SCOTT

2016
STANDARD POSTAGE
STAMP CATALOGUE

ONE HUNDRED AND SEVENTY-SECOND EDITION IN SIX VOLUMES

VOLUME 6
COUNTRIES OF THE WORLD
San-Z

EDITOR	Donna Houseman
MANAGING EDITOR	Charles Snee
EDITOR EMERITUS	James E. Kloetzel
SENIOR EDITOR /NEW ISSUES & VALUING	Martin J. Frankevicz
SENIOR VALUING ANALYST	Steven R. Myers
ADMINISTRATIVE ASSISTANT/CATALOGUE LAYOUT	Eric Wiessinger
PRINTING AND IMAGE COORDINATOR	Stacey Mahan
SENIOR GRAPHIC DESIGNER	Cinda McAlexander
ADVERTISING/SALES – EAST	Stephanie Campana
	David Pistello
ADVERTISING/SALES – MIDWEST	Mike Mandozzi
ADVERTISING/SALES – WEST & FL	Eric Roth
	Victoria Hardy
PRESIDENT	Jeff Greisch

Released September 2015

Includes New Stamp Listings through the July 2015 *Linn's Stamp News Monthly* Catalogue Update

Copyright© 2015 by

AMOS MEDIA

911 Vandemark Road, Sidney, OH 45365-4129

Publishers of *Linn's Stamp News, Linn's Stamp News Monthly, Coin World* and *Coin World Monthly*.

Table of Contents

See Volume 1 for United States, United Nations and Countries of the World A-B
See Volume 2, 3, 4, 5 for Countries of the World, C-Sam

Volume 2: C-F
Volume 3: G-I
Volume 4: J-M
Volume 5: N-Sam

Scott Catalogue Mission Statement

The Scott Catalogue Team exists to serve the recreational, educational and commercial hobby needs of stamp collectors and dealers.

We strive to set the industry standard for philatelic information and products by developing and providing goods that help collectors identify, value, organize and present their collections.

Quality customer service is, and will continue to be, our highest priority. We aspire toward achieving total customer satisfaction.

ISBN 0-89487-503-8

Library of Congress Card No. 2-3301

AMOS MEDIA

SCOTT. 911 VANDEMARK ROAD, SIDNEY, OHIO 45365   937-498-0802

Greetings, Fellow Scott Catalog User:

More than 2,150 value changes recorded for Singapore.
Welcome to Vol. 6 of the 2016 edition of the Scott *Standard Postage Stamp Catalogue*. The more than 9,900 value changes in this volume reflect the current market for countries of the world SAN (San Marino) through Z. Countries that received considerable attention from the Scott catalog editors this year include Singapore, Togo, Tristan da Cunha and Tunisia.

Singapore leads the way, with 2,154 value changes. A mixed bag of increases and decreases occur in the early issues. From 1966 on, the changes are overwhelmingly decreases, reflecting a stagnant market.

More than 1,550 value changes in Togo reflect a downward trend for this country. The decreases far outnumber the increases in this country located in western Africa. The first stamp issue under British rule shows a mixture of increases and decreases for stamps both with the first (wide) overprint setting (Scott 33-45) and second (narrow) setting. Significant increases occur in the inverted overprint varieties for the first setting. The unused value of Scott 37a moves from $9,000 to $10,000. The used value shows a decrease of $1,000, from $4,000 to $3,000. Scott 45a, another inverted overprint, jumps from $12,000 unused to $15,000. Values for many of the French occupation issues show general signs of weakening. The 1915 5-centime on 3-pfennig brown surcharged in sans-serif type (Scott 164) falls from $24,000 to $21,000 unused and $5,250 to $4,500 used. Similarly, the 50pf purple and black on salmon stamp (171) reflects a downward slide, from $24,000 unused to $21,000 and from $14,000 used to $12,500.

A thorough review of Tunisia yielded just north of 1,400 value changes. Moderate decreases prevail throughout, with a few increases interspersed. The 1928 10-centime on 15c brown on orange paper double surcharge (Scott 116c) slides from $140 to $125. The double surcharge, one inverted, variety of the 1938 65c on 50c with black surcharge (146) moves from $200 both mint and used to $175 both ways. The 1914 2-franc on 5fr black on yellow paper postage due (Scott J11) jumps from $1.60 mint and used to $3.50. Other back-of-the-book areas, including airmails and parcel post stamps, reflect a softening of the market.

A review of Ubangi-Shari resulted in 237 value changes. The first series of black overprints on Middle Congo stamps (Scott 1-22) show a mixed bag of increases and decreases. Decreases outnumber increases for the remainder of the country, and some of the decreases are significant. For example, the black "OUBANGUI CHARI" overprint omitted variety of the 1924-33 35-centime violet and green (Scott 54) falls from $525 to $275.

The 32 value changes in Southern Nigeria show solid gains, both unused and used.

The former French colony of Senegal reflects many decreases, with a sprinkling of increases within the 346 changes made in the classic period through 1944. The 1903 10-centime on 1-franc bronze green on straw paper (Scott 56) falls from $92.50 to $80 both unused and used.

The classic period of Southern Rhodesia exhibits significant gains, especially among the vertical pairs and horizontal pairs, imperf between. The horizontal pair, imperf between of the 6-penny lilac and black (Scott 7) rises from $40,000 unused to $45,000. The perf 11½ variety of the 1931-37 1-shilling turquoise blue and black (Scott 26) shows a $15 gain, from $125 unused to $140.

The 41 value changes in Sweden show a mix of increases and decreases. The sheet of nine of Scott 2545a rockets from $15 both mint and used to $40 both ways. Values have been added in footnotes for modern sheets.

While these comments tend to focus on those countries with larger numbers of value changes, there are changes to be found in many other countries, some of which are easy to overlook. The 98 value changes for Spain show a general weakening across the board. The 18 changes in Tobago and 28 changes in Timor reflect increases. Similarly, the 34 changes in the postage due section of Uruguay reflect upward movement. Scott J17, the 1922 10-centavo gray-green postage due stamp moves from 50¢ to $1. Take some time to look over these and other less-frequented areas for value updates.

Editorial enhancements for South Africa, Tripolitania.
Below we highlight some of the editorial changes that were made this year.

South Africa: An important footnote has been added following Scott 16, alerting catalog users that Scott values watermarked stamps of South Africa in the normal upright position. Frame-omitted varieties were added to the 3-penny blue green and black of the 1930-45 series (Scott 39d), and the 1p carmine and gray (48r) and 1-shilling chalky blue and light brown (62j) of the 1933-54 series. A new major number was added to the 1933-54 series: the 5sh blue green and black pair (Scott 64C) is valued at $42.50 unused and $21 used. Singles are valued at $1 unused and 40¢ used for both the English and Afrikaans inscribed stamps.

Serbia: A perf. 13¼ variety issued in 2011 is now listed as Scott 355a and valued at $1.25 both mint and used.

South Russia: Double impression varieties with the surcharge in the normal position were added for the 1918 25-kopeck on 2kop dull green (Scott 2b) and the imperforate 25kop on 2kop dull green (7a). Both varieties are valued at $150 unused.

Togo: A souvenir sheet of six was added to the 1961 set commemorating the 150th anniversary of UNICEF. The sheet is valued at $5 mint and $3.50 used.

Singapore: An imperf pair has been added for the 1977 10¢ orange and multicolor in the Sea Shells set. The mint pair is valued at $500. Another imperf pair was added to the 1980 $1 Coaster stamp (Scott 345a).

Tripolitania: Six minor listings were added, including double overprint varieties of the 1923 30-centesimi claret and brown orange (Scott 2a), value $2,250 unused; the 1923 2-lira brown (9a), value $1,650 unused; and the 1927 50c deep orange (26b), value $190 unused. A vertical pair, imperf between and at bottom is now listed as Scott 2b. An imperf variety has been added to the 1924 30c black and slate (13a) with a dash in the unused column. A double overprint, one inverted, variety is now listed as 26b for the 1927 50c deep orange. It is valued at $190 unused.

As always, we encourage you to pay special attention to the Number Additions, Deletions & Changes found on page 1713 in this volume.

While you settle in with your stamp album and Scott catalog, relax and enjoy the world's greatest hobby.

Donna Houseman
Donna Houseman/Catalogue Editor

Acknowledgments

Our appreciation and gratitude go to the following individuals who have assisted us in preparing information included in this year's Scott Catalogues. Some helpers prefer anonymity. These individuals have generously shared their stamp knowledge with others through the medium of the Scott Catalogue.

Those who follow provided information that is in addition to the hundreds of dealer price lists and advertisements and scores of auction catalogues and realizations that were used in producing the catalogue values. It is from those noted here that we have been able to obtain information on items not normally seen in published lists and advertisements. Support from these people goes beyond data leading to catalogue values, for they also are key to editorial changes.

> A special acknowledgment to Liane and Sergio Sismondo of The Classic Collector for their assistance and knowledge sharing that have aided in the preparation of this year's Standard and Classic Specialized Catalogues.

Michael Aldrich (Michael E. Aldrich, Inc.)
Roland Austin
Robert Ausubel (Great Britain Collectors Club)
Jack Hagop Barsoumian (International Stamp Co.)
John Birkinbine II
Brian M. Bleckwenn
Roger S. Brody
Keith & Margie Brown
Mahdi Bseiso
Josh Buchsbayew (Cherrystone Auctions)
Ronald A. Burns
Peter Bylen
Tina & John Carlson (JET Stamps)
Henry Chlanda
Frank D. Correl
Steven D. Crippe (Gradedstamps.com)
Tony L. Crumbley (Carolina Coin & Stamp, Inc.)
Christopher Dahle
Stephen R. Datz
Tony Davis
Charles Deaton
Ubaldo Del Toro
Bob & Rita Dumaine (Sam Houston Duck Co.)
Sister Theresa Durand
Mark Eastzer (Markest Stamp Co.)
Paul G. Eckman
George Epstein (Allkor Stamp Co.)
Mehdi Esmaili
George Eveleth (Spink Shreves Galleries)
Henry Fisher
Jeffrey M. Forster
Ernest E. Fricks (France & Colonies Philatelic Society)
Frank Geiger (Worldstamps.com)
Bob Genisol (Sultan Stamp Center)
Allan Grant (Rushstamps, Ltd.)
Daniel E. Grau
Jan E. Gronwall
Grosvenor Auctions
Chris Harmer (Harmer-Schau Auctions)
Robin Harris
Bruce Hecht (Bruce L. Hecht Co.)
Peter Hoffman
Armen Hovsepian (Armenstamp)
Philip J. Hughes
Doug Iams

John Jamieson (Saskatoon Stamp and Coin)
N. M. Janoowalla
Peter Jeannopoulos
Stephen Joe (International Stamp Service)
William A. Jones
Sheikh Shafiqul Islam
John Kardos
Allan Katz (Ventura Stamp Co.)
Stanford M. Katz
Lewis Kaufman (The Philatelic Foundation)
Patricia A. Kaufmann (Confederate Stamp Alliance)
William V. Kriebel (Brazil Philatelic Association)
George Krieger
Frederick P. Lawrence
Ken Lawrence
John R. Lewis (The William Henry Stamp Co.)
Ulf Lindahl
Ignacio Llach (Filatelia Llach S.L.)
Larry Martin (Crown Colony Stamp Co.)
Marilyn R. Mattke
William K. McDaniel
Mark S. Miller
Gary Morris (Pacific Midwest Co.)
Bruce M. Moyer (Moyer Stamps & Collectibles)
Richard H. Muller
Behruz Nassre
Nestor Nunez
Robert P. Odenweller
Nik & Lisa Oquist
Dr. Everett Parker
Donald J. Peterson (International Philippine Philatelic Society)
Stanley M. Piller (Stanley M. Piller & Associates)
Virgil Pirvulescu
Todor Drumev Popov
Philippe & Guido Poppe (Poppe Stamps, Inc.)
Siddique Mahmudur Rahman
Ghassan D. Riachi
Eric Roberts
Peter A. Robertson
Wilford H. Ross
Robert G. Rufe

Mehrdad Sadri (Persiphila)
Theodosios Sampson PhD
Michael Schreiber
Jacques C. Schiff, Jr. (Jacques C. Schiff, Jr., Inc.)
Vincent Sgro
Guy Shaw
Jeff Siddiqui
Sergio & Liane Sismondo (The Classic Collector)
Jay Smith
Frank J. Stanley, III
Kenneth Thompson
Peter Thy
Scott R. Trepel (Siegel Auction Galleries)
Dan Undersander (United Postal Stationery Society)
Steven Unkrich
Philip T. Wall
Kristian Wang
Daniel C. Warren
Giana Wayman
William R. Weiss, Jr. (Weiss Expertizing)
Don White (Dunedin Stamp Centre)
Ralph Yorio
Val Zabijaka
Michal Zika
Steven Zirinsky
Alfonso G. Zulueta
Steven Zwillinger

Addresses, Telephone Numbers, Web Sites, E-Mail Addresses of General & Specialized Philatelic Societies

Collectors can contact the following groups for information about the philately of the areas within the scope of these societies, or inquire about membership in these groups. Aside from the general societies, we limit this list to groups that specialize in particular fields of philately, particular areas covered by the Scott Standard Postage Stamp Catalogue, and topical groups. Many more specialized philatelic society exist than those listed below. These addresses are updated yearly, and they are, to the best of our knowledge, correct and current. Groups should inform the editors of address changes whenever they occur. The editors also want to hear from other such specialized groups not listed. Unless otherwise noted all website addresses begin with http://

American Philatelic Society
100 Match Factory Place
Bellefonte PA 16823-1367
Ph: (814) 933-3803
www.stamps.org
E-mail: apsinfo@stamps.org

American Stamp Dealers Association, Inc.
P.O. Box 692
Leesport PA 19553
Ph: (800) 369-8207
www.americanstampdealer.com
E-mail: asda@americanstampdealer.com

National Stamp Dealers Association
Dick Keiser, President
2916 NW Bucklin Hill Road #136
Silverdale WA 98383-8514
Ph: (800) 875-6633
www.nsdainc.org
E-mail: gail@nsdainc.org

International Society of Worldwide Stamp Collectors
Joanne Berkowitz, MD
P.O. Box 19006
Sacramento CA 95819
www.iswsc.org
E-mail: executivedirector@iswsc.org

Royal Philatelic Society
41 Devonshire Place
London, W1G 6JY
UNITED KINGDOM

www.rpsl.org.uk
E-mail: secretary@rpsl.org.uk

Royal Philatelic Society of Canada
P.O. Box 929, Station Q
Toronto, ON, M4T 2P1
CANADA
Ph: (888) 285-4143
www.rpsc.org
E-mail: info@rpsc.org

Young Stamp Collectors of America
Janet Houser
100 Match Factory Place
Bellefonte PA 16823-1367
Ph: (814) 933-3820
www.stamps.org/ysca/intro.htm
E-mail: ysca@stamps.org

Philatelic Research Resources
(The Scott editors encourage any additional research organizations to submit data for inclusion in this listing category)

American Philatelic Research Library
Tara Murray
100 Match Factory Place
Bellefonte PA 16823
Ph: (814) 933-3803
www.stamplibrary.org
E-mail: aprl@stamps.org

Institute for Analytical Philately, Inc.
P.O. Box 8035
Holland MI 49422-8035
Ph: (616) 399-9299
www.analyticalphilately.org
E-mail: info@analyticalphilately.org

The Western Philatelic Library
P.O. Box 2219
1500 Partridge Ave.
Sunnyvale CA 94087
Ph: (408) 733-0336
www.fwpf.org

Groups focusing on fields or aspects found in worldwide philately (some might cover U.S. area only)

American Air Mail Society
Stephen Reinhard
P.O. Box 110
Mineola NY 11501
www.americanairmailsociety.org
E-mail: sreinhard1@optonline.net

American First Day Cover Society
Douglas Kelsey
P.O. Box 16277
Tucson AZ 85732-6277
Ph: (520) 321-0880
www.afdcs.org
E-mail: afdcs@afdcs.org

American Revenue Association
Eric Jackson
P.O. Box 728
Leesport PA 19533-0728
Ph: (610) 926-6200
www.revenuer.org
E-mail: eric@revenuer.com

American Topical Association
Vera Felts
P.O. Box 8
Carterville IL 62918-0008
Ph: (618) 985-5100
www.americantopicalassn.org
E-mail: americantopical@msn.com

Christmas Seal & Charity Stamp Society
John Denune
234 E. Broadway
Granville OH 43023
Ph: (740) 587-0276
www.seal-society.org
E-mail: jdenune@roadrunner.com

Errors, Freaks and Oddities Collectors Club
Scott Shaulis
P.O. Box 549
Murrysville PA 15668-0549
Ph: (724) 733-4134
www.efocc.org

First Issues Collectors Club
Kurt Streepy, Secretary
3128 E. Mattatha Drive
Bloomington IN 47401
E-mail: secretary@firstissues.org

International Society of Reply Coupon Collectors
Peter Robin
P.O. Box 353
Bala Cynwyd PA 19004
E-mail: peterrobin@verizon.net

The Joint Stamp Issues Society
Richard Zimmermann
29A Rue Des Eviats
Lalaye F-67220
FRANCE
www.jointstampissues.net
E-mail: contact@jointstampissues.net

National Duck Stamp Collectors Society
Anthony J. Monico
P.O. Box 43
Harleysville PA 19438-0043
www.ndscs.org
E-mail: ndscs@ndscs.org

No Value Identified Club
Albert Sauvanet
Le Clos Royal B, Boulevard des Pas Enchantes
St. Sebastien-sur Loire, 44230
FRANCE
E-mail: alain.vailly@irin.univ nantes.fr

The Perfins Club
Jerry Hejduk
P.O. Box 490450
Leesburg FL 34749-0450
www.perfins.org
Ph: (352) 326-2117
E-mail: flprepers@comcast.net

Postage Due Mail Study Group
John Rawlins
13, Longacre
Chelmsford, CM1 3BJ
UNITED KINGDOM
E-mail: john.rawlins2@ukonline.co.uk.

Post Mark Collectors Club
Bob Milligan
7014 Woodland Oaks
Magnolia TX 77354
Ph: (281) 359-2735
www.postmarks.org
E-mail: bob.milligan@prodigy.net

Postal History Society
Joseph F. Frasch, Jr.
P.O. Box 20387
Columbus OH 43220-0387
www.stampclubs.com
E-mail: jfrasch@ix.netcom.com

Precancel Stamp Society
Rick Podwell
P.O. Box 85
Fawn Grove PA 17321
Ph: (717) 817-8807
www.precancels.com
E-mail: psspromosec@comcast.net

United Postal Stationery Society
Stuart Leven
P.O. Box 24764
San Jose CA 95154-4764
www.upss.org
E-mail: poststat@gmail.com

United States Possessions Philatelic Society
Daniel F. Ring
P.O. Box 113
Woodstock IL 60098
www.uspps.net
E-mail: danielfring@hotmail.com

Groups focusing on U.S. area philately as covered in the Standard Catalogue

Canal Zone Study Group
Tom Brougham
737 Neilson St.
Berkeley CA 94707
www.CanalZoneStudyGroup.com
E-mail: czsgsecretary@gmail.com

Carriers and Locals Society
Martin Richardson
P.O. Box 74
Grosse Ile MI 48138
www.pennypost.org
E-mail: martinr362@aol.com

Confederate Stamp Alliance
Patricia A. Kaufmann
10194 N. Old State Road
Lincoln DE 19960
Ph: (302) 422-2656
www.csalliance.org
E-mail: trishkauf@comcast.net

Hawaiian Philatelic Society
Kay H. Hoke
P.O. Box 10115
Honolulu HI 96816-0115
Ph: (808) 521-5721

Plate Number Coil Collectors Club
Gene Trinks
16415 W. Desert Wren Court
Surprise AZ 85374
Ph: (623) 322-4619
www.pnc3.org
E-mail: gctrinks@cox.net

Ryukyu Philatelic Specialist Society
Laura Edmonds, Secy.
P.O. Box 240177
Charlotte NC 28224-0177
Ph: (336) 509-3739
www.ryukyustamps.org
E-mail: secretary@ryukyustamps.org

United Nations Philatelists
Blanton Clement, Jr.
P.O. Box 146
Morrisville PA 19067-0146
www.unpi.com
E-mail: bclemjr@yahoo.com

United States Stamp Society
Executive Secretary
P.O. Box 6634
Katy TX 77491-6631
www.usstamps.org
E-mail: webmaster@usstamps.org

U.S. Cancellation Club
Arden Calleder
Houston TX 77077
Ph: (281) 589-1075
bob.trachimowicz.org/uscchome.htm
E-mail: callenderardy@secglobal.net

U.S. Philatelic Classics Society
Rob Lund
2913 Fulton St.
Everett WA 98201-3733
www.uspcs.org
E-mail: membershipchairman@uspcs.org

Groups focusing on philately of foreign countries or regions

Aden & Somaliland Study Group
Gary Brown
P.O. Box 106
Briar Hill, Victoria, 3088
AUSTRALIA
E-mail: garyjohn951@optushome.com.au

American Society of Polar Philatelists (Antarctic areas)
Alan Warren
P.O. Box 39
Exton PA 19341-0039
www.polarphilatelists.org

Andorran Philatelic Study Circle
D. Hope
17 Hawthorn Drive
Stalybridge, Cheshire, SK15 1UE
UNITED KINGDOM
apsc.free.fr
E-mail: apsc@free.fr

Australian States Study Circle of The Royal Sydney Philatelic Club
Ben Palmer
GPO 1751
Sydney, N.S.W., 2001
AUSTRALIA
www.philas.org.au/states

Austria Philatelic Society
Ralph Schneider
P.O. Box 23049
Belleville IL 62223
Ph: (618) 277-6152
www.austriaphilatelicsociety.com
E-mail: rschneiderstamps@att.net

American Belgian Philatelic Society
Edward de Bary
11 Wakefield Drive Apt. 2105
Asheville NC 28803

Bechuanalands and Botswana Society
Neville Midwood
69 Porlock Lane
Furzton, Milton Keynes, MK4 1JY
UNITED KINGDOM
www.nevsoft.com
E-mail: bbsoc@nevsoft.com

Bermuda Collectors Society
John Pare
405 Perimeter Road
Mount Horeb WI 53572
www.bermudacollectorssociety.org
E-mail: pare16@mhtc.net

Brazil Philatelic Association
William V. Kriebel
1923 Manning St.
Philadelphia PA 19103-5728
www.brazilphilatelic.org
E-mail: info@brazilphilatelic.org

British Caribbean Philatelic Study Group
Dr. Reuben Ramkissoon
11075 Benton St. #236
Loma Linda CA 92354-3812
Ph: (909) 796-6409
www.bcpsg.com
E-mail: rramkissoon@juno.com

The King George VI Collectors Society (British Commonwealth)
Brian Livingstone
21 York Mansions, Prince of Wales Drive
London, SW11 4DL
UNITED KINGDOM
www.kg6.info
E-mail: livingstone484@btinternet.com

British North America Philatelic Society (Canada & Provinces)
David G. Jones
184 Larkin Drive
Nepean, ON, K2J 1H9
CANADA
www.bnaps.org
E-mail: shibumi.management@gmail.com

British West Indies Study Circle
John Seidl
4324 Granby Way
Marietta GA 30062
Ph: (770) 642-6424
www.bwisc.org
E-mail: john.seidl@gmail.com

Burma Philatelic Study Circle
Michael Whittaker
1, Ecton Leys, Hillside
Rugby, Warwickshire, CV22 5SL
UNITED KINGDOM
www.burmastamps.homecall.co.uk
E-mail: manningham8@mypostoffice.co.uk

Cape and Natal Study Circle
Dr. Guy Dillaway
P.O. Box 181
Weston MA 02493
www.nzsc.demon.co.uk

Ceylon Study Circle
R. W. P. Frost
42 Lonsdale Road, Cannington
Bridgewater, Somerset, TA5 2JS
UNITED KINGDOM
www.ceylonsc.org
E-mail: rodney.frost@tiscali.co.uk

Channel Islands Specialists Society
Moira Edwards
86, Hall Lane, Sandon
Chelmsford, Essex, CM2 7RQ
UNITED KINGDOM
www.ciss1950.org.uk
E-mail: membership@ciss1950.org.uk

China Stamp Society
Paul H. Gault
P.O. Box 20711
Columbus OH 43220
www.chinastampsociety.org
E-mail: secretary@chinastampsociety.org

Colombia/Panama Philatelic Study Group (COPAPHIL)
Thomas P. Myers
P.O. Box 522
Gordonsville VA 22942
www.copaphil.org
E-mail: tpmphil@hotmail.com

Association Filatelic de Costa Rica
Giana Wayman
c/o Interlink 102, P.O. Box 52-6770
Miami FL 33152
E-mail: scotland@racsa.co.cr

Society for Costa Rica Collectors
Dr. Hector R. Mena
P.O. Box 14831
Baton Rouge LA 70808
www.socorico.org
E-mail: hrmena@aol.com

International Cuban Philatelic Society
Ernesto Cuesta
P.O. Box 34434
Bethesda MD 20827
www.cubafil.org
E-mail: ecuesta@philat.com

Cuban Philatelic Society of America ®
P.O. Box 141656
Coral Gables FL 33114-1656
www.cubapsa.com
E-mail: cpsa.usa@gmail.com

Cyprus Study Circle
Colin Dear
10 Marne Close, Wem
Shropshire, SY4 5YE
UNITED KINGDOM
www.cyprusstudycircle.org/index.htm
E-mail: colindear@talktalk.net

Society for Czechoslovak Philately
Tom Cassaboom
P.O. Box 4124
Prescott AZ 86302
www.csphilately.org
E-mail: klfck1@aol.com

Danish West Indies Study Unit of the Scandinavian Collectors Club
Arnold Sorensen
7666 Edgedale Drive
Newburgh IN 47630
Ph: (812) 480-6532
www.scc-online.org
E-mail: valbydwi@hotmail.com

East Africa Study Circle
Michael Vesey-Fitzgerald
Gambles Cottage, 18 Clarence Road
Lyndhurst, SO43 7AL
UNITED KINGDOM
www.easc.org.uk
E-mail: secretary@easc.org.uk

Egypt Study Circle
Mike Murphy
109 Chadwick Road
London, SE15 4PY
UNITED KINGDOM
Trent Ruebush: North American Agent
E-mail: truebrush@usaid.gov
egyptstudycircle.org.uk
E-mail: egyptstudycircle@hotmail.com

Estonian Philatelic Society
Juri Kirsimagi
29 Clifford Ave.
Pelham NY 10803
Ph: (914) 738-3713

Ethiopian Philatelic Society
Ulf Lindahl
21 Westview Place
Riverside CT 06878
Ph: (203) 722-0769
home.comcast.net/~fbheiser/ethiopia5.htm
E-mail: ulindahl@optonline.net

Falkland Islands Philatelic Study Group
Carl J. Faulkner
615 Taconic Trail
Williamstown MA 01267-2745
Ph: (413) 458-4421
www.fipsg.org.uk
E-mail: cfaulkner@taconicwilliamstown.com

Faroe Islands Study Circle
Norman Hudson
40 Queen's Road, Vicar's Cross
Chester, CH3 5HB
UNITED KINGDOM
www.faroeislandssc.org
E-mail: jntropics@hotmail.com

Former French Colonies Specialist Society
COLFRA
BP 628
75367 Paris, Cedex 08
FRANCE
www.colfra.org
E-mail: secretaire@colfra.org

France & Colonies Philatelic Society
Edward Grabowski
111 Prospect St., 4C
Westfield NJ 07090
www.franceandcols.org
E-mail: edjjg@alum.mit.edu

Germany Philatelic Society
P.O. Box 6547
Chesterfield MO 63006
www.germanyphilatelicusa.org

Gibraltar Study Circle

David R. Stirrups
152 The Rowans, Milton
Cambridge, CB24 6YX
UNITED KINGDOM
www.gibraltarstudycircle.wordpress.com
E-mail: beggloops@gmail.com

Great Britain Collectors Club
Steve McGill
10309 Brookhollow Circle
Highlands Ranch CO 80129
www.gbstamps.com/gbcc
E-mail: steve.mcgill@comcast.net

International Society of Guatemala Collectors
Jaime Marckwordt
449 St. Francis Blvd.
Daly City CA 94015-2136
www.guatemalastamps.com
E-mail: membership@guatamalastamps.com

Haiti Philatelic Society
Ubaldo Del Toro
5709 Marble Archway
Alexandria VA 22315
www.haitiphilately.org
E-mail: u007ubi@aol.com

Hong Kong Stamp Society
Ming W. Tsang
P.O. Box 206
Glenside PA 19038
www.hkss.org
E-mail: hkstamps@yahoo.com

Society for Hungarian Philately
Robert Morgan
2201 Roscomare Road
Los Angeles CA 90077-2222
Ph; (617) 645-4045
www.hungarianphilately.org
E-mail: alan@hungarianstamps.com

India Study Circle
John Warren
P.O. Box 7326
Washington DC 20044
Ph: (202) 564-6876
www.indiastudycircle.org
E-mail: warren.john@epa.gov

Indian Ocean Study Circle
E. S. Hutton
29 Paternoster Close
Waltham Abby, Essex, EN9 3JU
UNITED KINGDOM
www.indianoceanstudycircle.com
E-mail:
secretary@indianoceanstudycircle.com

Society of Indo-China Philatelists
Ron Bentley
2600 N. 24th St.
Arlington VA 22207
www.sicp-online.org
E-mail: ron.bentley@verizon.net

Iran Philatelic Study Circle
Mehdi Esmaili
P.O. Box 750096
Forest Hills NY 11375
www.iranphilatelic.org
E-mail: m.esmaili@earthlink.net

Eire Philatelic Association (Ireland)
David J. Brennan
P.O. Box 704
Bernardsville NJ 07924
www.eirephilatelicassoc.org
E-mail: brennan704@aol.com

Society of Israel Philatelists
Edwin Kroft
P.O. Box 507
Northfield OH 44067
www.israelstamps.com
E-mail: israelstamps@gmail.com

Italy and Colonies Study Circle
Richard Harlow
7 Duncombe House, 8 Manor Road
Teddington, TW11 8BE
UNITED KINGDOM
www.icsc.pwp.blueyonder.co.uk
E-mail: harlowr@gmail.com

International Society for Japanese Philately
William Eisenhauer
P.O. Box 230462
Tigard OR 97281
www.isjp.org
E-mail: secretary@isjp.org

Korea Stamp Society
John E. Talmage
P.O. Box 6889
Oak Ridge TN 37831
www.pennfamily.org/KSS-USA
E-mail: jtalmage@usit.net

Latin American Philatelic Society
Jules K. Beck
30½ St. #209
St. Louis Park MN 55426-3551

Liberian Philatelic Society
William Thomas Lockard
P.O. Box 106
Wellston OH 45692
Ph: (740) 384-2020
E-mail: tlockard@zoomnet.net

Liechtenstudy USA (Liechtenstein)
Paul Tremaine
410 SW Ninth St.
Dundee OR 97115
Ph: (503) 538-4500
www.liechtenstudy.org
E-mail: editor@liechtenstudy.org

Lithuania Philatelic Society
John Variakojis
8472 Carlisle Court.
Burr Ridge IL 60527
Ph: (630) 974-6525
www.lithuanianphilately.com/lps
E-mail: variakojis@sbcglobal.net

Luxembourg Collectors Club
Gary B. Little
7319 Beau Road
Sechelt, BC, V0N 3A8
CANADA
lcc.luxcentral.com
E-mail: gary@luxcentral.com

Malaya Study Group
David Tett
P.O. Box 34
Wheathampstead, Herts, AL4 8JY
UNITED KINGDOM
www.m-s-g.org.uk
E-mail: davidtett@aol.com

Malta Study Circle
Alec Webster
50 Worcester Road
Sutton, Surrey, SM2 6QB
UNITED KINGDOM
www.maltastudycircle.org.uk
E-mail: alecwebster50@hotmail.com

Mexico-Elmhurst Philatelic Society International
Thurston Bland
50 Regato
Rancho Santa Margarita CA 92688-3003
www.mepsi.org

Asociacion Mexicana de Filatelia AMEXFIL
Jose Maria Rico, 129, Col. Del Valle
Mexico City DF, 03100
MEXICO
www.amexfil.mx
E-mail: amexfil@gmail.com

Society for Moroccan and Tunisian Philately S.P.L.M.
206, bld. Pereire
75017 Paris
FRANCE
members.aol.com/Jhaik5814
E-mail: splm206@aol.com

Nepal & Tibet Philatelic Study Group
Roger D. Skinner
1020 Covington Road
Los Altos CA 94024-5003
Ph: (650) 968-4163
www.fuchs-online.com/ntpsc/
E-mail: colinhepper@hotmail.co.uk

American Society for Netherlands Philately
Hans Kremer
50 Rockport Court
Danville CA 94526
Ph: (925) 820-5841
www.asnp1975.com
E-mail: hkremer@usa.net

New Zealand Society of Great Britain
Michael Wilkinson
121 London Road
Sevenoaks, Kent, TN13 1BH
UNITED KINGDOM
www.nzsgb.org.uk
E-mail: mwilkin799@aol.com

Nicaragua Study Group
Erick Rodriguez
11817 SW 11th St.
Miami FL 33184-2501
clubs.yahoo.com/clubs/
nicaraguastudygroup
E-mail: nsgsec@yahoo.com

Society of Australasian Specialists/Oceania
David McNamee
P.O. Box 37
Alamo CA 94507
www.sasoceania.org
E-mail: dmcnamee@aol.com

Orange Free State Study Circle
J. R. Stroud
24 Hooper Close
Burnham-on-sea, Somerset, TA8 1JQ
UNITED KINGDOM
orangefreestatephilately.org.uk
E-mail: richardstroudph@gofast.co.uk

Pacific Islands Study Circle
John Ray
24 Woodvale Ave.
London, SE25 4AE
UNITED KINGDOM
www.pisc.org.uk
E-mail: info@pisc.org.uk

Pakistan Philatelic Study Circle
Jeff Siddiqui
P.O. Box 7002
Lynnwood WA 98046
E-mail: jeffsiddiqui@msn.com

Centro de Filatelistas Independientes de Panama
Vladimir Berrio-Lemm
Apartado 0823-02748
Plaza Concordia Panama
PANAMA
E-mail: panahistoria@gmail.com

Papuan Philatelic Society
Steven Zirinsky
P.O. Box 49, Ansonia Station
New York NY 10023
Ph: (718) 706-0616
www.communigate.co.uk/york/pps
E-mail: szirinsky@cs.com

International Philippine Philatelic Society
Donald J. Peterson
P.O. Box 122
Brunswick MD 21716
Ph: (301) 834-6419
www.theipps.info
E-mail: dpeterson4526@gmail.com

Pitcairn Islands Study Group
Dr. Everett L. Parker
249 NW Live Oak Place
Lake City FL 32055-8906
Ph: (386) 754-8524
www.pisg.net
E-mail: eparker@hughes.net

Polonus Philatelic Society (Poland)
Robert Ogrodnik
P.O. Box 240428
Ballwin MO 63024-0428
Ph: (314) 821-6130
www.polonus.org
E-mail: rvo1937@gmail.com

International Society for Portuguese Philately
Clyde Homen
1491 Bonnie View Road
Hollister CA 95023-5117
www.portugalstamps.com
E-mail: cjh1491@sbcglobal.net

Rhodesian Study Circle
William R. Wallace
P.O. Box 16381
San Francisco CA 94116
www.rhodesianstudycircle.org.uk
E-mail: bwall8rscr@earthlink.net

Rossica Society of Russian Philately
Alexander Kolchinsky
1506 Country Lake Drive
Champaign IL 6821-6428
www.rossica.org
E-mail: alexander.kolchinsky@rossica.org

St. Helena, Ascension & Tristan Da Cunha Philatelic Society
Dr. Everett L. Parker
249 NW Live Oak Place
Lake City FL 32055-8906
Ph: (386) 754-8524
www.atlanticislands.org
E-mail: eparker@hughes.net

St. Pierre & Miquelon Philatelic Society
James R. (Jim) Taylor
2335 Paliswood Road SW
Calgary, AB, T2V 3P6
CANADA
www.stamps.org/spm

Associated Collectors of El Salvador
Joseph D. Hahn
1015 Old Boalsburg Road Apt G-5
State College PA 16801-6149
www.elsalvadorphilately.org
E-mail: jdhahn2@gmail.com

Fellowship of Samoa Specialists
Donald Mee
23 Leo St.
Christchurch, 8051
NEW ZEALAND
www.samoaexpress.org
E-mail: donanm@xtra.co.nz

Sarawak Specialists' Society
Stu Leven
P.O. Box 24764
San Jose CA 95154-4764
Ph: (408) 978-0193
www.britborneostamps.org.uk
E-mail: stulev@ix.netcom.com

Scandinavian Collectors Club
Steve Lund
P.O. Box 16213
St. Paul MN 55116
www.scc-online.org
E-mail: steve88h@aol.com

Slovakia Stamp Society
Jack Benchik
P.O. Box 555
Notre Dame IN 46556

Philatelic Society for Greater Southern Africa
Alan Hanks
34 Seaton Drive
Aurora, ON, L4G 2KI
CANADA
Ph: (905) 727-6993
www.psgsa.thestampweb.com
Email: alan.hanks@sympatico.ca

South Sudan Philatelic Society
William Barclay
134A Spring Hill Road
South Londonerry VT 05155
E-mail: bill.barclay@wfp.org

Spanish Philatelic Society
Robert H. Penn
1108 Walnut Drive
Danielsville PA 18038
Ph: (610) 844-8963
E-mail: roberthpenn43@gmail.com

Sudan Study Group
David Sher
5 Ellis Park Road
Toronto, ON, M6S 2V2
CANADA
www.sudanstamps.org
E-mail: sh3603@hotmail.com

American Helvetia Philatelic Society (Switzerland, Liechtenstein)
Richard T. Hall
P.O. Box 15053
Asheville NC 28813-0053
www.swiss-stamps.org
E-mail: secretary2@swiss-stamps.org

Tannu Tuva Collectors Society
Ken R. Simon
P.O. Box 385
Lake Worth FL 33460-0385
Ph: (561) 588-5954
www.tuva.tk
E-mail: yurttuva@yahoo.com

Society for Thai Philately
H. R. Blakeney
P.O. Box 25644
Oklahoma City OK 73125
E-mail: HRBlakeney@aol.com

Transvaal Study Circle
Jeff Woolgar
c/o 9 Meadow Road
Gravesend, DA11 7LR
UNITED KINGDOM
www.transvaal.org.uk

Ottoman and Near East Philatelic Society (Turkey and related areas)
Bob Stuchell
193 Valley Stream Lane
Wayne PA 19087
www.oneps.org
E-mail: rstuchell@msn.com

Ukrainian Philatelic & Numismatic Society
Martin B. Tatuch
5117 8th Road N.
Arlington VA 22205-1201
www.upns.org
E-mail: treasurer@upns.org

Vatican Philatelic Society
Sal Quinonez
1 Aldersgate, Apt. 1002
Riverhead NY 11901-1830
Ph: (516) 727-6426
www.vaticanphilately.org

British Virgin Islands Philatelic Society
Giorgio Migliavacca
P.O. Box 7007
St. Thomas VI 00801-0007
www.islandsun.com/category/collectables/
E-mail: issun@candwbvi.net

West Africa Study Circle
Martin Bratzel
1233 Virginia Ave.
Windsor, ON, N8S 2Z1
CANADA
www.wasc.org.uk/
E-mail: marty_bratzel@yahoo.ca

Western Australia Study Group
Brian Pope
P.O. Box 423
Claremont, Western Australia, 6910
AUSTRALIA
www.wastudygroup.com
E-mail: black5swan@yahoo.com.au

**Yugoslavia Study Group of the Croatian
   Philatelic Society**
Michael Lenard
1514 N. Third Ave.
Wausau WI 54401
Ph: (715) 675-2833
E-mail: mjlenard@aol.com

Topical Groups

Americana Unit
Dennis Dengel
17 Peckham Road
Poughkeepsie NY 12603-2018
www.americanaunit.org
E-mail: info@americanaunit.org

Astronomy Study Unit
John W. G. Budd
728 Sugar Camp Way
Brooksville FL 34604
E-mail: jwgbudd@gmail.com

Bicycle Stamp Club
Steve Andreasen
2000 Alaskan Way, Unit 157
Seattle WA 98121
members.tripod.com/~bicyclestamps
E-mail: steven.w.andreasen@gmail.com

Biology Unit
Alan Hanks
34 Seaton Drive
Aurora, ON, L4G 2K1
CANADA
Ph: (905) 727-6993

Bird Stamp Society
S. A. H. (Tony) Statham
Ashlyns Lodge, Chesham Road,
Berkhamsted, Hertfordshire HP4 2ST
UNITED KINGDOM
www.bird-stamps.org/bss
E-mail: tony.statham@sky.com

Captain Cook Society
Jerry Yucht
8427 Leale Ave.
Stockton CA 95212
www.captaincooksociety.com
E-mail: US@captaincooksociety.com

The CartoPhilatelic Society
Marybeth Sulkowski
1117 Douglas Ave. #209
North Providence RI 02904-5374
www.mapsonstamps.org
E-mail: secretary@mapsonstamps.org

Casey Jones Railroad Unit
Roy W. Menninger MD
85 SW Pepper Tree Lane
Topeka KS 66611-2072
www.uqp.de/cjr/index.htm
E-mail: roymenn@sbcglobal.net

Cats on Stamps Study Unit
Mary Ann Brown
3006 Wade Road
Durham NC 27705
www.catsonstamps.org
E-mail: mabrown@nc.rr.com

Chemistry & Physics on Stamps Study Unit
Dr. Roland Hirsch
20458 Water Point Lane
Germantown MD 20874
www.cpossu.org
E-mail: rfhirsch@cpossu.org

Chess on Stamps Study Unit
Ray C. Alexis
608 Emery St.
Longmont CO 80501
E-mail: chessstuff911459@aol.com

Christmas Philatelic Club
Jim Balog
P.O. Box 774
Geneva OH 44041
www.web.295.ca/cpc/
E-mail: jpbstamps@windstream.net

Christopher Columbus Philatelic Society
Donald R. Ager
P.O. Box 71
Hillsboro NH 03244-0071
Ph: (603) 464-5379
ccps.maphist.nl/
E-mail: meganddon@tds.net

Collectors of Religion on Stamps
James Bailey
P.O. Box 937
Brownwood TX 76804
www.coros-society.org
E-mail: corosec@directtv.net

Cricket Philatelic Society
A.Melville-Brown, President
11 Weppons, Ravens Road
Shoreham-by-Sea
West Sussex, BN43 5AW
UNITED KINGDOM
www.cricketstamp.net
E-mail: mel.cricket.100@googlemail.com

Dogs on Stamps Study Unit
Morris Raskin
202A Newport Road
Monroe Township NJ 08831
Ph: (609) 655-7411
www.dossu.org
E-mail: mraskin@cellurian.com

Earth's Physical Features Study Group
Fred Klein
515 Magdalena Ave.
Los Altos CA 94024
epfsu.jeffhayward.com

**Ebony Society of Philatelic Events and
   Reflections, Inc. (African-American
   topicals)**
Manuel Gilyard
800 Riverside Drive, Suite 4H
New York NY 10032-7412
www.esperstamps.org
E-mail: gilyardmani@aol.com

Europa Study Unit
Tonny E. Van Loij
3002 S. Xanthia St.
Denver CO 80231-4237
www.europastudyunit.org/
E-mail: tvanloij@gmail.com

Fine & Performing Arts
Deborah L. Washington
6922 S. Jeffery Blvd., #7 - North
Chicago IL 60649
E-mail: brasslady@comcast.net

Fire Service in Philately
John Zaranek
81 Hillpine Road
Cheektowaga NY 14227-2259
Ph: (716) 668-3352
E-mail: jczaranek@roadrunner.com

Gay & Lesbian History on Stamps Club
Joe Petronie
P.O. Box 190842
Dallas TX 75219-0842
www.facebook.com/glhsc
E-mail: glhsc@aol.com

Gems, Minerals & Jewelry Study Unit
Mrs. Gilberte Proteau
138 Lafontaine
Beloeil QC J3G 2G7
CANADA
Ph: (978) 851-8283
E-mail: gilberte.ferland@sympatico.ca

Graphics Philately Association
Mark H. Winnegrad
P.O. Box 380
Bronx NY 10462-0380
www.graphics-stamps.org
E-mail: indybruce1@yahoo.com

Journalists, Authors & Poets on Stamps
Ms. Lee Straayer
P.O. Box 6808
Champaign IL 61826
E-mail: lstraayer@dcbnet.com

Lighthouse Stamp Society
Dalene Thomas
8612 W. Warren Lane
Lakewood CO 80227-2352
Ph: (303) 986-6620
www.lighthousestampsociety.org
E-mail: dalene@lighthousestampsociety.org

Lions International Stamp Club
John Bargus
108-2777 Barry Road RR 2
Mill Bay, BC, V0R 2P2
CANADA
Ph: (250) 743-5782

Mahatma Gandhi On Stamps Study Circle
Pramod Shivagunde
Pratik Clinic, Akluj
Solapur, Maharashtra, 413101
INDIA
E-mail: drnanda@bom6.vsnl.net.in

Masonic Study Unit
Stanley R. Longenecker
930 Wood St.
Mount Joy PA 17552-1926
Ph: (717) 669-9094
E-mail: natsco@usa.net

Mathematical Study Unit
Monty J. Strauss
4209 88th St.
Lubbock TX 79423-2041
www.mathstamps.org
E-mail: montystrauss@gmail.com

Medical Subjects Unit
Dr. Frederick C. Skvara
P.O. Box 6228
Bridgewater NJ 08807
E-mail: fcskvara@optonline.net

Military Postal History Society
Ed Dubin
1 S. Wacker Drive, Suite 3500
Chicago IL 60606
www.militaryPHS.org
E-mail: dubine@comcast.net

Mourning Stamps and Covers Club
James Bailey, Jr.
P.O. Box 937
Brownwood TX 76804
E-mail: jfbailey238@directtv.net

Napoleonic Age Philatelists
Ken Berry
4117 NW 146th St.
Oklahoma City OK 73134-1746
Ph: (405) 748-8646
www.nap-stamps.org
E-mail: krb4117@att.net

Old World Archeological Study Unit
Caroline Scannell
11 Dawn Drive
Smithtown NY 11787-1761
www.owasu.org
E-mail: editor@owasu.org

Petroleum Philatelic Society International
Dr. Chris Coggins
174 Old Bedford Road
Luton, England, LU2 7HW
UNITED KINGDOM
E-mail: WAMTECH@Luton174.fsnet.co.uk

Rotary on Stamps Unit
Gerald L. Fitzsimmons
105 Calla Ricardo
Victoria TX 77904
rotaryonstamps.org
E-mail: glfitz@suddenlink.net

Scouts on Stamps Society International
Lawrence Clay
P.O. Box 6228
Kennewick WA 99336
Ph: (509) 735-3731
www.sossi.org
E-mail: rfrank@sossi.org

Ships on Stamps Unit
Les Smith
302 Conklin Ave.
Penticton, BC, V2A 2T4
CANADA
Ph: (250) 493-7486
www.shipsonstamps.org
E-mail: lessmith440@shaw.ca

Space Unit
Carmine Torrisi
P.O. Box 780241
Maspeth NY 11378
Ph: (917) 620-5687
stargate.1usa.com/stamps/
E-mail: ctorrisi1@nyc.rr.com

Sports Philatelists International
Mark Maestrone
2824 Curie Place
San Diego CA 92122-4110
www.sportstamps.org
Email: president@sportstamps.org

Stamps on Stamps Collectors Club
Alf Jordan
156 W. Elm St.
Yarmouth ME 04096
www.stampsonstamps.org
E-mail: ajordan1@maine.rr.com

Windmill Study Unit
Walter J. Hollien
607 N. Porter St.
Watkins Glenn NY 14891-1345
Ph: (862) 812-0030
E-mail: whollien@earthlink.net

Wine On Stamps Study Unit
David Wolfersberger
768 Chain Ridge Road
St. Louis MO 63122-3259
Ph: (314) 961-5032
www.wine-on-stamps.org
E-mail: dewolf2@swbell.net

Women on Stamps Study Unit
Hugh Gottfried
2232 26th St.
Santa Monica CA 90405-1902
E-mail: hgottfried@adelphia.net

Expertizing Services

The following organizations will, for a fee, provide expert opinions about stamps submitted to them. Collectors should contact these organizations to find out about their fees and requirements before submiting philatelic material to them. The listing of these groups here is not intended as an endorsement by Amos Media Co.

General Expertizing Services

American Philatelic Expertizing Service (a service of the American Philatelic Society)
100 Match Factory Place
Bellefonte PA 16823-1367
Ph: (814) 237-3803
Fax: (814) 237-6128
www.stamps.org
E-mail: ambristo@stamps.org
Areas of Expertise: Worldwide

B. P. A. Expertising, Ltd.
P.O. Box 1141
Guildford, Surrey, GU5 0WR
UNITED KINGDOM
E-mail: sec@bpaexpertising.org
Areas of Expertise: British Commonwealth, Great Britain, Classics of Europe, South America and the Far East

Philatelic Foundation
341 W. 38th St., 5th Floor
New York NY 10018
Ph: (212) 221-6555
Fax: (212) 221-6208
www.philatelicfoundation.org
E-mail: philatelicfoundation@verizon.net
Areas of Expertise: U.S. & Worldwide

Philatelic Stamp Authentication and Grading, Inc.
P.O. Box 41-0880
Melbourne FL 32941-0880
Customer Service: (305) 345-9864
www.psaginc.com
E-mail: info@psaginc.com
Areas of Expertise: U.S., Canal Zone, Hawaii, Philippines, Canada & Provinces

Professional Stamp Experts
P.O. Box 6170
Newport Beach CA 92658
Ph: (877) STAMP-88
Fax: (949) 833-7955
www.collectors.com/pse
E-mail: pseinfo@collectors.com
Areas of Expertise: Stamps and covers of U.S., U.S. Possessions, British Commonwealth

Royal Philatelic Society Expert Committee
41 Devonshire Place
London, W1N 1PE
UNITED KINGDOM
www.rpsl.org.uk/experts.html
E-mail: experts@rpsl.org.uk
Areas of Expertise: Worldwide

Expertizing Services Covering Specific Fields Or Countries

China Stamp Society Expertizing Service
1050 W. Blue Ridge Blvd.
Kansas City MO 64145
Ph: (816) 942-6300
E-mail: hjmesq@aol.com
Areas of Expertise: China

Confederate Stamp Alliance Authentication Service
Gen. Frank Crown, Jr.
P.O. Box 278
Capshaw AL 35742-0396
Ph: (302) 422-2656
Fax: (302) 424-1990
www.csalliance.org
E-mail: csaas@knology.net
Areas of Expertise: Confederate stamps and postal history

Errors, Freaks and Oddities Collectors Club Expertizing Service
138 East Lakemont Drive
Kingsland GA 31548
Ph: (912) 729-1573
Areas of Expertise: U.S. errors, freaks and oddities

Estonian Philatelic Society Expertizing Service
39 Clafford Lane
Melville NY 11747
Ph: (516) 421-2078
E-mail: esto4@aol.com
Areas of Expertise: Estonia

Hawaiian Philatelic Society Expertizing Service
P.O. Box 10115
Honolulu HI 96816-0115
Areas of Expertise: Hawaii

Hong Kong Stamp Society Expertizing Service
P.O. Box 206
Glenside PA 19038
Fax: (215) 576-6850
Areas of Expertise: Hong Kong

International Association of Philatelic Experts United States Associate members:

Paul Buchsbayew
119 W. 57th St.
New York NY 10019
Ph: (212) 977-7734
Fax: (212) 977-8653
Areas of Expertise: Russia, Soviet Union

William T. Crowe
P.O. Box 2090
Danbury CT 06813-2090
E-mail: wtcrowe@aol.com
Areas of Expertise: United States

John Lievsay
(see American Philatelic Expertizing Service and Philatelic Foundation)
Areas of Expertise: France

Robert W. Lyman
P.O. Box 348
Irvington on Hudson NY 10533
Ph and Fax: (914) 591-6937
Areas of Expertise: British North America, New Zealand

Robert Odenweller
P.O. Box 401
Bernardsville NJ 07924-0401
Ph and Fax: (908) 766-5460
Areas of Expertise: New Zealand, Samoa to 1900

Sergio Sismondo
The Regency Tower, Suite 1109
770 James Street
Syracuse NY 13203
Ph: (315) 422-2331
Fax: (315) 422-2956
Areas of Expertise: British East Africa, Camerouns, Cape of Good Hope, Canada, British North America

International Society for Japanese Philately Expertizing Committee
132 North Pine Terrace
Staten Island NY 10312-4052
Ph: (718) 227-5229
Areas of Expertise: Japan and related areas, except WWII Japanese Occupation issues

International Society for Portuguese Philately Expertizing Service
P.O. Box 43146
Philadelphia PA 19129-3146
Ph and Fax: (215) 843-2106
E-mail: s.s.washburne@worldnet.att.net
Areas of Expertise: Portugal and Colonies

Mexico-Elmhurst Philatelic Society International Expert Committee
P.O. Box 1133
West Covina CA 91793
Areas of Expertise: Mexico

Ukrainian Philatelic & Numismatic Society Expertizing Service
30552 Dell Lane
Warren MI 48092-1862
Areas of Expertise: Ukraine, Western Ukraine

V. G. Greene Philatelic Research Foundation
P.O. Box 204, Station Q
Toronto, ON, M4T 2M1
CANADA
Ph: (416) 921-2073
Fax: (416) 921-1282
www.greenefoundation.ca
E-mail: vggfoundation@on.aibn.com
Areas of Expertise: British North America

Information on Catalogue Values, Grade and Condition

Catalogue Value

The Scott Catalogue value is a retail value; that is, an amount you could expect to pay for a stamp in the grade of Very Fine with no faults. Any exceptions to the grade valued will be noted in the text. The general introduction on the following pages and the individual section introductions further explain the type of material that is valued. The value listed for any given stamp is a reference that reflects recent actual dealer selling prices for that item.

Dealer retail price lists, public auction results, published prices in advertising and individual solicitation of retail prices from dealers, collectors and specialty organizations have been used in establishing the values found in this catalogue. Amos Media Co. values stamps, but Amos Media is not a company engaged in the business of buying and selling stamps as a dealer.

Use this catalogue as a guide for buying and selling. The actual price you pay for a stamp may be higher or lower than the catalogue value because of many different factors, including the amount of personal service a dealer offers, or increased or decreased interest in the country or topic represented by a stamp or set. An item may occasionally be offered at a lower price as a "loss leader," or as part of a special sale. You also may obtain an item inexpensively at public auction because of little interest at that time or as part of a large lot.

Stamps that are of a lesser grade than Very Fine, or those with condition problems, generally trade at lower prices than those given in this catalogue. Stamps of exceptional quality in both grade and condition often command higher prices than those listed.

Values for pre-1900 unused issues are for stamps with approximately half or more of their original gum. Stamps with most or all of their original gum may be expected to sell for more, and stamps with less than half of their original gum may be expected to sell for somewhat less than the values listed. On rarer stamps, it may be expected that the original gum will be somewhat more disturbed than it will be on more common issues. Post-1900 unused issues are assumed to have full original gum. From breakpoints in most countries' listings, stamps are valued as never hinged, due to the wide availability of stamps in that condition. These notations are prominently placed in the listings and in the country information preceding the listings. Some countries also feature listings with dual values for hinged and never-hinged stamps.

Grade

A stamp's grade and condition are crucial to its value. The accompanying illustrations show examples of Very Fine stamps from different time periods, along with examples of stamps in Fine to Very Fine and Extremely Fine grades as points of reference. When a stamp seller offers a stamp in any grade from fine to superb without further qualifying statements, that stamp should not only have the centering grade as defined, but it also should be free of faults or other condition problems.

FINE stamps (illustrations not shown) have designs that are quite off center, with the perforations on one or two sides very close to the design but not quite touching it. There is white space between the perforations and the design that is minimal but evident to the unaided eye. Imperforate stamps may have small margins, and earlier issues may show the design just touching one edge of the stamp design. Very early perforated issues normally will have the perforations slightly cutting into the design. Used stamps may have heavier than usual cancellations.

FINE-VERY FINE stamps will be somewhat off center on one side, or slightly off center on two sides. Imperforate stamps will have two margins of at least normal size, and the design will not touch any edge. For perforated stamps, the perfs are well clear of the design, but are still noticeably off center. *However, early issues of a country may be printed in such a way that the design naturally is very close to the edges. In these cases, the perforations may cut into the design very slightly.* Used stamps will not have a cancellation that detracts from the design.

VERY FINE stamps will be just slightly off center on one or two sides, but the design will be well clear of the edge. The stamp will present a nice, balanced appearance. Imperforate stamps will be well centered within normal-sized margins. *However, early issues of many countries may be printed in such a way that the perforations may touch the design on one or more sides. Where this is the case, a boxed note will be found defining the centering and margins of the stamps being valued.* Used stamps will have light or otherwise neat cancellations. This is the grade used to establish Scott Catalogue values.

EXTREMELY FINE stamps are close to being perfectly centered. Imperforate stamps will have even margins that are slightly larger than normal. Even the earliest perforated issues will have perforations clear of the design on all sides.

Amos Media Co. recognizes that there is no formally enforced grading scheme for postage stamps, and that the final price you pay or obtain for a stamp will be determined by individual agreement at the time of transaction.

Condition

Grade addresses only centering and (for used stamps) cancellation. *Condition* refers to factors other than grade that affect a stamp's desirability.

Factors that can increase the value of a stamp include exceptionally wide margins, particularly fresh color, the presence of selvage, and plate or die varieties. Unusual cancels on used stamps (particularly those of the 19th century) can greatly enhance their value as well.

Factors other than faults that decrease the value of a stamp include loss of original gum, regumming, a hinge remnant or foreign object adhering to the gum, natural inclusions, straight edges, and markings or notations applied by collectors or dealers.

Faults include missing pieces, tears, pin or other holes, surface scuffs, thin spots, creases, toning, short or pulled perforations, clipped perforations, oxidation or other forms of color changelings, soiling, stains, and such man-made changes as reperforations or the chemical removal or lightening of a cancellation.

Grading Illustrations

On the following two pages are illustrations of various stamps from countries appearing in this volume. These stamps are arranged by country, and they represent early or important issues that are often found in widely different grades in the marketplace. The editors believe the illustrations will prove useful in showing the margin size and centering that will be seen on the various issues.

In addition to the matters of margin size and centering, collectors are reminded that the very fine stamps valued in the Scott catalogues also will possess fresh color and intact perforations, and they will be free from defects.

Examples shown are computer-manipulated images made from single digitized master illustrations.

Stamp Illustrations Used in the Catalogue

It is important to note that the stamp images used for identification purposes in this catalogue may not be indicative of the grade of stamp being valued. Refer to the written discussion of grades on this page and to the grading illustrations on the following two pages for grading information.

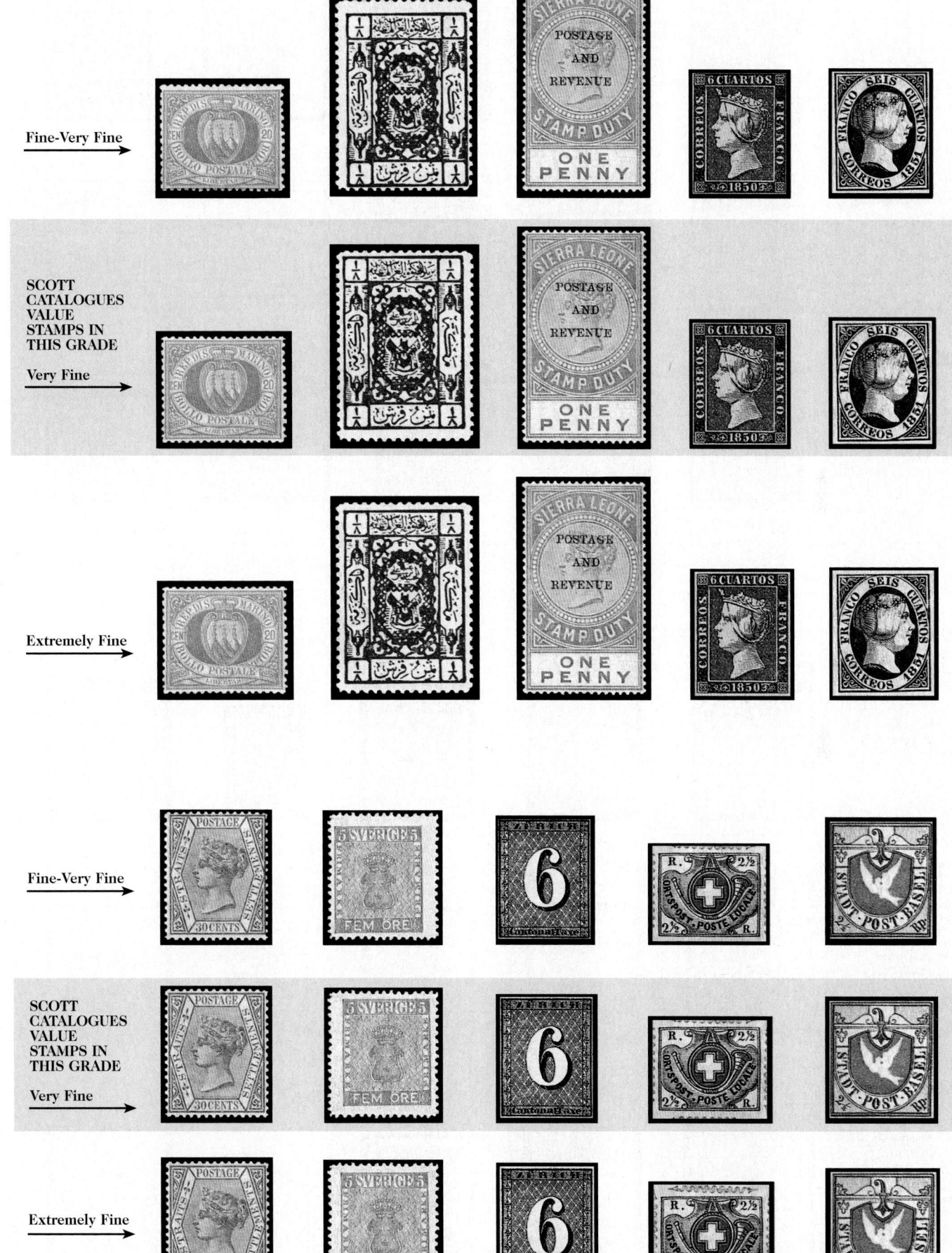

Fine-Very Fine

SCOTT
CATALOGUES
VALUE
STAMPS IN
THIS GRADE

Very Fine

Extremely Fine

Fine-Very Fine

SCOTT
CATALOGUES
VALUE
STAMPS IN
THIS GRADE

Very Fine

Extremely Fine

Fine-Very Fine →

    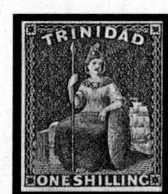

SCOTT CATALOGUES VALUE STAMPS IN THIS GRADE

Very Fine →

Extremely Fine →

    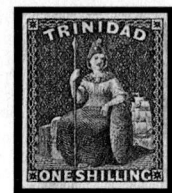

Fine-Very Fine →

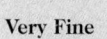

SCOTT CATALOGUES VALUE STAMPS IN THIS GRADE

Very Fine →

Extremely Fine →

For purposes of helping to determine the gum condition and value of an unused stamp, Scott presents the following chart which details different gum conditions and indicates how the conditions correlate with the Scott values for unused stamps. Used together, the Illustrated Grading Chart on the previous pages and this Illustrated Gum Chart should allow catalogue users to better understand the grade and gum condition of stamps valued in the Scott catalogues.

Gum Categories:	MINT N.H.	ORIGINAL GUM (O.G.)				NO GUM
	Mint Never Hinged *Free from any disturbance*	**Lightly Hinged** *Faint impression of a removed hinge over a small area*	**Hinge Mark or Remnant** *Prominent hinged spot with part or all of the hinge remaining*	**Large part o.g.** *Approximately half or more of the gum intact*	**Small part o.g.** *Approximately less than half of the gum intact*	**No gum** *Only if issued with gum*
Commonly Used Symbol:	★★	★	★	★	★	(★)
Pre-1900 Issues (Pre-1881 for U.S.)	*Very fine pre-1900 stamps in these categories trade at a premium over Scott value*			Scott Value for "Unused"		Scott "No Gum" listings for selected unused classic stamps
From 1900 to break-points for listings of never-hinged stamps	Scott "Never Hinged" listings for selected unused stamps	Scott Value for "Unused" (Actual value will be affected by the degree of hinging of the full o.g.)				
From breakpoints noted for many countries	Scott Value for "Unused"					

Never Hinged (NH; ★★): A never-hinged stamp will have full original gum that will have no hinge mark or disturbance. The presence of an expertizer's mark does not disqualify a stamp from this designation.

Original Gum (OG; ★): Pre-1900 stamps should have approximately half or more of their original gum. On rarer stamps, it may be expected that the original gum will be somewhat more disturbed than it will be on more common issues. Post-1900 stamps should have full original gum. Original gum will show some disturbance caused by a previous hinge(s) which may be present or entirely removed. The actual value of a post-1900 stamp will be affected by the degree of hinging of the full original gum.

Disturbed Original Gum: Gum showing noticeable effects of humidity, climate or hinging over more than half of the gum. The significance of gum disturbance in valuing a stamp in any of the Original Gum categories depends on the degree of disturbance, the rarity and normal gum condition of the issue and other variables affecting quality.

Regummed (RG; (★)): A regummed stamp is a stamp without gum that has had some type of gum privately applied at a time after it was issued. This normally is done to deceive collectors and/or dealers into thinking that the stamp has original gum and therefore has a higher value. A regummed stamp is considered the same as a stamp with none of its original gum for purposes of grading.

Understanding the Listings

On the opposite page is an enlarged "typical" listing from this catalogue. Below are detailed explanations of each of the highlighted parts of the listing.

1 **Scott number** — Scott catalogue numbers are used to identify specific items when buying, selling or trading stamps. Each listed postage stamp from every country has a unique Scott catalogue number. Therefore, Germany Scott 99, for example, can only refer to a single stamp. Although the Scott catalogue usually lists stamps in chronological order by date of issue, there are exceptions. When a country has issued a set of stamps over a period of time, those stamps within the set are kept together without regard to date of issue. This follows the normal collecting approach of keeping stamps in their natural sets.

When a country issues a set of stamps over a period of time, a group of consecutive catalogue numbers is reserved for the stamps in that set, as issued. If that group of numbers proves to be too few, capital-letter suffixes, such as "A" or "B," may be added to existing numbers to create enough catalogue numbers to cover all items in the set. A capital-letter suffix indicates a major Scott catalogue number listing. Scott generally uses a suffix letter only once. Therefore, a catalogue number listing with a capital-letter suffix will seldom be found with the same letter (lower case) used as a minor-letter listing. If there is a Scott 16A in a set, for example, there will seldom be a Scott 16a. However, a minor-letter "a" listing may be added to a major number containing an "A" suffix (Scott 16Aa, for example).

Suffix letters are cumulative. A minor "b" variety of Scott 16A would be Scott 16Ab, not Scott 16b.

There are times when a reserved block of Scott catalogue numbers is too large for a set, leaving some numbers unused. Such gaps in the numbering sequence also occur when the catalogue editors move an item's listing elsewhere or have removed it entirely from the catalogue. Scott does not attempt to account for every possible number, but rather attempts to assure that each stamp is assigned its own number.

Scott numbers designating regular postage normally are only numerals. Scott numbers for other types of stamps, such as air post, semi-postal, postal tax, postage due, occupation and others have a prefix consisting of one or more capital letters or a combination of numerals and capital letters.

2 **Illustration number** — Illustration or design-type numbers are used to identify each catalogue illustration. For most sets, the lowest face-value stamp is shown. It then serves as an example of the basic design approach for other stamps not illustrated. Where more than one stamp use the same illustration number, but have differences in design, the design paragraph or the description line clearly indicates the design on each stamp not illustrated. Where there are both vertical and horizontal designs in a set, a single illustration may be used, with the exceptions noted in the design paragraph or description line.

When an illustration is followed by a lower-case letter in parentheses, such as "A2(b)," the trailing letter indicates which overprint or surcharge illustration applies.

Illustrations normally are 70 percent of the original size of the stamp. Oversized stamps, blocks and souvenir sheets are reduced even more. Overprints and surcharges are shown at 100 percent of their original size if shown alone, but are 70 percent of original size if shown on stamps. In some cases, the illustration will be placed above the set, between listings or omitted completely. Overprint and surcharge illustrations are not placed in this catalogue for purposes of expertizing stamps.

3 **Paper color** — The color of a stamp's paper is noted in italic type when the paper used is not white.

4 **Listing styles** — There are two principal types of catalogue listings: major and minor.

Major listings are in a larger type style than minor listings. The catalogue number is a numeral that can be found with or without a capital-letter suffix, and with or without a prefix.

Minor listings are in a smaller type style and have a small-letter suffix or (if the listing immediately follows that of the major number) may show only the letter. These listings identify a variety of the major item. Examples include perforation and shade differences, multiples (some souvenir sheets, booklet panes and se-tenant combinations), and singles of multiples.

Examples of major number listings include 16, 28A, B97, C13A, 10N5, and 10N6A. Examples of minor numbers are 16a and C13Ab.

5 **Basic information about a stamp or set** — Introducing each stamp issue is a small section (usually a line listing) of basic information about a stamp or set. This section normally includes the date of issue, method of printing, perforation, watermark and, sometimes, some additional information of note. *Printing method, perforation and watermark apply to the following sets until a change is noted.* Stamps created by overprinting or surcharging previous issues are assumed to have the same perforation, watermark, printing method and other production characteristics as the original. Dates of issue are as precise as Scott is able to confirm and often reflect the dates on first-day covers, rather than the actual date of release.

6 **Denomination** — This normally refers to the face value of the stamp; that is, the cost of the unused stamp at the post office at the time of issue. When a denomination is shown in parentheses, it does not appear on the stamp. This includes the non-denominated stamps of the United States, Brazil and Great Britain, for example.

7 **Color or other description** — This area provides information to solidify identification of a stamp. In many recent cases, a description of the stamp design appears in this space, rather than a listing of colors.

8 **Year of issue** — In stamp sets that have been released in a period that spans more than a year, the number shown in parentheses is the year that stamp first appeared. Stamps without a date appeared during the first year of the issue. Dates are not always given for minor varieties.

9 **Value unused and Value used** — The Scott catalogue values are based on stamps that are in a grade of Very Fine unless stated otherwise. Unused values refer to items that have not seen postal, revenue or any other duty for which they were intended. Pre-1900 unused stamps that were issued with gum must have at least most of their original gum. Later issues are assumed to have full original gum. From breakpoints specified in most countries' listings, stamps are valued as never hinged. Stamps issued without gum are noted. Modern issues with PVA or other synthetic adhesives may appear ungummed. Unused self-adhesive stamps are valued as appearing undisturbed on their original backing paper. Values for used self-adhesive stamps are for examples either on piece or off piece. For a more detailed explanation of these values, please see the "Catalogue Value," "Condition" and "Understanding Valuing Notations" sections elsewhere in this introduction.

In some cases, where used stamps are more valuable than unused stamps, the value is for an example with a contemporaneous cancel, rather than a modern cancel or a smudge or other unclear marking. For those stamps that were released for postal and fiscal purposes, the used value represents a postally used stamp. Stamps with revenue cancels generally sell for less.

Stamps separated from a complete se-tenant multiple usually will be worth less than a pro-rated portion of the se-tenant multiple, and stamps lacking the attached labels that are noted in the listings will be worth less than the values shown.

10 **Changes in basic set information** — Bold type is used to show any changes in the basic data given for a set of stamps. These basic data categories include perforation gauge measurement, paper type, printing method and watermark.

11 **Total value of a set** — The total value of sets of three or more stamps issued after 1900 are shown. The set line also notes the range of Scott numbers and total number of stamps included in the grouping. The actual value of a set consisting predominantly of stamps having the minimum value of 25 cents may be less than the total value shown. Similarly, the actual value or catalogue value of se-tenant pairs or of blocks consisting of stamps having the minimum value of 25 cents may be less than the catalogue values of the component parts.

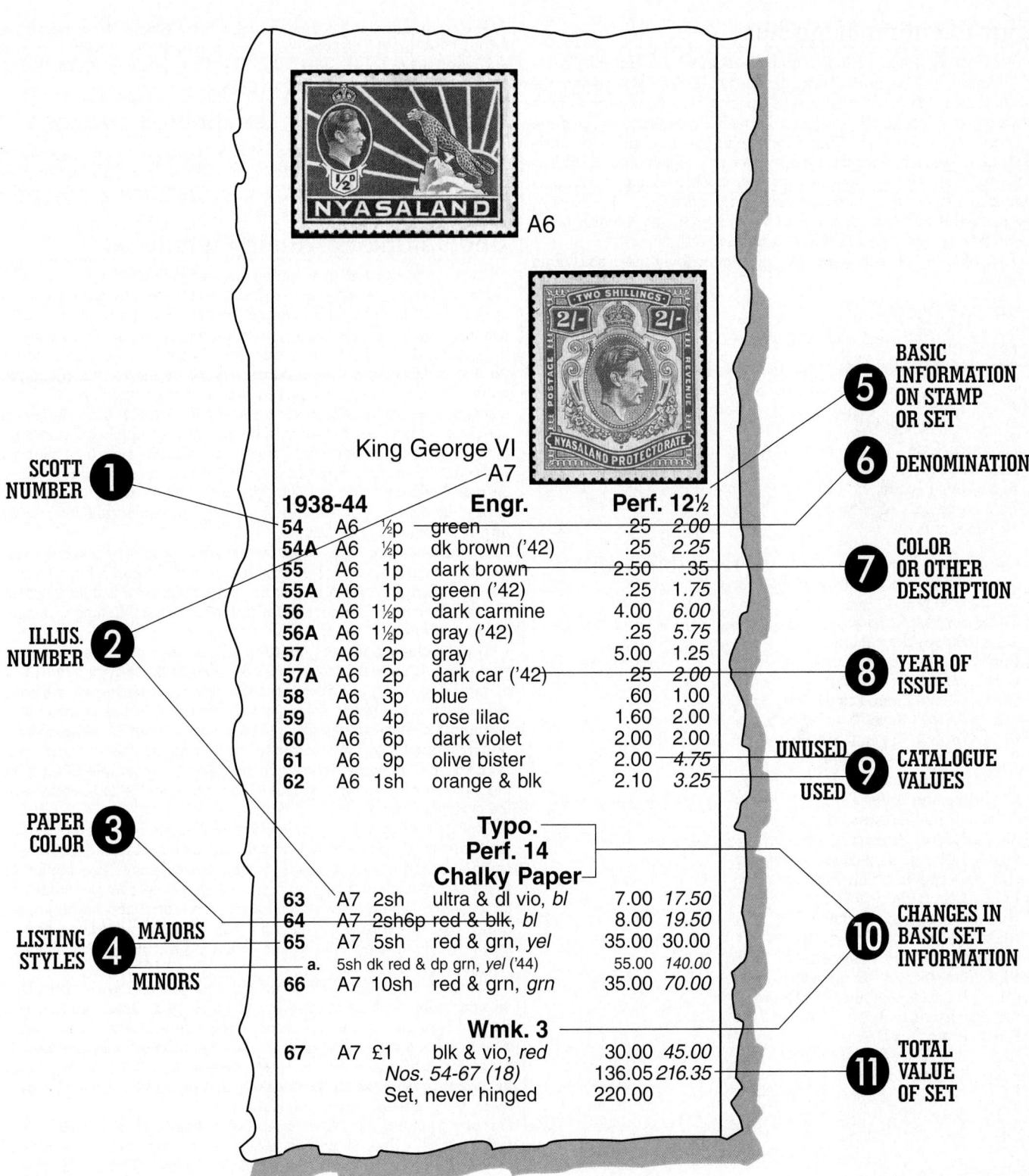

SCOTT NUMBER ❶

ILLUS. NUMBER ❷

PAPER COLOR ❸

LISTING STYLES ❹ MAJORS / MINORS

A6

King George VI
A7

				UNUSED	USED
1938-44			**Engr.**	**Perf. 12½**	
54	A6	½p	green	.25	2.00
54A	A6	½p	dk brown ('42)	.25	2.25
55	A6	1p	dark brown	2.50	.35
55A	A6	1p	green ('42)	.25	1.75
56	A6	1½p	dark carmine	4.00	6.00
56A	A6	1½p	gray ('42)	.25	5.75
57	A6	2p	gray	5.00	1.25
57A	A6	2p	dark car ('42)	.25	2.00
58	A6	3p	blue	.60	1.00
59	A6	4p	rose lilac	1.60	2.00
60	A6	6p	dark violet	2.00	2.00
61	A6	9p	olive bister	2.00	4.75
62	A6	1sh	orange & blk	2.10	3.25

Typo.
Perf. 14
Chalky Paper

63	A7	2sh	ultra & dl vio, *bl*	7.00	17.50
64	A7	2sh6p	red & blk, *bl*	8.00	19.50
65	A7	5sh	red & grn, *yel*	35.00	30.00
a.			5sh dk red & dp grn, *yel* ('44)	55.00	140.00
66	A7	10sh	red & grn, *grn*	35.00	70.00

Wmk. 3

67	A7	£1	blk & vio, *red*	30.00	45.00
			Nos. 54-67 (18)	136.05	216.35
			Set, never hinged	220.00	

❺ BASIC INFORMATION ON STAMP OR SET

❻ DENOMINATION

❼ COLOR OR OTHER DESCRIPTION

❽ YEAR OF ISSUE

❾ CATALOGUE VALUES

❿ CHANGES IN BASIC SET INFORMATION

⓫ TOTAL VALUE OF SET

Special Notices

Classification of stamps

The *Scott Standard Postage Stamp Catalogue* lists stamps by country of issue. The next level of organization is a listing by section on the basis of the function of the stamps. The principal sections cover regular postage, semi-postal, air post, special delivery, registration, postage due and other categories. Except for regular postage, catalogue numbers for all sections include a prefix letter (or number-letter combination) denoting the class to which a given stamp belongs. When some countries issue sets containing stamps from more than one category, the catalogue will at times list all of the stamps in one category (such as air post stamps listed as part of a postage set).

The following is a listing of the most commonly used catalogue prefixes.

Prefix .... Category
C.........Air Post
M........Military
P.........Newspaper
N...........Occupation - Regular Issues
O ....Official
Q ....Parcel Post
J ....Postage Due
RA ......Postal Tax
B ....Semi-Postal
E ....Special Delivery
MR......War Tax

Other prefixes used by more than one country include the following:
H.........Acknowledgment of Receipt
I ....Late Fee
CO......Air Post Official
CQ......Air Post Parcel Post
RAC....Air Post Postal Tax
CF ......Air Post Registration
CB ......Air Post Semi-Postal
CBO ...Air Post Semi-Postal Official
CE ......Air Post Special Delivery
EY.......Authorized Delivery
S.........Franchise
G ....Insured Letter
GY......Marine Insurance
MC .....Military Air Post
MQ .....Military Parcel Post
NC......Occupation - Air Post
NO......Occupation - Official
NJ........Occupation - Postage Due
NRA....Occupation - Postal Tax
NB ......Occupation - Semi-Postal
NE ......Occupation - Special Delivery
QY......Parcel Post Authorized Delivery
AR ......Postal-fiscal
RAJ .....Postal Tax Due
RAB ....Postal Tax Semi-Postal
F ....Registration
EB.......Semi-Postal Special Delivery
EO ......Special Delivery Official
QE......Special Handling

New issue listings

Updates to this catalogue appear each month in the *Linn's Stamp News* monthly magazine. Included in this update are additions to the listings of countries found in the *Scott Standard Postage Stamp Catalogue* and the *Specialized Catalogue of United States Stamps and Covers*, as well as corrections and updates to current editions of this catalogue.

From time to time there will be changes in the final listings of stamps from the *Linn's Stamp News* magazine to the next edition of the catalogue. This occurs as more information about certain stamps or sets becomes available.

The catalogue update section of the *Linn's Stamp News* magazine is the most timely presentation of this material available. Annual subscriptions to *Linn's Stamp News* are available from Linn's Stamp News, Box 926, Sidney, OH 45365-0926.

Number additions, deletions & changes

A listing of catalogue number additions, deletions and changes from the previous edition of the catalogue appears in each volume. See Catalogue Number Additions, Deletions & Changes in the table of contents for the location of this list.

Understanding valuing notations

The *minimum catalogue value* of an individual stamp or set is 25 cents. This represents a portion of the cost incurred by a dealer when he prepares an individual stamp for resale. As a point of philatelic-economic fact, the lower the value shown for an item in this catalogue, the greater the percentage of that value is attributed to dealer mark up and profit margin. In many cases, such as the 25-cent minimum value, that price does not cover the labor or other costs involved with stocking it as an individual stamp. The sum of minimum values in a set does not properly represent the value of a complete set primarily composed of a number of minimum-value stamps, nor does the sum represent the actual value of a packet made up of minimum-value stamps. Thus a packet of 1,000 different common stamps — each of which has a catalogue value of 25 cents — normally sells for considerably less than 250 dollars!

The *absence of a retail value* for a stamp does not necessarily suggest that a stamp is scarce or rare. A dash in the value column means that the stamp is known in a stated form or variety, but information is either lacking or insufficient for purposes of establishing a usable catalogue value.

Stamp values in *italics* generally refer to items that are difficult to value accurately. For expensive items, such as those priced at $1,000 or higher, a value in italics indicates that the affected item trades very seldom. For inexpensive items, a value in italics represents a warning. One example is a "blocked" issue where the issuing postal administration may have controlled one stamp in a set in an attempt to make the whole set more valuable. Another example is an item that sold at an extreme multiple of face value in the marketplace at the time of its issue.

One type of warning to collectors that appears in the catalogue is illustrated by a stamp that is valued considerably higher in used condition than it is as unused. In this case, collectors are cautioned to be certain the used version has a genuine and contemporaneous cancellation. The type of cancellation on a stamp can be an important factor in determining its sale price. Catalogue values do not apply to fiscal, telegraph or non-contemporaneous postal cancels, unless otherwise noted.

Some countries have released back issues of stamps in canceled-to-order form, sometimes covering as much as a 10-year period. The Scott Catalogue values for used stamps reflect canceled-to-order material when such stamps are found to predominate in the marketplace for the issue involved. Notes frequently appear in the stamp listings to specify which items are valued as canceled-to-order, or if there is a premium for postally used examples.

Many countries sell canceled-to-order stamps at a marked reduction of face value. Countries that sell or have sold canceled-to-order stamps at *full* face value include United Nations, Australia, Netherlands, France and Switzerland. It may be almost impossible to identify such stamps if the gum has been removed, because official government canceling devices are used. Postally used examples of these items on cover, however, are usually worth more than the canceled-to-order stamps with original gum.

Abbreviations

Scott uses a consistent set of abbreviations throughout this catalogue to conserve space, while still providing necessary information.

COLOR ABBREVIATIONS

amb. amber	crim. crimson	ol ..... olive
anil.. aniline	cr ..... cream	olvn . olivine
ap.... apple	dk..... dark	org... orange
aqua aquamarine	dl..... dull	pck .. peacock
az .... azure	dp.... deep	pnksh pinkish
bis ... bister	db.... drab	Prus. Prussian
bl..... blue	emer emerald	pur... purple
bld... blood	gldn. golden	redsh reddish
blk... black	gryshgrayish	res ... reseda
bril... brilliant	grn... green	ros ... rosine
brn... brown	grnsh greenish	ryl.... royal
brnsh brownish	hel... heliotrope	sal ... salmon
brnz. bronze	hn.... henna	saph sapphire
brt.... bright	ind... indigo	scar . scarlet
brnt . burnt	int .... intense	sep .. sepia
car... carmine	lav .. lavender	sien . sienna
cer ... cerise	lem .. lemon	sil..... silver
chlky chalky	lil ..... lilac	sl...... slate
chamchamois	lt ...... light	stl .... steel
chnt . chestnut	mag. magenta	turq.. turquoise
choc chocolate	man. manila	ultra ultramarine
chr... chrome	mar.. maroon	Ven.. Venetian
cit .... citron	mv ... mauve	ver ... vermilion
cl...... claret	multi multicolored	vio ... violet
cob .. cobalt	mlky milky	yel ... yellow
cop .. copper	myr.. myrtle	yelsh yellowish

When no color is given for an overprint or surcharge, black is the color used. Abbreviations for colors used for overprints and surcharges include: "(B)" or "(Blk)," black; "(Bl)," blue; "(R)," red; and "(G)," green.

Additional abbreviations in this catalogue are shown below:

Adm.	Administration
AFL................	American Federation of Labor
Anniv.............	Anniversary
APS	American Philatelic Society
Assoc.	Association
ASSR.	Autonomous Soviet Socialist Republic
b.	Born
BEP...............	Bureau of Engraving and Printing
Bicent............	Bicentennial
Bklt.	Booklet
Brit................	British
btwn.	Between
Bur................	Bureau
c. or ca.........	Circa
Cat.	Catalogue
Cent.	Centennial, century, centenary
CIO	Congress of Industrial Organizations
Conf.	Conference
Cong.............	Congress
Cpl.	Corporal
CTO	Canceled to order
d.	Died
Dbl.	Double
EDU..............	Earliest documented use
Engr.	Engraved
Exhib.............	Exhibition
Expo..............	Exposition
Fed.	Federation
GB................	Great Britain
Gen.	General
GPO	General post office
Horiz.	Horizontal
Imperf.	Imperforate
Impt...............	Imprint

Intl.	International
Invtd.............	Inverted
L	Left
Lieut., lt........	Lieutenant
Litho.............	Lithographed
LL	Lower left
LR	Lower right
mm	Millimeter
Ms.	Manuscript
Natl.	National
No................	Number
NY	New York
NYC	New York City
Ovpt.	Overprint
Ovptd...........	Overprinted
P	Plate number
Perf..............	Perforated, perforation
Phil..............	Philatelic
Photo...........	Photogravure
PO	Post office
Pr.	Pair
PR................	Puerto Rico
Prec..............	Precancel, precanceled
Pres..............	President
PTT..............	Post, Telephone and Telegraph
R	Right
Rio...............	Rio de Janeiro
Sgt................	Sergeant
Soc.	Society
Souv.	Souvenir
SSR..............	Soviet Socialist Republic, see ASSR
St.................	Saint, street
Surch.	Surcharge
Typo.	Typographed
UL................	Upper left
Unwmkd.	Unwatermarked
UPU..............	Universal Postal Union
UR	Upper Right
US	United States
USPOD	United States Post Office Department
USSR	Union of Soviet Socialist Republics
Vert..............	Vertical
VP................	Vice president
Wmk.............	Watermark
Wmkd.	Watermarked
WWI	World War I
WWII	World War II

Examination

Amos Media Co. will not comment upon the genuineness, grade or condition of stamps, because of the time and responsibility involved. Rather, there are several expertizing groups that undertake this work for both collectors and dealers. Neither will Amos Media Co. appraise or identify philatelic material. The company cannot take responsibility for unsolicited stamps or covers sent by individuals.

All letters, E-mails, etc. are read attentively, but they are not always answered due to time considerations.

How to order from your dealer

When ordering stamps from a dealer, it is not necessary to write the full description of a stamp as listed in this catalogue. All you need is the name of the country, the Scott catalogue number and whether the desired item is unused or used. For example, "Japan Scott 422 unused" is sufficient to identify the unused stamp of Japan listed as "422 A206 5y brown."

Catalogue Listing Policy

It is the intent of Amos Media Co. to list all postage stamps of the world in the *Scott Standard Postage Stamp Catalogue*. The only strict criteria for listing is that stamps be decreed legal for postage by the issuing country and that the issuing country actually have an operating postal system. Whether the primary intent of issuing a given stamp or set was for sale to postal patrons or to stamp collectors is not part of our listing criteria. Scott's role is to provide basic comprehensive postage stamp information. It is up to each stamp collector to choose which items to include in a collection.

It is Scott's objective to seek reasons why a stamp should be listed, rather than why it should not. Nevertheless, there are certain types of items that will not be listed. These include the following:

1. Unissued items that are not officially distributed or released by the issuing postal authority. If such items are officially issued at a later date by the country, they will be listed. Unissued items consist of those that have been printed and then held from sale for reasons such as change in government, errors found on stamps or something deemed objectionable about a stamp subject or design.

2. Stamps "issued" by non-existent postal entities or fantasy countries, such as Nagaland, Occusi-Ambeno, Staffa, Sedang, Torres Straits and others. Also, stamps "issued" in the names of legitimate, stamp-issuing countries that are not authorized by those countries.

3. Semi-official or unofficial items not required for postage. Examples include items issued by private agencies for their own express services. When such items are required for delivery, or are valid as prepayment of postage, they are listed.

4. Local stamps issued for local use only. Postage stamps issued by governments specifically for "domestic" use, such as Haiti Scott 219-228, or the United States non-denominated stamps, are not considered to be locals, since they are valid for postage throughout the country of origin.

5. Items not valid for postal use. For example, a few countries have issued souvenir sheets that are not valid for postage. This area also includes a number of worldwide charity labels (some denominated) that do not pay postage.

6. Intentional varieties, such as imperforate stamps that look like their perforated counterparts and are usually issued in very small quantities. Also, other egregiously exploitative issues such as stamps sold for far more than face value, stamps purposely issued in artificially small quantities or only against advance orders, stamps awarded only to a selected audience such as a philatelic bureau's standing order customers, or stamps sold only in conjunction with other products. All of these kinds of items are usually controlled issues and/or are intended for speculation. These items normally will be included in a footnote.

7. Items distributed by the issuing government only to a limited group, club, philatelic exhibition or a single stamp dealer or other private company. These items normally will be included in a footnote.

8. Stamps not available to collectors. These generally are rare items, all of which are held by public institutions such as museums. The existence of such items often will be cited in footnotes.

The fact that a stamp has been used successfully as postage, even on international mail, is not in itself sufficient proof that it was legitimately issued. Numerous examples of so-called stamps from non-existent countries are known to have been used to post letters that have successfully passed through the international mail system.

There are certain items that are subject to interpretation. When a stamp falls outside our specifications, it may be listed along with a cautionary footnote.

A number of factors are considered in our approach to analyzing how a stamp is listed. The following list of factors is presented to share with you, the catalogue user, the complexity of the listing process.

Additional printings — "Additional printings" of a previously issued stamp may range from an item that is totally different to cases where it is impossible to differentiate from the original. At least a minor number (a small-letter suffix) is assigned if there is a distinct change in stamp shade, noticeably redrawn design, or a significantly different perforation measurement. A major number (numeral or numeral and capital-letter combination) is assigned if the editors feel the "additional printing" is sufficiently different from the original that it constitutes a different issue.

Commemoratives — Where practical, commemoratives with the same theme are placed in a set. For example, the U.S. Civil War Centennial set of 1961-65 and the Constitution Bicentennial series of 1989-90 appear as sets. Countries such as Japan and Korea issue such material on a regular basis, with an announced, or at least predictable, number of stamps known in advance. Occasionally, however, stamp sets that were released over a period of years have been separated. Appropriately placed footnotes will guide you to each set's continuation.

Definitive sets — Blocks of numbers generally have been reserved for definitive sets, based on previous experience with any given country. If a few more stamps were issued in a set than originally expected,

they often have been inserted into the original set with a capital-letter suffix, such as U.S. Scott 1059A. If it appears that many more stamps than the originally allotted block will be released before the set is completed, a new block of numbers will be reserved, with the original one being closed off. In some cases, such as the U.S. Transportation and Great Americans series, several blocks of numbers exist. Appropriately placed footnotes will guide you to each set's continuation.

New country — Membership in the Universal Postal Union is not a consideration for listing status or order of placement within the catalogue. The index will tell you in what volume or page number the listings begin.

"No release date" items — The amount of information available for any given stamp issue varies greatly from country to country and even from time to time. Extremely comprehensive information about new stamps is available from some countries well before the stamps are released. By contrast some countries do not provide information about stamps or release dates. Most countries, however, fall between these extremes. A country may provide denominations or subjects of stamps from upcoming issues that are not issued as planned. Sometimes, philatelic agencies, those private firms hired to represent countries, add these later-issued items to sets well after the formal release date. This time period can range from weeks to years. If these items were officially released by the country, they will be added to the appropriate spot in the set. In many cases, the specific release date of a stamp or set of stamps may never be known.

Overprints — The color of an overprint is always noted if it is other than black. Where more than one color of ink has been used on overprints of a single set, the color used is noted. Early overprint and surcharge illustrations are altered to prevent their use by forgers.

Personalized Stamps — Since 1999, the special service of personalizing stamp vignettes, or labels attached to stamps, has been offered to customers by postal administrations of many countries. Sheets of these stamps are sold, singly or in quantity, only through special orders made by mail, in person, or through a sale on a computer website with the postal administrations or their agents for which an extra fee is charged, though some countries offer to collectors at face value personalized stamps having generic images in the vignettes or on the attached labels. It is impossible for any catalogue to know what images have been chosen by customers. Images can be 1) owned or created by the customer, 2) a generic image, or 3) an image pulled from a library of stock images on the stamp creation website. It is also impossible to know the quantity printed for any stamp having a particular image. So from a valuing standpoint, any image is equivalent to any other image for any personalized stamp having the same catalogue number. Illustrations of personalized stamps in the catalogue are not always those of stamps having generic images.

Personalized items are listed with some exceptions. These include:
1. Stamps or sheets that have attached labels that the customer cannot personalize, but which are nonetheless marketed as "personalized," and are sold for far more than the franking value.
2. Stamps or sheets that can be personalized by the customer, but where a portion of the print run must be ceded to the issuing country for sale to other customers.
3. Stamps or sheets that are created exclusively for a particular commercial client, or clients, including stamps that differ from any similar stamp that has been made available to the public.
4. Stamps or sheets that are deliberately conceived by the issuing authority that have been, or are likely to be, created with an excessive number of different face values, sizes, or other features that are changeable.
5. Stamps or sheets that are created by postal administrations using the same system of stamp personalization that has been put in place for use by the public that are printed in limited quantities and sold above face value.
6. Stamps or sheets that are created by licensees not directly affiliated or controlled by a postal administration.

Excluded items may or may not be footnoted.

Se-tenants — Connected stamps of differing features (se-tenants) will be listed in the format most commonly collected. This includes pairs, blocks or larger multiples. Se-tenant units are not always symmetrical. An example is Australia Scott 508, which is a block of seven stamps. If the stamps are primarily collected as a unit, the major number may be assigned to the multiple, with minors going to each component stamp. In cases where continuous-design or other unit se-tenants will receive significant postal use, each stamp is given a major Scott number listing. This includes issues from the United States, Canada, Germany and Great Britain, for example.

Basic Stamp Information

A stamp collector's knowledge of the combined elements that make a given stamp issue unique determines his or her ability to identify stamps. These elements include paper, watermark, method of separation, printing, design and gum. On the following pages each of these important areas is briefly described.

Paper

Paper is an organic material composed of a compacted weave of cellulose fibers and generally formed into sheets. Paper used to print stamps may be manufactured in sheets, or it may have been part of a large roll (called a web) before being cut to size. The fibers most often used to create paper on which stamps are printed include bark, wood, straw and certain grasses. In many cases, linen or cotton rags have been added for greater strength and durability. Grinding, bleaching, cooking and rinsing these raw fibers reduces them to a slushy pulp, referred to by paper makers as "stuff." Sizing and, sometimes, coloring matter is added to the pulp to make different types of finished paper.

After the stuff is prepared, it is poured onto sieve-like frames that allow the water to run off, while retaining the matted pulp. As fibers fall onto the screen and are held by gravity, they form a natural weave that will later hold the paper together. If the screen has metal bits that are formed into letters or images attached, it leaves slightly thinned areas on the paper. These are called watermarks.

When the stuff is almost dry, it is passed under pressure through smooth or engraved rollers - dandy rolls - or placed between cloth in a press to be flattened and dried.

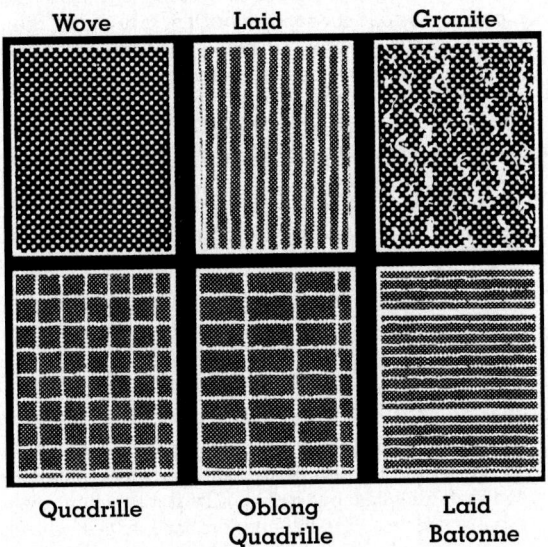

Stamp paper falls broadly into two types: wove and laid. The nature of the surface of the frame onto which the pulp is first deposited causes the differences in appearance between the two. If the surface is smooth and even, the paper will be of fairly uniform texture throughout. This is known as *wove paper*. Early papermaking machines poured the pulp onto a continuously circulating web of felt, but modern machines feed the pulp onto a cloth-like screen made of closely interwoven fine wires. This paper, when held to a light, will show little dots or points very close together. The proper name for this is "wire wove," but the type is still considered wove. Any U.S. or British stamp printed after 1880 will serve as an example of wire wove paper.

Closely spaced parallel wires, with cross wires at wider intervals, make up the frames used for what is known as *laid paper*. A greater thickness of the pulp will settle between the wires. The paper, when held to a light, will show alternate light and dark lines. The spacing and the thickness of the lines may vary, but on any one sheet of paper they are all alike. See Russia Scott 31-38 for examples of laid paper.

Batonne, from the French word meaning "a staff," is a term used if the lines in the paper are spaced quite far apart, like the printed ruling on a writing tablet. Batonne paper may be either wove or laid. If laid, fine laid lines can be seen between the batons.

Quadrille is the term used when the lines in the paper form little squares. *Oblong quadrille* is the term used when rectangles, rather than squares, are formed. Grid patterns vary from distinct to extremely faint. See Mexico-Guadalajara Scott 35-37 for examples of oblong quadrille paper.

Paper also is classified as thick or thin, hard or soft, and by color. Such colors may include yellowish, greenish, bluish and reddish.

Brief explanations of other types of paper used for printing stamps, as well as examples, follow.

Colored — Colored paper is created by the addition of dye in the paper-making process. Such colors may include shades of yellow, green, blue and red. *Surface-colored papers*, most commonly used for British colonial issues in 1913-14, are created when coloring is added only to the surface during the finishing process. Stamps printed on surface-colored paper have white or uncolored backs, while true colored papers are colored through. See Jamaica Scott 71-73.

Pelure — Pelure paper is a very thin, hard and often brittle paper that is sometimes bluish or grayish in appearance. See Serbia Scott 169-170.

Native — This is a term applied to handmade papers used to produce some of the early stamps of the Indian states. Stamps printed on native paper may be expected to display various natural inclusions that are normal and do not negatively affect value. Japanese paper, originally made of mulberry fibers and rice flour, is part of this group. See Japan Scott 1-18.

Manila — This type of paper is often used to make stamped envelopes and wrappers. It is a coarse-textured stock, usually smooth on one side and rough on the other. A variety of colors of manila paper exist, but the most common range is yellowish-brown.

Silk — Introduced by the British in 1847 as a safeguard against counterfeiting, silk paper contains bits of colored silk thread scattered throughout. The density of these fibers varies greatly and can include as few as one fiber per stamp or hundreds. U.S. revenue Scott R152 is a good example of an easy-to-identify silk paper stamp.

Silk-thread paper has uninterrupted threads of colored silk arranged so that one or more threads run through the stamp or postal stationery. See Great Britain Scott 5-6 and Switzerland Scott 14-19.

Granite — Filled with minute cloth or colored paper fibers of various colors and lengths, granite paper should not be confused with either type of silk paper. Austria Scott 172-175 and a number of Swiss stamps are examples of granite paper.

Chalky — A chalk-like substance coats the surface of chalky paper to discourage the cleaning and reuse of canceled stamps, as well as to provide a smoother, more acceptable printing surface. Because the designs of stamps printed on chalky paper are imprinted on what is often a water-soluble coating, any attempt to remove a cancellation will destroy the stamp. *Do not soak these stamps in any fluid.* To remove a stamp printed on chalky paper from an envelope, wet the paper from underneath the stamp until the gum dissolves enough to release the stamp from the paper. See St. Kitts-Nevis Scott 89-90 for examples of stamps printed on this type of chalky paper.

India — Another name for this paper, originally introduced from China about 1750, is "China Paper." It is a thin, opaque paper often used for plate and die proofs by many countries.

Double — In philately, the term double paper has two distinct meanings. The first is a two-ply paper, usually a combination of a thick and a thin sheet, joined during manufacture. This type was used experimentally as a means to discourage the reuse of stamps.

The design is printed on the thin paper. Any attempt to remove a cancellation would destroy the design. U.S. Scott 158 and other Banknote-era stamps exist on this form of double paper.

The second type of double paper occurs on a rotary press, when the end of one paper roll, or web, is affixed to the next roll to save

time feeding the paper through the press. Stamp designs are printed over the joined paper and, if overlooked by inspectors, may get into post office stocks.

Goldbeater's Skin — This type of paper was used for the 1866 issue of Prussia, and was a tough, translucent paper. The design was printed in reverse on the back of the stamp, and the gum applied over the printing. It is impossible to remove stamps printed on this type of paper from the paper to which they are affixed without destroying the design.

Ribbed — Ribbed paper has an uneven, corrugated surface made by passing the paper through ridged rollers. This type exists on some copies of U.S. Scott 156-165.

Various other substances, or substrates, have been used for stamp manufacture, including wood, aluminum, copper, silver and gold foil, plastic, and silk and cotton fabrics.

Watermarks

Watermarks are an integral part of some papers. They are formed in the process of paper manufacture. Watermarks consist of small designs, formed of wire or cut from metal and soldered to the surface of the mold or, sometimes, on the dandy roll. The designs may be in the form of crowns, stars, anchors, letters or other characters or symbols. These pieces of metal - known in the paper-making industry as "bits" - impress a design into the paper. The design sometimes may be seen by holding the stamp to the light. Some are more easily seen with a watermark detector. This important tool is a small black tray into which a stamp is placed face down and dampened with a fast-evaporating watermark detection fluid that brings up the watermark image in the form of dark lines against a lighter background. These dark lines are the thinner areas of the paper known as the watermark. Some watermarks are extremely difficult to locate, due to either a faint impression, watermark location or the color of the stamp. There also are electric watermark detectors that come with plastic filter disks of various colors. The disks neutralize the color of the stamp, permitting the watermark to be seen more easily.

Multiple watermarks of Crown Agents and Burma

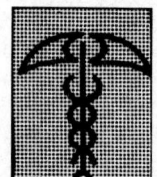  

Watermarks of Uruguay, Vatican City and Jamaica

WARNING: Some inks used in the photogravure process dissolve in watermark fluids (Please see the section on Soluble Printing Inks). Also, see "chalky paper."

Watermarks may be found normal, reversed, inverted, reversed and inverted, sideways or diagonal, as seen from the back of the stamp. The relationship of watermark to stamp design depends on the position of the printing plates or how paper is fed through the press. On machine-made paper, watermarks normally are read from right to left. The design is repeated closely throughout the sheet in a "multiple-watermark design." In a "sheet watermark," the design appears only once on the sheet, but extends over many stamps. Individual stamps

may carry only a small fraction or none of the watermark.

"Marginal watermarks" occur in the margins of sheets or panes of stamps. They occur on the outside border of paper (ostensibly outside the area where stamps are to be printed). A large row of letters may spell the name of the country or the manufacturer of the paper, or a border of lines may appear. Careless press feeding may cause parts of these letters and/or lines to show on stamps of the outer row of a pane.

Soluble Printing Inks

WARNING: Most stamp colors are permanent; that is, they are not seriously affected by short-term exposure to light or water. Many colors, especially of modern inks, fade from excessive exposure to light. There are stamps printed with inks that dissolve easily in water or in fluids used to detect watermarks. Use of these inks was intentional to prevent the removal of cancellations. Water affects all aniline inks, those on so-called safety paper and some photogravure printings - all such inks are known as fugitive colors. *Removal from paper of such stamps requires care and alternatives to traditional soaking.*

Separation

"Separation" is the general term used to describe methods used to separate stamps. The three standard forms currently in use are perforating, rouletting and die-cutting. These methods are done during the stamp production process, after printing. Sometimes these methods are done on-press or sometimes as a separate step. The earliest issues, such as the 1840 Penny Black of Great Britain (Scott 1), did not have any means provided for separation. It was expected the stamps would be cut apart with scissors or folded and torn. These are examples of imperforate stamps. Many stamps were first issued in imperforate formats and were later issued with perforations. Therefore, care must be observed in buying single imperforate stamps to be certain they were issued imperforate and are not perforated copies that have been altered by having the perforations trimmed away. Stamps issued imperforate usually are valued as singles. However, imperforate varieties of normally perforated stamps should be collected in pairs or larger pieces as indisputable evidence of their imperforate character.

PERFORATION

The chief style of separation of stamps, and the one that is in almost universal use today, is perforating. By this process, paper between the stamps is cut away in a line of holes, usually round, leaving little bridges of paper between the stamps to hold them together. Some types of perforation, such as hyphen-hole perfs, can be confused with roulettes, but a close visual inspection reveals that paper has been removed. The little perforation bridges, which project from the stamp when it is torn from the pane, are called the teeth of the perforation.

As the size of the perforation is sometimes the only way to differentiate between two otherwise identical stamps, it is necessary to be able to accurately measure and describe them. This is done with a perforation gauge, usually a ruler-like device that has dots or graduated lines to show how many perforations may be counted in the space of two centimeters. Two centimeters is the space universally adopted in which to measure perforations.

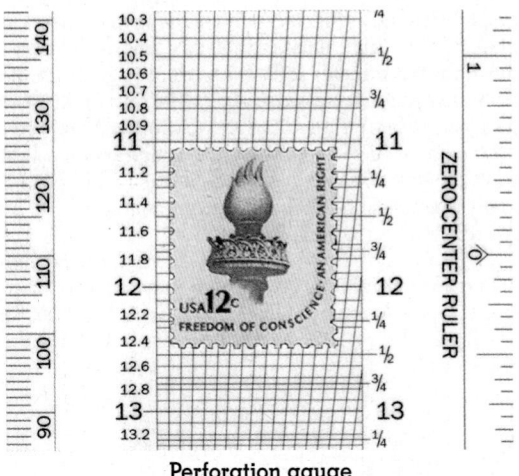

Perforation gauge

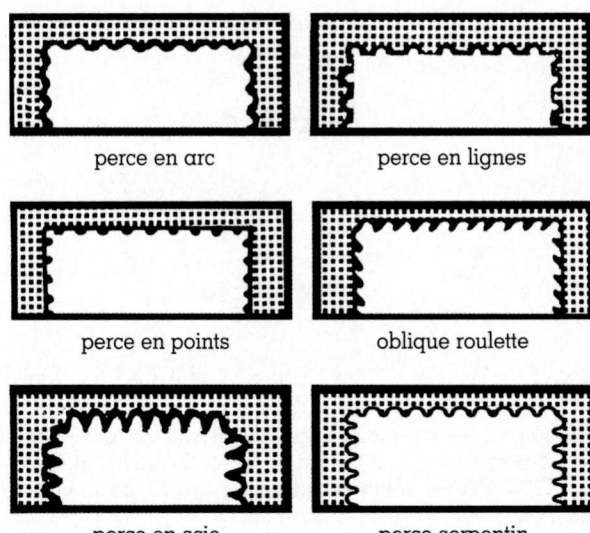

perce en arc   perce en lignes

perce en points   oblique roulette

perce en scie   perce serpentin

To measure a stamp, run it along the gauge until the dots on it fit exactly into the perforations of the stamp. If you are using a graduated-line perforation gauge, simply slide the stamp along the surface until the lines on the gauge perfectly project from the center of the bridges or holes. The number to the side of the line of dots or lines that fit the stamp's perforation is the measurement. For example, an "11" means that 11 perforations fit between two centimeters. The description of the stamp therefore is "perf. 11." If the gauge of the perforations on the top and bottom of a stamp differs from that on the sides, the result is what is known as *compound perforations*. In measuring compound perforations, the gauge at top and bottom is always given first, then the sides. Thus, a stamp that measures 11 at top and bottom and 10½ at the sides is "perf. 11 x 10½." See U.S. Scott 632-642 for examples of compound perforations.

Stamps also are known with perforations different on three or all four sides. Descriptions of such items are clockwise, beginning with the top of the stamp.

A perforation with small holes and teeth close together is a "fine perforation." One with large holes and teeth far apart is a "coarse perforation." Holes that are jagged, rather than clean-cut, are "rough perforations." *Blind perforations* are the slight impressions left by the perforating pins if they fail to puncture the paper. Multiples of stamps showing blind perforations may command a slight premium over normally perforated stamps.

The term *syncopated perfs* describes intentional irregularities in the perforations. The earliest form was used by the Netherlands from 1925-33, where holes were omitted to create distinctive patterns. Beginning in 1992, Great Britain has used an oval perforation to help prevent counterfeiting. Several other countries have started using the oval perfs or other syncopated perf patterns.

A new type of perforation, still primarily used for postal stationery, is known as microperfs. Microperfs are tiny perforations (in some cases hundreds of holes per two centimeters) that allows items to be intentionally separated very easily, while not accidentally breaking apart as easily as standard perforations. These are not currently measured or differentiated by size, as are standard perforations.

ROULETTING

In rouletting, the stamp paper is cut partly or wholly through, with no paper removed. In perforating, some paper is removed. Rouletting derives its name from the French roulette, a spur-like wheel. As the wheel is rolled over the paper, each point makes a small cut. The number of cuts made in a two-centimeter space determines the gauge of the roulette, just as the number of perforations in two centimeters determines the gauge of the perforation.

The shape and arrangement of the teeth on the wheels varies. Various roulette types generally carry French names:

Perce en lignes - rouletted in lines. The paper receives short, straight cuts in lines. This is the most common type of rouletting. See Mexico Scott 500.

Perce en points - pin-rouletted or pin-perfed. This differs from a small perforation because no paper is removed, although round, equidistant holes are pricked through the paper. See Mexico Scott 242-256.

Perce en arc and *perce en scie* - pierced in an arc or saw-toothed designs, forming half circles or small triangles. See Hanover (German States) Scott 25-29.

Perce en serpentin - serpentine roulettes. The cuts form a serpentine or wavy line. See Brunswick (German States) Scott 13-18.

Once again, no paper is removed by these processes, leaving the stamps easily separated, but closely attached.

DIE-CUTTING

The third major form of stamp separation is die-cutting. This is a method where a die in the pattern of separation is created that later cuts the stamp paper in a stroke motion. Although some standard stamps bear die-cut perforations, this process is primarily used for self-adhesive postage stamps. Die-cutting can appear in straight lines, such as U.S. Scott 2522, shapes, such as U.S. Scott 1551, or imitating the appearance of perforations, such as New Zealand Scott 935A and 935B.

Printing Processes

ENGRAVING (Intaglio, Line-engraving, Etching)

Master die — The initial operation in the process of line engraving is making the master die. The die is a small, flat block of softened steel upon which the stamp design is recess engraved in reverse.

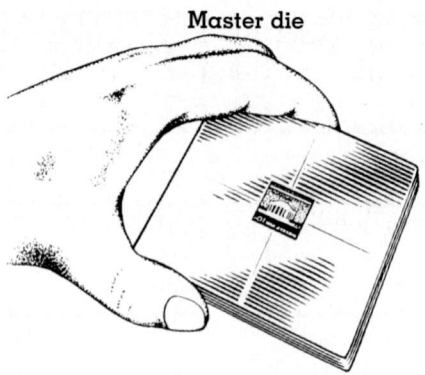

Master die

Photographic reduction of the original art is made to the appropriate size. It then serves as a tracing guide for the initial outline of the design. The engraver lightly traces the design on the steel with his graver, then slowly works the design until it is completed. At various points during the engraving process, the engraver hand-inks the die and makes an impression to check his progress. These are known as progressive die proofs. After completion of the engraving, the die is hardened to withstand the stress and pressures of later transfer operations.

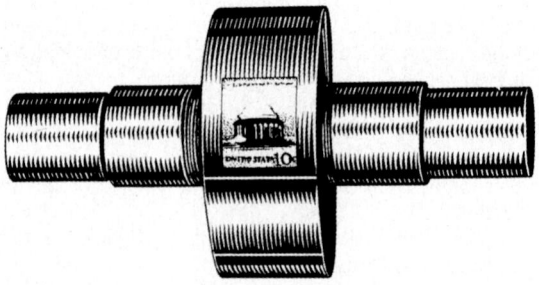

Transfer roll

Transfer roll — Next is production of the transfer roll that, as the name implies, is the medium used to transfer the subject from the master die to the printing plate. A blank roll of soft steel, mounted on a mandrel, is placed under the bearers of the transfer press to allow it to roll freely on its axis. The hardened die is placed on the bed of the press and the face of the transfer roll is applied to the die, under pressure. The bed or the roll is then rocked back and forth under increasing pressure, until the soft steel of the roll is forced into every engraved line of the die. The resulting impression on the roll is known as a "relief" or a "relief transfer." The engraved image is now positive in appearance and stands out from the steel. After the required number of reliefs are "rocked in," the soft steel transfer roll is hardened.

Different flaws may occur during the relief process. A defective relief may occur during the rocking in process because of a minute piece of foreign material lodging on the die, or some other cause. Imperfections in the steel of the transfer roll may result in a breaking away of parts of the design. This is known as a relief break, which will show up on finished stamps as small, unprinted areas. If a damaged relief remains in use, it will transfer a repeating defect to the plate. Deliberate alterations of reliefs sometimes occur. "Altered reliefs" designate these changed conditions.

Plate — The final step in pre-printing production is the making of the printing plate. A flat piece of soft steel replaces the die on the bed of the transfer press. One of the reliefs on the transfer roll is positioned over this soft steel. Position, or layout, dots determine the correct position on the plate. The dots have been lightly marked on the plate in advance. After the correct position of the relief is determined,

the design is rocked in by following the same method used in making the transfer roll. The difference is that this time the image is being transferred from the transfer roll, rather than to it. Once the design is entered on the plate, it appears in reverse and is recessed. There are as many transfers entered on the plate as there are subjects printed on the sheet of stamps. It is during this process that double and shifted transfers occur, as well as re-entries. These are the result of improperly entered images that have not been properly burnished out prior to rocking in a new image.

Modern siderography processes, such as those used by the U.S. Bureau of Engraving and Printing, involve an automated form of rocking designs in on preformed cylindrical printing sleeves. The same process also allows for easier removal and re-entry of worn images right on the sleeve.

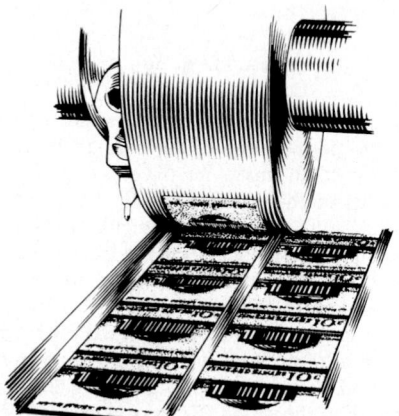

Transferring the design to the plate

Following the entering of the required transfers on the plate, the position dots, layout dots and lines, scratches and other markings generally are burnished out. Added at this time by the siderographer are any required *guide lines*, *plate numbers* or other *marginal markings*. The plate is then hand-inked and a proof impression is taken. This is known as a plate proof. If the impression is approved, the plate is machined for fitting onto the press, is hardened and sent to the plate vault ready for use.

On press, the plate is inked and the surface is automatically wiped clean, leaving ink only in the recessed lines. Paper is then forced under pressure into the engraved recessed lines, thereby receiving the ink. Thus, the ink lines on engraved stamps are slightly raised, and slight depressions (debossing) occur on the back of the stamp. Prior to the advent of modern high-speed presses and more advanced ink formulations, paper had to be dampened before receiving the ink. This sometimes led to uneven shrinkage by the time the stamps were perforated, resulting in improperly perforated stamps, or misperfs. Newer presses use drier paper, thus both *wet* and *dry printings* exist on some stamps.

Rotary Press — Until 1914, only flat plates were used to print engraved stamps. Rotary press printing was introduced in 1914, and slowly spread. Some countries still use flat-plate printing.

After approval of the plate proof, older *rotary press plates* require additional machining. They are curved to fit the press cylinder. "Gripper slots" are cut into the back of each plate to receive the "grippers," which hold the plate securely on the press. The plate is then hardened. Stamps printed from these bent rotary press plates are longer or wider than the same stamps printed from flat-plate presses. The stretching of the plate during the curving process is what causes this distortion.

Re-entry — To execute a re-entry on a flat plate, the transfer roll is re-applied to the plate, often at some time after its first use on the

press. Worn-out designs can be resharpened by carefully burnishing out the original image and re-entering it from the transfer roll. If the original impression has not been sufficiently removed and the transfer roll is not precisely in line with the remaining impression, the resulting double transfer will make the re-entry obvious. If the registration is true, a re-entry may be difficult or impossible to distinguish. Sometimes a stamp printed from a successful re-entry is identified by having a much sharper and clearer impression than its neighbors. With the advent of rotary presses, post-press re-entries were not possible. After a plate was curved for the rotary press, it was impossible to make a re-entry. This is because the plate had already been bent once (with the design distorted).

However, with the introduction of the previously mentioned modern-style siderography machines, entries are made to the preformed cylindrical printing sleeve. Such sleeves are dechromed and softened. This allows individual images to be burnished out and re-entered on the curved sleeve. The sleeve is then rechromed, resulting in longer press life.

Double Transfer — This is a description of the condition of a transfer on a plate that shows evidence of a duplication of all, or a portion of the design. It usually is the result of the changing of the registration between the transfer roll and the plate during the rocking in of the original entry. Double transfers also occur when only a portion of the design has been rocked in and improper positioning is noted. If the worker elected not to burnish out the partial or completed design, a strong double transfer will occur for part or all of the design.

It sometimes is necessary to remove the original transfer from a plate and repeat the process a second time. If the finished re-worked image shows traces of the original impression, attributable to incomplete burnishing, the result is a partial double transfer.

With the modern automatic machines mentioned previously, double transfers are all but impossible to create. Those partially doubled images on stamps printed from such sleeves are more than likely re-entries, rather than true double transfers.

Re-engraved — Alterations to a stamp design are sometimes necessary after some stamps have been printed. In some cases, either the original die or the actual printing plate may have its "temper" drawn (softened), and the design will be re-cut. The resulting impressions from such a re-engraved die or plate may differ slightly from the original issue, and are known as "re-engraved." If the alteration was made to the master die, all future printings will be consistently different from the original. If alterations were made to the printing plate, each altered stamp on the plate will be slightly different from each other, allowing specialists to reconstruct a complete printing plate.

Dropped Transfers — If an impression from the transfer roll has not been properly placed, a dropped transfer may occur. The final stamp image will appear obviously out of line with its neighbors.

Short Transfer — Sometimes a transfer roll is not rocked its entire length when entering a transfer onto a plate. As a result, the finished transfer on the plate fails to show the complete design, and the finished stamp will have an incomplete design printed. This is known as a "short transfer." U.S. Scott No. 8 is a good example of a short transfer.

TYPOGRAPHY (Letterpress, Surface Printing, Flexography, Dry Offset, High Etch)

Although the word "Typography" is obsolete as a term describing a printing method, it was the accepted term throughout the first century of postage stamps. Therefore, appropriate Scott listings in this catalogue refer to typographed stamps. The current term for this form of printing, however, is "letterpress."

As it relates to the production of postage stamps, letterpress printing is the reverse of engraving. Rather than having recessed areas trap the ink and deposit it on paper, only the raised areas of the design are inked. This is comparable to the type of printing seen by inking and using an ordinary rubber stamp. Letterpress includes all printing where the design is above the surface area, whether it is wood, metal or, in some instances, hardened rubber or polymer plastic.

For most letterpress-printed stamps, the engraved master is made in much the same manner as for engraved stamps. In this instance, however, an additional step is needed. The design is transferred to another surface before being transferred to the transfer roll. In this way, the transfer roll has a recessed stamp design, rather than one done in relief. This makes the printing areas on the final plate raised, or relief areas.

For less-detailed stamps of the 19th century, the area on the die not used as a printing surface was cut away, leaving the surface area raised. The original die was then reproduced by stereotyping or electrotyping. The resulting electrotypes were assembled in the required number and format of the desired sheet of stamps. The plate used in printing the stamps was an electroplate of these assembled electrotypes.

Once the final letterpress plates are created, ink is applied to the raised surface and the pressure of the press transfers the ink impression to the paper. In contrast to engraving, the fine lines of letterpress are impressed on the surface of the stamp, leaving a debossed surface. When viewed from the back (as on a typewritten page), the corresponding line work on the stamp will be raised slightly (embossed) above the surface.

PHOTOGRAVURE (Gravure, Rotogravure, Heliogravure)

In this process, the basic principles of photography are applied to a chemically sensitized metal plate, rather than photographic paper. The design is transferred photographically to the plate through a halftone, or dot-matrix screen, breaking the reproduction into tiny dots. The plate is treated chemically and the dots form depressions, called cells, of varying depths and diameters, depending on the degrees of shade in the design. Then, like engraving, ink is applied to the plate and the surface is wiped clean. This leaves ink in the tiny cells that is lifted out and deposited on the paper when it is pressed against the plate.

Gravure is most often used for multicolored stamps, generally using the three primary colors (red, yellow and blue) and black. By varying the dot matrix pattern and density of these colors, virtually any color can be reproduced. A typical full-color gravure stamp will be created from four printing cylinders (one for each color). The original multicolored image will have been photographically separated into its component colors.

Modern gravure printing may use computer-generated dot-matrix screens, and modern plates may be of various types including metal-coated plastic. The catalogue designation of Photogravure (or "Photo") covers any of these older and more modern gravure methods of printing.

For examples of the first photogravure stamps printed (1914), see Bavaria Scott 94-114.

LITHOGRAPHY (Offset Lithography, Stone Lithography, Dilitho, Planography, Collotype)

The principle that oil and water do not mix is the basis for lithography. The stamp design is drawn by hand or transferred from engraving to the surface of a lithographic stone or metal plate in a greasy (oily) substance. This oily substance holds the ink, which will later be transferred to the paper. The stone (or plate) is wet with an acid fluid, causing it to repel the printing ink in all areas not covered by the greasy substance.

Transfer paper is used to transfer the design from the original stone or plate. A series of duplicate transfers are grouped and, in turn, transferred to the final printing plate.

Photolithography — The application of photographic processes to

lithography. This process allows greater flexibility of design, related to use of halftone screens combined with line work. Unlike photogravure or engraving, this process can allow large, solid areas to be printed.

Offset — A refinement of the lithographic process. A rubber-covered blanket cylinder takes the impression from the inked lithographic plate. From the "blanket" the impression is *offset* or transferred to the paper. Greater flexibility and speed are the principal reasons offset printing has largely displaced lithography. The term "lithography" covers both processes, and results are almost identical.

EMBOSSED (Relief) Printing

Embossing, not considered one of the four main printing types, is a method in which the design first is sunk into the metal of the die. Printing is done against a yielding platen, such as leather or linoleum. The platen is forced into the depression of the die, thus forming the design on the paper in relief. This process is often used for metallic inks.

Embossing may be done without color (see Sardinia Scott 4-6); with color printed around the embossed area (see Great Britain Scott 5 and most U.S. envelopes); and with color in exact registration with the embossed subject (see Canada Scott 656-657).

HOLOGRAMS

For objects to appear as holograms on stamps, a model exactly the same size as it is to appear on the hologram must be created. Rather than using photographic film to capture the image, holography records an image on a photoresist material. In processing, chemicals eat away at certain exposed areas, leaving a pattern of constructive and destructive interference. When the photoresist is developed, the result is a pattern of uneven ridges that acts as a mold. This mold is then coated with metal, and the resulting form is used to press copies in much the same way phonograph records are produced.

A typical reflective hologram used for stamps consists of a reproduction of the uneven patterns on a plastic film that is applied to a reflective background, usually a silver or gold foil. Light is reflected off the background through the film, making the pattern present on the film visible. Because of the uneven pattern of the film, the viewer will perceive the objects in their proper three-dimensional relationships with appropriate brightness.

The first hologram on a stamp was produced by Austria in 1988 (Scott 1441).

FOIL APPLICATION

A modern technique of applying color to stamps involves the application of metallic foil to the stamp paper. A pattern of foil is applied to the stamp paper by use of a stamping die. The foil usually is flat, but it may be textured. Canada Scott 1735 has three different foil applications in pearl, bronze and gold. The gold foil was textured using a chemical-etch copper embossing die. The printing of this stamp also involved two-color offset lithography plus embossing.

THERMOGRAPHY

In the 1990s stamps began to be enhanced with thermographic printing. In this process, a powdered polymer is applied over a sheet that has just been printed. The powder adheres to ink that lacks drying or hardening agents and does not adhere to areas where the ink has these agents. The excess powder is removed and the sheet is briefly heated to melt the powder. The melted powder solidifies after cooling, producing a raised, shiny effect on the stamps. See Scott New Caledonia C239-C240.

COMBINATION PRINTINGS

Sometimes two or even three printing methods are combined in producing stamps. In these cases, such as Austria Scott 933 or Canada 1735 (described in the preceding paragraph), the multiple-printing technique can be determined by studying the individual characteristics of each printing type. A few stamps, such as Singapore Scott 684-684A, combine as many as three of the four major printing types (lithography, engraving and typography). When this is done it often indicates the incorporation of security devices against counterfeiting.

INK COLORS

Inks or colored papers used in stamp printing often are of mineral origin, although there are numerous examples of organic-based pigments. As a general rule, organic-based pigments are far more subject to varieties and change than those of mineral-based origin.

The appearance of any given color on a stamp may be affected by many aspects, including printing variations, light, color of paper, aging and chemical alterations.

Numerous printing variations may be observed. Heavier pressure or inking will cause a more intense color, while slight interruptions in the ink feed or lighter impressions will cause a lighter appearance. Stamps printed in the same color by water-based and solvent-based inks can differ significantly in appearance. This affects several stamps in the U.S. Prominent Americans series. Hand-mixed ink formulas (primarily from the 19th century) produced under different conditions (humidity and temperature) account for notable color variations in early printings of the same stamp (see U.S. Scott 248-250, 279B, for example). Different sources of pigment can also result in significant differences in color.

Light exposure and aging are closely related in the way they affect stamp color. Both eventually break down the ink and fade colors, so that a carefully kept stamp may differ significantly in color from an identical copy that has been exposed to light. If stamps are exposed to light either intentionally or accidentally, their colors can be faded or completely changed in some cases.

Papers of different quality and consistency used for the same stamp printing may affect color appearance. Most pelure papers, for example, show a richer color when compared with wove or laid papers. See Russia Scott 181a, for an example of this effect.

The very nature of the printing processes can cause a variety of differences in shades or hues of the same stamp. Some of these shades are scarcer than others, and are of particular interest to the advanced collector.

Luminescence

All forms of tagged stamps fall under the general category of luminescence. Within this broad category is fluorescence, dealing with forms of tagging visible under longwave ultraviolet light, and phosphorescence, which deals with tagging visible only under shortwave light. Phosphorescence leaves an afterglow and fluorescence does not. These treated stamps show up in a range of different colors when exposed to UV light. The differing wavelengths of the light activates the tagging material, making it glow in various colors that usually serve different mail processing purposes.

Intentional tagging is a post-World War II phenomenon, brought about by the increased literacy rate and rapidly growing mail volume. It was one of several answers to the problem of the need for more automated mail processes. Early tagged stamps served the purpose of triggering machines to separate different types of mail. A natural outgrowth was to also use the signal to trigger machines that faced all envelopes the same way and canceled them.

Tagged stamps come in many different forms. Some tagged stamps have luminescent shapes or images imprinted on them as a form of security device. Others have blocks (United States), stripes, frames (South Africa and Canada), overall coatings (United States), bars (Great Britain and Canada) and many other types. Some types of tagging are even mixed in with the pigmented printing ink (Australia Scott 366, Netherlands Scott 478 and U.S. Scott 1359 and 2443).

The means of applying taggant to stamps differs as much as the

intended purposes for the stamps. The most common form of tagging is a coating applied to the surface of the printed stamp. Since the taggant ink is frequently invisible except under UV light, it does not interfere with the appearance of the stamp. Another common application is the use of phosphored papers. In this case the paper itself either has a coating of taggant applied before the stamp is printed, has taggant applied during the papermaking process (incorporating it into the fibers), or has the taggant mixed into the coating of the paper. The latter method, among others, is currently in use in the United States.

Many countries now use tagging in various forms to either expedite mail handling or to serve as a printing security device against counterfeiting. Following the introduction of tagged stamps for public use in 1959 by Great Britain, other countries have steadily joined the parade. Among those are Germany (1961); Canada and Denmark (1962); United States, Australia, France and Switzerland (1963); Belgium and Japan (1966); Sweden and Norway (1967); Italy (1968); and Russia (1969). Since then, many other countries have begun using forms of tagging, including Brazil, China, Czechoslovakia, Hong Kong, Guatemala, Indonesia, Israel, Lithuania, Luxembourg, Netherlands, Penrhyn Islands, Portugal, St. Vincent, Singapore, South Africa, Spain and Sweden to name a few.

In some cases, including United States, Canada, Great Britain and Switzerland, stamps were released both with and without tagging. Many of these were released during each country's experimental period. Tagged and untagged versions are listed for the aforementioned countries and are noted in some other countries' listings. For at least a few stamps, the experimentally tagged version is worth far more than its untagged counterpart, such as the 1963 experimental tagged version of France Scott 1024.

In some cases, luminescent varieties of stamps were inadvertently created. Several Russian stamps, for example, sport highly fluorescent ink that was not intended as a form of tagging. Older stamps, such as early U.S. postage dues, can be positively identified by the use of UV light, since the organic ink used has become slightly fluorescent over time. Other stamps, such as Austria Scott 70a-82a (varnish bars) and Obock Scott 46-64 (printed quadrille lines), have become fluorescent over time.

Various fluorescent substances have been added to paper to make it appear brighter. These optical brighteners, as they are known, greatly affect the appearance of the stamp under UV light. The brightest of these is known as Hi-Brite paper. These paper varieties are beyond the scope of the Scott Catalogue.

Shortwave UV light also is used extensively in expertizing, since each form of paper has its own fluorescent characteristics that are impossible to perfectly match. It is therefore a simple matter to detect filled thins, added perforation teeth and other alterations that involve the addition of paper. UV light also is used to examine stamps that have had cancels chemically removed and for other purposes as well.

Gum

The Illustrated Gum Chart in the first part of this introduction shows and defines various types of gum condition. Because gum condition has an important impact on the value of unused stamps, we recommend studying this chart and the accompanying text carefully.

The gum on the back of a stamp may be shiny, dull, smooth, rough, dark, white, colored or tinted. Most stamp gumming adhesives use gum arabic or dextrine as a base. Certain polymers such as polyvinyl alcohol (PVA) have been used extensively since World War II.

The *Scott Standard Postage Stamp Catalogue* does not list items by types of gum. The *Scott Specialized Catalogue of United States Stamps and Covers* does differentiate among some types of gum for certain issues.

Reprints of stamps may have gum differing from the original issues. In addition, some countries have used different gum formulas for different seasons. These adhesives have different properties that may become more apparent over time.

Many stamps have been issued without gum, and the catalogue

will note this fact. See, for example, United States Scott 40-47. Sometimes, gum may have been removed to preserve the stamp. Germany Scott B68, for example, has a highly acidic gum that eventually destroys the stamps. This item is valued in the catalogue with gum removed.

Reprints and Reissues

These are impressions of stamps (usually obsolete) made from the original plates or stones. If they are valid for postage and reproduce obsolete issues (such as U.S. Scott 102-111), the stamps are *reissues*. If they are from current issues, they are designated as *second, third,* etc., *printing*. If designated for a particular purpose, they are called *special printings*.

When special printings are not valid for postage, but are made from original dies and plates by authorized persons, they are *official reprints*. *Private reprints* are made from the original plates and dies by private hands. An example of a private reprint is that of the 1871-1932 reprints made from the original die of the 1845 New Haven, Conn., postmaster's provisional. *Official reproductions* or imitations are made from new dies and plates by government authorization. Scott will list those reissues that are valid for postage if they differ significantly from the original printing.

The U.S. government made special printings of its first postage stamps in 1875. Produced were official imitations of the first two stamps (listed as Scott 3-4), reprints of the demonetized pre-1861 issues (Scott 40-47) and reissues of the 1861 stamps, the 1869 stamps and the then-current 1875 denominations. Even though the official imitations and the reprints were not valid for postage, Scott lists all of these U.S. special printings.

Most reprints or reissues differ slightly from the original stamp in some characteristic, such as gum, paper, perforation, color or watermark. Sometimes the details are followed so meticulously that only a student of that specific stamp is able to distinguish the reprint or reissue from the original.

Remainders and Canceled to Order

Some countries sell their stock of old stamps when a new issue replaces them. To avoid postal use, the *remainders* usually are canceled with a punch hole, a heavy line or bar, or a more-or-less regular-looking cancellation. The most famous merchant of remainders was Nicholas F. Seebeck. In the 1880s and 1890s, he arranged printing contracts between the Hamilton Bank Note Co., of which he was a director, and several Central and South American countries. The contracts provided that the plates and all remainders of the yearly issues became the property of Hamilton. Seebeck saw to it that ample stock remained. The "Seebecks," both remainders and reprints, were standard packet fillers for decades.

Some countries also issue stamps *canceled-to-order (CTO)*, either in sheets with original gum or stuck onto pieces of paper or envelopes and canceled. Such CTO items generally are worth less than postally used stamps. In cases where the CTO material is far more prevalent in the marketplace than postally used examples, the catalogue value relates to the CTO examples, with postally used examples noted as premium items. Most CTOs can be detected by the presence of gum. However, as the CTO practice goes back at least to 1885, the gum inevitably has been soaked off some stamps so they could pass as postally used. The normally applied postmarks usually differ slightly from standard postmarks, and specialists are able to tell the difference. When applied individually to envelopes by philatelically minded persons, CTO material is known as *favor canceled* and generally sells at large discounts.

Cinderellas and Facsimiles

Cinderella is a catch-all term used by stamp collectors to describe phantoms, fantasies, bogus items, municipal issues, exhibition seals, local revenues, transportation stamps, labels, poster stamps and many other types of items. Some cinderella collectors include in

their collections local postage issues, telegraph stamps, essays and proofs, forgeries and counterfeits.

A *fantasy* is an adhesive created for a nonexistent stamp-issuing authority. Fantasy items range from imaginary countries (Occusi-Ambeno, Kingdom of Sedang, Principality of Trinidad or Torres Straits), to non-existent locals (Winans City Post), or nonexistent transportation lines (McRobish & Co.'s Acapulco-San Francisco Line).

On the other hand, if the entity exists and could have issued stamps (but did not) or was known to have issued other stamps, the items are considered *bogus* stamps. These would include the Mormon postage stamps of Utah, S. Allan Taylor's Guatemala and Paraguay inventions, the propaganda issues for the South Moluccas and the adhesives of the Page & Keyes local post of Boston.

Phantoms is another term for both fantasy and bogus issues.

Facsimiles are copies or imitations made to represent original stamps, but which do not pretend to be originals. A catalogue illustration is such a facsimile. Illustrations from the Moens catalogue of the last century were occasionally colored and passed off as stamps. Since the beginning of stamp collecting, facsimiles have been made for collectors as space fillers or for reference. They often carry the word "facsimile," "falsch" (German), "sanko" or "mozo" (Japanese), or "faux" (French) overprinted on the face or stamped on the back. Unfortunately, over the years a number of these items have had fake cancels applied over the facsimile notation and have been passed off as genuine.

Forgeries and Counterfeits

Forgeries and counterfeits have been with philately virtually from the beginning of stamp production. Over time, the terminology for the two has been used interchangeably. Although both forgeries and counterfeits are reproductions of stamps, the purposes behind their creation differ considerably.

Among specialists there is an increasing movement to more specifically define such items. Although there is no universally accepted terminology, we feel the following definitions most closely mirror the items and their purposes as they are currently defined.

Forgeries (also often referred to as *Counterfeits*) are reproductions of genuine stamps that have been created to defraud collectors. Such spurious items first appeared on the market around 1860, and most old-time collections contain one or more. Many are crude and easily spotted, but some can deceive experts.

An important supplier of these early philatelic forgeries was the Hamburg printer Gebruder Spiro. Many others with reputations in this craft included S. Allan Taylor, George Hussey, James Chute, George Forune, Benjamin & Sarpy, Julius Goldner, E. Oneglia and L.H. Mercier. Among the noted 20th-century forgers were Francois Fournier, Jean Sperati and the prolific Raoul DeThuin.

Forgeries may be complete replications, or they may be genuine stamps altered to resemble a scarcer (and more valuable) type. Most forgeries, particularly those of rare stamps, are worth only a small fraction of the value of a genuine example, but a few types, created by some of the most notable forgers, such as Sperati, can be worth as much or more than the genuine. Fraudulently produced copies are known of most classic rarities and many medium-priced stamps.

In addition to rare stamps, large numbers of common 19th- and early 20th-century stamps were forged to supply stamps to the early packet trade. Many can still be easily found. Few new philatelic forgeries have appeared in recent decades. Successful imitation of well-engraved work is virtually impossible. It has proven far easier to produce a fake by altering a genuine stamp than to duplicate a stamp completely.

Counterfeit (also often referred to as *Postal Counterfeit* or *Postal Forgery*) is the term generally applied to reproductions of stamps that have been created to defraud the government of revenue. Such items usually are created at the time a stamp is current and, in some cases, are hard to detect. Because most counterfeits are seized when the perpetrator is captured, postal counterfeits, particularly used on cover, are usually worth much more than a genuine example to specialists. The first postal counterfeit was of Spain's 4-cuarto carmine of 1854 (the real one is Scott 25). Apparently, the counterfeiters were not satisfied with their first version, which is now very scarce, and they soon created an engraved counterfeit, which is common. Postal counterfeits quickly followed in Austria, Naples, Sardinia and the Roman States. They have since been created in many other countries as well, including the United States.

An infamous counterfeit to defraud the government is the 1-shilling Great Britain "Stock Exchange" forgery of 1872, used on telegraph forms at the exchange that year. The stamp escaped detection until a stamp dealer noticed it in 1898.

Fakes

Fakes are genuine stamps altered in some way to make them more desirable. One student of this part of stamp collecting has estimated that by the 1950s more than 30,000 varieties of fakes were known. That number has grown greatly since then. The widespread existence of fakes makes it important for stamp collectors to study their philatelic holdings and use relevant literature. Likewise, collectors should buy from reputable dealers who guarantee their stamps and make full and prompt refunds should a purchased item be declared faked or altered by some mutually agreed-upon authority. Because fakes always have some genuine characteristics, it is not always possible to obtain unanimous agreement among experts regarding specific items. These students may change their opinions as philatelic knowledge increases. More than 80 percent of all fakes on the philatelic market today are regummed, reperforated (or perforated for the first time), or bear forged overprints, surcharges or cancellations.

Stamps can be chemically treated to alter or eliminate colors. For example, a pale rose stamp can be re-colored to resemble a blue shade of high market value. In other cases, treated stamps can be made to resemble missing color varieties. Designs may be changed by painting, or a stroke or a dot added or bleached out to turn an ordinary variety into a seemingly scarcer stamp. Part of a stamp can be bleached and reprinted in a different version, achieving an inverted center or frame. Margins can be added or repairs done so deceptively that the stamps move from the "repaired" into the "fake" category.

Fakers have not left the backs of the stamps untouched either. They may create false watermarks, add fake grills or press out genuine grills. A thin India paper proof may be glued onto a thicker backing to create the appearance an issued stamp, or a proof printed on cardboard may be shaved down and perforated to resemble a stamp. Silk threads are impressed into paper and stamps have been split so that a rare paper variety is added to an otherwise inexpensive stamp. The most common treatment to the back of a stamp, however, is regumming.

Some in the business of faking stamps have openly advertised fool-proof application of "original gum" to stamps that lack it, although most publications now ban such ads from their pages. It is believed that very few early stamps have survived without being hinged. The large number of never-hinged examples of such earlier material offered for sale thus suggests the widespread extent of regumming activity. Regumming also may be used to hide repairs or thin spots. Dipping the stamp into watermark fluid, or examining it under longwave ultraviolet light often will reveal these flaws.

Fakers also tamper with separations. Ingenious ways to add margins are known. Perforated wide-margin stamps may be falsely represented as imperforate when trimmed. Reperforating is commonly done to create scarce coil or perforation varieties, and to eliminate the naturally occurring straight-edge stamps found in sheet margin positions of many earlier issues. Custom has made straight-edged stamps less desirable. Fakers have obliged by perforating straight-edged stamps so that many are now uncommon, if not rare.

Another fertile field for the faker is that of overprints, surcharges and cancellations. The forging of rare surcharges or overprints began in

the 1880s or 1890s. These forgeries are sometimes difficult to detect, but experts have identified almost all. Occasionally, overprints or cancellations are removed to create non-overprinted stamps or seemingly unused items. This is most commonly done by removing a manuscript cancel to make a stamp resemble an unused example. "SPECIMEN" overprints may be removed by scraping and repainting to create non-overprinted varieties. Fakers use inexpensive revenues or pen-canceled stamps to generate unused stamps for further faking by adding other markings. The quartz lamp or UV lamp and a high-powered magnifying glass help to easily detect removed cancellations.

The bigger problem, however, is the addition of overprints, surcharges or cancellations - many with such precision that they are very difficult to ascertain. Plating of the stamps or the overprint can be an important method of detection.

Fake postmarks may range from many spurious fancy cancellations to a host of markings applied to transatlantic covers, to adding normally appearing postmarks to definitives of some countries with stamps that are valued far higher used than unused. With the increased popularity of cover collecting, and the widespread interest in postal history, a fertile new field for fakers has come about. Some have tried to create entire covers. Others specialize in adding stamps, tied by fake cancellations, to genuine stampless covers, or replacing less expensive or damaged stamps with more valuable ones. Detailed study of postal rates in effect at the time a cover in question was mailed, including the analysis of each handstamp used during the period, ink analysis and similar techniques, usually will unmask the fraud.

Restoration and Repairs

Scott bases its catalogue values on stamps that are free of defects and otherwise meet the standards set forth earlier in this introduction. Most stamp collectors desire to have the finest copy of an item possible. Even within given grading categories there are variances. This leads to a controversial practice that is not defined in any universal manner: stamp *restoration*.

There are broad differences of opinion about what is permissible when it comes to restoration. Carefully applying a soft eraser to a stamp or cover to remove light soiling is one form of restoration, as is washing a stamp in mild soap and water to clean it. These are fairly accepted forms of restoration. More severe forms of restoration include pressing out creases or removing stains caused by tape. To what degree each of these is acceptable is dependent upon the individual situation. Further along the spectrum is the freshening of a stamp's color by removing oxide build-up or the effects of wax paper left next to stamps shipped to the tropics.

At some point in this spectrum the concept of *repair* replaces that of restoration. Repairs include filling thin spots, mending tears by reweaving or adding a missing perforation tooth. Regumming stamps may have been acceptable as a restoration or repair technique many decades ago, but today it is considered a form of fakery.

Restored stamps may or may not sell at a discount, and it is possible that the value of individual restored items may be enhanced over that of their pre-restoration state. Specific situations dictate the resultant value of such an item. Repaired stamps sell at substantial discounts from the value of sound stamps.

Terminology

Booklets — Many countries have issued stamps in small booklets for the convenience of users. This idea continues to become increasingly popular in many countries. Booklets have been issued in many sizes and forms, often with advertising on the covers, the panes of stamps or on the interleaving.

The panes used in booklets may be printed from special plates or made from regular sheets. All panes from booklets issued by the United States and many from those of other countries contain stamps that are straight edged on the sides, but perforated between. Others are distinguished by orientation of watermark or other identifying features. Any stamp-like unit in the pane, either printed or blank, that is not a postage stamp, is considered to be a *label* in the catalogue listings.

Scott lists and values booklet panes. Modern complete booklets also are listed and valued. Individual booklet panes are listed only when they are not fashioned from existing sheet stamps and, therefore, are identifiable from their sheet stamp counterparts.

Panes usually do not have a used value assigned to them because there is little market activity for used booklet panes, even though many exist used and there is some demand for them.

Cancellations — The marks or obliterations put on stamps by postal authorities to show that they have performed service and to prevent their reuse are known as cancellations. If the marking is made with a pen, it is considered a "pen cancel." When the location of the post office appears in the marking, it is a "town cancellation." A "postmark" is technically any postal marking, but in practice the term generally is applied to a town cancellation with a date. When calling attention to a cause or celebration, the marking is known as a "slogan cancellation." Many other types and styles of cancellations exist, such as duplex, numerals, targets, fancy and others. See also "precancels," below.

Coil Stamps — These are stamps that are issued in rolls for use in dispensers, affixing and vending machines. Those coils of the United States, Canada, Sweden and some other countries are perforated horizontally or vertically only, with the outer edges imperforate. Coil stamps of some countries, such as Great Britain and Germany, are perforated on all four sides and may in some cases be distinguished from their sheet stamp counterparts by watermarks, counting numbers on the reverse or other means.

Covers — Entire envelopes, with or without adhesive postage stamps, that have passed through the mail and bear postal or other markings of philatelic interest are known as covers. Before the introduction of envelopes in about 1840, people folded letters and wrote the address on the outside. Some people covered their letters with an extra sheet of paper on the outside for the address, producing the term "cover." Used airletter sheets, stamped envelopes and other items of postal stationery also are considered covers.

Errors — Stamps that have some major, consistent, unintentional deviation from the normal are considered errors. Errors include, but are not limited to, missing or wrong colors, wrong paper, wrong watermarks, inverted centers or frames on multicolor printing, inverted or missing surcharges or overprints, double impressions, missing perforations, unintentionally omitted tagging and others. Factually wrong or misspelled information, if it appears on all examples of a stamp, are not considered errors in the true sense of the word. They are errors of design. Inconsistent or randomly appearing items, such as misperfs or color shifts, are classified as freaks.

Color-Omitted Errors — This term refers to stamps where a missing color is caused by the complete failure of the printing plate to deliver ink to the stamp paper or any other paper. Generally, this is caused

by the printing plate not being engaged on the press or the ink station running dry of ink during printing.

Color-Missing Errors — This term refers to stamps where a color or colors were printed somewhere but do not appear on the finished stamp. There are four different classes of color-missing errors, and the catalog indicates with a two-letter code appended to each such listing what caused the color to be missing. These codes are used only for the United States' color-missing error listings.

FO = A *foldover* of the stamp sheet during printing may block ink from appearing on a stamp. Instead, the color will appear on the back of the foldover (where it might fall on the back of the selvage or perhaps on the back of the stamp or another stamp). FO also will be used in the case of foldunders, where the paper may fold underneath the other stamp paper and the color will print on the platen.

EP = A piece of *extraneous paper* falling across the plate or stamp paper will receive the printed ink. When the extraneous paper is removed, an unprinted portion of stamp paper remains and shows partially or totally missing colors.

CM = A misregistration of the printing plates during printing will result in a *color misregistration*, and such a misregistraion may result in a color not appearing on the finished stamp.

PS = A *perforation shift* after printing may remove a color from the finished stamp. Normally, this will occur on a row of stamps at the edge of the stamp pane.

Measurements – When measurements are given in the Scott catalogues for stamp size, grill size or any other reason, the first measurement given is always for the top and bottom dimension, while the second measurement will be for the sides (just as perforation gauges are measured). Thus, a stamp size of 15mm x 21mm will indicate a vertically oriented stamp 15mm wide at top and bottom, and 21mm tall at the sides. The same principle holds for measuring or counting items such as U.S. grills. A grill count of 22x18 points (B grill) indicates that there are 22 grill points across by 18 grill points down.

Overprints and Surcharges — Overprinting involves applying wording or design elements over an already existing stamp. Overprints can be used to alter the place of use (such as "Canal Zone" on U.S. stamps), to adapt them for a special purpose ("Porto" on Denmark's 1913-20 regular issues for use as postage due stamps, Scott J1-J7) or to commemorate a special occasion (United States Scott 647-648).

A *surcharge* is a form of overprint that changes or restates the face value of a stamp or piece of postal stationery.

Surcharges and overprints may be handstamped, typeset or, occasionally, lithographed or engraved. A few hand-written overprints and surcharges are known.

Personalized Stamps — In 1999, Australia issued stamps with se-tenant labels that could be personalized with pictures of the customer's choice. Other countries quickly followed suit, with some offering to print the selected picture on the stamp itself within a frame that was used exclusively for personalized issues. As the picture used on these stamps or labels vary, listings for such stamps are for any picture within the common frame (or any picture on a se-tenant label), be it a "generic" image or one produced especially for a customer, almost invariably at a premium price.

Precancels — Stamps that are canceled before they are placed in the mail are known as precancels. Precanceling usually is done to expedite the handling of large mailings and generally allow the affected mail pieces to skip certain phases of mail handling.

In the United States, precancellations generally identified the point of origin; that is, the city and state. This information appeared across the face of the stamp, usually centered between parallel lines. More recently, bureau precancels retained the parallel lines, but the city and state designations were dropped. Recent coils have a service inscription that is present on the original printing plate. These show the mail service paid for by the stamp. Since these stamps are not intended to receive further cancellations when used as intended, they are considered precancels. Such items often do not have parallel lines as part of the precancellation.

In France, the abbreviation *Affranchts* in a semicircle together with the word *Postes* is the general form of precancel in use. Belgian precancellations usually appear in a box in which the name of the city appears. Netherlands precancels have the name of the city enclosed between concentric circles, sometimes called a "lifesaver." Precancellations of other countries usually follow these patterns, but may be any arrangement of bars, boxes and city names.

Precancels are listed in the Scott catalogues only if the precancel changes the denomination (Belgium Scott 477-478); if the precanceled stamp is different from the non-precanceled version (such as untagged U.S. precancels); or if the stamp exists only precanceled (France Scott 1096-1099, U.S. Scott 2265).

Proofs and Essays — Proofs are impressions taken from an approved die, plate or stone in which the design and color are the same as the stamp issued to the public. Trial color proofs are impressions taken from approved dies, plates or stones in colors that vary from the final version. An essay is the impression of a design that differs in some way from the issued stamp. "Progressive die proofs" generally are considered to be essays.

Provisionals — These are stamps that are issued on short notice and intended for temporary use pending the arrival of regular issues. They usually are issued to meet such contingencies as changes in government or currency, shortage of necessary postage values or military occupation.

During the 1840s, postmasters in certain American cities issued stamps that were valid only at specific post offices. In 1861, postmasters of the Confederate States also issued stamps with limited validity. Both of these examples are known as "postmaster's provisionals."

Se-tenant — This term refers to an unsevered pair, strip or block of stamps that differ in design, denomination or overprint.

Unless the se-tenant item has a continuous design (see U.S. Scott 1451a, 1694a) the stamps do not have to be in the same order as shown in the catalogue (see U.S. Scott 2158a).

Specimens — The Universal Postal Union required member nations to send samples of all stamps they released into service to the International Bureau in Switzerland. Member nations of the UPU received these specimens as samples of what stamps were valid for postage. Many are overprinted, handstamped or initial-perforated "Specimen," "Canceled" or "Muestra." Some are marked with bars across the denominations (China-Taiwan), punched holes (Czechoslovakia) or back inscriptions (Mongolia).

Stamps distributed to government officials or for publicity purposes, and stamps submitted by private security printers for official approval, also may receive such defacements.

The previously described defacement markings prevent postal use, and all such items generally are known as "specimens."

Tete Beche — This term describes a pair of stamps in which one is upside down in relation to the other. Some of these are the result of intentional sheet arrangements, such as Morocco Scott B10-B11. Others occurred when one or more electrotypes accidentally were placed upside down on the plate, such as Colombia Scott 57a. Separation of the tete-beche stamps, of course, destroys the tete beche variety.

Currency Conversion

Country	Dollar	Pound	S Franc	Yen	HK $	Euro	Cdn $	Aus $
Australia	1.2481	1.9015	1.3559	0.0104	0.1610	1.4069	1.0403	–
Canada	1.1997	1.8277	1.3033	0.0100	0.1548	1.3524	–	0.9612
European Union	0.8871	1.3515	0.9637	0.0074	0.1144	–	0.7394	0.7108
Hong Kong	7.7517	11.810	8.4212	0.0648	–	8.7382	6.4614	6.2108
Japan	119.56	182.15	129.89	–	15.424	134.78	99.658	95.794
Switzerland	0.9205	1.4024	–	0.0077	0.1187	1.0377	0.7673	0.7375
United Kingdom	0.6564	–	0.7131	0.0055	0.0847	0.7399	0.5471	0.5259
United States	–	1.5235	1.0864	0.0084	0.1290	1.1273	0.8335	0.8012

Country	Currency	U.S. $ Equiv.
San Marino	euro	1.1273
Saudi Arabia	riyal	.2667
Senegal	Community of French Africa (CFA) franc	.0017
Serbia	dinar	.0094
Seychelles	rupee	.0735
Sierra Leone	leone	.0002
Singapore	dollar	.7541
Slovakia	euro	1.1273
Slovenia	euro	1.1273
Solomon Islands	dollar	.1288
Somalia	shilling	.0014
South Africa	rand	.0836
S. Georgia & S. Sandwich Isls	British pound	1.5235
Spain	euro	1.1273
South Sudan	pound	.1674
Sri Lanka	rupee	.0075
Sudan	pound	.1674
Surinam	dollar	.3086
Swaziland	emalangeni	.0836
Sweden	krona	.1210
Switzerland	franc	1.0864
Syria	pound	.0053
Tajikistan	somoni	.1589
Tanzania	shilling	.0005
Thailand	baht	.0300
Timor	U.S. dollar	1.0000
Togo	Community of French Africa (CFA) franc	.0017
Tokelau	New Zealand dollar	.7515
Tonga	pa'anga	.5044
Niuafoíou	pa'anga	.5044
Trinidad & Tobago	dollar	.1584
Tristan da Cunha	British pound	1.5235
Tunisia	dinar	.5247
Turkey	lira	.3702
Turk. Rep. of Northern Cyprus	lira	.3702
Turkmenistan	manat	.2857
Turks & Caicos Islands	U.S. dollar	1.0000
Tuvalu	Australian dollar	.8012
Uganda	shilling	.0003
Ukraine	hryvnia	.0478
United Arab Emirates	dirham	.2723
Uruguay	peso	.0378
Uzbekistan	sum	.0004
Vanuatu	vatu	.0098
Vatican City	euro	1.273
Venezuela	bolivar	.1587
Viet Nam	dong	.00005
Virgin Islands	U.S. dollar	1.0000
Wallis & Futuna Islands	Community of French Pacific (CFP) franc	.0094
Yemen	rial	.0047
Zambia	kwacha	.1368
Zaire (Congo Dem. Rep.)	franc	.0011
Zimbabwe	U.S. dollar	1.0000

*Source: **xe.com** May 6, 2015. Figures reflect values as of May 6, 2015.*

COMMON DESIGN TYPES

Pictured in this section are issues where one illustration has been used for a number of countries in the Catalogue. Not included in this section are overprinted stamps or those issues which are illustrated in each country. Because the location of Never Hinged breakpoints varies from country to country, some of the values in the listings below will be for unused stamps that were previously hinged.

EUROPA
Europa, 1956

The design symbolizing the cooperation among the six countries comprising the Coal and Steel Community is illustrated in each country.

Belgium	496-497
France	805-806
Germany	748-749
Italy	715-716
Luxembourg	318-320
Netherlands	368-369

Nos. 496-497 (2)	9.00	.70
Nos. 805-806 (2)	6.80	1.10
Nos. 748-749 (2)	7.30	1.20
Nos. 715-716 (2)	11.50	1.25
Nos. 318-320 (3)	102.50	56.35
Nos. 368-369 (2)	72.50	1.75
Set total (13) Stamps	209.60	62.35

Europa, 1958

"E" and Dove — CD1

European Postal Union at the service of European integration.

1958, Sept. 13

Belgium	527-528
France	889-890
Germany	790-791
Italy	750-751
Luxembourg	341-343
Netherlands	375-376
Saar	317-318

Nos. 527-528 (2)	4.25	.60
Nos. 889-890 (2)	1.65	.55
Nos. 790-791 (2)	3.65	.65
Nos. 750-751 (2)	1.85	.60
Nos. 341-343 (3)	2.35	1.15
Nos. 375-376 (2)	2.50	.75
Nos. 317-318 (2)	1.05	2.30
Set total (15) Stamps	17.30	6.60

Europa, 1959

6-Link Enless Chain — CD2

1959, Sept. 19

Belgium	536-537
France	929-930
Germany	805-806
Italy	791-792
Luxembourg	354-355
Netherlands	379-380

Nos. 536-537 (2)	1.55	.60
Nos. 929-930 (2)	1.85	.90
Nos. 805-806 (2)	1.55	.65
Nos. 791-792 (2)	.80	.50
Nos. 354-355 (2)	3.50	1.40
Nos. 379-380 (2)	9.90	1.25
Set total (12) Stamps	19.15	5.30

Europa, 1960

19-Spoke Wheel CD3

First anniverary of the establishment of C.E.P.T. (Conference Europeenne des Administrations des Postes et des Telecommunications.) The spokes symbolize the 19 founding members of the Conference.

1960, Sept.

Belgium	553-554
Denmark	379
Finland	376-377
France	970-971
Germany	818-820
Great Britain	377-378
Greece	688
Iceland	327-328
Ireland	175-176
Italy	809-810
Luxembourg	374-375
Netherlands	385-386
Norway	387
Portugal	866-867
Spain	941-942
Sweden	562-563
Switzerland	400-401
Turkey	1493-1494

Nos. 553-554 (2)	1.25	.55
No. 379 (1)	.65	.65
Nos. 376-377 (2)	1.70	1.80
Nos. 970-971 (2)	.55	.50
Nos. 818-820 (3)	2.25	1.50
Nos. 377-378 (2)	9.75	5.00
No. 688 (1)	5.00	2.00
Nos. 327-328 (2)	1.30	1.30
Nos. 175-176 (2)	75.00	14.00
Nos. 809-810 (2)	.70	.50
Nos. 374-375 (2)	1.00	.80
Nos. 385-386 (2)	3.65	1.50
No. 387 (1)	1.25	1.25
Nos. 866-867 (2)	2.25	1.25
Nos. 941-942 (2)	1.50	.75
Nos. 562-563 (2)	1.05	.55
Nos. 400-401 (2)	1.25	.65
Nos. 1493-1494 (2)	2.10	1.35
Set total (34) Stamps	112.20	35.90

Europa, 1961

19 Doves Flying as One — CD4

The 19 doves represent the 19 members of the Conference of European Postal and Telecommunications Administrations C.E.P.T.

1961-62

Belgium	572-573
Cyprus	201-203
France	1005-1006
Germany	844-845
Great Britain	382-384
Greece	718-719
Iceland	340-341
Italy	845-846
Luxembourg	382-383
Netherlands	387-388
Spain	1010-1011
Switzerland	410-411
Turkey	1518-1520

Nos. 572-573 (2)	.75	.50
Nos. 201-203 (3)	2.10	1.20
Nos. 1005-1006 (2)	.50	.50
Nos. 844-845 (2)	.60	.75
Nos. 382-384 (3)	.75	.90
Nos. 718-719 (2)	.80	.50
Nos. 340-341 (2)	.90	.90
Nos. 845-846 (2)	.55	.50
Nos. 382-383 (2)	.70	.70
Nos. 387-388 (2)	.55	.50
Nos. 1010-1011 (2)	.70	.55
Nos. 410-411 (2)	1.25	.60
Nos. 1518-1520 (3)	2.45	1.30
Set total (29) Stamps	12.60	9.40

Europa, 1962

Young Tree with 19 Leaves CD5

The 19 leaves represent the 19 original members of C.E.P.T.

1962-63

Belgium	582-583
Cyprus	219-221
France	1045-1046
Germany	852-853
Greece	739-740
Iceland	348-349
Ireland	184-185
Italy	860-861
Luxembourg	386-387
Netherlands	394-395
Norway	414-415
Switzerland	416-417
Turkey	1553-1555

Nos. 582-583 (2)	.65	.65
Nos. 219-221 (3)	76.25	4.40
Nos. 1045-1046 (2)	.60	.50
Nos. 852-853 (2)	.70	.80
Nos. 739-740 (2)	2.25	1.15
Nos. 348-349 (2)	.85	.85
Nos. 184-185 (2)	2.00	1.50
Nos. 860-861 (2)	1.35	.55
Nos. 386-387 (2)	.85	.70
Nos. 394-395 (2)	1.40	.75
Nos. 414-415 (2)	2.25	2.25
Nos. 416-417 (2)	1.65	1.00
Nos. 1553-1555 (3)	3.00	1.55
Set total (28) Stamps	93.80	16.65

Europa, 1963

Stylized Links, Symbolizing Unity — CD6

1963, Sept.

Belgium	598-599
Cyprus	229-231
Finland	419
France	1074-1075
Germany	867-868
Greece	768-769
Iceland	357-358
Ireland	188-189
Italy	880-881
Luxembourg	403-404
Netherlands	416-417
Norway	441-442
Switzerland	429
Turkey	1602-1603

Nos. 598-599 (2)	1.60	.55
Nos. 229-231 (3)	54.75	5.15
No. 419 (1)	1.60	.80
Nos. 1074-1075 (2)	.60	.50
Nos. 867-868 (2)	.50	.55
Nos. 768-769 (2)	5.25	1.90
Nos. 357-358 (2)	1.50	1.50
Nos. 188-189 (2)	4.75	3.25
Nos. 880-881 (2)	.65	.50
Nos. 403-404 (2)	1.00	.80
Nos. 416-417 (2)	2.25	1.00
Nos. 441-442 (2)	4.75	3.00
No. 429 (1)	.90	.60
Nos. 1602-1603 (2)	1.40	.60
Set total (27) Stamps	81.50	20.70

Europa, 1964

Symbolic Daisy — CD7

5th anniversary of the establishment of C.E.P.T. The 22 petals of the flower symbolize the 22 members of the Conference.

1964, Sept.

Austria	738
Belgium	614-615
Cyprus	244-246
France	1109-1110
Germany	897-898
Greece	801-802
Iceland	367-368
Ireland	196-197
Italy	894-895
Luxembourg	411-412
Monaco	590-591
Netherlands	428-429
Norway	458
Portugal	931-933
Spain	1262-1263
Switzerland	438-439
Turkey	1628-1629

No. 738 (1)	1.20	.80
Nos. 614-615 (2)	1.40	.80
Nos. 244-246 (3)	35.75	3.45
Nos. 1109-1110 (2)	.50	.50
Nos. 897-898 (2)	.50	.50
Nos. 801-802 (2)	5.00	1.90
Nos. 367-368 (2)	2.00	1.65
Nos. 196-197 (2)	20.00	4.25
Nos. 894-895 (2)	.55	.50
Nos. 411-412 (2)	.90	.55
Nos. 590-591 (2)	2.50	.70
Nos. 428-429 (2)	1.80	.60
No. 458 (1)	4.50	4.50
Nos. 931-933 (3)	10.00	2.00
Nos. 1262-1263 (2)	1.30	.80
Nos. 438-439 (2)	1.60	.50
Nos. 1628-1629 (2)	2.65	1.35
Set total (34) Stamps	92.15	25.15

Europa, 1965

Leaves and "Fruit" CD8

1965

Belgium	636-637
Cyprus	262-264
Finland	437
France	1131-1132
Germany	934-935
Greece	833-834
Iceland	375-376
Ireland	204-205
Italy	915-916
Luxembourg	432-433
Monaco	616-617
Netherlands	438-439
Norway	475-476
Portugal	958-960
Switzerland	469
Turkey	1665-1666

Nos. 636-637 (2)	.50	.50
Nos. 262-264 (3)	25.35	3.80
No. 437 (1)	1.50	.65
Nos. 1131-1132 (2)	.75	.80
Nos. 934-935 (2)	.50	.50
Nos. 833-834 (2)	2.25	1.15
Nos. 375-376 (2)	2.50	1.75
Nos. 204-205 (2)	20.00	3.35
Nos. 915-916 (2)	.50	.50
Nos. 432-433 (2)	.80	.60
Nos. 616-617 (2)	3.25	1.65
Nos. 438-439 (2)	.75	.55
Nos. 475-476 (2)	4.00	3.10
Nos. 958-960 (3)	10.00	2.75
No. 469 (1)	1.15	.25
Nos. 1665-1666 (2)	3.50	2.10
Set total (32) Stamps	77.30	24.00

Europa, 1966

Symbolic Sailboat — CD9

1966, Sept.

Andorra, French	172
Belgium	675-676
Cyprus	275-277
France	1163-1164
Germany	963-964

Greece	862-863
Iceland	384-385
Ireland	216-217
Italy	942-943
Liechtenstein	415
Luxembourg	440-441
Monaco	639-640
Netherlands	441-442
Norway	496-497
Portugal	980-982
Switzerland	477-478
Turkey	1718-1719

No. 172 (1)	3.00	3.00
Nos. 675-676 (2)	.80	.50
Nos. 275-277 (3)	*4.75*	*1.90*
Nos. 1163-1164 (2)	.60	.50
Nos. 963-964 (2)	.50	.55
Nos. 862-863 (2)	2.25	1.05
Nos. 384-385 (2)	5.00	3.80
Nos. 216-217 (2)	7.00	2.00
Nos. 942-943 (2)	.50	.50
No. 415 (1)	.40	.35
Nos. 440-441 (2)	.80	.60
Nos. 639-640 (2)	2.00	.65
Nos. 441-442 (2)	1.50	.65
Nos. 496-497 (2)	5.00	3.00
Nos. 980-982 (3)	*9.75*	2.25
Nos. 477-478 (2)	1.60	.60
Nos. 1718-1719 (2)	3.35	1.75
Set total (34) Stamps	48.80	23.65

Europa, 1967

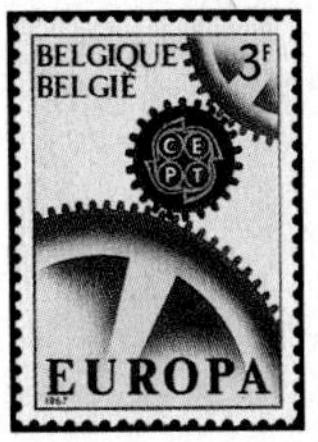

Cogwheels
CD10

1967

Andorra, French	174-175
Belgium	688-689
Cyprus	297-299
France	1178-1179
Germany	969-970
Greece	891-892
Iceland	389-390
Ireland	232-233
Italy	951-952
Liechtenstein	420
Luxembourg	449-450
Monaco	669-670
Netherlands	444-447
Norway	504-505
Portugal	994-996
Spain	1465-1466
Switzerland	482
Turkey	B120-B121

Nos. 174-175 (2)	10.75	6.25
Nos. 688-689 (2)	1.05	.55
Nos. 297-299 (3)	*4.25*	*1.75*
Nos. 1178-1179 (2)	.80	.70
Nos. 969-970 (2)	.55	.55
Nos. 891-892 (2)	3.75	1.00
Nos. 389-390 (2)	3.00	2.00
Nos. 232-233 (2)	6.15	2.30
Nos. 951-952 (2)	.60	.50
No. 420 (1)	.45	.40
Nos. 449-450 (2)	1.00	.70
Nos. 669-670 (2)	2.75	.70
Nos. 444-447 (4)	5.00	1.85
Nos. 504-505 (2)	3.25	2.75
Nos. 994-996 (3)	*9.50*	1.85
Nos. 1465-1466 (2)	.50	.50
No. 482 (1)	.70	.25
Nos. B120-B121 (2)	3.50	2.75
Set total (38) Stamps	57.55	27.35

Europa, 1968

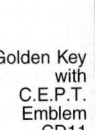

Golden Key
with
C.E.P.T.
Emblem
CD11

1968

Andorra, French	182-183
Belgium	705-706
Cyprus	314-316
France	1209-1210
Germany	983-984
Greece	916-917
Iceland	395-396
Ireland	242-243
Italy	979-980
Liechtenstein	442
Luxembourg	466-467
Monaco	689-691
Netherlands	452-453
Portugal	1019-1021
San Marino	687
Spain	1526
Switzerland	488
Turkey	1775-1776

Nos. 182-183 (2)	16.50	10.00
Nos. 705-706 (2)	1.25	.50
Nos. 314-316 (3)	*2.90*	*1.75*
Nos. 1209-1210 (2)	.90	.55
Nos. 983-984 (2)	.50	.55
Nos. 916-917 (2)	3.75	1.65
Nos. 395-396 (2)	3.00	2.50
Nos. 242-243 (2)	3.75	3.00
Nos. 979-980 (2)	.50	.50
No. 442 (1)	.45	.40
Nos. 466-467 (2)	.80	.70
Nos. 689-691 (3)	*5.40*	.95
Nos. 452-453 (2)	2.10	.70
Nos. 1019-1021 (3)	*9.75*	2.10
No. 687 (1)	.55	.35
No. 1526 (1)	.25	.25
No. 488 (1)	.45	.25
Nos. 1775-1776 (2)	5.00	2.00
Set total (35) Stamps	57.80	28.70

Europa, 1969

"EUROPA"
and "CEPT"
CD12

Tenth anniversary of C.E.P.T.

1969

Andorra, French	188-189
Austria	837
Belgium	718-719
Cyprus	326-328
Denmark	458
Finland	483
France	1245-1246
Germany	996-997
Great Britain	585
Greece	947-948
Iceland	406-407
Ireland	270-271
Italy	1000-1001
Liechtenstein	453
Luxembourg	475-476
Monaco	722-724
Netherlands	475-476
Norway	533-534
Portugal	1038-1040
San Marino	701-702
Spain	1567
Sweden	814-816
Switzerland	500-501
Turkey	1799-1800
Vatican	470-472
Yugoslavia	1003-1004

Nos. 188-189 (2)	18.50	12.00
No. 837 (1)	.65	.30
Nos. 718-719 (2)	.75	.50
Nos. 326-328 (3)	*3.00*	*1.35*
No. 458 (1)	1.10	.75
No. 483 (1)	4.50	1.00
Nos. 1245-1246 (2)	.55	.50
Nos. 996-997 (2)	.80	.50
No. 585 (1)	.25	.25
Nos. 947-948 (2)	5.00	1.50
Nos. 406-407 (2)	4.20	2.40
Nos. 270-271 (2)	4.00	2.00
Nos. 1000-1001 (2)	.70	.50
No. 453 (1)	.45	.45
Nos. 475-476 (2)	1.00	.70
Nos. 722-724 (3)	*10.50*	2.00
Nos. 475-476 (2)	2.60	1.15
Nos. 533-534 (2)	3.75	2.35
Nos. 1038-1040 (3)	17.85	2.40
Nos. 701-702 (2)	.90	.90
No. 1567 (1)	.25	.25
Nos. 814-816 (3)	4.00	2.85
Nos. 500-501 (2)	1.85	.60
Nos. 1799-1800 (2)	3.85	2.25
Nos. 470-472 (3)	.75	.75
Nos. 1003-1004 (2)	4.00	4.00
Set total (51) Stamps	95.75	44.20

Europa, 1970

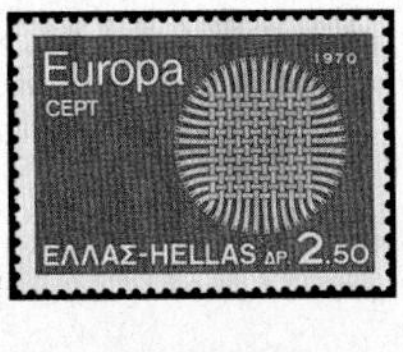

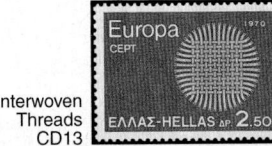

Interwoven
Threads
CD13

1970

Andorra, French	196-197
Belgium	741-742
Cyprus	340-342
France	1271-1272
Germany	1018-1019
Greece	985, 987
Iceland	420-421
Ireland	279-281
Italy	1013-1014
Liechtenstein	470
Luxembourg	489-490
Monaco	768-770
Netherlands	483-484
Portugal	1060-1062
San Marino	729-730
Spain	1607
Switzerland	515-516
Turkey	1848-1849
Yugoslavia	1024-1025

Nos. 196-197 (2)	20.00	8.50
Nos. 741-742 (2)	1.10	.55
Nos. 340-342 (3)	*2.70*	*1.90*
Nos. 1271-1272 (2)	.65	.50
Nos. 1018-1019 (2)	.60	.50
Nos. 985,987 (2)	7.75	2.00
Nos. 420-421 (2)	6.00	4.00
Nos. 279-281 (3)	9.50	3.30
Nos. 1013-1014 (2)	.65	.50
No. 470 (1)	.45	.45
Nos. 489-490 (2)	.80	.80
Nos. 768-770 (3)	*6.35*	2.10
Nos. 483-484 (2)	2.50	1.15
Nos. 1060-1062 (3)	*9.85*	2.35
Nos. 729-730 (2)	.90	.55
No. 1607 (1)	.25	.25
Nos. 515-516 (2)	1.85	.60
Nos. 1848-1849 (2)	5.00	2.25
Nos. 1024-1025 (2)	.80	.80
Set total (40) Stamps	77.70	33.05

Europa, 1971

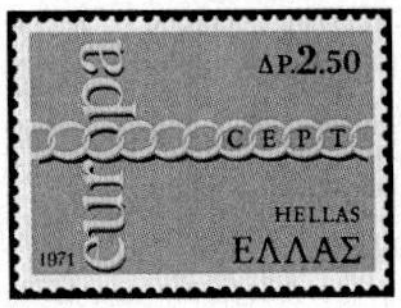

"Fraternity,
Cooperation,
Common
Effort"
CD14

1971

Andorra, French	205-206
Belgium	803-804
Cyprus	365-367
Finland	504
France	1304
Germany	1064-1065
Greece	1029-1030
Iceland	429-430
Ireland	305-306
Italy	1038-1039
Liechtenstein	485
Luxembourg	500-501
Malta	425-427
Monaco	797-799
Netherlands	488-489
Portugal	1094-1096
San Marino	749-750
Spain	1675-1676
Switzerland	531-532
Turkey	1876-1877
Yugoslavia	1052-1053

Nos. 205-206 (2)	20.00	7.75
Nos. 803-804 (2)	1.30	.55
Nos. 365-367 (3)	*2.60*	*1.75*
No. 504 (1)	5.00	.75
No. 1304 (1)	.45	.40
Nos. 1064-1065 (2)	.60	.50
Nos. 1029-1030 (2)	4.00	1.80
Nos. 429-430 (2)	5.00	3.75
Nos. 305-306 (2)	5.00	1.50
Nos. 1038-1039 (2)	.65	.50
No. 485 (1)	.45	.45
Nos. 500-501 (2)	1.00	.80
Nos. 425-427 (3)	*.80*	*.80*
Nos. 797-799 (3)	*15.00*	2.80
Nos. 488-489 (2)	2.50	1.15
Nos. 1094-1096 (3)	*9.75*	1.75
Nos. 749-750 (2)	.65	.55
Nos. 1675-1676 (2)	.75	.55
Nos. 531-532 (2)	1.85	.65
Nos. 1876-1877 (2)	5.60	2.50
Nos. 1052-1053 (2)	.50	.50
Set total (43) Stamps	83.45	31.75

Europa, 1972

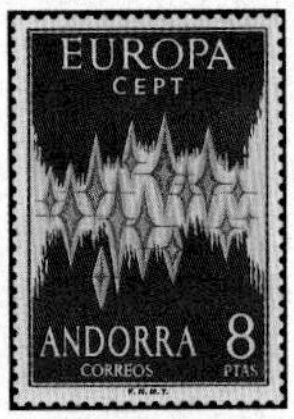

Sparkles, Symbolic
of Communications
CD15

1972

Andorra, French	210-211
Andorra, Spanish	62
Belgium	825-826
Cyprus	380-382
Finland	512-513
France	1341
Germany	1089-1090
Greece	1049-1050
Iceland	439-440
Ireland	316-317
Italy	1065-1066
Liechtenstein	504
Luxembourg	512-513
Malta	450-453
Monaco	831-832
Netherlands	494-495
Portugal	1141-1143
San Marino	771-772
Spain	1718
Switzerland	544-545
Turkey	1907-1908
Yugoslavia	1100-1101

Nos. 210-211 (2)	21.00	7.00
No. 62 (1)	65.00	45.00
Nos. 825-826 (2)	.95	.55
Nos. 380-382 (3)	*5.95*	*2.45*
Nos. 512-513 (2)	8.50	1.40
No. 1341 (1)	.50	.35
Nos. 1089-1090 (2)	1.30	.50
Nos. 1049-1050 (2)	2.00	1.55
Nos. 439-440 (2)	2.90	2.65
Nos. 316-317 (2)	13.00	4.50
Nos. 1065-1066 (2)	.65	.50
No. 504 (1)	.45	.45
Nos. 512-513 (2)	1.00	.80
Nos. 450-453 (4)	1.05	1.40
Nos. 831-832 (2)	5.00	1.40
Nos. 494-495 (2)	3.25	1.15
Nos. 1141-1143 (3)	*9.85*	1.50
Nos. 771-772 (2)	.70	.50
No. 1718 (1)	.50	.40
Nos. 544-545 (2)	1.65	.60
Nos. 1907-1908 (2)	7.50	3.00
Nos. 1100-1101 (2)	1.20	1.20
Set total (44) Stamps	153.90	78.85

Europa, 1973

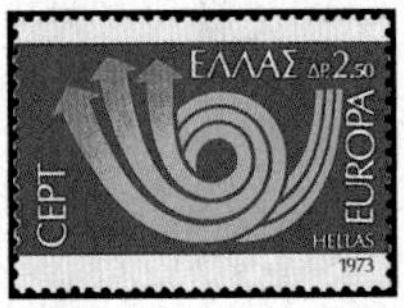

Post Horn
and Arrows
CD16

1973

Andorra, French	219-220
Andorra, Spanish	76
Belgium	839-840
Cyprus	396-398
Finland	526
France	1367
Germany	1114-1115
Greece	1090-1092
Iceland	447-448
Ireland	329-330
Italy	1108-1109
Liechtenstein	528-529
Luxembourg	523-524
Malta	469-471
Monaco	866-867
Netherlands	504-505
Norway	604-605
Portugal	1170-1172
San Marino	802-803
Spain	1753
Switzerland	580-581
Turkey	1935-1936
Yugoslavia	1138-1139

Nos. 219-220 (2)	20.00	11.00
No. 76 (1)	.65	.55
Nos. 839-840 (2)	1.00	.65
Nos. 396-398 (3)	*4.25*	*2.10*
No. 526 (1)	1.40	1.25
No. 1367 (1)	1.60	.75
Nos. 1114-1115 (2)	.90	.50
Nos. 1090-1092 (3)	2.10	1.40
Nos. 447-448 (2)	7.00	4.05

Nos. 329-330 (2)	5.25	2.00
Nos. 1108-1109 (2)	.65	.50
Nos. 528-529 (2)	.60	.60
Nos. 523-524 (2)	.90	1.00
Nos. 469-471 (3)	.90	1.20
Nos. 866-867 (2)	15.00	2.40
Nos. 504-505 (2)	2.85	1.10
Nos. 604-605 (2)	6.25	2.40
Nos. 1170-1172 (3)	13.00	2.15
Nos. 802-803 (2)	1.00	.60
No. 1753 (1)	.35	.25
Nos. 580-581 (2)	1.55	.60
Nos. 1935-1936 (2)	10.00	4.50
Nos. 1138-1139 (2)	1.15	1.10
Set total (46) Stamps	98.35	42.65

Europa, 2000

CD17

2000

Albania	2621-2622
Andorra, French	522
Andorra, Spanish	262
Armenia	610-611
Austria	1814
Azerbaijan	698-699
Belarus	350
Belgium	1818
Bosnia & Herzegovina (Moslem)	358
Bosnia & Herzegovina (Serb)	111-112
Croatia	428-429
Cyprus	959
Czech Republic	3120
Denmark	1189
Estonia	394
Faroe Islands	376
Finland	1129
Aland Islands	166
France	2771
Georgia	228-229
Germany	2086-2087
Gibraltar	837-840
Great Britain (Jersey)	935-936
Great Britain (Isle of Man)	883
Greece	1959
Greenland	363
Hungary	3699-3700
Iceland	910
Ireland	1230-1231
Italy	2349
Latvia	504
Liechtenstein	1178
Lithuania	668
Luxembourg	1035
Macedonia	187
Malta	1011-1012
Moldova	355
Monaco	2161-2162
Poland	3519
Portugal	2358
Portugal (Azores)	455
Portugal (Madeira)	208
Romania	4370
Russia	6589
San Marino	1480
Slovakia	355
Slovenia	424
Spain	3036
Sweden	2394
Switzerland	1074
Turkey	2762
Turkish Rep. of Northern Cyprus	500
Ukraine	379
Vatican City	1152

Nos. 2621-2622 (2)	13.00	13.00
No. 522 (1)	2.00	1.00
No. 262 (1)	1.60	.70
Nos. 610-611 (2)	9.00	9.00
No. 1814 (1)	1.40	1.40
Nos. 698-699 (2)	8.00	8.00
No. 350 (1)	2.00	2.00
No. 1818 (1)	1.40	.60
No. 358 (1)	4.75	4.75
Nos. 111-112 (2)	135.00	135.00
Nos. 428-429 (2)	4.40	3.50
No. 959 (1)	2.10	1.40
No. 3120 (1)	1.00	.40
No. 1189 (1)	3.50	2.25
No. 394 (1)	1.25	1.25
No. 376 (1)	3.00	3.00
No. 1129 (1)	2.00	.90
No. 166 (1)	1.75	1.50
No. 2771 (1)	1.40	.40
No. 228-229 (1)	9.00	9.00
Nos. 2086-2087 (2)	4.15	1.90
Nos. 837-840 (4)	6.25	6.25

Nos. 935-936 (2)	2.40	2.40
No. 883 (1)	1.50	1.50
No. 1959 (1)	3.00	3.00
No. 363 (1)	1.90	1.90
Nos. 3699-3700 (2)	6.50	2.50
No. 910 (1)	2.00	2.00
Nos. 1230-1231 (2)	4.75	4.75
No. 2349 (1)	1.50	.40
No. 504 (1)	5.00	2.40
No. 1178 (1)	2.25	1.75
No. 668 (1)	1.50	1.50
No. 1035 (1)	1.40	1.00
No. 187 (1)	3.25	3.25
Nos. 1011-1012 (2)	4.35	4.35
No. 355 (1)	3.50	3.50
Nos. 2161-2162 (2)	2.80	1.40
No. 3519 (1)	1.10	.50
No. 2358 (1)	1.25	.65
No. 455 (1)	1.25	.50
No. 208 (1)	1.25	.50
No. 4370 (1)	2.50	1.25
No. 6589 (1)	2.00	.85
No. 1480 (1)	1.00	1.00
No. 355 (1)	1.10	.55
No. 424 (1)	3.25	1.60
No. 3036 (1)	.75	.40
No. 2394 (1)	3.00	2.25
No. 1074 (1)	2.10	.75
No. 2762 (1)	2.00	2.00
No. 500 (1)	2.50	2.50
No. 379 (1)	4.50	3.00
No. 1152 (1)	1.25	1.25
Set total (68) Stamps	296.35	264.35

The Gibraltar stamps are similar to the stamp illustrated, but none have the design shown above. All other sets listed above include at least one stamp with the design shown, but some include stamps with entirely different designs. Bulgaria Nos. 4131-4132, Guernsey Nos. 802-803 and Yugoslavia Nos. 2485-2486 are Europa stamps with completely different designs.

PORTUGAL & COLONIES
Vasco da Gama

Fleet Departing CD20

Fleet Arriving at Calicut — CD21

Embarking at Rastello CD22

Muse of History CD23

San Gabriel, da Gama and Camoens CD24

Archangel Gabriel, the Patron Saint CD25

Flagship San Gabriel — CD26

Vasco da Gama — CD27

Fourth centenary of Vasco da Gama's discovery of the route to India.

1898

Azores	93-100
Macao	67-74
Madeira	37-44
Portugal	147-154
Port. Africa	1-8
Port. Congo	75-98
Port. India	189-196
St. Thomas & Prince Islands	170-193
Timor	45-52

Nos. 93-100 (8)	122.00	76.25
Nos. 67-74 (8)	136.00	96.75
Nos. 37-44 (8)	44.55	34.00
Nos. 147-154 (8)	169.30	43.45
Nos. 1-8 (8)	23.95	21.70
Nos. 75-98 (24)	34.45	34.45
Nos. 189-196 (8)	20.25	12.95
Nos. 170-193 (24)	37.85	34.30
Nos. 45-52 (8)	21.50	10.45
Set total (104) Stamps	609.85	364.30

Pombal
POSTAL TAX
POSTAL TAX DUES

Marquis de Pombal — CD28

Planning Reconstruction of Lisbon, 1755 — CD29

Pombal Monument, Lisbon — CD30

Sebastiao Jose de Carvalho e Mello, Marquis de Pombal (1699-1782), statesman, rebuilt Lisbon after earthquake of 1755. Tax was for the erection of Pombal monument. Obligatory on all mail on certain days throughout the year. Postal Tax Dues are inscribed "Multa."

1925

Angola	RA1-RA3, RAJ1-RAJ3
Azores	RA9-RA11, RAJ2-RAJ4
Cape Verde	RA1-RA3, RAJ1-RAJ3
Macao	RA1-RA3, RAJ1-RAJ3
Madeira	RA1-RA3, RAJ1-RAJ3
Mozambique	RA1-RA3, RAJ1-RAJ3
Nyassa	RA1-RA3, RAJ1-RAJ3
Portugal	RA11-RA13, RAJ2-RAJ4
Port. Guinea	RA1-RA3, RAJ1-RAJ3
Port. India	RA1-RA3, RAJ1-RAJ3
St. Thomas & Prince Islands	RA1-RA3, RAJ1-RAJ3
Timor	RA1-RA3, RAJ1-RAJ3

Nos. RA1-RA3,RAJ1-RAJ3 (6)	7.50	6.00
Nos. RA9-RA11,RAJ2-RAJ4 (6)	6.60	9.30
Nos. RA1-RA3,RAJ1-RAJ3 (6)	6.00	5.40
Nos. RA1-RA3,RAJ1-RAJ3 (6)	19.50	4.20
Nos. RA1-RA3,RAJ1-RAJ3 (6)	4.35	12.45
Nos. RA1-RA3,RAJ1-RAJ3 (6)	2.55	2.70
Nos. RA1-RA3,RAJ1-RAJ3 (6)	52.50	38.25
Nos. RA11-RA13,RAJ2-RAJ4 (6)	5.80	5.20
Nos. RA1-RA3,RAJ1-RAJ3 (6)	3.30	2.70
Nos. RA1-RA3,RAJ1-RAJ3 (6)	3.45	3.45
Nos. RA1-RA3,RAJ1-RAJ3 (6)	3.60	3.60
Nos. RA1-RA3,RAJ1-RAJ3 (6)	2.10	3.90
Set total (72) Stamps	117.25	97.15

Vasco da Gama CD34

Mousinho de Albuquerque CD35

Dam CD36

Prince Henry the Navigator CD37

Affonso de Albuquerque CD38

Plane over Globe CD39

1938-39

Angola	274-291, C1-C9
Cape Verde	234-251, C1-C9
Macao	289-305, C7-C15
Mozambique	270-287, C1-C9
Port. Guinea	233-250. C1-C9
Port. India	439-453, C1-C8
St. Thomas & Prince Islands	302-319, 323-340, C1-C18
Timor	223-239, C1-C9

Nos. 274-291,C1-C9 (27)	141.35	22.25
Nos. 234-251,C1-C9 (27)	100.00	31.20
Nos. 289-305,C7-C15 (26)	701.70	135.60
Nos. 270-287,C1-C9 (27)	60.95	11.20
Nos. 233-250,C1-C9 (27)	86.05	30.70
Nos. 439-453,C1-C8 (23)	74.75	25.50
Nos. 302-319,323-340,C1-C18 (54)	319.25	190.35
Nos. 223-239,C1-C9 (26)	149.25	73.15
Set total (237) Stamps	1,633	519.95

Lady of Fatima

Our Lady of the Rosary, Fatima, Portugal — CD40

1948-49

Angola	315-318
Cape Verde	266
Macao	336
Mozambique	325-328
Port. Guinea	271
Port. India	480
St. Thomas & Prince Islands	351
Timor	254

Nos. 315-318 (4)	88.50	17.90
No. 266 (1)	8.50	4.50
No. 336 (1)	40.00	12.00
Nos. 325-328 (4)	20.00	4.50
No. 271 (1)	3.25	3.00
No. 480 (1)	2.50	2.25
No. 351 (1)	7.25	6.50
No. 254 (1)	3.00	3.00
Set total (14) Stamps	173.00	53.65

A souvenir sheet of 9 stamps was issued in 1951 to mark the extension of the 1950 Holy Year. The sheet contains: Angola No. 316, Cape Verde No. 266, Macao No. 336, Mozambique No. 325, Portuguese Guinea No. 271, Portuguese India Nos. 480, 485, St. Thomas & Prince Islands No. 351, Timor No. 254. The sheet also contains a portrait of Pope Pius XII and is inscribed "Encerramento do"

Ano Santo, Fatima 1951." It was sold for 11 escudos.

Holy Year

Church Bells and Dove CD41

Angel Holding Candelabra CD42

Holy Year, 1950.

1950-51

Angola		331-332
Cape Verde		268-269
Macao		339-340
Mozambique		330-331
Port. Guinea		273-274
Port. India	490-491,	496-503
St. Thomas & Prince Islands		353-354
Timor		258-259

Nos. 331-332 (2)	7.60	1.35
Nos. 268-269 (2)	4.75	2.20
Nos. 339-340 (2)	55.00	12.50
Nos. 330-331 (2)	1.75	.85
Nos. 273-274 (2)	3.50	2.60
Nos. 490-491,496-503 (10)	12.80	5.40
Nos. 353-354 (2)	7.50	4.40
Nos. 258-259 (2)	3.75	3.25
Set total (24) Stamps	96.65	32.55

A souvenir sheet of 8 stamps was issued in 1951 to mark the extension of the Holy Year. The sheet contains: Angola No. 331, Cape Verde No. 269, Macao No. 340, Mozambique No. 331, Portuguese Guinea No. 275, Portuguese India No. 490, St. Thomas & Prince Islands No. 354, Timor No. 258, some with colors changed. The sheet contains doves and is inscribed 'Encerramento do Ano Santo, Fatima 1951.' It was sold for 17 escudos.

Holy Year Conclusion

Our Lady of Fatima — CD43

Conclusion of Holy Year. Sheets contain alternate vertical rows of stamps and labels bearing quotation from Pope Pius XII, different for each colony.

1951

Angola		357
Cape Verde		270
Macao		352
Mozambique		356
Port. Guinea		275
Port. India		506
St. Thomas & Prince Islands		355
Timor		270

No. 357 (1)	5.25	1.50
No. 270 (1)	1.50	1.25
No. 352 (1)	37.50	10.00
No. 356 (1)	2.25	1.00
No. 275 (1)	1.00	.65
No. 506 (1)	1.60	1.00
No. 355 (1)	2.50	2.00
No. 270 (1)	2.00	1.75
Set total (8) Stamps	53.60	19.15

Medical Congress

CD44

First National Congress of Tropical Medicine, Lisbon, 1952. Each stamp has a different design.

1952

Angola	358
Cape Verde	287
Macao	364

Mozambique	359
Port. Guinea	276
Port. India	516
St. Thomas & Prince Islands	356
Timor	271

No. 358 (1)	1.25	.45
No. 287 (1)	.70	.50
No. 364 (1)	9.75	4.25
No. 359 (1)	1.10	.55
No. 276 (1)	.45	.35
No. 516 (1)	4.75	2.00
No. 356 (1)	.30	.30
No. 271 (1)	1.00	1.00
Set total (8) Stamps	19.30	9.40

Postage Due Stamps

CD45

1952

Angola	J37-J42
Cape Verde	J31-J36
Macao	J53-J58
Mozambique	J51-J56
Port. Guinea	J40-J45
Port. India	J47-J52
St. Thomas & Prince Islands	J52-J57
Timor	J31-J36

Nos. J37-J42 (6)	4.05	3.15
Nos. J31-J36 (6)	2.80	2.30
Nos. J53-J58 (6)	17.45	6.85
Nos. J51-J56 (6)	1.80	1.55
Nos. J40-J45 (6)	2.55	2.55
Nos. J47-J52 (6)	6.10	6.10
Nos. J52-J57 (6)	4.15	4.15
Nos. J31-J36 (6)	3.50	3.50
Set total (48) Stamps	42.40	30.15

Sao Paulo

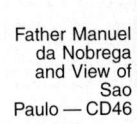 

Father Manuel da Nobrega and View of Sao Paulo — CD46

Founding of Sao Paulo, Brazil, 400th anniv.

1954

Angola	385
Cape Verde	297
Macao	382
Mozambique	395
Port. Guinea	291
Port. India	530
St. Thomas & Prince Islands	369
Timor	279

No. 385 (1)	.80	.50
No. 297 (1)	.70	.60
No. 382 (1)	14.00	3.00
No. 395 (1)	.40	.30
No. 291 (1)	.35	.25
No. 530 (1)	.80	.40
No. 369 (1)	.80	.60
No. 279 (1)	.85	.70
Set total (8) Stamps	18.70	6.35

Tropical Medicine Congress

CD47

Sixth International Congress for Tropical Medicine and Malaria, Lisbon, Sept. 1958. Each stamp shows a different plant.

1958

Angola	409
Cape Verde	303
Macao	392
Mozambique	404
Port. Guinea	295
Port. India	569
St. Thomas & Prince Islands	371

Timor	289

No. 409 (1)	3.50	1.10
No. 303 (1)	5.50	2.10
No. 392 (1)	8.00	3.00
No. 404 (1)	4.00	.85
No. 295 (1)	2.75	1.10
No. 569 (1)	1.75	.75
No. 371 (1)	2.75	2.25
No. 289 (1)	3.00	2.75
Set total (8) Stamps	31.25	13.90

Sports

CD48

Each stamp shows a different sport.

1962

Angola	433-438
Cape Verde	320-325
Macao	394-399
Mozambique	424-429
Port. Guinea	299-304
St. Thomas & Prince Islands	374-379
Timor	313-318

Nos. 433-438 (6)	6.50	3.20
Nos. 320-325 (6)	14.25	5.20
Nos. 394-399 (6)	74.00	14.60
Nos. 424-429 (6)	5.00	2.45
Nos. 299-304 (6)	4.95	2.15
Nos. 374-379 (6)	6.75	3.20
Nos. 313-318 (6)	6.40	3.70
Set total (42) Stamps	117.85	34.50

Anti-Malaria

Anopheles Funestus and Malaria Eradication Symbol — CD49

World Health Organization drive to eradicate malaria.

1962

Angola	439
Cape Verde	326
Macao	400
Mozambique	430
Port. Guinea	305
St. Thomas & Prince Islands	380
Timor	319

No. 439 (1)	2.00	.90
No. 326 (1)	1.40	.90
No. 400 (1)	6.50	2.00
No. 430 (1)	1.40	.40
No. 305 (1)	1.25	.45
No. 380 (1)	2.00	1.50
No. 319 (1)	.75	.60
Set total (7) Stamps	15.30	6.75

Airline Anniversary

Map of Africa, Super Constellation and Jet Liner — CD50

Tenth anniversary of Transportes Aereos Portugueses (TAP).

1963

Angola	490
Cape Verde	327
Mozambique	434
Port. Guinea	318
St. Thomas & Prince Islands	381

No. 490 (1)	1.25	.50
No. 327 (1)	1.10	.70
No. 434 (1)	.40	.25

No. 318 (1)	.65	.35
No. 381 (1)	.70	.60
Set total (5) Stamps	4.10	2.40

National Overseas Bank

Antonio Teixeira de Sousa — CD51

Centenary of the National Overseas Bank of Portugal.

1964, May 16

Angola	509
Cape Verde	328
Port. Guinea	319
St. Thomas & Prince Islands	382
Timor	320

No. 509 (1)	.90	.30
No. 328 (1)	1.10	.75
No. 319 (1)	.65	.40
No. 382 (1)	.70	.50
No. 320 (1)	.75	.60
Set total (5) Stamps	4.10	2.55

ITU

ITU Emblem and the Archangel Gabriel — CD52

International Communications Union, Cent.

1965, May 17

Angola	511
Cape Verde	329
Macao	402
Mozambique	464
Port. Guinea	320
St. Thomas & Prince Islands	383
Timor	321

No. 511 (1)	1.25	.65
No. 329 (1)	2.10	1.40
No. 402 (1)	5.00	2.00
No. 464 (1)	.40	.25
No. 320 (1)	1.90	1.00
No. 383 (1)	1.50	1.00
No. 321 (1)	1.50	.90
Set total (7) Stamps	13.65	6.95

National Revolution

CD53

40th anniv. of the National Revolution. Different buildings on each stamp.

1966, May 28

Angola	525
Cape Verde	338
Macao	403
Mozambique	465
Port. Guinea	329
St. Thomas & Prince Islands	392
Timor	322

No. 525 (1)	.45	.25
No. 338 (1)	.60	.45
No. 403 (1)	5.00	2.00
No. 465 (1)	.50	.30
No. 329 (1)	.55	.35
No. 392 (1)	.75	.50
No. 322 (1)	1.50	.90
Set total (7) Stamps	9.35	4.75

Navy Club

CD54

Centenary of Portugal's Navy Club. Each stamp has a different design.

1967, Jan. 31

Angola	527-528
Cape Verde	339-340
Macao	412-413
Mozambique	478-479
Port. Guinea	330-331
St. Thomas & Prince Islands	393-394
Timor	323-324

Nos. 527-528 (2)	2.25	1.00
Nos. 339-340 (2)	2.00	1.40
Nos. 412-413 (2)	9.50	3.75
Nos. 478-479 (2)	1.20	.65
Nos. 330-331 (2)	1.20	.90
Nos. 393-394 (2)	3.20	1.25
Nos. 323-324 (2)	4.00	2.00
Set total (14) Stamps	23.35	10.95

Admiral Coutinho

CD55

Centenary of the birth of Admiral Carlos Viegas Gago Coutinho (1869-1959), explorer and aviation pioneer. Each stamp has a different design.

1969, Feb. 17

Angola	547
Cape Verde	355
Macao	417
Mozambique	484
Port. Guinea	335
St. Thomas & Prince Islands	397
Timor	335

No. 547 (1)	1.00	.35
No. 355 (1)	.35	.25
No. 417 (1)	3.75	1.50
No. 484 (1)	.25	.25
No. 335 (1)	.35	.25
No. 397 (1)	.50	.35
No. 335 (1)	1.10	.85
Set total (7) Stamps	7.30	3.80

Administration Reform

Luiz Augusto Rebello da Silva — CD56

Centenary of the administration reforms of the overseas territories.

1969, Sept. 25

Angola	549
Cape Verde	357
Macao	419
Mozambique	491
Port. Guinea	337
St. Thomas & Prince Islands	399
Timor	338

No. 549 (1)	.25	.25
No. 357 (1)	.35	.25
No. 419 (1)	5.00	1.00
No. 491 (1)	.25	.25
No. 337 (1)	.25	.25
No. 399 (1)	.45	.45
No. 338 (1)	.40	.25
Set total (7) Stamps	6.95	2.70

Marshal Carmona

CD57

Birth centenary of Marshal Antonio Oscar Carmona de Fragoso (1869-1951), President of Portugal. Each stamp has a different design.

1970, Nov. 15

Angola	563
Cape Verde	359
Macao	422
Mozambique	493
Port. Guinea	340
St. Thomas & Prince Islands	403
Timor	341

No. 563 (1)	.45	.25
No. 359 (1)	.55	.35
No. 422 (1)	2.25	1.25
No. 493 (1)	.40	.25
No. 340 (1)	.35	.25
No. 403 (1)	.75	.45
No. 341 (1)	.25	.25
Set total (7) Stamps	5.00	3.05

Olympic Games

CD59

20th Olympic Games, Munich, Aug. 26-Sept. 11. Each stamp shows a different sport.

1972, June 20

Angola	569
Cape Verde	361
Macao	426
Mozambique	504
Port. Guinea	342
St. Thomas & Prince Islands	408
Timor	343

No. 569 (1)	.65	.25
No. 361 (1)	.65	.25
No. 426 (1)	3.25	1.00
No. 504 (1)	.30	.25
No. 342 (1)	.45	.25
No. 408 (1)	.35	.25
No. 343 (1)	.50	.50
Set total (7) Stamps	6.15	2.80

Lisbon-Rio de Janeiro Flight

CD60

50th anniversary of the Lisbon to Rio de Janeiro flight by Arturo de Sacadura and Coutinho, March 30-June 5, 1922. Each stamp shows a different stage of the flight.

1972, Sept. 20

Angola	570
Cape Verde	362
Macao	427
Mozambique	505
Port. Guinea	343
St. Thomas & Prince Islands	409
Timor	344

No. 570 (1)	.35	.25
No. 362 (1)	1.50	.30
No. 427 (1)	22.50	7.50
No. 505 (1)	.25	.25
No. 343 (1)	.25	.25
No. 409 (1)	.35	.25
No. 344 (1)	.25	.40
Set total (7) Stamps	25.45	9.20

WMO Centenary

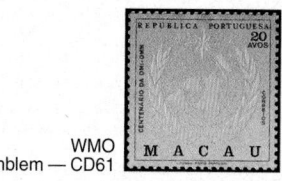

WMO Emblem — CD61

Centenary of international meterological cooperation.

1973, Dec. 15

Angola	571
Cape Verde	363
Macao	429
Mozambique	509
Port. Guinea	344
St. Thomas & Prince Islands	410
Timor	345

No. 571 (1)	.45	.25
No. 363 (1)	.65	.30
No. 429 (1)	6.25	1.75
No. 509 (1)	.30	.25
No. 344 (1)	.45	.35
No. 410 (1)	.60	.50
No. 345 (1)	1.75	2.00
Set total (7) Stamps	10.45	5.40

FRENCH COMMUNITY

Upper Volta can be found under Burkina Faso in Vol. 1
Madagascar can be found under Malagasy in Vol. 3

Colonial Exposition

People of French Empire CD70

Women's Heads CD71

France Showing Way to Civilization CD72

"Colonial Commerce" CD73

International Colonial Exposition, Paris.

1931

Cameroun	213-216
Chad	60-63
Dahomey	97-100
Fr. Guiana	152-155
Fr. Guinea	116-119
Fr. India	100-103
Fr. Polynesia	76-79
Fr. Sudan	102-105
Gabon	120-123
Guadeloupe	138-141
Indo-China	140-142
Ivory Coast	92-95
Madagascar	169-172
Martinique	129-132
Mauritania	65-68
Middle Congo	61-64
New Caledonia	176-179
Niger	73-76
Reunion	122-125
St. Pierre & Miquelon	132-135
Senegal	138-141
Somali Coast	135-138
Togo	254-257
Ubangi-Shari	82-85
Upper Volta	66-69
Wallis & Futuna Isls.	85-88

Nos. 213-216 (4)	23.00	18.25
Nos. 60-63 (4)	22.00	22.00
Nos. 97-100 (4)	26.00	26.00
Nos. 152-155 (4)	22.00	22.00
Nos. 116-119 (4)	19.75	19.75
Nos. 100-103 (4)	18.00	18.00
Nos. 76-79 (4)	30.00	30.00
Nos. 102-105 (4)	19.00	19.00
Nos. 120-123 (4)	17.50	17.50
Nos. 138-141 (4)	19.00	19.00
Nos. 140-142 (3)	11.50	11.50
Nos. 92-95 (4)	22.50	22.50
Nos. 169-172 (4)	7.90	5.00
Nos. 129-132 (4)	21.00	21.00
Nos. 65-68 (4)	22.00	22.00
Nos. 61-64 (4)	20.50	20.50
Nos. 176-179 (4)	24.00	24.00
Nos. 73-76 (4)	21.50	21.50
Nos. 122-125 (4)	22.00	22.00
Nos. 132-135 (4)	24.00	24.00
Nos. 138-141 (4)	20.00	20.00
Nos. 135-138 (4)	22.00	22.00
Nos. 254-257 (4)	22.00	22.00

Nos. 82-85 (4)	21.00	21.00
Nos. 66-69 (4)	19.00	19.00
Nos. 85-88 (4)	35.00	35.00
Set total (103) Stamps	552.15	544.50

Paris International Exposition
Colonial Arts Exposition

"Colonial Resources"
CD74   CD77

Overseas Commerce CD75

Exposition Building and Women CD76

"France and the Empire" CD78

Cultural Treasures of the Colonies CD79

Souvenir sheets contain one imperf. stamp.

1937

Cameroun	217-222A
Dahomey	101-107
Fr. Equatorial Africa	27-32, 73
Fr. Guiana	162-168
Fr. Guinea	120-126
Fr. India	104-110
Fr. Polynesia	117-123
Fr. Sudan	106-112
Guadeloupe	148-154
Indo-China	193-199
Inini	41
Ivory Coast	152-158
Kwangchowan	132
Madagascar	191-197
Martinique	179-185
Mauritania	69-75
New Caledonia	208-214
Niger	73-83
Reunion	167-173
St. Pierre & Miquelon	165-171
Senegal	172-178
Somali Coast	139-145
Togo	258-264
Wallis & Futuna Isls.	89

Nos. 217-222A (7)	18.95	20.45
Nos. 101-107 (7)	23.60	27.60
Nos. 27-32, 73 (7)	28.10	32.10
Nos. 162-168 (7)	22.50	24.50
Nos. 120-126 (7)	24.00	28.00
Nos. 104-110 (7)	21.15	24.40
Nos. 117-123 (7)	58.50	75.00
Nos. 106-112 (7)	23.60	27.60
Nos. 148-154 (7)	19.55	21.05
Nos. 193-199 (7)	17.70	19.70
No. 41 (1)	19.00	22.50
Nos. 152-158 (7)	22.20	26.20
No. 132 (1)	9.25	11.00
Nos. 191-197 (7)	17.55	18.30
Nos. 179-185 (7)	19.95	21.70
Nos. 69-75 (7)	20.50	24.50
Nos. 208-214 (7)	39.00	50.50
Nos. 73-83 (11)	42.70	46.70
Nos. 167-173 (7)	21.70	23.20
Nos. 165-171 (7)	49.60	64.00
Nos. 172-178 (7)	21.00	23.80
Nos. 139-145 (7)	25.60	32.60
Nos. 258-264 (7)	20.40	20.40
No. 89 (1)	28.50	37.50
Set total (154) Stamps	614.60	723.30

Curie

Pierre and Marie Curie CD80

40th anniversary of the discovery of radium. The surtax was for the benefit of the Intl. Union for the Control of Cancer.

1938

Cameroun	B1
Cuba	B1-B2
Dahomey	B2
France	B76
Fr. Equatorial Africa	B1
Fr. Guiana	B3
Fr. Guinea	B2
Fr. India	B6
Fr. Polynesia	B5
Fr. Sudan	B1
Guadeloupe	B3
Indo-China	B14
Ivory Coast	B2
Madagascar	B2
Martinique	B2
Mauritania	B3
New Caledonia	B4
Niger	B1
Reunion	B4
St. Pierre & Miquelon	B3
Senegal	B3
Somali Coast	B2
Togo	B1

No. B1 (1)	10.00	10.00
Nos. B1-B2 (2)	8.50	2.40
No. B2 (1)	9.50	9.50
No. B76 (1)	21.00	12.50
No. B1 (1)	24.00	24.00
No. B3 (1)	13.50	13.50
No. B2 (1)	8.75	8.75
No. B6 (1)	10.00	10.00
No. B5 (1)	20.00	20.00
No. B1 (1)	12.50	12.50
No. B3 (1)	11.00	10.50
No. B14 (1)	12.00	12.00
No. B2 (1)	11.00	7.50
No. B2 (1)	11.00	11.00
No. B2 (1)	13.00	13.00
No. B3 (1)	7.75	7.75
No. B4 (1)	16.50	17.50
No. B1 (1)	15.00	15.00
No. B4 (1)	14.00	14.00
No. B3 (1)	21.00	22.50
No. B3 (1)	10.50	10.50
No. B2 (1)	7.75	7.75
No. B1 (1)	20.00	20.00
Set total (24) Stamps	308.25	292.15

Caillie

Rene Caillie and Map of Northwestern Africa — CD81

Death centenary of Rene Caillie (1799-1838), French explorer. All three denominations exist with colony name omitted.

1939

Dahomey	108-110
Fr. Guinea	161-163
Fr. Sudan	113-115
Ivory Coast	160-162
Mauritania	109-111
Niger	84-86
Senegal	188-190
Togo	265-267

Nos. 108-110 (3)	1.20	3.60
Nos. 161-163 (3)	1.20	3.20
Nos. 113-115 (3)	1.20	3.20
Nos. 160-162 (3)	1.05	2.55
Nos. 109-111 (3)	1.05	3.80
Nos. 84-86 (3)	1.05	2.35
Nos. 188-190 (3)	1.05	2.90
Nos. 265-267 (3)	1.05	3.30
Set total (24) Stamps	8.85	24.90

New York World's Fair

Natives and New York Skyline CD82

1939

Cameroun	223-224
Dahomey	111-112
Fr. Equatorial Africa	78-79
Fr. Guiana	169-170
Fr. Guinea	164-165
Fr. India	111-112
Fr. Polynesia	124-125
Fr. Sudan	116-117
Guadeloupe	155-156
Indo-China	203-204
Inini	42-43
Ivory Coast	163-164
Kwangchowan	133-134
Madagascar	209-210
Martinique	186-187
Mauritania	112-113
New Caledonia	215-216
Niger	87-88
Reunion	174-175
St. Pierre & Miquelon	205-206
Senegal	191-192
Somali Coast	179-180
Togo	268-269
Wallis & Futuna Isls.	90-91

Nos. 223-224 (2)	2.80	2.40
Nos. 111-112 (2)	1.60	3.20
Nos. 78-79 (2)	1.60	3.20
Nos. 169-170 (2)	2.60	2.60
Nos. 164-165 (2)	1.60	3.20
Nos. 111-112 (2)	3.00	3.00
Nos. 124-125 (2)	4.80	4.80
Nos. 116-117 (2)	1.60	3.20
Nos. 155-156 (2)	2.50	2.50
Nos. 203-204 (2)	2.05	2.05
Nos. 42-43 (2)	7.50	9.00
Nos. 163-164 (2)	1.50	3.00
Nos. 133-134 (2)	2.50	2.50
Nos. 209-210 (2)	3.75	3.75
Nos. 186-187 (2)	2.35	2.35
Nos. 112-113 (2)	1.40	2.80
Nos. 215-216 (2)	3.35	3.35
Nos. 87-88 (2)	1.40	2.80
Nos. 174-175 (2)	2.80	2.80
Nos. 205-206 (2)	4.80	6.00
Nos. 191-192 (2)	1.40	2.80
Nos. 179-180 (2)	1.40	2.80
Nos. 268-269 (2)	1.40	2.80
Nos. 90-91 (2)	6.00	6.00
Set total (48) Stamps	65.70	82.90

French Revolution

Storming of the Bastille CD83

French Revolution, 150th anniv. The surtax was for the defense of the colonies.

1939

Cameroun	B2-B6
Dahomey	B3-B7
Fr. Equatorial Africa	B4-B8, CB1
Fr. Guiana	B4-B8, CB1
Fr. Guinea	B3-B7
Fr. India	B7-B11
Fr. Polynesia	B6-B10, CB1
Fr. Sudan	B2-B6
Guadeloupe	B4-B8
Indo-China	B15-B19, CB1
Inini	B1-B5
Ivory Coast	B3-B7
Kwangchowan	B1-B5
Madagascar	B3-B7, CB1
Martinique	B3-B7
Mauritania	B4-B8
New Caledonia	B5-B9, CB1
Niger	B2-B6
Reunion	B5-B9, CB1
St. Pierre & Miquelon	B4-B8
Senegal	B4-B8, CB1
Somali Coast	B3-B7
Togo	B2-B6
Wallis & Futuna Isls.	B1-B5

Nos. B2-B6 (5)	60.00	60.00
Nos. B3-B7 (5)	47.50	47.50
Nos. B4-B8,CB1 (6)	120.00	120.00
Nos. B4-B8,CB1 (6)	79.50	79.50
Nos. B3-B7 (5)	47.50	47.50
Nos. B7-B11 (5)	45.00	45.00
Nos. B6-B10,CB1 (6)	122.50	122.50
Nos. B2-B6 (5)	50.00	50.00
Nos. B4-B8 (5)	50.00	50.00
Nos. B15-B19,CB1 (6)	85.00	85.00
Nos. B1-B5 (5)	80.00	87.50
Nos. B3-B7 (5)	43.75	43.75
Nos. B1-B5 (5)	46.25	46.25
Nos. B3-B7,CB1 (6)	65.50	65.50
Nos. B3-B7 (5)	52.50	52.50
Nos. B4-B8 (5)	42.50	42.50
Nos. B5-B9,CB1 (6)	101.50	101.50
Nos. B2-B6 (5)	60.00	60.00
Nos. B5-B9,CB1 (6)	87.50	87.50
Nos. B4-B8 (5)	67.50	72.50
Nos. B4-B8,CB1 (6)	57.00	57.00
Nos. B3-B7 (5)	45.00	45.00
Nos. B2-B6 (5)	42.50	42.50
Nos. B1-B5 (5)	95.00	95.00
Set total (128) Stamps	1,594	1,606

Plane over Coastal Area CD85

All five denominations exist with colony name omitted.

1940

Dahomey	C1-C5
Fr. Guinea	C1-C5
Fr. Sudan	C1-C5
Ivory Coast	C1-C5
Mauritania	C1-C5
Niger	C1-C5
Senegal	C12-C16
Togo	C1-C5

Nos. C1-C5 (5)	4.00	4.00
Nos. C1-C5 (5)	4.00	4.00
Nos. C1-C5 (5)	4.00	4.00
Nos. C1-C5 (5)	3.80	3.80
Nos. C1-C5 (5)	3.50	3.50
Nos. C1-C5 (5)	3.50	3.50
Nos. C12-C16 (5)	3.50	3.50
Nos. C1-C5 (5)	3.15	3.15
Set total (40) Stamps	29.45	29.45

Defense of the Empire

Colonial Infantryman — CD86

1941

Cameroun	B13B
Dahomey	B13
Fr. Equatorial Africa	B8B
Fr. Guiana	B10
Fr. Guinea	B13
Fr. India	B13
Fr. Polynesia	B12
Fr. Sudan	B12
Guadeloupe	B10
Indo-China	B19B
Inini	B7
Ivory Coast	B13
Kwangchowan	B7
Madagascar	B9
Martinique	B9
Mauritania	B14
New Caledonia	B11
Niger	B12
Reunion	B11
St. Pierre & Miquelon	B8B
Senegal	B14
Somali Coast	B9
Togo	B10B
Wallis & Futuna Isls.	B7

No. B13B (1)	1.60
No. B13 (1)	1.20
No. B8B (1)	3.50
No. B10 (1)	1.40
No. B13 (1)	1.40
No. B13 (1)	1.25
No. B12 (1)	3.50
No. B12 (1)	1.40
No. B10 (1)	1.00
No. B19B (1)	1.60
No. B7 (1)	1.75
No. B13 (1)	1.25
No. B7 (1)	.85
No. B9 (1)	1.50
No. B9 (1)	1.40
No. B14 (1)	.95
No. B11 (1)	1.60
No. B12 (1)	1.40
No. B11 (1)	1.60
No. B8B (1)	3.75
No. B14 (1)	1.25
No. B9 (1)	1.60
No. B10B (1)	1.25
No. B7 (1)	2.40
Set total (24) Stamps	40.40

Each of the CD86 stamps listed above is part of a set of three stamps. The designs of the other two stamps in the set vary from country to country. Only the values of the Common Design stamps are listed here.

Colonial Education Fund

CD86a

1942

Cameroun	CB3
Dahomey	CB4
Fr. Equatorial Africa	CB5
Fr. Guiana	CB4
Fr. Guinea	CB4
Fr. India	CB3
Fr. Polynesia	CB4
Fr. Sudan	CB3
Guadeloupe	CB3
Indo-China	CB5
Inini	CB3
Ivory Coast	CB4
Kwangchowan	CB4
Malagasy	CB5
Martinique	CB3
Mauritania	CB4
New Caledonia	CB4
Niger	CB4
Reunion	CB4
St. Pierre & Miquelon	CB3
Senegal	CB5
Somali Coast	CB3
Togo	CB3
Wallis & Futuna	CB3

No. CB3 (1)	1.10	
No. CB4 (1)	.80	5.50
No. CB5 (1)	.80	
No. CB4 (1)	1.10	
No. CB4 (1)	.40	5.50
No. CB3 (1)	.90	
No. CB4 (1)	2.00	
No. CB4 (1)	.40	5.50
No. CB3 (1)	1.10	
No. CB5 (1)	1.10	
No. CB3 (1)	1.25	
No. CB4 (1)	1.00	5.50
No. CB4 (1)	1.00	
No. CB5 (1)	.65	
No. CB3 (1)	1.00	
No. CB4 (1)	.80	
No. CB4 (1)	1.60	
No. CB4 (1)	.35	
No. CB4 (1)	.90	
No. CB3 (1)	5.25	
No. CB5 (1)	.80	6.50
No. CB3 (1)	.70	
No. CB3 (1)	.35	
No. CB3 (1)	2.25	
Set total (24) Stamps	27.60	28.50

Cross of Lorraine & Four-motor Plane CD87

1941-5

Cameroun	C1-C7
Fr. Equatorial Africa	C17-C23
Fr. Guiana	C9-C10
Fr. India	C1-C6
Fr. Polynesia	C3-C9
Fr. West Africa	C1-C3
Guadeloupe	C1-C2
Madagascar	C37-C43

Martinique		C1-C2
New Caledonia		C7-C13
Reunion		C18-C24
St. Pierre & Miquelon		C1-C7
Somali Coast		C1-C7

Nos. C1-C7 (7)	6.30	6.30
Nos. C17-C23 (7)	10.40	6.35
Nos. C9-C10 (2)	3.80	3.10
Nos. C1-C6 (6)	9.30	9.30
Nos. C3-C9 (7)	13.75	10.00
Nos. C1-C3 (3)	9.50	3.90
Nos. C1-C2 (2)	3.75	2.50
Nos. C37-C43 (7)	5.60	3.80
Nos. C1-C2 (2)	3.00	1.60
Nos. C7-C13 (7)	8.35	8.35
Nos. C18-C24 (7)	7.05	5.00
Nos. C1-C7 (7)	11.60	9.40
Nos. C1-C7 (7)	13.95	11.10
Set total (71) Stamps	106.35	80.70

Transport Plane CD88

Caravan and Plane CD89

1942

Dahomey		C6-C13
Fr. Guinea		C6-C13
Fr. Sudan		C6-C13
Ivory Coast		C6-C13
Mauritania		C6-C13
Niger		C6-C13
Senegal		C17-C25
Togo		C6-C13

Nos. C6-C13 (8)	7.15
Nos. C6-C13 (8)	5.75
Nos. C6-C13 (8)	8.00
Nos. C6-C13 (8)	11.15
Nos. C6-C13 (8)	9.75
Nos. C6-C13 (8)	6.90
Nos. C17-C25 (9)	9.45
Nos. C6-C13 (8)	6.75
Set total (65) Stamps	64.90

Red Cross

Marianne CD90

The surtax was for the French Red Cross and national relief.

1944

Cameroun		B28
Fr. Equatorial Africa		B38
Fr. Guiana		B12
Fr. India		B14
Fr. Polynesia		B13
Fr. West Africa		B1
Guadeloupe		B12
Madagascar		B15
Martinique		B11
New Caledonia		B13
Reunion		B15
St. Pierre & Miquelon		B13
Somali Coast		B13
Wallis & Futuna Isls.		B9

No. B28 (1)	2.00	1.60
No. B38 (1)	1.60	1.20
No. B12 (1)	1.75	1.25
No. B14 (1)	1.50	1.25
No. B13 (1)	2.00	1.60
No. B1 (1)	6.50	4.75
No. B12 (1)	1.40	1.00
No. B15 (1)	.90	.90
No. B11 (1)	1.20	1.20
No. B13 (1)	1.50	1.50
No. B13 (1)	1.60	1.10
No. B13 (1)	2.75	2.40
No. B13 (1)	1.75	2.00
No. B9 (1)	4.50	3.25
Set total (14) Stamps	30.95	25.00

Eboue

CD91

Felix Eboue, first French colonial administrator to proclaim resistance to Germany after French surrender in World War II.

1945

Cameroun	296-297
Fr. Equatorial Africa	156-157
Fr. Guiana	171-172
Fr. India	210-211
Fr. Polynesia	150-151
Fr. West Africa	15-16
Guadeloupe	187-188
Madagascar	259-260
Martinique	196-197
New Caledonia	274-275
Reunion	238-239
St. Pierre & Miquelon	322-323
Somali Coast	238-239

Nos. 296-297 (2)	2.40	1.95
Nos. 156-157 (2)	2.55	2.00
Nos. 171-172 (2)	2.45	2.00
Nos. 210-211 (2)	2.20	1.95
Nos. 150-151 (2)	3.60	2.85
Nos. 15-16 (2)	2.40	2.40
Nos. 187-188 (2)	2.05	1.60
Nos. 259-260 (2)	1.70	1.45
Nos. 196-197 (2)	2.05	1.55
Nos. 274-275 (2)	3.40	3.00
Nos. 238-239 (2)	2.40	2.00
Nos. 322-323 (2)	4.40	3.45
Nos. 238-239 (2)	2.45	2.10
Set total (26) Stamps	34.05	28.30

Victory

Victory — CD92

European victory of the Allied Nations in World War II.

1946, May 8

Cameroun		C8
Fr. Equatorial Africa		C24
Fr. Guiana		C11
Fr. India		C7
Fr. Polynesia		C10
Fr. West Africa		C4
Guadeloupe		C3
Indo-China		C19
Madagascar		C44
Martinique		C3
New Caledonia		C14
Reunion		C25
St. Pierre & Miquelon		C8
Somali Coast		C8
Wallis & Futuna Isls.		C1

No. C8 (1)	1.60	1.20
No. C24 (1)	1.60	1.25
No. C11 (1)	1.75	1.25
No. C7 (1)	1.00	.95
No. C10 (1)	2.75	2.00
No. C4 (1)	1.60	1.20
No. C3 (1)	1.25	1.00
No. C19 (1)	1.00	.55
No. C44 (1)	.90	.35
No. C3 (1)	1.30	1.00
No. C14 (1)	2.25	1.25
No. C25 (1)	1.10	.90
No. C8 (1)	2.10	1.75
No. C8 (1)	1.75	1.40
No. C1 (1)	2.50	1.90
Set total (15) Stamps	24.45	17.95

Chad to Rhine

Leclerc's Departure from Chad — CD93

Battle at Cufra Oasis — CD94

Tanks in Action, Mareth — CD95

Normandy Invasion — CD96

Entering Paris — CD97

Liberation of Strasbourg — CD98

"Chad to the Rhine" march, 1942-44, by Gen. Jacques Leclerc's column, later French 2nd Armored Division.

1946, June 6

Cameroun	C9-C14
Fr. Equatorial Africa	C25-C30
Fr. Guiana	C12-C17
Fr. India	C8-C13
Fr. Polynesia	C11-C16
Fr. West Africa	C5-C10
Guadeloupe	C4-C9
Indo-China	C20-C25
Madagascar	C45-C50
Martinique	C4-C9
New Caledonia	C15-C20
Reunion	C26-C31
St. Pierre & Miquelon	C9-C14
Somali Coast	C9-C14
Wallis & Futuna Isls.	C2-C7

Nos. C9-C14 (6)	12.05	9.70
Nos. C25-C30 (6)	14.70	10.80
Nos. C12-C17 (6)	12.65	10.35
Nos. C8-C13 (6)	12.80	9.20
Nos. C11-C16 (6)	17.55	13.40
Nos. C5-C10 (6)	16.05	11.95
Nos. C4-C9 (6)	12.00	9.60
Nos. C20-C25 (6)	6.40	6.40
Nos. C45-C50 (6)	10.30	8.40
Nos. C4-C9 (6)	8.85	7.30
Nos. C15-C20 (6)	13.40	11.90
Nos. C26-C31 (6)	10.25	6.55
Nos. C9-C14 (6)	17.30	14.35

Nos. C9-C14 (6)	18.10	12.65
Nos. C2-C7 (6)	13.75	10.45
Set total (90) Stamps	196.15	153.00

UPU

French Colonials, Globe and Plane — CD99

Universal Postal Union, 75th anniv.

1949, July 4

Cameroun		C29
Fr. Equatorial Africa		C34
Fr. India		C17
Fr. Polynesia		C20
Fr. West Africa		C15
Indo-China		C26
Madagascar		C55
New Caledonia		C24
St. Pierre & Miquelon		C18
Somali Coast		C18
Togo		C18
Wallis & Futuna Isls.		C10

No. C29 (1)	8.00	4.75
No. C34 (1)	16.00	12.00
No. C20 (1)	11.50	8.75
No. C20 (1)	20.00	15.00
No. C15 (1)	12.00	8.75
No. C26 (1)	4.75	4.00
No. C55 (1)	4.00	2.75
No. C24 (1)	8.25	5.25
No. C18 (1)	20.00	12.00
No. C18 (1)	14.00	10.50
No. C18 (1)	8.50	7.00
No. C10 (1)	12.50	8.25
Set total (12) Stamps	139.50	99.00

Tropical Medicine

Doctor Treating Infant CD100

The surtax was for charitable work.

1950

Cameroun		B29
Fr. Equatorial Africa		B39
Fr. India		B15
Fr. Polynesia		B14
Fr. West Africa		B3
Madagascar		B17
New Caledonia		B14
St. Pierre & Miquelon		B14
Somali Coast		B14
Togo		B11

No. B29 (1)	7.25	5.50
No. B39 (1)	7.25	5.50
No. B15 (1)	6.00	4.00
No. B14 (1)	10.50	8.00
No. B3 (1)	9.50	7.25
No. B17 (1)	5.50	5.50
No. B14 (1)	6.75	5.25
No. B14 (1)	17.00	13.00
No. B14 (1)	7.75	6.25
No. B11 (1)	5.00	3.50
Set total (10) Stamps	82.50	63.75

Military Medal

Medal, Early Marine and Colonial Soldier — CD101

Centenary of the creation of the French Military Medal.

1952

Cameroun	322
Comoro Isls.	39
Fr. Equatorial Africa	186

Fr. India 233
Fr. Polynesia 179
Fr. West Africa 57
Madagascar 286
New Caledonia 295
St. Pierre & Miquelon 345
Somali Coast 267
Togo 327
Wallis & Futuna Isls. 149

No. 322 (1)	7.25	3.25
No. 39 (1)	50.00	40.00
No. 186 (1)	8.00	5.50
No. 233 (1)	7.00	4.75
No. 179 (1)	13.50	10.00
No. 57 (1)	8.75	6.50
No. 286 (1)	3.75	2.50
No. 295 (1)	7.50	6.00
No. 345 (1)	17.00	13.00
No. 267 (1)	9.00	8.00
No. 327 (1)	5.50	4.75
No. 149 (1)	9.50	7.00
Set total (12) Stamps	146.75	111.25

Liberation

Allied Landing, Victory Sign and Cross of Lorraine — CD102

Liberation of France, 10th anniv.

1954, June 6

Cameroun C32
Comoro Isls. C4
Fr. Equatorial Africa C38
Fr. India C18
Fr. Polynesia C22
Fr. West Africa C17
Madagascar C57
New Caledonia C25
St. Pierre & Miquelon C19
Somali Coast C19
Togo C19
Wallis & Futuna Isls. C11

No. C32 (1)	7.25	4.75
No. C4 (1)	35.00	20.00
No. C38 (1)	12.00	8.00
No. C18 (1)	11.00	8.00
No. C22 (1)	10.00	8.00
No. C17 (1)	12.00	5.50
No. C57 (1)	3.25	2.00
No. C25 (1)	8.25	5.00
No. C19 (1)	18.00	12.00
No. C19 (1)	10.50	8.50
No. C19 (1)	7.00	5.50
No. C11 (1)	12.50	8.25
Set total (12) Stamps	146.75	95.50

FIDES

Plowmen CD103

Efforts of FIDES, the Economic and Social Development Fund for Overseas Possessions (Fonds d' Investissement pour le Developpement Economique et Social). Each stamp has a different design.

1956

Cameroun 326-329
Comoro Isls. 43
Fr. Equatorial Africa 189-192
Fr. Polynesia 181
Fr. West Africa 65-72
Madagascar 292-295
New Caledonia 303
St. Pierre & Miquelon 350
Somali Coast 268-269
Togo 331

Nos. 326-329 (4)	6.90	3.20
No. 43 (1)	2.25	1.60
Nos. 189-192 (4)	3.20	1.65
No. 181 (1)	4.00	2.00
Nos. 65-72 (8)	16.00	6.35
Nos. 292-295 (4)	2.25	1.20
No. 303 (1)	1.90	1.10
No. 350 (1)	6.50	3.50
Nos. 268-269 (2)	5.35	3.15
No. 331 (1)	4.25	2.10
Set total (27) Stamps	52.60	25.85

Flower

CD104

Each stamp shows a different flower.

1958-9

Cameroun 333
Comoro Isls. 45
Fr. Equatorial Africa 200-201
Fr. Polynesia 192
Fr. So. & Antarctic Terr. 11
Fr. West Africa 79-83
Madagascar 301-302
New Caledonia 304-305
St. Pierre & Miquelon 357
Somali Coast 270
Togo 348-349
Wallis & Futuna Isls. 152

No. 333 (1)	1.60	.80
No. 45 (1)	5.50	4.50
Nos. 200-201 (2)	3.60	1.60
No. 192 (1)	6.50	4.00
No. 11 (1)	10.00	8.00
Nos. 79-83 (5)	10.45	5.60
Nos. 301-302 (2)	1.50	.55
Nos. 304-305 (2)	9.25	3.00
No. 357 (1)	4.50	2.40
No. 270 (1)	4.25	1.40
Nos. 348-349 (2)	1.10	.50
No. 152 (1)	4.50	2.50
Set total (20) Stamps	62.75	34.85

Human Rights

Sun, Dove and U.N. Emblem CD105

10th anniversary of the signing of the Universal Declaration of Human Rights.

1958

Comoro Isls. 44
Fr. Equatorial Africa 202
Fr. Polynesia 191
Fr. West Africa 85
Madagascar 300
New Caledonia 306
St. Pierre & Miquelon 356
Somali Coast 274
Wallis & Futuna Isls. 153

No. 44 (1)	11.00	11.00
No. 202 (1)	2.40	1.25
No. 191 (1)	13.00	8.75
No. 85 (1)	2.40	2.00
No. 300 (1)	.80	.40
No. 306 (1)	3.00	1.50
No. 356 (1)	3.50	2.50
No. 274 (1)	3.50	2.10
No. 153 (1)	5.75	4.00
Set total (9) Stamps	45.35	33.50

C.C.T.A.

CD106

Commission for Technical Cooperation in Africa south of the Sahara, 10th anniv.

1960

Cameroun 339
Cent. Africa 3
Chad 66
Congo, P.R. 90
Dahomey 138
Gabon 150
Ivory Coast 180
Madagascar 317
Mali 9
Mauritania 117
Niger 104
Upper Volta 89

No. 339 (1)	1.60	.75
No. 3 (1)	1.90	.65
No. 66 (1)	1.90	.50
No. 90 (1)	1.00	1.00
No. 138 (1)	.50	.25
No. 150 (1)	1.40	1.10
No. 180 (1)	1.10	.50
No. 317 (1)	.60	.30
No. 9 (1)	1.40	.50
No. 117 (1)	.75	.40
No. 104 (1)	.85	.45
No. 89 (1)	.45	.40
Set total (12) Stamps	13.45	6.80

Air Afrique, 1961

Modern and Ancient Africa, Map and Planes — CD107

Founding of Air Afrique (African Airlines).

1961-62

Cameroun C37
Cent. Africa C5
Chad C7
Congo, P.R. C5
Dahomey C17
Gabon C5
Ivory Coast C18
Mauritania C17
Niger C22
Senegal C31
Upper Volta C4

No. C37 (1)	1.00	.50
No. C5 (1)	1.00	.55
No. C7 (1)	1.00	.25
No. C5 (1)	1.75	.90
No. C17 (1)	.80	.40
No. C7 (1)	.75	.25
No. C18 (1)	2.00	1.25
No. C17 (1)	2.50	1.25
No. C22 (1)	1.75	.90
No. C31 (1)	.80	.30
No. C4 (1)	.65	.45
Set total (11) Stamps	14.00	7.00

Anti-Malaria

CD108

World Health Organization drive to eradicate malaria.

1962, Apr. 7

Cameroun B36
Cent. Africa B1
Chad B1
Comoro Isls. B1
Congo, P.R. B3
Dahomey B15
Gabon B4
Ivory Coast B15
Madagascar B19
Mali B1
Mauritania B16
Niger B14
Senegal B16
Somali Coast B15
Upper Volta B1

No. B36 (1)	1.00	.45
No. B1 (1)	1.40	1.40
No. B1 (1)	1.25	.50
No. B1 (1)	4.00	4.00
No. B3 (1)	1.40	1.00
No. B15 (1)	.75	.75
No. B4 (1)	1.00	1.00
No. B15 (1)	1.25	1.25
No. B19 (1)	.90	.50
No. B1 (1)	1.25	.60
No. B16 (1)	.80	.80
No. B14 (1)	.60	.60
No. B16 (1)	1.10	.65
No. B15 (1)	7.00	7.00
No. B1 (1)	.95	.95
Set total (15) Stamps	24.65	21.45

Abidjan Games

CD109

Abidjan Games, Ivory Coast, Dec. 24-31, 1961. Each stamp shows a different sport.

1962

Cent. Africa 19-20, C6
Chad 83-84, C8
Congo, P.R. 103-104, C7
Gabon 163-164, C6
Niger 109-111
Upper Volta 103-105

Nos. 19-20,C6 (3)	3.90	2.60
Nos. 83-84,C8 (3)	6.30	1.55
Nos. 103-104,C7 (3)	3.85	1.80
Nos. 163-164,C6 (3)	5.00	3.00
Nos. 109-111 (3)	2.60	1.10
Nos. 103-105 (3)	3.15	1.80
Set total (18) Stamps	24.80	11.85

African and Malagasy Union

Flag of Union CD110

First anniversary of the Union.

1962, Sept. 8

Cameroun 373
Cent. Africa 21
Chad 85
Congo, P.R. 105
Dahomey 155
Gabon 165
Ivory Coast 198
Madagascar 332
Mauritania 170
Niger 112
Senegal 211
Upper Volta 106

No. 373 (1)	2.00	.75
No. 21 (1)	1.25	.60
No. 85 (1)	1.25	.25
No. 105 (1)	1.50	.50
No. 155 (1)	1.25	.90
No. 165 (1)	1.60	1.25
No. 198 (1)	2.10	.75
No. 332 (1)	.80	.80
No. 170 (1)	.75	.50
No. 112 (1)	.80	.40
No. 211 (1)	.80	.50
No. 106 (1)	1.50	.90
Set total (12) Stamps	15.60	8.10

Telstar

Telstar and Globe Showing Andover and Pleumeur-Bodou — CD111

First television connection of the United States and Europe through the Telstar satellite, July 11-12, 1962.

1962-63

Andorra, French 154
Comoro Isls. C7
Fr. Polynesia C29
Fr. So. & Antarctic Terr. C5
New Caledonia C33
St. Pierre & Miquelon C26
Somali Coast C31
Wallis & Futuna Isls. C17

No. 154 (1)	2.00	1.60
No. C7 (1)	5.00	3.00
No. C29 (1)	11.50	8.00

No. C5 (1)	29.00	21.00
No. C33 (1)	30.00	18.50
No. C26 (1)	7.25	5.50
No. C31 (1)	1.00	1.00
No. C17 (1)	3.50	3.50
Set total (8) Stamps	89.25	62.10

Freedom From Hunger

World Map and Wheat Emblem CD112

U.N. Food and Agriculture Organization's "Freedom from Hunger" campaign.

1963, Mar. 21

Cameroun	B37-B38
Cent. Africa	B2
Chad	B2
Congo, P.R.	B4
Dahomey	B16
Gabon	B5
Ivory Coast	B16
Madagascar	B21
Mauritania	B17
Niger	B15
Senegal	B17
Upper Volta	B2

Nos. B37-B38 (2)	2.25	.75
No. B2 (1)	1.25	1.25
No. B2 (1)	2.00	.50
No. B4 (1)	1.40	1.00
No. B16 (1)	.80	.80
No. B5 (1)	1.00	1.00
No. B16 (1)	1.50	1.50
No. B21 (1)	.70	.45
No. B17 (1)	.80	.80
No. B15 (1)	.60	.60
No. B17 (1)	.80	.50
No. B2 (1)	.95	.95
Set total (13) Stamps	14.05	10.10

Red Cross Centenary

CD113

Centenary of the International Red Cross.

1963, Sept. 2

Comoro Isls.	55
Fr. Polynesia	205
New Caledonia	328
St. Pierre & Miquelon	367
Somali Coast	297
Wallis & Futuna Isls.	165

No. 55 (1)	9.50	7.00
No. 205 (1)	15.00	12.00
No. 328 (1)	9.00	6.75
No. 367 (1)	12.00	6.75
No. 297 (1)	6.25	6.25
No. 165 (1)	4.00	3.50
Set total (6) Stamps	55.75	42.25

African Postal Union, 1963

UAMPT Emblem, Radio Masts, Plane and Mail CD114

Establishment of the African and Malagasy Posts and Telecommunications Union.

1963, Sept. 8

Cameroun	C47
Cent. Africa	C10
Chad	C9
Congo, P.R.	C13

Dahomey	C19
Gabon	C13
Ivory Coast	C25
Madagascar	C75
Mauritania	C22
Niger	C27
Rwanda	36
Senegal	C32
Upper Volta	C9

No. C47 (1)	2.25	1.00
No. C10 (1)	1.90	.85
No. C9 (1)	2.40	.60
No. C13 (1)	1.40	.75
No. C19 (1)	.75	.25
No. C13 (1)	1.90	.80
No. C25 (1)	2.50	1.50
No. C75 (1)	1.25	.80
No. C22 (1)	1.50	.60
No. C27 (1)	1.25	.60
No. 36 (1)	.90	.55
No. C32 (1)	1.75	.50
No. C9 (1)	1.50	.75
Set total (13) Stamps	21.25	9.55

Air Afrique, 1963

Symbols of Flight — CD115

First anniversary of Air Afrique and inauguration of DC-8 service.

1963, Nov. 19

Cameroun	C48
Chad	C10
Congo, P.R.	C14
Gabon	C18
Ivory Coast	C26
Mauritania	C26
Niger	C35
Senegal	C33

No. C48 (1)	1.25	.40
No. C10 (1)	2.40	.60
No. C14 (1)	1.60	.60
No. C18 (1)	1.40	.65
No. C26 (1)	1.00	.50
No. C26 (1)	.70	.25
No. C35 (1)	.90	.50
No. C33 (1)	2.00	.65
Set total (8) Stamps	11.25	4.15

Europafrica

Europe and Africa Linked — CD116

Signing of an economic agreement between the European Economic Community and the African and Malagasy Union, Yaounde, Cameroun, July 20, 1963.

1963-64

Cameroun	402
Cent. Africa	C12
Chad	C11
Congo, P.R.	C16
Gabon	C19
Ivory Coast	217
Niger	C43
Upper Volta	C11

No. 402 (1)	2.25	.60
No. C12 (1)	2.50	1.75
No. C11 (1)	2.00	.50
No. C16 (1)	1.60	1.00
No. C19 (1)	1.40	.75
No. 217 (1)	1.10	.35
No. C43 (1)	.85	.50
No. C11 (1)	1.50	.80
Set total (8) Stamps	13.20	6.25

Human Rights

Scales of Justice and Globe CD117

15th anniversary of the Universal Declaration of Human Rights.

1963, Dec. 10

Comoro Isls.	56
Fr. Polynesia	206
New Caledonia	329
St. Pierre & Miquelon	368
Somali Coast	300
Wallis & Futuna Isls.	166

No. 56 (1)	9.50	7.50
No. 205 (1)	15.00	12.00
No. 329 (1)	8.00	6.00
No. 368 (1)	6.50	3.50
No. 166 (1)	8.00	7.50
Set total (5) Stamps	47.00	36.50

PHILATEC

Stamp Album, Champs Elysees Palace and Horses of Marly CD118

Intl. Philatelic and Postal Techniques Exhibition, Paris, June 5-21, 1964.

1963-64

Comoro Isls.	60
France	1078
Fr. Polynesia	207
New Caledonia	341
St. Pierre & Miquelon	369
Somali Coast	301
Wallis & Futuna Isls.	167

No. 60 (1)	4.50	4.00
No. 1078 (1)	.25	.25
No. 206 (1)	15.00	10.00
No. 341 (1)	8.50	6.75
No. 369 (1)	11.00	8.00
No. 167 (1)	3.50	3.50
Set total (6) Stamps	42.75	32.50

Cooperation

CD119

Cooperation between France and the French-speaking countries of Africa and Madagascar.

1964

Cameroun	409-410
Cent. Africa	39
Chad	103
Congo, P.R.	121
Dahomey	193
France	1111
Gabon	175
Ivory Coast	221
Madagascar	360
Mauritania	181
Niger	143
Senegal	236
Togo	495

Nos. 409-410 (2)	2.50	.50
No. 39 (1)	1.00	.55
No. 103 (1)	1.00	.25
No. 121 (1)	.80	.35
No. 193 (1)	.80	.35
No. 1111 (1)	.25	.25
No. 175 (1)	.90	.60
No. 221 (1)	1.10	.35
No. 360 (1)	.60	.25
No. 181 (1)	.60	.35

No. 143 (1)	.80	.40
No. 236 (1)	1.60	.85
No. 495 (1)	.70	.25
Set total (14) Stamps	12.65	5.30

ITU

Telegraph, Syncom Satellite and ITU Emblem CD120

Intl. Telecommunication Union, Cent.

1965, May 17

Comoro Isls.	C14
Fr. Polynesia	C33
Fr. So. & Antarctic Terr.	C8
New Caledonia	C40
New Hebrides	124-125
St. Pierre & Miquelon	C29
Somali Coast	C36
Wallis & Futuna Isls.	C20

No. C14 (1)	20.00	10.00
No. C33 (1)	80.00	52.50
No. C8 (1)	200.00	160.00
No. C40 (1)	12.00	9.00
Nos. 124-125 (2)	40.50	34.00
No. C29 (1)	24.00	11.00
No. C36 (1)	15.00	9.00
No. C20 (1)	21.00	15.00
Set total (9) Stamps	412.50	300.50

French Satellite A-1

Diamant Rocket and Launching Installation — CD121

Launching of France's first satellite, Nov. 26, 1965.

1965-66

Comoro Isls.	C16a
France	1138a
Reunion	359a
Fr. Polynesia	C41a
Fr. So. & Antarctic Terr.	C10a
New Caledonia	C45a
St. Pierre & Miquelon	C31a
Somali Coast	C40a
Wallis & Futuna Isls.	C23a

No. C16a (1)	11.00	11.00
No. 1138a (1)	.65	.65
No. 359a (1)	3.50	3.00
No. C41a (1)	14.00	14.00
No. C10a (1)	29.00	24.00
No. C45a (1)	8.25	7.00
No. C31a (1)	15.00	15.00
No. C40a (1)	7.00	7.00
No. C23a (1)	9.25	9.25
Set total (9) Stamps	97.65	90.90

French Satellite D-1

D-1 Satellite in Orbit — CD122

Launching of the D-1 satellite at Hammaguir, Algeria, Feb. 17, 1966.

1966

Comoro Isls.	C17
France	1148
Fr. Polynesia	C42
Fr. So. & Antarctic Terr.	C11

New Caledonia.........................C46
St. Pierre & Miquelon.................C32
Somali Coast..........................C49
Wallis & Futuna Isls. C24

No. C17 (1)	4.00	4.00
No. 1148 (1)	.25	.25
No. C42 (1)	7.00	4.75
No. C11 (1)	57.50	40.00
No. C46 (1)	3.00	2.00
No. C32 (1)	10.50	6.50
No. C49 (1)	4.25	2.75
No. C24 (1)	3.50	3.50
Set total (8) Stamps	90.00	63.75

Air Afrique, 1966

Planes and Air Afrique
Emblem — CD123

Introduction of DC-8F planes by Air Afrique.

1966

Cameroun...........................C79
Cent. Africa C35
Chad..............................C26
Congo, P.R........................C42
Dahomey...........................C42
Gabon.............................C47
Ivory Coast.......................C32
Mauritania........................C57
Niger.............................C63
Senegal...........................C47
Togo..............................C54
Upper Volta.......................C31

No. C79 (1)	.80	.25
No. C35 (1)	1.00	.40
No. C26 (1)	1.00	.25
No. C42 (1)	1.00	.25
No. C42 (1)	.75	.25
No. C47 (1)	.90	.35
No. C32 (1)	1.00	.60
No. C57 (1)	.80	.30
No. C63 (1)	.65	.35
No. C47 (1)	.80	.30
No. C54 (1)	.80	.25
No. C31 (1)	.75	.50
Set total (12) Stamps	10.25	4.05

African Postal Union, 1967

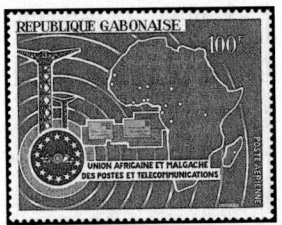

Telecommunications Symbols and Map
of Africa — CD124

Fifth anniversary of the establishment of the
African and Malagasy Union of Posts and
Telecommunications, UAMPT.

1967

Cameroun...........................C90
Cent. Africa C46
Chad..............................C37
Congo, P.R........................C57
Dahomey...........................C61
Gabon.............................C58
Ivory Coast.......................C34
Madagascar........................C85
Mauritania........................C65
Niger.............................C75
Rwanda............................C1-C3
Senegal...........................C60
Togo..............................C81
Upper Volta.......................C50

No. C90 (1)	2.40	.65
No. C46 (1)	2.25	.85
No. C37 (1)	2.00	.60
No. C57 (1)	1.60	.60
No. C61 (1)	1.75	.95
No. C58 (1)	2.25	.95
No. C34 (1)	3.50	1.50
No. C85 (1)	1.25	.60
No. C65 (1)	1.25	.60
No. C75 (1)	1.40	.60
Nos. C1-C3 (3)	2.30	1.25
No. C60 (1)	1.75	.50

No. C81 (1)	1.90	.30
No. C50 (1)	1.80	.70
Set total (16) Stamps	27.40	10.65

Monetary Union

Gold Token of the
Ashantis, 17-18th
Centuries — CD125

West African Monetary Union, 5th anniv.

1967, Nov. 4

Dahomey 244
Ivory Coast.......................259
Mauritania........................238
Niger.............................204
Senegal...........................294
Togo..............................623
Upper Volta.......................181

No. 244 (1)	.65	.65
No. 259 (1)	.85	.40
No. 238 (1)	.45	.25
No. 204 (1)	.45	.25
No. 294 (1)	.60	.25
No. 623 (1)	.60	.25
No. 181 (1)	.70	.35
Set total (7) Stamps	4.30	2.40

WHO Anniversary

Sun,
Flowers
and WHO
Emblem
CD126

World Health Organization, 20th anniv.

1968, May 4

Afars & Issas 317
Comoro Isls. 73
Fr. Polynesia.....................241-242
Fr. So. & Antarctic Terr. 31
New Caledonia 367
St. Pierre & Miquelon.............377
Wallis & Futuna Isls. 169

No. 317 (1)	3.25	2.25
No. 73 (1)	2.75	2.00
Nos. 241-242 (2)	22.00	12.75
No. 31 (1)	65.00	45.00
No. 367 (1)	4.50	2.25
No. 377 (1)	12.00	8.00
No. 169 (1)	6.50	4.50
Set total (8) Stamps	116.00	76.75

Human Rights Year

Human Rights
Flame — CD127

1968, Aug. 10

Afars & Issas 322-323
Comoro Isls. 76
Fr. Polynesia.....................243-244
Fr. So. & Antarctic Terr. 32
New Caledonia 369
St. Pierre & Miquelon.............382
Wallis & Futuna Isls. 170

Nos. 322-323 (2)	7.00	4.25
No. 76 (1)	3.50	3.50
Nos. 241-242 (2)	22.00	12.75
No. 31 (1)	65.00	45.00
No. 369 (1)	3.00	1.50
No. 382 (1)	10.00	5.50
No. 170 (1)	3.75	3.75
Set total (9) Stamps	114.25	76.25

2nd PHILEXAFRIQUE

CD128

Opening of PHILEXAFRIQUE, Abidjan, Feb.
14. Each stamp shows a local scene and
stamp.

1969, Feb. 14

Cameroun...........................C118
Cent. Africa C65
Chad..............................C48
Congo, P.R........................C77
Dahomey...........................C94
Gabon.............................C82
Ivory Coast.......................C38-C40
Madagascar........................C92
Mali..............................C65
Mauritania........................C80
Niger.............................C104
Senegal...........................C68
Togo..............................C104
Upper Volta.......................C62

No. C118 (1)	3.25	1.25
No. C65 (1)	1.90	1.90
No. C48 (1)	2.40	1.00
No. C77 (1)	2.00	1.75
No. C94 (1)	2.25	2.25
No. C82 (1)	2.25	2.25
Nos. C38-C40 (3)	14.50	14.50
No. C92 (1)	1.75	.85
No. C65 (1)	2.00	1.00
No. C80 (1)	1.90	.75
No. C104 (1)	2.75	1.90
No. C68 (1)	2.00	1.40
No. C104 (1)	2.25	.45
No. C62 (1)	4.00	3.75
Set total (16) Stamps	45.20	35.00

Concorde

Concorde in
Flight
CD129

First flight of the prototype Concorde supersonic plane at Toulouse, Mar. 1, 1969.

1969

Afars & Issas C56
Comoro Isls. C29
France............................C42
Fr. Polynesia.....................C50
Fr. So. & Antarctic Terr. C18
New Caledonia C63
St. Pierre & Miquelon.............C40
Wallis & Futuna Isls. C30

No. C56 (1)	30.00	18.00
No. C29 (1)	24.00	16.00
No. C42 (1)	1.00	.35
No. C50 (1)	55.00	35.00
No. C18 (1)	55.00	37.50
No. C63 (1)	35.00	20.00
No. C40 (1)	32.50	12.00
No. C30 (1)	15.00	10.00
Set total (8) Stamps	247.50	148.85

Development Bank

Bank
Emblem — CD130

African Development Bank, fifth anniv.

1969

Cameroun...........................499
Chad..............................217
Congo, P.R........................181-182

Ivory Coast.......................281
Mali..............................127-128
Mauritania........................267
Niger.............................220
Senegal...........................317-318
Upper Volta.......................201

No. 499 (1)	.80	.25
No. 217 (1)	.70	.25
Nos. 181-182 (2)	.80	.50
No. 281 (1)	.70	.40
Nos. 127-128 (2)	1.25	.50
No. 267 (1)	.60	.25
No. 220 (1)	.60	.30
Nos. 317-318 (2)	1.55	.50
No. 201 (1)	.70	.30
Set total (12) Stamps	7.70	3.25

ILO

ILO Headquarters, Geneva, and
Emblem — CD131

Intl. Labor Organization, 50th anniv.

1969-70

Afars & Issas 337
Comoro Isls. 83
Fr. Polynesia.....................251-252
Fr. So. & Antarctic Terr. 35
New Caledonia 379
St. Pierre & Miquelon.............396
Wallis & Futuna Isls. 172

No. 337 (1)	3.00	2.25
No. 83 (1)	1.25	.75
Nos. 251-252 (2)	24.00	12.50
No. 35 (1)	18.50	11.00
No. 379 (1)	2.25	1.10
No. 396 (1)	10.00	5.50
No. 172 (1)	3.00	2.90
Set total (8) Stamps	62.00	36.00

ASECNA

Map of
Africa,
Plane and
Airport
CD132

10th anniversary of the Agency for the
Security of Aerial Navigation in Africa and
Madagascar (ASECNA, Agence pour la
Securite de la Navigation Aerienne en Afrique
et a Madagascar).

1969-70

Cameroun...........................500
Cent. Africa 119
Chad..............................222
Congo, P.R........................197
Dahomey...........................269
Gabon.............................260
Ivory Coast.......................287
Mali..............................130
Niger.............................221
Senegal...........................321
Upper Volta.......................204

No. 500 (1)	2.00	.60
No. 119 (1)	2.25	.80
No. 222 (1)	1.00	.25
No. 197 (1)	2.00	.40
No. 269 (1)	.90	.55
No. 260 (1)	1.75	.75
No. 287 (1)	.90	.40
No. 130 (1)	1.00	.40
No. 221 (1)	1.25	.70
No. 321 (1)	1.60	.50
No. 204 (1)	1.75	1.00
Set total (11) Stamps	16.40	6.35

U.P.U. Headquarters

CD133

New Universal Postal Union headquarters,
Bern, Switzerland.

1970

Afars & Issas	342
Algeria	443
Cameroun	503-504
Cent. Africa	125
Chad	225
Comoro Isls.	84
Congo, P.R.	216
Fr. Polynesia	261-262
Fr. So. & Antarctic Terr.	36
Gabon	258
Ivory Coast	295
Madagascar	444
Mali	134-135
Mauritania	283
New Caledonia	382
Niger	231-232
St. Pierre & Miquelon	397-398
Senegal	328-329
Tunisia	535
Wallis & Futuna Isls.	173

No. 342 (1)	3.25	1.75
No. 443 (1)	1.10	.40
Nos. 503-504 (2)	2.60	.55
No. 125 (1)	1.90	.70
No. 225 (1)	1.00	.25
No. 84 (1)	5.50	2.00
No. 216 (1)	.80	.25
Nos. 261-262 (2)	20.00	10.00
No. 36 (1)	45.00	29.00
No. 258 (1)	.90	.55
No. 295 (1)	1.10	.50
No. 444 (1)	.55	.25
Nos. 134-135 (2)	1.25	.50
No. 283 (1)	.60	.30
No. 382 (1)	3.00	1.50
Nos. 231-232 (2)	1.20	.60
Nos. 397-398 (2)	34.00	17.50
Nos. 328-329 (2)	1.55	.55
No. 535 (1)	.60	.25
No. 173 (1)	4.00	4.00
Set total (26) Stamps	129.90	71.40

De Gaulle

CD134

First anniversay of the death of Charles de Gaulle, (1890-1970), President of France.

1971-72

Afars & Issas	356-357
Comoro Isls.	104-105
France	1325a
Fr. Polynesia	270-271
Fr. So. & Antarctic Terr.	52-53
New Caledonia	393-394
Reunion	380a
St. Pierre & Miquelon	417-418
Wallis & Futuna Isls.	177-178

Nos. 356-357 (2)	16.00	9.50
Nos. 104-105 (2)	9.00	5.75
No. 1325a (1)	4.50	4.00
Nos. 270-271 (2)	51.50	29.50
Nos. 52-53 (2)	47.00	33.50
Nos. 393-394 (2)	25.00	11.75
No. 380a (1)	9.25	8.00
Nos. 417-418 (2)	57.50	30.00
Nos. 177-178 (2)	24.00	16.25
Set total (16) Stamps	243.75	148.25

African Postal Union, 1971

UAMPT Building, Brazzaville, Congo — CD135

10th anniversary of the establishment of the African and Malagasy Posts and Telecommunications Union, UAMPT. Each stamp has a different native design.

1971, Nov. 13

Cameroun	C177
Cent. Africa	C89
Chad	C94

Congo, P.R.	C136
Dahomey	C146
Gabon	C120
Ivory Coast	C47
Mauritania	C113
Niger	C164
Rwanda	C8
Senegal	C105
Togo	C166
Upper Volta	C97

No. C177 (1)	2.00	.50
No. C89 (1)	2.25	.85
No. C94 (1)	1.50	.50
No. C136 (1)	1.60	.75
No. C146 (1)	1.75	.80
No. C120 (1)	1.75	.70
No. C47 (1)	2.00	1.00
No. C113 (1)	1.20	.65
No. C164 (1)	1.25	.60
No. C8 (1)	2.75	2.25
No. C105 (1)	1.60	.50
No. C166 (1)	1.25	.40
No. C97 (1)	1.50	.70
Set total (13) Stamps	22.40	10.20

West African Monetary Union

African Couple, City, Village and Commemorative Coin — CD136

West African Monetary Union, 10th anniv.

1972, Nov. 2

Dahomey	300
Ivory Coast	331
Mauritania	299
Niger	258
Senegal	374
Togo	825
Upper Volta	280

No. 300 (1)	.65	.25
No. 331 (1)	1.00	.50
No. 299 (1)	.75	.25
No. 258 (1)	.55	.30
No. 374 (1)	.50	.30
No. 825 (1)	.60	.25
No. 280 (1)	.60	.25
Set total (7) Stamps	4.65	2.10

African Postal Union, 1973

Telecommunications Symbols and Map of Africa — CD137

11th anniversary of the African and Malagasy Posts and Telecommunications Union (UAMPT).

1973, Sept. 12

Cameroun	574
Cent. Africa	194
Chad	294
Congo, P.R.	289
Dahomey	311
Gabon	320
Ivory Coast	361
Madagascar	500
Mauritania	304
Niger	287
Rwanda	540
Senegal	393
Togo	849
Upper Volta	297

No. 574 (1)	1.75	.40
No. 194 (1)	1.25	.75
No. 294 (1)	1.75	.40
No. 289 (1)	1.60	.60
No. 311 (1)	1.25	.55
No. 320 (1)	1.40	.75
No. 361 (1)	2.50	1.00
No. 500 (1)	1.00	.35
No. 304 (1)	1.10	.40
No. 287 (1)	.90	.60
No. 540 (1)	3.75	2.00
No. 393 (1)	1.60	.50

No. 849 (1)	1.00	.35
No. 297 (1)	1.25	.70
Set total (14) Stamps	22.10	9.25

Philexafrique II — Essen

CD138

CD139

Designs: Indigenous fauna, local and German stamps. Types CD138-CD139 printed horizontally and vertically se-tenant in sheets of 10 (2x5). Label between horizontal pairs alternately commemoratives Philexafrique II, Libreville, Gabon, June 1978, and 2nd International Stamp Fair, Essen, Germany, Nov. 1-5.

1978-1979

Benin	C286a
Central Africa	C201a
Chad	C239a
Congo Republic	C246a
Djibouti	C122a
Gabon	C216a
Ivory Coast	C65a
Mali	C357a
Mauritania	C186a
Niger	C292a
Rwanda	C13a
Senegal	C141a
Togo	C364a

No. C286a (1)	9.00	8.50
No. C201a (1)	7.50	7.50
No. C239a (1)	8.00	4.00
No. C246a (1)	7.00	7.00
No. C122a (1)	8.50	8.50
No. C216a (1)	6.50	4.00
No. C65a (1)	9.00	9.00
No. C357a (1)	7.50	3.00
No. C186a (1)	4.50	4.00
No. C292a (1)	6.00	5.00
No. C13a (1)	4.00	4.00
No. C147a (1)	10.00	4.00
No. C364a (1)	3.00	1.50
Set total (13) Stamps	90.50	70.00

BRITISH COMMONWEALTH OF NATIONS

The listings follow established trade practices when these issues are offered as units by dealers. The Peace issue, for example, includes only one stamp from the Indian state of Hyderabad. The U.P.U. issue includes the Egypt set. Pairs are included for those varieties issued with bilingual designs se-tenant.

Silver Jubilee

Windsor Castle and King George V
CD301

Reign of King George V, 25th anniv.

1935

Antigua	77-80
Ascension	33-36
Bahamas	92-95
Barbados	186-189
Basutoland	11-14

Bechuanaland Protectorate	117-120
Bermuda	100-103
British Guiana	223-226
British Honduras	108-111
Cayman Islands	81-84
Ceylon	260-263
Cyprus	136-139
Dominica	90-93
Falkland Islands	77-80
Fiji	110-113
Gambia	125-128
Gibraltar	100-103
Gilbert & Ellice Islands	33-36
Gold Coast	108-111
Grenada	124-127
Hong Kong	147-150
Jamaica	109-112
Kenya, Uganda, Tanzania	42-45
Leeward Islands	96-99
Malta	184-187
Mauritius	204-207
Montserrat	85-88
Newfoundland	226-229
Nigeria	34-37
Northern Rhodesia	18-21
Nyasaland Protectorate	47-50
St. Helena	111-114
St. Kitts-Nevis	72-75
St. Lucia	91-94
St. Vincent	134-137
Seychelles	118-121
Sierra Leone	166-169
Solomon Islands	60-63
Somaliland Protectorate	77-80
Straits Settlements	213-216
Swaziland	20-23
Trinidad & Tobago	43-46
Turks & Caicos Islands	71-74
Virgin Islands	69-72

The following have different designs but are included in the omnibus set:

Great Britain	226-229
Offices in Morocco (Sp. Curr.)	67-70
Offices in Morocco (Br. Curr.)	226-229
Offices in Morocco (Fr. Curr.)	422-425
Offices in Morocco (Tangier)	508-510
Australia	152-154
Canada	211-216
Cook Islands	98-100
India	142-148
Nauru	31-34
New Guinea	46-47
New Zealand	199-201
Niue	67-69
Papua	114-117
Samoa	163-165
South Africa	68-73
Southern Rhodesia	33-36
South-West Africa	121-124

Nos. 77-80 (4)	21.50	22.75
Nos. 33-36 (4)	61.00	127.50
Nos. 92-95 (4)	25.00	43.00
Nos. 186-189 (4)	30.15	49.30
Nos. 11-14 (4)	12.10	21.50
Nos. 117-120 (4)	17.00	29.25
Nos. 100-103 (4)	18.00	58.25
Nos. 223-226 (4)	18.35	35.50
Nos. 108-111 (4)	15.25	15.35
Nos. 81-84 (4)	16.95	17.75
Nos. 260-263 (4)	12.60	23.35
Nos. 136-139 (4)	39.75	34.40
Nos. 90-93 (4)	18.85	19.85
Nos. 77-80 (4)	51.00	13.75
Nos. 110-113 (4)	15.25	29.00
Nos. 125-128 (4)	12.65	29.25
Nos. 100-103 (4)	34.35	50.00
Nos. 33-36 (4)	37.00	53.50
Nos. 108-111 (4)	26.25	62.85
Nos. 124-127 (4)	18.60	45.00
Nos. 147-150 (4)	76.50	21.00
Nos. 109-112 (4)	22.80	42.00
Nos. 42-45 (4)	9.25	12.50
Nos. 96-99 (4)	35.75	49.60
Nos. 184-187 (4)	25.00	34.70
Nos. 204-207 (4)	47.60	58.25
Nos. 85-88 (4)	10.25	30.25
Nos. 226-229 (4)	17.50	12.05
Nos. 34-37 (4)	13.25	59.75
Nos. 18-21 (4)	16.75	16.25
Nos. 47-50 (4)	39.75	80.25
Nos. 111-114 (4)	31.15	33.25
Nos. 72-75 (4)	11.55	18.50
Nos. 91-94 (4)	16.00	20.80
Nos. 134-137 (4)	9.45	21.25
Nos. 118-121 (4)	17.50	31.00
Nos. 166-169 (4)	21.25	56.00
Nos. 60-63 (4)	30.00	38.00
Nos. 77-80 (4)	18.75	50.75
Nos. 213-216 (4)	15.00	25.10
Nos. 43-46 (4)	6.80	18.25
Nos. 71-74 (4)	12.30	27.75
Nos. 69-72 (4)	9.25	16.25
	22.20	47.50
Nos. 226-229 (4)	7.25	7.45

Nos. 67-70 (4)	14.35	*26.10*
Nos. 226-229 (4)	8.20	*28.90*
Nos. 422-425 (4)	3.90	2.00
Nos. 508-510 (3)	18.80	*23.85*
Nos. 152-154 (3)	45.75	60.35
Nos. 211-216 (6)	27.85	13.35
Nos. 98-100 (3)	6.75	*14.00*
Nos. 142-148 (7)	23.25	11.80
Nos. 31-34 (4)	12.60	*13.85*
Nos. 46-47 (2)	4.35	1.70
Nos. 199-201 (3)	21.75	*31.75*
Nos. 67-69 (3)	7.80	*22.50*
Nos. 114-117 (4)	9.20	*17.00*
Nos. 163-165 (3)	4.40	5.50
Nos. 68-71 (4)	57.00	*155.00*
Nos. 33-36 (4)	30.00	*45.25*
Nos. 121-124 (4)	14.50	*36.10*
Set total (245) Stamps	1,355	2,119

Coronation

Queen Elizabeth and King George VI CD302

1937

Aden....................13-15
Antigua....................81-83
Ascension....................37-39
Bahamas....................97-99
Barbados....................190-192
Basutoland....................15-17
Bechuanaland Protectorate......121-123
Bermuda....................115-117
British Guiana....................227-229
British Honduras....................112-114
Cayman Islands....................97-99
Ceylon....................275-277
Cyprus....................140-142
Dominica....................94-96
Falkland Islands....................81-83
Fiji....................114-116
Gambia....................129-131
Gibraltar....................104-106
Gilbert & Ellice Islands....................37-39
Gold Coast....................112-114
Grenada....................128-130
Hong Kong....................151-153
Jamaica....................113-115
Kenya, Uganda, Tanzania...........60-62
Leeward Islands....................100-102
Malta....................188-190
Mauritius....................208-210
Montserrat....................89-91
Newfoundland....................230-232
Nigeria....................50-52
Northern Rhodesia....................22-24
Nyasaland Protectorate....................51-53
St. Helena....................115-117
St. Kitts-Nevis....................76-78
St. Lucia....................107-109
St. Vincent....................138-140
Seychelles....................122-124
Sierra Leone....................170-172
Solomon Islands....................64-66
Somaliland Protectorate....................81-83
Straits Settlements....................235-237
Swaziland....................24-26
Trinidad & Tobago....................47-49
Turks & Caicos Islands....................75-77
Virgin Islands....................73-75

The following have different designs but are included in the omnibus set:

Great Britain....................234
Offices in Morocco (Sp. Curr.)..........82
Offices in Morocco (Fr. Curr.).........439
Offices in Morocco (Tangier)...........514
Canada....................237
Cook Islands....................109-111
Nauru....................35-38
Newfoundland....................233-243
New Guinea....................48-51
New Zealand....................223-225
Niue....................70-72
Papua....................118-121
South Africa....................74-78
Southern Rhodesia....................38-41
South-West Africa....................125-132

Nos. 13-15 (3)	3.00	*6.10*
Nos. 81-83 (3)	2.00	*4.50*
Nos. 37-39 (3)	2.75	*2.75*
Nos. 97-99 (3)	1.15	3.05
Nos. 190-192 (3)	1.10	1.95
Nos. 15-17 (3)	1.25	*3.00*
Nos. 121-123 (3)	.95	3.35
Nos. 115-117 (3)	1.25	5.00
Nos. 227-229 (3)	1.45	3.05
Nos. 112-114 (3)	1.20	2.35
Nos. 97-99 (3)	1.10	2.30
Nos. 275-277 (3)	8.25	10.35
Nos. 140-142 (3)	3.75	6.50
Nos. 94-96 (3)	.85	2.40
Nos. 81-83 (3)	2.90	*2.30*
Nos. 114-116 (3)	1.35	5.75
Nos. 129-131 (3)	1.00	4.70
Nos. 104-106 (3)	2.60	6.45
Nos. 37-39 (3)	.95	2.00
Nos. 112-114 (3)	3.10	*10.00*
Nos. 128-130 (3)	1.00	.85
Nos. 151-153 (3)	27.00	12.50
Nos. 113-115 (3)	1.95	1.25
Nos. 60-62 (3)	1.25	2.35
Nos. 100-102 (3)	1.55	4.00
Nos. 188-190 (3)	1.35	1.65
Nos. 208-210 (3)	2.05	3.75
Nos. 89-91 (3)	1.00	3.35
Nos. 230-232 (3)	7.00	2.80
Nos. 50-52 (3)	3.25	8.50
Nos. 22-24 (3)	.95	2.25
Nos. 51-53 (3)	1.05	1.30
Nos. 115-117 (3)	1.45	2.05
Nos. 76-78 (3)	.95	2.05
Nos. 107-109 (3)	1.05	2.05
Nos. 138-140 (3)	.80	*4.75*
Nos. 122-124 (3)	1.20	*1.90*
Nos. 170-172 (3)	1.95	5.65
Nos. 64-66 (3)	.90	2.00
Nos. 81-83 (3)	1.10	*3.40*
Nos. 235-237 (3)	3.25	1.60
Nos. 24-26 (3)	1.05	1.75
Nos. 47-49 (3)	1.00	1.00
Nos. 75-77 (3)	1.30	1.55
Nos. 73-75 (3)	1.20	5.00
No. 234 (1)	.25	.25
No. 82 (1)	.80	.80
No. 439 (1)	.35	.25
No. 514 (1)	.55	.55
No. 237 (1)	.35	.25
Nos. 109-111 (3)	.85	.80
Nos. 35-38 (4)	1.15	*5.50*
Nos. 233-243 (11)	34.50	30.40
Nos. 48-51 (4)	1.40	*7.90*
Nos. 223-225 (3)	1.40	*2.75*
Nos. 70-72 (3)	.80	*2.05*
Nos. 118-121 (4)	1.60	*5.25*
Nos. 74-78 (5)	9.25	10.80
Nos. 38-41 (4)	4.00	16.25
Nos. 125-132 (8)	5.50	8.45
Set total (189) Stamps	171.30	259.40

Peace

King George VI and Parliament Buildings, London CD303

Return to peace at the close of World War II.

1945-46

Aden....................28-29
Antigua....................96-97
Ascension....................50-51
Bahamas....................130-131
Barbados....................207-208
Bermuda....................131-132
British Guiana....................242-243
British Honduras....................127-128
Cayman Islands....................112-113
Ceylon....................293-294
Cyprus....................156-157
Dominica....................112-113
Falkland Islands....................97-98
Falkland Islands Dep.............1L9-1L10
Fiji....................137-138
Gambia....................144-145
Gibraltar....................119-120
Gilbert & Ellice Islands....................52-53
Gold Coast....................128-129
Grenada....................143-144
Jamaica....................136-137
Kenya, Uganda, Tanzania...........90-91
Leeward Islands....................116-117
Malta....................206-207
Mauritius....................223-224
Montserrat....................104-105
Nigeria....................71-72
Northern Rhodesia....................46-47
Nyasaland Protectorate....................82-83
Pitcairn Islands....................9-10
St. Helena....................128-129
St. Kitts-Nevis....................91-92
St. Lucia....................127-128
St. Vincent....................152-153
Seychelles....................149-150
Sierra Leone....................186-187
Solomon Islands....................80-81
Somaliland Protectorate...........108-109
Trinidad & Tobago....................62-63
Turks & Caicos Islands....................90-91
Virgin Islands....................88-89

The following have different designs but are included in the omnibus set:

Great Britain....................264-265
Offices in Morocco (Tangier)....523-524
Aden
Kathiri State of Seiyun..............12-13
Qu'aiti State of Shihr and Mukalla.....
....................12-13
Australia....................200-202
Basutoland....................29-31
Bechuanaland Protectorate......137-139
Burma....................66-69
Cook Islands....................127-130
Hong Kong....................174-175
India....................195-198
Hyderabad....................51-53
New Zealand....................247-257
Niue....................90-93
Pakistan-Bahawalpur....................O16
Samoa....................191-194
South Africa....................100-102
Southern Rhodesia....................67-70
South-West Africa....................153-155
Swaziland....................38-40
Zanzibar....................222-223

Nos. 28-29 (2)	.70	2.30
Nos. 96-97 (2)	.50	*.80*
Nos. 50-51 (2)	.90	1.75
Nos. 130-131 (2)	.50	1.40
Nos. 207-208 (2)	.50	1.10
Nos. 131-132 (2)	.55	.55
Nos. 242-243 (2)	1.05	*1.40*
Nos. 127-128 (2)	.50	.50
Nos. 112-113 (2)	.60	.80
Nos. 293-294 (2)	.60	*2.10*
Nos. 156-157 (2)	1.00	.70
Nos. 112-113 (2)	.50	.50
Nos. 97-98 (2)	.90	1.35
Nos. 1L9-1L10 (2)	1.40	1.00
Nos. 137-138 (2)	.50	*1.75*
Nos. 144-145 (2)	.50	.95
Nos. 119-120 (2)	.75	*1.00*
Nos. 52-53 (2)	.50	.50
Nos. 128-129 (2)	1.85	*3.75*
Nos. 143-144 (2)	.50	*.95*
Nos. 136-137 (2)	5.55	*7.50*
Nos. 90-91 (2)	.65	.65
Nos. 116-117 (2)	.50	1.50
Nos. 206-207 (2)	.65	2.00
Nos. 223-224 (2)	.50	1.05
Nos. 104-105 (2)	.50	.50
Nos. 71-72 (2)	.70	*2.75*
Nos. 46-47 (2)	1.25	*2.00*
Nos. 82-83 (2)	.50	.50
Nos. 9-10 (2)	1.40	1.40
Nos. 128-129 (2)	.65	.70
Nos. 91-92 (2)	.50	.50
Nos. 127-128 (2)	.50	.60
Nos. 152-153 (2)	.50	.50
Nos. 149-150 (2)	.55	.50
Nos. 186-187 (2)	.50	.50
Nos. 80-81 (2)	.50	1.30
Nos. 108-109 (2)	.70	.50
Nos. 62-63 (2)	.50	.50
Nos. 90-91 (2)	.50	.50
Nos. 88-89 (2)	.50	.50
Nos. 264-265 (2)	.50	.70
Nos. 523-524 (2)	1.50	3.00
Nos. 12-13 (2)	.50	*.90*
Nos. 12-13 (2)	.50	*1.05*
Nos. 200-202 (3)	1.60	*3.00*
Nos. 29-31 (3)	2.10	2.60
Nos. 137-139 (3)	2.05	*4.75*
Nos. 66-69 (4)	1.60	1.30
Nos. 127-130 (4)	2.20	2.00
Nos. 174-175 (2)	7.25	3.15
Nos. 195-198 (4)	4.75	3.60
Nos. 51-53 (3)	1.50	1.70
Nos. 247-257 (11)	3.95	3.90
Nos. 90-93 (4)	1.70	*2.20*
No. O16 (1)	5.50	*7.00*
Nos. 191-194 (4)	2.05	1.00
Nos. 100-102 (3)	1.20	4.00
Nos. 67-70 (4)	1.40	1.75
Nos. 153-155 (3)	2.55	3.50
Nos. 38-40 (3)	2.40	*5.50*
Nos. 222-223 (2)	.65	1.00
Set total (151) Stamps	80.35	109.20

Silver Wedding

King George VI and Queen Elizabeth

CD304 CD305

1948-49

Aden....................30-31
Kathiri State of Seiyun..............14-15
Qu'aiti State of Shihr and Mukalla.....
....................14-15
Antigua....................98-99
Ascension....................52-53
Bahamas....................148-149
Barbados....................210-211
Basutoland....................39-40
Bechuanaland Protectorate......147-148
Bermuda....................133-134
British Guiana....................244-245
British Honduras....................129-130
Cayman Islands....................116-117
Cyprus....................158-159
Dominica....................114-115
Falkland Islands....................99-100
Falkland Islands Dep............1L11-1L12
Fiji....................139-140
Gambia....................146-147
Gibraltar....................121-122
Gilbert & Ellice Islands....................54-55
Gold Coast....................142-143
Grenada....................145-146
Hong Kong....................178-179
Jamaica....................138-139
Kenya, Uganda, Tanzania...........92-93
Leeward Islands....................118-119
Malaya
Johore....................128-129
Kedah....................55-56
Kelantan....................44-45
Malacca....................1-2
Negri Sembilan....................36-37
Pahang....................44-45
Penang....................1-2
Perak....................99-100
Perlis....................1-2
Selangor....................74-75
Trengganu....................47-48
Malta....................223-224
Mauritius....................229-230
Montserrat....................106-107
Nigeria....................73-74
North Borneo....................238-239
Northern Rhodesia....................48-49
Nyasaland Protectorate....................85-86
Pitcairn Islands....................11-12
St. Helena....................130-131
St. Kitts-Nevis....................93-94
St. Lucia....................129-130
St. Vincent....................154-155
Sarawak....................174-175
Seychelles....................151-152
Sierra Leone....................188-189
Singapore....................21-22
Solomon Islands....................82-83
Somaliland Protectorate...........110-111
Swaziland....................48-49
Trinidad & Tobago....................64-65
Turks & Caicos Islands....................92-93
Virgin Islands....................90-91
Zanzibar....................224-225

The following have different designs but are included in the omnibus set:

Great Britain....................267-268
Offices in Morocco (Sp. Curr.)......93-94
Offices in Morocco (Tangier).......525-526
Bahrain....................62-63
Kuwait....................82-83
Oman....................25-26
South Africa....................106
South-West Africa....................159

Nos. 30-31 (2)	37.90	47.50
Nos. 14-15 (2)	21.50	*16.00*
Nos. 14-15 (2)	22.00	*18.50*
Nos. 98-99 (2)	15.00	*14.25*
Nos. 52-53 (2)	58.15	*60.60*
Nos. 148-149 (2)	45.25	40.30
Nos. 210-211 (2)	18.35	13.05
Nos. 39-40 (2)	50.30	*50.25*
Nos. 147-148 (2)	45.35	*50.25*
Nos. 133-134 (2)	47.75	*55.25*
Nos. 244-245 (2)	24.25	*28.45*
Nos. 129-130 (2)	22.75	*53.20*
Nos. 116-117 (2)	22.75	28.50
Nos. 158-159 (2)	58.50	*78.05*
Nos. 114-115 (2)	25.25	*32.75*
Nos. 99-100 (2)	112.10	83.60
Nos. 1L11-1L12 (2)	4.25	6.00
Nos. 139-140 (2)	18.20	10.75
Nos. 146-147 (2)	22.75	25.25
Nos. 121-122 (2)	71.00	*90.50*
Nos. 54-55 (2)	16.25	*24.25*
Nos. 142-143 (2)	35.25	37.75
Nos. 145-146 (2)	25.25	25.25
Nos. 178-179 (2)	363.90	136.60
Nos. 138-139 (2)	20.35	*77.75*
Nos. 92-93 (2)	52.75	*72.75*
Nos. 118-119 (2)	7.00	8.25
Nos. 128-129 (2)	29.25	*53.25*
Nos. 55-56 (2)	35.25	*50.25*
Nos. 44-45 (2)	35.75	*62.75*
Nos. 1-2 (2)	35.40	*49.75*
Nos. 36-37 (2)	28.10	*38.20*
Nos. 44-45 (2)	28.00	*38.05*
Nos. 1-2 (2)	40.50	37.80

Nos. 99-100 (2)	27.80	37.75
Nos. 1-2 (2)	33.50	58.00
Nos. 74-75 (2)	30.25	25.30
Nos. 47-48 (2)	35.25	62.75
Nos. 223-224 (2)	40.55	45.25
Nos. 229-230 (2)	17.75	45.25
Nos. 106-107 (2)	9.25	18.25
Nos. 73-74 (2)	17.85	22.80
Nos. 238-239 (2)	35.30	45.75
Nos. 48-49 (2)	92.80	90.25
Nos. 85-86 (2)	19.25	32.75
Nos. 11-12 (2)	51.75	53.50
Nos. 130-131 (2)	32.80	42.80
Nos. 93-94 (2)	11.25	7.25
Nos. 129-130 (2)	22.25	45.25
Nos. 154-155 (2)	27.75	30.25
Nos. 174-175 (2)	55.40	60.40
Nos. 151-152 (2)	16.25	45.75
Nos. 188-189 (2)	24.75	26.25
Nos. 21-22 (2)	131.25	45.40
Nos. 82-83 (2)	13.40	13.40
Nos. 110-111 (2)	8.40	8.75
Nos. 48-49 (2)	40.30	47.75
Nos. 64-65 (2)	32.75	38.25
Nos. 92-93 (2)	15.25	20.30
Nos. 90-91 (2)	18.85	21.35
Nos. 224-225 (2)	29.60	38.00
Nos. 267-268 (2)	40.40	40.25
Nos. 93-94 (2)	20.10	25.35
Nos. 525-526 (2)	23.10	29.25
Nos. 62-63 (2)	38.45	72.50
Nos. 82-83 (2)	45.50	45.50
Nos. 25-26 (2)	46.00	47.50
No. 106 (1)	.90	1.25
No. 159 (1)	1.25	.35
Set total (136) Stamps	2,604	2,806

U.P.U.

Mercury and Symbols of Communications — CD306

Plane, Ship and Hemispheres — CD307

Mercury Scattering Letters over Globe CD308

U.P.U. Monument, Bern CD309

Universal Postal Union, 75th anniversary.

1949

Aden	32-35
Kathiri State of Seiyun	16-19
Qu'aiti State of Shihr and Mukalla	16-19
Antigua	100-103
Ascension	57-60
Bahamas	150-153
Barbados	212-215
Basutoland	41-44
Bechuanaland Protectorate	149-152
Bermuda	138-141
British Guiana	246-249
British Honduras	137-140
Brunei	79-82
Cayman Islands	118-121
Cyprus	160-163
Dominica	116-119
Falkland Islands	103-106
Falkland Islands Dep.	1L14-1L17
Fiji	141-144
Gambia	148-151
Gibraltar	123-126

Gilbert & Ellice Islands	56-59
Gold Coast	144-147
Grenada	147-150
Hong Kong	180-183
Jamaica	142-145
Kenya, Uganda, Tanzania	94-97
Leeward Islands	126-129
Malaya	
Johore	151-154
Kedah	57-60
Kelantan	46-49
Malacca	18-21
Negri Sembilan	59-62
Pahang	46-49
Penang	23-26
Perak	101-104
Perlis	3-6
Selangor	76-79
Trengganu	49-52
Malta	225-228
Mauritius	231-234
Montserrat	108-111
New Hebrides, British	62-65
New Hebrides, French	79-82
Nigeria	75-78
North Borneo	240-243
Northern Rhodesia	50-53
Nyasaland Protectorate	87-90
Pitcairn Islands	13-16
St. Helena	132-135
St. Kitts-Nevis	95-98
St. Lucia	131-134
St. Vincent	170-173
Sarawak	176-179
Seychelles	153-156
Sierra Leone	190-193
Singapore	23-26
Solomon Islands	84-87
Somaliland Protectorate	112-115
Southern Rhodesia	71-72
Swaziland	50-53
Tonga	87-90
Trinidad & Tobago	66-69
Turks & Caicos Islands	101-104
Virgin Islands	92-95
Zanzibar	226-229

The following have different designs but are included in the omnibus set:

Great Britain	276-279
Offices in Morocco (Tangier)	546-549
Australia	223
Bahrain	68-71
Burma	116-121
Ceylon	304-306
Egypt	281-283
India	223-226
Kuwait	89-92
Oman	31-34
Pakistan-Bahawalpur	26-29, O25-O28
South Africa	109-111
South-West Africa	160-162

Nos. 32-35 (4)	6.60	8.95
Nos. 16-19 (4)	2.40	6.80
Nos. 16-19 (4)	2.55	3.25
Nos. 100-103 (4)	3.95	6.60
Nos. 57-60 (4)	10.90	9.00
Nos. 150-153 (4)	5.60	9.55
Nos. 212-215 (4)	4.40	14.15
Nos. 41-44 (4)	4.75	10.00
Nos. 149-152 (4)	3.35	7.25
Nos. 138-141 (4)	4.75	5.55
Nos. 246-249 (4)	2.65	4.20
Nos. 137-140 (4)	3.35	4.75
Nos. 79-82 (4)	7.75	6.75
Nos. 118-121 (4)	4.00	6.40
Nos. 160-163 (4)	4.60	8.30
Nos. 116-119 (4)	2.30	5.65
Nos. 103-106 (4)	14.90	17.10
Nos. 1L14-1L17 (4)	15.50	14.00
Nos. 141-144 (4)	3.35	14.00
Nos. 148-151 (4)	3.50	7.85
Nos. 123-126 (4)	6.75	9.50
Nos. 56-59 (4)	4.85	8.75
Nos. 144-147 (4)	3.05	6.95
Nos. 147-150 (4)	2.30	3.55
Nos. 180-183 (4)	74.25	23.60
Nos. 142-145 (4)	2.70	6.00
Nos. 94-97 (4)	2.90	3.40
Nos. 126-129 (4)	3.05	9.60
Nos. 151-154 (4)	4.70	8.90
Nos. 57-60 (4)	4.80	12.00
Nos. 46-49 (4)	4.25	12.65
Nos. 18-21 (4)	4.25	17.30
Nos. 59-62 (4)	3.50	10.75
Nos. 46-49 (4)	3.00	7.25
Nos. 23-26 (4)	5.10	11.75
Nos. 101-104 (4)	3.65	10.75
Nos. 3-6 (4)	3.95	14.25
Nos. 76-79 (4)	4.90	12.30
Nos. 49-52 (4)	4.95	9.75
Nos. 225-228 (4)	4.50	5.35
Nos. 231-234 (4)	4.35	6.70
Nos. 108-111 (4)	3.40	3.85
Nos. 62-65 (4)	1.60	4.10
Nos. 79-82 (4)	24.25	24.25

Nos. 75-78 (4)	2.80	9.25
Nos. 240-243 (4)	7.15	6.50
Nos. 50-53 (4)	5.00	6.50
Nos. 87-90 (4)	4.05	4.05
Nos. 13-16 (4)	21.25	17.00
Nos. 132-135 (4)	4.85	7.10
Nos. 95-98 (4)	3.35	4.70
Nos. 131-134 (4)	2.55	3.85
Nos. 170-173 (4)	2.20	5.05
Nos. 176-179 (4)	9.00	11.10
Nos. 153-156 (4)	3.25	4.10
Nos. 190-193 (4)	3.00	5.10
Nos. 23-26 (4)	20.75	14.20
Nos. 84-87 (4)	4.35	4.90
Nos. 112-115 (4)	3.95	8.70
Nos. 71-72 (4)	1.95	2.25
Nos. 50-53 (4)	2.80	4.65
Nos. 87-90 (4)	3.25	5.25
Nos. 66-69 (4)	3.15	3.15
Nos. 101-104 (4)	3.65	4.00
Nos. 92-95 (4)	2.60	4.60
Nos. 226-229 (4)	5.45	13.50
Nos. 276-279 (4)	1.85	2.40
Nos. 546-549 (4)	3.20	10.15
No. 223 (1)	.60	.55
Nos. 68-71 (4)	5.00	16.75
Nos. 116-121 (6)	7.15	5.30
Nos. 304-306 (3)	3.35	4.25
Nos. 281-283 (3)	5.75	2.70
Nos. 223-226 (4)	35.50	10.50
Nos. 89-92 (4)	6.10	10.25
Nos. 31-34 (4)	5.55	15.75
Nos. 26-29, O25-O28 (8)	2.00	42.00
Nos. 109-111 (3)	2.20	3.00
Nos. 160-162 (3)	3.95	6.00
Set total (313) Stamps	498.70	692.45

University

Arms of University College CD310

Alice, Princess of Athlone CD311

1948 opening of University College of the West Indies at Jamaica.

1951

Antigua	104-105
Barbados	228-229
British Guiana	250-251
British Honduras	141-142
Dominica	120-121
Grenada	164-165
Jamaica	146-147
Leeward Islands	130-131
Montserrat	112-113
St. Kitts-Nevis	105-106
St. Lucia	149-150
St. Vincent	174-175
Trinidad & Tobago	70-71
Virgin Islands	96-97

Nos. 104-105 (2)	1.35	3.25
Nos. 228-229 (2)	1.85	1.55
Nos. 250-251 (2)	1.10	1.25
Nos. 141-142 (2)	1.40	2.15
Nos. 120-121 (2)	1.40	1.75
Nos. 164-165 (2)	1.20	1.60
Nos. 146-147 (2)	.95	.85
Nos. 112-113 (2)	.85	1.50
Nos. 105-106 (2)	.90	1.50
Nos. 149-150 (2)	1.40	1.50
Nos. 174-175 (2)	1.00	2.15
Nos. 70-71 (2)	.75	.75
Nos. 96-97 (2)	1.50	3.40
Set total (26) Stamps	15.65	23.20

Coronation

Queen Elizabeth II — CD312

1953

Aden	47
Kathiri State of Seiyun	28
Qu'aiti State of Shihr and Mukalla	28

Antigua	106
Ascension	61
Bahamas	157
Barbados	234
Basutoland	45
Bechuanaland Protectorate	153
Bermuda	142
British Guiana	252
British Honduras	143
Cayman Islands	150
Cyprus	167
Dominica	141
Falkland Islands	121
Falkland Islands Dependencies	1L18
Fiji	145
Gambia	152
Gibraltar	131
Gilbert & Ellice Islands	60
Gold Coast	160
Grenada	170
Hong Kong	184
Jamaica	153
Kenya, Uganda, Tanzania	101
Leeward Islands	132
Malaya	
Johore	155
Kedah	82
Kelantan	71
Malacca	27
Negri Sembilan	63
Pahang	71
Penang	27
Perak	126
Perlis	28
Selangor	101
Trengganu	74
Malta	241
Mauritius	250
Montserrat	127
New Hebrides, British	77
Nigeria	79
North Borneo	260
Northern Rhodesia	60
Nyasaland Protectorate	96
Pitcairn Islands	19
St. Helena	139
St. Kitts-Nevis	119
St. Lucia	156
St. Vincent	185
Sarawak	196
Seychelles	172
Sierra Leone	194
Singapore	27
Solomon Islands	88
Somaliland Protectorate	127
Swaziland	54
Trinidad & Tobago	84
Tristan da Cunha	13
Turks & Caicos Islands	118
Virgin Islands	114

The following have different designs but are included in the omnibus set:

Great Britain	313-316
Offices in Morocco (Tangier)	579-582
Australia	259-261
Bahrain	92-95
Canada	330
Ceylon	317
Cook Islands	145-146
Kuwait	113-116
New Zealand	280-284
Niue	104-105
Oman	52-55
Samoa	214-215
South Africa	192
Southern Rhodesia	80
South-West Africa	244-248
Tokelau Islands	4

No. 47 (1)	1.25	1.25
No. 28 (1)	.40	1.50
No. 28 (1)	1.10	.60
No. 106 (1)	.50	.75
No. 61 (1)	1.25	2.50
No. 157 (1)	1.25	.75
No. 234 (1)	1.00	.25
No. 45 (1)	.50	.60
No. 153 (1)	.75	.35
No. 142 (1)	.85	.40
No. 252 (1)	.45	.25
No. 143 (1)	.55	.40
No. 150 (1)	.40	1.00
No. 167 (1)	1.50	1.00
No. 141 (1)	.40	.40
No. 121 (1)	.90	1.50
No. 1L18 (1)	1.50	1.50
No. 145 (1)	1.75	.60
No. 152 (1)	.50	.50
No. 131 (1)	.50	.50
No. 60 (1)	.65	2.25
No. 160 (1)	.95	.25
No. 170 (1)	.30	.25
No. 184 (1)	7.00	.35
No. 153 (1)	1.50	.25

No. 101 (1)	.40	.25
No. 132 (1)	1.00	2.25
No. 155 (1)	1.40	.30
No. 82 (1)	2.25	.60
No. 71 (1)	1.60	1.60
No. 27 (1)	1.10	1.50
No. 63 (1)	1.40	.65
No. 71 (1)	2.25	.25
No. 27 (1)	1.75	.30
No. 126 (1)	1.60	.25
No. 28 (1)	1.75	4.00
No. 101 (1)	1.75	.25
No. 74 (1)	1.50	1.00
No. 241 (1)	.55	.25
No. 250 (1)	1.00	.25
No. 127 (1)	.65	.50
No. 77 (1)	.75	.60
No. 79 (1)	.45	.25
No. 260 (1)	2.00	1.00
No. 60 (1)	.70	.25
No. 96 (1)	.75	.75
No. 19 (1)	2.50	2.50
No. 139 (1)	1.25	1.25
No. 119 (1)	.35	.25
No. 156 (1)	.70	.35
No. 185 (1)	.50	.30
No. 196 (1)	2.00	2.25
No. 172 (1)	.80	.80
No. 194 (1)	.40	.40
No. 27 (1)	2.50	.40
No. 88 (1)	1.10	1.10
No. 127 (1)	.40	.25
No. 54 (1)	.30	.25
No. 84 (1)	.25	.25
No. 13 (1)	1.00	1.75
No. 118 (1)	.40	1.10
No. 114 (1)	.40	1.00
Nos. 313-316 (4)	16.35	8.75
Nos. 579-582 (4)	7.40	5.20
Nos. 259-261 (3)	4.60	3.25
Nos. 92-95 (4)	15.25	12.75
No. 330 (1)	.25	.25
No. 317 (1)	1.50	.25
Nos. 145-146 (2)	2.90	2.90
Nos. 113-116 (4)	16.00	8.50
Nos. 280-284 (5)	5.65	6.85
Nos. 104-105 (2)	1.75	1.75
Nos. 52-55 (4)	15.25	6.50
Nos. 214-215 (2)	2.10	1.00
No. 192 (1)	.30	.25
No. 80 (1)	7.25	7.25
Nos. 244-248 (5)	4.90	3.50
No. 4 (1)	3.75	2.75
Set total (106) Stamps	174.35	122.90

Separate designs for each country for the visit of Queen Elizabeth II and the Duke of Edinburgh.

Royal Visit 1953

1953

Aden	62
Australia	267-269
Bermuda	163
Ceylon	318
Fiji	146
Gibraltar	146
Jamaica	154
Kenya, Uganda, Tanzania	102
Malta	242
New Zealand	286-287

No. 62 (1)	.65	2.00
Nos. 267-269 (3)	2.35	1.90
No. 163 (1)	.50	.25
No. 318 (1)	1.25	.25
No. 146 (1)	.65	.35
No. 146 (1)	.50	.35
No. 154 (1)	.55	.25
No. 102 (1)	.50	.25
No. 242 (1)	.35	.25
Nos. 286-287 (2)	.50	.50
Set total (13) Stamps	7.80	6.35

West Indies Federation

Map of the Caribbean
CD313

Federation of the West Indies, April 22, 1958.

1958

Antigua	122-124
Barbados	248-250
Dominica	161-163
Grenada	184-186
Jamaica	175-177
Montserrat	143-145
St. Kitts-Nevis	136-138
St. Lucia	170-172
St. Vincent	198-200

Trinidad & Tobago	86-88

Nos. 122-124 (3)	5.80	3.80
Nos. 248-250 (3)	1.60	2.90
Nos. 161-163 (3)	1.95	1.85
Nos. 184-186 (3)	1.50	1.20
Nos. 175-177 (3)	3.10	4.20
Nos. 143-145 (3)	2.35	1.35
Nos. 136-138 (3)	3.00	1.85
Nos. 170-172 (3)	2.05	2.80
Nos. 198-200 (3)	1.50	1.75
Nos. 86-88 (3)	.75	.90
Set total (30) Stamps	23.60	22.60

Freedom from Hunger

Protein Food
CD314

U.N. Food and Agricultural Organization's "Freedom from Hunger" campaign.

1963

Aden	65
Antigua	133
Ascension	89
Bahamas	180
Basutoland	83
Bechuanaland Protectorate	194
Bermuda	192
British Guiana	271
British Honduras	179
Brunei	100
Cayman Islands	168
Dominica	181
Falkland Islands	146
Fiji	198
Gambia	172
Gibraltar	161
Gilbert & Ellice Islands	76
Grenada	190
Hong Kong	218
Malta	291
Mauritius	270
Montserrat	150
New Hebrides, British	93
North Borneo	296
Pitcairn Islands	35
St. Helena	173
St. Lucia	179
St. Vincent	201
Sarawak	212
Seychelles	213
Solomon Islands	109
Swaziland	108
Tonga	127
Tristan da Cunha	68
Turks & Caicos Islands	138
Virgin Islands	140
Zanzibar	280

No. 65 (1)	1.75	1.75
No. 133 (1)	.35	.35
No. 89 (1)	1.00	1.00
No. 180 (1)	.65	.65
No. 83 (1)	.50	.25
No. 194 (1)	1.00	.50
No. 192 (1)	.45	.25
No. 271 (1)	.65	.25
No. 179 (1)	3.25	2.25
No. 100 (1)	.50	.30
No. 168 (1)	.30	.30
No. 181 (1)	11.50	3.50
No. 146 (1)	5.25	2.75
No. 198 (1)	.50	.25
No. 172 (1)	4.00	2.25
No. 161 (1)	1.40	.40
No. 76 (1)	.30	.25
No. 190 (1)	57.50	8.75
No. 218 (1)	2.25	2.75
No. 291 (1)	.50	.50
No. 270 (1)	.55	.45
No. 150 (1)	.60	.25
No. 93 (1)	1.90	.95
No. 296 (1)	12.50	5.00
No. 35 (1)	2.25	1.10
No. 173 (1)	.40	.40
No. 179 (1)	.90	.50
No. 201 (1)	1.60	1.75
No. 212 (1)	.85	.35
No. 213 (1)	2.00	.85
No. 109 (1)	.50	.50
No. 108 (1)	.70	.35
No. 127 (1)	.90	.40
No. 68 (1)	.50	.50
No. 138 (1)	.50	.50
No. 140 (1)	1.50	.80
No. 280 (1)		
Set total (37) Stamps	122.25	44.20

Red Cross Centenary

Red Cross and Elizabeth II
CD315

1963

Antigua	134-135
Ascension	90-91
Bahamas	183-184
Basutoland	84-85
Bechuanaland Protectorate	195-196
Bermuda	193-194
British Guiana	272-273
British Honduras	180-181
Cayman Islands	169-170
Dominica	182-183
Falkland Islands	147-148
Fiji	203-204
Gambia	173-174
Gibraltar	162-163
Gilbert & Ellice Islands	77-78
Grenada	191-192
Hong Kong	219-220
Jamaica	203-204
Malta	292-293
Mauritius	271-272
Montserrat	151-152
New Hebrides, British	94-95
Pitcairn Islands	36-37
St. Helena	174-175
St. Kitts-Nevis	143-144
St. Lucia	180-181
St. Vincent	202-203
Seychelles	214-215
Solomon Islands	110-111
South Arabia	1-2
Swaziland	109-110
Tonga	134-135
Tristan da Cunha	69-70
Turks & Caicos Islands	139-140
Virgin Islands	141-142

Nos. 134-135 (2)	1.10	1.50
Nos. 90-91 (2)	8.25	2.70
Nos. 183-184 (2)	2.30	2.55
Nos. 84-85 (2)	1.20	.90
Nos. 195-196 (2)	1.05	1.05
Nos. 193-194 (2)	2.75	2.55
Nos. 272-273 (2)	1.05	.80
Nos. 180-181 (2)	1.00	2.25
Nos. 169-170 (2)	.95	2.00
Nos. 182-183 (2)	.70	1.05
Nos. 147-148 (2)	19.75	6.00
Nos. 203-204 (2)	4.00	3.55
Nos. 173-174 (2)	.85	.85
Nos. 162-163 (2)	7.05	5.40
Nos. 77-78 (2)	2.25	3.25
Nos. 191-192 (2)	.80	.50
Nos. 219-220 (2)	39.50	8.85
Nos. 203-204 (2)	.75	1.65
Nos. 292-293 (2)	3.25	5.00
Nos. 271-272 (2)	.90	.90
Nos. 151-152 (2)	1.00	.80
Nos. 94-95 (2)	1.00	.50
Nos. 36-37 (2)	8.50	6.50
Nos. 174-175 (2)	1.70	2.30
Nos. 143-144 (2)	.90	.90
Nos. 180-181 (2)	1.25	1.25
Nos. 202-203 (2)	.90	.90
Nos. 214-215 (2)	1.10	.90
Nos. 110-111 (2)	1.25	1.15
Nos. 1-2 (2)	1.25	1.25
Nos. 109-110 (2)	1.10	1.10
Nos. 134-135 (2)	1.00	1.25
Nos. 69-70 (2)	1.50	1.00
Nos. 139-140 (2)	.95	1.10
Nos. 141-142 (2)	.80	.80
Set total (70) Stamps	123.65	75.00

Shakespeare

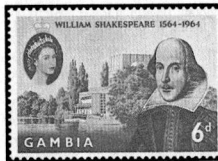

Shakespeare Memorial Theatre, Stratford-on-Avon — CD316

400th anniversary of the birth of William Shakespeare.

1964

Antigua	151
Bahamas	201
Bechuanaland Protectorate	197
Cayman Islands	171

Dominica	184
Falkland Islands	149
Gambia	192
Gibraltar	164
Montserrat	153
St. Lucia	196
Turks & Caicos Islands	141
Virgin Islands	143

No. 151 (1)	.40	.25
No. 201 (1)	.60	.35
No. 197 (1)	.35	.35
No. 171 (1)	.35	.30
No. 184 (1)	.35	.35
No. 149 (1)	1.75	.50
No. 192 (1)	.35	.25
No. 164 (1)	.65	.55
No. 153 (1)	.35	.25
No. 196 (1)	.45	.25
No. 141 (1)	.40	.40
No. 143 (1)	.45	.45
Set total (12) Stamps	6.45	4.25

ITU

ITU Emblem
CD317

Intl. Telecommunication Union, cent.

1965

Antigua	153-154
Ascension	92-93
Bahamas	219-220
Barbados	265-266
Basutoland	101-102
Bechuanaland Protectorate	202-203
Bermuda	196-197
British Guiana	293-294
British Honduras	187-188
Brunei	116-117
Cayman Islands	172-173
Dominica	185-186
Falkland Islands	154-155
Fiji	211-212
Gibraltar	167-168
Gilbert & Ellice Islands	87-88
Grenada	205-206
Hong Kong	221-222
Mauritius	291-292
Montserrat	157-158
New Hebrides, British	108-109
Pitcairn Islands	52-53
St. Helena	180-181
St. Kitts-Nevis	163-164
St. Lucia	197-198
St. Vincent	224-225
Seychelles	218-219
Solomon Islands	126-127
Swaziland	115-116
Tristan da Cunha	85-86
Turks & Caicos Islands	142-143
Virgin Islands	159-160

Nos. 153-154 (2)	1.65	1.35
Nos. 92-93 (2)	1.90	1.50
Nos. 219-220 (2)	1.35	1.35
Nos. 265-266 (2)	1.50	1.25
Nos. 101-102 (2)	.85	.65
Nos. 202-203 (2)	1.20	.75
Nos. 196-197 (2)	2.15	2.25
Nos. 293-294 (2)	.60	.55
Nos. 187-188 (2)	.85	.85
Nos. 116-117 (2)	1.75	1.75
Nos. 172-173 (2)	1.00	1.00
Nos. 185-186 (2)	.55	.55
Nos. 154-155 (2)	7.75	3.65
Nos. 211-212 (2)	2.70	2.70
Nos. 167-168 (2)	11.25	5.95
Nos. 87-88 (2)	.95	.75
Nos. 205-206 (2)	.50	.50
Nos. 221-222 (2)	32.00	4.55
Nos. 291-292 (2)	1.20	.65
Nos. 157-158 (2)	1.25	1.15
Nos. 108-109 (2)	.65	.50
Nos. 52-53 (2)	10.00	7.55
Nos. 180-181 (2)	.80	.60
Nos. 163-164 (2)	.60	.60
Nos. 197-198 (2)	1.25	1.25
Nos. 224-225 (2)	.80	.90
Nos. 218-219 (2)	.90	.60
Nos. 126-127 (2)	.70	.55
Nos. 115-116 (2)	.75	.75
Nos. 85-86 (2)	1.15	.65
Nos. 142-143 (2)	.90	.90
Nos. 159-160 (2)	.95	.95
Set total (64) Stamps	92.40	49.50

Intl. Cooperation Year

ICY Emblem CD318

1965

Antigua	155-156
Ascension	94-95
Bahamas	222-223
Basutoland	103-104
Bechuanaland Protectorate	204-205
Bermuda	199-200
British Guiana	295-296
British Honduras	189-190
Brunei	118-119
Cayman Islands	174-175
Dominica	187-188
Falkland Islands	156-157
Fiji	213-214
Gibraltar	169-170
Gilbert & Ellice Islands	104-105
Grenada	207-208
Hong Kong	223-224
Mauritius	293-294
Montserrat	176-177
New Hebrides, British	110-111
New Hebrides, French	126-127
Pitcairn Islands	54-55
St. Helena	182-183
St. Kitts-Nevis	165-166
St. Lucia	199-200
Seychelles	220-221
Solomon Islands	143-144
South Arabia	17-18
Swaziland	117-118
Tristan da Cunha	87-88
Turks & Caicos Islands	144-145
Virgin Islands	161-162

Nos. 155-156 (2)	.60	.50
Nos. 94-95 (2)	1.30	1.50
Nos. 222-223 (2)	.65	1.40
Nos. 103-104 (2)	.75	.85
Nos. 204-205 (2)	1.00	1.15
Nos. 199-200 (2)	2.25	1.25
Nos. 295-296 (2)	.65	.60
Nos. 189-190 (2)	.60	.55
Nos. 118-119 (2)	.85	.85
Nos. 174-175 (2)	1.00	.95
Nos. 187-188 (2)	.55	.55
Nos. 156-157 (2)	7.00	1.90
Nos. 213-214 (2)	2.60	2.35
Nos. 169-170 (2)	1.35	3.00
Nos. 104-105 (2)	.95	.60
Nos. 207-208 (2)	.50	.50
Nos. 223-224 (2)	26.00	4.10
Nos. 293-294 (2)	.70	.70
Nos. 176-177 (2)	.80	.65
Nos. 110-111 (2)	.50	.50
Nos. 126-127 (2)	12.00	12.00
Nos. 54-55 (2)	9.85	5.25
Nos. 182-183 (2)	.95	.50
Nos. 165-166 (2)	.70	.60
Nos. 199-200 (2)	.55	.55
Nos. 220-221 (2)	.90	.65
Nos. 143-144 (2)	.70	.60
Nos. 17-18 (2)	1.20	.50
Nos. 117-118 (2)	.75	.75
Nos. 87-88 (2)	1.35	.75
Nos. 144-145 (2)	.85	.85
Nos. 161-162 (2)	.80	.80
Set total (64) Stamps	81.20	48.25

Churchill Memorial

Winston Churchill and St. Paul's, London, During Air Attack CD319

1966

Antigua	157-160
Ascension	96-99
Bahamas	224-227
Barbados	281-284
Basutoland	105-108
Bechuanaland Protectorate	206-209
Bermuda	201-204
British Antarctic Territory	16-19
British Honduras	191-194
Brunei	120-123
Cayman Islands	176-179
Dominica	189-192
Falkland Islands	158-161
Fiji	215-218

Gibraltar	171-174
Gilbert & Ellice Islands	106-109
Grenada	209-212
Hong Kong	225-228
Mauritius	295-298
Montserrat	178-181
New Hebrides, British	112-115
New Hebrides, French	128-131
Pitcairn Islands	56-59
St. Helena	184-187
St. Kitts-Nevis	167-170
St. Lucia	201-204
St. Vincent	241-244
Seychelles	222-225
Solomon Islands	145-148
South Arabia	19-22
Swaziland	119-122
Tristan da Cunha	89-92
Turks & Caicos Islands	146-149
Virgin Islands	163-166

Nos. 157-160 (4)	3.05	2.55
Nos. 96-99 (4)	10.00	7.15
Nos. 224-227 (4)	2.30	3.20
Nos. 281-284 (4)	3.00	4.45
Nos. 105-108 (4)	2.80	2.75
Nos. 206-209 (4)	2.80	2.30
Nos. 201-204 (4)	4.00	4.00
Nos. 16-19 (4)	46.35	20.00
Nos. 191-194 (4)	2.55	1.80
Nos. 120-123 (4)	8.00	7.25
Nos. 176-179 (4)	3.40	3.55
Nos. 189-192 (4)	1.15	1.15
Nos. 158-161 (4)	12.75	7.80
Nos. 215-218 (4)	5.15	3.45
Nos. 171-174 (4)	3.80	5.45
Nos. 106-109 (4)	1.75	1.30
Nos. 209-212 (4)	1.10	1.10
Nos. 225-228 (4)	68.00	12.15
Nos. 295-298 (4)	4.05	4.05
Nos. 178-181 (4)	1.60	1.55
Nos. 112-115 (4)	2.30	1.00
Nos. 128-131 (4)	10.25	10.25
Nos. 56-59 (4)	15.00	10.50
Nos. 184-187 (4)	1.85	1.95
Nos. 167-170 (4)	1.70	1.70
Nos. 201-204 (4)	1.50	1.50
Nos. 241-244 (4)	1.50	1.75
Nos. 222-225 (4)	3.20	3.60
Nos. 145-148 (4)	1.75	1.75
Nos. 19-22 (4)	3.80	2.50
Nos. 119-122 (4)	1.70	2.55
Nos. 89-92 (4)	5.95	2.70
Nos. 146-149 (4)	1.60	1.75
Nos. 163-166 (4)	1.90	1.90
Set total (136) Stamps	241.60	142.40

Royal Visit, 1966

Queen Elizabeth II and Prince Philip CD320

Caribbean visit, Feb. 4 - Mar. 6, 1966.

1966

Antigua	161-162
Bahamas	228-229
Barbados	285-286
British Guiana	299-300
Cayman Islands	180-181
Dominica	193-194
Grenada	213-214
Montserrat	182-183
St. Kitts-Nevis	171-172
St. Lucia	205-206
St. Vincent	245-246
Turks & Caicos Islands	150-151
Virgin Islands	167-168

Nos. 161-162 (2)	3.80	2.60
Nos. 228-229 (2)	3.05	3.05
Nos. 285-286 (2)	3.00	2.00
Nos. 299-300 (2)	3.35	1.60
Nos. 180-181 (2)	3.45	1.80
Nos. 193-194 (2)	3.00	4.00
Nos. 213-214 (2)	.90	.50
Nos. 182-183 (2)	1.70	1.00
Nos. 171-172 (2)	.80	.75
Nos. 205-206 (2)	1.50	1.35
Nos. 245-246 (2)	2.75	1.35
Nos. 150-151 (2)	1.20	.70
Nos. 167-168 (2)	2.25	2.25
Set total (26) Stamps	30.75	19.55

World Cup Soccer

Soccer Player and Jules Rimet Cup CD321

World Cup Soccer Championship, Wembley, England, July 11-30.

1966

Antigua	163-164
Ascension	100-101
Bahamas	245-246
Bermuda	205-206
Brunei	124-125
Cayman Islands	182-183
Dominica	195-196
Fiji	219-220
Gibraltar	175-176
Gilbert & Ellice Islands	125-126
Grenada	230-231
New Hebrides, British	116-117
New Hebrides, French	132-133
Pitcairn Islands	60-61
St. Helena	188-189
St. Kitts-Nevis	173-174
St. Lucia	207-208
Seychelles	226-227
Solomon Islands	167-168
South Arabia	23-24
Tristan da Cunha	93-94

Nos. 163-164 (2)	.85	.50
Nos. 100-101 (2)	2.50	1.80
Nos. 245-246 (2)	.65	.65
Nos. 205-206 (2)	1.75	1.75
Nos. 124-125 (2)	1.40	1.00
Nos. 182-183 (2)	.75	.75
Nos. 195-196 (2)	1.20	.75
Nos. 219-220 (2)	2.00	1.20
Nos. 175-176 (2)	2.00	1.80
Nos. 125-126 (2)	.80	.60
Nos. 230-231 (2)	.65	.95
Nos. 116-117 (2)	1.00	1.00
Nos. 132-133 (2)	7.00	7.00
Nos. 60-61 (2)	8.00	4.75
Nos. 188-189 (2)	1.25	.60
Nos. 173-174 (2)	.85	.80
Nos. 207-208 (2)	1.15	.90
Nos. 226-227 (2)	.85	.85
Nos. 167-168 (2)	.70	.70
Nos. 23-24 (2)	1.90	.55
Nos. 93-94 (2)	1.25	.80
Set total (42) Stamps	38.50	29.70

WHO Headquarters

World Health Organization Headquarters, Geneva — CD322

1966

Antigua	165-166
Ascension	102-103
Bahamas	247-248
Brunei	126-127
Cayman Islands	184-185
Dominica	197-198
Fiji	224-225
Gibraltar	180-181
Gilbert & Ellice Islands	127-128
Grenada	232-233
Hong Kong	229-230
Montserrat	184-185
New Hebrides, British	118-119
New Hebrides, French	134-135
Pitcairn Islands	62-63
St. Helena	190-191
St. Kitts-Nevis	177-178
St. Lucia	209-210
St. Vincent	247-248
Seychelles	228-229
Solomon Islands	169-170
South Arabia	25-26
Tristan da Cunha	99-100

Nos. 165-166 (2)	1.05	.55
Nos. 102-103 (2)	6.60	3.50
Nos. 247-248 (2)	.80	.80
Nos. 126-127 (2)	1.35	1.00
Nos. 184-185 (2)	2.25	1.40
Nos. 197-198 (2)	.75	.75
Nos. 224-225 (2)	5.10	3.90
Nos. 180-181 (2)	7.50	4.75
Nos. 127-128 (2)	.80	.70
Nos. 232-233 (2)	.80	.50
Nos. 229-230 (2)	14.25	2.30
Nos. 184-185 (2)	1.00	1.00
Nos. 118-119 (2)	.75	.50
Nos. 134-135 (2)	8.75	8.75
Nos. 62-63 (2)	10.00	6.50
Nos. 190-191 (2)	3.50	1.50
Nos. 177-178 (2)	.65	.65
Nos. 209-210 (2)	.80	.80
Nos. 247-248 (2)	1.15	1.05
Nos. 228-229 (2)	1.25	.75
Nos. 169-170 (2)	.80	.80

Nos. 25-26 (2)	2.10	.70
Nos. 99-100 (2)	1.90	1.25
Set total (46) Stamps	73.90	44.40

UNESCO Anniversary

"Education" — CD323

"Science" (Wheat ears & flask enclosing globe). "Culture" (lyre & columns). 20th anniversary of the UNESCO.

1966-67

Antigua	183-185
Ascension	108-110
Bahamas	249-251
Barbados	287-289
Bermuda	207-209
Brunei	128-130
Cayman Islands	186-188
Dominica	199-201
Gibraltar	183-185
Gilbert & Ellice Islands	129-131
Grenada	234-236
Hong Kong	231-233
Mauritius	299-301
Montserrat	186-188
New Hebrides, British	120-122
New Hebrides, French	136-138
Pitcairn Islands	64-66
St. Helena	192-194
St. Kitts-Nevis	179-181
St. Lucia	211-213
St. Vincent	249-251
Seychelles	230-232
Solomon Islands	171-173
South Arabia	27-29
Swaziland	123-125
Tristan da Cunha	101-103
Turks & Caicos Islands	155-157
Virgin Islands	176-178

Nos. 183-185 (3)	1.90	2.50
Nos. 108-110 (3)	11.00	6.15
Nos. 249-251 (3)	2.35	2.35
Nos. 287-289 (3)	2.50	2.15
Nos. 207-209 (3)	4.30	3.90
Nos. 128-130 (3)	5.00	7.40
Nos. 186-188 (3)	2.50	1.70
Nos. 199-201 (3)	1.60	.75
Nos. 183-185 (3)	7.50	3.75
Nos. 129-131 (3)	2.50	1.65
Nos. 234-236 (3)	1.10	1.20
Nos. 231-233 (3)	89.00	20.00
Nos. 186-188 (3)	2.10	1.50
Nos. 120-122 (3)	1.90	1.90
Nos. 136-138 (3)	7.75	7.75
Nos. 64-66 (3)	9.35	6.35
Nos. 192-194 (3)	5.25	3.65
Nos. 179-181 (3)	.90	.90
Nos. 211-213 (3)	1.15	1.15
Nos. 249-251 (3)	2.30	1.35
Nos. 230-232 (3)	2.40	2.40
Nos. 171-173 (3)	2.00	1.50
Nos. 27-29 (3)	5.90	3.05
Nos. 123-125 (3)	1.45	1.45
Nos. 101-103 (3)	2.00	1.40
Nos. 155-157 (3)	1.05	1.05
Nos. 176-178 (3)	1.30	1.30
Set total (84) Stamps	180.45	92.60

Silver Wedding, 1972

Queen Elizabeth II and Prince Philip — CD324

Designs: borders differ for each country.

1972

Anguilla	161-162
Antigua	295-296
Ascension	164-165
Bahamas	344-345
Bermuda	296-297
British Antarctic Territory	43-44
British Honduras	306-307
British Indian Ocean Territory	48-49

Brunei	186-187
Cayman Islands	304-305
Dominica	352-353
Falkland Islands	223-224
Fiji	328-329
Gibraltar	292-293
Gilbert & Ellice Islands	206-207
Grenada	466-467
Hong Kong	271-272
Montserrat	286-287
New Hebrides, British	169-170
Pitcairn Islands	127-128
St. Helena	271-272
St. Kitts-Nevis	257-258
St. Lucia	328-329
St.Vincent	344-345
Seychelles	309-310
Solomon Islands	248-249
South Georgia	35-36
Tristan da Cunha	178-179
Turks & Caicos Islands	257-258
Virgin Islands	241-242

Nos. 161-162 (2)	1.80	1.50
Nos. 295-296 (2)	.50	.50
Nos. 164-165 (2)	.80	.80
Nos. 344-345 (2)	.60	.60
Nos. 296-297 (2)	.50	.50
Nos. 43-44 (2)	7.75	6.10
Nos. 306-307 (2)	.90	.90
Nos. 48-49 (2)	2.30	1.00
Nos. 186-187 (2)	.65	.85
Nos. 304-305 (2)	.75	.75
Nos. 352-353 (2)	.65	.65
Nos. 223-224 (2)	1.10	1.10
Nos. 328-329 (2)	1.00	1.00
Nos. 292-293 (2)	.50	.50
Nos. 206-207 (2)	.50	.50
Nos. 466-467 (2)	.70	.70
Nos. 271-272 (2)	2.10	1.75
Nos. 286-287 (2)	.55	.55
Nos. 169-170 (2)	.50	.50
Nos. 127-128 (2)	1.15	.80
Nos. 271-272 (2)	.70	1.20
Nos. 257-258 (2)	.65	.50
Nos. 328-329 (2)	.75	.75
Nos. 344-345 (2)	.55	.55
Nos. 309-310 (2)	.95	.95
Nos. 248-249 (2)	.60	.60
Nos. 35-36 (2)	1.40	1.40
Nos. 178-179 (2)	.70	.70
Nos. 257-258 (2)	.50	.50
Nos. 241-242 (2)	.50	.50
Set total (60) Stamps	32.60	29.20

Princess Anne's Wedding

Princess Anne and Mark Phillips — CD325

Wedding of Princess Anne and Mark Phillips, Nov. 14, 1973.

1973

Anguilla	179-180
Ascension	177-178
Belize	325-326
Bermuda	302-303
British Antarctic Territory	60-61
Cayman Islands	320-321
Falkland Islands	225-226
Gibraltar	305-306
Gilbert & Ellice Islands	216-217
Hong Kong	289-290
Montserrat	300-301
Pitcairn Islands	135-136
St. Helena	277-278
St. Kitts-Nevis	274-275
St. Lucia	349-350
St. Vincent	358-359
St. Vincent Grenadines	1-2
Seychelles	311-312
Solomon Islands	259-260
South Georgia	37-38
Tristan da Cunha	189-190
Turks & Caicos Islands	286-287
Virgin Islands	260-261

Nos. 179-180 (2)	.55	.55
Nos. 177-178 (2)	.65	.65
Nos. 325-326 (2)	.50	.50
Nos. 302-303 (2)	.50	.50
Nos. 60-61 (2)	1.10	1.10
Nos. 320-321 (2)	.55	.55
Nos. 225-226 (2)	.75	.75
Nos. 305-306 (2)	.70	.70
Nos. 216-217 (2)	.50	.50
Nos. 289-290 (2)	3.25	2.25
Nos. 300-301 (2)	.65	.65
Nos. 135-136 (2)	.90	.60
Nos. 277-278 (2)	.50	.50
Nos. 274-275 (2)	.50	.50
Nos. 349-350 (2)	.50	.50
Nos. 358-359 (2)	.50	.50
Nos. 1-2 (2)	.65	.65
Nos. 311-312 (2)	.70	.70
Nos. 259-260 (2)	.70	.70
Nos. 37-38 (2)	.75	.75
Nos. 189-190 (2)	.50	.50
Nos. 286-287 (2)	.50	.50
Nos. 260-261 (2)	.50	.50
Set total (46) Stamps	16.90	15.60

Elizabeth II Coronation Anniv.

CD326

CD327

CD328

Designs: Royal and local beasts in heraldic form and simulated stonework. Portrait of Elizabeth II by Peter Grugeon. 25th anniversary of coronation of Queen Elizabeth II.

1978

Ascension	229
Barbados	474
Belize	397
British Antarctic Territory	71
Cayman Islands	404
Christmas Island	87
Falkland Islands	275
Fiji	384
Gambia	380
Gilbert Islands	312
Mauritius	464
New Hebrides, British	258
St. Helena	317
St. Kitts-Nevis	354
Samoa	472
Solomon Islands	368
South Georgia	51
Swaziland	302
Tristan da Cunha	238
Virgin Islands	337

No. 229 (1)	2.25	2.25
No. 474 (1)	1.35	1.35
No. 397 (1)	1.75	1.75
No. 71 (1)	6.00	6.00
No. 404 (1)	2.00	2.50
No. 87 (1)	3.75	4.25
No. 275 (1)	4.00	4.00
No. 384 (1)	2.75	2.75
No. 380 (1)	1.50	1.50
No. 312 (1)	1.25	1.25
No. 464 (1)	2.75	2.75
No. 258 (1)	1.75	1.75
No. 317 (1)	1.75	1.75
No. 354 (1)	1.00	1.00
No. 472 (1)	2.00	2.00
No. 368 (1)	3.00	3.00
No. 51 (1)	3.00	3.00
No. 302 (1)	1.75	1.75
No. 238 (1)	1.50	1.50
No. 337 (1)	2.25	2.25
Set total (20) Stamps	47.35	48.35

Queen Mother Elizabeth's 80th Birthday

CD330

Designs: Photographs of Queen Mother Elizabeth. Falkland Islands issued in sheets of 50; others in sheets of 9.

1980

Ascension	261
Bermuda	401
Cayman Islands	443
Falkland Islands	305
Gambia	412
Gibraltar	393
Hong Kong	364
Pitcairn Islands	193
St. Helena	341
Samoa	532
Solomon Islands	426
Tristan da Cunha	277

No. 261 (1)	.50	.50
No. 401 (1)	.45	.45
No. 443 (1)	.45	.45
No. 305 (1)	.40	.40
No. 412 (1)	.40	.50
No. 393 (1)	.35	.35
No. 364 (1)	1.10	1.00
No. 193 (1)	.70	.70
No. 341 (1)	.50	.50
No. 532 (1)	.55	.55
No. 426 (1)	.50	.50
No. 277 (1)	.45	.45
Set total (12) Stamps	6.35	6.35

Royal Wedding, 1981

Prince Charles and Lady Diana — CD331

CD331a

Wedding of Charles, Prince of Wales, and Lady Diana Spencer, St. Paul's Cathedral, London, July 29, 1981.

1981

Antigua	623-627
Ascension	294-296
Barbados	547-549
Barbuda	497-501
Bermuda	412-414
Brunei	268-270
Cayman Islands	471-473
Dominica	701-705
Falkland Islands	324-326
Falkland Islands Dep.	1L59-1L61
Fiji	442-444
Gambia	426-428
Ghana	759-764
Grenada	1051-1055
Grenada Grenadines	440-443
Hong Kong	373-375
Jamaica	500-503
Lesotho	335-337
Maldive Islands	906-909
Mauritius	520-522
Norfolk Island	280-282
Pitcairn Islands	206-208
St. Helena	353-355
St. Lucia	543-549
Samoa	558-560
Sierra Leone	509-518
Solomon Islands	450-452
Swaziland	382-384
Tristan da Cunha	294-296
Turks & Caicos Islands	486-489
Caicos Island	8-11
Uganda	314-317
Vanuatu	308-310
Virgin Islands	406-408

Nos. 623-627 (5)	7.55	2.55
Nos. 294-296 (3)	1.10	1.10
Nos. 547-549 (3)	.90	.90
Nos. 497-501 (5)	10.95	10.95
Nos. 412-414 (3)	2.00	2.00
Nos. 268-270 (3)	2.15	4.50
Nos. 471-473 (3)	1.35	1.35
Nos. 701-705 (5)	8.35	2.35
Nos. 324-326 (3)	1.65	1.70
Nos. 1L59-1L61 (3)	1.45	1.45
Nos. 442-444 (3)	1.70	1.70
Nos. 426-428 (3)	.80	.80
Nos. 759-764 (9)	5.00	5.00
Nos. 1051-1055 (5)	9.85	1.85
Nos. 440-443 (4)	2.35	2.35
Nos. 373-375 (3)	3.30	3.10
Nos. 500-503 (4)	1.50	1.25
Nos. 335-337 (3)	1.10	1.10
Nos. 906-909 (4)	1.70	1.80
Nos. 520-522 (3)	2.75	2.75
Nos. 280-282 (3)	1.35	1.35
Nos. 206-208 (3)	1.35	1.35
Nos. 353-355 (3)	.85	.85
Nos. 543-549 (5)	8.50	8.50
Nos. 558-560 (3)	.85	.85
Nos. 509-518 (10)	15.50	15.50
Nos. 450-452 (3)	1.05	1.05
Nos. 382-384 (3)	1.30	1.25
Nos. 294-296 (3)	.90	.90
Nos. 486-489 (4)	2.20	2.20
Nos. 8-11 (4)	6.25	6.25
Nos. 314-317 (4)	3.30	3.00
Nos. 308-310 (3)	1.15	1.15
Nos. 406-408 (3)	1.30	1.30
Set total (131) Stamps	113.35	96.05

Princess Diana

CD332

CD333

Designs: Photographs and portrait of Princess Diana, wedding or honeymoon photographs, royal residences, arms of issuing country. Portrait photograph by Clive Friend. Souvenir sheet margins show family tree, various people related to the princess. 21st birthday of Princess Diana of Wales, July 1.

1982

Antigua	663-666
Ascension	313-316
Bahamas	510-513
Barbados	585-588
Barbuda	544-547
British Antarctic Territory	92-95
Cayman Islands	486-489
Dominica	773-776
Falkland Islands	348-351
Falkland Islands Dep.	1L72-1L75
Fiji	470-473
Gambia	447-450
Grenada	1101A-1105
Grenada Grenadines	485-491
Lesotho	372-375
Maldive Islands	952-955
Mauritius	548-551
Pitcairn Islands	213-216
St. Helena	372-375
St. Lucia	591-594
Sierra Leone	531-534
Solomon Islands	471-474
Swaziland	406-409
Tristan da Cunha	310-313
Turks and Caicos Islands	531-534
Virgin Islands	430-433

Nos. 663-666 (4)	9.70	9.70
Nos. 313-316 (4)	3.95	3.95
Nos. 510-513 (4)	6.00	3.85
Nos. 585-588 (4)	3.40	3.25
Nos. 544-547 (4)	9.75	7.70
Nos. 92-95 (4)	5.30	3.45
Nos. 486-489 (4)	5.40	2.70
Nos. 773-776 (4)	7.05	7.05
Nos. 348-351 (4)	3.10	3.10
Nos. 1L72-1L75 (4)	2.50	2.60
Nos. 470-473 (4)	4.50	4.50
Nos. 447-450 (4)	2.85	2.85
Nos. 1101A-1105 (7)	16.05	15.55
Nos. 485-491 (7)	17.65	17.65
Nos. 372-375 (4)	4.00	4.00
Nos. 952-955 (4)	7.25	7.25
Nos. 548-551 (4)	5.50	5.50
Nos. 213-216 (4)	3.40	3.40
Nos. 372-375 (4)	2.95	2.95
Nos. 591-594 (4)	9.90	9.90
Nos. 531-534 (4)	7.60	7.60
Nos. 471-474 (4)	2.90	2.90
Nos. 406-409 (4)	3.85	2.25
Nos. 310-313 (4)	3.65	1.45
Nos. 486-489 (4)	2.20	2.20
Nos. 430-433 (4)	3.55	3.55
Set total (110) Stamps	153.95	140.85

250th anniv. of first edition of Lloyd's List (shipping news publication) & of Lloyd's marine insurance.

CD335

Designs: First page of early edition of the list; historical ships, modern transportation or harbor scenes.

1984

Ascension	351-354
Bahamas	555-558
Barbados	627-630
Cayes of Belize	10-13
Cayman Islands	522-526
Falkland Islands	404-407
Fiji	509-512
Gambia	519-522
Mauritius	587-590
Nauru	280-283
St. Helena	412-415
Samoa	624-627
Seychelles	538-541
Solomon Islands	521-524
Vanuatu	368-371
Virgin Islands	466-469

Nos. 351-354 (4)	3.30	2.55
Nos. 555-558 (4)	4.55	2.95
Nos. 627-630 (4)	6.10	5.15
Nos. 10-13 (4)	3.05	3.05
Nos. 522-526 (5)	9.30	8.45
Nos. 404-407 (4)	3.65	4.00
Nos. 509-512 (4)	6.15	6.15
Nos. 519-522 (4)	4.20	4.30
Nos. 587-590 (4)	8.95	8.95
Nos. 280-283 (4)	2.40	2.35
Nos. 412-415 (4)	2.40	2.40
Nos. 624-627 (4)	2.75	2.55
Nos. 538-541 (4)	5.25	5.25
Nos. 521-524 (4)	4.65	3.95
Nos. 368-371 (4)	2.40	2.40
Nos. 466-469 (4)	5.00	5.00
Set total (65) Stamps	74.10	69.45

Queen Mother 85th Birthday

CD336

Designs: Photographs tracing the life of the Queen Mother, Elizabeth. The high value in each set pictures the same photograph taken of the Queen Mother holding the infant Prince Henry.

1985

Ascension	372-376
Bahamas	580-584
Barbados	660-664
Bermuda	469-473
Falkland Islands	420-424
Falkland Islands Dep	1L92-1L96
Fiji	531-535
Hong Kong	447-450
Jamaica	599-603
Mauritius	604-608
Norfolk Island	364-368
Pitcairn Islands	253-257
St. Helena	428-432
Samoa	649-653
Seychelles	567-571
Zil Elwannyen Sesel	101-105
Solomon Islands	543-547
Swaziland	476-480
Tristan da Cunha	372-376
Vanuatu	392-396

Nos. 372-376 (5)	5.35	5.35
Nos. 580-584 (5)	7.95	6.45
Nos. 660-664 (5)	8.00	6.70
Nos. 469-473 (5)	9.90	9.90
Nos. 420-424 (5)	8.80	8.80
Nos. 1L92-1L96 (5)	8.25	8.25
Nos. 531-535 (5)	7.05	7.05

Nos. 447-450 (4)	10.25	8.50
Nos. 599-603 (5)	7.50	8.00
Nos. 604-608 (5)	11.80	11.80
Nos. 364-368 (5)	5.05	5.05
Nos. 253-257 (5)	6.00	6.15
Nos. 428-432 (5)	5.25	5.25
Nos. 649-653 (5)	8.65	7.80
Nos. 567-571 (5)	8.70	8.70
Nos. 101-105 (5)	7.15	7.15
Nos. 543-547 (5)	4.45	4.45
Nos. 476-480 (5)	8.00	7.50
Nos. 372-376 (5)	5.40	5.40
Nos. 392-396 (5)	5.25	5.25
Set total (99) Stamps	148.75	143.50

Queen Elizabeth II, 60th Birthday

CD337

1986, April 21

Ascension	389-393
Bahamas	592-596
Barbados	675-679
Bermuda	499-503
Cayman Islands	555-559
Falkland Islands	441-445
Fiji	544-548
Hong Kong	465-469
Jamaica	620-624
Kiribati	470-474
Mauritius	629-633
Papua New Guinea	640-644
Pitcairn Islands	270-274
St. Helena	451-455
Samoa	670-674
Seychelles	592-596
Zil Elwannyen Sesel	114-118
Solomon Islands	562-566
South Georgia	101-105
Swaziland	490-494
Tristan da Cunha	388-392
Vanuatu	414-418
Zambia	343-347

Nos. 389-393 (5)	2.80	2.80
Nos. 592-596 (5)	2.75	3.70
Nos. 675-679 (5)	3.35	3.20
Nos. 499-503 (5)	4.90	4.90
Nos. 555-559 (5)	4.55	4.45
Nos. 441-445 (5)	3.95	4.95
Nos. 544-548 (5)	4.05	4.05
Nos. 465-469 (5)	9.60	6.85
Nos. 620-624 (5)	2.95	3.05
Nos. 470-474 (5)	2.10	2.10
Nos. 629-633 (5)	3.70	3.70
Nos. 640-644 (5)	4.50	4.50
Nos. 270-274 (5)	3.85	3.85
Nos. 451-455 (5)	3.05	3.05
Nos. 670-674 (5)	2.90	2.90
Nos. 592-596 (5)	2.70	2.70
Nos. 114-118 (5)	2.25	2.25
Nos. 562-566 (5)	2.50	2.50
Nos. 101-105 (5)	3.55	3.55
Nos. 490-494 (5)	2.30	2.30
Nos. 388-392 (5)	3.00	3.00
Nos. 414-418 (5)	3.10	3.10
Nos. 343-347 (5)	1.75	1.75
Set total (115) Stamps	80.15	79.20

Royal Wedding

Marriage of Prince Andrew and Sarah Ferguson
CD338

1986, July 23

Ascension	399-400
Bahamas	602-603
Barbados	687-688
Cayman Islands	560-561
Jamaica	629-630
Pitcairn Islands	275-276
St. Helena	460-461
St. Kitts	181-182
Seychelles	602-603
Zil Elwannyen Sesel	119-120
Solomon Islands	567-568
Tristan da Cunha	397-398
Zambia	348-349

Nos. 399-400 (2)	1.60	1.60
Nos. 602-603 (2)	2.75	2.75

Nos. 687-688 (2)	2.25	1.25
Nos. 560-561 (2)	1.50	2.15
Nos. 629-630 (2)	1.75	1.75
Nos. 275-276 (2)	2.75	2.75
Nos. 460-461 (2)	1.05	1.05
Nos. 181-182 (2)	1.50	1.50
Nos. 602-603 (2)	2.50	2.50
Nos. 119-120 (2)	2.30	2.30
Nos. 567-568 (2)	1.00	1.00
Nos. 397-398 (2)	1.40	1.40
Nos. 348-349 (2)	1.10	1.30
Set total (26) Stamps	23.45	23.30

Queen Elizabeth II, 60th Birthday

Queen Elizabeth II & Prince Philip, 1947 Wedding Portrait — CD339

Designs: Photographs tracing the life of Queen Elizabeth II.

1986

Anguilla	674-677
Antigua	925-928
Barbuda	783-786
Dominica	950-953
Gambia	611-614
Grenada	1371-1374
Grenada Grenadines	749-752
Lesotho	531-534
Maldive Islands	1172-1175
Sierra Leone	760-763
Uganda	495-498

Nos. 674-677 (4)	8.00	8.00
Nos. 925-928 (4)	6.75	6.75
Nos. 783-786 (4)	25.60	25.60
Nos. 950-953 (4)	7.15	7.15
Nos. 611-614 (4)	8.25	7.90
Nos. 1371-1374 (4)	6.80	6.80
Nos. 749-752 (4)	6.75	6.75
Nos. 531-534 (4)	5.50	5.50
Nos. 1172-1175 (4)	7.00	7.00
Nos. 760-763 (4)	6.30	6.30
Nos. 495-498 (4)	8.50	8.50
Set total (44) Stamps	96.60	96.25

Royal Wedding, 1986

CD340

Designs: Photographs of Prince Andrew and Sarah Ferguson during courtship, engagement and marriage.

1986

Antigua	939-942
Barbuda	809-812
Dominica	970-973
Gambia	635-638
Grenada	1385-1388
Grenada Grenadines	758-761
Lesotho	545-548
Maldive Islands	1181-1184
Sierra Leone	769-772
Uganda	510-513

Nos. 939-942 (4)	8.25	8.25
Nos. 809-812 (4)	15.90	15.80
Nos. 970-973 (4)	7.25	7.25
Nos. 635-638 (4)	8.55	8.55
Nos. 1385-1388 (4)	8.30	8.30
Nos. 758-761 (4)	9.00	9.00
Nos. 545-548 (4)	7.95	7.95
Nos. 1181-1184 (4)	10.20	10.20
Nos. 769-772 (4)	5.55	5.55
Nos. 510-513 (4)	9.50	10.25
Set total (40) Stamps	90.45	91.10

Lloyds of London, 300th Anniv.

CD341

Designs: 17th century aspects of Lloyds, representations of each country's individual connections with Lloyds and publicized disasters insured by the organization.

1986

Ascension	454-457
Bahamas	655-658
Barbados	731-734
Bermuda	541-544
Falkland Islands	481-484
Liberia	1101-1104
Malawi	534-537
Nevis	571-574
St. Helena	501-504
St. Lucia	923-926
Seychelles	649-652
Zil Elwannyen Sesel	146-149
Solomon Islands	627-630
South Georgia	131-134
Trinidad & Tobago	484-487
Tristan da Cunha	439-442
Vanuatu	485-488

Nos. 454-457 (4)	5.00	5.00
Nos. 655-658 (4)	8.90	4.95
Nos. 731-734 (4)	12.50	8.35
Nos. 541-544 (4)	8.25	5.60
Nos. 481-484 (4)	6.30	4.55
Nos. 1101-1104 (4)	5.25	5.25
Nos. 534-537 (4)	11.00	7.85
Nos. 571-574 (4)	8.35	8.35
Nos. 501-504 (4)	8.70	7.15
Nos. 923-926 (4)	9.40	9.40
Nos. 649-652 (4)	13.10	13.10
Nos. 146-149 (4)	11.25	11.25
Nos. 627-630 (4)	7.90	4.45
Nos. 131-134 (4)	6.30	3.70
Nos. 484-487 (4)	11.85	8.50
Nos. 439-442 (4)	7.60	7.60
Nos. 485-488 (4)	5.90	5.90
Set total (68) Stamps	147.55	120.95

Moon Landing, 20th Anniv.

CD342

Designs: Equipment, crew photographs, spacecraft, official emblems and report profiles created for the Apollo Missions. Two stamps in each set are square in format rather than like the stamp shown; see individual country listings for more information.

1989

Ascension	468-472
Bahamas	674-678
Belize	916-920
Kiribati	517-521
Liberia	1125-1129
Nevis	586-590
St. Kitts	248-252
Samoa	760-764
Seychelles	676-680
Zil Elwannyen Sesel	154-158
Solomon Islands	643-647
Vanuatu	507-511

Nos. 468-472 (5)	9.40	8.60
Nos. 674-678 (5)	23.00	19.70
Nos. 916-920 (5)	27.40	23.50
Nos. 517-521 (5)	12.50	12.50
Nos. 1125-1129 (5)	10.65	10.65
Nos. 586-590 (5)	7.50	7.50
Nos. 248-252 (5)	8.00	8.00
Nos. 760-764 (5)	9.60	9.05
Nos. 676-680 (5)	16.65	16.65
Nos. 154-158 (5)	26.85	26.85

Nos. 643-647 (5)	12.75	11.60
Nos. 507-511 (5)	9.90	9.90
Set total (60) Stamps	174.20	164.50

Queen Mother, 90th Birthday

CD343   CD344

Designs: Portraits of Queen Elizabeth, the Queen Mother. See individual country listings for more information.

1990

Ascension	491-492
Bahamas	698-699
Barbados	782-783
British Antarctic Territory	170-171
British Indian Ocean Territory	106-107
Cayman Islands	622-623
Falkland Islands	524-525
Kenya	527-528
Kiribati	555-556
Liberia	1145-1146
Pitcairn Islands	336-337
St. Helena	532-533
St. Lucia	969-970
Seychelles	710-711
Zil Elwannyen Sesel	171-172
Solomon Islands	671-672
South Georgia	143-144
Swaziland	565-566
Tristan da Cunha	480-481

Nos. 491-492 (2)	4.75	5.65
Nos. 698-699 (2)	5.65	5.65
Nos. 782-783 (2)	4.00	3.70
Nos. 170-171 (2)	6.75	6.75
Nos. 106-107 (2)	20.75	21.25
Nos. 622-623 (2)	5.10	6.75
Nos. 524-525 (2)	5.25	5.25
Nos. 527-528 (2)	7.00	7.00
Nos. 555-556 (2)	5.60	5.60
Nos. 1145-1146 (2)	4.25	4.25
Nos. 336-337 (2)	5.25	5.25
Nos. 532-533 (2)	5.25	5.25
Nos. 969-970 (2)	5.25	5.25
Nos. 710-711 (2)	6.60	6.60
Nos. 171-172 (2)	8.25	8.25
Nos. 671-672 (2)	6.50	6.40
Nos. 143-144 (2)	5.75	5.75
Nos. 565-566 (2)	4.35	4.35
Nos. 480-481 (2)	5.60	5.60
Set total (38) Stamps	121.90	124.55

Queen Elizabeth II, 65th Birthday, and Prince Philip, 70th Birthday

CD345

CD346

Designs: Portraits of Queen Elizabeth II and Prince Philip differ for each country. Printed in sheets of 10 + 5 labels (3 different) between. Stamps alternate, producing 5 different triptychs.

1991

Ascension	506a
Bahamas	731a
Belize	970a
Bermuda	618a
Kiribati	572a

Mauritius	734a
Pitcairn Islands	349a
St. Helena	555a
St. Kitts	319a
Samoa	791a
Seychelles	724a
Zil Elwannyen Sesel	178a
Solomon Islands	689a
South Georgia	150a
Swaziland	587a
Vanuatu	541a

No. 506a (1)	3.50	3.75
No. 731a (1)	4.00	4.00
No. 970a (1)	3.75	3.75
No. 618a (1)	4.00	4.00
No. 572a (1)	4.00	4.00
No. 734a (1)	3.75	3.75
No. 349a (1)	3.50	3.50
No. 555a (1)	2.75	2.75
No. 319a (1)	3.00	3.00
No. 791a (1)	4.25	4.25
No. 724a (1)	5.00	5.00
No. 178a (1)	6.50	6.50
No. 689a (1)	4.50	4.50
No. 150a (1)	7.00	7.00
No. 587a (1)	4.25	4.25
No. 541a (1)	2.50	2.50
Set total (16) Stamps	66.25	66.50

Royal Family Birthday, Anniversary

CD347

Queen Elizabeth II, 65th birthday, Charles and Diana, 10th wedding anniversary: Various photographs of Queen Elizabeth II, Prince Philip, Prince Charles, Princess Diana and their sons William and Henry.

1991

Antigua	1446-1455
Barbuda	1229-1238
Dominica	1328-1337
Gambia	1080-1089
Grenada	2006-2015
Grenada Grenadines	1331-1340
Guyana	2440-2451
Lesotho	871-875
Maldive Islands	1533-1542
Nevis	666-675
St. Vincent	1485-1494
St. Vincent Grenadines	769-778
Sierra Leone	1387-1396
Turks & Caicos Islands	913-922
Uganda	918-927

Nos. 1446-1455 (10)	21.95	20.30
Nos. 1229-1238 (10)	146.25	139.90
Nos. 1328-1337 (10)	29.85	29.85
Nos. 1080-1089 (10)	24.65	24.40
Nos. 2006-2015 (10)	25.45	22.10
Nos. 1331-1340 (10)	23.85	23.35
Nos. 2440-2451 (12)	37.05	36.70
Nos. 871-875 (5)	13.55	13.55
Nos. 1533-1542 (10)	29.60	29.60
Nos. 666-675 (10)	25.65	25.65
Nos. 1485-1494 (10)	26.75	25.90
Nos. 769-778 (10)	27.10	27.10
Nos. 1387-1396 (10)	26.55	26.55
Nos. 913-922 (10)	31.65	30.00
Nos. 918-927 (10)	26.60	26.60
Set total (147) Stamps	516.50	501.55

Queen Elizabeth II's Accession to the Throne, 40th Anniv.

CD348

CD349

Various photographs of Queen Elizabeth II with local Scenes.

1992 - CD348

Antigua	1513-1518

Barbuda	1306-1311
Dominica	1414-1419
Gambia	1172-1177
Grenada	2047-2052
Grenada Grenadines	1368-1373
Lesotho	881-885
Maldive Islands	1637-1642
Nevis	702-707
St. Vincent	1582-1587
St. Vincent Grenadines	829-834
Sierra Leone	1482-1487
Turks and Caicos Islands	978-987
Uganda	990-995
Virgin Islands	742-746

Nos. 1513-1518 (6)	16.00	14.10
Nos. 1306-1311 (6)	144.50	98.75
Nos. 1414-1419 (6)	12.50	12.50
Nos. 1172-1177 (6)	16.60	16.35
Nos. 2047-2052 (6)	15.95	15.95
Nos. 1368-1373 (6)	17.00	15.35
Nos. 881-885 (5)	11.90	11.90
Nos. 1637-1642 (6)	17.55	17.55
Nos. 702-707 (6)	13.80	13.80
Nos. 1582-1587 (6)	14.40	14.40
Nos. 829-834 (6)	20.55	20.55
Nos. 1482-1487 (6)	22.50	22.50
Nos. 913-922 (10)	31.65	30.00
Nos. 990-995 (6)	19.50	19.50
Nos. 742-746 (5)	15.50	15.50
Set total (92) Stamps	389.90	338.70

1992 - CD349

Ascension	531-535
Bahamas	744-748
Bermuda	623-627
British Indian Ocean Territory	119-123
Cayman Islands	648-652
Falkland Islands	549-553
Gibraltar	605-609
Hong Kong	619-623
Kenya	563-567
Kiribati	582-586
Pitcairn Islands	362-366
St. Helena	570-574
St. Kitts	332-336
Samoa	805-809
Seychelles	734-738
Zil Elwannyen Sesel	183-187
Solomon Islands	708-712
South Georgia	157-161
Tristan da Cunha	508-512
Vanuatu	555-559
Zambia	561-565

Nos. 531-535 (5)	6.35	6.35
Nos. 744-748 (5)	6.90	4.70
Nos. 623-627 (5)	8.20	7.30
Nos. 119-123 (5)	24.75	21.00
Nos. 648-652 (5)	7.60	7.10
Nos. 549-553 (5)	6.80	8.20
Nos. 605-609 (5)	6.55	7.00
Nos. 619-623 (5)	5.65	2.65
Nos. 563-567 (5)	9.10	9.10
Nos. 582-586 (5)	3.85	3.85
Nos. 362-366 (5)	6.55	6.55
Nos. 570-574 (5)	5.70	5.70
Nos. 332-336 (5)	6.60	5.50
Nos. 805-809 (5)	8.10	6.15
Nos. 734-738 (5)	10.80	10.80
Nos. 183-187 (5)	9.40	9.40
Nos. 708-712 (5)	7.95	7.30
Nos. 157-161 (5)	5.85	5.75
Nos. 508-512 (5)	8.75	8.30
Nos. 555-559 (5)	3.65	3.65
Nos. 561-565 (5)	5.60	5.60
Set total (105) Stamps	164.70	151.95

Royal Air Force, 75th Anniversary

CD350

1993

Ascension	557-561
Bahamas	771-775
Barbados	842-846
Belize	1003-1008
Bermuda	648-651
British Indian Ocean Territory	136-140
Falkland Is.	573-577
Fiji	687-691
Montserrat	830-834
St. Kitts	351-355

Nos. 557-561 (5)	15.55	14.05
Nos. 771-775 (5)	26.00	22.20
Nos. 842-846 (5)	12.90	11.60
Nos. 1003-1008 (6)	19.40	18.70
Nos. 648-651 (4)	10.50	9.95
Nos. 136-140 (5)	17.50	17.50
Nos. 549-553 (5)	6.80	8.20
Nos. 687-691 (5)	18.95	18.95

Nos. 830-834 (5)	14.35	14.35
Nos. 351-355 (5)	24.45	23.95
Set total (50) Stamps	166.40	159.45

Royal Air Force, 80th Anniv.

Design CD350 Re-inscribed

1998

Ascension	697-701
Bahamas	907-911
British Indian Ocean Terr	198-202
Cayman Islands	754-758
Fiji	814-818
Gibraltar	755-759
Samoa	957-961
Turks & Caicos Islands	1258-1265
Tuvalu	763-767
Virgin Islands	879-883

Nos. 697-701 (5)	17.35	17.35
Nos. 907-911 (5)	14.25	13.55
Nos. 136-140 (5)	17.50	17.50
Nos. 754-758 (5)	15.75	15.75
Nos. 814-818 (5)	15.50	15.50
Nos. 755-759 (5)	12.20	12.20
Nos. 957-961 (5)	16.70	15.90
Nos. 1258-1265 (2)	32.00	32.00
Nos. 763-767 (5)	9.75	9.75
Nos. 879-883 (5)	17.00	17.00
Set total (47) Stamps	168.00	166.50

End of World War II, 50th Anniv.

CD351

CD352

1995

Ascension	613-617
Bahamas	824-828
Barbados	891-895
Belize	1047-1050
British Indian Ocean Territory	163-167
Cayman Islands	704-708
Falkland Islands	634-638
Fiji	720-724
Kiribati	662-668
Liberia	1175-1179
Mauritius	803-805
St. Helena	646-654
St. Kitts	389-393
St. Lucia	1018-1022
Samoa	890-894
Solomon Islands	799-803
South Georgia	198-200
Tristan da Cunha	562-566

Nos. 613-617 (5)	21.50	21.50
Nos. 824-828 (5)	22.00	18.70
Nos. 891-895 (5)	14.20	11.90
Nos. 1047-1050 (4)	7.45	6.75
Nos. 163-167 (5)	16.25	16.25
Nos. 704-708 (5)	18.15	14.45
Nos. 634-638 (5)	17.90	17.40
Nos. 720-724 (5)	21.35	21.35
Nos. 662-668 (7)	16.30	16.30
Nos. 1175-1179 (5)	19.60	19.60
Nos. 803-805 (3)	7.50	7.50

Nos. 646-654 (9)	26.10	26.10
Nos. 389-393 (5)	13.60	13.60
Nos. 1018-1022 (5)	14.25	11.15
Nos. 890-894 (5)	14.25	13.50
Nos. 799-803 (5)	17.50	17.50
Nos. 198-200 (3)	14.00	14.00
Nos. 562-566 (5)	20.10	20.10
Set total (91) Stamps	302.00	287.65

UN, 50th Anniv.

CD353

1995

Bahamas	839-842
Barbados	901-904
Belize	1055-1058
Jamaica	847-851
Liberia	1187-1190
Mauritius	813-816
Pitcairn Islands	436-439
St. Kitts	398-401
St. Lucia	1023-1026
Samoa	900-903
Tristan da Cunha	568-571
Virgin Islands	807-810

Nos. 839-842 (4)	8.00	7.05
Nos. 901-904 (4)	7.00	5.75
Nos. 1055-1058 (4)	5.70	5.60
Nos. 847-851 (5)	6.30	5.85
Nos. 1187-1190 (4)	15.00	15.00
Nos. 813-816 (4)	3.90	3.90
Nos. 436-439 (4)	11.25	11.25
Nos. 398-401 (4)	6.15	6.15
Nos. 1023-1026 (4)	7.50	7.25
Nos. 900-903 (4)	9.35	8.20
Nos. 568-571 (4)	13.50	13.50
Nos. 807-810 (4)	9.45	9.45
Set total (49) Stamps	103.10	98.95

Queen Elizabeth, 70th Birthday

CD354

1996

Ascension	632-635
British Antarctic Territory	240-243
British Indian Ocean Territory	176-180
Falkland Islands	653-657
Pitcairn Islands	446-449
St. Helena	672-676
Samoa	912-916
Tokelau	223-227
Tristan da Cunha	576-579
Virgin Islands	824-828

Nos. 632-635 (4)	5.90	5.90
Nos. 240-243 (4)	10.50	8.90
Nos. 176-180 (5)	11.50	11.50
Nos. 653-657 (5)	13.75	13.75
Nos. 446-449 (4)	10.50	10.50
Nos. 672-676 (5)	12.70	12.70
Nos. 912-916 (5)	11.50	11.50
Nos. 223-227 (5)	11.35	11.35
Nos. 576-579 (4)	8.35	8.35
Nos. 824-828 (5)	11.80	11.80
Set total (46) Stamps	107.85	106.25

Diana, Princess of Wales (1961-97)

BAHAMAS 15c   CD355

1998

Ascension	696

Bahamas	901A-902
Barbados	950
Belize	1091
Bermuda	753
Botswana	659-663
British Antarctic Territory	258
British Indian Ocean Terr.	197
Cayman Islands	752A-753
Falkland Islands	694
Fiji	819-820
Gibraltar	754
Kiribati	719A-720
Namibia	909
Niue	706
Norfolk Island	644-645
Papua New Guinea	937
Pitcairn Islands	487
St. Helena	711
St. Kitts	437A-438
Samoa	955A-956
Seycelles	802
Solomon Islands	866-867
South Georgia	220
Tokelau	252B-253
Tonga	980
Niuafo'ou	201
Tristan da Cunha	618
Tuvalu	762
Vanuatu	718A-719
Virgin Islands	878

No. 696 (1)	5.50	5.50
Nos. 901A-902 (2)	5.30	5.30
No. 950 (1)	5.00	5.00
No. 1091 (1)	5.50	5.50
No. 753 (1)	5.50	5.50
Nos. 659-663 (5)	10.25	10.10
No. 258 (1)	6.25	6.25
No. 197 (1)	6.50	6.50
Nos. 752A-753 (3)	7.75	7.75
No. 694 (1)	4.75	4.75
Nos. 819-820 (2)	6.00	6.00
No. 754 (1)	5.50	5.50
Nos. 719A-720 (2)	4.85	4.85
No. 909 (1)	1.90	1.90
No. 706 (1)	5.50	5.50
Nos. 644-645 (2)	5.25	5.25
No. 937 (1)	6.50	6.50
No. 487 (1)	5.25	5.25
No. 711 (1)	4.25	4.25
Nos. 437A-438 (2)	5.15	5.15
Nos. 955A-956 (2)	7.00	7.00
No. 802 (1)	6.25	6.25
Nos. 866-867 (2)	6.90	6.90
No. 220 (1)	5.25	5.25
Nos. 252B-253 (2)	6.75	6.75
No. 980 (1)	5.75	5.75
No. 201 (1)	7.75	7.75
No. 618 (1)	5.00	5.00
No. 762 (1)	4.00	4.00
Nos. 718A-719 (2)	8.00	8.00
No. 878 (1)	5.50	5.50
Set total (46) Stamps	180.60	180.45

Wedding of Prince Edward and Sophie Rhys-Jones

CD356

1999

Ascension	729-730
Cayman Islands	775-776
Falkland Islands	729-730
Pitcairn Islands	505-506
St. Helena	733-734
Samoa	971-972
Tristan da Cunha	636-637
Virgin Islands	908-909

Nos. 729-730 (2)	5.90	5.90
Nos. 775-776 (2)	5.50	5.50
Nos. 729-730 (2)	15.00	15.00
Nos. 505-506 (2)	9.00	9.00
Nos. 733-734 (2)	5.00	5.00
Nos. 971-972 (2)	5.00	5.00
Nos. 636-637 (2)	7.50	7.50
Nos. 908-909 (2)	8.30	8.30
Set total (16) Stamps	61.20	61.20

1st Manned Moon Landing, 30th Anniv.

CD357

1999

Ascension	731-735
Bahamas	942-946
Barbados	967-971
Bermuda	778
Cayman Islands	777-781
Fiji	853-857
Jamaica	889-893
Kirbati	746-750
Nauru	465-469
St. Kitts	460-464
Samoa	973-977
Solomon Islands	875-879
Tuvalu	800-804
Virgin Islands	910-914

Nos. 731-735 (5)	13.90	13.90
Nos. 942-946 (5)	14.10	14.10
Nos. 967-971 (5)	8.65	7.75
No. 778 (1)	8.00	8.00
Nos. 777-781 (5)	10.30	10.30
Nos. 853-857 (5)	10.40	10.40
Nos. 889-893 (5)	10.20	10.00
Nos. 746-750 (5)	8.85	8.85
Nos. 465-469 (5)	8.90	10.15
Nos. 460-464 (5)	12.00	12.00
Nos. 973-977 (5)	13.45	13.30
Nos. 875-879 (5)	10.00	9.85
Nos. 800-804 (5)	7.45	7.45
Nos. 910-914 (5)	15.00	15.00
Set total (66) Stamps	151.20	151.05

Queen Mother's Century

CD358

1999

Ascension	736-740
Bahamas	951-955
Cayman Islands	782-786
Falkland Islands	734-738
Fiji	858-862
Norfolk Island	688-692
St. Helena	740-744
Samoa	978-982
Solomon Islands	880-884
South Georgia	231-235
Tristan da Cunha	638-642
Tuvalu	805-809

Nos. 736-740 (5)	17.00	17.00
Nos. 951-955 (5)	14.00	12.90
Nos. 782-786 (5)	9.15	9.15
Nos. 734-738 (5)	29.85	29.85
Nos. 858-862 (5)	15.00	15.00
Nos. 688-692 (5)	10.30	10.30
Nos. 740-744 (5)	16.15	16.15
Nos. 978-982 (5)	13.25	13.25
Nos. 880-884 (5)	10.00	9.45
Nos. 231-235 (5)	30.25	29.75
Nos. 638-642 (5)	18.00	18.00
Nos. 805-809 (5)	8.65	8.65
Set total (60) Stamps	191.60	189.45

Prince William, 18th Birthday

CD359

2000

Ascension	755-759
Cayman Islands	797-801
Falkland Islands	762-766
Fiji	889-893
South Georgia	257-261
Tristan da Cunha	664-668
Virgin Islands	925-929

Nos. 755-759 (5)	17.75	17.75
Nos. 797-801 (5)	13.05	12.75
Nos. 762-766 (5)	27.15	23.75
Nos. 889-893 (5)	14.00	14.00
Nos. 257-261 (5)	29.00	29.00
Nos. 664-668 (5)	21.50	21.50
Nos. 925-929 (5)	14.75	14.75
Set total (35) Stamps	137.20	133.50

Reign of Queen Elizabeth II, 50th Anniv.

CD360

2002

Ascension	790-794
Bahamas	1033-1037
Barbados	1019-1023
Belize	1152-1156
Bermuda	822-826
British Antarctic Territory	307-311
British Indian Ocean Territory	239-243
Cayman Islands	844-848
Falkland Islands	804-808
Gibraltar	896-900
Jamaica	952-956
Nauru	491-495
Norfolk Island	758-762
Papua New Guinea	1019-1023
Pitcairn Islands	552
St. Helena	788-792
St. Lucia	1146-1150
Solomon Islands	931-935
South Georgia	274-278
Swaziland	706-710
Tokelau	302-306
Tonga	1059
Niuafo'ou	239
Tristan da Cunha	706-710
Virgin Islands	967-971

Nos. 790-794 (5)	16.25	16.25
Nos. 1033-1037 (5)	15.75	15.75
Nos. 1019-1023 (5)	13.15	13.15
Nos. 1152-1156 (5)	15.50	15.15
Nos. 822-826 (5)	18.50	18.50
Nos. 307-311 (5)	25.00	25.00
Nos. 239-243 (5)	22.00	22.00
Nos. 844-848 (5)	14.25	14.25
Nos. 804-808 (5)	23.50	22.50
Nos. 896-900 (5)	8.00	8.00
Nos. 952-956 (5)	18.25	18.25
Nos. 491-495 (5)	18.75	18.75
Nos. 758-762 (5)	19.50	19.50
Nos. 1019-1023 (5)	14.50	14.50
No. 552 (1)	11.50	11.50
Nos. 788-792 (5)	19.75	19.75
Nos. 1146-1150 (5)	12.25	12.25
Nos. 931-935 (5)	16.00	16.00
Nos. 274-278 (5)	28.50	28.50
Nos. 706-710 (5)	12.75	12.75
Nos. 302-306 (5)	17.00	17.00
No. 1059 (1)	8.00	8.00
No. 239 (1)	7.00	7.00
Nos. 706-710 (5)	18.50	18.50
Nos. 967-971 (5)	19.00	19.00
Set total (113) Stamps	413.15	411.80

Queen Mother Elizabeth (1900-2002)

CD361

2002

Ascension	799-801
Bahamas	1044-1046
Bermuda	834-836
British Antarctic Territory	312-314

British Indian Ocean Territory 245-247
Cayman Islands......................857-861
Falkland Islands 812-816
Nauru....................................499-501
Pitcairn Islands.......................561-565
St. Helena 808-812
St. Lucia 1155-1159
Seychelles 830
Solomon Islands......................945-947
South Georgia 281-285
Tokelau 312-314
Tristan da Cunha.....................715-717
Virgin Islands.........................979-983

Nos. 799-801 (3)	9.75	9.75
Nos. 1044-1046 (3)	9.35	9.35
Nos. 834-836 (3)	12.50	12.50
Nos. 312-314 (3)	19.25	19.25
Nos. 245-247 (3)	19.50	19.50
Nos. 857-861 (5)	15.00	15.00
Nos. 812-816 (5)	32.00	32.00
Nos. 499-501 (3)	16.00	16.00
Nos. 561-565 (5)	18.50	18.50
Nos. 808-812 (5)	12.00	12.00
Nos. 1155-1159 (5)	13.00	13.00
No. 830 (1)	6.50	6.50
Nos. 945-947 (3)	11.00	11.00
Nos. 281-285 (5)	20.00	20.00
Nos. 312-314 (3)	14.25	13.75
Nos. 715-717 (3)	16.25	16.25
Nos. 979-983 (5)	26.50	26.50
Set total (63) Stamps	271.35	270.85

Head of Queen Elizabeth II

CD362

2003

Ascension...822
Bermuda..865
British Antarctic Territory.................322
British Indian Ocean Territory 261
Cayman Islands...............................878
Falkland Islands 828
St. Helena 820
South Georgia 294
Tristan da Cunha.............................731
Virgin Islands.................................1003

No. 822 (1)	13.50	13.50
No. 865 (1)	55.00	55.00
No. 322 (1)	10.00	10.00
No. 261 (1)	12.50	12.50
No. 878 (1)	17.00	17.00
No. 828 (1)	10.00	10.00
No. 820 (1)	9.00	9.00
No. 294 (1)	9.00	9.00
No. 731 (1)	10.00	10.00
No. 1003 (1)	10.00	10.00
Set total (10) Stamps	156.00	156.00

Coronation of Queen Elizabeth II, 50th Anniv.

CD363

2003

Ascension 823-825
Bahamas 1073-1075
Bermuda.................................866-868
British Antarctic Territory.........323-325
British Indian Ocean Territory 262-264
Cayman Islands.......................879-881
Jamaica 970-972
Kiribati 825-827
Pitcairn Islands.......................577-581
St. Helena 821-823
St. Lucia 1171-1173
Tokelau 320-322
Tristan da Cunha.....................732-734
Virgin Islands.......................1004-1006

Nos. 823-825 (3)	13.50	13.50
Nos. 1073-1075 (3)	13.00	13.00
Nos. 866-868 (3)	14.25	14.25
Nos. 323-325 (3)	26.00	26.00
Nos. 262-264 (3)	31.00	31.00
Nos. 879-881 (3)	20.25	20.25

Nos. 970-972 (3)	11.75	11.75
Nos. 825-827 (3)	13.50	13.50
Nos. 577-581 (5)	18.50	18.50
Nos. 821-823 (3)	7.25	7.25
Nos. 1171-1173 (3)	8.75	8.75
Nos. 320-322 (3)	20.00	20.00
Nos. 732-734 (3)	16.75	16.75
Nos. 1004-1006 (3)	25.00	25.00
Set total (44) Stamps	239.50	239.50

Prince William, 21st Birthday

CD364

2003

Ascension 826
British Indian Ocean Territory 265
Cayman Islands......................882-884
Falkland Islands 829
South Georgia 295
Tokelau 323
Tristan da Cunha.............................735
Virgin Islands.....................1007-1009

No. 826 (1)	7.50	7.50
No. 265 (1)	9.00	9.00
Nos. 882-884 (3)	7.65	7.65
No. 829 (1)	14.50	14.50
No. 295 (1)	9.00	9.00
No. 323 (1)	7.25	7.25
No. 735 (1)	6.00	6.00
Nos. 1007-1009 (3)	10.00	10.00
Set total (12) Stamps	70.90	70.90

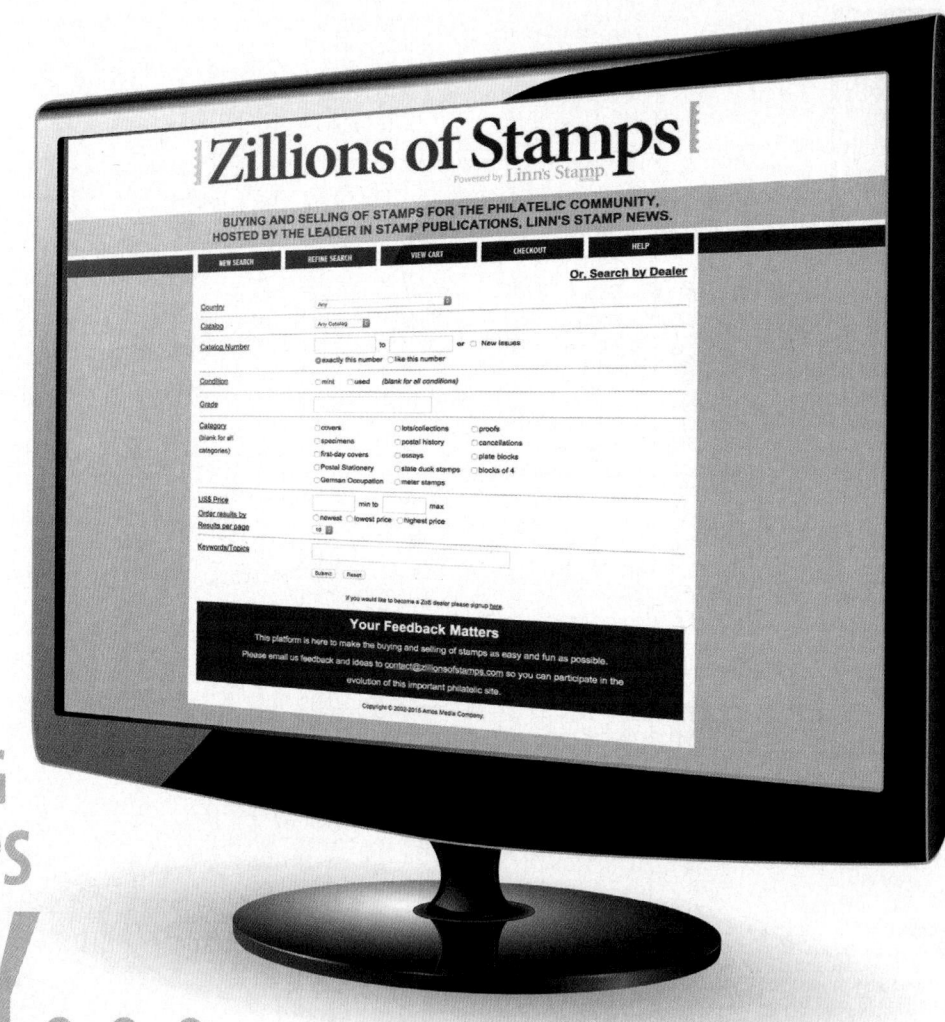

British Commonwealth of Nations

Dominions, Colonies, Territories, Offices and Independent Members

Comprising stamps of the British Commonwealth and associated nations.

A strict observance of technicalities would bar some or all of the stamps listed under Burma, Ireland, Kuwait, Nepal, New Republic, Orange Free State, Samoa, South Africa, South-West Africa, Stellaland, Sudan, Swaziland, the two Transvaal Republics and others but these are included for the convenience of collectors.

1. Great Britain

Great Britain: Including England, Scotland, Wales and Northern Ireland.

2. The Dominions, Present and Past

AUSTRALIA

The Commonwealth of Australia was proclaimed on January 1, 1901. It consists of six former colonies as follows:

New South Wales	Victoria
Queensland	Tasmania
South Australia	Western Australia

The following islands and territories are, or have been, administered by Australia: Australian Antarctic Territory, Christmas Island, Cocos (Keeling) Islands, Nauru, New Guinea, Norfolk Island, Papua.

CANADA

The Dominion of Canada was created by the British North America Act in 1867. The following provinces were former sepa- rate colonies and issued postage stamps:

British Columbia and	Newfoundland
Vancouver Island	Nova Scotia
New Brunswick	Prince Edward Island

FIJI

The colony of Fiji became an independent nation with dominion status on Oct. 10, 1970.

GHANA

This state came into existence Mar. 6, 1957, with dominion status. It consists of the former colony of the Gold Coast and the Trusteeship Territory of Togoland. Ghana became a republic July 1, 1960.

INDIA

The Republic of India was inaugurated on January 26, 1950. It succeeded the Dominion of India which was proclaimed August 15, 1947, when the former Empire of India was divided into Pakistan and the Union of India. The Republic is composed of about 40 predominantly Hindu states of three classes: governor's provinces, chief commissioner's provinces and princely states. India also has various territories, such as the Andaman and Nicobar Islands.

The old Empire of India was a federation of British India and the native states. The more important princely states were autonomous. Of the more than 700 Indian states, these 43 are familiar names to philatelists because of their postage stamps.

CONVENTION STATES

Chamba	Jhind
Faridkot	Nabha
Gwalior	Patiala

FEUDATORY STATES

Alwar	Jammu and Kashmir
Bahawalpur	Jasdan
Bamra	Jhalawar
Barwani	Jhind (1875-76)
Bhopal	Kashmir
Bhor	Kishangarh
Bijawar	Kotah
Bundi	Las Bela
Bussahir	Morvi
Charkhari	Nandgaon
Cochin	Nowanuggur
Dhar	Orchha
Dungarpur	Poonch
Duttia	Rajasthan
Faridkot (1879-85)	Rajpeepla
Hyderabad	Sirmur
Idar	Soruth
Indore	Tonk
Jaipur	Travancore
Jammu	Wadhwan

NEW ZEALAND

Became a dominion on September 26, 1907. The following islands and territories are, or have been, administered by New Zealand:

Aitutaki	Ross Dependency
Cook Islands (Rarotonga)	Samoa (Western Samoa)
Niue	Tokelau Islands
Penrhyn	

PAKISTAN

The Republic of Pakistan was proclaimed March 23, 1956. It succeeded the Dominion which was proclaimed August 15, 1947. It is made up of all or part of several Moslem provinces and various districts of the former Empire of India, including Bahawalpur and Las Bela. Pakistan withdrew from the Commonwealth in 1972.

SOUTH AFRICA

Under the terms of the South African Act (1909) the self-governing colonies of Cape of Good Hope, Natal, Orange River Colony and Transvaal united on May 31, 1910, to form the Union of South Africa. It became an independent republic May 3, 1961.

Under the terms of the Treaty of Versailles, South-West Africa, formerly German South-West Africa, was mandated to the Union of South Africa.

SRI LANKA (CEYLON)

The Dominion of Ceylon was proclaimed February 4, 1948. The island had been a Crown Colony from 1802 until then. On May 22, 1972, Ceylon became the Republic of Sri Lanka.

3. Colonies, Past and Present; Controlled Territory and Independent Members of the Commonwealth

Aden	Bechuanaland
Aitutaki	Bechuanaland Prot.
Antigua	Belize
Ascension	Bermuda
Bahamas	Botswana
Bahrain	British Antarctic Territory
Bangladesh	British Central Africa
Barbados	British Columbia and
Barbuda	Vancouver Island
Basutoland	British East Africa
Batum	British Guiana

British Honduras
British Indian Ocean Territory
British New Guinea
British Solomon Islands
British Somaliland
Brunei
Burma
Bushire
Cameroons
Cape of Good Hope
Cayman Islands
Christmas Island
Cocos (Keeling) Islands
Cook Islands
Crete,
   British Administration
Cyprus
Dominica
East Africa & Uganda
   Protectorates
Egypt
Falkland Islands
Fiji
Gambia
German East Africa
Gibraltar
Gilbert Islands
Gilbert & Ellice Islands
Gold Coast
Grenada
Griqualand West
Guernsey
Guyana
Heligoland
Hong Kong
Indian Native States
   (see India)
Ionian Islands
Jamaica
Jersey

Kenya
Kenya, Uganda & Tanzania
Kuwait
Labuan
Lagos
Leeward Islands
Lesotho
Madagascar
Malawi
Malaya
   Federated Malay States
   Johore
   Kedah
   Kelantan
   Malacca
   Negri Sembilan
   Pahang
   Penang
   Perak
   Perlis
   Selangor
   Singapore
   Sungei Ujong
   Trengganu
Malaysia
Maldive Islands
Malta
Man, Isle of
Mauritius
Mesopotamia
Montserrat
Muscat
Namibia
Natal
Nauru
Nevis
New Britain
New Brunswick
Newfoundland
New Guinea

New Hebrides
New Republic
New South Wales
Niger Coast Protectorate
Nigeria
Niue
Norfolk Island
North Borneo
Northern Nigeria
Northern Rhodesia
North West Pacific Islands
Nova Scotia
Nyasaland Protectorate
Oman
Orange River Colony
Palestine
Papua New Guinea
Penrhyn Island
Pitcairn Islands
Prince Edward Island
Queensland
Rhodesia
Rhodesia & Nyasaland
Ross Dependency
Sabah
St. Christopher
St. Helena
St. Kitts
St. Kitts-Nevis-Anguilla
St. Lucia
St. Vincent
Samoa
Sarawak
Seychelles
Sierra Leone
Solomon Islands
Somaliland Protectorate
South Arabia
South Australia
South Georgia

Southern Nigeria
Southern Rhodesia
South-West Africa
Stellaland
Straits Settlements
Sudan
Swaziland
Tanganyika
Tanzania
Tasmania
Tobago
Togo
Tokelau Islands
Tonga
Transvaal
Trinidad
Trinidad and Tobago
Tristan da Cunha
Trucial States
Turks and Caicos
Turks Islands
Tuvalu
Uganda
United Arab Emirates
Victoria
Virgin Islands
Western Australia
Zambia
Zanzibar
Zululand

POST OFFICES IN FOREIGN COUNTRIES
Africa
   East Africa Forces
   Middle East Forces
Bangkok
China
Morocco
Turkish Empire

Colonies, Former Colonies, Offices, Territories Controlled by Parent States

Belgium
Belgian Congo
Ruanda-Urundi

Denmark
Danish West Indies
Faroe Islands
Greenland
Iceland

Finland
Aland Islands

France

COLONIES PAST AND PRESENT, CONTROLLED TERRITORIES
Afars & Issas, Territory of
Alaouites
Alexandretta
Algeria
Alsace & Lorraine
Anjouan
Annam & Tonkin
Benin
Cambodia (Khmer)
Cameroun
Castellorizo
Chad
Cilicia
Cochin China
Comoro Islands
Dahomey
Diego Suarez
Djibouti (Somali Coast)
Fezzan
French Congo
French Equatorial Africa
French Guiana
French Guinea
French India
French Morocco
French Polynesia (Oceania)
French Southern & Antarctic Territories
French Sudan
French West Africa
Gabon
Germany
Ghadames
Grand Comoro
Guadeloupe
Indo-China
Inini
Ivory Coast
Laos
Latakia
Lebanon
Madagascar
Martinique
Mauritania
Mayotte
Memel
Middle Congo
Moheli
New Caledonia
New Hebrides
Niger Territory

Nossi-Be
Obock
Reunion
Rouad, Ile
Ste.-Marie de Madagascar
St. Pierre & Miquelon
Senegal
Senegambia & Niger
Somali Coast
Syria
Tahiti
Togo
Tunisia
Ubangi-Shari
Upper Senegal & Niger
Upper Volta
Viet Nam
Wallis & Futuna Islands

POST OFFICES IN FOREIGN COUNTRIES
China
Crete
Egypt
Turkish Empire
Zanzibar

Germany

EARLY STATES
Baden
Bavaria
Bergedorf
Bremen
Brunswick
Hamburg
Hanover
Lubeck
Mecklenburg-Schwerin
Mecklenburg-Strelitz
Oldenburg
Prussia
Saxony
Schleswig-Holstein
Wurttemberg

FORMER COLONIES
Cameroun (Kamerun)
Caroline Islands
German East Africa
German New Guinea
German South-West Africa
Kiauchau
Mariana Islands
Marshall Islands
Samoa
Togo

Italy

EARLY STATES
Modena
Parma
Romagna
Roman States
Sardinia
Tuscany
Two Sicilies
  Naples
  Neapolitan Provinces
  Sicily

FORMER COLONIES, CONTROLLED TERRITORIES, OCCUPATION AREAS
Aegean Islands
  Calimno (Calino)
  Caso
  Cos (Coo)
  Karki (Carchi)
  Leros (Lero)
  Lipso
  Nisiros (Nisiro)
  Patmos (Patmo)
  Piscopi
  Rodi (Rhodes)
  Scarpanto
  Simi
  Stampalia
Castellorizo
Corfu
Cyrenaica
Eritrea
Ethiopia (Abyssinia)
Fiume
Ionian Islands
  Cephalonia
  Ithaca
  Paxos
Italian East Africa
Libya
Oltre Giuba
Saseno
Somalia (Italian Somaliland)
Tripolitania

POST OFFICES IN FOREIGN COUNTRIES
"ESTERO"*
Austria
China
  Peking
  Tientsin
Crete
Tripoli
Turkish Empire
  Constantinople
  Durazzo
  Janina
Jerusalem
Salonika
Scutari
Smyrna
Valona
*Stamps overprinted "ESTERO" were used in various parts of the world.

Netherlands
Aruba
Caribbean Netherlands
Curacao
Netherlands Antilles (Curacao)
Netherlands Indies
Netherlands New Guinea
St. Martin
Surinam (Dutch Guiana)

Portugal

COLONIES PAST AND PRESENT, CONTROLLED TERRITORIES
Angola
Angra
Azores

Cape Verde
Funchal
Horta
Inhambane
Kionga
Lourenco Marques
Macao
Madeira
Mozambique
Mozambique Co.
Nyassa
Ponta Delgada
Portuguese Africa
Portuguese Congo
Portuguese Guinea
Portuguese India
Quelimane
St. Thomas & Prince Islands
Tete
Timor
Zambezia

Russia

ALLIED TERRITORIES AND REPUBLICS, OCCUPATION AREAS
Armenia
Aunus (Olonets)
Azerbaijan
Batum
Estonia
Far Eastern Republic
Georgia
Karelia
Latvia
Lithuania
North Ingermanland
Ostland
Russian Turkestan
Siberia
South Russia
Tannu Tuva
Transcaucasian Fed. Republics
Ukraine
Wenden (Livonia)
Western Ukraine

Spain

COLONIES PAST AND PRESENT, CONTROLLED TERRITORIES
Aguera, La
Cape Juby
Cuba
Elobey, Annobon & Corisco
Fernando Po
Ifni
Mariana Islands
Philippines
Puerto Rico
Rio de Oro
Rio Muni
Spanish Guinea
Spanish Morocco
Spanish Sahara
Spanish West Africa

POST OFFICES IN FOREIGN COUNTRIES
Morocco
Tangier
Tetuan

Dies of British Colonial Stamps

DIE A:

1. The lines in the groundwork vary in thickness and are not uniformly straight.

2. The seventh and eighth lines from the top, in the groundwork, converge where they meet the head.

3. There is a small dash in the upper part of the second jewel in the band of the crown.

4. The vertical color line in front of the throat stops at the sixth line of shading on the neck.

DIE B:

1. The lines in the groundwork are all thin and straight.

2. All the lines of the background are parallel.

3. There is no dash in the upper part of the second jewel in the band of the crown.

4. The vertical color line in front of the throat stops at the eighth line of shading on the neck.

DIE I:

1. The base of the crown is well below the level of the inner white line around the vignette.

2. The labels inscribed "POSTAGE" and "REVENUE" are cut square at the top.

3. There is a white "bud" on the outer side of the main stem of the curved ornaments in each lower corner.

4. The second (thick) line below the country name has the ends next to the crown cut diagonally.

DIE Ia.
1 as die II.
2 and 3 as die I.

DIE Ib.
1 and 3 as die II.
2 as die I.

DIE II:

1. The base of the crown is aligned with the underside of the white line around the vignette.

2. The labels curve inward at the top inner corners.

3. The "bud" has been removed from the outer curve of the ornaments in each corner.

4. The second line below the country name has the ends next to the crown cut vertically.

Wmk. 1
Crown and C C

Wmk. 2
Crown and C A

Wmk. 3
Multiple Crown
and C A

Wmk. 4
Multiple Crown
and Script C A

Wmk. 4a

Wmk. 314
St. Edward's Crown
and C A Multiple

Wmk. 373

Wmk. 384

Wmk. 406

British Colonial and Crown Agents Watermarks

Watermarks 1 to 4, 314, 373, 384 and 406, common to many British territories, are illustrated here to avoid duplication.

The letters "CC" of Wmk. 1 identify the paper as having been made for the use of the Crown Colonies, while the letters "CA" of the others stand for "Crown Agents." Both Wmks. 1 and 2 were used on stamps printed by De La Rue & Co.

Wmk. 3 was adopted in 1904; Wmk. 4 in 1921; Wmk. 314 in 1957; Wmk. 373 in 1974; Wmk. 384 in 1985; Wmk 406 in 2008.

In Wmk. 4a, a non-matching crown of the general St. Edwards type (bulging on both sides at top) was substituted for one of the Wmk. 4 crowns which fell off the dandy roll. The non-matching crown occurs in 1950-52 printings in a horizontal row of crowns on certain regular stamps of Johore and Seychelles, and on various postage due stamps of Barbados, Basutoland, British Guiana, Gold Coast, Grenada, Northern Rhodesia, St. Lucia, Swaziland and Trinidad and Tobago. A variation of Wmk. 4a, with the non-matching crown in a horizontal row of crown-CA-crown, occurs on regular stamps of Bahamas, St. Kitts-Nevis and Singapore.

Wmk. 314 was intentionally used sideways, starting in 1966. When a stamp was issued with Wmk. 314 both upright and sideways, the sideways varieties usually are listed also – with minor numbers. In many of the later issues, Wmk. 314 is slightly visible.

Wmk. 373 is usually only faintly visible.

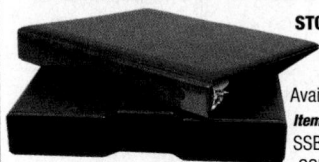

New World of Technology

6-IN-1 LED POCKET MAGNIFIER/ MICROSCOPE (55X)

A powerful LED microscope (up to 55X magnification) teams up with two aspheric Perspex lenses (3X magnification large and 10X magnification small) to examine objects at various levels of detail. Built-in focus wheel ensures clarity. View objects even in low-light conditions with three lighting functions: three LED flashlight, simple UV light, one white LED. Black composite housing.

Item	Retail	AA*
MG61LED	21.95	19.95

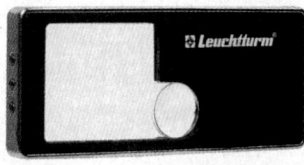

5-IN-1 MULTI-FUNCTION POCKET MAGNIFIER 2.5X-10X LED

A sturdy stainless steel frame houses two aspheric lenses: 2.5X rectangular and 10X round, plus three lighting functions: 3-LED side flashlight, 1-LED research light, simple 395nm long-wave UV light. A mini ballpoint pen, available to take notes, tucks inside the acrylic housing. Leatherette case and 3 #LR927 batteries included.

Item	Retail	AA*
MG51	15.95	13.95

3.2X LED ILLUMINATED MAGNIFIER

This 7" aluminum 3.2X magnifier is both beautiful and functional. Six LEDs surround the 1.375" lens to provide glare-free illumination. Zippered protective case and 2 AA batteries included.

Item	Retail	AA*
MG32XL	35.95	31.95

SCHAUBEK 10X LED & UV COMBO MAGNIFIER

This pocket-sized magnifier boasts 10X magnification with both LED and UV longwave light. Battery powered for maximum portability. Handy carrying case protects the 21mm magnifier while on the go.

Item	Retail	AA*
MG10XLUV	39.99	34.99

LIGHTHOUSE DIGITAL CALIPERS 6"

Sliding calipers measure from 1-150mm (0"-6") in .01mm increments with accuracy to 0.3mm. Six-digit LCD display easily switches from millimeters to inches. Batteries and padded case included.

Item	Retail	AA*
LHSL1	49.95	42.95

LHSCOPE

Clip this compact Lighthouse Phonescope lens on your smartphone or tablet to transform it into a powerful digital microscope. See the smallest details and instantly capture high-quality images and videos. The precision macro glass lens offers up to 60X magnification and requires no batteries. Field of view: 1/2" (13mm). Phonescope works with all popular smartphones without scratching display. Image resolution and zoom function dependent upon your device.

Item	Retail	AA*
LHSCOPE	25.99	21.99

ZOOM 20X-40X MICROSCOPE WITH LED

This practical zoom microscope provides what collectors have been waiting for – outstanding clarity and resolution. Magnification is continuously adjustable between 20X and 40X. Powerful LED lighting illuminates the stage (3 #LR44 batteries included). Stand, examination slides, and slide covers also included.

Item	Retail	AA*
LHPM3	29.95	21.95

LIGHTHOUSE DUAL WAVE ULTRAVIOLET LAMP

Examine your collectibles for both fluorescence (long wave) and phosphorescence (short wave) using one versatile ultraviolet lamp. Flip a switch to change quickly and easily between short and long UV rays (254 and 380nm). Short wave exposes tagging, while long wave reveals faults, tears, and repairs. Battery operated; requires 4x AA batteries (not included).

Item	Retail	AA*
LHL81	71.95	59.95

LIGHTHOUSE .1-500G DIGITAL SCALE

This portable-sized digital scale displays weight in six different units: g, oz, ozt, dwt, ct, gn. Illuminated LCD display with tare function is great for gold coins. Weight range 0.1-500 g with +/- 0.03 g tolerance. Requires 2 AA batteries, included.

Item	Retail	AA*
LHDW4	29.95	24.95

ZOOM 20X-200X USB DIGITAL MICROSCOPE, 2.0 MEGAPIXELS

Powered by your computer's USB port, this digital microscope offers amazing 2.0 megapixel resolution. Examine objects, take photos, and shoot short videos all with the same device. 20X-200X magnification enhanced with 8 adjustable LED lights will show the smallest details. Microscope comes complete with CD-ROM software, stand and USB cable. Compatible with Windows 2000 / XP / Vista / Win7 / Win8 and Mac OS X 10.5 and higher. Web based updates available.

Item	Retail	AA*
LHDM1	169.95	137.95

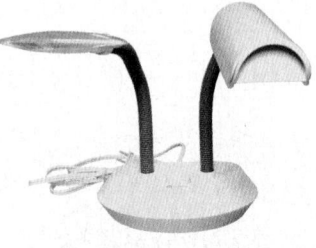

ACC213W

The OttLite DuoFlex has a two-pronged approach to enhance your vision. First, the large 3X-5X magnifier enlarges your subject. Then the energy-efficient 13w "E" bulb spotlights the field. Flexible arms allow nearly infinite positioning. Long-term bulb is rated to last up to 10,000 hours.

Item	Retail	AA*
ACC213W	109.99	59.99

ORDERING INFORMATION: *AA prices apply to paid subscribers of Amos Hobby titles, or for orders placed online. Prices, terms and product availability subject to change.

Call: **1-800-572-6885**
Outside U.S. & Canada Call: **1-800-572-6885**
Visit: **www.amosadvantage.com**

AMOS ADVANTAGE

SAN MARINO

ˌsan mə-ˈrē-ˌnō

LOCATION — Eastern Italy, about 20 miles inland from the Adriatic Sea
GOVT. — Republic
AREA — 24.1 sq. mi.
POP. — 25,061 (1999 est.)
CAPITAL — San Marino

100 Centesimi = 1 Lira
100 Cents = 1 Euro (2002)

> Catalogue values for unused stamps in this country are for Never Hinged items, beginning with Scott 412 in the regular postage section, Scott B39 in the semipostal section, Scott C97 in the airpost section, Scott E26 in the special delivery section, and Scott Q40 in the parcel post section.

Watermarks

Wmk. 140 — Crown

Wmk. 174 — Coat of Arms

Wmk. 217 — Three Plumes

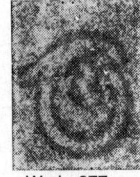

Wmk. 277 — Winged Wheel

Wmk. 303 — Multiple Stars

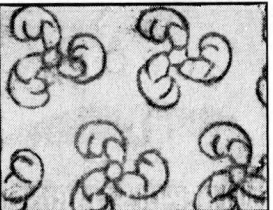

Wmk. 339 — Triskelion

> Nos. 1-28 were spaced very narrowly on the plates, so that perforations often cut into the design on one or two sides. Values are for stamps with perforations clear of the design. Examples with perfs cutting in the design sell for less, while examples with four clear, full margins sell for substantially more than the values shown.

Numeral — A1

Coat of Arms — A2

Coat of Arms — A3

1877-99 Typo. Wmk. 140 Perf. 14

1	A1	2c green	37.50	19.00
2	A1	2c blue ('94)	15.00	19.00
3	A1	2c claret ('95)	13.50	19.00
4	A2	5c orange ('90)	180.00	50.00
5	A2	5c olive grn ('92)	9.00	9.25
6	A2	5c green ('99)	9.25	14.00
7	A2	10c ultra	350.00	115.00
a.		10c blue ('90)	3,600.	300.00
8	A2	10c dk green ('92)	9.25	11.00
9	A2	10c claret ('99)	9.25	13.50
10	A2	15c claret ('94)	170.00	120.00
11	A2	20c vermilion	45.00	19.00
12	A2	20c lilac ('95)	9.25	19.00
13	A2	25c maroon ('90)	150.00	90.00
14	A2	25c blue ('99)	9.25	17.00
15	A2	30c brown	925.00	125.00
16	A2	30c org yel ('92)	9.25	19.00
17	A2	40c violet	925.00	125.00
18	A2	40c dk brn ('92)	9.25	19.00
19	A2	45c gray grn ('92)	9.25	19.00
20	A2	65c red brn ('92)	9.25	19.00
21	A3	1 l car & yel ('92)	1,825.	950.00
22	A3	1 l lt blue ('95)	1,675.	750.00
23	A3	2 l brn & yel ('94)	90.00	120.00
24	A3	5 l vio & grn ('94)	225.00	450.00

See Nos. 911-915.

Nos. 7a, 15, 11 Surcharged in Black

1892

25	A2	5c on 10c blue	90.00	26.00
a.		Inverted surcharge	110.00	34.00
b.		5c on 10c ultramarine	50,000.	12,000.
c.		As "b," inverted surch.		
d.		Double surcharge, one inverted	—	
e.		Pair, one without surcharge	2,250.	
f.		Pair, one without surcharge, surcharge inverted	2,250.	
26	A2	5c on 30c brn	300.00	135.00
a.		Inverted surcharge	375.00	170.00
b.		Double surch., one inverted	375.00	210.00
c.		Double invtd. surcharge	375.00	210.00
27	A2	10c on 20c ver	67.50	15.00
a.		Inverted surcharge	75.00	22.50
b.		Double surch., one inverted	82.50	30.00
c.		Double surcharge	82.50	30.00

Ten to twelve varieties of each surcharge.

No. 11 Surcharged

28	A2	10c on 20c ver	300.00	19.00

Government Palace and Portraits of Regents, Tonnini and Marcucci
A6 · A7

Portraits of Regents and View of Interior of Palace — A8

Wmk. 174
1894, Sept. 30 Litho. Perf. 15½

29	A6	25c blue & dk brn	7.50	3.00
30	A7	50c dull red & dk brn	45.00	9.50
31	A8	1 l green & dk brown	35.00	11.50
		Nos. 29-31 (3)	87.50	24.00

Opening of the new Government Palace and the installation of the new Regents.

Statue of Liberty — A9

Wmk. 140
1899-1922 Typo. Perf. 14

32	A9	2c brown	3.75	1.90
33	A9	2c claret ('22)	.75	.75
34	A9	5c brown org	7.50	4.50
35	A9	5c olive grn ('22)	.75	.75
36	A9	10c brown org ('22)	.75	.75
37	A9	20c dp brown ('22)	.75	.75
38	A9	25c ultra ('22)	1.50	1.50
39	A9	45c red brown ('22)	3.00	3.00
		Nos. 32-39 (8)	18.75	13.90

Numeral of Value — A10 · Mt. Titano — A11

1903-25 Perf. 14, 14½x14

40	A10	2c violet	22.50	12.00
41	A10	2c org brn ('21)	1.50	1.10
42	A11	5c brown	11.00	7.50
43	A11	5c olive grn ('21)	1.50	1.10
a.		Imperforate	85.00	
44	A11	5c red brn ('25)	.75	.75
45	A11	10c claret	11.50	7.50
46	A11	10c brown org ('21)	1.50	1.20
47	A11	10c olive grn ('25)	.75	.75
48	A11	15c blue grn ('22)	1.50	1.10
49	A11	15c brown vio ('25)	.75	.75
50	A11	20c brown orange	150.00	60.00
51	A11	20c brown ('21)	1.50	1.20
52	A11	20c blue grn ('25)	.75	.75
53	A11	25c blue	27.50	12.00
54	A11	25c gray ('21)	1.50	1.10
55	A11	25c violet ('25)	.75	.75
56	A11	30c brown red	12.00	18.50
57	A11	30c claret ('21)	1.50	1.20
58	A11	30c orange ('25)	22.50	3.75
59	A11	40c orange red	22.50	18.50
60	A11	40c dp rose ('21)	1.50	1.20
61	A11	40c brown ('25)	.75	.75
62	A11	45c yellow	16.50	18.50
63	A11	50c brown vio ('23)	3.00	3.00
64	A11	50c gray blk ('25)	.75	.75
65	A11	60c brown red ('25)	1.50	.75
66	A11	65c chocolate	17.00	18.50
67	A11	80c blue ('21)	6.00	6.00
68	A11	90c brown ('23)	6.00	6.00
69	A11	1 l olive green	60.00	30.00
70	A11	1 l ultra ('21)	6.00	6.00
71	A11	1 l lt blue ('25)	1.50	.75
72	A11	2 l violet	1,000.	425.00
73	A11	2 l orange ('21)	22.50	27.00
74	A11	2 l lt green ('25)	7.50	7.50
75	A11	5 l slate	275.00	300.00
76	A11	5 l ultra ('25)	16.50	19.00
		Nos. 40-76 (37)	1,735.	1,022.

For overprints and surcharges see Nos. 77, 93-96, 103, 107, 188-189, B1-B2, E2, E4.

No. 50 Surcharged

1905, Sept. 1

77	A11	15c on 20c brown org	15.00	10.50
a.		Large 5 in 1905 on level with 9	92.50	45.00

Coat of Arms
A12 · A13

Two types:
I — Width 18½mm.
II — Width 19mm.

1907-10 Unwmk. Engr. Perf. 12

78	A12	1c brown, II ('10)	8.00	2.00
a.		Type I	16.00	3.00
79	A13	15c gray, I	37.50	6.00
a.		Imperforate	140.00	140.00
b.		Type II ('10)	300.00	32.50
c.		As "b," imperforate	600.00	600.00

No. 79a Surcharged in Brown

1918, Mar. 15

80	A13	20c on 15c gray	6.00	3.75

St. Marinus — A14

Perf. 14½x14, 14x14½

1923, Aug. 11   Typo.   Wmk. 140
81   A14   30c dark brown   .75   .75

San Marino Intl. Exhib. of 1923. Proceeds from the sale of this stamp went to a mutual aid society.

Imperforate examples on chalky paper are proofs. Value, $175.

Italian Flag and Views of Arbe and Mt. Titano A15

1923, Aug. 6
82   A15   50c olive green   .75   .75
   a.   Reverse printing omitted   215.00

Presentation to San Marino of the Italian flag which had flown over the island of Arbe, the birthplace of the founder of San Marino. Inscribed on back: "V. Moraldi dis. Blasi inc. Petiti impr.-Roma."

Imperfroate examples on chalky paper are proofs. Value, $175.

Mt. Titano and Sword — A16

1923, Sept. 29   *Perf. 14x14½*
83   A16   1 l dark brown   22.50   22.50

In honor of the San Marino Volunteers who were killed or wounded in WWI.

Giuseppe Garibaldi A17

Allegory-San Marino Sheltering Garibaldi A18

1924, Sept. 25   *Perf. 14*
84   A17   30c dark violet   3.75   4.00
85   A17   50c olive brown   3.75   4.00
86   A17   60c dull red   5.00   5.00
87   A18   1 l deep blue   9.00   9.00
88   A18   2 l gray green   11.00   11.00
   Nos. 84-88 (5)   32.50   33.00

75th anniv. of Garibaldi's taking refuge in San Marino.

No. B8 Surcharged in Black

1924, Oct. 9
89   SP1   30c on 45c yel brn
      & blk   3.00   3.00

Nos. B9-B11 Surcharged

90   SP2   60c on 1 l bl grn &
      blk   10.50   10.50
91   SP2   1 l on 2 l vio & blk   29.00   29.00
92   SP2   2 l on 3 l claret &
      blk   22.00   22.00
   Nos. 89-92 (4)   64.50   64.50

Nos. 67 and 68 Surcharged in Black or Red

1926, July 1
93   A11   75c on 80c blue   2.25   2.50
94   A11   1.20 l on 90c brown   2.25   2.50
95   A11   1.25 l on 90c brn (R)   3.75   3.75
96   A11   2.50 l on 80c blue (R)   8.00   8.00
   Nos. 93-96 (4)   16.25   16.75

Antonio Onofri — A19

Unwmk.

1926, July 29   Engr.   *Perf. 11*
97   A19   10c dk blue & blk   .75   .75
98   A19   20c olive grn & blk   1.50   1.50
99   A19   45c dk vio & blk   .75   .75
100   A19   65c green & blk   .75   .75
101   A19   1 l orange & blk   5.50   5.50
102   A19   2 l red vio & blk   5.50   5.50
   Nos. 97-102 (6)   14.75   14.75

For surcharges see Nos. 104-106, 181-182.

Special Delivery Stamp No. E2 Surcharged

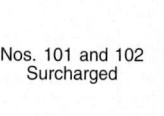

Perf. 14½x14

1926, Nov. 25   Wmk. 140
103   A11   1.85 l on 60c violet   .80   .80

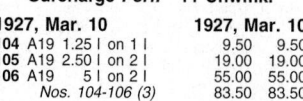

Nos. 101 and 102 Surcharged

13 Dots in Curved Row in Surcharge *Perf.* 11 Unwmk.

1927, Mar. 10   1927, Mar. 10
104   A19   1.25 l on 1 l   9.50   9.50
105   A19   2.50 l on 2 l   19.00   19.00
106   A19   5 l on 2 l   55.00   55.00
   Nos. 104-106 (3)   83.50   83.50

Type of Special Delivery Stamp of 1923 Surcharged

1927, Sept. 15   Wmk. 140   *Perf. 14*
107   A11   1.75 l on 50c on 25c
      vio   1.25   1.25

13 Dots in Curved Row in Surcharge

War Memorial A21

Unwmk.

1927, Sept. 28   Engr.   *Perf. 12*
108   A21   50c brown violet   2.25   2.25
109   A21   1.25 l blue   3.25   3.25
110   A21   10 l gray   30.00   30.00
   Nos. 108-110 (3)   35.50   35.50

Erection of a cenotaph in memory of the San Marino volunteers in WWI.

Capuchin Church and Convent A22

Design: 2.50 l, 5 l, Death of St. Francis.

1928, Jan. 2
111   A22   50c red   27.50   10.50
112   A22   1.25 l dp blue   12.00   12.00
113   A22   2.50 l dk brown   12.00   12.00
114   A22   5 l dull violet   37.50   35.00
   Nos. 111-114 (4)   89.00   69.50

7th centenary of the death of St. Francis of Assisi.

For surcharges see Nos. 183-184.

The Rocca (State Prison) A24

Government Palace A25

Statue of Liberty — A26

1929-35   Wmk. 217
115   A24   5c vio brn & ul-
      tra   1.50   .75
116   A24   10c grnsh blue &
      red vio   2.00   1.25
117   A24   15c dp org & em-
      er   1.50   .75
118   A24   20c dk bl & org
      red   1.50   .75
119   A24   25c grn & gray
      blk   1.50   .75
120   A24   30c gray brn &
      red   1.50   .75
121   A24   50c red vio & ol
      gray   1.50   .75
122   A24   75c dp red &
      gray blk   1.50   .75
123   A25   1 l dk brn & em-
      er   1.50   .75
124   A25   1.25 l dk blue & blk   1.50   .75
125   A25   1.75 l green & org   4.00   2.00
126   A25   2 l bl gray & red   2.00   1.25
127   A25   2.50 l car rose &
      ultra   2.00   1.25
128   A25   3 l dp org & bl   2.00   1.25
129   A25   3.70 l ol blk & red
      brn ('35)   2.00   1.25
130   A26   5 l dk vio & dk
      grn   4.00   3.75
131   A26   10 l bis brn & dk
      bl   16.00   15.00
132   A26   15 l grn & red vio   90.00   90.00
133   A26   20 l dk bl & red   350.00   350.00
   Nos. 115-133 (19)   472.50   473.75

General Post Office — A27

1932, Feb. 4
134   A27   20c blue green   35.00   22.50
135   A27   50c dark red   42.50   26.00
136   A27   1.25 l dark blue   275.00   190.00
137   A27   1.75 l dark brown   170.00   105.00
138   A27   2.75 l dark violet   85.00   60.00
   Nos. 134-138 (5)   607.50   403.50

Opening of new General Post Office. For surcharges see Nos. 151-160.

San Marino-Rimini Electric Railway — A28

1932, June 11
139   A28   20c deep green   4.50   4.50
140   A28   50c dark red   7.50   7.50
141   A28   1.25 l dark blue   19.00   19.00
142   A28   5 l deep brown   105.00   105.00
   Nos. 139-142 (4)   136.00   136.00

Opening of the new electric railway between San Marino and Rimini.

Giuseppe Garibaldi — A29

Garibaldi's Arrival at San Marino — A30

1932, July 30
143   A29   10c violet brown   12.50   5.00
144   A29   20c violet   12.50   5.00
145   A29   25c green   12.50   5.00
146   A29   50c yellow brn   17.00   10.00
147   A30   75c dark red   42.50   21.00
148   A30   1.25 l dark blue   50.00   30.00
149   A30   2.75 l brown org   100.00   60.00
150   A30   5 l olive green   340.00   425.00
   Nos. 143-150 (8)   587.00   561.00

Garibaldi (1807-1882), Italian patriot.

Nos. 138 and 137 Surcharged

1933, May 27
151   A27   25c on 2.75 l   16.00   16.00
152   A27   50c on 1.75 l   32.50   32.50
153   A27   75c on 1.75 l   65.00   65.00
154   A27   1.25 l on 1.75 l   425.00   425.00
   Nos. 151-154 (4)   538.50   538.50

Convention of philatelists, San Marino, May 28.

Nos. 134-137
Surcharged in Black

1934, Apr. 12
155	A27	25c on 1.25 l	3.25	3.25
156	A27	50c on 1.75 l	4.75	4.75
157	A27	75c on 50c	11.00	11.00
158	A27	1.25 l on 20c	40.00	40.00
		Nos. 155-158 (4)	59.00	59.00

San Marino's participation (with a philatelic pavilion) in the 15th annual Trade Fair at Milan, Apr. 12-27.

Nos. 136 and 138 Surcharged Wheel and New Value

1934, Apr. 12
| 159 | A27 | 3.70 l on 1.25 l | 67.50 | 67.50 |
| 160 | A27 | 3.70 l on 2.75 l | 82.50 | 82.50 |

Ascent to
Mt.
Titano
A31

Unwmk.
1935, Feb. 7   Engr.   Perf. 14
161	A31	5c choc & blk	.75	.75
162	A31	10c dk vio & blk	.75	.75
163	A31	20c orange & blk	.75	.75
164	A31	25c green & blk	.75	.75
165	A31	50c olive bis & blk	.75	.75
166	A31	75c brown red & blk	3.50	3.50
167	A31	1.25 l blue & blk	7.00	7.00
		Nos. 161-167 (7)	14.25	14.25

12th anniv. of the founding of the Fascist Movement.

Melchiorre
Delfico — A32

Statue of
Delfico — A33

1935, Apr. 15   Wmk. 217   Perf. 12
Center in Black
169	A32	5c brown lake	2.50	2.50
170	A32	7½c lt brown	2.50	2.50
171	A32	10c dk blue grn	2.50	2.50
172	A32	15c rose carmine	50.00	25.00
173	A32	20c orange	3.25	3.00
174	A32	25c green	3.25	3.00
175	A33	30c dull violet	3.25	3.00
176	A33	50c olive green	5.00	5.00
177	A33	75c red	15.00	15.00
178	A33	1.25 l dark blue	4.25	4.25
179	A33	1.50 l dk brown	70.00	70.00
180	A33	1.75 l brown org	100.00	105.00
		Nos. 169-180 (12)	261.50	240.75

Melchiorre Delfico (1744-1835), historian. For surcharges see Nos. 202, 277.

Nos. 99-100
Surcharged in Black

Nos. 112-113 Surcharged in Black

1936   Unwmk.   Perf. 11
181	A19	80c on 45c dk vio & blk	4.00	4.00
182	A19	80c on 65c grn & blk	4.00	4.00
		Perf. 12		
183	A22	2.05 l on 1.25 l	9.50	9.50
184	A22	2.75 l on 2.50 l	25.00	25.00
		Nos. 181-184 (4)	42.50	42.50

Issued: Nos. 181-182, 4/14; Nos. 183-184, 8/23.

Souvenir Sheet

Design from Base of Roman
Column — A34

1937, Aug. 23   Engr.   Wmk. 217
| 185 | A34 | 5 l steel blue | 15.00 | 12.50 |

Unveiling of the Roman Column at San Marino. The date "1636 d. F. R." means the 1,636th year since the founding of the republic.

No. 185 was privately surcharged "+ 10 L 1941."

Souvenir Sheets

Abraham Lincoln — A35

1938, Apr. 7   Wmk. 217   Perf. 13
| 186 | A35 | 3 l dark blue | 2.75 | 2.75 |
| 187 | A35 | 5 l rose red | 18.00 | 18.00 |

Dedication of a Lincoln bust, Sept. 3, 1937.

No. 49 and Type of 1925 Surcharged with New Value in Black
1941   Wmk. 140   Perf. 14
| 188 | A11 | 10c on 15c brown vio | .50 | .50 |
| 189 | A11 | 10c on 30c brown org | 1.00 | 1.00 |

Flags of Italy and
San
Marino — A36

Harbor of
Arbe
A37

1942   Photo.
190	A36	10c yel brn & brn org	.35	.35
191	A36	15c brn & red brn	.35	.35
192	A36	20c gray grn & gray blk	.35	.35
193	A36	25c green & blue	.35	.35
194	A36	50c brn red & brn	.35	.35
195	A36	75c red & gray blk	.35	.35
196	A37	1.25 l bl & gray bl	.35	.35
197	A37	1.75 l brn & grnsh bl	.35	.35
198	A37	2.75 l bis brn & gray bl	.90	.90
199	A37	5 l green & brown	4.75	4.75
		Nos. 190-199 (10)	8.45	8.45

Return of the Italian flag to Arbe.

No. 190
Surcharged in
Black

1942, July 30
| 200 | A36 | 30c on 10c | .30 | .30 |

Rimini-San Marino Stamp Day, Aug. 3.

No. 192
Surcharged in
Black

1942, Sept. 14
| 201 | A36 | 30c on 20c | .30 | .30 |

No. 177 Surcharged with New Value in Black
1942, Sept. 28   Wmk. 217   Perf. 12
| 202 | A33 | 20 l on 75c red & blk | 17.50 | 17.50 |

Printing
Press and
Newspaper
A38

Newspapers
A39

Wmk. 140
1943, Apr. 12   Photo.   Perf. 14
203	A38	10c deep green	.30	.30
204	A38	15c bister	.30	.30
205	A38	20c dk orange brn	.30	.30
206	A38	30c dk rose vio	.30	.30
207	A38	50c blue black	.30	.30
208	A38	75c red orange	.30	.30
209	A39	1.25 l blue	.30	.30
210	A39	1.75 l deep violet	.30	.30
211	A39	5 l slate	1.25	1.25
212	A39	10 l dark brown	4.50	4.50
		Nos. 203-212 (10)	8.15	8.15

Nos. 206
and 207
Overprinted
in Red

1943, July 1
| 213 | A38 | 30c dk rose vio | .25 | .25 |
| 214 | A38 | 50c blue black | .25 | .25 |

Rimini-San Marino Stamp Day, July 5.

A40

A41

Overprinted in Black: "28 LVGLIO 1943 1642 F. R."

1943, Aug. 27
215	A40	5c brown	.30	.30
216	A40	10c orange red	.30	.30
217	A40	20c ultra	.30	.30
218	A40	25c deep green	.30	.30
219	A40	30c brown carmine	.30	.30
220	A40	50c deep violet	.30	.30
221	A40	75c car rose	.30	.30
222	A41	1.25 l sapphire	.30	.30
223	A41	1.75 l red org	.30	.30
224	A41	2.75 l dk red brn	1.25	1.25
225	A41	5 l green	1.50	1.50
226	A41	10 l violet	2.40	2.40
227	A41	20 l slate blue	6.50	6.50
		Nos. 215-227,C26-C33 (21)	27.10	27.10

This series was prepared for the 20th anniv. of fascism, but as Mussolini was overthrown July 25, 1943, it was overprinted for the downfall of fascism.

Overprint on Nos. 222-227 adds "d." before "F.R."

Exist without overprint. Value of set $55.

A42

A43

Overprinted "Governo Provvisorio" in Black

1943, Aug. 27
228	A42	5c brown	.30	.30
229	A42	10c orange red	.30	.30
230	A42	20c ultra	.30	.30
231	A42	25c deep green	.30	.30
232	A42	30c brown carmine	.30	.30
233	A42	50c deep violet	.30	.30
234	A42	75c carmine rose	.30	.30
235	A43	1.25 l sapphire	.30	.30
236	A43	1.75 l red orange	.30	.30

237	A43	5 l green	.80	.80
238	A43	20 l slate blue	2.00	2.00
	Nos. 228-238,C34-C39 (17)		11.20	11.20

Souvenir Sheets

A44

Perf. 14, Imperf.
1945, Mar. 15   Photo.   Unwmk.

239	A44	Sheet of 3	95.00	90.00
		Never hinged	130.00	
a.		10 l dull blue	27.50	22.50
b.		15 l dull green	27.50	22.50
c.		25 l dull red brown	27.50	22.50

Sheets contain a papermaker's watermark, "Hammermill Bond, Made in U.S.A."
Nos. 239, 241 and C40 were issued to commemorate the 50th anniv. of the reconstruction of the Government Palace.

Government Palace — A45

1945, Mar. 15   Wmk. 140   Perf. 14

241	A45	25 l brown violet	6.50	6.50
		Never hinged	13.00	

Coat of Arms of Faetano — A46

Coats of Arms: 20c, 60c, 25 l, Montegiardino. 40c, 5 l, San Marino. 80c, 2 l-4 l, Fiorentino. 10 l, Borgomaggiore. 20 l, Serravalle.

1945-46   Wmk. 277

242	A46	10c dark blue	.30	.30
243	A46	20c vermilion	.30	.30
244	A46	40c deep orange	.30	.30
245	A46	60c slate black	.30	.30
246	A46	80c dark green	.30	.30
247	A46	1 l dk car rose	.30	.30
248	A46	1.20 l deep violet	.30	.30
249	A46	2 l chestnut	.30	.30
250	A46	3 l dp blue ('46)	.30	.30
250A	A46	4 l red org ('46)	.30	.30
251	A46	5 l dark brown	.30	.30
251A	A46	15 l dp blue ('46)	2.25	2.75

Lithographed and Engraved

252	A46	10 l brt red & brn	2.25	2.75
253	A46	20 l brt red & ultra	6.00	4.75
254	A46	20 l org brn & ultra ('46)	12.00	5.00
a.		Vert. pair, imperf. btwn.	425.00	
		Never hinged	600.00	
255	A46	25 l hn brn & ultra ('46)	11.00	7.00

Size: 22x27mm

256	A46	50 l ol brn & ultra ('46)	17.00	14.00
	Nos. 242-256 (17)		53.80	39.55
	Set, never hinged		100.00	

Nos. 252-256 are in sheets of 10 (2x5). Values: Nos. 252, 254-255, $90 each. No. 253, $125, No. 256, $300.
For surcharges see Nos. 258-259, B26.

"Dawn of New Hope" — A52

Engr. & Litho.
1946   Unwmk.   Perf. 14

257	A52	100 l dull yel & brn vio	8.75	8.75
		Never hinged	20.00	
j.		Vert. pair, imperf. btwn.	1,100.	
		Never hinged	1,800.	

UN Relief and Rehabilitation Administration. Sheets of 10 with blue coat of arms in top margin.

Franklin D. Roosevelt and Flags of San Marino and US — A52a

Designs: 1 l, 50 l, Quotation on Liberty, from Franklin D. Roosevelt. 2 l, 100 l, Roosevelt portrait, vert. 5 l, 15 l, Roosevelt and flags (as shown).

Wmk. 277
1947, May 3   Photo.   Perf. 14

257A	A52a	1 l bister & brn	.25	.25
257B	A52a	2 l blue & sepia	.25	.25
257C	A52a	5 l violet & multi	.25	.25
257D	A52a	15 l green & multi	.25	.25
257E	A52a	50 l ver & brn	.80	.70
257F	A52a	100 l violet & sepia	1.25	1.10
	Nos. 257A-257F,C51A-C51H (14)		26.95	21.95
	Set, never hinged		60.00	

For surcharges see Nos. 257G-257I, C51I-C51K.

Nos. 257A-257C Surcharged with New Value
1947, June 16

257G	A52a	3 l on 1 l	.40	.40
257H	A52a	4 l on 2 l	.40	.40
257I	A52a	6 l on 5 l	.40	.40
	Nos. 257G-257I,C51I-C51K (6)		2.40	2.40
	Set, never hinged		4.75	

No. 250A Surcharged with New Value in Black
1947, June 16   Wmk. 277

258	A46	6(l) on 4 l red org	.25	.25
		Never hinged	.30	

No. 250A Surcharged in Black

259	A46	21 l on 4 l red org	.90	1.00
		Never hinged	2.00	

"St. Marinus Raising the Republic" by Girolamo Batoni — A53

Wmk. 217
1947, July 18   Engr.   Perf. 12

260	A53	1 l brt grn & vio	.30	.30
261	A53	2 l purple & olive	.30	.30
262	A53	4 l vio brn & dk bl grn	.30	.30
263	A53	10 l org & bl blk	.30	.30
264	A53	25 l carmine & purple	.90	.75
265	A53	50 l dk bl grn & brn	20.00	16.00
	Nos. 260-265,C52-C53 (8)		26.10	21.70
	Set, never hinged		55.00	

For overprints and surcharges see Nos. 294-295, B27-B38, C56.

United States 1847 Stamp A54

United States Stamps of 1847 and 1869 A55

A56

Wmk. 277
1947, Dec. 24   Photo.   Perf. 14

266	A54	2 l red vio & dk brn	.30	.30
267	A55	3 l sl gray, dp ultra & car	.30	.30
268	A54	6 l dp bl & dk gray grn	.30	.30
269	A56	15 l vio, dp ultra & car	.45	.60
270	A55	35 l dk brn, dp ultra & car	1.75	1.50
271	A56	50 l sl grn, dp ultra & car	1.75	1.50
	Nos. 266-271,C55 (7)		14.85	14.50
	Set, never hinged		35.00	

1st United States postage stamps, cent.

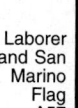 

Laborer and San Marino Flag A57

1948, June 3

272	A57	5 l brown	1.50	1.00
273	A57	8 l green	1.50	1.00
274	A57	30 l crimson	3.50	1.00
275	A57	50 l red brn & rose lil	5.00	4.50

Engr.

276	A57	100 l dk bl & dp vio	52.50	52.50
	Nos. 272-276 (5)		64.00	60.00
	Set, never hinged		125.00	

See Nos. 373-374.

No. 172 Surcharged with New Value and Ornaments in Black
1948   Wmk. 217   Perf. 12

277	A32	100 l on 15c	57.50	50.00
		Never hinged	110.00	

Government Palace — A58

Mt. Titano, Distant View — A59

Various Views of San Marino.

1949-50   Wmk. 277   Photo.   Perf. 14

278	A58	1 l black & blue	.40	.30
279	A58	2 l violet & car	.40	.30
280	A58	3 l violet & ultra	.40	.30
281	A58	4 l black & vio	.40	.30
282	A58	5 l violet & brn	.40	.30
283	A58	6 l dp blue & sep	1.40	.60
284	A59	8 l blk brn & yel brn	.90	.30
285	A59	10 l brn blk & bl	1.40	.30
286	A58	12 l brt rose & vio	2.75	.85
287	A58	15 l vio & brt rose	5.00	2.25

288	A58	20 l dp bl & brn ('50)	15.00	2.10
289	A58	35 l green & violet	9.50	5.50
290	A58	50 l brt rose & yel brn	4.75	1.60
291	A58	55 l dp bl & dl grn ('50)	60.00	35.00

Perf. 14x13½
Engr.

292	A59	100 l blk brn & dk grn	80.00	60.00
293	A59	200 l dp blue & brn	80.00	65.00
	Nos. 278-293 (16)		262.70	175.00
	Set, never hinged		525.00	

Nos. 260 and 261 Overprinted in Black

Giornata Filatelica San Marino-Riccione 28-6-1949

1949, June 28   Wmk. 217

294	A53	1 l brt green & vio	.40	.40
295	A53	2 l purple & olive	.40	.40
	Set, never hinged		1.60	

San Marino-Riccione Stamp Day, June 28.

Francesco Nullo — A60

1 l, 20 l, Francesco Nullo. 2 l, 5 l, Anita Garibaldi. 3 l, 50 l, Giuseppe Garibaldi. 4 l, 15 l, Ugo Bassi.

Wmk. 277
1949, July 31   Photo.   Perf. 14
Size: 22x28mm

296	A60	1 l blk & car lake	.25	.25
297	A60	2 l red brn & blue	.25	.25
298	A60	3 l car lake & dk grn	.25	.25
299	A60	4 l violet & dk brn	.25	.25

Size: 26½x36½mm

300	A60	5 l purple & dk brn	.25	.25
301	A60	15 l car lake & gray bl	.80	.80
302	A60	20 l violet & car lake	1.50	1.50
303	A60	50 l red brn & violet	15.00	13.00
	Nos. 296-303,C57-C61 (13)		34.20	28.20
	Set, never hinged			

Centenary of Garibaldi's escape to San Marino.
See Nos. C57-C61, 404-410.

Stagecoach on Road from San Marino — A61

1949, Dec. 29   Engr.

304	A61	100 l bl & gray vio	11.00	11.00
		Never hinged	22.50	
		Sheet of 6	200.00	200.00
		Never hinged	300.00	

UPU, 75th anniversary.

A62

A63

A63a

Perf. 13½x14, 14x13½
1951, Mar. 15   Engr.   Wmk. 277
Sky and Cross in Carmine

305	A62	25 l dk brn & red vio	7.00	6.75
306	A63	75 l org brn & dk brn	9.00	9.00
307	A63a	100 l dk brn & gray blk	12.00	12.00
		Nos. 305-307 (3)	28.00	27.75
		Set, never hinged	55.00	

Issued to honor the San Marino Red Cross.

Christopher Columbus A64

Designs: 2 l, 25 l, Columbus on his ship. 3 l, 10 l, 20 l, Landing of Columbus. 4 l, 15 l, 80 l, Pioneers trading with Indians. 5 l, 200 l, Columbus and map of Americas.

1952, Jan. 28   Photo.   Perf. 14

308	A64	1 l brn org & dk grn	.30	.30
309	A64	2 l dk brn & vio	.30	.30
310	A64	3 l vio & dk brn	.30	.30
311	A64	4 l bl & org brn	.30	.30
312	A64	5 l grn & dk bl grn	.45	.45
313	A64	10 l dk brn & blk	.65	.65
314	A64	15 l carmine & blk	.95	.95

Engr.

315	A64	20 l dp bl & dk bl grn	1.40	1.40
316	A64	25 l vio brn & blk brn	6.00	6.00
317	A64	60 l choc & vio bl	8.25	8.25
318	A64	80 l gray & blk	26.00	26.00
319	A64	200 l Prus grn & dp ultra	47.50	47.50
		Nos. 308-319,C80 (13)	119.90	119.90
		Set, never hinged	250.00	

Issued to honor Christopher Columbus.

Type of 1952 in New Colors Overprinted in Black or Red

1952, June 29   Photo.

320	A64	1 l vio & dk brn	.25	.25
321	A64	2 l carmine & blk	.25	.25
322	A64	3 l dk & dk bl grn (R)	.25	.25
323	A64	4 l dk brn & blk	.25	.25
324	A64	5 l purple & vio	.30	.30
325	A64	10 l bl & org brn (R)	.70	.70
326	A64	15 l org brn & blue	2.75	2.50
		Nos. 320-326,C81 (8)	39.75	39.50
		Set, never hinged	80.00	

4th Intl. Sample Fair of Trieste.

Discobolus — A65

Tennis A66

Model Airplane — A67

Designs: 3 l, Runner. 4 l, Cyclist. 5 l, Soccer. 25 l, Shooting. 100 l, Roller skating.

1953, Apr. 20   Wmk. 277   Perf. 14

327	A65	1 l dk brn & blk	.25	.25
328	A66	2 l black & brown	.25	.25
329	A65	3 l blk & grnsh bl	.25	.25
330	A66	4 l blk & brt bl	.25	.25
331	A66	5 l dk brn & sl grn	.25	.25
332	A67	10 l dp blue & crim	.35	.35
333	A67	25 l blk & dk brn	1.75	1.75
334	A66	100 l dk brn & slate	6.50	6.50
		Nos. 327-334,C90 (9)	54.85	54.85
		Set, never hinged	125.00	

See No. 438.

Type of 1953 Overprinted in Black

1953, Aug. 24

335	A66	100 l grn & dk bl grn	16.00	16.00
		Never hinged	35.00	

San Marino-Riccione Stamp Day, Aug. 24.

Narcissus A68

Flowers: 2 l, Tulips. 3 l, Oleanders. 4 l, Cornflowers. 5 l, Carnations. 10 l, Irises. 25 l, Cyclamen. 80 l, Geraniums. 100 l, Roses.

1953, Dec. 28   Photo.

336	A68	1 l multicolored	.25	.25
337	A68	2 l multicolored	.25	.25
338	A68	3 l multicolored	.25	.25
339	A68	4 l multicolored	.25	.25
340	A68	5 l multicolored	.25	.25
341	A68	10 l multicolored	.25	.25
342	A68	25 l multicolored	2.00	1.75
343	A68	80 l multicolored	12.50	12.50
344	A68	100 l multicolored	20.00	20.00
		Nos. 336-344 (9)	36.00	35.75
		Set, never hinged	70.00	

Walking Racer — A69

Fencing A70

Sports: 3 l, Boxing. 4 l, 200 l, 250 l, Gymnastics. 5 l, Motorcycling. 8 l, Javelin-throwing. 12 l, Automobiling. 25 l, Wrestling. 80 l, Walk racer.

1954-55   Photo.   Wmk. 277

345	A69	1 l violet & cer	.25	.25
346	A70	2 l dk grn & vio	.25	.25
347	A70	3 l brn & brn org	.25	.25
348	A70	4 l dk bl & brt bl	.25	.25
349	A70	5 l dk grn & dk brn	.25	.25
350	A70	8 l lil rose & pur	.25	.25
351	A70	12 l black & crim	.25	.25
352	A69	25 l bl & dk bl grn	.75	.35
353	A69	80 l dk bl & bl grn	2.00	1.00
354	A69	200 l violet & brn	4.75	4.00

Perf. 12½x13
Engr.

355	A69	250 l multi ('55)	32.50	32.50
		Sheet of 4 (#355)	250.00	250.00
		Nos. 345-355 (11)	41.75	39.60
		Set, never hinged	80.00	

A71

Liberty statue and Government palace.

1954, Dec. 16   Photo.   Perf. 13x13½

356	A71	20 l choc & blue	.40	.40
357	A71	60 l car & dk grn	.80	.80
		Nos. 356-357,C92 (3)	2.30	2.30
		Set, never hinged	4.50	

A72

1955, Aug. 27   Wmk. 303   Perf. 14

358	A72	100 l gray blk & bl	2.00	2.00
		Never hinged	4.00	

7th San Marino-Riccione Stamp Fair. See No. 385.

Murata Nuova Bridge — A73   View of La Rocca — A74

Design: 15 l, Government Palace.

Size: 22x27½mm; 27½x22mm
1955, Nov. 15   Perf. 14

359	A73	5 l blue & brown	.25	.25
360	A74	10 l org & bl grn	.25	.25
361	A74	15 l Prus grn & car	.25	.25
362	A73	25 l dk brn & vio	.25	.25
363	A74	35 l vio & red car	.30	.25
		Nos. 359-363 (5)	1.30	1.25
		Set, never hinged	1.40	

See Nos. 386-388, 636-638.

Ice Skater — A75

Skier A76

3 l, 50 l, Tobogganing. 4 l, Skier going downhill. 5 l, 100 l, Ice Hockey player. 10 l, Girl ice skater.

1955, Dec. 15   Wmk. 303   Perf. 14

364	A75	1 l brown & yellow	.25	.25
365	A76	2 l brt blue & red	.25	.25
366	A76	3 l blk brn & lt brn	.25	.25
367	A75	4 l brown & green	.25	.25
368	A76	5 l ultra & sal pink	.25	.25
369	A75	10 l ultra & pink	.25	.25
370	A76	25 l gray blk & red	.50	.50
371	A76	50 l brown & indigo	1.40	1.40
372	A76	100 l blk & Prus grn	4.25	4.25
		Nos. 364-372,C95 (10)	25.15	25.15
		Set, never hinged	47.50	

7th Winter Olympic Games at Cortina d'Ampezzo, Jan. 26-Feb. 5, 1956. For surcharge see No. C96.

Type of 1948 Inscribed: "50th Anniversario Arengo 25 Marzo 1906"
1956, Mar. 24   Wmk. 303   Perf. 14

373	A57	50 l sapphire	5.50	5.50
		Never hinged	11.00	

50th anniv. of the meeting of the heads of families (Arengo), the beginning of the democratic era in San Marino.

Type of 1948 inscribed: "Assistenza Invernale"
1956, Mar. 24   Photo.

374	A57	50 l dark green	5.50	5.50
		Never hinged	11.00	

Issued to publicize the Winterhelp charity.

Pointer and Arms A77

Dogs: 2 l, Russian greyhound. 3 l, Sheep dog. 4 l, English greyhound. 5 l, Boxer. 10 l, Great Dane. 25 l, Irish setter. 60 l, German shepherd. 80 l, Scotch collie. 100 l, Hunting hound.

1956, June 8   Wmk. 303   Perf. 14

375	A77	1 l ultra & brown	.25	.25
376	A77	2 l car lake & bl gray	.25	.25
377	A77	3 l ultra & brown	.25	.25
378	A77	4 l grnsh bl & gray vio	.25	.25
379	A77	5 l car lake & dk brn	.25	.25
380	A77	10 l ultra & brown	.25	.25
381	A77	25 l dk blue & multi	1.00	1.00
382	A77	60 l car lake & multi	4.00	4.00
383	A77	80 l dk blue & multi	6.50	4.50
384	A77	100 l car lake & multi	10.00	7.50
		Nos. 375-384 (10)	23.00	18.50
		Set, never hinged	50.00	

Sailboat Type of 1955
1956   Wmk. 303   Perf. 14

385	A72	100 l brown & bl grn	1.25	*1.75*
		Never hinged	2.50	

8th San Marino-Riccione Stamp Fair.

Types of 1955 with added inscription: "Congresso Internaz. Periti Filatelici San Marino-Salsomaggiore 6-8 Ottobre 1956."

Designs: 20 l, La Rocca. 80 l, Murata Nuova Bridge. 100 l, Government palace.

1956, Oct. 6 ***Perf. 14***

Size: 26x36mm; 36x26mm

386 A74 20 l blue & brown .60 .60
387 A73 80 l vio & red car 1.50 *2.25*
388 A74 100 l org & bl grn 2.50 *3.00*
Nos. 386-388 (3) 4.60 5.85
Set, never hinged 9.50

Intl. Philatelic Cong., San Marino, 10/6-8.

Street and Borgo Maggiore Church — A78

Hospital Street — A79

Views: 3 l, Gate tower. 20 l, Covered Market of Borgo Maggiore. 125 l, View from South Bastion.

1957, May 9 **Photo.** **Wmk. 303**

389 A78 2 l dk grn & rose red .25 .25
390 A78 3 l blue & brown .25 .25
391 A78 20 l dk blue green .25 .25
392 A79 60 l brn & blue vio .90 *1.50*

Engr.

393 A78 125 l dk blue & blk .40 .25
Nos. 389-393 (5) 2.05 2.50
Set, never hinged 3.00

See Nos. 473-476, 633-635.

Daisies and View of San Marino — A80

Flowers: 2 l, Primrose. 3 l, Lily. 4 l Orchid. 5 l, Lily of the Valley. 10 l, Poppy. 25 l, Pansy. 60 l, Gladiolus. 80 l, Wild Rose. 100 l, Anemone.

Wmk. 303

1957, Aug. 31 **Photo.** ***Perf. 14***

Flowers in Natural Colors

394 A80 1 l dk vio blue .25 .25
395 A80 2 l dk vio blue .25 .25
396 A80 3 l dk vio blue .25 .25
397 A80 4 l dk vio blue .25 .25
398 A80 5 l dk vio blue .25 .25
399 A80 10 l blue, buff & lilac .25 .25
400 A80 25 l blue, yel & lilac .25 .25
401 A80 60 l blue, yel & dl red brn .35 *.35*
402 A80 80 l blue & dl red brn .80 *.90*
403 A80 100 l bl, yel & dl red brn 1.00 *1.75*
Nos. 394-403 (10) 3.90 4.75
Set, never hinged 6.50

Type of 1949 Inscribed: "Commemorazione 150 Nascita G. Garibaldi."

Portraits: 2 l, 50 l, Anita Garibaldi. 3 l, 25 l, Francesco Nullo. 5 l, 100 l, Giuseppe Garibaldi. 15 l, Ugo Bassi.

1957, Dec. 12 **Wmk. 303** ***Perf. 14***

Size: 22x28mm

404 A60 2 l vio & dull bl .25 .25
405 A60 3 l lake & dk grn .25 .25
406 A60 5 l brn & ol gray .25 .25

Size: 26½x37mm

407 A60 15 l blue & vio .25 .25
408 A60 25 l green & dk gray .25 .25
409 A60 50 l violet & brn .85 *1.25*
410 A60 100 l brown & vio .85 *1.25*
Nos. 404-410 (7) 2.95 3.75
Set, never hinged 5.50

Nos. 409-410 are printed se-tenant.
Birth of Giuseppe Garibaldi, 150th anniv.

Panoramic View A81

1958, Feb. 27 **Engr.** ***Perf. 14***

411 A81 500 l green & blk 70.00 70.00
Never hinged 110.00
Sheet of 6 550.00 550.00
Never hinged 850.00

Catalogue values for unused stamps in this section, from this point to the end of the section, are for Never Hinged items.

Fair Emblem and San Marino Peaks — A82

1958, Apr. 12 **Photo.** ***Perf. 14***

412 A82 40 l yel green & brn .25 .25
413 A82 60 l brt blue & mar .55 .55

World's Fair, Brussels, Apr. 17-Oct. 19.

Madonna and Fair Entrance A83

Design: 60 l, View of Fair Grounds.

1958, Apr. 12

414 A83 15 l yellow, grn & bl .25 .25
415 A83 60 l green & rose red .60 .50
Nos. 414-415,C97 (3) 4.10 4.00

San Marino's 10th participation in the Milan Fair.

Wheat — A84

Designs: 2 l, 125 l, Corn. 3 l, 80 l, Grapes. 4 l, 25 l, Peaches. 5 l, 40 l, Plums.

1958, Aug. 30 **Wmk. 303** ***Perf. 14***

416 A84 1 l dk blue & yel org .25 .25
417 A84 2 l dk grn & red org .25 .25
418 A84 3 l blue & ocher .25 .25
419 A84 4 l grn & rose car .25 .25
420 A84 5 l blue, yel & grn .25 .25
421 A84 15 l ultra & brn org .25 .25
422 A84 25 l multicolored .25 .25
423 A84 40 l multicolored .75 .50
424 A84 80 l multicolored 1.10 .60
425 A84 125 l bl, grn & org ver 4.50 3.00
Nos. 416-425 (10) 8.10 5.85

Bay and Stamp of Naples A85

1958, Oct. 8 **Photo.**

426 A85 25 l lilac & red brn .25 .25

Cent. of the stamps of Naples. See No. C100.

Pierre de Coubertin — A86

Portraits: 3 l, Count Alberto Bonacossa. 5 l, Avery Brundage. 30 l, Gen. Carlo Montu. 60 l, J. Sigfrid Edstrom. 80 l, Henri de Baillet Latour.

1959, May 19 **Wmk. 303** ***Perf. 14***

427 A86 2 l brn org & blk .25 .25
428 A86 3 l lilac & gray brn .25 .25
429 A86 5 l blue & dk grn .25 .25
430 A86 30 l violet & blk .25 .25
431 A86 60 l dk grn & gray brn .25 .25
432 A86 80 l car rose & dp grn .25 .25
Nos. 427-432,C106 (7) 6.00 4.75

Leaders of the Olympic movement; 1960 Olympic Games, Rome.
See Nos. 1060-1062.

Lincoln and his Praise of San Marino, May 7, 1861 A87

Lincoln Portraits and: 10 l, Map of San Marino. 15 l, Government palace. 70 l, San Marino peaks, vert.

1959, July 1 ***Perf. 14***

433 A87 5 l brown & blk .25 .25
434 A87 10 l blue grn & ultra .25 .25
435 A87 15 l gray & green .25 .25

Perf. 13x13½

Engr.

436 A87 70 l violet .45 .45
Nos. 433-436,C108 (5) 6.95 6.20

Birth sesquicentennial of Abraham Lincoln.

Arch of Augustus, Rimini, and Romagna ½b Stamp A88

1959, Aug. 29 **Photo.** ***Perf. 14***

437 A88 30 l black & brown .25 .25

Centenary of the first stamps of Romagna. See No. C109.

Type of 1953 Inscribed: "Universiade Torino"

1959, Aug. 29 **Wmk. 303** ***Perf. 14***

438 A65 30 l red orange .75 .50

Turin University Sports Meet, 8/27-9/6.

Messina Cathedral Portal and Stamp of Sicily 1859 — A89

Stamp of Sicily and: 2 l, Greek temple, Selinus. 3 l, Erice Church. 4 l, Temple of Concordia, Agrigento. 5 l, Ruins of Castor and Pollux Temple, Agrigento. 25 l, San Giovanni degli Eremiti Church. 60 l, Greek theater, Taormina, horiz.

1959, Oct. 16

439 A89 1 l ocher & dk brn .25 .25
440 A89 2 l olive & dk red .25 .25
441 A89 3 l blue & slate .25 .25
442 A89 4 l red & brown .25 .25
443 A89 5 l dull bl & rose lil .25 .25
444 A89 25 l multicolored .25 .25
445 A89 60 l multicolored .25 .25
Nos. 439-445,C110 (8) 4.25 4.00

Centenary of stamps of Sicily.

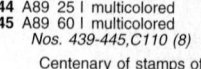

Golden Oriole A90

Nightingale — A91

Birds: 3 l, Woodcock. 4 l, Hoopoe. 5 l, Red-legged partridge. 10 l, Goldfinch. 25 l, European Kingfisher. 60 l, Ringnecked pheasant. 80 l, Green woodpecker. 110 l, Red-breasted flycatcher.

1960, Jan. 28 **Photo.** ***Perf. 14***

Centers in Natural Colors

446 A90 1 l blue .25 .25
447 A91 2 l green & red .25 .25
448 A90 3 l green & red .25 .25
449 A91 4 l dk green & red .25 .25
450 A90 5 l dark green .25 .25
451 A91 10 l blue & red .25 .25
452 A91 25 l grnsh blue .75 .40
453 A90 60 l blue & red 2.25 1.50
454 A91 80 l Prus blue & red 4.50 3.00
455 A91 110 l blue & red 5.50 4.50
Nos. 446-455 (10) 14.50 10.90

Shot Put — A92

Sports: 2 l, Gymnastics. 3 l, Walking. 4 l, Boxing. 5 l, Fencing, horiz. 10 l, Bicycling. 15 l, Hockey, horiz. 25 l, Rowing, horiz. 60 l, Soccer. 110 l, Equestrian, horiz.

1960, May 23 **Wmk. 303** ***Perf. 14***

456 A92 1 l car rose & vio .25 .25
457 A92 2 l gray & org .25 .25
458 A92 3 l brn ol & pur .25 .25
459 A92 4 l rose red & brn .25 .25
460 A92 5 l brown & blue .25 .25
461 A92 10 l red brn & bl .25 .25
462 A92 15 l emer & lilac .25 .25
463 A92 25 l bl grn & org .25 .25
464 A92 60 l dp grn & org .25 .25
465 A92 110 l emer, red & blk .30 .25
Set of 3 souvenir sheets, imperf. 11.00 11.00
Nos. 456-465,C111-C114 (14) 3.65 3.50

17th Olympic Games, Rome, 8/25-9/11.
Souvenir sheets are: (1.) Sheet of 4, one each of 1 l, 2 l, 3 l and 60 l, all printed in deep green and brown. (2.) Sheet of 4, one each of 4 l and 10 l plus a 20 l and 40 l in designs of Nos. C111-C112 but without "Posta Aerea" inscribed-all 4 printed in rose red and brown. (3.) Sheet of 6, one each of 5 l, 15 l, 25 l and 110 l plus an 80 l and 125 l in designs of Nos. C113-C114 but without "Posta Aerea"- all 6 printed in emerald and brown.

Mt. Titano — A93

Founder Melvin Jones and Lions Headquarters — A94

60 l, Government Palace and statue of Liberty. 115 l, Clarence L. Sturm, president. 150 l, Finis E. Davis, vice president.

1960, July 1 Photo. Wmk. 303

466	A93	30 l	red brn & dk bl	.25	.25
467	A94	45 l	bl vio & bis brn	.50	.50
468	A93	60 l	dull rose & bl	.25	.25
469	A94	115 l	green & blk	.50	.50
470	A94	150 l	brn & dk bl	2.75	2.75
			Nos. 466-470,C115 (6)	11.75	11.75

Lions Intl.; founding of the Lions Club of San Marino.

Beach of Riccione and San Marino Peaks A95

1960, Aug. 27 ***Perf. 14***

471	A95	30 l	multicolored	.30	.25

12th San Marino-Riccione Stamp Day, Aug. 27. See No. C116.

Boy with Basket of Fruit, by Caravaggio — A96

1960, Dec. 29 Wmk. 303 ***Perf. 14***

472	A96	200 l	multicolored	9.00	8.50

350th anniversary of the death of Michelangelo da Caravaggio (Merisi), painter.

Types of 1957

Views: 1 l, Hospital street. 4 l, Government building. 30 l, Gate tower. 115 l, Covered market of Borgo Maggiore.

1961, Feb. 16 ***Perf. 14***

473	A79	1 l	dk blue grn	.25	.25
474	A78	4 l	dk blue & blk	.25	.25
475	A78	30 l	brt vio & brn	.60	.40
476	A78	115 l	brown & blue	.60	.40
			Nos. 473-476 (4)	1.70	1.30

Hunting Roebuck A97

Hunting Scenes (16th-18th century): 2 l, Falconer, vert. 3 l, Wild boar hunt. 4 l, Duck shooting with crossbow. 5 l, Stag hunt. 10 l, Mounted falconer, vert. 30 l, Hunter with horn and dogs. 60 l, Hunter with rifle and dog, vert. 70 l, Hunter and beater. 115 l, Duck hunt.

Wmk. 303

1961, May 4 Photo. ***Perf. 14***

477	A97	1 l	lil rose & vio bl	.25	.25
478	A97	2 l	gray, dk red & blk	.25	.25
479	A97	3 l	red org, brn & blk	.25	.25
480	A97	4 l	lt bl, red & blk	.25	.25
481	A97	5 l	yellow grn & brn	.25	.25
482	A97	10 l	org, blk, brn & vio	.25	.25
483	A97	30 l	yel, bl & dk grn	.25	.25
484	A97	60 l	ocher, brn, blk & red	.25	.25
485	A97	70 l	green, blk & car	.25	.25
486	A97	115 l	brt pink, blk & dk bl	.50	.50
			Nos. 477-486 (10)	2.75	2.75

Mt. Titano and Cancelled Stamp of Sardinia, 1862 — A98

Photogravure and Embossed

1961, Sept. 5 Wmk. 303 ***Perf. 13***

487	A98	30 l	multicolored	.50	.50
488	A98	70 l	multicolored	.70	.70
489	A98	200 l	multicolored	.75	.75
			Nos. 487-489 (3)	1.95	1.95

Cent. of Independence Phil. Exhib., Turin, 1961.

Europa Issue

View of San Marino A99

Wmk. 339

1961, Oct. 20 Photo. ***Perf. 13***

490	A99	500 l	brn & blue grn	*30.00*	*15.00*
			Sheet of 6	*225.00*	*150.00*

King Enzo's Palace and Neptune Fountain, Bologna — A100

Views of Bologna: 70 l, Loggia dei Mercanti. 100 l, Two Towers.

1961, Nov. 25 Wmk. 339 ***Perf. 14***

491	A100	30 l	grnsh bl & blk	.25	.25
492	A100	70 l	dk ol grn & blk	.25	.25
493	A100	100 l	red brown & blk	.25	.25
			Nos. 491-493 (3)	.75	.75

Bophilex, philatelic exhibition, Bologna.

Duryea, 1892 A101

Automobiles (pre-1910): 2 l, Panhard-Levassor. 3 l, Peugeot. 4 l, Daimler. 5 l, Fiat, vert. 10 l, Decauville. 15 l, Wolseley. 20 l, Benz. 25 l, Napier. 30 l, White, vert. 50 l, Oldsmobile. 70 l, Renault, vert. 100 l, Isotta Fraschini. 115 l, Bianchi. 150 l, Alfa.

1962, Jan. 23 Wmk. 303 ***Perf. 14***

494	A101	1 l	red brn & bl	.25	.25
495	A101	2 l	ultra & org brn	.25	.25
496	A101	3 l	black, brn & org	.25	.25
497	A101	4 l	gray & dk red	.25	.25
498	A101	5 l	violet & org	.25	.25
499	A101	10 l	black & org	.25	.25
500	A101	15 l	black & ver	.25	.25
501	A101	20 l	black & ultra	.25	.25
502	A101	25 l	gray & org	.25	.25
503	A101	30 l	black & ocher	.25	.25
504	A101	50 l	black & brt pink	.25	.25
505	A101	70 l	black, gray & grn	.25	.25
506	A101	100 l	black, yel & car	.30	.30
507	A101	115 l	blk, org & bl grn	.40	.40
508	A101	150 l	multicolored	.50	.50
			Nos. 494-508 (15)	4.20	4.20

Wright Plane, 1904 A102

Historic Planes (1907-1910): 2 l, Ernest Archdeacon. 3 l, Albert and Emile Bonnet-Labranche. 4 l, Glenn Curtiss. 5 l, Farman. 10 l, Louis Bleriot. 30 l, Hubert Latham. 60 l, Alberto Santos Dumont. 70 l, Alliott Verdon Roe. 115 l, Faccioli.

Wmk. 339

1962, Apr. 4 Photo. ***Perf. 14***

509	A102	1 l	blk & dull yel	.25	.25
510	A102	2 l	red brn & grn	.25	.25
511	A102	3 l	red brn & gray grn	.25	.25
512	A102	4 l	brown & blk	.25	.25
513	A102	5 l	magenta & blue	.25	.25
514	A102	10 l	ocher & bl grn	.25	.25
515	A102	30 l	ocher & ultra	.25	.25
516	A102	60 l	black & ocher	.30	.30
517	A102	70 l	dp orange & blk	.35	.35
518	A102	115 l	blk, grn & ocher	.70	.70
			Nos. 509-518 (10)	3.10	3.10

Mountaineer Descending A103

Designs: 2 l, View of Sassolungo. 3 l, Mt. Titano. 4 l, Three Peaks of Lavaredo. 5 l, Matterhorn. 15 l, Skier on downhill run. 30 l, Climbing an overhang. 40 l, Cutting steps in ice. 85 l, Giant's Tooth. 115 l, Mt. Titano.

1962, June 14 Wmk. 339 ***Perf. 14***

519	A103	1 l	bis brn & blk	.25	.25
520	A103	2 l	Prus grn & blk	.25	.25
521	A103	3 l	lilac & blk	.25	.25
522	A103	4 l	brt bl & blk	.25	.25
523	A103	5 l	dp org & blk	.25	.25
524	A103	15 l	org yel & blk	.25	.25
525	A103	30 l	carmine & blk	.25	.25
526	A103	40 l	grnsh bl & blk	.25	.25
527	A103	85 l	lt green & blk	.25	.25
528	A103	115 l	vio bl & blk	.40	.40
			Nos. 519-528 (10)	2.65	2.65

Hunter with Dog A104

Modern Hunting Scenes: 2 l, Hound master on horseback, vert. 3 l, Duck hunt. 4 l, Stag hunt. 5 l, Partridge hunt. 15 l, Lapwing (hunt). 50 l, Wild duck hunt. 70 l, Duck hunt from boat. 100 l, Boar hunt. 150 l, Pheasant hunt, vert.

1962, Aug. 25 Photo. ***Perf. 14***

529	A104	1 l	brown & yel grn	.25	.25
530	A104	2 l	dk bl & org	.25	.25
531	A104	3 l	blk & Prus bl	.25	.25
532	A104	4 l	black & brown	.25	.25
533	A104	5 l	brn & yel grn	.25	.25
534	A104	15 l	blk & org brn	.25	.25
535	A104	50 l	brn, dp grn & blk	.25	.25
536	A104	70 l	grn, sal pink & blk	.25	.25
537	A104	100 l	blk, brick red & sep	.25	.25
538	A104	150 l	grn, lil & blk	.40	.40
			Nos. 529-538 (10)	2.65	2.65

Europa Issue

Mt. Titano and "Europa" A105

1962, Oct. 25 Wmk. 339

539	A105	200 l	gray & car	*1.40*	*1.25*
			Sheet of 6	*9.50*	*9.50*

Egyptian Cargo Ship A106

Ancient Ships: 2 l, Greece, 2nd Cent. B.C. 3 l, Roman galley. 4 l, Vikings, 10th Cent. 5 l, "Santa Maria," 1492. 10 l, Cypriote galleon, vert. 30 l, Galley, 1600. 60 l, "Sovereign of the Seas," 1637, vert. 70 l, Danish ship, 1750, vert. 115 l, Frigate, 1850.

1963, Jan. 10

540	A106	1 l	blue & org yel	.25	.25
541	A106	2 l	mag, tan & brn	.25	.25
542	A106	3 l	brown & lil rose	.25	.25
543	A106	4 l	vio brn & gray	.25	.25
544	A106	5 l	brown & yellow	.25	.25
545	A106	10 l	brn & brt yel grn	.25	.25
546	A106	30 l	blk, bl & sep	.60	.60
547	A106	60 l	lt vio bl & yel grn	.60	.60
548	A106	70 l	blk, gray & dl red	.95	.95
549	A106	115 l	blk, brn & gray bl	1.50	1.50
			Nos. 540-549 (10)	5.15	5.15

Lady with Veil, by Raphael — A107

Paintings by Raphael: 70 l, Self-portrait. 100 l, St. Barbara from Sistine Madonna. 200 l, Portrait of a Young Woman (Maddalena Strozzi).

Size: 26½x37mm

Wmk. 339

1963, Mar. 28 Photo. ***Perf. 14***

550	A107	30 l	multicolored	.35	.35
551	A107	70 l	multicolored	.25	.25
552	A107	100 l	multicolored	.30	.25

Size: 26½x44mm

553	A107	200 l	multicolored	.35	.35
			Nos. 550-553 (4)	1.25	1.20

Jousting with "Saracen," Arezzo — A108

Medieval "Knightly Games": 2 l, French knights, horiz. 3 l, Crossbow contest. 4 l, English knight receiving lance, horiz. 5 l, Tournament, Florence. 10 l, Jousting with "Quintana," Ascoli Piceno. 30 l, "Quintana," Foligno, horiz. 60 l, Race through Siena. 70 l, Tournament, Malpaga, horiz. 115 l, Knights challenging.

1963, June 22 Wmk. 339 ***Perf. 14***

554	A108	1 l	lilac rose	.25	.25
555	A108	2 l	slate	.25	.25
556	A108	3 l	black	.25	.25
557	A108	4 l	violet	.25	.25
558	A108	5 l	rose violet	.25	.25
559	A108	10 l	dull green	.25	.25
560	A108	30 l	red brown	.25	.25
561	A108	60 l	Prus green	.25	.25
562	A108	70 l	brown	.25	.25
563	A108	115 l	black	.25	.25
			Nos. 554-563 (10)	2.50	2.50

Butterfly — A109

Various butterflies. 70 l, 115 l, horiz.

Wmk. 339

1963, Aug. 31 Photo. *Perf. 14*

564	A109	25 l multicolored	.25	.25
565	A109	30 l multicolored	.25	.25
566	A109	60 l multicolored	.25	.25
567	A109	70 l multicolored	.30	.30
568	A109	115 l multicolored	.45	.45
		Nos. 564-568 (5)	1.50	1.50

St. Marinus Statue, Government Palace — A110

1963, Aug. 31

569	A110	100 l shown	.25	.25
570	A110	100 l Modern fountain	.25	.25

San Marino-Riccione Stamp Fair.

Europa Issue

Flag and "E" — A111

1963, Sept. 21 Wmk. 339 *Perf. 14*

571	A111	200 l blue & brn org	*.60*	*.50*

Women's Hurdles A112

Sports: 2 l, Pole vaulting, vert. 3 l, Women's relay race. 4 l, Men's high jump. 5 l, Soccer. 10 l, Women's high jump. 30 l, Women's discus throw, vert. 60 l, Women's javelin throw. 70 l, Water polo. 115 l, Hammer throw.

1963, Sept. 21

572	A112	1 l org & red brn	.25	.25
573	A112	2 l lt grn & dk brn	.25	.25
574	A112	3 l bl & dk brn	.25	.25
575	A112	4 l dp bl & dk brn	.25	.25
576	A112	5 l red & dk brn	.25	.25
577	A112	10 l lil rose & claret	.25	.25
578	A112	30 l gray & red brn	.25	.25
579	A112	60 l brt yel & dk brn	.25	.25
580	A112	70 l brt bl & dk brn	.25	.25
581	A112	115 l grn & dk brn	.25	.25
		Nos. 572-581 (10)	2.50	2.50

Publicity for 1964 Olympic Games.

Modern Pentathlon A113

Designs: 1 l, Runner, vert. 2 l, Woman gymnast, vert. 3 l, Basketball, vert. 5 l, Dual rowing. 15 l, Broad jumper. 30 l, Swimmer in racing dive. 70 l, Woman sprinter. 120 l, Bicycle racers, vert. 150 l, Fencers, vert.

Inscribed "Tokio, 1964"

1964, June 25 Wmk. 339 *Perf. 14*

582	A113	1 l brn & yel grn	.25	.25
583	A113	2 l blk & red brn	.25	.25
584	A113	3 l blk & brown	.25	.25
585	A113	4 l blk & org red	.25	.25
586	A113	5 l blk & brt bl	.25	.25
587	A113	15 l dk brn & org	.25	.25
588	A113	30 l dk vio & bl	.25	.25
589	A113	70 l red brn & grn	.25	.25
590	A113	120 l brn & brt bl	.25	.25
591	A113	150 l blk & crimson	.25	.25
		Nos. 582-591 (10)	2.50	2.50

18th Olympic Games, Tokyo, Oct. 10-25.

Same Inscribed "Verso Tokio"

1964, June 25 Photo.

592	A113	30 l indigo & lilac	.25	.25
593	A113	70 l brn & Prus grn	.25	.25

"Verso Tokyo" Stamp Exhibition at Rimini, Italy, June 25-July 6.

Murray-Blenkinsop Locomotive, 1812 — A114

History of Locomotive: 2 l, Puffing Billy, 1813. 3 l, Locomotion I, 1825. 4 l, Rocket, 1829. 5 l, Lion, 1838. 15 l, Bayard, 1839. 20 l, Crampton, 1849. 50 l, Little England, 1851. 90 l, Spitfire, c. 1860. 110 l, Rogers, c. 1865.

1964, Aug. 29 Wmk. 339 *Perf. 14*

594	A114	1 l blk & buff	.25	.25
595	A114	2 l blk & green	.25	.25
596	A114	3 l blk & rose lilac	.25	.25
597	A114	4 l blk & yellow	.25	.25
598	A114	5 l blk & salmon	.25	.25
599	A114	15 l blk & yel grn	.25	.25
600	A114	20 l blk & dp pink	.25	.25
601	A114	50 l blk & pale bl	.25	.25
602	A114	90 l blk & yel org	.25	.25
603	A114	110 l blk & brt bl	.35	.35
		Nos. 594-603 (10)	2.60	2.60

Baseball Players A115

1964, Aug. 29 Photo.

604	A115	30 l shown	.30	.30
605	A115	70 l Pitcher	.30	.30

8th European Baseball Championship, Milan.

Europa Issue

"E" and Globe A116

1964, Oct. 15 Wmk. 339 *Perf. 14*

606	A116	200 l dk blue & red	*1.50*	*1.00*

President John F. Kennedy (1917-1963) — A117

130 l, Kennedy and American flag, vert.

1964, Nov. 22 Photo. *Perf. 14*

607	A117	70 l multicolored	.25	.25
608	A117	130 l multicolored	.25	.25

Start of Bicycle Race from Government Palace — A118

Designs: 70 l, Cyclists (going right) and view of San Marino. 200 l, Cyclists (going left) and view of San Marino.

1965, May 15 Photo. Wmk. 339

609	A118	30 l sepia	.25	.25
610	A118	70 l deep claret	.25	.25
611	A118	200 l rose red	.25	.25
		Nos. 609-611 (3)	.75	.75

48th Bicycle Tour of Italy.

Brontosaurus — A119

Dinosaurs: 2 l, Brachiosaurus, vert. 3 l, Pteranodon. 4 l, Elasmosaurus. 5 l, Tyrannosaurus. 10 l, Stegosaurus. 75 l, Thaumatosaurus victor. 100 l, Iguanodon. 200 l, Triceratops.

1965, June 30 Wmk. 339 *Perf. 14*

612	A119	1 l dk brn & emer	.25	.25
613	A119	2 l blk & sl bl	.25	.25
614	A119	3 l sl grn, ol grn & yel	.25	.25
615	A119	4 l brn & slate bl	.25	.25
616	A119	5 l claret & grn	.25	.25
617	A119	10 l claret & grn	.25	.25
618	A119	75 l dk bl & bl grn	.25	.25
619	A119	100 l green & claret	.40	.40
620	A119	200 l brown & grn	.50	.50
		Nos. 612-620 (9)	2.65	2.65

Europa Issue

Rooks on Chessboard A120

1965, Aug. 28 Photo. *Perf. 14*

621	A120	200 l brown & multi	*1.10*	*.65*

Dante by Gustave Doré A121

Doré's Illustrations for Divina Commedia: 90 l, Charon ferrying boat across Acheron. 130 l, Eagle carrying Dante from Purgatory to Paradise. 140 l, Dante with Beatrice examined by Sts. Peter, James and John on faith.

Perf. 14x14½

1965, Nov. 20 Engr. Wmk. 339

Center in Brown Black

622	A121	40 l indigo	.25	.25
623	A121	90 l car rose	.25	.25
624	A121	130 l red brown	.25	.25
625	A121	140 l ultra	.25	.25
		Nos. 622-625 (4)	1.00	1.00

Dante Alighieri (1265-1321), poet.

Stylized Peaks, Flags of Italy and San Marino A122

1965, Nov. 25 Photo. *Perf. 14*

626	A122	115 l grn, red, ocher & bl	.30	.30

Visit of Giuseppe Saragat, president of Italy.

Trotter A123

Horses: 20 l, Cross Country, vert. 40 l, Hurdling. 70 l, Gallop. 90 l, Steeplechase. 170 l, Polo, vert.

Perf. 14x13, 13x14

1966, Feb. 28 Photo. Wmk. 339

627	A123	10 l multicolored	.25	.25
628	A123	20 l multicolored	.25	.25
629	A123	40 l multicolored	.25	.25
630	A123	70 l multicolored	.25	.25
631	A123	90 l multicolored	.25	.25
632	A123	170 l multicolored	.25	.25
		Nos. 627-632 (6)	1.50	1.50

Scenic Types of 1955-57

5 l, Hospital Street. 10 l, Gate tower. 15 l, View from South Bastion. 40 l, Murata Nuova Bridge. 90 l, View of La Rocca. 140 l, Government Palace.

1966, Mar. 29 Wmk. 339 *Perf. 14*

633	A79	5 l blue & brn	.25	.25
634	A78	10 l dk sl grn & bl grn	.25	.25
635	A78	15 l dk brn & vio	.25	.25
636	A73	40 l dk pur & brick red	.25	.25
637	A74	90 l blk & dull bl	.25	.25
638	A74	140 l violet & org	.25	.25
		Nos. 633-638 (6)	1.50	1.50

"Bella" by Titian A124

Titian Paintings: 90 l, 100 l, Details from "The Education of Love." 170 l, Detail from "Sacred and Profane Love."

1966, June 16 Wmk. 339 *Perf. 14*

639	A124	40 l multicolored	.25	.25
640	A124	90 l multicolored	.25	.25
641	A124	100 l multicolored	.25	.25
642	A124	170 l multicolored	.25	.25
		Nos. 639-642 (4)	1.00	1.00

Stone Bass A125

Fish: 2 l, Cuckoo wrasse. 3 l, Dolphin. 4 l, John Dory. 5 l, Octopus, vert. 10 l, Orange scorpionfish. 40 l, Electric ray, vert. 90 l, Jellyfish, vert. 115 l, Sea Horse, vert. 130 l, Dentex.

Perf. 14x13½, 13½x14

1966, Aug. 27 Photo. Wmk. 339

643	A125	1 l multicolored	.25	.25
644	A125	2 l multicolored	.25	.25
645	A125	3 l multicolored	.25	.25
646	A125	4 l multicolored	.25	.25
647	A125	5 l multicolored	.25	.25
648	A125	10 l multicolored	.25	.25
649	A125	40 l multicolored	.25	.25
650	A125	90 l multicolored	.25	.25

651 A125 115 l multicolored   .25   .25
652 A125 130 l multicolored   .25   .25
   Nos. 643-652 (10)   2.50 2.50

Europa Issue

Our Lady of Europe
A126

1966, Sept. 24   Wmk. 339   Perf. 14
653 A126 200 l multicolored   .45   .35

Peony and Mt. Titano — A127

Flowers and Various Views of Mt. Titano: 10 l, Bell flowers. 15 l, Pyrenean poppy. 20 l, Purple nettle. 40 l, Day lily. 140 l, Gentian. 170 l, Thistle.

Wmk. 339
1967, Jan. 12   Photo.   Perf. 14
654 A127   5 l multicolored   .25   .25
655 A127 10 l multicolored   .25   .25
656 A127 15 l multicolored   .25   .25
657 A127 20 l multicolored   .25   .25
658 A127 40 l multicolored   .25   .25
659 A127 140 l multicolored   .25   .25
660 A127 170 l multicolored   .25   .25
   Nos. 654-660 (7)   1.75 1.75

St. Marinus — A128

The Return of the Prodigal Son — A129

Design: 170 l, St. Francis. The paintings are by Giovanni Francesco Barbieri (1591-1666).

Wmk. 339
1967, Mar. 16   Photo.   Perf. 14
661 A128 40 l multicolored   .25   .25
662 A128 170 l multicolored   .25   .25
663 A129 190 l multicolored   .25   .25
 a.   Strip of 3, #661-663   .75   .75

Europa Issue

Map Showing Members of CEPT — A130

1967, May 5   Wmk. 339   Perf. 14
664 A130 200 l sl grn & brn org   *.75*   .45

Amanita Caesarea — A131

Various Mushrooms.

1967, June 15   Photo.   Perf. 14
665 A131   5 l multicolored   .25   .25
666 A131 15 l multicolored   .25   .25
667 A131 20 l multicolored   .25   .25
668 A131 40 l multicolored   .25   .25
669 A131 50 l multicolored   .25   .25
670 A131 170 l multicolored   .25   .25
   Nos. 665-670 (6)   1.50 1.50

Amiens Cathedral A132

Designs: 40 l, Siena Cathedral. 80 l, Toledo Cathedral. 90 l, Salisbury Cathedral. 170 l, Cologne Cathedral.

Wmk. 339
1967, Sept. 21   Engr.   Perf. 14
671 A132 20 l dk vio, *bister*   .25   .25
672 A132 40 l slate grn, *bister*   .25   .25
673 A132 80 l slate bl, *bister*   .25   .25
674 A132 90 l sepia, *bister*   .25   .25
675 A132 170 l deep plum, *bister*   .25   .25
   Nos. 671-675 (5)   1.25 1.25

Crucifix of Santa Croce, by Cimabue A133

1967, Dec. 5   Wmk. 339   Perf. 15
676 A133 300 l brn & vio blue   .60   .60

The Crucifix of Santa Croce, by Giovanni Cimabue (1240-1302), was severely damaged in the Florentine flood of Nov. 1966.

Coat of Arms — A134

Coats of Arms: 3 l, Penna Rossa. 5 l, Fiorentino. 10 l, Montecerreto. 25 l, Serravalle. 35 l, Montegiardino. 50 l, Faetano. 90 l, Borgo Maggiore. 180 l, Montelupo. 500 l, State arms of San Marino.

Perf. 13x13½
1968, Mar. 14   Litho.   Wmk. 339
677 A134   2 l multi   .25   .25
678 A134   3 l multi   .25   .25
679 A134   5 l multi   .25   .25
680 A134 10 l multi   .25   .25
681 A134 25 l multi   .25   .25
682 A134 35 l multi   .25   .25
683 A134 50 l multi   .25   .25
684 A134 90 l multi   .25   .25
685 A134 180 l multi   .25   .25
686 A134 500 l multi   .45   .25
   Nos. 677-686 (10)   2.70 2.50

Common Design Types pictured following the introduction.

Europa Issue, 1968
Common Design Type
1968, Apr. 29   Engr.   Perf. 14x13½
Size: 37x27½mm
687 CD11 250 l claret brown   *.55*   .35

"Battle of San Romano" (Detail), by Paolo Uccello — A135

Designs: Details from "The Battle of San Romano," by Paolo Uccello (1397-1475).

Photogravure and Engraved
1968, June 14   Wmk. 339   Perf. 14
688 A135 50 l pale lil & blk   .25   .25
689 A135 90 l pale lil & blk,
             vert.   .25   .25
690 A135 130 l pale lil & blk   .25   .25
691 A135 230 l pale pink & blk   .25   .25
   Nos. 688-691 (4)   1.00 1.00

The Mystic Nativity, by Botticelli, Detail A136

1968, Dec. 5   Wmk. 339
1968, Dec. 5   Engr.   Perf. 14
692 A136 50 l dark blue   .25   .25
693 A136 90 l deep claret   .25   .25
694 A136 180 l sepia   .25   .25
   Nos. 692-694 (3)   .75   .75

Christmas.

"Peace" by Lorenzetti A137

Designs: 80 l, "Justice." 90 l, "Moderation." 180 l, View of Siena, 14th century, horiz. All designs are from the "Good Government" frescoes by Ambrogio Lorenzetti in the Town Hall of Siena.

Wmk. 339
1969, Feb. 13   Engr.   Perf. 14
695 A137 50 l dark blue   .25   .25
696 A137 80 l brown   .25   .25
697 A137 90 l dk blue vio   .25   .25
698 A137 180 l magenta   .25   .25
   Nos. 695-698 (4)   1.00 1.00

Young Soldier, by Bramante — A138

Designs: 90 l, Old Soldier, by Bramante. Designs are from murals in the Pinakotheke of Brear, Milan.

1969, Apr. 28   Photo.   Perf. 14
699 A138 50 l multicolored   .25   .25
700 A138 90 l multicolored   .25   .25

Bramante (1444-1514), Italian architect and painter.

Europa Issue
Common Design Type
1969, Apr. 28   Engr.   Perf. 14x13
Size: 37x27mm
701 CD12 50 l dull green   *.45*   .45
702 CD12 180 l rose claret   *.45*   .45

Charabanc A139

Coaches, 19th Century: 10 l, Barouche. 25 l, Private drag. 40 l, Hansom cab. 50 l, Curricle. 90 l, Wagonette. 180 l, Spider phaeton.

Perf. 14½x14
1969, June 25   Photo.   Unwmk.
703 A139   5 l blk, ocher & dk bl   .25   .25
704 A139 10 l blk, grn & pur   .25   .25
705 A139 25 l dk grn, pink &
             brn   .25   .25
706 A139 40 l ind, lil & lt brn   .25   .25
707 A139 50 l blk, dl yel & dk bl   .25   .25
708 A139 90 l blk, yel grn & brn   .25   .25
709 A139 180 l multi   .25   .25
   Nos. 703-709 (7)   1.75 1.75

Pier at Rimini A140

Paintings by R. Viola: 20 l, Mt. Titano. 200 l, Pier at Riccione, horiz.

1969, Sept. 17   Unwmk.   Perf. 14
710 A140 20 l multicolored   .25   .25
711 A140 180 l multicolored   .25   .25
712 A140 200 l multicolored   .30   .30
   Nos. 710-712 (3)   .80   .80

"Faith" by Raphael — A141

Designs: 180 l, "Hope" by Raphael. 200 l, "Charity" by Raphael.

Perf. 13½x14
1969, Dec. 10   Engr.   Wmk. 339
713 A141   20 l dl pur & sal   .25   .25
714 A141   180 l dl pur & lt grn   .25   .25
715 A141   200 l dp pur & bis   .25   .25
    Nos. 713-715 (3)   .75   .75

Signs of
the Zodiac
A142

Perf. 14x13½
1970, Feb. 18   Photo.   Unwmk.
716 A142   1 l Aries   .25   .25
717 A142   2 l Taurus   .25   .25
718 A142   3 l Gemini   .25   .25
719 A142   4 l Cancer   .25   .25
720 A142   5 l Leo   .25   .25
721 A142   10 l Virgo   .25   .25
722 A142   15 l Libra   .25   .25
723 A142   20 l Scorpio   .25   .25
724 A142   70 l Sagittarius   .25   .25
725 A142   90 l Capricorn   .25   .25
726 A142   100 l Aquarius   .25   .25
727 A142   180 l Pisces   .30   .30
    Nos. 716-727 (12)   3.05   3.05

Fleet in Bay of Naples, by Peter
Brueghel, the Elder — A143

Unwmk.
1970, Apr. 30   Photo.   Perf. 14
728 A143   230 l multi   .40   .40

10th Europa Phil. Exhib., Naples, May 2-10.

Europa Issue
Common Design Type
1970, Apr. 30   Perf. 14x13½
Size: 36x27mm
729 CD13   90 l brt yel grn & red   .45   .25
730 CD13   180 l ocher & red   .45   .30

St. Francis' Gate
and Rotary
Emblem — A144

220 l, Rocca (State Prison) and Rotary
emblem.

1970, June 25   Photo.   Perf. 13½x14
731 A144   180 l multi   .25   .25
732 A144   220 l multi   .45   .45

65th anniv. of Rotary Intl.; 10th anniv. of the
San Marino Rotary Club.

Woman with Mandolin, by
Tiepolo — A145

Paintings by Tiepolo: 180 l, Woman with
Parrot. 220 l, Rinaldo and Armida Surprised,
horiz.

Size: 26½x37½mm
1970, Sept. 10   Unwmk.   Perf. 14
733   50 l multi   .25   .25

---

734   180 l multi   .25   .25

Size: 56x37½mm
735   220 l multi   .25   .25
  a. A145 Strip of 3, #733-735   1.00   1.00

Giambattista Tiepolo (1696-1770), Venetian
painter.

Black
Pete — A146

Walt
Disney and
Jungle
Book
Scene
A147

Disney Characters: 2 l, Gyro Gearloose. 3 l,
Pluto. 4 l, Minnie Mouse. 5 l, Donald Duck.
10 l, Goofy. 15 l, Scrooge McDuck. 50 l, Huey,
Louey and Dewey. 90 l, Mickey Mouse.

Perf. 13x14, 14x13
1970, Dec. 22   Photo.
736 A146   1 l multi   .25   .25
737 A146   2 l multi   .25   .25
738 A146   3 l multi   .25   .25
739 A146   4 l multi   .25   .25
740 A146   5 l multi   .25   .25
741 A146   10 l multi   .25   .25
742 A146   15 l multi   .25   .25
743 A146   50 l multi   .30   .30
744 A146   90 l multi   .75   .75
745 A147   220 l multi   5.25   5.25
    Nos. 736-745 (10)   8.05   8.05

Walt Disney (1901-66), cartoonist & film
maker.

Customhouse Dock, by
Canaletto — A148

Paintings by Canaletto: 180 l, Grand Canal
between Balbi Palace and Rialto Bridge. 200 l,
St. Mark's and Doges' Palace.

1971, Mar. 23   Unwmk.   Perf. 14
746 A148   20 l multi   .25   .25
747 A148   180 l multi   .40   .40
748 A148   200 l multi   .40   .40
    Nos. 746-748 (3)   1.05   1.05

Save Venice campaign.

Europa Issue, 1971
Common Design Type
1971, May 29   Perf. 13½x14
Size: 27½x23mm
749 CD14   50 l org & blue   .25   .25
750 CD14   90 l blue & org   .40   .30

Congress Emblem and Hall, San
Marino Flag — A149

Design: 90 l, Detail from Government Palace door, Congress and San Marino emblems,
vert.

1971, May 29   Photo.   Perf. 12
751 A149   20 l violet & multi   .25   .25
752 A149   90 l olive & multi   .25   .25
753 A149   180 l multi   .25   .25
    Nos. 751-753 (3)   .75   .75

Italian Philatelic Press Union Congress, San
Marino, May 29-30.

Duck-shaped Jug with Flying
Lasa — A150

Etruscan Art, 6th-3rd Centuries B.C.: 80 l,
Head of Mercury, vert. 90 l, Sarcophagus of a
married couple, vert. 180 l, Chimera.

Photo. & Engr.
1971, Sept. 16   Perf. 14
754 A150   50 l blk & org   .25   .25
755 A150   80 l blk & lt grn   .25   .25
756 A150   90 l blk & lt bl   .25   .25
757 A150   180 l blk & org   .35   .35
    Nos. 754-757 (4)   1.10   1.10

Tiger Lily — A151

1971, Dec. 2   Photo.   Perf. 11½
758 A151   1 l shown   .25   .25
759 A151   2 l Phlox   .25   .25
760 A151   3 l Carnations   .25   .25
761 A151   4 l Globe flowers   .25   .25
762 A151   5 l Thistles   .25   .25
763 A151   10 l Peonies   .25   .25
764 A151   15 l Hellebore   .25   .25
765 A151   50 l Anemones   .25   .25
766 A151   90 l Gaillardia   .25   .25
767 A151   220 l Asters   .25   .25
    Nos. 758-767 (10)   2.50   2.50

Venus, by
Botticelli — A152

Details from La Primavera, by Sandro Botticelli: 180 l, Three Graces. 220 l, Spring.

Sizes: 50 l, 220 l, 21x37mm; 180 l, 27x37mm
1972, Feb. 23   Perf. 14, 13x14 (180 l)
768 A152   50 l gold & multi   .25   .25
769 A152   180 l gold & multi   .50   .50
770 A152   220 l gold & multi   .50   .50
    Nos. 768-770 (3)   1.25   1.25

Europa Issue
Common Design Type
1972, Apr. 27   Perf. 11½
Granite Paper
Size: 22½x33mm
771 CD15   50 l org & multi   .30   .25
772 CD15   90 l lt bl & multi   .40   .25

St. Marinus
Taming
Bear
A153

Designs: 55 l, Donna Felicissima asking St.
Marinus for mercy for her sons. 100 l, St.
Marinus turning archers to stone. 130 l,
Felicissima giving mountains to St. Marinus to
establish Republic.

Photo. & Engr.
1972, Apr. 27   Perf. 14
773 A153   25 l dl yel & blk   .25   .25
774 A153   55 l sal pink & blk   .25   .25
775 A153   100 l dl bl & blk   .25   .25
776 A153   130 l citron & blk   .25   .25
    Nos. 773-776 (4)   1.00   1.00

Allegories of San Marino after 16th century
paintings.

Italian House
Sparrow — A154

1972, June 30   Photo.   Perf. 11½
Granite Paper
777 A154   1 l shown   .25   .25
778 A154   2 l Firecrest   .25   .25
779 A154   3 l Blue tit   .25   .25
780 A154   4 l Ortolan bunting   .25   .25
781 A154   5 l White-spotted
    bluethroat   .25   .25
782 A154   10 l Bullfinch   .25   .25
783 A154   25 l Linnet   .25   .25
784 A154   50 l Black-eared
    wheater   .25   .25
785 A154   90 l Sardinian warbler   .25   .25
786 A154   220 l Greenfinch   .25   .25
    Nos. 777-786 (10)   2.50   2.50

Young Man,
Heart,
Emblem — A155

Design: 90 l, Heart disease victim, horiz.

Perf. 13½x14, 14x13½
1972, Aug. 26
787 A155   50 l lt bl & multi   .25   .25
788 A155   90 l ocher & multi   .25   .25

World Heart Month.

Italian Philatelic
Federation
Emblem — A156

1972, Aug. 26   Perf. 13½x14
789 A156   25 l gold & ultra   .25   .25

Honoring veterans of Philately.

5c Coin,
1864
A157

Coins: 10 l, 10c coin, 1935. 15 l, 1 lira, 1906.
20 l, 5 lire, 1898. 25 l, 5 lire, 1937. 50 l, 10 lire,
1932. 55 l, 5 lire, 1938. 220 l, 20 lire, 1925.

1972, Dec. 15   Litho.   Perf. 12½x13
790 A157   5 l gray, blk & brn   .25   .25
791 A157   10 l org, blk & sil   .25   .25
792 A157   15 l brt rose, blk & sil   .25   .25
793 A157   20 l lil, blk & sil   .25   .25
794 A157   25 l vio, blk & sil   .25   .25
795 A157   50 l brt bl, blk & sil   .25   .25

796 A157 55 l ocher, blk & sil .25 .25
797 A157 220 l emer, blk & gold .25 .25
Nos. 790-797 (8) 2.00 2.00

New York, 1673 — A158

300 l, View of New York from East River, 1973.

1973, Mar. 9 Photo. Perf. 11½
Granite Paper
798 200 l bis, och & ol grn .40 .40
799 300 l bl, lil & blk .75 .75
a. A158 Pair, #798-799 1.50 1.50

New York, 300th anniv. Printed checkerwise.

Rotary Press, San Marino Towers — A159

1973, May 10 Photo. Perf. 13x14
800 A159 50 l multi .25 .25

Tourist Press Congress, San Marino.

Gymnasts and Olympic Rings — A160

1973, May 10 Unwmk.
801 A160 100 l grn & multi .25 .25

5th Youth Games.

Europa Issue
Common Design Type

1973, May 10 Perf. 11½
Size: 32½x23mm
802 CD16 20 l salmon & multi .40 .25
803 CD16 180 l lt bl & multi .60 .35

Grapes — A161

1973, July 11 Photo. Perf. 11½
804 A161 1 l shown .25 .25
805 A161 2 l Tangerines .25 .25
806 A161 3 l Apples .25 .25
807 A161 4 l Plums .25 .25
808 A161 5 l Strawberries .25 .25
809 A161 10 l Pears .25 .25
810 A161 25 l Cherries .25 .25
811 A161 50 l Pomegranate .25 .25
812 A161 90 l Apricots .25 .25
813 A161 220 l Peaches .25 .25
Nos. 804-813 (10) 2.50 2.50

Arc-en-Ciel, France — A162

Famous Aircraft: 55 l, Macchi Castoldi, Italy. 60 l, Antonov, USSR. 90 l, Spirit of St. Louis, US. 220 l, Handley Page, Great Britain.

1973, Aug. 31 Photo. Perf. 14x13½
814 A162 25 l ocher, vio bl & gold .25 .25
815 A162 55 l gray, vio bl & gold .25 .25
816 A162 60 l rose, vio bl & gold .25 .25
817 A162 90 l lem, vio bl & gold .25 .25
818 A162 220 l org, vio bl & gold .35 .35
Nos. 814-818 (5) 1.35 1.35

Crossbowman, Serravalle Castle — A163

Designs: 10 l, Crossbowman, Pennarossa Castle. 15 l, Drummer, Montegiardino Castle. 20 l, Trumpeter, Fiorentino Castle. 30 l, Crossbowman, Borga Maggiore Castle. 50 l, Trumpeter, Guaita Castle. 80 l, Crossbowman, Faetano Castle. 200 l, Crossbowman, Montelupo Castle.

1973, Nov. 7 Photo. Perf. 13½
819 A163 5 l black & multi .25 .25
820 A163 10 l black & multi .25 .25
821 A163 15 l black & multi .25 .25
822 A163 20 l black & multi .25 .25
823 A163 30 l black & multi .25 .25
824 A163 40 l black & multi .25 .25
825 A163 50 l black & multi .25 .25
826 A163 80 l black & multi .25 .25
827 A163 200 l black & multi .30 .30
Nos. 819-827 (9) 2.30 2.30

San Marino victories in the Crossbow Tournament, Massa Marittima, July 15, 1973.

Attendants, by Gentile Fabriano — A164

Christmas: Details from Adoration of the Kings, by Gentile Fabriano (1370-1427).

1973, Dec. 19 Photo. Perf. 11½
828 A164 5 l shown .25 .25
829 A164 30 l King .25 .25
830 A164 115 l King .25 .25
831 A164 250 l Horses .30 .30
Nos. 828-831 (4) 1.05 1.05

Shield, 16th Century A165

16th Century Armor: 5 l, Round shield. 10 l, German full armor. 15 l, Helmet with intricate etching. 20 l, Horse's head armor "Massimiliano." 30 l, Decorated helmet with Sphinx statuette on top. 50 l, Pommeled sword and gauntlets. 80 l, Sparrow-beaked helmet. 250 l, Sforza round shield.

Engr. & Litho.
1974, Mar. 12 Perf. 13
832 A165 5 l blk, lt grn & buff .25 .25
833 A165 10 l blk, buff & bl .25 .25
834 A165 15 l blk, bl & ultra .25 .25
835 A165 20 l blk, tan & ultra .25 .25
836 A165 30 l blk & lt bl .25 .25
837 A165 50 l blk, rose & ultra .25 .25
838 A165 80 l blk, gray & grn .25 .25
839 A165 250 l blk & yel .35 .35
Nos. 832-839 (8) 2.10 2.10

Head of Woman, by Emilio Greco — A166

Europa: 200 l, Nude, by Emilio Greco (head shown on 100 l).

Engr. & Litho.
1974, May 9 Perf. 13x14
840 A166 100 l buff & blk .45 .40
841 A166 200 l pale grn & blk .65 .50

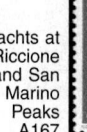

Yachts at Riccione and San Marino Peaks A167

1974, July 18 Photo. Perf. 11½
Granite Paper
842 A167 50 l ultra & multi .25 .25

26th San Marino-Riccione Stamp Day.

Arms of Lucia — A168

Coats of arms of participating cities.

1974, July 18 Perf. 12
843 A168 15 l shown .50 .50
844 A168 20 l Massa Marittima .50 .50
845 A168 50 l San Marino .50 .50
846 A168 115 l Gubbio .75 .75
847 A168 300 l Lucca .75 .75
a. Strip of 5, #843-847 4.00 4.00

9th Crossbow Tournament, San Marino.

UPU Emblem — A169

1974, Oct. 9 Photo. Perf. 11½
Granite Paper
848 A169 50 l multi .25 .25
849 A169 90 l grn & multi .30 .30

Centenary of Universal Postal Union.

Mt. Titano and Hymn by Tommaseo A170

Niccolo Tommaseo A171

1974, Dec. 12 Photo. Perf. 13½x14
850 A170 50 l lt grn, blk & red .30 .30
851 A171 150 l yel, grn & blk .30 .30

Tommaseo (1802-1874), Italian writer.

Virgin and Child, 14th Century Wood Panel — A172

1974, Dec. 12 Perf. 11½
852 A172 250 l gold & multi .50 .50

Christmas.

"Refuge in San Marino" — A173

1975, Feb. 20 Photo. Perf. 13½x14
853 A173 50 l multi .25 .25

Flight of 100,000 refugees from Romagna to San Marino, 30th anniversary.

Musicians, from Leopard Tomb, Tarquinia — A174

Etruscan Art: 30 l, Chariot race, from Tomb on the Hill, Chiusi. 180 l, Achilles and Troilus, from Bulls' Tomb, Tarquinia. 220 l, Dancers, from Triclinium Tomb, Tarquinia.

Litho. & Engr.
1975, Feb. 20 Perf. 14
854 A174 20 l multi .25 .25
855 A174 30 l multi .25 .25
856 A174 180 l multi .25 .25
857 A174 220 l multi .30 .30
Nos. 854-857 (4) 1.05 1.05

Europa Issue

St. Marinus, by Guercino (Francesco Barbieri)
A175   A176

1975, May 14 Photo. Perf. 11½
Granite Paper
858 A175 100 l multi .55 .25
859 A176 200 l multi .75 .35

The Lamentation, by Giotto — A177

Frescoes by Giotto (details): 40 l, Mary and Jesus (Flight into Egypt). 50 l, Heads of four angels (Flight into Egypt). 100 l, Mary Magdalene (Noli Me Tangere), horiz. 500 l, Angel and the elect (Last Judgment), horiz.

1975, July 10   Photo.   Perf. 11½
Granite Paper

860	A177	10 l gold & multi	.25	.25
861	A177	40 l gold & multi	.25	.25
862	A177	50 l gold & multi	.25	.25
863	A177	100 l gold & multi	.25	.25
864	A177	500 l gold & multi	.65	.65
	Nos. 860-864 (5)		1.65	1.65

Holy Year.

Tokyo, 1835, Woodcut by Hiroshige — A178

300 l, Tokyo, Business District, 1975.

1975, Sept. 5   Photo.   Perf. 11½
Granite Paper

865	A178	200 l multi	.35	.35
866	A178	300 l multi	.35	.35
a.	Pair, #865-866		1.10	1.10

Printed checkerwise.

Aphrodite A179

1975, Sept. 19   Photo.   Perf. 11½
867 A179 50 l vio, blk & gray   .30 .30

Europa '75 Philatelic Exhibition, Naples.

Multiple Crosses A180

1975, Sept. 19
868 A180 100 l blk, dp org & vio   .30 .30

EUROCOPHAR Intl. Pharmaceutical Cong.

Christmas — A181

Christmas: Paintings by Michelangelo: 50 l, Angel. 100 l, Head of Virgin. 250 l, Doni Madonna.

1975, Dec. 3   Photo.   Perf. 11½
Granite Paper

869	50 l multi		.25	.25
870	100 l multi		.30	.30
871	250 l multi		.30	.30
a.	A181 Strip of 3, #869-871		1.25	1.25

Woman on Balcony, by Gentilini — A183

Two Women, by Gentilini A184

230 l, Woman (same as right head on 150 l) & IWY emblem, by Franco Gentilini.

1975, Dec. 3   Granite Paper

872	A183	70 l bl & multi	.25	.25
873	A184	150 l multi	.50	.50
874	A183	230 l multi	.50	.50
	Nos. 872-874 (3)		1.25	1.25

International Women's Year.

Modesty, by Emilio Greco — A185

"Civic Virtues": 20 l, Temperance. 50 l, Fortitude. 100 l, Altruism. 150 l, Hope. 220 l, Prudence. 250 l, Justice. 300 l, Faith. 500 l, Honesty. 1000 l, Industry. Designs show drawings of women's heads by Emilio Greco.

1976, Mar. 4   Photo.   Perf. 11½
Granite Paper

875	A185	10 l buff & blk	.25	.25
876	A185	20 l pink & blk	.25	.25
877	A185	50 l grnsh & blk	.25	.25
878	A185	100 l salmon & blk	.25	.25
879	A185	150 l lilac & blk	.25	.25
880	A185	220 l gray & blk	.25	.25
881	A185	250 l yel & multi	.25	.25
882	A185	300 l gray & blk	.30	.30
883	A185	500 l yel & blk	.40	.40
884	A185	1000 l gray & blk	1.00	1.00
	Nos. 875-884 (10)		3.45	3.45

See Nos. 900-905, 931-933.

Capitol, Washington, D.C. — A186

Arms of San Marino and: 150 l, Statue of Liberty. 180 l, Independence Hall, Philadelphia.

1976, May 29   Photo.   Perf. 11½

885	A186	70 l multi	.25	.25
886	A186	150 l multi	.25	.25
887	A186	180 l multi	.30	.30
	Nos. 885-887 (3)		.80	.80

American Bicentennial.

Montreal Olympic Games Emblem A187

1976, May 29
888 A187 150 l crimson & blk   .30 .30

21st Olympic Games, Montreal, Canada, 7/17-8/1.

Decorated Plate — A188

Europa: 180 l, Seal of San Marino.

1976, July 8   Photo.   Perf. 11½
Granite Paper

889	A188	150 l multi	.40	.40
890	A188	180 l bl, sil & blk	.60	.60

"Unity" — A189

1976, July 8   Perf. 13½x14
891 A189 150 l vio blk, yel & red   .25 .25

United Mutual Aid Society, centenary.

"Peaks of San Marino" — A190

1976, Oct. 14   Photo.   Perf. 13x14
892 A190 150 l blk & multi   .30 .30

ITALIA 76 Intl. Phil. Exhib., Milan, 10/14-24.

Children and UNESCO Emblem A191

1976, Oct. 14   Perf. 11½
Granite Paper

893	A191	180 l multi	.25	.25
894	A191	220 l multi	.25	.25

UNESCO, 30th anniv.

Christmas — A192

Design: 150 l, Annunciation (detail), by Titian. 300 l, Virgin and Child, by Titian.

Litho. & Engr.
1976, Dec. 15   Perf. 13x14

895	150 l multi		.30	.30
896	300 l multi		.50	.50
a.	A192 Pair, #895-896		1.00	1.00

Exhibition Emblem A193

1977, Jan. 28   Photo.   Perf. 11½
Granite Paper

897	A193	80 l grn, ol grn & red	.25	.25
898	A193	170 l pur, blue, yel	.25	.25
899	A193	200 l blue, lt bl & org	.30	.30
	Nos. 897-899,C133 (4)		1.10	1.10

San Marino 77 Phil. Exhib.
See No. C133.

Civic Virtues Type of 1976

70 l, Fortitude. 90 l, Prudence. 120 l, Altruism. 160 l, Temperance. 170 l, Hope. 320 l, Faith.

1977, Apr. 14   Photo.   Perf. 11½
Granite Paper

900	A185	70 l pink & blk	.25	.25
901	A185	90 l buff & blk	.25	.25
902	A185	120 l lt bl & blk	.25	.25
903	A185	160 l lt grn & blk	.25	.25
904	A185	170 l cream & blk	.25	.25
905	A185	320 l lil & blk	.35	.35
	Nos. 900-905 (6)		1.60	1.60

San Marino, after Ghirlandaio A194

Europa: 200 l, San Marino, detail from painting by Guercino.

1977, Apr. 14   Granite Paper

906	A194	170 l multi	.50	.35
907	A194	200 l multi	.50	.35

Vertical Flying Machine, by da Vinci — A195

Litho. & Engr.
1977, June 6   Perf. 13x14
908 A195 120 l multi   .30 .30

Centenary of Enrico Forlanini's experiments with vertical flight.

University Square, Bucharest, 1877 — A196

Design: 400 l, National Theater and Intercontinental Hotel, 1977.

1977, June 6   Photo.   *Perf. 11½*
Granite Paper
909   200 l bis & multi   .35 .35
910   400 l lt bl & multi   .50 .50
  a. A196 Pair, #909-910   1.25 1.25
  Centenary of Romanian independence.
Printed checkerwise.

Type A2 of
1877 — A197

1977, June 15   Engr.   *Perf. 15x14½*
911   A197   40 l slate grn   .25 .25
912   A197   70 l deep blue   .25 .25
913   A197   170 l red   .25 .25
914   A197   500 l brown   .40 .40
915   A197   1000 l purple   1.00 1.00
      Nos. 911-915 (5)   2.15 2.15
  Centenary of San Marino stamps.

Souvenir Sheet

St. Marinus, by
Retrosi — A198

1977, Aug. 28   Photo.   *Perf. 11½*
Granite Paper
916   Sheet of 5   9.00 9.00
  a. A198 1000 l single stamp   1.75 1.75
  Centenary of San Marino stamps; San
Marino '77 Phil. Exhib., Aug. 28-Sept. 4.

Medicinal
Plants — A199

1977, Oct. 19   Photo.   *Perf. 11½*
917   A199 170 l multi   .30 .30
  Congress of Italian Pharmacists' Union.
Design shows high mallow, tilia, camomile,
borage, centaury and juniper.

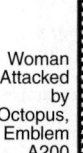

Woman
Attacked
by
Octopus,
Emblem
A200

1977, Oct. 19
918   A200 200 l multi   .30 .30
  World Rheumatism Year.

Virgin
Mary — A201

Christmas: 230 l, Palm, olive and star. 300 l,
Angel.

1977, Dec. 5   Photo.   *Perf. 11½*
919   A201 170 l sil, gray & blk   .25 .25
920   A201 230 l sil, gray & blk   .30 .30
921   A201 300 l sil, gray & blk   .40 .40
  a.   Strip of 3, #919-921   1.10 1.10

San Francisco
Gate — A202

Europa: 200 l, Ripa Gate.

1978, May 30   Photo.   *Perf. 11½*
922   A202 170 l lt bl & dk bl   .50 .40
923   A202 200 l buff & brn   .50 .50

Baseball Player
and
Diamond — A203

1978, May 30
924   A203   90 l multi   .25 .25
925   A203   120 l multi   .25 .25
  World Baseball Championships.

Feather, WHO
Emblem — A204

1978, May 30
926   A204 320 l multi   .50 .50
  Fight against hypertension.

ITU Emblem,
Waves Coming
from 3
Peaks — A205

1978, July 26   Photo.   *Perf. 11½*
927   A205   10 l car & yel   .25 .25
928   A205   200 l vio bl & lt bl   .25 .25
  Membership in ITU.

Seagull and
Falcon, 3
Peaks
A206

1978, July 26
929   A206 120 l multi   .25 .25
930   A206 170 l multi   .30 .30
  30th San Marino-Riccione Stamp Day.

Civic Virtues Type of 1976
  Drawings by Emilio Greco: 5 l, Wisdom. 35 l,
Love. 2000 l, Faithfulness.

1978, Sept. 28   Photo.   *Perf. 11½*
Granite Paper
931   A185   5 l lt vio & blk   .25 .25
932   A185   35 l gray & blk   .25 .25
933   A185   2000 l yel & blk   2.00 2.00
      Nos. 931-933 (3)   2.50 2.50

Christmas
A207

1978, Dec. 6   Photo.   *Perf. 14x13½*
941   A207   10 l Holly leaves   .25 .25
942   A207   120 l Stars   .25 .25
943   A207   170 l Snowflakes   .25 .25
      Nos. 941-943 (3)   .75 .75

Globe and Woman
Holding
Torch — A208

1978, Dec. 6   *Perf. 11½x12*
944   A208 200 l multi   .30 .30
  Universal Declaration of Human Rights,
30th anniversary.

First San
Marino
Autobus,
1915
A209

Europa: 220 l, Mail coach, 1895.

1979, Mar. 29   Photo.   *Perf. 11½x12*
945   A209 170 l multi   1.25 .75
946   A209 220 l multi   1.75 1.00

Albert Einstein (1879-1955),
Theoretical Physicist — A210

1979, Mar. 29   *Perf. 11½*
947   A210 120 l gray, lt & dk brn   .40 .40

San Marino
Crossbow
Federation
Emblem — A211

1979, July 12   Litho.   *Perf. 14x13*
948   A211 120 l multi   .25 .25
  14th Crossbow Tournament.

Maigret — A212

Fictional Detectives: 80 l, Perry Mason. 150
l, Nero Wolfe. 170 l, Ellery Queen. 220 l, Sherlock Holmes.

Litho. & Engr.
1979, July 12   *Perf. 13x14*
949   A212   10 l multi   .25 .25
950   A212   80 l multi   .25 .25
951   A212   150 l multi   .25 .25

952   A212   170 l multi   .25 .25
953   A212   220 l multi   .25 .25
      Nos. 949-953 (5)   1.25 1.25

Girl Holding
Book — A213

  IYC Emblem, Paintings by Marina
Busignani: 120 l, 170 l, 220 l, Children and
birds, diff. 350 l, Mother nursing child.

1979, Sept. 6   Litho.   *Perf. 11½*
954   A213   20 l multi   .25 .25
955   A213   120 l multi   .25 .25
956   A213   170 l multi   .25 .25
957   A213   220 l multi   .25 .25
958   A213   350 l multi   .35 .35
      Nos. 954-958 (5)   1.35 1.35

St. Apollonia, 15th
Century
Woodcut — A214

1979, Sept. 6   Photo.
959   A214 170 l multi   .25 .25
  13th Biennial Intl. Congress of Stomatology.

Waterskier
A215

1979, Sept. 6
960   A215 150 l multi   .25 .25
  European Waterskiing Championship.

Chestnut Tree,
Deer — A216

  Protected Trees and Animals or Birds: 10 l,
Cedar of Lebanon, falcon. 35 l, Dogwood,
racoon. 50 l, Banyan, tiger. 70 l, Umbrella
pine, hoopoe. 90 l, Siberian spruce, marten.
100 l, Eucalyptus, koala bear. 120 l, Date
palm, camel. 150 l, Sugar maple, beaver.
170 l, Adansonia, elephant.

1979, Oct. 25   Photo.   *Perf. 11½*
961   A216   5 l multi   .25 .25
962   A216   10 l multi   .25 .25
963   A216   35 l multi   .25 .25
964   A216   50 l multi   .25 .25
965   A216   70 l multi   .25 .25
966   A216   90 l multi   .25 .25
967   A216   100 l multi   .25 .25
968   A216   120 l multi   .25 .25
969   A216   150 l multi   .25 .25
970   A216   170 l multi   .25 .25
      Nos. 961-970 (10)   2.50 2.50

Holy Family, by Antonio Alberto de Ferrara, 15th Century Fresco A217

Christmas (de Ferrara Fresco): 80 l, St. Joseph. 170 l, Infant Jesus. 220 l, One of the Three Kings.

1979, Dec. 6   Photo.   Perf. 12
971 A217   80 l multi   .25 .25
972 A217 170 l multi   .25 .25
973 A217 220 l multi   .30 .30
974 A217 320 l multi   .50 .50
       Nos. 971-974 (4)   1.30 1.30

Disturbing Muses, by Giorgio de Chirico — A218

1979, Dec.
975 A218   40 l shown   .25 .25
976 A218 150 l Ancient horses   .25 .25
977 A218 170 l Self-portrait   .25 .25
       Nos. 975-977 (3)   .75 .75

Giorgio de Chirico, Italian surrealist painter.

St. Benedict, 15th Century Fresco — A219

Granite Paper
1980, Mar. 27 Photo. Perf. 12x11½
978 A219 170 l multi   .35 .35

St. Benedict of Nursia, 1500th birth anniversary.

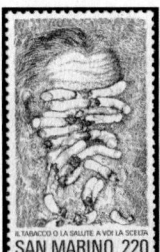

Fight Against Cigarette Smoking — A220

Designs: Sketches of smokers and cigarettes by Giuliana Consilivio.

1980, Mar. 27
979 A220 120 l multi   .25 .25
980 A220 220 l multi   .30 .30
981 A220 520 l multi   .50 .50
       Nos. 979-981 (3)   1.05 1.05

Naples, 17th Century Engraving A221

1980, Mar. 27   Perf. 14x13½
982 A221 170 l multi   .30 .30

20th Intl. Phil. Exhib., Europa '80, Naples, Apr. 26-May 4.

View of London, 1850 — A222

1980, May 8   Perf. 11½x12
983   200 l shown   .30 .30
984   400 l London, 1980   .50 .50
   a. A222 Pair, #983-984   1.25 1.25

London 1980 Intl. Stamp Exhib., May 6-14. Printed checkerwise.
   See Nos. 1001-1002, 1032-1033, 1054-1055, 1069-1070, 1098-1099, 1110-1111, 1141-1142, 1339-1340.

A223

Europa: 170 l, Giovanbattista Belluzzi (1506-54), military architect. 220 l, Antonio Orafo (1460-1552), goldsmith and jeweler.

1980, May 8   Perf. 11½
985 A223 170 l multi   .90 .60
986 A223 220 l multi   1.00 .85

A224

Granite Paper
1980, July 7   Photo.   Perf. 11½
987 A224   70 l Bicycling   .25 .25
988 A224   90 l Basketball   .25 .25
989 A224 170 l Running   .25 .25
990 A224 350 l Gymnast   .35 .35
991 A224 450 l High jump   .55 .55
       Nos. 987-991 (5)   1.65 1.65

22nd Summer Olympic Games, Moscow, July 19-Aug. 3.

Ancient Fortifications A225

Photogravure and Engraved
1980, Sept. 18   Perf. 13½x14
992 A225 220 l multi   .35 .35

World Tourism Conf., Manila, Sept. 27.

Weight Lifting — A226

1980, Sept. 18 Photo.   Perf. 14x13½
993 A226 170 l multi   .30 .30

European Junior Weight Lifting Championship, Sept.

Robert Stolz, "Philatelic Waltz" Score A227

Photo. & Engr.
1980, Sept. 18   Perf. 14
994 A227 120 l lt bl & blk   .30 .30

Robert Stolz (1880-1975) composer.

Madonna of the Harpies, by Andrea Del Sarto — A228

Annunciation by Del Sarto (Details): 250 l, Virgin Mary. 500 l Angel.

1980, Dec. 11   Perf. 13½
995 A228 180 l multi   .30 .30
996 A228 250 l multi   .35 .35
997 A228 500 l multi   .85 .85
       Nos. 995-997 (3)   1.50 1.50

Christmas; 450th death anniv. of Del Sarto.

Europa Issue

St. Joseph's Eve Bonfire — A229

1981, Mar. 24   Photo.   Perf. 12
Granite Paper
998 A229 200 l shown   .55 .40
999 A229 300 l San Marino Day
             fireworks   1.50 .55

Intl. Year of the Disabled — A230

1981, May 15   Photo.   Perf. 11½
Granite Paper
1000 A230 300 l multi   .40 .40

Exhibition Type of 1980
St. Charles' Square, Vienna, by Jakob Alt, 1817.

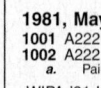

1981, May 15   Granite Paper
1001 A222 200 l shown   .30 .30
1002 A222 300 l Vienna, 1981   .40 .40
   a.   Pair, #1001-1002   1.00 1.00

WIPA '81 Intl. Phil. Exhib., Vienna, 5/22-31.

Woman Playing Flute — A232

Drawings based on Roman sculptures.

1981, July 10   Photo.   Perf. 11½
Granite Paper
1003 A232 300 l shown   .35 .35
1004 A232 550 l Soldier   .60 .60
1005 A232 1500 l Shepherd   1.75 1.70
   a.   Souv. sheet of 3, #1003-1005   4.50 4.50

Virgil's death bimillennium. No. 1005a has continuous design.

Grand Prix Motorcycle Race — A233

1981, July 10   Litho.   Perf. 14x15
1006 A233 200 l multi   .30 .30

Natl. Urban Development Plan (Housing) — A234

1981, Sept. 22   Photo.
Granite Paper
1007 A234 20 l shown   .25 .25
1008 A234 80 l Parks   .25 .25
1009 A234 400 l Energy plants   .40 .40
       Nos. 1007-1009 (3)   .90 .90

European Junior Judo Championship, Oct. 30-Nov. 1 — A235

1981, Sept. 22   Photo.   Perf. 11½
Granite Paper
1010 A235 300 l multi   .40 .40

World Food Day — A236

1981, Oct. 23   Granite Paper
1011 A236 300 l multi   .50 .50

A237

Designs: 150 l, Child Holding a Dove, by Pablo Picasso (1881-1973). 200 l, Homage to Picasso, by Renato Guttuso.

1981, Oct. 23　　　　**Granite Paper**
| 1012 | A237 | 150 l multi | .25 | .25 |
| 1013 | A237 | 200 l multi | .40 | .40 |

A238

Christmas; 500th Birth Anniv. of Benvenuto Tisi da Garofalo (Adoration of the Kings and St. Bartholomew): 200 l, One of the Three Kings with Goblet, by Garafalo. 300 l, King with a Jar. 600 l, Virgin and Child.

Photo. & Engr.
1981, Dec. 15　　　　**Perf. 13½**
1014	A238	200 l multi	.25	.25
1015	A238	300 l multi	.40	.40
1016	A238	600 l multi	.75	.75
		Nos. 1014-1016 (3)	1.40	1.40

Postal Stationery Centenary A239

1982, Feb. 19　　**Photo.**　　**Perf. 12**
| 1017 | A239 | 200 l multi | | .30 | .30 |

Savings Bank Centenary A240

1982, Feb. 19
| 1018 | A240 | 300 l multi | | .40 | .40 |

Europa 1982 — A241

Designs: 300 l, Convocation of the Assembly of Heads of Families, 1906. 450 l, Napoleons's Treaty of Friendship offer, 1797.

1982, Apr. 21　　**Photo.**　　**Perf. 11½**
Granite Paper
| 1019 | A241 | 300 l multi | 2.00 | 1.25 |
| 1020 | A241 | 450 l multi | 3.25 | 1.50 |

Archimedes — A242

1982, Apr. 21　**Photo.**　**Perf. 14x13½**
1021	A242	20 l shown	.25	.25
1022	A242	30 l Copernicus	.25	.25
1023	A242	40 l Newton	.25	.25
1024	A242	50 l Lavoisier	.25	.25
1025	A242	60 l Marie Curie	.25	.25
1026	A242	100 l Robert Koch	.25	.25

Litho. & Engr.
1027	A242	200 l Thomas Edison	.25	.25
1028	A242	300 l Guglielmo Marconi	.25	.25
1029	A242	450 l Hippocrates	.45	.45

Engr.
| 1030 | A242 | 5000 l Galileo | 5.00 | 5.00 |
| | | Nos. 1021-1030 (10) | 7.45 | 7.45 |

See Nos. 1041-1046.

800th Birth Anniv. of St. Francis of Assisi — A243

1982, June 10　　　　　**Photo.**
| 1031 | A243 | 200 l multi | | .30 | .30 |

Exhibition Type of 1980
1982, June 10
1032	A222	300 l Notre Dame, 1806	.35	.35
1033	A222	450 l 1982	.55	.55
a.		Pair, #1032-1033	1.25	1.25

PHILEXFRANCE '82 Stamp Exhibition, Paris, June 11-21.

Visit of Pope John Paul II — A245

1982, Aug. 29　**Litho.**　**Perf. 13½x14**
| 1034 | A245 | 900 l multi | 1.10 | 1.10 |

Natl. Flags of ASCAT Members — A246

Granite Paper
1982, Sept. 1　　**Photo.**　　**Perf. 11½**
| 1035 | A246 | 300 l multi | .40 | .40 |

Inaugural Meeting of ASCAT (Assoc. of Editors of Philatelic Catalogues), 1977.

A247

1982, Sept. 1　　　　　　**Unwmk.**
| 1036 | A247 | 700 l blk & red | .85 | .85 |

15th Amnesty Intl. Congress, Rimini, Italy, Sept. 9-15.

A248

Christmas: Paintings by Gregorio Sciltian (1900-85).

Photo. & Engr.
1982, Dec. 15　　　　**Perf. 13½**
1037	A248	200 l Angel	.30	.30
1038	A248	400 l Virgin and Child	.40	.40
1039	A248	450 l Angel, diff.	.55	.55
		Nos. 1037-1039 (3)	1.25	1.25

Secondary School Centenary A249

1983, Feb. 24　**Photo.**　**Perf. 13½x14**
| 1040 | A249 | 300 l Begni Building | .45 | .45 |

Scientist Type of 1982

150 l, Alexander Fleming. 250 l, Alessandro Volta. 350 l, Evangelista Torricelli. 400 l, Carolus Linnaeus. 1000 l, Pythagoras. 1400 l, Leonardo da Vinci.

1983, Apr. 21　　　　**Perf. 14x13½**
1041	A242	150 l multi	.25	.25
1042	A242	250 l multi	.30	.30
1043	A242	350 l multi	.35	.35
1044	A242	400 l multi	.50	.50
1045	A242	1000 l multi	1.00	1.00
1046	A242	1400 l multi	1.50	1.50
		Nos. 1041-1046 (6)	3.90	3.90

3rd Formula One Grand Prix A250

1983, Apr. 20　**Photo.**　**Perf. 14x13½**
| 1047 | A250 | 50 l multi | .25 | .25 |
| 1048 | A250 | 350 l multi | .70 | .70 |

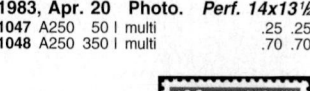

Auguste Piccard — A251

1983, Apr. 20　　　　**Perf. 12x11½**
Granite Paper
| 1049 | A251 | 400 l Aerostat | 1.75 | 1.10 |
| 1050 | A251 | 500 l Bathyscaph | 2.50 | 1.75 |

Europa. Piccard (1884-1962), Swiss scientist.

World Communications Year — A252

1983, Apr. 28　　**Engr.**　　**Perf. 14x13**
| 1051 | A252 | 400 l Ham radio operator | .65 | .65 |
| 1052 | A252 | 500 l Mailman | .80 | .80 |

Manned Flight Bicentenary A253

Lithographed and Engraved
1983, May 22　　　　**Perf. 13½x14**
| 1053 | A253 | 500 l Montgolfiere, 1783 | .65 | .65 |

Exhibition Type of 1980

Designs: Botafogo Bay and Monte Corcovado, Rio de Janeiro.

1983, July 29　**Photo.**　**Perf. 11½x12**
Granite Paper
1054	A222	400 l 1845	.40	.40
1055	A222	1400 l 1983	1.50	1.50
a.		Pair, #1054-1055	2.75	2.75

BRASILIANA '83 Intl. Stamp Show, Rio de Janeiro, July 29-Aug. 7.

20th Anniv. of World Food Program A255

1983, Sept. 29　**Photo.**　**Perf. 14x13½**
| 1056 | A255 | 500 l multi | | .70 | .70 |

Christmas A256

Paintings, Raphael (1483-1520): 300 l, Our Lady of the Grand Duke. 400 l, Our Lady of the Goldfinch. 500 l, Our Lady of the Chair.

Photo. & Engr.
1983, Dec. 1　　　　**Perf. 13½**
1057	A256	300 l multi	.35	.35
1058	A256	400 l multi	.45	.45
1059	A256	500 l multi	.65	.65
a.		Strip of 3, #1057-1059	2.00	2.00

Olympic Type of 1959

IOC Presidents: 300 l, Demetrius Vikelas, 1894-96. 400 l, Lord Killanin. 550 l, Antonio Samaranch, 1984.

1984, Feb. 8　**Photo.**　**Perf. 14x13½**
1060	A86	300 l multi	.45	.45
1061	A86	400 l multi	.55	.55
1062	A86	550 l multi	1.00	1.00
		Nos. 1060-1062 (3)	2.00	2.00

Flag-wavers
Group, 2nd
Anniv. — A257

Litho. & Engr.

1984, Apr. 27   *Perf. 13x14*
1063 A257 300 l Flag   .40 .40
1064 A257 400 l Flags   .60 .60

Europa
(1959-1984)
A258

1984, Apr. 27   Photo.   *Perf. 11½*
Granite Paper
1065 A258 400 l multi   1.75 1.00
1066 A258 550 l multi   2.50 1.50

A259

1984, June 14   Photo.   *Perf. 13½x14*
1067 A259 450 l multi   .70 .70

Motorcross Grand Prix, Baldasserona.

Souvenir Sheet

A260

1984, June 14   Litho.   *Perf. 13x14*
1068   Sheet of 2   3.00 3.00
a. A260 550 l Man   .60   .60
b. A260 1000 l Woman   1.20 1.20

1984 Summer Olympics.

Exhibition Type of 1980

Ausipex '84: Views of Melbourne. Se-tenant.

1984, Sept. 21   Photo.   *Perf. 11½*
Granite Paper
1069 A222 1500 l 1839   1.75 1.75
1070 A222 2000 l 1984   2.25 2.25
a.   Pair, #1069-1070   4.75 4.75

Visit of
Italian Pres.
Pertini
A262

1984, Oct. 20   Photo.   *Perf. 14x13½*
1071 A262 1950 l multi   2.75 2.75

School and
Philately — A263

Sketches by Jacovitti.

1984, Oct. 30   *Perf. 13½x14*
1072 A263   50 l Universe   .25   .25
1073 A263 100 l Evolution   .25   .25
1074 A263 150 l Environment   .25   .25
1075 A263 200 l Mankind   .25   .25
1076 A263 450 l Science   .55   .55
1077 A263 550 l Philosophy   .65   .65
        Nos. 1072-1077 (6)   2.20 2.20

Christmas — A264

Details of Madonna of San Girolamo by Correggio, 1527.

1984, Dec. 5   Litho.   *Perf. 13½x14*
1078   400 l multi   .55   .55
1079   450 l multi   .75   .75
1080   550 l multi   .85   .85
a. A264 Strip of 3, #1078-1080   2.75 2.75

Composers and
Music — A265

Europa: 450 l, Johann Sebastian Bach (1685-1750), Toccata and Fugue. 600 l, Vincenzo Bellini (1801-1835), Norma.

1985, Mar. 18   Photo.   *Perf. 12*
1081 A265 450 l ocher & gray blk *1.75* .90
1082 A265 600 l yel grn & gray
                   blk   2.25 1.40

Olympiad of the
Small States, May
23-26 — A266

Sportphilex '85: Natl. Olympic Committee and Sportphilex '85 emblems, flags of Andorra, Cyprus, Iceland, Liechtenstein, Luxembourg, Malta, Monaco, San Marino.

1985, May 16   Litho.   *Perf. 13½x14*
1083 A266   50 l Diving   .25   .25
1084 A266 350 l Running   .45   .45
1085 A266 400 l Rifle shooting   .55   .55
1086 A266 450 l Cycling   .60   .60
1087 A266 600 l Basketball   .90   .90
        Nos. 1083-1087 (5)   2.75 2.75

Emigration
A267

1985, May 16
1088 A267 600 l Birds migrating   1.00 1.00

Intl. Youth
Year — A268

1985, June 24   Photo.   *Perf. 12*
Granite Paper
1089 A268 400 l Boy, dove   .50   .50
1090 A268 600 l Girl, dove, horse 1.00 1.00

Helsinki
Conference, 10th
Anniv. — A269

1985, June 24   *Perf. 13½x14*
1091 A269 600 l Sapling, sun-
                   burst, clouds   .80   .80

City Hall, by
Renzo Bonelli,
Camera
Lens. — A270

1985, June 24   *Perf. 13½x14½*
1092 A270 450 l multi   .75   .75

Intl. Fed. of Photographic Art, 18th Congress.

World Angling
Championships,
Arno River,
Florence, Sept.
14-15 — A271

1985, Sept. 11   Photo.   *Perf. 14½x15*
1093 A271 600 l Hooked fish   1.00 1.00

Alessandro Manzoni (1785-1873),
Novelist & Poet — A272

19th century engravings from Manzoni's I Promessi Sposi (1825-27): 400 l, Don Abbondio encounters Don Rodrigo's henchmen. 450 l, The attempt to force the curate to perform a dubious marriage ceremony. 600 l, The Plague at Milan.

1985, Sept. 11   Engr.   *Perf. 14x13½*
1094 A272 400 l multi   .50   .50
1095 A272 450 l multi   .60   .60
1096 A272 600 l multi   .90   .90
        Nos. 1094-1096 (3)   2.00 2.00

Intl. Feline
Fed.
Congress
A273

Mosaic detail: Cat, Natl. Museum, Naples.

1985, Oct. 25   Photo.   *Perf. 12*
Granite Paper
1097 A273 600 l multi   1.00 1.00

Exhibition Type of 1980

ITALIA '85: Views of the Colosseum, Rome.

1985, Oct. 25   *Perf. 11½x12*
Granite Paper
1098 A222 1000 l multi   1.10 1.10
1099 A222 1500 l multi   1.90 1.90
a.   Pair, #1098-1099   4.00 4.00

Christmas
A275

Photo. & Engr.

1985, Dec. 3   *Perf. 14*
1100 A275 400 l Angel   .80   .80
1101 A275 450 l Mother and
                   Child   1.25 1.25
1102 A275 600 l Angel, diff.   1.50 1.50
a.   Strip of 3, #1100-1102   4.25 4.25

Hospital,
Cailungo
A276

1986, Mar. 6   Photo.   *Perf. 12x11½*
1103 A276 450 l multi   .60   .60
1104 A276 650 l multi   .85   .85

Natl. social security org., ISS, 30th anniv., and World Health Day.

Halley's
Comet — A277

Designs: 550 l, Giotto space probe. 1000 l, Adoration of the Magi, by Giotto (1276-1337).

1986, Mar. 6   *Perf. 11½x12*
1105 A277 550 l multi   1.00 1.00
1106 A277 1000 l multi   1.50 1.50

Europa Issue

Deer — A278

1986, May 22   Photo.   Perf. 13½x14
1107 A278 550 l shown   8.50 7.00
1108 A278 650 l Falcon   10.00 8.00

3rd Veterans World Table Tennis Championships A279

1986, May 22   Engr.
1109 A279 450 l multicolored   .80   .80

AMERIPEX '86, Chicago, May 22-June 1 — A280

Views of Old Water Tower, Chicago: 2000 l, Lithograph, 1870, by Charles Shober. 3000 l, Photograph, 1986.

Perf. 11½x12
1986, May 22   Photo.   Unwmk.
1110   2000 l multi   2.25 2.25
1111   3000 l multi   3.25 3.25
  a.   A280 Pair, #1110-1111   7.00 7.00

Intl. Peace Year — A281

1986, July 10   Photo.   Perf. 11½x12
1112 A281 550 l multi   .75   .75

Souvenir Sheet

Terra Cotta Statuary, Tomb of Emperor Qin Shi Huang Di (259-210 B.C.) — A282

Litho. & Engr.
1986, July 10   Perf. 13½
1113 A282   Sheet of 3   5.00 5.00
  a.   550 l Bearded man   .90   .90
  b.   650 l Horse, horiz.   1.25 1.25
  c.   2000 l Bearded man, diff.   2.00 2.00

Normalization of diplomatic relations with the People's Republic of China, 15th anniv.

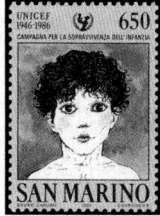

UNICEF, 40th Anniv. — A283

1986, Sept 16   Photo.   Perf. 12
1114 A283 650 l multi   .90   .90

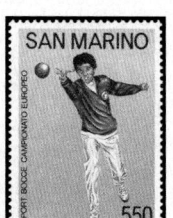

European Boccie Championships A284

1986, Sept. 16   Perf. 14x15
1115 A284 550 l multi   .75   .75

Choral Society, 25th Anniv. — A285

Painting (detail): Apollo Dancing with the Muses, by Giulio Romano (1492-1546).

1986, Sept. 16
1116 A285 450 l multi   .70   .70

Christmas A286

Design: Oil on wood triptych, 15th cent., by Hans Memling (1435-1494), Kunsthistorisches Museum, Vienna.

Photo. & Engr.
1986, Nov. 26   Perf. 14
1117 A286 450 l St. John the
                  Baptist   .85   .85
1118 A286 550 l Virgin and Child   1.00 1.00
1119 A286 650 l St. John the
                  Evangelist   1.25 1.25
  a.   Strip of 3, #1117-1119   3.75 3.75

Europa Issue

Our Lady of Consolation Church, Borgomaggiore A287

Church designed by Giovanni Michelucci, architect: 600 l, Architect's sketch of interior. 700 l, Actual interior.

1987, Mar. 12   Photo.   Perf. 12
1120 A287 600 l multi   7.50 4.00
1121 A287 700 l multi   10.00 5.00

Motoring Events A288

Designs: 500 l, 80th anniv., Peking-Paris Race. 600 l, 15th San Marino Rally. 700 l, Mille Miglia Race, 60th anniv.

1987, Mar. 12   Perf. 11½
1122 A288 500 l multi   .70   .70
1123 A288 600 l multi   .85   .85
1124 A288 700 l multi   1.00 1.00
       Nos. 1122-1124 (3)   2.55 2.55

Sculptures, Open-air Museum — A289

Perf. 14½x13½
1987, June 13   Photo.
1125 A289   50 l Reffi
                  Busignani   .25   .25
1126 A289   100 l Bini   .25   .25
1127 A289   200 l Guguianu   .30   .30
1128 A289   300 l Berti   .50   .50
1129 A289   400 l Crocetti   .60   .60
1130 A289   500 l Berti, diff.   .80   .80
1131 A289   600 l Messina   1.00 1.00
1132 A289 1000 l Minguzzi   1.25 1.25
1133 A289 2200 l Greco   3.25 3.25
1134 A289 10000 l Sassu   15.00 15.00
       Nos. 1125-1134 (10)   23.20 23.20

Seventh Natl. Art Biennale — A290

Abstract works: 500 l, Dal Diario del Brasile-foresta Vergine, by Emilio Vedova. 600 l, Invenzione Cromatica con Brio, by Corrado Cagli.

Granite Paper
1987, June 13   Perf. 11½
1135 A290 500 l multi   .70   .70
1136 A290 600 l multi   .80   .80

Air Club of San Marino Ultra-lightweight Aircraft — A291

1987, June 13   Granite Paper
1137 A291 600 l multi   1.00 1.00

Mahatma Gandhi A292

1987, Aug. 2   Photo.   Perf. 14x13½
1138 A292 500 l Gandhi Square,
                  bust   .85   .85

Olympic Emblem, Athlete — A293

1987, Aug. 29   Perf. 12
Granite Paper
1139 A293 600 l multi   1.00 1.00
       OLYMPHILEX '87, Rome.

A294

1987, Aug. 29   Granite Paper
1140 A294 700 l ultra, blk & red   1.10 1.10

First Representation of San Marino at the Mediterranean Games, Syria, Sept. 11-15.

Exhibition Type of 1980

HAFNIA '87: Views of Copenhagen (1836-1986), as seen from the Round Tower.

1987, Oct. 16   Photo.   Perf. 11½x12
Granite Paper
1141 A222 1200 l multi   1.90 1.90
1142 A222 2200 l multi, diff.   2.75 2.75
  a.   Pair, #1141-1142   6.00 6.00

Christmas A296

Details from Triptych of Cortona and The Annunciation, by Fra Angelico (c. 1400-1455), Diocesan Museum of Cortona: No. 1143, Angel. No. 1144, Madonna and child. No. 1145, Saint. Printed se-tenant.

Photo. & Engr.
1987, Nov. 12   Perf. 13½
1143 A296 600 l multi   1.10 1.10
1144 A296 600 l multi   1.10 1.10
1145 A296 600 l multi   1.10 1.10
  a.   Strip of 3, #1143-1145   4.25 4.25

High Speed Train — A297

Europa Issue 1988
Granite Paper

1988, Mar. 17   Photo.   Perf. 12
1146 A297 600 l shown   5.00 3.50
1147 A297 700 l Fiber optics   6.50 4.00

Promote
Stamp
Collecting
A298

Stamps, cancellations, covers: 50 l, Nos. 81, B25 and 859. 150 l, No. C11. 300 l, Nos. 349 and 1006. 350 l, Nos. 944 and 1031. 1000 l, Nos. 303, 1081 and 308.

1988, Mar. 17   Perf. 11½
Granite Paper
1148	A298	50 l multi	.25	.25
1149	A298	150 l multi	.25	.25
1150	A298	300 l multi	.45	.45
1151	A298	350 l multi	.60	.60
1152	A298	1000 l multi	1.50	1.50
		Nos. 1148-1152 (5)	3.05	3.05

See Nos. 1179-1183, 1225-1229.

A299

Historic sites and distinguished professors: 550 l, Carlo Malagola. 650 l, Pietro Ellero. 1300 l, Giosue Carducci (1835-1907), professor of literary history, 1861-1904, and Nobel Prize winner for literature, 1906. 1700 l, Giovanni Pascoli (1855-1912), lyric poet, Pascoli's successor as professor at Bologna.

1988, May 7   Photo.   Perf. 13½x14
1153	A299	550 l multi	.75	.75
1154	A299	650 l multi	.90	.90
1155	A299	1300 l multi	1.60	1.60
1156	A299	1700 l multi	2.25	2.25
		Nos. 1153-1156 (4)	5.50	5.50

Bologna University, 900th anniv.

A300

Posters from Fellini Films: 300 l, La Strada. 900 l, La Dolce Vita. 1200 l, Amarcord.

1988, July 8   Photo.   Perf. 13½x14
1157	A300	300 l multi	.40	.40
1158	A300	900 l multi	1.25	1.25
1159	A300	1200 l multi	1.75	1.75
		Nos. 1157-1159 (3)	3.40	3.40

Federico Fellini, Italian film director and winner of the 1988 San Marino Prize.
See Nos. 1187-1189, 1202-1204.

Mt. Titano and Sand Dunes of the Adriatic Coast
A301

1988, July 8   Perf. 14x13½
| 1160 | A301 | 750 l multi | 1.00 | 1.00 |

40th Stamp Fair, Riccione.

Souvenir Sheet

1988 Summer Olympics, Seoul — A302

1988, Sept. 19 Photo. Perf. 13½x14
1161	A302	Sheet of 3	3.75	3.75
a.		650 l Running	.80	.80
b.		750 l Hurdles	.90	.90
c.		1300 l Gymnastics	1.25	1.25

Intl. AIDS Congress, San Marino, Oct. 10-14
A303

1988, Sept. 19   Perf. 14x13½
1162	A303	250 l shown	.45	.45
1163	A303	350 l "AIDS"	.55	.55
1164	A303	650 l Virus, knot	1.00	1.00
1165	A303	1000 l Newspaper	1.60	1.60
		Nos. 1162-1165 (4)	3.60	3.60

Kurhaus Scheveningen, The Hague — A304

1988, Oct. 18   Photo.   Perf. 11½x12
Granite Paper
1166		1600 l Lithograph, c. 1885	2.25	2.25
1167		3000 l 1988	4.25	4.25
a.	A304	Pair, #1166-1167	7.25	7.25

FILACEPT '88, Holland.
See Nos. 1190-1191.

Christmas — A305

Paintings by Melozzo da Forli (1438-1494): No. 1168, Angel with Violin, Vatican Art Gallery. No. 1169, Angel of the Annunciation, Uffizi Gallery, Florence. No. 1170, Angel with Lute, Vatican Art Gallery.

1988, Dec. 9   Photo.   Perf. 13½
Size of No. 1169: 21x40mm
1168		650 l multi	1.25	1.25
1169		650 l multi	1.25	1.25
1170		650 l multi	1.25	1.25
a.	A305	Strip of 3, #1168-1168	4.50	4.50

Europa Issue
Souvenir Sheet

Children's Games — A306

1989, Mar. 31 Photo.   Perf. 13½x14
1171		Sheet of 2	18.00	15.00
a.	A306	650 l Sledding	5.00	5.00
b.	A306	750 l Hopscotch	5.00	5.00

Nature Conservation — A307

Illustrations by contest-winning youth: 200 l, Federica Sparagna. 500 l, Giovanni Monteduro. 650 l, Rosa Mannarino.

1989, Mar. 31   Perf. 14x13½
1172	A307	200 l multi	.35	.35
1173	A307	500 l multi	.75	.75
1174	A307	650 l multi	.90	.90
		Nos. 1172-1174 (3)	2.00	2.00

Sporting Anniversaries and Events — A308

1989, May 13   Photo.   Perf. 12
Granite Paper
1175	A308	650 l Olympics	.80	.80
1176	A308	750 l Soccer	.90	.90
1177	A308	850 l Tennis	1.00	1.00
1178	A308	1300 l Car racing	1.50	1.50
		Nos. 1175-1178 (4)	4.20	4.20

Natl. Olympic Committee, 30th anniv. (650 l); admission of San Marino Soccer Federation to the UEFA and FIFA (750 l); San Marino '89, the tennis grand prix (850 l); Grand Prix of San Marino, Imola (1300 l).

Stamp Collecting Type of 1988
Covers and canceled stamps (postal history): 100 l, No. 916a with Iserravalle cancel, Sept. 1, 1977. 200 l, No. 1151 with Montegiardino cancel, May 3, 1986. 400 l, Italy No. 47 canceled on San Marino parcel card #422, 1895. 500 l, Type SP3 essay proposed by Martin Riester di Parigi, March 1865. 1000 l, Stampless cover, 1862.

1989, May 13   Perf. 12
Granite Paper
1179	A298	100 l multi	.30	.30
1180	A298	200 l multi	.40	.40
1181	A298	400 l multi	.60	.60
1182	A298	500 l multi	.90	.90
1183	A298	1000 l multi	1.25	1.25
		Nos. 1179-1183 (5)	3.45	3.45

French Revolution, Bicent. — A309

700 l, The Tennis Court Oath. 1000 l, Arrest of Louis XVI. 1800 l, Napoleon.

1989, July 7   Litho.   Perf. 12½x13
1184	A309	700 l multicolored	.90	.90
1185	A309	1000 l multicolored	1.50	1.50
1186	A309	1800 l multicolored	1.75	1.75
		Nos. 1184-1186 (3)	4.15	4.15

Show Business Type of 1988
Scenes from: 1200 l, Marguerite et Armand. 1500 l, Apollon Musagete. 1700 l, Valentino.

1989, Sept. 18 Photo. Perf. 13½x14
1187	A300	1200 l multi	1.50	1.50
1188	A300	1500 l multi	2.00	2.00
1189	A300	1700 l multi	2.50	2.50
		Nos. 1187-1189 (3)	6.00	6.00

Rudolf Nureyev, Russian ballet dancer and winner of the 1989 San Marino Prize.

Exhibition Type of 1988
Views of The Capitol, Washington, DC.: 2000 l, In 1850. 2500 l, In 1989.

1989, Nov. 17   Photo.   Perf. 11½
Granite Paper
1190	A304	2000 l multi	2.50	2.50
1191	A304	2500 l multi	3.25	3.25
a.		Pair, #1190-1191	7.00	7.00

World Stamp Expo '89.

A310

Christmas: Panels from a Polyptych, c. 1540, by Coda Studio of Rimini, in the Church of the Servants of Mary, Valdragone.

Size of No. 1193: 50x40mm

1989, Nov. 17   Granite Paper
1192		650 l Angel	1.00	1.00
1193		650 l Holy family	1.00	1.00
1194		650 l Praying Madonna	1.00	1.00
a.	A310	Strip of 3, #1192-1194	3.75	3.75

Palazzeto delle Poste, 1842 — A311

Europa — Post offices: 800 l, Dogana.

1990, Feb. 22 Photo. Perf. 13½x14
| 1195 | A311 | 700 l multicolored | 1.50 | 1.10 |
| 1196 | A311 | 800 l multicolored | 2.00 | 1.40 |

A312

Design: The Martyrdom of Saint Agatha, by Giambattista Tiepolo, and occupation force departing by the Porta del Loco.

1990, Feb. 22   Perf. 12
Granite Paper
| 1197 | A312 | 3500 l multicolored | 6.25 | 5.00 |

Liberation from Cardinal Alberoni's occupation force, 250th anniv.

A313

European Tourism Year: No. 1198, The republic pinpointed on a map of Italy. No. 1199, San Marino atop Mt. Titano in proximity to other cities in the region. No. 1200, Rocca Guaita, San Marino.

1990, Mar. 23 Photo. *Perf. 11½x12*
Granite Paper
1198	A313	600 l	shown	.75 .75
1199	A313	600 l	multicolored	.75 .75
1200	A313	600 l	multicolored	.75 .75
		Nos. 1198-1200 (3)		2.25 2.25

See Nos. 1209a, 1260-1262.

Souvenir Sheet

1990 World Cup Soccer
Championships, Italy — A314

Various athletes: a, Germany. b, Italy. c, Great Britain. d, Uruguay. e, Brazil. f, Argentina.

1990, Mar. 23 *Perf. 13½x14*
1201	A314	Sheet of 6	6.25 6.25
a.-f.		700 l any single	.80 .80

Show Business Type of 1988
Scenes from: 600 l, *Hamlet.* 700 l, *Richard III.* 1500 l, *Marathon Man.*

1990, May 3 Photo. *Perf. 13½x14*
1202	A300	600 l	multi	1.00 1.00
1203	A300	700 l	multi	1.25 1.25
1204	A300	1500 l	multi	2.75 2.75
		Nos. 1202-1204 (3)		5.00 5.00

Sir Laurence Olivier (1907-1989), British actor, winner of the 1990 San Marino Prize. Name misspelled "Lawrence" on the stamps.

President
of Italy,
State Visit
A315

1990, June 11 Litho. *Perf. 13x12½*
1205	A315	600 l	multicolored	.90 .90

Statue of Saint
Marinus — A316

No. 1207, Liberty statue. No. 1208, Government Palace. No. 1209, Flag of San Marino.
Granite Paper
Booklet Stamps
1990, June 11 Photo. *Perf. 11½*
1206	A316	50 l	multicolored	.25 .25
1207	A316	50 l	multicolored	.25 .25
1208	A316	50 l	multicolored	.25 .25

1209	A316	50 l	multicolored	.25 .25
a.		Bklt. pane of 7, #1198-1200, perf. 11½ vert., #1206-1209		4.00
		Nos. 1206-1209 (4)		1.00 1.00

See Nos. 1256-1259.

Discovery
of America,
500th
Anniv. (in
1992)
A317

1990, Sept. 6 Litho. *Perf. 13x12½*
1210	A317	1500 l	Artifacts, map	2.25 2.25
1211	A317	2000 l	Native plants, map	3.00 3.00

See Nos. 1230-1231.

Pinocchio, by
Carlo Collodi
(1826-1890)
A318

Cartoon style drawings from Pinocchio.

1990, Sept. 6 Photo. *Perf. 11½x12*
Granite Paper
1212	A318	250 l	shown	.40 .40
1213	A318	400 l	Geppetto	.55 .55
1214	A318	450 l	Blue fairy	.60 .60
1215	A318	600 l	Cat & wolf	1.25 1.25
		Nos. 1212-1215 (4)		2.80 2.80

Flora and
Fauna — A319

Designs: 200 l, Papilio machaon, Ephedra major. 300 l, Apoderus coryli, Corylus avellana. 500 l, Eliomys quercinus, Quercus ilex. 1000 l, Lacerta viridis, Ophrys bertolonii. 2000 l, Regulus ignicapillus, Pinus nigra.

1990, Oct. 31 Photo. *Perf. 14x13½*
1216	A319	200 l	multicolored	.30 .30
1217	A319	300 l	multicolored	.50 .50
1218	A319	500 l	multicolored	.90 .90
1219	A319	1000 l	multicolored	1.50 1.50
1220	A319	2000 l	multicolored	2.75 2.75
		Nos. 1216-1220 (5)		5.95 5.95

A320

Christmas: Cuciniello Crib, San Martino Museum of Naples.

1990, Oct. 31 *Perf. 11½*
Granite Paper
1221	750 l	shown	1.25 1.25
1222	750 l	Nativity, diff.	1.25 1.25
a.	A320	Pair, #1221-1222	3.25 3.25

A321

1991, Feb. 12 Photo. *Perf. 13½x14*
1223	A321	750 l	Ariane 4 rocket	3.75 3.75
1224	A321	800 l	ERS-1 satellite	3.75 3.75

Europa.

Stamp Collecting Type of 1988
Areas of philately: 100 l, Stamp store. 150 l, Clubs. 200 l, Exhibitions. 450 l, Albums, catalogues. 1500 l, Magazines, books.

1991, Feb. 12 *Perf. 12*
Granite Paper
1225	A298	100 l	multicolored	.25 .25
1226	A298	150 l	multicolored	.25 .25
1227	A298	200 l	multicolored	.35 .35
1228	A298	450 l	multicolored	.75 .75
1229	A298	1500 l	multicolored	2.00 2.00
		Nos. 1225-1229 (5)		3.60 3.60

Italian Philatelic Press Union, 25th anniv. (No. 1229).

Discovery of America Type
750 l, Map, instruments. 3000 l, Columbus' fleet.

1991, Mar. 22 Litho. *Perf. 13x12½*
1230	A317	750 l	multicolored	1.25 1.25
1231	A317	3000 l	multicolored	4.75 4.75

1992
Summer
Olympics,
Barcelona
A323

Olympic torch relay.

1991, Mar. 22 *Perf. 15x14*
1232	A323	400 l	Athens	.60 .60
1233	A323	600 l	San Marino	.80 .80
1234	A323	2000 l	Barcelona	3.00 3.00
		Nos. 1232-1234 (3)		4.40 4.40

Basketball,
Cent. — A324

Designs: 750 l, James Naismith (1861-1939), creator of basketball, players.

1991, June 4 Photo. *Perf. 13½x14*
1235	A324	650 l	multicolored	1.00 1.00
1236	A324	750 l	multicolored	1.25 1.25

Fauna — A325

500 l, House cat. 550 l, Hamster on wheel. 750 l, Great Dane, poodle. 1000 l, Tropical fish. 1200 l, Birds in cage.

1991, June 4 *Perf. 14x13½*
1237	A325	500 l	multi	.75 .75
1238	A325	550 l	multi	.80 .80
1239	A325	750 l	multi	1.10 1.10
1240	A325	1000 l	multi	1.50 1.50
1241	A325	1200 l	multi	1.75 1.75
		Nos. 1237-1241 (5)		5.90 5.90

Children's Day.
See Nos. 1251-1255.

James Clerk Maxwell (1831-1879),
Physicist — A326

1991, Sept. 24 Photo. *Perf. 14x13½*
1242	A326	750 l	multicolored	1.00 1.00

Radio, cent. (in 1995).
See Nos. 1263, 1279, 1300.

Souvenir Sheet

Birth of New Europe — A327

Designs: No. 1243a, Dove, broken chains, Brandenburg Gate. b, Pres. Gorbachev, rainbow, Pres. Bush. c, Flower, broken barbed wire, map.

1991, Sept. 24 *Litho.*
1243	A327	1500 l	Sheet of 3, #a.-c.	7.00 7.00

La Rocca
Fortress — A328

Christmas: Diff. winter views of 10th cent.

1991, Nov. 13 Litho. *Perf. 14½*
1244	A328	600 l	multicolored	1.00 1.00
1245	A328	750 l	multicolored	1.25 1.25
1246	A328	1200 l	multicolored	1.75 1.75
		Nos. 1244-1246 (3)		4.00 4.00

No. 1246 is airmail.

Gioacchino Rossini (1792-1868),
Composer — A329

Designs: 750 l, Bianca e Falliero, Rossini opera festival 1989. 1200 l, The Barber of Seville, La Scala 1982-83.

1992, Feb. 3 Photo. *Perf. 14x13½*
1247	A329	750 l	multicolored	1.25 1.25
1248	A329	1200 l	multicolored	1.75 1.75

Discovery
of America,
500th
Anniv.
A330

Designs: 1500 l, Columbus, ships at anchor, natives. 2000 l, Map of voyages.

1992, Feb. 3 Litho. *Perf. 12*
1249	A330	1500 l	multicolored	2.10 2.10
1250	A330	2000 l	multicolored	3.25 3.25

Fauna Type of 1991

Flora.

			Perf. 13½	
1992, Mar. 26		**Litho.**		
1251	A325	50 l	Roses	.25 .25
1252	A325	200 l	House plant	.30 .30
1253	A325	300 l	Orchids	.40 .40
1254	A325	450 l	Cacti	.60 .60
1255	A325	5000 l	Geraniums	6.00 6.00
	Nos. 1251-1255 (5)			*7.55 7.55*

Tourism Types of 1990

Designs: No. 1256, Crossbowman. No. 1257, Tennis player. No. 1258, Motorcyclist. No. 1259, Race car. No. 1260, Couple in moonlight. No. 1261, Man in restaurant. No. 1262, Woman reading beneath umbrella.

			Perf. 14½x13½	
1992, Mar. 26				
		Booklet Stamps		
1256	A316	50 l	multicolored	.25 .25
1257	A316	50 l	multicolored	.25 .25
1258	A316	50 l	multicolored	.25 .25
1259	A316	50 l	multicolored	.25 .25
		Perf. 13½ Vert.		
1260	A313	600 l	multicolored	1.00 1.00
1261	A313	600 l	multicolored	1.00 1.00
1262	A313	600 l	multicolored	1.00 1.00
a.		Bklt. pane of 7, #1256-1262+label		4.00

Physicist Type of 1991

Design: Heinrich Rudolf Hertz (1857-94).

1263	A326	750 l	multicolored	1.00 1.00

Radio, cent. (in 1995).

Discovery of America, 500th Anniv. — A331

1992, May 22		**Photo.**	**Perf. 12x11½**	
		Granite Paper		
1264	A331	750 l	Globe, ship at sea	1.75 1.75
1265	A331	850 l	Ship in egg	2.25 2.25

Europa.

Souvenir Sheet

1992 Summer Olympics, Barcelona — A332

a, Soccer. b, Shooting. c, Swimming. d, Running.

			Perf. 14	
1992, May 22		**Litho.**		
1266	A332	1250 l	Sheet of 4, #a.-d.	7.25 7.25

Mushrooms — A333

Designs: Nos. 1267, Poisonous mushrooms. No. 1268a, Edible mushrooms in bowl. No. 1268b, Edible mushrooms on table.

1992, Sept. 18		**Photo.**	**Perf. 11½x12**	
		Granite Paper		
1267	A333	Pair		1.25 1.25

a.-b.		250 l	any single	.55 .55
1268	A333	Pair		1.50 1.50
a.-b.		350 l	any single	.70 .70

Admission to the UN — A334

Designs: a, Arms of San Marino, buildings. b, UN emblem, buildings.

1992, Sept. 18		**Litho.**	**Perf. 12x12½**	
1269	A334	Pair		2.50 2.50
a.-b.		1000 l	any single	1.00 1.00

The Sacred Conversation, by Piero della Francesca (1420-1492) A335

Christmas: a, Entire painting. b, Detail of faces. c, Detail of dome.

1992, Nov. 16		**Litho.**	**Perf. 14½**	
1270		Triptych		4.00 4.00
a.-c.	A335	750 l	any single	1.00 1.00

Contemporary Art — A336

Paintings: 750 l, Stars, by Nicola de Maria. 850 l, Abstract face, by Mimmo Paladino.

1993, Jan. 29		**Litho.**	**Perf. 11½**	
1271	A336	750 l	multicolored	.95 .95
1272	A336	850 l	multicolored	1.10 1.10

Europa.

1993 Sporting Events — A337

300 l, Tennis. 400 l, Cross-country skiing. 550 l, Women running. 600 l, Fisherman. 700 l, Men running. 1300 l, Sailboat, runners.

			Perf. 13½x14	
1993, Jan. 29				
1273	A337	300 l	multicolored	.40 .40
1274	A337	400 l	multicolored	.50 .50
1275	A337	550 l	multicolored	.70 .70
1276	A337	600 l	multicolored	.75 .75
1277	A337	700 l	multicolored	.80 .80
1278	A337	1300 l	multicolored	1.75 1.75
	Nos. 1273-1278 (6)			*4.90 4.90*

No. 1273, Youth Games. No. 1274-1275, European Youth Olympic Days. No. 1276, World Championships for Freshwater Angling Clubs, Ostellato, Italy. No. 1277, Games of Small European Countries, Malta. No. 1278, Mediterranean Games, Roussillon, France.

Physicists Type of 1991

Design: 750 l, Edouard Branly (1844-1940).

1993, Mar. 26		**Photo.**	**Perf. 14x13½**	
1279	A326	750 l	multicolored	1.00 1.00

Radio, cent. (in 1995).

Souvenir Sheet

Inauguration of State Television — A338

Designs: a, 100-meter finals, World Track Championships, Tokyo, 1991. b, San Marino. c, Neil Armstrong on moon, 1969.

1993, Mar. 26		**Litho.**	**Perf. 13½**	
1280	A338	Sheet of 3		7.75 7.75
a.-c.		2000 l	any single	2.25 2.25

Soaking may affect the hologram on No. 1280b.

Butterflies A339

No. 1281, Iphiclides podalirius. No. 1282, Colias crocea. No. 1283, Nymphalis antiopa. No. 1284, Melitaea cinxia.

1993, May 26		**Litho.**	**Perf. 14x15**	
1281	A339	250 l	multicolored	.75 .75
1282	A339	250 l	multicolored	.75 .75
1283	A339	250 l	multicolored	.75 .75
1284	A339	250 l	multicolored	.75 .75
a.		Block or strip of 4, #1281-1284		3.75 3.75

World Wildlife Fund.

Miniature Sheet

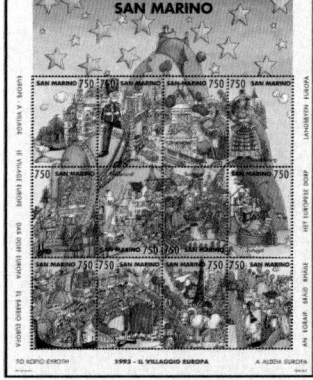

United Europe — A340

Village of Europe: No. 1285a, Denmark. b, England. c, Ireland. d, Luxembourg. e, Germany. f, Netherlands. g, Belgium. h, Portugal. i, Italy. j, Spain. k, France. l, Greece.

1993, May 26			**Perf. 13½x14**	
1285	A340	750 l	Sheet of 12	11.50 11.50
a.		Any single, #a.-l.		.80 .80

Famous Men A341

Designs: 550 l, Carlo Goldoni (1707-93), playwright, vert. 650 l, Horace (65-8 BC), poet and satirist, vert. 850 l, Claudio Monteverdi (1567-1643), composer. 1850 l, Guy de Maupassant (1850-93), writer.

1993, Sept. 17		**Litho.**	**Perf. 13½x14**	
1286	A341	550 l	multicolored	.70 .70
1287	A341	650 l	multicolored	.80 .80
1288	A341	850 l	multicolored	.90 .90
1289	A341	1850 l	multicolored	2.25 2.25
	Nos. 1286-1289 (4)			*4.65 4.65*

Christmas A342

Designs: 600 l, San Marino in winter, vert. Paintings by Gerard van Honthorst: 750 l, Adoration of the Child. 850 l, Adoration of the Shepherds, vert.

1993, Nov. 12		**Litho.**	**Perf. 14½**	
1290	A342	600 l	multicolored	.70 .70
1291	A342	750 l	multicolored	.90 .90
1292	A342	850 l	multicolored	1.10 1.10
	Nos. 1290-1292 (3)			*2.70 2.70*

10th Intl. Dog Show A343

Designs: 350 l, Dachshund. 400 l, Afghan hound. 450 l, Belgian tervueren shepherd dog. 500 l, Boston terrier. 550 l, Mastiff. 600 l, Alaskan malamute.

1994, Jan. 31		**Litho.**	**Perf. 15x14**	
1293	A343	350 l	multicolored	.45 .45
1294	A343	400 l	multicolored	.50 .50
1295	A343	450 l	multicolored	.55 .55
1296	A343	500 l	multicolored	.60 .60
1297	A343	550 l	multicolored	.65 .65
1298	A343	600 l	multicolored	.70 .70
	Nos. 1293-1298 (6)			*3.45 3.45*

Souvenir Sheet

1994 Winter Olympics, Lillehammer — A344

a, 90-meter ski jump. b, Downhill skiing. c, Giant slalom skiing. d, Pairs figure skating.

1994, Jan. 31			**Perf. 13½**	
1299	A344	750 l	2 each #a.-d.	7.00 7.00

Physicists Type of 1991

Aleksandr Stepanovich Popov (1859-1905).

1994, Mar. 11		**Photo.**	**Perf. 14x13½**	
1300	A326	750 l	multicolored	1.00 1.00

Radio cent. (in 1995).

Gardens — A345

1994, Mar. 11		**Litho.**	**Perf. 13**	
1301	A345	100 l	Gate	.25 .25
1302	A345	200 l	Grape arbor	.25 .25
1303	A345	300 l	Well	.40 .40
1304	A345	450 l	Gazebo	.60 .60
1305	A345	1850 l	Pond	2.00 2.00
	Nos. 1301-1305 (5)			*3.50 3.50*

Intl. Olympic Committee, Cent. A346

1994, Mar. 11 Photo. Perf. 14x13½
1306 A346 600 l multicolored 1.10 1.10

A347

Various soccer plays: a, Two players, one with #8 on shirt. b, Player in blue shirt kicking ball upward. c, Player heading ball. d, Players, one with #6 on shirt. e, Goal keeper.

1994, May 23 Litho. Perf. 14
1307 A347 600 l Strip of 5, #a.-e. 3.50 3.50

1994 World Cup Soccer Championships, US. No. 1307 has a continuous design.

A348

Europa (Ulysses spacecraft and: 750 l, Flight path around Sun and Jupiter. 850 l, Sun.

1994, May 23
1308 A348 750 l multicolored .95 .95
1309 A348 850 l multicolored 1.10 1.10

Inauguration of Government Building, Cent. — A349

Designs: 150 l, Exterior in shade, vert. 600 l, Exterior in sunshine, vert. 650 l, Clock tower. 1000 l, Interior.

Perf. 13½x13, 13x13½
1994, Sept. 30 Litho.
1310 A349 150 l multicolored .25 .25
1311 A349 600 l multicolored .70 .70
1312 A349 650 l multicolored .80 .80
1313 A349 1000 l multicolored 1.10 1.10
    Nos. 1310-1313 (4) 2.85 2.85

Dedication of St. Mark's Basilica, 900th Anniv. A350

1994, Oct. 8 Photo. Perf. 13½x13
1314 A350 750 l multicolored 3.50 3.50
  a. Souvenir sheet of 2, tete beche 4.50 4.50

No. 1314 printed with se-tenant label. No. 1314a contains No. 1314 and Italy No. 2003. Only No. 1314 was valid for postage in San Marino.

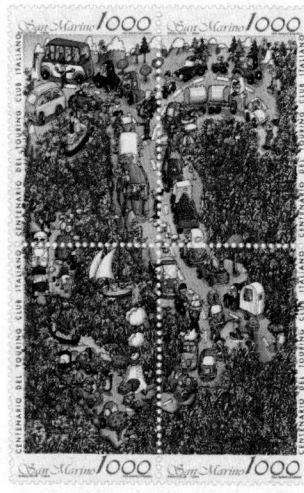

Touring Club of Italy, Cent. — A351

Vehicles traveling on road in middle of flower field: a, Traffic cop, bus. b, Tandem tanker truck. c, Sailboat, volcano. d, Truck loaded with animals, camper, fish in lake.

1994, Nov. 18 Litho. Perf. 14x13½
1315 A351 Block of 4 4.75 4.75
  a.-d. 1000 l any single 1.00 1.00

No. 1315 is a continuous design.

A352

The Enthroned Madonna and Child with Saints, by Giovanni Santi (1440-1494) (Christmas): 600 l, Drummer, piper. 750 l, Madonna and Child. 850 l, Piper, harpist.

1994, Nov. 18 Perf. 14x15
1316 A352 600 l multicolored .70 .70
1317 A352 750 l multicolored .85 .85
1318 A352 850 l multicolored 1.00 1.00
    Nos. 1316-1318 (3) 2.55 2.55

A353

Sporting Events of 1995: 1319, Junior World Cycling Championships, Forli, San Marino. 1320, Volleyball, cent. 1321, Men's Speed Skating World Championships, Baselga di Pine, Italy. 1322, World Track & Field Championships, Goteborg, Sweden.

1995, Feb. 10 Photo. Perf. 13x14
1319 A353 100 l Cycling .25 .25
1320 A353 500 l Volleyball .60 .60
1321 A353 650 l Speed skater .80 .80
1322 A353 850 l Runner 1.00 1.00
    Nos. 1319-1322 (4) 2.65 2.65

European Nature Conservation Year — A354

Nature scenes with flowers, water: a, Snails, dragonfly, fish. b, Frog, snake. c, Ladybugs, butterfly. d, Ducklings, frog. e, Ducks, snail.

1995, Feb. 10
1323 A354 600 l Strip of 5, #a.-e. 3.75 3.75

No. 1323 is a continuous design.

UN, 50th Anniv. — A355

Designs: 550 l, UN emblem surrounded by people. 600 l, Emblem in center of rose. 650 l, Hourglass shaped from halves of globe. 1200 l, "50," Emblem, rainbow.

1995, Mar. 24 Litho. Perf. 14x15
1324 A355 550 l multicolored .60 .60
1325 A355 600 l multicolored .75 .75
1326 A355 650 l multicolored .85 .85
1327 A355 1200 l multicolored 1.25 1.25
    Nos. 1324-1327 (4) 3.45 3.45

Peace & Freedom A356

1995, Mar. 24 Perf. 15x14
1328 A356 750 l shown .95 .95
1329 A356 850 l Sheep, meadow 1.00 1.00

Europa.

World Tourism Organization, 20th Anniv. — A357

Designs: 750 l, Mt. Titano encircled by five colored lines symbolizing continents. 850 l, Airplane over globe. 1200 l, Five lines encircling earth.

1995, May 5 Litho. Perf. 15x14
1330 A357 600 l multicolored .80 .80
1331 A357 750 l multicolored .95 .95
1332 A357 850 l multicolored 1.00 1.00
1333 A357 1200 l multicolored 1.25 1.25
    Nos. 1330-1333 (4) 4.00 4.00

Santa Croce Basilica, Florence, 700th Anniv. A358

1200 l, Detail from fresco, The Legend of the True Cross, by Agnolo Gaddi, facade of the basilica. 1250 l, Painting, The Madonna and Child with Saints, by Andrea della Robbia, Santa Croce Cloister, Pazzi Chapel.

1995, May 5
1334 A358 1200 l multicolored 1.40 1.40
1335 A358 1250 l multicolored 1.50 1.50

Radio, Cent. — A359

Designs: No. 1336, Stations on radio dial. No. 1337, Guglielmo Marconi (1874-1937), transmitting equipment.

1995, June 8 Litho. Perf. 14
1336 850 l multicolored 1.00 1.00
1337 850 l multicolored 1.00 1.00
  a. A359 Pair, #1336-1337 2.50 2.50

Printed in sheets of 10 stamps.
See Germany No. 1900, Ireland Nos. 973-974, Italy Nos. 2038-2039, Vatican City Nos. 978-979.

Miniature Sheet

Motion Picture, Cent. — A360

Different frames from films:
The General: a, 1. b, 2. c, 3. d, 4.
Il Gattopardo: e, 1. f, 2. g, 3. h, 4.
Allegro Non Troppo: i, 1. j, 2. k, 3. l, 4.
Braveheart: m, 1. n, 2. o, 3. p, 4.

1995, Sept. 14 Litho. Perf. 15x14
1338 Sheet of 16 5.00 5.00
  a.-p. A360 250 l any single .30 .30

Exhibition Type of 1980
Qianmen complex of Zhengyangmen Rostrum, Embrasured Watchtower, Beijing: No. 1339, In 1914. No. 1340, In 1995.

1995, Sept. 14 Perf. 14
1339 A222 1500 l multicolored 1.50 1.50
1340 A222 1500 l multicolored 1.50 1.50
  a. Pair, #1339-1340 3.75 3.75

Beijing '95.

Neri of Rimini, 14th Cent. Artist — A361

Designs: 650 l, The Annunciation.

1995, Nov. 6 Litho. Perf. 14x15
1341 A361 650 l multicolored 1.00 1.00

Christmas — A362

Designs: a, Santa, sleigh, reindeer. b, Children, Christmas tree. c, Nativity, star.

1995, Nov. 6 Litho. Perf. 14x15
1342 A362 Strip of 3 3.50 3.50
  a.-c. 750 l any single .75 .75

No. 1342 is a continuous design.

Express Mail Service A363

1995, Nov. 6 Perf. 15x14
1343 A363 6000 l multicolored 6.75 6.75

A364

1996, Feb. 12 Litho. Perf. 14x15
1344 A364 100 l Discus .25 .25
1345 A364 500 l Wrestling .70 .70
1346 A364 650 l Athletics .80 .80

1347	A364	1500 l	Javelin	1.75	1.75
1348	A364	2500 l	Running	3.00	3.00
		Nos. 1344-1348 (5)		6.50	6.50

1996 Summer Olympics, Atlanta.

A365

Portrait of Mother Teresa of Calcutta, by Gina Lollobrigida.

Granite Paper

1996, Mar. 22   Photo.   *Perf. 12*

1349	A365	750 l	multicolored	1.75	1.75

Europa.

China '96 Philatelic Exhibition, Beijing A366

1996, Mar. 22   *Perf. 14x13½*

1350	A366	1250 l	multicolored	1.90	1.90

Marco Polo's return from China, 700th anniv. (in 1995).
See Italy No. 2070.

Nature World Exhibition A367

Photographs of wildlife: 50 l, Dolphin. 100 l, Frog. 150 l, Penguins. 1000 l, Butterfly. 3000 l, Ducks.

1996, Mar. 22   *Perf. 12*
Granite Paper

1351	A367	50 l	multicolored	.25	.25
1352	A367	100 l	multicolored	.25	.25
1353	A367	150 l	multicolored	.25	.25
1354	A367	1000 l	multicolored	1.00	1.00
1355	A367	3000 l	multicolored	3.00	3.00
		Nos. 1351-1355 (5)		4.75	4.75

China-San Marino Relations, 25th Anniv. A368

No. 1356, Great Wall of China. No. 1357, Wall surrounding Mount Titano, San Marino.

1996, May 6   Litho.   *Perf. 12*

1356	A368	750 l	multicolored	.75	.75
1357	A368	750 l	multicolored	.75	.75
a.		Pair, Nos. 1356-1357		2.50	2.50
b.		Souvenir sheet, No. 1357a		2.75	2.75

No. 1357a is a continuous design.
See People's Republic of China Nos. 2675-2676.

Medieval Days Celebration A369

Festival activities: No. 1358, Woman weaving yarn, vert. No. 1359, Potter, vert. No. 1360, Woman making brushes, vert. No. 1361, Man

playing checkers, vert. No. 1362, Group blowing trumpets. No. 1363, Group holding banners. No. 1364, Men seated with crossbows. No. 1365, Street performers.

Perf. 14 on 2 Sides

1996, May 6   Litho. & Photo.
Booklet Stamps

1358	A369	750 l	multicolored	.80	.80
1359	A369	750 l	multicolored	.80	.80
1360	A369	750 l	multicolored	.80	.80
1361	A369	750 l	multicolored	.80	.80
1362	A369	750 l	multicolored	.80	.80
1363	A369	750 l	multicolored	.80	.80
1364	A369	750 l	multicolored	.80	.80
1365	A369	750 l	multicolored	.80	.80
a.		Booklet pane, #1358-1365		9.00	
		Complete booklet, #1365a		11.00	

Festival Bar A370

History of Italian Songs — A371

Singer, allegory of song: a, Enrico Caruso, "O Sole Mio." b, Armando Gill, "Come Pioveva." c, Ettore Petrolini, "Gastone." d, Vittorio de Sica, "Parlami D'Amore Mariu." e, Odoardo Spadaro, "La Porti un Bacione a Firenze." f, Alberto Rabagliati, "O Mia Bela Madonina." g, Beniamino Gigli, "Mamma." h, Claudio Villa, "Luna Rossa." i, Secondo Casadei, "Romagna Mia." j, Renato Rascel, "Arrivederci Roma." k, Fred Buscaglione, "Guarda Che Luna." l, Domenico Modugno, "Nel Blu Dipinto di Blu."

1996, May 25   Litho.   *Perf. 14x13½*

1366	A370	2000 l	shown	2.50	2.50

Granite Paper
Photo.
Perf. 12x11½

1367	A371	750 l	Sheet of 12, #a.-l.	10.00	10.00

Gazzetta Dello Sport, Cent. — A372

1996, May 25   *Perf. 12*
Granite Paper

1368	A372	1850 l	multicolored	2.25	2.25

UNICEF, 50th Anniv. A373

1996, Sept. 20   Photo.   *Perf. 12*
Granite Paper

1369	A373	550 l	Hen, chicks	.60	.60
1370	A373	1000 l	Baby birds	1.40	1.40

UNESCO, 50th Anniv. A374

World Heritage Sites: 450 l, Yellowstone Natl. Park, US. 500 l, Prehistoric caves, Vézère Valley, France. 650 l, Old town center, San Gimignano, Italy. 1450 l, Church of the Wies Pilgrimage, Germany.

1996, Sept. 20   Granite Paper

1371	A374	450 l	multicolored	.60	.60
1372	A374	500 l	multicolored	.65	.65
1373	A374	650 l	multicolored	.80	.80
1374	A374	1450 l	multicolored	1.75	1.75
		Nos. 1371-1374 (4)		3.80	3.80

Christmas — A375

Scenes looking through windows of a home: a, Playing game underneath Christmas tree. b, Tags draped from holly branch. c, Girl reading book, Santa in sleigh. d, Christmas tree. e, Fruits, candles, nuts. f, Streaking star, snowflakes. g, Toys. h, Presents. i, Santa Claus puppet. j, Nativity. k, Mistletoe. l, Stocking hung by fireplace. m, Family eating, drinking. n, Christmas tree, silhouettes of mother, father, wreath. o, Wreath, silhouettes of children & grandmother, snowman. p, Calendar, champaigne bottle popping cork.

1996, Nov. 8   Photo.   *Perf. 14½*

1375	A375	750 l	Sheet of 16, #a.-p.	14.00	14.00

Souvenir Sheet

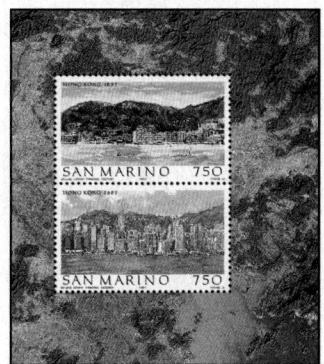

Hong Kong — A376

View from harbor: a, 1897. b, 1997.

1997, Feb. 12   Litho.   *Perf. 12½*

1376	A376	750 l	Sheet of 2, #a.-		
			b.	1.90	1.90

World Alpine Skiing Championships, Sestrière, Italy — A377

Scene of people skiing on mountain: a, Skier jumping left, birds. b, Ski lift, bird in sky. c, Coming down mountain, sleigh. d, Coming down mountain, Sestrière sign.

1997, Feb. 12   *Perf. 12*
Granite Paper

1377	A377	1000 l	Block of 4, #a.-		
			d.	5.00	5.00

No. 1377 is a continuous design.

San Marino Townships (Castelli) A378

100 l, Acquaviva. 200 l, Borgomaggiore. 250 l, Chiesanuova. 400 l, Domagnano. 500 l, Faetano. 550 l, Fiorentino. 650 l, Montegiardino. 750 l, Serravalle. 5000 l, San Marino.

1997, Mar. 21   Photo.   *Perf. 12*
Granite Paper

1378	A378	100 l	multi	.25	.25
1379	A378	200 l	multi	.25	.25
1380	A378	250 l	multi	.35	.35
1381	A378	400 l	multi	.50	.50
1382	A378	500 l	multi	.60	.60
1383	A378	550 l	multi	.70	.70
1384	A378	650 l	multi	.80	.80
1385	A378	750 l	multi	.90	.90
1386	A378	5000 l	multi	5.50	5.50
		Nos. 1378-1386 (9)		9.85	9.85

Stories and Legends — A379

St. Marinus, Mt. Titano: 650 l, St. Marinus talking to bear that killed the mule. 750 l, Mother begging St. Marinus to forgive her son for trying to kill him.

1997, Mar. 21   Granite Paper

1387	A379	650 l	multicolored	.85	.85
1388	A379	750 l	multicolored	.95	.95

Europa.

Sporting Events A380

500 l, Giro d'Italia cycling event. 550 l, 10th Tennis Intl. 750 l, Formula 1 San Marino Grand Prix. 850 l, Republic of San Marino (Soccer) Trophy. 1000 l, Bowls (pétanque) World Championship. 1250 l, Motorcross 250cc World Championship. 1500 l, Mille Miglia classic car spectacle.

1997, May 19   Photo.   *Perf. 12*
Granite Paper

1389	A380	500 l	multicolored	.50	.50
1390	A380	550 l	multicolored	.60	.60
1391	A380	750 l	multicolored	.85	.85
1392	A380	850 l	multicolored	.95	.95
1393	A380	1000 l	multicolored	1.10	1.10
1394	A380	1250 l	multicolored	1.50	1.50
1395	A380	1500 l	multicolored	1.75	1.75
		Nos. 1389-1395 (7)		7.25	7.25

5th Intl. Symposium on UFO's and Associated Phenomena A381

1997, May 19   Granite Paper

1396	A381	750 l	multicolored	1.00	1.00

Trees — A382

50 l, Pinus pinea. 800 l, Quercus pubescens. 1800 l, Juglans regia. 2000 l, Pirus communis.

1997, June 27   **Photo.**   *Perf. 12*
Granite Paper

1397	A382	50 l	multicolored	.25	.25
1398	A382	800 l	multicolored	.90	.90
1399	A382	1800 l	multicolored	2.00	2.00
1400	A382	2000 l	multicolored	2.50	2.50
	Nos. 1397-1400 (4)			5.65	5.65

First Stamps of
San Marino,
120th
Anniv. — A383

Designs: No. 1401, G. Battista Barbavara di Gravellona, director general of Sardinian Post Office. No. 1402, Enrico Repettati, chief engraver for Officina Carte Valori, Turin. No. 1403, Otto Bickel, German stamp dealer, promoter of San Marino-Philatelist. No. 1404, Alfredo Reffi, San Marino stamp dealer, publisher of post cards, stamp catalogue.

1997, June 27   *Perf. 11½*
Granite Paper

1401	A383	800 l	multicolored	.75	.75
1402	A383	800 l	multicolored	.75	.75
1403	A383	800 l	multicolored	.75	.75
1404	A383	800 l	multicolored	.75	.75
a.	Strip of 4, #1401-1404			4.00	4.00

Beatification
of
Bartolomeo
Maria Dal
Monte
(1726-78)
A384

1997, Sept. 18   **Photo.**   *Perf. 12*
Granite Paper

1405	A384	800 l	multicolored	1.00	1.00

Italian
Comic Book
Characters
A385

Designs: a, "Quadratino," by Antonio Rubino. b, "Signor Bonaventura," by Sergio Tofano. c, "Kit Carson," by Rino Albertarelli. d, "Cocco Bill," by Benito Jacovitti. e, "Tex Willer," by Gian Luigi Bonelli and Arelio Galleppini. f, "Diabolik," by Angela and Luciana Giussani and Franco Paludetti. g, "Valentina," by Guido Crepax. h, "Corto Maltese," by Hugo Pratt. i, "Sturmtruppen," by Franco Bonvicini. j, "Alan Ford," by Max Bunker. k, "Lupo Alberto," by Guido Silvestri. l, "Pimpa," by Francesco Tullio Altan. m, "Bobo," by Sergio Staino. n, "Zanardi," by Andrea Pazienza. o, "Martin Mystère," by Alfredo Castelli and Giancarlo Alessandrini. p, "Dylan Dog," by Tiziano Sclavi and Angelo Stano.

1997, Sept. 18   **Granite Paper**
Sheet of 16

1406	A385	800 l	#a.-p.	15.00	15.00

Adoration of the
Magi, by Georgio
Vasari (1511-
74) — A386

1997, Nov. 14   **Photo.**   *Perf. 12*
Granite Paper

1407	A386	800 l	multicolored	1.10	1.10

Volunteer
Service,
Solidarity
A387

Designs: 550 l, St. Francis of Assisi, doves. 650 l, Mariele Ventre, children. 800 l, Children circling hands around world, Zecchino d'Oro song festival.

1997, Nov. 14   **Granite Paper**

1408	A387	550 l	multicolored	.70	.70
1409	A387	650 l	multicolored	.85	.85
1410	A387	800 l	multicolored	1.00	1.00
	Nos. 1408-1410 (3)			2.55	2.55

Volkswagen
Beetle
A388

Designs: a, Maggiolino (old Beetle). b, Golf I. c, New Beetle. d, Golf IV.

1997, Nov. 14   **Granite Paper**

1411	A388	800 l	Sheet of 4, #a.-d.	4.50	4.50

No. 1411 was issued with attached entry form for drawing to win a new Beetle car. Entry form is rouletted at top to separate from bottom of sheet. Values are for sheets with entry form attached.

Ferrari's
Formula 1
Race Cars,
50th Anniv.
A389

Model number, year: a, 125S, 1947. b, 500F2, 1952. c, 801, 1956. d, 246 Dino, 1958. e, 156, 1961. f, 158, 1964. g, 312T, 1975. h, 312T4, 1979. i, 126C, 1981. j, 156/85, 1985. k, 639, 1989. l, F310, 1996.

1998, Feb. 11   **Litho.**   *Perf. 13*

1412	A389	800 l	Sheet of 12, #a.-l.	12.00	12.00

6th World Day of the Sick: 1500 l, Rainbow pulled over earth by dove.

1998, Feb. 11   *Perf. 14x14½*

1413	A390	650 l	shown	.75	.75
1414	A390	1500 l	multicolored	1.75	1.75

A391

Europa (Natl. Feasts and Festivals): 650 l, Installation of the Captains Regent. 1200 l, Feast Day of the Republic's Patron Saint.

1998, Mar. 31   **Litho.**   *Perf. 14x15*

1415	A391	650 l	multicolored	*.85*	*.85*
1416	A391	1200 l	multicolored	*1.60*	*1.60*

Giacomo Leopardi (1798-1837),
Poet — A392

Words from poem, illustration: 550 l, "The Infinite," 1819, hedges, hill. 650 l, "A Village Saturday," 1829, woman walking. 900 l, "Nocturne of a Wandering Asian Shepherd," 1822-30, man looking at moon. 2000 l, "To Sylvia," woman's face.

1998, Mar. 31   *Perf. 15x14*

1417	A392	550 l	multicolored	.75	.75
1418	A392	650 l	multicolored	.85	.85
1419	A392	900 l	multicolored	1.00	1.00
1420	A392	2000 l	multicolored	2.50	2.50
	Nos. 1417-1420 (4)			5.10	5.10

1998 World Cup
Soccer
Championships,
France — A393

Soccer players: 650 l, At goal. 800 l, In black & yellow, in blue. 900 l, In red, in black & blue.

1998, May 28   **Photo.**   *Perf. 11½x12*
Granite Paper

1421	A393	900 l	multicolored	1.00	1.00
a.	Booklet pane of 4			4.00	
1422	A393	800 l	multicolored	1.25	1.25
a.	Booklet pane of 4			5.00	
1423	A393	900 l	multicolored	1.75	1.75
a.	Booklet pane of 4			7.00	
	Complete booklet, #1421a, 1422a, 1423a			19.00	
	Nos. 1421-1423 (3)			4.00	4.00

Emigration
A394

Designs: 800 l, People on ship's deck, group photograph in front of Mt. Titano, 3rd class ticket to New York, passport. 1500 l, People at work, work permit, residency permit, pay slip, US dollar.

1998, May 28   **Granite Paper**

1424	A394	800 l	multicolored	.80	.80
1425	A394	1500 l	multicolored	1.75	1.75

Souvenir Sheet

San Marino Natl. Flag in
Space — A395

Designs: a, Launch of US space shuttle. b, Shuttle in orbit, flag of San Marino. c, Earth, space shuttle.

1998, May 28   **Granite Paper**

1426	A395	2000 l	Sheet of 3, #a.-c.	7.50	7.50

A396

Riccione 1998, Intl. Stamp Fair: 800 l, Sun, sail on boat as canceled stamp. 1500 l, Dolphin diving through canceled stamp.

1998, Aug. 28   **Photo.**   *Perf. 12x11½*

1427	A396	800 l	multicolored	.90	.90
1428	A396	1500 l	multicolored	1.75	1.75

A397

Science Fiction: a, Twenty Thousand Leagues Under the Sea, by Jules Verne (1828-1905). b, War of the Worlds, by H.G. Wells (1866-1946). c, Brave New World, by Aldous Huxley (1894-1963). d, 1984, by George Orwell (1903-50). e, Chronicles of the Galaxy, by Isaac Asimov (1920-92). f, City without End, by Clifford D. Simak (1904-88). g, Fahrenheit 451, by Ray Bradbury (b. 1920). h, The Seventh Victim, by Robert Sheckley (b. 1928). i, The Space Merchants, by Frederik Pohl (b. 1919) and C.M. Kornbluth (1923-58). j, Neighbors from the Middle Ages and the Future, by Roberto Vacca (b. 1927). k, Stranger in a Strange Land, by Robert Heinlein (1907-88). l, A Clockwork Orange, by Anthony Burgess (1917-93). m, Drowned World, by James G. Ballard (b. 1930). n, Dune, by Frank Herbert (1920-86). o, 2001, A Space Odessy, by Arthur Clarke (b. 1917). p, Blade Runner (Do Androids Dream of Electric Sheep), by Phillip K. Dick (1928-82).

Granite Paper

1998, Aug. 28   *Perf. 14½*

1429	A397	800 l	Sheet of 16, #a.-p.	15.00	15.00

Italia
'98
A398

1998, Oct. 23   **Photo.**   *Perf. 14*

1430	A398	800 l	Pope John Paul II	1.40	1.40

See Italy No. 2265, Vatican City No. 1085.

A399

Christmas (Children of different races, Christmas tree made up of Santa Clauses, gifts): a, Boy running left, star on tree. b, Child from tropical region, star on tree. c, Child, rabbit, bottom of tree. d, Dog, girl, bottom of tree.

1998, Oct. 23   *Perf. 12x11½*
Granite Paper

1431	A399	800 l	Block of 4, #a.-d.	4.25	4.25

No. 1431 is a continuous design.

A400

1998, Oct. 23 **Granite Paper**
1432 A400 900 l Woman　　　1.00 1.00
1433 A400 900 l Man　　　　1.00 1.00
　a.　Pair, #1432-1433　　　2.25 2.25
Universal Declaration of Human Rights, 50th Anniv. No. 1433a is a continuous design.

A401

Italia '98: Statue, "Girl," by Emilio Greco.

1998, Oct. 23 **Granite Paper**
1434 A401 1800 l multicolored　　2.25 2.25

For Nos. 1435-1521, denominations are shown in euros and lira. For listing purposes, face values in lira are shown.

A402

1999 World Hang Gliding Championships, Italy: 800 l, Hand using feather to write in sky. 1800 l, Man on glider, holding balloon.

1999, Feb. 12 **Litho.** **Perf. 13½x13**
1435 A402 800 l multicolored　　1.00 1.00
1436 A402 1800 l multicolored　　2.25 2.25

Operas in San Marino, 400th Anniv. — A403

Opera, composer: a, "L'incoronazione di Poppea," by Monteverdi. b, "Dido and Aeneas," by Purcell. c, "Orpheus and Euridice," by Gluck. d, "Don Giovanni," by Mozart. e, "The Barber of Seville," by Rossini. f, "Norma," by Bellini. g, "Lucia di Lammermour," by Donizetti. h, "Aida," by Verdi. i, "Faust," by Gounod. j, "Carmen," by Bizet. k, "The Ring of the Nibelungen," by Wagner. l, "Boris Godonov," by Mussorgski. m, "Tosca," by Puccini. n, "Love for Three Oranges," by Prokofiev. o, "Porgy and Bess," by Gershwin. p, "West Side Story," by Bernstein.

1999, Feb. 12 **Perf. 13x13½**
Sheet of 16
1437 A403 800 l #a.-p.　　16.00 16.00

Bonsai '99, San Marino Bonsai Exhibition A404

50 l, Pinus mugo. 300 l, Olea europaea. 350 l, Pinus silvestris. 500 l, Quercus robar.

1999, Mar. 27 **Litho.** **Perf. 13x13½**
1438 A404　50 l multicolored　　.25 .25
1439 A404 300 l multicolored　　.35 .35
1440 A404 350 l multicolored　　.40 .40
1441 A404 500 l multicolored　　.60 .60
　Nos. 1438-1441 (4)　　　1.60 1.60

Mount Titano Natl. Park A405

Europa: 650 l, Eastern slopes, fortress tower. 1250 l, Walled enclosure, Cesta tower.

1999, Mar. 27
1442 A405　650 l multicolored　　.80 .80
1443 A405 1250 l multicolored　　1.75 1.75

1999 World Cycling Championships, Veneto, Italy — A406

900 l, Building, emblem. 3000 l, Colosseum, emblem.

1999, Mar. 27
1444 A406　900 l multicolored　　1.00 1.00
1445 A406 3000 l multicolored　　3.75 3.75

2nd Roman Republic, Garibaldi's Escape to San Marino, 150th Anniv. A407

1999, May 12 **Litho.** **Perf. 13x13¼**
1446 A407 1250 l multicolored　　1.60 1.60

Council of Europe, 50th Anniv. — A408

1999, May 12 **Perf. 13¼x13**
1447 A408 1300 l multicolored　　1.75 1.75

UPU, 125th Anniv. A409

800 l, Text from original UPU Treaty, Swiss Parliament Building, Bern. 3000 l, World map highlighting UPU's 22 founding countries.

1999, May 12 **Perf. 13x13¼**
1448 A409　800 l multicolored　　.90 .90
1449 A409 3000 l multicolored　　3.75 3.75

Holy Year 2000 A410

650 l, Map of route of 15th cent. European pilgrims, Canterbury Cathedral. 800 l, Fresco of priest blessing pilgrim, 11th cent., Reims Cathedral. 900 l, Fresco of hospice welcoming pilgrims, 15th cent., Duomo de Pavia. 1250 l, Bas-relief of pilgrims on the road, Cathedral of Fidenza, 12th cent. 1500 l, View of Rome from Monte Mario, by Sir Charles Eastlake. St. Peter's Basilica, Rome.

1999, June 5
1450 A410　650 l multicolored　　.65 .65
1451 A410　800 l multicolored　　.90 .90
1452 A410　900 l multicolored　　1.00 1.00
1453 A410 1250 l multicolored　　1.50 1.50
1454 A410 1500 l multicolored　　2.00 2.00
　Nos. 1450-1454 (5)　　　6.05 6.05

Fauna of San Marino A411

500 l, Lepus europaeus. 650 l, Sciurus vulgaris. 1100 l, Meles meles. 1250 l, Vulpes vulpes. 1850 l, Hystrix cristata.

1999, June 5
1455 A411　500 l multicolored　　.60 .60
1456 A411　650 l multicolored　　.75 .75
1457 A411 1100 l multicolored　　1.10 1.10
1458 A411 1250 l multicolored　　1.50 1.50
1459 A411 1850 l multicolored　　2.50 2.50
　Nos. 1455-1459 (5)　　　6.45 6.45

Architecture — A412

Designs: 50 l, Sant'Agata Feltria, Rocca Fregosa. 250 l, San Leo, Rocca Feltresca. 650 l, Urbino, Ducal Palace. 1300 l, Sassocorvaro, Rocca Ubaldinesca. 6000 l, Montale and Rocca towers, San Marino.

1999, Sept. 20 **Litho.** **Perf. 13x13¼**
1460 A412　50 l multicolored　　.25 .25
1461 A412　250 l multicolored　　.35 .35
1462 A412　650 l multicolored　　.85 .85
1463 A412 1300 l multicolored　　1.60 1.60
1464 A412 6000 l multicolored　　7.50 7.50
　Nos. 1460-1464 (5)　　　10.55 10.55

San Marino Red Cross, 50th Anniv. A413

1999, Sept. 20
1465 A413 800 l St. Martin of Tours　　　1.10 1.10

Souvenir Sheet

Milan Soccer Club, 100th Anniv. — A414

Designs: a, 1901 team, trophy on table. b, Players Gren, Nordahl and Liedholm. c, 1963 team, black and white photograph. d, 1990 team, white shirts. e, 1994 team, hanging banners. f, 1999 team, player holding trophy.

1999, Sept. 20
1466 A414 800 l Sheet of 6, #a.-f.　　6.75 6.75

Souvenir Sheet

Audi Automobiles — A415

Designs: a, Horch. b, Audi TT. c, Audi A8. d, Auto Union.

1999, Nov. 5 **Litho.** **Perf. 13x13¼**
1467 A415 1500 l Sheet of 4, #a.-d.　　7.75 7.75

No. 1467 was issued with attached entry form for drawing to win a new Audi A3 car. Entry form is rouletted at top to separate from bottom of sheet. Values are for sheets with entry form attached.

Christmas A416

1999, Nov. 5
1468 A416 800 l multicolored　　1.10 1.10

Millennium — A417

Designs: a, Tank, soldiers and refugees of World Wars. b, Syringe and vial, MRI machine, DNA molecule. c, Washing machine, subway, Tiffany lamp. d, Radio, telephone operators, person at computer. e, Airplanes, airship, astronaut on moon. f, Pollution, g, Automobiles and truck. h, Atomic diagram, nuclear submarine, mushroom cloud. i, Charlie Chaplin in "Modern Times," comic strip, chair. j, Crossword puzzle, art gallery visitors, car and trailer, people exercising. k, Advertisements and slogans. l, Cyclist, soccer players, stadium.

2000, Feb. 2 **Litho.** **Perf. 13x13¼**
1469 A417 650 l Sheet of 12, #a.-l.　　11.00 11.00

Souvenir Sheet

Holy Year 2000 — A418

Designs: a, St. John Lateran Basilica, St. Marinus and Mt. Titano. b, Basilica of St. Paul, statue of St. Marinus, the Rocca. c, Basilica of St. Mary Major, Basilica of San Marino. d, St. Peter's Basilica, St. Marinus.

2000, Feb. 2
1470 A418 1000 l Sheet of 4,
#a.-d.   5.25 5.25

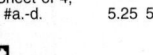

A419

Designs: 650 l, Rotary emblem and towers.
800 l, Palace, coat of arms, Statue of Liberty,
Rotary emblem.

2000, Apr. 27   Litho.   *Perf. 13¼x13*
1471 A419 650 l multi   .90   .90
1472 A419 800 l multi   1.10 1.10
Rotary Club of San Marino, 40th anniv.

A420

Bologna, European City of Culture: 650 l,
Government Palace and Statue of Liberty, San
Marino, and Fiera Towers, Bologna. 800 l,
Marconi's workbench, radio antenna, Bologna
buildings. 1200 l, Microchip, drums, key-
boards, Bologna buildings. 1500 l, Still Life, by
Giorgio Morandi, antique books, Bologna
buildings.

2000, Apr. 27
1473 A420 650 l multi   .70   .70
1474 A420 800 l multi   .90   .90
1475 A420 1200 l multi   1.50 1.50
1476 A420 1500 l multi   2.00 2.00
    Nos. 1473-1476 (4)   5.10 5.10

Community of San Patrignano's Fight
Against Drug Abuse — A421

Designs: 650 l, Vincenzo Muccioli, community's founder. 1200 l, Rainbow emblem.
2400 l, Muccioli and community residents.

2000, Apr. 27   *Perf. 13x13¼*
1477 A421 650 l multi   .85   .85
1478 A421 1200 l multi   1.50 1.50
1479 A421 2400 l multi   2.75 2.75
    Nos. 1477-1479 (3)   5.10 5.10

Europa Issue
Common Design Type

2000, Apr. 27   *Perf. 13¼x13*
1480 CD17 800 l multi   *1.00 1.00*

Stampin'
the Future
Children's
Stamp
Design
Contest
Winner
A422

2000, May 31   *Perf. 13x13¼*
1481 A422 800 l multi   1.00 1.00

Intl. Cycling
Union,
Cent.
A423

2000, May 31
1482 A423 1200 l multi   1.50 1.50

2000 Summer Olympics,
Sydney — A424

Designs: a, Dog, butterfly. b, Hippopotamus,
penguin. c, Elephant, ladybug. d, Rabbit, snail.

2000, May 31   *Perf. 13¼x13*
1483 A424 1000 l Block of 4,
#a-d   5.50 5.50

European
Convention
on Human
Rights,
50th Anniv.
A425

2000, Sept. 15   Litho.   *Perf. 13x13¼*
1484 A425 800 l multi   1.00 1.00

Intl. Rights
of the Child
Convention,
10th Anniv.
A426

Child: 650 l, And army helmet. 800 l, In corner of room. 1200 l, As flower. 1500 l, With
book.

2000, Sept. 15
1485-1488 A426   Set of 4   5.50 5.50

Art of the
Montefeltro
A427

650 l, Basilica of San Marino, Statue of St.
Marinus, by Adamo Tadolini. 800 l, Santa
Maria d'Antico Church, Madonna and Child
statue, by Luca Della Robbia. 1000 l, San
Lorenzo Church, church door. 1500 l, Interior
and exterior of San Leo Church. 1800 l, Frescoes, Santuario Madonna della Grazie.

2000, Sept. 15
1489-1493 A427   Set of 5   7.25 7.25

Republic of San
Marino, 1700th
Anniv. — A428

No. 1494: a, Melchiorre Delfico (1744-
1835), historian. b, Giuseppe Garibaldi. c,
Abraham Lincoln. d, World War II refugees. e,
Jewels from Treasure of Domagnano. f, Map
after 1643 war. g, Napoleon Bonaparte's offer
to extend territory. h, Arengo of 1906. i, Child's
head. j, Young man's head. k, Woman's head.
l, Old man's head. m, St. Marinus, by Francesco Manzocchi di Forli, left half of arms. n,
Right half of arms, St. Marinus, work attributed
to Ghirlandaio. o, St. Marinus, by School of
Guercino (blue denomination at top). p, St.
Marinus in Glory, by anonymous artist. q,
Double throne of Regents. r, Republican statutes, 17th cent. s, Palace Guards on parade. t,
Flags of San Marino and other countries.

2000, Nov. 14   Photo.   *Perf. 11¾*
1494   Souvenir booklet   25.00
  a.-l. A428 800 l Any single   1.00   1.00
  m.-t. A428 1200 l Any single   1.50   1.50
  u. Booklet pane, #1494a-1494d 4.00
  v. Booklet pane, #1494e-1494h 4.00
  w. Booklet pane, #1494i-1494l 4.00
  x. Booklet pane, #1494m-1494p 6.00
  y. Booklet pane, #1494q-1494t 6.00
No. 1494 includes an 800 l postal card.

Virgin With
the Infant
Jesus, by
Ludovico
Carracci
A429

2000, Nov. 14   Litho.   *Perf. 13x13½*
1495 A429 800 l multi   2.75 2.75
Christmas.

Souvenir Sheet

Ferrari, 2000 Formula 1 Racing
Champion — A430

a, Car on track. b, Car, track wall.

2001, Jan. 10
1496 A430 1500 l #a-b   4.00 4.00

Heritage of
the
Malatesta
Family
A431

Sigismondo Malatesta and: 800 l, Malates-
tian Temple, by Leon Battista Alberti. 1200 l,
Pieta by Giovanni Bellini.

2001, Feb. 19   Litho.   *Perf. 13x13¼*
1497-1498 A431   Set of 2   4.00 4.00

24 Hours of San Marino
Regatta — A432

Hull colors: a, Green. b, Orange. c, Black. d,
Brown.

2001, Feb. 19   *Perf. 13¼x13*
1499 A432 1200 l Block or
strip of 4,
#a-d   7.00 7.00

Giuseppe Verdi (1813-1901),
Composer — A433

Verdi and scenes from operas: a, Nabucco.
b, Ernani. c, Rigoletto. d, Il Trovatore. e, La
Traviata. f, I Vespri Siciliani. g, Un Ballo in
Maschera. h, La Forza del Destino. i, Don Carlos. j, Aida. k, Otello. l, Falstaff.

2001, Feb. 19   *Perf. 13x13¼*
1500   Sheet of 12   13.00 13.00
  a.-l. A433 800 l Any single   1.00   1.00

Europa — A434

Designs: 800 l, Safe in forest. 1200 l, Faucet
on mountain.

2001, Apr. 17   Litho.   *Perf. 13¼x13*
1501-1502 A434   Set of 2   *2.60 2.60*

Emigration
to the
US — A435

Immigrants viewing Statue of Liberty and:
1200 l, Ellis Island Immigration Museum, New
York. 2400 l, San Marino Social Club, Detroit.

2001, Apr. 17   *Perf. 13x13¼*
1503-1504 A435   Set of 2   4.50 4.50

Euroflora 2001,
Genoa — A436

Designs: 800 l, Dahlia variabilis, ship. 1200 l, Zantedeschia aethiopica, ship. 1500 l, Helen Troubel rose, ship. 2400 l, Amaryllis hippeastrum, Lanterna.

2001, Apr. 17 ***Perf. 13¼x13***
1505-1508 A436 Set of 4 7.75 7.75

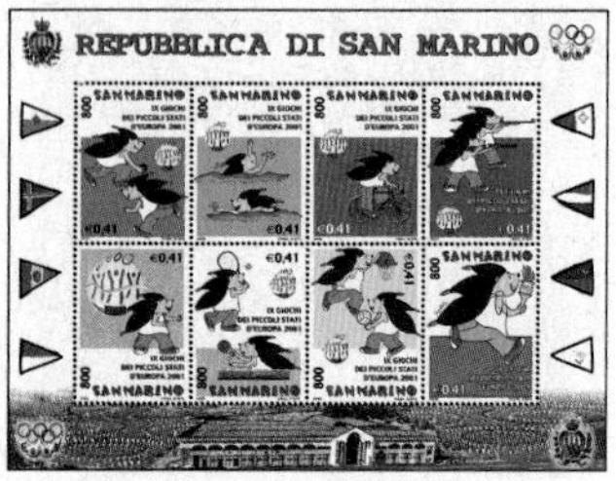

9th Games of the Small European States — A437

No. 1509: a, Bocce, running. b, Swimming. c, Cycling. d, Shooting. e, Judo. f, Tennis, table tennis. g, Basketball and volleyball. h, Mascot carrying torch.

2001, Apr. 17
1509 A437 800 l Sheet of 8, #a-h 8.25 8.25

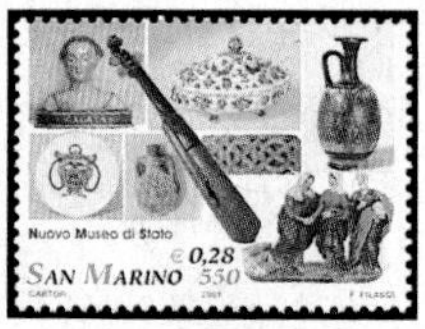

Opening of New State Museum A438

Various holdings: 550 l, 800 l, 1500 l, 2000 l.

2001, June 23 ***Perf. 13x13¼***
1510-1513 A438 Set of 4 6.50 6.50

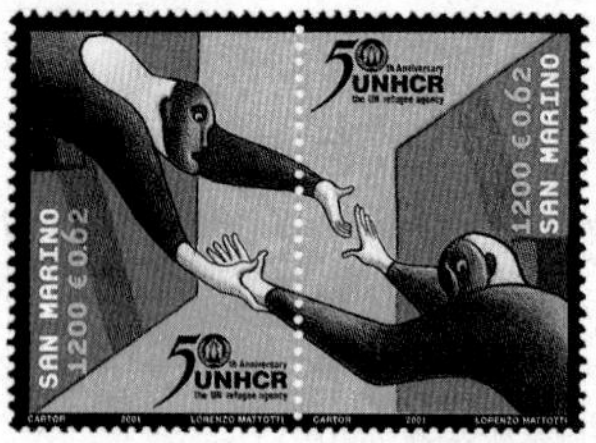

UN High Commisioner for Refugees, 50th Anniv. — A439

No. 1514: a, Emblem at bottom. b, Emblem at top.

2001, June 23 ***Perf. 13¼x13***
1514 A439 1200 l Horiz. pair, #a-b 3.50 3.50

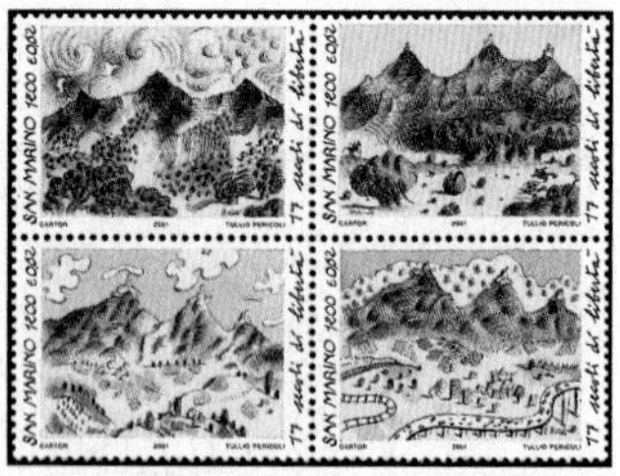

Foundation of the Republic, 1700th Anniv. — A440

No. 1515: a, Uninhabited land. b, People on horses. c, Small community. d, Town with highway.

2001, June 23 ***Perf. 13x13¼***
1515 A440 1200 l Block of 4, #a-d 6.25 6.25

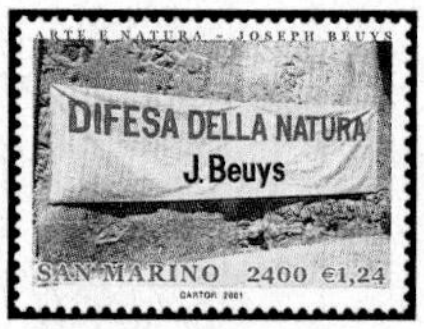

Homage to Artist Joseph Beuys A441

2001, Sept. 10
1516 A441 2400 l multi 3.25 3.25

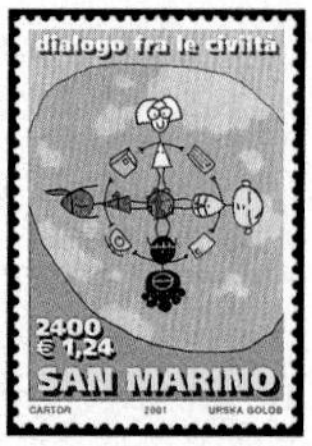

Year of Dialogue Among Civilizations A442

2001, Sept. 10 ***Perf. 13¼x13***
1517 A442 2400 l multi 3.25 3.25

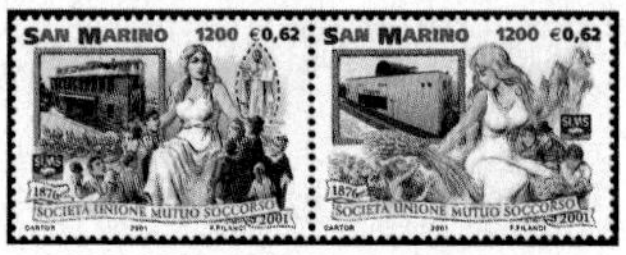

United Mutual Aid Society, 125th Anniv. — A443

Allegory of assistance and: a, Old building. b, Modern building.

2001, Sept. 10 ***Perf. 13x13¼***
1518 A443 1200 l Horiz. pair, #a-b 3.00 3.00

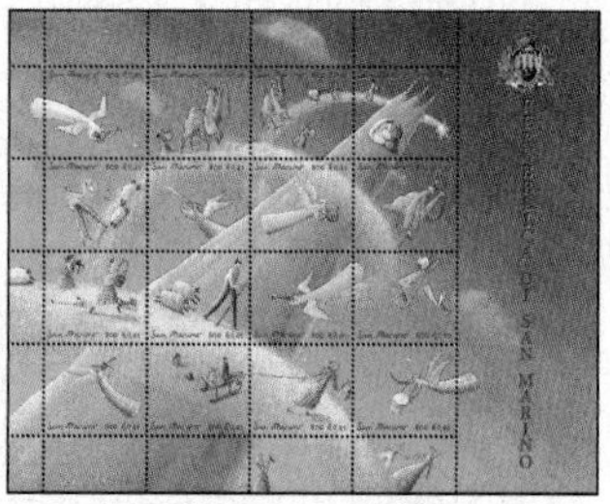

Christmas — A444

No. 1519: a, Angel with lute. b, Woman with basket, Magus on camel. c, Magus on camel, shepherd with sheep, woman with gift. d, Man with gift, castles, star, Holy Family. e, Man with lantern, goose, chicken, sheep. f, Angel with long, thin-mouthed, horn. g, Angel with harp. h, Magus on camel. i, Two women with baskets, dog. j, Shepherd with two sheep. k, Angel with short, wide-mouthed horn. l, Woman with gift, angel with horn. m, Angel with violin. n, Man, sleigh, gifts. o, Woman with gift, pulling sleigh. p, Angel with drum.

2001, Oct. 18 **Litho.** ***Perf. 13***
1519 A444 800 l Sheet of 16, #a-p 17.50 17.50

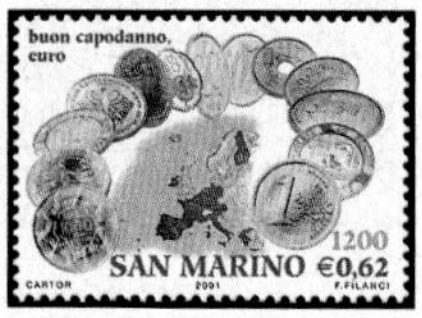

Introduction of the Euro (in 2002) A445

Map of Europe and: 1200 l, Coins of various countries, 1-euro coin. 2400 l, Banknotes of various countries, 100-euro banknote.

2001, Oct. 18 ***Perf. 13x13¼***
1520-1521 A445 Set of 2 4.50 4.50

100 Cents = 1 Euro (€)

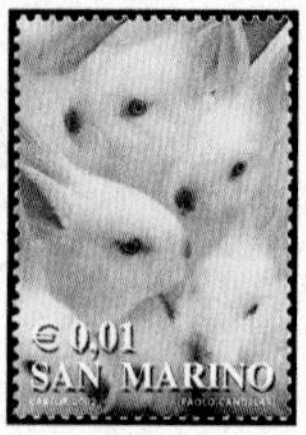

A446

Designs: 1c, Rabbits. 2c, Sunset over San Marino. 5c, Cactus. 10c, Field of grain. 25c, Aerial view of alpine landscape. 50c, Wet olive branches. €1, Sparrows. €5, Baby.

2002, Jan. 16 **Litho.** ***Perf. 13¼x13***

1522	A446	1c multi	.25	.25
1523	A446	2c multi	.25	.25
1524	A446	5c multi	.25	.25
1525	A446	10c multi	.30	.30
1526	A446	25c multi	.65	.65
1527	A446	50c multi	1.50	1.50
1528	A446	€1 multi	2.00	2.00
1529	A446	€5 multi	13.00	13.00
		Nos. 1522-1529 (8)	18.20	18.20

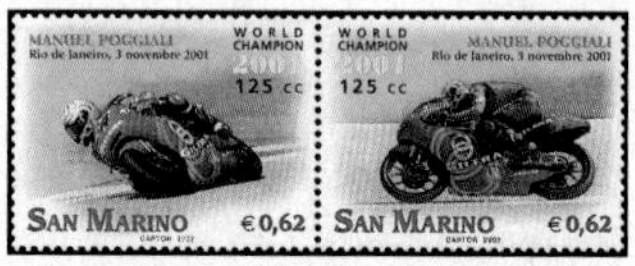

Manuel Poggiali, 2001 World 125cc Class Motorcycling Champion — A447

No. 1530: a, "2001" at UR. b, "2001" at UL.

2002, Jan. 16 ***Perf. 13x13¼***
1530 A447 62c Horiz. pair, #a-b 4.00 4.00

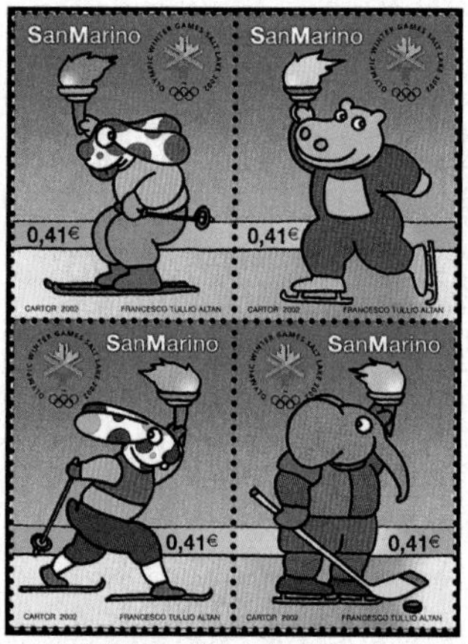

2002 Winter Olympics, Salt Lake City — A448

No. 1531: a, Dog skiing. b, Hippopotamus skating. c, Rabbit skiing. d, Elephant playing ice hockey.

2002, Jan. 16 ***Perf. 13¼x13***
1531 A448 41c Block of 4, #a-d 5.00 5.00

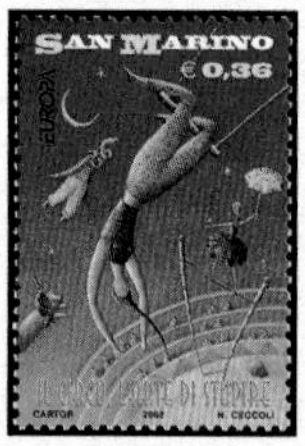

Europa — A449

Designs: 36c, Lion tamer, clown, trapeze artist, tightrope walker. 62c, Trapeze artist, horse act, clown, acrobat.

2002, Mar. 22 **Litho.** ***Perf. 13¼x13***
1532-1533 A449 Set of 2 *10.00 10.00*

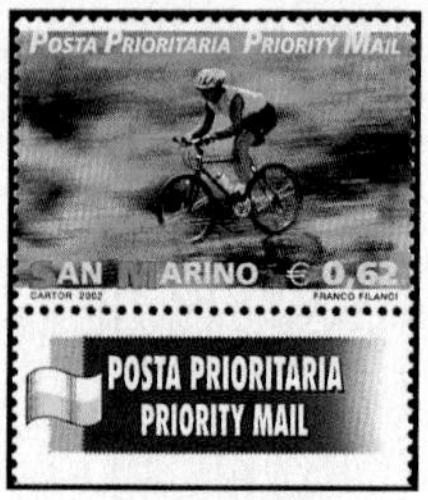

Priority Mail A450

Designs: 62c, Cyclist. €1.24, Hurdler.

2002, Mar. 22 ***Perf. 13x13¼***
Stamp + Etiquette
1534-1535 A450 Set of 2 4.75 4.75

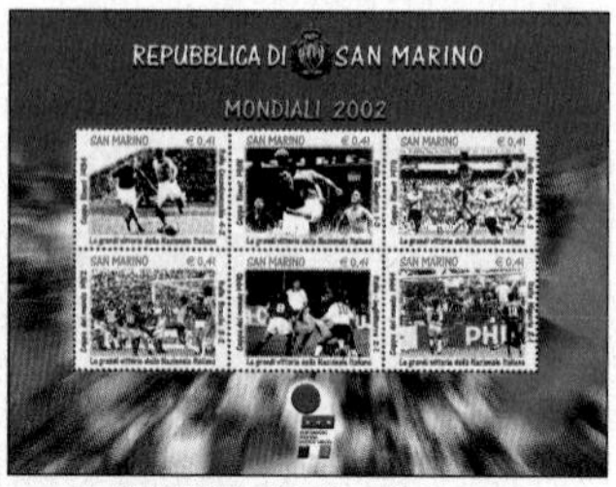

2002 World Cup Soccer Championships, Japan and Korea — A451

Scenes from Italian team's victorious matches in: a, 1934. b, 1938. c, 1970. d, 1982. e, 1990. f, 1994.

2002, Mar. 22
1536 A451 41c Sheet of 6, #a-f 6.00 6.00

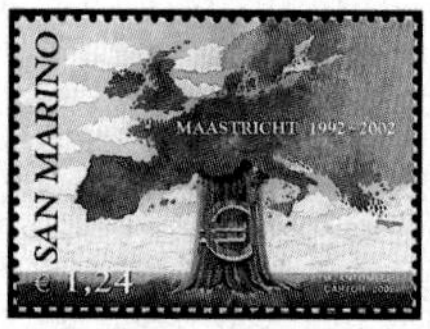

Maastricht Treaty, 10th Anniv. A452

2002, June 3 **Litho.** ***Perf. 13x13¼***
1537 A452 €1.24 multi 3.00 3.00

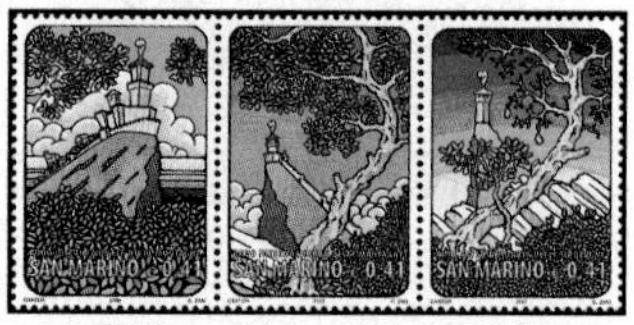

Intl. Year of Mountains — A453

No. 1538: a, Clouds at and above level of Mt. Titano. b, Clouds below Mt. Titano. c, Mt. Titano with no clouds.

2002, June 3 ***Perf. 13¼x13***
1538 A453 41c Horiz. strip of 3, #a-c 3.50 3.50

Souvenir Sheet

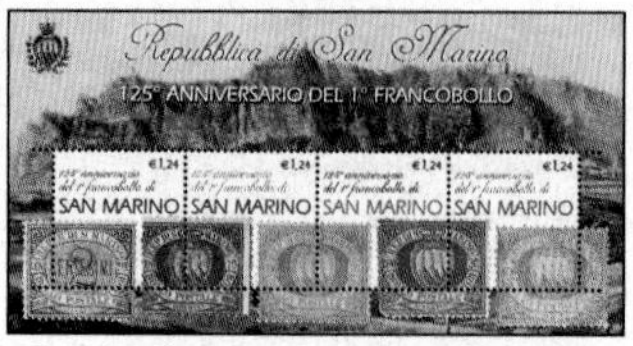

San Marino Postage Stamps, 125th Anniv. — A454

No. 1539: a, Parts of #1, 7. b, Parts of #7, 11. c, Parts of #11, 15. d, Parts of #15, 17.

2002, June 3 ***Perf. 13¼***
1539 A454 €1.24 Sheet of 4, #a-d 12.00 12.00

Intl. Amateur
Radio Conference
A455

Emblems of San Marino and International
Amateur Radio Associations, Morse code and
map in: 36c, Green. 62c, Orange.

2002, Sept. 19   **Perf. 13¼x13**
1540-1541 A455   Set of 2   2.25 2.25

Craftsmen — A456

Designs: 26c, Blacksmith. 36c, Broom
maker. 41c, Chair mender. 77c, Scribe. €1.24,
Knife grinder. €1.55, Charcoal maker.

2002, Sept. 19
1542-1547 A456   Set of 6   11.00 11.00

Souvenir Sheet

Tourist Attractions — A457

No. 1548: a, Public Palace (30x52mm). b,
Guaita (First Tower), buildings at bottom
(45x30mm). c, Cesta and Montale (Second
and Third Towers) (45x30mm). d, Basilica del
Santo (building with steps at left) (45x30mm).
e, Cappucini Church (building with steps at
center) (45x30mm). f, Gate of San Francesco
(40x40mm).

2002, Sept. 19   **Perf. 12½**
1548 A457 62c Sheet of 6, #a-
     f   9.50 9.50

Greetings — A458

Designs: No. 1549, 41c, "Da mi basia
mille. . . " No. 1550, 41c, "Hello." No. 1551,
41c, "Best Wishes." No. 1552, 41c, "Ehi! Ci
sono anch'io." No. 1553, 41c, "?????!!!!!" No.
1554, 41c, "Sorry."

2002, Oct. 31   **Perf. 13¼x13**
1549-1554 A458   Set of 6   6.00 6.00

Christmas — A459

No. 1555: a, Baby's hands grasping adult's
hands. b, Baby looking up towards mother. c,
Baby breastfeeding. d, Mother and baby
asleep. e, Hands cradling baby. f, Baby and
mother in blanket. g, Mother kissing baby. h,
Mother showing open mouth to baby. i, Baby
on mother's shoulder. j, Mother smiling at
baby. k, Mother nuzzling baby's hand. l, Two
babies.

2002, Oct. 31   **Perf. 12½**
1555 A459 41c Sheet of 12,
     #a-l   12.00 12.00

Paintings — A460

Designs: 52c, Woman with Mango, by Paul
Gauguin (1848-1903). 62c, Wheatfield with
Flight of Crows, by Vincent Van Gogh (1853-
90). €1.55, Portrait of a Young Woman, by Il
Parmigianino (1503-40).

2003, Jan. 24 Litho. Perf. 13¼x13
1556-1558 A460   Set of 3   6.50 6.50

2003 World Nordic Skiing
Championships, Val di Fiemme,
Italy — A461

No. 1559: a, Skiers #4, 13. b, Skier #37. c,
Skiers #6, 7.

2003, Jan. 24
1559 A461 77c Sheet of 3, #a-c 6.00 6.00

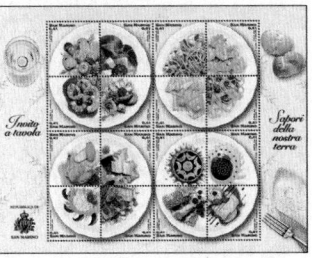

Cuisine — A462

No. 1560: a, Artichoke and mushroom
salad. b, Prosciutto, sausage and cheese. c,
Spaghetti with chopped tomatoes. d, Tortellini
with ham. e, Shrimp. f, Octopus. g, Ravioli. h,
Fettucini with tomato sauce. i, Breast of fowl. j,
Fish, shrimp and salad greens. k, Dessert with
red sauce in starburst design. l, Dessert with
yellow sauce. m, Salad with cherry tomato
garnish. n, Meat on bed of vegetables. o, Dessert with raspberry, grape and whipped cream
garnishes. p, Custard in shell with lines of
chocolate sauce.

2003, Jan. 24   **Perf. 12½**
1560 A462 41c Sheet of 16,
     #a-p   20.00 17.50

Girolamo Fracastoro (1478-1553),
Physician and Verona, Italy — A463

2003, Mar. 18 Litho. Perf. 13x13¼
1561 A463 77c multi   2.00 2.00

100th Veronafil Philatelic Exhibition, Verona,
Italy.

Europa — A464

Poster art by: 28c, Armando Testa. 77c,
Henri de Toulouse-Lautrec.

2003, Mar. 18   **Perf. 13¼x13**
1562-1563 A464   Set of 2   10.00 10.00

Race
Horses — A465

Designs: 11c, Molvedo. 15c, Tornese. 26c,
Ribot. €1.55, Varenne.

2003, Mar. 18
1564-1567 A465   Set of 4   5.50 5.50

Start of
Stagecoach
Mail
Service,
120th Anniv.
A466

Designs: 41c, Stagecoach going to Rimini.
77c, Stagecoach drawn by four horses.

2003, June 7   **Perf. 13x13¼**
1568-1569 A466   Set of 2   3.00 3.00

Powered
Flight, Cent.
A467

Designs: 36c, Wright Flyer. 41c, Bleriot XI.
62c, Aermacchi MB339. 77c, Italian 313th
Acrobatic Training Group (Frecce Tricolori).

2003, June 7
1570-1573 A467   Set of 4   5.00 5.00

St.
Petersburg,
Russia,
300th Anniv.
A468

Designs: 15c, Bridge across Winter Canal,
Fortress, Cathedral of Sts. Peter and Paul.
26c, Architect Bartolomeo Francesco Rastrelli,
Opera House. 36c, View of city from Trinity
Bridge. 41c, Aleksandr Pushkin. 77c, Empress

Catherine II (the Great). €1.55, Czar Peter I
(the Great).

2003, June 7
1574-1579 A468   Set of 6   9.00 9.00

Souvenir Sheet

Bicycle Races — A469

No. 1580: a, Tour de France, cent. b, 2003
Road Cycling World Championships, Hamilton, Ont., Canada.

2003, June 7   **Perf.**
1580 A469 77c Sheet of 2, #a-b 4.00 4.00

No. 1580 contains two 38mm diameter
stamps.

2003 Rugby World
Cup,
Australia — A470

Various rugby players: 41c, 62c, 77c, €1.55.

2003, Sept. 15 Litho. Perf. 13¼x13
1581-1584 A470   Set of 4   8.00 8.00

Children's
Games
A471

Designs: 36c, Cart racing. 41c, Blind man's
buff. 62c, Hoop rolling. 77c, Marbles. €1.24,
Handkerchief game. €1.55, Tug-of-war.

2003, Sept. 15   **Perf. 13x13¼**
1585-1590 A471   Set of 6   12.00 12.00

Puppetry — A472

No. 1591: a, Puppets with drum and cymbals. b, Puppet with horn. c, Audience, puppet
with flower. d, Audience, puppets with sticks.

2003, Sept. 15
1591 A472 41c Block of 4, #a-d 4.00 4.00

Reconstruction of
La Fenice Theater,
Venice — A473

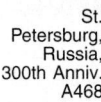

Litho. & Embossed
2003, Oct. 24　　　*Perf. 13¼x13*
1592　A473　€3.72 multi　　　15.00 15.00

Christmas — A474

No. 1593: a, Christmas cards. b, Holy Family c, Shepherds and Magi. d, Angel. e, Christmas tree, vert. f, Girl and games. g, Children, fruit and cake. h, Carolers. i, Stocking on Christmas tree, vert. j, Cornucopia. k, Arms of San Marino. l, Girl, toys and gift, vert. m, Wreath. n, Boy, sled and snowman. o, Santa Claus. p, Children, toys and Christmas tree.

2003, Oct. 24　Litho.　*Perf. 13½*
1593　A474　41c Sheet of 16,
　　　#a-p　　　16.00 16.00

Manuel
Poggiali,
2003
250cc
Motorcycle
World
Champion
A475

2004, Feb. 6　Litho.　*Perf. 13x13¼*
1594　A475　€1.55 multi　　　3.50 3.50

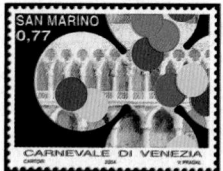

Venice
Carnival
A476

Designs: 77c, Doges' Palace. €1.55, Costumed carnival participant, canal and bridge.

2004, Feb. 6
1595-1596　A476　Set of 2　　5.50 5.50

Latin
Union,
50th Anniv.
A477

Designs: 41c, Ballerina, by Edgar Degas, tango dancers. 77c, Illustration from *Don Quixote*, scene from *Dona Flor and Her Two Husbands*. €1.55, Susanna and the Elders, by Tintoretto, and Sunday Afternoon, by Fernando Botero.

2004, Feb. 6
1597-1599　A477　Set of 3　　6.50 6.50

FIFA (Fédération
Internationale de
Football
Association),
Cent. — A478

2004, Apr. 16　Litho.　*Perf. 13¼x13*
1600　A478　€2.80 multi　　　6.50 6.50

European Bonsai
Association, 20th
Convention
A479

Trees and: 45c, Black Japanese pine bonsai, by Kunjo Kobayashi. 60c, Dwarf pine bonsai, by Pius Notter.

2004, Apr. 16
1601-1602　A479　Set of 2　　3.00 3.00

Souvenir Sheet

People's Republic of China, 55th
Anniv. — A480

No. 1603: a, Tien-an-men Palace, Beijing, and Government Palace, San Marino. b, Mount San Marino, Great Wall of China. c, Tower of San Marino, Pagoda of the Temple of Heaven, Peace Statue, vert.

Perf. 13x13¼, 13¼x13 (#1603c)
2004, Apr. 16
1603　A480　80c Sheet of 3, #a-c　6.00 6.00

Europa — A481

Fantasy vacation vehicles made up of: 45c, Automobile, airplane and boat. 80c, Boat, camper, train and bus.

Perf. 13¼x13, 13x13¼
2004, May 21　　　　　**Litho.**
1604-1605　A481　Set of 2　　3.25 3.25

2004 Summer Olympics,
Athens — A482

No. 1606: a, Chariot, boxers, javelin thrower. b, Discus thrower, wrestlers, torch bearer. c, Relay race runner, cyclist, golfer. d, Tennis player, weight lifter, gymnasts.

2004, May 21　　　*Perf. 13x13¼*
1606　A482　Horiz. strip of 4　9.50 9.50
　a.-d.　　　90c Any single　　2.00 2.00

Volkswagen Automobiles in Italy, 50th
Anniv. — A483

No. 1607: a, Blue Volkswagen Golf. b, Old and new Volkswagen Beetles, blue denomination. c, Old and new Volkswagen Beetles, green denomination. d, Silver Volkswagen Golf.

2004, May 21　　　*Perf. 13x13¼*
1607　A483　Booklet pane of
　　　　　4　　　　14.00 14.00
　a.-d.　€1.50 Any single　　3.00 3.00
　　　Complete booklet, #1607　15.00

Sao Paolo,
Brazil,
450th
Anniv.
A484

Designs: 60c, Founding of city by Jesuits Manuel de Nobrega and José Anchieta. 80c, Mario de Andrade, artist, Antonio Alcantara Machado, writer, and Municipal Theater. €1.40, City skyline, monastery building.

2004, Aug. 20
1608-1610　A484　Set of 3　　7.00 7.00

Writers — A485

Designs: 45c, Petrarch (1304-74). €1.50, Oscar Wilde (1854-1900). €2.20, Anton Chekhov (1860-1904).

2004, Aug. 20　　　*Perf. 13¼x13*
1611-1613　A485　Set of 3　　10.00 10.00

Fairy
Tales — A486

Designs: 45c, Hansel and Gretel. 60c, Little Red Riding Hood. 80c, Pinocchio. €1, Puss in Boots.

2004, Aug. 20
1614-1617　A486　Set of 4　　7.00 7.00

Souvenir Sheet

Meeting of Rimini, 25th Anniv. — A487

No. 1618: a, Man with tie, two men with construction helmets. b, Woman wearing glasses, child, woman. c, Child, woman and man. d, Priest, rabbi and man.

2004, Aug. 20　　　*Perf. 13½*
1618　A487　€1 Sheet of 4,
　　　　　#a-d　　　9.00 9.00

Christmas — A488

No. 1619 — Angels and: a, Musical instruments. b, Bag of toys. c, Christmas tree. d, Cornucopia and "2005."

2004, Nov. 12　　　*Perf. 13¼x13*
1619　A488　60c Block of 4, #a-d　6.00 6.00

Paintings
A489

Designs: 45c, Rebecca at the Well, by Giovanni Battista Piazzetta (1682-1754). €1.40, Piazza Navona, by Scipione Gino Bonichi (1904-33). €1.70, The Persistence of Memory, by Salvador Dali (1904-89).

2004, Nov. 12　　　*Perf. 14¾x14¼*
1620-1622　A489　Set of 3　　8.50 8.50

Souvenir Sheet

Reopening of La Scala Theater,
Milan — A490

No. 1623: a, Composer Antonio Salieri, theater's stage. b, Theater's facade. c, Conductor Riccardo Muti, audience.

2004, Nov. 12　　　*Perf. 13¼*
1623　A490　€1.50 Sheet of 3,
　　　　　#a-c　　　11.00 11.00

Dec. 26,
2004
Tsunami
Relief
A491

2005, Feb. 28　Litho.　*Perf. 13x13¼*
1624　A491　€1.50 multi　　　4.00 4.00

Profits from the sale of this stamp went to charities involved with tsunami relief.

Intl. Weight Lifting Federation, Cent. — A492

2005, Feb. 28   *Perf. 13¼x13*
1625 A492 €2.20 multi   5.25 5.25

2004 Beatification of Alberto Marvelli — A493

Designs: 90c, Marvelli assisting injured man. €1.80, Marvelli, Pope John Paul II, Loreto Basilica.

2005, Feb. 28
1626-1627 A493 Set of 2   6.50 6.50

Ferrari Race Cars — A494

Race cars and: 1c, Juan Manuel Fangio. 4c, Niki Lauda. 5c, John Surtees. 45c, Michael Schumacher. 62c, Ferrari emblem. €1.50, Alberto Ascari.

2005, Feb. 28
1628-1633 A494 Set of 6   6.50 6.50

Europa — A495

Designs: 62c, Bread. €1.20, Wine.

2005, Apr. 25   **Litho.**   *Perf. 13¼x13*
1634-1635 A495 Set of 2   5.00 5.00

78th Annual Reunion of Italian Alpine Troops — A496

Soldier: 36c, Climbing mountain. 45c, Picking flower. 62c, Assisting mother and child. €1, With other soldiers at reunion.

2005, Apr. 25
1636-1639 A496 Set of 4   6.00 6.00

Uniformed Militia — A497

Designs: 36c, Officer with saber, Third Tower. 45c, Soldier with musket, Second Tower. 62c, Standard bearer, Palazzo Pubblico. €1.50, Officer with saber, member of Military Band, First Tower.

2005, Apr. 25   *Perf. 13¼x14*
1640-1643 A497 Set of 4   7.00 7.00

History of Mail Service A498

Designs: 36c, Courier, ship, train. 45c, Man reading letter. 60c, Men reading letter. 62c, Man and woman.

2005, June 4   *Perf. 13x13¼*
1644-1647 A498 Set of 4   5.00 5.00

Coins A499

Designs: 36c, 1864 copper 5-centisimi coin. 45c, 1898 silver 5-lire coin. €1, Gold 10 and 20-lire coins, euro coins. €2.20, Euro coins.

2005, June 4
1648-1651 A499 Set of 4   9.50 9.50

Miniature Sheet

Musical Theater — A500

No. 1652: a, Erminio Macario in *Made in Italy*. b, Wanda Osiris in *Gran Baraonda*. c, Toto in *A Prescindere*. d, Anna Magnani in *Volumeide*. e, Aldo Fabrizzi in *Rugantino*. f, Renato Rascel in *Rascelinaria*. g, Nino Taranto in *Napoli che Ride*. h, Delia Scala in *Il Delia Scala Show*. i, Tino Scotti in *Ghe Pensi Mi*. j, Carlo Dapporto in *Giove in Doppiopetto*.

2005, June 4   *Perf. 13¼x13*
1652 A500 45c Sheet of 10, #a-j   11.00 11.00

Giovanni Pascoli (1855-1912), Poet — A501

Poetry and: 36c, Kite and child. 45c, Mt. Titano. €1, Tower and horse. €2, Pascoli and church bell tower.

2005, Aug. 26   *Perf. 13x13¼*
1653-1656 A501 Set of 4   9.00 9.00

Venice Gondola Regatta A502

Designs: €1.40, Statues of angel and devil as racing gondoliers. €2, Gondolier, vert.

Perf. 13x13¼, 13¼x13
2005, Aug. 26   **Litho.**
1657-1658 A502 Set of 2   8.50 8.50

Miniature Sheet

Italian Wine Bottle Labels — A503

No. 1659: a, Ferrari Brut. b, Amarone della Valpolicella. c, Canevel. d, Biondi-Santi. e, Vecchioflorio. f, Fazi Battaglia. g, Sassicaia, vert. h, Piano di Monte Vergine dei Feudi di San Gregorio, vert. i, Schiopetto, vert. j, Barolo, vert.

Perf. 13x13¼, 13¼x13 (vert. stamps)
2005, Aug. 26
1659 A503 45c Sheet of 10, #a-j   12.00 12.00

Dahlia — A504

Serpentine Die Cut 6¾ Vert.
2005, Nov. 17   **Photo.**
Self-Adhesive
Coil Stamp
1660 A504 (45c) multi   1.25 1.25

Pope Clement XIV (1705-74) A505

Designs: 80c, Wearing monk's habit and cardinal's biretta. €1, Giving blessing.

2005, Nov. 17   **Litho.**   *Perf. 13x13¼*
1661-1662 A505 Set of 2   4.50 4.50

Artists and Writers — A506

Designs: 36c, Baptistry door panel by Lorenzo Ghiberti (1378-1455), sculptor. 62c, The Annunciation, by Fra Angelico (c. 1400-1455). €1, Jules Verne (1828-1905), writer.

€1.30, Hans Christian Andersen (1805-75), writer.

2005, Nov. 17   *Perf. 13¼x13*
1663-1666 A506 Set of 4   8.50 8.50

Christmas A507

Designs: 62c, Annunciation. €1.55, Holy Family. €2.20, Adoration of the Magi.

2005, Nov. 17   *Perf. 13x13¼*
1667-1669 A507 Set of 3   11.00 11.00

2004 Winter Olympics, Turin — A508

No. 1670 — Ski slope with: a, American flag at left. b, Eagle and airplane at right. c, Finish line. d, Skaters at right.

2006, Feb. 1   *Perf. 12½x12¾*
1670 A508 45c Block of 4, #a-d   5.00 5.00

Christopher Columbus (1451-1506), Explorer — A509

Columbus and: 90c, Native American. €1.80, Ship and globe.

2006, Feb. 1   *Perf. 13x13¼*
1671-1672 A509 Set of 2   6.75 6.75

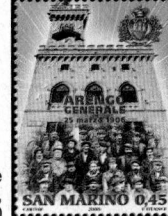

Assembly of the Patriarchs, Cent. — A510

Assembled patriarchs and: 45c, Government Palace. 62c, Statue of Liberty. €1.50, Basilica.

2006, Feb. 1   *Perf. 13¼x13*
1673-1675 A510 Set of 3   6.50 6.50

Souvenir Sheet

"Two Republics" Philatelic Exhibition — A511

2006, Apr. 5   Photo.   *Perf. 13x13¼*
1676 A511   Sheet, #1676a, Italy
     #2740   4.00   4.00
   a.   62c multi   2.00   2.00

See Italy No. 2740. On No. 1676, the San Marino stamp is on the left. On Italy No. 2740a, the San Marino stamp is on the right. Both stamps in No. 1676 have text printed on reverse.

2006 World Cup Soccer Championships, Germany
A512

2006, Apr. 5   Litho.   *Perf. 13¼x13*
1677 A512   €2.20 multi   5.50   5.50

Art — A513

Designs: 36c, Bathers, by Paul Cézanne (1839-1906). 45c, Bathsheba With King David's Letter, by Rembrandt (1606-69). 60c, Coronation of the Virgin, by Gentile da Fabriano (c. 1370-1427). €1.80, The Bridal Chamber, fresco by Andrea Mantegna (1431-c. 1506).

2006, Apr. 5   *Perf. 13x13¼*
1678-1681 A513   Set of 4   8.00   8.00

Children's Health — A514

2006, June 19   *Perf. 13¼*
1682 A514   €2.20 multi + label   6.50   6.50

Europa
A515

Designs: 45c, Butterfly with children's faces. 62c, Leonardo da Vinci's Vitruvian Man as jigsaw puzzle.

2006, June 19   *Perf. 13x13¼*
1683-1684 A515   Set of 2   *2.75   2.75*

Crossbow Federation, 50th Anniv. — A516

Designs: 36c, Flag bearers, drummer. 45c, Flag bearers carrying flags of the nine San Marino castles. 62c, Crossbowman preparing to shoot, flag of Federation. €1, Two crossbowmen positioning weapons. € 1.50, Flag-throwers and drummers. €2.80, Flags of Federation and San Marino, man holding target with shot arrows.

2006, June 19   *Perf. 13¼x13*
1685-1690 A516   Set of 6   16.50   16.50

Italy's Victory in 2006 World Cup Soccer Championships
A517

2006, Aug. 21
1691 A517   €1 multi   3.00   3.00

Intl. Gymnastics Federation, 125th Anniv. — A518

Emblem and: 15c, Rings. €2.80, Female gymnast.

2006, Aug. 21
1692-1693 A518   Set of 2   7.00   7.00

Italian Philatelic Press Union, 40th Anniv. — A519

Emblem and: 90c, Castle turrets. €2.20, Arch and statues.

2006, Aug. 21
1694-1695 A519   Set of 2   7.50   7.50

Duke Guidubaldo, Carlo Bo and University of Urbino — A520

2006, Nov. 13   Litho.   *Perf. 13*
1696 A520   €2.20 multi   5.50   5.50
    University of Urbino, 500th anniv.

Famous Men — A521

Artist's interpretations of famous works by: 5c, Roberto Rossellini (1906-77), film director. 65c, Luchino Visconti (1906-76), film director. 85c, Jacopone da Todi (c. 1236-1306), poet. €1.40, Wolfgang Amadeus Mozart (1756-91), composer.

2006, Nov. 13   *Perf. 13¼x13*
1697-1700 A521   Set of 4   7.25   7.25

A522

Christmas
A523

The Nativity, by Tiepolo: No. 1701, Joseph (detail). No. 1702, Angel (detail). No. 1703, Infant Jesus (detail). No. 1704, Virgin Mary (detail). €2.80, Entire painting.

2006, Nov. 13   Litho.   *Perf. 13¼*
1701 A522   60c multi + label   1.75   1.75
1702 A522   60c multi + label   1.75   1.75
1703 A522   65c multi + label   1.90   1.90
1704 A522   65c multi + label   1.90   1.90
1705 A523   €2.80 multi   8.50   8.50
   a.   Booklet pane, #1701-1705,
      + label, perf. 13¼ on 3
      sides   16.00   —
     Complete booklet, #1705a   16.00
     Nos. 1701-1705 (5)   15.80   15.80

No. 1705a lacks the small labels attached to Nos. 1701-1704.

San Marino's Presidency of the Council of Europe Committee of Ministers — A524

2007, Jan. 23   Litho.   *Perf. 13¼*
1706 A524   65c multi   1.75   1.75
     Printed in sheets of 4.

Alessandro Glaray, San Marino Philatelic Expert
A525

2007, Jan. 23   *Perf. 13x13¼*
1707 A525   €1.80 multi   4.50   4.50

Gina Lollobrigida, Actress and Artist — A526

Designs: 65c, Self-portrait. 85c, "Potato Seller," photograph by Lollobrigida. €1, "Esmerelda," sculpture by Lollobrigida. €3.20, Lollobrigida and Mother Teresa.

2007, Jan. 23   *Perf. 13¼x13*
1708-1711 A526   Set of 4   14.00   14.00

25th San Gabriel Intl. Philatelic Art Award — A527

2007, Apr. 20
1712 A527   €1.50 multi   3.75   3.75

Items Designed by Bruno Munari (1907-98) A528

Designs: 36c, Window-dresser's tool. 65c, Milk carton. €1.40, Shutter lock. €2, Hangable shop light.

2007, Apr. 20   *Perf. 12½x12¾*
1713-1716 A528   Set of 4   11.00   11.00

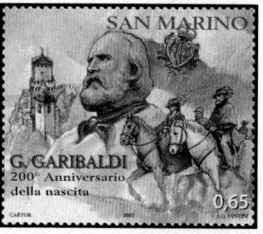

Giuseppe Garibaldi (1807-82), Italian Nationalist Leader — A529

Designs: 65c, Garibaldi, San Marino flag, men on horseback. €1.40, Garibaldi landing at Marsala, battle scene. €2, Garibaldi on horseback, Garibaldi shaking hands with King Victor Emmanuel II of Italy.

2007, Apr. 20   Litho.   *Perf. 13¼x13*
1717-1719 A529   Set of 3   10.00   10.00

Europa — A530

Designs: 60c, Scouts, stylized globe, compass. 65c, Scouts, stylized globe, map of San Marino.

2007, June 2
1720-1721 A530   Set of 2   3.25   3.25
     Scouting, cent.

2007 European Baseball Cup, San Marino — A531

Designs: 65c, Batter, catcher and umpire. €1, Pitcher.

2007, June 2
1722-1723 A531   Set of 2   4.25   4.25

2007 World Track and Field Championships, Osaka, Japan — A532

Designs: 60c, High jump. 85c, Long jump, horiz. €1.50, Runners, horiz.

2007, June 2   **Perf. 13**
1724-1726 A532   Set of 3   6.50 6.50

Souvenir Sheet

Postilions, 400th Anniv. — A533

Litho. & Engr.
2007, June 2   **Perf. 13¼**
1727 A533 €4.50 multi   11.00 11.00

Intl. Assoc. of Editors of Stamp Catalogues, Albums and Philatelic Publications (ASCAT), 30th Anniv. — A534

2007, Aug. 24   Litho.   Perf. 13¼x13
1728 A534 65c multi   1.75 1.75

Castles — A535

No. 1729: a, Rocca, San Marino. b, Orava Castle, Slovakia.

Litho. & Engr.
2007, Aug. 24   **Perf. 13**
1729 A535 65c Horiz. pair, #a-b   3.25 3.25
No. 1729 was printed in sheets containing four pairs. See Slovakia No. 525.

Miniature Sheet

European Wine Labels — A536

No. 1730: a, 1996 Porto Quinta do Estanho. b, Tarlant Cuvée Louis Brut Champagne, horiz. c, Bauget-Jouette Champagne, horiz. d, 2006 Zlahtina. e, 2006 Petri Riesling. f, 1999 Tokaji, horiz. g, Carmelo Rodero Ribera de Duero, horiz. h, Teodor Belo Simcic.

Perf. 13¼x13, 13x13¼ (horiz. stamps)
2007, Aug. 24   **Litho.**
1730 A536 65c Sheet of 8, #a-h, + 2 labels   12.50 12.50

Equal Opportunity To All — A537

2007, Dec. 3   Litho.   Perf. 13¼x13
1731 A537 €1 multi   6.50 6.50

Famous People — A538

Designs: 60c, Arturo Toscanini (1867-1957), conductor. 65c, Sculpture of Paolina Borghese, by Antonio Canova (1757-1822). €1, Carlo Goldoni (1707-93), playwright. €1.80, Via Toscanella, painting by Ottone Rosai (1895-1957).

2007, Dec. 3
1732-1735 A538   Set of 4   10.00 10.00

Christmas — A539

Designs: 60c, Government Palace, Christmas tree, and Star of Bethlehem. 65c, Santa Claus. 85c, Holy Family.

2007, Dec. 3
1736-1738 A539   Set of 3   5.25 5.25

Milan International Soccer Team, Cent. — A540

2008, Feb. 26   Litho.   Perf. 13¼x13
1739 A540 €1 multi   2.50 2.50

San Marino Post Office, 175th Anniv. A541

2008, Feb. 26   **Perf. 13x13¼**
1740 A541 €1.80 multi   4.50 4.50

Paintings — A542

Designs: 36c, The Crucifixion, by Giovanni Bellini. 60c, Madonna and Child with St. John, by Jacopo Bassano. 65c, Venus and Love, by Gian Antonio Pellegrini. 85c, Old Man's Face, by Giandomenico Tiepolo.

2008, Feb. 26   **Perf. 13¼x13**
1741-1744 A542   Set of 4   6.00 6.00

Intl. Year of Planet Earth A543

Designs: 60c, Stylized skeleton and car emitting exhaust. 85c, Stylized sun and person. €1.40, Drop of water and tipped glass. €2, Earth on fire.

2008, Feb. 26   **Perf. 13x13¼**
1745-1748 A543   Set of 4   12.00 12.00

European Year of Intercultural Dialogue — A544

2008, Apr. 8   Litho.   Perf. 14¼x14½
1749 A544 65c multi   1.75 1.75
Printed in sheets of 3.

Concetto Marchesi (1878-1957), Historian of Italian and Latin Literature — A545

2008, Apr. 8   **Perf. 13x13¼**
1750 A545 €1 multi   2.50 2.50

Apparition at Lourdes, 150th Anniv. — A546

Designs: 36c, Bernadette Soubirous, first miracle healing. 60c, Procession of faithful at Lourdes. €2, Apparition of Virgin Mary before Soubirous.

2008, Apr. 8   **Perf. 13¼x13**
1751-1753 A546   Set of 3   7.25 7.25

Our Lady of Mercy, Bas-relief by Leonardo Blanco — A547

Litho. & Embossed
2008, June 13   **Perf. 13¼x13**
1754 A547 €1 multi   2.75 2.75

San Marino-America Friendship Association, 30th Anniv. — A548

2008, June 13   **Litho.**
1755 A548 €1.50 multi   3.75 3.75

Europa A549

Boy and girl: 60c, On ships. 65c, On globe releasing doves.

2008, June 13   **Perf. 13x13¼**
1756-1757 A549   Set of 2   3.25 3.25

Souvenir Sheet

2008 Summer Olympics, Beijing — A550

No. 1758: a, 36c, Table tennis. b, 65c, Fencing. c, 85c, Swimming.

2008, June 13
1758 A550   Sheet of 3, #a-c   4.75 4.75

Andrea Palladio (1508-80), Architect A551

2008, Aug. 22   Litho.   Perf. 13x13¼
1759 A551 €1 multi   2.75 2.75

A552

Road Cycling World Championships, Varese, Italy — A553

2008, Aug. 22   *Perf. 13¼x13*
1760 A552   85c multi   2.25 2.25
1761 A553   €3.25 multi   8.75 8.75

Famous People — A554

Designs: 60c (No. 1762), Posters for operas by Giacomo Puccini (1858-1924). 60c (No. 1763), Scenes from *Cuore*, by Edmondo De Amicis (1846-1908). €1, Rotonda di Palmieri and Vita Militare, paintings by Giovanni Fattori (1825-1908). €1.40, Book cover designs and actors in movie based on works by Giovannino Guareschi (1908-68), writer. €1.70, Piece of pottery and painting, The Print Collectors, by Honoré Daumier (1808-79), artist. €2.20, Scene from *La Luna e i Falò*, by Cesare Pavese (1908-50).

2008
1762-1767 A554   Set of 6   12.00 12.00
   Issued: No. 1762, €1, €1.40, €1.70, 8/22; No. 1763, €2.20, 11/18.

International Polar Year — A555

Designs: 60c, Mountain. €1, Penguins. €1.20, Helicopter over ice sheet.

2008, Nov. 18   *Perf. 13x13¼*
1768-1770 A555   Set of 3   7.25 7.25

Miniature Sheet

Addition of San Marino Historic Center and Mt. Titano to UNESCO World Heritage List — A556

No. 1771: a, Cesta Tower. b, Basilica. c, Statue of Liberty, Government Palace. d, Omerelli neighborhood. e, Buildings near wall. f, Guaita Tower.

2008, Nov. 18   *Perf. 13¼x13*
1771 A556   €1 Sheet of 6, #a-
           f   13.50 13.50

Christmas A557

Designs: 36c, Angel playing trumpet. 60c, Holy Family. €1, Angel with gift.

2008, Nov. 18
1772-1774 A557   Set of 3   5.00 5.00

San Marino Olympic Committee, 50th Anniv. — A558

2009, Feb. 20   Litho.   *Perf. 13¼x14*
1775 A558   €1.80 multi   4.25 4.25

Ceramics A559

Designs: 36c, Amphora, by Libero Cellarosi. 60c, Amphora, by Umberto Masi. 85c, Vase, by Giorgio Monti.

2009, Feb. 20   *Perf. 13x13¼*
1776-1778 A559   Set of 3   4.25 4.25

Miniature Sheet

Futurist Manifesto, by Filippo Tomasso Marinetti, Cent. — A560

No. 1779: a, Dog on a Leash, painting by Giacomo Balla (40x30mm). b, Armored Train, painting by Giono Severini (30x40mm). c, Electric Power Plant, painting by Antonio Sant'Elia (30x45mm). d, Zang Tumb Tumb, by Marinetti (45x30mm). e, Red Horseman, painting by Carlo Carra (40x30mm). f, Noise machine, by Luigi Russolo (53x30mm). g, Cyclist, painting by Umberto Boccioni (40x30mm). h, Still Life with Red Egg, by Ardeng Soffici (30x38mm). i, Unique Forms of Continuity in Space, sculpture by Boccioni (30x38mm). j, Futurist Evening, drawing by Boccioni (45x30mm).

2009, Feb. 20   *Perf. 12½ to 13¼*
1779 A560   60c Sheet of 10,
          #a-j, + label   14.50 14.50

38th Intl. Criminal Police Organization and Interpol European Regional Conference, San Marino — A561

2009, May 8   Litho.   *Perf. 14x13¼*
1780 A561   €2 multi   5.00 5.00

San Marino Expo 2010 Pavilion and Shanghai Skyline — A562

2009, May 8   Litho.   *Perf. 13*
1781 A562   €2.20 multi   5.50 5.50

Europa — A563

Designs: 60c, Earth, Saturn, Neptune, astronomical instruments. 65c, Solar System, star ring of European Union flag, Mount Titano.

2009, May 8   Litho.   *Perf. 13½x14*
1782-1783 A563   Set of 2   3.25 3.25
        Intl. Year of Astronomy.

World Air Games, Turin — A564

Doves and: 60c, Hot-air balloon. 85c, Glider. €1.50, Helicopter. €1.80, Airplane.

2009, May 8   Litho.   *Perf. 13¼*
1784-1787 A564   Set of 4   11.00 11.00

Louis Braille (1809-52), Educator of the Blind — A565

Litho. & Embossed
2009, June 16   *Perf. 13¼x13*
1788 A565   €1.50 multi   3.75 3.75

Writers of Detective Stories A566

Designs relating to and names of characters from stories by: 36c, Edgar Allan Poe (1809-49). 85c, Arthur Conan Doyle (1859-1930). €1.40, Raymond Chandler (1888-1959).

2009, June 16   Litho.   *Perf. 14x13¼*
1789-1791 A566   Set of 3   6.00 6.00

16th Mediterranean Games, Pescara, Italy — A567

Designs: 60c, Running. €1.40, Cycling. €1.70, Wrestling.

2009, June 16
1792-1794 A567   Set of 3   9.75 9.75

Miniature Sheet

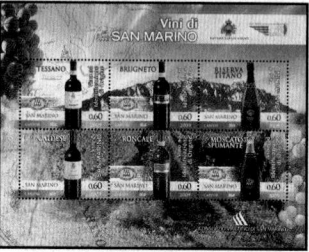

Wines of San Marino — A568

No. 1795: a, Tessano. b, Brugneto. c, Riserva Titano. d, Caldese. e, Roncale. f, Moscato Spumante.

2009, June 16   *Perf. 13x13¼*
1795 A568   60c Sheet of 6, #a-
          f   8.00 8.00

Bologna Soccer Club, Cent. A569

2009, Aug. 25
1796 A569   €1 multi   2.50 2.50

30th Rimini Meeting — A570

2009, Aug. 25   Litho.   *Perf. 13½x14*
1797 A570   €1.80 multi   4.50 4.50

Souvenir Sheets

Attractions of San Marino — A571

No. 1798, €1 — Interior of Palazzo Pubblico with: a, Entire denomination on vignette. b, Part of final "0" of denomination on black frame.
No. 1799, €1 — Statue of St. Marinus with: a, Entire denomination on vignette. b, Part of final "0" of denomination on black frame.

No. 1800, €1 — Statue of Liberty and Piazza della Libertà with: a, "1" of denomination below "a" of "San." b, "1" of denomination below "S."

2009, Aug. 25   Litho.   Perf. 13¾x14
1798-1800 A571   Set of 3   15.00 15.00

European Year of Creativity and Innovation. Nos. 1798-1800 were sold as a set with a €1.40 postal card that opened up to serve as a stereoscope for the stamp sheets. The set included a pair of plastic lenses for the stereoscope, an instruction card for assembling the stereoscope, a self-adhesive seal for the postal card, and an imperforate sample stereoscope card depicting the vignette shown on the postal card that was not valid for postage. Values are for the set of 3 sheets only.

Italian Language Day — A572

2009, Oct. 21   Photo.   Perf. 13¼x13
1801 A572 60c multi + label   2.50 2.50

Issued in sheets of 5 + 5 labels. See Italy No. 2966; Vatican City No. 1426.

Pets A573

Winning photographs in pet photography contest: 36c, Cat, by Natascia Stefanelli. 60c, Poodle, by Tina Woodcock. 65c, Duck, by Ettore Zonzini. 75c, Kid, foal and dog, by Anna Rosa Francioni. 85c, Turtle, by Maria Eleonora Vaglio. €1.20, Dog and butterfly, by Lorenzo Zamagni.

2009, Oct. 21   Litho.   Perf. 14x13¼
1802-1807 A573   Set of 6   11.50 11.50

Souvenir Sheet

Christmas — A574

No. 1808 — Rest on the Flight Into Egypt, by Caravaggio: a, €1.50, Joseph and angel. b, €2, Madonna and Child, horiz.

2009, Oct. 21   Perf. 13¾
1808 A574   Sheet of 2, #a-b   8.75 8.75

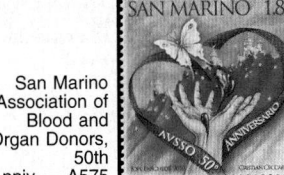

San Marino Association of Blood and Organ Donors, 50th Anniv. — A575

2010, Feb. 9   Litho.   Perf. 13¾
1809 A575   €1.80 multi   4.50 4.50

Flowers — A576

No. 1810: a, 10c, Daffodils. b, 85c, Hyacinths. c, €1, Grape hyacinths. d, €1.50, Tulips.

2010, Feb. 9   Perf. 13¼x13
1810 A576   Block or strip of 4, #a-d   8.75 8.75

Souvenir Sheet

2010 Winter Olympics, Vancouver — A577

No. 1811: a, 65c, Ski jumping, snowboarding, ice hockey, speed skating. b, 85c, Downhill skiing, cross-country skiing, curling, bobsledding. c, €1, Speed skating, figure skating, downhill skiing.

2010, Feb. 9   Perf. 13x13¼
1811 A577   Sheet of 3, #a-c   6.25 6.25

Miniature Sheet

Expo 2010, Shanghai — A578

No. 1812: a, 65c, San Marino flag, Third Tower on Mt. Titano (30x40mm). b, €1, Second Tower, Great Wall of China (30x40mm). c, €1.50, First Tower, spear of Statue of Liberty (30x40mm). d, €1.80, San Marino Government Building, Statue of Liberty (36x51mm).

Perf. 13¼x13, 13¼ (#1812d)
2010, Feb. 9
1812 A578   Sheet of 4, #a-d   12.00 12.00

Men's Volleyball World Championships, Italy — A579

2010, Mar. 17   Perf. 13¼x14
1813 A579 €1 multi   2.50 2.50

2010 World Cup Soccer Championships, South Africa — A580

2010, Mar. 17   Perf. 14x13¼
1814 A580   €1.50 multi   3.50 3.50

Italian Cyclists — A581

No. 1815: a, €1.40, Gino Bartali (1914-2000). b, €1.50, Fausto Coppi (1919-60).

2010, Mar. 17
1815 A581   Horiz. pair, #a-b   7.25 7.25

Europa A582

Designs: 60c, Girl with wings of book pages. 65c, Girl asleep on a book in space.

2010, Mar. 17   Perf. 14¾x14
1816-1817 A582   Set of 2   3.00 3.00

Miniature Sheet

Friendship Between San Marino and Japan — A583

No. 1818: a, Statue of La Repubblica, by Vittorio Pochini, La Rocca tower, San Marino. b, Himeji Castle, Japan. c, Apparition of Saint Marinus to His People, mural by Emilio Retrosi. d, Nihonbashi Bridge in the Morning, painting by Hiroshige.

2010, Mar. 17   Perf. 13x13¼
1818 A583   €1.50 Sheet of 4, #a-d   14.00 14.00

See Japan No. 3217.

San Marino Lions Club, 50th Anniv. A584

Various photos of San Marino with country name in: 36c, Red violet. 60c, Orange brown.

2010, July 26   Litho.   Perf. 14x13¼
1819-1820 A584   Set of 2   2.25 2.25

F.C. Internazionale, 2009-10 Italian Soccer Champions — A585

No. 1821: a, Italian flag, soccer ball, F.C. Internazionale emblem. b, Shield inscribed "18," part of soccer ball. c, Part of soccer ball, European Union flag.

2010, July 26
1821   Horiz. strip of 3   7.50 7.50
a.-c.   A585 €1 Any single   2.40 2.40

Miniature Sheet

Sites in San Marino and Gibraltar — A586

No. 1822: a, Second Tower, San Marino. b, Moorish Castle, Gibraltar. c, Mt. Titano, San Marino. d, Rock of Gibraltar.

2010, July 26
1822 A586   €1.50 Sheet of 4, #a-d   15.00 15.00

See Gibraltar No. 1237.

Famous People A587

Designs: 60c, Moon, hands of Frédéric Chopin (1810-49), composer. 65c, Scenes from movies, *The Seven Samurai, Ran,* and *Dersu Uzala,* directed by Akira Kurosawa (1910-98). 85c, Symphony orchestra and conductor Gustav Mahler (1860-1911), composer. €1, *The Birth of Venus,* by Sandro Botticelli (1445-1510), vert. €1.40, *The Tempest,* by Giorgione da Castelfranco (c. 1477-1510), vert. €1.45, *The Supper at Emmaus,* by Caravaggio (1571-1610), vert. €1.50, *The Football Players,* by Henri Rousseau (1844-1910), vert. €4.95, Characters from "The Adventures of Huckleberry Finn," and Mark Twain (1835-1910), author.

2010   Perf. 14x13¼, 13¼x14
1823-1830 A587   Set of 8   30.00 30.00

Issued: 60c, 65c, 85c, €4.95, 10/5; others, 7/26.

Luciano Pavarotti (1935-2007), Opera Singer — A588

2010, Oct. 5   **Perf. 14x13¼**
1831 A588 €2.20 multi   5.25 5.25

Christmas A589

Christmas tree with background color of: 60c, Blue. 65c, Green. 85c, Red.

Litho. With Foil Application
2010, Oct. 5   **Perf. 13x13¼**
1832-1834 A589   Set of 3   5.00 5.00

Sport in the Philately of San Marino Exhibition A590

2011, Feb. 8 Litho.   **Perf. 14¼x14¾**
1835 A590 €1.50 multi   3.50 3.50

San Marino Choir, 50th Anniv. — A591

2011, Feb. 8
1836 A591 €2.20 multi   5.25 5.25

Luigi Einaudi (1874-1961), President of Italy — A592

2011, Feb. 8   **Perf. 14¾x14¼**
1837 A592 €3.30 multi   7.75 7.75

Paintings A593

Designs: 10c, Self-portrait with a Beret, by Paul Cézanne. 50c, Horse Racing at Longchamp, by Edgar Degas. 85c, View from the Artist's Window, by Camille Pissarro. €1, Flower Beds at Vétheuil, by Claude Monet.

€2.50, Jacques Bergeret as a Child, by Pierre-Auguste Renoir.

2011, Feb. 8   **Perf. 13¾**
1838-1842 A593   Set of 5   11.00 11.00

Europa A594

Designs: 60c, Forest. 65c, Stacked logs.

2011, Apr. 5 Litho.   **Perf. 14¾x14¼**
1843-1844 A594   Set of 2   3.00 3.00

Intl. Year of Forests.

First Men in Space, 50th Anniv. A595

Designs: 50c, Yuri Gagarin (1934-68), Soviet cosmonaut. €2.40, Alan B. Shepard, Jr. (1923-98), American astronaut.

2011, Apr. 5
1845-1846 A595   Set of 2   6.75 6.75

Souvenir Sheet

Flowers — A596

No. 1847: a, Delphinium "Verissimo del Titano." b, Dianthus "Sant'Agata." c, Rosa "Repubblica di San Marino."

2011, Apr. 5
1847 A596 €1.50 Sheet of 3,   11.00 11.00
        #a-c

Miniature Sheet

Tourism — A597

No. 1848 — Sites in San Marino: a, Prima Torre (First Tower). b, Basilica del Santo, horiz. c, Chiesa dei Cappuccini (Church of the Capuchin), horiz. d, Palazzo del Governo (Government Building). e, Chiesa di San Francesco (San Francesco Church). f, Porta San Francesco (San Francesco Gate).

2011, Apr. 5   **Perf. 14¾**
1848 A597 65c Sheet of 6, #a-   9.50 9.50
      f

Brescia Soccer Team, Cent. — A598

2011, June 4   **Perf. 14x14¾**
1849 A598 €1 multi   2.75 2.75

Visit of Pope Benedict XVI to San Marino A599

2011, June 4   **Perf. 14¾x14**
1850 A599 €1 multi   2.75 2.75

Souvenir Sheet

Anita and Giuseppe Garibaldi, First Tower of San Marino — A600

2011, June 4   **Perf. 14x13¼**
1851 A600 €1.50 multi   3.75 3.75
Granting of San Marino citizenship to Garibaldis. See Italy No. 3070.

Miniature Sheet

World Theater Day — A601

No. 1852: a, Statue of Liberty, San Marino, buildings. b, Mask with tassels, buildings. c, Character with arms extended. d, Face, three towers of San Marino. e, Face, dancers in ring. f, Dancers in ring.

2011, June 4   **Perf. 13¾x13¼**
1852 A601 85c Sheet of 6, #a-   12.00 12.00
      f

A.C. Milan, 2010-11 Italian Soccer Champions A602

2011, Oct. 11   **Perf. 14**
1853 A602 €1 multi   2.50 2.50

Alcide De Gasperi (1881-1954), Italian Prime Minister — A603

No. 1854 — De Gasperi and: a, 50c, Family, scales, war damage. b, €2.64, Torch, map of Europe.

2011, Oct. 11   **Perf. 14x13½**
1854 A603   Horiz. pair, #a-b   7.50 7.50

Souvenir Sheet

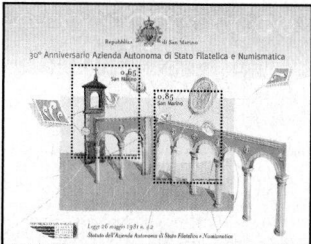

European Year of Volunteering — A604

2011, Oct. 11   **Perf. 14¾x14¼**
1855 A604 €4.95 multi   12.00 12.00

Souvenir Sheet

Philatelic and Numismatic Bureau of San Marino, 30th Anniv. — A605

No. 1856: a, 65c, Tower, arches, stamp and coins. b, 85c, Arches, stamp and coins.

2011, Oct. 11   **Perf. 13½x14**
1856 A605   Sheet of 2, #a-b   3.50 3.50

Miniature Sheet

Christmas — A606

No. 1857: a, 85c, Angels. b, €1, Magi. c, €1.50, Shepherd and Mary. d, €2.50, Mary and infant Jesus.

2011, Oct. 11
1857 A606   Sheet of 4, #a-d   14.00 14.00

Milano Marittima,
Italy,
Cent. — A607

2012, Feb. 29
1858 A607 €1 multi — 2.75 2.75

Miniature Sheet

Paintings by Gustav Klimt (1862-
1918) — A608

No. 1859: a, 85c, The Embrace
(L'abbraccio). b, €1, The Kiss (Il bacio). c,
€1.40, The Three Ages of Woman (Le tre età
della donna). d, €1.50, Hope II (La speranza
II).

2012, Feb. 29 **Perf. 13¼x13**
1859 A608 Sheet of 4, #a-d — 12.50 12.50

Souvenir Sheet

New San Marino Coat of
Arms — A609

No. 1860: a, 60c, Crown, arms in blue. b,
85c, Berry on branch, arms in silver. c, €4.95,
Old arms in circle, new arms in gold.

Litho. With Foil Application
2012, Feb. 29 **Perf. 13x13¼**
1860 A609 Sheet of 3, #a-c — 17.00 17.00

Faetano
Ceramics,
50th Anniv.
A610

2012, May 9 **Litho.** **Perf. 14**
1861 A610 65c multi — 1.75 1.75

Santos Soccer
Team,
Cent. — A611

2012, May 9 **Perf. 14x14¾**
1862 A611 €1 multi — 2.50 2.50

Intl. Year of Sustainable Energy For
All — A612

No. 1863: a, Biomass energy. b, Geother-
mic energy. c, Hydroelectric and marine
energy. d, Wind and solar energy.

2012, May 9 **Perf. 13x13¼**
1863 A612 50c Block of 4, #a-d — 5.00 5.00

Miniature Sheet

United Nations Convention on
Preservation of World Heritage, 40th
Anniv. — A613

No. 1864: a, Mt. Titano, construction workers, rose, painter holding brush, woman looking through binoculars. b, Painter, Pyramid,
Egyptian statues, volcano. c, Charles Darwin,
man and woman in water, pteranosaur,
Galapagos sea tortoise. d, Scroll, rainbow,
sailboat, man on ladder, cyclist, Eiffel Tower,
building, sculpture.

2012, May 9 **Perf. 13**
1864 A613 €1.50 Sheet of 4,
#a-d — 15.00 15.00

Juvenus, 2011-
12 Italian Soccer
Champions
A614

2012, May 29 **Perf. 13¼x13**
1865 A614 €1 multi — 2.50 2.50

Europa — A616

2012, June 13 **Perf. 13¼x13**
1867 A616 65c multi — 1.60 1.60

2012 Summer Olympics,
London — A617

No. 1868: a, Olympic flame, woman wearing
laurel garland. b, Swimmer wearing goggles
and swim cap. c, Male athlete. d, Shooter
wearing cap and ear protection.

2012, June 13 **Perf. 13¼x13¾**
1868 A617 Horiz. strip of 4 — 5.00 5.00
a.-d. 50c Any single — 1.25 1.25

Souvenir Sheet

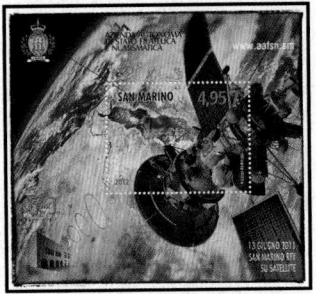

San Marino Television on
Satellite — A618

2012, June 13 **Perf. 13¾x14**
1869 A618 €4.95 multi — 12.50 12.50

Italian Earthquake Relief — A619

2012, Aug. 30 **Perf. 14**
1870 A619 €1 multi — 2.60 2.60

San Marino-
Rimini Electric
Railway, 80th
Anniv. — A620

2012, Oct. 16
1871 A620 €2.64 multi — 6.75 6.75

Italian Socialist Politicians — A621

No. 1872: a, Filippo Turati (1857-1932). b,
Giacomo Matteotti (1885-1924).

2012, Oct. 16 **Perf. 13¼**
1872 A621 Horiz. pair + central label — 11.50 11.50
a. €1.74 multi — 4.50 4.50
b. €2.64 multi — 6.75 6.75

Miniature Sheet

International Wine Labels — A622

No. 1873: a, Kendall-Jackson Chardonnay,
United States. b, Casillero del Diablo
Cabernet Sauvignon, Chile. c, Mission Hill
Family Estate Pinot Noir, Canada. d, Octagon
Red Table Wine, United States. e, Jacob's
Creek Shiraz Cabernet, Australia. f, Luigi
Bosca Malbec, Argentina. g, Groot Constantia
Landgoed, South Africa.

2012, Oct. 16 **Perf. 13¼x13**
1873 A622 €1 Sheet of 7, #a-
g — 18.00 18.00

Souvenir Sheet

Diplomatic Relations Between San
Marino and Croatia, 20th
Anniv. — A623

No. 1874 — Traditional costumes with
denomination at: a, LR. b, LL.

2012, Oct. 16 **Perf. 14**
1874 A623 85c Sheet of 2, #a-b — 4.50 4.50
See Croatia No. 851.

Madonna and
Child, by Marco
Ventura — A624

2012, Oct. 16
1875 A624 85c multi — 2.25 2.25
Christmas.

San Marino World Symposium on
Unidentified Flying Objects, 20th
Anniv.
A625

2013, Feb. 13 **Perf. 13x13¼**
1876 A625 85c multi — 2.25 2.25

2012, June 13 **Perf. 13x13¼**
1866 A615 60c multi — 1.50 1.50

25th San Marino CEPU Open Tennis
Championships — A615

Souvenir Sheet

Edict of Milan, 1700th Anniv. — A626

No. 1877: a, Men and women, bas-reliefs of Roman Emperors Constantine and Licinius. b, Map of Europe, chrismon, medal.

2013, Feb. 13
1877 A626 €2.50 Sheet of 2,
#a-b   13.00 13.00

Souvenir Sheet

2013 World Nordic Skiing Championships, Val di Fiemme, Italy — A627

No. 1878: a, 85c, Ski jumper. b, €1.74, Boots of Nordic combined skier. c, €2.64, Cross-country skiers, vert.

2013, Feb. 13   **Perf. 13**
1878 A627   Sheet of 3, #a-c 13.50 13.50

Tre Monti Cake and Emblem of La Serenissima Cake Company A628

2013, Apr. 3   **Perf. 13x13¼**
1879 A628 70c multi   1.90 1.90

Rimini to San Marino Flight of Gianni Widmer, Cent. — A629

2013, Apr. 3   **Perf. 14**
1880 A629 €1.90 multi   5.00 5.00

Campaign to Prevent Cardiovascular Disease — A630

2013, Apr. 3
1881 A630 €2 multi   5.25 5.25

Europa A631

Designs: 70c, Porta San Francesco, automobile from early 20th cent., envelope. 85c, Parva Domus, Volkswagen van, 1950s, stamped cover.

2013, Apr. 3   **Perf. 13x13¼**
1882-1883 A631   Set of 2   4.00 4.00

Souvenir Sheet

Donation of Mount La Verna to St. Francis of Assisi, 800th Anniv. — A632

2013, Apr. 3   **Perf. 13¼x13½**
1884 A632 €3.50 multi   9.00 9.00

Genoa Cricket and Soccer Team, 120th Anniv. — A633

2013, Apr. 13   **Perf. 14x14¾**
1885 A633 €1 multi   2.60 2.60

European Patent Convention, 40th Anniv. — A634

2013, June 7   **Perf. 13¼x13**
1886 A634 85c multi   2.25 2.25

Juventus, 2012-13 Italian Soccer Champions A635

2013, June 7   **Perf. 14**
1887 A635 €1 multi   2.75 2.75

Assistance of San Marino in Building of Nursery School in Matola, Malawi — A636

Rainbow and: 10c, Children, map of Africa. 70c, School building, horiz.

2013, June 7
1888-1889 A636   Set of 2   2.25 2.25

Souvenir Sheet

Church of St. John the Baptist, San Marino — A637

No. 1890: a, €1.90, Church exterior. b, €3.20, Church altar.

2013, June 7   **Perf. 13¼x13**
1890 A637   Sheet of 2, #a-b 14.00 14.00

Miniature Sheet

Determination of San Marino Borders, 550th Anniv. — A638

No. 1891 — Map of various border areas of San Marino, and: a, 70c, Insect. b, 85c, Bird. c, €1.90, Bird and flowers. d, €2, Bird, flowers, wax seal.

2013, June 7   **Perf. 14x13¼**
1891 A638   Sheet of 4, #a-d 15.00 15.00
See Italy No. 3191.

Italian Thematic Philately Center, 50th Anniv. — A639

2013, Oct. 9   Litho.   Perf. 13½x14
1892 A639 €1 multi   2.75 2.75

Scenes From Operas A640

Scene from: 70c, Aida, by Giuseppe Verdi (1813-1901). 85c, The Ring of the Nibelung, by Richard Wagner (1813-83).

2013, Oct. 9   Litho.   Perf. 13x13¼
1893-1894 A640   Set of 2   4.25 4.25

Rally Legend, 10th Anniv. — A641

No. 1895: a, Lancia Delta, emblem at UL. b, Volkswagen Golf, emblem at UR.

2013, Oct. 9   Litho.   Perf. 13x13¼
1895 A641 €1 Horiz. pair, #a-b 5.50 5.50

Miniature Sheet

UNESCO World Heritage Sites in Italy — A642

No. 1896: a, Basilica of St. Francis, Assisi (990). b, Ducal Palace, Urbino (828). c, Mausoleum of Theodoric, Ravenna (788). d, Estense Castle, Ferrara (733bis).

2013, Oct. 9   Litho.   Perf. 13x13¼
1896 A642 €1.40 Sheet of 4,
#a-d   15.50 15.50

Souvenir Sheet

Admission of San Marino to Council of Europe, 25th Anniv. — A643

No. 1897 — Arms of San Marino, ring of stars and "25" with: a, Dark blue background at left. b, White background at right.

2013, Oct. 9   Litho.   Perf. 13x13¼
1897 A643 85c Sheet of 2, #a-b 4.75 4.75

Souvenir Sheet

Christmas — A644

No. 1898 — Various creche figures made by children with denominations in: a, Black, at LL. b, Brown, at LL. c, Black, at UL.

2013, Oct. 9   Litho.   Perf. 13x13¼
1898 A644 70c Sheet of 3, #a-c 5.75 5.75

Colorificio Sammarinese Paint Manufacturer, 70th Anniv. — A645

2014, Mar. 17   Litho.   Perf. 13x13¼
1899 A645 70c multi   2.00 2.00

Special Olympics Federation of San Marino, 30th Anniv. A646

2014, Mar. 17   Litho.   Perf. 13x13¼
1900 A646 70c multi   2.00 2.00

35th World Convention of the Intl. Confederation of Sport Fishing, San Marino — A647

2014, Mar. 17   Litho.   Perf. 13x13¼
1901 A647 85c multi   2.40 2.40

Soroptimist International Single Club San Marino, 25th Anniv. — A648

2014, Mar. 17   Litho.   Perf. 13¼x13
1902 A648 85c multi   2.40 2.40

Europa A649

Designs: 70c, Trumpet. 85c, French horn.

2014, Mar. 17   Litho.   Perf. 13¼
1903-1904 A649 Set of 2   4.25 4.25

Campaign Against Gender-Based Violence — A650

Designs: 5c, Girl covering her eyes. 85c, Boy breaking stones (child labor). €1.90, Boy carrying military rifle, vert. €3.60, Frightened woman, vert.

Perf. 13x13¼, 13¼x13
2014, Mar. 17   Litho.
1905-1908 A650 Set of 4   17.50 17.50

Souvenir Sheet

Declaration of Rights Law, 40th Anniv. — A651

No. 1909 — Extended arms with denomination at: a, Center. b, Right.

2014, Mar. 17   Litho.   Perf. 13
1909 A651 €2.50 Sheet of 2,
            #a-b   14.00 14.00

Convention of Friendship Between San Marino and Italy, 75th Anniv. A652

2014, June 5   Litho.   Perf. 13x13¼
1910 A652 70c multi   1.90 1.90

See Italy No. 3243.

58th Plenary Assembly of PostEurop, San Marino A653

2014, June 5   Litho.   Perf. 13x13¼
1911 A653 85c multi   2.40 2.40

Juventus, 2013-14 Italian Soccer Champions A654

2014, June 5   Litho.   Perf. 13x13¼
1912 A654 €1 multi   2.75 2.75

Ayrton Senna (1960-94), Formula 1 Race Car Driver A655

2014, June 5   Litho.   Perf. 13x13¼
1913 A655 €2.50 multi   7.00 7.00

Renata Tebaldi (1922-2004), Opera Singer — A656

No. 1914 — Tebaldi and: a, La Scala Theater, Milan. b, Titano Theater, Titano. c, San Carlo Theater, Naples.

2014, June 5   Litho.   Perf. 13x13¼
1914   Horiz. strip of 3   19.00 19.00
  a. A656 70c multi   1.90 1.90
  b. A656 €2.50 multi   7.00 7.00
  c. A656 €3.60 multi   10.00 10.00

Miniature Sheet

Municipalities in San Marino — A657

No. 1915 — Municipal arms and: a, Bell tower and cable car, Borgo Maggiore. b, Fountain, Acquaviva. c, Church, Faetano. d, Castellaccio of Mount Seghizzo, Fiorentino. e, Government Building, Città. f, Town Hall, Chiesanuova. g, Church, Domagnano. h, Church of St. Laurence, Montegiardino. i, Clock tower, Serravalle.

2014, June 5   Litho.   Perf. 14x14¼
1915 A657 70c Sheet of 9, #a-i 17.50 17.50

Pitti Tondo, by Michelangelo (1475-1564) A658

2014, Oct. 22   Litho.   Perf. 13¼x13
1916 A658 €5.35 multi   13.50 13.50

Galileo Galilei (1564-1642), Astronomer — A659

Designs: No. 1917, 70c, Globe, orrery, trial of Galileo. No. 1918, 70c, Telescope and compass.

2014, Oct. 22   Litho.   Perf. 13x13¼
1917-1918 A659 Set of 2   3.50 3.50

Miniature Sheet

UNESCO World Heritage Sites in Italy — A660

No. 1919: a, €1, Verona Arena, Verona (797rev). b, €1.40, Piazza Ducale, Sabbioneta (1287). c, €2, Cathedral of Modena (827). d, €2.50, Palazzo Comunale and tower, San Gimignano (550).

2014, Oct. 22   Litho.   Perf. 13x13¼
1919 A660 Sheet of 4, #a-d   17.50 17.50

Christmas — A661

Designs: 50c, Angel, Government Building, San Marino. 70c, Holy Family, Three Towers. 85c, Magi, Basilica of San Marino.

2014, Oct. 22   Litho.   Perf. 13¼x13
1920-1922 A661 Set of 3   5.25 5.25

Europa A662

Designs: 80c, Rocking horse. 95c, Toy car.

2015, Mar. 10   Litho.   Perf. 13x13¼
1923-1924 A662 Set of 2   4.00 4.00

Intl. Day of Happiness — A663

Happy children on: 95c, Globe. €2.30, Bird.

2015, Mar. 10   Litho.   Perf. 13¼x13
1925-1926 A663 Set of 2   7.25 7.25

Revolution in Three-Dimensional Printing — A664

Designs: 10c, Apple in printer. 80c, Sphere in printer. €2.15, Woman's head in printer.

2015, Mar. 10   Litho.   Perf. 13¼x13
1927-1929 A664 Set of 3   6.75 6.75

Buildings Designed by Gino Zani (1883-1964) — A665

Designs: 20c, Puntone della Murata Nuova. 30c, Portici del Mercato. €4, Portici e Cripta di Sant'Agata.

2015, Mar. 10   Litho.   Perf. 13x13¼
1930-1932 A665 Set of 3   10.00 10.00

Souvenir Sheet

Expo 2015, Milan — A666

No. 1933: a, Man, grapes. b, Woman, jar of olive oil. c, Man, wheat.

Litho. With Foil Application
2015, Mar. 10   Perf. 13¼x13
1933 A666 €1 Sheet of 3, #a-c 6.75 6.75

SEMI-POSTAL STAMPS

Regular Issue of 1903 Surcharged

a   b

1917, Dec. 15   Wmk. 140   *Perf. 14*

| B1 | A10(a) | 25c on 2c violet | 15.00 | 15.00 |
| B2 | A11(b) | 50c on 2 l violet | 60.00 | 60.00 |

Statue of
Liberty — SP1

View of
San Marino
SP2

1918, June 1   Typo.

B3	SP1	2c dl vio & blk	3.75	3.75
B4	SP1	5c bl grn & blk	3.75	3.75
B5	SP1	10c lake & blk	3.75	3.75
B6	SP1	20c brn org & blk	3.75	3.75
B7	SP1	25c ultra & blk	3.75	3.75
B8	SP1	45c yel brn & blk	3.75	3.75
B9	SP1	1 l bl grn & blk	20.00	24.00
B10	SP2	2 l vio & blk	17.00	21.00
B11	SP2	3 l claret & blk	17.00	21.00
		Nos. B3-B11 (9)	76.50	88.50

These stamps were sold at an advance of 5c each over face value, the receipts from that source being devoted to the support of a hospital for Italian soldiers.

For surcharges see Nos. 89-92.

Nos. B6-B8
Overprinted

1918, Dec. 12

B12	SP1	20c brn org & blk	6.00	6.00
B13	SP1	25c ultra & blk	6.00	6.00
B14	SP1	45c yel brn & blk	6.00	6.00

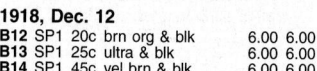

Nos. B9-
B11 Ovptd.

B15	SP2	1 l blue grn & blk	10.50	10.50
B16	SP2	2 l violet & blk	19.00	20.00
B17	SP2	3 l claret & blk	19.00	20.00
		Nos. B12-B17 (6)	66.50	68.50

Celebration of Italian Victory over Austria. Inverted overprints were privately produced.

Coat of   Liberty
Arms   SP4
SP3

1923, Sept. 20   Engr.

B18	SP3	5c + 5c olive grn	.80	.80
B19	SP3	10c + 5c orange	.80	.80
B20	SP3	15c + 5c dk green	.80	.80
B21	SP3	25c + 5c brn lake	.80	.80
B22	SP3	40c + 5c vio brn	4.00	4.00
B23	SP3	50c + 5c gray	2.40	.80
B24	SP4	1 l + 5c blk & bl	8.00	8.00
		Nos. B18-B24 (7)	17.60	16.00

St. Marinus
SP5

Wmk. 140

1944, Apr. 25   Photo.   *Perf. 14*

B25	SP5	20 l + 10 l gldn brn	2.40	2.40
		Never hinged	5.00	5.00
		Sheet of 8	110.00	110.00
		Never hinged	225.00	

The surtax was used for workers' houses. See No. CB1.

No. 256 Surcharged in Red "L. 10"

1946, Aug. 24   Unwmk.

B26	A46	50 l + 10 l	20.00	20.00
		Never hinged	40.00	
		Sheet of 10	800.00	800.00
		Never hinged	1,500.	

Third Philatelic Day, Rimini. The surtax was for the exhibition.

Air Post Types of 1946 Surcharged "CONVEGNO FILATELICO / 30 NOVEMBRE 1946 / + LIRE 25" (or "LIRE 50") in Red or Violet

1946, Nov. 30   Wmk. 277

B26A	AP7	3 l + 25 l dk brn (R)	.95	.95
B26B	AP8	5 l + 25 l red org		
		(V)	.95	.95
B26C	AP6	10 l + 50 l ultra (R)	7.25	6.75
		Nos. B26A-B26C (3)	9.15	8.65
		Set, never hinged	20.00	

Inscription "Posta Aerea" does not appear on these stamps.

No. 260 Surcharged
in Black

1947, Nov. 13   Wmk. 217   *Perf. 12*

B27	A53	1 l + 1 l brt grn & vio	.30	.30
B28	A53	1 l + 2 l brt grn & vio	.30	.30
B29	A53	1 l + 3 l brt grn & vio	.30	.30
B30	A53	1 l + 4 l brt grn & vio	.30	.30
B31	A53	1 l + 5 l brt grn & vio	.30	.30
a.		Strip of 5, #B27-B31	2.00	2.00

Surcharged on No. 261

B32	A53	2 l + 1 l pur & olive	.30	.30
B33	A53	2 l + 2 l pur & olive	.30	.30
B34	A53	2 l + 3 l pur & olive	.30	.30
B35	A53	2 l + 4 l pur & olive	.30	.30
B36	A53	2 l + 5 l pur & olive	.30	.30
a.		Strip of 5, #B32-B36	2.00	2.00

Surcharged on No. 262

B37	A53	4 l + 1 l	2.10	2.10
B38	A53	4 l + 2 l	2.10	2.10
a.		Pair, #B37-B38	14.50	14.50
		Nos. B27-B38 (12)	7.20	7.20
		Set, never hinged	18.00	

Surcharges on Nos. B27-B38 are arranged consecutively, changing from ascending to descending order of denomination on alternate rows in the sheet.

> **Catalogue values for unused stamps in this section, from this point to the end of the section, are for Never Hinged items.**

Refugee
Boy — SP6

1982, Dec. 15   Photo.   *Perf. 11½*

| B39 | SP6 | 300 l + 100 l multi | .40 | .40 |

Surcharge was for refugee support.

AIR POST STAMPS

View of
San Marino
AP1

Wmk. 217

1931, June 11   Engr.   *Perf. 12*

C1	AP1	50c blue grn	32.50	22.50
C2	AP1	80c red	32.50	22.50
C3	AP1	1 l bister brn	9.50	11.00
C4	AP1	2 l brt violet	9.50	11.00
C5	AP1	2.60 l Prus bl	65.00	80.00
C6	AP1	3 l dk gray	55.00	62.50
C7	AP1	5 l olive grn	9.50	11.00
C8	AP1	7.70 l dk brown	19.00	22.50
C9	AP1	9 l dp orange	19.00	22.50
C10	AP1	10 l dk blue	400.00	525.00
		Nos. C1-C10 (10)	651.50	790.50
		Set, never hinged	1,625.	

Exist imperf.

Graf Zeppelin Issue

Stamps of Type AP1 Surcharged in Blue or Black

1933, Apr. 28

C11	AP1	3 l on 50c org	9.50	165.00
C12	AP1	5 l on 80c ol grn	47.50	165.00
C13	AP1	10 l on 1 l dk bl		
		(Bk)	47.50	210.00
C14	AP1	12 l on 2 l yel brn	47.50	260.00
C15	AP1	15 l on 2.60 l dl		
		red (Bk)	47.50	280.00
C16	AP1	20 l on 3 l bl grn		
		(Bk)	47.50	450.00
		Nos. C11-C16 (6)	247.00	1,530.
		Set, never hinged	600.00	

Exist imperf.

Nos. C1 and C2 Surcharged

1936, Apr. 14

C17	AP1	75c on 50c blue grn	2.40	2.40
C18	AP1	75c on 80c red	14.00	14.00
		Set, never hinged	40.00	

Nos. C5 and C6 Surcharged with New Value and Bars

1941, Jan. 12

C19	AP1	10 l on 2.60 l	95.00	95.00
C20	AP1	10 l on 3 l	30.00	30.00
		Set, never hinged	250.00	

View of
Arbe — AP2

Wmk. 140

1942, Mar. 16   Photo.   *Perf. 14*

C21	AP2	25c brn & gray blk	.30	.30
C22	AP2	50c grn & brn	.30	.30
C23	AP2	75c gray bl & red brn	.30	.30
C24	AP2	1 l ocher & brn	.75	.75
C25	AP2	5 l bis brn & bl	7.00	7.00
		Nos. C21-C25 (5)	8.65	8.65
		Set, never hinged	16.00	

Return of the Italian flag to Arbe.

AP3

Overprinted in Black

1943, Aug. 27

C26	AP3	25c yellow org	.30	.30
C27	AP3	50c car rose	.30	.30
C28	AP3	75c dark brown	.30	.30
C29	AP3	1 l dk rose vio	.30	.30
C30	AP3	2 l sapphire	.30	.30
C31	AP3	5 l orange red	1.50	1.50
C32	AP3	10 l deep green	2.25	2.25
C33	AP3	20 l black	7.50	7.50
		Nos. C26-C33 (8)	12.75	12.75
		Set, never hinged	25.00	

See footnote after No. 227. Nos. C26-C33 exist without overprint (not regularly issued). Value $1,500.

San Marino Map,
Fasces and
Wing — AP4

Overprinted in Black

1943, Aug. 27

C34	AP4	25c yellow org	.30	.30
C35	AP4	50c car rose	.30	.30
C36	AP4	75c dark brown	.30	.30
C37	AP4	1 l dk rose vio	.30	.30
C38	AP4	5 l orange red	1.25	1.25
C39	AP4	20 l black	3.25	3.25
		Nos. C34-C39 (6)	5.70	5.70
		Set, never hinged	9.50	

Government
Palace — AP5

1945, Mar. 15   Photo.

| C40 | AP5 | 25 l bister brn | 6.50 | 6.50 |

See note after No. 239.

Gulls and
San Marino
Skyline
AP6

Plane and View of San Marino AP7

Planes over Mt. Titano — AP8

Plane over Globe AP9

Photo., Engr. (20 l, 50 l)
1946-47   **Unwmk.**   *Perf. 14*
C41	AP6	25c blue blk	.25	.25
C42	AP7	75c red org	.25	.25
C43	AP6	1 l brown	.25	.25
C44	AP7	2 l dull green	.25	.25
C45	AP7	3 l violet	.25	.25
C46	AP8	5 l violet blue	.25	.25
C47	AP6	10 l crimson	.25	.25
C48	AP8	20 l brown lake	1.60	1.60
C49	AP8	35 l orange red	4.75	6.00
C50	AP8	50 l dk yellow grn	8.00	9.00
C51	AP9	100 l sepia ('47)	1.25	1.25
		Nos. C41-C51 (11)	17.35	19.60
		Set, never hinged	30.00	

Some values exist imperforate.
Issue dates: 35 l, Nov. 3, 1946; 100 l, Mar. 27, 1947; others, Aug. 8, 1946.
For surcharges and overprint see Nos. B26A-B26C, C54.

Roosevelt Type of Regular Issue, 1947

F. D. Roosevelt and: 1 l, 31 l, 50 l, Eagle. 2 l, 20 l, 100 l, San Marino arms. 5 l, 200 l, Flags of San Marino and US, vert.

Wmk. 277
1947, May 3   **Photo.**   *Perf. 14*
C51A	A52a	1 l dp ultra & sep	.25	.25
C51B	A52a	2 l org red & sep	.25	.25
C51C	A52a	5 l multicolored	.25	.25
C51D	A52a	20 l choc & sep	.25	.25
C51E	A52a	31 l org & sep	.50	.50
C51F	A52a	50 l dk car & sep	.90	.90
C51G	A52a	100 l bl & sepia	3.00	1.75
C51H	A52a	200 l multicolored	18.50	15.00
		Nos. C51A-C51H (8)	23.90	19.15
		Set, never hinged	50.00	

Nos. C51A-C51E, C51H exist imperf. Value, set $150.

Nos. C51A-C51C Surcharged

1947, June 16
C51I	A52a	3 l on 1 l dp ultra & sep	.40	.40
C51J	A52a	4 l on 2 l org red & sep	.40	.40
C51K	A52a	6 l on 5 l multicolored	.40	.40
		Nos. C51I-C51K (3)	1.20	1.20
		Set, never hinged	2.50	

St. Marinus Type of Regular Issue, 1947
Wmk. 217
1947, July 18   **Engr.**   *Perf. 12*
Center in Bright Blue
C52	A53	25 l deep orange	1.25	1.25
C53	A53	50 l red brown	2.75	2.50
		Set, never hinged	8.00	

No. C51 Overprinted in Red

1947, July 18   **Unwmk.**   *Perf. 14*
C54	AP9	100 l sepia	1.25	1.25
		Never hinged	2.00	
a.		Double overprint	160.00	

	Never hinged	260.00
b.	Inverted overprint	160.00
	Never hinged	260.00

Rimini Phil. Exhib., July 18-20.

US No. 1 and Mt. Titano AP11

Wmk. 277
1947, Dec. 24   **Engr.**   *Perf. 14*
C55	AP11	100 l dk pur & dk brn	10.00	10.00
		Never hinged	20.00	
		Sheet of 10	2,500.	
a.		Imperf.	160.00	
		Never hinged	300.00	
		As "a," sheet of 10	8,000.	

1st US postage stamps, cent.

No. 264 Surcharged "POSTA AEREA" and New Value in Black
1948, Oct. 9   **Wmk. 217**   *Perf. 12*
C56	A53	200 l on 25 l	30.00	30.00
		Never hinged	60.00	

Giuseppe and Anita Garibaldi Entering San Marino — AP12

Wmk. 277
1949, June 28   **Photo.**   *Perf. 14*
Size: 27½x22mm
C57	AP12	2 l brn red & ultra	.30	.30
C58	AP12	3 l dk grn & sep	.30	.30
C59	AP12	5 l dk bl grn & ultra	.30	.30

Size: 37x22mm
C60	AP12	25 l dk green & vio	2.75	1.75
C61	AP12	65 l grnsh blk & gray blk	12.00	9.00
		Nos. C57-C61 (5)	15.65	11.65
		Set, never hinged	30.00	

Garibaldi's escape to San Marino, cent.

Stagecoach on Road from San Marino AP13

1950, Feb. 9   **Engr.**   *Perf. 14*
C62	AP13	200 l deep blue	1.50	1.50
		Never hinged	2.50	
a.		Perf. 13½x14 ('51)	3.50	3.50
		Never hinged	5.00	
		As "a," sheet of 6	40.00	40.00
		Never hinged	70.00	
b.		Imperf ('51)	22.50	20.00
		As "b," sheet of 6	275.00	275.00
		Never hinged	450.00	

UPU, 75th anniv. No. C62 was issued in sheets of 25; Nos. C62a & C62b in sheets of 6. See No. C75.

AP14   AP15

AP16

Various Views of San Marino.

1950, Apr. 12   **Photo.**   *Perf. 14*
Size: 27½x21½mm, 21½x27½mm
C63	AP14	2 l vio & dp grn	.35	.25
C64	AP14	3 l blue & brn	.35	.25
C65	AP15	5 l brn blk & rose red	.35	.25
C66	AP14	10 l grnsh blk & bl	1.40	.60
C67	AP14	15 l grnsh blk & vio	1.60	.75

Size: 36x26½mm, 26½x36mm
C68	AP15	55 l dp bl & dp grn	24.00	18.00
C69	AP15	100 l car & gray	18.00	15.00
C70	AP15	250 l violet & brn	77.50	40.00

Engr.
C71	AP16	500 l bl, dk grn & vio brn	65.00	85.00
		Nos. C63-C71 (9)	188.55	160.10
		Set, never hinged	425.00	

See No. C78. For overprints and surcharges see Nos. C72-C74, C76, C79.

Types of 1950 Overprinted in Black, Blue or Brown

1950, Apr. 12   **Photo.**
New Colors; Sizes as Before
C72	AP15	5 l dp bl & dp grn	.25	.25
C73	AP14	15 l car & gray (Bl)	.55	.55
C74	AP15	55 l vio & brn (Br)	4.00	4.00
		Nos. C72-C74 (3)	4.80	4.80
		Set, never hinged	7.50	

The overprint is arranged differently on each denomination.
San Marino's participation in the 28th Intl. Fair of Milan, Apr., 1950.

Stagecoach Type of 1950
1951, Jan. 31   **Engr.**   *Perf. 13½x14*
C75	AP13	300 l rose brn & brn	19.00	19.00
		Never hinged	30.00	
		Sheet of 6	200.00	225.00
		Never hinged	400.00	
a.		Imperf.	800.00	
		Never hinged	1,400.	
		Sheet of 6	4,500.	5,000.
		Never hinged	8,000.	

No. C71 Surcharged in Black "Giornata Filatelica San Marino-Riccione 20-8-1951," New Value and Bars
1951, Aug. 20   *Perf. 14*
C76	AP16	300 l on 500 l	35.00	35.00
		Never hinged	80.00	

Flag and Plane AP17

Perf. 13½x14
1951, Nov. 22   **Engr.**   **Wmk. 277**
C77	AP17	1000 l multi	500.00	500.00
		Never hinged	700.00	
		Sheet of 6	7,000.	7,000.
		Never hinged	9,000.	

Type of 1950
1951, Apr. 28   **Photo.**   *Perf. 14*
Size: 36x26½mm
C78	AP16	500 l dk grn & brn	110.00	110.00
		Never hinged	250.00	
		Sheet of 6	2,250.	2,250.
		Never hinged	3,000.	

No. C78 exists imperf.

No. C70 Surcharged in Black

1951, Dec. 6
C79	AP15	100 l on 250 l	4.00	4.00
		Never hinged	6.50	

Issued to raise funds for flood victims in northern Italy.

Columbus, Globe, Statue of Liberty and Buildings AP18

1952, Jan. 28   **Engr.**
C80	AP18	200 l dk bl & blk	27.50	27.50
		Never hinged	55.00	

Issued to honor Christopher Columbus.

No. C80 Overprinted in Red

1952, June 29
C81	AP18	200 l blk brn & choc	35.00	35.00
		Never hinged	70.00	

4th Intl. Sample Fair of Trieste.

Cyclamen — AP19

Flowers and Seacoast — AP20

2 l, As Nos. C85-C87 with flowers omitted. 3 l, Rose.

1952, Aug. 25   **Photo.**   *Perf. 10x14*
C82	AP19	1 l pur & lil rose	.25	.25
C83	AP19	2 l blue & bl grn	.25	.25
C84	AP19	3 l dk brn & red	.25	.25

Perf. 14
C85	AP20	5 l rose lil & brn	.25	.25
C86	AP20	25 l vio & bl grn	.25	.25

Perf. 13
Engr.
C87	AP20	200 l multi	40.00	40.00
		Sheet of 6, #C87	800.00	800.00
		Never hinged	1,000.	
		Nos. C82-C87 (6)	41.25	41.25
		Set, never hinged	80.00	

Riccione Phil. Exhib., Aug. 25, 1952.

Plane Making Photographic Survey — AP21

75 l, Aerial survey, seen through window.

1952, Nov. 17   **Photo.**   *Perf. 14*
C88	AP21	25 l olive green	1.25	1.25
C89	AP21	75 l red brn & pur	4.25	4.25
		Set, never hinged	8.00	

Aerial photographic survey of San Marino, 1952.

Skier
AP22

1953, Apr. 20   **Engr.**
C90 AP22 200 l bl grn &
  dk grn   45.00   45.00
  Never hinged   90.00
  Sheet of 6   1,000.   800.00
  Never hinged   1,250.

Plane and
Arms of
San Marino
AP23

1954, Apr. 5
C91 AP23 1000 l dk blue
  & brn   100.00   100.00
  Never hinged   150.00
  Sheet of 6   1,000.   1,000.
  Never hinged   1,250.

Type of Regular Issue, 1954
1954, Dec. 16   Photo.   Perf. 13
C92 A71 120 l dp bl & red
  brn   1.10   1.10
  Never hinged   2.25

Hurdler
AP25

1955, June 26   Wmk. 303   Perf. 14
C93 AP25 80 l shown   1.00 1.00
C94 AP25 120 l Relay   1.50 1.25
  Set, never hinged   4.75

San Marino's first Intl. Exhib. of Olympic
Stamps, June.

Ski Jumper
AP26

1955, Dec. 15
C95 AP26 200 l blk & red org 17.50 17.50
  Never hinged   35.00

7th Winter Olympic Games at Cortina
d'Ampezzo, Jan. 26-Feb. 5, 1956.

**No. 372 Overprinted in Upper Right
Corner with Plane and "Posta
Aerea"**

1956, Dec. 10
C96 A76 100 l blk & Prus grn 1.40 2.00
  Never hinged   2.75

┌─────────────────────────────────┐
│ Catalogue values for unused   │
│ stamps in this section, from this│
│ point to the end of the section, are│
│ for Never Hinged items.   │
└─────────────────────────────────┘

Helicopter, Plane
and Modernistic
Building — AP27

Wmk. 303
1958, Apr. 12   Photo.   Perf. 14
C97 AP27 125 l lt blue & brn   3.25 3.25

10th participation in Milan Fair.
See Nos. 414-415.

View of San Marino — AP28

Design: 300 l, Road from Mt. Titano.

Wmk. 303
1958, June 23   Engr.   Perf. 13
C98 AP28 200 l brn & dk blue   4.75 4.75
C99   300 l magenta & vio   4.75 4.75
  a. AP28 Strip, Nos. C98, C99 +
    label   10.00 10.00

Printed in sheets containing 20 each of Nos.
C98 and C99 flanking a center label with San
Marino coat of arms. Nos. C98 and C99 also
come se-tenant in sheet.

**Naples Stamps Type of Regular
Issue**

Design: Bay of Naples and 50g stamp of
Naples.

1958, Oct. 8   Photo.   Perf. 14
C100 A85 125 l brn & red brn   2.75 2.75

Sea Gull
AP29

Birds: 10 l, Falcon. 15 l, Mallard. 120 l, Stock
dove. 250 l, Barn swallow.

1959, Feb. 12   **Perf. 14**
C101 AP29   5 l green & gray   .25   .25
C102 AP29 10 l blue & org brn .25   .25
C103 AP29 15 l red & multi   .25   .25
C104 AP29 120 l rose red, yel &
  gray blk   1.25   .60
C105 AP29 250 l dp grn, yel &
  blk   4.00 2.25
  Nos. C101-C105 (5) 6.00 3.60

Pierre de
Coubertin
AP30

Wmk. 303
1959, May 19   Engr.   Perf. 13
C106 AP30 120 l sepia   4.50 3.25

Pierre de Coubertin; 1960 Olympic Games
in Rome.

Alitalia
Viscount
Over San
Marino
AP31

1959, June 3   Photo.   Perf. 14
C107 AP31 120 l bright violet 2.00 2.00

First flight San Marino-Rimini-London.

Lincoln Type of Regular Issue, 1959

Design: Abraham Lincoln and San Marino
peaks.

1959, July 1   Engr.   Perf. 14x13
C108 A87 200 l dark blue   5.75 5.00

Romagna Stamps Type

Design: Bologna view, 3b Romagna stamp.

Wmk. 303
1959, Aug. 29   Photo.   Perf. 14
C109 A88 120 l blk & blue grn 2.00 1.75

Sicily Stamps Type
Design: Fishing boats, Monte Pellegrino
and 50g stamp of Sicily, horiz.

1959, Oct. 16
C110 A89 200 l multicolored   2.50 2.25

Olympic Games Type
Sports: 20 l, Basketball. 40 l, Sprint race.
80 l, Swimming, horiz. 125 l, Target shooting,
horiz.

1960, May 23   Wmk. 303   Perf. 14
C111 A92 20 l lilac   .25   .25
C112 A92 40 l bis brn & dk red .25   .25
C113 A92 80 l ultra & buff   .25   .25
C114 A92 125 l ver & dk brn   .35   .25
  Nos. C111-C114 (4)   1.10 1.00

Souvenir sheets are valued and described
below No. 465.

Lions Intl. Type
Design: 200 l, Globe and Lions emblem.

1960, July 1   **Photo.**
C115 A94 200 l ol grn, brn & ul-
  tra   7.50 7.50

12th Stamp Fair Type
1960, Aug. 27   Wmk. 303   Perf. 14
C116 A95 125 l multicolored   1.30 1.30

Helicopter
and Mt.
Titano
AP32

1961, July 6   Engr.   Perf. 14
C117 AP32 1000 l rose car   52.50 35.00
  Sheet of 6   350.00 250.00

Tupolev TU-
104A
AP33

Planes: 10 l, Boeing 707, vert. 15 l, Douglas
DC-8. 25 l, Boeing 707. 50 l, Vickers Viscount
837. 75 l, Caravelle, vert. 120 l, Vickers VC10.
200 l, D. H. Comet 4C. 300 l, Boeing 727.
500 l, Rolls Royce Dart turbo-prop. 1000 l,
Boeing 707.

1963-65   Wmk. 339   Photo.   Perf. 14
C118 AP33   5 l bl & vio brn   .30   .30
C119 AP33 10 l org & dk bl   .30   .30
C120 AP33 15 l violet & red   .30   .30
C121 AP33 25 l violet & car   .30   .30
C122 AP33 50 l grnsh bl &
  red   .30   .30
C123 AP33 75 l emer & dp
  org   .30   .30
C124 AP33 120 l vio bl & red   .30   .30
C125 AP33 200 l brt yel & blk   .50   .50
C126 AP33 300 l org & blk   .50   .50
Perf. 13
C127 AP33 500 l multicolored   5.75 5.75
  Sheet of 4   22.50 22.50
C128 AP33 1000 l lil rose, ultra
  & yel   2.75 2.75
  Sheet of 4   25.00 25.00
  Nos. C118-C128 (11) 11.60 11.60

Issued: Nos. C118-C126, Dec. 5, 1963. No.
C127, Mar. 4, 1965. No. C128, Mar. 12, 1964.
No. C128 exists imperf.

Mt. Titano and
Flight
Symbolized
AP34

1972, Oct. 25   Unwmk.   Perf. 11½
Granite Paper
C129 AP34 1000 l multi   1.75 1.75

Glider
AP35

Designs: Each stamp shows a different type
of air current in background.

1974, Oct. 9   Photo.   Perf. 11½
Granite Paper
C130 AP35 40 l multicolored   .25   .25
C131 AP35 50 l multicolored   .25   .25
C132 AP35 500 l multicolored   .55   .55
  Nos. C130-C132 (3)   1.05 1.05

50th anniversary of gliding in Italy.

San Marino 77 Type of 1977
1977, Jan. 28   Photo.   Perf. 11½
C133 A193 200 l grn, blue & yel .30   .30

See Nos. 897-899.

Wright Brothers'
Flyer A — AP36

1978, Sept. 28   Photo.   Perf. 11½
C134 AP36 10 l multicolored   .25   .25
C135 AP36 50 l multicolored   .25   .25
C136 AP36 200 l multicolored   .25   .25
  Nos. C134-C136 (3)   .75   .75

75th anniversary of first powered flight.

AIR POST SEMI-POSTAL STAMP

View of San
Marino
APSP1

Wmk. 140
1944, Apr. 25   Photo.   Perf. 14
CB1 APSP1 20 l + 10 l ol
  grn   2.40 2.40
  Never hinged   4.75
  Sheet of 8   100.00 100.00
  Never hinged   175.00

The surtax was used for workers' houses.
No. CB1 exists imperf.

SPECIAL DELIVERY STAMPS

SD1

Unwmk.
1907, Apr. 25   Engr.   Perf. 12
E1 SD1 25c carmine   35.00 17.50

For surcharges see Nos. E3, E5.

ESPRESSO

Type of Regular Issue
of 1903 Overprinted

Perf. 14½x14
1923, May 30   Wmk. 140
E2 A11 60c violet   1.75 1.25

For surcharge see No. 103.

Type of 1907 Issue Surcharged

1923, July 26   *Perf. 14*
E3   SD1 60c on 25c carmine   1.50 1.25
   a.   Vert. pair, imperf. between   275.00

No. E2 Surcharged

1926, Nov. 25   *Perf. 14½x14*
E4   A11 1.25 l on 60c violet   1.90 1.90

No. E3 Surcharged

1927, Sept. 15
E5   SD1 1.25 l on 60c on 25c   1.50 1.25
   a.   Inverted surcharge   175.00
   b.   Vert. pair, imperf. between   800.00
   c.   Double surcharge   190.00

Statue of Liberty and View of San
Marino — SD2

Wmk. 217
1929, Aug. 29   Engr.   *Perf. 12*
E6   SD2 1.25 l green   .65 .50

Overprinted in Red

E7   SD2 2.50 l deep blue   1.00 1.00

Arms of
San Marino
SD3

Wmk. 140
1943, Sept.   Photo.   *Perf. 14*
E8   SD3 1.25 l green   .25 .25
E9   SD3 2.50 l reddish orange   .25 .25

View of
San Marino
SD4

Pegasus
SD5

1945-46   Photo.   Wmk. 140
E12   SD4 2.50 l deep green   .25 .25
E13   SD4 5 l deep orange   .25 .25
    Unwmk.
E14   SD4 5 l carmine rose   1.00 .50
    Wmk. 277
    Engr.
E15   SD4 10 l sapphire ('46)   2.00 2.00
    Engr.
    Unwmk.
E16   SD5 30 l deep ultra ('46)   3.50 4.00
    Nos. E12-E16 (5)   7.00 7.00
See Nos. E22-E23. For surcharges see
Nos. E17-E21, E24-E25.
No. E16 exists imperf.

Nos. E14
and E15
Srchd. in
Black

1947   Unwmk.   *Perf. 14*
E17   SD4 15 l on 5 l car rose   .25 .25
    Wmk. 277
E18   SD4 15 l on 10 l saph   .25 .25

No. E16 Surcharged with New Value and Bars in Carmine

1947-48   Unwmk.
E19   SD5 35 l on 30 l ('48)   35.00 30.00
E20   SD5 60 l on 30 l   2.00 3.00
E21   SD5 80 l on 30 l ('48)   17.50 17.50
    Nos. E19-E21 (3)   54.50 51.00
    Set, never hinged   100.00

Types of 1945-46

1950, Dec. 11   Photo.   Wmk. 277
E22   SD4 60 l rose brown   7.50 7.50
E23   SD5 80 l deep blue   7.50 7.50
    Set, never hinged   30.00

Nos. E22-E23 Surcharged with New Value and Three Bars

1957, Dec. 12   *Perf. 14*
E24   SD4 75 l on 60 l rose brn   1.75 2.75
E25   SD5 100 l on 80 l dp blue   1.75 2.75
    Set, never hinged   7.00

> **Catalogue values for unused stamps in this section, from this point to the end of the section, are for Never Hinged items.**

Crossbow
SD6

Design: No. E27, "Espresso" at left; crossbow casts two shadows.

1965, Aug. 28   Photo.   Wmk. 339
E26   SD6 120 l on 75 l blk, gray & yel   .25 .25
E27   SD6 135 l on 100 l blk & org   .25 .25

Design: 80 l, 100 l, "Espresso" at left; crossbow casts two shadows.

1966, Mar. 29   Without Surcharge
E28   SD6 75 l blk, gray & yel   .25 .25
E29   SD6 80 l blk & lilac   .25 .25
E30   SD6 100 l blk & orange   .25 .25
    Nos. E28-E30 (3)   .75 .75

SEMI-POSTAL SPECIAL DELIVERY STAMP

SPSD1

Wmk. 140
1923, Sept. 20   Engr.   *Perf. 14*
EB1   SPSD1 60c + 5c brown red   1.75 1.75

POSTAGE DUE STAMPS

C.5	C.10	
D1	D2	
L.1	L.5	
D3	D4	

Wmk. 140
1897-1920   Typo.   *Perf. 14*
J1   D1 5c bl grn & dk brn   1.25 1.25
J2   D2 10c bl grn & dk brn   1.25 1.25
   a.   Numerals inverted   375.00
J3   D2 30c bl grn & dk brn   3.25 3.00
J4   D2 50c bl grn & dk brn   3.50 3.50
   a.   Numerals inverted   375.00
J5   D2 60c bl grn & dk brn   40.00 20.00
J6   D3 1 l claret & dk brn   7.50 7.50
J7   D4 3 l claret & brn ('20)   20.00 20.00
J8   D4 5 l claret & dk brn   80.00 55.00
J9   D2 10 l claret & dk brn   40.00 35.00
    Nos. J1-J9 (9)   196.75 151.50

See Nos. J10-J36, J61. For surcharges see
Nos. J37-J60, J64.

1924
J10   D1 5c rose & brown   1.75 1.75
J11   D2 10c rose & brown   1.75 1.75
J12   D2 30c rose & brown   3.00 3.00
J13   D2 50c rose & brown   3.25 3.25
J14   D2 60c rose & brown   12.00 12.00
J15   D3 1 l green & brown   20.00 20.00
J16   D4 3 l green & brown   55.00 55.00
J17   D4 5 l green & brown   70.00 70.00
J18   D2 10 l green & brown   325.00 325.00
    Nos. J10-J18 (9)   491.75 491.75

Postage Due Types of 1897 and

L.50
D5

1925-39   *Perf. 14*
J19   D1 5c blue & brn   1.50 .75
   a.   Numerals inverted   300.00
J20   D2 10c blue & brn   1.50 .75
   a.   Numerals inverted   300.00
J21   D2 15c blue & brn ('39)   1.00 .80
J22   D2 20c blue & brn ('39)   1.00 .80
J23   D2 25c blue & brn ('39)   1.50 1.25
J24   D2 30c blue & brn   1.50 .80
J25   D2 40c blue & brn ('39)   7.50 9.00
J26   D2 50c blue & brn   2.50 1.25
   a.   Numerals inverted   300.00
J27   D2 60c blue & brn   6.50 1.60
J28   D3 1 l buff & brn   9.50 1.60
J29   D2 2 l buff & brn ('39)   4.00 3.00
J30   D4 3 l buff & brn   125.00 50.00
J31   D4 5 l buff & brn   35.00 7.50
J32   D2 10 l buff & brn   47.50 20.00
J33   D5 15 l buff & brn ('28)   5.50 2.00
J34   D5 25 l buff & brn ('28)   67.50 40.00
J35   D5 30 l buff & brn ('28)   11.50 18.00
J36   D5 50 l buff & brn ('28)   13.50 18.00
    Nos. J19-J36 (18)   343.50 177.10

Postage Due Stamps
of 1925 Surcharged
in Black and Silver

1931, May 18
J37   D1 15c on 5c bl & brn   1.50 1.50
J38   D2 15c on 10c bl & brn   1.50 1.50
J39   D2 15c on 30c bl & brn   1.50 1.50
J40   D1 20c on 5c bl & brn   1.50 1.50
J41   D2 20c on 10c bl & brn   1.50 1.50
J42   D2 20c on 30c bl & brn   1.50 1.50
J43   D1 25c on 5c bl & brn   4.50 3.00
J44   D2 25c on 10c bl & brn   4.50 3.00
J45   D2 25c on 30c bl & brn   25.00 20.00
J46   D1 40c on 5c bl & brn   4.50 1.50
J47   D2 40c on 10c bl & brn   5.50 1.50
J48   D2 40c on 30c bl & brn   5.50 1.50
J49   D1 2 l on 5c bl & brn   55.00 55.00
J50   D2 2 l on 10c bl & brn   140.00 100.00
J51   D2 2 l on 30c bl & brn   90.00 75.00
    Nos. J37-J51 (15)   343.50 269.50

Nos. J19, J24-J25,
J30, J34, J33, J22
Surcharged in Black

Perf. 14, 14½x14
1936-40   Wmk. 140
J52   D1 10c on 5c ('38)   5.50 3.00
J53   D2 25c on 30c ('38)   17.50 16.00
J54   D1 50c on 5c ('37)   17.50 16.00
J55   D2 1 l on 30c   67.50 11.00
J56   D2 1 l on 40c ('40)   11.50 12.00
J57   D4 1 l on 3 l ('37)   67.50 4.75
J58   D5 1 l on 25 l ('39)   110.00 30.00
J59   D5 2 l on 15 l ('38)   55.00 35.00
J60   D2 3 l on 20c ('40)   35.00 35.00
    Nos. J52-J60 (9)   387.00 162.75

Postage Due Type of 1897

1939   Typo.   *Perf. 14*
J61   D2 5c blue & brown   1.25 .50

Nos. J61 and J36 Surcharged

1940-43
J62   D2 10c on 5c   .80 .40
J63   D2 50c on 5c   4.00 1.50
J64   D5 25 l on 50 l ('43)   3.50 3.50
    Nos. J62-J64 (3)   8.30 5.40

Coat of Arms — D6

Unwmk.
1945, June 7   Photo.   *Perf. 14*
J65   D6 5c dk green   .25 .25
J66   D6 10c orange brn   .25 .25
J67   D6 15c rose red   .25 .25
J68   D6 20c dp ultra   .25 .25
J69   D6 25c dk purple   .25 .25
J70   D6 30c rose lake   .25 .25
J71   D6 40c bister   .25 .25
J72   D6 50c slate blk   .25 .25
J73   D6 60c chestnut   .25 .25
J74   D6 1 l dp orange   .25 .25
J75   D6 2 l carmine   .25 .25
J76   D6 5 l dull violet   .25 .25
J77   D6 10 l dark blue   .50 .35
J78   D6 20 l dark green   7.00 8.00
J79   D6 25 l red orange   7.00 8.00
J80   D6 50 l dark brown   7.00 8.00
    Nos. J65-J80 (16)   24.50 27.35

PARCEL POST STAMPS

These stamps were used by affixing them to the way bill so that one half remained on it following the parcel, the other half staying on the receipt given the sender. Most used halves are right halves. Complete stamps were and are obtainable canceled, probably to order. Both unused and used values are for complete stamps. Most exist imperf and are scarce to rare thus.

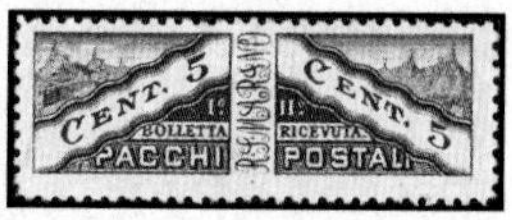
PP1

Engraved, Typographed

1928, Nov. 22 Unwmk. *Perf. 12*

Pairs are imperforate between

Q1	PP1	5c blk brn & bl	.60	.60
a.		Imperf.	75.00	
Q2	PP1	10c dk bl & bl	.60	.60
Q3	PP1	20c gray blk & bl	.60	.60
a.		Imperf.	75.00	
Q4	PP1	25c car & blue	.60	.60
Q5	PP1	30c ultra & blue	.60	.60
Q6	PP1	50c orange & bl	.60	.60
Q7	PP1	60c rose & blue	.60	.60
Q8	PP1	1 l violet & brn	.60	.60
a.		Imperf.	75.00	
Q9	PP1	2 l green & brn	1.50	1.00
Q10	PP1	3 l bister & brn	1.75	1.25
Q11	PP1	4 l gray & brn	2.25	1.50
Q12	PP1	10 l rose lilac & brn	4.75	3.00
Q13	PP1	12 l red brn & brn	18.00	18.00
Q14	PP1	15 l olive grn & brn	27.50	27.50
a.		Imperf.	75.00	
Q15	PP1	20 l brn vio & brn	45.00	45.00
		Nos. Q1-Q15 (15)	105.55	102.05

Halves Used

Q1-Q8	.25
Q9-Q10	.25
Q11	.25
Q12	.35
Q13	.65
Q14	2.75
Q15	3.00

1945-46 Wmk. 140 *Perf. 14*

Pairs are perforated between

Q16	PP1	5c rose vio & red org	.25	.25
Q17	PP1	10c red org & blk	.25	.25
Q18	PP1	20c dark red & grn	.25	.25
Q19	PP1	25c yel & blk	.25	.25
Q20	PP1	30c red vio & org red	.25	.25
Q21	PP1	50c dull pur & blk	.25	.25
Q22	PP1	60c rose lake & blk	.25	.25
Q23	PP1	1 l brown & dp bl	.25	.25
Q24	PP1	2 l dk brn & dk bl	.25	.25
Q25	PP1	3 l olive brn & brn	.25	.25
Q26	PP1	4 l blue grn & brn	.25	.25
Q27	PP1	10 l bl blk & brt pur	.25	.25
Q28	PP1	12 l myr grn & dl bl	3.00	2.00
Q29	PP1	15 l green & purple	2.00	1.75
Q30	PP1	20 l rose lil & brn	1.50	1.75
Q31	PP1	25 l dp car & ultra ('46)	27.50	27.50
Q32	PP1	50 l yel & dp org ('46)	42.50	*55.00*
		Nos. Q16-Q32 (17)	79.50	91.00

Halves Used

Q16-Q27	.25
Q28	.25
Q29	.25
Q30	.25
Q31	.30
Q32	.60

Nos. Q32 and Q31 Surcharged with New Value and Wavy Lines in Black

1948-50

Q33	PP1	100 l on 50 l	42.50	42.50
		Half, used		1.00
Q34	PP1	200 l on 25 l ('50)	140.00	125.00
		Half, used		1.00

1953, Mar. 5 Wmk. 277 *Perf. 13½*

Pairs Perforated Between

Q35	PP1	10 l dk grn & rose lil	32.50	19.00
		Half, used		1.40
Q36	PP1	300 l pur & lake	110.00	110.00
		Half, used		1.40

1956 Wmk. 303 *Perf. 13½*

Q37	PP1	10 l gray & brt pur	.25	.25
		Half, used		.25
Q38	PP1	50 l yel & dp org	.60	.80
		Half, used		.25

No. Q38 Surcharged with New Value and Wavy Lines In Black

Q39	PP1	100 l on 50 l	.50	*.70*
		Half, used		.25

Catalogue values for unused stamps in this section, from this point to the end of the section, are for Never Hinged items.

1960-61

Q40	PP1	300 l violet & brn	52.50	37.50
		Half, used		.75
Q41	PP1	500 l dk brn & car ('61)	2.40	2.40
		Half, used		.30

1965-72 Wmk. 339 *Perf. 13½*

Pairs Perforated Between

Q42	PP1	10 l gray & brt pur	.25	.25
Q43	PP1	50 l yel & red org	.25	.25
Q44	PP1	100 l on 50 l yel & red org	.80	.80
Q45	PP1	300 l violet & brown	.30	.30
Q46	PP1	500 l brn & red ('72)	6.00	6.00
Q47	PP1	1000 l bl grn & lt red brn ('67)	.80	.80
		Nos. Q42-Q47 (6)	8.40	8.40

Halves Used

Q42-Q43	.25
Q44-Q45	.25
Q46	.50
Q47	.25

SARAWAK

sə-'rä-ˌwä‚k

LOCATION — Northwestern part of the island of Borneo, bordering on the South China Sea

GOVT. — Former British Crown Colony

AREA — 48,250 sq. mi. (approx.)

POP. — 1,954,300 (1997 est.)

CAPITAL — Kuching

The last ruling Raja, who retired in 1946 when he ceded Sarawak to the British Crown, was Sir Charles Vyner Brooke, an Englishman. He inherited the title from his father, Sir Charles Johnson Brooke, who in turn received it from his uncle, Sir James Brooke. The title of Raja was conferred on Sir James by Raja Muda Hassim after Sir James had aided him in subduing a rebellion. The title and right of succession were duly recognized by the Sultan of Brunei and by Great Britain.

Sarawak joined the Federation of Malaysia in 1963.

100 Cents = 1 Dollar

Catalogue values for unused stamps in this country are for Never Hinged items, beginning with Scott 155.

Watermarks

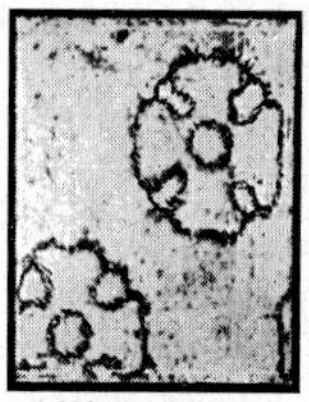
Wmk. 47 — Multiple Rosettes

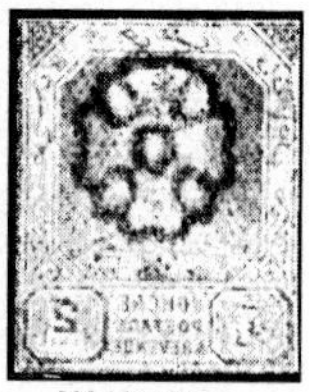
Wmk. 71 — Rosette

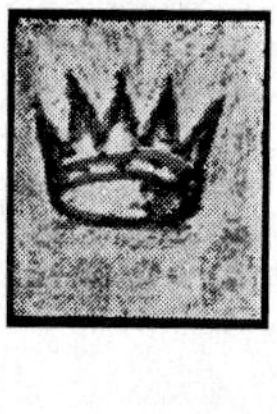
Wmk. 231 — Oriental Crown

Unused examples of Nos. 1-7, 25 and 32-35 are valued without gum. Stamps with original gum are worth more.

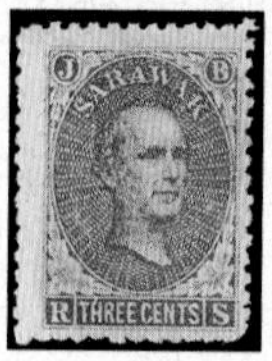
Sir James Brooke — A1

Unwmk.

1869, Mar. 1 Litho. *Perf. 11*

1	A1	3c brown, *yellow*	60.00	*240.00*

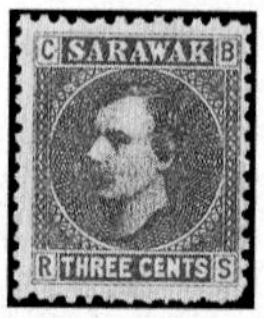
Sir Charles Johnson Brooke — A2

1871, Jan.

2	A2	3c brown, *yellow*	3.00	*4.00*
a.		Vertical pair, imperf between	*600.00*	
b.		Horizontal pair, imperf between	*1,000.*	
c.		Period after "THREE"	70.00	*85.00*

No. 2 surcharged "TWO CENTS" is believed to be bogus.

There are a number of lithographic flaws, including narrow A, "period" after THREE, etc.

Imperfs. of Nos. 1, 2 are proofs.

A papermaker's watermark, "LNL," usually appears once or twice in each pane.

For surcharges see Nos. 25, 32.

1875, Jan. 1 *Perf. 12*

3	A2	2c gray lilac, *lilac*	25.00	*22.00*
4	A2	4c brown, *yellow*	7.00	4.00
b.		Vertical pair, imperf between	*925.00*	*975.00*
5	A2	6c green, *green*	5.25	4.75
6	A2	8c blue, *blue*	6.00	*6.75*
7	A2	12c red, *rose*	12.00	*9.00*
		Nos. 3-7 (5)	55.25	*46.50*

Nos. 3-7 have each five varieties of the words of value.

Imperfs are proofs.

A papermaker's watermark usually appears once or twice in each pane of Nos. 3-7, "LNT" on No. 5, "LNL" on others.

Some examples of No. 7 have the appearance of being on laid paper, but the lines are accidental and not constant within the sheets.

For surcharges see Nos. 33-35.

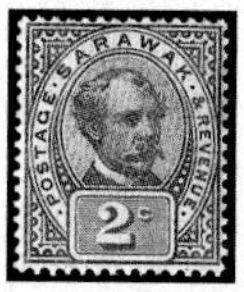
Sir Charles Johnson Brooke — A4

1888-97 Typo. *Perf. 14*

8	A4	1c lilac & blk ('92)	5.50	1.60
9	A4	2c lilac & carmine	7.00	5.00
10	A4	3c lilac & blue	9.25	*5.50*
11	A4	4c lilac & yellow	40.00	*70.00*
12	A4	5c lilac & grn ('91)	35.00	5.00
13	A4	6c lilac & brown	29.00	*70.00*
14	A4	8c green & car	19.50	6.00
a.		8c green & rose ('97)	35.00	17.50
15	A4	10c grn & vio ('91)	55.00	16.50
16	A4	12c green & blue	20.00	*15.00*
17	A4	16c gray grn & org ('97)	70.00	*95.00*
18	A4	25c green & brown	75.00	*52.50*
19	A4	32c gray grn & blk ('97)	60.00	*75.00*
20	A4	50c gray green ('97)	80.00	*130.00*
21	A4	$1 gray grn & blk ('97)	110.00	*110.00*
		Nos. 8-21 (14)	615.25	*657.10*

No. 21 shows the numeral on white tablet.

Three higher values — $2, $5, $10 — were prepared but not issued. Value $950 each.

For surcharges see Nos. 22-24, 26-27.

Nos. 14 and 16 Surcharged in Black

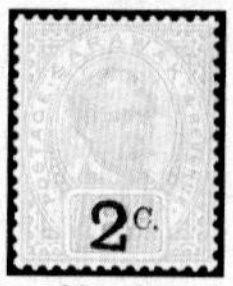

No. 22

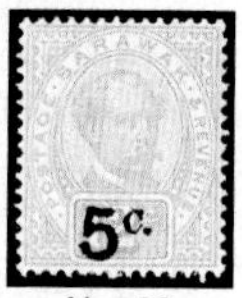

No. 23

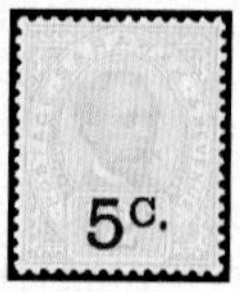

No. 24

1889-91

22	A4	2c on 8c	4.25	*10.00*
a.		Double surcharge	525.00	
b.		Pair, one without surcharge	8,500.	
c.		Inverted surcharge	4,500.	
23	A4	5c on 12c ('91)	35.00	*60.00*
a.		Double surcharge	1,400.	*1,400.*
b.		Pair, one without surcharge	*13,000.*	
c.		No period after "C"	45.00	*70.00*
d.		Without "C"	850.00	975.00
e.		Double surch., one vert.	4,250.	
24	A4	5c on 12c ('91)	350.00	*375.00*
a.		No period after "C"	190.00	*200.00*
b.		Double surcharge	1,500.	
c.		"C" omitted	1,200.	*1,300.*

No. 2 Surcharged in Black

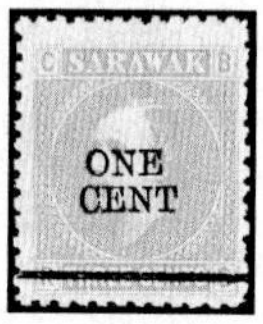

1892, May 23 *Perf. 11*

25	A2	1c on 3c brown, *yel*	2.50	*3.00*
b.		Without bar	375.00	*275.00*
c.		Period after "THREE"	57.50	*70.00*
d.		Double surcharge	475.00	550.00
e.		Vertical pair, imperf between	*800.00*	
f.		Vertical pair, imperf horiz.	*800.00*	

Examples of No. 25b must be from the first printing, wherein the bar was applied after the surcharge. Examples of No. 25 with parts of the surcharge and/or bar omitted are stamps that had gum on the face prior to the surcharging operation. The ink was removed when the gum was washed off.

No. 10 Surcharged in Black

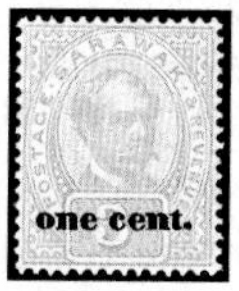

e

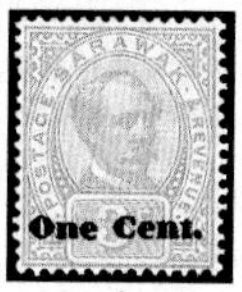

f

1892 *Perf. 14*

26	A4(e)	1c on 3c lil & bl	3.75	*3.75*
a.		No period after "cent"	275.00	*300.00*
27	A4(f)	1c on 3c lil & bl	80.00	50.00
b.		Double surcharge	800.00	850.00

Issued: #26, Feb.; #27, Jan. 12.

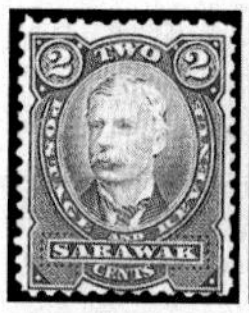
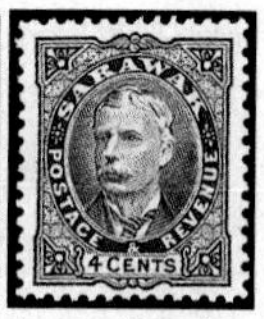
Sir Charles Johnson Brooke
A11 A12

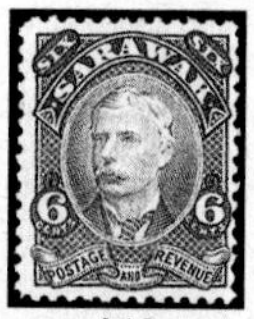
A13

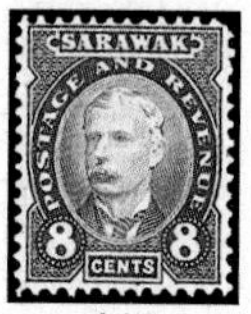
A14

1895, Jan. 1 Engr. *Perf. 11½, 12*

28	A11	2c red brn	17.50	*9.75*
a.		Perf. 12½	27.00	5.00
b.		Vertical pair, imperf between	*650.00*	
c.		Horizontal pair, imperf between	*500.00*	
d.		As "a," horiz. pair, imperf between	*750.00*	

29 A12 4c black 17.50 3.75
a. Horizontal pair, imperf between 875.00
30 A13 6c violet 20.00 *9.75*
31 A14 8c deep green 45.00 6.00
Nos. 28-31 (4) 100.00 29.25

The 2c and 8c imperf are proofs. Perforated stamps of these designs in other colors are color trials, which exist surcharged with new values in pence. These surcharged varieties were used in trial printings of a British South African issue.

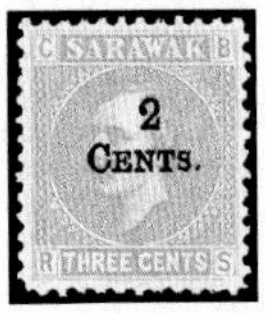

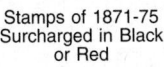

Stamps of 1871-75 Surcharged in Black or Red

1899 ***Perf. 11***
32 A2 2c on 3c brown, *yel* 3.75 *2.00*
a. Period after "THREE" 90.00 *90.00*
b. Vertical pair, imperf between 1,000.

Perf. 12
33 A2 2c on 12c red, *rose* 3.75 *4.50*
a. Inverted surcharge 1,000. *1,400.*
34 A2 4c on 6c grn, *grn* (R) 60.00 *110.00*
35 A2 4c on 8c blue, *bl* (R) 9.25 *14.00*
Nos. 32-35 (4) 76.75 *130.50*

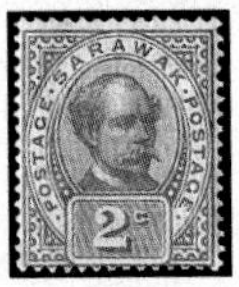

Sir Charles J. Brooke — A16

1899-1908 **Typo.** ***Perf. 14***
36 A16 1c blue & car ('01) 1.75 *1.75*
37 A16 2c gray green 2.25 1.00
38 A16 3c dull violet ('08) 24.00 .75
39 A16 4c aniline car 2.75 .25
40 A16 8c yellow & black 2.75 .90
41 A16 10c ultra 5.50 1.10
42 A16 12c light violet ('99) 7.00 5.00
43 A16 16c org brn & grn 8.50 1.90
44 A16 20c brn ol & vio ('00) 7.00 7.50
45 A16 25c brown & ultra 11.00 *7.00*
46 A16 50c ol grn & rose 30.00 *40.00*
47 A16 $1 rose & green 100.00 *130.00*
Nos. 36-47 (12) 202.50 *197.15*

A 5c was prepared but not issued. Value $13.50.

See the *Scott Classic Catalogue* for listings of shades.

1901 **Wmk. 71**
48 A16 2c gray green 60.00 21.00

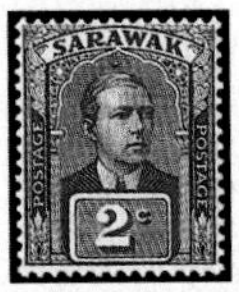

Sir Charles Vyner Brooke — A17

1918-23 **Unwmk.**
50 A17 1c slate bl & rose 2.60 *3.25*
51 A17 2c deep green 3.00 1.75
52 A17 2c violet ('23) 2.25 *3.00*
53 A17 3c violet brown 3.75 3.00
54 A17 3c dp grn ('22) 4.50 1.40
55 A17 4c carmine rose 9.00 4.00
56 A17 4c purple brn ('23) 2.50 *2.75*
57 A17 5c orange ('23) 3.00 2.75
58 A17 6c lake brn ('22) 2.25 *1.60*
59 A17 8c yellow & blk 16.00 *70.00*
60 A17 8c car rose ('22) 5.25 *35.00*
61 A17 10c ultra 6.50 6.50
a. 10c blue 6.50 6.50
62 A17 10c black ('23) 4.50 *5.00*
63 A17 12c violet 21.00 *50.00*
64 A17 12c ultra ('22) 12.50 *21.00*
65 A17 16c brn & blue grn 7.00 *8.50*
66 A17 20c olive bis & vio 9.50 *7.50*
a. 20c olive green & violet 9.50 *7.50*
67 A17 25c brown & blue 4.75 *23.00*
68 A17 30c bis & gray ('22) 4.25 *4.75*
69 A17 50c ol grn & rose 11.50 *17.00*
70 A17 $1 car rose & grn 37.50 *32.50*
Nos. 50-70 (21) 173.10 *304.25*

In 1918 a supply of the 1c (No. 50) had the value tablet printed, by error, in slate blue instead of rose. It is officially stated that this stamp was never issued and had no franking power. Value $22.

The $1 denomination shows numeral of value in color on white tablet.

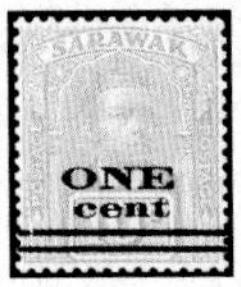

Nos. 61 and 63 Surcharged

1st Printing — Bars 1¼mm apart.
2nd Printing — Bars ¾mm apart.

1923, Jan.
77 A17 1c on 10c ultra 16.50 *62.50*
a. "cnet" 450.00 *975.00*
b. Bars ¾mm apart 160.00 *450.00*
78 A17 2c on 12c violet 11.00 *47.50*
a. Bars ¾mm apart 92.50 *300.00*

Type of 1918 Issue

1928-29 **Typo.** **Wmk. 47**
79 A17 1c slate blue & rose 1.75 .40
80 A17 2c dull violet 2.75 1.40
81 A17 3c deep green 4.50 *5.75*
82 A17 4c purple brown 2.10 .25
83 A17 5c orange ('29) 14.00 5.75
84 A17 6c brown lake 1.50 .35
85 A17 8c carmine 4.00 *27.50*
86 A17 10c black 2.00 1.40
87 A17 12c ultra 4.00 *37.50*
88 A17 16c dp brn & bl grn 4.00 *4.50*
89 A17 20c dp olive & vio 4.00 *9.00*
90 A17 25c dk brown & ultra 7.00 *9.75*
91 A17 30c olive bis & gray 5.50 *11.50*
92 A17 50c olive grn & rose 15.00 *24.00*
93 A17 $1 car rose & grn 22.50 *27.50*
Nos. 79-93 (15) 94.60 *166.55*
Set, never hinged 170.00

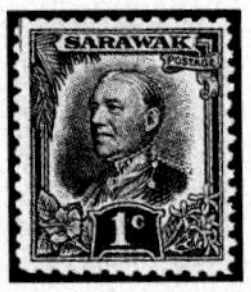

Sir Charles Vyner Brooke — A18

Wmk. 231

1932, Jan. 1 **Engr.** ***Perf. 12½***
94 A18 1c indigo 1.00 1.10
95 A18 2c dark green 1.25 *2.25*
96 A18 3c deep violet 5.00 1.10
97 A18 4c deep orange 12.00 .85
98 A18 5c brown lake 8.50 1.40
99 A18 6c deep red 9.75 *11.00*
100 A18 8c orange yel 11.00 *9.75*
101 A18 10c black 2.75 *3.75*
102 A18 12c violet blue 5.00 *11.00*
103 A18 15c orange brown 8.25 *11.00*
104 A18 20c violet & org 8.00 *9.00*
105 A18 25c org brn & yel 15.00 *25.00*
106 A18 30c org red & ol brn 12.50 *42.50*
107 A18 50c olive grn & red 17.50 *15.00*
108 A18 $1 car & green 25.00 *40.00*
Nos. 94-108 (15) 142.50 *184.70*

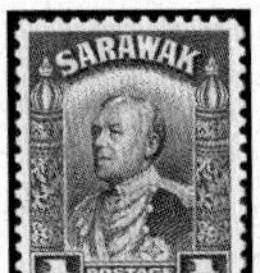

Sir Charles Vyner Brooke — A19

1934-41 **Unwmk.** ***Perf. 12***
109 A19 1c brown violet 1.50 .25
110 A19 2c blue green 1.75 .25
111 A19 2c black ('41) 4.75 *1.75*
112 A19 3c black 1.40 .25
113 A19 3c blue grn ('41) 8.00 *5.00*
114 A19 4c magenta 2.25 .25
115 A19 5c violet 2.25 .25
116 A19 6c deep rose 3.00 .70
117 A19 6c red brn ('41) 8.75 *9.00*
118 A19 8c red brown 2.50 .25
119 A19 8c dp rose ('41) 9.25 .25
120 A19 10c red 5.00 .45
121 A19 12c deep ultra 3.50 .30
122 A19 12c orange ('41) 7.50 *6.25*
123 A19 15c orange 8.00 *12.00*
124 A19 15c deep blue ('41) 9.75 *20.00*
125 A19 20c dp rose & olive 8.00 1.50
126 A19 25c orange & vio 8.00 *2.00*
127 A19 30c vio & red brn 8.00 *3.25*
128 A19 50c red & violet 12.00 1.00
129 A19 $1 dk brn & red 6.00 1.00
130 A19 $2 violet & mag 30.00 30.00
131 A19 $3 bl grn & rose 50.00 *55.00*
132 A19 $4 red & ultra 50.00 *80.00*
133 A19 $5 red brn & red 70.00 *85.00*
134 A19 $10 orange & blk 35.00 *85.00*
Nos. 109-134 (26) 356.15 *400.95*

Issue dates: May 1, 1934, Mar. 1, 1941.
For overprints see #135-154, 159-173, N1-N22.

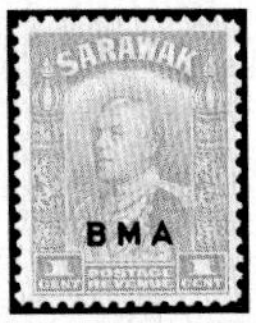

Stamps of 1934-41 Overprinted in Black or Red

1945, Dec. 17
135 A19 1c brown violet .85 *.70*
136 A19 2c black (R) 3.00 *1.50*
137 A19 3c blue green .85 *2.00*
138 A19 4c magenta 2.25 .35
139 A19 5c violet (R) 3.00 1.50
140 A19 6c red brown 3.50 .90
141 A19 8c deep rose 11.50 *25.00*
142 A19 10c red 1.50 .80
143 A19 12c orange 4.00 *4.25*
144 A19 15c deep blue 6.00 .45
145 A19 20c dp rose & ol 4.00 *5.50*
146 A19 25c org & vio (R) 4.50 *3.50*
147 A19 30c vio & red brn 4.75 *4.25*
148 A19 50c red & violet 1.50 .40
149 A19 $1 dk brn & red 2.00 *5.00*
150 A19 $2 violet & mag 6.75 *22.50*
151 A19 $3 bl grn & rose 20.00 *100.00*
152 A19 $4 red & ultra 26.00 *70.00*
153 A19 $5 red brn & red 140.00 *300.00*
154 A19 $10 org & blk (R) 125.00 *275.00*
Nos. 135-154 (20) 370.95 *823.60*
Set, never hinged 575.00

Catalogue values for unused stamps in this section, from this point to the end of the section, are for Never Hinged items.

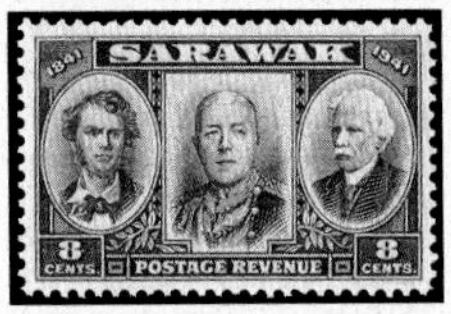

Sir James Brooke, Sir Charles V. Brooke and Sir Charles J. Brooke A20

1946, May 18
155 A20 8c dark carmine 4.75 1.75
156 A20 15c dark blue 5.25 2.50
157 A20 50c red & black 5.25 *3.50*
158 A20 $1 sepia & black 5.25 *40.00*
Nos. 155-158 (4) 20.50 *47.75*

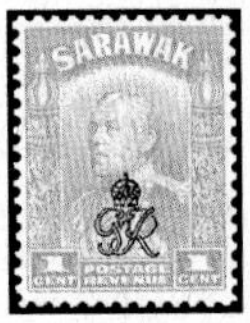

Type of 1934-41 Overprinted in Blue or Red

1947, Apr. 16 **Wmk. 4** ***Perf. 12***
159 A19 1c brown violet .25 *.30*
160 A19 2c black (R) .25 .25
161 A19 3c blue green (R) .25 .25
162 A19 4c magenta .30 .25
163 A19 6c red brown .50 *1.00*
164 A19 8c deep rose 1.00 .25
165 A19 10c red .50 .25
166 A19 12c orange .70 *1.10*
167 A19 15c deep blue (R) .50 *.55*
168 A19 20c dp rose & ol (R) 2.25 .65
169 A19 25c orange & vio (R) .65 .55
170 A19 50c red & violet (R) 1.25 .90
171 A19 $1 dk brown & red 1.50 *1.50*
172 A19 $2 violet & magenta 4.00 *6.50*
173 A19 $5 red brown & red 8.50 4.00
Nos. 159-173 (15) 22.40 18.30

Common Design Types pictured following the introduction.

Silver Wedding Issue
Common Design Types

1948, Oct. 25 **Photo.** ***Perf. 14x14½***
174 CD304 8c scarlet .40 .40

Perf. 11½x11

Engraved; Name Typographed
175 CD305 $5 light brown 55.00 *60.00*

UPU Issue
Common Design Types
Engr.; Name Typo. on 15c, 25c
Perf. 13½, 11x11½

1949, Oct. 10 **Wmk. 4**
176 CD306 8c rose carmine 1.50 .60
177 CD307 15c indigo 3.50 2.50
178 CD308 25c green 2.00 1.50
179 CD309 50c violet 2.00 *6.50*
Nos. 176-179 (4) 9.00 11.10

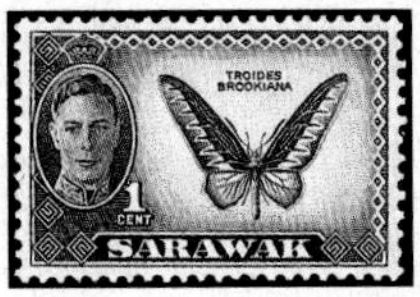

Troides Brookiana A21

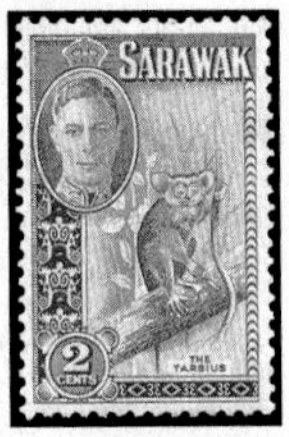

Western Tarsier — A22

Designs: 3c, Kayan tomb. 4c, Kayan girl and boy. 6c, Bead work. 8c, Dyak dancer. 10c, Scaly anteater. 12c, Kenyah boys. 15c, Fire making. 20c, Kelemantan rice barn. 25c, Pepper vines. 50c, Iban woman. $1, Kelabit smithy. $2, Map of Sarawak. $5, Arms of Sarawak.

Perf. 11½x11, 11x11½

1950, Jan. 3 **Engr.**
180 A21 1c black .75 .30
181 A22 2c orange red .45 *.50*
182 A22 3c green .60 *1.25*
183 A22 4c brown 1.00 .25
184 A22 6c aquamarine .75 .25
185 A21 8c red 1.00 .30
186 A21 10c orange 3.25 *6.00*
187 A21 12c purple 3.50 1.75
188 A21 15c deep blue 4.50 .25
189 A21 20c red org & brn 2.75 .50
190 A21 25c carmine & grn 4.25 .60
191 A22 50c purple & brn 8.50 .45
192 A21 $1 dk brn & bl grn 27.50 5.00
193 A21 $2 rose car & blue 45.00 18.50

Engr. and Typo.
194 A21 $5 dp vio, blk, red & yel 30.00 18.50
Nos. 180-194 (15) 133.80 54.40

1952, Feb. 1
195 A21 10c orange *(Map)* 2.75 .80

Coronation Issue
Common Design Type

1953, June 3 **Engr.** ***Perf. 13½x13***
196 CD312 10c ultra & black 2.00 *2.25*

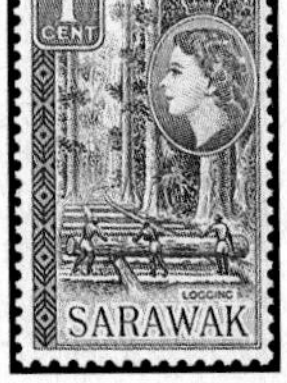

Logging — A23

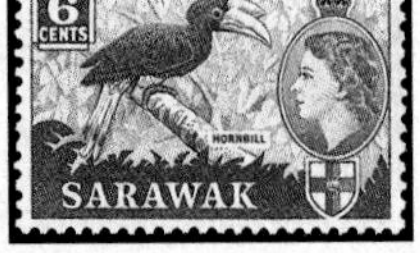

Hornbill A24

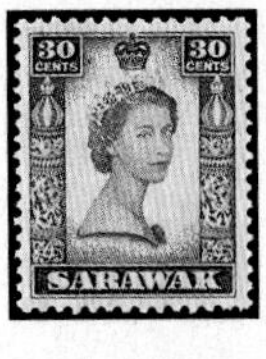

Elizabeth II — A25

Designs: 2c, Young Orangutan. 4c, Kayan Dancing. 8c, Shield with spears. 10c, Kenyah

ceremonial carving. 12c, Barong Panau (sailboat). 15c, Turtles. 20c, Melanau basket making. 25c, Astana, Kuching (Governor's Residence). $1, $2, Queen Elizabeth II (Portrait like Fiji A39). $5, Arms.

Perf. 11x11½, 11½x11, 12x12½ (A25)

1955-57 Wmk. 4 Engr.

197	A23	1c green	.25	*.30*
198	A23	2c red orange	.35	*.55*
199	A23	4c brown carmine	1.50	.60
200	A24	6c greenish blue	3.75	3.50
201	A24	8c rose red	.40	.30
202	A24	10c dark green	.30	.25
203	A24	12c purple	4.25	.55
204	A24	15c ultra	2.25	.30
205	A24	20c brown & olive	1.25	.25
206	A24	25c brt green & brn	7.50	.25
207	A25	30c violet & red brn	9.00	.30
208	A25	50c car rose & blk	3.00	.40
209	A25	$1 org brn & grn	16.00	2.50
210	A25	$2 green & violet	27.50	3.75

Engr. and Typo.

211	A24	$5 dp vio, blk, red & yel	40.00	23.00
		Nos. 197-211 (15)	117.30	36.80

Issued: 30c, 6/1/55; others, 10/1/57.
See Nos. 215-222.

Freedom from Hunger Issue
Common Design Type
Perf. 14x14½

1963, June 4 Photo. Wmk. 314

212	CD314	12c sepia	1.60	*1.75*

OCCUPATION STAMPS

Issued under Japanese Occupation

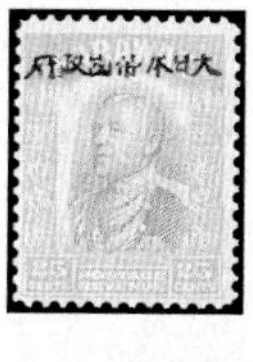

Stamps of 1934-41 Handstamped in Violet

1942 Unwmk. *Perf. 12*

N1	A19	1c brown vio	45.00	*85.00*
N2	A19	2c blue green	125.00	*200.00*
N3	A19	2c black	170.00	*200.00*
N3A	A19	3c black	*500.00*	*500.00*
N4	A19	3c blue green	96.00	*110.00*
N5	A19	4c magenta	130.00	*140.00*
N6	A19	5c violet	160.00	*170.00*
N7	A19	6c deep rose	225.00	180.00
N8	A19	6c red brown	120.00	*160.00*
N8A	A19	8c red brown	*500.00*	*500.00*
N9	A19	8c deep rose	100.00	*120.00*
N10	A19	10c red	130.00	*150.00*
N11	A19	12c deep ultra	250.00	*250.00*
N12	A19	12c orange	200.00	*200.00*
N12A	A19	15c orange	*600.00*	*600.00*
N13	A19	15c deep blue	180.00	*190.00*
N14	A19	20c dp rose & ol	90.00	*120.00*
N15	A19	25c org & vio	130.00	*150.00*
N16	A19	30c vio & red brn	90.00	*120.00*
N17	A19	50c red & vio	100.00	*120.00*
N18	A19	$1 dk brn & red	150.00	*170.00*
N19	A19	$2 vio & mag	375.00	*475.00*
N19A	A19	$3 blue grn & rose	*3,750.*	*3,750.*
N20	A19	$4 red & ultra	325.00	*475.00*
N21	A19	$5 red brn & red	325.00	*475.00*
N22	A19	$10 org & blk	325.00	*475.00*
		Nos. N1-N22 (26)	*9,191.*	*10,085.*

Stamps overprinted with Japanese characters in oval frame or between 2 vertical black lines were not for paying postage.

SASENO

'sə-'zā-ˌnō

LOCATION — An island in the Adriatic Sea, lying at the entrance of Valona Bay, Albania.
GOVT. — Italian possession
AREA — 2 sq. mi.

Italy occupied this Albanian islet in 1914, and returned it to Albania in 1947.

100 Centesimi = 1 Lira

Used values in italics are for postally used stamps. CTO's or stamps with fake cancels sell for about the same as unused, hinged stamps.

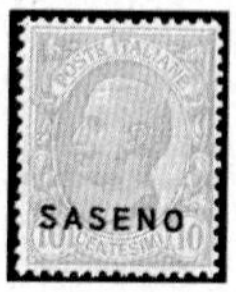

Italian Stamps of 1901-22 Overprinted

1923 Wmk. 140 *Perf. 14*

1	A48	10c claret	30.00	*82.50*
2	A48	15c slate	30.00	*82.50*
3	A50	20c brown orange	30.00	*82.50*
4	A49	25c blue	30.00	*82.50*
5	A49	30c yellow brown	30.00	*82.50*
6	A49	50c violet	30.00	*82.50*
7	A49	60c carmine	30.00	*82.50*
8	A46	1 l brown & green	30.00	*82.50*
a.		Double overprint	450.00	
		Nos. 1-8 (8)	240.00	*660.00*
		Set, never hinged	575.00	

Superseded by postage stamps of Italy.

SAUDI ARABIA

'sau̇-dē ə-'rā-bē-ə

LOCATION — Southwestern Asia, on the Arabian Peninsula between the Red Sea and the Persian Gulf
GOVT. — Kingdom
AREA — 849,400 sq. mi.
POP. — 17,880,000 (1995 est.)
CAPITAL — Riyadh

In 1916 the Grand Sherif of Mecca declared the Sanjak of Hejaz independent of Turkish rule. In 1925, Ibn Saud, then Sultan of the Nejd, captured the Hejaz after a prolonged siege of Jedda, the last Hejaz stronghold.

The resulting Kingdom of the Hejaz and Nejd was renamed Saudi Arabia in 1932.

40 Paras = 1 Piaster = 1 Guerche (Garch, Qirsh)
11 Guerche = 1 Riyal (1928)
110 Guerche = 1 Sovereign (1931)
440 Guerche = 1 Sovereign (1952)
20 Piasters (Guerche) = 1 Riyal (1960)
100 Halalas = 1 Riyal (1976)

Catalogue values for unused stamps in this country are for Never Hinged items, beginning with Scott 178 in the regular postage section, Scott C1 in the airpost section, Scott J28 in the postage due section, Scott O7 in official section, and Scott RA6 in the postal tax section.

Watermarks

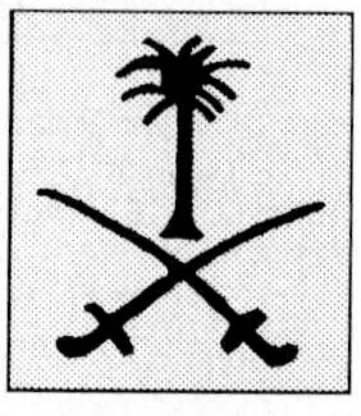

Wmk. 337 — Crossed Swords and Palm Tree

Watermark lines are thicker than the paper.

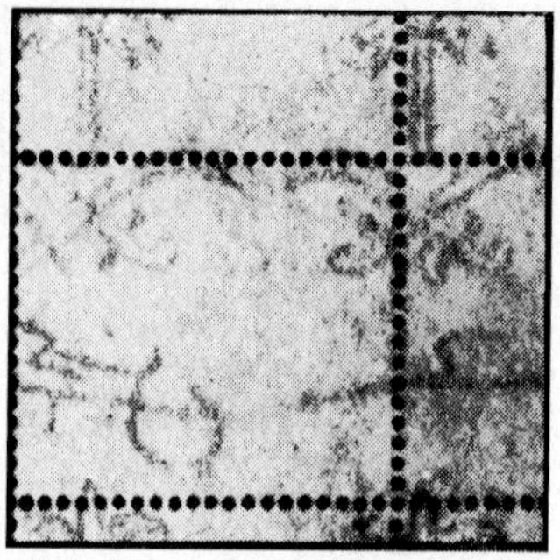

Wmk. 361 — Crossed Swords, Palm Tree and Arabic Inscription

HEJAZ

Sherifate of Mecca

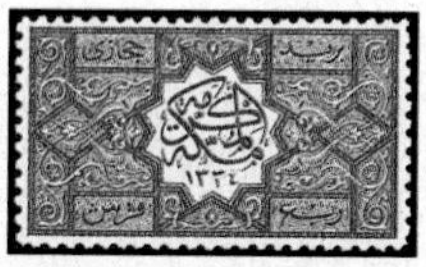

Adapted from Carved Door Panels of Mosque El Salih Talay, Cairo — A1

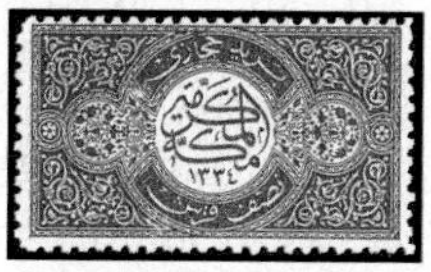

Taken from Page of Koran in Mosque of El Sultan Barquq, Cairo — A2

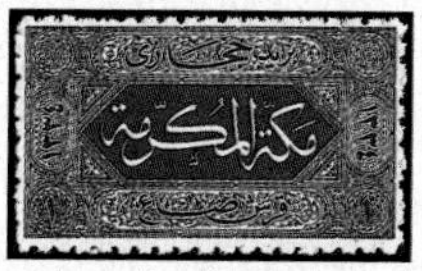

Taken from Details of an Ancient Prayer Niche in the Mosque of El Amri at Qus in Upper Egypt — A3

Perf. 10, 12

1916, Oct. Unwmk. Typo.

L1	A1	¼pi green	50.00	32.50
L2	A2	½pi red	50.00	30.00
a.		Perf. 10	225.00	90.00
L3	A3	1pi blue	20.00	11.00
a.		Perf. 12	160.00	140.00
b.		Perf. 10x12		1,200.
		Nos. L1-L3 (3)	120.00	73.50

Exist imperf. Forged perf. exist.

See Nos. L5-L7, L10-L12. For overprints see Nos. L16-L18, L26-L28, L52-L54, L57-L59, L61-L66, L67, L70-L72, L77-L81, 37.

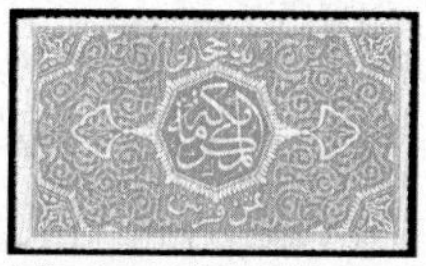

Central Design Adapted from a Koran Design for a Tomb. Background is from Stone Carving on Entrance Arch to the Ministry of Wakfs — A4

1916-17 *Roulette 20*

L4	A4	⅛pi orange ('17)	5.00	1.40
L5	A1	¼pi green	6.00	1.40
L6	A2	½pi red	9.00	1.40
L7	A3	1pi blue	9.50	1.40
		Nos. L4-L7 (4)	29.50	5.60

See No. L9. For overprints & surcharge see Nos. L15a, L16c, L17b, L18d, L25, L51, L56, L69, 33.

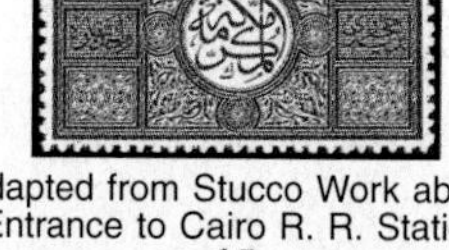

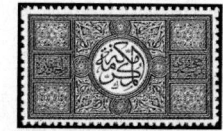

Adapted from Stucco Work above Entrance to Cairo R. R. Station A5

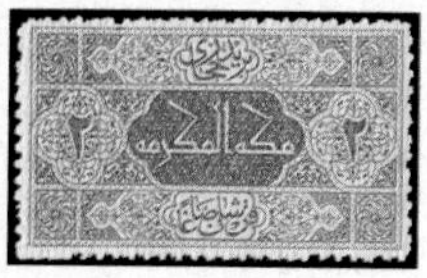

Adapted from First Page of the Koran of Sultan Farag — A6

1917 *Serrate Roulette 13*

L8	A5	1pa lilac brown	4.10	1.40
L9	A4	⅛pi orange	4.75	1.40
L10	A1	¼pi green	5.25	1.40
L11	A2	½pi red	5.75	1.40
L12	A3	1pi blue	6.00	1.40
L13	A6	2pi magenta	10.00	9.00
		Nos. L8-L13 (6)	35.85	16.00

Designs A1-A6 are inscribed "Hejaz Postage."

For overprints and surcharge see Nos. L14-L31, L55-60, L62, L65--L75, L79a-81.

Kingdom of the Hejaz

Stamps of 1917-18 Overprinted in Black, Red or Brown

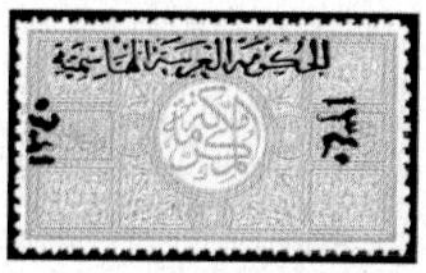

1921, Dec. 21 *Serrate Roulette 13*

L14	A5	1pa lilac brown	65.00	14.00
a.		Date omitted at right	150.00	
b.		Date omitted at left	275.00	
L15	A4	⅛pi orange	35.00	16.00
a.		Inverted overprint	110.00	
b.		Double overprint	225.00	
c.		Roulette 20	800.00	
d.		As "c," invtd. overprint	1,750.	*1,400.*
e.		Double overprint, one inverted	500.00	
f.		Double overprint, both inverted	500.00	
g.		Date omitted at right	100.00	
g.		Date omitted at right	100.00	
L16	A1	¼pi green	35.00	5.50
a.		Inverted overprint	110.00	
b.		Double overprint	225.00	
c.		Roulette 20	800.00	
d.		As "c," invtd. overprint	1,750.	
e.		Double overprint, one inverted	600.00	
f.		Double overprint, both inverted	200.00	
g.		Date omitted at right	100.00	
L17	A2	½pi red	35.00	6.75
a.		Inverted overprint	200.00	77.50
b.		Roulette 20	800.00	
c.		Double overprint	500.00	
d.		Double overprint, both inverted	500.00	
e.		Date omitted at right	100.00	
L18	A3	1pi blue (R)	35.00	6.25
a.		Brown overprint	30.00	18.00
b.		Black overprint	40.00	27.50
c.		As "b," invtd. overprint	400.00	
d.		Roulette 20	800.00	
e.		Date omitted at right	100.00	
L19	A6	2pi magenta	35.00	9.00
a.		Double overprint	*3,500.*	
b.		Date omitted at right	100.00	
c.		As "a," date omitted at right	12,500.	
		Nos. L14-L19 (6)	240.00	57.50

Nos. L15-L17, L18b and L19 exist with date (1340) omitted at left or right side.

All values except No. L15 exist with gold overprint.

No. L19c is unique.

No. L14 With Additional Surcharge

a

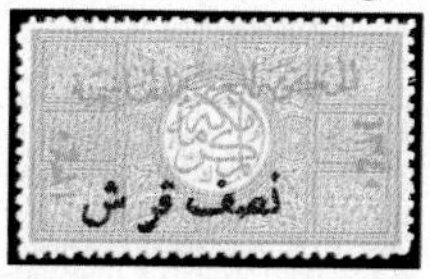

b

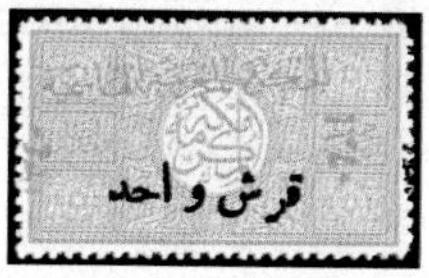

L22	A5(a)	½pi on 1pa	350.00	125.00
L23	A5(b)	1pi on 1pa	350.00	125.00

Forgeries of Nos. L14-L23 abound.

Stamps of 1917-18 Overprinted in Black

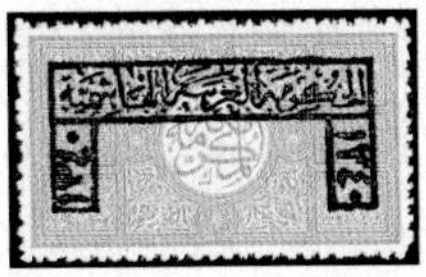

1922, Jan. 7

L24 A5 1pa lilac brown 12.50 2.75
a. Inverted overprint 150.00
b. Double overprint 110.00
c. Double ovpt., one inverted 225.00
L25 A4 ⅛pi orange 20.00 6.25
a. Inverted overprint 110.00
b. Double ovpt., one inverted 225.00
L26 A1 ¼pi green 8.00 2.75
a. Inverted overprint 110.00
b. Double ovpt., one inverted 225.00
L27 A2 ½pi red 10.00 1.75
a. Inverted overprint 110.00
b. Double ovpt., one inverted 225.00
L28 A3 1pi blue 5.00 .80
a. Double overprint 95.00
b. Inverted overprint 175.00
L29 A6 2pi magenta 9.00 5.50
a. Double overprint 175.00

With Additional Surcharge of New Value

L30 A5(a) ½pi on 1pa lil brn 40.00 14.00
L31 A5(b) 1pi on 1pa lil brn 4.00 .90
a. Inverted surcharge 105.00
b. Double surcharge 100.00
c. Dbl. surch., one invtd., ovpt. invtd. 300.00
d. Inverted overprint 115.00
e. Inverted overprint and surcharge 225.00
f. Inverted overprint, double surcharge 225.00
g. Words of surcharge transposed 225.00
h. Overprint and surcharge inverted, words of surcharge transposed 500.00
i. Right hand character of surcharge inverted 100.00
Nos. L24-L31 (8) 108.50 34.70

The 1921 and 1922 overprints read: "The Arab Hashemite Government, 1340."
The overprint on No. L28 in red is bogus.
Forgeries abound.

Types A7 and A8
Very fine examples will be somewhat off center but perforations will be clear of the framelines.

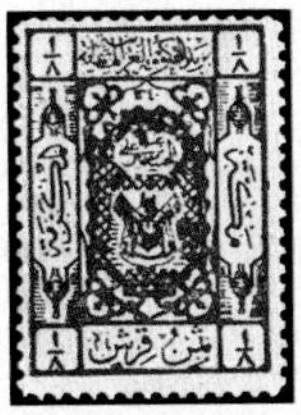

Arms of Sherif of Mecca — A7

1922, Feb. Typo. *Perf. 11½*

L32 A7 ⅛pi red brown 3.00 .45
L34 A7 ½pi red 3.25 .45
L35 A7 1pi dark blue 3.50 .45
L36 A7 1½pi violet 4.00 .45
L37 A7 2pi orange 5.00 .45
L38 A7 3pi olive brown 4.00 .45
a. 3pi brown 3.00 .25
L39 A7 5pi olive green 4.25 .55
Nos. L32-L39 (7) 27.00 3.25

Numerous shades exist. Some values were printed in other colors in 1925 for handstamping by the Nejdi authorities in Mecca. These exist without handstamps.
Exist imperf.
Forgeries exist, usually perf. 11.
Reprints of Nos. L32, L35 exist; paper and shades differ.
See Nos. L48A-L49. For surcharges and overprints see Nos. L40-L48, L76, L82-L159, 7-20, 38A-48, 55A-58A, LJ11-LJ16, LJ26-LJ39, J1-J8, J10-J11, P1-P3, Jordan 64-72, 91, 103-120, J1-J17, O1.

Stamps of 1922 Surcharged with New Values in Arabic

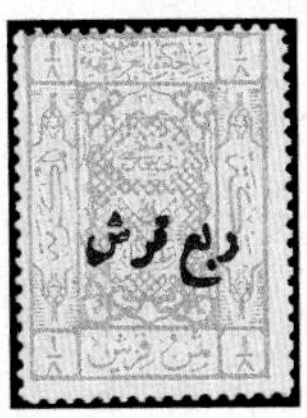

c

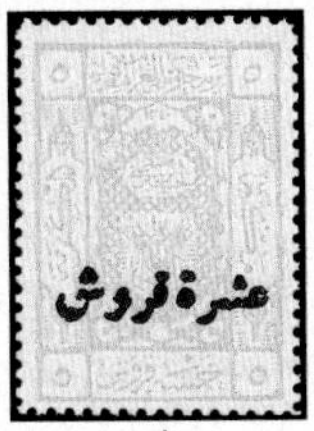

d

1923

L40 A7(c) ¼pi on ⅛pi org brn 40.00 32.50
Never hinged 60.00
a. Double surcharge 150.00
b. Double inverted surcharge 375.00
c. Double surch., one invtd. 400.00
L41 A7(d) 10pi on 5pi ol grn 45.00 27.50
Never hinged 70.00
a. Double surch., one invtd. 200.00
b. Inverted surcharge 175.00

Forgeries exist.

Caliphate Issue

Stamps of 1922 Overprinted in Gold

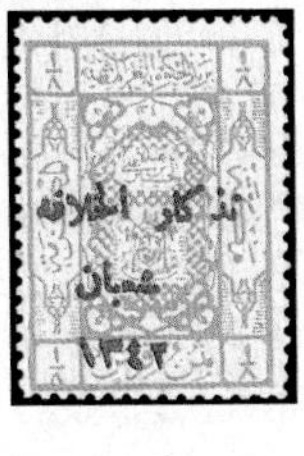

1924

L42 A7 ⅛pi orange brown 5.50
L43 A7 ½pi red 4.00
L44 A7 1pi dark blue 6.00 —
a. Inverted overprint 225.00
L45 A7 1½pi violet 5.75
L46 A7 2pi orange 5.25
a. Inverted overprint 225.00
L47 A7 3pi olive brown 6.00
L48 A7 5pi olive green 7.00
a. Inverted overprint 225.00
Nos. L42-L48 (7) 39.50

Assumption of the Caliphate by King Hussein in Mar., 1924. The overprint reads "In commemoration of the Caliphate, Shaaban, 1342."
The overprint was typographed in black and dusted with "gold" powder while wet. Inverted overprints on other values are forgeries. So-called black overprints are either forgeries or gold overprints with the gold rubbed off. No genuine black overprints are known.
The overprint is 18-20mm wide. The 1st setting of the ½p is 16mm.
Forgeries exist.
Nos. L43-L44, L46 exist with postage due overprint as on Nos. LJ11-LJ13.

Type of 1922 and

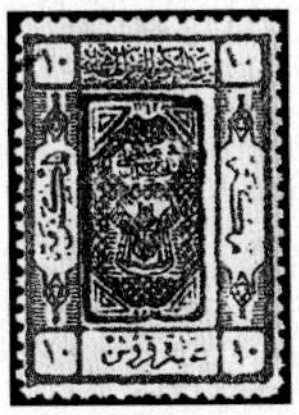

Arms of Sherif of Mecca — A8

1924 *Perf. 11½*

L48A A7 ¼pi yellow green 7.50 5.75
b. Tête bêche pair 50.00
L49 A7 3pi brown red 11.00 9.00
a. 3pi dull red 3.50 4.50
L50 A8 10pi vio & dk brn 7.00 4.50
a. Center inverted 60.00 55.00
c. 10pi purple & sepia 4.00 4.50
Nos. L48A-L50 (3) 25.50 19.25

Nos. L48A, L50, L50a exist imperf.
Several printings of Nos. L48A-L50 exist; paper and shades differ.
A plate flaw in position 13 of No. L48A, which appears as a large white gash in the upper left portion of the stamp, exists. Values: unused single, $50; unused tête-bêche pair, $250.
Forgeries exist, usually perf. 11.
For overprint see Nos. L76A, Jordan 121.

Jedda Issues

Stamps of 1916-17 Overprinted

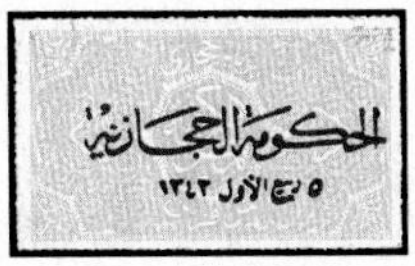

The Jedda overprints on Nos. L51-L159 read: "Al-hukuma al Hejaziyeh, 5 Rabi al'awwal 1343"
(The Hejaz Government, October 4, 1924). This is the date of the accession of King Ali.
Counterfeits exist of all Jedda overprints.

Jedda issues were also used in Medina and Yambo.
Used values for #L51-L186 and LJ17-LJ39 are for genuine cancels. Privately applied cancels exist for "Mekke" (Mecca, bilingual or all Arabic), Khartoum, Cairo, as well as for Jeddah. Many private cancels have wrong dates, some as early as 1916. These are worth half the used values.

Red Overprint

1925, Jan. *Roulette 20*

L51 A4 ⅛pi orange 40.00 *14.00*
a. Inverted overprint 110.00
b. Ovptd. on face and back 225.00
c. Normal ovpt. on face, double ovpt. on back 325.00
L52 A1 ¼pi green 40.00 *14.00*
a. Inverted overprint 75.00
b. Double overprint 75.00
c. Double overprint, one invtd. 175.00
L53 A2 ½pi red 90.00 *67.50*
a. Inverted overprint 175.00
L54 A3 1pi blue 40.00 *32.50*
a. Inverted overprint *175.00*
b. Double ovpt., one invtd. 175.00
Nos. L51-L53 (3) 170.00 *95.50*

Serrate Roulette 13

L55 A5 1pa lilac brown 30.00 *12.50*
a. Inverted overprint 75.00
b. Double overprint 70.00
c. Ovptd. on face and back *200.00*
d. Normal ovpt. on face, double ovpt. on back 150.00
L56 A4 ⅛pi orange 60.00 *35.00*
L57 A1 ¼pi green 37.50 *20.00*
a. Pair, one without overprint *2,000.*
b. Inverted overprint 55.00
c. Double ovpt., one inverted 300.00
L58 A2 ½pi red 55.00 *27.50*
a. Inverted overprint *175.00*
L59 A3 1pi blue 60.00 *32.50*
a. Inverted overprint *125.00*
L60 A6 2pi magenta 45.00 *35.00*
a. Inverted overprint *150.00*
Nos. L55-L60 (6) 287.50 *162.50*

Gold Overprint

Roulette 20

L61 A1 ¼pi green, gold on red ovpt. *2,250.*
Never hinged 3,000.
No gum 1,000.
a. Gold on blue ovpt. 4,000. *7,000.*

Serrate Roulette 13

L62 A1 ¼pi green, gold on red ovpt. 45.00 *22.50*
a. Inverted overprint *300.00*

The overprint on No. L61 was typographed in red or blue (No. L62 only in red) and dusted with "gold" powder while wet.

Blue Overprint

Roulette 20

L63 A1 ¼pi green 150.00 *22.50*
a. Inverted overprint 175.00
b. Ovptd. on face and back 250.00 *550.00*
L64 A2 ½pi red, invtd. ovpt. 150.00 *80.00*
a. Upright overprint 200.00

Serrate Roulette 13

L65 A1 ¼pi green 35.00 *16.00*
a. Inverted overprint 75.00
b. Vertical overprint 1,100.
L66 A2 ½pi red 55.00 *27.50*
a. Inverted overprint *110.00*
L66B A6 2pi mag, invtd. ovpt. *1,900.*

Blue overprint on Nos. L4, L8, L9 are bogus.

Same Overprint in Blue on Provisional Stamps of 1922

Overprinted on No. L17

L67 A2 ½pi red *2,750.*

Overprinted on Nos. L24-L29

L68 A5 1pa lilac brn 225.00 *160.00*
L69 A4 ⅛pi orange *2,500.* *1,800.*
a. Inverted overprint 4,500.
L70 A1 ¼pi green 80.00 *65.00*
a. Inverted overprint 800.00
L71 A2 ½pi red 100.00 *85.00*
a. Inverted overprint 900.00
L72 A3 1pi blue 125.00 *110.00*
L73 A6 2pi magenta 175.00 *160.00*
a. Inverted overprint 1,500.

Same Overprint on Nos. L30 and L31

L74 A5(a) ½pi on 1pa 105.00 *90.00*
L75 A5(b) 1pi on 1pa 90.00 *75.00*
a. Inverted overprint 800.00

Same Overprint in Blue Vertically, Reading Up or Down, on Stamps of 1922-24

Perf. 11½

L76 A7 ½pi red *900.00 900.00*
L76A A8 10pi vio & dk brn *1,800.* *1,800.*

Nos. L5, L10 Overprinted Reading Up in Blue or Red

(Overprint reads up in illustration.)

Roulette 20

L77a A1 ¼pi green (Bl) *550.00 500.00*
L78 A1 ¼pi green (R) *500.00 450.00*

Serrate Roulette 13

L79a A1 ¼pi green (Bl) 350.00 *300.00*
L80 A1 ¼pi green (R) 75.00 *60.00*

Overprint Reading Down

Roulette 20

L77 A1 ¼pi green (Bl) *200.00 175.00*

Serrate Roulette 13

L79 A1 ¼pi green (Bl) 105.00 *90.00*
L80a A1 ¼pi green (R) 225.00 *200.00*
L80b A1 ¼pi green (R), double ovpt. 450.00
L80c A1 ¼pi green (R), double ovpt., 1 reading up and 1 reading down 500.00
L80d A1 ¼pi green (R), triple ovpt., all reading up 600.00

Nos. L10, L32-L39, L48A, L49a, L50 Overprinted

Serrate Roulette 13

Red Overprint (vertical, reading down)

L81 A1 ¼pi green *1,350.*
a. Overprint reading up 1,500.
b. Overprint horizontal 1,750.
c. As "b," overprint inverted 1,750.

Perf. 11½

Blue Overprint

L82 A7 ⅛pi red brown 13.00 *5.50*
a. Inverted overprint 55.00
L83 A7 ½pi red 15.00 *7.25*
a. Double overprint 75.00
b. Inverted overprint 50.00 *45.00*
c. Double ovpt., one invtd. 100.00
d. Overprint reading up 175.00
L84 A7 1pi dark blue *600.00*
a. Inverted overprint *600.00*
L85 A7 1½pi violet 22.50 *11.00*
a. Inverted overprint 50.00 *45.00*
L86 A7 2pi orange 22.50 *11.00*
On cover, single franking *200.00*
a. Double ovpt., one invtd. 75.00
b. Inverted overprint 50.00
c. Double overprint 75.00
L87 A7 3pi olive brown 20.00 *9.00*
a. Inverted overprint 50.00
b. Double ovpt., one invtd. 75.00
c. Overprint reading up 180.00
d. Dbl. ovpt., both invtd. 105.00
L88 A7 3pi dull red 24.00 *11.00*
a. Inverted overprint 50.00
b. Double ovpt., one invtd. 75.00
L89 A7 5pi olive green 21.00 *11.00*
a. Inverted overprint 55.00

Some values exist in pairs, one without overprint.

Black Overprint

L90 A7 ⅛pi red brown *90.00*
a. Inverted overprint *175.00*
L91 A7 ½pi red 11.00 *4.50*
a. Inverted overprint 75.00
L92 A7 1pi dark blue *600.00*
a. Inverted overprint *600.00*
L93 A7 1½pi violet 26.00 *12.00*
a. Inverted overprint 75.00
L94 A7 2pi orange 15.00 *7.25*
a. Inverted overprint 50.00
L95 A7 3pi olive brown 12.00 *5.50*
a. Inverted overprint 75.00 *67.50*
L96 A7 3pi dull red 15.00 *7.25*
a. Inverted overprint 50.00

L97 A7 5pi olive green 20.00 9.00
a. Inverted overprint 50.00

Red Overprint

L98 A7 ⅛pi red brn, invtd. 950.00
L99 A7 ¼pi yellow grn 35.00 16.00
a. Tête bêche pair 100.00
b. Inverted overprint 50.00
c. Tête bêche pair, one with inverted overprint 125.00
L100 A7 ½pi red 1,000. 500.00
a. Inverted overprint 1,100. 500.00
L101 A7 1pi dark blue 20.00 8.00
a. Inverted overprint 50.00
b. Double ovpt., one invtd. 40.00
L102 A7 1½pi violet 11.00 4.50
a. Inverted overprint 50.00
L103 A7 2pi orange 27.50 12.00
a. Inverted overprint 50.00
b. Overprint reading up 200.00
L104 A7 3pi olive brown 27.50 12.00
a. Inverted overprint 50.00
L105 A7 3pi dull red, invtd. 1,700.
L106 A7 5pi olive green 20.00 7.25
a. Inverted overprint 50.00
b. Overprint reading up 175.00
c. Overprint reading down 175.00
L107 A8 10pi vio & dk brn 35.00 16.00
a. Inverted overprint 50.00
b. Center inverted 125.00
c. As "b," invtd. ovpt. 175.00

Nos. L98, L105 with normal overprint are fakes.

Gold Overprint

L108 A7 ⅛pi red brown 35.00 27.50
L109 A7 ½pi red 35.00 27.50
L110 A7 1pi dark blue 40.00 27.50
L111 A7 1½pi violet 125.00 110.00
L112 A7 2pi orange 110.00 90.00
L113 A7 3pi olive brown 45.00 35.00
L114 A7 3pi dull red 130.00 100.00
L115 A7 5pi olive green 105.00 85.00
Nos. L108-L115 (8) 625.00 502.50

Inverted overprints are forgeries.

Same Overprint on Nos. L42-L48

Blue Overprint

L116 A7 ⅛pi red brown 50.00 42.50
a. Double ovpt., one invtd. 300.00
L117 A7 ½pi red 95.00 80.00
L118 A7 1pi dark blue 80.00 55.00
L119 A7 1½pi violet 90.00 65.00
L120 A7 2pi orange 300.00 275.00
a. Inverted overprint 500.00
L121 A7 3pi olive brown 125.00 110.00
a. Inverted overprint 225.00
L122 A7 5pi olive green 50.00 37.50
a. Inverted overprint 250.00
Nos. L116-L122 (7) 790.00 665.00

Black Overprint

L123 A7 ⅛pi red brown 50.00 42.50
a. Inverted overprint 275.00
L125 A7 1½pi violet 150.00 140.00
a. Inverted overprint 300.00
L127 A7 3pi olive brown 125.00 110.00
a. Inverted overprint 300.00
L128 A7 5pi olive green 155.00 140.00
a. Inverted overprint 300.00
Nos. L123-L128 (4) 480.00 432.50

Red Overprint

L129 A7 1pi dark blue 125.00 90.00
L130 A7 1½pi violet 135.00 110.00
L131 A7 2pi orange 150.00 90.00
Nos. L129-L131 (3) 410.00 290.00

Overprints on stamps or in colors other than those listed are forgeries.

Stamps of 1922-24 Surcharged

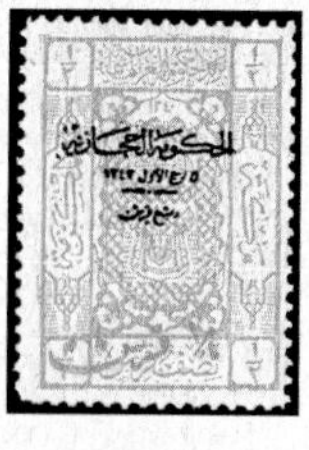

a

and Handstamp Surcharged

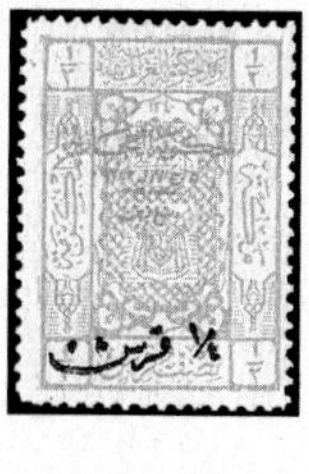

b — 1/4pi

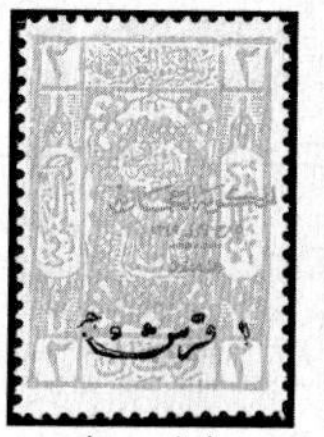

b — 1pi

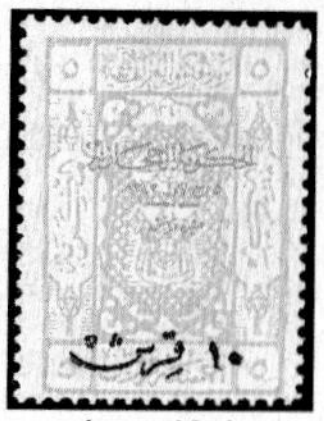

b — 10pi

1925 Litho. *Perf. 11½*

L135 A7 ¼pi on ¼pi on ⅛pi red brn 75.00 47.50
b. 1pi on ¼pi on ⅛pi red brown 225.00
L136 A7 ¼pi on ¼pi on ½pi red 50.00 30.00
c. 1pi on ¼pi on ½pi 125.00 55.00
L138 A7 1pi on 1pi on 2pi orange 50.00 30.00
a. ¼pi on ¼pi on 2pi org 125.00
b. 10pi on 1pi on 2pi org 105.00
c. ¼pi on 1pi on 2pi org 55.00
d. 1pi on ¼pi on 2pi org 105.00
L139 A7 1pi on 1pi on 3pi ol brn 30.00 22.50
L140 A7 1pi on 1pi on 3pi dl red 45.00 35.00
b. ¼pi on 1pi on 3pi dl red 125.00
L141 A7 10pi on 10pi on 5pi ol grn 25.00 16.00
b. 1pi on 10 pi on 5 pi 110.00
Nos. L135-L141 (6) 275.00 181.00

The printed surcharge (a) reads "The Hejaz Government. October 4, 1924." with new denomination in third line. This surcharge alone was used for the first issue (Nos. L135a-L141a). The new denomination was so small and indistinct that its equivalent in larger characters was soon added by handstamp (b) at bottom of each stamp for the second issue (Nos. L135-L141).

The handstamped surcharge (b) is found double, inverted, etc. It is also known in dark violet.

Without Handstamp "b"

L135a A7 ¼pi on ⅛pi red brn 110.00
L136b A7 ¼pi on ½pi red 110.00
L138e A7 1pi on 2pi orange 110.00
L139a A7 1pi on 3pi olive brn 110.00
L140a A7 1pi on 3pi dull red 110.00
L141a A7 10pi on 5pi olive grn 110.00
Nos. L135a-L141a (6) 660.00

Stamps of 1922-24 Surcharged

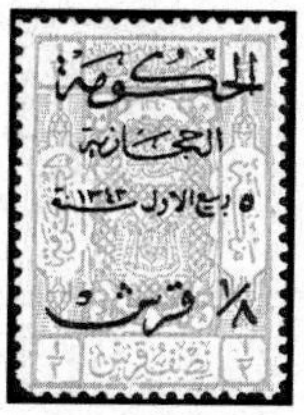

Black Surcharge

L142 A7 ⅛pi on ½pi red 10.00 7.25
a. Inverted surcharge 40.00
L143 A7 ¼pi on ½pi red 11.00 7.25
a. Inverted surcharge 40.00
L144 A7 1pi on ½pi red 12.50 7.25
a. Inverted surcharge 25.00
L145 A7 1pi on 1½pi vio 12.50 7.25
a. Inverted surcharge 40.00
L146 A7 1pi on 2pi org 10.00 7.25
a. "10pi" 100.00
b. Inverted surcharge 50.00
c. As "a," inverted surcharge 150.00
L147 A7 1pi on 3pi olive brn 12.50 7.25
a. "10pi" 100.00
b. Inverted surcharge 55.00
c. As "a," inverted surcharge 150.00
L148 A7 10pi on 5pi olive grn 20.00 14.00
a. Inverted surcharge 75.00
Nos. L142-L148 (7) 88.50 57.50

Blue Surcharge

L149 A7 ⅛pi on ½pi red 17.50 11.00
a. Inverted surcharge 75.00
b. Double surcharge 225.00
L150 A7 ¼pi on ½pi red 15.00 11.00
a. Inverted surcharge 75.00
L151 A7 1pi on ½pi red 15.00 11.00
a. Inverted surcharge 75.00
b. Double surcharge 125.00
L152 A7 1pi on 1½pi vio 20.00 11.00
a. Inverted surcharge 75.00
L153 A7 1pi on 2pi org 17.50 11.00
a. "10pi" 100.00
b. Inverted surcharge 90.00
L154 A7 1pi on 3pi olive brn 30.00 22.50
a. "10pi" 110.00
b. Inverted surcharge 75.00
L155 A7 10pi on 5pi olive grn 35.00 25.00
a. Inverted surcharge 75.00
Nos. L149-L155 (7) 150.00 102.50

Red Surcharge

L156 A7 1pi on 1½pi vio 30.00 22.50
a. Inverted surcharge 90.00
L157 A7 1pi on 2pi org 30.00 22.50
a. "10pi" 100.00
b. Inverted surcharge 90.00
L158 A7 1pi on 3pi olive brn 32.50 22.50
a. "10pi" 125.00
b. Inverted surcharge 90.00
L159 A7 10pi on 5pi olive grn 32.50 22.50
a. Inverted surcharge 90.00
Nos. L156-L159 (4) 125.00 90.00
Nos. L142-L159 (18) 363.50 250.00

The "10pi" surcharge is found inverted on Nos. L146a, L147a. The existence of genuine inverted "10pi" surcharges on Nos. L153a, L154a, L157a and L158a is in doubt.

The 10pi on 1½pi is bogus.

King Ali Issue

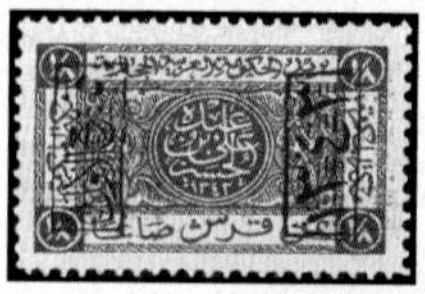

A9

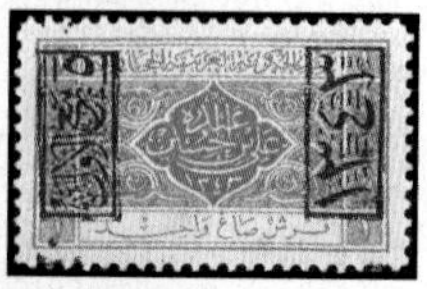

A10

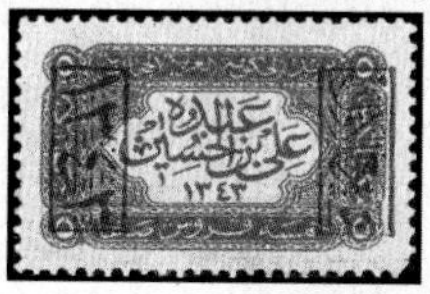

A11

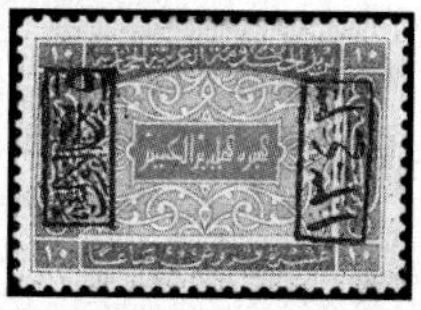

A12

1925, May-June *Perf. 11½*

Black Overprint

L160 A9 ⅛pi chocolate 2.25 1.50
L161 A9 ¼pi ultra 2.25 1.50
L162 A9 ½pi car rose 2.25 1.50
L163 A10 1pi yellow green 3.00 1.75
L164 A10 1½pi orange 3.00 1.75
L165 A10 2pi blue 3.50 2.25
L166 A11 3pi dark green 3.50 2.25
L167 A11 5pi orange brn 3.50 2.25
L168 A12 10pi red & green 6.00 4.50
a. Center inverted 90.00
Nos. L160-L168 (9) 29.25 19.25

Red Overprint

L169 A9 ⅛pi chocolate 4.00 2.75
L170 A9 ¼pi ultra 2.50 1.60
L171 A10 1pi yellow green 3.00 2.00
L172 A10 1½pi orange 3.00 2.00
L173 A10 2pi deep blue 3.50 2.50
L174 A11 3pi dark green 3.25 2.75
a. Horiz. pair, imperf. vert. 75.00
L175 A11 5pi org brn 4.00 2.75
L176 A12 10pi red & green 6.50 5.50
Nos. L169-L176 (8) 29.75 21.85

Blue Overprint

L177 A9 ⅛pi chocolate 2.75 1.75
L179 A9 ½pi car rose 2.75 1.75
L180 A10 1pi yellow green 2.75 1.75
L181 A10 1½pi orange 2.75 1.75
L182 A11 3pi dark green 2.75 1.75
L183 A11 5pi orange brn 6.75 5.50
L184 A12 10pi red & green 9.00 7.25
L185 A12 10pi red & org 275.00
Nos. L177-L184 (7) 29.50 21.50

Without Overprint

L186 A12 10pi red & green 8.00 6.75
a. Dbl. impression of center 90.00

The overprint in the tablets on Nos. L160-L185 reads: "5 Rabi al'awwal, 1343" (Oct. 4, 1924), the date of the accession of King Ali.

The tablet overprints vary slightly in size. Each is found reading upward or downward and at either side of the stamp. These control overprints were first applied in Jedda by the government press.

They were later made from new plates by the stamp printer in Cairo. In the Jedda overprint, the bar over the "0" figure extends to the left.

Some values exist with 13m or 15mm instead of 18mm between tablets. They sell for more. The lines of the Cairo overprinting are generally wider, but more lightly printed, usually appearing slightly grayish and the bar is at center right. The Cairo overprints are believed not to have been placed in use.

Imperforates exist.

Nos. L160-L168 are known with the overprints spaced as on type D3 and aligned horizontally.

Examples of these stamps (perforated or imperforate) without the overprint, except No. L186 were not regularly issued and not available for postage.

No. L185 exists only with Cairo overprint. Imperfs of No. L185 sell for much less than No. L185. Fake perfs have been added to the imperfs.

The ¼pi with blue overprint is bogus.

No. L186 in other colors are color trials.

For overprints see #58B-58D, Jordan 122-129.

NEJDI ADMINISTRATION OF HEJAZ

Handstamped in Blue, Red, Black or Violet

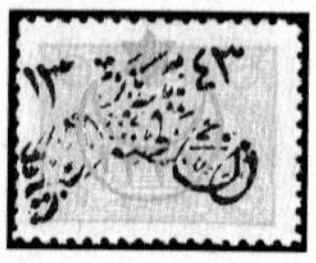

The overprint reads: "1343. Barid al Sultanat an Nejdia" (1925. Post of the Sultanate of Nejd).

The overprints on this and succeeding issues are handstamped and, as usual, are found double, inverted, etc. These variations are scarce.

On Stamp of Turkey, 1915, With Crescent and Star in Red

1925, Mar.-Apr. Unwmk. *Perf. 12*

1 A22 5pa ocher (Bl) 30.00 27.50
2 A22 5pa ocher (R) 30.00 20.00
3 A22 5pa ocher (Bk) 30.00 22.50
4 A22 5pa ocher (V) 30.00 18.00

On Stamp of Turkey, 1913

5 A28 10pa green (Bl) 40.00 16.00
a. Inverted overprint 500.00
6 A28 10pa green (R) 40.00 12.50

On Stamps of Hejaz, 1922-24

Perf. 11½

7 A7 ⅛pi red brn (R) 70.00 24.00
8 A7 ⅛pi red brn (Bk) 70.00 35.00
9 A7 ⅛pi red brn (V) 50.00 24.00
10 A7 ⅛pi car (R) 70.00 30.00
11 A7 ⅛pi car (Bk) 70.00 35.00
12 A7 ⅛pi car (V) 50.00 27.50
13 A7 ½pi red (Bl) 40.00 22.50
14 A7 ½pi red (V) 40.00 18.00
15 A7 1½pi vio (R) 60.00 24.00
16 A7 2pi yel buff (R) 85.00 57.50
a. 2pi orange (R) 110.00
17 A7 2pi yel buff (V) 85.00 57.50
a. 2pi orange (V) 100.00 32.50
18 A7 3pi brn red (Bl) 70.00 30.00
19 A7 3pi brn red (R) 70.00 22.50
20 A7 3pi brn red (V) 70.00 25.00

Many Hejaz stamps of the 1922 type were especially printed for this and following issues. The re-impressions are usually more clearly printed, in lighter shades than the 1922 stamps, and some are in new colors.

Counterfeits exist.

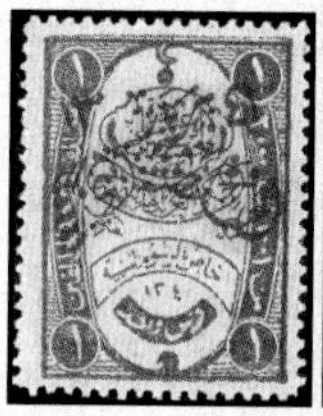

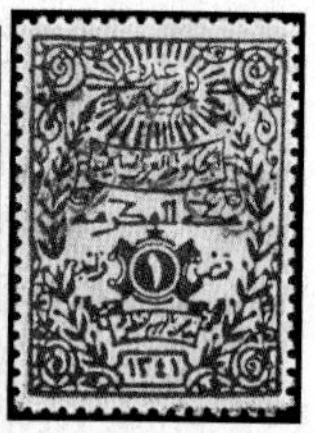

Arabic Inscriptions

R1 R2

On Hejaz Bill Stamp

22 R1 1pi violet (R) 40.00 15.00

On Hejaz Notarial Stamps

23 R2 1pi violet (R) 50.00 20.00
24 R2 2pi blue (R) 50.00 30.00
25 R2 2pi blue (V) 50.00 27.50

For overprint see No. 49.

On Hejaz Railway Tax Stamps

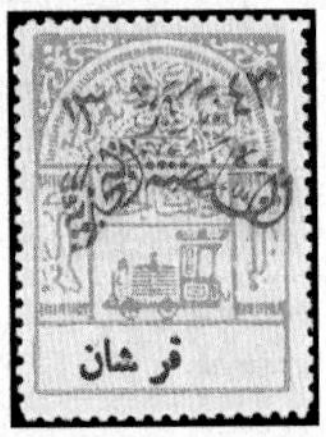

Locomotive — R3

Type I

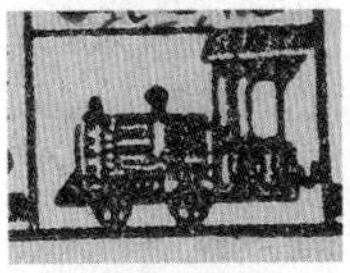

Type II

Two design types appear on the basic revenue stamps. Type 1 depicts the cab's window and the band at the center of the boiler as a series of horizontal lines, the top of the cab does not touch the frame line above it, and the coupler at rear of car appears as a fine hook that does not touch the right frame. Type 2 depicts the cab's window and band on boiler as open vertical spaces, the top of the cab touches the frame line above it, and the coupler appears as a blob connected to the right frame line. Type 2 appears in position 12 in the sheet of 18 (6x3) of the 500pi value, and in position 30 in the 36-stamp (6x6) sheets in which the other values were printed.

Type 1

26	R3 1pi blue (R)	40.00	9.00
a.	Type 2	60.00	
27	R3 2pi ocher (R)	60.00	14.00
a.	Type 2	90.00	
28	R3 2pi ocher (V)	60.00	14.00
a.	Type 2	90.00	
29	R3 3pi lilac (R)	60.00	20.00
a.	Type 2	90.00	
	Nos. 1-20,22-29 (28)	1,510.	698.50

For overprints and surcharges see Nos. 34, 50-54, 55, 59-68, J12-J15.

Pilgrimage Issue

Various Stamps Handstamp Surcharged in Blue and Red in Types "a" and "b" and with Tablets with New Values

a

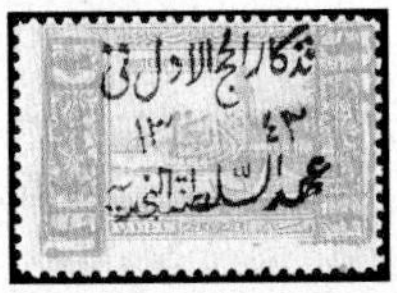

b

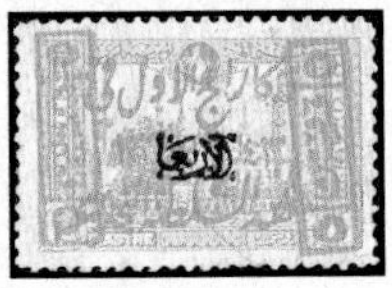

Surcharge "a" reads: "Tezkar al Hajj al Awwal Fi 'ahd al Sultanat al Nejdia, 1343" (Commemorating the first pilgrimage under the Nejdi Sultanate, 1925).

"b" reads: "Al Arba" (Wednesday.)

On Stamps of Turkey, 1913

1925, July 1 *Perf. 12*

30	A28 1pi on 10pa grn (Bl & R)	100.00	55.00
31	A30 5pi on 1pi bl (Bl & R)	100.00	55.00

On Stamps of Hejaz, 1917-18

Serrate Roulette 13

32	A5 2pi on 1pa lil brn (R & Bl)	125.00	67.50
33	A4 4pi on ⅛pi org (R & Bl)	400.00	350.00

On Hejaz Railway Tax Stamp

Perf. 11½

34	R3 3pi lilac, type 1 (Bl & R)	200.00	40.00
a.	Type 2	300.00	
	Nos. 30-34 (5)	925.00	567.50

No. 30 with handstamp "a" in black was a favor item. Nos. 30 and 33 with both handstamps in red are forgeries.

Handstamped in Blue, Red, Black or Violet

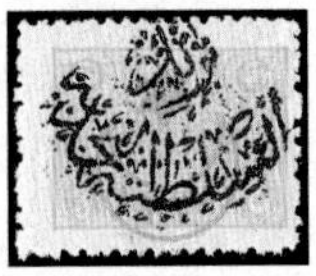

This overprint has practically the same meaning as that described over No. 1. The Mohammedan year (1343) is omitted.

This handstamp is said to be in private hands at this time. Extreme caution is advised before buying rare items.

On Stamp of Turkey, 1915, with Crescent and Star in Red

1925, July-Aug. *Perf. 12*

35	A22	5pa ocher (Bl)	50.00	24.00

On Stamps of Turkey, 1913

36	A28	10pa green (Bl)	60.00	20.00
a.		Black overprint	120.00	
b.		As "a," overprint inverted	650.00	

On Stamps of Hejaz, 1922 (Nos. L28-L29)

Serrate Roulette 13

37	A3	1pi blue (R)	120.00	*67.50*
38	A6	2pi magenta (Bl)	120.00	*67.50*

On Stamps of Hejaz, 1922-24

Perf. 11½

38A	A7	⅛pi red brn (Bk)	*4,500.*	
38B	A7	⅛pi red brn (Bl)	*3,750.*	
39	A7	½pi red (Bl)	12.50	10.00
a.		Imperf., pair	25.00	22.50
39B	A7	½pi red (Bk)	20.00	18.00
c.		Imperf., pair	50.00	37.50
40	A7	1pi gray vio (R)	50.00	29.00
a.		1pi black violet (R)	*50.00*	
41	A7	1½pi dk red (Bk)	50.00	30.00
a.		1½pi brick red (Bk)	50.00	
42	A7	2pi yel buff (Bl)	80.00	47.50
a.		2pi orange (Bl)	110.00	55.00
43	A7	2pi deep vio (Bl)	85.00	52.50
44	A7	3pi brown red (Bl)	50.00	30.00
45	A7	5pi scarlet (Bl)	70.00	37.50
		Never hinged	110.00	
		Nos. 35-38,39-45 (12)	767.50	*433.50*

Overprint on Nos. 38A, 39B, 39C is blue-black.

See note above No. 35.

With Additional Surcharge of New Value Typo. in Black

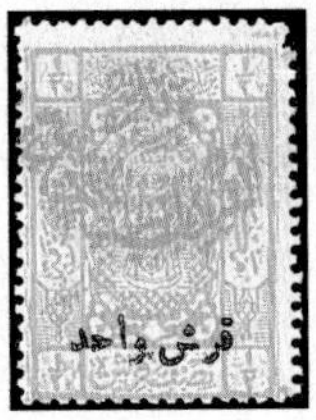

c

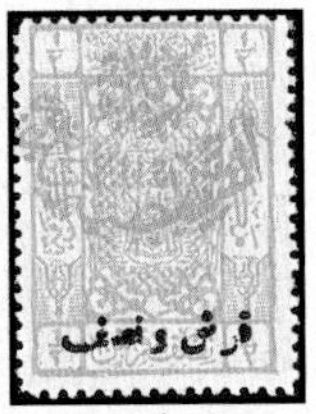

d

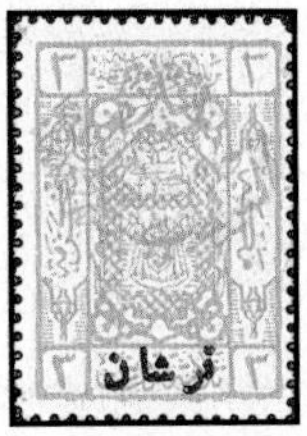

e

Color in parenthesis is that of overprint on basic stamp.

46	A7(c)	1pi on ½pi (Bl)	12.50	1.75
a.		Imperf, pair	40.00	
b.		Ovpt. & surch. inverted	90.00	
47	A7(d)	1½pi on ½pi (Bl)	17.50	7.25
a.		Imperf., pair	30.00	
b.		Black overprint	20.00	
48	A7(e)	2pi on 3pi (Bl)	17.50	16.00
		Nos. 46-48 (3)	47.50	25.00

Several variations in type settings of "c," "d" and "e" exist, including inverted letters and values.

On Hejaz Notarial Stamp

49	R2 2pi blue (Bk)	50.00	20.00

On Hejaz Railway Tax Stamps

50	R3 1pi blue, type 1 (R)	40.00	25.00
a.	Type 2	60.00	
51	R3 1pi blue, type 1 (Bk)	60.00	9.00
a.	Type 2	90.00	
52	R3 2pi ocher, type 1 (Bl)	60.00	9.00
a.	Type 2	90.00	
53	R3 3pi lilac, type 1 (Bl)	70.00	22.50
a.	Type 2	100.00	
54	R3 5pi green, type 1 (Bl)	60.00	20.00
a.	Type 2	90.00	
	Nos. 49-54 (6)	340.00	105.50

Hejaz Railway Tax Stamp Handstamped in Black

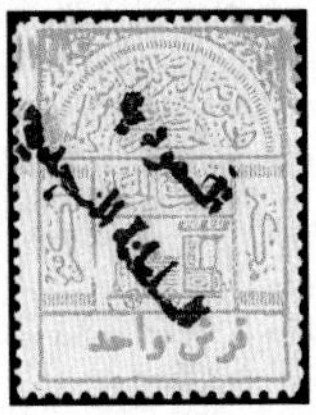

This overprint reads: "Al Saudia. — Al Sultanat al Nejdia." (The Saudi Sultanate of Nejd.)

1925-26 **Small Handstamp**

55	R3	1pi blue, type 1	—	*200.00*
b.		Type 2		400.00

On Nos. L34, L36-L37, L41

55A	A7	½ pi red	—	*350.00*
56	A7	1½pi violet	—	*375.00*
57	A7	2pi orange	—	*375.00*
57A	A7	10pi on 5pi ol green	—	*375.00*

On Nos. L95 and L97

58	A7	3pi olive brown	—	*400.00*
58A	A7	5pi olive green	—	*400.00*

On Nos. L162-L163, L173

Perf. 11½

58B	A9	½pi car rose	350.00	—
58C	A10	1pi yel grn	—	*225.00*
58D	A10	2pi blue	—	*350.00*

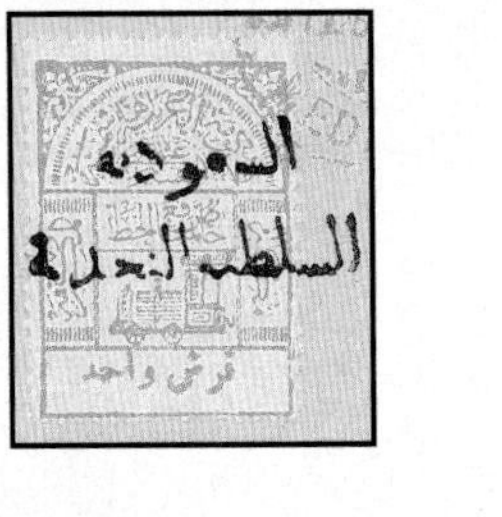

Large Handstamp

58K	R3	1pi blue		*7,000.*
58L	A7	3pi brn (#L95b) reading up		*1,000.*
a.		Overprint reading down		1,000.
58M	A10	1pi yel grn (#L163)	1,500.	*1,000.*

Nos. 55-58M were provisionally issued at Medina after its capitulation.

Only one example of No. 58K, a single stamp used on piece, is known.

This overprint exists on Nos. L160-L161, L164-L172, L174-L175, L180-L183. These 17 are known as bogus items, but may exist genuine.

Lithographed overprints are forgeries.

Medina Issue

Hejaz Railway Tax Stamps Handstamped

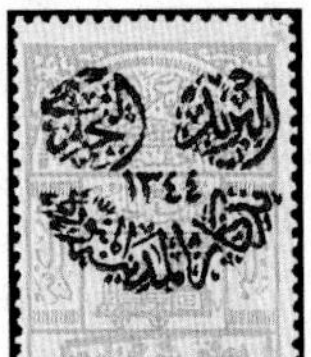

and Handstamp Surcharged in Various Colors

The large overprint reads: "The Nejdi Posts — 1344 — Commemorating Medina, the Illustrious." The tablet shows the new value.

1925

59	R3 1pi on 10pi vio, type 1 (Bk & V)	70.00	70.00
a.	Type 2	100.00	
60	R3 2pi on 50pi lt bl, type 1 (R & Bl)	70.00	70.00
a.	Type 2	100.00	
61	R3 3pi on 100pi red brn, type 1 (Bl & Bk)	70.00	70.00
a.	Type 2	100.00	
62	R3 4pi on 500pi dull red, type 1 (Bl & Bk)	70.00	70.00
a.	Type 2	100.00	
63	R3 5pi on 1000pi dp red, type 1 (Bl & Bk)	70.00	70.00
a.	Type 2	100.00	
	Nos. 59-63 (5)	350.00	350.00

JEDDA ISSUE

Hejaz Railway Tax Stamps Handstamped and Tablet with New Value in Various Colors

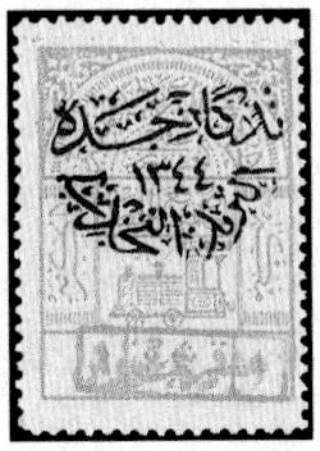

This handstamp reads: "Commemorating Jedda — 1344 — The Nejdi Posts."

1925

64	R3 1pi on 10pi vio, type 1 (Bk & Bl)	70.00	70.00
b.	Type 2	100.00	
65	R3 2pi on 50pi lt bl, type 1 (R & Bk)	70.00	70.00
a.	Type 2	100.00	
66	R3 3pi on 100pi red brn, type 1 (R & Bl)	70.00	70.00
a.	Type 2	100.00	
67	R3 4pi on 500pi dl red, type 1 (Bk & Bl)	70.00	70.00
a.	Type 2	100.00	
68	R3 5pi on 1000pi dp red, type 1 (Bk & Bl)	70.00	70.00
a.	Type 2	100.00	
	Nos. 64-68 (5)	350.00	350.00

Nos. 59-63 and 64-68 were prepared in anticipation of the surrender of Medina and Jedda.

Kingdom of Hejaz-Nejd

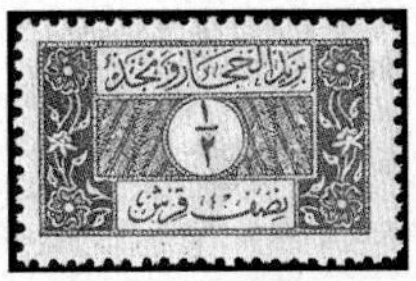

Arabic Inscriptions and Value — A1

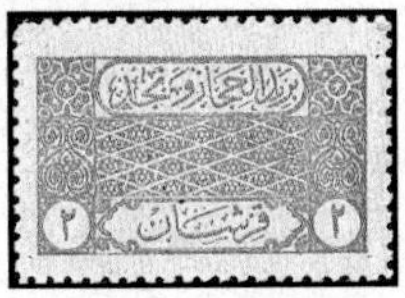

A2

Inscriptions in upper tablets: "Barid al Hejaz wa Nejd" (Posts of the Hejaz and Nejd)

1926, Feb. Typo. Unwmk. ***Perf. 11***

69	A1	¼pi violet	45.00	17.00
70	A1	½pi gray	45.00	17.00
71	A1	1pi deep blue	45.00	21.00
72	A2	2pi blue green	45.00	17.00
73	A2	3pi carmine	45.00	18.00
74	A2	5pi maroon	45.00	12.00
		Nos. 69-74 (6)	270.00	102.00

Nos. 69-72, 74 exist imperf. Value, each $40.

Used values are for favor cancels.

1926, Mar. *Perf. 11*

75	A1	¼pi orange	12.00	10.00
a.		Horiz. pair, imperf between	100.00	
76	A1	½pi blue green	5.25	*15.00*
a.		Horiz. pair, imperf between	100.00	
b.		Vertz. pair, imperf between	100.00	
77	A1	1pi carmine	4.25	*7.50*
a.		Horiz. pair, imperf between	100.00	
b.		Vert. pair, imperf between	100.00	

78 A2 2pi violet 5.25 *12.50*
   a. Horiz. pair, imperf between 100.00
   b. Vert. pair, imperf between 100.00
79 A3 3pi dark blue 5.25 *7.50*
   a. Horiz. pair, imperf between 100.00
   b. Vert. pair, imperf between 100.00
80 A3 5pi lt brown 10.00 *20.00*
   a. 5pi olive brown
   b. Horiz. pair, imperf between 100.00
   c. Vert. pair, imperf between 100.00
   Nos. 75-80 (6) 42.00 *72.50*

Nos. 75-80 also exist imperf. Value, twice the values shown above. Examples that are perforated 14, 14x11 and 11x14 were privately produced.

Counterfeits of types A1 and A2 are perf. 11½. They exist with and without overprints.

Types A1 and A2 in colors other than listed are proofs.

Pan-Islamic Congress Issue

Stamps of 1926 Hstmpd.

1926 *Perf. 11*
92 A1 ¼pi orange 12.00 4.00
93 A1 ½pi blue green 12.00 4.00
94 A1 1pi carmine 12.00 4.00
95 A2 2pi violet 12.00 4.00
96 A2 3pi dark blue 12.00 4.00
97 A2 5pi light brown 12.00 4.00
   Nos. 92-97 (6) 72.00

The overprint reads: "al Mootamar al Islami 20 Zilkada, Sanat 1344." (The Islamic Congress, June 1, 1926.)
See counterfeit note after No. 80.

Tughra of King Abdul Aziz — A3

1926-27 **Typo.** *Perf. 11½*
98 A3 ⅛pi ocher 5.00 .60
99 A3 ¼pi gray green 6.00 1.50
100 A3 ½pi dull red 6.00 1.50
   On paper wrapper 75.00
   On cover 100.00
   On cover, single franking 200.00
   b. Horiz. pair, imperf between 400.00
101 A3 1pi deep violet 6.50 1.50
102 A3 1½pi gray blue 18.00 2.25
103 A3 3pi olive green 14.00 4.75
104 A3 5pi brown orange 27.50 5.00
105 A3 10pi dark brown 70.00 11.00
   Nos. 98-105 (8) 153.00 24.10

Inscription at top reads: "Al Hukumat al Arabia" (The Arabian Government). Inscription below tughra reads: "Barid al Hejaz wa Nejd" (Post of the Hejaz and Nejd).

Stamps of 1926-27 Handstamped in Black or Red

1927
107 A3 ⅛pi ocher 13.00 4.75
108 A3 ¼pi gray grn 13.00 4.75
109 A3 ½pi dull red 13.00 4.75
110 A3 1pi deep violet 13.00 4.75
111 A3 1½pi gray bl (R) 13.00 4.75
112 A3 3pi olive green 13.00 4.75
113 A3 5pi brown orange 14.50 4.75
114 A3 10pi dark brown 16.00 4.75
   Nos. 107-114 (8) 108.50 38.00
   Set, never hinged 175.00

The overprint reads: "In commemoration of the Kingdom of Nejd and Dependencies, 25th Rajab 1345."
Inverted varieties have not been authenticated.

Turkey No. 258 Surcharged in Violet

1925 *Perf. 12*
115 A28 1g on 10pa green 175.00

Similar surcharges of 6g and 20g were made in red, but were not known to have been issued. Values: 6g, $350; 20g, $500.

A4

1929-30 **Typo.** *Perf. 11½*
117 A4 1¾g gray blue 40.00 4.50
119 A4 20g violet 50.00 10.00
120 A4 30g green 80.00 22.50

A5

1930 *Perf. 11, 11½*
125 A5 ½g rose 19.00 3.25
126 A5 1½g violet 19.00 2.10
127 A5 1¾g ultra 19.00 2.75
128 A5 3½g emerald 19.00 4.25

Perf. 11
129 A5 5g black brown 30.00 6.50
   Nos. 125-129 (5) 106.00 18.85

Anniversary of King Ibn Saud's accession to the throne of the Hejaz, January 8, 1926.

A6

1931-32 *Perf. 11½*
130 A6 ⅛g ocher ('32) 22.50 3.25
131 A6 ¼g blue green 22.50 2.50
133 A6 1¾g ultra 37.50 3.25
   Nos. 130-133 (3) 82.50 9.00

A7

1932 *Perf. 11½*
135 A7 ¼g blue green 16.00 32.50
136 A7 ½g scarlet 47.50 5.25
   a. Perf 11
137 A7 2¼g ultra 90.00 8.50
   a. Perf 11
   Nos. 135-137 (3) 153.50 46.25

Kingdom of Saudi Arabia

A8

1934, Jan. *Perf. 11½, Imperf.*
138 A8 ¼g yellow green 11.00 10.00
   Never hinged 15.00
139 A8 ½g red 11.00 10.00
   Never hinged 15.00

---

140 A8 1½g light blue 21.00 19.00
   Never hinged 27.50
141 A8 3g blue green 21.00 19.00
   Never hinged 27.50
142 A8 3½g ultra 37.50 7.75
   Never hinged 47.50
143 A8 5g yellow 50.00 37.50
   Never hinged 65.00
144 A8 10g red orange 90.00
   Never hinged 120.00
145 A8 20g bright violet 110.00
   Never hinged 150.00
146 A8 ¼s claret 225.00
   Never hinged 300.00
147 A8 30g dull violet 140.00
   Never hinged 180.00
148 A8 ½s chocolate 475.00
   Never hinged 700.00
149 A8 1s violet brown 1,075.
   Never hinged 1,750.
   Nos. 138-149 (12) 2,266.

Proclamation of Emir Saud as Heir Apparent of Arabia. Perf. and imperf. stamps were issued in equal quantities.
Favor cancels exist on Nos. 144-149.

Tughra of King Abdul Aziz — A9

1934-57 *Perf. 11, 11½*
159 A9 ⅛g yellow 5.25 .45
160 A9 ¼g yellow grn 5.25 .45
161 A9 ½g rose red ('43) 3.75 .25
   a. ½g dark carmine 12.00 1.40
162 A9 ⅞g lt blue ('56) 6.50 .55
163 A9 1g blue green 5.25 .45
164 A9 2g olive grn ('57) 9.00 2.25
   a. 2g olive bister ('57) 25.00 7.25
165 A9 2⅞g violet ('57) 6.50 .55
166 A9 3g ultra ('38) 6.50 .25
   a. 3g light blue 20.00 1.75
167 A9 3½g lt ultra 35.00 2.25
168 A9 5g orange 6.50 .55
169 A9 10g violet 19.00 1.75
170 A9 20g purple brn 32.50 1.10
   a. 20g purple black 25.00 2.25
171 A9 100g red vio ('42) 90.00 5.25
172 A9 200g vio brn ('42) 115.00 7.00
   Nos. 159-172 (14) 346.00 23.10
   Set, never hinged 450.00

The ½g has two types differing in position of the tughra.
No. 162 measures 31x22mm. No. 164 30½x21½mm. No. 165, 30½x22mm. No. 166 30x21mm. No. 171, 31x22mm. No. 172, 30½x21½mm. Rest of set, 29x20½mm. Grayish paper was used in 1946-49 printings.
No. 168 exists with pin-perf 6.
For overprint see No. J24.

Yanbu Harbor near Radwa — A10

1945 **Typo.** *Perf. 11½*
173 A10 ½g brt carmine 7.75 .35
174 A10 3g lt ultra 10.00 1.10
175 A10 5g purple 27.50 1.40
176 A10 10g dk brown vio 60.00 3.25
   Nos. 173-176 (4) 105.25 6.10
   Set, never hinged 145.00

Meeting of King Abdul Aziz and King Farouk of Egypt at Jebal Radwa, Saudi Arabia, Jan. 24, 1945.

> **Catalogue values for unused stamps in this section, from this point to the end of the section, are for Never Hinged items.**

Arms of Saudi Arabia and Afghanistan A12

1950, Mar. *Perf. 11*
178 A12 ½g carmine 9.00 1.10
179 A12 3g violet blue 13.50 1.10

Visit of Zahir Shah of Afghanistan, March 1950. One 3g in each sheet inscribed POSTFS, value $45.

Old City Walls, Riyadh A13

1950 **Center in Red Brown**
180 A13 ½g magenta 67.50 .40
181 A13 1g lt blue 13.00 .40
182 A13 3g violet 19.00 .90
183 A13 5g vermilion 42.50 1.75
184 A13 10g green 77.50 4.50
   a. Singular "guerche" in Arabic 575.00 75.00
   Nos. 180-184 (5) 219.50 7.95

50th lunar anniversary of King Ibn Saud's capture of Riyadh, Jan. 16, 1902.
No. 184a: On the 3g, 5g and 10g the currency is expressed in the plural in both French (grouche) and Arabic. One stamp in each sheet of 20 (4x5), position 11, of the 10g shows the Arabic characters in the singular form of "guerche," as on the ½g and 1g.

Arms of Saudi Arabia and Jordan — A14

1951, Nov. *Perf. 11*
185 A14 ½g carmine 15.00 1.75
   a. "BOYAUME" 275.00 100.00
186 A14 3g violet blue 20.00 2.75
   a. "BOYAUME" 275.00 100.00

Visit of King Tallal of Jordan, Nov. 1951.

Bedouins and Train — A15

1952, June **Engr.** *Perf. 12*
187 A15 ½q redsh brown 9.75 1.50
188 A15 1q deep green 9.75 1.50
189 A15 3q violet 20.00 1.00
190 A15 10q rose pink 40.00 7.50
191 A15 20q blue 82.50 16.00
   Nos. 187-191 (5) 162.00 27.50

Inaugural trip over the Saudi Government Railroad between Riyadh and Dammam.

Saudi Arabia Arms and Lebanon Emblem — A16

1953, Feb. **Typo.** *Perf. 11*
192 A16 ½g carmine 9.00 1.25
193 A16 3g violet blue 17.50 2.00

Visit of President Camille Chamoun of Lebanon.

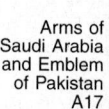

Arms of Saudi Arabia and Emblem of Pakistan A17

1953, Mar.
194 A17 ½g dark carmine 10.00 1.25
195 A17 3g violet blue 20.00 1.90

Visit of Gov.-Gen. Ghulam Mohammed of Pakistan.

Arms of Saudi Arabia and Jordan — A18

1953, July   **Unwmk.**
196 A18	½g carmine	9.00	1.25
a.	"GOERCHE"	75.00	
197 A18	3g violet blue	21.00	1.90

Visit of King Hussein of Jordan, July, 1953.

Globe — A18a

1955, July   **Litho.**
198 A18a	½g emerald	5.00	.60
199 A18a	3g violet	12.50	1.25
200 A18a	4g orange	17.50	3.00
	Nos. 198-200 (3)	35.00	4.85

Founding of the Arab Postal Union, July 1, 1954.

Ministry of Communications Building, Riyadh — A19

1960, Apr. 12   **Photo.**   **Perf. 13**
201 A19	2p bright blue	1.40	.25
202 A19	5p deep claret	2.75	.25
203 A19	10p dark green	7.50	.95
	Nos. 201-203 (3)	11.65	1.45

Arab Postal Union Conference, at Riyadh, Apr. 11. Imperfs. exist.

Arab League Center, Cairo A20

1960, Mar. 22   **Perf. 13x13½**
204 A20	2p dull grn & blk	2.50	.30

Opening of the Arab League Center and the Arab Postal Museum in Cairo. Exists imperf.

Radio Tower and Waves A21

1960, June 4
205 A21	2p red & black	2.50	.35
206 A21	5p brown blk & mar	4.25	.40
207 A21	10p bluish blk & ultra	6.75	.95
	Nos. 205-207 (3)	13.50	1.70

1st international radio station in Saudi Arabia. Imperfs. exist.

Map of Palestine, Refugee Camp and WRY Emblem — A22

1960, Oct. 30   **Litho.**   **Perf. 13**
208 A22	2p dark blue	.45	.30
209 A22	8p lilac	.45	.30
210 A22	10p green	1.40	.30
	Nos. 208-210 (3)	2.30	.90

World Refugee Year, July 1, 1959-June 30, 1960. Imperfs. exist.

Wadi Hanifa Dam, near Riyadh — A23

Type I (Saud Cartouche) (Illustrated over No. 286)

1960-62   **Unwmk.**   **Photo.**   **Perf. 14**
Size: 27½x22mm
211 A23	½p bis brn & org	1.75	.30
212 A23	1p ol bis & pur	1.75	.30
213 A23	2p blue & sepia	1.75	.30
214 A23	3p sepia & blue	1.75	.30
215 A23	4p sepia & ocher	1.75	.30
216 A23	5p blk & dk violet	1.75	.30
217 A23	6p brn blk & car rose ('62)	1.75	.50
a.	6p black & carmine rose	1.75	.40
218 A23	7p red & gray ol	1.75	.30
219 A23	8p dk bl & brn blk	1.75	.35
220 A23	9p org brn & scar	1.75	.40
c.	9p yel brn & metallic red	1.75	.55
221 A23	10p emer grn & mar ('62)	2.10	.50
a.	10p blue green & maroon	2.10	.40
222 A23	20p brown & green	5.00	.50
223 A23	50p black & brown	27.50	2.50
224 A23	75p brown & gray	77.50	2.75
225 A23	100p dk bl & grn bl	72.50	3.25
226 A23	200p lilac & green	110.00	8.50
	Nos. 211-226 (16)	312.10	21.35

Gas-Oil Separating Plant, Buqqa — A24

1960-61
227 A24	½p maroon & org	1.50	1.50
228 A24	1p blue & red org	1.50	1.50
229 A24	2p ver & blue	1.50	1.50
230 A24	3p lilac & brt grn	1.50	1.50
231 A24	4p yel grn & lilac	1.50	1.50
232 A24	5p dk gray & brn red	1.50	1.50
233 A24	6p brn org & dk vio	1.50	1.50
234 A24	7p vio & dull grn	1.50	1.50
235 A24	8p blue grn & gray	1.50	1.50
236 A24	9p ultra & sepia	4.75	1.50
237 A24	10p dk blue & rose	2.50	.45
238 A24	20p org brn & blk	8.75	.65
239 A24	50p red & brn grn	25.00	1.90
240 A24	75p red & blk	40.00	4.00
241 A24	100p dk bl & red brn	60.00	3.50
242 A24	200p dk gray & ol grn	100.00	8.00
	Nos. 227-242 (16)	254.50	33.50

Nearly all of Nos. 211-242 exist imperf; probably not regularly issued.
See Nos. 258-273, 286-341, 393-450, 461-483.

Dammam Port — A25

Wmk. 337
1961, Aug. 16   **Litho.**   **Perf. 13**
243 A25	3p lilac	1.75	.30
244 A25	6p light blue	2.50	.40
245 A25	8p dark green	4.25	.40
	Nos. 243-245 (3)	8.50	1.10

Expansion of the port of Dammam. Imperf min. sheets of 4 were for presentation purposes and have wmk. sideways. Value, set $425. Imperforate pairs or margined imperfs with upright watermark come from full sheets not perforated by the print shop.

Globe, Radio and Telegraph A26

Perf. 13x13½
1961, Aug. 7   **Photo.**   **Unwmk.**
246 A26	3p dull purple	1.50	.25
247 A26	6p gray black	2.75	.40
248 A26	8p brown	4.25	.65
	Nos. 246-248 (3)	8.50	1.30

Arab Union of Telecommunications. Imperfs. exist.

Arab League Building, Cairo — A27

1962, Apr. 22   **Wmk. 337**   **Perf. 13**
249 A27	3p olive green	1.50	.30
250 A27	6p carmine rose	3.00	.40
251 A27	8p slate blue	4.75	.45
	Nos. 249-251 (3)	9.25	1.15

Arab League Week, Mar. 22-28.

Imperforate or missing-color varieties of Nos. 249-285 and 344-353 were not regularly issued.

Malaria Eradication Emblem — A28

1962, May 7   **Litho.**   **Wmk. 337**
252 A28	3p red org & blue	1.50	.30
253 A28	6p emerald & Prus bl	2.00	.35
254 A28	8p black & lil rose	3.00	.60
a.	Souv. sheet of 3, #252-254, imperf.	32.50	32.50
	Nos. 252-254 (3)	6.50	1.25

WHO drive to eradicate malaria.
Nos. 252-254 are known unofficially overprinted with new dates only or with "AIR MAIL" and two plane silhouettes.
A 4p exists as an essay.

Koran A29

1963, Mar. 12   **Wmk. 337**   **Perf. 11**
255 A29	2½p lilac rose & pink	1.00	.25
256 A29	7½p blue & pale grn	2.10	.40
257 A29	9½p green & gray	3.25	.40
	Nos. 255-257 (3)	6.35	1.05

First anniversary of the Islamic Institute, Medina. A 3p exists as an essay. Copies of the 2½p exist with virtually all the pink background omitted. No copies are known with the pink completely omitted.

Dam Type of 1960 Redrawn
Type I (Saud Cartouche)
Perf. 13½x13
1963-65   **Wmk. 337**   **Litho.**
Size: 28½x23mm
258 A23	½p bis brn & org	15.00	1.10

Nos. 258, 264-265 are widely spaced in the sheet, producing large margins.

Perf. 14
Photo.
Size: 27½x22mm
259 A23	½p bis brn & org ('65)	22.50	1.75
260 A23	3p sepia & blue	9.00	.65
261 A23	4p sepia & ocher ('64)	12.50	.80

---

262 A23	5p black & dk vio	12.50	.80
263 A23	20p dk car & grn	22.50	1.60
	Nos. 258-263 (6)	94.00	6.70

A 1p was prepared but not issued. It is known only imperf.

Gas-Oil Plant Type of 1960 Redrawn
Type I (Saud Cartouche)
Perf. 13½x13
1963-65   **Wmk. 337**   **Litho.**
Size: 28½x23mm
264 A24	½p mar & org	13.50	1.25
265 A24	1p bl & red org ('64)	7.25	.45

Photo.
Perf. 14
Size: 27½x22mm
266 A24	½p mar & org ('64)	11.50	.60
267 A24	1p blue & red org	9.75	.45
268 A24	3p lilac & brt grn	22.50	1.10
269 A24	4p yel grn & lilac	17.50	.60
270 A24	5p dk gray & brn red	13.50	.60
271 A24	6p brn org & dk vio ('65)	19.00	.75
272 A24	8p dull grn & blk	50.00	1.40
273 A24	9p blue & sepia	35.00	1.75
	Nos. 264-273 (10)	199.50	8.95

The 3p, 4p and 6p exist imperf.

Hands Holding Wheat Emblem A30

1963, Mar. 21   **Litho.**   **Perf. 11**
274 A30	2½p lilac rose & rose	1.10	.25
275 A30	7½p brt lilac & pink	1.10	.35
276 A30	9p red brn & lt blue	2.75	.45
	Nos. 274-276 (3)	4.95	1.05

FAO "Freedom from Hunger" campaign. The 3p imperf in various colors are essays.

Jet over Dhahran Airport — A31

1963, July 27   **Litho.**   **Perf. 13**
277 A31	1p blue gray & ocher	1.60	.35
278 A31	3½p ultra & emer	3.25	.35
279 A31	6p emerald & rose	5.75	.45
a.	"Thahran" for "Dharan" in Arabic	8.75	
280 A31	7½p lilac rose & lt bl	5.75	.55
281 A31	9½p ver & dull vio	8.25	.60
	Nos. 277-281 (5)	24.60	2.30

Opening of the US-financed terminal of the Dhahran Airport and inauguration of international jet service.
On No. 279a the misspelling consists of an omitted dot over character near top left in one horiz. row of five.
Nos. 277-281 with a second impression of the frame are forgeries.

Flame — A32

1964, Apr.   **Wmk. 337**   **Perf. 13x13½**
282 A32	3p lil, pink & Prus bl	3.50	.30
283 A32	6p yel grn, lt bl & Prus bl	4.00	.35
284 A32	9p brn, buff & Prus bl	9.00	.45
	Nos. 282-284 (3)	16.50	1.10

15th anniv. of the signing of the Universal Declaration of Human Rights.
The 3p in other colors is an essay.

King Faisal and Arms of Saudi Arabia A33

1964, Nov. Litho. *Perf. 13*

285	A33	4p dk blue & emerald	7.50	.60

Installation of Prince Faisal ibn Abdul Aziz as King, Nov. 2, 1964.

King Saud's Cartouche — Type I

King Faisal's Cartouche — Type II

Dam Type of 1960 Redrawn Type I (Saud Cartouche)

1965-70 Litho. Unwmk. *Perf. 14*

Size: 27x22mm

286	A23	1p ol bis & pur	32.50	1.60
287	A23	2p dk blue & sep	6.25	.45
288	A23	3p sepia & blue	4.75	.50
289	A23	4p sepia & ocher	9.00	.50
290	A23	5p blk & dk vio	8.00	.50
291	A23	6p blk & car rose	19.00	.90
292	A23	7p brn & gray	19.00	.50
293	A23	8p dk bl & gray	*125.00*	8.00
294	A23	9p org brn & scar	*100.00*	8.00
295	A23	10p bl grn & mar	*92.50*	5.00
296	A23	11p red & yel grn	8.75	3.25
297	A23	12p org & dk bl	8.75	.50
298	A23	13p dk ol & rose	8.75	.60
299	A23	14p org brn & yel grn	8.75	.60
300	A23	15p sepia & gray grn	8.75	3.25
301	A23	16p dk red & dl vio	10.50	.70
302	A23	17p rose lil & dk bl	10.50	3.50
303	A23	18p grn & brt bl	10.50	.70
304	A23	19p blk & bis	14.50	.85
305	A23	20p brn & grn	13.50	1.60
306	A23	23p mar & lilac	11.50	3.25
307	A23	24p ver & blue	14.50	.95
308	A23	26p olive & yel	18.00	1.10
309	A23	27p ultra & red brn	18.00	1.10
310	A23	31p gray & dull bl	18.00	1.25
311	A23	33p ol grn & lilac	18.00	1.25
312	A23	100p dk bl & grnsh bl	*650.00*	*80.00*
313	A23	200p dull lil & grn	*650.00*	*80.00*
		Nos. 286-313 (28)	*1,917.*	*210.40*

A 50p exists but was never placed in use.
Issue years: 1966, 2p, 4p, 10p-20p, 1968, 6p-9p. 1970, 100p-200p.

Gas-Oil Plant Type of 1960 Redrawn Type I (Saud Cartouche)

1964-70 Litho. Unwmk.

Size: 27x22mm

314	A24	1p bl & red org	7.25	.25
315	A24	2p vermilion & bl	11.00	.25
316	A24	3p lilac & brt grn	4.50	.25
317	A24	4p yel grn & lilac	6.50	.25
318	A24	5p dl gray vio & dk red brn	24.00	1.75
319	A24	6p brn org & dk vio	50.00	4.50
320	A24	7p vio & dull grn	27.50	1.75
321	A24	8p bl grn & gray	6.00	.30
322	A24	9p ultra & sepia	12.50	.70
323	A24	10p dk blue & rose	*650.00*	32.50
324	A24	11p olive & org	4.00	.30
325	A24	12p bister & grn	4.00	.30
326	A24	13p rose red & dk bl	4.00	.35
327	A24	14p vio & lt brown	5.50	.35
328	A24	15p rose red & sep	6.00	.45
329	A24	16p grn & rose red	8.00	.45
330	A24	17p car rose & red brn	12.50	1.40
331	A24	18p gray & ultra	8.00	.55
332	A24	19p brown & yel	8.00	.55
333	A24	20p dull org & dk gray	27.50	1.75
334	A24	23p orange & car	7.25	.65
335	A24	24p emer & org yel	8.00	.70
336	A24	26p lil & red brn	11.00	.70
337	A24	27p ver & dk gray	11.00	.70
338	A24	31p dull grn & car	19.00	1.40
339	A24	33p red brn & gray	17.00	1.40
340	A24	50p red brn & dull grn	*650.00*	*45.00*
341	A24	200p dk gray & ol gray	*650.00*	*45.00*
		Nos. 314-341 (28)	*2,260.*	*144.50*

A 100p exists but was never placed in use.
Issue years: 1965, 4p, 8p, 9p, 23p-33p. 1966, 1p, 2p, 5p, 11p-14p, 16p-20p. 1967, 15p. 1968, 6p, 7p. 1969, 50p. 1970, 200p. Others, 1964.

Holy Ka'aba, Mecca — A34

1965, Apr. 17 Wmk. 337 *Perf. 13*

344	A34	4p salmon & blk	4.50	.30
345	A34	6p brt pink & blk	6.50	.35
346	A34	10p yel grn & blk	9.00	.45
		Nos. 344-346 (3)	20.00	1.10

Mecca Conf. of the Moslem World League.

Arms of Saudi Arabia and Tunisia A35

1965, Apr. Litho.

347	A35	4p car rose & silver	3.50	.30
348	A35	8p red lilac & silver	4.50	.45
349	A35	10p ultra & silver	6.50	.45
		Nos. 347-349 (3)	14.50	1.20

Visit of Pres. Habib Bourguiba of Tunisia, Feb. 22-26.

Highway, Hejaz Mountains — A36

1965, June 2 Wmk. 337 *Perf. 13*

350	A36	2p red & blk	2.00	.35
351	A36	4p blue & blk	4.00	.50
352	A36	6p lilac & blk	5.75	.85
353	A36	8p brt green & blk	7.25	1.00
		Nos. 350-353 (4)	19.00	2.70

Opening of highway from Mecca to Tayif.

ICY Emblem A37

1965, Nov. 13 Unwmk. *Perf. 13*

354	A37	1p yellow & dk brn	1.75	.25
355	A37	2p orange & ol grn	1.75	.25
356	A37	3p lt blue & gray	1.75	.25
357	A37	4p yel grn & dk sl grn	2.00	.25
358	A37	10p orange & magenta	4.50	1.25
		Nos. 354-358 (5)	11.75	2.25

International Cooperation Year, 1965.

ITU Emblem, Old and New Communication Equipment — A38

1965, Dec. 22 Litho. *Perf. 13*

359	A38	3p blue & blk	2.25	.25
360	A38	4p lilac & dk grn	2.25	.25
361	A38	8p emerald & dk brn	2.25	.40
362	A38	10p dull org & dk grn	2.25	.40
		Nos. 359-362 (4)	9.00	1.30

Centenary of the ITU.

Library Aflame and Lamp A39

1966, Jan. Litho. *Perf. 12x12½*

363	A39	1p orange	1.90	.25
364	A39	2p dark red	1.90	.25
365	A39	3p red violet	2.50	.25
366	A39	4p violet	3.00	.25
367	A39	5p lilac rose	4.50	.35
368	A39	6p vermilion	9.50	.45
		Nos. 363-368 (6)	23.30	1.80

Burning of the Library of Algiers, June 7, 1962. Nos. 363-368 were withdrawn from sale Jan. 26, 1966, due to incorrect Arabic inscriptions. Later some values were inadvertently again placed in use.

Arab Postal Union Emblem — A40

1966, Mar. 15 Litho. *Perf. 14*

369	A40	3p dull pur & olive	1.25	.30
370	A40	4p deep blue & olive	1.25	.30
371	A40	6p maroon & olive	4.50	.30
372	A40	7p deep green & olive	4.50	.45
		Nos. 369-372 (4)	11.50	1.35

10th anniv. (in 1964) of the APU. Printed in sheets of two panes, so horizontal gutter pairs exist.

Dagger in Map of Palestine — A41

1966, Mar. 19 Litho. *Perf. 13*

373	A41	2p yel grn & blk	2.25	.50
374	A41	4p lt brown & blk	4.00	1.00
375	A41	6p dull blue & blk	5.00	1.25
376	A41	8p ocher & blk	8.00	1.50
		Nos. 373-376 (4)	19.25	4.25

Deir Yassin massacre, Apr. 9, 1948.

Emblems of World Boy Scout Conference and Saudi Arabian Scout Association A42

1966, Mar. 23 Unwmk.

377	A42	4p yel, blk, grn & gray	4.75	.55
378	A42	8p yel, blk, org & lt bl	4.75	.55
379	A42	10p yel, blk, sal & bl	10.00	.80
		Nos. 377-379 (3)	19.50	1.90

Arab League Rover Moot (Boy Scout Jamboree).

WHO Headquarters, Geneva, and Flag — A43

1966, May Litho. *Perf. 13*

380	A43	4p aqua & multi	1.75	.50
381	A43	6p yel brn & multi	3.50	1.00
382	A43	10p pink & multi	6.75	1.25
		Nos. 380-382 (3)	12.00	2.75

Opening of the WHO Headquarters, Geneva.

UNESCO Emblem — A44

1966, Sept. Unwmk. *Perf. 12*

383	A44	1p apple grn & multi	1.75	.25
384	A44	2p dull org & multi	1.75	.30
385	A44	3p lilac rose & multi	2.50	.40
386	A44	4p pale green & multi	2.50	.50
387	A44	10p gray & multi	3.50	1.00
		Nos. 383-387 (5)	12.00	2.45

20th anniv. of UNESCO.

Radio Tower, Telephone and Map of Arab Countries — A45

1966, Nov. 7 Litho. *Perf. 12½*

Design in Black, Carmine & Yellow

388	A45	1p vio blue	1.90	.25
389	A45	2p bluish lilac	1.90	.25
390	A45	4p rose lilac	3.75	.25
391	A45	6p lt olive grn	3.75	.35
392	A45	7p gray green	5.00	.50
		Nos. 388-392 (5)	16.30	1.60

Issued to publicize the 8th Congress of the Arab Telecommunications Union, Riyadh.

Dam Type of 1960 Redrawn Type II (Faisal Cartouche) (Illustrated over No. 286)

1966-76 Litho. Unwmk. *Perf. 14*

Size: 27x22mm

393	A23	1p ol bis & pur	*225.00*	*22.50*
394	A23	2p dk blue & sep	19.00	1.50
395	A23	3p blk & dk bl	11.00	.80
396	A23	4p sepia & ocher	15.00	.40
397	A23	5p blk & dk vio	40.00	7.50
398	A23	6p blk & car rose	32.50	6.75
399	A23	7p sepia & gray	18.00	1.75
400	A23	8p dk bl & gray	11.00	.45
401	A23	9p org brn & scar	7.50	.80
402	A23	10p bl grn & mar	15.00	1.40
403	A23	11p red & yel grn	11.00	1.40
404	A23	12p org & dk bl	6.50	1.40
405	A23	13p blk & rose	22.50	1.40
406	A23	14p org brn & yel grn	19.00	1.40
407	A23	15p sep & gray grn	19.00	1.75
408	A23	16p dk red & dl vio	27.50	3.25
409	A23	17p rose lil & dk bl	32.50	1.75
410	A23	18p grn & brt bl	22.50	2.50
411	A23	19p blk & bis	7.25	.80
412	A23	20p brown & grn	72.50	*2.25*
413	A23	23p maroon & lil	*375.00*	*4.50*
414	A23	24p ver & blue	52.50	5.50
415	A23	26p olive & yel	6.75	.70
416	A23	27p ultra & red brn	7.75	.70
417	A23	33p ol grn & lilac	42.50	2.25
419	A23	50p blk & brn	*300.00*	*35.00*

420	A23	100p dk bl & grnsh bl	*500.00*	*45.00*
421	A23	200p dl lil & grn	*500.00*	*72.50*
		Nos. 393-421 (28)	*2,418.*	*227.90*

A 31p has been reported.

Issue years: 1966, 1p. 1967, 2p, 10p. 1968, 3p, 4p, 6p, 7p, 20p; 1969, 5p, 8p. 1970, 9p, 23p; 1972, 12p, 15p, 16p. 1973, 11p; 1974, 17p, 50p-200p; 1975, 13p, 14p, 19p, 24p-33p; 1976, 18p.

Gas-Oil Plant Type of 1960 Redrawn Type II (Faisal Cartouche) (Illustrated over No. 286)

1966-78 **Unwmk.**

Size: 27x22mm

422	A24	1p bl & red org	37.50	*3.00*
423	A24	2p ver & dull bl	7.75	.35
424	A24	3p lilac & brt grn	15.00	.60
425	A24	4p grn & dull lil	9.00	.35
426	A24	5p dl gray vio & dk red brn	40.00	1.90
427	A24	6p brn org & dull pur	25.00	3.75
428	A24	7p vio & dull grn	35.00	1.90
429	A24	8p bl grn & grnsh gray	6.00	.35
430	A24	9p ultra & sep	4.25	.35
431	A24	10p dk bl & rose	5.00	.60
432	A24	11p olive & org	80.00	8.00
433	A24	12p bister & grn	5.00	.75
434	A24	13p rose red & dk bl	47.50	.35
435	A24	14p vio & lt brn	45.00	2.50
436	A24	15p car & sepia	11.50	.65
437	A24	16p grn & rose red	15.50	.75
438	A24	17p car rose & red brn	11.00	.60
439	A24	18p gray & ultra	15.50	1.60
440	A24	19p brown & yel	17.50	1.60
441	A24	20p brn org & gray	13.00	1.60
442	A24	23p orange & car	22.50	1.90
443	A24	24p emer & org yel	10.00	.75
444	A24	26p lilac & red brn	*225.00*	
445	A24	27p ver & dk gray	37.50	3.75
446	A24	31p grn & rose car	12.00	.75
447	A24	33p brown & gray	22.50	1.25
448	A24	50p red brn & dl grn	500.00	*150.00*
449	A24	100p dk bl & red brn	500.00	*50.00*
450	A24	200p dk gray & ol gray	500.00	*62.50*
		Nos. 422-450 (29)	2,275.	302.45

Issue years: 1967, 20p; 1968, 3p, 5p-9p, 15p, 16p; 1969, 100p; 1970, 11p, 14p, 200p; 1973, 13p, 18p, 24p; 1974, 19p, 50p; 1975, 12p, 17p, 27p-33p; 1978, 26p; others, 1966.

No. 442 with a double impression of the frame is a forgery.

Emblem of Saudi Arabian Scout Association A46

1967, Mar. 28 **Litho.** ***Perf. 13½***

Emblem in Green, Red, Yellow & Black

451	A46	1p dk blue & blk	2.25	.75
452	A46	2p blue grn & blk	2.75	.75
453	A46	3p lt blue & blk	4.25	.75
454	A46	4p rose brn & blk	5.25	.75
455	A46	10p brown & blk	12.50	2.00
		Nos. 451-455 (5)	27.00	5.00

2nd Arabic League Rover Moot, Mecca, March 13-28.

Meteorological Instruments and WMO Emblem — A47

1967, July **Unwmk.** ***Perf. 13***

456	A47	1p brt magenta	1.25	.30
457	A47	2p violet	2.50	.30
458	A47	3p olive	2.50	.35
459	A47	4p blue green	9.00	.35
460	A47	10p blue	13.00	.75
		Nos. 456-460 (5)	28.25	2.05

Issued for World Meteorological Day.

Dam Type of 1960 Redrawn Type II (Faisal Cartouche)

1968-76 **Wmk. 361** **Litho.** ***Perf. 14***

461	A23	1p ol bis & pur ('68)	*1,250.*	*300.00*
462	A23	2p dk blue & sep	110.00	*6.50*
463	A23	3p blk & dk bl	70.00	*3.50*
464	A23	4p sepia & ocher	625.00	*110.00*
465	A23	5p blk & dk vio	92.50	*6.50*
466	A23	6p blk & car rose	85.00	*5.00*
467	A23	7p sepia & gray	125.00	*10.00*
468	A23	8p dk bl & gray	65.00	3.25
469	A23	9p org brn & ver	240.00	*22.50*
470	A23	10p bl grn & mar	160.00	*13.00*
471	A23	11p red & yel grn	200.00	*20.00*
472	A23	12p org & sl bl	175.00	*16.00*
473	A23	13p black & rose	240.00	*24.50*
		Nos. 462-473 (12)	2,187.	*240.75*

Issue years: 1968, 2p, 10p; 1969, 3p; 1970, 8p; 1971, 1p, 5p; 1972, 6p, 9p, 11p, 12p; 1973, 4p; 1974, 13p; 1976, 9p.

Gas-Oil Plant Type of 1960 Redrawn Type II (Faisal Cartouche)

1968-76 ***Perf. 14***

474	A24	1p bl & red org	9.50	.90
475	A24	2p ver & dl bl	5.75	.45
476	A24	4p grn & dl lil	95.00	*9.50*
477	A24	5p dk brn & red brn ('73)	26.00	1.75
478	A24	6p brn org & dk vio ('73)	32.50	2.25
479	A24	9p dk bl & sep ('76)	52.50	4.50
480	A24	10p dk bl & rose	8.50	.60
481	A24	11p ol & org ('72)	40.00	2.25
482	A24	12p bis & grn ('72)	42.50	3.50
483	A24	23p org & car ('74)	70.00	3.50
		Nos. 474-483 (10)	382.25	29.20

Map Showing Dammam to Jedda Road, and Dates — A48

Wmk. 361

1968, Aug. **Litho.** ***Perf. 14***

484	A48	1p yellow & multi	1.60	.25
485	A48	2p orange & multi	1.60	.25
486	A48	3p multicolored	3.25	.25
487	A48	4p multicolored	3.25	.25
488	A48	10p multicolored	10.00	.45
		Nos. 484-488 (5)	19.70	1.45

Issued to commemorate the completion of the trans-Saudi Arabia highway in 1967.

Several positions in the sheet have the dots representing Dammam and Riyadh omitted. Most had the dots added by pen before issuance.

Prophet's Mosque, Medina — A49

Wmk. 361, 337 (#489, 493)

1968-76 **Litho.** ***Perf. 13½x14***

Design A49

489	A49	1p org & grn ('70)	2.10	.30
490	A49	2p red brn & grn, redrawn ('72)	3.50	.35
a.		2p red brn & grn, wmk. 337	6.25	.30
b.		As "a," redrawn	*200.00*	
491	A49	3p vio & grn ('72)	3.25	.35
a.		3p vio & grn, wmk. 337 ('70)	2.75	.30
492	A49	4p ocher & grn	3.50	.35
a.		Redrawn ('71)	5.50	.45
b.		4p ocher & green, redrawn, wmk. 337	6.25	
493	A49	5p dp lil rose & grn ('71)	7.75	.90
494	A49	6p blk & grn ('73)	9.75	.90
a.		6p gray & green ('76)	18.00	.90
495	A49	10p brown & grn	12.00	.90
a.		Redrawn	9.00	
496	A49	20p dk brn & grn ('70)	15.00	1.75
a.		Redrawn	18.00	
497	A49	50p sepia & grn ('75)	19.00	5.75
498	A49	100p dk bl & grn ('75)	15.00	4.50
499	A49	200p red & grn ('75)	19.00	6.25
		Nos. 489-499 (11)	109.85	22.30

See redrawn note following design A55. No. 494 exists imperf.

Warning: Stamps of design A49 in other colors, double frames, inverted centers or centers omitted are forgeries. They are printed on sheet selvage.

New Arcade, Mecca Mosque — A50

1968-69 **Wmk. 361**

500	A50	3p dp org & gray ('69)	375.00	95.00
501	A50	4p green & gray	5.75	.45
502	A50	10p mag & gray	8.25	.90
		Nos. 500-502 (3)	389.00	96.35

Expansion of Prophet's Mosque — A51

1968-76 **Wmk. 361**

503	A51	1p org & grn ('72)	4.50	.25
504	A51	2p brn & grn ('72)	7.25	.25
c.		As No. 504, redrawn		
505	A51	3p blk & grn ('69)	6.25	.35
b.		3p gray & green ('76)	18.00	1.75
c.		As No. 505, redrawn	4.50	
506	A51	4p org & grn ('70)	6.25	.45
a.		Redrawn	4.50	.45
507	A51	5p red & grn, redrawn ('74)	6.75	.75
508	A51	6p Prus bl & grn ('72)	9.00	.90
509	A51	8p rose red & grn ('76)	22.50	1.75
510	A51	10p brn red & grn ('70)	8.25	.55
b.		10p org & grn, redrawn ('76)	18.00	.90
511	A51	20p vio & grn ('74)	18.00	2.25
		Nos. 503-511 (9)	88.75	7.50

Wmk. 337

503a	A51	1p	5.00	.35
504a	A51	2p ('70)	6.75	.35
b.		As "a," redrawn	35.00	
505a	A51	3p ('71)	7.25	.70
d.		As "a," redrawn	—	
506b	A51	4p Redrawn ('72)	9.00	
507a	A51	5p ('70)	4.50	.45
508a	A51	6p ('72)	6.25	.55
510a	A51	10p ('70)	11.00	.60
c.		As "a," redrawn	18.00	
511a	A51	20p ('72)	8.25	.70
		Nos. 503a-511a (8)	58.00	3.70

See redrawn note following design A55.

Madayin Saleh — A52

1968-75

512	A52	2p ultra & bis brn ('70)	26.00	4.50
513	A52	4p dk & lt brown	6.50	.90
514	A52	7p org & lt brn ('75)	50.00	*1.10*
515	A52	10p sl grn & lt brn	16.00	2.25
516	A52	20p lil rose & brn ('71)	18.00	1.75
		Nos. 512-516 (5)	116.50	*10.50*

Arabian Stallion — A53

517	A53	4p mag & org brn	7.25	.95
518	A53	10p blk & org brn	20.00	3.75
519	A53	14p bl & ocher ('71)	30.00	7.50
520	A53	20p ol grn & ocher ('71)	11.00	2.40
		Nos. 517-520 (4)	68.25	14.60

Camels and Oil Derrick — A54

1969-71

521	A54	4p dk pur & redsh brn ('71)	32.50	5.00
522	A54	10p ultra & hn brn	29.00	3.75

Holy Ka'aba, Mecca — A55

Original

Redrawn

On the original stamps the knob-shaped Arabic letter, located under the two square dots in the middle of the top panel, has a small central dot. The dot often is missing.

On the redrawn stamps the dot has been enlarged into a conspicuous irregular oval. The 3p also has a period added after the value and the 4p has the "4" under the "T" instead of the "S." There are other small differences.

Numeral & "Postage" on Gray Background, 8p on White

1969-75

523	A55	4p dp grn & blk ('70)	7.75	.70
a.		Redrawn, value corner white ('74)	16.00	1.75
b.		Redrawn ('75)	14.00	
524	A55	6p dp lil rose & blk ('71)	4.50	.35
a.		Value corner white ('74)	22.50	2.75
525	A55	8p red & blk ('75)	27.50	2.75
526	A55	10p org & blk ('69)	16.00	1.40
a.		Redrawn, value corner white ('74)	14.00	1.75
b.		Redrawn ('75)	18.00	
		Nos. 523-526 (4)	55.75	5.20

Rover Moot Badge — A56

Perf. 13½x14

1969, Feb. 19 **Litho.** **Wmk. 337**

607	A56	1p orange & multi	2.00	.25
608	A56	4p dull purple & multi	7.00	.25
609	A56	10p orange brn & multi	17.50	.85
		Nos. 607-609 (3)	26.50	1.35

3rd Arab League Rover Moot, Mecca, Feb. 19-Mar. 3.

Traffic Light and Intersection — A57

1969, Feb.   Wmk. 361   Perf. 13½
610	A57	3p dl bl, red & brt bl grn	2.75	.25
a.		3p dull blue, red & gray green	30.00	1.25
611	A57	4p org brn, red & gray grn	2.75	.25
612	A57	10p dl pur, red & gray grn	5.50	.60
		Nos. 610-612 (3)	11.00	1.10

Issued for Traffic Day.

WHO Emblem — A58

1969, Oct. 20   Wmk. 337   Perf. 14
613	A58	4p lt bl, vio bl & yel	13.00	.25

20th anniv. (in 1968) of WHO.

Islamic Conference Emblem A59

1970, Mar. 23   Litho.   Wmk. 361
614	A59	4p blue & black	3.50	.25
615	A59	10p yellow bis & blk	5.25	.55

Islamic Conference of Foreign Ministers, Jedda, March 1970.

Open Book and Satellite Earth Receiving Station — A60

Perf. 14x13½
1970, Aug. 1   Litho.   Wmk. 337
616	A60	4p violet bl & multi	5.75	.25
617	A60	10p green & multi	11.50	.60

World Telecommunications Day.

Steel Rolling Mill, Jedda A61

1970, Oct. 26   Wmk. 337   Perf. 13½
618	A61	3p yellow org & multi	5.25	.25
619	A61	4p violet & multi	8.00	.25
620	A61	10p brt green & multi	14.00	.95
		Nos. 618-620 (3)	27.25	1.45

Inauguration of 1st steel mill in Saudi Arabia.

Rover Moot Emblem — A62

1971, Feb.   Litho.   Perf. 14
621	A62	10p brt blue & multi	10.50	.80

4th Arab League Rover Moot, 1971.

Telecommunications Symbol — A63

1971, May 17   Wmk. 337   Perf. 14
622	A63	4p blue & blk	2.50	.25
623	A63	10p lilac & blk	6.00	.50

World Telecommunications Day.

University Emblem — A64

Wmk. 337; Wmk. 361 (4p)
1971, Aug.   Litho.   Perf. 14
624	A64	3p brt green & black	2.10	.25
625	A64	4p brown & black	4.25	.25
626	A64	10p blue & black	7.75	.60
		Nos. 624-626 (3)	14.10	1.10

King Abdul Aziz National University.

Arab League Emblem — A65

1971, Nov.   Wmk. 337   Perf. 13½
627	A65	10p multicolored	8.00	.45

Arab League Week.

Education Year Emblem — A66

1971, Nov.   Litho.
628	A66	4p apple grn & brn red	7.25	.25

International Education Year 1970.

OPEC Emblem — A67

1971, Dec.   Perf. 14
629	A67	4p light blue	8.00	.25

10th anniversary of OPEC (Organization of Petroleum Exporting Countries).

Globe A68

1972, Aug.   Wmk. 361   Perf. 14
630	A68	4p multicolored	8.00	.25

4th World Telecommunications Day.

Telephone — A69

1972, Oct.   Wmk. 337, 361 (5p)
631	A69	1p red, blk & grn	2.50	.25
632	A69	4p dk grn, blk & grn	2.50	.25
633	A69	5p lil, blk & grn	4.75	.25
634	A69	10p tan, blk & grn	10.50	.50
		Nos. 631-634 (4)	20.25	1.25

Inauguration of automatic telephone system (1969).

Writing Hand — A70

1972, Sept. 8   Litho.   Wmk. 361
635	A70	10p multicolored	10.50	.45

World Literacy Day, Sept. 8.

Holy Ka'aba and Grand Mosque, Mecca A71

Rover Moot Emblem and: 4p, Prophet's Mosque, Medina. 10p, Plains of Arafat.

1973
636	A71	4p lt blue & multi	4.50	.25
637	A71	6p lilac & multi	9.00	.25
638	A71	10p salmon & multi	13.50	.75
		Nos. 636-638 (3)	27.00	1.45

5th Arab League Rover Moot.

Globe and Map of Palestine A71a

1973   Litho.   Wmk. 361   Perf. 14
639	A71a	4p black, yel & red	4.50	.25
640	A71a	10p blue, yel & red	9.25	.50

Palestine Week.

Leaf and Emblem — A72

1973
641	A72	4p yellow & multi	8.00	.35

International Hydrological Decade 1965-74.

Arab Postal Union Emblem — A73

1973, Dec.   Litho.   Perf. 14
642	A73	4p sepia & multi	5.50	.40
643	A73	10p purple & multi	13.50	.65

25th anniversary (in 1971) of the Conference of Sofar, Lebanon, establishing the Arab Postal Union.

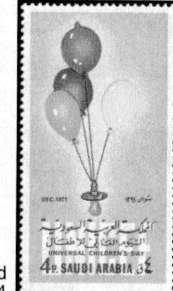

Balloons and Pacifier — A74

1973, Dec.
644	A74	4p lt blue & multi	10.00	.25

Universal Children's Day (stamp dated 1971).

Arab Postal and UPU Emblems A75

1974, July 7   Wmk. 361   Perf. 14
645	A75	3p yellow & multi	62.50	3.50
646	A75	4p rose & multi	62.50	6.75
647	A75	10p lt green & multi	62.50	10.50
		Nos. 645-647 (3)	187.50	20.75

Centenary of the Universal Postal Union.

Handshake and UNESCO
Emblem — A76

1974, May 21   *Perf. 13½*
648 A76   4p orange & multi   3.00 .30
649 A76   10p green & multi   14.00 .80
International Book Year, 1972.

Desalination Plant — A77

1974, Sept. 3   **Wmk. 361**   *Perf. 14*
650 A77   4p dp orange & bl   2.75 .25
651 A77   6p emerald & vio   5.75 .30
652 A77   10p rose red & blk   8.75 .65
     Nos. 650-652 (3)   17.25 1.20
Opening (in 1971) of sea water desalination
plant, Jedda.

A78

Design: INTERPOL emblem.

1974, Nov. 1
653 A78   4p ocher & ultra   9.50 .25
654 A78   10p emerald & ultra   17.50 .60
50th anniversary (in 1973) of International
Criminal Police Organization.

A79

APU emblem, tower and letter.

1974, Oct. 26   **Litho.**   **Wmk. 361**
655 A79   4p multicolored   9.00 .25
Arab Consultative Council for Postal Studies, 3rd session.

UPU Headquarters, Bern — A80

1974, Nov. 15   *Perf. 13½*
656 A80   3p orange & multi   4.50 .30
657 A80   4p lilac & multi   7.50 .60
658 A80   10p blue & multi   10.50 1.50
     Nos. 656-658 (3)   22.50 2.40
Opening of new Universal Postal Union
Headquarters, Bern, May 1970.

Tank,
Planes,
Rockets
and Flame
A81

1974, Dec. 15   *Perf. 14*
659 A81   3p slate & multi   2.50 .25
660 A81   4p brown & multi   5.00 .30
661 A81   10p lilac & multi   13.50 .85
     Nos. 659-661 (3)   21.00 1.40
King Faisal Military Cantonment, 1971.

A82

Red Crescent flower.

1974, Dec. 17   *Perf. 14x14½*
662 A82   4p gray & multi   2.25 .30
663 A82   6p lt green & multi   5.75 .60
664 A82   10p lt blue & multi   11.50 1.10
     Nos. 662-664 (3)   19.50 2.00
Saudi Arabian Red Crescent Society, 10th
anniversary (in 1973).

A83

Saudi Arabian scout emblem and minarets.

1974, Dec. 23   **Wmk. 361**   *Perf. 14*
665 A83   4p brown & multi   6.00 .25
666 A83   6p blue blk & multi   11.50 .40
667 A83   10p purple & multi   17.50 .70
     Nos. 665-667 (3)   35.00 1.35
6th Arab League Rover Moot, Mecca.

BLINDS' DAY — A84

Design: Reading braille.

1975, Mar. 31   *Perf. 14x13½*
668 A84   4p multicolored   14.00 .30
669 A84   10p multicolored   10.00 .50
     Day of the Blind.

Anemometer and Weather Balloon
with WMO Emblem — A85

Perf. 13½x14
1975, May 8   **Litho.**   **Wmk. 361**
670 A85   4p multicolored   10.50 .30
Centenary (in 1973) of International Meteorological Cooperation.

King
Faisal — A86

1975, July 6   **Unwmk.**   *Perf. 14*
671 A86   4p green & rose brn   3.50 .35
672 A86   16p violet & green   4.50 .90
673 A86   23p dk green & vio   9.25 1.50
     Nos. 671-673 (3)   17.25 2.75

Imperf
674 A86   40p Prus bl & ocher   400.00
King Faisal ibn Abdul-Aziz Al Saud (1906-
1975). Size of No. 674: 71x80mm.

Conference
Emblem — A87

1975, July 11   *Perf. 14*
675 A87   10p rose brn & blk   6.25 .55
6th Islamic Conference of Foreign Ministers,
Jedda, July 12.

Wheat and
Sun — A88

1975, Sept. 17   **Litho.**   **Wmk. 361**
676 A88   4p lilac & multi   4.00 .25
677 A88   10p blue & multi   11.00 .50
Charity Society, 20th anniversary.

Holy Ka'aba, Globe, Clasped
Hands — A89

1975, Sept. 17   *Perf. 14*
678 A89   4p olive bis & multi   9.50 .30
679 A89   10p orange & multi   19.00 .55
Conference of Moslem Organizations,
Mecca, Apr. 6-10, 1974.

Saudia Tri-Star and DC-3 — A90

1975, Sept.   **Litho.**   **Unwmk.**
680 A90   4p buff & multi   9.50 .35
681 A90   10p lt blue & multi   19.00 .65
Saudia, Saudi Arabian Airline, 30th
anniversary.

Conference
Centers in
Mecca and
Riyadh
A91

1975, Sept.   *Perf. 14*
682 A91   10p multicolored   14.50 .70

Friday Mosque, Medina, and Juwatha
Mosque, al-Hasa — A92

1975, Oct. 26   **Litho.**   **Unwmk.**
683 A92   4p green & multi   8.00 .40
684 A92   10p vermilion & multi   11.00 .70
Ancient Islamic holy places.

FAO Emblem — A93

1975, Oct. 26
685 A93   4p gray & multi   5.50 .25
686 A93   10p buff & multi   16.00 .65
World Food Program, 10th anniversary (in
1973). Stamps are dated 1973.

Conference Emblem — A94

1976, Mar. 20　Unwmk.　Perf. 14
687　A94　4p multicolored　　　19.00　.35
Islamic Solidarity Conference of Science and Technology.

Saudi Arabia Map, Transmission Tower, TV Screen — A95

1976, May 26　Litho.　Perf. 14
688　A95　4p multicolored　　　26.00　.35
Saudi Arabian television, 10th anniversary.

Grain, Atom Symbol, Graph A96

1976, June 28　Litho.　Perf. 14
689　A96　20h yellow & multi　　5.00　.40
690　A96　50h yellow & multi　　9.50　.80
Second Five-year Plan.

Holy Ka'aba A97

Type I

Two types:
I — "White" minarets. Gray vignette.
II — Black minarets and vignette. Design redrawn, strengthened, darkened, clarified.

1976-79　Litho.　Wmk. 361　Perf. 14
Type II
691　A97　5h lilac & blk　　　　.25　.25
692　A97　10h lt violet & blk　　.35　.25
693　A97　15h salmon & blk　　.50　.25
　a.　Type I　　　　　　　　4.25　.25
694　A97　20h lt bl & blk, II　　5.50　.25
　a.　Type I　　　　　　　　5.00　.25
695　A97　25h yellow & blk　　1.50　.25
696　A97　30h gray grn & blk　2.10　.25
697　A97　35h bister & blk　　1.25　.25
698　A97　40h lt green & blk　4.75　.25
　a.　Type I ('77)　　　　　6.00　.30
699　A97　45h dull rose & blk　1.60　.25
700　A97　50h pink & blk　　1.50　.25
703　A97　65h gray blue & blk　1.90　.25
710　A97　1r lt yel grn & blk　2.50　.25
711　A97　2r green & black　9.75　.50
　　Nos. 691-711 (13)　　33.45　3.50

No. 698 imperf exists as an issued error. Value, $110. Nos. 691-711 also exist as imperfs not regularly issued.

Issue years: 20h, 1977; 5h-15h, 25h-50h, 1r, 1978; 65h, 2r, 1979.
See Nos. 872-882, 961-968.

Quba Mosque, Medina, built 622 — A98

1976-77
719　A98　20h orange & blk　　2.25　.25
720　A98　50h emer & lilac ('77)　4.00　.25
Reissued in 1978 in different shades.
No. 720 exists imperf as an issued error.

Globe, Telephones 1876 and 1976 A100

1976, July 17　Unwmk.　Perf. 13½
721　A100　50h multicolored　　9.00　.35
Centenary of first telephone call by Alexander Graham Bell, Mar. 10, 1876.

Arab Leaders A101

1976, Oct. 30　Litho.　Perf. 14
722　A101　20h ultra & emerald　5.50　.30

Arab Summit Conference, Riyadh, October. Leaders pictured: Pres. Elias Sarkis, Lebanon; Pres. Anwar Sadat, Egypt; Pres. Hafez al Assad, Syria; King Khalid, Saudi Arabia; Amir Sabah, Kuwait; Yasir Arafat, Palestine Liberation Organization chairman.

WHO Emblem and Eye A102

1976, Nov. 28　Litho.　Perf. 14
723　A102　20h multicolored　14.50　.25
World Health Day; Prevention of Blindness.

Holy Ka'aba — A103

1976, Nov. 28　Unwmk.
724　A103　20h multicolored　10.00　.30
50th anniversary of installation of new covering of Holy Ka'aba, Mecca.

Conference Emblem A104

Unwmk.
1977, Feb. 18　Litho.　Perf. 14
725　A104　20h multicolored　10.00　.25
Islamic Jurisprudence Conference, Riyadh, Oct. 24-Nov. 2, 1976.

A105

Design: Sharia College emblem.

1977, Feb. 25　　　　Perf. 14
726　A105　4p multicolored　　9.00　.25
25th anniversary (in 1974) of the founding of Sharia (Islamic Law) College, Mecca.

A106

1977
727　A106　20h dk brn & brt grn　2.50　.25
　a.　Incorrect date　　　　22.50
728　A106　80h bl blk & brt grn　4.75　.65
　a.　Incorrect date　　　　22.50

2nd anniversary of installation of King Khalid ibn Abdul-Aziz. Nos. 727a-728a, issued Mar. 3, have incorrect Arabic date in bottom panel, last characters of 2nd and 3rd rows identical "ir." Stamps withdrawn after a few days and replaced Aug. 14 with corrected date, last characters in 3rd row changed to "ro."

Diesel Train and Map of Route A107

1977, May 23　Litho.　Perf. 14
729　A107　20h multicolored　30.00　.25
Dammam-Riyadh railroad, 25th anniversary.

Arabic Ornament and Names — A108

Designs (Names from Left to Right): UL, Malik Ben Anas (715-795). UR, Mohammad Ben Idris Al-Shafi'i (767-820). LL, Abu Hanifa an-Nu'man (699-767). LR, Ahmed Ben Hanbal (780-855).

1977, Aug. 15　Litho.　Perf. 14
730　A108　Block of 4　　　65.00　3.75
　a.-d.　20h, single stamp　　9.00　.70

Famous Imams (7th-9th centuries), founders of traditional schools of Islamic jurisprudence. Sheets of 60 stamps (15 blocks).
No. 730 exists with a double impression of the blue color. Stamps with double impressions of the black color are forgeries.

Al Khafji Oil Rig — A109

1976-80　　　　　　Wmk. 361
731　A109　5h vio blue & org　.25　.25
732　A109　10h yel grn & org　.25　.25
733　A109　15h brown & org　.25　.25
734　A109　20h green & org　.25　.25
735　A109　25h dk pur & org　.25　.25
736　A109　30h blue & orange　.30　.25
737　A109　35h sepia & org　.40　.25
738　A109　40h mag & org　.40　.25
　a.　40h dull purple & org　175.00
739　A109　45h violet & orange　.50　.25
740　A109　50h rose & orange　.65　.25
　a.　50h dull org & org (error)　75.00　6.75
741　A109　55h grnsh bl & org　27.50　4.25
743　A109　65h sepia & org　1.50　.25
750　A109　1r gray & orange　1.90　.65
751　A109　2r dk vio & org　4.25　1.25
　　　　　　　　　　　　　('80)
　　Nos. 731-751 (14)　38.65　9.05

All values exist with extra dot in Arabic "Al Khafji." The 20h, 25h, 50h, 65h and 1r were retouched to remove the dot.
Color of flame varies from light orange to vermilion.
No. 737 imperf exists as an issued error. Value, $275. Nos. 731-751 also exist as imperfs not regularly issued.
See Nos. 885-892, 1300A.

Mohenjo-Daro Ruins — A110

1977, Oct. 23　Litho.　Unwmk.
761　A110　50h multicolored　10.00　.40
UNESCO campaign to save Mohenjo-Daro excavations in Pakistan.

Idrisi's World Map, 1154 — A111

1977, Nov. 1   **Litho.**   **Perf. 14**
762 A111 20h multicolored   3.50   .40
763 A111 50h multicolored   7.00   .70

First International Symposium on Studies in the History of Arabia at the University of Riyadh, Apr. 23-26, 1977.

King Faisal Specialist Hospital, Riyadh — A112

1977, Nov. 13   **Litho.**   **Unwmk.**
764 A112 20h multicolored   4.25   .30
765 A112 50h multicolored   6.75   .50

Conference Emblem — A113

1978, Jan. 24   **Litho.**   **Perf. 14**
766 A113 20h vio blue & yel   5.50   .25

1st World Conf. on Moslem Education.

APU Emblem, Members' Flags A114

1978, Jan. 21
767 A114 20h multicolored   2.50   .25
768 A114 80h multicolored   4.75   .60

25th anniversary of Arab Postal Union.

Taif-Abha-Jizan Highway — A115

1978, Oct. 15   **Litho.**   **Perf. 14**
769 A115 20h multicolored   2.50   .25
770 A115 80h multicolored   4.75   .50

Inauguration of Taif-Abha-Gizan highway. No. 770 exists with black (road) missing and with black double.

Pilgrims, Mt. Arafat and Holy Ka'aba — A116

Unwmk.
1978, Nov. 6   **Litho.**   **Perf. 14**
771 A116 20h multicolored   2.50   .25
772 A116 80h multicolored   4.75   .50

Pilgrimage to Mecca. No. 772 exists with inscriptions (black and blue colors) omitted.

Gulf Postal Organization Emblem — A117

1979, Feb. 6   **Litho.**   **Perf. 14**
773 A117 20h multicolored   1.75   .25
774 A117 50h multicolored   3.25   .40

1st Conf. of Gulf Postal Organization, Baghdad.

Saudi Arabia No. 129, King Abdul Aziz ibn Saud A118

Unwmk.
1979, June 4   **Litho.**   **Perf. 14**
775 A118   20h multicolored   2.00   .25
776 A118   50h multicolored   4.25   .35
777 A118 115h multicolored   6.75   .75
   Nos. 775-777 (3)   13.00   1.35

Imperf
778 A118 100h multicolored   110.00

1st commemorative stamp, 50th anniv. No. 778 contains one stamp with simulated perforations. Size: 101x76mm.

Crown Prince Fahd A119

1979, June 25   **Perf. 14**
779 A119 20h multicolored   2.50   .25
780 A119 50h multicolored   4.70   .35

Crown Prince Fahd ibn Abdul Aziz.

Dome of the Rock, Jerusalem A120

1979, July 2   **Wmk. 361**
781 A120 20h multi (shades)   2.75   .55

No. 781 exists with inscriptions (green and mauve colors) omitted. Imperfs. exist. See No. 866.

Gold Door, Holy Ka'aba — A121

1979, Oct. 13   **Litho.**   **Perf. 14**
782 A121 20h multicolored   2.25   .25
783 A121 80h multicolored   4.25   .50

Installation of new gold doors. Imperfs. exist.

Pilgrims at Holy Ka'aba, Mecca Mosque — A122

1979, Oct. 27
784 A122 20h multicolored   1.50   .25
785 A122 50h multicolored   3.25   .35

Pilgrimage to Mecca. Imperfs. exist.

Birds in Trees, IYC Emblem — A123

IYC Emblem and: 50h, Child's drawing.

1980, Feb. 17   **Litho.**   **Perf. 14**
786 A123 20h multicolored   12.50   .25
787 A123 50h multicolored   19.00   .40

Intl. Year of the Child (1979). Imperfs. exist.

King Abdul Aziz ibn Saud on Horseback, Saudi Flag A124

1980, Apr. 5   **Litho.**   **Perf. 14**
788 A124 20h multicolored   1.75   .25
789 A124 80h multicolored   4.25   .40

Saudi Arabian Army, 80th anniv. (1979). Imperfs. exist.

Arab League, 35th Anniversary A125

1980, Apr. 27   **Litho.**   **Perf. 14**
790 A125 20h multicolored   2.25   .25

Imperfs. exist.

International Bureau of Education, 50th Anniversary — A126

1980, May 4
791 A126 50h multicolored   2.75   .35

Imperfs. exist.

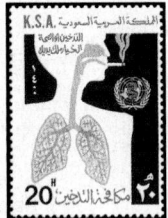

Smoke Entering Lungs, WHO Emblem — A127

1980, May 20
792 A127 20h shown   1.75   .25
793 A127 50h Cigarette, horiz.   4.25   .30

Anti-smoking campaign. Imperfs. exist.

20th Anniversary of OPEC A128

Design: 50h, Workers holding OPEC emblem (Organization of Petroleum Exporting Countries).

1980, Sept. 1   **Litho.**   **Perf. 14**
794 A128 20h multicolored   1.75   .25
795 A128 50h multi, vert.   3.25   .35

Pilgrims Arriving at Jedda Airport A129

1980, Oct. 18
796 A129 20h multicolored   1.10   .25
797 A129 50h multicolored   2.50   .40

Pilgrimage to Mecca.

Conference Emblem A130

Holy Ka'aba, Mecca Mosque — A131

1981, Jan. 25   **Litho.**   **Perf. 14**
798 A130 20h shown   1.25   .25
799 A131 20h shown   1.25   .25
800 A131 20h Prophet's Mosque, Medina   1.25   .25

801 A131 20h Dome of the Rock,
Jerusalem 1.25 .25
Nos. 798-801 (4) 5.00 1.00
Third Islamic Summit Conference, Mecca.

Hegira,
1500th
Anniv.
A132

1981, Jan. 26
802 A132 20h multicolored 1.10 .25
803 A132 50h multicolored 2.10 .35
804 A132 80h multicolored 4.00 .60
Nos. 802-804 (3) 7.20 1.20
Souvenir Sheet
805 A132 300h multicolored 125.00

Industry
Week
A133

1981, Feb. 21
806 A133 20h multicolored 1.00 .25
807 A133 80h multicolored 3.25 .55

Line Graph
and
Telephone
A134

Map of
Saudi
Arabia,
Microwave
Tower
A135

1981, Feb. 28
808 A134 20h shown .75 .30
809 A135 80h shown 3.25 .55
810 A134 115h Earth satellite
station 4.00 .85
Nos. 808-810 (3) 8.00 1.70
Imperf
811 A134 100h like #808 65.00
812 A135 100h like #809 65.00
813 A134 100h like #810 65.00
Ministry of Posts and Telecommunications
achievements.

Arab City
Day — A135a

1981, Apr. 2 Litho. Perf. 14
814 A135a 20h multicolored .50 .25
815 A135a 65h multicolored 1.50 .50
816 A135a 80h multicolored 2.25 .50
817 A135a 115d multicolored 3.00 .90
Nos. 814-817 (4) 7.25 2.15

Jedda
Airport
Opening
A136

1981, Apr. 12
818 A136 20h shown .75 .25
819 A136 80h Plane over airport,
diff. 3.75 .65

1982 World Cup
Soccer
Preliminary
Games — A137

1981, July 26 Litho. Perf. 14
820 A137 20h multicolored 2.75 .35
821 A137 80h multicolored 5.50 .55

Intl. Year of the
Disabled — A138

1981, Aug. 5
822 A138 20h Reading braille 2.00 .25
823 A138 50h Man weaving rug 4.00 .35

3rd Five-year Plan (1981-
1985) — A139

1981, Sept. 5
824 A139 20h multicolored 1.75 .25

King Abdul
Aziz, Map
of Saudi
Arabia
A140

1981, Sept. 23 Litho. Perf. 14
825 A140 5h multicolored .25 .25
826 A140 10h multicolored .25 .25
827 A140 15h multicolored .25 .25
828 A140 20h multicolored .45 .25
829 A140 50h multicolored .90 .35
830 A140 65h multicolored 1.25 .50
831 A140 80h multicolored 3.25 .50
832 A140 115h multicolored 4.25 .75
Nos. 825-832 (8) 10.85 3.10
Imperf
833 A140 10r multicolored 110.00
50th anniv. of kingdom. No. 833 shows king,
map, document. Size: 100x75mm.

Pilgrimage
to Mecca
A141

1981, Oct. 7
834 A141 20h multicolored 2.25 .25
835 A141 65h multicolored 3.75 .60

World Food
Day
A142

1981, Oct. 16
836 A142 20h multicolored 3.00 .50

2nd Session of
the Gulf
Cooperative
Council Summit
Conference,
Riyadh, Nov.
10 — A143

1981, Nov. 10 Litho. Perf. 14
837 A143 20h multicolored 1.25 .35
838 A143 80h multicolored 3.50 .75

King Saud
University,
25th Anniv.
A144

1982, Mar. 10 Litho. Perf. 14
839 A144 20h multicolored 1.10 .30
840 A144 50h multicolored 2.40 .40

New
Regional
Postal
Centers
A145

1982, July 14 Litho. Perf. 14
841 A145 20h Riyadh P.O. .45 .25
842 A145 65h Jedda 1.50 .40
843 A145 80h Dammam 1.90 .40
844 A145 115h Automated sorting 2.25 .65
Nos. 841-844 (4) 6.10 1.70
Four 300h souvenir sheets exist in same
designs as Nos. 841-844 respectively. Value,
$26.50 each.

Riyadh Television
Center — A146

1982, Sept. 4
845 A146 20h multicolored 1.50 .25

25th Anniv.
of King's
Soccer Cup
A147

1982, Sept. 8
846 A147 20h multicolored 1.00 .25
847 A147 65h multicolored 2.25 .40

30th Anniv.
of Arab
Postal
Union
A148

1982, Sept. 8
848 A148 20h Emblem 1.00 .25
849 A148 65h Map, vert. 2.25 .50

Pilgrimage
to Mecca
A149

1982, Sept. 26
850 A149 20h multicolored 1.00 .25
851 A149 50h multicolored 2.25 .50

World
Standards
Day
A150

1982, Oct. 14
852 A150 20h multicolored 1.75 .25

World Food
Day
A151

1982, Oct. 16
853 A151 20h multicolored 1.50 .25

Coronation
of King
Fahd, June
14, 1982
A152

Installation
of Crown
Prince
Abdullah,
June 14,
1982
A153

1983, Feb. 12 Litho. Perf. 14
854 A152 20h multicolored .45 .25
855 A153 20h multicolored .45 .25
856 A152 50h multicolored .90 .40
857 A153 50h multicolored .90 .40
858 A152 65h multicolored 1.40 .45
859 A153 65h multicolored 1.40 .45

860	A152	80h multicolored	1.60	.50
861	A153	80h multicolored	1.60	.50
862	A152	115h multicolored	2.50	.80
863	A153	115h multicolored	2.50	.80
	Nos. 854-863 (10)		13.70	4.80

Two one-stamp souvenir sheets contain Nos. 862-863, perf. 12½. Value $300.

6th Anniv. of United Arab Shipping Co. — A154

Various freighters.

1983, Aug. 9   Litho.   Perf. 14

864	A154	20h multicolored	.75	.25
865	A154	65h multicolored	2.50	.25

Dome of the Rock, Jerusalem A155

1983, Sept.   Wmk. 361   Perf. 12

866	A155	20h multicolored	.90	.25

See No. 781.

Pilgrimage to Mecca A156

1983, Sept. 16   Litho.   Perf. 14

867	A156	20h brt blue & multi	.50	.25
868	A156	65h dk black & multi	1.75	.25

World Communications Year — A157

20h, Post and UPU emblems. 80h, Telephone and ITU emblems.

1983, Oct. 8   Litho.   Perf. 14

869	A157	20h multicolored	.35	.25
870	A157	80h multicolored	1.90	.35

Holy Ka'aba Type of 1976
Type II
Perf. 14x13½
1982-86   Litho.   Wmk. 361
Size: 26x21mm

872	A97	10h lt vio & blk ('83)	.25	.25
874	A97	20h lt blue & blk	.25	.25
880	A97	50h pink & blk ('83)	.45	.25
881	A97	65h gray bl & blk	.60	.25
882	A97	1r lt yel grn & blk	1.40	.25

Perf. 13½

874c	A97	20h lt blue & blk	.25	.25
880a	A97	50h pink & blk ('83)	.45	.25
881a	A97	65h gray bl & blk	.60	.25
882a	A97	1r lt yel grn & blk	1.40	.25

Perf. 12

872b	A97	10h lt vio & blk		—
873	A97	15h sal & blk ('85)	.25	.25
874a	A97	20h lt blue & blk ('84)	.25	.25
880b	A97	50h pink & blk ('86)	.30	.25
881b	A97	65h gray bl & blk ('84)	.60	.25
882b	A97	1r lt yel grn & blk ('83)	1.40	.25

Perf. 12
Unwmk.

872a	A97	10h lt vio & blk ('87)	.25	.25
874b	A97	20h lt blue & blk	.25	.25
881c	A97	65h gray bl & blk ('84)	.25	.25
882c	A97	1r lt yel grn & blk ('85)	1.40	.25
	Nos. 872-882c (7)		4.60	1.75

Counterfeits of the 1r are perf. 11.

Al Khafji Oil Rig Type of 1976
Perf. 14x13½
1982-84   Litho.   Wmk. 361
Size: 26x21mm

885	A109	5h vio bl & org	.25	.25
886	A109	10h yel grn & org	.25	.25
887	A109	15h bis brn & org	.25	.25
888	A109	20h green & org	.25	.25
890	A109	50h rose & org	.30	.25
891a	A109	65h sepia & orange	2.75	1.40
892	A109	1r gray & org	.60	.30

Perf. 13½

885a	A109	5h	.25	.25
886a	A109	10h	.25	.25
887a	A109	15h	.25	.25
888a	A109	20h	.25	.25
890a	A109	50h	.30	.25
891	A109	65h sepia & org ('84)	.55	.25
892a	A109	1r	.55	.30

1983   Perf. 12

886b	A109	10h	.25	.25
887b	A109	15h	.25	.25
888b	A109	20h	.25	.25
889	A109	25h dk pur & org	.25	.25
890b	A109	50h	.30	.25
891b	A109	65h	.35	.25
892b	A109	1r	.45	.30
	Nos. 885-892b (8)		2.50	2.05

Opening of King Khalid International Airport — A158

1983, Nov. 16   Litho.   Perf. 13½x14

893	A158	20h shown	.60	.25
894	A158	65h blue & multi	2.10	.25

World Food Day — A159

1983, Nov. 29   Litho.   Perf. 14

895	A159	20h Wheat, Irrigation, Silos	1.75	.25

Aqsa Mosque, Jerusalem A160

1983, Dec. 13   Litho.   Perf. 14

896	A160	20h multicolored	.70	.30

Old and Modern Riyadh — A161

Shobra Palace, Taif — A162

Old and New Jedda (Waterfront) — A163

Damman — A164

1984-95   Litho.   Wmk. 361   Perf. 12

897	A161	20h lilac rose & multi	.25	.25
898	A162	20h Prus grn & multi	.25	.25
899	A161	50h black & multi	.50	.25
900	A162	50h brn & multi	1.00	.55

Unwmk.

901	A161	50h multicolored	.70	.40
902	A162	50h multicolored	1.00	.55
903	A163	50h multicolored	1.40	.70
904	A164	50h grn & multi	.65	.25
905	A161	75h grn & multi	1.00	.55
906	A162	75h multicolored	1.00	.55
907	A163	75h pink & multi	1.40	.70
908	A164	75h blue & multi	.95	.55
909	A161	150h pink & multi	2.40	1.10
910	A162	150h grn & multi	2.40	1.10
911	A163	150h grn & multi	2.50	1.10
911A	A164	150h red lilac & multi	2.00	.95
	Nos. 897-911A (16)		19.40	9.80

Issued: #897, 6/27/84; #898, 10/13/84; #899, 8/29/84; #900, 3/10/87; #910, 9/3/87; #902, 11/3/87; #909, 5/4/88; #903, 911, 1/31/89; #906, 1990, 907, 1991; #901, 1992; #904, 908, 911A, 1995.

Estate Development Fund, 10th Anniv. — A165

1984, July 28   Unwmk.

912	A165	20h multicolored	.80	.30

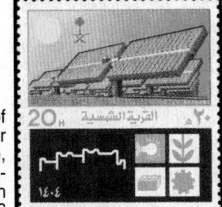

Opening of Solar Village, near Al-Eyenah A166

1984, Aug. 14   Litho.   Perf. 12

913	A166	20h multicolored	.50	.25
914	A166	80h Stylized sun, solar panels	1.50	.35

Imperf
Size: 81x81mm

915	A166	100h like 20h	35.00	
916	A166	100h like 80h	35.00	

Pilgrimage to Mecca — A167

Al-Kheef Mosque: 65h, Aerial view.

1984, Sept. 4   Litho.   Perf. 14

917	A167	20h brown & multi	.60	.25

Perf. 12

918	A167	65h olive gray & multi	2.10	.25

Participation of Saudi Arabian Soccer Team in 1984 Olympics — A168

1984, Sept. 25   Litho.   Perf. 12

919	A168	20h blue & multi	2.00	1.25
920	A168	115h green & multi	6.50	2.00

"Games" and "Olympiad" are misspelled on both stamps.

World Food Day A169

1984, Oct. 16   Litho.   Perf. 12

921	A169	20h multicolored	.70	.30

Beginning with Nos. 922-923 some issues are printed in sheets that have labels inscribed in Arabic. Generally there are from 2 to 6 labels per sheet. Stamps with label attached command a premium.

90th Anniv. International Olympic Committee — A170

1984, Dec. 23   Litho.   Perf. 12

922	A170	20h multicolored	.75	.50
923	A170	50h multicolored	3.75	.50

Launch of ARABSAT — A171

1985, Feb. 9   Litho.   Perf. 12

924	A171	20h ARABSAT, view of Earth	2.40	.25

7th Holy Koran Competition — A172

1985, Feb. 10   Litho.   Perf. 12
925 A172 20h multicolored   .55   .25
926 A172 65h multicolored   1.25   .25

4th Five-Year Development Plan,
1985-1990 — A173

Portrait of King Fahd, industry emblems
and: 20h, Dhahran Harbor, Jubail. 50h, Television
tower, earth receiver, microwave tower.
65h, Agriculture. 80h, Harbor, Yanbu.

1985, Mar. 23   Litho.   Perf. 13x12
927   20h multicolored   .50   .25
928   50h multicolored   1.25   .25
929   65h multicolored   1.50   .25
930   80h multicolored   2.10   .35
  a. A173 Block of 4, #927-930   6.25 1.25

Intl. Youth
Year
A174

1985, May 4   Perf. 12
931 A174 20h multicolored   .55   .25
932 A174 80h multicolored   1.25   .35

Self-sufficiency in
Wheat Production
A175

1985, May 4
933 A175 20h multicolored   .70   .30

East-West Pipeline — A176

1985, June 9
934 A176 20h Tanker loading
                berth, Yanbu   .75   .25
935 A176 65h Pipeline, map   1.75   .25

Shuttle
Launch — A177

Shuttle, Missions Emblem — A178

1985, July 7
936 A177 20h multicolored   1.25   .55
937 A178 115h multicolored   6.00 1.10
Prince Sultan Ibn Salman Al-Saud, 1st
Arab-Moslem astronaut, on Discovery 51-G.

UN, 40th
Anniv.
A179

1985, July 15
938 A179 20h multicolored   .80   .30

Highway, Map, Holy Ka'aba in Mecca
to Prophet's Mosque in
Medina — A180

1985, July 22
939 A180 20h multicolored   .60   .30
940 A180 65h multicolored   1.40   .30
Mecca-Medina Highway opening, 10/11/84.

Post Code Inauguration — A181

1985, July 24
941 A181 20h Covers   .75   .30

1984 Asian
Soccer
Cup
Victory
A182

1985, July 30
942 A182 20h multicolored   .50   .40
943 A182 65h multicolored   1.25   .40
944 A182 115h multicolored   3.25   .70
    Nos. 942-944 (3)   5.00 1.50

Pilgrimage to Mecca — A183

1985, Aug. 25   Litho.   Perf. 12
945 A183 10h multicolored   .30   .30
946 A183 15h multicolored   .30   .30
947 A183 20h multicolored   .45   .30
948 A183 65h multicolored   1.00   .30
    Nos. 945-948 (4)   2.05 1.20

1st Gulf
Olympics
Day,
Riyadh,
May 2
A184

1985, Sept. 8
949 A184 20h multicolored   .50   .25
950 A184 115h multicolored   2.40   .50

World Food
Day
A185

1985, Oct. 16
951 A185 20h multicolored   1.00   .50
952 A185 65h multicolored   3.50   .50

King Abdul Aziz, Masmak Fort and
Horsemen — A186

1985, Dec. 1
953 A186 15h multicolored   .30   .30
954 A186 20h multicolored   .30   .30
955 A186 65h multicolored   1.00   .30
956 A186 80h multicolored   1.25   .35
    Nos. 953-956 (4)   2.85 1.25
Intl. Conference on the History of King
Abdul Aziz Al-Sa'ud, Riyadh. An imperf. souvenir sheet showing smaller versions of Nos.
953-956 and the conference emblem exists.
Sold for 10r. Value $26.50.

King Fahd Koran Publishing Center,
Medina — A187

1985, Dec. 18
957 A187 20h multicolored   .30   .30
958 A187 65h multicolored   1.50   .30

OPEC,
25th Anniv.
A188

1985, Dec. 24
959 A188 20h multicolored   .40   .30
960 A188 65h multicolored   2.10   .30

**Holy Ka'aba Type of 1976
Booklet Stamps
Size: 29x19mm
Type II**

1986, Feb. 17   Litho.   Perf. 12
961 A97 10h lt vio & blk   8.00
  a. Booklet pane of 4   37.50
965 A97 20h bluish grn & blk   13.50
968 A97 50h pink & black   27.50
  a. Bkt. pane of 4, #961, 2 #965,
       #968   60.00
    Nos. 961-968 (3)   49.00
Due to vending machine breakdowns, distribution of this set has been very limited. The
government does have stocks of these stamps
but they are not currently being sold.

A189

1986, Jan. 8   Litho.   Perf. 12
971 A189 20h multicolored   1.40   .30
Intl. Peace Year.

A190

1986, Mar. 24   Perf. 14, 12 (65h)
972 A190 20h multicolored   .60   .25
  a. Perf. 12   .60   .25
973 A190 65h multicolored   1.40   .25
Riyadh Municipality, 50th aAnniv.

A191

1986, Apr. 21   Perf. 12
974 A191 20h multicolored   .75   .25
975 A191 50h multicolored   1.25   .25
UN child survival campaign.

General Establishment for Electric
Power, 10th Anniv. — A192

1986, Apr. 26
976 A192 20h multicolored   .40   .30
977 A192 65h multicolored   1.60   .30

Continental Maritime Cable
Inauguration — A193

1986, June 1   Litho.   Perf. 12
978 A193 20h multicolored   .75 .35
979 A193 50h multicolored   1.50 .35

Natl. Guard Housing Project, Riyadh, Inauguration — A194

1986, July 19
980 A194 20h multicolored   .50 .25
981 A194 65h multicolored   1.50 .25

Islamic Arch, Holy Ka'aba — A195

1986-99   Litho.   Perf. 12
984 A195 30h blk & bluish
            grn   .25 .25
985 A195 40h blk & lil rose   .45 .25
986 A195 50h blk & brt grn   1.10 .60
987 A195 75h blk & Prus bl   1.40 .70
  a.   Perf. 13½x14   1.10 .60
987B A195 100h black & red
988 A195 100h blk & bl green   1.60 .80
989 A195 150h blk & rose lil   2.75 1.40
  a.   Perf. 13½x14   2.50 1.25
990 A195 2r blk & vio blue   3.00 1.60
  a.   Perf. 13½x14
         Nos. 984-990 (8)   10.55 5.60

Issued: 30h, 40h, 8/5; 75h, 150h, 7/30/90; 50h, 10/9/90; #987a, 6/13/92; #989a, 6/6/92; 2r, 4/99; #987B, 988, 9/21/96; No. 990a, 1999 ?

Pilgrimage to Mecca — A196

Designs of: a, A116. b, A129. c, A156. d, A149. e, A141. f, A122. g, A183. h, A167.

1986, Aug. 13   Litho.   Perf. 12
1002 A196 Block of 8   22.50 22.50
  a.-h.   20h, any single

Discovery of Oil, 50th Anniv. — A197

1986, Sept. 16
1003 A197 20h Well, refinery   .50 .25
1004 A197 65h Well, map   2.25 .25

Because of difficulty in separation most stamps have damaged perfs.

World Food Day — A198

1986, Oct. 18
1005 A198 20h shown   .35 .35
1006 A198 115h Stylized plant   1.90 .65

Massacre of Palestinian Refugees, Sept. 17, 1982 — A199

1986, Nov. 1   Litho.   Perf. 12
1007 A199 80h multicolored   1.25 .60
1008 A199 115h multicolored   1.90 .95

Definitive stamps generally do not have an official date of issue. Any dates shown probably reflect sales at the Riyadh or Dammam post offices only.

Saudi Universities

Imam Mohammed ibn Saud — A200

Umm al-Qura — A201

King Saud — A202

King Fahd Petroleum and Minerals — A203

King Faisal — A204

King Abdul Aziz — A205

Medina Islamic — A206

1986-91
1009 A200 15h sage grn &
            blk   .25 .25
1010 A200 20h ultra & black   .25 .25
1011 A200 50h ultra & black   .65 .40
1012 A200 65h brt bl & blk   .80 .40
1013 A200 75h brt bl & blk   1.00 .55
1014 A200 100h rose & black   1.10 .55
1015 A200 150h rose cl & blk   2.00 .95
1016 A201 50h ultra & black   .80 .50
1017 A201 65h brt bl & blk   1.00 .40
1018 A201 75h brt bl & blk   1.00 .55
1019 A201 100h dull rose &
            blk   1.60 .80
1020 A201 150h rose cl & blk   2.40 1.10
1021 A202 50h ultra & black   .85 .50
1022 A202 75h brt bl & blk   1.00 .55
1023 A202 100h dull rose &
            blk   1.60 .80
1024 A202 150h rose cl & blk   2.25 1.00
1025 A203 50h ultra & black   .65 .40
1026 A203 75h brt bl & blk   1.00 .55
1027 A203 150h rose cl & blk   2.00 .95
1028 A204 50h ultra & black   .65 .40
1029 A204 75h brt bl & blk   1.00 .55
1030 A204 150h rose cl & blk   2.25 .70
1031 A205 50h ultra & black   .65 .40
1032 A205 75h brt bl & blk   1.00 .65
1033 A205 150h rose cl & blk   2.25 1.00
1034 A206 50h ultra & black   .70 .25
1035 A206 75h brt bl & blk   1.00 .55
1036 A206 150h rose cl & blk   2.00 .40
         Nos. 1009-1036 (28)   33.70 16.35

Issued: #1009-1010, 1012, 1014, 11/26; #1019, 3/29; #1023, 7/22; #1016, 1020, 8/8; #1015, 1027, 1036, 1/31/89; #1011, 1025, 1028, 1031, 2/25/89; #1017, 3/89; #1024, 1030, 1033, 4/29/89; #1034, 7/4/89; #1021, 1989; #1013, 1018, 1026, 1990; #1022, 1029, 1032, 1035, 1991.

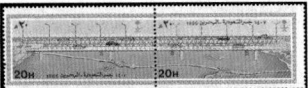

Saudi-Bahrain Highway Inauguration — A207

1986, Nov. 26   Perf. 14
1039 A207 Strip of 2   3.25 .45
  a.-b.   20h any single   1.40 .25

Printed se-tenant in a continuous design.

1st Modern Olympic Games, Athens, 90th Anniv. A208

1986, Dec. 27
1040 A208 20h multicolored   1.50 .70
1041 A208 100h multicolored   8.00 1.25

General Petroleum and Minerals Organization (Petromin), 25th Anniv. — A209

1987, Feb. 23   Litho.   Perf. 12
1042 A209 50h multicolored   .80 .45
1043 A209 100h multicolored   1.90 .80

Restoration and Expansion of Quba Mosque, Medina — A210

Design: View of mosque and model of expanded mosque.

1987, Mar. 21
1044 A210 50h multicolored   1.00 .40
1045 A210 75h multicolored   1.50 .55

Vocational Training — A211

Designs: a, Welding. b, Drill press operation. c, Lathe operation. d, Electrician.

Unwmk.
1987, Apr. 8   Litho.   Perf. 12
1046 A211 Block of 4   8.50 8.50
  a.-d.   50h any single   1.75 1.75

Cairo Exhibition A212

Design: Desert fortifications in silhouette, Riyadh television tower, King Khalid Intl. Airport hangars and pyramid of Giza.

Unwmk.
1987, June 17   Litho.   Perf. 12
1047 A212 50h multicolored   .90 .50
1048 A212 75h multicolored   1.60 .65

A213

Inauguration of King Fahd Telecommunications Center, Jedda — A214

1987, July 21
1049 A213 50h multicolored   .90 .50
1050 A214 75h multicolored   1.60 .65

Afghan Resistance Movement A215

1987, July 25
1051 A215 50h multicolored   .90 .50
1052 A215 100h multicolored   1.60 .90

Pilgrimage to Mecca — A216

Design: View of Ihram and Meqat Wadi Muhrim Mosque from Wadi Muhrim Meqat.

1987, Aug. 3
1053	A216	50h multicolored	1.00	.50
1054	A216	75h multicolored	1.50	.60
1055	A216	100h multicolored	1.75	.90
	Nos. 1053-1055 (3)		4.25	2.00

Home for Disabled Children, 1st Anniv. — A217

1987, Oct. 3
1056	A217	50h multicolored	1.10	.55
1057	A217	75h multicolored	1.75	.75

World Post Day — A218

1987, Oct. 10
1058	A218	50h multicolored	.70	.40
1059	A218	150h multicolored	2.00	.95

World Food Day A219

1987, Oct. 17
1060	A219	50h multicolored	.85	.40
1061	A219	75h multicolored	1.40	.50

Social Welfare Society, 25th Anniv. — A220

1987, Oct. 26
1062	A220	50h multicolored	.95	.45
1063	A220	100h multicolored	1.75	.75

Dome of the Rock — A221

1987, Dec. 5
1064	A221	75h multicolored	2.25	.60
1065	A221	150h multicolored	4.25	1.10

Restoration and Expansion of the Prophet's Mosque, Medina — A222

1987, Dec. 15   **Perf. 14**
1066	A222	50h multicolored	.90	.35
1067	A222	75h multicolored	1.25	.50
1068	A222	150h multicolored	2.50	.95
	Nos. 1066-1068 (3)		4.65	1.80

An imperf. 300h souvenir sheet exists. Value $52.50.

Battle of Hattin, 800th Anniv. A223

Warriors in silhouette and Dome of the Rock.

1987, Dec. 21   **Perf. 12**
1069	A223	75h multicolored	2.25	.50
1070	A223	150h multicolored	4.25	1.10

Saladin's conquest of Jerusalem.

A224

1987, Dec. 26
1071	A224	50h multicolored	1.00	.50
1072	A224	75h multicolored	1.50	.60

8th session of the Supreme Council of the Gulf Cooperation Council.

A225

1988, Feb. 13   **Litho.**   **Perf. 12**
1073	A225	50h multicolored	1.10	.60
1074	A225	75h multicolored	1.75	.85

3rd Regional Highways Conf. of the Middle East.

A226

Inauguration of King Fahd Intl. Stadium — A227

1988, Mar. 2
1075	A226	50h multicolored	1.00	.45
1076	A227	150h multicolored	2.75	1.25

Blood Donation — A228

1988, Apr. 13   **Litho.**   **Perf. 12**
1077	A228	50h multicolored	1.00	.45
1078	A228	75h multicolored	1.25	.60

WHO, 40th Anniv. — A229

1988, Apr. 7
1079	A229	50h multicolored	1.10	.50
1080	A229	75h multicolored	1.40	.60

King Fahd, Custodian of the Holy Mosques — A230

King Fahd and mosques at Medina and Mecca.

1988, Apr. 23   **Litho.**   **Perf. 12**
1081	A230	50h multicolored	.65	.40
1082	A230	75h multicolored	.95	.50
1083	A230	150h multicolored	2.10	.95
	Nos. 1081-1083 (3)		3.70	1.85

A 75h souvenir sheet exists containing an enlarged version of No. 1082. Sold for 3r. Value $67.50.

Environmental Protection A231

1988, June 5
1084	A231	50h multicolored	1.00	.35
1085	A231	75h multicolored	1.50	.55

Palestinian Uprising, Gaza and the West Bank A232

1988, July 10
1086	A232	75h multicolored	1.50	.60
1087	A232	150h multicolored	3.00	1.10

Pilgrimage to Mecca — A233

1988, July 23   **Litho.**   **Perf. 12**
1088	A233	50h multicolored	1.10	.40
1089	A233	75h multicolored	1.60	.55

World Food Day A234

1988, Oct. 16   **Litho.**   **Perf. 12**
1090	A234	50h multicolored	1.25	.50
1091	A234	75h multicolored	1.90	.70

Qiblatain Mosque Expansion — A235

1988, Nov. 9
1092	A235	50h multicolored	1.00	.35
1093	A235	75h multicolored	1.50	.55

5th World Youth Soccer Championships, Riyadh, Dammam, Jedda and Taif — A250

1989, Feb. 16   **Litho.**   **Perf. 12**
1094	A250	75h multicolored	1.75	.65
1095	A250	150h multicolored	3.25	1.25

World Health Day — A251

1989, Apr. 8   **Litho.**   **Perf. 12**
1096	A251	50h multicolored	1.10	.35
1097	A251	75h multicolored	1.60	.55

Sea Water Desalination Plant — A252

1989, May 30   **Litho.**   **Perf. 12**
1098	A252	50h multicolored	.70	.40
1099	A252	75h multicolored	1.10	.60

Proclamation of the State of Palestine,
Nov. 15, 1988 — A253

1989, June 6   Litho.   Perf. 12
1100 A253 50h multicolored   1.00 .25
1101 A253 75h multicolored   1.50 .35

Pilgrimage to Mecca — A254

Design: Al-Tan'eem Mosque, Mecca.

1989, July 12   Litho.   Perf. 12
1102 A254 50h multicolored   .90 .25
1103 A254 75h multicolored   1.40 .40

World Food
Day
A255

1989, Oct. 16   Litho.   Perf. 12
1104 A255 75h multicolored   .75 .50
1105 A255 150h multicolored   1.50 1.00

Holy Mosque Expansion — A256

1989, Dec. 30   Litho.   Perf. 12
1106 A256 50h multicolored   .75 .35
1107 A256 75h multicolored   1.10 .55
1108 A256 150h multicolored   2.10 1.10
    Nos. 1106-1108 (3)   3.95 2.00

A souvenir sheet containing an enlarged
version of design A256 exists. Sold for 5r.
Value, perf or imperf, each $35.00.

Youth Soccer
Cup
Championships
A257

1989, Dec. 20
1109 A257 75h multicolored   1.10 .45
1110 A257 150h multicolored   2.10 .95

UNESCO World
Literacy
Year — A258

1990, Jan. 9
1111 A258 50h multicolored   .95 .40
1112 A258 75h multicolored   1.50 .55

World Health Day — A259

Unwmk.
1990, Apr. 7   Litho.   Perf. 12
1113 A259 75h multicolored   1.00 .50
1114 A259 150h multicolored   2.10 .95

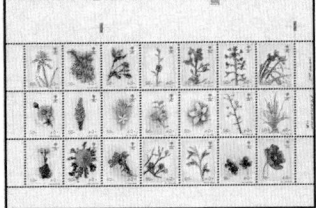

Flowers — A262

1990
1115 A262 Sheet of 21   12.00
  a.-u. 50h any single   .60 .25
1116 A262 Sheet of 21   18.00
  a.-u. 75h any single   .75 .40
1117 A262 Sheet of 21   35.00
  a.-u. 150h any single   1.50 .80
    Nos. 1115-1117 (3)   65.00

21 Different species pictured on the sheets.
Issued: 50h, 75h, Feb. 6; 150h, Jan. 17.
See No. 1292A.

Islamic Conference, 20th
Anniv. — A263

1990, Feb. 7   Litho.   Perf. 12
1118 A263 75h blue & multi   .70 .35
1119 A263 150h gray & multi   1.50 .70

Islamic Heritage — A264

Designs: b, Arabic script in rectangle. c, Circular design. d, Mosque and minaret.

1990, July 29
1120 A264 Block of 4   4.50 2.50
  a.-d.   75h any single   1.00 .60

Horses — A265

1990, Apr. 14   Color of Horse
1121 A265   Block of 4   4.00 1.40
  a. 50h white, red tassels on bri-
      dle   .95 .35
  b. 50h black   .95 .35
  c. 50h white, brown bridle   .95 .35
  d. 50h chestnut   .95 .35
1122 A265 50h like #1121d   .65 .35
1123 A265 75h like #1121b   1.00 .50
1124 A265 100h like #1121a   1.40 .65
1125 A265 150h like #1121c   2.00 1.00
    Nos. 1121-1125 (5)   9.05 3.90

No. 1121 has white border on two sides.
Nos. 1122-1125 have white border on four
sides.

Pilgrimage to Mecca — A266

1990, June 28
1126 A266 75h multicolored   1.00 .50
1127 A266 150h multicolored   2.10 1.00

Television
Tower — A267

1990, July 21
1128 A267 75h multicolored   1.00 .50
1129 A267 150h multicolored   2.10 1.00

Saudi Arabian Airlines Route
Map — A268

1990, Sept. 3
1130   75h Global routes   .75 .40
1131   75h Domestic routes   .75 .40
  a. A268 Pair, #1130-1131   1.75 1.00
1132   150h like #1130   1.50 .90
1133   150h like #1131   1.50 .90
  a. A268 Pair, #1132-1133   3.25 2.10
    Nos. 1130-1133 (4)   4.50 2.60

World Food
Day
A269

1990, Oct. 16   Litho.   Perf. 12
1134 A269 75h multicolored   1.10 .65
1135 A269 150h multicolored   2.50 1.25

Organization of Petroleum Exporting
Countries (OPEC), 30th
Anniv. — A270

1990, Sept. 26
1136 A270 75h multicolored   1.75 .60
1137 A270 150h multicolored   2.75 1.10

Fifth Five Year Development
Plan — A271

Designs: a, Oil refinery, irrigation, and oil
storage tanks. b, Radio tower, highway, and
mine. c, Monument, sports stadium, and vocational training. d, Television tower, environmental protection, and modern architecture.

1990, Oct. 30
1138 A271 75h Block of 4, #a.-d. 5.50 2.10

Battle of
Badr,
624 — A272

1991, Apr. 3   Litho.   Perf. 12
1139 A272 75h org, dk grn &
            grn   1.00 .50
1140 A272 150h lt bl, dk bl & grn 1.90 .95

A273

1991, Apr. 9
1141 A273 75h multicolored   1.00 .45
1142 A273 150h multicolored   1.90 .90

World Health Day.

A274

Animals: a, k, Impala. b, l, Ibex. c, m, Oryx.
d, n, Fox. e, o, Bat. f, p, Hyena. g, q, Cat. h, r,
Dugong. i, s, Leopard.

Blocks of 9

1991   Litho.   Perf. 12
1143 A274 25h Block, #a.-i.   3.50 1.75
1144 A274 50h Block, #a.-i.   8.00 4.00
1145 A274 75h Block, #a.-i.   11.50 6.25
1146 A274 100h Block, #a.-i.   16.00 7.75
1146J A274 150h Block, #k.-s.   22.50 18.00
  f.   Perf 14x13½   27.50 19.00
    Nos. 1143-1146J (5)   61.50 37.75

Issued: #1143-1146, May 1; #1146J, Dec. 1.
No. 1146J exists imperf.

Pilgrimage to Mecca — A275

1991, June 20   Litho.   *Perf. 14*
1147 A275 75h blue & multi   .90   .45
1148 A275 150h green & multi   1.60   .80

World Telecommunications
Day — A276

1991, June 3   *Perf. 12*
1149 A276 75h multicolored   .90   .45
1150 A276 150h multicolored   1.60   .80

A277

1991, May 11
1151 A277 75h multicolored   1.10   .70
1152 A277 150h multicolored   2.25 1.40

Liberation of Kuwait.

A278

1991, Sept. 8   Litho.   *Perf. 12*
1153 A278 75h blue & multi   1.50   .75
1154 A278 150h buff & multi   3.00 1.50

Literacy Day.

A279

1991, Oct. 16   Litho.   *Perf. 12*
1155 A279 75h green & multi   .90   .50
1156 A279 150h orange & multi   1.60 1.00

World Food Day.

A280

1991, Dec. 7
1157 A280 75h green & multi   1.75   .75
1158 A280 150h dk blue & multi   2.75 1.75

Childrens' Day.

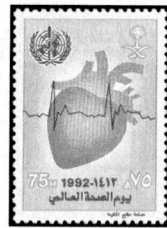

A281

1992, Apr. 8   Litho.   *Perf. 12*
1159 A281 75h lt blue & multi   1.00   .60
1160 A281 150h lt org & multi   2.10 1.10

World Health Day.

War
Between
the Arabs
of Medina
and
Mecca,
624-630
A282

1992, Apr. 18
1161 A282 75h lt org & grn   .90   .55
1162 A282 150h lt bl, dk bl & grn 2.00   .95

Pilgrimage
to Mecca
A283

Unwmk.
1992, June 9   Litho.   *Perf. 12*
1163 A283 75h lt blue & multi   1.00   .60
1164 A283 150h lt orange & multi   2.10 1.10

Population and Housing
Census — A284

1992, Sept. 26   Litho.   *Perf. 14*
1165 A284 75h blue & multi   .75   .50
1166 A284 150h org yel & multi   1.50   .95

World Food
Day
A285

1992, Oct. 17   *Perf. 12*
1167 A285 75h Vegetables   1.25   .65
1168 A285 150h Fruits   2.40 1.25

Consultative Council — A286

Document: d, g, 12 lines. e, h, 13 lines. f, i,
11 lines. 5r, Scrolls of 12, 11, & 13 lines.

1992, Dec. 12   Litho.   *Perf. 12*
1168A A286 75h Strip of 3,
                 #d.-f.   2.25 1.40
1168B A286 150h Strip of 3,
                 #g.-i.   5.75 3.00

Imperf
Size: 120x79mm
1168C A286 5r multicolored   27.50 13.50

Birds — A287

a, k, Woodpecker. b, l, Arabian bustard. c,
m, Lark. d, n, Turtle dove. e, o, Heron. f, p,
Partridge. g, q, Hoopoe. h, r, Falcon. i, s,
Houbara bustard.

1992-97   Blocks of 9   *Perf. 14x13½*
1169   A287 25h #a.-i.   5.25   5.25
  j.   Perf. 12, #k.-s.   27.50
1170   A287 50h #a.-i.   10.00
  j.   Perf. 12, #k.-s.
1171   A287 75h #a.-i.   11.50   5.50
  j.   Perf. 12, #k.-s.   11.50   5.75
1172   A287 100h #a.-i.   24.50 12.00
  j.   Perf. 12, #k.-s.   24.50 12.00
1173   A287 150h #a.-i.   40.00 19.00
  j.   Perf. 12, #k.-s.   40.00 19.00
      Nos. 1169-1173 (5)   91.25 41.75

Issued: 150h, 3/18/92; 75h, 7/14/92; 100h,
3/1/93; 25h, 50h, 11/6/94; #1171j, 1173j, 8/94;
1169j, 1996; 1170j, 1997(?).

World
Health Day
A288

1993, Apr. 7   Litho.   *Perf. 12*
1175   A288 75h red & multi   .90   .50
1175A A288 150h blue & multi   2.00   .90

King Fahd
Championship
Soccer
Cup — A289

1993, Mar. 15
1176   A289 75h green & multi   1.75   .70
1176A A289 150h rose red &
                  multi   2.75 1.75

Pilgrimage to Mecca — A290

1993, May 30   Litho.   *Perf. 12*
1177 A290 75h green & multi   .90   .50
1178 A290 150h blue & multi   1.60 1.00

Intl. Telecommunications Day — A291

1993, May 17   Inscription Color
1179 A291 75h dark blue   .90   .50
1180 A291 150h red lilac   1.60 1.00

Battle of
Alkandk
A292

1993, May 15
1181 A292 75h lt org & grn   .90   .50
1182 A292 150h lt bl, dk bl & grn 1.60 1.00

World Food
Day — A293

1993, Dec. 14   Litho.   *Perf. 12*
1183 A293 75h black & multi   1.10   .55
1184 A293 150h red & multi   2.50 1.10

World
Dental
Health Day
A294

1994, Apr. 9   Litho.   *Perf. 12*
1185 A294 75h multicolored   1.00   .50
1186 A294 150h multicolored   1.90 1.00

Intl.
Olympic
Committee,
Cent.
A295

1994, Apr. 23   Litho.   *Perf. 12*
1187 A295 75h blue & multi   1.10   .65
1188 A295 150h red & multi   2.50 1.10

Battle of
Khaybar
A296

1994, June 14   Litho.   *Perf. 12*
1189 A296 75h bister & green   1.00   .50
1190 A296 150h sil, bl & grn   1.90 1.00

Pilgrimage to Mecca — A297

1994, May 14
| 1191 | A297 | 75h green & multi | .90 | .50 |
| 1192 | A297 | 150h red & multi | 1.60 | 1.10 |

Consultative Council — A298

Design: 150h, Different view of building, inscription tablet at right.

1994, July 12   **Litho.**   **Perf. 12**
1193	A298	75h multicolored	.90	.50
1194	A298	150h multicolored	2.00	.90
a.		Souv. sheet of 2, #1193-1194, imperf.	32.50	

No. 1194a sold for 5r.

A299

1994 World Soccer Cup Championships, U.S. — A300

1994, June 18
| 1195 | A299 | 75h multicolored | .90 | .50 |
| 1196 | A300 | 150h multicolored | 2.00 | .90 |

King Abdul Aziz Port, Dammam — A301

1994-95   **Litho.**   **Perf. 12**
1198	A301	25h multicolored	.75	.50
1199	A301	50h multicolored	.75	.50
1200	A301	75h multicolored	1.00	.65
1201	A301	100h multicolored	1.40	.75
1202	A301	150h multicolored	2.10	1.00
		Nos. 1198-1202 (5)	6.00	3.40

Issued: 75h, 8/22/94; 150h, 11/5/94; 100h, 3/11/95; 50h, 11/28/95; 25h, 12/27/95.

A304

World Food Day A305

1994, Oct. 16   **Litho.**   **Perf. 12**
| 1212 | A304 | 75h Green house | 1.75 | .70 |
| 1213 | A305 | 150h Foods | 2.75 | 1.75 |

A306

Arab League, 50th Anniv. A307

1995, Mar. 25   **Litho.**   **Perf. 12**
| 1214 | A306 | 75h multicolored | .95 | .50 |
| 1215 | A307 | 150h multicolored | 1.75 | 1.00 |

A308

UN, 50th Anniv. — A309

1995, Feb. 19
| 1216 | A308 | 75h multicolored | 1.00 | .50 |
| 1217 | A309 | 150h multicolored | 1.90 | 1.00 |

Refugee Care A310

1995, Apr. 9   **Litho.**   **Perf. 12**
| 1218 | A310 | 75h green & multi | .95 | .50 |
| 1219 | A310 | 150h tan & multi | 1.75 | 1.00 |

Pilgrimage to Mecca A311

1995, May 3   **Litho.**   **Perf. 12**
| 1220 | A311 | 75h blue & multi | .95 | .50 |
| 1221 | A311 | 150h tan & multi | 1.75 | 1.00 |

Deaf Week — A312

1995, May 3   **Litho.**   **Perf. 12**
| 1222 | A312 | 75h shown | 1.00 | .50 |
| 1223 | A312 | 150h Hand sign, ear | 1.90 | 1.00 |

Saudi Arabian Airlines, 50th Anniv. A313

1995, Aug. 21
| 1224 | A313 | 75h Anniv. emblem, vert. | 1.00 | .50 |
| 1225 | A313 | 150h shown | 1.90 | 1.00 |

FAO, 50th Anniv. — A314

1995, Oct. 16   **Litho.**   **Perf. 12**
| 1226 | A314 | 75h shown | 1.75 | .70 |
| 1227 | A314 | 150h Emblem over globe | 2.75 | 1.75 |

Jeddah Port — A315

1996   **Litho.**   **Perf. 12**
1228	A315	25h multicolored	.45	.35
1229	A315	50h multicolored	.90	.45
1230	A315	75h multicolored	1.40	.70
1230A	A315	100h multicolored	2.25	2.25
1230B	A315	150h multicolored	3.00	1.75
		Nos. 1228-1230B (5)	8.00	5.50

Issued: 25h and 50h, 1/27/96; 75h, 2/7/96; 100h, 11/25/96; 150h, 3/30/96.

1996 Summer Olympics, Atlanta A316

1996, June 23
| 1231 | A316 | 150h orange & multi | 2.10 | 1.10 |
| 1232 | A316 | 2r blue & multi | 3.25 | 1.50 |

Pilgrimage to Mecca — A317

1996, Apr. 21
1233	A317	150h black & multi	2.10	1.10
1234	A317	2r rose red & multi	3.00	1.40
1235	A317	3r green & multi	4.25	2.10
		Nos. 1233-1235 (3)	9.35	4.60

World Health Organization A318

1996, July 14   **Litho.**   **Perf. 12**
| 1236 | A318 | 2r green & multi | 2.50 | 1.25 |
| 1237 | A318 | 3r red & multi | 4.00 | 2.00 |

FAO, 50th Anniv. A319

1996, Oct. 16   **Litho.**   **Perf. 12**
| 1238 | A319 | 2r blue & multi | 3.75 | 1.60 |
| 1239 | A319 | 3r red & multi | 5.25 | 2.50 |

UNICEF, 50th Anniv. A320

1996, Nov. 12
| 1240 | A320 | 150h buff & multi | 2.00 | 1.00 |
| 1241 | A320 | 2r blue & multi | 2.75 | 1.25 |

King Abdul Aziz Research Center, 25th Anniv. A321

1997, Jan. 8   **Litho.**   **Perf. 12**
| 1242 | A321 | 150h brown & multi | 2.00 | 1.00 |
| 1243 | A321 | 2r green & multi | 2.75 | 1.25 |

Rabigh Steam Power Plant A322

Designs: 150h, Power plant. 2r, Power plant, electrical power lines.

1996, Dec. 31
1244 A322 150h multicolored 2.00 1.00
Size: 51x26mm
1245 A322 2r multicolored 2.75 1.25

Yanbu Port — A323

1996 Litho. Perf. 12
1245A A323 50h multicolored 1.10 .60
1246 A323 2r multicolored 3.75 1.90

Issued: 1245A, 12/21; 1246 11/25.
See No. 1273.

Opening Mecca A324

1997, Jan. 30
1247 A324 1r brt grn & multi 1.40 .65
1248 A324 2r lt yel grn & multi 2.75 1.40

King Fahd, Birthday A325

1997, Mar. 10
1249 A325 100h green & multi 1.40 .60
1250 A325 150h pink & multi 1.90 .95
1251 A325 2r tan & multi 2.50 1.40
Nos. 1249-1251 (3) 5.80 2.95

An imperf souvenir sheet containing an enlarged version of design A325 exists. Sold for 5r. Value $18.

Jubail Port — A326

1996-97
1251A A326 50h multicolored .85 .50
1251B A326 100h multicolored .85 .40
1252 A326 150h multicolored 1.25 .65
1252A A326 2r multicolored 3.00 1.50
1252B A326 4r multicolored 3.50 1.75
Nos. 1251A-1252B (5) 9.45 4.80

Issued: 50h, 10/17/96; 100h, 6/29/96; 150h, 7/8/96; 2r, 9/97(?); 4r, 7/24/96.

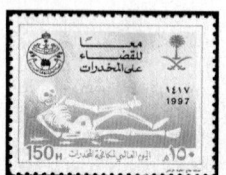

Campaign Against Use of Illegal Drugs A327

1997, Feb. 26
1253 A327 150h blue & multi 4.00 2.00
1254 A327 2r red & multi 5.50 2.75

Battle of Hunain A328

1997, Mar. 10 Litho. Perf. 12
1255 A328 150h multicolored 1.90 1.00
1256 A328 2r multicolored 2.75 1.40

World Health Day A329

1997, Apr. 7 Litho. Perf. 14
1257 A329 150h multicolored 1.90 1.00
1258 A329 2r multicolored 2.75 1.40

A330

Al-Hijjah A331

1997, Apr. 8
1259 A330 1r multicolored 1.25 .65
1260 A331 2r multicolored 2.75 1.25

King Fahd Natl. Library A332

1997, July 9 Litho. Perf. 12
1261 A332 1r shown 1.25 .65
1262 A332 2r Open book 2.75 1.25

A333

1997, July 26
1263 A333 150h Emblem, rays 2.10 1.10
1264 A333 2r shown 3.25 1.50
King Abdul Aziz Public Library.

A334

1997, July 15 Litho. Perf. 12
1265 A334 1r red & multi 1.25 .70
1266 A334 2r green & multi 2.75 1.25
Montreal Protocol on Substances that Deplete Ozone Layer, 10th anniv.

3rd GCC Stamp Exhibition, Riyadh A335

1997, Sept. 30 Litho. Perf. 12
1267 A335 1r multicolored 1.50 .70

Prince Salman Center — A336

1997, Dec. 27 Litho. Perf. 12
1268 A336 1r multicolored 1.50 .70

Battle of Tabuk A337

1998, Jan. 24 Litho. Perf. 12
1269 A337 1r multicolored 1.40 .70

World Food Day — A338

1998, Feb. 22
1270 A338 2r multicolored 2.75 1.50

Disabled Persons Day — A339

1998, Mar. 8 Litho. Perf. 12
1271 A339 1r multicolored 1.40 .70

Al Hijjah — A340

1998, Mar. 29
1272 A340 2r multicolored 2.75 1.40

Yanbu Port Type of 1997
1996, Sept. 3 Litho. Perf. 12
1273 A323 100h multicolored 1.90 .90
1273A A323 150h multicolored 3.00 1.90
1273B A323 4r multicolored 4.00 1.75
Nos. 1273-1273B (3) 8.90 4.55

Issued: 150h, 8/28/96; 4r, 11/8/97.

WHO, 50th Anniv. — A341

1998, May 18
1274 A341 1r multicolored 1.25 .60

Dam — A342

1998, May 9
1275 A342 1r multicolored 1.25 .60

A343

1998, May 31 Litho. Perf. 12
1276 A343 1r multicolored 1.25 .60
Islamic Organization for Education and Science.

A344

1998, Sept. 30
1277 A344 2r multicolored 2.50 1.25
Arab Stamp Day.

A345

KSA, Cent.
A346

Designs: No. 1278, Forts. No. 1279, Military equipment. No. 1280, Entrance to fort, vert. 2r, King Fahd, KSA emblem, outline of map of Saudi Arabia, vert.

1999, Jan 22   Litho.   Perf. 12
1278	A345	1r multicolored	2.25 1.10
1279	A346	1r multicolored	2.25 1.10
1280	A345	1r multicolored	2.25 1.10
1281	A345	2r multicolored	4.50 2.25
		Nos. 1278-1281 (4)	11.25 5.55

#1278-1279 exist imperf in souvenir sheets of 1. There are some color variations. #1280-1281 exist imperf in a souvenir sheet of 2. The three sheets sold for 5r each. Value, set of three sheets $55.

King Fahd Intl. Airport — A347

1999, Feb. 6
1282	A347	1r multicolored	1.25 .65

Size: 26x38mm
1283	A347	2r Jet, control tower	2.50 1.25

Development of Palace of Justice Area — A348

1999, Jan. 22
1284	A348	1r multicolored	2.25 1.10

Exists imperf in a souvenir sheet of 1. It sold for 5r. Value $18.

World Food Day — A348a

1999, Mar. 16   Litho.   Perf. 12
1285	A348a	1r multicolored	2.50 1.25

Al-Hijjah — A349

1999, Mar. 18   Litho.   Perf. 12
1286	A349	2r multicolored	2.50 1.10

A350

1999, Mar. 6
1287	A350	1r multicolored	2.25 1.10

Kingdom of Saudi Arabia, cent. Exists in an imperf. souvenir sheet of 1. It sold for 5r. Value $18.

A351

1999, May 22   Litho.   Perf. 12
1288	A351	1r Traffic signals	1.40 .70

Academy for Security Sciences — A352

1999, May 29   Litho.   Perf. 12
1289	A352	150h multicolored	2.00 1.00

Intl. Holy Koran Competition — A353

1999, Oct. 3   Litho.   Perf. 12
1290	A353	1r multicolored	1.40 .70

UPU, 125th Anniv. — A354

1999, Oct. 26   Litho.   Perf. 12
1291	A354	1r multi	2.50 1.10

World Meteorological Organization, 50th Anniv. — A355

2000, Mar. 23   Litho.   Perf. 12
1292	A355	1r multi	1.40 .70

Flowers Type of 1990
Designs like Nos. 1115a-1115u.

2000, Feb. 1   Litho.   Perf. 12
1292A		Block of 21	40.00
b.-v.		A262 1r Any single	
w.		Sheet of 21, #1292Ab-1292Av, perf. 13½x14	— —

Pilgrimage to Mecca
A356

2000, Mar. 11   Perf. 14x14¼
1293	A356	1r black & multi	1.10 .60
1294	A356	2r red & multi	2.10 1.10

Scouting — A357

2000, July 18   Litho.   Perf. 14
1295	A357	1r multi	1.10 .50

Riyadh, Arabian Cultural Capital, 2000 — A358

2000, July 4   Litho.   Perf. 14
1296	A358	1r multi	1.60 1.00

Water Conservation
A359

2000, June 18
1297	A359	1r multi	1.60 1.00

Consultative Council, 75th Anniv. — A360

2000, June 7
1298	A360	1r multi	1.60 1.00

UN High Commissioner for Refugees, 50th Anniv. — A361

2000, Sept. 23
1299	A361	2r multi	2.00 1.00

Jizan Port — A362

2000, Sept. 16   Litho.   Perf. 14
1299A	A362	50h multi	.50 .50
1299B	A362	1r multi	1.00 1.00
1300	A362	2r multi	1.90 1.90
		Nos. 1299A-1300 (3)	3.40 3.40

Al Khafji Oil Rig Type of 1976-80 Redrawn With Palm Trees and Swords at Upper Right
Perf. 14x13½

2000, Sept. 13   Litho.   Unwmk.
Size: 26x21mm
1300A	A109	25h dk pur & org	.35 .35

King Abdul Aziz City for Science and Technology
A363

2000, Oct. 28
1301	A363	1r multi	1.10 .50

King Khalid University
A364

2000, Dec. 5   Perf. 14
1302	A364	1r multi	1.10 .50

Buraydah — A365

2000   Perf. 13¾x14
1303	A365	50h blue & multi	.50 .50
1304	A365	1r grn & multi	1.00 1.00
1305	A365	2r blk & multi	1.90 1.90
		Nos. 1303-1305 (3)	3.40 3.40

Buraydah — A366

2000-01   **Perf. 13¾x14**
1306 A366 50h blue & multi   .50   .50
1307 A366 1r grn & multi   1.00 1.00
1308 A366 2r blk & multi   1.90 1.90
    Nos. 1306-1308 (3)   3.40 3.40
    No. 1308 issued 2/2/01.

King Fahd
Printing
Press
A367

Denomination color: 50h, Pink. 1r, Blue. 2r, Black.

2001, Apr. 25   **Litho.**   **Perf. 14**
1309-1311 A367   Set of 3   3.25 3.25

King Abdul Aziz
Center for Gifted
Care — A368

2001, May 13
1312 A368 1r multi   1.00 .50

Pilgrimage to Mecca — A369

No. 1313: a, Mosque, tower at center, b, Holy Ka'aba. c, Mosque, tower at left and center. d, Mosque, tower and two men at left. e, Mosque, tower at right, mountain in background. f, Mosque, tower and five pilgrims at left. g, Mosque, tower at right. h, Mosque, orange background.

2001, Feb. 28   **Perf. 13¾x14**
1313 A369 1r Block of 8, #a-h   8.00 8.00

Palestinian
Intifada
A370

Designs: 1r, Map of Israel, Palestinian boy and father. 2r, Barbed wire, boy and father, vert.

2001, May 30   **Litho.**   **Perf. 14**
1314-1315 A370   Set of 2   3.25 3.25
   A souvenir sheet containing an imperforate 49x36mm example of No. 1314 sold for 5r. Value $35.

King Abdul Aziz Historical
Center — A371

No. 1316: a, Building with curved, pointed wall. b, Building with one tree in front. c, Building with towers. d, Aerial view of building.

2001, June 25
1316 A371 1r Block of 4, #a-d   4.00 4.00

World Teacher's
Day — A372

2001, Oct. 6
1317 A372 1r multi   1.00 1.00

Paintings
A373

No. 1318: a, Abstract cityscape in green and yellow. b, Horse and geometric designs. c, Building windows. d, Landscape in yellow, orange and brown. e, Building with blue sky.

2001, Oct. 15
1318   Horiz. strip of 5   5.00 5.00
   a.-e. A373 1r Any single   .95 .95

7th Five-
Year Plan
A374

2002, Jan. 19   **Litho.**   **Perf. 14**
1319 A374 1r multi   .95 .95

A375

Abha — A376

2002, Jan. 19
1320 A375 1r blue & multi   1.00 1.00
1321 A376 2r green & multi   1.90 1.90

Islamic Educational, Scientific and
Cultural Organization — A377

2002, Jan. 29
1322 A377 1r multi   .95 .95

Pilgrimage
to Mecca
A378

2002, Feb. 13
1323 A378 1r multi   .95 .95

20 Years of
Achievements
Under King
Fahd — A379

Litho. with Foil Application
2002, Apr. 13
1324 A379 1r multi   .95 .95
   An imperforate 3r souvenir sheet overprinted in gold and depicting an example of No. 1324 and various other stamps, in whole or in part, exists. Value $3.

King Fahd
Port, Yanbu
A380

2002, May 26   **Litho.**   **Perf. 14**
1325 A380 1r yel & multi   1.00 1.00
1326 A380 2r gray & multi   1.90 1.90

King Fahd
Port, Al
Jubail
A381

2002, May 26
1327 A381 1r black & multi   1.00 1.00
1328 A381 2r multi   1.90 1.90
    Issued: 1r, 7/13.

Pilgrimage
to Mecca
A382

2003, Feb. 7   **Litho.**   **Perf. 14**
1329 A382 1r multi   .95 .95

Water Conservation — A383

Designs: No. 1330, 1r, Two water drops. No. 1331, 1r, One water drop, vert.

2003, Mar. 30   **Litho.**   **Perf. 14**
1330-1331 A383   Set of 2   2.00 2.00

Civil
Defense
A384

2003, Apr. 29
1332 A384 1r multi   .95 .95

Saudi
Arabian Red
Cresecent
Society
A385

2003, May 20
1333 A385 1r multi   .95 .95

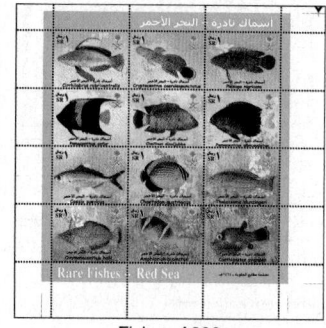

Fish — A386

Designs: Nos. 1334a, 1335a, Cirrhilabrus rubriventralis. Nos. 1334b, 1335b, Cryptocentrus caeruleopunctatus. Nos. 1334c, 1335c, Plesiops nigricans. Nos. 1334d, 1335d, Pomacanthus asfur. Nos. 1334e, 1335e, Cheilinus abudjubbe. Nos. 1334f, 1335f, Pomacentrus albicaudatus. Nos. 1334g, 1335g, Caesio suevicus. Nos. 1334h, 1335h, Chaetodon austriacus. Nos. 1334i, 1335i, Thalassoma klunzingeri. Nos. 1334j, 1335j, Oxymonacanthus halli. Nos. 1334k, 1335k, Amphiprion bicinctus. Nos. 1334l, 1335l, Canthigaster pygmaea.

2003
1334 A386 1r Sheet of 12, #a-l 13.50 13.50
1335 A386 2r Sheet of 12, #a-l 22.50 18.00
    Issued: No. 1334, 5/26; No. 1335, 6/21.

Dialogue
Among
Civilizations
A387

2003, July 1
1336 A387 1r multi   .95 .95

Electricity Conservation — A388

2003, Sept. 27
1337 A388 1r multi .95 .95

World Post
Day — A389

2003, Oct. 9
1338 A389 1r multi .95 .95

Ninth Gulf
Cooperation
Council Stamp
Exhibition — A390

2003, Oct. 18
1339 A390 1r multi .95 .95

First Saudi Commemorative Stamp,
75th Islamic Year Anniv. — A391

2003, Oct. 20
1340 A391 1r No. 129 .95 .95

Supreme Council
for Handicapped
Affairs — A392

2003, Nov. 11
1341 A392 1r multi .95 .95

King Abdul
Aziz
Equestrian
Race
Course,
Janadriyah
A393

2003, Dec. 17
1342 A393 1r multi .95 .95

Pilgrimage
to Mecca
A394

2003, Dec. 24
1343 A394 1r multi .95 .95
  a.   Arabian "1" missing in de-
    nomination 20.00 —

Mosque,
Buraydah
A395

Mosque,
Medina
A396

Mosque,
Riyadh
A397

Mosque,
Dammam
A398

Mosque,
Baha
A399

Mosque,
Khobar
A400

Mosque,
Taif — A401

Mosque,
Najran
A402

2003, Dec. 24
1344   Sheet of 8 6.25 6.25
  a. A395 1r bl & multi .80 .80
  b. A396 1r bl & multi .80 .80
  c. A397 1r bl & multi .80 .80
  d. A398 1r bl & multi .80 .80
  e. A399 1r bl & multi .80 .80
  f. A400 1r bl & multi .80 .80
  g. A401 1r bl & multi .80 .80
  h. A402 1r bl & multi .80 .80
1345   Sheet of 8 13.50 13.50
  a. A395 2r red & multi 1.60 1.60
  b. A396 2r red & multi 1.60 1.60
  c. A397 2r red & multi 1.60 1.60
  d. A398 2r red & multi 1.60 1.60
  e. A399 2r red & multi 1.60 1.60
  f. A400 2r red & multi 1.60 1.60
  g. A401 2r red & multi 1.60 1.60
  h. A402 2r red & multi 1.60 1.60

Mosques built in reign of King Fahd.

Tabouk — A403

2004, Jan. 19
1346 A403 1r blk & multi 1.00 1.00
1347 A403 2r red & multi 1.90 1.90

MD-11
A404

Boeing
747 — A405

Boeing
777 — A406

MD-90
A407

2004, Jan. 19
1348   Block of 4 4.00 4.00
  a. A404 1r multi .90 .90
  b. A405 1r multi .90 .90
  c. A406 1r multi .90 .90
  d. A407 1r multi .90 .90

New airplanes of Saudi Arabian Airlines.

Judicial
Systems
A408

2004, Apr. 5   Litho.   *Perf. 14*
1349 A408 1r multi .95 .95

Hail — A409

2004, Oct. 16   Litho.   *Perf. 13¾x14*
1350 A409 1r blk & multi 1.00 1.00
1351 A409 2r red & multi 1.90 1.90

World
Summit on
the
Information
Society
A410

2004, Nov. 1   *Perf. 14*
1352 A410 1r multi .95 .95

Tourism — A411

No. 1353: a, Sand dune. b, Funicular cars.
c, Sea coast. d, Rock climbers.

2004, Nov. 1
1353 A411 2r Block of 4, #a-d 8.00 8.00

"Islam is
Peace"
A412

2004, Dec. 27
1354 A412 2r multi 2.00 2.00

Pilgrimage
to Mecca
A413

2005, Jan. 4
1355 A413 1r multi .95 .95

Municipal
Elections — A414

2005, Jan. 8   Litho.   *Perf. 14*
1356 A414 1r multi .95 .95

Islamic Solidarity Games — A415

2005, Apr. 2
1357 A415 1r multi   .95   .95

Anti-Terrorism
Campaign
A416

2005, July 9   Litho.   Perf. 14
1358 A416 1r multi   .95   .95
An imperf. souvenir sheet with simulated
perfs sold for 3r. Value $9.

Arar
A417

2005, July 16   Litho.   Perf. 14
1359 A417 1r multi   .95   .95
a.   Missing Arabian "1" at right
No. 1359a appears in position 10 on some
sheets.

Ancient Artifacts — A418

Ruins — A419

No. 1360: a, Bowl. b, Head of animal. c,
Head of human. d, Inscribed tablet.
No. 1361: a, Ruin with two towers, walls in
foreground, year in black. b, Building with one
tower, year in white. c, Fort with towers at
corners, year in white. d, Ruins on hilltop, year
in black.

2005, Aug. 20
1360 A418 1r Block of 4, #a-d   4.25   4.25
1361 A419 2r Block of 4, #a-d   7.75   7.75

Mecca, Capital of
Islamic
Culture — A420

2005, July 16   Litho.   Perf. 14
1362 A420 3r multi   2.50   2.50
A souvenir sheet of one exists. Value, $20.

King Fahd (1921-
2005)
A421

Denominations: 2r, 3r.

2005, Dec. 21
1363-1364 A421   Set of 2   4.00   4.00
An imperf 105x80mm stamp with picture
reversed sold for 5r. Value $18.

Pilgrimage
to Mecca
A422

2005, Dec. 28
1365 A422 2r multi   1.50   1.50
An imperf 80x105mm stamp depicting pilgrims to Mecca sold for 5r.

King
Abdullah — A423

Crown Prince
Sultan — A424

Litho. with Foil Application
2006, Jan. 18
1366 A423 2r multi   1.60   1.60
1367 A424 2r multi   1.60   1.60
1368 A423 3r multi   2.50   2.50
1369 A424 3r multi   2.50   2.50
     Nos. 1366-1369 (4)   8.20   8.20
Installation of new king and crown prince.
An imperf 106x80mm stamp depicting the new
king and crown prince sold for 5r. Value
$22.50.

National
Society for
Human
Rights
A425

2006, Jan. 30   Litho.   Perf. 14
1370 A425 2r multi   1.60   1.60
An 80x105mm imperforate stamp depicting
a stylized person sold for 5r. Value $22.50.

OPEC Intl. Development Fund, 30th
Anniv. — A426

2006, Mar. 13
1371 A426 2r multi   1.60   1.60

King Faisal International Prize — A427

Color of denomination: 2r, Blue. 3r, Green.

2006, Apr. 3
1372-1373 A427   Set of 2   4.00   4.00

Saudi Post
Mailboxes
A428

2006, Apr. 22
1374 A428 2r multi   1.60   1.60

King Saud
University
A429

2006, May 14
1375 A429 2r multi   1.60   1.60

2006 World Cup
Soccer
Championships,
Germany
A430

Emblem and: 2r, Players. 3r, World map.

2006, May 20
1376-1377 A430   Set of 2   4.00   4.00

Gulf Cooperation Council, 25th
Anniv. — A431

Litho. With Foil Application
2006, May 25
1378 A431 2r multi   1.60   1.60
An imperf. 165x105mm stamp depicting
flags of Gulf Cooperation council members
sold for 5r. Value $13.50.
See Bahrain Nos. 628-629, Kuwait Nos.
1646-1647, Oman Nos. 477-478, and Qatar
Nos. 1007-1008.

Saudi Center for
Organ
Transplantation
A432

2006, June 17   Litho.
1379 A432 2r multi   1.60   1.60

Al Medina
Al
Munawara
A433

2006, Sept. 5
1380 A433 2r multi   1.50   1.50
An imperf. 105x80mm stamp depicting a
smaller version of No. 1380 and the doorway
shown at the lower left of No. 1380 sold for 5r.

Riyadh Intl.
Book Fair
A434

2006, Sept. 9
1381 A434 2r multi   1.50   1.50

National
Day
A435

2006, Sept. 23
1382 A435 2r multi   1.50   1.50

Arabian
Horses
A436

No. 1383: a, Brown horse facing right, no
shadow. b, Brown horse facing left, no
shadow. c, Brown horse facing right, with
shadow. d, Brown horse facing left, with
shadow. e, White horse. f, Horse and colt.

2006, Nov. 13
1383 Block of 6 9.00 9.00
a.-f. A436 2r Any single 1.50 1.50

Pilgrimage to Mecca A437

2006, Dec. 11
1384 A437 2r multi 1.50 1.50

Kingdom of Humanity A438

2007, Apr. 23
1385 A438 2r multi 1.50 1.50

An imperf. 105x80mm stamp depicting flag and King Abdullah sold for 5r.

2006 World Cup Soccer Championships, Germany A439

2007, May 14
1386 A439 2r multi 1.50 1.50

Elimination of Poliomyelitis From Saudi Arabia — A440

2007, June 9
1387 A440 2r multi 1.50 1.50

Butterflies A441

Nos. 1388 and 1389: a, Junonia hierta. b, Melitaea desenticola. c, Junonia orithya cheesmani. d, Eurema hecabe. e, Papilio demoleus. f, Colotis calais. g, Colotis phisadia. h, Vanessa cardui. Backgrounds differ on Nos. 1388 and 1389.

2007, Aug. 20
1388 Sheet of 8 12.00 12.00
a.-h. A441 2r Any single 1.50 1.50
1389 Sheet of 8 18.00 18.00
a.-h. A441 3r Any single 2.25 2.25

The Latin names of the butterflies on Nos. 1388c, 1388d, 1388f, 1389c, 1389d and 1389f are incorrect on the stamps.

Direct Mail Conference, Riyadh — A442

No. 1390: a, PosTech 2007 emblem. b, Flags and emblems of postal services of Gulf Cooperation Council countries. c, Emblem of 13th Gulf Cooperation Council Postage Stamp Exhibition. d, Emblem for UPU Regional Roundtable and map.

2007, Nov. 11
1390 A442 2r Block of 4, #a-d 6.00 6.00

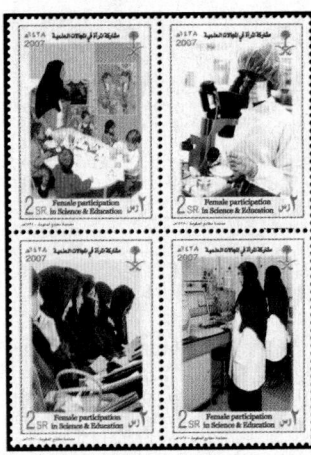

Women in Science and Education — A443

No. 1391: a, Woman teaching children. b, Woman at microscope. c, Women in classroom. d, Woman at computer in laboratory.

2007, Nov. 11
1391 A443 2r Block of 4, #a-d 6.00 6.00

Third OPEC Summit, Riyadh A444

2007, Nov. 17
1392 A444 2r multi 1.50 1.50

National Day A445

2007, Dec. 1
1393 A445 2r multi 1.50 1.50

Pilgrimage to Mecca A446

2007, Dec. 9 Litho. Perf. 14
1394 A446 2r multi 1.50 1.50

Harmony Through Intellectual Dialogue — A447

2007, Dec. 29
1395 A447 2r multi 1.50 1.50

Camels — A448

No. 1396: a, Al majaheem. b, Al wad'h. c, Al shog'h. d, Al shoe'l.

2008, Apr. 21
1396 A448 2r Block of 4, #a-d 6.00 6.00

An imperf. 105x75mm stamp depicting smaller versions of Nos. 1396a-1396d sold for 5r.

Aramco, 75th Anniv. — A449

No. 1397: a, Workmen on oil drilling platform. b, Scuba diver and fish. c, Child's drawing of oil drilling. d, Child's drawing of Saudi people.

2008, May 20 Perf. 13¾x14
1397 A449 2r Block of 4, #a-d 6.00 6.00

Development of Riyadh, 50th Anniv. — A450

2008, June 21 Perf. 14
1398 A450 2r multi 1.50 1.50

An imperf. 105x80mm stamp depicting Riyadh and King Abdullah sold for 5r.

Intl. Electrotechnical Commission, Cent. — A451

2008, July 19
1399 A451 2r multi 1.50 1.50

A souvenir sheet containing two perf. 13¾x13¼ stamps for Arab Postal Day sold for 10r.

Pilgrimage to Mecca A452

2008, Dec. 1 Litho. Perf. 14
1400 A452 2r multi 1.50 1.50

Compare with types A437 and A446.

King Abdullah University of Science and Technology — A453

2009, Sept. 23 Perf. 13¾x14
1401 A453 2r multi 1.50 1.50

An imperf. 105x75mm stamp depicting King Abdullah and the university sold for 5r.

Jerusalem, Capital of Arab Culture — A454

2009, Oct. 25 Perf. 14
1402 A454 2r multi 1.50 1.50

National Day A455

2009, Nov. 18
1403 A455 2r multi 1.50 1.50

Pilgrimage to Mecca — A456

2009, Nov. 18   *Perf. 13¾x14*
1404 A456 2r multi   1.50 1.50

Organization of Petroleum Exporting
Countries, 50th Anniv. — A457

2010, Jan. 9   *Perf. 14*
1405 A457 2r multi   1.50 1.50

Janandriyah
Festival, 25th
Anniv. — A458

2010, Nov. 9   *Perf. 14*
1406 A458 2r multi   1.50 1.50

National Day — A459

2010, Nov. 10   *Perf. 13¾x14*
1407 A459 2r multi   1.50 1.50

Souvenir Sheet

Pilgrimage to Mecca — A460

No. 1408: a, Pilgrims and train. b, Pilgrims,
train, King Abdullah, Mecca Royal Clock Hotel
Tower, Holy Ka'aba. c, Mecca Royal Clock
Hotel Tower, Holy Ka'aba, clock.

2010, Nov. 10   *Perf. 14*
1408 A460 2r Sheet of 3, #a-c, +
    3 labels   4.50 4.50

Miniature Sheets

Jewelry — A461

No. 1409: a, Bracelet with ruby. b, Gold
bracelet. c, Three horseshoe bracelets. d, Silver armlets. e, Silver bangles. f, Two bracelets.
No. 1410 — Stamps with gray brown background: a, Headdress ornament. b, Earrings.

c, Earrings with hooks visible at top. d, Head
ornament. e, Rings. f, Forehead ornament.
No. 1411 — Stamps with pink background:
a, Gold, cornelian and ruby necklace. b, Silver
necklace. c, Necklace with red stone. d, Waist
belt. e, Necklace. f, Silver necklace with large
square pendants.

2010-11   *Perf. 14*
1409 A461 2r Sheet of 6, #a-f   9.00 9.00
1410 A461 2r Sheet of 6, #a-f   9.00 9.00
1411 A461 2r Sheet of 6, #a-f   9.00 9.00
    Nos. 1409-1411 (3)   27.00 27.00

Issued: No. 1409, 12/29. No. 1410, 4/4/11;
No. 1411, 9/12/11.

World Map, Dove and Scouting
Emblem — A462

2011   *Perf. 13¾x14*
1412 A462 2r multi   1.50 1.50

King Abdullah Haram Expansion
Project — A463

2011
1413 A463 2r multi   1.50 1.50

Prince
Sultan
(1928-2011)
A464

2012, Sept. 15   *Perf. 14*
1414 A464 2r multi   1.50 1.50
An imperforate 105x75mm stamp depicting
Prince Sultan sold for 5r.

Installation
of Crown
Prince Nayef
A465

2012, Sept. 15
1415 A465 2r multi   1.50 1.50
An imperforate 105x75mm stamp depicting
Crown Prince Nayef sold for 5r.

Crown
Prince
Nayef
(1934-2012)
A466

2012, Sept. 15
1416 A466 2r multi   1.50 1.50
An imperforate 106x75mm stamp depicting
Crown Prince Nayaf sold for 5r.

Installation
of Crown
Prince
Suleiman
A467

2012, Sept. 23
1417 A467 2r multi   1.50 1.50
An imperforate 105x75mm stamp depicting
Crown Prince Suleiman sold for 5r.

National
Day — A468

2012, Sept. 23
1418 A468 2r multi   1.50 1.50

Arab Postal Day — A469

2012, Oct. 17   *Perf. 13¾x14*
1419 A469 2r multi   1.50 1.50

18th Gulf Cooperation Council Stamp
Exhibition, Jeddah — A470

2012, Oct. 17   *Perf. 14*
1420 A470 2r multi   1.50 1.50

Souvenir Sheet

Pilgrimage to Mecca — A471

No. 1421: a, Aerial view of mosque and surrounding plaza. b, Aerial view of Grand
Mosque and Holy Ka'aba, Mecca.

2012, Oct. 22   *Perf. 13¾x14*
1421 A471 2r Sheet of 2, #a-b   3.00 3.00

A472

Princess
Nora Bint
Abdul
Rahman
University,
Riyadh
A473

2013, Feb. 16   *Perf. 14*
1422 A472 2r multi   1.50 1.50
1423 A473 3r multi   2.25 2.25

A474

King Abdullah Prize for
Translation — A475

2013, Mar. 3   *Perf. 14*
1424 A474 2r multi   1.50 1.50
    Perf. 13¾x14
1425 A475 3r multi   2.25 2.25

Arabian
Fatherhood
Symbol
A476

2013, Apr. 6   *Perf. 14*
1426 A476 2r multi   1.50 1.50

Pilgrimage
to Mecca
A477

2013, Aug. 3
1427 A477 2r multi   1.50 1.50

Souvenir Sheet

Medina, 2013 Capital of Islamic
Culture — A478

No. 1428: a, Emblem for Third Arab Stamps
Exhibition. b, Emblem for Medina as Capital of
Islamic Culture

2013, Sept. 1   Litho.   *Perf. 14*
1428 A478 2r Sheet of 2, #a-b   3.00 3.00

National
Day
A479

2013, Sept. 23   Litho.   *Perf. 14*
1429 A479 2r multi   1.50 1.50

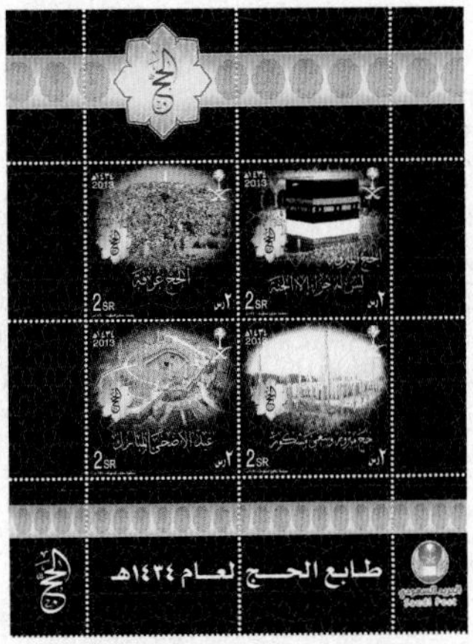

Pilgrimage to Mecca — A480

No. 1430: a, Worshipers on pilgrimage. b, Worshipers and Holy Ka'aba. c, Aerial view of Grand Mosque. d, Worshipers outside of mosque.

2013, Oct. 9 Litho. *Perf. 14*

1430	A480	2r	Sheet of 4, #a-d, + 2 labels	6.00	6.00

Charity Committee for Orphans Care A481

2014, Jan. 13 Litho. *Perf. 14*

1431	A481	2r	multi	1.50	1.50

Souvenir Sheet

King Abdullah Sports City — A482

No. 1432: a, Interior of stadium. b, Emblem. c, Aerial view of stadium.

2014, May 1 Litho. *Perf. 13¾x14*

1432	A482	2r	Sheet of 3, #a-c, + 6 labels	4.50	4.50

AIR POST STAMPS

Catalogue values for unused stamps in this section are for Never Hinged items.

Airspeed Ambassador Airliner — AP1

1949-58 Unwmk. Typo. *Perf. 11*

C1	AP1	1g	blue green	4.50	.50
C2	AP1	3g	ultra	5.75	.50
a.			3g blue ('58)	20.00	1.75
C3	AP1	4g	orange	5.75	.50
C4	AP1	10g	purple	16.00	1.00
C5	AP1	20g	brn vio ('58+)	13.50	2.25
a.			20g chocolate ('49)	25.00	2.40
C6	AP1	100g	violet rose	175.00	22.50
			Nos. C1-C6 (6)	220.50	27.25

Imperfs. exist, not regularly issued.

The 1st printings are on grayish paper and sell for more.

No. C3 exists with pin-perf 6.

+ The date for No. C5 is not definite.

Saudi Airlines Convair 440 — AP2

Type I (Saud Cartouche) (Illustrated over No. 286)

1960-61 Photo. *Perf. 14*

C7	AP2	1p	dull pur & grn	.80	.30
C8	AP2	2p	grn & dull pur	.80	.30
C9	AP2	3p	brn red & bl	.80	.30
C10	AP2	4p	bl & dull pur	.80	.30
C11	AP2	5p	grn & rose red	.80	.30
C12	AP2	6p	ocher & slate	1.40	.30
C13	AP2	8p	rose & gray ol	1.50	.30
C14	AP2	9p	pur & red brn	2.25	.30
C15	AP2	10p	blk & dl red brn	6.50	.60
C16	AP2	15p	bl & bis brn	6.50	.30
C17	AP2	20p	bis brn & emer	6.50	.45
C18	AP2	30p	sep & Prus grn	15.00	1.40
C19	AP2	50p	green & indigo	35.00	.95
C20	AP2	100p	gray & dk brn	70.00	2.50
C21	AP2	200p	dk vio & black	115.00	3.75
			Nos. C7-C21 (15)	263.65	12.35

Nos. C7-C18 exist imperf., probably not regularly issued.

1963-64 Photo. Wmk. 337

Size: 27½x22mm

C24	AP2	1p	lilac & green	3.25	.30
C25	AP2	2p	green & dull pur	12.00	.30
C26	AP2	4p	blue & dull pur	4.50	.30
C27	AP2	6p	ocher & slate	12.00	.95
C28	AP2	8p	rose & gray olive	22.50	1.90
C29	AP2	9p	pur & red brn ('64)	17.50	1.25
			Nos. C24-C29 (6)	71.75	5.00

Redrawn

Perf. 13½x13

1964 Wmk. 337 Litho.

Size: 28½x23mm

C30	AP2	3p	brn red & dull bl	10.00	1.00
C31	AP2	10p	blk & dk red brn	17.50	1.50
C32	AP2	20p	bis brn & emer	37.50	3.50
			Nos. C30-C32 (3)	65.00	6.00

Nos. C30-C32 are widely spaced in the sheet, producing large margins.

Saudi Airline Boeing 720-B Jet — AP3

Type I (Saud Cartouche) (Illustrated over No. 286)

1965-70 Unwmk. Litho. *Perf. 14*

C33	AP3	1p	lilac & green	125.00	3.75
C34	AP3	2p	grn & dull pur	3,850.	150.00
C35	AP3	3p	rose lil & dull bl	13.00	.25
C36	AP3	4p	blue & dull pur	7.75	.25
C37	AP3	5p	ol & rose red	2,525.	550.00
C38	AP3	6p	ocher & slate	140.00	2.40
C39	AP3	7p	rose & ol gray	8.75	.45
C40	AP3	8p	rose & gray ol	125.00	2.40
C41	AP3	9p	purple & red brn	7.25	.40
C42	AP3	10p	blk & dk red brn	110.00	7.75
C43	AP3	11p	grn & bis	110.00	25.00
C44	AP3	12p	org & gray	7.75	.40
C45	AP3	13p	dk grn & yel grn	6.00	.40
C46	AP3	14p	dk blue & org	6.00	.45
C47	AP3	15p	blue & bis brn	100.00	7.75
C48	AP3	16p	black & ultra	8.75	.60
C49	AP3	17p	bis & sep	7.00	.45
C50	AP3	18p	dk bl & yel grn	7.00	.45
C51	AP3	19p	car & dp org	7.75	.60
C52	AP3	20p	bis brn & emer	190.00	8.75
C53	AP3	23p	olive & bister	210.00	15.00
C54	AP3	24p	dk bl & sep	7.00	.60
C55	AP3	26p	ver & bl grn	7.00	.60
C56	AP3	27p	ol brn & ap grn	8.00	.60
C57	AP3	31p	car rose & rose red	10.00	.75
C58	AP3	33p	red & dull pur	13.00	.75

The 50p, 100p and 200p exist but were not placed in use.

Issue years: 1966, 1p, 3p, 7p, 10p, 12p-14p, 16p-19p; 1969, 5p, 11p; 1970, 2p, 6p, 8p, 15p, 20p; others, 1965.

Type II (Faisal Cartouche)

1966-78 Unwmk. Litho. *Perf. 14*

C59	AP3	1p	dull pur & grn	25.00	1.10
C60	AP3	2p	grn & dl pur	25.00	1.75
C61	AP3	3p	brn red & dull bl	25.00	.55
C62	AP3	4p	blue & dull pur	12.50	.30
C63	AP3	5p	ol & rose red	2,250.	550.00
C64	AP3	6p	ocher & slate	150.00	11.00
C65	AP3	7p	rose & ol gray	70.00	7.75
C66	AP3	8p	rose & gray ol	95.00	13.50
C67	AP3	9p	purple & red brn	6.25	.65
C68	AP3	10p	blk & dull red brn	20.00	1.10
C69	AP3	11p	grn & bis	15.00	.55
C70	AP3	12p	org & gray	55.00	4.25
C71	AP3	13p	dk grn & yel grn	17.50	1.10
C72	AP3	14p	dk blue & org	16.00	1.75
C73	AP3	15p	blue & bis brn	13.50	.85
C74	AP3	16p	blk & ultra	20.00	3.25
C75	AP3	17p	bis & sep	17.50	1.75
C76	AP3	18p	dk bl & yel grn	16.00	2.75
C77	AP3	19p	car & org	22.50	1.10
C78	AP3	20p	brn & brt grn	210.00	15.00
C79	AP3	23p	ol & bis	27.50	3.25
C80	AP3	24p	dk blue & blk	32.50	3.25
C83	AP3	31p	car rose & rose red	—	
C84	AP3	33p	red & dull pur	13.50	.55
C85	AP3	50p	emer & ind	800.00	210.00
C86	AP3	100p	gray & dk brn	1,050.	325.00
C87	AP3	200p	dk vio & blk	1,125.	210.00

The existence of 26p and 27p denominations has been reported.

The status of the 31p has been questioned. If it exists it may not have been issued.

Issue years: 1968, 4p, 33p; 1969, 7p; 1970, 8p, 9p, 20p; 1971, 13p, 16p; 1974, 50p, 200p; 1975, 12p, 14p, 15p, 17p, 19p, 24p; 1976, 18p; 1978, 31p, 100p; others, 1966.

1968-71 Wmk. 361 Litho. *Perf. 14*

C88	AP3	1p	lilac & green	8.25	.25
C89	AP3	2p	green & lilac	10.50	.25
C90	AP3	3p	rose lil & dull bl	50.00	2.40
C91	AP3	4p	blue & dull pur	13.00	1.50
C92	AP3	7p	rose & gray	13.00	2.10
C93	AP3	8p	red & gray ol	52.50	8.25
C94	AP3	9p	pur & red brn	72.50	10.00
C95	AP3	10p	blk & dull red brn	45.00	4.75
			Nos. C88-C95 (8)	264.75	29.50

Issue years: 1969, 3p, 10p; 1970, 4p; 1971, 7p-9p; others, 1968.

Falcon — AP4

Perf. 13½x14

1968-71 Litho. Wmk. 361

C96	AP4	1p	green & red brn	18.50	.30
C97	AP4	4p	dk red & red brn	300.00	19.00
C98	AP4	10p	blue & red brn	32.50	4.75
C99	AP4	20p	green & red brn ('71)	60.00	9.75
			Nos. C96-C99 (4)	411.00	33.80

Nine other denominations were printed but are not known to have been issued.

HEJAZ POSTAGE DUE STAMPS

From Old Door at El Ashraf Barsbai in Shari el Ashrafiya, Cairo — D1

Serrate Roulette 13

1917, June 27 Typo. Unwmk.

LJ1	D1	20pa	red	3.25	2.00
LJ2	D1	1pi	blue	3.50	2.00
LJ3	D1	2pi	magenta	3.75	2.00
			Nos. LJ1-LJ3 (3)	10.50	6.00

For overprints see Nos. LJ4-LJ10, LJ17-LJ25, J9.

Nos. LJ1-LJ3 Overprinted in Black or Red — a

1921, Dec. Type a

LJ4	D1	20pa	red	20.00	2.75
			Never hinged	30.00	
a.			Double overprint, one at left	140.00	
b.			Overprint at left	30.00	20.00
			Never hinged	45.00	
LJ5	D1	1pi	blue (R)	7.00	3.50
			Never hinged	11.00	
LJ6	D1	1pi	bl, ovpt. at left	30.00	18.00
			Never hinged	45.00	
a.			Overprint at right	27.50	32.50
			Never hinged	40.00	
LJ7	D1	2pi	magenta	12.50	7.25
			Never hinged	19.00	
a.			Double overprint, one at left	62.50	
b.			Overprint at left	27.50	
			Never hinged	40.00	
			Nos. LJ4-LJ7 (4)	69.50	31.50

Nos. LJ1-LJ3 Overprinted in Black — b

1922, Jan. Type b

LJ8	D1	20pa	red	25.00	27.50
			Never hinged	37.50	
a.			Overprint at left	35.00	
LJ9	D1	1pi	blue	5.00	3.25
			Never hinged	7.50	
a.			Overprint at left	45.00	
LJ10	D1	2pi	magenta	5.00	3.25
			Never hinged	7.50	
a.			Overprint at left	32.50	
			Nos. LJ8-LJ10 (3)	35.00	34.00

Regular issue of 1922 Overprinted

1923 Black Overprint *Perf. 11½*

LJ11	A7	½pi	red	4.25	1.40
a.			Inverted overprint	50.00	
LJ12	A7	1pi	dark blue	7.50	1.40
a.			Inverted overprint	80.00	
b.			Double overprint	125.00	
LJ13	A7	2pi	orange	5.00	1.75
a.			Inverted overprint	47.50	
			Nos. LJ11-LJ13 (3)	16.75	4.55

1924 Blue Overprint

LJ14	A7	½pi	red	17.50	2.75
a.			Inverted overprint	80.00	
LJ15	A7	1pi	dark blue	37.50	2.75
a.			Inverted overprint	100.00	

LJ16 A7 2pi orange 27.50 4.50
a. Inverted overprint 40.00
Nos. LJ14-LJ16 (3) 82.50 10.00

This overprint reads "Mustahaq" (Due).

Jedda Issues

Nos. LJ1-LJ3 Overprinted in Red or Blue (Overprint reads up in illustration)

Jedda issues were also used in Medina and Yambo. **Used values for #L51-L186 and LJ17-LJ39 are for genuine cancels. Privately applied cancels exist for "Mekke" (Mecca, bilingual or all Arabic), Khartoum, Cairo, as well as for Jeddah. Many private cancels have wrong dates, some as early as 1916. These are worth half the used values.**

1925, Jan. ***Serrate Roulette 13***

LJ17 D1 20pa red (R) 400.00 *350.00*
LJ18 D1 20pa red (Bl) *75.00*
LJ19 D1 1pi blue (R) 20.00 *18.00*
LJ20 D1 1pi blue (Bl) 27.50 *25.00*
LJ21 D1 2pi mag (Bl) 15.00 *14.00*

Overprint Reading Down

LJ17a D1 20pa *550.00 550.00*
LJ18a D1 20pa 450.00
LJ19a D1 1pi 18.00 *18.00*
LJ20a D1 1pi 67.50 *80.00*
LJ21a D1 2pi 60.00 *60.00*

Nos. LJ1-LJ3 Overprinted in Blue or Red

1925

LJ22 D1 20pa red (Bl) 475.00 *425.00*
a. Inverted overprint 325.00 *325.00*
LJ24 D1 1pi blue (R) 25.00 *27.50*
a. Inverted overprint 32.50 *32.50*
LJ25 D1 2pi magenta (Bl) 20.00 *18.00*
a. Inverted overprint 35.00 *45.00*
b. Double overprint 350.00

No. LJ2 with this overprint in blue is bogus.

Regular Issues of 1922-24 Overprinted

and Handstamped — b

1925 ***Perf. 11½***

LJ26 A7 ⅛pi red brown 20.00 *18.00*
Never hinged 30.00
b. Pair, one without handstamp 100.00 —
c. Overprint inverted 60.00 —
d. Violet handstamp 75.00 —
LJ27 A7 ¼pi red 27.50 *25.00*
Never hinged 42.50
b. Pair, one without handstamp 100.00 —
c. Overprint inverted 60.00 —
LJ28 A7 1pi dark blue 20.00 *18.00*
Never hinged 30.00
b. Pair, one without handstamp 100.00 —
c. Overprint inverted 60.00 —
LJ29 A7 1½pi violet 22.50 *18.00*
Never hinged 35.00
b. Pair, one without handstamp 100.00 —
c. Overprint inverted 60.00 —
d. Violet handstamp 75.00 —
LJ30 A7 2pi orange 25.00 *20.00*
Never hinged 37.50
b. Pair, one without handstamp 100.00 —
c. Overprint inverted 60.00 —
d. Violet handstamp 75.00 —
LJ31 A7 3pi olive brown 25.00 *20.00*
Never hinged 37.50
b. Pair, one without handstamp 100.00 —
c. Overprint inverted 60.00 —
LJ32 A7 3pi dull red 50.00 *45.00*
Never hinged 75.00
b. Pair, one without handstamp 100.00 —
c. Overprint inverted 60.00 —
d. Violet handstamp 75.00 —
LJ33 A7 5pi olive green 25.00 *20.00*
Never hinged 37.50
b. Pair, one without handstamp 100.00 —
c. Overprint inverted 60.00 —
LJ34 A7 10pi vio & dk brn 30.00 *25.00*
Never hinged 45.00
b. Pair, one without handstamp 100.00 —
c. Overprint inverted 60.00 —
d. Violet handstamp 75.00 —
Nos. LJ26-LJ34 (9) 245.00 *209.00*

The printed overprint *(a)*, consisting of the three top lines of Arabic, was used alone for the first issue (Nos. LJ26a-LJ34a). The "postage due" box was so small and indistinct that its equivalent in larger characters was added by boxed handstamp *(b)* at bottom of each stamp for the second issue (Nos. LJ26-LJ34).

The handstamped overprint *(b)* is found double, inverted, etc. It is also known in dark violet.

Counterfeits exist of both overprint and handstamp.

Without Boxed Handstamp "b"

LJ26a A7 ⅛pi red brown 42.50
LJ27a A7 ¼pi red 42.50
LJ28a A7 1pi dark blue 42.50
LJ29a A7 1½pi violet 42.50
LJ30a A7 2pi orange 42.50
LJ31a A7 3pi olive brown 42.50
LJ32a A7 3pi dull red 42.50
LJ33a A7 5pi olive green 55.00
LJ34a A7 10pi vio & dk brn 55.00
Nos. LJ26a-LJ34a (9) 407.50

Regular Issue of 1922 Overprinted

and Handstamped

LJ35 A7 ½pi red *150.00 140.00*
LJ36 A7 1½pi violet *150.00 140.00*
a. Overprint in red, boxed handstamp violet *1,400.*
LJ37 A7 2pi orange *200.00 175.00*
LJ38 A7 3pi olive brown *150.00 140.00*
LJ39 A7 5pi olive green *150.00 140.00*
Nos. LJ35-LJ39 (5) *800.00 735.00*
Set, never hinged 1,000.

Counterfeits exist of Nos. LJ4-LJ39.

Arabic Numeral of Value — D2

1925, May-June ***Perf. 11½***

LJ40 D2 ½pi light blue 3.00
LJ41 D2 1pi orange 3.00
LJ42 D2 2pi lt brown 3.00
LJ43 D2 3pi pink 3.00
Nos. LJ40-LJ43 (4) 12.00

Nos. LJ40-LJ43 have no overprint and were not officially issued. No. LJ40 exists only on cover.

Nos. LJ40-LJ43 exist imperforate. Impressions in colors other than issued are trial color proofs.

Arabic Numeral of Value — D3

1925 **Black Overprint**

LJ44 D3 ½pi light blue 3.00
Never hinged 4.50
LJ45 D3 1pi orange 3.00
Never hinged 4.50
LJ46 D3 2pi light brown 3.00
Never hinged 4.50
LJ47 D3 3pi pink 3.75
Never hinged 6.00
Nos. LJ44-LJ47 (4) 12.75

Nos. LJ44-LJ47 exist with either Jedda or Cairo overprints and the tablets normally read upward. Values are for Cairo overprints; Jedda overprints sell for more.

Red Overprint

LJ48 D3 ½pi light blue 3.75
Never hinged 6.00
LJ49 D3 1pi orange 3.75
Never hinged 6.00
LJ50 D3 2pi light brown 3.75
Never hinged 6.00
LJ51 D3 3pi pink 3.75
Never hinged 6.00

Blue Overprint

LJ52 D3 ½pi light blue 3.75
Never hinged 6.00
LJ53 D3 1pi orange 3.75
Never hinged 6.00
LJ54 D3 2pi light brown 3.75
Never hinged 6.00
LJ55 D3 3pi pink 3.75
Never hinged 6.00
Nos. LJ40-LJ55 (16) 54.75

Red and blue overprints are from Cairo. Nos. LJ44-LJ55 exist imperf.

NEJDI ADMINISTRATION OF HEJAZ POSTAGE DUE STAMPS

Nos. LJ11-LJ16 Handstamped in Blue, Red or Black

1925, Apr.-June **Unwmk.** ***Perf. 11½***

J1 A7 ½pi red (Bl) 27.50 27.50
J2 A7 1pi lt blue (R) 55.00 55.00
a. 1pi dark blue (R) 35.00 35.00
J3 A7 2pi yel buff (Bl) 55.00 55.00
a. 2pi orange (Bl) 47.50 47.50
Nos. J1-J3 (3) 137.50 137.50

The original boxed overprint is printed on Nos. J1, J2a and J3a. Nos. J2-J3 are overprinted on a new printing of the basic stamps with handstamped boxed overprints.

Same, with Postage Due Overprint in Blue

J4 A7 ½pi red (Bl) *140.00*
J5 A7 1pi dk blue (R) *550.00*
J6 A7 2pi orange (Bl) *175.00*

On Hejaz Stamps of 1922-24 Handstamped in Blue

J7 A7 ½pi red (Bl & Bl) 16.00 16.00
J8 A7 3pi brn red (Bl & Bl) 19.00 19.00

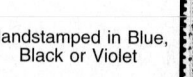

Handstamped in Blue, Black or Violet

On Hejaz No. LJ9

Serrate Roulette 13½

J9 D1 1pi blue (V) 60.00 27.50

Same Overprint on Hejaz Stamps of 1924 with additional Handstamp in Black, Blue or Red

Perf. 11½

J10 A7 3pi brn red (Bl & Bk) 11.00 11.00
J11 A7 3pi brn red (Bk & Bl) 11.00 11.00

Same Handstamps on Hejaz Railway Tax Stamps

J12 R3 1pi blue, type 1 (Bk & R) 12.00 12.00
a. Type 2 40.00
Never hinged 60.00
J13 R3 2pi ocher, type 1 (Bl & Bk) 12.00 12.00
a. Type 2 40.00
Never hinged 60.00
J14 R3 5pi green, type 1 (Bk & R) 20.00 20.00
a. Type 2 60.00
Never hinged 90.00
J15 R3 5pi green, type 1 (V & BK) 20.00 9.00
a. Type 2 60.00
Never hinged 90.00
Nos. J10-J15 (6) 86.00 75.00

The second handstamp, which is struck on the lower part of the Postage Due Stamps, is the word Mustahaq (Due) in various forms.

#J13 exists with 2nd handstamp in blue.

Hejaz-Nejd

D1

1926 **Typo.** ***Perf. 11***

J16 D1 ½pi carmine 4.00 *10.00*
J17 D1 2pi orange 4.00 *10.00*
J18 D1 6pi light brown 4.00 *10.00*
Nos. J16-J18 (3) 12.00 *30.00*

Nos. J16-J18 exist with perf. 14, 14x11 and 11x14, and imperf. These sell for six times the values quoted.

Nos. J16-J18 in colors other than listed (both perf. and imperf.) are proofs.

Counterfeit note after No. 80 also applies to Nos. J16-J21.

Pan-Islamic Congress Issue
Postage Due Stamps of 1926
Handstamped like Regular Issue

J19	D1	½pi carmine	5.50	4.50
		Never hinged	8.00	
J20	D1	2pi orange	5.50	4.50
		Never hinged	8.00	
J21	D1	6pi light brown	5.50	4.50
		Never hinged	8.00	
		Nos. J19-J21 (3)	16.50	13.50

D2

1927   **Perf. 11½**

J22	D2	1pi slate	18.00	.45
a.	Inscription reads "2 piastres" in upper right circle		200.00	100.00
J23	D2	2pi dark violet	5.75	.45

Saudi Arabia

Saudi Arabia
No. 161
Handstamped
in Black

1935

J24	A9	½g dark carmine	350.00

Two types of overprint.

D3

1937-39   **Unwmk.**

J25	D3	½g org brn ('39)	20.00	20.00
		Never hinged	20.00	
J26	D3	1g light blue	20.00	20.00
		Never hinged	20.00	
J27	D3	2g rose vio ('39)	29.00	13.50
		Never hinged	25.00	
		Nos. J25-J27 (3)	69.00	53.50

> **Catalogue values for unused stamps in this section, from this point to the end of the section, are for Never Hinged items.**

D4

1961   **Litho.**   **Perf. 13x13½**

J28	D4	1p purple	5.00	5.00
J29	D4	2p green	8.50	4.00
J30	D4	4p rose red	10.00	10.00
		Nos. J28-J30 (3)	23.50	19.00

The use of Postage Due stamps ceased in 1963.

OFFICIAL STAMPS

Official stamps were normally used only on external correspondence.

O1

1939   **Unwmk.**   **Typo.**   **Perf. 11½**

O1	O1	3g deep ultra	5.25	2.40

Perf. 11, 11½

O2	O1	5g red violet	6.75	3.00

Perf. 11

O3	O1	20g brown	14.00	6.25
O4	O1	50g blue green	27.50	13.00
O5	O1	100g olive grn	110.00	60.00
O6	O1	200g purple	90.00	40.00
		Nos. O1-O6 (6)	253.50	124.65

> **Catalogue values for unused stamps in this section, from this point to the end of the section, are for Never Hinged items.**

O2

1961   **Litho.**   **Perf. 13x13½**
Size: 18x22-22½mm

O7	O2	1p black	2.00	.30
O8	O2	2p dark green	3.00	.50
O9	O2	3p bister	3.75	.60
O10	O2	4p dark blue	5.50	.75
O11	O2	5p rose red	6.50	.90
O12	O2	10p maroon	10.00	2.75
O13	O2	20p violet blue	17.50	5.25
O14	O2	50p dull brown	40.00	14.50
O15	O2	100p dull green	85.00	25.00
		Nos. O7-O15 (9)	173.25	50.55

Nos. O8, O10-O15 exist imperf., probably not regularly issued.

1964-65   **Wmk. 337**   **Perf. 13½x13**
Size: 21x26mm

O16	O2	1p black	3.00	.55
O17	O2	2p green ('65)	5.00	1.10
O18	O2	3p bister	15.00	3.75
O19	O2	4p dark blue	11.00	2.75
O20	O2	5p rose red	14.00	1.60
		Nos. O16-O20 (5)	48.00	9.75

1965-70   **Wmk. 337**   **Typo.**   **Perf. 11**

O21	O2	1p dark brn	8.00	2.40
O22	O2	2p green	8.00	2.40
O23	O2	3p bister	8.00	2.40
O24	O2	4p dark blue	8.00	2.40
O25	O2	5p deep org	14.00	3.00
O26	O2	6p red lilac	14.00	3.00
O27	O2	7p emerald	14.00	3.00
O28	O2	8p car rose	14.00	3.00
O29	O2	9p red	250.00	50.00
O30	O2	10p red brown	55.00	3.00
O31	O2	11p pale green	105.00	
O32	O2	12p violet	450.00	
O33	O2	13p blue	19.00	4.50
O34	O2	14p purple	19.00	4.50
O35	O2	15p orange	275.00	
O36	O2	16p black	275.00	
a.	"19" instead of "16"		750.00	
O37	O2	17p gray green	275.00	
O38	O2	18p yellow	275.00	
O39	O2	19p dp red lil	275.00	
O39A	O2	20p lt bl grn		2,750.
O40	O2	23p ultra	375.00	
O41	O2	24p yel grn	275.00	
O42	O2	26p bister	300.00	
O43	O2	27p pale lilac	375.00	
O44	O2	31p pale sal	375.00	
O45	O2	33p yel grn	300.00	
O46	O2	50p olive bister	900.00	300.00
O47	O2	100p ol gray ('70)	1,450.	500.00
		Nos. O21-O39,O40-O47 (27)	6,636.	

Nos. O21-O28, O30 and O33-O34 were released to the philatelic trade in 1964. Nos. O21-O47 were printed from new plates; lines of the design are heavier. The numerals have been enlarged and the P's are smaller. Head of "P" 2mm wide on 1964-65 issue, 1mm wide on 1965-70 issue.

No. O39A is only known used. All known examples are faulty.

O3

Wmk. 361, 337 (7p, 8p, 9p, 11p, 12p, 23p)

1970-72   **Litho.**   **Perf. 13½x14**

O48	O3	1p red brown	4.50	1.50
O49	O3	2p deep green	4.50	1.50
O50	O3	3p rose red	6.00	2.40
O51	O3	4p bright blue	7.50	3.00
O52	O3	5p brick red	7.50	3.00
O53	O3	6p orange	7.50	3.00
a.	Wmk. 337		200.00	45.00
O54	O3	7p deep salmon	175.00	
O55	O3	8p violet	325.00	
O56	O3	9p dk blue grn	325.00	
O57	O3	10p blue	9.50	9.50
a.	Wmk. 337		175.00	
O58	O3	11p olive green	325.00	
O58A	O3	12p black brown	400.00	
O59	O3	20p gray violet	24.00	7.75
a.	Wmk. 337		200.00	90.00
O59B	O3	23p ocher ('72)	375.00	
O60	O3	31p deep plum	75.00	29.00
O61	O3	50p light brown	750.00	200.00
O62	O3	100p green	750.00	325.00

Use of official stamps ceased in 1974.

NEWSPAPER STAMPS

Nos. 8, 9 and 14
with Additional
Overprint in Black

1925   **Unwmk.**   **Perf. 11½**

P1	A7	⅛pi red brown (Bk)	1,800.	1,800.
P2	A7	⅛pi red brown (V)	1,400.	900.
P3	A7	½pi red (V)	2,750.	1,800.

Overprint reads: "Matbu'a" (Newspaper), but these stamps were normally used for regular postage. Counterfeits exist.

The status of this set in question. The government may have declared it to be unauthorized.

POSTAL TAX STAMPS

PT1

1934, May 15   **Unwmk.**   **Perf. 11½**

RA1	PT1	½g scarlet	100.00	4.50

No. RA1 collected a "war tax" to aid wounded of the 1934 Saudi-Yemen war.

Nos. RA2-RA8 raised funds for the Medical Aid Society.

General
Hospital,
Mecca
PT2

PT2a

1936, Oct.   **Size: 37x20mm**

RA2	PT2	⅛g scarlet	400.00	9.00

Type of 1936, Redrawn

1937-42   **Size: 30½x18mm**

RA3	PT2a	⅛g scarlet	35.00	.90
a.	⅛g rose ('39)		60.00	1.75
b.	⅛g rose car, perf. 11 ('42)		125.00	6.75

General
Hospital,
Mecca — PT3

1943   **Typo.**   **Perf. 11½, 11**
Grayish Paper

RA4	PT3	⅛g car rose	35.00	.25
a.	⅛g scarlet		35.00	.25

The 1g green and 5g indigo were not for postal use.
See Nos. RA5-RA8.

Map of Saudi
Arabia Type I
— (Flag
inscriptions
intact) — PT4

Type II —
(Flag
inscriptions
scratched out)

1946   **Unwmk.**   **Perf. 11½**

RA4B	PT4	½g magenta (II)	16.00	1.00
c.	Type I		55.00	1.00
d.	Type I, perf. 11		45.00	9.00
e.	Type II, perf. 11		67.50	

Return of King Ibn Saud from Egypt. This stamp was required on all mail during Jan.-July.

Type of 1943, Redrawn

1948-53   **Litho.**   **Perf. 10**

RA5	PT3	⅛g rose brn ('53)	20.00	.30
c.	Perf. 11x10		27.50	3.00

> **Catalogue values for unused stamps in this section, from this point to the end of the section, are for Never Hinged items.**

1950   **Rouletted**

RA6	PT3	⅛g red brown	5.50	.30
a.	⅛g rose		7.25	.30
b.	⅛g carmine		9.00	.30

All lines in lithographed design considerably finer; some shading in center eliminated.

Type of 1943

1955-56   **Photo.**   **Perf. 11**

RA7	PT3	⅛g rose car	8.00	.30
RA8	PT3	¼g car rose ('56)	4.75	.30

The tax on postal matter was discontinued in May, 1964.

Coat of Arms, Waves and View — PT5

Wmk. 361

1974, Oct.   **Litho.**   **Perf. 14**

RA9	PT5	1r blue & multi	200.00	

Obligatory on all mailed entries in a government television contest during month of Ramadan in 1974 and 1975. The tax aided a benevolent society.

SCHLESWIG

ˈshles-ˌwig

LOCATION — In the northern part of the former Schleswig-Holstein Province, in northern Germany.

Schleswig was divided into North and South Schleswig after the Versailles Treaty, and plebiscites were held in 1920. North Schleswig (Zone 1) voted to join Denmark, South Schleswig to stay German.

100 Pfennig = 1 Mark
100 Ore = 1 Krone

Watermark

Wmk. 114 —
Multiple Crosses

Plebiscite Issue

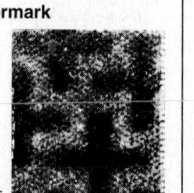

Arms — A11

View of
Schleswig
A12

Perf. 14x15

1920, Jan. 25   **Typo.**   **Wmk. 114**

1	A11	2½pf gray	.25	.80
2	A11	5pf green	.25	.80
3	A11	7½pf yellow brown	.25	.80
4	A11	10pf deep rose	.25	.80
5	A11	15pf red violet	.25	.80
6	A11	20pf deep blue	.25	.80
7	A11	25pf orange	.35	.80
8	A11	35pf brown	.45	1.00
9	A11	40pf violet	.35	.80
10	A11	75pf greenish blue	.45	.80
11	A12	1m dark brown	.45	.80
12	A12	2m deep blue	.70	1.20
13	A12	5m green	1.50	1.60
14	A12	10m red	2.75	3.25
		Nos. 1-14 (14)	8.50	15.05
		Set, never hinged	40.00	

The colored areas of type A11 are white, and the white areas are colored, on Nos. 7-10.

Types of 1920
Overprinted in Blue

1920, May 20

15	A11	1o dark gray	.25	2.40
16	A11	5o green	.25	1.60
17	A11	7o yellow brn	.25	1.60
18	A11	10o rose red	.25	1.60
19	A11	15o lilac rose	.25	2.40
20	A11	20o dark blue	.25	2.75
21	A11	25o orange	.25	8.00
22	A11	35o brown	.85	14.50
23	A11	40o violet	.25	4.75
24	A11	75o greenish blue	.45	8.00
25	A12	1k dark brown	.65	13.00
26	A12	2k deep blue	7.00	47.50
27	A12	5k green	3.50	47.50
28	A12	10k red	8.00	87.50
		Nos. 15-28 (14)	22.45	243.10
		Set, never hinged	165.00	

OFFICIAL STAMPS

Nos. 1-14 Overprinted

1920   **Wmk. 114**   **Perf. 14x15**

O1	A11	2½pf gray	65.00	92.50
O2	A11	5pf green	65.00	110.00
O3	A11	7½pf yellow brn	65.00	92.50
O4	A11	10pf deep rose	65.00	120.00
O5	A11	15pf red violet	42.50	60.00
O6	A11	20pf dp blue	65.00	67.50
a.		Double overprint	1,500.	
O7	A11	25pf orange	125.00	175.00
a.		Inverted overprint	1,050.	
O8	A11	35pf brown	125.00	175.00
O9	A11	40pf violet	110.00	100.00
O10	A11	75pf grnsh blue	125.00	250.00
O11	A12	1m dark brown	125.00	250.00
O12	A12	2m deep blue	185.00	275.00
O13	A12	5m green	275.00	425.00
O14	A12	10m red	500.00	625.00
		Nos. O1-O14 (14)	1,937.	2,817.
		Set, never hinged	3,800.	

The letters "C.I.S." are the initials of "Commission Interalliée Slesvig," under whose auspices the plebiscites took place.
Counterfeit overprints exist.

SENEGAL

ˌse-ni-ˈgäl

LOCATION — West coast of Africa, bordering on the Atlantic Ocean
GOVT. — Republic
AREA — 76,000 sq. mi.
POP. — 10,051,930 (1999 est.)
CAPITAL — Dakar

The former French colony of Senegal became part of French West Africa in 1943. The Republic of Senegal was established Nov. 25, 1958. From Apr. 4, 1959, to June 20, 1960, the Republic of Senegal and the Sudanese Republic together formed the Mali Federation. After its breakup, Senegal resumed issuing its own stamps in 1960.

100 Centimes = 1 Franc

> Catalogue values for unused stamps in this country are for Never Hinged items, beginning with Scott 193 in the regular postage section, Scott B16 in the the semi-postal section, Scott C26 in the airpost section, Scott CB2 in the airpost semi-postal section, Scott J32 in the postage due section, and Scott O1 in the official section.

French Colonies Nos. 48, 49, 51, 52, 55, Type A9, Surcharged

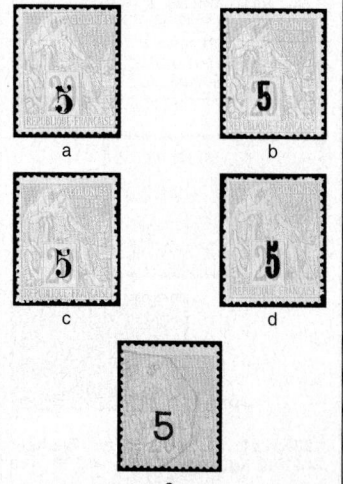

1887   **Unwmk.**   **Perf. 14x13½**
Black Surcharge

1	(a)	5c on 20c red, grn	210.00	210.00
a.		Double surcharge	500.00	
2	(b)	5c on 20c red, grn	375.00	375.00
3	(c)	5c on 20c red, grn	1,250.	1,250.
4	(d)	5c on 20c red, grn	260.00	260.00
5	(e)	5c on 20c red, grn	475.00	475.00
6	(a)	5c on 30c brn, bis	325.00	325.00
7	(b)	5c on 30c brn, bis	1,400.	1,400.
8	(d)	5c on 30c brn, bis	475.00	475.00
		Nos. 1-8 (8)	4,770.	4,770.

See Madagascar #6-7 for stamps with surcharge like "d" on 10c and 25c stamps.

9	(f)	10c on 4c cl, lav	160.00	160.00
10	(g)	10c on 4c cl, lav	240.00	240.00
11	(h)	10c on 4c cl, lav	120.00	120.00
12	(i)	10c on 4c cl, lav	120.00	120.00
a.		"1" without top stroke		
13	(f)	10c on 20c red, grn	725.00	725.00
14	(g)	10c on 20c red, grn	750.00	750.00
15	(h)	10c on 20c red, grn	650.00	650.00
16	(i)	10c on 20c red, grn	3,750.	3,750.
17	(j)	10c on 20c red, grn	750.00	750.00
18	(k)	10c on 20c red, grn	2,500.	2,500.
19	(l)	10c on 20c red, grn	750.00	750.00
20	(m)	10c on 20c red, grn	750.00	750.00

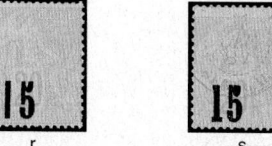

v

w

21	(n)	15c on 20c red, grn	130.00	130.00
22	(o)	15c on 20c red, grn	110.00	110.00
23	(p)	15c on 20c red, grn	87.50	87.50
24	(q)	15c on 20c red, grn	160.00	160.00
25	(r)	15c on 20c red, grn	100.00	100.00
26	(s)	15c on 20c red, grn	100.00	100.00
27	(t)	15c on 20c red, grn	260.00	260.00
28	(u)	15c on 20c red, grn	87.50	87.50
29	(v)	15c on 20c red, grn	120.00	120.00
30	(w)	15c on 20c red, grn	425.00	425.00
		Nos. 21-30 (10)	1,580.	1,580.

Counterfeits exist of Nos. 1-34.

French Colonies Stamps of 1881-86 Surcharged

1892   **Black Surcharge**

31	A9	75c on 15c blue	450.00	200.00
a.		"SENEGAL" double		950.00
32	A9	1fr on 5c grn, grnsh	450.00	200.00
a.		"SENEGAL" double		14,750.
b.		"SENEGAL" omitted		2,800.
c.		"1F" double		325.00

"SENEGAL" in Red

33	A9	75c on 15c blue	15,250.	5,500.
34	A9	1fr on 5c grn, grnsh	6,500.	1,600.

Navigation and
Commerce — A24

Name of Colony in Blue or Carmine

1892-1900   **Typo.**   **Perf. 14x13½**

35	A24	1c blk, lil bl	1.60	1.20
36	A24	2c brn, buff	2.25	2.25
37	A24	4c claret, lav	3.50	1.75
38	A24	5c grn, grnsh	3.50	2.25
39	A24	5c yel grn ('00)	3.50	1.40
40	A24	10c blk, lav	10.00	5.50
41	A24	10c red ('00)	7.00	1.40
42	A24	15c bl, quadrille paper	15.00	2.25
43	A24	15c gray ('00)	7.25	2.50
44	A24	20c red, grn	10.50	7.00
45	A24	25c blk, rose	17.50	7.25
46	A24	25c blue ('00)	40.00	35.00
47	A24	30c brn, bis	17.50	10.00
48	A24	40c red, straw	25.00	21.00
49	A24	50c car, rose	45.00	30.00
50	A24	50c brn, az ('00)	50.00	45.00
51	A24	75c vio, org	22.50	17.50
52	A24	1fr brnz grn, straw	25.00	21.00
		Nos. 35-52 (18)	306.60	214.25

Perf. 13½x14 stamps are counterfeits.
For surcharges see Nos. 53-56, 73-78.

Stamps of 1892 Surcharged

1903

53	A24	5c on 40c red, straw	17.50	17.50
54	A24	10c on 50c car, rose	25.00	25.00
55	A24	10c on 75c vio, org	25.00	25.00
56	A24	10c on 1fr brnz grn, straw	80.00	80.00
		Nos. 53-56 (4)	147.50	147.50

General Louis Faidherbe A25

Oil Palms — A26

Dr. Noel Eugène Ballay A27

1906 **Typo.**

"SÉNÉGAL" in Red or Blue

57	A25	1c slate	1.40	1.40
a.		"SENEGAL" omitted	140.00	140.00
58	A25	2c choc (R)	1.40	1.40
58A	A25	2c choc (Bl)	2.75	2.10
59	A25	4c choc, *gray bl*	2.75	2.10
60	A25	5c green	2.75	1.20
a.		"SENEGAL" omitted		130.00
61	A25	10c car (Bl)	14.00	1.20
a.		"SENEGAL" omitted	450.00	450.00
62	A25	15c violet	7.00	3.50
63	A26	20c blk, *az*	10.50	4.25
64	A26	25c bl, *pnksh*	3.50	2.75
65	A26	30c choc, *pnksh*	10.50	5.50
66	A26	35c blk, *yellow*	27.50	2.75
a.		"SENEGAL" double	210.00	*225.00*
67	A26	40c car, *az* (Bl)	14.00	6.25
67A	A26	45c choc, *grnsh*	25.00	15.00
68	A26	50c dp violet	14.00	6.25
69	A26	75c bl, *org*	10.50	7.75
70	A27	1fr blk, *azure*	27.50	27.50
71	A27	2fr blue, *pink*	35.00	35.00
72	A27	5fr car, *straw* (Bl)	72.50	62.50
		Nos. 57-72 (18)	282.55	188.40

Stamps of 1892-1900 Surcharged in Carmine or Black

1912

73	A24	5c on 15c gray (C)	1.10	1.10
74	A24	5c on 20c red, *grn*	2.10	*2.10*
75	A24	5c on 30c brn, *bis* (C)	1.40	1.40
76	A24	10c on 40c red, *straw*	1.75	1.75
77	A24	10c on 50c car, *rose*	4.25	*5.00*
78	A24	10c on 75c vio, *org*	7.00	*7.75*
		Nos. 73-78 (6)	17.60	19.10

Two spacings between the surcharged numerals found on Nos. 73 to 78. For detailed listings, see the *Scott Classic Specialized Catalogue of Stamps and Covers.*

Senegalese Preparing Food A28

1914-33 **Typo.**

79	A28	1c ol brn & vio	.25	.25
80	A28	2c black & blue	.25	.30
81	A28	4c gray & brn	.25	.25
82	A28	5c yel grn & bl grn	.35	.25
83	A28	5c blk & rose ('22)	.25	.25
a.		Center double	300.00	
84	A28	10c org red & rose	1.45	.25
85	A28	10c yel grn & bl grn ('22)	.35	.30
86	A28	10c red brn & bl ('25)	.35	.35
87	A28	15c red org & brn vio ('17)	.35	.35
88	A28	20c choc & blk	.35	.30
89	A28	20c grn & bl grn ('26)	.35	.35
90	A28	20c db & lt bl ('27)	.70	.70
91	A28	25c ultra & bl	1.10	.45
92	A28	25c red & blk ('22)	.70	.30
93	A28	30c black & rose	.75	.35
94	A28	30c red org & rose ('22)	.70	.30
95	A28	30c gray & bl ('26)	.35	.35
96	A28	30c dl grn & dp grn ('28)	.70	.70
97	A28	35c orange & vio	.70	.45
98	A28	40c violet & grn	1.10	.45
99	A28	45c bl & ol brn	1.75	1.40
100	A28	45c rose & bl ('22)	1.10	.45
101	A28	45c rose & ver ('25)	.70	.70
102	A28	45c ol brn & org ('28)	3.50	2.75
103	A28	50c vio brn & bl	1.75	1.10
104	A28	50c ultra & bl ('22)	2.75	1.75
105	A28	50c red org & grn ('26)	.70	.35
106	A28	60c vio, *pnksh* ('26)	.70	.35
107	A28	65c rose red & dp grn ('28)	2.10	1.40
108	A28	75c gray & rose	1.40	.70
109	A28	75c dk bl & lt bl ('25)	1.10	1.10
110	A28	75c rose & gray bl ('26)	2.10	1.05
111	A28	90c brn red & rose ('30)	5.00	5.00
112	A28	1fr violet & blk	1.40	.70
113	A28	1fr blue ('26)	1.05	1.05
114	A28	1fr blk & gray bl ('26)	1.75	1.05
115	A28	1.10fr bl grn & blk ('28)	4.25	*4.50*
116	A28	1.25fr dp grn & dp org ('33)	1.40	1.40
117	A28	1.50fr dk bl & bl ('30)	3.25	3.25
118	A28	1.75fr dk brn & Prus bl ('33)	7.25	1.40
119	A28	2fr carmine & bl	3.50	2.50
120	A28	2fr lt bl & brn ('22)	2.75	.90
121	A28	3fr red vio ('30)	3.50	2.10
122	A28	5fr green & vio	5.00	1.75
		Nos. 79-122 (44)	71.10	45.95

Nos. 79, 82, 84 and 97 are on both ordinary and chalky paper.

For surcharges see Nos. 123-137, B1-B2.

No. 108 and Type of 1914 Srchd.

1922-25

123	A28	60c on 75c vio, *pnksh*	1.40	.90
a.		Double surcharge	125.00	
124	A28	65c on 15c red org & dl vio ('25)	1.40	1.40
125	A28	85c on 15c red org & dl vio ('25)	1.40	1.40
126	A28	85c on 75c ('25)	1.40	1.40

No. 87 Srchd. in Various Colors

1922

127	A28	1c on 15c (Bk)	.70	.70
128	A28	2c on 15c (Bl)	.70	.70
129	A28	4c on 15c (G)	.70	.70
130	A28	5c on 15c (R)	.70	.70
		Nos. 123-130 (8)	8.40	7.90

Stamps and Type of 1914 Surcharged with New Value and Bars in Black or Red

1924-27

131	A28	25c on 5fr grn & vio	.85	.85
132	A28	90c on 75c brn red & cer ('27)	1.40	1.10
a.		Double surcharge	125.00	
133	A28	1.25fr on 1fr bl & lt bl (R) ('26)	1.40	1.10
134	A28	1.50fr on 1fr dk bl & ultra ('27)	1.40	1.10
135	A28	3fr on 5fr mag & ol brn ('27)	3.50	2.50
136	A28	10fr on 5fr dk bl & red org ('27)	7.75	3.50
137	A28	20fr on 5fr vio & ol bis ('27)	7.00	7.00
		Nos. 131-137 (7)	23.30	17.15

Common Design Types pictured following the introduction

Colonial Exposition Issue

Common Design Types

Name of Country Typographed in Black

1931 **Engr.** ***Perf. 12½***

138	CD70	40c deep green	5.00	5.00
139	CD71	50c violet	5.00	5.00
140	CD72	90c red orange	5.00	5.00
a.		"SENEGAL" double	175.00	
141	CD73	1.50fr dull blue	5.00	5.00
		Nos. 138-141 (4)	20.00	20.00

Faidherbe Bridge, St. Louis A29

Diourbel Mosque A30

1935-40 ***Perf. 12½x12***

142	A29	1c violet blue	.25	.25
143	A29	2c brown	.25	.25
144	A29	3c violet ('40)	.25	.25
145	A29	4c gray blue	.25	.25
146	A29	5c orange red	.25	.25
147	A29	10c violet	.25	.25
148	A29	15c black	.25	.25
149	A29	20c dk carmine	.30	.25
150	A29	25c black brn	.30	.25
151	A29	30c green	.30	.30
152	A29	40c rose lake	.35	.30
153	A29	45c dk blue grn	.35	.30
154	A30	50c red orange	.35	.25
155	A30	60c violet ('40)	.25	.30
156	A30	65c dk violet	.35	.30
157	A30	70c red brn ('40)	.70	.70
158	A30	75c brown	.70	.55
159	A30	90c rose car	2.10	1.40
160	A30	1fr violet	10.50	2.50
161	A30	1.25fr redsh brn	1.40	1.10
162	A30	1.25fr rose car ('39)	.85	.85
163	A30	1.40fr dk bl grn ('40)	.70	.85
164	A30	1.50fr dk blue	.35	.35
165	A30	1.60fr pck bl ('40)	.70	.85
166	A30	1.75fr dk blue grn	.35	.35
167	A30	2fr blue	.70	.35
168	A30	3fr green	.70	.45
169	A30	5fr black brn	.70	.70
170	A30	10fr rose lake	1.75	1.10
171	A30	20fr grnsh slate	1.75	1.10
		Nos. 142-171 (30)	28.25	17.20

Nos. 143, 148 and 156 surcharged with new values are listed under French West Africa.

For surcharges see Nos. B9, B11-B12.

Paris International Exposition Issue

Common Design Types

1937 ***Perf. 13***

172	CD74	20c deep violet	1.75	1.75
a.		Sénégal omitted	90.00	*100.00*
173	CD75	30c dark green	1.75	1.75
174	CD76	40c car rose	1.75	1.75
175	CD77	50c dark brown	1.75	1.40
176	CD78	90c red	1.75	1.40
177	CD79	1.50fr ultra	1.75	1.75
		Nos. 172-177 (6)	10.50	9.80

Colonial Arts Exhibition Issue

Souvenir Sheet

Common Design Type

1937 **Unwmk.** ***Imperf.***

178	CD76	3fr rose violet	10.50	14.00
a.		Inscriptions inverted	1,400.	

Senegalese Woman — A31

1938-40 ***Perf. 12x12½, 12½x12***

179	A31	35c green	.35	.55
180	A31	55c chocolate	.70	.55
181	A31	80c violet	1.10	.65
182	A31	90c lt rose vio ('39)	.70	.70
183	A31	1fr car lake	1.75	1.10
184	A31	1fr cop brn ('40)	.35	.65
185	A31	1.75fr ultra	1.10	.70
186	A31	2.25fr ultra ('39)	.90	.90
187	A31	2.50fr black ('40)	1.40	1.40
		Nos. 179-187 (9)	8.35	7.20

For surcharge see No. B10.

Caillié Issue

Common Design Type

1939 **Engr.** ***Perf. 12½x12***

188	CD81	90c org brn & org	.35	.70
189	CD81	2fr brt vio	.35	1.10
190	CD81	2.25fr ultra & dk bl	.35	1.10
		Nos. 188-190 (3)	1.05	2.90
		Set, never hinged	2.40	

For No. 188 surcharged 20fr and 50fr, see French West Africa.

New York World's Fair Issue

Common Design Type

1939 ***Perf. 12½x12***

191	CD82	1.25fr car lake	.70	1.40
192	CD82	2.25fr ultra	.70	1.40
		Set, never hinged	2.10	

Catalogue values for unused stamps in this section, from this point to the end of the section, are for Never Hinged items.

Diourbel Mosque and Marshal Pétain A32

1941 **Engr.**

193	A32	1fr green	.70	
194	A32	2.50fr blue	.70	

Nos. 193-194 were issued by the Vichy government in France, but were not placed on sale in Senegal.

For surcharges, see Nos. B15A-B15B.

Types of 1935-38 Without "RF"

1943-44 ***Perf. 12½***

194A	A29	40c rose lake	1.00	
194B	A31	1fr red brn & dk blue	1.40	
194C	A30	1.50fr bl grn & blk	.70	
194D	A30	2fr Prus blue & red	1.10	
194E	A30	3fr grn & red vio	1.40	
194F	A30	5fr dp ol brn & lake	1.40	
194G	A30	10fr rose lake & blue	1.40	
194H	A30	20fr gray bl & red	3.50	
		Nos. 194A-194H (8)	11.90	

Nos. 194A-194H were issued by the Vichy government in France, but were not placed on sale in Senegal.

See French West Africa No. 69 for additional stamp inscribed "Senegal" and "Afrique Occidentale Francaise."

Republic

Roan Antelope — A33

Animals: 10fr, Savannah buffalo, horiz. 15fr, Wart hog. 20fr, Giant eland. 25fr, Bushbuck, horiz. 85fr, Defassa waterbuck.

1960 **Unwmk.** **Engr.** ***Perf. 13***

195	A33	5fr brn, grn & claret	.30	.25
196	A33	10fr grn & brn	.55	.25
197	A33	15fr blk, claret & org brn	.65	.30
198	A33	20fr brn, grn, ocher & sal	.85	.40

199 A33 25fr brn, lt grn & org   1.40   .60
200 A33 85fr brn, grn, olive & bis 3.25 1.40
       Nos. 195-200 (6)   7.00 3.20

Imperforates
Most Senegal stamps from 1960 onward exist imperforate in issued and trial colors, and also in small presentation sheets in issued colors.

Allegory of Independent State — A34

1961, Apr. 4
201 A34 25fr bl, choc & grn   .80 .25

Independence Day, Apr. 4.

Wrestling A35

1fr, Pirogues racing. 2fr, Horse race. 30fr, Male tribal dance. 45fr, Lion game.

1961, Sept. 30   Perf. 13
202 A35 50c ol, bl & choc   .25 .25
203 A35 1fr grn, bl & maroon   .25 .25
204 A35 2fr ultra, bis & sepia .70 .25
205 A35 30fr carmine & claret 1.10 .55
206 A35 30fr indigo & brn org 1.75 .65
       Nos. 202-206 (5)   4.05 1.95

UN Headquarters, New York and Flag — A36

1962, Jan. 6   Engr.   Perf. 13
207 A36 10fr grn, ocher & car   .35 .25
208 A36 30fr car, ocher & grn   .65 .40
209 A36 85fr grn, ocher & car 2.25 .65
       Nos. 207-209 (3)   3.25 1.30

1st anniv. of Senegal's admission to the United Nations, Sept. 28, 1960.

Map of Africa, ITU Emblem and Man with Telephone A37

1962, Jan. 22 Photo. Perf. 12½x12
210 A37 25fr blk, grn, red & ocher .80 .30

Meeting of the Commission for the Africa Plan of the ITU, Dakar.

African and Malgache Union Issue
Common Design Type

1962, Sept. 8   Unwmk.
211 CD110 30fr grn, bluish grn, red & gold   .80 .50

Boxing — A38

15fr, Diving, horiz. 20fr, High jump, horiz. 25fr, Soccer. 30fr, Basketball. 85fr, Running.

1963, Apr. 11   Engr.   Perf. 13
Athletes in Dark Brown
212 A38 10fr ver & emer   .30 .25
213 A38 15fr dk bl & bis   .40 .25
214 A38 20fr ver & dk bl   .45 .25
215 A38 30fr grn & dk bl   .65 .25
216 A38 30fr ver & grn   1.25 .50
217 A38 85fr vio bl   2.75 1.10
       Nos. 212-217 (6)   5.80 2.60

Friendship Games, Dakar, Apr. 11-21.

UPU Monument, Bern A39

1963, June 14   Unwmk.   Perf. 13
218 A39 10fr grn & ver   .45 .25
219 A39 15fr dk bl & red brn .45 .25
220 A39 30fr red brn & dk bl 1.00 .40
       Nos. 218-220 (3)   1.90 .90

2nd anniv. of Senegal's admission to the UPU.

Charaxes Varanes — A40

Butterflies: 45fr, Papilio nireus. 50fr, Colotis danae. 85fr, Epiphora bauhiniae. 100fr, Junonia hierta. 500fr, Danaus chrysippus.

Butterflies in Natural Colors

1963, July 20 Photo. Perf. 12½x13
221 A40 30fr bl gray & blk   1.25   .50
222 A40 45fr org & blk   1.75   .75
223 A40 50fr brt yel & blk   2.00   .95
224 A40 85fr red & blk   4.50 1.25
225 A40 100fr bl & blk   5.25 2.00
226 A40 500fr emer & blk   18.00 6.50
       Nos. 221-226 (6)   32.75 11.95

Prof. Gaston Berger (1896-1960), Philosopher, and Owl — A41

1963, Nov. 13   Perf. 12½x12
227 A41 25fr multi   .75 .30

Scales, Globe, Flag and UNESCO Emblem A42

1963, Dec. 10
228 A42 60fr multi   1.25 .50

15th anniv. of the Universal Declaration of Human Rights.

Flag, Mother and Child — A43

1963, Dec. 21   Perf. 12x12½
229 A43 25fr multi   .80 .30

Issued for the Senegalese Red Cross.

Dredging of Titanium-bearing Sand — A44

Designs: 10fr, Titanium extraction works. 15fr, Cement works at Rufisque. 20fr, Phosphate quarry at Pallo. 25fr, Extraction of phosphate ore at Taiba. 85fr, Mineral dock, Dakar.

1964, July 4   Engr.   Perf. 13
230 A44 5fr grnsh bl, car & dk brn   .25 .25
231 A44 10fr ocher, grn & ind   .25 .25
232 A44 15fr dk bl, brt grn & dk brn .35 .25
233 A44 20fr ultra, ol & pur   .55 .25
234 A44 25fr dk bl, yel & blk   .70 .25
235 A44 85fr bl, red & brn   2.00 .85
       Nos. 230-235 (6)   4.10 2.10

Cooperation Issue
Common Design Type

1964, Nov. 7   Engr.   Perf. 13
236 CD119 100fr dk grn, dk brn & car 1.60 .85

St. Theresa's Church, Dakar A45

10fr, Mosque, Touba. 15fr, Mosque, Dakar, vert.

1964, Nov. 28   Unwmk.   Perf. 13
237 A45 5fr bl, grn & red brn   .25 .25
238 A45 10fr dk bl, ocher & blk .25 .25
239 A45 15fr brn, bl & sl grn   .90 .25
       Nos. 237-239 (3)   1.40 .75

Leprosy Examination — A46

Leprosarium, Peycouk Village — A47

1965, Jan. 30   Engr.   Perf. 13
240 A46 20fr brn red, grn & blk .50 .30
241 A47 65fr org, dk bl & grn   1.50 .55

Issued to publicize the fight against leprosy.

Upper Casamance Region — A48

Views: 30fr, Sangalkam. 45fr, Forest along Senegal River.

1965, Feb. 27   Unwmk.   Perf. 13
242 A48 25fr red brn, sl bl & grn .55 .25
243 A48 30fr indigo & lt brn   .65 .30
244 A48 45fr yel grn, red brn & dk brn 1.40 .50
       Nos. 242-244,C41 (4)   5.10 2.05

Abdoulaye Seck — A49

General Post Office, Dakar A50

1965, Apr. 24   Unwmk.   Perf. 13
245 A49 10fr dk brn & blk   .35 .25
246 A50 15fr brn & dk sl grn   .45 .25

Berthon-Ader Telephone — A51

Designs: 60fr, Cable laying ship "Alsace." 85fr, Picard's cable relay for submarine telegraph.

1965, May 17   Engr.
247 A51 50fr bl grn & org brn   .65 .30
248 A51 60fr mag & dk bl   1.25 .45
249 A51 85fr ver, bl & red brn 1.40 .50
       Nos. 247-249 (3)   3.30 1.25

ITU, centenary.

Plowing with Ox Team A52

Designs: 60fr, Harvesting millet, vert. 85fr, Men working in rice field.

1965, July 3   Unwmk.   Perf. 13
250 A52 25fr dk ol grn, brn & pur .55 .30
251 A52 60fr ind, sl grn & dk brn 1.25 .50
252 A52 85fr dp car, sl grn & brt grn 1.75 .55
       Nos. 250-252 (3)   3.55 1.35

Gorée Sailboat A53

Designs: 20fr, Large Seumbediou canoe. 30fr, Fadiouth one-man canoe. 45fr, One-man canoe on Senegal River.

1965, Aug. 7   Photo.   Perf. 12½x13
253	A53	10fr multi	.25	.25
254	A53	20fr multi	.55	.25
255	A53	30fr multi	1.00	.30
256	A53	45fr multi	1.75	.60
		Nos. 253-256 (4)	3.55	1.40

Cashew — A54

1965   Photo.   Perf. 12½
257	A54	10fr shown	.25	.25
258	A54	15fr Papaya	.45	.25
259	A54	20fr Mango	.65	.25
260	A54	30fr Peanuts	1.25	.30
		Nos. 257-260 (4)	2.60	1.10

Issued: 10fr, 15fr, 20fr, Nov. 6. 30fr, Dec. 18.

"Elegant Man" — A55

Dolls of Gorée: 2fr, "Elegant Woman." 3fr, Woman peddling fruit. 4fr, Woman pounding grain.

1966, Jan. 22   Engr.   Perf. 13
261	A55	1fr brn, rose car & ultra	.25	.25
262	A55	2fr brn, bl & org	.25	.25
263	A55	3fr brn, red & bl	.25	.25
264	A55	4fr brn, lil & emer	.25	.25
		Nos. 261-264 (4)	1.00	1.00

Drummer and Map of Africa — A56

15fr, Sculpture; mother & child. #267, Music; stringed instrument. 75fr, Dance; carved antelope headpiece (Bambara). 90fr, Ideogram.

1966
265	A56	15fr dk red brn, bl & ocher	.35	.25
266	A56	30fr brn, red & grn	.70	.25
267	A56	30fr dk red brn, bl & yel	1.10	.60
268	A56	75fr dk red brn, bl & blk	1.75	.60
269	A56	90fr dk red brn, org & sl grn	2.10	.65
a.		Souv. sheet of 4, #265, 267-269	6.25	6.25
		Nos. 265-269 (5)	6.00	2.35

Intl. Negro Arts Festival, Dakar, Apr. 1-24.
Issued: #266, 2/5; others, 4/2. See #364.

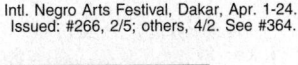

Fish — A57

1966, Feb. 26   Photo.   Perf. 12½x13
270	A57	20fr Tuna	.50	.25
271	A57	30fr Merou	.60	.30
272	A57	50fr Girella	1.25	.65
273	A57	100fr Parrot fish	2.75	.85
		Nos. 270-273 (4)	5.10	2.05

Arms of Senegal — A58

1966, July 2   Litho.   Perf. 13x12½
274	A58	30fr multi	.80	.25

Flowers — A59

1966, Nov. 19   Photo.   Perf. 11½
275	A59	45fr Mexican poppy	1.25	.25
276	A59	55fr Mimosa	1.25	.35
277	A59	60fr Haemanthus	1.60	.45
278	A59	90fr Baobab	2.10	.65
		Nos. 275-278 (4)	6.20	1.70

Harbor, Gorée Island A60

Designs: 25fr, S.S. France in roadstead, Dakar and seagulls. 30fr, Hotel and tourist village, N'Gor. 50fr, Hotel and bay, N'Gor.

1966, Dec. 25   Engr.   Perf. 13
279	A60	20fr mar & vio bl	.25	.25
280	A60	25fr red, grn & blk	2.00	.30
281	A60	30fr dk red & dp bl	.40	.25
282	A60	50fr brn, sl grn & emer	.65	.30
		Nos. 279-282 (4)	3.30	1.10

Laying Urban Water Pipes A61

Symbolic Water Cycle — A62

20fr, Cattle at water trough. 50fr, Village well.

1967, Mar. 25   Engr.   Perf. 13
283	A61	10fr org brn, grn & dk bl	.25	.25
284	A61	20fr brn, brt bl & org brn	.65	.25

Typo.
Perf. 13x14
285	A62	30fr sky bl, blk & org	.70	.25

Engr.
Perf. 13
286	A62	50fr brn red, brt bl & bis	1.50	.35
		Nos. 283-286 (4)	3.10	1.10

Intl. Hydrological Decade (UNESCO), 1965-74.

Lions Emblem A63

1967, May 27   Photo.   Perf. 12½x13
287	A63	30fr lt ultra & multi	1.00	.40

50th anniversary of Lions International.

Blaise Diagne A64

1967, June 10   Engr.   Perf. 13
288	A64	30fr ocher, sl grn & dk red brn	.80	.30

Blaise Diagne (1872-1934), member of French Chamber of Deputies and Colonial Minister.
For surcharge see No. 380.

City Hall and Arms, Dakar A65

1967, June 10
289	A65	90fr bl, dk grn & blk	1.75	.50

Eagle and Antelope Carvings — A66

150fr, Flags, maple leaf and EXPO '67 emblem.

1967, Sept. 2   Photo.   Perf. 13x12½
290	A66	90fr red & blk	2.00	.50
291	A66	150fr red & multi	2.50	.80

EXPO '67 Intl. Exhib., Montreal, 4/28-10/27.

International Tourist Year Emblem — A67

Tourist Photographing Hippopotamus and Siminti Hotel — A68

1967, Oct. 7   Typo.   Perf. 14x13
292	A67	50fr blk & bl	.90	.40

Perf. 13
Engr.
293	A68	100fr blk, sl grn & ocher	3.50	1.10

International Tourist Year.

Monetary Union Issue
Common Design Type

1967, Nov. 4   Engr.   Perf. 13
294	CD125	30fr multi	.60	.25

West African Monetary Union, 5th anniv.

Lyre-shaped Megalith, Kaffrine — A69

70fr, Ancient covered bowl, Bandiala.

1967, Dec. 2   Engr.   Perf. 13
295	A69	30fr grn, grnsh bl & red brn	1.25	.35
296	A69	70fr red brn, ocher & brt bl	2.10	.85

Nurse Feeding Child — A70

1967, Dec. 23
297	A70	50fr bl grn, red & red brn	1.00	.40

Issued for the Senegalese Red Cross.

Human Rights Flame — A71

1968, Jan. 20   Photo.   Perf. 13x12½
298	A71	30fr brt grn & gold	.80	.30

International Human Rights Year.

Parliament, Dakar A72

1968, Apr. 16   Photo.   Perf. 12½x13
299	A72	30fr car rose	.80	.25

Inter-Parliamentary Union Meeting, Dakar.

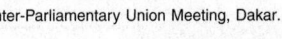

Pied Kingfisher — A73

Goose Barnacles A74

10fr, Green lobster. 15fr, African jacana. 20fr, Sea cicada. 35fr, Shrimp. 70fr, African anhinga.

1968-69   Photo.   Perf. 11½
Dated "1968" or (70fr) "1969"
Granite Paper
300	A73	5fr brn & multi	.35	.25
301	A74	10fr red & multi	.50	.25
302	A73	15fr yel & multi	.75	.35
303	A74	20fr ultra & multi	.90	.35
304	A74	35fr car rose & ol grn	2.25	.40

305 A73 70fr Prus bl & multi   2.75 1.00
306 A74 100fr yel grn & multi   6.50 1.75
   Nos. 300-306 (7)   14.00 4.35
   Issued: 5fr, 7/13/68; 15fr, 12/21/68; 70fr,
4/26/69; others 5/18/68. Nos. 300-306 exist as
tete-beche pairs. Value, set of pairs $30.
   See Nos. C53-C57.

Steer and Hypodermic Syringe — A75

1968, Aug. 17   Engr.   Perf. 13
307 A75 30fr dk grn, dp bl & brn
              red   1.00 .40
   Campaign against cattle plague.

Boy and WHO
Emblem — A76

1968, Nov. 16   Engr.   Perf. 13
308 A76 30fr blk, grn & car   .55 .30
309 A76 45fr red brn, grn & blk   1.10 .30
   WHO, 20th anniversary.

Bambara Antelope
Symbol — A77

   Design: 30fr, School of Medicine and Phar-
macology, Dakar, horiz.

1969, Jan. 13   Engr.   Perf. 13
310 A77 30fr emer, brt bl & ind   .80 .30
311 A77 50fr red, gray ol & bl grn   .90 .30
   6th Medical Meeting, Dakar, Jan. 13-18.

Panet, Camels
and Mogador-St.
Louis
Route — A78

1969, Feb. 15   Engr.   Perf. 13
312 A78 75fr ultra, Prus bl & brn   2.50 .80
   Leopold Panet (1819-1859), first explorer of
the Mauritanian Sahara.

ILO
Emblem
A79

1969, May 3   Photo.   Perf. 12½x13
313 A79 30fr blk & grnsh bl   .55 .25
314 A79 45fr blk & dp car   .80 .25
   ILO, 50th anniversary.

Arms of
Casamance — A80

   Design: 20fr, Arms of Gorée Island.

1969, July 26   Litho.   Perf. 13½
315 A80 15fr rose & multi   .25 .25
316 A80 20fr bl & multi   .75 .25

Development Bank Issue
Common Design Type
1969, Sept. 10   Engr.   Perf. 13
317 CD130 30fr gray, grn & ocher   .65 .25
318 CD130 45fr brn, grn & ocher   .90 .25

Mahatma
Gandhi — A81

1969, Oct. 2   Engr.   Perf. 13
319 A81 50fr multi   1.50 .35
   a.   Miniature sheet of 4   6.00 3.00
   Mohandas K. Gandhi (1869-1948), leader in
India's fight for independence.

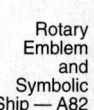

Rotary
Emblem
and
Symbolic
Ship — A82

1969, Nov. 29 Photo. Perf. 12½x13
320 A82 30fr ultra, yel & blk   .80 .30
   Dakar Rotary Club, 30th anniversary.

ASECNA Issue
Common Design Type
1969, Dec. 12   Engr.   Perf. 13
321 CD132 100fr dark gray   1.60 .50

Niokolo-Koba Campsite — A83

   Tourism: 20fr, Cape Skiring, Casamance.
35fr, Elephants at Niokolo-Koba National Park.
45fr, Millet granaries, pigs and boats, Fadiouth
Island.

1969, Dec. 27
322 A83 20fr bl, red brn & ol   .75 .25
323 A83 30fr bl, red brn & ocher   1.00 .25
324 A83 35fr grnsh bl, blk &
              ocher   4.00 .65
325 A83 45fr vio bl & hn brn   2.00 .55
   Nos. 322-325 (4)   7.75 1.70

Bottle-nosed
Dolphins — A84

1970, Feb. 21   Photo.   Perf. 12x12½
326 A84 50fr dl bl, blk & red   7.50 1.50

Lenin (1870-1924)
A85

1970, Apr. 22   Photo.   Perf. 11½
327 A85 30fr brn, buff & ver   2.50 .65
Souvenir Sheet
Perf. 12x11½
327A A85 50fr brn, buff & ver   4.00 1.75
   No. 327A contains one 32x48mm stamp.

UPU Headquarters Issue
Common Design Type
1970, May 20   Engr.   Perf. 13
328 CD133 30fr dk red, ind & dp
               cl   .55 .25
329 CD133 45fr dl brn, dk car &
               bl grn   1.00 .30

Textile Plant, Thies — A86

   Design: 45fr, Fertilizer plant, Dakar.

1970, Nov. 21   Engr.   Perf. 13
330 A86 30fr grn, brt bl & brn red   .65 .25
331 A86 45fr brn red & brt bl   1.00 .30
   Industrialization of Senegal.

Boy Scouts — A87

   Design: 100fr, Lord Baden-Powell, map of
Africa with Dakar, and fleur-de-lis.

1970, Dec. 11   Photo.   Perf. 11½
332 A87 30fr multi   .55 .25
333 A87 100fr multi   2.25 .60
   1st African Boy Scout Conf., Dakar, Dec.
11-14.

Three Heads and
Sun — A88

   Design: 40fr, African man and woman,
globe with map of Africa.

1970, Dec. 19   Engr.   Perf. 13
334 A88 25fr ultra, org & vio brn   .65 .25
335 A88 40fr brn ol, dk brn & org   1.00 .40
   International Education Year.

Senegal Arms — A89

1970-76   Photo.   Perf. 12
336 A89 30fr yel grn & multi   .50 .25
336A A89 35fr brt pink & multi
               ('71)   .50 .25
   b.   Bklt. pane of 10 ('72)   5.00
336C A89 50fr bl & multi ('75)   .50 .25
336D A89 65fr lil rose & multi
               ('76)   .50 .25
   Nos. 336-336D (4)   2.00 1.00
   The booklet pane has a control number in
the margin.
   See No. 654.

Refugees
and UN
Emblem
A90

1971, Jan. 16   Perf. 12½x12
337 A90 40fr ver, blk, yel & grn   1.00 .30
   High Commissioner for Refugees, 20th
anniversary. See No. C94.

Mare
"Mbayang"
A91

   Horses: 25fr, Mare Madjiguene. 100fr,
Stallion Pass. 125fr, Stallion Pepe.

1971   Photo.   Perf. 11½
338 A91 25fr multi   1.00 .50
339 A91 40fr multi   1.50 .65
340 A91 100fr multi   4.00 2.25
341 A91 125fr multi   5.25 1.90
   Nos. 338-341 (4)   11.75 5.30
   Improvements in horse breeding.
   For surcharge see No. 392.

UN Emblem,
Black and White
Children — A92

UN
Emblem,
Four Races
A93

Perf. 13x12½, 12½x11
1971, Mar. 21   Litho.
342 A92 30fr multi   .85 .35
343 A93 50fr multi   1.40 .60
   Intl. Year against Racial Discrimination.

Globe and
Telephone — A94

   Design: 40fr, Radar, satellite, orbits.

1971, May 17   Engr.   Perf. 13
344 A94 30fr pur, grn & brn   .45 .25
345 A94 40fr Prus bl, dk brn &
               red brn   1.10 .30
   3rd World Telecommunications Day.

Drummer (Hayashida) — A95

50fr, Dwarf Japanese quince and grape hyacinth. 65fr, Judo. 75fr, Mt. Fuji.

1971, Aug. 7   Photo.   Perf. 13½
346 A95 35fr lt ultra & multi   1.25   .30
347 A95 50fr yel & multi   1.50   .45
348 A95 65fr dp org & multi   2.25   .60
349 A95 75fr grn & multi   2.75   .95
       Nos. 346-349 (4)   7.75 2.30

13th Boy Scout World Jamboree, Asagiri Plain, Japan, Aug. 2-10.

Map of West Africa with Senegal, UNICEF Emblem A97

100fr, Nurse, children, UNICEF emblem.

1971, Oct. 30   Perf. 12½
352 A97 35fr dl bl, org & blk   .90   .35
353 A97 100fr multi   3.00   .65

UNICEF, 25th anniv.

Basketball and Games' Emblem — A98

40fr, Basketball. 75fr, Emblem.

1971, Dec. 24   Photo.   Perf. 13½x13
354 A98 35fr lt vio & multi   .70   .25
355 A98 40fr emer & multi   1.00   .30
356 A98 75fr ocher & multi   1.60   .65
       Nos. 354-356 (3)   3.30 1.20

6th African Basketball Championships, Dakar, Dec. 25, 1971-Jan. 2, 1972.

"The Exile of Albouri" — A99

Design: 40fr, "The Merchant of Venice."

1972, Mar. 25   Perf. 13x12½
357 A99 35fr dk red & multi   .55   .30
358 A99 40fr dk red & multi   .90   .30

Intl. Theater Day. See No. C112.

WHO Emblem and Heart A100

Design: 40fr, Physician with patient, WHO emblem and electrocardiogram.

1972, Apr. 7   Engr.   Perf. 13
359 A100 35fr brt bl & red brn   .50   .25
360 A100 40fr slate grn & brn   1.00   .25

"Your heart is your health," World Health Month.

Containment of the Desert, Environment Emblem — A101

1972, June 3   Photo.   Perf. 13x12½
361 A101 35fr multi   1.60   .60

UN Conference on Human Environment, Stockholm, June 5-16. See No. C113.

Tartarin Shooting the Lion — A102

Design: 100fr, Alphonse Daudet.

1972, June 24   Engr.   Perf. 13
362 A102 40fr brt grn, rose car
                & brn   2.00 1.10
363 A102 100fr Prus bl, bl & brn   3.00 1.10

Alphonse Daudet (1840-1897), French novelist, and centenary of the publication of his "Tartarin de Tarascon."

Souvenir Sheet

Stringed Instrument — A103

1972, July 1   Engr.   Perf. 11½
364 A103 150fr rose red   4.00 3.00

Belgica 72, Intl. Phil. Exhib., Brussels, June 24-July 9. No. 364 contains one stamp in design similar to No. 267.

Wrestling, Olympic Rings — A104

1972, July 22   Photo.   Perf. 14x13½
365 A104 15fr shown   .35   .25
366 A104 20fr 100-meter dash   .80   .25
367 A104 100fr Basketball   2.50   .50
368 A104 125fr Judo   3.00   .65
       Nos. 365-368 (4)   6.65 1.65

Souvenir Sheet
Perf. 13½x14½
369 A104 240fr Torchbearer and
                Munich   6.25 3.25

20th Olympic Games, Munich, 8/26-9/11.

Book Year Emblem, Children Reading A105

1972, Sept. 16   Photo.   Perf. 13
370 A105 50fr gray & multi   .90   .35

International Book Year.

Senegalese Fashion — A106

1972-76   Engr.
371 A106 25fr black   .35   .25
   a.   Booklet pane of 5   2.00
   b.   Booklet pane of 10   5.00
372 A106 40fr brt ultra   .50   .25
   a.   Booklet pane of 5   3.00
   b.   Booklet pane of 10   7.50
372C A106 60fr brt grn ('76)   .50   .25
372D A106 75fr lil rose   .50   .25
       Nos. 371-372D (4)   1.85 1.00

See Nos. 563-573, 1153-1164, 1249-1257D, 1345A-1345C.

Aleksander Pushkin — A107

1972, Oct. 28   Photo.   Perf. 11½
373 A107 100fr salmon & purple   3.00   .65

Aleksander Pushkin (1799-1837), Russian writer.

West African Monetary Union Issue
Common Design Type

Design: 40fr, African couple, city, village and commemorative coin.

1972, Nov. 2   Engr.   Perf. 13
374 CD136 40fr ol brn, bl & gray   .50   .30

Amphicra-sphedum Murrayanum A108

Marine Life: 10fr, Pterocanium tricolpum. 15fr, Ceratospyris polygona. 20fr, Cortiniscus typicus. 30fr, Theopera cortina.

1972-73   Perf. 11½
**   Photo.**
375 A108 5fr multi   1.00   .35
376 A108 10fr multi   1.25   .40
377 A108 15fr multi   2.50   .40
378 A108 20fr multi   1.50   .40
379 A108 30fr multi   4.00   .50
     Nos. 375-379,C115-C118 (9)   34.75 7.30

Issued: #375-377, 11/25/72; #378-379, 7/28/73.

No. 288 Surcharged in Vermilion

1972, Dec. 9   Engr.   Perf. 13
380 A64 100fr on 30fr multi   2.25   .60

Blaise Diagne (1872-1934).

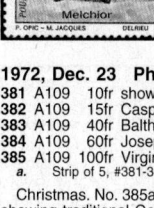

Melchior — A109

1972, Dec. 23   Photo.   Perf. 13x13½
381 A109 10fr shown   .25   .25
382 A109 15fr Caspar   .25   .25
383 A109 40fr Balthasar   .80   .35
384 A109 60fr Joseph   .85   .40
385 A109 100fr Virgin and Child   1.50   .65
   a.   Strip of 5, #381-385   5.25 2.00

Christmas. No. 385a has continuous design, showing traditional Gorée dolls.

Black and White Men Carrying Emblem — A110

Europafrica Issue
1973, Jan. 20   Engr.   Perf. 13
386 A110 65fr blk & grn   1.40   .40

Earth Station, Gandoul A111

1973, May 17   Engr.   Perf. 13
387 A111 40fr multi   .80   .30

Phases of Solar Eclipse A112

Designs: 65fr, Moon between earth and sun casting shadow on earth. 150fr, Diagram of areas of partial and total eclipse, satellite in space.

1973, June 30   Photo.   Perf. 13x14
388 A112 35fr dk bl & multi   .75   .30
389 A112 65fr dk bl & multi   1.25   .45
390 A112 150fr dk bl & multi   2.75 1.00
       Nos. 388-390 (3)   4.75 1.75

Total solar eclipse over Africa, June 30.

Men Holding Torch over Africa — A113

1973, July 7   Perf. 12½x13
391 A113 75fr multi   1.00   .40

Org. for African Unity, 10th anniv.

No. 338 Srchd. with New Value, 2 Bars, and Ovptd. in Ultramarine "SECHERESSE / SOLIDARITE AFRICAINE"

1973, July 21   Photo.   Perf. 11½
392 A91 100fr on 25fr multi   2.25 .85
African solidarity in drought emergency.

African Postal Union Issue
Common Design Type

1973, Sept. 12   Engr.   Perf. 13
393 CD137 100fr dk grn, vio & dk
           red   1.60 .50

Child, Map of Senegal, WMO Emblem — A114

1973, Sept. 22
394 A114 50fr multi   .80 .35
Intl. meteorological cooperation, cent.

INTERPOL Headquarters, Paris — A115

1973, Oct. 6   Engr.   Perf. 13
395 A115 75fr ultra, bis & slate
           grn   1.60 .50
50th anniv. of Intl. Criminal Police Org.

Souvenir Sheet

John F. Kennedy (1917-1963) — A116

1973, Nov. 22   Engr.   Perf. 13
396 A116 150fr ultra   2.75 2.75

Amilcar Cabral — A117

1973, Dec. 15   Photo.   Perf. 12½x13
397 A117 75fr multi   1.25 .40
Cabral (1924-1973), leader of anti-Portuguese guerrilla movement in Portuguese Guinea.

Victorious Athletes and Flag — A118

1974, Apr. 6   Photo.   Perf. 12½x13
398 A118 35fr shown   .80 .25
399 A118 40fr Folk theater   .80 .25
National Youth Week.

Soccer Cup, Yugoslavia-Brazil Game, Our Lady's Church, Munich — A119

Soccer Cup and Games: 40fr, Australia-Germany (Fed. Rep.) and Belltower, Hamburg. 65fr, Netherlands-Uruguay and Tower, Hanover. 70fr, Zaire-Italy and Church, Stuttgart.

1974, June 29   Photo.   Perf. 13x14
400 A119 25fr car & multi   .35 .25
401 A119 40fr car & multi   .65 .25
402 A119 65fr car & multi   .90 .30
403 A119 70fr car & multi   1.50 .40
       Nos. 400-403 (4)   3.40 1.20
World Cup Soccer Championship, Munich, June 13-July 7.
For surcharge see No. 406.

UPU Emblem, Envelopes and Means of Transportation — A120

1974, Oct. 9   Engr.   Perf. 13
404 A120 100fr multi   3.00 .85
Centenary of Universal Postal Union.

Fair Emblem — A121

1974, Nov. 28   Engr.   Perf. 12½x13
405 A121 100fr bl, org & dk brn 1.75 .50
Dakar International Fair.

No. 401 Surcharged in Black on Gold

1975, Feb. 1   Photo.   Perf. 13x14
406 A119 200fr on 40fr multi   3.25 1.25
World Cup Soccer Championships, 1974, victory of German Federal Republic.

Pres. Senghor and King Baudouin — A122

1975, Feb. 28   Photo.   Perf. 13x13½
407 A122 65fr lil & dk bl   .80 .35
408 A122 100fr org & grn   2.00 .50
Visit of King Baudouin of Belgium.

ILO Emblem — A123

1975, Apr. 30   Photo.   Perf. 13½x13
409 A123 125fr multi   1.75 .50
International Labor Festival.

Globe, Stamp, Letters, España 75 Emblem — A124

1975, June 6   Engr.   Perf. 13
410 A124 55fr indigo, grn & red 1.25 .40
Espana 75 Intl. Phil. Exhib., Madrid, 4/4-13.

Apollo of Belvedere, Arphila 75 Emblem, Stamps — A125

1975, June 6
411 A125 95fr dk brn, brn & bis 2.25 .80
Arphila 75 International Philatelic Exhibition, Paris, June 6-16.

Professional Instruction — A126

1975, June 28   Engr.   Perf. 13
412 A126 85fr multi   1.25 .40

Dr. Albert Schweitzer (1875-1965), Medical Missionary, Lambarene Hospital — A127

1975, July 5
413 A127 85fr grn & vio brn   1.75 .65

Senegalese Soldier, Batallion Flag, Map of Sinai — A128

1975, July 10   Litho.   Perf. 12½
414 A128 100fr multi   1.75 .50
Senegalese Battalion of the UN' Sinai Service, 1973-74.

Women and Child — A129

55fr, Women pounding grain, vert.

1975, Oct. 18   Photo.   Perf. 13½
415 A129 55fr silver & multi   1.75 .35
416 A129 75fr silver & multi   2.25 .50
International Women's Year.

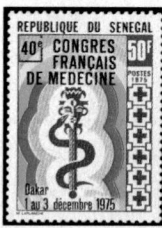

Staff of Aesculapius and African Mask — A130

1975, Dec. 1   Photo.   Perf. 12½x13
417 A130 50fr multi   .80 .30
40th French Medical Cong., Dakar, Dec. 1-3.

Map of Africa with Senegal and Namibia, UN Emblem A131

1976, Jan. 5   Photo.   Perf. 13
418 A131 125fr vio bl & multi   1.00 .35
International Human Rights and Namibia Conference, Dakar, Jan. 5-8.

Sailfish Fishing A132

200fr, Racing yachts & Oceanexpo 75 emblem.

1976, Jan. 28   Photo.   Perf. 13½x13
419 A132 140fr multi   5.25 1.50
420 A132 200fr multi   3.50 1.60
Oceanexpo 75, 1st Intl. Oceanographic Exhib., Okinawa, July 20, 1975-Jan. 1976.

Servals — A133

Designs: 3fr, Black-tailed godwits. 4fr, River hogs. 5fr, African fish eagles. No. 425, Okapis. No. 426, Sitatungas.

1976, Feb. 26   Photo.   Perf. 13
421	A133	2fr gold & multi	.30	.25
422	A133	3fr gold & multi	.65	.25
423	A133	4fr gold & multi	.30	.25
424	A133	5fr gold & multi	1.00	.50
425	A133	250fr gold & multi	6.25	1.75
426	A133	250fr gold & multi	6.25	1.75
a.		Strip of 2, #425-426 + label	14.50	
		Nos. 421-426 (6)	14.75	4.75

Basse Casamance National Park.
See Nos. 473-478.

A. G. Bell, Telephone, ITU
Emblem — A134

1976, Mar. 31   Litho.   Perf. 12½x13
427 A134 175fr multi   2.50 .80

Centenary of first telephone call by Alexander Graham Bell, Mar. 10, 1876.

Map of African French-speaking
Countries — A135

1976, Apr. 12   Litho.   Perf. 13½
428 A135 60fr yel grn & multi   .80 .30

Scientific and Cultural Meeting of the African Dental Association, Dakar, Apr. 12-17.

Family and
Graph
A136

1976, Apr. 26
429 A136 65fr multi   1.00 .40

1st population census in Senegal, Apr. 1976.

Thomas Jefferson and 13-star
Flag — A137

1976, June 19   Engr.   Perf. 13
430 A137 50fr bl, red & blk   1.00 .30

American Bicentennial.

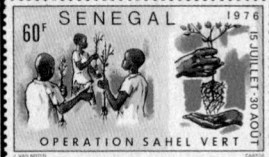

Planting Seedlings — A138

1976, Aug. 21   Litho.   Perf. 12
431 A138 60fr yel & multi   1.00 .25

Reclamation of Sahel region.

Campfire
A139

Jamboree
Emblem, Map of
Africa — A140

1976, Aug. 30   Litho.   Perf. 12½
432	A139	80fr multi	.90	.40
433	A140	100fr multi	1.75	.55

1st All Africa Scout Jamboree, Sherehills, Jos, Nigeria, Apr. 2-8, 1977.

A140a

1976 Summer Olympics,
Montreal — A140b

5fr, Swimming. 10fr, Weightlifting. 15fr, Hurdles, horiz. 20fr, Equestrian, horiz. 25fr, Steeplechase, horiz. 50fr, Wrestling, horiz. 60fr, Field hockey. 65fr, Track. 70fr, Women's gymnastics. 100fr, Cycling, horiz. 400fr, Boxing. 500fr, Judo.
No. 433M, Basketball. No. 433Q, Boxers, city skyline.

1976, Sept. 11   Litho.   Perf. 13½
433A	A140a	5fr multi	.25	.25
433B	A140a	10fr multi	.25	.25
433C	A140a	15fr multi	.25	.25
433D	A140a	20fr multi	.25	.25
433E	A140a	25fr multi	.35	.25
433F	A140a	50fr multi	.55	.25
433G	A140a	60fr multi	.70	.25
433H	A140a	65fr multi	.80	.25
433I	A140a	70fr multi	1.00	.40
433J	A140a	100fr multi	1.25	.50
433K	A140a	400fr multi	4.50	.95
433L	A140a	500fr multi	5.75	1.10
		Nos. 433A-433L (12)	15.90	4.95

Litho. & Embossed
433M A140b 1000fr multi   9.00 3.75
Souvenir Sheet
433Q A140b 1000fr multi   9.00 3.75

Nos. 433K-433Q are airmail.

Mechanized Tomato Harvest — A141

1976, Oct. 23   Photo.   Perf. 13
434 A141 180fr multi   3.00 1.25

Map of
Dakar and
Gorée
A142

Designs: 60fr, Star over Africa. 70fr, Students in laboratory and library. 200fr, Handshake over world map, Pres. Senghor.

1976, Oct. 9   Litho.   Perf. 13½x14
435	A142	40fr multi	.35	.25
436	A142	60fr multi	.50	.25
437	A142	70fr multi	1.00	.25
438	A142	200fr multi	2.75	.85
		Nos. 435-438 (4)	4.60	1.60

70th birthday of Pres. Leopold Sedar Senghor.

Scroll with Map of
Africa,
Senegalese
People — A143

1977, Jan. 8   Perf. 12½
439 A143 60fr multi   .80 .30

Day of the Black People.

Joe Frazier and Muhammad
Ali — A144

Design: 60fr, Ali and Frazier in ring, vert.

1977, Jan. 7   Photo.   Perf. 13x13½
440	A144	60fr blue & blk	.65	.25
441	A144	150fr emerald & blk	2.25	.60

World boxing champion Muhammad Ali.

Dancer
and
Musician
A145

Festival Emblem and: 75fr, Wood carving and masks. 100fr, Dancers and ancestor statuette.

1977, Feb. 10   Litho.   Perf. 12½
442	A145	50fr yellow & multi	.55	.25
443	A145	75fr green & multi	1.25	.30
444	A145	100fr rose & multi	1.40	.50
		Nos. 442-444 (3)	3.20	1.05

2nd World Black and African Festival, Lagos, Nigeria, Jan. 15-Feb. 12.

Cogwheels and Symbols of
Industry — A146

1977, Mar. 28   Engr.   Perf. 13
445 A146 70fr yel grn & ocher   .80 .30

Dakar Industrial Zone, 1st anniversary.

Burning Match
and Burnt
Trees — A147

60fr, Burnt trees and house, fire-truck, horiz.

1977, Apr. 30   Litho.   Perf. 12½
446	A147	40fr green & multi	1.00	.35
447	A147	60fr slate & multi	1.75	.55

Prevention of forest fires.

Drummer, Telephone, Agriculture and
Industry — A148

Electronic Tree
and ITU
Emblem — A149

1977, May 17   Litho.   Perf. 13
448	A148	80fr multi	.80	.40
449	A149	100fr multi	1.25	.60

World Telecommunications Day.

Symbol of
Language
Studies — A150

Sassenage Castle, Grenoble — A151

Perf. 12x12½, 12½

1977, May 21   Litho.
450 A150 65fr multi   .65   .25
451 A151 250fr multi   2.75 1.00
10th anniv. of Intl. French Language Council.

Woman in Boat, Wooden Shoe A152

Design: 125fr, Senegalese woman, symbolic tulip and stamp, vert.

1977, June 4   Perf. 13½x14, 14x13½
452 A152 50fr blue grn & multi   .50   .25
453 A152 125fr ocher & multi   1.50   .45
Amphilex '77 International Philatelic Exhibition, Amsterdam, May 26-June 5.

Adult Reading Class A153

Design: 65fr, Man learning to read.

1977, Sept. 10   Litho.   Perf. 12½
454 A153 60fr multi   .70   .25
455 A153 65fr multi   .70   .25
National Literacy Week, Sept. 8-14.

A154

Paintings: 20fr, Mercury, by Rubens. 25fr, Daniel in the Lions' Den, by Peter Paul Rubens (1577-1640). 40fr, The Empress, by Titian (1477-1576). 60fr, Flora, by Titian. 65fr, Jo, the Beautiful Irish Woman, by Gustave Courbet (1819-1877). 100fr, The Painter's Studio, by Courbet.

1977, Nov.   Photo.   Perf. 13x13½
456 A154 20fr multi   .55   .25
457 A154 25fr multi   .55   .25
458 A154 40fr multi   .55   .25
459 A154 60fr multi   1.00   .25
460 A154 65fr multi   1.40   .55
461 A154 100fr multi   3.00 1.00
      Nos. 456-461 (6)   7.05 2.55

A155

Christmas: 20fr, Adoration by People of Various Races. 25fr, Decorated arch and procession. 40fr, Christmas tree, mother and child. 100fr, Adoration of the Kings, horiz.

1977, Dec. 22   Litho.   Perf. 12½
462 A155 20fr multi   .25   .25
463 A155 25fr multi   .40   .25
464 A155 40fr multi   .65   .25
465 A155 100fr multi   1.25   .65
      Nos. 462-465 (4)   2.55 1.40

Regatta at Soumbedioun A156

Tourism: 10fr, Senegalese wrestlers. 65fr, Regatta at Soumbedioun. 100fr, Dancers.

1978, Jan. 7   Litho.   Perf. 12½
466 A156 10fr multi   .25   .25
467 A156 30fr multi   .35   .25
468 A156 65fr multi, horiz.   .80   .40
469 A156 100fr multi, horiz.   1.75   .50
      Nos. 466-469 (4)   3.15 1.40

Acropolis, Athens, and African Buildings A157

1978, Jan. 30
470 A157 75fr multi   .80   .30
UNESCO campaign to save world's cultural heritage.

Solar-powered Pump, Field and Sheep — A158

Energy in Senegal: 95fr, Pylon bringing electricity to villages and factories.

1978, Feb. 25
471 A158 50fr multi   .55   .25
472 A158 95fr multi   1.25   .40

Park Type of 1976

5fr, Caspian terns in flight, royal terns on ground. 10fr, Pink-backed pelicans. 15fr, Wart hog & gray heron. 20fr, Greater flamingoes, nests, eggs & young. #477, Gray heron & royal terns. #478, Abyssinian ground hornbill & wart hog.

1978, Apr. 22   Photo.   Perf. 13
473 A133 5fr gold & multi   .25   .25
474 A133 10fr gold & multi   .55   .25
475 A133 15fr gold & multi   1.10   .25
476 A133 20fr gold & multi   1.25   .40
477 A133 150fr gold & multi   5.25 1.00
478 A133 150fr gold & multi   5.25 1.00
  a.   Strip of 2, #477-478 + label   11.50
      Nos. 473-478 (6)   13.65 3.15
Salum Delta National Park.

Dome of the Rock, Jerusalem A159

1978, May 15   Litho.   Perf. 12½
479 A159 60fr multi   .80   .25
Palestinian fighters and their families.

Vaccination, Dr. Jenner, WHO Emblem — A160

1978, June 3
480 A160 60fr multi   .80   .35
Eradication of smallpox.

Soccer, Flags: Argentina, Hungary, France, Italy — A161

Soccer, Cup, Argentina '78 Emblem and Flags of: 40fr, No. 486a, Poland, German Democratic Rep., Tunisia, Mexico. 65fr, 125fr, Austria, Spain, Sweden, Brazil. 75fr, No. 484, Netherlands, Iran, Peru, Scotland. 150fr, like 25fr.

1978, June 24   Photo.   Perf. 13
481 A161 25fr multi   .25   .25
482 A161 40fr multi   .55   .25
483 A161 65fr multi   .80   .30
484 A161 100fr multi   1.50   .30
      Nos. 481-484 (4)   3.10 1.10
          Souvenir Sheets
485   Sheet of 2   2.75
  a.   A161 75fr multi   .60
  b.   A161 125fr multi   1.10
486   Sheet of 2   2.75
  a.   A161 100fr multi   .85
  b.   A161 150fr multi   1.10
11th World Cup Soccer Championship, Argentina, June 1-25.

Mahatma Gandhi — A162

Design: 150fr, No. 489a, Martin Luther King. No. 489b, like 125fr.

1978, June 27   Perf. 12
487 A162 125fr multi   1.75   .35
488 A162 150fr multi   2.25   .60
          Souvenir Sheet
489   Sheet of 2   4.00
  a.   A162 200fr multi   1.60
  b.   A162 200fr multi   1.60
Mahatma Gandhi and Martin Luther King, advocates of non-violence.

Homes and Industry — A163

1978, Aug. 5   Litho.   Perf. 12½
490 A163 110fr multi   1.25   .40
3rd Intl. Fair, Dakar, Nov. 28-Dec. 10.

Wright Brothers and Flyer — A164

Designs: 150fr, like 75fr. 100fr, 250fr, Yuri Gagarin and spacecraft. 200fr, 300fr, US astronauts Frank Borman, William Anders, James Lovell Jr. and spacecraft.

1978, Sept. 25   Litho.   Perf. 13½x14
491 A164 75fr multi   .90   .25
492 A164 125fr multi   1.25   .40
493 A164 200fr multi   2.25   .85
      Nos. 491-493 (3)   4.40 1.50
          Souvenir Sheet
494   Sheet of 3   6.25
  a.   A164 150fr multi   .60
  b.   A164 250fr multi   1.40
  c.   A164 300fr multi   1.40
75th anniv. of 1st powered flight; 10th anniv. of the death of Yuri Gagarin, first man in space; 10th anniv. of Apollo 8 flight around moon.

Henri Dunant (1828-1910), Founder of Red Cross, and Patients — A165

Design: 20fr, Henri Dunant, First Aid station, Red Cross flag.

1978, Oct. 28   Photo.   Perf. 11½
495 A165 5fr brt blue & red   .25   .25
496 A165 20fr multi   .45   .25

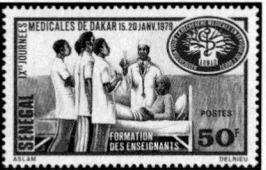

Bedside Lecture and Emblem — A166

100fr, Pollution, fish and mercury bottles.

1979, Jan. 15   Litho.   Perf. 13½x13
497 A166 75fr multi   .45   .25
498 A166 100fr multi   1.10   .30
9th Medical Days, Dakar, Jan. 15-20.

Map of Senegal with Shortwave Stations A167

60fr, Children on vacation, ambulance, soccer player. 65fr, Rural mobile post office.

1978, Dec. 27   Litho.   Perf. 13½x13
499	A167 50fr multi	.55	.25
500	A167 60fr multi	.55	.25
501	A167 65fr multi	.70	.25
	Nos. 499-501 (3)	1.80	.75

Achievements of postal service.

Farmer
A168

Design: 150fr, Factories, communication, transportation, fish, physician and worker.

1979, Feb. 17   Litho.   Perf. 12½
| 502 | A168 30fr multi | .35 | .25 |
| 503 | A168 150fr multi | 1.40 | .50 |

Pride in workmanship.

Children's Village and
Children — A169

Design: 60fr, Different view of village.

1979, Mar. 30   Perf. 12x12½
| 504 | A169 40fr multi | .45 | .25 |
| 505 | A169 60fr multi | .70 | .25 |

Children's SOS villages.

Infant, Physician
Vaccinating Child,
IYC
Emblem — A170

65fr, Boys with book, globe, IYC emblem.

1979, Apr. 21   Litho.   Perf. 13½x13
| 506 | A170 60fr multi | .65 | .25 |
| 507 | A170 65fr multi | .65 | .25 |

International Year of the Child.

Drum, Carrier Pigeon,
Satellite — A171

Design: 60fr, Baobab tree and flower, Independence monument with lion, vert.

1979, June 8   Perf. 12½x13
Size: 36x48mm
| 508 | A171 60fr multi | 1.75 | .85 |
Perf. 12½
Size: 36x36mm
| 509 | A171 150fr multi | 3.50 | 1.50 |

Philexafrique II, Libreville, Gabon, June 8-17. Nos. 508, 509 each printed with labels showing UAPT '79 emblem.

People
Walking
through
Open Book
A172

1979, Sept. 15   Photo.   Perf. 11½x12
| 510 | A172 250fr multi | 2.50 | .80 |

Intl. Bureau of Education, Geneva, 50th anniv.

Sir Rowland Hill (1795-1879),
Originator of Penny Postage, Type
AP3 with Exhibition Cancel — A173

1979, Oct. 9   Perf. 11½
| 511 | A173 500fr multi | 5.25 | 2.00 |

Black Trees, by
Hundertwasser
A174

Litho. & Engr.
1979, Dec. 10   Perf. 13½x14
512	A174 60fr shown	45.00	11.00
a.	Souvenir sheet of 4	175.00	175.00
513	A174 100fr Head of a man	45.00	13.00
a.	Souvenir sheet of 4	175.00	175.00
514	A174 200fr Rainbow windows	45.00	15.00
a.	Souvenir sheet of 4	175.00	175.00
	Nos. 512-514 (3)	135.00	39.00

Paintings by Friedensreich Hundertwasser, pseudonym of Friedrich Stowasser (b. 1928).

Running,
Championship
Emblem
A175

1980, Jan. 14   Litho.   Perf. 13
515	A175 20fr shown	.25	.25
516	A175 25fr Javelin	.25	.25
517	A175 50fr Relay race	.55	.25
518	A175 100fr Discus	1.25	.45
	Nos. 515-518 (4)	2.30	1.20

1st African Athletic Championships.

Mudra
Afrique
Arts
Festival
A176

50fr, Musicians. 100fr, Dancers, festival building. 200fr, Drummer, dancers.

1980, Mar. 22   Photo.   Perf. 14
519	A176 50fr multi	.45	.25
520	A176 100fr multi	1.00	.45
521	A176 200fr multi	1.75	.85
	Nos. 519-521 (3)	3.20	1.55

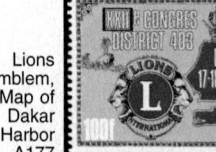

Lions
Emblem,
Map of
Dakar
Harbor
A177

1980, May 17   Litho.   Perf. 13
| 522 | A177 100fr multi | 1.10 | .40 |

22nd Cong., Lions Intl. District 403, Dakar.

Chimpanzees — A178

1980, June 2   Photo.   Perf. 13½
523	A178 40fr shown	.85	.25
524	A178 60fr Elephants	1.25	.40
525	A178 65fr Derby's elands	1.50	.45
526	A178 100fr Hyenas	2.25	.50
527	Pair	9.00	5.00
a.	A178 200fr Herd	4.25	1.00
b.	A178 200fr Guest house	4.25	1.00
	Nos. 523-527 (5)	14.85	6.60

Souvenir Sheet
528	Sheet of 4	8.00	8.00
a.	A178 125fr like #523	1.50	1.50
b.	A178 125fr like #524	1.50	1.50
c.	A178 125fr like #525	1.50	1.50
d.	A178 125fr like #526	1.50	1.50

Niokolo Koba National Park. No. 527 printed in continuous design with label showing location of park.

Tree Planting
Year — A179

1980, June 27   Litho.   Perf. 13
| 529 | A179 60fr multi | .90 | .40 |
| 530 | A179 65fr multi | 1.00 | .40 |

Rural Women
Workers
A180

Rural women workers. 50fr, 200fr, horiz.

1980, July 19
531	A180 50fr multi	.35	.25
532	A180 100fr multi	1.25	.50
533	A180 200fr multi	2.00	.80
	Nos. 531-533 (3)	3.60	1.40

Wrestling,
Moscow '80
Emblem — A181

60fr, Wrestling. 65fr, Running. 70fr, Sports, map showing Moscow. 100fr, Judo. 200fr, Basketball.

1980, Aug. 21   Perf. 14½
534	A181 60fr multicolored	.45	.25
535	A181 65fr multicolored	.55	.30
536	A181 70fr multicolored	.55	.30
537	A181 100fr multicolored	.80	.40
538	A181 200fr multicolored	1.75	.80
	Nos. 534-538 (5)	4.10	2.05

Souvenir Sheet
539	Sheet of 2	2.00	
a.	A181 75fr like #534	.65	.25
b.	A181 125fr like #535	1.00	.35
540	Sheet of 2	2.00	
a.	A181 75fr like #527	.65	.25
b.	A181 125fr like #538	1.00	.35

22nd Summer Olympic Games, Moscow, July 19-Aug. 3.

Caspian
Tern and
Sea Gulls,
Kalissaye
Bird
Sanctuary
A182

National Park Wildlife: 70fr, Laughing gulls and Hansel's tern, Barbarie Spit. 85fr, Turtle and crab, Madeleine Islands. 150fr, Cormorant, Madeleine Islands.

1981, Jan. 31   Litho.   Perf. 14½x14
541	A182 50fr multi	3.50	.50
542	A182 70fr multi	3.50	.70
543	A182 85fr multi	1.75	.70
544	A182 150fr multi	7.00	1.75
	Nos. 541-544 (4)	15.75	3.65

Souvenir Sheet
545	Sheet of 4	22.50	22.50
a.	A182 125fr like #541	3.50	2.75
b.	A182 125fr like #542	3.50	2.75
c.	A182 125fr like #543	3.50	2.75
d.	A182 125fr like #544	3.50	2.75

Anti-Tobacco
Campaign — A183

1981, June 20   Litho.   Perf. 13
| 546 | A183 75fr Healthy people | .70 | .30 |
| 547 | A183 80fr shown | .90 | .30 |

4th Intl.
Dakar Fair,
Nov. 25-
Dec. 7
A184

1981, Sept. 19   Litho.   Perf. 12½
| 548 | A184 80fr multi | .80 | .30 |

Natl.
Hero Lat
Dior
A185

1982, Jan. 11   Photo.   Perf. 14
| 549 | A185 80fr Portrait, vert. | .55 | .35 |
| 550 | A185 500fr Battle | 4.50 | 1.40 |

Local
Flora — A186

50fr, Nymphaea lotus. 75fr, Strophanthus sarmentosus. 200fr, Crinum moorei. 225fr, Cochlospermum tinctorium.

1982, Feb. 1   *Perf. 11½*
551	A186	50fr multicolored	.55	.25
552	A186	75fr multicolored	.90	.30
553	A186	200fr multicolored	2.25	.65
554	A186	225fr multicolored	2.25	.85
		Nos. 551-554 (4)	5.95	2.05

Inscribed 1981.

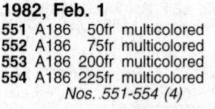

Euryphrene Senegalensis — A187

55fr, Hypolimnas salmacis. 75fr, Cymothoe caenis. 80fr, Precis cebrene.

1982, Feb. 27   **Litho.**   *Perf. 14*
555	A187	45fr multicolored	2.25	.50
556	A187	55fr multicolored	3.00	.60
557	A187	75fr multicolored	3.25	.75
558	A187	80fr multicolored	4.00	.90
		Nos. 555-558 (4)	12.50	2.75

Souvenir Sheet
Perf. 14½
559		Sheet of 4	20.00	20.00
a.	A187	100fr like 45fr	2.00	1.50
b.	A187	150fr like 55fr	3.00	2.50
c.	A187	200fr like 75fr	4.00	3.50
d.	A187	250fr like 80fr	5.00	4.00

Destructive Insects — A188

Various insects. 80fr, 100fr horiz.

1982, Apr. 7   **Litho.**   *Perf. 14*
560	A188	75fr multi	1.75	.40
561	A188	80fr multi	3.25	.70
562	A188	100fr multi	2.50	.90
		Nos. 560-562 (3)	7.50	2.00

Fashion Type of 1972

1982-93   **Engr.**   *Perf. 13*
563	A106	5fr Prus blue	.25	.25
564	A106	10fr dull red	.25	.25
565	A106	15fr orange	.25	.25
566	A106	20fr dk purple	.25	.25
567	A106	30fr henna brn	.25	.25
568	A106	45fr orange yellow	.35	.25
569	A106	50fr bright magenta	.40	.25
570	A106	90fr brt carmine	.50	.30
571	A106	125fr ultramarine	.95	.50
572	A106	145fr orange	.85	.35
573	A106	180fr gray blue	1.40	.70
		Nos. 563-573 (11)	5.70	3.60

Issued: 5, 10, 15, 20, 30fr, Apr. 30; 90fr, Dec., 1984; 180fr, 1991; 45, 50, 125fr, 1993; 145fr, 1995.

Banner and Stamp — A189

1982, Dec. 30   **Photo.**   *Perf. 13*
575	A189	100fr shown	.70	.35
576	A189	500fr Stamp, arrows	4.50	1.50

PHILEXFRANCE Intl. Stamp Exhibition, Paris, June 11-21.

Senegambia Confederation, Feb. 1 — A190

1982, Nov. 15   **Litho.**   *Perf. 12½*
577	A190	225fr Map, flags	2.00	.65
578	A190	350fr Arms	2.75	1.00

Local Birds — A191

1982, Dec. 1   **Photo.**
Granite Paper   *Perf. 11½*
579	A191	45fr Godwit	.65	.25
580	A191	75fr Jabiru	1.10	.35
581	A191	80fr Francolin	1.25	.55
582	A191	500fr Eagle	6.25	2.25
		Nos. 579-582 (4)	9.25	3.40

1982 World Cup — A192

1982, Dec. 11   **Litho.**   *Perf. 12½x13*
583	A192	30fr Player	.25	.25
584	A192	50fr Player, diff.	.35	.25
585	A192	75fr Ball	.80	.35
586	A192	80fr Cup	.90	.35
		Nos. 583-586 (4)	2.30	1.10

Souvenir Sheets
Perf. 12½
587	A192	75fr like 30fr	.80	.80
588	A192	100fr like 50fr	1.10	1.10
589	A192	150fr like 75fr	1.50	1.50
590	A192	200fr like 80fr	2.25	2.25
		Nos. 587-590 (4)	5.65	5.65

A193

Designs: 60fr, Exhibition poster, viewers, horiz. 70fr, Simulated butterfly stamps. 90fr, Simulated stamps under magnifying glass. 95fr, Coat of Arms over Exhibition Building.

1983, Aug. 6   **Litho.**   *Perf. 12½*
591	A193	60fr multi	.55	.25
592	A193	70fr multi	1.40	.30
593	A193	90fr multi	1.75	.30
594	A193	95fr multi	1.75	.40
		Nos. 591-594 (4)	5.45	1.25

Dakar '82 Stamp Exhibition.

A194

1983, Oct. 25   **Litho.**   *Perf. 12½x13*
595	A194	90fr Electricity	.85	.40
596	A194	95fr Gasoline	1.00	.45
597	A194	260fr Coal, wood	2.25	.65
		Nos. 595-597 (3)	4.10	1.50

Energy conservation.

Namibia Day — A195

1983, Nov. 14   **Litho.**   *Perf. 13½x13*
598	A195	90fr Torch	.80	.35
599	A195	95fr Chain, fist	.90	.35
600	A195	260fr Woman bearing torch	2.75	.65
		Nos. 598-600 (3)	4.45	1.35

West African Monetary Union, 20th Anniv. — A196

Designs: 60fr, Mask emblem, Ziguinchor Agency building, Dakar, horiz. 65fr, Monetary Union headquarters, emblem.

Perf. 13½x13, 13x13½
1983, Nov. 28
601	A196	60fr multi	.65	.25
602	A196	65fr multi	.65	.25

Dakar Alizes Rotary Club, First Anniv. — A197

1983, Dec. 5   *Perf. 13x13½*
603	A197	70fr green & multi	.90	.35
604	A197	500fr blue & multi	4.50	1.75

Customs Cooperation Council, 30th Anniv. — A198

1983, Dec. 23   *Perf. 12½x13*
605	A198	90fr multi	.65	.25
606	A198	300fr multi	3.00	.80

Economic Comm. for Africa, 25th Anniv. — A199

1984, Jan. 10   *Perf. 12½*
607	A199	90fr multi	.70	.35
608	A199	95fr multi	.90	.35

SOS Children's Village A200

90fr, Village. 95fr, Mother & child, vert. 115fr, Brothers & sisters. 260fr, House, vert.

1984, Mar. 29   *Perf. 13½x13, 13x13½*
609	A200	90fr multicolored	.80	.25
610	A200	95fr multicolored	1.00	.40
611	A200	115fr multicolored	1.10	.40
612	A200	260fr multicolored	2.50	.85
		Nos. 609-612 (4)	5.40	1.90

Scouting Year A201

1984, May 28   **Litho.**   *Perf. 13*
613	A201	60fr Sign	.55	.25
614	A201	70fr Emblem	.55	.25
615	A201	90fr Scouts	.70	.30
616	A201	95fr Baden-Powell	.90	.30
		Nos. 613-616 (4)	2.70	1.10

1984 Olympic Games — A202

1984, July 28   **Litho.**   *Perf. 13*
617	A202	90fr Javelin	.70	.25
618	A202	95fr Hurdles	.90	.35
619	A202	165fr Soccer	1.50	.50
		Nos. 617-619 (3)	3.10	1.10

Souvenir Sheet
Perf. 13x12½
620		Sheet of 3	4.50	4.50
a.	A202	125fr like 90fr	.95	.95
b.	A202	175fr like 95fr	1.50	1.50
c.	A202	250fr like 165fr	1.75	1.75

World Food Day A203

Perf. 13x12½, 12½x13
1984, Dec. 16   **Litho.**
621	A203	65fr Food production	.55	.30
622	A203	70fr Cooking, vert.	.70	.30
623	A203	225fr Dining	2.25	.85
		Nos. 621-623 (3)	3.50	1.45

No. 612 Overprinted "AIDE AU SAHEL 84"

1984, Dec.   *Perf. 13x13½*
624	A200	260fr multi	2.25	1.25

Drought relief.

UNESCO World
Heritage
Campaign
A204

90fr, William Ponty School. 95fr, Island map, horiz. 250fr, History Museum. 500fr, Slave Prison, horiz.

1984, Dec. 6   Litho.   Perf. 13½
625	A204	90fr multi	1.10	.40
626	A204	95fr multi	1.10	.40
627	A204	250fr multi	3.25	1.00
628	A204	500fr multi	6.00	2.25
	Nos. 625-628 (4)		11.45	4.05

Souvenir Sheet
Perf. 13x12½, 12½x13
629		Sheet of 4	11.00	11.00
a.	A204	125fr like No. 625	1.00	.75
b.	A204	150fr like No. 626	1.25	1.00
c.	A204	325fr like No. 627	2.25	2.00
d.	A204	675fr like No. 628	5.25	5.00

Restoration of historic sites, Goree Island.

Water Emergency
Plan — A205

1985, Mar. 28   Perf. 13x12½, 12½x13
630	A205	40fr Well and pump	.60	.25
631	A205	50fr Spigot and crops	.70	.35
632	A205	90fr Water tanks, live-stock	1.40	.55
633	A205	250fr Women at well	3.00	1.10
	Nos. 630-633 (4)		5.70	2.25

Nos. 631-633 horiz.

World Communications Year — A206

Designs: 95fr, Maps of Africa and Senegal, transmission tower. 350fr, Globe, pigeon with letter.

1985, Apr. 13   Litho.   Perf. 13
634	A206	90fr multi	.70	.35
635	A206	95fr multi	.90	.35
636	A206	350fr multi	3.25	1.25
	Nos. 634-636 (3)		4.85	1.95

Traditional Musical
Instruments — A207

50fr, Gourd fiddle, bamboo flute. 85fr, Drums, stringed instrument. 125fr, Musician playing balaphone, drums. 250fr, Rabab, shawm & single-string fiddles.

1985, May 4   Perf. 12½x13, 13x12½
637	A207	50fr multi	.75	.25
638	A207	85fr multi	1.10	.45
639	A207	125fr multi	1.60	.60
640	A207	250fr multi	3.25	1.00
	Nos. 637-640 (4)		6.70	2.30

Nos. 638-640 vert. For surcharge see No. 676.

PHILEXAFRICA '85, Lome, Togo, Nov.
16-24 — A208

100fr, Political and civic education. 125fr, Vocational training. 150fr, Culture, space exploration. 175fr, Self-sufficiency in food production.

1985, Oct. 21   Perf. 13
641	A208	100fr multi	.70	.25
642	A208	125fr multi	1.00	.40
643	A208	150fr multi	1.25	.50
644	A208	175fr multi	2.25	.85
	Nos. 641-644 (4)		5.20	2.00

Intl. Youth
Year
A209

40fr, Vocational training. 50fr, Communications. 90fr, World peace. 125fr, Cultural exchange.

1985, Nov. 30   Perf. 14
645	A209	40fr multicolored	.35	.25
646	A209	50fr multicolored	.45	.25
647	A209	90fr multicolored	.80	.30
648	A209	125fr multicolored	1.25	.35
	Nos. 645-648 (4)		2.85	1.15

Senegal Arms Type of 1970
1985, Dec.   Litho.   Perf. 13
Background Color
654	A89	95fr bright orange	.80	.25

Fishing at
Kayar
A210

1986, Jan. 28   Litho.   Perf. 14
659	A210	40fr Hauling boat	.35	.25
660	A210	50fr Women on beach	.55	.25
661	A210	100fr Fisherman, catch	1.00	.35
662	A210	125fr Women buying fish	1.40	.50
663	A210	150fr Unloading fish	1.60	.60
	Nos. 659-663 (5)		4.90	1.95

Nos. 661-662 vert.

Folk Costumes — A211

1985, Dec. 28   Litho.   Perf. 13½
664	A211	40fr multi	.25	.25
665	A211	95fr multi, vert., diff.	.80	.30
666	A211	100fr multi, vert., diff.	.90	.30
667	A211	150fr multi, vert., diff.	1.25	.50
	Nos. 664-667 (4)		3.20	1.35

Coiffures — A212

90fr, Perruque, Ceeli. 125fr, Ndungu, Kearly, Rasta. 250fr, Jamono Kura, Kooraa. 300fr, Mbaram, Jeere.

1986, Mar. 3   Perf. 13
668	A212	90fr multicolored	.70	.35
669	A212	125fr multicolored	1.00	.40
670	A212	225fr multicolored	2.25	.75
671	A212	300fr multicolored	2.75	.90
	Nos. 668-671 (4)		6.70	2.40

1986 Africa
Soccer Cup,
Cairo — A213

1986, Mar. 7   Perf. 13½
672	A213	115fr Soccer ball, flags	1.00	.30
673	A213	125fr Athlete, map	1.00	.35
674	A213	135fr Pyramid, heraldic lion	1.10	.40
675	A213	165fr Flag, lions, map	1.40	.50
	Nos. 672-675 (4)		4.50	1.55

**No. 638 Surcharged with Lions Intl.
Emblem, Two Bars, and "Ve
CONVENTION / MULTI-DISTRICT /
403 / 8-10 / MAI / 1986" in Dark
Ultramarine**
1986, May 8   Litho.   Perf. 13x12½
676	A207	165fr on 85fr multi	1.40	.50

World Wildlife Fund — A214

Ndama gazelles.

1986, June 30   Perf. 13
677	A214	15fr multi	1.00	.40
678	A214	45fr multi	1.75	.60
679	A214	85fr multi	3.00	1.25
680	A214	125fr multi	5.00	2.00
	Nos. 677-680 (4)		10.75	4.25

UN Child Survival
Campaign — A215

1986, Sept. 5   Litho.   Perf. 14
681	A215	50fr Immunization	.45	.25
682	A215	85fr Nutrition	.70	.30

1986 World Cup Soccer
Championships, Mexico — A216

Various plays, world cup and artifacts: 125fr, Ceremonial vase. 135fr, Mayan mask, Palenque. 165fr, Gold breastplate. 340fr, Porcelain mask, Teofihuacan, 7th cent. B.C.

1986, Nov. 17   Perf. 12½x12
683	A216	125fr multi	1.00	.40
684	A216	135fr multi	1.10	.40
685	A216	165fr multi	1.40	.55
686	A216	340fr multi	2.75	1.10
	Nos. 683-686 (4)		6.25	2.45

**Nos. 683-686 Overprinted
"ARGENTINE 3 / R.F.A. 2" in Scarlet**
1986, Nov. 17
687	A216	125fr multi	1.00	.40
688	A216	135fr multi	1.10	.45
689	A216	165fr multi	1.40	.55
690	A216	340fr multi	2.75	1.10
	Nos. 687-690 (4)		6.25	2.50

Guembeul
Nature
Reserve
A217

1986, Dec. 4   Litho.   Perf. 13½
691	A217	50fr Ostriches	1.25	.25
692	A217	65fr Kob antelopes	.45	.25
693	A217	85fr Giraffes	.60	.40
694	A217	100fr Ostrich, buffalo, kob, giraffe	2.00	.50
695	A217	150fr Buffaloes	1.25	.60
	Nos. 691-695 (5)		5.55	2.00

Christmas
A218

70fr, Puppet, vert. 85fr, Folk musicians. 150fr, Outdoor celebration, vert. 250fr, Boy praying, creche.

1986, Dec. 22   Litho.   Perf. 14
696	A218	70fr multicolored	.55	.25
697	A218	85fr multicolored	.80	.25
698	A218	150fr multicolored	1.25	.50
699	A218	250fr multicolored	2.25	.85
	Nos. 696-699 (4)		4.85	1.85

Inscribed 1985.

Statue of Liberty,
Cent. — A219

1986, Dec. 30   Litho.   Perf. 12½
700	A219	225fr multi	2.00	.65

Marine
Life
A220

1987, Jan. 2   Perf. 14
701	A220	50fr Jellyfish, coral	.55	.25
702	A220	85fr Sea urchin, starfish	1.00	.25
703	A220	100fr Spiny lobster	1.60	.50
704	A220	150fr Dolphin	2.10	.65
705	A220	200fr Octopus	3.25	.90
	Nos. 701-705 (5)		8.50	2.55

Senegal Stamp Cent. — A221

1987, Apr. 8   Perf. 13
706	A221	100fr Intl. express mail	1.40	.30
707	A221	130fr #37	1.60	.40
708	A221	140fr Similar to #201	1.75	.40

709 A221 145fr #151, similar to
#154 1.75 .50
710 A221 320fr #27 5.00 1.10
Nos. 706-710 (5) 11.50 2.70

Designs of Nos. 37, 151 and 27 same as
originally released but perfs simulated.
For overprint see No. 784.

Paris-Dakar Rally — A222

1987, Jan. 22 *Perf. 14*
711 A222 115fr Motorcycle, truck,
vert. 1.25 .40
712 A222 125fr Official, race 1.75 .40
713 A222 135fr Sabine, truck 1.75 .55
714 A222 340fr Eiffel Tower, Dakar huts, vert. 3.25 1.25
Nos. 711-714 (4) 8.00 2.60

Homage to Thierry Sabine. Inscribed 1986.

Ferlo Nature
Reserve — A223

1987, Feb. 5 *Perf. 13½*
715 A223 55fr Antelope .80 .30
716 A223 70fr Ostrich 1.10 .45
717 A223 85fr Warthog 1.10 .45
718 A223 90fr Elephant 1.25 .50
Nos. 715-718 (4) 4.25 1.70

Inscribed 1986.

Agena-Gemini 8 Link-up in Outer
Space, 20th Anniv. — A224

1987, Feb. 27 **Litho.** *Perf. 13*
719 A224 320fr multi 2.75 1.25

Souvenir Sheet
Perf. 12½

720 A224 500fr multi 6.25 6.25

Nos. 719-720 inscribed 1986 and have erroneous "10e Anniversaire" inscription.

Solidarity Against South African
Apartheid — A225

140fr, Mandela, hand, broken chain, vert.
145fr, Mandela, dove, death.

1987, July 31 **Litho.** *Perf. 13*
721 A225 130fr multicolored 1.00 .40
722 A225 140fr multicolored 1.10 .45
723 A225 145fr multicolored 1.10 .50
Nos. 721-723 (3) 3.20 1.35

Inscribed 1986.

Intelsat,
20th
Anniv.
A226

1987, Aug. 31 *Perf. 14*
724 A226 50fr Emblem .45 .25
725 A226 125fr Satellite 1.00 .40
726 A226 150fr Emblem, globe 1.10 .50
727 A226 200fr Earth, satellite in
space 2.00 .70
Nos. 724-727 (4) 4.55 1.85

Inscribed 1985. Nos. 726-727 vert.

West African
Union, 10th
Anniv. — A227

1987, Sept. 7
728 A227 40fr shown .35 .25
729 A227 125fr Emblem, handshake 1.00 .45

Inscribed 1985.

Dakar Rotary
Club, 45th
Anniv. — A228

1987, Sept. 29 *Perf. 13*
730 A228 500fr multi 4.50 1.75

Inscribed 1985.

United Nations,
40th
Anniv. — A229

1987, Oct. 8 *Perf. 14*
731 A229 85fr Emblem, NYC office .90 .30
732 A229 95fr Emblem .90 .30
733 A229 150fr Hands, emblem 1.25 .55
Nos. 731-733 (3) 3.05 1.15

Inscribed 1985.

Cathedral
of African
Memory,
50th Anniv.
A230

130fr, Statue of saint, Fr. Daniel Brottier,
vert.

1987, Oct. 16 *Perf. 12½x13, 13x12½*
734 A230 130fr multi 1.25 .65
735 A230 140fr multi 1.25 .65

Inscribed 1986.

Lat Dior,
King of
Cayor (d.
1887)
A231

1987, Oct. 27 **Litho.** *Perf. 14*
736 A231 130fr Battle of Dekhele 1.25 .50
737 A231 160fr Lat Dior 1.25 .50

World Food
Day
A232

1987, Oct. 30 **Litho.** *Perf. 12½*
738 A232 130fr Earth storing
grain, vert. 1.00 .60
739 A232 140fr shown 1.25 .60
740 A232 145fr Emblem, vert. 1.50 .60
Nos. 738-740 (3) 3.75 1.80

Inscribed 1986.

A233

Fauna, Bassa Casamance Natl.
Park — A234

No. 741, Felis servaline. No. 742, Gala-
goides demi-dovii. No. 743, Potamochoerus
porcus. No. 744, Panthera pardus. No. 745,
Aigrette. No. 746, Guepier.

1987, Nov. 9 *Perf. 13*
741 A233 115fr multi 1.00 .55
742 A233 135fr multi 1.40 .60
743 A233 150fr multi 1.50 .65
744 A233 250fr multi 2.75 1.25
745 300fr multi 12.50 3.75
746 300fr multi 12.50 3.75
a. A234 Pair, #745-746 + label 27.50 8.00
Nos. 741-746 (6) 31.65 10.55

Inscribed 1986. No. 745-746 has continuous design with corner label picturing map of
Senegal with park highlighted.

Traditional
Wrestling — A235

Various moves.

1987, Nov. 30 **Litho.** *Perf. 14*
747 A235 115fr multi, horiz. 1.10 .45
748 A235 125fr multi, diff., horiz. 1.10 .50
749 A235 135fr multi, diff. 1.25 .55
750 A235 165fr multi, diff. 1.60 .75
Nos. 747-750 (4) 5.05 2.25

Birds in Djoudj
Natl. Park — A236

115fr, Stork. 125fr, Pink flamingos, horiz.
135fr, White pelicans, horiz. 300fr, Pelicans in
water. No. 755, like 125fr, horiz. No. 756, like
135fr, horiz.

1987, Dec. 4
751 A236 115fr multi 1.75 .40
752 A236 125fr multi 2.00 .40
753 A236 135fr multi 2.50 .65
754 A236 300fr multi 5.00 1.25
755 A236 350fr multi 5.25 1.75
756 A236 350fr multi 5.25 1.75
a. Pair, #755-756 + label 11.50 11.50
Nos. 751-756 (6) 21.75 6.20

Christmas
A237

Designs: 145fr, Youth dreaming of presents.
150fr, Madonna and child. 180fr, Holy Family,
congregation praying. 200fr, Holy Family, candle and Christmas tree.

1987, Dec. 24 *Perf. 12½x13*
757 A237 145fr multi 1.25 .40
758 A237 150fr multi 1.25 .40
759 A237 180fr multi 1.75 .65
760 A237 200fr multi 2.00 .65
Nos. 757-760 (4) 6.25 2.10

Dakar Intl. Fair, 10th Anniv. (in
1985) — A238

1988, Feb. 27 **Litho.** *Perf. 13*
761 A238 125fr multi .90 .45

Inscribed 1985.

Fish — A239

5fr, Amelurus nebulosus. 100fr, Heniochus
acuminatus. 145fr, Anthias anthias. 180fr,
Cyprinus carpio.

1988, Feb. 29 **Litho.** *Perf. 13*
762 A239 5fr multicolored .30 .30
763 A239 100fr multicolored 1.25 .60
764 A239 145fr multicolored 2.25 .90
765 A239 180fr multicolored 4.00 1.50
Nos. 762-765 (4) 7.80 3.30

World Meteorology Day — A240

1988, Mar. 15   **Perf. 13½**
766 A240 145fr multi   1.25 .55

Paris-Dakar Rally, 10th Anniv. (in
1987) — A241

Various motorcycle and automobile entries
in desert settings.

1988   **Perf. 13**
767 A241 145fr Motorcycle   1.60 .55
768 A241 180fr Race car   2.00 .60
769 A241 200fr Race car, truck   2.10 .90
770 A241 410fr Thierry Sabine   4.50 1.75
    Nos. 767-770 (4)   10.20 3.80

Inscribed 1987. For surcharges, see Nos.
1051, 1194A.

Mollusks
A242

1988, Apr. 20   **Perf. 12½**
771 A242 10fr Squid   .25 .25
772 A242 20fr Donax trunculus   .25 .25
773 A242 145fr Achatina fulica,
    vert.   1.75 .65
774 A242 165fr Helix nemoralis   2.25 .85
    Nos. 771-774 (4)   4.50 2.00

1988 African Soccer Cup
Championships, Rabat — A243

80fr, Cameroun (winner). 100fr, Kick, CAF
emblem. 145fr, Map, players, final score.
180fr, Trophy.

1988, May 10   **Litho.**   **Perf. 13**
775 A243 80fr multi   .70 .30
776 A243 100fr multi   .90 .35
777 A243 145fr multi   1.25 .40
778 A243 180fr multi   1.75 .60
    Nos. 775-778 (4)   4.60 1.65
    Nos. 776-778 vert.

US Peace
Corps in
Senegal, 25th
Anniv. — A244

1988, May 11   **Litho.**   **Perf. 13**
779 A244 190fr multi   1.50 .65

Marine
Flora — A245

10fr, Dictyota atomaria. 65fr, Agarum gme-
lini. 145fr, Saccorrhiza bulbosa. 180fr,
Rhodymenia palmetta.

1988, June 13   **Litho.**   **Perf. 12½**
780 A245 10fr multicolored   .25 .25
781 A245 65fr multicolored   .65 .25
782 A245 145fr multicolored   1.40 .50
783 A245 180fr multicolored   1.75 .65
    Nos. 780-783 (4)   4.05 1.65

Inscribed 1987.

No. 710 Overprinted

1988, Aug. 27   **Litho.**   **Perf. 13**
784 A221 320fr multi   2.75 1.25

Stamp Fair, Riccione, Aug. 27-29, 1988.
Stamp incorrectly overprinted "89," instead of
"88."

ENDA — A246

125fr, Thierno Saidou Nourou Tall Center.

1988   **Litho.**   **Perf. 13**
785 A246 125fr multi   1.00 .50

For surcharge, see No. 824.

1988 Summer
Olympics,
Seoul — A247

75fr, Running, swimming, soccer. 300fr,
Character trademark, torch. 410fr, Emblems,
running.

1988, Sept. 17   **Litho.**   **Perf. 13**
786 A247 5fr multi   .25 .25
787 A247 75fr multi   .70 .35
788 A247 300fr multi   2.75 1.00
789 A247 410fr multi   3.50 1.40
    Nos. 786-789 (4)   7.20 3.00

Industries
A248

5fr, Phosphate, Thies. 20fr, I.C.S. 145fr,
Seib Mill, Diourbel. 410fr, Mbao refinery.

1988, Nov. 7   **Litho.**   **Perf. 13**
790 A248 5fr multi   .25 .25
791 A248 20fr multi   .25 .25
792 A248 145fr multi   1.25 .45
793 A248 410fr multi   3.75 1.60
    Nos. 790-793 (4)   5.50 2.55

Postcards, c. 1900 — A249

20fr, Boys, Government Palace. 145fr,
Wrestlers, St. Louis Great Mosque. 180fr,
Dakar Depot, young woman in folk costume.
200fr, Governor's Residence, housewife using
mortar & pestle.

1988, Nov. 26
794 A249 20fr red brn & blk   .25 .25
795 A249 145fr red brn & blk   1.25 .55
796 A249 180fr red brn & blk   1.60 .75
797 A249 200fr red brn & blk   1.90 1.00
    Nos. 794-797 (4)   5.00 2.55

Indigenous
Flowers — A250

20fr, Packia biglobosa. 60fr, Eurphorbia
pulcherrima. 65fr, Cyrtosperma senegalense.
410fr, Bombax costatum.

1988, Dec. 4   **Perf. 13x12½**
798 A250 20fr multi   .25 .25
799 A250 60fr multi   .55 .25
800 A250 65fr multi   .65 .25
801 A250 410fr multi   3.75 1.50
    Nos. 798-801 (4)   5.20 2.25

11th Paris-
Dakar Rally
A251

10fr, Mask, vehicle, Eiffel Tower. 145fr, Helmet, desert scene. 180fr, Turban, rallyist in
desert. 220fr, Thierry Sabine.

1989, Jan. 13   **Perf. 13½**
802 A251 10fr multi   .25 .25
803 A251 145fr multi   1.50 .50
804 A251 180fr multi   1.75 .65
805 A251 220fr multi   2.25 .85
    Nos. 802-805 (4)   5.75 2.25

For surcharge see No. 1050.

Tourism
A252

1989, Feb. 15   **Perf. 13**
806 A252 10fr Teranga   .25 .25
807 A252 80fr Campement   .70 .30
808 A252 100fr Saly   .90 .40
809 A252 350fr Dior   2.75 1.10
    Nos. 806-809 (4)   4.60 2.05

Inscribed 1988.

Tourism — A253

130fr, Natl. tourism emblem, vert. 140fr, Visiting rural community. 145fr, Sport fishing.
180fr, Water skiing, polo.

1989, Mar. 11
810 A253 130fr multi   1.00 .40
811 A253 140fr multi   1.10 .45
812 A253 145fr multi   1.40 .65
813 A253 180fr multi   1.40 .80
    Nos. 810-813 (4)   4.90 2.30

Inscribed 1987.

French Revolution, Bicent. — A254

Designs: 180fr, Governor's Palace, St.
Louis. 220fr, Declaration of Human Rights and
Citizenship, vert. 300fr, Flag, revolutionaries.

1989, May 24   **Litho.**   **Perf. 13**
814 A254 180fr shown   1.75 1.00
815 A254 220fr multi   2.00 1.00
816 A254 300fr multi   3.00 1.60
    Nos. 814-816 (3)   6.75 3.60

PHILEXFRANCE
'89 — A255

1989, July 7   **Litho.**   **Perf. 13x12½**
817 A255 10fr shown   .25 .25
818 A255 25fr Simulated stamp,
      map of France   .25 .25
819 A255 75fr Exhibit   .65 .30
820 A255 145fr Affixing stamp   1.25 .50
    Nos. 817-820 (4)   2.40 1.30

Antoine de Saint-Exupery (1900-
1944), French Aviator and
Writer — A256

Scenes from novels: 180fr, *Southern Courier*, 1929. 220fr, *Night flier*, 1931. 410fr, *Bomber pilot*, 1942.

1989, Aug. 30   Litho.   Perf. 13

821	A256	180fr multi	1.50	.50
822	A256	220fr multi	1.75	.85
823	A256	410fr multi	4.00	1.40
		Nos. 821-823 (3)	7.25	2.75

No. 785 Surcharged in Bright Green

1989   Litho.   Perf. 13

824	A246	555fr on 125fr multi	4.25	2.00

3rd Francophone Summit on the Arts
and Culture — A257

Designs: 5fr, Palette, quill pen in ink pot, dancer, vert. 30fr, Children reading. 100fr, Architecture, women, Earth. 200fr, Artist sketching, easel, gear wheels, chemist, computer operator.

1989   Perf. 13x13½, 13½x13

825	A257	5fr multicolored	.25	.25
826	A257	30fr multicolored	.25	.25
827	A257	100fr multicolored	.80	.45
828	A257	200fr multicolored	1.75	.95
		Nos. 825-828 (4)	3.05	1.90

Pottery
A258

30fr, Potter, three-handled urn. 75fr, Vases. 145fr, Woman carrying pottery.

1989, Nov. 1   Perf. 13

829	A258	15fr shown	.25	.25
830	A258	30fr multicolored	.35	.25
831	A258	75fr multicolored	.65	.35
832	A258	145fr multicolored	1.25	.45
		Nos. 829-832 (4)	2.50	1.30

"30," Dakar
Cancel — A259

30fr, Telephone handset, map. 180fr, Map, simulated stamp, phone handset. 220fr, Telecommunications satellite, globe, map.

1989, Oct. 9   Perf. 13½

833	A259	25fr multicolored	.25	.25
834	A259	30fr multicolored	.25	.25
835	A259	180fr multicolored	1.50	.50
836	A259	220fr multicolored	1.75	.65
		Nos. 833-836 (4)	3.75	1.65

Conference of Postal and Telecommunication Administrations of West African Nations (CAPTEAO), 30th anniv.

Natl. Archives, 75th
Anniv. — A260

Designs: 15fr, Stacks, postal card of 1922. 40fr, Document, 1825. 145fr, Document, Archives building. 180fr, Tome.

1989, Oct. 23   Perf. 11½

837	A260	15fr multicolored	.25	.25
838	A260	40fr multicolored	.35	.25
839	A260	145fr multicolored	1.25	.55
840	A260	180fr multicolored	1.40	.65
		Nos. 837-840 (4)	3.25	1.70

Jawarharlal Nehru, 1st Prime Minister
of Independent India — A261

1989, Nov. 14   Perf. 13

841	A261	220fr Portrait, vert.	1.75	.65
842	A261	410fr shown	3.75	1.40

Marine
Life
A262

10fr, Grapsus grapsus. 60fr, Hippocampus guttulatus. 145fr, Lepas anatifera. 220fr, Beach flea.

1989, Nov. 27

843	A262	10fr multicolored	.25	.25
844	A262	60fr multicolored	.85	.30
845	A262	145fr multicolored	1.75	.55
846	A262	220fr multicolored	1.90	.95
		Nos. 843-846 (4)	4.75	2.05

Children's March
to the Sanctuary
A263

1989, Dec. 9   Litho.   Perf. 13½

847	A263	145fr shown	1.10	.40
848	A263	180fr Church	1.50	.60

Pilgrimage to Notre Dame de Popenguine, cent.

Birds
A263a

Designs: 10fr, Phalacrocovax carbolucidus, Anhinga rufa. 45fr, Lavius cirrocephalus. 100fr, Dwarf bee-eater, Lophogetus occipitalis. 180fr, Egretta gularis.

1989, Dec. 11   Perf. 13

849	A263a	10fr multicolored	.35	.30
850	A263a	45fr multicolored	1.00	.40
851	A263a	100fr multicolored	2.00	.60
852	A263a	180fr multicolored	6.00	1.00
		Nos. 849-852 (4)	9.35	2.30

Natl. parks: Djoudj (10fr), Langue de Barbarie (45fr), Basse Casamance (100fr) and Saloum (180fr).

Christmas — A264

1989, Dec. 22   Litho.   Perf. 13

853	A264	10fr shown	.25	.25
854	A264	25fr Teddy bear	.25	.25
855	A264	30fr Manger	.25	.25
856	A264	200fr Mother and child	1.75	.80
		Nos. 853-856 (4)	2.50	1.55

Joan of Arc
Institute, 50th
Anniv. — A265

1989, Dec. 26   Perf. 13½

857	A265	20fr shown	.25	.25
858	A265	500fr Institute	4.25	1.40

Flight of the 1st Seaplane, Mar. 28,
1910 — A266

Perf. 13x12½, 12½x13

1989, Dec. 30   Litho.

859	A266	125fr shown	1.00	.30
860	A266	130fr Seaplane, Fabre	1.10	.40
861	A266	475fr Fabre, schematic of aircraft, vert.	4.25	1.00
		Nos. 859-861 (3)	6.35	1.70

Souvneir Sheet

862	A266	700fr like 475fr, vert.	6.00	5.00

Henri Fabre (1882-1984), aviator.

1992 Summer Olympics,
Barcelona — A267

Various athletes and monuments or architecture.

1990, Jan. 8   Perf. 12½

863	A267	10fr Basketball	.25	.25
864	A267	130fr High jump	.90	.25
865	A267	180fr Discus	1.25	.30
866	A267	190fr Running	1.50	.40
867	A267	315fr Tennis	2.25	.50
868	A267	475fr Equestrian	3.75	.60
		Nos. 863-868 (6)	9.90	2.30

Souvenir Sheet

869	A267	600fr Soccer	4.50	1.00

Fight AIDS
Worldwide
A268

100fr, Umbrella. 145fr, Fist crushing virus. 180fr, Hammering away at virus.

1989, Dec. 1   Litho.   Perf. 13½

870	A268	5fr shown	.25	.25
871	A268	100fr multicolored	.90	.35
872	A268	145fr multicolored	1.10	.50
873	A268	180fr multicolored	1.50	.65
		Nos. 870-873 (4)	3.75	1.75

12th Paris-Dakar Rally — A269

1990, Jan. 16   Perf. 13

874	A269	20fr shown	.25	.25
875	A269	25fr Motorcycle	.25	.25
876	A269	180fr Trophy winner, crowd	1.60	.65
877	A269	200fr Thierry Sabine	1.60	.80
		Nos. 874-877 (4)	3.70	1.95

1990 World Cup Soccer
Championships, Italy — A270

Various athletes and: 45fr, Trophy, the Piazza Della Signoria, Florence. 140fr, Piazza Navona, Rome. 180fr, *The Virgin with St. Anne and the Infant Jesus*, by Leonardo da Vinci. 220fr, Portrait of Giuseppe Garibaldi (1807-1882), Risorgimento Museum, Turin. 300fr, *The Sistine Madonna*, by Raphael. 415fr, *The Virgin and Child*, by Daniele da Volterra. 700fr, Columbus Monument, Milan.

1990, Jan. 31   Litho.   Perf. 13x12½

878	A270	45fr multicolored	.35	.25
879	A270	140fr multicolored	1.00	.40
880	A270	180fr multicolored	1.40	.45
881	A270	220fr multicolored	1.50	.55
882	A270	300fr multicolored	2.50	.75
883	A270	415fr multicolored	3.50	1.25
		Nos. 878-883 (6)	10.25	3.65

Nos. 878-883 exist in souvenir sheets of 1.

Souvenir Sheet

884	A270	700fr multicolored	6.00	3.00

1990 African Soccer
Cup
Championships,
Algeria — A271

1990, Mar. 2   Litho.   Perf. 13

885	A271	20f shown	.25	.25
886	A271	60f Goalie	.55	.25
887	A271	100f Exchange of flags	.90	.40
888	A271	500f Ball, trophy	4.50	1.75
		Nos. 885-888 (4)	6.20	2.65

Postal Services A272

5fr, Facsimile transmission. 15fr, Express mail. 100fr, Postal money orders. 180fr, CNE.

1990, Apr. 30   Litho.   Perf. 13
889 A272 5fr multicolored   .25 .25
890 A272 15fr multicolored   .25 .25
891 A272 100fr multicolored   .75 .30
892 A272 180fr multicolored   1.25 .50
　　Nos. 889-892 (4)   2.50 1.30

A273

1990, May 31   Perf. 13½
893 A273 145fr shown   1.25 .45
894 A273 180fr Hand, wreath,
　　envelope   1.50 .75

Multinational Postal School, 20th anniv.

A274

1990, May 31
895 A274 5fr shown   .25 .25
896 A274 500fr Family   3.75 1.25

S.O.S. Children's Village appeal for aid.

Boy Scouts A275

Scouting emblems and: 30fr, Camping. 100fr, Hiking at lakeshore. 145fr, Following trail. 200fr, Scout, vert.

1990, Nov. 5   Litho.   Perf. 11½
897 A275 30fr multicolored   .25 .25
898 A275 100fr multicolored   .70 .30
899 A275 145fr multicolored   1.00 .50
900 A275 200fr multicolored   1.60 .60
　　Nos. 897-900 (4)   3.55 1.65

Medicinal Plants — A276

95fr, Cassia tora. 105fr, Tamarindus indica. 125fr, Cassia occidentalis. 175fr, Leptadenia hastata.

1990, Nov. 30   Perf. 13x13½
901 A276 95fr multi   1.00 .40
902 A276 105fr multi   1.10 .45
903 A276 125fr multi   1.40 .55
904 A276 175fr multi   1.75 .65
　　Nos. 901-904 (4)   5.25 2.05

A277

145fr, Angel, stars, people. 180fr, Adoration of the Magi. 200fr, Animals, baby in manger.

1990, Dec. 24   Litho.   Perf. 13½
905 A277 25fr multi   .25 .25
906 A277 145fr multicolored   1.25 .65
907 A277 180fr multi   1.60 .65
908 A277 200fr multi   1.75 .65
　　Nos. 905-908 (4)   4.85 2.20

Christmas.

A278

1991, Jan. 2   Litho.   Perf. 13x12½
909 A278 180fr multicolored   1.50 .65

Intl. Red Cross, 125th Anniv., Senegalese Red Cross, 25th anniv. No. 909 inscribed 1988.

Paris-Dakar Rally — A279

125fr, Car, motorcycle. 180fr, Car racing in water. 220fr, Two motorcycles, beach.

1991, Jan. 17
910 A279 15fr shown   .25 .25
911 A279 125fr multicolored   .90 .40
912 A279 180fr multicolored 1.50 .60
913 A279 220fr multicolored 2.00 .85
　　Nos. 910-913 (4)   4.65 2.15

Reptiles A280

15fr, Python sebae. 60fr, Chelonia mydas. 100fr, Crocolylus niloticus. 180fr, Chameleo senegalensis.

1991, Jan. 31   Perf. 13½x13
914 A280 15fr multicolored   .25 .25
915 A280 60fr multicolored   .90 .25
916 A280 100fr multicolored 1.50 .50
917 A280 180fr multicolored 2.50 .85
　　Nos. 914-917 (4)   5.15 1.85

Inscribed 1990.

African Film Festival A281

Designs: 30fr, Sphinx, slave house, cave paintings, tomb of Mohammed. 60fr, Dogon mask, mosque of Dioulasso, drawing of Osiris, man on camel. 100fr, Ruins, drum, statue of

scribe, camels. 180fr, mask, mosque of Djenne, pyramids, Moroccan architecture.

1991, Feb. 23   Perf. 11½
918 A281 30fr org & multi   .25 .25
919 A281 60fr org & multi   .50 .25
920 A281 100fr org & multi   1.00 .45
921 A281 180fr org & multi   1.75 .65
　　Nos. 918-921 (4)   3.50 1.60

Alfred Nobel (1833-1896), Industrialist — A282

Designs: 145fr, Drawing of Nobel.

1991, Mar. 29   Litho.   Die Cut
Self-adhesive
922 A282 145fr multi, vert.   2.00 .65
923 A282 180fr shown   2.50 .85

Antelope — A283

1991, Apr. 24   Litho.   Perf. 13½x13
924 A283 5fr Ouerbia ourebi   .25 .25
925 A283 10fr Gazella dorcas   .25 .25
926 A283 180fr Kobos kob kob 1.40 .60
927 A283 555fr Alcelaphus buce-
　　laphus major   5.00 2.00
　　Nos. 924-927 (4)   6.90 3.10

Trees A284

90fr, Ancardium occidentalus. 100fr, Mangifera indica. 125fr, Borassus flabellifer, vert. 145fr, Elaeis guineensis, vert.

1991, May 30   Perf. 13½x13, 13x13½
928 A284 90fr multicolored   .75 .40
929 A284 100fr multicolored 1.00 .50
930 A284 125fr multicolored 1.00 .50
931 A284 145fr multicolored 1.25 .60
　　Nos. 928-931 (4)   4.00 2.00

Christopher Columbus — A285

100fr, Meeting Haitian natives. 145fr, Columbus' personal coat of arms, vert. 180fr, Santa Maria, Columbus. 200fr, 220fr, Columbus, ships. 500fr, Details of voyages. 625fr, Columbus at chart table.

1991, July 8   Litho.   Perf. 13
932 A285 100fr multicolored   .90 .40
　a.　　Sheet of 1, perf. 12½ .90 .40
933 A285 145fr multicolored 1.25 .55
　a.　　Sheet of 1, perf. 12½ 1.25 .60
934 A285 180fr multicolored 1.60 .65
　a.　　Sheet of 1, perf. 12½ 1.75 .75
935 A285 200fr multicolored 1.75 .75
　a.　　Sheet of 1, perf. 12½ 1.75 .75
936 A285 220fr multicolored 2.00 .80
　a.　　Sheet of 1, perf. 12½ 2.00 .80
937 A285 500fr multicolored 4.50 1.90
　a.　　Sheet of 1, perf. 12½ 4.50 2.00
938 A285 625fr multicolored 5.75 2.25
　a.　　Sheet of 1, perf. 12½ 5.75 2.50
　　Nos. 932-938 (7)   17.75 7.30

Tourism A286

Designs: 10fr, Canoe excursion, Basse-Casamance. 25fr, Shore at Boufflers Hotel, Goree Island. 30fr, Huts built on stilts, Fadiouth Island. 40fr, Salt collecting on lake.

1991, July 30   Litho.   Perf. 13
939 A286 10fr multicolored   .25 .25
940 A286 25fr multicolored   .25 .25
941 A286 30fr multicolored   .35 .25
942 A286 40fr multicolored   .35 .25
　　Nos. 939-942 (4)   1.20 1.00

Dated 1989.

Louis Armstrong, Jazz Musician, 20th Death Anniv. — A287

1991, Oct. 7   Perf. 13½
943 A287 10fr shown   .25 .25
944 A287 145fr Singing   1.25 .60
945 A287 180fr With trumpets 1.50 .75
946 A287 220fr Playing trumpet 1.75 .90
　　Nos. 943-946 (4)   4.75 2.50

Yuri Gagarin, First Man in Space, 30th Anniv. — A288

Various portraits of Gagarin with Vostok I in Earth orbit.

1991, Nov. 25   Litho.   Perf. 13½
947 A288 15fr multicolored   .25 .25
948 A288 145fr multicolored 1.25 .60
949 A288 180fr multicolored 1.50 .75
950 A288 220fr multicolored 1.75 .90
　　Nos. 947-950 (4)   4.75 2.50

Rural Water Supply Project — A289

30fr, Bowl of water. 145fr, Water faucet, huts. 180fr, Dripping faucet, flags. 220fr, Water tower, huts.

1991, Dec. 2   Litho.   Perf. 13½
951 A289 30fr multicolored   .25 .25
952 A289 145fr multicolored 1.25 .65
953 A289 180fr multicolored 1.60 .80
954 A289 220fr multicolored 1.90 .95
　　Nos. 951-954 (4)   5.00 2.65

6th Islamic Summit — A290

145fr, Upraised hands. 180fr, Congress Center, Dakar. 220fr, Grand Mosque, Dakar.

1991, Dec. 9
955	A290	15fr shown	.25	.25
956	A290	145fr multicolored	1.25	.65
957	A290	160fr multicolored	1.60	.80
958	A290	220fr multicolored	1.90	.95
		Nos. 955-958 (4)	5.00	2.65

A291

Basketball, Cent.: 145fr, Player dribbling ball. 180fr, Couple holding trophy. 220fr, Lion, basketball, trophies.

1991, Dec. 21   Litho.   Perf. 13½
959	A291	125fr multicolored	1.00	.50
960	A291	145fr multicolored	1.25	.60
961	A291	180fr multicolored	1.50	.75
962	A291	220fr multicolored	1.75	.90
		Nos. 959-962 (4)	5.50	2.75

A292

5fr, Jesus. 145fr, Madonna and Child. 160fr, Angels. 220fr, Christ Child, animals.

1991, Dec. 24   Litho.   Perf. 13½
963	A292	5fr multicolored	.25	.25
964	A292	145fr multicolored	1.25	.60
965	A292	160fr multicolored	1.40	.70
966	A292	220fr multicolored	1.90	.95
		Nos. 963-966 (4)	4.80	2.50

Christmas. For surcharge see No. 975.

A293

Musical score and: 5fr, Bust of Mozart. 150fr, Mozart conducting. 180fr, Mozart at piano. 220fr, Portrait.

1991, Dec. 31
967	A293	5fr multicolored	.25	.25
968	A293	150fr multicolored	1.25	.65
969	A293	180fr multicolored	1.60	.80
970	A293	220fr multicolored	1.90	.95
		Nos. 967-970 (4)	5.00	2.65

Wolfgang Amadeus Mozart, death bicent.

A293a

Mermoz and: 145fr, Outline maps of South America, Africa. 180fr, Airplane. 200fr, Aiplane in flight.

1991?   Litho.   Perf. 13½
970A	A293a	15fr multicolored	.25	.25
970B	A293a	145fr multicolored	1.00	.35
970C	A293a	180fr multicolored	1.50	.35
970D	A293a	200fr multicolored	2.00	.65
		Nos. 970A-970D (4)	4.75	1.60

Jean Mermoz (1901-36), pilot.
Nos. 970A-970D exist in imperf. souvenir sheets of 1.

A294

1992, Jan. 12   Litho.   Perf. 13½
971	A294	10fr shown	.25	.25
972	A294	145fr Map, soccer balls	1.25	.60
973	A294	200fr Lion, trophy	1.60	.85
974	A294	220fr Players	1.75	.90
		Nos. 971-974 (4)	4.85	2.60

18th African Soccer Cup Championships.

No. 965
Surcharged

1992, Feb. 19   Litho.   Perf. 13½
975	A292	180fr on 160fr	2.00	1.00

Natl.
Parks
A295

1992, Mar. 20   Perf. 13½x13
976	A295	10fr Delta Du Saloum	.45	.25
977	A295	125fr Djoudj	1.60	.50
978	A295	145fr Niokolo-Koba	2.25	.60
979	A295	220fr Basse Casamance	2.75	.90
		Nos. 976-979 (4)	7.05	2.25

Senegal's
Participation in
Gulf War — A296

Designs: 30fr, Oil wells, flag and missiles. 145fr, Oil wells, soldier. 180fr, Holy Ka'aba, soldier with gun. 220fr, Peace dove with flag, map.

1992, Apr. 4   Perf. 13½
980	A296	30fr multicolored	.25	.25
981	A296	145fr multicolored	1.25	.60
982	A296	180fr multicolored	1.50	.75
983	A296	220fr multicolored	1.75	.90
		Nos. 980-983 (4)	4.75	2.50

Fish
Industry
A297

Stylized designs: 5fr, Catching fish. 60fr, Retail outlets. 100fr, Processing plant. 150fr, Packaging.

1992, Apr. 6   Litho.   Perf. 13½
984	A297	5fr multicolored	.25	.25
985	A297	60fr multicolored	.55	.30
986	A297	100fr multicolored	.90	.45
987	A297	150fr multicolored	1.25	.65
		Nos. 984-987 (4)	2.95	1.65

Tourism — A298

1992, May 5   Perf. 13½x13
988	A298	5fr Niokolo complex	.25	.25
989	A298	10fr Casamance River	.25	.25
990	A298	150fr Dakar region	1.25	.65
991	A298	200fr Saint-Louis excursion	1.75	.95
		Nos. 988-991 (4)	3.50	2.10

Planting
Trees
A299

Various designs showing children planting trees.

1992, May 29   Perf. 13½x13, 13x13½
992	A299	145fr multi	1.25	.65
993	A299	180fr multi	1.60	.80
994	A299	200fr multi	1.75	.90
995	A299	220fr multi, vert.	1.90	.95
		Nos. 992-995 (4)	6.50	3.30

Public
Works
Projects
A300

Various scenes of people cleaning and repairing public walkways.

Perf. 13½x13, 13x13½
1992, June 1   Litho.
996	A300	25fr multi	.25	.25
997	A300	145fr multi	1.25	.65
998	A300	180fr multi, vert.	1.60	.80
999	A300	220fr multi, vert.	2.00	1.00
		Nos. 996-999 (4)	5.10	2.70

Children's Rights — A301

1992, June 12   Perf. 13
1000	A301	20fr Education	.25	.25
1001	A301	45fr Guidance	.40	.25
1002	A301	165fr Instruction	1.40	.70
1003	A301	180fr Health care	1.60	.80
		Nos. 1000-1003 (4)	3.65	2.00

African
Integration
A302

1992, June 29   Litho.   Perf. 13
1004	A302	10fr Free trade	.25	.25
1005	A302	30fr Youth activities	.25	.25
1006	A302	145fr Communications	1.25	.60
1007	A302	220fr Women's movements	2.00	1.00
		Nos. 1004-1007 (4)	3.75	2.10

1992 Summer
Olympics,
Barcelona
A303

1992, July 25   Litho.   Perf. 13½
1008	A303	145fr Map, horiz.	1.10	.55
1009	A303	180fr Runner	1.50	.70
1010	A303	200fr Sprinter, horiz.	2.00	.75
1011	A303	300fr Torch bearer	2.75	1.10
		Nos. 1008-1011 (4)	7.35	3.10

Blue
Train — A304

1992, Aug. 3
1012	A304	70fr shown	.70	.30
1013	A304	145fr Train yard	1.40	.55
1014	A304	200fr Train, passengers	2.00	.75
1015	A304	220fr Station	2.10	.85
		Nos. 1012-1015 (4)	6.20	2.45

Intl. Maritime
Heritage
Year — A305

25fr, Map of Antarctica. 100fr, Ocean, sea life. 180fr, Man addressing UN. 220fr, Hands holding globe, flags, ship, fish.

1992, Sept. 4
1016	A305	25fr multi, horiz.	.25	.25
1017	A305	100fr multi	1.00	.40
1018	A305	180fr multi	2.00	.70
1019	A305	220fr multi	2.25	.85
		Nos. 1016-1019 (4)	5.50	2.20

Corals
A306

Various coral formations.

Perf. 13½x13, 13x13½
1992, Sept. 18   Litho.
1020	A306	50fr multicolored	.40	.25
1021	A306	100fr multicolored	1.10	.40
1022	A306	145fr multi, vert.	1.50	1.10
1023	A306	220fr multicolored	2.25	.90
		Nos. 1020-1023 (4)	5.25	2.65

Konrad Adenauer (1876-1967) — A307

Designs: 5fr, Portrait, vert. 145fr, Schaumburg Palace, Bonn. 180fr, Hands clasped. 220fr, Map of West Germany.

SENEGAL

Perf. 13x13½, 13½x13

1992, Sept. 30   Litho.
1024	A307	5fr multicolored	.25	.25
1025	A307	145fr multicolored	1.25	.60
1026	A307	180fr multicolored	1.50	.75
1027	A307	220fr multicolored	1.75	.90
		Nos. 1024-1027 (4)	4.75	2.50

Shellfish — A308

1992, Oct. 1   Litho.   *Perf. 13½*
1028	A308	20fr Crab	.25	.25
1029	A308	30fr Spider crab	.35	.25
1030	A308	180fr Lobster	1.75	.70
1031	A308	200fr Shrimp	2.10	.75
		Nos. 1028-1031 (4)	4.45	1.95

Fruit-bearing Plants — A309

10fr, Parkia biglobosa. 50fr, Balanites aegyptiaca. 200fr, Parinari macrophylla. 220fr, Opuntiatuna.

1992, Oct. 16   Litho.   *Perf. 13x13½*
1032	A309	10fr multicolored	.25	.25
1033	A309	50fr multicolored	.45	.25
1034	A309	200fr multicolored	1.60	.70
1035	A309	220fr multicolored	1.75	.90
		Nos. 1032-1035 (4)	4.05	2.10

John Glenn's Orbital Flight, 30th Anniv. — A310

15fr, Astronaut in spacesuit, flag, map, spacecraft, horiz. 145fr, American flag, Glenn, horiz. 180fr, Flag, lift-off of rocket, Glenn in spacesuit, horiz. 200fr, Astronaut in spacesuit, spacecraft.

1992, Nov. 30   Litho.   *Perf. 13½*
1036	A310	15fr multicolored	.25	.25
1037	A310	145fr multicolored	1.25	.60
1038	A310	180fr multicolored	1.60	.70
1039	A310	200fr multicolored	1.75	.80
		Nos. 1036-1039 (4)	4.85	2.35

Maps Featuring Bakari II — A311

100fr, Map from Spanish Atlas, 1375. 145fr, Stone head, Vera Cruz, Mexico, world map, 1413.

1992, Dec. 2   *Perf. 13*
| 1040 | A311 | 100fr multicolored | 1.50 | .40 |
| 1041 | A311 | 145fr multicolored | 2.25 | .60 |

No. 1041 issued only with black bar obliterating "Mecades."

Biennial of Dakar — A312

20fr, Picture frame. 50fr, Puppet head, stage. 145fr, Open book. 220fr, Musical instrument.

1992, Dec. 14   *Perf. 13½*
1042	A312	20fr multicolored	.25	.25
1043	A312	50fr multicolored	.45	.25
1044	A312	145fr multicolored	1.25	.60
1045	A312	220fr multicolored	2.10	.90
		Nos. 1042-1045 (4)	4.05	2.00

Christmas A313

Designs: 15fr, Children dancing around large ornament, horiz. 145fr, Christmas tree. 180fr, Jesus Christ. 200fr, Santa Claus.

1992, Dec. 24   *Perf. 13½*
1046	A313	15fr multicolored	.25	.25
1047	A313	145fr multicolored	2.00	.60
1048	A313	180fr multicolored	2.50	.70
1049	A313	200fr multicolored	2.75	.90
		Nos. 1046-1049 (4)	7.50	2.45

Nos. 770, 804 Srchd. in Red

1993, Jan. 17   Litho.   *Perf. 13½*
| 1050 | A251 | 145fr on 180fr #804 | 1.75 | 1.00 |

Perf. 13
| 1051 | A241 | 220fr on 410fr #770 | 2.75 | 1.25 |

Size and location of surcharge varies.

Environmental Protection — A314

Accident Prevention A315

Designs: 20fr, Medical clinic. 25fr, Preventing industrial accidents. 145fr, Preventing chemical spills. 200fr, Red Cross helicopter, airline crash.

Perf. 13 (#1052, 1055), 13½

1993, Mar. 22   Litho.
1052	A314	20fr multicolored	.25	.25
1053	A315	25fr multicolored	.25	.25
1054	A315	145fr multicolored	1.10	.60
1055	A314	200fr multicolored	1.60	.80
		Nos. 1052-1055 (4)	3.20	1.90

Abdoulaye Seck Marie Parsine (1873-1931), PTT Director — A316

1993, Apr. 21   Litho.   *Perf. 13½*
| 1056 | A316 | 220fr multicolored | 2.10 | .90 |

Wild Animals A317

30fr, Crocuta crocuta. 50fr, Panthera leo. 70fr, Panthera pardus. 150fr, Giraffa camelo-pardalis peratta, vert. 180fr, Cervus.

1993, Nov. 26   Litho.   *Perf. 13½*
1057	A317	30fr multicolored	.25	.25
1058	A317	50fr multicolored	.25	.25
1059	A317	70fr multicolored	.55	.25
1060	A317	150fr multicolored	1.00	.30
1061	A317	180fr multicolored	1.60	.35
		Nos. 1057-1061 (5)	3.65	1.40

Christmas A318

Designs: 80fr, Two children seated by Christmas tree. 145fr, Santa holding presents, three children. 150fr, Girl, Santa with present.

1993, Dec. 24   Litho.   *Perf. 13x13½*
1062	A318	5fr multicolored	.25	.25
1063	A318	80fr multicolored	.30	.25
1064	A318	145fr multicolored	.55	.30
1065	A318	150fr multicolored	.60	.30
		Nos. 1062-1065 (4)	1.70	1.10

Paris-Dakar Rally, 16th Anniv. — A319

Designs: 145fr, Truck, car, motorcycle racing by tree. 180fr, Racing through desert, men with camel. 220fr, Car, truck, village.

1994, Jan. 5   *Perf. 13½*
1066	A319	145fr multicolored	.70	.30
1067	A319	180fr multicolored	.90	.35
1068	A319	220fr multicolored	1.00	.45
		Nos. 1066-1068 (3)	2.60	1.10

Assassination of John F. Kennedy, 30th Anniv. — A320

1993, Dec. 31   Litho.   *Perf. 13*
| 1069 | A320 | 80fr shown | .30 | .25 |
| 1070 | A320 | 555fr Kennedy, White House | 2.25 | 1.10 |

Fishing Industry A321

5fr, Drying eels. 90fr, Sifting for shellfish. 100fr, Salting fish. 200fr, Cooking fish.

1994, Feb. 28
1071	A321	5fr multicolored	.25	.25
1072	A321	90fr multicolored	.35	.25
1073	A321	100fr multicolored	.40	.25
1074	A321	200fr multicolored	.80	.40
		Nos. 1071-1074 (4)	1.80	1.15

Flowers — A321a

Design: 80fr, Gloriosa superba. 100fr, Erythrina senegalensis. 145fr, Spathodea campanulata. 220fr, Hibiscus rosa-sinensis. 250fr, Satanocrater berhautii.

Perf. 13¼x13½

1994, Feb. 28   Litho.
1074A	A321a	80fr multi	4.00	—
1074B	A321a	100fr multi	5.00	—
1074C	A321a	145fr multi	7.25	—
1074D	A321a	220fr multi		
1074E	A321a	250fr multi	11.00	

Dated 1993.

Conservation of the Seashore — A322

Stylized designs: 5fr, Halting removal of sand. 75fr, Fight against drifting sand dunes. 100fr, Dams, dikes against beach erosion. 200fr, Healthy, aesthetic environment.

1994, Mar. 7
1075	A322	5fr multicolored	.25	.25
1076	A322	75fr multicolored	.30	.25
1077	A322	100fr multicolored	.55	.40
1078	A322	200fr multicolored	.80	.60
		Nos. 1075-1078 (4)	1.90	1.50

Save the Elephant A323

60fr, Elephant in "SOS". 90fr, Elephants forming "SOS". 145fr, Elephant, tusks.

1994, Apr. 18
1079	A323	30fr shown	.25	.25
1080	A323	60fr multicolored	.65	.25
1081	A323	90fr multicolored	1.25	.45
1082	A323	145fr multicolored	1.60	.50
		Nos. 1079-1082 (4)	3.75	1.45

Arrival of
Portuguese
in Senegal,
550th
Anniv.
A324

1994, Nov. 17   Litho.   Perf. 12
1083 A324 175fr multicolored   .80   .40
See Portugal No. 2036.

A325

Shells: 20fr, Murex saxatilis, horiz. 45fr, Nerita senegalensis. 75fr, Polymita picea, horiz. 175fr, Scalaria pretiosa. 215fr, Conus gloria maris.

1994, Oct. 3   Litho.   Perf. 13½
1084 A325 20fr multicolored   .25   .25
1085 A325 45fr multicolored   .25   .25
1086 A325 75fr multicolored   .30   .25
1087 A325 175fr multicolored   .75   .40
1088 A325 215fr multicolored   .95   .50
        Nos. 1084-1088 (5)   2.50 1.65

A326

1994, Nov. 4
1089 A326 175fr multi, horiz.   .75   .40
1090 A326 215fr multi, horiz.   .95   .50
1091 A326 275fr multicolored   1.25   .60
1092 A326 275fr multi, diff.   1.25   .65
        Nos. 1089-1092 (4)   4.20 2.15

Intl. Olympic Committee, Cent.

Wild
Animals
A327

60fr, Canis aureus. 70fr, Aonyx capensis. 100fr, Herpestes ichneumon. 175fr, Manis gigantea. 215fr, Varanus niloticus.

1994, Oct. 28   Litho.   Perf. 13½
1093 A327 60fr multicolored   .30   .25
1094 A327 70fr multicolored   .30   .25
1095 A327 100fr multicolored   .45   .25
1096 A327 175fr multicolored   .75   .40
1097 A327 215fr multicolored   .95   .45
        Nos. 1093-1097 (5)   2.75 1.60

Lions Club Intl., 13th Multidistrict
Convention, Dakar — A328

1994, May 5   Litho.   Perf. 13½x13
1098 A328 30fr shown   .25   .25
1099 A328 60fr Emblem, butterfly   .30   .25

1100 A328 175fr Emblem, "L's"   .85   .40
1101 A328 215fr Colors, emblem   1.00   .50
        Nos. 1098-1101 (4)   2.40 1.40

African
Children's
Day
A329

UNICEF emblem and: 175fr, Children playing. 215fr, Family, huts.

1994, June 16   Litho.   Perf. 13½
1102 A329 175fr multicolored   2.00   .40
1103 A329 215fr multicolored   2.25   .50

1994 World Cup Soccer
Championships, US — A330

Designs: 45fr, Flags of participants, soccer ball, vert. 175fr, Top of globe, bottom of soccer ball, vert. 215fr, Player. 665fr, Two players.

1994, June 17
1104 A330 45fr multicolored   .25   .25
1105 A330 175fr multicolored   .80   .40
1106 A330 215fr multicolored   1.00   .50
1107 A330 665fr multicolored   3.00 1.50
        Nos. 1104-1107 (4)   5.05 2.65

UPU Congress, Seoul — A331

Designs: 10fr, Rainbow. 175fr, Dove with wings like postage stamp. 300fr, 260fr, Stylized stamp. Stylized globe, air mail envelope, hands.

1994, Aug. 16   Litho.   Perf. 13½x13
1108 A331 10fr multicolored   .30   .25
1109 A331 175fr multicolored   1.50 1.00
1110 A331 260fr multicolored   2.00 1.10
1111 A331 300fr multicolored   2.25 1.25

Intl.
Year of
the
Family
A333

UN emblem and: 5fr, People of different races, national flags, peace dove, globe, sun. 175fr, Globe, flags, people. 215fr, Globe, mother & child. 290fr, Buildings, family, dove, sun, globe.

1994, Aug. 19   Perf. 13½x13
1113 A333 5fr multicolored   .25   .25
1114 A333 175fr multicolored   .80   .40
1115 A333 215fr multicolored   1.00   .50
1116 A333 290fr multicolored   1.40   .70
        Nos. 1113-1116 (4)   3.45 1.85

10th Toulouse to
Saint-Louis Air
Rally — A334

1994, Apr. 10   Perf. 13½
1117 A334 100fr Breguet 14   .50   .25
1118 A334 145fr Guillaumet   .65   .35
1119 A334 180fr Jean Mermoz   .85   .40
1120 A334 220fr Saint-Exupery   1.00   .50
        Nos. 1117-1120 (4)   3.00 1.50
        Dated 1993.

Christmas — A335

175fr, Santa Claus, Christ, children, presents. 215fr, Christmas trees, religious scenes. 275fr, Magi, Christ Child. 290fr, Madonna & Child.

Perf. 13x13½, 13½x13
1994, Nov. 24
1121 A335 175fr multi, vert.   .80   .40
1122 A335 215fr multi, vert.   1.00   .50
1123 A335 275fr multi   1.25   .65
1124 A335 290fr multi, vert.   1.40   .70
        Nos. 1121-1124 (4)   4.45 2.25

Historical Sites — A336

Designs: 100fr, Goree Chateau. 175fr, Soudan Mansion. 215fr, Goree Island. 275fr, Pinet Laprade fort, Sedhiou.

1994, Mar. 20   Litho.   Perf. 13½x13
1125 A336 100fr multicolored   .45   .25
1126 A336 175fr multicolored   .80   .40
1127 A336 215fr multicolored   1.00   .50
1128 A336 275fr multicolored   1.25   .65
        Nos. 1125-1128 (4)   3.50 1.80

Kallisaye
Natl. Park
A337

Water birds: 100fr, Ardea melanocephala, vert. 275fr, Sterna caspia, vert. 290fr, Egretta gularis, vert. 380fr, Pelecanus rufescens.

1995, Feb. 2   Perf. 13½
1129 A337 100fr multicolored   .50   .25
1130 A337 275fr multicolored   1.40   .70
1131 A337 290fr multicolored   1.60   .75
1132 A337 380fr multicolored   2.00   .95
        Nos. 1129-1132 (4)   5.50 2.65

Dinosaurs
A338

1995, Jan. 27
1133 A338 100fr Diplodocus   .45   .25
1134 A338 175fr Brontosaurus   .75   .40
1135 A338 215fr Triceratops   1.00   .50
1136 A338 290fr Stegosaurus   1.75   .70
1137 A338 300fr Tyrannosaurus   2.50 1.00
        Nos. 1133-1137 (5)   6.45 2.85

House of
Slaves,
Goree
A339

1994   Litho.   Perf. 13½
1138 A339 500fr multicolored   2.50 1.25

Flowers — A340

Designs: 30fr, Bombax costatum. 75fr, Allamanda cathartica. 100fr, Catharantus roseus. 1000fr, Clerodendron speciossimum.

1995, Apr. 9
1139 A340 30fr multicolored   .25   .25
1140 A340 75fr multicolored   .40   .25
1141 A340 100fr multicolored   .50   .25
1142 A340 1000fr multicolored   5.00 2.50
        Nos. 1139-1142 (4)   6.15 3.25

A341

1995, May 11   Litho.   Perf. 11½
1143 A341 260fr shown   1.25   .65
1144 A341 275fr Emblem, dove   1.40   .70

District 9100 Conference of Rotary, Intl.

A342

Map of Africa with countries highlighted, native item or animal: 10fr, Sudan, musical instrument. 15fr, Dahomey (Benin), huts, canoes. 30fr, Ivory Coast, elephant. 70fr, Mauritania, camel. 175fr, Guinea, string instrument, bananas. 180fr, Upper Volta (Burkina Faso), ox, vegetables, drum. 215fr, Niger, Cross of Agadès. 225fr, Senegal, lions.

1995, June 17
1145 A342 10fr multicolored   .25   .25
1146 A342 15fr multicolored   .25   .25
1147 A342 30fr multicolored   .25   .25
1148 A342 70fr multicolored   .35   .25
1149 A342 175fr multicolored   .90   .45
1150 A342 180fr multicolored   .95   .45
1151 A342 215fr multicolored   1.10   .55
1152 A342 225fr multicolored   1.25   .60
        Nos. 1145-1152 (8)   5.30 3.05

Fashion Type of 1972
1995, June 30   Perf. 13½x13
Size: 21x26mm
1153 A106 5fr yel brown   .25   .25
1154 A106 10fr bright green   .25   .25
1155 A106 20fr henna brown   .25   .25
1156 A106 25fr olive   .25   .25
1157 A106 30fr light olive   .25   .25
1158 A106 40fr yellow green   .25   .25
1159 A106 100fr slate blue   .50   .25
1160 A106 150fr deep blue   .75   .35
1161 A106 175fr dull brown   .90   .45
1162 A106 200fr black   1.00   .50
1163 A106 250fr red   1.25   .60
1164 A106 275fr rose carmine   1.40   .80
        Nos. 1153-1164 (12)   7.30 4.45

Economic Community of West African States (ECOWAS), 20th Anniv. — A343

Designs: 175fr, Satellite dish, telephone, computer, map, dam, vert. 215fr, Flags of member nations, fruits, vegetables.

1995, Sept. 11   Litho.   Perf. 13½
1165 A343 175fr multicolored   .90   .45
1166 A343 215fr multicolored   1.10   .55

Louis Pasteur (1822-95) — A345

275fr, Holding vial. 500fr, In laboratory.

1995, Sept. 28   Litho.   Perf. 11½
1168 A345 275fr multicolored   1.25   .60
1169 A345 500fr multicolored   2.25 1.25

Motion Pictures, Cent. A346

Early developments by Lumiere Brothers: 100fr, Scene from "The Water Sprinkler." 200fr, First pulbic showing of motion picture. 250fr, Auguste, Louis Lumiere watching picture of train arriving at station. 275fr, Demonstrating cinematography.

1995, Oct. 2   Perf. 13½
1170 A346 100fr multicolored   .45   .25
1171 A346 200fr multicolored   1.00   .45
1172 A346 250fr multicolored   1.25   .55
1173 A346 275fr multicolored   1.75   .70
       Nos. 1170-1173 (4)   4.45 1.95

FAO, 50th Anniv. A347

Designs: 175fr, Farmer, oxen. 215fr, Technician, bringing water to arid regions. 260fr, Gathering fish. 275fr, Nutrition of infants.

1995, Oct. 16
1174 A347 175fr multicolored   .80   .40
1175 A347 215fr multicolored   .95   .50
1176 A347 260fr multicolored   1.10   .55
1177 A347 275fr multicolored   1.25   .60
       Nos. 1174-1177 (4)   4.10 2.05

A348

1995, Oct. 24   Perf. 11½
1178 A348 275fr shown   1.25   .60
1179 A348 1000fr Building   4.25 2.00
       UN, 50th anniv.

A349

1995, Nov. 2
1180 A349 150fr shown   .70   .35
1181 A349 500fr Contestants   2.25 1.10

La Francophonie, 25th anniv.

Wild Animals — A350

Designs: a, 90fr, Syncerus nanus savanensis. b, 150fr, Phacochoerus aethiopicus. c, 175fr, Tragelaphus scriptus. d, 275fr, Goechelone sulcata. e, 300fr, Hystrix cristata.

1995, Nov. 13   Perf. 13½
1182 A350 Strip of 5, #a.-e.   5.75 5.75

Endangered Birds — A351

90fr, Hydroprogne caspia. 145fr, Gelochelidon nilotica. 150fr, Sterna maxima. 180fr, Sterna hirunda.

1995, Nov. 30   Perf. 13½x13
1183 A351 90fr multicolored   .45   .25
1184 A351 145fr multicolored   .80   .30
1185 A351 150fr multicolored   1.40   .35
1186 A351 180fr multicolored   1.75   .55
       Nos. 1183-1186 (4)   4.40 1.45

Butterflies A352

Designs: 45fr, Meganostoma eurydice. 100fr, Luehdorfia japonica. 200fr, Hebomoia glaucippe. 220fr, Aglais urticae.

1995, Dec. 4   Perf. 13
1187 A352 45fr multicolored   .40   .25
1188 A352 100fr multicolored   .80   .30
1189 A352 200fr multicolored   1.90   .50
1190 A352 220fr multicolored   2.25   .80
       Nos. 1187-1190 (4)   5.35 1.85

Tourism A353

1995, Dec. 28   Perf. 13½
1191 A353 100fr Bassari Festival .45   .25
1192 A353 175fr Baawnaan, vert.   .80   .40
1193 A353 220fr Traditional huts 1.00   .50
1194 A353 500fr Turu   2.25 1.10
       Nos. 1191-1194 (4)   4.50 2.25

No. 770 Surcharged

1995 ?   Litho.   Perf. 13
1194A A241 275fr on 410fr #770   —

A354

Paris-Granada-Dakar Rally, 17th Anniv.: 215fr, Car, silhouettes of three people. 275fr, Man racing on motorcycle, vert. 290fr, Car under Eiffel Tower, car racing toward finish line. 665fr, Two cars going over hill.

1996, Jan. 16   Litho.   Perf. 11½
1195 A354 215fr multicolored   1.10   .60
1196 A354 275fr multicolored   1.50   .75
1197 A354 290fr multicolored   1.60   .80
1198 A354 665fr multicolored   3.50 1.75
       Nos. 1195-1198 (4)   7.70 3.90

A355

Flowers: 175fr, Gossypium barbadense. 275fr, Hibiscus sabdariffa. 290fr, Hibiscus asper. 500fr, Nymphaea lotus.

1996, Feb.2
1199 A355 175fr multicolored   .95   .45
1200 A355 275fr multicolored   1.50   .75
1201 A355 290fr multicolored   1.60   .80
1202 A355 500fr multicolored   2.75 1.40
       Nos. 1199-1202 (4)   6.80 3.40

Sports A356

1996, Mar. 29   Litho.   Perf. 11½
1203 A356 125fr Boxing   .65   .35
1204 A356 215fr Judo   1.10   .60
1205 A356 275fr Javelin   1.50   .75
1206 A356 320fr Discus   1.75   .90
       Nos. 1203-1206 (4)   5.00 2.60

Art by Serge Correa, Hall of Pearls A357

1996,Apr. 18
1207 A357 260fr Corridor 1   1.25   .70
1208 A357 320fr Symphony 1   1.75   .85

National Parks A358

Designs: 175fr, Dolphin, flamingo, heron, Saloum Delta. 200fr, Chimpanzee, giraffe, elephant, Niokolo-Koba. 220fr, Crustaceans, bird in cave, Madeleine Island. 275fr, Abyssinia hornbill, crocodile, hippopotamus, Basse Casamance.

1996, Mar. 4
1209 A358 175fr multicolored   .95   .50
1210 A358 200fr multicolored   1.10   .55
1211 A358 220fr multicolored   1.25   .60
1212 A358 275fr multicolored   1.50   .75
       Nos. 1209-1212 (4)   4.80 2.40

Intl. Olympic Committee, Cent. A359

1996, July 1   Litho.   Perf. 12½
1213 A359 215fr multicolored   1.25   .60

1996 Summer Olympic Games, Atlanta A360

1996, July 15   Perf. 13
1214 A360 10fr Swimming   .25   .25
1215 A360 80fr Gymnastics   .40   .25
1216 A360 175fr Running   1.00   .50
1217 A360 260fr Hurdles   1.40   .75
       Nos. 1214-1217 (4)   3.05 1.70

Decade of UN Against Illegal Drug Abuse and Trafficking A361

215fr, UN emblem, hand holding red stop sign, drug paraphernalia.

1996, June 21   Perf. 13½
1218 A361 175fr multicolored   .95   .50
1219 A361 215fr multicolored   1.10   .60

Red Cross of Senegal — A362

1996, Oct. 21   Perf. 12½
1220 A362 275fr multicolored   1.50   .75

Primates A363

Designs: 10fr, Cercopithecus aethiops. 30fr, Erthrocebus patas. 90fr, Cercopithecus campbelli. 215fr, Pantroglodytes verus. 260fr, Papio papio.

1996, Nov. 29   Litho.   Perf. 13x13½
1221 A363 10fr multicolored   .30   .25
1222 A363 30fr multicolored   .30   .25
1223 A363 90fr multicolored   .50   .25
1224 A363 215fr multicolored   .90   .50
1225 A363 260fr multicolored   1.00   .60
   a. Strip of 5, #1221-1225   4.00 3.00

UNICEF,
50th
Anniv.
A364

1996, Dec. 11   Perf. 13½x13
1226 A364 75fr shown   .30   .25
1227 A364 275fr Child, diff. 1.25   .60

19th Dakar-Agades-Dakar
Rally — A365

25fr, Semi-truck. 75fr, Man pushing car, figure of man. 215fr, Race car. 300fr, Man on motorcycle.

1997, Jan. 19   Litho.   Perf. 13x13½
1228 A365 25fr multicolored   .25   .25
1229 A365 75fr multicolored   .30   .25
1230 A365 215fr multicolored   .90   .45
1231 A365 300fr multicolored   1.25   .65
      Nos. 1228-1231 (4)   2.70   1.60

Trees — A366

Designs: 80fr, Faidherbia albida. 175fr, Eucalyptus. 220fr, Khaya senegalensis. 260fr, Casuarina equisetifolia.

1997, Mar. 31
1232 A366 80fr multicolored   .35   .25
1233 A366 175fr multicolored   .75   .35
1234 A366 220fr multicolored   .90   .45
1235 A366 260fr multicolored   1.00   .50
      Nos. 1232-1235 (4)   3.00   1.55

Birds — A367

25fr, Platalea leucorodia. 70fr, Leptilos crumeniferus. 175fr, Balcarica pavonina. 215fr, Ephippiarhychus senegalensis. 220fr, Numenius arquata.

1997, Feb. 28
1236 A367 25fr multicolored   .25   .25
1237 A367 70fr multicolored   .30   .25
1238 A367 175fr multicolored   .75   .35
1239 A367 215fr multicolored   .90   .45
1240 A367 220fr multicolored   .95   .50
  a. Strip of 5, #1236-1240   5.00   5.00

Insects
A368

Designs: 10fr, Mantis religiosa. 50fr, Forficula auricularia. 75fr, Schistocerca gregaria. 215fr, Cicindela lunulata. 220fr, Gryllus campestris.

1997, Jan. 31   Perf. 13½x13
1241 A368 10fr multicolored   .25   .25
1243 A368 50fr multicolored   .25   .25
1244 A368 75fr multicolored   .30   .25
1245 A368 215fr multicolored   .90   .45
1246 A368 220fr multicolored   .95   .45
  a. Strip of 5, #1241-1246   4.00   4.00

Postal officials in Senegal have declared Greenpeace sheets of nine with values of 250fr and 425fr "fake" and "illegal".

Cheikh Anta Diop (1923-86),
Historian — A369

Diop: 175fr, And Egyptian hieroglyphs, Sphinx. 215fr, Performing carbon 14 test.

1996, Feb. 26   Litho.   Perf. 13¼
1247-1248 A369 Set of 2   3.50   1.50

Fashion Type of 1972
1996-97   Engr.   Perf. 13½x13
Size: 21x26mm
1249   A106 15fr green
1250   A106 50fr green   .25   .25
1251   A106 60fr olive grn   .40
1251A A108 70fr olive green   .40
1252   A106 80fr green   .60   —
1253   A106 190fr olive green   .75
1254   A106 215fr dark blue   .80   .40
1254A A106 225fr dark blue   1.00   —
1255   A106 240fr brown   1.40
1256   A106 260fr red brown   1.00   .50
1256A A106 300fr red lilac   1.40
1256B A106 320fr rose lilac   1.50
1257   A106 350fr henna brown   1.60
1257B A106 410fr lake   1.75
1257C A106 500fr brn violet   2.25
1257D A106 1000fr carmine   4.50

Issued: 80fr, 225fr, 4/13/96. 50fr, 70fr, 215fr, 260fr, 4/13; 190fr, 240fr, 300fr, 350fr, 1000fr, 6/97.
Additional stamps were released in this set. The editors would like to examine them. Numbers will change if necessary.

Third World
A370

Design: 500fr, Hot air balloon in flight.

1996, Apr. 13   Litho.   Perf. 13½
1258 A370 215fr shown   .75   .40
1259 A370 500fr multicolored 1.75   .90

See Mali Nos. 812-813.

Pres.
Leopold
Senghor,
90th
Birthday
A371

Pictures of Senghor and: 175fr, Map of Senegal. 275fr, Quotation, vert.

1996, Oct. 9   Litho.   Perf. 13¼
1260-1261 A371 Set of 2   1.75   1.75

Niokolo-Badiar Natl. Park — A372

Designs: 30fr, Haliaetus vacifer. 90fr, Hippopotamus amphibius. 240fr, Loxindonta africana oxyotis. 300fr, Taurotragus derbianus.

1997, July 21   Litho.   Perf. 13½x13
1262 A372 30fr multicolored   .65   .25
1263 A372 90fr multicolored   .65   .25
1264 A372 240fr multicolored 1.00   .50
1265 A372 300fr multicolored 1.25   .65
      Nos. 1262-1265 (4)   3.55   1.65

Shells — A373

Designs: a, 15fr, Cassis tesselata. b, 40fr, Pugilina meria. c, 190fr, Cyprea mappa. d, 200fr, Natica adansoni. e, 300fr, Bullia miran.

1997, Aug. 19   Perf. 13x13½
1266 A373 Strip of 5, #a.-e. 4.00   4.00

Wild Animals — A374

a, 25fr, African buffaloes. b, 90fr, Gazelles. c, 100fr, Gnu. d, 200fr, Wild dogs. e, 240fr, Cheetah.

1997, June 27
1267 A374 Strip of 5, #a.-e. 4.00   4.00

Goree
Island
A375

1997, May 30   Perf. 13½
1268 A375 180fr multicolored .75   .40

No. 1268 is dated 1992 and has word "almadies" obliterated.

Dakar-Dakar Rally, 20th
Anniv. — A376

Designs: 20fr, Truck traveling across Sahel. 45fr, Motorcycle arriving at Lake Rose. 190fr, Sports utility vehicle crossing Mauritanian Desert. 240fr, Car at Senegal River.

1998, Jan. 1   Litho.   Perf. 13½x13
1269 A376 20fr multicolored   .25   .25
1270 A376 45fr multicolored   .25   .25
1271 A376 190fr multicolored .80   .40
1272 A376 240fr multicolored 1.00   .50
      Nos. 1269-1272 (4)   2.30   1.40

Food
Day
A377

190fr, Receiving grain through cereal bank. 200fr, Proper nutrition for women.

1997, Oct. 16
1273 A377 190fr multicolored .80   .40
1274 A377 200fr multicolored .85   .45

A378

Masks: 45fr, Planche, Burkina Faso. 90fr, Kpeliyehe, Ivory Coast. 200fr, Nimba, Guinea Bissau. 240fr, Walu, Mali. 300fr, Dogon, Mali.

1997, Nov. 28
1275 A378 45fr multicolored   .25   .25
1276 A378 90fr multicolored   .45   .25
1277 A378 200fr multicolored .85   .40
1278 A378 240fr multicolored 1.00   .50
1279 A378 300fr multicolored 1.25   .65
  a. Strip of 5, #1275-1279   4.00   2.50

A379

1997   Perf. 11½
1280 A379 310fr multicolored 1.25   .65

Heinrich von Stephan (1831-97).

Vasco de Gama (1460-1524),
Expedition Around Cape of Good
Hope, 500th Anniv.
A380

De Gama and: 40fr, Route of spices. 75fr, Port of Zanzibar. 190fr, Caravel revolution. 200fr, Maps being printed.

1997, Nov. 22
1281 A380 40fr multicolored   .35   .25
1282 A380 75fr multicolored   .35   .25
1283 A380 190fr multicolored 1.40   .40
1284 A380 200fr multicolored 1.40   .40
      Nos. 1281-1284 (4)   3.50   1.30

Trains
A381

Designs: 15fr, CC2400. 90fr, Loco-tractor. 100fr, Mountain train. 240fr, Maquinista. 310fr, Freight train, series 151-A.

1997, Dec. 16   Perf. 13x13½
1285 A381 15fr multicolored   .25   .25
1286 A381 90fr multicolored   .50   .25
1287 A381 100fr multicolored .55   .30
1288 A381 240fr multicolored 1.00   .55
1289 A381 310fr multicolored 1.25   .70
  a. Strip of 5, #1285-1289   3.50   2.75

Musical
Instruments
A382

1997, Nov. 22   *Perf. 13x13½*
1290	A382	125fr Riiti	.75	.25
1291	A382	190fr Kora	1.00	.40
1292	A382	200fr Fama	1.25	.45
1293	A382	240fr Dioung dioung	1.50	.50
	Nos. 1290-1293 (4)		4.50	1.60

World
Wildlife
Fund
A383

Profelis aurata: 100fr, Climbing on tree limb.
240fr, Lying on tree limb. 300fr, Two cubs.

1997, Dec. 24   **Litho.**   *Perf. 11½*
1294	A383	45fr multicolored	.50	.30
1295	A383	100fr multicolored	.75	.40
1296	A383	240fr multicolored	1.25	.95
1297	A383	300fr multicolored	1.75	1.25
	Nos. 1294-1297 (4)		4.25	2.90

SOS
Children's
Village,
Ziguinchor
A384

1998, Jan. 14   **Litho.**   *Perf. 11½*
1298	A384	190fr shown	.80	.40
1299	A384	240fr Child, buildings	1.00	.50

Club Aldiana,
25th
Anniv. — A385

Designs: 290fr, Hut, people at market,
mother and baby. 320fr, People on boats,
woman in traditional dress, fish in basket.

1998, Jan. 12   *Perf. 13½*
1300	A385	290fr multicolored	2.25	.60
1301	A385	320fr multicolored	2.50	.65

Diana,
Princess of
Wales (1967-
97)
A386

Various portraits.

1998
1302	A386	240fr like #1304g	1.00	.50

Sheets of 9
1303	A386	200fr #a.-i.	7.50	3.75
1304	A386	250fr #a.-i.	9.50	4.75

Nos. 1303-1304 are continuous designs.

Souvenir Sheets
1305	A386	1000fr Portrait	4.25	2.10
1306	A386	1500fr With her sons	6.25	3.25
1307	A386	2000fr Wearing tiara	8.25	4.25

1998 World Cup Soccer Cup
Championships, France — A387

Designs: 25fr, Soccer players. 50fr, Player's
legs kicking ball. 150fr, Mascot, ball in air.
300fr, Country flags in shape of soccer
players.

1998, June 10   **Litho.**   *Perf. 13x13½*
1308	A387	25fr multicolored	.25	.25
1309	A387	50fr multicolored	.25	.25
1310	A387	190fr multicolored	.60	.25
1311	A387	300fr multicolored	1.00	.50
	Nos. 1308-1311 (4)		2.10	1.25

Henriette
Bathily
Women's
Museum
A388

1998, May 16   **Litho.**   *Perf. 13*
1312	A388	190fr shown	1.25	.60
1313	A388	270fr Emblem at right	1.90	.90

Abolition of
Slavery, 150th
Anniv. — A389

Designs: 20fr, Slavery Museum, Goree.
40fr, Frederick Douglass. 190fr, Mother, child.
290fr, Victor Schoelcher.

1998, Apr. 27
1314	A389	20fr multicolored	.25	.25
1315	A389	40fr multicolored	.25	.25
1316	A389	190fr multicolored	1.40	.65
1317	A389	290fr multicolored	2.00	1.00
	Nos. 1314-1317 (4)		3.90	2.15

SOS Children's Village — A390

Children's drawings: 30fr, House, car. 50fr,
shown. 180fr, Sun, flowers. 300fr, Lakes,
trees.

1998, June 16
1318	A390	30fr multicolored	.25	.25
1319	A390	50fr multicolored	.25	.25
1320	A390	180fr multicolored	.70	.35
1321	A390	300fr multicolored	1.10	.55
	Nos. 1318-1321 (4)		2.30	1.40

Navigational
Aids — A391

Designs: 50fr, Red buoy. 100fr, Mamelles
Lighthouse. 190fr, Lighted buoy. 240fr, Port
entrance lighthouse.

1998, July 3   *Perf. 12*
1322	A391	50fr multicolored	.25	.25
1323	A391	100fr multicolored	.40	.25
1324	A391	190fr multicolored	.70	.35
1325	A391	240fr multicolored	.90	.45
	Nos. 1322-1325 (4)		2.25	1.30

21st Paris-
Dakar
Rally — A392

Designs: 150fr, Race car broken down,
hood up, helicopter, rescue van. 175fr, Man
with shovels, vehicle stuck in sand, helicopter.
240fr, Motorcycles racing, one down, camel.
290fr, Motorcycle racing, man walking, vehicle
broken down.

1999, Jan. 17   **Litho.**   *Perf. 11½*
1326	A392	150fr multicolored	.55	.30
1327	A392	175fr multicolored	.65	.35
1328	A392	240fr multicolored	.90	.45
1329	A392	290fr multicolored	1.00	.50
	Nos. 1326-1329 (4)		3.10	1.60

Women's Hair
Styles,
Headdresses
A393

Designs: 100fr, Long hair over shoulders.
240fr, Shorter hair. 300fr, Head wrapped.

1998, Nov. 30
1330	A393	40fr red brn & blk	.25	.25
1331	A393	100fr brt grn & blk	.35	.25
1332	A393	240fr violet & black	.90	.45
1333	A393	300fr blue & black	1.10	.55
	Nos. 1330-1333 (4)		2.60	1.50

Endangering
Marine Fauna
A394

Designs: 50fr, Intensive net fishing. 100fr,
Sewage and pollutants in sea. 310fr, Use of
dynamite for fishing. 365fr, Oil slicks released
from tanker ships.

1998, Dec. 29
1334	A394	50fr multicolored	.25	.25
1335	A394	100fr multicolored	.40	.25
1336	A394	310fr multicolored	1.25	.65
1337	A394	365fr multicolored	1.50	.75
	Nos. 1334-1337 (4)		3.40	1.90

Intl. Year of
the Ocean
A395

1998, Oct. 30   *Perf. 13x13½*
1338	A395	190fr shown	.70	.35
1339	A395	790fr Sea life, diff.	2.75	1.50

Universal
Declaration
of Human
Rights,
50th Anniv.
A396

1998, Dec. 9
1340	A396	200fr Prisoner	1.25	.70
1341	A396	350fr Free people	2.25	1.10

Hotel
Palm
Beach,
Voyages
of Fram,
50th
Anniv.
A397

Designs: 240fr, Huts, trees, aerial view of
hotel grounds. 300fr, Woman braiding
another's hair, beach at hotel.

1998, Nov. 6   **Litho.**   *Perf. 13½x13*
1342	A397	240fr multicolored	1.60	.80
1343	A397	300fr multicolored	2.00	1.00

Italia '98 Intl. Philatelic
Exhibition — A398

Design: Leaning Tower of Pisa.

1998, Oct. 23
1344	A398	290fr multicolored	1.00	.50

Italia '98 Intl Philatelic Exhibition
A398a

No. 1344A — Race drivers and automo-
biles: b, Alberto Ascari. c, Giuseppe Farina. d,
Ricardo Patrese. e, Michele Alboreto. f, Elio de
Angelis. g, Andrea de Cesaris.

1998, Oct. 23   **Litho.**   *Perf. 13¼*
1344A	A398a	100fr Sheet of 6, #b-g	8.00	8.00

Souvenir Sheet

Ferrari Automobiles, 50th
Anniv. — A399

1998, Oct. 23   **Litho.**   *Perf. 13½*
1345	A399	1000fr multicolored	4.75	4.75

Italia '98.

Fashion Type of 1972
1998		**Engr.**	*Perf. 13½x13*	
		Size: 21x26mm		
1345A	A106	125fr dark olive	.50	.40
1345B	A106	290fr violet	1.25	1.00
1345C	A106	310fr purple brown	1.40	1.10

Souvenir Sheet

De Tomaso Automobiles, 40th
Anniv. — A400

Automobile colors: a, black, shown. b, silver.
c, black, diff. d, red.

1999, Feb. 28   Litho.   Perf. 12¼
1346   A400   250fr Sheet of 4, #a.-
      d.   9.50   9.50

Italia '98. Dated 1998.

Actors & Actresses — A401

No. 1347: a, Romy Schneider. b, Yves Montand. c, Catherine Deneuve. d, Gina Lollobrigida. e, Marcello Mastroianni. f, Sophia Loren. g, Frank Sinatra. h, Dean Martin. i, Marilyn Monroe.

1500fr, Monroe, diff. 2000fr, Mastroianni, diff.

1999, Feb. 28   Litho.   Perf. 12x12¼
1347   A401   200fr Sheet of 9,
      #a.-i.   7.00   7.00

Souvenir Sheets
Perf. 13½
1348   A401   1500fr multicolored   6.00   6.00
1349   A401   2000fr multicolored   9.50   9.50

Italia '98. Dated 1998.

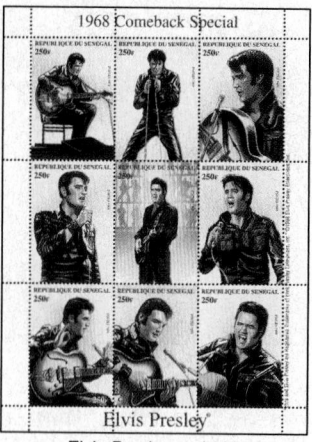

Elvis Presley — A402

Various portraits.

1999, Feb. 28   Litho.   Perf. 12x12¼
1350   A402   250fr Sheet of 9, #a.-
      i.   9.50   9.50

Dated 1998.
A sheet similar to No. 1350 exists. Stamps are perf 13¼ and have Italia '98 logo. The top margins of the sheet are not inscribed.

PhilexFrance 99 — A403

1999, July 2   Litho.   Perf. 13
1351   A403   240fr multicolored   1.25   1.10

No. 1351 has a holographic image. Soaking in water may affect hologram.

Chess Pieces and Scenes of the Crusades A404

Designs: No. 1353, Pope Urban II, 1053.
No. 1354: a, Muslim army. b, Bishopric of St. George. c, Army of Karbugha. d, Muslim troops attacking Christians. e, Baldwin I, King of Jerusalem. f, Christian Army. g, Third crusade, Richard the Lion-Hearted. h, Capture of Acre, 1191. i, Crusaders leave for Jaffa, 1191.
No. 1355: a, Pope Urban II, diff. b, Peter the Hermit. c, Byzantine Emperor Alexius. d, People's Crusade, 1096. e, Godfrey of Bouillon. f, Crusaders at Constantinople, 1097. g, Knights of St. John. h, Crusaders cross Alps. i, Capture of Jerusalem.
No. 1356: a, Chateau-gaillard of Richard the Lion-Hearted. b, Capture of Arsuf, 1191. c, Truce between Richard the Lion-Hearted and Saladin, 1192. d, Arrival of Louis IX at Damietta, 1248. e, Children's Crusade. f, Capture of Louis IX. g, Flood at El Mansurah. h, Treaty between Sultan al-Kamil and Frederick II. i, Monks record history of Crusades.

1999, July 16   Litho.   Perf. 13½
1353   A404   250fr multicolored   1.25   1.25
Sheets of 9
1354   A404   200fr #a.-i.   7.50   7.50
1355   A404   250fr #a.-i.   9.25   9.25
1356   A404   400fr #a.-i.   15.00   15.00

Athletes — A405

No. 1357, Jackie Robinson with bat behind back. No. 1358, Muhammad Ali, arm raised by referee.
No. 1359: a-h, various portraits of Jackie Robinson.
No. 1360: a-h, various portraits of Muhammad Ali.
1000fr, Muhammad Ali in robe. 1500fr, Close-up of Jackie Robinson like No. 1359g. No. 1363, Robinson at bat. No. 1364, Ali with both fists clenched.

1999, July 16   Litho.   Perf. 13½
1357   A405   250fr multicolored   1.00   1.00
1358   A405   300fr multicolored   1.25   1.25
Sheets of 9
1359   A405   250fr #1357,
           1359a.-h.   9.25   9.25
1360   A405   300fr #1358,
           1360a.-h.   11.50   11.50

Souvenir Sheets
1361   A405   1000fr multicolored   4.25   4.25
1362   A405   1500fr multicolored   6.25   6.25
1363   A405   2000fr multicolored   8.25   8.25
1364   A405   2000fr multicolored   8.25   8.25

Nos. 1361-1364 each contain one 36x42mm stamp.

Sports A405a

Designs: 200fr, Ayrton Senna, Formula 1 racing champion. 300fr, Ludger Beerbaum, equestrian competitor, vert. 400fr, Pete Sampras, tennis player, vert.
No. 1366 — Formula 1 racing champions: a, Juan Manuel Fangio. b, Alberto Ascari. c, Graham Hill. d, Jim Clark. e, Jack Brabham. f, Jackie Stewart. g, Niki Lauda. h, Like No. 1365, no white margin. i, Alain Prost.
No. 1367 — Equestrian competitors, vert.: a, Martin Schaudt. b, Klaus Balkenhol. c, Nadine Capellman-Biffar. d, Willi Melliger. e, Like No. 1365A, without printer's name at LL. f, Ulrich Kirchhoff. g, Sally Clark. h, Bettina Overesch-Boker. i, Karen O'Conner.
No. 1368 — Tennis and table tennis players, vert.: a, Liu Guoliang. b, Martina Hingis. c, Deng Yaping. d, Andre Agassi. e, Jean-Philippe Gatien. f, Anna Kournikova. g, Mikael Appelgren. h, Like No. 1365B, no white margin. i, Jan-Ove Waldner.
1500fr, German Equestrian jumping team. No. 1370, Ayrton Senna. No. 1370A, Table tennis players Vladimir Samsonov, Deng Yaping, Jörg Rosskopf.

1999, July 16   Litho.   Perf. 13½
1365-1365B A405a   Set of 3   3.75   3.75
Sheets of 9, #a-i
1366   A405a   200fr multi   7.50   7.50
1367   A405a   300fr multi   11.00   11.00
1368   A405a   400fr multi   15.00   15.00
Souvenir Sheets
1369   A405a   1500fr multi   6.25   6.25
1370   A405a   2000fr multi   8.00   8.00
1370A A405a   2000fr multi   8.00   8.00

Transportation — A406

Designs: 250fr, Sailboat of Sir Thomas Lipton. 300fr, Sinking of Titanic. 325fr, Bentley coupe. 350fr, Prussian locomotive. 375fr, Ducati Motorcycle. 500fr, Concorde.

1999, July 23   Litho.   Perf. 13½
1371   A406   250fr multicolored   1.00   1.00
1372   A406   300fr multicolored   1.25   1.25
1373   A406   325fr multicolored   1.40   1.40
1374   A406   350fr multicolored   1.40   1.40
1375   A406   375fr multicolored   1.50   1.50
1376   A406   500fr multicolored   2.00   2.00
    Nos. 1371-1376 (6)   8.55   8.55

See Nos. 1385-1399.

Intl. Year of Older Persons A407

30fr, Picture in book. 150fr, Man with mallet. 290fr, Musicians. 300fr, Scientists, vert.

Perf. 13¼x13, 13x13¼
1999, Aug. 10   Litho.
1377   A407   30fr multicolored   .25   .25
1378   A407   150fr multicolored   .60   .60
1379   A407   290fr multicolored   1.10   1.10
1380   A407   300fr multicolored   1.25   1.25
    Nos. 1377-1380 (4)   3.20   3.20

Mushrooms A408

Scouting emblem and: 60fr, "Amanite phalloide." 175fr, Coprinus atramantarius. 220fr, "Amanite vireuse." 250fr, Agaricus campester.

Perf. 13¼x13½
1999, Aug. 27   Litho.
1381   A408   60fr multicolored   .30   .30
1382   A408   175fr multicolored   .75   .75
1383   A408   220fr multicolored   1.00   1.00
1384   A408   250fr multicolored   1.10   1.10
    Nos. 1381-1384 (4)   3.15   3.15

Transportation Type of 1999

No. 1385 — Boats and ships: a, France. b, United States. c, Finnjet. d, Chusan. e, Sheers. f, Vendredi 13. g, Like No. 1371 without white margin. h, Pen Duick 11. i, Jester.
No. 1386 — Titanic: a, Construction. b, Launching. c, Departing. d, At start of voyage. e, Collision with iceberg. f, Like No. 1372 without white margin. g, Exploration of wreckage. h, Bow, passengers. i, Captain Edward John Smith.
No. 1387 — Automobiles: a, Duryea. b, Menon. c, Petite Renault. d, Zero Fiat. e, Spa. f, Packard. g, Like No. 1373 without white margin. h, Mercedes-Benz. i, Morris Minor.
No. 1388 — Trains: a, Mikado. b, 241P. c, Ten-wheeler. d, The Milwaukee. e, Class 1.S. f, Prussian locomotive G12. g, Like No. 1374 without white margin. h, KK-SEB Series 310. i, Outrance.
No. 1389 — Motorcycles and bicycles: a, Brooklands. b, Moto Brough Superior. c, 1903 race. d, Like No. 1375 without inscription at LL. e, Dave Thorpe Moto-cross Yamaha. f, Kevin Schwantz Moto Suzuki. g, Michaux bicycle. h, Racing bicycle with helmeted rider. i, Women on bicycles.
No. 1390 — Rockets, vert.: a, R.D. 107, USSR. b, Soyuz, USSR. c, Proton, USSR. d, Atlas-Centaur, US. e, Atlas-Agena, US. f, Atlas-Mercury, US. g, Titan 2, US. h, Juno 2, US. i, Saturn 1, US.
No. 1391 — Express trains: a, Acela, US. b, Class 332, Great Britain. c, ICE, Germany. d, TEE, Luembourg. e, Nevada Super Speed, US. f, Inter City 250, Great Britain. g, Korean High Speed. h, Eurostar, France & Great Britain. i, Thalys PBA, France.
No. 1392 — Supersonic aircraft or prototypes: a, SR-71. b, Maglifter. c, S.M. d, Super Concorde. e, TU-144. f, Boeing X. g, X-33. h, Like No. 1376 without white margin. i, X-34.
1000fr, Eric Tabarly and Pen Duick IV. No. 1394, Marc Seguin, arrival of train at Mont-Saint-Michel, vert. No. 1395, Walter P. Chrysler, 1924 Chrysler. No. 1396, Etienne Chambron, TGV trains, vert. No. 1397, Bobby Julich on racing bicycle. No. 1398, Concorde, diff. 2500fr, Neil Armstrong.

Sheets of 9
1999, July 23   Litho.   Perf. 13½
1385   A406   250fr #a.-i.   9.25   9.25
1386   A406   300fr #a.-i.   11.00   11.00
1387   A406   325fr #a.-i.   12.00   12.00
1388   A406   350fr #a.-i.   13.00   13.00
1389   A406   375fr #a.-i.   14.00   14.00
1390   A406   400fr #a.-i.   15.00   15.00
1391   A406   450fr #a.-i.   17.00   17.00
1392   A406   500fr #a.-i.   18.00   18.00

Souvenir Sheets
1393   A406   1000fr multicolored   4.25   4.25
1394   A406   1500fr multicolored   5.50   5.50
1395   A406   1500fr multicolored   6.00   6.00
1396   A406   2000fr multicolored   8.25   8.25
1397   A406   2000fr multicolored   8.25   8.25
1398   A406   2000fr multicolored   8.25   8.25
1399   A406   2500fr multicolored   10.50   10.50

No. 1390 contains nine 35x50mm stamps. Nos. 1393, 1395, 1397-1399 each contain one 50x35 stamp. Nos. 1394 and 1396 each contain one 35x50mm stamp.

UPU, 125th Anniv. — A409

UPU emblem and: 270fr, Rainbows, envelope. 350fr, "125."

1999, Oct. 9   Litho.   Perf. 11½x11¾
1400	A409	270fr multi	1.10 1.10
1401	A409	350fr multi	1.40 1.40

First Manned Moon Landing, 30th Anniv. — A410

Designs: 25fr, Two astronauts on moon, flag. 145fr, Neil Armstrong, flag, astronaut on moon, vert. 180fr, Astronaut, flag, rocket, vert. 500fr, Astronaut on moon, space shuttle, vert.

1999, Oct. 9   Perf. 13½x13, 13x13½
1402	A410	25fr multi	.25 .25
1403	A410	145fr multi	.60 .60
1404	A410	180fr multi	.70 .70
1405	A410	500fr multi	2.00 2.00
		Nos. 1402-1405 (4)	3.55 3.55

Mother Teresa — A411

Mother Teresa and: 75fr, Child, facing away. 100fr, Three children. 290fr, Priest. 300fr, Child.

1999, Oct. 9   Perf. 11½x11¾
1406	A411	75fr multi	.25 .25
1407	A411	100fr multi	.40 .40
1408	A411	290fr multi	1.10 1.10
1409	A411	300fr multi	1.25 1.25
		Nos. 1406-1409 (4)	3.00 3.00

Awarding of Nobel Peace Prize to Mother Teresa, 20th anniv.

Fauna A412

Designs: 60fr, Hippotragus equinus. 90fr, Haematopus ostralegus. 300fr, Dendrocygna viduada. 320fr, Demochelys coriacea.

1999, Oct. 9   Perf. 13½x13
1410	A412	60fr multi	.25 .25
1411	A412	90fr multi	.35 .35
1412	A412	125fr multi	1.25 1.25
1413	A412	320fr multi	1.25 1.25
		Nos. 1410-1413 (4)	3.10 3.10

Paintings by Paul Cézanne — A413

Various paintings.

1999   Perf. 13¼
1414	A413	200fr Sheet of 9, #a.-i.	8.00 8.00

Betty Boop — A414

Designs: No. 1415, 250fr, With red guitar. No. 1416, 250fr, With microphone. No. 1417, 400fr, On chair.
No. 1418, 250fr: a, With saxophone. b, With tambourine. c, Like #1415 (continuous design). d, With pink guitar. e, On piano keys. f, With drumsticks. g, With earphones. h, Like #1416 (continuous design). i, With purple jacket.
No. 1419, 400fr: a, With red dress. b, With flowers. c, With blue pants. d, With purple dress. e, Like #1417 (continuous design). f, With black pants. g, With ankh earrings. h, With black dress. i, With purple shirt and pants.
No. 1420, 1000fr, With saxophone. No. 1421, 1500fr, With red dress. No. 1422, 2000fr, With purple shirt.

1999   Litho.   Perf. 13¼
1415-1417	A414	Set of 3	3.75 3.75
Sheets of 9, #a-i			
1418-1419	A414	Set of 2	24.00 24.00
Souvenir Sheets			
1420-1422	A414	Set of 3	12.00 12.00

Actors and Actresses — A415

No. 1423, 250fr: a, Clark Gable. b, Rudolph Valentino. c, Errol Flynn. d, Cary Grant. e, Robert Taylor. f, Gary Cooper. g, James Dean. h, Humphrey Bogart. i, Marlon Brando.
No. 1424, 425fr: a, Grace Kelly. b, Marilyn Monroe. c, Audrey Hepburn. d, Greta Garbo. e, Jean Harlow. f, Loretta Young. g, Jane Russell. h, Dorothy Lamour. i, Veronica Lake.
No. 1425, 450fr: a, Ginger Rogers, Fred Astaire. b, Cary Grant, Katharine Hepburn, James Stewart. c, Melvyn Douglas, Greta Garbo. d, Vivien Leigh, Clark Gable. e, Burt Lancaster, Deborah Kerr. f, Humphrey Bogart, Lauren Bacall. g, Steve McQueen, Jacqueline Bisset. h, Gene Kelly, Rita Hayworth. i, Ingrid Bergman, Cary Grant.

1999   Sheets of 9, #a-i
1423-1425	A415	Set of 3	32.50 32.50

I Love Lucy — A416

Designs: No. 1426, 300fr, Fred, Ethel and Lucy with chick boxes. No. 1427, 300fr, Lucy reading murder mystery, vert.

No. 1428: a, Ethel, Lucy holding box. b, Ricky, Lucy, Fred and Ethel. c, Fred, Ethel and Lucy standing. d, Lucy with chicks. e, Fred, Ethel, Lucy and Ricky at table. f, Ethel and Lucy bending over. g, Lucy. h, Lucy, Ethel and Fred at table.
No. 1429, vert. — Lucy with: a, Telephone. b, Green dress. c, Black vest. d, Black hair bow. e, Spoon and bottle. f, Salad. g, Lilac jacket. h, Tan coat.
No. 1430, 1000fr, Lucy holding box, vert. No. 1431, 2000fr, Lucy holding bag, vert.

1999
1426-1427	A416	Set of 2	2.40 2.40
1428	A416	300fr Sheet of 9, #1426, 1428a-1428h	11.00 11.00
1429	A416	300fr Sheet of 9, #1427, 1429a-1429h	11.00 11.00
Souvenir Sheets			
1430-1431	A416	Set of 2	12.00 12.00

The Three Stooges — A417

Designs: No. 1432, Larry with scissors, Curly, Moe with drill.
No. 1433: a, Larry and Moe on bed. b, Larry, Moe, Curly in police uniforms. c, Moe, Larry on telephone. d, Larry and Moe with scissors, Curly. e, Larry, Curly, Moe behind operating room equipment. f, Moe on floor, Larry, Curly. g, Moe, Curly, Larry with ladder. h, Moe with plank, Larry, Curly.
No. 1434, 1000fr, Moe with feathers in hair, Curly, vert. No. 1435, 1500fr, Curly with hat, vert.

1999
1432	A417	400fr multi	1.60 1.60
1433	A417	400fr Sheet of 9, #1432, 1433a-1433h	14.50 14.50
Souvenir Sheets			
1434-1435	A417	Set of 2	10.00 10.00

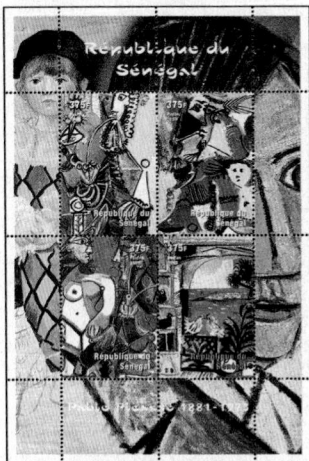

Picasso Paintings — A418

No. 1436: a, Country name in yellow, denomination at UL. b, Country name in white. c, Country name in yellow, denomination at UR. d, Country name in red.

1999
1436	A418	375fr Sheet of 4, #a-d	5.50 5.50

22nd Paris-Cairo-Dakar Rally — A419

Designs: 75fr, Motorcycles, car, truck, helicopter, Pyramids. 100fr, Cars, truck, Sphinx, Pyramid, camel and driver. 220fr, Motorcycle, truck, helicopter. 320fr, Camel and driver, motorcycle, car, Pyramids.

2000   Litho.   Perf. 11¾x11½
1437-1440	A419	Set of 4	3.50 3.50

World Meteorological Organization, 50th Anniv. A420

Designs: 100fr, Satellite dish, map, weather station. 790fr, Weather measuring equipment, vert.

2000   Perf. 11¾x11½, 11½x11¾
1441-1442	A420	Set of 2	3.25 3.25

23rd Paris-Cairo-Dakar Rally — A421

Stylized head and: 190fr, Motorcyclist. 220fr, Facial features with text, vert. 240fr, Camel, car. 790fr, Car.

Perf. 13½x13¼, 13¼x13½
2001, Jan. 6
1443-1446	A421	Set of 4	6.50 6.50

Advent of New Millennium A422

Millennium emblem and: 20fr, National Festival of Arts and Culture. 100fr, Pan-African Plastic Arts. 150fr, National Heritage Day. 300fr, Goree Memorial, horiz.

2001, Feb. 13   Perf. 13½x13, 13x13½
1447-1450	A422	Set of 4	2.50 2.50
		Dated 2000.	

2000 Summer Olympics, Sydney — A423

Designs: 40fr, Swimming, weight lifting. 80fr, Taekwondo. 240fr, 200-meter race. 290fr, Handball.

2001, Feb. 28   Perf. 13¼x13½
1451-1454	A423	Set of 4	3.25 3.25
		Dated 2000.	

Kermel Artisan Market — A424

Building and: 50fr, Woman, flowers. 90fr, Mask, drum. 250fr, Masks, bowls, horiz. 350fr, Woman, carvings.

Perf. 13¼x13½, 13½x13¼

2001, Mar. 15

1455-1458 A424 Set of 4 3.25 3.25

Medicinal Plants — A425

Designs: 240fr, Maytenus senegalensis. 320fr, Boscia senegalensis. 350fr, Euphorbia hirta. 500fr, Guierra senegalensis.

2001, Apr. 16 Litho. ***Perf. 13¼x13***

1459-1462 A425 Set of 4 6.00 6.00

19th Lions Intl. Convention, Dakar A426

Lions Intl. emblem and: 190fr, People in canoe, map of Senegal. 300fr, Lion, vert.

Perf. 13½x13¼, 13¼x13½

2001, May 21

1463-1464 A426 Set of 2 2.40 2.40

UN High Commissioner for Refugees, 50th Anniv. — A427

Emblem and: 240fr, Tank, refugees. 320fr, Refugee, globe, vert.

Perf. 13½x13¼, 13¼x13½

2001, June 20

1465-1466 A427 Set of 2 2.00 2.00

Intl. Teacher's Day — A428

UNESCO emblem and: 225fr, Book, teacher, vert. 290fr, Teacher, world map.

Perf. 13¼x13, 13x13¼

2001, Oct. 5 Litho.

1467-1468 A428 Set of 2 1.75 1.75

Dated 2000.

National Parks A429

Designs: 75fr, Antelope, lion. 125fr, Heron and marabou stork. 275fr, Cranes and elephant. 300fr, Zebras, vert.

Perf. 13¾x13½

2001, Nov. 12 Litho.

1469	A429	75fr	multicolored	.50	.25
1470	A429	125fr	multicolored	.90	.25
1471	A429	275fr	multicolored	1.75	1.00
1472	A429	300fr	multicolored	1.90	1.00
		Nos. 1469-1472 (4)		5.05	2.50

Dated 2000.

Tourism A430

Tourism emblem and: 145fr, Drummer and dancer. 290fr, Tree, windsurfer, person on air mattress, vert.

Perf. 13x13¼, 13¼x13

2001, Dec. 3 Litho.

1473-1474 A430 Set of 2 1.60 1.60

Dated 2000.

2002 African Cup Soccer Tournament, Mali A431

Tournament emblem and: 250fr, Flags, player holding cup, players and soccer ball. 380fr, Players near goal. 425fr, Players kicking ball at goal. 440fr, Player, cup, vert.

2002, Jan. 9

1475-1478 A431 Set of 4 5.25 5.25

24th Paris-Dakar Rally A432

Designs: 250fr, Two motorcyclists. 360fr, Two cars in rally. 370fr, Motorcyclist, Eiffel Tower, map of Africa, vert. 425fr, Motorcyclist, vert.

Perf. 13x13¼, 13¼x13

2002, Jan. 13 Litho.

1479-1482 A432 Set of 4 — —

Peulh Woman — A433a A433

Linguère — A434a A434

On types A433a and A434a, the numerals in the denominations have thin serifs and zeroes that are thin at top and bottom. On types A433 and A434 the lines of these numerals are the same thickness.

2002 Litho. ***Perf. 13½x13***

1483	A433	5fr	lilac rose	—	—
1483A	A433a	5fr	lilac rose		—
1484	A433	10fr	brt orange	—	—
1484A	A433a	10fr	orange	—	—
1485	A433	20fr	orange	—	—
1485A	A433a	20fr	orange		—
1486	A433	25fr	rose red	—	—
1486A	A433a	25fr	rose red		—
1487	A433	40fr	bright pink	—	—
1488	A433	50fr	light blue	—	—
1488A	A433a	50fr	light blue	—	—
1489	A433	60fr	lt bl grn	—	—
1490	A433	70fr	lt yel grn	—	—
1490A	A433	75fr	dark green	—	—
1490B	A433	80fr	dark blue		—
1490C	A433	90fr	brown		—
1491	A433	100fr	brt yel grn	—	—
1491A	A433	125fr	silver		—
1491B	A433a	125fr	silver		—
1492	A433	150fr	olive green	—	—
1493	A433	175fr	yel brn	—	—
1494	A434	200fr	olive green	—	—
1494A	A434	225fr	lilac	—	—
1495	A434	250fr	ocher	—	—
1496	A434	290fr	red brown	—	—
1497	A434	300fr	brt rose lil	—	—
1497A	A434a	350fr	brt rose lil	—	—
1498	A434	360fr	violet	—	—
1499	A434	370fr	blue		—
1499A	A434	380fr	brt green		—
1500	A434	390fr	Prus blue	—	—
1500A	A434	400fr	light brown	—	—
1501	A434	425fr	bright green	—	—
1501A	A434	450fr	green		—
1502	A434	500fr	olive brown	—	—
1502A	A434a	600fr	gray	—	—
1502B	A434a	700fr	bright lilac	—	—
1503	A434	800fr	black	—	—
1504	A434	1000fr	brt blue	—	—
1504A	A434a	1000fr	brt blue		—

Issued: 10fr (#1484), 10fr (#1484A), 50fr (#1488A), 75fr, 100fr, 300fr, 500fr, 1000fr, 2002; 5fr, 20fr, 25fr, 40fr, 50fr (#1488), 60fr, 150fr, 175fr, 200fr, 250fr, 290fr, 360fr, 370fr, 390fr, 425fr, 800fr, 3/12/02; 225fr, 400fr, 2003; 125fr, 350fr, 600fr, 700fr, 4/5/04; No. 1501A, 2007. Issue dates for Nos. 1483A, 1485A, 1486A, 1490B, 1490C, 1491B, 1499, 1499A and 1504A are uncertain, because examples seen used are from 2005 and 2006. Nos. 1490B, 1490C, 1491B, and 1499A have "2003" year dates, while others have "2002" year dates. No. 1501A has "2007" year date.

Proclamation of the Act of African Union — A435

Map of Africa and: 330fr, Handshake, vert. 390fr, Hands, flags.

2002 Litho. ***Perf. 13¼x13, 13x13¼***

1505-1506 A435 Set of 2 2.50 2.50

Door of the Third Millennium A436

Various depictions with frame colors of: 200fr, Orange. 290fr, Blue. 390fr, Olive green. 725fr, Rose pink.

2002 ***Perf. 13¼x13***

1507-1510 A436 Set of 4 4.50 4.50

Dak'Art 2002 A437

Art by: 200fr, Zehirum Yetmgeta. 380fr, Moustapha Dime, vert. 400fr, Abdoulaye Konate. 425fr, Gora Mbengue.

2002, Apr. 30 ***Perf. 13x13¼, 13¼x13***

1511-1514 A437 Set of 4 5.00 5.00

Star and Map of Senegal — A438

Denomination color: 200fr, Green. 380fr, Red.

2002, May 15 ***Perf. 13¼x13***

1515-1516 A438 Set of 2 2.00 2.00

Year of Dialogue Among Civilizations A439

UPU and United Nations emblems and: 290fr, Globe, building, native shelters. 380fr, Stylized people and methods of communications.

2002, June 26 Litho. ***Perf. 13¼x13***

1517-1518 A439 Set of 2 — —

Horses A440

Designs: 30fr, Mbayar du Baol. 200fr, Mpar du Cayor. 250fr, Narougor. 300fr, Foutanke.

2002, Dec. 20 Litho. ***Perf. 13x13¼***

1519-1522 A440 Set of 4 2.50 2.50

Ecotourism A441

Designs: 90fr, Sacred baobab tree. 250fr, Birds, Djoudj National Park. 300fr, Mangroves. 380fr, Wood and vine bridge.

2002, Dec. 20 Litho. ***Perf. 13x13¼***

1523-1526 A441 Set of 4 7.75 7.75

Fauna A442

Designs: 75fr, Gorilla gorilla. 290fr, Ceratotherium simum. 360fr, Geochelone sulcata, ostrich and snake. 380fr, Giraffa camelopardalis, vert.

2002, Dec. 26 ***Perf. 13x13¼, 13¼x13***

1527-1530 A442 Set of 4 5.75 5.75

25th Paris-Dakar Rally A443

Designs: 360fr, Automobiles, man with camel. 425fr, Motorcyclists.

2003, Jan. 19 Litho. ***Perf. 13x13¼***

1531-1532 A443 Set of 2 4.25 4.25

Dated 2002.

A444

A445

New Partnership for African Development — A446

Designs: 250fr, Map of Africa, symbols of industry. 290fr, Map of Africa, bird, model of atom.

Perf. 13¼x13, 13x13¼

2003, June 22 Litho.

1533 A444 200fr shown	.70	.70
1534 A444 250fr multi	.85	.85
1535 A445 250fr shown	.85	.85
1536 A444 290fr multi	1.00	1.00
1537 A446 360fr shown	1.25	1.25
Nos. 1533-1537 (5)	4.65	4.65

Traditional Costumes — A447

Designs: 250fr, Goumbé Lébou. 360fr, Badiaranké. 390fr, Grand Boubou. 500fr, Bowede.

2003, July 16 ***Perf. 13¼x13***

1538-1541 A447 Set of 4 5.25 5.25

Marine Life A448

Designs: 290fr, Cymbium cymbium. 370fr, Herring. 380fr, Catfish. 400fr, Chelonia mydas.

2003, July 16 Litho. ***Perf. 13x13¼***

1542-1545 A448 Set of 4 5.00 5.00

Sculptures A449

Designs: 200fr, Le Cailcédrat Mort. 300fr, Tete d'un Sorcier. 380fr, Le Laard. 440fr, Le Thioury.

2003, July 16 Litho. ***Perf. 13¼x13***

1546-1549 A449 Set of 4 *11.50 11.50*

Léopold Sédar Senghor (1906-2001), First President of Senegal — A450

Senghor: 200fr, Seated in front of flag of Senegal. 300fr, Holding book of poetry and diploma. 1000fr, Standing in front of fireworks.

2003, Dec. 17 Litho. ***Perf. 13¼x13***

Booklet Stamps

1550 A450 200fr multi — —
1551 A450 300fr multi — —
a. Booklet pane of 2, #1550-1551 — —

Size: 40x52mm

Perf. 13

1552 A450 1000fr multi — —
a. Booklet pane of 1 —
Complete booklet, #1551a, 1552a —

26th Paris-Dakar Rally — A451

Designs: 390fr, Motorcyclists. 500fr, Motorcyclist and car.

2004, Jan. 14 Litho. ***Perf. 13x13¼***

1553-1554 A451 Set of 2 3.50 3.50

Dated 2003.

Intl. Cycling Union, Cent. (in 2000) A452

Designs: 45fr, Stylized cyclists facing left. 275fr, Two cyclists, vert. 290fr, Two cyclists on road. 310fr, Victorious cyclist celebrating, vert.

2004? Litho. ***Perf. 13¼x13, 13x13¼***

1555 A452 45fr multi — —
1556 A452 275fr multi — —
1557 A452 290fr multi — —
1558 A452 310fr multi — —

Dated 2000.

Historic Sites A453

Designs: 240fr, Dakar Railroad Station. 370fr, Fort Podor. 390fr, Dakar City Hall. 500fr, Notre Dame des Victoires Cathedral.

2004, Apr. 29 Litho. ***Perf. 13x13¼***

1559-1562 A453 Set of 4 5.50 5.50

Dated 2003.

Land Transportation — A453a

Design: 200fr, Small bus (Car rapide). 250fr, Horse-drawn wagon (Charrette). 290fr, Dakar Dem Dikk bus. 380fr, Automobile, buses, truck, motorcycle and train.

2004 Litho. ***Perf. 13x13¼***

1562A A453a 200fr multi — —
1562B A453a 250fr multi — —
1562C A453a 290fr multi — —
1562D A453a 380fr multi — —

African Cup of Nations Soccer Tournament A454

Designs: 200fr, Cup, emblem. 300fr, Cup, soccer ball, stadium, television, horiz. 400fr, Emblems, players shaking hands, horiz. 425fr, Players in action, horiz.

2004 ***Perf. 13¼x13, 13x13¼***

1563-1566 A454 Set of 4 5.50 5.50

Art — A454a

Designs: 300fr, Dak'art, by Amadou Sow. 400fr, Chaise, by Vincent Amian Niamen. 450fr, Prototype I, by Issa Diabaté. 525fr, Choses au Mur, by Viyé Diba.

2004 Litho. ***Perf. 13¼x13***

1566A-1566D A454a Set of 4 — —

Houses of Worship A455

Designs: 200fr, Omarienne de Guédé Mosque. 225fr, Popenguine Basilica, vert. 250fr, Grand Mosque, Touba. 300fr, Grand Mosque, Tivaouane.

Perf. 13x13¼, 13¼x13

2004, Oct. 9 Litho.

1567-1570 A455 Set of 4 3.75 3.75

Locally Produced Crops — A456

Designs: 100fr, Millet. 150fr, Cowpeas, millet and corn, horiz. 200fr, Corn. 300fr, Rice.

2004, Dec. 6 ***Perf. 13¼x13, 13x13¼***

1571-1574 A456 Set of 4 3.00 3.00

27th Paris-Dakar Rally — A457

Designs: 450fr, Automobile, motorcycle and truck. 550fr, Motorcycle, vert.

Perf. 13x13¼, 13¼x13

2005, Jan. 16 Litho.

1575-1576 A457 Set of 2 4.00 4.00

Children's Art — A458

Various drawings by: 50fr, Mbaye Gnilane. 75fr, Pape Cheick Diack, horiz. 100fr, Aly Gueye, horiz. 425fr, Abdourahim Diallo, horiz.

Perf. 13¼x13, 13x13¼

2005, Feb. 28 Litho.

1577-1580 A458 Set of 4 2.75 2.75

28th Paris-Dakar Rally A459

Design: 500fr, Rally emblem, camels, tents, automobile. 1000fr, Rally emblem, helicopter, man repairing car, men carrying car doors.

2006, Jan. 14 Litho. ***Perf. 13x13¼***

1581 A459 500fr multi — —
1582 A459 1000fr multi —

Dolls — A460

Designs: 200fr, Tooiodo Peulh. 250fr, La Reine Siguare. 375fr, Zulu doll. 425fr, Woloff stuffed dolls.

Litho., Litho & Engr. (375fr)

2006, Apr. 5 ***Perf. 13¼x13***

1583-1586 A460 Set of 4 7.25 7.25

Campaign Against HIV
A461

Designs: 200fr, Family discussing HIV and AIDS, map of Senegal. 250fr, Woman, molecular model, drop of water, vert. 290fr, Couples with thought balloons. 425fr, Group of seated men, huts.

Perf. 13x13¼, 13¼x13
2006, Apr. 5 Litho.
1587-1590 A461 Set of 4 4.50 4.50
Dated 2004.

World Numerical Solidarity Day — A462

Designs: 200fr, Satellite, computer screen, Earth's hemispheres. 250fr, Earth, people using telephones, clasped arms. 370fr, Satellite, map of Senegal, city skyline, horiz. 380fr, Satellite, computer screen, hand with computer disk, horiz.

Perf. 13½x13, 13x13½
2006, May 3 Litho.
1591-1594 A462 Set of 4 4.75 4.75

Flowers
A463

Designs: 100fr, Malva silvestris. 150fr, Moringa olifera, vert. 300fr, Cichorum intybus, vert. 450fr, Dandelion.

Perf. 13x13¼, 13¼x13
2006, July 10 Litho.
1595-1598 A463 Set of 4 9.00 9.00
Dated 2005.

Wrestling
A464

Designs: 100fr, Two wrestlers standing. 200fr, Two wrestlers in ring. 250fr, Wrestler, vert. 500fr, Wrestler pouring water on himself, vert.

Perf. 13x13¼, 13¼x13
2007, July 10 Litho.
1599-1602 A464 Set of 4 9.50 9.50

Demba and Dupont Memorial, Dakar — A465

Various views of statue: 200fr, 450fr.

2006, Aug. 23 Litho. **Perf. 13¼x13**
1603-1604 A465 Set of 2 3.75 3.75

Pres. Léopold Sedar Senghor (1906-2001)
A466

Denomination color: 200fr, Red. 450fr, Green.

2006, Oct. 9 Litho. **Perf. 13¼x13**
1605-1606 A466 Set of 2 5.75 5.75

Campaign Against Mutilation of Female Genitalia — A467

Designs: 50fr, Woman grabbing another woman, man holding sign. 200fr, Two women, two children, razor blade. 350fr, Woman, health workers, razor blade. 370fr, Women, girl with raised hand.

2006, Dec. 8 Litho. **Perf. 13¼x13**
1607-1610 A467 Set of 4 4.00 4.00

Air Transport
A468

Design: 100fr, Earth, Map of Africa, jet, Concorde in flight. 250fr, Airship and airplane. 500fr, Airplane and passengers. 370fr, Airplane on runway, control tower.

2006 Litho. **Perf. 13x13¼**
1611 A468 100fr multi — —
1612 A468 250fr multi — —
1613 A468 370fr multi — —
1614 A468 500fr multi — —

Birds
A469

Designs: 30fr, Luscinia phoenicurus. 75fr, Rouge-gorge bleu (robin), vert. 200fr, Pica pica, vert. 400fr, Corneille (crow), vert.

2006 Litho. **Perf. 13x13¼, 13¼x13**
1615-1618 A469 Set of 4 12.50 12.50

Fishing — A469a

Design: 15fr, Fishermen removing catch from boat. 50fr, Fishermen in boat pulling in net. 150fr, Fisherman in boat casting net. 300fr, Fishermen in boat and in water drawing in net.

2006 **Perf. 13x13¼**
1618A A469a 15fr multi — —
1618B A469a 50fr multi — —
1618C A469a 150fr multi — —
1618D A469a 300fr multi — —

29th Paris-Dakar Rally
A470

Designs: 450fr, Two automobiles, two motorcycles. 550fr, Motorcyclist passing rally watchers.

2007, Jan. 20 Litho. **Perf. 13x13¼**
1619-1620 A470 Set of 2 — —

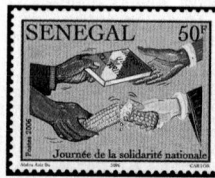

National Solidarity Day
A471

Designs: 50fr, Exchange of books and corn. 100fr, Shell, hands, star, map of Senegal. 200fr, Map of Senegal, hands, bowl. 500fr, Map of Senegal, items produced in Senegal.

2007, Sept. 11 Litho. **Perf. 13x13¼**
1621-1624 A471 Set of 4 3.75 3.75
Dated 2006.

Gorée Diaspora Festival — A472

Designs: 50fr, Emblem. 200fr, Emblem, pendant and prism, horiz. 450fr, Hands with quill pen, building. 525fr, Ship, emblem, Gorée Island.

Perf. 13¼x13, 13x13¼
2007, Sept. 11
1625-1628 A472 Set of 4 5.50 5.50

Tourism
A473

Designs: 75fr, Patas monkey, flamingos, Sine Saloum Park. 125fr, Wildlife, Niokolo-koba Park. 200fr, Lion, elephant and giraffes, Niokolo-koba Park. 450fr, Pelicans, Faidherbe Bridge, Saint-Louis.

2008, Feb. 27 Litho. **Perf. 13x13¼**
1629 A473 75fr multi — —
1630 A473 125fr multi — —
1631 A473 200fr multi — —
1632 A473 450fr multi — —
Dated 2007.

Environmental Protection — A474

Designs: 100fr, Do not cut down trees. 200fr, Fire is dangerous, vert. 300fr, Man picking up litter. 450fr, Protect the vegetation.

Perf. 13x13¼, 13¼x13
2008, June 5 Litho.
1633-1636 A474 Set of 4 5.00 5.00
Dated 2007.

Flora
A475

Designs: 200fr, Strichnos nux vomica. 290fr, Conium maculatum, vert. 300fr, Tree bud, vert. 450fr, Pitcher plant, vert.

Perf. 13x13¼, 13¼x13
2008, Sept. 5 Litho.
1637-1640 A475 Set of 4 5.50 5.50
Dated 2007.

Miniature Sheet

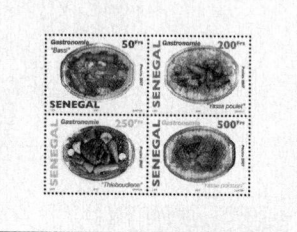

Native Dishes — A476

No. 1641: a, 50fr, Bassi (seasoned meat and vegetables). b, 200fr, Yassa poulet (marinated chicken and vegetables). c, 250fr, Thieboudiene (marinated fish. d, 500fr, Yassa poisson (marinated fish and vegetables).

2008, Sept. 5 Litho. **Perf. 13x13¼**
1641 A476 Sheet of 4, #a-d 4.50 4.50

30th Paris-Dakar Rally — A476a

Designs: 450fr, Motorcyclist, van, camel. 550fr, Motorcyclist, car, horiz.

Perf. 13¼x13, 13x13¼
2009, Jan. 29 Litho.
1643-1644 A476a Set of 2 4.00 4.00
Dated 2008.

Mother's Day
A477

Mothers receiving flowers from daughters, with background color of: 200fr, Lilac. 450fr, Yellow, vert.

Perf. 13x13¼, 13¼x13
2009, June 3 Litho.
1645-1646 A477 Set of 2 2.75 2.75

Blind Boy Reading Braille Book — A478

Designs: 200fr, Shown. 450fr, "9" in Braille text.

Litho. & Embossed
2009, May 20 Perf. 13¼x13
1647-1648 A478 Set of 2 2.75 2.75
Louis Braille (1809-52), educator of the blind.

Independence, 50th Anniv. — A479

Denomination color: 300fr, Green. 500fr, Red.

2010, Apr. 4 Litho. Perf. 13x13¼
1649-1650 A479 Set of 2 3.50 3.50

West African Economic and Monetary Union, 11th Anniv. (in 2005) — A480

Designs: 500fr, Coin, balls and emblem. 790fr, Map of member countries, emblems, building, birthday cake with candle, horiz.

2010, Apr. 5 Perf. 13¼x13, 13x13¼
1651-1652 A480 Set of 2 5.50 5.50
Dated 2006.

Democracy and Liberty — A481

Designs: 150fr, Peaceful protest. 250fr, Woman holding election card. 400fr, Woman casting ballot. 450fr, Newspapers, radio, television.

2010, Apr. 5 Litho. Perf. 13¼x13
1653-1656 A481 Set of 4 5.25 5.25
Dated 2006.

Dances — A482

Designs: 100fr, Ndaw rabine. 200fr, Niary gorom, horiz. 250fr, Daganthe. 450fr, Ndaa daly.

2010, Apr. 21 Perf. 13¼x13, 13x13¼
Granite Paper
1657-1660 A482 Set of 4 4.25 4.25

Insects A483

Grand Agricultural Offensive for Food Security — A484

Designs: 150fr, Praying mantis. 200fr, Wasp. 250fr, Grasshopper. 500fr, Ant.

2010, Apr. 21 Litho. Perf. 13x13¼
1661-1664 A483 Set of 4 4.50 4.50

Designs: 100fr, Map of Africa, farmers with team of oxen, fruits and vegetables. 200fr, Map of Senegal, farmers with plow and crops, horiz. 250fr, Maps of Africa and Senegal, crops, people with grain sacks. 500fr, People and vegetables.

Perf. 13¼x13, 13x13¼
2010, Aug. 5 Litho.
1665-1668 A484 Set of 4 — —
Dated 2009.

SOS Children's Village A485

Denomination in: 300fr, Orange. 400fr, Yellow.

2010, Sept. 15 Litho. Perf. 13x13¼
1669-1670 A485 Set of 2 3.00 3.00

Fifth Gorée Diaspora Festival A486

Festival emblem on: 190fr, Men and buildings. 200fr, Dancers, Gorée Island, Aimé Césaire (1913-2008), poet. 250fr, Girls dancing.

2010, Nov. 4 Litho. Perf. 13x13¼
1671 A486 190fr multi — —
1672 A486 200fr multi — —
1673 A486 250fr multi — —
Dated 2009. One additional stamp was issued in this set. The editors would like to examine any examples.

World Festival of Negro Arts — A487

Designs: 200fr, Woman with arms raised, vert. 300fr, Map of Africa. 450fr, Sphere, stylized people with arms raised, vert. 500fr, Carving of woman smoking pipe, table, vert.

Perf. 13x13¼, 13¼x13
2010, Dec. 21 Litho.
1675 A487 200fr multi — —
1676 A487 300fr multi — —
1677 A487 450fr multi — —
1678 A487 500fr multi — —
Dated 2007.

Birds — A488

Designs: 10fr, Ibis religionas, horiz. 200fr, Ardea pavonia. 450fr, Spoonbill (spatule). 500fr, Himantopus himantopus.

2011, Apr. 6 Litho. Perf. 13x13¼
1679 A488 10fr multi — —
Perf. 13¼x13
1680 A488 200fr multi — —
1681 A488 450fr multi — —
1682 A488 500fr multi — —
Dated 2009.

Pottery — A489

Design: 150fr, Water container and lid (canari réservoir d'eau). 200fr, Drinking cup (canari de libation). 225fr, Clay stove (fourneau athé). 425fr, Censer (encensoir).

2011, Apr. 6 Litho. Perf. 13¼x13
1683 A489 150fr multi — —
1684 A489 200fr multi — —
1685 A489 225fr multi — —
1686 A489 425fr multi — —
Dated 2007.

Islands A490

Design: 50fr, Ile du Sine Saloume. 100fr, Ile aux Oiseaux (Bird Island). 450fr, Ilot Sarpant. 500fr, Ile de Carabane.

2011 Litho. Perf. 13x13¼
1687 A490 50fr multi — —
1688 A490 100fr multi — —
1689 A490 450fr multi — —
1690 A490 500fr multi — —
Dated 2009.

Horses in Sports A491

Designs: 10fr, Steeplechase. 50fr, Dressage. 250fr, Horse and jockey. 500fr, Horse race.

2012, June 5 Litho. Perf. 13x13¼
1691-1694 A491 Set of 4 — —

Diplomatic Relations Between Senegal and Vatican City, 50th Anniv. A492

Designs: 50fr, Flags of Senegal and Vatican City. 200fr, Christ Giving the Keys to St. Peter, by Pietro Perugino, vert.

2012 Litho. Perf. 13x13¼, 13¼x13
1695-1696 A492 Set of 2 1.40 1.40

Weaving — A493

Designs: 50fr, Weaver winding yarn on bobbin. 150fr, Yarn on swift and shuttles, horiz. 300fr, Weaver at loom. 500fr, Weaver with finished fabric, horiz.

Perf. 13¼x13, 13x13¼
2012, Sept. 18 Litho.
1697-1700 A493 Set of 4 4.00 4.00
Dated 2009.

2002 Sinking of the Joola Ferry A494

Joola Ferry: 75fr, Afloat near Ziguinchor, and sinking (in inset). 100fr, At sea. 200fr, At dock with door open. 250fr, Next to small boat near Ile de Carabane.

2012 ? Litho. Perf. 13x13¼
1701 A494 75fr multi — —
1702 A494 100fr multi — —
1703 A494 200fr multi — —
1704 A494 250fr multi — —
Dated 2003.

Fruits — A495

Designs: 25fr, Balanites aegyptiaca. 200fr, Citrullus vulgaris, horiz. 450fr, Cashew. 500fr, Saba senegalensis.

2013 Litho. Perf. 13¼x13, 13x13¼
1705-1708 A495 Set of 4 — —

Keur Moussa Benedictine Abbey, 50th Anniv. — A496

Designs: 200fr, Cross, heart, monk praying. 450fr, Fiftieth anniversary emblem.

2013 Litho. Perf. 13¼x13
1709-1710 A496 Set of 2 — —

Gueumbeul Reserve A497

Designs: 25fr, Reptiles, mushrooms, birds and flowers near pond. 50fr, Antelopes at pond. 200fr, Mammals, birds and fruit. 450fr, Birds on Senegal River.

2013, Dec. 18   Litho.   Perf. 13x13¼
1711-1714 A497   Set of 4   3.00 3.00

Blaise Diagne (1872-1934), Mayor of Dakar — A498

2014   Litho.   Perf. 13¼x13
1715 A498 25fr multi

World War I, Cent. A499

Designs: 200fr, Assassination of Archduke Franz Ferdinand. 450fr, Soldiers in trenches, vert. 500fr, Senegalese soldiers.

2014   Litho.   Perf. 13x13¼, 13¼x13
1716-1718 A499   Set of 3

A souvenir sheet containing one 2000fr air post stamp depicting Senegalese soldiers was produced in limited quantities.

Bodies of Water A500

Designs: 100fr, Lake Rétba. 1000fr, Dindefelo Falls, vert.

2014   Litho.   Perf. 13x13¼
1719 A500 100fr multi

Perf. 13¼x13
1720 A500 1000fr multi

SEMI-POSTAL STAMPS

No. 84 Surcharged in Red

1915   Unwmk.   Perf. 14x13½
B1 A28 10c + 5c org red &
             rose   1.75 1.75
 a. Chalky paper   1.75 1.75

No. B1 is on both ordinary and chalky paper.

Same Surcharge on No. 87
1918
B2 A28 15c + 5c org red &
             brn vio   1.75 1.75

Curie Issue
Common Design Type
1938   Engr.   Perf. 13
B3 CD80 1.75fr + 50c brt ul-
             tra   10.50 10.50

French Revolution Issue
Common Design Type
Photo., Name & Value Typo. in Black
1939
B4 CD83 45c + 25c green   8.50 8.50
B5 CD83 70c + 30c brown   8.50 8.50
B6 CD83 90c + 35c red
             org   8.50 8.50
B7 CD83 1.25fr + 1fr rose
             pink   8.50 8.50
B8 CD83 2.25fr + 2fr blue   9.00 9.00
     Nos. B4-B8 (5)   43.00 43.00

Stamps of 1935-38 Surcharged in Red or Black

1941   Perf. 12x12½, 12
B9   A30 50c + 1fr red org   3.25
B10 A31 80c + 2fr vio (R)   7.25
B11 A30 1.50fr + 2fr dk bl   7.25
B12 A30 2fr + 3fr blue   7.25
     Nos. B9-B12 (4)   25.00

Common Design Type and

Bambara Sharpshooter SP1   Colonial Soldier SP2

1941   Photo.   Perf. 13½
B13 SP1   1fr + 1fr red   1.25
B14 CD86 1.50fr + 3fr maroon 1.25
B15 SP2   2.50fr + 1fr blue   1.25
     Nos. B13-B15 (3)   3.75

The surtax was for the defense of the colonies.

Nos. B13-B15 were issued by the Vichy government, but it is doubtful whether they were placed in use in Senegal.

Nos. 193-194 Srchd. in Black or Red

1944   Engr.   Perf. 12½x12
B15A 50c + 1.50fr on 2.50fr bl
             (R)   .80
B15B + 2.50fr on 1fr green   .80
Colonial Development Fund.

Nos. B15A-B15B were issued by the Vichy government in France, but were not placed on sale in Senegal.

Catalogue values for unused stamps in this section, from this point to the end of the section, are for Never Hinged items.

Republic
Anti-Malaria Issue
Common Design Type
Perf. 12½x12
1962, Apr. 7   Engr.   Unwmk.
B16 CD108 25fr + 5fr brt grn   1.10 .65

Freedom from Hunger Issue
Common Design Type
1963, Mar. 21   Perf. 13
B17 CD112 25fr + 5fr dp vio, grn &
             brn   .80 .50

SP3

2002 World Cup Soccer Championships, Japan and Korea — SP4

World Cup: 290fr+50fr, Soccer ball and stadium. 360fr+50fr, Soccer field and crowd.

2002   Litho.   Perf. 13½
B18 SP3 75fr +100fr shown   .75 .75
          Perf. 13x13¼
B19 SP4 200fr +100fr shown   1.25 1.25
B20 SP4 290fr + 50fr multi   1.40 1.40
B21 SP4 360fr + 50fr multi   1.60 1.60
     Nos. B18-B21 (4)   5.00 5.00

Value for No. B18 is for example with surrounding selvage.

AIR POST STAMPS

Landscape AP1

Caravan AP2

Perf. 12½x12, 12x12½
1935   Engr.   Unwmk.
C1   AP1 25c dk brown   .30   .30
C2   AP1 50c red orange   .35   .45
C3   AP1 1fr rose lilac   .30   .30
C4   AP1 1.25fr yellow grn   .30   .30
C5   AP1 2fr blue   .30   .30
C6   AP1 3fr olive grn   .30   .30
C7   AP2 3.50fr violet   .35   .30
C8   AP2 4.75fr orange   .35   .45
C9   AP2 6.50fr dk blue   1.10 1.10
C10 AP2 8fr black   1.10 1.75
C11 AP2 15fr rose lake   1.40 1.40
     Nos. C1-C11 (11)   6.15 6.95

No. C8 surcharged "ENTR' AIDE FRANCAIS + 95f 25" in green, red violet or blue, was never issued in this colony.

Common Design Type
1940   Engr.   Perf. 12½x12
C12 CD85 1.90fr ultra   .50   .50
C13 CD85 2.90fr dk red   .50   .50
C14 CD85 4.50fr dk gray
             grn   .55   .55
C15 CD85 4.90fr yellow bis   .85   .85
C16 CD85 6.90fr dp orange   1.10 1.10
     Nos. C12-C16 (5)   3.50 3.50

Common Design Types
1942
C17 CD88 50c car & bl   .30
C18 CD88 1fr brn & blk   .50
C19 CD88 2fr dk grn & red
             brn   .50
C20 CD88 3fr dk bl & scar   1.05
C21 CD88 5fr vio & brn red   .70

Frame Engr., Center Typo.
C22 CD89 10fr ultra, ind & hn   .70
C23 CD89 20fr rose car, mag
             & choc   1.10
C24 CD89 50fr yel grn, dl grn
             & yel   2.10 2.75
Engr. & Photo.
Size: 47x26mm
C25 CD88 100fr dk red & bl   2.50 3.75
     Nos. C17-C25 (9)   9.45

There is doubt whether Nos. C17 to C23 were officially placed in use.

Catalogue values for unused stamps in this section, from this point to the end of the section, are for Never Hinged items.

Republic

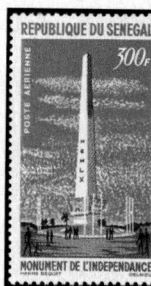

Abyssinian Roller — AP3

Designs: 50fr, Carmine bee-eater, vert. 200fr, Violet touraco, vert. 250fr, Red bishop, vert. 500fr, Fish eagle, vert.

Perf. 12½x13, 13x12½
1960-63   Photo.   Unwmk.
Birds in Natural Colors
C26 AP3 50fr blk & gray bl
             ('61)   2.25 .50
C27 AP3 100fr blk, yel & lil
                               4.00 1.00
C28 AP3 200fr blk, grn & bl
             ('61)   9.00 2.50
C29 AP3 250fr blk & pale grn
             ('63)   9.00 3.00
C30 AP3 500fr blk & bl   25.00 5.25
     Nos. C26-C30 (5)   49.25 12.25

Air Afrique Issue
Common Design Type
1962, Feb. 17   Engr.   Perf. 13
C31 CD107 25fr vio brn, sl grn &
             ocher   .80   .30

African Postal Union Issue
Common Design Type
1963, Sept. 8   Photo.   Perf. 12½
C32 CD114 85fr choc, ocher &
             red   1.75   .50

Air Afrique Issue
Common Design Type
1963, Nov. 19   Unwmk.   Perf. 13x12
C33 CD115 50fr multicolored 2.00   .65

Independence Monument — AP4

1964, Apr. 4   Photo.   Perf. 12x13
C34 AP4 300fr ultra, tan, ocher &
             grn   5.00 1.75

Symbolic European and African
Cities — AP5

1964, Apr. 18   Engr.   *Perf. 13*
C35 AP5 150fr grn, brn red & blk 4.00 1.40
Congress of the Intl. Federation of Twin Cities, Dakar.

Europafrica Issue

Peanuts, Globe, Factory, Figures of
"Africa," and "Europe" — AP6

1964, July 20   Photo.   *Perf. 13x12*
C36 AP6 50fr multicolored   2.00 .60
See note after Madagascar No. 357.

Basketball
AP7

1964, Aug. 22   Engr.   *Perf. 13*
C37 AP7 85fr shown   2.50 .65
C38 AP7 100fr Pole vault   2.75 1.00
18th Olympic Games, Tokyo, Oct. 10-25.

Launching of
Syncom
2 — AP8

1964, Oct. 24   Unwmk.   *Perf. 13*
C39 AP8 150fr grn, red brn & ultra   3.00 1.00
Communication through space.

Pres. John F.
Kennedy (1917-
1963)
AP9

1964, Dec. 5   Photo.   *Perf. 13*
C40 AP9 100fr brt yel, dk grn
& brn red   2.75 1.00
  a. Souvenir sheet of 4   12.00 12.00

Scenic Type of Regular Issue
View: 100fr, Shore of Gambia River in Eastern Senegal.

1965, Feb. 27   Engr.   *Perf. 13*
Size: 48x27mm
C41 A48 100fr brn blk, grn & bis 2.50 1.00

Mother and
Child, Globe and
Emblems
AP10

1965, Sept. 25   Unwmk.   *Perf. 13*
C42 AP10 50fr choc, brt bl & grn 1.25 .40
International Cooperation Year.

A-1 Satellite and Earth — AP11

Designs: No. C44, Diamant rocket. 90fr,
Scout rocket and FR-1 satellite.

1966, Feb. 19   Engr.   *Perf. 13*
C43 AP11 50fr yel brn, dk grn &
blk   1.00 .40
C44 AP11 50fr Prus bl, lt red brn
& car rose   1.00 .40
C45 AP11 90fr dk red brn, dk
gray & Prus bl 2.50 .85
  Nos. C43-C45 (3)   4.50 1.65
French achievements in space.

D-1 Satellite over Globe — AP12

1966, June 11   Engr.   *Perf. 13*
C46 AP12 100fr dk car, sl & vio 2.50 .80
Launching of the D-1 satellite at Hammaguir, Algeria, Feb. 17, 1966.

Air Afrique Issue
Common Design Type
1966, Aug. 31   Photo.   *Perf. 13*
C47 CD123 30fr red brn, blk & lem .80 .30

Mermoz Plane "Arc-en-Ciel" — AP13

Jean
Mermoz — AP14

Designs: 35fr, Latecoére 300 "Croix du
Sud." 100fr, Map showing last flight from
Dakar to Brazil.

1966, Dec. 7   Engr.   *Perf. 13*
C48 AP13 20fr bl, rose lil & indigo   .80 .25
C49 AP13 35fr slate, brn & grn 1.00 .40
C50 AP13 100fr grn, lt grn & mar 1.75 .50
C51 AP14 150fr blk, ultra & mar 3.50 1.00
  Nos. C48-C51 (4)   7.05 2.05
Jean Mermoz (1901-36), French aviator, on
the 30th anniv. of his last flight.

Dakar-Yoff Airport — AP15

1967, Apr. 22   Engr.   *Perf. 13*
C52 AP15 200fr red brn, ind &
brt bl   3.50 1.00

Knob-billed Goose — AP16

Flowers and Birds: 100fr, Mimosa. 150fr,
Flowering cactus. 250fr, Village weaver. 500fr,
Bateleur.

1967-69   Photo.   *Perf. 11½*
Granite Paper
Dated "1967"
C53 AP16 100fr gray, yel & grn 3.00 1.00
C54 AP16 150fr multicolored 5.00 1.50
Dated "1969"
C55 AP16 250fr gray & multi 8.00 1.75
Dated "1968"
C56 AP16 300fr brt bl & multi 12.50 3.00
C57 AP16 500fr orange & multi 17.50 4.25
  Nos. C53-C57 (5)   46.00 11.50
Issued: 100fr, 150fr, 6/24/67; 500fr, 7/13/68;
300fr, 12/21/68; 250fr, 4/26/69.

The Girls
from
Avignon,
by Picasso
AP17

1967, July 22   *Perf. 12x13*
C59 AP17 100fr multicolored   3.50 1.00

African Postal Union Issue
Common Design Type
1967, Sept. 9   Engr.   *Perf. 13*
C60 CD124 100fr brt grn, vio &
car lake   1.75 .50

Konrad Adenauer
AP18

1968, Feb. 17   Photo.   *Perf. 12½*
C61 AP18 100fr dk red, ol &
blk   2.25 .60
  a. Souvenir sheet of 4   10.00 10.00
Konrad Adenauer (1876-1967), chancellor
of West Germany (1949-63).

Weather Balloon,
Vegetation and
WMO
Emblem — AP19

1968, Mar. 23   Engr.   *Perf. 13*
C62 AP19 50fr blk, ultra & bl grn 1.25 .40
8th World Meteorological Day, Mar. 23.

19th Olympic
Games, Mexico
City, Oct. 12-
27 — AP20

1968, Oct. 12   Engr.   *Perf. 13*
C63 AP20 20fr Hurdling   .55 .25
C64 AP20 30fr Javelin   .70 .30
C65 AP20 50fr Judo   1.40 .35
C66 AP20 75fr Basketball 2.25 .65
  Nos. C63-C66 (4)   4.90 1.55

PHILEXAFRIQUE Issue

Young
Woman
Reading
Letter, by
Jean
Raoux
AP21

1968, Oct. 26   Photo.   *Perf. 12½*
C67 AP21 100fr buff & multi 3.50 2.00
PHILEXAFRIQUE, Phil. Exhib. in Abidjan,
Feb. 14-23, 1969. Printed with alternating buff
label.

2nd PHILEXAFRIQUE Issue
Common Design Type
Senegal #160 and Boulevard, Dakar.

1969, Feb. 14   Engr.   *Perf. 13*
C68 CD128 50fr grn, gray & pur 2.00 1.40

Tourist Emblem with Map of Africa and
Dove — AP22

1969   Photo.   Perf. 13
C69 AP22 100fr red, lt grn & lt bl   1.75 .50
Year of African Tourism, 1969.

Pres. Lamine
Gueye (1891-
1968)
AP23

Design: 45fr, Pres. Gueye wearing fez.

1969, June 10   Photo.   Perf. 12½
C70 AP23 30fr brn, org & blk   .45 .25
C71 AP23 45fr brn, lt grnsh bl &
            blk   1.25 .30
 a.   Min. sheet, 2 ea #C70-C71   3.50 3.50

"Transmission of
Thought"
Tapestry by Ousmane
Faye — AP24

Fari, Tapestry by Allaye
N'Diaye — AP25

1969, Oct. 25   Photo.   Perf. 12½
C72 AP24 25fr multicolored   .90 .35
            Perf. 12x12½
C73 AP25 50fr multicolored   2.00 .65

Europafrica Issue

Baila Bridge — AP26

1969, Nov. 15   Photo.   Perf. 13x12
C74 AP26 100fr multicolored   2.00 .50

Emile Lécrivain, Plane and Toulouse-
Dakar Route — AP27

1970, Jan. 31   Engr.   Perf. 13
C75 AP27 50fr grn, slate & rose
            brn   1.25 .40
40th anniv. of the disappearance of the aviator Emile Lécrivain (1897-1929).

René Maran,
Martinique
AP28

Portraits: 45fr, Marcus Garvey, Jamaica.
50fr, Dr. Price Mars, Haiti.

1970, Mar. 21   Photo.   Perf. 12½
C76 AP28 30fr red brn, lt grn &
            blk   .35 .25
C77 AP28 45fr blue, pink & blk   1.00 .25
C78 AP28 50fr grn, buff & blk   1.10 .40
            Nos. C76-C78 (3)   2.45 .90

Issued to honor prominent Negro leaders.

"One People,
One Purpose,
One Faith"
AP29

1970, Apr. 3   Photo.   Perf. 11½
C79 AP29 500fr gold & multi   7.50 3.00
 a.   Souvenir sheet   10.00 10.00
10th anniv. of independence. No. C79 sold
for 600fr.

Bay of Naples and Dakar Post
Office — AP30

1970, May 2   Photo.   Perf. 13x12½
C80 AP30 100fr multicolored   2.00 .60
10th Europa Phil. Exhib., Naples, May 2-10.

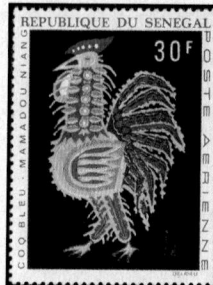

Blue Cock,
by
Mamadou
Niang
AP31

Tapestries: 45fr, Fairy. 75fr, "Lunaris," by
Jean Lurçat.

1970, June 20 Photo. Perf. 12½x12
C81 AP31 30fr black & multi   .55 .35
C82 AP31 45fr dk red brn & multi 2.00 .50
C83 AP31 75fr yellow & multi   3.00 .65
            Nos. C81-C83 (3)   5.55 1.50

Head of the Courtesan Nagakawa, by
Chobunsai Yeishi, and Mt. Fuji, by
Hokusai — AP32

EXPO Emblem and: 25fr, Woman Playing
Guitar, by Hokusai, and Sun Tower, vert.
150fr, "One of the Present-day Beauties of
Nanboku" by Katsukawa Shuncho, vert.

1970, July 18   Photo.   Perf. 13
C84 AP32 25fr red & green   .65 .25
C85 AP32 75fr yel grn, dk bl &
            red brn   1.75 .35
C86 AP32 150fr bl, red brn &
            ocher   2.75 .80
            Nos. C84-C86 (3)   5.15 1.40
EXPO '70 Intl. Exhib., Osaka, Japan, Mar.
15-Sept. 13.

Tuna, Processing Plant and
Ship — AP33

Urban Development in Dakar — AP34

1970, Aug. 22   Engr.   Perf. 13
C87 AP33 30fr dl red, blk & brt bl 1.00 .25
C88 AP34 100fr chocolate & grn   1.75 .60
Progress in industrialization and urbaniza-
tion in Dakar.

Beethoven;
Napoleon and
Allegory of
Eroica
Symphony
AP35

Design: 100fr, Beethoven holding quill.

1970, Sept. 26   Engr.   Perf. 13
C89 AP35 50fr ol, brn & ocher   2.25 .50
C90 AP35 100fr Prus grn & dp
            claret   4.50 1.10
Ludwig van Beethoven (1770-1827),
composer.

Globe, Scales and Women of Four
Races — AP36

1970, Oct. 24   Engr.   Perf. 13
C91 AP36 100fr grn, ocher & red 2.25 .80
25th anniversary of United Nations.

De Gaulle, Map
of Africa,
Symbols — AP37

100fr, Charles de Gaulle & map of Senegal.

1970, Dec. 31   Photo.   Perf. 12½
C92 AP37 50fr multicolored   1.75 .85
C93 AP37 100fr blue & multi   3.50 1.60
Honoring Pres. Charles de Gaulle as libera-
tor of the colonies.

"A Roof for Every Refugee" — AP38

1971, Jan. 16
C94 AP38 100fr multicolored   1.75 .65
High Commissioner for Refugees, 20th
anniv.

Phillis Wheatley,
American
Poet — AP39

Prominent Blacks: 40fr, James E. K. Aggrey,
Methodist missionary, Ghana. 60fr, Alain Le
Roy Locke, American educator. 100fr, Booker
T. Washington, American educator.

1971, Apr. 10   Photo.   Perf. 12½
C95 AP39 25fr multicolored   .25 .25
C96 AP39 40fr blk, bl & bis   .45 .30
C97 AP39 60fr blk, bl & emer   1.00 .40
C98 AP39 100fr blk, bl & red   1.50 .60
            Nos. C95-C98 (4)   3.20 1.55

Napoleon
as First
Consul, by
Ingres
AP40

Designs: 25fr, Napoleon in 1809, by Robert Lefevre. 35fr, Napoleon on his death bed, by Georges Rouget. 50fr, Awakening into Immortality, sculpture by Francois Rude.

1971, June 19   Photo.   Perf. 13
C99 AP40 15fr gold & multi   .70   .40
C100 AP40 25fr gold & multi   1.00   .50
C101 AP40 35fr gold & multi   1.40   .60
C102 AP40 50fr gold & multi   2.75 1.00
  Nos. C99-C102 (4)   5.85 2.50
Napoleon Bonaparte (1769-1821).

Gamal Abdel
Nasser — AP41

1971, July 17   Perf. 12½
C103 AP41 50fr multicolored   1.00   .30
Nasser (1918-1970), President of Egypt.

Alfred Nobel —
AP41a

1971, Sept. 25 Photo. Perf. 13½x13
C103A AP41a 100fr multicolored 2.25   .60
Alfred Nobel (1833-1896), inventor of dynamite who established the Nobel Prizes.

Iranian Flag and Senegal Coat of Arms — AP42

1971, Oct. 15   Perf. 13x12½
C104 AP42 200fr multicolored   3.00 1.00
2500th anniversary of the founding of the Persian empire by Cyrus the Great.

African Postal Union Issue
Common Design Type
Design: 100fr, Arms of Senegal and UAMPT Building, Brazzaville, Congo.

1971, Nov. 13   Perf. 13x13½
C105 CD135 100fr blue & multi   1.60   .50

Louis Armstrong (1900-1971),
American Jazz Musician — AP43

1971, Nov. 27   Photo.   Perf. 12½
C106 AP43 150fr gold & dk brn   6.75 1.60

Sapporo Olympic Emblem and Speed Skating — AP44

Sapporo '72 Emblem and: 10fr, Bobsledding. 125fr, Skiing.

1972, Jan. 22   Perf. 13
C107 AP44 5fr multicolored   .25   .25
C108 AP44 10fr multicolored   .25   .25
C109 AP44 125fr multicolored   3.00   .60
  Nos. C107-C109 (3)   3.50 1.10
11th Winter Olympic Games, Sapporo, Japan, Feb. 3-13.

Fonteghetto della Farina, by Canaletto — AP45

Design: 100fr, San Giorgio Maggiore, by Giovanni Antonio Guardi, vert.

1972, Feb. 26
C110 AP45 50fr gold & multi   1.25   .65
C111 AP45 100fr gold & multi   2.50 1.25
UNESCO campaign to save Venice.

Theater Type of Regular Issue
150fr, Daniel Sorano as Shylock, vert.

1972, Mar. 25 Photo. Perf. 12½x13
C112 A99 150fr multicolored   4.00 1.50

Environment Type of Regular Issue
100fr, Protection of the ocean (oil slick).

1972, June 3 Photo. Perf. 13x12½
C113 A101 100fr multicolored   2.25   .60

Emperor Haile Selassie, Ethiopian and Senegalese Flags — AP46

1972, July 23 Photo. Perf. 13½x13
C114 AP46 100fr gold & multi   1.75   .60
80th birthday of Emperor Haile Selassie of Ethiopia.

Swordfish — AP47

Designs: 65fr, Killer whale. 75fr, Rhincodon. 125fr, Common rorqual (whale).

1972-73   Photo.   Perf. 11½
C115 AP47 50fr multi   3.75   .75
C116 AP47 65fr multi   5.00 1.25
C117 AP47 75fr multi   7.25 1.50
C118 AP47 125fr multi   8.50 1.75
  Nos. c115-c118 (4)   24.50 5.25
Issued: #C115, C118, 11/25/72; #C116-C117, 7/28/73.

Palace of the Republic — AP48

1973, Apr. 3   Photo.   Perf. 13
C119 AP48 100fr multi   1.75   .60

Hotel Teranga, Dakar — AP49

1973, May 26   Photo.   Perf. 13
C120 AP49 100fr multi   1.75   .60

Emblem of African Lions Club — AP50

1973, June 2
C121 AP50 150fr multi   2.50   .80
15th Congress of Lions Intl., District 403, Dakar, June 1-2.

"Couple
with
Mimosa,"
by Marc
Chagall
AP51

1973, Aug. 11   Photo.   Perf. 13
C122 AP51 200fr multi   7.00 2.75

Map of Italy with Riccione — AP52

1973, Aug. 25   Engr.
C123 AP52 100fr dk grn, red & pur   2.25 .60
Intl. Phil. Exhib., Riccione 1973.

Raoul Follereau and World Map — AP53

100fr, Dr. Armauer G. Hansen & leprosy bacilli.

1973, Dec. 22   Engr.   Perf. 13
C124 AP53 40fr sl grn, pur & red brn   1.10 .25
C125 AP53 100fr sl grn, mag & plum   2.40 .75
Centenary of the discovery of the Hansen bacillus, the cause of leprosy.

Human Rights Flame and People — AP54

65fr, Human Rights flame and drummer.

1973, Dec. 15   Photo.   Perf. 13½
C126 AP54 35fr grn & multi   .70   .25
C127 AP54 65fr org & multi   1.00   .40
25th anniv. of the Universal Declaration of Human Rights.

Men of Four Races, Arms of Dakar, Congress Emblem — AP55

50fr, Key joining twin cities & emblem, vert.

1973, Dec. 26   Photo.
C128 AP55 50fr org & multi   .90   .35
C129 AP55 125fr red & multi   1.75   .50
8th Congress of the World Federation of Twin Cities, Dakar, Dec. 26-29.

Finfoots — AP56

1974, Feb. 9　　Photo.　　*Perf. 13*

C130	AP56	1fr shown	.25	.25
C131	AP56	2fr Spoonbills	.25	.25
C132	AP56	3fr Crested cranes	.30	.25
C133	AP56	4fr Egrets	.30	.25
C134	AP56	250fr Flamingos	7.00	1.60
C135	AP56	250fr Flamingos	7.00	1.60
a.		Strip of 2 + label	12.50	
		Nos. C130-C135 (6)	15.10	4.20

Djoudj Park bird sanctuary. Denomination in gold on No. C134, in black on No. C135.

Tiger Attacking Wild Horse, by Delacroix — AP57

Design: 200fr, Tiger Hunt, by Eugéne Delacroix (1798-1863).

1974, Mar. 23　　Photo.　　*Perf. 13*

C136	AP57	150fr gold & multi	3.00	.80
C137	AP57	200fr gold & multi	3.75	1.25

Intl. Fair, Dakar — AP57a

1974, Nov. 28　Embossed　*Perf. 10½*

C137A	AP57a	350fr silver	5.75	4.50
C137B	AP57a	1500fr gold	27.50	18.00

Soyuz and Apollo, Space Docking Emblem — AP58

1975, May 23　　Engr.　　*Perf. 13*

C138	AP58	125fr multi	2.00	.60

US-USSR space cooperation.
For overprint see No. C140.

Senegal Type D6, Tuscany Type A1, Map of Italy AP59

1975, Aug. 23　　Engr.　　*Perf. 13*

C139	AP59	125fr org, vio & dk red	2.00	.65

Intl. Phil. Exhib., Riccione 1975.

No. C138 Overprinted "JONCTION / 17 Juil. 1975"

1975, Oct. 21　　Engr.　　*Perf. 13*

C140	AP58	125fr multi	2.00	.60

Apollo-Soyuz link-up in space, July 17, 1975.

Boston Massacre — AP60

Design: 500fr, Lafayette, Washington, Rochambeau and Battle of Yorktown.

1975, Dec. 20　　Engr.　　*Perf. 13*

C141	AP60	250fr ultra, red & brn	3.00	1.10
C142	AP60	500fr bl & ver	6.75	2.50

American Bicentennial.

Concorde and Map — AP61

1976, Jan. 21　　Litho.　　*Perf. 13*

C143	AP61	300fr multi	4.00	2.00

First commercial flight of supersonic jet Concorde, Paris to Rio de Janeiro, Jan. 21. For overprint see No. C145.

2nd Intl. Fair, Dakar — AP61a

1976, Dec. 3　Embossed　*Perf. 10½*

C143A	AP61a	500fr silver	6.50	6.50
C143B	AP61a	1500fr gold	27.50	27.50

Spaceship and Control Room — AP62

1977, June 25　　Litho.　　*Perf. 12½*

C144	AP62	300fr multi	3.25	1.25

Viking space mission to Mars.

No. C143 Overprinted in Red "22.11.77 / PARIS NEW-YORK"

1977, Nov. 22　　　　　　*Perf. 13*

C145	AP61	300fr multi	4.00	2.00

Concorde, 1st commercial flight, Paris-New York.

Evolution of Fishing — AP62a

Designs: 10fr, Fishermen hauling in netted catch. 15fr, Two fishermen in canoe. 20fr, Ship, man holding fish. 25fr, Fisherman holding net.

1977　　　Litho.　　　*Perf. 12¾*

C145A	AP62a	5fr shown	—	—
C145B	AP62a	10fr multi	—	—
C145C	AP62a	15fr multi	—	—
C145D	AP62a	20fr multi	—	—
C145E	AP62a	25fr multi	—	—

Philexafrique II-Essen Issue
Common Design Types

Designs: No. C146, Lion & Senegal #C28. No. C147, Capercaillie & Schleswig-Holstein #1.

1978, Nov. 1　　Litho.　　*Perf. 12½*

C146	CD138	100fr multi	2.00	1.50
C147	CD139	100fr multi	2.00	1.50
a.		Pair, #C146-C147	10.00	4.00

J. Dabry, L. Gimie, and J. Mermoz, Airplane, Map of Route (St. Louis-Natal) — AP63

1980, Dec.　　Photo.　　*Perf. 13*

C148	AP63	300fr multi	3.25	1.00

1st airmail crossing of So. Atlantic, 50th anniv.

1st Transatlantic Commercial Airmail Flight, 55th Anniv. — AP64

1985, May 12　　Litho.　　*Perf. 13*

C149	AP64	250fr multi	2.75	1.00

Clement Ader (1841-1926), Engineer and Aviation Pioneer — AP65

Ader and: 145fr, Automobile, microphone. 180fr, 615fr, 940fr, Bat-winged steam powered airplane.

1991, June 7　　Litho.　　*Perf. 13*

C150	AP65	145fr multicolored	2.00	.40
C151	AP65	180fr multicolored	2.25	.65
C152	AP65	615fr multi, vert.	7.50	2.25
		Nos. C150-C152 (3)	11.75	3.30

Souvenir Sheet

C153	AP65	940fr multi, vert.	7.00	3.50

AIR POST SEMI-POSTAL STAMPS

French Revolution Issue
Common Design Type

1939　　Unwmk.　Photo.　*Perf. 13*
Name and Value Typo. in Orange

CB1	CD83	4.75 + 4fr brn blk	14.00	14.00

Surtax used for the defense of the colonies.

Dahomey Types SPAP1-SPAP3 Inscribed Senegal
Perf. 13½x12½, 13 (#CB4)
Photo, Engr. (#CB4)

1942, June 22

CB2	SPAP1	1.50fr + 3.50fr grn	.80	6.50
CB3	SPAP2	2fr + 6fr brown	.80	6.50
CB4	SPAP3	3fr + 9fr car red	.80	6.50
		Nos. CB2-CB4 (3)	2.40	19.50

Native children's welfare fund.

Colonial Education Fund
Common Design Type
Perf. 12½x13½

1942, June 22　　　　　　Engr.

CB5	CD86a	1.20fr + 1.80fr blue & red	.80	6.50

> Catalogue values for unused stamps in this section, from this point to the end of the section, are for Never Hinged items.

Republic

Nile Gods Uniting Upper and Lower Egypt (Abu Simbel) — SPAP1

1964, Mar. 7　　Engr.　　*Perf. 13*

CB6	SPAP1	25fr + 5fr Prus bl, red brn & sl grn	1.60	.65

UNESCO campaign to save historic monuments in Nubia.

POSTAGE DUE STAMPS

Postage Due Stamps of French Colonies Surcharged

1903　　Unwmk.　　*Imperf.*

J1	D1	10c on 50c lilac	105.00	105.00
J2	D1	10c on 60c brown, buff	105.00	105.00
J3	D1	10c on 1fr rose, buff	425.00	425.00
		Nos. J1-J3 (3)	635.00	635.00

D2

1906　　Typo.　　*Perf. 14x13½*

J4	D2	5c green, grnsh	7.00	4.25
J5	D2	10c red brown	7.00	5.00
J6	D2	15c dark blue	7.00	6.25
J7	D2	20c black, yellow	10.50	6.25
J8	D2	30c red, straw	10.50	10.00
J9	D2	50c violet	10.50	7.50
J10	D2	60c black, buff	17.00	15.00
J11	D2	1fr black, pinkish	27.50	22.50
		Nos. J4-J11 (8)	97.00	76.75

D3

1914

J12	D3	5c green	.70	.45
J13	D3	10c rose	.70	.45
J14	D3	15c gray	1.10	.70
J15	D3	20c brown	1.10	1.10
J16	D3	30c blue	1.40	1.10
J17	D3	50c black	1.75	1.40
J18	D3	60c orange	2.10	1.40
J19	D3	1fr violet	2.10	1.75
		Nos. J12-J19 (8)	10.95	8.35

Type of 1914 Issue Surcharged

1927

J20	D3	2fr on 1fr lilac rose	10.50	7.00
J21	D3	3fr on 1fr org brn	10.50	7.00

D4

1935 **Engr.** **Perf. 12½x12**

J22	D4	5c yellow green	.25	.25
J23	D4	10c red orange	.25	.25
J24	D4	15c violet	.25	.25
J25	D4	20c olive green	.25	.25
J26	D4	30c reddish brown	.25	.25
J27	D4	50c rose lilac	1.40	1.40
J28	D4	60c orange	1.50	1.50
J29	D4	1fr black	1.10	1.10
J30	D4	2fr dark blue	1.10	1.10
J31	D4	3fr dark carmine	1.40	1.40
		Nos. J22-J31 (10)	7.75	7.75

> **Catalogue values for unused stamps in this section, from this point to the end of the section, are for Never Hinged items.**

Republic

D5

1961, Feb. 20 **Typo.** **Perf. 14x13½**

J32	D5	1fr orange & red	.25	.25
J33	D5	2fr ultra & red	.25	.25
J34	D5	5fr brown & red	.25	.25
J35	D5	20fr green & red	.60	.60
J36	D5	25fr red lilac & red	1.25	1.25
		Nos. J32-J36 (5)	2.60	2.60

Lion — D6

1966-83 **Typo.** **Perf. 14x13**
Lion in Gold

J37	D6	1fr red & black	.25	.25
J38	D6	2fr yel brn & black	.25	.25
J39	D6	5fr red lilac & black	.25	.25
J40	D6	10fr brt blue & black	.25	.25
J41	D6	20fr emerald & black	.40	.40
J42	D6	30fr gray & black	.80	.80
J43	D6	60fr blue & black	.40	.40
J44	D6	90fr rose & black	.60	.40
		Nos. J37-J44 (8)	3.20	3.00

Issued: 1fr-30fr, 12/1/66; others, 10/1983.

OFFICIAL STAMPS

> **Catalogue values for unused stamps in this section are for Never Hinged items.**

Arms — O1

Perf. 14x13½
1961, Sept. 18 **Typo.** **Unwmk.**
Denominations in Black

O1	O1	1fr sepia & bl	.25	.25
O2	O1	2fr dk bl & org	.25	.25
O3	O1	5fr maroon & grn	.25	.25
O4	O1	10fr ver & bl	.25	.25
O5	O1	25fr vio bl & ver	.65	.25
O6	O1	50fr ver & gray	1.00	.45
O7	O1	85fr lilac & org	2.00	.60
O8	O1	100fr ver & yel grn	2.75	1.10
		Nos. O1-O8 (8)	7.40	3.40

Baobab Tree — O2

1966-77 **Typo.** **Perf. 14x13**

O9	O2	1fr yel & blk	.25	.25
O10	O2	5fr org & blk	.25	.25
O11	O2	10fr red & blk	.25	.25
O12	O2	20fr dp red lil & blk	.25	.25
O13	O2	25fr dp lil & blk ('75)	.45	.25
O14	O2	30fr bl & blk	.45	.25
O15	O2	35fr bl & blk ('73)	.55	.25
O16	O2	40fr grnsh bl & blk ('75)	.55	.25
O17	O2	55fr emer & blk	1.00	.45
O18	O2	60fr emer & blk ('77)	.55	.25
O19	O2	90fr dk bl grn & blk	1.40	.25
O20	O2	100fr brn & blk	1.75	.25
		Nos. O9-O20 (12)	7.70	3.20

See Nos. O22-O25.

No. O17 Surcharged with New Value and Two Bars

1969

O21	O2	60fr on 55fr emer & blk	1.75	.25

1983, Oct. **Typo.** **Perf. 14x13**

O22	O2	90fr dk grn & blk	.60	.25

"90F" is shorter and wider than on No. O19.

Types of 1966-77 Official Stamps
1991 **Litho.** **Perf. 13x13¼**

O22B	O2	45fr blue & black		
O23	O2	50fr red & blk	1.00	1.00
O24	O2	145fr brt grn & blk	2.75	2.75
O25	O2	180fr org yel & blk	3.25	3.25
		Nos. O23-O25 (3)	7.00	7.00

An additional stamp was issued in this set. The editors would like to examine an example.

No. O22B Surcharged

2010 ? **Litho.** **Perf. 13x13¼**

O26	O2	100fr on 45fr #O22B		—

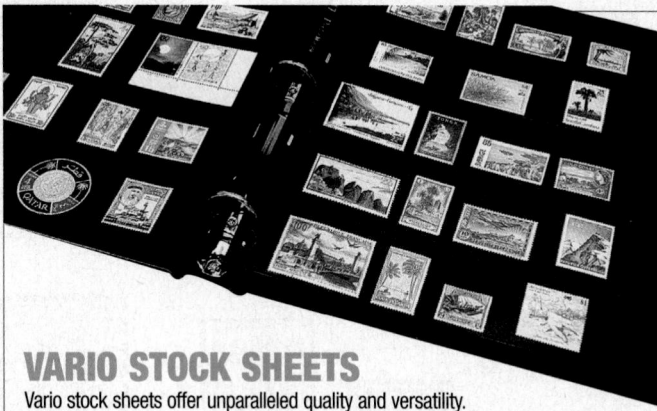
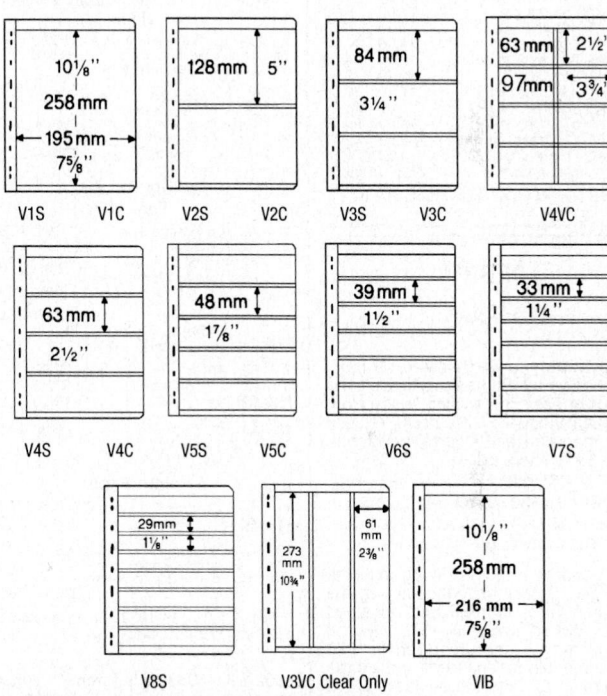

SENEGAMBIA & NIGER

ˌse-nə-ˈgam-bē-ə and ˈnī-jər

A French Administrative unit for the Senegal and Niger possessions in Africa during the period when the French possessions in Africa were being definitively divided into colonies and protectorates. The name was dropped in 1904 when this territory was consolidated with part of French Sudan, under the name Upper Senegal and Niger.

100 Centimes = 1 Franc

Navigation and Commerce — A1

1903 Unwmk. Typo. *Perf. 14x13½*

Name of Colony in Blue or Carmine

1	A1	1c black, *lil bl*	2.10	*2.75*
2	A1	2c brown, *buff*	2.10	*2.75*
3	A1	4c claret, *lav*	7.00	*6.25*
4	A1	5c yel grn	7.00	*7.00*
5	A1	10c red	7.00	*7.75*
6	A1	15c gray	14.00	14.00
7	A1	20c red, *green*	10.50	*14.00*
8	A1	25c blue	21.00	17.50
9	A1	30c brn, *bister*	17.50	*19.00*
10	A1	40c red, *straw*	21.00	*25.00*
11	A1	50c brn, *azure*	45.00	*50.00*
12	A1	75c deep vio, *org*	52.50	*62.50*
13	A1	1fr brnz grn, *straw*	70.00	*70.00*
		Nos. 1-13 (13)	276.70	298.50

Perf. 13½x14 stamps are counterfeits.

SERBIA

ˈsər-bē-ə

LOCATION — In southeastern Europe, bounded by Romania and Bulgaria on the east, the former Austro-Hungarian Empire on the north, Greece on the south, and Albania and Montenegro on the west

GOVT. — Kingdom

AREA — 18,650 sq. mi.

POP. — 2,911,701 (1910)

CAPITAL — Belgrade

A powerful kingdom during the Middle Ages, Serbia was conquered by the Ottoman Turks in 1389 and remained under Turkish rule until 1829, when it became an autonomous region. In 1878 it became fully independent and led the movement to unite the southern Slavs into a single state under Serbian rule. Occupied by Germany, Austria-Hungary and Bulgaria during World War I, the collapse of Austria-Hungary in the autumn of 1918 made it possible for Serbia to realize its national ambitions.

On December 1, 1918, Serbia absorbed Montenegro, Bosnia and Herzegovina, Croatia, Dalmatia and Slovenia, to form the Kingdom of the Serbs, Croats and Slovenes, which became the Kingdom of Yugoslavia in 1929.

During World War II, Yugoslavia was broken up by its Axis occupiers, and a German satellite regime was established in Serbia. After the war, it became one of the constituent republics of the Socialist Federal Republic of Yugoslavia.

In 1992, with the dissolution of the greater Yugoslav republic, only Montenegro remained associated with Serbia, first in the Federal Republic of Yugoslavia and, after 2002, in the looser federation of Serbia & Montenegro.

After a referendum on independence on May 21, 2006, Montenegro seceded from Serbia and Montenegro, declaring independence on June 3, 2006. Serbia formally accepted this secession on June 7. While some stamps issued after June 7 bear the "Serbia and Montenegro" inscription, they were sold only in Serbia.

100 Paras = 1 Dinar

Catalogue values for unused stamps in this country are for Never Hinged items, beginning with Scott 180 in the regular postage section and Scott RA2 in the postal tax section.

Coat of Arms — A1

Prince Michael (Obrenovich III) — A2

1866 Unwmk. Typo. *Imperf.*

Paper colored Through

1	A1	1p dk green, *dk vio rose*	55.00	

Surface Colored Paper, Thin or Thick

2	A1	1p dk green, *lil rose*	55.00	
a.		1p olive green, *rose*	55.00	
b.		1p yel grn, *pale rose* (thick paper)	375.00	
3	A1	2p red brown, *lilac*	75.00	
a.		2p red brn, *lil gray* (thick paper)	250.00	
b.		2p dl grn, *lil gray* (thick paper)	800.00	
		Nos. 1-3 (3)	185.00	

Vienna Printing

Perf. 12

4	A2	10p orange	1,100.	675.00
5	A2	20p rose	750.00	30.00
6	A2	40p blue	750.00	125.00
a.		Half used as 20p on cover		
		Nos. 4-6 (3)	2,600.	830.00

Belgrade Printing

Perf. 9½

7	A2	1p green	22.50	
8	A2	2p bister brn	32.50	
9	A2	20p rose	15.00	22.50
a.		Pair, imperf. between		
10	A2	40p ultra	240.00	275.00
a.		Half used as 20p on cover		
		Nos. 7-10 (4)	310.00	

Pelure Paper

11	A2	10p orange	90.00	110.00
12	A2	20p rose	75.00	15.00
a.		Pair, imperf. between		
13	A2	40p ultra	55.00	37.50
a.		Pair, imperf. between		
b.		Half used as 20p on cover		
		Nos. 11-13 (3)	220.00	162.50

Nos. 1-3, 7-8, 14-16, 25-26 were used only as newspaper tax stamps.

1868-69 Ordinary Paper *Imperf.*

14	A2	1p green	37.50	
a.		1p olive green ('69)	*3,750.*	
15	A2	2p brown	75.00	
a.		2p bister brown ('69)	260.00	

Counterfeits of type A2 are common.

Prince Milan (Obrenovich IV) — A3

Perf. 9½, 12 and Compound

1869-78

16	A3	1p yellow	5.50	*110.00*
17	A3	10p red brown	9.00	4.75
a.		10p yellow brown	*475.00*	75.00
18	A3	10p orange ('78)	2.25	6.00
19	A3	15p orange	85.00	30.00
20	A3	20p gray blue	1.50	2.50
a.		20p ultramarine	4.50	2.25
b.		Half used as 10p on cover		
21	A3	25p rose	2.25	7.50
22	A3	35p lt green	4.50	4.50
23	A3	40p violet	2.25	3.00
a.		Half used as 20p on cover		
24	A3	50p blue green	11.00	7.50
		Nos. 16-24 (9)	123.25	*175.75*

The first setting, which included all values except No. 18, had the stamps 2-2½mm apart.

A new setting, introduced in 1878, had the stamps 3-4mm apart, providing wider margins. Only Nos. 17, 18, 20 and 21 exist in this new setting, which differs also in shades from the earlier setting.

The narrow-spaced Nos. 17, 20 and 21 are rarer, especially unused, as are the early shades of Nos. 23 and 24.

All values except Nos. 19 and 24 are known in various partly perforated varieties.

Counterfeits exist.

See No. 25.

Prince Milan (Obrenovich IV) — A4

1872-79 *Imperf.*

25	A3	1p yellow	6.75	19.00
a.		Tête bêche pair		
26	A4	2p blk, thin paper ('79)	.75	.75
a.		Thick paper ('73)	2.25	*19.00*

Used value of No. 26 is for canceled-to-order.

King Milan I — A5

1880 *Perf. 13x13½*

27	A5	5p green	1.90	.35
a.		5p olive green	550.00	3.75
28	A5	10p rose	2.25	.35
29	A5	20p orange	1.10	.75
a.		20p yellow	4.50	1.90
30	A5	25p ultra	1.50	1.10
a.		25p blue	1.90	1.10
31	A5	50p brown	1.50	*5.50*
a.		50p brown violet	210.00	4.50
32	A5	1d violet	6.75	6.00
		Nos. 27-32 (6)	15.00	14.05

King Alexander (Obrenovich V) — A6

1890

33	A6	5p green	.35	.25
34	A6	10p rose red	1.30	.25
35	A6	15p red violet	1.10	.25
36	A6	20p orange	.75	.25
37	A6	25p blue	.90	.35
38	A6	50p brown	2.25	2.25
39	A6	1d dull lilac	11.00	9.00
		Nos. 33-39 (7)	17.65	12.60

King Alexander — A7

1894-96 *Perf. 13x13½*

Granite Paper

40	A7	5p green	4.00	.25
a.		Perf. 11½	7.50	.40
41	A7	10p car rose	5.50	.25
b.		Perf. 11½	90.00	1.50
42	A7	15p violet	9.00	.25
43	A7	20p orange	67.50	.75
a.		Half used as 10p on cover		*375.00*
44	A7	25p blue	19.00	.35
45	A7	50p brown	22.50	.75
46	A7	1d dk green	1.50	3.00
47	A7	1d red brn, *bl* ('96)	19.00	3.75
		Nos. 40-47 (8)	148.00	9.35

1898-1900 *Perf. 13x13½, 11½*

Ordinary Paper

48	A7	1p dull red	.30	.25
49	A7	5p green	3.75	.25
50	A7	10p rose	60.00	.25
51	A7	15p violet	7.50	.25
52	A7	20p orange	6.25	.25
53	A7	25p deep blue	7.00	.35
54	A7	50p brown	15.00	3.00
		Nos. 48-54 (7)	99.80	4.60

Nos. 49-54 exist imperf.

Nos. 49-51, 53 and 56-57 exist with perf. 13x13½x11½x13½.

Type of 1900 Stamp Surcharged

1900

56	A7	10p on 20p rose	5.50	.75

Same, Surcharged

1901

57	A7	10p on 20p rose	1.75	.25
58	A7	15p on 1d red brn, *bl*	5.25	1.00
a.		Inverted surcharge	*100.00*	*110.00*

King Alexander (Obrenovich V)

A8 A9

1901-03 Typo. *Perf. 11½*

59	A8	5p green	.35	.35
60	A8	10p rose	.35	.35
61	A8	15p red violet	.35	.35
62	A8	20p orange	.35	.35
63	A8	25p ultra	.35	.35
64	A8	50p bister	.75	.75
65	A9	1d brown	1.10	1.90
66	A9	3d brt rose	11.00	15.00
67	A9	5d deep violet	11.00	15.00
		Nos. 59-67 (9)	25.60	34.40

Counterfeits of Nos. 66-67 exist. Nos. 59-67 imperf. value of set of pairs, $100.

Arms of Serbia on Head of King Alexander — A10

Type I

Type II

Two Types of the Overprint

Type I — Overprint 12mm wide. Bottom of mantle defined by a single line. Wide crown above shield.

Type II — Overprint 10mm wide. Double line at bottom of mantle. Smaller crown above shield.

Arms Overprinted in Blue, Black, Red and Red Brown

1903-04 Type I *Perf. 13½*

68	A10	1p red lil & blk (Bl)	.90	1.10
a.		Inverted overprint	10.00	
69	A10	5p yel grn & blk (Bl)	.75	.35
70	A10	10p car & blk (Bk)	.50	.35
a.		Double overprint	8.75	
71	A10	15p ol gray & blk (Bk)	.50	.35
a.		Double overprint	8.75	
72	A10	20p org & blk (Bk)	.75	.35
73	A10	25p bl & blk (Bk)	.75	.35
a.		Double overprint	10.00	
74	A10	50p gray & blk (R)	4.50	1.10

There were two printings of the type I overprint on Nos. 68-74, one typographed and one lithographed.

Type II

75	A10	1d bl grn & blk (Bk)	11.00	4.50

#68-75 with overprint omitted, value, set $75.

Perf. 11½
Type I

75A	A10	5p (Bl)	.75	1.50
75B	A10	50p (R)	2.25	7.50
75C	A10	1d (Bk)	2.25	15.00

Type II

76	A10	3d vio & blk (R Br)	3.00	3.75
a.		Perf. 13½	110.00	110.00
77	A10	5d lt brn & blk (Bl)	3.00	3.75

Type I With Additional Surcharge

78	A10	1p on 5d (R)	2.25	11.00
a.		Perf. 13½	750.00	750.00
		Nos. 68-78 (14)	33.15	50.95

Karageorge and Peter I — A11

Insurgents, 1804 A12

1904   Typo.

79	A11	5p yellow green	1.50	.75
80	A11	10p rose red	.75	.75
81	A11	15p red violet	.75	.75
82	A11	25p blue	1.50	1.50
83	A11	50p gray brown	1.50	1.50
84	A12	1d bister	2.25	5.25
85	A12	3d blue green	3.00	7.50
86	A12	5d violet	3.75	9.00
		Nos. 79-86 (8)	15.00	27.00

Centenary of the Karageorgevich dynasty and the coronation of King Peter. Counterfeits of Nos. 79-86 exist.

King Peter I Karageorgevich — A13

Perf. 11½, 12x11½
1905   Wove Paper

87	A13	1p gray & blk	.25	.25
88	A13	5p yel grn & blk	.90	.25
89	A13	10p red & blk	2.50	.25
90	A13	15p red lil & blk	3.00	.25
91	A13	20p yellow & blk	5.25	.25
92	A13	25p ultra & blk	6.25	.25
93	A13	30p sl grn & blk	4.50	.25
94	A13	50p dk brown & blk	5.50	.50
95	A13	1d bister & blk	.90	.35
96	A13	3d blue grn & blk	.90	.90
97	A13	5d violet & blk	3.75	2.75
		Nos. 87-97 (11)	33.70	6.25

Counterfeits of Nos. 87-97 abound. The stamps of this issue may be found on both thick and thin paper.

1908   Laid Paper

98	A13	1p gray & blk	.35	.25
99	A13	5p yel grn & blk	2.25	.25
100	A13	10p red & blk	6.75	.25
101	A13	15p red lilac & blk	9.00	.25
102	A13	20p yellow & blk	9.00	.35
103	A13	25p ultra & blk	6.75	.35
104	A13	30p gray grn & blk	10.00	.35
105	A13	50p dk brn & blk	13.00	.75
		Nos. 98-105 (8)	57.10	2.80

Nos. 90, 98-100, 102-104 are known imperforate but are not believed to have been issued in this condition.
Values of Nos. 98-105 are for horizontally laid paper. Four values also exist on vertically laid paper (1p, 5p, 10p, 30p).

King Peter I Karageorgevich A14

1911-14   Thick Wove Paper

108	A14	1p slate green	.25	.25
109	A14	2p dark violet	.25	.25
110	A14	5p green	.25	.25
111	A14	5p pale yel grn ('14)	.25	.25
112	A14	10p carmine	.25	.25
113	A14	10p red ('14)	.25	.25
114	A14	15p red violet	.35	.25
115	A14	15p slate blk ('14)	.25	.25
a.		15p red (error)	900.00	—
116	A14	20p yellow	.30	.25
117	A14	20p brown ('14)	.50	.30
118	A14	25p deep blue	.45	.25
119	A14	25p indigo ('14)	.25	.25
120	A14	30p blue green	.30	.30
121	A14	30p olive grn ('14)	.25	.30
122	A14	50p dk brown	.50	.35
123	A14	50p brn red ('14)	.45	.35
124	A14	1d orange	22.50	45.00
125	A14	1d slate ('14)	2.50	7.50
126	A14	3d lake	30.00	90.00
127	A14	3d olive yel ('14)	140.00	1,100.
128	A14	5d violet	27.50	62.50
129	A14	5d dk violet ('14)	5.00	19.00
		Nos. 108-129 (22)	232.60	1,328.

Counterfeits exist.

King Peter and Military Staff — A15

1915   Perf. 11½

132	A15	5p yellow green	.35	—
133	A15	10p scarlet	.35	—
134	A15	15p slate	5.50	
135	A15	20p brown	1.50	
136	A15	25p blue	11.00	
137	A15	30p olive green	7.50	
138	A15	50p orange brown	30.00	
		Nos. 132-138 (7)	56.20	

Nos. 134-138 were prepared but not issued for postal use. Instead they were permitted to be used as wartime emergency currency. Some are known imperf. The 15p also exists in blue from an erroneous cliche in the 25p plate; value $325.

Stamps of France, 1900-1907, with this handstamped control were used in 1916-1918 by the Serbian Postal Bureau on the Island of Corfu. On the 1c to 35c, the handstamp covers 2 or 3 stamps. It was applied after the stamps were on the cover.

King Peter and Prince Alexander — A16

1918-20   Typo.   Perf. 11, 11½

155	A16	1p black	.25	.25
156	A16	2p olive brown	.25	.25
157	A16	5p apple green	.25	.25
158	A16	10p red	.25	.25
159	A16	15p black brown	.25	.25
160	A16	20p red brown	.25	.25
161	A16	20p violet ('20)	1.50	.90
162	A16	25p deep blue	.25	.25
163	A16	30p olive green	.25	.25
164	A16	50p violet	.25	.25
165	A16	1d violet brown	.90	.25

King Peter I Karageorgevich A14

166	A16	3d slate green	1.10	.90
167	A16	5d red brown	1.60	1.10
		Nos. 155-167 (13)	7.35	5.40

Nos. 157-160, 164 exist imperf. Value each $9.

1920   Pelure Paper   Perf. 11½

169	A16	1p black	.25	.25
170	A16	2p olive brown	.25	.25

Catalogue values for unused stamps in this section, from this point to the end of the section, are for Never Hinged items.

SERBIA & MONTENEGRO
100 Paras = 1 Dinar

Yugoslavia became Serbia & Montenegro Feb. 4, 2003, with each section of the country maintaining and operating their own postal service, and each having their own currency. After a referendum on independence on May 21, 2006, Montenegro seceded from Serbia and Montenegro, declaring independence on June 3. On June 7, Serbia recognized the dissolution of the union.

The listings below contain stamps bearing the dinar currency, for use in Serbia, or those bearing both the dinar and euro currencies, which were issued for use in either Serbia or Montenegro. Stamps inscribed in euro currency only were used in Montenegro and may be found in listings for that country.

Council of Europe — A20

Map color: 16d, Red violet. 28.70d, Blue.

2003, Apr. 3   Litho.   Perf. 13¾
180-181	A20	Set of 2	2.75	2.75

Easter — A21

Religious paintings: 12d, From 16th cent. 16d, By D. Bacevic. 26.20d, From 1616. 28.70d, By Giovanni Bellini.

2003, Apr. 18
182-185	A21	Set of 4	4.75	4.75

Belgrade Choral Society, 150th Anniv. A22

2003, Apr. 22   Perf. 13¼ Syncopated
186	A22	16d multi	2.00	2.00

Europa — A23

Man pasting poster on: 28.70d, Pillar. 50d, Wall.

2003, May 9   Perf. 13¾
187-188	A23	Set of 2	4.50	4.50

Flowers — A24

2003, May 13
189		Horiz. strip of 4 + central label	4.75	4.75
a.	A24	16d Galanthus nivalis	.75	.75
b.	A24	24d Erythronium dens-canis	1.00	1.00
c.	A24	26.20d Hepatica nobilis	1.10	1.10
d.	A24	28.70d Anemone ramunculoides	1.25	1.25

Actors and Actresses — A25

No. 190: a, Ilija Stanojevic (1859-1930). b, Dobrivoje Dobrica Milutinovic (1880-1956). c, Zivana Zanka Stokic (1887-1947). d, Ljubinka Bobic (1897-1978). e, Radomir-Rasa Plaovic (1899-1977). f, Milivoje Zivanovic (1900-76). g, Miloslav Mija Aleksic (1923-95). h, Zoran Radmilovic (1933-85).

2003, May 20
190	A25	16d Sheet of 8, #a-h, + 8 labels	6.00	6.00

First Automobile in Belgrade, Cent. — A26

2003, June 3   Perf. 13¼ Syncopated
191	A26	16d multi	7.00	7.00

Nature Protection A27

Views of Zasavicz Nature Reserve: 28.70d, River. 50d, Swamp, vert.

2003, June 12
192-193	A27	Set of 2	4.50	4.50

Yugoslavia No. F1 and Type of Yugoslavia No. 2258 Surcharged

2003, July 3   Litho.   Perf. 12½
194	RL1	1d on (R) ultra	2.10	2.10
195	A751	12d on 20p lil rose & pale vio	3.75	3.75

No. 189b Under Magnifying Glass — A28

Postal Van and Parcels — A29

Woman With Headset A30

Postal Van A31

Cable Television System — A32

2003		Litho.	Perf. 12½	
196	A28	1d multi	.60	.60
197	A29	8d multi	.80	.80
198	A30	12d multi	1.20	1.20
199	A31	16d multi	1.60	1.60
200	A32	32d multi	3.75	3.75
	Nos. 196-200 (5)		7.95	7.95

Issued: 16d, 8/4; others 8/7.

Military Museum, Belgrade, 125th Anniv. — A33

2003, Aug. 27   *Perf. 13x13¾*
201 A33 16d (25c) multi   .90 .90

Serbian Women's Circle, Cent. — A34

Perf. 13¼ Syncopated
2003, Aug. 28
202 A34 16d (25c) multi   .90 .90

Serbian and Montenegrin States, 125th Anniv. — A35

Designs: No. 203, 16d (25c), Serbian arms, denomination at UR. No. 204, 16d (25c), Montenegrin arms, denomination at UL.

2003, Sept. 10
203-204 A35   Set of 2   1.50 1.50

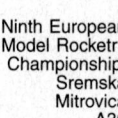

Ninth European Model Rocketry Championship, Sremska Mitrovica A36

2003, Sept. 12   *Perf. 13x13¾*
205 A36 16d (25c) multi   .90 .90

Second Danube Countries Conference on Art and Culture — A37

Carved rocks with: No. 206, 16d (25c), Denomination at UL. No. 207, 16d (25c), Denomination at UR.

2003, Sept. 17
206-207 A37   Set of 2   1.50 1.50

Nos. 206-207 were each printed in sheets of 8 + label.

Souvenir Sheet

Serbiafila XIII Philatelic Exhibition — A38

No. 208: a, Belgrade in the 17th century. b, Sculpture.

2003, Sept. 22   *Perf. 13½*
208 A38 32d (50c) Sheet of 2, #a-b   4.25 4.25

Joy of Europe — A39

Children's drawings: 28.70d (50c), Man, woman, bird and flower. 50d (80c), Rabbit, flowers, horiz.

2003, Oct. 14   *Perf. 13¼*
209-210 A39   Set of 2   4.25 4.25

Vecernje Novosti Newspaper, 50th Anniv. — A40

2003, Oct. 16
211 A40 32d (50c) multi   1.75 1.75

Stamp Day — A41

2003, Oct. 24
212 A41 16d (25c) multi   3.75 3.75

Association of Applied Artists and Designers, 50th Anniv. — A42

2003, Oct. 29
213 A42 16d (25c) multi   .90 .90

National Theater of Montenegro, 50th Anniv. — A43

2003, Nov. 1   *Perf. 13¾x13*
214 A43 32d (50c) multi   1.75 1.75

City of Pancevo, 850th Anniv. — A44

2003, Nov. 12   *Perf. 13x13¾*
215 A44 32d (50c) multi   2.00 2.00

Christmas — A45

Designs: 10d, Santa Claus and reindeer. 13.50d, Ornaments. 26.20d, Snowflakes.

2003, Nov. 24   *Perf. 13¼*
216-218 A45   Set of 3   3.00 3.00
    Complete booklet, 10 #216   7.00
    Complete booklet, 10 #217   8.00

Serbian Orthodox Church Museum Exhibits — A46

No. 219: a, Painting of St. John the Baptist, 1645. b, Cross, 1602. c, Miter, 15th cent. d, Tabernacle, 1550-51.

2003, Nov. 26   *Perf. 13¾x13*
219	Horiz. strip of 4 + central label	5.25	5.25
a.	A46 16d (25c) multi	.90	.90
b.	A46 24d (35c) multi	1.20	1.20
c.	A46 26.20d (40c) multi	1.40	1.40
d.	A46 28.70d (50c) multi	1.50	1.50

Christmas A47

Religious paintings: 12d (20c), Nativity, 1983. 16d (25c), Nativity, 18th cent. 26.20d (40c), Madonna and Child, 2000. 28.70d

(50c), Adoration of the Magi, by Albrecht Durer.

2003, Dec. 2   *Perf. 13x13¼*
220-223 A47   Set of 4   4.25 4.25

Submarine Units, 75th Anniv. — A48

2003, Dec. 10   *Perf. 13¼*
224 A48 32d (50c) multi   3.00 3.00

Printed in sheets of 8 + label.

Powered Flight, Cent. — A49

Designs: 16d (25c), Wright Brothers and airplane. 28.70d (50c), Airplane in flight, horse-drawn carriages.

2003, Dec. 17
225-226 A49   Set of 2   10.00 10.00

Politika Newspaper, Cent. — A50

Centenary emblem and: No. 227, 16d (25c), Typewriter. No. 228, 16d, (25c), Office building, vert.

2004, Jan. 21
227-228 A50   Set of 2   2.00 2.00

Worldwide Fund for Nature (WWF) A51

No. 229 — Insects: a, Parnassius apollo. b, Rosalia alpina. c, Aeshna viridis. d, Saga pedo.

2004, Jan. 30   *Perf. 13¼*
229	Horiz. strip of 4 + central label	5.00	5.00
a.	A51 12d (20c) multi	.60	.60
b.	A51 16d (25c) multi	.75	.75
c.	A51 26.20d (40c) multi	1.25	1.25
d.	A51 28.70d (50c) multi	1.50	1.50

First Serbian Rebellion, Bicent. — A52

Bicentennial emblem and: No. 230, 16d (25c), Flag, Karageorge (George Petrovic). No. 231, 16d (25c), Children and map of Europe.

2004, Feb. 13   *Perf. 13x13¾*
230-231 A52   Set of 2   1.50 1.50

Flora and Butterflies — A53

No. 232: a, Ramonda serbica. b, Ramonda nathaliae. c, Heodes virgaureae. d, Lysandra bellargus.

2004, Feb. 16   **Perf. 13¾x13**
232   Horiz. strip of 4 + central
    label   5.25 5.25
   a.   A53 16d (25c) multi   .80 .80
   b.   A53 24d (35c) multi   1.10 1.10
   c.   A53 26.20d (40c) multi   1.25 1.25
   d.   A53 28.70d (50c) multi   1.60 1.60

2004 Summer Olympics, Athens — A54

Serbia and Montenegro Olympic Committee emblem and: 32d (50c), Runner. 56d (80c), Wrestlers.

2004, Feb. 27   **Perf. 13x13¾**
233-234 A54   Set of 2   4.25 4.25

First Serbian Rebellion, Bicent. A55

Designs: 12d, Rebels. 16d, Flag, gun, vert. 28.70d, Karageorge (George Petrovic), vert. 32d, Children, globe, vert.

2004, Mar. 1   **Litho.**   **Perf. 13¼**
235-238 A55   Set of 4   4.75 4.75

Campaign Against Terrorism — A56

2004, Mar. 12   **Perf. 13¾x13**
239 A56 16d (25c) multi   1.25 1.25

Easter — A57

Designs: 16d (25c), The Crucifixion, by Vlasios Coconis. 28.70d (50c), The Resurrection, by Klemens Katounakis.

2004, Mar. 15   **Perf. 13x13¾**
240-241 A57   Set of 2   2.50 2.50

Milutin Milankovic (1879-1958), Climatologist A58

2004, Mar. 22
242 A58 16d (25c) multi   1.10 1.10

Albert Einstein (1879-1955), Physicist — A59

2004, Mar. 31   **Perf. 13¾x13**
243 A59 16d (25c) multi   7.75 7.75
   Printed in sheets of 8 + label.

Selection of Kotor as World Heritage Site, 25th Anniv. — A60

2004, Apr. 7   **Perf. 13x13¾**
244 A60 16d (25c) multi   .95 .95

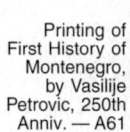 

Printing of First History of Montenegro, by Vasilije Petrovic, 250th Anniv. — A61

2004, Apr. 29
245 A61 16d (25c) multi   1.50 1.50

Europa — A62

Designs: 16d (25c), Paragliders. No. 247, 56d (80c), Sailboat, swimmer, horiz. No. 248: a, 32d (50c), Sailboats, paraglider, horiz. b, 56d (80c), Rowboats, horiz.

2004, May 5   **Perf. 13¾x13, 13x13¾**
246-247 A62   Set of 2   4.00 4.00
    Souvenir Sheet
248 A62   Sheet of 2, #a-b   8.00 8.00

Church of St. Sava, Belgrade — A63

Designs: 16d (25c), Church, St. Sava. 28.70d (50c), Church, statue of St. Sava, horiz.

2004, May 10   **Perf. 13¾x13, 13x13¼**
249-250 A63   Set of 2   2.50 2.50

Michael Pupin (1854-1935), Inventor — A64

2004, May 13   **Engr.**   **Perf. 13¼**
251 A64 16d (25c) violet   .95 .95

FIFA (Fédération Internationale de Football Association), Cent. — A65

2004, May 21   **Litho.**   **Perf. 13x13¾**
252 A65 28.70d (50c) multi   1.75 1.75

Nature Protection A66

Designs: 32d (50c), Ravnjak River. 56d (80c), Sara National Park.

2004, June 10
253-254 A66   Set of 2   5.00 5.00
   Each stamp printed in sheet of 8 + label.

    Souvenir Sheet

JUFIZ XII Philatelic Exhibition, Belgrade — A67

No. 255: a, Lion from Terazije Fountain. b, Entire fountain.

2004, June 21   **Perf. 13¼**
255 A67 32d (50c) Sheet of 2, #a-b   4.50 4.50

2004 Summer Olympics, Athens — A68

Athens Olympics emblem, ancient Greek ruins and: 16d (25c), Runners. 28.70d (50c), Runners, diff. 32d (50c), Long jumper. 57.40d (80c), Hurdlers.

2004, June 24   **Perf. 13x13¾**
256-259 A68   Set of 4   7.75 7.75
   Each stamp printed in sheets of 8 + label.

Yugoslavia Nos. 2255-2256 Surcharged

Methods as Before
2004, June 25   **Perf. 12½**
260 A751 12d on 1p #2255a   2.50 2.50
   a.   on #2255, perf. 13¼   150.00 150.00
261 A751 32d on 5p #2256a   5.00 5.00
   a.   on #2256, perf. 13¼   450.00 450.00
   See Yugoslavia No. 2577 for stamp similar to No. 260, but with violet surcharge.

Volujica Telegraph Station, Cent. — A69

2004, Aug. 3   **Litho.**   **Perf. 13x13¾**
262 A69 16d (25c) multi   1.75 1.75

Joy of Europe — A70

Children's drawings: 32d (50c) Bridge and city skyline. 56d (80c), City buildings, vert.

2004, Oct. 2   **Perf. 13¾**
263-264 A70   Set of 2   4.75 4.75
   Each stamp printed in sheets of 8 + label.

Port of Bar, 125th Anniv. — A71

2004, Oct. 12
265 A71 32d (50c) multi   1.75 1.75

Stamp Day — A72

2004, Oct. 22   **Perf. 13¾x13**
266 A72 16d (25c) multi   2.40 2.40

National Bank of Serbia, 120th Anniv. — A73

Designs: 16d (25c), Bank building. 32d (50c), Bank building, George Vajfert.

    Perf. 13¼ Syncopated
2004, Oct. 28   **Engr.**
267-268 A73   Set of 2   2.50 2.50
   Each stamp printed in sheet of 8 + label.

Silver Objects From 1899 — A74

2004, Nov. 2   Litho.   *Perf. 13¾x13*

269   Horiz. strip of 4 + central
     label   5.00   5.00
a.   A74 16d (25c) Plate on pedestal   .75   .75
b.   A74 24d (35c) Box   1.10   1.10
c.   A74 26.20d (40c) Bowl   1.25   1.25
d.   A74 28.70d (50c) Bowl with lid   1.50   1.50

Buildings
A75

2004, Nov. 15   *Perf. 13x13¾*

270   Horiz. strip of 4 + central
     label   5.00   5.00
a.   A75 16d (25c) Lombardic Palace   .75   .75
b.   A75 24d (35c) Pima Palace   1.10   1.10
c.   A75 26.20d (40c) Grgurina Palace   1.25   1.25
d.   A75 28.70d (50c) Bizanti Palace   1.50   1.50

Christmas
A76

Designs: 16d (25c), Nativity, by Vasilis
Leurac. 28.70d (50c), Nativity, by Ememija
Profeta.

2004, Dec. 1

271-272 A76   Set of 2   2.50   2.50

Endangered
Birds — A77

2005, Jan. 31   Litho.   *Perf. 13¼*

273   Horiz. strip of 4 + central
     label   6.00   6.00
a.   A77 16.50d (25c) Egretta alba   .70   .70
b.   A77 33d (40c) Podiceps nigricollis   1.25   1.25
c.   A77 41.50d (50c) Aythya nyroca   1.75   1.75
d.   A77 49.50d (60c) Ciconia nigra   2.00   2.00

Yugoslavia No. F1,
Serbia Nos. 199,
200 Surcharged in
Blue or Black

2005, Feb. 3   Litho.   *Perf. 12½*

274 RL1   50p on R #F1
            (Bl)   60.00   15.00
275 A31   16.50d on 16d #199   30.00   7.50
276 A32   33d on 32d #200   45.00   7.50
     Nos. 274-276 (3)   135.00   30.00
         Surcharge styles differ.

Stamp
Collecting — A78

2005, Feb. 3   Litho.   *Perf. 12½*

277 A78   50p multi   1.40   1.40

Flora and
Fauna — A79

2005, Feb. 16   *Perf. 13x13¾*

278   Horiz. strip of 4 + central
     label   6.00   6.00
a.   A79 16.50d (25c) Capparis spinosa   .70   .70
b.   A79 33d (40c) Mustela erminea   1.25   1.25
c.   A79 41.50d (50c) Trollius
     europaeus   1.75   1.75
d.   A79 49.50d (60c) Rupicapra rupi-
     capra   2.00   2.00

Montenegrin
Table Tennis
Assoc., 50th
Anniv. — A80

2005, Feb. 28

279 A80   16.50d (25c) multi   15.00   15.00

Easter — A81

Designs: 16.50d (25c), Fresco, 18th cent.
28.70d (50c), Crucifixion, 1602.

2005, Mar. 1

280-281 A81   Set of 2   2.75   2.75

Mountain
Scenes — A82

2005, Mar. 7   Litho.   *Perf. 12½*

282 A82   16.50d Zlatibor   1.10   1.10
283 A82   33d Kopaonik   3.25   3.25

Serbian Law
University,
Cent. — A83

2005, Mar. 12   *Perf. 13x13¾*

284 A83   16.50d (25c) multi   .95   .95

Miniature Sheet

Theater Celebrities — A84

No. 285: a, Jovan Djordjevic (1826-1900). b,
Milan Predic (1881-1972). c, Milan Grol (1876-
1952). d, Mira Trailovic (1924-89). e, Soja
Jovanovich (1922-2002). f, Hugo Klajn (1894-
1981). g, Mata Milosevic (1901-97). h, Bojan
Stupica (1910-70).

2005, Mar. 25   *Perf. 13¾x13*

285 A84   16.50d (25c) Sheet of 8,
     #a-h, + central
     label   7.00   7.00

European
Philatelic
Cooperation,
50th Anniv.
(in
2006) — A85

Elements of Europa common design types
(CD) or Yugoslavian stamps: No. 286, CD12.
No. 287, CD13. No. 288, CD14. No. 289,
CD15. No. 290, CD16. No. 291, Yugoslavia
#1206. No. 292, Yugoslavia #1678. No. 293,
CD13, CD15 and Yugoslavia #1678.

2005, Mar. 31   *Perf. 13x13¾*
Background Color

286 A85   16.50d (25c) green   .70   .70
287 A85   16.50d (25c) claret   .70   .70
288 A85   16.50d (25c) claret   .70   .70
289 A85   16.50d (25c) blue   .70   .70
a.   Souvenir sheet, #286-289   7.50   7.50
290 A85   41.50d (50c) claret   1.75   1.75
291 A85   41.50d (50c) olive
     gray   1.75   1.75
292 A85   41.50d (50c) blue   1.75   1.75
293 A85   41.50d (50c) orange   1.75   1.75
a.   Souvenir sheet, #290-293   11.00   11.00
     Nos. 286-293 (8)   9.80   9.80
     Europa stamps, 50th anniv. (in 2006).

Hans Christian
Andersen (1805-
75),
Author — A86

Silhouette of Andersen and: 41.50d (50c),
The Little Mermaid. 58d (70c), The Snow
Queen.

2005, Apr. 1   *Perf. 13¾x13*

294-295 A86   Set of 2   4.00   4.00

Mountain Scenes Type of 2005

Design: 5d, Goc, 13d, Jastrebac.

2005, Apr. 1   Litho.   *Perf. 12¾x12¼*

295A A82   5d multi   1.10   .25
295B A82   13d multi   2.25   .45

Europa — A87

Designs: No. 296, 41.50d (50c), Dumplings
and rolls. No. 297, 73d (90c), Fish dish,
tomato, lettuce, garlic, oil cruet, pepper mill.
No. 298: a, 41.50d (50c), Cake, flower, cup
of coffee. b, 73d (90c), Slice of pie, apples.

2005, May 5   *Perf. 13x13¾*

296-297 A87   Set of 2   4.75   4.75

Souvenir Sheet

298 A87   Sheet of 2, #a-b   4.75   4.75

Captains
and Their
Ships
A88

2005, May 13   *Perf. 13¼*

299   Horiz. strip of 4 + central
     label   6.00   6.00
a.   A88 16.50d (25c) Marko Ivanovic   .70   .70
b.   A88 33d (40c) Petar Zelalic   1.40   1.40
c.   A88 41.50d (50c) Matija Balovic   1.75   1.75
d.   A88 49.50d (60c) Ivan Bronza   2.00   2.00

Emblem of
Red Star
Sports
Club — A89

Emblem of
Partisan
Sports
Club — A90

No. 302 — Knight with shield with emblem
of: a, Red Star. b, Partisan.

2005, May 23   *Perf. 13x13¾*

300 A89   16.50d (25c) multi   .90   .90
301 A90   16.50d (25c) multi   .90   .90

Souvenir Sheet

302   Sheet of 2   2.00   2.00
a.   A89 16.50d (25c) multi   .90   .90
b.   A90 16.50d (25c) multi   .90   .90

Souvenir Sheet

Danube Regatta, 50th Anniv. — A91

No. 303: a, 41.50d (50c), Rowers in boats.
b, 49.50d (60c), Rowers in boats, map.

2005, June 6

303 A91   Sheet of 2, #a-b   4.00   4.00

Intl. Year of
Physics
A92

Theory of
Relativity,
Cent. — A93

2005, June 10

304 A92   41.50d (50c) multi   1.75   1.75
305 A93   58d (70c) multi   2.50   2.50

European
Nature
Protection
A94

Various views of Koviljsko-Petrovaradinski
Rit Special Nature Reserve: 41.50d (50c), 58d
(70c).

2005, June 20

306-307 A94   Set of 2   4.25   4.25

European Volleyball Championships, Belgrade and Rome — A95

2005, Sept. 2   Litho.   Perf. 13x13¾
310 A95 16.50d (25c) multi   3.00 3.00
Printed in sheets of 8 + label.

European Basketball Championships, Serbia & Montenegro — A96

2005, Sept. 16
311 A96 16.50d (25c) multi   3.00 3.00
Printed in sheets of 8 + label.

A97

Joy of Europe — A98

Perf. 13¾x13, 13x13¾
2005, Sept. 21
312 A97 41.50d (50c) multi   1.60 1.60
313 A98 58d (70c) multi   2.40 2.40
Each stamp printed in sheets of 8 + label.

World Youth Day — A99

2005, Sept. 30   Perf. 13x13¾
314 A99 41.50d (50c) multi   1.75 1.75
Printed in sheets of 8 + label.

Start of European Union Accession Negotiations — A100

2005, Oct. 10   Perf. 13¾x13
315 A100 16.50d (25c) multi   .90 .90

World Air Sports Federation, Cent. — A101

Emblem and: 49.50d (60c), Alberto Santos-Dumont's 14-bis airplane. 58d (70c), Parachute, glider, ultra-light aircraft.

2005, Oct. 14   Perf. 13x13¾
316-317 A101   Set of 2   4.50 4.50
Each stamp printed in sheets of 8 + label.

Stamp Day — A102

2005, Oct. 24
318 A102 16.50d (25c) multi   .90 .90

United Nations, 60th Anniv. A103

2005, Oct. 24
319 A103 16.50d (25c) multi   .90 .90

St. Petar of Cetinje (1782-1830), Montenegrin Leader A104

2005, Oct. 28
320 A104 16.50d (25c) multi   .90 .90

First Montenegrin Constitution, Cent. — A105

2005, Nov. 14
321 A105 16.50d (25c) multi   .90 .90

Stevan Sremac (1855-1906), Humorist — A106

2005, Nov. 23   Perf. 13¼
322 A106 16.50d (25c) multi   .90 .90

Paintings of Monasteries A107

No. 323: a, Studenica Monastery, by Djordje Krstic. b, Sopocani Monastery, by Paja Jovanovic. c, Zica Monastery, by Krstic. d, Gracanica Monastery, by Milan Milanovic.

2005, Nov. 28
323   Horiz. strip of 4 + central
         label   6.00 6.00
a. A107 16.50d (25c) multi   .70 .70
b. A107 33d (40c) multi   1.40 1.40
c. A107 41.50d (50c) multi 1.75 1.75
d. A107 49.50d (60c) multi 2.00 2.00

Paintings in Museums A108

No. 324: a, Girl with a Blue Ribbon, by F. X. Winterhalter. b, Adoration of the Child, by Andrea Alovidi. c, Madonna and Child with Saints, by Biagio d'Antonio. d, Remorse, by Vlaho Bukovac.

2005, Dec. 9
324   Horiz. strip of 4 + central
         label   6.00 6.00
a. A108 16.50d (25c) multi   .70 .70
b. A108 33d (40c) multi   1.40 1.40
c. A108 41.50d (50c) multi 1.75 1.75
d. A108 49.50d (60c) multi 2.00 2.00

Christmas A109

Designs: 16.50d (25c), Nativity. 46d (50c), Nativity, diff.

2005, Dec. 12   Perf. 13x13¾
325-326 A109   Set of 2   2.75 2.75

Stevan Stojanovic Mokranjac (1856-1914), Composer A110

2006, Jan. 9   Perf. 13¾x13
327 A110 46d (50c) multi   2.00 2.00

Jovan Sterija Popovic (1806-56), Writer — A111

2006, Jan. 13
328 A111 33d (40c) multi   1.50 1.50

2006 Winter Olympics, Turin — A112

Designs: 53d (60c), Ski jumping. 73d (80c), Downhill skiing.

2006, Feb. 10   Perf. 13x13¾
329-330 A112   Set of 2   5.00 5.00
Each stamp printed in sheets of 8 + label.

National Theater, Belgrade — A113

2006, Feb. 1   Litho.   Perf. 13¼
331 A113 46d multi   2.00 2.00

Easter — A114

Designs: 16.50d (20c), Easter egg with Cyrillic inscription. 46d (50c), Basket of Easter eggs.

2006, Mar. 1   Perf. 13¾x13¼
332-333 A114   Set of 2   2.50 2.50

Danube Commission, 150th Anniv. A115

No. 334: a, Novi Sad (shown). b, Smederevo. c, Belgrade. d, Tabula Traiana.

2006, Mar. 6   Perf. 13¼x13¾
334   Horiz. strip of 4 + cen-
         tral label   5.25 5.25
a.-b. A115 16.50d (20c) Either single .70 .70
c.-d. A115 46d (50c) Either single   1.90 1.90

Fauna A116

No. 335: a, Canis lupus. b, Otis tarda. c, Vormela peregusna. d, Ursus arctos.

2006, Apr. 3
335   Horiz. strip of 4 + cen-
         tral label   5.25 5.25
a.-b. A116 16.50d (20c) Either single .70 .70
c.-d. A116 46d (50c) Either single   1.90 1.90

2006 World Cup Soccer Championships, Germany — A117

2006 World Cup emblem and: 33d (40c), Soccer players. 46d (50c), Soccer player and stadium.
No. 338, horiz.: a, Stadium, text in Cyrillic letters. b, Stadium, text in Latin letters.

2006, Apr. 12   Perf. 13¾x13¼
336-337 A117   Set of 2   20.00 20.00
Souvenir Sheet
Perf. 13¼x13¾
338 A117 46d (50c) Sheet of
         2, #a-b   25.00 25.00

Europa
A118

Children's drawings: No. 339, 46d (50c), Beach umbrella, person in winter jacket on beach towel, penguin. No. 340, 73d (80c), Lion and lamb.
No. 341: a, 46d (50c), Girls talking. b, 73d (80c), Children at open door, rainbow.

2006, May 4   *Perf. 13¼x13¾*
339-340 A118   Set of 2   5.00 5.00
     Souvenir Sheet
341 A118   Sheet of 2, #a-b   6.00 6.00

Nikola Tesla (1856-1943), Electrical Engineer — A119

Designs: 16.50d (20c), Tesla, lightning. No. 343, 46d (50c), Tesla, electrical generator. No. 344, horiz.: a, 46d (50c), Tesla. b, 112d (€1.30), Turbine.

2006, May 26   *Perf. 13¾x13¼*
342-343 A119   Set of 2   2.75 2.75
     Souvenir Sheet
     Perf. 13¾
344 A119   Sheet of 2, #a-b   7.50 7.50

Rose Varieties
A120

No. 345: a, Aqua. b, Vendela. c, Sphinx. d, Red Berlin.

     Perf. 13¼x13¾
2006, June 20   **Litho.**
345   Horiz. strip of 4 + central label   5.25 5.25
   a.-b.   A120 16.50d Either single   .70 .70
   c.-d.   A120 46d Either single   1.90 1.90

As these stamps were released after the breakup of Serbia and Montenegro, they were sold only in Serbia.

Nature Protection
A121

Designs: 46d, Fususki Park, Novi Sad. 58d, Gradski Park, Vrsac.

2006, June 20
346-347 A121   Set of 2   4.00 4.00

As these stamps were released after the breakup of Serbia and Montenegro, they were sold only in Serbia. Each stamp was printed in a sheet of 8 + label.

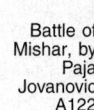 

Battle of Mishar, by Paja Jovanovic
A122

2006, June 30
348 A122 46d multi   2.00 2.00

Battle of Mishar, 200th anniv.

Flag — A123   Coat of Arms — A124

2006, June 30   *Perf. 12½*
349 A123 16.50d multi   1.10 .70
350 A124 20d multi   1.20 .90

European Water Polo Championships, Belgrade — A125

2006, Sept. 1   *Perf. 13¼x13¾*
351 A125 46d multi   1.90 1.90

Serbian Victory at European Water Polo Championships — A126

2006, Sept. 13
352 A126 46d mult   2.25 2.25

Joy of Europe
A127

Children's drawings: 46d, Buildings. 73d, Girl touching bird.

2006, Sept. 29
353-354 A127   Set of 2   5.25 5.25

Zhica Monastery — A128

2006, Oct. 7   *Perf. 12½*
355 A128 8d multi   1.00 1.00
   a.   Perf. 13¼ (2011)   1.25 1.25

Stamp Day — A129

2006, Oct. 24   *Perf. 13¾x13¼*
356 A129 46d Serbia #1   2.25 2.25

First Serbian postage stamps, 140th anniv.

Bridal Jewelry
A130

No. 357: a, Bracelet, 19th cent. b, Ring, 17th-19th cent. c, Earrings, 20th cent. d, Necklace, 19th cent.

2006, Oct. 30   *Perf. 13¼x13¾*
357   Horiz. strip of 4 + central label   6.00 6.00
   a.-b.   A130 16.50d Either single   .80 .80
   c.-d.   A130 46d Either single   2.10 2.10

Atelie 212 Theater, 50th Anniv. — A131

2006, Nov. 10   *Perf. 13¾x13¼*
358 A131 46d multi   1.90 1.90

Wolfgang Amadeus Mozart (1756-91), Composer
A132

Rembrandt (1606-69), Painter — A133

2006, Nov. 16
359 A132 46d multi   2.25 2.25
360 A133 46d multi   2.25 2.25

A134

Christmas
A135

2006, Nov. 20   *Perf. 13¼x13¾*
361 A134 16.50d multi   .80 .80
362 A135 46d multi   2.10 2.10

New Year 2007 — A136

2006, Dec. 1
363 A136 46d multi   2.10 2.10

UNICEF, 60th Anniv.
A137

2006, Dec. 11
364 A137 16.50d multi   .80 .80

Liberation of Belgrade, 200th Anniv.
A138

2006, Dec. 13
365 A138 16.50d multi   .80 .80

Flower — A139

Flowers
A140

Apple Orchard
A141

River — A142

Goc
A143

Zlatibor
A144

Kopaonik
A145

Belgrade — A146

2007, Jan. 1   Litho.   Perf. 13¾x13¼
366 A139 50p multi .35 .35
Perf. 13¼x13¾
367 A140 1d multi .35 .35
368 A141 5d multi .35 .35
369 A142 10d multi .50 .50
Perf. 13¼
370 A143 13d multi .65 .65
371 A144 33d multi 1.60 1.60
372 A145 50d multi 2.60 2.60
373 A146 100d multi 5.25 5.25
   Nos. 366-373 (8) 11.65 11.65

Intl. Polar
Year — A147

2007, Jan. 30   Perf. 13¼x13¾
374 A147 46d multi 2.00 2.00

Miniature Sheet

Actors and Actresses — A148

No. 375: a, Petar Dobrinovic (1853-1923). b, Milka Grgurova Aleksic (1840-1924). c, Ljubisa Jovanovic (1908-71). d, Rahela Ferari (1911-94). e, Miodrag Petrovic Ckalja (1924-2003). f, Branko Plesa (1926-2001). g, Ljuba Tadic (1929-2005). h, Danila Bata Stojkovic (1934-2002).

2007, Feb. 16
375 A148 16.50d Sheet of 8, #a-
         h, + central la-
         bel 6.00 6.00

Easter — A149

Designs: 20d, Crucifixion. 46d, Crucifixion in silhouette.

2007, Mar. 1   Perf. 13¾x13¼
376-377 A149 Set of 2 3.00 3.00

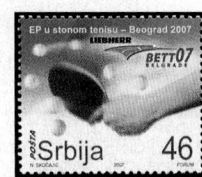

2007 European Table Tennis Championships, Belgrade — A150

2007, Mar. 23   Perf. 13¼x13¾
378 A150 46d multi 2.25 2.25
Souvenir Sheet
Perf. 13¾
379 A150 112d Player, net 5.00 5.00
No. 378 printed in sheets of 8 + label.

Art From St.
Sava Church
— A150a

2007, Apr. 1   Litho.   Perf. 13¼
379A A150a 10d multi .50 .50

Rose — A151

2007, Apr. 4   Perf. 13¼
380 A151 40d multi 2.00 2.00

Worldwide Fund
for Nature
(WWF) — A152

No. 381 — Dryocopus martius: a, Facing right. b, Facing right, feeding chicks. c, Facing left, feeding chicks. d, Facing left.

2007, Apr. 6   Perf. 13¾x13¼
381   Horiz. strip of 4 + cen-
            tral label 5.75 5.75
a.-b. A152 20d Either single .85 .85
c.-d. A152 40d Either single 1.75 1.75

Parks — A153

Designs: 40d, Vrnacka Banja Park. 46d, Pionirski Park, Belgrade.

2007, Apr. 20   Perf. 13¼x13¾
382-383 A153 Set of 2 4.00 4.00

Europa
A154

International and Serbian Scouting emblems and: No. 384, 20d, Scouts, tents and compass. 46d, Scouts in canoe, Scout hat, neckerchief and backpack.
No. 386: a, c, e, Milos Popovic and compass. b, d, f, Lord Robert Baden-Powell, Scout hat, neckerchief and backpack.

2007, May 3   Litho.   Perf. 13¼x13¾
384-385 A154 Set of 2 3.00 3.00
Miniature Sheet
386   Sheet of 6 5.25 5.25
a. A154 20d multi, perf. 13¼x13¾,
         imperf. at top .85 .85
b. A154 20d multi, perf. 13¼x13¾,
         imperf. at top .85 .85
c. A154 20d multi, perf. 13¼x13¾,
         imperf. at top and right .85 .85
d. A154 20d multi, perf. 13¼x13¾,
         imperf. at bottom .85 .85
e. A154 20d multi, perf. 13¼x13¾,
         imperf. at bottom .85 .85
f. A154 20d multi, perf. 13¼x13¾,
         imperf. at bottom and right .85 .85

Scouting, cent. Nos. 384-385 each printed in sheets of 8 + label. No. 386 was sold with but not attached to a booklet cover.

Serbian
Chairmanship
of Council of
Europe
A155

2007, May 10   Perf. 13¼x13¾
387 A155 20d multi 1.10 1.10

First Air
Crossing of
Atlantic by
Amelia
Earhart, 75th
Anniv.
A156

2007, May 21   Litho.
388 A156 50d multi 2.50 2.50
Printed in sheets of 8 + label.

Dositej
Obradovic's
Arrival in Serbia,
Bicent. — A157

2007, May 28   Perf. 13¾x13¼
389 A157 20d multi .80 .80

Jovan Zmaj's
Children's
Games, 50th
Anniv.
A158

2007, June 1   Perf. 13¼x13¾
390 A158 20d multi .80 .80

Souvenir Sheet

Srbijafila XIV, Belgrade — A159

No. 391: a, 20d, Stefan Lazarevic. b, 46d, Castle.

2007, June 11   Perf. 13¾
391 A159 Sheet of 2, #a-b 2.50 2.50

Souvenir Sheet

European Olympic Youth Festival,
Belgrade — A160

No. 392: a, Swimmer. b, Runner.

2007, June 20
392 A160 46d Sheet of 2, #a-d 3.75 3.75

Equestrian
Events
A161

No. 393: a, Endurance jumping. b, Carriage pull. c, Dressage. d, Show jumping.

2007, June 28   Perf. 13¼x13¾
393   Horiz. strip of 4 + cen-
            tral label 5.50 5.50
a.-b. A161 20d Either single .85 .85
c.-d. A161 40d Either single 1.75 1.75

Scientists — A162

Designs: 40d, William Thomson, Lord Kelvin (1824-1907), physicist. No. 395, 46d, Giuseppe Occhialini (1907-93), physicist. No. 396, 46d, Dmitri Mendeleev (1834-1907), chemist.

2007, July 10   Perf. 13¾x13¼
394-396 A162 Set of 3 6.00 6.00

Petar
Lubarda
(1907-74),
Painter
A163

2007, July 27   Perf. 13¼
397 A163 20d multi .90 .90

Kalenic Monastery, 600th Anniv. — A164

2007, Aug. 28   *Perf. 13¾x13¼*
398 A164 20d multi   .90 .90

Haliaeetus Albicilla A165

2007, Sept. 7   **Photo.**   *Perf. 13¾*
399 A165 46d multi   1.90 1.90
See Austria No. 2116.

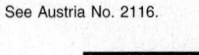

Ozone Layer Protection A166

Perf. 13¾x13¼
2007, Sept. 17   **Litho.**
400 A166 20d multi   .90 .90
Printed in sheets of 8 + label.

Archaeological Sites — A167

Gamzigrad-Romulijana site: 46d, No. 401, Cyrillic inscriptions, denomination at UL. No. 402, Latin inscriptions, denomination at UR.

2007, Sept. 21   *Perf. 13¼x13¾*
401-402 A167   Set of 2   4.75 4.75
Nos. 401-402 each were printed in sheets of 9 + label.

Joy of Europe A168

2007, Sept. 28
403 A168 46d multi   1.90 1.90

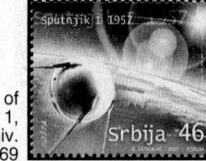

Launch of Sputnik 1, 50th Anniv. A169

2007, Oct. 4
404 A169 46d multi   2.25 2.25

Belgrade Observatory, 120th Anniv. — A170

2007, Oct. 15
405 A170 20d multi   .90 .90
Printed in sheets of 24 + label.

Evzhen Deroko (1860-1944) and Serbia No. 24 — A171

2007, Oct. 24
406 A171 46d multi   2.25 2.25
Stamp Day.

Paintings — A172

Paintings by: 20d, Dura Jaksic (1832-78). No. 408, 46d, Uros Predic (1857-1953). No. 409, 46d, Frida Kahlo (1907-54).

2007, Nov. 1   *Perf. 13¾x13¼*
407-409 A172   Set of 3   4.75 4.75

Christmas A173

Nativity paintings: 20d, 46d.

2007, Nov. 9   *Perf. 13¼x13¾*
410-411 A173   Set of 2   3.25 3.25

Danube River Harbors and Ships — A174

Ships and: 20d, Novi Sad, Serbia. 46d, Orsova, Romania.
No. 414 — Ships: a, 40d, Sirona. b, 50d, Orsova.

2007, Nov. 14   *Perf. 13¼x13¾*
412-413 A174   Set of 2   3.25 3.25
Souvenir Sheet
Perf. 13¾
414 A174   Sheet of 2, #a-d   4.25 4.25
See Romania Nos. 5003-5005.

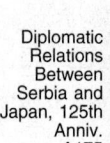 

Diplomatic Relations Between Serbia and Japan, 125th Anniv. A175

Perf. 13¼x13¾
2007, Dec. 23   **Litho.**
415 A175 46d multi   2.25 2.25
Printed in sheets of 8 + label.

Vinca Archaeological Excavations, Cent. — A176

2008, Jan. 28
416 A176 20d multi   1.00 1.00

Paintings of Predrag-Peda Milosavljevic (1908-87) A177

Designs: 20d, Cluny Museum, Paris. 46d, Notre Dame Cathedral, Paris.

2008, Feb. 4
417-418 A177   Set of 2   2.75 2.75

Intl. Swimming Federation (FINA), Cent. — A178

2008, Feb. 18
419 A178 50d multi   2.25 2.25
Printed in sheets of 8 + label.

2008 Summer Olympics, Beijing A179

Designs: 46d, Tennis. 50d, Hurdlers.

2008, Mar. 7
420-421 A179   Set of 2   3.75 3.75
Nos. 420-421 each were printed in sheets of 8 + label.

Easter — A180

Designs: 20d, Shown. 46d, Jesus, cross, diff.

2008, Mar. 21   *Perf. 13¾x13¼*
422-423 A180   Set of 2   3.00 3.00

2008 Serbian Olympic Tennis Team — A181

Designs: 20d, Janko Tipsarevic. No. 425, 30d, Nenad Zimonjic. No. 426, 30d, Jelena Jankovic. 40d, Ana Ivanovic. 46d, Novak Djokovic.

2008, Apr. 8   *Perf. 13¼x13¾*
424-428 A181   Set of 5   10.00 10.00

Endangered Animals — A182

No. 429: a, Cervus elaphus. b, Meles meles. c, Felis silvestris. d, Sus scrofa.

2008, Apr. 7   *Perf. 13¾x13¼*
429   Horiz. strip of 4 + central label   6.00 6.00
a.-b. A182 20d Either single   .90 .90
c.-d. A182 46d Either single   2.00 2.00

Souvenir Sheet

2008 Eurovision Song Contest, Belgrade — A183

2008, Apr. 11   *Perf. 13¾*
430 A183 177d multi   8.00 8.00

Europa A184

Stamped cover, letter and: 46d, Quill pen. 50d, Letter opener.

2008, May 5   *Perf. 13¼x13¾*
431-432 A184   Set of 2   4.00 4.00
Nos. 431-432 each were printed in sheets of 8 + label.

European Nature Protection A185

Designs: 20d, Vlasina Lake. 46d, Djavolja Varos rock formations.

2008, May 23
433-434 A185   Set of 2   3.00 3.00
Nos. 433-434 each were printed in sheets of 8 + label.

Oriental Express, 125th Anniv. — A186

Train and: 20d, Eiffel Tower and Arc de Triomphe. 50d, Hagia Sophia, Istanbul.

2008, June 9
435-436 A186   Set of 2   3.00 3.00
Nos. 435-436 each were printed in sheets of 8 + label.

Television Belgrade, 50th Anniv. — A187

2008, June 16 Litho.
437 A187 46d multi 1.90 1.90
Printed in sheets of 8 + label.

University of Belgrade, Bicent. A188

2008, July 10 Perf. 13¼x13¾
438 A188 20d multi .90 .90

Grapes and Vineyards A189

No. 439: a, Riesling grapes, vineyard in Fruska Gora (grapes at left). b, Sauvignon Blanc grapes, vineyard in Oplenac (grapes at right). c, Prokupac grapes, vineyard in Zupa. d, Frankovka grapes, vineyard in Vrsac.

2008, Sept. 25
439 Horiz. strip of 4 + central label 6.25 6.25
a.-b. A189 20d Either single 1.00 1.00
c.-d. A189 46d Either single 2.00 2.00

Joy of Europe A190

2008, Sept. 26
440 A190 46d multi 1.90 1.90
Printed in sheets of 8 + label.

First Telephone Station in Belgrade, 125th Anniv. — A191

2008, Oct. 24
441 A191 46d multi 1.90 1.90
Stamp Day.

Traditional Children's Costumes A192

Girl from: 46d, Sumadija. 50d, Kumodraz.

2008, Nov. 10 Perf. 13¾x13¼
442-443 A192 Set of 2 3.75 3.75
Nos. 442-443 each were printed in sheets of 9 + label.

Danube Navigation Convention, 60th Anniv. — A193

2008, Nov. 20 Perf. 13¼x13¾
444 A193 46d multi 1.90 1.90
Printed in sheets of 8 + label.

Christmas A194

Designs: 20d, Nativity, by unknown artist. 46d, Nativity, by Dimitrije Bacevic.

2008, Nov. 28 Perf. 13¾x13¼
445-446 A194 Set of 2 2.75 2.75

Dadov Theater, Belgrade, 50th Anniv. — A195

2008, Dec. 5
447 A195 20d multi .90 .90

Osisani Jez Magazine, 75th Anniv. — A196

2009, Jan. 5 Litho. Perf. 13¾x13¼
448 A196 20d multi .90 .90
Printed in sheets of 8 + central label.

Louis Braille (1809-52), Educator of the Blind — A197

2009, Jan. 5 Perf. 13¼x13¾
449 A197 46d multi 1.90 1.90

Coat of Arms Type of 2006 Surcharged

2009, Jan. 28 Litho. Perf. 13¼
450 A124 22d on 20d multi .90 .90

Belt and Buckle — A198

Ring — A199

Embroidery A200

Kalemegdan, Belgrade A201

2009, Jan. 28 Perf. 13¾
451 A198 11d multi .45 .45
a. Dated 2012 .25 .25
b. Dated "2013" .25 .25
c. Perf. 13¼, dated "2010"
452 A199 22d multi .90 .90
453 A200 44d multi 1.90 1.90
454 A201 55d multi 2.25 2.25
454a Dated "2013" 1.40 1.40
Nos. 451-454 (4) 5.50 5.50

Issued: No. 451a, 2012; No. 451b, 4/18/13; No. 454a, 4/12/13.

Protected Mammals — A202

No. 455: a, Mustela ermina. b, Micromys minutus. c, Sicista subtilis. d, Spermophilus citellus.

2009, Feb. 16 Perf. 13¾x13¼
455 Horiz. strip of 4 + central label 4.50 4.50
a.-b. A202 22d Either single .70 .70
c.-d. A202 46d Either single 1.50 1.50

Politikin Zabavnik Magazine, 70th Anniv. — A203

2009, Feb. 28 Perf. 13¼x13¾
456 A203 22d multi .90 .90
Printed in sheets of 8 + central label.

Birds A204

Designs: 22d, Scolopax rusticola. 46d, Monticola saxatilis.

2009, Mar. 2 Perf. 13¾x13¼
457-458 A204 Set of 2 2.25 2.25
458a Souvenir sheet, #457-458 2.25 2.25
See Bulgaria Nos. 4498-4499.

Easter A205

Icons from church in Topola: 22d, Last Supper. 46d, Entombment of Jesus.

2009, Mar. 9 Perf. 13¼
459-460 A205 Set of 2 2.25 2.25

Miniature Sheet

Actors and Actresses — A206

No. 461: a, Vela Nigrinova (1862-1908). b, Milan Ajvaz (1897-1980). c, Nevenka Urbanova (1909-2007). d, Stevo Zigon (1926-2005). e, Slobodan Perovic (1926-78). f, Stevan Salajic (1929-2002). g, Neda Spasojevic (1941-81). h, Milos Zutic (1939-93).

2009, Mar. 27 Perf. 13¼x13¾
461 A206 22d Sheet of 8, #a-h, + central label 6.50 6.50

25th Summer Universiade, Belgrade A207

Belgrade skyline, emblem, and birds in sports: 22d, Diving, fencing, basketball, soccer, swimming. 46d, Handball, gymnastics, tennis, judo, hurdling.

2009, Mar. 31 Litho.
462-463 A207 Set of 2 2.25 2.25

Paintings — A208

Designs: 22d, Self-portrait with a Veil, by Milena Pavlovic Barili (1909-45). No. 465, 46d, Young Woman in a Pink Dress, by Paja Jovanovic (1859-1957). No. 466, 46d, Still Life with Parrot, by Jovan Bijelic (1884-1964).

2009, Apr. 6 Perf. 13¾x13¼
464-466 A208 Set of 3 4.00 4.00

Europa A209

Designs: 46d, Goddess Urania, Galileo's telescope, Milky Way. 50d, Radio telescope, Horsehead Nebula.

2009, May 5 Perf. 13¼x13¾
467-468 A209 Set of 2 3.50 3.50
Intl. Year of Astronomy. Nos. 467-468 were each printed in sheets of 8 + central label.

Laying of Cornerstone of St. Sava Cathedral, 70th Anniv. A210

2009, May 9   *Perf. 13¼*
469 A210 22d multi   .90 .90

European Nature Protection A211

Designs: 22d, Gyps fulvus over Uvac River. 46d, Pcinja Valley.

2009, May 20   *Perf. 13¾x13¼*
470-471 A211   Set of 2   2.50 2.50
Nos. 470-471 were each printed in sheets of 8 + central label.

Miniature Sheet

Composers — A212

No. 472: a, Kornelije Stankovic (1831-65). b, Josif Marinkovic (1851-1931). c, Petar Konjovic (1883-1970). d, Stevan Hristic (1885-1958). e, Miloje Milojevic (1884-1946). f, Mihovil Logar (1902-98). g, Lyubica Maric (1909-2003). h, Vasilije Mokranjac (1923-84).

2009, May 29
472 A212 22d Sheet of 8, #a-h, + central label   6.00 6.00

Battle of Cegar, 200th Anniv. A213

Designs: 22d, Battle of Cegar, painting by Boza Ilic. 46d, Stevan Sindelic, soldiers at Skull Tower.

2009, May 29   *Perf. 13¼x13¾*
473-474 A213   Set of 2   2.50 2.50

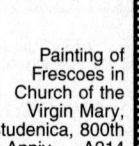

Painting of Frescoes in Church of the Virgin Mary, Studenica, 800th Anniv. — A214

2009, June 8   *Perf. 13¼*
475 A214 22d multi   .90 .90

Famous Men — A215

Designs: No. 476, 22d, Pavle Savic (1909-94), physicist. No. 477, 22d, Dimitrije Putnikovic (1859-1910), educator. No. 478, 46d, Pierre Curie (1859-1906), physicist. No. 479, 46d, Charles Darwin (1809-82), naturalist.

2009, June 22   *Perf. 13¾x13¼*
476-479 A215   Set of 4   5.00 5.00

Railroads in Serbia, 125th Anniv. — A216

Designs: 22d, CS No. 1 steam locomotive, Belgrade Station. 46d, JZ 441 electric locomotive, Nis Station.

2009, Sept. 8   Litho.   *Perf. 13¼*
480-481 A216   Set of 2   2.25 2.25

Golden Pen International Biennale of Illustrations, 50th Anniv. — A217

2009, Sept. 21   *Perf. 13¾x13¼*
482 A217 22d gold & black   .90 .90

Joy of Europe A218

2009, Sept. 30   *Perf. 13¼x13¾*
483 A218 46d multi   1.90 1.90
Printed in sheets of 8 + label.

Gold Medalists at 2009 FINA World Swimming Championships, Rome — A219

Designs: No. 484, 46d, Nadja Higl (shown). No. 485, 46d, Milorad Cavic. 50d, Serbian Water Polo team.

2009, Oct. 9
484-486 A219   Set of 3   5.50 5.50
Nos. 484-486 each were printed in sheets of 8 + label.

Stamp Day — A220

2009, Oct. 23   *Perf. 13¾x13¼*
487 A220 46d multi   1.90 1.90
Michel Stamp Catalogs, Cent.

Exhibition of Dinosaurs From Argentina, Belgrade A221

Designs: 22d, Herrerasaurus ischigualastensis. 46d, Giganotosaurus carolinii.

2009, Nov. 9   *Perf. 13¼x13¾*
488-489 A221   Set of 2   2.50 2.50
Nos. 488-489 each were printed in sheets of 9 + label.

Christmas A222

Frescoes from Krusedol Monastery by Jov Vasilijevic: 22d, Christ's Birth. 46d, Epiphany.

2009, Nov. 23   Litho.   *Perf. 13¼*
490-491 A222   Set of 2   2.50 2.50

NIN Magazine, 75th Anniv. — A223

2010, Jan. 26   *Perf. 13¾x13¼*
492 A223 22d multi   .75 .75

New Year 2010 (Year of the Tiger) — A224

Tiger at: 22d, Right. 50d, Left.

2010, Jan. 27   *Perf. 13¼x13¾*
493-494 A224   Set of 2   2.40 2.40

European Nature Protection A225

Paeonia officinalis and: 22d, Deliblato Sands. 46d, Vrsac Mountains.

2010, Feb. 10   *Perf. 13¼x13¾*
495-496 A225   Set of 2   2.25 2.25
496a   Souvenir sheet, #495-496, perf. 13¾   2.25 2.25

2010 Winter Olympics, Vancouver A226

Designs: 22d, Cross-country skiing. 50d, Downhill skier.

2010, Feb. 12   *Perf. 13¾*
497-498 A226   Set of 2   2.50 2.50
Nos. 497-498 each were printed in sheets of 8 + central label.

Serbian Olympic Committee, Cent. — A227

2010, Feb. 23   Litho.   *Perf. 13¾*
499 A227 22d multi   .80 .80

Expo 2010, Shanghai A228

Serbian Pavilion and: 22d, People, birds. 50d, Shanghai buildings.

2010, Feb. 26   *Perf. 13¾x13¼*
500-501 A228   Set of 2   2.50 2.50

Frédéric Chopin (1810-49), Composer A229

2010, Mar. 1
502 A229 50d multi   1.75 1.75
Printed in sheets of 8 + central label.

Easter — A230

Red Easter egg and: 22d, Crucifixion painting. 46d, Egg depicting resurrected Jesus.

2010, Mar. 2   *Perf. 13¼x13¾*
503-504 A230   Set of 2   2.25 2.25

Military Academy, Belgrade, 160th Anniv. A231

Perf. 13¼x13¾
2010, Mar. 18   Litho.
505 A231 22d multi   .60 .60

Zastava 750,
55th
Anniv. — A232

2010, Apr. 8
506   A232   22d multi   .80   .80

Birds
A233

No. 507: a, Passer domesticus. b,
Phoenicurus ochruros. c, Columba livia. d,
Parus major.

2010, Apr. 12   **Perf. 13¾**
507   Horiz. strip of 4 + central
            label   5.00   5.00
  a.   A233 22d multi   .70   .70
  b.   A233 33d multi   1.00   1.00
  c.   A233 46d multi   1.40   1.40
  d.   A233 50d multi   1.60   1.60

Industrialization of Serbia, 140th
Anniv. — A234

2010, Apr. 19   **Perf. 13¾**
508   A234   22d multi   .80   .80

Europa — A235

Designs: 66d, Girl reading on stack of
books, vine, house, rabbit, giraffe, chicks. 77d,
Girl standing on stack of books, boy in sling
under moon, pumpkins, fairies.

2010, May 5
509-510 A235   Set of 2   4.00   4.00
Nos. 509-510 each were printed in sheets of
8 + central label.

2010 World Cup
Soccer
Championships,
South
Africa — A236

Emblem of 2010 World Cup and: 22d, Map
of Africa, two players. 50d, Map of Africa, two
players, flags of South Africa and Serbia.
177d, Feet of soccer player, soccer balls,
horiz.

2010, May 6   **Perf. 13¾**
511-512 A236   Set of 2   2.25   2.25
Souvenir Sheet
Perf. 13¾x¼
513   A236   177d multi   4.50   4.50
No. 513 contains one 43x35mm stamp.
Nos. 511-512 each were printed in sheets of 8
+ label.

50th Tour de Serbie Bicycle
Race — A237

2010, June 1   **Perf. 13¾x13¼**
514   A237   50d multi   1.75   1.75
Printed in sheets of 8 + label.

Icons — A238

No. 515: a, Archangel Michael, by Andrei
Rublev, 15th cent., Russia. b, Odigitria Virgin,
Belgrade, 14th cent.

2010, June 28   **Perf. 13¼x13¾**
515   A238   50d Pair, #a-b   2.75   2.75
No. 515 was printed in sheets of 8, containing 4 of each stamp, + central label. See Russia No. 7221.

50th
Trumpet
Festival,
Guca
A239

2010, Aug. 13   **Perf. 13¾**
516   A239   44d multi   1.50   1.50
Printed in sheets of 8 + label. See Bosnia &
Herzegovina (Serb Administration) No. 402.

2010 Youth Olympics,
Singapore — A240

2010, Aug. 14
517   A240   51d multi   1.50   1.50
Printed in sheets of 8 + label.

Mother Teresa
(1910-97),
Humanitarian
A241

2010, Aug. 26   **Perf. 13¾x13¼**
518   A241   50d multi   1.50   1.50

Miniature Sheet

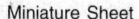

Writers — A242

No. 519: a, Laza Kostic (1841-1910). b,
Branislav Nusic (1864-1938). c, Borisav
Stankovic (1876-1927). d, Ivo Andric (1892-
1975). e, Milos Crnjanski (1893-1977). f, Mesa
Selimovic (1910-82). g, Borislav Pekic (1930-
92). h, Danilo Kis (1935-89).

2010, Nov. 26   **Perf. 13¼**
519   A242   22d Sheet of 8, #a-h, +
                    central label   5.25   5.25

Plate, 16th
Cent. — A243

Figurine, 19th
Cent. — A244

2010, Nov. 26
520   A243   22d multi   .65   .65
521   A244   44d multi   1.30   1.30
Belgrade Art Museum, 60th anniv.

Serbian
Postal
Service,
170th Anniv.
A245

2010, Nov. 26   **Perf. 13¼**
522   A245   46d multi   1.50   1.50
Stamp Day.

Joy of
Europe
A246

2010, Nov. 26
523   A246   46d multi   1.50   1.50
Printed in sheets of 8 + central label.

Christmas
A247

Nativity paintings from church in Zemun by:
22d, Arsenija Teodorovic. 46d, Unknown artist.

2010, Nov. 30
524-525 A247   Set of 2   2.00   2.00

Ivan Saric
(1876-1966),
Aviation
Pioneer, and
Saric No. 1
Airplane
A248

Airplanes — A249

No. 527: a, 44d, Breguet 14. b, 55d, Spartan
Cruiser. c, 66d, Rogozarski IK-3. d, 77d,
McDonnell Douglas DC-9.

2010, Dec. 9   **Perf. 13¼**
526   A248   22d multi   .65   .65
                                      Perf. 13¾
527   A249   Sheet of 4, #a-d   6.75   6.75

Souvenir Sheet

Preservation of Polar Regions and
Glaciers — A250

No. 528: a, 46d, Iceberg. b, 66d, Glacier.

2011, Jan. 31   Litho.   Perf. 13¼
528   A250   Sheet of 2, #a-b   3.00   3.00

New Year
2011 (Year
of the
Rabbit)
A251

Rabbit, ring of Chinese Zodiac animals and:
22d, Geometric design. 55d, Chinese character for "rabbit."

2011, Feb. 7
529-530 A251   Set of 2   2.00   2.00

Serbian Membership in Intl. Telecommunications Union, 145th Anniv. — A252

2011, Feb. 9   **Perf. 13¼x13¾**
531 A252 46d multi   1.25 1.25
Printed in sheets of 8 + label.

Rebuilding of Avala Telecommunications Tower, Belgrade — A253

2011, Feb. 14   **Perf. 13¼**
532 A253 44d multi   1.25 1.25
532a   Dated "2013"   1.10 1.10
Issued: No. 532a, 4/11/13.

Art — A254

Designs: 22p, Self-portrait of Katarina Ivanovic (1811-82). 33d, Woman in Traditional Dress, by Uros Knezevic (1811-76). 44d, Self-portrait, sculpture, by Djordje Jovanovic (1861-1953). 66d, Self-portrait with Wife and Son, by Bora Baruh (1911-42).

2011, Feb. 25   **Perf. 13¾x13¼**
533-536 A254   Set of 4   4.50 4.50

Kornelije Stankovic (1831-65), Composer A255

2011, Mar. 15   **Perf. 13¼x13¾**
537 A255 22d multi   .65 .65
Stankovic Music School, cent.

Easter — A256

Religious paintings by Arsenije Teodorovic (1767-1826): 22d, Christ's Arrival in Jerusalem. 112d, Resurrection.

2011, Mar. 25   **Perf. 13¾**
538-539 A256   Set of 2   4.00 4.00

Serbian National Theater, Novi Sad, 150th Anniv. A257

2011, Mar. 28
540 A257 22d multi   .65 .65
Printed in sheets of 24 + central label.

Rotary International Polio Plus Program A258

2011, Mar. 31   **Perf. 13¾x13¼**
541 A258 50d multi   1.50 1.50

Worldwide Fund for Nature (WWF) A259

No. 542 — Phalacrocorax pygmaeus: a, Two birds, one on branch. b, Bird on rock. c, Two birds in flight. d, Two birds in water.

2011, Apr. 11   **Perf. 13¼x13¾**
542   Horiz. strip of 4 + central
    label   4.75 4.75
a. A259 22d multi   .65 .65
b. A259 33d multi   .95 .95
c. A259 44d multi   1.25 1.25
d. A259 66d multi   1.90 1.90

Intl. Year of Biodiversity — A260

2011, Apr. 15   **Perf. 13¾**
543 A260 50d multi   1.50 1.50

Europa A261

Forest and: 33d, Logs. 66d, Tree leaves.

2011, May 5   **Litho.**
544-545 A261   Set of 2   3.00 3.00
Intl. Year of Forests. Nos. 544-545 each were printed in sheets of 8 + central label.

Scouting in Serbia, Cent. — A262

2011, May 6   **Perf. 13¼x13¾**
546 A262 22d multi   .65 .65

Bora Stankovic Gymnasium, Vranje, 130th Anniv. — A263

2011, May 10   **Perf. 13¾x13¼**
547 A263 22d multi   .65 .65

Dr. Laza Lazarevic (1851-91), Writer and Psychiatrist A264

2011, May 13
548 A264 22d multi   .65 .65

Berries A265

No. 549: a, Rubus idaeus. b, Fragaria vesca. c, Ribes rubrum. d, Vaccinium macrocarpon.

2011, May 27   **Perf. 13¼x13¾**
549   Horiz. strip of 4 + central
    label   5.00 5.00
a. A265 22d multi   .65 .65
b. A265 33d multi   .95 .95
c. A265 44d multi   1.40 1.40
d. A265 66d multi   2.00 2.00

Campaign Against AIDS, 30th Anniv. — A266

2011, June 1   **Perf. 13¾x13¼**
550 A266 50d multi   1.50 1.50

Digital Serbia — A267

Designs: 22d, Keyhole on Earth, key. 44d, Stylized eye, "@" and "www."

2011, June 3   **Perf. 13¼**
551-552 A267   Set of 2   2.00 2.00

European Nature Protection A268

Waterfalls: 22d, Mokranjska Stena. 46d, Beli Izvorac.

2011, June 13   **Perf. 13¾x13¼**
553-554 A268   Set of 2   2.00 2.00

Franz Liszt (1811-86), Composer — A269

2011, June 14   **Perf. 13¾**
555 A269 50d multi   1.40 1.40

Bridges A270

Designs: 22d, Danube River Bridge, near Beska. 44d, Sava River Railway Bridge, Belgrade. 46d, Danube River Bridge, Novi Sad.

2011, June 20   **Litho.**
556-558 A270   Set of 3   3.25 3.25

Duzijanca Harvest Festival, Cent. — A271

Designs: 22d, Model of cathedral in Subotica. 55d, Centenary wheat crown.

2011, July 1
559-560 A271   Set of 2   2.25 2.25
Nos. 559-560 each were printed in sheets of 9 + label.

Belgrade Zoo, 75th Anniv. A272

Designs: 22d, Lion, white lion and cubs. No. 562, vert. — White or albino animals: a, 33d, Panthera tigris tigris. b, 44d, Neophron percnopterus. c, 46d, Macropus rufogriseus. d, 50d, Panthera leo.

2011, July 12   **Perf. 13¾**
561 A272 22d multi   .65 .65
562 A272   Sheet of 4, #a-d   5.00 5.00
No. 562 was sold with, but unattached to, a booklet cover.

Computer Mouse Flower — A273

2011, July 13
563 A273 22d multi   .65 .65
563a   Dated 2013   .50 .50
Issued: No. 563a, 2/19/13.

Soko Galeb Jet, 50th Anniv. A274

2011, July 20   **Perf. 13¼x13¾**
564 A274 50d multi   1.40 1.40
Printed in sheets of 8 + central label.

First Conference of Non-Aligned Countries, 50th Anniv. — A275

2011, Sept. 1   **Perf. 13¾x13¼**
565 A275 22d multi   .60 .60

European Women's Volleyball Championships, Italy and Serbia — A276

2011, Sept. 20   **Perf. 13¾**
566 A276 46d multi   1.25 1.25
Printed in sheets of 8 + central label.

Joy of Europe A277

2011, Sept. 30   **Perf. 13¼x13¾**
567 A277 46d multi   1.25 1.25
Printed in sheets of 8 + central label.

First Serbian Motion Picture, Cent. A278

2011, Oct. 3   **Perf. 13¾**
568 A278 22d multi   .60 .60

Stamp Day — A279

2011, Oct. 25   **Perf. 13¾x13¼**
569 A279 46d multi   1.25 1.25
Beogradfila Stamp Exhibition, Belgrade.

Writers A280

Designs: 22d, Rachel de Queiroz (1910-2003), Brazilian writer. 46d, Ivo Andric (1892-1975), Yugoslvian writer, and Nobel medal.

2011, Oct. 26   **Perf. 13¾**
570-571 A280 Set of 2   1.90 1.90
See Brazil No. 3198.

Christmas A281

Designs: 22d, Birth of Christ, icon, c. 1780. 112d, Birth of Christ, by Arsenije Teodorovic.

2011, Nov. 15
572-573 A281 Set of 2   3.50 3.50

Journalist's Association of Serbia, 130th Anniv. — A282

2011, Nov. 25
574 A282 22d multi   .60 .60

Moravica Hydroelectric Plant, Cent. — A283

2011, Dec. 19   **Perf. 13¼x13¾**
575 A283 22d multi   .55 .55

Serbian Victories at 2011 Men's and Women's European Volleyball Championships A284

Designs: No. 576, 22d, Two male players. No. 577, 22d, Three female players.

2011, Dec. 20   **Perf. 13¾x13¼**
576-577 A284 Set of 2   1.10 1.10

African National Congress, Cent. — A285

2012, Jan. 6   **Litho.**
578 A285 46d multi   1.25 1.25

New Year 2012 (Year of the Dragon) A286

Designs: 22d, Dragon. 55d, Dragon, diff.

2012, Feb. 6   **Perf. 13¼x13¾**
579-580 A286 Set of 2   1.90 1.90

Architecture A287

Designs: 22d, Department store, Belgrade. 33d, Telephone Exchange Building, Belgrade, horiz. 46d, Hotel Moskva, Belgrade, horiz. 55d, City Hall, Subotica, horiz.

Perf. 13¾x13¼, 13¼x13¾
2012, Mar. 2
581-584 A287 Set of 4   3.75 3.75

National Theater, Nis, 125th Anniv. A288

2012, Mar. 9   **Perf. 13¼**
585 A288 22d multi   .55 .55

Easter — A289

Designs: 22d, Ceremonial cross. 46d, Resurrection of Christ.

2012, Mar. 15   **Perf. 13¾**
586-587 A289 Set of 2   1.60 1.60

Academy Anniversaries — A290

Woman and building: 22d, Music Academy, Belgrade, 75th anniv. 33d, Art Academy, Belgrade, 75th anniv. 44d, Science Academy, Pozarevac, 150th anniv.

2012, Mar. 30
588-590 A290 Set of 3   2.40 2.40

Ján Koniarek (1878-1952), Sculptor — A291

2012, Apr. 13
591 A291 50d multi   1.25 1.25
Printed in sheets of 8 + central label. See Slovakia No. 636.

25th Belgrade Marathon A292

2012, Apr. 21
592 A292 22d multi   .55 .55

Europa A293

Designs: 44d, Church and angel. 77d, Snowboarder, mountainside forest in winter, cottage, lakefront building.

2012, May 4
593-594 A293 Set of 2   2.60 2.60
Nos. 593-594 each were printed in sheets of 8 + central label

Reptiles A294

No. 595: a, Coronella austriaca. b, Podarcis taurica. c, Lacerta viridis. d, Emys orbicularis.

2012, May 21   **Perf. 13¼x13¾**
595   Horiz. strip of 4 + central
     label   3.75 3.75
   a.   A294 22d multi   .50 .50
   b.   A294 33d multi   .75 .75
   c.   A294 44d multi   .95 .95
   d.   A294 66d multi   1.50 1.50

European Nature Protection A295

Forest and: 22d, Pinus nigra. 46d, Acer heldreichii.

2012, June 1   **Perf. 13¾**
596-597 A295 Set of 2   1.50 1.50
Nos. 596-597 each were printed in sheets of 8 + central label.

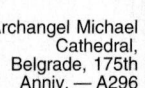

Archangel Michael Cathedral, Belgrade, 175th Anniv. — A296

2012, July 13   **Perf. 13¾x13¼**
598 A296 22d multi   .45 .45

No. 598 was printed in sheets of 8 + central label.

2012 Summer Olympics, London — A297

Emblem of 2012 Summer Olympics and: 44d, Torch and stadium. 77d, London landmarks.

2012, July 27
599-600 A297 Set of 2   2.50 2.50

Nos. 599-600 each were printed in sheets of 8 + central label.

Writers A298

Designs: 22d, Vojislav Ilic (1860-94), poet. 33d, Janko Veselinovic (1862-1905), novelist. 44d, Vuk Stefanovic Karadzic (1787-1864), linguist.

2012, Sept. 3   **Perf. 13x13¾**
601-603 A298 Set of 3   2.25 2.25

Items in National Museum A299

Designs: 22d, Statue, 4th cent. 55d, Sword, 20th cent.

2012, Sept. 27
604-605 A299 Set of 2   1.75 1.75

Nos. 604-605 each were printed in sheets of 9 + label.

Joy of Europe A300

2012, Oct. 1
606 A300 46d multi   1.10 1.10

No. 606 was printed in sheets of 8 + central label.

Digital Television — A301

2012, Oct. 4   **Perf. 13¾**
607 A301 50d multi   1.10 1.10

Battle of Kumanovo, Cent. — A302

Designs: 22d, Gen. Radomir Putnik, Gen. Stepa Stepanovic, Col. Zivojin Misic, and Prince Regent Alexander Karageorgevich. 50d, Revenge of Kosovo, painting by Paja Jovanovic.

2012, Oct. 24
608-609 A302 Set of 2   1.60 1.60

Nos. 608-609 each were printed in sheets of 8 + central label.

Stamp Day A303

2012, Oct. 25
610 A303 22d multi   .50 .50

First Serbian stamp exhibition, 75th anniv.

Christmas A304

Nativity icons by, 22d, Dimitrije Bacevic. 46d, Dimitrije Bratoglic.

2012, Nov. 1
611-612 A304 Set of 2   1.60 1.60

Miniature Sheet

Serbian Air Force, Cent. — A305

No. 613: a, 22d, Military balloon. b, 22d, Rogozarski IK-3 propeller airplane. c, 22d, Soko Jastreb jet fighter. d, 55d, Fizir FN biplane. e, 55d, Ikarus S-49. f, 55d, Lasta 95.

2012, Dec. 24   **Perf. 13¼x13¾**
613 A305 Sheet of 6, #a-f   5.50 5.50

New Year 2013 (Year of the Snake) — A306

Designs: 22d, Snake and lotus flower. 46d, Snake.

2013, Feb. 8   **Perf. 13¾**
614-615 A306 Set of 2   1.60 1.60

Serbian Historical Museum, 50th Anniv. A307

Museum exhibits: 22d, Gospel of King Alexander Obrenovich. 50d, Crown of King Peter I Karageorgevich.

2013, Feb. 20   **Litho.**
616-617 A307 Set of 2   1.75 1.75

Nos. 616-617 each were printed in sheets of 9 + label.

Easter — A308

Frescos from Most Holy Theotokos Monastery Church: 22d, Crucifixion. 46d, Descent to Hell.

2013, Mar. 1
618-619 A308 Set of 2   1.60 1.60

Composers — A309

Designs: 22d, Oskar Danon (1913-2009). 46d, Richard Wagner (1813-83). 50d, Giuseppe Verdi (1813-1901).

2013, Mar. 4   **Perf. 13¾**
620-622 A309 Set of 3   2.75 2.75

Edict of Milan, 1700th Anniv. — A310

Bust of Emperor Constantine and: 50d, Chrismon. 112d, Ship, map of Adriatic area, horiz.

2013, Apr. 5   **Perf. 13¾x13¼**
623 A310 50d multi   1.25 1.25

Souvenir Sheet
Perf. 13¾
624 A310 112d multi   2.75 2.75

No. 623 was printed in sheets of 8 + central label.

Intl. Red Cross, 150th Anniv. — A311

2013, May 8   **Perf. 13¾**
625 A311 50d black & red   1.25 1.25

No. 625 was printed in sheets of 9 + label.

Europa A312

Postal vehicles: 44d, Old postal truck. 112d, Modern postal van.

2013, May 9   **Perf. 13¼x13¾**
626-627 A312 Set of 2   3.75 3.75

Nos. 626-627 each were printed in sheets of 8 + central label.

European Nature Protection A313

Designs: 46d, Man with scythe in meadow near Mt. Rajac. 50d, Resava Cave.

2013, May 13
628-629 A313 Set of 2   2.25 2.25

Nos. 628-629 each were printed in sheets of 8 + central label.

Miniature Sheet

Actors and Actresses — A314

No. 630: a, Zivojin Zika Milenkovic (1927-2008). b, Radmila Rada Savicevic (1926-2001). c, Petar Kralj (1941-2011). d, Radomir Rade Markovic (1921-2010). e, Ksenija Jovanovic (1928-2012). f, Predrag Tasovac (1922-2010). g, Pavle Paja Vujisic (1926-88). h, Dragan Lakovic (1929-90).

2013, May 24   **Perf. 13¾x13¼**
630 A314 22d Sheet of 8, #a-h, +
    central label   4.25 4.25

Diplomatic Relations Between Serbia and Cuba, 70th Anniv. — A315

2013, May 29   **Perf. 13¼x13¾**
631 A315 46d multi   1.10 1.10

Orchids
A316

No. 632: a, Cymbidium Burgundium. b, Masdevallia kimballiana. c, Angraecum leonis. d, Cymbidium Fort George.

2013, June 14
632   Horiz. strip of 4 + central
       label   4.00 4.00
  a.   A316 22d multi   .55   .55
  b.   A316 33d multi   .75   .75
  c.   A316 46d multi   1.10 1.10
  d.   A316 66d multi   1.60 1.60

50th Ljubicevo Equestrian
Games — A317

No. 633: a, Joceky with helmet on horse facing right. b, Rider with crop on horse, bullseye target. c, Rider with crop on horse, watermelon on stand. d, Rider on horse facing left.

2013, Aug. 30   Litho.   Perf. 13¾
633   Horiz. strip of 4 + cen-
       tral label   2.00 2.00
  a.-d. A317 22d Any single   .50   .50

Joy of
Europe — A318

Children's drawings of: 22d, Children and bicycle. 46d, Boy and girl playing musical instruments, vert.

Perf. 13¼x13¾, 13¾x13¼
2013, Sept. 2   Litho.
634-635 A318   Set of 2   1.60 1.60
  Nos. 634-635 are each printed in sheets of 8 + central label.

Constitutional
Court, 50th
Anniv. — A319

2013, Oct. 14   Litho.   Perf. 13¼x13¾
636 A319 22d multi   .50   .50

Stamp
Day — A320

2013, Oct. 25   Litho.   Perf. 13¼x13¾
637 A320 22d multi   .50   .50
  a.   With "NS" in oval handstamp
       near top left corner of envel-
       ope   .50   .50
  First postal law in Serbia, 170th anniv. No. 637a is the 7th stamp in the sheet of 25.

Christmas — A321

Icons depicting the Nativity from: 22d, 1866-67. 46d, 1868.

2013, Oct. 28   Litho.   Perf. 13¾
638-639 A321   Set of 2   1.60 1.60

Petar II Petrovic-
Njegos (1813-51),
Prince of
Montenegro
A322

2013, Nov. 13   Litho.   Perf. 13¼
640 A322 46d multi   1.10 1.10
  No. 640 was printed in sheets of 8 + central label.

Mitrovica High
School, 175th
Anniv. — A323

Pancevo
High School,
150th Anniv.
A324

Novi Pazar
High School,
Cent.
A325

Prijepolje
High School,
Cent.
A326

2013, Nov. 20   Litho.   Perf. 13¼
641 A323 22d multi   .55   .55
642 A324 22d multi   .55   .55
643 A325 22d multi   .55   .55
644 A326 22d multi   .55   .55
       Nos. 641-644 (4)   2.20 2.20

King Alexander of
Yugoslavia (1888-
1934)
A327

2013, Nov. 25   Litho.   Perf. 13¼
645 A327 50d multi   1.25 1.25
  No. 645 was printed in sheets of 8 + central label.

Zastava
Arms
Factory,
Kragujevac,
160th Anniv.
A328

2013, Nov. 28   Litho.   Perf. 13¼
646 A328 22d multi   .55   .55

Souvenir Sheet

Rugs — A329

No. 647 — Rugs with inscriptions in: a, Latin letters. b, Cyrillic letters.

2013, Dec. 2   Litho.   Perf. 13¾
647 A329 46d Sheet of 2, #a-b   2.25 2.25
       See Algeria No.

Grand Prince
Stefan Namanja
(c. 1113-
99) — A330

2013, Dec. 6   Litho.   Perf. 13¼
648 A330 22d multi   .55   .55

Start of
Negotiations
for Serbian
Admittance
to European
Union
A331

2014, Jan. 21   Litho.   Perf. 13¼
649 A331 22d multi   .50   .50

New Year
2014 (Year
of the Horse)
A332

Ring of Chinese Zodiac animals and: 22d, Horse. 46d, Pegasus.

2014, Jan. 31   Litho.   Perf. 13¼
650-651 A332   Set of 2   1.60 1.60

2014 Winter
Olympics, Sochi,
Russia — A333

Designs: 22d, Figure skating. 46d, Ski jumping.

2014, Feb. 7   Litho.   Perf. 13¼
652-653 A333   Set of 2   1.60 1.60
  Nos. 652-653 are each printed in sheets of 8 + central label.

Easter
A334

Icons depicting: 22d, The Last Supper. 46d, Entombment of Christ.

2014, Feb. 17   Litho.   Perf. 13¼
654-655 A334   Set of 2   1.60 1.60

Writers — A335

Designs: 22d, Branislav Nusic (1864-1938). 46d, Mikhail Lermontov (1814-41). 50d, William Shakespeare (1564-1616).

2014, Mar. 28   Litho.   Perf. 13¼
656-658 A335   Set of 3   3.00 3.00

Electronic
Communications
A336

2014, Apr. 1   Litho.   Perf. 13½
659 A336 1d multi   .25   .25

Mileva Maric-Einstein
(1875-1948),
Physicist — A337

2014, Apr. 1   Litho.   Perf. 13½
660 A337 23d multi   .55   .55

Europa
A338

Musician playing: 69d, Fife. 74d, Bagpipes.

2014, Apr. 26   Litho.   Perf. 13¼
661-662 A338   Set of 2   3.50 3.50
  Nos. 661-662 were each printed in sheets of 8 + central label.

European
Nature
Protection
A339

Animals at: 35d, Stara Planina Nature Park. 70d, Zaovine Lake.

2014, May 22 Litho. Perf. 13¼
663-664 A339 Set of 2 2.50 2.50

Nos. 663-664 were each printed in sheets of 8 + central label.

World War I, Cent. A340

Paintings and objects: 23d, Serbian Army Crossing Albania, by Milos Golubovic, 1915, and regiment flag. 35d, Another View, by Golubovic, 1915-16, swords and war medal. 46d, Serbian Army Arriving at the Sea, bu Vasa Eskicevic, 1916, army helmet and regiment flag. 70d, Goodbye, My Children, by Golubovic, 1915-16, Order of the Star with Swords.

2014, June 24 Litho. Perf. 13¼
665-668 A340 Set of 4 4.25 4.25

Nos. 665-668 were each printed in sheets of 9 + label.

Wild Animals A341

2014, June 30 Litho. Perf. 13¼
669 Horiz. strip + central label 4.25 4.25
a. A341 23d Felis silvestris .55 .55
b. A341 35d Vulpes vulpes .85 .85
c. A341 46d Canis lupus 1.10 1.10
d. A341 70d Lynx lynx 1.75 1.75

Joy of Europe A342

2014, Sept. 2 Litho. Perf. 13¼
670 A342 70d multi 1.60 1.60

No. 670 was printed in sheets of 8 + central label.

Patriarch Pavle (1914-2009) A343

2014, Sept. 11 Litho. Perf. 13¼
671 A343 23d multi .50 .50

No. 671 was printed in sheets of 8 + central label.

Stamp Day — A344

2014, Sept. 23 Litho. Perf. 13¼
672 A344 23d multi .50 .50

Museum Exhibits — A345

Coats of Arms in Museum of Applied Arts, Belgrade: 23d, Arms of the Nemajic Dynasty. 69d, Arms of the Brankovic Dynasty.

2014, Oct. 1 Litho. Perf. 13¼
673-674 A345 Set of 2 2.00 2.00

Nos. 673-674 were each printed in sheets of 9 + label.

Scientists A346

Designs: 23d, Petar Stevanovic (1914-99), geologist and paleontologist. 74d, Josef Pancic (1814-88), botanist.

2014, Oct. 8 Litho. Perf. 13¼
675-676 A346 Set of 2 2.00 2.00

Christmas A347

Designs: 23d, Fresco from Zica Monastery, 1309-16. 70d, Fresco from Zica Monastery, music for hymn *Slava Vo Visnjih Bogu*.

2014, Oct. 17 Litho. Perf. 13¼
677-678 A347 Set of 2 2.00 2.00

Souvenir Sheet

Liberation of Belgrade, 70th Anniv. — A348

No. 679: a, 50d, Belgrade war damage. b, 170d. Rebuilt buildings in Belgrade.

2014, Oct. 20 Litho. Perf. 14x13¾
679 A348 Sheet of 2, #a-b 4.75 4.75

POSTAGE DUE STAMPS

Coat of Arms — D1

1895 Unwmk. Typo. Perf. 13x13½
Granite Paper

J1 D1 5p red lilac 6.00 1.00
J2 D1 10p blue 6.00 .40
J3 D1 20p orange brown 47.50 8.00
J4 D1 30p green .40 .80
J5 D1 50p rose .40 1.10
a. Cliché of 5p in plate of 50p 80.00 100.00
Nos. J1-J5 (5) 60.30 11.30

No. J1 exists imperf. Value $75.

1898-1904 Ordinary Paper
J6 D1 5p magenta ('04) .70 .70
J7 D1 20p brown 6.00 1.00
a. Tête bêche pair 150.00 150.00
J8 D1 20p dp brn ('04) 6.00 1.00
Nos. J6-J8 (3) 12.70 2.70

1906 Granite Paper Perf. 11½
J9 D1 5p magenta 5.25 1.00

1909 Laid Paper
J10 D1 5p magenta .80 .60
J11 D1 10p pale blue 4.75 7.50
J12 D1 20p pale brown .40 .80
Nos. J10-J12 (3) 5.95 8.90

1914 White Wove Paper
J13 D1 5p rose .40 2.00
J14 D1 10p deep blue 6.00 9.00

Coat of Arms — D2

1918-20 Perf. 11
J15 D2 5p red .40 .85
J16 D2 5p red brown ('20) .40 .85
J17 D2 10p yellow green .40 .85
J18 D2 20p olive brown .40 .85
J19 D2 30p slate green .40 .85
J20 D2 50p chocolate .90 1.50
Nos. J15-J20 (6) 2.90 5.75

NEWSPAPER STAMPS

N1

Overprinted with Crown-topped Shield in Black

1911 Unwmk. Typo. Perf. 11½
P1 N1 1p gray .80 .80
P2 N1 5p green .80 .80
P3 N1 10p orange .80 .80
a. Cliché of 1p in plate of 10p 225.00
P4 N1 15p violet .80 .80
P5 N1 20p yellow .80 .80
a. Cliché of 50p in plate of 20p 85.00 140.00
P6 N1 25p blue .80 .80
P7 N1 30p slate 7.50 7.50
P8 N1 50p brown 6.25 6.25
P9 N1 1d bister 6.25 6.25
P10 N1 3d rose red 7.50 7.50
P11 N1 5d gray vio 6.25 6.25
Nos. P1-P11 (11) 38.55 38.55

POSTAL TAX STAMPS

> Catalogue values for unused stamps in this section, from this point to the end of the section, are for Never Hinged items.

Ksenofon Sahovic (1898-1956), Pathologist — PT1

2006, July 10 Litho. Perf. 12½
RA1 PT1 8d multi .25 .25

Campaign against cancer. Obligatory on mail July 10-Aug. 5.

Red Cross and Disabled People — PT2

2006, Sept. 14 Perf. 13¾
RA2 PT2 8d multi .25 .25

Obligatory on mail Sept. 14-21.

Red Cross and Children — PT3

2006, Sept. 22
RA3 PT3 8d multi .25 .25

Obligatory on mail Sept. 22-29.

Children's Week — PT4

2006, Oct. 2 Litho. Perf. 12½
RA4 PT4 8d multi .25 .25

Obligatory on mail Oct. 2-8.

AIDS Prevention — PT5

2006, Oct. 9 Perf. 13¾
RA5 PT5 8d multi .25 .25

Obligatory on mail Oct. 9-31.

European Olympic Youth Festival, Belgrade — PT6

2006, Dec. 1 Litho. Perf. 13¾
RA6 PT6 8d multi .30 .30

Obligatory on mail Dec. 1-31.

2007 European Judo Championships, Belgrade — PT7

2007, Jan. 22
RA7 PT7 8d multi .30 .30

Obligatory on mail Jan. 22-27.

Dr. Blagoje Neskovic (1907-86), Politician — PT8

2007, Mar. 5 Perf. 12½
RA8 PT8 8d multi .30 .30

Campaign against cancer. Obligatory on mail Mar. 5-31.

Red Cross
Week — PT9

2007, May 8   *Perf. 13¾*
RA9 PT9 10d multi   .35 .35
Obligatory on mail May 8-15.

Fresco of
St. Sava in
St. Sava's
Cathedral,
Belgrade
PT10

2007, May 16   *Perf. 13¼*
RA10 PT10 10d multi   .35 .35
Restoration of St. Sava Cathedral. Obligatory on mail May 16-Sept. 13.

Red Cross Solidarity
Week — PT11

2007, Sept. 14   *Perf. 13¾*
RA11 PT11 10d multi   .40 .40
Obligatory on mail Sept. 14-21.

Children's
Week — PT12

2007, Oct. 1   *Perf. 13¼*
RA12 PT12 10d multi   .40 .40
Obligatory on mail Oct. 1-7.

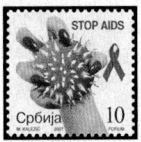

Campaign Against
AIDS — PT13

2007, Nov. 1   *Perf. 13¾*
RA13 PT13 10d multi   .40 .40
Obligatory on mail Nov. 1-30.

Ana and Vlade Divac
Foundation — PT14

2007, Dec. 24
RA14 PT14 10d multi   .40 .40
Obligatory on mail Dec. 24-29.

Campaign
Against Sex
Slavery
PT15

2008, Jan. 21   *Perf. 13¼*
RA15 PT15 10d multi   .35 .35
Obligatory on mail Jan. 21-26.

Zivojin Misic Statue,
Mionica, 90th
Anniv. — PT16

2008, Apr. 21   *Perf. 13¾*
RA16 PT16 10d multi   .40 .40
Obligatory on mail Apr. 21-May 7.

Red Cross
Week — PT17

2008, May 8   *Dated "2008"*   *Perf. 13¾*
RA17 PT17 10d multi   .40 .40
Obligatory on mail May 8-15. See Nos.
RA25, RA35, RA40, RA58.

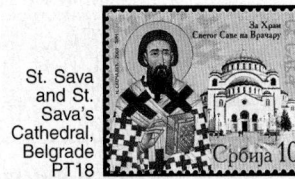

St. Sava
and St.
Sava's
Cathedral,
Belgrade
PT18

St. Sava's
Cathedral
PT19

2008, May 16   *Perf. 13¼*
RA18 PT18 10d multi   .40 .40
RA19 PT19 10d multi   .40 .40
Obligatory on mail May 16-Sept. 13.

Red Cross Solidarity
Week — PT20

2008, Sept. 14   *Perf. 13¾*
RA20 PT20 10d multi   .35 .35
Obligatory on mail Sept. 14-21.

Children's
Week — PT21

2008, Oct. 6   *Perf. 13¼*
RA21 PT21 10d multi   .35 .35
Obligatory on mail Oct. 6-12.

Avram Josif Vinaver
(1862-1915,
Physician — PT22

2008, Oct. 13
RA22 PT22 10d multi   .30 .30
Campaign against cancer. Obligatory on
mail Oct. 13-31.

Avala
Telecommunications
Tower,
Belgrade — PT23

2008, Nov. 3   *Perf. 13¾*
RA23 PT23 10d multi   .30 .30
Obligatory on mail Nov. 3-29.

Dr. Aleksandar Simic
(1899-1966) — PT24

2009, Apr. 6   *Perf. 13¼*
RA24 PT24 10d multi   .30 .30
Campaign against cancer. Obligatory on
mail Apr. 6-25.

Red Cross Week Type of 2008
2009, May 8   *Perf. 13¾*
Dated "2009"
RA25 PT17 10d multi   .30 .30
Obligatory on mail May 8-15.

King Alexander I
(1888-1934) — PT26

2009, June 8
RA26 PT26 10d multi   .30 .30
Obligatory on mail June 8-13.

St. Sava Cathedral,
Belgrade — PT27

2009, June 29
RA27 PT27 10d multi   .30 .30
Obligatory on mail June 29-Aug. 29.

Red Cross Solidarity
Week — PT28

2009, Sept. 14
RA28 PT28 10d multi   .35 .35
Obligatory on mail Sept. 14-21.

Children's
Week — PT29

2009, Oct. 5   *Perf. 13¼*
RA29 PT29 10d multi   .35 .35
Obligatory on mail Oct. 5-11.

Monument
PT30

2009, Nov. 9   *Perf. 13¼x13¾*
RA30 PT30 10d multi   .35 .35
Cultural preservation. Obligatory on mail
Nov. 9-14.

Homeless
Children — PT31

2009, Dec. 23   *Perf. 13¾*
RA31 PT31 10d multi   .30 .30
Obligatory on mail Dec. 23-31.

Refugees — PT32

2010, Feb. 1
RA32 PT32 10d multi   .30 .30
Obligatory on mail Feb. 1-6.

Dragoljub Jovanovic
(1895-1977),
Politician — PT33

2010, Mar. 8   *Litho.*   *Perf. 13½*
RA33 PT33 10d multi   — —
Obligatory on mail Mar. 8-31.

European Water Polo Championships,
Zagreb — PT34

2010, Apr. 16   *Litho.*   *Perf. 13¼x13¾*
RA34 PT34 10d multi   .30 .30
Obligatory on mail Apr. 16-24.

Red Cross Week Type of 2009
Dated "2010"
2010, May 8   *Perf. 13¾*
RA35 PT17 10d multi   .25 .25
Obligatory on mail May 8-15.

Bells and St.
Sava's
Cathedral,
Belgrade
PT36

2010, Aug. 2   *Perf. 13x13¾*
RA36 PT36 10d multi   .25 .25
Restoration of St. Sava's Catahedral. Obligatory on mail Aug. 2-Sept. 13.

Red Cross Solidarity
Week — PT37

Dated "2010"

2010, Sept. 14　　　**Perf. 13¾**
RA37 PT37 10d multi　　　.25　.25
Obligatory on mail Sept. 14-21. See Nos. RA42, RA52, RA61.

Children's Week — PT38

2010, Oct. 4　　　**Perf. 13¼**
RA38 PT38 10d multi　　　.30　.30
Obligatory on mail Oct. 4-10.

Dr. Dimitrije Miodragovic (1888-1959) — PT39

2011, Apr. 4
RA39 PT39 10d multi　　　.30　.30
Campaign against cancer. Obligatory on mail Apr. 4-30.

Red Cross Week Type of 2008
Dated "2011"

2011, May 8　　**Litho.**　　**Perf. 13¼**
RA40 PT17 10d multi　　　.30　.30
Obligatory on mail May 8-15.

Bells and St. Sava's Cathedral, Belgrade — PT40

2011, June 6　　　**Perf. 13¾**
RA41 PT40 10d multi　　　.30　.30
Restoration of St. Sava's Cathedral. Obligatory on mail, June 6-Aug. 20.

Red Cross Solidarity Week Type of 2010
Dated "2011"

2011, Sept. 14　　　**Perf. 13¼**
RA42 PT37 10d multi　　　.30　.30
Obligatory on mail Sept. 14-21.

Children's Week — PT41

2011, Oct. 3
RA43 PT41 10d multi　　　.30　.30
Obligatory on mail Oct. 3-9.

UNICEF — PT42

2011, Nov. 21
RA44 PT42 10d blue & black　　.30　.30
Obligatory on mail Nov. 21-27.

Refugee Assistance — PT43

2011, Dec. 19
RA45 PT43 10d multi　　　.25　.25
Obligatory on mail Dec. 19-25.

European Wrestling Championships, Belgrade — PT45

2012, Feb. 27　　**Litho.**　　**Perf. 13¼**
RA47 PT45 10d multi　　　.25　.25
Obligatory on mail Feb. 27.

Aleksije Milosavljevic (1919-2002), Physician — PT46

2012, Mar. 26　　**Litho.**　　**Perf. 13½**
RA48 PT46 10d multi　　　—　—
Obligatory on mail Mar. 26-Apr. 14.

St. Sava's Cathedral, Belgrade — PT48

2012, June 11　　**Litho.**　　**Perf. 13¾**
RA51 PT48 10d multi　　　—　—
Obligatory on mail June 11-Aug. 31.

Red Cross Solidarity Week Type of 2010

2012, Sept. 14　　**Litho.**　　**Perf. 13¼**
Dated "2012"
RA52 PT37 10d multi　　　.25　.25
Obligatory on mail Sept. 14-21.

Children's Week — PT49

2012, Oct. 1　　**Litho.**　　**Perf. 13¼**
RA53 PT49 10d multi　　　.25　.25
Obligatory on mail Oct. 1-7.

National Library, 180th Anniv. — PT50

2012, Oct. 29　　**Litho.**　　**Perf. 13¾**
RA54 PT50 10d multi　　　.25　.25
Obligatory on mail Oct. 29-Nov. 17.

European Women's Handball Championships, Serbia — PT51

2012, Dec. 4　　**Litho.**　　**Perf. 13¾**
RA55 PT51 10d multi　　　.25　.25
Obligatory on mail Dec. 4-16.

Refugee Assistance — PT52

2013, Jan. 30　　**Litho.**　　**Perf. 13¼**
RA56 PT52 10d multi　　　.25　.25
Obligatory on mail Jan. 30-Feb. 14.

Dr. Zlatko Merkas (1920-98), Radiologist — PT53

2013, Apr. 10　　**Litho.**　　**Perf. 13¼**
RA57 PT53 10d multi　　　.25　.25
Campaign against cancer. Obligatory on mail Apr. 10-30.

Red Cross Week Type of 2008
2013, May 8　　**Litho.**　　**Perf. 13¾**
Dated "2012"
RA58 PT17 10d multi　　　.25　.25
Obligatory on mail May 6-15.

2013 World Cadet Wrestling Championships, Zrenjanin — PT54

2013, May 20　　**Litho.**　　**Perf. 13¾**
RA59 PT54 10d multi　　　.25　.25
Obligatory on mail May 20-26.

St. Sava's Cathedral, Belgrade — PT55

2013, June 18　　**Litho.**　　**Perf. 13¾**
RA60 PT55 10d multi　　　.25　.25
Obligatory on mail June 18-Aug. 31.

Red Cross Solidarity Week Type of 2010

2013, Sept. 14　　**Litho.**　　**Perf. 13¼**
Dated "2013"
RA61 PT37 10d multi　　　.25　.25
Obligatory on mail Sept. 14-21.

Children's Week — PT56

2013, Oct. 7　　**Litho.**　　**Perf. 13¼**
RA62 PT56 10d multi　　　.25　.25
Obligatory on mail Oct. 7-14.

2013 Women's World Handball Championships, Serbia — PT57

2013, Nov. 4　　**Litho.**　　**Perf. 13¼**
RA63 PT57 10d multi　　　.25　.25
Obligatory on mail Nov. 4-10.

Renovation of National Library, 40th Anniv. — PT58

2013, Nov. 18　　**Litho.**　　**Perf. 13¾**
RA64 PT58 10d multi　　　.25　.25
Obligatory on mail Nov. 18-Dec. 12.

Environmental Protection — PT59

2014, Feb. 10　　**Litho.**　　**Perf. 13¼**
RA65 PT59 10d multi　　　.25　.25
Obligatory on mail Feb. 10-23.

2014 European Men's Rowing Championships, Belgrade — PT60

2014, Mar. 10　　**Litho.**　　**Perf. 13¾**
RA66 PT60 10d multi　　　.25　.25
Obligatory on mail Mar. 10-16.

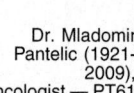

Dr. Mladomir Pantelic (1921-2009), Oncologist — PT61

2014, Apr. 9　　**Litho.**　　**Perf. 13¼**
RA67 PT61 10d multi　　　.25　.25
Campaign against cancer. Obligatory on mail Apr. 9-30.

Tour de Serbie Bicycle Race — PT62

2014, June 9　　**Litho.**　　**Perf. 13¾**
RA68 PT62 10d multi　　　.25　.25

St. Sava's Cathedral, Belgrade — PT63

2014, June 16　　**Litho.**　　**Perf. 13¾**
RA69 PT63 10d multi　　　.25　.25

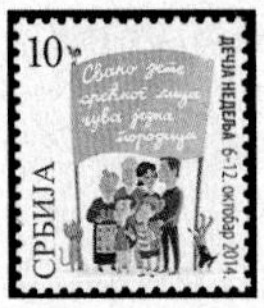

Children's Week — PT64

2014, Oct. 6 Litho. *Perf. 13¼*

RA70	PT64	10d multi	.25	.25

Obligatory on mail Oct. 6-12.

ISSUED UNDER AUSTRIAN OCCUPATION

100 Heller = 1 Krone

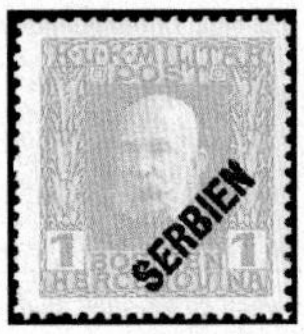

Stamps of Bosnia, 1912-14, Overprinted

1916 Unwmk. *Perf. 12½*

1N1	A23	1h olive green	2.25	5.25
1N2	A23	2h brt blue	2.25	5.25
1N3	A23	3h claret	2.25	5.25
1N4	A23	5h green	.40	.75
1N5	A23	6h dk gray	1.50	3.75
1N6	A23	10h rose carmine	.40	.75
1N7	A23	12h dp olive grn	.80	2.25
1N8	A23	20h orange brown	.80	1.40
1N9	A23	25h ultra	.80	2.25
1N10	A23	30h orange red	.80	2.25
1N11	A24	35h myrtle grn	.80	2.25
1N12	A24	40h dk violet	.80	2.25
1N13	A24	45h olive brown	.80	2.25
1N14	A24	50h slate blue	.80	2.25
1N15	A24	60h brown violet	.80	2.25
1N16	A24	72h dark blue	.80	2.25
1N17	A25	1k brn vio, *straw*	1.50	2.25
1N18	A25	2k dk gray, *bl*	1.50	2.25
1N19	A26	3k carmine, *grn*	1.50	2.25
1N20	A26	5k dk vio, *gray*	1.50	2.25
1N21	A25	10k dk ultra, *gray*	15.00	30.00
		Nos. 1N1-1N21 (21)	38.05	81.65

Stamps of Bosnia, 1912-14, Overprinted "SERBIEN" Horizontally at Bottom

1916

1N22	A23	1h olive green	8.00	19.00
1N23	A23	2h bright blue	8.00	19.00
1N24	A23	3h claret	8.00	19.00
1N25	A23	5h green	.50	3.00
1N26	A23	6h dark gray	8.00	19.00
1N27	A23	10h rose carmine	.50	3.00
1N28	A23	12h dp olive grn	8.00	19.00
1N29	A23	20h orange brn	8.00	19.00
1N30	A23	25h ultra	8.00	19.00
1N31	A23	30h orange red	8.00	19.00
1N32	A24	35h myrtle green	8.00	19.00
1N33	A24	40h dark violet	8.00	19.00
1N34	A24	45h olive brown	8.00	19.00
1N35	A24	50h slate blue	8.00	19.00
1N36	A24	60h brown violet	8.00	19.00
1N37	A24	72h dark blue	8.00	19.00
1N38	A25	1k brn vio, *straw*	19.00	40.00
1N39	A25	2k dk gray, *bl*	19.00	40.00
1N40	A26	3k carmine, *grn*	22.50	47.50
1N41	A26	5k dk vio, *gray*	27.50	60.00
1N42	A25	10k dk ultra, *gray*	52.50	100.00
		Nos. 1N22-1N42 (21)	253.50	559.50

Nos. 1N22-1N42 were prepared in 1914, at the time of the 1st Austrian occupation of Serbia. They were not issued at that time because of the retreat. The stamps were put on sale in 1916, at the same time as Nos. 1N1-1N21.

ISSUED UNDER GERMAN OCCUPATION

In occupied Serbia, authority was ostensibly in the hands of a government created by the former Yugoslav General, Milan Nedich, supported by the Chetniks, a nationalist organization which turned fascist. Actually the German military ran the country.

Types of Yugoslavia, 1939-40, Overprinted in Black

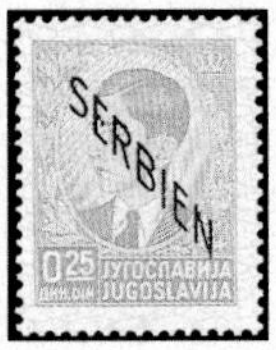

1941 Unwmk. Typo. *Perf. 12½*

Paper with colored network

2N1	A16	25p blk *(lt grn)*	.30	*7.50*
2N2	A16	50p org *(pink)*	.30	3.75
2N3	A16	1d yel grn *(lt grn)*	.30	3.75
2N4	A16	1.50d red *(pink)*	.30	3.75
2N5	A16	2d dp mag *(pink)*	.30	3.75
2N6	A16	3d dl red brn *(pink)*	1.10	*30.00*
2N7	A16	4d ultra *(lt grn)*	.75	*6.00*
2N8	A16	5d dk bl *(lt grn)*	1.10	*15.00*
2N9	A16	5.50d dk vio brn *(pink)*	1.10	*15.00*
2N10	A16	6d sl bl *(pink)*	1.10	*15.00*
2N11	A16	8d sep *(lt grn)*	1.50	*22.50*
2N12	A16	12d brt vio *(lt grn)*	1.50	*22.50*
2N13	A16	16d dl vio *(pink)*	2.10	*75.00*
2N14	A16	20d bl *(lt grn)*	3.50	*275.00*
2N15	A16	30d brt pink *(lt grn)*	13.50	*1,000.*
		Nos. 2N1-2N15 (15)	28.75	*1,498.*
		Set, never hinged	72.50	

Double overprints exist on 50p, 1d, 5d, 5.50d and 12d. Value, $250.

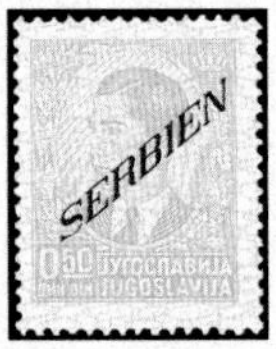

Stamps of Yugoslavia, 1939-40, Overprinted in Black

Paper with colored network

2N16	A16	25p blk *(lt grn)*	.25	*22.50*
2N17	A16	50p org *(pink)*	.25	*5.25*
2N18	A16	1d yel grn *(lt grn)*	.25	*5.25*
2N19	A16	1.50d red *(pink)*	.25	*5.25*
2N20	A16	2d dp mag *(pink)*	.25	*5.25*
2N21	A16	3d dl red brn *(pink)*	.60	*20.00*
2N22	A16	4d ultra *(lt grn)*	.65	*5.25*
2N23	A16	5d dk bl *(lt grn)*	.65	*9.75*
2N24	A16	5.50d dk vio brn *(pink)*	1.00	*20.00*
2N25	A16	6d sl bl *(pink)*	1.00	*20.00*
2N26	A16	8d sep *(lt grn)*	1.25	*30.00*
2N27	A16	12d brt vio *(lt grn)*	1.75	*30.00*
2N28	A16	16d dl vio *(pink)*	1.75	*97.50*
2N29	A16	20d bl *(lt grn)*	1.75	*300.00*
2N30	A16	30d brt pink *(lt grn)*	9.00	*975.00*
		Nos. 2N16-2N30 (15)	20.65	*1,551.*
		Set, never hinged	47.50	

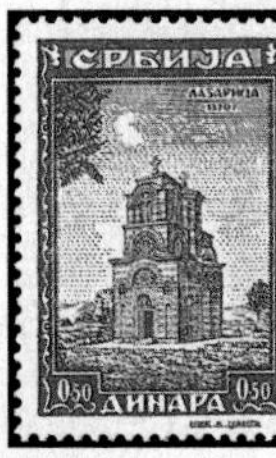

Lazaritza Monastery — OS1

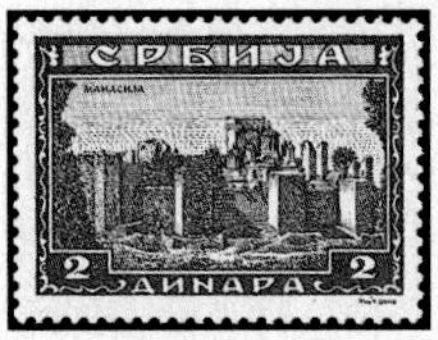

Ruins of Manassia Monastery OS4

Designs: 1d, Kalenica Monastery. 1.50d, Ravanica Monastery. 3d, Ljubostinja Monastery. 4d, Sopocane Monastery. 7d, Tsitsa Monastery. 12d, Goriak Monastery. 16d, Studenica Monastery.

1942-43 Typo. *Perf. 11½*

2N31	OS1	50p brt violet	.25	*.40*
2N32	OS1	1d red	.25	*.40*
2N33	OS1	1.50d red brn	.75	*5.25*
2N34	OS1	1.50d green ('43)	.25	*.40*
2N35	OS4	2d dl rose violet	.25	*.40*
2N36	OS4	3d brt blue	.75	*5.25*
2N37	OS4	3d rose pink ('43)	.25	*.40*
2N38	OS4	4d ultra	.25	*.40*
2N39	OS4	7d dk slate grn	.25	*.40*
2N40	OS1	12d lake	.25	*2.50*
2N41	OS1	16d grnsh blk	1.00	*3.00*
		Nos. 2N31-2N41 (11)	4.50	*18.80*
		Set, never hinged	5.25	

For surcharges see Nos. 2NB29-2NB37.

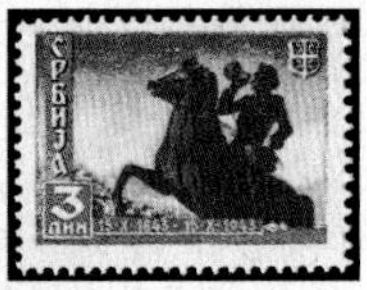

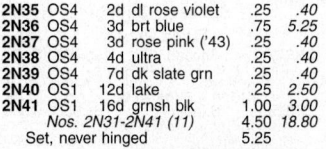

Post Rider — OS10

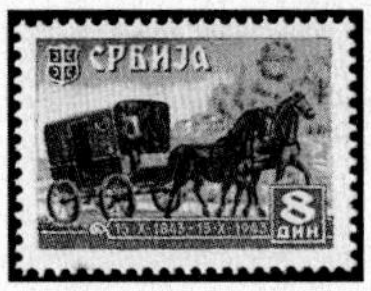

Post Wagon — OS11

9d, Mail train. 30d, Mail truck. 50d, Mail plane.

1943, Oct. 15 Photo. *Perf. 12½*

2N42	OS10	3d copper red & gray lilac	.80	*4.50*
2N43	OS11	8d vio rose & gray	.80	*4.50*
2N44	OS10	9d dk bl grn & sep	.80	*4.50*
2N45	OS10	30d chnt & sl grn	.80	*4.50*
2N46	OS10	50d dp bl & red brn	.80	*4.50*
		Nos. 2N42-2N46 (5)	4.00	*22.50*
		Set, never hinged	8.00	

Centenary of postal service in Serbia. Printed in sheets of 24 containing 4 of each stamp and 4 labels.

OCCUPATION SEMI-POSTAL STAMPS

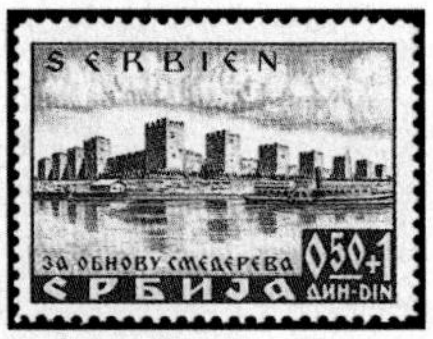

Smederevo Fortress on the Danube OSP1

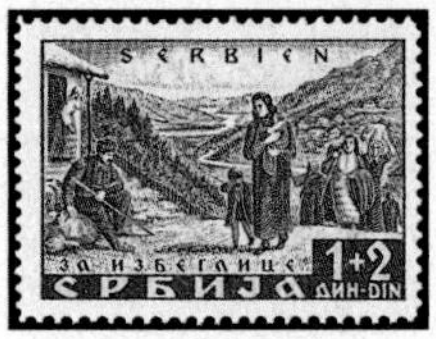

Refugees OSP2

Perf. 11½x12½

1941, Sept. 22 Typo. Unwmk.

2NB1	OSP1	50p + 1d dk brn	.30	*1.60*
2NB2	OSP2	1d + 2d dk gray grn	.30	*2.00*
2NB3	OSP2	1.50d + 3d dp cl	.55	*3.50*
a.		Perf. 12½	4.25	*16.00*
		Never hinged	8.50	
2NB4	OSP1	2d + 4d dk bl	.80	*4.75*
		Nos. 2NB1-2NB4 (4)	1.95	*11.85*
		Set, never hinged	4.25	

Souvenir Sheets

2NB5		Sheet of 2	55.00	*450.00*
		Never hinged	110.00	
a.		OSP2 1d + 49d rose lake	19.00	*45.00*
b.		OSP1 2d + 48d gray	19.00	*45.00*

Imperf

2NB6		Sheet of 2	55.00	*450.00*
		Never hinged	110.00	
a.		OSP2 1d + 49d gray	19.00	*45.00*
b.		OSP1 2d + 48d rose lake	19.00	*45.00*

The surtax aided the victims of an explosion at Smederevo and was used for the reconstruction of the town.

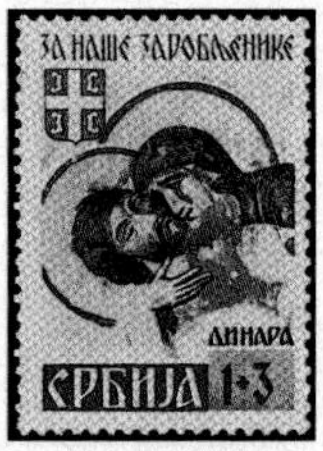

Christ and Virgin Mary — OSP4

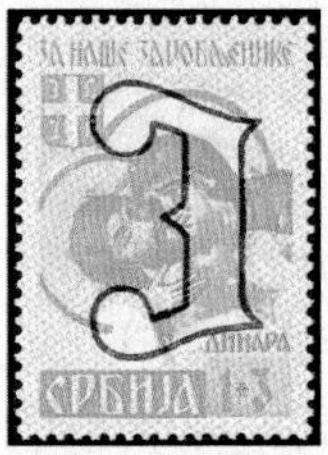

a

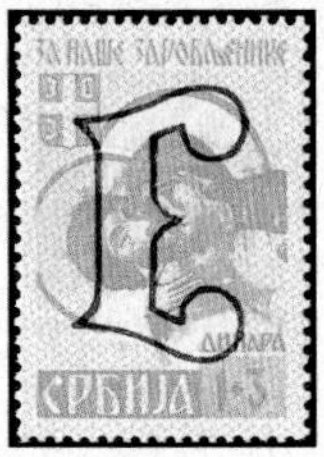

b

With Rose Burelage

1941, Dec. 5 Photo. *Perf. 11½*

2NB7	OSP4	50p + 1.50d brn red	.35	*6.25*
2NB8	OSP4	1d + 3d sl grn	.35	*6.25*
2NB9	OSP4	2d + 6d dp red	.35	*6.25*
2NB10	OSP4	4d + 12d dp bl	.35	*6.25*
		Nos. 2NB7-2NB10 (4)	1.40	*25.00*
		Set, never hinged	3.00	

With Symbol "a" Outlined in Cerise

2NB7a	OSP4	50p	11.00	*72.50*
2NB8a	OSP4	1d	11.00	*72.50*
2NB9a	OSP4	2d	11.00	*72.50*
2NB10a	OSP4	4d	11.00	*72.50*
		Nos. 2NB7a-2NB10a (4)	44.00	*290.00*
		Set, never hinged	87.50	

With Symbol "b" Outlined in Cerise

2NB7b	OSP4	50p	11.00	*72.50*
2NB8b	OSP4	1d	11.00	*72.50*
2NB9b	OSP4	2d	11.00	*72.50*
2NB10b	OSP4	4d	11.00	*72.50*
		Nos. 2NB7b-2NB10b (4)	44.00	*290.00*
		Set, never hinged	87.50	

Without Burelage

2NB7c	OSP4	50p	1.60	*20.00*
2NB8c	OSP4	1d	1.60	*20.00*
2NB9c	OSP4	2d	1.60	*20.00*
2NB10c	OSP4	4d	1.60	*20.00*
		Nos. 2NB7c-2NB10c (4)	6.40	*80.00*
		Set, never hinged	12.40	

These stamps were printed in sheets of 50, in 2 panes of 25. In the panes, #8, 12, 13, 14, 18, forming a cross, are without burelage. #7, 17 are type "a," #9, 19 type "b." 16 of the 25 stamps have overall burelage.

Surtax aided prisoners of war.

Thicker Paper, Without Burelage

1942, Mar. 26

2NB11	OSP4	50p + 1.50d brn	1.00	*4.00*
2NB12	OSP4	1d + 3d bl grn	1.00	*4.00*
2NB13	OSP4	2d + 6d mag	1.00	*4.00*
2NB14	OSP4	4d + 12d ultra	1.00	*4.00*
		Nos. 2NB11-2NB14 (4)	4.00	*16.00*
		Set, never hinged	8.50	

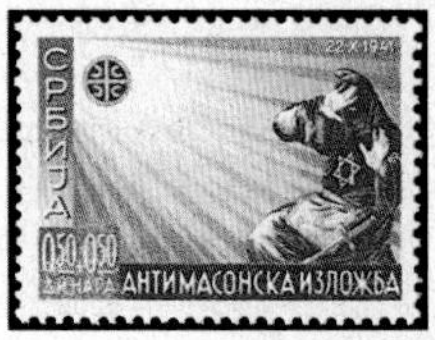

OSP5

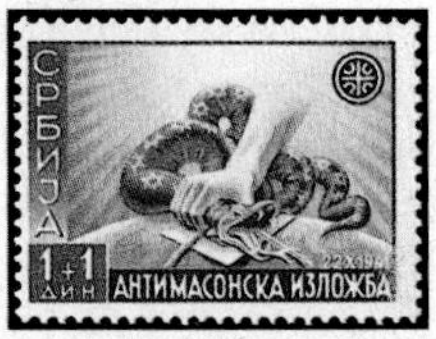

OSP6

OSP7

OOS1

OSP8

Designs: Anti-Masonic symbolisms.

1942, Jan. 1
2NB15	OSP5	50p + 50p yel brn	.30	3.50
2NB16	OSP6	1d + 1d dk grn	.30	3.50
2NB17	OSP7	2d + 2d rose car	.40	6.25
2NB18	OSP8	4d + 4d indigo	.40	6.25
	Nos. 2NB15-2NB18 (4)		1.40	19.50
	Set, never hinged		3.00	

Anti-Masonic Exposition of Oct. 22, 1941. The surtax was used for anti-Masonic propaganda.

Souvenir Sheets
Thick Paper
2NB27	Sheet of 2	50.00	3,000.
a.	OSP10 1.50d + 48.50d dk brn	16.00	1,350.
b.	OSP10 4d + 46d dp bl	16.00	1,350.
2NB28	Sheet of 2	55.00	3,000.
a.	OSP11 2d + 48d dk bl grn	18.00	1,350.
b.	OSP11 3d + 47d dp rose vio	18.00	1,350.

The sheets measure 150x110mm. The surtax aided war victims.

No. 2NC14

Stamps of 1942-43 Surcharged in Black

1943   Unwmk.   Typo.   *Perf. 12½*
2NO1	OOS1 3d red lilac	.80	2.00
	Never hinged	1.60	

Without colored network
2NC11	AP7	1d on 10d	3.00	200.00
2NC12	AP8	3d on 20d	3.00	200.00
2NC13	AP9	6d on 30d	3.00	200.00
2NC14	AP10	8d on 40d	6.00	400.00
2NC15	AP11	12d on 50d	10.00	850.00
	Nos. 2NC11-2NC15 (5)		25.00	1,850.
	Set, never hinged		60.00	

Mother and Children — OSP9

1942
2NB19	OSP9	2d + 6d brt pur	4.75	10.50
2NB20	OSP9	4d + 8d dp bl	4.75	10.50
2NB21	OSP9	7d + 13d dk bl grn	4.75	10.50
2NB22	OSP9	20d + 40d dp rose lake	4.75	10.50
	Nos. 2NB19-2NB22 (4)		19.00	42.00
	Set, never hinged		40.00	

Nos. 2NB19-2NB22 were issued in sheets of 16 consisting of a block of four of each denomination. The surtax aided war orphans.

Pale Green Burelage
1943, Dec. 11
2NB29	OS1	50p + 2d brt vio	.25	47.50
2NB30	OS1	1d + 3d red	.25	47.50
2NB31	OS1	1.50d + 4d dp grn	.25	47.50
2NB32	OS4	2d + 5d dl rose vio	.25	47.50
2NB33	OS4	3d + 7d rose pink	.25	47.50
2NB34	OS4	4d + 9d ultra	.25	47.50
2NB35	OS4	7d + 15d dk sl grn	.50	47.50
2NB36	OS1	12d + 25d lake	.50	225.00
2NB37	OS1	16d + 33d grnsh blk	1.10	350.00
	Nos. 2NB29-2NB37 (9)		3.60	907.50
	Set, never hinged		7.00	

The surtax aided victims of the bombing of Nisch.

Regular Issue of Yugoslavia, 1939-40, Surcharged in Black

1942   **Green Network**
2NC16	A16	2d on 2d dp mag	.25	2.00
2NC17	A16	4d on 4d ultra	.25	2.00
2NC18	A16	10d on 12d brt vio	.25	4.00
2NC19	A16	14d on 20d blue	.25	4.00
2NC20	A16	20d on 30d brt pink	.50	16.00
	Nos. 2NC16-2NC20 (5)		1.50	28.00
	Set, never hinged		3.00	

OCCUPATION AIR POST STAMPS

Types of Yugoslavia, 1937-40, Overprinted in Carmine or Maroon

Nos. 2NC1-2NC3, 2NC5-2NC7, 2NC9

OCCUPATION POSTAGE DUE STAMPS

Nos. 2NC4, 2NC8, 2NC10

Paper with colored network
1941   Unwmk.   *Perf. 12½*
2NC1	AP6	50p brown	4.00	175.00
2NC2	AP7	1d yel grn	4.00	175.00
2NC3	AP8	2d bl gray	4.00	175.00
2NC4	AP9	2.50d rose red (M)	4.00	175.00
2NC5	AP6	5d brn vio	4.00	175.00
2NC6	AP7	10d brn lake (M)	4.00	175.00
2NC7	AP8	20d dk green	4.00	175.00
2NC8	AP9	30d ultra	4.00	175.00
2NC9	AP10	40d Prus grn & pale grn (C)	9.50	625.00
2NC10	AP11	50d sl bl & gray bl (C)	13.50	1,100.
	Nos. 2NC1-2NC10 (10)		55.00	3,125.
	Set, never hinged		125.00	

Nos. 2NC1-2NC2 exist without network.

Types of Yugoslavia Similar to OD3-OD4 Overprinted

1941   Unwmk.   Typo.   *Perf. 12½*
2NJ1	OD3	50p violet	.80	40.00
2NJ2	OD3	1d lake	.80	40.00
2NJ3	OD3	2d dark blue	.80	40.00
2NJ4	OD3	3d red	1.25	60.00
2NJ5	OD4	4d lt blue	1.60	140.00
2NJ6	OD4	5d orange	1.60	140.00
2NJ7	OD4	10d violet	2.75	350.00
2NJ8	OD4	20d green	6.75	950.00
	Nos. 2NJ1-2NJ8 (8)		16.35	1,760.
	Set, never hinged		32.50	

Broken Sword — OSP10

OD3   OD4

1942   *Perf. 12½*
2NJ9	OD3	1d mar & grn	1.25	8.00
2NJ10	OD3	2d dk bl & red	1.25	8.00
2NJ11	OD3	3d ver & bl	1.25	12.00
2NJ12	OD4	4d blue & red	1.25	12.00
2NJ13	OD4	5d orange & bl	1.60	16.00
2NJ14	OD4	10d violet & red	1.60	24.00
2NJ15	OD4	20d green & red	8.00	95.00
	Nos. 2NJ9-2NJ15 (7)		16.20	175.00
	Set, never hinged		32.50	

Wounded Flag-bearer OSP11

Designs: 1.50d+48.50d, Broken sword. 3d+5d, 2d+48d, Wounded soldier. 3d+47d, Wounded flag-bearer. 4d+10d, 4d+46d, Tending casualty.

1943
2NB23	OSP10	1.50d + 1.50d dk brn	1.00	3.25
2NB24	OSP11	2d + 3d dk bl grn	1.00	3.25
2NB25	OSP11	3d + 5d dp rose vio	2.00	4.75
2NB26	OSP10	4d + 10d dp bl	2.00	5.75
	Nos. 2NB23-2NB26 (4)		6.00	17.00
	Set, never hinged		13.00	

Same Surcharged in Maroon or Carmine

No. 2NC13

OD5

2NJ16	OD5	50p black	.75	6.25
2NJ17	OD5	3d violet	.75	6.25
2NJ18	OD5	4d blue	.75	6.25
2NJ19	OD5	5d dk slate grn	.75	6.25
2NJ20	OD5	6d orange	1.25	16.00
2NJ21	OD5	10d red	1.60	20.00
2NJ22	OD5	20d ultra	4.00	60.00
	Nos. 2NJ16-2NJ22 (7)		9.85	121.00
	Set, never hinged		22.50	

SEYCHELLES

sā-'shel̦z̦

LOCATION — A group of islands in the Indian Ocean, off the coast of Africa north of Madagascar.
GOVT. — Republic
AREA — 175 sq. mi.
POP. — 79,164 (1999 est.)
CAPITAL — Victoria

The islands were attached to the British colony of Mauritius from 1810 to 1903, when they became a separate colony. Seychelles achieved internal self-government in October 1975 and independence on June 29, 1976.

100 Cents = 1 Rupee

Catalogue values for unused stamps in this country are for Never Hinged items, beginning with Scott 149 in the regular postage section and Scott J1 in the postage due section.

Watermark

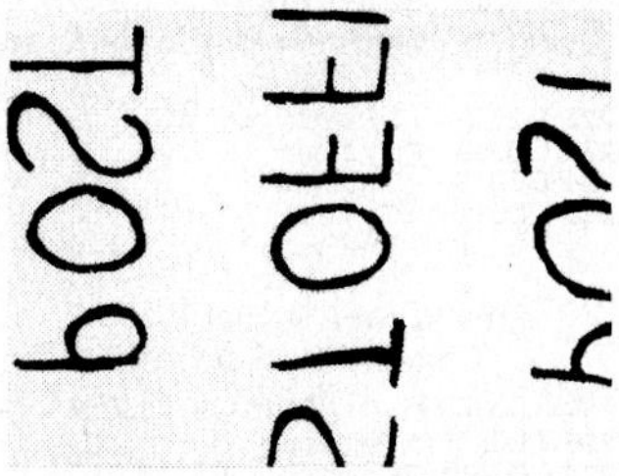

Wmk. 380 — "POST OFFICE"

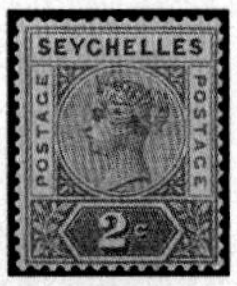

Queen Victoria — A1

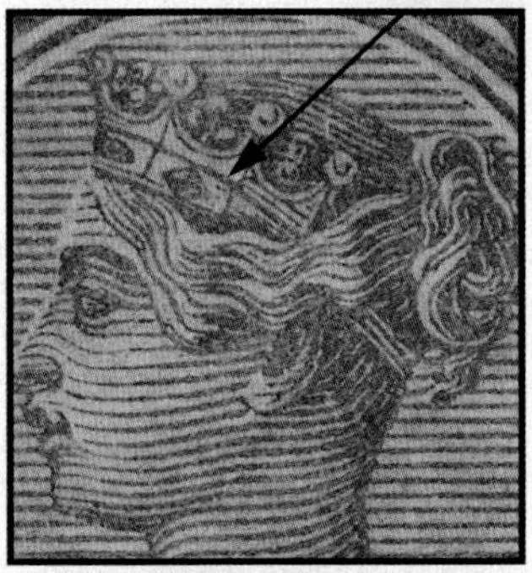

Die I

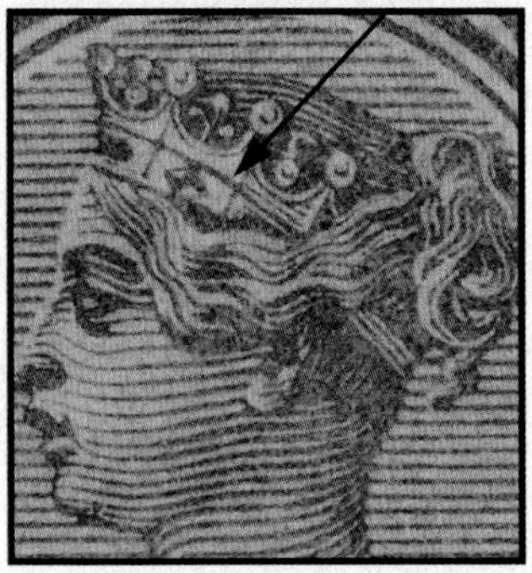

Die II

Two dies of 2c, 4c, 8c, 10c, 13c, 16c:

Die I — Shading lines at right of diamond in tiara band.

Die II — No shading lines in this rectangle.

1890-1900 Typo. Wmk. 2 *Perf. 14*

1	A1	2c grn & rose (II)	3.50	1.25
a.		Die I	7.00	18.00
2	A1	2c org brn & grn ('00)	2.50	1.75
3	A1	3c dk vio & org ('93)	2.00	.75
4	A1	4c car rose & grn (II)	3.50	1.75
a.		Die I	45.00	17.00
5	A1	6c car rose ('00)	4.50	.75
6	A1	8c brn vio & ultra (II)	15.00	2.50
a.		8c brn vio & bl (I)	15.00	4.50
7	A1	10c ultra & brn (II)	15.00	4.25
a.		10c bl & brn (I)	13.00	32.00
8	A1	12c ol gray & grn ('93)	3.50	.85
9	A1	13c slate & blk (II)	5.00	2.50
a.		Die I	8.00	17.00
10	A1	15c ol grn & vio ('93)	6.00	2.75
11	A1	15c ultra ('00)	11.00	7.00
12	A1	16c org brn & bl (I)	12.00	5.50
a.		16c org brn & ultra (II)	52.50	14.50
13	A1	18c ultra ('97)	10.00	1.50
14	A1	36c brn & rose ('97)	45.00	7.00
15	A1	45c brn & rose ('93)	30.00	45.00
16	A1	48c ocher & green	25.00	15.00
17	A1	75c yel & pur ('00)	70.00	87.50
18	A1	96c violet & car	67.50	60.00
19	A1	1r vio & red ('97)	16.00	6.50
20	A1	1.50r blk & rose ('00)	90.00	110.00
21	A1	2.25r vio & grn ('00)	125.00	110.00
		Nos. 1-21 (21)	562.00	474.10

Numerals of 75c, 1r, 1.50r and 2.25r of type A1 are in color on plain tablet.

For surcharges see Nos. 22-37.

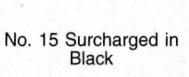

Surcharged in Black

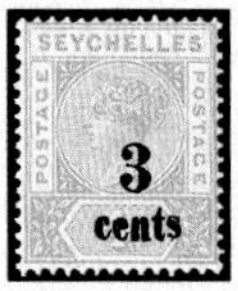

1893

22	A1	3c on 4c car rose & grn (II)	1.50	2.00
a.		Inverted surcharge	375.00	450.00
b.		Double surcharge	600.00	
d.		Pair, one without surcharge	14,000.	
23	A1	12c on 16c org brn & ultra (II)	21.00	3.50
a.		12c on 16c org brn & bl (I)	6.50	7.50
b.		Inverted surcharge (I)	575.00	
d.		Double surcharge (I)	15,750.	11,000.
e.		Double surcharge (II)	5,500.	5,500.
24	A1	15c on 16c org brn & ultra (II)	23.00	4.00
a.		15c on 16c org brn & bl (I)	12.00	17.50
b.		Inverted surcharge (I)	400.00	375.00
c.		Inverted surcharge (II)	1,100.	1,250.
d.		Double surcharge (I)	1,500.	1,500.
e.		Double surcharge (II)	825.00	875.00
f.		Triple surcharge (II)	5,000.	
25	A1	45c on 48c ocher & grn	35.00	7.00
26	A1	90c on 96c vio & car	70.00	45.00
		Nos. 22-26 (5)	150.50	61.50

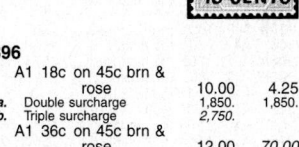

No. 15 Surcharged in Black

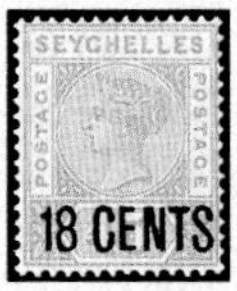

1896

27	A1	18c on 45c brn & rose	10.00	4.25
a.		Double surcharge	1,850.	1,850.
b.		Triple surcharge	2,750.	
28	A1	36c on 45c brn & rose	12.00	70.00
a.		Double surcharge	1,850.	

Surcharged in Black

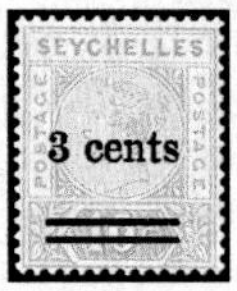

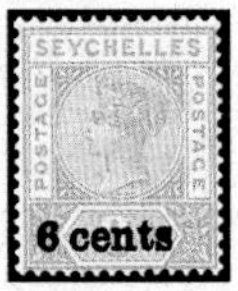

1901

29	A1	3c on 10c bl & brn (II)	2.25	.90
a.		Double surcharge	950.00	
b.		Triple surcharge	3,250.	
30	A1	3c on 16c org brn & ultra (II)	6.00	8.50
a.		"3 cents" omitted (II)	675.00	675.00
b.		Inverted surcharge (II)	800.00	800.00
c.		Double surcharge (II)	625.00	650.00
31	A1	3c on 36c brn & rose	1.75	1.10
a.		Without bars	—	—
b.		Double surcharge	950.00	1,100.
c.		"3 cents" omitted	800.00	850.00
32	A1	6c on 8c brn vio & ultra (II)	6.00	4.00
a.		Inverted surcharge	800.00	925.00
		Nos. 29-32 (4)	16.00	14.50

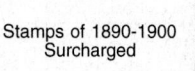

Stamps of 1890-1900 Surcharged

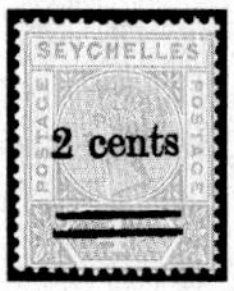

1902, June

33	A1	2c on 4c car rose & grn (II)	3.75	3.50
34	A1	30c on 75c yel & pur	2.25	5.50
a.		Narrow "0" in "30"	12.50	57.50
35	A1	30c on 1r vio & red	18.00	47.50
a.		Narrow "0" in "30"	37.50	110.00
b.		Double surcharge	1,750.	
36	A1	45c on 1r vio & red	8.50	60.00
37	A1	45c on 2.25r vio & grn	52.50	160.00
a.		Narrow "5" in "45"	250.00	450.00
		Nos. 33-37 (5)	85.00	276.50

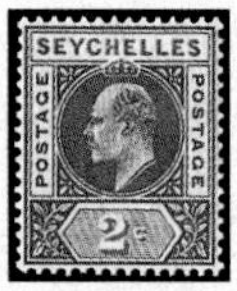

King Edward VII — A6

Numerals of 75c, 1.50r and 2.25r of type A6 are in color on plain tablet.

1903, May 26 Typo. Wmk. 2

38	A6	2c red brn & grn	2.25	2.50
39	A6	3c green	1.25	1.60
40	A6	6c carmine rose	3.50	1.60
41	A6	12c ol gray & grn	3.75	3.25
42	A6	15c ultra	5.00	3.25
43	A6	18c pale yel grn & rose	5.25	8.25
44	A6	30c purple & grn	8.75	15.00
45	A6	45c brown & rose	8.75	15.00
46	A6	75c yel & pur	12.50	35.00
47	A6	1.50r black & rose	55.00	87.50
48	A6	2.25r red vio & grn	50.00	110.00
		Nos. 38-48 (11)	156.00	282.95

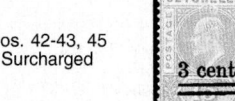

Nos. 42-43, 45 Surcharged

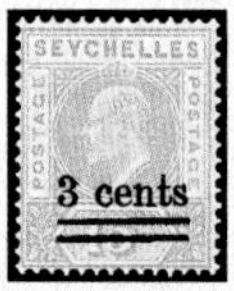

1903

49	A6	3c on 15c	1.40	4.25
50	A6	3c on 18c	4.00	52.50
51	A6	3c on 45c	4.25	4.25
		Nos. 49-51 (3)	9.65	61.00

Type of 1903

1906 Wmk. 3

52	A6	2c red brn & grn	1.90	5.50
53	A6	3c green	1.90	1.90
54	A6	6c car rose	2.50	1.00
55	A6	12c ol gray & grn	4.00	4.00
56	A6	15c ultra	4.00	2.50
57	A6	18c pale yel grn & rose	4.00	8.00
58	A6	30c purple & grn	7.75	10.00
59	A6	45c brown & rose	4.00	10.00
60	A6	75c yellow & pur	11.00	67.50
61	A6	1.50r black & rose	65.00	72.50
62	A6	2.25r red vio & grn	55.00	72.50
		Nos. 52-62 (11)	161.05	255.40

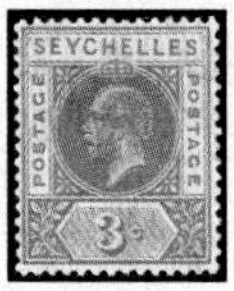

King George V — A7

Numerals of 75c, 1.50r and 2.25r of type A7 are in color on plain tablet.

1912 *Perf. 14*

63	A7	2c org brn & grn	1.00	7.50
64	A7	3c green	4.50	.70
65	A7	6c car rose	4.75	2.00
66	A7	12c ol gray & grn	1.50	5.00
67	A7	15c ultra	4.00	1.75
68	A7	18c pl yel grn & rose	3.50	9.00
69	A7	30c pur & grn	12.00	2.25
70	A7	45c brn & rose	3.00	50.00
71	A7	75c yell & pur	3.25	6.00
72	A7	1.50r blk & rose	11.00	1.10
73	A7	2.25r vio & grn	75.00	2.75
		Nos. 63-73 (11)	123.50	88.05

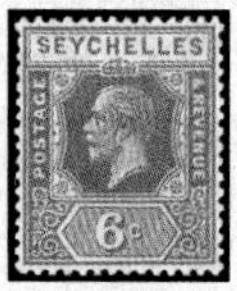

King George V — A8

For description of dies I and II see Dies of British Colonial Stamps in the Table of Contents.

The 5c of type A8 has a colorless numeral on solid-color tablet. Numerals of 9c, 20c, 25c, 50c, 75c, and 1r to 5r of type A8 are in color on plain tablet.

1917-20 Die I

74	A8	2c org brn & grn	.55	3.00
75	A8	3c green	2.25	1.40
76	A8	5c brown ('20)	4.00	12.00
77	A8	6c carmine rose	4.25	1.60
78	A8	12c gray	2.50	1.10
79	A8	15c ultra	1.90	1.60
80	A8	18c violet, *yel*	4.25	60.00
a.		Die II ('20)	3.75	25.00
81	A8	25c blk & red, *yel* ('20)	3.75	47.50
a.		Die II ('20)	3.75	20.00
82	A8	30c dull vio & ol grn	1.60	12.00
83	A8	45c dull vio & org	3.50	42.50
84	A8	50c dull vio & blk ('20)	11.00	55.00
85	A8	75c blk, *bl grn*, ol back	1.75	27.50
a.		75c blk, *emer* (Die II) ('20)	1.50	23.00
86	A8	1r dl vio & red ('20)	21.00	70.00
87	A8	1.50r vio & bl, *bl*	10.00	57.50
a.		Die II ('20)	22.00	35.00
88	A8	2.25r gray grn & dp vio	55.00	160.00
89	A8	5r gray grn & ultra ('20)	140.00	275.00
		Nos. 74-89 (16)	267.30	827.70

Die II

1921-32 Ordinary Paper Wmk. 4

91	A8	2c org brn & grn	.30	.25
92	A8	3c green	1.90	.25
93	A8	3c black ('22)	1.10	.35
94	A8	4c green ('22)	1.10	2.75
95	A8	4c ol grn & rose red ('28)	7.25	19.00
96	A8	5c dk brown	1.25	6.00
97	A8	6c car rose	3.00	10.00
98	A8	6c violet ('22)	1.25	.25
99	A8	9c rose red ('27)	3.50	4.75
100	A8	12c gray	3.00	.25
a.		Die I ('32)	25.00	.65
101	A8	12c carmine ('22)	1.50	.35
102	A8	15c ultra	2.25	65.00
103	A8	15c yellow ('22)	1.10	3.00
104	A8	18c violet, *yel*	2.75	17.00
105	A8	20c ultra ('22)	1.60	.40

Chalky Paper

106	A8	25c blk & red, *yel* ('25)	3.00	25.00
107	A8	30c dull vio & ol grn	1.60	17.00
108	A8	45c dull vio & org	1.40	5.75
109	A8	50c dull vio & blk	2.75	2.50
110	A8	75c blk, *emer* ('24)	9.00	24.00
111	A8	1r dull vio & red	24.00	20.00
a.		Die I ('32)	12.00	37.50
112	A8	1.50r vio & bl, *bl* ('24)	15.00	25.00
113	A8	2.25r green & vio	19.00	16.00
114	A8	5r green & ultra	120.00	175.00
		Nos. 91-114 (24)	228.60	439.85

Common Design Types pictured following the introduction.

Silver Jubilee Issue
Common Design Type

1935, May 6 Engr. *Perf. 11x12*

118	CD301	6c black & ultra	1.25	3.00
119	CD301	12c indigo & grn	4.75	2.25
120	CD301	20c ultra & brown	3.50	3.75
121	CD301	1r brn vio & indigo	8.00	22.00
		Nos. 118-121 (4)	17.50	31.00
		Set, never hinged	30.00	

Coronation Issue
Common Design Type

1937, May 12 *Perf. 11x11½*

122	CD302	6c olive green	.30	.25
123	CD302	12c deep orange	.45	.55
124	CD302	20c deep ultra	.45	1.10
		Nos. 122-124 (3)	1.20	1.90
		Set, never hinged	2.00	

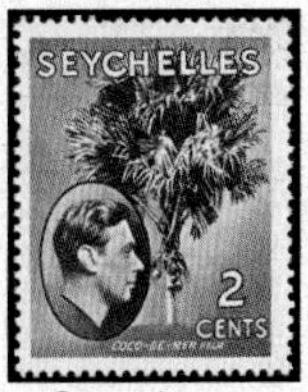

Coco-de-mer Palm — A9

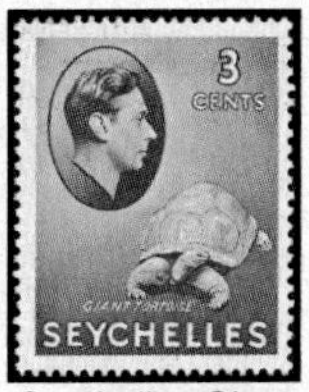

Seychelles Giant Tortoise — A10

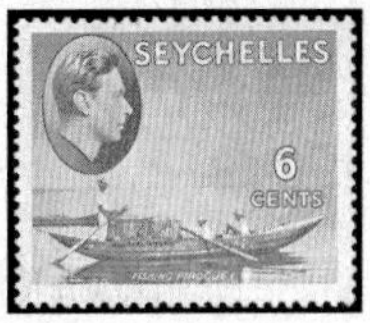

Fishing Canoe — A11

Ordinary or Chalky Paper

Perf. 13½x14½, 14½x13½

1938-41 Photo. Wmk. 4

125	A9	2c violet brown	.40	*1.75*
126	A10	3c green	5.50	2.50
127	A10	3c orange	.50	1.50
128	A11	6c orange	8.50	3.75
129b	A11	6c green	.45	*2.40*
130	A9	9c rose red	9.50	3.25
131	A9	9c peacock blue ('45)	4.25	3.25
132	A10	12c violet	30.00	1.75
133	A10	15c copper red	4.00	*4.25*
134	A9	18c rose lake	4.75	3.00
135	A11	20c brt bl ('41)	25.00	6.50
136	A11	20c ocher	1.90	*3.25*
137	A9	25c ocher	30.00	15.00
138	A10	30c rose lake	30.00	10.00
139	A9	30c bright blue	1.90	*5.50*
140	A11	45c brown	2.25	2.50
141	A9	50c dl lil ('49)	2.50	3.00
142	A10	75c gray blue	50.00	45.00
143	A10	75c dull violet	2.00	*5.00*
144	A11	1r yel grn	72.50	*70.00*
145	A11	1r gray	2.00	*5.00*
146	A9	1.50r ultra	3.75	*13.00*
147	A10	2.25r olive bister	16.00	*29.00*
148	A11	5r copper red	13.00	*11.00*
		Nos. 125-148 (24)	320.65	251.15
		Set, never hinged	600.00	

Issued: Nos. 126, 128, 132, 135, 137, 1/1; Nos. 125, 130, 138, 140-142, 144, 146-148, 2/10; others, 8/8/41.

See Nos. 158-169, 174-188.

For detailed listings, see the Scott Classic Specialized catalogue.

Catalogue values for unused stamps in this section, from this point to the end of the section, are for Never Hinged items.

Peace Issue

Common Design Type

Perf. 13½x14

1946, Sept. 23 Engr. Wmk. 4

149	CD303	9c light blue	.25	.25
150	CD303	30c dark blue	.30	.25

Silver Wedding Issue

Common Design Types

1948, Nov. 11 Photo. *Perf. 14x14½*

151	CD304	9c bright ultra	.25	.75

Engraved; Name Typographed

Perf. 11½x11

152	CD305	5r rose carmine	16.00	*45.00*

UPU Issue

Common Design Types

Perf. 13½, 11x11½

1949, Oct. 10 Engr.

153	CD306	18c red violet	.25	.25
154	CD307	50c dp rose violet	2.00	2.25
155	CD308	1r gray	.55	.35
156	CD309	2.25r olive	.45	*1.25*
		Nos. 153-156 (4)	3.25	4.10

Types of 1938-41 Redrawn and

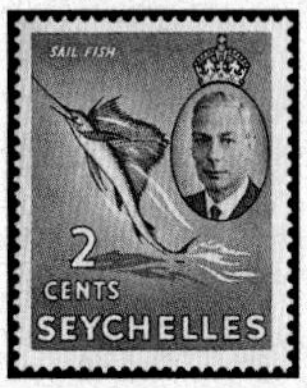

Sailfish — A12

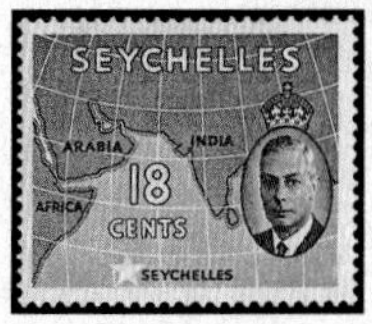

Map — A13

Perf. 14½x13½, 13½x14½

1952, Mar. 3 Photo. Wmk. 4

157	A12	2c violet	.75	.75
158	A10	3c orange	.75	.30
159	A9	9c peacock blue	.70	*1.75*
160	A11	15c yellow green	.60	*1.00*
161	A13	18c rose lake	1.75	.25
162	A11	20c ocher	2.00	1.50
163	A10	25c bright red	.80	2.25
164	A12	40c ultra	1.25	2.00
165	A11	45c violet brown	1.50	.35
166	A9	50c brt violet	1.40	1.75
167	A13	1r gray	4.75	4.25
168	A9	1.50r brt blue	11.00	*16.00*
169	A10	2.25r olive bister	17.50	*18.00*
170	A13	5r copper red	18.00	*19.00*
171	A12	10r green	25.00	*45.00*
		Nos. 157-171 (15)	87.75	*114.15*

The redrawn design shows a new portrait of King George VI surmounted by crown, as on type A12.

Nos. 157-170 exist with watermark 4a (error). See the *Scott Classic Specialized Catalogue of Stamps and Covers* for listings.

Coronation Issue

Common Design Type

1953, June 2 Engr. *Perf. 13½x13*

172	CD312	9c dark blue & blk	.80	.80

Types of 1938-52 with Portrait of Queen Elizabeth II

Perf. 14½x13½, 13½x14½

1954-56 Photo.

173	A12	2c violet	.25	.25
174	A10	3c orange	.25	.25
175	A9	9c peacock blue	.25	.25
176	A9	10c blue ('56)	.70	*2.25*
177	A11	15c yellow grn	2.50	.30
178	A13	18c rose lake	.25	.25
179	A11	20c ocher	1.50	.50
180	A10	25c bright red	2.50	1.25
181	A13	35c mag ('56)	6.50	1.75
182	A12	40c ultra	1.00	.25
183	A11	45c violet brn	.25	.25
184	A9	50c brt violet	.35	.80
185	A11	70c vio brn ('56)	7.50	2.25
186	A13	1r gray	1.75	.60
187	A9	1.50r brt blue	6.00	*10.00*
188	A10	2.25r olive bister	6.00	*8.50*
189	A13	5r copper red	18.00	10.00
190	A12	10r green	28.00	18.00
		Nos. 173-190 (18)	83.55	57.70

Issued: 10c, 35c, 70c, 9/15/56; others, 2/1/54.

For surcharge see No. 193.

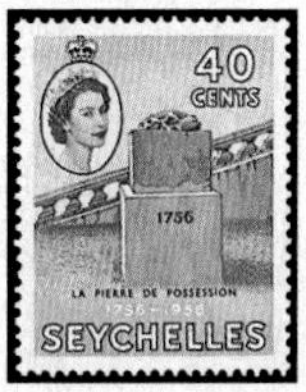

"Stone of Possession" — A14

Perf. 14½x14

1956, Nov. 15 Wmk. 4

191	A14	40c ultra	.25	.25
192	A14	1r gray black	.30	.30

Bicentenary of French colonization.

No. 183 Surcharged "5 cents" and Bars

1957, Sept. 16 *Perf. 13½x14½*

193	A11	5c on 45c violet brn	.50	.50
a.		Double surcharge	*550.00*	
b.		Thick bars omitted	*1,100.*	

The "c," "e" or "s" of surcharge may be found in italic.

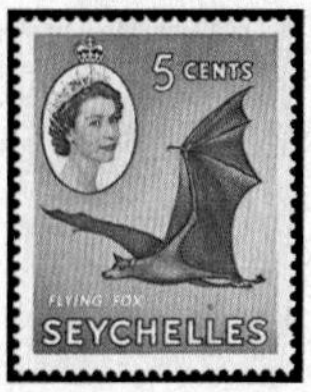

Flying Fox — A15

1957, Oct. 25 *Perf. 14½x13½*

194	A15	5c light violet	2.75	.30

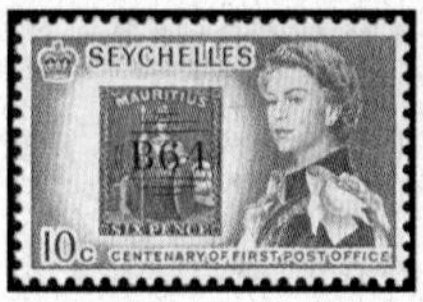

Mauritius Stamp of 1859 with Seychelles "B64" Cancellation A16

Engr. & Typo.

Perf. 11½x11

1961, Dec. 11 Wmk. 314

Stamp in Dull Blue & Black

195	A16	10c lilac	.30	.30
196	A16	35c dull green	.40	.40
197	A16	2.25r orange brown	1.25	1.25
		Nos. 195-197 (3)	1.95	1.95

1st post office in Victoria, Seychelles, cent.

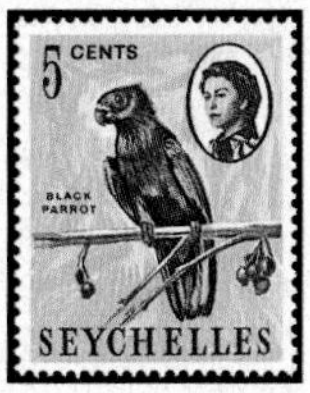

Black Parrot — A17

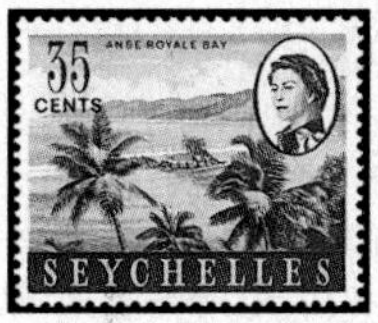

Anse Royal Bay — A18

Designs: 10c, Vanilla. 15c, Fisherman. 20c, Denis Island Lighthouse. 25c, Clock Tower, Victoria. 30c, 35c, Anse Royal Bay. 40c, Government House. 45c, Fishing boat. 50c, Cascade Church. 60c, Flying fox. 70c, 85c, Sailfish. 75c, Coco-de-mer palm. 1r, Cinnamon. 1.50r, Copra. 2.25r, Map of Indian Ocean. 3.50r, Settlers' homes. 5r, Regina Mundi Convent. 10r, Badge of Seychelles.

Perf. 14½x13½, 13½x14½

1962-69 Photo. Wmk. 314

Size: 24x31mm, 31x24mm

198	A17	5c multicolored	3.25	2.00
a.		Wmkd. sideways ('67)	.35	*1.75*
199	A17	10c multicolore	1.50	.25
a.		Wmkd. sideways ('68)	.30	.25
200	A17	15c multicolored	.35	.25
201	A17	20c multicolored	.40	.25
202	A17	25c multicolored	.50	.25
202A	A18	30c multicolored	8.50	*5.50*
203	A18	35c multicolored	2.00	2.25
204	A18	40c multicolored	.25	*1.00*
204A	A18	45c multicolore	3.75	*5.75*
205	A17	50c multicolored	.45	.30
b.		Wmkd. sideways ('69)	1.75	3.75
205A	A17	60c multicolored	2.00	.50
206	A17	70c multicolored	6.50	3.25
206A	A17	75c multicolored	2.75	*4.25*
206B	A17	85c multicolored	1.25	.45
207	A18	1r multicolored	.40	.25
208	A18	1.50r multicolored	5.50	*7.00*
209	A18	2.25r multicolored	5.50	8.00
210	A18	3.50r multicolored	2.50	*7.00*
211	A18	5r multicolored	5.00	2.75

Perf. 13x14

Size: 22½x39mm

212	A17	10r multicolored	14.00	4.00
		Nos. 198-212 (20)	66.35	55.25

Issued: 45c, 75c, 8/1/66; No. 198a, 2/7/67; 30c, 60c, 85c, 7/15/68; others 2/21/62.

The 60c and 85c have watermark sideways.

For surcharges and overprints see Nos. 216-217, 233-236, 241-243.

For overprints see British Indian Ocean Territory Nos. 1-15.

Freedom from Hunger Issue

Common Design Type

1963, June 4 *Perf. 14x14½*

213	CD314	70c lilac	.85	.35

Red Cross Centenary Issue

Common Design Type

1963, Sept. 2 Litho. *Perf. 13*

214	CD315	10c black & red	.25	.25
215	CD315	75c ultra & red	.85	.65

Nos. 203 and 206 Surcharged with New Value and Bars

Perf. 14x14½, 14½x14

1965, Apr. Photo. Wmk. 314

216	A18	45c on 35c	.25	.25
217	A17	75c on 70c	.60	.60

ITU Issue

Common Design Type

Perf. 11x11½

1965, June 1 Litho. Wmk. 314

218	CD317	5c orange & vio bl	.25	.25
219	CD317	1.50r red lil & apple grn	.65	.35

Intl. Cooperation Year Issue

Common Design Type

1965, Oct. 25 *Perf. 14½*

220	CD318	5c blue grn & claret	.25	.25
221	CD318	40c lt violet & green	.65	.40

Churchill Memorial Issue

Common Design Type

1966, Jan. 24 Photo. *Perf. 14*

Design in Black, Gold and Carmine Rose

222	CD319	5c bright blue	.25	.40
223	CD319	15c green	.35	.30
224	CD319	75c brown	1.00	.40
225	CD319	1.50r violet	1.60	2.50
		Nos. 222-225 (4)	3.20	3.60

World Cup Soccer Issue

Common Design Type

1966, July 1 Litho. *Perf. 14*

226	CD321	15c multicolored	.25	.25
227	CD321	1r multicolored	.60	.60

WHO Headquarters Issue

Common Design Type

1966, Sept. 20 Litho. *Perf. 14*

228	CD322	20c multicolored	.45	.30
229	CD322	50c multicolored	.80	.45

UNESCO Anniversary Issue

Common Design Type

1966, Dec. 1 Litho. *Perf. 14*

230	CD323	15c "Education"	.25	.25
231	CD323	1r "Science"	.55	.55
232	CD323	5r "Culture"	1.60	1.60
		Nos. 230-232 (3)	2.40	2.40

Nos. 200, 204A, 206A and 210 Overprinted "UNIVERSAL / ADULT / SUFFRAGE / 1967"

Perf. 14½x14, 14x14½

1967, Sept. 18 Photo. Wmk. 314

233	A17	15c multicolored	.25	.25
234	A18	45c brt blue & yel	.25	.25
235	A17	75c multicolored	.25	.25
236	A18	3.50r multicolored	.25	*.50*
		Nos. 233-236 (4)	1.00	1.25

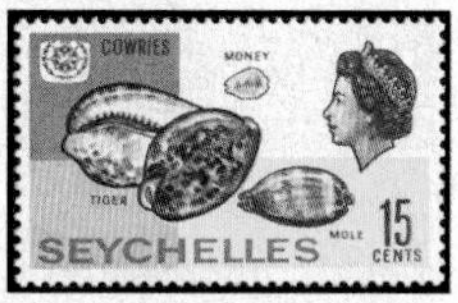

Cowries: Tiger, Mole, Money A19

Sea Shells (ITY Emblem and): 40c, Textile, betulinus and virgin cones. 1r, Arthritic spider conch. 2.25r, Triton and subulate auger.

Perf. 14x13½

1967, Dec. 4 Photo. Wmk. 314

237	A19	15c multicolored	.30	.25
238	A19	40c multicolored	.45	.25
239	A19	1r multicolored	.65	.40
240	A19	2.25r multicolored	1.10	1.10
		Nos. 237-240 (4)	2.50	2.00

Issued for International Tourist Year, 1967.

Nos. 204, 204A and 206A Surcharged
Perf. 14x14½, 14½x14

1968, Apr. 16   Photo.   Wmk. 314
241	A18	30c on 40c multicolored	.25	.25
242	A18	60c on 45c blue & yel	.25	.25
243	A17	85c on 75c multicolored	.30	.30
		Nos. 241-243 (3)	.80	.80

The surcharge on No. 241 includes 2 bars; on Nos. 242-243 it includes 3 bars and "CENTS."

Family, Rising Sun and Human Rights Flame A20

Perf. 14½x14
1968, Sept. 2   Litho.   Wmk. 314
244	A20	20c chocolate & multi	.25	.25
245	A20	50c vio blue & multi	.25	.25
246	A20	85c black & multi	.25	.25
247	A20	2.25r brown & multi	.25	1.25
		Nos. 244-247 (4)	1.00	2.00

International Human Rights Year.

First Landing on Praslin Island — A21

Designs: 50c, La Digue and La Curieuse at anchor, vert. 85c, Coco-de-mer and black parrot, vert. 2.25r, La Digue and La Curieuse under sail.

Litho.; Head Embossed in Gold
Perf. 14x14½
1968, Dec. 30   Wmk. 314
248	A21	20c multicolored	.30	.25
249	A21	50c dk blue, blk & red	.40	.35
250	A21	85c rose red & multi	1.00	.40
251	A21	2.25r ultra & multi	1.50	2.50
		Nos. 248-251 (4)	3.20	3.50

Landing on Praslin Island of the Chevalier Marion Dufresne expedition, 200th anniv.

Separation of Rocket and Spacecraft — A22

5c, Launching of Apollo XI, vert. 50c, Landing module & men on the moon. 85c, Seychelles tracking station. 2.25r, Moonscape & earth.

1969, Sept. 9   Litho.   Perf. 13½
252	A22	5c multicolored	.25	.25
253	A22	20c multicolored	.25	.25
254	A22	50c multicolored	.30	.25
255	A22	85c multicolored	.45	.35
256	A22	2.25r multicolored	.70	1.50
		Nos. 252-256 (5)	1.95	2.60

See note after US No. C76.

Lazare Picault Landing in 1741 — A23

History of Seychelles: 10c, US satellite tracking station. 15c, German cruiser Königsberg at Aldabra, 1915. 20c, British fleet refueling, St. Anne, 1939-45. 25c, Ashanti King Prempeh in exile, 1896. 30c, 40c, Stone of Possession placed, 1756. 50c, 65c, Pirates. 60c, Corsairs. 85c, 95c, Jet and airport. 1r, First capitulation of the French to the British, 1794. 1.50r, Battle between the sailing vessels

Sybille and Chiffone, 1801. 3.50r, Visit of Duke of Edinburgh, 1956. 5r, Chevalier Queau de Quincy. 10r, Map of Indian Ocean, 1574. 15r, Seychelles coat of arms.

Perf. 13x12½
1969-72   Litho.   Wmk. 314
257	A23	5c multicolored	.25	.25
258	A23	10c multicolored	.25	.25
259	A23	15c multicolored	3.00	2.25
260	A23	20c multicolored	2.00	.25
261	A23	25c multicolored	.25	.25
262	A23	30c multicolored	1.25	4.00
262A	A23	40c multicolored	3.00	1.25
263	A23	50c multicolored	.40	.25
264	A23	60c multicolored	1.25	1.50
264A	A23	65c multicolored	6.00	8.00
265	A23	85c multicolored	3.50	2.00
265A	A23	95c multicolored	5.50	3.25
266	A23	1r multicolored	.40	.25
267	A23	1.50r multicolored	2.00	2.25
268	A23	3.50r multicolored	1.25	2.25
269	A23	5r multicolored	1.25	3.00
270	A23	10r multicolored	2.75	8.00
271	A23	15r multicolored	4.50	14.00
		Nos. 257-271 (18)	38.80	53.25

Issued: 40, 65, 95c, 12/11/72; others, 11/3/69.
For overprints & surcharges see Nos. 294-298, 323-330, 361-369.

St. Anne Island, Ship and Gulls A24

Designs: 50c, Flying fish, island and ship. 85c, Map of Seychelles and compass rose. 3.50r, Anchor, chain on sea bottom.

1970, Apr. 27   Perf. 14
272	A24	20c multicolored	1.00	.60
273	A24	50c multicolored	.55	.45
274	A24	85c multicolored	.55	.45
275	A24	3.50r multicolored	.80	.80
		Nos. 272-275 (4)	2.90	2.30

Bicentenary of first settlement on St. Anne.

Girl and Eye Chart A25

Designs: 50c, Infant on scales and milk bottles. 85c, Mother and child, vert. 3.50r, Red Cross branch headquarters.

1970, Aug. 4   Litho.   Wmk. 314
276	A25	20c lt blue & multi	.35	.25
277	A25	50c multicolored	.50	.50
278	A25	85c multicolored	.70	.70
279	A25	3.50r multicolored	1.75	2.40
		Nos. 276-279 (4)	3.30	3.85

Centenary of British Red Cross Society.

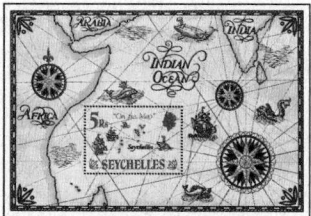

Pitcher Plant — A26

Flowers: 50c, Wild vanilla. 85c, Tropic-bird flower. 3.50r, Vare hibiscus.

1970, Dec. 29   Perf. 14½
280	A26	20c multicolored	.35	.25
281	A26	50c multicolored	.45	.45
282	A26	85c multicolored	1.00	1.00
283	A26	3.50r multicolored	3.50	2.25
a.		Souvenir sheet of 4, #280-283	9.00	13.00
		Nos. 280-283 (4)	5.30	3.95

Souvenir Sheet

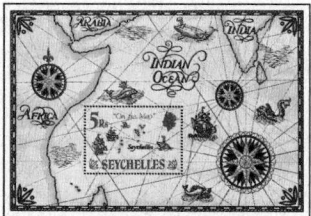

Map Showing Location of Seychelles — A27

Perf. 13½x14
1971, Apr. 20   Litho.   Wmk. 314
284	A27	5r yellow grn & multi	4.00	9.50

Issued to publicize Seychelles' location.

Consolidated Catalina Amphibian — A28

Designs: 5c, Piper Navajo, vert. 20c, Westland Wessex, vert. 60c, Grumman Albatross amphibian, vert. 85c, "G" class Short Brothers flying boat. 3.50r, Vickers supermarine "Walrus" amphibian.

Perf. 14x14½, 14½x14
1971, June 28   Litho.   Wmk. 314
285	A28	5c orange & multi	.25	.25
286	A28	20c purple & multi	.25	.25
287	A28	50c olive & multi	.65	.25
288	A28	60c sepia & multi	.80	.30
289	A28	85c brown & multi	1.10	.40
290	A28	3.50r blue & multi	7.00	3.00
		Nos. 285-290 (6)	10.05	4.45

Completion of Seychelles Airport.

Santa Claus, by Jean-Claude Waye Hive — A29

Christmas (Children's Drawings): 15c, Santa Claus riding a tortoise, by Edison Thérésine. 3.50r, Santa Claus on the seashore, by Isabelle Tirant.

1971, Oct. 12   Perf. 13½
291	A29	10c dark blue & multi	.25	.25
292	A29	15c dark green & multi	.25	.25
293	A29	3.50r violet & multi	.50	1.50
		Nos. 291-293 (3)	1.00	2.00

Nos. 262, 264-265 Surcharged with New Value and 5 Bars
1971, Dec. 21   Perf. 13x12½
294	A23	40c on 30c multicolored	.55	.75
295	A23	65c on 60c multicolored	.65	.90
296	A23	95c on 85c multicolored	.80	1.25
		Nos. 294-296 (3)	2.00	2.90

Nos. 260, 269 Overprinted in Black or Gold "ROYAL VISIT 1972"
1972, Mar. 21   Litho.   Wmk. 314
297	A23	20c multicolored	.25	.25
298	A23	5r multicolored (G)	1.40	2.50

Visit of Elizabeth II and Prince Philip.

Brush Warbler — A30

1972, July 15   Perf. 14x13½
299	A30	5c shown	1.00	.50
300	A30	20c Scops owl	2.50	.50
301	A30	50c Blue pigeons	2.75	.60
302	A30	65c Magpie robin	3.00	.65
303	A30	95c Paradise flycatchers	3.00	2.75
304	A30	3.50r Kestrel	8.00	12.00
a.		Souvenir sheet of 6, #299-304	37.50	40.00
		Nos. 299-304 (6)	20.25	17.00

Fireworks — A31

1972, Sept. 18   Litho.   Perf. 14
305	A31	10c shown	.30	.25
306	A31	15c Canoe race, horiz.	.30	.25
307	A31	25c Women in local costumes	.30	.25
308	A31	5r Water-skiing, horiz.	.80	1.00
		Nos. 305-308 (4)	1.70	1.75

Seychelles Festival 1972.

Silver Wedding Issue, 1972
Common Design Type

Design: Queen Elizabeth II, Prince Philip, giant tortoise and leaping sailfish.

1972, Nov. 20   Photo.   Perf. 14x14½
309	CD324	95c multicolored	.25	.25
310	CD324	1.50r multicolored	.70	.70

Princess Anne's Wedding Issue
Common Design Type

1973, Nov. 14   Perf. 14
311	CD325	95c ocher & multi	.30	.30
312	CD325	1.50r slate & multi	.40	.40

Soldierfish — A32

Wmk. 314
1974, Mar. 5   Litho.   Perf. 14
313	A32	20c shown	.30	.25
314	A32	50c Filefish	.55	.25
315	A32	95c Butterflyfish	1.10	.70
316	A32	1.50r Gaterin	2.75	2.75
		Nos. 313-316 (4)	4.70	3.95

Envelope and Globe — A33

UPU, cent.: 50c, Globe with location of Seychelles and radio tower. 95c, Cancellation and globe. 1.50r, "UPU" with emblems.

Perf. 12½x12

1974, Oct. 9 **Wmk. 314**

317	A33	20c multicolored	.25	.25
318	A33	50c multicolored	.25	.25
319	A33	95c multicolored	.35	.35
320	A33	1.50r multicolored	.55	.55
		Nos. 317-320 (4)	1.40	1.40

Winston Churchill A34

Design: 1.50r, Churchill, different portrait.

1974, Nov. 30 **Litho.** ***Perf. 14½***

321	A34	95c lt blue & multi	.25	.25
322	A34	1.50r lt green & multi	.60	.60
a.		Souvenir sheet of 2, #321-322	.90	*1.60*

Sir Winston Churchill (1874-1965).

Nos. 260, 263, 265A and 267 Overprinted in Black or Silver

Perf. 13x12½

1975, Feb. 8 **Wmk. 314**

323	A23	20c multi (B)	.30	.25
324	A23	50c multi (B)	.30	.25
325	A23	95c multi (S)	.40	.40
326	A23	1.50r multi (B)	.55	*1.25*
		Nos. 323-326 (4)	1.55	2.15

Visit of cruise ship Queen Elizabeth II, Mahe, Seychelles.

Nos. 260, 264A, 266, 268 Overprinted in Gold

1975, Oct. 1 **Litho.** **Wmk. 314**

327	A23	20c multicolored	.25	.25
328	A23	65c multicolored	.35	.35
329	A23	1r multicolored	.65	.55
330	A23	3.50r multicolored	1.75	2.00
		Nos. 327-330 (4)	3.00	3.15

Queen Elizabeth I A35

Portraits: 15c, Gladys Aylward. 20c, Elizabeth Fry. 25c, Emmeline Pankhurst. 65c, Florence Nightingale. 1r, Amy Johnson. 1.50r, Joan of Arc. 3.50r, Eleanor Roosevelt.

Wmk. 314

1975, Dec. 15 **Litho.** ***Perf. 13½***

331	A35	10c dp brown & multi	.25	.25
332	A35	15c dk brown & multi	.25	.25
333	A35	20c dk green & multi	.25	.25
334	A35	25c purple & multi	.25	.25
335	A35	65c dk blue & multi	.50	.40
336	A35	1r Prus blue & multi	.75	.65
337	A35	1.50r dp violet & multi	1.00	*1.25*
338	A35	3.50r dk olive & multi	2.00	*3.00*
		Nos. 331-338 (8)	5.25	6.30

International Women's Year.

Praslin Map and Grand Anse Postmark, 1907 — A36

Designs: 65c, La Digue map and postmark, 1916. 1r, Partial map of Mahé and Victoria postmark, 1917. 1.50r, Southern part of Mahé and Anse Royale postmark, 1938.

1976, Mar. 30 **Wmk. 373** ***Perf. 14***

339	A36	20c lt blue & multi	.25	.25
340	A36	65c lt blue & multi	.40	.40
341	A36	1r lt blue & multi	.55	.55
342	A36	1.50r lt blue & multi	.75	.75
a.		Souvenir sheet of 4, #339-342	3.25	*3.50*
		Nos. 339-342 (4)	1.95	1.95

Rural posts of Seychelles.

First Landing, 1609, and James Mancham — A37

Designs: 25c, Stone of Possession. 40c, Arrival of 1st settlers, 1770 (ship). 75c, Le Chevalier Quéau de Quincy. 1r, Sir Bickham Sweet-Escott. 1.25r, Government House. 1.50r, Coat of arms of Internal Self-government. 3.50r, Seychelles flag.

1976, June 29 ***Perf. 14***

343	A37	20c rose & multi	.25	.25
344	A37	25c yellow & multi	.25	.25
345	A37	40c lilac & multi	.25	.25
346	A37	75c green & multi	.40	.40
347	A37	1r salmon & multi	.65	.65
348	A37	1.25r multicolored	.75	.75
349	A37	1.50r ocher & multi	.90	.90
350	A37	3.50r blue & multi	2.00	2.00
		Nos. 343-350 (8)	5.45	5.45

Seychelles' independence, June 29, 1976.

Flags of Seychelles and US — A38

US bicent.: 10r, State House, Seychelles, and Independence Hall, Philadelphia.

1976, July 12 **Litho.**

351	A38	1r blue & multi	.30	.30
352	A38	10r red & multi	1.40	*3.00*

Swimming — A39

Designs (Olympic Rings and): 65c, Hockey. 1r, Basketball. 3.50r, Soccer.

1976, July 26 ***Perf. 14½***

353	A39	20c vio blue & blk	.30	.25
354	A39	65c dk grn, yel grn & blk	.50	.25
355	A39	1r brown, grn & blk	.50	.25
356	A39	3.50r car rose & blk	.75	*2.25*
		Nos. 353-356 (4)	2.05	3.00

21st Olympic Games, Montreal, Canada, July 17-Aug. 1.

Seychelles Sunbird — A40

Seychelles Birds (James R. Mancham, Congress Emblem and): 20c, Paradise flycatcher, vert. 1.50r, Gray white-eye. 5r, Black parrot, vert.

Wmk. 373

1976, Nov. 8 **Litho.** ***Perf. 14½***

357	A40	20c multicolored	.25	.25
358	A40	1.25r multicolored	1.25	.80
359	A40	1.50r multicolored	1.60	1.10
360	A40	5r multicolored	2.75	*3.75*
a.		Souvenir sheet of 4, #357-360	8.00	*10.50*
		Nos. 357-360 (4)	5.85	5.90

4th Pan-African Ornithological Cong., Mahe Beach Hotel, Nov. 6-13.

Nos. 260, 263, 265A-266, 268-271, 264A Ovptd. or Srchd. "Independence / 1976"

Perf. 13x12½

1976, Nov. 22 **Litho.** **Wmk. 314**

361	A23	20c multicolored	1.00	*1.90*
362	A23	50c multicolored	.90	*2.25*
363	A23	95c multicolored	2.50	2.25
364	A23	1r multicolored	.90	*2.25*
365	A23	3.50r multicolored	4.00	4.75
366	A23	5r multicolored	3.50	*6.50*
367	A23	10r multicolored	4.75	*12.00*
368	A23	15r multicolored	5.25	*12.00*
369	A23	25r on 65c multi	6.50	*18.00*
		Nos. 361-369 (9)	29.30	61.90

Washington's Inauguration — A41

American Bicentennial: 2c, Jefferson and map of Louisiana Purchase. 3c, Seward and map of Alaska Purchase. 4c, Pony Express, 1860. 5c, Lincoln's Emancipation Proclamation, 1863. 1.50r, Completion of Transcontinental Railroad, 1869. 3.50r, Wright Brothers' 1st flight, 1903. 5r, Ford assembly line, 1913. 10r, Kennedy and Apollo 11 moon landing, 1969. 25r, Declaration of Independence, 1776.

Perf. 14x13½

1976, Dec. 21 **Wmk. 373**

370	A41	1c rose & plum	.25	.25
371	A41	2c lilac & vio	.25	.25
372	A41	3c blue & vio bl	.25	.25
373	A41	4c yellow & brn	.25	.25
374	A41	5c brt yel & grn	.25	.25
375	A41	1.50r yel brn & brn	.60	.60
376	A41	3.50r brt grn & bl grn	.90	.90
377	A41	5r yellow & brn	1.25	1.25
378	A41	10r dull bl & dk bl	2.00	2.00
		Nos. 370-378 (9)	6.00	6.00

Souvenir Sheet

379	A41	25r lilac rose & pur	5.50	5.50

Seychelles Islands and Arms — A42

The Orb — A43

Designs: 40c, 5r, 10r, similar to 20c. 1r, St. Edward's Crown. 1.25r, Ampulla and Spoon. 1.50r, Scepter with Cross.

1977, Sept. 5 **Litho.** ***Perf. 14***

380	A42	20c multicolored	.25	.25
381	A42	40c multicolored	.25	.25
382	A43	50c multicolored	.25	.25
383	A43	1r multicolored	.25	.25
384	A43	1.25r multicolored	.25	.25
385	A43	1.50r multicolored	.25	.25
386	A42	5r multicolored	.35	.35
387	A42	10r multicolored	.65	.65
a.		Souv. sheet of 4, #380, 382, 383, 387	2.00	2.25
		Nos. 380-387 (8)	2.50	2.50

25th anniv. of reign of Elizabeth II.

Coral Reef — A44

Sizes: 40c, 1, 1.25, 1.50r, 30x25mm, Others 28x23mm

Without Date Imprint

Perf. 14, 14x14½ (40c, 1, 1.25, 1.50r)

1977-91 **Litho.** **Wmk. 373**

388	A44	5c Reef fish	.25	1.00
389	A44	10c Hawksbill turtle	.25	.25
a.		Inscribed "1979"	.30	.25
c.		Inscribed "1982"	.30	.25
d.		Inscribed "1988"	.35	.35
390	A44	15c Coco de mer	.25	1.00
a.		Inscribed "1979"	.30	.25
391	A44	20c Wild vanilla	1.20	.25
c.		Inscribed "1982"	4.00	3.25
392	A44	25c Butterfly	1.20	.50
a.		Inscribed "1979"	3.25	3.25
d.		Inscribed "1988"	1.50	1.50
393	A44	40c Coral reef	.25	.25
a.		Inscribed "1979"	.30	.25
b.		Inscribed "1981"	.30	.25
c.		Inscribed "1982"	.30	.25
394	A44	50c Giant tortoise	.25	.25
a.		Inscribed "1979"	.60	.25
d.		Inscribed "1988"	.60	.25
e.		Inscribed "1991"	.60	.25
f.		Wmk. 384, perf. 14x14½, inscr. "1991"	.30	.30
395	A44	75c Crayfish	.25	.25
a.		Inscribed "1979"	.75	.45
396	A44	1r Madagascar cardinal	.35	.30
a.		Inscribed "1979"	12.00	1.10
d.		Inscribed "1988"	1.50	1.10
397	A44	1.25r Fairy tern	1.00	.40
398	A44	1.50r Flying fox	1.00	.45
b.		Inscribed "1979"	3.00	.75
398A	A44	3r like #399, wmk. 384	2.00	1.75
399	A44	3.50r Green gecko	1.25	2.50

Perf. 13

Size: 27x35mm

400	A44	5r Octopus, vert.	1.90	1.60
401	A44	10r Tiger cowrie, vert.	3.75	3.25
402	A44	15r Pitcher plant, vert.	5.25	3.25
403	A44	20r Arms, vert.	5.75	3.25
		Nos. 388-403 (17)	26.15	20.50

Issued: 40c, 1r, 1.25r, 1.50r, 10/31/77; Nos. 394a, 398A, 11/1991; others, 1978.

For surcharge see No. 446.

Denomination "R" Instead of "Re." or "Rs."

"1980" Imprint Beneath Design

Sizes: 1.10r, 28x23mm, Others, 30x25mm

Perf. 14x14½, 14 (1.10r)

1981, Jan. 6 **Litho.**

403A	A44	1r like No. 396	.55	.55
b.		Inscribed "1982"	.55	.55
d.		Inscribed "1986"	.55	.55
e.		Inscribed "1988"	.55	.55
f.		Inscribed "1990"	.55	.55
g.		Inscribed "1991"	1.75	1.25
403B	A44	1.10r like No. 399	1.00	1.00
a.		Inscribed "1981"	2.10	1.75
403C	A44	1.25r like No. 397	.75	.75
i.		Wmk. 384 ('89)	.80	.80
403D	A44	1.50r like No. 398	.80	.80
b.		Inscribed "1982"	.90	1.25
g.		Inscribed "1991"	.90	1.25

Perf. 13

k.		Inscribed "1981"	—	—
403E	A44	5r like No. 400	3.00	3.00
c.		Inscribed "1985"	2.25	2.25
j.		Perf. 14x14½, Wmk 384 ('90)	4.00	4.00
403F	A44	10r like No. 401	6.25	6.25
403G	A44	15r like No. 402	9.00	9.00
403H	A44	20r like No. 403	12.50	12.50
		Nos. 403A-403H (8)	33.85	33.85

See No. 576 for No. 403C with commemorative inscription. For overprint see No. 605.

Cruiser Aurora, Star and Flag — A45

1977, Nov. 7   Unwmk.   Perf. 12
404   A45   1.50r red, black & gold   .80   .65
a.   Souvenir sheet   2.00   2.00

60th anniv. of Russian Oct. Revolution.

St. Roch Roman Catholic Church, Bel Ombre — A46

Christmas: 1r, Anglican Cathedral, Victoria. 1.50r, R. C. Cathedral, Victoria. 5r, St. Mark's Anglican Church, Praslin.

Perf. 13½x14
1977, Dec. 5   Wmk. 373
405   A46   20c multicolored   .25   .25
406   A46   1r multicolored   .25   .25
407   A46   1.50r multicolored   .25   .25
408   A46   5r multicolored   .30   .40
    Nos. 405-408 (4)   1.05   1.15

Calendar Page, June 5, 1977 — A47

1.25r, Hands holding rifle, torch & Seychelles flag. 1.50r, Fisherman & farmer holding hands. 5r, Soldiers & waving children.

Perf. 14x13½
1978, June 5   Litho.   Wmk. 373
409   A47   40c multicolored   .25   .25
410   A47   1.25r multicolored   .25   .25
411   A47   1.50r multicolored   .25   .25
412   A47   5r multicolored   .50   .50
    Nos. 409-412 (4)   1.25   1.25

First anniversary of Liberation Day.

Edward VII, George V, George VI — A48

Designs: 1.50r, Queens Victoria and Elizabeth II. 3r, Queen Victoria Monument, Seychelles. 5r, Queen's Building, Victoria, Seychelles.

1978, Aug. 21   Litho.   Perf. 14
413   A48   40c multicolored   .25   .25
414   A48   1.50r multicolored   .25   .25
415   A48   3r multicolored   .25   .25
416   A48   5r multicolored   .35   .35
a.   Souvenir sheet of 4, #413-416   1.40   1.40
    Nos. 413-416 (4)   1.10   1.10

25th anniv. of coronation of Elizabeth II.

Gardenia from Aride Island — A49

Designs (Coat of Arms and): 1.25r, Magpie robin of Fregate Island. 1.50r, Seychelles paradise flycatchers. 5r, Green turtle.

Perf. 13½x14
1978, Oct. 16   Litho.   Wmk. 373
417   A49   40c multicolored   .25   .25
418   A49   1.25r multicolored   2.00   .75
419   A49   1.50r multicolored   2.00   .75
420   A49   5r multicolored   2.00   1.90
    Nos. 417-420 (4)   6.25   3.65

"Stone of Possession" — A50

1978, Dec. 15   Litho.   Perf. 13½
421   A50   20c shown   .25   .25
422   A50   1.25r Map, 1782   .25   .25
423   A50   1.50r Clock tower   .25   .25
424   A50   5r Pierre Poivre   .25   .50
    Nos. 421-424 (4)   1.00   1.25

Bicentennary of the founding of Victoria.

Seychelles Fody — A51

Birds: No. 426, Green-backed heron. No. 427, Seychelles bulbul. No. 428, Seychelles cave swiftlets. No. 429, Grayheaded lovebirds.

1979, Feb. 27   Litho.   Perf. 14
425   A51   2r multicolored   .90   .90
426   A51   2r multicolored   .90   .90
427   A51   2r multicolored   .90   .90
428   A51   2r multicolored   .90   .90
429   A51   2r multicolored   .90   .90
a.   Strip of 5, #425-429   4.75   4.75
    Nos. 425-429 (5)   4.50   4.50

Patrice Lumumba — A52

African Liberation Heroes: 2r, Kwame Nkrumah. 2.25r, Dr. Eduardo Mondlane. 5r, Amilcar Cabral.

1979, June 5   Litho.   Perf. 14½
430   A52   40c violet & blk   .25   .25
431   A52   2r dark blue & blk   .25   .25
432   A52   2.25r orange brn & blk   .25   .25
433   A52   5r olive grn & blk   .30   .75
    Nos. 430-433 (4)   1.05   1.50

Coat of Arms, Rowland Hill, Seychelles No. 412 — A53

Coat of Arms, Hill, Seychelles stamps: 2.25r, No. 301. 3r, No. 205. 5r, No. 4.

1979, Aug. 27   Litho.   Perf. 14x14½
434   A53   40c multicolored   .25   .25
435   A53   2.25r multicolored   .30   .30
436   A53   3r multicolored   .35   .35
    Nos. 434-436 (3)   .90   .90

Souvenir Sheet
437   A53   5r multicolored   .80   1.25

Sir Rowland Hill (1795-1879), originator of penny postage.

Schoolboy, IYC Emblem — A54

IYC Emblem and: 2.25r, Children. 3r, Boy with ball, vert. 5r, Girl with puppet, vert.

Perf. 14½x14, 14x14½
1979, Oct. 25   Litho.
438   A54   40c multicolored   .25   .25
439   A54   2.25r multicolored   .25   .25
440   A54   3r multicolored   .25   .25
441   A54   5r multicolored   .25   .50
    Nos. 438-441 (4)   1.00   1.25

International Year of the Child.

Three Kings Bearing Gifts A55

Christmas (Stained Glass Windows): 20c, Angel, vert. 2.25r, Virgin and Child, vert. 5r, Flight into Egypt.

1979, Dec. 3   Litho.   Perf. 14½
442   A55   20c multicolored   .25   .25
443   A55   2.25r multicolored   .35   .35
444   A55   3r multicolored   .45   .45
    Nos. 442-444 (3)   1.05   1.05

Souvenir Sheet
445   A55   5r multicolored   .80   .80

No. 399 Surcharged

Wmk. 373
1979, Dec. 7   Litho.   Perf. 14
446   A44   1.10r on 3.50r multicolored   .50   .50

Seychelles Kestrel — A56

Seychelles Kestrel: a, shown. b, Pair. c, Female, eggs. d, Mother and chick. e, Chicks nesting.

1980, Feb. 29   Litho.   Perf. 14
447   Strip of 5   6.00   6.00
a.-e.   A56 2r any single   1.15   1.15
    See Nos. 468, 483.

50-Rupee Bank Note, London 1980 Emblem — A57

New Currency: 40c, 1.50r, horiz.

1980, Apr. 18   Litho.   Perf. 14
448   A57   40c multicolored   .25   .25
449   A57   1.50r multicolored   .40   .40
450   A57   2.25r multicolored   .50   .50
451   A57   5r multicolored   .85   .85
a.   Souvenir sheet of 4, #448-451   2.25   2.25
    Nos. 448-451 (4)   2.00   2.00

London 1980 Intl. Stamp Exhib., May 6-14.

Sprinting, Moscow '80 Emblem — A58

IYC Emblem and: 2.25r, Weight lifting

1980, June 13   Perf. 14½
452   A58   40c shown   .25   .25
453   A58   2.25r Weight lifting   .25   .25
454   A58   3r Boxing   .35   .35
455   A58   5r Yachting   .85   .85
a.   Souvenir sheet of 4, #452-455   2.75   2.75
    Nos. 452-455 (4)   1.70   1.70

22nd Summer Olympic Games, Moscow, July 19-Aug. 3.

Boeing 747 A59

2.25r, Tour bus. 3r, Ocean liner, pirogue. 5r, Tour motor boat.

1980, Aug. 22   Litho.   Perf. 14
456   A59   40c shown   .25   .25
457   A59   2.25r multicolored   .30   .30
458   A59   3r multicolored   .50   .50
459   A59   5r multicolored   .85   .85
    Nos. 456-459 (4)   1.90   1.90

World Tourism Conf., Manila, Sept. 27.

Female Coco-de-Mer Palm Tree — A60

1980, Oct. 31   Litho.   Perf. 14
460   A60   40c shown   .25   .25
461   A60   2.25r Male tree   .35   .35
462   A60   3r Bowls   .50   .50
463   A60   5r Gourds, canoes   .80   .80
a.   Souvenir sheet of 4, #460-463   3.25   3.25
    Nos. 460-463 (4)   1.90   1.90

Vasco da Gama's San Gabriel, 1497 A61

2.25r, Mascarenhas' Caravel, 1505. 3.50r, Darwin's Beagle, 1831. 5r, Queen Elizabeth 2, 1968.

Wmk. 373

1981, Feb.	Litho.	Perf. 14½	
464	A61	40c multi	.25 .25
465	A61	2.25r multi	.55 .55
466	A61	3.50r multi	.75 .75
467	A61	5r multi	.95 .95
a.	Souvenir sheet of 4, #464-467		3.75 3.75
	Nos. 464-467 (4)		2.50 2.50

Bird Type of 1980

1981, Apr. 10	Litho.	Perf. 14	
468	Strip of 5, multi		6.75 6.75
a.	A56 2r Male fairy tern		1.30 1.30
b.	A56 2r Pair		1.30 1.30
c.	A56 2r Female on nest		1.30 1.30
d.	A56 2r Female on nest, egg		1.30 1.30
e.	A56 2r Adult bird, chick		1.30 1.30

Prince Charles, Lady Diana, Royal Yacht Charlotte A61a

Prince Charles and Lady Diana — A61b

Wmk. 380

1981, June 23	Litho.	Perf. 14	
469	A61a 1.50r Couple, Victoria & Albert I		.25 .25
a.	Bklt. pane of 4, perf. 12		1.10
470	A61b 1.50r Couple		.50 .50
471	A61a 5r Cleveland		.60 .60
472	A61b 5r like #470		1.75 1.75
a.	Bklt. pane of 2, perf. 12		2.00
473	A61b 10r Britannia		1.50 1.50
474	A61b 10r like #470		3.50 3.50
	Nos. 469-474 (6)		8.10 8.10

Each denomination issued in sheets of 7 (6 type A61a, 1 type A61b).
For surcharges see Nos. 528-533.

Souvenir Sheet

1981	Litho.	Perf. 12	
474A	A61b 7.50r Couple		2.50 2.50

Seychelles Intl. Airport, 10th Anniv. — A62

40c, Britten-Norman Islander. 2.25r, Britten-Norman Trislander. 3.50r, Vickers VC-10. 5r, Boeing 747.

Wmk. 373

1981, July 27	Litho.	Perf. 14½	
475	A62	40c multicolored	.25 .25
476	A62	2.25r multicolored	.65 .65
477	A62	3.50r multicolored	.90 .90
478	A62	5r multicolored	1.25 1.25
	Nos. 475-478 (4)		3.05 3.05

A63

Designs: Various flying foxes.

1981, Oct. 9	Litho.	Perf. 14	
479	A63	40c multicolored	.25 .25
480	A63	2.25r multicolored	.35 .35
481	A63	3r multicolored	.55 .55
482	A63	3r multicolored	1.00 1.00
a.	Souvenir sheet, #479-482		3.75 3.75
	Nos. 479-482 (4)		2.15 2.15

Bird Type of 1980

a, Male Chinese bittern. b, Female. c, Hen on nest. d, Nest, eggs. e, Hen, chicks.

Wmk. 373

1982, Feb. 4	Litho.	Perf. 14	
483	Strip of 5		16.00 16.00
a.-e.	A56 3r any single		3.00 3.00

A65

40c, Map of Silhouette Island and La Digue. 1.50r, Denis & Bird Islands. 2.75r, Curieuse Island, Praslin. 7r, Mahe.

1982, Apr. 22	Litho.	Perf. 14½	
487	A65	40c multicolored	.25 .25
488	A65	1.50r multicolored	.35 .35
489	A65	2.75r multicolored	.60 .60
490	A65	7r multicolored	1.50 1.50
a.	Souvenir sheet of 4, #487-490		4.00 4.00
	Nos. 487-490 (4)		2.70 2.70

5th Anniv. of Liberation A66

40c, Bookmobile. 1.75r, Mobile dental clinic. 2.75r, Farming. 7r, Construction site.

1982, June 5		Perf. 14	
491	A66	40c multicolored	.25 .25
492	A66	1.75r multicolored	.25 .25
493	A66	2.75r multicolored	.40 .40
494	A66	7r multicolored	1.25 1.25
a.	Souvenir sheet of 4, #491-494		5.00 5.00
	Nos. 491-494 (4)		2.15 2.15

Tourism A67

Hotels.

1982, Sept. 1			
495	A67 1.75r Northolme		.35 .35
496	A67 1.75r Reef		.35 .35
497	A67 1.75r Barbarons Beach		.35 .35
498	A67 1.75r Coral Strand		.35 .35
499	A67 1.75r Beau Vallon Bay		.35 .35
500	A67 1.75r Fisherman's Cove		.35 .35
501	A67 1.75r Mahe Beach		.35 .35
502	A67 1.75r Island scene		.35 .35
	Nos. 495-502 (8)		2.80 2.80

Tata Bus A68

Wmk. 373

1982, Nov. 18	Litho.	Perf. 14	
503	A68	20c shown	.25 .25
504	A68	1.75r Mini moke	.35 .35
505	A68	2.75r Ox cart	.55 .55
506	A68	7r Truck	1.40 1.40
	Nos. 503-506 (4)		2.55 2.55

World Communications Year — A69

40c, Radio control room. 2.75r, Satellite earth station. 3.50fr, TV control room. 5r, Postal services.

1983, Feb. 25			
507	A69	40c multicolored	.25 .25
508	A69	2.75r multicolored	.45 .45
509	A69	3.50r multicolored	.60 .60
510	A69	5r multicolored	.85 .85
	Nos. 507-510 (4)		2.15 2.15

Commonwealth Day — A70

40c, Agricultural research. 2.75r, Food processing plant. 3.50r, Fishing industry. 7r, Flag.

1983, Mar. 14			
511	A70	40c multicolored	.25 .25
512	A70	2.75r multicolored	.25 .25
513	A70	3.50r multicolored	.35 .35
514	A70	7r multicolored	1.00 1.00
	Nos. 511-514 (4)		1.85 1.85

Denis Isld. Lighthouse, 1910 — A71

2.75r, Seychelles Hospital, 1924. 3.50r, Supreme Court, 1894. 7r, State House, 1911.

1983, July 14		Perf. 14x13½	
515	A71	40c shown	.25 .25
516	A71	2.75r multicolored	.25 .25
517	A71	3.50r multicolored	.45 .45
518	A71	7r multicolored	.90 .90
a.	Souvenir sheet of 4, #515-518		5.00 5.00
	Nos. 515-518 (4)		1.85 1.85

Manned Flight Bicentenary — A72

40c, Royal Vauxhall balloon, 1836. 1.75r, DeHavilland D.H.-50j. 2.75r, Grumman Albatross. 7r, Swearingen Merlin.

1983, Sept. 15		Perf. 14	
519	A72	40c multicolored	.25 .25
520	A72	1.75r multicolored	.55 .55
521	A72	2.75r multicolored	.80 .80
522	A72	7r multicolored	1.40 1.40
	Nos. 519-522 (4)		3.00 3.00

First Intl. Air Seychelles Flight — A73

1983, Oct. 26		Litho.	
523	A73	2r DC10 aircraft	2.50 2.50

Paintings, Marianne North — A74

40c, Swamp Plant and Moorhen. 1.75r, Wormia flagellaria. 2.75r, Asiatic Pancratium. 7r, Pitcher Plant.

1983, Nov. 17	Litho.	Perf. 14	
524	A74	40c multicolored	.25 .25
525	A74	1.75r multicolored	.45 .45
526	A74	2.75r multicolored	.70 .70
527	A74	7r multicolored	1.60 1.60
a.	Souvenir sheet of 4, #524-527		6.25 6.25
	Nos. 524-527 (4)		3.00 3.00

Nos. 469-474 Surcharged
Wmk. 380

1983, Dec. 28	Litho.	Perf. 14	
528	A61a	50c on 1.50r multi	.25 .25
529	A61b	50c on 1.50r multi	.25 .25
530	A61a	2.25r on 5r multi	1.40 1.40
531	A61b	2.25r on 5r multi	1.40 1.40
532	A61a	3.75r on 10r multi	2.25 2.25
533	A61b	3.75r on 10r multi	2.25 2.25
	Nos. 528-533 (6)		7.80 7.80

Handicrafts — A75

Wmk. 373

1984, Feb. 29	Litho.	Perf. 14	
534	A75	50c Coconut kettle	.25 .25
535	A75	2r Scarf, doll	.50 .70
536	A75	3r Coconut-fiber roses	.75 1.00
537	A75	10r Carved fishing boat, doll	2.25 3.75
	Nos. 534-537 (4)		3.75 5.70

Lloyd's List Issue
Common Design Type

1984, May 21	Litho.	Perf. 14½x14	
538	CD335	50c Port Victoria	.25 .25
539	CD335	2r Steamship, 1930s	.75 .75
540	CD335	3r Cruise liner	1.00 1.00
541	CD335	10r Ennerdale	3.25 3.25
	Nos. 538-541 (4)		5.25 5.25

People's United Party, 20th Anniv. A76

50c, Original headquarters. 2r, Liberation statue, vert. 3r, New headquarters. 10r, Pres. Rene, vert.

1984, June 2	Litho.	Perf. 14	
542	A76	50c multicolored	.25 .25
543	A76	2r multicolored	.40 .40
544	A76	3r multicolored	.60 .60
545	A76	10r multicolored	1.50 1.50
	Nos. 542-545 (4)		2.75 2.75

Souvenir Sheet

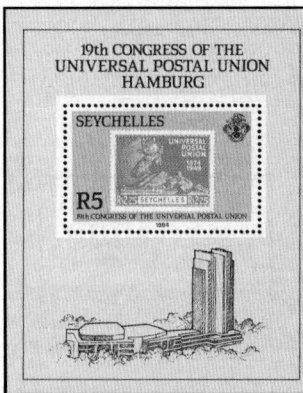

19th CONGRESS OF THE UNIVERSAL POSTAL UNION HAMBURG

UPU Congress — A77

1984, June 18   *Perf. 14½*
546 A77 5r No. 156   3.00 3.00

1984 Summer Olympics A78

1984, July 28   *Perf. 14*
547 A78 50c Long jump   .25 .25
548 A78 2r Boxing   .45 .45
549 A78 3r Diving   .60 .60
550 A78 10r Weight lifting   2.25 2.25
 a. Souvenir sheet of 4, #547-550   4.00 4.00
   Nos. 547-550 (4)   3.55 3.55

Scuba Diving A79

1984, Sept. 24
551 A79 50c shown   .25 .25
552 A79 2r Paragliding   .90 .90
553 A79 3r Sailing   1.25 1.25
554 A79 10r Water skiing   4.50 4.50
   Nos. 551-554 (4)   6.90 6.90

Whale Conservation — A80

1984, Nov.   *Litho.*
555 A80 50c Humpback whale   3.00 3.00
556 A80 2r Sperm whale   5.00 5.00
557 A80 3r Right whale   6.00 6.00
558 A80 10r Blue whale   10.00 10.00
   Nos. 555-558 (4)   24.00 24.00

Audubon Birth Bicent. — A81

Bare-legged scops owls.

1985, Mar. 11   *Litho.*   *Perf. 14*
559 A81 50c multicolored   2.75 2.75
560 A81 2r multicolored   4.50 4.50
561 A81 3r multicolored   4.75 4.75
562 A81 10r multicolored   8.00 8.00
   Nos. 559-562 (4)   20.00 20.00

EXPO '85, Tsukuba — A82

Wmk. 373
1985, Mar. 15   *Litho.*   *Perf. 14*
563 A82 50c Giant tortoise   .30 .30
564 A82 2r Fairy tern   1.60 1.60
565 A82 3r Wind surfing   2.25 2.25
566 A82 5r Coco de mer   3.75 3.75
 a. Souvenir sheet of 4, #563-566   9.50 9.50
   Nos. 563-566 (4)   7.90 7.90

See No. 604.

Queen Mother 85th Birthday
Common Design Type

50c, Queen Elizabeth, 1930. 2r, With grandchildren, 1970. 3r, 75th birthday celebration. 5r, Holding Prince Henry. 10r, Exiting from helicopter.

Perf. 14½x14
1985, June 7   *Litho.*   **Wmk. 384**
567 CD336 50c multi   .25 .25
568 CD336 2r multi   .75 .75
569 CD336 3r multi   1.10 1.10
570 CD336 5r multi   1.60 1.60
   Nos. 567-570 (4)   3.70 3.70

Souvenir Sheet
571 CD336 10r multi   5.00 5.00

2nd Indian Ocean Islands Games A83

1985, Aug. 24
572 A83 50c Boxing   .25 .25
573 A83 2r Soccer   .80 .80
574 A83 3r Swimming   1.25 1.25
575 A83 10r Wind surfing   4.25 4.25
   Nos. 572-575 (4)   6.55 6.55

A83a

1985, Nov. 1   **Wmk. 384**
576 A83a 1.25r Fairy tern   3.50 3.50
Air Seychelles 1st Airbus.

A84

1985, Nov. 28
577 A84 50c Agriculture   .25 .25
578 A84 2r Construction   .70 .70
579 A84 3r Carpentry   1.10 1.10
580 A84 10r Science education   3.50 3.50
   Nos. 577-580 (4)   5.55 5.55

Intl. Youth Year.

Vintage Cars A85

1985, Dec. 18
581 A85 50c 1919 Ford Model T   .25 .25
582 A85 2r 1922 Austin Seven   1.40 1.40
583 A85 3r 1924 Morris Bull-nose Oxford   1.60 1.60
584 A85 10r 1929 Humber Coupe   5.50 5.50
   Nos. 581-584 (4)   8.75 8.75

Halley's Comet — A86

Perf. 14x14½
1986, Feb. 28   **Wmk. 384**
585 A86 50c Transit instrument   .25 .25
586 A86 2r Quadrant   .75 .75
587 A86 3r Trajectory diagram   1.25 1.25
588 A86 10r Edmond Halley   3.75 3.75
   Nos. 585-588 (4)   6.00 6.00

Giselle, Performed by the Ballet Louvre, Apr. 4-8 — A87

Wmk. 384
1986, Apr. 4   *Litho.*   *Perf. 14*
589 A87 2r Heroine   .80 .80
590 A87 3r Hero   1.10 1.10

Souvenir Sheet
591 A87 10r United   4.00 4.00

First ballet performed in the Seychelles.

Queen Elizabeth II 60th Birthday
Common Design Type

Designs: 50c, Marrying the Duke of Edinburgh, 1947. 1.25r, State opening of Parliament, 1982. 2r, Greeting child aboard the Britannia, Qatar Harbor. 3r, Silver Jubilee celebration. 5r, Visiting Crown Agents' offices, 1983.

1986, Apr. 21   *Perf. 14½*
592 CD337 50c scarlet, blk & sil   .25 .25
593 CD337 1.25r ultra & multi   .25 .25
594 CD337 2r green & multi   .45 .45
595 CD337 3r violet & multi   .65 .65
596 CD337 5r rose vio & multi   1.10 1.10
   Nos. 592-596 (5)   2.70 2.70

For overprints see Nos. 625-629.

AMERIPEX '86, Inter-island Communications — A88

Wmk. 384
1986, May 22   *Litho.*   *Perf. 14*
597 A88 50c La Digue Ferry   .35 .35
598 A88 2r Phone booth, vert.   1.40 1.40
599 A88 3r Victoria P.O., vert.   2.40 2.40
600 A88 7r Air Seychelles trislander   5.50 5.50
   Nos. 597-600 (4)   9.65 9.65

Coptic Catholic Knights of Malta Celebration Day — A89

Perf. 14½x14
1986, June 7   *Litho.*   **Wmk. 384**
601 A89 5r Natl. arms, assoc. emblem   2.00 2.00
 a. Souvenir sheet of 1   4.25 4.25

Royal Wedding Issue, 1986
Common Design Type

2r, Informal portrait. 10r, Andrew, helicopter.

1986, July 23   *Litho.*   *Perf. 14*
602 CD338 2r multicolored   .50 .50
603 CD338 10r multicolored   2.00 2.00

Tsukuba Expo Type of 1985
Souvenir Sheet
Wmk. 384
1986, July 12   *Litho.*   *Perf. 14*
604 Sheet of 4   6.50 6.50
 a. A82 50c multicolored   .25 .25
 b. A82 2r multicolored   1.25 1.25
 c. A82 3r multicolored   1.75 1.75
 d. A82 5r multicolored   3.00 3.00

No. 604 inscribed "Seychelles Philatelic Exhibition-Tokyo-1986" and printed without EXPO '85 emblem on margin or on individual stamps. Nos. 604a-604d inscribed "1986."

No. 403Ad Overprinted

Perf. 14½x14
1986, Oct. 28   **Wmk. 373**
605 A44 1r multicolored   6.00 6.00

Intl. Creole Day.

State Visit of Pope John Paul II — A90

Pope and: 50c, Seychelles Airport. 2r, Cathedral. 3r, Baie Lazare parish church. 10r, People's Stadium.

1986, Dec. 1   **Wmk. 384**   *Perf. 14½*
606 A90 50c multicolored   .25 .25
607 A90 2r multicolored   1.75 1.75
608 A90 3r multicolored   2.50 2.50
609 A90 10r multicolored   8.50 8.50
 a. Souvenir sheet of 4, #606-609   19.00 19.00
   Nos. 606-609 (4)   13.00 13.00

Butterflies — A91

Wmk. 384
1987, Feb. 18   *Litho.*   *Perf. 14½*
610 A91 1r Melanitis leda   .90 .90
611 A91 2r Phalanta philiberti   1.75 1.75
612 A91 3r Danaus chrysippus   2.50 2.50
613 A91 10r Euploea mitra   8.75 8.75
   Nos. 610-613 (4)   13.90 13.90

Seashells — A92

1r, Gloripallium pallium. 2r, Spondylus aurantius. 3r, Harpa ventricosa, Lioconcha ornata. 10r, Strombus lentiginosus.

1987, May 7   **Wmk. 373**
614	A92	1r multi	1.10	1.10
615	A92	2r multi	2.25	2.25
616	A92	3r multi	3.25	3.25
617	A92	10r multi	10.00	10.00
		Nos. 614-617 (4)	16.60	16.60

Liberation, 10th Anniv. — A93

Perf. 14x14½, 14½x14
1987, June 5   **Wmk. 384**
618	A93	1r Liberation monument	.25	.25
619	A93	2r Hospital, horiz.	.45	.45
620	A93	3r Orphanage, horiz.	.75	.75
621	A93	10r Fish monument	1.90	1.90
		Nos. 618-621 (4)	3.35	3.35

Natl. Banking Cent. — A94

1987, June 25   **Perf. 14½x14**
622	A94	1r Savings Bank, Praslin	.25	.25
623	A94	2r Development Bank	.40	.40
624	A94	10r Central Bank	1.50	1.50
		Nos. 622-624 (3)	2.15	2.15

Nos. 592-596 Ovptd. in Silver

Wmk. 384
1987, Dec. 9   **Litho.**   **Perf. 14½**
625	CD337	50c scar, blk & sil	.25	.25
626	CD337	1.25r ultra & multi	.25	.25
627	CD337	2r green & multi	.50	.50
628	CD337	3r violet & multi	.75	.75
629	CD337	5r rose vio & multi	1.25	1.25
		Nos. 625-629 (5)	3.00	3.00

Fishing Industry A95

Wmk. 384
1987, Dec. 11   **Litho.**   **Perf. 14**
630	A95	50c Tuna cannery	.25	.25
631	A95	2r Fishing trawler	.75	.75
632	A95	3r Weighing fish	1.10	1.10

633	A95	10r Hauling catch from net	4.25	4.25
		Nos. 630-633 (4)	6.35	6.35

Beach Scenes A96

Wmk. 384
1988, Feb. 9   **Litho.**   **Perf. 14½**
634	A96	1r Para-sailing, wind-surfing, kayaks	.45	.45
635	A96	2r Boating	1.10	1.10
636	A96	3r Yacht at anchor	1.50	1.50
637	A96	10r Hotel, cabanas	5.00	5.00
		Nos. 634-637 (4)	8.05	8.05

Green Turtles — A97

No. 638, Newly hatched turtles headed toward ocean. No. 639, Offspring hatching. No. 640, Female emerging from ocean. No. 641, Female laying eggs in sand. Stamps of same denomination printed se-tenant in a continuous design.

1988, Apr. 22   **Wmk. 373**
638	A97	2r multicolored	2.75	2.75
639	A97	2r multicolored	2.75	2.75
640	A97	3r multicolored	3.50	3.50
641	A97	3r multicolored	3.50	3.50
		Nos. 638-641 (4)	12.50	12.50

A98

Designs: 1r, No. 647a, Shot put. Nos. 643, 647b, High jump. 3r, No. 647c, Medal winner, grandstand and flags. 4r, No. 647d, Running. 5r, No. 647e, Javelin. 10r, Tennis.

1988, July 29   **Wmk. 384**   **Perf. 14½**
642	A98	1r multicolored	.30	.30
643	A98	2r multicolored	.70	.70
644	A98	3r multicolored	1.00	1.00
645	A98	4r multicolored	1.40	1.40
646	A98	5r multicolored	1.60	1.60
647		Strip of 5	3.25	3.25
a.-e.		A98 2r any single	.65	.65
		Nos. 642-647 (6)	8.25	8.25

Souvenir Sheet
Wmk. 373
648	A98	10r multicolored	7.50	7.50

No. 647 has a continuous design.
1988 Summer Olympics, Seoul, (1r-5r). Intl. Tennis Fed., 75th anniv. (10r). No. 648 contains one stamp, size: 28x39mm.

Lloyds of London, 300th Anniv.
Common Design Type

Designs: 1r, Leadenhall Street, London, 1928. 2r, Cinq Juin, horiz. 3r, Queen Elizabeth II, horiz. 10r, Explosion of the Hindenburg, Lakehurst, New Jersey, 1937.

Wmk. 384
1988, Sept. 30   **Litho.**   **Perf. 14**
649	CD341	1r multicolored	1.00	1.00
650	CD341	2r multicolored	1.10	1.10
651	CD341	3r multicolored	2.25	2.25
652	CD341	10r multicolored	8.75	8.75
		Nos. 649-652 (4)	13.10	13.10

Defense Forces Day, 1st Anniv. A99

1988, Nov. 25   **Litho.**   **Wmk. 373**
653	A99	1r Motorcycle police	1.20	1.20
654	A99	2r Air force helicopter	2.40	2.40
655	A99	5r Navy patrol boat	3.75	3.75
656	A99	10r Tank	12.50	12.50
		Nos. 653-656 (4)	19.85	19.85

Christmas A100

Illustrations by local artists.

1988, Dec. 1   **Litho.**   **Wmk. 373**
657	A100	50c Selwyn Hoareau	.25	.25
658	A100	2r Robin Leste	.75	.75
659	A100	3r France Anacoura	1.25	1.25
660	A100	10r Andre McGaw	4.25	4.25
		Nos. 657-660 (4)	6.50	6.50

Orchids A101

1r, Dendrobium, vert. 2r, Arachnis hybrid. 3r, Vanda caerulea, vert. 10r, Dendrobium phalaenopsis.

Wmk. 384
1988, Dec. 21   **Litho.**   **Perf. 14**
661	A101	1r multi	.70	.70
662	A101	2r multi	1.40	1.40
663	A101	3r multi	2.00	2.00
664	A101	10r multi	6.75	6.75
		Nos. 661-664 (4)	10.85	10.85

Jawaharlal Nehru (1889-1964), 1st Prime Minister of Independent India A102

1989, Mar. 30   **Perf. 13½**
665	A102	2r India Type A409	1.40	1.40
666	A102	10r Portrait	7.25	7.25

People's United Party (SPUP), 25th Anniv. — A103

1989, June 5   **Perf. 14**
667	A103	1r Rally, old office	.35	.35
668	A103	2r Maison Du Peuple	.65	.65
669	A103	3r Pres. Rene, banner, torch	1.00	1.00
670	A103	10r Torch, flag, Rene	3.25	3.25
		Nos. 667-670 (4)	5.25	5.25

Moon Landing, 20th Anniv.
Common Design Type

Apollo 15: 1r, Saturn 5 lift-off. 2r, David R. Scott, Alfred M. Worden and James B. Irwin. 3r, Mission emblem. 5r, Irwin salutes flag in front of the Hadley Delta. 10r, Buzz Aldrin about to step onto the Moon, Apollo 11 mission.

Size of Nos. 677-678: 29x29mm
1989, July 20
676	CD342	1r multicolored	.45	.45
677	CD342	2r multicolored	1.10	1.10
678	CD342	3r multicolored	1.75	1.75
679	CD342	5r multicolored	2.75	2.75
		Nos. 676-679 (4)	6.05	6.05

Souvenir Sheet
680	CD342	10r multicolored	10.00	10.00

Intl. Red Cross and Red Crescent Organizations, 125th Annivs. — A104

1r, Ambulance, 1870. 2r, H.M. Hospital Ship Liberty, 1914-18. 3r, Sunbeam Standard Army Ambulance, 1914-18. 10r, The White Train, 1899-1902.

1989, Sept. 12   **Perf. 14½**
681	A104	1r multi	1.40	1.40
682	A104	2r multi	3.00	3.00
683	A104	3r multi	5.00	5.00
684	A104	10r multi	16.00	16.00
		Nos. 681-684 (4)	25.40	25.40

Island Birds — A105

1989, Oct. 16   **Perf. 14½x14**
685	A105	50c Black parrot	.35	.35
686	A105	2r Sooty tern	3.75	3.75
687	A105	3r Magpie robin	5.50	5.50
688	A105	5r Roseate tern	9.00	9.00
a.		Souvenir sheet of 4, #685-688	20.00	20.00
		Nos. 685-688 (4)	18.60	18.60

French Revolution Bicent., World Stamp Expo '89 — A106

2r, Flags. 5r, Storming of the Bastille. 10r, Raising French flag, Seychelles, 1791.

1989, Nov. 17   **Perf. 14**
689	A106	2r multicolored	2.25	2.25
690	A106	5r multicolored	5.50	5.50

Souvenir Sheet
691	A106	10r multicolored	10.50	10.50

African Development Bank, 25th Anniv. — A107

1r, Beau Vallon School, horiz. 2r, Fishing Authority headquarters, horiz. 3r, Variola. 10r, Deneb.

1989, Dec. 29   **Wmk. 384**
692	A107	1r multicolored	1.00	1.00
693	A107	2r multicolored	1.90	1.90
694	A107	3r multicolored	3.00	3.00
695	A107	10r multicolored	11.00	11.00
		Nos. 692-695 (4)	16.90	16.90

Orchids — A108

1r, Disperis tripetaloides. 2r, Vanilla phalae-nopsis. 3r, Angraecum eburneum superbum. 10r, Polystachya concreta.

1990, Jan. 26
696	A108	1r multi	1.40	1.40
697	A108	2r multi	3.00	3.00
698	A108	3r multi	4.25	4.25
699	A108	10r multi	15.00	15.00
	Nos. 696-699 (4)		23.65	23.65

Expo '90 (International Garden & Greenery Exposition), Japan — A109

Designs: 2r, Fumiyo Sako. 3r, Coco-de-mer, male and female plants. 5r, Pitcher plant, Aldabra lily. 7r, Gardenia, Arms of Seychelles.

1990, June 8   Litho.   Wmk. 373
700	A109	2r multicolored	1.60	1.60
701	A109	3r multicolored	2.25	2.25
702	A109	5r multicolored	4.00	4.00
703	A109	7r multicolored	5.50	5.50
a.		Souvenir sheet of 4, #700-703	14.50	14.50
	Nos. 700-703 (4)		13.35	13.35

Penny Black 150th Anniv., Stamp World London '90 A110

Exhibition emblem and stamps on stamps: 1r, Seychelles #38, Great Britain #80 canceled. 2r, Seychelles #81, Great Britain #64 canceled. 3r, Seychelles #74, Great Britain #62 canceled. 5r, Seychelles #2, Great Britain #3 canceled. 10r, Seychelles #197, Great Britain #1 canceled.

1990, May 3   Perf. 12½
704	A110	1r multicolored	1.00	1.00
705	A110	2r multicolored	2.10	2.10
706	A110	3r multicolored	2.75	2.75
707	A110	5r multicolored	5.00	5.00
	Nos. 704-707 (4)		10.85	10.85

Souvenir Sheet
708	A110	10r multicolored	14.50	14.50

Boeing 767-200ER A111

Wmk. 384
1990, July 27   Litho.   Perf. 14½
709	A111	3r multicolored	5.50	5.50

Printed in panes of 10 (2 strips of 5 separated by pictorial gutter).

Queen Mother, 90th Birthday
Common Design Types

2r, Queen Elizabeth in coronation robes, 1937. 10r, Visiting workshops, 1947.

1990, Aug. 4   Wmk. 384   Perf. 14x15
710	CD343	2r multicolored	1.10	1.10

Perf. 14½
711	CD344	10r multicolored	5.50	5.50

A112

1r, Blackboard. 2r, Reading mail. 3r, Reading directions. 10r, Crossword puzzle.

1990, Sept. 8   Wmk. 373   Perf. 14
712	A112	1r multicolored	.90	.90
713	A112	2r multicolored	1.90	1.90
714	A112	3r multicolored	2.75	2.75
715	A112	10r multicolored	9.00	9.00
	Nos. 712-715 (4)		14.55	14.55

Intl. Literacy Year.

A113

Various Sega Dancers: a, Pink and white skirt, white blouse. b, Yellow dress. c, Blue, sky blue and pink dress. d, Yellow, green and pink dress. e, White and pink skirt, green blouse.

1990, Oct. 27   Perf. 13½x14
716		Strip of 5	15.00	15.00
a.-e.		A113 2r any single	2.75	2.75

Festival Kreol 1990.

First Regional Seminar, Indian Ocean Petroleum Exploration A114

1990, Dec. 10   Wmk. 384   Perf. 14½
717	A114	3r Beach	3.00	3.00
718	A114	10r Geological map	10.50	10.50

Orchids — A115

1r, Bulbophyllum intertextum. 2r, Agrostophyllum occidentale. 3r, Vanilla planifolia. 10r, Malaxis seychellarum.

1991, Feb. 1   Perf. 14
719	A115	1r multi	1.10	1.10
720	A115	2r multi	2.25	2.25
721	A115	3r multi	3.50	3.50
722	A115	10r multi	11.00	11.00
	Nos. 719-722 (4)		17.85	17.85

Elizabeth & Philip, Birthdays
Common Design Types

1991, June 17   Perf. 14½
723	CD345	4r multicolored	2.00	2.00
724	CD346	4r multicolored	2.00	2.00
a.		Pair, #723-724 + label	5.00	5.00

Butterflies A116

1.50r, Precis rhadama. 3r, Lampides boeticus. 3.50r, Zizeeria knysna. 10r, Phalanta phalanta aethiopica.
No. 729, Eagris sabadius.

Perf. 14½x14
1991, Nov. 15   Litho.   Wmk. 373
725	A116	1.50r multi	1.75	1.75
726	A116	3r multi	3.75	3.75
727	A116	3.50r multi	4.75	4.75
728	A116	10r multi	13.50	13.50
	Nos. 725-728 (4)		23.75	23.75

Souvenir Sheet
729	A116	10r multi	14.50	14.50

Phila Nippon '91.

Christmas A117

Woodcuts: 50c, The Holy Virgin, Joseph, the Holy Child and St. John by Raphael, engraved by S. Vouillemont. 1r, The Holy Virgin, the Child and an Angel by Van Dyck, engraved by A. Blooting. 2r, The Holy Family, St. John and St. Anna by Rubens, engraved by Lucas Vorsterman. 7r, The Holy Family, an Angel and St. Catherine, painting and engraving by Cornelius Bloemaert.

1991, Dec. 2   Wmk. 384   Perf. 14
730	A117	50c multicolored	.25	.25
731	A117	1r multicolored	1.25	1.25
732	A117	2r multicolored	2.75	2.75
733	A117	7r multicolored	9.00	9.00
	Nos. 730-733 (4)		13.25	13.25

Queen Elizabeth II's Accession to the Throne, 40th Anniv.
Common Design Type

1992, Feb. 6   Wmk. 373
734	CD349	1r multicolored	.80	.80
735	CD349	1.50r multicolored	1.10	1.10
736	CD349	3r multicolored	2.40	2.40
737	CD349	3.50r multicolored	2.50	2.50
738	CD349	5r multicolored	4.00	4.00
	Nos. 734-738 (5)		10.80	10.80

Flora and Fauna A118

Designs: 10c, Brush warbler. 25c, Bronze gecko, vert. 50c, Seychelles tree frog. 1r, Seychelles splendid palm, vert. 1.50r, Seychelles skink, vert. 2r, Giant tenebrionid beetle. 3r, Seychelles sunbird. 3.50r, Seychelles killifish. 4r, Magpie robin. 5r, Seychelles vanilla, vert. 10r, Tiger chameleon. 15r, Coco-de-mer, vert. 25r, Paradise flycatcher, vert. 50r, Giant tortoise.

Wmk. 373
1993, Mar. 1   Litho.   Perf. 13½
"1993" Date Imprint Beneath Design
739	A118	10c multicolored	.30	.30
b.		Inscribed "1996"	.50	
d.		Inscribed "2000"	—	
740	A118	25c multicolored	.30	.30
b.		Inscribed "1996"	.50	
d.		Inscribed "2000"	—	
741	A118	50c multicolored	.30	.30
b.		Inscribed "1996"	.50	
d.		Inscribed "2000"	—	
742	A118	1r multicolored	.40	.40
a.		Inscribed "1994"	1.20	1.20
d.		Inscribed "2000"		
743	A118	1.50r multicolored	.65	.65
744	A118	2r multicolored	.90	.90
b.		Inscribed "1996"	1.75	1.75
745	A118	3r multicolored	1.35	1.35
c.		Inscribed "1998"	3.50	3.50
d.		Inscribed "2000"		

746	A118	3.50r multicolored	1.75	1.75
d.		Inscribed "2000"	—	
e.		Perf. 14x13¾	—	18.00
747	A118	4r multicolored	1.75	1.75
748	A118	5r multicolored	2.25	2.25
a.		Inscribed "1994"	7.25	7.25
749	A118	10r multicolored	4.50	4.50
a.		Inscribed "1994"	13.00	13.00
750	A118	15r multicolored	6.50	6.50
b.		Inscribed "1996"	13.00	13.00
d.		Inscribed "2000"		
751	A118	25r multicolored	11.00	11.00
752	A118	50r multicolored	22.50	22.50
	Nos. 739-752 (14)		54.45	54.45

No. 746e is dated 2000.
For surcharges see Nos. 844-850.

First Visit to Seychelles by Archbishop of Canterbury — A119

Archbishop and: 3r, Anglican Cathedral, Victoria. 10r, Air France, Air Seychelles airplanes.

1993, June 8   Perf. 13½
753	A119	3r multicolored	2.50	1.25
754	A119	10r multicolored	8.75	4.50

4th Indian Ocean Island Games — A120

1993, Aug. 21   Perf. 14½
755	A120	1.50r Running	1.10	1.10
756	A120	3r Soccer	2.00	2.00
757	A120	3.50r Cycling	2.40	2.40
758	A120	10r Sailing	6.00	6.00
	Nos. 755-758 (4)		11.50	11.50

Telecommunications, Cent. — A121

Designs: 1r, Cable ship Scotia, Victoria, 1893. 3r, Eastern Telegraph Company's Office, Victoria, 1904. 4r, HF Transmitting Station, operational 1971. 10r, New Telecoms House, Victoria, 1993.

1993, Nov. 12   Perf. 13
759	A121	1r multicolored	.85	.85
760	A121	3r multicolored	2.50	2.50
761	A121	4r multicolored	3.75	3.75
762	A121	10r multicolored	9.50	9.50
	Nos. 759-762 (4)		16.60	16.60

Zil Elwannyen Sesel Nos. 59, 61, 63, 64 Srchd.

1994, Feb. 18   Perf. 14x14½
763	A9	1r on 2.10r #59	.70	.70
764	A9	1.50r on 2.75r #61	1.10	1.10
765	A9	3.50r on 7r #63	2.10	2.10
766	A9	10r on 15r #64	6.75	6.75
	Nos. 763-766 (4)		10.65	10.65

Hong Kong '94. Size and location of surcharge varies.

Butterflies
A122

1.50r, Eurema floricola. 3r, Coeliades forestan. 3.50r, Borbo borbonica. 10r, Zizula hylax.

1994, Aug. 16　Wmk. 384　Perf. 14

767	A122	1.50r multi	1.50	1.50
768	A122	3r multi	3.25	3.25
769	A122	3.50r multi	3.50	3.50
770	A122	10r multi	11.00	11.00
		Nos. 767-770 (4)	19.25	19.25

A123

1995, Sept. 26　Wmk. 373

771	A123	1.50r Age 9	.95	.95
772	A123	3r Wedding day	1.75	1.75
773	A123	3.50r 1936 Portrait	2.00	2.00
774	A123	10r 1975 Photograph	5.75	5.75
		Nos. 771-774 (4)	10.45	10.45

Queen Mother, 95th birthday.

A124

Black Paradise Flycatcher.

1996, July 12　Wmk. 384　Litho.　Perf. 14

775	A124	1r Female on branch	1.00	1.00
776	A124	1r Male in flight	1.00	1.00
777	A124	1r Male on branch	1.00	1.00
778	A124	1r Female, young	1.00	1.00
a.		Strip of 4, #775-778	4.75	4.75

Souvenir Sheet

779	A124	10r Female, male birds	8.50	8.50

World Wildlife Fund.
Stamps in No. 778a may be out of Scott number sequence.

A125

1996, July 15

780	A125	50c Swimming	.25	.25
781	A125	1.50r Running	.95	.95
782	A125	3r Sailing	2.10	2.10
783	A125	5r Boxing	3.50	3.50
		Nos. 780-783 (4)	6.80	6.80

Modern Olympic Games, cent.

A126

1996, Aug. 19　Wmk. 373　Litho.　Perf. 14

784	A126	3r shown	2.00	2.00
785	A126	10r Portrait up close	6.25	6.25

Archbishop Makarios of Cyprus, Exiled in Seychelles, 40th anniv.

Birds — A127

No. 786, Aldabra souimanga sunbird. No. 787, Seychelles sunbird. No. 788, Aldabra blue pigeon. No. 789, Seychelles blue pigeon. No. 790, Aldabra red headed fody. No. 791, Seychelles fody. No. 792, Aldabra white-eye. No. 793, Seychelles white-eye.

Wmk. 373

1996, Nov. 11　Litho.　Perf. 14½

786		3r multicolored	2.50	2.50
787		3r multicolored	2.50	2.50
a.		A127 Pair, #786-787	5.00	5.00
788		3r multicolored	2.50	2.50
789		3r multicolored	2.50	2.50
a.		A127 Pair, #788-789	5.00	5.00
790		3r multicolored	2.50	2.50
791		3r multicolored	2.50	2.50
a.		A127 Pair, #790-791	5.00	5.00
792		3r multicolored	2.50	2.50
793		3r multicolored	2.50	2.50
a.		A127 Pair, #792-793	5.00	5.00
		Nos. 786-793 (8)	20.00	20.00

Zil Elwannyen Sesel No. 58 Srchd.

1997, Feb. 12　Perf. 14x14½

794	A9	1.50r on 2r	3.50	3.50

Hong Kong '97.

Queen Elizabeth II and Prince Philip, 50th Wedding Anniv. — A128

Designs: No. 795, Queen in red & white dress. No. 796, Prince driving four-in-hand team. No. 797, Prince in business suit. No. 798, Queen, horse. No. 799, Prince Charles, Princess Anne. No. 800, Prince, Queen.
10r, Queen and Prince in open carriage, horiz.

Wmk. 373

1997, Nov. 20　Litho.　Perf. 13

795		1r multicolored	.85	.85
796		1r multicolored	.85	.85
a.		A128 Pair, #795-796	1.75	1.75
797		1.50r multicolored	1.10	1.10
798		1.50r multicolored	1.10	1.10
a.		A128 Pair, #797-798	2.25	2.25

799		3r multicolored	2.25	2.25
800		3r multicolored	2.25	2.25
a.		A128 Pair, #799-800	4.50	4.50
		Nos. 795-800 (6)	8.40	8.40

Souvenir Sheet

801	A128	10r multicolored	7.50	7.50

Diana, Princess of Wales (1961-97)
Common Design Type

Designs: a, In red dress. b, Wearing white blouse, printed vest. c, In blue dress, flowers. d, Wearing white dress.

Perf. 14½x14

1998, Mar. 31　Litho.　Wmk. 373

802	CD355	3r Sheet of 4, #a.-d.	6.25	6.25

No. 802 sold for 12r + 3r, with surtax from international sales being donated to the Princess Diana Memorial Fund and surtax from national sales being donated to designated local charity.

Intl. Year of the Ocean — A129

Designs: a, Blue and yellow fish. b, School of gold-colored fish. c, Lionfish. d, Various small fish. e, Anemones. f, Turtle.

1998　Litho.　Perf. 14

803	A129	3r Strip of 6, #a.-f.	9.50	9.50
		Complete booklet, 2 #803	20.00	

Australia '99, World Stamp Expo A130

18th Cent. ships: 1.50r, Vierge du Cap, 1721. 3r, Elizabeth, 1741. 3.50r, Curieuse, 1768. 10r, Le Flèche, 1801.
20r, The Cheval Marin, 1774, vert.

1999　Litho.　Perf. 14

804	A130	1.50r multicolored	.75	.75
805	A130	3r multicolored	1.50	1.50
806	A130	3.50r multicolored	1.75	1.75
807	A130	10r multicolored	5.25	5.25
		Nos. 804-807 (4)	9.25	9.25

Souvenir Sheet

808	A130	20r multicolored	12.00	12.00

Nos. 804-807 each issued with se-tenant label.

Wedding of Prince Edward and Sophie Rhys-Jones A131

Wmk. 373

1999, Sept. 1　Litho.　Perf. 13¼

809	A131	3r shown	2.25	2.25
810	A131	15r In carriage	7.25	7.25

Christmas and Millennium A132

1r, Cathedral of the Immaculate Conception. 1.50r, Fairy tern. 2.50r, Dolphin. 10r, Comet.

Perf. 14x14½

1999, Dec. 14　Litho.　Wmk. 373

811	A132	1r multi	.75	.75
812	A132	1.50r multi	1.10	1.10
813	A132	2.50r multi	1.75	1.75
814	A132	10r multi	6.75	6.75
		Nos. 811-814 (4)	10.35	10.35

Queen Mother, 100th Birthday — A133

Designs: 3r, As child. 5r, As young woman. 7r, With King George VI. 10r, As old woman.

Wmk. 373

2000, Aug. 4　Litho.　Perf. 14¼

815	A133	3r multi	1.50	1.50
816	A133	5r multi	2.50	2.50
817	A133	7r multi	3.50	3.50
818	A133	10r multi	5.00	5.00
		Nos. 815-818 (4)	12.50	12.50

Anniversaries — A134

Designs: 1r, Arrival of the Jacobin deportees, 200th anniv. 1.50r, Victoria as capital of Seychelles, 160th anniv. 3r, Arrival of Father Leon Des Avanchers, 150th anniv. 3.50r, Victoria Fountain, cent., vert. 5r, Botanical Gardens, cent. 10r, Independence, 25th anniv., vert.

Wmk. 373

2001, July 25　Litho.　Perf. 14

819-824	A134	Set of 6	8.75	8.75

Nos. 819 and 824 lack Age of Victoria emblem.

Ducks A135

Designs: No. 825, 3r, Garganey. No. 826, 3r, Northern shoveler. No. 827, 3r, Ruddy shelduck. No. 828, 3r, White-faced whistling duck.

Wmk. 384

2001, Oct. 4　Litho.　Perf. 14

825-828	A135	Set of 4	9.00	9.00

Birdlife International World Bird Festival — A136

Seychelles Scops owl: a, In flight. b, In tree. c, Standing on branch, vert. d, Standing on tip of broken branch, vert. e, Standing on branch.

Perf. 14¼x14½, 14½x14¼

2001, Oct. 4

829	A136	3r Sheet of 5, #a-e	14.00	14.00

Queen Mother Elizabeth (1900-2002)
Common Design Type
Souvenir Sheet

No. 830: a, 5r, As young woman, without hat. b, 10r, As old woman, wearing hat.

Perf. 14½x14¼

2002, Aug. 5　Litho.　Wmk. 373
Without Purple Frames

830	CD361	Sheet of 2, #a-b	6.50	6.50

Worldwide Fund for Nature (WWF) A137

Frogs: No. 831, 1r, Seychelles frog. No. 832, 1r, Palm frog. No. 833, 1r, Thomasset's frog. No. 834, 1r, Gardiner's frog. 20r, Seychelles tree frog.

Wmk. 373
2003, Feb. 3   Litho.   *Perf. 14*
831-834 A137   Set of 4   4.00 4.00
Souvenir Sheet
835 A137 20r multi   11.50 11.50

Fish A138

Designs: 10c, Seychelles blenny. 50c, Seychelles anemonefish. 1r, Indian butterflyfish. 1.50r, Goldbar wrasse. 3r, Seychelles squirrelfish. 5r, Greenthroat parrotfish. 50r, Whale shark.

Wmk. 373
2003, Nov. 3   Litho.   *Perf. 14*
836 A138   10c multi   .30 .30
837 A138   50c multi   .30 .30
838 A138   1r multi   .55 .55
839 A138   1.50r multi   .80 .80
840 A138   3r multi   1.30 1.30
841 A138   5r multi   2.10 2.10
  a.   Wmk. 406, dated "2010"   .95 .95
842 A138   50r multi   21.00 21.00
  a.   Wmk. 406, dated "2010" 9.50 9.50
      Nos. 836-842 (7)   26.35 26.35

See Nos. 852-858, 893-896.
Issued: Nos. 841a, 842a, 7/5/10.

Indian Ocean Commission, 20th Anniv. — A139

Wmk. 373
2004, Feb. 16   Litho.   *Perf. 13¼*
843 A139 15r multi   5.75 5.75

Nos. 743, 745, 748-752 Surcharged

Methods and Perfs As Before
2004, July 1   Wmk. 373
844 A118   1r on 1.50r #743   .70 .70
845 A118   2r on 3r #745   1.30 1.30
846 A118   3.50r on 5r #748 2.50 2.50
847 A118   3.50r on 10r #749 2.50 2.50
848 A118   3.50r on 15r #750 2.50 2.50
849 A118   4r on 25r #751   2.75 2.75
850 A118   4r on 50r #752   2.75 2.75
      Nos. 844-850 (7)   15.00 15.00

Pope John Paul II (1920-2005) A140

Wmk. 373
2005, Aug. 18   Litho.   *Perf. 14*
851 A140 5r multi   3.75 3.75

Fish Type of 2003

Designs: 25c, African pygmy angelfish. 2r, Picasso triggerfish. 3.50r, Palette surgeonfish. 4r, Longfin batfish. 10r, Masked moray eel. 15r, Lyretail grouper. 25r, Emperor snapper.

2005, Oct. 3   Wmk. 373   *Perf. 14*
852 A138   25c multi   .30 .30
853 A138   1r multi   1.00 1.00
  a.   Wmk. 406, dated "2012"   .55 .55
854 A138   3.50r multi 1.90 1.90
  a.   Wmk. 406, dated "2010"   .65 .65
855 A138   4r multi   2.10 2.10
  a.   Wmk. 406, dated "2010"   .80 .80
  b.   Wmk. 406, dated "2012"   .65 .65
856 A138   10r multi   4.25 4.25
  a.   Wmk. 406, dated "2010" 1.90 1.90
857 A138   15r multi   5.75 5.75
  a.   Wmk. 406, dated "2010" 2.75 2.75
858 A138   25r multi   9.50 9.50
  a.   Wmk. 406, dated "2010" 4.75 4.75
      Nos. 852-858 (7)   24.80 24.80

Issued: Nos. 854a, 855a, 856a, 857a, 858a, 7/5/10. Nos. 853a, 855b, 12/1/12.

Exile of Archbishop Makarios in Seychelles, 50th Anniv. — A141

Designs: 3.50r, Archbishop Makarios and Seychelles natives. 15r, Archbishop Makarios.

Wmk. 373
2006, June 28   Litho.   *Perf. 14*
859-860 A141   Set of 2   11.50 11.50

Independence, 30th Anniv. — A142

Designs: 50c, Possesion Stone. 1r, Seychelles flag. 1.50r, Valee de Mai World Heritage Site. 2r, School children. 3.50r, Jacob Marie holding bonm. 4r, Ship "Seychelles Progress." 15r, Independence anniversary emblem.

Wmk. 373
2006, June 28   Litho.   *Perf. 14*
861-867 A142   Set of 7   17.50 17.50

Selection of Aldabra as UNESCO World Heritage Site, 25th Anniv. — A143

Designs: 2r, Zangiv flowers. 3.50r, Dugongs. 10r, Giant tortoises.

Perf. 12½x13
2007, Nov. 19   Litho.   Wmk. 373
868-870 A143   Set of 3   6.00 6.00

2008 Summer Olympics, Beijing A144

Designs: 1r, Bamboo, kayaking. 1.50r, Dragon, swimming. 2r, Lantern, sailing. 3.50r, Fish, javelin.

Wmk. 373
2008, Apr. 30   Litho.   *Perf. 13¼*
871-874 A144   Set of 4   2.75 2.75

Aldabra Drongos A145

Aldabra Red-headed Fodies — A146

Wmk. 373
2008, Oct. 1   Litho.   *Perf. 14*
875 A145   1r shown   .45 .45
876 A145   1r Drongos, diff. .45 .45
877 A146   1r shown   .45 .45
878 A146   1r Fodies, diff. .45 .45
      Nos. 875-878 (4)   1.80 1.80
Souvenir Sheet
879 A146 20r Fody and drongo 6.50 6.50

Worldwide Fund for Nature (WWF).

Explorers and Ships — A147

Designs: 1.50r, Ferdinand Magellan. 3.50r, Sir Martin Frobisher. 6.50r, Sir Francis Drake. 8r, Henry Hudson. 15r, Abel Tasman. 27r, Sir John Franklin.
7r, The Ascension.

Wmk. 406
2009, May 25   Litho.   *Perf. 14*
880-885 A147   Set of 6   9.50 9.50
Souvenir Sheet
886 A147   7r multi   2.00 2.00

Space Exploration A148

Designs: 3.50r, X-1 jet being loaded under Superfortress, 1951. 7r, Lunar landing research vehicle, 1964. 8r, Apollo 11 launch site, 1969. 13r, Space Shuttle flight STS-86 on launch pad, 1997. 20r, Soyuz TMA-13 rolls out to launch pad, 2008.
24r, Astronaut on Moon, painting by Capt. Alan Bean, vert.

Wmk. 406
2009, July 20   Litho.   *Perf. 13¼*
887-891 A148   Set of 5   9.00 9.00
Souvenir Sheet
Perf. 13x13¼
892 A148 24r multi   4.75 4.75

No. 892 contains one 40x60mm stamp. Nos. 887-891 each were printed in sheets of 6.

Fish Type of 2003

Designs: 6.50r, Queen coris. 7r, White-lined goatfish. 8r, Three-spot angelfish. 100r, Coral grouper.

Wmk. 406
2010, July 5   Litho.   *Perf. 14*
893 A138   6.50r multi   1.00 1.00
894 A138   7r multi   1.10 1.10
895 A138   8r multi   1.25 1.25
  a.   Dated "2012"   1.25 1.25
896 A138   100r multi   16.00 16.00
      Nos. 893-896 (4) 19.35 19.35

Issued: No. 895a, 12/1/12.

Wedding of Prince William and Catherine Middleton — A149

Couple: 3.50r, Waving in coach. 4r, Kissing, vert. 7r, Standing and waving, vert. 25r, Holding hands, vert.

2011, Aug. 1
897-900 A149   Set of 4   6.50 6.50

State House, Cent. A150

2011, Nov. 11
901 A150 3.50r multi   .55 .55

Seychelles Post Office, 150th Anniv. — A151

Designs: 3.50r, Post Office, Victoria, 2011. 7r, Old Post Office, Victoria, 1900s.

2011, Dec. 12
902-903 A151   Set of 2   1.60 1.60

Green Turtle A152

2014, Oct. 9   Litho.   *Perf. 13x13¼*
904 A152 50r multi   7.00 7.00

See Comoro Islands No. , France No. 4695, French Southern & Antarctic Territories No. 511, Malagasy Republic No. , Mauritius No. 1144.

POSTAGE DUE STAMPS

Catalogue values for unused stamps in this section are for **Never Hinged** items.

D1

Engr.; Denomination Typo. in Carmine

1951, Mar. 1 Wmk. 4 *Perf. 11½*

J1	D1	2c carmine	1.50	*3.00*
J2	D1	3c blue green	2.25	*3.00*
J3	D1	6c ocher	2.25	*2.25*
J4	D1	9c brown orange	2.25	*4.00*
J5	D1	15c purple	2.10	*12.50*
J6	D1	18c deep blue	2.75	*12.50*
J7	D1	20c black brown	2.75	*12.50*
J8	D1	30c red brown	2.75	*9.00*
		Nos. J1-J8 (8)	18.60	*58.75*

Engr.; Denomination Typo.

1964-65 Wmk. 314

J9	D1	2c carmine	2.00	*14.00*
J10	D1	3c green & red	2.00	*16.00*

Issue dates: July 7, 1964, Sept. 14, 1965.

Dated "1980"

1980 Litho. *Perf. 14*

J11	D1	5c lilac rose & red	.30	*1.60*
J12	D1	10c dk green & red	.30	*1.60*
J13	D1	15c bister & red	.30	*1.60*
J14	D1	20c brown org & red	.30	*1.60*
J15	D1	25c violet & red	.30	*1.60*
J16	D1	75c dk red brown & red	.35	*1.60*
J17	D1	80c dk blue & red	.40	*1.75*
J18	D1	1r claret & red	.40	*1.75*
		Nos. J11-J18 (8)	2.65	13.10

ZIL ELWANNYEN SESEL

LOCATION — South of Seychelles

The islands of Aldabra, Farquhar and Des Roches. Formerly part of the British Indian Ocean Territory.

Catalogue values for unused stamps in this country are for Never Hinged items.

Type of Seychelles, 1977-78

Imprinted "1980" Beneath Design

Size: 30x26mm (40c, 1r, 1.25r, 1.50r)

Perf. 14, 14½x14 (40c, 1r, 1.25r, 1.50r)

1980-81 Litho. Wmk. 373

1	A44	5c Reef fish	.25	.25
2	A44	10c Hawksbill turtle	.25	.25
3	A44	15c Coco-de-mer	.25	.25
4	A44	20c Wild vanilla	.30	.25
5	A44	25c Butterfly	1.25	.25
6	A44	40c Coral reef	.45	.25
7	A44	50c Giant tortoise	.45	.25
8	A44	75c Crayfish	.55	.25
9	A44	1r Madagascar fody	1.50	.75
10	A44	1.10r Green gecko	.60	*.75*
11	A44	1.25r Fairy tern	2.00	.80
12	A44	1.50r Flying fox	.75	.60

Size: 27x35mm

13	A44	5r Octopus, vert.	1.10	*1.40*
a.		Perf. 13 ('81)	1.50	1.50
14	A44	10r Giant tiger cowrie, vert.	1.25	*2.25*
a.		Perf. 13 ('81)	2.50	2.50
15	A44	15r Pitcher plant, vert.	1.50	*3.50*
a.		Perf. 13 ('81)	3.50	3.50
16	A44	20r Natl. arms, vert.	1.50	*4.75*
a.		Perf. 13 ('81)	4.75	4.75
		Nos. 1-16 (16)	13.95	16.80

Nos. 13a-16a have "1981" date imprint beneath design.

1981 Inscribed "1981"

1a	A44	5c multicolored	.25	.25
2a	A44	10c multicolored	.25	.25
3a	A44	15c multicolored	.25	.25
4a	A44	20c multicolored	.30	.25
5a	A44	25c multicolored	1.50	.25
6a	A44	40c multicolored	.60	.25
7a	A44	50c multicolored	.60	.25
8a	A44	75c multicolored	.60	.25
9a	A44	1r multicolored	1.50	.75
10a	A44	1.10r multicolored	.90	.75
11a	A44	1.25r multicolored	2.00	.80
12a	A44	1.50r multicolored	.90	.60
		Nos. 1a-12a (12)	9.65	4.90

Traveling Post Office A1

1980, Oct. 24 *Perf. 14*

17	A1	1.50r Cinq Juin	.25	.25
18	A1	2.10r Canceling letters	.25	.25
19	A1	5r Map	.50	.50
		Nos. 17-19 (3)	1.00	1.00

The 5r showing Agalega as part of the Seychelles was not issued.

Marine Life — A2

1980, Nov. 28

20	A2	1.50r Yellowfin Tuna	.50	.50
21	A2	2.10r Blue marlin	.55	.55
22	A2	5r Sperm whale	1.05	1.05
		Nos. 20-22 (3)	2.10	2.10

Royal Wedding Types of Seychelles

1981, June 23 Wmk. 380 *Perf. 14*

23	A61a	40c Royal Escape	.25	.25
a.		Bklt. pane of 4, perf. 12½x12, unwmkd.	1.10	1.10
24	A61b	40c Couple	.40	.40
25	A61a	5r Victoria & Albert II	.80	.80
26	A61b	5r like #24	1.25	1.25
a.		Bklt pane of 2, perf. 12½x12, unwmkd.	3.00	3.00
27	A61a	10r Britannia	1.50	1.50
28	A61b	10r like #24	2.50	2.50
		Nos. 23-28 (6)	6.70	6.70

Souvenir Sheet

Perf. 12½x12

29	A61b	7.50r like #24	2.50	2.50

Each denomination issued in sheets of 7 (6 type A61a, 1 type A61b).

For surcharges see Nos. 70-75.

Wildlife A3

1981, Dec. 11 Wmk. 373 *Perf. 14*

30	A3	1.40r Wright's skink	.30	.30
31	A3	2.25r Tree frog	.40	.40
32	A3	5r Robber crab	.65	.65
		Nos. 30-32 (3)	1.35	1.35

Workboats — A4

1982, Mar. 11 *Perf. 14x14½*

33	A4	1.75r Cinq Juin	.55	.45
34	A4	2.10r Junon	.65	.55
35	A4	5r Diamond M. Dragon	.80	.70
		Nos. 33-35 (3)	2.00	1.70

Mailboats A5

1982, July 22 Wmk. 373 *Perf. 14*

36	A5	40c Paulette	.40	.30
37	A5	1.75r Janette	.55	.55
38	A5	2.75r Lady Esme	.70	.75
39	A5	3.50r Cinq Juin	.75	.90
		Nos. 36-39 (4)	2.40	2.50

Aldabra, World Heritage Site — A6

1982, Nov. 19

40	A6	40c Birds flying over island	.30	.30
41	A6	2.75r Map	.65	.65
42	A6	7r Giant tortoises	1.40	1.40
		Nos. 40-42 (3)	2.35	2.35

Wildlife A7

1983, Feb. 25 *Perf. 14x14½*

43	A7	1.75r Red land crab	.45	.45
44	A7	2.75r Black terrapin	.80	.80
45	A7	7r Madagascar green gecko	2.00	2.00
		Nos. 43-45 (3)	3.25	3.25

Maps — A8

1983, Apr. 27 *Perf. 14½*

46	A8	40c Poivre Island, Ile du Sud	.30	.30
47	A8	1.50r Ile des Roches	.30	.30
48	A8	2.75r Astove Island	.60	.60
49	A8	7r Coetivy Island	1.50	1.50
a.		Souvenir sheet of 4, #46-49	4.25	4.25
		Nos. 46-49 (4)	2.70	2.70

Birds — A9

5c, Aldabra brush warbler. 10c, Barred ground dove. 15c, Aldabra nightjar. 20c, Malagasy grass warbler. 25c, Aldabra white-eye. 40c, Aldabra fody. 50c, Aldabra rail. 75c, Aldabra bulbul. 2r, Dimorphic little egret. 2.10r, Aldabra sunbird. 2.50r, Aldabra turtle dove. 2.75r, Aldabra sacred ibis. 3.50r, Aldabra coucal. 7r, Aldabra kestrel. 15r, Aldabra blue pigeon. 20r, Greater flamingo.

Perf. 14x14½

1983, July 13 Wmk. 373

50	A9	5c multicolored	.25	.25
51	A9	10c multicolored	.25	.25
52	A9	15c multicolored	.25	.25
53	A9	20c multicolored	.25	.25
54	A9	25c multicolored	.25	.25
55	A9	40c multicolored	.25	.25
56	A9	50c multicolored	.25	.25
57	A9	75c multicolored	.30	.30
58	A9	2r multicolored	1.10	1.10
59	A9	2.10r multicolored	1.25	1.40
60	A9	2.50r multicolored	1.50	1.50
61	A9	2.75r multicolored	1.60	1.75

Perf. 14½x14

62	A9	3.50r multicolored	2.00	2.10
63	A9	7r multicolored	4.25	4.50
64	A9	15r multicolored	9.00	9.50
65	A9	20r multicolored	11.50	12.00
		Nos. 50-65 (16)	34.25	35.90

Nos. 62-65 vert. See Nos. 96-100. For surcharges see Seychelles Nos. 763-766.

World Tourism Day A10

1983, Sept. 27 *Perf. 14*

66	A10	50c Windsurfing	.30	.30
67	A10	2r Hotel	.30	.30
68	A10	3r Beach	.50	.50
69	A10	10r Sunset	1.50	1.50
		Nos. 66-69 (4)	2.60	2.60

Nos. 23-28 Surcharged

1983 Wmk. 380 *Perf. 14*

70	A61a	30c on 40c multi	.35	.35
71	A61b	30c on 40c multi	.35	.35
72	A61a	2r on 5r multi	1.40	1.40
73	A61b	2r on 5r multi	1.40	1.40
74	A61a	3r on 10r multi	2.00	2.00
75	A61b	3r on 10r multi	2.00	2.00
		Nos. 70-75 (6)	7.50	7.50

Each denomination issued in sheets of 7 (6 type A61a, 1 type A61b).

Aldabra Post Office, Reopening — A11

1984, Mar. 30 Wmk. 373 *Perf. 14*

76	A11	50c Map, postmark	.25	.25
77	A11	2.75r Aldabra rail	.80	.80
78	A11	3r Giant tortoise	.90	.90
79	A11	10r Red-footed booby	3.25	3.25
		Nos. 76-79 (4)	5.20	5.20

Game Fishing A12

50c, Fishing boat. 2r, Hooked fish, vert. 3r, Weighing catch, vert. 10r, Fishing boat, stern view.

1984, May 31

80	A12	50c multicolored	.25	.25
81	A12	2r multicolored	.60	.60
82	A12	3r multicolored	.80	.80
83	A12	10r multicolored	2.75	2.75
		Nos. 80-83 (4)	4.40	4.40

Crabs A13

1984, Aug. 24 *Perf. 14½*

84	A13	50c Giant hermit crab	.25	.25
85	A13	2r Fiddler crabs	.75	.75
86	A13	3r Ghost crab	1.00	1.00
87	A13	10r Spotted pebble crab	3.50	3.50
		Nos. 84-87 (4)	5.50	5.50

Constellations A14

1984, Oct. 16 *Perf. 14*

88	A14	50c Orion	.25	.25
89	A14	2r Cygnus	.65	.65
90	A14	3r Virgo	.90	.90
91	A14	10r Scorpio	2.50	2.50
		Nos. 88-91 (4)	4.30	4.30

Mushrooms — A15

Wmk. 373

1985, Jan. 31   Litho.   Perf. 14

92	A15	50c	Lenzites elegans	.25 .25
93	A15	2r	Xylaria telfairei	1.60 1.60
94	A15	3r	Lentinus sajor-caju	2.25 2.25
95	A15	10r	Hexagonia tenuis	7.75 7.75
		Nos. 92-95 (4)		11.85 11.85

Bird Type of 1983
Year Imprint ( ) Beneath Design
Inscribed "Zil Elwannyen Sesel"
Wmk. 373, 384 (5c)

1985-88   Perf. 14x14½

96	A9	5c	Like #50 (1988)		5.50 5.50
			('88)		
97	A9	10c	Like #51 (1985)		5.50 5.50
a.			Inscribed "1987"		5.50 5.50
b.			Wmk. 384 (1988) ('88)		5.50 5.50
98	A9	25c	Like #54 (1985)		5.50 5.50
99	A9	50c	Like #56 (1987)		
			('87)		5.50 5.50
a.			Wmk. 384 ('88)		5.50 5.50
100	A9	2r	Like #58		7.50 7.50
a.			Wmk. 384 ('88)		7.50 7.50
b.			As "a," inscribed "1990"		7.50 7.50
		Nos. 96-100 (5)			29.50 29.50

Common Design Types
pictured following the introduction.

Queen Mother 85th Birthday
Common Design Type

1r, Coronation portrait. 2r, With Princess Anne. 3r, Wearing tiara. 5r, Holding Prince Henry. 10r, In river taxi, Venice.

Perf. 14½x14

1985, June 1   Wmk. 384

101	CD336	1r	multicolored	.25 .25
102	CD336	2r	multicolored	.65 .65
103	CD336	3r	multicolored	1.00 1.00
104	CD336	5r	multicolored	1.75 1.75
		Nos. 101-104 (4)		3.65 3.65

Souvenir Sheet

105	CD336	10r	multicolored	3.50 3.50

World Wildlife Fund A16

50c, Giant tortoise. 75c, Tortoises crossing stream. 1r, Three tortoises. 2r, Tortoise facing right.

10r, Two tortoises.

1985, Sept. 27   Perf. 14

106	A16	50c	multicolored	8.25 3.00
107	A16	75c	multicolored	9.00 1.00
108	A16	1r	multicolored	9.75 4.00
109	A16	2r	multicolored	13.00 5.50
		Nos. 106-109 (4)		40.00 13.50

Souvenir Sheet
Perf. 13x13½

110	A16	10r	multicolored	29.00 29.00

See Nos. 131-134.

Famous Visitors A17

Visitors and their ships: 50c, Phoenician trader, 600 B.C. 2r, Sir Hugh Scott, HMS Sealark, 1908. 10r, Vasco de Gama, Sao Gabriel, 1502.

1985, Oct. 25   Wmk. 373   Perf. 14

111	A17	50c	multicolored	.30 .30
112	A17	2r	multicolored	1.25 1.25
113	A17	10r	multicolored	6.25 6.25
		Nos. 111-113 (3)		7.80 7.80

Queen Elizabeth II, 60th Birthday
Common Design Type

Designs: 75c, As princess. 1r, With Prince Philip. 1.50r, Wearing blue cape. 3.75r, Portrait. 5r, Wearing red hat.

Perf. 14½x14

1986, Apr. 21   Wmk. 384

114	CD337	75c	scar, blk & sil	.25 .25
115	CD337	1r	blue & multi	.25 .25
116	CD337	1.50r	grn & multi	.25 .25
117	CD337	3.75r	vio & multi	.60 .60
118	CD337	5r	rose vio & multi	.90 .90
		Nos. 114-118 (5)		2.25 2.25

For overprints see Nos. 135-139.

Royal Wedding
Common Design Type

3r, Sarah Ferguson, Prince Andrew. 7r, Andrew.

1986, July 23   Perf. 14

119	CD338	3r	multicolored	.70 .70
120	CD338	7r	multicolored	1.60 1.60

Coral — A18

Continuous design: a, Acropora palifera, Tubastraea coccinea. b, Echinopora lamellosa, Favia pallida. c, Sarcophyton sp, Porites lutea. d, Goniopora sp, Goniastrea retiformis. e, Tubipora musica, Fungia fungites.

1986, Sept. 17

121	A18	2r	Strip of 5, #a.-e.	13.00 13.00

Flowers — A19

1986, Nov. 12

122	A19	50c	Hibiscus tiliaceus	.30 .30
123	A19	2r	Crinum angustum	1.50 1.50
124	A19	3r	Phaius tetragonus	2.25 2.25
125	A19	10r	Rothmannia annae	7.75 7.75
		Nos. 122-125 (4)		11.80 11.80

Fish — A20

Continuous design: a, Chaetodon unimaculatus. b, Ostorhincus fleurieu. c, Platax orbicularis. d, abudefduf annulatus. e, Chaetodon lineolatus.

1987, Mar. 26

126	A20	2r	Strip of #126a-126e	9.50 9.50

Trees — A21

1987, Aug. 26   Perf. 14½

127	A21	1r	Coconut	.80 .80
128	A21	2r	Mangrove	1.75 1.75
129	A21	3r	Pandanus palm	3.00 3.00
130	A21	5r	Indian almond	5.00 5.00
		Nos. 127-130 (4)		10.55 10.55

Nos. 106-109 Redrawn
World Wildlife Fund Emblem
without Circle

1987, Sept. 9   Wmk. 384   Perf. 14

131	A16	50c	multicolored	9.75 5.50
132	A16	75c	multicolored	12.50 7.00
133	A16	1r	multicolored	15.00 8.50
134	A16	2r	multicolored	20.00 11.50
		Nos. 131-134 (4)		57.25 32.50

Nos. 114-118 Ovptd. in Silver "40TH WEDDING ANNIVERSARY"

1987, Dec. 9   Perf. 14½x14

135	CD337	75c	scar, blk & sil	.25 .25
136	CD337	1r	blue & multi	.30 .30
137	CD337	1.50r	grn & multi	.50 .50
138	CD337	3.75r	vio & multi	1.25 1.25
139	CD337	5r	rose vio & multi	1.75 1.75
		Nos. 135-139 (5)		4.05 4.05

Mai Valley Tropical Forest — A22

Continuous design: b, Trunk of palm tree at right. c, Bamboo.

1987, Dec. 16   Perf. 14

140	A22	3r	Strip of 3, #a.-c.	11.00 11.00

Insects A23

1r, Yanga seychellensis. 2r, Belenois aldabraensis. 3r, Polyspilota seychelliana. 5r, Polposipus herculeanus.

1988, July 28   Wmk. 373

141	A23	1r	multi	2.10 2.10
142	A23	2r	multi	3.50 3.50
143	A23	3r	multi	4.25 4.25
144	A23	5r	multi	5.25 5.25
		Nos. 141-144 (4)		15.10 15.10

Souvenir Sheet

1988 Summer Olympics, Seoul — A24

1988, Aug. 31   Wmk. 384

145	A24	10r	multicolored	7.50 7.50

Lloyds' of London, 300th Anniv.
Common Design Type

Designs: 1r, Lloyd's building, 1988. 2r, Cable ship Retriever, horiz. 3r, Chantel, horiz. 5r, Torrey Canyon aground off Cornwall, 1967.

1988, Oct. 28   Wmk. 373

146	CD341	1r	multicolored	1.10 1.10
147	CD341	2r	multicolored	1.90 1.90
148	CD341	3r	multicolored	3.00 3.00
149	CD341	5r	multicolored	5.25 5.25
		Nos. 146-149 (4)		11.25 11.25

Christmas — A25

Perf. 13½x14, 14x13½

1988, Nov. 18   Wmk. 384

150	A25	1r	Santa, toys in canoe	.45 .45
151	A25	2r	Church, vert.	.75 .75
152	A25	3r	Santa riding bird, vert.	1.15 1.15
153	A25	5r	Sleigh over island	1.90 1.90
		Nos. 150-153 (4)		4.25 4.25

Moon Landing, 20th Anniv.
Common Design Type

Apollo 18: 1r, Firing room, Launch Control Center. 2r, Astronauts Slayton, Stafford, Brand and cosmonauts Leonov and Kubasov. 3r, Mission emblem. 5r, Apollo and Soyuz docking in space. 10r, Apollo 11 lifted aboard USS Hornet.

Size of Nos. 155-156: 29x29mm

Perf. 14x13½, 14 (#155-156)

1989, July 20

154	CD342	1r	multicolored	1.25 1.25
155	CD342	2r	multicolored	2.10 2.10
156	CD342	3r	multicolored	3.25 3.25
157	CD342	5r	multicolored	5.25 5.25
		Nos. 154-157 (4)		11.85 11.85

Souvenir Sheet

158	CD342	10r	multicolored	15.00 15.00

Poisonous Plants — A26

1989, Oct. 9   Perf. 14

159	A26	1r	Dumb cane	1.40 1.40
160	A26	2r	Star of Bethlehem	3.00 3.00
161	A26	3r	Indian licorice	4.50 4.50
162	A26	5r	Black nightshade	7.00 7.00
		Nos. 159-162 (4)		15.90 15.90

See Nos. 173-176.

Creole Cooking — A27

1r, Tec-tec broth. 2r, Pilaf a la Seychelloise. 3r, Mullet grilled in banana leaves. 5r, Daube.

1989, Dec. 18

163	A27	1r	multi	1.40 1.40
164	A27	2r	multi	2.75 2.75
165	A27	3r	multi	4.00 4.00
166	A27	5r	multi	6.50 6.50
a.			Souvenir sheet of 4, #163-166	16.00 16.00
		Nos. 163-166 (4)		14.65 14.65

No. 166a has continuous design.

Stamp World London '90 A28

Designs: 1r, #22. 2r, #13. 3r, #61. 5r, #32.

Wmk. 373

1990, May 3   Litho.   Perf. 12½

167	A28	1r	multicolored	1.40 1.40
168	A28	2r	multicolored	3.00 3.00
169	A28	3r	multicolored	4.25 4.25
170	A28	5r	multicolored	7.75 7.75
a.			Souvenir sheet of 4, #167-170	15.00 15.00
		Nos. 167-170 (4)		16.40 16.40

Queen Mother 90th Birthday
Common Design Types

Designs: 2r, As Duchess of York with infant Elizabeth. 10r, With King George VI viewing bomb-damaged London, 1940.

1990, Aug. 4 Wmk. 384 *Perf. 14x15*
171 CD343 2r multi 1.25 1.25

Perf. 14½
172 CD344 10r yel brn & blk 7.00 7.00

Poisonous Plants Type of 1989
Wmk. 373

1990, Nov. 5 Litho. *Perf. 12½*
173 A26 1r Ordeal plant 1.40 1.40
174 A26 2r Thorn apple 2.75 2.75
175 A26 3r Strychnine tree 4.00 4.00
176 A26 5r Bwa zasmen 7.25 7.25
Nos. 173-176 (4) 15.40 15.40

Elizabeth & Philip, Birthdays
Common Design Types
Wmk. 384

1991, June 17 Litho. *Perf. 14½*
177 CD345 4r multicolored 3.00 3.00
178 CD346 4r multicolored 3.00 3.00
a. Pair, #177-178 + label 6.50 6.50

Shipwrecks — A29

Wmk. 373

1991, Oct. 28 Litho. *Perf. 14*
179 A29 1.50r St. Abbs, 1860 2.25 2.25
180 A29 3r Norden, 1862 4.00 4.00
181 A29 3.50r Clan Mackay, 1894 4.50 4.50
182 A29 10r Glenlyon, 1905 11.50 11.50
Nos. 179-182 (4) 22.25 22.25

Queen Elizabeth II's Accession to the Throne, 40th Anniv.
Common Design Type

1992, Feb. 6
183 CD349 1r multicolored .75 .75
184 CD349 1.50r multicolored 1.00 1.00
185 CD349 3r multicolored 1.90 1.90
186 CD349 3.50r multicolored 2.25 2.25
187 CD349 5r multicolored 3.50 3.50
Nos. 183-187 (5) 9.40 9.40

Aldabra World Heritage Site, 10th Anniv. — A30

Designs: 1.50r, Lomatopyllum aldabrense. 3r, Dryolimnas cuvieri aldabranus. 3.50r, Birgus latro. 10r, Dicrurus aldabranus.

1992, Nov. 19 *Perf. 14½*
188 A30 1.50r multicolored 2.00 2.00
189 A30 3r multicolored 4.00 4.00
190 A30 3.50r multicolored 4.75 4.75
191 A30 10r multicolored 13.00 13.00
Nos. 188-191 (4) 23.75 23.75

SHANGHAI

shaŋ-hī

LOCATION — A city on the Whangpoo River, Kiangsu Province, China
POP. — 3,489,998

A British settlement was founded there in 1843 and by agreement with China settlements were established by France and the United States. Special areas were set aside for the foreign settlements and a postal system independent of China was organized which was continued until 1898.

16 Cash = 1 Candareen
100 Candareens = 1 Tael
100 Cents = 1 Dollar (1890)

Watermark

Wmk. 175 — Kung Pu (Municipal Council)

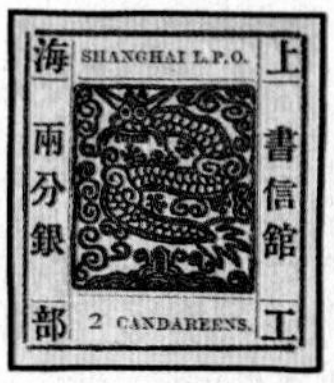
Dragon — A1

Antique Numerals
Roman "I" in "I6"
"Candareens" Plural

1865-66 Unwmk. Typo. *Imperf.*
Wove Paper
1 A1 2ca black 775.00 *6,750.*
a. Pelure paper 825.00
2 A1 4ca yellow 1,000. *5,250.*
a. Pelure paper 1,000. —
b. Double impression —
3 A1 8ca green 650.00 *6,000.*
a. 8ca yellow green 775.00 —
4 A1 16ca scarlet 2,250. *6,000.*
a. 16ca vermilion 2,250.
b. Pelure paper 2,250.
Nos. 1-4 (4) 4,675. 24,000.

No. 1: top character of three in left panel as illustrated. No. 5: top character is two horiz. lines.

Nos. 2, 3: center character of three in left panel as illustrated. Nos. 6, 7: center character much more complex.

Antique Numerals
"Candareens" Plural
Pelure Paper
5 A1 2ca black 650.00
a. Wove paper 650.00 6,250.
6 A1 4ca yellow 825.00 3,750.
7 A1 8ca dp grn 875.00 —
Nos. 5-7 (3) 2,350.

Antique Numerals
"Candareen" Singular
Laid Paper
8 A1 1ca blue 700.00 *5,500.*
9 A1 2ca black 10,000.
10 A1 4ca yellow 2,750.
Nos. 8-10 (3) 13,450.

Wove Paper
11 A1 1ca blue 500.00 *7,750.*
12 A1 2ca black 650.00 *7,750.*
13 A1 4ca yellow 775.00 8,000.
14 A1 8ca ol grn 650.00 —
15 A1 16ca vermilion 700.00 —
a. "1" of "16" omitted 26,000.
Nos. 11-15 (5) 3,275.

Roman "I," Antique "2"
"Candareens" Plural Except on 1ca
Wove Paper
16 A1 1ca blue 950.00 *3,800.*
17 A1 12ca fawn 375.00
18 A1 12ca choc 550.00
Nos. 16-18 (3) 1,875.

Antique Numerals
"Candareens" Plural Except on 1ca
Wove Paper
19 A1 1ca indigo, pelure paper 450.00 *5,500.*
a. 1ca blue, wove paper 425.00 *5,750.*
20 A1 3ca org brn 500.00 *4,250.*
a. Pelure paper 525.00 *3,750.*
21 A1 6ca red brn 350.00
22 A1 6ca fawn 875.00 —
23 A1 6ca vermilion 500.00
24 A1 12ca org brn 325.00
25 A1 16ca vermilion 325.00 *1,500.*
a. "1" of "16" omitted *500.00*
Nos. 19-25 (7) 3,325.

Examples of No. 22 usually have the straight lines cutting through the paper.

Antique Numerals
Roman "I"
"Candareens" Plural Except on 1ca
Laid Paper
26 A1 1ca blue *32,000.*
27 A1 2ca black *7,000.*
28 A1 3ca red brn *28,000.* —

Examples of No. 28 usually have the straight lines cutting through the paper.

Modern Numerals
"Candareen" Singular
29 A1 1ca sl bl 250.00 *4,500.*
a. 1ca dark blue 250.00 *4,250.*
30 A1 3ca red brn 250.00 *5,000.*

"Candareens" Plural Except the 1c
31 A1 2ca gray 225.00
32 A1 3ca red brn 225.00 *3,400.*

Coarse Porous Wove Paper
33a A1 1ca blue 160.00
34a A1 2ca black 210.00
b. Grayish paper 275.00
35a A1 3ca red brown 150.00
36a A1 4ca yellow 350.00
37a A1 6ca olive green 190.00
38a A1 8ca emerald 225.00
39a A1 12ca org ver 160.00
40a A1 16ca red 250.00 *875.00*
41a A1 16ca red brown 225.00 *875.00*
Nos. 33a-41a (9) 1,920.

Chinese characters change on same denomination stamps.

Nos. 1, 2, 11 and 32 exist on thicker paper, usually toned. Most authorities consider these four stamps and Nos. 33a-41a to be official reprints made to present sample sets to other post offices. The tone in this paper is an acquired characteristic, due to various causes. Many shades and minor varieties exist of Nos. 1-41a.

A2

A3

A4

A5

1866 Litho. *Perf. 12*
42 A2 2c rose 27.50 *35.00*
43 A3 4c lilac 47.50 *60.00*
44 A4 8c gray blue 52.50 *55.00*
45 A5 16c green 82.50 *110.00*
Nos. 42-45 (4) 210.00 260.00

Nos. 42-45 imperf. are proofs. See No. 50. For surcharges see Nos. 51-61, 67.

A6

A7

A8

A9

1866 *Perf. 15*
46 A6 1ca brown 11.00 15.50
a. "CANDS" 200.00 200.00
47 A7 3ca orange 45.00 *60.00*
48 A8 6ca slate 47.50 *55.00*
49 A9 12ca olive gray 72.50 *110.00*
Nos. 46-49 (4) 176.00 240.50

See Nos. 69-77. For surcharges see Nos. 62-66, 68, 78-83.

1872
50 A2 2c rose 170.00 *200.00*

Handstamp Surcharged in Blue, Red or Black — a

1873 *Perf. 12*
51 A2 1ca on 2c rose 60.00 *65.00*
52 A3 1ca on 4c lilac 25.00 *37.50*
a. Inverted surcharge 625.00
b. Double surcharge 725.00
53 A3 1ca on 4c lilac (R) *9,000.* *3,750.*
54 A3 1ca on 4c lil (Bk) 25.00 *37.50*
a. Inverted surcharge 300.00
55 A4 1ca on 8c gray bl 52.50 *55.00*
a. Double surcharge 625.00
56 A4 1ca on 8c gray bl (R) *22,000.* *16,000.*
57 A5 1ca on 16c green *4,250.* *3,250.*
a. Double surcharge *10,000.*
58 A5 1ca on 16c green (R) *32,000.* *13,500.*

Perf. 15
59 A2 1ca on 2c rose 72.50 *75.00*

1875 *Perf. 12*
60 A2 3ca on 2c rose 300.00 250.00
61 A5 3ca on 16c green *4,250.* *3,250.*

Perf. 15
62 A7 1ca on 3ca org *38,000.* *18,000.*
63 A8 1ca on 6ca slate 875.00 650.00
64 A8 1ca on 6ca slate (R) *12,000.* *4,500.*
65 A9 1ca on 12ca ol gray 1,100. 900.00
66 A9 1ca on 12ca ol gray (R) *8,000.* *4,000.*
67 A2 3ca on 2c rose 875.00 750.00
68 A9 3ca on 12ca olive gray *6,000.* *6,000.*

Counterfeits exist of Nos. 51-68.

Types of 1866

1875 *Perf. 15*
69 A6 1ca yel, *yel* 42.50 37.50
70 A7 3ca rose, *rose* 42.50 37.50

Perf. 11½
71 A6 1ca yel, *yel* 900.00 650.00

1876 *Perf. 15*
72 A6 1ca yellow 25.00 *30.00*
73 A7 3ca rose 95.00 *95.00*
74 A8 6ca green 140.00 *160.00*
75 A9 9ca blue 250.00 300.00
76 A9 12ca light brown 275.00 325.00
Nos. 72-76 (5) 785.00 910.00

1877 Engr. *Perf. 12½*
77 A6 1ca rose 2,250. *3,000.*

Stamps of 1875-76 Surcharged type "a" in Blue or Red

1877 Litho. *Perf. 15*
78 A7 1ca on 3ca rose, *rose* 550.00 475.00
79 A7 1ca on 3ca rose 170.00 150.00
a. Double surcharge 2,250.
80 A8 1ca on 6ca green 300.00 250.00
81 A9 1ca on 9ca blue 550.00 550.00
82 A9 1ca on 12ca lt brn 3,250. 2,000.
83 A9 1ca on 12ca lt brn (R) *8,500.* *5,500.*

Counterfeits exist of Nos. 78-83.

A11

A12

A13

A14

1877 *Perf. 15*
84 A11 20 cash blue vio 16.50 *15.00*
a. 20 cash violet 13.00 10.00
85 A12 40 cash rose 22.50 20.00
86 A13 60 cash green 25.00 23.00
87 A14 80 cash blue 32.50 35.00
88 A14 100 cash brown 30.00 *32.50*
Nos. 84-88 (5) 126.50 125.50

Handstamp Surcharged in Blue — b

1879 *Perf. 15*

89 A12 20 cash on 40c rose 45.00 37.50
a. Inverted surcharge 550.00
90 A14 60 cash on 80c blue 55.00 *70.00*
91 A14 60 cash on 100c brn 65.00 *65.00*
Nos. 89-91 (3) 165.00 172.50

Types of 1877

1880 *Perf. 11½*

92 A11 20 cash violet 11.00 *11.00*
a. Horiz. pair, imperf. btwn. 800.00
b. Vert. pair, imperf. horiz. 850.00
93 A12 40 cash rose 17.50 15.00
a. Horiz. pair, imperf. btwn. 900.00
94 A13 60 cash green 20.00 *20.00*
95 A14 80 cash blue 21.00 *20.00*
96 A14 100 cash brown 24.00 *22.50*

Perf. 15x11½

97 A11 20 cash lilac 170.00 *150.00*
Nos. 92-97 (6) 263.50 238.50

Surcharged type "b" in Blue

1884 *Perf. 11½*

98 A12 20 cash on 40c rose 24.00 22.00
a. Double surcharge 700.00
99 A14 60 cash on 80c blue 35.00 *36.00*
100 A14 60 cash on 100c brn 42.50 42.50
Nos. 98-100 (3) 101.50 100.50

Types of 1877

1884

101 A11 20 cash green 10.50 10.00

1885 *Perf. 15*

102 A11 20 cash green 8.25 5.00
103 A12 40 cash brown 10.00 9.00
104 A13 60 cash violet 17.50 17.00
a. 60 cash red violet 22.50 *25.00*
b. Vert. pair, imperf. btwn. 1,000.
105 A14 80 cash buff 16.50 15.00
a. Horiz. pair, imperf. btwn. 800.00
106 A14 100 cash yellow 20.00 *20.00*

Perf. 11½x15

107 A11 20 cash green 16.50 15.00
108 A13 60 cash red vio 17.50 15.00
Nos. 102-108 (7) 106.25 96.00

Surcharged type "b" in Blue or Red

1886 *Perf. 15*

109 A14 40 cash on 80c buff 13.50 12.00
a. Inverted surcharge 20.00 18.00
b. Red surcharge 550.00
110 A14 60 cash on 100c yellow 20.00 18.00
a. Inverted surcharge 100.00 100.00
b. Double surcharge 225.00
c. Red surcharge 600.00

Types of 1877

1888 *Perf. 15*

111 A11 20 cash gray 9.50 5.50
112 A12 40 cash black 9.50 *9.50*
113 A13 60 cash rose 13.00 12.00
a. Third character at left lacks dot at top 27.50 *20.00*
114 A14 80 cash green 14.00 10.00
115 A14 100 cash lt blue 17.50 *17.50*
Nos. 111-115 (5) 63.50 54.50

Nos. 106, 103, 105 Handstamp Surcharged in Blue or Red Type "b" or

c

d

1888 *Perf. 15*

116 A14(b) 40 cash on 100c yel 16.50 16.00
a. Inverted surcharge 125.00
b. Double surcharge 140.00
c. Red surcharge 32.50 30.00
118 A12(c) 20 cash on 40c brn 27.50 25.00
a. Inverted surcharge 200.00 175.00
b. Double surcharge 350.00
c. Red surcharge 400.00
119 A14(c) 20 cash on 80c buff 14.50 12.00
a. Inverted surcharge 250.00 140.00
b. Double surcharge 650.00 550.00
c. Red surcharge 425.00
120 A12(d) 20 cash on 40c brn 27.50 *26.00*
a. Inverted surcharge 300.00 275.00
Nos. 116-120 (4) 86.00 79.00

Omitted surcharges paired with normal stamp exist on Nos. 116, 119.

Handstamp Surcharged in Black and Red (100 cash) or Red (20 cash) — e

1889 **Unwmk.**

121 A14(e) 100 cash on 20c on 100c yel 200.00 *225.00*
a. Without the surcharge "100 cash" 500.00
b. Blue & red surcharge 1,800. —
122 A14(c) 20 cash on 80c grn 16.50 15.00
a. Inverted surcharge 140.00
123 A14(c) 20 cash on 100c bl 16.50 15.00
a. Double surcharge 350.00
Nos. 121-123 (3) 233.00 255.00

Counterfeits exist of Nos. 116-123.

1889 **Wmk. 175** *Perf. 15*

124 A11 20 cash gray 5.75 4.25
125 A12 40 cash black 8.50 7.00
126 A13 60 cash rose 27.50 *27.50*
a. Third character at left lacks dot at top 30.00 *30.00*

Perf. 12

127 A14 80 cash green 11.00 *22.00*
a. Horiz. pair, imperf. btwn. 2,000.
128 A14 100 cash dk bl 17.50 22.00
Nos. 124-128 (5) 70.25 82.75

Nos. 124-126 are sometimes found without watermark. This is caused by the sheet being misplaced in the printing press, so that the stamps are printed on the unwatermarked margin of the sheet.

Shield with Dragon Supporters — A20

1890 **Unwmk.** **Litho.** *Perf. 15*

129 A20 2c brown 4.25 *4.75*
130 A20 5c rose 12.00 8.00
131 A20 15c blue 27.50 15.00

Nos. 129-131 imperforate are proofs.

Wmk. 175

132 A20 10c black 17.50 12.00
a. Perf. 12 1,000. 550.00
133 A20 15c blue 25.00 18.00
134 A20 20c violet 17.50 14.00
Nos. 129-134 (6) 103.75 71.75

See Nos. 135-141. For surcharges and overprints see Nos. 142-152, J1-J13.

1891 *Perf. 12*

135 A20 2c brown 3.00 2.00
136 A20 5c rose 13.00 7.00

1892

137 A20 2c green 3.50 2.50
138 A20 5c red 8.25 7.25
139 A20 10c orange 22.00 *22.00*
140 A20 15c violet 13.50 10.00
141 A20 20c brown 14.50 13.00
Nos. 137-141 (5) 61.75 54.75

No. 130 Handstamp Surcharged in Blue — f

1892 **Unwmk.** *Perf. 15*

142 A20 2c on 5c rose 130.00 80.00
a. Inverted surcharge 850.00 750.00

Counterfeits exist of Nos. 142-152.

Stamps of 1892 Handstamp Surcharged in Blue

g

h

1893 **Wmk. 175** *Perf. 12*

143 A20 ½c on 15c violet 20.00 13.00
a. Double surcharge 375.00
b. Vert. pair, imperf. btwn. 350.00 325.00
144 A20 1c on 20c brown 20.00 13.00
a. ½c on 20c brown (error) *26,000.*

Nos. 144 and 144a exist in se-tenant pairs. Example pairs with black surcharge come from a trial printing.

Surcharged in Blue or Red (#152) on Halves of #136 (#145-147), #138 (#148-150), #135 (#151), #137 (#152)

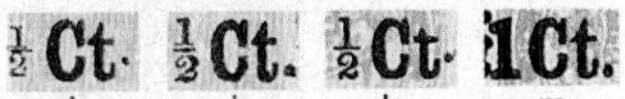

i j k m

145 A20(i) ½c on half of 5c 13.50 10.00
146 A20(j) ½c on half of 5c 13.50 10.00
147 A20(k) ½c on half of 5c 275.00 200.00
148 A20(i) ½c on half of 5c 13.50 10.00
149 A20(j) ½c on half of 5c 13.50 10.00
150 A20(k) ½c on half of 5c 225.00 160.00
151 A20(m) 1c on half of 2c 3.50 3.00
c. Dbl. surch., one in green 1,600. *350.00*
d. Dbl. surch., one in black 1,700. *350.00*
152 A20(m) 1c on half of 2c 16.50 12.00
Nos. 145-152 (8) 574.00 415.00

The ½c surcharge setting of 20 (2x10) covers a vertical strip of 10 unsevered stamps, with horizontal gutter midway. This setting has 11 of type "i," 8 of type "j" and 1 of type "k." Nos. 145-152 are perforated vertically down the middle.

Inverted surcharges exist on Nos. 145-151. Double surcharges, one inverted, are also found in this issue.

Handstamped provisionals somewhat similar to Nos. 145-152 were issued in Foochow by the Shanghai Agency.

Coat of Arms — A24

Typo. (Dot)

Litho. (No Dot)

Frame Inscriptions in Black

1893 **Litho.** *Perf. 13½x14*

153 A24 ½c orange 7.25 3.00
b. Horiz. pair, imperf vert. 225.00
154 A24 1c brown 7.25 1.75
155 A24 2c vermilion 8.00 2.50
a. Imperf, pair 225.00
156 A24 5c blue 1.10 .65
a. Black inscriptions inverted 1,800.
b. Black inscriptions double 900.00
157 A24 10c green 10.00 *11.00*
158 A24 15c yellow 1.10 .90
159 A24 20c lilac 11.00 9.00
Nos. 153-159 (7) 45.70 28.80

Typographed

153a A24 ½c orange .55 .50
154a A24 1c brown .55 .50

Typo & Litho

157a A24 10c green 2.75 *3.00*
159a A24 20c lilac 3.00 *5.00*

On Nos. 157 and 159, frame inscriptions are lithographed, rest of design typographed.

See Nos. 170-172. For overprints and surcharges see Nos. 160-166, 168-169.

Stamps of 1893 Overprinted in Black

1893, Dec. 14

160 A24 ½c (On #153a) .50 .50
a. Inverted overprint 165.00 150.00
161 A24 1c (On #154a) .65 .65
a. Double overprint 67.50 50.00
162 A24 2c (On #155) .90 .90
a. Inverted overprint 165.00 120.00
163 A24 5c (On #156) 3.50 *5.00*
a. Inverted overprint 325.00
164 A24 10c (On #157a) 11.00 *12.00*
165 A24 15c (On #158) 7.25 6.50
166 A24 20c (On #159) 9.50 *10.00*
Nos. 160-166 (7) 33.30 35.55

50th anniv. of the first foreign settlement in Shanghai.

Mercury — A26

1893, Nov. 11 **Litho.** *Perf. 13½*

167 A26 2c vermilion & black 1.10 1.00

Nos. 158 and 159 Handstamp Surcharged in Black

1896 *Perf. 13½x14*

168 A24 4c on 15c yel & blk 11.00 8.00
169 A24 6c on 20c lil & blk (#159) 11.00 8.00
a. On #159a 55.00 25.00

Surcharge occurs inverted or double on Nos. 168-169.

Arms Type of 1893

1896

170 A24 2c scarlet & blk .30 *1.60*
a. Black inscriptions inverted 2,000. 1,800.
b. Black inscriptions double 1,400. 1,200.
171 A24 4c org & blk, *yel* 7.25 *5.50*
172 A24 6c car & blk, *rose* 8.25 *8.50*
Nos. 170-172 (3) 15.80 *15.60*

POSTAGE DUE STAMPS

Postage Stamps of 1890-92 Handstamped in Black, Red or Blue

1892 **Unwmk.** *Perf. 15*

J1 A20 2c brown (Bk) 900.00 *900.00*
a. Inverted overprint 2,500.
J2 A20 5c rose (Bk) 25.00 *14.00*
a. Inverted overprint 425.00
J3 A20 15c blue (Bk) 52.50 47.50
a. Inverted overprint 400.00

b.	Blue overprint		425.00	

Wmk. 175

J4	A20	10c black (R)	35.00	32.50
J5	A20	15c blue (Bk)	30.00	27.50
a.	Inverted overprint		600.00	
b.	Double overprint		300.00	
c.	Pair, one without ovpt.		1,300.	
J6	A20	20c violet (Bk)	22.50	20.00
	Nos. J1-J6 (6)		1,065.	1,041.

1892-93   Perf. 12

J7	A20	2c brown (Bk)	3.75	3.75
a.	Inverted overprint		175.00	160.00
b.	Double overprint		400.00	
c.	Pair, one without ovpt.		1,000.	
J8	A20	2c brown (Bl)	3.50	3.00
J9	A20	5c rose (Bl)	15.50	9.00
a.	Inverted overprint		225.00	
J10	A20	10c orange (Bk)	250.00	225.00
J11	A20	10c orange (Bl)	20.00	15.00
a.	Inverted overprint		325.00	
J12	A20	15c violet (R)	32.50	30.00
J13	A20	20c brown (R)	32.50	30.00
	Nos. J7-J13 (7)		357.75	315.75

D2

1893   Litho.   Perf. 13½

J14	D2	½c orange & blk	.55	.55

Perf. 14x13½

J15	D2	1c brown & black	.65	.55
a.	Horiz. pair, imperf. vert.		350.00	
J16	D2	2c ver & blk	.65	.55
a.	Horiz. pair, imperf. vert.		350.00	
J17	D2	5c blue & black	1.00	.90
J18	D2	10c green & black	6.00	2.00
J19	D2	15c yellow & black	4.75	4.00
J20	D2	20c violet & black	1.75	1.50
	Nos. J14-J20 (7)		15.35	10.05

Stamps of Shanghai were discontinued in 1898.

SHARJAH & DEPENDENCIES

'shär-jə

LOCATION — Oman Peninsula, Arabia, on Persian Gulf
GOVT. — Sheikdom under British protection
POP. — 5,000 (estimated)
CAPITAL — Sharjah

The dependencies on the Gulf of Oman are Dhiba, Khor Fakkan, and Kalba.

Sharjah is one of six Persian Gulf sheikdoms to join the United Arab Emirates which proclaimed independence Dec. 2, 1971. See United Arab Emirates.

100 Naye Paise = 1 Rupee

Catalogue values for all unused stamps in this country are for Never Hinged items.

Sheik Saqr bin Sultan al Qasimi, Flag and Map — A1

Perf. 14½x14

1963, July 10   Photo.   Unwmk.
Black Portrait and Inscriptions; Lilac Rose Flag

1	A1	1np lt bl grn & pink	.25	.25
2	A1	2np grnsh bl & sal	.25	.25
3	A1	3np violet & yel	.25	.25
4	A1	4np emerald & gray	.25	.25
5	A1	5np aqua & lt grn	.25	.25
6	A1	6np dl grn & brt yel	.30	.25
7	A1	8np Prus bl & bis	.30	.25
8	A1	10np aqua & tan	.30	.25
9	A1	16np ultra & bis	.40	.25
10	A1	20np lt vio & lem	.50	.30
11	A1	30np rose lil & brt yel grn	1.10	.35
12	A1	40np dk bl & yel grn	1.75	.50
13	A1	50np green & fawn	2.25	.75
14	A1	75np ultra & fawn	4.00	1.00
15	A1	100np ol bis & rose	5.00	1.50
	Nos. 1-15 (15)		17.15	6.65

Exist imperf. Value, set $14.

Malaria Eradication Emblem — A2

1963, Aug. 8

16	A2	1np grnsh blue	.25	.25
17	A2	2np dull blue	.25	.25
18	A2	3np violet blue	.30	.25
19	A2	4np emerald	.40	.25
20	A2	90np yellow brown	3.50	1.50
	Nos. 16-20 (5)		4.70	2.50

Miniature Sheet
Imperf

21	A2	100np bright blue	8.50	3.75

WHO drive to eradicate malaria. No. 21 contains one 39x67mm stamp.
See Nos. C1-C6. For surcharge and overprints see Nos. 35, C7-C12, O1-O9.

Red Crescent and Sheik — A3

1963, Aug. 25   Perf. 14x14½

22	A3	1np purple & red	.25	.25
23	A3	2np brt green & red	.25	.25
24	A3	3np dark blue & red	.25	.25
25	A3	4np dark green & red	.25	.25
26	A3	5np dark brown & red	.25	.25
27	A3	85np green & red	2.75	.90
	Nos. 22-27 (6)		4.00	2.15

Miniature Sheet
Imperf

28	A3	100np plum & red	6.50	3.75

Cent. of the Intl. Red Cross. Imperfs. exist. Value, set $12. No. 28 contains one 67x39m stamp.

Nos. 36-40 and No. 20 Surcharged

Nos. 29-34

No. 35

1963, Oct. 6   Photo.   Perf. 14½x14

29	A4	10np on 1np brt grn	.40	.30
30	A4	20np on 2np red brn	.80	.60
31	A4	30np on 3np ol grn	1.25	1.00
32	A4	40np on 4np dp ultra	1.60	1.25
33	A4	75np on 90np carmine	3.00	2.00
34	A4	80np on 90np carmine	3.75	2.50
35	A2	1r on 90np yel brn	4.75	3.75
	Nos. 29-35 (7)		15.55	11.40

Due to a stamp shortage the surcharged set appeared before the commemorative issue.

Wheat Emblem and Hands with Broken Chains — A4

1963, Oct. 15   Perf. 14½x14

36	A4	1np brt green	.25	.25
37	A4	2np red brown	.25	.25
38	A4	3np olive green	.25	.25
39	A4	4np deep ultra	.25	.25
40	A4	90np carmine	3.00	1.00
	Nos. 36-40 (5)		4.00	2.00

Miniature Sheet
Imperf

41	A4	100np purple	5.00	3.00

"Freedom from Hunger" campaign of the FAO. Imperfs. exist. Value, set $12. No. 41 contains one 39x67mm stamp.
For surcharges see Nos. 29-34.

Orbiting Astronomical Observatory — A5

Satellites: 2np, Nimbus weather satellite. 3np, Pioneer V space probe. 4np, Explorer XIII. 5np, Explorer XII. 35np, Relay satellite. 50np, Orbiting Solar Observatory.

1964, Feb. 5   Photo.   Perf. 14

42	A5	1np blue	.25	.25
43	A5	2np red brn & yel grn	.25	.25
44	A5	3np blk & grnsh bl	.25	.25
45	A5	4np lemon & blk	.25	.25
46	A5	5np brt pur & lem	.25	.25
47	A5	35np grnsh bl & pur	1.25	.80
48	A5	50np ol grn & redsh brn	2.75	1.25
	Nos. 42-48 (7)		5.25	3.30

Space research. Exist imperf. Value, set $8.
A 100np imperf. souvenir sheet shows various satellites, the Earth and stars. Colors: dark blue, gold, green & pink. Size: 112x80mm. Value $9.

Runner — A6

1964, Mar. 3   Unwmk.

49	A6	1np shown	.25	.25
50	A6	2np Discus	.25	.25
51	A6	3np Hurdler	.25	.25
52	A6	4np Shot put	.25	.25
53	A6	20np High jump	.40	.25
54	A6	30np Weight lifting	.90	.25
55	A6	40np Javelin	1.25	.30
56	A6	1r Diving	2.75	1.00
	Nos. 49-56 (8)		6.30	2.80

18th Olympic Games, Tokyo, Oct. 10-25, 1964.
Exist imperf. Value, set $10.
An imperf. souvenir sheet contains one 1r stamp similar to No. 56. Size of stamp: 67x67mm, size of sheet: 102x102mm. Value $10.

Girl Scouts A7

1964, June 30   Perf. 14x14½

57	A7	1np grnsh gray	.25	.25
58	A7	2np emerald	.25	.25
59	A7	3np brt blue	.25	.25
60	A7	4np brt violet	.25	.25
61	A7	5np carmine rose	.40	.25
62	A7	2r dark red brown	4.00	2.00
	Nos. 57-62 (6)		5.40	3.25

Exist imperf. Value, set $9.
An imperf. souvenir sheet contains one 2r bright red stamp. Size of stamp: 67x40mm. Size of sheet: 102½x76mm. Value $7.

Sharjah Boy Scout — A8

Marching Scouts With Drummers — A9

Designs: 3np, 2r, Boy Scout portrait.

Perf. 14½x14, 14x14½

1964, June 30   Photo.   Unwmk.

63	A8	1np gray green	.25	.25
64	A9	2np emerald	.25	.25
65	A8	3np brt blue	.25	.25
66	A8	4np brt violet	.40	.30
67	A9	5np brt carmine rose	.60	.40
68	A8	2r dk red brown	3.00	1.25
	Nos. 63-68 (6)		4.75	2.70

Issued to honor the Sharjah Boy Scouts.
Exist imperf. Value, set $4.10.
An imperf. souvenir sheet exists with one 2r bright red stamp in design of No. 68. Size of stamp: 39½x67mm. Size of sheet: 77x103mm. Value $7.

Olympic Torch and Rings — A10

1964, Oct. 15   Litho.   Perf. 14

69	A10	1np olive green	.25	.25
70	A10	2np ultra	.25	.25
71	A10	3np orange brown	.25	.25
72	A10	4np blue green	.25	.25
73	A10	5np dark violet	.30	.25
74	A10	40np brt blue	.50	.30
75	A10	50np dark red brown	.80	.40
76	A10	2r bister	4.25	1.25
		Nos. 69-76 (8)	6.85	3.20

18th Olympic Games, Tokyo, Oct. 10-25. Exist imperf. Value, set $12.

An imperf. souvenir sheet exists with one 2r yellow green stamp. Size of stamp: 82mm at base. Size of sheet: 107x76mm. Value $12.

Early Telephone — A11

Designs: No. 78, Modern telewriter. No. 79, 1895 car. No. 80, American automobile, 1964. No. 81, Early X-ray. No. 82, Modern X-ray. No. 83, Mail coach. No. 84, Telstar and Delta rocket. No. 85, Sailing vessel. No. 86, Nuclear ship "Savannah." No. 87, Early astronomers. No. 88, Jodrell Bank telescope. No. 89, Greek messengers. No. 90, Relay satellite, Delta rocket and globe. No. 91, Early flying machine. No. 92, Caravelle plane. No. 93, Persian water wheel. No. 94, Hydroelectric dam. No. 95, Old steam locomotive. No. 96, Diesel locomotive.

Unwmk.
1965, Apr. 23   Litho.   Perf. 14

77	A11	1np rose red & blk	.25	.25
78	A11	1np rose red & blk	.25	.25
79	A11	2np orange & indigo	.25	.25
80	A11	2np orange & indigo	.25	.25
81	A11	3np dk brn & emer	.25	.25
82	A11	3np emer & dk brn	.25	.25
83	A11	4np yel grn & dk vio	.25	.25
84	A11	4np dk vio & yel grn	.25	.25
85	A11	5np bl grn & brn	.25	.25
86	A11	5np bl grn & brn	.25	.25
87	A11	30np gray & bl	.25	.25
88	A11	30np blue & gray	.25	.25
89	A11	40np vio bl & yel	.45	.25
90	A11	40np vio bl & yel	.45	.25
91	A11	50np blue & sepia	.55	.30
92	A11	50np blue & sepia	.55	.30
93	A11	75np brt grn & dk brn	.65	.40
94	A11	75np brt grn & dk brn	.65	.40
95	A11	1r yellow & vio bl	3.25	1.25
96	A11	1r yellow & vio bl	3.25	1.25
		Nos. 77-96 (20)	12.80	7.40

Issued to show progress in science, transport and communications. Each two stamps of same denomination are printed se tenant. Exist imperf.

Two imperf. souvenir sheets exist. One contains one each of Nos. 89-90 and the other, of Nos. 95-96. Size: 102x75mm.

Stamps of Sharjah & Dependencies were replaced in 1972 by those of United Arab Emirates.

AIR POST STAMPS

Type of Regular Issue, 1963

Black Portrait and Inscriptions; Lilac Rose Flag

Perf. 14½x14

1963, July 10   Photo.   Unwmk.

C1	A1	1r ultra & fawn	1.75	.40
C2	A1	2r lt violet & lemon	3.25	.70
C3	A1	3r dl grn & brt yel	4.00	1.00
C4	A1	4r grnsh bl & sal	6.50	1.40
C5	A1	5r emerald & gray	8.00	1.60
C6	A1	10r olive bis & rose	15.00	3.50
		Nos. C1-C6 (6)	38.50	8.60

Exist imperf.

Nos. C1-C6 Overprinted

Black Portrait and Inscriptions; Lilac Rose Flag

1964, Apr. 7

C7	A1	1r ultra & fawn	3.50	3.50
C8	A1	2r lt violet & lem	7.00	7.00
C9	A1	3r dull grn & brt yel	12.00	12.00
C10	A1	4r grnsh blue & sal	15.00	15.00
C11	A1	5r emerald & gray	22.50	22.50
C12	A1	10r olive bis & rose	32.50	32.50
		Nos. C7-C12 (6)	92.50	92.50

Pres. John F. Kennedy (1917-63). Exist imperf. Value, set $100.

World Map and Flame AP1

1964, Apr. 15   Perf. 14x14½

C13	AP1	50np red brown	.75	.35
C14	AP1	1r purple	1.50	.85
C15	AP1	150np Prus green	2.75	1.40
		Nos. C13-C15 (3)	5.00	2.60

Issued for Human Rights Day. Exist imperf. Value, set $7.

An imperf. souvenir sheet contains one 3r carmine rose stamp. Size of stamp: 67x40mm. Size of sheet: 89x64mm. Value $6.

View of Khor Fakkan — AP2

Designs: 20np, Beni Qatab Bedouin camp near Dhaid. 30np, Oasis of Dhaid. 40np, Kalba Castle. 75np, Sharjah street with wind tower. 100np, Sharjah Fortress.

1964, Aug. 13   Photo.   Unwmk.

C16	AP2	10np multi	.25	.25
C17	AP2	20np multi	.35	.25
C18	AP2	30np multi	.45	.25
C19	AP2	40np multi	.65	.35
C20	AP2	75np multi	1.40	.45
C21	AP2	100np multi	2.25	.65
		Nos. C16-C21 (6)	5.35	2.20

Unisphere and Sheik Saqr — AP3

20np, Offshore oil rig. 1r, New York skyline.

Perf. 14½x14

1964, Sept. 5   Photo.   Unwmk.

Size: 26x45mm

C22	AP3	20np multi	.40	.25
C23	AP3	40np multi	.75	.25

Size: 86x45mm

C24	AP3	1r multi, horiz.	2.50	.60
a.		Strip of 3, Nos. C22-C24	5.00	5.00

New York World's Fair, 1964-65. Exist imperf. Value, strip $6.

An imperf. souvenir sheet exists with one 40np stamp in AP3 design. Size of stamp: 40x68mm. Size of sheet: 76x108mm. Value $6.

J. F. Kennedy, Statue of Liberty — AP4

1964, Nov. 22   Perf. 14x13½

C25	AP4	40np multicolored	1.50	.85
C26	AP4	60np multicolored	1.75	.85
C27	AP4	100np multicolored	1.75	.85
		Nos. C25-C27 (3)	5.00	2.55

Pres. John F. Kennedy. Exist imperf. Value, set $17.50.

A souvenir sheet contains one each of Nos. C25-C27, imperf. Size: 107x76mm. Value $11.50.

Rock Dove AP5

Birds: 40np, 2r, Red jungle fowl. 75np, 3r, Hoopoe.

Perf. 14x14½

1965, Feb. 20   Photo.   Unwmk.

C28	AP5	30np gray & multi	.85	.25
C29	AP5	40np multicolored	1.00	.35
C30	AP5	75np brt blue & multi	1.50	.50
C31	AP5	150np blue & multi	2.75	.90
C32	AP5	2r multicolored	3.50	1.25
C33	AP5	3r red & multi	5.25	1.75
		Nos. C28-C33 (6)	14.85	5.00

Exist imperf. Value, set $17.50.

OFFICIAL STAMPS

Nos. 7-15 Overprinted

Perf. 14½x14

1965, Jan. 13   Photo.   Unwmk.

O1	A1	8np multi	.25	.25
O2	A1	10np multi	.25	.25
O3	A1	16np multi	.25	.25
O4	A1	20np multi	.35	.35
O5	A1	30np multi	.40	.40
O6	A1	40np multi	.60	.60
O7	A1	75np multi	1.50	1.50
O8	A1	75np multi	4.00	4.00
O9	A1	100np multi	7.00	7.00
		Nos. O1-O9 (9)	14.60	14.60

SIBERIA

sī-ˈbir-ē-ə

LOCATION — A vast territory of Russia lying between the Ural Mountains and the Pacific Ocean.

The anti-Bolshevist provisional government set up at Omsk by Adm. Aleksandr V. Kolchak issued Nos. 1-10 in 1919. The monarchist, anti-Soviet government in Priamur province issued Nos. 51-118 in 1921-22.

(Stamps of the Czechoslovak Legion are listed under Czechoslovakia.)

100 Kopecks = 1 Ruble

Russian Stamps of 1909-18 Surcharged

a

b

On Stamps of 1909-12

1919 Unwmk. *Perf. 14x14½*

Wove Paper

Lozenges of Varnish on Face

1	A14(a)	35k on 2k dull grn	.60	*2.00*
a.		Inverted surcharge	100.00	
b.		"5" omitted	*150.00*	
c.		Double surcharge	—	
2	A14(a)	50k on 3k car	.60	*2.00*
a.		Inverted surcharge	100.00	
3	A14(a)	70k on 1k dl org yel	1.00	*4.50*
a.		Inverted surcharge	100.00	
4	A15(b)	1r on 4k car	1.25	*2.00*
a.		Dbl. surch., one inverted	200.00	*110.00*
b.		Inverted surcharge	100.00	
c.		Double surcharge	200.00	
5	A14(b)	3r on 7k blue	7.00	*9.50*
a.		Double surcharge	100.00	*30.00*
b.		Inverted surcharge	100.00	*25.00*
c.		Pair, one without surcharge	400.00	
d.		"3" omitted	—	
6	A11(b)	5r on 14k dk bl & car	9.50	*20.00*
a.		Double surcharge	100.00	*40.00*
b.		Inverted surcharge	100.00	*40.00*

On Stamps of 1917

Imperf

7	A14(a)	35k on 2k gray grn	1.25	*4.50*
a.		Inverted surcharge	*100.00*	
8	A14(a)	50k on 3k red	1.00	*4.50*
a.		Inverted surcharge	200.00	
b.		Double surcharge	*100.00*	
9	A14(a)	70k on 1k orange	.75	*4.50*
a.		Inverted surcharge	100.00	
b.		Dbl. surch., one inverted	—	
10	A15(b)	1r on 4k car	9.50	*16.00*
		Nos. 1-10 (10)	32.45	*69.50*

Nos. 1-10 were first issued in Omsk during the regime of Admiral Kolchak. Later they were used along the line of the Trans-Siberian railway to Vladivostok.

Some experts question the postal use of most off-cover canceled examples of Nos. 1-10.

25 P 1-

Similar surcharges, handstamped as above are bogus.

Priamur Government Issues Nikolaevsk Issue

A5

A6

A7

1909-17 Russian Stamps Handstamp Surcharged or Overprinted

1921 Unwmk. *Perf. 14x14½, 13½*

51	A5	10k on 4k carmine	*250.00*	
52	A5	10k on 10k dark blue	*1,750.*	
53	A6	15k on 14k dk blue & car	*200.00*	
54	A6	15k on 15k red brn & dp blue	*80.00*	
55	A6	15k on 35k red brn & grn	*80.00*	
56	A6	15k on 50k brn vio & grn	*80.00*	
57	A6	15k on 70k brn & red org	*200.00*	
58	A7	15k on 1r brn & org	*200.00*	
59	A5	on 20k dl bl & dk car	*300.00*	
60	A5	on 20k on 14k dk bl & car (#118)	*200.00*	
a.		15k on 20k on 14k dk bl & car (error)	*1,100.*	
61	A7	20k on 3½r mar & lt grn	*250.00*	
62	A7	20k on 5r indigo, grn & lt bl	*950.00*	
63	A7	20k on 7r dk grn & pink	*950.00*	

Nos. 59-60 are overprinted with initials but original denominations remain.

A 10k on 5k claret (Russia No. 77) and a 15k on 20k blue & carmine (Russia No. 82a) were not officially issued. Some authorities consider them bogus.

Reprints exist.

On Semi-Postal Stamp of 1914

64	SP6	20k on 3k mar & gray grn, *pink*	*800.00*	

On Stamps of 1917

Imperf

65	A5	10k on 1k orange	*100.00*	
66	A5	10k on 2k gray green	*100.00*	
67	A5	10k on 3k red	*100.00*	
68	A5	10k on 5k claret	*700.00*	
69	A6	15k on 1r pale brn, brn & red org	*150.00*	
70	A7	20k on 1r pale brn, brn & red org	*200.00*	
71	A7	20k on 3½r mar & lt grn	*350.00*	
72	A7	20k on 7r dk grn & pink	*950.00*	

The letters of the overprint are the initials of the Russian words for "Nikolaevsk on Amur Priamur Provisional Government."

As the surcharges on Nos. 51-72 are handstamped, a number exist inverted or double.

A 20k blue & carmine (Russia No. 126) with Priamur overprint and a 15k on 20k (Russia No. 126) were not officially issued. Some authorities consider them bogus.

No evidence found of genuine usage of Nos. 51-72.

Stamps of Far Eastern Republic Overprinted

1922

78	A2	2k gray green	25.00	25.00
a.		Inverted overprint	200.00	
79	A2a	4k rose	25.00	25.00
a.		Inverted overprint	*250.00*	
80	A2	5k claret	25.00	25.00
81	A2a	10k blue	25.00	25.00
		Nos. 78-81 (4)	100.00	100.00

Anniv. of the overthrow of the Bolshevik power in the Priamur district.

The letters of the overprint are the initials of "Vremeno Priamurski Pravitel'stvo" i.e. Provisional Priamur Government, 26th May.

Russian Stamps of 1909-21 Overprinted in Dark Blue or Vermilion

On Stamps of 1909-18

1922 *Perf. 14x14½*

85	A14	1k dull org yel	75.00	100.00
86	A14	2k dull green	125.00	110.00
87	A14	3k carmine	35.00	50.00
88	A15	4k carmine	25.00	35.00
89	A14	5k dk claret	35.00	40.00
90	A14	7k blue (V)	100.00	45.00
91	A15	10k dark blue (V)	65.00	70.00
92	A11	14k dk bl & car	75.00	85.00
93	A11	15k red brn & dp bl	15.00	25.00
94	A8	20k dl bl & dk car	50.00	25.00
95	A11	20k on 14k dk bl & car	120.00	150.00
96	A11	25k dl grn & dk vio (V)	50.00	50.00
97	A11	35k red brn & grn	10.00	15.00
a.		Inverted overprint	200.00	
98	A8	50k brn vio & grn	20.00	30.00
99	A11	70k brn & red org	55.00	55.00
		Nos. 85-99 (15)	855.00	885.00

On Stamps of 1917

Imperf

100	A14	1k orange	10.00	*25.00*
a.		Inverted overprint	250.00	100.00
101	A14	2k gray green	15.00	25.00
102	A14	3k red	20.00	25.00
103	A15	4k carmine	100.00	100.00
104	A14	5k claret	35.00	25.00
105	A11	15k red brn & dp bl	*100.00*	125.00
106	A8	20k blue & car	125.00	75.00
107	A9	1r pale brn, brn & red org	30.00	40.00
		Nos. 100-107 (8)	435.00	440.00

On Stamps of Siberia, 1919

Perf. 14½x15

108	A14	35k on 2k green	100.00	100.00

Imperf

109	A14	70k on 1k orange	110.00	120.00

On Stamps of Far Eastern Republic, 1921

110	A2	2k gray green	20.00	20.00
111	A2a	4k rose	20.00	7.00
112	A2	5k claret	20.00	*25.00*
a.		Inverted overprint	100.00	
113	A2a	10k blue (R)	20.00	*30.00*
		Nos. 109-113 (5)	190.00	202.00

Same, Surcharged with New Values

114	A2	1k on 2k gray grn	20.00	*25.00*
115	A2a	3k on 4k rose	20.00	*25.00*

The overprint is in a rectangular frame on stamps of 1k to 10k and 1r; on the other values the frame is omitted. It is larger on the 1 ruble than on the smaller stamps.

The overprint reads "Priamurski Zemski Krai," Priamur Rural Province.

Far Eastern Republic Nos. 30-32 Overprinted in Blue

Perf. 14½x15

116	A14	35k on 2k green	20.00	*25.00*

Imperf

117	A14	35k on 2k green	60.00	*120.00*
118	A14	70k on 1k orange	30.00	15.00
		Nos. 116-118 (3)	110.00	160.00

Counterfeits of Nos. 51-118 abound.

SIERRA LEONE

sē-ˌer-ə lē-ˈōn

LOCATION — West coast of Africa, between Guinea and Liberia

GOVT. — Republic in British Commonwealth

AREA — 27,925 sq. mi.

POP. — 5,296,651 (1999 est.)

CAPITAL — Freetown

Sierra Leone was a British colony and protectorate. In 1961 it became fully independent, remaining within the Commonwealth. It became a republic April 19, 1971.

12 Pence = 1 Shilling
20 Shillings = 1 Pound
100 Cents = 1 Leone (1964)

Catalogue values for unused stamps in this country are for Never Hinged items, beginning with Scott 186 in the regular postage section and Scott C1 in the air post section.

Watermark

Wmk. 336 — St. Edwards Crown & SL, Multiple

Queen Victoria — A1

1859-74 Unwmk. Typo. *Perf. 14*

1	A1	6p bright violet ('74)	77.50	30.00
a.		6p dull violet ('59)	275.00	55.00
b.		6p gray lilac ('65)	300.00	45.00

1872 *Perf. 12½*

5	A1	6p violet	425.00	70.00

Queen Victoria — A2

1872 Wmk. 1 Sideways *Perf. 12½*

6	A2	1p rose	85.00	50.00
8	A2	3p yellow buff	160.00	42.50
9	A2	4p blue	200.00	45.00
10	A2	1sh yellow green	525.00	62.50

1873 Wmk. 1 Upright

6a	A2	1p	140.00	35.00
7	A2	2p magenta	150.00	55.00
8a	A2	3p	550.00	95.00
9a	A2	4p	375.00	57.50
10a	A2	1sh	675.00	110.00

1876-96 Wmk. 1 Upright *Perf. 14*

11	A2	½p bister	5.50	14.50
12	A2	1p rose	60.00	16.00
13	A2	1½p violet ('77)	55.00	10.00
14	A2	2p magenta	75.00	4.50
15	A2	3p yellow buff	65.00	8.00
16	A2	4p blue	225.00	7.25
17	A1	6p brt violet ('85)	72.50	27.50
a.		Half used as 3p on cover		2,750.
18	A1	6p violet brn ('90)	27.50	16.00
19	A1	6p brown vio ('96)	3.00	7.75
20	A2	1sh green	92.50	7.25
		Nos. 11-20 (10)	681.00	118.75

For surcharge see No. 32.

1883-93 Wmk. Crown and C A (2)

21	A2	½p bister	45.00	62.50
22	A2	½p dull green ('84)	3.50	2.25
23	A2	1p carmine ('84)	15.00	1.10
a.		1p rose carmine	32.50	9.50
b.		1p rose	225.00	40.00
24	A2	1½p violet ('93)	3.50	7.25
25	A2	2p magenta	77.50	9.50
26	A2	2p slate ('84)	62.50	4.50
27	A2	2½p ultra ('91)	18.50	1.75
28	A2	3p org yel ('92)	4.00	11.00
29	A2	4p blue	1,000.	32.50
30	A2	4p bister ('84)	2.75	3.00
31	A2	1sh org brn ('88)	26.00	17.00
		Nos. 21-28,30-31 (10)	258.25	119.85

For surcharge see No. 33.

Nos. 13 and 24
Surcharged in Black

1893   **Wmk. 1**
32 A2 ½p on 1½p violet 525.00 800.00
a. "PFNNY" 3,750. 4,500.

Wmk. 2
33 A2 ½p on 1½p violet 8.50 3.75
a. "PFNNY" 85.00 82.50
b. Inverted surcharge 125.00 125.00
c. Same as "a," inverted 8,000. 5,500.
d. Double surcharge 1,200.

A4

1896-97
34 A4 ½p lilac & grn ('97) 2.75 3.50
35 A4 1p lilac & car 5.00 2.00
36 A4 1½p lilac & blk ('97) 4.50 24.00
37 A4 2p lilac & org 2.75 5.50
38 A4 2½p lilac & ultra 2.75 1.40
39 A4 3p lilac & sl ('97) 9.50 7.75
40 A4 4p lilac & car ('97) 10.50 14.50
41 A4 5p lilac & blk 14.50 16.00
42 A4 6p lilac ('97) 9.00 27.50
43 A4 1sh green & blk 6.75 22.50
44 A4 2sh green & ultra 30.00 75.00
45 A4 5sh green & car 90.00 250.00
46 A4 £1 violet, red 325.00 600.00
Nos. 34-46 (13) 513.00 1,049.

Numerals of Nos. 39-46 of type A4 are in color on plain tablet.

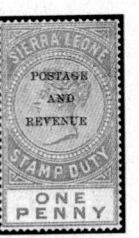
A5

a

b
A6

c

d

e

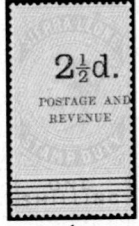
f

1897   **Wmk. C A over Crown (46)**
47 A5 1p lilac & grn 6.50 4.25
a. Double overprint 2,000. 2,000.

---

48 A6(a) 2½p on 3p lil & grn 13.50 19.00
a. Double surcharge 40,000.
b. Double surcharge, types "a" and "b" 32,000.
c. Double surcharge, types "a" and "c" 55,000.
49 A6(b) 2½p on 3p 70.00 95.00
50 A6(c) 2½p on 3p 200.00 250.00
51 A6(d) 2½p on 3p 400.00 525.00
52 A6(a) 2½p on 6p lil & grn 10.50 21.00
53 A6(b) 2½p on 6p 55.00 85.00
54 A6(c) 2½p on 6p 150.00 190.00
55 A6(d) 2½p on 6p 325.00 400.00
56 A6(a) 2½p on 1sh lilac 110.00 80.00
57 A6(b) 2½p on 1sh lilac 1,100. 1,100.
58 A6(c) 2½p on 1sh lilac 550.00 500.00
59 A6(e) 2½p on 1sh lilac 1,750. 2,000.
59A A6(f) 2½p on 1sh lilac 1,800. 1,500.
60 A6(a) 2½p on 2sh lilac 4,000. 2,750.
61 A6(b) 2½p on 2sh lilac 20,000.
62 A6(c) 2½p on 2sh lilac 12,000. 17,000.
a. Italic "N" in "REVENUE" 50,000. 50,000.
63 A6(e) 2½p on 2sh lilac 47,500.
63A A6(f) 2½p on 2sh lilac 47,500. 50,000.

The words "POSTAGE AND REVENUE" on Nos. 56-63A are set in two lines and overprinted below instead of above "2½d."
The "d" in type "f" is 3½mm wide; that in type "a" is 3mm.
Very fine examples of Nos. 47-63A will have perforations touching the frameline on one or more sides.
Nos. 56-59A are often found discolored. Such stamps sell for about half the values quoted.

King Edward VII — A7

Numerals of 3p to £1 of type A7 are in color on plain tablet.

1903   **Wmk. Crown and C A (2)**
64 A7 ½p violet & grn 3.25 6.50
65 A7 1p violet & car 2.25 1.10
66 A7 1½p violet & blk 1.50 19.00
67 A7 2p violet & brn org 4.50 17.50
68 A7 2½p violet & ultra 5.00 9.00
69 A7 3p violet & gray 15.00 17.00
70 A7 4p violet & car 8.00 19.00
71 A7 5p violet & blk 13.00 50.00
72 A7 6p violet & dull vio 12.50 28.00
73 A7 1sh green & blk 24.00 75.00
74 A7 2sh green & car 50.00 75.00
75 A7 5sh green & car 80.00 130.00
76 A7 £1 violet, red 275.00 325.00
Nos. 64-76 (13) 494.00 772.10

1904-05   **Wmk. 3**   **Chalky Paper**
77 A7 ½p violet & grn 5.75 5.25
78 A7 1p violet & car 6.00 1.75
79 A7 1½p violet & blk 3.50 15.00
80 A7 2p violet & brn org 4.75 4.50
81 A7 2½p violet & ultra 6.50 2.25
82 A7 3p violet & gray 50.00 4.00
83 A7 4p violet & car 11.00 8.00
84 A7 5p violet & blk 13.00 32.00
85 A7 6p violet & dl vio 7.50 3.75
86 A7 1sh green & blk 8.50 10.00
87 A7 2sh green & ultra 30.00 32.50
88 A7 5sh green & car 47.50 65.00
89 A7 £1 violet, red 275.00 325.00
Nos. 77-89 (13) 469.00 509.00

The 1p also exists on ordinary paper. Value, $1.50

1907-10   **Ordinary Paper**
90 A7 ½p green 1.00 .60
91 A7 1p carmine 17.00 .80
92 A7 1½p orange ('10) 3.00 2.25
93 A7 2p gray 2.25 1.75
94 A7 2½p ultra 4.00 3.25

Chalky Paper
95 A7 3p violet, yel 11.00 3.25
96 A7 4p blk & red, yel 2.60 1.75
97 A7 5p vio & ol grn 22.50 6.00
98 A7 6p vio & red vio 20.00 9.00
99 A7 1sh black, green 6.25 5.75
100 A7 2sh vio & bl, bl 25.00 22.50
101 A7 5sh grn & red, yel 47.50 70.00
102 A7 £1 vio & blk, red 300.00 250.00
Nos. 90-102 (13) 462.10 376.90

The 3p also exists on ordinary paper. Value, unused $24, used $15.

King George V and Seal of the Colony
A8   A9

Die I

For description of dies I and II see "Dies of British Colonial Stamps" in Table of Contents.
Numerals of 3p, 4p, 5p, 6p and 10p of type A8 are in color on plain tablet. Numerals of 7p and 9p are on solid-color tablet.

1912-24   **Ordinary Paper**   **Wmk. 3**
103 A8 ½p green 4.25 3.50
104 A8 1p scarlet 9.50 1.00
a. 1p carmine 2.25 .45
105 A8 1½p orange 2.25 2.75
106 A8 2p gray 1.50 .25
107 A8 2½p ultra 1.25 1.00

Chalky Paper
108 A9 3p violet, yel 5.00 3.75
109 A9 4p blk & red, yel 3.25 16.00
a. Die II ('24) 5.50 6.00
110 A8 5p violet & ol grn 1.50 7.00
111 A8 6p vio & red vio 4.50 6.75
112 A8 7p violet & org 3.50 10.00
113 A8 9p violet & blk 5.75 14.00
114 A8 10p violet & red 3.50 20.00
115 A9 1sh black, green 8.50 5.25
a. 1sh black, emerald 190.00
116 A9 2sh vio & ultra, bl 26.00 6.25
117 A9 5sh grn & red, yel 24.00 35.00
118 A9 10sh grn & red, grn 110.00 150.00
119 A9 £1 vio & blk, red 225.00 300.00
120 A9 £2 violet & ultra 950.00 1,100.
121 A9 £5 gray grn & org 3,250. 4,250.
Nos. 103-119 (17) 439.25 582.50

The status of #115a has been questioned.

Die II
1921-27   **Ordinary Paper**   **Wmk. 4**
122 A8 ½p green 2.25 1.10
123 A8 1p violet ('26) 7.00 .25
a. Die I ('24) 4.25 2.50
124 A8 1½p scarlet 2.00 1.50
125 A8 2p gray ('22) 1.25 .25
126 A8 2½p ultra 3.00 19.00
127 A8 3p ultra ('22) 1.75 1.40
128 A8 4p blk & red, yel 4.75 3.75
129 A8 5p vio & ol grn 1.50 1.40

Chalky Paper
130 A8 6p dp vio & red vio 1.50 3.25
131 A8 7p vio & org ('27) 3.75 27.00
132 A8 9p dl vio & blk ('22) 5.00 24.00
133 A8 10p violet & red 5.00 32.00
134 A9 1sh blk, emerald 14.00 8.00
135 A9 2sh vio & ultra, bl 11.00 11.50
136 A9 5sh grn & red, yel 11.00 57.50
137 A9 10sh grn & red, grn 150.00 275.00
138 A9 £2 violet & ultra 850.00 1,200.
139 A9 £5 gray grn & org 2,750. 4,000.
Nos. 122-137 (16) 224.75 466.90

Rice Field — A10
Palms and Kola Tree — A11

1932, Mar. 1   **Engr.**   **Perf. 12½**
140 A10 ½p green .25 .50
141 A10 1p dk violet .40 .30
142 A10 1½p rose car .50 2.25
143 A10 2p yellow brn 1.50 .30
144 A10 3p ultra 1.75 2.75
145 A10 4p orange 1.50 13.00
146 A10 5p olive green 2.50 7.50
147 A10 6p light blue 1.50 4.75
148 A10 1sh red brown 6.50 13.00

Perf. 12
149 A11 2sh dk brown 6.00 8.25
150 A11 5sh indigo 19.00 26.00
151 A11 10sh deep green 90.00 160.00
152 A11 £1 deep violet 180.00 275.00
Nos. 140-152 (13) 311.40 508.85

Wilberforce Issue

Arms of Sierra Leone — A12 
Slave Throwing Off Shackles — A13

Map of Sierra Leone — A14

Old Slave Market, Freetown A15

Fruit Seller — A16

Government Sanatorium — A17

Bullom Canoe — A18

Punting near Banana Islands — A19

Government Buildings, Freetown A20

Old Slavers' Resort, Bunce Island — A21

African Elephant — A22

George V
A23

Freetown
Harbor — A24

1933, Oct. 2

153	A12	½p dp grn	1.00	1.25
154	A13	1p brn & blk	.85	.25
155	A14	1½p org brn	7.50	4.75
156	A15	2p violet	3.50	.25
157	A16	3p ultra	6.50	1.75
158	A17	4p dk brn	7.00	10.00
159	A18	5p red brn & sl grn	7.50	11.00
160	A19	6p dp org & blk	12.00	7.00
161	A20	1sh dk vio	5.00	18.00
162	A21	2sh bl & dk vio	40.00	50.00
163	A22	5sh red vio & blk	160.00	200.00
164	A23	10sh grn & blk	300.00	475.00
165	A24	£1 yel & dk vio	650.00	800.00
		Nos. 153-165 (13)	1,200.	1,579.

Abolition of slavery in the British colonies and cent. of the death of William Wilberforce, English philanthropist and agitator against the slave trade.

Common Design Types
pictured following the introduction.

Silver Jubilee Issue
Common Design Type

1935, May 6   ***Perf. 11x12***

166	CD301	1p black & ultra	1.25	2.50
167	CD301	3p ultra & brown	2.75	8.50
168	CD301	5p indigo & green	3.75	25.00
169	CD301	1sh brn vio & ind	13.50	20.00
		Nos. 166-169 (4)	21.25	56.00
		Set, never hinged	32.50	

Coronation Issue
Common Design Type

1937, May 12   ***Perf. 11x11½***

170	CD302	1p deep orange	.40	.90
171	CD302	2p dark violet	.65	1.00
172	CD302	3p deep ultra	.90	3.75
		Nos. 170-172 (3)	1.95	5.65
		Set, never hinged	3.75	

Freetown
Harbor
A25

Rice
Harvesting
A26

1938-44   ***Perf. 12½***

173	A25	½p grn & blk	.25	.50
174	A25	1p dp cl & blk	.30	.70
175	A26	1½p rose red	12.50	1.25
175A	A26	1½p red vio ('41)	.25	.70
176	A26	2p red violet	30.00	3.00
176A	A26	2p dk red ('41)	.25	2.10
177	A25	3p ultra & blk	.30	.60
178	A25	4p red brn & blk	.55	4.50
179	A26	5p olive green	3.75	4.00
180	A26	6p gray	.55	.60
181	A25	1sh ol grn & blk	1.40	.90
181A	A26	1sh3p org yel ('44)	.30	.60
182	A25	2sh sepia & blk	2.75	2.75
183	A26	5sh red brown	6.00	14.00

184	A26	10sh emerald	15.00	16.00
185	A25	£1 dk blue	11.00	30.00
		Nos. 173-185 (16)	85.15	82.20
		Set, never hinged	150.00	

Catalogue values for unused stamps in this section, from this point to the end of the section, are for Never Hinged items.

Peace Issue
Common Design Type
Perf. 13½x14

1946, Oct. 1   **Engr.**   **Wmk. 4**

186	CD303	1½p lilac	.25	.25
187	CD303	3p bright ultra	.25	.25

Silver Wedding Issue
Common Design Types

1948, Dec. 1   **Photo.**   ***Perf. 14x14½***

188	CD304	1½p brt red violet	.25	.25

Engraved; Name Typographed
Perf. 11½x11

189	CD305	£1 dark blue	24.50	26.00

UPU Issue
Common Design Types
Engr.; Name Typo. on 3p, 6p

1949, Oct. 10   ***Perf. 13½, 11x11½***

190	CD306	1½p rose violet	.25	.35
191	CD307	3p indigo	.50	1.75
192	CD308	6p gray	.85	2.00
193	CD309	1sh olive	1.40	1.00
		Nos. 190-193 (4)	3.00	5.10

Coronation Issue
Common Design Type

1953, June 2   **Engr.**   ***Perf. 13½x13***

194	CD312	1½p purple & black	.40	.40

Cape
Lighthouse
A27

Cotton Tree,
Freetown — A28

1p, Queen Elizabeth II Quay. 1½d, Piassava workers. 3p, Rice harvesting. 4p, Iron ore production, Marampa. 6p, Whale Bay, York Village. 1sh, Bullom boat. 1sh3p, Map of Sierra Leone & plane. 2sh6p, Orugu Bridge. 5sh, Kuranko chief. 10sh, Law Courts, Freetown. £1, Government House.

Perf. 13 (A27), 13½ (A28)

1956, Jan. 2   **Engr.**   **Wmk. 4**
Center in Black

195	A27	½p lt violet	1.10	2.25
196	A27	1p reseda	.75	.30
197	A27	1½p ultra	1.90	5.50
198	A28	2p lt brown	.60	.30
199	A28	3p ultra	1.05	.90
a.		Perf 13x13½	1.90	11.00
200	A27	4p gray blue	2.75	2.25
201	A27	6p violet	1.10	.35
202	A28	1sh carmine	1.40	.55
203	A27	1sh3p gray brown	13.00	.55
204	A28	2sh6p brown org	16.50	11.00
205	A27	5sh green	4.25	4.50
206	A27	10sh red violet	4.50	3.25
207	A27	£1 orange	19.00	25.00
		Nos. 195-207 (13)	67.90	56.10

For surcharges and overprints see Nos. 242-247, 251-253, 255-256, 319, 322, C1-C7, C13.

Independent State

Carrying Oil Palm
Fruit — A29

Diamond
Miner and
Badge
A30

Badge and: 1½p, 5sh, Bundu mask. 2p, 10sh, Bishop Crowther and Old Fourah Bay College. 3p, 6p, Sir Milton Margai. 4p, 1sh3p, Lumley Beach, Freetown. £1, Bugler.

Perf. 13x13½, 13½x13

1961, Apr. 27   **Wmk. 336**

208	A29	½p bl grn & dk brn	.25	.25
209	A30	1p gray grn & brn org	1.50	.25
210	A29	1½p green & blk	.25	.25
211	A29	2p vio blue & blk	.25	.25
212	A30	3p brn org & ultra	.25	.25
213	A30	4p rose red & grnsh bl	.25	.25
214	A30	6p lilac & gray	.25	.25
215	A29	1sh org & dk brn	.35	.25
216	A30	1sh3p vio & grnsh bl	.35	.25
217	A30	2sh6p black & grn	2.75	.40
218	A29	5sh rose red & blk	1.00	1.50
219	A29	10sh emerald & blk	1.25	1.50
220	A29	£1 carmine & yel	8.50	10.00
		Nos. 208-220 (13)	17.20	15.65

Sierra Leone's Independence.
For surcharges see Nos. 254, 274, 279-280, 285-286, 290-291, 294, 296, 299, C10, C29-C31, C132-C133.

Royal Charter,
1799 — A31

House of Representatives, Freetown,
1924 — A32

Designs: 4p, King's Yard Gate, Freetown, 1817. 1sh3p, Yacht "Britannia."

1961, Nov. 25   **Engr.**   **Wmk. 336**

221	A31	3p vermilion & blk	.25	.25
222	A31	4p violet & blk	.75	.75
223	A32	6p orange & blk	.90	.90
224	A32	1sh3p blue & blk	1.75	1.75
		Nos. 221-224 (4)	3.65	3.65

Visit of Elizabeth II to Sierra Leone, Nov., 1961.
For overprints and surcharges see Nos. 272, 278, C8-C9, C11-C12.

Malaria Eradication
Emblem — A33

1962, Apr. 7   ***Perf. 11x11½***

225	A33	3p crimson	.25	.25
226	A33	1sh3p green	.40	.40

WHO drive to eradicate malaria.

Fireball
Lily — A34

Jina
Gbo — A35

Plants: 1½p, Stereospermum. 2p, Black-eyed Susan. 3p, Beniseed. 4p, Blushing hibiscus. 6p, Climbing lily. 1sh, Beautiful crinum. 1sh3p, Bluebells. 2sh6p, Broken hearts. 5sh, Ra-ponthi. 12sh, Blue plumbago. £1, African tulip tree.

1963, Jan. 1   **Photo.**   ***Perf. 14***
Flowers in Natural Colors

227	A34	½p olive brown	.25	.25
228	A35	1p org ver & dk red	.25	.25
229	A34	1½p green	.25	.25
230	A35	2p lemon	.25	.25
231	A34	3p dark green	.25	.25
232	A34	4p lt violet blue	.25	.25
233	A35	6p indigo	.25	.25
234	A34	1sh brt yel grn & red	.50	.25
235	A35	1sh3p dk yellow grn	1.20	.25
236	A34	2sh6p dk gray	1.50	.60
237	A34	5sh deep violet	1.75	.80
238	A34	10sh red lilac	3.75	1.25
239	A34	£1 bright blue	6.50	5.50
		Nos. 227-239 (13)	16.95	10.40

For surcharges see Nos. 271, 273, 276-277, 283-284, 289, 295, 300-305, 317-318, 320-321, 329-332, C37-C41, C57-C60, C134.

Wheat
Emblem,
Grain Bin
and
Threshing
Machine
A36

1sh3p, Bullom woman examining onion crop.

Perf. 11½x11

1963, Mar. 21   **Engr.**   **Wmk. 336**

240	A36	3p orange yel & blk	.25	.25
241	A36	1sh3p green & brown	.45	.45

FAO "Freedom from Hunger" campaign.
For surcharges see Nos. 275, C28.

Nos. 195, 197 and 199 Surcharged in Red, Brown, Orange, Violet or Blue

On A27

On A28

Perf. 13, 13½

1963, Apr. 27 Wmk. 4

Center in Black

242	A27	3p on ½p lt vio (R)	.40	.25
243	A27	4p on 1½p ultra (Br)	.25	.25
244	A27	6p on ½p lt vio (O)	.30	.25
245	A28	10p on 3p ultra (R)	.50	.50
246	A28	1sh6p on 3p ultra (V)	.40	.40
247	A28	3sh6p on 3p ultra (Bl)	.50	.50
		Nos. 242-247 (6)	2.35	2.15

Type "a" exists in two settings, varying in the width of the line "19 Progress 63." In each sheet of 60, this line measures 19½-21mm on 55 stamps, and 17½-18mm on 5 stamps. See Nos. C1-C7.

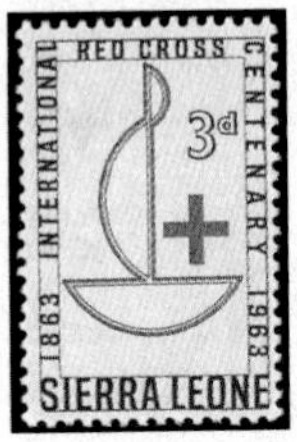

Centenary Emblem — A37

Design: 6p, Red Cross. 1sh3p, Centenary Emblem with curved-lines background.

Perf. 11x11½

1963, Nov. 1 Engr. Wmk. 336

248	A37	3p purple & red	.25	.25
249	A37	6p black & red	.25	.25
250	A37	1sh3p dark green & red	1.10	1.10
		Nos. 248-250 (3)	1.60	1.60

Centenary of International Red Cross.
For surcharge see No. C56.

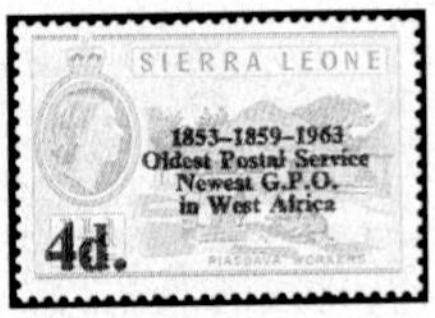

Nos. 199, 197, 216 and 195 Ovptd. or Srchd. in Pink, Red, Violet or Brown

Perf. 13, 13½, 13½x13

1963, Nov. 4 Engr. Wmk. 4

Center in Black except No. 254

251	A28	3p (P)	.25	.25
252	A27	4p on 1½p (R)	.25	.25
253	A27	9p on 1½p (V)	.25	.25
254	A30	1sh on 1sh3p (R)	.25	.25
255	A27	1sh6p on ½p (P)	.40	.30
256	A28	2sh on 3p (Br)	.40	.30
		Nos. 251-256,C8-C13 (12)	39.05	37.60

Oldest postal service (1st stamps in 1859) and the newest GPO in West Africa. Overprint in 5 lines on Nos. 251 and 256. A number of surcharge varieties and errors exist.

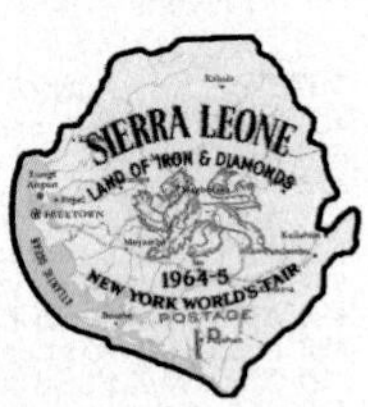

Map and Lion of Sierra Leone — A38

Engraved and Lithographed

1964, Feb. 10 Unwmk. *Die Cut*

Self-adhesive

257	A38	1p multicolored	.25	.25
258	A38	3p multicolored	.25	.25
259	A38	4p multicolored	.25	.25
260	A38	6p multicolored	.25	.25
261	A38	1sh multicolored	.25	.25
262	A38	2sh multicolored	.30	.30
263	A38	5sh multicolored	.60	.60
		Nos. 257-263,C14-C20 (14)	5.30	5.80

New York World's Fair, 1964-65.
For surcharges see Nos. 288, 297, 335 and note under No. 299.

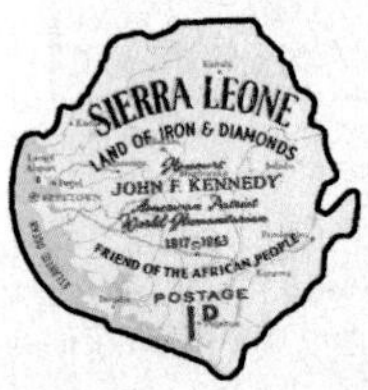

"John F. Kennedy, American Patriot, World Humanitarian" A39

1964, May 11 Self-adhesive

264	A39	1p multicolored	.25	.25
265	A39	3p multicolored	.25	.25
266	A39	4p multicolored	.25	.25
267	A39	6p multicolored	.25	.25
268	A39	1sh multicolored	.25	.25
269	A39	2sh multicolored	.35	.35
270	A39	5sh multicolored	.60	*1.25*
		Nos. 264-270,C21-C27 (14)	5.15	8.00

For surcharges see Nos. 281-282, 287, 292-293, 298, 333, 336, and note under No. 299.

Issues of 1961-63 Srchd. in Red, Black, Dark Blue, Violet or Orange

1964, Aug. 4

271	A35	1c on 6p (#233) (R)	.25	.25
272	A31	2c on 3p (#221)	.25	.25
273	A34	3c on 3p (#231)	.25	.25
274	A29	5c on ½p (#208) (DB)	.25	.25
275	A36	8c on 3p (#240) (R)	.25	.25
276	A35	10c on 1sh3p (#235) (R)	.30	.25
277	A34	15c on 1sh (#234)	.40	.40
278	A32	25c on 6p (#223) (V)	.60	.60
279	A30	50c on 2sh6p (#217) (O)	1.20	1.20
		Nos. 271-279,C28-C31 (13)	5.70	5.65

Issues of 1961-64 Surcharged in Black or Gold

1965, Jan. 20

280	A30	1c on 3p (#212)	.25	.25
281	A39	2c on 1p (#264)	.25	.25
282	A39	4c on 3p (#265)	.25	.25
283	A35	5c on 2p (#230)	.25	.25
284	A34	1 le on 5sh (#237) (G)	2.50	2.50
285	A29	2 le on £1 (#220)	5.25	5.25
		Nos. 280-285 (6)	8.75	8.75

The surcharges on Nos. 284-285 are given in numerals and spelled out in two lines; numeral on Nos. 280-283.

Issues of 1961-64 Srchd. in Red, Black, Orange, Blue or Pink

1965, Apr.

286	A29	1c on 1½p (#210) (R)	.25	.25
287	A39	2c on 3p (#265)	.25	.25
288	A38	2c on 4p (#259)	.25	.25
289	A35	3c on 1p (#228)	.25	.25
290	A29	3c on 2p (#211) (O)	.25	.25
291	A30	5c on 1sh3p (#216) (O)	.25	.25
292	A39	15c on 6p (#267)	2.75	2.75
293	A39	15c on 1sh (#268) (O)	5.00	5.00
294	A30	20c on 6p (#214) (O)	1.25	1.25
295	A35	25c on 6p (#233) (R)	1.60	1.60
296	A30	50c on 3p (#212) (R)	3.25	3.25
297	A38	60c on 5sh(#263) (Bl)	7.50	7.50
298	A39	1 le on 4p (#266) (P)	9.75	9.75
299	A29	2 le on £1 (#220) (Bl)	18.00	18.00
		Nos. 286-299 (14)	50.60	50.60

Additional surcharges exist: "1c" on Nos. 260, 262, 269-270. See note after No. C41 for airmails. Value $4 each.
For surcharges see Nos. 333, 335-336.

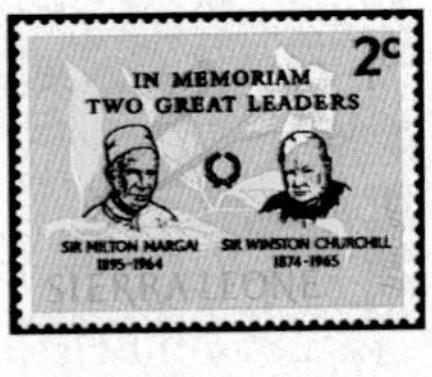

Nos. 228, 231, 234, 235, 232, 237 Srchd.

Designs of Surcharge: Nos. 301, 304, Sir Milton Margai. Nos. 302, 305, Sir Winston Churchill.

Wmk. 336

1965, May 19 Photo. *Perf. 14*

300	A35	2c on 1p multi	.40	.25
301	A34	3c on 3p multi	.25	.25
302	A34	10c on 1sh multi	.60	.30
303	A35	20c on 1sh3p multi	1.10	.30
304	A34	50c on 4p multi	1.00	.50
305	A34	75c on 5sh multi	4.00	2.00
		Nos. 300-305,C37-C41 (11)	27.35	12.35

For surcharges see Nos. 329-332.

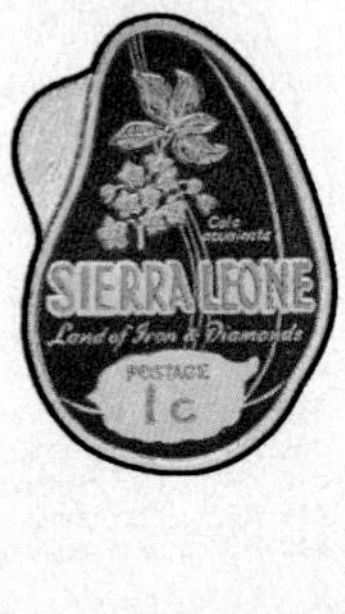

Cola Nut and Plant — A40

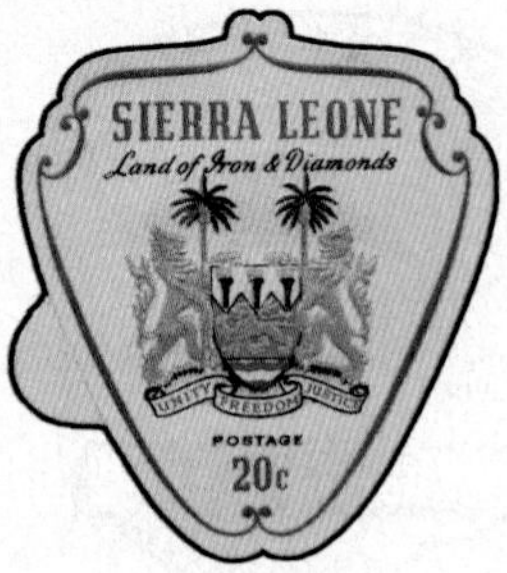

Coat of Arms A41

Typographed; Embossed on Silver Foil

1965 Unwmk. *Die Cut*

Self-adhesive

310	A40	1c multicolored	.25	.25
311	A40	2c multicolored	.25	.25
312	A40	3c multicolored	.25	.25
313	A40	4c multicolored	.50	.40
314	A40	5c multicolored	.50	.40

Engr.; Embossed on Paper

315	A41	20c multi, *cream*	2.00	.75
316	A41	50c multi, *cream*	4.00	4.00
		Nos. 310-316,C53-C55 (10)	14.30	11.80

Various advertisements printed on peelable paper backing. Nos. 310-316 have side tabs for handling and come packed in boxes of 100. Nos. 310-312 and 314 were released during November due to a stamp shortage; official release date for set, Dec. 17, 1965. See #338-356, C67, C97. For surcharges see #334, 337, 364-368.

Nos. 197-198, and 232-234, 236 Srchd. with New Value in Black or Ultramarine and Ovptd. "FIVE YEARS / INDEPENDENCE / 1961-1966"

1966, Apr. 27 Wmk. 4, 336

317	A35	1c on 6p multi	.25	.25
318	A34	2c on 4p multi	.25	.25
319	A27	3c on 1½p ultra & blk (U)	.25	.25
320	A34	8c on 1sh multi (U)	.25	.25
321	A34	10c on 2sh6p multi (U)	.25	.25
322	A28	20c on 2p lt brown (U)	.55	.55
		Nos. 317-322,C56-C60 (11)	7.60	7.60

5th anniv. of independence. The surcharge on No. 317 includes an "X" over old denomination.

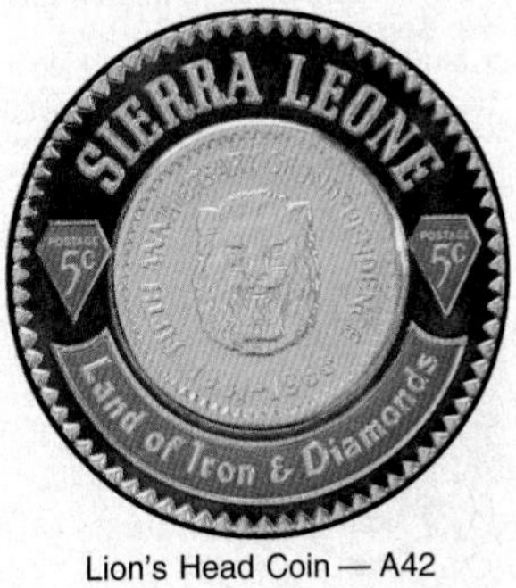

Lion's Head Coin — A42

Designs: 2c, 3c, ¼ Golde coin. 5c, 8c, ½ Golde coin. 25c, 1 le, 1 Golde coin. (3c, 8c, 1 le, Map of Sierra Leone.)

Diameter: 2c, 3c, 38mm; 5c, 8c, 54mm; 25c, 1 le, 82mm

Self-adhesive

Litho.; Embossed on Gilt Foil

1966, Nov. 12 Unwmk. *Die Cut*

323	A42	2c org & dp plum	.25	.25
324	A42	3c red lil & emer	.25	.25
325	A42	5c vio bl & red org	.25	.25
326	A42	8c black & Prus blue	.25	.25
327	A42	25c emerald & violet	.50	.50
328	A42	1 le red & orange	2.75	2.75
		Nos. 323-328,C61-C66 (12)	11.05	11.15

1st gold coinage of Sierra Leone. Advertising printed on paper backing.

Nos. 297-298, 303-305 and 316 Surcharged in Red, Silver, Violet, Green, Blue or Black

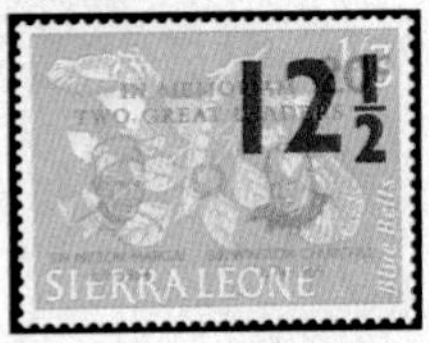

on A34, A35

on A38, A39

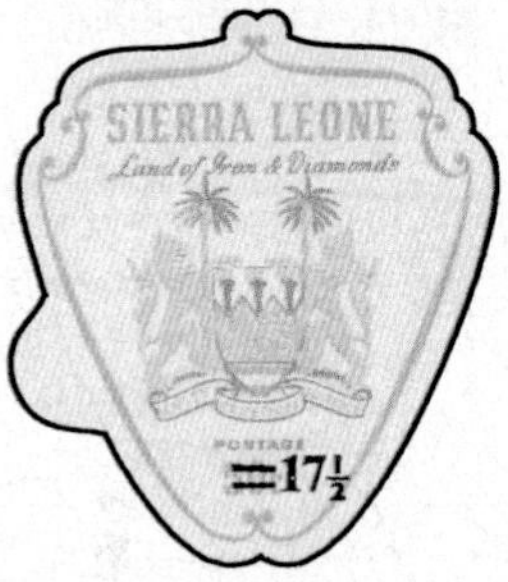

on A41

1967, Dec. 2

329	A34	6½c on 75c on 5sh (R)	.30	.30
330	A34	7½c on 75c on 5sh (S)	.30	.30
331	A34	9½c on 50c on 4p (G)	.40	.40
332	A35	12½c on 20c on 1sh3p (V)	.50	.50
333	A39	17½c on 1 le on 4p (Bl)	3.50	3.50
334	A41	17½c on 50c	3.50	3.50
335	A38	18½c on 60c on 5sh	10.00	10.00
336	A39	18½c on 1 le on 4p	3.50	3.50
337	A41	25c on 50c	1.00	1.00
		Nos. 329-337,C67-C69 (12)	24.90	24.90

Self-adhesive & Die Cut
Nos. 338-421 are self-adhesive and die cut.

Cola Nut Type of 1965
White Numeral Tablet

Typographed; Embossed on White Paper

1967-68 Unwmk.

338	A40	½c brt car, grn & yel	.25	.25
339	A40	1c brt car, grn & yel	.25	.25
340	A40	1½c orange, grn & yel	.25	.25
341	A40	2c brt car, grn & yel	.25	.25
342	A40	2½c emer, bl grn & yel	.40	.40
343	A40	3c brt car, grn & yel	.25	.25
344	A40	3½c olive, rose & ultra	.25	.25
345	A40	4½c gray ol, grn & yel	.40	.40
346	A40	5c brt car, grn & yel	.40	.40
347	A40	5½c red brn, grn & yel	.45	.45
		Nos. 338-347 (10)	3.15	3.15

Advertisements printed on peelable backing except on the 2c, 3c, 3½c and 5c.

Colored Numeral Tablet

348	A40	½c brt car, grn & yel	.25	.25
349	A40	1c brt car, grn & yel	.25	.25
350	A40	2c pink, brn & car	.25	.25
351	A40	2c brt car, grn & yel	.75	.60
352	A40	2½c bl grn, vio & org	1.00	.75
353	A40	2½c emer, bl grn & yel	.30	.25
354	A40	3c brt car, grn & yel	.25	.25
355	A40	3½c lilac rose, grn & yel	.30	.30
356	A40	4c brt car, grn & yel	.25	.25
		Nos. 348-356 (9)	3.60	3.15

Nos. 344, 348-354 issued in 1968.
Advertisements printed on peelable backing on the 3½c and 4c.

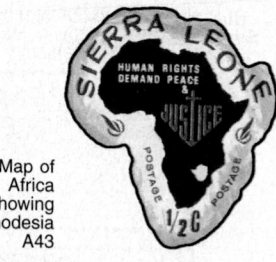

Map of
Africa
Showing
Rhodesia
A43

Each denomination shows map of Africa
with map of one of the following countries —
Portuguese Guinea, South Africa,
Mozambique, Rhodesia, South West Africa or
Angola.

1968, Sept. 25   Unwmk.   Litho.

357	A43	½c multicolored	.25	.25
358	A43	2c multicolored	.25	.25
359	A43	2½c multicolored	.25	.25
360	A43	3½c multicolored	.25	.25
361	A43	10c multicolored	.30	.30
362	A43	11½c multicolored	.35	.35
363	A43	15c multicolored	.40	.40
		Nos. 357-363 (7)	2.05	2.05
		7 Strips of 6 (1 of each design)		
		(42)		17.50

Intl. Human Rights Year. Sheets of 30 have
5 horizontal rows containing one stamp of
each design. Advertisements printed on peelable backing.
   See #C72-C78. For surcharges see #C106-
C111.

No. 316 Surcharged

Engraved; Embossed on Paper
1968, Nov. 30

364	A41	6½c on 50c multi	.25	.25
365	A41	17½c on 50c multi	.30	.30
366	A41	22½c on 50c multi	.60	.60
367	A41	28½c on 50c multi	.75	.75
368	A41	50c on 50c multi	1.10	1.10
		Nos. 364-368,C79-C83 (10)	6.20	6.20

19th Olympic Games, Mexico City, 10/12-27.

Sierra
Leone
Type A1,
1859
A44

2c, Design A40, 2c, 1965. 3½c, #220. 5c,
#315. 12½c, #189. 1 le, Design A9, #2, 1912.

1969, Mar. 1   Litho.

369	A44	1c multicolored	.25	.25
370	A44	2c multicolored	.25	.25
371	A44	3½c multicolored	.25	.25
372	A44	5c multicolored	.25	.25
373	A44	12½c multicolored	.40	.40
374	A44	1 le multicolored	2.75	2.75
		Nos. 369-374,C84-C89 (12)	16.40	16.40

5th anniv. of free-form self-adhesive postage stamps. Various advertisements printed
on peelable paper backing. No. 369 has side
tab for handling and comes packed in boxes of
50. Nos. 370-374 are without side tabs and
come 20 stamps attached to one sheet.

Globe, Freighter, Flags of Sierra
Leone and Japan — A45

Map of Europe and Africa, Freighter,
Flags of Sierra Leone and
Netherlands — A46

Anvil Shape with Flags of Sierra Leone and:
3½c, Union Jack. 10c, 50c, West Germany.
18½c, Netherlands.

1969, July 10

375	A45	1c multicolored	.25	.25
376	A46	2c multicolored	.25	.25
377	A46	3½c multicolored	.25	.25
378	A46	10c multicolored	.25	.25
379	A46	18½c multicolored	.45	.45
380	A46	50c multicolored	1.00	1.00
		Nos. 375-380,C90-C95 (12)	8.20	8.20

Completion of the Pepel Port iron ore carrier
terminal. Various advertisements printed on
peelable paper backing. No. 375 has side tab
for handling and comes packed in boxes of 50.
Nos. 376-380 are without side tabs and come
20 stamps attached to one sheet.

African Development
Bank Emblem — A47

Lithographed; Gold Impressed
1969, Sept. 10

381	A47	3½c lt blue, grn & gold	1.00	1.00

5th anniv. of the African Development Bank.
Advertising printed on peelable paper backing,
20 imperf. stamps to a sheet of backing, roulette 10. See No. C96.

Diamond and
Boy Scout
Emblem
A48

1969, Dec. 6   Litho.

382	A48	1c multicolored	.25	.25
383	A48	2c multicolored	.25	.25
384	A48	3½c multicolored	.25	.25
385	A48	4½c multicolored	.25	.25
386	A48	5c multicolored	.30	.30
387	A48	75c multicolored	8.00	8.00
		Nos. 382-387,C100-C105		
		(12)	77.55	62.35

60th anniv. of the Sierra Leone Boy Scouts.
Various advertising printed on peelable paper
backing. No. 382 has side tab for handling and
comes packed in boxes of 100. Nos. 383-387
are without side tabs and come 20 stamps
attached to one sheet.

EXPO '70 Emblems, Torii, Maps of
Sierra Leone and Japan — A49

1970, June 22

388	A49	2c multicolored	.25	.25
389	A49	3½c multicolored	.25	.25
390	A49	10c multicolored	.25	.25
391	A49	12½c multicolored	.30	.30
392	A49	20c multicolored	.35	.35
393	A49	45c multicolored	.60	.60
		Nos. 388-393,C112-C117 (12)	6.15	6.15

EXPO '70 Intl. Exhib., Osaka, Japan, Mar.
15-Sept. 13. Various advertising printed on
peelable paper backing.

Diamond
A50

Palm
Kernel — A51

Lithographed and Embossed
1970, Oct. 3   Unwmk.
Light Blue Background

394	A50	1c carmine & blk	.25	.25
395	A50	1½c brt green & car	.25	.25
396	A50	2c lilac & yel grn	.25	.25
397	A50	2½c ocher & dk bl	.25	.25
398	A50	3c vio bl & org red	.45	.25
399	A50	3½c dk blue & grn	.50	.25
400	A50	4c olive & ultra	.50	.25
401	A50	5c black & lilac	.50	.25

Orange Brown Background

402	A51	6c bright green	.60	.25
403	A51	7c rose lilac	.65	.30
404	A51	8½c orange	.70	.30
405	A51	9c lilac	.70	.30
406	A51	10c dark blue	.75	.30
407	A51	11½c blue	1.00	.50
408	A51	18½c yellow green	2.00	.75
		Nos. 394-408,C118-C124 (22)	51.05	44.90

Advertisements printed on peelable paper
backing. Packed in boxes of 500.

Sewa Diadem in Jewelry Box — A52

1970, Dec. 30

409	A52	2c multicolored	.50	.25
410	A52	3½c multicolored	.50	.25
411	A52	10c multicolored	.90	.35
412	A52	12½c multicolored	1.00	.45

413	A52	40c multicolored	2.75	1.50
414	A52	1 le multicolored	13.00	11.00
		Nos. 409-414,C125-C130 (12)	58.30	51.60

Diamond industry. Advertisement printed on
peelable paper backing. Sheets of 20.

Traffic
Pattern — A53

1971, Mar. 1   Litho.

415	A53	3½c orange & vio blue	3.00	3.00

Right hand traffic change-over. See No.
C131. Advertisements printed on peelable
paper backing.

Flag and
Lion's
Head — A54

Litho.; Embossed in Silver
1971, Apr. 27

416	A54	2c multicolored	.25	.25
417	A54	3½c multicolored	.25	.25
418	A54	10c multicolored	.25	.25
419	A54	12½c multicolored	.25	.25
420	A54	40c multicolored	.80	.80
421	A54	1 le multicolored	1.75	1.75
		Nos. 416-421,C137-C142 (12)	9.75	9.75

10th anniversary of independence. Advertisements printed on peelable paper backing.
Stamps are in shape of Sierra Leone map.

Pres. Siaka
Stevens — A55

1972   Litho.   Perf. 13

422	A55	1c pink & multi	.25	.25
423	A55	2c violet & multi	.25	.25
424	A55	4c lt ultra & multi	.25	.25
425	A55	5c buff & multi	.25	.25
426	A55	7c rose & multi	.25	.25
427	A55	10c olive & multi	.25	.25
428	A55	15c emerald & multi	.25	.25
429	A55	18c yellow & multi	.30	.30
430	A55	20c lt blue & multi	.35	.35
431	A55	25c orange & multi	.40	.40
432	A55	50c brt green & multi	1.00	.60
433	A55	1 le multicolored	1.60	1.25
434	A55	2 le red org & multi	2.50	2.50
435	A55	5 le multicolored	4.00	8.50
		Nos. 422-435 (14)	11.90	15.65

Shades from later printings are found on
several denominations including 1c, 2c, 7c,
10c, 1 le, 2 le.

Guma Valley Dam and Bank
Emblem — A56

1975, Jan. 14   Litho.   Perf. 13½

436	A56	4c multicolored	125.00	50.00

African Development Bank, 10th anniversary. See No. C143.

Pres. Siaka Stevens and Opening of
Congo Bridge — A57

1975, Aug. 24 Litho. Perf. 13x13½
437 A57 5c multicolored 15.00 15.00
Congo Bridge opening and Pres. Siaka Stevens' 70th birthday. See No. C144.

Pres. Tolbert and Stevens, Hands
across Mano River — A58

1975, Oct. 3 Litho. Perf. 13x13½
438 A58 4c multicolored 1.25 1.25
Mano River Union Agreement between Liberia and Sierra Leone, signed Oct. 3, 1973. See No. C145.

Mohammed Ali
Jinnah, Flags of
Sierra Leone
and
Pakistan — A59

1977, Jan. 28 Litho. Perf. 13 rough
439 A59 30c multicolored 1.10 1.10
Mohammed Ali Jinnah (1876-1948), First Governor General of Pakistan.

Elizabeth II — A60

1977, Nov. 28 Litho. Perf. 12½x12
440 A60 5c multicolored .25 .25
441 A60 1 le multicolored 1.10 1.10
25th anniv. of the reign of Elizabeth II.

Fourah Bay College — A61

Design: 20c, Old College, vert.

Perf. 12x12½, 12½x12
1977, Dec. 19 Litho.
442 A61 5c multicolored .25 .25
443 A61 20c multicolored .35 .35
Fourah Bay College, Mt. Aureol, Freetown, founded 1827.

St. Edward's Crown
and Scepters — A62

Designs: 50c, Elizabeth II in coronation coach. 1 le, Elizabeth II and Prince Philip on coronation day.

1978, Sept. 14 Litho. Perf. 14½x14
444 A62 5c multicolored .25 .25
445 A62 50c multicolored .45 .45
446 A62 1 le multicolored .60 .60
Nos. 444-446 (3) 1.30 1.30
25th anniv. of coronation of Elizabeth II.

Fig Tree
Blue
A63

Butterflies: 15c, Narrow blue-banded swallowtail. 25c, Pirate. 1 le, African giant swallowtail.

1979, Apr. 9 Litho. Perf. 14½
447 A63 5c multicolored .30 .30
448 A63 15c multicolored .65 .65
449 A63 25c multicolored 1.05 1.05
450 A63 1 le multicolored 4.00 4.00
Nos. 447-450 (4) 6.00 6.00

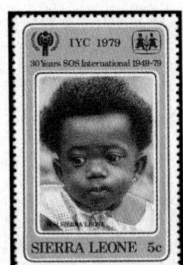

Child, IYC and
SOS
Emblems — A64

Designs (Emblems and): 27c, Girl and infant. 1 le, Mother and infant.

Perf. 14x13½
1979, Aug. 13 Litho. Wmk. 373
451 A64 5c multicolored .25 .25
452 A64 27c multicolored .45 .45
453 A64 1 le multicolored .80 .80
a. Souvenir sheet of 1 2.00 2.00
Nos. 451-453 (3) 1.50 1.50
Intl. Year of the Child and 30th anniv. of SOS villages (villages for homeless children).

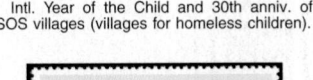

Presidents Stevens and Tolbert,
Pigeon Post, Mano River — A65

1979, Oct. 3 Perf. 13½
454 A65 5c multicolored .25 .25
455 A65 22c multicolored .25 .25
456 A65 27c multicolored .30 .30
457 A65 35c multicolored .35 .35
458 A65 1 le multicolored 1.05 1.05
a. Souvenir sheet of 1 1.25 1.25
Nos. 454-458 (5) 2.20 2.20
Mano River Union, 5th anniv.; Postal Union, 1st anniv.

Sierra Leone No.
9, Hill — A66

1979, Dec. 19 Litho. Perf. 14½x14
459 A66 10c Grt. Britain #6 .25 .25
460 A66 15c shown .25 .25
461 A66 50c Sierra Leone #220 .50 .50
Nos. 459-461 (3) 1.00 1.00
Souvenir Sheet
462 A66 1 le Sierra Leone #119 .70 .70
Sir Rowland Hill (1795-1879), originator.

Touraco
A67

2c, Olive-bellied sunbird. 3c, Black-headed oriole. 5c, Spur-winged goose. 7c, White-bellied didric cuckoo. 10c, Gray parrot, vert. 15c, African blue quail, vert. 20c, West African wood owl, vert. 30c, Blue plantain eater, vert. 40c, Nigerian blue-breasted kingfisher, vert. 50c, Black crake, vert. 1 le, Hartlaub's duck. 2 le, Black bee-eater. 5 le, Denham's bustard.

1980, Jan. 29 Perf. 14
No Date Inscription Below Design
463 A67 1c multicolored .25 .25
464 A67 2c multicolored .25 .25
465 A67 3c multicolored .25 .25
466 A67 5c multicolored .25 .25
467 A67 7c multicolored .25 .25
468 A67 10c multicolored .25 .25
469 A67 15c multicolored .45 .45
470 A67 20c multicolored .60 .60
471 A67 30c multicolored .90 .90
472 A67 40c multicolored 1.10 1.10
473 A67 50c multicolored 1.60 1.60
474 A67 1 le multicolored 3.00 3.00
475 A67 2 le multicolored 6.00 6.00
476 A67 5 le multicolored 15.00 15.00
Nos. 463-476 (14) 30.15 30.15
For surcharges see Nos. 632-636. For overprints see Nos. 637-638.

1981 Inscribed "1981"
463a A67 1c multicolored 1.20 1.20
464a A67 2c multicolored 1.20 1.20
465a A67 3c multicolored 1.20 1.20
466a A67 5c multicolored 1.20 1.20
468a A67 10c multicolored .90 .90
469a A67 15c multicolored 2.10 2.10
470a A67 20c multicolored 3.00 3.00
471a A67 30c multicolored 2.40 2.40
472a A67 40c multicolored 2.40 2.40
473a A67 50c multicolored 2.40 2.40
474a A67 1 le multicolored 3.50 3.50
475a A67 2 le multicolored 7.25 7.25
476a A67 5 le multicolored 14.00 14.00
Nos. 463a-476a (13) 42.75 42.75
For surcharges see Nos. 632a-636a. For overprints see Nos. 637a, 638a.

1982 Inscribed "1982"
463b A67 1c multicolored 1.20 1.20
464b A67 2c multicolored 1.20 1.20
465b A67 3c multicolored 1.20 1.20
466b A67 5c multicolored 1.20 1.20
467b A67 7c multicolored 12.00 12.00
468b A67 10c multicolored .90 .90
469b A67 15c multicolored 2.10 2.10
470b A67 20c multicolored 3.00 3.00
471b A67 30c multicolored 2.40 2.40
472b A67 40c multicolored 2.40 2.40
473b A67 50c multicolored 2.40 2.40
474b A67 1 le multicolored 3.50 3.50
475b A67 2 le multicolored 7.25 7.25
476b A67 5 le multicolored 14.00 14.00
Nos. 463b-476b (14) 54.75 54.75
For surcharges see Nos. 632b-636b. For overprints see Nos. 637b, 638b.
For this design dated 1983, without watermark, see Nos. 600A-600K.

Rotary
Intl.,
75th
Anniv.
A68

1980, Feb. 23 Perf. 14
477 A68 5c orange & multi .25 .25
478 A68 27c red & multi .25 .25
479 A68 50c green & multi .40 .40
480 A68 1 le blue & multi .80 .80
Nos. 477-480 (4) 1.70 1.70

Mail Ship
"Maria,"
1884,
London
'80
Emblem
A69

1980, May 6 Litho. Perf. 14
481 A69 6c shown .25 .25
482 A69 31c "Tarquah," 1902 .45 .45
483 A69 50c "Aureol," 1951 1.00 1.00
484 A69 1 le "Africa Palm," 1974 1.60 1.60
Nos. 481-484 (4) 3.30 3.30
London 80 Intl. Stamp Exhib., May 6-14.

Conf.
Emblem — A70

1980, July 1 Litho. Perf. 14½
485 A70 20c multicolored .25 .25
486 A70 1 le multicolored 1.00 1.00
17th African Summit Conf., Freetown, July 1-4.

Small Striped
Swordtail — A71

1980, Oct. 6 Litho. Perf. 14
487 A71 5c shown .25 .25
488 A71 27c Pearl charaxes .90 .90
489 A71 35c White barred charaxes 1.10 1.10
490 A71 1 le Zaddach's forester 3.25 3.25
Nos. 487-490 (4) 5.50 5.50

Freetown
Airport — A72

1980, Dec. 5 Litho. Perf. 13½
491 A72 6c shown .25 .25
492 A72 26c Mammy Yoko Hotel .30 .30
493 A72 31c Freetown Cotton Tree .35 .35
494 A72 40c Beindomgo Falls .50 .50
495 A72 50c Water skiing .60 .60
496 A72 1 le Elephant 1.25 1.25
Nos. 491-496 (6) 3.25 3.25

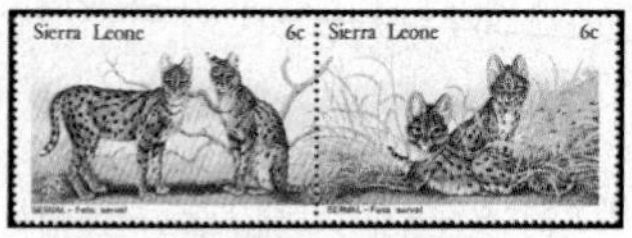

Servals — A73

Cats and Kittens: No. 498, Serval kittens. No. 500a, African golden cats. No. 502a, Leopards. No. 504a, Lions. Pairs have continuous design.

1981, Feb. 23 Litho. *Perf. 14*

497	6c multicolored	.25	.25
498	6c multicolored	.25	.25
a.	A73 Pair, #497-498	.25	.25
499	31c multicolored	.65	.65
500	31c multicolored	.65	.65
a.	A73 Pair, #499-500	1.60	1.60
501	50c multicolored	1.25	1.25
502	50c multicolored	1.25	1.25
a.	A73 Pair, #501-502	3.00	3.00
503	1 le multicolored	3.00	3.00
504	1 le multicolored	3.00	3.00
a.	A73 Pair, #503-504	6.00	6.00
	Nos. 497-504 (8)	10.30	10.30

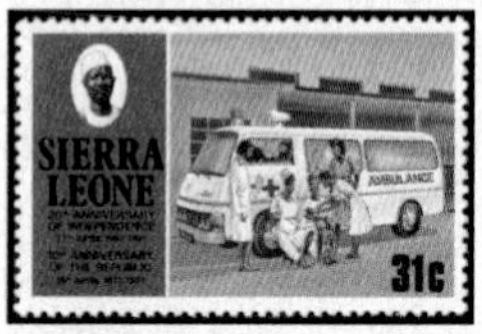

Ambulance Clinic — A74

Wmk. 373

1981, Apr. 18 Litho. *Perf. 14½*

505	A74 6c Soldiers, vert.	.30	.30
506	A74 31c shown	1.60	1.60
507	A74 40c Traffic policeman, vert.	2.10	2.10
508	A74 1 le Coast Guard ship	5.00	5.00
	Nos. 505-508 (4)	9.00	9.00

Anniv.: independence, 20th; republic, 10th.

Royal Wedding Issue

Common Design Type

1981 Litho. *Perf. 12, 14*

509	CD331 31c Bouquet	.40	.40
510	CD331a 35c Sandringham	.60	.60
511	CD331 45c Charles	.75	.75
512	CD331a 60c Charles	.75	.75
513	CD331a 70c like 35c	2.00	2.00
514	CD331 1 le Couple	1.00	1.00
515	CD331a 1.30 le Charles	2.00	2.00
516	CD331a 1.50 le Couple	1.00	1.00
517	CD331a 2 le Couple	4.00	4.00
	Nos. 509-517 (9)	12.50	12.50

Souvenir Sheet

518	CD331 3 le Royal landau	3.00	3.00

31c, 45c, 1 le, 3 le issued July 22, perf. 14. 35c, 60c, 1.50 le issued in sheets of 5 plus label; perf. 12, Sept. 9. 70c, 1.30 le, 2 le issued in booklets only, perf. 14.

For surcharges see #540-546, 714, 716, 721.

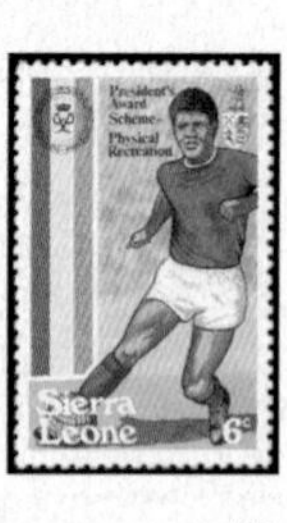

Soccer Player — A75

Wmk. 373

1981, Sept. 30 Litho. *Perf. 14*

519	A75 6c shown	.25	.25
520	A75 31c Boys planting trees	.40	.40
521	A75 1 le Duke of Edinburgh	.80	.80
522	A75 1 le Pres. Stevens	.80	.80
	Nos. 519-522 (4)	2.25	2.25

Duke of Edinburgh's Awards and Pres. Steven's Awards, 25th anniv.

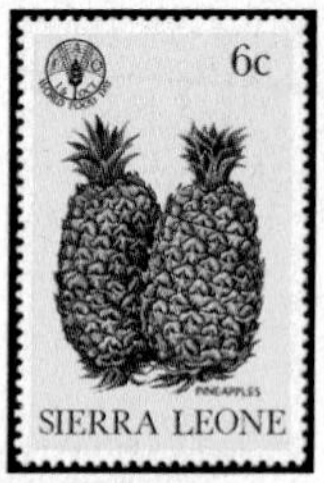

Pineapples — A76

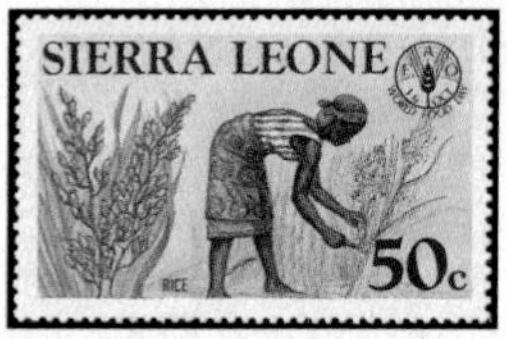

Woman Tending Rice Plants — A77

Perf. 14, 14½ (A77)

1981 Litho. Wmk. 373

523	A76 6c shown	.25	.25
524	A77 6c Peanuts for export	.25	.25
525	A76 31c Peanuts	.50	.50
526	A77 31c Crushing, eating cassava	.50	.50
527	A76 50c Cassava fruits	.85	.85
528	A77 50c shown	.85	.85
529	A76 1 le Rice plants	1.25	1.25
530	A77 1 le Men tending pineapple plants	1.25	1.25
	Nos. 523-530 (8)	5.70	5.70

World Food Day. Issue dates: Nos. 523, 525, 527, 529, Oct. 16; others, Nov. 2.

Princess Diana Issue

Common Design Type

1982, July Litho. *Perf. 14½*

531	CD332 31c Caernarvon Castle	.45	.45
532	CD332 50c Honeymoon	.75	.75
533	CD332 2 le Wedding	2.25	2.25
	Nos. 531-533 (3)	3.45	3.45

Souvenir Sheet

534	CD332 3 le Diana	3.75	3.75

Also issued in sheetlets of 5 + label.

For overprints and surcharges see Nos. 552-555, 713, 715, 717-720, 722-723.

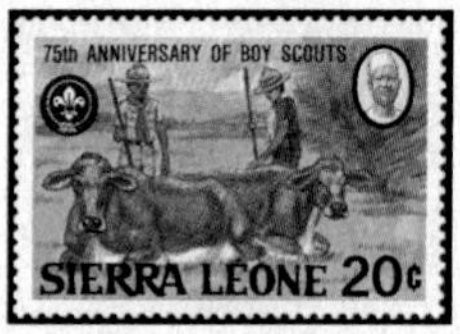

Scouting Year A78

1982, Aug. 23 *Perf. 14*

535	A78 20c Studying animal husbandry	.30	.30
536	A78 50c Botanical study	.85	.85
537	A78 1 le Baden-Powell	1.60	1.60
538	A78 2 le Fishing at campsite	2.50	2.50
	Nos. 535-538 (4)	5.25	5.25

Souvenir Sheet

539	A78 3 le Raising flag	4.25	4.25

For surcharges see Nos. 694-698.

Nos. 509-512, 514, 516, 518 Surcharged

1982, Aug. 30 Wmk. 373

540	CD331 50c on 31c	1.60	1.60
541	CD331 50c on 35c	1.60	1.60
542	CD331 50c on 45c	1.60	1.60
543	CD331 50c on 60c	1.60	1.60
544	CD331 90c on 1 le	2.75	2.75
545	CD331 2 le on 1.50 le	6.00	6.00
	Nos. 540-545 (6)	15.15	15.15

Souvenir Sheet

546	CD331 3.50 le on 3 le	2.50	2.50

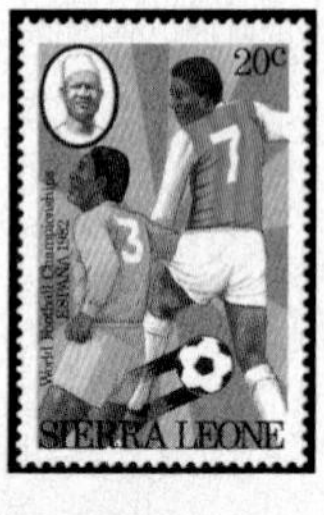

1982 World Cup — A79

Designs: Various soccer players.

1982, Sept. 7

547	A79 20c multicolored	.50	.50
548	A79 30c multicolored	.70	.70
549	A79 1 le multicolored	2.50	2.50
550	A79 2 le multicolored	4.50	4.50
	Nos. 547-550 (4)	8.20	8.20

Souvenir Sheet

551	A79 3 le multicolored	6.75	6.75

For overprints see Nos. 561-565.

Nos. 531-534 Overprinted: "ROYAL BABY/ 21.6.82"

1982, Oct. 15 Litho. *Perf. 14½*

552	CD332 31c multicolored	.30	.30
553	CD332 50c multicolored	.50	.50
554	CD332 2 le multicolored	1.25	1.00
	Nos. 552-554 (3)	2.05	1.80

Souvenir Sheet

555	CD332 3 le multicolored	2.25	2.25

Birth of Prince William of Wales, June 21.

Also issued in sheetlets of 5 + label.

For surcharges see #715, 719-720, 723.

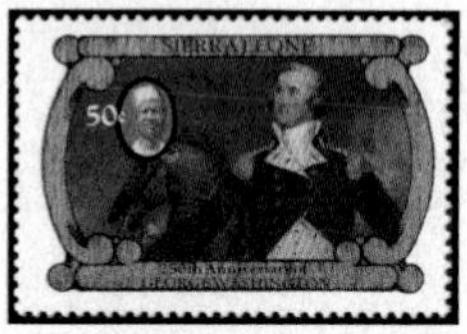

George Washington — A80

Various paintings of Washington. 31c, 1 le, vert.

1982, Oct. 30 Litho. *Perf. 14*

556	A80 6c multicolored	.25	.25
557	A80 31c multicolored	.40	.40
558	A80 50c multicolored	.50	.50
559	A80 1 le multicolored	.85	.85
	Nos. 556-559 (4)	2.00	2.00

Souvenir Sheet

560	A80 2 le multicolored	2.00	2.00

Nos. 547-551 Overprinted with Finalists and Score

1982, Nov. 9 *Perf. 14*

561	A79 20c multicolored	.30	.30
562	A79 30c multicolored	.45	.45
563	A79 1 le multicolored	1.25	1.25
564	A79 2 le multicolored	1.75	1.75
	Nos. 561-564 (4)	3.75	3.75

Souvenir Sheet

565	A79 3 le multicolored	2.25	2.25

Italy's victory in 1982 World Cup.

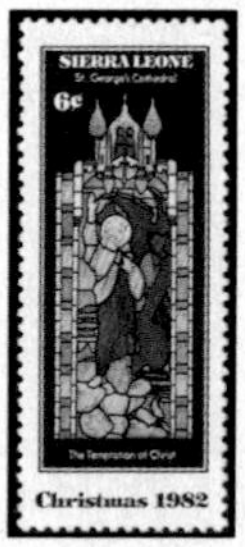

Christmas — A81

Stained-glass Windows, St. George's Cathedral, Freetown.

1982, Nov. 18 *Perf. 14*

566	A81 6c Temptation of Christ	.25	.25
567	A81 31c Baptism of Christ	.35	.35
568	A81 50c Annunciation	.45	.45
569	A81 1 le Nativity	.75	.75
	Nos. 566-569 (4)	1.80	1.80

Souvenir Sheet

570	A81 2 le Mary and Joseph	2.00	2.00

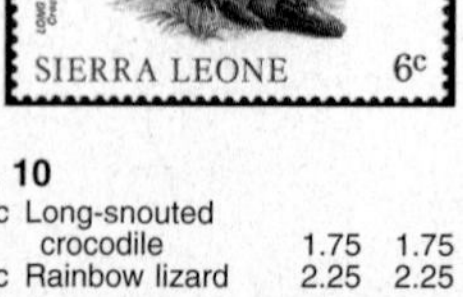

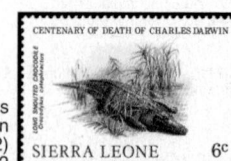

Charles Darwin (1809-82) A82

1982, Dec. 10

571	A82 6c Long-snouted crocodile	1.75	1.75
572	A82 31c Rainbow lizard	2.25	2.25
573	A82 50c River turtle	3.25	3.25
574	A82 1 le Chameleon	4.75	4.75
	Nos. 571-574 (4)	12.00	12.00

Souvenir Sheet

575	A82 2 le Royal python, vert.	3.75	3.75

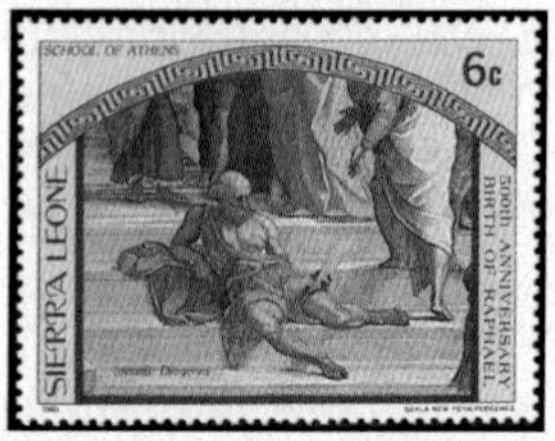

500th Birth Anniv. of Raphael — A83

School of Athens, Fresco, Vatican. Nos. 576-579 show details.

1983, Jan. 28 Litho. *Perf. 14*

576	A83 6c Diogenes	.25	.25
577	A83 31c Euclid, Ptolemy	.45	.45
578	A83 50c Euclid and his Students	.75	.75
579	A83 2 le Pythagoras, Heraclitus	2.00	2.00
	Nos. 576-579 (4)	3.45	3.45

Souvenir Sheet

580	A83 3 le Entire painting	2.60	2.60

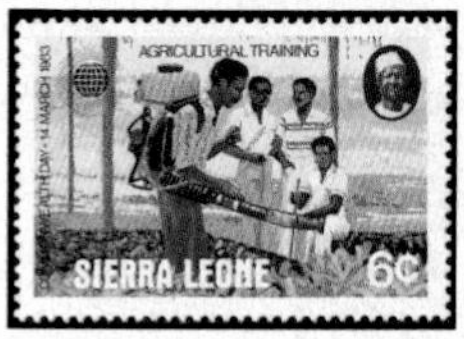

A83a

6c, Agricultural training. 10c, Tourism development. 50c, Broadcast training. 1 le, Airport services.

1983, Mar. 14 Litho. *Perf. 14*

581	A83a 6c multicolored	.25	.25
582	A83a 10c multicolored	.25	.25
583	A83a 50c multicolored	.65	.65
584	A83a 1 le multicolored	1.25	1.25
	Nos. 581-584 (4)	2.40	2.40

Commonwealth Day.

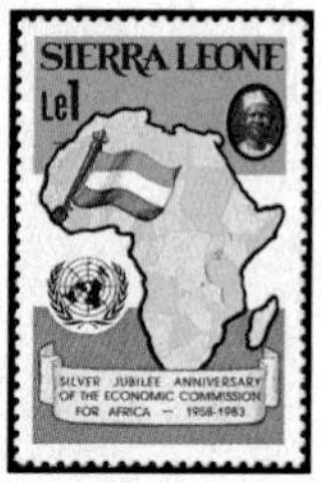

25th Anniv. of Economic Commission for Africa — A84

1983, Apr. 29 Litho. *Perf. 13½x13*

585	A84 1 le multicolored	1.10	1.10

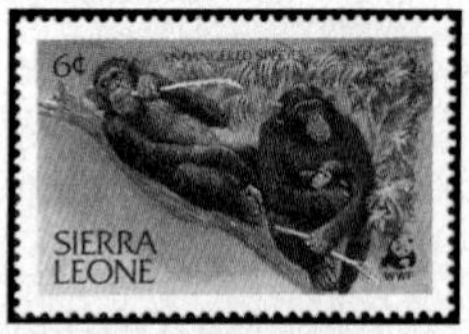

Endangered Chimpanzees, World Wildlife Fund Emblem — A85

Various chimpanzees from Outamba-Kilimi Natl. Park. 10c, 31c, vert.

1983, May Litho. *Perf. 14*

586	A85 6c multicolored	*2.00*	*2.00*
587	A85 10c multicolored	*2.50*	*2.50*
588	A85 31c multicolored	*4.50*	*4.50*
589	A85 60c multicolored	*7.25*	*7.25*
	Nos. 586-589 (4)	*16.25*	*16.25*

Souvenir Sheet

590	A85 3 le Elephants	*6.75*	*6.75*

For surcharges see No. 2906-2909.

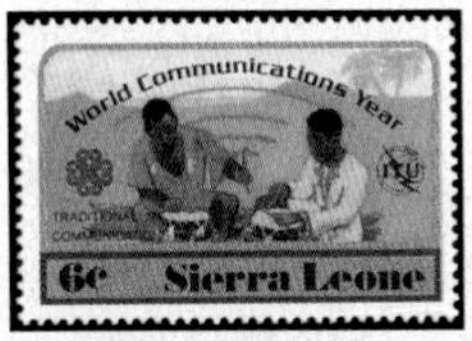

World Communications Year — A86

6c, Traditional communications. 10c, Mano River mail. 20c, Satellite ground station. 1 le, English packet, 1805.
2 le, Map, phone, envelope.

1983, July 14 *Perf. 14*

591	A86	6c multicolored	.25	.25
592	A86	10c multicolored	.25	.25
593	A86	20c multicolored	.25	.25
594	A86	1 le multicolored	1.10	1.10
		Nos. 591-594 (4)	1.85	1.85

Souvenir Sheet

595	A86	2 le multicolored	1.75	1.75

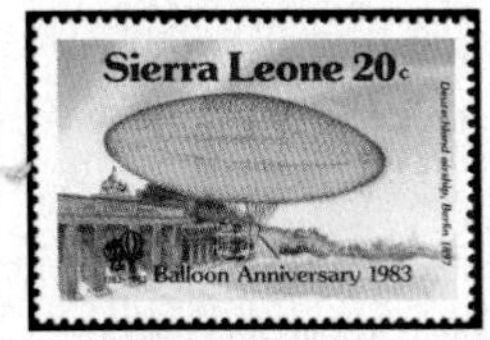

Manned Flight Bicentenary — A87

6c, Montgolfiere, 1783, vert. 20c, Deutschland blimp, 1897. 50c, Norge I blimp, North Pole, 1926. 1 le, Cape Sierra sport balloon, Freetown, 1983, vert.
2 le, Futuristic airship.

1983, Aug. 31 Litho. *Perf. 14*

596	A87	6c multicolored	.30	.30
597	A87	20c multicolored	.80	.80
598	A87	50c multicolored	1.90	1.90
599	A87	1 le multicolored	3.75	3.75
		Nos. 596-599 (4)	6.75	6.75

Souvenir Sheet

600	A87	2 le multicolored	2.75	2.75

Birds Type of 1980

1c, Touraco. 2c, Olive-bellied sunbird. 5c, Spur-winged goose. 10c, Gray parrot, vert. 15c, African blue quail, vert. 20c, West African wood owl, vert. 30c, Blue plantain eater, vert. 40c, Nigerian blue-breasted kingfisher, vert. 50c, Black crake, vert. 2 le, Black bee-eater. 5 le, Denham's bustard.

1983, Oct. 1 Unwmk. *Perf. 14*
Inscribed "1983"

600A	A67	1c multi	1.50	1.50
600B	A67	2c multi	1.50	1.50
600C	A67	5c multi	1.00	1.00
600D	A67	10c multi	1.25	1.25
600E	A67	15c multi	1.75	1.75
600F	A67	20c multi	2.75	2.75
600G	A67	30c multi	2.50	2.50
600H	A67	40c multi	3.50	3.50
600I	A67	50c multi	3.50	3.50
600J	A67	2 le multi	10.00	10.00
600K	A67	5 le multi	15.00	15.00
		Nos. 600A-600K (11)	44.25	44.25

For surcharges see Nos. 632A-636E. For overprints see Nos. 638C-638D.

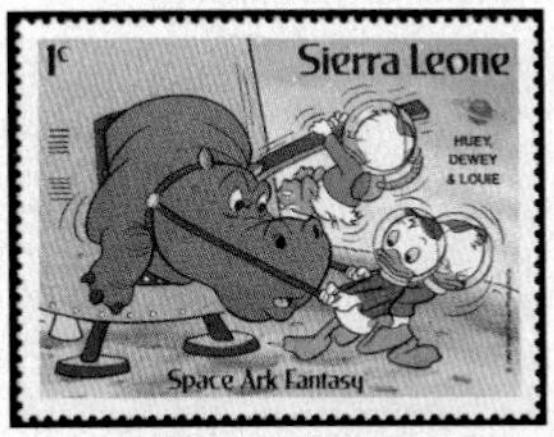

Walt Disney, Space Ark Fantasy — A88

No. 601, Hippopotamus, Huey, Dewey and Louie. No. 602, Mickey Mouse and Snake. No. 603, Elephant and Donald Duck. No. 604, Zebra and Goofy. No. 605, Lion and Ludwig von Drake. No. 606, Rhinoceros and Goofy. No. 607, Giraffe and Mickey Mouse. No. 608, Monkey and Donald Duck.
No. 609, Mickey Mouse and animals.

1983, Nov.

601	A88	1c multicolored	.25	.25
602	A88	1c multicolored	.25	.25
603	A88	3c multicolored	.25	.25
604	A88	3c multicolored	.25	.25
605	A88	10c multicolored	.25	.25
606	A88	10c multicolored	.25	.25
607	A88	2 le multicolored	1.60	1.60
608	A88	3 le multicolored	2.25	2.25
		Nos. 601-608 (8)	5.35	5.35

Souvenir Sheet

609	A88	5 le multicolored	5.25	5.25

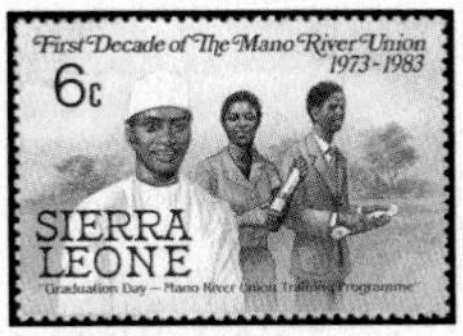

10th Anniv. of Mano River Union A89

1984, Feb. 8 Litho. *Perf. 15*

610	A89	6c Teaching Program graduates	.25	.25
611	A89	25c Emblem	.25	.25
612	A89	31c Map, presidents	.25	.25
613	A89	41c Guinea Accession signing	.35	.35
a.		Souvenir sheet of 1	.60	.60
		Nos. 610-613 (4)	1.10	1.10

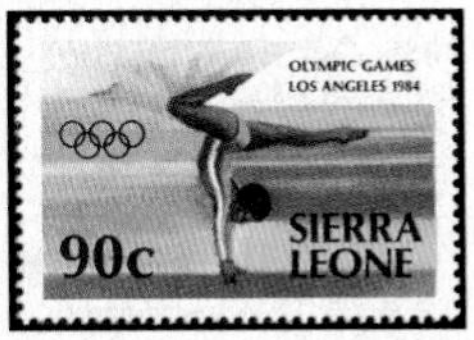

23rd Olympic Games, Los Angeles, July 28-Aug. 12 — A90

1984, Mar. 15 *Perf. 14*

614	A90	90c Gymnastics	.50	.50
615	A90	1 le Hurdles	.65	.65
616	A90	3 le Javelin	1.10	1.10
		Nos. 614-616 (3)	2.25	2.25

Souvenir Sheet

617	A90	7 le Boxing	3.25	3.25

For surcharges see Nos. 699-702.

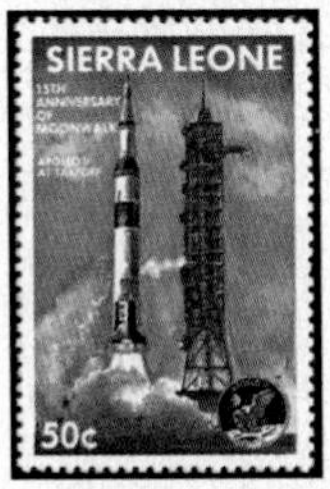

Apollo 11, 15th Anniv. — A91

50c, Lift off. 75c, Lunar landing. 1.25 le, 1st step on moon. 2.50 le, Walking on moon.
5 le, TV transmission, horiz.

1984, May 14 Litho. *Perf. 14*

618	A91	50c multicolored	.40	.40
619	A91	75c multicolored	.60	.60
620	A91	1.25 le multicolored	1.00	1.00
621	A91	2.50 le multicolored	2.00	2.00
		Nos. 618-621 (4)	4.00	4.00

Souvenir Sheet

622	A91	5 le multicolored	3.50	3.50

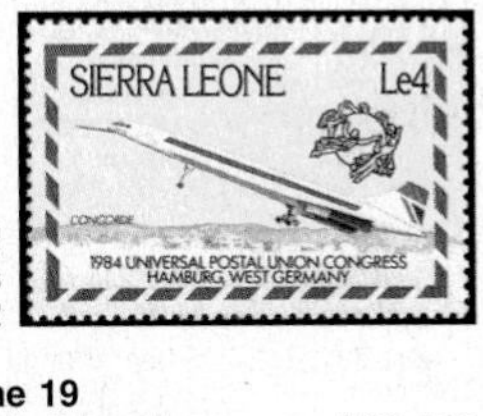

UPU Congress A92

1984, June 19

623	A92	4 le Concorde	5.00	5.00

Souvenir Sheet

624	A92	4 le UPU emblem, von Stephan	3.00	3.00

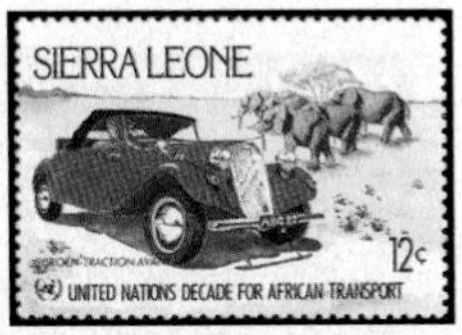

UN Decade for African Transportation — A93

Various cars.

1984, July 16 *Perf. 14½x15*

625	A93	12c Citroen	.25	.25
626	A93	60c Locomobile	.65	.65
627	A93	90c AC Ace	.85	.85
628	A93	1 le Vauxhall Prince Henry	1.10	1.10
629	A93	1.50 le Delahaye-185	1.60	1.60
630	A93	2 le Mazda	2.00	2.00
		Nos. 625-630 (6)	6.45	6.45

Souvenir Sheet
Perf. 15

631	A93	6 le Volkswagon Beetle	6.00	6.00

Nos. 466, 468, 475 Surcharged
Wmk. 373

1984, Aug. 3 Litho. *Perf. 14*

632	A67	25c on 10c multi	*7.50*	*7.50*
633	A67	40c on 10c multi	*7.50*	*7.50*
634	A67	50c on 2 le multi	*7.50*	*7.50*
635	A67	70c on 5c multi	*7.50*	*7.50*
636	A67	10 le on 5c multi	*7.50*	*7.50*
		Nos. 632-636 (5)	*37.50*	*37.50*

Nos. 466a, 468a, 475a Surcharged

632a	A67	25c on 10c multi	*7.50*	*7.50*
633a	A67	40c on 10c multi	*7.50*	*7.50*
634a	A67	50c on 2 le	*7.50*	*7.50*
635a	A67	70c on 5c	*7.50*	*7.50*
636a	A67	10 le on 5c	*7.50*	*7.50*
		Nos. 632a-636a (5)	*37.50*	*37.50*

Nos. 466b, 468b, 475b Surcharged

632b	A67	25c on 10c multi	*7.50*	*7.50*
633b	A67	40c on 10c multi	*7.50*	*7.50*
634b	A67	50c on 2 le	*7.50*	*7.50*
635b	A67	70c on 5c	*7.50*	*7.50*
636b	A67	10 le on 5c	*7.50*	*7.50*
		Nos. 632b-636b (5)	*37.50*	*37.50*

Nos. 600C, 600D, 600J Surcharged

1984, Aug. 3 Unwmk. *Perf.*

636A	A67	25c on 10c multi	1.40	1.40
636B	A67	40c on 10c multi	1.00	1.00
636C	A67	50c on 2 le multi	1.00	1.00
636D	A67	70c on 5c multi	1.00	1.00
636E	A67	10 le on 5c multi	4.50	4.50
		Nos. 636A-636E (5)	8.90	8.90

#473, 476 Ovptd.: "AUSIPEX 84"
Wmk. 373

1984, Aug. 22 Litho. *Perf. 14*

637	A67	50c multi (#473)	8.00	8.00
a.		On #473a	8.00	8.00
b.		On #473b	8.00	8.00
638	A67	5 le multi (#476)	22.00	22.00
a.		On #476a	22.00	22.00
b.		On #476b	22.00	22.00

On Nos. 600I, 600K

638C	A67	50c multicolored	2.00	2.00
638D	A67	5 le multicolored	4.00	4.00

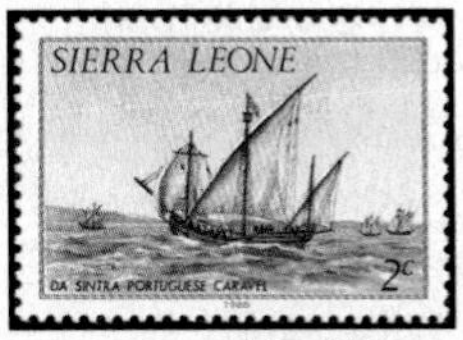

Portuguese Caravel Da Sintra — A94

5c, Merlin of Bristol. 10c, Golden Hind. 15c, Interloper Morduant. 20c, Navy Board Transport Atlantic. 25c, Navy Vessel Lapwing. 30c, Brig Traveller. 40c, Schooner Amistad. 50c, Teazer. 70c, Cable Ship Scotia. 1 le, Alecto. 2 le, Blonde. 5 le, Fox. 10 le, Mail ship Accra.

1984

639	A94	2c multi	.95	1.75
640	A94	5c multi	.95	.95
641	A94	10c multi	1.50	.70
642	A94	15c multi	2.40	.70
643	A94	20c multi	1.75	.70
644	A94	25c multi	1.75	.70
645	A94	30c multi	1.75	.70
646	A94	40c multi	1.90	1.05
647	A94	50c multi	2.10	1.30
648	A94	70c multi	2.40	1.90
649	A94	1 le multi	3.00	2.75
650	A94	2 le multi	6.00	5.50
651	A94	5 le multi	16.00	14.00
652	A94	10 le multi	28.00	28.00
		Nos. 639-652 (14)	70.45	60.70

Issued: Nos. 639-649, 9/5; Nos. 650-651, 10/9; 10 le, 11/7.
See Nos. 739-740. For surcharges see Nos. 809-812.

1985 *Perf. 12½x12*

639a	A94	2c	.30	.30
640a	A94	5c	.30	.30
641a	A94	10c	.30	.30
643a	A94	20c	.30	.30
644a	A94	25c	.30	.30
645a	A94	30c	.30	.30
646a	A94	40c	.30	.30
647a	A94	50c	.30	.30
648a	A94	70c	.30	.30
649a	A94	1 le	1.75	1.75
650a	A94	2 le	3.50	3.50
651a	A94	5 le	8.50	8.50
652a	A94	10 le	16.00	16.00
		Nos. 639a-652a (13)	32.45	32.45

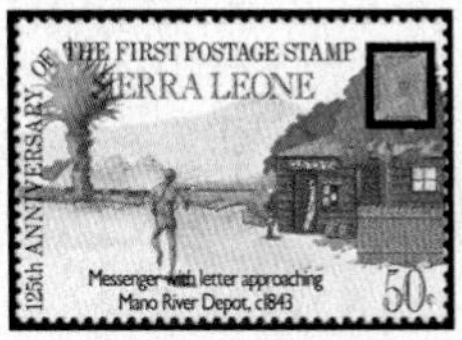

125th Anniv. of Sierra Leone Postage Stamps A95

50c, Mail messenger, No. 2. 2 le, Post Master receiving letters, No. 2. 3 le, Cover.
5 le, Penny Black, No. 2.

1984, Oct. 9

653	A95	50c multicolored	.45	.45
654	A95	2 le multicolored	2.00	2.00
655	A95	3 le multicolored	3.00	3.00
		Nos. 653-655 (3)	5.45	5.45

Souvenir Sheet

656	A95	5 le multicolored	3.00	3.00

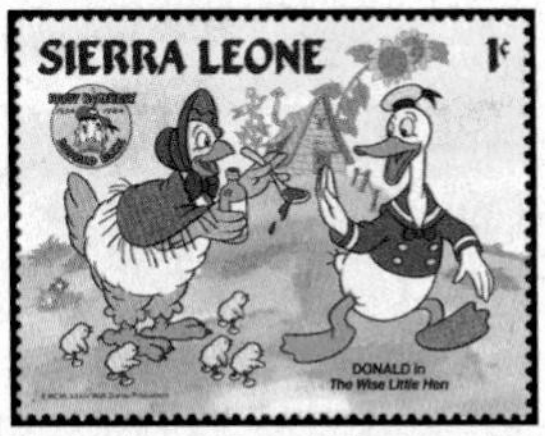

50th Anniv. of Donald Duck — A95a

1c, Wise Little Hen. 2c, Boat Builders. 3c, Three Caballeros. 4c, Mathmagic Land. 5c, Mickey Mouse Club. 10c, On Parade. 1 le, Don Donald. 2 le, Donald gets drafted, p. 12½x12. 4 le, Tokyo Disneyland.
5 le, Sketches.

1984, Nov. Litho. *Perf. 14x13½*

657	A95a	1c multi	.25	.25
658	A95a	2c multi	.25	.25
659	A95a	3c multi	.25	.25
660	A95a	4c multi	.25	.25
661	A95a	5c multi	.25	.25
662	A95a	10c multi	.25	.25
663	A95a	1 le multi	1.25	1.25
663A	A95a	2 le multi	2.75	2.75
664	A95a	4 le multi	5.50	5.50
		Nos. 657-664 (9)	11.00	11.00

Souvenir Sheet

665	A95a	5 le multi	8.50	8.50

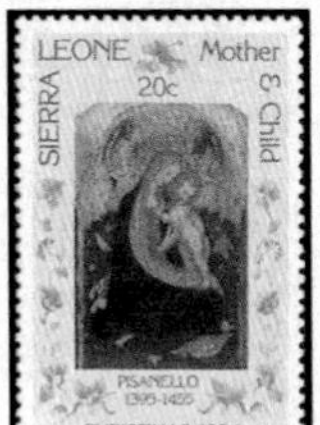

Christmas — A96

Mother and Child paintings.

1984, Nov. 28 *Perf. 14*

666	A96	20c Pisanello	.30	.30
667	A96	1 le Memling	.60	.60
668	A96	2 le Raphael	1.10	1.10
669	A96	3 le van der Werff	1.40	1.40
		Nos. 666-669 (4)	3.40	3.40

Souvenir Sheet

670	A96	6 le Picasso	4.25	4.25

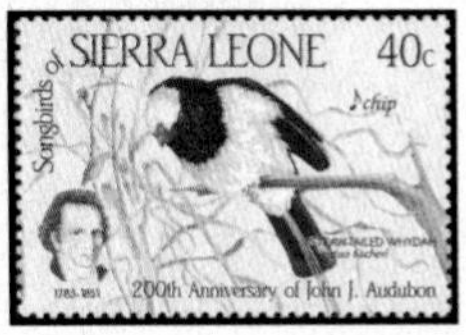

Songbirds A97

40c, Straw-tailed whydah. 90c, Spotted flycatcher. 1.30 le, Garden warbler. 3 le, Speke's weaver.
5 le, Great gray shrike.

1985, Jan. 31　　　　　Litho.
671 A97　40c multi　　　　　　.95　　.95
672 A97　90c multi　　　　　2.10　2.10
673 A97　1.30 le multi　　　　3.25　3.25
674 A97　3 le multi　　　　　5.75　5.75
　　　Nos. 671-674 (4)　　　12.05　12.05

Souvenir Sheet
675 A97　5 le multi　　　　　6.00　6.00

International Youth Year — A98

1985, Feb. 14　　　　　Litho.
676 A98　1.15 le Fishing　　　.70　　.70
677 A98　1.50 le Timber　　　.80　　.80
678 A98　2.15 le Rice farming　1.25　1.25
　　　Nos. 676-678 (3)　　　2.75　2.75

Souvenir Sheet
679 A98　5 le Diamond polish-
　　　　　　ing　　　　　4.25　4.25

Intl. Civil
Aviation
Org.,
40th
Anniv.
A100

Early aviators and their aircraft: 70c, Eddie Rickenbacker, Spad XIII (1918). 1.25 le, Samuel P. Langley, Aerodrome No. 5. 1.30 le, Orville and Wilbur Wright, Flyer 1. 2 le, Charles Lindbergh, Spirit of St. Louis.

1985, Feb. 28　　Litho.　　Perf. 14
680 A100　70c multicolored　　1.40　1.40
681 A100　1.25 le multicolored　2.40　2.40
682 A100　1.30 le multicolored　2.40　2.40
683 A100　2 le multicolored　　4.50　4.50
　　　Nos. 680-683 (4)　　　10.70　10.70

Souvenir Sheet
684 A100　5 le Jet over
　　　　　Freetown　　　3.75　3.75

Easter
A101

Religious paintings — 45c, The Temptation of Christ. 70c, Christ at the Column. 1.55 le, Pieta. 10 le, Christ on the Cross. 12 le, Man of Sorrows
Nos. 685, 687, 689 by Botticelli (1445-1510). Nos. 686, 688 by Velazquez (1599-1660).

1985, Apr. 29
685 A101　45c multicolored　　.25　　.25
686 A101　70c multicolored　　.30　　.30
687 A101　1.55 le multicolored　.85　　.85
688 A101　10 le multicolored　6.50　6.50
　　　Nos. 685-688 (4)　　　7.90　7.90

Souvenir Sheet
689 A101　12 le multicolored　6.25　6.25

Queen Mother,
85th
Birthday — A102

Designs: 1 le, Queen Mother at St. Peter's Cathedral, London, vert. 1.70 le, With Double Star at Sandown Racetrack. 10 le, Attending the gala ballet at Covent Garden, 1971, vert. 12 le, With Princess Anne at Ascot, vert.

1985, July 8　　Litho.　　Perf. 14
690 A102　1 le multicolored　　.25　　.25
691 A102　1.70 le multicolored　.50　　.50
692 A102　10 le multicolored　3.00　3.00
　　　Nos. 690-692 (3)　　　3.75　3.75

Souvenir Sheet
693 A102　12 le multicolored　3.75　3.75

Nos. 535-539 Surcharged "75th Anniversary / of Girl Guides," Black Bar and New Value

1985, July 25
694 A78　70c on 20c multi　　1.00　1.00
695 A78　1.30 le on 50c multi　2.25　2.25
696 A78　5 le on 1 le multi　　1.50　1.50
697 A78　7 le on 2 le multi　　2.75　2.75
　　　Nos. 694-697 (4)　　　7.50　7.50

Souvenir Sheet
698 A78　15 le on 3 le multi　5.75　5.75

Nos. 614-617 Surcharged with Winners Names, Country, "Gold Medal," Black Bar and New Value

No. 699, Ma Yanhonjg, China. No. 700, E. Moses, USA. No. 701, A. Haerkoenen, Finland.
No. 702, M. Taylor, USA.

1985, July 25
699 A90　2 le on 90c multi　　.90　　.90
700 A90　4 le on 1 le multi　　1.60　1.60
701 A90　8 le on 3 le multi　　3.25　3.25
　　　Nos. 699-701 (3)　　　5.75　5.75

Souvenir Sheet
702 A90　15 le on 7 le multi　6.00　6.00

1905 Chater-Lea, Hill Station
House — A103

Designs: 2 le, Honda XR 350 R, QE II Quay. 4 le, Kawasaki Vulcan, Bo Clock Tower. 5 le, Harley-Davidson Electra-Glide, Makeni. 12 le, 1893 Millet.

1985, Aug. 15
703 A103　1.40 le multicolored　1.10　1.10
704 A103　2 le multicolored　　1.50　1.50
705 A103　4 le multicolored　　3.00　3.00
706 A103　5 le multicolored　　3.75　3.75
　　　Nos. 703-706 (4)　　　9.35　9.35

Souvenir Sheet
707 A103　12 le multicolored　8.00　8.00

Motorcycle cent., Decade for African Transport.

A104

1985, Sept. 3
708 A104　70c Viola pomposa　.50　　.50
709 A104　3 le Spinet　　　　2.50　2.50
710 A104　4 le Lute　　　　　3.25　3.25
711 A104　5 le Oboe　　　　　3.50　3.50
　　　Nos. 708-711 (4)　　　9.75　9.75

Souvenir Sheet
712 A104　12 le Portrait　　　8.00　8.00

Johann Sebastian Bach (1685-1750), composer. Nos. 708-712 show music from "Clavier Ubang."

Nos. 510, 512, 516, 531-534, 552-555 Surcharged

1985, Sept. 30　　Perfs. as Before
Designs CD331-CD332
713　　70c on 31c #531　　　.65　　.65
714　　1.30 le on 60c #512　3.00　3.00
715　　1.30 le on 31c #552　1.40　1.40
716　　2 le on 35c #510　　4.00　4.00
717　　4 le on 50c #532　　4.00　4.00
718　　5 le on 2 le #533　　4.75　4.75
719　　5 le on 50c #553　　4.75　4.75

720　　7 le on 2 le #554　　6.75　6.75
721　　8 le on 1.50 le #516　12.50　12.50
　　　Nos. 713-721 (9)　　41.80　41.80

Souvenir Sheets
722　　15 le on 3 le #534　12.00　12.00
723　　15 le on 3 le #555　12.00　12.00

Christmas — A105

Madonna and child paintings by: 70c, Carlo Crivelli (c. 1430-1494). 3 le, Dirk Bouts (c. 1400-1475). 4 le, Antonello de Messina (c. 1430-1479). 5 le, Stefan Lochner (c. 1400-1451). 12 le, Miniature from the Book of Kells, 9th cent., Ireland.

1985, Oct. 18　　Litho.　　Perf. 14
724 A105　70c multicolored　　.25　　.25
725 A105　3 le multicolored　　1.10　1.10
726 A105　4 le multicolored　　1.25　1.25
727 A105　5 le multicolored　　1.75　1.75
　　　Nos. 724-727 (4)　　　4.35　4.35

Miniature Sheet
728 A105　12 le multicolored　3.25　3.25

Jacob and Wilhelm Grimm,
Fabulists — A106

Mark Twain,
American
Humorist
A107

Walt Disney characters acting out Twain quotes (A107) or in Rumpelstiltskin (A106).

1985, Oct. 30　　Litho.　　Perf. 14
729 A106　70c multicolored　　.30　　.30
730 A106　1.30 le multicolored　.45　　.45
731 A107　1.50 le multicolored　1.15　1.15
732 A106　2 le multicolored　　.65　　.65
733 A107　3 le multicolored　　1.35　1.35
734 A107　4 le multicolored　　1.45　1.45
735 A107　5 le multicolored　　1.60　1.60
736 A106　10 le multicolored　3.00　3.00
　　　Nos. 729-736 (8)　　　9.95　9.95

Souvenir Sheets
737 A106　15 le multicolored　4.75　4.75
738 A107　15 le multicolored　6.00　6.00

Nos. 731, 733-735 bear the Intl. Youth Year emblem.

Ship Type of 1984
1985, Nov. 15
739 A94　15 le Favourite　　　4.50　4.50
740 A94　25 le Euryalus　　　7.50　7.50

UN,
40th
Anniv.
A108

Stamps of UN and famous men: 2 le, No. 30, Kennedy. 4 le, No. 59, Einstein. 7 le, No.

44, Maimonides (1135-1204), medieval Judaic scholar. 12 le, Martin Luther King, Jr. (1929-1968), civil rights leader, vert.

1985, Nov. 28　　Litho.　　Perf. 14½
741 A108　2 le multicolored　　1.25　1.25
742 A108　4 le multicolored　　2.25　2.25
743 A108　7 le multicolored　　4.50　4.50
　　　Nos. 741-743 (3)　　　8.00　8.00

Souvenir Sheet
744 A108　12 le multicolored　3.25　3.25

1986 World Cup
Soccer
Championships
A109

Various soccer plays.

1986, Mar. 3　　　　　Perf. 14
745 A109　70c multicolored　　.40　　.40
746 A109　3 le multicolored　　1.50　1.50
747 A109　4 le multicolored　　2.10　2.10
748 A109　5 le multicolored　　2.75　2.75
　　　Nos. 745-748 (4)　　　6.75　6.75

Souvenir Sheet
749 A109　12 le multicolored　3.25　3.25

For overprints and surcharges see Nos. 788-792.

Statue of Liberty,
Cent. — A110

New York City: 40c, Times Square, 1905. 70c, Times Square, 1986. 1 le, Tally Ho Coach, c. 1880, horiz. 10 le, Liberty Lines express bus, 1986. 12 le, Statue of Liberty.

1986, Mar. 11
750 A110　40c multicolored　　.25　　.25
751 A110　70c multicolored　　.25　　.25
752 A110　1 le multicolored　　.55　　.55
753 A110　10 le multicolored　3.00　3.00
　　　Nos. 750-753 (4)　　　4.05　4.05

Souvenir Sheet
754 A110　12 le multicolored　4.25　4.25

A111

Halley's Comet — A112

15c, Johannes Kepler (1571-1630), German astronomer, & Paris Observatory. 50c, US space shuttle landing, 1986. 70c, Bayeux Tapestry (detail), 1066 sighting. 10 le, Arthurian magician, Merlin, sights comet, 530. 12 le, Comet over Sierra Leone.

1986, Apr. 1
755	A111	15c multicolored	.25	.25
756	A111	50c multicolored	.25	.25
757	A111	70c multicolored	.35	.35
758	A111	10 le multicolored	5.25	5.25
		Nos. 755-758 (4)	6.10	6.10

Souvenir Sheet

759	A112	12 le multicolored	3.25	3.25

For overprints and surcharges see Nos. 813-817.

Queen Elizabeth II, 60th Birthday
Common Design Type

10c, Cranwell, 1951. 1.70 le, Garter Ceremony. 10 le, Braemar Games, 1970. 12 le, Windsor Castle, 1943.

1986, Apr. 21
760	CD339	10c multi	.25	.25
761	CD339	1.70 le multi	.55	.55
762	CD339	10 le multi	2.75	2.75
		Nos. 760-762 (3)	3.55	3.55

Souvenir Sheet

763	CD339	12 le multi	2.75	2.75

For surcharges see Nos. 793-795.

AMERIPEX '86 — A113

Locomotives — 50c, Hiawatha, Milwaukee. 2 le, The Rocket, Rock Is. 4 le, Prospector, Rio Grande. 7 le, Daylight, So. Pacific. 12 le, Broadway, Pennsylvania.

1986, May 22
764	A113	50c multi	1.25	1.25
765	A113	2 le multi	2.25	2.25
766	A113	4 le multi	3.75	3.75
767	A113	7 le multi	4.50	4.50
		Nos. 764-767 (4)	11.75	11.75

Souvenir Sheet

768	A113	12 le multi	6.50	6.50

Royal Wedding Issue, 1986
Common Design Type

Designs: 10c, Prince Andrew and Sarah Ferguson. 1.70 le, Andrew with shotgun. 10 le, Andrew saluting.
12 le, Couple, diff.

1986, July 23
769	CD340	10c multi	.25	.25
770	CD340	1.70 le multi	.35	.35
771	CD340	10 le multi	1.75	1.75
		Nos. 769-771 (3)	2.35	2.35

Souvenir Sheet

772	CD340	12 le multi	3.00	3.00

For surcharges see Nos. 796-798.

Indigenous
Flowers — A114

70c, Monodora myristica. 1.50 le, Gloriosa simplex. 4 le, Mussaenda erythrophylla. 6 le, Crinum ornatum. 8 le, Bauhinia purpurea. 10 le, Bombax costatum. 20 le, Hibiscus rosasinensis. 30 le, Cassia fistula.
No. 781, Clitoria ternatea. No. 782, Plumbago auriculata.

1986, Aug. 25   Litho.   Perf. 14
773	A114	70c multi	.25	.25
774	A114	1.50 le multi	1.00	1.00
775	A114	4 le multi	.45	.45
776	A114	6 le multi	.70	.70
777	A114	8 le multi	.80	.80
778	A114	10 le multi	1.00	1.00
779	A114	20 le multi	1.75	1.75
780	A114	30 le multi	2.25	2.25
		Nos. 773-780 (8)	8.20	8.20

Souvenir Sheets

781	A114	40 le multi	4.25	4.25
782	A114	40 le multi	4.25	4.25

US Peace Corps in Sierra Leone, 25th Anniv. A115

1986, Aug. 26   Litho.   Perf. 14
783	A115	10 le multi	1.40	1.40

Intl. Peace Year A116

1986, Sept. 1
784	A116	1 le Transportation	.40	.40
785	A116	2 le Education	.60	.60
786	A116	5 le Communications	1.25	1.25
787	A116	10 le Fishing	2.00	2.00
		Nos. 784-787 (4)	4.25	4.25

Nos. 745-749 Ovptd. or Surcharged "WINNERS / Argentina 3 / West Germany 2" in Gold

1986, Sept. 15   Perf. 14
788	A109	70c multi	.35	.35
789	A109	3 le multi	.80	.80
790	A109	4 le multi	1.10	1.10
791	A109	40 le on 5 le multi	9.50	9.50
		Nos. 788-791 (4)	11.75	11.75

Souvenir Sheet

792	A109	40 le on 12 le multi	4.75	4.75

Nos. 760, 762-763 Surcharged in Silver or Black

1986, Sept. 15
793	CD339	70c on 10c multi	.50	.25
794	CD339	45 le on 10 le multi	4.00	4.00

Souvenir Sheet

795	CD339	50 le on 12 le (B)	5.00	5.00

Nos. 769, 771-772 Surcharged in Silver

1986, Sept. 15
796	CD340	70c on 10c multi	.25	.25
797	CD340	45 le on 10 le multi	2.50	2.50

Souvenir Sheet

798	CD340	50 le on 12 le multi	5.00	5.00

STOCKHOLMIA '86 — A117

Disney characters in Mother Goose fairy tales — 70c, Jack and Jill. 1 le, Wee Willie Winkie. 2 le, Little Miss Muffet. 4 le, Old King Cole. 5 le, Mary Quite Contrary. 10 le, Little Bo Peep. 25 le, Polly Put the Kettle On. 35 le, Rub-a-Dub-Dub.
No. 807, Old Woman in the Shoe. No. 808, Simple Simon.

1986, Sept. 22   Perf. 11
799	A117	70c multi	.25	.25
800	A117	1 le multi	.25	.25
801	A117	2 le multi	.25	.25
802	A117	4 le multi	.55	.55
803	A117	5 le multi	.85	.85
804	A117	10 le multi	1.25	1.25
805	A117	25 le multi	3.25	3.25
806	A117	35 le multi	4.50	4.50
		Nos. 799-806 (8)	11.15	11.15

Souvenir Sheets

807	A117	40 le multi	5.25	5.25
808	A117	40 le multi	5.25	5.25

Nos. 639, 645-646 and 648 Surcharged

1986, Oct. 15
809	A94	30 le on 2c multi	2.75	2.75
810	A94	40 le on 30c multi	3.00	3.00
811	A94	45 le on 40c multi	3.50	3.50
812	A94	50 le on 70c multi	3.50	3.50
		Nos. 809-812 (4)	12.75	12.75

Nos. 755-759 Ovptd. or Srchd. with Halley's Comet Emblem in Black or Silver

1986, Oct. 15
813	A111	50c multi	.35	.35
814	A111	70c multi	.35	.35
815	A111	1.50 le on 15c multi	.35	.35
816	A111	45 le on 10 le multi	7.50	7.50
		Nos. 813-816 (4)	8.55	8.55

Souvenir Sheet

817	A112	50 le on 12 le multi (S)	6.00	6.00

Christmas A118

Paintings by Titian: 70c, Virgin and Child with St. Dorothy. $1.50 le, The Gypsy Madonna, vert. 20 le, The Holy Family. 30 le, Virgin and Child in an Evening Landscape, vert. 40 le, Madonna with the Pesaro Family.

1986, Nov. 17   Litho.   Perf. 14
818	A118	70c multi	.25	.25
819	A118	1.50 le multi	.25	.25
820	A118	20 le multi	3.00	3.00
821	A118	30 le multi	4.00	4.00
		Nos. 818-821 (4)	7.50	7.50

Souvenir Sheet

822	A118	40 le multi	12.00	12.00

Statue of Liberty, Cent. A119

Pictures of the statue by Peter B. Kaplan before and after renovation — 70c, Torch assembly. 1.50 le, Liberty holding torch. 2 le, Torch assembly, diff. 3 le, Man, torch. 4 le, Crown. 5 le, Lighting of the statue. 10 le, Lighting, diff. 25 le, Liberty Island. 30 le, Face.
Nos. 823, 825-826, 828-829, 831, vert.

1987, Jan. 2   Perf. 14
823	A119	70c multicolored	.25	.25
824	A119	1.50 le multicolored	.25	.25
825	A119	2 le multicolored	.25	.25
826	A119	3 le multicolored	.25	.25
827	A119	4 le multicolored	.25	.25
828	A119	5 le multicolored	.30	.30
829	A119	10 le multicolored	.60	.60
830	A119	25 le multicolored	1.50	1.50
831	A119	30 le multicolored	1.75	1.75
		Nos. 823-831 (9)	5.40	5.40

UNICEF, 40th Anniv. A120

1987, Mar. 18   Litho.   Perf. 14
832	A120	10 le multi	.70	.70

Nomoli Soapstone Sculpture — A121

Tall Ship in Harbor, Freetown — A122

An early view of Freetown

1987, Jan. 2   Perf. 15
833	A121	2 le shown	.25	.25
834	A121	5 le King's Yard Gate, 1817	.30	.30

Souvenir Sheet

835	A122	60 le shown	4.00	4.00

First settlement of liberated slaves returned to the African continent by the British, Freetown, bicent.

America's Cup — A123

Constellation, 1964 — A124

No. 836, USA, 1987. No. 837, New Zealand, 1987. No. 838, French Kiss, 1987. No. 839, Stars & Stripes, 1987. No. 840, Australia II, 1983. No. 841, Freedom, 1980. No. 842, Kookaburra III, 1987.

1987, June 15   Litho.   Perf. 14
836	A123	1 le multi	.25	.25
837	A123	1.50 le multi	.25	.25
838	A123	2.50 le multi	.25	.25
839	A123	10 le multi	1.10	1.10
840	A123	15 le multi	1.50	1.50
841	A123	25 le multi	2.40	2.40
842	A123	30 le multi	2.40	2.40
		Nos. 836-842 (7)	8.15	8.15

Souvenir Sheet

843	A124	50 le multi	3.75	3.75

Nos. 837, 839 and 842 horiz.
For overprint see No. 964.

CAPEX '87 — A125

Disney characters, Canadian sights — 2 le, Parliament. 5 le, Totem poles. 10 le, Perce Rock. 20 le, Canadian Rockies. 25 le, Old Quebec City. 45 le, Aurora Borealis. 50 le, Yukon P.O. 75 le, Niagara Falls.
No. 857, Exploring Newfoundland. No. 858, Calgary Exhibition and Stampede.

1987, June 15   Perf. 11
849	A125	2 le multi	.25	.25
850	A125	5 le multi	.45	.45
851	A125	10 le multi	.75	.75
852	A125	20 le multi	1.30	1.30
853	A125	25 le multi	1.75	1.75
854	A125	45 le multi	2.75	2.75
855	A125	50 le multi	3.00	3.00
856	A125	75 le multi	5.25	5.25
		Nos. 849-856 (8)	15.50	15.50

Souvenir Sheets

857	A125	100 le multi	6.00	6.00
858	A125	100 le multi	6.00	6.00

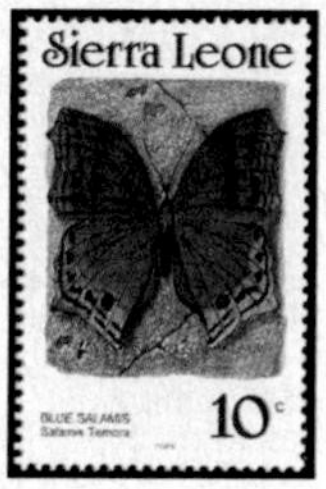

Butterflies — A126

10c, Blue salamis. 20c, Pale-tailed blue. 40c, Acraea swallowtail. 1 le, Broad blue-banded swallowtail. 2 le, Giant blue swallowtail. 3 le, Blood-red cymothoe. 5 le, Green-spotted swallowtail. 10 le, Small-striped swordtail. 20 le, Congo long-tailed blue. 25 le, Blue monarch. 30 le, Black and yellow swallowtail. 45 le, Western blue charaxes. 60 le, Violet-washed charaxes. 75 le, Orange admiral. 100 le, Blue-patched judy.

1987, Aug. 4 *Perf. 14*

859	A126	10c multi	2.10	.70
b.		Inscribed "1989"	1.75	1.00
860	A126	20c multi	2.10	.70
b.		Inscribed "1989"	1.75	1.00
861	A126	40c multi	2.10	.70
b.		Inscribed "1989"	1.75	.75
862	A126	1 le multi	2.10	.70
b.		Inscribed "1989"	2.50	1.10
863	A126	2 le multi	2.10	.70
b.		Inscribed "1989"	3.00	1.50
864	A126	3 le multi	2.50	1.10
b.		Inscribed "1989"	4.25	2.25
865	A126	5 le multi	2.50	1.10
866	A126	10 le multi	4.25	1.50
867	A126	20 le multi	7.75	3.50
868	A126	25 le multi	8.00	4.50
869	A126	30 le multi	8.00	4.75
870	A126	45 le multi	13.50	6.50
871	A126	60 le multi	3.25	*5.25*
872	A126	75 le multi	3.75	*4.75*
873	A126	100 le multi	5.75	*9.00*
		Nos. 859-873 (15)	69.75	45.45

See Nos. 1257-1260, 1332A-1332L.

1988-89 *Perf. 12x12½*

859a	A126	10c	.60	.25
860a	A126	20c	.90	.25
861a	A126	40c	.90	.25
862a	A126	1 le	.90	.25
863a	A126	2 le	1.10	.25
864a	A126	3 le	1.10	.25
865a	A126	5 le	1.10	.25
866a	A126	10 le	1.10	.40
867a	A126	20 le	1.40	.80
868a	A126	25 le	1.40	1.00
869a	A126	30 le	1.50	1.25
870a	A126	45 le	1.75	1.75
871a	A126	60 le	—	—
872a	A126	75 le	—	—
873a	A126	100 le	6.25	5.00
		Nos. 859a-873a (15)	20.00	11.95

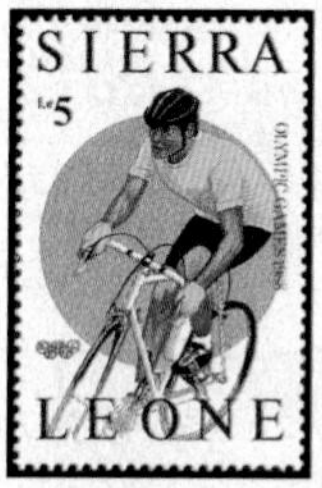

1988 Summer Olympics, Seoul — A127

1987, Aug. 10

874	A127	5 le Cycling	.25	.25
875	A127	10 le Equestrian	.60	.60
876	A127	45 le Running	2.60	2.60
877	A127	50 le Tennis	2.75	2.75
		Nos. 874-877 (4)	6.20	6.20

Souvenir Sheet

878	A127	100 le Gold medal, map	6.75	6.75

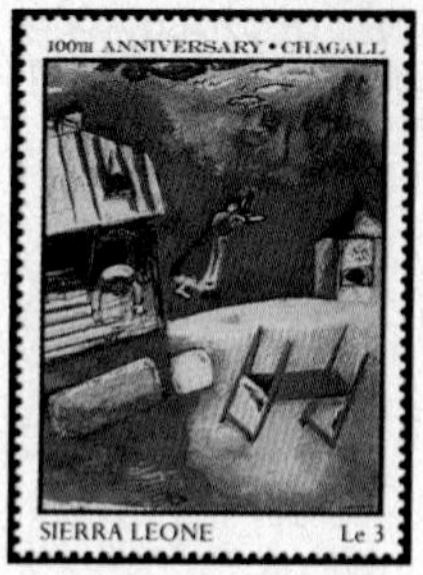

Works of Art by Marc Chagall, (1887-1985) A128

3 le, The Quarrel, 1911-1912. 5 le, Rebecca Giving Abraham's Servant a Drink. 10 le, The Village. 20 le, Ida at the Window, 1924. 25 le, Promenade, 1913. 45 le, Peasants. 50 le, Turquoise Plate. 75 le, Cemetery Gate, 1917.

No. 887, Wedding Feast, Stravinsky's Ballet, 1945. No. 888, The Falling Angel.

1987, Aug. 17 *Perf. 14*

879	A128	3 le multi	.25	.25
880	A128	5 le multi	.25	.25
881	A128	10 le multi	.50	.50
882	A128	20 le multi	.85	.85
883	A128	25 le multi	1.50	1.50
884	A128	45 le multi	3.25	3.25
885	A128	50 le multi	4.00	4.00
886	A128	75 le multi	5.50	5.50
		Nos. 879-886 (8)	16.10	16.10

Size: 111x95mm

Imperf

887	A128	100 le multi	8.00	8.00
888	A128	100 le multi	8.00	8.00

Nos. 879-886 printed in sheets of 10 (5x2). Stamp selvage inscribed with name of painting.

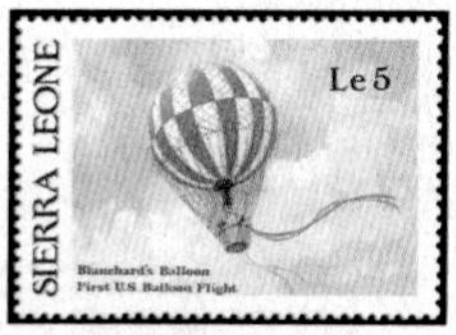

Transportation Innovations — A129

3 le, Apollo 8, 1968, vert. 5 le, Blanchard's Balloon, 1793. 10 le, Lockheed Vega, 1932. 15 le, Vicker's Vimy, 1919. 20 le, Tank Mk1, c. 1918. 25 le, Sikorsky VS-300, 1939. 30 le, Flyer 1, 1903. 35 le, Bleriot XI, 1909. 40 le, Paraplane, 1983, vert. 50 le, Daimler's motorcycle, 1885.

1987, Aug. 28 *Perf. 15*

889	A129	3 le multi	.25	.25
890	A129	5 le multi	.25	.25
891	A129	10 le multi	.50	.50
892	A129	15 le multi	.80	.80
893	A129	20 le multi	1.40	1.40
894	A129	25 le multi	1.60	1.60
895	A129	30 le multi	2.10	2.10
896	A129	35 le multi	2.25	2.25
897	A129	40 le multi	2.75	2.75
898	A129	50 le multi	3.25	3.25
		Nos. 889-898 (10)	15.15	15.15

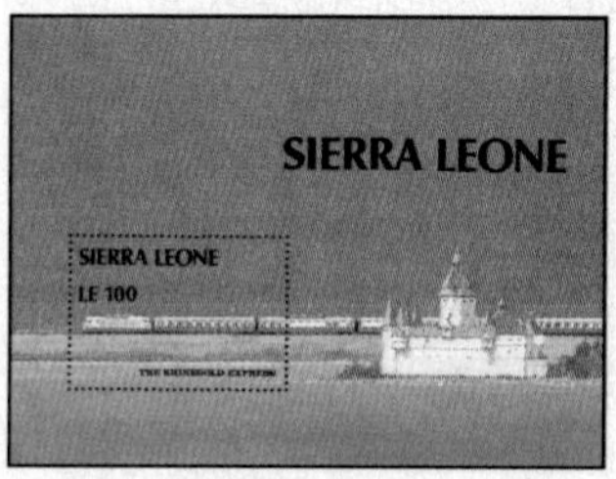

Rhinegold Express, Ireland (1st Electric Railroad, 1884) — A129a

1987, Aug. 28 **Litho.** *Perf. 15*

898A	A129a	100 le multi	6.75	6.75

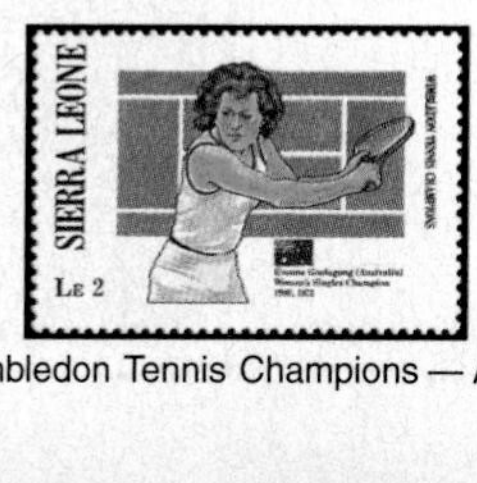

Wimbledon Tennis Champions — A130

2 le, Evonne Goolagong, Australia. 5 le, Martina Navratilova, US-Czechoslovakia. 10 le, Jimmy Connors, US. 15 le, Bjorn Borg, Sweden. 30 le, Boris Becker, West Germany. 40 le, John McEnroe, US. 50 le, Chris Evert Lloyd, US. 75 le, Virgina Wade, Great Britain.

#907, Steffi Graf, German Open 1986. #908, Boris Becker.

1987, Sept. 4 *Perf. 14*

899	A130	2 le multicolored	.30	.30
900	A130	5 le multicolored	.75	.75
901	A130	10 le multicolored	1.10	1.10
902	A130	15 le multicolored	1.50	1.50
903	A130	30 le multicolored	2.75	2.75
904	A130	40 le multicolored	3.00	3.00
905	A130	50 le multicolored	3.25	3.25
906	A130	75 le multicolored	4.50	4.50
		Nos. 899-906 (8)	17.15	17.15

Souvenir Sheets

907	A130	100 le multicolored	8.50	8.50
908	A130	100 le multicolored	8.50	8.50

For overprints see Nos. 965, 1023-1024.

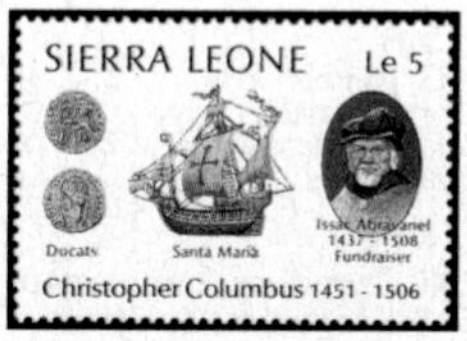

Discovery of America, 500th Anniv. (in 1992) A131

5 le, Ducats, Santa Maria, Issac Abravanel (1437-1508), fund raiser. 10 le, Astrolabe, Pinta, Abraham Zacuto (1452-1515), astronomer. 45 le, Maravedis (coins), Nina, Luis de Santangel (1448-1498), fund raiser. 50 le, Tobacco leaves, plant, Luis de Torres (1453-1522), translator.

1987, Sept. 11

909	A131	5 le multicolored	1.00	1.00
910	A131	10 le multicolored	1.25	1.25
911	A131	45 le multicolored	3.75	3.75
912	A131	50 le multicolored	4.50	4.50
		Nos. 909-912 (4)	10.50	10.50

Souvenir Sheet

913	A131	100 le Columbus, map	6.00	6.00

For overprint see No. 966.

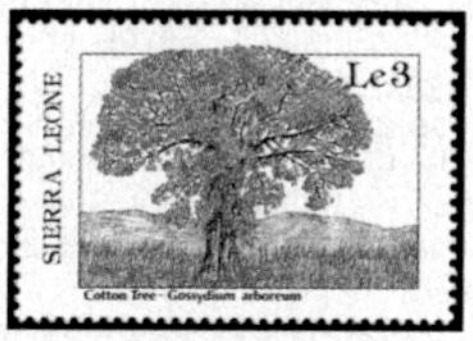

Fauna and Flora A132

3 le, Cotton tree. 5 le, Dwarf crocodile. 10 le, Kudu. 20 le, Yellowbells. 25 le, Hippopotamus. 45 le, Comet orchid. 50 le, Baobab tree. 75 le, Elephant.

No. 922, Banana, papaya, coconut, pineapple. No. 923, Leopard.

1987, Sept. 15

914	A132	3 le multi	.25	.25
915	A132	5 le multi	.25	.25
916	A132	10 le multi	.65	.65
917	A132	20 le multi	1.60	1.60
918	A132	25 le multi	2.10	2.10
919	A132	45 le multi	3.50	3.50
920	A132	50 le multi	4.00	4.00
921	A132	75 le multi	6.25	6.25
		Nos. 914-921 (8)	18.60	18.60

Souvenir Sheets

922	A132	100 le multi	5.00	5.00
923	A132	100 le multi	5.00	5.00

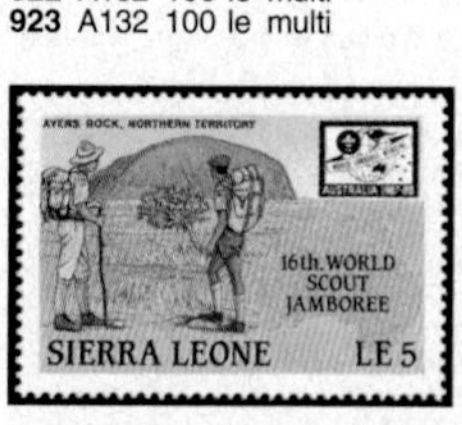

16th World Scout Jamboree, Australia, 1987-88 A133

Scouts, jamboree emblem, map of Australia and: 5 le, Ayers Rock. 15 le, Sailing. 40 le, Sydney skyline. 50 le, Sydney Harbour Bridge, Opera House. 100 le, Flags of Sierra Leone, Australia and Scouts.

1987, Oct. 5 **Litho.** *Perf. 15*

924	A133	5 le multicolored	.45	.45
925	A133	15 le multicolored	1.10	1.10
926	A133	40 le multicolored	2.25	2.25
927	A133	50 le multicolored	3.50	3.50
		Nos. 924-927 (4)	7.30	7.30

Souvenir Sheet

928	A133	100 le multicolored	5.25	5.25

1.50 le stamps like the 50 le were printed but not issued.

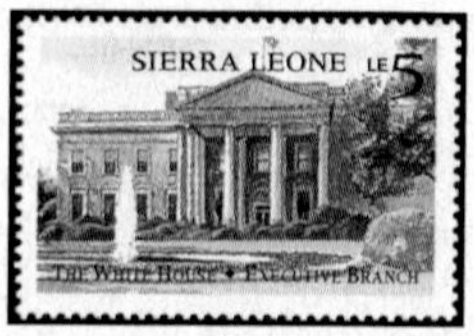

US Constitution Bicentennial — A134

Designs: 5 le, White House. 10 le, George Washington. 30 le, Patrick Henry. 65 le, New Hampshire state flag. 100 le, John Jay.

1987, Nov. 9 *Perf. 14*

929	A134	5 le multi	.25	.25
930	A134	10 le multi, vert.	.85	.85
931	A134	30 le multi, vert.	1.25	1.25
932	A134	65 le multi	2.75	2.75
		Nos. 929-932 (4)	5.10	5.10

Souvenir Sheet

933	A134	100 le multi, vert.	5.00	5.00

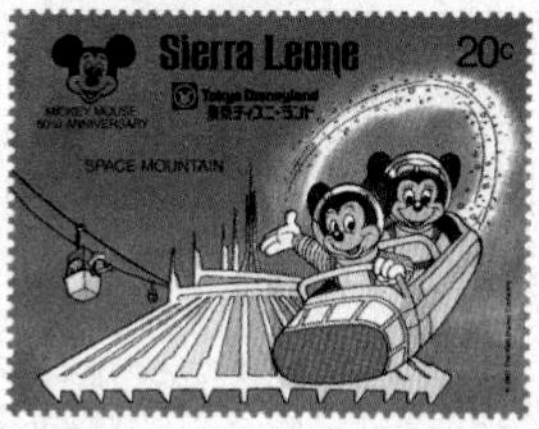

Tokyo Disneyland, 5th Anniv. — A135

Disney animated characters and attractions at Tokyo Disneyland — 20c, Space Mountain. 40c, Country Bear Jamboree. 80c, Mickey Mouse Review. 1 le, Mark Twain's River Boat. 2 le, Western River Railroad. 3 le, Pirates of the Caribbean. 10 le, Big Thunder Mountain train. 20 le, It's a Small World. 30 le, Park entrance.

65 le, Cinderella's Castle.

1987, Dec. 9 **Litho.** *Perf. 14*

934	A135	20c multicolored	.25	.25
935	A135	40c multicolored	.25	.25
936	A135	80c multicolored	.25	.25
937	A135	1 le multicolored	.25	.25
938	A135	2 le multicolored	.25	.25
939	A135	3 le multicolored	.25	.25
940	A135	10 le multicolored	.75	.75
941	A135	20 le multicolored	1.60	1.60
942	A135	30 le multicolored	2.25	2.25
		Nos. 934-942 (9)	6.10	6.10

Souvenir Sheet

943	A135	65 le multicolored	9.50	9.50

Mickey Mouse, 60th anniv.

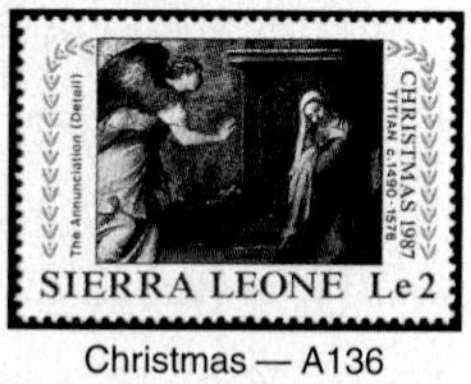

Christmas — A136

Paintings by Titian: 2 le, The Annunciation. 10 le, Madonna and Child with Saints. 20 le, Madonna and Child with Saints Ulfus and Brigid. 35 le, Madonna of the Cherries. 65 le, Pesaro Altarpiece, vert.

1987, Dec. 21

944	A136	2 le multicolored	.30	.30
945	A136	10 le multicolored	1.00	1.00
946	A136	20 le multicolored	1.75	1.75
947	A136	35 le multicolored	2.75	2.75
		Nos. 944-947 (4)	5.80	5.80

Souvenir Sheet

948	A136	65 le multicolored	6.25	6.25

40th Wedding
Anniv. of Queen
Elizabeth II and
Prince
Philip — A137

2 le, Ceremony, 1947. 3 le, Elizabeth,
Charles, 1948. 10 le, Elizabeth, Anne,
Charles, c. 1950. 50 le, Elizabeth, c. 1970.
65 le, Wedding portrait.

1988, Feb. 15   Litho.   Perf. 14
949	A137	2 le multicolored	.30	.30
950	A137	3 le multicolored	.30	.30
951	A137	10 le multicolored	.80	.80
952	A137	50 le multicolored	4.00	4.00
		Nos. 949-952 (4)	5.40	5.40

Souvenir Sheet
953	A137	65 le multicolored	5.00	5.00

Mushrooms
A138

3 le, Russula cyanoxantha. 10 le,
Lycoperdon perlatum. 20 le, Lactarius deliciosus. 30 le, Boletus edulis.
65 le, Amanita muscaria.

1988, Feb. 29
954	A138	3 le multicolored	.25	.25
955	A138	10 le multicolored	1.60	1.60
956	A138	20 le multicolored	3.25	3.25
957	A138	30 le multicolored	5.00	5.00
		Nos. 954-957 (4)	10.10	10.10

Miniature Sheet
958	A138	65 le multicolored	9.25	9.25

Fish
A139

1988, Apr. 13   Perf. 15
959	A139	3 le Golden pheasant	.30	.30
960	A139	10 le Banded toothcarp	.55	.55
961	A139	20 le Jewel fish	.85	.85
962	A139	35 le Butterfly fish	1.30	1.30
		Nos. 959-962 (4)	3.00	3.00

Miniature Sheet
963	A139	65 le African longfin	4.00	4.00

**Nos. 841, 903 and 911 Ovptd. for
Philatelic Exhibitions in Black**

1988, Apr. 19   Litho.   Perf. 14
964	A123(a)	25 le multicolored	2.75	2.75
965	A130(b)	30 le multicolored	3.25	3.25
966	A131(c)	45 le multicolored	4.50	4.50
		Nos. 964-966 (3)	10.50	10.50

Intl. Fund for Agricultural Development
(IFAD), 10th Anniv. — A140

1988, May 3   Litho.   Perf. 14
967	A140	3 le Cocoa, coffee	.25	.25
968	A140	15 le Tropical fruit	.85	.85
969	A140	25 le Rice harvest	1.40	1.40
		Nos. 967-969 (3)	2.50	2.50

1988 Summer
Olympics,
Seoul — A141

1988, June 15
970	A141	3 le Basketball	.25	.25
971	A141	10 le Judo	.50	.50
972	A141	15 le Gymnastics	.60	.60
973	A141	40 le Synchronized swimming	1.75	1.75
		Nos. 970-973 (4)	3.10	3.10

Souvenir Sheet
974	A141	65 le Torch-bearer	2.75	2.75

Birds — A142

3 le, Swallow-tailed bee-eater. 5 le, Tooth-
billed barbet. 8 le, African golden oriole. 10 le,
Red bishop. 12 le, Red-billed shrike. 20 le,
European bee-eater. 35 le, Barbary shrike. 40
le, Black-headed oriole.
No. 983, Saddlebill stork. No. 984, Purple
heron.

1988, June 25
975	A142	3 le multicolored	1.10	1.10
976	A142	5 le multicolored	1.35	1.35
977	A142	8 le multicolored	1.75	1.75
978	A142	10 le multicolored	1.75	1.75
979	A142	12 le multicolored	1.75	1.75
980	A142	20 le multicolored	2.00	2.00
981	A142	35 le multicolored	2.75	2.75
982	A142	40 le multicolored	3.25	3.25
		Nos. 975-982 (8)	15.70	15.70

Souvenir Sheets
983	A142	65 le multicolored	3.50	3.50
984	A142	65 le multicolored	3.50	3.50

For surcharges see Nos. 2892-2896.

Merchant
Marine
A143

1988, July 1
985	A143	3 le Aureol	.85	.85
986	A143	10 le Dunkwa	2.25	2.25
987	A143	15 le Melampus	3.00	3.00
988	A143	30 le Dumbaia	3.75	3.75
		Nos. 985-988 (4)	9.85	9.85

Souvenir Sheet
989	A143	65 le Loading containers	4.25	4.25

Paintings by
Titian
A144

1 le, The Concert, 1512. 2 le, Philip II of
Spain, c. 1550-51. 3 le, St. Sebastian, c. 1520-
22. 5 le, Martyrdom of St. Peter Martyr, c.
1528-30. 15 le, St. Jerome, 1560. 20 le, St.
Mark Enthroned with Saints Cosmas and
Damian, Roch & Sebastian, c. 1508-09. 25 le,
Portrait of a Young Man, 1506. 30 le, St.
Jerome in Penitence, 1555. #998, Self-por-
trait, 1567. #999, Orpheus and Eurydice,
1508.

1988, Aug. 22   Litho.   Perf. 13½x14
990	A144	1 le multicolored	.25	.25
991	A144	2 le multicolored	.25	.25
992	A144	3 le multicolored	.25	.25
993	A144	5 le multicolored	.55	.55
994	A144	15 le multicolored	1.40	1.40
995	A144	20 le multicolored	1.60	1.60
996	A144	25 le multicolored	1.90	1.90
997	A144	30 le multicolored	2.25	2.25
		Nos. 990-997 (8)	8.45	8.45

Souvenir Sheets
998	A144	25 le multicolored	3.25	3.25
999	A144	50 le multicolored	3.25	3.25

John F.
Kennedy
A145

Kennedy half-dollar and space achievements: 3 le, Recovery of a Mercury capsule by
the US Navy. 5 le, Splashdown and recovery
of Liberty Bell 7, July 21, 1961, piloted by Virgil
"Gus" Grissom, vert. 15 le, Launch of Freedom
7, piloted by Alan B. Shepard, May 5, 1961,
vert. 40 le, Friendship 7 in orbit, piloted by
John Glenn, Feb. 20, 1962. 65 le, Kennedy,
speech excerpt.

1988, Sept. 26   Litho.   Perf. 14
1000	A145	3 le multicolored	.30	.30
1001	A145	5 le multicolored	.80	.80
1002	A145	15 le multicolored	2.60	2.60
1003	A145	40 le multicolored	3.25	3.25
		Nos. 1000-1003 (4)	6.95	6.95

Souvenir Sheet
1004	A145	65 le multicolored	4.25	4.25

Intl. Red Cross
and Red Crescent
Organizations,
125th
Annivs. — A146

3 le, Africa food relief. 10 le, Battle of Solferino. 20 le, WWII Pacific. 40 le, WWI Europe.
65 le, Alfred Nobel, Dunant, horiz.

1988, Nov. 1
1005	A146	3 le multicolored	.90	.90
1006	A146	10 le multicolored	3.00	3.00
1007	A146	20 le multicolored	4.00	4.00
1008	A146	40 le multicolored	5.00	5.00
		Nos. 1005-1008 (4)	12.90	12.90

**Souvenir Sheet
Size: 41x28mm**
1009	A146	65 le multicolored	6.00	6.00

Miniature Sheet

Christmas, Mickey Mouse 60th
Anniv. — A147

Walt Disney characters dancing: No. 1010a,
Huey, Dewey and Louie. No. 1010b,
Clarabelle Cow. No. 1010c, Goofy. No. 1010d,
Scrooge McDuck and Grandma Duck. No.
1010e, Donald Duck. No. 1010f, Daisy Duck.
No. 1010g, Minnie Mouse. No. 1010h, Mickey
Mouse. No. 1011, Dance, c. 1920. No. 1012,
Dance, c. 1950.

1988, Dec. 1   Perf. 13½x14
1010	A147	Sheet of 8	7.00	7.00
a.-h.		10 le any single	.65	.65

Souvenir Sheets
1011	A147	70 le multicolored	4.50	4.50
1012	A147	70 le multicolored	4.50	4.50

Christmas
A148

Paintings by Rubens (details): 3 le, Adora-
tion of the Magi (Virgin and Child). 3.60 le,
Adoration of the Shepherds (shepherds and
child). 5 le, Adoration of the Magi (Magi). 10 le,
Adoration of the Shepherds (Virgin and Child).
20 le, Virgin and Child Surrounded by Flowers.
40 le, St. Gregory the Great and Other Saints
(Virgin and Child). 60 le, Adoration of the
Magi, (Virgin, Child and Magi), diff. 80 le,
Madonna and Child with Saints. No. 1021, St.
Gregory the Great and Other Saints. No.
1022, Virgin and Child Enthroned with Saints.

1988, Dec. 15   Litho.   Perf. 13½x14
1013	A148	3 le multicolored	.25	.25
1014	A148	3.60 le multicolored	.25	.25
1015	A148	5 le multicolored	.45	.45
1016	A148	10 le multicolored	.65	.65
1017	A148	20 le multicolored	1.25	1.25
1018	A148	40 le multicolored	2.50	2.50
1019	A148	60 le multicolored	3.50	3.50
1020	A148	80 le multicolored	4.75	4.75
		Nos. 1013-1020 (8)	13.60	13.60

Souvenir Sheets
1021	A148	100 le multicolored	6.00	6.00
1022	A148	100 le multicolored	6.00	6.00

**No. 907 Ovptd. "GRAND SLAM
WINNER" in Gold
Set of 4**

**1989, Jan. 16   Perf. 14
Souvenir Sheets**
1023A-1023D	A130	100 le	20.00	20.00

Gold marginal overprints: No. 1023A, "AUS-
TRALIAN OPEN / JANUARY 11-24, 1988 /
GRAF v EVERET / 6-1 / 7-6." 1023B,
"FRENCH OPEN / MAY 23-JUNE 5, 1988 /
GRAF v ZVEREVA / 6-0 / 6-0." 1023C, "WIM-
BLEDON / JUNE 20-JULY 4, 1988 / GRAF v
NAVRATILOVA / 5-7 / 6-2 / 6-1." 1023D, "U.S.
OPEN / AUGUST 29-SEPTEMBER 11, 1988 /
GRAF v SABATINI / 6-3 / 3-6 / 6-1."

**No. 907 Ovptd. "GOLD MEDALIST"
in Gold**

1989, Jan. 16   Litho.   Perf. 14
1024	A130	100 le multi	6.00	6.00

Marginal overprint: "SEOUL OLYMPICS
1988 / GRAF v SABATINI / 6-3 / 6-3."

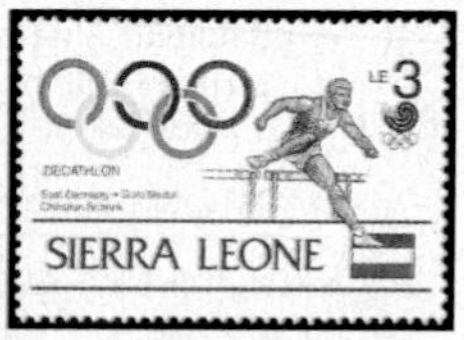

Medalists of the 1988 Summer Olympics, Seoul A149

Designs: 3 le, Christian Schenk, German Democratic Republic, decathlon. 6 le, Hitoshi Saito, Japan, heavyweight judo. 10 le, Jutta Niehaus, Federal Republic of Germany, women's road race. 15 le, Tomas Lange, German Democratic Republic, single sculls. 20 le, Matthew Biondi, US, 50m and 100m freestyle. 30 le, Carl Lewis, US, 100m sprint. 40 le, Nicole Uphoff, Federal Republic of Germany, individual dressage. 50 le, Andras Sike, Hungary, 126-pound Greco-Roman wrestling. No. 1033, Gold medal, five-ring emblem. No. 1034, Torch, five-ring emblem.

1989, Apr. 28 Litho. *Perf. 14*

1025	A149	3 le multicolored	.95	.95
1026	A149	6 le multicolored	1.25	1.25
1027	A149	10 le multicolored	1.90	1.90
1028	A149	15 le multicolored	1.90	1.90
1029	A149	20 le multicolored	1.90	1.90
1030	A149	30 le multicolored	2.40	2.40
1031	A149	40 le multicolored	3.00	3.00
1032	A149	50 le multicolored	3.00	3.00
		Nos. 1025-1032 (8)	16.30	16.30

Souvenir Sheets

1033	A149	100 le multicolored	6.50	6.50
1034	A149	100 le multicolored	6.50	6.50

Name of athlete not inscribed on No. 1031.

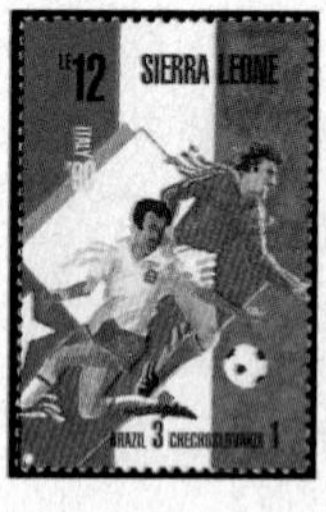

1990 World Cup Soccer Championships, Italy — A150

3 le, Brazil vs. Sweden. 6 le, Germany vs. Hungary. 8 le, England vs. Germany. 10 le, Argentina vs. The Netherlands. 12 le, Brazil vs. Czechoslovakia. 20 le, Germany vs. The Netherlands. 30 le, Italy vs. Germany. 40 le, Brazil vs. Italy.

No. 1043, Uruguay vs. Brazil. No. 1044, Argentina vs. Germany.

1989, May 8

1035	A150	3 le multi	.25	.25
1036	A150	6 le multi	.55	.55
1037	A150	8 le multi	.70	.70
1038	A150	10 le multi	.90	.90
1039	A150	12 le multi	1.10	1.10
1040	A150	20 le multi	1.75	1.75
1041	A150	30 le multi	2.75	2.75
1042	A150	40 le multi	3.50	3.50
		Nos. 1035-1042 (8)	11.50	11.50

Souvenir Sheets

1043	A150	100 le multi	5.00	5.00
1044	A150	100 le multi	5.00	5.00

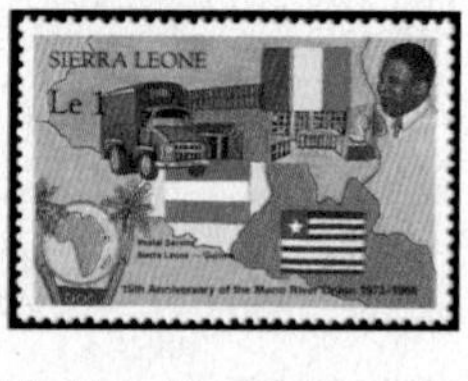

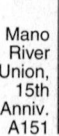

Mano River Union, 15th Anniv. A151

Designs: 1 le, Sierra Leone-Guinea postal service. 3 le, Presidents Momoh, Conte of Guinea and Doe of Liberia. 10 le, Freetown-Monrovia Highway under construction. 15 le, Presidents signing the Communique at a 1988 summit.

1989, May 19 *Perf. 14*

1045	A151	1 le multicolored	.80	.80
1046	A151	3 le multicolored	1.40	1.40
1047	A151	10 le multicolored	2.25	2.25
		Nos. 1045-1047 (3)	4.45	4.45

Souvenir Sheet

1048	A151	15 le multicolored	3.50	3.50

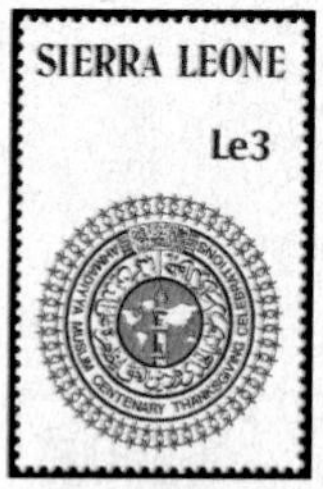

Ahmadiyya Muslim Centenary Thanksgiving Celebrations A152

1989, June 8

1049	A152	3 le black & brt blue	.60	.60

Miniature Sheets

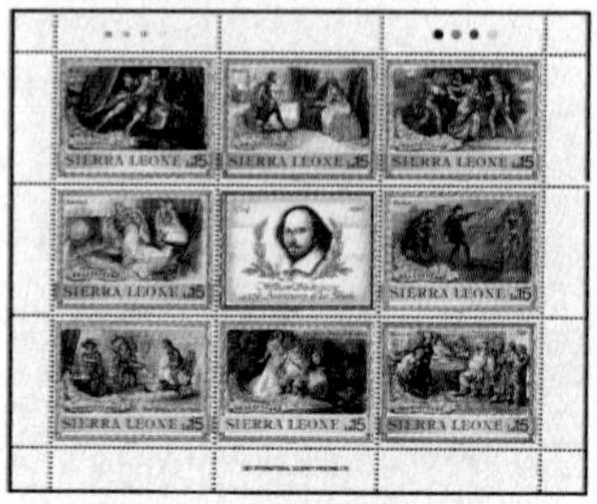

Shakespeare's 425th Birth Anniv. — A153

Scenes from the playwright's works.

No. 1050: a, Richard III. b, Othello (Desdemona and two men). c, The Two Gentlemen of Verona. d, Macbeth (chamber). e, Hamlet. f, Taming of the Shrew (scene with dog). g, The Merry Wives of Windsor. h, Henry IV (assembly room).

No. 1051: a, Macbeth (horsemen). b, Romeo and Juliet. c, Merchant of Venice. d, As You Like It. e, Taming of the Shrew (ruined meal). f, King Lear. g, Othello (death scene). h, Henry IV (street scene).

1989, May 30 *Perf. 13*

1050		Sheet of 8 + label	9.00	9.00
a.-h.	A153	15 le any single	1.00	1.00
1051		Sheet of 8 + label	9.00	9.00
a.-h.	A153	15 le any single	1.00	1.00

Souvenir Sheets

1052	A153	100 le Portrait	7.25	7.25
1053	A153	100 le Portrait, coat of arms	7.25	7.25

Nos. 1050-1051 contain center label picturing Shakespeare's portrait (No. 1050) or his birthplace in Stratford (No. 1051).

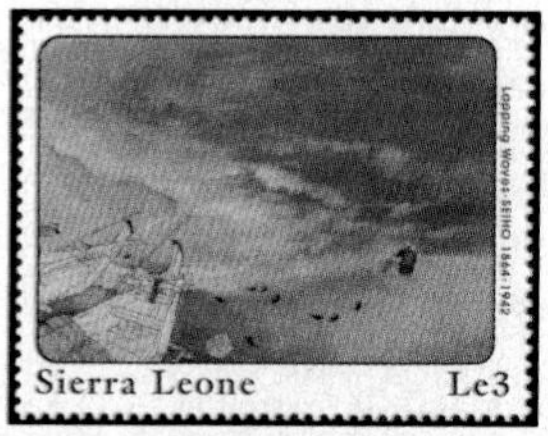

Paintings by Takeuchi Seiho (1864-1942) — A154

Designs: 3 le, Lapping Waves. 6 le, Hazy Moon, vert. 8 le, Passing Spring, vert. 10 le, Mackerels. 12 le, Calico Cat. 30 le, The First Time To Be a Model, vert. 40 le, Kingly Lion. 75 le, After a Shower, vert. No. 1062, Domesticated Monkeys and Rabbits. No. 1063, Dozing in the Midst of All the Chirping, vert.

Perf. 14x13½, 13½x14

1989, July 3 Litho.

1054	A154	3 le multicolored	.25	.25
1055	A154	6 le multicolored	.30	.30
1056	A154	8 le multicolored	.45	.45
1057	A154	10 le multicolored	.55	.55
1058	A154	12 le multicolored	.60	.60
1059	A154	30 le multicolored	1.60	1.60
1060	A154	40 le multicolored	2.25	2.25
1061	A154	75 le multicolored	4.25	4.25
		Nos. 1054-1061 (8)	10.25	10.25

Souvenir Sheets

1062	A154	150 le multicolored	7.00	7.00
1063	A154	150 le multicolored	7.00	7.00

Hirohito (1901-89) and enthronement of Akihito as emperor of Japan.

See Nos. 1098-1129.

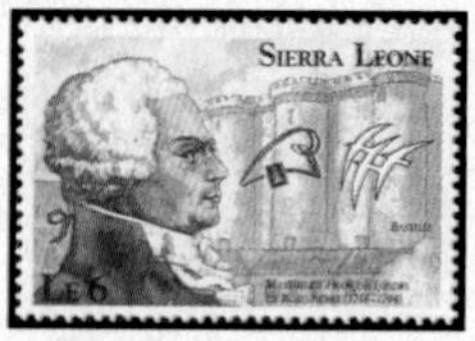

PHILEXFRANCE '89, French Revolution Bicent. — A155

Famous people, sites, exhibition and anniv. emblems: 6 le, Robespierre (1758-94), the Bastille. 20 le, Georges Jacques Danton (1759-94), the Louvre. 45 le, Marie Antoinette (1755-93), Notre Dame Cathedral interior. 80 le, Louis XVI (1754-93), Palace of Versailles. 150 le, Revolutionaries in Paris, vert.

1989, July 14 Litho. *Perf. 14*

1064	A155	6 le multicolored	.65	.65
1065	A155	20 le multicolored	1.25	1.25
1066	A155	45 le multicolored	2.25	2.25
1067	A155	80 le multicolored	3.75	3.75
		Nos. 1064-1067 (4)	7.90	7.90

Souvenir Sheet

1068	A155	150 le multicolored	6.00	6.00

Miniature Sheets

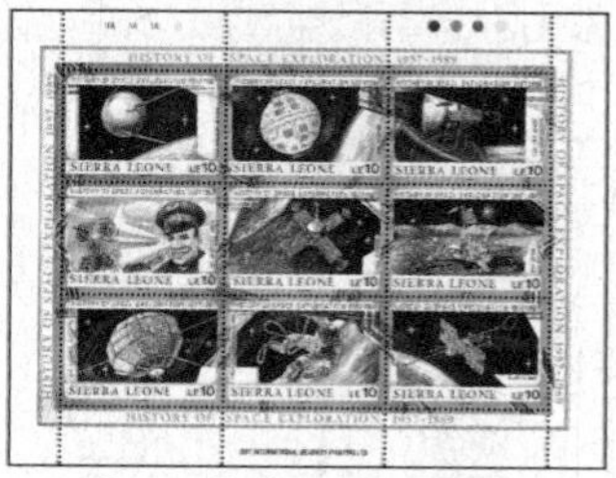

Space Exploration — A156

Satellites, probes and spacecraft.

No. 1069: a, Sputnik, 1957. b, Telstar, 1962. c, Rendezvous of Gemini 6 and 7, 1965. d, Yuri Gagarin, 1st man in space, 1961. e, Mariner, 1964. f, Surveyor on Mars, 1966. g, US-Canadian Alouette satellite, 1962. h, Edward White, 1st American to walk in space, 1965. i, OGO-4 satellite, 1967.

No. 1070: a, Buzz Aldrin on the Moon, Apollo 11 mission, 1969. b, Apollo 15 mission lunar rover. c, Apollo 15 crew member. d, Conducting experiments on the lunar surface. e, Splitrock, Valley of Taurus-Littrow. f, Saluting the flag, Apollo 15 lunar module. g, Solar wind experiment. h, Lunar rover, diff. i, Apollo command module.

No. 1071: a, Module separation. b, Docking maneuvers. c, Lunar module in space. d, Second stage separation. e, Module transposition. f, Lunar module controlled descent, Moon's surface. g, Apollo 11 liftoff, 1969. h, Lunar module separates from command module. i, Neil Armstrong's first step on the Moon.

No. 1072: a, Mariner-Mars, 1971. b, Mariner 10, 1973. c, Viking, 1975. d, Skylab, 1974. e, Soyuz-Salyut, 1974. f, Viking robot craft, 1974. g, Pioneer 2, 1973. h, Apollo-Soyuz, 1975. i, Pioneer-Venus, 1978.

No. 1073: a, Apollo 17 lunar module, 1972. b, Command module jettison of service module before reentry. c, Soyuz 11, 1971. d, Lunar module liftoff. e, U.S. Navy recovery operation. f, Mars 2, 1971. g, Command module in docking position. h, Luna 17, 1970. i, Mars 3, 1971.

No. 1074: a, Voyager 1 and 2, 1977. b, Columbia space shuttle, 1981. c, Mir space station, 1986. d, IUE-Ultraviolet Explorer, US, U.K. and the European Space Agency, 1978. e, Astronaut operating out of shuttle cargo bay, 1983. f, Magellan, 1989. g, Soyuz-Salyut, 1978. h, STS-10, 1984. i, Shuttle, space telescope, 1989.

No. 1075, Spacelab. No. 1076, Future space station. No. 1077, Voyager.

1989, July 20 Litho. *Perf. 14*

1069		Sheet of 9	5.00	5.00
a.-i.	A156	10 le any single	.55	.55
1070		Sheet of 9	5.00	5.00
a.-i.	A156	10 le any single	.55	.55
1071		Sheet of 9	5.00	5.00
a.-i.	A156	10 le any single	.55	.55
1072		Sheet of 9	8.00	8.00
a.-i.	A156	15 le any single	.85	.85
1073		Sheet of 9	8.00	8.00
a.-i.	A156	15 le any single	.85	.85
1074		Sheet of 9	8.00	8.00
a.-i.	A156	15 le any single	.85	.85

Souvenir Sheets

1075	A156	100 le multicolored	7.00	7.00
1076	A156	100 le multicolored	7.00	7.00
1077	A156	100 le multicolored	7.00	7.00

Nos. 1069f is incorrectly inscribed "Mars" instead of "Moon."

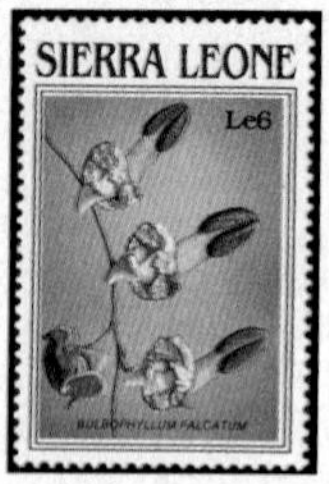

Orchids — A157

3 le, Bulbophyllum barbigerum. 6 le, Bulbophyllum falcatum. 12 le, Habenaria macrara. 20 le, Eurychone rothchildiana. 50 le, Calyptrochilum christyanum. 60 le, Bulbophyllum distans. 70 le, Eulophia guineensis. 80 le, Diapha-nanthe pellu-cida.

No. 1086, Cyrtorchis arcuata. No. 1087, Butterflies, Eulophia cucullata.

1989, Sept. 8 Litho. *Perf. 14*

1078	A157	3 le multi	.85	.85
1079	A157	6 le multi	1.25	1.25
1080	A157	12 le multi	1.75	1.75
1081	A157	20 le multi	2.25	2.25
1082	A157	50 le multi	3.25	3.25
1083	A157	60 le multi	3.75	3.75
1084	A157	70 le multi	3.75	3.75
1085	A157	80 le multi	4.50	4.50
		Nos. 1078-1085 (8)	21.35	21.35

Souvenir Sheets

1086	A157	100 le multi	12.00	12.00
1087	A157	100 le multi	12.00	12.00

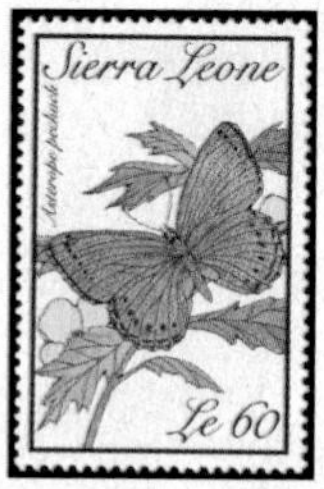

Butterflies — A158

6 le, Salamis temora. 12 le, Pseudacraea lucretia. 18 le, Charaxes boueti. 30 le, Graphium antheus. 40 le, Colotis protomedia. 60 le, Asterope pechueli. 72 le, Coenura aurantiaca. 80 le, Precis octavia.

No. 1096, Charaxes cithaeron. No. 1097, Euphaedra themis.

1989, Sept. 11

1088	A158	6 le multi	1.25	1.25
1089	A158	12 le multi	1.60	1.60
1090	A158	18 le multi	2.10	2.10
1091	A158	30 le multi	3.50	3.50
1092	A158	40 le multi	4.50	4.50
1093	A158	60 le multi	5.00	5.00
1094	A158	72 le multi	5.75	5.75
1095	A158	80 le multi	5.75	5.75
		Nos. 1088-1095 (8)	29.45	29.45

Souvenir Sheets

1096	A158	100 le multi	12.00	12.00
1097	A158	100 le multi	12.00	12.00

Nos. 1088-1090, 1095 and 1097 horiz.

Art Type of 1989

Paintings by Hiroshige in the series Fifty-three Stations on the Tokaido: No. 1098, Coolies Warming Themselves at Hamamatsu. No. 1099, Imakiri Ford at Maisaka. No. 1100, Pacific Ocean Seen from Shirasuka. No. 1101, Futakawa Street Singers. No. 1102, Repairing Yoshida Castle. No. 1103, The Inn at Akasaka. No. 1104, The Bridge to Okazaki. No. 1105, Samurai's Wife Entering Narumi. No. 1106, Harbour at Kuwana. No. 1107, Autumn in Ishiyakushi. No. 1108, Snowfall at Kameyama. No. 1109, The Frontier Station of Seki. No. 1110, Teahouse at Sakanoshita. No. 1111, Kansai Houses at Minakushi. No. 1112, Kusatsu Station. No. 1113, Ferry to Kawasaki. No. 1114, The Hilly Town of Hodogaya. No. 1115, Lute Players at Fujisawa. No. 1116, Mild Rainstorm at Oiso. No. 1117, Lake Ashi and Mountains of Hakone. No. 1118, Twilight at Numazu. No. 1119, Mount Fuji From Hara. No. 1120, Samurai's Children Riding Through Yoshiwara. No. 1121, Mountain Pass at Yui. No. 1122, Harbour at Ejiri. No. 1123, Stopping at Fujieda. No. 1124, Misty Kanaya on the Oi River. No. 1125, The Bridge to Kakegawa. No. 1126, Teahouse at Fukuroi. No. 1127, The Ford at Mistuke. No. 1128, Sanjo Bridge in Kyoto. No. 1129, Nibonbashi Bridge in Edo.

1989, Nov. 13 Litho. Perf. 14x13½
1098-1127 A154 25 le Set of
30 37.50 37.50

Souvenir sheets
1128-1129 A154 120 le each 14.00 14.00

Hirohito (1901-1989) and enthronement of Akihito as emperor of Japan.

Souvenir Sheet

Jefferson Memorial, Washington, DC — A159

1989, Nov. 17 Litho. Perf. 14
1136 A159 100 le multicolored 2.00 2.00

World Stamp Expo '89.

Endangered Species — A160

6 le, Humpback whale. 9 le, Formosan sika deer. 16 le, Spanish lynx. 20 le, Goitered gazelle. 30 le, Japanese sea lion. 50 le, Long-eared owl. 70 le, Chinese copper pheasant. 100 le, Siberian tiger.
No. 1145, Mauritius kestrel falcon. No. 1146, Crested ibis.

1989, Nov. 29 Perf. 14
1137 A160 6 le multi .25 .25
1138 A160 9 le multi .30 .30
1139 A160 16 le multi .65 .65
1140 A160 20 le multi .95 .95
1141 A160 30 le multi 1.40 1.40
1142 A160 50 le multi 2.25 2.25
1143 A160 70 le multi 3.25 3.25
1144 A160 100 le multi 4.50 4.50
  Nos. 1137-1144 (8) 13.55 13.55

Souvenir Sheets
1145 A160 150 le multi 8.50 8.50
1146 A160 150 le multi 8.50 8.50

World Stamp Expo '89.

Christmas — A161

Disney characters and classic automobiles: 3 le, 1934 Phantom II Rolls-Royce Roadstar. 6 le, 1935 Mercedes-Benz 500K. 10 le, 1938 Jaguar SS-100. 12 le, 1941 Jeep. 20 le, 1937 Buick Roadmaster Sedan Model 91. 30 le, 1948 Tucker. 40 le, 1933 Alfa Romeo. 50 le, 1937 Cord. No. 1155, 1938 Fiat Topolino. No. 1156, 1931 Pontiac Model 401, 1929 Pontiac Landau.

1989, Dec. 18 Perf. 14x13½
1147 A161 3 le multicolored .90 .90
1148 A161 6 le multicolored 1.10 1.10
1149 A161 10 le multicolored 1.40 1.40
1150 A161 12 le multicolored 1.60 1.60
1151 A161 20 le multicolored 2.25 2.25
1152 A161 30 le multicolored 2.50 2.50
1153 A161 40 le multicolored 2.75 2.75
1154 A161 50 le multicolored 3.00 3.00
  Nos. 1147-1154 (8) 15.50 15.50

Souvenir Sheets
1155 A161 100 le multicolored 6.00 6.00
1156 A161 100 le multicolored 6.00 6.00

Christmas — A162

Religious paintings by Rembrandt: 3 le, Adoration of the Magi. 6 le, The Holy Family with a Cat. 10 le, The Holy Family with Angels. 15 le, Simeon in the Temple. 30 le, The Circumcision. 90 le, The Holy Family. 100 le, The Visitation. 120 le, The Flight into Egypt. No. 1165, The Adoration of the Shepherds. No. 1166, The Presentation of Jesus in the Temple.

1989, Dec. 22 Perf. 14
1157 A162 3 le multicolored .60 .60
1158 A162 6 le multicolored .75 .75
1159 A162 10 le multicolored 1.10 1.10
1160 A162 15 le multicolored 1.25 1.25
1161 A162 30 le multicolored 1.90 1.90
1162 A162 90 le multicolored 3.50 3.50
1163 A162 100 le multicolored 3.50 3.50
1164 A162 120 le multicolored 3.50 3.50
  Nos. 1157-1164 (8) 16.10 16.10

Souvenir Sheets
1165 A162 150 le multicolored 5.00 5.00
1166 A162 150 le multicolored 5.00 5.00

Miniature Sheets

Exploration of Mars — A163

No. 1167: a, Kepler. b, Galileo. c, Drawings by Huygens in 1672 and Schiaparelli in 1886. d, Sir W. Herschel. e, Percival Lowell in Arizona, 1896-1907. f, Mars. g, Mariner 4, 1965. h, Mars 2, 1971. i, Mars 3, 1971.
No. 1168: a, Mariner 9, 1971. b, Mariner 9, Phobos. c, Cydonia Region. d, South polar cap. e, Profile of Mars. f, Polar cap, diff. g, Nix Olympica. h, Grand Canyon of Mars. i, North Pole.
No. 1169: a, Olympus Mons. b, Viking 1, July 1976. c, Viking 2 releases Lander, Sept. 1976. d, Lander entering Mars's atmosphere. e, Parachute deployed. f, Terminal descent. g, Viking Lander on Mars. h, Soil sampler (robotic arm). i, Soil Sampler (US flag, machine).
No. 1170: a, Martian dusk. b, Project Deimos. c, Exploration of Mars (astronauts surveying land). d, Return to Rombus. e, US rocket bound for Mars. f, Spacecraft bound for Mars. g, Spacecraft in Martian orbit. h, Mission to Mars (astronauts weightless in spacecraft cabin). i, Space station.
No. 1171, "The Face," Mars.

1990 Litho. Perf. 14
1167 Sheet of 9 17.50 17.50
  a.-i. A163 175 le any single 1.90 1.90
1168 Sheet of 9 17.50 17.50
  a.-i. A163 175 le any single 1.90 1.90
1169 Sheet of 9 17.50 17.50
  a.-i. A163 175 le any single 1.90 1.90
1170 Sheet of 9 17.50 17.50
  a.-i. A163 175 le any single 1.90 1.90

Souvenir Sheet
1171 A163 150 le multicolored 5.50 5.50
1171A A163 150 le Space station 5.50 5.50

Issued: No. 1171A, Dec. 24; others, Jan. 15. Extreme speculation has occured with this issue, centered around No. 1171, the face on Mars stamp.

World War II — A164

USAF aircraft — No. 1172, Doolittle Raid B-25. No. 1173, B-24 Liberator. No. 1174, A-20 Boston. No. 1175, P-38 Lightning. No. 1176,

B-26. No. 1177, B-17 F. No. 1178, B-25 D Mitchell. No. 1179, Boeing B-29. No. 1180, B-17 G. No. 1181, The Enola Gay.
No. 1182, B-25, USS Hornet. No. 1183, B-17 G.

1990, Feb. 5 Litho. Perf. 14
1172 A164 1 le multi .25 .25
1173 A164 2 le multi .25 .25
1174 A164 3 le multi .25 .25
1175 A164 9 le multi .50 .50
1176 A164 12 le multi .55 .55
1177 A164 16 le multi .80 .80
1178 A164 50 le multi 2.40 2.40
1179 A164 80 le multi 3.50 3.50
1180 A164 90 le multi 4.25 4.25
1181 A164 100 le multi 4.75 4.75
  Nos. 1172-1181 (10) 17.50 17.50

Souvenir Sheets
1182 A164 150 le multi 7.00 7.00
1183 A164 150 le multi 7.00 7.00

Stage and Screen Roles Played by Sir Laurence Olivier (1907-1989) — A165

3 le, Antony & Cleopatra, 1951. 9 le, Henry V, 1943. 16 le, Oedipus, 1945. 20 le, Wuthering Heights, 1939. 30 le, Marathon Man, 1976. 70 le, Othello, 1964. 175 le, Beau Geste, 1929. 200 le, Richard III, 1956.
No. 1192, The Battle of Britain, 1969. No. 1193, Hamlet, 1947.

1990, Apr. 27
1184 A165 3 le multi .25 .25
1185 A165 9 le multi .25 .25
1186 A165 16 le multi .40 .40
1187 A165 20 le multi .60 .60
1188 A165 30 le multi .80 .80
1189 A165 70 le multi 1.90 1.90
1190 A165 175 le multi 5.00 5.00
1191 A165 200 le multi 5.75 5.75
  Nos. 1184-1191 (8) 14.95 14.95

Souvenir Sheets
1192 A165 250 le multi 6.75 6.75
1193 A165 250 le multi 6.75 6.75

Walt Disney Characters, Settings in Sierra Leone — A166

3 le, Bauxite mine. 6 le, Panning for gold. 10 le, Lungi Intl. Airport. 12 le, Old Fourah Bay College. 16 le, Mining bauxite. 20 le, Rice harvest. 30 le, The Cotton Tree. 100 le, Rutile Mine. 200 le, Fishing at Goderich. 225 le, Bintumani Hotel.
No. 1204, Market Place, King Jimmy. No. 1205, Diamond mining.

1990, Apr. 23
1194 A166 3 le multi .25 .25
1195 A166 6 le multi .25 .25
1196 A166 10 le multi .25 .25
1197 A166 12 le multi .25 .25
1198 A166 16 le multi .30 .30
1199 A166 20 le multi .40 .40
1200 A166 30 le multi .75 .75
1201 A166 100 le multi 2.60 2.60
1202 A166 200 le multi 5.25 5.25
1203 A166 225 le multi 5.50 5.50
  Nos. 1194-1203 (10) 15.80 15.80

Souvenir Sheets
1204 A166 250 le multi 6.00 6.00
1205 A166 250 le multi 6.00 6.00

Penny Black, 150th Anniv. — A167

1990, May 3 Perf. 14
1206 A167 50 le deep ultra 2.00 2.00
1207 A167 100 le violet brown 4.75 4.75

Souvenir Sheet
1208 A167 250 le black 6.75 6.75

World Cup Soccer Championships, Italy — A168

Team photographs.

1990, May 11 Litho. Perf. 14
1209 A168 15 le Colombia .55 .55
1210 A168 15 le United Arab Emirates .55 .55
1211 A168 15 le South Korea .55 .55
1212 A168 15 le Cameroun .55 .55
1213 A168 15 le Costa Rica .55 .55
1214 A168 15 le Romania .55 .55
1215 A168 15 le Yugoslavia .55 .55
1216 A168 15 le Egypt .55 .55
1217 A168 30 le Netherlands 1.10 1.10
1218 A168 30 le Uruguay 1.10 1.10
1219 A168 30 le USSR 1.10 1.10
1220 A168 30 le Czechoslova-kia 1.10 1.10
1221 A168 30 le Scotland 1.10 1.10
1222 A168 30 le Belgium 1.10 1.10
1223 A168 30 le Austria 1.10 1.10
1224 A168 30 le Sweden 1.10 1.10
1225 A168 45 le W. Germany 1.50 1.50
1226 A168 45 le England 1.50 1.50
1227 A168 45 le United States 1.50 1.50
1228 A168 45 le Ireland 1.50 1.50
1229 A168 45 le Spain 1.50 1.50
1230 A168 45 le Brazil 1.50 1.50
1231 A168 45 le Italy 1.50 1.50
1232 A168 45 le Argentina 1.50 1.50
  Nos. 1209-1232 (24) 25.20 25.20

No. 1209 spelled "Columbia," No. 1218 "Uruaguay," No. 1220 "Czecheslovakia" on stamps.

Great Crested Grebe A169

6 le, Green woodhoopoe. 10 le, African jacana. 12 le, Avocet. 20 le, African finfoot. 80 le, Glossy ibis. 150 le, Hamerkop. 200 le, Greater honey guide.
No. 1241, Painted snipe. No. 1242, Palm swift.

1990, June 4
1233 A169 3 le multi .25 .25
1234 A169 6 le multi .25 .25
1235 A169 10 le multi .25 .25
1236 A169 12 le multi .25 .25
1237 A169 20 le multi .40 .40
1238 A169 80 le multi 1.75 1.75
1239 A169 150 le multi 3.00 3.00
1240 A169 200 le multi 4.00 4.00
  Nos. 1233-1240 (8) 10.15 10.15

Souvenir Sheets
1241 A169 250 le multi 5.25 5.25
1242 A169 250 le multi 5.25 5.25

Mickey as Yeoman Warder A170

Disney characters: 6 le, Scrooge as lamplighter. 12 le, Knight Goofy. 15 le, Clarabell as Anne Boleyn. 75 le, Minnie Mouse as Queen Elizabeth I. 100 le, Donald Duck as chimmey sweep. 125 le, Pete as King Henry VIII. 150 le,

May dancers in Salisbury. No. 1251, Boadicea, Queen of the Iceni. No. 1252, Lawyers at Parliament House.

1990, June 6 *Perf. 13½x14*

1243	A170	3 le	multicolored	.25	.25
1244	A170	6 le	multicolored	.25	.25
1245	A170	12 le	multicolored	.25	.25
1246	A170	15 le	multicolored	.30	.30
1247	A170	75 le	multicolored	2.10	2.10
1248	A170	100 le	multicolored	2.75	2.75
1249	A170	125 le	multicolored	3.50	3.50
1250	A170	150 le	multicolored	4.25	4.25
			Nos. 1243-1250 (8)	13.65	13.65

Souvenir Sheets

1251	A170	250 le	multicolored	5.25	5.25
1252	A170	250 le	multicolored	5.25	5.25

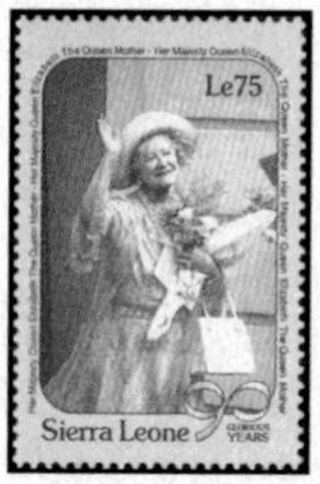

Queen Mother, 90th Birthday — A171

1990, July 5 *Perf. 14*

1253	75 le	shown	1.60	1.60
1254	75 le	Wearing black hat	1.60	1.60
1255	75 le	Wearing yellow hat	1.60	1.60
a.	A171	Strip of 3, #1253-1255	5.25	5.25
		Nos. 1253-1255 (3)	4.80	4.80

Souvenir Sheet

1256	A171	250 le Like No. 1253	5.00	5.00

Butterfly Type of 1987

1990 *Perf. 12½x11½*

1257	A126	3 le	like No. 861	.25	.25
1258	A126	9 le	like No. 864	.25	.25
1259	A126	12 le	like No. 859	.25	.25
1260	A126	16 le	like No. 860	.30	.30
			Nos. 1257-1260 (4)	1.05	1.05

Inscribed 1989.

Miniature Sheet

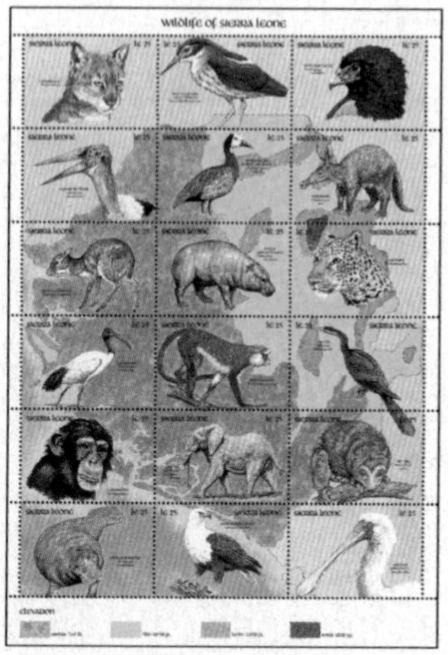

Wildlife — A172

Designs: No. 1261a, Golden cat. b, White-backed night heron. c, Bateleur eagle. d, Marabou stork. e, White-faced whistling duck. f, Aardvark. g, Royal antelope. h, Pygmy hippopotamus. i, Leopard. j, Sacred ibis. k, Mona monkey. l, Darter. m, Chimpanzee. n, African elephant. o, Potto. p, African manatee. q, African fish eagle. r, African spoonbill.

1990, Sept. 24 **Litho.** *Perf. 14*

1261	Sheet of 18	19.00	19.00
a.-r.	A172 25 le any single	.85	.85

Souvenir Sheet

1262	A172 150 le Crowned eagle, vert.	10.50	10.50

No. 1261 printed in continuous design showing map of Sierra Leone in background.

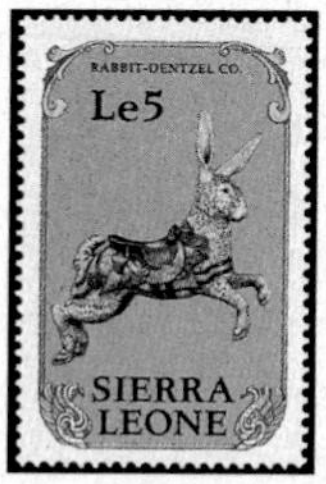

A173

Carousel animals — 5 le, Rabbit. 10 le, Horse with panther saddle. 20 le, Ostrich. 30 le, Zebra. 50 le, White horse. 80 le, Sea monster. 100 le, Giraffe. 150 le, Armored horse. 200 le, Camel.

No. 1272, Centaur, Lord Baden-Powell. No. 1273, Horse head.

1990, Oct. 22 **Litho.** *Perf. 14*

1263	A173	5 le	multi	.25	.25
1264	A173	10 le	multi	.25	.25
1265	A173	20 le	multi	.35	.35
1266	A173	30 le	multi	.55	.55
1267	A173	50 le	multi	.90	.90
1268	A173	80 le	multi	1.25	1.25
1269	A173	100 le	multi	1.60	1.60
1270	A173	150 le	multi	2.50	2.50
1271	A173	200 le	multi	3.25	3.25
			Nos. 1263-1271 (9)	10.90	10.90

Souvenir Sheets

1272	A173	300 le	multi	6.75	6.75
1273	A173	300 le	multi	6.75	6.75

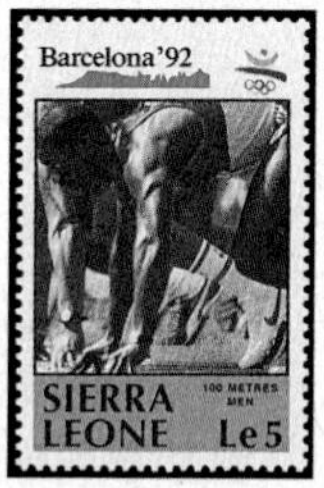

A174

5 le, Men's 100-meter race. 10 le, Men's 4x400-meter relay. 20 le, Men's 100-meter race, diff. 30 le, Weight lifting. 40 le, Freestyle wrestling. 80 le, Water polo. 150 le, Women's gymnastics. 200 le, Cycling.

No. 1282, Boxing. No. 1283, Olympic flag.

1990, Nov. 12 **Litho.** *Perf. 14*

1274	A174	5 le	multi	.25	.25
1275	A174	10 le	multi	.25	.25
1276	A174	20 le	multi	.35	.35
1277	A174	30 le	multi	.60	.60
1278	A174	40 le	multi	.85	.85
1279	A174	80 le	multi	1.75	1.75
1280	A174	150 le	multi	3.00	3.00
1281	A174	200 le	multi	4.25	4.25
			Nos. 1274-1281 (8)	11.30	11.30

Souvenir Sheets

1282	A174	400 le	multi	6.50	6.50
1283	A174	400 le	multi	6.50	6.50

1992 Summer Olympics, Barcelona.

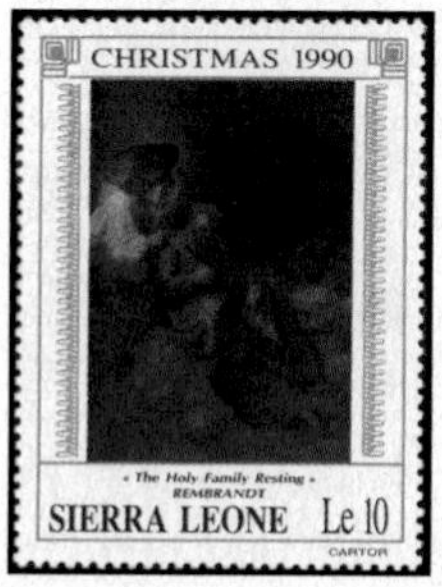

Christmas A175

Paintings: 10 le, The Holy Family Resting by Rembrandt. 20 le, The Holy Family with St. Elizabeth by Andrea Mantegna. 30 le, Virgin and Child with an Angel by Correggio. 50 le, The Annunciation by Bernardo Strozzi. 100 le, Madonna and Child Appearing to St. Anthony by Filippino Lippi. 175 le, Virgin and Child by Giovanni Boltraffio. 200 le, The Esterhazy Madonna by Raphael. 300 le, Coronation of Mary by Orcagna. No. 1292, Adoration of the Shepherds by Bronzino. No. 1293, Adoration of the Shepherds by Gerard David.

1990, Dec. 17 *Perf. 13*

1284	A175	10 le	multicolored	.25	.25
1285	A175	20 le	multicolored	.30	.30
1286	A175	30 le	multicolored	.50	.50
1287	A175	50 le	multicolored	.80	.80
1288	A175	100 le	multicolored	2.00	2.00
1289	A175	175 le	multicolored	4.00	4.00
1290	A175	200 le	multicolored	4.25	4.25
1291	A175	300 le	multicolored	6.00	6.00
			Nos. 1284-1291 (8)	18.10	18.10

Souvenir Sheets

1292	A175	400 le	multicolored	7.50	7.50
1293	A175	400 le	multicolored	7.50	7.50

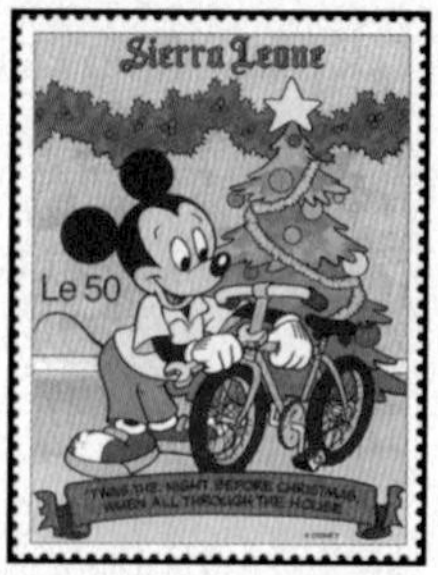

Christmas A176

Walt Disney characters in "The Night Before Christmas."

No. 1294a, 'Twas the night. . . b, Not a creature. . . c, The stockings were hung. . . d, And Mama in her kerchief. . . e, When out on the lawn. . . f, I sprang from my bed. . . g, Away to the window. . . h, Tore open the shutter. . .

No. 1295a, The moon on the breast. . . b, When what to my wondering. . . c, With a little old driver. . . d, More rapid than eagles. . . e, To the top of the porch. . . f, And then in a twinkling. . . g, As I drew in my head. . . h, He was dressed. . .

No. 1296a, A bundle of toys. . . b, The stump of a pipe. . . c, He had a broad face. . . d, He was chubby and plump. . . e, A wink of his eye. . . f, Then turned with a jerk. . . g, And giving a nod. . . h, He sprang to his sleigh. . .

No. 1297, The children were nestled. . . No. 1298, His eyes, how they twinkled. . . No. 1299, He spoke not a word. . . No. 1300, And he whistled. . . No. 1301, As dry leaves. . . No. 1302, But I heard him exclaim. . .

1990, Dec. 17 **Litho.** *Perf. 13*

Miniature Sheets of 8

1294	A176	50 le	#a.-h.	5.50	5.50
1295	A176	75 le	#a.-h.	16.00	16.00
1296	A176	100 le	#a.-h.	8.25	8.25

Souvenir Sheets

1297	A176	400 le	multi	4.50	4.50
1298	A176	400 le	multi, horiz.	4.50	4.50
1299	A176	400 le	multi	4.50	4.50
1300	A176	400 le	multi, horiz.	4.50	4.50
1301	A176	400 le	multi, horiz.	4.50	4.50
1302	A176	400 le	multi	4.50	4.50

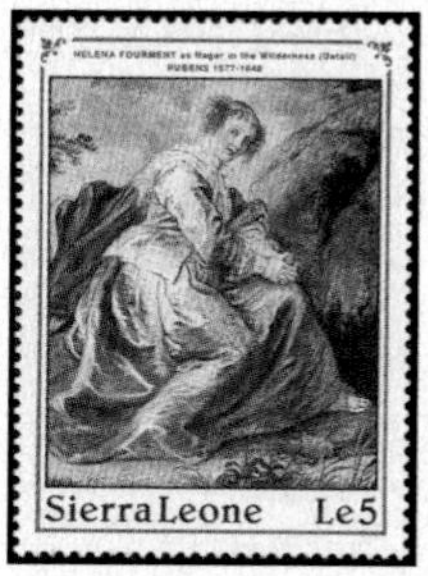

Peter Paul Rubens (1577-1640), Painter A177

Entire paintings or different details from: 5 le, Helena Fourment as Hagar in the Wilderness. 10 le, Isabella Brant. 20 le, 60 le, Countess of Arundel and Her Party. 80 le, Nicolaas Rockox. 100 le, Adriana Perez. 150 le, George Villiers, Duke of Buckingham. 300 le, Countess of Buckingham. No. 1311, Veronica Spinola Doria. No. 1312, Giovanni Carlo Dorio.

1990, Dec. 24 *Perf. 14*

1303	A177	5 le	multicolored	.25	.25
1304	A177	10 le	multicolored	.25	.25
1305	A177	20 le	multicolored	.25	.25
1306	A177	60 le	multicolored	.85	.85
1307	A177	80 le	multicolored	1.10	1.10
1308	A177	100 le	multicolored	1.40	1.40
1309	A177	150 le	multicolored	2.40	2.40
1310	A177	300 le	multicolored	4.50	4.50
			Nos. 1303-1310 (8)	11.00	11.00

Souvenir Sheets

1311	A177	350 le	multicolored	6.25	6.25
1312	A177	350 le	multicolored	6.25	6.25

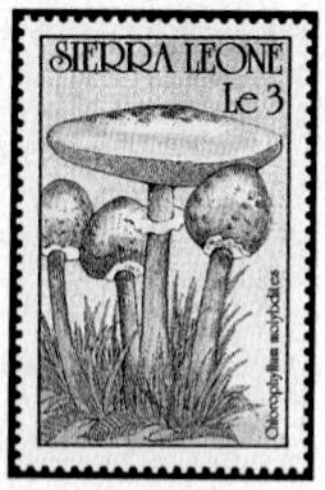

Mushrooms A178

Designs: 3 le, Chlorophyllum molybdites. 5 le, Lepista nuda. 10 le, Clitocybe nebularis. 15 le, Cyathus striatus. 20 le, Bolbitius vitellinus. 25 le, Leucoagaricus naucinus. 30 le, Suillus luteus. 40 le, Podaxis pistillaris. 50 le, Oudemansiella radicata. 60 le, Phallus indusiatus. 80 le, Macrolepiota rhacodes. 100 le, Mycena pura. 150 le, Volvariella volvacea. 175 le, Omphalotus olearius. 200 le, Sphaerobolus stellatus. 250 le, Schizophyllum commune.

Each 350 le: No. 1329, Agaricus campestris. No. 1330, Hypholama fasciculare. No. 1331, Suillus granulatus. No. 1332, Psilocybe coprophila.

1990, Dec. 31 *Perf. 14*

1313	A178	3 le	multicolored	.25	.25
1314	A178	5 le	multicolored	.25	.25
1315	A178	10 le	multicolored	.25	.25
1316	A178	15 le	multicolored	.25	.25
1317	A178	20 le	multicolored	.30	.30
1318	A178	25 le	multicolored	.45	.45
1319	A178	30 le	multicolored	.55	.55
1320	A178	40 le	multicolored	.70	.70
1321	A178	50 le	multicolored	.85	.85
1322	A178	60 le	multicolored	.95	.95
1323	A178	80 le	multicolored	1.40	1.40
1324	A178	100 le	multicolored	2.25	2.25
1325	A178	150 le	multicolored	2.75	2.75
1326	A178	175 le	multicolored	3.50	3.50
1327	A178	200 le	multicolored	4.25	4.25
1328	A178	250 le	multicolored	5.00	5.00
			Nos. 1313-1328 (16)	23.95	23.95

Souvenir Sheets

1329-1332	A178	Set of 4	24.00	24.00

Butterfly Type of 1987 With "Sierra Leone" in Blue

1991 **Litho.** *Perf. 14*

1332A	A126	50c	Like #861		—
m.			Perf. 12½x11½	—	
1332B	A126	1 le	Like #862		—
1332C	A126	2 le	Like #863		—
1332D	A126	5 le	Like #865		—
1332E	A126	10 le	Like #866		—
1332F	A126	20 le	Like #867		—
1332G	A126	30 le	Like #864		—
1332H	A126	50 le	Like #859		—
n.			Perf. 12½x11½	—	
1332I	A126	60 le	Like #871		—
1332J	A126	80 le	Like #860		—
o.			Perf. 12½x11½	—	
1332K	A126	100 le	Like #873		—
1332L	A126	300 le	Like #869		—
p.			Perf. 12½x11½	—	

Every sixth perforation hole on Nos. 1332Am, 1332Hn, 1132Jo, and 1332Lp is larger. These stamps are not known used. All stamps are dated "1990."

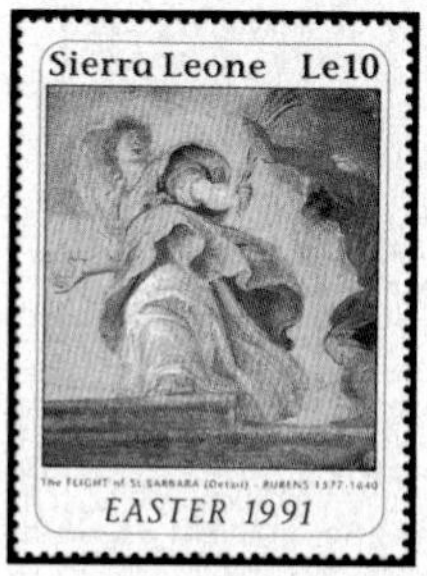

Easter A179

Entire works or details from paintings by Rubens: 10 le, Flight of St. Barbara. 20 le, No. 1341, The Last Judgement. 30 le, St. Gregory of Nazianzus. 50 le, Doubting Thomas. 80 le, No. 1342, The Way to Calvary. 100 le, St. Gregory with Sts. Domitilla, Maurus and Papianus. 175 le, Sts. Gregory, Maurus and Papianus. 300 le, Christ and the Penitent Sinners.

1991, Apr. 8 **Litho.** *Perf. 13½x14*

1333	A179	10 le	multicolored	.25	.25
1334	A179	20 le	multicolored	.40	.40
1335	A179	30 le	multicolored	.65	.65
1336	A179	50 le	multicolored	1.10	1.10
1337	A179	80 le	multicolored	1.60	1.60
1338	A179	100 le	multicolored	2.10	2.10
1339	A179	175 le	multicolored	3.50	3.50
1340	A179	300 le	multicolored	6.00	6.00
			Nos. 1333-1340 (8)	15.60	15.60

Souvenir Sheets

1341-1342	A179	400 le	Set of 2	14.00	14.00

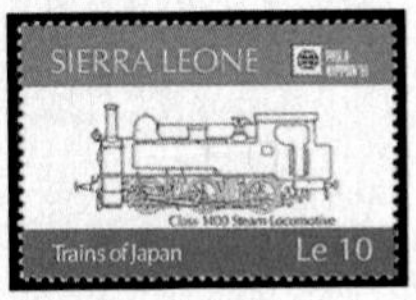

Phila Nippon '91 — A180

Japanese locomotives: 10 le, Class 1400 steam. 20 le, Streamlined C55 steam. 30 le, ED17 electric. 60 le, EF13 electric. 100 le, Baldwin Mikado steam. 150 le, C62 steam. 200 le, KiHa 81 class diesel. 300 le, Class 8550 steam.

Each 400 le: No. 1351, Hikari bullet train. No. 1352, Class 7000 electric. No. 1353, D51 steam. No. 1354, Class 9600 steam.

1991, May 13 Litho. *Perf. 14*

1343	A180	10 le	multicolored	.25	.25
1344	A180	20 le	multicolored	.35	.35
1345	A180	30 le	multicolored	.55	.55
1346	A180	60 le	multicolored	1.00	1.00
1347	A180	100 le	multicolored	1.75	1.75
1348	A180	150 le	multicolored	2.50	2.50
1349	A180	200 le	multicolored	3.50	3.50
1350	A180	300 le	multicolored	5.25	5.25
			Nos. 1343-1350 (8)	15.15	15.15

Souvenir Sheets

1351-1354	A180	Set of 4	22.00	22.00

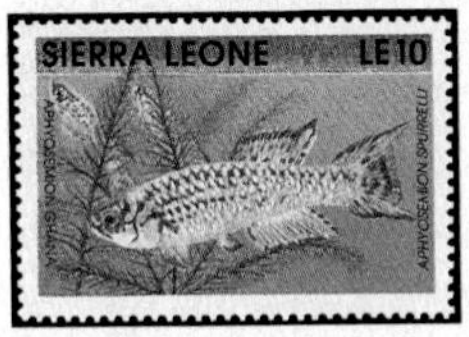

Fish A181

10 le, Aphyosemion ghana. 20 le, Black-lipped panchax. 30 le, Peter's killie. 60 le, Micro-walkeri killie. 100 le, Butterfly fish. 150 le, Green panchax. 200 le, Six-barred panchax. 300 le, Banded puffer.

No. 1363, Spotfin synodontis. No. 1364, Two-striped panchax.

1991, June 3 Litho. *Perf. 14*

1355	A181	10 le	multi	.25	.25
1356	A181	20 le	multi	.35	.35
1357	A181	30 le	multi	.65	.65
1358	A181	60 le	multi	1.25	1.25
1359	A181	100 le	multi	2.25	2.25
1360	A181	150 le	multi	3.00	3.00
1361	A181	200 le	multi	4.25	4.25
1362	A181	300 le	multi	6.00	6.00
			Nos. 1355-1362 (8)	18.00	18.00

Souvenir Sheets

1363	A181	400 le	multi	8.00	8.00
1364	A181	400 le	multi	8.00	8.00

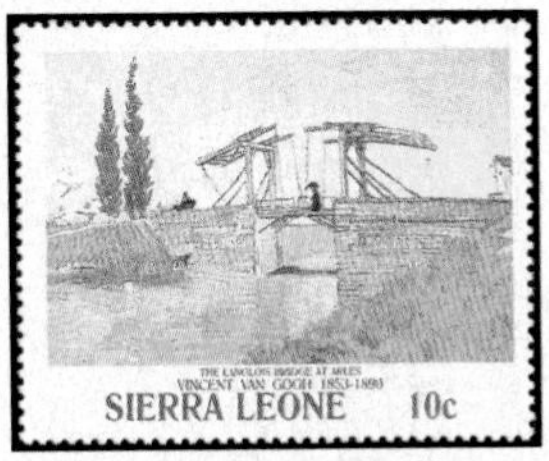

Paintings by Vincent Van Gogh — A182

Designs: 10c, The Langlois Bridge at Arles. 50c, Trees in the Garden of Saint-Paul Hospital, vert. 1 le, Wild Flowers and Thistles in a Vase, vert. 2 le, Still Life: Vase with Oleanders and Books. 5 le, Farmhouses in a Wheat Field Near Arles. 10 le, Self-Portrait, Sept. 1889, vert. 20 le, Portrait of Patience Escalier, vert. 30 le, Portrait of Doctor Felix Rey, vert. 50 le, The Iris, vert. 60 le, The Shepherdess, vert. 80 le, Vincent's House in Arles (The Yellow House). 100 le, The Road Menders. 150 le, The Garden of Saint-Paul Hospital, vert. 200 le, View of the Church of Saint-Paul-De-Mausole. 250 le, Seascape at Saintes-Maries. 300 le, Pieta, vert.

Each 400 le: No. 1381, Church at Auvers Sur Dise, vert. No. 1382, Vineyards with a View of Auvers. No. 1383, The Trinquetaille Bridge. No. 1384, Two Poplars on a Road Through the Hills, vert. No. 1385, Haystacks in Provence. No. 1386, The Garden of Saint-Paul Hospital, diff.

1991, June 28 Litho. *Perf. 13½*

1365	A182	10c	multicolored	.30	.30
1366	A182	50c	multicolored	.30	.30
1367	A182	1 le	multicolored	.30	.30
1368	A182	2 le	multicolored	.30	.30
1369	A182	5 le	multicolored	.30	.30
1370	A182	10 le	multicolored	.30	.30
1371	A182	20 le	multicolored	.30	.30
1372	A182	30 le	multicolored	.45	.45
1373	A182	50 le	multicolored	.85	.85
1374	A182	60 le	multicolored	1.00	1.00
1375	A182	80 le	multicolored	1.40	1.40
1376	A182	100 le	multicolored	1.75	1.75
1377	A182	150 le	multicolored	2.60	2.60
1378	A182	200 le	multicolored	3.75	3.75
1379	A182	250 le	multicolored	4.75	4.75
1380	A182	300 le	multicolored	5.25	5.25
			Nos. 1365-1380 (16)	23.90	23.90

Size: 102x76mm

Imperf

1381-1386	A182	Set of 6	27.00	27.00

Royal Family Birthday, Anniversary

Common Design Type

1991, July 5 Litho. *Perf. 14*

1387	CD347	10 le	multi	.25	.25
1388	CD347	20 le	multi	.25	.25
1389	CD347	30 le	multi	.45	.45
1390	CD347	80 le	multi	1.10	1.10
1391	CD347	100 le	multi	1.50	1.50
1392	CD347	200 le	multi	3.00	3.00
1393	CD347	250 le	multi	3.75	3.75
1394	CD347	300 le	multi	4.25	4.25
			Nos. 1387-1394 (8)	14.55	14.55

Souvenir Sheets

1395	CD347	400 le	Elizabeth, Philip	6.00	6.00
1396	CD347	400 le	Charles, Diana, sons	6.00	6.00

10 le, 30 le, 200 le, 250 le, No. 1395, Queen Elizabeth II, 65th birthday. Others, Charles and Diana, 10th wedding anniversary.

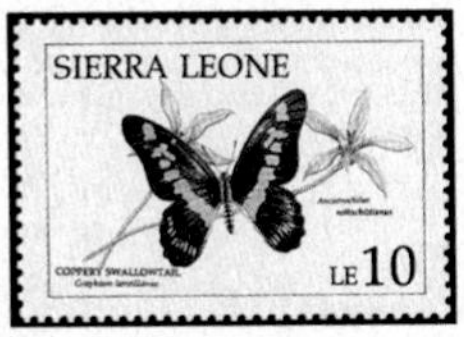

Butterflies A183

10 le, Coppery swallowtail. 30 le, Orange forester. 50 le, Large striped swordtail. 60 le, Lilac beauty. 80 le, African leaf. 100 le, Blue diadem. 200 le, Beautiful monarch. 300 le, Veined swallowtail.

No. 1405, Blue banded nymph. No. 1406, Western red charaxes. No. 1407, Broad-bordered grass yellow. No. 1408, African clouded yellow.

1991, Aug. 5 Litho. *Perf. 14x13½*

1397	A183	10 le	multi	.25	.25
1398	A183	30 le	multi	.80	.80
1399	A183	50 le	multi	1.35	1.35
1400	A183	60 le	multi	1.60	1.60
1401	A183	80 le	multi	2.00	2.00
1402	A183	100 le	multi	2.75	2.75
1403	A183	200 le	multi	5.50	5.50
1404	A183	300 le	multi	7.75	7.75
			Nos. 1397-1404 (8)	22.00	22.00

Souvenir Sheets

Perf. 13x12

1405	A183	400 le	multi	7.50	7.50
1406	A183	400 le	multi	4.00	4.00
1407	A183	400 le	multi	4.00	4.00
1408	A183	400 le	multi	5.00	5.00

While numbers 1406-1407 have the same issue date as Nos. 1397-1405, the dollar value of Nos. 1406-1407 was lower when they were released. While No. 1408 has the same issue date as Nos. 1397-1407, the value of No. 1408 was different when released.

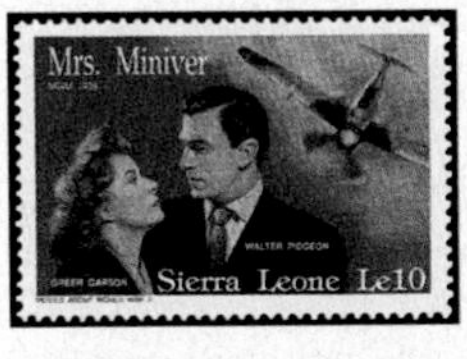

World War II Motion Pictures A184

Designs: 2 le, To Hell and Back, Audie Murphy. 5 le, Attack, Jack Palance. 10 le, Mrs. Miniver, Greer Garson and Walter Pidgeon. 20 le, The Guns of Navarone. 30 le, The Great Dictator, Paulette Goddard and Charlie Chaplin. 50 le, The Train. 60 le, The Diary of Anne Frank. 80 le, The Bridge on the River Kwai, William Holden. 100 le, Lifeboat, Alfred Hitchcock, Tallulah Bankhead. 200 le, Sands of Iwo Jima, John Wayne. 300 le, Thirty Seconds Over Tokyo, Van Johnson and Spencer Tracy. 350 le, Casablanca, Humphrey Bogart and Ingrid Bergman. No. 1421, Twelve O'Clock High, Gregory Peck. No. 1422, Tora! Tora! Tora!. No. 1423, Patton, George C. Scott.

1991, Oct. 14 Litho. *Perf. 14*

1409	A184	2 le	multicolored	.25	.25
1410	A184	5 le	multicolored	.25	.25
1411	A184	10 le	multicolored	.25	.25
1412	A184	20 le	multicolored	.25	.25
1413	A184	30 le	multicolored	.40	.40
1414	A184	50 le	multicolored	.90	.90
1415	A184	60 le	multicolored	1.00	1.00
1416	A184	80 le	multicolored	1.40	1.40
1417	A184	100 le	multicolored	1.90	1.90
1418	A184	200 le	multicolored	3.50	3.50
1419	A184	300 le	multicolored	5.25	5.25
1420	A184	350 le	multicolored	6.00	6.00
			Nos. 1409-1420 (12)	21.35	21.35

Souvenir Sheets

1421	A184	450 le	multicolored	6.25	6.25
1422	A184	450 le	multicolored	6.25	6.25
1423	A184	450 le	multicolored	6.25	6.25

Miniature Sheets

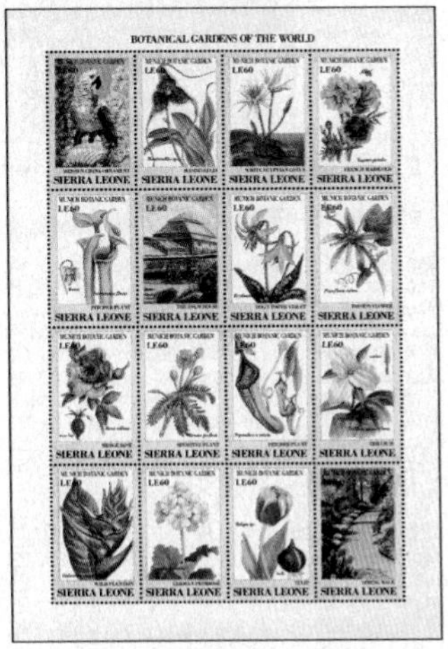

Botanic Gardens — A185

Munich Botanic Garden: No. 1424a, Meissen China ornament. b, Masdevallia. c, White Egyptian lotus. d, French marigold. e, Pitcher plant. f, The Palm House. g, Dog's tooth violet. h, Passion flower. i, Hedge rose. j, Sensitive plant. k, Pitcher plant, diff. l, Trillium. m, Wild plantain. n, German primrose. o, Tulip. p, Spring walk.

Kyoto Botanic Garden: No. 1425a, Flowering cherry. b, Gardenia. c, The Domed Conservatory. d, Chrysanthemums. e, Bleeding heart. f, Hibiscus. g, Hiryu azalea. h, Sweet honeysuckle. i, Goldband lily. j, Non-traditional garden art. k, Viburnum. l, Japanese iris. m, Orchid. n, Hydrangea. o, View of Kyoto Botanic Garden. p, Camelia.

Brooklyn Botanic Garden: No. 1426a, The Palm House. b, Kurume azalea. c, Southern magnolia. d, Oleander. e, Chinese wisteria. f, Sourwood tree. g, Cattleya orchid. h, Gingko tree. i, Japanese Hill and Pond Garden. j, Rose. k, German iris. l, East Indian lotus. m, Speciosum lily. n, Lilac. o, Rose bay. p, Cranford Rose Garden.

Each 600 le: No. 1427, Rhododendron, Munich, horiz. No. 1428, Chrysanthemum, Kyoto, horiz. No. 1429, Magnolia soulangeana, Brooklyn, horiz.

1991, Oct. 28 Sheets of 16

1424	A185	60 le	#a.-p.	12.50	12.50
1425	A185	60 le	#a.-p.	12.50	12.50
1426	A185	60 le	#a.-p.	12.50	12.50

Souvenir Sheets

1427-1429	A185	Set of 3	20.00	20.00

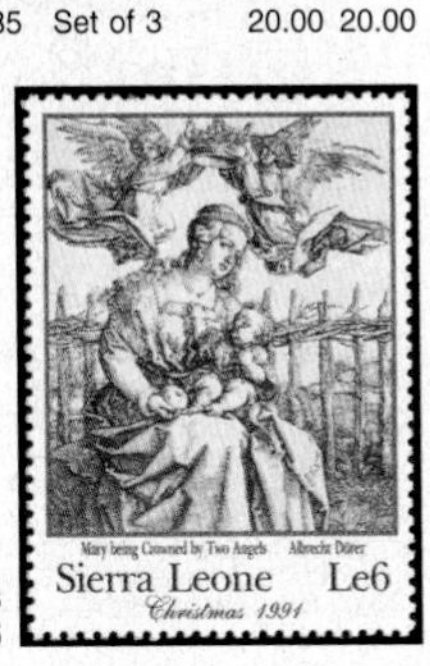

Christmas A186

Details from paintings or engravings by Albrecht Durer: 6 le, Mary being Crowned by Two Angels. 60 le, St. Christopher. 80 le, Virgin and Child. 100 le, Madonna and Child (Virgin with the Pear). 200 le, Madonna and Child. 300 le, The Virgin in Half-Length. 700 le, The Madonna with the Siskin.

Each 600 le: No. 1437, The Feast of the Rose Garlands. No. 1438, Virgin and Child with St. Anne.

1991, Dec. 9 Litho. *Perf. 12*

1430	A186	6 le	pink & black	.25	.25
1431	A186	60 le	blue & black	.65	.65
1432	A186	80 le	multicolored	.80	.80
1433	A186	100 le	multicolored	1.00	1.00
1434	A186	200 le	multicolored	2.00	2.00
1435	A186	300 le	multicolored	3.00	3.00
1436	A186	700 le	multicolored	7.00	7.00
			Nos. 1430-1436 (7)	14.70	14.70

Souvenir Sheets

Perf. 14½

1437-1438	A186	Set of 2	13.50	13.50

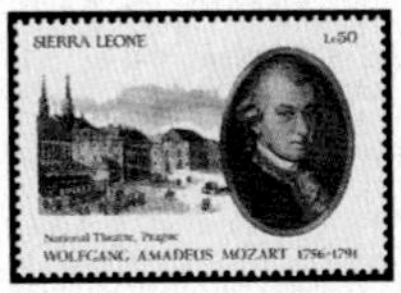

Wolfgang Amadeus Mozart, Death Bicent. A187

Mozart and: 50 le, National Theatre, Prague. 100 le, St. Peter's Abbey, Salzburg. 500 le, Scene from opera, "Idomeneo."

1991, Dec. 20 *Perf. 14*

1439	A187	50 le	multicolored	.50	.50
1440	A187	100 le	multicolored	1.00	1.00
1441	A187	500 le	multicolored	5.00	5.00
			Nos. 1439-1441 (3)	6.50	6.50

Souvenir Sheet

1442	A187	600 le	Bust, vert.	7.50	7.50

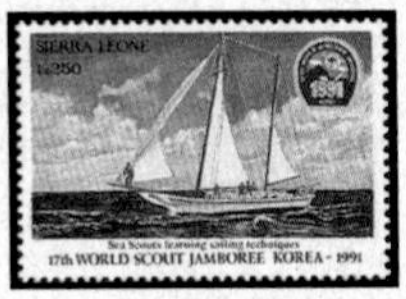

17th World Scout Jamboree, Korea A188

Designs: 250 le, Scouts learning to sail. 300 le, Lord Robert Baden-Powell, founder. 400 le, Scouts playing baseball. 750 le, Jamboree emblem, vert.

1991, Dec. 20

1443	A188	250 le	multicolored	1.75	1.75
1444	A188	300 le	multicolored	2.25	2.25
1445	A188	400 le	multicolored	3.25	3.25
			Nos. 1443-1445 (3)	7.25	7.25

Souvenir Sheet

1446	A188	750 le	multicolored	7.50	7.50

Miniature Sheet

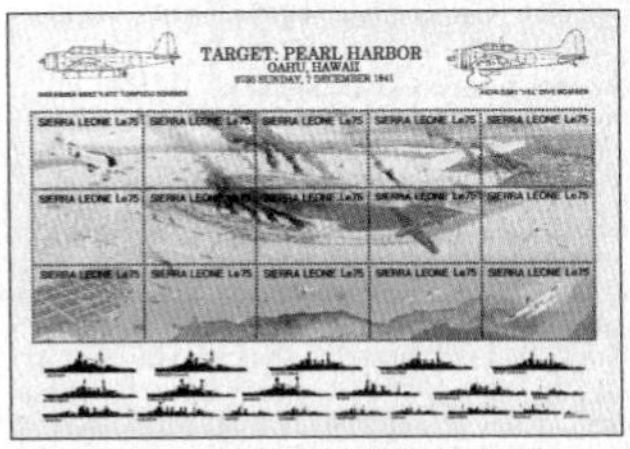

Attack on Pearl Harbor, 50th Anniv. — A189

Designs: a, Japanese D3A1 Val dive bomber. b, Plane amid rising smoke over Ford Island. c, Battleships ablaze. d, Naval station, three planes. e, Drydock ablaze, tank farm. f, Two Vals over water, ships. g, USS Utah and Ford Island installations ablaze, ship underway. h, Installations on Ford Island ablaze. i, US P-40 Warhawk fighter plane. j, Two Japanese torpedo bombers, plane on fire falling from sky. k, Three Japanese bombers over Pearl City. l, Two Japanese bombers diving on four ships, one burning ship. m, Japanese plane on fire. n, Two Japanese planes. o, One Japanese plane over Waipio Peninsula.

1991, Dec. 20 *Perf. 14½x15*

1447	A189	75 le	Sheet of 15, #a.-o.	18.00	18.00

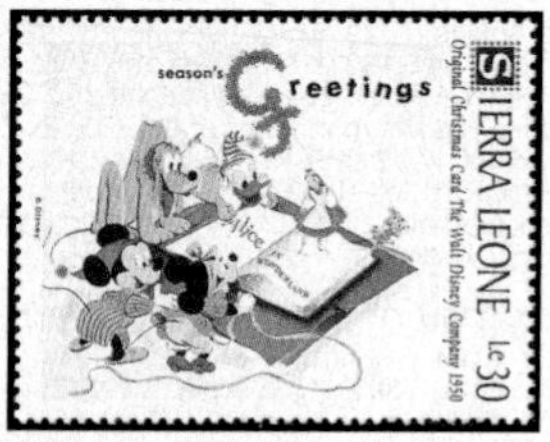

Walt Disney Christmas Cards — A190

Designs and year of issue: 12 le, Mickey and Donald decorating tree, 1952. 30 le, Characters surrounding book with "Alice in Wonderland", 1950. 60 le, Dwarf asleep with hare and tortoise, 1938. 75 le, Minnie, Donald, Mickey and Pluto mailing Christmas card, 1936. 100 le, Costumed characters in front of Magic Kingdom, 1984. 125 le, Mickey singing, Donald's nephews and Pluto reading 20,000 Leagues Under the Sea, 1954. 150 le, 101 Dalmations with season's greetings, 1960. 200 le, Donald and Mickey among gifts, 1948. 300 le, Mickey, Minnie at home for Christmas, 1983. 400 le, Donald and ducks preparing for Christmas watching Mickey Mouse Club, 1956. Characters on parade with Christmas cheer. 500 le, Disney characters, 50th birthday of Walt Disney Productions, 1972.

Each 900 le: No. 1460, Map of Magic Kingdom, 1955, vert. No. 1461, Seven dwarfs in bobsled, 1959, vert. No. 1462, Alice in Wonderland at tea party, 1950, vert.

1991, Dec. 24 Litho. *Perf. 14x13½*

1448	A190	12 le multicolored	.25	.25
1449	A190	30 le multicolored	.25	.25
1450	A190	60 le multicolored	.45	.45
1451	A190	75 le multicolored	.50	.50
1452	A190	100 le multicolored	.70	.70
1453	A190	125 le multicolored	1.00	1.00
1454	A190	150 le multicolored	1.10	1.10
1455	A190	200 le multicolored	1.60	1.60
1456	A190	300 le multicolored	2.10	2.10
1457	A190	400 le multicolored	2.75	2.75
1458	A190	500 le multicolored	3.50	3.50
1459	A190	600 le multicolored	4.25	4.25
		Nos. 1448-1459 (12)	18.45	18.45

Souvenir Sheets

Perf. 13½x14

1460-1462	A190	Set of 3	18.00	18.00

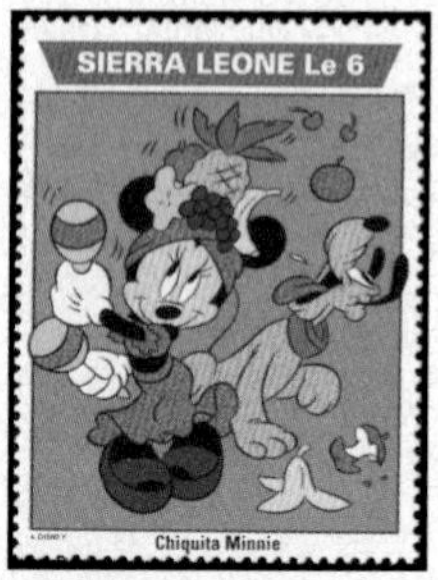

Disney Characters on World Tour A192

Designs: 6 le, Chiquita Minnie in Central America. 10 le, Gold Medal Goofy in Ancient Greece. 20 le, Donald, Daisy having Flamenco Fun in Spain. 30 le, Goofy guarding Donald at London's Buckingham Palace. 50 le, Mickey and Minnie dressed in Paris originals. 100 le, Goofy with mountain goat in Switzerland. 200 le, Daisy, Minnie as luau ladies in Hawaii. 350 le, Mickey, Donald and Goofy as ancient Egyptian comic strips, horiz. 500 le, Daisy and Minnie as can-can dancers in Paris, horiz.

Each 700 le: No. 1479, Mickey playing bagpipes in Scotland. No. 1480, Goofy fishes from Donald's gondola in Venice, Italy. No. 1481, Mickey and Goofy taking crash course in Greek.

Perf. 13x13½, 13½x13

1992, Feb. Litho.

1470	A192	6 le multicolored	.25	.25
1471	A192	10 le multicolored	.25	.25
1472	A192	20 le multicolored	.25	.25
1473	A192	30 le multicolored	.30	.30
1474	A192	50 le multicolored	.50	.50
1475	A192	100 le multicolored	.95	.95
1476	A192	200 le multicolored	1.90	1.90
1477	A192	350 le multicolored	3.25	3.25
1478	A192	500 le multicolored	4.75	4.75
		Nos. 1470-1478 (9)	12.40	12.40

Souvenir Sheets

1479-1481	A192	Set of 3	19.00	19.00

Queen Elizabeth II's Accession to the Throne, 40th Anniv.

Common Design Type

1992, Feb. 6 Litho. *Perf. 14*

1482	CD348	60 le multi	.65	.65
1483	CD348	100 le multi	1.10	1.10
1484	CD348	300 le multi	3.00	3.00
1485	CD348	400 le multi	4.25	4.25
		Nos. 1482-1485 (4)	9.00	9.00

Souvenir Sheets

1486	CD348	700 le Queen, hillside	6.75	6.75
1487	CD348	700 le Queen, houses	6.75	6.75

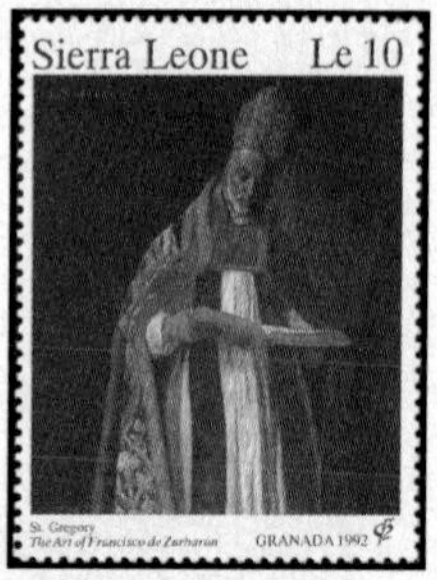

Spanish Art — A193

Paintings by Francisco de Zurbaran: 1 le, The Visit of St. Thomas Aquinas to St. Bonaventure. 10 le, St. Gregory. 30 le, St. Andrew. 50 le, St. Gabriel the Archangel. 60 le, The Blessed Henry Suso. 100 le, St. Lucy. 300 le, St. Casilda. 400 le, St. Margaret of Antioch. 500 le, St. Apollonia. 600 le, St. Bonaventure at the Council of Lyons. 700 le, St. Bonaventure on His Bier. 800 le, The Martyrdom of St. James (detail). No. 1496, St. Hugh in the Refectory, horiz. No. 1497, The Martyrdom of St. James. No. 1497A, The Young Virgin.

1992, May 25 Litho. *Perf. 13*

1487A	A193	1 le multi	.25	.25
1488	A193	10 le multi	.25	.25
1489	A193	30 le multi	.25	.25
1490	A193	50 le multi	.25	.25
1491	A193	60 le multi	.25	.25
1491A	A193	100 le multi	.30	.30
1491B	A193	300 le multi	.85	.85
1492	A193	400 le multi	1.60	1.60
1493	A193	500 le multi	2.25	2.25
1494	A193	600 le multi	2.60	2.60
1495	A193	700 le multi	1.90	1.90
1495A	A193	800 le multi	2.25	2.25

Size: 120x95mm

Imperf

1496	A193	900 le multi	4.00	4.00
1497	A193	900 le multi	3.75	3.75
1497A	A193	900 le multi	2.60	2.60
		Nos. 1487A-1497A (15)	23.35	23.35

Granada '92.

While Nos. 1487A-1497A all have the same issue date, the dollar value of Nos. 1487A, 1489-1490, 1491A-1491B, 1492, 1495, 1497-1497A was lower when they were released.

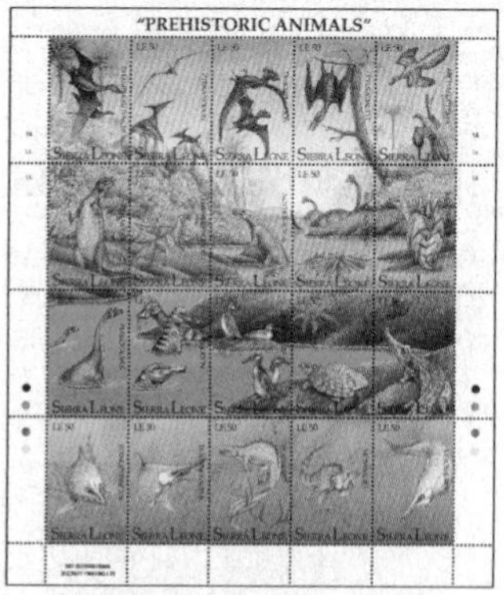

Prehistoric Animals — A194

Designs: No. 1498a, Rhamphorhynchus. b, Pteranodon. c, Dimorphodon. d, Pterodactyl. e, Archaeopteryx. f, Iguanodon. g, Hypsilophodon. h, Nothosaurus. i, Brachiosaurus. j, Kentrosaurus. k, Plesiosaurus. l, Trachodon. m, Hesperornis. n, Henodus. o, Steneosaurus. p, Stenopterygius. q, Eurhinosaurus r, Placodus. s, Mosasaurus. t, Mixosaurus. No. 1499, Herperornis, diff.

1992, June 8 *Perf. 14*

1498	A194	50 le Sheet of 20, #a.-t.	20.00	20.00

Souvenir Sheet

1499	A194	50 le multicolored	2.50	2.50

"Sierra Leone" is 22mm wide on No. 1499.

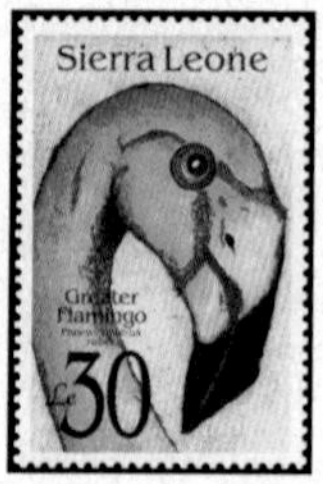

A195

Tropical Birds: 30 le, Greater flamingo. 50 le, White-crested hornbill. 100 le, Verreaux's touraco. 170 le, Yellow-spotted barbet. 200 le, African spoonbill. 250 le, Saddlebill stork. 300 le, Red-headed lovebird. 600 le, Yellow-billed barbet. No. 1508, Fire-bellied woodpecker. No. 1509, Swallow-tailed bee-eater.

1992, July 20 Litho. *Perf. 14*

1500	A195	30 le multi	.40	.40
1501	A195	50 le multi	.65	.65
1502	A195	100 le multi	.80	.80
1503	A195	170 le multi	1.50	1.50
1504	A195	200 le multi	2.40	2.40
1505	A195	250 le multi	2.00	2.00
1506	A195	300 le multi	2.50	2.50
1507	A195	600 le multi	7.50	7.50
		Nos. 1500-1507 (8)	17.75	17.75

Souvenir Sheets

1508	A195	1000 le multi	11.00	11.00
1509	A195	1000 le multi	7.00	7.00

While Nos. 1500-1509 all have the same release date, the value of Nos. 1502-1503, 1505-1506, 1509 was lower when they were released.

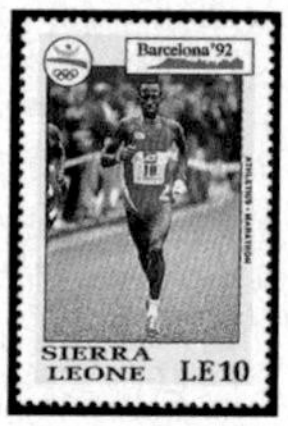

A196

1992 Summer Olympics, Barcelona: 10 le, Marathon. 20 le, Gymnastics, parallel bars. 30 le, Discus. 50 le, 110-meter hurdles, horiz. 60 le, Women's long jump. 100 le, Gymnastics, floor exercise, horiz. 200 le, Windsurfing. 300 le, Road race cycling. 400 le, Weight lifting. 900 le, Soccer, horiz.

1992 Litho. *Perf. 14*

1510	A196	10 le multicolored	.25	.25
1511	A196	20 le multicolored	.25	.25
1512	A196	30 le multicolored	.40	.40
1513	A196	50 le multicolored	.55	.55
1514	A196	60 le multicolored	.75	.75
1515	A196	100 le multicolored	1.25	1.25
1516	A196	200 le multicolored	2.40	2.40
1517	A196	300 le multicolored	3.50	3.50
1518	A196	400 le multicolored	4.75	4.75
		Nos. 1510-1518 (9)	14.10	14.10

Souvenir Sheet

1519	A196	900 le multicolored	8.00	8.00

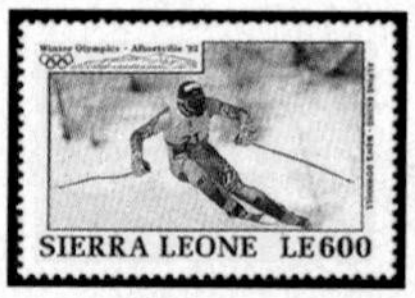

1992 Winter Olympics, Albertville A197

Designs: 250 le, Women's biathlon, vert. 500 le, Speed skating, vert. 600 le, Men's downhill skiing.

Each 900 le: No. 1523, Men's single luge. No. 1524, Ice dancing, vert.

1992, Sept. 8 Litho. *Perf. 14*

1520	A197	250 le multicolored	2.00	2.00
1521	A197	500 le multicolored	4.00	4.00
1522	A197	600 le multicolored	4.75	4.75
		Nos. 1520-1522 (3)	10.75	10.75

Souvenir Sheets

1523-1524	A197	Set of 2	10.00	10.00

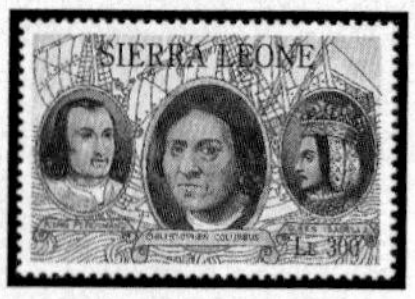

Discovery of America, 500th Anniv. A198

Designs: 300 le, Ferdinand, Isabella, Columbus. 500 le, Landing in New World. 900 le, Columbus, vert.

1992, Oct. Litho. *Perf. 14*

1525	A198	300 le multicolored	2.00	2.00
1526	A198	500 le multicolored	3.00	3.00

Souvenir Sheet

1527	A198	900 le multicolored	4.50	4.50

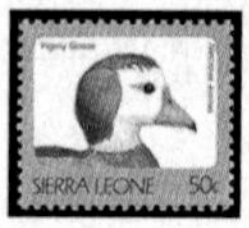

Birds — A199

Designs: 50c, Pygmy goose. 1 le, Spotted eagle owl. 2 le, Verreaux's touraco. 5 le, Saddlebill stork. 10 le, African golden oriole. 20 le, Malachite kingfisher. 30 le, Fire-crowned bishop. 40 le, Fire-bellied woodpecker. 50 le, Red-billed fire-finch. 80 le, Blue fairy flycatcher. 100 le, Crested malimbe. 150 le, Vitelline masked weaver. 170 le, Blue plantain-eater. 200 le, Superb sunbird. 250 le, Swallow-tailed bee-eater. 300 le, Cabani's yellow bunting. 500 le, Crocodile bird. 750 le, White-faced owl. 1000 le, Blue cuckoo-shrike. 2000 le, Bare-headed rock-fowl. 3000 le, Red-tailed buzzard.

No Date Imprint

1992-93 Litho. *Perf. 14x15*

1528	A199	50c multi	.25	.25
1529	A199	1 le multi	.25	.25
1530	A199	2 le multi	.25	.25
1531	A199	5 le multi	.25	.25
1532	A199	10 le multi	.25	.25
1533	A199	20 le multi	.25	.25
1534	A199	30 le multi	.25	.25
1535	A199	40 le multi	.25	.25
1536	A199	50 le multi	.25	.25
a.		Inscribed "1994"	—	—
c.		Inscribed "1997"	—	—
1537	A199	80 le multi	.40	.40
1538	A199	100 le multi	.50	.50
a.		Inscribed "1994"	—	—
b.		Inscribed "1996"	—	—
c.		Inscribed "1997"	—	—
d.		Inscribed "1999"	—	—
e.		Inscribed "2000"	—	—
1539	A199	150 le multi	.80	.80
a.		Inscribed "1994"	—	—
1540	A199	170 le multi	.90	.90
1541	A199	200 le multi	1.00	1.00
a.		Inscribed "1994"	—	—
b.		Inscribed "1996"	—	—
c.		Inscribed "1997"	—	—
d.		Inscribed "1999"	—	—
e.		Inscribed "2000"	—	—
g.		Inscribed "2006"	—	—
1542	A199	250 le multi	1.25	1.25
c.		Inscribed "1997"	—	—
e.		Inscribed "2000"	—	—
f.		Inscribed "2002"	—	—
g.		Inscribed "2006"	—	—
1543	A199	300 le multi	1.90	1.90
a.		Inscribed "1994"	—	—
b.		Inscribed "1996"	—	—
c.		Inscribed "1997"	—	—
d.		Inscribed "1999"	—	—
e.		Inscribed "2000"	—	—
g.		Inscribed "2006"	—	—
1544	A199	500 le multi	3.25	3.25
b.		Inscribed "1996"	—	—
c.		Inscribed "1997"	—	—
e.		Inscribed "2000"	—	—
f.		Inscribed "2002"	—	—
g.		Inscribed "2006"	—	—
1545	A199	750 le multi	4.75	4.75
e.		Inscribed "2000"	—	—
g.		Inscribed "2006"	—	—
1546	A199	1000 le multi	6.25	6.25
b.		Inscribed "1996"	—	—
d.		Inscribed "1999"	—	—
e.		Inscribed "2000"	—	—
f.		Inscribed "2002"	—	—
g.		Inscribed "2006"	—	—
1546A	A199	2000 le multi	19.00	19.00
e.		Inscribed "2000"	—	—
f.		Inscribed "2002"	—	—
g.		Inscribed "2006"	—	—
1546B	A199	3000 le multi	19.00	19.00
b.		Inscribed "1996"	—	—
e.		Inscribed "2000"	—	—
f.		Inscribed "2002"	—	—
g.		Inscribed "2006"	—	—
		Nos. 1528-1546B (21)	61.25	61.25

Issued: #1528-1546, 9/92; #1546A-1546B, 1993.

See Nos. 2152-2155.

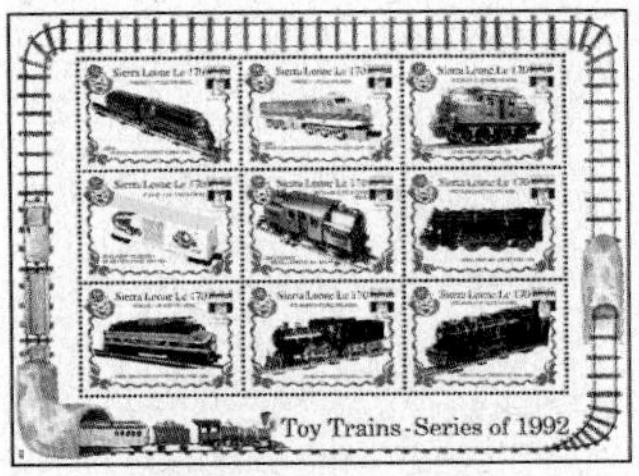

Model Trains — A200

Lionel models: No. 1547a, Pennsylvannia RR GG-1 electric #6-18306, O gauge, 1992. b, Wabash RR Hudson #8610, O gauge, 1985. c, Locomotive #1911, standard gauge, 1911. d, Chesapeake & Ohio 4-4-2 #6-18627, O gauge, 1992. e, Gang car #50, O gauge, 1954. f, #8004, 1980 model of Rock Island & Peoria RR engine built for Columbian Exposition of 1893, O gauge. g, Western Maryland RR Shay #6-18023, O gauge, 1992. h, (Kenner-Parker) Boston & Albany Hudson #784, O gauge, 1986. i, Locomotive #6, standard gauge, 1906.

No. 1548a, Pennsylvania RR Torpedo #238EW, O gauge, 1936. b, Denver & Rio Grande Western Alco Pa No. 6-18107, O gauge, 1992. c, #408E Locomotive, standard gauge, 1930. d, Mickey Mouse 60th birthday boxcar No. 19241, O gauge, 1991. e, Polished brass locomotive, No. 54, standard gauge, 1913. f, Broadway limited #392E, standard gauge, 1936. g, Great Northern RR EP-5 #18302, O gauge, 1988. h, 4-4-0 Locomotive #6, standard gauge, 1918. i, 4-4-4 Locomotive No. 400E, standard gauge, 1933.

No. 1549a, Special F-3 diesel engine, O gauge, 1947. b, Pennsylvania RR GE 44-ton switcher #6-18905, O gauge, 1992. c, #1 trolley, standard gauge, 1913. d, Seaboard RR freight diesel, O gauge, 1958. e, Pennsylvania S-2 turbine, O gauge, 1991. f, Western Pacific RR GP-9 diesel #6-18822, O gauge, 1992. g, #10 with Ives plates transition model, standrad gauge, 1929. h, 4-4-4 locomotive #400E, standard gauge, 1931. i, #384E, standard gauge, 1928.

Each 1000 le: No. 1550, Hudson No. 8210 Special, O gauge. No. 1551, #381E, standard gauge, 1928. No. 1552, 2-Rail electric model #300 trolley with converse body, 2 7/8-inch gauge.

Sheets of 9

1992, Nov. 23 Litho. *Perf. 14*

1547	A200	150 le #a.-i.	12.00	12.00
1548	A200	170 le #a.-i.	14.00	14.00
1549	A200	170 le #a.-i.	14.00	14.00

Souvenir Sheets

Perf. 13

1550-1552	A200	Set of 3	22.50	22.50

Genoa '92 (#1547-1549). Nos. 1550-1552 contains one 51x39mm stamp.

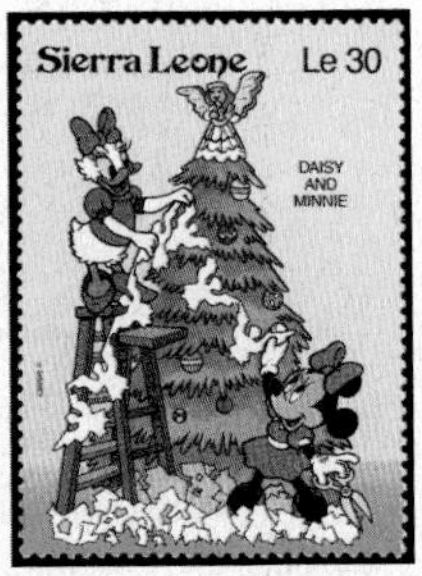

Walt Disney Characters in Christmas Scenes A201

10 le, Minnie & Chip. 20 le, Goofy as Santa. 30 le, Daisy, Minnie. 50 le, Mickey, Goofy. 80 le, Pete. 100 le, Donald Duck. 150 le, Morty & Ferdie. 200 le, Mickey. 300 le, Goofy with ornament. 500 le, Chip & Dale. 600 le, Donald & Dale. 800 le, Huey, Dewey & Louie.

No. 1565, Mickey Mouse. No. 1566, Angel with Chip, horiz. No. 1567, Mickey & Minnie, horiz.

1992, Nov. 16 *Perf. 13½x14*

1553	A201	10 le multi	.25	.25
1554	A201	20 le multi	.25	.25
1555	A201	30 le multi	.25	.25
1556	A201	50 le multi	.35	.35
1557	A201	80 le multi	.55	.55
1558	A201	100 le multi	.70	.70
1559	A201	150 le multi	1.10	1.10
1560	A201	200 le multi	1.40	1.40
1561	A201	300 le multi	2.25	2.25
1562	A201	500 le multi	3.50	3.50
1563	A201	600 le multi	5.00	5.00
1564	A201	800 le multi	6.00	6.00
		Nos. 1553-1564 (12)	21.60	21.60

Souvenir Sheets

1565	A201	900 le multi	6.75	6.75

Perf. 14x13½

1566	A201	900 le multi	6.75	6.75
1567	A201	900 le multi	6.75	6.75

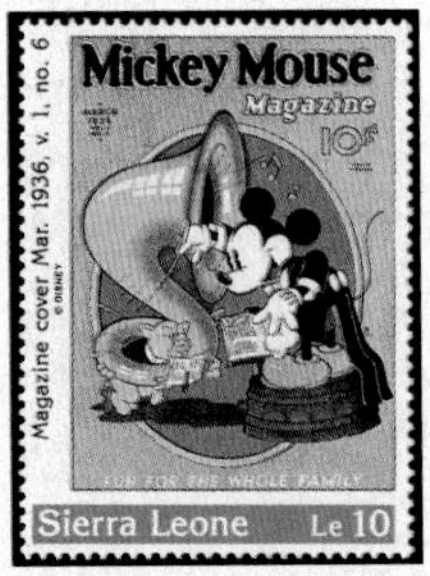

Mickey Mouse Magazines and Books A202

10 le, Magazine cover, Mar. 1936, v. 1, #6. 20 le, Magazine cover, June 1936, v. 1, #9. 30 le, Magazine cover, Nov. 1936, v. 2, #2. 40 le, Magazine cover, Aug. 1937, v. 2, #11. 50 le, Magazine cover, Oct. 1937, v. 2, #13. 60 le, Magazine cover, Dec. 1937, v. 3, #3. 70 le, Magazine cover, Jan. 1938, v. 3, #4. 150 le, Cover, Big Book #4062, 1935. 170 le, Story book cover, 1936. 200 le, Comic book cover, unnumbered. 300 le, Comic book cover, No. 181. 400 le, Comic book cover #194. 500 le, Story book cover, Book 1, 1931. No. 1581, Boys' and Girls' March of Comics cover, 1948. No. 1582, First Mickey Mouse Magazine cover for June-Aug. 1935, v. 1, #1, horiz. No. 1583, Cover of early Mickey Mouse story book published in England, 1933, horiz.

1992 *Perf. 13½x14*

1568	A202	10 le multicolored	.25	.25
1569	A202	20 le multicolored	.25	.25
1570	A202	30 le multicolored	.25	.25
1571	A202	40 le multicolored	.25	.25
1572	A202	50 le multicolored	.30	.30
1573	A202	60 le multicolored	.35	.35
1574	A202	70 le multicolored	.40	.40
1575	A202	150 le multicolored	.80	.80
1576	A202	170 le multicolored	1.10	1.10
1577	A202	200 le multicolored	1.25	1.25
1578	A202	300 le multicolored	1.90	1.90
1579	A202	400 le multicolored	2.40	2.40
1580	A202	500 le multicolored	3.25	3.25
		Nos. 1568-1580 (13)	12.75	12.75

Souvenir Sheets

1581	A202	900 le multicolored	5.50	5.50

Perf. 14x13½

1582	A202	900 le multicolored	5.50	5.50
1583	A202	900 le multicolored	5.50	5.50

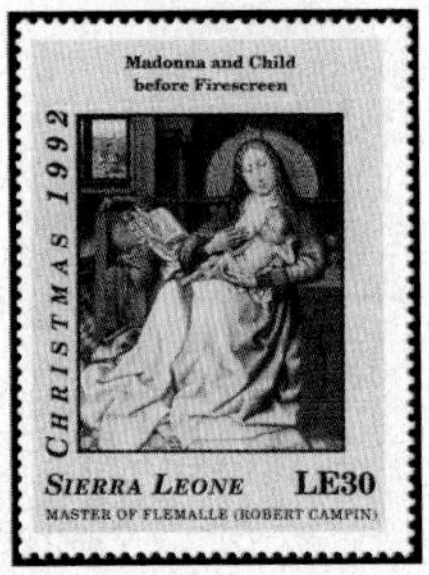

Christmas A203

Details or entire paintings: 1 le, Virgin and Child, by Fiorenzo di Lorenzo. 10 le, Madonna and Child on a Wall, by Circle of Dirk Bouts. 20 le, Virgin and Child with the Flight into Egypt, by Master of Hoogstraeten. 30 le, Madonna and Child before Firescreen, by Master of Flemalle. 50 le, Mary in a Rose Garden, by Hans Memling. 100 le, Virgin Mary and Child, by Lucas Cranach the Elder. 170 le, Virgin and Child, by Rogier van der Weyden. 200 le, Madonna and Saints, by Perugino. 250 le, Madonna Enthroned with Saints Catherine and Barbara, by Master of Hoogstraeten. 300 le, The Virgin in a Rose Arbor, by Stefan Lochner. 500 le, Madonna and Child with Angels, by Sandro Botticelli. 1000 le, Madonna and Child with Young St. John the Baptist, by Fra Bartolemmeo.

Each 900 le: No. 1596, The Virgin with the Green Cushion, by Andrea Solario. No. 1597, The Virgin and Child, by Jan Gossaert. No. 1598, The Virgin and Child, by Lucas Cranach the Younger.

1992, Dec. 7 Litho. *Perf. 13½x14*

1584	A203	1 le multi	.25	.25
1585	A203	10 le multi	.25	.25
1586	A203	20 le multi	.25	.25
1587	A203	30 le multi	.25	.25
1588	A203	50 le multi	.40	.40
1589	A203	100 le multi	.70	.70
1590	A203	170 le multi	1.25	1.25
1591	A203	200 le multi	1.40	1.40
1592	A203	250 le multi	1.75	1.75
1593	A203	300 le multi	2.25	2.25
1594	A203	500 le multi	3.75	3.75
1595	A203	1000 le multi	7.25	7.25
		Nos. 1584-1595 (12)	19.75	19.75

Souvenir Sheets

1596-1598	A203	Set of 3	20.00	20.00

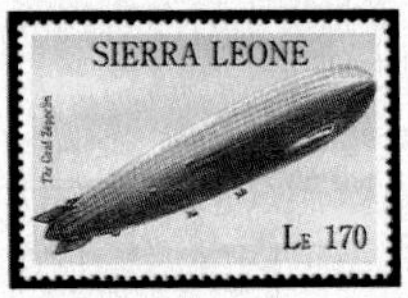

Anniversaries and Events A204

150 le, Emblems of FAO, ICN, WHO. No. 1600, Graf Zeppelin. No. 1601, Cow, emblems, grain stalk. 200 le, Starving child. No. 1603, Lions Intl. emblem, map. No. 1604, Cottonwood tree. 300 le, African elephant. 600 le, Space Shuttle. 700 le, Graf Zeppelin LZ 127, specifications.

Each 900 le: No. 1608, Astronaut. No. 1609, Count Zeppelin.

1992, Dec. Litho. *Perf. 14*

1599	A204	150 le multicolored	.65	.65
1600	A204	170 le multicolored	.75	.75
1601	A204	170 le multicolored	.75	.75
1602	A204	200 le multicolored	1.05	1.05
1603	A204	250 le multicolored	1.05	1.05
1604	A204	250 le multicolored	1.20	1.20
1605	A204	300 le multicolored	1.50	1.50
1606	A204	600 le multicolored	2.25	2.25
1607	A204	700 le multicolored	2.50	2.50
		Nos. 1599-1607 (9)	11.70	11.70

Souvenir Sheets

1608-1609	A204	Set of 2	8.50	8.50

Intl. Conference on Nutrition, Rome (#1599, 1601). Count Zeppelin, 75th anniv. of death (#1600, 1607, 1609). World Health Organization (#1602). Lions Intl., 75th anniv. (#1603). Earth Summit, Rio de Janeiro (#1604-1605). Intl. Space Year (#1606, 1608).

Miniature Sheet

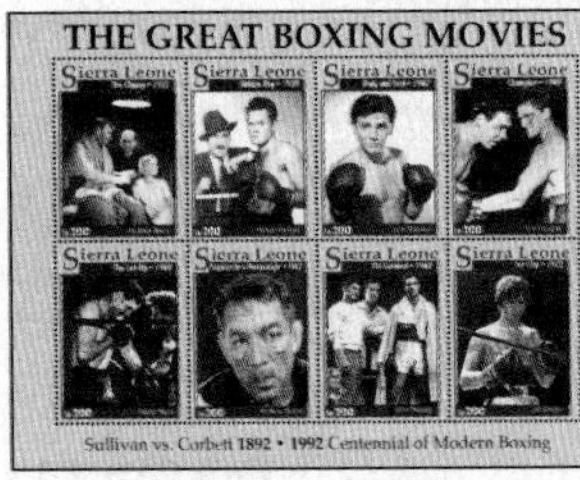

Boxing — A205

Boxing movies, stars, each 200 le: No. 1610a, The Champ, Wallace Beery. b, Golden Boy, William Holden. c, Body and Soul, John Garfield. d, Champion, Kirk Douglas. e, The Set-Up, Robert Ryan. f. Requiem for a Heavyweight, Anthony Quinn. g, Kid Galahad, Elvis Presley. h, Fat City, Jeff Bridges.

Boxing champions, each 200 le: No. 1611a, Joe Louis. b, Archie Moore. c, Muhammad Ali. d, George Foreman. e, Joe Frazier. f, Marvin Hagler. g, Sugar Ray Leonard. h, Evander Holyfield.

Each 1000 le: No. 1612, Gentlemen Jim, Errol Flynn. No. 1613, Muhammad Ali, diff. No. 1614, Rocky III, Sylvester Stallone.

1993, Feb. 8 Litho. *Perf. 13½x14*

1610	A205	Sheet of 8, #a.-h.	10.50	10.50
1611	A205	Sheet of 8, #a.-h.	10.50	10.50

Souvenir Sheets

1612-1614	A205	Set of 3	17.00	17.00

Miniature Sheets

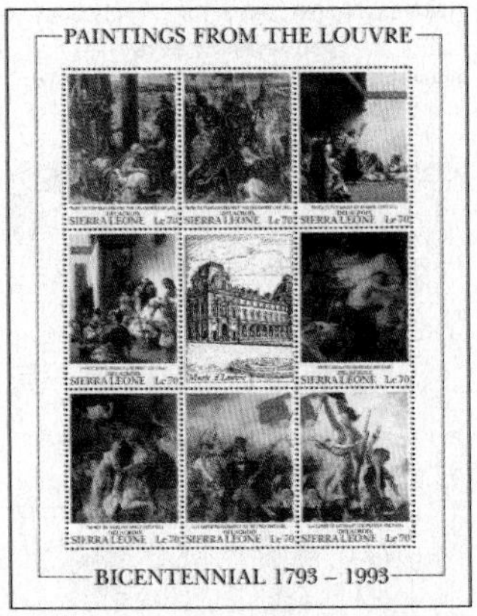

Louvre Museum, Bicent. — A206

Details or entire paintings by Eugene Delacroix (1798-1863): Nos. 1615a-1615b, Entry of the Crusaders into Constantinople (left, right). c-d, Jews Purchasing Brides in Morocco (left, right). e-f, The Death of Sardanapalus (left, right). g-h, Liberty Guiding the People (left, right).

No. 1616a, An Orphan at the Cemetery. b-c, Women of Algiers in their Apartment (left, right). d, Dante and Virgil in the Infernal Regions. e, Self-Portrait. f-g, Massacre at Chios (left, right). h, Frederic Chopin.

No. 1617, Rape of the Sabine Women, by Jacques-Louis David (1748-1825).

1993, Mar. 8 Litho. *Perf. 12x12½*

1615	A206	70 le Sheet of 8, #a.-h. + label	6.00	6.00
1616	A206	70 le Sheet of 8, #a.-h. + label	6.00	6.00

Souvenir Sheet

Perf. 14½

1617	A206	900 le multicolored	8.00	8.00

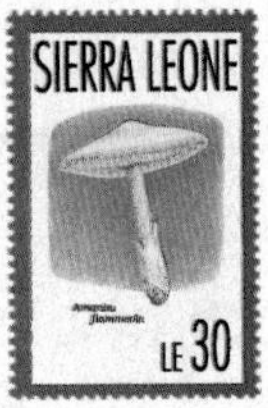

Mushrooms — A207

Designs: 30 le, Amanita flammeola. 50 le, Cantharellus pseudocibarius. 100 le, Volvariella volvacea. 200 le, Termitomyces microcarpus. 300 le, Auricularia auricula. 400 le, Pleurotus tuberregium. 500 le, Schizophyllum commune. 600 le, Termitomyces robustus.

Each 1000 le: No. 1626, Phallus rubicundus. No. 1627, Daldina concentrica.

1993, May 5 *Perf. 14*

1618	A207	30 le multi	.25	.25
1619	A207	50 le multi	.25	.25
1620	A207	100 le multi	.50	.50
1621	A207	200 le multi	1.00	1.00
1622	A207	300 le multi	1.50	1.50
1623	A207	400 le multi	2.00	2.00
1624	A207	500 le multi	2.50	2.50
1625	A207	600 le multi	3.25	3.25
		Nos. 1618-1625 (8)	11.25	11.25

Souvenir Sheets

1626-1627	A207	Set of 2	15.00	15.00

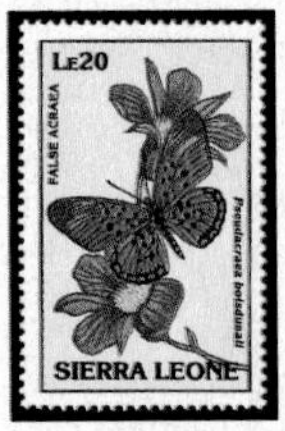

Butterflies — A208

20 le, False acraea. 30 le, Blue temora. 50 le, Foxy charaxes. 100 le, Leaf blue. 150 le, Blue-banded swallowtail. 170 le, African monarch. 200 le, Mountain beauty. 250 le, Gaudy commodore. 300 le, Palla butterfly. 500 le, Pirate butterfly. 600 le, Painted lady. 700 le, Gold-banded forester.

Each 1000 le: No. #1640, Blue diadem. #1641, Blue swallowtail. #1642, African leaf butterfly.

1993, May 5
1628-1639 A208   Set of 12   15.00 15.00
Souvenir Sheets
1640-1642 A208   Set of 3   14.00 14.00

Miniature Sheets

Cats — A209

Designs, each 150 le: No. 1643a, Somali. b, Egyptian Mau smoke. c, Chocolate-point Siamese. d, Mi-Ke Japanese bobtail. e, Chinchilla. f, Red Burmese. g, British shorthair brown tabby. h, Blue Persian. i, British silver classic tabby. j, Oriental ebony. k, Red Persian. l, British calico shorthair.
Each 150 le: No. 1644a, Black Persian. b, Blue-point Siamese. c, American wirehair. d, Birman. e, Scottish fold (silver tabby). f, American shorthair red tabby. g, Blue & white Persian bicolor. h, Havana brown. i, Norwegian forest cat. j, Brown tortie Burmese. k. Angora. l, Exotic shorthair.
Each 1000 le: No. 1645, American shorthair blue tabby, horiz. No. 1646, Seal-point colorpoint, horiz.

1993, May 17   Litho.   **Perf. 14**
1643 A209   Sheet of 12, #a.-l.   15.00 15.00
1644 A209   Sheet of 12, #a.-l.   15.00 15.00
Souvenir Sheets
1645-1646 A209   Set of 2   16.00 16.00

Nos. 1643-1646 Ovptd. with Hong Kong '94 Emblem

1994   **Perf. 14**
1643m   On #1643b & in sheet margin   9.50 9.50
1644m   On #1644b & in sheet margin   9.50 9.50
1645a   Ovptd. in sheet margin   5.25 5.25
1646a   Ovptd. in sheet margin   5.25 5.25

Wild Animals
A210

30 le, Gorilla. 100 le, Bongo. 150 le, Potto. 170 le, Chimpanzee. 200 le, Dwarf galago. 300 le, African linsang. 500 le, Banded duiker. 750 le, Diana monkey.
No. 1655, Leopard. No. 1656, Elephant.

1993, June 17
1647 A210   30 le multi   .25   .25
1648 A210   100 le multi   .50   .50
1649 A210   150 le multi   .75   .75
1650 A210   170 le multi   .85   .85
1651 A210   200 le multi   .95   .95
1652 A210   300 le multi   1.50 1.50
1653 A210   500 le multi   2.75 2.75
1654 A210   750 le multi   4.00 4.00
    Nos. 1647-1654 (8)   11.55 11.55
Souvenir Sheets
1655 A210   1200 le multi   7.00 7.00
1656 A210   1200 le multi   7.00 7.00

Flowers
A211

30 le, Bleeding-heart vine. 40 le, Passion vine. 50 le, Hydrangea. 60 le, Wax begonia. 100 le, Hibiscus. 150 le, Crape-myrtle. 170 le, Bougainvillea. 200 le, Leadwort. 250 le, Gerbera daisy. 300 le, Black-eyed susan. 500 le, Gloriosa lily. 900 le, Sweet violet.
Each 1200 le: #1669, Gloriosa lily, diff. #1670, Passion vine, diff. #1671, Hibiscus, diff.

1993, July 15   Litho.   **Perf. 14**
1657 A211   30 le multi   .25   .25
1658 A211   40 le multi   .25   .25
1659 A211   50 le multi   .25   .25
1660 A211   60 le multi   .25   .25
1661 A211   100 le multi   .55   .55
1662 A211   150 le multi   .90   .90
1663 A211   170 le multi   1.00 1.00
1664 A211   200 le multi   1.10 1.10
1665 A211   250 le multi   1.40 1.40
1666 A211   300 le multi   1.75 1.75
1667 A211   500 le multi   2.75 2.75
1668 A211   900 le multi   3.50 3.50
    Nos. 1657-1668 (12)   13.95 13.95
Souvenir Sheets
1669-1671 A211   Set of 3   18.00 18.00

Coronation of Queen Elizabeth II, 40th Anniv. — A212

100 le, Queen, Princess Anne. 200 le, Coronation procession. 600 le, Official coronation photograph. 1500 le, Portrait, by Pietro Annigoni, 1954-55.

1993, Oct.   Litho.   **Perf. 14**
1672 A212   100 le multi   .45   .45
1673 A212   200 le multi   1.10 1.10
1674 A212   600 le multi   3.75 3.75
    Nos. 1672-1674 (3)   5.30 5.30
Souvenir Sheet
1675 A212   1500 le multi   11.50 11.50

Copernicus (1473-1543) — A213

250 le, Early telescope. 800 le, Moon's surface.

1993, Oct.
1676 A213   250 le multicolored   1.50 1.50
1677 A213   800 le multicolored   5.00 5.00

Picasso (1881-1973) — A214

Sculpture: 170 le, Woman with Hat, 1961. Paintings: 200 le, Buste de Femme, 1958. 800 le, Maya with a Doll, 1938. 1000 le, Women of Algiers (after Delacroix), 1955.

1993, Oct.
1678 A214   170 le multicolored   1.00 1.00
1679 A214   200 le multicolored   1.10 1.10
1680 A214   800 le multicolored   5.00 5.00
    Nos. 1678-1680 (3)   7.10 7.10
Souvenir Sheet
1681 A214   1000 le multicolored   6.50 6.50

Christmas
A215

Details or entire paintings, by Raphael: 50 le, 100 le, 1200 le (No. 1690), Madonna of the Fish. 150 le, Madonna & Child Enthroned with Five Saints. 800 le, The Holy Family with the Lamb.
Details or entire woodcuts, by Durer: 200 le, 250 le, 300 le, The Circumcision. 500 le, 1200 le (No. 1691), Holy Clan with Saints and Two Angels Playing Music.

1993, Dec.   **Perf. 13½x14**
1682 A215   50 le multi   .25   .25
1683 A215   100 le multi   .40   .40
1684 A215   150 le multi   .65   .65
1685 A215   200 le multi   1.00 1.00
1686 A215   250 le multi   1.20 1.20
1687 A215   300 le multi   1.40 1.40
1688 A215   500 le multi   2.40 2.40
1689 A215   800 le multi   4.00 4.00
    Nos. 1682-1689 (8)   11.30 11.30
Souvenir Sheets
1690-1691 A215   Set of 2   12.00 12.00

Christmas
A216

Disney characters celebrate Christmas: different.
Each 1200 le: #1700, Santa. #1701, Elves, horiz. #1702, Santa, horiz. #1703, Mickey, Minnie, horiz.

1993, Dec. 17   **Perf. 13½x14**
1692 A216   50 le multi   .25   .25
1693 A216   100 le multi   .50   .50
1694 A216   170 le multi   .90   .90
1695 A216   200 le multi   1.00 1.00
1696 A216   250 le multi   1.40 1.40
1697 A216   500 le multi   2.75 2.75
1698 A216   600 le multi   3.25 3.25
1699 A216   900 le multi   4.50 4.50
    Nos. 1692-1699 (8)   14.55 14.55
Souvenir Sheets
Perf. 13½x14, 14x13½
1700-1703 A216   Set of 4   24.00 24.00

1994 World Cup Soccer Championships, US — A217

Players, country: 30 le, Jose Luis Brown (R), Argentina. 50 le, Gary Lineker, England. 100 le, Carlos Valderrama, Colombia. 250 le, Skuhravy, Czechoslovakia. 300 le, Marchena, Costa Rica. 300 le, Butragueno, Spain. 400 le, Roger Milla, Cameroun. 500 le, Roberto Donadoni, Italy. 700 le, Enzo Scifo, Belgium.
Each 1200 le: No. 1712, 1200 le, Socrates, Brazil. No. 1713, 1200 le, Wright, England; Demol, Belgium.

1993   **Perf. 13½x14**
1704-1711 A217   Set of 8   12.00 12.00
Souvenir Sheets
1712-1713 A217   Set of 2   18.00 18.00

A218

Hong Kong '94 — A219

Stamps and: No. 1714, Hong Kong #455, pagoda, Tiger Baum Garden. No. 1715, Ai Par Garden, #1084.
Carved lacquer, Qing Dynasty: No. 1716a, Bowl with "Wan-Sui-Ch'ang-Chun." b, Four-wheeled box. c, Flower container. d, Box with human figure design. e, Shishi dog (not lacquer). f, Persimmon.

1994, Feb. 18   Litho.   **Perf. 14**
1714   200 le multicolored   1.00 1.00
1715   200 le multicolored   1.00 1.00
  a.   A218 Pair, #1714-1715   2.00 2.00
Miniature Sheet
1716 A219   100 le Sheet of 6,   #a.-f.   6.50 6.50

Nos. 1714-1715 issued in sheets of 5 pairs. No. 1715a is a continuous design.
New Year 1994 (Year of the Dog) (#1716e).

Miniature Sheet

New Year 1994 (Year of the Dog) — A220

a, 100 le, Pekingese. b, 150 le, Doberman pinscher. c, 200 le, Tibetan terrier. d, 250 le, Weimaraner. e, 400 le, Rottweiler. f, 500 le, Akita. g, 600 le, Schnauzer. h, 1000 le, Tibetan spaniel.
Each 1200 le: No. 1718, Wire-haired pointing Griffon. No. 1719, Shih Tzu.

1994, June 20   Litho.   **Perf. 14**
1717 A220   Sheet of 8, #a.-h.   14.50 14.50
Souvenir Sheets
1718-1719 A220   Set of 2   11.50 11.50

D-Day, 50th Anniv.
A221

Designs: 500 le, British paratroops drop behind enemy lines. 750 le, US paratrooper jumps from C47 transport.
1000 le, C47 Douglas Dakota, paratroops.

1994, July 11   Litho.   **Perf. 14**
1720 A221   500 le multicolored   2.25 2.25
1721 A221   750 le multicolored   3.25 3.25
Souvenir Sheet
1722 A221   1000 le multicolored   6.00 6.00

A222

PHILAKOREA
'94 — A223

100 le, Traditional wedding, Korea House, Seoul. 400 le, Royal tombs, Koryo Dynasty, Kaesong. 600 le, Terraced farm land, near Chungmu.

Tiger paintings, Choson Dynasty: No. 1726: a, Tiger, cubs, 19th cent. b, Munsa-pasal seated on lion. c, Extinct Korean tiger. d, Tiger, bamboo. e, Tiger guarding 3 cubs, 4 magpies. f, Tiger, 19th cent. g, Mountain Spirit. h, Tiger, bird in tree.

No. 1727, Wall painting of mounted hunters from Tomb of the Dancers of Kungnaesong, Koguryo period.

Perf. 14, 13½ (#1726)

1994, July 11			**Litho.**	
1723-1725	A222	Set of 3	6.00	6.00
Miniature Sheet of 8				
1726	A223	200 le #a.-h.	7.00	7.00
Souvenir Sheet				
1727	A222	1200 le multi	10.00	10.00

Miniature Sheets of 6

First Manned Moon Landing, 25th Anniv. — A224

No. 1728, each 200 le: a, Edwin E. Aldrin, Jr. b, Michael Collins. c, Neil A. Armstrong. d, Apollo 11 liftoff. e, Aldrin descending to lunar surface. f, Armstrong, lunar module Eagle reflected in Aldrin's face shield.

No. 1729, each 200 le: a, Aldrin gathering soil samples. b, Eagle with Aldrin deploying solar wind experiment. c, Aldrin, ALSEP & Eagle at Tranquility Base. d, US flag, Aldrin, Tranquility Base. e, Plaque on moon. f, Apollo 11 crew, stamp ceremony.

1000 le, First footprint on moon.

Sheets of 6, #a-f

1994, July 11			**Perf. 14**	
1728-1729	A224	Set of 2	9.00	9.00
Souvenir Sheet				
1730	A224	1000 le multicolored	6.00	6.00

Miniature Sheet of 6

A225

1994 World Cup Soccer Championships, U.S. — A226

Players: No. 1731a, Kim Ho, South Korea. b, Cobi Jones, U.S. c, Claudio Suarez, Mexico. d, Tomas Brolin, Sweden. e, Ruud Gullit, Netherlands. f, Andreas Herzog, Austria.

Each 1500 le: No. 1732, Sierra Leone team. No. 1733, Giants Stadium, New Jersey.

1994, July 15

1731	A225	250 le #a.-f.	8.50	8.50
Souvenir Sheets				
1732-1733	A226	Set of 2	13.00	13.00

Birds — A227

250 le, Black kite. 300 le, Superb sunbird. 500 le, Martial eagle. 800 le, Red bishop.

No. 1738 - White-necked picathartes: a, 50 le, Feeding young. b, 100 le, On brown tree limb. c, 150 le, Two at nest. d, 200 le, On gray limb, green leaves.

No. 1739, 1200 le, Greater flamingo, vert. No. 1740, 1200 le, White-necked picathartes up close, vert.

1994, Aug. 10

1734-1737	A227	Set of 4	11.00	11.00
1738	A227	Vert. Strip of 4, #a.-d.	5.00	5.00
Souvenir Sheets				
1739-1740	A227	Set of 2	15.00	15.00

World Wildlife Fund (#1738). For surcharge see No. 2903.

Orchids — A228

Designs: 50 le, Aerangis kotschyana. 100 le, Brachycorythis kalbreyeri. 150 le, Diaphananthe pellucida. 200 le, Eulophia guineensis. 300 le, Eurychone rothschildana. 500 le, Tridactyle tridactylites. 750 le, Cyrtorchis arcuata. 900 le, Ancistrochilus rothschildianus.

Each 1500 le: No. 1749, Plectrelminthus caudatus. No. 1750, Polystachaya affinis.

1994, Sept. 1

1741-1748	A228	Set of 8	17.00	17.00
Souvenir Sheets				
1749-1750	A228	Set of 2	15.00	15.00

Christmas A229

Details or entire paintings: 50 le, The Birth of the Virgin, by Murillo. 100 le, Education of the Virgin, by Murillo. 150 le, Annunciation, by Filippino Lippi. 200 le, Marriage of the Virgin, by Bernard van Orley. 250 le, The Visitation, by Nicolas Vleughels. 300 le, Holy Infant from Castelfranco altarpiece, by Giorgione. 400 le, Adoration of the Magi, Workshop of Bartholome Zeitblom. 600 le, Presentation of Infant Jesus in the Temple, by Memling.

Each 1500 le: No. 1759, Nativity Altarpiece, by Lorenzo Monado. No. 1760, Allendale Nativity, by Giorgione.

1994, Dec. 1   Litho.   Perf. 13½x14

1751-1758	A229	Set of 8	9.00	9.00
Souvenir Sheets				
1759-1760	A229	Set of 2	11.00	11.00

Intl. Year of the Family A230

1994, Dec. 20   Litho.   Perf. 14

1761	A230	300 le Working in field	1.25	1.25
1762	A230	350 le At beach	1.40	1.40

Disney Christmas — A231

Designs: 50 le, Mickey's Christmas cat. 100 le, Goofy's Christmas tree, vert. 150 le, Daisy's Christmas gift. 200 le, Donald's Christmas surprise, vert. 250 le, Minnie's Christmas flight. 300 le, Goofy's Christmas snowball, vert. 400 le, Goofy's Christmas letters. 500 le, Christmas sled ride, vert. 600 le, Mickey's Christmas snowman. 800 le, Pluto's Christmas treat, vert.

Each 1500 le: No. 1773, Goofy hanging outdoor lights. No. 1774, Mickey asleep in chair, vert.

Perf. 14x13½, 13½x14

1995, Jan. 23			**Litho.**	
1763-1772	A231	Set of 10	13.00	13.00
Souvenir Sheets				
1773-1774	A231	Set of 2	12.00	12.00

Donald Duck's Gallery of Old Masters A232

Name of painting, inspiration: 50 le, Madonna Duck, Leonardo da Vinci. 100 le, Portrait of a Venetian Duck, Tintoretto. 150 le, Duck with a Glove, Frans Hals. 200 le, Donald with a Pink, Quentin Massys. 250 le, Pinkie Daisy, Sir Thomas Lawrence. 300 le, Donald's Whistling Mother, Whistler. 400 le, El Quacko, El Greco. 500 le, The Noble Snob, Rembrandt. 600 le, The Blue Duck, by Gainsborough. 800 le, Modern Quack, Picasso.

Each 1500 le: No. 1785, Soup's On, Brueghel. No. 1786, Duck Dancers, Degas, horiz.

1995, Jan. 23   Perf. 13½x14, 14x13½

1775-1784	A232	Set of 10	11.00	11.00
Souvenir Sheets				
1785-1786	A232	Set of 2	11.00	11.00

Miniature Sheets of 12

Olympic Medal Winners — A233

Summer Olympics: No. 1787a, Ragnar Lundberg, 1952 men's pole vault. b, Karin Janz, 1972 all-round gymnastics. c, Matthias Volz, 1936 gymnastics. d, Carl Lewis, 1988 long jump. e, Sara Simeoni, 1976 high jump. f, Daley Thompson, 1980 decathlon. g, Japan vs. Britain, 1964 soccer. h, Gabriella Dorio, 1984 1500-meters run. i, Daniela Hunger, 1988 200-meters individual medley swimming. j, Kyoko Iwasaki, 1992 200-meters breast stroke. k, Italian team member, 1960 water

polo. l, David Wilkie, 1976 200-meters breast stroke.

1994 Winter Olympics, Lillehammer: No. 1788a, Katja Seizinger, downhill skiing. b, Hot air balloon (no medalist). c, Elvis Stojko, figure skating. d, Jens Weissflog, individual large hill ski jump. e, Bjorn Daehlie, 10k cross-country skiing. f, Germany, four-man bobsled. g, Markus Wasmeier, men's super giant slalom. h, Georg Hackl, luge. i, Trovill & Dean, ice dancing. j, Bonnie Blair, speed skating. k, Nancy Kerrigan, figure skating. l, Team Sweden, hockey.

Each 1000 le: No. 1789, torchbearer, horiz. No. 1790, Oksana Baiul, Nancy Kerrigan, Chen Lu, 1994 figure skating, horiz.

1995, Feb. 6   Litho.   Perf. 14

1787	A233	75 le #a.-l.	3.50	3.50
1788	A233	200 le #a.-l.	8.50	8.50
Souvenir Sheets				
1789-1790	A233	Set of 2	8.00	8.00

Miniature Sheets

Dinosaurs — A234

No. 1791, each 200 le: a, Ceratosaurus (d). b, Brachiosaurus. c, Pteranodon (b). d, Stegoceras. e, Saurolophus (h). f, Ornithomumus. g, Compsognathus (j). h, Deinonychus (i). i, Ornitholestes. j, Archaeopteryx. k, Heterodontosaurus (l). l, Lesothosaurus.

No. 1792: a, 100 le, Triceratops. b, 250 le, Protoceratops (c). c, 400 le, Monoclonius (b). d, 800 le, Styracosaurus (c).

Each 2500 le: No. 1793, Deinonychus. No. 1794, Rhamphorynchus.

1995, May 4   Litho.   Perf. 14

1791	A234	Sheet of 12, #a.-l.	8.00	8.00
1792	A234	Sheet of 4, #a.-d.	5.25	5.25
Souvenir Sheets				
1793-1794	A234	Set of 2	12.00	12.00

Sierra Club, Cent. A235

No. 1795, vert, each 150 le: a, L'Hoest's guenon. b, Black-footed cat. c, Colobus monkey up close. d, Colobus monkey in tree. e, Mandrill facing forward. f, Bonobo with young. g, Bonobo lying down. h, Mandrill facing right. i, Colobus monkey standing.

No. 1796, each 150 le: a, Black-faced impala facing forward. b, Herd of black-faced impala. c, Black-faced impala drinking. d, Bonobo. e, Black-footed cat. f, Black-footed cat up close. g, L'Hoest's guenon. h, L'Hoest's guenon, seated. i, Mandrills.

1995, May 10   Sheets of 9, #a-i

1795-1796	A235	Set of 2	11.00	11.00

Nos. 1795-1796 exist imperf. Value, set of 2, $25.

New Year 1995 (Year of the Boar) — A236

Stylized boars, each 100 le: No. 1797a, red & multi, facing left. b, green & multi, facing right. c, green & multi, facing left. d, red & multi, facing right.

500 le, Two boars, vert.

1995, May 8   **Litho.**   ***Perf. 14***
1797 A236   Block of 4, #a.-d.   6.00 6.00
Souvenir Sheet
1798 A236   500 le multicolored   8.00 8.00

Singapore
'95 — A237

Marine life, each 300 le: No. 1799a, Pufferfish. b, Coral grouper. c, Hawksbill turtle. d, Hogfish. e, Emperor angelfish. f, Butterflyfish. g, Lemon butterflyfish. h, Parrotfish. i, Moray eel.
Water birds, marine life, each 300 le: No. 1800a, Cape pigeons. b, Pelican. c, Puffin. d, Humpback whale. e, Greater shearwater. f, Bottlenose dolphin. g, Gurnard. h, Salmon. i, John dory.
Each 1500 le: #1801, Surgeonfish. #1802, Angelfish, vert.

1995   **Sheets of 9, #a-i**
1799-1800 A237   Set of 2   20.00 20.00
Souvenir Sheets
1801-1802 A237   Set of 2   12.00 12.00

Miniature Sheets of 6 or 8

A238

End of World War II, 50th
Anniv. — A239

No. 1803: a, USS Idaho. b, HMS Ark Royal. c, Admiral Graf Spee. d, Destroyer. e, HMS Nelson. f, PT 109. g, USS Iowa. h, Bismark.
No. 1804: a, B-17. b, B-25. c, B-24 Liberator. d, USS Missouri. e, A-20 Boston. f, Pennsylvania, Colorado, Louisville, Portland, Columbia enter Lingayen Gulf.
No. 1805, HMS Indomitable launching aircraft. No. 1806, B-29 bomber.

1995, July 10
1803 A238   250 le #a.-h. + label   8.00 8.00
1804 A239   300 le #a.-f. + label   8.00 8.00
Souvenir Sheet
1805 A238   1500 le multi   4.75 4.75
1806 A239   1500 le multi   6.50 6.50
No. 1805 contains one 57x42mm stamp.

UN, 50th
Anniv. — A240

No. 1807: a, 300 le, Dais, UN General Assembly. 400 le, Sec. Gen. U. Thant. 500 le, UN building, dove.
1500 le, Sec. Gen. Dag Hammarskjold.

1995, July 10   **Litho.**   ***Perf. 14***
1807 A240   Strip of 3, #a.-c.   3.50 3.50
Souvenir Sheet
1808 A240   1500 le multicolored   4.25 4.25
No. 1807 is a continuous design.

1995 Boy
Scout
Jamboree,
Holland
A241

No. 1809: a, 400 le, Natl. flag. b, 500 le, Lord Baden-Powell. c, 600 le, Scout sign.
1500 le, Scout salute.

1995, July 10
1809 A241   Strip of 3, #a.-c.   4.50 4.50
Souvenir Sheet
1810 A241   1500 le multicolored   4.50 4.50

Queen
Mother, 95th
Birthday
A242

No. 1811: a, Drawing. b, Holding bouquet of flowers. c, Formal portrait. d, Without hat.
1500 le, Blue hat, dress.

1995, July 10   ***Perf. 13½x14***
1811 A242   400 le Block or strip of 4, #a.-d.   5.00 5.00
Souvenir Sheet
1812 A242   1500 le multicolored   4.75 4.75
No. 1811 was issued in sheets of 8 stamps.
For surcharges see Nos. 2544-2545.

FAO, 50th
Anniv.
A243

No. 1813: a, 300 le, Man working with sack of food. b, 400 le, Boy carrying bundle of sticks on head. c, 500 le, Woman holding bowl of fruit.
1500 le, Woman holding baby, vert.

1995, July 10   ***Perf. 14***
1813 A243   Strip of 3, #a.-c.   3.50 3.50
Souvenir Sheet
1814 A243   1500 le multicolored   4.00 4.00

Rotary Intl.,
90th Anniv.
A244

Designs: 500 le, Natl. flag, Rotary emblem. 1000 le, Paul Harris, Rotary emblem.

1995, July 10
1815 A244   500 le multicolored   2.50 2.50
Souvenir Sheet
1816 A244   1000 le multicolored   3.75 3.75

Singapore
'95 — A245

Flora & fauna, each 300 le: No. 1817a, African tulip tree. b, Senegal bush locust. c, Killifish. d, Bird of paradise. e, Mandrill. f, Painted reed frog. g, Large spotted acraea. h, Carmine bee-eater.
No. 1818, each 300 le: a, Flame lily. b, Grants gazelle. c, Dogbane. d, Gold-banded forester. e, Horned chameleon. f, Malachite kingfisher. g, Leaf beetle. h, Acanthus.
Each 1500 le: No. 1819, Lion. No. 1820, African elephant.

1995, Sept. 5   **Litho.**   ***Perf. 14***
   Sheets of 8, #a-h
1817-1818 A245   Set of 2   24.00 24.00
Souvenir Sheets
1819-1820 A245   Set of 2   9.00 9.00

Third UN Decade for
Advancement of
Women — A246

Designs: 300 le, Development. 500 le, Peace. 700 le, Equality.

1995   **Litho.**   ***Perf. 14***
1821-1823 A246   Set of 3   5.00 5.00

Sierra Leone
Grammar
School,
150th Anniv.
A247

1995, Sept. 27   **Litho.**   ***Perf. 14***
1824 A247   300 le multicolored   1.00 1.00

Christmas
A248

Details or entire paintings: 50 le, Holy Family, by Beccafumi. 100 le, Rest on Flight into Egypt, by Barocci. 150 le, La Vierge, by Bellini. 200 le, The Flight, by d'Arpino. 600 le, Adoration of the Magi, by Francken. 800 le, The Annunciation, by da Conegliano.
Each 1500 le: No. 1831, Virgin and child, by Cranach. No. 1832, Madonna and Child, by Berlinghiero.

1995, Dec. 1   **Litho.**   ***Perf. 13½x14***
1825-1830 A248   Set of 6   5.50 5.50
Souvenir Sheets
1831-1832 A248   Set of 2   8.50 8.50

Disney
Christmas
A249

Antique Disney toys: 5 le, Mickey Mouse doll. 10 le, Donald rag drum major. 15 le, Donald wind up. 20 le, Toothbrush holder. 25 le, Mickey telephone. 30 le, Walking wind-up. 800 le, Movie projector. 1000 le, Goofy tricycle.
Each 1500 le: No. 1841, Black Mickey Mouse. No. 1842, First Mickey book.

1995, Dec. 4   ***Perf. 13½x14***
1833-1840 A249   Set of 8   8.25 8.25
Souvenir Sheets
1841-1842 A249   Set of 2   10.00 10.00

Nobel Prize Fund
Established,
Cent. — A250

Recipients, each 250 le: No. 1843a, Andrew Huxley, medicine, 1963. b, Nelson Mandela, peace, 1993. c, Gabriela Mistral, literature, 1945. d, Otto Diels, chemistry, 1950. e, Hannes Alfven, physics, 1970. f, Wole Soyinka, literature, 1986. g, Hans G. Dehmelt, physics, 1989. h, Desmond Tutu, peace, 1984. i, Leo Esaki, physics, 1973.
No. 1844, each 250 le: a, Maria Goeppert Mayer, physics, 1963. b, Irène Joliot-Curie, chemistry, 1935. c, Mother Teresa, peace, 1979. d, Selma Lagerlöf, literature, 1909. e, Rosalyn Yalow, medicine, 1977. f, Dorothy Hodgkin, chemistry, 1964. g, Rita Levi-Montalcini, medicine, 1986. h, Mairead Corrigan, peace, 1976. i, Betty Williams, peace, 1976.
No. 1845, each 250 le: a, Tobias Asser, peace, 1911. b, Andrei Sakharov, peace, 1975. c, Frederic Passy, peace, 1901. d, Dag Hammarskjöld, peace, 1961. e, Aung San Suu Kyi, peace, 1991. f, Ludwig Quidde, peace, 1927. g, Elie Wiesel, peace, 1986. h, Bertha von Suttner, peace, 1905. i, Dalai Lama, peace, 1989.
No. 1846, each 250 le: a, Richard Zsigmondy, chemistry, 1925. b, Robert Huber, chemistry, 1988. c, Wilhelm Ostwald, chemistry, 1909. d, Johann Deisenhofer, chemistry, 1988. e, Heinrich Wieland, chemistry, 1927. f, Gerhard Herzberg, chemistry, 1971. g, Hans von Euler-Chelpin, chemistry, 1929. h, Richard Willstätter, chemistry, 1915. i, Fritz Haber, chemistry, 1918.
Each 1500 le: No. 1847, Albert Einstein, physics, 1921. No. 1848, Wilhelm Röentgen, physics, 1901. No. 1849, Sin-Itiro Tomonaga, physics, 1965.

Sheets of 9, #a-i

1995, Dec. 29   **Litho.**   ***Perf. 14***
1843-1846 A250   Set of 4   40.00 40.00
Souvenir Sheets
1847-1849 A250   Set of 3   12.50 12.50

Railways of
the World
A251

No. 1850, each 200 le: a, Denver and Rio Grande Western. b, Central of Georgia. c, Seaboard Air Line. d, Missouri Pacific Lines. e, Atchison, Topeka and Santa Fe. f, Chicago, Milwaukee, St. Paul and Pacific. g, Texas and Pacific. h, Minneapolis, St. Paul & Sault Saint Marie. (Soo Line). i, Western Pacific. j, Great Northern. k, Baltimore & Ohio. l, Chicago, Rock Island and Pacific.
No. 1851, each 200 le: a, Southern Pacific 4-8-4 "Daylight" express, US. b, Belgian National 4-4-2 express. c, Indian Railways 4-6-2 "WP" express. d, South Australian 4-8-4

express. e, Union Pacific 4-8-8-4 "Big Boy," US. f, UK 4-6-2 "Royal Scot" streamlined. g, German Federal, class 052 2-10-0. h, Japanese National, 4-6-4 express. i, Pennsylvania, 4-4-4-4 streamlined, US. j, East African 4-8-2+2-8-4 Beyer-Garratt. k, Milwaukee Road 4-6-4 "Hiawatha" express, US. l, Paris-Orleans, 4-6-2 Pacific, France.

No. 1852, each 250 le: a, "Eurostar" express. b, ETR 401 Pendolino four-car tilting train, Italy. c, HST 125 inter-city high speed train, UK. d, "Virgin" B-B class high speed diesel-hydraulic express, Spain. e, French Natl. Railways TGV. f, Amtrak "Southwest Chief," US. g, TGV "Atlantique," France. h, "Peloponnese Express," Greece. i, "Shin-Kansen" high-speed electric train, Japan. j, Canadian Natl. turbo train. k, XPT high-speed diesel-electric train, Australia. l, SS1 Co-Co electric locomotive, China.

No. 1853, each 300 le: a, Canadian Natl. U1-F. b, Central Pacific No. 119 at Promontory, US. c, LNER "A4" class streamlined 4-6-2, UK. d, New York Central J32 "Empire State Express," US. e, Canadian Natl. 4-8-4. f, Class 38 Pacific 4-6-2 express, Australia. g, Canadian Pacific 4-6-2 express. h, Southern "West Country" class 4-6-2, UK.i, Norfolk & Western Class J 4-8-4, US. j, RM Class 4-6-0 Pacific, China. k, P-36 class 4-8-4 express, USSR. l, Great Western "King" class 4-6-0, UK.

Each 1500 le: No. 1853M, British Railways Jubilee class 4-6-0, No. 45627 named "Sierra Leone." No. 1853N, Denver & Rio Grande Western "California Zephyr," US. No. 1853O, 1st train to cross newly opened bridge over Yangtze River, 1968, China. No. 1853P, Beijing-Shanghai Express, China. No. 1853Q, China Railways, "QJ" class 2-10-2.

Sheets of 12, #a-l

1995, May 23 Litho. *Perf. 14*

1850-1851	A251	Set of 2	15.00	15.00
1852	A251	250 le multi	9.00	9.00
1853	A251	300 le multi	11.00	11.00

Souvenir Sheets

1853M-1853Q	A251	Set of 5	22.00	22.00

Nos. 1853M-1853Q each contain one 56x43mm stamp. No. 1850 exists with two different top margin inscriptions, "THE COLOURFUL RAILROADS OF NORTH AMERICA" and "THE COLOURFUL RAILROADS OF THE WORLD."

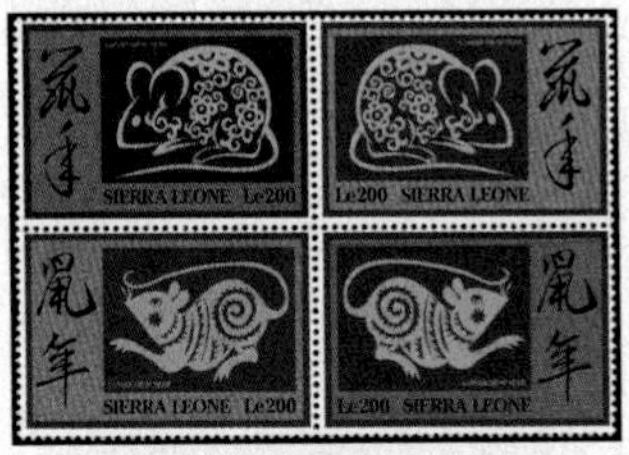

New Year 1996 (Year of the Rat) — A252

Different stylized rats: No. 1854a, Facing left, purple & multi. b, Facing right, blue green & multi. c, Facing left, blue green & multi. d, Facing right, blue & multi.

No. 1856, Rat, vert.

1996, Jan. 6

1854	A252	200 le Block of 4, #a.-d.	3.75	3.75

Miniature Sheet of 4

1855	A252	200 le #1854a-1854d	3.75	3.75

Souvenir Sheet

1856	A252	500 le multicolored	3.75	3.75

No. 1854 was issued in sheets of 16 stamps.

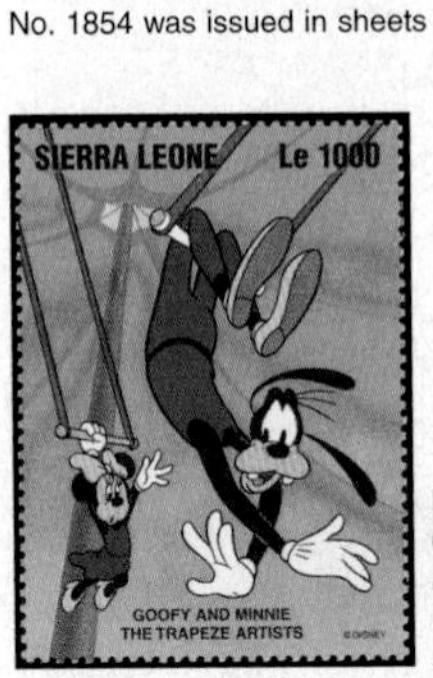

Disney Characters as Circus Performers A253

Designs: 100 le, Mickey, the magician. 200 le, Clarabelle Cow, the tightrope walker. 250 le, The clowns, Donald and Huey, Dewey and Louie. 300 le, Donald, the lion tamer. 800 le, Minnie, the bareback rider. 1000 le, Goofy and Minnie, the trapeze artists.

Each 1500 le: #1863, Mickey, horiz. #1864, Pluto, horiz.

1996, Jan. 29 Litho. *Perf. 14x13½*

1857-1862	A253	Set of 6	9.00	9.00

Souvenir Sheets

Perf. 13½x14½

1863-1864	A253	Set of 2	9.00	9.00

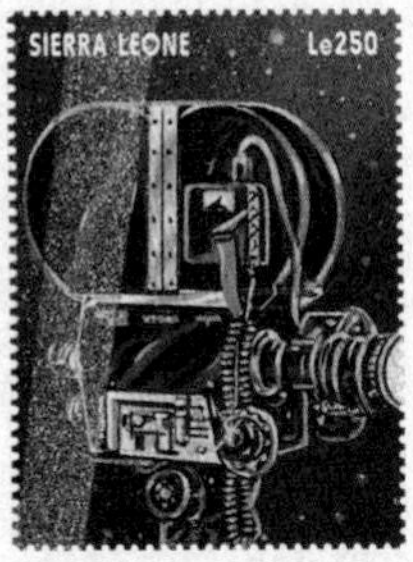

Motion Pictures, Cent. A254

No. 1865, each 250 le: a, Film projector. b, Pete. c, Silver. d, Rin-Tin-Tin. e, King Kong. f, Flipper. g, Jaws. h, Elsa. i, Moby Dick.

No. 1866, Directors or stars, scene from movie, each 250 le: a, Lumière Brothers. b, George Méliès. c, Toshiro Mifune d, Clark Gable, Vivian Leigh, David O. Selznick. e, Fritz Lang, Metropolis. f, Akira Kurosawa, Ran. g, Charlie Chaplin. h, Marlène Dietrich. i, Steven Spielberg, ET.

Each 1500 le: #1867, Lassie. #1868, Cecil B. de Mille.

Sheets of 9, #a-i

1996, Feb. 26 Litho. *Perf. 14*

1865-1866	A254	Set of 2	16.00	16.00

Souvenir Sheets

1867-1868	A254	Set of 2	9.50	9.50

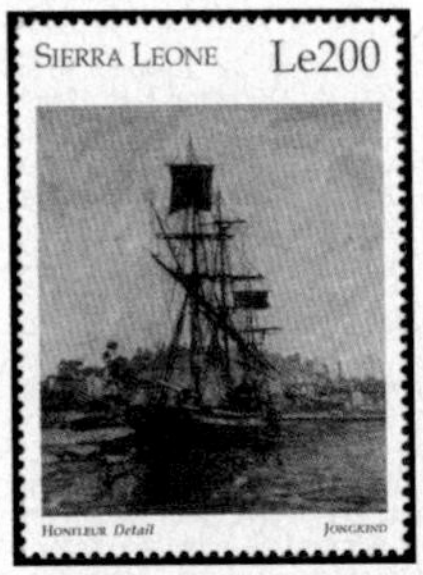

Paintings from Metropolitan Museum of Art — A255

Entire paintings or details: No. 1869, each 200 le: a, Honfleur, by Jongkind. b, A Boat on the Shore, by Courbet. c, Barges at Pontoise, by Pissarro. d, The Dead Christ with Angels, by Manet. e, Salisbury Cathedral, by Constable. f, A Lady with a Setter Dog, by Eakins. g, Tahitian Women Bathing, by Gaugin. h, Majas on a Balcony, by Goya.

By Renoir: No. 1870, each 200 le: a, In the Meadow. b, By the Seashore. c, Still Life with Peaches and Grapes. d, Marguerite (Margot) Bérard. e, Young Girl in Pink and Black Hat. f, A Waitrress at Duval's Restaurant. g, A Road in Louveciennes. h, Two Young Girls at the Piano.

No. 1871, each 200 le: a, Morning, an Overcast Day, Rouen, by Pissarro. b, The Horse Fair, by Bonheur. c, High Tide: the Bathers, by Homer. d, The Dance Class, by Degas. e, The Brioche, by Manet. f, The Grand Canal, Venice, by Turner. g, St. Thecla Interceding for Plague-stricken Este, by G. B. Tiepolo. h, Bridge at Villeneuve, by Sisley.

No. 1872, each 200 le: a, Madame Charpentier, by Renoir. b, Head of Christ, by Rembrandt. c, The Standard-Bearer, by Rembrandt. d, Girl Asleep, by Vermeer. e, Lady with a Lute, by Vermeer. f, Portrait of a Woman, by Rembrandt. g, La Grenouillère, by Monet. h, Woman with Chrysanthemums, by Degas.

Each 1500 le: No. 1873, The Death of Socrates, by J.L. David. No. 1874, Battle of Constantine and Maxentius, by Rubens. No. 1875, Samson and Delilah, by Rubens. No. 1876, The Emblem of Christ Appearing to Constantine, by Rubens.

Sheets of 8, #a-h, + label

1996 Litho. *Perf. 13½x14*

1869-1872	A255	Set of 4	22.00	22.00

Souvenir Sheets

Perf. 14

1873-1876	A255	Set of 4	12.00	12.00

Nos. 1873-1876 each contain one 85x57mm.

Nos. 1874-1876 are not in the Metropolitan.

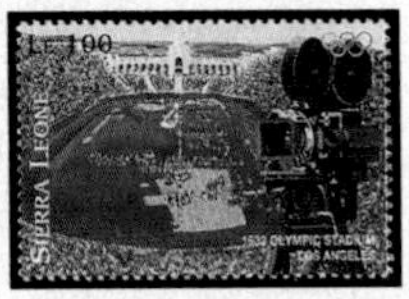

1996 Summer Olympic Games, Atlanta A256

100 le, 1932 Olympic Stadium, Los Angeles. 150 le, Archery. 500 le, Rings (gymnastics). 600 le, Pole vault.

No. 1881: a, Field hockey. b, Swimming. c, Equestrian. d, Boxing. e, Pommel horse. f, 100-meter dash.

1996, June 11 Litho. *Perf. 14*

1877-1880	A256	Set of 4	4.75	4.75
1881	A256	300 le Sheet of 6, #a.-f.	6.25	6.25

Souvenir Sheet

1882	A256	1500 le Runner	5.50	5.50

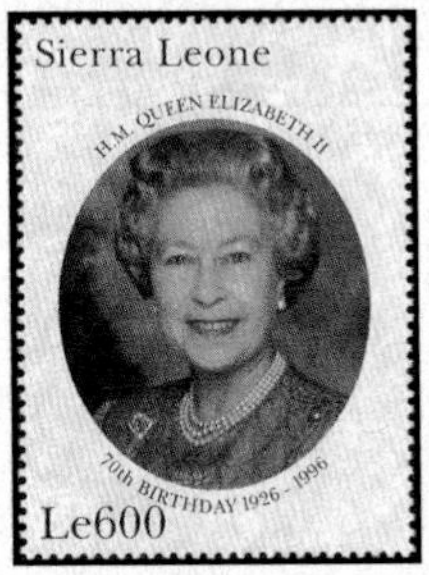

Queen Elizabeth II, 70th Birthday A257

Designs: a, Portrait. b, Receiving flowers. c, Holding flowers, wearing black hat, coat.

1500 le, Waving from balcony.

1996, July 15 Litho. *Perf. 13½x14*

1886	A257	600 le Strip of 3, #a.-c.	4.75	4.75

Souvenir Sheet

1887	A257	1500 le multicolored	4.75	4.75

No. 1886 was issued in sheets of 9 stamps.

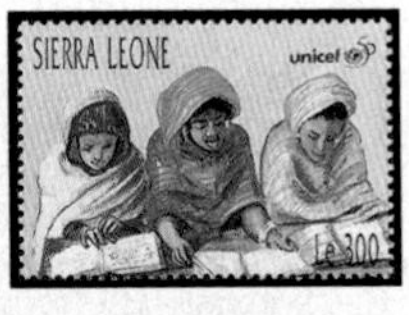

UNICEF, 50th Anniv. A258

Designs: 300 le, Children reading. 400 le, Young man, woman reading. 500 le, Children in class.

1500 le, Children's faces.

1996, July 15 *Perf. 14*

1888-1890	A258	Set of 3	3.50	3.50

Souvenir Sheet

1891	A258	1500 le multicolored	5.00	5.00

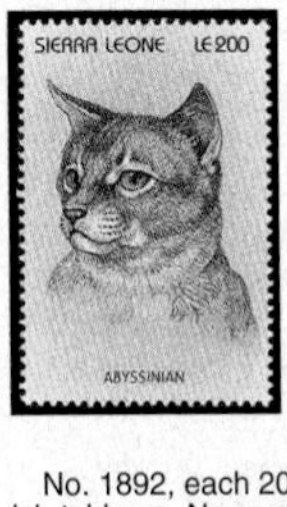

Cats — A259

No. 1892, each 200 le a, Abyssinian. b, British tabby. c, Norwegian forest. d, Maine coon. e, Bengal. f, Asian. g, American curl. h, Devon rex. i, Tonkinese. j, Egyptian mau. k, Burmese. l, Siamese.

No. 1893, each 200 le: a, British shorthair. b, Tiffany. c, Birman. d, Somali. e, Malayan. f, Japanese bobtail. g, Himalayan. h, Tortoiseshell. i, Oriental. j, Ocicat. k, Chartreux. l, Ragdoll.

Each 2000 le: No. 1894, Persian. No. 1895, Burmilla.

1996, June 17 Sheets of 12, #a-l

1892-1893	A259	Set of 2	17.50	17.50

Souvenir Sheets

1894-1895	A259	Set of 2	10.00	10.00

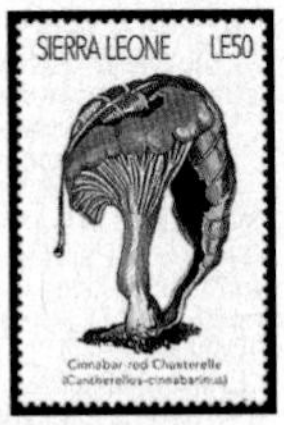

Mushrooms — A260

50 le, Cinnabar-red chanterelle. 300 le, Larch suillus. 400 le, Yellow more. 500 le, Variable cort.

No. 1900, each 250 le: a, African driver ant, Indigo milky, Marshall's false monarch (e). b, Scally inky cap. c, Pyxie cup (b). d, Barometer earthstar (c), rainbow grasshopper (h). e, Felt-ringed agaricus, long-horned longhorn. f, Spotted mycena. g, Orange latex milky. h, Tawny grissett amanita fulva, lamellicorn larva.

No. 1901, each 250 le: a, Millar tiger, little nest polymore. b, Coral slime. c, Red-gilled cort. d, Parasitic volvamella, veined tiger. e, Onion-stalked lepiota. f, Blusher. g. Orange mock oyster. h, Lizard claw, red and yellow barbet.

Each 1500 le: No. 1902, Netted rhodotus. No. 1903, Parasitic psathyrella.

1996, June 17

1896-1899	A260	Set of 4	4.00	4.00

Sheets of 8, #a.-h.

1900-1901	A260	Set of 2	10.00	10.00

Souvenir Sheets

1902-1903	A260	Set of 2	9.00	9.00

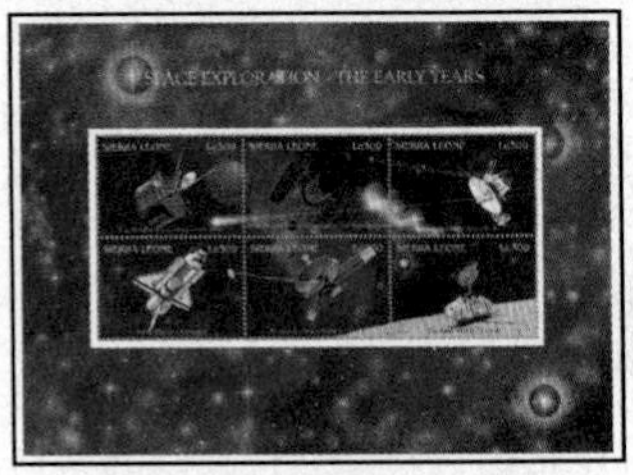

Space Exploration — A261

Designs: a, Pioneer-Venus orbiter, 1986-92. b, Hubble space telescope. c, Voyager probe. d, Space Shuttle Challenger in orbit. e, Pioneer II. f, Mars-Viking 1 lander.

1500 le, Shuttle Challenger landing.

1996

1904	A261	300 le Sheet of 6, #a.-f.	5.25	5.25

Souvenir Sheet

1905	A261	1500 le multicolored	5.75	5.75

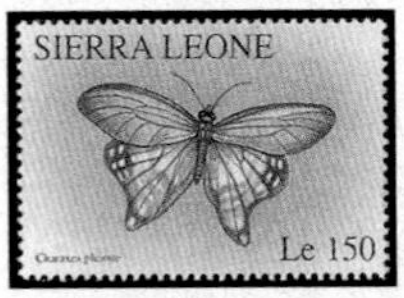

Butterflies A262

Designs: 150 le, Charaxes pleione. 200 le, Eurema brigitta. 300 le, Charaxes ameliae. 500 le, Kallimoides rumia.

No. 1910, each 250 le: a, Precis orithya. b, Palla ussheri. c, Junonia orithya. d, Cymothoe sangaris. e, Cyrestis camillus. f, Precis rhadama. g, Precis cebrene. h, Hypolimnas misippus. i, Colotis danae.

Each 1500 le: No. 1911, Charaxes bohemani. No. 1912, Papilio antimachus.

1996, Aug. 15 Litho. *Perf. 14*

1906-1909	A262	Set of 4	4.25	4.25
1910	A262	Sheet of 9, #a.-i.	7.75	7.75

Souvenir Sheets

1911-1912	A262	Set of 2	9.50	9.50

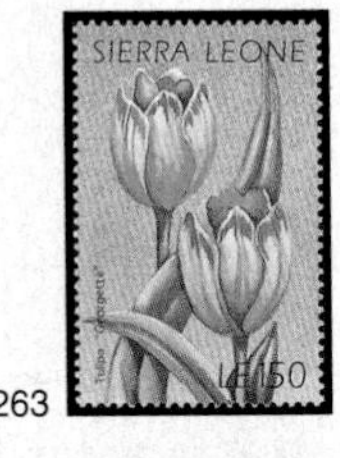

Flowers — A263

Designs: 150 le, Tulipa. 200 le, Helichrysum bracteatum. 400 le, Viola. 500 le, Phalaenopsis.

No. 1917, each 200 le: a, Fountain. b, Begonia multiflora. c, Narcissus. d, Crocus speciosus. e, Chrysanthemum frutescens. Petunia. f, Cosmos pipinnatus. g, Anemone coronaria. h, Convolvulus minor.

No. 1918, each 300 le: a, Paphiopedilum. b, Cymbidium "Peach bloom." c, Sailboat. d, Miltonia. e, Parides gundalachianus. f, Laeliocatt leya. g, Lycaste aromatica. h, Brassolaeliocatt leya. i, Cymbidium "Southern Lace," Catastica teutila.

Each 1500 le: No. 1919, Helianthus annuus. No. 1920, Cymbidium "Lucifer."

1996, Aug. 19
1913-1916	A263	Set of 4	4.00	4.00
1917	A263	Sheet of 9, #a.-i.	5.50	5.50
1918	A263	Sheet of 9, #a.-i.	8.00	8.00

Souvenir Sheets
1919-1920	A263	Set of 2	9.00	9.00

Chinese Lunar Calendar A264

Year of the: a, Rat. b, Ox. c, Tiger. d, Hare. e, Dragon. f, Snake. g, Horse. h, Sheep. i, Monkey. j, Rooster. k, Dog. l, Pig.

1996, July 15   Litho.   Perf. 13½x14
1921	A264	150 le Sheet of 12, #a.-l.	8.00	8.00

Ships — A265

No. 1922, each 300 le: a, Clipper ship, "Cutty Sark," 19th cent. b, SS Great Britain, 1846. c, "Dreadnaught," 1906. d, RMS Queen Elizabeth, 1940-72. e, Ocean-going racing yacht, 1962. f, SS United States, 1952. g, Nuclear powered submarine, 1950's. h, Super tanker, 1960's. i, USS Enterprise, 1980s.

No. 1923, each 300 le: a, Greek war galley, 4th cent. BC. b, Roman war galley, 50AD. c, Viking ship, 9th cent. d, Flemish carrack, 15th cent. e, Merchant man, 16th cent. f, Tudor warship, 16th cent. g, Elizabethan galleon, 17th cent. h, Dutch Man of War, 17th cent. i, "Maestrale," Maltese galley, 18th cent.

Each 1500 le: No. 1924, Cruise ship "Legend of the Seas," 1996 Panama Canal. No. 1925, Egyptian ocean-going ship, 1480BC.

Sheets of 9, #a-i
1996, Oct. 29   Litho.   Perf. 14
1922-1923	A265	Set of 2	15.00	15.00

Souvenir Sheets
1924-1925	A265	Set of 2	8.00	8.00

Nos. 1924-1925 each contain one 56x43mm stamp.

Christmas A266

Details or entire paintings, by Filippo Lippi: 200 le, Madonna of Humility. 250 le, Coronation of the Virgin. 400 le, 500 le, Annunciation.

---

600 le, Barbadori Altarpiece. 800 le, Coronation of the Virgin, diff.

Each 2000 le: Paintings by Rubens: No. 1932, Adoration of the Magi. No. 1933, Holy Family with St. Anne.

1996, Dec. 12   Litho.   Perf. 13½x14
1926-1931	A266	Set of 6	8.00	8.00

Souvenir Sheets
1932-1933	A266	Set of 2	9.25	9.25

Souvenir Sheets

Fantasies of the Sea — A267

Each 1500 le: #1934, Sea Dragon's Daughter. #1935, Homo Aquaticus. #1936, Chinese Sea Fairy. #1937, Sea Totem. #1938, The Turtle, horiz. #1939, Mermaid, horiz. #1940, How the Whale Got its Throat, horiz. #1941, Killer Whale Crest. #1942, Aphrodite. #1943, Ship Figurehead. #1944, Lilith. #1945, Queen of the Orkney Islands. #1946, Haida Eagle. #1947, Captain Ahab. #1948, Waskos. #1949, Jonah. #1950, Odysseus. #1951, The Little Mermaid. #1952, Squamish Indians. #1953, Boy on a Dolphin. $1954, Airship to Atlantis. #1955, Sea Bishop. #1956, 20,000 Leagues Under the Sea. #1957, Whale Song. #1958, Arion. #1959, Dragonrider of Pern. #1960, Kelpie. #1961, Natsilhane. #1962, Merman. #1963, Albatross. #1964, City under polar ice melt. #1965, Tom Swift. #1966, The Flying Dutchman, horiz. #1967, Sea Centaur. #1968, Lang (dragon), horiz. #1969, Triton. #1970, Sea Serpent. #1971, Arthropod sea monster. #1972, The Ancient Mariner. #1973, Poseidon.

1996, Dec. 19   Litho.   Perf. 14
1934-1973	A267	Set of 40	150.00	150.00

New Year 1997 (Year of the Ox) — A268

Various stylized oxen, background color: Nos. 1975-1976: a, purple. b, green. c, blue. d, claret.

800 le, like #1975d, vert.

1997, Jan. 8   Litho.   Perf. 14
1975	A268	150 le Block of 4, #a.-d.	1.50	1.50
1976	A268	250 le Sheet of 4, #a.-d.	6.50	6.50

Souvenir Sheet
1977	A268	800 le multicolored	2.75	2.75

No. 1975 was issued in sheets of 16 stamps.

Disney's Aladdin in Christmas Scenes A269

Designs: 10 le, Aladdin, Jasmine. 15 le, Santa, Genie. 20 le, Aladdin, Jasmine on magic carpet. 25 le, Genie as Christmas tree. 30 le, Aladdin, Genie "Santa." 100 le, Jasmine, Aladdin, Genie. 800 le, Genie's letter to Santa. 1000 le, Genie's Christmas carol.

Each 2000 le: No. 1986, Aladdin, Abu. No. 1987, Jasmine, Aladdin, horiz.

1997, Jan. 27   Perf. 14x13½
1978-1985	A269	Set of 8	9.50	9.50

Souvenir Sheets
Perf. 14x13½, 13½x14
1986-1987	A269	Set of 2	10.00	10.00

Hong Kong — A270

Panoramic view of Hong Kong, each 500 le: No. 1988, in daytime. No. 1989, at night.

1997, Feb. 12   Litho.   Perf. 14
Sheets of 4, #a-d
1988-1989	A270	Set of 2	10.50	10.50

UNESCO, 50th Anniv. A271

World Heritage Sites: 60 le, Town of Kizhi Pogost, Russia. 200 le, Durmitor Natl. Park, Yugoslavia. 250 le, City of Nessebar, Bulgaria. 400 le, City of Bukhara, Uzbekistan. 500 le, Monastery of Kiev-Pechersk, Ukraine. 700 le, Mountain Walks, Vlkolinec, Slovakia.

No. 1996, each 300 le: a, Town of Roros, Norway. b, City of Warsaw, Poland. c, Cathedral of Notre Dame, Luxembourg. d, City of Vilnius, Lithuania. e, Jelling, Denmark. f, Old Church of Petäjävesi, Finland. g, Sweden. h, Cathedral City of Bern, Switzerland.

No. 1997, each 500 le: a, Area surrounding Mt. Kilimanjaro, Tanzania. b, Monument, Fasil Ghebbi, Ethiopia. c, Natl. Park, Mt. Ruwenzori, Uganda. d, Abu Simbel, Egypt. e, Tsingy Bemaraha Strict Nature Reserve, Madagascar. f, House, Djenne, Mali. g, Traditional house construction, Ghana. h, Large house, Aromey.

Various views of Himeji-Jo, Japan, vert: No. 1998: a, b, c, d, e.

Each 2000 le: No. 1999, Natl. Bird Sanctuary, Djudj, Senegal, horiz. No. 2000, Acropolis, Athens, Greece, horiz.

1997, Mar. 24   Litho.   Perf. 13½x14
1990-1995	A271	Set of 6	6.00	6.00

Sheets of 8, #a-h, + Label
1996-1997	A271	Set of 2	13.50	13.50

Sheet of 5 + Label
1998	A271	500 le #a.-e.	6.75	6.75

Souvenir Sheets
1999-2000	A271	Set of 2	12.50	12.50

Paintings by Hiroshige (1797-1858) — A272

No. 2001, each 400 le: a, Hatsune Riding Grounds, Bakuro-cho. b, Mannen Bridge, Fukagawa. c, Ryogoku Bridge and the Great Riverbank. d, Asakusa River, Great Riverbank, Miyato River. e, Silk-goods Lane, Odenmacho. f, Mokuboji Temple, Uchigawa Inlet, Gozensaihata.

Each 1500 le: No. 2002, Tsukudajima from Eitai Bridge. No. 2003, Nihonbashi Bridge and Edobashi Bridge.

1997   Litho.   Perf. 13½x14
2001	A272	Sheet of 6, #a.-f.	6.75	6.75

Souvenir Sheets
2002-2003	A272	Set of 2	7.50	7.50

Chernobyl Disaster, 10th Anniv. A273

Designs: 1000 le, UNESCO. 1500 le, Chabad's Children of Chernobyl.

1997, June 23
2004	A273	1000 le multicolored	3.00	3.00
2005	A273	1500 le multicolored	4.25	4.25

Queen Elizabeth II and Prince Philip, 50th Wedding Anniv. — A274

No. 2006: a, Queen. b, Royal arms. c, Black & white photograph, Prince in dress uniform. d, Black & white photograph, Prince in tuxedo, bow tie. e, Palace of Holyroodhouse. f, Prince in hat guiding horses.

1500 le, Queen, Prince in colored photograph.

1997, June 23   Perf. 14
2006	A274	400 le Sheet of 6, #a.-f.	12.00	12.00

Souvenir Sheet
2007	A274	1500 le multi	3.50	3.50

Return of Hong Kong to China — A275

Designs: 400 le, Flag of China, map of China, Hong Kong, Victoria at night. 500 le, 650 le, Flag of China, July 1, 1997, city scene inside letters spelling "Hong Kong." 550 le, 600 le, Flag of China, Victoria harbor inside letters spelling "Hong Kong '97." 800 le, Victoria harbor, Deng Xiaoping (1904-97).

1997, June 23
2008-2013	A275	Set of 6	8.75	8.75

Nos. 2008-2013 were each issued in sheets of 3.

Souvenir Sheets

Mother Goose — A276

Designs, each 1500 le: No. 2014, Three Blind Mice. No. 2015, Woman holding out full skirt as "Myself."

1997, June 23   Litho.   Perf. 14
2014-2015 A276 Set of 2   8.00 8.00

1998 Winter Olympic Games, Nagano — A277

Designs: 250 le, Stadium, Calgary, 1988, American Indian. 300 le, Freestyle aerial skiing, vert. 500 le, Ice hockey, vert. 800 le, Dan Jansen, 1000-meter speed skater, vert.

No. 2022, vert, each 300 le: a, Peggy Fleming, figure skating. b, Japanese ski jumper, Nordic combined. c, 2-man luge, Germany. d, Frank-Peter Roetsch, biathlon, E. Germany.

Each 1500 le: No. 2023, Jamaican bobsled team, vert. No. 2024, Johann Olav Koss, Norway, vert.

1997, July 16   Litho.   Perf. 14
2018-2021 A277 Set of 4   5.00 5.00
2022   A276 Strip of 4, #a.-d. 4.00 4.00
Souvenir Sheets
2023-2024 A277 Set of 2   8.50 8.50

No. 2022 was issued in sheets of 8 stamps.

1998 World Cup Soccer Championships, France — A278

Players: 100 le, Stabile, Uruguay. 150 le, Schiavio, Italy. 200 le, Kocsis, Hungary. 250 le, Nejedly, Czechoslovakia. 500 le, Leonidas, Brazil. 600 le, Ademir, Brazil.

No. 2031, each 300 le: a, Dwight Yorke, Trinidad & Tobago. b, Dennis Bergkamp, Holland. c, Steve McManaman, England. d, Ryan Giggs, Wales. e, Romario, Brazil, f, Faustino Asprilla, Colombia. g, Roy Keane, Ireland. h, Peter Schmeichel, Denmark.

Each 1500 le: No. 2032, Pele, Brazil, horiz. No. 2033, Lato, Poland, horiz.

1997, July 23   Perf. 13½x14, 14x13½
2025-2030 A278 Set of 6   5.00 5.00
Sheet of 8
2031   A278 #a.-h. + 2 labels 7.00 7.00
Souvenir Sheets
2032-2033 A278 Set of 2   10.00 10.00

Classic Horror Movies — A279

Lead character, movie: No. 2034, each 300 le: a, Lon Chaney, "Phantom of the Opera," 1934. b, Boris Karloff, "The Mummy," 1932. c,

Fredric March, "Dr. Jekyll & Mr. Hyde, " 1932. d, Lon Chaney, Jr., "The Wolf Man," 1941. e, Charles Laughton, "Island of Lost Souls," 1933. f, Lionel Atwill, "Mystery of the Wax Museum," 1933. g, Bela Lugosi, "Dracula," 1931. h, Vincent Price, "The Haunted Palace," 1963. i, Elsa Lanchester, "Bride of Frankenstein," 1935.

3000 le, Bela Lugosi, Boris Karloff, "Son of Frankenstein," 1939.

1997, Aug. 15   Perf. 14
2034 A279 Sheet of 9, #a.-i. 10.00 10.00
Souvenir Sheet
2035 A279 3000 le multi   9.00 9.00

Domestic Cats — A280

Designs: 150 le, American short hair tabby. 200 le, British short hair. 500 le, Turkish angora.

No. 2039, each 400 le: a, Chartreux. b, Abyssinian. c, Burmese. d, White angora. e, Japanese bobtail. f, Cymric.

1500 le, Egyptian mau.

1997, Aug. 29
2036-2038 A280 Set of 3   2.25 2.25
2039   A280 Sheet of 6, #a.-f. 6.50 6.50
Souvenir Sheet
2040   A280 1500 le multicolored 4.00 4.00

No. 2040 contains one 64x32mm stamp.

Butterflies — A281

Designs: 150 le, Vindula erota. 200 le, Pereutel leucodrosime. 250 le, Dynstor napolean. 300 le, Thauria aliris. 600 le, Papilio aegeus. 800 le, Amblypodia anita. 1500 le, Kallimoides rumia. 2000 le, Papilio dardanas.

No. 2049: a, Lycaena dispar. b, Graphium sarpedon. c, Euploe core. d, Papilio cresphontes. e, Colotis danae. f, Battus philenor.

No. 2050: a, Mylothris chloris. b, Argynnis lathonia. c, Elymnias agondas. d, Palla ussheri. e, Papilio glaucus. f, Cercyonis pegala.

Each 3000 le: No. 2051, Hebomoia glaucippe, horiz. No. 2052, Colias eurytheme, horiz.

1997, Aug. 1   Litho.   Perf. 14
2041-2048 A281 Set of 8   15.00 15.00
Sheets of 6
2049 A281 500 le #a.-f.   8.00 8.00
2050 A281 600 le #a.-f.   9.75 9.75
Souvenir Sheets
2051-2052 A281 Set of 2   16.00 16.00

For surcharges see Nos. 2897-2898.

Orchids — A282

Designs: 150 le, Ansellia africana. 200 le, Maxillaria praestans. 250 le, Cymbidium mimi. 300 le, Dendrobium bigibbum. 500 le, Encyclia vitellina. 800 le, Epidendrum prismatocarpum.

No. 2059, each 400 le: a, Laelia anceps. b, Paphiopedilum fairrieanum. c, Restrepia lansbergii. d, Yamadara cattleya. e, Cleistes divaricata. f, Calypso bulbosa.

Each 1500 le: No. 2060, Odontoglossum schlieperianum. No. 2061, Paphiopedilum tonsum.

1997, Sept. 1
2053-2058 A282 Set of 6   6.00 6.00

2059 A282 Sheet of 6, #a.-f.   6.50 6.50
Souvenir Sheets
2060-2061 A282 Set of 2   8.00 8.00

Motion Pictures Directed by Alfred Hitchcock — A283

No. 2062, each 350 le: a, Ray Milland in "Dial M for Murder." b, James Stewart, Kim Novak in "Vertigo." c, Cary Grant, Ingrid Bergman in "Notorious." d, John Dall, James Stewart in "Rope." e, Cary Grant in "North by Northwest." f, Grace Kelly, James Stewart in "Rear Window." g, Joan Fontaine, Laurence Olivier in "Rebecca." h, Tippi Hedren in "The Birds." i, Janet Leigh in "Psycho."

1500 le, Alfred Hitchcock.

1997, Aug. 15   Litho.   Perf. 14
2062 A283 Sheet of 9, #a.-i. 10.00 10.00
Souvenir Sheet
2063 A283 1500 le multi   4.50 4.50

Dogs — A284

Designs: 100 le, Shetland sheep dog. 250 le, Alaskan husky. 600 le, Jack Russell terrier.

No. 2067, each 400 le: a, Basset hound. b, Irish setter. c, St. Bernard. d, German shepherd. e, Dalmatian. f, Cocker spaniel.

1500 le, Boxer.

1997, Aug. 29
2064-2066 A284 Set of 3   2.50 2.50
2067   A284 Sheet of 6, #a.-f. 6.50 6.50
Souvenir Sheet
2068   A284 1500 le multicolored 4.00 4.00

No. 2068 contains one 31x63mm stamp.

Disney Christmas Stamps A285

Designs: 150 le, Huey, Dewey, & Louie. 200 le, Mickey's kids. 250 le, Daisy Duck. 300 le, Minnie. 400 le, Mickey. 500 le, Donald Duck. 600 le, Pluto. 800 le, Goofy.

No. 2077, each 50 le: a, like #2071. b, like #2069. c, like #2074. d, like #2072. e, like #2070. f, like #2073.

Each 2000 le: No. 2078, Mickey in sleigh. No. 2079, Mickey, Donald, Daisy in Santa suits, horiz.

1997, Oct. 1   Perf. 13½x14, 14x13½
2069-2076 A285 Set of 8   8.75 8.75
2077   A285 Sheet of 6, #a.-f. 1.75 1.75
Souvenir Sheets
2078-2079 A285 Set of 2   12.00 12.00

For overprints see Nos. 2117-2119.

Civilian Airliners — A286

No. 2080, each 600 le: a, SUD Caravelle 6. b, DeHavilland comet. c, Boeing 707. d, Airbus industrie A-300.

No. 2080E, each 600 le: f, Benoist Type XIV. g, Junkers JU52/3m. h, Douglas DC-3. i, Sikorsky S-42.

Each 600 le: #2081, Concorde. #2081A, Lockheed L-1649A Starliner.

1997, Oct. 6   Perf. 14
2080   A286 Sheet of 4, #a.-d.
             + label   6.25 6.25
2080E A286 Sheet of 4, #f.-i.
             + label   6.25 6.25
2081-2081A A286 Set of 2   11.00 11.00

Nos. 2081-2081A contain one 91x34mm stamp.

Christmas A287

Entire paintings or details: 100 le, 150 le, The Annunciation, by Titian (diff. details). 200 le, Madonna of Folingo, by Raphael. 250 le, The Annunciation, by Michelino. 500 le, The Prophet Isaiah, by Michelangelo. 600 le, Three Angels, by Master of the Rhenish Housebook.

Each 2000 le: No. 2088, The Fall of the Rebel Angels, by Peter Bruegel the Elder, horiz. No. 2089, Unidentified painting of Angel pointing hand in air, man with book, horiz.

1997, Dec. 24
2082-2087 A287 Set of 6   5.25 5.25
Souvenir Sheets
2088-2089 A287 Set of 2   9.75 9.75

Diana, Princess of Wales (1961-97) — A288

Various portraits, each 400 le, color of sheet margin: No. 2090, Pale pink. No. 2091, Pale blue. No. 2092, Pale yellow.

Each 1500 le: No. 2093, Wearing wide-brimmed hat. No. 2094, With Prince Harry (in margin). No. 2095, Helping to feed needy.

1998, Jan. 12   Litho.   Perf. 14
Sheets of 6, #a.-f.
2090-2092 A288 Set of 3   17.50 17.50
Souvenir Sheets
2093-2095 A288 Set of 3   11.00 11.00

New Year 1998 (Year of the Tiger) — A289

Various stylized tigers in: No. 2096: a, purple. b, maroon. c, bright lilac rose. d, orange. 800 le, maroon, vert.

1998, Jan. 26   Litho.   Perf. 14
2096 A289 250 le Sheet of 4,
    #a.-d.   2.75 2.75

Souvenir Sheet
2097 A289 800 le red org & multi 2.25 2.25

Flora and Fauna A290

Designs: 200 le, Metagyrphus nitens, vert. 250 le, Lord Derby's parakeet, vert. 300 le, Narcissus, vert. 400 le, Barbus tetrazona. 500 le, Agalychnis callidryas. 600 le, Wolverine.

No. 2104, each 450 le: a, Japanese white-eyes. b, Rhododendron. c, Slow loris. d, Violet flowers. e, Orthetrum albistylum. f, Coluber jugularis.

No. 2105, each 450 le: a, Cheetah. b, Ornithogalum thyrsoides. c, Ostrich. d, Common chameleon. e, Fennec fox. f, Junonia hierta cebrene.

Each 2000 le: No. 2106, Tricolored heron, vert. No. 2107, Atheris squamiger.

1998, Aug. 4   Litho.   Perf. 14
2098-2103 A290 Set of 6   4.50 4.50

Sheets of 6, #a.-f.
2104-2105 A290 Set of 2   13.50 13.50

Souvenir Sheets
2106-2107 A290 Set of 2   8.50 8.50

Dinosaurs A291

Designs: 200 le, Hypsilophodon, vert. 400 le, Lambeosaurus, vert. 500 le, Corythosaurus, vert. 600 le, Stegosaurus, vert. 800 le, Antrodemus.

No. 2113, each 500 le: vert: a, Plateosaurus. b, Tyrannosaurus. c, Brachiosaurus. d, Iguanodon. e, Styracosaurus. f, Hadrosaurus.

No. 2114, each 500 le: a, Tyrannosaurus. b, Tenontosaurus. c, Deinonychus. d, Triceratops. e, Maiasaura. f, Struthiomimus.

Each 2000 le: No. 2115, Tyrannosaurus. No. 2116, Triceratops.

1998, Aug. 18   Litho.   Perf. 14
2108-2112 A291 Set of 5   5.00 5.00

Sheets of 6, #a.-f.
2113-2114 A291 Set of 2   12.50 12.50

Souvenir Sheets
2115-2116 A291 Set of 2   8.75 8.75

Nos. 2077-2079 Ovptd.

Perf. 13½x14, 14x13½
1998, Aug. 31
2117 A285 50 le Sheet of 6,
    #a.-f.   6.00 6.00

Souvenir Sheets
2118-2119 A285 Set of 2   12.00 12.00
Emblem and "MICKEY & MINNIE — 70TH ANNIVERSARY" appear in sheet margin on Nos. 2118-2119.

Ships of the World — A292

No. 2120, each 300 le: a, Phoenician, 8th cent. BC. b, Drakkar, 6th cent. c, Carrack, 14th cent. d, Venetian Galley, 16th cent. e, Galeasse, 17th cent. f, Chebeck, 17th cent.

No. 2121, each 300 le: a, Junk, 19th cent. b, HMS Victory, 19th cent. c, Savanna, 19th cent. d, Gaissa, 19th cent. e, Warrior, 19th cent. f, Preussen, 20th cent.

Each 2000 le: No. 2122, Santa Maria, 1492. No. 2123, Titanic, 1912.

Sheets of 6, #a.-f.
1998, Sept. 1   Perf. 14
2120-2121 A292 Set of 2   16.00 16.00

Souvenir Sheets
2122-2123 A292 Set of 2   9.00 9.00
Nos. 2122-2123 each contain one 57x43mm stamp.
For surcharges see Nos. 2899-2900.

Disney's The Lion King, Simba's Pride — A293

No. 2124, each 500 le: a, Kiara (with bird). b, Pumbaa. c, Kiara & Kovu. d, Kovu. e, Kiara & Kovu (red background). f, Timon (orange background).

No. 2125, each 500 le: a, Kiara (with butterfly). b, Timon & Pumbaa. c, Kiara. d, Kiara & Kovu (green background). e, Kovu (with bird). f, Kiara & Kovu (pink background).

Each 2500 le: No. 2126, Pumbaa & Timon. No. 2127, Kiara & Kovu, horiz.

Perf. 13½x14, 14x13½
1998, Sept. 15   Sheets of 6, #a.-f.
2124-2125 A293 Set of 2   16.00 16.00

Souvenir Sheets
2126-2127 A293 Set of 2   13.50 13.50

Paintings by Picasso — A294

Paintings: 400 le, Man with Straw Hat and Ice Cream Cone, 1938. 600 le, Woman in Red Armchair, 1932. 800 le, Nude in a Garden, 1934.
2000 le, Child Holding a Dove, 1901.

1998, Dec. 15   Litho.   Perf. 14½
2128-2130 A294 Set of 3   6.50 6.50

Souvenir Sheet
2131 A294 2000 le multicolored 3.75 3.75

Gandhi — A295

1998, Dec. 15   Perf. 14
2132 A295 600 le Portrait   5.00 5.00

Souvenir Sheet
2133 A295 2000 le Close-up   5.50 5.50
No. 2132 printed in sheets of 4.
For surcharge see No. 2904.

Royal Air Force, 80th Anniv. — A296

No. 2134, each 800 le: a, McDonnell Douglas Phantom FRG2. b, Two Panavia Tornado GR1. c, Jaguar GR1A. d, Hercules C-130.

Each 2000 le: No. 2135, Eagle, biplane. No. 2136, Lysander, Eurofighter.

1998, Dec. 15
2134 A296 Sheet of 4, #a.-d. 11.50 11.50

Souvenir Sheets
2135-2136 A296 Set of 2   13.00 13.00

19th World Scouting Jamboree, Chile — A297

No. 2137, each 1500 le: a, Dan Beard, Robert Baden-Powell, 1937. b, Kuwaiti Scouts. c, Scout leader bottle feeding bear cub.

No. 2138, each 1500 le, vert.: a, William D. Boyce, Lone Scouts founder. b, Guion S. Bluford. c, Ellison S. Onizuka.

Each 3000 le: No. 2139, Lord, Lady Robert Baden-Powell. No. 2140, Bear cub drinking from bottle.

1998, Dec. 15   Sheets of 3, #a.-c.
2137-2138 A297 Set of 2   16.00 16.00

Souvenir Sheets
2139-2140 A297 Set of 2   12.00 12.00
For surcharge see No. 2901.

Christmas A298

Entire paintings or details: 200 le, Penitent of Mary Magdalen, by Titian. 500 le, Lamentation of Christ, by Veronese. 1500 le, The Building of Noah's Ark, by Guido Reni. 2000 le, Abraham and Isaac, by Rembrandt.

Each 3000 le: No. 2145, Adoration of the Shepherds, by Bartolomé Estéban Murillo. No. 2146, The Assumption of the Virgin, by Murillo.

1998, Dec. 14   Litho.   Perf. 14
2141-2144 A298 Set of 4   6.75 6.75

Souvenir Sheets
2145-2146 A298 Set of 2   10.50 10.50

Ferrari Automobiles — A298a

No. 2146A, each 800 le: c, 400 Superamerica. d, 250 GT Lusso. e, 342 America. 2000 le, 330 GTC.

1998, Dec. 15   Litho.   Perf. 14
2146A A298a Sheet of 3, #c-e 2.75 2.75

Souvenir Sheet
2146B A298a multi   2.40 2.40
No. 2146A contains three 39x25mm stamps.

Diana, Princess of Wales (1961-97) — A299

1998, Dec. 15   Perf. 14½x14
2147 A299 600 le multicolored 1.75 1.75
No. 2147 was issued in sheets of 6.

New Year 1999 (Year of the Rabbit) — A300

Color of stylized rabbits — #2148: a, red. b, red violet. c, blue. d, light violet. 1500 le, Rabbit, vert.

1998, Dec. 24   Perf. 14
2148 A300 700 le Sheet of 4,
    #a.-d.   6.50 6.50

Souvenir Sheet
2149 A300 1500 le multicolored 5.50 5.50

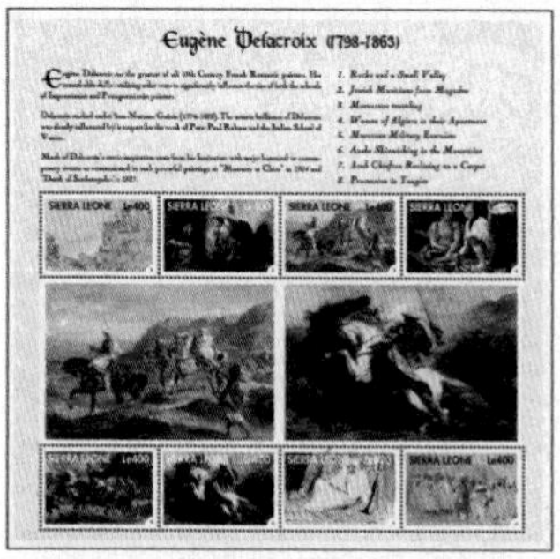

Paintings by Eugène Delacroix (1798-1863) — A301

Designs: a, Rocks and a Small Valley. b, Jewish Musicians from Magador. c, Moroccans Traveling. d, Women of Algiers in their Apartment. e, Moroccan Military Exercises. f, Arabs Skirmishing in the Mountains. g, Arab Chieftan Reclining on a Carpet. h, Procession in Tangier.

No. 2151, Chopin, vert.

1998

2150 A301 400 le Sheet of 8, #a.-h. 11.00 11.00

Souvenir Sheet

2151 A301 400 le multicolored 5.50 5.50

Bird Type of 1992

Designs: 4000 le, Gray-headed bush-shrike. 5000 le, Black-backed puffback. 6000 le, Crimson-breasted shrike. 10,000 le, Northern shrike.

1999 Litho. *Perf. 14x15*

No Date Imprint

2152	A199 4000 le multi		12.00	12.00
2153	A199 5000 le multi		14.00	14.00
a.	Inscribed "2002"		14.00	14.00
b.	Inscribed "2006"		14.00	14.00
2154	A199 6000 le multi		18.00	18.00
2155	A199 10,000 le multi		22.50	22.50
b.	Inscribed "2006"		22.50	22.50
	Nos. 2152-2155 (4)		66.50	66.50

Issued: 4000 le, 5000 le, 2/18/99.

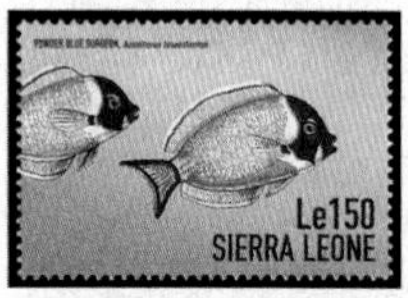

Birds, Marine Life — A302

150 le, Powder blue surgeon. 250 le, Frilled anemone. 600 le, Red beard sponge. 800 le, Red-finned batfish.

No. 2160, each 400 le: a, Eastern reef egret. b, Dolphins. c, Sailing ship, Humpback whale. d, Red and green macaw. e, Blue tangs. f, Guitarfish. g, Manatees. h, Hammerhead shark. i, Blue shark. j, Lemon goby, moorish idol. k, Ribbon eels. l, Loggerhead turtle.

Sharks — #2161, each 500 le: a, Blue shark. b, Tiger shark. c, Bull shark. d, Great white. e, Scalloped hammerhead. f, Oceanic whitetip. g, Zebra shark. h, Leopard shark. i, Horn shark.

Dolphins, whales — #2162, each 500 le: a, Hector's dolphin. b, Tucuxi. c, Hourglass dolphin. d, Bottlenose dolphin. e, Gray's beaked whale. f, Bowhead whale. g, Fin whale. h, Gray whale. i, Blue whale.

Each 3000 le: No. 2163, Purple firefish. No. 2164, Spotted eagle ray. No. 2165, Leatherback turtle.

1999, Feb. 22 *Perf. 14*

2156-2159 A302 Set of 4 3.75 3.75
2160 A302 Sheet of 12, #a.-l. 9.50 9.50

Sheets of 9, #a.-i.

2161-2162 A302 Set of 2 18.00 18.00

Souvenir Sheets

2163-2165 A302 Set of 3 24.00 24.00

Intl. Year of the Ocean (#2160-2162, #2164-2165).

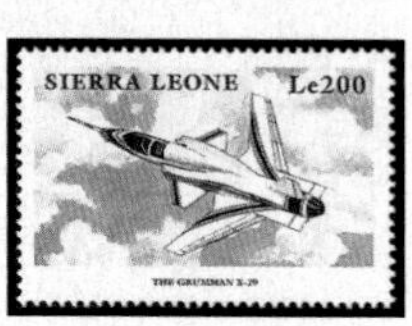

Airplanes A303

200 le, Grumman X-29. 300 le, Rocket-powered Bell X-1. 400 le, MiG-21 Fishbed, 1956, USSR. 600 le, Blériot X1 Monoplane, 1909. 800 le, Southern Cross, Fokker F.VII, 1928. 1500 le, Supermarine S.6B.

No. 2172, each 600 le: a, Grumman F3F-1, 1940. b, North American F-86A Sabre Jet, 1949. c, Cessna 377 Super Skymaster. d, F-16 Fighting Falcon, 1973. e, Voyager, Experimental Aircraft, Dick Rutan, Jeana Yeager. f, Fairchild A10A Thunderbolt II, 1975. g, Lockheed Vega, 1933. h, Lockheed Vega, 1930.

No. 2173, each 600 le: a, Sopwith Tabloid, 1914, UK. b, Vickers F.B.5 Gun Bus, 1915. c, Savoia Marchetti S.M. 79-II Sparviero, 1940. d, Mitsubishi A6M3 Zero Sen, 1942. e, Morane-Saulnier L, 1915. f, Shorts 360. g, Tupolev TU-160, 1988. h, Mikoyan-Gurevich MiG-15, 1948.

No. 2174, each 600 le: a, Nieuport 11C. 1, 1915. b, D.H. Vampire N.F. 10, 1951. c, Aerospatiale-Aeritalia ATR 72. d, Fiat CR.32, 1933. e, Curtiss P-6E Hawk, 1932. f, Saab JA 37 Viggen, 1977. g, Piper Pa-46 Malibu. h, F-14 Tomcat.

Each 3000 le: No. 2175, Spirit of St. Louis. No. 2176, Canadair CL-215.

1999, Mar. 22 Litho. *Perf. 14*

2166-2171 A303 Set of 6 6.00 6.00

Sheets of 8, #a.-h.

2172-2174 A303 Set of 3 26.00 26.00

Souvenir Sheets

2175-2176 A303 Set of 2 13.00 13.00

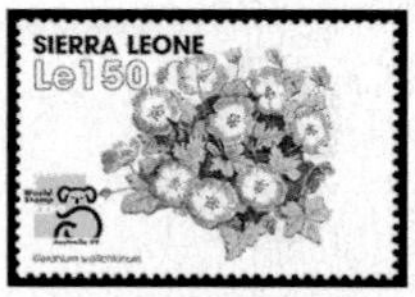

Australia '99 World Stamp Expo A304

Flowers: 150 le, Geranium wallchianum. 200 le, Osmanthus x burkwoodu. 250 le, Iris pallida, vert. 500 le, Rhododendron, vert. 600 le, Rose, vert. 800 le, Papoose, vert. 1500 le, Viola labradorica, vert. 2000 le, Rosa banksiae, vert.

No. 2185, each 600 le: a, Jack snipe. b, Alstroemeria ligtu. c, Lilium (yellow). d, Marjorie fair. e, Aemone coranaria. f, Clematis ranncu.

No. 2186, each 600 le: a, Aquilegiaa olympica. b, Lilium (orange). c, Magnolia grandiflora. d, Polygonatum x hybridum. e, Clematis montana. f, Vinca minor.

No. 2187, each 600 le: a, Colchicum speciosum. b, Scandere. c, Helianthus annuus. d, Lady Kerkrade. e, Clematix x durandil. f, Lilium regale.

No. 2188, each 600 le, vert.: a, Clematis hybrida. b, Cardiospermum halicacabum. c, Fritillaria imperialis. d, Iris ibetidiisima. e, Pyracantina. f, Hepatica transsilvanica.

Each 4000 le: No. 2189, Clerodendrum trichotomum. No. 2190, Holboellia. No. 2191, Crocus angustifolius, vert. No. 2192, Rubus fruitcosus, vert.

1999, Apr. 14

2177-2184 A304 Set of 8 9.00 9.00

Sheets of 6, #a-f

2185-2188 A304 Set of 4 23.00 23.00

Souvenir Sheets

2189-2192 A304 Set of 4 27.00 27.00

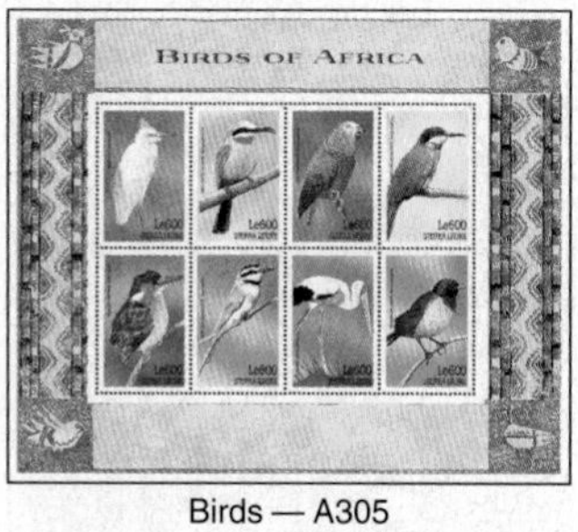

Birds — A305

No. 2193, each 600 le: a, Cattle egret. b, White-fronted bee-eater. c, African gray parrot. d, Cinnamon-chested bee-eater. e, Malachite kingfisher. f, White-throated bee-eater. g, Yellow-billed stork. h, Hildebrandt's starling.

No. 2194, each 600 le: a, Great white pelican. b, Superb starling. c, Red-throated bee-eater. d, Woodland kingfisher. e, Purple swamphen. f, Pied kingfisher. g, African spoonbill. h, Crocodile bird.

Each 3000 le: No. 2195, African fish-eagle. No. 2196, Richenow's weaver.

1999, May 18 Litho. *Perf. 14*

Sheets of 8, #a.-h.

2193-2194 A305 Set of 2 19.00 19.00

Souvenir Sheets

2195-2196 A305 Set of 2 12.00 12.00

For surcharge see No. 2902.

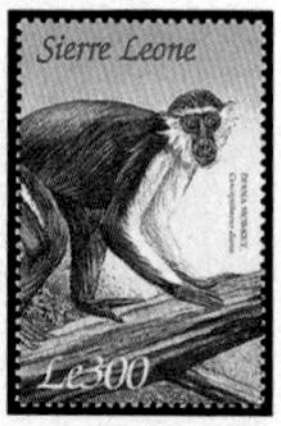

Fauna — A306

Designs: 300 le, Diana monkey. 400 le, Red-vented malimbe. 500 le, Eurasian kestrel. 600 le, Little owl. 800 le, Bush pig. 1500 le, Lion.

No. 2203, each 900 le: a, Flap-necked chameleon. b, Golden oriole (c). c, Europeon bee-eater. d, Leopard. e, Lion (d). f, Chimpanzee (e).

No. 2204, each 900 le: a, Senagal galago. b, Hoopoe. c, Long-tailed pangolin (f). d, Hippopotamus. e, African elephant (d). f, Red-billed hornbill.

Each 3000 le: No. 2205, West African linsang. No. 2206, Gray parrot.

1999, May 31 Litho.

2197-2202 A306 Set of 6 9.00 9.00

Sheets of 6, #a-f

2203-2204 A306 Set of 2 19.00 19.00

Souvenir Sheets

2205-2206 A306 Set of 2 13.50 13.50

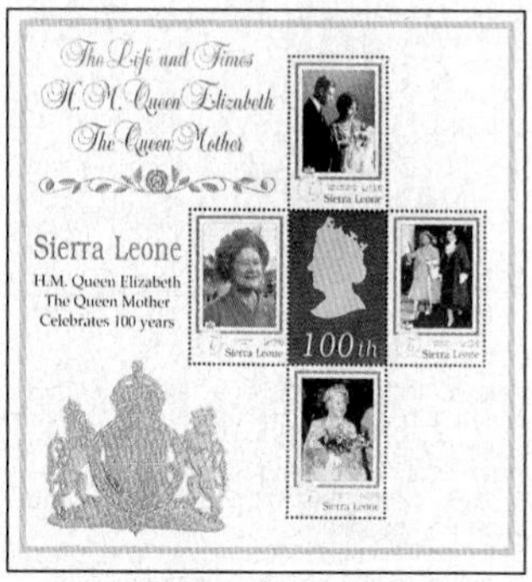

Queen Mother (b. 1900) — A307

No. 2207, each 1300 le: a, With Duke of York and Princess Elizabeth, 1926. b, In 1979. c, In Nairobi, 1959. d, In 1991.

4000 le, With crown, 1937.

1999, Aug. 4 Litho. *Perf. 14*

Gold Frames

2207 A307 Sheet of 4, #a.-d. + label 10.00 10.00

Souvenir Sheet

Perf. 13½

2208 A307 4000 le multi 9.00 9.00

No. 2208 contains one 38x51mm stamp.

See Nos. 2512-2513.

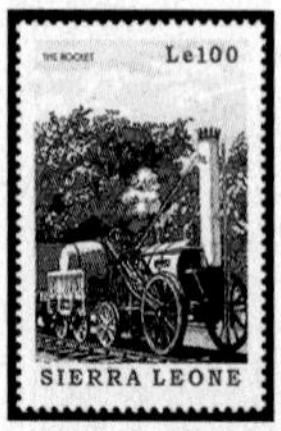

Trains — A308

Designs: 100 le, Rocket. 150 le, Benguela Railway, horiz. 200 le, Sudan Railways 310 2-8-2, horiz. 250 le, Chicago, Burlington & Quincy Railroad, horiz. 300 le, Terrier, horiz. 400 le, Dublin-Cork Express, horiz. 500 le, George Stephenson, horiz. 600 le, Shay, horiz. 1500 le, South Wind, horiz.

No. 2218, each 800 le, horiz.: a, American. b, Flying Scotsman. c, Lord Nelson. d, Mallard. e, Evening Star. f, Britannia.

No. 2219, each 800 le, horiz.: a, Class 19D 4-8-2. b, Double-headed train. c, Egyptian Railways Bo-Bo. d, GMAM Garratt 4-8-2+2-8-4. e, Passenger train, Rabat. f, Rhodesian Railway 14A Class 2-2 Garratt.

Each 3000 le: No. 2220, Mountain Class Garratt. No. 2221, Royal train.

1999, Aug. 4 *Perf. 14*

2209-2217 A308 Set of 9 6.50 6.50

Sheets of 6, #a-f

2218-2219 A308 Set of 2 16.00 16.00

Souvenir Sheets

2220-2221 A308 Set of 2 12.00 12.00

Inscription on No. 2218f is misspelled.

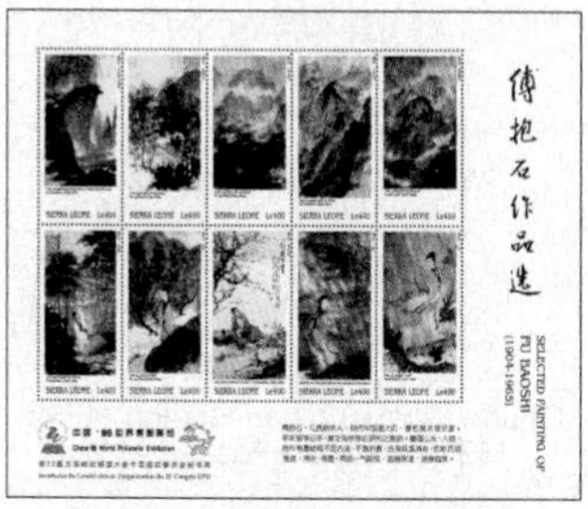

Paintings of Fu Baoshi (1904-65) — A309

No. 2222: a, Interpretation of a Poem of Shi-Tao. b, Autumn of Ho-Pao. c, Landscape in Rain (bridge). d, Landscape in Rain, diff. e, Landscape in Rain (house on mountain). f, Portrait of To-Fu. g, Classic Lady (trees with leaves). h, Portrait of Li-Pai. i, Sprite of the Mountain. j, Classic Lady (bare trees).

No. 2223: a, 800 le, Four Seasons — Winter, horiz. b, 1500 le, Four Seasons — Summer, horiz.

1999, Aug. 4 *Perf. 12¾*

2222 A309 400 le Sheet of 10, #a.-j. 9.00 9.00

Perf. 13

2223 A309 Sheet of 2, #a.-b. 7.25 7.25

China 1999 World Philatelic Exhibition. No. 2223 contains 51x38mm stamps.

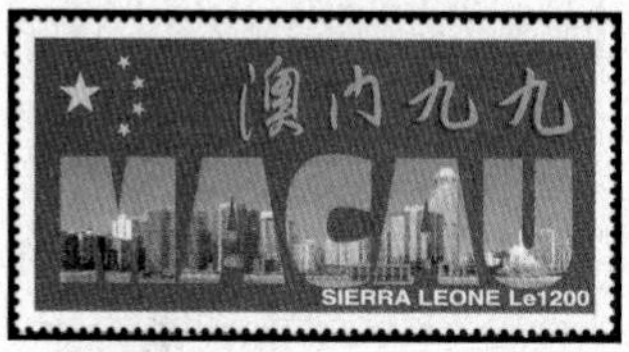

1999 Return of Macao to People's Republic of China — A310

1999, Aug. 4 *Perf. 14*

2224 A310 1200 le multi 3.75 3.75

China 1999 World Philatelic Exhibition. Issued in sheets of 3 stamps.

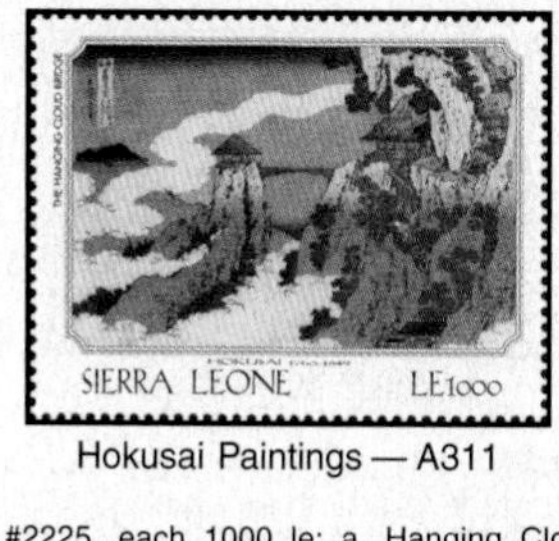

Hokusai Paintings — A311

#2225, each 1000 le: a, Hanging Cloud Bridge. b, Timber Yard by the Tate River. c, Bird Drawings (owl). d, As "c," (ducks). e, Travelers Crossing the Oi River. f, Travelers on the Tokaido Road at Hodogaya.

No. 2226, each 1000 le: a, People Admiring Mount Fuji from a Tea House. b, People on a Temple Balcony. c, Sea Life (crustacean). d, Sea Life (clam). e, Pontoon Bridge at Sano in Winter. f, A Shower Below the Summit.

Each 3000 le: No. 2227, A View of Mount Fuji and Travelers by a Bridge, vert. No. 2228, A Sudden Gust of Wind at Eijiri, vert.

1999, Aug. 4 *Perf. 13¾*

Sheets of 6, #a.-f.

2225-2226 A311 Set of 2 17.00 17.00
2227-2228 A311 Set of 2 11.00 11.00

Johann Wolfgang von Goethe (1749-
1832), German Poet — A312

No. 2229: a, Witch besieges faust. b, Goe-
the and Friedrich von Schiller. c, Margaret
places flowers before the niche of Mater
Dolorosa.
No. 2230: a, Helena with her chorus. b,
Faust takes a seat beside Helena.
Each 3000 le: #2231, Angelic spirit. #2232,
Ariel, vert.

1999, Aug. 4   Sheets of 3   Perf. 14
2229 A312 1600 le #a.-c.   8.00   8.00
2230 A312 1600 le #a.-b.,
              2229b   8.00   8.00
Souvenir Sheets
2231-2232 A312 Set of 2   12.00 12.00

Souvenir Sheets

PhilexFrance '99 — A313

Designs, each 3000 le: No. 2233, Crampton
locomotive. No. 2234, De Glehn compound
with Lemaitre front end 4-4-2.

1999, Aug. 4   Perf. 13¾
2233-2234 A313 Set of 2   11.00 11.00

IBRA '99 — A314

1999   Perf. 14x14½
2235 A314 1500 le Class 4-4-0   3.50   3.50
2236 A314 2000 le Class 05   4.50   4.50

Rights of the Child — A315

No. 2237: a, Girl holding candle. b, Two children. c, Girl, diff.
2000 le, Child, horiz.

1999, Aug. 4   Litho.   Perf. 14
2237 A315 1600 le Sheet of 3,
              #a.-c.   9.00   9.00
Souvenir Sheet
2238 A315 3000 le multi   7.50   7.50

Wedding of Prince Edward and Sophie
Rhys-Jones — A316

No. 2239: a, Sophie, close-up. b, Edward
(shirt and tie). c, Sophie, diff. d, edward, diff.
4000 le, Couple.

1999, Aug. 4   Perf. 13¾x13¼
2239 A316 2000 le Sheet of 4,
              #a.-d.   10.00 10.00
Souvenir Sheet
Perf. 13¼x13¾
2240 A316 4000 le multi   10.00 10.00

Birds of Africa — A317

No. 2241, each 600 le: a, African paradise
monarch. b, Lilac-breasted roller. c, Common
Scops owl. d, African emerald cuckoo. e, Blue
monarch. f, African golden oriole. g, White-
throated bee eater. h, Black-bellied seed-
cracker. i, Hoopoe.
No. 2242, each 600 le: a, White-faced
whistling duck. b, Black-headed heron. c,
Black-headed gonolek. d, Malachite kingfisher. e, Fish eagle. f, African spoonbill. g,
African skimmer. h, Black heron. i, Allen's
gallinule.
No. 2243, each 600 le: a, Scimitarbill. b,
Bateleur. c, Black-headed weaver. d, Variable
sunbird. e, Blue swallow. f, Black-winged red
bishop. g, Namaqua dove. h, Golden-breasted
bunting. i, Hartlaub's bustard.
No. 2244, each 600 le: a, Montagu's harrier.
b, Booted eagle. c, Yellow crested helmet-
shrike. d, Scarlet-tufted malachite sunbird. e,
Pin-tailed whydah. f, Red-headed malimbe. g,
Western violet-backed sunbird. h, Yellow white
eye. i, Brubru.
Each 4000 le: No. 2245, Rwenzori turaco,
vert. No. 2246, African pygmy kingfisher, vert.
No. 2247, Gray crowned crane, vert. No. 2248,
Shoebill, vert.

1999   Litho.   Perf. 14
Sheets of 9, #a.-i.
2241-2244 A317 Set of 4   32.50 32.50
Souvenir Sheets
2245-2248 A317 Set of 4   24.00 24.00
For surcharge see No. 2905.

New Year 2000 (Year of the
Dragon) — A318

No. 2249 (dragon color): a, Brown red. b,
Blue green. c, Bright red. d, Lilac.
4000 le, Red dragon, vert.

2000, Feb. 5   Litho.   Perf. 14
2249 A318 1500 le Sheet of 4,
              #a.-d.   8.00   8.00
Souvenir Sheet
2250 A318 4000 le multi   7.50   7.50

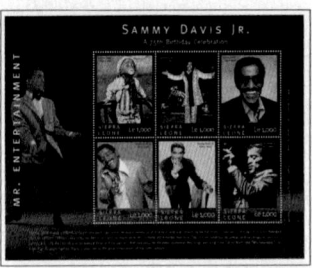

Sammy Davis, Jr. — A319

No. 2251: a, As child. b, With motorcycle. c,
With red checked shirt. d, With microphone. e,
With leg on chair. f, Holding cigarette.
5000 le, With other people.

2000, Mar. 8   Perf. 13¾
2251 A319 1000 le Sheet of 6,
              #a.-f.   5.75   5.75
Souvenir Sheet
2252 A319 5000 le multi   4.75   4.75

Flowers — A320

Various flowers making up a photomosaic of
Princess Diana.

2000, Mar. 28
2253 A320 800 le Sheet of 8,
              #a.-h.   6.50   6.50
See Nos. 2359-2360.

Millennium — A321

Highlights of 1600-1650: a, Election of
Michael Romanov as Russian tsar. b, William
Shakespeare publishes "Hamlet." c, Kung
Hsien paints "Thousand Peaks and Myriad
Ravines." d, Francis Bacon publishes his
works. e, Founding of Jamestown, Virginia. f,
Reign of Louis XIV of France. g, Founding of
Quebec. h, Birth of Isaac Newton. i, Nicholas
Poussin paints "Rape of the Sabine Women."
j, Johannes Kepler publishes "The New
Astronomy." k, The Mayflower arrives in
America. l, King James Bible is published. m,
Dutch East India Company introduces tea to
Europe. n, René Descartes develops his phi-
losophy. o, Galileo defends Copernican sys-
tem. p, Queen Elizabeth I dies (60x40mm). q,
Miguel de Cervantes publishes "Don Quixote."

2000, Mar. 28   Perf. 12¾x12½
2254 A321 400 le Sheet of 17,
              #a.-q., + label 6.50   6.50

Paintings of Anthony Van
Dyck — A322

No. 2255, each 1000 le: a, Portrait of a Man.
b, Anna Wake, Wife of Peter Stevens. c, Peter
Stevens. d, Adriaen Stevens. e, Maria Boss-
chaerts, Wife of Adriaen Stevens. f, Portrait of
a Woman.
No. 2256, each 1000 le: a, Self-portrait,
1617-18. b, Self-portrait, 1620-21. c, Self-por-
trait, 1622-23. d, Andromeda Chained to the
Rock. e, Self-portrait, late 1620s-early 1630s.
f, Mary Ruthven.
No. 2257, each 1000 le: a, The Betrayal of
Judas (detail of The Taking of Christ.) b, Ecce
Homo, 1625-26. c, Christ Carrying the Cross
(showing woman with blue garment). d, The
Raising of Christ on the Cross. e, The Crucifixion, c. 1627 f, The Lamentation, c. 1616 (actually the "Mocking of Christ").
No. 2258, each 1000 le: a, The Taking of
Christ. b, The Mocking of Christ. c, Ecce
Homo, 1628-32. d, Christ Carrying the Cross
(showing poleax). e, The Crucifixion, c. 1629-
30. f, The Lamentation 1618-20.
No. 2258G, each 1000 le: h, The Duchess
of Crow With Her Son. i, Susanna Fourment
and Her Daughter. j, Geronima Brignole-Sale
With Her Daughter Maria Aurelia. k, A Woman
With Her Daughter. l, A Genoese Noblewo-
man With Her Child. m, A Genoese Noblewo-
man (Paola Adorno) and Her Son.
Each 5000 le: No. 2259, Self-portrait With a
Sunflower. No. 2260, Self-portrait with Endym-
ion Porter. No. 2261, Young Woman With a
Child. No. 2262, Porzia Imperiale With Her
Daughter Maria Francesca. No. 2263, Portrait
of a Mother and Her Daughter. No. 2264, A
Woman and a Child, horiz.

2000, Apr. 10   Perf. 13¾
Sheets of 6, #a.-f.
2255-2258G A322 Set of 5   29.00 29.00
Souvenir Sheets
2259-2264 A322 Set of 6   29.00 29.00
Easter (Nos. 2257-2258).

Mario Andretti — A323

No. 2265: a, Behind wheel. b, With helmet,
facing left. c, In pits. d, In crash. e, Inspecting
tire. f, With white shirt. g, Without shirt. h, In
car #50.

5000 le, With others in front of old car.

2000, Mar. 28   Litho.   Perf. 13¾
2265 A323 600 le Sheet of 8,
              #a-h   5.00 5.00
Souvenir Sheet
2266 A323 5000 le multi   5.00 5.00

Scenes from "The Little Colonel" with
Shirley Temple — A324

Temple — No. 2267: a, With Colonel Lloyd
(Lionel Barrymore), standing. b, With Walker
(Bill Robinson). c, With two children. d, With
soldiers. e, With mother (Evelyn Venable),
Becky (Hattie McDaniel). f, Hugging Colonel
Lloyd.
No. 2268: a, With Becky and Walker. b, With
Walker, diff. c, Alone. d, Tugging Colonel
Lloyd's coat.
No. 2269, Holding chair.

2000, Mar. 28   Sheets of 6 and 4
2267 A324 1200 le #a-f   7.50 7.50
2268 A324 1500 le #a-d   6.25 6.25
Souvenir Sheet
2269 A324 5000 le multi   5.00 5.00
    See also Nos. 2550-2552.

Parrots — A325

Designs: 200 le, African gray parrot.
1500 le, Sulfur-crested cockatoo, horiz.
No. 2272, each 800 le: a, Monk parakeet. b,
Citron-crested cockatoo. c, Queen-of-Bavaria
conure. d, Budgerigar. e, Yellow-chevroned
parakeet. f, Cockatiel. g, Amazon parrot. h,
Sun conure. i, Malabar parakeet.
No. 2273, each 800 le: a, Grand eclectus
parrot. b, Sun parakeet. c, Red fan parakeet.
d, Fischer's lovebird. e, Blue masked lovebird.
f, White belly rosella. g, Plum-headed parakeet. h, Striated lorikeet. i, Gold-mantled
rosella.
4000 le, Blue and gold macaw.

2000, May 16   Perf. 13¾x14, 14x13¾
2270-2271 A325 Set of 2   1.90 1.90
Sheets of 9, #a-i
2272-2273 A325 Set of 2   16.00 16.00
Souvenir Sheet
2274 A325 multi   4.50 4.50
The Stamp Show 2000, London (Nos. 2272-
2274). Size of stamps: Nos. 2272-2273,
28x42mm; No. 2274, 38x50mm.

Orchids
A326

Designs: 300 le, Aeranthes henrici. 500 le,
Ophrys apifera. 600 le, Disa crassicornis.
2000 le, Aeranthes grandiflora.
No. 2279, each 1100 le: a, Oeleoclades
maculata. b, Polystachya campyloglossa. c,
Polystachya pubescens. d, Tridactyle
bicaudata. e, Angraecum veitcii. f, Sobennikof-
fia robusta.
No. 2280, each 1100 le: a, Aerangis
curnowiana. b, Aerangis fastudsa. c,
Angraecum magdalenae. d, Angraecum
sororium. e, Eulophia speciosa. f, Ansellia
africana.

Each 4000 le: No. 2281, Angraecum com-
pactum. No. 2282, Angraecum eburneum.

2000, May 16   Perf. 14
2275-2278 A326 Set of 4   3.75 3.75
Sheets of 6, #a-f
2279-2280 A326 Set of 2   15.00 15.00
Souvenir Sheets
2281-2282 A326 Set of 2   9.00 9.00

Prince William, 18th Birthday — A327

Various photos.

2000, May 29   Perf. 14
2283 A327 1100 le Sheet of 4,
              #a-d   5.00 5.00
Souvenir Sheet
Perf. 13¾
2284 A327 5000 le multi   5.50 5.50
No. 2284 contains one 38x50mm stamp.

Souvenir Sheet

2000 Summer Olympics,
Sydney — A328

Designs: a, Hurdler. b, Soccer player. c,
Finnish flag, Helsinki Stadium. d, Ancient
Greek wrestlers.

2000, May 29   Perf. 14
2285 A328 1500 le Sheet of 4.
              #a-d   6.25 6.25

First Zeppelin Flight, Cent. — A329

No. 2286: a, LZ-129. b, LZ-4. c, LZ-6.
4000 le, LZ-127.

2000, May 29   Perf. 14
2286 A329 2000 le Sheet of 3,
              #a-c   6.25 6.25
Souvenir Sheet
Perf. 14¼
2287 A329 4000 le multi   4.25 4.25
Size of stamps: No. 2286, 38x24mm.

Betty Boop — A330

No. 2288: a, Wearing flowered dress. b,
Carrying shopping bags. c, Wearing baseball
cap. d, Holding shoes. e, Sitting in chair. f,
Wearing jacket. g, Playing guitar. h, Holding
lasso. i, Holding flower.
Each 5000 le: No. 2289, Pointing at dog.
No. 2290, Riding bicycle.

2000, Mar. 8   Litho.   Perf. 13¾
2288 A330 800 le Sheet of 9,
              #a-i   8.25 8.25
Souvenir Sheets
2289-2290 A330 Set of 2   11.50 11.50

I Love Lucy — A331

No. 2291, each 800 le — Lucy: a, Wearing
blue cap. b, With arms in front, with
Vitameatavegamin bottle. c, Wearing pink
nightgown. d, Wearing pink nightgown, stick-
ing out tongue. e, Wearing blue cap on television screen. f, Holding bottle near table. g,
With arms at side, with bottle. h, Holding bottle
near cheek. i, Pouring out liquid in bottle.
Each 5000 le: No. 2292, Wearing blue cap
on television, Ricky touching television. No.
2293, Lucy and Fred Mertz.

2000, Mar. 8
2291 A331 Sheet of 9, #a-i   8.25 8.25
Souvenir Sheets
2292-2293 A331 Set of 2   11.50 11.50

Berlin Film Festival, 50th
Anniv. — A332

No. 2294, each 1100 le: a, Las Palabras de
Max. b, Ascendancy. c, Deprisa, Deprisa. d,
Die Sehnsucht der Veronika Voss. e, Heart-
land. f, La Colmena.
5000 le, Las Truchas.

2000, May 29   Perf. 14
2294 A332 Sheet of 6, #a-f   7.50 7.50
Souvenir Sheet
2295 A332 5000 le multi   5.75 5.75

Souvenir Sheet

Public Railways, 175th Anniv. — A333

No. 2296, each 3000 le: a, Locomotion No.
1, George Stephenson. b, James Watt's original design for a separate condenser engine.

2000, May 29
2296 A333 Sheet of 2, #a-b   7.00 7.00

Souvenir Sheet

Johann Sebastian Bach (1685-
1750) — A334

2000, May 29
2297 A334 5000 le multi   5.75 5.75

Sea Birds
A335

Designs: 400 le, Herring gull. 600 le, Caspian tern. 800 le, Red phalarope. 2000 le,
Magnificent frigatebird.
No. 2302, each 1000 le: a, Caspian tern,
diff. b, Glaucous gull. c, Northern gannet. d,
Long-tailed jaeger. e, Brown pelican. f, Great
skua.
No. 2303, each 1000 le: a, Wandering albatross. b, Fork-tailed storm petrel. c, Great
shearwater. d, Blue-footed booby. e, Great
cormorant. f, Atlantic puffin.
Each 5000 le: No. 2304, Brown booby, vert.
No. 2305, Red-tailed tropicbird, vert.

2000, May 16   Litho.   Perf. 14
2298-2301 A335 Set of 4   3.75 3.75
Sheets of 6, #a-f
2302-2303 A335 Set of 2   12.00 12.00
Souvenir Sheets
2304-2305 A335 Set of 2   10.00 10.00

Richard Petty, Stock Car
Racer — A336

No. 2306, each 800 le: a, Car in pits. b, With family. c, Wearing red jacket. d, Wearing Pontiac cap. e, Wearing white hat, uniform with two STP logos. f, Wearing STP cap. g, Standing in car. h, Profile, wearing STP logos on shoulder. i, Wearing headphones.

No. 2307, each 800 le: a, Holding trophy. b, Wearing Winston cap. c, Wearing black hat. d, Hatless, blue background. e, Wearing shirt with red collar. f, Holding helmet. g, Leaning on blue and red car. h, With arm in car. i, Leaning head out of car.

No. 2308, each 800 le: a, Wearing red shirt, white hat. b, Hatless, orange background. c, Wearing Pontiac cap. d, Strapped in car, without helmet. e, Holding timer. f, Wearing red and blue helmet. g, Wearing white hat, blue uniform. h, With trophy, wearing STP cap. i, With white hat, reclining.

Each 5000 le: No. 2309, Standing in car, diff. No, 2310, In race, horiz.

2000, Aug. 15   **Perf. 13¾**
Sheets of 9, #a-i
2306-2308 A336 Set of 3   21.00 21.00
Souvenir Sheets
2309-2310 A336 Set of 2   10.00 10.00

Popes — A337

No. 2311, each 1100 le: a, Gregory VI (1045-46). b, Celestine V (1294). c, Honorius IV (1285-87). d, Innocent IV (1243-54). e, Innocent VII (1404-06). f, John XXII (1316-34).

No. 2312, each 1100 le: a, Martin IV (1281-85). b, Nicholas II (1059-61). c, Nicholas IV (1288-92). d, Urban IV (1261-64). e, Urban V (1362-70). f, Urban VI (1378-89).

Each 5000 le: No. 2313, Nicholas IV (1288-92), diff. No. 2314, Clement XI (1700-21).

2000, Aug. 21   **Sheets of 6, #a-f**
2311-2312 A337 Set of 2   13.00 13.00
Souvenir Sheets
2313-2314 A337 Set of 2   10.00 10.00

Monarchs — A338

No. 2315, each 1100 le: a, Emperor Hung Wu of China. b, Emperor Hsuan Te of China. c, King Sejong of Korea. d, Emperor T'ung Chih of China. e, Emperor T'ai Tsu (Chao K'uang-yin) of Chin. f, Empress Yung Ching of China.

No. 2316, Kublai Khan of China.

2000, Aug. 21
2315 A338 Sheet of 6, #a-f   6.50 6.50
Souvenir Sheet
2316 A338 5000 le multi   5.00 5.00

European Soccer
Championships — A339

No. 2317, each 1300 le — Germany: a, Worns. b, Team photo. c, Babbel. d, Franz Beckenbauer. e, Selessin Stadium, Liege, Belgium. f, Stefan Kuntz.

No. 2318, each 1300 le — Italy: a, Walter Zenga. b, Team photo. c, Roberto Bettega. d, Totti. e, Philips Stadium, Eindhoven, Netherlands. f, Vieri.

No. 2319, each 1300 le — Portugal: a, Dimas. b, Team photo. c, Pinto. d, Santos. e, Gelredome Stadium, Arnhem, Netherlands. f, Sousa.

No. 2320, each 1300 le — Romania: a, Munteanu. b, Team photo. c, Petre. d, Petrescu. e, Popescu.

Each 5000 le: No. 2321, German coach Erich Ribbeck, vert. No. 2322, Italian coach Dino Zoff, vert. No. 2323, Portuguese coach Humberto Coelho, vert. No. 2324, Romanian coach Emerich Jenei, vert.

Sheets of 6, #a-f (#2317-2319);
Sheet of 6 #a-e, #2319e (#2320)
2000, Aug. 21
2317-2320 A339 Set of 4   30.00 30.00
Souvenir Sheets
2321-2324 A339 Set of 4   20.00 20.00

Souvenir Sheet

Albert Einstein (1879-1955) — A340

2000, May 29   **Litho.**   **Perf. 14**
2325 A340 5000 le multi   5.00 5.00

Apollo-Soyuz Mission, 25th
Anniv. — A341

No. 2326, each 1200 le, vert.: a, Apollo 18. b, Soyuz 19. c, Apollo and Soyuz docked. 5000 le, Apollo and Soyuz docking.

2000, May 29
2326 A341 Sheet of 3, #a-c   3.50 3.50
Souvenir Sheet
2327 A341 5000 le multi   5.00 5.00

Queen Mother, 100th Birthday — A342

Litho. & Embossed
2000, Aug. 4   **Die Cut Perf. 8¾**
Without Gum
2328 A342 18,000 le gold & multi

Dogs and
Cats
A343

500 le, Bulldog. 800 le, Brown tabby. 1500 le, Burmese. 2000 le, Dachshund.

No. 2333, 1000 le: a, Beagle. b, Scottish terrier. c, Bloodhound. d, Greyhound. e, German shepherd. f, Cocker spaniel.

No. 2334, 1000 le: a, Red tabby stumpy Manx. b, Red self. c, Maine Coon cat. d, Black smoke. e, Chinchilla. f, Russian Blue.

No. 2335, 1100 le: a, Pointer. b, Doberman pinscher. c, Collie. d, Chihuahua. e, Afghan hound. f, Boxer.

No. 2336, 1100 le: a, Singapura. b, Himalayan. c, Abyssinian. d, Black cat. e, Siamese. f, North African wild cat.

No. 2337, 5000 le, Fox terrier, vert. No. 2338, 5000 le, Calico, vert.

2000, Oct. 2   **Litho.**   **Perf. 14**
2329-2332 A343 Set of 4   5.00 5.00
Sheets of 6, #a-f
2333-2336 A343 Set of 4   26.00 26.00
Souvenir Sheets
2337-2338 A343 Set of 2   10.50 10.50

Paintings from the Prado — A344

No. 2339, 1000 le: a, The Transport of Mary Magdalen, by José Antolinez. b, The Holy Family, by Francisco de Goya. c, Our Lady of the Immaculate Conception, by Antolinez. d, Charles IV as Prince, by Anton Raphael Mengs. e, Louis XIII of France, by Philippe de Champaigne. f, Prince Ferdinand VI by Jean Ranc.

No. 2340, 1000 le: a, Adam, by Albrecht Dürer. b, Moor, by Manuel Benedito Vives. c, Eve, by Dürer. d, A Gypsy, by Raimundo Madrazo y Garreta. e, Maria Guerrero, by Joaquin Sorolla y Bastida. f, The Model Aline Masson with a White Mantilla, by Madrazo y Garreta.

No. 2341, 1000 le: a, Figure in yellow robe from Madonna and Child Between Saints Catherine and Ursula, by Giovanni Bellini. b, Madonna and Child from Madonna and Child

Between Saints Catherine and Ursula. c, Figure in red robe from Madonna and Child Between Saints Catherine and Ursula. d, Giovanni Mateo Ghiberti, by Agustín Esteve. e, The Marchioness of Santa Cruz, by Agustín Esteve. f, Self-portrait, by Orazio Borgianni.

No. 2342, 1000 le: a, Mary from The Holy Family with a Bird, by Bartolomé Esteban Murillo. b, Jesus from The Holy Family with a Bird. c, Joseph, from The Holy Family with a Bird. d, Cardinal Carlos de Borja, by Andrea Procaccini. e, St. Dominic de Guzmán, by Claudio Coello. f, Christ Supported by an Angel, by Alonso Cano.

No. 2343, 1000 le: a, Woman from The Seller of Fans, by José del Castillo. b, Allegory of Summer, by Mariano Salvador Maella. c, Man with basket from The Seller of Fans. d, Portrait of a Girl, by Carlos Luis de Ribera y Fieve. e, The Poultry Keeper, by Pensionante del Saraceni. f, The Death of Cleopatra, by Guido Reni.

No. 2344, 1000 le; a, Feliciana Bayeu, by Francisco Bayeu y Subias. b, Tomás de Iriarte by Joaquín Inza. c, St. Elizabeth of Portugal, by Francisco de Zurbarán. d, Christ from The Vision of St. Francis at Porziuncola, by Murillo. e, Monk from The Vision of St. Francis at Porziuncola. f, Woman from The Vision of St. Francis at Porziuncola.

No. 2345, 5000 le, Lot and His Daughters, by Francesco Furini. No. 2346, 5000 le, The Execution of Torrijos and His Companions, by Antonio Gisbert Pérez. No. 2347, 5000 le, the Concert, by Vicente Palmaroli y González. No. 2348, 5000 le, The Finding of Joseph's Cup in Benjamin's Bag, by Jacopo Amigoni. No. 2349, 5000 le, Vulcan's Forge, by Diego Velázquez. No. 2350, 5000 le, The Two Friends, by Joaquin Agrasot y Juan, horiz.

2000, Oct. 6   **Perf. 12x12¼, 12¼x12**
Sheets of 6, #a-f
2339-2344 A344 Set of 6   37.50 37.50
Souvenir Sheets
2345-2350 A344 Set of 6   32.50 32.50

Espana 2000 Intl. Philatelic Exhibition.

Mushrooms — A345

Designs: 600 le, Tuberous polyphore. 900 le, Cultivated agaricus. 1200 le, Scarlet wax cap. 2500 le, Blue-green psilocybe.

No. 2355, 1000 le, vert.: a, Armed stinkhorn. b, Red-staining inocybe. c, Amanitopsis vaginata. d, Inocybe jurana. e, Xerula longipes. f, Tricholoma matsutake.

No. 2356, 1000 le, vert.: a, Orange-staining mycena. b, Russula amoema. c, Cinnabar chanterelle. d, Calodon aurantiacum. e, Lentinus lepidus. f, Gomphidius roseus.

No. 2357, 5000 le, Orange latex lactarius. No. 2358, 5000 le, Common morel, vert.

2000, Oct. 30   **Litho.**   **Perf. 14**
2351-2354 A345 Set of 4   5.50 5.50
Sheets of 6, #a-f
2355-2356 A345 Set of 2   12.50 12.50
Souvenir Sheets
2357-2358 A345 Set of 2   10.50 10.50

Flower Photomosaic Type of 2000

No. 2359, 800 le: Various flowers making up a photomosaic of the Queen Mother.

No. 2360, 900 le: Various photographs of religious scenes making up a photomosaic of Pope John Paul II.

2000, Oct. 30   **Perf. 13¾**
Sheets of 8, #a-h
2359-2360 A320 Set of 2   14.50 14.50

Massacre of Israeli Olympic Athletes,
1972 — A346

No. 2361, horiz.: a, Kahat Shor. b, Andrei Schpitzer. c, Joseph Romano. d, Yaakov Springer. e, Eliazer Halffin. f, Amitsur Shapira. g, Moshe Weinberg. h, Torchbearer, Israeli flag. j, Joseph Gottfreund. k, Ze'ev Friedman. l, David Berger.

2000, Nov. 9   *Perf. 14*
2361 A346   500 le Sheet of 12,
    #a-l   6.25 6.25
Souvenir Sheet
2362 A346 5000 le Torchbearer   5.25 5.25

Circus
A347

Designs: 800 le, Tightrope rider. 1000 le, Bear and ball. 1500 le, Tiger on ball. 2000 le, Camels.
No. 2367, 1100 le: a, Polar bear on roller. b, Ape. c, Clown, green background. d, Tightrope walker. e, Seals. f, Camel.
No. 2368, 1100 le: a, Clown, brown background. b, Tiger on wires. c, Monkey. d, Dogs. e, Bear on skates. f, Trapeze artists.
No. 2369, 1100 le, vert.: a, Acrobat. b, Giraffe. c, Bear on poles. d, Elephant. e, Horse. f, Fire eater.
No. 2370, 5000 le, Trainer on elephant's trunk, vert. No. 2371, 5000 le, Tiger jumping through flaming hoop, vert. No. 2372, 5000 le, Cannon flyer, vert.

2000, Dec. 1   *Litho.*
2363-2366 A347   Set of 4   5.75 5.75
Sheets of 6, #a-f
2367-2369 A347   Set of 3   21.00 21.00
Souvenir Sheets
2370-2372 A347   Set of 3   16.00 16.00

Queen Mother,
100th
Birthday — A348

2000, Dec. 18
2373 A348 1100 le multi   1.10 1.10
Issued in sheets of 6.

New Year 2001 (Year of the
Snake) — A349

No. 2374, horiz.: a, Blue snake. b, Red snake. c, Purple snake. d, Green snake.

2001, Jan. 2
2374 A349   800 le Sheet of 4,
    #a-d   3.50 3.50
Souvenir Sheet
2375 A349 2500 le Green snake   2.60 2.60

History of the Orient Express — A350

No. 2376, 1000 le: a, First sleeping car, 1872. b, Dining car #193, 1886. c, Dining car #2422, 1913. d, Sleeping car Type S1. e, Metal sleeping car #2645. f, Metal sleeping car #2644, 1922.
No. 2377, 1000 le: a, Dining car, Series #8341. b, Dining car, Series #3342. c, Sleeping car, Series #3312 Type Z. d, Sleeping car, Series #3879, 1950. e, Sleeping car, Series #3311 Type Z. f, Dining car, Series #3785, 1932.
No. 2378, 1100 le: a, Ostend-Vienna. b, Engine East 230, #3175. c, Dual cylinder locomotive. d, Simplon Orient Express, 1919. e, Engine East 220, #2405. f, Caboose of Simplon Express, c. 1906.
No. 2379, 1100 le: a, Sleeping car #507, 1897. b, Sleeping car #438, 1894. c, Sleeping car #313, 1880. d, Sleeping car #190, 1886. e, Sleeping car #102, 1882. f, Sleeping car #77, 1881.
No. 2380, 5000 le, Locomotive. No. 2381, 5000 le, Georges Nagelmackers, vert. No. 2382, 5000 le, Mata Hari, vert. No. 2383, 5000 le, Agatha Christie, vert.

2001, Jan. 15   *Perf. 14*
    Sheets of 6, #a-f
2376-2379 A350   Set of 4   26.00 26.00
    Souvenir Sheets
2380-2383 A350   Set of 4   21.00 21.00

Reptiles
A351

Designs: 250 le, Natal Mixands dwarf chameleon. 400 le, Cape cobra. 500 le, Western sand lizard. 600 le, Pan-hinged terrapin. 800 le, Many-horned adder. 1500 le, Hawequa flat gecko.
No. 2390, 1200 le: a, Reticulated desert lizard. b, Ball python. c, Gaboon viper. d, Dumeril's boa. e, Common egg-eater. f, Helmet turtle.
No. 2391, 1200 le: a, Asian saw-scaled viper. b, Namibian sand snake. c, Angolan garter snake. d, Striped skaapsteker. e, Brown house snake. f, Shield-nosed cobra.
No. 2392, 5000 le, Green water snake. No. 2393, 5000 le, Flap-necked chameleon.

2001, Jan. 15
2384-2389 A351   Set of 6   4.25 4.25
    Sheets of 6, #a-f
2390-2391 A351   Set of 2   15.00 15.00
    Souvenir Sheets
2392-2393 A351   Set of 2   10.50 10.50

Rijksmuseum, Amsterdam, Bicent. (in
2000) — A352

No. 2394, 1100 le, vert.: a, Gentleman Writing a Letter, by Gabriel Metsu. b, Self-portrait, by Carel Fabritius. c, The Windmill at Wijk bij Duurstede, by Jacob van Ruisdael. d, Bentheim Castle, by van Ruisdael. e, Ships on a Stormy Sea, by Willem van de Velde, the Younger. f, David from David Playing the Harp, by Jan de Bray.
No. 2395, 1100 le, vert.: a, St. Paul from St. Paul Healing the Cripple at Lystra, by Karel Dujardin. b, Two hatless men from The Meagre Company, by Frans Hals and Pieter Codde. c, Man from Elegant Couple in an Interior, by Eglon van der Neer. d, Laid Table With

Cheese and Fruit, by Floris van Dijck. e, Bacchanal, by Moses van Uyttenbroeck. f, Kneeling woman from St. Paul Healing the Cripple at Lystra.
No. 2396, 1100 le, vert.: a, Lady Reading a Letter, by Metsu. b, Portrait of Titus, by Rembrandt. c, Portrait of Gerard de Lairesse, by Rembrandt. d, Portrait of a Family in an Interior, by Emanuel de Witte. e, The Letter, by Gerard Terborch. f, Three Women and a Man in a Courtyard Behind a House, by Pieter de Hooch.
No. 2397, 1100 le, vert.: a, Candlebearers from David Playing the Harp. b, Hand of St. Paul from St. Paul Healing the Cripple at Lystra. c, Two men, one with hat, from The Meagre Company. d, The Gray, by Ohilips Wouwerman. e, Couple from Elegant Couple in an Interior. f, The Hut, by Adriaen van de Velde.
No. 2398, 5000 le, Road in the Dunes With a Passenger Coach, by Salomon van Ruysdael. No. 2399, 5000 le, Cows in the Meadow, by Albert Gerard Bilders. No. 2400, 5000 le, Lot and His Daughters, by Hendrick Goltzius. No. 2401, 5000 le, Arrival of Queen Wilhelmina at the Frederiksplein in Amsterdam, by Otto Eerelman.

2001, Jan. 15   *Perf. 13¾*
    Sheets of 6, #a-f
2394-2397 A352   Set of 4   27.50 27.50
    Souvenir Sheets
2398-2401 A352   Set of 4   21.00 21.00

Battle of Britain, 60th Anniv. — A353

No. 2402, 1000 le: a, Bombed village near London. b, The Underground as a bomb shelter. c, Firemen. d, Home Guard. e, Setting lights out time. f, Pilots resting between flights. g, Brendan "Paddy" Finucane, ace pilot. h, Hawk 75.
No. 2403, 1000 le: a, St. Paul's Cathedral. b, Eastenders leaving London. c, Winston Churchill being cheered by British crew. d, Rescue pilot. e, Boy Scouts helping children. f, Big gunners, 1940. g, Plane spotter lights. h, Survey watchers.
No. 2404, 1000 le: a, Post Office Engineer, WAFF. b, Women munitions workers. c, Churchill as prime minister and defense minister. d, German Dornier DO17. e, Church fires from Nazi bombs, London, 1940. f, All-night raid on London, 1940. g, Lunchtime in the Underground, 1940. h, People in the Underground, 1940.
No. 2405, 1000 le: a, London Bridge. b, Surrey Home Guard. c, British Cruiser tank MK III. d, Newfoundland men at the guns, 1940. e, Lady Astor's Constituency hit, 1940. f, Churchill worried with war, 1940. g, Bomb blast at Parliament. h, Development of radar, 1940.
No. 2406, 6000 le, Churchill and wife inspecting harbor damage. No. 2407, 6000 le, London, 1940. No. 2408, 6000 le, British Supermarine Spitfire. No. 2409, 6000 le, Bombing crew preparing for flight, 1940, vert.

2001, Jan. 30   *Perf. 14*
    Sheets of 8, #a-h
2402-2405 A353   Set of 4   35.00 35.00
    Souvenir Sheets
2406-2409 A353   Set of 4   25.00 25.00

Biblical Scenes by Rembrandt — A354

No. 2410, 1000 le: a, The Song of Simeon. b, Study for Adoration of the Magi. c, Mary With the Child by a Window. d, The Rest on the Flight Into Egypt. e, The Circumcision. f, The Shepherds Worship the Child.
No. 2411, 1000 le: a, The Angel Rises Up in the Flame of Manoah's Sacrifice. b, Tobias Frighterned by the Fish. c, The Angel of the Lord Stands in Balaam's Path. d, The Angel Appears to Hagar in the Desert. e, Jacob's Dream. f, The Healing of Tobit.
No. 2412, 5000 le, Simeon's Prophecy to Mary. No. 2413, 5000 le, The Angel Prevents the Sacrifice of Isaac. No. 2414, 5000 le, The Angel Leaves Tobit and His Family, vert. No. 2415, 5000 le, The Adoration of the Magi, vert.

2001, Feb. 13   *Perf. 13¾*
    Sheets of 6, #a-f
2410-2411 A354   Set of 2   12.50 12.50
    Souvenir Sheets
2412-2415 A354   Set of 4   21.00 21.00

Racehorses
A355

Designs: 200 le, Native Dancer. 500 le, Citation. 1500 le, Spectre. 2000 le, Carbine.
No. 2420, 1200 le: a, Arkle. b, Golden Miller. c, Phar Lap. d, Battleship. e, Kelso. f, Nijinsky.
No. 2421, 1200 le: a, Red Rum. b, Sir Ken. c, War Admiral. d, Troytown. e, Shergar. f, Allez France.
No. 2422, 5000 le, Cigar. No. 2423, 5000 le, Desert Orchid. No. 2424, 5000 le, Trophy. No. 2425, 5000 le, Horses on turf track, horiz.

2001, Feb. 27   *Perf. 14*
2416-2419 A355   Set of 4   4.50 4.50
    Sheets of 6, #a-f
2420-2421 A355   Set of 2   15.00 15.00
    Souvenir Sheets
2422-2425 A355   Set of 4   21.00 21.00

Automobiles — A356

No. 2426, 1000 le: a, 1898 Benz Velo. b, 1909 Rolls-Royce Silver Ghost. c, 1912 Ford Model T. d, 1937 Duesenberg SJ. e, 1938-40 Grosser Mercedes. f, 1938 Citroen Light 15.
No. 2427, 1000 le: a, 1939 Lincoln Zephyr. b, 1947 Volkswagen Beetle. c, 1959 Jaguar Mark II. d, 1968 Ford Shelby Mustang GT500. e, 1987-94 Opel/Vauxhall Senator. f, 2002 Mercedes Maybach.
No. 2428, 5000 le, 1928 Bentley 3-liter short chassis Tourer. No. 2429, 5000 le, 1999 Ferrari 360 Modena.

2001, Apr. 30   **Perf. 13¾**
Sheets of 6, #a-f, + 6 labels
2426-2427   A356   Set of 2   12.50 12.50
    Souvenir Sheets
2428-2429   A356   Set of 2   10.50 10.50

Butterflies
A357

Designs: 250 le, Eurema floricola. 400 le, Papilio dardanus. 800 le, Amauris nossima. 1500 le, Gideona lucasi.
No. 2434, 1100 le: a, Papilio dardanus. b, Cymothoe sangaris. c, Epiphora albida. d, African giant swallowtail. e, Papilio nobilis nobilis. f, Charaxes hadnanus.
No. 2435, 1100 le: a, Charaxes lucretia. b, Euxanthe closslex. c, Charaxes phenix. d, Charaxes acraeades. e, Charaxes protoclea azota. f, Charaxes lydiae.
No. 2436, 5000 le, Clotis zoe. No. 2437, 5000 le, Acraea ranaualona, vert.

Perf. 13¼x13½, 13½x13¼
2001, Apr. 30   **Litho.**
2430-2433   A357   Set of 4   3.25 3.25
    Sheets of 6, #a-f
2434-2435   A357   Set of 2   14.50 14.50
    Souvenir Sheets
2436-2437   A357   Set of 2   11.00 11.00

Queen Elizabeth II, 75th
Birthday — A358

No. 2438: a, Wearing hat. b, With infant. c, Wearing crown. d, Wearing black blouse.

2001, June 18   **Litho.**   **Perf. 14**
2438   A358   2000 le Sheet of 4,
       #a-d   8.25 8.25
    Souvenir Sheet
       Perf. 13¾
2439   A358   5000 le As older wo-
       man   5.25 5.25
No. 2438 contains four 28x42mm stamps.

Japanese
Art — A359

Designs: 50 le, Iziu Chinuki No Hi, by Hokkei, horiz. 100 le, A Visit to Enoshima, by Kiyonaga Torii, horiz. 150 le, Inn on a Harbor, by Sadahide, horiz. 200 le, Entrance to Foreigner's Establishment, by Sadahide, horiz. 250 le, Courtesans at Cherry Blossom Time, by Kiyonaga, horiz. 300 le, Cherry Blossom Viewing at Ueno, by Toyohara Chikanobu, horiz. 400 le, A Summer Evening at a Restaurant by the Sumida River, by Torii, horiz.

500 le, Ichikana Yaozo I As Samurai, by Buncho. 600 le, The Actor Nakamura Noshoi II as a Street Walker, by Shunzan Katsukawa. 800 le, Arashi Sangoro II, by Shokosai. 1500 le, bando Mitsugoro I by Shunko. No. 2451, 2000 le, Matsumoto Koshiro II, by Masanobu.
No. 2452, 2000 le: a, Nakamura Shikan II and Nakamura Baiko, by Shigeharu. b, Women Making Rice Cakes, by Shunsho. c, Youth Sending Letter by Arrow, by Harushige. d, Woman with green sash from Six Girls, by Eisho.
No. 2453, 2000 le: a, Woman with checked kimono, from Six Girls. b, Courtesan on a Bench, by Eiri. c, Courtesan and Her Two Kamuro, by Suzuki Harunobu. d, Clearing Weather at Awazu, by Shigemasa.
No. 2454, 2000 le — Paintings by Harunobu: a, Promenade. b, Wine Tasters. c, Rain in May. d, Lovers by the Wall.
No. 2455, 2000 le — Paintings by Harunobu: a, Young Woman Attended by Maid. b, Lovers by Lespedeza Bush. c, Girl Contemplating a Landscape. d, Young Man Unrolling a Hanging Scroll.
No. 2456, 5000 le, Searching for the Hermit, by Harunobu. No. 2457, 5000 le, Courtesan and Two Kamuro, by Harunobu. No. 2458, 5000 le, Drying Clothes, by Harunobu. No. 2459, 5000 le, Komachi Praying For Rain, by Harunobu. No. 2460, 5000 le, Girl Contemplating Landscape, by Harunobu.

2001, July 2   **Perf. 13½**
2440-2451   A359   Set of 12   7.25 7.25
    Sheets of 4, #a-d
2452-2455   A359   Set of 4   32.50 32.50
    Souvenir Sheets
2456-2460   A359   Set of 5   26.00 26.00
Phila Nippon '01, Japan (#2452-2460).

Marlene Dietrich — A360

No. 2461: a, Looking over shoulder. b, Wearing necklace. c, Wearing coat with flower. d, Holding cigarette.

2001, June 18   **Litho.**   **Perf. 13¾**
2461   A360   2000 le Sheet of 4,
       #a-d   8.25 8.25

Toulouse-Lautrec Paintings — A361

No. 2462, horiz.: a, A La Mie. b, A Corner of the Moulin de la Gallete. c, The Start of the Quadrille.

5000 le, La Goulue.

2001, June 18
2462   A361   2200 le Sheet of 3,
       #a-c   7.00 7.00
    Souvenir Sheet
2463   A361   5000 le multi   5.25 5.25

Monet Paintings — A362

No. 2464, horiz.: a, The Road to Vétheuil, Winter. b, The Church at Vétheuil, Snow. c, Breakup of the Ice Near Vétheuil. d, The Boulevard de Pontoise at Argenteuil, Snow.
5000 le, Irises by the Pond.

2001, June 18
2464   A362   1500 le Sheet of 4,
       #a-d   6.25 6.25
    Souvenir Sheet
2465   A362   5000 le multi   5.25 5.25

Giuseppe Verdi (1813-1901), Opera
Composer — A363

No. 2466: a, Vladimir Popov. b, Enrico Caruso. c, Rudolf Bockelmann. d, Stage.
5000 le, Aprile Millo and Barseg Tumanyan.

2001, June 18   **Perf. 14**
2466   A363   1700 le Sheet of 4,
       #a-d   7.00 7.00
    Souvenir Sheet
2467   A363   5000 le multi   5.25 5.25

Royal Navy Submarines,
Cent. — A364

No. 2468: a, C Class submarine. b, HMS Spartan. c, HMS Exeter. d, HMS Chatham. e, HMS Verdun. f, HMS Marlborough.
5000 le, HMS Vanguard.

2001, June 18
2468   A364   1100 le Sheet of 6,
       #a-f   7.00 7.00
    Souvenir Sheet
2469   A364   5000 le multi   5.25 5.25

U.S. Civil War — A365

No. 2470, 2000 le — Generals: a, Ulysses S. Grant. b, John Bell Hood. c, Jeb Stuart. d, Robert E. Lee.
No. 2471, 2000 le: a, Gen. Joshua Chamberlain. b, Gen. Stonewall Jackson. c, Gen. George McClellan. d, Adm. David Farragut.
No. 2472, 2000 le — Battle scenes: a, Shiloh. b, Bull Run. c, Fair Oaks. d, Chattanooga.
No. 2473, 2000 le — Battle scenes: a, Fredericksburg. b, Gettysburg. c, Mobile Bay. d, Fort Sumter.
No. 2474, 5000 le, Gen. William Tecumseh Sherman. 2475, 5000 le, Gen. George A. Custer. No. 2476, 5000 le, Battle of Vicksburg. No. 2477, 5000 le, Battle of Antietam.

2001, Aug. 27
    Sheets of 4, #a-d
2470-2473   A365   Set of 4   32.50 32.50
    Souvenir Sheets
2474-2477   A365   Set of 4   21.00 21.00

Horses in Literature and
Mythology — A366

No. 2478, 1100 le: a, Piebald, from National Velvet, by Enid Bagnold. b, Strider, by Leo Tolstoy. c, Black Beauty, by Anna Sewell. d, Red Pony, by John Steinbeck. e, Black Stallion, by Walter Farley. f, Misty of Chincoteague, by Marguerite Henry.
No. 2479, 1100 le: a, Arvak Alsvid. b, Pegasus. c, Sleipnir. d, Veillanfif. e, Grani. f, Galathe, from Troilus and Cressida, by William Shakespeare.
No. 2480, 5000 le, Rosinante, from Don Quixote, by Miguel de Cervantes. No. 2481, 5000 le, Xanthus and Balius.

2001, Feb. 27   **Litho.**   **Perf. 14**
    Sheets of 6, #a-f
2478-2479   A366   Set of 2   14.00 14.00
    Souvenir Sheets
2480-2481   A366   Set of 2   10.50 10.50

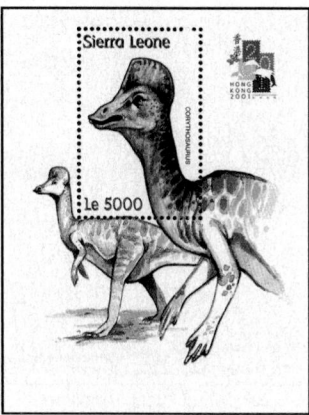

Dinosaurs — A367

No. 2482, 1000 le: a, Acrocanthosaurus. b, Edmontosaurus. c, Archaeopteryx. d, Hadrosaurus. e, Mongolian avimimus. f, Pachyrhinosaurus. g, Iguanodons (with tree trunk). h, Iguanodons, diff.
No. 2483, 1000 le, horiz.: a, Albertosaurus. b, Pteranodon ingens. c, Asiatic iguanodon. d, Sordes. e, Coelophysis. f, Saichania. g, Bactrosaurus. h, Triceratops.
No. 2484, 5000 le, Corythosaurus. No. 2485, 5000 le, Stenonychosaurus.

2001, Mar. 1   *Perf. 13½*
Sheets of 8, #a-h
2482-2483 A367   Set of 2   17.00 17.00
Souvenir Sheets
2484-2485 A367   Set of 2   10.50 10.50
Hong Kong 2001 Stamp Exhibition.

Souvenir Sheets

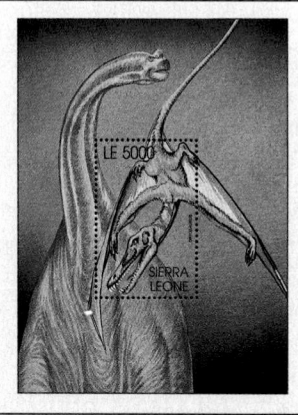

Dinosaurs — A367a

Designs: No. 2485A, 5000 le, Dryosaurus. No. 2485B, 5000 le, Diplodocids. No. 2485C, 5000 le, Allosaurus.

2001, Mar. 1   **Litho.**   *Perf. 13½*
2485A-2485C   A367a   Set of
        3   15.00 15.00
Nos. 2485A-2485C were not available in the marketplace until 2002.

Butterflies — A368

No. 2486, 1100 le: a, Teinopalpus imperialis. b, Swallowtail. c, Doris. d, Northern Jezebel. e, Beautiful monarch. f, Gaudy commodore.
No. 2487, 1100 le: a, Plain tiger. b, Tiger. c, Morpho cypris. d, Castnia litus. e, Dismorphia nemesis. f, Blue and yellow butterfly (inscribed African violets).

No. 2488, 5000 le, Scarce swallowtail. No. 2489, 5000 le, Clouded yellow, vert.

2001, Apr. 30   **Sheets of 6, #a-f**
2486-2487 A368   Set of 2   14.50 14.50
Souvenir Sheets
2488-2489 A368   Set of 2   11.00 11.00

Photomosaic of
Queen Elizabeth
II — A369

2001, June 18   *Perf. 14*
2490 A369 1000 le multi   1.10 1.10
Printed in sheets of 8.

Mao Zedong (1893-1976) — A370

No. 2492, 1100 le — Map of China and Mao: a, Without hat. b, With green cap. c, With blue cap.
No. 2493, 1100 le — Red frame and Mao with: a, Uniform. b, Shirt with open collar. d, Cap.
No. 2493, 5000 le, Mao wearing black suit. No. 2494, 5000 le, Mao in white.

2001, June 18   **Sheets of 3, #a-c**
2491-2492 A370   Set of 2   7.00 7.00
Souvenir Sheets
2493-2494 A370   Set of 2   10.50 10.50

Ferrari Automobiles — A371

Designs: 100 le, 2001 360 Challenge. 500 le, 1971 712 Can Am. 600 le, 1970 512M. 1000 le, 1988 F40. 1500 le, 1982 365 GT4/BB. 2000 le, 1972 365 GTB/4.

2001, Oct. 8   *Perf. 13¾*
2495-2500 A371   Set of 6   6.00 6.00

Souvenir Sheets

Horses — A372

Chinese Character for Horse — A373

No. 2501: a, Green background. b, Blue background.
No. 2502 — "2002" in: a, Green. b, Red. c, Orange. d, Purple.

2001, Nov. 29   *Perf. 13*
2501 A372 1200 le Sheet of 2,
           #a-b   2.50 2.50
        Perf. 13x13¼
2502 A373 1200 le Sheet of 4,
           #a-d   5.00 5.00
New Year 2002 (Year of the Horse).

2002 World Cup Soccer
Championships, Japan and
Korea — A374

No. 2503, 1400 le: a, Newspaper article, 1950. b, Jules Rimet, 1954. c, Pele and teammates, 1958. d, Vava and Schroiff, 1962. e, Bobby Charlton, 1966. f, Pele, 1970.
No. 2504, 1400 le: a, Daniel Passarella, 1978. b, Karl-Heinz Rummenigge, 1982. c, Diego Maradona, 1986. d, Roger Milla, 1990. e, Romario, 1994. f, Zinedine Zidane, 1998.
No. 2505, 5000 le, Head from Jules Rimet trophy, 1930. No. 2506, 5000 le, Head and globe from World Cup trophy, 2002.

2001, Dec. 7   *Perf. 13¾x14¼*
Sheets of 6, #a-f
2503-2504 A374   Set of 2   17.00 17.00
Souvenir Sheets
       Perf. 14½x14¼
2505-2506 A374   Set of 2   10.00 10.00

Christmas
A375

Paintings by Filippo Lippi: 300 le, Madonna of Humility. 600 le, Annunciation. 1500 le, Annunciation, vert. 2000 le, Adoration of the Child and Saints, vert.
5000 le, Barbadori Altarpeice, vert.

2001, Dec. 26   *Perf. 14*
2507-2510 A375   Set of 4   4.50 4.50
Souvenir Sheet
2511 A375 5000 le multi   5.00 5.00

**Queen Mother Type of 1999
Redrawn**

No. 2512: a, With Duke of York and Princess Elizabeth, 1926. b, In 1979. c, In Nairobi, 1959. d, In 1991.
4000 le, With crown, 1937.

2001, Dec.   *Perf. 14*
Yellow Orange Frames
2512 A307 1300 le Sheet of 4,
          #a-d, + label 5.25 5.25

Souvenir Sheet
       Perf. 13¾
2513 A307 4000 le multi   4.00 4.00
Queen Mother's 101st birthday. No. 2513 contains one 38x51mm stamp with a slightly darker backdrop than that found on No. 2208. Sheet margins of Nos. 2512-2513 lack embossing and gold arms and frames found on Nos. 2207-2208.

SOS Children's
Village — A376

2002, Jan. 24   *Perf. 14*
2514 A376 2000 le multi   2.00 2.00

Steam and Electric Inventions and
Their Inventors — A377

No. 2515, 1100 le: a, The Rocket steam locomotive, 1829. b, High-speed electric passenger train. c, 1863 Steam pumper. d, Early electric trolley. e, 1893 Steam automobile. f, Electric monorail.
No. 2516, 1100 le: a, Early steam pumper. b, Telephone. c, Steam liner. d, Battery and light bulb. e, 1770 Steam carriage. f, Electric passenger train.
No. 2517, 1100 le: a, Robert Fulton and steamboat. b, Thomas Edison and light bulb. c, 1899 T9 steam locomotive. d, Radio and antennae. e, James Watt, and steam engine diagram. f, Alexander Graham Bell and telephone.
No. 2518, 5000 le, 1899 Steam locomotive. No. 2519, 5000 le, Telephone, radio and light bulb. No. 2520, 5000 le, Benjamin Franklin, vert.

     Perf. 13¼x13½, 13½x13¼
2002, Jan. 24   **Sheets of 6, #a-f**
2515-2517 A377   Set of 3   20.00 20.00
Souvenir Sheets
2518-2520 A377   Set of 3   15.00 15.00

United We
Stand — A378

2002, Feb. 6   *Perf. 13½x13¼*
2521 A378 2000 le multi   2.25 2.25

Reign of Queen Elizabeth II, 50th
Anniv. — A379

No. 2522: a, With young Prince Charles and
Princess Anne. b, Wearing tiara and stole,
looking forward. c, Wearing tiara and stole,
looking right. d, Wearing hat.
5000 le, Wearing hat and gloves.

2002, Feb. 6   **Perf. 14¼**
2522 A379 2000 le Sheet of 4,
        #a-d   9.00 9.00
Souvenir Sheet
2523 A379 5000 le multi   5.50 5.50

2002
Winter
Olympics,
Salt Lake
City
A380

Designs: Nos. 2524, 2525, 2000 le, Curling.
Nos. 2524A, 2525A, 2000 le, Ice hockey.

2002, Apr. 22   Litho.   Perf. 14
Olympic Rings in Color
2524-2524A A380 Set of 2   4.00 4.00
2524Ab   Souvenir sheet, #2524-
            2524A   4.00 4.00
Olympic Rings in White on Black
Background
Perf. 13¼x13½
2525-2525A A380 Set of 2   4.00 4.00
2525Ab   Souvenir sheet, #2525-
            2525A   4.00 4.00

Flowers — A381

Designs: 400 le, Jerusalem artichoke.
500 le, Painted trillium. 600 le, Bluebells.
1000 le, Rough-fruited cinquefoil. 1500 le,
Wake robin. 2000 le, Seashore mallow.
No. 2532, 1300 le, horiz.: a, Hepatica. b,
Star of Bethlehem. c, Wood lily. d, Wild gera-
nium. e, Hedge bindweed. f, Gloxinias.
No. 2533, 1300 le, horiz.: a, Laevigata iris.
b, Dietes. c, Day lily. d, Cardinal flower. e,
Mountain pink. f, Seaside gentian.
No. 2534, 5000 le, Dame's rocket. No. 2535,
5000 le, Pinxter flower.

2002, Apr. 29   Litho.   Perf. 14x14½
2526-2531 A381 Set of 6   6.00 6.00
Perf. 14
Sheets of 6, #a-f
2532-2533 A381 Set of 2   15.00 15.00
Souvenir Sheets
2534-2535 A381 Set of 2   10.00 10.00
Nos. 2532-2533 contain six 42x38mm
stamps; Nos. 2534-2535 contain one
38x42mm stamp.

Wildlife — A382

Designs: 200 le, Giraffe. 400 le, L'Host's
guenon. 1500 le, Jentik's duiker.
No. 2539, 1100 le, horiz.: a, Kudu. b, Caracal. c, Oribi. d, Aardwolf. e, Bushpig. f,
Suricates.
No. 2540, 1100 le, horiz.: a, African buffalo.
b, Wild dog. c, Black-backed jackal. d, Aardvark. e, Impala. f, Waterbuck.
No. 2541, 8000 le, Vervet monkey. No.
2542, 8000 le, Springbok.

2002, Apr. 29   **Perf. 14**
2536-2538 A382 Set of 3   2.10 2.10
Sheets of 6, #a-f
2539-2540 A382 Set of 2   13.00 13.00
Souvenir Sheets
2541-2542 A382 Set of 2   16.00 16.00

Chiune Sugihara,
Japanese Diplomat
Who Saved Jews
in World War
II — A383

2002, July 1   Litho.   Perf. 14
2543 A383 2000 le multi   2.00 2.00
Printed in sheets of 4.

Nos. 1811-
1812
Surcharged

Methods & Perfs. As Before
2002, July 1
2544 A242 800 le on 400 le
           Block or
           strip of 4,
           #a-d   3.25 3.25
Souvenir Sheet
2545 A242 5000 le on 1500 le
           multi   5.00 5.00
Queen Mother Elizabeth (1900-2002). No.
2544 was issued in sheets of eight stamps.
Sheet margins of 2544-2544 were overprinted
with black border and "In Memoriam / 1900-
2002."

Intl Year of Ecotourism — A384

No. 2546: a, Bullom boats. b, Dinkongor
Falls. c, Rokel River. d, Pygmy hippopotamus.
e, Hills of Soa Chiefdom. f, Long Beach.
5000 le, Photo safari.

2002, July 1   Litho.   Perf. 14
2546 A384 1300 le Sheet of 6,
        #a-f   7.75 7.75
Souvenir Sheet
2547 A384 5000 le multi   5.00 5.00

First Non-stop Solo Transatlantic
Flight, 75th Anniv. — A385

No. 2548, horiz. — The Spirit of St. Louis: a,
Being towed from Ryan Airlines factory. b,
Being towed May 20, 1927. c, Taking off, May
20, 1927.
No. 2549, Charles Lindbergh.

2002, July 1
2548 A385 2500 le Sheet of 3,
        #a-c   7.50 7.50
Souvenir Sheet
2549 A385 2500 le multi   2.50 2.50

Shirley Temple Movie Type of 2000
Temple in scenes from "Wee Willie Winkie"
— No. 2550: a, With woman, man in army
uniform, two men wearing turbans. b, Resting
head near mirror. c, With boy wearing army
uniform and kilt. d, With man wearing turban.
e, With man in army uniform. f, Giving note to
man in prison.
No. 2551, vert.: a, With woman. b, With man
wearing turban. c, With woman and man. d,
With man in army uniform.
5000 le, With man in army uniform, vert.

2002, July 1   **Perf. 12¼**
2550 A324 1100 le Sheet of 6,
        #a-f   6.50 6.50
2551 A324 1300 le Sheet of 4,
        #a-d   5.25 5.25
Souvenir Sheet
2552 A324 5000 le multi   5.00 5.00

20th World Scout Jamboree,
Thailand — A386

No. 2553: a, Boys on rocks fishing. b,
Scouts without caps. c, Scouts in water holding fish. d, Scouts with caps.
5000 le, Scouts in sailboat.

2002, July 1   **Perf. 14**
2553 A386 2000 le Sheet of 4,
        #a-d   8.00 8.00
Souvenir Sheet
2554 A386 5000 le multi   5.00 5.00

Intl. Year of Mountains — A387

No. 2555: a, Mt. Etna, Italy. b, Cotopaxi,
Ecuador. c, Mt. Everest, Nepal. d, Mt. Popo-
catepetl, Mexico.
5000 le, Mt. Machhapuchare, Nepal.

2002, July 1
2555 A387 2000 le Sheet of 4,
        #a-d   8.00 8.00
Souvenir Sheet
2556 A387 5000 le multi   5.00 5.00

Pokémon — A388

No. 2557, vert.: a, Sudowoodo. b, Aipom. c,
Shuckle. d, Miltank. e, Hitmontop. f, Ledian.
5000 le, Lugia.

2002, Aug. 26   **Perf. 13¾**
2557 A388 1500 le Sheet of 6,
        #a-f   9.25 9.25
Souvenir Sheet
2558 A388 5000 le multi   5.25 5.25

Popeye in New York — A389

No. 2559, vert. — Popeye and: a, And Olive Oyl on river tour. b, And Olive Oyl in Central Park. c, And Olive Oyl near Brooklyn Bridge. d, Statue of Liberty. e, Flatiron Building. f, Empire State Building.

5000 le, Popeye and Olive Oyl skating at Rockefeller Center.

2002, Aug. 26   **Perf. 12¼**
2559 A389 1300 le Sheet of 6,
      #a-f   8.00 8.00
Souvenir Sheet
2560 A389 5000 le multi   5.25 5.25

No. 2559 contains six 38x50mm stamps.

A390

Teddy Bears, Cent. — A391

No. 2561: a, Bear with green bow. b, Bears with harlequin costumes. c, Bear with red headdress. d, Bear with black and gold neckband.

No. 2562: a, Baby girl bear. b, School girl bear. c, Bear in overalls. d, Bear in pajamas.

2002, Sept. 23   **Perf. 14**
2561 A390 1700 le Sheet of 4,
      #a-d   6.50 6.50
2562 A391 2000 le Sheet of 4,
      #a-d   7.75 7.75

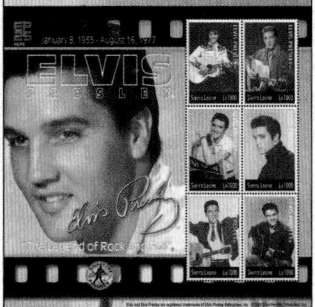

Elvis Presley (1935-77) — A392

No. 2563: a, Wearing flowered shirt. b, Wearing jacket, holding light-colored guitar. c, Seated in chair. d, Wearing sweater. e, With arms raised. f, With black guitar.

2002, Oct. 7   **Litho.**
2563 A392 1000 le Sheet of 6,
      #a-f   5.75 5.75

2002 World Cup Soccer Championships, Japan and Korea — A393

No. 2564, 1400 le — Germany vs. Paraguay: a, Michael Ballack. b, Oliver Kahn. c, Miroslav Klose. d, Diego Gacilan. e, Jose Luis Chilavert. f, Guido Alvarenga.

No. 2565, 1400 le — Denmark vs. England: a, Jesper Gronkjaer. b, Thomas Helveg. c, Dennis Rommedahl. d, Michael Owen. e, David Seaman. f, Rio Ferdinand.

No. 2566, 1400 le — Mexico vs. U.S.: a, Rafael Marquez. b, Oscar Perez. c, Jared Borgetti. d, Landon Donovan. e, Brad Friedel. f, DaMarcus Beasley.

No. 2567, 1400 le — Japan vs. Turkey: a, Ryuzo Morioka. b, Kazuyuki Toda. c, Atsushi Yanagisawa. d, Fatih Akyel. e, Yildiray Basturk. f, Umit Davala.

No. 2568, 2500 le — Germany: a, Coach Rudi Voeller. b, Dietmar Hamann.

No. 2569, 2500 le — Paraguay: a, Julio Cesar Caceres. b, Coach Cesare Maldini.

No. 2570, 2500 le — Denmark: a, Coach Morten Olsen. b, Jon Dahl Tomasson.

No. 2571, 2500 le — England: a, David Beckham. b, Coach Sven Goran Eriksson.

No. 2572, 2500 le — Mexico: a, Coach Javier Aguirre. b, Jesus Arellano.

No. 2573, 2500 le — United States: a, Brian McBride. b, Coach Bruce Arena.

No. 2574, 2500 le — Japan: a, Coach Philippe Troussier. b, Junichi Inamoto.

No. 2575, 2500 le — Turkey: a, Vildiray Basturk. b, Coach Senol Gunes.

2002, Nov. 18   **Perf. 13¼**
Sheets of 6, #a-f
2564-2567 A393 Set of 4 40.00 40.00
Souvenir Sheets of 2, #a-b
2568-2575 A393 Set of 8 47.50 47.50

Christmas — A394

Designs: 50 le, Madonna and Child Between Saints John the Baptist and Catherine of Alexandria, by Perugino. 100 le, Madonna and Child Enthroned Between Angels and Saints, by Domenico Ghirlandaio. 150 le, The Virgin, by Giovanni Bellini. 500 le, Stories of the Virgin Birth of Mary, by Ghirlandaio. 5000 le, Adoration of the Magi, by Ghirlandaio.

6000 le, Madonna Enthroned with Saints, by Ghirlandaio.

2002, Nov. 18   **Perf. 14**
2576-2580 A394 Set of 5 6.75 6.75
Souvenir Sheet
2581 A394 6000 le multi 7.00 7.00

Pres. Ronald Reagan — A395

No. 2582, 1700 le — Country name in black: a, Wearing brown tie. b, Wearing red tie.

No. 2583, 1700 le — Country name in white: a, Wearing spotted tie. b, Wearing striped tie.

2002, Dec. 30 **Pairs, #a-b** **Litho.**
2582-2583 A395 Set of 2 6.75 6.75

Nos. 2582-2583 each were printed in sheets containing two pairs.

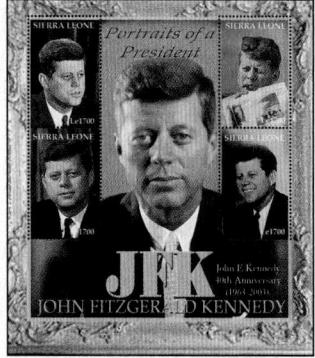

Pres. John F. Kennedy (1917-63) — A396

No. 2584, 1700 le: a, Wearing red tie. b, With newspaper. c, In front on brown curtain. d, In front of brown and tan background.

No. 2585, 1700 le — John and Jacqueline: a, In formal wear greeting man. b, With purple background. c, Playing with child. d, At Love Field, Nov. 22, 1963.

2002, Dec. 30   **Perf. 14**
Sheets of 4, #a-d
2584-2585 A396 Set of 2 13.50 13.50

Princess Diana (1961-97) — A397

Designs: No. 2586, 1700 le, Wearing black dress. No. 2587, 1700 le, Wearing blue dress and tiara.

2002, Dec. 30
2586-2587 A397 Set of 2 3.50 3.50

Nos. 2586-2587 each were printed in sheets of 4.

Birds, Flowers and Insects of Africa — A398

No. 2588, 1300 le — Birds: a, Great blue turaco. b, Helmet vanga. c, Scarlet-tufted malachite sunbird. d, African pitta. e, African jacana. f, Southern carmine bee-eater.

No. 2589, 1300 le — Flowers: a, Ancistrochilus rothschildianus. b, Oeceoclades maculata. c, Eulophia guineensis. d, Angraecum distichum. e, Disa uniflora. f, Vanilla imperialis.

No. 2590, 1300 le — Insects: a, Panther-spotted grasshopper. b, Basker moth. c, Charaxes samagdalis. d, Carpenter ant. e, Worker bee. f, Ten-spot dragonfly.

No. 2591, 5000 le, European robin. No. 2592, 5000 le, Bulbophyllum lepidum. No. 2593, 5000 le, Common dotted border butterfly, horiz.

2003, Jan. 13   **Sheets of 6, #a-f**
2588-2590 A398 Set of 3 25.00 25.00
Souvenir Sheets
2591-2593 A398 Set of 3 16.00 16.00

New Year 2003 (Year of the Ram) — A399

No. 2594 — Color of ram: a, Green. b, Orange. c, Red violet. d, Orange brown.

2003, Feb. 10
2594 A399 900 le Sheet of 6, #a-
      c, 3 #d   5.75 5.75

Astronauts Killed in Space Shuttle Columbia Accident — A400

No. 2595: a, Mission Specialist 1 David M. Brown. b, Commander Rick D. Husband. c, Mission Specialist 4 Laurel Blair Salton Clark. d, Mission Specialist 4 Kalpana Chawla. e, Payload Commander Michael P. Anderson. f, Pilot William C. McCool. g, Payload Specialist 4 Ilan Ramon.

2003, Apr. 7　　　*Perf. 13½x13¼*
2595　A400　1000 le Sheet of 7,
　　　　　#a-g　　　6.25　6.25

A401

Teddy Bears, Cent. — A402

No. 2596, vert.: a, Bear with umbrella. b, Bear with belt. c, Bear with pink dress. d, Bear with horn.
　5000 le, Bear in automobile.
　12,000 le, Bear with flower.

2003　　　**Litho.**　　*Perf. 14¼*
2596　A401　1500 le Sheet of
　　　　　4, #a-d　　5.25　5.25
　　　Souvenir Sheet
2597　A401　5000 le multi　　4.25　4.25
　　　Embroidered
　　　　Imperf
2598　A402　12,000 le multi　10.50　10.50
　Issued: Nos. 2596, 2597, 7/1, No. 2598, Apr. No. 2598 issued in sheets of 4.

A403

Coronation of Queen Elizabeth II, 50th Anniv. — A404

Designs: No. 2599, 1500 le, Crowning of the Queen. No. 2600, 1500 le, Queen signs the oath. No. 2601, 1500 le, Sovereign's sword. No. 2602, 1500 le, Anointing of the Queen. No. 2603, 1500 le, Queen presented with Holy Bible. No. 2604, 1500 le, Royal onlookers. No. 2605, 1500 le, Ampulla and spoon. No. 2606, 1500 le, Orb and scepter.
　5000 le, Queen with crown. 15,000 le, Queen with hat.

2003　　　**Litho.**　　*Perf. 13¼*
2599-2606　A403　Set of 8　　10.50　10.50
　　　Souvenir Sheet
　　　　Perf. 14¼
2607　A403　5000 le multi　　4.25　4.25
　　　Miniature Sheet
　　　Litho. & Embossed
　　　　Perf. 13¼x13
2608　A404　15,000 le multi　13.00　13.00
　Issued: Nos. 2599-2607, 7/1; No. 2608, 4/7. No. 2607 contains one 37x50mm stamp.

Rembrandt Paintings A405

Designs: 800 le, Young Man with Pointed Beard. 1000 le, Old Man with Book. 1200 le, The Shipbuilder Jan Rijcksen and His Wife, Griet Jans, horiz. 2000 le, Portrait of a Young Jew.
　No. 2613: a, Juno. b, Bellona, Goddess of War. c, Artemesia. d, Esther Preparing to Intercede with Ahasuerus.
　5000 le, Two Scholars Disputing.

　　Perf. 14¼, 13¼ (#2613)
2003, May 13　　　　**Litho.**
2609-2612　A405　Set of 4　　4.50　4.50
2613　A405　1700 le Sheet of 4,
　　　　　#a-d　　　6.00　6.00
　　　Souvenir Sheet
2614　A405　5000 le multi　　4.50　4.50

Japanese Art — A406

Designs: 800 le, Priest Raigo Transformed Into a Rat, by Yoshitoshi Tsukioka. 1000 le, The Spirit of Tamichi as a Great Snake, by Yoshitoshi Tsukioka. 1500 le, The Gathering and Gossiping of Various Tools, by Kuniyoshi Utagawa. 2500 le, Caricatures of Actors as

---

Three Animals Playing Ken, by Kuniyoshi Utagawa.
　No. 2619 — Paintings by Yoshitoshi Tsukioka: a, The Fox Woman Leaving Her Child. b, Fox Cry. c, The Lucky Teakettle of Morin Temple. d, The Ghost of Okiku.
　5000 le, Fox in a Thunderstorm, by Kunisada Utagawa.

2003, May 13　　　*Perf. 14¼*
2615-2618　A406　Set of 4　　5.25　5.25
2619　A406　2000 le Sheet of 4,
　　　　　#a-d　　　7.25　7.25
　　　Souvenir Sheet
2620　A406　5000 le multi　　4.50　4.50

Paintings by Pablo Picasso A407

Designs: 400 le, Glass, Pipe and Playing Card. 500 le, Still-Life on a Pedestal in front of a Window. 600 le, Woman in a Feathered Hat. 700 le, Pedestal and Guitar. 1000 le, The Bread Carrier. 3000 le, Female Acrobat.
　No. 2627: a, Portrait of a Woman. b, Woman in a Red Armchair. c, Seated Woman with Small Round Hat (Dora Maar). d, Woman with Crossed Hands.
　No. 2628, Boy in Black Shorts. No. 2629, Bathers, horiz.

2003, May 13　　　*Perf. 14¼*
2621-2626　A407　Set of 6　　5.50　5.50
2627　A407　2000 le Sheet of 4,
　　　　　#a-d　　　7.25　7.25
　　　　Imperf
　　　Size: 82x105mm
2628　A407　5000 le multi　　4.50　4.50
　　　Size: 103x82mm
2629　A407　5000 le multi　　4.50　4.50

Painting of Mona Lisa, 500th Anniv. — A408

No. 2629A, 500th Anniversary of Mona Lisa (complete painting).
　No. 2630 — Inscribed: a, Chartier: Mona Lisa — Mistress of Francis I. b, Copy of Mona Lisa, Cheramy Collection.
　5000 le, 500th Anniversary of Mona Lisa (face).

2003, July 1　　　*Perf. 14*
2629A　A408　2000 le multi　　1.75　1.75
2630　A408　2000 le Sheet of 3,
　　　　　#a-b, No.
　　　　　2629A　　　5.25　5.25
　　　Souvenir Sheet
2631　A408　5000 le multi　　4.25　4.25
　No. 2629A was issued in two sheets of six with different selvage in 2004.

Intl. Year of Fresh Water — A409

No. 2632 a, Waterfalls of Mount Tonkoui. b, Tagbaladougou Falls. c, Cascades d'Ouzoud. 5000 le, Little Scarcies.

2003, July 1
2632　A409　2000 le Sheet of 3,
　　　　　#a-c　　　5.25　5.25
　　　Souvenir Sheet
2633　A409　5000 le multi　　4.25　4.25

Rotary Club of Sierra Leone, 40th Anniv. — A410

No. 2634 — Rotarians and: a, People in canoe. b, Cacheted first day cover envelope, Sierra Leone natives. c, Girl with flowers.
　6000 le, Bhichal Rattakul, Rotary President.

2003, July 1
2634　A410　2500 le Sheet of 3,
　　　　　#a-c　　　6.50　6.50
　　　Souvenir Sheet
2635　A410　6000 le multi　　5.25　5.25

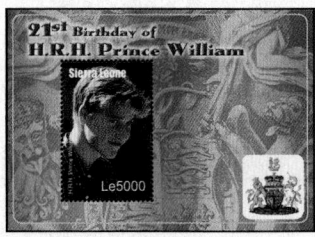

Prince William, 21st Birthday — A411

No. 2636: a, Wearing solid shirt. b, Wearing striped shirt. c, Wearing sweater.
　5000 le, Wearing plaid shirt.

2003, July 1
2636　A411　2500 le Sheet of 3,
　　　　　#a-c　　　6.50　6.50
　　　Souvenir Sheet
2637　A411　5000 le multi　　4.25　4.25

Circus Performers — A412

No. 2638, 2000 le: a, Peggy Williams. b, Nico. c, Steve T. J. Tatter Smith. d, Uncle Dippy.

No. 2639, 2000 le: a, Caracal. b, Chairs. c, Elena Panova. d, Chinese Circus.

Sheets of 4, #a-d

2003, July 1 **Litho.**
2638-2639 A412 Set of 2 13.50 13.50

Powered Flight, Cent. — A413

No. 2640, 1500 le: a, Wright Brothers first plane (gray background). b, Voisin-Farmin (blue background). c, Levavasseur Antoinette (pink background). d, Nieuport (numbered 345).

No. 2641, 1500 le: a, Wright Brothers first plane (blue background). b, Voisin-Farmin (gray background). c, Levavasseur Antoinette (blue background). d, Nieuport (no number on plane).

No. 2642, 5000 le, Henri Farmin Crossing Finish Line in Voisin-Farmin plane. No. 2643, 5000 le, Roland Garros and others around airplane.

2003, July 14 **Sheets of 4, #a-d**
2640-2641 A413 Set of 2 10.50 10.50
Souvenir Sheets
2642-2643 A413 Set of 2 8.50 8.50

Inscriptions on No. 2640 are incorrect. See also No. 2751.

Tour de France Bicycle Race, Cent. — A414

No. 2644, 1500 le: a, Ferdinand Kubler, 1950. b, Hugo Koblet, 1951. c, Fausto Coppi, 1952. d, Louison Bobet, 1953.

No. 2645, 1500 le: a, Bobet, 1954. b, Bobet, 1955. c, Roger Walkowiak, 1956. d, Jacques Anquetil, 1957.

No. 2646, 1500 le: a, Eddy Merckx, 1970. b, Merckx, 1971. c, Merckx, 1972. d, Luis Ocana, 1973.

No. 2647, 5000 le, Bobet, 1953-55. No. 2648, 5000 le, Anquetil, 1957, diff. No. 2649, 5000 le, Bernard Hinault, 1978.

Sheets of 4, #a-d

2003, July 14 **Perf. 13¼**
2644-2646 A414 Set of 3 15.50 15.50
Souvenir Sheets
2647-2649 A414 Set of 3 13.00 13.00

Olympic Medalists A415

Designs: 300 le, Forrest Smithson, 1908. 400 le, Hannes Kolehmainen, 1912. 500 le, Larissa Latynina, 1964. 800 le, Klaus Dibiasi, 1976. 1000 le, Archie Hahn, 1904. 1500 le, M. Hurley. 2000 le, Ray Ewry, 1900. 3000 le, Henry Taylor, 1908.

2003, Nov. 17 **Perf. 13¼**
2650-2657 A415 Set of 8 7.75 7.75

Inscription on No. 2655 is incorrect as there were no cycling events in 1904 and no cycling medalists in any year named Hurley.

Christmas A416

Paintings by Pontormo Rosso Fiorentino: 100 le, Madonna and Child with St. Anne and Four Saints. 150 le, Madonna and Child with Two Saints. 500 le, Madonna and Child Enthroned with Four Saints (Ognissanti Altarpiece). 4000 le, Madonna Enthroned Between Two Saints.

5000 le, Madonna with Saints.

2003, Nov. 17 **Perf. 14¼**
2658-2661 A416 Set of 4 4.00 4.00
Souvenir Sheet
2662 A416 5000 le multi 4.25 4.25

New Year 2004 (Year of the Monkey) — A417

No. 2663 — Background color: a, Yellow orange. b, Blue. c, Rose pink. d, Dark orange 2500 le, Pink.

2004, Jan. 15 **Perf. 13¾**
2663 A417 1200 le Sheet of 4, #a-d 4.00 4.00
Souvenir Sheet
Perf. 14
2664 A417 2500 le multi 2.10 2.10

No. 2664 contains one 42x28mm stamp.

Paintings of Chiao Ping-chen (1689-1726) — A418

No. 2665: a, Untitled painting depicting courtyard. b, Untitled landscape. c, Court Ladies (woman with purple robe at LR). d, Court Ladies (woman with purple robe at center)

5000 le, The Beauty of Traditional Chinese Architecture in Painting.

2004, Jan. 21 **Perf. 13¼**
2665 A418 2000 le Sheet of 4, #a-d 6.50 6.50
Imperf
2666 A418 5000 le shown 4.25 4.25

No. 2665 contains four 38x50mm stamps.

British Council, 60th Anniv. A419

Frame colors: 500 le, Gray green. 1000 le, Dull green. 2000 le, Purple. 3000 le, Red.

2004, Jan. 29 **Perf. 14**
2667-2670 A419 Set of 4 5.50 5.50

Map & Lion Type of 1964 Redrawn
2004, Feb. 4 Self-Adhesive Die Cut
2671 A38 1000 le multi .85 .85

Printed in sheets of 10.

Paintings by Norman Rockwell — A420

No. 2672: a, Ice Cream Carrier. b, The Voyeur. c, Teacher's Birthday. d, Fisk Tires Advertisement.

5000 le, Cousin Reginald Plays Pirate.

2004, Feb. 24 Litho. Perf. 13½
2672 A420 2000 le Sheet of 4, #a-d 6.50 6.50
Souvenir Sheet
2673 A420 5000 le multi 4.25 4.25

The Concorde G-BOAA flew a total of 22,769 hours. One of it's many stops was in Rio de Janeiro.

Cessation of Concorde Flights in 2003 — A421

No. 2674, 3000 le — Concorde 206-G BOAA and: a, Blue background. b, Top half of Brazilian flag. c, Bottom half of Brazilian flag.

No. 2675, 3000 le — Concorde G-AXDN and: a, Pink background. b, Top half of Egyptian flag (red stripe). c, Bottom half of Egyptian flag.

No. 2676, 3000 le — Concorde G-ADXN Aircraft 101 and: a, City skyline. b, Top half of Kenyan flag (black stripe). c, Bottom half of Kenyan flag.

2004, Feb. 24 **Perf. 13¼x13½**
Sheets of 3, #a-c
2674-2676 A421 Set of 3 22.50 22.50

Paintings from the Hermitage, St. Petersburg, Russia — A422

No. 2677: a, The Birth of St. John the Baptist, by Jacopo Tintoretto. b, Penitent Mary Magdalene, by Titian. c, The Death of St. Petronilla, by Simone Pignoni. d, The Assumption of the Virgin, by Bartolomé Esteban Murillo. e, St. Jerome Hears the Trumpet, by Jusepe de Ribera. f, St. George and the Dragon, by Tintoretto.

No. 2678 — Paintings by Elisabeth Vigée-Lebrun: a, Countess A. S. Stroganova and Her Son. b, Count G. I. Chernyshev Holding a Mask. c, Self-portrait. d, Baron G. A. Stroganov.

No. 2679, The Apostles Peter and Paul, by El Greco. No. 2680, A Visit to the Priest, by Jean-Baptiste Greuze, horiz.

2004, Feb. 24 Litho. Perf. 13¼
2677 A422 1400 le Sheet of 6, #a-f 7.00 7.00
2678 A422 2000 le Sheet of 4, #a-d 6.50 6.50
Imperf
2679 A422 5000 le shown 4.25 4.25
Size: 100x69mm
2680 A422 5000 le multi 4.25 4.25

Marilyn Monroe (Larger Final Zero) — A423

Marilyn Monroe (Zeroes Same Size) — A424

Marilyn Monroe — A425

2004, May 3   **Perf. 14**
2681 A423 1000 le Pair, #a-b   1.60 1.60

Perf. 13½x13¼
2682 A424 1000 le Pair, #a-b   1.60 1.60
2683 A425 2000 le Sheet of 4,
      #a-d   6.50 6.50

First Orbiting Astronauts of China, US and Russia — A426

No. 2684, horiz. — Yang Lewei: a, Wearing flight jumpsuit. b, Wearing uniform. c, Wearing space suit. d, Wearing space suit, giving hand gesture.
No. 2685: a, Vostok 1. b, John Glenn. c, Friendship 7. d, Yuri Gagarin. e, Shenzhou 5. f, Yang Lewei, diff.
No. 2686, 5000 le, Yang Lewei, diff. No. 2687, 5000 le, Glenn, diff.

2004, May 10   **Perf. 13¼x13½**
2684 A426 900 le Horiz. strip of
      4, #a-d   2.75 2.75

Perf. 13½x13¼
2685 A426 1200 le Sheet of 6,
      #a-f   5.50 5.50
Souvenir Sheets
2686-2687 A426 Set of 2   7.75 7.75
No. 2684 printed in sheets containing two strips.

Cats
A427

Designs: 100 le, Ruddy Somali. 800 le, Bombay. 1200 le, Burmese. 3000 le, Blue British Shorthair.
No. 2692, vert.: a, Persian. b, Colorpoint Shorthair. c, Cornish Rex. d, Blue Point Balinese.
5000 le, Devon Rex.

Perf. 13¼x13½, 13½x13¼
2004, May 17
2688-2691 A427   Set of 4   4.25 4.25
2692 A427 1700 le Sheet of 4,
       5.50 5.50
Souvenir Sheet
2693 A427 5000 le multi   4.00 4.00

Moths and Butterflies A428

Designs: 200 le, Io moth. 300 le, Hackberry butterfly. 400 le, Red admiral butterfly. 4000 le, Spangled fritillary butterfly.
No. 2698: a, Pearl crescent butterfly. b, Pipevine swallowtail butterfly. c, Alfalfa looper moth. d, Tiger swallowtail butterfly.
5000 le, Cecropia moth.

2004, May 17   **Perf. 13¼x13½**
2694-2697 A428   Set of 4   4.00 4.00
2698 A428 1700 le Sheet of 4,
      #a-d   5.50 5.50
Souvenir Sheet
2699 A428 5000 le multi   4.00 4.00

Birds — A429

Designs: 500 le, Belted kingfisher. 1000 le, Burrowing owl. 1500 le, Crested caracara. 2000 le, Red-headed finch.
No. 2704, horiz.: a, Snail kite. b, Avocet. c, Greater flamingo. d, Bald eagle.
5000 le, Ring-necked pheasant, horiz.

Perf. 13½x13¼, 13¼x13½
2004, May 17
2700-2703 A429   Set of 4   4.00 4.00
2704 A429 1700 le Sheet of 4,
      #a-d   5.50 5.50
Souvenir Sheet
2705 A429 5000 le multi   4.00 4.00

Fish A430

Designs: 800 le, Banded sculpin. 1100 le, Black durgon. No. 2708, 1400 le, Atlantic spadefish. No. 2709, 1400 le, Queen triggerfish.
No. 2710: a, Peacock flounder. b, Northern puffer. c, Sea raven. d, Tiger shark.
5000 le, Sea lamprey, vert.

Perf. 13¼x13½, 13½x13¼
2004, May 17
2706-2709 A430   Set of 4   4.00 4.00
2710 A430 1700 le Sheet of 4,
      #a-d   5.50 5.50
Souvenir Sheet
2711 A430 5000 le multi   4.00 4.00

Election of Pope John Paul II, 25th Anniv. (in 2003) — A431

No. 2712 — Pope John Paul II: a, Visiting Australia, 1986. b, With John Bonica, 1987. c, Visiting Croatia, 2003. d, Celebrating 25th anniversary mass, 2003.

2004, May 24   **Perf. 13¼x13½**
2712 A431 2000 le Sheet of 4,
      #a-d   6.50 6.50
Souvenir Sheet

Deng Xiaoping (1904-97), Chinese Leader — A432

2004, June 1   **Perf. 14**
2713 A432 5000 le multi   4.00 4.00

2004 Summer Olympics, Athens A433

Designs: 250 le, Marathon, 1908. 300 le, Dimitrios Vikelas, first president of Intl. Olympic Committee. 1500 le, 1896 Olympic medal. 2000 le, Discus thrower.

2004, June 6   **Perf. 14¼**
2714-2717 A433   Set of 4   3.25 3.25

A434

D-Day, 60th Anniv. — A435

No. 2718: a, Gen. Dwight D. Eisenhower. b, Rear Adm. Don P. Moon. c, Lt. Gen. Omar N. Bradley. d, Rear Adm. Alan G. Kirk. e, Maj. Gen. Clarence R. Huebner. f, Maj. Gen. Maxwell D. Taylor.
No. 2719, 950 le: a, LST landing craft. b, M4 Sherman tank. c, M4 Sherman tank and soldier. d, Tank cannon. e, 70th Tank Battalion patch. f, Soldier with rifle. g, 743rd Tank Battalion patch. h, 741st Tank Battalion patch.
No. 2720, 1000 le: a, P-51 Mustang over battle. b, Paratroopers, map. c, Map. d, P-38 Lightning. e, M4 Sherman tank, diff. f, Soldiers. g, LCM landing craft, map. h, US light cruiser, map with numbers.
No. 2721, 1000 le: a, P-47 Thunderbolt. b, Paratroopers, airplanes, map. c, Tank, map. d, Soldier with rifle, map. e, US heavy cruiser. f, US light cruiser, map. g, Ships. h, US destroyer escorts.
No. 2722, 1000 le: a, Spitfire. b, Typhoon. c, Tail of Typhoon, wing of P-38 Lightning, other airplane. d, P-51 Mustang. e, C-47 Skytrain. f, Wing of Typhoon, fuselage of C-47 Skytrain, other airplane. g, P-38 Lightning. h, US Air Force patch.
No. 2723, 1100 le: a, US light cruiser, blimps. b, LST landing craft, blimps. c, Landing craft with door open. d, LST landing craft. e, US armored car. f, Soldiers, tank. g, US medical transport vehicle. h, US armored car leaving landing craft.
No. 2724, 1100 le: a, Soldier with rifle, map, diff. b, Paratrooper, 101st Airborne Division patch. c, Paratrooper, tail of plane. d, Nose of airplane. e, Gen. Eisenhower. f, Gen. Bernard Montgomery. g, Paratrooper, 82nd Airborne Division patch. h, Two paratroopers, C-47 Skytrain.

2004, June 1   **Perf. 14**
2718 A434 1400 le Sheet of 6,
      #a-f   7.00 7.00
Sheets of 8, #a-h
2719-2724 A435   Set of 6   40.00 40.00

British Lighthouses A436

Designs: 1800 le, Smalls Lighthouse. 2000 le, Needles Rocks Lighthouse. 2500 le, St. John's Point Lighhouse. 3500 le, Bell Rock Lighthouse. 4000 le, Eddystone Lighthouse.

2004, June 17   **Perf. 14¾x14**
2725-2729 A436   Set of 5   11.50 11.50

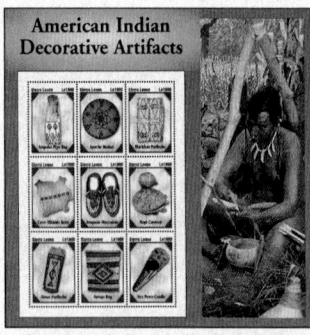

American Indian Artifacts — A437

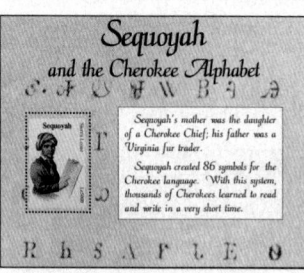

American Indians — A438

No. 2730: a, Arapaho pipe bag. b, Apache basket. c, Blackfoot parfleche. d, Crow elkhide robe. e, Iroquois moccasins. f, Hopi canteen. g, Sioux parfleche. h, Navajo rug. i, Nez Perce cradle.

No. 2731 — Ioway chiefs and warriors: a, Ne-O-Mon-Ne. b, Ma-Has-Kah. c, Moa-Na-Hon-Ga. d, Tah-Ro-Hon. e, Not-Chi-Mi-Ne. f, Shau-Hau-Napo-Tinia.

No. 2732, horiz. — Paintings by Charles Russell: a, Medicine Man. b, War Party. c, Signal Smoke.

5000 le, Sequoyah.

2004, July 5			Perf. 14	
2730	A437	1000 le Sheet of 9, #a-i	7.50	7.50
2731	A438	1500 le Sheet of 6, #a-f	7.50	7.50
2732	A438	3000 le Sheet of 3, #a-c	7.50	7.50
		Nos. 2730-2732 (3)	22.50	22.50
		Souvenir Sheet		
2733	A438	5000 le multi	4.00	4.00

Prehistoric Animals — A439

No. 2734, 2000 le: a, Apatosaurus. b, Styracosaurus. c, Plateosaurus. d, Pachyrhinosaurus.

No. 2735, 2000 le, horiz.: a, Camarasaurus. b, Iystrosaurus. c, Ankylosaurus. d, Herrerasaurus.

No. 2736, 5000 le, Dunklosteus. No. 2737, 5000 le, Archaeopteryx, horiz.

2004		Sheets of 4, #a-d	Perf. 14	
2734-2735	A439	Set of 2	13.00	13.00
		Souvenir Sheets		
2736-2737	A439	Set of 2	8.25	8.25
		No. 2734 has two labels.		

Orchids — A440

Designs: 150 le, Catasetum pileatum. No. 2739, 400 le, Cattleya araguainsis. No. 2740, 400 le, Barkeria spectabilis. 3500 le, Catasetum fimbriatum.

No. 2742: a, Odontonia vesta. b, Ancistro rothschildianus. c, Ansellia africana. d, Aspasia epidendroides.

5000 le, Bulbophyllum lobbii.

2004, May 17		Litho.	Perf. 12½	
2738-2741	A440	Set of 4	3.75	3.75

2742	A440	1700 le Sheet of 4, #a-d	5.50	5.50
		Souvenir Sheet		
2743	A440	5000 le multi	4.25	4.25

Dogs — A441

Designs: 250 le, Great Pyrenees. 600 le, Kerry Blue terrier. 1300 le, Mastiff. 1800 le, English sheepdog.

No. 2748: a, Sealyham terrier. b, Norwich terrier. c, Wheaton terrier. d, Bull terrier. 5000 le, Greyhound.

2004, May 17		Set of 4		
2744-2747	A441	Set of 4	3.25	3.25
2748	A441	1700 le Sheet of 4, #a-d	5.50	5.50
		Souvenir Sheet		
2749	A441	5000 le multi	4.25	4.25

Souvenir Sheet

Intl. Year of Peace — A442

No. 2750 — Position of olive branch carried by dove: a, Below last two zeros of denomination. b, Below three and first two zeros of denomination. c, Covered by last two zeros of denomination.

2004, June 1			Perf. 14	
2750	A442	3000 le Sheet of 3, #a-c	7.50	7.50

Powered Flight Type of 2003

No. 2751: a, Curtiss Triad. b, Avro Biplane. c, Curtiss America. d, Farnborought Be-2.

2004, July 17				
2751	A413	1500 le Sheet of 4, #a-d	5.00	5.00

Worldwide Fund for Nature (WWF) — A443

No. 2752 — Patas monkey: a, Monkey grooming another. b, Monkeys and flower. c, Adult and juvenile. d, Head of monkey.

2004, Oct. 11			Perf. 13¼x13½	
2752	A443	1000 le Block of 4, #a-d	3.75	3.75
e.		Miniature sheet, 2 each #2752a-2752d	8.00	8.00
		for surcharge see No. 2910.		

National Basketball Association Players — A444

Designs: No. 2753, 700 le, Kobe Bryant, Los Angeles Lakers. No. 2754, 700 le,

Carmelo Anthony, Denver Nuggets. No. 2755, 700 le, Yao Ming, Houston Rockets. No. 2756, 700 le, Jermaine O'Neal, Indiana Pacers. No. 2757, 700 le, Leandro Barbosa, Phoenix Suns. 2000 le, Vlade Divac, Sacramento Kings.

2004			Perf. 14	
2753-2758	A444	Set of 6	4.50	4.50

Issued: Nos. 2753, 2758, 11/2; No. 2754, 11/4; Nos. 2755-2756, 11/6; No. 2757, 12/13. Each stamp printed in a sheet of 12.

George Herman "Babe" Ruth (1895-1948), Baseball Player — A445

2004, Dec. 13				
2759	A445	500 le multi	.40	.40
		Printed in sheet of 16.		

National Soccer Team — A446

2004, Dec. 13			Perf. 12	
2760	A446	2000 le multi	1.75	1.75

Pres. Ronald Reagan and Queen Elizabeth II — A447

No. 2761, Reagan and Queen: a, With spouses. b, Making a toast.

2004, Dec. 13			Perf. 13½	
2761	A447	2000 le Horiz. pair, #a-b	3.25	3.25

Printed in sheets containing three each of Nos. 2761a and 2761b.

Ocean Liners A448

Designs: 600 le, Paris. 800 le, Statendam. 1000 le, Stavengerfjord. 1500 le, Campania. 2000 le, Drottningholm. 3000 le, Lusitania. 5000 le, United States, horiz.

2004, Dec. 13			Perf. 14¼	
2762-2767	A448	Set of 6	7.25	7.25
		Souvenir Sheet		
2768	A448	5000 le multi	4.25	4.25

Christmas A449

Designs: 1000 le, Nativity with the Annunciation to the Shepherds, by Follower of Jan Joest. 1500 le, Christmas Snow, by Norman Rockwell. 2000 le, The Christmas Tree, by E. Osborn. 5000 le, The Spirit of Christmas, by Rockwell.

8000 le, Madonna and Child Enthroned with Two Angels, by Fra Filippo Lippi.

2004, Dec. 13			Perf. 12¼x12	
2769-2772	A449	Set of 4	7.75	7.75
		Souvenir Sheet		
2773	A449	8000 le multi	6.50	6.50

Miniature Sheet

Yasujiro Ozu (1903-63), Film Director — A450

No. 2774 — Posters or scenes from: a, Tokyo Story. b, Late Spring. c, Early Summer. d, Equinox Flower. e, Good Morning. f, An Autumn Afternoon.

2004, Dec. 13			Perf. 13¼	
2774	A450	1400 le Sheet of 6, #a-f	7.00	7.00

Miniature Sheets

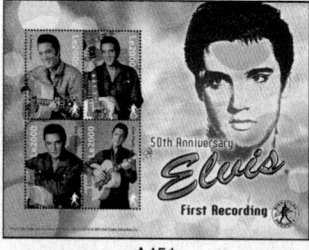

A451

Elvis Presley (1935-77) — A452

Various depictions of Presley.

2004, Dec. 13			Perf. 13½	
2775	A451	2000 le Sheet of 4, #a-d	6.50	6.50
2776	A452	2000 le Sheet of 4, #a-d	6.50	6.50

FIFA (Fédération Internationale de Football Association), Cent. — A453

No. 2777: a, Diego Simeone. b, Careca. c, Oliver Bierhoff. d, Kevin Keegan. 5000 le, David Ginola.

2004, Dec. 13   **Perf. 12¾x12½**
2777 A453 2000 le Sheet of 4,
   #a-d   6.50 6.50
Souvenir Sheet
2778 A453 5000 le multi   4.25 4.25

Locomotives, 200th Anniv. — A454

No. 2779, 1000 le: a, Stephenson's Rocket. b, Indonesian State Railway B50 class 2-4-0. c, Eurostar Paris-London train. d, China Railways SY Class 2-8-2. e, Baldwin 0-6-0. f, Hunsle 0-4-2T. g, Bagnall 0-6-0 ST Progress. h, North British-built 4-8-2T. i, Baldwin 0-6-2l.

No. 2780, 1000 le, vert.: a, GWR Mogul, Severn Valley Railway. b, Kitson Meyer 0-6-6-0. c, China Railways SL7 Class Pacific. d, Fireman fueling Yugoslav Class 20 2-6-0. e, Lookout man with flag. f, Workers filling sandboxes. g, Indian Railways locomotive taking water. h, Man on Indian Railways ZP Pacific Pulgeon. i, Worker cleaning smokebox.

No. 2781, 1000 le, vert.: a, LMS 8F 2-8-0, Great Central Railway. b, Rhodesia Railways 12 Class 4-8-2. c, DR German Railways 01 Class Pacific. d, Indian Railways McArthur 2-8-2. e, USATC 0-6-0T. f, China Railways KD6 2-8-0. g, Polish Feldbahn 0-8-0T, h, Indian Railways Mawd 2-8-2. i, North British 2-10-0.

No. 2782, 1000 le, vert.: a, B12 Class 4-6-0. b, Uruguay Railways Beyer Peacock Mogul 2-6-0. c, Ghana Railways Diesel-electric locomotive. d, Bagnall 0-4-0. e, Ledo Brickworks, Upper Assam. f, Train at Indian sugar mill. g, Carbon converter, Tangshan Locomotive Works, China. h, Crane loading timber on train car, Lanxiang, China. i, Worker carrying clay to train at Ledo Brickworks.

No. 2783, 5000 le, Ghan. No. 2784, 5000 le, Hudson Line. No. 2785, 5000 le, Blue Train. No. 2786, 5000 le, Bullet Train.

    Perf. 13¼x13½, 13½x13¼
2004, Dec. 13   **Sheets of 9, #a-i**
2779-2782 A454 Set of 4   30.00 30.00
Souvenir Sheets
2783-2786 A454 Set of 4   16.50 16.50

New Year 2005 (Year of the Rooster) — A455

No. 2787: a, Country name in blue. b, Country name in red.

2005, Feb. 23   **Perf. 12**
2787 A455 600 le Pair, #a-b   1.00 1.00
Printed in sheets containing two pairs.

Pope John Paul II (1920-2005) and French President Jacques Chirac — A456

2005, May 24 Litho.   **Perf. 13½x13¼**
2788 A456 1800 le multi   1.60 1.60
Printed in sheet of 6.

Maimonides (1135-1204), Philosopher — A457

2005, May 24   **Perf. 12**
2789 A457 2000 le multi   1.75 1.75
Printed in sheets of 4.

Rotary International, Cent. — A458

No. 2790: a, Map, handshake. b, Map, people, "Service Above Self." c, Emblem. d, Founder Paul P. Harris.

2005, May 24   **Perf. 12¾**
2790 A458 1800 le Sheet of 4,
   #a-d   6.25 6.25

Expo 2005, Aichi, Japan — A459

No. 2791: a, Glacial polish, Toiyabe National Forest, Nevada. b, African gorilla. c, Rock climber, Yosemite Valley, California. d, Nassau grouper spawning, Caribbean Sea. e, Ladybug swarm. f, Evolution Valley, California.

2005, May 24   **Perf. 12**
2791 A459 1500 le Sheet of 6,
   #a-f   7.75 7.75

Hans Christian Andersen (1805-75), Author — A460

No. 2792: a, Little Claus and Big Claus. b, Little Ida's Flowers. c, The Tinderbox. 5000 le, The Princess and the Pea.

2005, May 24   **Perf. 12¾**
2792 A460 3000 le Sheet of 3,
   #a-c   7.75 7.75
Souvenir Sheet
    Perf. 12
2793 A460 5000 le multi   4.25 4.25
No. 2792 contains three 42x28mm stamps.

Friedrich von Schiller (1759-1805), Writer — A461

No. 2794: a, Statue of Schiller, Berlin. b, Statue of Schiller, Munich. c, Statue of Schiller and Johann Wolfgang von Goethe. 5000 le, Schiller.

2005, May 24   **Perf. 12¾**
2794 A461 3000 le Sheet of 3,
   #a-c   7.75 7.75
Souvenir Sheet
2795 A461 5000 le multi   4.25 4.25

Jules Verne (1828-1905), Writer — A462

No. 2796: a, Verne's tomb, Amiens, France. b, Michael Arden, From the Earth to the Moon. c, Verne, Moon. 5000 le, Verne, hot air balloon.

2005, May 24
2796 A462 3000 le Sheet of 3,
   #a-c   7.75 7.75
Souvenir Sheet
2797 A462 5000 le multi   4.25 4.25

Battle of Trafalgar, Bicent. — A463

Paintings of various battle scenes: 500 le, 1000 le, 2000 le, 5000 le. 8000 le, Battle scene, diff.

2005, May 24   **Perf. 12¾**
2798-2801 A463 Set of 4   7.25 7.25
Souvenir Sheet
    Perf. 12
2802 A463 8000 le multi   7.00 7.00

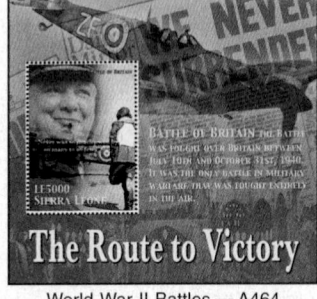

World War II Battles — A464

No. 2803, 2000 le, horiz. — Battle of Britain: a, Luftwaffe launches air strikes on Britain. b, Civilians take cover on underground station platform. c, Pilots race to planes. d, War in the sky.

No. 2804, 2000 le, horiz. — Battle of Stalingrad: a, Russians counterattack. b, Destroyed German tank. c, End of the German 6th Army. d, German prisoners of war.

No. 2805, 5000 le, Winston Churchill. No. 2806, 5000 le, Russian victory at Stalingrad, horiz.

2005, May 24   **Perf. 13¼**
    Sheets of 4, #a-d
2803-2804 A464 Set of 2   14.00 14.00
Souvenir Sheets
2805-2806 A464 Set of 2   8.50 8.50

End of World War II, 60th Anniv. — A465

No. 2807, 2000 le: a, Franklin D. Roosevelt, Winston Churchill. b, Secretary of Defense Louis Johnson, Generals Douglas MacArthur and Omar Bradley. c, Meeting of Allied Expeditionary Force commanders. d, Winston Churchill.

No. 2808, 2000 le: a, Roosevelt's address to Congress after Pearl Harbor attack. b, "Little Boy" atomic bomb. c, "Fat Man" atomic bomb. d, Japanese surrender ceremony.

No. 2809, 5000 le, Winston Churchill on V-E Day. No. 2810, 5000 le, Women reading newspapers.

2005, May 24   **Perf. 12¾**
    Sheets of 4, #a-d
2807-2808 A465 Set of 2   14.00 14.00
Souvenir Sheets
2809-2810 A465 Set of 2   8.50 8.50
The picture used for No. 2807b is not from the World War II era as Johnson was not Secretary of Defense until 1949.

Fire Fighting Apparatus — A466

Designs: 900 le, Boss Hoss Limited Edition fire motorcycle, German flag. 1200 le, Pumper

8 by 10, Austrian flag. 1500 le, Hydraulic platform truck, Germany, Ireland flag. 1800 le, Scania fire appliance, Australian flag.

No. 2815, 2000 le — Trucks from: a, Japan. b, Germany. c, Canada. d, Ireland.

No. 2816, 2000 le: a, Mercedes-Benz 2635 Thoma, Germany. b, 1997 Dennis Sabre water tender, Ireland. c, Microscopic fire truck, Japan. d, Scania fire appliance, Australia, diff.

No. 2817, 2000 le: a, 1935 Chevrolet fire truck. b, 1914 International fire truck. c, 1885 Chemical fire engine. d, 1963 Mason FD1.

No. 2818, 5000 le, Fire engine, US flag. No. 2819, 5000 le, 1890 horse-driven fire wagon, British flag.

2005, May 24   **Perf. 12¾**
2811-2814 A466   Set of 4   4.75   4.75
     Sheets of 4, #a-d
2815-2817 A466   Set of 3   21.00 21.00
     Souvenir Sheets
2818-2819 A466   Set of 2   8.50   8.50

Quesnard Lighthouse, Alderney — A467

2005, June 17
2820 A467 4500 le multi   4.00   4.00

Wedding of Prince Charles and Camilla Parker Bowles A468

Designs: No. 2821, 2000 le, Families of bride and groom. No. 2822, 2000 le, Charles and Camilla, vert. No. 2823, 2000 le, Charles, Camilla and bookstand, vert.

     Perf. 13¼x13½, 13½x13¼
2005, Sept. 22   **Litho.**
2821-2823 A468   Set of 3   5.25   5.25

A469

Elvis Presley (1935-70) — A470

No. 2824, 2000 le — Elvis with microphone with background colors of: a, Blue. b, Dark green. c, Yellow green. d, Red and violet.

No. 2825, 2000 le — Elvis: a, Playing guitar, blue denomination. b, Holding guitar, pale olive denomination. c, Holding guitar, pink denomination. d, Playing guitar, lilac denomination.

2005, Dec. 1   **Litho.**   **Perf. 13¼**
     Sheets of 4, #a-d
2824-2825 A469   Set of 2   13.50 13.50
     Litho. & Embossed
     Serpentine Die Cut 8¾
2826 A470 18,000 le gold &
         multi   15.50 15.50

Christmas — A471

Paintings: 500 le, The Virgin with Grapes, by Pierre Mignard. 1500 le, Adoration of the Shepherds, by Bartolomé Esteban Murillo. 2000 le, Madonna with the Child, by Murillo. 3000 le, Fountain of Life, by Hans Holbein the Elder.

6000 le, Adoration of the Shepherds, by Murillo, diff.

2005, Dec. 13   **Litho.**   **Perf. 12½**
2827-2830 A471   Set of 4   6.00   6.00
     Souvenir Sheet
2831 A471 6000 le multi   5.25   5.25

     Souvenir Sheet

Intl. Year of Microcredit — A472

No. 2832 — Woman at left and: a, Man and woman. b, Man holding stick. c, Man with scales. d, Woman and cow.

2005
2832 A472 2500 le Sheet of 4,
       #a-d   8.50   8.50

New Year 2006 (Year of the Dog) — A473

In its Position, by Xu Beihong: 600 le, Detail. 2000 le, Entire painting.

2006   **Perf. 13¼**
2833 A473   600 le multi   .50   .50
     Souvenir Sheet
     Perf. 11¼x11½
2834 A473 2000 le multi   1.75   1.75

No. 2833 printed in sheets of 4. No. 2834 contains one 26x60mm stamp.

Pope Benedict XVI — A474

2006, Jan. 24   **Perf. 13¼**
2835 A474 10,000 le multi   8.50   8.50

Printed in sheets of 4.

     Miniature Sheet

Indian Chiefs — A475

No. 2836 — Chief and tribe: a, Medicine Crow, Crow. b, Quanah Parker, Comanche. c, Garfield, Jicarilla. d, Pretty Eagle, Crow. e, Plenty Coups, Crow. f, He Dog, Oglala. g, Crow King, Hunkpapa. h, Pontiac, Ottawa. i, Naiche, Chiricahua. j, Gall, Hunkpapa.

2006, Jan. 31
2836 A475 1250 le Sheet of
      10, #a-j   11.00 11.00

Travels of Pope John Paul II in 2003-04 — A476

No. 2837, 2500 le: a, Madrid, Spain. b, Croatia. c, Banja Luka, Bosnia & Herzegovina. d, Slovakia.

No. 2838, 2500 le: a, Pompeii, Italy. b, Bern Switzerland. c, Lourdes, France. d, Loreto, Italy.

2006, Feb. 27   **Perf. 13½**
     Sheets of 4, #a-d, + 4 Labels
2837-2838 A476   Set of 2   17.00 17.00

Children's Art — A477

No. 2839, 2000 le — Circus animals: a, Monkey. b, Red-toed elephant. c, Colored giraffe. d, Colored bird.

No. 2840, 2000 le — Reptiles: a, Green gecko. b, Frog. c, Spotted lizard. d, Orange lizard.

No. 2841, 2000 le — Flowers: a, Yellow flowers. b, Poppies. c, Orange flowers. d, Lilies.

2006   **Sheets of 4, #a-d**   **Perf. 13¼**
2839-2841 A477   Set of 3   21.00 21.00

2006 Winter Olympics, Turin A478

Designs: 1000 le, US #1146. 1300 le, Canada #1152. 2000 le, Poster for 1988 Calgary Winter Olympics. 3000 le, Poster for 1960 Squaw Valley Winter Olympics.

2006, Apr. 7   **Litho.**   **Perf. 13¼**
2842-2845 A478   Set of 4   6.25   6.25

Messengers of Peace — A479

No. 2846: a, Michael Douglas, actor. b, United Nations Building, New York.

2006, May 29
2846 A479 2000 le Pair, #a-b   3.50   3.50

Printed in sheets containing 3 each #2846a-2846b.

     Souvenir Sheet

US #300, Benjamin Franklin — A480

2006, May 29
2847 A480 6000 le multi   5.25   5.25

Washington 2006 World Stamp Exhibition.

Queen Elizabeth II, 80th Birthday — A481

No. 2848 — Queen wearing: a, Green hat. b, Blue hat. c, No hat. d, Yellow hat. 6000 le, Wearing tiara.

2006, June 13   **Perf. 14¼**
2848 A481 3000 le Sheet of 4,
       #a-d   10.50 10.50
     Souvenir Sheet
2849 A481 6000 le multi   5.25   5.25

Souvenir Sheet

Ludwig Durr (1878-1956), Engineer,
and Zeppelins — A482

No. 2850 — Durr and: a, Zeppelin L30. b,
The Hindenburg. c, Graf Zeppelin.

2006, July 26   **Perf. 12¾**
2850 A482 4000 le Sheet of 3,
         #a-c   10.50 10.50

Rembrandt
(1606-69),
Painter
A483

Designs: 800 le, Abraham Frans. 1000 le,
The Rat Catcher. 2000 le, Young Man with
Velvet Cap. 8000 le, The Flute Player.
No. 2855, 3000 le: a, Abraham and Isaac. b,
Abraham Entertaining the Angels. c, Return of
the Prodigal Son. d, Adam and Eve.
No. 2856, 3000 le — Details from The Night
Watch: a, Man with black hat, neck ruffle and
sash. b, Man holding gun below chin. c, Man
with white hat. d, Man with red hat holdiing
gun.
No. 2857, 6000 le, Portrait of an Amsterdam
Citizen as a Militiaman. No. 2858, 6000 le,
Maria Trip, Daughter of Alotte Adriaenson. No.
2859, 6000 le, Homer Dictating to a Scribe.

2006, July 26   **Perf. 12, 13¼ (#2855)**
2851-2854 A483   Set of 4   10.00 10.00
Sheets of 4, #a-d
2855-2856 A483   Set of 2   21.00 21.00
Imperf
Size: 70x100mm
2857-2859 A483   Set of 3   15.50 15.50

Souvenir Sheet

Elvis Presley (1935-77) — A484

No. 2860 — Presley in: a, White costume. b,
Black and white cape. c, Army uniform. d, Blue
jacket.

2006, Dec. 21   **Perf. 13¼**
2860 A484 2000 le Sheet of 4,
         #a-d   6.75 6.75

Christmas — A485

Details from Main Altar of the Jesuit Church,
Antwerp, by Peter Paul Rubens: 1000 le,
Angel. 1500 le, Madonna and Child. No. 2863,
2000 le, Angel, diff., with denomination in
white at UL. 3000 le, Angel, diff.
No. 2865, 2000 le: a, Like 1000 le. b, Like
1500 le. c, Like No. 2863, with denomination in
black at LR. d, Like 3000 le.

2006, Dec. 21   **Perf. 14**
2861-2864 A485   Set of 4   6.50 6.50
Souvenir Sheet
2865 A485 2000 le Sheet of 4,
         #a-d   6.75 6.75

Souvenir Sheet

Wolfgang Amadeus Mozart (1756-91),
Composer — A486

2006, Dec. 21   **Litho.**   **Perf. 13¼**
2866 A486 7000 le multi   6.00 6.00

Miniature Sheets

Pres. John F. Kennedy (1917-
63) — A487

No. 2867, 2000 le — Kennedy: a, At microphones on inauguration day. b, Portrait and
cover of inaugural program. c, Taking oath,
medal depicting Kennedy. d, And Robert Frost
and poem.
No. 2868, 2000 le: a, Kennedy and map of
Cuba. b, Map of US, Soviet Premier Nikita
Khrushchev, and Soviet R-12 missile. c, Map
of Cuba, Kennedy meeting with Soviet Foreign
Minister Andrei Gromyko. d, Cuban President
Fidel Castro, John and Robert Kennedy.

2006, Dec. 21   **Perf. 13¼**
Sheets of 4, #a-d
2867-2868 A487   Set of 2   14.00 14.00

Miniature Sheet

Marilyn Monroe (1926-62),
Actress — A488

No. 2869: a, With hand on shoulder. b, With
straps of brown dress showing. c, With hand
behind head. d, Leaning to left.

2006, Dec. 21
2869 A488 2000 le Sheet of 4,
         #a-d   7.00 7.00

Space Achievements — A489

No. 2870: a, Mir Space Station. b, Space
Shuttle Challenger. c, Giotto Comet Probe. d,
Luna 9. e, Viking 1. f, International Space
Station.
No. 2871, 3000 le: a, Launch of Boeing
Delta II rocket. b, Calipso. c, CloudSat. d,
Aura, Parasol, Calipso, CloudSat, Aqua and
OCO satellites in orbit.
No. 2872, 3000 le, vert. — Artist's concep-
tions of: a, NASA's crew launch. b, New
spacecraft to rendezvous with International
Space Station. c, New lunar lander. d,
Parachutes deploying after reentry.
No. 2873, 3000 le, vert. — Photos of Inter-
national Space Station from: a, June 3, 1999.
b, Dec. 2, 2000. c, June 15, 2002. d, Aug. 6,
2005.
No. 2874, 6000 le, Apollo 11 Lunar Module.
No. 2875, 6000 le, Impactor with Deep Impact
Probe. No. 2876, 6000 le, Mars Reconnais-
sance Orbiter. No. 2877, 6000 le, Space Shuttle Columbia, vert.

2006, Dec. 21
2870 A489 2000 le Sheet of 6,
         #a-f   10.50 10.50
Sheets of 4, #a-d
2871-2873 A489   Set of 3   32.50 32.50
Souvenir Sheets
2874-2877 A489   Set of 4   21.00 21.00

New Year
2007
(Year of
the Pig)
A490

2007, Jan. 3   **Perf. 13¼**
2878 A490 2000 le multi   1.75 1.75
         Printed in sheets of 4.

Scouting, Cent. — A491

Designs: 3000 le, Dove, inscriptions in various languages. 6000 le, Dove, inscriptions in
various languages, symbols.

2007, Feb. 15
2879 A491 3000 le multi   2.60 2.60
Souvenir Sheet
2880 A491 6000 le multi   5.25 5.25
No. 2867 was printed in sheets of 4 with
stamps having slightly different gradations of
background color.

Princess Diana (1961-97) — A492

No. 2881, vert. — Diana wearing: a, Yellow
dress, country name in red. b, Blue dress,
country name in red. c, White dress, country
name in green at bottom. d, Yellow dress,

---

country name in green. e, No dress shown,
country name in green. f, White dress, country
name in green at top.
7000 le, Diana with blue hat.

2007, Mar. 15   **Litho.**   **Perf. 13¼**
2881 A492 1500 le Sheet of 6,
         #a-f   7.75 7.75
Souvenir Sheet
2882 A492 7000 le multi   6.00 6.00

Concorde — A493

No. 2883, 2000 le: a, Air speed indicator
showng speed record. b, Concorde in flight.
No. 2884, 2000 le, horiz.: a, Concorde,
Royal Air Force Red Arrows and British flag. b,
Concorde over Buckingham Palace.

2007, Mar. 15   **Litho.**
Pairs, #a-b
2883-2884 A493   Set of 2   7.00 7.00
Nos. 2883-2884 each printed in sheets containing three of each stamp.

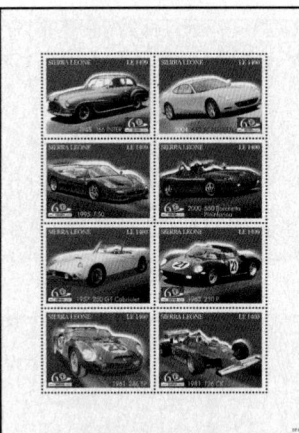

Pope Benedict
XVI — A494

2007, July 12
2885 A494 1500 le multi   1.00 1.00
         Printed in sheets of 8.

Miniature Sheet

Ferrari Automobiles, 60th
Anniv. — A495

No. 2886: a, 1948 166 Inter. b, 2004 612
Scaguetti. c, 1995 F50. d, 2000 550 Barchetta
Pininfarina. e, 1957 250 GT Cabriolet. f, 1963
250 P. g, 1961 246 SP. h, 1981 126 CK.

2007, July 12
2886 A495 1400 le Sheet of 8,
         #a-h   7.75 7.75

Christmas
A496

Painting details: 1000 le, The Annunciation, by Raphael. 1500 le, The Adoration of the Magi, by Raphael. 2000 le, The Presentation of the Christ Child in the Temple, by Raphael. 3000 le, The Nativity and the Arrival of the Magi, by Giovanni di Pietro.

2007, Nov. 28   **Perf. 14¾x14**
2887-2890 A496   Set of 4   5.00 5.00

Miniature Sheet

2008 Summer Olympics, Beijing — A497

No. 2891 — 1956 Melbourne Summer Olympics: a, Murray Rose, swimming gold medalist. b, Poster for 1956 Summer Olympics. c, Vladimir Kuts, track gold medalist. d, Laszlo Papp, boxing gold medalist.

2008, Jan. 8   **Litho.**   **Perf. 14**
2891 A497 1500 le Sheet of 4,
     #a-d   4.00 4.00

Nos. 975-977, 980-981 Surcharged

Methods and Perfs. As Before
2008, Mar. 10
2892	A142	800 le on 3 le #975		.55	.55
2893	A142	800 le on 5 le #976		.55	.55
2894	A142	800 le on 8 le #977		.55	.55
2895	A142	800 le on 20 le #980		.55	.55
2896	A142	800 le on 35 le #981		.55	.55
		Nos. 2892-2896 (5)		2.75	2.75

Nos. 2049-2050 Surcharged

Methods and Perfs. As Before
2008, Mar. 10
2897 A281 2500 le on 500 le
     Sheet of
     6, #a-f,
     #2049   10.00 10.00
2898 A281 2500 le on 600 le
     Sheet of
     6, #a-f,
     #2050   10.00 10.00

Nos. 2120-2121 Surcharged

Methods and Perfs. As Before
2008, Mar. 10
2899 A292 2800 le on 300 le
     Sheet of
     6, #a-f,
     #2120   11.50 11.50
2900 A292 4000 le on 300 le
     Sheet of
     6, #a-f,
     #2121   16.00 16.00

No. 2138 Surcharged

Methods and Perfs As Before
2008, Mar. 10
2901 A297 2800 le on 1500 le
     Sheet of 3,
     #a-c   5.75 5.75

No. 2193 Surcharged

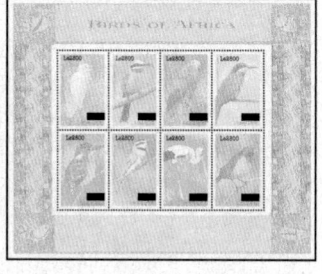

Methods and Perfs As Before
2008, Mar. 10
2902 A305 2800 le on 600 le
     Sheet of
     8, #a-h,
     #2193   15.00 15.00

Nos. 1738a-1738d Surcharged

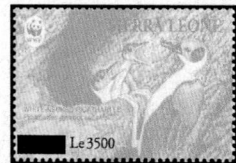

Methods and Perfs. As Before
2008, Mar. 10
2903		Vert. strip of 4	9.75	9.75
a.	A227	3500 le on 50 le #1738a	2.40	2.40
b.	A227	3500 le on 100 le #1738b	2.40	2.40
c.	A227	3500 le on 150 le #1738c	2.40	2.40
d.	A227	3500 le on 200 le #1738d	2.40	

No. 2903 amd a miniature sheet of 3 vertical strips of 4 exist imperf.

No. 2132 Surcharged

Methods and Perfs. As Before
2008, Mar. 10
2904 A295 3500 le on 600 le
     #2132   2.40 2.40

No. 2241 Surcharged

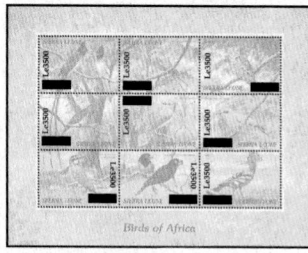

Birds of Africa

Methods and Perfs. As Before
2008, Mar. 10
2905 A317 3500 le on 600 le
     Sheet of
     9, #a-i,
     #2241   21.00 21.00

Nos. 586-589 Surcharged

Methods and Perfs. As Before
2008, Mar. 10
2906	A85	4000 le on 6c #586	2.75	2.75
2907	A85	4000 le on 10c #587	2.75	2.75
2908	A85	4000 le on 31c #588	2.75	2.75
2909	A85	4000 le on 60c #589	2.75	2.75
		Nos. 2906-2909 (4)	11.00	11.00

No. 2752 Surcharged in Black and Red

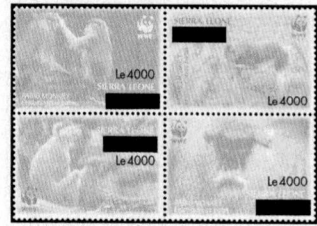

Methods and Perfs. As Before
2008, Mar. 10
2910 A443 4000 le on 1000 le
     Block of
     4, #a-d,
     #2752   11.00

No. 2910 exists imperf. in a souvenir sheet of 8 and miniature sheet of 16.

2008 World Stamp Championship, Israel — A498

2008, May 14   **Litho.**   **Imperf.**
2911 A498 7500 le multi   5.25 5.25

Miniature Sheet

Discovery and Exploration of Oregon — A499

No. 2912: a, Joel Palmer locates pass through the Cascades (30x50mm). b, Sir Francis Drake, first European to view Oregon coast, horiz. (40x25mm). c, Capt. Robert Gray, discoverer of the Columbia River, horiz. (40x25mm). d, Meriwether Lewis, William Clark and Multnomah Falls (30x50mm).

2008, June 13   **Perf. 13¼**
2912 A499 1500 le Sheet of 4,
     #a-d   4.25 4.25

2008 National Topical Stamp Show, Portland, Oregon.

Wedding of Queen Elizabeth II and Prince Philip, 60th Anniv. — A500

No. 2913: a, Couple. b, Queen.

2008, June 19
2913 A500 1500 le Pair, #a-b   2.10 2.10

Printed in sheets containing three of each stamp.

32nd America's Cup Yacht Races — A501

Various yachts with large panel in: a, Blue. b, Orange. c, Red. d, Olive brown.

2008, June 19
2914		Strip of 4	8.00 8.00
a.	A501	200 le multi	.25 .25
b.	A501	500 le multi	.35 .35
c.	A501	1000 le multi	.70 .70
d.	A501	10,000 le multi	6.75 6.75

Seven Wonders of the Modern World — A502

No. 2915, vert.: a, Statue of Christ the Redeemer, Brazil. b, Roman Colosseum, Italy. c, Great Wall of China. d, Machu Picchu, Peru. e, Petra, Jordan. f, Chichén Itzá, Mexico. 7000 le, Taj Mahal, India.

2008, June 19
2915	A502	1500 le Sheet of 6, #a-f	6.25 6.25

Souvenir Sheet
2916	A502	7000 le multi	4.75 4.75

Khilafat Ahmadiyya, Cent. — A503

Denominations: 800 le, 1000 le, 2000 le, 3000 le.

2008, June 20   *Perf. 12¾*
2917-2920	A503	Set of 4	4.75 4.75

A504

Elvis Presley (1935-77) — A505

No. 2921 — Presley: a, Both shoulders showing. b, Right shoulder showing. c, Left shoulder showing.
No. 2922: a, Denomination in yellow green, country name in blue. b, Denomination in red, country name in yellow green. c, Denomination in blue, country name in red. d, Denomination in blue, country name in yellow green. e, Denomination in yellow green, country name in red. f, Denomination in red, country name in blue.

2008, Oct. 28   *Perf. 11½*
2921		Horiz. strip of 3	3.00 3.00
a.-c.	A504 1500 le Any single		1.00 1.00

Perf. 13¼
2922	A505	1500 le Sheet of 6, #a-f	6.00 6.00

No. 2921 was printed in sheets containing two of each stamp.

Intl. Polar Year — A506

No. 2923 — Penguins with background color of: a, Red. b, Purple. c, Blue green. d, Orange.
7000 le, Penguins on ice.

2008, Oct. 28   *Perf. 13¼*
2923	A506	3000 le Sheet of 4, #a-d	8.00 8.00

Souvenir Sheet
2924	A506	7000 le multi	4.75 4.75

Christmas
A507

Designs: 1000 le, Nativity. 1500 le, Virgin Mary and Jesus. 2000 le, Joseph and Jesus. 3000 le, Angels and Jesus.

2008, Dec. 11   *Perf. 14¼x14¾*
2925-2928	A507	Set of 4	5.00 5.00

Inauguration of Barack Obama as US President — A508

2009, Jan. 20   *Perf. 12¼x11¾*
2929	A508	3000 le multi	2.00 2.00

Printed in sheets of 4.

Miniature Sheets

Space Exploration, 50th Anniv. (in 2007) — A509

No. 2930, 2200 le: a, Martian North Pole dust storms. b, Saturn. c, Jupiter's atmosphere. d, Craters on Mercury. e, Venus. f, Mercury.
No. 2931, 2200 le, horiz.: a, Spitzer Space Telescope. b, Galaxy M81. c, Hubble Space Telescope. d, Evil Eye Galaxy (M64). e, Cat's Eye Nebula. f, Hoag's Object.
No. 2932, 3000 le: a, Apollo 11 Lunar Module. b, Mercury Redstone rocket. c, Space Shuttle Atlantis on launch pad. d, Space Shuttle Endeavour.
No. 2933, 3000 le, horiz.: a, Sun shining, astronaut. b, South Pole of the Sun. c, Solar eruption. d, Solar eclipse.

2009, Jan. 27   *Perf. 12*
Sheets of 6, #a-f
2930-2931	A509	Set of 2	17.00 17.00

Sheets of 4, #a-d
2932-2933	A509	Set of 2	15.50 15.50

Miniature Sheet

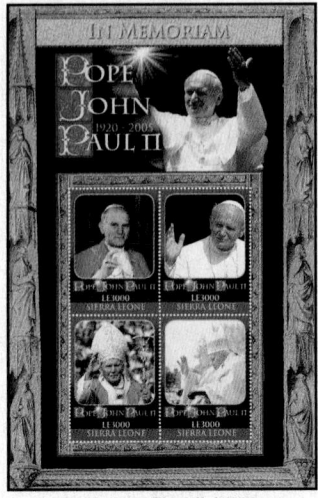

Pope John Paul II (1920-2005) — A510

No. 2934 — Color of vestments: a, Red. b, White. c, Green. d, Yellow.

2009, Feb. 4   *Litho.*   *Perf. 13¼*
2934	A510	3000 le Sheet of 4, #a-d	7.75 7.75

Yi Jianlian, National Basketball Association Player — A511

No. 2935: a, Wearing white uniform, holding basketball. b, Wearing dark uniform, holding basketball. c, Wearing white uniform, without basketball.

2009, Feb. 20
2935		Vert. strip of 3	3.00 3.00
a.-c.	A511 1500 le Any single		1.00 1.00

Printed in sheets of 6, containing two each Nos. 2935a-2935c.

Miniature Sheets

A512

A513

China 2009 World Stamp Exhibition, Luoyang — A514

No. 2936 — Art of Chang Dai-chien (1899-1983): a, Landscape of Yangshuo. b, Scholar Admiring Plum Blossoms. c, The Golden Summit of Mount Emei. d, Lotuses After the Rain.
No. 2937 — Chinese landmarks: a, Temple of Heaven, Beijing. b, Dalian Exhibition Center, Dalian. c, Xian South Gate, Shaanxi Province. d, National Grand Theater, Beijing.
No. 2938 — Sports: a, Javelin. b, Fencing. c, Soccer. d, Weight lifting.

2009   *Litho.*   *Perf. 12¾*
2936	A512	1500 le Sheet of 4, #a-d	4.00 4.00

Perf. 12½
2937	A513	1500 le Sheet of 4, #a-d	4.00 4.00

Perf. 11½
2938	A514	2000 le Sheet of 4, #a-d	5.25 5.25

Issued: No. 2938, 2/16; Nos. 2936-2937, 4/10.

Peonies
A515

2009, Apr. 10   *Perf. 13¼*
2939	A515	1500 le multi	.95 .95

Printed in sheets of 6.

Miniature Sheet

U.S. Inaugural Bibles of 1861 and 2009 — A516

No. 2940: a, Abraham Lincoln taking oath of office, 1861. b, Barack Obama taking oath of office, 2009. c, Obama's hand on Bible. d, Lincoln's inaugural Bible.

2009, May 14 *Perf. 11½*
2940 A516 3000 le Sheet of 4,
#a-d 7.50 7.50

Miniature Sheet

Elvis Presley (1935-77) — A517

No. 2941 — Presley and: a, Light blue denomination, purple background. b, Yellow denomination, brown background. c, Light blue denomination, green and black background. d, Yellow denomination, dull purple background.

2009, May 14 *Perf. 13¼*
2941 A517 3000 le Sheet of 4,
#a-d 7.50 7.50

Miniature Sheet

George Frideric Handel (1685-1759), Composer — A518

No. 2942: a, Handel's birthplace, Halle, Germany. b, Foundling Hospital where Handel directed concerts. c, Portrait of Handel, by Thomas Hudson. d, Ranelagh Gardens. e, Statue of Handel, by Louis-François Roubiliac. f, Farinelli and Senesino from opera, "Flavio."

2009, May 14 *Perf. 11½*
2942 A518 2500 le Sheet of 6,
#a-f 9.50 9.50

Miniature Sheets

2009 National Basketball Association All-Star Teams — A519

No. 2943, 1250 le — Eastern Division All-Stars: a, Ray Allen. b, Kevin Garnett. c, Danny Granger. d, Devin Harris. e, Dwight Howard. f, Allen Iverson. g, LeBron James. h, Joe Johnson. i, Rashard Lewis. j, Paul Pierce. k, Dwyane Wade. l, Mo Williams.
No. 2944, 1250 le — Western Division All-Stars: a, Chauncey Billups. b, Kobe Bryant. c, Tim Duncan. d, Pau Gasol. e, Yao Ming. f, Dirk Nowitzki. g, Shaquille O'Neal. h, Tony Parker. i, Chris Paul. j, Brandon Ray. k, Amare Stoudemire. l, David West.

2009, May 14 *Perf. 14¼x14¾*
Sheets of 12, #a-l
2943-2944 A519 Set of 2 19.00 19.00

Miniature Sheet

Ferrari Race Cars — A520

No. 2945: a, 1977 312 T2. b, 1982 126 C2. c, 1983 126 C3. d, 2007 F2007.

2009, July 6 *Perf. 14¼*
2945 A520 3000 le Sheet of 4,
#a-d 7.50 7.50

Miniature Sheet

First Man on the Moon, 40th Anniv. — A521

No. 2946: a, Apollo 11 Command and Lunar Modules. b, Astronaut Neil Armstrong. c, Apollo 11 plaque. d, Apollo 11 Command Module. e, Apollo 11 Lunar Module. f, Apollo 11 crew in quarantine.

2009, July 20 *Litho.* *Perf. 13¼*
2946 A521 2500 le Sheet of 6,
#a-f 8.75 8.75

Souvenir Sheet

35th G8 Summit, L'Aquila, Italy — A522

2009, Sept. 30
2947 A522 8000 le multi 4.25 4.25

Miniature Sheet

Pope Benedict XVI — A523

No. 2948 — Pope Benedict XVI: a, 2600 le, Facing forward. b, 2600 le, Facing left. c, 2800 le, As "a." d, 2800 le, As "b."

2009, Sept. 30 *Perf. 11½*
2948 A523 Sheet of 4, #a-d 5.75 5.75

Miniature Sheets

Dogs — A524

No. 2949, 3000 le — Cavalier King Charles spaniel: a, In front of fence. b, In bucket. c, With head on ground. d, With flowers at left.
No. 2950, 3000 le — English Springer spaniel: a, On wooden planks. b, Head. c, Standing. d, In front of overturned bucket.

2009, Sept. 30 *Perf. 11½x12*
Sheets of 4, #a-d
2949-2950 A524 Set of 2 13.00 13.00

Cats A525

Designs: 1000 le, Birman lilac point. 1500 le, Singapura sepia agouti. No. 2953, 2000 le, Scottish Fold blue tortie tabby and white. 3000 le, Asian Shaded lilac shaded silver.
No. 2955, 2000 le: a, Somali lilac. b, British Angora red shaded silver. c, Maine coon Maine wave. d, Turkish Van tortie and white.

2009, Sept. 30 *Perf. 14¾x14¼*
2951-2954 A525 Set of 4 4.00 4.00
2955 A525 2000 le Sheet of 4,
#a-d 4.25 4.25

Wildlife — A527

Designs: 1000 le, Giraffe. 1500 le, Bonobo. No. 2958, 2000 le, African bush elephant. 3000 le, Zebra.
No. 2960, 2000 le: a, Cheetah. b, Red colobus monkey. c, Hippopotamus. d, Lion.

2009, Sept. 30 *Perf. 14*
2956-2959 A526 Set of 4 4.00 4.00
2960 A527 2000 le Sheet of 4,
#a-d 4.25 4.25

Birds — A529

Designs: 1000 le, Pied kingfisher. 1500 le, House sparrow. No. 2963, 2000 le, Skylark. 3000 le, Black-chested snake-eagle.
No. 2965, 2000 le: a, Greenfinch. b, Pangani longclaw. c, Barn swallow. d, Namaqua sandgrouse.

2009, Sept. 30 *Perf. 14¾x14¼*
2961-2964 A528 Set of 4 4.00 4.00
2965 A529 2000 le Sheet of 4,
#a-d 4.25 4.25

A530

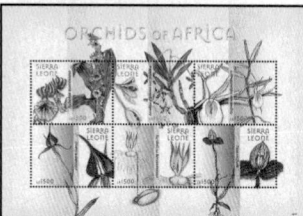

Orchids — A531

Designs: 1000 le, Penthea filicornis. No. 2967, 1500 le, Herschelia graminifolia. 2000 le, Satyrium princeps. 3000 le, Herschelia charpentieriana.
No. 2970, 1500 le: a, Eulophia quartiniana. b, Ansellia gigantea. c, Angraecum infundibulare. d, Disperis capensis. e, Bartholina burmanniana. f, Disa uniflora.

2009, Sept. 30 *Perf. 14¼x14¾*
2966-2969 A530 Set of 4 4.00 4.00
Perf. 14¾x14¼
2970 A531 1500 le Sheet of 6,
#a-f 5.00 5.00

A532

Mushrooms — A533

Designs: 1000 le, Fringed panaeolus. 1500 le, Orange latex lactarius. 2000 le, Purple laccaria. 3000 le, Liver lactarius.

No. 2975: a, Death cap. b, Cinnabar polypore. c, King bolete. d, Panther amanita. e, Fly amanita. f, Mica inky cap.

2009, Sept. 30   **Perf. 14**
2971-2974 A532 Set of 4   4.00   4.00
          Perf. 14¾x14¼
2975 A533 1700 le Sheet of 6,
      #a-f   5.50   5.50

Chinese Aviation, Cent. — A534

No. 2976 — Feng Ru (1884-1912), pilot: a, And newspaper story. b, With airplane in Auckland. c, With airplane in 1912. d, And Feng Ru II airplane.

7500 le, Feng Ru and airplane.

2009, Nov. 12   **Perf. 14¼**
2976 A534 2700 le Sheet of 4,
      #a-d   5.75   5.75
     Souvenir Sheet
2977 A534 7500 le multi   4.00   4.00

Aeropex 2009, Beijing. No. 2976 contains four 42x28mm stamps.

Miniature Sheet

The Three Stooges — A535

No. 2978 — Moe, Larry and Curly: a, Looking over the back of a sofa. b, Holding bottles. c, With wringer washer. d, Holding glasses.

2009, Dec. 9   **Perf. 11½x11¼**
2978 A535 2700 le Sheet of 4,
      #a-d   5.50   5.50

Bridges — A536

No. 2979: a, Tower Bridge, London. b, Hangzhou Bay Bridge, Zhejiang, China. c, Juscelino Kubitschek Bridge, Brasilia, Brazil. d, Sydney Harbour Bridge, Sydney, Australia. e, Ponte Vecchio, Florence, Italy. f, Bosporus Bridge, Istanbul.

7000 le, Golden Gate Bridge, San Francisco.

2009, Dec. 9
2979 A536 2000 le Sheet of 6,
      #a-f   6.25   6.25
     Souvenir Sheet
2980 A536 7000 le multi   3.75   3.75

Miniature Sheet

Chinese Zodiac Animals — A537

No. 2981: a, Rat. b, Ox. c, Tiger. d, Rabbit. e, Dragon. f, Snake. g, Horse. h, Ram. i, Monkey. j, Rooster. k, Dog. l, Pig.

2010, Jan. 4   **Litho.**   **Perf. 12**
2981 A537 800 le Sheet of 12,
      #a-l   5.00   5.00

Souvenir Sheet

New Year 2010 (Year of the Tiger) — A538

No. 2982 — Tiger with denomination at: a, Right. b, Left.

2010, Jan. 4   **Perf. 11½x12**
2982 A538 8000 le Sheet of 2,
      #a-b   8.25   8.25

Flag, Coat of Arms and Title of National Anthem of Sierra Leone A539

2010, Mar. 1   **Perf. 13½**
2983 A539 2000 le multi   1.10   1.10

Pres. Abraham Lincoln (1809-65) A540

2010, Mar. 1   **Perf. 12x11½**
2984 A540 2700 le multi   1.40   1.40

Printed in sheets of 4.

Miniature Sheet

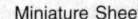

Election of Pres. John F. Kennedy, 50th Anniv. — A541

No. 2985 — Kennedy: a, Standing in limousine. b, Pointing. c, Sitting in chair. d, On campaign button.

2010, Mar. 1   **Perf. 12x11½**
2985 A541 4000 le Sheet of 4,
      #a-d   8.50   8.50

Miniature Sheet

Charles Darwin (1809-82), Naturalist — A542

No. 2986: a, Darwin's frog. b, Darwin's fox. c, Galapagos tortoise. d, Galapagos marine iguana.

2010, Mar. 1   **Perf. 13¼**
2986 A542 2500 le Sheet of 4,
      #a-d   5.25   5.25

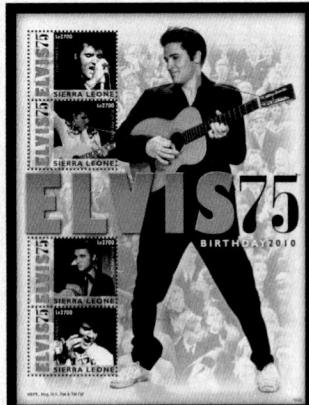

A543

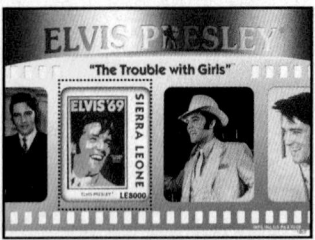

A544

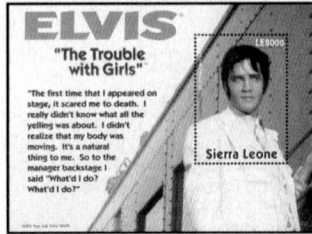

A545

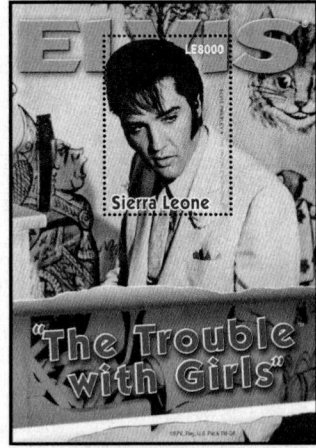

A546

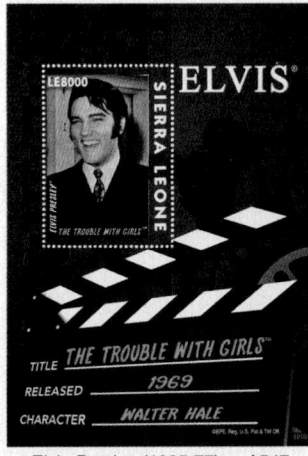

Elvis Presley (1935-77) — A547

No. 2987 — Presley: a, Holding microphone on stand. b, With arm raised and other on neck of guitar. c, With hand resting on guitar. d, Singing, not holding microphone.

2010, Mar. 1   **Perf. 11½x12**
2987 A543 2700 le Sheet of 4,
      #a-d   5.75   5.75
     Souvenir Sheets
        Perf. 13¼
2988 A544 8000 le multi   4.25   4.25
2989 A545 8000 le multi   4.25   4.25
2990 A546 8000 le multi   4.25   4.25
2991 A547 8000 le multi   4.25   4.25
   Nos. 2988-2991 (4)   17.00 17.00

Teams Participating in 2010 World Cup Soccer Championships, South Africa — A548

Team and flag of: No. 2992, 1900 le, Algeria. No. 2993, 1900 le, Argentina. No. 2994, 1900 le, Australia. No. 2995, 1900 le, Brazil. No. 2996, 1900 le, Cameroun. No. 2997, 1900 le, Chile. No. 2998, 1900 le, Denmark. No. 2999, 1900 le, England. No. 3000, 1900 le, France. No. 3001, 1900 le, Germany. No. 3002, 1900 le, Ghana. No. 3003, 1900 le, Greece. No. 3004, 1900 le, Honduras. No. 3005, 1900 le, Italy. No. 3006, 1900 le, Ivory Coast. No. 3007, 1900 le, Japan. No. 3008, 1900 le, North Korea. No. 3009, 1900 le, South Korea. No. 3010, 1900 le, Mexico. No. 3011, 1900 le, Netherlands. No. 3012, 1900 le, New Zealand. No. 3013, 1900 le, Nigeria. No. 3014, 1900 le, Paraguay. No. 3015, 1900 le, Portugal. No. 3016, 1900 le, Serbia. No. 3017, 1900 le, Slovakia. No. 3018, 1900 le, Slovenia. No. 3019, 1900 le, South Africa. No. 3020, 1900 le, Spain. No. 3021, 1900 le, Switzerland. No. 3022, 1900 le, United States. No. 3023, 1900 le, Uruguay.

2010, Mar. 1   *Perf. 14¼*
2992-3023 A548   Set of 32   32.00 32.00

Nos. 2992-3023 each were printed in sheets of 6.
An imperf. set 32 exists. Value, $400.

Miniature Sheets

A549

Pope John Paul II (1920-2005) — A550

No. 3024 — Country name in yellow with Pope John Paul II: a, Waving. b, Wearing miter with large cross. c, Wearing miter with central panel of hexagons and triangles. d, With candlestick at right.
No. 3025 — Country name in black with Pope John Paul II: a, Praying. b, Wearing red vestments. c, With both arms raised. d, Wearing miter.

2010, Apr. 26   *Perf. 11½x12*
3024 A549 4000 le Sheet of 4,
    #a-d   8.25 8.25
3025 A550 4000 le Sheet of 4,
    #a-d   8.25 8.25

Miniature Sheets

A551

Michael Jackson (1958-2009), Singer — A552

No. 3026 — Blue background with Jackson: a, Looking right. b, Holding microphone with silver head. c, Holding microphone with black head. d, Wearing red shirt.
No. 3027 — Purple background with Jackson: a, Facing left, wearing shiny costume. b, Wearing white jacket. c, With head raised. d, Holding microphone.

2010, Apr. 26   *Perf. 12*
3026 A551 4000 le Sheet of 4,
    #a-d   8.25 8.25
3027 A552 4000 le Sheet of 4,
    #a-d   8.25 8.25

Miniature Sheets

A553

Boy Scouts of America, Cent. — A554

No. 3028 — Eagle-shaped cloud and: a, Eagle Scout badge, Dog Care, Small Boat Sailing, Law and Botany merit badges. b, Eagle Scout badge, Astronomy, Energy, Theater and Home Repairs merit badges. c, Boy Scouts of America emblem, Scout holding branch.
No. 3029: a, Badges for Tenderfoot, Second Class and First Class Scout ranks. b, Badges for Star, Life and Eagle Scout ranks. c, Boy Scouts of America emblem, Scout holding branch, eagle-shaped cloud.

2010, Apr. 26   *Perf. 13¼*
3028 A553 4000 le Sheet of 4,
    #3028a-
    3028b, 2
    #3028c   8.25 8.25
3029 A554 4000 le Sheet of 4,
    #3029a-
    3029b, 2
    #3029c   8.25 8.25

Butterflies — A555

No. 3030: a, Protogoniomorpha parhassus. b, Kallimoides rumia rumia. c, Precis pelarga. d, Salamis cacta cacta.
No. 3031, 6000 le: a, Hypolimnas misippus. b, Hypolimnas salmacis salmacis.
No. 3032, 6000 le: a, Junonia sophia sophia. b, Junonia oenone.

2010, Apr. 26   *Perf. 12*
3030 A555 4000 le Sheet of 4,
    #a-d   8.25 8.25
Souvenir Sheets of 2, #a-b
3031-3032 A555   Set of 2   12.50 12.50

Girl Guides, Cent. — A556

No. 3033 — Pictures of Girl Guides of the past in frames and: a, Three Girl Guides. b, Two Girl Guides blowing bubbles, Girl Guide wearing balloon sculpture. c, Four Girl Guides. d, Eight Girl Guides.
8000 le, Brownie saluting, vert.

2010, June 17   *Perf. 11½x12*
3033 A556 2700 le Sheet of 4,
    #a-d   5.50 5.50
Souvenir Sheet
Perf. 11½
3034 A556 8000 le multi   4.25 4.25

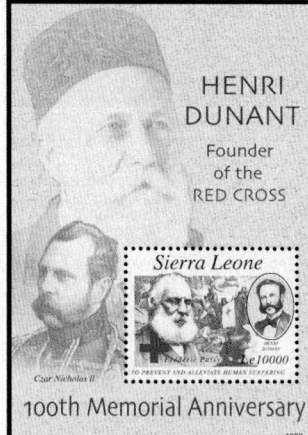

Henri Dunant (1828-1910), Founder of the Red Cross — A557

No. 3035 — Dunant, Red Cross and: a, Harriet Beecher Stowe (1811-96), writer. b, Charles Dickens (1812-70), writer. c, Bertha von Suttner (1843-1914), writer. d, Victor Hugo (1802-85), writer.
10,000 le, Dunant and Frédéric Passy (1822-1912), co-winner of 1901 Nobel Peace Prize.

2010, Oct. 14   *Perf. 11½x12*
3035 A557   4000 le Sheet of 4,
    #a-d   7.75 7.75
Souvenir Sheet
Perf. 11½
3036 A557 10,000 le multi   5.00 5.00

Miniature Sheets

A558

Mother Teresa (1910-97), Humanitarian — A559

No. 3037 — Mother Teresa at left with: a, Five children, child at left in red. b, Three children. c, Five children, all with head coverings. d, With four children.
No. 3025 — Mother Teresa: a, Holding child and wrapping hand around another child. b, Speaking to woman. c, Holding child. d, Holding baby, children near hut.

2010, Oct. 14   *Perf. 13x13¼*
3037 A558 4000 le Sheet of 4,
    #a-d   7.75 7.75
3038 A559 4000 le Sheet of 4,
    #a-d   7.75 7.75

Princess Diana (1961-97) — A560

No. 3039 — Background color: a, Red violet. b, Green. c, Blue violet. d, Orange.
No. 3040, 10,000 le, Red violet background. No. 3041, 10,000 le, Blue violet background.

2010, Oct. 14   *Perf. 12*
3039 A560 4000 le Sheet of 4,
    #a-d   7.75 7.75
Souvenir Sheets
3040-3041 A560   Set of 2   9.75 9.75

Souvenir Sheet

New Year 2011 (Year of the Rabbit) — A561

No. 3042 — Rabbit with: a, Head lowered. b, Head raised.

2010, Nov. 7
3042 A561 6000 le Sheet of 2,
    #a-b   5.75 5.75

Miniature Sheets

Chinese Emperors — A562

No. 3043: a, Text "Emperor / Gaozu / Han Dynasty" and Chinese characters. b, Portrait of Emperor Gaozu (c. 256-195 B.C.).

No. 3044: a, Text "Emperor / Hongwu / Ming Dynasty" and Chinese characters. b, Color portrait of Emperor Hongwu (1328-98). c, Ink drawing of Emperor Hongwu. d, Empress Ma (1333-82).

No. 3045: a, Text "Emperor / Kangxi / Qing Dynasty" and Chinese characters. b, Emperor Kangxi (1654-1722), wearing purple robe. c, Emperor Kangxi on throne. d, Emperor Kangxi holding calligrapher's brush.

2010, Nov. 7   **Perf. 12**
3043 A562 3000 le Sheet of 4,
              #3043a, 3
              #3043b   5.75 5.75
3044 A562 3000 le Sheet of 4,
              #a-d   5.75 5.75
3045 A562 3000 le Sheet of 4,
              #a-d   5.75 5.75
      Nos. 3043-3045 (3)   17.25 17.25
China 2010 World Philatelic Exhibition, Beijing.

Miniature Sheets

A563

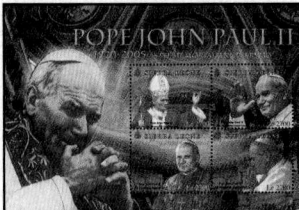

Pope John Paul II (1920-2005) — A564

No. 3046 — Denominations at left with Pope John Paul II: a, Wearing miter with large cross. b, Wearing zucchetto and red vestments, denomination in black. c, Wearing zucchetto and red vestments, denomination in orange. d, Wearing miter with central panel of hexagons and triangles.

No. 3047 — Denominations at right with Pope John Paul II: a, Holding cross. b, Waving. c, Wearing red vestments. d, Praying.

2010, Dec. 30   **Perf. 12**
3046 A563 2700 le Sheet of 4,
              #a-d   5.25 5.25
3047 A564 2700 le Sheet of 4,
              #a-d   5.25 5.25

Miniature Sheets

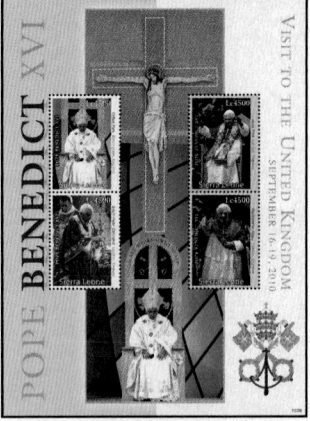

A565

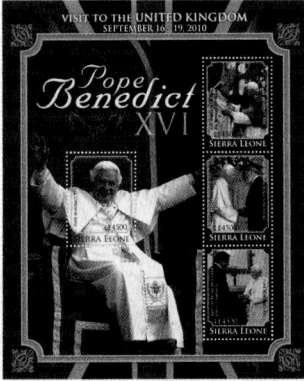

Visit of Pope Benedict XVI to United Kingdom — A566

No. 3048 — Pope Benedict XVI: a, At Cotton Park, Birmingham. b, At Hyde Park, London. c, Celebrating mass at Westminster Cathedral, London. d, Waving at Westminster Abbey, London.

No. 3049 — Pope Benedict XVI: a, Meeting Archbishop of Canterbury Rowan Williams. b, Seated. c, Meeting Chief Rabbi Jonathan Sacks. d, Meeting British Prime Minister David Cameron.

2010, Dec. 30   **Perf. 12x12½**
3048 A565 4500 le Sheet of 4,
              #a-d   8.75 8.75
                                Perf. 12x11½
3049 A566 4500 le Sheet of 4,
              #a-d   8.75 8.75

Souvenir Sheets

Popes and Their Coats of Arms — A567

No. 3050, 14,000 le: a, Pope Paul VI. b, Arms of Pope Paul VI.

No. 3051, 14,000 le: a, Pope John Paul I. b, Arms of Pope John Paul I.

2010, Dec. 30   Litho.   Imperf.
                Without Gum
              Sheets of 2, #a-b
3050-3051 A567 Set of 2   27.00 27.00

A568

Whales — A569

No. 3052: a, Southern minke whale. b, Common minke whale. c, Blue whale. d, Sei whale.

No. 3053, Bryde's whale. No. 3054, Fin whale.

2011, Jan. 12   **Perf. 12**
3052 A568 4000 le Sheet of 4,
              #a-d   7.75 7.75
              Souvenir Sheets
            Perf. 13 Syncopated
3053 A568 8000 le multi   4.00 4.00
3054 A569 8000 le multi   4.00 4.00

Lotus Flowers — A570

No. 3055: a, Country name at LL, denomination at top right, Latin name at right reading down. b, Country name at LL, denomination at top right, Latin name at top. c, Country name at UL, denomination at LR. Latin name at right reading down. d, Country name at LR. denomination at UL, Latin name at top right.

10,000 le, Lotus flower, vert.

2011, Feb. 1   **Perf. 14¾x114¼**
3055 A570 4000 le Sheet of 4,
              #a-d   7.50 7.50
              Souvenir Sheet
            Perf. 14¼x14¾
3056 A570 10,000 le multi 4.75 4.75
Indipex Intl. Philatelic Exhibition, New Delhi.

Miniature Sheet

Jewish Anti-apartheid Activists — A571

No. 3057: a, Ray Alexander (1914-2004). b, Baruch Hirson (1921-99). c, Norma Kitson (1933-2002). d, Yetta Barenblatt (1913-99).

2011, Mar. 1   **Perf. 12**
3057 A571 4500 le Sheet of 4,
              #a-d   8.50 8.50

Reptiles and Amphibians — A572

No. 3058, 4000 le — Reptiles: a, Nile crocodile. b, African clawed gecko. c, African spurred tortoise. d, Rainbow agama.

No. 3059, 4000 le — Frogs and toads: a, Big-eyed tree frog. b, Marbled reed frog. c, African red toad. d, African clawed frog.

No. 3060, 8000 le, Eastern green mamba. No. 3061, 8000 le, African bullfrog.

2011, Mar. 25   Perf. 13 Syncopated
            Sheets of 4, #a-d
3058-3059 A572 Set of 2   15.00 15.00
              Souvenir Sheets
3060-3061 A572 Set of 2   7.50 7.50

Paintings by Sandro Botticelli (c. 1445-1510) — A573

No. 3062: a, Portrait of a Young Man. b, Flight into Egypt. c, Crucified Christ. d, Three Miracles of Saint Zenobius.

8000 le, The Annunciation, horiz.

2011, Mar. 25   **Perf. 12**
3062 A573 4000 le Sheet of 4,
              #a-d   7.50 7.50
              Souvenir Sheet
                Perf. 12¾
3063 A573 8000 le multi   3.75 3.75
No. 3063 contains one 51x38mm stamp.

Miniature Sheets

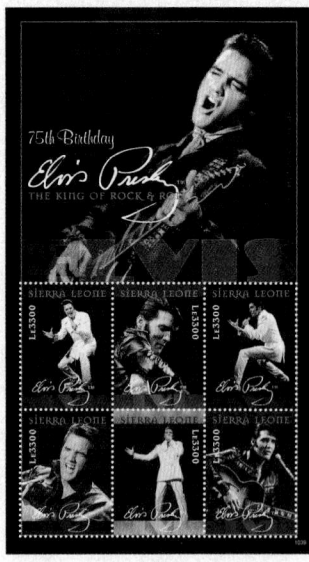

A574

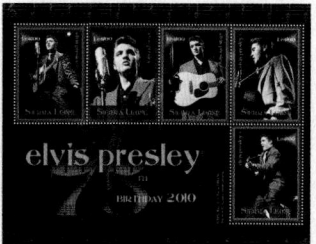

Elvis Presley (1935-77) — A575

No. 3064 — Presley wearing: a, White suit, with knees bent, facing forward. b, Leather jacket, no microphone visible. c, White suit with knees bent, facing left. d, Leather jacket, with microphone at left. e, White suit, legs straight. f, Leather jacket, microphone at right.
No. 3065 — Presley with frame in: a, Bright blue. b, Dark brown. c, Green. d, Yellow brown. e, Blue.

2011, Mar. 25   **Perf. 12**
3064 A574 3300 le Sheet of 6,
    #a-f   9.25 9.25
    Perf. 12½
3065 A575 4100 le Sheet of 5,
    #a-e   9.50 9.50

Miniature Sheets

President Barack Obama — A576

No. 3066, 4000 le: a, Afghanistan Pres. Hamid Karzai. b, Presidents Karzai and Obama seated. c, Presidents Karzai and Obama shaking hands. d, Pres. Obama.
No. 3067, 4000 le: a, Pres. Obama at left, flag at right. b, Pres Obama and Representative Nancy Pelosi. c, Pres. Obama and Senator Harry Reid. d, Pres. Obama in center, unidentified people in background, flag at right.

2011, Mar. 25   **Perf. 13 Syncopated**
    Sheets of 4, #a-d
3066-3067 A576 Set of 2   15.00 15.00

Miniature Sheets

Soviet Union General Secretary Mikhail Gorbachev — A577

No. 3068: a, Gorbachev standing next to Pres. Ronald Reagan. b, Gorbachev and Reagan shaking hands. c, Gorbachev looking forward.
No. 3069: a, Gorbachev wearing hat. b, Gorbachev looking left. c, Gorbachev and Reagan seated. d, Gorbachev and Pres. George H. W. Bush.

2011, Mar. 25   **Litho.**
3068 A577 5000 le Sheet of 4,
    #3068a-
    3068b, 2
    #3068c   9.25 9.25
3069 A577 5000 le Sheet of 4,
    #a-d   9.25 9.25

Engagement of Prince William and Catherine Middleton — A578

Designs: No. 3070, 4000 le, Couple.
No. 3071, vert.: a, Prince William. b, Middleton. c, Couple, hands visible. d, Couple, hands not visible.
No. 3072, 5000 le: a, Middleton. b, Prince William.
No. 3073, 5000 le, vert: a, Middleton. b, Prince William.

2011, Mar. 25   **Perf. 12**
3070 A578 4000 le multi   1.90 1.90
3071 A578 4000 le Sheet of 4,
    #a-d   7.50 7.50
  Souvenir Sheets of 2, #a-b
    Perf. 13 Syncopated
3072-3073 A578 Set of 2   9.25 9.25
No. 3070 was printed in sheets of 4.

Wedding of Prince William and Catherine Middleton — A579

No. 3074: a, Prince William. b, Catherine Middleton. c, Prince Charles. d, Princess Diana. e, Prince Philip. f, Queen Elizabeth II.
No. 3075, 5500 le: a, Prince William. b, Couple in coach.
No. 3076, 5500 le: a, Middleton. b, Couple kissing.

2011   **Perf. 13 Syncopated**
3074 A579 3500 le Sheet of 6,
    #a-f, + 5
    labels   9.75 9.75
Souvenir Sheets of 2, #a-b, + Central Label
3075-3076 A579 Set of 2   10.50 10.50
The stated day of issue of Apr. 29 for this issue is incorrect as the stamps show photographs from the wedding held that day.

Miniature Sheets

Dr. Sun Yat-sen (1866-1925), President of China — A580

No. 3077A: b, Sun Yat-sen, diff. c, Flag of People's Republic of China.

2011, Oct. 3   **Perf. 12**
3077 A580 4000 le multi   1.90 1.90
    Without Gum
       Imperf
3077A A580 8000 le Sheet of 2,
    #a-b   7.25 7.25
  Printed in sheets of 4.

Miniature Sheet

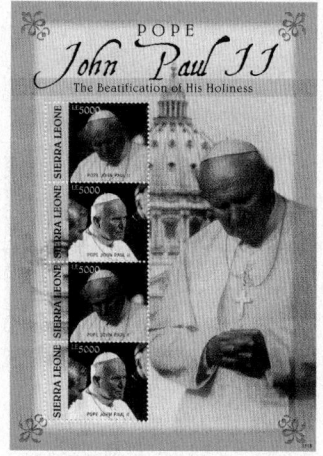

Beatification of Pope John Paul II — A581

No. 3078: a, Pope John Paul II looking down, beige under country name. b, Pope John Paul II, cardinal at right, beige area under "Leone" only. c, As "a," dark areas under country name. d, As "b," beige area under "Sierra" only.

2011, Oct. 3   **Litho.**
3078 A581 5000 le Sheet of 4,
    #a-d   9.00 9.00

Worldwide Fund for Nature (WWF) — A582

No. 3079 — Forest puff adder with country name and denomination in: a, Red. b, Purple. c, Yellow. d, Blue.

2011, Oct. 3   **Perf. 13¼**
3079   Strip of 4   5.75 5.75
 a.-d. A582 3100 le Any single   1.40 1.40
  e.   Souvenir sheet of 8, 2 each
    #a-d   11.50 11.50

Miniature Sheets

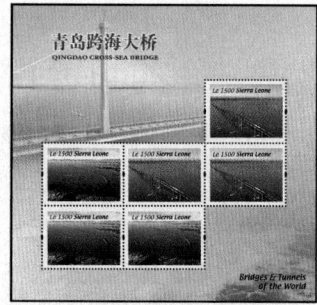

Chinese Civil Engineering Projects — A583

No. 3080 — Qingdao Cross-sea Bridge: a, Bridge, both shores visible. b, Bridge span.
No. 3081 — Qingdao-Jiaozhouwan Undersea Tunnel: a, Tunnel entrance. b, Tunnel cross-section.

2011, Oct. 3   **Perf. 13 Syncopated**
3080 A583 1500 le Sheet of 6, 3
    each #a-b   4.25 4.25
3081 A583 2500 le Sheet of 4, 2
    each #a-b   4.50 4.50

Intl. Year of Forests — A584

No. 3082: a, Forest. b, Boy in forest. c, Red-eyed tree frog. d, Red-crested turaco. e, Logger with chain saw. f, U.N. Secretary-General Ban Ki-moon.
No. 3083: a, Intl. Year of Forests emblem. b, Forest, diff.

2011, Oct. 3   **Perf. 12x11½**
3082 A584 2500 le Sheet of 6,
    #a-f, + 3 labels   6.75 6.75
    Souvenir Sheet
      Perf. 11½
3083 A584 5000 le Sheet of 2,
    #a-b   4.50 4.50

Miniature Sheets

Jane Goodall Institute, 50th Anniv. — A585

No. 3084, 5000 le: a, Black-and-white photograph of Goodall. b, Color photograph of Goodall extending arm towards chimpanzee. c, Black-and-white photograph of Goodall and chimpanzee. d, Color photograph of Goodall.
No. 3085, 5000 le: a, Goodall writing in journal. b, Goodall, holding camera, observing chimpanzee. c, Goodall extending arm toward three chimpanzees. d, Goodall holding cup with sun on horizon.

2011, Oct. 3   **Perf. 13 Syncopated**
    Sheets of 4, #a-d
3084-3085 A585 Set of 2   18.00 18.00

Princess Diana (1961-97) — A586

No. 3086 — Various photographs of Princess Diana with upper and lower panels in: a, Black. b, Pale pink. c, Red. d, Orange red. 11,000 le, Princess Diana, diff.

2011, Oct. 3   **Perf. 12**
3086 A586 5000 le Sheet of 4,
    #a-d   9.00 9.00
    Souvenir Sheet
3087 A586 11,000 le multi   5.00 5.00

Sept. 11, 2001 Terrorist Attacks, 10th Anniv. — A587

No. 3088: a, Memorial wall dedicated to firefighters. b, Tribute in light, Brooklyn Bridge in foreground. c, Pentagon memorial. d, Commemorative flag. e, Field with American flags. f, Cross of steel beams at Ground Zero.

11,000 le, Tribute in light, vert.

2011, Oct. 3   *Perf. 12*
3088 A587   3400 le Sheet of 6,
     #a-f   9.25   9.25

Souvenir Sheet
Perf. 12½
3089 A587 11,000 le multi   5.00   5.00

No. 3089 contains one 38x51mm stamp.

Pres. Abraham Lincoln (1809-65) — A588

No. 3090: a, US flag, bust of Lincoln. b, Painting of Lincoln.
No. 3091 — Photograph of Lincoln and: a, Union soldier's cap. b, Lincoln's stovepipe hat. c, Confederate soldier's cap.

2011, Oct. 3   *Perf. 11½*
3090 A588 4000 le Sheet of 4, 2
     each #a-b   7.25   7.25

Perf. 11½x12
3091 A588 6000 le Sheet of 3,
     #a-c   8.25   8.25

American Civil War, 150th anniv.

First Man in Space, 50th Anniv. — A589

No. 3092, 4000 le, horiz.: a, Vostok rocket on pedestal. b, MiG 15. c, Yuri Gagarin, first man in space. d, Alan Shepard, Jr., first American in Space.
No. 3093, 4000 le, horiz.: a, Vostok rocket in space. b, Vostok capsule. c, Vostok mission patch for Gagarin's space flight. d, L. Gordon Cooper, American astronaut.
No. 3094, 8000 le, Gagarin. No. 3095, 8000 le, Vostok capsule.

2011, Oct. 3   *Perf. 12½x12*
Sheets of 4, #a-d
3092-3093 A589   Set of 2   14.50 14.50
Souvenir Sheets
Perf. 12x12½
3094-3095 A589   Set of 2   7.25   7.25

Orchids — A590

No. 3096: a, Bolusiella imbricata. b, Bulbophyllum scaberulum. c, Oeceoclades maculata. d, Ancistrochilus rothschildianus. e, Sarracenia flava. f, Phaius.
No. 3097: a, Ancistrochilus rothschildianus, diff. b, Angraecum subulatum. c, Eulophia guineensis. d, Eurychone rothschildiana.
No. 3098, 11,000 le, Monodora myristica.
No. 3099, 11,000 le, Polystachya galeata.

Perf. 11½, 12x12½ (#3097)
2011, Oct. 3
3096 A590   3400 le Sheet of 6,
     #a-f   9.25   9.25
3097 A590   4800 le Sheet of 4,
     #a-d   8.75   8.75
Souvenir Sheets
3098-3099 A590   Set of 2   10.00 10.00

Intl. Year of Forests.

Marine Life — A591

No. 3100, 5000 le: a, Comb jellyfish. b, Benthocodon pedunculata. c, Glowing sucker octopus. d, Hatchetfish.
No. 3101, 5000 le, vert.: a, Dumbo octopus. b, Vampire squid. c, Gulper eel. d, Ping pong tree sponge.
No. 3102, 11,000 le, Dana octopus squid.
No. 3103, 11,000 le, Anglerfish.

2011, Oct. 3   *Perf. 12*
Sheets of 4, #a-d
3100-3101 A591   Set of 2   18.00 18.00
Souvenir Sheets
Perf. 12½
3102-3103 A591   Set of 2   10.00 10.00

Nos. 3102-3103 each contain one 51x38mm stamp.

Miniature Sheet

Chinese Zodiac Animals — A592

No. 3104: a, Rat. b, Ox. c, Tiger. d, Snake. e, Dragon. f, Rabbit. g, Horse. h, Ram. i, Monkey. j, Boar. k, Dog. l, Rooster.

2011, Oct. 3
3104 A592 1250 le Sheet of 12,
     #a-l   6.75   6.75

Miniature Sheet

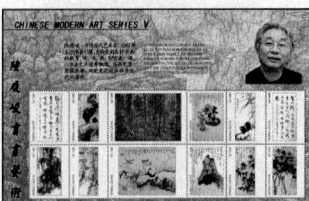

Chinese Art by Lu Lujun — A593

No. 3105: a, Calligraphy with two red chops below left column of characters (30x40mm). b, Two birds on tree branch (30x40mm). c, Forest (60x40mm). d, Flowers, calligraphy at top red chop at left (30x40mm). e, Two birds on ground below tree (30x40mm). f, Calligraphy with two red chops to left of left column of characters (30x40mm). g, 18mm wide abstract work (30x40mm). h, Trees with red chop at lower right (30x40mm). i, Calligraphy and cat (60x40mm). j, Calligraphy and Chinese person (30x40mm). k, Flowers, calligraphy at top, two red chops at left (30x40mm). l, Flowers, calligraphy at right (30x40mm).

2011, Oct. 22   *Perf. 14*
3105 A593 1300 le Sheet of 12,
     #a-l   7.25   7.25

Miniature Sheet

Freddy Will, Musician — A594

No. 3106 — Will wearing: a, T-shirt, black background. b, Suit, with hands clasped. c, Suit, brick wall in background. d, T-shirt, chain link fence in background.

2011, Oct. 22   *Perf. 13 Syncopated*
3106 A594 4000 le Sheet of 4,
     #a-d   7.50   7.50

Birds — A595

No. 3107, 4000 le: a, Greater flamingo. b, Fulvous whistling duck. c, Cory's shearwater. d, Purple heron.
No. 3108, 4000 le: a, Pink-backed pelican. b, Abdim's stork. c, Western reef heron. d, African spoonbill.
No. 3109, 10,000 le, African sacred ibis, horiz. No. 3110, 10,000 le, Squacco heron, horiz.

2011, Sept. 26   **Sheets of 4, #a-d**
3107-3108 A595   Set of 2   14.50 14.50
Souvenir Sheets
3109-3110 A595   Set of 2   9.00   9.00

Miniature Sheet

Binhai New Area, People's Republic of China — A596

No. 3111: a, Waterfront buildings and pagoda. b, Skyscrapers, shoreline, airplanes. c, Aircraft carrier. d, Birds over buildings. e, Windmill, trees, plaque. f, Building with curved roof.

2011, Oct. 26   *Perf. 13 Syncopated*
3111 A596 1500 le Sheet of 6,
     #a-f   4.25   4.25

Christmas A597

Paintings: 1000 le, The Adoration of the Magi, by Stefano da Verona. 2000 le, Madonna and Child, by Taddeo di Bartolo. 3000 le, Madonna, by Lorenzo Monaco. 3500 le, Virgin and Child, by Gentile da Fabriano.

2011, Dec. 20   *Perf. 14*
3112-3115 A597   Set of 4   4.50   4.50

Mao Zedong (1893-1976), Chinese Leader — A598

Mao Zedong: No. 3116, 1100 le, On beach. No. 3117, 1100 le, As young man, wearing cap. No. 3118, 1100 le, Seated. No. 3119, 1100 le, In airplane door, waving hat (35x35mm).
No. 3120: a, Like No. 3116. b, Like No. 3117. c, Like No. 3118.
10,000 le, Like No. 3119.

Perf. 14, 13¾ (#3119, 3121)
2012, Feb. 22
3116-3119 A598   Set of 4   2.10   2.10
3120 A598   5200 le Sheet of 3,
     #a-c   7.25   7.25
Souvenir Sheet
3121 A598 10,000 le multi   4.75   4.75

Miniature Sheet

2012 Summer Olympics, London — A599

No. 3122: a, Runners in blue, emblem at UL. b, Runners in blue, emblem at LR. c, Runners in red, emblem at UL. d, Runners in red, emblem at LR.

2012, May 30 — *Perf. 14*
3122 A599 3600 le Sheet of 4,
#a-d 6.75
No. 3122 exists imperf. Value, $12.50.

A600

Chinese Zodiac Animals — A601

Designs: No. 3123, 1000 le, Dog. No. 3124, 1000 le, Boar.
No. 3125: a, Rat. b, Ox. c, Tiger. d, Rabbit. e, Dragon. f, Snake. g, Horse. h, Sheep. i, Monkey. j, Rooster. k, Dog. l, Boar.

2012, July 25 — *Perf. 13¼x13*
3123-3124 A600 Set of 2 .95 .95
Perf. 14
3125 A601 15,000 le Sheet of
12, #a-l 82.50 82.50
Beijing 2012 Intl. Stamp Exhibition (#3125).

Sinking of the Titanic, Cent. — A602

No. 3126: a, John J. Astor IV, passenger who died. b, Sidney Goodwin, passenger who died. c, William T. Stead, passenger who died. d, Stern of Titanic. e, Bow of Titanic. f, Capt. Edward J. Smith.
3127, horiz.: a, J. P. Morgan, financier of Titanic. b, Titanic under construction. c, Titanic sets sail.

2012, July 25 — *Perf. 14*
3126 A602 3000 le Sheet of 6,
#a-f 8.25 8.25
Souvenir Sheet
3127 A602 7000 le Sheet of 3,
#a-c 9.75 9.75

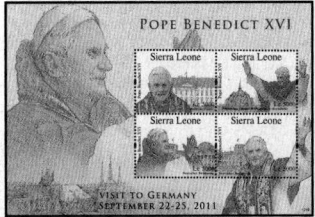
2011 Visit of Pope Benedict XVI to Germany — A603

No. 3128 — Pope Benedict XVI and: a, Bellevue Castle. b, Pilgrimage Church of Etzelsbach. c, Bundestag (Pope facing right with hands together). d, Bundestag (Pope facing forward, arm raised).
15,000 le, Pope Benedict XVI, vert.

2012, Sept. 25 — *Perf. 13 Syncopated*
3128 A603 5000 le Sheet of 4,
#a-d 9.25 9.25
Souvenir Sheet
3129 A603 15,000 le multi 7.00 7.00

Pres. John F. Kennedy (1917-63) — A604

No. 3130 — Pres. Kennedy: a, Seated. b, Pointing. c, With group of people.
15,000 le, Pres. Kennedy at desk, horiz.

2012, July 25 — *Perf. 12*
3130 A604 6000 le Sheet of 3,
#a-c 8.25 8.25
Souvenir Sheet
3131 A604 15,000 le multi 7.00 7.00
No. 3131 contains one 50x30mm stamp.

Dedication of the Lincoln Memorial, 90th Anniv. — A605

No. 3132: Lincoln Memorial and various depictions of Pres. Lincoln, as shown.
No. 3133, 15,000 le, Photograph of Pres. Lincoln, arms visible. No. 3134, 15,000 le, Photograph of Pres. Lincoln, arms not visible.

2012, July 25 — *Perf. 14*
3132 A605 5000 le Sheet of 4,
#a-d 9.25 9.25
Souvenir Sheets
3133-3134 A605 Set of 2 14.00 14.00

Christmas — A606

Paintings: 1000 le, Nativity, by Hans Memling. 1500 le, Nativity, by unattributed artist. 2000 le, The Presentation of Christ, by Melchior Broederlam. 3000 le, Madonna and Child, by Fra Angelico. 3900 le, Adoration of the Shepherds, by Correggio. 6000 le, Holy Family on the Steps, by Nicolas Poussin.

2012, July 25 — *Litho.*
3135-3140 A606 Set of 6 8.00 8.00

2012 UEFA European Soccer Championships, Poland and Ukraine — A607

No. 3141: a, Poland team. b, Greece team. c, Russia team. d, Netherlands team. e, Czech Republic team. f, Denmark team. g, Germany team. h, Portugal team. i, Soccer ball and upper deck of stadium.
No. 3142: a, Spain team. b, Italy team. c, Ireland team. d, Ukraine team. e, Croatia team. f, Sweden team. g, France team. h, England team.
No. 3143a, National Stadium, Poland. No. 3143b, Municipal Stadium, Poland (field visible at bottom). No. 3144a, PGE Arena, Poland. No. 3145a, Metalist Stadium, Ukraine. No. 3146a, Arena Lviv, Ukraine. No. 3147a, Donbass Arena, Ukraine. No. 3148a, Municipal Stadium, Poland (field not visible at bottom). No. 3148b, Olympic Stadium, Ukraine.

2012, July 26 — *Perf. 14*
3141 A607 Sheet of 9 11.50 11.50
a.-i. 2500 le Any single 1.25 1.25
3142 A607 Sheet of 9,
#3141i, 3142a-
3142h 11.50 11.50
a.-h. 2500 le Any single 1.25 1.25
3143 A607 Sheet of 6,
#3143a-3143b,
4 #3141a (Po-
land) 7.50 7.50
a.-b. 2500 le Either single 1.25 1.25
c. Sheet of 6, #3143a, 3143b,
4 #3141b (Greece) 7.50 7.50
d. Sheet of 6, #3143a, 3143b,
4 #3141e (Czech Repub-
lic) 7.50 7.50
3144 A607 Sheet of 6,
#3143a, 3144a,
4 #3141c (Rus-
sia) 7.50 7.50
a. 2500 le multi 1.25 1.25
3145 A607 Sheet of 6,
#3144a, 3145a,
4 #3141d
(Netherlands) 7.50 7.50
a. 2500 le multi 1.25 1.25
3146 A607 Sheet of 6,
#3143a, 3146a,
4 #3141f (Den-
mark) 7.50 7.50
a. 2500 le multi 1.25 1.25
b. Sheet of 6, #3145a, 3146a,
4 #3141g (Germany) 7.50 7.50
c. Sheet of 6, #3145a, 3146a,
4 #3141h (Portugal) 7.50 7.50
3147 A607 Sheet of 6,
#3144a, 3147a,
4 #3142a
(Spain) 7.50 7.50
a. 2500 le multi 1.25 1.25
3148 A607 Sheet of 6,
#3148a-3148b,
4 #3142b (Italy) 7.50 7.50
a.-b. 2500 le Either single 1.25 1.25
c. Sheet of 6, #3144a, 3148a,
4 #3142c (Ireland) 7.50 7.50
d. Sheet of 6, #3147a, 3148b,
4 #3142d (Ukraine) 7.50 7.50
e. Sheet of 6, #3143a, 3148a,
4 #3142e (Croatia) 7.50 7.50
f. Sheet of 6, #3143a, 3148b,
4 #3142f (Sweden) 7.50 7.50
g. Sheet of 6, #3143a, 3148b,
4 #3142g (France) 7.50 7.50
h. Sheet of 6, #3147a, 3148b,
4 #3142h (England) 7.50 7.50
Nos. 3141-3148 (8) 68.00 68.00

Miniature Sheet

Bees
A608

No. 3149: a, African honey bee. b, Honey bee. c, Leafcutter bee. d, Maranga bee. e, Stingless bee.

2012, Aug. 7 — *Litho.*
3149 A608 5000 le Sheet of 5,
#a-e 12.00 12.00

Souvenir Sheets

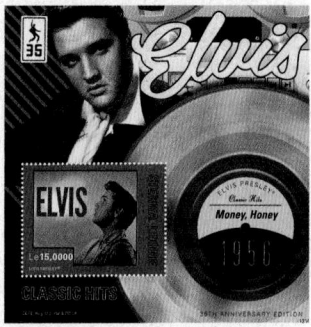
Elvis Presley (1935-77) — A609

Presley: No. 3150, 15,000 le, Facing left, red frame. No. 3151, 15,000 le, On *One Night* and *I Got Stung* record cover, black frame. No. 3152, 15,000 le, Holding microphone, purple frame. No. 3153, 15,000 le, Holding microphone, diff., gray frame. No. 3154, 15,000 le, Holding microphone, spotlight in background, red frame.

2012, Sept. 27 — *Perf. 12¾*
3150-3154 A609 Set of 5 35.00 35.00

Miniature Sheet

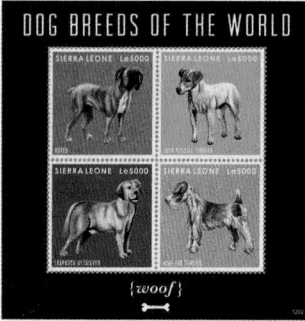

Dogs — A610

No. 3155: a, Boxer. b, Jack Russell terrier. c, Labrador retriever. d, Wire fox terrier.

2012, Nov. 28		**Perf. 13¾**
3155 A610 5000 le Sheet of 4, #a-d	9.25	9.25

Carnivorous Plants — A611

No. 3156: a, Dewy pine. b, Nepenthes pitcher. c, Waterwheel plant. d, Pitcher plant. 16,000 le, African sundew, vert.

2012, Nov. 28		**Perf. 13¾**
3156 A611 5000 le Sheet of 4, #a-d	9.25	9.25
Souvenir Sheet		
Perf. 12¾		
3157 A611 16,000 le multi	7.50	7.50

No. 3157 contains one 38x51mm stamp.

Primates — A612

No. 3158: a, Eastern chimpanzee. b, Nigeria-Cameroon chimpanzee. c, Western lowland gorilla. d, Western chimpanzee. 15,000 le, Sumatran orangutan, horiz.

2012, Nov. 28		**Perf. 12**
3158 A612 5500 le Sheet of 4, #a-d	10.50	10.50
Souvenir Sheet		
Perf. 12¾		
3159 A612 15,000 le multi	7.00	7.00

No. 3159 contains one 51x38mm stamp.

Miniature Sheets

Completion of Painting of Sistine Chapel Ceiling by Michelangelo, 500th Anniv. — A613

No. 3160, 5000 le: a, The Prophet Jonah. b, The Creation of Eve. c, The Downfall of Adam and Eve. d, The Sacrifice of Noah.

No. 3161, 5000 le, vert.: a, Deluge. b, Detail from the Eleazar lunette. c, The Ezechias spandrel. d, First Day of Creation.

2012, Nov. 28		**Perf. 12¾**
Sheets of 4, #a-d		
3160-3161 A613 Set of 2	18.50	18.50

Souvenir Sheet

Elvis Presley (1935-77) — A614

Litho., Sheet Margin Embossed		
With Foil Application		
2013, July 23		**Imperf.**
3162 A614 42,500 le multi	20.00	20.00

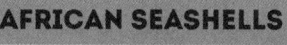

Shells — A615

No. 3163: a, Conus algoensis scitulus. b, Columbarium radiale. c, Fusivoluta clarkei. d, Burnupena cincta. 16,000 le, Melapium lineatum.

2013, Sept. 9 **Litho.**		**Perf. 14**
3163 A615 5000 le Sheet of 4, #a-d	9.25	9.25
Souvenir Sheet		
Perf. 12		
3164 A615 16,000 le multi	7.50	7.50

Turtles — A616

No. 3165: a, Pelomedusa subrufa. b, Geochelone sulcata. c, Geochelone pardalis. d, Astrochelys radiata. 16,000 le, Pelusios castanoides.

2013, Sept. 9 **Litho.**		**Perf. 12**
3165 A616 5000 le Sheet of 4, #a-d	9.25	9.25
Souvenir Sheet		
3166 A616 16,000 le multi	7.50	7.50

Insects — A617

No. 3167: a, Analeptes trifasciata. b, Eotithoes palinii. c, Hecphora latefasciata. d, Gnathoenia flavovariegata. 16,000 le, Goliathus regius.

2013, Sept. 9 **Litho.**		**Perf. 12**
3167 A617 5000 le Sheet of 4, #a-d	9.25	9.25
Souvenir Sheet		
Perf. 14		
3168 A617 16,000 le multi	7.50	7.50

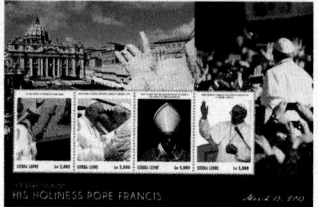

Election of Pope Francis — A618

No. 3169: a, Pope Francis celebrating mass. b, Pope Francis with Pope Emeritus Benedict XVI. c, Pope Francis attending celebration of the Lord's Passion in the Vatican Basilica. d, Pope Francis addressing weekly audience. 16,000 le, Pope Francis at Inauguration Mass.

2013, Sept. 9 **Litho.**		**Perf. 14**
3169 A618 5000 le Sheet of 4, #a-d	9.25	9.25
Souvenir Sheet		
Perf. 12½		
3170 A618 16,000 le multi	7.50	7.50

No. 3170 contains one 38x51mm stamp.

Pres. John F. Kennedy (1917-63) — A619

No. 3171 — Pres. Kennedy: a, On telephone. b, Behind microphones. c, Holding daughter, Caroline. d, Holding microphone, waving. 16,000 le, Pres. Kennedy reading, horiz.

2013, Sept. 9 **Litho.**		**Perf. 13¾**
3171 A619 5000 le Sheet of 4, #a-d	9.25	9.25
Souvenir Sheet		
Perf. 12½		
3172 A619 16,000 le multi	7.50	7.50

No. 3172 contains one 51x38mm stamp.

World Environment Day — A620

No. 3173 — Inscriptions: a, Buy local to cut back on emissions. b, Save water. c, Limit food waste. 16,000 le, Think before you eat and help save the environment!

2013, Sept. 9 **Litho.**		**Perf. 13¾**
3173 A620 6000 le Sheet of 3, #a-c	8.50	8.50
Souvenir Sheet		
3174 A620 16,000 le multi	7.50	7.50

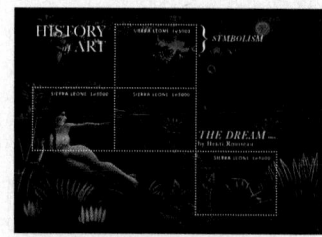

History of Art — A621

No. 3175 — Details from The Dream, by Henri Rousseau: a, Bird and fruit in tree. b, Nude woman. c, Flowers and head of cat. d, Head of cat, foliage, tail.

No. 3176, vert.: a, The Yellow Tree, by Emile Bernard. b, Woman Holding a Fruit, by Paul Gauguin. c, Vase with Oleanders and Books, by Vincent van Gogh.

No. 3177, vert. — Paintings by Henri de Toulouse-Lautrec: a, Aristide Bruant. b, Moulin Rouge. c, Jane Avril. 16,000 le, Arrangement in Gray and Black, No. 1, by James Abbott McNeill Whistler.

2013, Sept. 9 **Litho.**		**Perf. 12½**
3175 A621 5000 le Sheet of 4, #a-d	9.25	9.25
3176 A621 6000 le Sheet of 3, #a-c	8.50	8.50
3177 A621 6000 le Sheet of 3, #a-c	8.50	8.50
Nos. 3175-3177 (3)	26.25	26.25
Souvenir Sheet		
3178 A621 16,000 le multi	7.50	7.50

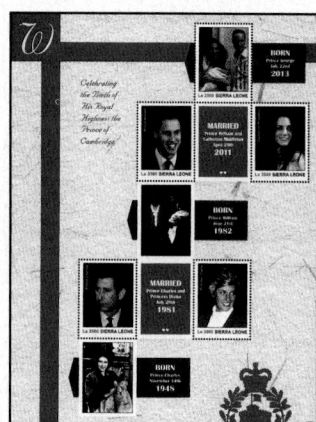

Birth of Prince George of Cambirdge — A622

No. 3179: a, Duke and Duchess of Cambridge with Prince George. b, Prince William (Duke of Cambridge). c, Catherine Middleton (Duchess of Cambridge). d, Prince Charles. e, Princess Diana. 16,000 le, Duke and Duchess of Cambridge with Prince George, diff.

2013, Sept. 10 **Litho.**		**Perf. 14**
3179 A622 3500 le Sheet of 5, #a-e	8.25	8.25
Souvenir Sheet		
Perf. 12		
3180 A622 16,000 le multi	7.50	7.50

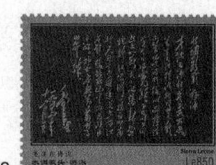

A623

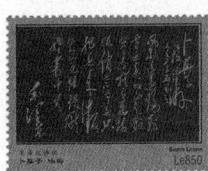

Poetry of
Mao
Zedong
A625

A626

Mao Zedong (1893-1976), Chinese
Communist Leader — A627

No. 3182 — Paintings depicting Mao
Zedong: a, Standing behind tree, extending
hand to old man. b, At table, with scribe at
side. c, With child in lap. d, Standing with old
man.

No. 3183: a, Painting of Mao Zedong in
library. b, Poem by Mao Zedong, half line of
Chinese text at right. c, Poem by Mao Zedong,
half line of Chinese text in second vertical column, with bottom character in that line being
two curved lines that do not touch. d, As "c,"
with bottom character in second line having
crossed lines.

2013, Sept. 10   Litho.   Perf. 14
3181		Horiz. strip of 3	1.20	1.20
	a.	A623 850 le multi	.40	.40
	b.	A624 850 le multi	.40	.40
	c.	A625 850 le multi	.40	.40

Miniature Sheets
3182	A626 850 le Sheet of 4, #a-d	1.60	1.60
3183	A627 850 le Sheet of 4, #a-d	1.60	1.60

No. 3181 was printed in sheets of 6 containing two of each stamp.

Parrots — A628

No. 3184, 5000 le: a, African gray parrot. b,
Senegal parrot. c, Meyer's parrot. d, Cape
parrot.

No. 3185, 5000 le: a, Madagascar lovebird.
b, Rosy-faced lovebird. c, Masked lovebird. d,
Fischer's lovebird.

No. 3186, 16,000 le, Jardine's parrot. No.
3187, 16,000 le, Lilian's lovebird.

2013, Sept. 17   Litho.   Perf. 12½
Sheets of 4, #a-d
3184-3185	A628 Set of 2	18.50	18.50

Souvenir Sheets
3186-3187	A628 Set of 2	15.00	15.00

Miniature Sheet

Brasiliana 2013 World Stamp
Exhibition, Rio de Janeiro — A629

No. 3188 — Brazilan landscapes: a, Sugar-
loaf Mountain. b, Fernando de Noronha. c,
Amazon rainforest. d, Iguaçu Falls.

Perf. 13½x12½
2013, Nov. 18   Litho.
3188	A629 5000 le Sheet of 4, #a-d	9.25	9.25

New Year
2014 (Year
of the
Horse)
A630

2013, Nov. 25 Embroidered Imperf.
Self-Adhesive
3189	A630 34,000 le multi	16.00	16.00

Christmas
A631

Paintings: 1000 le, *Toppling of the Pagan
Idols*, by Bedford Master. 2000 le, *The Flight
into Egypt*, by Vittore Carpaccio. 3000 le, *The
Annunciation*, by Melchior Broederlam.
6000 le, *The Virgin*, by Carlo Dolci.
16,000 le, *The Adoration of the Shepherds*,
by Giorgione.

2013, Dec. 2   Litho.   Perf. 12½
3190-3193	A631 Set of 4	5.50	5.50

Souvenir Sheet
3194	A631 16,000 le multi	7.50	7.50

A632

Nelson Mandela (1918-2013),
President of South Africa — A633

Nos. 3195, 3196: Various photographs of
Mandela, as shown.
16,000 le, Mandela, diff.
43,000 le, Mandela, diff.

2013, Dec. 15   Litho.   Perf. 14
3195	A632 5000 le Sheet of 6, #a-f	14.00	14.00
3196	A633 5000 le Sheet of 6, #a-f	14.00	14.00

Souvenir Sheets
3197	A633 16,000 le multi	7.50	7.50

**Litho., Margin Embossed With Foil
Application**
Imperf
3198	A633 43,000 le multi	20.00	20.00

No. 3198 contains one 40x40mm stamp.

Games — A634

No. 3199: a, Backgammon. b, Go. c, Mah
Jongg. d, Mancala.
16,000 le, Chess.

2013, Dec. 18   Litho.   Perf. 13¾
3199	A634 5000 le Sheet of 4, #a-d	9.25	9.25

Souvenir Sheet
3200	A634 16,000 le multi	7.50	7.50

Birds — A635

No. 3201: a, Crested barbet. b, White-
fronted bee-eater. c, Starling. d, Crimson-
breasted shrike.
16,000 le, Lilac-breasted roller.

2013, Dec. 23   Litho.   Perf. 14
3201	A635 5000 le Sheet of 4, #a-d	9.25	9.25

Souvenir Sheet
Perf. 12
3202	A635 16,000 le multi	7.50	7.50

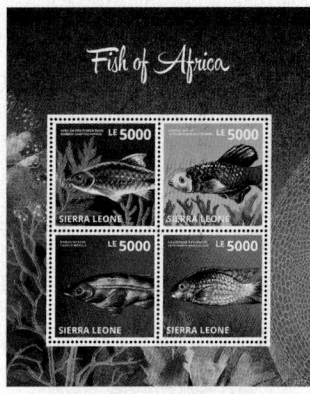

Fish — A636

No. 3203: a, African red-finned barb. b,
Redtail notho. c, Brown wrasse. d, Roundhead
sandeater.
16,000 le, Broadhead sleeper, African butter
catfish, horiz.

2013, Dec. 23   Litho.   Perf. 13¾
3203	A636 5000 le Sheet of 4, #a-d	9.25	9.25

Souvenir Sheet
Perf. 12½
3204	A636 16,000 le multi	7.50	7.50

No. 3204 contains one 51x38mm stamp.

Miniature Sheet

Mushrooms — A637

No. 3205: a, Delicious milk cap. b, Amethyst
deceiver. c, Penny bun. d, Japanese umbrella.
e, Glistening ink cap. f, Panther cap.

2013, Dec. 23   Litho.   Perf. 13¾
3205	A637 4000 le Sheet of 6, #a-f	11.00	11.00

Worldwide Fund for Nature
(WWF) — A638

Nos. 3206 and 3207: Various photographs
of Western Bongo, as shown.

2014, Apr. 2   Litho.   Perf. 14
3206	A638 3900 le Block or vert. strip of 4, #a-d	7.25	7.25
3207	A638 4300 le Block or vert. strip of 4, #a-d	8.00	8.00

AIR POST STAMPS

Catalogue values for unused
stamps in this section are for
Never Hinged items.

Independence — Progress Issue

Nos. 197, 199, 204 and 206 Surcharged Like Nos. 242-247 plus "AIRMAIL" in Carmine, Red, Violet, Blue or Orange

Perf. 13, 13½

1963, Apr. 27 Wmk. 4 Engr.

Center in Black

C1 A27 7p on 1½p (C) .25 .25
C2 A27 1sh3p on 1½p (R) .25 .25
C3 A28 2sh6p brn org (V) 2.50 .55
C4 A28 3sh on 3p (Bl) .55 .55
C5 A28 6sh on 3p (O) 1.00 .40
C6 A27 11sh on 10sh (C) 2.00 1.40
C7 A27 11sh on £1 (C) 700.00 240.00
Nos. C1-C6 (6) 6.55 3.40

Nos. 221, 224, 213, 223 and 207 Srchd. or Ovptd. in Brown, Red, Black, Violet, Ultra or Orange

Perf. 13x13½, 13½x13, 13

1963, Nov. 4 Wmk. 4, 336

C8 A31 7p on 3p (Br) .25 .25
C9 A32 1sh3p blue & blk (R) 2.00 1.50
C10 A30 2sh6p on 4p (Bk) 1.25 1.00
C11 A31 3sh on 3p (V) 2.50 2.00
C12 A32 6sh on 6p (U) 1.25 1.25
C13 A27 £1 org & blk (O) 30.00 30.00
Nos. C8-C13 (6) 31.70 31.20

Overprint is in 6 lines on Nos. C8, C11 and C12. A number of surcharge varieties and errors exist.

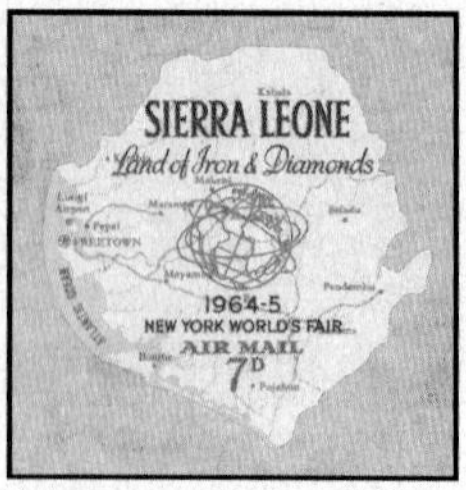

Unisphere and Map of Sierra Leone — AP1

Engraved and Lithographed

1964, Feb. 10 Unwmk. *Die Cut*

Self-adhesive

C14 AP1 7p multicolored .25 .25
C15 AP1 9p multicolored .25 .25
C16 AP1 1sh3p multicolored .25 .25
C17 AP1 2sh6p multicolored .35 .35
C18 AP1 3sh6p multicolored .50 .50
C19 AP1 6sh multicolored .65 .65
C20 AP1 11sh multicolored .90 1.40
Nos. C14-C20 (7) 3.10 3.10

New York World's Fair, 1964-65.
For surcharge see No. C33.

John F. Kennedy AP2

1964, May 11 Self-adhesive

C21 AP2 7p multicolored .25 .25
C22 AP2 9p multicolored .25 .25
C23 AP2 1sh3p multicolored .25 .25
C24 AP2 2sh6p multicolored .35 .30
C25 AP2 3sh6p multicolored .40 .60
C26 AP2 6sh multicolored .65 1.25
C27 AP2 11sh multicolored .80 2.25
Nos. C21-C27 (7) 2.65 3.80

For surcharges see Nos. C32, C34-C36.

Nos. 241, 213, 219 and 218 Srchd. in Dark Blue, Black, Red or Violet Blue

Perf. 11½x11, 13½x13, 13x13½

1964, Aug. 4 Engr. Wmk. 336

C28 A36 7c on 1sh3p (#241) (DB) .25 .25
C29 A30 20c on 4p (#213) .40 .40
C30 A29 30c on 10sh (#219) (R) .60 .60
C31 A29 40c on 5sh (#218) (VB) .70 .70
Nos. C28-C31 (4) 2.20 2.20

Map-shaped Issues of 1964 Surcharged in Red or Black

Engraved and Lithographed

1964-65 Unwmk. *Die Cut*

C32 AP2 7c on 7p (#C21) (R) .25 .25
C33 AP1 7c on 9p (#C15) .85 .85
C34 AP2 60c on 9p (#C22) 1.25 1.25
C35 AP2 1 le on 1sh3p (#C23) (R) 1.00 2.00
C36 AP2 2 le on 11sh (#C27) 2.00 3.75
Nos. C32-C36 (5) 5.35 8.10

Issue dates: Aug. 4, 1964, Nos. C35-C36. Jan. 20, 1965, Nos. C32, C34. April, 1965, No. C33.

Regular Issue of 1963 Surcharged like Nos. 300-305 with "AIRMAIL" added

Wmk. 336

1965, May 19 Photo. *Perf. 14*

Designs of Surcharge: No. C37, C39-C40, Sir Milton Margai and Sir Winston Churchill. No. C38, Margai. No. C41, Churchill.

C37 A35 7c on 2p (#230) .65 .25
C38 A34 15c on ½p (#227) .45 .75
C39 A35 30c on 6p (#233) 1.90 .50
C40 A35 1 le on £1 (#239) 5.50 1.75
C41 A34 2 le on 10sh (#238) 11.50 5.50
Nos. C37-C41 (5) 18.55 8.70

The portraits and inscription on No. C39 are white, the denomination and "AIRMAIL" are orange.

Ten more surcharges were issued Nov. 9, 1965: "2c" on Nos. C16, C23 and C25. "3c" on Nos. C14 and C22. "5c" on Nos. C17-C19, C24, and C26. Value $4 each.

One further surcharge was issued Jan. 28, 1966: "TWO/Leones" on No. C39. Value $10.

Type of Regular Issue and

Diamond Necklace AP3

Litho.; Reversed Embossing

1965, Dec. 17 Unwmk. *Die Cut*

Self-adhesive

C53 AP3 7c blk, grn, gold & bl .80 .25
C54 AP3 15c blk, brnz, car & bl 1.75 1.25

Engr. and Embossed on Paper

C55 A41 40c multi, *cream* 4.00 4.00
Nos. C53-C55 (3) 7.05 6.40

Various advertisements printed on peelable paper backing. Nos. C54-C55 have side tabs for handling and come packed in boxes of 100. No. C53 is without side tab and comes 25 stamps attached to one sheet.

For overprints and surcharges see Nos. C68-C69, C79-C83.

Nos. 248, 229, 232, 234 and 236 Srchd. and Ovptd. "AIRMAIL/FIVE YEARS/INDEPENDENCE/1961-1966"

1966, Apr. 27 Wmk. 336

C56 A37 7c on 3p pur & red .25 .25
C57 A34 15c on 1sh multi .40 .40
C58 A34 25c on 2sh6p multi .65 .65
C59 A34 50c on 1½p multi 1.25 1.25
C60 A34 1 le on 4p multi 3.25 3.25
Nos. C56-C60 (5) 6.45 6.45

The denomination on No. C60 is spelled out "One Leone."

Self-adhesive & Die Cut

Nos. C61-C131, C135-C142 are self-adhesive and die cut.

Gold Coin Type of Regular Issue

Designs: 7c, 10c, ¼ Golde coin. 15c, 30c, ½ Golde coin. 50c, 2 le, 1 Golde coin. (7c, 15c, 50c, Map of Sierra Leone. 10c, 30c, 2 le, Lion's head.)

Diameter: 7c, 10c, 38mm; 15c, 30c, 54mm; 50c, 2 le, 82mm.

Lithographed; Embossed on Gilt Foil

1966, Nov. 12 Unwmk.

C61 A42 7c red & orange .25 .25
C62 A42 10c dull blue & red .25 .25
C63 A42 15c red & orange .30 .30
C64 A42 30c black & rose lilac .50 .60
C65 A42 50c rose lilac & emer 1.00 1.00
C66 A42 2 le green & black 4.50 4.50
Nos. C61-C66 (6) 7.80 7.80

Advertising printed on paper backing.

Type of Regular Issue, 1965 and No. C55 Surcharged

1967, Dec. 2 Engr. & Embossed

C67 A41 10c multi (red frame), *cream* .50 .50
a. Black frame .50 .50
C68 A41 11½c on 40c multi, *cr* .40 .40
C69 A41 25c on 40c multi, *cr* 1.00 1.00
Nos. C67-C69 (3) 1.90 1.90

Eagle — AP4

Embossed Foil on Black Paper

1967, Dec. 2 Unwmk.

C70 AP4 9½c black, gold & red .70 .70
C71 AP4 15c black, gold & grn 1.00 1.00

Various advertisements printed on peelable paper backing. See Nos. C98-C99, C118-C124.

Map Type of Regular Issue

Designs: Each denomination shows map of Africa with map of one of the following countries — Portuguese Guinea, South Africa, Mozambique, Rhodesia, South West Africa or Angola. Sheets of 30 (6x5) have 5 horizontal rows containing one stamp of each design.

1968, Sept. 25 Litho.

C72 A43 7½c multicolored .25 .25
C73 A43 9½c multicolored .30 .30
C74 A43 14½c multicolored .35 .35
C75 A43 18½c multicolored .35 .35
C76 A43 25c multicolored .45 .45
C77 A43 1 le multicolored 3.25 4.50
C78 A43 2 le multicolored 9.00 10.50
Nos. C72-C78 (7) 13.95 16.70
7 Strips of 6, 1 of each design (42) 122.50

No. C55 Ovptd. and Srchd. in Red Similar to Nos. 364-368

Engraved and Embossed on Paper

1968, Nov. 30

C79 A41 6½c on 40c multi .25 .25
C80 A41 17½c on 40c multi .55 .55
C81 A41 22½c on 40c multi .55 .55
C82 A41 28½c on 40c multi .75 .75
C83 A41 40c multicolored 1.10 1.10
Nos. C79-C83 (5) 3.50 3.50

Scroll Type of Regular Issue

7½c, #C54. 9½c, #C70. 20c, #C16. 30c, #C26. 50c, #165. 2 le, #207 with "2nd Year of Independence" overprint. All are horiz.

1969, Mar. 1 Litho.

C84 A44 7½c multicolored .25 .25
C85 A44 9½c multicolored .30 .30
C86 A44 20c multicolored .50 .50
C87 A44 30c multicolored .70 .70
C88 A44 50c multicolored 1.50 1.50
C89 A44 2 le multicolored 9.00 9.00
Nos. C84-C89 (6) 13.50 13.50

Various advertisements printed on peelable paper backing. No. C84 has side tab for handling and comes packed in boxes of 50. Nos. C85-C89 are without side tabs and come 20 stamps attached to one sheet.

For surcharges see Nos. C135-C136.

Pepel Port Types of Regular Issue

Designs: 7½c, 15c, Globe, tanker, flags of Sierra Leone and Japan. Anvil Shape with Flags of Sierra Leone and: 9½c, 2 le, Union Jack. 25c, Netherlands. 1 le, West Germany.

1969, July 10

C90 A45 7½c multicolored .25 .25
C91 A46 9½c multicolored .25 .25
C92 A45 15c multicolored .40 .40
C93 A46 25c multicolored .60 .60
C94 A46 1 le multicolored 1.75 1.75
C95 A46 2 le multicolored 2.50 2.50
Nos. C90-C95 (6) 5.65 5.65

Various advertisements printed on peelable paper backing. No. C90 has side tab for handling and comes packed in boxes of 50. Nos. C91-C95 are without side tabs and come 20 stamps attached to one sheet.

Bank Type of Regular Issue

Lithographed; Gold Impressed

1969, Sept. 10

C96 A47 9½c yel grn, vio & gold .90 .90

Advertising printed on peelable paper backing; 20 imperf. stamps to a sheet of backing, roulette 10.

Cola Nut Type of Regular Issue and Type of 1967

Typo.; Embossed on White Paper

1969, Sept. 10

C97 A40 7c yel, mar & car .40 .40

Embossed Foil on Black Paper

C98 AP4 9½c blk, gold & bl 7.00 7.00
C99 AP4 15c blk, gold & red 9.00 9.00
Nos. C97-C99 (3) 16.40 16.40

No. C97 has side tab for handling and comes packed in boxes of 100. Nos. C98-C99 have advertisements printed on peelable paper backing, side tabs and come packed in boxes of 50.

Boy Scout, Lord Baden-Powell and Scout Emblem — AP5

1969, Dec. 6 Litho.

C100 AP5 7½c multicolored .50 .40
C101 AP5 9½c multicolored .60 .50
C102 AP5 15c multicolored .90 .90
C103 AP5 22c multicolored 1.25 1.25
C104 AP5 55c multicolored 5.00 5.00
C105 AP5 3 le multicolored 60.00 45.00
Nos. C100-C105 (6) 73.25 58.05

60th anniv. of the Sierra Leone Boy Scouts. Various advertising printed on peelable paper backing. No. C100 has side tab for handling and comes packed in boxes of 100. Nos. C101-C105 are without side tabs and come 20 stamps attached to one sheet.

No. 357 Srchd. "AIRMAIL" and New Denomination in Metallic Emerald, Lilac, Blue, Green, Bronze or Silver

1970, Mar 28

C106 A43 7½c on ½c (E) .30 .30
C107 A43 9½c on ½c (L) .40 .40
C108 A43 15c on ½c (Bl) .55 .55
C109 A43 28c on ½c (G) 1.00 1.00

C110	A43	40c on ½c (Br)	1.75	1.75
C111	A43	2 le on ½c (S)	9.00	9.00
		Nos. C106-C111 (6)	13.00	13.00

See design paragraph over No. 357.

EXPO Type of Regular Issue

Maps of Sierra Leone and Japan.

1970, June 22   **Litho.**

C112	A49	7½c multicolored	.25	.25
C113	A49	9½c multicolored	.25	.25
C114	A49	15c multicolored	.35	.35
C115	A49	25c multicolored	.60	.60
C116	A49	50c multicolored	.70	.70
C117	A49	3 le multicolored	2.00	2.00
		Nos. C112-C117 (6)	4.05	4.05

Various advertising printed on peelable paper backing.

Eagle Type of 1967

1970, Oct. 3   **Embossed Foil**

C118	AP4	7½c crim & gold	.55	.55
C119	AP4	9½c emer & cop	.65	.65
C120	AP4	15c grnsh bl & sil	1.25	1.25
C121	AP4	25c brt red lil & gold	2.75	2.25
C122	AP4	50c gold & emer	5.50	4.50
C123	AP4	1 le silver & dk bl	12.00	12.00
C124	AP4	2 le gold & brt bl	19.00	19.00
		Nos. C118-C124 (7)	39.20	35.70

Advertisements printed on peelable paper backing. Issued in sheets of 10.

"Treasure of Sierra Leone"
Diamond — AP6

Lithographed and Embossed
1970, Dec. 30

C125	AP6	7½c multicolored	.75	.25
C126	AP6	9½c multicolored	.90	.30
C127	AP6	15c multicolored	1.25	.50
C128	AP6	25c multicolored	1.75	1.75
C129	AP6	75c multicolored	7.50	7.50
C130	AP6	2 le multicolored	27.50	27.50
		Nos. C125-C130 (6)	39.65	37.75

Diamond industry. Advertisement printed on peelable paper backing. Sheets of 20.

Traffic Type of Regular Issue
1971, Mar. 1   **Litho.**

C131	A53	9½c vio blue & org	3.00	3.00

Advertisements printed on peelable paper backing.

Nos. 211, 215, 228 and C87
Surcharged in Dark Red, Dark Blue
or Black

a

b

1971, Mar. 1   **Engr.**   **Wmk. 336**

C132	A29(a)	10c on 2p (DR)	.35	.30
C133	A29(a)	20c on 1sh (DB)	.70	.65

        Photo.   **Perf. 14**

C134	A35(a)	50c on 1p (Bk)	1.75	1.50

        Unwmk.
        Litho.   **Imperf.**

C135	A44(b)	70c on 30c (DB)	2.75	2.75
C136	A44(b)	1 le on 30c (Bk)	4.00	4.00
		Nos. C132-C136 (5)	9.55	9.20

Lion's
Head
and
Bugles
AP7

Lithographed and Embossed (Gold)
1971, Apr. 27

C137	AP7	7½c multicolored	.25	.25
C138	AP7	9½c multicolored	.25	.25
C139	AP7	15c multicolored	.25	.25
C140	AP7	25c multicolored	.45	.45
C141	AP7	75c multicolored	1.50	1.50
C142	AP7	2 le multicolored	3.50	3.50
		Nos. C137-C142 (6)	6.10	6.10

10th anniversary of independence. Advertisements printed on peelable paper backing. Stamps are in shape of Sierra Leone map and in flag colors.

Guma Valley Dam and Bank
Emblem — AP8

1975, Jan. 14   **Litho.**   **Perf. 13½**

C143	AP8	15c multicolored	1.00	1.00

African Development Bank, 10th anniv.

Congo River Type of 1975
1975, Aug. 24   **Litho.**   **Perf. 13x13½**

C144	A57	20c multicolored	.50	.50

Mano River Type of 1975
1975, Oct. 3   **Perf. 13x13½**

C145	A58	15c multicolored	.30	.30

SINGAPORE

'siŋ-ə-ˌpor

LOCATION — An island just off the southern tip of the Malay Peninsula, south of Johore

GOVT. — Republic in British Commonwealth

AREA — 250 sq. mi.

POP. — 3,531,600 (1999 est.)

CAPITAL — Singapore

Singapore, Malacca and Penang were the British settlements which, together with the Federated Malay States, composed the former colony of Straits Settlements. On April 1, 1946, Singapore became a separate colony when the Straits Settlements colony was dissolved. Malacca and Penang joined the Malayan Union, which was renamed the Federation of Malaya in 1948. In 1959 Singapore became a state with internal self-government.

Singapore joined the Federation of Malaysia in 1963 and withdrew in 1965.

100 Cents = 1 Dollar

Catalogue values for all unused stamps in this country are for Never Hinged items.

Watermark

Wmk. 366 — S multiple

King George VI — A1

1948   Wmk. 4   Typo.   Perf. 14

1	A1	1c black	.25	.50
2	A1	2c orange	.25	.50
3	A1	3c green	.75	.80
4	A1	4c chocolate	.50	.50
6	A1	6c gray	.60	.65
7	A1	8c rose red	1.25	.95
9	A1	10c plum	.50	.25
11	A1	15c ultra	8.50	.40
12	A1	20c dk green & blk	5.00	.55
14	A1	25c org & rose lilac	6.00	.60
16	A1	40c dk vio & rose red	11.00	9.50
17	A1	50c ultra & black	5.50	.40
18	A1	$1 vio brn & ultra	21.00	4.50
19	A1	$2 rose red & emer	70.00	6.75
20	A1	$5 chocolate & emer	150.00	9.00
		Nos. 1-20 (15)	281.10	35.85
		Set, hinged	140.00	

1949-52   Perf. 18

1a	A1	1c black ('52)	.75	1.75
2a	A1	2c orange	1.50	1.50
4a	A1	4c chocolate	2.00	.25
5	A1	5c rose violet ('52)	4.75	1.00
6a	A1	6c gray ('52)	2.00	2.00
8	A1	8c green ('52)	9.00	3.00
9a	A1	10c plum ('50)	.70	.25
10	A1	12c rose red ('52)	14.00	9.50
11a	A1	15c ultra ('50)	22.50	.50
12a	A1	20c dark green & black	12.00	4.00
13	A1	20c ultra ('52)	10.00	.75
14a	A1	25c org & rose lil ('50)	4.00	.25
15	A1	35c dk vio & rose red ('52)	10.00	2.50
16a	A1	40c dk vio & rose red ('51)	45.00	20.00
17a	A1	50c ultra & black ('50)	7.50	.20
18a	A1	$1 violet brown & ultra	20.00	.90
b.		Wmk. 4a (error)	15,000.	
19a	A1	$2 rose red & emer ('51)	125.00	3.25
b.		Wmk. 4a (error)	18,000.	
20a	A1	$5 choc & emerald ('51)	150.00	9.00
		Nos. 1a-20a (18)	540.70	55.70
		Set, hinged	300.00	

Common Design Types pictured following the introduction.

Silver Wedding Issue
Common Design Types
Inscribed: "Singapore"

1948, Oct. 25   Photo.   Perf. 14x14½

21	CD304	10c purple	1.25	.40

Perf. 11½x11
Engraved; Name Typographed

22	CD305	$5 light brown	130.00	45.00

UPU Issue
Common Design Types
Inscribed: "Malaya-Singapore"
Engr.; Name Typo. on 15c, 25c
Perf. 13½, 11x11½

1949, Oct. 10   Wmk. 4

23	CD306	10c rose violet	1.00	.70
24	CD307	15c indigo	4.50	2.50
25	CD308	25c orange	5.75	4.50
26	CD309	50c slate	9.50	6.50
		Nos. 23-26 (4)	20.75	14.20

Coronation Issue
Common Design Type

1953, June 2   Engr.   Perf. 13½x13

27	CD312	10c mag & blk	2.50	.40

Chinese Sampans — A2

Sir Stamford Raffles Statue — A3

Singapore River — A4

Designs: 2c, Malay kolek. 4c, Twa-kow. 5c, Lombok sloop. 6c, Trengganu pinas. 8c, Palari. 10c, Timber tongkong. 12c, Hylam trader. 20c, Cocos-Keeling schooner. 25c, Argonaut plane. 30c, Oil tanker. 50c, Liner (M.S. Chusan). $5, Arms of Singapore.

Perf. 13½x14½

1955, Sept. 4   Photo.   Wmk. 4

28	A2	1c sepia	.25	.80
29	A2	2c orange yellow	1.75	1.25
30	A2	4c orange brown	1.25	.25
31	A2	5c magenta	.90	.30
32	A2	6c gray blue	1.00	.40
33	A2	8c aqua	1.25	1.00
34	A2	10c dark purple	2.75	.25
35	A2	12c rose red	3.50	3.00
36	A2	20c violet blue	2.25	.30
37	A2	25c orange & purple	2.50	.50
38	A2	30c purple & plum	3.75	.25
39	A2	50c brt blue & black	2.50	.35

Perf. 13½x14, 14x13½
Engr.

40	A3	$1 blue & purple	32.50	1.00
a.		Purple (Queen's head) omitted	26,000.	
41	A4	$2 blue green & red	47.50	2.75

Engr.; Arms Typo.

42	A3	$5 multicolored	52.50	7.00
		Nos. 28-42 (15)	156.15	19.40

For a later printing of the 10c and 50c, plates with finer screen (250) than normal (200) were used.

Singapore Lion and Administrative Center — A5

Perf. 11½x12

1959, June 1   Photo.   Wmk. 314
Lion in Gold

43	A5	4c deep rose red	.85	.75
44	A5	10c magenta	1.25	.50
45	A5	20c ultra	2.75	2.75
46	A5	25c yellow green	2.75	2.75
47	A5	30c bright violet	3.00	3.25
48	A5	50c bluish gray	4.25	4.25
		Nos. 43-48 (6)	14.85	14.25

New Constitution of Singapore.

State Flag of Singapore A6

1960, June 3   Litho.   Perf. 13½

49	A6	4c blue, red & yellow	1.75	.75
50	A6	10c gray, red & yellow	3.25	1.10

Issued for National Day, June 3, 1960.

Hands and Map of Singapore A7

1961, June 3   Photo.

51	A7	4c brown, yellow & gray	1.25	1.10
52	A7	10c green, yellow & gray	2.00	.25

Issued for National Day, June 3, 1961.

Sea Horse — A8

Malayan Fish: 4c, Tiger barb, horiz. 5c, Anemone fish, horiz. 6c, Archerfish. 10c, Harlequin fish, horiz. 20c, Butterflyfish. 25c, Two-spot gournami, horiz.

Perf. 14½x13½, 13½x14½

1962, Mar. 31   Wmk. 314

53	A8	2c lt grn & red brn	.40	.60
54	A8	4c red orange & blk	.40	.60
a.		Black omitted	1,200.	
55	A8	5c gray & red org	.30	.25
a.		Red orange omitted	650.00	
b.		Wmkd. sideways ('67)	3.25	1.00
56	A8	6c yellow & blk	.55	.55
57	A8	10c dk gray & red org	.75	.25
a.		Red orange omitted	425.00	300.00
b.		Wmkd. sideways ('67)	1.60	.50
c.		Black omitted	6,000.	
58	A8	20c blue & orange	1.50	.25
a.		Orange omitted	1,100.	
59	A8	25c orange & black	1.25	.25
a.		Black omitted	1,200.	
b.		Wmkd. sideways ('67)	2.50	.25
		Nos. 53-59 (7)	5.15	2.75

For surcharge see No. 370.

Symbolic of Labor's Role in Building the Nation — A9

1962, June 3   Unwmk.   Perf. 11½

60	A9	4c brt rose, blk & yel	1.40	1.40
61	A9	10c brt blue, blk & yel	1.75	.75

Issued for National Day, June 3, 1962.

Vanda Tan Chay Yan — A10

Yellow-Breasted Sunbird — A11

Designs: 1c, Arachnis Maggie Oei, horiz. 12c, Grammatophyllum speciosum. 30c, Vanda Miss Joaquim. 50c, Shama, horiz. $1, White-breasted kingfisher, horiz. $5, White-tailed sea eagle.

Perf. 12½, 13½x13 (50c, $1), 13x13½ ($2, $5)

1963, Mar. 10   Photo.   Wmk. 314
Flowers and Birds in Natural Colors
Size: 37x26mm, 26x37mm

62	A10	1c brt pink & ultra	.30	.25
a.		Wmkd. sideways ('67)	1.50	.50
63	A10	8c lt blue & mag	1.00	1.00
64	A10	12c salmon & brown	1.25	1.25
65	A10	30c tan & ol green	1.50	.40
a.		Tan omitted	150.00	

Size: 35½x25½mm, 25½x35½mm

66	A11	50c yel green & blk	1.60	.40
a.		Wmkd. sideways ('66)	8.00	4.50
67	A11	$1 yellow & blk	19.00	.80
a.		Wmkd. sideways ('67)	24.00	6.50
68	A11	$2 dull blue & blk	15.00	2.00
69	A11	$5 pale blue & blk	37.50	5.50
		Nos. 62-69 (8)	77.15	11.60

See No. 76.

Government Housing Project — A12

1963, June 3   Perf. 12½

70	A12	4c multicolored	1.00	.70
71	A12	10c multicolored	2.00	.40

Issued for National Day, June 3, 1963.

Folk Dancers — A13

1963, Aug. 8   Photo.   Perf. 14x14½

72	A13	5c multicolored	.85	.50

Southeast Asia Cultural Festival.

Workers, Factory and Apartment House A14

Wmk. 314 (30c), Unwmd. (15, 20c)

1966, Aug. 9 Photo. Perf. 12½x13
73	A14	15c ultra & multi	.75	.30
74	A14	20c red & multi	1.25	.25
75	A14	30c yellow & multi	2.25	1.50
		Nos. 73-75 (3)	4.25	2.05

First anniversary of the Republic.

Bird Type of 1963

Design: 15c, Black-naped tern (sterna).

1966, Nov. 9 Wmk. 314 Perf. 12½
Bird in Natural Colors
Size: 26x37mm
76	A11	15c blue & black	3.50	.25
a.		Orange (eye) omitted	80.00	

Marching Women, Chinese
Inscription — A15

15c, Malay inscription. 50c, Tamil inscription.

Perf. 14x14½
1967, Aug. 9 Photo. Unwmk.
77	A15	6c lt brn, gray & red	.70	.75
78	A15	15c multicolored	1.00	.25
79	A15	50c multicolored	2.25	1.75
		Nos. 77-79 (3)	3.95	2.75

"Build a Vigorous Singapore" campaign.

Buildings
and Map of
Africa and
Southeast
Asia — A16

1967, Oct. 7 Perf. 14x13½
Black Overprint
80	A16	10c multicolored	.55	.30
81	A16	25c multicolored	1.00	1.10
82	A16	50c multicolored	1.75	1.50
		Nos. 80-82 (3)	3.30	2.90

2nd Afro-Asian Housing Cong., Oct. 7-15. No. 80 exists without overprint. Value, $1,500.

Map of Singapore
and Symbolic
Worker — A17

Stamps are inscribed "Work for Prosperity" in English and: 6c, Chinese. 15c, Malay. 50c, Tamil.

Perf. 13½x14½
1968, Aug. 9 Photo. Unwmk.
83	A17	6c red, black & gold	.35	.25
84	A17	15c brt yel grn, blk & gold	.50	.40
85	A17	50c brt blue, blk & gold	1.50	1.50
		Nos. 83-85 (3)	2.35	2.15

Issued for National Day, 1968.

Sword Dance — A18

Designs: 6c, Lion dance. 10c, Bharatha Natyam, Indian dance. 15c, Tari Payong, Sumatran dance. 20c, Kathak Kali, Indian dance mask. 25c, Lu Chih Shen and Lin

Chung, Chinese opera masks. 30c, Dragon dance, horiz. 50c, Tari Lilin, Malayan candle dance. 75c, Tarian Kuda Kepang, Javanese dance. $1, Yao Chi, Chinese opera mask.

Wmk. Rectangles (334)
1968 Photo. Perf. 14
86	A18	5c yellow & multi	.50	.75
87	A18	6c orange & multi	1.00	1.00
88	A18	10c bl grn & multi	.40	.25
89	A18	15c lt brown & multi	.60	.25
a.		Booklet pane of 4 ('69)	50.00	
90	A18	20c brown & multi	.90	.30
91	A18	25c dp car & multi	1.10	.50
92	A18	30c pink & multi	.50	.50
93	A18	50c brown org & multi	.75	.75
94	A18	75c brt rose & multi	3.00	1.25
95	A18	$1 olive grn & multi	3.75	1.25
		Nos. 86-95 (10)	12.50	6.80

Issue dates: 6c, 20c, 30c, 50c, 75c, Dec. 1; 5c, 10c, 15c, 25c, $1, Dec. 29.

1973 Perf. 13
86a	A18	5c yellow & multi	7.00	6.00
88a	A18	10c blue green & multi	10.00	7.00
90a	A18	20c brown & multi	14.00	8.00
91a	A18	25c deep car & multi	12.00	10.00
92a	A18	30c pink & multi	10.00	10.00
93a	A18	50c brown org & multi	15.00	11.00
95a	A18	$1 olive green & multi	25.00	22.50
		Nos. 86a-95a (7)	97.00	74.50

Cogwheel
and Emblem
A19

1969, Apr. 15 Unwmk. Perf. 13
96	A19	15c blue, black & silver	.50	.25
97	A19	30c red, black & silver	1.00	1.00
98	A19	75c violet, black & silver	1.50	2.00
		Nos. 96-98 (3)	3.00	3.25

25th Plenary Session of the Economic Commission for Asia and the Far East (ECAFE), Singapore, Apr. 15-28.

"Homes for the
People" — A20

Perf. 13x13½
1969, July 20 Litho. Unwmk.
99	A20	25c emerald & black	1.40	.50
100	A20	50c dark blue & black	2.00	1.50

1960-69 building program of the Housing and Development Board.

Plane over Docks of
Singapore — A21

30c, UN emblem and map of Singapore. 75c, Flags and map of Malaya and Borneo. $1, Uplifted hands and Singapore flag. $5, Tail of Japanese plane and searchlights. $10, Statue of Sir Thomas Stamford Raffles.

1969, Aug. 9 Perf. 14x14½
101	A21	15c yel, blk & org	2.50	1.50
102	A21	30c brt blue & blk	2.50	2.00
103	A21	75c orange & multi	4.50	3.00
104	A21	$1 red & black	10.00	10.00
105	A21	$5 gray, blk & red	24.00	30.00
106	A21	$10 emerald & blk	37.50	37.50
a.		Souv. sheet of 6, #101-106	700.00	500.00
		Nos. 101-106 (6)	81.00	84.00

Sesquicent. of the founding of Singapore.

Mirudhangam, South Indian
Drum — A22

Musical Instruments: 4c, Pi Pa, Chinese, 4 strings, vert. $2, Rebab, Malay violin, 3 strings, vert. $5, Vina, Indian, 7 strings. $10, Ta Ku, Chinese drum, vert.

1969 Photo. Wmk. 366 Perf. 13
107	A22	1c multicolored	.25	1.25
108	A22	4c multicolored	.60	1.25
109	A22	$2 multicolored	4.25	1.50
110	A22	$5 multicolored	16.00	3.00
111	A22	$10 multicolored	40.00	16.00
		Nos. 107-111 (5)	61.10	23.00

Issued: 1c, 4c, $2, $5, Nov. 10; $10, Dec. 6.

Sea
Shells — A23

Designs: 30c, Tropical fish. 75c, Greater flamingo and helmeted hornbill. $1, Orchids.

Perf. 13½
1970, Mar. 15 Unwmk. Litho.
112	A23	15c pale vio & multi	1.00	.25
113	A23	30c lt blue & multi	2.50	1.25
114	A23	75c yellow & multi	6.50	4.25
115	A23	$1 lt green & multi	8.50	6.00
a.		Souvenir sheet of 4, #112-115	30.00	30.00
		Nos. 112-115 (4)	18.50	11.75

EXPO '70 International Exposition, Osaka, Japan, Mar. 15-Sept. 13. Compare with type A396.

Child Playing (Kindergarten) — A24

50c, Sports activities. 75c, Cultural activities.

1970, July 1 Unwmk. Perf. 13½
116	A24	15c dp org & blk	1.00	.25
117	A24	50c org, blk & vio bl	2.50	2.50
118	A24	75c blk & dp lilac rose	4.25	4.25
		Nos. 116-118 (3)	7.75	7.00

People's Association, 10th anniversary.

Soldier and Map of
Singapore — A25

Map and soldiers in various positions.

1970, Aug. 9 Litho. Unwmk.
119	A25	15c emer, blk & org	1.50	.25
120	A25	50c org, blk & brt mag	4.25	3.75
121	A25	$1 brt mag, blk & emer	5.75	5.75
		Nos. 119-121 (3)	11.50	9.75

National military service.

Runners
A26

1970, Aug. 23 Photo. Perf. 13
122	A26	10c shown	1.25	1.25
123	A26	15c Swimmers	2.50	2.50
124	A26	25c Badminton	2.75	2.75
125	A26	50c Automobile race	3.50	3.50
a.		Strip of 4, #122-125	14.00	14.00

1970 Festival of Sports.

Ship and Emblem of National Line
(Neptune Oriental Lines) — A27

Designs: 30c, Ship in first container berth. 75c, Ship repairing and ship building.

1970, Nov. 1 Litho. Perf. 12
126	A27	15c vio bl, lem & red	3.00	1.75
127	A27	30c dp ultra & lemon	6.00	6.00
128	A27	75c red & lemon	12.00	11.00
		Nos. 126-128 (3)	21.00	17.75

Singapore shipping industry.

Flags of Commonwealth
Nations — A28

Designs: 15c, Circular arrangement of names of Commonwealth members. 30c, Flags arranged in circle. $1, Flags (different arrangement).

1971, Jan. 14 Perf. 15½x14½
Size: 46½x31mm
129	A28	15c gold & multi	1.25	.50
130	A28	30c gold & multi	2.00	1.00
131	A28	75c gold & multi	3.00	3.00

Size: 67x31mm
Perf. 14
132	A28	$1 gold & multi	4.00	4.00
		Nos. 129-132 (4)	10.25	8.50

Commonwealth Heads of Government Meeting, Singapore, Jan. 12-14.

Cycle
Rickshaws
A29

Houses of Worship in
Singapore — A30

Perf. 11½
1971, Apr. 4 Unwmk. Litho.
133	A29	15c shown	1.00	.25
134	A29	20c Sampans	1.50	.60
135	A29	30c Market place	2.00	1.40

Perf. 13x13½
136	A30	50c Waterfront	4.50	5.50
137	A30	75c shown	6.75	6.75
		Nos. 133-137 (5)	15.75	14.50

Tourist publicity.

Chinese New Year — A31

Singapore Festivals: 30c, Hari Raya Puasa (Moslem). 50c, Deepavali (Hindu). 75c, Christmas.

1971, Aug. 9   **Litho.**   *Perf. 14*

138	A31	15c multicolored	1.75	1.50
139	A31	30c multicolored	2.75	3.75
140	A31	50c multicolored	4.25	4.25
141	A31	75c multicolored	6.25	6.25
a.		Souvenir sheet of 4, #138-141	130.00	110.00
		Nos. 138-141 (4)	15.00	15.75

Satellite Earth Station, Sentosa Island — A32

No. 143 as 15c, enlarged to cover 4 stamps.

1971, Oct. 23   **Unwmk.**   *Perf. 13½*

142	A32	15c red & multi	2.75	2.75
143	A32	Block of 4	42.50	42.50
a.		30c (yellow numeral)	10.00	10.00
b.		30c (green numeral)	10.00	10.00
c.		30c (rose numeral)	10.00	10.00
d.		30c (orange numeral)	10.00	10.00

Establishment of Singapore's satellite earth station, Sentosa Island.

Singapore River and Fort Canning, 1843-1847 — A33

Views of Singapore, from 19th century art works: 15c, The Padang, 1851. 20c, Waterfront, 1848-1849. 35c, View from Fort Canning, 1846. 50c, View from Mount Wallich, 1857. $1, Waterfront with ships, from the sea, 1861.

1971, Dec. 5   **Unwmk.**   *Perf. 13x12½*

Size: 52x45mm

144	A33	10c gold & multi	3.75	3.00
145	A33	15c gold & multi	4.50	2.00
146	A33	20c gold & multi	5.00	5.00
147	A33	35c gold & multi	9.50	9.50

Perf. 12½x13

Size: 68x47mm

148	A33	50c gold & multi	11.00	11.00
149	A33	$1 gold & multi	20.00	20.00
		Nos. 144-149 (6)	53.75	50.50

George V 1c Copper Coin, 1920 A34

Singapore Coins: 35c, Silver dollar, 1969. $1, Gold $150, 1969 commemorative coin for sesquicentennial of founding of Singapore.

1972, June 4   **Litho.**   *Perf. 13½*

150	A34	15c dk grn, dp org & blk	1.25	1.25
151	A34	35c red & black	2.75	2.75
152	A34	$1 ultra, yellow & blk	4.50	4.50
		Nos. 150-152 (3)	8.50	8.50

"Moon Festival," by Seah Kim Joo — A35

Paintings by Singapore Artists: 35c, "Complimentary Force," by Thomas Yeo. 50c, "Rhythm in Blue," by Yusman Aman. $1, "Gibbons," by Chen Wen Hsi.

1972, July 9   **Litho.**   *Perf. 12½*

Size: 40x43½mm

153	A35	15c brown org & multi	1.00	.50

Size: 35½x53½mm

154	A35	35c bl grn & multi	2.00	2.00
155	A35	50c dull violet & multi	2.25	2.25

Size: 40x43½mm

156	A35	$1 bister & multi	6.00	6.00
		Nos. 153-156 (4)	11.25	10.75

Chinese New Year — A36

Festivals: 35c, Hari Raya Puasa (candles and ornament). 50c, Deepavali (incense and teapot). 75c, Christmas (candle and stained glass window).

1972, Aug. 9   **Litho.**   *Perf. 13x12½*

157	A36	15c deep rose & multi	1.00	.25
158	A36	35c violet & multi	1.25	1.25
159	A36	50c green & multi	2.50	2.50
160	A36	75c blue & multi	3.50	3.50
		Nos. 157-160 (4)	8.25	7.50

Technical and Scientific Training — A37

Designs: 35c, Sport. $1, Art and culture.

1972, Oct. 1   **Photo.**   *Perf. 12*

161	A37	15c orange & multi	1.00	.75
162	A37	35c blue & multi	2.25	2.25
163	A37	$1 orange & multi	3.75	3.75
		Nos. 161-163 (3)	7.00	6.75

Youth of Singapore.

Neptune Ruby A38

1972, Dec. 17   **Litho.**   *Perf. 14x14½*

Size: 42x28½mm

164	A38	15c shown	2.50	.80

Size: 29½x28½mm

165	A38	75c Maria Rickmers	6.00	6.00
166	A38	$1 Chinese junk	9.00	9.00
a.		Souvenir sheet of 3, #164-166	47.50	47.50
		Nos. 164-166 (3)	17.50	15.80

Singapore shipping industry.

Quality and Reliability Emblem — A39

15c, Emblem & initials of participating organizations: Singapore Institute of Standards & Industrial Research, Singapore Manufacturers' Association, Natl. Trades Union Congress. 75c, Emblem & "Prosperity through Quality & Reliability" in multiple rows. $1, Quality & Reliability emblem.

1973, Feb. 25   **Litho.**   *Perf. 14½x14*

167	A39	15c gold & multi	.75	.40
168	A39	35c gold & multi	1.75	1.75
169	A39	75c gold & multi	2.00	2.00
170	A39	$1 gold & multi	2.50	2.25
		Nos. 167-170 (4)	7.00	6.40

Prosperity through Quality and Reliability campaign.

Birds, Jurong Bird Park — A40

Landmarks: 35c, Dancers, National Theater. 50c, City Hall and ballplayers. $1, Singapore River with boats and buildings.

1973, Apr. 29   *Perf. 12½*

171	A40	15c vermilion & blk	1.10	.50
172	A40	35c dull green & blk	2.00	2.00
173	A40	50c brown & blk	3.50	3.50
174	A40	$1 dark violet & blk	4.50	4.50
		Nos. 171-174 (4)	11.10	10.50

Airline Emblems A41

35c, Emblem of Singapore Airlines and intl. destinations. 75c, SIA emblem on stylized tail of Boeing jet. $1, SIA emblems circling globe.

1973, June 24   **Litho.**   *Perf. 13½*

175	A41	10c multicolored	.80	.30
176	A41	35c multicolored	2.00	2.00
177	A41	75c multicolored	2.25	2.25
178	A41	$1 multicolored	3.25	3.25
		Nos. 175-178 (4)	8.30	7.80

Singapore Intl. Airport at Paya Lebar.

Entertainers A42

Composite of various forms of entertainment.

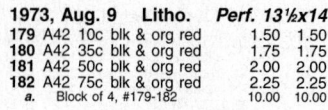

Running, Judo, Boxing — A43

Designs: 15c, Bicycling, weight lifting, pistol shoot, yachting. 25c, Various balls. 35c, Tennis racket, ball, hockey stick. 50c, Swimming. $1, Singapore National Stadium.

Size: 25x25mm

1973, Sept. 1   **Photo.**   *Perf. 14*

183	A43	10c gold, silver & ind	.75	.75
184	A43	15c gold & dk brown	2.00	2.00
185	A43	25c silver, gold & blk	1.75	1.75
186	A43	35c gold, silver & dk pur	2.75	2.75

Perf. 13x14

Size: 40½x25mm

187	A43	50c gold & multi	3.00	3.00
188	A43	$1 sil, vio bl & emer	5.00	5.00
a.		Souvenir sheet of 6, #183-188	47.50	47.50
		Nos. 183-188 (6)	15.25	15.25

7th South East Asia (SEAP) Games, Singapore.

Agave A44

Mangosteen A45

Designs: Stylized flowers and fruit.

1973, Sept. 30   **Photo.**   *Perf. 13*

189	A44	1c shown	.25	.70
190	A44	5c Coleus blumei	.25	.25
a.		Booklet pane of 10 (4 #190, 4 #191 + 2 #193)	15.00	
191	A44	10c Madagascar periwinkle	.25	.25
192	A44	15c Sunflower	.80	.25
193	A44	20c Dwarf palm	.50	.50
194	A44	25c Yellow daisy	1.50	.45
195	A44	35c Chrysanthemum	.75	.65
196	A44	50c Costus	1.00	.25
197	A44	75c Transvaal daisy	2.00	.75
198	A45	$1 shown	2.50	.75
199	A45	$2 Jackfruit	3.00	1.25
200	A45	$5 Coconuts	7.00	7.00
201	A45	$10 Pineapple	14.00	14.00
		Nos. 189-201 (13)	33.80	27.05

Nos. 189-201 have fluorescent underprint "Singapore" in multiple rows.

Tiger and Orangutans — A46

1973, Dec. 16   **Litho.**   *Perf. 13*

202	A46	5c shown	1.00	1.00
203	A46	10c Leopard and deer	1.25	1.25
204	A46	35c Panther and stag	3.75	3.75
205	A46	75c White horse & lion	5.25	5.25
		Nos. 202-205 (4)	11.25	10.75

Opening of Singapore Zoo.

Tropical Fish — A47

1973, Aug. 9   **Litho.**   *Perf. 13½x14*

179	A42	10c blk & org red	1.50	1.50
180	A42	35c blk & org red	1.75	1.75
181	A42	50c blk & org red	2.00	2.00
182	A42	75c blk & org red	2.25	2.25
a.		Block of 4, #179-182	10.00	10.00

National Day 1973.

Designs: Various poecilia reticulata fish.

1974, Apr. 21 **Perf. 13½x14**
206 A47 5c apple grn & multi 1.00 1.00
207 A47 10c pink & multi 1.25 .40
208 A47 35c brt blue & multi 3.00 3.00
209 A47 $1 brt green & multi 5.00 5.00
Nos. 206-209 (4) 10.25 9.40

Scout Conference Emblem A48

1974, June 9 **Perf. 13½x14½**
210 A48 10c multicolored .50 .50
211 A48 75c multicolored 1.75 1.75

9th Asia-Pacific Boy Scout Conf., Singapore.

UPU Emblem, Circle and "Centenary" Multiple — A49

UPU, cent.: 35c, Circle and UN emblems, multiple. 75c, Circle and pigeons, multiple.

1974, July 7 **Litho.** **Perf. 14½x13½**
212 A49 10c orange brn & multi .35 .35
213 A49 35c blue & multi 1.00 1.00
214 A49 75c emerald & multi 1.25 *2.50*
Nos. 212-214 (3) 2.60 3.85

Family — A50

35c, Symbols for male & female. 75c, World map and WPY emblem.

1974, Aug. 9 **Litho.** **Perf. 13x13½**
215 A50 10c shown .50 .50
216 A50 35c multicolored 1.10 1.10
217 A50 75c multicolored 1.50 *2.75*
Nos. 215-217 (3) 3.10 4.35

Natl. Day and World Population Year 1974.

"Sun and Tree" — A51

Children's Drawings: 10c, "My Daddy and Mommy." 35c, "A Dump Truck." 50c, "My Aunt."

1974, Oct. 1 **Photo.** **Perf. 14x13½**
218 A51 5c multicolored .50 .50
219 A51 10c multicolored .60 .40
220 A51 35c multicolored 2.25 2.25
221 A51 50c multicolored 2.75 2.75
a. Souv. sheet, #218-221, perf 13 27.50 27.50
Nos. 218-221 (4) 6.10 5.90

Children's drawings for Children's Day (UNICEF).

Alfresco Dining A52

Tourist publicity: 20c, Singapore River. $1, "Kelong" fish traps.

1975, Jan. 26 **Litho.** **Perf. 14**
222 A52 15c multicolored .80 .50
223 A52 20c multicolored 1.50 1.50
224 A52 $1 multicolored 4.00 4.00
Nos. 222-224 (3) 6.30 6.00

Prows of Barges and Wave Design A53

25c, Cargo ships & ship's wheel. 50c, Tanker & signal flags. $1, Container ship & propellers.

1975, Mar. 10 **Litho.** **Perf. 13½**
225 A53 5c multicolored .50 .25
226 A53 25c multicolored 1.75 1.75
227 A53 50c multicolored 2.50 2.50
228 A53 $1 multicolored 3.75 3.75
Nos. 225-228 (4) 8.50 8.25

9th Biennial Conf. of the Intl. Assoc. of Ports and Harbors, Singapore, Mar. 8-15.

Satellite Earth Stations, Sentosa Island — A54

Oil Refinery — A55

Science and Industry: 75c, Brain surgery, Medical Center, Jurong.

1975, June 29 **Photo.** **Perf. 13½**
229 A54 10c multicolored .50 .50
230 A55 35c multicolored 2.50 2.50
231 A54 75c multicolored 2.75 2.75
Nos. 229-231 (3) 5.75 5.50

"10" and "Homes and Gardens for the People" — A56

Tenth Natl. Day ("10" and): 35c, "Shipping and ship building." 75c, "Communications and technology." $1, "Trade, commerce and industry."

1975, Aug. 9 **Litho.** **Perf. 13½**
232 A56 10c multicolored .50 .45
233 A56 35c multicolored 1.25 1.25
234 A56 75c multicolored 2.50 2.50
235 A56 $1 multicolored 2.75 2.75
Nos. 232-235 (4) 7.00 6.95

Crowned Cranes — A57

Birds: 10c, Great hornbill. 35c, White-breasted and white-collared kingfishers. $1, Sulphur-crested cockatoo and blue and yellow macaw.

1975, Oct. 5 **Litho.** **Perf. 14½x13½**
236 A57 5c emerald & multi 2.25 2.25
237 A57 10c emerald & multi 2.50 2.50
238 A57 35c emerald & multi 8.50 8.50
239 A57 $1 emerald & multi 11.00 11.00
Nos. 236-239 (4) 24.25 24.25

IWY Emblem, Peace Dove as "Equality" — A58

IWY Emblem: 35c, Peace dove with eggs in basket, symbolizing "Development." 75c, Peace dove & young, symbolizing "Peace."

1975, Dec. 7 **Litho.** **Perf. 13½**
240 A58 10c blk, blue & pink .30 .30
241 A58 35c orange & multi 2.00 2.00
242 A58 75c dp violet & multi 2.75 2.75
a. Souvenir sheet of 3, #240-242 20.00 20.00
Nos. 240-242 (3) 5.05 5.05

International Women's Year 1975.

Yellow Flame — A59

Wayside Trees: 35c, Cabbage tree. 50c, Rose of India. 75c, Variegated coral tree.

1976, Apr. 18 **Litho.** **Perf. 14**
243 A59 10c multicolored .75 .25
244 A59 35c multicolored 2.00 2.00
245 A59 50c multicolored 2.50 2.50
246 A59 75c multicolored 3.50 3.50
Nos. 243-246 (4) 8.75 8.25

Aranda Hybrid — A60

Designs: Varieties of aranda orchids.

1976, June 20 **Litho.** **Perf. 14**
247 A60 10c black & multi 1.25 .50
248 A60 35c black & multi 3.25 3.25
249 A60 50c black & multi 3.50 3.50
250 A60 75c black & multi 5.25 5.25
Nos. 247-250 (4) 13.25 12.50

"10" and Children's Band A61

35c, Running boys. 75c, Dancing children.

1976, Aug. 9 **Litho.** **Perf. 12½**
251 A61 10c multicolored .40 .30
252 A61 35c multicolored 1.50 1.50
253 A61 75c multicolored 1.75 1.75
Nos. 251-253 (3) 3.65 3.55

Singapore Youth Festival, 10th anniversary.

Queen Elizabeth Walk — A62

Paintings of Old Singapore, c. 1905-10: 50c, The Padang. $1, Raffles Place.

1976, Nov. 14 **Litho.** **Perf. 14**
254 A62 10c multicolored 1.00 1.00
255 A62 50c multicolored 2.25 2.25
256 A62 $1 multicolored 4.75 4.75
a. Souvenir sheet of 3, #254-256, perf. 13½ 21.00 21.00
Nos. 254-256 (3) 8.00 8.00

Chinese Bridal Costume — A63

Designs: 35c, Indian bridal costume. 75c, Malay bridal costume.

1976, Dec. 19 **Litho.** **Perf. 14½**
257 A63 10c lt green & multi .75 .55
258 A63 35c lilac & multi 1.75 1.75
259 A63 75c yellow & multi 3.00 3.00
Nos. 257-259 (3) 5.50 5.30

Radar, Surface to Air Missile, Soldiers — A64

50c, Infantry soldiers and tank. 75c, Jet fighter, pilot, telecommunications center.

1977, Mar. 12 **Litho.** **Perf. 14½**
260 A64 10c multicolored .75 .50
261 A64 50c multicolored 2.75 2.50
262 A64 75c multicolored 4.00 4.00
Nos. 260-262 (3) 7.50 7.00

National Service, 10th anniversary.

Lyrate Cockle A65 Spotted Hermit Crab A66

Sea Shells: 5c, Folded scallop. 10c, Marble cone. 15c, Scorpion conch. 20c, Amplustre bubble. 25c, Spiral Babylon. 35c, Regal thorny oyster. 50c, Winged frog shell. 75c, Troschel's murex.
Marine Life: $2, Stingray. $5, Cuttlefish. $10, Lionfish.

1977 **Perf. 13½**
263 A65 1c orange & multi 1.10 *1.60*
264 A65 5c orange & multi .25 .25
a. Bklt. pane, 4 #264, 8 #265 9.00 *12.00*
265 A65 10c orange & multi .25 .25
a. Imperf., pair 500.00
266 A65 15c orange & multi 1.00 .40
267 A65 20c orange & multi 1.00 .25
268 A65 25c orange & multi 1.25 *2.25*
269 A65 35c orange & multi 1.50 1.40
270 A65 50c orange & multi 2.00 .25
271 A65 75c orange & multi 2.75 .25

Perf. 14
272 A66 $1 multicolored 2.50 .25
273 A66 $2 multicolored 2.50 .75
274 A66 $5 multicolored 4.00 4.00
275 A66 $10 multicolored 7.50 6.00
Nos. 263-275 (13) 27.60 17.90

No. 264a has a large inscribed selvage, the size of 6 stamps.
Issued: #263-271, Apr. 9; others, June 4.

Singapore Harbor Improvements A67

Labor Day: 50c, Construction workers. 75c, Road workers.

1977, May 1   Litho.   Perf. 13x12½
276 A67 10c multicolored   .60   .50
277 A67 50c multicolored   1.50   1.50
278 A67 75c multicolored   2.00   2.00
      Nos. 276-278 (3)   4.10   4.00

"Key to
Savings" — A68

Designs: 35c, "On-line Banking Service." 75c, "GIRO Service."

1977, July 16   Litho.   Perf. 13, 14
279 A68 10c multicolored   .30   .25
  a.   Perf 14   25.00 25.00
280 A68 35c multicolored   1.00   1.00
  a.   Perf 14   100.00 100.00
281 A68 75c multicolored   2.10   2.10
  a.   Perf 14   130.00 130.00
      Nos. 279-281 (3)   3.40   3.35

Centenary of Post Office Savings Bank.

Grain and
Cattle — A69

10c, Flags of founding members: Thailand, Indonesia, Singapore, Malaysia, Philippines. 75c, Steel, oil & chemical industries.

1977, Aug. 8   Litho.   Perf. 14
282 A69 10c multicolored   .35   .25
283 A69 35c multicolored   1.00   1.00
284 A69 75c multicolored   2.10   2.10
      Nos. 282-284 (3)   3.45   3.35

Association of South East Asian Nations (ASEAN), 10th anniversary.

Bus
Stop — A70

Children's Drawings: 10c, Chingay procession, vert. 75c, Playground.

1977, Oct. 1   Perf. 12½
285 A70 10c multicolored   .35   .35
286 A70 35c multicolored   1.00   .65
287 A70 75c multicolored   2.50   2.00
  a.   Souvenir sheet of 3, #285-287 13.50 13.50
      Nos. 285-287 (3)   3.85   2.90

Symbols of Life
Sciences — A71

Singapore Science Center: 35c, "Physical sciences." 75c, "Science and technology." $1, Science Center.

1977, Dec. 10   Litho.   Perf. 14½x14
288 A71 10c multicolored   .45   .40
289 A71 35c multicolored   .50   .45
290 A71 75c multicolored   1.25   1.40
291 A71 $1 multicolored   2.00   2.00
      Nos. 288-291 (4)   4.20   4.25

Botanical
Gardens — A72

Singapore Parks and Gardens: 10c, Jurong Bird Park, horiz. 35c, East Coast Lagoon and Park.

1978, Apr. 22   Litho.   Perf. 14½
292 A72 10c multicolored   .25   .25
293 A72 35c multicolored   .85   .85
294 A72 75c multicolored   1.75   1.75
      Nos. 292-294 (3)   2.85   2.85

Red-whiskered
Bulbul — A73

Songbirds: 35c, White eyes. 50c, White-rumped shama. 75c, White-crested laughing thrush.

1978, July 1   Litho.   Perf. 13½
295 A73 10c multicolored   .75   .75
296 A73 35c multicolored   2.00   2.00
297 A73 50c multicolored   2.25   2.25
298 A73 75c multicolored   3.00   3.00
      Nos. 295-298 (4)   8.00   8.00

Thian Hock Keng Temple — A74

National Monuments: No. 303a, like No. 299. Nos. 300, 303b, Hajjah Fatimah Mosque. Nos. 301, 303c, Armenian Church. Nos. 302, 303d, Sri Mariamman Temple.

1978, Aug. 9
299 A74 10c tan & multi   .70   .70
300 A74 10c green & multi   .70   .70
301 A74 10c blue & multi   .70   .70
302 A74 10c lilac & multi   .70   .70
      Nos. 299-302 (4)   2.80   2.80
          Souvenir Sheet
303   Sheet of 4   6.50   6.50
  a.   A74 35c tan & multi   1.00
  b.   A74 35c green & multi   1.00
  c.   A74 35c blue & multi   1.00
  d.   A74 35c lilac & multi   1.00

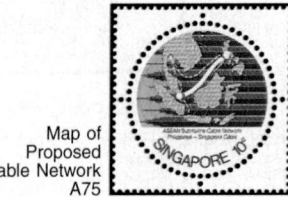

Map of
Proposed
Cable Network
A75

1978, Oct. 30   Litho.   Perf. 14
304 A75 10c multicolored   .25   .25
305 A75 35c multicolored   1.00   1.00
306 A75 50c multicolored   1.00   1.10
307 A75 75c multicolored   1.25   1.25
      Nos. 304-307 (4)   3.50   3.60

ASEAN Submarine Cable Network. Nos. 304-307 printed in sheets of 100. Stamps have perforations around design and around edges. See No. 429a.

Neptune Spinel — A76

Ships: 35c, Neptune Aries. 50c, Arno Temasek. 75c, Neptune Pearl.

1978, Nov. 18   Litho.   Perf. 13½x14
308 A76 10c multicolored   1.00   .65
309 A76 35c multicolored   1.75   1.75
310 A76 50c multicolored   2.00   2.00
311 A76 75c multicolored   2.75   2.75
      Nos. 308-311 (4)   7.50   7.15

Neptune Oriental Shipping Lines, 10th anniv.

Concorde
A77

Aviation Development: 35c, Boeing 747B. 50c, Vickers-Vimy, 1st aircraft to land in Singapore. 75c, Wright Brothers' Flyer I.

1978, Dec. 16   Perf. 13½
312 A77 10c yellow green & blk   .60   .40
313 A77 35c blue & black   1.40   1.25
314 A77 50c carmine & black   1.60   1.60
315 A77 75c brown & black   2.50   2.50
      Nos. 312-315 (4)   6.10   5.75

75th anniversary of 1st powered flight.

Distance Marker in
Kilometers — A78

Designs: 35c, Tape measure in centimeters. 75c, Scales in grams and kilograms.

1979, Jan. 24   Litho.   Perf. 13x13½
316 A78 10c multicolored   .25   .25
317 A78 35c multicolored   .50   .50
318 A78 75c multicolored   1.25   1.25
      Nos. 316-318 (3)   2.00   2.00

Introduction of metric system.

Vanda
Orchids — A79

Varieties of vanda hybrids. 10c, 35c, horiz.

Perf. 14½x14, 14x14½
1979, Apr. 14   Litho.
319 A79 10c multicolored   .30   .30
320 A79 35c multicolored   .75   .75
321 A79 50c multicolored   1.25   1.25
322 A79 75c multicolored   1.50   1.50
      Nos. 319-322 (4)   3.80   3.80

Envelope
Addressed
to
Postmaster
A80

50c, Envelope addressed to Philatelic Bureau.

1979, July 1   Litho.   Perf. 12½x13
323 A80 10c orange & multi   .25   .25
324 A80 50c dark blue & multi   1.00   1.00

Singapore's postal code system.

Old Phone,
Telephone
Lines — A81

Designs: 35c, Dial, world map. 50c, Push-button phone, skyline. 75c, Line network.

1979, Oct. 5   Litho.   Perf. 13½
325 A81 10c multicolored   .25   .25
326 A81 35c multicolored   .60   .60
327 A81 50c multicolored   .75   .75
328 A81 75c multicolored   1.25   1.25
      Nos. 325-328 (4)   2.85   2.85

Telephone service centenary.

IYC
Emblem,
Lanterns
Festival
A82

IYC Emblem, Children's Drawings: 35c, Singapore Harbor. 50c, "Use Your Hands." 75c, Soccer.

1979, Nov. 10   Litho.   Perf. 13
329 A82 10c multicolored   .25   .25
330 A82 35c multicolored   .60   .60
331 A82 50c multicolored   .75   .75
332 A82 75c multicolored   1.25   1.25
  a.   Souvenir sheet of 4, #329-332 5.50 5.50
      Nos. 329-332 (4)   2.85   2.85

International Year of the Child.

Botanic Gardens, 120th
Anniversary — A83

1979, Dec. 15   Perf. 13½
333 A83 10c shown   .25   .25
334 A83 50c Gazebo   1.25   1.25
335 A83 $1 Greenhouse   1.80   1.80
      Nos. 333-335 (3)   3.30   3.30

Hainan
Junk — A84

1980   Litho.   Perf. 14
336 A84 1c shown   .30   .30
337 A84 5c Clipper   .25   .25
338 A84 10c Fujian junk   .25   .25
  a.   Booklet pane of 10   4.00
339 A84 15c Golekkan   .25   .25
340 A84 20c Palari   .25   .25
341 A84 25c East Indiaman   .30   .25
342 A84 35c Galleon   .50   .25
343 A84 50c Caravel   .60   .25
344 A84 75c Jiangsu trader   1.00   .30
          Size: 41½x24½mm
              Perf. 13½
345 A84 $1 Coaster   1.25   .35
  a.   Imperf., pair   350.00
346 A84 $2 Oil tanker   2.50   .60
347 A84 $5 Screw steamer   4.50   1.75
348 A84 $10 Paddle wheel
            steamer   10.00   6.00
      Nos. 336-348 (13)   21.95 11.05

Issued: #336-344, Apr. 26; others, Apr. 5.

Straits Settlements No. 1, Old
Singapore Map, London 1980
Emblem — A85

London 1980 Emblem and: 35c, Straits Settlements No. 146, letter. $1, Singapore No. 19, map of Straits. $2, Singapore No. 106, letter, 1819.

1980, May 6   Litho.   Perf. 13
349	A85	10c multicolored	.30	.30
350	A85	35c multicolored	.60	.35
351	A85	$1 multicolored	1.10	1.10
352	A85	$2 multicolored	1.50	1.50
a.		Souvenir sheet of 4, #349-352	4.00	4.00
		Nos. 349-352 (4)	3.50	3.25

London 1980 Intl. Stamp Exhib., May 6-14.

Fund Board Emblem,
Keys to
Retirement — A86

1980, July 1   Litho.   Perf. 13
353	A86	10c shown	.25	.25
354	A86	50c Home ownership savings	.50	.50
355	A86	$1 Old age savings	1.25	1.25
		Nos. 353-355 (3)	2.00	2.00

Central Provident Fund Board, 25th anniv.

Map Showing Singapore-Indonesia
Cable Route — A87

1980, Aug. 8   Litho.   Perf. 14
356	A87	10c multicolored	.25	.25
357	A87	35c multicolored	.80	.80
358	A87	50c multicolored	1.10	1.10
359	A87	75c multicolored	1.50	1.50
		Nos. 356-359 (4)	3.65	3.65

ASEAN Submarine Cable Network extension. Stamps perforated around design and around edges. See No. 429a.

Fair
Emblem
A88

1980, Oct. 3   Litho.   Perf. 13
360	A88	10c multicolored	.25	.25
361	A88	35c multicolored	.40	.40
362	A88	75c multicolored	.85	.85
		Nos. 360-362 (3)	1.50	1.50

Asean Trade Fair, Oct. 3-12.

A89

1980, Nov. 2   Litho.   Perf. 13½
363	A89	10c Flame of the wood	.25	.25
364	A89	35c Golden trumpet	.55	.55
365	A89	50c Sky vine	.65	.65
366	A89	75c Bougainvillea	1.25	1.25
		Nos. 363-366 (4)	2.70	2.70

A90

1981, Jan. 24   Litho.   Perf. 14x14½
367	A90	10c multicolored	.30	.30
368	A90	35c multicolored	.40	.40
369	A90	75c multicolored	.75	.75
		Nos. 367-369 (3)	1.45	1.45

Monetary Authority of Singapore, 10th anniv.

No. 54
Surcharged

Perf. 13½x14½
1981, Mar. 5   Photo.   Wmk. 314
| 370 | A8 | 10c on 4c red org & blk | .45 | .45 |

A91

10c, Technical Training (Woodworking). 35c, Building construction. 50c, Electronics. 75c, Precision machinery.

Unwmk.
1981, Apr. 11   Litho.   Perf. 13
371	A91	10c multicolored	.30	.30
372	A91	35c multicolored	.55	.55
373	A91	50c multicolored	.65	.65
374	A91	75c multicolored	.85	.85
		Nos. 371-374 (4)	2.35	2.35

A92

Sports For All: Various sports.

1981, Aug. 25   Litho.   Perf. 14
375	A92	10c multicolored	.55	.55
376	A92	75c multicolored	2.00	2.00
377	A92	$1 multicolored	2.50	2.50
		Nos. 375-377 (3)	5.05	4.75

A93

1981, Nov. 24   Litho.   Perf. 14½
378	A93	10c Man in wheelchair	.25	.25
379	A93	35c Group	.60	.60
380	A93	50c Teacher, student	.70	.70
381	A93	75c Blind communications worker	.80	.80
		Nos. 378-381 (4)	2.35	2.35

Intl. Year of the Disabled.

A94

1981, Dec. 29   Litho.   Perf. 14x13½
382	A94	10c multicolored	.30	.30
383	A94	35c multicolored	.40	.40
384	A94	50c multicolored	.50	.50
385	A94	75c multicolored	.70	.70
386	A94	$1 multicolored	.90	.90
a.		Souvenir sheet of 5, #382-386	4.00	4.00
		Nos. 382-386 (5)	2.80	2.80

Changi airport opening.

A95

1982, Mar. 3   Litho.   Perf. 14x14½
387	A95	10c Clipper	.50	.50
388	A95	50c Blue grassy tiger	1.50	1.50
389	A95	$1 Raja Brooke's birdwing	2.00	2.00
		Nos. 387-389 (3)	4.00	4.00

A96

1982, June 14   Litho.   Perf. 14
390	A96	10c multicolored	.25	.25
391	A96	35c multicolored	.55	.55
392	A96	50c multicolored	.65	.65
393	A96	75c multicolored	.85	.85
		Nos. 390-393 (4)	2.30	2.30

15th ASEAN Ministerial meeting.

A97

1982, July 9   Litho.   Perf. 12
394	A97	10c multicolored	.25	.25
395	A97	75c multicolored	.85	.85
396	A97	$1 multicolored	1.25	1.25
		Nos. 394-396 (3)	2.35	2.35

1982 World Cup.

Sultan Shoal
Lighthouse,
1896 — A98

1982, Aug. 7
397	A98	10c shown	.65	.65
398	A98	75c Horsburgh, 1851	1.40	1.40
399	A98	$1 Raffles, 1855	1.75	1.75
a.		Souvenir sheet of 3, #397-399	5.50	5.50
		Nos. 397-399 (3)	3.80	3.80

10th Anniv.
of PSA
Container
Terminal
A99

1982, Sept. 15   Litho.   Perf. 13½
400	A99	10c Yard gantry cranes	.25	.25
401	A99	35c Computer	.50	.50
402	A99	50c Freightlifter	.65	.65
403	A99	75c Straddle carrier	1.00	1.00
		Nos. 400-403 (4)	2.40	2.40

Scouting
Year — A100

1982, Oct. 15   Litho.   Perf. 14x13½
404	A100	10c Color guard	.25	.25
405	A100	35c Hiking	.55	.55
406	A100	50c Building tower	.65	.65
407	A100	75c Kayaking	1.10	1.10
		Nos. 404-407 (4)	2.55	2.55

Productivity
Movement
A101

1982, Nov. 17   Perf. 13½
408	A101	10c Text	.25	.25
409	A101	35c Housing	.45	.45
410	A101	50c Quality control meeting	.55	.55
411	A101	75c Participation	.90	.90
		Nos. 408-411 (4)	2.15	2.15

Commonwealth
Day — A102

1983, May 14   Litho.   Perf. 13½x13
412	A102	10c multicolored	.25	.25
413	A102	35c multicolored	.45	.45
414	A102	75c multicolored	.50	.50
415	A102	$1 multicolored	.85	.85
		Nos. 412-415 (4)	2.05	2.05

12th Southeast Asia
Games — A103

1983, May 28   Litho.   Perf. 14x13½
416	A103	10c Soccer	.25	.25
417	A103	35c Racket games	.45	.45
418	A103	75c Athletics	.90	.90
419	A103	$1 Swimming	1.10	1.10
		Nos. 416-419 (4)	2.70	2.70

Neighborhood
Watch Safety
Campaign
A104

1983, June 24   Litho.   Perf. 14
420	A104	10c Family	.40	.25
421	A104	35c Children	.70	.70
422	A104	75c Community	1.10	1.10
		Nos. 420-422 (3)	2.20	2.05

BANGKOK '83
Intl. Stamp
Show, Aug. 4-
13 — A105

10c, #282-284, statue of King Chu-lalongkorn (1868-1910). 35c, #304-307, map of southeast Asia. $1, #390-393, Declaration of ASEAN (Assoc. of South East Asian Nations) signatures, 1976.

1983, Aug. 4   Litho.   Perf. 14x14½
423 A105 10c multicolored   .35   .25
424 A105 35c multicolored   .65   .65
425 A105 $1 multicolored   1.40 1.40
  a.   Souvenir sheet of 3, #423-425   4.75 4.75
      Nos. 423-425 (3)   2.40 2.30

ASEAN
Submarine
Cable Network
A106

1983, Sept. 27   Litho.   Perf. 14
426 A106 10c multicolored   .30   .25
427 A106 35c multicolored   .90   .90
428 A106 50c multicolored   1.10 1.10
429 A106 75c multicolored   1.75 1.75
  a.   Souv. sheet of 6, #304, 359,
        426-429   7.00 7.00
      Nos. 426-429 (4)   4.05 4.00

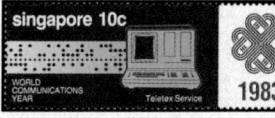

World Communications Year — A107

10c, Telex service. 35c, Telephone numbering plan. 75c, Satellite transmission. $1, Sea communications.

1983, Nov. 10   Litho.   Perf. 13
430 A107 10c multicolored   .35   .25
431 A107 35c multicolored   .70   .70
432 A107 75c multicolored   1.25 1.25
433 A107 $1 multicolored   1.75 1.75
      Nos. 430-433 (4)   4.05 3.95

Coastal
Birds — A108

Perf. 14½x13½
1984, Mar. 15   Litho.
434 A108 10c Slaty-breasted rail   .50   .25
435 A108 35c Black bittern   1.25 1.25
436 A108 50c Brahminy kite   1.75 1.75
437 A108 75c Common moor-
           hens   2.75 2.75
      Nos. 434-437 (4)   6.25 6.00

Natl. Monuments
A109

10c, House of Tan Yeok Nee (merchant), 1885. 35c, Thong Chai Building (former hospital), 1892. 50c, Telok Ayer Market, 1894. $1, Nagore Durgha Muslim Shrine, 1828.

1984, June 7   Litho.   Perf. 12
438 A109 10c multicolored   .25   .25
439 A109 35c multicolored   .50   .50
440 A109 50c multicolored   .75   .75
441 A109 $1 multicolored   1.75 1.75
      Nos. 438-441 (4)   3.25 3.25

A110

1984, Aug. 9   Litho.   Perf. 14
442 A110 10c No. 121   .25   .25
443 A110 35c No. 377   .45   .45
444 A110 50c No. 99   .65   .65
445 A110 75c No. 243   1.00 1.00
446 A110 $1 No. 386   1.40 1.40
447 A110 $2 No. 367   2.50 2.50
  a.   Souvenir sheet of 6, #442-
        447   9.00 9.00
      Nos. 442-447 (6)   6.25 6.25

25th anniv. of self-government.

A111

Total Defense: a, This is our country. b, We are one. c, We work together. d, We are prepared. e, We are ready.

1984, Oct. 26   Litho.   Perf. 12
448   Strip of 5   1.00 1.00
  a.-e. A111 10c any single   .25   .25

Bridges
A112

1985, Mar. 15   Engr.   Perf. 14½x14
449 A112 10c Coleman   .25   .25
450 A112 35c Cavenagh   .40   .40
451 A112 75c Elgin   1.00 1.00
452 A112 $1 Benjamin Sheares   1.50 1.50
      Nos. 449-452 (4)   3.15 3.15

Insects — A113

5c, Ceriagrion cerinorubellum. 10c, Apis javana. 15c, Delta arcuata. 20c, Xylocopa caerulea. 25c, Donacia javana. 35c, Heteroneda reticulata. 50c, Catacanthus nigripes. 75c, Chremistica pontianaka. $1, Homoeoxipha lycoides. $2, Traulia azureipennis. $5, Trithemis aurora. $10, Scambophyllum sangiunolentum.

1985   Litho.   Perf. 13x13½
453 A113 5c multicolored   .25   .25
454 A113 10c multicolored   .25   .25
455 A113 15c multicolored   .25   .25
456 A113 20c multicolored   .25   .25
457 A113 25c multicolored   .30   .30
458 A113 35c multicolored   .50   .50
459 A113 50c multicolored   .65   .65
460 A113 75c multicolored   1.25 1.25

Litho. & Engr.
Size: 35x30mm
461 A113 $1 multicolored   2.25   .60
462 A113 $2 multicolored   3.00 2.00
463 A113 $5 multicolored   7.00 5.00
464 A113 $10 multicolored   13.50 8.00
      Nos. 453-464 (12)   29.45 19.30

Issued: #453-460, 4/24; #461-464, 6/5.

Redrawn
1988   Perf. 13x13½
453a A113 5c   2.75 2.00
454a A113 10c   3.25 1.00
455a A113 15c   15.00 2.00
456a A113 20c   18.00 2.00
457a A113 25c   20.00 3.00
458a A113 35c   47.50 2.50
459a A113 50c   57.50 57.50
460a A113 75c   75.00 10.00
      Nos. 453a-460a (8)   239.00 80.00

Singapore is 20½mm long on Nos. 453a-454a; 21mm long on Nos. 453-454. Rock is 1½mm from bottom right on No. 455; 2½mm on No. 455a. Pink flower touches frame on No. 456; is clear of the frame on No. 456a. Feelers indistinct and left one touches frame on No. 457; feelers sharp and left one ends just below frame on No. 457a.
Vein of leaf at lower left stops short of frame on No. 458; vein touches frame on No. 458a. Leaf at top touches frame on No. 459; leaf is below frame on No. 459a. Wing ends 1½mm above frame on No. 460; wing touches frame at bottom on No. 460a.
Other differences exist in the position and sharpness of the design and colors.

People's Assoc., 25th Anniv. — A114

Montage of public services.

1985, July 1   Perf. 13½x14
465 A114 10c multicolored   .25   .25
466 A114 35c multicolored   .40   .40
467 A114 50c multicolored   .70   .75
468 A114 75c multicolored   1.00 1.00
      Nos. 465-468 (4)   2.35 2.40

Public Housing, 25th Anniv. — A115

Modern housing developments.

1985, Aug. 9
469 A115 10c multicolored   .25   .25
470 A115 35c multicolored   .45   .45
471 A115 50c multicolored   .60   .60
472 A115 75c multicolored   .90   .90
  a.   Souv. sheet of 4, #469-472   4.50 4.50
      Nos. 469-472 (4)   2.20 2.20

Girl Guides, 75th
Anniv. — A116

Activities.

1985, Nov 6   Perf. 14½x14
473 A116 10c Brownies   .25   .25
474 A116 35c Guides   .50   .50
475 A116 50c Seniors   .65   .65
476 A116 75c Guide leaders   1.10 1.10
      Nos. 473-476 (4)   2.50 2.50

Intl. Youth
Year — A117

10c, Youth assoc. emblems. 75c, Hand, sapling. $1, Dove, stick figures.

1985, Dec. 18   Perf. 13
477 A117 10c multicolored   .25   .25
478 A117 75c multicolored   .90   .75
479 A117 $1 multicolored   1.10 1.10
      Nos. 477-479 (3)   2.25 2.10

Indigenous
Fruit — A118

1986, Feb. 26   Litho.   Perf. 14½x14
480 A118 10c Psidium guajava   .40   .25
481 A118 35c Eugenia aquea   .95   .75
482 A118 50c Nephelium lap-
           paceum   1.25 1.25
483 A118 75c Manilkara zapota   1.75 1.75
      Nos. 480-483 (4)   4.35 4.00

Natl. Trade Unions Cong., 25th
Anniv. — A119

Progress: a, Science and technology. b, Communications. c, Industry. d, Education.

1986, May 1   Perf. 13½
484 A119 Strip of 4   1.75 1.75
  a.-d. 10c any single   .25   .25
      Souvenir Sheet
485   Sheet of 4   4.75 4.75
  a.-d. A119 35c any single   .50   .50

EXPO '86,
Vancouver
A120

1986, May 2   Perf. 14½x14
486   Strip of 3   3.75 3.75
  a.   A120 50c Calligraphy   .60   .60
  b.   A120 75c Garland making   1.10 1.10
  c.   A120 $1 Batik printing   1.25 1.25

Economic
Development Board,
25th Anniv. — A121

1986, Aug. 1   Perf. 15
487 A121 10c Automation   .25   .25
488 A121 35c Precision engi-
           neering   .40   .40
489 A121 50c Electronics   .60   .60
490 A121 75c Biotechnology   .70   .70
      Nos. 487-490 (4)   1.95 1.95

Submarine Cable — A122

1986, Sept. 8   Perf. 13½
491 A122 10c multicolored   .45   .25
492 A122 35c multicolored   .90   .60
493 A122 50c multicolored   1.25 1.00
494 A122 75c multicolored   1.50 1.50
      Nos. 491-494 (4)   4.10 3.35

Citizens' Consultative Committees, 21st Anniv. — A123

1986, Oct 15 **Perf. 12**
495 A123 Block of 4 2.75 2.75
 a. 10c multicolored .25 .25
 b. 35c multicolored .50 .50
 c. 50c multicolored .75 .75
 d. 75c multicolored 1.10 1.10

Intl. Peace Year — A124

1986, Dec. 17 Litho. Perf. 14x13½
496 A124 10c People .30 .25
497 A124 35c Southeast Asia
 map .70 .70
498 A124 $1 Globe 1.40 1.40
 Nos. 496-498 (3) 2.40 2.35

Views of Singapore A125

10c, Orchard Road. 50c, Central business district. 75c, Marina Center, Raffles City.

1987, Feb. 25 Perf. 12x12½
499 A125 10c multicolored .25 .25
500 A125 50c multicolored .75 .75
501 A125 $1 multicolored 1.00 1.00
 Nos. 499-501 (3) 2.00 2.00

Assoc. of Southeast Asian Nations (ASEAN), 20th Anniv. — A126

1987, June 15 Perf. 12
502 A126 10c multicolored .25 .25
503 A126 35c multicolored .45 .45
504 A126 50c multicolored .70 .70
505 A126 75c multicolored 1.00 1.00
 Nos. 502-505 (4) 2.40 2.40

National Service, 20th Anniv. — A127

Designs: a, Army. b, Navy. c, Air Force. d, Pledge of Allegiance. e, Singapore Lion.

1987, July 1 Perf. 15x14
506 A127 Strip of 4 2.25 2.25
 a.-d. 10c any single .25 .25
507 A127 Sheet of 5 5.00 5.00
 a.-e. 35c any single .45 .45

River Life — A128

1987, Sept. 2 Perf. 14
508 A128 10c Singapore River .30 .25
509 A128 50c Kallang Basin .90 .90
510 A128 $1 Kranji Reservoir 2.75 2.75
 Nos. 508-510 (3) 3.95 3.90

Natl. Museum Cent. A129

Views of the museum and artifacts: 10c, Majapahis gold bracelet, 14th-15th cent. 75c, Ming fluted kendi (water jar). $1, Seventeen-wave kris (sword with silver hilt, sheath), property of Sultan Abdul Jalil Sabat, 1699.

1987, Oct. 12 Litho. Perf. 13½x14
511 A129 10c multicolored .45 .25
512 A129 75c multicolored 1.50 1.50
513 A129 $1 multicolored 1.75 1.75
 Nos. 511-513 (3) 3.70 3.50

Singapore Science Center, 10th Anniv. A130

Attractions.

1987, Dec. 10 Perf. 14½
514 A130 10c Omni Theater .35 .25
515 A130 35c Omni Planetarium 1.00 1.00
516 A130 75c Cellular model 2.00 2.00
517 A130 $1 Science exhibits 2.60 2.60
 Nos. 514-517 (4) 5.95 5.85

Artillery, Cent. A131

Designs: 10c, 155-Gun Howitzer and Khatib Camp, headquarters of the Singapore Gunners. 35c, 25-Pound gun salute and Singapore City Hall. 50c, 4.5-inch Howitzer and Singapore Cricket Club, c. 1928. $1, Ft. Fullerton Drill Hall, c. 1893, and .405 Maxim gun.

1988, Feb. 22 Litho. Perf. 13½x14
518 A131 10c multicolored .60 .25
519 A131 35c multicolored 1.75 1.25
520 A131 50c multicolored 2.00 2.00
521 A131 $1 multicolored 2.75 2.40
 Nos. 518-521 (4) 7.10 5.90

Mass Transit A132

1988, Mar. 12 Perf. 14
522 A132 10c Rail car, map 1.20 .25
523 A132 50c Elevated train 2.75 2.50
524 A132 $1 Urban subway 4.50 4.00
 Nos. 522-524 (3) 8.45 6.75

See No. 1064.

Natl. Television Broadcast System, 25th Anniv. A133

35c, Studio. 75c, Television, transmission tower. $1, Screen, satellite dish.

1988, Apr. 4 Litho. Perf. 13½x14
525 A133 10c shown .40 .25
526 A133 35c multicolored .85 .85
527 A133 75c multicolored 1.25 1.25
528 A133 $1 multicolored 2.25 2.25
 Nos. 525-528 (4) 4.75 4.60

Public Utilities Board, 25th Anniv. — A134

1988, May 4 Litho. Perf. 13½
529 A134 10c Water works .35 .25
530 A134 50c Electric company 1.20 1.20
531 A134 $1 Fossil fuels 2.10 2.00
 a. Souvenir sheet of 3, #529-531 6.00 6.00
 Nos. 529-531 (3) 3.65 3.45

Courtesy Campaign, 10th Anniv. — A135

Singa the lion (character trademark) and: 10c, Neighbors. 30c, Store service counter. $1, Helping the elderly.

1988, July 6 Litho. Perf. 14½
532 A135 10c multicolored .35 .25
533 A135 30c multicolored .70 .70
534 A135 $1 multicolored 1.90 1.90
 Nos. 532-534 (3) 2.95 2.85

Fire Service, Cent. A136

10c, Turntable ladder truck. $1, 1890s Steam pump.

1988, Nov. 1 Litho. Perf. 13½
535 A136 10c multicolored 1.00 .25
536 A136 $1 multicolored 4.75 4.75

Port Authority, 25th Anniv. — A137

Various facilities.

1989, Apr. 3 Litho. Perf. 14x13½
537 A137 10c multicolored .80 .25
538 A137 30c multi, diff. 1.20 .60
539 A137 75c multi, diff. 1.75 1.75
540 A137 $1 multi, diff. 2.00 2.00
 Nos. 537-540 (4) 5.75 4.60

Old Chinatown A138

1989, May 17 Litho. Perf. 14½
541 A138 10c Sago St. .55 .30
542 A138 35c Pagoda St. 1.40 1.00
543 A138 75c Trengganu St. 2.50 2.50
544 A138 $1 Temple St. 2.75 2.75
 Nos. 541-544 (4) 7.20 6.55

Maps of Singapore — A139

Early 19th cent. map Singapore Showing Principal Residences and Places of Interest: No. 545a, Upper left. No. 545b, Upper right. No. 545c, Lower left. No. 545d, Lower right. No. 546, Singapore and Dependencies. No. 547, Plan of the British Settlement.

1989, July 26 Litho. Perf. 14½
545 A139 Block of 4 7.00 7.00
 a.-d. 15c any single 1.75 1.60
 Size: 33x31mm
 Perf. 12½x13
546 A139 50c multi 3.00 2.50
547 A139 $1 multi 3.50 3.50
 Nos. 545-547 (3) 13.50 13.00

Fish — A140

15c, Clown triggerfish. 30c, Majestic angelfish. 75c, Emperor angelfish. $1, Royal empress angelfish.

1989, Sept. 6 Perf. 14
548 A140 15c multicolored 2.00 2.00
549 A140 30c multicolored 2.10 2.50
550 A140 75c multicolored 4.00 4.00
551 A140 $1 multicolored 4.50 4.25
 Nos. 548-551 (4) 12.60 12.75

Festivals — A141

Children's drawings: 15c, Hari Raya Puasa, by Loke Yoke Yen. 35c, Chinese New Year, by Simon Koh. 75c, Thaipusam, by Henry Setiono. $1, Christmas, by Wendy Ang Lin.

1989, Oct. 25 Litho. Perf. 14½
552 A141 15c multicolored .45 .25
553 A141 35c multicolored .80 .60
554 A141 75c multicolored 1.50 1.50
555 A141 $1 multicolored 2.00 2.00
 a. Souv. sheet of 4, #552-555, perf. 14 5.50 5.50
 Nos. 552-555 (4) 4.75 4.35

Singapore Indoor Stadium — A142

1989, Dec. 27   Litho.   Perf. 14½
556　A142　30c North entrance　　1.00　.35
557　A142　75c Interior　　　　　2.00　1.50
558　A142　$1 East entrance　　　2.25　1.75
　a.　Souvenir sheet of 3, #556-558　5.75　5.75
　　Nos. 556-558 (3)　　　　　5.25　3.60

Sports issue.

Lithographs of
19th Cent.
Singapore
A143

15c, Singapore River, 1839. 30c, Chinatown, 1837. 75c, Waterfront, 1837. $1, View
from Ft. Canning, 1824.

1990, Feb. 21   Litho.   Perf. 13
559　A143　15c multicolored　　　.90　.25
　　Complete booklet, 10 #559　12.00
560　A143　30c multicolored　　　1.25　.75
561　A143　75c multicolored　　　2.25　2.25
562　A143　$1 multicolored　　　2.75　2.75
　　Nos. 559-562 (4)　　　　　7.15　6.00

First Postage Stamps, 150th
Anniv. — A144

Maps and: 50c, Nos. 101-106. 75c, Cover to
Scotland. $1, Cover to Ireland $2, Great Britain Nos. 1, 2.

1990, May 3   Litho.   Perf. 13½
563　A144　50c multicolored　　　1.10　.70
564　A144　75c multicolored　　　1.25　1.25
565　A144　$1 multicolored　　　2.00　2.00
566　A144　$2 multicolored　　　3.00　3.00
　a.　Souvenir sheet of 4, #563-
　　566　　　　　　　　　10.50　10.50
　　Nos. 563-566 (4)　　　　　7.35　6.95

Tourism
A145

1990, July 4   Perf. 14½
567　A145　5c Zoo　　　　　　　.25　.25
568　A145　15c Resort　　　　　.25　.25
　a.　Booklet pane of 10　　　12.00
569　A145　20c City　　　　　　.25　.25
　a.　Booklet pane of 10
　　Complete booklet, #569a　　—
570　A145　25c Dragon boat race　.25　.25
571　A145　30c Hotel　　　　　.35　.35
572　A145　35c Caged birds　　　.45　.40
573　A145　40c Park　　　　　　.50　.45
574　A145　50c Festival　　　　.60　.50
575　A145　75c Building, diff.　　.90　.60
　　Nos. 567-575 (9)　　　　　3.80　3.30

Issued: No. 569a, 3/6/91.

Independence,
25th
Anniv. — A146

1990, Aug. 16   Litho.   Perf. 14x14½
576　A146　15c shown　　　　　1.25　.40
　a.　Booklet pane of 10　　　17.50
577　A146　35c One Singapore　　1.40　1.00
578　A146　75c One hope　　　　2.25　2.25
579　A146　$1 One people　　　2.75　2.75
　　Nos. 576-579 (4)　　　　　7.65　6.40

Tourism
A147

$1, Chinese opera singer, Siong Lim Tem-
ple. $2, Malay dancer, Sultan Mosque. $5,
Indian dancer, Sri Mariamman Temple. $10,
Ballet dancer, Victoria Memorial Hall.

Photo. & Engr.
1990, Oct. 10   Perf. 15x14
580　A147　$1 multicolored　　　1.75　1.60
581　A147　$2 multicolored　　　3.25　2.50
582　A147　$5 multicolored　　　7.50　6.50
583　A147　$10 multicolored　　14.00　14.00
　　Nos. 580-583 (4)　　　　26.50　24.60

Ferns
A148

1990, Nov. 14   Litho.   Perf. 14
584　A148　15c Stag's horn　　　.35　.25
585　A148　35c Maiden hair　　　.75　.75
586　A148　75c Bird's nest　　　1.50　1.50
587　A148　$1 Rabbit's foot　　1.90　1.90
　　Nos. 584-587 (4)　　　　　4.50　4.40

Houses of
Worship
A149

Designs: 20c, Hong San See Temple, 1912.
50c, Abdul Gattoor Mosque, 1910. 75c, Sri
Perumal Temple, 1961. $1, St. Andrew's
Cathedral, 1863.

1991, Jan. 23   Litho.   Perf. 14½
588　20c multicolored　　　　.35　.35
589　20c multicolored　　　　.35　.35
　a.　A149 Pair, #588-589　　.90　.90
590　50c multicolored　　　　.85　.85
591　50c multicolored　　　　.85　.85
　a.　A149 Pair, #590-591　　2.00　2.00
592　75c multicolored　　　　1.25　1.25
593　75c multicolored　　　　1.25　1.25
　a.　A149 Pair, #592-593　　3.00　3.00
594　$1 multicolored　　　　1.50　1.50
595　$1 multicolored　　　　1.50　1.50
　a.　A149 Pair, #594-595　　4.50　4.50
　　Nos. 588-595 (8)　　　　7.90　7.90

Singapore '95 Intl. Philatelic
Exhibition — A151

No. 596, Vanda Miss Joaquim. No. 597,
Dendrobium Anocha.

1991, Apr. 24   Litho.   Perf. 14
596　$2 multicolored　　　　2.50　2.50
597　$2 multicolored　　　　2.50　2.50
　a.　A151 Pair, #596-597 + label　7.00　7.00
　b.　Souvenir sheet of #596-597　11.00　11.00

See Nos. 615-616, 664-665, 685-686, 716-
717.

Civilian
Airports
A152

Designs: 20c, Boeing 747, Changi Terminal
II, 1991. 75c, Boeing 747, Changi Terminal I,
1981. $1, Concorde, Paya Lebar, 1955-1981.
$2, DC-3, Kallang, 1937-1955.

Perf. 13½x14½
1991, July 1   Litho. & Engr.
598　A152　20c multicolored　　.50　.40
599　A152　75c multicolored　　1.75　1.50
600　A152　$1 multicolored　　2.25　2.25
601　A152　$2 multicolored　　6.00　6.00
　　Nos. 598-601 (4)　　　　10.50　10.15

Arachnopsis
Eric Holttum
A153

Orchids: 30c, Cattleya Meadii. $1, Calanthe
vestita.

1991, Aug. 8   Litho.   Perf. 14½x13½
602　A153　20c multicolored　　1.00　.50
603　A153　30c multicolored　　1.40　1.40
604　A153　$1 multicolored　　3.50　3.50
　　Nos. 602-604 (3)　　　　5.90　5.40

Birds — A154

Designs: 20c, Common tailorbird. 35c, Scar-
let-backed flowerpecker. 75c, Black-naped oriole. $1, Common tora.

1991, Sept. 19   Perf. 14
605　A154　20c multicolored　　.45　.25
　a.　Booklet pane of 10　　22.50　22.50
606　A154　35c multicolored　　1.50　1.50
607　A154　75c multicolored　　2.50　2.50
608　A154　$1 multicolored　　3.75　3.75
　　Nos. 605-608 (4)　　　　8.20　8.00

10 Years of
Productivity
A155

1991, Nov. 1   Litho.   Perf. 14x14½
609　A155　20c shown　　　　.25　.25
610　A155　$1 Construction engi-
　　neers　　　　　　　1.60　1.60

Phila Nippon
'91 — A156

Flowers: 30c, Railway creeper. 75c, Asysta-
sia. $1, Singapore rhododendron. $2, Coat
buttons.

1991, Nov. 16   Perf. 14½x14
611　A156　30c multicolored　　.90　.45
612　A156　75c multicolored　　1.40　1.40
613　A156　$1 multicolored　　1.75　1.75
614　A156　$2 multicolored　　3.25　3.25
　a.　Souvenir sheet of 4, #611-
　　614　　　　　　　　9.50　9.50
　　Nos. 611-614 (4)　　　　7.30　6.85

Flower Type of 1991

Designs: No. 615, Dendrobium Sharifah
Fatimah. No. 616, Phalaenopsis Shim Beauty.

1992, Jan. 22   Litho.   Perf. 14
615　A151　$2 multicolored　　3.00　3.00
616　A151　$2 multicolored　　3.00　3.00
　a.　Pair, #615-616 + label　　7.25　7.25
　b.　Souvenir sheet of 2, #615-
　　616　　　　　　　　13.00　13.00

Singapore '95 Intl. Philatelic Exhibition.

Paintings
A157

20c, Singapore Waterfront, 1958. 75c,
Kampung Hut, 1973. $1, Bridge, 1983. $2,

1992, Mar. 11   Litho.   Perf. 14
617　A157　20c multicolored　　.50　.30
618　A157　75c multicolored　　1.00　1.00
619　A157　$1 multicolored　　2.00　2.00
620　A157　$2 multicolored　　2.75　2.75
　　Nos. 617-620 (4)　　　　6.25　6.05

1992
Summer
Olympics,
Barcelona
A158

1992, Apr. 24   Perf. 14
621　A158　20c Soccer　　　　.35　.30
622　A158　35c Relay races　　.45　.35
623　A158　50c Swimming　　　.70　.70
624　A158　75c Basketball　　1.25　1.25
625　A158　$1 Tennis　　　　1.75　1.75
626　A158　$2 Sailing　　　　2.40　2.40
　a.　Souvenir sheet of 6, #621-
　　626　　　　　　　　11.00　11.00
　　Nos. 621-626 (6)　　　　6.90　6.75

No. 626a exists with two different inscrip-
tions in the bottom selvage: "XXVth Olympic
Games 1992 Barcelona" and "Games of the
XXVth Olympiad."

Costumes,
1910 — A159

1992, Apr. 24   Litho.   Perf. 14½
627　A159　20c Chinese family　　.45　.30
628　A159　35c Malay family　　.70　.55
629　A159　75c Indian family　　1.50　1.50
630　A159　$2 Straits Chinese
　　family　　　　　　2.25　2.25
　　Nos. 627-630 (4)　　　　4.90　4.60

Natl. Military
Forces, 25th
Anniv. — A160

Designs: 35c, Frogman with gun, fighter
plane, artillery. $1, Fighter, tank, ship.

1992, July 1
631　A160　20c multicolored　　.40　.40
632　A160　35c multicolored　　1.25　1.25
633　A160　$1 multicolored　　3.25　3.25
　　Nos. 631-633 (3)　　　　4.90　4.90

Visit ASEAN Year, 25th Anniv. A161

Designs: 20c, Mask, bird, sea life. 35c, Costumed women. $1, Outdoor scenery.

1992, Aug. 8
634	A161	20c multicolored	.45	.30
635	A161	35c multicolored	1.25	1.25
636	A161	$1 multicolored	2.40	2.40
		Nos. 634-636 (3)	4.10	3.95

Crabs A162

Designs: 20c, Mosaic crab. 50c, Johnson's freshwater crab. 75c, Singapore freshwater crab. $1, Swamp forest crab.

1992, Aug. 21   Perf. 14½x15
637	A162	20c multicolored	.45	.30
a.		Booklet pane of 10	13.00	
638	A162	50c multicolored	1.00	1.00
639	A162	75c multicolored	1.75	1.75
640	A162	$1 multicolored	2.25	2.25
		Nos. 637-640 (4)	5.45	5.30

Currency, Notes and Coins — A163

1992, Oct. 2   Litho.   Perf. 14½
641	A163	20c Coins	.75	.40
642		75c Coin, flowers on note	1.50	1.50
643		$1 Boat on note, coins	2.00	2.00
644		$2 Bird on note	3.00	3.00
a.	A163	Block of 4, #641-644	8.25	8.25
		Nos. 641-644 (4)	7.25	6.90

Wild Animals A164

1993, Jan. 13   Litho.   Perf. 14½x15
645	A164	20c Sun bear	.30	.30
646	A164	30c Orangutan	.60	.60
647	A164	75c Slow loris	1.40	1.40
648	A164	$2 Large mouse deer	4.00	4.00
		Nos. 645-648 (4)	6.30	6.30

Greetings Stamps — A165

a, Thank you. b, Congratulations. c, Best wishes. d, Happy birthday. e, Get well soon.

Perf. 14½x14 on 3 Sides
1993, Feb. 10   Booklet Stamps
649	A165	20c Strip of 5, #a.-e.	3.50	3.50
f.		Booklet pane of 2 #649	7.25	7.25

Preservation of Tanjong Pagar — A166

1993, Mar. 10   Litho.   Perf. 14
650	A166	20c shown	.40	.30
651	A166	30c Building facade, tower	1.50	1.50
652	A166	$2 Aerial view	4.50	4.50
		Nos. 650-652 (3)	6.40	6.30

Cranes, by Chen Wen Hsi — A167

1993, May 29   Perf. 12x11½
653	A167	$2 multicolored	3.00	3.00
		Indopex '93.		

A168

1993, June 12   Litho.   Perf. 14
654	A168	20c Soccer	.40	.30
655	A168	35c Basketball	.70	.60
656	A168	50c Badminton	.90	.90
657	A168	75c Running	1.00	1.00
658	A168	$1 Water polo	1.40	1.40
659	A168	$2 Yachting	2.25	2.00
		Nos. 654-659 (6)	6.65	6.20

17th Southeast Asian (SEA) Games, Singapore.

Butterflies A169

1993, Aug. 21   Litho.   Perf. 14½
660	A169	20c Plain tiger	.30	.30
a.		Booklet pane of 10	11.50	
661	A169	50c Malay lacewing	.80	.80
662	A169	75c Palm king	1.50	1.50
663	A169	$1 Banded swallow-tail	2.00	2.00
		Nos. 660-663 (4)	4.60	4.60

Flower Type of 1991
1993, Aug. 13   Size: 26x34mm
664	A151	$2 Phalaenopsis amabilis	3.00	3.00
665	A151	$2 Vanda sumatrana	3.00	3.00
a.		Pair, #664-665 + label	7.50	7.50
b.		Souvenir sheet of 2, #664-665, perf. 15x14½	8.00	8.00

Singapore '95 World Stamp Exhibition and Taipei '93, Asian Intl. Invitation Stamp Exhibition (#665b).

Fruits — A170

1993, Oct. 1   Litho.   Perf. 14½x14
666	A170	20c Papaya	.50	.30
667	A170	35c Pomegranate	.75	.60
668	A170	75c Starfruit	1.50	1.50
669	A170	$2 Durian	2.25	2.25
a.		Souvenir sheet of 4, #666-669	6.00	6.00
		Nos. 666-669 (4)	5.00	4.65

Bangkok '93 (#669a).

Chinese Egrets — A171

Designs: 20c, Two, one with bill in water. 25c, Two, one with fish in mouth. 30c, Two facing opposite directions. 35c, In flight.

1993, Nov. 10   Litho.   Perf. 13½x14
670	A171	20c multicolored	.75	.40
671	A171	25c multicolored	.80	.80
672	A171	30c multicolored	1.25	1.25
673	A171	35c multicolored	1.50	1.50
a.		Strip of 4, #670-673	5.25	5.25

World Wildlife Fund.

Palm Tree — A171a

1993, Nov. 24   Photo.   Die Cut
Self-Adhesive
Booklet Stamp
673B	A171a	(20c) multicolored	.75	.75
c.		Booklet pane of 15	13.50	13.50

By its nature, No. 673c is a complete booklet. The peelable backing serves as a booklet cover.

Marine Life — A172

5c, Tiger cowrie. 20c, Sea fan. (20c), Blue-spotted stingray. 25c, Tunicate. 30c, Clownfish. 35c, Nudibranch. 40c, Sea urchin. 50c, Soft coral. 75c, Pin cushion star. $1, Knob coral. $2, Mushroom coral. $5, Bubble coral. $10, Octopus coral. No. 684B, Blue-spotted stingray.

Perf. 13x13½, 13½x14 (#675B)
1994			**Litho.**	
674	A172	5c multi	.25	.25
675	A172	20c multi	.35	.25
a.		Booklet pane of 10	4.00	
675B	A172	(20c) multi	.40	.25
676	A172	25c multi	.50	.40
677	A172	30c multi	.55	.55
678	A172	35c multi	.65	.65
679	A172	40c multi	.70	.70
680	A172	50c multi	.90	.90
681	A172	75c multi	1.40	1.40

Litho. & Engraved
Perf. 14 Syncopated
682	A172	$1 multi	2.00	2.00
683	A172	$2 multi	3.75	3.75
684	A172	$5 multi	9.00	9.00
684A	A172	$10 multi	16.00	16.00
		Nos. 674-684A (13)	36.45	36.10

Self-Adhesive
Die Cut Perf. 8½
684B	A172	(20c) multi	.75	.75
c.		Booklet pane of 10	13.00	

Nos. 675B, 684B inscribed "FOR LOCAL ADDRESSES ONLY." By its nature, No. 684c is a complete booklet. The peelable paper backing serves as a booklet cover.
Issued: 5c-75c, 1/12/94; $1-$10, 3/23/94; #675B, 684B, 11/16/94.
See Nos. 816-824.

Flower Type of 1991

Designs: No. 685, Paphiopedilum vicotriaregina. No. 686, Dendrobium smillieae.

1994, Feb. 18   Litho.   Perf. 14½
Size: 26x35mm
685	A151	$2 multicolored	3.50	3.50
686	A151	$2 multicolored	3.50	3.50
a.		Pair, #685-686 + label	8.50	8.50
b.		Souvenir sheet of 2, #685-686	9.00	9.00

Singapore '95 and Hong Kong '94 (#686b).

Spring Festival — A173

1994, May 18   Litho.   Perf. 13½
687	A173	20c Ballet	.40	.25
688	A173	30c Mime, puppets	.80	.80
689	A173	50c Musicians	1.00	1.00
690	A173	$1 Crafts	2.00	2.00
		Nos. 687-690 (4)	4.20	4.05

Operationally Ready Natl. Servicemen, 25th Anniv. — A174

Civilian-soldiers: 20c, Saluting flag, aiming anti-tank missile. 30c, With family, on jungle patrol with automatic rifle. 35c, Reading newspaper, aiming machine gun. 75c, Working with computer, and as commander, looking through binoculars.

1994, July 1   Litho.   Perf. 13½
691	A174	20c multicolored	.75	.40
692	A174	30c multicolored	1.00	1.00
693	A174	35c multicolored	1.25	1.25
694	A174	75c multicolored	2.00	2.00
		Nos. 691-694 (4)	5.00	4.65

Herons — A175

1994, Aug. 16   Litho.   Perf. 14
695		20c Black-crowned night heron	.65	.65
a.		Booklet pane of 10	11.50	
696		50c Little heron	.95	.95
697		75c Purple heron	1.00	1.00
698		$1 Gray heron	1.40	1.40
a.	A175	Block of 4, #695-698	5.50	5.50
		Nos. 695-698 (4)	4.00	4.00

Greetings Stamps — A175a

#698B, Birthday cake. #698C, Bouquet of flowers. #698D, Gift-wrapped present. #698E, Fireworks. #698F, Balloons.

Die Cut Perf. 11½

1994, Sept. 14 Litho.

Self-Adhesive

Booklet Stamps

698B	A175a (20c) multicolored	.75	*.85*
698C	A175a (20c) multicolored	.75	*.85*
698D	A175a (20c) multicolored	.75	*.85*
698E	A175a (20c) multicolored	.75	*.85*
698F	A175a (20c) multicolored	.75	*.85*
g.	Bklt. pane, 2 ea #698B-698F	7.50	*8.50*
	Nos. 698B-698F (5)	3.75	*4.25*

Nos. 698B-693F inscribed "For Local Addresses Only." By its nature, No. 698Fg is a complete booklet. The peelable paper backing serves as a booklet cover. The outside of the cover contains 10 peelable labels.

Modern Singapore, 175th Anniv. — A176

Early, modern scenes: 20c, Schoolchildren reading, graduating seniors. 50c, Horse-drawn carriages, high-speed train. 75c, Small boats, container ship dock. $1, Skyline.

1994, Sept. 30 ***Perf. 13½x14***

699	A176 20c multicolored	.55	.55
700	A176 50c multicolored	.90	.90
701	A176 75c multicolored	1.10	1.10
702	A176 $1 multicolored	1.50	1.50
a.	Souvenir sheet of 4, #699-702	5.00	5.00
	Nos. 699-702 (4)	4.05	4.05

No. 702a exists with Singpex '94 overprint. Value $25.

ICAO, 50th Anniv. A177

Designs: 35c, Control tower, passenger jet. 75c, Terminal, Concord jet. $2, Control tower, communication satellite, passenger jet.

1994, Oct. 5 Litho. ***Perf. 14***

703	A177 20c multicolored	.35	.35
704	A177 35c multicolored	.65	.65
705	A177 75c multicolored	1.00	1.00
706	A177 $2 multicolored	2.75	2.75
	Nos. 703-706 (4)	4.75	4.75

Love Stamps — A178

#707, "Love" in three different inscriptions. #708, Spiral of "Love." #709, "Love" on two lines. #710, "Love" in different languages. #711, Geometrical "Love."

Die Cut Perf. 11½

1995, Feb. 8 Litho.

Self-Adhesive

Booklet Stamps

707	A178 (20c) multicolored	1.10	1.10
708	A178 (20c) multicolored	1.10	1.10
709	A178 (20c) multicolored	1.10	1.10
710	A178 (20c) multicolored	1.10	1.10
711	A178 (20c) multicolored	1.10	1.10
a.	Booklet pane, 2 each #707-711	12.50	
	Nos. 707-711 (5)	5.50	5.50

Nos. 707-711 inscribed "FOR LOCAL ADDRESSES ONLY." By its nature, No. 711a is a complete booklet. The peelable paper backing serves as a booklet cover. The outside of the cover contains 10 peelable labels.

Meet in Singapore — A179

Scenes in Suntec City: (20c), Intl. Convention & Exhibition Center. 75c, High rise buildings. $1, Temasek Boulevard. $2, Fountain Terrace.

1995, Jan. 11 ***Perf. 13½x14***

712	A179 (20c) multicolored	.40	.30
713	A179 75c multicolored	1.00	1.00
714	A179 $1 multicolored	1.50	1.50
715	A179 $2 multicolored	3.00	3.00
	Nos. 712-715 (4)	5.90	5.80

Singapore '95. No. 712 inscribed "FOR LOCAL ADDRESSES ONLY."

Souvenir Sheets of 2, #712, 715 Inscribed:

715a	FIP DAY	8.50	8.50
715b	OLYMPIC DAY-YOUTH	8.50	8.50
715c	FIAP DAY	8.50	8.50
715d	LETTER WRITING DAY	8.50	8.50
715e	STAMP COLLECTING DAY	8.50	8.50
715f	SINGAPORE '95 DAY	8.50	8.50
715g	PHILATELIC MUSEUM DAY	8.50	8.50
715h	SINGAPORE POST DAY	8.50	8.50
715i	AWARDS DAY	8.50	8.50
715j	THEMATIC PHILATELY DAY	8.50	8.50

Flower Type of 1991

Designs: No. 716, Vanda Marlie Dolera, No. 717, Vanda limbata.

1995, Mar. 15 Litho. ***Perf. 14***

716	A151 $2 multicolored	2.50	2.50
717	A151 $2 multicolored	2.50	2.50
a.	Pair, #716-717 + label	6.00	*6.00*
b.	Souvenir sheet, #716-717	11.50	11.50
c.	Souvenir sheet, #716-717	10.00	10.00

Singapore '95 (#717a-717c).

The margin of No. 717b pictures a chimpanzee in the jungle and No. 717c pictures a fish.

No. 717b exists imperf. Value, $50.

Three limited edition sheets were issued 9/1/95 at the show. They sold for 50, 12.5 and 2.9 times face. Values, $550, $220, $350.

Independence, 30th Anniv. — A180

"My Singapore, My Country, Happy Birthday" in various languages and: 20c, "30" formed in ribbon, vert. 50c, #471, flower. 75c, #598, Music sheet. $1, Natl. flag, #489, music sheets, vert.

Perf. 14x13½, 13½x14

1995, Apr. 19 Litho.

718	A180 (20c) multicolored	.40	.30
719	A180 50c multicolored	.80	.80
720	A180 75c multicolored	1.25	1.25
721	A180 $1 multicolored	1.50	1.50
a.	Souvenir sheet of 4, #718-721	6.00	6.00
	Nos. 718-721 (4)	3.95	3.85

No. 718 inscribed "For Local Addresses Only." No. 721a is a continuous design.

End of World War II, 50th Anniv. A181

Designs: (20c), Crowd celebrating, Straits Settlements #271, vert. 60c, Lord Mountbatten receiving Japanese surrender of Singapore, Straits Settlements #265, vert. 70c, Food kitchen. $2, Police road block.

Perf. 14x13½, 13½x14

1995, June 21 Litho.

723	A181 (20c) multicolored	.30	.30
724	A181 60c multicolored	.90	.90
725	A181 70c multicolored	1.00	1.00
726	A181 $2 multicolored	2.75	2.75
	Nos. 723-726 (4)	4.95	4.95

No. 723 inscribed "For Local Addresses Only" and sold for 20c on day of issue.

New Six Digit Postal Code A182

1995, Sept. 1 Litho. ***Perf. 14x14½***

727	A182 (20c) shown	.40	.30
728	A182 $2 Six boxes, numbers	2.75	2.75

No. 728 inscribed "For Local Addresses Only."

Philatelic Museum, Singapore A183

Museum building, various stamps, featuring: 20c, #12. 50c, #157. 60c, #661. $2, Displays of stamps.

1995, Aug. 19 ***Perf. 13x13½***

729	A183 (20c) multicolored	1.00	1.00
730	A183 50c multicolored	1.10	1.10
731	A183 60c multicolored	1.25	1.25
732	A183 $2 multicolored	3.25	3.25
	Nos. 729-732 (4)	6.60	6.60

No. 729 inscribed "For Local Addresses Only."

Fish A184

(20c), Yellow-faced angelfish. 60c, Harlequin sweetlips. 70c, Lionfish. $1, Longfin bannerfish.

1995, July 19 Litho. ***Perf. 13½x14***

733	A184 (20c) multi	.40	.40
	Complete booklet, 10 #733	5.00	
734	A184 60c multi	1.00	1.00
735	A184 70c multi	1.25	1.25
736	A184 $1 multi	1.75	1.75
	Nos. 733-736 (4)	4.40	4.40

No. 733 inscribed "For Local Addresses Only."

Paintings in Singapore Art Museum A185

Designs: (20c), Tropical Fruits, by Georgette Chen. 30c, Bali Beach, by Cheong Soo Pieng. 70c, Gibbons, by Chen Wen Hsi. $2, Shi (Lion), by Pan Shou (calligraphy).

1995, Oct. 20 Litho. ***Perf. 12½***

737	A185 (20c) multicolored	.40	.40
738	A185 30c multicolored	.60	.60
739	A185 70c multicolored	1.25	1.25

Perf. 13½x13

740	A185 $2 multicolored	3.75	3.75
	Nos. 737-740 (4)	6.00	6.00

No. 737 inscribed "For Local Addresses Only." No. 740 is 22½x39mm.

New Year 1996 (Year of the Rat) — A186

1996, Feb. 9 Litho. ***Perf. 12***

741	A186 (20c) shown	.40	.30
742	A186 $2 Rat with orange	3.50	3.50

Souvenir Sheet

742A	A186 Sheet of 2, #742, 742Ab	40.00	40.00
b.	22c like #741	.25	.25
c.	As #742A, diff. sheet margin	22.50	22.50
d.	As #742A, diff. sheet margin	25.00	25.00

No. 741 inscribed "For Local Addresses Only."

Sheet margins contain exhibition emblems for: #742A: Indonesia '96; #742Ac, China '96; #742Ad, CAPEX '96.

Issued: #742A, 3/21; #742Ac, 5/18; #742Ad, 6/8.

Architectural Styles — A187

Designs: (20c), Bukit Pasoh, Chinatown. 35c, Jalan Sultan, Kampong Glam. 70c, Dalhousie Lane, Little India. $1, Supreme Court, Civic District.

1996, Jan. 17 ***Perf. 13½x14***

743	A187 (20c) multicolored	.45	.30
744	A187 35c multicolored	.65	.65
745	A187 70c multicolored	1.25	1.25
746	A187 $1 multicolored	1.75	1.75
	Nos. 743-746 (4)	4.10	3.95

No. 743 inscribed "For Local Addresses Only."

Old Maps of Singapore A188

Designs: (20c), Old Straits. 60c, Detail of town. $1, Part of Malay Penisula, Singapore. $2, Town and entrance.

1996, Mar. 13 Litho. ***Perf. 12***

747	A188 (20c) multicolored	.50	.25
748	A188 60c multicolored	1.00	1.00
749	A188 $1 multicolored	1.50	1.50
750	A188 $2 multicolored	2.75	2.75
	Nos. 747-750 (4)	5.75	5.50

No. 747 inscribed "For Local Addresses Only."

Greetings Stamps — A189

Children's drawings about courtesy: (22c), #755Bc, Child telling another to be quiet in library. 35c, Children helping elderly during outdoor activities. 50c, Giving seat at bus stop to expectant mother. 60c, Sharing umbrella. $1, Giving up seat on bus to senior citizen.

Booklet Stamps

Die Cut Perf. 11

1996, July 10 Litho.

Self-Adhesive

751	A189 (22c) multicolored	.40	.30
a.	Booklet pane of 10	4.50	
752	A189 35c multicolored	.75	.75
753	A189 50c multicolored	1.00	1.00
754	A189 60c multicolored	1.25	1.25

755 A189 $1 multicolored 1.75 1.75
a. Booklet pane of 10, 5 #751, 2 #752, 1 each #753-755 9.50
Nos. 751-755 (5) 5.15 5.05

Souvenir Sheet

755B A189 Sheet of 5, #752-755, 755Bc 6.50 6.50
c. 22c multicolored *1.25 1.25*

No. 751 inscribed "For Local Addresses Only." By their nature Nos. 751a and 755a are complete booklets. The peelable paper backing serves as a booklet cover. The outside of the cover contains 10 peelable labels.

1996 Summer Olympic Games, Atlanta — A190

Designs: (22c), #759Ab, Board, dinghy sailing. 60c, Soccer, tennis. 70c, Pole vault, hurdles. $2, Diving, swimming.

1996, July 19 Litho. *Perf. 14½*
756 A190 (22c) multicolored .50 .30
757 A190 60c multicolored 1.00 1.00
758 A190 70c multicolored 1.25 1.25
759 A190 $2 multicolored 2.50 2.50
Nos. 756-759 (4) 5.25 5.05

Souvenir Sheet

759A A190 Sheet of 4, #757-759, 759Ab 5.75 5.75
b. 22c multicolored 1.00 1.00

No. 756 inscribed "For Local Addresses Only."

Asian Civilizations Museum — A191

(22c), Calligraphy in Caoshu, Ming Dynasty, 17th cent. 60c, Javanese Divination manuscript, Surkarta (Solo), Indonesia, 1842. 70c, Temple hanging, Tamilnadu, South India, 19th cent. $2, Calligraphic implements, Persia and Turkey, 17th-19th cent.

1996, June 5 Litho. *Perf. 13½x14*
760 A191 (22c) multicolored .50 .50
761 A191 60c multicolored 1.00 1.00
762 A191 70c multicolored 1.25 1.25
763 A191 $2 multicolored 2.75 2.75
Nos. 760-763 (4) 5.50 5.50

No. 760 inscribed "For Local Addresses Only."

Care for Nature — A192

Native trees: (22c), Cinnamomum iners. 60c, Hibiscus tiliaceus. 70c, Parkia speciosa. $1, Terminalia catappa.

1996, Sept. 11 Litho. *Perf. 13½*
764 A192 (22c) multicolored .35 .30
a. Booklet pane of 10 7.00
Complete booklet, #764a 7.50
765 A192 60c multicolored .90 .90
766 A192 70c multicolored 1.00 1.00
767 A192 $1 multicolored 1.50 1.50
Nos. 764-767 (4) 3.75 3.70

No. 764 inscribed "For Local Addresses Only."

Panmen, Suzhou, China — A193

Design: 60c, Singapore waterfront.

1996, Oct. 9 Litho. *Perf. 13x13½*
768 A193 (22c) multicolored .35 .30
769 A193 60c multicolored 1.60 1.60

Souvenir Sheet

769A A193 Sheet of 2, #769, 769Ab 4.00 4.00
b. 22c like #768 .75 .75
c. As #769A, ovptd. in sheet margin 30.00 30.00

No. 768 inscribed "For Local Addresses Only."

No. 769Ac is ovptd. in sheet margin with violet on gold Singapore-China Stamp Exhibition emblem.

See People's Republic of China Nos. 2733-2734.

First World Trade Organization Ministerial Conference — A194

1996, Nov. 20 Litho. *Perf. 14*
770 A194 (22c) pink, vio & multi .50 .40
771 A194 60c ver, grn & multi 1.00 1.00
772 A194 $1 bl, yel org & multi 1.50 1.50
773 A194 $2 grn, car & multi 2.50 2.50
Nos. 770-773 (4) 5.50 5.40

No. 770 inscribed "For Local Addresses Only."

New Year 1997 (Year of the Ox) A195

Nos. 774, 775, Different stylized oxen.

1997, Jan. 10 *Perf. 13½x14*
774 A195 (22c) multicolored .65 .65
775 A195 $2 multicolored 3.00 3.00
a. Sheet, 9 each #774-775 45.00
b. Souvenir sheet, #775, #775d 12.50 12.50
c. As "b," diff. sheet margin 12.00 12.00
d. 22c like #774 *4.50 5.00*
e. As "b," diff. sheet margin 10.00 10.00

No. 774 inscribed "For Local Addresses Only."

Sheet margin contains exhibition emblem: #775b Hong Kong '97; #775c Pacific '97; #775e Shanghai 1997.

Issued: #775b, 2/12/97; #775c, 5/29/97; #775e, 11/19/97.

Traditional Games — A196

1997, Feb. 21 Litho. *Perf. 14½*
776 A196 (22c) Shuttlecock .30 .30
777 A196 35c Marbles .50 .50
778 A196 60c Tops .80 .80
779 A196 $1 Fivestones 1.40 1.40
a. Souvenir sheet of 4, #776-779 3.50 3.50
Nos. 776-779 (4) 3.00 3.00

No. 776 inscribed "For Local Addresses Only." Singpex '97 (#779a).

Ground Transportation — A197

1997, Mar. 19 *Perf. 13½*
780 A197 5c Bullock cart .25 .25
781 A197 20c Bicycle .30 .25
782 A197 (22c) Rickshaw .30 .25
783 A197 30c Electric tram .40 .40
784 A197 35c Trolley bus .50 .50
785 A197 40c Trishaw .55 .55
786 A197 50c Vintage car .70 .70
787 A197 60c Horse-drawn carriage .85 .85
788 A197 70c Fire engine .95 .95
Nos. 780-788 (9) 4.80 4.70

Souvenir Sheet

788A A197 Sheet, #780-781, 783-788, 788Ab 6.50 6.50
b. 22c like #782 .90 .90

Self-Adhesive

Serpentine Die Cut Perf. 11½

Booklet Stamp

789 A197 (22c) like #782 .40 .40
a. Booklet pane of 10 7.00

Nos. 782, 789 are inscribed "For Local Addresses Only." Nos. 780, 783-784, 787-788 are horiz.

By its nature No. 789a is a complete booklet. The peelable paper backing serves as a booklet cover.

Size: 28x35mm (#790, 792), 43x24mm (#791, 793)

$1, Taxi. $2, Bus, horiz. $5, Mass rapid transit system. $10, Light rapid transit system, horiz.

Litho. & Engr.

1997, Apr. 23 *Perf. 13*
790 A197 $1 multicolored 1.25 1.00
791 A197 $2 multicolored 3.00 2.00
792 A197 $5 multicolored 6.00 5.00
793 A197 $10 multicolored 12.00 12.00
a. Souvenir sheet, #790-793 25.00 25.00
Nos. 790-793 (4) 22.25 20.00

Greetings Stamps — A198

Word "Friends" used in making designs: #794, Man's head. #795, Sharing umbrella. #796, Penguins. #797, Butterflies, hand. #798, Coffee cup. #799, Flower. #800, Candle. #801, Tree. #802, Jar holding stars. #803, Two cans connected by string.

Serpentine Die Cut 14½

1997, May 14 Litho.

Self-Adhesive

Booklet Stamps

794 A198 (22c) multicolored .55 .55
795 A198 (22c) multicolored .55 .55
796 A198 (22c) multicolored .55 .55
797 A198 (22c) multicolored .55 .55
798 A198 (22c) multicolored .55 .55
a. Booklet pane, 2 each #794-798 5.50 *5.50*
Nos. 794-798 (5) 2.75 2.75
799 A198 (22c) multicolored .55 .55
800 A198 (22c) multicolored .55 .55
801 A198 (22c) multicolored .55 .55
802 A198 (22c) multicolored .55 .55
803 A198 (22c) multicolored .55 .55
a. Booklet pane, 2 each #799-803 5.50 *5.50*
Nos. 799-803 (5) 2.75 2.75

Nos. 794-803 are inscribed "For Local Addresses Only." By their nature Nos. 798a and 803a are complete booklets. The peelable paper backing serves as a booklet cover. The outside cover contains 10 peelable labels.

Upgrading of Public Housing — A199

Designs: (22c) New look for the precinct. 30c, Outdoor facilities. 70c, Landscaped gardens. $1, Additional space, balcony.

1997, July 16 Litho. *Perf. 14*
804 A199 (22c) multicolored .35 .25
805 A199 30c multicolored .45 .45
806 A199 70c multicolored 1.00 1.00
807 A199 $1 multicolored 1.25 1.25
Nos. 804-807 (4) 3.05 2.95

No. 804 is inscribed "For Local Addresses Only."

ASEAN, 30th Anniv. — A200

Designs: (22c), 30 years of "dates," globe, hands clasped, sky. 35c, Southeast Asian cultures. 60c, Satellite dish, circuit board, map of Southeast Asia, sky. $1, Tourist attractions in ASEAN countries.

1997, Aug. 8 Litho. *Perf. 14*
808 A200 (22c) multicolored .40 .25
809 A200 35c multicolored .55 .55
810 A200 60c multicolored .90 .90
811 A200 $1 multicolored 1.40 1.40
Nos. 808-811 (4) 3.25 3.10

No. 808 is inscribed "For Local Addresses Only."

Value is for stamp with surrounding selvage.

Protection of the Environment — A201

(22c), Clean Environment. 60c, Clean waters. 70c, Clean air. $1, Clean homes.

1997, Sept. 13 Litho. *Perf. 14x13½*
812 A201 (22c) multicolored .30 .25
a. Booklet pane of 10 3.75
Complete booklet, #812a 3.75
813 A201 60c multicolored .70 .70
814 A201 70c multicolored .80 .80
815 A201 $1 multicolored 1.00 1.00
Nos. 812-815 (4) 2.80 2.75

No. 812 is inscribed "For Local Addresses Only."

Marine Life Type of 1994

1997 Photo. *Perf. 13x13½*
816 A172 5c like #674 7.00 3.00
816A A172 (20c) like #675B 3.50 2.50
817 A172 25c like #676 50.00 2.00
818 A172 30c like #677 4.00 1.50
819 A172 35c like #678 5.00 1.75
820 A172 40c like #679 5.00 2.00
821 A172 50c like #680 6.00 1.50

Photo. & Embossed

Perf. 14 Syncopated Type A (2 Sides)

822 A172 $1 like #682 16.00 3.50
822A A172 $2 like #683 11.00 11.00
823 A172 $5 like #684 37.50 20.00
824 A172 $10 like #684A 47.50 25.00
Nos. 816-824 (11) 192.50 73.75

No. 816A is inscribed "For Local Addresses Only."

Nos. 822-824 have embossed logo in center of stamp and denomination and country are white. Nos. 682, 684, 684A have embossed lettering for country name and denomination.

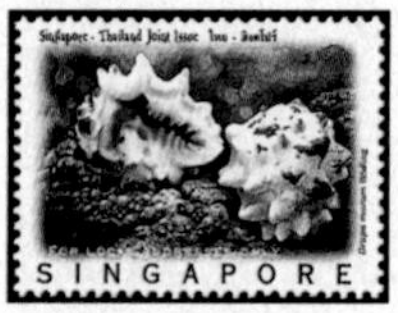

Shells of Singapore and Thailand
A202

Designs: (22c), Drupa morum. 35c, Nerita chamaeleon. 60c, Littoraria melanostoma. $1, Cryptospira elegans.

1997, Oct. 9 Litho. *Perf. 13x14*

825 A202 (22c) multicolored .40 .25
826 A202 35c multicolored .45 .45
827 A202 60c multicolored .80 .80
828 A202 $1 multicolored 1.50 1.50
Nos. 825-828 (4) 3.15 3.00

Souvenir Sheet

828A A202 Sheet of 4, #826-828, #828Ab 3.50 3.50
b. 22c like #825 .85 *.85*

No. 825 inscribed "For Local Addresses Only."
See Thailand Nos. 1771-1774.

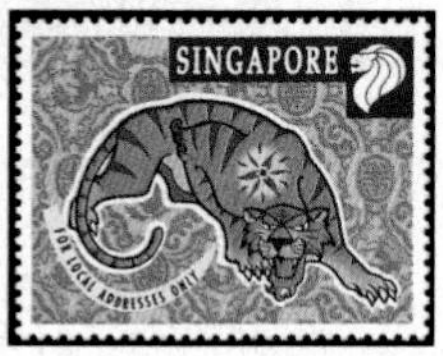

New Year 1998 (Year of the Tiger)
A203

Different stylized tigers.

1998, Jan. 9 Litho. *Perf. 13x14*

829 A203 (22c) multicolored .35 .30
830 A203 $2 multicolored 2.25 2.25
a. Horiz. or vert. pair, #829-830 3.00 *3.00*
b. Sheet of 9 each, #829-830 27.50 *27.50*

Souvenir Sheet

830C A203 Sheet of 2, #830, #830Cd 5.00 5.00
d. 22c like #829 .90 *.90*
e. As #830C, diff. inscription 5.25 5.25

Israel '98 (#830C). Italia '98 (#830Ce).
No. 829 inscribed "For Local Addresses Only."
Stamps in No. 830b are arranged in a checkerboard fashion.
Issued: #830Ce, 10/23/98.

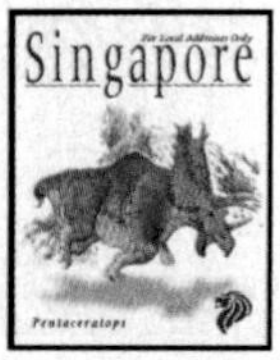

Dinosaurs — A204

Self-Adhesive

1998, Apr. 22 Photo. *Die Cut*

831 A204 (22c) Pentaceratops .35 .35
832 A204 (22c) Apatosaurus .35 .35
833 A204 (22c) Albertosaurus .35 .35
a. Pane, 5 each #831-833 7.00
Nos. 831-833 (3) 1.05 1.05

Nos. 831-833 are inscribed "For Local Addresses Only."

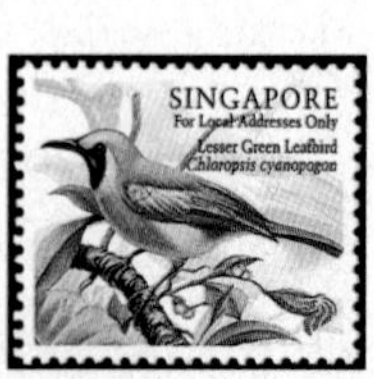

A205

Songbirds: (22c), Lesser green leafbird. 60c, Magpie robin. 70c, Straw-headed bulbul. $2, Yellow-bellied prinia.

Granite Paper

1998, May 6 Photo. *Perf. 11½*

834 A205 (22c) multicolored .50 .30
835 A205 60c multicolored 1.00 1.00
836 A205 70c multicolored 1.10 1.10
837 A205 $2 multicolored 2.00 2.00
Nos. 834-837 (4) 4.60 4.40

No. 834 is inscribed "For Local Addresses Only."

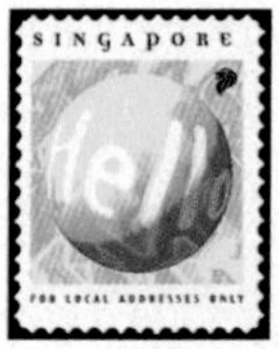

A206

"Hello" stamps.

Self-Adhesive
Booklet Stamps

Serpentine Die Cut 11

1998, May 20 Litho.

838 A206 (22c) yellow & multi .65 .65
839 A206 (22c) orange & multi .65 .65
840 A206 (22c) green & multi .65 .65
841 A206 (22c) blue & multi .65 .65
842 A206 (22c) black & multi .65 .65
a. Booklet pane, 2 each #838-842 6.50

Nos. 838-842 are inscribed "For Local Addresses Only."
By its nature No. 842a is a complete booklet. The peelable paper backing serves as a booklet cover. The outside cover contains 10 peelable labels.

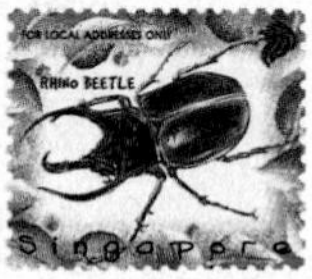

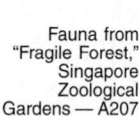

Fauna from "Fragile Forest," Singapore Zoological Gardens — A207

No. 843, Rhino beetle. No. 844, Surinam horned frog. No. 845, Atlas moth. No. 846, Green iguana. No. 847, Giant scorpion. No. 848, Hissing cockroach. No. 849, Two-toed sloth. No. 850, Archer fish. No. 851, Cobalt blue tarantula. No. 852, Greater mousedeer.

Self-Adhesive
Booklet Stamps

Serpentine Die Cut 11½

1998, June 5 Litho.

843 A207 (22c) multicolored .50 .50
844 A207 (22c) multicolored .50 .50
845 A207 (22c) multicolored .50 .50
846 A207 (22c) multicolored .50 .50
847 A207 (22c) multicolored .50 .50
a. Booklet, 2 each #843-847 5.00
848 A207 (22c) multicolored .50 .50
849 A207 (22c) multicolored .50 .50
850 A207 (22c) multicolored .50 .50
851 A207 (22c) multicolored .50 .50
852 A207 (22c) multicolored .50 .50
a. Booklet, 2 each #848-852 5.00

Nos. 843-852 are inscribed "For Local Addresses Only."
The peelable paper backing of Nos. 847a & 852a serves as a booklet cover. In the margins of Nos. 847a & 852a there is a leaf-shaped scratch-off that reveals an animal.

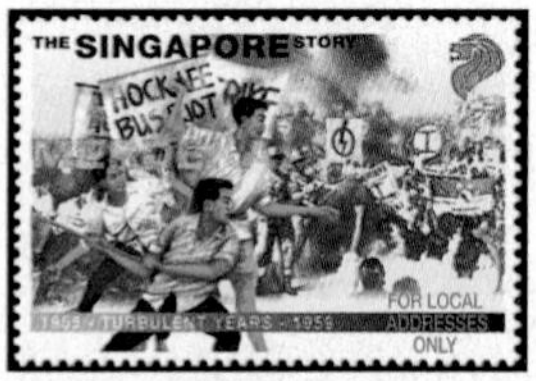

The Singapore Story (Moments in History) — A208

(22c), 22c, "Turbulent years," 1955-59. 60c, "Self-government," 1959-63. $1, "Towards merger and independence," 1961-65. $2, "A nation is born," 1965.

1998, July 7 *Perf. 13x13½*

853 A208 (22c) multicolored .35 .30
854 A208 60c multicolored .65 .65
855 A208 $1 multicolored 1.10 1.10
856 A208 $2 multicolored 2.40 2.40
Nos. 853-856 (4) 4.50 4.45

Souvenir Sheet

857 Souvenir sheet of 4 12.00 12.00
a. 22c multicolored 1.50 1.50
b. 60c multicolored 1.75 1.75
c. $1 multicolored 2.50 2.50
d. $2 multicolored 4.75 4.75

Issued: #853-856, 7/7/98; #857, 7/23/98.
No. 853 is inscribed "For Local Addresses Only." No. 857 has a UV varnish producing a shiny effect on portions of the design. No. 857 sold for $7.
Singpex '98 (#857).

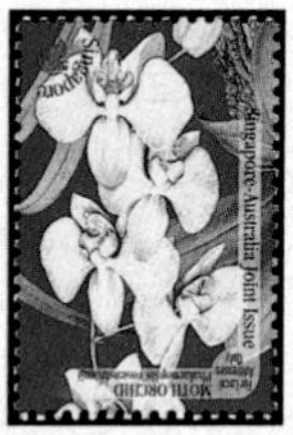

Orchids of Singapore and Australia — A209

1998, Aug. 6 Photo. *Perf. 11½*

858 A209 (22c) Moth orchid .65 .40
859 A209 70c Bamboo orchid 1.50 1.50
860 A209 $1 Tiger orchid 2.25 2.25
861 A209 $2 Cooktown orchid 3.50 3.50
Nos. 858-861 (4) 7.90 7.65

Souvenir Sheet

861A A209 Sheet of 4, #859-861, #861Ab 8.25 8.25
b. 22c like #858 2.00 *2.00*

No. 858 is inscribed "For Local Addresses Only."
See Australia Nos. 1681-1684.

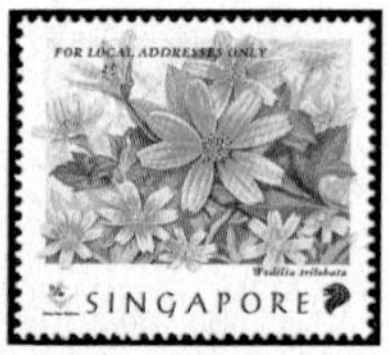

Flowers
A210

Designs: No. 862, Wedilia trilobata. No. 863, Dillenia suffruticosa. No. 864, Canna hybrid. No. 865, Caesalpinia pulcherrima.
No. 866, Zephyranthes rosea. No. 867, Cassia alata. No. 868, Heliconia rostrata. No. 869, Allamanda cathartica.

1998, Sept. 9 Litho. *Perf. 14*

862 A210 (22c) multicolored .45 .35
863 A210 (22c) multicolored .45 .35
864 A210 (22c) multicolored .45 .35
865 A210 (22c) multicolored .45 .35
a. Strip of 4, #862-865 2.00 2.00
b. Booklet pane, 3 each #864-865, 2 each #862-863 5.00
Complete booklet, #865b 5.00
866 A210 35c multicolored .60 .60
867 A210 35c multicolored .60 .60
868 A210 60c multicolored .85 .85
869 A210 60c multicolored .85 .85
a. Strip of 4, #866-869 3.00 3.00
b. Souvenir sheet of 8, #862-869 4.75 4.75

Stamps in #869b are in pairs, #864-863, 862/865 horiz., #866-867, 868, 869 vert.

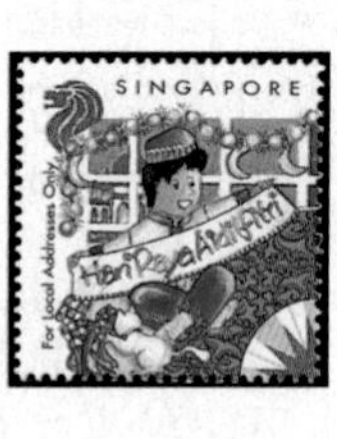

A211

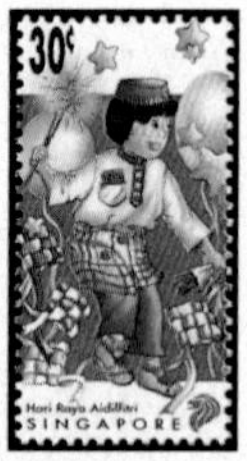

Festivals — A212

#870, 874 Eid al-Fitr. #871, 875, Christmas. #872, 876, Chinese New Year. #873, 877, Deepavali.

1998, Oct. 7 Litho. *Perf. 13x14*

870 A211 (22c) multicolored .30 .30
871 A211 (22c) multicolored .30 .30
872 A211 (22c) multicolored .30 .30
873 A211 (22c) multicolored .30 .30
a. Block of 4, #870-873 1.75 1.75
874 A212 30c multicolored .45 .45
875 A212 30c multicolored .45 .45
876 A212 30c multicolored .45 .45
877 A212 30c multicolored .45 .45
Nos. 870-877 (8) 3.00 3.00

Nos. 870-873 are inscribed "For Local Addresses Only."

Serpentine Die Cut

878 A211 (22c) like #870 .80 .80
879 A211 (22c) like #871 .80 .80
880 A211 (22c) like #872 .80 .80
881 A211 (22c) like #873 .80 .80
Nos. 878-881 (4) 3.20 3.20

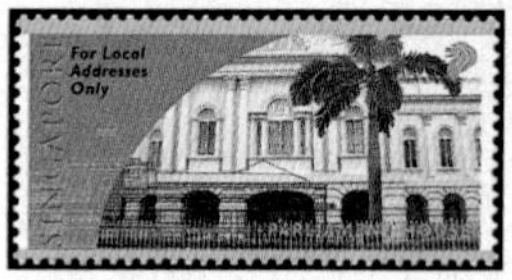

Historical Buildings — A213

(22c), Parliament House. 70c, Former Convent of the Holy Infant Jesus Chapel. $1, Hill Street Building. $2, Sun Yat Sen Nanyang Memorial Hall.

1998, Nov. 4 *Perf. 13½*

882 A213 (22c) multicolored .35 .35
883 A213 70c multicolored .90 .90
884 A213 $1 multicolored 1.40 1.40
885 A213 $2 multicolored 3.00 3.00
Nos. 882-885 (4) 5.65 5.65

No. 882 inscribed "For Local Addresses Only."

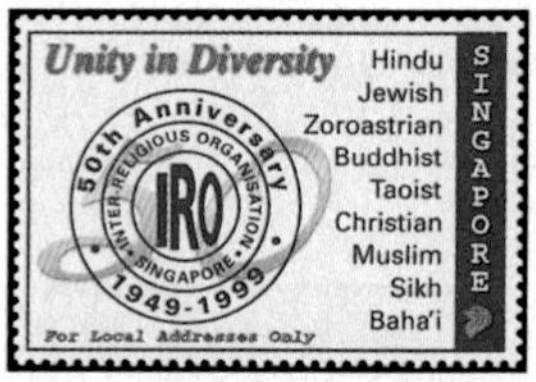

Inter-Religious Organization, 50th Anniv. — A214

1999, Jan. 15 Litho. *Perf. 13x13½*

886 A214 (22c) cream & multi .35 .25
887 A214 60c pink & multi .85 .85
888 A214 $1 blue & multi 1.40 1.40
Nos. 886-888 (3) 2.60 2.50

No. 886 is inscribed "For Local Addresses Only."

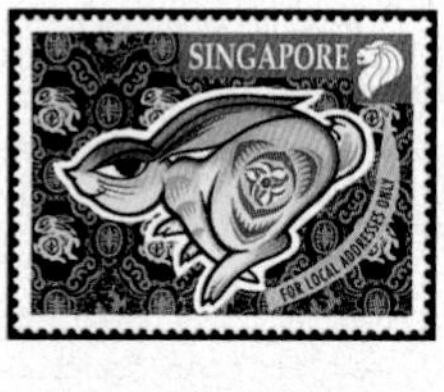

New Year 1999 (Year of the Rabbit)
A215

Various stylized rabbits.

1999, Jan. 15 *Perf. 14*

889 A215 (22c) multicolored .50 .50
890 A215 $2 multicolored 2.00 2.00
a. Horiz. or vert. pair, #889-890 2.75 2.75
b. Sheet, 9 each #829-830 27.50

Souvenir Sheet

890C Sheet of 2, #890 & 890Cd 4.00 4.00
d. A215 22c like #889 1.25 *1.25*
e. As #890C, with PhilexFrance 99 margin 4.25 4.25
f. As #890C, with China 1999 World Phil. Exhib. margin 4.25 4.25

No. 889 is inscribed "For Local Addresses Only."
No. 890C was issued 4/27 for IBRA '99, World Philatelic Exhibition, Nuremberg.
Issued: #890Ce, 7/2/99; #890Cf, 8/21/99.

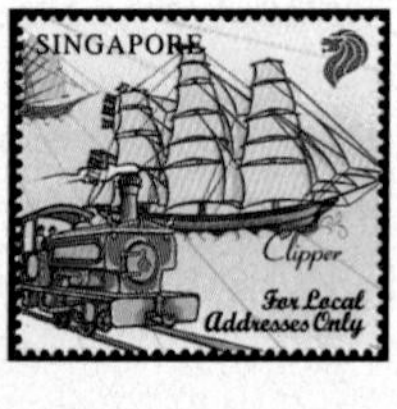

19th Century Sailing Ships — A216

1999, Mar. 19   Litho.   Perf. 14½
891	A216	(22c) Clipper	.60	.35
892	A216	70c Twakow, vert.	1.00	1.00
893	A216	$1 Fujian junk, vert.	1.50	1.50
894	A216	$2 Golekkan	2.50	2.50
		Nos. 891-894 (4)	5.60	5.35

Souvenir Sheet
894A	A216	Sheet of 4, #892-894, #894Ab	5.75	5.75
b.		22c like #891	1.50	1.50

Australia '99 World Stamp Expo (#894A). No. 891 is inscribed "For Local Address Only."

Greetings Stamps — A217

Expressions of kindness: a, "Think of others." b, "Do not litter." c, "Be kind to animals." d, "Be considerate." e, "Be generous."

Serpentine Die Cut 9½
1999, May 12   Litho.
Self-Adhesive
Booklet Stamps
895	A217	(22c) Booklet pane, 2 each #a.-e.	4.25	4.25

Nos. 895a-895e are inscribed "For Local Addresses Only."
No. 895 is a complete booklet. The peelable paper backing serves as a booklet cover. Stamps are printed 2 each #895a-895c on one side, 2 each #895d-895e on the other with 3 labels on each side.

Hong Kong and Singapore Tourism — A218

(22c), Hong Kong Harbor. 35c, Skyline of Singapore. 50c, Giant Buddha, Hong Kong. 60c, Merlion Sentosa Island, Singapore. 70c, Hong Kong Street scene. $1, Bugis Junction, Singapore.

1999, July 1   Litho.   Perf. 13½x13¼
896	A218	(22c) multicolored	.40	.40
897	A218	35c multicolored	.50	.50
898	A218	50c multicolored	.80	.80
899	A218	60c multicolored	1.00	1.00
900	A218	70c multicolored	1.10	1.10
901	A218	$1 multicolored	1.60	1.60
		Nos. 896-901 (6)	5.40	5.40

Souvenir Sheet
902		Sheet of 6, #897-901, #902a	5.50	5.50
a.	A218	22c like #896	.90	.90

No. 896 is inscribed for "For Local Addresses Only."
See Hong Kong Nos. 849-854.

Butterflies A219

Perf. 12½x12¾
1999, Aug. 12   Litho. & Engr.
903	A219	(22c) Peacock	.60	.40
904	A219	70c Blue pansy	1.00	1.00
905	A219	$1 Great egg-fly	1.75	1.75
906	A219	$2 Red admiral	3.00	3.00
		Nos. 903-906 (4)	6.35	6.15

Souvenir Sheet
907	A219	Sheet of 4, #904-906, #907a	6.75	6.75
a.	A219	22c like #903	1.75	1.75

No. 903 is inscribed "For Local Addresses Only."
See Sweden No. 2356.

Yusof bin Ishak (1910-70), First President of Singapore A220

Perf. 13¼x13¾
1999, Sept. 9   Litho. & Engr.
908	A220	$2 multicolored	2.75	2.75

Issued in sheets of 4.

Amphibians & Reptiles — A221

(22c), Green turtle. 60c, Green crested lizard. 70c, Copper-cheeked frog. $1, Water monitor.

1999, Oct. 13   Litho.   Perf. 14
909	A221	(22c) multi	.30	.30
		Complete booklet, 10 #909	3.50	
910	A221	60c multi	.90	.90
911	A221	70c multi	1.00	1.00
912	A221	$1 multi	1.40	1.40
		Nos. 909-912 (4)	3.60	3.60

No. 909 inscribed "For Local Addresses Only."

New Parliament House — A222

Perf. 13¼x13¾
1999, Nov. 17   Litho.
913	A222	(22c) North view	.45	.35
914	A222	60c Northeast view	.75	.75
915	A222	$1 Southeast view	1.25	1.25
916	A222	$2 West view	2.75	2.75
		Nos. 913-916 (4)	5.20	5.10

#913 inscribed "For Local Address Only."

Singapore in the 20th Century A223

No. 917: a, Colonialism. b, Education. c, Immigration. d, Government. e, Japanese occupation. f, National service. g, Transportation. h, Tourism. i, Housing. j, Economic progress.

Perf. 13¼x12½
1999, Dec. 31   Litho.
917		Sheet of 10 + 5 labels	8.50	8.50
a.-b.	A223	(22c) Any single	.35	.35
c.-d.	A223	35c Any single	.45	.45
e.-f.	A223	60c Any single	.85	.85
g.-h.	A223	70c Any single	1.00	1.00
i.-j.	A223	$1 Any single	1.50	1.50

Nos. 917a-917b inscribed "For Local Addresses Only."

Millennium — A224

No. 918: a, (22c), Information technology. b, 60c, Arts and culture. c, $1, Heritage. d, $2, Globalization.

2000, Jan. 1   Photo.   Perf. 14¼x14¾
Granite Paper
918	A224	Horiz. strip of 4, #a-d	5.00	5.00
e.		Souvenir sheet, #918	5.00	5.00

No. 918a inscribed "For Local Addresses Only."

New Year 2000 (Year of the Dragon) A225

Dragon: (22c), 22c, Facing left. $2, $10, Facing right.

2000   Litho.   Perf. 13x13¼
919	A225	(22c) multi	.50	.50
920	A225	$2 multi	2.75	2.75
a.		Horiz. pair, #919-920	3.50	3.50
b.		Souvenir sheet, #920a	3.50	3.50

Souvenir Sheets
921		Sheet of 2, #920, 922a, with Bangkok 2000 margin	4.00	4.00
a.		A225 22c multi	1.00	1.00
b.		As No. 921, with The Stamp Show 2000 margin	4.00	4.00
c.		As No. 921, with Naba 2000 margin	5.50	5.50

Litho. & Embossed
922	A225	$10 gold & multi	14.00	14.00

Issued: No. 920b, 10/30; No. 921, 3/25; No. 921b, 5/22; No. 921c, 6/21; others, 1/1. No. 919 inscribed "For Local Addresses Only."

Millennium Personalized Stamp — A225a

2000, Mar. 8   Litho.   Perf. 14x14¼
923	A225a	(22c) multi + label	1.25	1.25

No. 923 printed in sheets of 20 stamps + labels that could be personalized. Sheets sold for $20 for the first sheet with additional sheets available for $10. The design on No. 923 is similar to that on No. 918a, but is 19x46mm and lacks frame.

Post Offices and Cancels A226

Designs: (22c), Original post office, B172 cancel. 60c, General Post Office, c. 1873, 1875 cancel. $1, General Post Office, 1928, 1935 cancel. $2, Singapore Post Center, 1998 cancel.

2000, Mar. 8   Litho.   Perf. 13½
935	A226	(22c) multi	.40	.40
936	A226	60c multi	.85	.85
a.		Booklet pane, 4 #935, 2 #936	3.25	
937	A226	$1 multi	1.25	1.25
938	A226	$2 multi	3.00	3.00
a.		Booklet pane, 4 #937, 2 #938	12.00	
		Complete bklt., #936a, 938a	15.25	
		Nos. 935-938 (4)	5.50	5.50

Souvenir Sheet
939	A226	Sheet of 4, #936-938, 939a	4.50	4.50
a.		A226 22c like No. 935	1.00	1.00

No. 935 is inscribed "For Local Addresses Only."

Celebrations A227

Designs: No. 940, (22c), Yipee. No. 940A, (22c), Yeah. No. 940B, (22c), Hurray. No. 940C, (22c), Yes. No. 941, (22c), Happy.

Serpentine Die Cut 9½
2000, May 10   Litho.
Self-Adhesive
940-941	A227	Set of 5	2.75	2.75
941a		Booklet, 2 each #940-941	5.50	

Nos. 940-941 are inscribed "For Local Addresses Only." Eight self-adhesive die cut labels are affixed to the opposite side of the peelable backing paper.

Singapore River — A228

No. 942: a, River community, 1920s. b, South Boat Quay, 1930s. c, Social gathering, 1950s. d, Changing skyline, 1980s. e, River Regatta, 1990s. f, At the river mouth, 1900s. g, Stevedores, 1910s. h, Lighters, 1940s. i, Men at work, 1960s. j, Working with cranes, 1970s.

2000, June 21   Perf. 14
942	A228	Sheet of 10	6.00	6.00
a.-e.		(22c) Any single	.35	.35
f.-j.		60c Any single	.80	.80

Nos. 942a-942e are inscribed "For Local Addresses Only."

Stampin' the Future A229

Children's Stamp Design Contest Winners: (22c), Future lifestyle, art by Liu Jiang Wen. 60c, Future homes, art by Shaun Yew Chuan Bin. $1, Home automation, art by Gwendolyn Soh Shihui. $2, Floating city, art by Dawn Koh.

2000, July 7   Litho.   Perf. 14x12¾
943-946	A229	Set of 4	5.00	5.00
946a		Souvenir sheet, #943-946	5.25	5.25

World Stamp Expo 2000, Anaheim (No. 946a). No. 943 is inscribed "For Local Addresses Only."

Care for Nature — A230

No. 947: a, Archer fish. b, Smooth otter. c, Collared kingfisher. d, Orange fiddler crab.

2000, Aug. 11   Photo.   Perf. 14½
Granite Paper
947	A230	Block of 4	4.50	4.50
a.-b.		(22c) Any single	.40	.40
c.-d.		$1 Any single	1.80	1.80
e.		Booklet pane, 5 each #947a, 947b	7.00	
		Booklet #947e	7.00	
f.		Souv. sheet, #947, 947 imperf	8.00	8.00

Nos. 947a-947b are inscribed "For Local Addresses Only."
No. 947f sold for $5.

2000 Summer Olympics,
Sydney — A231

Designs: (22c), Swimming and high jump. 60c, Badminton and discus. $1, Soccer and hurdles. $2, Table tennis and gymnastics.

2000, Sept. 15   Litho.   Perf. 13½
948-951 A231 Set of 4   5.50 5.50
No. 948 is inscribed "For Local Addresses Only."

A232

Festivals
and
Holidays
A233

Designs: Nos. 952, 960, (22c), 956, 30c, Christmas. Nos. 953, 961, (22c), 957, 30c, Eid ul-Fitr. Nos. 954, 962, (22c), 958, 30c, Chinese New Year. Nos. 955, 963, (22c), 959, 30c, Deepavali.

2000, Oct. 11   Litho.   Perf. 13
952-955 A232 Set of 4   2.75 2.75
956-959 A233 Set of 4   2.75 2.75

Serpentine Die Cut 12¾x13¼
Self-Adhesive
960-963 A232 Set of 4   3.75 3.75
Nos. 952-955, 960-963 are inscribed "For Local Addresses Only."

New Year
2001 (Year
of the
Snake)
A234

Designs: (22c), Snake and branch. $2, Two snakes.

2001, Jan. 12   Perf. 14½x14
964 A234 (22c) multi   .50 .50
965 A234 $2 multi   2.50 2.50
  a. Horiz. pair, #964-965   3.50 3.50
  b. Souvenir sheet, #964-965, with
       Hong Kong 2001 margin   5.00 5.00
  c. Souvenir sheet, #964-965, with
       Belgica 2001 margin   5.00 5.00
  d. Souvenir sheet, #964-965, with
       Phila Nippon '01 margin   5.00 5.00

Issued: No. 965c, 6/9; No. 965d, 7/1.

Early
Singaporeans
A235

Designs: No. 966, $1, Tan Tock Seng (1798-1850), philanthropist. No. 967, $1, P. Govindasamy Pillai (1887-1980), business-man. No. 968, $1, Edwin John Tessensohn (1857-1926), politician. No. 969, $1, Eunos bin Abdullah (1876-1941), politician.

2001, Feb. 28   Photo.   Perf. 11¾
Granite Paper
966-969 A235 Set of 4   5.50 5.50

Commonwealth
Day, 25th
Anniv. — A236

Designs: (22c), Co-operation. 60c, Education. $1, Sports. $2, Arts and culture.

2001, Mar. 12   Litho.   Perf. 14x14¼
970-973 A236 Set of 4   5.75 5.75
No. 970 inscribed "For Local Addresses Only."

Greetings — A237

Serpentine Die Cut 10
2001, Apr. 25   Litho.
Self-Adhesive
974 A237 (22c) Balloons   .45 .45
975 A237 (22c) Fireworks   .45 .45
976 A237 (22c) Roses   .45 .45
977 A237 (22c) Gifts   .45 .45
978 A237 (22c) Musical instru-
               ments   .45 .45
  a. Booklet, 2 each #974-978 + 10
       labels   4.50
       Nos. 974-978 (5)   2.25 2.25
Nos. 974-978 inscribed "For Local Addresses Only."

Perf. 14
Water-Activated Gum
978B A237 (22c) Fireworks   1.00 1.00
978C A237 (22c) Musical instru-
                ments   1.00 1.00
978D A237 (22c) Roses   1.00 1.00
978E A237 (22c) Balloons   1.00 1.00
978F A237 (22c) Gifts   1.00 1.00
  g. Vert. strip, #978B-978F + 5
       labels   5.00 5.00
Nos. 978B-978F were printed in sheets containing four of each stamp and 20 labels that could be personalized. Sheets sold for $11 for the first sheet with additional sheets available for $10. At least three different sheets of 6 of No. 978B and 6 non-personalizable labels exist. These sheets sold as part of a set of 8 sheets with various face values that sold for $8.50 per sheet, and later as part of another set of 8 sheets, for $9 per sheet..

Singapore Arts Festival — A238

No. 979: a, (22c), "a." b, 60c, "r." c, $1, "t." d, $2, "s."

2001, May 16   Perf. 14
979 A238 Block of 4, #a-d   4.75 4.75
No. 979a inscribed "For Local Addresses Only."

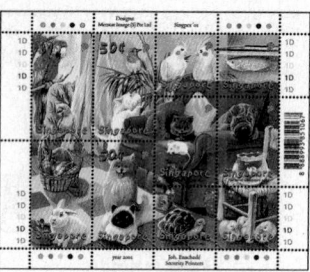

Pets — A239

No. 980: a, Fish. b, Cockatoos. c, Chicks. d, Turtle. e, Dog and fish. f, Cat and mice. g, Bird and dog. h, Dog and cat. i, Parrots. j, Cat and rabbit.

2001, July 26   Perf. 13½
980   A239   Sheet of 10   7.00 7.00
  a.-d. (22c) Any single, 25x25mm   .40 .40
  e.-f. (22c) Any single, 25x35mm   .40 .40
  g.-h. 50c Any single, 25x42mm   .90 .90
  i.-j. $1 Any single, 25x42mm   1.60 1.60
Nos. 980a-980f are inscribed "For Local Addresses Only." Singpex '01.

Frame — A240

Serpentine Die Cut 15x14½
2001, July 26   Self-Adhesive
981 A240 (22c) multi   .80 .80
Size: 24x34mm
982 A240 (22c) multi   .80 .80
  a. Pane, 6 #981, 4 #982 +16 la-
       bels   8.00
Nos. 981-982 inscribed "For Local Addresses Only." No. 982a contains three examples of No. 982 with differing white paw prints, and one example without paw print. Singpex '01.

Care for Nature — A241

Orangutans: (22c), Adult hanging on tree. 60c, Two adults. No. 983c, Adult and child. No. 983d, Two adults and child.

2001, Sept. 5   Perf. 13½x13
983   A241   Horiz. strip of 4   3.75 3.75
  a. (22c) multi   .30 .30
  b. 60c multi   .75 .75
  c.-d. $1 Any single   1.25 1.25
  e. Souvenir sheet, #983   6.00 6.00
  f. Sheet, 2 each #983c-983d, +
       8 labels, perf. 12¾('05) 8.75 8.75

Self-Adhesive
Booklet Stamp
Serpentine Die Cut 12½
984 A241 (22c) multi   .50 .50
  a. Booklet of 10   5.00
Nos. 983a, 984 inscribed "For Local Addresses Only."
No. 983e sold for $3.90, with 50c of that donated to the Care for Nature Trust Fund.
No. 983f issued 5/1/05. No. 983f sold for $6.

Flowers
A242

Designs: (22c), Melastoma malabathricum. 60c, Leontopodium alpinum. $1, Saraca cauliflora. $2, Gentiana clusii.

2001, Sept. 20   Perf. 13¼x12¾
985-988 A242 Set of 4   5.50 5.50
  988a Souvenir sheet, #985-988   5.50 5.50
No. 985 inscribed "For Local Addresses Only." See Switzerland No. 1107.

Tropical
Fish — A243

Designs: 5c, Moorish idol. 20c, Threadfin butterflyfish. (22c), Copperband butterflyfish. (23c), Copperband butterflyfish. 30c, Pearl-scale butterflyfish. 31c, Eight-banded butterflyfish. 40c, Rainbow butterflyfish. 50c, Yellow-faced angelfish. 60c, Emperor angelfish. 70c, Striped sailfin tang. 80c, Palette tang.

2001-05   Perf. 13x13¼
989   A243   5c multi   .25 .35
990   A243   20c multi   .30 .25
991   A243   (22c) multi   .35 .25
992   A243   30c multi   .50 .45
992A A243   31c multi   .50 .25
992B A243   (31c) multi   .50 .25
993   A243   40c multi   .75 .40
994   A243   50c multi   1.00 1.00
995   A243   60c multi   1.10 1.10
996   A243   70c multi   1.40 1.40
997   A243   80c multi   1.50 1.50
  a. Sheet of 9, #989-997   8.25 8.25
       Nos. 989-997 (11)   8.15 7.20

Self-Adhesive
Serpentine Die Cut 12½
998   A243   (22c) multi   .40 .40
  a. Booklet of 10   4.00
998B A243   (23c) multi   .50 .50
  c. Booklet pane of 10   5.00

Issued: Nos. 989-992, 993-998 issued 10/24/01. 31c, 2/3/04; (23c), 7/7/04; No. 992B, 3/18/05.
Nos. 991, 998 inscribed "For Local Addresses Only." No. 998B is inscribed "1st Local." No. 992B is inscribed "2nd Local."
See Nos. 1018-1021.

New Year
2002 (Year
of the
Horse)
A244

Designs: Nos. 999, 1001a, (22c), One horse. Nos. 1000, 1001b, $2, Two horses.

Litho., Litho & Embossed with Foil
Application (#1001a, 1001b)
2002, Jan. 10   Perf. 13½x13¼
999-1000 A244 Set of 2   4.00 4.00
  1000a Souvenir sheet, #999-1000,
          perf. 13x13¼   4.00 4.00
1001   Sheet, #1001a-1001b, 8
        each #999-1000   26.00 26.00
  a. A244 (22c) silver & multi .30 .30
  b. A244 $2 gold & multi   2.50 2.50
A souvenir sheet containing one each of Nos. 1001a and 1001b exists. It was sold only in year sets.
No. 1000a issued 8/2/02, for Philakorea.

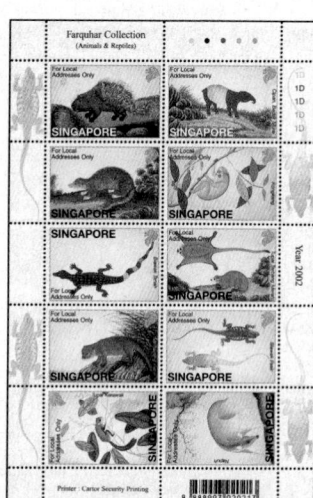

William Farquhar Collection of Natural History Drawings — A245

No. 1002, (22c) — Animals and Reptiles: a, Landak raya. b, Cipan, Badak murai. c, Landak kelubu. d, Kongkang. e, Biawak tanah. f, Tupai terbang merah. g, Memerang kecil. h,

Biawak pasir. i, Tupai kerawak, vert. j, Napuh, vert.

No. 1003, (22c) — Fruits and Plants: a, Buah rumenia. b, Manggis hutan. c, Cempedak. d, Bunga dedap. e, Jeringau, vert. f, Rotang, vert. g, Tuba, vert. h, Tebu gagak, vert. i, Temu kunci, vert. j, Rambutan, vert.

No. 1004, (22c) — Birds: a, Burung gaji-gaji. b, Kuau cermin. c, Ayam kolam. d, Kelengking. e, Burung kuang. f, Puhung. g, Burung kunyit, vert. h, Burung pacat sayap biru, vert. i, Burung mural, vert. j, Burung berek-berek, vert.

No. 1005, (22c) — Fish: a, Ikan tenggiri papan. b, Ikan kertang. c, Ikan kakatua. d, Ikan bambangan. e, Ikan parang. f, Ikan buntai pisang. g, Ikan ketang. h, Pari hitam. i, Telinga gajah. j, Ikan babi.

Designs: No. 1006, Like No. 1002. No. 1007, Like No. 1003. No. 1008, Like No. 1004. No. 1009, Like No. 1005.

Perf. 13¼x13¾, 13¾x13¼

2002	Sheets of 10, #a-j	Litho.	
1002-1005	A245	Set of 4	13.50 13.50

Serpentine Die Cut 12½
Sheets of 10, #a-j
Self-Adhesive

| 1006-1009 | A245 | Set of 4 | 16.50 16.50 |

Issued: Nos. 1002-1003, 2/20; Nos. 1004-1005, 3/20. Nos. 1006-1007, 2/20; Nos. 1008-1009, 3/20. Nos. 1002-1009 inscribed "For Local Addresses Only."

Toys
A246

Designs: (22c), Lego blocks. 60c, Cowboys and Indians, robot. 70c, Dolls. $1, Racing cars.

2002, May 22		Perf. 14½x14	
1010-1013	A246	Set of 4	3.50 3.50

No. 1010 inscribed "For local addresses only."

Tropical Birds — A247

Designs: (22c), Red-throated sunbird. 40c, Asian fairy bluebird. $1, Black-naped oriole. $2, White-bellied woodpecker.

2002, June 27		Perf. 13¼x14	
1014-1017	A247	Set of 4	5.00 5.00
1017a		Souvenir sheet, #1014-1017	6.00 6.00

No. 1014 inscribed "For local addresses only." See Malaysia Nos. 886-888.

Fish Type of 2001

Discus fish: $1, Blue turquoise. $2, Brown discus. $5, Red alenquer. $10, Red turquoise.

2002, July 24		Perf. 13½x13¼	
		Size: 29x25mm	
1018	A243	$1 multi	1.75 1.75
1019	A243	$2 multi	3.00 3.00
1020	A243	$5 multi	7.00 7.00
1021	A243	$10 multi	14.00 14.00
a.		Souvenir sheet, #1018-1021	27.50 27.50
		Nos. 1018-1021 (4)	25.75 25.75

A248

Festivals and Holidays
A249

Designs: Nos. 1022, 50c; 1026, 1030, (22c), Christmas. Nos. 1023, 50c; 1027, 1031, (22c), Chinese New Year. Nos. 1024, 50c; 1028, 1032, (22c), Deepavali. Nos. 1025, 50c; 1029, 1033, (22c), Eid ul-Fitr.

Litho. with Hologram Affixed

2002, Aug. 21		Perf. 13¼x13¾	
1022-1025	A248	Set of 4	3.00 3.00
1026-1029	A249	Set of 4	1.75 1.75

Self-Adhesive
Serpentine Die Cut 13¼x13¾

| 1030-1033 | A249 | Set of 4 | 3.75 3.75 |

Nos. 1026-1033 are inscribed "For Local Addresses Only."

Trees — A250

Designs: Nos. 1034, 1038, (22c), Flame of the forest. 60c, Rain tree. No. 1036, $1, Tembusu. No. 1037, $1, Kapok tree.

2002, Sept. 25	Litho.	Perf. 13½x13	
1034-1037	A250	Set of 4	3.50 3.50

Self-Adhesive
Booklet Stamp
Serpentine Die Cut 12½

1038	A250	(22c) multi		.50 .50
a.		Booklet of 10		5.00

Nos. 1034, 1038 are inscribed "For Local Addresses Only."

A sheet containing 2 each Nos. 1035-1036 and 2 stamps similar to No. 1034 but inscribed "1st Local" + 6 non-personalizable labels sold for $9.90.

Opening of Esplanade Performing Arts Center
A251

Various views of complex with background colors of: (22c), Orange. 60c, Brown. $1, Blue green. $2, Dark blue.

2002, Oct. 12	Litho.	Perf. 13¼x13¾	
1039-1042	A251	Set of 4	5.00 5.00
1042a		Souvenir sheet, #1039-1042	5.00 5.00

No. 1039 is inscribed "For Local Addresses only."

Singapore, A Global City — A252

No. 1043: a, Sailboats. b, Conductor's hands.

2002-04		Perf. 14¼x14	
1043	A252	$2 Horiz. pair, #a-b + central label	5.25 5.25
1043c		Souvenir sheet, #1043a-1043b, + American Express label	6.25 6.25
d.		As "c," with Coca-Cola label	6.25 6.25
e.		As "c," with McDonald's label	6.25 6.25
f.		As "c," with Reader's Digest label	6.25 6.25
g.		As "c," with Swatch label	6.25 6.25
h.		As "c," ovptd. in margin with World Stamp Championship emblem in silver	6.25 6.25
i.		As "d," ovptd. in margin with World Stamp Championship emblem in silver	6.25 6.25
j.		As "e," ovptd. in margin with World Stamp Championship emblem in silver	6.25 6.25
k.		As "f," ovptd. in margin with World Stamp Championship emblem in silver	6.25 6.25
l.		As "g," ovptd. in margin with World Stamp Championship emblem in silver	6.25 6.25

Issued: Nos. 1043-1043g, 11/20/02. Nos. 1043h-1043l, 6/23/04. Nos. 1043h-1043l sold for $4.53 each.

New Year 2003 (Year of the Ram)
A253

Designs: (22c) Red violet ram. $2, Tree and yellow green ram.

2003, Jan. 10	Litho.	Perf. 13x13½	
1044-1045	A253	Set of 2	2.75 2.75
1045a		Sheet, 9 each #1044-1045	22.50 22.50
1045b		Souvenir sheet, #1044-1045, with Bangkok 2003 margin	4.00 4.00
1045c		Souvenir sheet, #1044-1045, with China 2003 margin	4.00 4.00

No. 1044 inscribed "For Local Addresses Only."

Issued: No. 1045b, 10/4; No. 1045c, 11/20.

History of Empress Place Building
A254

Designs: (22c), Government offices. 60c, Government offices, diff. $1, Empress Place Museum. $2, Asian Civilizations Museum.

2003, Feb. 26		Perf. 14½	
1046-1049	A254	Set of 4	5.25 5.25

No. 1046 inscribed "For local addresses only."

Nocturnal Animals
A255

Designs: (22c), Tarsier. 40c, Barn owl. $1, Babirusa. $2, Clouded leopard.

2003, Mar. 20	Litho.	Perf. 13¼	
1050-1053	A255	Set of 4	5.00 5.00
1053a		Souvenir sheet, #1050-1053	6.00 6.00

No. 1050 inscribed "For Local Addresses Only." Glow-in-the-dark ink was applied to portions of No. 1053a by silk-screening.

Singapore Police Force — A256

Designs: (22c), Community policing. 40c, Traffic policing. $1, Maritime policing. $2, International peacekeeping.

2003, Apr. 23	Litho.	Perf. 13¼x13	
1054-1057	A256	Set of 4	5.75 5.75

No. 1054 inscribed "For Local Addresses Only."

Singapore, A Global City — A257

No. 1058: a, Spacecraft. b, Robot.

2003, May 21	Litho.	Perf. 14¼x14	
1058	A257	$2 Horiz. pair, #a-b + central label	5.50 5.50
c.		Souvenir sheet, #1058a-1058b + CNN label	6.00 6.00
d.		As "c," with Creative Technology label	6.00 6.00
e.		As "c," with Microsoft label	6.00 6.00
f.		As "c," with Siemens label	6.00 6.00
g.		As "c," with Singapore Airlines label	6.00 6.00
h.		As "c," ovptd. in margin with World Stamp Championship emblem in silver	6.00 6.00
i.		As "d," ovptd. in margin with World Stamp Championship emblem in silver	6.00 6.00
j.		As "e," ovptd. in margin with World Stamp Championship emblem in silver	6.00 6.00
k.		As "f," ovptd. in margin with World Stamp Championship emblem in silver	6.00 6.00
l.		As "g," ovptd. in margin with World Stamp Championship emblem in silver	6.00 6.00

Issued: Nos. 1058-1058g, 5/21/03. Nos. 1058h-1058l, 6/23/04. Nos. 1058h-1058l sold for $4.53 each.

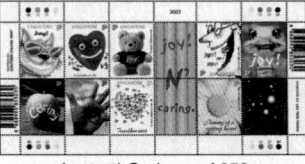

Joy and Caring — A258

Designs and inscriptions: Nos. 1059a, 1060a, Cat (Joy). Nos. 1059b, 1060b, Running heart (Joy). Nos. 1059c, 1060c, Teddy bear (Joy). Nos. 1059d, 1060d, Laughing man (Joy). Nos. 1059e, 1060e, Ostrich head (Joy). Nos. 1059f, 1060f, Apple (Caring). Nos. 1059g, 1060g, Hand and heart (A helping hand). Nos. 1059h, 1060h, Hearts (Togetherness). Nos. 1059i, 1060i, Flower (Beauty of a caring heart). Nos. 1059j, 1060j, Stars (Keeping in touch keeps us going).

2003, June 25		Perf. 14½	
1059	A258	Sheet of 10 + 2 labels	4.75 4.75
a.-j.		(22c) Any single	.45 .45
k.		Sheet, 10 each #1059c, 1059h + 20 labels	12.00 12.00
l.		Sheet of 20 #1059i + 20 labels	12.50 12.50
m.		Sheet, 10 each #1059c, 1059h + 20 labels	14.00 14.00

Self-Adhesive
Serpentine Die Cut 10x9¾

1060	A258	Booklet of 10 + 6 labels	5.00 5.00
a.-j.	A258	(22c) Any single	.50 .50

Inscribed "For Local Addresses Only." Labels on No. 1059k could be personalized for an additional fee.

Issued: No. 1059l, 8/8; No. 1059m, 11/25/04. Nos. 1059l and 1059m each sold for $8. A sheet of 5 #1059j and 5 non-personalizable labels sold for $9.90.

See Nos. 1119-1121.

Opening of North East Line of Rapid Transit System
A259

Designs: (22c), Map of Rapid Transit System, train. 60c, Entrance gates, station cross-section, train. $2, System control room, train. No. 1064: a, (22c), Like No. 522. b, 60c, Like No. 523. c, $2, Like No. 524.

2003, July 18		Perf. 13¾	
1061-1063	A259	Set of 3	4.00 4.00

Souvenir Sheet

1064	A259	Sheet of 6, #1061-1063, 1064a-1064c	7.00 7.00

Nos. 1061, 1064a are inscribed "For Local Addresses Only."

National Day — A260

Designs: (22c), Flag. 60c, National flower, Vanda Miss Joaquim orchid. $1, Merlion and buildings. $2, People of Singapore.

2003, Aug. 9 *Perf. 13¼x13½*

1065-1068	A260 Set of 4		4.75	4.75
1065a	Sheet of 20 + 20 labels		12.50	12.50
1068a	Souvenir sheet, #1065-1068		5.00	5.00
1068B	Sheet, 3 #1068Bc, 2#1068Bd + 10 labels		10.00	10.00
c.	A260 60c Like #1066, 35x28mm		1.50	1.50
d.	A260 $1 Like #1067, 35x28mm		2.50	2.50

No. 1065 is inscribed "For local addresses only."

No. 1065a sold for $8. Labels could be personalized.

Numerous different sheets containing 5 stamps similar to No. 1065 but inscribed "1st Local" + 10 non-personalizable labels (sheets having various labels and margins) exist. Sheets sold for $6. A sheet containing 3 stamps similar to No. 1068Bc exists, sold as part of a series of sheets sold with a book for $39.90.

Size of Nos. 1066-1067: 33x28mm. No. 1068B sold for $6.

Aircraft — A261

No. 1069 — Military aircraft: a, Alouette III helicopter. b, E-2C Hawkeye. c, Hawker Hunter. d, Super Puma AS-332M helicopter. e, Hercules C-130H. f, F-16 C/D Fighting Falcon. g, AH-64D Apache helicopter. h, KC-135R Stratotanker. i, Cessna 172. j, F-5E Tiger II.

No. 1070 — Civil aircraft: a, Airbus 340-500. b, Boeing 747-400. c, Boeing 777-200. d, Boeing 747-400 Freighter. e, Airbus 320. f, Concorde. g, Boeing 737-100. h, Comet IV. i, Viscount. j, Airspeed Consul.

2003, Sept. 3 *Perf. 13¼x13½*

1069	A261 Sheet of 10	3.75	3.75
a.-j.	(22c) Any single	.35	.35
1070	A261 Sheet of 10	3.75	3.75
a.-j.	(22c) Any single	.35	.35
k.	Sheet of 20, #1069a-1069j, 1070a-1070j	8.00	8.00

Self-Adhesive

Serpentine Die Cut 12½

1071	A261 Sheet of 10	5.00	
a.-j.	(22c) Any single	.50	.50
1072	A261 Sheet of 10	5.00	
a.-j.	(22c) Any single	.50	.50

Inscribed "For local addresses only." Powered flight, cent.; Singapore Air Force, 35th anniv.

Singapore, A Garden City — A262

Designs: Nos. 1073, 1077, (22c), Singapore Botanic Gardens. 60c, Fort Canning Park. No. 1075, $1, Marina City Park. No. 1076, $1, Sungei Buloh Wetland Reserve.

2003, Oct. 22 **Litho.** *Perf. 13½*

1073-1076	A262 Set of 4	4.00	4.00

Booklet Stamp

Self-Adhesive

Serpentine Die Cut 10x9½

1077	A262 (22c) multi	.55	.55
a.	Booklet pane of 10	5.50	*5.50*

Nos. 1073, 1077 are inscribed "For Local Addresses Only."

A sheet containing Nos. 1075, 1076, 2 No. 1074 and 2 stamps similar to No. 1073 inscribed "1st Local" + 6 non-personalizable labels sold for $9.90.

New Year 2004 (Year of the Monkey) A263

Designs: (22c), Monkey and heart. $2, Two monkeys.

2004, Jan. 9 *Perf. 14x13¼*

1078-1079	A263 Set of 2	2.75	2.75
1079a	Sheet, 9 each #1078-1079	32.50	32.50
1079b	Souvenir sheet, #1078-1079, with Hong Kong 2004 Stamp Expo margin	3.50	3.50

No. 1078 is inscribed "For Local Addresses Only." No. 1079a is reserved.

Paintings — A264

Nos. 1080, 1082 — Paintings of Liu Kang: a, Farmer's House. b, Artist and Model. c, Lanterns Galore. d, Enjoying a Smoke, Kashmir. e, Life by the River. f, Tenth Trip Up to Huangshan. g, My Young Wife, vert. h, Kek Lok Si, Penang, vert. i, Souri, vert. j, Siesta in Bali, vert.

Nos. 1081, 1083 — Paintings of Ong Kim Seng: a, Kampong Tengah, Singapore. b, Gyantse Market. c, Sebatu Spring, Bali. d, Jetty, Bangkok. e, Resort, Bali. f, Dance Studio, Bali. g, Telok Ayer Market. h, Kathmandu, Nepal. i, Portofino, Italy, vert. j, Boats at Rest, vert.

Perf. 13¼x13½, 13½x13¼ (Vert. stamps)

2004, Feb. 18

1080	A264 Sheet of 10	3.75	3.75
a.-j.	(23c) Any single	.35	.35
1081	A264 Sheet of 10	3.75	3.75
a.-j.	(23c) Any single	.35	.35

Self-Adhesive

Serpentine Die Cut 12½x12¼, 12¼x12½ (Vert. stamps)

1082	A264 Sheet of 10	4.50	4.50
a.-j.	(23c) Any single	.45	.45
1083	A264 Sheet of 10	4.50	4.50
a.-j.	(23c) Any single	.45	.45
	Nos. 1080-1083 (4)	16.50	16.50

Inscribed "For local addresses only."

Suzhou, China Industrial Park, 10th Anniv. A265

2004, Mar. 1 **Litho.** *Perf. 13x13½*

1084	A265 60c multi	1.25	1.25
a.	Sheet of 8	10.00	10.00

Singapore Skyline A266

Designs: (23c), Buildings as seen from street level. 60c, Fountain. 70c, Buildings as seen from distance.

$1, Singapore, circa 1900. $5, Singapore, 2004.

Perf. 14¼x14½

2004, Mar. 24 **Litho.**

1085-1087	A266 Set of 3	2.50	2.50
1087a	Sheet, 3 #1086, 2 #1087, + 10 labels, perf. 12¾x13 ('05)	8.75	8.75

Souvenir Sheets

Perf. 14¼x14

1088	A266 $1 multi	1.75	1.75

Litho. & Engr.

1089	A266 $5 multi	8.00	8.00

No. 1085 is inscribed "1st Local." Nos. 1088 and 1089 each contain one 95x35mm stamp

No. 1087a issued 5/1/05. No. 1087a sold for $6.

Singapore, A Global City — A267

No. 1090: a, Cargo containers. b, Gas tanks.

2004 **Litho.** *Perf. 14½x14¼*

1090	A267 Horiz. pair with central label	6.00	6.00
a.-b.	$2 Either single	2.75	2.75
c.	Souvenir sheet, #1090a-1090b + AIA label	6.00	6.00
d.	As "c," with GlaxoSmithKline label	6.00	6.00
e.	As "c," with HSBC label	6.00	6.00
f.	As "c," with Shell Oil label	6.00	6.00
g.	As "c," with Sony label	6.00	6.00
h.	As "c," ovptd. in margin with World Stamp Championship emblem in silver	6.00	6.00
i.	As "d," ovptd. in margin with World Stamp Championship emblem in silver	6.00	6.00
j.	As "e," ovptd. in margin with World Stamp Championship emblem in silver	6.00	6.00
k.	As "f," ovptd. in margin with World Stamp Championship emblem in silver	6.00	6.00
l.	As "g," ovptd. in margin with World Stamp Championship emblem in silver	6.00	6.00
m.	Souvenir sheet, #1043a, 1043b, 1058a, 1058b, 1090a, 1090b	22.50	22.50

Issued: Nos. 1090, 1090c-1090g, 4/21; 1090h-1090l, 6/23; No. 1090m, 8/28. Nos. 1090h-1090l sold for $4.53 each. No. 1090m sold for $12.60 and exists imperf.

FIFA (Fédération Internationale de Football Association), Cent. — A268

FIFA emblem and: 30c, Soccer field. 60c, Soccer ball. $1, Player's shirt. $2, World map.

Litho. & Embossed

2004, May 21 *Perf. 13*

Flocked Paper

1091-1094	A268 Set of 4	6.00	6.00

Festivals and Holidays — A269

Designs: Nos. 1095, 1103, (23c), Santa Claus, reindeer (Christmas). Nos. 1096, 1104, (23c), Flowers, fruit (Chinese New Year). Nos. 1097, 1105, (23c), Candles (Deepavali). Nos. 1098, 1106, Candle (Eid ul-Fitr). No. 1099, 50c, Carolers (Christmas). No. 1100, 50c, Woman (Chinese New Year). No. 1101, 50c, Woman and candle (Deepavali). No. 1102, 50c, Child with sparkler (Eid ul-Fitr).

2004, July 7 **Litho.** *Perf. 13*

1095-1102	A269 Set of 8	4.25	4.25
1095a	Perf. 12¾x13 + label	.35	.35
1099a	Perf. 12¾x13 + label	.80	.80
1102a	Sheet, #1099-1102, + 8 labels, perf. 12¾x13	8.00	8.00

Self-Adhesive

Serpentine Die Cut 12½

1103-1106	A269 Set of 4	2.75	2.75

Nos. 1103-1106 were each printed in sheets of 10. Nos. 1095-1098, 1103-1106 are inscribed "1st Local."

Nos. 1095a, 1099a issued 11/7/05. Nos. 1095a, 1099a issued in sheets of 8 + 8 labels.

No. 1102a issued 5/1/05. No. 1102a sold for $6.

National Monuments — A270

No. 1107, (23c): a, Column, City Hall. b, City Hall.

No. 1108, 30c: a, Tower, Victoria Theater and Concert Hall. b, Victoria Theater and Concert Hall.

No. 1109, 60c: a, Dome, Supreme Court. b, Supreme Court.

No. 1110, $1: a, Decoration, Istana (President's residence). b, Istana.

Sizes: Nos. 1107a-1110a, 41x46mm. Nos. 1107b-1110b, 41x27mm.

2004, Aug. 9 *Perf. 13¼x13¾*

Vert. Pairs, #a-b

1107-1110	A270 Set of 4	6.25	6.25
1110c	Souvenir sheet, #1107b, 1108b, 1109b, 1110b	3.50	3.50

No. 1107 is inscribed "1st Local."

2004 Summer Olympics, Athens A271

Carved rocks with stylized: (23c), Runners. 30c, Swimmers. $1, Weight lifter. $2, Sailor.

2004, Aug. 13 *Perf. 13¾*

1111-1114	A271 Set of 4	5.25	5.25

No. 1111 is inscribed "1st Local."

Nos. 1111-1114 exist imperf. Value, set $225.

Use of Postage Stamps in Singapore, 150th Anniv. — A272

Cancels, buildings, stamp vignettes and: (23c), Singapore #27, 49, 1067. 60c, Straits Settlements #N27, 271, Singapore #11. $1, Straits Settlements #124, 167, 251. $2, India #6, Straits Settlements #1, 18.

2004, Aug. 28 ***Perf. 12¼x11¾***

1115-1118 A272 Set of 4 5.25 5.25
1115a Sheet of 15 + 15 labels 9.50 9.50
1118a Souvenir sheet, #1115-1118 6.00 6.00

No. 1115a sold for $6 and labels could be personalized for an additional fee.

Joy and Caring Type of 2003 Inscribed "1st Local"

Designs: No. 1119, Flower (Beauty of a Caring Heart). No. 1120, Hearts (Togetherness). No. 1121, Teddy bear (Joy).

2004 **Litho.** ***Perf. 14½***

1119 A258 (23c) multi + label 1.75 1.75
1120 A258 (23c) multi + label .50 .50
a. Pair, #1119-1120 + 2 labels 3.50 3.50
1121 A258 (23c) multi + label .50 .50
a. Pair, #1120-1121 + 2 labels 1.00 1.00
Nos. 1119-1121 (3) 2.75 2.75

Issued: Nos. 1119, 1120, 8/28; No. 1121, 8/30. Nos. 1119 and 1120 were printed in a sheet containing five of each stamp and ten labels that sold for $15. Nos. 1120 and 1121 were printed in a sheet containing ten of each stamp and 20 labels that sold for $8, and a sheet containing 8 No. 1120 and 6 No. 1121 and 18 labels that sold for $20.

Three sheets containing 4 smaller-sized versions of No. 1120 + 4 labels (each sheet with different label and margin) sold for $5 per sheet.

A sheet with 6 No. 1120 with smaller "1st Local" inscriptions and 6 non-personalizable labels sold for $9.90. A similar sheet later sold as part of a set of 8 sheets with various face values for $8.50 per sheet. A similar set of sheets with various face values containing similar sheets containing 6 No. 1120 and 6 non-personalizable labels later sold for $9 per sheet.

Care For Nature — A273

Designs: Nos. 1122a, 1123 Seashore nutmeg. Nos. 1122b, 1124, Oriental pied hornbill. No. 1122c, Knobby sea star. No. 1122d, Common seahorse.

2004, Oct. 20 ***Perf. 14***

1122 A273 Horiz. strip of 4 4.00 4.00
a.-b. (23c) Either single .35 .35
c.-d. $1 Either single 1.60 1.60

Booklet Stamps
Self-Adhesive
Serpentine Die Cut 10¼x9½

1123 A273 (23c) multi .45 .45
1124 A273 (23c) multi .45 .45
a. Booklet pane, 5 each #1123-1124 4.50

Nos. 1122a-1122b, 1123-1124 are inscribed "1st Local."

New Year 2005 (Year of the Rooster) A274

Designs: (23c), Rooster. $2, Rooster and hen.

2005, Jan. 14 ***Perf. 13¼x13½***

1125-1126 A274 Set of 2 3.50 3.50
1126a Sheet, 9 each #1125-1126 32.50 32.50
1126b Souvenir sheet, #1125-1126, perf. 12¾, with Pacific Explorer emblem in margin 3.75 3.75
1126c Souvenir sheet, #1125-1126, perf. 12¾, with Taipei 2005 emblem in margin 3.75 3.75

No. 1125 is inscribed "1st Local."
No. 1126b issued 4/21; No. 1126c, 8/19.

Greetings A275

Designs: Nos. 1127a, 1132, Balloon animal. Nos. 1127a, 1131, Orchid. Nos. 1127c, 1130, Gift. Nos. 1127d, 1129, Flowers and teddy bears. Nos. 1127e, 1128, Candle and goblets.

2005, Feb. 23 ***Perf. 13½x13¾***

1127 Vert. strip of 5 1.80 1.80
a.-e. A275 (23c) Any single .35 .35

Booklet Stamps
Self-Adhesive
Serpentine Die Cut 11¼

1128 A275 (23c) multi .35 .35
1129 A275 (23c) multi .35 .35
1130 A275 (23c) multi .35 .35
1131 A275 (23c) multi .35 .35
1132 A275 (23c) multi .35 .35
a. Booklet pane, 2 each #1128-1132 3.50

Inscribed "1st Local." Two sheets, each containing 4 each of Nos. 1127c and 1127d and 5 non-personalizable labels sold for $10. The labels on these sheets could be personalized for an additional fee.

Hans Christian Andersen (1805-75), Author A276

Stories: (23c), Thumbelina. 60c, The Ugly Duckling. $1, The Emperor's New Clothes. $2, The Little Mermaid.

2005, Mar. 30 **Litho.** ***Perf. 13x12¾***

1133-1136 A276 Set of 4 5.50 5.50
1136a Souvenir sheet, #1133-1136 5.50 5.50

No. 1133 is inscribed "1st Local."

University Education in Singapore, Cent. — A277

Designs: (23c), Global knowledge enterprise. 60c, Quality education. 70c, Artistic and cultural hub. $1, Research excellence.

2005, Apr. 20 ***Perf. 12¼***

1137-1140 A277 Set of 4 3.75 3.75

No. 1137 is inscribed "1st Local."

A278

A279

A280

A281

"Uniquely Singapore" — A282

2005, May 1 ***Perf. 12¾***

1141 Miniature sheet of 5 + 10 labels 8.00 8.00
a. A278 $1 multi 1.60 1.60
b. A279 $1 multi 1.60 1.60
c. A280 $1 multi 1.60 1.60
d. A281 $1 multi 1.60 1.60
e. A282 $1 multi 1.60 1.60

No. 1141 sold for $6. Labels could be personalized.

Sheets containing one each of stamps similar to Nos. 1141a-1141e, lacking "Uniquely" and containing 5 or 10 non-personalizable labels sold for a variety of prices. A sheet of three stamps similar to No. 1141a, lacking "Uniquely" and containing three non-personalizable labels sold for $8.50.

Numerous sheets containing $1.10 stamps of types A278-A282 and two similar types showing other geometric designs, all lacking "Uniquely," and with different colors, exist. Various combinations and quantities of stamps exist on such sheets and all such sheets have non-personalizable labels in various quantities. All of these sheets sold for prices well above face value. Some sheets were sold only together with a variety of other non-philatelic products.

Malay Heritage Center A283

Designs: (31c), Building, drummers. 60c, Fountain pen, seal, manuscript. $1, Stringed instrument, man and woman. $2, Sailor, boat.

2005, May 31 ***Perf. 13¾***

1142-1145 A283 Set of 4 5.75 5.75

No. 1142 is inscribed "2nd Local."

Admiral Zheng He's Voyages, 600th Anniv. A284

Map and: No. 1146, (23c), Admiral Zheng He, ship. No. 1147 (23c), Ships. 60c, Ships, diff. $1, Ships, diff.

2005, June 28 ***Perf. 13¼x13½***

1146-1149 A284 Set of 4 3.25 3.25
1147a Sheet, 5 each #1146-1147, perf. 12¾ 3.75 3.75

Nos. 1146 and 1147 are inscribed "1st Local."

117th International Olympic Committee Session, Singapore — A285

Emblem, world map showing Singapore and candidates for hosting 2012 Olympics and: (23c), Cycling, running, table tennis. 50c, Running, basketball, tennis. 60c, Soccer, tennis, javelin. $1, Gymnastics, weight lifting.

2005, July 5 ***Perf. 14¼***

Size: 44x25mm

1150-1153 A285 Set of 4 3.25 3.25

Perf. 12¼

1154 Miniature sheet, #1154a-1154b, 2 each #1154c-1154d, + 6 labels 7.25 7.25
a. A285 (23c) multi, 44x28mm .45 .45
b. A285 50c multi, 44x28mm .95 .95
c. A285 60c multi, 44x28mm 1.10 1.10
d. A285 $1 multi, 44x28mm 1.75 1.75

Nos. 1150, 1154a are inscribed "1st Local." No. 1154 sold for $6, and labels could be personalized.

A286

A287

National Day — A288

Nos. 1155 and 1157 — Patchwork quilt blocks depicting: a, Stylized people, nine hearts. b, Hearts in a block of nine. c, Flower with face. d, Tower and hearts. e, Red orchid on green patterned background. f, Sun and rainbow. g, "Peace." h, Crescent and heart on Singapore map. i, White and purple orchid. j, Heart with red lace border. k, "Happy Birthday." l, Hands, "One Singapore," and "United We Stand." m, Cats and dog, "Singapore Is Our Home Too." n, Five stars around large star. o, Clothes on line, "One Nation Many Colors." p, Airplane, clouds. q, Love, star, dove, smiling face, "Love, Hope, Peace, Joy." r, Plate of food. s, Hearts and "Many Hearts One Nation." t, Stylized buildings and trees.

Nos. 1156 and 1158 — Patchwork quilt blocks depicting: a, "1" and flowers. b, Children with arms raised, "Home. . . Everyone Fits In!" c, Heads around flag. d, Rainbow and clouds. e, Person looking up, butterflies. f, Sun, butterflies, flowers, "Love Singapore." g, "One People, One Nation, One S'pore." h, Heart and durian. i, Frog on lily pad. j, Bird kites and flowers, "Flying High, My Singapore." k, Hands and heart. l, Singapore skyline, "Singapore My Home." m, Yellow, purple and green orchid on red background. n, Tree, hearts, "Racial Harmony." o, "I", heart, map of Singapore. p, Hand with buttons, child. q, Heart, stars, "Singapore." r, Four hearts in squares. s, Stars, hearts, stylized people in block of four. t, The Pledge.

$1, Entire quilt.

2005, Aug. 9 ***Perf. 14¼x14½***

1155 A286 (23c) Sheet of 20, #a-t, + label 6.50 6.50
1156 A287 (23c) Sheet of 20, #a-t, + label 6.50 6.50

Self-Adhesive (#1157-1158)
Serpentine Die Cut 10x9½

1157 A286 (23c) Sheet of 20, #a-t, + label 7.50 7.50
1158 A287 (23c) Sheet of 20, #a-t, + label 7.50 7.50

Souvenir Sheet
Perf. 14

1159 A288 $1 multi 1.75 1.75
a. Sheet of 4 #1159 9.25 9.25

Each stamp on Nos. 1155-1158 inscribed "1st Local." No. 1159a sold for $5.50.

A sheet containing 2 each Nos. 1155b, 1155c, 1155j, 1155n, 1156d, 1156r, and 12 labels that could not be personalized sold for $6. This sheet was available with personalized labels for an additional fee. Three different sheets of 6 Nos. 1155n, 1156d or 1156r, and 6 non-personalizable labels each sold as part of

a set of 8 sheets with various face values for $8.50 per sheet. A sheet containing 3 each of Nos. 1156d and 1156r and 5 non-personalizable labels sold for $10.50.

Buildings in Belgium and Singapore A289

Designs: (23c), Belgian Center for Comic Strip Art, Brussels. 60c, Shop on Kandahar Street, Singapore. $1, Shops on Bukit Pasoh Road, Singapore. $2, Museum of Musical Instruments, Brussels.

2005, Sept. 9   *Perf. 12¾*
1160-1163	A289	Set of 4	5.50 5.50
1160a		Perf. 13½x13¼ + label	.70 .70
1161a		Perf. 13½x13¼ + label	1.00 1.00
1162a		Perf. 13½x13¼ + label	1.75 1.75
1163a		Souvenir sheet, #1160-1163	5.25 5.25

No. 1160 is inscribed "1st Local." See Belgium Nos. 2104-2107.
Nos. 1160a, 1161a, 1162a issued 11/7/05. Nos. 1160a issued in sheets of 8 + 8 labels that sold for $5. Nos. 1161a and 1162a were issued in sheets containing four of each stamp + eight labels that sold for $9.

HSBC Tree Top Walk — A290

No. 1164: a, (23c), Colugo. b, 60c, Adenia. c, $1, Red-crowned barbet. d, $1, Common tree nymph butterfly.

2005, Oct. 19   *Perf. 14*
1164	A290	Horiz. strip of 4, #a-d	4.50 4.50

Booklet Stamp
Self-Adhesive
Serpentine Die Cut 10x9½
1165	A290 (23c)	Like #1164a	.60 .60
a.		Booklet pane of 10	5.00 5.00

New Year 2006 (Year of the Dog) A291

Designs: (23c), Dog. $2, Two dogs.

2006, Jan. 6   Litho.   Perf. 13x13¼
1167-1168	A291	Set of 2	3.25 3.25
1167a		Perf. 13x12¾, + label	.35 .35
1168a		Sheet, 9 each #1167-1168	30.00 30.00
1168b		Souvenir sheet, #1167-1168, with Washington 2006 World Philatelic Exhibition emblem in sheet margin	3.50 3.50
1168c		Souvenir sheet, #1167-1168, with Belgica '06 emblem in sheet margin	3.50 3.50

Issued: Nos. 1167-1168, 1167a, 1168a, 1/6; No. 1168b, 5/27; No. 1168c, 11/16. No. 1167a printed in sheets of 10 + 10 labels. No. 1167 is inscribed "1st Local."

Art by Tan Swie Hian A292

No. 1169: a, White Cloud. b, Ganges. c, Soaring over the Flower Field. d, Kuta is a Song. e, The Winged Steed.

No. 1170, vert.: a, Black Panther (Pine). b, Ginkgo (Male). c, White Elephant. d, Summer Lotus. e, Water Dhyana.
$2, Calligraphy, vert.

2006, Feb. 22   *Perf. 12*
1169		Horiz. strip of 5	1.75 1.75
a.-e.		A292 (23c) Any single	.35 .35

Perf. 12¾
Size: 27x57mm
1170		Horiz. strip of 5	4.25 4.25
a.-e.		A292 50c Any single	.85 .85

Souvenir Sheet
1171	A292	$2 multi	3.50 3.50

Nos. 1169a-1169e are inscribed "1st Local." No. 1171 contains one 40x60mm stamp.

Marine Mammals — A293

Designs: (23c), Indo-Pacific bottlenose dolphin. (31c), Indo-Pacific humpbacked dolphin. $1, Finless porpoise. $2, Dugong.

2006, Mar. 22   *Perf. 13¼*
1172-1175	A293	Set of 4	5.50 5.50
1175a		Souvenir sheet, #1172-1175	5.50 5.50

Self-Adhesive
1175B	A293 (23c)	Like #1172	.35 .35

Nos. 1172 and 1175B are inscribed "1st Local;" No. 1173, "2nd Local."

A294    Festivals and Holidays — A295

Designs: Nos. 1176, 1184, (23c), Dove (Christmas). Nos. 1177, 1185, (23c), Fruit (Chinese New Year). Nos. 1178, 1186, (23c), Candle (Deepavali). Nos. 1179, 1187 (23c), Crescent and star (Eid ul-Fitr).
No. 1180, 50c, Dove (Christmas), diff. No. 1181, 50c, Fruit (Chinese New Year), diff. No. 1182, 50c, Candle (Deepavali), diff. No. 1183, 50c, Crescent and star (Eid ul-Fitr), diff.

2006, Apr. 19   *Perf. 14½x14*
1176-1179	A294	Set of 4	1.25 1.25
1180-1183	A295	Set of 4	3.00 3.00

Self-Adhesive
Die Cut Perf. 14½x14
1184-1187	A294	Set of 4	1.60 1.60

Nos. 1176-1179, 1184-1187 are inscribed "1st Local." Nos. 1184-1187 were each issued in sheets of 10.

Traveler's Palm — A296

2006, May 2   Litho.   Perf. 12¾
1188		Vert. strip of 5 + 5 labels	2.40 2.40
a.		A296 (23c) beige & multi + label	.40 .40
b.		A296 (23c) light green & multi + label	.40 .40
c.		A296 (23c) yellow & multi + label	.40 .40
d.		A296 (23c) lt blue & multi + label	.40 .40
e.		A296 (23c) pale rose & multi + label	.40 .40

No. 1188 was printed in sheets containing 2 strips of stamps and labels. The sheet sold for $3. Nos. 1188a-1188e are inscribed "1st Local." Two sheets containing 4 examples of Nos. 1188c and 1188d, each with four non-personalizable labels sold as part of a set of

eight sheets with various face values that sold for $9 each.

Orchid — A297

2006, May 2
1189		Vert. strip of 4 + 4 labels	3.25 3.25
a.		A297 50c black, red & pink + label	.80 .80
b.		A297 50c lilac, black & purple + label	.80 .80
c.		A297 50c org yel, black & brown + label	.80 .80
d.		A297 50c lt grn, black & dark grn + label	.80 .80

No. 1189 was printed in sheets containing 2 strips of stamps and labels. Two sheets, differing in label and marginal image, were created. Each sheet sold for $5.
Sheets containing five No. 1189a or five No. 1189c, and five non-personalizable labels sold for $8.50 per sheet. A sheet containing 2 each of Nos. 1189b, 1189c, and 1189d and 6 non-personalizable labels sold as part of a set of 8 sheets with various face values for $8.50 per sheet. A sheet containing two each of Nos. 1189c and 1189d and 4 non-personalizable labels sold as part of a set of 8 sheets with various face values that sold for $9 per sheet.

Vanishing Occupations A298

Designs: Nos. 1190, 1200, (23c), Clog maker. Nos. 1191, 1201, (23c), Wooden bucket maker. Nos. 1192, 1202, (23c), Spice grinder. Nos. 1193, 1203, (23c), Snake charmer. Nos. 1194, 1204, (23c), Satay man. No. 1195, 80c, Mama store worker. No. 1196, 80c, Roti man. No. 1197, 80c, Backlane barber. No. 1198, 80c, Chinese medicinal tea shop worker. No. 1199, 80c, Tin bucket maker.

2006, May 24   *Perf. 13*
1190-1199	A298	Set of 10	7.50 7.50

Self-Adhesive
Serpentine Die Cut 10
1200-1204	A298	Set of 5	1.75 1.75

Nos. 1190-1194, 1200-1204 are inscribed "1st Local."

National Computerization Program, 25th Anniv. — A299

Use of computer technology in: (23c), Government. 60c, Trade. 80c, Education. $1, Telecommunications.

2006, June 20   *Perf. 12¾*
1205-1208	A299	Set of 4	4.00 4.00

No. 1205 is inscribed "1st Local."

Singapore Chinese Chamber of Commerce and Industry, Cent. — A300

Map, centenary emblem, Chinese characters and: (23c), Chamber building. (31c),

Orchids. 80c, Emblem of World Chinese Entrepreneurs Convention. $1, Nanyang University Administration Building. $2, War Memorial and Sun Yat-sen Nanyang Memorial Hall.

2006, July 19   *Perf. 12¾x12*
1209-1213	A300	Set of 5	6.75 6.75
1213a		Souvenir sheet, #1209-1213	6.75 6.75

No. 1209 is inscribed "1st Local;" No. 1210 is inscribed "2nd Local."

National Day — A301

Globe and: (23c), Buildings (partial globe). 60c, People. 80c, Shipping containers. $1, Entertainers and fireworks. $2, Buildings (full globe).

2006, Aug. 9   *Perf. 12¾*
1214-1217	A301	Set of 4	3.75 3.75

Souvenir Sheet
Perf. 12¾x13
1218	A301	$2 multi	3.50 3.50

No. 1214 is inscribed "1st Local." No. 1218 contains one 49x49mm stamp. A sheet containing 3 #1214 exists, sold as part of a series of sheets sold with a book for $39.90.

Singapore Biennale 2006 — A302

2006, Sept. 13   *Perf. 14¼x14*
1219	A302	$2 multi	3.25 3.25

A303

Intl. Monetary Fund World Bank Group Board of Governors Annual Meeting A304

Designs: 50c, Orchids. 80c, Esplanade Performing Arts Center. No. 1222, Buildings. No. 1223, Coin depicting orchid. $5, Coin depicting traveler's palm.

Perf. 13½x13¾
2006, Sept. 13   *Litho.*
1220	A303	50c multi	.80 .80
1221	A303	80c multi	1.25 1.25
1222	A303	$1 multi	1.75 1.75
a.		Miniature sheet, 4 each #1220, 1222, perf. 13½x13¼, + 4 labels	16.50 16.50

Litho. With Foil Application
Perf. 13¼
1223	A304	$1 gold & blk	1.75 1.75
1224	A304	$5 silver & blk	8.50 8.50
		Nos. 1220-1224 (5)	14.05 14.05

Orchids and Paintings — A305

Designs: Nos. 1225, 1231a, (23c), Vanda Mimi Palmer orchid. Nos. 1226, 1231b, (23c), Renanthera Singaporean orchid. Nos. 1227, 1231c, 70c, Vanda Miss Joaquim orchid. Nos. 1228, 1231d, 70c, Mokara Lion's Gold orchid. $1, Hollyhocks and Egret, by Hoitsu Sakai, horiz. (49x34mm). Nos. 1230, 1231e, $2, Irises and Moorhens, by Sakai, horiz. (49x34mm).

2006, Oct. 3   Litho.   Perf. 14¼
1225-1230 A305   Set of 6   7.25   7.25
1230a   Miniature sheet, #1229-
1230, 3 each #1227-
1228, perf. 13½x13¼,
+ 6 labels   16.00 16.00

Litho. With Foil Application (#1231a-1231e)
Perf. 14¼
1231 A305   Miniature sheet,
#1229, 1231a-
1231e   7.75 7.75

Nos. 1225-1226, 1231a-1231e are inscribed "1st Local." No. 1230a sold for $8; No. 1231 sold for $5.10. See Japan No. 2966.
A sheet containing 3 perf. 13¼ examples of No. 1230 and three labels that could not be personalized sold for $8.50.

Diplomatic Relations Between Singapore and Vatican City, 25th Anniv. — A306

Designs: 50c, Merlion and St. Peter's Basilica. $2, Flags of Singapore and Vatican City.

2006, Oct. 12   Litho.   Perf. 13½x13¼
1232-1233 A306   Set of 2   4.25   4.25
1233a   Souvenir sheet, #1232-
1233, perf. 12¾   4.25   4.25

See Vatican City Nos. 1336-1337.

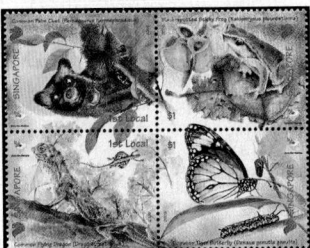

Care for Nature — A307

Designs: Nos. 1234a, 1235, Common palm civet. Nos. 1234b, 1236, Common flying dragon. No. 1234c, Black-spotted sticky frog. No. 1234d, Common tiger butterfly.

2006, Oct. 31   Perf. 13x13¼
1234 A307   Block of 4   3.75   3.75
a.-b.   (23c) Either single   .35   .35
c.-d. $1 Either single   1.50   1.50

Booklet Stamps
Self-Adhesive
Serpentine Die Cut 11x11¼
1235 A307   (23c) multi   .50   .50
1236 A307   (23c) multi   .50   .50
a.   Booklet pane, 5 each #1235-
1236   5.00

Nos. 1234a, 1234b, 1235 and 1236 are inscribed "1st Local."

New Year 2007 (Year of the Pig) — A308

Designs: (25c), One pig. $2, Two pigs.

2007, Jan. 19   Perf. 13½x13¼
1237-1238 A308   Set of 2   3.25   3.25
1238a   Miniature sheet, 9 each
#1237-1238, perf. 12¾   32.50 32.50
1238b   Souvenir sheet, #1237-
1238, perf. 12¾   3.50   3.50

No. 1237 is inscribed "1st Local." Bangkok 2007 World Stamp Exhibition (#1238b).
A collector's souvenir sheet exists with No. 1237-1238 including previous 12 sets of Chinese Zodiac stamps. Value, $60.

Kindness Movement, 10th Anniv. — A309

Children's drawings: Nos. 1239a, 1240a, Boy in wheelchair, children with joined hands. Nos. 1239b, 1240b, Child opening elevator door. Nos. 1239c, 1240c, Girl assisting fallen girl, horiz. Nos. 1239d, 1240h, Red Cross volunteers helping people, horiz. Nos. 1239e, 1240g, Four people under open umbrella, horiz. Nos. 1239f, 1240f, Children visiting people at hospital, horiz. Nos. 1239g, 1240j, People in subway car, horiz. Nos. 1239h, 1240e, Boy assisting person slipping in rain, horiz. Nos. 1239i, 1240i, Boy helping blind man, horiz. Nos. 1239j, 1240d, People in crosswalk, horiz.

Perf. 13¼x13, 13x13¼ (horiz. stamps)
2007, Feb. 8
1239 A309   Sheet of 10   4.00   4.00
a.-j.   (25c) Any single   .40   .40

Booklet Stamps
Self-Adhesive
Serpentine Die Cut 10x10½, 10½x10 (horiz. stamps)
1240 A309   Booklet pane of 10   4.00
a.-j.   (25c) Any single   .40   .40

Each stamp is inscribed "1st Local."

Traditional Wedding Costumes — A310

No. 1241: a, Korean (mountains in background). b, Korean (flowers in background). c, Chinese. d, Indian. e, Malay. f, Eurasian. g, Korean (flowers in background). h, Korean (ducks in background).

Perf. 13½x13¼
2007, Mar. 30   Litho.
1241 A310   Block of 8   8.50   8.50
a.-b.   (25c) Either single   .40   .40
c.-f.   65c Any single   1.05   1.05
g.-h. $1.10 Either single   1.75   1.75
i.   Souvenir sheet, #1241   8.50   8.50

Nos. 1241a-1241b are inscribed "1st Local." See South Korea No. 2250.

Cultural Dances — A311

Dancers from: (25c), Chinese culture. (31c), Indian culture. $1.10, Eurasian and Western cultures. $2, Malay culture.

2007, May 16   Perf. 15x14¾
1242-1245 A311   Set of 4   5.75 5.75

No. 1242 is inscribed "1st Local;" No. 1243, "2nd Local."

Birds A312

Flowers — A313

Mammals — A314

Designs: 5c, Crimson sunbird. 20c, Yellow-rumped flycatcher. (25c), Frangipani. 30c, Blue-throated bee-eater. (31c), Torch ginger. 45c, Yellow wagtail. 50c, Stork-billed kingfisher. 55c, Blue-crowned hanging parrot. 65c, Common goldenback. 80c, Jambu fruit dove. $1.10, Large Indian civet. $2, Banded leaf monkey. $5, Malayan pangolin. $10, Cream-colored giant squirrel.

2007, June 6   Litho.   Perf. 14
1246 A312   5c multi   .25   .25
a.   Dated "2007C"   .25   .25
b.   Dated "2007C"   .25   .25
1247 A312   20c multi   .30   .30
a.   Dated "2007B"   .30   .30
b.   Dated "2007C"   .30   .30
c.   Dated "2007D"   .30   .30
d.   Dated "2007E"   .25   .25
e.   Dated "2007F"   .25   .25
f.   Dated "2007G"   .25   .25
1248 A313   (25c) multi   .40   .40
1249 A312   30c multi   .45   .45
a.   Dated "2007B"   .35   .35
b.   Dated "2007C"   .35   .35
c.   Dated "2007D"   .35   .35
d.   Dated "2007E"   .35   .35
1250 A313   (31c) multi   .50   .50
a.   Dated "2007C"   .50   .50
b.   Dated "2007D"   .50   .50
c.   Dated "2007E"   .40   .40
1251 A312   45c multi   .70   .70
a.   Dated "2007B"   .70   .70
b.   Dated "2007C"   .70   .70
c.   Dated "2007D"   .60   .60
d.   Dated "2007E"   .60   .60
e.   Dated "2007F"   .60   .60
f.   Dated "2007G"   .60   .60
1252 A312   50c multi   .80   .80
a.   Dated "2007B"   .80   .80
b.   Dated "2007C"   .80   .80
c.   Dated "2007D"   .65   .65
d.   Dated "2007E"   .65   .65
e.   Dated "2007F"   .65   .65
f.   Dated "2007G"   .65   .65
1253 A312   55c multi   .90   .90
a.   Dated "2007B"   .90   .90
b.   Dated "2007C"   .70   .70
c.   Dated "2007D"   .70   .70
1254 A312   65c multi   1.05   1.05
a.   Dated "2007C"   1.05   1.05
b.   Dated "2007D"   1.05   1.05
c.   Dated "2007D"   .85   .85
d.   Dated "2007E"   .85   .85
e.   Dated "2007F"   .85   .85
1255 A312   80c multi   1.25   1.25
a.   Dated "2007B"   1.25   1.25
b.   Dated "2007C"   1.25   1.25
c.   Dated "2007D"   1.00   1.00
d.   Dated "2007E"   1.00   1.00
e.   Dated "2007F"   1.00   1.00

f.   Dated "2007G"   1.00   1.00
Perf. 15x14¾
1256 A314 $1.10 multi   1.75   1.75
a.   Dated "2007B"   1.75   1.75
b.   Dated "2007C"   1.75   1.75
c.   Dated "2007D"   1.40   1.40
d.   Dated "2007E"   1.40   1.40
1257 A314 $2 multi   3.25   3.25
1258 A314 $5 multi   8.00   8.00
a.   Dated "2007B"   8.00   8.00
b.   Dated "2007C"   8.00   8.00
c.   Dated "2007D"   6.50   6.50
1259 A314 $10 multi   16.00 16.00
a.   Miniature sheet, #1246-1259   40.00 40.00
b.   Dated "2007B"   16.00 16.00
c.   Dated "2007C"   16.00 16.00
d.   Dated "2007D"   13.00 13.00
Nos. 1246-1259 (14)   35.60 35.60

Serpentine Die Cut 9½x10
Self-Adhesive
1260 A313   (25c) multi   .40   .40
a.   Booklet pane of 10   4.00
b.   Dated "2007B"   .40   .40
c.   Dated "2007C"   .40   .40
d.   Dated "2007D"   .40   .40
e.   Dated "2007E"   .30   .30
f.   Booklet pane of 10 #1260e   .30   .30

Nos. 1248 and 1260 are inscribed "1st Local;" No. 1250, "2nd Local." No. 1260a sold for $2.55. No. 1259a sold for $28.
See Nos. 1370-1374, 1439-1441.

National Service Act, 40th Anniv. — A315

Designs: (26c), Enlistees taking oath of allegiance. (32c), Soldiers in basic training. $1.10, Soldiers in drill. $2, Soldiers in action.

2007, July 2   Perf. 14½x14
1261-1264 A315   Set of 4   6.00 6.00

No. 1261 is inscribed "1st Local;" No. 1262, "2nd Local."

Miniature Sheet

Association of South East Asian Nations (ASEAN), 40th Anniv. — A316

No. 1265: a, Secretariat Building, Bandar Seri Begawan, Brunei. b, National Museum of Cambodia. c, Fatahillah Museum, Jakarta, Indonesia. d, Typical house, Laos. e, Malayan Railway Headquarters Building, Kuala Lumpur, Malaysia. f, Yangon Post Office, Myanmar (Burma). g, Malacañang Palace, Philippines. h, National Museum of Singapore. i, Vimanmek Mansion, Bangkok, Thailand. j, Presidential Palace, Hanoi, Viet Nam.

2007, Aug. 8   Perf. 13¼
1265 A316   (26c) Sheet of 10, #a-
j   4.00 4.00

Each stamp on No. 1265 is inscribed "1st Local." No. 1265 sold for $2.55.
See Brunei No. 607, Burma No. 370, Cambodia No. 2339, Indonesia Nos. 2120-2121, Laos Nos. 1717-1718, Malaysia No. 1170, Philippines Nos. 3103-3105, Thailand No. 2315, and Viet Nam Nos. 3302-3311.

Tourist Attractions — A317

Designs: (26c), Chinatown. 65c, Kampong Glam. 80c, Little India. $1.10, Orchard Road. $5, Merlion, vert.

2007, Aug. 9   Litho.   Perf. 12¼
1266-1269 A317 Set of 4   4.50 4.50
Souvenir Sheet
Litho. & Embossed
1270 A317 $5 multi   8.00 8.00
No. 1266 is inscribed "1st Local."

Uniforms of Youth Organizations A318

Organization: No. 1271, (32c), National Cadet Corps. No. 1272, (32c), Singapore Scout Association. No. 1273, (32c), Girl Guides Singapore. No. 1274, (32c), Girls' Brigade Singapore. No. 1275, (32c), Boys' Brigade in Singapore. No. 1276, (32c), St. John Ambulance Brigade Singapore. No. 1277, (32c), Red Cross Youth. No. 1278, (32c), National Police Cadet Corps. No. 1279, (32c), National Civil Defense Cadet Corps.

2007, Sept. 19   Litho.   Perf. 13¼x13
1271-1279 A318 Set of 9   4.25 4.25
Nos. 1271-1279 are each inscribed "2nd Local."

Coral Reef Inhabitants — A319

Designs: Nos. 1280a, 1281, False clown anemonefish, Sea anemone. Nos. 1280b, 1282, Singapore goby, Blind shrimp. No. 1280c, Hawksbill turtle, Remora. No. 1280d, Razorfish, Sea urchin.

2007, Oct. 17   Perf. 13x13¼
1280 A319 Block of 4   4.50 4.50
a.-b.   (26c) Either single   .40   .40
c.-d. $1.10 Either single   1.75 1.75
Booklet Stamps
Self-Adhesive
1281 A319 (26c) multi   .40   .40
1282 A319 (26c) multi   .40   .40
a.   Booklet pane of 10, 5 each
      #1281-1282   4.25
Nos. 1280a, 1280b, 1281, 1282 are each inscribed "1st Local."

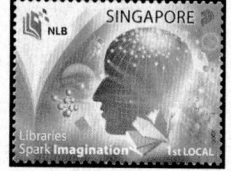

National Library Board A320

Slogans: (26c), Libraries Spark Imagination. 80c, Libraries Bring Knowledge Alive. $1.10,

Libraries Create Possibilities. $2, Libraries for Life, Knowledge for Success.

2007, Nov. 12
1283-1286 A320 Set of 4   6.75 6.75
No. 1283 is inscribed "1st Local."

Opening of Changi Airport Terminal 3 — A321

Designs: (26c), Clouds, Interior of Terminal 3. 65c, Exterior of Terminal 3, Airbus A380. $1.10, Plant leaves, Terminal 3 Vertical Garden. $2, Airplane in flight, Airport control tower, baggage handlers outside Terminal 3.

2008, Jan. 9   Perf. 14¼x14
1287-1290 A321 Set of 4   6.50 6.50
No. 1287 is inscribed "1st Local."

New Year 2008 (Year of the Rat) A322

Designs: (26c), Rat. 65c, Rat and tangerine. $1.10, Two rats, vert.
No. 1294: a, Rat (pig hologram). b, Rat and tangerine (ox hologram).

2008, Jan. 18   Litho.   Perf. 14
1291 A322 (26c) multi   .40   .40
a.   Perf. 13½x13¼   .40   .40
1292 A322 65c multi   1.05 1.05
a.   Perf. 13½x13¼   1.05 1.05
Size: 35x45mm
Perf. 14¼x14½
1293 A322 $1.10 multi   1.75 1.75
a.   Souvenir sheet, #1291a,
      1292a, 1293, with Taiwan
      2008 emblem in sheet
      margin   3.25 3.25
b.   As "a," with Olympex 2008
      sheet margin   3.25 3.25
c.   As "a," with Jakarta 2008
      emblem in sheet margin   3.25 3.25
Nos. 1291-1293 (3)   3.20 3.20
Souvenir Sheet
Litho. With Transparent Holographic Film
Perf. 13x13¼
1294   Sheet of 2   22.50 22.50
a.   A322 $5 multi   7.00 7.00
b.   A322 $10 multi   14.00 14.00
Litho.
Self-Adhesive
Serpentine Die Cut 10
1295 A322 (26c) multi   .40   .40
Nos. 1291 and 1295 are inscribed "1st Local."
Issued: Nos. 1291a, 1292a, 1293a, 3/7; No. 1293b, 8/18; No. 1293c, 10/23.

Festivals — A323

Designs: Nos. 1296, 1308, (26c), Christmas. Nos. 1297, 1309, (26c), Chinese New Year. Nos. 1298, 1310, (26c), Deepavali. Nos. 1299, 1311, (26c), Eid ul-Fitr. No. 1300, (32c), Easter. No. 1301, (32c), Mid-autumn festival. No. 1302, (32c), Pongal. No. 1303, (32c), Hari Raya Haji. No. 1304, 55c, Christmas, diff. No. 1305, 55c, Chinese New Year, diff. No. 1306, 55c, Deepavali, diff. No. 1307, 55c, Eid ul-Fitr, diff.

2008, Feb. 29   Litho.   Perf. 14x14½
1296-1307 A323 Set of 12   7.00 7.00

Self-Adhesive
Die Cut Perf. 14x14½
1308-1311 A323 Set of 4   1.60 1.60
Nos. 1296-1299, 1308-1311 are inscribed "1st Local;" Nos. 1300-1303, "2nd Local."

Embroidery, Beadwork and Porcelain Designs of Peranakan Culture — A324

No. 1312, (26c) — Various designs with bottom panel color of: a, Orange. b, Red.
No. 1313, (32c) — Various designs with bottom panel color of: a, Red violet. b, Green.
No. 1314, 65c — Various designs with bottom panel color of: a, Green. b, Blue.
No. 1315, $1.10 — Various designs with bottom panel color of: a, Olive green. b, Dark red.
$5, Deer with red violet top panel.

2008, Apr. 8   Litho.   Perf. 13x13½
Horiz. Pairs, #a-b
1312-1315 A324 Set of 4   7.00 7.00
Souvenir Sheet
Litho. With Beads Applied
Perf. 13¾
1316 A324 $5 multi   55.00 55.00
Nos. 1312a-1312b each inscribed "1st Local;" Nos. 1313a-1313b each inscribed "2nd Local." No. 1316 sold for $8 and contains one 44x44mm stamp.

Selection of Singapore as Host of 2010 Youth Olympic Games — A325

No. 1317: a, (26c), People celebrating. b, $2, People, flag, building.

2008, June 25   Litho.   Perf. 12¾
1317 A325 Horiz. pair, #a-b   3.50 3.50
No. 1317a is inscribed "1st Local."

Native Cuisine of Singapore and Macao — A326

No. 1318, (26c) — Macao dishes: a, Carne de porco à Alentejana. b, Lombo de bacalhau braseado em lascas. c, Yangzhou fried rice. d, Crispy fried chicken.
No. 1319, 65c — Singapore dishes: a, Roti Prata. b, Hainanese chicken rice. c, Laksa. d, Satay.
No. 1320, vert.: a, Clay pot rice, Macao. b, Chili crab, Singapore.

2008, July 4   Perf. 14x13¼
Blocks of 4, #a-d
1318-1319 A326 Set of 2   5.50 5.50
Souvenir Sheet
Perf. 13¼x14
1320 A326 $2 Sheet of 2, #a-b   5.50 5.50
Nos. 1318a-1318d are each inscribed "1st Local." See Macao Nos. 1248-1249.

2008 Summer Olympics, Beijing — A327

Designs: (26c), Table tennis. (32c), Sailing. No. 1323, $1.10, Shooting. No. 1324, $1.10, Badminton.

2008, Aug. 8   Perf. 13
1321-1324 A327 Set of 4   4.00 4.00
No. 1321 is inscribed "1st Local;" No. 1322, "2nd Local."

National Day — A328

Various photographs of buildings and Singapore daily life by: No. 1325, (26c), No. 1330, 50c, David Tay Poey Cher. No. 1326, (26c), No. 1331, 50c, Tan Lip Seng. No. 1327, (26c), No. 1332, 50c, Chua Soo Bin. No. 1328, (26c), No. 1333, 50c, Foo Tee Jun. No. 1329, (26c), No. 1334, 50c, Teo Bee Yen.
$2, Photographs by the various photographers.

2008, Aug. 9   Perf. 14¼
1325-1334 A328 Set of 10   6.00 6.00
Souvenir Sheet
Perf. 14½
1335 A328 $2 multi   3.25 3.25
Nos. 1325-1329 each are inscribed "1st Local." No. 1335 contains one 61x61mm stamp.

Singapore Air Force, 40th Anniv. A329

Designs: (26c), Pilots, airplane, helicopter. (32c), Weapon systems officers, plane. 65c, Unmanned aerial vehicle pilot, drone. 80c, Air engineering officer, Senior technician, helicopter. $1.10, Weapons system officers, missiles.

2008, Aug. 28   Perf. 14
1336-1340 A329 Set of 5   5.00 5.00
No. 1336 is inscribed "1st Local;" No. 1337, "2nd Local."

2008 Formula 1 Singapore Grand Prix — A330

No. 1341 — Formula 1 race car and: a, Singapore skyline. b, Checkered flag.

2008, Sept. 26   Perf. 13½
1341 A330 $2 Horiz. pair, #a-b   6.00 6.00
No. 1341 exists imperf.

Singapore Post Office, 150th Anniv. — A331

Postman: (26c), On scooter, 2008. (32c), And scooter, c. 1980. 50c, And bicycle, c. 1970. 80c, And mailbox, c. 1950. $1.10, And post office, c. 1910.

2008, Oct. 29   *Perf. 12¾x13¼*
1342-1346 A331   Set of 5   4.25 4.25

No. 1342 is inscribed "1st Local;" No. 1343, "2nd Local."

Cash Crops — A332

Designs: (26c), Pepper. 65c, Tapioca. $1.10, Rubber. $2, Nutmeg.

2008, Nov. 12   *Perf. 13½*
1347-1350 A332   Set of 4   6.50 6.50

Booklet Stamp
Self-Adhesive
Serpentine Die Cut 10x9½
1351 A332 (26c) multi   .40 .40
    a.   Booklet pane of 10   4.00

Nos. 1347 and 1351 are inscribed "1st Local."

Fruit — A333

Designs: 65c, Dragon fruit. $1.10, Durian.

2008, Nov. 18   *Perf. 13¾*
1352-1353 A333   Set of 2   2.75 2.75
  1353a   Souvenir sheet, #1352-1353   2.75 2.75

See Viet Nam Nos. 3345-3346.

New Year 2009 (Year of the Ox) A334

Designs: Nos. 1354, 1357a, 1358, Ox facing right. Nos. 1355, 1357b, Ox facing left. $1.10, Two oxen, vert. (35x45mm).

2009, Jan. 9   Litho.   *Perf. 13x13¼*
1354 A334 (26c) multi   .40 .40
1355 A334 65c multi   1.05 1.05

    Perf. 13
1356 A334 $1.10 multi   1.75 1.75
    a.   Souvenir sheet, #1354-1356, with China 2009 emblem in sheet margin   3.25 3.25
    b.   As "a," with Hong Kong 2009 emblem in sheet margin   3.25 3.25
    Nos. 1354-1356 (3)   3.20 3.20

Souvenir Sheet
Litho. With Hologram
Perf. 13x13¼
1357   Sheet of 2   22.50 22.50
    a.   A334 $5 multi   7.00 7.00
    b.   A334 $10 multi   14.00 14.00

Self-Adhesive
Litho.
Serpentine Die Cut 12
1358 A334 (26c) multi   .40 .40

Nos. 1354 and 1358 are inscribed "1st Local."

Issued: No. 1356a, 4/10; No. 1356b, 5/14.

Greetings A335

Designs: Nos. 1359a, 1364, Man and woman kissing, bowl and umbrella. Nos. 1359b, 1360, Girl blowing out candles. Nos. 1359c, 1361, Boy and girl in frame. Nos. 1359d, 1362, Girl, teddy bear, gift boxes. Nos. 1359e, 1363, Boy with balloons.

2009, Feb. 11   Litho.   *Perf. 14x14½*
1359   Horiz. strip of 5   2.10 2.10
    a.-e.   A335 (26c) Any single   .40 .40

Booklet Stamps
Self-Adhesive
Serpentine Die Cut 11¼x10½
1360 A335 (26c) multi   .40 .40
1361 A335 (26c) multi   .40 .40
1362 A335 (26c) multi   .40 .40
1363 A335 (26c) multi   .40 .40
1364 A335 (26c) multi   .40 .40
    a.   Booklet pane of 10, 2 each #1360-1364   4.00
    Nos. 1360-1364 (5)   2.00 2.00

Nos. 1359a-1359e, 1360-1364 are each inscribed "1st Local."

Old Movie Theaters A336

Designs: (26c), Cathay Theater, 1939. 50c, Majestic Theater, 1928. 80c, Capitol Theater, 1933. No. 1368, $1.10, Queens Theater, c. 1920. No. 1369, $1.10, Rex Theater, 1946.

2009, Mar. 20   Litho.   *Perf. 14¼*
1365-1369 A336   Set of 5   6.00 6.00

No. 1365 is inscribed "1st Local."

Flower Type of 2007
Designs: Nos. 1370, 1373, Blue pea vine. Nos. 1371, 1372, 1374, Pigeon orchid.

2009, May 6   Litho.   *Perf. 14*
1370 A313 (26c) multi   .40 .40
1371 A313 (26c) multi   .40 .40

Souvenir Sheet
Litho. With Embroidered Flower Affixed
1372 A313 $5 multi   11.00 11.00

Self-Adhesive
Litho.
Serpentine Die Cut 9¾x10
1373 A313 (26c) multi   .40 .40
    a.   Booklet pane of 10   4.00
    b.   Dated "2009B"   .40 .40
    c.   Booklet pane of 10 #1373b   4.00
    d.   Dated "2009C"   .35 .35
    e.   Booklet pane of 10 #1373d   3.50
1374 A313 (26c) multi   .40 .40
    a.   Booklet pane of 10   4.00
    b.   Dated "2009B"   .35 .35
    c.   Booklet pane of 10 #1374b   3.50
    d.   Dated "2009C"   .35 .35
    e.   Booklet pane of 10 #1374d   3.50

Nos. 1370-1371, 1373-1374 are inscribed "1st Local." No. 1372 sold for $8.

Opening of First Stations on Singapore Mass Rapid Transit Circle Line — A337

Designs: (26c), Map of Singapore and Circle Line. 80c, People in station. $1.10, Circle

Line train. $2, People in operation control center.

2009, May 28   Litho.   *Perf. 13¾*
1375-1378 A337   Set of 4   6.25 6.25

No. 1375 is inscribed "1st Local." Values are for stamps with surrounding selvage.

Singapore Botanic Gardens, 150th Anniv. A338

No. 1379: a, Visitor Center. b, Bandstand. c, Burkill Hall, Girl on a Swing sculpture. d, Swans in flight, bridge.
$2, Swans on lake, bridge

2009, June 19   *Perf. 14*
1379   Horiz. strip of 4   3.75 3.75
    a.-b.   A338 (26c) Either single   .35 .35
    c.-d.   A338 $1.10 Either single   1.50 1.50

Souvenir Sheet
Perf. 15x14½
1380 A338 $2 multi   3.25 3.25

Nos. 1379a-1379b are inscribed "1st Local." No. 1380 contains one 48x48mm stamp.

Desserts — A339

Designs: (26c), Ice kacang. (32c), Ondeh-ondeh. 65c, Ang ku kueh. 80c, Lapis sagu. $1.10, Mithai.

2009, July 17   *Perf. 12¾*
1381-1385 A339   Set of 5   5.00 5.00

No. 1381 is inscribed "1st Local;" No. 1382, "2nd Local."

Sculpture — A340

Works by: No. 1386, 50c, Teo Eng Seng. No. 1387, 50c, Anthony Poon. No. 1388, 50c, Han Sai Por. No. 1389, 50c, Wee Beng Chong. No. 1390, 50c, Ng Eng Teng, horiz. No. 1391, 50c, Brother Joseph McNally, horiz. No. 1392, 50c, Tay Chee Toh.
$2, All 7 sculptures, horiz.

    Perf. 13¼x13¾, 13¾x13¼
2009, Aug. 9
1386-1392 A340   Set of 7   5.00 5.00

Souvenir Sheet
Perf. 14¾x14
1393 A340 $2 multi   3.00 3.00

No. 1393 contains one 96x37mm stamp.

2010 Youth Olympic Games, Singapore — A341

Designs: (26c), Diver. 65c, Two women athletes. $1.10, Four men. $2, Hurdler.

2009, Aug. 14   *Perf. 13¼*
1394-1397 A341   Set of 4   6.50 6.50

No. 1394 is inscribed "1st Local."

Diplomatic Relations Between Singapore and the Philippines, 40th Anniv. — A342

Bridges: (26c), Bamban Bridge, Philippines. 65c, Cavenagh Bridge, Singapore. 80c, Henderson Waves and Alexandra Arch Bridges, Singapore. $1.10, Marcelo B. Fernan Bridge, Philippines.

2009, Aug. 28   *Perf. 12¾*
1398-1401 A342   Set of 4   4.25 4.25
  1401a   Souvenir sheet, #1398-1401   4.25 4.25

No. 1398 is inscribed "1st Local." See Philippines No. 3231.

Tourist Sites in Singapore and Indonesia A343

Designs: (26c), Singaraja Statue, Indonesia. 65c, Merlion, Singapore. 80c, Taman Mini Indonesia Indah (Beautiful Indonesia Miniature Park). $1.10, Sentosa, Singapore.

2009, Oct. 28   *Perf. 14x13½*
1402-1405 A343   Set of 4   4.50 4.50
  1405a   Souvenir sheet, #1402-1405   4.50 4.50

No. 1402 is inscribed "1st Local." See Indonesia Nos. 2213-2216.

Asia-Pacific Economic Cooperation 2009 Meetings, Singapore — A344

No. 1406: a, Singapore skyline. b, Port of Singapore.
No. 1407: a, Singapore at night. b, Singapore Airport.

2009, Nov. 9   *Perf. 14x14½*
1406 A344   Horiz. pair, #a-b, + central label   3.75 3.75
    a.   (26c) multi   .40 .40
    b. $2 multi   3.25 3.25
1407 A344   Horiz. pair, #a-b, + central label   3.25 3.25
    a.   80c multi   1.25 1.25
    b. $1.10 multi   1.75 1.75

No. 1406a is inscribed "1st Local."

New Year 2010 (Year of the Tiger) A345

Designs: (26c), $5, Tiger, yellow green and yellow background. 65c, $10, Tiger, pink and rose background. $1.10, Two tigers, vert. (35x40mm).

2010, Jan. 8   Litho.   *Perf. 13½*
1408 A345 (26c) multi   .40 .40
1409 A345 65c multi   1.05 1.05

    Perf. 13x13¼
1410 A345 $1.10 multi   1.75 1.75
    a.   Souvenir sheet of 3, #1408-1410, with London 2010 emblem in sheet margin   3.00 3.00
    b.   Souvenir sheet of 3, #1408-1410, with Bangkok 2010 emblem in sheet margin   3.00 3.00
    Nos. 1408-1410 (3)   3.20 3.20

Souvenir Sheet
Litho. With Transparent Holographic Film

1411	Sheet of 2	22.50	22.50
a.	A345 $5 multi	7.00	7.00
b.	A345 $10 multi	14.00	14.00

Self-Adhesive
Litho.
Serpentine Die Cut 9¾x10½

1412	A345 (26c) multi	.40	.40

Nos. 1408 and 1412 are inscribed "1st Local."

Issued: No. 1410a, 5/8; No. 1410b, 8/4.

Anniversaries
A346

Designs: No. 1413, 50c, Housing and Development Board, 50th anniv. No. 1414, 50c, People's Association, 50th anniv. No. 1415, $1, Customs Department, cent., horiz. No. 1416, $1, Singapore Scout Association, cent., horiz.

2010, Jan. 26	**Litho.**	**Perf. 13**	
1413-1416	A346	Set of 4	4.25 4.25

Playgrounds — A347

Various playgrounds in Singapore: (26c), 50c, 65c, 80c, $1.10, $2.

2010, Mar. 9		**Perf. 13½**	
1417-1422	A347	Set of 6	8.50 8.50

No. 1417 is inscribed "1st Local."

Butterflies
A348

Designs: Nos. 1423, 1427, (26c), Common birdwing. 80c, Tailed jay. $1.10, Common posy. $2, Blue glassy tiger.

2010, Apr. 21		**Litho.**	**Perf. 14**
1423-1426	A348	Set of 4	6.75 6.75

Booklet Stamp
Self-Adhesive
Serpentine Die Cut 9½x10

1427	A348 (26c) multi	.40	.40
a.	Booklet pane of 10	4.00	

Trees
A349

Designs: Nos. 1428, 1438a, (26c), Saga tree. Nos. 1429, 1438b, (26c), Rain tree. Nos. 1430, 1438c, (26c), Yellow flame tree. Nos. 1431, 1438d, (26c), Tembusu tree. Nos. 1432, 1438e, (26c), Angsana tree. Nos. 1433, 1438f, (26c), Sea almond tree, vert. Nos. 1434, 1438g, (26c), Broad-leafed mahogany tree, vert. Nos. 1435, 1438h, (26c), Sea apple tree, vert. Nos. 1436, 1438i, (26c), Senegal mahogany tree, vert. Nos. 1437, 1438j, (26c), Trumpet tree, vert.

Perf. 14x14¼, 14¼x14			
2010, May 26			**Litho.**
1428-1437	A349	Set of 10	3.75 3.75

Booklet Stamps
Self-Adhesive
Serpentine Die Cut 9½x10, 10x9½

1438	Booklet pane of 10	3.75	
a.-j.	A349 (26c) Any single	.35	.35

Nos. 1428-1437, 1438a-1438j are inscribed "1st Local."

Flower Type of 2007

Designs: (26c), Simpoh air. (32c), Singapore rhododendron.

2010, June 23		**Perf. 14**	
1439	A313 (26c) multi	.40	.40
1440	A313 (32c) multi	.50	.50
a.	Dated "2010B"	.50	.50
b.	Dated "2010C"	.50	.50

Self-Adhesive
Serpentine Die Cut 9¾x10

1441	A313 (26c) multi	.40	.40
a.	Booklet pane of 10	4.00	
b.	Dated "2010B"	.40	.40
c.	Booklet pane of 10 #1441b	4.00	

Nos. 1439, 1441 are inscribed "1st Local." No. 1440 is inscribed "2nd Local."

National Monuments — A350

Buildings and their architectural features: (26c), Bowyer Block. (32c), College of Medicine Building. 55c, Command House. 65c, Hwa-Chong Institution Clock Tower. 80c, Former Raffles College. $1.10, Tan Teck Guan Building. $2, Architectural features of the aforementioned buildings.

2010, Aug. 4		**Perf. 13½x13¾**	
1442-1447	A350	Set of 6	5.50 5.50

Souvenir Sheet
Perf. 14x13¼

1448	A350 $2 multi	3.00	3.00

No. 1442 is inscribed "1st Local." No. 1443 is inscribed "2nd Local."

2010 Youth Olympics, Singapore — A351

Lyo and Merly, Youth Olympics Mascots: (26c) Sitting on globe. 65c, Sitting under palm tree. $1.10, Merly swimming. $2, Lyo playing basketball.

2010, Aug. 14		**Perf. 13½x13¾**	
1449-1452	A351	Set of 4	5.50 5.50
1452a		Sheet of 4, #1449-1452, + 2 labels, perf. 13½x13¼	22.00 22.00

No. 1449 is inscribed "1st Local." No. 1452a with personalized labels sold for $15.50, and for $19.90 with generic labels depicting the 2010 Youth Olympics emblem and mascots.

Heritage Trail and Kent Ridge Park Trail
A352

No. 1453: a, Flowers, Bukit Chandu War Museum, sculpture of soldiers. b, Bird, flowers, elevated walkway. c, Flowers, sheltered walkway, eagle. d, Flowers, gazebo.

2010, Sept. 22		**Perf. 12¾**	
1453	Horiz. strip of 4	4.50	4.50
a.	A352 (32c) multi	.50	.50
b.	A352 65c multi	1.00	1.00
c.	A352 80c multi	1.25	1.25
d.	A352 $1.10 multi	1.75	1.75

No. 1453a is inscribed "2nd Local."

Festivals — A353

Designs: Nos. 1454, 1463, (26c), Lion and fish (Chinese New Year). Nos. 1455, 1464, (26c), Candles (Christmas). Nos. 1456, 1465, (26c), Oil lamps (Eid ul-Fitr). Nos. 1457, 1466 (26c), Peacocks (Deepavali). Nos. 1458, 1462a, 55c, Chinese characters, fruit (Chinese New Year). Nos. 1459, 1462b, 55c, Ornaments (Christmas). Nos. 1460, 1462c, 55c, Crescent moon and star, diamonds (Eid ul-Fitr). Nos. 1461, 1462d, 55c, Oil lamp (Deepavali). No. 1462e, Lion, fish, Chinese character, flowers (Chinese New Year). No. 1462f, Ornaments and stars (Christmas). No. 1462g, Oil lamps (Eid ul-Fitr). No. 1462h, Peacocks (Deepavali).

2010, Oct. 20	**Litho.**	**Perf. 14½**	
Stamps With White Frames			
1454-1461	A353	Set of 8	5.00 5.00

Litho. With Foil Application
Stamps Without White Frames

1462	Sheet of 8	17.00	17.00
a.-d.	A353 55c Any single	1.40	1.40
e.-h.	A353 $1.10 Any single	2.75	2.75

Litho.
Booklet Stamps
Self-Adhesive
Stamps With White Frames
Serpentine Die Cut 10x9¾

1463	A353 (26c) multi	.40	.40
a.	Booklet pane of 10	4.00	
1464	A353 (26c) multi	.40	.40
a.	Booklet pane of 10	4.00	
1465	A353 (26c) multi	.40	.40
a.	Booklet pane of 10	4.00	
1466	A353 (26c) multi	.40	.40
a.	Booklet pane of 10	4.00	
	Nos. 1463-1466 (4)	1.60	1.60

Nos. 1454-1457, 1463-1466 are inscribed "1st Local." No. 1462 sold for $10.80.

New Year 2011 (Year of the Rabbit)
A354

Designs: (26c), $5, Rabbit facing right. 65c, $10, Rabbit facing left. $1.10, Two rabbits, vert. (35x40mm).

2011		**Litho.**	**Perf. 13½**
1467	A354 (26c) multi	.40	.40
1468	A354 65c multi	1.00	1.00
		Perf. 13x13¼	
1469	A354 $1.10 multi	1.75	1.75
a.	Souvenir sheet of 3, #1467-1469, with Indipex 2011 emblem in sheet margin	3.25	3.25
b.	As "a," with PhilaNippon '11 emblem in sheet margin	3.50	3.50
c.	As "a," with China 2011 exhibition emblem in sheet margin	3.25	3.25
	Nos. 1467-1469 (3)	3.15	3.15

Souvenir Sheet
Litho. With Transparent Holographic Film

1470	Sheet of 2	22.50	22.50
a.	A354 $5 multi	7.00	7.00
b.	A354 $10 multi	14.00	14.00

Self-Adhesive
Litho.
Serpentine Die Cut 9¾x10½

1471	A354 (26c) multi	.40	.40

Nos. 1467 and 1471 are inscribed "1st Local." Issued: No. 1469a, 2/12; No. 1469b, 7/28; No. 1469c, 11/11; others, 1/7.

Spirit of Giving — A355

Children's art with panel at bottom in: $1.10, Blue. $2, Purple.

2011, Jan. 24	**Litho.**	**Perf. 12¾x13¼**	
1472-1473	A355	Set of 2	4.25 4.25

Intl. Association of Volunteer Efforts World Volunteer Conference, Singapore.

Pond Life
A356

Flora and fauna: 5c, White-collared kingfisher. 20c, Diving beetle. (26c), Water lily (30x27mm). 30c, Common redbolt. (32c), Water hyacinth (30x27mm). 45c, Ornate coraltail. 50c, Black marsh terrapin. 55c, White-breasted waterhen. 65c, Common greenback. 80c, Common toad. $1.10, Common tilapia (50x30mm). $2, Pond wolf spider (50x30mm). $5, Water strider (50x30mm). $10, Water scorpion (50x30mm).

Perf. 13x13¼ Syncopated, 13¼ Syncopated (#1476, 1478, 1484-1487)

2011			**Photo.**
1474	A356	5c multi	.25 .25
1475	A356	20c multi	.35 .35
1476	A356	(26c) multi	.45 .45
1477	A356	30c multi	.50 .50
1478	A356	(32c) multi	.55 .55
1479	A356	45c multi	.75 .75
1480	A356	50c multi	.80 .80
1481	A356	55c multi	.90 .90
1482	A356	65c multi	1.10 1.10
1483	A356	80c multi	1.25 1.25
1484	A356	$1.10 multi	1.75 1.75
1485	A356	$2 multi	3.25 3.25
1486	A356	$5 multi	8.00 8.00
1487	A356	$10 multi	16.00 16.00
a.	Miniature sheet of 14, #1474-1487	36.00	36.00
	Nos. 1474-1487 (14)	35.90	35.90

Booklet Stamp
Self-Adhesive
Die Cut Perf. 13¼ Syncopated

1488	A356 (26c) multi	.45	.45
a.	Booklet pane of 10	4.50	

Nos. 1476 and 1488 are inscribed "1st Local." No. 1478 is inscribed "2nd Local." Issued: Nos. 1484-1487, 2/16; others, 4/13. See Nos. 1532-1534, 1597-1599.

Aviation in Singapore, Cent.
A357

Silhouettes of people with airplanes and airports: (26c), Bristol Box Kite airplane, Old Racecourse. 45c, Fokker F7-A, Seletar Airport. 65c, Airspeed Consul, Kallang Airport. 80c, F-15SG, Paya Lebar Air Base. $1.10, Airbus A380, Singapore Changi Airport.

2011, Mar. 16	**Litho.**	**Perf. 13¼**	
1489-1493	A357	Set of 5	5.25 5.25

No. 1489 is inscribed "1st Local."

Hawker Centers A358

Hawker centers: No. 1494, 80c, Lau Pa Sat. No. 1495, 80c, East Coast. No. 1496, 80c, Maxwell. No. 1497, 80c, Newton.

2011, May 18 — Perf. 13x13¼
1494-1497 A358 Set of 4 — 5.25 5.25

Oriental Small-clawed Otter — A359

No. 1498 — Otter: a, Underwater. b, On log with crab. c, Pair looking at dragonfly. d, Head.

2011, June 3 — Perf. 12¾
1498 A359 Horiz. strip of 4 — 5.25 5.25
a.-b. 50c Either single — .80 .80
c.-d. $1.10 Either single — 1.75 1.75

Spices and Dishes They Are In — A360

Designs: (26c), Cinnamon, Masala teh. (32c), Coriander, Satay. 65c, Star anise, Braised duck. 80c, Tamarind, Assam prawns. $1.10, Turmeric, Fish head curry.

2011, July 15 — Perf. 14
1499-1503 A360 Set of 5 — 5.25 5.25

No. 1499 is inscribed "1st Local." No. 1500 is inscribed "2nd Local."

Economic Development in Singapore, 50th Anniv — A361

Designs: (26c), "HOME." $2, Stylized tree.

2011, Aug. 1 — Perf. 12¾x13
1504-1505 A361 Set of 2 — 3.75 3.75

No. 1504 is inscribed "1st Local."

Historic Areas of Singapore — A362

Designs: No. 1506, 50c, Joo Chiat. No. 1507, 50c, Taman Jurong. No. 1508, $1.10, Old Joo Chiat. No. 1509, $1.10, Old Taman Jurong.
$2, Old and new Joo Chiat and Taman Jurong.

2011, Aug. 8 — Perf. 13¼
1506-1509 A362 Set of 4 — 5.50 5.50
Souvenir Sheet
1510 A362 $2 multi — 3.50 3.50

No. 1510 contains one 72x51mm stamp.

 A363
 A364
 A365
 A366
 A367 
 A368
 A369
 A370
 A371
 Your Singapore A372

2011, Sept. 14 — Perf. 12¾
1511 Sheet of 10 — 4.50 4.50
a. A363 (26c) multi — .45 .45
b. A364 (26c) multi — .45 .45
c. A365 (26c) multi — .45 .45
d. A366 (26c) multi — .45 .45
e. A367 (26c) multi — .45 .45
f. A368 (26c) multi — .45 .45
g. A369 (26c) multi — .45 .45
h. A370 (26c) multi — .45 .45
i. A371 (26c) multi — .45 .45
j. A372 (26c) multi — .45 .45

Self-Adhesive
Serpentine Die Cut 13½x13¼
1512 Booklet pane of 10 — 4.50
a. A363 (26c) multi — .45 .45
b. A364 (26c) multi — .45 .45
c. A365 (26c) multi — .45 .45
d. A366 (26c) multi — .45 .45
e. A367 (26c) multi — .45 .45
f. A368 (26c) multi — .45 .45
g. A369 (26c) multi — .45 .45
h. A370 (26c) multi — .45 .45
i. A371 (26c) multi — .45 .45
j. A372 (26c) multi — .45 .45

Nos. 1511a-1511j, 1512a-1512j each are inscribed "1st Local."

Rivers — A373

Designs: $1.10, Singapore River. $2, Nile River.

2011, Oct. 17 — Perf. 13¼
Size: 163x30mm
1513 A373 $1.10 multi — 1.75 1.75
1514 A373 $2 multi — 3.25 3.25
Souvenir Sheet
Perf. 12¾
1515 A373 Sheet of 2 — 5.00 5.00
a. $1.10 multi, 120x22mm — 1.75 1.75
b. $2 multi, 120x22mm — 3.25 3.25

See Egypt No. 2080.

20th World Orchid Conference, Singapore A374

Orchid varieties: (26c), Vanda Miss Joaquim. 45c, Renanthera 20th WOC Singapore 2011. 65c, Dendrobium World Peace. 80c, Cyrtocidium goldiana. $2, Grammatophyllum speciosum.
$5, Grammatophyllum speciosum, Renanthera 20th WOC Singapore, 2011, Dendrobium World Peace, Vanda Miss Joaquim, Cyrtocidiuim goldiana, horiz.

2011, Nov. 12 — Litho. — Perf. 14
1516-1520 A374 Set of 5 — 6.50 6.50
Souvenir Sheet
Perf. 14½
1521 A374 $5 multi — 7.75 7.75

No. 1516 is inscribed "1st Local." No. 1521 contains one 78x40mm stamp.

New Year 2012 (Year of the Dragon) A375

Designs: (26c), $5, Dragon facing right. 65c, $10, Dragon facing left. $1.10, Two dragons, vert. (35x45mm).

2012, Jan. 5 — Perf. 13½
1522 A375 (26c) multi — .45 .45
1523 A375 65c multi — 1.10 1.10

Perf. 13x13¼
1524 A375 $1.10 multi — 1.75 1.75
a. Souvenir sheet of 3, #1522-1524 — 3.25 3.25
b. As "a," with Beijing Intl. Stamp and Coin Expo emblem in sheet margin — 3.25 3.25
Nos. 1522-1524 (3) — 3.30 3.30
Souvenir Sheet
1525 Sheet of 2 — 22.50 22.50
a. A375 $5 multi — 7.50 7.50
b. A375 $10 multi — 14.00 14.00
Self-Adhesive
Serpentine Die Cut 9¾x10½
1526 A375 (26c) multi — .45 .45

Nos. 1522 and 1526 are inscribed "1st Local." No. 1525 sold for $15.70.
Issued: No. 1524a, 6/18. Indonesia 2012 World Stamp Exhibition, Jakarta (#1524a.) No. 1524b, 11/2.

Local Tea Time Snacks — A376

Designs: Nos. 1527, 1531, (26c), Lapis Sagu (nine-layered kueh). 50c, Kueh Dadar (coconut pancake). 80c, Bao (Chinee buns). $1.10, Kueh Tutu.

2012, Feb. 8 — Perf. 13¼x13½
1527-1530 A376 Set of 4 — 4.25 4.25
Booklet Stamp
Self-Adhesive
Serpentine Die Cut 10x9½
1531 A376 (26c) multi — .45 .45
a. Booklet pane of 10 — 4.50

Nos. 1527 and 1531 each are inscribed "1st Local."

Pond Life Type of 2011

Designs: (26c), Yellow burhead flower (30x27mm). (32c), Water lettuce (30x27mm).

Perf. 13¼ Syncopated
2012, Mar. 12 — Photo.
1532 A356 (26c) multi — .45 .45
1533 A356 (32c) multi — .50 .50
Booklet Stamp
Self-Adhesive
Die Cut Perf. 13¼ Syncopated
1534 A356 (26c) multi — .45 .45
a. Booklet pane of 10 — 4.50

Nos. 1532 and 1534 are inscribed "1st Local." No. 1533 is inscribed "2nd Local."

Reservoirs — A377

Designs: No. 1535, (26c), Serangoon Reservoir. No. 1536, (26c), Marina Reservoir. No. 1537, (26c), Lower Selatar Reservoir. No. 1538, (26c), Punggol Reservoir. No. 1539, (26c), Jurong Lake. No. 1540, 50c, Upper Selatar Reservoir. No. 1541, 50c, Pandan Reservoir. No. 1542, 50c, Bedok Reservoir. No. 1543, 50c, MacRitchie Reservoir. No. 1544, 50c, Lower Peirce Reservoir.

2012, Mar. 22 — Litho. — Perf. 14¼x14
1535-1544 A377 Set of 10 — 5.50 5.50

Nos. 1535-1539 are each inscribed "1st Local."

A378

A379

A380

Local
Markets
A381

2012, Apr. 18 **Perf. 14x13¼**
1545 A378 80c multi 1.40 1.40
1546 A379 80c multi 1.40 1.40
1547 A380 80c multi 1.40 1.40
1548 A381 80c multi 1.40 1.40
 Nos. 1545-1548 (4) 5.60 5.60

Intl. Year of Cooperatives — A382

Designs: No. 1549, (26c), Singapore sky-line, 2012. No. 1550, (26c), Birth of Singapore National Cooperative Federation, 1980. 50c, Birth of National Trade Unions Congress Cooperatives, 1969. No. 1552, $1.10, Birth of Singapore's first cooperative, the Singapore Government Staff Credit Cooperative Society, 1925. No. 1553, $1.10, Founders of the Coop-erative Principles, 1844.

2012, May 31 **Perf. 14½**
1549-1553 A382 Set of 5 5.00 5.00
 Nos. 1549-1550 are inscribed "1st Local."

Gardens by the Bay — A383

Designs: No. 1554, $1.10, Conservatory, flowers and trees. No. 1555, $1.10, Tree, king-fisher and dragonfly.

2012, June 28 **Perf. 12¾**
1554-1555 A383 Set of 2 3.50 3.50

2012 Summer Olympics,
London — A384

Designs: (26c), Table tennis. 65c, Swim-ming. $1.10, Sailing. $2, Badminton.

2012, July 27 **Perf. 13¼**
1556-1559 A384 Set of 4 6.50 6.50
 No. 1556 is inscribed "1st Local."

Historical Places in Singapore — A385

Designs: (32c), Tiong Bahru in 2012. 50c, Balestier in 2012. 80c, Tiong Bahru in the past. $1.10, Balestier in the past. $2, Tiong Bahru and Balestier.

2012, Aug. 2 **Perf. 14x13¼**
1560-1563 A385 Set of 4 4.50 4.50
 Souvenir Sheet
1564 A385 $2 multi 3.25 3.25
 No. 1560 is inscribed "2nd Local." No. 1564 contains one 100x41mm stamp.

Birds — A386

Designs: Nos. 1565a, 1566a, Haliaeetus leucogaster. Nos. 1565b, 1566b, Leptocoma jugularis.

2012, Aug. 31 **Photo.** **Perf. 13**
1565 A386 Horiz. pair +
 central label 6.50 6.50
 a.-b. $2 Either single 3.25 3.25
 Souvenir Sheet
 Litho. & Embossed
 Perf. 13¼x13
1566 A386 Sheet of 2 16.50 16.50
 a.-b. $5 Either single 8.25 8.25
 Singapore 2015 World Philatelic Exhibition.

Giant
Pandas — A387

Designs: Nos. 1567, 1571, 50c, Head of Giant panda. 65c, Giant panda in tree. $2, Two Giant pandas (39x74mm). $10, Like $2, with different colors in background.

Perf. 12¾, 12x12¼ ($2)
2012, Sept. 6 **Litho.**
1567-1569 A387 Set of 3 5.25 5.25
 Souvenir Sheet
 Perf. 12¾x13
1570 A387 $10 multi 16.50 16.50
 Booklet Stamp
 Self-Adhesive
 Serpentine Die Cut 10x9½
1571 A387 50c multi .85 .85
 a. Booklet pane of 10 8.50
 Diplomatic relations between Singapore and People's Republic of China, 22nd anniv. No. 1570 contains one 39x74mm stamp.

Festivals — A388

Designs: Nos. 1572, 1581, (26c), Christ-mas. No. 1573, 1582, (26c), Deepavali. Nos. 1574, 1583, (26c), Chinese New Year. Nos. 1575, 1584, (26c), Eid ul-Fitr. No. 1576, 55c, Christmas, diff. No. 1577, 55c, Deepavali, diff. No. 1578, 55c, Chinese New Year, diff. No. 1579, 55c, Eid ul-Fitr, diff.
 $5, Celebrants of the various festivals.

2012, Oct. 17 **Perf. 13¼x12¾**
1572-1579 A388 Set of 8 5.25 5.25
 Souvenir Sheet
 Perf. 12¾x13¼
1580 A388 $5 multi 8.25 8.25
 Booklet Stamps
 Self-Adhesive
 Serpentine Die Cut 13¾x14
1581 A388 (26c) multi .45 .45
 a. Booklet pane of 10 4.50
1582 A388 (26c) multi .45 .45
 a. Booklet pane of 10 4.50
1583 A388 (26c) multi .45 .45
 a. Booklet pane of 10 4.50
1584 A388 (26c) multi .45 .45
 a. Booklet pane of 10 4.50
 Nos. 1581-1584 (4) 1.80 1.80
 Nos. 1572-1575, 1581-1584 each are inscribed "1st Local." No. 1580 contains one 100x36mm stamp.

Currency Interchangeability Agreement Between Singapore and Brunei, 45th Anniv. — A389

Designs: No. 1585, $1, Images from Singa-pore banknotes issued in 1967, 1976, 1984 and 1999. $2, Singapore Skyline, and Mosque, Brunei.
 No. 1587a, $1, Images from Brunei banknotes issued in 1967, 1989, 1996 and 2007.

2012, Nov. 27 **Perf. 12¾**
1585-1586 A389 Set of 2 5.00 5.00
 Souvenir Sheet
1587 A389 Sheet of 3, #1585-
 1586, 1587a 6.50 6.50
 a. $1 multi 1.60 1.60
 See Brunei Nos. 633-634.

New Year
2013 (Year
of the
Snake)
A390

Designs: Nos. 1588, 1591a, 1592, Snake facing right. No. 1589, 1591b, Snake facing left. $1.10, Two snakes, vert. (35x45mm).

2013, Jan. 4 **Perf. 12¾**
1588 A390 (26c) multi .45 .45
1589 A390 65c multi 1.10 1.10
 Perf. 13
1590 A390 $1.10 multi 1.75 1.75
 a. Souvenir sheet of 3, #1588-
 1590, with Australia 2013
 Stamp Exhibition emblem
 in sheet margin 3.25 3.25
 b. Souvenir sheet of 3, #1588-
 1590, with Thailand 2013
 Stamp Exhibition emblem
 in sheet margin 3.25 3.25
 Nos. 1588-1590 (3) 3.30 3.30
 Souvenir Sheet
 Perf. 13x13¼
1591 Sheet of 2 24.00 24.00
 a. A390 $5 multi 8.00 8.00
 b. A390 $10 multi 16.00 16.00
 Self-Adhesive
 Serpentine Die Cut 13¾x13½
1592 A390 (26c) multi .45 .45
 Nos. 1588 and 1592 are each inscribed "1st Local."
 A sheet containing perf. 13 examples of Nos. 1293, 1356, 1410, 1469, 1524 and 1590 sold for $15.70.
 Issued: No. 1590a, 5/10; No. 1590b, 8/2.

History of
Singapore
Railroads — A391

Designs: (26c), Tanjong Pagar Station exte-rior. 65c, Bukit Timah Station. $1.10, Tanjong Pagar Station interior. $2, Bukit Timah Railway track and bridge.

2013, Feb. 28 **Perf. 13½**
1593-1596 A391 Set of 4 6.50 6.50
 No. 1593 is inscribed "1st Local."

Pond Life Type of 2011

Designs: (26c), Geli geli (30x27mm). (32c), Water gentian (30x27mm).

Perf. 13¼ Syncopated
2013, Mar. 20 **Photo.**
1597 A356 (26c) multi .45 .45
1598 A356 (32c) multi .50 .50
 Booklet Stamp
 Self-Adhesive
 Die Cut Perf. 13¼ Syncopated
1599 A356 (26c) multi .45 .45
 a. Booklet pane of 10 4.50
 Nos. 1597 and 1599 are inscribed "1st Local." No. 1598 is inscribed "2nd Local."

Marina Bay Skyline — A392

No. 1600: a, Fullerton Hotel. b, Singapore Flyer (Ferris wheel). c, Esplanade —Theaters on the Bay. d, Marina Bay Sands Resort. $5, Marina Bay skyline.

2013, May 28 **Litho.** **Perf. 14¼**
1600 A392 Block of 4 5.25 5.25
 a. (26c) multi .40 .40
 b. (32c) multi .50 .50
 c. 65c multi 1.10 1.10
 d. $2 multi 3.25 3.25
 Souvenir Sheet
 Litho. With Foil Application
 Perf. 14¼x14
1601 A392 $5 multi 12.00 12.00
 No. 1600a is inscribed "1st Local"; No. 1600b, "2nd Local." No. 1601 contains one 50x50mm stamp and sold for $7.48.

Sign Language — A393

Frequently-used signs: Nos. 1602a, 1603, Hi. Nos. 1602b, 1604, Welcome. Nos. 1602c, 1605, I love you. Nos. 1602d, 1606, Thanks. Nos. 1602e, 1607, Goodbye.

2013, June 17 **Litho.** **Perf. 12¾**
1602 A393 Horiz. strip of 5 2.00 2.00
 a.-e. (26c) Any single .40 .40
 Booklet Stamps
 Self-Adhesive
 Serpentine Die Cut 13¼x13½
1603 A393 (26c) multi .40 .40
1604 A393 (26c) multi .40 .40
1605 A393 (26c) multi .40 .40
1606 A393 (26c) multi .40 .40

1607 A393 (26c) multi .40 .40
    a. Booklet pane of 10, 2 each 4.00
    #1603-1607
    Nos. 1603-1607 (5) 2.00 2.00
Nos. 1602a-1602e and 1603-1607 are each inscribed "1st Local."

"Our City in a Garden" A394

City buildings and: Nos. 1608, 1613a, (26c), Sunda pangolin, Green-crested lizard, Collared kingfisher, Dendrobium leonis, Moss rose. Nos. 1609, 1613b, 50c, Oriental pied hornbill, Pink mempat, Cymbidium bicolor, Tree-climbing crab, Crimson sunbird. 80c, Crepe myrtle, Dragon scales, Blue-spotted crow caterpillar, Blue pansy butterfly, Torch ginger, Magpie robin, Ferns, Heliconias, Tiger orchid. $1.10, Crimson dropwing, Baya weaver, Ridley's staghorn fern, Smooth otter, Cannonball tree flower and fruits, Yellow flame, Knobbly sea star, Angsana tree, Rain trees.
$5, Composite of Nos. 1608-1611.

2013, July 13 Litho. Perf. 13¼
1608-1611 A394 Set of 4 4.25 4.25
Souvenir Sheet
Litho., Sheet Margin Litho. & Embossed
1612 A394 $5 multi 13.00 13.00
Self-Adhesive
Serpentine Die Cut 12½
1613 Sheet of 4, 2 each
    #1613a-1613b 2.50
    a. A394 (26c) multi .40 .40
    b. A394 50c multi .85 .85
Nos. 1608 and 1613a are inscribed "1st Local." No. 1612 contains one 140x35mm stamp, and sold for $8. No. 1613 sold for $1.55. Portulaca grandiflora seeds are found under gummed plastic circles affixed to Nos. 1612 and 1613a.

Independence, 48th Anniv. — A395

Inscriptions: (26c), Beating SARS together. 50c, Cleaning and greening our city. 65c, Conquering our water challenges. 80c, Living together in harmony. $1.10, Forging a vibrant economy.
$2, 48 years of independence.

2013, Aug. 5 Litho. Perf. 13¾
1614-1618 A395 Set of 5 5.25 5.25
Souvenir Sheet
Litho. With Foil Application
Perf. 13¼
1619 A395 $2 multi 3.25 3.25
No. 1614 is inscribed "1st Local." No. 1619 contains one 48x48mm stamp.

Singapore 2015 World Stamp Exhibition — A396

Nos. 1620 and 1621: a, Sea shells. b, Tropical fish.

2013, Aug. 23 Litho. Perf. 14x14½
1620 A396 $2 Horiz. pair, #a-b, + central label 6.50 6.50
Souvenir Sheet
Litho. & Embossed With Transparent Holographic Film
1621 A396 $5 Sheet of 2, #a-b 19.00 19.00
Compare types A396 and A23. No. 1621 sold for $12. Imperforate examples of No. 1621 were offered in a folder that sold for $46.73.

Singapore's Globalization Journey — A397

Designs: (26c), Truck and agricultural products. 65c, Ship, cranes and containers. 80c, Airplane and Singapore skyline. $1.10, Train, people, and flags.

2013, Sept. 10 Litho. Perf. 13x13¼
1622-1625 A397 Set of 4 4.50 4.50
No. 1622 is inscribed "1st Local."

Birds A398

Designs: (26c), Gray peacock pheasants. $2, Red juunglefowl.

2013, Sept. 12 Litho. Perf. 12¾
1626-1627 A398 Set of 2 3.75 3.75
1627a Souvenir sheet of 2, #1626-1627 3.75 3.75
Diplomatic relations between Singapore and Viet Nam, 40th anniv. No. 1626 is inscribed "1st Local." See Viet Nam Nos. 3485-3486.

Vanishing Trades — A399

Designs: (26c), Dairy man. (32c), Maker of beaded slippers.
5c, Kachung puteh (nuts and legumes) seller. 20c, Lantern maker. 30c, Songkok (religious head covering) maker. 45c, Goldsmith. 50c, Cobbler. 55c, Knife sharpener. 65c, Ice ball seller. 80c, Parrot astrologer.

2013, Oct. 16 Litho. Perf. 14
1628 A399 (26c) multi .40 .40
1629 A399 (32c) multi .50 .50
Size: 32x28mm
Perf. 13¼x13½
1630 A399 5c multi .25 .25
1631 A399 20c multi .35 .35
1632 A399 30c multi .50 .50
1633 A399 45c multi .75 .75
1634 A399 50c multi .80 .80
1635 A399 55c multi .90 .90
1636 A399 65c multi 1.10 1.10
1637 A399 80c multi 1.25 1.25
    Nos. 1628-1637 (10) 6.80 6.80
Booklet Stamps
Self-Adhesive
Size: 30x27mm
1638 A399 (26c) multi .40 .40
    a. Booklet pane of 10 4.00
Size: 32x28mm
1639 A399 50c multi .80 .80
    a. Booklet pane of 10 8.00
Nos. 1628 and 1638 are inscribed "1st Local." No. 1629 is inscribed "2nd Local."

Fashion A400

Designs: (26c), Three women wearing white dresses. 65c, Three dress forms. $1.10, Flower, three women wearing white dresses. $2, Finished dresses on three dress forms.

2013, Nov. 8 Litho. Perf. 13x13¼
1640-1643 A400 Set of 4 6.50 6.50
1643a Souvenir sheet of 4, #1640-1643 6.50 6.50
No. 1640 is inscribed "1st Local." See France Nos. 4528-4531.

Television Broadcasting in Singapore, 50th Anniv — A401

Designs: (26c), People with high definition and tablet televisions. 50c, People looking at on-screen programming guide. 65c, Cameraman and television performers. 80c, People watching soccer game on color television. $1.10, People watching black-and-white television.

2013, Nov. 22 Litho. Perf. 14x13¼
1644-1648 A401 Set of 5 5.25 5.25
No. 1644 is inscribed "1st Local."

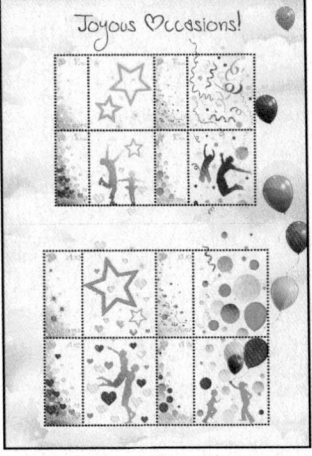

This sheet, released Dec. 7, 2013, containing four "1st Local" stamps with a franking value of 26c each, and four $1.10 stamps, plus eight non-personalizable labels sold for $11.22.

New Year 2014 (Year of the Horse) A402

Designs: Nos. 1649, 1652a, 1653, Horse facing left. Nos. 1650, 1652b, Horse facing right. $1.10, Two horses, vert. (35x45mm).

2014, Jan. 3 Litho. Perf. 13½
1649 A402 (26c) multi .40 .40
1650 A402 65c multi 1.00 1.00
Perf. 13
1651 A402 $1.10 multi 1.75 1.75
    a. Souvenir sheet of 3, #1649-1651, with Philakorea 2014 emblem in sheet margin 3.25 3.25

---

    a. Souvenir sheet of 3, #1649-1651, with World Youth Stamp Exhibition emblem in sheet margin 3.25 3.25
    Nos. 1649-1651 (3) 3.15 3.15
Souvenir Sheet
Litho. With Transparent Holographic Film
Perf. 13x13¼
1652 Sheet of 2 25.00 25.00
    a. A402 $5 multi 8.50 8.50
    b. A402 $10 multi 16.50 16.50
Litho.
Self-Adhesive
Serpentine Die Cut 9¾x10½
1653 A402 (26c) multi .40 .40
Issued: No. 1651a, 8/7; No. 1651b, 12/1. Nos. 1649 and 1653 are inscribed "1st Local." No. 1652 sold for $15.70.

Happy Occasions

This sheet, released Jan. 3, 2014, containing four "1st Local" stamps in two different designs, each with a franking value of 26c each, two 50c stamps, two $1.10 stamps, and eight non-personalizable labels sold for $11.22. A sheet containing three examples of the $1.10 stamp and three examples of one of the "1st Local" stamps and six non-personalizable labels, also was released on that day, and also sold for $11.22.

Ferns — A403

Designs: (26c), Angiopteris evecta. 50c, Angiopteris evecta, diff. 80c, Cibotium barometz. Nos. 1657, 1658, $1, Cibotium barometz, diff.

2014, Feb. 26 Litho. Perf. 12¾
1654-1657 A403 Set of 4 4.00 4.00
Booklet Stamp
Self-Adhesive
Serpentine Die Cut 13¼x13½
1658 A403 $1 multi 1.60 1.60
    a. Booklet pane of 10 16.00
No. 1654 is inscribed "1st Local."

Greetings — A404

Designs: Nos. 1659, 1666, Cupcake and candle. Nos. 1660, 1667, Heart and "love."

Nos. 1661, 1668, Wedding rings. 50c, Champagne flutes. $1, Pinwheel.

2014, Mar. 26   **Litho.**   **Perf. 12¾**
1659 A404 (26c) multi	.40	.40
1660 A404 (26c) multi	.40	.40
1661 A404 (26c) multi	.40	.40
1662 A404 50c multi	.80	.80
1663 A404 $1 multi	1.60	1.60
Nos. 1659-1663 (5)	3.60	3.60

Size: 28x33mm
Self-Adhesive
Serpentine Die Cut 13¼x13
1664 A404 50c multi	.80	.80
1665 A404 $1 multi	1.60	1.60

Booklet Stamps
1666 A404 (26c) multi	.40	.40
1667 A404 (26c) multi	.40	.40
1668 A404 (26c) multi	.40	.40
a. Booklet pane of 10, 3 each #1666, 1668, 4 #1667	4.00	
Nos. 1664-1668 (5)	3.60	3.60

Nos. 1659-1661, 1666-1668 are inscribed "1st Local." Nos. 1664 and 1665 are each printed in sheets of 4.

Street Scenes — A405

Designs: $1.10, Woman carrying baby, street stalls. $1.15, Bicyclist, children walking near harbor. $1.30, Street stalls. $2, Cyclist, trolley, pedicab. $5, Ice cream vendor, street performance. $10, Crowded street, building with advertisement sign on roof.

2014   **Litho.**   **Perf. 14x13¼**
1669 A405 $1.10 multi	1.75	1.75
1670 A405 $1.15 multi	1.75	1.75
1671 A405 $1.30 multi	2.00	2.00
1672 A405 $2 multi	3.25	3.25
1673 A405 $5 multi	8.00	8.00
1674 A405 $10 multi	16.00	16.00
a. Souvenir sheet of 6, #1669-1674	33.00	33.00
Nos. 1669-1674 (6)	32.75	32.75

Issued: $1.10, $2, $5, $10, 5/28; $1.15, $1.30, 11/26.

Festivals — A406

Designs: Nos. 1675, 1683, (26c), Christmas. Nos. 1676, 1684, (26c), Chinese New Year. No. 1677, (26c), Eid ul-Fitr. No. 1678, (26c), Deepavali. No. 1679, 55c, Christmas, diff. No. 1680, 55c, Chinese New Year, diff. No. 1681, 55c, Eid ul-Fitr, diff. No. 1682, 55c, Deepavali, diff.

2014, June 25   **Litho.**   **Perf. 12½**
1675-1682 A406 Set of 8	5.25	5.25

Booklet Stamps
Self-Adhesive
Die Cut
1683 A406 (26c) multi	.45	.45
a. Booklet pane of 10	4.50	
1684 A406 (26c) multi	.45	.45
a. Booklet pane of 10	4.50	

Nos. 1675-1678, 1683-1684 are inscribed "1st Local."

Pulau Ubin
A407

Designs: (32c), Jetty. 65c, Chek Jawa. 80c, Wayang Stage. $1.10, Quarry.

2014, July 18   **Litho.**   **Perf. 13x13¼**
1685-1688 A407 Set of 4	4.75	4.75

No. 1685 is inscribed "2nd Local."

POSTAGE DUE STAMPS

D1

Wmk. 314
1968, Feb. 1   **Litho.**   **Perf. 9**
J1 D1 1c emerald	.50	.50
J2 D1 2c red org	.80	.80
J3 D1 4c yel org	2.00	2.00
J4 D1 8c brown	1.25	1.25
J5 D1 10c rose mag	2.00	2.00
J6 D1 12c dl vio	3.00	3.00
J7 D1 20c brt bl	3.75	3.75
J8 D1 50c gray grn	11.50	11.50
Nos. J1-J8 (8)	24.80	24.80

1973-77   **Perf. 13x13½**
J1a D1 1c Unwmkd. ('77)	85.00	85.00
J3a D1 4c Unwmkd. ('77)	85.00	85.00
J5a D1 10c	1.50	4.00
b. Unwmkd. ('77)	90.00	90.00
J7a D1 20c Unwmkd. ('77)	95.00	95.00
J8a D1 50c	14.00	15.00
b. Unwmkd. ('77)	110.00	110.00

D2

1981   **Unwmk.**   **Perf. 12x11½**
J9 D2 1c emerald	.35	1.00
J10 D2 4c orange	.35	1.00
J11 D2 10c carmine	1.00	3.00
J12 D2 20c light blue	2.00	3.00
J13 D2 50c light yellow green	3.00	4.00
Nos. J9-J13 (5)	6.70	12.00

1978, Sept. 25   **Perf. 13x13½**
J9a D2 1c	1.25	1.50
J10a D2 4c	1.25	1.50
J11a D2 10c	1.60	1.60
J12a D2 20c	1.90	1.90
J13a D2 50c	2.75	2.75
Nos. J9a-J13a (5)	8.75	9.25

D3

1989, July 12   **Litho.**   **Perf. 13x13½**
J14 D3 5c red lilac	.25	.25
J15 D3 10c red	.25	.25
J16 D3 20c light blue	1.00	1.00
J17 D3 50c yellow green	2.75	2.75
J18 D3 $1 brown	5.75	5.75
Nos. J14-J18 (5)	10.00	10.00

Issued: $1, 4/30/93; others, 7/12/89.

1997, Nov. 7   **Litho.**   **Perf. 13x13½**
J19 D3 1c green	65.00	—
J20 D3 4c brown orange	90.00	—

A small quantity of Nos. J19-J20 were produced, which was sold locally only, in late 1997. Postage due stamps were replaced by machine-generated labels on Dec. 31, 1997.

SLOVAKIA

slō-'vä-kē-ə

LOCATION — Central Europe
GOVT. — Republic
AREA — 18,932 sq. mi.
POP. — 5,396,193 (1999 est.)
CAPITAL — Bratislava

Formerly a province of Czechoslovakia, Slovakia declared its independence in Mar., 1939. A treaty was immediately concluded with Germany guaranteeing Slovakian independence but providing for German "protection" for 25 years.

In 1945 the republic ended and Slovakia again became a part of Czechoslovakia.

On January 1, 1993, Czechoslovakia split into the Czech Republic and Slovakia.

100 Halierov = 1 Koruna

> **Catalogue values for unused stamps in this country are for never hinged items, beginning with Scott 26 in the regular postage section, Scott B1 in the semi-postal section, Scott C1 in the airmail section, Scott EX1 in the personal delivery section, Scott J1 in the postage due section, and Scott P10 in the newspaper section.**

Watermark

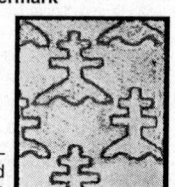

Wmk. 263 —
Double-Barred
Cross Multiple

Stamps of
Czechoslovakia, 1928-39, Overprinted in Red or Blue

1939   **Perf. 10, 12½, 12x12½**
2 A29 5h dk ultra	1.50	1.40
3 A29 10h brown	.25	.25
4 A29 20h red (Bl)	.25	.25
5 A29 25h green	6.00	5.00
6 A29 30h red vio (Bl)	.25	.25
7 A61a 40h dark blue	.25	.25
8 A73 50h deep green	.25	.25
9 A63 50h deep green	.25	.25
10 A63 60h dull violet	.25	.25
11 A63 60h dull blue	9.50	10.25
12 A60 1k rose lake (Bl) (On No. 212)	.25	.25

Overprinted Diagonally
13 A64 1.20k rose lil (Bl)	1.25	1.25
14 A65 1.50k carmine (Bl)	1.25	1.25
15 A79 1.60k ol grn (Bl)	2.00	2.75
16 A66 2k dk bl grn	2.00	2.75
17 A67 2.50k dark blue	1.25	1.25
18 A68 3k brown	1.25	1.25
19 A69 3.50k dk violet	27.50	27.50
20 A69 3.50k dk vio (Bl)	40.00	40.00
21 A70 4k dk violet	17.50	17.50
22 A71 5k green	22.50	22.50
23 A72 10k blue	200.00	175.00
Nos. 2-23 (22)	335.50	311.65

Excellent counterfeit overprints exist.

Stefánik Type of Czechoslovakia

Gen. Milan Stefánik

1939, Mar. 30   **Engr.**   **Perf. 12½**
23A A63 60h dark blue	45.00	37.50

Prepared by Czechoslovakia prior to the German occupation March 15, 1939. Subsequently issued for use in Slovakia.

Andrej Hlinka — A1

Overprinted in Red or Blue
Perf. 12½
1939, Apr.   **Unwmk.**   **Photo.**
24 A1 50h dark green (R)	.70	.70
a. Perf. 10½	5.00	2.50
b. Perf. 10½x12½	25.00	12.50
25 A1 1k dk car rose (Bl)	.75	.65
a. Perf. 10½	1,200.	1,000.
Never hinged	2,000.	
b. Perf. 10½x12½	30.00	17.50

> **Catalogue values for unused stamps in this section, from this point to the end of the section, are for Never Hinged items.**

Andrej Hlinka — A2

1939   **Unwmk.**   **Perf. 12½**
26 A2 5h brt ultra	.55	.45
27 A2 10h olive green	.90	.70
a. Perf. 10½x12½	150.00	50.00
b. Perf. 10½	600.00	80.00
28 A2 20h orange red	.90	.70
a. Imperf.	.85	.80
29 A2 30h dp violet	.90	.70
a. Imperf.	1.00	1.25
b. Perf. 10½x12½	20.00	10.00
c. Perf. 10½	50.00	12.00
30 A2 50h dk green	.90	.70
31 A2 1k dk carmine rose	1.25	.70
32 A2 2.50k brt blue	1.25	.30
a. Perf. 10½x12½	200.00	70.00
33 A2 3k black brown	3.00	.50
a. Perf. 10½x12½	15.00	5.00
b. Perf. 10½	15.00	1.50
Nos. 26-33 (8)	9.65	4.75

On Nos. 32 and 33 a pearl frame surrounds the medallion. See Nos. 55-57, 69.

General Stefánik and Memorial Tomb — A3

1939, May   **Perf. 12½**
Size: 25x20mm
34 A3 40h dark blue	1.10	
35 A3 60h slate green	1.10	
36 A3 1k gray violet	1.10	

Size: 30x23¾mm
37 A3 2k bl vio & sepia	1.25	
Nos. 34-37 (4)	4.55	

20th anniv. of the death of Gen. Milan Stefánik, but not issued.

Rev. Josef Murgas and Radio Towers — A4

1939   **Unwmk.**
38 A4 60h purple	.30	.30
39 A4 1.20k slate black	.75	.25

10th anniv. of the death of Rev. Josef Murgas. See No. 65.

Girl
Embroidering
A5

Woodcutter
A6

Girl at
Spring — A7

1939-44   Wmk. 263   Perf. 12½
40	A5	2k dk blue green	6.25	.50
41	A6	4k copper brown	1.40	1.00
42	A7	5k orange red	1.00	.50
a.		Perf. 10 ('44)	1.25	1.00
		Nos. 40-42 (3)	8.65	2.00

Dr. Josef Tiso — A8

1939-44   Wmk. 263   Perf. 12½
43	A8	50h slate green	.45	.30
43A	A8	70h dk red brn ('42)	.35	.25
b.		Perf. 10½ ('44)	.50	.35

See No. 88.

Presidential
Residence — A9

1940, Mar. 14
| 44 | A9 | 10k deep blue | 1.00 | .75 |

Tatra
Mountains
A10

Krivan Peak
A11

Edelweiss in
the Tatra
Mountains
A12

Chamois
A13

Church at
Javorina — A14

1940-43   Wmk. 263   Perf. 12½
Size: 17x21mm
45	A10	5h dk olive grn	.30	.25
46	A11	10h deep brown	.25	.25
47	A12	20h blue black	.25	.25
48	A13	25h olive brown	.55	.25
49	A14	30h chestnut brown	.35	.25
a.		Perf. 10½ ('43)	2.50	1.00
		Nos. 45-49 (5)	1.70	1.25

See Nos. 84-87, 103-107.

Hlinka Type of 1939
1940-42   Wmk. 263   Perf. 12½
55	A2	1k dk car rose	.90	.60
56	A2	2.50k brt blue ('42)	1.25	.75
a.		Perf. 10½	.60	.60
57	A2	3k black brn ('41)	2.00	1.00
a.		Perf. 10½	2.00	.90

On Nos. 56 and 57 a pearl frame surrounds
the medallion.

Stiavnica
A15

Lietava
A16

Spissky
Hrad — A17

Bojnice — A18

1941   Perf. 12½
58	A15	1.20k rose lake	.25	.25
59	A16	1.50k rose pink	.25	.25
60	A17	1.60k royal blue	.25	.25
61	A18	2k dk gray green	.25	.25
		Nos. 58-61 (4)	1.00	1.00

Slovakian Castles.

S. M. Daxner
and Stefan
Moyses
A19

1941, May 26   Photo.   Wmk. 263
62	A19	50h olive green	2.25	1.50
63	A19	1k slate blue	7.50	6.25
64	A19	2k black	6.00	5.00
		Nos. 62-64 (3)	15.75	12.75

80th anniv. of the Memorandum of the
Slovak Nation.

Murgas Type of 1939
1941   Wmk. 263
| 65 | A4 | 60h purple | .40 | .25 |

Andrej Hlinka — A20

1942
| 69 | A20 | 1.30k dark purple | .45 | .25 |

Post Horn and
Miniature
Stamp — A21

Philatelist — A22

Philatelist — A23

1942, May 23
70	A21	30h dark green	1.10	.95
71	A22	70h dk car rose	1.10	.95
72	A23	80h purple	1.10	.95
73	A21	1.30k dark brown	1.10	.95
		Nos. 70-73 (4)	4.40	3.80

Natl. Philatelic Exhibition at Bratislava.
On No. 70 the miniature stamp bears the
coat-of-arms of Bratislava; on No. 73 it shows
the National arms of Slovakia.

St. Stephen's
Cathedral,
Vienna — A24

1942, Oct. 12   Perf. 14
74	A24	70h blue green	.75	.75
75	A24	1.30k olive green	1.50	1.50
76	A24	2k sapphire	2.50	2.50
		Nos. 74-76 (3)	4.75	4.75

European Postal Congress held in Vienna.

Slovakian Educational Society — A25

1942, Dec. 14
77	A25	70h black	.25	.25
78	A25	1k rose red	.30	.25
79	A25	1.30k sapphire	.30	.25
80	A25	2k chestnut brown	.35	.25
81	A25	3k dark green	.50	.30
82	A25	4k dull purple	.50	.30
		Nos. 77-82 (6)	2.20	1.60

Slovakian Educational Soc., 150th anniv.

Andrej Hlinka — A26

1943   Wmk. 263
| 83 | A26 | 1.30k brt ultra | .75 | .35 |

See Nos. 93-94A.

Types of 1939-40
1943   Unwmk.   Perf. 12½
84	A11	10h deep brown	.25	.25
85	A12	20h blue black	.70	.50
86	A13	25h olive brown	.70	.50
87	A14	30h chestnut brown	.50	.35
88	A8	70h dk red brown	.85	.95
		Nos. 84-88 (5)	3.00	2.55

Presov
Church — A27

Locomotive
A28

Railway Tunnel
A29

Viaduct — A30

1943, Sept. 5   Perf. 14
89	A27	70h dk rose violet	.60	.50
90	A28	80h sapphire	.60	.50
91	A29	1.30k black	.60	.50
92	A30	2k dk violet brn	.60	.50
		Nos. 89-92 (4)	2.40	2.00

Inauguration of the new railroad line
between Presov and Strazske.

Hlinka Type of 1943 and

Ludovit
Stur — A31

Martin
Razus — A32

1944   Unwmk.
93	A31	80h slate green	.35	.25
94	A32	1k brown red	.35	.25
94A	A26	1.30k brt ultra	.50	.25
		Nos. 93-94A (3)	1.20	.75

Prince
Pribina — A33

Designs: 70h, Prince Mojmir. 80h, Prince
Ratislav. 1.30k, King Svatopluk. 2k, Prince
Kocel. 3k, Prince Mojmir II. 5k, Prince
Svatopluk II. 10k, Prince Braslav.

1944, Mar. 14
95	A33	50h dark green	.25	.25
96	A33	70h lilac rose	.25	.25
97	A33	80h red brown	.25	.25
98	A33	1.30k brt ultra	.30	.25
99	A33	2k Prus blue	.30	.25
100	A33	3k dark brown	.45	.30
101	A33	5k violet	.95	.70
102	A33	10k black	2.50	2.00
		Nos. 95-102 (8)	5.25	4.25

Scenic Types of 1940
1944, Apr. 1   Perf. 14
Size: 18x23mm
103	A11	10h bright carmine	.25	.30
104	A12	20h bright blue	.25	.30
105	A13	25h brown red	.25	.30
106	A14	30h red violet	.25	.30
107	A10	50h deep green	.25	.30
		Nos. 103-107 (5)	1.25	1.50

5th anniv. of Slovakia's independence.
See Nos. B25-B26.

Symbolic of
National
Protection
A41

1944, Oct. 6   Wmk. 263
| 108 | A41 | 2k green | .50 | .60 |
| 109 | A41 | 3.80k red violet | .50 | .90 |

President Josef
Tiso — A42

1945   **Unwmk.**
110 A42   1k orange   .55   .40
111 A42   1.50k brown   .30   .25
112 A42   2k green   .30   .40
113 A42   4k rose red   .90   .55
114 A42   5k sapphire   .80   .40
              Wmk. 263
115 A42   10k red violet   .75   .40
   Nos. 110-115 (6)   3.60 2.40

6th anniv. of the Republic of Slovakia's declaration of independence, Mar. 14, 1939.

Natl. Arms — A50

1993   Photo. & Engr.   Perf. 11½
150 A50 3k multicolored   .60   .30
              Engr.
              Perf. 12
           Size: 30x44mm
151 A50 8k multicolored   6.00 4.00

Issued: 3k, Jan. 2; 8k, Jan. 1. No. 151 does
not have black frameline.
No. 151 was issued in sheets of 6.

Castles &
Churches — A51

Nos. 152-155 are churches, Nos. 156-157
castles.

   Perf. 11½x12, 12x11½
1993-95   Photo. & Engr.
152 A51 2k Nitra   .25   .25
153 A51 3k Banska Bystrica   .30   .25
154 A51 5k Ruzomberok,
              horiz.   .50   .25
155 A51 10k Kosice   .90   .45
156 A51 30k Zvolen, horiz.   3.00 1.50
157 A51 50k Bratislava   6.50 3.25
   Nos. 152-157 (6)   11.45 5.95

Issued: 5k, 10k, 1993; 30k, 9/12/93; 50k,
12/31/93; 3k, 11/15/94; 2k, 3/15/95.
See Nos. 218-227.

St. John
Nepomuk,
600th Death
Anniv.
A57

Photo. & Engr.
1993, Mar. 11   Perf. 12x11½
158 A57 8k multicolored   1.10   .50

See Czech Republic #2880; Germany #1776.

President Michal Kovac

1993   Engr.   Perf. 12x11½
159 A58 2k dark gray blue   .25   .25
159A A58 3k red brown & red   .30   .25

Issued: 2k, 3/2/93; 3k, 11/3/93.

A59

Trees.
         Photo. & Engr.
1993, May 14   Perf. 11½
160 A59 3k Quercus robur   .65   .25
161 A59 4k Carpinus betulus   .65   .30
162 A59 10k Pinus silvestris .85   .50
   Nos. 160-162 (3)   2.15 1.05

A60

Famous Men: 5k, Jan Levoslav Bella (1843-
1936), composer. 8k, Alexander Dubcek
(1921-92), politician. 20k, Jan Kollar (1793-
1852), writer.

Photo. & Engr.
1993, May 20   Perf. 12x11½
163 A60 5k red brown & blue   .75   .40
164 A60 8k brown & lilac red 1.25   .60
165 A60 20k gray blue & orange 3.00 1.50
   Nos. 163-165 (3)   5.00 2.50

A61

Woman with Pitcher, by Marian Cunderlik.

1993, May 31   Engr.   Perf. 12
166 A61 14k multicolored   6.00 5.00

Europa. Issued in sheets of 4.

Literary
Slovak
Language,
150th Anniv.
A62

Design: 8k, Arrival of St. Cyril and St.
Methodius, 1130th Anniv.

Photo. & Engr.
1993, June 22   Perf. 12x11½
167 A62 2k multicolored   .25   .25
168 A62 8k multicolored   .90   .50

See Czech Republic No. 2886.

A63

Arms of Dubnica nad Vahom.

Photo. & Engr.
1993, July 8   Perf. 12x11½
169 A63 1k multicolored   .25   .25

A64

The Big Pets, by Lane Smith.

Photo. & Engr.
1993, Sept. 2   Perf. 11½
170 A64 5k multicolored   .50   .25

Bratislava Biennial of Illustrators.

Gabcikovo Dam — A65

Photo. & Engr.
1993, Nov. 12   Perf. 11½
172 A65 10k multicolored   1.25   .60

No. 172 issued se-tenant with label.

Madonna and Child,
by J. B. Klemens
(1817-83) — A66

Photo. & Engr.
1993, Dec. 1   Perf. 11½
173 A66 2k multicolored   .30   .25

Christmas.

Souvenir Sheet

Monument to Gen. Milan
Stefanik — A67

1993, Dec. 17   Engr.   Perf. 11½x12
174 A67 16k multicolored   2.75 1.25

Art from Bratislava Natl.
Gallery — A68

Sculpture: 9k, Plough of Springtime, by
Josef Kostka.

1993, Dec. 31
175 A68 9k multicolored   2.25 2.00

Issued in sheets of 4.
See Nos. 199-200, 237-238, 255.

A69

Photo. & Engr.
1994, Jan. 26   Perf. 11x11½
176 A69 2k multicolored   .50   .25
   Complete booklet, 10 #176   6.00

1994 Winter Olympics, Lillehammer.

A70

Photo. & Engr.
1994, Apr. 29   Perf. 11x11½
177 A70 3k multicolored   .35   .25
   Complete booklet, 5 #177   2.75

Intl. Year of the Family.

Jan Andrej Segner
(1704-77),
Physicist — A71

Design: 9k, Antoine de Saint-Exupery
(1900-44), aviator, author.

Photo. & Engr.
1994, May 25   Perf. 11½x11
178 A71 8k red brown & blue   1.00   .45
179 A71 9k black, blue & pink 1.00   .45

See Nos. 196-198.

Josef Murgas
(1864-1929),
Inventor of Radio
Transmitters — A72

1994, May 27   Engr.   Perf. 11½
180 A72 28k multicolored   3.25 2.50

Europa. Issued in sheets of 4

A73

Photo. & Engr.
1994, May 31   Perf. 11½x11
181 A73 3k multicolored   .30   .25

Intl. Stop Smoking Day.

A74

Photo. & Engr.
1994, June 10   Perf. 11½
182 A74 2k blue, black & green .35   .25

1994 World Cup Soccer Championships, US.

Intl. Olympic
Committee,
Cent. — A75

Photo. & Engr.
1994, June 23   *Perf. 12x11½*
183 A75 3k multicolored   .40 .25
No. 183 issued with se-tenant label.

Raptors — A76

Photo. & Engr.
1994, July 4   *Perf. 11½x12*
184 A76 4k Aquila chrysaetos   .65 .25
185 A76 5k Falco peregrinus   .75 .25
186 A76 7k Bubo bubo   .95 .40
    Nos. 184-186 (3)   2.35 .90

Prince Svatopluk of Moravia (870-894) — A77

1994, July 20   **Engr.**   *Perf. 12*
187 A77 12k red brn, buff & blk   1.60 1.00
    Issued in sheets of 4.

UPU, 120th Anniv. — A78

Photo. & Engr.
1994, Aug. 1   *Perf. 11½x12*
188 A78 8k multicolored   .90 .45

Slovak Uprising, 50th Anniv. — A79

Design: 6k, Gen. Rudolf Viest, Gen. Jan. Golian. 8k, French Volunteers' Memorial, Strecno hill.

Photo. & Engr.
1994, Aug. 27   *Perf. 12x11½*
189 A79 6k multicolored   .75 .40
190 A79 8k multicolored   .75 .40
Nos. 189-190 printed with se-tenant label.

Souvenir Sheet

Janko Matuska, Lyricist, 150th Death Anniv. — A80

Design: 34k, Matuska, woman with pitcher, verse of "A Well She Dug."

Photo. & Engr.
1994, Sept. 1   *Perf. 12x11½*
191 A80 34k multicolored   3.50 1.75

Comenius University, 75th Anniv. — A81

Photo. & Engr.
1994, Oct. 18   *Perf. 11½x12*
192 A81 12k multicolored   1.25 .60

Mojmirovce Horse Race, 180th Anniv. A82

1994, Oct. 25   *Perf. 12x11½*
193 A82 2k multicolored   .40 .25

St. George's Church, Kostotany pod Tribecom — A83

1994, Nov. 8   *Perf. 11*
194 A83 20k multicolored   2.00 1.00

Christmas — A84

1994, Nov. 29   *Perf. 11½*
195 A84 2k multicolored   .35 .25

Personalities Type of 1994

Designs: 5k, Chatam Sofer (1762-1839), rabbi. 6k, Wolfgang Kempelen (1734-1804), polytechnician. 10k, Stefan Banic (1870-1941), inventor of aviation parachute.

1994, Dec. 12   *Perf. 11½x11*
196 A71 5k multicolored   .60 .30
    Complete booklet, 5 #196   8.00
197 A71 6k multicolored   .70 .35
198 A71 10k multicolored   1.25 .60
    Nos. 196-198 (3)   2.55 1.25

Bratislava Art Type of 1993

Designs: 7k, Girls, by Janko Alexy, horiz. 14k, The Bulls, by Vincent Hloznik.

Perf. 12x11½, 11½x12
1994, Dec. 15   **Engr.**
199 A68 7k multicolored   1.00 .75
200 A68 14k multicolored   2.00 1.50

Ships — A85

5k, Cargo ship, NL EMS. 8k, Cargo ship, Ryn. 10k, 400-passenger cruise ship.

Photo. & Engr.
1994, Dec. 30   *Perf. 12x11½*
201 A85 5k multicolored   .55 .30
202 A85 8k multicolored   1.00 .60
203 A85 10k multicolored   1.00 .60
    Nos. 201-203 (3)   2.55 1.50

Samuel Jurkovic, Founder of of Landlords Assoc., 1845 — A86

Photo. & Engr.
1995, Feb. 8   *Perf. 11½*
204 A86 9k multicolored   1.10 .45

European Nature Conservation Year — A87

Protected plants: 2k, Ciminalis clusii. 3k, Pulsatilla slavica. 8k, Onosma tornense.

1995, Feb. 28
205 A87 2k multicolored   .55 .25
    Complete booklet, 10 #205   15.00
206 A87 3k multicolored   .55 .25
    Complete booklet, 5 #206   15.00
207 A87 8k multicolored   1.10 .50
    Nos. 205-207 (3)   2.20 1.00

Slovak Natl. Theatre, 75th Anniv. A88

1995, Feb. 28   *Perf. 12x11½*
208 A88 10k multicolored   1.10 .45

1995 Group B World Cup Ice Hockey Championships, Bratislava — A89

1995, Mar. 29   *Perf. 11½*
209 A89 5k blue & yellow   .55 .25

Bela Bartok (1881-1945), Composer A90

6k, Jan Bahyl (1856-1916), inventor.

Photo. & Engr.
1995, Apr. 20   *Perf. 12x11½*
210 A90 3k multicolored   .35 .25
211 A90 6k multicolored   .75 .35

Souvenir Sheet

Ludovit Stur (1815-56), Writer — A91

1995, Apr. 20   *Perf. 11½*
212 A91 16k multicolored   1.75 .85

Europa A92

1995, May 5   **Engr.**   *Perf. 12*
213 A92 8k multicolored   1.40 1.10

Liberation of the Concentration Camps, 50th Anniv. — A93

Photo. & Engr.
1995, May 5   *Perf. 11*
214 A93 12k multicolored   1.25 .60

Slovak Scouting — A94

1995, May 18   *Perf. 11½x11*
215 A94 5k multicolored   1.00 .30

Visit of Pope John Paul II — A95

1995, May 29   **Engr.**
216 A95 3k red   .35 .25
    Complete booklet, 10 #216   9.00

Organized Philately in Slovakia, Cent. — A96

Photo. & Engr.
1995, June 1   *Perf. 11½x12*
217 A96 3k blue, black & gray   .60 .35
    a. Souv. sheet of 2   2.25 1.50
    Dunafila '95.

Castles &
Churches — A100

Perf. 11¾x11¼, 11¼x11¾ (#218, 225-226)

1995-2001   Photo. & Engr.
218 A100 50h Bardejov, horiz.   .25   .25
219 A100 4k Nova Bana   .50   .25
220 A100 4k Presov   .40   .25
221 A100 5k Trnava   .50   .25
222 A100 7k Martin   .65   .30
223 A100 8k Trencin Castle   1.25   .60
224 A100 9k Zilina   .85   .40
225 A100 20k Roznava, horiz.   1.90   .95
226 A100 40k Piestany, horiz.   4.00 2.00
227 A100 50k Komarno   5.00 2.50
       Nos. 218-227 (10)   15.30 7.75

Issued: 4k (#219), 6/15/95; 8k, 9/12/95. 9k, 4/15/97. 7k, 7/17/97. 5k. 9/12/98. 4k (#220), 11/3/98. 50h, 2/1/00. 20k, 7/26/00. 40k, 5/25/01. 50k, 4/26/01.

See Nos. 401-402, 424-425, 447.

UNESCO
World
Heritage
Sites
A107

Perf. 11½x12, 12x11½
1995, July 19   Photo. & Engr.
228 A107 7k Banska Stiavnica,
            vert.   .70   .35
229 A107 10k Spissky Hrad   1.00   .50
230 A107 15k Vlkolinec   1.60   .80
       Nos. 228-230 (3)   3.30 1.65

Volleyball,
Cent. — A108

1995, Aug. 16   Perf. 11½
231 A108 9k multicolored   1.25   .70

A109

Bratislava Biennial of Illustrators: 2k, Clown, by Lorenzo Mattotti, Italy. 3k, Two characters, by Dusan Kallay, Slovakia.

Photo. & Engr.
1995, Sept. 5   Perf. 11½
232 A109 2k multicolored   .25   .25
    Complete booklet, 10 #232   2.50
233 A109 3k multicolored   .30   .25
    Complete booklet, 10 #233   3.50

St. Adalbert
Assoc. — A110

1995, Sept. 14
234 A110 4k multicolored   .45   .25

The
Cleveland
Agreement,
80th Anniv.
A111

Photo. & Engr.
1995, Oct. 20   Perf. 12x11½
235 A111 5k multicolored   .55   .25

UN, 50th
Anniv.
A112

1995, Oct. 24   Engr.   Perf. 11½x12
235A A112 8k multicolored   1.10   .55
Issued in sheets of 8 + 2 labels.

Christmas
A113

Photo. & Engr.
1995, Oct. 27   Perf. 11½
236 A113 2k multicolored   .25   .25

Bratislava Art Type of 1993

Designs: 8k, The Hlohovec Nativity. 16k, Two Women, by Mikulás Galanda.

Photo. & Engr.
1995, Nov. 30   Perf. 11½x12
237 A68 8k multicolored   .80   .40
238 A68 16k multicolored   1.75   .85

Issued in sheets of 4 + 2 labels.

Jozef Cíger-
Hronsky (1896-
1960)
A114

4k, Jozef L'udovít Holuby (1836-1923).

Photo. & Engr.
1996, Feb. 15   Perf. 11½
239 A114 3k multicolored   .40   .25
240 A114 4k multicolored   .60   .35

See Nos. 293-295, 320-322.

Olympic Games,
Cent. — A115

1996, Feb. 15
241 A115 9k multicolored   1.25   .50

Folk
Traditions — A116

Easter tradition of dousing women with water

Photo. & Engr.
1996, Mar. 15   Perf. 11½
242 A116 2k multicolored   .35   .25
    Complete booklet, 10 #242   3.50

Souvenir Sheet

Year for the Eradication of
Poverty — A117

1996, Apr. 15   Engr.   Perf. 12
243 A117 7k multicolored   1.25   .90

A118

Europa: a, Holding thistle, carduus textori-anus marg. b, Portrait, daphne cneorum.

1996, May 3   Engr.   Perf. 11½
244 A118 8k Pair, #a.-b.   1.75   .85

Izabela Textorisová (1866-1949), Slovakia's 1st female botanist. Issued in sheets of 4.

Souvenir Sheet

A119

Motion Pictures, Cent.: Two frames from 1936 film, Jánosík.

1996, May 15   Perf. 11½x12
245 A119 16k multicolored   2.00 2.00
Printed se-tenant with label.

Round Slovakia
Cycle
Race — A120

1996, May 30   Engr.   Perf. 11½
246 A120 3k multicolored   .45   .25
    Complete booklet, 10 #246   5.50

Slovak
Perspectives,
150th
Anniv. — A121

1996, May 30
247 A121 18k multicolored   2.00 1.00

A122

Photo. & Engr.
1996, June 14   Perf. 12x11½
248 A122 6k Coat of arms   .65   .35

Town of Senica.

A123

Nature protection: No. 249, Ovis musimon. No. 250, Bison bonasus. No. 251, Rupicapra rupicapra.

1996, July 16   Perf. 11½x12
249 A123 4k multicolored   .50   .25
    Complete booklet, 10 #249   5.50
250 A123 4k multicolored   .50   .25
    Complete booklet, 10 #250   5.50
251 A123 4k multicolored   .50   .25
    Complete booklet, 10 #251   5.50
       Nos. 249-251 (3)   1.50   .75

Splendors of
Homeland — A124

Photo. & Engr.
1996, Sept. 25   Perf. 11½x12
252 A124 4k Popradské Lake   .40   .25
253 A124 8k Skalnaté Lake   .75   .35
254 A124 12k Strbské Lake   1.10   .55
       Nos. 252-254 (3)   2.25 1.15

Bratislava Art Type of 1993

The Baroque Chair, by Endre Nemes (1909-85).

1996, Oct. 5   Engr.   Perf. 11½x12
255 A68 14k multicolored   2.00 2.00

See Czech Republic #2995, Sweden #2199. Issued in sheets of 4 + label.

Technological
Advances
A125

4k, Bratislava-Trnava horse-drawn railway. 6k, Andrej Kvasz's (1883-1974) airplane.

Photo. & Engr.
1996, Oct. 15   Perf. 11
256 A125 4k multicolored   .45   .25
    Complete booklet, 10 #256   6.00
257 A125 6k multicolored   .70   .30
    Complete booklet, 10 #257   8.00

Queen Ntombi Twala, by Andy Warhol (1928-87) — A126

Design: 10k, Suppressed Laughter, by Franz Xaver Messerschmidt (1736-83).

1996   **Engr.**   *Perf. 11½*
258 A126 7k multicolored   .85 .70
259 A126 10k multicolored   1.25 1.00

Each issued in sheets of 4.
Issued: 7k, 11/13/96; 10k, 10/5/96.
See Nos. 284-286, 311, 314-315, 340-341, 366-367, 389-391, 417-418, 430, 443-445, 465-466, 488-489, 508-509, 530-531, 555-556, 584-585, 605-606, 628, 650, 676-677, 703-704.

Christmas, Kysuce Village — A127

Photo. & Engr.
1996, Nov. 5   *Perf. 11½*
260 A127 2k multicolored   .25 .25

Michael Martikén, Olympic Gold Medalist, Canoeing A128

Photo. & Engr.
1996, Dec. 18   *Perf. 12x11½*
261 A128 3k brown & yellow   .50 .25

Stamp Day — A129

Designs: Unexecuted 1938 stamp design of a woman with patriarchal cross, dove, Martin Benka, stamp designer.

1996, Dec. 18
262 A129 3k violet & buff   .45 .45
   Complete booklet, 9 #262   9.00

No. 262 was printed se-tenant with label.

Bishop Stefan Moyses (1797-1869) — A130

Design: 4k, Svetozar Hurban Vajansky (1847-1916), politician.

Photo. & Engr.
1997, Jan. 16   *Perf. 11½*
263 A130 3k multicolored   .30 .25
264 A130 4k multicolored   .35 .25

A131

Photo. & Engr.
1997, Jan. 31   *Perf. 11½*
265 A131 6k multicolored   .55 .25

1997 World Biathlon Championships, Osrblie.

A132

Photo. & Engr.
1997, Feb. 15   *Perf. 11½*
266 A132 3k multicolored   .35 .25
   Complete booklet, 10 #266   3.50

Folk Tradition of collecting dew.

Franciscan Church, Bratislava, 700th Anniv. — A133

Photo. & Engr.
1997, Mar. 25   *Perf. 11½x12*
267 A133 16k multicolored   1.50 .75

Radio, Cent. A135

Photo. & Engr.
1997, Apr. 15   *Perf. 12x11½*
269 A135 10k multicolored   .95 .45

A136

Europa (Stories and Legends): Miraculous rain near Hron.

1997, May 5   **Engr.**   *Perf. 12x11½*
270 A136 9k multicolored   1.10 .55

Issued in sheets of 7 + 3 labels.

A137

Limestone Formations: 6k, Domica Cavern, Silická. 8k, Aragonit Cavern, Octiná.

1997, June 12   **Engr.**   *Perf. 12x11½*
271 A137 6k multicolored   .55 .25
272 A137 8k multicolored   .75 .35

Nos. 271-272 issued in sheets of 8 + label.

Souvenir Sheet

Folklore Festival, Vychodná — A138

1997, June 12   **Photo. & Engr.**
273 A138 11k multicolored   1.10 .90

Triennale of Naive Art, Bratislava A139

Photo. & Engr.
1996, June 26   *Perf. 12x11½*
274 A139 3k multicolored   .35 .25
   Complete booklet, 10 #274   3.50

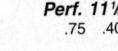

World Year of Slovaks — A140

1997, July 17   *Perf. 11½*
276 A140 9k multicolored   .75 .40

Bratislava Biennale of Illustrators — A141

Photo. & Engr.
1997, Aug. 5   *Perf. 11½*
277 A141 3k multicolored   .30 .25
   Complete booklet, 10 #277   3.25

Water Mill, Jelka — A142

1997, Aug. 5
278 A142 4k multicolored   .40 .25
   Complete booklet, 10 #278   4.00

A143

Photo. & Engr.
1997, Sept. 1   *Perf. 11½*
279 A143 4k multicolored   .40 .25

Constitution, 5th anniv.

A144

1997, Sept. 17
280 A144 9k multicolored   .85 .40

6th Half Marathon World Championships, Kosice.

Mushrooms — A145

Designs: #281, Boletus aereus. #282, Morchella esculenta. #283, Catathelasma imperiale.

1997, Sept. 17   *Perf. 12*
281 A145 9k multicolored   1.10 .80
282 A145 9k multicolored   1.10 .80
283 A145 9k multicolored   1.10 .80
   a.   Souvenir sheet, #281-283   3.50 3.00
   Nos. 281-283 (3)   3.30 2.40

Art Type of 1996

Designs: 9k, Self-portrait, by Ján Kupecky (1667-1740). 10k, Bojnice Altar, St. Peter and St. Lucia, by Nardo Di Cione, 14th cent., horiz. 12k, Towards the Goal (The Miners), by Koloman Sokol (b. 1902).

1997, Oct. 15   **Engr.**   *Perf. 11½*
284 A126 9k multicolored   .90 .45
285 A126 10k multicolored   1.10 .55
286 A126 12k multicolored   1.40 .70
   Nos. 284-286 (3)   3.40 1.70

Cernova 1907 — A146

Photo. & Engr.
1997, Oct. 24   *Perf. 11½x12*
287 A146 4k Lamenting woman, church   .40 .25

Christmas — A147

1997, Nov. 3   *Perf. 11½*
288 A147 3k Nativity   .30 .25

Ondrej Nepala, Figure Skater — A148

1997, Nov. 3
289 A148 5k multicolored   .60 .30

A149

Photo. & Engr.
1997, Dec. 1   **Perf. 11½**
290 A149 4k Resurrection of
           Christ   .40   .25
   Complete booklet, 10 #290   4.00
Spiritual renewal. See #301, 327.

Stamp
Day — A150

1997, Dec. 18
291 A150 4k dark brown & blue   .55   .25
   Complete booklet, 9 #291 + 12
   labels   7.00
No. 291 was printed se-tenant with label.

Slovak Republic, 5th Anniv. — A151

Photo. & Engr.
1998, Jan. 1   **Perf. 11½**
292 A151 4k multicolored   .40   .25
   Complete booklet, 10 #292   6.00

Personality Type of 1996
Writers: No. 293, Martin Rázus (1888-
1937), politician. No. 294, Ján Smrek (1898-
1982), poet. No. 295, Jozef Skultéty (1853-
1948), linquist, editor.

1998, Jan. 19
293 A114 4k multicolored   .40   .25
294 A114 4k multicolored   .40   .25
295 A114 4k multicolored   .40   .25
   Nos. 293-295 (3)   1.20   .75

1998 Winter
Olympic
Games,
Nagano
A152

1998, Jan. 19   **Perf. 12x11½**
296 A152 19k Hockey player   1.75   .70

Folk Tradition,
Banishing of
Winter — A153

Photo. & Engr.
1998, Mar. 3   **Perf. 11½**
297 A153 3k multicolored   .30   .25
   Complete booklet, 10 #297   4.00

Castles
A154

1998, Mar. 3
298 A154 6k Budatin   .60   .35
299 A154 11k Krásna Horka   1.25   .55
Souvenir Sheet
300 A154 18k Nitra   2.00 1.50

Spiritual Renewal Type of 1997
Design: Descent of the Holy Spirit, flames
above peoples' heads.

Photo. & Engr.
1998, May 5   **Perf. 11½**
301 A149 4k multicolored   .40   .25
   Complete booklet, 10 #301   4.00

Folklore
Festivals — A155

1998, May 5
302 A155 12k Tekov wedding   1.25   .60
   Europa. Issued in sheet of 8 + label.

A156

Photo. & Engr.
1998, June 1   **Perf. 11½**
303 A156 3k Child's drawing   .45   .25
   Complete booklet, 10 #303   4.50
The Children's Center, Ruzomberok.

A157

Design: Viktor Kolibik (1890-1918),
wireworker, leader of revolt.

1998, June 1
304 A157 3k multicolored   .30   .25
   Mutiny at Kragujevac, 80th anniv.

Slovak
Uprising of
1848-49
A158

1998, June 1
305 A158 4k multi, with 1 or 2 la-
           bels   2.00   .40

Railways in Slovakia,
Cent. — A159

Designs: 4k, Bihar steam locomotive. 10k,
Lubochna-Mocidla electrified narrow-gauge
trolley. 15k, Diesel locomotive.

Photo. & Engr.
1998, Aug. 20   **Perf. 11½**
306 A159 4k multicolored   .50   .25
307 A159 10k multicolored   .95   .45
308 A159 15k multicolored   1.40   .70
   Nos. 306-308 (3)   2.85 1.40

Fish
A160

Designs: a, 4k, Umbra krameri. b, 11k,
Zingel zingel. c, 16k, Cyprinus carpio.

1998, Sept. 7   **Sheet of 3**
309 A160 #a.-c. + label   3.25 2.75

Art Type of 1996
1564 Wooden "Pieta" statue, by unknown
artist, Sastín.

1998, Sept. 14   **Perf. 11½x12**
311 A126 18k multicolored   2.25 2.00
   Issued in sheets of 4.

"No" to Drugs — A161

Photo. & Engr.
1998, Oct. 5   **Perf. 11x11½**
312 A161 3k multicolored   .30   .25

Ektopfilm, Ecology-Related Film
Festival, 25th Anniv. — A162

1998, Oct. 5   **Perf. 11**
313 A162 4k multicolored   .40   .25
   Complete booklet, 10 #313   5.00

Art Type of 1996
Designs: 10k, Terchova Landscape, by Mar-
tin Benka (1888-1971). 12k, Fishermen, by
L'udovít Fulla (1902-80).

1998, Oct. 15   **Engr.**   **Perf. 11½x12**
314 A126 10k multicolored   .85   .75
315 A126 12k multicolored   1.25 1.00

Adoration of the
Magi — A163

1998, Nov. 3   **Perf. 11x11½**
317 A163 3k Christmas   .30   .25
   Complete booklet, 10 #317   3.50

Stamp Day — A164

Photo. & Engr.
1998, Dec. 18   **Perf. 12x11½**
318 A164 4k multi, with 1 or 2 la-
           bels   .75   .25
   Complete booklet, 9 #318 + 12
   labels   9.00

19th World Winter Universiad Games,
4th European Youth Olympic
Days — A165

Photo. & Engr.
1999, Jan. 12   **Perf. 12x11½**
319 A165 12k multicolored   2.50   .40
No. 319 is printed se-tenant with 2 labels.

Personality Type of 1996
Designs: 3k, Matej Bel (1684-1749),
teacher, pastor. 4k, Juraj Haulik (1788-1869),
1st cardinal of Croatia. 11k, Pavol Országh-
Hviezdoslav (1849-1921), poet, dramatist.

1999, Jan. 28   **Perf. 11½**
320 A114 3k multicolored   .30   .25
321 A114 4k multicolored   .40   .25
322 A114 11k multicolored   1.00   .40
   Nos. 320-322 (3)   1.70   .90
         See Croatia 388.

UPU, 125th
Anniv. — A166

Photo. & Engr.
1999, Mar. 12   **Perf. 11½**
323 A166 4k multicolored   .40   .25
   Complete booklet, 10 #323   4.00

A167

Traditional bonnets.

Litho. & Engr.
1999, Mar. 12   **Perf. 11½x12**
324 A167 4k Cajkov   .40   .30
325 A167 15k Helpa   1.25 1.00
326 A167 18k Madunice   1.50 1.10
   Nos. 324-326 (3)   3.15 2.40
Nos. 324-326 were each issued in sheets of
10.

Spiritual Renewal Type of 1997
Design: "Transfiguration," by Vincent
Hloznik, depicting ascension of Christ.

Photo. & Engr.
1999, May 5   **Perf. 11½**
327 A149 5k multicolored   .50   .25
   Complete booklet, 10 #327   5.00

Tatra
National
Park
A168

1999, May 5   **Engr.**   **Perf. 11½**
328 A168 9k shown   .90   .55
329 A168 11k Mountains, diff.   1.10   .75
   a. Pair, #328-329   2.25 2.25
Europa. No. 329a is a continuous design.
Issued in sheets of 8 + label.

Council of
Europe,
50th Anniv.
A169

1999, May 5   **Engr.**   **Perf. 12x11½**
330 A169 16k multicolored   1.50 1.50
   a. Souvenir sheet of 1   2.00 2.00

A170

Photo. & Engr.
1999, June 15   **Perf. 11½x11¾**
331 A170 4k multicolored   .35 .25
Slovak Philharmonic Orchestra, 50th anniv.

A171

1999, June 15   **Perf. 11½**
332 A171 5k multicolored   .60 .30
Intl. Year of Older Persons.

Souvenir Sheet

Astronaut Ivan Bella, First Slovak in
Space — A172

1999, June 15   **Perf. 11¾x11½**
333 A172 12k multicolored   1.25 .90

UPU, 125th
Anniv. — A173

Photo. & Engr.
1999, July 15   **Perf. 11½**
334 A173 12k Zilina University   1.00 .50
335 A173 16k Globe   1.25 .60

A174

Photo. & Engr.
1999, Sept. 3   **Perf. 11¼x11¾**
336 A174 4k multicolored   .35 .25
Bratislava Univ. of Fine Arts, 50th anniv.

A175

1999, Sept. 3   **Perf. 11¼x11½**
337 A175 5k multicolored   .50 .30
Complete booklet, 10 #337   5.00
Bratislava Biennale of Illustrators.

Mine Water
Pump Invented
By Jozef Hell
(1713-89)
A176

1999, Sept. 21   **Perf. 11x11¼**
338 A176 7k sepia & yellow   .95 .25

Souvenir Sheet

Birds — A177

a, 14k, Panurus biarmicus. b, 15k, Lanius
collurio. c, 16k, Phoenicurus phoenicurus.

Litho. & Engr.
1999, Sept. 21   **Perf. 11¾**
339 A177 Sheet of 3, #a.-c.   4.75 4.00

Art Type of 1996

Designs: 13k, Malatiná, by Milos Alexander
Bazovsky (1899-1968), horiz. 14k, Study of
the Blacksmith, by Dominik Skutecky.

1999, Oct. 5   **Engr.**   **Perf. 11¾**
340 A126 13k multicolored   1.25 1.00
341 A126 14k multicolored   1.25 1.00
Each issued in sheets of 4.

Christmas — A178

Photo. & Engr.
1999, Nov. 3   **Perf. 11¾x11¼**
342 A178 4k multicolored   .35 .25
Complete booklet, 10 #342   3.50

Czechoslovakia's "Velvet Revolution,"
10th Anniv. — A179

1999, Nov. 17   **Perf. 12x11¼**
343 A179 5k multicolored   .80 .25

Ceramic Urns, Museum of Jewish
Culture — A180

Litho. & Engr.
1999, Nov. 23   **Perf. 11¾**
344 12k 1776 urn   1.10 .55
345 18k 1734 urn   1.75 .85
a. A180 Pair, #344-345   3.00 1.50
Issued in sheets of 8.
See Israel #1380-1381.

Albín
Brunovsky
(1935-97),
Stamp
Designer
A181

Photo. & Engr.
1999, Dec. 18   **Perf. 12x11¼**
346 A181 5k multi   .60 .25
Complete booklet, 9 #346   8.00
Stamp Day. Issued se-tenant with label.

Rivers and Gaps — A182

Designs: a, 10k, Dunajec. b, 12k, Váh.

Litho. & Engr.
2000, Jan. 1   **Perf. 11¾**
347 A182 Pair, #a.-b.   2.25 1.75
Issued in sheets of 8.

Famous
People — A183

4k, Hana Melickova (1900-78), actress. 5k,
Stefan Anián Jedlik (1800-95), inventor.

Photo. & Engr.
2000, Jan. 11   **Perf. 11½x11¼**
348 A183 4k multi   .40 .25
349 A183 5k multi   .60 .25

Basketball — A184

Photo. & Engr.
2000, Feb. 15   **Perf. 11¼x11½**
351 A184 4k multi   .40 .25
Ruzomberok team, 1999 European
Women's Basketball League champions.

World Mathematics Year — A185

2000, Feb. 15   **Perf. 11¾x11¼**
352 A185 5k multi   .55 .25
Juraj Hronec (1881-1959), Stefan Schwarz
(1914-96), mathematicians.

Easter — A186

2000, Feb. 15 Engr. Perf. 11¼x11½
353 A186 4k brown   .40 .25
Complete booklet, 10 #353   4.00

Ján Holly
(1785-1849),
Poet — A187

Photo. & Engr.
2000, Mar. 24   **Perf. 11½x11¼**
354 A187 5.50k multi   .55 .25

Europa, 2000
Common Design Type
Litho. & Engr.
2000, May 9   **Perf. 11¾**
355 CD17 12k multi   1.10 .55

UNICEF
A188

Photo. & Engr.
2000, June 1   **Perf. 11½x11¼**
356 A188 5.50k multi   .55 .25

A189

Postman and Austria design A1.

Photo. & Engr.
2000, June 1   **Perf. 11¼x11¾**
357 A189 10k multi   1.10 .45
First postage stamp used in Slovakia, 150th
anniv.

Pres. Rudolf
Schuster — A190

Perf. 11¾x11¼
2000, June 15   **Engr.**
358 A190 5.50k brown   .80 .25
See also No. 421.

2000 Summer Olympics,
Sydney — A191

Photo. & Engr.
2000, June 27   *Perf. 11¼x11½*
359 A191 18k multi + label   3.50 3.50

Organization for
Security and
Cooperation in
Europe, 25th
Anniv. — A192

2000, Aug. 18   *Perf. 11½x11¼*
361 A192 4k black & blue   .40 .25

Wooden
Bridge,
Kluknava
A193

2000, Sept. 14   *Perf. 11¼*
362 A193 6k multi   .60 .30

Souvenir Sheet

Berries — A194

No. 363: a, 11k, Rubus idaeus. b, 13k, Fragaria vesca. c, 15k, Vaccinium myrtillus.

Litho. & Engr.
2000, Sept. 14   *Perf. 11¾*
363 A194 Sheet of 3, #a-c   4.50 4.50

Holy Year
2000 — A195

Photo. & Engr.
2000, Oct. 5   *Perf. 11¼x11½*
364 A195 4k multi   .40 .25
    Booklet, 10 #364   4.00

Postal Agreement
with Sovereign
Military Order of
Malta — A196

2000, Oct. 13   *Perf. 11¼x11¾*
365 A196 10k multi   1.10 .45

Art Type of 1996
Designs: 18k, Nativity, from church in
Spisska Stara Ves. 20k, Crucifixion, from
church in Kocelovce, horiz.

Perf. 11½x11¾, 11¾x11½
2000, Oct. 17   **Engr.**
366-367 A126 Set of 2   3.50 2.50

Stamp Day — A197

Photo. & Engr.
2000, Dec. 18   *Perf. 11¾x11½*
368 A197 5.50k multi + label   1.10 .25
    Booklet, 9 #368   11.00

POFIS, 50th Anniv.

History of
Postal
Law
A198

2000, Dec. 18   **Engr.**   *Perf. 11¾*
369 A198 20k multi   2.75 2.00

Issued in sheets of 4.

Mantel Clock, c.
1780 — A199

Photo. & Engr.
2001, Jan. 1   *Perf. 11¼x11½*
370 A199 13k multi   1.25 .60

Janko Blaho (1901-
81), Singer — A200

2001, Jan. 15
371 A200 5.50k multi   .55 .25

2001 European
Figure Skating
Championships,
Bratislava — A201

2001, Jan. 16
372 A201 16k multi   1.40 .70

Agricultural Control Institute, 50th
Anniv. — A202

2001, Feb. 22   *Perf. 11¾x11¼*
373 A202 12k multi   1.10 .55

Traditional
Costumes — A203

Designs: 5.50k, Man from Detva. 6k,
Woman and child from Detva.

2001, Feb. 22   *Perf. 11¼x11½*
374 A203 5.50k multi   .50 .25
    Booklet, 10 #374   5.00
375 A203   6k multi   .60 .30
    Booklet, 10 #375   6.50

Archaeological Sites — A204

No. 376: a, 12k. Havránok. b, 15k, Ducové.

2001, Apr. 10   **Engr.**   *Perf. 11¾*
376 A204 Horiz. pair, #a-b   2.10 1.75

Issued in sheets of 4 pairs + 1 label.

Europa
A205

2001, May 5   **Engr.**   *Perf. 11¾*
379 A205 18k multi   1.40 .85

Issued in sheets of 10.

Souvenir Sheet

Princes of Great Moravia — A206

No. 380: a, 6k, Pribina. b, 9k, Rastislav. c,
11k, Kocel. d, 14k, Svatopluk.

Litho. & Engr.
2001, July 4   *Perf. 11¾*
380 A206 Sheet of 4, #a-d   3.25 3.00

Souvenir Sheet

Wild Animals — A207

No. 381: a, 14k, Ursus arctos. b, 15k, Canis
lupus. c, 16k, Lynx lynx.

2001, July 10   *Perf. 11¾x11½*
381 A207 Sheet of 3, #a-c   4.25 4.25

Dobro Resonator Guitar and US
Map — A208

Photo. & Engr.
2001, Aug. 1   *Perf. 11¾x11¼*
382 A208 19k multi   1.75 .85

Bratislava
Biennale of
Illustrators
A209

2001, Aug. 15   *Perf. 11½x11¼*
383 A209 7k multi   .65 .30
    Booklet, 10 #383   6.50

The
Righteous
Among
Nations
A210

2001, Sept. 9   *Perf. 11¾x11¼*
384 A210 14k multi   1.25 .60

Souvenir Sheet

Alexander Dubcek (1921-92),
Czechoslovakian Communist
Leader — A211

Litho. & Engr.
2001, Sept. 18   **Perf. 11¾**
385 A211 18k multi   1.60 1.25

Banská Bystrica
Postal
Museum — A212

Photo. & Engr.
2001, Oct. 9   **Perf. 11¼x11½**
386 A212 6k multi   .55 .25

Remembrance of
Political Trial
Victims — A213

2001, Oct. 9
387 A213 10k multi   1.10 .45

Maria Valeria Bridge
Reconstruction — A214

2001, Oct. 11   **Perf. 11¾x11¼**
388 A214 10k multi   1.10 .45

See Hungary No. 3776.

Art Type of 1996
Designs: 16k, Raftsman's Dream, by Imrich Weiner-Král'. 18k, Light of the Soul, by Albín Brunovsky. 20k, St. Michael the Archangel with Saints, by unknown artist.

2001, Oct. 15   **Engr.**   **Perf. 11¾**
389-391 A126 Set of 3   4.50 3.50

Christmas
A215

Photo. & Engr.
2001, Oct. 15   **Perf. 11½x11¼**
392 A215 5.50k multi   .55 .25
    Booklet, 10 #392   5.50

Famous
Men — A216

Designs: 10k, Juraj Papánek (1738-1802), historian. 14k, Bjornsterne Bjornson (1832-1910), 1903 Nobel laureate for Literature.

2002, Jan. 15
393-394 A216 Set of 2   2.25 1.00

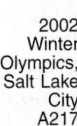

2002
Winter
Olympics,
Salt Lake
City
A217

2002, Jan. 25   **Perf. 11¾x11¼**
395 A217 18k multi   1.60 .80

European Dog Sled
Championships
A218

2002, Feb. 8   **Perf. 11¼x11½**
396 A218 6k multi   .55 .25

Easter — A219

2002, Feb. 15
397 A219 5.50k multi   .55 .25
    Booklet, 10 #397   5.50

First Slovakian
High
Schools — A220

Designs: 12k, Martin, 1866. 13k, Revuca, 1862. 15k, Klástor pod Znievom, 1869.

2002, Mar. 20   **Perf. 11½x11¼**
398-400 A220 Set of 3   3.50 1.50

Castles and Churches Type of 1995
Perf. 11¾x11¼, 11¼x11¾
2002   **Photo. & Engr.**
401 A100 10k Kezmarok   1.25 .55
402 A100 16k Levoca, horiz.   1.50 .75

Issued: 10k, 5/6; 16k, 4/18.

Europa — A221

2002, May 6   **Engr.**   **Perf. 11¾**
403 A221 18k multi   1.75 .85

Issued in sheets of 8.

Wine Production — A222

Designs: 7k, Barrels. 9k, Wine press.

Photo. & Engr.
2002, June 24   **Perf. 11¾x11¼**
Stamps + labels
404-405 A222 Set of 2   1.60 1.00

Souvenir Sheet

Butterflies — A223

No. 406: a, 10k, Zerynthia polyxena. b, 16k, Inachis io. c, 25k, Papilio machaon.

Litho. & Engr.
2002, June 26   **Perf. 11¾**
406 A223 Sheet of 3, #a-c, + 4   8.00 5.00
    labels

Souvenir Sheet

Alexander Cardinal Rudnay (1760-1831) — A224

2002, July 4   **Engr.**
407 A224 17k multi   2.25 2.00

Doves and Roses — A225

Photo. & Engr.
2002, July 4   **Perf. 11¾x11¼**
408 A225 6k multi + label   .90 .55

Issued in sheets of 12 stamps + 12 labels which could be personalized.

Victory at 2002 World Ice Hockey
Championships — A226

2002, July 4
409 A226 10k multi   1.10 .45

Architecture in Slovakia and
China — A227

No. 410: a, 6k, Handan Congtai Pavilion, People's Republic of China. b, 12k, Bojnice Castle, Slovakia.

2002, Oct. 12   **Perf. 11¾x11½**
410 A227 Horiz. pair, #a-b   1.75 .85

Issued in sheets of 4 pairs.
See People's Republic of China No. 3239.

Kosice Technological
University, 50th
Anniv. — A228

Photo. & Engr.
2002, Oct. 17   **Perf. 11¼x11½**
411 A228 6k multi   .55 .25

Christmas — A229

2002, Nov. 8
412 A229 5.50k multi   .55 .25
    Complete booklet, 10 #412   6.00

Churches — A230

Designs: 7k, St. Michael's Church, Klizske Hradiste. 14k, St. George's Rotunda, Skalica. 22k, St. Martin's Cathedral, Spisska Kapitula.

2002, Nov. 15   **Engr.**   **Perf. 11¾x11½**
413-415 A230 Set of 3   4.00 2.00

Issued in sheets of 10.

Miniature Sheet

Astronaut Eugene Cernan and Lunar Rover — A231

Photo. & Engr.
2002, Dec. 6 **Perf. 11¾x11¼**
416 A231 20k multi + label 2.25 1.75
Apollo 17 mission, 30th anniv.

Art Type of 1996
Designs: 20k, The Beheading of St. John the Baptist, by Master Pavol of Levoca. 23k, In the Studio, by Koloman Sokol.
2002 **Engr.** **Perf. 11¾**
417-418 A126 Set of 2 4.00 2.00
Nos. 417-418 issued in sheets of 4.
Issued: 20k, 12/18; 23k, 12/12.

Stamp Day — A232

Photo. & Engr.
2002, Dec. 18 **Perf. 11¾x11¼**
419 A232 10k multi + 2 labels 1.10 .45
Nitrafila Stamp Exhibition, Nitra.

Independent Slovakia, 10th Anniv. — A233

Perf. 11¾x11½
2003, Jan. 1 **Litho. & Engr.**
420 A233 20k multi 1.75 .85
Issued in sheets of 6.

Pres. Schuster Type of 2000
2003, Feb. 5 **Engr.** **Perf. 11¾x11¼**
421 A190 7k blue .65 .30

Roses — A234

Photo. & Engr.
2003, Feb. 14 **Perf. 11½x11¼**
422 A234 7k multi .65 .30
a. Sheet of 8 + 8 labels 12.00 6.00
No. 422a issued 4/30. Labels on No. 422a could be personalized.

Easter — A235

2003, Mar. 10 **Perf. 11¼x11½**
423 A235 7k multi .65 .30
Booklet, 10 #423 6.50

Churches and Castles Type of 1995-2001
Photo. & Engr.
2003 **Perf. 11¾x11¼**
424 A100 18k Kremnica 1.35 .75
425 A100 100k Pezinok 7.75 3.75
Issued: 18k, 3/20, 100k, 9/18.

Souvenir Sheet

Saints Cyril and Methodius — A236

No. 426: a, 17k, St. Cyril. b, 22k, St. Methodius.

Litho. & Engr.
2003, Apr. 6 **Perf. 11¾**
426 A236 Sheet of 2, #a-b, + 2 labels 3.75 3.00

Ludwig van Beethoven (1770-1827), Composer A237

Photo. & Engr.
2003, Apr. 24 **Perf. 11½x11¼**
427 A237 15k multi 1.25 .60

Milan Stefánik (1880-1919), Czechoslovakian General — A238

Litho. & Engr.
2003, May 3 **Perf. 11¾**
428 A238 14k multi 1.40 .75
Issued in sheets of 8.
See France No. 2942.

Europa — A239

2003, May 9
429 A239 14k multi 1.25 .60
Issued in sheets of 10.

Art Type of 1996
Design: The Brook, by Ladislav Mednansky, horiz.
2003, May 9 **Engr.** **Perf. 11¾**
430 A126 18k multi 1.60 .80
Issued in sheets of 4.

Sts. Benedict and Andrej Svorad — A240

Photo. & Engr.
2003, May 16 **Perf. 11½x11¼**
431 A240 13k multi 1.25 .60

Third Place Finish of Slovakian Ice Hockey Team at World Championships, Finland — A241

2003, May 30 **Litho.** **Perf. 13½**
432 A241 20k multi 1.90 .95
Issued in sheets of 4.

Matko and Kubko — A242

Photo. & Engr.
2003, June 1 **Perf. 11¼x11½**
433 A242 7k multi .65 .30
Complete booklet, 10 #433 6.50
Intl. Children's Day.

Worldwide Fund for Nature (WWF) — A243

Various views of Felis silvestris silvestris: a, 13k. b, 14k. c, 16k. d, 18k.

Litho. & Engr.
2003, June 25 **Perf. 11¾**
434 A243 Sheet of 4, #a-d 5.75 3.50

World Swimming Championships, Barcelona A244

Photo. & Engr.
2003, July 7 **Perf. 11½x11¼**
435 A244 11k multi 1.10 .50

Banska Stiavnica Reservoirs — A245

No. 436: a, 9k, Lake Klinger. b, 12k, Rozgrund Reservoir.
2003, July 15 **Engr.** **Perf. 11¾**
436 A245 Pair, #a-b 2.00 1.00
Issued in sheets of 4 pairs + 1 label.

Bratislava Biennale of Illustrators — A246

Photo. & Engr.
2003, Aug. 15 **Perf. 11¼x11½**
437 A246 12k multi 1.10 .55
Complete booklet, 10 # 437 11.00

Visit of Pope John Paul II — A247

Die Cut Perf. 14¾x14½
2003, Sept. 7 **Litho.**
Self-Adhesive
438 A247 12k violet 1.10 .55
Issued in sheets of 4.

Father Ján Baltazár Magin (1681-1734), Poet — A248

Photo. & Engr.
2003, Sept. 17 **Perf. 11½x11¼**
439 A248 8k multi .75 .35

Christmas A249

2003, Oct. 30
440 A249 7k multi .65 .30
Complete booklet, 10 #440 6.50

Bronze Buttons, Sword Hilt and Cross A250

2003, Nov. 17 **Perf. 11¾x11¼**
441 A250 18k multi 1.75 .85
"Travel of History" exhibit of archaeological treasures.

Powered Flight, Cent. — A251

2003, Nov. 17 **Perf. 11½x11¼**
442 A251 18k multi 1.75 .85

Art Type of 1996

Designs: 14k, St. Catherine, by Simon Vouet. 16k, Bagpipes, by Rudolf Krivos, horiz. 21k, The Annunciation, by Master Jan.

2003, Nov. 28   Engr.   Perf. 11¾
443-445 A126   Set of 3   4.50 2.25
Nos. 443-445 issued in sheets of 4.

Marginal Design from Czechoslovakia No. 2517 Sheet, by Josef Baláz — A252

Photo. & Engr.
2003, Nov. 28   Perf. 11¾x11¼
446 A252 12k multi + label   1.10 .55
Stamp Day.

Castles and Churches Type of 1995-2001
2004, Jan. 30   Litho.   Perf. 14¼x14
447 A100 9k Liptovsky Mikulás, horiz.   .85 .40

St. Valentine's Day — A253

Litho. & Embossed
2004, Jan. 30   Perf. 11¾
448 A253 8k multi   .75 .35

Lilium Royal Parade — A254

Perf. 14¾x14½ Syncopated
2004, Feb. 12   Litho.
449 A254 8k multi   .75 .35

Tulip Kaufmanniana — A255

2004, Feb. 12   Perf. 13¼
450 A255 9k multi + label   .85 .40
Printed in sheets of 8 + 8 labels which could be personalized. Value (any label picture), mint $8, used $6.

Easter Egg — A256

2004, Mar. 10   Die Cut Perf. 14½
Self-Adhesive
451 A256 8k multi   1.25 .80
a.   Booklet pane of 10   12.50

Wedding Clothing From Pata — A257

Designs: 15k, Groom. 28k, Bride.

2004, Apr. 16   Perf. 13¼
452-453 A257 Set of 2   4.00 2.00

Europa — A258

Perf. 14x14¼ Syncopated
2004, Apr. 23
454 A258 20k multi   1.90 .95
Issued in sheets of 10.

Admission Into European Union A259

2004, May 1   Perf. 13½
455 A259 18k multi   1.75 .85
Issued in sheets of 10.

Admission Into NATO — A260

2004, May 1   Perf. 14
456 A260 60k multi   5.00 2.50

Grandfather, From Evening Tales Television Program — A261

2004, May 21   Perf. 13¼
Granite Paper
457 A261 8k multi   1.00 .35

2004 Paralympics, Athens — A262

2004, May 31   Perf. 13¼x13½
458 A262 34k multi   3.00 1.50

Pres. Ivan Gasparovic — A263

2004, June 15   Perf. 13
Granite Paper
459 A263 8k multi   .90 .35

Dobroc Forest A264

2004, June 17   Perf. 14
Granite Paper
460 A264 12k multi   1.10 .55

Tatra Omnibus, 1904-06 A265

2004, June 30   Perf. 13¼x13½
Granite Paper
461 A265 14k multi   1.25 .60
Issued in sheets of 8.

Spania Valley Mining Water System A266

2004, June 30   Granite Paper
462 A266 24k multi   2.25 1.10
Issued in sheets of 8.

Dunajec River Raftsmen — A267

2004, Sept. 3   Perf. 13¼x13
463 A267 21k multi   2.00 1.00
See Poland No. 3752.

Roman Legions in Trencin — A268

2004, Oct. 15   Perf. 13
464 A268 26k multi   2.25 1.10

Art Type of 1996
Designs: 33k, Cock Fight, by Jakub Bogdan, horiz. 35k, Don Quixote, by Július Jakoby.

Litho. & Engr.
2004, Oct. 20   Perf. 11¾
465-466 A126 Set of 2   6.50 5.50
Nos. 465-466 issued in sheets of 4.

Christmas A269

2004, Nov. 5   Litho.   Perf. 13
467 A269 8k multi   .75 .35
Complete booklet, 10 #467   7.50

Medalists at 2004 Summer Olympics — A270

No. 468: a, Jozef Gonci, air rifle bronze medalist. b, Kayak 1000-meter fours team, bronze medalists. c, Jozef Krnac, 66-kilogram judo silver medalist. d, Michal Martikán, men's canoe slalom silver medalist. e, Elena Kaliská,

women's canoe slalom gold medalist. f, Pavol and Peter Hochschornerovci, canoe slalom doubles gold medalists.

Serpentine Die Cut 12½
2004, Nov. 5 Self-Adhesive Litho.
468   Booklet of 6   10.00
a.-b.   A270 8k Either single   1.00 .75
c.-d.   A270 14k Either single   1.25 .85
e.-f.   A270 20k Either single   2.50 1.10

Stamp Day — A271

2004, Dec. 18   Perf. 13
469 A271 9k multi   1.00 .40

St. Valentine's Day — A272

2005, Jan. 31   Litho.   Perf. 13½
470 A272 9k multi   1.00 .40

Family — A273

2005, Feb. 14   Perf. 13½x13
471 A273 9k multi   1.00 .40

Banska Bystrica, 750th Anniv. A274

2005, Feb. 14   Perf. 13½
472 A274 16k multi   1.50 .75

Summit Meeting of Presidents George W. Bush and Vladimir Putin A275

2005, Feb. 24   Perf. 13
473 A275 25k multi   2.40 1.25

Easter — A276

2005, Mar. 10   Litho.   Perf. 13½
474 A276 9k multi   .85 .40
Complete booklet, 10 #474   8.50

Souvenir Sheet

Beatification of Sister Zdenka
Schelingová — A277

2005, Mar. 10   **Perf. 13x13¼**
475 A277 34k multi   3.25 3.75

Cycling for the
Handicapped
A278

2005, Mar. 30   **Perf. 13½**
476 A278 22k multi   2.00 .95

Poor Mother, by
Frantisek
Studeny — A279

    Perf. 11¾x11½
2005, Mar. 30   **Litho. & Engr.**
477 A279 25k blk & lt grn   2.25 1.50

    Issued in sheets of 8.
An unstated portion of the receipts were donated to UNICEF for relief works for the Dec. 26, 2004 tsunami.

Europa
A280

2005, Apr. 22   **Litho.**   **Perf. 13¾**
478 A280 19k multi   1.75 .85
    Issued in sheets of 8.

Peace of Bratislava
(Pressburg),
Bicent. — A281

2005, Apr. 29   **Perf. 13½**
479 A281 23k multi   2.00 1.00

Intl. Year of
Physics
A282

2005, May 16   **Litho.**   **Perf. 13½**
480 A282 18k multi   1.90 .85

Fish — A283

2005, May 23   **Litho.**   **Perf. 13½**
481 A283 9k multi   .85 .40
    Complete booklet, 10 #481   13.00

Biennale of
Children's Book
Illustrations,
Bratislava — A284

2005, May 23   **Perf. 13½**
482 A284 30k multi   2.75 1.40

Holic and Town
Arms — A285

2005, June 3   **Litho.**   **Perf. 13¼x13**
483 A285 22k multi   2.10 1.00

Pres. Ivan
Gasparovic — A286

    Perf. 11¾x11¼
2005, June 15   **Litho. & Engr.**
484 A286 9k brn & buff   .85 .40

Souvenir Sheet

Horses — A287

No. 485: a, 29k, Lippizaners, carriage. b, 31k, Slovak warm-bloods, rider.

2005, June 30   **Perf. 11¾**
485 A287   Sheet of 2, #a.-b.   12.00 4.50

Locomotives — A288

Designs: 24k, Ciernohronska Railroad. 33k, Vychylovka.

    Litho. & Engr.
2005, Sept. 22   **Perf. 11¾**
486-487 A288   Set of 2   8.00 5.00
Nos. 486-487 issued in sheets of 8 + 1 label.

Art Type of 1996

Designs: 28k, Supper at Emmaus, by Rembrandt. 35k, Magic of Still Life Paintings V, by Karol Baron, horiz.

2005, Oct. 20   **Engr.**
488-489 A126   Set of 2   5.50 2.75
    Nos. 488-489 issued in sheets of 4.

Christmas — A289

2005, Nov. 16   **Litho.**   **Perf. 13¼**
490 A289 9k multi   1.00 .40
    Complete booklet, 10 #490   10.00

Stamp Day — A290

2005, Nov. 25   **Perf. 13¼x13½**
491 A290 15k multi + label   2.00 .70

Karol Kuzmány
(1806-66),
Writer — A291

2006, Feb. 3   **Perf. 13½**
492 A291 16k multi   1.10 .75

2006 Winter Olympics, Turin — A292

2006, Feb. 3   **Perf. 13¼x13½**
493 A292 21k multi + label   5.00 3.00

Poprad and Town
Arms — A293

2006, Feb. 3   **Perf. 13¼**
494 A293 23k multi   1.60 1.10

Narcissus — A294

2006, Mar. 24   **Litho.**   **Perf. 13¼**
495 A294 10k multi   .85 .55

Easter — A295

2006, Mar. 31   **Perf. 13½**
496 A295 10k multi   .75 .55
    Complete booklet, 10 #496   8.00

Souvenir Sheet

Geological Formations — A296

No. 497: a, 32k, Sandberg. b, 35k, Somoska.

    Litho. & Engr.
2006, Apr. 21   **Perf. 11¾**
497 A296   Sheet of 2, #a-b   7.50 6.00

Europa
A297

    Litho. & Embossed
2006, May 5   **Perf. 13¼x13**
498 A297 18k multi   1.75 .85
    Issued in sheets of 10.

Belfries — A298

Designs: 27k, Kezmarok. 29k, Podolinec.

    Photo. & Engr.
2006, May 19   **Perf. 11½x11¾**
499-500 A298   Set of 2   4.50 3.50

Children's
Art — A299

2006, May 31   **Litho.**   **Perf. 11¼**
501 A299 10k multi   1.00 .55
    Complete booklet, 10 #501   10.00

Shepherd's Pipe — A300

2006, June 9   *Perf. 11¼x12¼*
502 A300 25k multi   2.00 1.50

Devín Castle — A301

2006, June 9   **Litho.**   *Perf. 12¾x12¼*
503 A301 10k multi + label   3.00 2.00
   Printed in sheets of 8 + 8 labels which could be personalized.

Objects in Museums — A302

   Designs: 28k, Blue cobalt glass goblet, 16th cent. 31k, Copper measuring cup, 1576.

Litho. & Engr.
2006, June 23   *Perf. 11¾*
504-505 A302   Set of 2   5.25 4.00
   Nos. 504-505 issued in sheets of 8 containing 4 of each stamp.

Puppets — A303

   Designs: 22k, Indonesian puppet. 25k, Slovakian marionette.

2006, July 27   **Litho.**   *Perf. 13¼x13*
506-507 A303   Set of 2   4.00 3.00
   Nos. 506-507 issued in sheets of 6 containing 3 of each stamp.
   See Indonesia No. 2092.

Art Type of 1996
   Designs: 37k, Krivy Jarok, by Dezider Milly, horiz. 38k, Moravian Venus sculpture fragment.

2006, Oct. 20   **Engr.**   *Perf. 11¾*
508-509 A126   Set of 2   7.00 4.25
   Nos. 508-509 issued in sheets of 4.

Christmas A304

2006, Nov. 10   **Litho.**   *Perf. 11*
510 A304 10k multi   .75 .50
   Complete booklet, 10 #510   8.00

Jozef Cincík (1909-92), Stamp Designer — A305

2006, Nov. 24   *Perf. 13¼x12½*
511 A305 19k multi   1.75 .85
   Stamp Day.

Modra and Town Arms — A306

2007, Feb. 7   **Litho.**   *Perf. 12¼x11½*
512 A306 14k multi   1.25 .75

Terézia Vansová (1857-1942), Writer — A307

2007, Feb. 7   *Perf. 11*
513 A307 19k multi   1.60 .80

Flowers — A308

2007, Feb. 14   *Perf. 12x11½*
514 A308 (10k) multi   1.00 .55

Easter — A309

2007, Mar. 15   *Perf. 11x11¼*
515 A309 10k multi   1.00 .50
   Complete booklet, 10 #515   12.00

Women's Tennis — A310

2007, Mar. 21   *Perf. 11*
516 A310 16k multi   1.30 .80

Souvenir Sheet

Dogs — A311

No. 517: a, Slovakian cuvac. b, Slovakian kopov.

Litho. & Engr.
2007, Apr. 18   *Perf. 11¾*
517 A311 31k Sheet of 2, #a-b 10.00 10.00

Slovak League of America, Cent. — A312

2007, May 15   **Litho.**   *Perf. 11¾x11½*
518 A312 22k multi   1.60 1.10

Janko Hrasko, by Stefan Cpin — A313

2007, May 30   *Perf. 13½*
519 A313 10k multi   1.25 .55
   Complete booklet, 10 #519   13.00

Europa A314

2007, May 30   *Perf. 13¾*
520 A314 18k multi   1.60 .80
   Issued in sheets of 10.

Monasteries A315

   Designs: 30k, Jasov Monastery. 34k, Hronsky Benadik Monastery.

Photo. & Engr.
2007, June 6   *Perf. 11¼x11¾*
521-522 A315   Set of 2   7.50 4.75

Biennale of Children's Book Illlustrations, Bratislava — A316

2007, June 27   **Litho.**   *Perf. 13½*
523 A316 25k multi   2.25 1.75

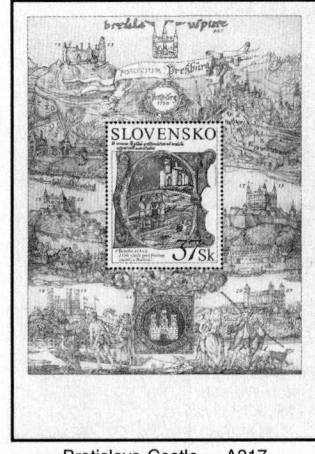

Bratislava Castle — A317

Litho. & Engr.
2007, June 27   *Perf. 11¾x12*
524 A317 37k multi   13.00 3.00

Castles — A318

   No. 525: a, Rocca, San Marino. b, Orava Castle, Slovakia.

2007, Aug. 24   *Perf. 11¾*
525 A318 21k Horiz. pair, #a-b   6.00 4.00
   No. 525 was printed in sheets containing four pairs. See San Marino No. 1729.

Jozef Miloslav Hurban (1817-88), Nationalist Leader — A319

2007, Sept. 1   **Litho.**   *Perf. 11¼x11¾*
526 A319 31k multi   2.25 1.75

Král'ova Bridge, Senec A320

Photo. & Engr.
2007, Sept. 5   *Perf. 11¼*
527 A320 29k multi   3.00 1.75

Gospel Book of Nitra — A321

2007, Sept. 22   *Perf. 11¼x11¾*
528 A321 15k multi   1.10   .75

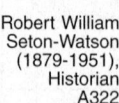

Robert William Seton-Watson (1879-1951), Historian A322

2007, Oct. 26 Litho. *Perf. 11¾x11¼*
529 A322 24k multi   1.90 1.50

Art Type of 1996

Designs: No. 530, 33k, St. Elizabeth of Hungary, by Frantisek X. K. Palko. No. 531, 33k, Bouquet of Chrysanthemums, by Ján Zelibsky, horiz.

2007, Nov. 14 Engr. *Perf. 11¾*
530-531 A126 Set of 2   6.00 4.25

Each stamp printed in sheets of 4.

Christmas — A323

Perf. 11¼x11¾
2007, Nov. 14   **Litho.**
532 A323 10k multi   1.00   .50
     Complete booklet, 10 #532   12.00

Field Post — A324

2007, Nov. 28   *Perf. 11¾x11¼*
533 A324 28k multi + label   3.00 1.75
     Stamp Day.

Independence, 15th Anniv. — A325

2008, Jan. 1 Litho. *Perf. 11¾x11¼*
534 A325 (16k) multi   1.40   .70

Easter — A326

2008, Feb. 28   *Perf. 11¼x11¾*
535 A326 (10k) multi   .75   .55
     Complete booklet, 10 #535   8.00

Krupina Arms and Church — A327

2008, Mar. 6   *Perf. 11¾x11¼*
536 A327 (14k) multi   1.25   .80

Dahlias — A328

2008, Mar. 20
537 A328 (10k) multi + label 2.50 1.50

Printed in sheets of 8 stamps + 8 labels that could be personalized.

Constitutional Court, 15th Anniv. — A329

2008, Apr. 3   *Perf. 11¼x11¾*
538 A329 25k multi   2.50 1.75

Eugen Suchon (1908-93), Composer — A330

2008, Apr. 17
539 A330 (15k) multi   1.50 1.10

Masa Hal'amová (1908-86), Poet — A331

2008, Apr. 17   *Perf. 11¾x11¼*
540 A331 (18k) multi   1.75 1.25

1872 Smekal Fire Pumper A332

1880 Seltenhofer Fire Pumper — A333

2008, Apr. 30   **Litho. & Engr.**
541 A332 (19k) multi   1.50 1.10
542 A333 (31k) multi   2.50 2.00

Europa — A334

2008, May 5 Litho. *Perf. 11¼x11¾*
543 A334 21k multi   2.50 2.00

Multi-headed Dragon from Stories by Pavol Dobsinsky — A335

2008, May 29   *Perf. 11¼x11½*
544 A335 (10k) multi   .75   .55
     Complete booklet, 10 #544   7.50

2008 Summer Olympics, Beijing — A336

2008, June 4   *Perf. 11¾x11¼*
545 A336 25k multi   4.00 1.50

2008 Paralympics, Beijing — A337

2008, June 6
546 A337 30k multi   4.00 2.00

9th Cent. Copper Plaque Found at Bojná — A338

Litho. & Engr.
2008, June 30   *Perf. 11¾*
547 A338 33k multi + label   5.00 3.00

Printed in sheets of 3 stamps + 3 labels.

Karol Plicka (1894-1987), Photographer — A339

2008, Sept. 12
548 A339 40k multi + 2 labels 4.50 3.00
     See Czech Republic No. 3397.

Coronation of King Matthias Corvinus, 550th Anniv. A340

2008, Sept. 25 Litho. *Perf. 11¼*
549 A340 (16k) multi   1.50   .75

Wooden Churches — A341

No. 550 — Church in: a, Hervartov. b, Dobroslava.

Litho. & Engr.
2008, Oct. 9   *Perf. 11¾*
550 A341 (18k) Horiz. pair, #a-b,
           + central label   6.00 5.00

Printed in sheets containing two of each stamp + 2 labels.

Orchids A342

Designs: (14k), Cypripedium calceolus. (15k), Ophrys apifera.

Photo. & Engr.
2008, Oct. 23   *Perf. 12x11¼*
551-552 A342 Set of 2   4.00 3.00

No. 551 is inscribed "T2 100g;" No. 552, "T2 500g."

Christmas — A343

Perf. 11¼x11¾
2008, Nov. 13   **Litho.**
553 A343 (10k) multi   .85   .40
     Complete booklet, 10 #553   8.50

Post Rider For Bratislava-Ruzomberok-
Kosice Mail Route — A344

2008, Nov. 27   **Perf. 11¾x11¼**
554 A344 (16k) multi + label   1.90   .70
Stamp Day.

Art Type of 1996

Designs: (31k), Illustration by Josef Baláz, from book *The Seven-colored Flower*. (37k), A Girl in White with Factory Chimneys and Flowers, by Zoltán Palugyay.

2008, Nov. 27   Engr.   Perf. 11¾
555-556 A126   Set of 2   5.75 3.00
Nos. 555-556 each were printed in sheets of 4. No. 555 is inscribed "T2 1000g"; No. 556, "T1 1000g."

100 Cents = 1 Euro

Euro Symbol and
Map of
Slovakia — A345

Perf. 11¾x11½
2009, Jan. 1   **Litho. & Engr.**
557 A345 €1 multi   2.75 1.40
Introduction of Euro currency.
Issued in sheets of 6.

A346

Churches and Their
Decorations — A347

Designs: 1c, Chapel of St. Margaret, Kopcany. 2c, Sculpture from Church of the Virgin Mary, Boldog. 5c, Rotunda of Church of St. Margaret, Sivetice. 10c, Altar from Church of St. John the Baptist, Pominovce. 20c, Church, Svätuse. 33c, Church, Cierny Brod. 50c, Sculpture of lion from Church of St. Martin, Spisská Kapitula, horiz. 66c, Columns, Church of St. Egidius, Ilija, vert. 83c, Mural from Church of St. Stephen the King, Zilina-Zavodie, vert. €1, Capital from Church of the Virgin Mary, Bina. €2, Church of St. Michael the Archangel, Drazovce.
€1.33, Church of the Holy Cross, Hamuliakovo.

Photo. & Engr., Litho. (33c, 66c, 83c)
Perf. 11¾x11¼, 11¼x11¾
2009, Jan. 2
558 A346   1c multi   .25   .25
559 A346   2c multi   .25   .25
560 A346   5c multi   .25   .25
561 A346   10c multi   .30   .25
562 A346   20c multi   .55   .25
563 A347   33c multi   .95   .45
564 A346   50c multi   1.40   .70
565 A347   66c multi   1.90   .95
566 A347   83c multi   2.40 1.25
567 A346   €1 multi   2.75 1.40
568 A346   €2 multi   5.50 2.75
   Nos. 558-568 (11)   16.50 8.75

Souvenir Sheet
Perf. 11¾
569 A346 €1.33 multi   3.75 1.90
See Nos. 587, 610, 631, 654, 679.

Easter — A348

Perf. 11¾x11¼
2009, Feb. 27   **Litho.**
570 A348 33c multi   2.50   .40
Serpentine Die Cut 16½x15
Booklet Stamp
Self-Adhesive
570A A348 33c multi   3.00   .40
  b.   Booklet pane of 10   30.00

Karate — A349

2009, Mar. 13   **Perf. 11¼x11¾**
571 A349 60c multi   1.60   .80

Aurel Stodola
(1859-1942),
Engineer
A350

2009, Apr. 17   **Perf. 11¾x11¼**
572 A350 33c multi   .90   .45

Union of Slovak Philatelists, 40th
Anniv. — A351

Perf. 11½x11¼
2009, Apr. 29   **Litho. & Engr.**
573 A351 (33c) multi + label   .90   .45

Supreme Audit
Office, 40th
Anniv. — A352

Photo. & Engr.
2009, May 7   **Perf. 11½x11¼**
574 A352 80c multi   2.25 1.10

Europa
A353

2009, May 28 Litho.   Perf. 11¾x11¼
575 A353 90c multi   2.50 1.25
Intl. Year of Astronomy.
Issued in sheets of 8.

Souvenir Sheet

Zofia Bosniaková (1609-44), Founder
of Poorhouse — A354

Litho. & Engr.
2009, June 2   **Perf. 11¾**
576 A354 80c multi   2.25 1.10

Souvenir Sheet

Pres. Ivan Gasparovic — A355

Litho. With Foil Application
2009, June 15   **Perf. 11¾x12**
577 A355 €1 gold + 2 labels   3.00 1.50

2009 Biennale of
Illustrations,
Bratislava — A356

2009, Aug. 14 Engr.   Perf. 11¼x11¾
578 A356 (33c) brown   .95   .45

Souvenir Sheet

Archaeological Excavations of Roman
Military Camps — A357

No. 579: a, Carnuntum. b, Gerulata.

Perf. 11½x11¾
2009, Sept. 11   **Litho. & Engr.**
579 A357 60c Sheet of 2, #a-b   3.50 1.75
See Austria No. 2220.

Souvenir Sheet

Nature
Preservation
A358

Designs: No. 580, €1.10, Salamandra salamandra. No. 581, €1.10, Emys orbicularis.

2009, Oct. 23   **Perf. 11¾x11½**
580-581 A358   Set of 2   6.50 3.25
Nos. 580-581 were printed in sheets of 6 containing 3 of each stamp.

Christmas — A359

Perf. 11¼x11¾
2009, Nov. 11   **Litho.**
582 A359 40c multi   1.25   .60
Booklet Stamp
Self-Adhesive
Serpentine Die Cut 15x16½
583 A359 40c multi   2.00   .60
  a.   Booklet pane of 10   20.00

Art Type of 1996

Designs: No. 584, €1.20, Madonna with Black Nimbus, by Ján Mudroch. No. 585, €1.20, Don Quixote, by Cyprián Majerník.

2009, Nov. 27   Engr.   Perf. 11¾
584-585 A126   Set of 2   7.25 3.75
Nos. 584-585 were each printed in sheets of 4 + 2 labels.

Louis Braille (1809-52), Educator of
the Blind — A360

2009, Dec. 4   Litho.   Perf. 11¾x11¼
586 A360 70c multi + label   2.10 1.10
Stamp Day.

Church Art and Architecture Type of 2009

Design: Cross, Church of the Assumption of the Virgin Mary, Spisská Nová Ves.

Photo. & Engr.
2010, Jan. 4   **Perf. 11¾x11¼**
587 A346 60c multi   1.75   .85

2010 Winter Olympics,
Vancouver — A361

2010, Jan. 15   **Litho.**
588 A361 €1 multi   2.75 1.40

Pres. Ivan
Gasparovic — A362

2010, Jan. 29   **Photo. & Engr.**
589 A362 40c multi   1.10 .55

Easter — A363

Perf. 11¼x11¾
2010, Feb. 26   **Litho.**
590 A363 40c multi   1.10 .55
Serpentine Die Cut 15x16½
Booklet Stamp
Self-Adhesive
591 A363 40c multi   1.10 .55
a.   Booklet pane of 10   11.00

Count
Matthew
Csák of
Trencin (c.
1260-1321),
Palatine
A364

2010, Mar. 12   **Litho.**   **Perf. 11¼**
592 A364 70c multi   1.90 .95

Souvenir Sheet

Zilina Synod, 400th Anniv. — A365

Litho. & Engr.
2010, Mar. 30   **Perf. 11¾**
593 A365 €1.10 multi   3.00 1.50

Milan Hodza
(1878-1944),
Journalist
A366

2010, Apr. 16   **Litho.**   **Perf. 11¾x11¼**
594 A366 40c multi   1.10 .55

Europa — A367

2010, May 4   **Perf. 11¼x11¾**
595 A367 90c multi   2.40 1.25
Issued in sheets of 8.

Souvenir Sheet

2010 World Cup Soccer
Championships, South Africa — A368

Litho. With Three-Dimensional
Plastic Affixed
2010, June 8   *Die Cut*
Self-Adhesive
596 A368   Sheet of 2   11.00 5.50
a.   €2.30 Single stamp   5.50 2.75

Topol'cianky Castle — A369

Betliar
Castle
A370

Photo. & Engr.
2010, June 18   **Perf. 11¾x11¼**
597 A369 40c multi   1.00 .50
598 A370 40c multi   1.00 .50

Miniature Sheet

Saints — A371

No. 599: a, St. Gorazd. b. St. Clement.

2010, July 16   **Perf. 11¾**
599   A371   Sheet of 5, 3
    #599a, 2 #599b, +
    5 labels   8.00 4.00
a.-b.   60c Either single   1.60 .80

Topol'cany Castle — A372

Perf. 11¾x11¼
2010, Sept. 17   **Litho.**
600 A372 40c multi + label   1.10 .55
Printed in sheets of 8 stamps + 8 labels that
could be personalized.

Egyptian Alabaster
Canopic
Jar — A373

2010, Oct. 8   **Litho. & Engr.**
601 A373 €1 multi   2.75 1.40
See Egypt No. 2069.

Miniature Sheet

Protected Flowers of the Muránska
Plain — A374

No. 602: a, Primula auricula. b, Daphne
arbuscula.

2010, Oct. 15   **Perf. 11½x11¾**
602   A374   Sheet of 4, 2 each
    #a-b, + 2 labels   9.00 4.50
a.-b.   80c Either single   2.25 1.10

Christmas — A375

Perf. 11¼x11¾
2010, Nov. 12   **Litho.**
603 A375 40c multi   1.10 .55
Self-Adhesive
Booklet Stamp
Serpentine Die Cut 15x16½
604 A375 40c multi   1.10 .55
a.   Booklet pane of 10   11.00

Art Type of 1996

Designs: No. 605, €1.20, Coronation of
Charles I of Hungary (Charles Robert), by
unknown artist, St. Martin Cathedral, Spisská
Kapitula (denomination in black). No. 606,
€1.20, Madonna and Child, statue by Master
Paul of Levoca, Assumption of the Virgin Mary
Church, L'ubica (denomination in blue).

2010, Nov. 26   **Engr.**   **Perf. 11¾**
605-606 A126   Set of 2   6.50 3.25
Nos. 605-606 each were printed in sheets of
4 + 2 labels

Campaign
Against
AIDS — A376

2010, Dec. 1   **Litho.**   **Perf. 11¼**
607 A376 40c multi   1.10 .55
No. 607 has a die cut cross-shaped hole at
lower left.

Karol Ondreicka (1944-2003), Stamp
Designer — A377

Perf. 11¾x11¼
2010, Dec. 3   **Litho. & Engr.**
608 A377 70c multi + label   1.90 .95
Stamp Day.

Intl. Year of Chemistry — A378

2011, Jan. 17   **Litho.**   **Perf. 11¾x11¼**
609 A378 80c multi + label   2.25 1.10

Churches and Their Decorations
Type of 2009

Designs: Sculpture of St. George Killing
Dragon, Church of St. George, Svaty Jur.

2011, Jan. 28   **Photo. & Engr.**
610 A346 70c multi   1.90 .95

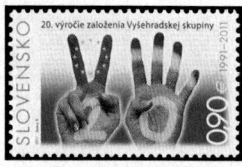

Visegrád Group, 20th Anniv. — A379

2011, Feb. 11   **Litho.**
611 A379 90c multi   2.50 1.25
Issued in sheets of 8.
See Czech Republic No. 3490, Hungary No.
4183, Poland No. 4001.

Meringue
Lamb — A380

2011, Mar. 4   **Perf. 11¾x11¼**
612 A380 40c multi   1.10 .55
Booklet Stamp
Self-Adhesive
Serpentine Die Cut 16½x15
613 A380 40c multi   1.10 .55
a.   Booklet pane of 10   11.00
Easter.

2011 World Ice Hockey
Championships, Slovakia — A381

No. 614: a, 40c, Slovakian player Pavol
Demitra (1974-2011). b, 50c, Russian
goaltender.

Perf. 11¼x11¾
2011, Mar. 25   **Litho.**
614 A381   Horiz. pair, #a-b   2.60 1.25

Dobsinská Ice Cave UNESCO World Heritage Site — A382

Perf. 11¾x11½
2011, Apr. 15   **Litho. & Engr.**
615 A382 €1.10 multi   3.25 1.60
Issued in sheets of 6.

Beatification of Pope John Paul II — A383

2011, Apr. 29   **Perf. 11¾**
616 A383 40c multi   1.25 .60
Pritned in sheets of 4 + label.

Europa — A384

2011, May 6
617 A384 90c multi   2.60 1.25
Intl. Year of Forests.
Issued in sheets of 8.

Flower — A385

2011, June 3 Litho.   **Perf. 11¼x11¾**
618 A385 (40c) multi + label   1.25 .60
Printed in sheets of 8 stamps + 8 labels that could be personalized.

Souvenir Sheet

Memorandum of the Slovak Nation, 150th Anniv. — A386

Litho. & Engr.
2011, June 6   **Perf. 11¾**
619 A386 €1.20 multi   3.50 1.75

Old Automobiles — A387

Designs: 40c, Aero 30. 80c, Tatra 87.

Photo. & Engr.
2011, July 1   **Perf. 11¾x11¼**
620-621 A387   Set of 2   3.50 1.75

Ján Cikker (1911-89), Composer A388

2011, July 29   **Litho.**
622 A388 50c multi   1.50 .75

2011 Biennale of Illustrations, Bratislava — A389

2011, Sept. 2   **Perf. 11¼x11¾**
623 A389 40c multi   1.10 .55

Michal Miloslav Hodza (1811-70), Nationalist Leader and Poet — A390

Photo. & Engr.
2011, Sept. 22   **Perf. 11½x11¼**
624 A390 40c multi   1.10 .55

Otis Tarda — A391

Litho. & Engr.
2011, Oct. 14   **Perf. 11¾**
625 A391 €1.10 multi   3.00 1.50
Printed in sheets of 4 + 2 labels.

Fish-shaped Honey Cake — A392

Perf. 11¾x11¼
2011, Nov. 11   **Litho.**
626 A392 40c multi   1.10 .55
Booklet Stamp
Self-Adhesive
Serpentine Die Cut 16½x15
627 A392 40c multi   1.10 .55
   a.   Booklet pane of 10   11.00
Christmas. No. 626 is impregnated with a cinnamon scent.

Art Type of 1996
Design: Woodcut of Historian Ján Sambucus (1534-81), by Tobias Stimmer.

Litho. & Engr.
2011, Nov. 25   **Perf. 11¾**
628 A126 €1.20 blk & beige   3.25 1.60

Mailbox and Postrider — A393

2011, Dec. 2 Litho.   **Perf. 11¾x11¼**
629 A393 50c multi + label   1.40 .70
Stamp Day.

Souvenir Sheet

Virgin and Child with St. Anne (Roznava Metercia), by Unknown Artist — A394

Litho. & Engr.
2011, Dec. 13   **Perf. 11¾**
630 A394 €1.60 multi   4.25 2.10

Churches and Their Decorations
Type of 2009
Design: Angel, Piarist Church, Prievidza.

Photo. & Engr.
2012, Jan. 27   **Perf. 11¾x11¼**
631 A346 80c multi   2.10 1.10

Jonás Záborsky (1812-76), Writer — A395

2012, Feb. 3   **Litho.**
632 A395 40c multi   1.10 .55

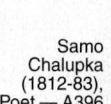

Samo Chalupka (1812-83), Poet — A396

2012, Feb. 27
633 A396 50c multi   1.40 .70

Christ Carrying the Cross, by Hans von Aachen A397

2012, Mar. 9   **Perf. 11¾x11¼**
634 A397 40c multi   1.10 .55
Booklet Stamp
Self-Adhesive
Serpentine Die Cut 16½x15
635 A397 40c multi   1.10 .55
   a.   Booklet pane of 10   11.00

Souvenir Sheet

Ján Koniarek (1878-1952), Sculptor — A398

Perf. 11¾x11½
2012, Apr. 13   **Litho. & Engr.**
636 A398   Sheet of 2, #636a + central label   6.50 3.25
   a.   €1.20 Single stamp   3.25 1.60
See Serbia No. 591.

Europa A399

2012, May 4 Litho.   **Perf. 11¾x11¼**
637 A399 90c multi   2.25 1.10
Printed in sheets of 8 + 4 labels.

Slovakian Men's Ice Hockey Team's Second-Place Finish in 2012 World Championships A400

2012, May 25   *Perf. 11¼x11¾*
638 A400 40c multi   1.00 .50

Intl. Children's Day — A401

2012, June 1   *Perf. 11¼x11¾*
639 A401 (40c) multi + label   1.00 .50
Booklet Stamp
Self-Adhesive
Serpentine Die Cut 15x16½
640 A401 (40c) multi   1.00 .50
a.   Booklet pane of 10   10.00

No. 639 was printed in sheets of 8 stamps + 8 labels that could be personalized.

Souvenir Sheet

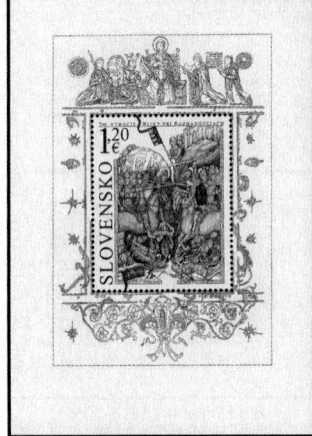

Battle of Rozhanovce, 700th Anniv. — A402

Litho. & Engr.
2012, June 15   *Perf. 11¾*
641 A402 €1.20 multi   3.00 1.50

2012 Summer Olympics and Paralympics, London — A403

No. 642: a, Runners, Nike with sword, Greek bronze statue. b, London Eye, wheelchair racer, Slovakian Paralympics emblem.

Perf. 11¾x11¼
2012, June 28   **Litho.**
642 A403 90c Pair, #a-b   4.50 2.25

Church, Skalka A404

2012, July 13   **Photo. & Engr.**
643 A404 40c multi   1.00 .50

Basilica of Our Lady of Sorrows, Sastín — A405

2012, Sept. 14   *Perf. 11½x11¾*
644 A405 40c lt blue & blue   1.10 .55

Souvenir Sheet

Anton Bernolák (1762-1813). Linguist — A406

2012, Oct. 3   **Litho. & Engr.**
645 A406 €1.10 multi   3.00 1.50

Souvenir Sheet

Flowers of the Low Tatras National Park — A407

No. 646: a, Loiseleuria procumbens. b, Saxifraga mutata.

2012, Oct. 12   *Perf. 11¾*
646 A407 70c Sheet of 2, #a-b, + 3 labels   3.75 1.90

L'ubovna Castle A408

2012, Nov. 8
647 A408 90c multi   2.40 1.25

Christmas A409

Perf. 11¾x11¼
2012, Nov. 16   **Litho.**
648 A409 40c multi   1.10 .55

Booklet Stamp
Self-Adhesive
Serpentine Die Cut 16½x15
649 A409 40c multi   1.10 .55
a.   Booklet pane of 10   11.00

Art Type of 1996

Design: Untitled painting by Viera Zilincanová, horiz.

2012, Nov. 23   **Engr.**   *Perf. 11¾*
650 A126 €1.20 multi   3.25 1.60

No.. 650 was printed in sheets of 4 + central label.

Souvenir Sheet

Sala Terrena Fresco, Cerveny Kamen Castle — A410

2012, Nov. 23   **Litho. & Engr.**
651 A410 €1.60 multi   4.25 2.10

Pavol Sochán (1862-1941), Photographer — A411

2012, Dec. 3   **Litho.**   *Perf. 11¾x11¼*
652 A411 50c multi + label   1.40 .70

Slovak Republic, 20th Anniv. — A412

2013, Jan. 1
653 A412 (65c) multi + label   1.75 .90

Churches and Decorations Type of 2009

Design: Putti with theater mask, Empire Theater, Hlohovec.

2013, Jan. 25   **Photo. & Engr.**
654 A346 90c multi   2.50 1.25

Ján Popluhár (1935-2011), Soccer Player — A413

2013, Feb. 14   **Litho.**
655 A413 65c multi   1.75 .85

Easter — A414

2013, Mar. 1   *Perf. 11¼x11¾*
656 A414 45c multi   1.25 .60

Booklet Stamp
Self-Adhesive
Serpentine Die Cut 15x16½
657 A414 45c multi   1.25 .60
a.   Booklet pane of 10   12.50

Dominik Tatarka (1913-89), Writer — A415

2013, Mar. 14   *Perf. 11¾x11¼*
658 A415 65c multi   1.75 .85

Breast Cancer Awareness — A416

2013, Apr. 12   *Perf. 11¼x11¾*
659 A416 €1.10 multi   3.00 1.50

Windmill, Holic — A417

2013, Apr. 26   **Photo. & Engr.**
660 A417 (45c) multi   1.25 .60

Europa A418

2013, May 9   **Litho.**   *Perf. 11¾x11¼*
661 A418 90c multi   2.40 1.25
Booklet Stamp
Self-Adhesive
Serpentine Die Cut 16½x15
662 A418 90c multi   2.40 1.25
a.   Booklet pane of 6   14.50

Lúcnica Art Ensemble Dancers, Slovakia — A419

Pansori Performers, South Korea — A420

Perf. 11½x11¾

2013, May 31   **Litho. & Engr.**
663 A419 €1 multi   2.75 1.40
664 A420 €1 multi   2.75 1.40

Nos. 663-664 were printed in sheets of 6 containing 3 of each stamp. See South Korea No. 2405.

Sun and Zodiac Symbols — A421

2013, June 7   **Litho.**   **Perf. 11¼x11¾**
665 A421 (45c) multi + label   1.25 .60

No. 665 was printed in sheets of 8 + 8 labels that could be personalized.

Souvenir Sheet

Mission of Sts. Cyril and Methodius to Slavic Lands, 1150th Anniv. — A422

Litho. & Engr.
2013, June 12   **Perf. 11¾**
666 A422 €1.60 multi   4.50 2.25

See Bulgaria No. 4647, Czech Republic No. 3573, Vatican City No. 1536.

Gorazd Zvonicky (1913-95), Missionary and Poet — A423

Perf. 11¾x11¼

2013, June 28   **Litho.**
667 A423 65c multi   1.75 .85

Matica Slovenská Foundation, 150th Anniv. — A424

2013, Aug. 2   **Litho.**   **Perf. 11¾**
668 A424 80c multi   2.25 1.10

Printed in sheets of 8 + 1 label

2013 Biennale of Illustrations, Bratislava — A425

2013, Sept. 2   **Litho.**   **Perf. 11¼x11¾**
669 A425 (45c) multi   1.25 .60

Tatra Mountains — A426

Designs: €1.25, Small Cold Valley. €1.45, Chalet at Zelene Pleso.

Photo. & Engr.

2013, Sept. 20   **Perf. 11¼x11¾**
670-671 A426   Set of 2   7.50 3.75

Minerals — A427

No. 672: a, Scepter quartz crystal from Sobova (denomination at UL). b, Opal from Dubnik (denomination at LR).

Perf. 11¾x11½

2013, Oct. 11   **Litho. & Engr.**
672 A427 60c Horiz. pair, #a-b   3.25 1.60

Printed in sheets of 6, containing 3 each #672a and 672b.

A428

Christmas — A429

2013   **Litho.**   **Perf. 11¼x11¾**
673 A428 45c multi + label   1.25 .60
674 A429 45c multi   1.25 .60

Booklet Stamp
Self-Adhesive
Serpentine Die Cut 15x16½

675 A428 45c multi   1.25 .60
   a.   Booklet pane of 10   12.50

Issued: Nos. 673, 675, 11/4; No. 674, 11/13. No. 673 was printed in sheets of 8 + 8 labels that could be personalized.
No. 675 is impregnated with a baked apple scent.

Art Type of 1996

Designs: €1.20, Po Dojeni (After Milking), photograph by Martin Martincek. €1.25, Portrait of Count Jan Joseph Hadik de Futak, by Ján Jakub Stunder.

2013, Nov. 29   **Engr.**   **Perf. 11¾**
676-677 A126   Set of 2   6.75 3.50

Drawing by Igor Rumansky (1946-2006), Stamp Designer — A430

Photo. & Engr.

2013, Dec. 6   **Perf. 11¾x11¼**
678 A430 65c multi + label   1.90 .95

Stamp Day.

Churches and Their Decorations Type of 2009

Design: Synagogue, Levice, horiz.

Photo. & Engr.

2014, Jan. 2   **Perf. 11¼x11¾**
679 A346 65c multi   1.75 .90

2014 Winter Olympics, Sochi, Russia — A431

2014, Jan. 15   **Litho.**   **Perf. 11¾x11¼**
680 A431 90c multi   2.50 1.25

2014 Winter Paralympics, Sochi, Russia — A432

2014, Jan. 15   **Litho.**   **Perf. 11¾x11¼**
681 A432 90c multi   2.50 1.25

International Year of Crystallography — A433

Perf. 11¾x11¼

2014, Feb. 14   **Litho.**
682 A433 €1 multi + label   2.75 1.40

Easter — A434

Perf. 11¼x11¾

2014, Mar. 10   **Litho.**
683 A434 45c multi   1.25 .60

Booklet Stamp
Self-Adhesive
Serpentine Die Cut 11½x11¼
Syncopated

684 A434 45c multi   1.25 .60
   a.   Booklet pane of 10   12.50

Stefan Osusky (1889-1973), Diplomat A435

Photo. & Engr.

2014, Mar. 31   **Perf. 11¾x11¼**
685 A435 45c multi   1.25 .60

Motorcycles — A436

Designs: €1.10, Manet M90. €1.25, Jawa 50/550 Pionier.

Photo. & Engr.

2014, Apr. 17   **Perf. 11¾x11¼**
686-687 A436   Set of 2   6.50 3.25

Bagpipes — A437

2014, May 5   **Litho.**   **Perf. 11¼x11¾**
688 A437 90c multi   2.50 1.25

Booklet Stamp
Self-Adhesive
Serpentine Die Cut 16½x15

689 A437 90c multi   2.50 1.25
   a.   Booklet pane of 6   15.00

Europa.

Pavol Horov (1914-75), Poet — A438

2014, May 23   **Litho.**   **Perf. 11¾x11½**
690 A438 45c multi   1.25 .60

Regietów, Poland World War I Cemetery Memorials Designed by Dusan Jurkovic — A439

2014, June 2   **Litho.**   **Perf. 11¾x11½**
691 A439 65c multi   1.75 .90

Dandelion and Ladybug — A440

2014, June 6   **Litho.**   **Perf. 11¼x11¾**
692 A440 (45c) multi + label   1.25 .60

No. 692 was printed in sheets of 8 + 8 labels that could be personalized.

Pres. Andrej Kiska — A441

Photo. & Engr.
2014, June 13 *Perf. 11¾x11¼*
693 A441 45c multi 1.25 .60

Slovak National Uprising Monument, Banská Bystrica A442

2014, Aug. 29 Litho. *Perf. 11¼*
694 A442 65c multi 1.75 .85
Slovak National Uprising, 70th anniv.

Wedding Palace, Bytca A443

Litho. & Engr.
2014, Sept. 19 *Perf. 11¾*
695 A443 €1.30 blk & gray 3.25 1.60
No. 695 was printed in sheets of 8 + label.

Father Andrej Hlinka (1864-1938), Politician — A444

2014, Sept. 26 Litho. *Perf. 11¾*
696 A444 80c multi 2.10 1.10
No. 696 was printed in sheets of 4 + label.

International Peace Marathon, Kosice, 90th Anniv. — A445

2014, Oct. 5 Litho. *Perf. 12*
697 A445 45c multi 1.10 .55

Souvenir Sheet

Insects in Sitno National Nature Reserve — A446

No. 698: a, Oryctes nasicornis. b, Lucanus cervus.

Litho. & Engr.
2014, Oct. 10 *Perf. 11¾*
698 A446 80c Sheet of 2, #a-b, + 2 labels 4.00 2.00

Obverse and Reverse of Silver Half Denarius of King Charles II of Western Francia — A447

Litho. & Engr.
2014, Nov. 6 *Perf. 11¾*
699 A447 €1 multi + 2 labels 2.50 1.25
History of customs in central Europe.

Christmas
A448 A449
2014 Litho. *Perf. 11¼x11¾*
700 A448 45c multi 1.10 .55
701 A449 (45c) multi 1.10 .55
Booklet Stamp
Self-Adhesive
Serpentine Die Cut 15x16½
702 A449 (45c) multi 1.10 .55
a. Booklet pane of 10 11.00
Issued: No. 700, 11/14; Nos. 701-702, 11/13.

Art Type of 1996
Designs: €1.30, Portrait of the Artist's Wife, by Peter Michal Bohún. €1.65, Dying Deer, sculpture by Alojz Stróbl, horiz.

Litho. & Engr.
2014, Nov. 25 *Perf. 11¾*
703 A126 €1.30 multi 3.25 1.60
Souvenir Sheet
704 A126 €1.65 multi 4.25 2.10

Severín Zrubec (1921-2011), Philatelist — A450

Photo. & Engr.
2014, Dec. 5 *Perf. 11¼x11½*
705 A450 60c multi + 2 labels 1.50 .75
Stamp Day.

SEMI-POSTAL STAMPS

Catalogue values for unused stamps in this section are for Never Hinged items.

Josef Tiso — SP1

Wmk. 263
1939, Nov. 6 Photo. *Perf. 12½*
B1 SP1 2.50k + 2.50k royal blue 3.75 *4.00*
The surtax was used for Child Welfare.

Medical Corpsman and Wounded Soldier — SP2

1941, Nov. 10
B2 SP2 50h + 50h dull green .60 .60
B3 SP2 1k + 1k rose lake .60 .60
B4 SP2 2k + 1k brt blue 1.90 1.50
Nos. B2-B4 (3) 3.10 2.70

Mother and Child — SP3

1941, Dec. 10
B5 SP3 50h + 50h dull green 1.00 .90
B6 SP3 1k + 1k brown 1.00 .90
B7 SP3 2k + 1k violet 1.00 .90
Nos. B5-B7 (3) 3.00 2.70
Surtax for the benefit of child welfare.

Soldier and Hlinka Youth — SP4

1942, Mar. 14
B8 SP4 70h + 1k brown org .50 .30
B9 SP4 1.30k + 1k brt blue .50 .30
B10 SP4 2k + 1k rose red 1.50 1.10
Nos. B8-B10 (3) 2.50 1.70
The surtax aided the Hlinka Youth Society "Hlinkova Mladez."

SP5 SP6

National Costumes — SP7

1943 *Perf. 14*
B11 SP5 50h + 50h dk slate grn .30 .25
B12 SP6 70h + 1k dp carmine .30 .25
B13 SP7 80h + 2k dark blue .40 .40
Nos. B11-B13 (3) 1.00 .90
The surtax was for the benefit of children, the Red Cross and winter relief of the Slovakian popular party.

Infantrymen — SP8

Aviator — SP9

Tank and Gun Crew SP10

1943, July 28
B14 SP8 70h + 2k rose brown .80 *.95*
B15 SP9 1.30k + 2k sapphire .80 *.95*
B16 SP10 2k + 2k olive green .80 *.95*
Nos. B14-B16 (3) 2.40 2.85
The surtax was for soldiers' welfare.

"The Slovak Language Is Our Life" — L. Stur — SP11

Slovakian National Museum SP12

Slovakian Foundation SP13

Slovakian Peasant — SP14

1943, Oct. 16

B17	SP11	30h + 1k brown red	.50	.35
B18	SP12	70h + 1k slate green	.50	.35
B19	SP13	80h + 2k slate blue	.50	.35
B20	SP14	1.30k + 2k dull brown	.50	.35
		Nos. B17-B20 (4)	2.00	1.40

The surtax was for the benefit of Slovakian cultural institutions.

Soccer Player — SP15

Skier — SP16   Diver — SP17

Relay Race — SP18

1944, Apr. 30   Unwmk.

B21	SP15	70h + 70h slate grn	.75	.90
B22	SP16	1k + 1k violet	.75	.90
B23	SP17	1.30k + 1.30k Prus bl	.75	.90
B24	SP18	2k + 2k chnt brn	.75	.90
		Nos. B21-B24 (4)	3.00	3.60

Symbolic of National Protection SP19

1944, Oct. 6   Wmk. 263

B25	SP19	70h + 4h sapphire	.90	1.00
B26	SP19	1.30k + 4k red brown	.90	1.00

The surtax was for the benefit of social institutions.

Children — SP20

1944, Dec. 18

B27	SP20	2k + 4k light blue	3.00	4.00
a.		Sheet of 8 + Label	50.00	70.00

The surtax was to aid social work for Slovak youth.

Red Cross — SP21

Photo. & Engr.
1993, Nov. 15   Perf. 11x11½

B28	SP21	3k +1k red & gray blue	.40	.40

Souvenir Sheet

1996 Summer Olympics, Atlanta — SP22

Photo. & Engr.
1996, May 15   Perf. 12x11½

B29	SP22	12k +2k multi	1.50	1.50

Surcharge for Slovak Olympic Committee.

AIR POST STAMPS

Catalogue values for unused stamps in this section are for Never Hinged items.

Planes over Tatra Mountains
AP1   AP2

Perf. 12½
1939, Nov. 20   Photo.   Unwmk.

C1	AP1	30h violet	.40	.40
C2	AP1	50h dark green	.40	.40
C3	AP1	1k vermilion	.40	.40
C4	AP2	2k grnsh black	.65	.65
C5	AP2	3k dark brown	1.00	1.00
C6	AP2	4k slate blue	1.90	1.90
		Nos. C1-C6 (6)	4.75	4.75

See No. C10.

Plane in Flight — AP3

1940, Nov. 30   Wmk. 263   Perf. 12½

C7	AP3	5k dk violet brn	1.50	1.50
C8	AP3	10k gray black	1.75	1.75
C9	AP3	20k myrtle green	2.25	2.25
		Nos. C7-C9 (3)	5.50	5.50

Type of 1939
1944, Sept. 15   Wmk. 263

C10	AP1	1k vermilion	1.50	1.50

PERSONAL DELIVERY STAMPS

Catalogue values for unused stamps in this section are for Never Hinged items.

PD1

1940   Wmk. 263   Photo.   Imperf.

EX1	PD1	50h indigo & blue	1.00	1.75
EX2	PD1	50h carmine & rose	1.00	1.75

POSTAGE DUE STAMPS

Catalogue values for unused stamps in this section are for Never Hinged items.

D1

1939   Unwmk.   Photo.   Perf. 12½

J1	D1	5h bright blue	1.00	.55
J2	D1	10h bright blue	.50	.55
J3	D1	20h bright blue	.50	.55
J4	D1	30h bright blue	3.00	1.00
J5	D1	40h bright blue	.70	.75
J6	D1	50h bright blue	2.50	.80
J7	D1	60h bright blue	2.00	.80
J8	D1	1k dark carmine	14.00	8.25
J9	D1	2k dark carmine	14.00	2.50
J10	D1	5k dark carmine	8.00	2.50
J11	D1	10k dark carmine	55.00	7.50
J12	D1	20k dark carmine	18.00	9.25
		Nos. J1-J12 (12)	119.20	35.00

1940-41   Wmk. 263

J13	D1	5h bright blue ('41)	.75	.55
J14	D1	10h bright blue ('41)	.30	.30
J15	D1	20h bright blue ('41)	.50	.30
J16	D1	30h bright blue ('41)	4.00	2.00
J17	D1	40h bright blue ('41)	.60	.55
J18	D1	50h bright blue ('41)	.75	.95
J19	D1	60h bright blue	.90	.95
J20	D1	1k dark carmine ('41)	.90	1.10
J21	D1	2k dark carmine ('41)	20.00	9.00
J22	D1	5k dark carmine ('41)	4.00	2.75
J23	D1	10k dark carmine ('41)	3.00	3.25
		Nos. J13-J23 (11)	35.70	21.70

Letter, Post Horn — D2

1942   Unwmk.   Perf. 14

J24	D2	10h deep brown	.25	.25
J25	D2	20h deep brown	.25	.25
J26	D2	40h deep brown	.25	.25
J27	D2	50h deep brown	1.00	.60
J28	D2	60h deep brown	.25	.25
J29	D2	80h deep brown	.30	.25
J30	D2	1k rose red	.35	.25
J31	D2	1.10k rose red	.70	.60
J32	D2	1.30k rose red	.50	.25
J33	D2	1.60k rose red	.50	.25
J34	D2	2k rose red	1.00	.25
J35	D2	2.60k rose red	1.50	1.25
J36	D2	3.50k rose red	11.00	9.00
J37	D2	5k rose red	3.00	2.25
J38	D2	10k rose red	4.00	3.25
		Nos. J24-J38 (15)	24.85	19.20

NEWSPAPER STAMPS

Newspaper Stamps of Czechoslovakia, 1937, Overprinted in Red or Blue

1939, Apr.   Unwmk.   Imperf.

P1	N2	2h bister brn (Bl)	.50	.40
P2	N2	5h dull blue (R)	.50	.40
P3	N2	7h red org (Bl)	.50	.40
P4	N2	9h emerald (R)	.50	.40
P5	N2	10h henna brn (Bl)	.50	.40
P6	N2	12h ultra (R)	.50	.40
P7	N2	20h dk green (R)	1.10	.95

P8	N2	50h dk brown (Bl)	3.00	2.50
P9	N2	1k grnsh gray (R)	11.00	10.00
		Nos. P1-P9 (9)	18.10	15.85

Excellent counterfeits exist of Nos. P1-P9.

Catalogue values for unused stamps in this section, from this point to the end of the section, are for Never Hinged items.

Arms of Slovakia — N1

1939   Typo.

P10	N1	2h ocher	.30	.25
P11	N1	5h ultra	.45	.40
P12	N1	7h red orange	.35	.30
P13	N1	9h emerald	.35	.30
P14	N1	10h henna brown	1.60	1.10
P15	N1	12h dk ultra	.40	.35
P16	N1	20h dark green	1.60	1.10
P17	N1	50h red brown	1.90	1.25
P18	N1	1k grnsh gray	1.60	1.10
		Nos. P10-P18 (9)	8.55	6.15

1940-41   Wmk. 263

P20	N1	5h ultra	.25	.25
P23	N1	10h henna brown	.25	.25
P24	N1	15h brt purple ('41)	.30	.25
P25	N1	20h dark green	.60	.50
P26	N1	25h lt blue ('41)	.60	.50
P27	N1	40h red org ('41)	.60	.50
P28	N1	50h chocolate	1.10	.75
P29	N1	1k grnsh gray ('41)	1.10	.75
P30	N1	2k emerald ('41)	2.25	1.60
		Nos. P20-P30 (9)	7.05	5.35

Type Block "N" (for "Noviny" - Newspaper) — N2

1943   Photo.   Unwmk.

P31	N2	10h green	.25	.25
P32	N2	15h dark brown	.25	.25
P33	N2	20h ultra	.35	.35
P34	N2	50h rose red	.35	.35
P35	N2	1k slate green	.45	.45
P36	N2	2k intense blue	.65	.65
		Nos. P31-P36 (6)	2.30	2.30

SLOVENIA

slō-'vē-nē-ə

LOCATION — Southeastern Europe
GOVT. — Independent state
AREA — 7,819 sq. mi.
POP. — 1,970,570 (1999 est.)
CAPITAL — Ljubljana

A constituent republic of Yugoslavia since 1945, Slovenia declared its independence on June 25, 1991.

100 Paras = 1 Dinar
100 Stotin = 1 Tolar
100 Cents = 1 Euro (2007)

Catalogue values for unused stamps in this country are for Never Hinged items, beginning with Scott 100 in the regular postage section and Scott RA1 in the postal tax section.

Declaration of
Independence
A18

1991, June 26   Litho.   Perf. 10½
100 A18 5d Parliament building   1.10 1.10

National Arms
A19   A20

1991-92   Perf. 14
Background Color
101 A19   1t brown   .35   .35
102 A20   1t brown   .35   .35
103 A20   2t lilac rose   .35   .35
104 A19   4t green   .35   .35
105 A20   4t green   .35   .35
106 A19   5t salmon   .35   .35
107 A20   5t salmon   .35   .35
108 A20   6t yellow   .50   .50
109 A19 11t orange   .70   .70
110 A20 11t orange   .50   .50
111 A20 15t blue   .50   .50
112 A20 20t purple   1.10 1.10
113 A20 50t dark green   1.60 1.60
114 A20 100t gray   2.60 2.60
       Nos. 101-114 (14)   9.95 9.95

Issued: #107, 3/6/91; #101, 104, 106, 109, 12/26/91; #102, 6t, 20t, 50t, 100t, 2/12/92; 2t, 15t, #105, 110, 3/16/92.

1992 Winter Olympics,
Albertville — A21

a, 30t, Ski jumper. b, 50t, Alpine skier.

1992, Feb. 8
134 A21 Pair, #a.-b., + 1 or 2 labels   7.50 7.50

Rhomboid stamps issued in sheets of 3 #134 plus 4 labels. See No. 143.

Ljubljana
Opera
House,
Cent.
A22

1992, Mar. 31
135 A22 20t multicolored   1.40 1.40

Giuseppe Tartini
(1692-1770),
Italian Violinist
and Composer
A23

1992, Apr. 8
136 A23 27t multicolored   1.50 1.50

Discovery of America, 500th
Anniv. — A24

Designs: a, 27t, Map of northwestern Mexico and Gulf of California, Marko Anton Kappus preaching to natives. b, 47t, Map of parts of North and South America, sailing ship.

1992, Apr. 21
137 A24 Pair, #a.-b.   8.00 8.00
   Issued in sheets containing 6 No. 137.

Intl. Conference of Interior Designers,
Ljubljana — A25

1992, May 17
138 A25 41t multicolored   1.50 1.50

A. M. Slomsek
(1800-1862), Bishop
of Maribor — A26

1992, May 29
139 A26 6t multicolored   .65   .65

Mountain Rescue
Service, 80th
Anniv. — A27

1992, June 12
140 A27 41t multicolored   1.50 1.50

A28

1992, June 20
141 A28 6t multicolored   .40   .40
   Ljubljana Boatmen's Competition, 900th anniv.

A29

1992, June 25
142 A29 41t multicolored   1.50 1.50
   Independence, 1st anniv.

Olympic Type of 1992

a, 40t, Leon Stukelj, triple medalist in 1924, 1928. b, 46t, Olympic rings, three heads of Apollo.

1992, July 25
143 A21 Pair, #a.-b. +1 or 2 labels   3.75 3.75

1992 Summer Olympics, Barcelona. Rhomboid stamps issued in sheets of 3 #143 plus 4 labels.

World
Championship of
Registered
Dogs,
Ljubljana — A30

1992, Sept. 4
144 A30 40t Slovenian sheep dog 1.50 1.50

Marij Kogoj
(1892-1956),
Composer
A31

1992, Sept. 30
145 A31 40t multicolored   1.50 1.50

Self-Portrait, by
Matevz Langus
(1792-1855),
Painter — A32

1992, Oct. 30
146 A32 40t multicolored   1.50 1.50

Christmas
A33

Designs: 6t, 7t, Nativity Scene, Ljubljana. 41t, Stained glass window of Madonna and Child, St. Mary's Church, Bovec, vert.

1992
147   A33   6t multicolored   .25   .25
147A A33   7t multicolored   .50   .50
148   A33 41t multicolored   1.25 1.25
       Nos. 147-148 (3)   2.00 2.00

   Issued: 6t, 41t, Nov. 20. 7t, Dec. 15.

Herman Potocnik, Theoretician of
Geosynchronous Satellite Orbit, Birth
Cent. — A34

1992, Nov. 27   Litho.   Perf. 14
149 A34 46t multicolored   1.50 1.50

Prezihov Voranc (1893-1950),
Writer — A35

1993, Jan. 22   Litho.   Perf. 14
150 A35 7t multicolored   .35   .35

Rihard Jakopic (1869-1943),
Painter — A36

1993, Jan. 22
151 A36 44t multicolored   1.25 1.25

Jozef
Stefan
(1835-93),
Physicist
A37

1993, Jan. 22
152 A37 51t multicolored   1.40 1.40

A38

Designs: 1t, Early cake. 2t, Pan pipes. 5t, Kozolec. 6t, Early building. 7t, Zither. 8t, Water mill. 9t, Sled. 10t, Lonceni bajs. 11t, Kraski kos. 12t, Statue of boy on horseback, Ribnica. 20t, Cross-section of house. 44t, Stone building. 50t, Wind-powered pump. 100t, Potica.

1993-94

153	A38	1t multicolored	.35	.35
154	A38	2t multicolored	.35	.35
155	A38	5t multicolored	.35	.35
156	A38	6t multicolored	.35	.35
157	A38	7t multicolored	.35	.35
158	A38	8t multicolored	.35	.35
159	A38	9t multicolored	.35	.35
160	A38	10t multicolored	.35	.35
160A	A38	11t multicolored	.35	.35
160B	A38	12t multicolored	.35	.35
161	A38	20t multicolored	.45	.45
162	A38	44t multicolored	.70	.70
163	A38	50t multicolored	.95	.95
164	A38	100t multicolored	1.75	1.75
		Nos. 153-164 (14)	7.35	7.35

Issued: 1t, 6t, 7t, 44t, 2/18/93; 2t, 5t, 10t, 20t, 50t, 5/14/93; 8t, 9t, 8/25/93; 11t, 12t, 7/8/94.

See #208A-220, 370, 373-379, 616-623. For surcharge see #371.

Mountain Climbers A39

1993, Feb. 27
165	A39	7t shown	.30	.30
166	A39	44t Route map, mountain	1.10	1.10

Slovenian Alpine Club, centennial (#165). Joza Cop (1893-1975), mountain climber (#166).

A40

1993, Mar. 19
167	A40	7t multicolored	.30	.30

Slovenian Post Office, 75th anniv.

A41

7t, Altarpiece, by Tintoretto. 44t, Coat of arms.

1993, Apr. 9   Litho.   Perf. 14
168	A41	7t multicolored	.30	.30
169	A41	44t multicolored	1.10	1.10

Collegiate Church of Novo Mesto, 500th anniv.

Contemporary Art — A42

Europa: 44t, Round Table of Pompeii, by Marij Pregelj (1913-1967). 159t, Little Girl at Play, by Gabrijel Stupica (1913-1990).

1993, Apr. 29   Litho.   Perf. 14
170		44t multicolored	1.50	1.50
171		159t multicolored	3.75	3.75
a.		A42 Pair, #170-171	6.00	6.00

Schwagerina Carniolica — A43

1993, May 7
172	A43	44t multicolored	1.10	1.10

Admission of Slovenia to UN, 1st Anniv. A44

1993, May 21   Litho.   Perf. 14
173	A44	62t multicolored	1.50	1.50

Mediterranean Youth Games, Agde, France — A45

1993, June 8
174	A45	36t multicolored	1.00	1.00

Battle of Sisak, 400th Anniv. A46

1993, June 22   Litho.   Perf. 14
175	A46	49t multicolored	1.40	1.40

Aphaenopidius Kamnikensis — A47

Designs: 7t, Monolistra spinosissima. 55t, Proteus anguinus. 65t, Zospeum spelaeum.

1993, July 12   Litho.   Perf. 14
176	A47	7t multicolored	.30	.30
177	A47	40t multicolored	.80	.80
178	A47	55t multicolored	1.25	1.25
179	A47	65t multicolored	1.60	1.60
		Nos. 176-179 (4)	3.95	3.95

A48

1993, July 30
180	A48	65t multicolored	1.50	1.50

World dressage competition.

A49

Coats of Arms: 9t, Janez Vajkard Valvasor. 65t, Citizen's Academy of Ljubljana.

1993, Oct. 29   Litho.   Perf. 14
181	A49	9t multicolored	.30	.30
182	A49	65t multicolored	1.40	1.40

Christmas A50

Designs: 9t, Slovenian Family Viewing Nativity, by Maxim Gaspari (1883-1980). 65t, Archbishop Joze Pogacnik (1902-80), writer.

1993, Nov. 15
183	A50	9t multicolored	.30	.30
184	A50	65t multicolored	1.40	1.40

Famous People — A51

Works by: 8t, Josip Jurcic (1844-81), writer. 9t, Simon Gregorcic (1844-1906), poet. 55t, Stanislav Skrabec (1844-1918), linguist. 65t, Jernej Kopitar (1780-1844), linguist.

1994, Jan. 14   Litho.   Perf. 14
185	A51	8t multicolored	.30	.30
186	A51	9t multicolored	.30	.30
187	A51	55t multicolored	1.25	1.25
188	A51	65t multicolored	1.40	1.40
		Nos. 185-188 (4)	3.25	3.25

Love — A52

1994, Jan. 25
189	A52	9t multicolored	.35	.35

1994 Winter Olympics, Lillehammer — A53

1994, Feb. 4
190		9t Cross-country skiing	.25	.25
191		65t Slalom skiing	1.25	1.25
a.		A53 Pair, #190-191	1.50	1.50

World Ski Jumping Championships, Planica — A54

1994, Mar. 11   Litho.   Perf. 14
192	A54	70t multicolored	1.60	1.60

City of Ljubljana, 850th Anniv. A55

1994, Mar. 25   Litho.   Perf. 14
193	A55	9t multicolored	.25	.25

Europa — A56

70t, Janez Puhar, camera. 215t, Moon, Jurij Vega.

1994, Apr. 22
194		70t multicolored	1.10	1.10
195		215t multicolored	3.75	3.75
a.		A56 Pair, #194-195	5.00	5.00

Miniature Sheet

Flowers of Slovenia — A57

Designs: a, 9t, Primula carniolica. b, 44t, Hladnikia pastinacifolia. c, 60t, Daphne blagayana. d, 70t, Campanula zoysii.

1994, May 20   Litho.   Perf. 14
196	A57	Sheet of 4 + 2 labels	4.25	4.25

1994 World Cup Soccer Championships, U.S. — A58

1994, June 10
197	A58	44t multicolored	.90	.90

Intl. Olympic Committee, Cent. A59

1994, June 10
198	A59	100t multicolored	2.25	2.25

Mt. Ojstrica — A60

1994, July 1   Litho.   Perf. 14
199 A60 12t multicolored   .40   .40

Max Pletersnik,
Professors — A61

1994, July 22
200 A61 70t multicolored   1.50 1.50

First Slovenian-German dictionary published by Max Pletersnik (1840-1932), cent.

Battle of
the
Frigidus,
1600th
Anniv.
A62

1994, Sept. 1   Litho.   Perf. 14
201 A62 60t multicolored   1.50 1.50

Maribor
Post Office,
Cent.
A63

1994, Sept. 23   Litho.   Perf. 14
202 A63 70t multicolored   1.50 1.50

Ljubljana-Novo Mesto Railway,
Cent. — A64

1994, Sept. 24   Litho.   Perf. 14
203 A64 70t Locomotive 5722,
1893   1.50 1.50

See Nos. 233, 243, 291, 325, 363.

Philharmonic Assoc., Bicent. — A65

Designs: 12t, Building, Ljubljana. 70t, Beethoven, Brahms, Dvorak, Haydn, Paganini.

1994, Oct. 20
204 A65 12t multicolored   .30   .30
205 A65 70t multicolored   1.40 1.40

Black Madonna of
Loreto, 700th
Anniv. — A66

1994, Nov. 18
206 A66 70t multicolored   1.50 1.50

Christmas — A67

1994, Nov. 18
207 A67 12t multicolored   .30   .30

Intl. Year of the
Family — A68

1994, Nov. 18
208 A68 70t multicolored   1.40 1.40

Type of 1993

13t, Wind rattle, Prlekija. 14t, Sentjernej pottery cock. 15t, Blast furnace, Zelezniki. 16t, Windmill, Stara Gora. 17t, Corn storage building. 55t, Easter eggs, Bela Krajina. 65t, Cobbler's lamp with glass spheres, Trzic. 70t, Snow skis. 75t, 1812 Iron window lattice, Srednja vas, Bohinj. 80t, Palm Sunday bundle. 90t, Beehive. 200t, "Zajec," insect-shaped bootjack, Dvor. 300t, Slamnati doznjek. 400t, Wine press. 500t, Kumer family's table, Koprivna, Carinthia.

1994-99   Litho.   Perf. 14
Size 25x34mm
208A A38 13t multicolored   .50   .25
208B A38 14t multicolored   .25   .25
209   A38 15t multicolored   .25   .25
210   A38 16t multicolored   .25   .25
210A A38 17t multicolored   .25   .25
211   A38 55t multicolored   .60   .60
212   A38 65t multicolored   .80   .80
213   A38 70t multicolored   1.00   1.00
214   A38 75t multicolored   1.00   1.00
215   A38 80t multicolored   1.25   1.25
216   A38 90t multicolored   1.40   1.40
217   A38 200t multicolored 2.50   2.50
218   A38 300t brown   5.00   5.00
219   A38 400t brown & lake 7.25   7.25
220   A38 500t multicolored 7.00   7.00
Nos. 208A-220 (15)   29.30 29.05

Issued: 300t, 400t, 11/7/94; 70t, 11/16/95; 55t, 65t, 75t, 3/22/96; 80t, 3/20/97; 13t, 14t, 8/8/97; 90t, 5/30/97; 15t, 6/23/98; 200t, 500t, 11/12/98; 16t, 2/5/99; 17t, 5/7/99.

Ljubljana
University,
75th Anniv.
A69

Design: 70t, Provincial palace buildings, founders, I. Hribar, M. Rostohar, D. Majaron.

1994, Dec. 3   Litho.   Perf. 14
221 A69 70t multicolored   1.50 1.50

Postal Service
Emblem — A70

1995, Jan. 27
222 A70 13t multicolored   .40   .40

Love — A71

1995, Feb. 7
223 A71 20t multicolored   .50   .50

Famous
People — A72

Works by: 20t, Anton Tomaz Linhart (1756-95), playwright, horiz. No. 225, Ivan Vurnik (1884-1971), architect. No. 226, Lili Novy (1885-1958), poet, horiz.

1995, Feb. 7
224 A72 20t multicolored   .50   .50
225 A72 70t multicolored   1.50 1.50
226 A72 70t multicolored   1.50 1.50
Nos. 224-226 (3)   3.50 3.50

A73

1995, Mar. 29   Litho.   Perf. 14
227 A73 13t multicolored   .45   .45

End of World War II, 50th anniv.

Karavankina
schellwieni — A74

1995, Mar. 29
228 A74 70t multicolored   1.60 1.60

Liberation of the Concentration
Camps, 50th Anniv. — A75

Europa: 60t, Skeleton of Death lying on bride. 70t, Nike going from dark to light.

1995, Mar. 29
229 A75 60t multicolored   1.50 1.50
230 A75 70t multicolored   1.50 1.50
  a. Pair, #229-230   4.00 4.00

#230a was issued in sheets of 4.

European Nature Conservation
Year — A76

1995, Mar. 29
231 A76 70t Triglav Natl. Park   1.60 1.60

Town of
Radovljica,
500th
Anniv.
A77

1995, June 8   Litho.   Perf. 14
232 A77 44t multicolored   1.00 1.00

Railways Type of 1994

Design: 70t, Locomotive KRB 37, Podnart.

1995, June 8
233 A64 70t multicolored   1.50 1.50

Ljubljana-Jesenice Line, 125th anniv.

Aljaz Tower,
Cent. — A78

1995, June 8   Perf. 13½
234 A78 100t multicolored   2.10 2.10

Portions of the design on No. 234 were applied by a thermogrphic process producing a shiny, raised effect.

Endangered Birds — A79

Designs: a, 13t, Falco naumanni. b, 60t, Coracias garrulus. c, 70t, Lanius minor. d, 215t, Emberiza melanocephala.

1995, June 8   Perf. 14
235 A79 Block of 4, #a.-d.   7.00 7.00

Slovenian
Boy Scouts
A80

1995, Sept. 26   Litho.   Perf. 14
236 A80 70t multicolored   1.50 1.50

Comtemporary Art, by France
Kralj — A81

No. 237, Death of a Genius, 1921. No. 238,
Family of Horses, 1959.

1995, Sept. 26
237 A81 60t multicolored   1.40 1.40
238 A81 70t multicolored   1.60 1.60
  a.   Pair, #237-238   3.00 3.00

A82

UN, FAO, 50th Anniv.: No. 239, Stylized pictures of food products, faces of people from
many nations. No. 240, Black & white figures
touching hands, faces of people from many
nations.

1995, Sept. 26
239 A82 70t multicolored   1.50 1.50
240 A82 70t multicolored   1.50 1.50
  a.   Pair, #239-240   3.25 3.25

Issued in miniature sheets of 4 stamps.

A83

Christmas (Paintings): 13t, Winter, by
Marlenka Stupica. 70t, St. Mary of Succour,
Brezje, by Leopold Layer.

1995, Nov. 16
241 A83 13t multicolored   .30 .30
  a.   Booklet pane of 10 + 2 labels   3.50 3.50
     Complete booklet   3.50 3.50
242 A83 70t multicolored   1.50 1.50
  a.   Booklet pane of 10 + 2 labels   16.00 16.00
     Complete booklet   16.00 16.00

Railways Type of 1994

Design: 70t, Locomotive "Aussee."

1996, Jan. 31   Litho.   Perf. 14
243 A64 70t multicolored   1.50 1.50

The Graz-Celje Line, 150th anniv.

St.
Gregory's
Day — A84

1996, Jan. 31   Litho.   Perf. 14
244 A84 13t multicolored   .50 .50

Carnival
Costumes
A85

1996, Jan. 31
245 A85 13t Ptujsko region   .30 .30
246 A85 70t Dravsko region   1.50 1.50

See Nos. 281-282, 384-385.

Emys
Orbicularis
A86

World Wildlife Fund: a, 13t, Peeking head
out of water. b, 50t, Laying eggs. c, 60t, Adult
crawling though water. d, 70t, Two juveniles.

1996, Jan. 31
247 A86   Strip of 4, #a.-d.   4.25 4.25

No. 247 printed in sheets of 4 vertical or
horizontal strips, each having a different order.

Fran Saleski Finzgar (1871-1962),
Writer, Priest — A87

1996, Apr. 18   Litho.   Perf. 14
248 A87 13t multicolored   .30 .30

A88

1996, Apr. 18
249 A88 65t multicolored   1.40 1.40

UNICEF, 50th anniv.

A89

Paintings: 65t, Children on Grass (detail).
75t, Bouquet of Dahlias.

1996, Apr. 18
250   65t multicolored   1.50 1.50
251   75t multicolored   1.50 1.50
  a.   A89 Pair, Nos. 250-251   3.00 3.00

Ivana Kobilca (1861-1926), painter.
Issued in sheets of 8 stamps. Europa.

Ita Rina
(1907-79),
Film
Actress
A90

1996, Apr. 18
252 A90 100t multicolored   1.60 1.60

Visit of Pope John
Paul II, May 17-
19 — A91

1996, Apr. 18
253 A91 75t multicolored   1.50 1.50

Souvenir Sheet
254 A91 200t multicolored   3.75 3.75

City of
Zagorje ob
Savi, 700th
Anniv.
A92

1996, June 6   Litho.   Perf. 14
255 A92 24t Gallenberg Castle   .50 .50

World Junior Cycling Championships,
Novo Mesto — A93

1996, June 6
256 A93 55t multicolored   1.00 1.00

Independence, 5th
Anniv. — A94

1996, June 6
257 A94 75t multicolored   1.50 1.50

Mushrooms — A95

Designs: a, 65t, Cantharellus cibarius. b,
75t, Boletus aestivalis.

1996, June 6
258 A95   Sheet of 2, #a.-b.   3.00 3.00

Modern Olympic
Games, Cent.,
1996 Summer
Olympics,
Atlanta — A96

Designs: 75t, Iztok Cop, rower; Fredja Mar-
sic, kayaker. 100t, Britta Bilac, high jumper;
Brigita Bukovec, hurdler.

1996, June 6
259 A96 75t multicolored   *1.50* 1.50
260 A96 100t multicolored   *2.00* 2.00
  a.   Pair, #259-260 + label   3.75 3.75

No. 260a issued in sheets of 6 stamps + 3
labels.

Two versions of the sheet exist. One with
white, red & blue flag, the other with white,
blue & red flag.

A97   A98

A99   A100

Idrijan Lace
A101   A102

1996, June 21   Litho.   Perf. 14
261 A97   1t shown   .25 .25
262 A97   1t olive gray, diff.   .25 .25
  a.   Pair, #261-262   .50 .50
263 A98   2t shown   .25 .25
264 A98   2t carmine, diff.   .25 .25
  a.   Pair, #263-264   .50 .50
265 A99   5t shown   .25 .25
266 A99   5t square   .25 .25
  a.   Pair, #265-266   .50 .50
267 A100   12t shown   .25 .25
268 A100   12t diamond   .25 .25
  a.   Pair, #267-268   .50 .50
269 A101   13t shown   .25 .25
270 A101   13t red, diff.   .25 .25
  a.   Pair, #269-270   .50 .50
271 A102   50t shown   .55 .55
272 A102   50t lilac, diff.   .55 .55
  a.   Pair, #272-272   1.10 1.10
     Nos. 261-272 (12)   3.60 3.60

Nos. 261-272 were originally issued with a
background containing "1996," posthorn, and
security lettering that appear under UV light,
values as shown above. In 1997 Nos. 261-270
were reissued, with date within fluorescent
inscription changed to "1997." Value, set,
$150.

In their final form, Nos. 261-272 were issued
later in 1997 without fluorescent inscription.
Value same as for 1996 issue.

See Nos. 297-304.

Modern
Cardiology,
Cent. — A103

1996, Sept. 6   **Litho.**   **Perf. 14**
273 A103 12t multicolored   .40   .40

Grammar
School,
Novo
Mesto,
250th
Anniv.
A104

1996, Sept. 6
274 A104 55t multicolored   1.00   .55

Skocjan Caves, Karst Region,
UNESCO World Heritage Site
A105

1996, Sept. 6
275 A105 55t multicolored   1.00   .55

Moscon Family Portrait, by Jozef
Tominc (1790-1866) — A106

1996, Sept. 6
276 A106 65t multicolored   1.40   .90

Post Office,
Ljubljana,
Cent. — A107

1996, Oct. 18   **Litho.**   **Perf. 14**
277 A107 100t multicolored   1.75   .75

A108

1996, Oct. 20
278 A108 12t multicolored   .40   .40
Introduction of automatic letter sorting
machines, Maribor.

Children
Sledding
A109

Nativity
A110

1996, Nov. 20   **Litho.**   **Perf. 14**
279 A109 12t multicolored   .25   .25
   a.   Booklet pane of 10   3.00   3.00
    Complete booklet, #279a   3.00
280 A110 65t multicolored   1.25   1.25
   a.   Booklet pane of 10   15.00   15.00
    Complete booklet, #280a   15.00
      Christmas.

Carnival Costumes Type of 1996

From Cerkno region: 20t, "Ta terjast." 80t,
"Pust."

1997, Jan. 21   **Litho.**   **Perf. 14**
281 A85 20t multicolored   .25   .25
282 A85 80t multicolored   1.25   1.25

Love
A111

1997, Jan. 21   **Litho.**   **Perf. 14**
283 A111 15t multicolored   .30   .30

Sneznik
Mountain
A112

1997, Jan. 21
284 A112 20t multicolored   .60   .60

Legend of the
Goldenhorn
A113

1997, Mar. 27   **Litho.**   **Perf. 14**
285 A113 80t multicolored   3.50   3.50
      Europa.

Wulfenite — A114

1997, Mar. 27
286 A114 80t multicolored   1.25   .75

A115

Endangered Fish — A115a

1997, Mar. 27
287 A115 12t Salmo marmoratus   .35   .35
288 A115 13t Zingel streber   .60   .60
289 A115 80t Vimba vimba   1.40   1.40
290 A115 90t Umbra krameri   2.00   2.00
    Nos. 287-290 (4)   4.35   4.35

Miniature Sheet

290A A115a Sheet of 4, #a-d   5.00   5.00
   a.   12t Salmo marmoratus   .35   .35
   b.   13t Zingel streber   .60   .60
   c.   80t Vimba vimba   1.40   1.40
   d.   90t Umbra krameri   2.00   2.00

Railways Type of 1994

Design: 80t, Locomotive SZ 03-002,
Ljubljana-Trieste Railway Line, 140th anniv.

1997, May 30   **Litho.**   **Perf. 14**
291 A64 80t multicolored   1.40   .80

A116

1997, May 30
292 A116 70t multicolored   1.25   .70
Volunteer fire fighting brigades in Slovenia.

A117

Famous People: 13t, Matija Cop (1797-
1835), literary expert. 24t, Sigismundus Zois
(1747-1819), economist, natural scientist. 80t,
Bishop Frederic Baraga (1797-1868), missionary, linguist.

1997, May 30
293 A117 13t multicolored   .25   .25
294 A117 24t multicolored   .55   .25
295 A117 80t multicolored   1.25   .75
    Nos. 293-295 (3)   2.05   1.25

Souvenir Sheet

4th Meeting of the Presidents of
Central European Countries,
Piran — A118

Designs: a, 100t, Tartini Square. b, 200t,
Coats of arms from eight countries.

1997, June 6
296 A118 Sheet of 2, #a.-b.   5.25   5.25

Idrijan Lace Type of 1996

Shape of lace: No. 297, Flower in center of
oval. No. 298, Circular outside with swirl at
bottom. No. 299, Butterfly. No. 300, Diamond.
No. 301, Square. No. 302, Circle. No. 303,
Leaves. No. 304, Tulip.

1997, June 20   **Litho.**   **Perf. 14**
297 A97 10t magenta   .30   .30
298 A97 10t magenta   .30   .30
   a.   Pair, #297-298   .65   .65
299 A97 20t violet   .35   .35
300 A97 20t violet   .35   .35
   a.   Pair, #299-300   .75   .75
301 A97 44t bright blue   .75   .50
302 A97 44t bright blue   .75   .50
   a.   Pair, #301-302   1.75   1.75
303 A97 100t gray brown   1.60   1.60
304 A97 100t gray brown   1.60   1.60
   a.   Pair, #303-304   3.50   3.50
    Nos. 297-304 (8)   6.00   5.50

A119

1997, Sept. 9
305 A119 14t multicolored   .40   .25
Children's Week.

Return of
Primorska, 50th
Anniv. — A120

1997, Sept. 9
306 A120 50t multicolored   .80   .50

France Gorse (1897-1986),
Sculptor — A121

1997, Sept. 9
307 A121 70t "Bashful Armor"   1.00   1.00
308 A121 80t "Peasant Woman"   1.25   1.25
   a.   Pair, #307-308   2.50   2.50

A122

1997, Sept. 9
309 A122 90t multicolored   1.50 1.50

MEJP '97, European Youth Judo Championship.

A123

1997, Nov. 18   **Litho.**   **Perf. 14**
310 A123 90t multicolored   1.25 .80

Golden Fox World Cup Ski Competition for Women, 35th anniv.

Christmas & New Year
A124

Designs: 14t, Children watching birds and snow outside window. 90t, Sculptured Nativity scene, by Liza Hribar (1913-96).

1997, Nov. 18
311 A124 14t multicolored   .25 .25
312 A124 90t multicolored   1.50 1.00
  a.   Booklet pane of 8, 5 #311, 3 #312   6.25
     Complete booklet, #312a   6.25

New Mail Center, Ljubljana — A125

1997, Nov. 28
313 A125 30t multicolored   .50 .25

Borovo Gostüvanje (Pine Wedding) — A126

20t, Participating "players," tree. 80t, Participants, "bride & groom," top of pine tree.

1998, Jan. 22   **Litho.**   **Perf. 14**
314 A126 20t multicolored   .35 .25
315 A126 80t multicolored   .95 .75
  a.   Pair, #314-315   1.50 1.50

See Nos. 338-339.

1998 Winter Olympic Games, Nagano A127

1998, Jan. 22
316 A127 70t Woman skater   .75 .50
317 A127 90t Biathlete   1.25 .75
  a.   Vert. pair, #316-317 + label   3.00 3.00

Issued in sheets of 6 stamps + 3 labels.

EUROCONTROL (European Organization for Safety of Air Navigation), 35th Anniv. — A128

1998, Jan. 22
318 A128 90t multicolored   1.40 .80

Louis Adamic (1898-1951), Writer — A129

90t, Francesco Robba (1698-1757), sculptor.

1998, Mar. 25   **Litho.**   **Perf. 14**
319 A129 26t multicolored   .30 .25
320 A129 90t multicolored   1.40 .90

Jurjevanje (Green George's Festival) A130

1998, Mar. 25
321 A130 90t multicolored   3.00 1.75

Europa.

Comic Strip Characters, by Miki Muster — A131

1998, Mar. 25
322 A131 14t Fox   .50 .50
323 A131 105t Turtle   1.75 1.75
324 A131 118t Wolf   2.25 2.25
  a.   Sheet, 2 each #322-324   8.00 8.00
     Nos. 322-324 (3)   4.50 4.50

Railways Type of 1994

Design: Steam locomotive SZ 06-018.

1998, June 10   **Litho.**   **Perf. 14**
325 A64 80t multicolored   1.25 .75

Boc Mountain, Pulsatilla Grandis — A132

1998, June 10
326 A132 14t multicolored   .40 .25

A133

Conifers: a, 14t, Juniperus communis. b, 15t, Picea abies. c, 80t, Pinus nigra. d, 90t, Larix decidua.

1998, June 10
327 A133   Sheet of 4, #a.-d.   4.75 4.75

A134

1998, June 23   **Litho.**   **Perf. 14**
328 A134 15t multicolored   .40 .25

Committee for the Protection of Human Rights, 10th anniv.

United Slovenia, 150th Anniv. A135

1998, June 23
329 A135 80t multicolored   1.25 .75

Cistercian Order, 900th Anniv. and Sticna Revival, Cent. A136

1998, Sept. 11   **Litho.**   **Perf. 14**
330 A136 14t multicolored   .40 .25

Radio Ljubljana, 70th Anniv. A137

1998, Sept. 11
331 A137 50t Cuckoo   .80 .50

Avgust Cernigoj (1898-1985), Artist — A138

Designs: 70t, Abstract painting, "Banker." 80t, Sculpture, "El."

1998, Sept. 11
332 A138 70t multicolored   .90 .60
333 A138 80t multicolored   1.00 .70
  a.   Pair, #332-333   2.25 2.25

Universal Declaration of Human Rights, 50th Anniv. — A139

1998, Sept. 11
334 A139 100t multicolored   1.50 1.00

Christmas A140

Designs: 15t, Children walking through snow, candle. 90t, Fresco of "Bow of the Three Wise Men of the East," Church of St. Nicholas, Mace, 1476.

1998, Nov. 12   **Litho.**   **Perf. 14**
335 A140 15t multicolored   .30 .25
  a.   Booklet pane of 10   3.25 *3.25*
     Complete booklet, #335a   3.25
336 A140 90t multicolored   1.40 .80
  a.   Bkt. pane, 6 #335, 4 #336   7.50 *7.50*
     Complete booklet, #336a   7.50

Leon Stukelj, Olympic Gymnastics Champion, 100th Birthday — A141

Designs: a, Portrait. b, As a gymnast. c, With IOC Pres. Juan Antonio Samaranch, horiz. (58x40mm).

1998, Nov. 12
337 A141 100t Sheet of 3, #a.-c.   4.75 4.75

Wedding, Festival Type of 1998

Skoromati carnival mask characters: 20t, Wearing tall hats, Skopit character in black. 80t, Skopit character blowing horn.

1999, Jan. 22   **Litho.**   **Perf. 14**
338 A126 20t multicolored   .25 .25
339 A126 80t multicolored   1.00 .65
  a.   Pair, #338-339   1.60 1.60

Greetings A142

1999, Jan. 22
340 A142 15t multicolored   .40 .25

Famous Men — A143

14t, Peter Kozler (1824-79), geographer.
15t, Bozidar Lavric (1899-1961), surgeon. 70t,
Rudolf Maister (1874-1934), general, poet.
80t, France Preseren (1800-49), poet.

1999, Jan. 22
341	A143	14t multicolored	.40	.25
342	A143	15t multicolored	.40	.25
343	A143	70t multicolored	1.10	.55
344	A143	80t multicolored	1.40	.70
		Nos. 341-344 (4)	3.30	1.75

Golica
Mountain,
Narcissus
Flowers
A144

1999, Mar. 23   Litho.   Perf. 14
345 A144 15t multicolored   .40   .25

Slovenian Philatelic Assoc., 50th
Anniv. — A145

1999, Mar. 23
346 A145 16t Yugoslavia #3L5 &
#305   .40   .25

Mercury &
Cinnabar,
Idrija Mine
A146

1999, Mar. 23
347 A146 80t multicolored   1.25   .60

Council of
Europe,
50th Anniv.
A147

1999, Mar. 23
348 A147 80t multicolored   1.25   .60

Triglav
Natl. Park
A148

1999, Mar. 23
349 A148 90t multicolored   2.50 1.25
Europa.

5th Rescue Dog World
Championships — A149

1999, May 21   Litho.   Perf. 14
350 A149 80t multicolored   1.25   .60

UPU, 125th
Anniv. — A150

Designs: 30t, Early postman with backpack.
90t, Astronaut on moon with backpack.

1999, May 21
351	A150	30t multicolored	.60	.30
352	A150	90t multicolored	1.00	.50
a.		Pair, #351-352	1.60	.80

Horses
A151

Designs: 60t, Slovenian cold-blooded horse.
70t, Ljutomer trotter. 120t, Slovenian warm-
blooded horse (show jumper). 350t,
Lipizzaner.

1999, May 21
353	A151	60t multicolored	.95	.45
354	A151	70t multicolored	1.10	.55
355	A151	120t multicolored	1.75	.85
356	A151	350t multicolored	5.50	2.75
a.		Sheet of 4, #353-356	11.00	7.00
		Nos. 353-356 (4)	9.30	4.60

Towards A New Millennium — A152

Designs: 20t, Balanced objects. 70t, Roadway, earth. 80t, Cogwheels. 90t, Tree.

1999, Sept. 16   Litho.   Perf. 13¾
357	A152	20t multicolored	.25	.25
358	A152	70t multicolored	.90	.45
359	A152	80t multicolored	1.00	.50
360	A152	90t multicolored	1.25	.60
a.		Block of 4, #357-360	3.50	1.75

Bozidar Jakac (1899-1989),
Painter — A153

Self-portraits and: 70t, Girl drawing curtain.
80t, Landscape.

1999, Sept. 16
361	A153	70t multicolored	.95	.45
362	A153	80t multicolored	1.10	.55
a.		Pair, #361-362	2.25	1.10

Railway Type of 1994
1999, Sept. 16
363 A64 80t multicolored   1.25   .60
Rail Line to Ljubljana, 150th anniv.

Bishop Anton M.
Slomsek (1800-
62) — A154

1999, Sept. 16
364 A154 90t multicolored   1.40   .70

Millennium
A155

Christmas — A156

1999, Nov. 18   Litho.   Perf. 14
365	A155	17t multicolored	.55	.55
a.		Booklet pane of 10	5.50	
		Complete booklet, #365a	5.50	
366	A155	18t multicolored	.55	.55
367	A156	80t multicolored	2.25	1.10
a.		Booklet pane, 5 #365, 3 #367 + 2 labels	9.50	
		Complete booklet, #367a	9.50	
368	A156	90t multicolored	2.50	1.25
		Nos. 365-368 (4)	5.85	3.45

Nos. 365 and 367 were issued only in
booklets.

Types of 1993-94
Overprinted & No.
210A Surcharged

Design: 18t, Accordion. 19t on 17t, Corn
storage building. A, Post office door, Zgornji
Otok. No. 373, Easter eggs. No. 374, Fishing
boat. No. 375, Miner's house, Trbovlje. C,
Scythe. No. 377, Ljubljana Palm Sunday bundle. No. 378, Horse collar comb. No. 379,
Fishing boat and oars.

1999-2004   Litho.   Perf. 14
Size 25x34mm
370	A38	18t multi	.45	.25
371	A38	19t on 17t multi	.45	.25
372	A38	A multi	.95	.45
373	A38	B multi	.60	.30
374	A38	B multi	1.10	.55
375	A38	B multi	1.25	.60
376	A38	C multi	2.50	1.25
377	A38	D multi	2.50	1.25
378	A38	D multi	3.00	1.50
379	A38	D multi	3.00	1.50
		Nos. 370-379 (10)	15.80	7.90

Issued: 18t, 12/17/99. No. 371, 4/20/2000.
Nos. 373, 377, 2/28/02. Nos. 372, 374, 376,
378, 11/19/03. No. 375, 7/3/04. No. 379,
9/22/04.
Nos. 373 and 377 sold for 31t and 107t
respectively on day of issue. Nos. 372, 374,
376 and 378 sold for 38t, 44t, 95t and 107t
respectively on day of issue. No. 375 sold for
48t on day of issue. No. 379 sold for 107t on
day of issue.

Issued: No. 371, 4/20/00.

Love — A158

2000, Jan. 20   Litho.   Perf. 14
383 A158 34t multi   .60   .30

Carnival Costume Type of 1996
Pustovi masks: 34t, Two masks, horiz. 80t,
Four masks, horiz.

2000, Jan. 20
384	A85	34t multi	.60	.30
385	A85	80t multi	1.40	.70

A159

2000, Jan. 20
386 A159 64t multi   1.00   .50
Tone Seliskar (1900-69), poet.

A160

2000, Jan. 20
387 A160 120t multi   2.00 1.00
Elvira Kralj (1900-78), actress.

Postal Service in
Slovenia, 500th
Anniv. — A161

2000, Jan. 20
388 A161 500t multi   9.00 7.00

Mt. Storzic
A162

2000, Mar. 21   Litho.   Perf. 14
389 A162 18t multi   .70   .35

Return of
World War
II Exiles
A163

2000, Mar. 21
390 A163 25t multi   .70   .35

Characters from
Children's
Books — A164

#391, 394, Pedenjped. #392, 395, Mojca
Pokrajculja. #393, 396, Macek Muri.

2000, Mar. 21   *Perf. 14*
391	A164	20t multi	1.50	.75
392	A164	20t multi	1.50	.75
393	A164	20t multi	1.50	.75

Booklet Stamps
Self-Adhesive
Serpentine Die Cut 7½
394	A164	20t multi	1.25	.55
395	A164	20t multi	1.25	.55
396	A164	20t multi	1.25	.55
a.		Booklet pane, 3 each #394-396 + 9 labels	12.00	
		Nos. 391-396 (6)	8.25	3.90

No. 396a is a complete booklet.

Fossils and
Minerals
A165

2000, Mar. 21   *Perf. 14*
397	A165	80t Trilobite	1.60	.80
398	A165	90t Dravite	1.60	.80

See Nos. 453-454, 517.

Souvenir Sheet

Holy Year 2000 — A166

2000, Mar. 21
399	A166	2000t multi	35.00	22.50

Castles — A167

2000-04   *Litho.*   *Perf. 14*
Size 23x32mm
400	A167	1t	Predjama	.35	.25
401	A167	1t	Velenje	.35	.25
a.		Pair, #400-401		.70	.35
404	A167	A	Ptuj	.60	.30
405	A167	A	Otocec	.60	.30
a.		Pair, #404-405		1.25	.90
406	A167	B	Zuzemberk	.60	.30
407	A167	B	Turjak	.60	.30
a.		Pair, #406-407		1.25	.90

410	A167	C	Dobrovo	1.50	.75
411	A167	C	Breziski	1.50	.75
a.		Pair, #410-411		3.00	1.75
411B	A167	C	Gewerkenegg	1.50	.75
412	A167	100t	Podsreda	1.50	.75
413	A167	100t	Bled	1.50	.75
a.		Pair, #412-413		3.00	1.75
414	A167	D	Olimje	1.50	.75
415	A167	D	Murska Sobota	1.50	.75
a.		Pair, #414-415		3.00	1.75

Size: 38x26mm
415B	A167	1000t Kamen	15.00	7.25
		Nos. 400-415B (14)	28.60	14.20

Nos. 404-405 each sold for 20t; Nos. 406-
407 for 21t; Nos. 410-411 for 95t; No. 411B
sold for 95t on day of issue; Nos. 414-415 for
107t on day of issue.
Issued: Nos. 1t, 100t, 4/20; A, B, 6/23; Nos.
410-411, 414-415, 10/4/01. 1000t, 3/24/03.
No. 411B, 11/18/04.
See Nos. 624-628.

Fruits, Blossoms and
Insects — A168

Designs: No. 416, Apple blossom weevil.
No. 417, Apple blossom. No. 418, Apple.

2000, Apr. 20   *Perf. 13¾*
Vignette Frame Size 20x26½mm
416	A168	10t multi	.25	.25
417	A168	10t multi	.25	.25
418	A168	10t multi	.25	.25
a.		Strip, #416-418	.75	.35

Printed in sheets of 15 stamps + 5 labels.
See Nos. 426-428, 464-466, 502-504, 528-
530, 568-570, 606-608, 629-646, 676-678.

Amateur
Radio
A169

2000, May 9   *Litho.*   *Perf. 14*
419	A169	20t multi	1.75	.85

Slovenian Team
Qualification for
European Soccer
Championships
A170

2000, May 9
420	A170	40t multi	1.50	.75

2000 Summer Olympics,
Sydney — A171

2000, May 9
421		80t Sailboats	2.50	1.25
422		90t Sydney Opera House	2.50	1.25
a.		A171 Pair, #421-422	5.00	2.50

World Environment Day — A172

2000, May 9
423	A172	90t multi	30.00	15.00

Issued in sheets of 10 + 5 labels.

Europa, 2000
Common Design Type
2000, May 9   *Litho.*   *Perf. 14*
424	CD17	90t multi	3.25	1.60

Issued in sheets of 8 + 1 label.

Meteorology
A173

2000, May 9   *Perf. 13¾*
425	A173	150t multi	30.00	15.00

Issued in sheets of 9 + 1 label.

Fruits, Blossoms and Insects Type
of 2000

No. 426, Cherry blossom. No. 427, European cherry fruit fly. No. 428, Cherries.

Vignette Frame Size 20x26½mm
2000, June 23   *Litho.*   *Perf. 13¾*
426	A168	5t multi	.25	.25
427	A168	5t multi	.25	.25
428	A168	5t multi	.25	.25
a.		Strip, #426-428	.75	.35

Printed in sheets of 15 stamps + 5 labels.

Paintings by Tone Kralj (1900-
75) — A174

2000, Sept. 15   *Litho.*   *Perf. 14*
429		Horiz. pair	3.00	1.25
a.		A174 70t multi	1.25	.50
b.		A174 80t multi, diff.	1.40	.60

Grape
Varieties — A175

Designs: 20t, Zelen. 40t, Ranfol. 80t,
Zametovka. 130t, Rumeni Plavec.

2000, Sept. 15
430-433	A175	Set of 4	6.00	3.00
a.		Souvenir sheet, #430-433	6.00	3.00

Gold
Medalists
at 2000
Summer
Olympics
A176

Winners and events: No. 434, 21t, Iztok
Cop, Luka Spik, double sculls. No. 435, 21t,
Rajmond Debevec, Men's three-position rifle.

2000, Oct. 16
434-435	A176	Set of 2	.80	.40

First Book Printed
in Slovenian,
450th
Anniv. — A177

2000, Nov. 21
436	A177	50t multi	.90	.45

Christmas
A178

Designs: B, Children in snow. 90t, Christ in
manger.

2000, Nov. 21
437	A178	B multicolored	.50	.25
438	A178	90t multicolored	2.00	1.00

Booklet Stamps
Self-Adhesive
Serpentine Die Cut 7¼
439	A178	B multi	.60	.30
a.		Booklet of 10 + 2 labels	6.00	
440	A178	90t multi	2.40	1.25
a.		Booklet, 6 #439, 4 #440 + 2 labels	13.50	
		Nos. 437-440 (4)	5.50	2.80

Nos. 437 and 439 sold for 21t on day of
issue.

Advent of New Millennium — A179

2000, Nov. 21   *Litho.*   *Perf. 14*
441	A179	40t multi	.80	.40

Wedding
Greetings
A180

2001, Jan. 19   *Litho.*   *Perf. 14*
442	A180	B multi	.60	.30

No. 442 sold for 25t on day of issue.

Carnival Masks, Dobrepolje — A181

Mask wearers including: 50t, Woman with flowers. 95t, Woman in box on cart.

2001, Jan. 19
443-444 A181   Set of 2   2.25 1.10

Writers — A182

Objects symbolic of writer's works: A, Bucket (Dragotin Kette, 1876-99). 95t, Flowers in jar (Ivan Tavcar, 1851-1923). 107t, Coffee cup (Ivan Cankar, 1876-1918).

2001, Jan. 19
445-447 A182   Set of 3   4.00 1.60
No. 445 sold for 24t on day of issue.

Mt. Jalovec and Triglav Flowers — A183

2001, Mar. 21   Litho.   Perf. 14
448 A183 B multi   1.00 .50
No. 448 sold for 25t on day of issue.

Comic Strip Characters by Bozo Kos — A184

Designs: Nos. 449, 451, Cowboy. Nos. 450, 452, Indian.

2001, Mar. 21
449 A184 B multicolored   1.00 .50
450 A184 B multicolored   1.00 .50

Booklet Stamps
Self-Adhesive
Serpentine Die Cut 7¼
451 A184 B multicolored   1.25 .60
452 A184 B multicolored   1.25 .60
 a.   Booklet, 4 each #451-452   9.50
      Nos. 449-452 (4)   4.50 2.20
Nos. 449-452 each sold for 25t on day of issue.

Fossil and Mineral Type of 2000
No. 453 — Stereoscopic image of fluorite crystal with arrow at: a, Right. b, Left. 107t, Starfish fossil.

2001, Mar. 21   Litho.   Perf. 14
453   Horiz. pair   3.25 1.60
 a.-b. A165 95t Any single   1.60 .80
454 A165 107t Starfish fossil   1.60 .80

Europe Day A185

2001, Mar. 21
455 A185 221t multi   3.50 1.75

Solkan, 1000th Anniv. — A186

2001, Mar. 21
456 A186 261t multi   4.00 2.25

Formation of Liberation Front, 60th Anniv. — A187

2001, Apr. 24   Litho.   Perf. 14
457 A187 24t multi   .95 .45

Independence, 10th Anniv. — A188

2001, May 23
458 A188 100t multi   3.50 2.00
Issued in sheets of 10 + 2 labels.

Europa — A189

2001, May 23
459 A189 107t multi   3.50 1.75
Issued in sheets of 8 + 1 label.

Ljubljana Tram System, Cent. A190

2001, May 23
460 A190 113t multi   2.10 .85

6th World Maxi Basketball Championships, Ljubljana — A191

2001, May 23
461 A191 261t multi   4.00 1.75

Souvenir Sheet

Apiculture — A192

No. 462: a, 24t, Bee on flower. b, 48t, Queen and drones. c, 95t, Worker bees. d, 170t, Hive and apiary.

2001, May 23
462 A192   Sheet of 4, #a-d   6.25 4.00

Flags of US and Russia, Dragon Bridge, Ljubljana — A193

2001, June 14
463 A193 107t multi   1.75 .85
 a.   Souvenir sheet of 1   2.25 1.10
First meeting of US Pres. George W. Bush and Russian Pres. Vladimir Putin, Brdo Castle, June 16.

Fruit, Blossoms and Insects Type of 2000
Designs: No. 464, Peach blossom. No. 465, Green peach aphid. No. 466, Peach.

2001, July 21   Perf. 13¾
Vignette Frame Size 20x26mm
464 A168 50t multi   .70 .35
465 A168 50t multi   .70 .35
466 A168 50t multi   .70 .35
 a.   Strip, #464-466   2.10 1.00
Printed in sheets of 15 strips + 5 labels.

Mohorjeve Druzbe Publishing House, 150th Anniv. — A194

2001, Sept. 4   Perf. 14
467 A194 B multi   .70 .35
No. 467 sold for 27t on day of issue.

Foundation of First Technical High School, Cent. A195

2001, Sept. 21
468 A195 A multi   .70 .35
No. 468 sold for 26t on day of issue.

World Animal Day — A196

2001, Sept. 21
469 A196 107t multi   2.00 1.00

Year of Dialogue Among Civilizations A197

2001, Sept. 21   Litho.   Perf. 14
470 A197 107t multi   2.50 1.25

Composers — A198

Designs: 95t, Blaz Arnic (1901-70). 107t, Lucijan Marija Skerjanc (1900-73).

2001, Sept. 21   Litho.   Perf. 14
471-472 A198   Set of 2   3.25 1.60

New Year's Greetings A199   Christmas A200

2001, Nov. 16   Litho.   Perf. 14
473 A199 B multi   .35 .25
474 A200 D multi   1.90 .95

Self-Adhesive
Booklet Stamps
Serpentine Die Cut 7¼
475 A199 B multi   .35 .25
 a.   Booklet pane of 12   4.25
476 A200 D multi   2.10 1.00
 a.   Booklet pane, 6 each #475-476 15.00
Nos. 473 and 475 sold for 31t, Nos. 474 and 476 for 107t on day of issue.

Love — A201

2002, Jan. 23   Litho.   Perf. 14
477 A201 B multi   .70 .35
No. 477 sold for 31t on day of issue.

Masks — A202

Designs: 56t, Rusa. 95t, Picek.

2002, Jan. 23
478-479 A202   Set of 2   2.25 1.10

Famous
Slovenians — A203

Designs: 95t, Joze Plecnik (1872-1957),
architect. 107t, Janko Kersnik (1852-97), poet.

2002, Jan. 23
480-481 A203   Set of 2   2.75 1.40

2002 Winter Olympics, Salt Lake
City — A204

No. 482: a, 95t, Sledder. b, 107t, Skier.

2002, Jan. 23
482 A204   Horiz. pair, #a-b, +
            label   3.25 1.60

No. 482 printed in sheets of three pairs.
Labels, which have different designs, appear
at left and center in other pairs on the sheet.

Insect Fossil
A205

2002, Mar. 21
485 A205 C multi   1.75 .85

No. 485 sold for 95t on day of issue.

Kostanjevica
on the Krka,
750th Anniv.
A206

2002, Mar. 21
486 A206 D multi   1.75 .85

No. 486 sold for 107t on day of issue.

Intl. Year of
Mountains
A207

Flowers and mountains: A, Clematis alpina
and Martuljek Group. D, Lilium carniolicum
and Mt. Spik.

2002, Mar. 21
487-488 A207   Set of 2   3.00 1.50

Nos. 487-488 sold for 30t and 107t respectively on day of issue.

Martin Krpan from
Vrh, by Fran
Levstik — A208

Designs: No. 489, B, Krpan carrying horse.
No. 490, B, Krpan at blacksmith's shop. No.
491, B, Krpan in Ljubljana. No. 492, B, Like
#489. No. 493, B, Like #490. No. 494, B, Like
No. 491.

2002, Mar. 21   **Perf. 14**
489-491 A208   Set of 3   2.50 1.25
Self-Adhesive
Booklet Stamps
Serpentine Die Cut 7¼
492-494 A208   Set of 3   2.50 1.25
494a   Booklet pane, 3 each #492-
            494   7.00

Nos. 489-494 each sold for 31t on day of
issue.

Europa — A209

2002, May 22   **Perf. 14**
495 A209 D multi   15.00 7.50

No. 495 sold for 107t on day of issue.

2002 World Cup Soccer
Championships, Japan and
Korea — A210

2002, May 22
496 A210 D multi   1.75 .85

No. 496 sold for 107t on day of issue.

Medicinal
Plants — A211

Designs: A, Rosa canina. B, Chamomilla
recutita. C, Valeriana officinalis.
D, Viola odorata.

2002, May 22
497-499 A211   Set of 3   4.00 2.00
Souvenir Sheet
500 A211 D multi   1.75 .85

Nos. 497-500 each sold for 30t, 31t, 95t and
107t respectively on day of issue.

Souvenir Sheet

9th Summit of Presidents of Central
European States, Bled — A212

No. 501: a, D, Bled Island in map of Europe.
b, D, Map of Europe, Brdo Castle.

2002, May 22
501 A212   Sheet of 2, #a-b   3.50 1.75

Nos. 501a and 501b each sold for 107t on
day of issue.

**Fruit, Blossoms and Insects Type of
2000**

Designs: No. 502, Bilberry blossoms. No.
503, Winter moth. No. 504, Bilberries.

2002, July 19   **Perf. 13¾**
Vignette Frame Size 20x26mm
502 A168 150t multi   2.25 1.10
503 A168 150t multi   2.25 1.10
504 A168 150t multi   2.25 1.10
    a.   Horiz. strip, #502-504   6.75 3.50

Paintings by Matija Jama (1872-
1947) — A213

Designs: 95t, Kolo — A National Dance.
214t, A Village in Winter.

2002, Sept. 19   **Perf. 14**
505-506 A213   Set of 2   4.50 2.25

Souvenir Sheet

35th Chess Olympiad, Bled — A214

No. 507: a, C, Horse, Bled Castle. b, D,
Fields in checkerboard pattern.

2002, Sept. 19
507 A214   Sheet of 2, #a-b   4.00 2.00

Nos. 507a and 507b each sold for 95t and
107t respectively on day of issue.

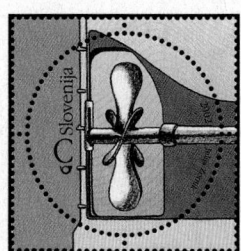

Screw Propeller Invented by Josef
Ressel (1793-1857) — A215

2002, Nov. 15 **Litho.** **Perf. 13¾**
508 A215 C multi   2.10 1.00

No. 508 sold for 95t on day of issue. Values
are for stamps with surrounding selvage.

Christmas and
New Year's
Greetings — A216

Designs: Nos. 509, 511, Snowman. Nos.
510, 512, Girl with evergreen branch.

2002, Nov. 15 **Litho.** **Perf. 14**
509 A216 B multi   .70 .35
510 A216 D multi   1.90 .95
Booklet Stamps
Self-Adhesive
Serpentine Die Cut 7¼
511 A216 B multi   .75 .35
512 A216 D multi   2.25 1.10
    a.   Booklet, 6 each #511-512   18.00
          Nos. 509-512 (4)   5.60 2.75

Nos. 509 and 511 each sold for 36t, and
Nos. 510 and 512 each sold for 107t on day of
issue.

Traditional
Istrian
Clothing
A217

2003, Jan. 21 **Litho.** **Perf. 14**
513 A217 A multi   1.10 .55

No. 513 sold for 38t on day of issue.

Love
A218

2003, Jan. 21   **Perf. 11**
514 A218 180t multi   2.75 1.40

No. 514 is impregnated with a rose scent.
Values are for examples with surrounding
selvage.

Famous Men
A219

Designs: 107t, Ferdinand Avgustin Hallerstein (1703-74), astronomer and Chinese missionary. 221t, Alfonz Paulin (1853-1942), director of Ljubljana Botanical Gardens.

2003, Jan. 21
515-516 A219 Set of 2 4.50 2.25

Mineral Type of 2000
2003, Mar. 24
517 A165 D Barite 1.60 .80
No. 517 sold for 107t on day of issue.

Vilenica Cave — A220

2003, Mar. 24
518 A220 D multi 1.60 .80
No. 518 sold for 107t on day of issue.

Fairy Tales
A221

Designs: No. 519, B, The Three Vixens. No. 520, B, The Golden Bird, vert.

2003, Mar. 24   **Perf. 14**
519-520 A221 Set of 2 1.60 .80

Serpentine Die Cut 7¼
Booklet Stamps
Self-Adhesive
521 A221 B Like #519 1.00 .50
522 A221 B Like #520 1.00 .50
  a. Booklet, 4 each #521-522 8.50

Nos. 519-522 each sold for 44t on day of issue.

Europa — A222

2003, May 22 Litho. Perf. 14
523 A222 D multi 1.75 .85
No. 523 sold for 107t on day of issue. Printed in sheets of 8 + 1 label.

Kresnik, Mythological Character — A223

2003, May 22
524 A223 110t multi 1.75 .85

Souvenir Sheet

Slavko and Vilko Avsenik, Musicians — A224

2003, May 22
525 A224 180t multi 3.00 1.50

European Water Polo Championships, Kranj and Ljubljana — A225

2003, May 22
526 A225 180t multi 3.00 1.50

Painted Beehive Panel
A226

2003, May 22
527 A226 218t multi 3.25 1.60

Fruit, Blossom and Insect Type of 2000

Designs: No. 528, Olive blossom. No. 529, Olive fruit fly. No. 530, Olives on branch.

2003, Sept. 18   Perf. 13¾x14
Vignette Frame Size 20x26½mm
528 A168 B multi .75 .35
529 A168 B multi .75 .35
530 A168 B multi .75 .35
  a. Horiz. strip, #528-530 2.25 1.10

Nos. 528-530 each sold for 44t on day of issue.

Stampless Covers, 1830
A227

2003, Sept. 18   Perf. 14
531 A227 A multi .90 .45
No. 531 sold for 38t on day of issue.

Illustration from the Tournament Book of Gasper Lamberger — A228

Jousting contest: a, 76t, Riderless horse. b, 570t, Horse with rider.

2003, Sept. 18   Perf. 13¾
532 A228 Horiz. pair, #a-b 9.00 4.75

Farm Animals
A229

Designs: 95t, Krsko Polje pig. 107t, Cika cattle. 148t, Jezersko-Solcava sheep. 368t, Styrian hen and rooster, vert.

2003, Sept. 18   Perf. 14
533-535 A229 Set of 3 5.00 2.50
Souvenir Sheet
536 A229 368t multi 5.00 2.50

Opening of Mail Sorting and Logistics Center, Maribor
A230

Litho. with Hologram Applied
2003, Nov. 11   Perf. 13¾x14¼
537 A230 221t multi 3.00 1.50

Franja Partisan Hospital, 60th Anniv.
A231

2003, Nov. 19 Litho. Perf. 14
538 A231 76t brown & bronze 1.25 .60

Wooden Cart
A232

2003, Nov. 19
539 A232 221t multi 3.25 1.60

Christmas
A233

2003, Nov. 19   Perf. 14
540 A233 D multi 1.50 .75

Serpentine Die Cut 7¼
Booklet Stamp
Self-Adhesive
541 A233 D multi 2.00 1.00
  a. Booklet pane of 12 24.00
No. 540 and 541 each sold for 107t on day of issue.

New Year's Greetings
A234

2003, Nov. 19 Litho. Perf. 14
542 A234 B multi 1.00 .50

Serpentine Die Cut 7¼
Booklet Stamp
Self-Adhesive
543 A234 B multi 1.25 .60
  a. Booklet pane of 12 15.00
No. 542 and 543 each sold for 44t on day of issue.

Traditional Clothing from Vipava Valley — A235

2004, Jan. 22 Litho. Perf. 13¾
544 A235 A multi .75 .35
No. 544 sold for 38t on day of issue.

March of the 14th Division to the Styria, 60th Anniv.
A236

2004, Jan. 22   Perf. 14
545 A236 B multi .75 .35

Edvard Kocbek (1904-81), Writer
A237

2004, Jan. 22
546 A237 D multi 1.40 .70
No. 546 sold for 107t on day of issue.

Love
A238

2004, Jan. 22   Perf. 11
547 A238 180t multi 3.00 1.50

Values are for examples with surrounding selvage.

Srecko Kosovel (1904-26), Writer
A239

2004, Jan. 22   Perf. 14
548 A239 221t black & red 3.25 1.60

Sixth Men's European Handball Championships A240

2004, Jan. 22
549 A240 221t multi   3.25 1.60

Fossil Type of 2000
2004, Mar. 24   Litho.   Perf. 14
550 A165 D Fish   1.40 .70
  No. 541 sold for 107t on day of issue.

European Men's Gymnastic Championships, Ljubljana — A241

2004, Mar. 24
551 A241 D multi   1.50 .75
  No. 551 sold for 107t on day of issue.

Bled, 1000th Anniv. — A242

2004, Mar. 24
552 A242 218t multi   3.25 1.60

Kekec, the Shepherd Boy, by Josip Vandot — A243

  Designs: No. 553, B, Kekec. No. 554, B, Pehta. No. 555, B, Kosobrin. No. 556, B, Kekec. No. 557, B, Pehta. No. 558, B, Kosobrin.

2004, Mar. 24   Perf. 14
553-555 A243   Set of 3   2.00 1.00

Serpentine Die Cut 7¼
Booklet Stamps
556-558 A243   Set of 3   2.00 1.00
558a   Booklet pane, 3 each #556-
     558   6.00
  Nos. 553-558 each sold for 44t on day of issue.

Admission to NATO A244

2004, Apr. 2   Litho.   Perf. 14
559 A244 D multi   1.50 .75
  No. 559 sold for 107t on day of issue.

Admission to the European Union — A245

2004, May 1
560 A245 95t multi   1.25 .60

Laurenz Koschier (1804-79), Proposer of Postage Stamps A246

2004, May 21
561 A246 B multi   .70 .35
  No. 561 sold for 48t on day of issue.

Posthorns — A247

Booklet Stamp
Serpentine Die Cut 12½
2004, May 21   Self-Adhesive
562 A247 B multi   .75 .35
a.   Booklet pane of 8   6.00
  No. 562 sold for 48t on day of issue. See Nos. 583-583A.

Europa — A248

2004, May 21   Perf. 14
563 A248 D multi   1.50 .75
  No. 563 sold for 107t on day of issue.

Puch Bicycle, Chainwheel and Chain — A249

2004, May 21
564 A249 110t multi   1.25 .60

Painted Beehive Panel and Bee A250

2004, May 21
565 A250 218t multi   3.00 1.50
  See also No. 600.

2004 Summer Olympics, Athens — A251

  No. 566: a, C, Discus thrower, silhouette of gymnast. b, Long jumper, silhouette of pole vaulter.

2004, May 21
566 A251   Horiz. pair, #a-b   2.75 1.40
  No. 566a sold for 95t; No. 566b sold for 107t on day of issue.

Souvenir Sheet

Opening of Crni Kal Viaduct — A252

2004, Sept. 15   Litho.   Perf. 14
567 A252 95t multi   1.25 .60

Fruit, Blossoms and Insect Type of 2000

  Designs: No. 568, Pear blossom. No. 569, Pear psylla. No. 570, Pear.

Vignette Frame Size 19x26½mm
2004, Sept. 22   Perf. 13¾
568 A168 A multi   .65 .30
569 A168 A multi   .65 .30
570 A168 A multi   .65 .30
a.   Horiz. strip, #568-570   2.00 1.00
  Nos. 568-570 each sold for 45t on day of issue.

First Mention of Town of Maribor in Document, 750th Anniv. A253

2004, Sept. 22   Perf. 13
571 A253 C multi   1.25 .60
  No. 571 sold for 95t on day of issue.

Orchids A254

  Designs: B, Epipactis palustris. D, Ophrys holosericea.

2004, Sept. 22   Perf. 14
572 A254 B multi   1.00 .50
Souvenir Sheet
573 A254 D multi   1.75 .85
  Nos. 572 and 573 sold for 52t and 107t respectively on day of issue.
  See also Nos. 609-610.

Illuminated Manuscripts — A255

  No. 574: a, Illuminated "P." b, Illuminated "Q."

2004, Sept. 22
574 A255 107t Pair, #a-b   2.75 1.40

Souvenir Sheet

Signing of Second London Memorandum, 50th Anniv. — A256

2004, Sept. 22
575 A256 221t multi   3.25 1.60

Christmas A257

2004, Nov. 18   Perf. 14
576 A257 C multi   1.50 .75
Booklet Stamp
Self-Adhesive
Serpentine Die Cut 7¼
577 A257 C multi   1.75 .85
a.   Booklet pane of 12   21.00
  Nos. 576 and 577 each sold for 95t of issue.

New Year's Greetings — A258

2004, Nov. 18   Perf. 14
578 A258 A multi   .70 .35
Booklet Stamp
Self-Adhesive
Serpentine Die Cut 7¼
579 A258 A multi   .80 .40
a.   Booklet pane of 12   9.50
  Nos. 578 and 579 each sold for 45t on day of issue.

Native Dishes — A259

  No. 580 — Map and cuisine of the Prekmurje region: a, Prekmurska gibanica

(pie). b, Bograc, butja repa (goulash, pickled turnips).

2004, Nov. 18   *Perf. 13¾*
580 A259 52t Pair, #a-b   1.75   .85

Birth Fairies Rojenice and Sojenice — A260

2004, Nov. 18   *Perf. 14*
581 A260 180t multi   2.75 1.40

Traditional Clothing From Pohorje and Kobansko Areas A261

2005, Jan. 21   *Perf. 11¾x11¼*
582 A261 A multi   .75   .35
   No. 582 sold for 45t on day of issue.

Posthorn Type of 2004
2005   *Perf. 14, 11¼x11¾ (#583A)*
583   A247 83t multi   1.40   .70
583A A247 83t multi   1.40   .70
   Issued: No. 583, 1/21; No. 583A, 4/2. Size of No. 583: 25x34mm.

Janez Sigismund Valentin Popovic (1705-74), Linguist, Scientist — A262

2005, Jan. 21   *Perf. 11¼x11¾*
584 A262 107t multi   1.40   .70

Love A263

2005, Jan. 21   *Perf. 11*
585 A263 180t multi   2.50 1.25
   Values are for stamps with surrounding selvage.

Janez Trdina (1830-1905), Writer — A264

2005, Jan. 21   *Perf. 11¼x11¾*
586 A264 221t multi   3.50 1.75

Return of Slovenian Exiles, 60th Anniv. A265

2005, Mar. 18   *Perf. 11¾x11¼*
587 A265 A multi   .80   .40
   No. 587 sold for 49t on day of issue.

Victory in World War II, 60th Anniv. A266

2005, Mar. 18
588 A266 B multi   .90   .50
   No. 588 sold for 57t on day of issue.

Souvenir Sheet

National Tourist Association, Cent. — A267

2005, Mar. 18   *Perf. 11¼*
589 A267 100t multi   1.50   .75

Zoisite A268

2005, Mar. 18   *Perf. 11¾x11¼*
590 A268 D multi   1.50   .75
   No. 590 sold for 107t on day of issue.

Folk Tales — A269

   Designs: No. 591, A, The Golden Fish. No. 592, A, The Grateful Bear.

2005, Mar. 18   *Perf. 11¼x11¾*
591-592 A269   Set of 2   1.50   .75
   Nos. 591 and 592 each sold for 49t on day of issue.

Folk Tales Type of 2005
Serpentine Die Cut 7¼
2005, Mar. 18   **Litho.**
Booklet Stamps
Self-Adhesive
593   A269 A Like #591   .75   .30
594   A269 A Like #592   .75   .30
   a.   Booklet pane, 4 each #593, 594   6.00
   Nos. 593 and 594 each sold for 49t on day of issue.

Child and Sunflower — A270

Die Cut Perf. 12½x12¼
2005, May 20   **Litho.**
Self-Adhesive
595   A270 A multi   .75   .35
   a.   Serpentine die cut 13¾x14½   .65   .35
   No. 595 sold for 49t on day of issue.
   No. 595a sold for 23c when issued in 2008.

1910 Puch Motorcycle A271

2005, May 20   *Perf. 11¾x11¼*
596 A271 98t multi   1.40   .70

Europa A272

2005, May 20
597 A272 D multi   1.50   .75
   No. 597 sold for 107t on day of issue.

Postal Wagon and Mail Box — A273

2005, May 20
598 A273 107t multi   1.50   .75

Vesna, Goddess of Spring — A274

2005, May 20   *Perf. 11¼x11¾*
599 A274 180t multi   2.40 1.25

Painted Beehive Panel Type of 2004
2005, May 20   *Perf. 11¾x11¼*
600 A250 221t Hunter and bird   3.25 1.60

Bishop Anton Jeglic and St. Stanislav's Institute A275

2005, May 20
601 A275 221t multi   3.00 1.50
   St. Stanislav's Institute, cent.

European Philatelic Cooperation, 50th Anniv. (in 2006) — A276

   Magnifying glass and details from Slovenian stamps: No. 602, 60t, #495 (circus elephant). No. 603, 60t, #285 (ram), and stamp tongs. No. 604, 60t, #349 (river). #605, 60t, #195 (Jurij Vega).

2005, May 20   *Perf. 14x13½*
602-605 A276   Set of 4   3.50 1.75
605a   Souvenir sheet #602-605, perf. 14   3.50 1.75

Fruit, Blossoms and Insects Type of 2000
   Designs: No. 606, Apricot blossom. No. 607, Apricots on branch. No. 608, San José scale on branch.

2005, July 5   *Perf. 11¾x11¼*
Size 19x23mm
606   A168 D multi   1.50   .75
607   A168 D multi   1.50   .75
608   A168 D multi   1.50   .75
   a.   Horiz. strip, #606-608   4.50 2.25
   Nos. 606-608 each sold for 107t on day of issue.

Orchids Type of 2004
   Designs: B, Dactylorhiza sambucina. D, Platanithera bifolia.

2005, Sept. 23   *Perf. 11¾x11¼*
Size: 37x26mm
609 A254 B multi   .90   .45

Souvenir Sheet
610 A254 D multi   1.60   .80
   No. 609 sold for 57t and No. 610 sold for 107t on day of issue. No. 610 contains one 41x28mm stamp.

Dance of Death Fresco, by Janez of Kastav — A277

   No. 611: a, Denomination in gray. b, Denomination in brown.

Litho. & Embossed
2005, Sept. 23   *Perf. 13½x13¾*
611 A277 107t Horiz. pair, #a-b   3.25 1.60

Dogs A278

   Designs: A, Posavec hound. B, Istrian rough-coated hound. C, Slovenian mountain hound.
   D, Istrian smooth-coated hound, vert.

2005, Sept. 23   *Perf. 11¾x11¼*
612-614 A278   Set of 3   3.00 1.50
Souvenir Sheet
Perf. 11¼
615 A278 D multi   1.60   .80
   On day of issue, No. 612 sold for 49t, No. 613, 57t, No. 614, 95t, and No. 615, 107t. No. 615 contains one 28x41mm stamp.

Types of 1993 Redrawn
2005   **Litho.**   *Perf. 11¼x11¾*
Size: 26x36mm
616   A38   A Like #374   .60   .30
617   A38   B Like #373   .70   .35
618   A38   B Like #375   .70   .35
619   A38   B Like #375A   .70   .35
620   A38   90t Like #216   1.25   .60
621   A38   C Like #376   1.25   .60

622	A38	D Like #378	1.50	.75
623	A38	D Like #379	1.50	.75
		Nos. 616-623 (8)	8.20	4.05

Issued: Nos. 616-617, 3/18; Nos. 618, 622, 4/2; Nos. 619-621, 623, 5/4. On day of issue No. 616 sold for 49t, Nos. 618-619 each sold for 57t, No. 621 sold for 95t, and Nos. 622-623 each sold for 107t.

Size of Nos. 216, 373-375, 375A, 376, 378-379: 25x34mm.

Castles Type of 2000-04 Redrawn
2005 Litho. Perf. 11¼x11¾
Size: 24x34mm

624	A167	1t Predjama	.25	.25
625	A167	1t Velenje	.25	.25
a.		Pair, #624-625	.50	.50
626	A167	C Gewerkenegg	1.25	.60
627	A167	100t Podsreda	1.25	.60
628	A167	100t Bled	1.25	.60
a.		Pair, #626-627	2.50	1.25
		Nos. 624-628 (5)	4.25	2.30

Issued: Nos. 626, 4/2; others 5/4. No. 626 sold for 95t on day of issue.

Size of Nos. 400-401, 411B, 412-413: 23x32mm.

Fruits, Blossoms and Insects Type of 2000 Redrawn
2005 Litho. Perf. 11¾x11¼
Vignette Frame Size: 19x23mm

629	A168	5t Like #426	.25	.25
630	A168	5t Like #427	.25	.25
631	A168	5t Like #428	.25	.25
a.		Strip of 3, #629-631	.50	.25
632	A168	10t Like #416	.25	.25
633	A168	10t Like #417	.25	.25
634	A168	10t Like #418	.25	.25
a.		Strip of 3, #632-634	.50	.25
635	A168	A Like #568	.60	.30
636	A168	A Like #569	.60	.30
637	A168	A Like #570	.60	.30
a.		Strip of 3, #635-637	1.75	.90
638	A168	50t Like #464	.65	.30
639	A168	50t Like #465	.65	.30
640	A168	50t Like #466	.65	.30
a.		Strip of 3, #638-640	2.00	.90
641	A168	B Like #528	.80	.40
642	A168	B Like #529	.80	.40
643	A168	B Like #530	.80	.40
a.		Strip of 3, #641-643	2.40	1.20
644	A168	150t Like #502	1.75	.85
645	A168	150t Like #503	1.75	.85
646	A168	150t Like #504	1.75	.85
a.		Strip of 3, #644-646	5.25	2.50
		Nos. 629-646 (18)	12.90	7.05

Issued: Nos. 629-631, 638-640, 5/4; Nos. 632-634, 4/2; Nos. 635-637, 7/22; Nos. 641-643, 6/30; Nos. 644-646, 7/5. On day of issue Nos. 635-637 each sold for 49t; Nos. 641-643 each sold for 57t.

Sizes of vignette frames of Nos. 426-428, 416-418, 568-570, 464-466, 528-530, and 502-504 vary from 19 to 20x26 to 26½mm. Some designs extend beyond vignette frames.

Slovenian Chairmanship of Organization for Security and Cooperation in Europe — A279

2005, Nov. 18 Perf. 11¼x11¾
647 A279 107t multi 1.60 .80

Traditional Foods — A280

No. 648: a, Prleska Gibanica and Ajdov Krapec. b, Prleska Tunka (bread, meat, lard and onion on wooden barrel).

2005, Nov. 18
648 A280 107t Pair, #a-b 3.25 1.60

New Year's Day — A281

2005, Nov. 18 Perf. 11¾x11¼
649 A281 A multi .85 .40
Size: 40x28mm
Self-Adhesive
Serpentine Die Cut 7¼
650 A281 A multi .85 .40
a. Booklet pane of 12 10.50

Nos. 649-650 each sold for 49t on day of issue.

Christmas A282

2005, Nov. 18 Perf. 11¾x11¼
651 A282 C multi 1.40 .70
Size: 40x28mm
Self-Adhesive
Serpentine Die Cut 7¼
652 A282 C multi 1.40 .70
a. Booklet pane of 12 17.00

Nos. 651-652 each sold for 95t on day of issue.

Traditional Carinthian Clothing A283

2006, Jan. 20 Perf. 14
653 A283 A multi .75 .35

No. 653 sold for 49t on day of issue.

Love A284

2006, Jan. 20 Perf. 11
654 A284 B multi .90 .45

No. 654 sold for 57t on day of issue. Values are for stamps with surrounding selvage.

Dr. Anton Trstenjak (1906-96), Psychologist — A285

2006, Jan. 20 Perf. 14
655 A285 B multi .80 .40

No. 655 sold for 57t on day of issue.

Ponikve Carnival — A286

2006, Jan. 20
656 A286 420t multi 5.00 2.50

2006 Winter Olympics, Turin — A287

No. 657: a, 95t, Ski jumper. b, 107t, Snowboarder.

2006, Jan. 20
657 A287 Horiz. pair, #a-b, + label at right 3.00 1.50

Printed in sheets containing 3 pairs and labels.

Pericnik Waterfall — A288

2006, Mar. 24
658 A288 D multi 1.60 .80

No. 658 sold for 107t on day of issue.

Pereiraea Gervaisi Fossil — A289

2006, Mar. 24
659 A289 D multi 1.60 .80

No. 659 sold for 107t on day of issue.

Butterflies A290

Designs: B, Erannis ankeraria. D, Erebia calcaria.

2006, Mar. 24 Perf. 14
660 A290 B multi .80 .40
Souvenir Sheet
Perf. 14x14x13x14
661 A290 D multi 1.60 .80

On day of issue No. 660 sold for 57t; No. 661 for 107t.

Children's Book Characters — A291

Designs: Nos. 662, 664, A, Zvezdica Zaspanka, by Frane Milicinski Jezek. No. 663, 665, A, Zogica Nogica, by Jan Malik.

2006, Mar. 24 Litho. Perf. 14
662-663 A291 Set of 2 1.40 .70
Booklet Stamps
Self-Adhesive
Serpentine Die Cut 7¼
664-665 A291 Set of 2 2.00 1.00
a. Booklet pane, 4 each #664-665 8.00

On day of issue Nos. 662-663, 664-665 each sold for 49t.

World Junior Slalom Kayaking Championships, Solkan — A292

2006, May 19 Perf. 14
666 A292 C multi 1.50 .75

No. 666 sold for 95t on day of issue.

Greetings — A293

Serpentine Die Cut 9¼x9
2006, May 19 Self-Adhesive
667 A293 C multi 1.50 .75

No. 667 sold for 95t on day of issue.

Painted Beehive Type of 2004
2006, May 19 Perf. 14
668 A250 D Hay rake fighters 1.60 .80

No. 668 sold for 107t on day of issue.

Europa — A294

2006, May 19
669 A294 D multi 1.60 .80

No. 669 sold for 107t on day of issue. Printed in sheets of 8 + label.

Svarog, Slavic
Sun God — A295

2006, May 19
670 A295 D multi 1.75 .85
No. 670 sold for 107t on day of issue.

Souvenir Sheet

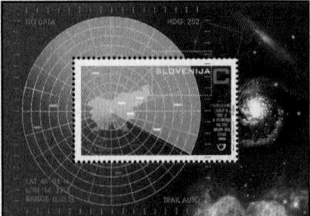

Slovenian Air Traffic Control, 15th
Anniv. — A296

2006, June 25 *Perf. 13¼x14*
671 A296 C multi 1.50 .75
No. 671 sold for 95t on day of issue.

Ox-drawn
Farm
Wagon
A297

2006, Sept. 22 *Perf. 14*
672 A297 D multi 1.75 .85
No. 672 sold for 107t on day of issue.

Souvenir Sheet

Ceiling Painting, Celje
Mansion — A298

No. 673 — Text "Masa Kozjek, Tomaz
Lauko" at: a, LL. b, LR. c, UL. d, UR.

2006, Sept. 22
673 A298 D Sheet of 4, #a-d 5.25 2.50
Nos. 673a-673d each sold for 107t on day of
issue.

Aquatic
Plants — A299

Designs: A, Salvinia natans and silhouette
of frog. D, Marsilea quadrifolia and silhouette
of dragonfly.

2006, Sept. 22
674 A299 A multi .85 .40

Souvenir Sheet
675 A299 D multi 1.75 .85
On day of issue No. 674 sold for 49t and No.
675 sold for 107t.

**Fruit, Blossoms and Insects Type of
2000**
Designs: No. 676, Persimmon blossom (cvet
kakija). No. 677, Persimmon (kaki). No. 678,
Citrus flatid planthopper (Medeci skrzat).

2006, Nov. 17 *Perf. 11¾x11¼*
Vignette Size: 19x23mm
676 A168 D multi 1.50 .75
677 A168 D multi 1.50 .75
678 A168 D multi 1.50 .75
a. Horiz. strip of 3, #676-678 4.50 2.25
On day of issue Nos. 676-678 each sold for
107t.

Partisan Couriers
of World War
II — A300

2006, Nov. 17 *Perf. 14*
679 A300 C multi 1.50 .75
No. 679 sold for 95t on day of issue.

Traditional Foods — A301

No. 680: a, Roast turkey, bread, corn, apple.
b, Yeast cake (kvaseníca).

2006, Nov. 17
680 A301 D Horiz. pair, #a-b 2.75 1.40
On day of issue Nos. 680a-680b each sold
for 107t.

Souvenir Sheet

Father Simon Asic (1906-92),
Herbalist — A302

2006, Nov. 17
681 A302 D multi 1.50 .75
No. 681 sold for 107t on day of issue.

Christmas — A303

Designs: A, Snowman and bird. C, Carolers.

2006, Nov. 17 *Perf. 14*
682 A303 A multi .70 .35
683 A303 C multi 1.40 .70

Booklet Stamps
Self-Adhesive
Serpentine Die Cut 7¼
684 A303 A multi .70 .35
a. Booklet pane of 12 8.50
685 A303 C multi 1.40 .70
a. Booklet pane of 12 17.00
Nos. 682-685 (4) 4.20 2.10
On day of issue Nos. 682 and 684 each sold
for 49t, and Nos. 683 and 685 each sold for
95t.

100 Cents = 1 Euro

Flora — A304

Designs: 1c, Asplenium adulterinum. 2c,
Moehringia tommasinii. 5c, Himantoglossum
adriaticum. 10c, Pulsatilla grandis. 20c,
Primula carniolica. A, Campanula zoysii. B,
Cypripedium calceolus. 25c, Gladiolus palus-
tris. 35c, Cerastium dinaricum. C, Serratula
lycopifolia. D, Genisia holopetala. 48c, Ade-
nophora liliifolia. 50c, Aquilegia bertolonii. 75c,
Liparis loeselii. 92c, Scilla litardierei. €1,
Eryngium alpinum. €2, Rhododendron luteum.

2007, Jan. 1 Litho. *Perf. 11¼x11¾*
686 A304 1c multi .25 .25
687 A304 2c multi .25 .25
688 A304 5c multi .25 .25
689 A304 10c multi .35 .25
690 A304 20c multi .65 .30
691 A304 A multi .65 .30
692 A304 B multi .75 .35
693 A304 25c multi .80 .35
694 A304 35c multi 1.10 .50
695 A304 C multi 1.40 .60
696 A304 D multi 1.50 .70
697 A304 48c multi 1.50 .70
698 A304 50c multi 1.60 .75
699 A304 75c multi 2.40 1.10
700 A304 92c multi 3.00 1.90
701 A304 €1 multi 3.25 1.50
702 A304 €2 multi 6.50 3.00
Nos. 686-702 (17) 26.20 13.05
On day of issue No. 691 sold for 20c; No.
692 for 24c; No. 695 for 40c; No. 696 for 45c.
See Nos. 787-797, 881-882.

Souvenir Sheet

Introduction of Euro Currency — A305

Perf. 13¼x13 Syncopated
2007, Jan. 1
703 A305 €1 multi 3.50 1.75

Traditional
Clothing
From
Smlednik
A306

2007, Jan. 24 *Perf. 11¾x11¼*
704 A306 20c multi .70 .35

Bride
and
Groom
A307

2007, Jan. 24 *Perf. 11*
705 A307 24c multi .85 .40
Values are for stamps with surrounding
selvage.

Vasja Pirc (1907-80), Chess
Grandmaster — A308

2007, Jan. 24 *Perf. 14*
706 A308 48c multi 1.60 .80

A309

A310

A311

Generic
Personalized
Stamps
A312

Serpentine Die Cut 12x11½, 11½x12
2007, Jan. 24 **Self-Adhesive**
707 A309 A multi .75 .35
708 A310 A multi .75 .35
709 A311 A multi .75 .35
710 A312 A multi .75 .35
Nos. 707-710 (4) 3.00 1.40
On day of issue Nos. 707-710 each sold for
20c. Images within the frames shown above
are generic images and were the only stamps
with these frames sold at 20c. Stamps with
these frames and other images are personalized stamps, created starting on Mar. 8, which
sold in sheets of 20 for €12.51 per sheet.

Aragonite
A313

2007, Mar. 23   *Perf. 11¾x11¼*
711 A313 45c multi   1.60 .80

Mt. Mangart and Geum Reptans
A314

2007, Mar. 23   *Perf. 14*
712 A314 45c multi   1.60 .80

Europa
A315

2007, Mar. 23
713 A315 50c multi   4.25 1.75
Scouting, cent. Printed in sheets of 8 + label.

Worldwide Fund for Nature (WWF)
A316

Sciurus vulgaris: Nos. 714, 718a, 48c, Adult. Nos. 715, 718b, 48c, Adult eating acorn. Nos. 716, 718c, 48c, Two adults. Nos. 717, 718d, 48c, Adult and young.

2007, Mar. 23   *Perf. 11¾x11¼*
     Size: 33x24mm
714-717 A316   Set of 4   5.75 2.75
     Miniature Sheet
     Perf. 13x13¼
     Size: 36x26mm
718 A316 48c Sheet, 2 each
       #a-d   11.50 5.75

Elves — A317

2007, May 25   Litho.   *Perf. 14*
719 A317 45c multi   1.50 .75

Treaty of Rome, 50th Anniv. — A318

2007, May 25   *Perf. 11¼x11¾*
720 A318 45c multi   1.50 .75

Horse-drawn Wagon — A319

2007, May 25   *Perf. 14*
721 A319 92c multi   2.75 1.40

Butterflies
A320

Designs: 24c, Callimorpha quadripunctaria. 45c, Colias myrmidone, vert.

2007, May 25
722 A320 24c multi   .75 .35
     Souvenir Sheet
723 A320 45c multi   1.50 .75

Souvenir Sheet

Year of the Bible — A321

2007, May 25
724 A321 75c multi   2.50 1.25

Lent Festival, Maribor
A322

2007, June 22   *Perf. 14x13¼*
725 A322 €1 multi   3.25 1.60
Printed in sheets of 6 + 3 labels.

Wall Climbing
A323

2007, Sept. 26   *Perf. 14*
726 A323 48c multi   1.50 .75
Printed in sheets of 6 + 3 labels.

Ceiling Fresco, Church of St. Nicholas, Ljubljana, by Giulio Quaglio
A324

2007, Sept. 26   *Perf. 11¾x11¼*
727 A324 92c multi   2.75 1.40

Aquatic Flowers — A325

Designs: 20c, Nuphar luteum. 24c, Hydrocharis morsus-ranae. 40c, Nymphoides peltata.
     45c, Nymphaea alba, horiz.

2007, Sept. 26   *Perf. 14*
728-730 A325   Set of 3   2.75 1.40
     Souvenir Sheet
731 A325 45c multi   1.50 .75

Slovenian Entry Into Schengen Border-Free Zone — A326

2007, Nov. 23   *Perf. 11¾x11¼*
732 A326 45c multi   1.50 .75

Slovenian Food — A327

No. 733: a, Stajerska sour soup, Pohorski stew. b, Pohorje omelet.

2007, Nov. 23   *Perf. 11¼x11¾*
733 A327 45c Horiz. pair, #a-b   3.00 1.50

Souvenir Sheet

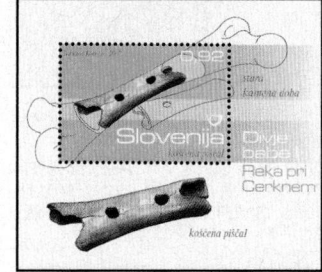

Bear Bone Flute From Divje Babe I Archaeological Site — A328

2007, Nov. 23   *Perf. 14*
734 A328 92c multi   3.00 1.50

A329

A330

A331

Personalized Stamps
A332

Serpentine Die Cut 12x11½, 11½x12
2007, Nov. 23   Litho.
735 A329   A green & org   .65 .30
736 A330   A green & org   .60 .30
737 A331   C gray & org   1.40 .70
738 A332   C gray & org   1.40 .70
    Nos. 735-738 (4)   4.05 2.00

On day of issue, Nos. 735-736 each sold for 20c, and Nos. 737-738 each sold for 40c. Images within the frames shown above are generic images and were the only stamps sold at these prices. Stamps with these frames and other images are personalized stamps, which sold for more.

Christmas — A333

     Perf. 13½x13¼
2007, Nov. 23   Litho.
739 A333 C multi   1.25 .60
No. 739 sold for 40c on day of issue.

New Year 2008 — A334

2007, Nov. 23   *Perf. 13x13¼*
740 A334 A multi   .60 .30
No. 740 sold for 20c on day of issue.

Slovenian postal authorities have declared illegal two sheetlets of six stamps with a denomination of "45" and bearing the name of "Slovenia" in Cyrillic lettering depicting Marilyn Monroe.

Souvenir Sheet

Slovenian Presidency of the European Union Council of Ministers — A335

Litho. With Foil Application
2008, Jan. 1   **Perf. 14x13½**
741 A335 €2.38 multi   7.00 3.50

Traditional Clothing From Pesnica and Scavnica A336

2008, Jan. 29 Litho. Perf. 11¾x11½
742 A336 20c multi   .70 .35

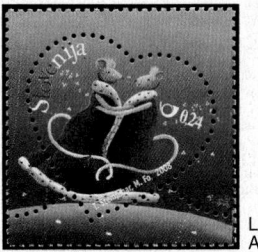

Love A337

2008, Jan. 29   **Perf. 11**
743 A337 24c multi   .75 .35
Values are for stamps with surrounding selvage.

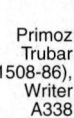

Primoz Trubar (1508-86), Writer A338

2008, Jan. 29   **Perf. 14**
744 A338 48c multi   1.50 .75

Vrbica Carnival Masks — A339

2008, Jan. 29   **Perf. 11¼x11¾**
745 A339 €1.75 multi   5.25 2.60

Dr. Julius Kugy (1858-1944), Botanist, and Scabiosa Trenta — A340

2008, Mar. 28   **Litho.**   **Perf. 14**
746 A340 45c multi   1.40 .70

Flowers — A341

Designs: 20c, Paeonia officinalis. 24c, Pulsatilla montana. 40c, Iris illyrica. 45c, Gentiana tergestina.

2008, Mar. 28
747-749 A341   Set of 3   2.75 1.40
Souvenir Sheet
750 A341 45c multi   1.40 .70

Slovenian Academy of Arts and Sciences, 70th Anniv. A342

2008, May 29   **Litho.**   **Perf. 14**
751 A342 40c multi   1.25 1.25

Mokos, Slavic Goddess — A343

2008, May 29
752 A343 45c multi   1.50 1.50

Europa A344

Designs: 45c, Winged letters, postal card, parcel. 92c, Letters as townspeople.

2008, May 29   **Perf. 11¾x11¼**
753-754 A344   Set of 2   4.50 4.50
Nos. 753-754 were each printed in sheets of 8 + label.

2008 Summer Olympics, Beijing — A345

No. 755: a, 40c, Combat sports. b, 45c, Sailing.

2008, May 29
755 A345   Horiz. pair, #a-b   2.75 2.75

Stamp Day — A346

2008, Sept. 29   **Perf. 11¼x11¾**
756 A346 23c multi   .65 .65

Dr. Alojzij Sustar (1920-2007), Archbishop of Ljubljana — A347

2008, Sept. 29   **Perf. 14**
757 A347 45c multi   1.25 1.25

Rococo Decorations, Gruber Palace — A348

2008, Sept. 29   **Perf. 11¼x11¾**
758 A348 92c multi   2.60 2.60

Horse-drawn Sledge — A349

2008, Sept. 29   **Perf. 14**
759 A349 92c multi   2.60 2.60

Souvenir Sheet

Slovenian Radio, 80th Anniv. and Slovenian Television, 50th Anniv. — A350

Perf. 13¼x14¼ Syncopated
2008, Sept. 29
760 A350 92c multi   2.60 2.60

Amphibians and Reptiles — A351

Designs: 23c, Rana latastei. 27c, Bombina bombina. 40c, Triturus carnifex.

45c, Elaphe quatuorlineata.

2008, Sept. 29   **Perf. 14**
761-763 A351   Set of 3   2.50 2.50
Souvenir Sheet
764 A351 45c multi   1.25 1.25

Primoz Kozmus, 2008 Hammer Throw Olympic Gold Medalist A352

2008, Oct. 14   **Litho.**
765 A352 45c multi   1.25 1.25

Introduction of the Euro, 10th Anniv. (in 2009) — A353

2008, Nov. 27
766 A353 45c multi   1.25 1.25

End of World War I, 90th Anniv. A354

2008, Nov. 27
767 A354 92c multi   2.40 2.40

Souvenir Sheet

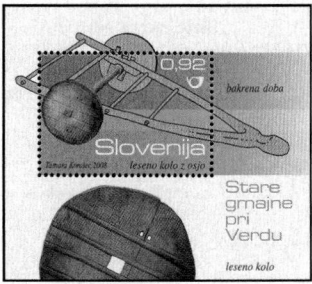

Wheel and Axle, c. 3200 B. C. — A355

2008, Nov. 27
768 A355 92c multi   2.40 2.40

Traditional Foods — A356

No. 769: a, Zgornjesavinjski zelodec (dried sausage), bread. b, Ubrnenik (dumpling), Solcavski sirnek (spiced cheese).

2008, Nov. 27   **Perf. 11¼x11¾**
769 A356 45c Horiz. pair, #a-b   2.40 2.40

A357

Christmas
A358

2008, Nov. 27　　**Perf. 11¼x11¾**
770 A357 A multi　　　　.60　.60
　　Perf. 11¾x11¼
771 A358 C multi　　　　1.00 1.00
　On day of issue, Nos. 770 and 771 sold for 23c and 40c, respectively.

Traditional Clothing From Bela Krajina A359

2009, Jan. 30　　**Perf. 11¾x11¼**
772 A359 23c multi　　　.60　.60

Love
A360

2009, Jan. 30　　**Perf. 11**
773 A360 27c multi　　　.70　.70
　Values are for stamps with surrounding selvage.

Alojz Knafelc (1859-1937), Mountain Cartographer A361

2009, Jan. 30　　**Perf. 13¼x13**
774 A361 45c multi　　　1.25 1.25

Jozef Mrak (1709-86), Geodesist A362

2009, Jan. 30　　**Perf. 13x13¼**
775 A362 92c multi　　　2.40 2.40

Selma Carnival Costumes — A363

2009, Jan. 30　　**Perf. 11¼x11¾**
776 A363 €1.60 multi　　4.25 4.25

Souvenir Sheet

Eye and Braille Letters — A364

Litho. & Embossed
2009, Jan. 30　　**Perf. 13x13¼**
777 A364 €2.38 multi　　6.25 6.25
Louis Braille (1809-52), educator of the blind.

Essay for First Stamps of Slovenia A365

Perf. 11¾x11½
2009, Mar. 27　　**Litho.**
778 A365 23c multi　　　.65　.65
　First Slovenian stamps (Yugoslavia Nos. 3L1-3L8), 90th anniv.

Lovrenc Lakes A366

2009, Mar. 27　　**Perf. 13x13¼**
779 A366 35c multi　　　.95　.95

Zice Charterhouse — A367

2009, Mar. 27
780 A367 92c multi　　　2.50 2.50

Flowers
A368

　Designs: 23c, Centaurea cyanus. 27c, Papaver rhoeas. 40c, Agrostemma githago. 45c, Ranunculus arvensis.

2009, Mar. 27　　**Perf. 13x13¼**
781-783 A368　Set of 3　　2.50 2.50
Souvenir Sheet
Perf. 14x13½
784 A368 45c multi　　　1.25 1.25

Souvenir Sheet

Preservation of Polar Regions and Glaciers — A369

　No. 785: a, Polar bear and puffins. b, Killer whale and polar bears.

2009, Mar. 27　　**Perf. 13x13¼**
785 A369 45c Sheet of 2, #a-b　2.50 2.50

Council of Europe, 60th Anniv. A370

2009, May 8　　**Perf. 11¾x11¼**
786 A370 45c multi　　　1.25 1.25

Flora Type of 2007
Designs as before.
Self-Adhesive
Size: 23x30mm
Serpentine Die Cut 14x15
2009, May 29　　　**Litho.**
787 A304　1c multi　　　.25　.25
788 A304　10c multi　　　.30　.30
789 A304　20c multi　　　.55　.55
790 A304　25c multi　　　.70　.70
791 A304　A multi　　　.75　.75
792 A304　B multi　　　.85　.85
793 A304　35c multi　　　1.00 1.00
794 A304　C multi　　　1.10 1.10
795 A304　D multi　　　1.25 1.25
796 A304　75c multi　　　2.10 2.10
797 A304　€1 multi　　　2.75 2.75
　　Nos. 787-797 (11)　　11.60 11.60
　On day of issue, No. 791 sold for 26c; No. 792, 30c; No. 794, 40c, No. 795, 45c.

Bread in Heart-shaped Loaf — A371

Serpentine Die Cut 14x15
2009, May 29　　**Self-Adhesive**
798 A371 C multi　　　1.10 1.10
　No. 798 sold for 40c on day of issue.

World Track and Field Championships, Berlin — A372

2009, May 29　　**Perf. 13¼x13**
799 A372 45c multi　　　1.25 1.25
　Printed in sheets of 6 + 3 labels.

World Plowing Championships, Tesanovci — A373

2009, May 29　　**Perf. 13x13¼**
800 A373 45c multi　　　1.25 1.25

Werewolf A374

2009, May 29　　**Perf. 13¼x13**
801 A374 70c multi　　　2.00 2.00

Ljubljana Jazz Festival, 50th Anniv. — A375

2009, May 29　　**Perf. 11½x11¾**
802 A375 92c black & yellow　2.60 2.60

Europa A376

　Designs: 45c, Stargazers. 92c, Observatory.

2009, May 29　　**Perf. 13x13¼**
803-804 A376　Set of 2　　4.00 4.00
　Intl. Year of Astronomy. Nos. 803-804 were each printed in sheets of 8 + label.

Trolleybus, Piran A377

2009, Sept. 25　　**Litho.**
805 A377 92c multi　　　2.75 2.75

Transfer of Seat of the Lavant
Diocese, 150th Anniv. — A378

2009, Sept. 25   *Perf. 11½x11¾*
806   A378   92c multi   2.75 2.75

Bohinj Lake, by Anton
Karinger — A379

2009, Sept. 25
807   A379   €1.50 multi   4.50 4.50

Beetles
A380

Designs: 26c, Lucanus cervus. 30c, Rosalia
alpina. 40c, Osmoderma eremita.
45c, Carabus variolosus.

2009, Sept. 25   *Perf. 13x13¼*
808-810   A380   Set of 3   3.00 3.00
    Souvenir Sheet
811   A380   45c multi   1.40 1.40

Souvenir Sheet

Stone Buildings — A381

No. 812 — Stone buildings in: a, Pazin, Croatia. b, Kopriva na Krasu, Slovenia.

2009, Sept. 25   *Perf. 13 Syncopated*
812   A381   92c Sheet of 2, #a-b   5.50 5.50
    See Croatia No. 743.

Souvenir Sheet

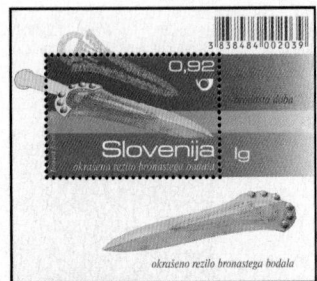

Bronze Age Dagger — A382

2009, Nov. 27   *Perf. 13x14*
813   A382   92c multi   2.75 2.75

Traditional Foods — A383

No. 814: a, Funsterc ali knapovsko sonce
(omelet) and Grenadirmars (potatoes and
pasta). b, Zasavska jetrnica (sausage).

2009, Nov. 27   *Perf. 11½x11¾*
814   A383   45c Horiz. pair, #a-b   2.75 2.75

Christmas

A384   A385

2009, Nov. 27   *Perf. 11½x11¾*
815   A384   A multi   .80 .80
816   A385   C multi   1.25 1.25

Booklet Stamps
Self-Adhesive
Serpentine Die Cut 12¾
817   A384   A multi   .80 .80
   a.   Booklet pane of 12   9.75
818   A385   C multi   1.25 1.25
   a.   Booklet pane of 12   15.00

On day of issue, Nos. 815 and 817 each
sold for 26c, and Nos. 816 and 818 each sold
for 40c.

Vertical
Orientation,
Plain
Frame — A386

Vertical
Orientation,
Candles in
Frame — A387

Vertical
Orientation,
Flower in
Frame — A388

Vertical
Orientation,
Book in
Frame — A389

Horizontal Orientation, Plain
Frame — A390

Horizontal Orientation, Candles in
Frame — A391

Horizontal Orientation, Flower in
Frame — A392

Horizontal Orientation, Book in
Frame — A393

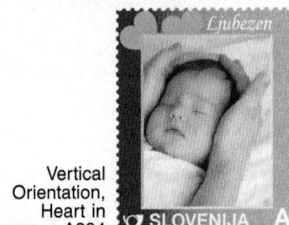

Vertical
Orientation,
Heart in
Frame — A394

Vertical
Orientation,
Envleopes in
Frame — A395

Horizontal Orientation, Heart in
Frame — A396

Horizontal Orientation, Envelopes in
Frame — A397

Serpentine Die Cut 11½x11¾ (#819,
821), 11¾x11½ (#820, 822)
2009, Nov. 27   **Litho.**
       Self-Adhesive
819   Sheet of 20   22.00
   a.   A386 A red frame   .80   .80
   b.   A387 A green frame   .80   .80
   c.   A386 A white frame   .80   .80
   d.   A388 A purple frame   .80   .80
   e.   A389 A orange frame   .80   .80
   f.   A386 B white frame   .90   .90
   g.   A389 B orange frame   .90   .90
   h.   A386 B red frame   .90   .90
   i.   A388 B purple frame   .90   .90
   j.   A387 B green frame   .90   .90
   k.   A386 C red frame   1.25   1.25
   l.   A389 C orange frame   1.25   1.25
   m.   A386 C white frame   1.25   1.25
   n.   A387 C green frame   1.25   1.25
   o.   A388 C purple frame   1.25   1.25
   p.   A389 D orange frame   1.40   1.40
   q.   A387 D green frame   1.40   1.40
   r.   A388 D purple frame   1.40   1.40
   s.   A386 D white frame   1.40   1.40
   t.   A386 D red frame   1.40   1.40
820   Sheet of 20   22.00
   a.   A390 A white frame   .80   .80
   b.   A392 A purple frame   .80   .80
   c.   A393 A orange frame   .80   .80
   d.   A391 A green frame   .80   .80
   e.   A390 A red frame   .80   .80
   f.   A390 B white frame   .90   .90
   g.   A390 B red frame   .90   .90
   h.   A391 B green frame   .90   .90
   i.   A392 B purple frame   .90   .90
   j.   A393 B orange frame   .90   .90
   k.   A390 C red frame   1.25   1.25
   l.   A393 C orange frame   1.25   1.25
   m.   A392 C purple frame   1.25   1.25
   n.   A391 C green frame   1.25   1.25
   o.   A390 C white frame   1.25   1.25
   p.   A391 D green frame   1.40   1.40
   q.   A393 D orange frame   1.40   1.40
   r.   A392 D purple frame   1.40   1.40
   s.   A390 D white frame   1.40   1.40
   t.   A390 D red frame   1.40   1.40
821   Sheet of 20   22.50
   a.   A394 A red frame   .80   .80
   b.   A386 A gray frame   .80   .80
   c.   A395 A blue frame   .80   .80
   d.   A386 B dark blue frame   .90   .90
   e.   A386 B orange frame   .90   .90
   f.   A386 B green frame   .90   .90
   g.   A395 B blue frame   .90   .90
   h.   A386 B gray frame   .90   .90
   i.   A394 B red frame   .90   .90
   j.   A386 C orange frame   1.25   1.25
   k.   A386 C green frame   1.25   1.25
   l.   A395 C blue frame   1.25   1.25
   m.   A386 C dark blue frame   1.25   1.25
   n.   A394 C red frame   1.25   1.25
   o.   A394 D red frame   1.40   1.40
   p.   A386 D green frame   1.40   1.40
   q.   A386 D dark blue frame   1.40   1.40
   r.   A386 D orange frame   1.40   1.40
   s.   A386 D gray frame   1.40   1.40
   t.   A395 D blue frame   1.40   1.40
822   Sheet of 20   22.50
   a.   A390 A gray frame   .80   .80
   b.   A397 A blue frame   .80   .80
   c.   A396 A red frame   .80   .80
   d.   A390 B green frame   .90   .90
   e.   A396 B red frame   .90   .90
   f.   A390 B dark blue frame   .90   .90
   g.   A390 B gray frame   .90   .90
   h.   A390 B orange frame   .90   .90
   i.   A397 B blue frame   .90   .90
   j.   A397 C blue frame   1.25   1.25
   k.   A390 C orange frame   1.25   1.25
   l.   A390 C green frame   1.25   1.25
   m.   A396 C red frame   1.25   1.25
   n.   A390 C dark blue frame   1.25   1.25
   o.   A396 D red frame   1.40   1.40
   p.   A390 D dark blue frame   1.40   1.40
   q.   A397 D blue frame   1.40   1.40
   r.   A390 D gray frame   1.40   1.40
   s.   A390 D green frame   1.40   1.40
   t.   A390 D orange frame   1.40   1.40
    Nos. 819-822 (4)   89.00

On day of issue, stamps inscribed "A" sold
for 26c; "B" sold for 30c; "C" sold for 40c; and
"D" sold for 45c. Each vignette on Nos. 819-
822 is in sepia. All sepia vignettes are different
on the four sheets and are generic images
found only on those sheets. Stamps can be
personalized, printed in sheets of 20 stamps
that have one type of frame and frame color
and one personalized image in the vignette
area.

Traditional Clothing From Prekmurje A398

2010, Jan. 29   Litho.   Perf. 13¾
823 A398 26c multi   .75   .75

Love A399

2010, Jan. 29   Perf. 11
824 A399 30c multi   .85   .85

Values are for stamps with surrounding selvage.

Arrows — A400

Serpentine Die Cut 15x14
2010, Jan. 29   Self-Adhesive
825 A400 D multi   2.40 2.40

No. 825 sold for 85c on day of issue and is for international priority mail.

New Year 2010 (Year of the Tiger) A401

2010, Jan. 29   Perf. 12¾x13
826 A401 92c multi   2.60 2.60

Stanko Vraz (1810-51), Poet — A402

2010, Jan. 29   Perf. 13x12¾
827 A402 €1.10 multi   3.25 3.25

Pustnaki Procession, Mozirje — A403

2010, Jan. 29   Perf. 13½x13¾
828 A403 €1.60 multi   4.50 4.50

2010 Winter Olympics, Vancouver — A404

2010, Jan. 29   Perf. 12¾x13
829 A404 Horiz. pair + label   2.40 2.40
  a.   40c Ski flags   1.10 1.10
  b.   45c Hockey puck and stick   1.25 1.25

Braided Palm Branches
A406   A407

Serpentine Die Cut 14x15
2010, Mar. 18   Self-Adhesive
830 A406 B multi   .80   .80
831 A407 D multi   1.25 1.25

On day of issue, No. 830 sold for 30c and No. 831 sold for 45c.

Souvenir Sheet

World Ski Jumping Championships, Planica — A408

2010, Mar. 18   Perf. 13½x13¾
832 A408 €2.38 multi   6.50 6.50

No. 832 has holes in the sheet margin reading "Planica 2010."

Izola A409

2010, Mar. 26   Perf. 12¾x13
833 A409 92c multi   2.50 2.50

Jurkloster Monastery A410

2010, Mar. 26   Litho.
834 A410 92c multi   2.50 2.50

Peonies A411

Designs: 45c, Paeonia officinalis. 92c, Paeonia rockii.

2010, Mar. 26   Perf. 12¾x13
835 A411 45c multi   1.25 1.25
  a.   Perf. 14¼x13¾   1.25 1.25
836 A411 92c multi   2.50 2.50
  a.   Perf. 14¼x13¾   2.50 2.50
  b.   Souvenir sheet, #835a-836a   3.75 3.75

Flowers A412

Designs: 26c, Dianthus sanguineus. 30c, Dianthus sternbergii. 40c, Dianthus deltoides. 92c, Dianthus carthusianorum.

2010, Mar. 26   Perf. 12¾x13
837-839 A412   Set of 3   2.60 2.60

Souvenir Sheet
Perf. 14¼x13¾
840 A412 92c multi   2.50 2.50

Carved Wooden Pigeon — A413

Self-Adhesive
Serpentine Die Cut 14x15
2010, May 28   Litho.
841 A413 D multi   1.10 1.10

No. 841 sold for 45c on day of issue.

Kurent, Slovenian Deity — A414

2010, May 28   Perf. 13x12¾
842 A414 70c multi   1.75 1.75

Sports World Championships — A415

Designs: No. 843, 92c, Soccer player, 2010 World Cup Soccer Championships, South Africa. No. 844, 92c, Basketball player, 2010 World Basketball Championships, Turkey.

2010, May 28   Perf. 13¾
843-844 A415   Set of 2   4.50 4.50

Values are for stamps with surrounding selvage. Nos. 843-844 were printed in sheets containing four of each stamp and 2 central labels.

Europa A416

Designs: D, Boy reading book. 92c, Girl reading book.

2010, May 28   Perf. 13x13¼
845-846 A416   Set of 2   3.25 3.25

No. 845 sold for 45c on day of issue. Nos. 845-846 each were printed in sheets of 8 + label.

Puppets — A417

Designs: No. 847, 92c, Martin Krpan puppet made by Matjaz Schmidt. No. 848, 92c, Pavilha puppet made by Mara Kralj. No. 849, 92c, Gaspercek puppet made by Milan Klemencic. No. 850, 92c, Desetnica puppet made by Alenka Sotler. No. 851, 92c, Tincek Petelincek puppet made by Matej Vogrincic.

2010, May 28   Perf. 13½x13¾
847-851 A417   Set of 5   11.00 11.00

Souvenir Sheet

Medalists at 2010 Winter Olympics, Vancouver — A418

No. 852: a, Tina Maze, Giant Slalom and Super-G skiing silver medalist. b, Petra Majdic, Individual Sprint Classic cross-country skiing bronze medalist

2010, June 24   Perf. 13¾x14¼
852 A418 70c Sheet of 2, #a-b   3.50 3.50

Design of First UNICEF Greeting Card — A419

Die Cut Perf. 10¼x10
2010, Sept. 24   Self-Adhesive
853 A419 A multi   .80   .80

No. 853 sold for 29c on day of issue.

Ljubljana Trolleybus A420

2010, Sept. 24   Perf. 12¾x13
854 A420 €1.50 multi   4.25 4.25

The Letter, by Janez Subic — A421

2010, Sept. 24   Perf. 13½x13¾
855 A421 €1.50 multi   4.25 4.25

Snakes A422

Designs: A, Vipera aspis. B, Coronella austriaca. C, Natrix natrix. 92c, Vipera ammodytes, vert.

2010, Sept. 24   **Perf. 12¾x13**
856-858 A422   Set of 3   3.00 3.00

Souvenir Sheet
Perf. 13¾x14¼

859 A422 92c multi   2.60 2.60

On day of issue, Nos. 856-858 sold for 29c, 33c and 44c, respectively.

Souvenir Sheet

Glass Bead Necklace From Early Iron Age — A423

2010, Nov. 26   Litho.   **Perf. 13x14**
860 A423 92c multi   2.50 2.50

Traditional Foods — A424

No. 861: a, Mezerli (chopped pork ball). b, Koroska skuta (cottage cheese with onions and pumpkin seed oil).

2010, Nov. 26   **Perf. 13½**
861 A424 49c Horiz. pair, #a-b   2.75 2.75

Christmas
A425   A426

2010, Nov. 26   **Perf. 11¼x11¾**
862 A425 A multi   .80 .80
863 A426 C multi   1.25 1.25

Booklet Stamps
Self-Adhesive

Serpentine Die Cut 12¾

864 A425 A multi   .80 .80
  a.   Booklet pane of 12   9.75
865 A426 C multi   1.25 1.25
  a.   Booklet pane of 12   15.00

On day of issue, Nos. 862 and 864 each sold for 29c and Nos. 863 and 865 each sold for 44c.

Traditional Clothing From Notranjska A427

2011, Jan. 28   **Perf. 13½x14**
866 A427 A multi   .65 .65

No. 866 sold for 24c on day of issue.

Lips
A428

2011, Jan. 28   **Perf. 13¼**
867 A428 B multi   .80 .80

No. 867 sold for 28c on day of issue. Values are for stamp with surrounding selvage.

Dr. Matija Murko (1861-1952), Ethnologist — A429

2011, Jan. 28   **Perf. 14x13¼**
868 A429 41c multi   1.10 1.10

New Year 2011 (Year of the Rabbit) A430

2011, Jan. 28   **Perf. 14x13¼**
869 A430 77c multi   2.10 2.10

Lieutenant General Franc Rozman (Commander Stane) (1911-43) — A431

2011, Jan. 28   **Litho.**
870 A431 92c multi   2.50 2.50

Godlar Stirring Pot, Sencur A432

2011, Jan. 28   **Perf. 13¼x14**
871 A432 €1.33 multi   3.75 3.75

Souvenir Sheet

Maribor Post Office Brass Band, 80th Anniv. — A433

2011, Mar. 25   **Perf. 14**
872 A433 B multi   .90 .90

No. 872 sold for 31c on day of issue.

Easter Egg — A434

Serpentine Die Cut 14x15
2011, Mar. 25   **Self-Adhesive**
873 A434 D multi   1.25 1.25

No. 434 sold for 44c on day of issue.

Church of the Holy Spirit, Javorca A435

2011, Mar. 25   **Perf. 14x13½**
874 A435 44c multi   1.25 1.25

Carthusian Monastery, Bistra A436

2011, Mar. 25   **Litho.**
875 A436 92c multi   2.75 2.75

Treaty of Paris, 60th Anniv. — A437

2011, Mar. 25   **Perf. 13¼x12¾**
876 A437 92c multi   2.75 2.75

Marsh Plants A438

Designs: A, Drosera rotundifolia. B, Oxycoccus palustris. C, Eriophorum vaginatum. 92c, Andromeda polifolia.

2011, Mar. 25   **Perf. 14x13½**
877-879 A438   Set of 3   3.00 3.00

Souvenir Sheet
Perf. 13x13¼
880 A438 92c multi   2.75 2.75

On day of issue, Nos. 877-879 sold for 27c, 31c and 40c, respectively.

Flowers Type of 2007
Designs as before.

Size: 23x30mm

Serpentine Die Cut 14x15
2011, Mar. 31   **Litho.**
Self-Adhesive
881 A304 2c multi   .25 .25
882 A304 5c multi   .25 .25

First Slovenian Motion Picture, 80th Anniv. A439

2011, May 27   **Perf. 14¼x13¾**
883 A439 44c multi   1.25 1.25

Organization for Economic Cooperation and Development, 50th Anniv. — A440

2011, May 27   **Perf. 14x13½**
884 A440 D multi   1.25 1.25

No. 884 sold for 44c on day of issue.

Water Man — A441

2011, May 27   **Perf. 13¼x14**
885 A441 77c multi   2.25 2.25

2011 World Rowing Championships, Bled — A442

2011, May 27   **Perf. 13¾x14¼**
886 A442 92c multi   2.75 2.75

Printed in sheets of 6 + 3 labels.

Postman Pavli — A443

Postman Pavli: A, Riding bicycle. B, Inserting letter into mailbox.

Serpentine Die Cut 14x15

2011, May 27   **Self-Adhesive**
| 887 | A443 | A multi | .80 | .80 |
| 888 | A443 | B multi | .90 | .90 |

On day of issue, No. 887 sold for 27c and No. 888 sold for 31c.
See Nos. 934-935, 971-972.

Europa
A444

Designs: D, Fagus sylvatica. 92c, Tallest pine tree in central Europe.

2011, May 27   **Perf. 13x13¼**
| 889-890 | A444 | Set of 2 | 4.00 | 4.00 |

Intl. Year of Forests. No. 889 sold for 44c on day of issue. Nos. 889-890 each were printed in sheets of 8 + label.

Souvenir Sheet

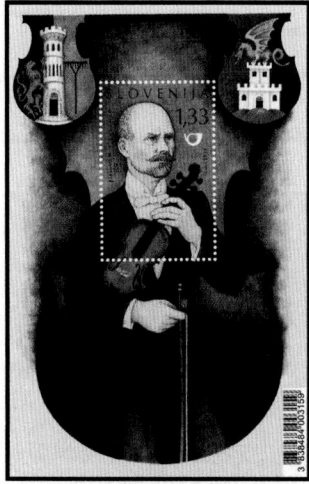

Johann Gerstner (1851-1939), Violinist — A445

Litho. & Engr.

2011, May 27   **Perf. 13¼**
| 891 | A445 | €1.33 multi | 4.00 | 4.00 |

See Czech Republic No. 3501.

Souvenir Sheet

Independence, 20th Anniv. — A446

Litho. & Embossed With Foil Application

2011, June 25   **Perf. 13¼x13¾**
| 892 | A446 | €3.11 multi | 8.75 | 8.75 |

First University Chair for Slovene Studies, Bicent. A447

2011, Sept. 23   **Litho.**   **Perf. 14x13¼**
| 893 | A447 | C multi | 1.10 | 1.10 |

No. 893 sold for 40c on day of issue.

Tomos Colibri T 12 Moped A448

2011, Sept. 23
| 894 | A448 | €1.33 multi | 3.75 | 3.75 |

The Green Veil, by Rihard Jakopic (1896-1943) A449

2011, Sept. 23   **Perf. 13¼x14**
| 895 | A449 | €1.33 multi | 3.75 | 3.75 |

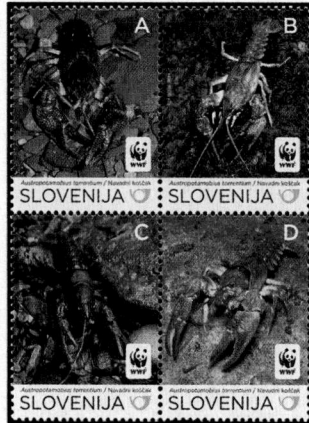

Worldwide Fund for Nature (WWF) — A450

No. 896 — Various depictions of Austropotamobius torrentium: a, A. b, B. c, C. d, D.

2011, Sept. 23   **Perf. 13¼x13**
| 896 | A450 | Block of 4, 3a-d | 4.00 | 4.00 |

On day of issue, Nos. 896a-896d sold for 27c, 31c, 40c and 44c, respectively.

Birds — A451

Designs: A, Numenius arquata. B, Dendrocopos leucotos. C, Emberiza hortulana. 92c, Ciconia ciconia.

2011, Sept. 23   **Perf. 13¼x14**
| 897-899 | A451 | Set of 3 | 2.75 | 2.75 |

Souvenir Sheet
Perf. 13¼x13
| 900 | A451 | 92c multi | 2.50 | 2.50 |

On day of issue, Nos. 897-899 sold for 27c, 31c and 40c, respectively.

MKS-Exclusive Microphone, Designed, by Marko Turk (1920-99) — A452

2011, Nov. 25   **Perf. 14¼x13¾**
| 901 | A452 | 58c multi | 1.60 | 1.60 |

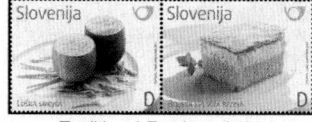

Traditional Foods — A453

No. 902: a, Loska smojka (stuffed turnips). b, Blejska kremna rezina (Bled cream slice).

2011, Nov. 25   **Perf. 14x13¼**
| 902 | A453 | D Horiz. pair, #a-b | 2.40 | 2.40 |

On day of issue Nos. 902a-902b each sold for 44c.

Souvenir Sheet

Secovlje Salina Nature Park — A454

2011, Nov. 25   **Perf. 13x13¼**
| 903 | A454 | 77c multi | 2.10 | 2.10 |

Souvenir Sheet

Bronze Belt Plate With Hunting Motif, 7th-4th Cent. B.C. — A455

2011, Nov. 25   **Litho.**   **Perf. 14**
| 904 | A455 | 92c multi | 2.50 | 2.50 |

Personalized Stamps — A456

Frame designs: Nos. 905-912, Christmas gifts, ornaments, bells, crackers and holly. Nos. 913-920, Holly and ribbon.

Country Name in Red
Horizontal Stamps

Serpentine Die Cut 12x11¾, 11¾x12
2011, Nov. 25   **Self-Adhesive**
905	A456	A multi	.75	.75
906	A456	B multi	.85	.85
907	A456	C multi	1.10	1.10

| 908 | A456 | D multi | 1.25 | 1.25 |
| a. | | Horiz. strip of 4, #905-908 | 4.00 | |

Vertical Stamps
909	A456	A multi	.75	.75
910	A456	B multi	.85	.85
911	A456	C multi	1.10	1.10
912	A456	D multi	1.25	1.25
a.		Vert. strip of 4, #909-912	4.00	

Country Name in Green
Horizontal Stamps
913	A456	A multi	.75	.75
914	A456	B multi	.85	.85
915	A456	C multi	1.10	1.10
916	A456	D multi	1.25	1.25
a.		Horiz. strip of 4, #913-916	4.00	

Vertical Stamps
917	A456	A multi	.75	.75
918	A456	B multi	.85	.85
919	A456	C multi	1.10	1.10
920	A456	D multi	1.25	1.25
a.		Vert. strip of 4, #917-920	4.00	
		Nos. 905-920 (16)	15.80	15.80

On day of issue, stamps inscribed "A" each sold for 27c; stamps inscribed "B" each sold for 31c; stamps inscribed "C" each sold for 40c; and stamps inscribed "D" each sold for 44c. The generic images for each stamp, an example of which is shown, depicts a different work of children's art, with stamps with the same color of country name and orientation issued in sheets of 20 containing five of each stamp. The vignettes of these stamps could be personalized, being printed in sheets of 20 containing the same denomination, frame and orientation.

Christmas Bread — A457

Serpentine Die Cut 14x15

2011, Nov. 25   **Litho.**
Self-Adhesive
| 921 | A457 | A multi | .75 | .75 |
| 922 | A457 | C multi | 1.10 | 1.10 |

Booklet Stamps
Size: 26x35mm
Serpentine Die Cut 12¾
923	A457	A multi	.75	.75
924	A457	C multi	1.10	1.10
a.		Booklet pane of 12, 8 #923, 4 #924	10.50	

Christmas. On day of issue, Nos. 921 and 923 each sold for 27c, and Nos. 922 and 924 each sold for 40c.

Four-leaf Clover — A458

Serpentine Die Cut 14x15

2011, Nov. 25   **Self-Adhesive**
| 925 | A458 | A multi | .75 | .75 |
| 926 | A458 | C multi | 1.10 | 1.10 |

Booklet Stamps
Size: 26x35mm
Serpentine Die Cut 12¾
927	A458	A multi	.75	.75
928	A458	C multi	1.10	1.10
a.		Booklet pane of 12, 8 #927, 4 #928	10.50	

New Year 2012. On day of issue, Nos. 925 and 927 each sold for 27c, and Nos. 926 and 928 each sold for 40c.

Traditional Clothing From Bohinj A459

2012, Jan. 27   **Perf. 11¾x11¼**
929 A459 27c multi   .70 .70

Heart Carved in Tree A460

2012, Jan. 27   **Perf. 13x13¼**
930 A460 31c multi   .85 .85
Values are for stamps with surrounding selvage.

New Year 2012 (Year of the Dragon) A461

2012, Jan. 27   **Perf. 14¼x13¾**
931 A461 92c multi   2.50 2.50

Mira Mihelic (1912-85), Writer — A462

2012, Jan. 27   **Perf. 13¾x14¼**
932 A462 €1.25 multi   3.25 3.25

Souvenir Sheet

Enclosure of Ljubljana Inside Barbed Wire Fence, 70th Anniv. — A463

2012, Jan. 27   **Perf. 14¼x13¾**
933 A463 €1.33 multi   3.50 3.50

Postman Pavli Type of 2011
Postman Pavli: C, With children at school. D, With dog and bicycle.

Serpentine Die Cut 14x15
2012, Mar. 30   **Self-Adhesive**
934 A443 C multi   1.10 1.10

---

935 A443 D multi   1.25 1.25
On day of issue, No. 934 sold for 40c and No. 935 sold for 44c.

Heart-shaped Honey Biscuit — A464

2012, Mar. 30   **Litho.**
Self-Adhesive
936 A464 A multi   .75 .75
No. 936 sold for 27c on day of issue.

Valleys, Solcavsko District A465

2012, Mar. 30   **Perf. 14¼x13¾**
937 A465 €1.25 multi   3.50 3.50

Sts. Peter and Paul Minorite Monastery, Ptuj — A466

2012, Mar. 30
938 A466 €1.33 multi   3.50 3.50

Europa A467

Abstract design with: 44c, Spiral. 92c, Atomic orbits.
2012, Mar. 30   **Perf. 11¾x11¼**
939-940 A467   Set of 2   3.75 3.75
Maribor, 2012 European Capital of Culture. Nos. 939-940 each were printed in sheets of 8 + label.

Flowers in Ljubljana Botanical Gardens A468

Designs: 40c, Pastinaca sativa var. fleischmanni. 44c, Primula x venusta. 77c, Scabiosa hladnikiana. 92c, Scopolia carniolica f. hladnikiana.
2012, Mar. 30   **Perf. 14¼x13¾**
941-943 A468   Set of 3   4.25 4.25
Souvenir Sheet
944 A468 92c multi   2.50 2.50

2012 Summer Olympics, London — A469

No. 945: a, 77c, Judo, sailing. b, 92c, Swimming, handball.
2012, May 25 Litho.   Perf. 14¼x13¾
945 A469   Horiz. pair, #a-b   4.25 4.25

Souvenir Sheet

Maribofila 2012 Philatelic Exhibition, Maribor — A470

2012, May 25
946 A470 D multi   1.10 1.10
No. 946 sold for 44c on day of issue.

Souvenir Sheet

Goricko Regional Park — A471

2012, May 25
947 A471 €1.25 multi   3.25 3.25

Souvenir Sheet

Smokehouses and Pottery — A472

No. 948: a, Felsoszölnök, Hungary smokehouse at left, pitcher, two lidded jars. b, Filovci, Slovenia smokehouse at right, jug, colander.
2012, May 25   **Perf. 14x13¼**
948 A472 92c Sheet of 2, #a-b   4.75 4.75
See Hungary No. 4244.

Urska Zolnir, Judo Gold Medalist in 2012 Summer Olympics, London A473

Perf. 14¼x13¾
2012, Sept. 28   **Litho.**
949 A473 92c multi   2.40 2.40

Lacemaker, by Veno Pilon (1896-1970) A474

2012, Sept. 28   **Perf. 11¾x11¼**
950 A474 €1.33 multi   3.50 3.50

Bees A475

Designs: 40c, Bombus lapidarius. 44c, Bombus pascuorum. 77c, Bombus humilis. 92c, Bombus lucorum.
2012, Sept. 28   **Perf. 14¼x13¾**
951-953 A475   Set of 3   4.25 4.25
Souvenir Sheet
954 A475 92c multi   2.40 2.40

Souvenir Sheet

World Youth Chess Championships, Maribor — A476

2012, Sept. 28   **Perf. 13¾x14¼**
955 A476 €1.33 multi   3.50 3.50

Premiere of Film *The Slopes of Triglav*, 80th Anniv. — A477

2012, Nov. 23
956 A477 58c multi   1.50 1.50

ETA 80 Telephone, Designed by Davorin Savnik A478

2012, Nov. 23   **Perf. 14¼x13¾**
957 A478 58c multi   1.50 1.50

Traditional Foods — A479

No. 958: a, Carniolan sausage, roll and mustard (Kranjska klobasa). b, Sauteed potatoes (Prazen komprir).

2012, Nov. 23   **Perf. 11½x11¾**
958 A479 77c Horiz. pair, #a-b   4.00 4.00

Angel
A480

Creche
Figures
A481

Serpentine Die Cut 14x15
2012, Nov. 23   **Litho.**
   Self-Adhesive
959 A480 A multi   .70 .70
960 A481 C multi   1.10 1.10
   Booklet Stamps
   Size: 26x35mm
Serpentine Die Cut 12¾
961 A480 A multi   .70 .70
  a.   Booklet pane of 12   8.50
962 A481 C multi   1.10 1.10
  a.   Booklet pane of 12   13.50

Christmas. On day of issue, Nos. 959 and 961 each sold for 27c, and Nos. 960 and 962 each sold for 40c.

Fairy — A482    Pig — A483

Serpentine Die Cut 14x15
2012, Nov. 23   **Litho.**
   Self-Adhesive
963 A482 A multi   .70 .70
964 A483 C multi   1.10 1.10
   Booklet Stamps
   Size: 26x35mm
Serpentine Die Cut 12¾
965 A482 A multi   .70 .70
  a.   Booklet pane of 12   8.50
966 A483 C multi   1.10 1.10
  a.   Booklet pane of 12   13.50

New Year 2013. On day of issue, Nos. 963 and 965 each sold for 27c, and Nos. 964 and 966 each sold for 40c.

Traditional
Clothing
From
Ljubljana
A484

2013, Jan. 25   **Perf. 11¾x11¼**
967 A484 27c multi   .75 .75

Heart-shaped Lock — A485

2013, Jan. 25   **Perf. 13¼**
968 A485 31c multi   .85 .85
  Values are for stamps with surrounding selvage.

New Year
2013 (Year of
the Snake)
A486

2013, Jan. 25   **Litho.**
969 A486 92c multi   2.50 2.50

Fran Miklosic
(1813-91),
Linguist
A487

2013, Jan. 25
970 A487 €1.33 multi   3.75 3.75

Postman Pavli Type of 2011

Postman Pavli and dog with: A, Posthorn, flowers, horiz. B, Watermelon slice, horiz.

Serpentine Die Cut 11½
2013, Mar. 22
   Self-Adhesive
971 A443 A multi   .70 .70
972 A443 B multi   .80 .80
  On day of issue, No. 971 sold for 27c and No. 972 sold for 31c.

Clay Anthropomorphic
Vessel, 3000
B.C. — A488

2013, Mar. 22   **Litho.**
   Self-Adhesive
973 A488 D multi   1.75 1.75
  No. 973 sold for 64c on day of issue.

Kolpa Valley
A489

2013, Mar. 22   **Perf. 13¼**
974 A489 €1.25 multi   3.25 3.25

Capuchin
Monastery,
Vipavski
Kriz — A490

2013, Mar. 22
975 A490 €1.33 multi   3.50 3.50

Europa
A491

Postal vehicles: 64c, Krpan bicycle. 92c, Diligence mail coach, 18th cent.

2013, Mar. 22   **Perf. 11¾x11½**
976-977 A491   Set of 2   4.00 4.00

Fruit — A492

Designs: 60c, Ziziphus jujuba. 64c, Ficus carica. 92c, Eriobotrya japonica. 97c, Sorbus domestica.

2013, Mar. 22   **Perf. 13¼**
978-980 A492   Set of 3   5.50 5.50
   Souvenir Sheet
981 A492 97c multi   2.50 2.50

   Souvenir Sheet

Underground Post Office in Postojna
Cave — A493

2013, Mar. 22   **Perf. 14x13¼**
982 A493 64c multi   1.75 1.75
  See Austria No. 2431.

   Souvenir Sheet

Tolmin Peasant Rebellion, 300th
Anniv. — A494

2013, Mar. 22   **Perf. 13¼**
983 A494 €2.18 multi   5.75 5.75

2013 European Basketball
Championships, Slovenia — A495

2013, May 24   **Perf. 14¼x13¾**
984 A495 €1.33 multi   3.75 3.75
  No. 984 was printed in sheets of 6 + 3 labels.

Bridges — A496

Designs: 27c, Old Bridge, Maribor. 31c, Rail Bridges, Zidani Most. 60c, Triple Bridge, Ljubljana. 64c, Kandija Bridge, Novo Mesto. 97c, Soca River Bridge, Kanal.

2013, May 24   **Perf. 14¼**
985-989 A496   Set of 5   7.50 7.50

Personalized Stamps — A497

Serpentine Die Cut 12x11¾, 11¾x12
2013, May 24   **Self-Adhesive**
Animal Tracks in Upper Left Corner
   Horizontal Stamps
990 A497 A brown   .75 .75
991 A497 B brown   .85 .85
992 A497 C brown   1.60 1.60
993 A497 D brown   1.75 1.75
  a.   Horiz. strip of 4, #990-993   5.00
   Vertical Stamps
994 A497 A brown   .75 .75
995 A497 B brown   .85 .85
996 A497 C brown   1.60 1.60
997 A497 D brown   1.75 1.75
  a.   Vert. strip of 4, #994-997   5.00
Various Pets in Upper Left Corner
   Horizontal Stamps
998 A497 A gray   .75 .75
999 A497 B gray   .85 .85
1000 A497 C gray   1.60 1.60
1001 A497 D gray   1.75 1.75
  a.   Horiz. strip of 4, #998-1001   5.00
   Vertical Stamps
1002 A497 A gray   .75 .75
1003 A497 B gray   .85 .85
1004 A497 C gray   1.60 1.60
1005 A497 D gray   1.75 1.75
  a.   Vert. strip of 4, #1002-1005   5.00
   Nos. 990-1005 (16)   19.80 19.80

On day of issue, stamps inscribed "A" each sold for 27c; stamps inscribed "B" each sold for 31c; stamps inscribed "C" each sold for 60c; and stamps inscribed "D" each sold for 64c, The generic images for each stamp, an example of which is shown, depicts a different pet, with stamps with the same frame color and orientation issued in sheets of 20 containing five of each stamp. The vignettes of these stamps could be personalized, being printed in sheets of 20 containing the same denomination, frame and orientation.

Marine Life
A498

Designs: 60c, Chromis chromis. 64c, Sepia officinalis. 92c, Caretta caretta. 97c, Liza aurata.

Litho. & Thermography
2013, Sept. 27   *Perf. 13x13¼*
1006-1008 A498   Set of 3   6.00 6.00
Souvenir Sheet
1009 A498 97c multi   2.75 2.75

Sea salt was added to the thermographic portions on Nos. 1006-1009, producing a rough texture.

Souvenir Sheet

Kozjansko Apple Tree in Kozjansko Regional Park — A499

Perf. 13¼x13½
2013, Sept. 27   Litho.
1010 A499 €1.25 multi   3.50 3.50

K67 Kiosks
A500

Perf. 14¼x13¾
2013, Nov. 22   Litho.
1011 A500 92c multi   2.60 2.60

Premiere of First Slovene Film *Vesna*, 60th Anniv. A501

2013, Nov. 22   Litho.   *Perf. 14x13¾*
1012 A501 97c multi   2.75 2.75

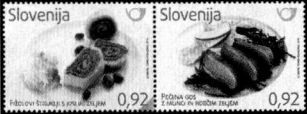

Traditional Foods — A502

No. 1013: a, Fizolovi struklji s kislim zeljem (bean roll with sauerkraut). b, Pecena gos z mlinci in rdecim zeljem (roast goose with bread and red cabbage).

Perf. 11½x11¾
2013, Nov. 22   Litho.
1013 A502 92c Horiz. pair, #a-b   5.25 5.25

Christmas
A503   A504
Serpentine Die Cut 11¼x11½
2013, Nov. 22   Litho.
Self-Adhesive
1014 A503 A multi   .80 .80
1015 A504 C multi   1.75 1.75

Booklet Stamps
Self-Adhesive
Size: 26x35mm
Serpentine Die Cut 12½x12¾
1016 A503 A multi   .80 .80
   a. Booklet pane of 12   9.75
1017 A504 C multi   1.75 1.75
   a. Booklet pane of 12   21.00

On day of issue, Nos. 1014, 1016 each sold for 29c, Nos. 1015, 1017 each sold for 60c.

New Year's Day 2014
A505   A506
Serpentine Die Cut 11¼x11½   Litho.
2013, Nov. 22
Self-Adhesive
1018 A505 A multi   .80 .80
1019 A506 C multi   1.75 1.75

Booklet Stamps
Self-Adhesive
Size: 26x35mm
Serpentine Die Cut 12½x12¾
1020 A505 A multi   .80 .80
   a. Booklet pane of 12   9.75
1021 A506 C multi   1.75 1.75
   a. Booklet pane of 12   21.00

On day of issue, Nos. 1018, 1020 each sold for 29c and Nos. 1019, 1021 each sold for 60c.

Mehdi Huseynzade (1918-44), Soldier — A507

2013, Dec. 12   Litho.   *Perf. 13¼*
1022 A507 97c multi   2.75 2.75
See Azerbaijan No. 1042.

Traditional Clothing From Trieste Area — A508

2014, Jan. 31   Litho.   *Perf. 11¾x11¼*
1023 A508 29c multi   .80 .80

Silver Ring
A509
2014, Jan. 31   Litho.   *Perf. 13¼*
1024 A509 33c multi   .90 .90
Values are for stamps with surrounding selvage.

New Year 2014 (Year of the Horse) — A510

2014, Jan. 31   Litho.   *Perf. 13¼*
1025 A510 92c multi   2.50 2.50

Rado Simoniti (1914-81), Composer A511

2014, Jan. 31   Litho.   *Perf. 13¼*
1026 A511 €1.33 multi   3.75 3.75

2014 Winter Olympics, Sochi, Russia A512

No. 1027: a, 64c, Ski jumping. b, 97c, Ice hockey.

2014, Jan. 31   Litho.   *Perf. 12*
1027 A512   Vert. pair, #a-b, + central label   4.50 4.50

Souvenir Sheet

Enthronement of Duke Ernst the Iron (1377-1422), 600th Anniv. — A513

2014, Jan. 31   Litho.   *Perf. 13¼*
1028 A513 €1.25 multi   3.50 3.50

Mortar and Pestle — A514

Serpentine Die Cut 11½
2014, Mar. 28   Litho.
Self-Adhesive
1029 A514 B multi   .90 .90
No. 1029 sold for 33c on day of issue.

Easter Eggs — A515

The Crucified, Painting by Tone Kralj — A516

Serpentine Die Cut 11½x11
2014, Mar. 28   Litho.
Self-Adhesive
1030 A515 A multi   .80 .80
1031 A516 C multi   1.75 1.75
Easter. On day of issue, No. 1030 sold for 29c and No. 1031 sold for 60c.

Idrija Tourism — A517

2014, Mar. 28   Litho.   *Perf. 13¼*
1032 A517 €1.25 multi   3.50 3.50

Carthusian Monastery, Pleterje A518

2014, Mar. 28   Litho.   *Perf. 13¼*
1033 A518 €1.33 multi   3.75 3.75

Old Grapevines A519

Grapevine in: 60c, Sepulje. 64c, Merce. 92c, Brje pri Komnu.
97c, Grapevine in Maribor, horiz.

2014, Mar. 28   Litho.   *Perf. 13¼*
1034-1036 A519   Set of 3   6.00 6.00
Souvenir Sheet
1037 A519 97c multi   2.75 2.75

Rescue of Allied Airmen, 70th Anniv. A520

2014, May 30   Litho.   *Perf. 13¼*
1038 A520 60c multi   1.60 1.60

Scouting
A521

2014, May 30   Litho.   Perf. 12
1039 A521 77c multi   2.10 2.10

40th World Scout Conference, Ljubljana, 12th World Scout Youth Forum, Ragla. No. 1039 was printed in sheets of 6 + 3 labels.

Tina Maze, Two-time Gold Medalist in Skiing at 2014 Winter Olympics, Sochi, Russia — A522

2014, May 30   Litho.   Perf. 13¼
1040 A522 €1.33 multi   3.75 3.75

Europa
A523

Musical instruments: 64c, Haloze flutes. 97c, Rattles.

2014, May 30   Litho.   Perf. 13¼
1041-1042 A523   Set of 2   4.50 4.50

Birds — A524

Designs: A, Hirundo rupestris. B, Mergus merganser. 36c, Botaurus stellaris. C, Falco naumanni. D, Strix uralensis.

Serpentine Die Cut 11¼x11½
2014, May 30   Litho.
Self-Adhesive
1043 A524   A multi   .80 .80
1044 A524   B multi   .90 .90
1045 A524   36c multi   1.00 1.00
1046 A524   C multi   1.60 1.60
1047 A524   D multi   1.75 1.75
    Nos. 1043-1047 (5)   6.05 6.05

On day of issue, No. 1043 sold for 29c; No. 1044, 33c; No. 1046, 60c; No. 1047, 64c.

Souvenir Sheet

Kolpa Nature Park — A525

2014, May 30   Litho.   Perf. 13¼
1048 A525 €1.25 multi   3.50 3.50

Souvenir Sheet

Cargo Ship Martin Krpan — A526

2014, May 30   Litho.   Perf. 13¼
1049 A526 €1.33 multi   3.75 3.75

Souvenir Sheet

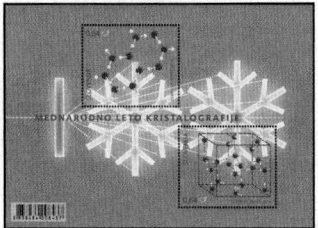

International Year of Crystallography — A527

No. 1050 — Snowflake and molecular diagrams for ice with: a, 10 red atoms. b, 20 red atoms in cube.

2014, May 30   Litho.   Perf. 14x13¼
1050 A527 64c Sheet of 2, #a-b   3.50 3.50
    See Belgium No. 2702.

Euromed Postal Emblem and Mediterranean Area — A528

2014, July 9   Litho.   Perf. 13¼
1051 A528 64c multi   1.75 1.75

Coat of Arms of the Nobility — A529

Arms of the House of: 34c, Attems. 40c, Lamberg. 46c, Auersperg. 58c, Herberstein. 60c, Thurn-Valsassina.

Perf. 12¾x13¼
2014, Sept. 26   Litho.
1052-1056 A529   Set of 5   6.00 6.00

Bats — A530

Designs: 60c, Myotis bechsteinii. 64c, Rhinolophus hipposideros. 92c, Pipistrellus kuhlii. 97c, Miniopterus schreibersii.

2014, Sept. 26   Litho.   Perf. 13¼
1057-1059 A530   Set of 3   5.50 5.50
Souvenir Sheet
1060 A530 97c multi   2.50 2.50

Souvenir Sheet

Coronation of Barbara of Cilli, 600th Anniv. — A531

2014, Sept. 26   Litho.   Perf. 13¼
1061 A531 €2.25 multi   5.75 5.75

Personalized Stamps — A532

Serpentine Die Cut 12x11¾, 11¾x12
2014, Nov. 28   Litho.
Self-Adhesive
Lace in Upper Right and Lower Left Corners
Horizontal Stamps
1062 A532   A multi   .85 .85
1063 A532   B multi   1.00 1.00
1064 A532   C multi   1.50 1.50
1065 A532   D multi   1.60 1.60
  a.   Horiz. strip of 4, #1062-1065   5.00

Vertical Stamps
1066 A532   A multi   .85 .85
1067 A532   B multi   1.00 1.00
1068 A532   C multi   1.50 1.50
1069 A532   D multi   1.60 1.60
  a.   Vert. strip of 4, #1066-1069   5.00

With Green Flowers at Top, Bottom and Right
Horizontal Stamps
1070 A532   A multi   .85 .85
1071 A532   B multi   1.00 1.00
1072 A532   C multi   1.50 1.50
1073 A532   D multi   1.60 1.60
  a.   Horiz. strip of 4, #1070-1073   5.00

Vertical Stamps
1074 A532   A multi   .85 .85
1075 A532   B multi   1.00 1.00
1076 A532   C multi   1.50 1.50
1077 A532   D multi   1.60 1.60
  a.   Vert. strip of 4, #1074-1077   5.00

With Blue Nautilus Shells in Top Left and Bottom Right Corners
Horizontal Stamps
1078 A532   A multi   .85 .85
1079 A532   B multi   1.00 1.00
1080 A532   C multi   1.50 1.50
1081 A532   D multi   1.60 1.60
  a.   Horiz. strip of 4, #1078-1081   5.00

Vertical Stamps
1082 A532   A multi   .85 .85
1083 A532   B multi   1.00 1.00
1084 A532   C multi   1.50 1.50
1085 A532   D multi   1.60 1.60
  a.   Vert. strip of 4, #1082-1085   5.00

With Brown and Yellow Brown Leaves At Top and Sides
Horizontal Stamps
1086 A532   A multi   .85 .85
1087 A532   B multi   1.00 1.00
1088 A532   C multi   1.50 1.50

1089 A532   D multi   1.60 1.60
  a.   Horiz. strip of 4, #1086-1089   5.00

Vertical Stamps
1090 A532   A multi   .85 .85
1091 A532   B multi   1.00 1.00
1092 A532   C multi   1.50 1.50
1093 A532   D multi   1.60 1.60
  a.   Vert. strip of 4, #1090-1093   5.00
    Nos. 1062-1093 (32)   39.60 39.60

On day of issue, stamps inscribed "A" each sold for 34c; stamps inscribed "B" each sold for 40c; stamps inscribed "C" each sold for 60c; and stamps inscribed "D" each sold for 64c. Each stamp was printed in sheets of 20 in which vignettes could be personalized. The generic images for each stamp, an example of which is shown, depicts a different picture of winter scenes on Nos. 1062-1069, a different picture of flowers on Nos. 1070-1077, a different picture of seashore scenes on Nos. 1078-1085, and a different picture of autumnal scenes on Nos. 1086-1093.

Monument to Unknown Soldiers, Ljubljana — A533

2014, Nov. 28   Litho.   Perf. 13¼
1094 A533 40c multi   1.00 1.00

World War I, cent.

Tomos 4 Outboard Motor
A534

2014, Nov. 28   Litho.   Perf. 13¼
1095 A534 58c multi   1.50 1.50

Scene From Film *Don't Cry, Peter* — A535

2014, Nov. 28   Litho.   Perf. 13¼
1096 A535 92c multi   2.25 2.25

Children's Art — A536

No. 1097: a, 34c, Indian family and house, by Roshan V. Anvekar, India. b, 60c, Dancers, by Sara Zivkovic, Slovenia.

Perf. 11¼x11¾
2014, Nov. 28   Litho.
1097 A536   Horiz. pair, #a-b   2.40 2.40
    See India Nos. 2706-2707.

Traditional Foods — A537

No. 1098: a, Fizolova minestra (minestrone soup). b, Vipavski struklji (sweet dumpling rolls).

Perf. 11¼x11¾
2014, Nov. 28   Litho.
1098 A537 77c Horiz. pair, #a-b   4.00 4.00

Christmas
A538   A539

Serpentine Die Cut 11¼x11½
2014, Nov. 28   **Litho.**
Self-Adhesive
1099 A538 B multi   1.00 1.00
1100 A539 C multi   1.50 1.50

Booklet Stamps
Self-Adhesive
Size: 26x35mm
Serpentine Die Cut 12½x12¼
1101 A538 B multi   1.00 1.00
 a.   Booklet pane of 12   12.00
1102 A539 C multi   1.50 1.50
 a.   Booklet pane of 12   18.00

On day of issue, Nos. 1099 and 1101 each sold for 40c; Nos. 1100 and 1102 each sold for 60c.

New Year's Day 2015
A540   A541

Serpentine Die Cut 11¼x11½
2014, Nov. 28   **Litho.**
Self-Adhesive
1103 A540 A multi   .85 .85
1104 A541 C multi   1.50 1.50

Booklet Stamps
Self-Adhesive
Size: 26x35mm
Serpentine Die Cut 12½x12¼
1105 A540 A multi   .85 .85
 a.   Booklet pane of 12   10.50
1106 A541 C multi   1.50 1.50
 a.   Booklet pane of 12   18.00

On day of issue, Nos. 1103 and 1105 each sold for 34c; Nos. 1104 and 1106 each sold for 60c.

Traditional Clothing From Prem and the Cicarija Plateau
A542

2015, Jan. 30 Litho. *Perf. 11¾x11¼*
1107 A542 34c multi   .80 .80

Marriage Spoons on Chain
A543

2015, Jan. 30 Litho. *Perf. 13¼*
1108 A543 40c multi   .90 .90

Values are for stamps with surrounding selvage.

New Year 2015 (Year of the Goat)
A544

2015, Jan. 30   **Litho.**   ***Perf. 13¼***
1109 A544 92c multi   2.10 2.10

Max Fabiani (1865-1962), Architect
A545

2015, Jan. 30   **Litho.**   ***Perf. 13¼***
1110 A545 €1.25 multi   3.00 3.00

Balthazar Hacquet (c. 1739-1815), Scientist — A546

2015, Jan. 30   **Litho.**   ***Perf. 13¼***
1111 A546 €1.33 multi   3.00 3.00

Souvenir Sheet

Slovenia Post, 20th Anniv. — A547

2015, Jan. 30   **Litho.**   ***Perf. 13¼***
1112 A547 €2.25 multi   5.25 5.25

Lasko
A548

2015, Mar. 27   **Litho.**   ***Perf. 13¼***
1113 A548 €1.25 multi   2.75 2.75

Cistercian Abbey, Sticna
A549

2015, Mar. 27   **Litho.**   ***Perf. 13¼***
1114 A549 €1.33 multi   3.00 3.00

Orchids
A550

Designs: 60c, Orchis pallens. 64c, Orchis simla. 92c, Orchis ustulata. 97c, Orchis purpurea.

2015, Mar. 27   **Litho.**   ***Perf. 13¼***
1115-1117 A550 Set of 3   4.75 4.75
Souvenir Sheet
1118 A550 97c multi   2.25 2.25

Birds and Letters — A551

Designs: 1c, Podiceps cristatus and "P." 2c, Columba oenas and "O." 5c, Ciconia nigra and "S." 10c, Charadrius alexandrinus and "T." 20c, Montifringilla nivalis and "A."

Serpentine Die Cut 14¾x14
2015, May 29   **Litho.**
Self-Adhesive
1119 A551 1c multi   .25 .25
1120 A551 2c multi   .25 .25
1121 A551 5c multi   .25 .25
1122 A551 10c multi   .25 .25
1123 A551 20c multi   .45 .45
       Nos. 1119-1123 (5)   1.45 1.45

Postcrossing
A552

2015, May 29   **Litho.**   ***Perf. 13¼***
1124 A552 60c multi   1.40 1.40

World Track and Field Championships, Beijing — A553

2015, May 29   **Litho.**   ***Perf. 12***
1125 A553 €1.33 multi   3.00 3.00

No. 1125 was printed in sheets of 6 + 3 labels.

Europa — A554

Designs: 64c, Rocking horse. 97c, Wind-up car.

2015, May 29   **Litho.**   ***Perf. 13¼***
1126-1127 A554 Set of 2   3.50 3.50

Nos. 1126-1127 each were printed in sheets of 8 + central label.

Mountain Huts — A555

Designs: 34c, Oroznova Koca. 40c, Aljazev Dom. 60c, Presernova Koca. 64c, Ceska Koca. 97c, Ruska Koca.

2015, May 29 Litho. *Perf. 12¾x13¼*
1128-1132 A555 Set of 5   6.50 6.50

Souvenir Sheet

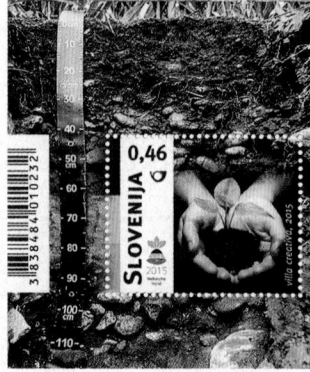

Intl. Year of Soils — A556

2015, May 29   **Litho.**   ***Perf. 13¼***
1133 A556 46c multi   1.00 1.00

Souvenir Sheet

Cargo Steamer Rog — A557

2015, May 29   **Litho.**   ***Perf. 13¼***
1134 A557 €1.33 multi   3.00 3.00

POSTAL TAX STAMPS

Catalogue values for unused stamps in this section are for Never Hinged items.

Red Cross — PT1

1992, May 8   **Litho.**   ***Perf. 14***
RA1 PT1 3t blue, black & red   1.00 1.00

PT2

1992, June 2   ***Perf. 14½x14***
RA2 PT2 3t multicolored   .60 .60

Red Cross, Solidarity.

PT3

1992, Sept. 14   Litho.   *Perf. 14*
RA3 PT3 3t multicolored   .50 .50
Stop Smoking Week, Sept. 14-21.

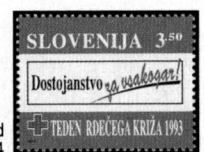

Red
Cross — PT4

1993, May 8   Litho.   *Perf. 14*
RA4 PT4 3.50t blue, black & red   .50 .50

Rescue
Team — PT5

1993, June 1
RA5 PT5 3.50t multicolored   .40 .40

Anti-Smoking
Campaign
PT6

1993, Sept. 14   Litho.   *Perf. 14*
RA6 PT6 4.50t multicolored   .40 .40

PT7

1994, May 8   Litho.   *Perf. 14*
RA7 PT7 4.50t multicolored   .40 .40
Obligatory on mail May 8-15.

Red Cross
Worker,
Child — PT8

1994, June 1
RA8 PT8 4.50t multicolored   .40 .40
Obligatory on mail June 1-7.

PT9

1995, May 8   Litho.   *Perf. 14*
RA9 PT9 6.50t multicolored   .50 .50
Obligatory on mail May 8-15.

Red Cross,
Solidarity
PT10

1995, June 1   Litho.   *Perf. 14*
RA10 PT10 6.50t multicolored   .50 .50
Obligatory on mail June 1-7.

Red Cross,
Solidarity — PT11

1996, May 8   Litho.   *Perf. 14*
RA11 PT11 7t multicolored   .45 .45
Obligatory on mail May 8-15.

Red Cross,
Solidarity
PT12

1996, June 1   Litho.   *Perf. 14*
RA12 PT12 7t multicolored   .45 .45
Obligatory on mail June 1-7.

Red Cross,
Solidarity
PT13

1997, May 8   Litho.   *Perf. 14*
RA13 PT13 7t multicolored   .45 .45
Obligatory on mail May 8-14.

Red Cross,
Solidarity
PT14

1997, June 1   Litho.   *Perf. 14*
RA14 PT14 7t multicolored   .45 .45
Obligatory on mail June 1-7.

PT15

1998, May 8   Litho.   *Perf. 14*
RA15 PT15 7t black & red   .50 .50
Obligatory on mail May 8-14.

Red Cross, Solidarity — PT16

Design: No. RA16a, "7" at lower left. No. RA16b, "7" at upper right.

1998, June 1
RA16 PT16 7t Pair, #a.-b.   .65 .65
Obligatory on mail June 1-7.
See also Nos. RA18, RA20.

Red
Cross — PT17

1999, May 8   Litho.   *Perf. 14*
RA17 PT17 8t black & red   .50 .50
Obligatory on mail May 8-15.

Solidarity Type of 1998

a, 9t at LL. b, 9t at UR.

1999, Nov. 1   Litho.   *Perf. 14*
RA18 PT16 9t Pair, #a.-b.   .65 .65
Obligatory on mail Nov. 1-7.

Red
Cross — PT19

2000, May 8   Litho.   *Perf. 14*
RA19 PT19 10t blk & red   .70 .70
Obligatory on mail May 8-15.

Red Cross Solidarity Type of 1998

No. RA20: a, 10 at LL. b, 10 at UR.

2000, Nov. 1   Litho.   *Perf. 14*
RA20 PT16 10t Horiz. pair, #a-b   2.40 2.40
Obligatory on mail Nov. 1-7.

Red
Cross — PT20

2001, May 8
RA21 PT20 12t multi   .75 .75
Obligatory on mail May 8-15.

Red Cross
Solidarity
Week — PT21

2001, Nov. 1   Litho.   *Perf. 14*
RA22 PT21 13t multi   .75 .75
Obligatory on mail Nov. 1-7.

Red Cross
Week — PT22

2002, May 8
RA23 PT22 15t multi   1.10 1.10
Obligatory on mail May 8-15.

Red Cross
Solidarity
Week — PT23

2002, Nov. 1
RA24 PT23 15t multi   1.10 1.10
Obligatory on mail Nov. 1-7.

Red Cross
Week — PT24

2003, May 8   *Perf. 14*
RA25 PT24 19t multi   .75 .75

Self-Adhesive
Imperf

RA25A PT24 19t multi   .75 .75
Obligatory on mail May 8-15.

Red Cross Solidarity
Week — PT25

2003, Nov. 1   Litho.   *Perf. 14*
RA26 PT25 19t multi   .50 .50

Imperf
Self-Adhesive

RA26A PT25 19t multi   .50 .50
Obligatory on mail Nov. 1-7.

Red Cross — PT26

No. RA27: a, Blood droplet. b, Girl. c, Injured boy. d, Old woman.

2004, May 8   Litho.   *Perf. 14*
RA27 PT26 19t Block of 4, #a-d   2.25 2.25
Obligatory on mail May 8-15.

Red Cross Solidarity Week — PT27

No. RA28: a, Airplane dropping aid packages. b, House on fire. c, Aid packages landing on ground. d, Damaged building.

2004, Nov. 1   Litho.   *Perf. 14*
RA28 PT27 23t Block of 4, #a-d   2.25 2.25
Obligatory on mail Nov. 1-7.

Red Cross
Week — PT28

2005, May 8　　Litho.　　Perf. 14
RA29 PT28 25t black & red　　　.75　.75
Obligatory on mail May 8-15.

Red Cross Solidarity — PT29

No. RA30: a, House in flood. b, Flood
gauge.

2005, Nov. 1　　Litho.　　Perf. 14
RA30 PT29 25t Horiz. pair, #a-b　.85　.85
Obligatory on mail Nov. 1-7.

Red Cross
Week — PT30

2006, May 8　　Litho.　　Perf. 14
RA31 PT30 25t multi　　　　　.60　.60
Obligatory on mail May 8-15.

Fire Protection
Week — PT31

2006, Oct. 9
RA32 PT31 25t multi　　　　.70　.70
Obligatory on mail Oct. 9-14.

Red Cross Solidarity
Week — PT32

2006, Nov. 1
RA33 PT32 25t multi　　　　.60　.60
Obligatory on mail Nov. 1-7.

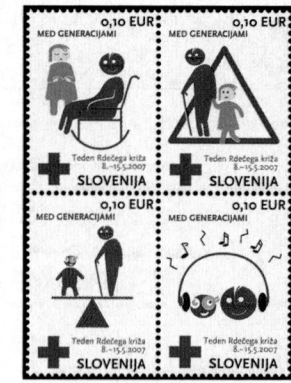

Red Cross Week — PT33

No. RA34: a, Woman, man in rocking chair.
b, Man with cane, child, large triangle. c, Child
and man with cane on seesaw. d, Man and
child with earphones.

2007, May 8　　Litho.　　Perf. 14
RA34 PT33 10c Block of 4, #a-d　1.50 1.50
Obligatory on mail May 8-15.

Fire Protection
Week — PT34

2007, Oct. 8　　Litho.　　Perf. 14
RA35 PT34 11c multi　　　　　1.50 1.50
Obligatory on mail Oct. 8-13.

Red Cross Solidarity Week — PT35

No. RA36 — Circle in upper left in: a, Green.
b, Yellow orange. c, Pink. d, Blue.

2007, Nov. 1
RA36 PT35 10c Block of 4, #a-d　1.50 1.50
Obligatory on mail Nov. 1-7.

Red Cross Week — PT36

No. RA37: a, Girl in water, fish. b, Boy in
water, ship.

2008, May 8　　Litho.　　Perf. 14
RA37 PT36 10c Horiz. pair, #a-b　.65　.65
Obligatory on mail May 8-15.

Fire Prevention
Week — PT37

2008, Oct. 6
RA38 PT37 12c multi　　　　　.35　.35
Obligatory on mail Oct. 6-11.

Red Cross
Solidarity
Week — PT38

2008, Nov. 1　　Litho.　　Perf. 14
RA39 PT38 12c multi　　　　　.30　.30
Obligatory on mail Nov. 1-7.

Battle of
Solferino,
150th
Anniv. — PT39

2009, May 8
RA40 PT39 13c multi　　　　　.40　.40
Red Cross Week. Obligatory on mail May 8-
15.

Fire Prevention
Week — PT40

2009, Oct. 5
RA41 PT40 14c multi　　　　　.45　.45
Obligatory on mail Oct. 5-10.

Red Cross
Solidarity
Week — PT41

2009, Nov. 1
RA42 PT41 13c multi　　　　　.40　.40
Obligatory on mail Nov. 1-7.

Red Cross
Week — PT42

2010, May 8　　　　　　Perf. 14
RA43 PT42 13c multi　　　　　.35　.35
Obligatory on mail May 8-15.

Fire Prevention
Week — PT43

2010, Oct. 4
RA44 PT43 14c multi　　　　　.40　.40
Obligatory on mail Oct. 4-9.

Henri Dunant (1828-
1910), Founder of
the Red
Cross — PT44

2010, Nov. 1
RA45 PT44 13c multi　　　　　.40　.40
Obligatory on mail Nov. 1-7.

Red Cross
Week
PT45

2011, May 8
RA46 PT45 15c multi　　　　　.45　.45
Obligatory on mail May 8-15.

Fire Prevention
Week — PT46

2011, Oct. 3　　　　　Perf. 11¼x12
RA47 PT46 15c multi　　　　　.45　.45
Obligatory on mail Oct. 3-8.

Red Cross
Solidarity
Week
PT47

2011, Nov. 1　　　　　　Perf. 14
RA48 PT47 15c multi　　　　　.45　.45
Obligatory on mail Nov. 1-7.

Red Cross
Week — PT48

2012, May 8　　　　　Perf. 14¼x14
RA49 PT48 15c multi　　　　　.40　.40
Obligatory on mail May 8-15.

Fire Prevention Week — PT49

2012, Oct. 1 Litho. Perf. 11¼x11¾
RA50 PT49 15c multi .40 .40
Obligatory on mail Oct. 1-6.

Red Cross Solidarity Week — PT50

2012, Nov. 1 Litho. Perf. 14x14¼
RA51 PT50 15c multi .40 .40
Obligatory on mail Nov. 1-7.

Red Cross Week — PT51

2013, May 8 Litho. Perf. 14¼x14
RA52 PT51 17c multi .45 .45
Obligatory on mail May 8-15.

Fire Prevention Week — PT52

2013, Oct. 7 Litho. Perf. 13¼x13
RA53 PT52 15c multi .40 .40
Obligatory on mail Oct. 7-12.

Red Cross Solidarity Week — PT53

2013, Nov. 1 Litho. Perf. 14
RA54 PT53 17c multi .45 .45
Obligatory on mail Nov. 1-7.

Red Cross Week — PT54

2014, May 8 Litho. Perf. 14
RA55 PT54 17c multi .50 .50
Obligatory on mail May 8-15.

Fire Prevention Week PT55

2014, Oct. 6 Litho. Perf. 13½x12¾
RA56 PT55 15c multi .40 .40
Obligatory on mail Oct. 6-11.

SOLOMON ISLANDS

ˈsä-lə-mən ˈī-lənds

British Solomon Islands

LOCATION — West Pacific Ocean, east of Papua
GOVT. — Independent state in British Commonwealth
AREA — 10,954 sq. mi.
POP. — 455,429 (1999 est.)
CAPITAL — Honiara

The Solomons include 10 large islands and four groups of small islands extending over an area of 375,000 square miles.

The British protectorate of British Solomon Islands changed its name to Solomon Islands in 1975 and achieved independence July 7, 1978.

12 Pence = 1 Shilling
20 Shillings = 1 Pound
100 Cents = 1 Dollar (1966)

> Catalogue values for unused stamps in this country are for Never Hinged items, beginning with Scott 80 in the regular postage section and Scott B1 in the semi-postal section.

Watermark

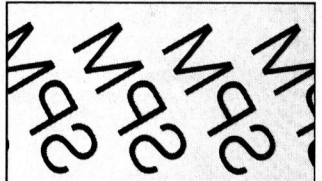

Wmk. 388 — Multiple "SPM"

War Canoe — A1

Unwmk.

1907, Feb. 14 Litho. Perf. 11
1	A1	½p ultra	11.00	16.00
2	A1	1p red	27.50	30.00
3	A1	2p dull blue	45.00	35.00
a.		Horiz. pair, imperf. btwn.	15,000.	
4	A1	2½p orange	38.50	50.00
a.		Vert. pair, imperf. btwn.	7,500.	
b.		Horiz. pair, imperf. btwn.	12,000.	7,000.
5	A1	5p yellow green	67.50	80.00
6	A1	6p chocolate	75.00	77.50
a.		Vertical pair, imperf. btwn.	7,000.	
7	A1	1sh violet	97.50	110.00
		Nos. 1-7 (7)	362.00	398.50

Imperf. between varieties should be accompanied by certificates of authenticity issued by competent authorities. Excellent counterfeits are plentiful.

War Canoe — A2

Wmk. Multiple Crown and CA (3)

1908-11 Engr. Perf. 14
8	A2	½p green	1.75	1.25
9	A2	1p carmine	1.50	1.25
10	A2	2p gray	1.50	1.25
11	A2	2½p ultra	4.25	2.50
12	A2	4p red, yel ('11)	3.75	13.50
13	A2	5p olive green	10.50	8.75
14	A2	6p claret	11.50	8.25
15	A2	1sh black, green	9.75	9.25
16	A2	2sh vio, bl ('10)	50.00	70.00
17	A2	2sh6p red, bl ('10)	62.50	95.00
18	A2	5sh bl, yel ('10)	115.00	140.00
		Nos. 8-18 (11)	272.00	351.00

George V — A3

Inscribed "POSTAGE - POSTAGE"

1913-24 Typo.
19	A3	½p green	.95	4.00
20	A3	1p carmine	3.50	16.50
21	A3	3p violet, yel	1.00	4.75
a.		3p violet, orange buff	9.25	27.50
22	A3	11p dull violet & red	5.75	14.00

Wmk. 4
23	A3	1½p scarlet ('24)	2.50	.80
		Nos. 19-23 (5)	13.70	40.05

Inscribed "POSTAGE - REVENUE"

1914-23 Wmk. 3
28	A3	½p green	1.50	13.50
a.		½p yellow green ('17)	6.50	21.00
29	A3	1p carmine	1.75	1.50
a.		1p scarlet ('17)	6.00	7.50
30	A3	2p gray	4.25	10.50
31	A3	2½p ultra	4.50	5.75

Chalky Paper
32	A3	3p vio, yel ('23)	27.50	140.00
33	A3	4p blk & red, yel	2.25	3.00
34	A3	5p dull vio & ol grn	24.00	35.00
a.		5p brown purple & olive green	24.00	35.00
35	A3	6p dull vio & red vio	7.00	16.00
36	A3	1sh blk, green	5.50	8.00
a.		1sh blk, bl grn, ol back	8.50	27.50
37	A3	2sh dull vio & ultra, bl	8.00	11.50
38	A3	2sh6p blk & red, bl	11.00	22.50
39	A3	5sh grn & red, yel	50.00	55.00
a.		5sh green & red, orange buff	55.00	80.00
40	A3	10sh grn & red, grn	97.50	100.00
41	A3	£1 vio & blk, red	300.00	150.00
		Nos. 28-41 (14)	544.75	572.25

Inscribed "POSTAGE - REVENUE"

1922-31 Wmk. 4
43	A3	½p green	.50	4.00
44	A3	1p carmine ('23)	12.50	12.50
45	A3	1p violet ('27)	1.10	8.50
46	A3	2p gray ('23)	5.50	17.00
47	A3	3p ultra ('23)	.85	5.25

Chalky Paper
48	A3	4p blk & red, yel ('27)	4.25	26.00
49	A3	4½p red brn ('31)	3.75	22.50
50	A3	5p dull vio & ol grn	3.75	32.50
51	A3	6p dull vio & red vio	4.50	32.50
52	A3	1sh black, emer	5.00	15.00
53	A3	2sh dull vio & ultra, bl ('27)	23.00	45.00
54	A3	2sh6p blk & red, bl	8.75	55.00
55	A3	5sh grn & red, yel	40.00	65.00
56	A3	10sh grn & red, emer ('25)	140.00	130.00
		Nos. 43-56 (14)	253.45	470.75

No. 49 is on ordinary paper.

Common Design Types pictured following the introduction.

Silver Jubilee Issue
Common Design Type

1935, May 6 Engr. Perf. 13½x14
60	CD301	1½p car & dk bl	1.50	1.50
61	CD301	3p bl & brn	6.00	7.50
62	CD301	6p ol grn & lt bl	15.00	12.00
63	CD301	1sh brt vio & ind	7.50	17.00
		Nos. 60-63 (4)	30.00	38.00
		Set, never hinged	46.00	

Coronation Issue
Common Design Type

1937, May 13 Perf. 11x11½
64	CD302	1p dark purple	.25	1.00
65	CD302	1½p dk car	.25	.55
66	CD302	3p deep ultra	.40	.45
		Nos. 64-66 (3)	.90	2.00
		Set, never hinged	1.40	

Spears and Shield — A4

Policeman and Chief — A5

Artificial Island, Malaita — A6

Canoe House, New Georgia A7

Roviana War Canoe — A8

View of Munda Point — A9

Meeting House, Reef Islands A10

Coconut Plantation A11

Breadfruit A12

Tinakula Volcano, Santa Cruz Islands A13

Scrub Fowl — A14

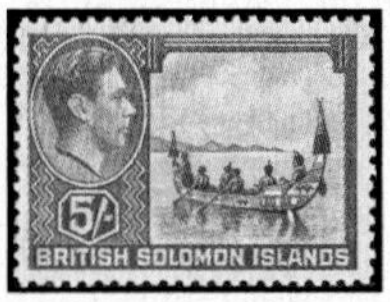

Malaita Canoe — A15

Perf. 12½, 13½ (A7, A13, A14)

1939-51 Wmk. 4

67 A4 ½p deep grn & ultra .25 *1.10*
68 A5 1p dk pur & choc .25 *1.75*
69 A6 1½p car & sl grn .30 *1.50*
70 A7 2p blk & org brn .35 *1.60*
a. 2p black & red brown ('43) .35 *1.75*
Never hinged .70
b. Perf. 12 ('51) .25 *1.60*
Never hinged .40
71 A8 2½p ol grn & rose vio 1.25 *2.75*
a. Vert. pair, imperf. horiz. *24,000.*
72 A9 3p ultra & blk, perf. 13½ .60 *2.00*
a. Perf. 12 ('51) .85 *3.00*
Never hinged 2.00
73 A10 4½p dk brn & yel grn 3.25 *13.00*
74 A11 6p rose lil & dk pur .40 *1.25*
75 A12 1sh blk & grn .80 *1.25*
76 A13 2sh dp org & blk 4.75 *6.00*
a. 2sh dp org & vio blk ('43) 4.75 *6.50*
Never hinged 13.00
77 A14 2sh6p dull vio & blk 17.50 5.00
78 A15 5sh red & brt bl grn 20.00 12.00
79 A10 10sh red lil & ol ('42) 4.00 *8.00*
Nos. 67-79 (13) 53.70 57.20
Set, never hinged 110.00

Catalogue values for unused stamps in this section, from this point to the end of the section, are for Never Hinged items.

Peace Issue

Common Design Type

Perf. 13½x14

1946, Oct. 15 Wmk. 4 Engr.

80 CD303 1½p carmine .25 1.00
81 CD303 3p deep blue .25 .30

Silver Wedding Issue

Common Design Types

1949, Mar. 14 Photo. *Perf. 14x14½*

82 CD304 2p black .40 .40

Perf. 11½x11

Engr.; Name Typo.

83 CD305 10sh red violet 13.00 13.00

UPU Issue

Common Design Types

Engr.; Name Typo. on 3p and 5p

Perf. 13½, 11x11½

1949, Oct. 10 Wmk. 4

84 CD306 2p red brown .75 .85
85 CD307 3p indigo 2.10 1.25
86 CD308 5p green .75 *1.40*
87 CD309 1sh slate .75 *1.40*
Nos. 84-87 (4) 4.35 4.90

Coronation Issue

Common Design Type

1953, June 2 Engr. *Perf. 13½x13*

88 CD312 2p gray & black 1.10 1.10

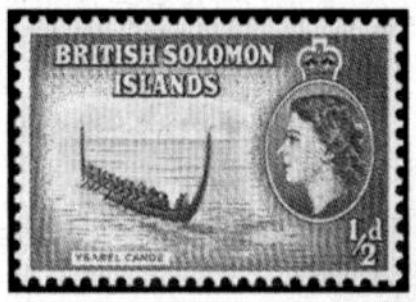

Ysabel Canoe A16

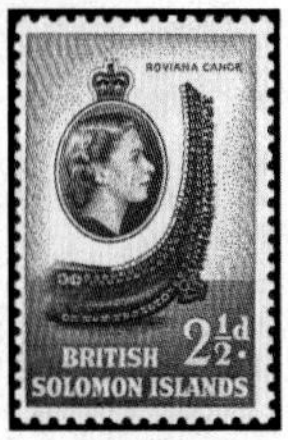

Prow of Roviana Canoe — A17

Designs: 1p, Roviana canoe. 1½p, Artificial Island, Malaita. 2p, Canoe house. 3p, Malaita canoe. 5p, 1sh3p, Map. 6p, Trading schooner. 8p, 9p, Henderson Field, Guadalcanal. 1sh, Chart of Solomons and H.M.S. Swallow, recalling Capt. Philip Carteret's voyage of 1767. 2sh, Tinakula Volcano. 2sh6p, Meeting house, Reef Islands. 5sh, Alvaro de Mendana de Neyra and Caravel. 10sh, Constable and Chief. £1, Coat of Arms.

Perf. 11½x11, 11x11½, 12, 13

1956-60 Engr. Wmk. 4

89 A16 ½p lilac & orange .25 *.55*
90 A16 1p red brn & ol grn .25 .25
91 A16 1½p dk car & sl bl .25 *1.10*
92 A16 2p gray grn & choc .35 *.30*
93 A17 2½p gray bl & blk .90 *.90*
94 A16 3p dull red & grn .80 .25
95 A16 5p blue & black .30 *.65*
96 A16 6p bluish grn & blk .65 .30
97 A16 8p blue & ultra .45 .25
98 A16 9p black & brt grn 3.50 1.00
99 A16 1sh brn org & sl bl 1.75 .75
100 A16 1sh3p blue & black 6.50 2.00
101 A16 2sh car rose & blk 13.50 3.00
102 A17 2sh6p rose lil & emer 7.50 .55
103 A16 5sh red brown 16.00 5.50
104 A17 10sh black brown 25.00 7.25
105 A16 £1 lt blue & blk 32.50 *35.00*
Nos. 89-105 (17) 110.45 59.60

Issued: £1, 11/5/58; 9p, 1sh3p, 1/28/60; others, 3/1/56.
See Nos. 113-125.

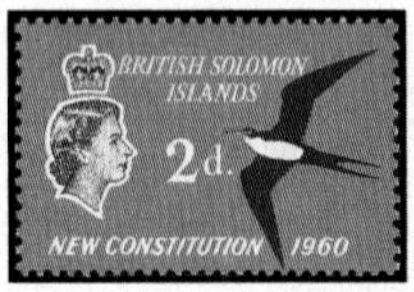

Great Frigate Bird — A18

Perf. 13x12½

1961, Jan. 19 Litho. Wmk. 314

106 A18 2p blue grn & blk .25 *.30*
107 A18 3p rose red & black .25 .25
108 A18 9p lilac & black .30 *.40*
Nos. 106-108 (3) .80 .95

New constitution, brought into operation Oct. 18, 1960. The watermark is sideways and may be found facing both left and right.

Freedom from Hunger Issue

Common Design Type

1963, June 4 Photo. *Perf. 14x14½*

109 CD314 1sh3p ultra 2.00 .85

Red Cross Centenary Issue

Common Design Type

1963, Sept. 2 Litho. *Perf. 13*

110 CD315 2p black & red .25 .25
111 CD315 9p ultra & red 1.00 .90

Types of 1956-60

Perf. 12, 13, 11½x11

1963-64 Engr. Wmk. 314

113 A16 1p red brn & ol grn .40 *.45*
114 A16 1½p dk car & sl bl 1.00 *.80*
115 A16 2p gray grn & choc .30 .25
117 A16 3p dull red & grn .80 .25
119 A16 6p bluish grn & blk 1.00 .65
121 A16 9p black & brt grn 1.10 .55
123 A16 1sh3p blue & blk 1.25 *1.75*
124 A16 2sh car rose & blk 3.00 *6.00*
125 A17 2sh6p rose lil & emer 18.00 16.50
Nos. 113-125 (9) 26.85 27.20

Issued: 3p, 11/16; 6p, 9p, 1sh3p, 7/7/64; 1p, 1½p, 2p, 2sh, 2sh6p, 7/9/64.

ITU Issue

Common Design Type

Perf. 11x11½

1965, June 28 Litho. Wmk. 314

126 CD317 2p ver & grnsh blue .30 .25
127 CD317 3p grnsh bl & ol bis .40 .30

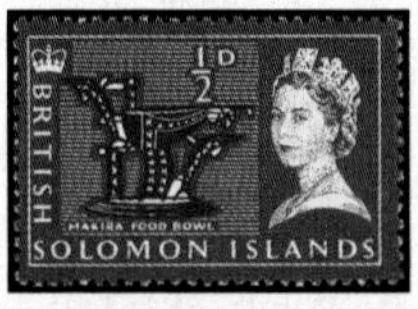

Makira Food Bowl — A19

Designs: 1p, 1sh, 1sh3p, Various orchids. 1½p, Scorpion shell. 2p, Papuan hornbill. 2½p, Ysabel shield. 3p, Rennellese club. 6p, Moorish idol (fish). 9p, Great frigate bird. 2sh, Sanford's sea eagle. 2sh6p, Malaita belt. 5sh, Ornithoptera Victoreae (butterfly). 10sh, White cockatoo. £1, Figurehead, western canoe.

Perf. 13x12½

1965, May 24 Litho. Wmk. 314

Design Subject in Black

128 A19 ½p sl blue & lt bl .25 *1.50*
129 A19 1p orange & yel .35 .60
130 A19 1½p blue & yel grn .25 *1.25*
131 A19 2p vio bl & lt bl .25 *1.60*
132 A19 2½p red brn & buff .25 *1.25*
133 A19 3p grn & lt grn .25 .25
134 A19 6p brt car rose & org .25 *.85*
135 A19 9p slate grn & buff .40 .25
136 A19 1sh dp cl & rose .85 .25
137 A19 1sh3p ver & buff 3.75 2.50
138 A19 2sh dp mag & lil 7.00 3.00
139 A19 2sh6p ol brn & buff .85 .75
140 A19 5sh dk vio bl & lil 10.50 4.75
141 A19 10sh ol grn & yel 12.50 3.75
142 A19 £1 purple & red 7.75 4.75
Nos. 128-142 (15) 45.45 27.30

For surcharges see Nos. 149-166.

Intl. Cooperation Year Issue

Common Design Type

1965, Oct. 25 Litho. *Perf. 14½*

143 CD318 1p bl grn & cl .25 .25
144 CD318 2sh6p lt vio & grn .45 .35

Churchill Memorial Issue

Common Design Type

1966, Jan. 24 Photo. *Perf. 14*

145 CD319 2p multicolored .25 *.30*
146 CD319 9p multicolored .40 .30
147 CD319 1sh3p multicolored .50 .30
148 CD319 2sh6p multicolored .60 *.85*
Nos. 145-148 (4) 1.75 1.75

Nos. 128-142 Srchd. with New Value and Three Bars in Black or Red

Perf. 13x12½

1966-67 Litho. Wmk. 314

149 A19 1c on ½p multi .25 .25
150 A19 2c on 1p multi .25 .25
151 A19 3c on 1½p multi .25 .25
152 A19 4c on 2p multi .25 .25
153 A19 5c on 6p multi .25 .25
154 A19 6c on 2½p multi .25 .25
155 A19 7c on 3p multi .25 .25
156 A19 8c on 9p multi .25 .25
b. "8" inverted 45.00 22.50
157 A19 10c on 1sh .35 .35
158 A19 12c on 1sh3p multi .65 .45
159 A19 13c on 1sh3p multi 2.10 .50
160 A19 14c on 3p multi .55 .50
161 A19 20c on 2sh multi 2.10 .85
162 A19 25c on 2sh6p multi .80 .75
163 A19 35c on 2p multi 2.10 .40
164 A19 50c on 5sh multi (R) 4.00 1.75
165 A19 $1 on 10sh multi 2.00 1.50
166 A19 $2 on £1 multi 1.75 3.00
Nos. 149-166 (18) 18.40 12.05

The 12c, 14c, 35c have watermark sideways.
Issued: 12c, 14c, 35c, 3/1/67; others, 2/14/66.

1966 Wmk. 314 Sideways

149a A19 1c on ½p .25 .25
150a A19 2c on 1p .25 .25
151a A19 3c on 1½p .25 .25
152a A19 4c on 2p .25 .25
153a A19 5c on 6p .30 .30
154a A19 6c on 2½p .35 .35
155a A19 7c on 3p .40 .40
156a A19 8c on 9p .45 .45
157a A19 10c on 1sh .60 .60
159a A19 13c on 1sh3p 4.25 2.75
161a A19 20c on 2sh 3.00 .35
162a A19 25c on 2sh6p 2.25 .35
164a A19 50c on 5sh (R) 9.00 4.75
165a A19 $1 on 10sh 7.00 2.00
166a A19 $2 on £1 6.00 3.00
Nos. 149a-166a (15) 34.60 16.30

World Cup Soccer Issue

Common Design Type

1966, July 1 Litho. *Perf. 14*

167 CD321 8c multicolored .30 .30
168 CD321 35c multicolored .40 .40

WHO Headquarters Issue

Common Design Type

1966, Sept. 20 Litho. *Perf. 14*

169 CD322 3c multicolored .25 .25
170 CD322 50c multicolored .55 .55

UNESCO Anniversary Issue

Common Design Type

1966, Dec. 1 Litho. *Perf. 14*

171 CD323 3c "Education" .25 .25
172 CD323 25c "Science" .50 .25
173 CD323 $1 "Culture" 1.25 1.00
Nos. 171-173 (3) 2.00 1.50

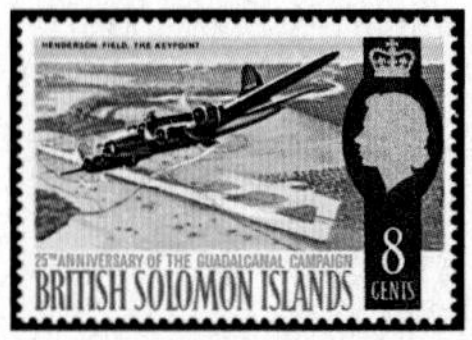

Henderson Field, Guadalcanal — A20

Design: 35c, US Marines landing, Red Beach, Guadalcanal, 1942.

Perf. 14x14½

1967, Aug. 28 Photo. Wmk. 314

174 A20 8c multi & silver .25 .25
175 A20 35c multi & gold .35 .35

Guadalcanal campaign in WW II, 25th anniv.

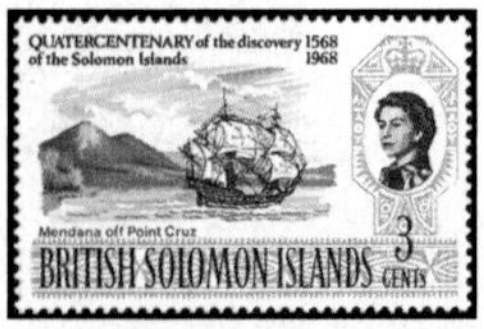

Mendana's Ship Off Puerta de la Cruz (Honiara), Guadalcanal, 1568 — A21

Designs: 8c, Arrival of Missionaries. 35c, Naval battle during World War II. $1, Honor guard raising Union Jack during proclamation of Protectorate.

1968, Feb. 2 Photo. *Perf. 14½*

176 A21 3c pink & multi .30 .25
177 A21 8c emerald & multi .30 .25
178 A21 35c multicolored .60 .25
179 A21 $1 blue & multi .80 *1.25*
Nos. 176-179 (4) 2.00 2.00

400th anniv. of the discovery of the British Solomon Islands by the Spanish navigator Alvaro de Mendana de Neyra.

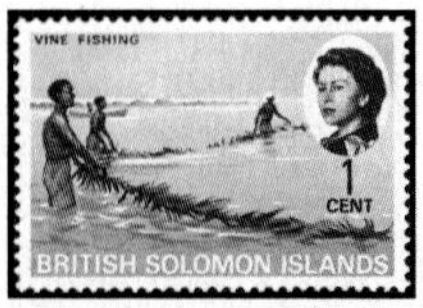

Vine Fishing A22

Designs: 2c, Kite fishing. 3c, Platform fishing. 4c, Net fishing. 6c, Gold lip shell diving. 8c, Night fishing. 12c, Boat building. 14c, Cocoa harvest. 15c, Road building. 20c, Geological survey by plane. 24c, Hauling timber. 35c, Copra. 45c, Harvesting rice. $1, Honiara Port. $2, Map of the Islands, plane and route of Internal Air Service.

Wmk. 314

1968, May 20 Photo. *Perf. 14½*

180 A22 1c aqua, brn & blk .25 .25
181 A22 2c lt yel grn, brn & blk .25 .25
182 A22 3c brt grn, dk grn & blk .25 .25
183 A22 4c brt rose lil, brn & blk .25 .25
184 A22 6c multicolored .25 .25
185 A22 8c dp ultra, org & blk .25 .30
186 A22 12c bister, red & blk .55 .35
187 A22 14c red org, brn & blk 1.75 *2.25*
188 A22 15c multicolored .60 .70
189 A22 20c ultra, red & blk 3.00 3.25
190 A22 24c scarlet, yel & blk 1.60 *3.75*
191 A22 35c multicolored 1.60 .45
192 A22 45c yellow, red & blk 1.30 .45
193 A22 $1 vio bl, emer & blk 1.90 1.75
194 A22 $2 multicolored 4.75 4.00
Nos. 180-194 (15) 18.55 18.50

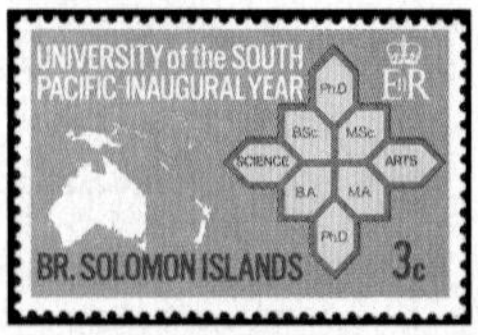

Map of South Pacific and University Degrees — A23

Perf. 12½x12
1969, Feb. 10   Litho.   Unwmk.
195 A23 3c multicolored   .25   .25
196 A23 12c multicolored   .25   .25
197 A23 35c multicolored   .25   .25
   Nos. 195-197 (3)   .75   .75

Inauguration of the University of the South Pacific in 1969, at the Royal New Zealand Air Force Seaplane Station, Laucala Bay, Fiji.

Field Ball and Games' Emblem — A24

Perf. 14½x14
1969, Aug. 13   Photo.   Wmk. 314
198 A24 3c shown   .25   .25
199 A24 8c Soccer   .25   .25
200 A24 14c Running   .25   .25
201 A24 45c Rugby   .40   .40
a.   Souvenir sheet of 4, #198-201   5.50   5.50
   Nos. 198-201 (4)   1.15   1.15

3rd S. Pacific Games, Port Moresby, Aug. 13-23.

In No. 201a, shading was added below athlete's foot on 14c, and strengthened on 8c and 45c.

Stained Glass Window with Melanesian Peace Symbol — A25

Christmas: 8c, South Sea Islands scene with palms and Star of Bethlehem.

1969, Nov. 21   Photo.   Wmk. 314
202 A25 8c vio, grnsh bl & blk   .25   .25
203 A25 35c black & multi   .30   .30

C. M. Woodford and Stamp of 1907 — A26

Designs: 7c, British Solomon Islands 1906 handstamp and cancellation, and New South Wales No. 99. 18c, British Solomon Islands No. 18 and 1913 Tulagi cancellation. 23c, New General Post Office, Honiara.

1970, Apr. 15   Litho.   Perf. 13
204 A26 7c lilac rose & black   .25   .25
205 A26 14c lt olive & black   .25   .25
206 A26 18c orange, yel & blk   .30   .30
207 A26 23c multicolored   .35   .35
   Nos. 204-207 (4)   1.15   1.15

Issued to publicize the opening of the new General Post Office in Honiara.

Map of Solomon Islands A27

18c, British Solomon Islands coat of arms, vert.

Perf. 14½x14, 14x14½
1970, June 15   Litho.   Wmk. 314
208 A27 18c multicolored   .30   .30
209 A27 35c multicolored   .65   .65

Adoption of the new 1970 Constitution.

Red Cross Headquarters, Honiara — A28

35c, Map of British Solomon Islands showing Red Cross stations, wheelchair.

1970, Aug. 17   Perf. 14½x14
210 A28 3c multicolored   .25   .25
211 A28 35c multicolored   .65   .65

Centenary of British Red Cross Society.

Carved Angel and Southern Cross — A29

Reredos: Symbols of Trinity and Light at St. Luke's Church, Kia — A30

Perf. 14x13½, 13½x14
1970, Oct. 19   Litho.   Wmk. 314
212 A29 8c violet & bister brn   .25   .25
213 A30 45c multicolored   .75   .75

Christmas 1970.

Count de La Pérouse and "La Boussole" — A31

4c, Astrolabe, Polynesian reed map. 12c, Abel Tasman, sailing ship Heemskerk, 1643. 35c, Te Puki canoe, Santa Cruz.

1971, Jan. 28   Perf. 14½x14
214 A31 3c multicolored   .90   .50
215 A31 4c multicolored   .90   .50
216 A31 12c multicolored   1.10   .75
217 A31 35c multicolored   1.25   1.25
   Nos. 214-217 (4)   4.15   3.00

In honor of famous explorers and ships. See Nos. 228-231, 250-253.

Bishop Patteson, J. Atkin and S. Taroniara — A32

Designs: 4c, Last landing of the "Southern Cross" at Nukapu. 14c, Memorial for Bishop Patteson and map of Nukapu. 45c, Ceremonial leaf tag (had been attached to Bishop's body), vert.

Perf. 14½x14, 14x14½
1971, Apr. 5   Litho.   Wmk. 314
218 A32 2c lt green & multi   .25   .25
219 A32 4c blue green & multi   .25   .25
220 A32 14c brt pink & multi   .25   .25
221 A32 45c brown & multi   .35   .35
   Nos. 218-221 (4)   1.10   1.10

Bishop John Coleridge Patteson (1827-71), head of the Melanesian mission.

Boxing, Games Emblem A33

8c, Soccer. 12c, Running. 35c, Spearfishing.

1971, Aug. 9   Perf. 14½x14
222 A33 3c orange & multi   .25   .25
223 A33 8c emerald & multi   .25   .25
224 A33 12c yellow & multi   .25   .25
225 A33 35c blue & multi   .40   .40
   Nos. 222-225 (4)   1.15   1.15

4th South Pacific Games, Papeete, French Polynesia, Sept. 8-19.

Melanesian Lectern (wood carving) — A34

Christmas: 45c, Stylized birds, painted by school girl Margarita Bara.

1971, Nov. 15   Litho.   Wmk. 314
226 A34 9c orange & multi   .25   .25
227 A34 45c blue & multi   .55   .55

Explorer Type of 1971

4c, Louis Antoine de Bougainville, La Boudeuse, 1776. 9c, Horizontal planisphere, 1574, ivory backstaff, 1695. 15c, Philip Carteret, H.M.S. Swallow, 1707. 45c, Small canoe of Malaita.

1972, Feb. 1   Perf. 14½
228 A31 4c brown & multi   .35   .25
229 A31 9c green & multi   .55   .25
230 A31 15c lt blue & multi   .90   .50
231 A31 45c blue & multi   2.00   2.00
   Nos. 228-231 (4)   3.80   3.00

Cupha Woodfordi A35

2c, Ornithoptera priamus. 3c, Vindula sapor. 4c, Papilio orssippus. 5c, Great trevally. 8c, Little bonito. 9c, Sapphire demoiselle. 12c, Costus speciosus. 15c, Orange anemone. 20c, Spathoglottis plicata. 25c, Ephemerantha comata. 35c, Dendrobium cuthbertsonii. 45c, Heliconia salomonica. $1, Blue-finned triggerfish. $2, Ornithoptera allotti. $5, Great frigate bird. Designs: 1c, 2c, 3c, 4c, $2, Butterflies. 5c, 8c, 9c, 15c, $1. Fishes. 12c, 20c, 25c, 35c, 45c, Orchids. $5, Birds.

1972-73   Perf. 14
232 A35 1c shown   .25   .25
233 A35 2c multicolored   .30   .30
234 A35 3c multicolored   .30   .30
235 A35 4c multicolored   .30   .30
236 A35 5c multicolored   .40   .40
237 A35 8c multicolored   .50   .50
238 A35 9c multicolored   .60   .70
239 A35 12c multicolored   1.50   .80
240 A35 15c multicolored   1.50   1.00
241 A35 20c multicolored   3.50   1.25
242 A35 25c multicolored   3.50   1.50
243 A35 35c multicolored   3.75   2.00
244 A35 45c multicolored   3.00   3.00
245 A35 $1 multicolored   3.75   5.00

246 A35 $2 multicolored   11.00   17.50
247 A35 $5 multicolored   18.50   19.50
   Nos. 232-247 (16)   52.65   54.30

Issued: $5, 7/2/73; others, 7/2/72.
For overprints see Nos. 300-311.

Silver Wedding Issue, 1972
Common Design Type

Design: Queen Elizabeth II, Prince Philip, scroll and message drum on woven mat.

1972, Nov. 20   Photo.   Perf. 14x14½
248 CD324 8c car rose & multi   .25   .25
249 CD324 45c olive & multi   .35   .35

Explorer Type of 1971

Designs: 4c, Antoine R. J. d'Entrecasteaux and "The Recherche," 1791. 9c, Ship's hourglass, 17th century, and chronometer, 1761. 15c, Lieutenant Shortland and "The Alexander," 1788. 35c, Tomoko (war canoe).

Wmk. 314
1973, Mar. 9   Litho.   Perf. 14½
250 A31 4c blue & multi   .25   .25
251 A31 9c blue & multi   .45   .45
252 A31 15c blue & multi   .80   .80
253 A31 35c blue & multi   2.50   2.50
   Nos. 250-253 (4)   4.00   4.00

Pan Pipes A36

Musical Instruments: 9c, Castanets. 15c, Bamboo flute. 35c, Bauro gongs. 45c, Bamboo band.

1973, Oct. 1   Perf. 13½x14
254 A36 4c brick red & multi   .25   .25
255 A36 9c yellow bis & multi   .25   .25
256 A36 15c pink & multi   .35   .35
257 A36 35c blue green & multi   .75   .75
258 A36 45c multicolored   1.05   1.05
   Nos. 254-258 (5)   2.65   2.65

Princess Anne's Wedding Issue
Common Design Type

1973, Nov. 14   Perf. 14
259 CD325 4c slate & multi   .30   .30
260 CD325 35c multicolored   .40   .40

Adoration of the Kings, by Jan Brueghel A37

Adoration of the Kings by: 22c, Peter Brueghel, vert. 45c, Botticelli.

1973, Nov. 26   Litho.   Perf. 14
Size: 39x25mm, 25x39mm
261 A37 8c pink & multi   .25   .25
262 A37 22c lilac & multi   .30   .30

Perf. 13½
Size: 47x35mm
263 A37 45c gray & multi   .65   .65
   Nos. 261-263 (3)   1.20   1.20

Christmas 1973.

Map of Solomon Islands — A38

1974, Feb. 18   Litho.   Perf. 13½
264 A38 4c blue & multi   .25   .25
265 A38 9c citron & multi   .25   .25
266 A38 15c violet gray & multi   .40   .40
267 A38 35c emerald & multi   1.10   1.10
   Nos. 264-267 (4)   2.00   2.00

Visit of British Royal Family.

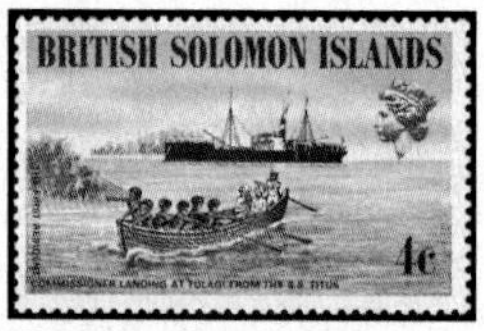

First Resident Commissioner Landing at Tulagi — A39

Designs: 9c, Marine radar and scanner unit, map of Islands. 15c, Islanders taken to "Blackbirder" ship. 45c, John F. Kennedy's P.T. 109 off Lumbari Island, 1943.

1974, May 15 Litho. *Perf. 14½*

268	A39	4c multicolored	.25	.25
269	A39	9c multicolored	.35	.35
270	A39	15c multicolored	.45	.45
271	A39	45c multicolored	2.00	2.00
		Nos. 268-271 (4)	3.05	3.05

Ships and navigators.

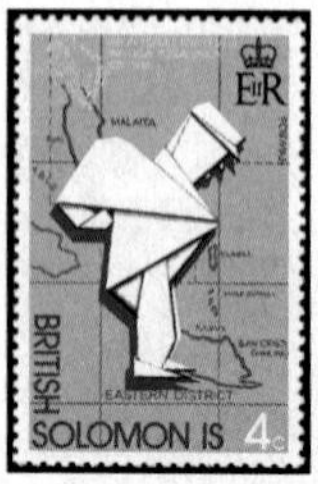

Mailman, Map of Islands — A40

9c, Carrier pigeon, horiz. 15c, Angel Gabriel. 45c, Pegasus, horiz. Designs based on origami (folded paper) figures.

1974, Aug. 29 Wmk. 314 *Perf. 14*

272	A40	4c brt green & multi	.25	.25
273	A40	9c lemon & multi	.25	.25
274	A40	15c multicolored	.30	.30
275	A40	45c blue & multi	1.00	1.25
		Nos. 272-275 (4)	1.80	2.05

Centenary of Universal Postal Union.

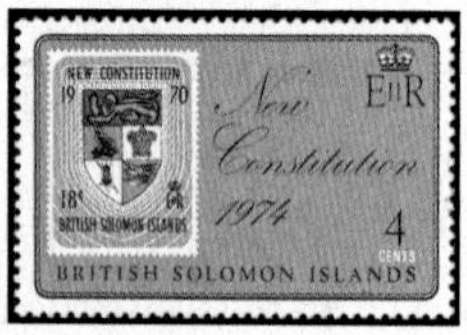

Solomon Islands No. 208 A41

1974, Dec. 16 Litho. *Perf. 14½*

276	A41	4c shown	.25	.25
277	A41	9c No. 107	.25	.25
278	A41	15c same	.45	.45
279	A41	35c like 4c	.80	.80
a.		Souvenir sheet of 4, #276-279	4.50	4.50
		Nos. 276-279 (4)	1.75	1.75

New Constitution, inaugurated Oct. 18, 1960.

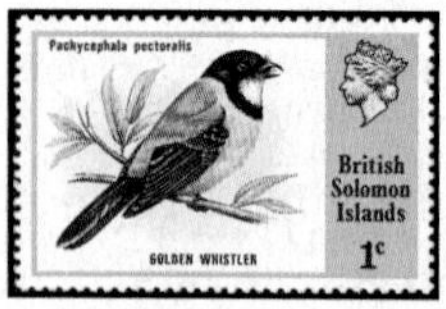

Golden Whistler A42

Birds: 2c, River kingfisher. 3c, Red-throated fruit dove. 4c, Button quail. $2, Duchess lorikeet.

1975, Apr. 7 Wmk. 314 *Perf. 14*

280	A42	1c yellow grn & multi	.60	*.75*
281	A42	2c lt blue & multi	.70	*1.00*
282	A42	3c brt pink & multi	.80	*1.00*
283	A42	4c orange & multi	.90	*1.00*
284	A42	$2 dp orange & multi	15.00	15.00
		Nos. 280-284 (5)	18.00	18.75

See Nos. 316-320, 323, 330-331. For overprints see Nos. 296-299, 310.

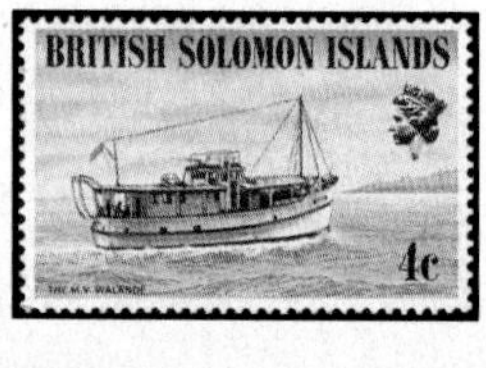

Motor Vessel Walande A43

No. 286, M. V. Melanesian. No. 287, Ship Marsina, house flag. No. 288, S. S. Himalaya.

1975, May 29 *Perf. 13½*

285	A43	4c multicolored	.40	.25
286	A43	9c multicolored	.55	.25
287	A43	15c multicolored	.75	.25
288	A43	45c multicolored	1.30	1.50
		Nos. 285-288 (4)	3.00	2.25

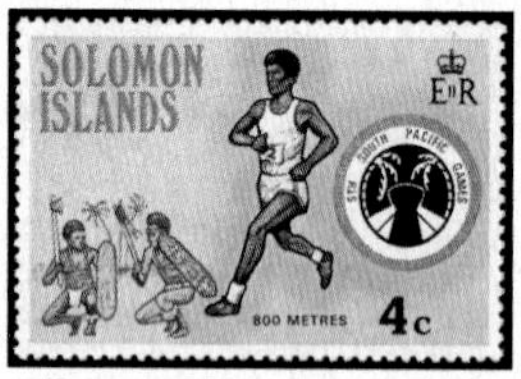

Runner, 800-meters — A44

1975, Aug. 4 Litho. *Perf. 13½*

289	A44	4c shown	.25	.25
290	A44	9c Long jump	.25	.25
291	A44	15c Javelin	.25	.25
292	A44	45c Soccer	.75	.75
a.		Souvenir sheet of 4, #289-292	5.00	5.00
		Nos. 289-292 (4)	1.50	1.50

5th South Pacific Games, Guam, Aug. 1-10.

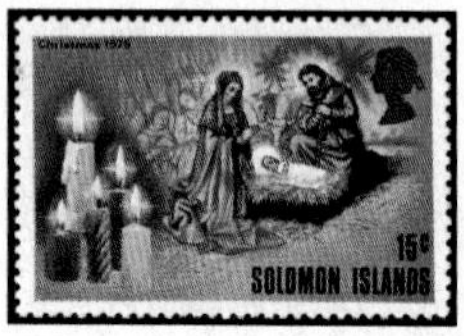

Nativity and Candles A45

Christmas: 35c, Angels, shepherds and candles. 45c, Three Kings approaching Bethlehem, and candles.

1975, Oct. 13 Wmk. 373 *Perf. 14*

293	A45	15c multicolored	.25	.25
294	A45	35c multicolored	.50	.50
295	A45	45c multicolored	.75	.75
a.		Souvenir sheet of 3, #293-295	5.75	5.75
		Nos. 293-295 (3)	1.50	1.50

Nos. 236-245, 247, 280-284 Ovptd. with Bar Obliterating "British" in Black or Silver

1975, Nov. 12 Litho. Wmk. 314

296	A42	1c multicolored	.85	.70
297	A42	2c multicolored	1.50	.70
298	A42	3c multicolored	.95	.70
299	A42	4c multicolored	1.50	.70
300	A35	5c multicolored	.75	.70
301	A35	8c multicolored	.75	.70
302	A35	9c multicolored	.75	.70
303	A35	12c multicolored	2.50	1.25
304	A35	15c multicolored	2.50	1.75
305	A35	20c multicolored	3.00	2.25
306	A35	25c multicolored	3.00	2.25
307	A35	35c multicolored	3.25	2.00
308	A35	45c multicolored	3.00	2.75
309	A35	$1 multicolored	2.50	*4.00*
310	A42	$2 multicolored	7.50	*9.00*
311	A35	$5 multicolored (S)	7.25	*18.00*
		Nos. 296-311 (16)	41.55	*48.15*

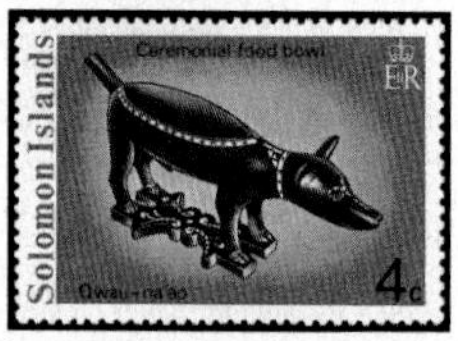

Ceremonial Food Bowl — A46

Artifacts: 15c, Barava, chief's money. 35c, Nguzu-nguzu, canoe protector spirit, vert. 45c, Nguzu-nguzu on canoe prow.

Wmk. 314

1976, Jan. 12 Litho. *Perf. 14*

312	A46	4c scarlet & black	.25	.25
313	A46	15c lt violet & multi	.25	.25
314	A46	35c multicolored	.60	.60
315	A46	45c multicolored	.75	.75
		Nos. 312-315 (4)	1.85	1.85

Type of 1975 Inscribed "Solomon Islands" and

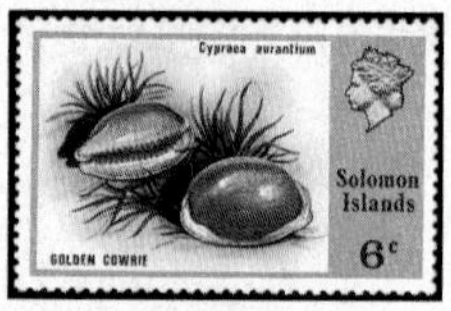

Golden Cowries A47

1c, Golden whistler. 2c, River kingfisher. 3c, Red-throated fruit dove. 4c, Button quail. 5c, Willie wagtail. 10c, Glory-of-the-sea cones. 12c, Rainbow lory. 15c, Pearly nautilus. 20c, Venus comb murex. 25c, Commercial trochus. 35c, Melon or baler shell. 45c, Orange spider conch. $1, Pacific triton. $2, Duchess lorikeet. $5, Great frigate bird.

1976 Wmk. 373 *Perf. 14*

316	A42	1c yel grn & multi	.40	.35
317	A42	2c lt blue & multi	1.00	.70
318	A42	3c pink & multi	.45	.35
319	A42	4c orange & multi	.45	.40
320	A42	5c red brown & multi	1.00	.70
321	A47	6c rose & multi	.60	.50
322	A47	10c multicolored	.60	.50
323	A42	12c yel grn & multi	1.00	.80
324	A47	15c lilac & multi	.55	.35
325	A47	20c ultra & multi	1.00	.75
326	A47	25c dull grn & multi	.80	.65
327	A47	35c bister & multi	.95	.95
328	A47	45c fawn & multi	1.10	1.10
329	A47	$1 olive & multi	2.50	2.50
330	A42	$2 multicolored	5.00	5.00
331	A42	$5 multicolored	9.75	9.75
		Nos. 316-331 (16)	27.15	25.35

Issue dates: $5, Dec. 6; others Mar. 8.

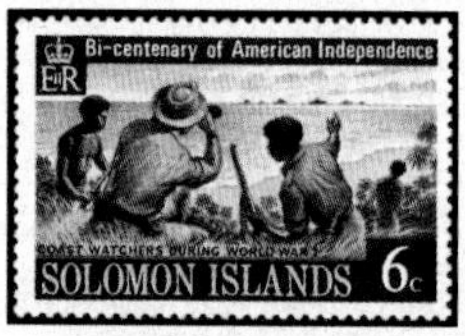

Coast Watchers, World War II A48

American Bicentennial: 20c, "Amagiri" ramming "P.T.109" and Lt. John F. Kennedy. 35c, Plane on Henderson Airfield. 45c, Map showing landing of US forces on Guadalcanal.

1976, May 24 *Perf. 14*

333	A48	6c black & multi	.35	.25
334	A48	20c black & multi	.90	.55
335	A48	35c black & multi	1.25	.90
336	A48	45c black & multi	1.25	1.10
a.		Souvenir sheet of 4, #333-336	7.75	7.75
		Nos. 333-336 (4)	3.75	2.80

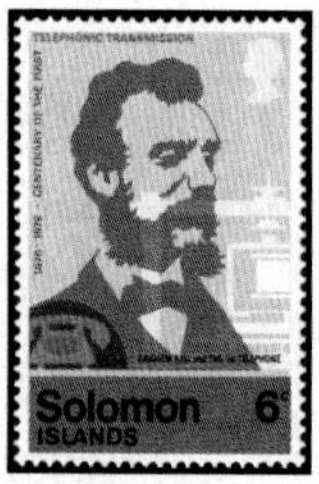

Alexander Graham Bell — A49

Designs: 20c, Radio-telephone and satellite. 35c, Ericsson's magneto telephone. 45c, Telephone, 1876, and stick telephone.

1976, July 26 Litho. *Perf. 14½x14*

337	A49	6c lt ultra & multi	.25	.25
338	A49	20c multicolored	.30	.30
339	A49	35c orange & multi	.45	.45
340	A49	45c bister & multi	.60	.60
		Nos. 337-340 (4)	1.60	1.60

Centenary of first telephone call by Alexander Graham Bell, Mar. 10, 1876.

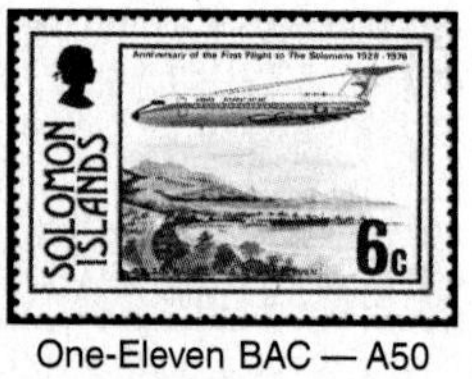

One-Eleven BAC — A50

Planes: 20c, Solair Britten Norman Islander. 35c, DC-3 Dakota. 45c, De Havilland DH50A.

1976, Sept. 13 Wmk. 373 *Perf. 14*

341	A50	6c black & multi	.25	.25
342	A50	20c black & multi	.65	.65
343	A50	35c black & multi	1.10	1.10
344	A50	45c black & multi	1.25	1.25
		Nos. 341-344 (4)	3.25	3.25

1st flight to Solomon Islands, 50th anniv.

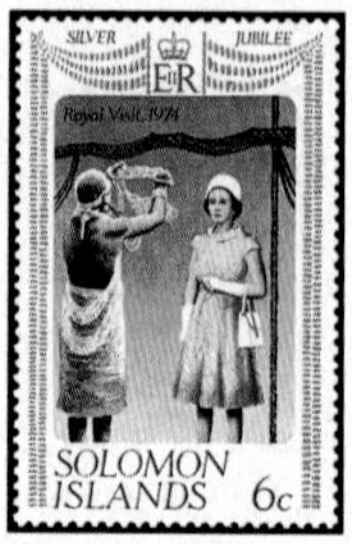

Queen Receiving Lei, 1974 Visit — A51

35c, Communion plate, cup. 45c, Communion.

1977, Feb. 7 Litho. *Perf. 14x13½*

345	A51	6c multicolored	.25	.25
346	A51	35c multicolored	.30	.30
347	A51	45c multicolored	.45	.45
		Nos. 345-347 (3)	1.00	1.00

25th anniv. of the reign of Elizabeth II.

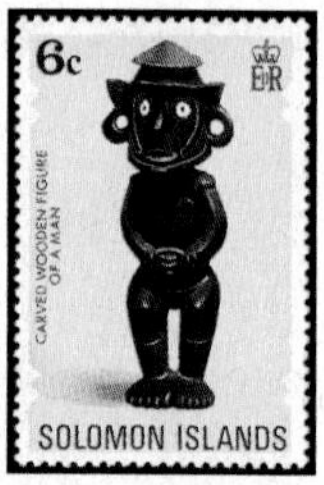

Carved Wooden Figure — A52

Artifacts: 20c, Sea adaro or spirit. 35c, Shark-headed man. 45c, Seated man.

1977, May 9 *Perf. 14*

348	A52	6c yellow & multi	.25	.25
349	A52	20c blue & multi	.25	.25
350	A52	35c rose & multi	.30	.30
351	A52	45c multicolored	.35	.35
		Nos. 348-351 (4)	1.15	1.15

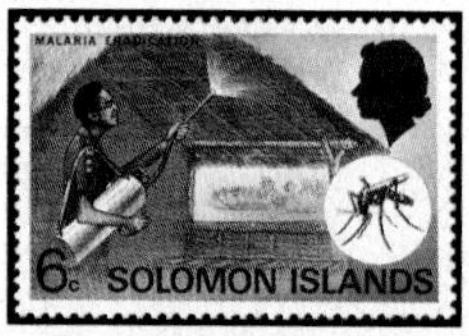

Man Spraying House, Anopheles Mosquito — A53

Designs: 20c, Taking blood samples. 35c, Microscope, map of Solomon Islands, Malaria Eradication Program emblem. 45c, Messenger delivering medicine to malaria patient.

1977, July 27 Litho. Wmk. 373

352	A53	6c multicolored	.25	.25
353	A53	20c multicolored	.25	.25
354	A53	35c multicolored	.40	.40
355	A53	45c multicolored	.60	.60
		Nos. 352-355 (4)	1.50	1.50

Malaria eradication.

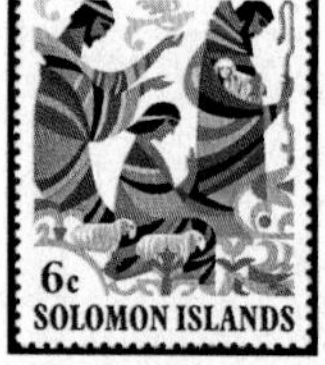

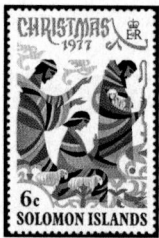

Adoration of the Shepherds — A54

Christmas: 20c, Nativity. 35c, Adoration of the Kings. 45c, Flight into Egypt.

Wmk. 373
1977, Sept. 12   Litho.   Perf. 14

356	A54	6c multicolored	.25	.25
357	A54	20c multicolored	.25	.25
358	A54	40c multicolored	.40	.40
359	A54	45c multicolored	.60	.60
		Nos. 356-359 (4)	1.50	1.50

Traditional Feather Money — A55

Designs: No. 361, New coins. No. 362, Banknotes. No. 363, Traditional shell money.

1977, Oct. 24   Litho.   Perf. 14x14½

360		6c brt green & multi	.25	.25
361		6c brt green & multi	.25	.25
a.		A55 Pair, #360-361	.30	.30
362		45c buff & multi	.60	.60
363		45c buff & multi	.60	.60
a.		A55 Pair, #362-363	1.20	1.20
		Nos. 360-363 (4)	1.70	1.70

New coinage.

Shortland Islands
Figure — A56

Artifacts: 20c, Ceremonial shield. 35c, Santa Cruz ritual figure. 45c, Decorative combs.

1978, Jan. 11   Perf. 14

364	A56	6c multicolored	.25	.25
365	A56	20c multicolored	.25	.25
366	A56	35c multicolored	.50	.50
367	A56	45c multicolored	.60	.60
		Nos. 364-367 (4)	1.60	1.60

Elizabeth II Coronation Anniversary Issue
Common Design Types
Souvenir Sheet
Unwmk.

1978, Apr. 21   Perf. 15

368		Sheet of 6	3.00	3.00
a.	CD326	45c King's dragon	.50	.50
b.	CD327	45c Elizabeth II	.50	.50
c.	CD328	45c Sandford eagle	.50	.50

No. 368 contains 2 se-tenant strips of Nos. 368a-368c, separated by horizontal gutter with commemorative and descriptive inscriptions and showing central part of coronation procession with coach.

National
Flag — A57

Independence: 15c, Governor General's flag. 35c, Cenotaph, Honiara, flags of U.S., Great Britain, New Zealand and Australia. 45c, Coat of Arms.

Wmk. 373
1978, July 7   Litho.   Perf. 14

369	A57	6c multicolored	.25	.25
370	A57	15c multicolored	.25	.25
371	A57	35c multicolored	.60	.60
372	A57	45c multicolored	.75	.75
		Nos. 369-372 (4)	1.85	1.85

Apostles by
Dürer — A58

1978, Oct. 4   Litho.   Perf. 14

373	A58	6c John	.25	.25
374	A58	20c Peter	.35	.35
375	A58	35c Paul	.60	.60
376	A58	45c Mark	.80	.80
		Nos. 373-376 (4)	2.00	2.00

Albrecht Dürer (1471-1528), German painter, 450th death anniversary.

Scouts
Making
Fire — A59

Designs: 20c, Camping. 35c, Solomon Islands Scouts. 45c, Canoeing.

1978, Nov. 15   Litho.   Perf. 14

377	A59	6c multicolored	.25	.25
378	A59	20c multicolored	.25	.25
379	A59	35c multicolored	.50	.50
380	A59	45c multicolored	.60	.60
		Nos. 377-380 (4)	1.60	1.60

50 years of Scouting in Solomon Islands.

Discovery
A60

Designs: 18c, Capt. Cook, 1776, painting by Nathaniel Dance. 35c, Sextant. 45c, Capt. Cook after Flaxman / Wedgwood medallion.

Wmk. 373
1979, Jan. 16   Litho.   Perf. 11

381	A60	8c multicolored	.25	.25
382	A60	18c multicolored	.30	.30
383	A60	35c multicolored	.65	.65

Litho.; Embossed

384	A60	45c multicolored	.80	.80
		Nos. 381-384 (4)	2.00	2.00

Capt. Cook's voyages.

Fish Net
Float
A61

Artifacts: 20c, Armband made of shell money, vert. 35c, Ceremonial food bowl. 45c, Forehead ornament, vert.

1979, Mar. 21   Litho.   Perf. 14

385	A61	8c multicolored	.25	.25
386	A61	20c multicolored	.25	.25
387	A61	35c multicolored	.40	.40
388	A61	45c multicolored	.50	.50
		Nos. 385-388 (4)	1.40	1.40

6th South
Pacific
Games
A62

1979, June 4   Litho.   Wmk. 373

389	A62	8c Running	.25	.25
390	A62	20c Hurdles	.25	.25
391	A62	35c Soccer	.25	.25
392	A62	45c Swimming	.35	.35
		Nos. 389-392 (4)	1.10	1.10

Solomon Islands
No. 14 — A63

Designs (Rowland Hill and): 20c, Great Britain No. 27. 35c, Solomon Islands No. 372. 45c, Solomon Islands No. 40.

1979, Aug. 16   Litho.   Perf. 14

393	A63	8c multicolored	.25	.25
394	A63	20c multicolored	.30	.30
395	A63	35c multicolored	.50	.50
		Nos. 393-395 (3)	1.05	1.05

Souvenir Sheet

396	A63	45c multicolored	1.10	1.10

Sir Rowland Hill (1795-1879), originator of penny postage.

Sea Snake — A64

Perf. 13½x13
1979-83   Litho.   Wmk. 373

397	A64	1c Sea snake	.25	.50
398	A64	3c Red-banded tree snake	.25	.75
399	A64	4c Whip snake	.25	.75
400	A64	6c Pacific boa	.25	.75
401	A64	8c Skink	.25	.45
402	A64	10c Gecko	.25	.50
403	A64	12c Monitor	.30	.50
404	A64	15c Angelhead	.30	.75
405	A64	20c Giant toad	.40	.35
406	A64	25c Marsh frog	.45	.60
407	A64	30c Horned frog	1.50	.60
408	A64	35c Tree frog	.50	.60
408A	A64	40c Burrowing snake	1.50	1.40
409	A64	45c Guppy's snake	.65	.85
409A	A64	50c Tree gecko	1.50	.85
410	A64	$1 Large skink	2.00	1.25
411	A64	$2 Guppy's frog	2.50	2.50
412	A64	$5 Estuarine crocodile	6.50	6.50
412A	A64	$10 Hawksbill turtle	13.00	13.00
		Nos. 397-412A (19)	32.60	33.45

Issued: $10, 9/20/82; 40c, 50c, 1/24/83; others, 9/1979 (undated).
Nos. 403, 406, 410, 412 reissued inscribed "1982." No. 407, "1983."

Madonna and
Child, by
Morando — A65

IYC Emblem and Madonna and Child: 20c, Bernardino Luini. 35c, Bellini. 50c, Raphael.

1979, Nov. 15   Perf. 14½

413	A65	4c multicolored	.25	.25
414	A65	20c multicolored	.25	.25
415	A65	35c multicolored	.25	.25
416	A65	50c multicolored	.50	.50
a.		Souvenir sheet of 4, #413-416	1.75	1.75
		Nos. 413-416 (4)	1.25	1.25

Christmas 1979, Intl. Year of the Child.

Curacoa
and Crest
A66

Ships and Crests: 20c, Herald, 1854. 35c, Royalist, 1889. 45c, Beagle, 1878.

Wmk. 373
1980, Jan. 23   Litho.   Perf. 14

417	A66	8c multicolored	.25	.25
418	A66	20c multicolored	.45	.45
419	A66	35c multicolored	.70	.70
420	A66	45c multicolored	.95	1.40
		Nos. 417-420 (4)	2.35	2.80

See Nos. 435-438.

Steel Fishery Training Ship — A67

1980, Mar. 27   Litho.   Perf. 13½

421	A67	8c shown	.25	.25
422	A67	20c Fishery training ship	.25	.25
423	A67	45c Refrigerated carrier	.45	.40
424	A67	80c Research ship	.85	1.75
		Nos. 421-424 (4)	1.80	2.65

"Comliebank," Tulag Cancel — A68

1980, May 6   Litho.   Perf. 14½

425		Sheet of 4	2.00	2.00
a.		A68 45c shown	.50	.50
b.		A68 45c Douglas C-47	.50	.50
c.		A68 45c BAC 1-11, Honiara cancel	.50	.50
d.		A68 45c "Corabank," Auki cancel	.50	.50

London 1980 Intl. Stamp Exhib., May 6-14.

Queen Mother Elizabeth Birthday Issue
Common Design Type
Wmk. 373

1980, Aug. 4   Litho.   Perf. 14

426	CD330	45c multicolored	.50	.50

Angel with
Trumpet — A69

Christmas: 20c, Angel with violin. 45c, Angel with trumpet. 80c, Angel with lute.

Wmk. 373
1980, Sept. 2   Litho.   Perf. 14½

427	A69	8c multicolored	.25	.25
428	A69	20c multicolored	.25	.25
429	A69	45c multicolored	.25	.25
430	A69	80c multicolored	.35	.35
		Nos. 427-430 (4)	1.10	1.10

Parthenos Sylvia — A70

No. 432, Delias schoenbergi. No. 433, Jamides cephion. No. 434, Ornithoptera victoriae.

Wmk. 373

1980, Nov. 12   Litho.   Perf. 13½
431 A70 8c multicolored   .75   .45
432 A70 20c multicolored   1.00   .65
433 A70 45c multicolored   1.75 1.25
434 A70 80c multicolored   3.00 3.00
     Nos. 431-434 (4)   6.50 5.35

See Nos. 461-464.

Ship & Crest Type of 1980

8c, Mounts Bay, 1959. 20c, Charybdis, 1970. 45c, Hydra, 1972-73. $1, Britannia, 1974.

1981, Jan. 14
435 A66 8c multicolored   .25   .25
436 A66 20c multicolored   .25   .25
437 A66 45c multicolored   .40   .40
438 A66 $1 multicolored   1.10 1.10
     Nos. 435-438 (4)   2.00 2.00

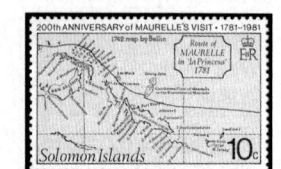

Maurelle's Map, 1742 — A71

No. 439, Francisco Maurelle, vert. No. 441, La Princesa. No. 442, Compass cards, vert.

Wmk. 373

1981, Mar. 23   Litho.   Perf. 14
439 A71 8c multicolored   .25   .25
440 A71 10c multicolored   .25   .25
441 A71 45c multicolored   .50   .50
442 A71 $1 multicolored   .75   .75
     Nos. 439-442 (4)   1.75 1.75

Souvenir Sheet
443   Sheet of 4   1.25 1.25
  a. A71 25c any single   .30   .30

Bicent. of arrival of Francisco Antonio Maurelle and of charts of mapmaker Jean Nicholas Buache (1741-1825). No. 443 contains 4 44x28mm stamps, perf. 14½.

Women's
Basketball — A72

Wmk. 373

1981, July 7   Litho.   Perf. 12
444 A72 8c shown   .25   .25
445 A72 10c Tennis   .25   .25
446 A72 25c Women's running   .30   .30
447 A72 30c Soccer   .30   .30
448 A72 45c Boxing   .40   .40
     Nos. 444-448 (5)   1.50 1.50

Souvenir Sheet
449 A72 $1 Emblem   1.25 1.25

Mini South Pacific Games, July.

Royal Wedding Issue
Common Design Type

1981, July 22   Perf. 13½x13
450 CD331 8c Bouquet   .25   .25
451 CD331 45c Charles   .25   .25
452 CD331 $1 Couple   .55   .55
     Nos. 450-452 (3)   1.05 1.05

For surcharge see No. B1.

Duke of Edinburgh's
Awards, 25th
Anniv. — A73

Wmk. 373

1981, Sept. 28   Litho.   Perf. 14
453 A73 8c Music   .25   .25
454 A73 25c Handicrafts   .25   .25
455 A73 45c Canoeing   .30   .30
456 A73 $1 Duke of Edinburgh   .70   .70
     Nos. 453-456 (4)   1.50 1.50

Holy Cross Cathedral, Honiara — A74

Christmas: 8c, 25c, Old churches, diff. 10c, St. Barnabas Anglican Cathedral, Honiara.

1981, Oct. 12
457 A74 8c multicolored   .25   .25
458 A74 10c multicolored   .25   .25
459 A74 25c multicolored   .30   .30
460 A74 $2 multicolored   1.10 1.10
     Nos. 457-460 (4)   1.90 1.90

Butterfly Type of 1980

No. 461, Doleschallia bisaltide. No. 462, Papilio bridgei hecataeus. No. 463, Taenaris phorcas. No. 464, Graphium sarpedon.

Wmk. 373

1982, Jan. 5   Litho.   Perf. 13½
461 A70 10c multicolored   .75   .40
462 A70 25c multicolored   1.00   .75
463 A70 35c multicolored   1.50 1.25
464 A70 $1 multicolored   3.75 3.75
     Nos. 461-464 (4)   7.00 6.15

Sanford's
Eagle — A75

1982, May 15   Litho.   Perf. 14
465 A75 12c Pair facing left   .60   .60
466 A75 12c Chick   .60   .60
467 A75 12c Mother feeding
              chicks   .60   .60
468 A75 12c Pair facing right   .60   .60
469 A75 12c Male flying   .60   .60
470 A75 12c Pair flying   .60   .60
     Nos. 465-470 (6)   3.60 3.60

Se-tenant in sheets of 24. Value of complete sheet, $25. The center horiz. row consists of 4 No. 470 + label. No block of 6 contains all 6 designs.

Princess Diana Issue
Common Design Type

Perf. 14½x14

1982, July 1   Litho.   Wmk. 373
471 CD333 12c Arms   .25   .25
472 CD333 40c Diana   .50   .50
473 CD333 50c Wedding   .75   .75
474 CD333 $1 Portrait   1.40 1.40
     Nos. 471-474 (4)   2.90 2.90

A76

1982, Oct. 11   Litho.   Perf. 14
475 A76 25c Running   .40   .40
476 A76 25c Boxing   .40   .40

Souvenir Sheet
477   Sheet of 3, #475-476, 477a 3.75 3.75
  a. A76 $1 Britannia facing left 2.75 2.75

12th Commonwealth Games, Brisbane, Australia, Sept. 30-Oct. 9.

1982, Oct. 11
478 A76 12c Royal couple   .25   .25
479 A76 12c Flags   .25   .25

Souvenir Sheet
480   Sheet of 3, #478-479, 480a 4.00 4.00
  a. A76 $1 Britannia facing right 3.50 3.50

Visit of Queen Elizabeth II and Prince Philip.

Scouting
Year
A78

Designs: Nos. 481, 485, Scout patroller. Nos. 482, 486, Brigade bugler. Nos. 483, 487, Baden-Powell. Nos. 484, 488, William Smith.

1982, Nov. 30
481 A78 12c dark blue & multi   .25   .25
482 A78 12c brown & multi   .25   .25
483 A78 25c dark blue & multi   .25   .25
484 A78 25c brown & multi   .25   .25
485 A78 35c green & multi   .25   .25
486 A78 35c red & multi   .25   .25
487 A78 50c green & multi   .40   .40
488 A78 50c red & multi   .40   .40
     Nos. 481-488 (8)   2.30 2.30

Turtles
A79

1983, Jan. 5   Perf. 14
489 A79 18c Leatherback   .75   .75
490 A79 35c Loggerhead   1.10 1.10
491 A79 45c Pacific Ridley   1.50 1.50
492 A79 50c Green   1.50 1.50
     Nos. 489-492 (4)   4.85 4.85

Commonwealth Day — A80

No. 493, Oliva vidum, conus generalis, murex tribulus. No. 494, Romu, kurila, kakadu, money belt. No. 495, Shells, bride necklaces. No. 496, Trochus niloticus, natural, polished.

1983, Mar. 14
493 A80 12c multicolored   .25   .25
494 A80 35c multicolored   .55   .55
495 A80 45c multicolored   .70   .70
496 A80 50c multicolored   .75   .75
     Nos. 493-496 (4)   2.25 2.25

Manned Flight Bicentenary — A81

No. 497, Montgolfliere, 1783. No. 498, Lockheed Hercules. No. 499, Wright Brothers' Flyer III, 1905. No. 500, Columbia space shuttle. No. 501, Beechcraft Baron-Solair.

Wmk. 373

1983, June 30   Litho.   Perf. 14
497 A81 30c multicolored   .45   .45
498 A81 35c multicolored   .50   .50
499 A81 40c multicolored   .55   .55

500 A81 45c multicolored   .60   .60
501 A81 50c multicolored   .75   .75
     Nos. 497-501 (5)   2.85 2.85

Christmas 1983 — A82

1983, Aug. 25
502 A82 12c Weto dance   .25   .25
503 A82 15c Custom wrestling   .25   .25
504 A82 15c Girl dancers   .25   .25
505 A82 20c Devil dancers   .25   .25
506 A82 25c Bamboo band   .30   .30
507 A82 35c Gilbertese dancers   .45   .45
508 A82 40c Pan pipers   .55   .55
509 A82 45c Afufu girl dancers   .60   .60
510 A82 50c Cross, flowers   .65   .65
  a. Souvenir sheet of 9, #502-510 4.00 4.00
     Nos. 502-510 (9)   3.55 3.55

Stamps in #510a do not have "Christmas 1983."
For overprints see Nos. 519-520.

World Communications Year — A83

Wmk. 373

1983, Dec. 19   Litho.   Perf. 14
511 A83 12c Telephone Ex-
              change building   .25   .25
512 A83 18c Ham radio operator   .25   .25
513 A83 25c No. 11   .30   .30
514 A83 $1 No. 14   1.10 1.10
  a. Souvenir sheet of 1   2.25 2.25
     Nos. 511-514 (4)   1.90 1.90

No. 514a is inscribed "1908-1983." See No. 525 for sheet inscribed "1907-1984."

Local
Fungi — A84

6c, Calvatia gardneri. 18c, Marasmiellus inoderma. 35c, Pycnoporus sanguineus. $2, Filoboletus manipularis.

1984, Jan. 30   Perf. 13½
515 A84 6c multicolored   .30   .30
516 A84 18c multicolored   .50   .50
517 A84 35c multicolored   .75   .75
518 A84 $2 multicolored   3.00 3.00
     Nos. 515-518 (4)   4.55 4.55

Type of No. 510 overprinted "VISIT OF POPE JOHN PAUL II May 9th, 1984"

1984, Apr. 16   Wmk. 373
519 A82 12c multicolored   .30   .30
520 A82 50c multicolored   .80   .80

Lloyd's List Issue
Common Design Type

1984, Apr. 21   Litho.   Perf. 14½x14
521 CD335 12c Olivebank, 1892   .65   .65
522 CD335 15c Tinhow, 1906   .85   .65
523 CD335 18c Oriana, Point
                Cruz   .90   .80
524 CD335 $1 Point Cruz view   2.25 2.25
     Nos. 521-524 (4)   4.65 3.95

WCY Type of 1983
Souvenir Sheet

Wmk. 373

1984, June 18   Litho.   Perf. 14
525 A83 $1 multicolored   2.25 2.25

UPU Congress. No. 514a is inscribed "1908-1983," No. 525 inscribed "1907-1984."

Asia-Pacific Broadcasting Union, 20th Anniv. — A86

1984, July 2   **Perf. 13½**
526 A86 12c Village drums   .25 .25
527 A86 45c Radio City Guadal-
     canal   .50 .50
528 A86 60c Broadcasting studio   .70 .70
529 A86 $1 Broadcasting station   1.10 1.10
     Nos. 526-529 (4)   2.55 2.55

1984 Summer Olympics — A87

Perf. 13½x14
1984, Aug. 4   **Litho.**   **Wmk. 373**
530 A87 12c Flag, vert.   .25 .25
531 A87 25c Lawson Tama Stadi-
     um, Honiara   .30 .30
532 A87 50c Honiara Community
     Center   .65 .65
   a.   Booklet pane, 2 ea #531-532   3.00
533 A87 $1 Olympic Stadium   1.30 1.30
     Nos. 530-533 (4)   2.50 2.50

Souvenir Sheet
534 A87 95c Bronte Baths   8.50 8.50

Solomon Islds. first olympic participation. No. 534 available in booklet only. Margin shows swimmer A. Wickham (1886-1976).

Little Pied Cormorant (Ausipex '84) A88

Wmk. 373
1984, Sept. 21   **Litho.**   **Perf. 14½**
535 A88 12c shown   .75 .75
536 A88 18c Australian grey
     duck   1.00 1.00
537 A88 35c Nankeen night-
     heron   1.50 1.50
538 A88 $1 Dollarbird   2.50 2.50
   a.   Souvenir sheet of 4, #535-538   6.50 6.50
     Nos. 535-538 (4)   5.75 5.75

EXPO '85, Tsukuba, Japan A89

Designs: 12c, Japanese Memorial Shrine, Mt. Austen, Guadalcanal. 25c, Digital telephone exchange equipment. 45c, Soltai No. 7 fishing vessel. 85c, Coastal village.

Wmk. 373
1985, June 28   **Litho.**   **Perf. 14**
539 A89 12c multicolored   .25 .25
540 A89 25c multicolored   .30 .30
541 A89 45c multicolored   .55 .55
542 A89 85c multicolored   1.15 1.15
     Nos. 539-542 (4)   2.25 2.25

Queen Mother 85th Birthday
Common Design Type

12c, VE Day, 1945. 25c, With Margaret. 35c, St. Patrick's Day celebration. $1, Holding Prince Henry.
$1.50, In a gondola, Venice.

Perf. 14½x14
1985, June 7   **Litho.**   **Wmk. 384**
543 CD336 12c multicolored   .25 .25
544 CD336 25c multicolored   .25 .25
545 CD336 35c multicolored   .35 .35
546 CD336 $1 multicolored   1.10 1.10
     Nos. 543-546 (4)   1.95 1.95

Souvenir Sheet
547 CD336 $1.50 multicolored   2.25 2.25

For surcharge see No. B2.

Christmas — A90

12c, Titiana Village. 25c, Sigana, Santa Isabel. 35c, Artificial Island, Langa Lagoon.

1985, Aug. 30   **Wmk. 373**   **Perf. 14½**
548 A90 12c multicolored   .25 .25
549 A90 25c multicolored   .35 .35
550 A90 35c multicolored   .45 .45
     Nos. 548-550 (3)   1.05 1.05

A $1 stamp is known to exist, but it was not issued by the Solomon Islands Postal Administration.

Intl. Youth Year — A91

12c, Girl Guide activities. 15c, Stop Polio Campaign. 25c, Relay runners, views of the islands. 35c, Relay runners, views of Australia. 45c, Saluting natl. flag, badges.

1985, Sept. 30   **Perf. 14**
551 A91 12c multicolored   .90 .25
552 A91 15c multicolored   1.00 .60
553 A91 25c multicolored   1.25 .90
554 A91 35c multicolored   1.40 1.00
   a.   Souvenir sheet of 2, #553-554   2.25 2.25
555 A91 45c multicolored   2.50 1.50
     Nos. 551-555 (5)   7.05 4.25

Girl Guides 75th anniv., 12c, 45c; IYY, others.

Souvenir Sheet

Audubon Birth Bicent. — A92

Bird illustration by Audubon.

1985, Nov. 25   **Wmk. 384**
556 A92   Sheet of 3, 45c, 2
     50c   6.50 6.50
   a.   Portrait   1.75 1.75
   b.   Osprey   2.25 2.25

Souvenir Sheet

Mini Hydro-Electric Project, Iriri Village — A93

Designs: 30c, Water-driven generator. 60c, Illuminated village house.

1986, Jan. 24   **Perf. 14**
557 A93   Sheet of 2   2.25 2.25
   a.   30c multicolored   .75 .75
   b.   60c multicolored   1.30 1.30

Halley's Comet A94

Operation Raleigh, 1986: 18c, Construction of Red Cross Center, Gizo. 30c, Exploring rain forest. 60c, Observing Halley's Comet. $1, Ships Sir Walter Raleigh and Zebu.

Perf. 14½x14
1986, Mar. 27   **Wmk. 373**
558 A94 18c multicolored   .90 .25
559 A94 30c multicolored   1.50 .50
560 A94 60c multicolored   2.75 1.50
561 A94 $1 multicolored   3.25 2.25
     Nos. 558-561 (4)   8.40 4.50

Queen Elizabeth II 60th Birthday
Common Design Type

Designs: 5c, Visiting Clydebank Town Hall with Prince Philip, 1947. 18c, At Queen Mother's 80th birthday, St. Paul's Cathedral, 1980. 22c, Walking among children of the islands, Pacific tour, 1982. 55c, 50th birthday, Windsor Castle, 1976. $2, Visiting Crown Agents' offices, 1983.

1986, Apr. 21   **Wmk. 384**   **Perf. 14½**
562 CD337 5c scarlet, blk & sil   .25 .25
563 CD337 18c ultra & multi   .25 .25
564 CD337 22c green & multi   .25 .25
565 CD337 55c violet & multi   .35 .35
566 CD337 $2 rose vio & multi   1.40 1.40
     Nos. 562-566 (5)   2.50 2.50

Royal Wedding Issue, 1986
Common Design Type

Designs: 55c, Informal portrait. 60c, Andrew aboard royal navy vessel.

Wmk. 384
1986, July 23   **Perf. 14**
567 CD338 55c multicolored   .45 .45
568 CD338 60c multicolored   .55 .55

Souvenir Sheet

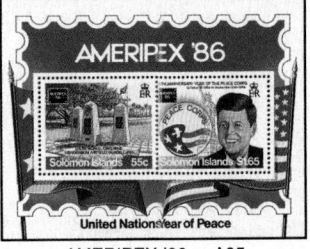

AMERIPEX '86 — A95

55c, U.S. Memorial, Henderson Field, Guadalcanal. $1.65, Peace Corps emblem, Statue of Liberty, Pres. John F. Kennedy.

1986, May 22   **Litho.**   **Perf. 13½**
569 A95   Sheet of 2   2.50 2.50
   a.   55c multicolored   .60 .60
   b. $1.65 multicolored   1.75 1.75

Intl. Peace Year, Peace Corps 25th anniv. For surcharge see No. B3.

1987 America's Cup — A96

Previous winners, challengers, maps and club emblems: No. 570a, America, US, 1851. b, Magic, US, 1870. c, Madeleine, US, 1876. d, Mischief, US, 1881. e, Columbia, US, 1871. f, British Cup course, 1851. g, America II, US, 1987. h, America's Cup. i, Heart of America, US, 1987. j, French Kiss, France, 1987.
No. 571a, Puritan, US, 1885. b, Mayflower, US, 1886. c, Defender, US, 1895. d, Vigilant, US, 1893. e, Volunteer, US, 1887. f, America Cup course, Newport, 1930-1962. g, South Australia, Australia, 1987. h, KA14, Australia, 1987. i, New Zealand II, New Zealand, 1987. j, St. Francis IX, US, 1987.
No. 572a, Columbia, US, 1899. b, Columbia, US, 1901. c, Enterprise, US, 1930. d, Resolute, US, 1920. e, Reliance, US, 1903. f, America Cup course, 1964-1983. g, Kookaburra, Australia, 1987. h, Eagle, US, 1987. i, True North, Canada, 1987. j, Italia, Italy, 1987.
No. 573a, Rainbow, US, 1934. b, Ranger, US, 1937. c, Constellation, US, 1964. d, Weatherly, US, 1962. e, Columbia, US, 1958. f, Western Australia Cup course, 1987. g, Secret Cove, syndicate, 1987. h, Courageous III, US, 1987. i, France, France, 1987. j, Azzurra, Italy, 1987.
No. 574a, Intrepid, US, 1967. b, Intrepid, US, 1970. c, Freedom, US, 1980. d, Courageous, US, 1977. e, Courageous, US, 1974. f, Australia II, Australia, 1983. g, Crusader, Great Britain, 1987. h, Sail America, US, 1987. i, Australia III, Australia, 1987. j, Royal Perth Yacht Club/America's Cup '87 emblem, 1987.

1986, Aug. 22   **Litho.**   **Perf. 14½**
570   Strip of 10 + label   4.00 4.00
  a.-d.   A96 18c any single   .25 .25
  e.-f.   A96 30c any single   .25 .25
  g.-j.   A96 $1 any single   .60 .60
571   Strip of 10 + label   4.00 4.00
  a.-d.   A96 18c any single   .25 .25
  e.-f.   A96 30c any single   .25 .25
  g.-j.   A96 $1 any single   .60 .60
572   Strip of 10 + label   4.00 4.00
  a.-d.   A96 18c any single   .25 .25
  e.-f.   A96 30c any single   .25 .25
  g.-j.   A96 $1 any single   .60 .60
573   Strip of 10 + label   4.00 4.00
  a.-d.   A96 18c any single   .25 .25
  e.-f.   A96 30c any single   .25 .25
  g.-j.   A96 $1 any single   .60 .60
574   Strip of 10 + label   4.00 4.00
  a.-d.   A96 18c any single   .25 .25
  e.-f.   A96 30c any single   .25 .25
  g.-j.   A96 $1 any single   .60 .60
     Nos. 570-574 (5)   20.00 20.00

Nos. 570-574 printed se-tenant with center labels picturing natl. arms, 1987 America's Cup emblem and trophy in sheets of 50.

Souvenir Sheet

1987, Feb. 4   **Litho.**   **Perf. 14½**
575 A96 $5 Stars and Stripes,
     U.S., victor   5.50 5.50

Coral — A97

No. 576, Dendrophyllia gracilis. No. 577, Dendronephthya. No. 578, Clavularia. No. 579, Melithaea squamata.

Perf. 14½x14
1987, Feb. 11   **Litho.**   **Wmk. 384**
576 A97 18c multicolored   .40 .25
577 A97 45c multicolored   .80 .50
578 A97 60c multicolored   1.00 1.00
579 A97 $1.50 multicolored   2.25 2.25
     Nos. 576-579 (4)   4.45 4.00

Flowering Plants — A98

No. 580, Cassia fistula. No. 581, Allamanda cathartica. No. 582, Catharanthus roseus. No. 583, Mimosa pudica. No. 584, Hibiscus rosa-sinensis. No. 585, Clerodendrum thomsonae. No. 586, Bauhinia variegata. No. 587, Gloriosa rothschildiana. No. 588, Heliconia solomonensis. No. 589, Episcia hybrid. No. 590, Bougainvillea hybrid. No. 591, Alpinia purpurata. No. 592, Plumeria rubra. No. 593, Acacia farnesiana. No. 594, Ipomea purpurea. No. 595, Dianella ensifolia. No. 596, Passiflora foetida. No. 596A, Hemigraphis specie ('88).

1987-88

580	A98	1c multicolored	.25	.25
581	A98	5c multicolored	.25	.25
582	A98	10c multicolored	.25	.25
583	A98	18c multicolored	.40	.25
584	A98	20c multicolored	.40	.25
585	A98	22c multicolored	.45	.25
586	A98	25c multicolored	.50	.30
587	A98	28c multicolored	.55	.30
588	A98	30c multicolored	.60	.35
589	A98	40c multicolored	.70	.45
590	A98	45c multicolored	.75	.50
591	A98	50c multicolored	.80	.60
592	A98	55c multicolored	.90	.60
593	A98	60c multicolored	1.00	.70
594	A98	$1 multicolored	2.50	1.10
595	A98	$2 multicolored	3.50	3.50
596	A98	$5 multicolored	5.75	5.75
596A	A98	$10 multicolored	9.00	9.00
		Nos. 580-596A (18)	28.55	24.65

Issue dates: $10, Mar. 1; others, May 12.

Mangrove Kingfisher — A99

Designs: a, Perched on root. b, Diving. c, Landing in water. d, Emerging with fish.

Perf. 14x14½

1987, July 15   **Wmk. 373**
597		Strip of 4	16.00 16.00
a.-d.	A99 60c any single		3.50 3.50

No. 597 has a continuous design.

Orchids — A100

No. 598, Dendrobium conanthum. No. 599, Spathoglottis plicata. No. 600, Dendrobium gouldii. No. 601, Dendrobium goldfinchii.

Perf. 13½x13

1987, Sept. 23   **Wmk. 384**
598	A100	18c multi	1.40	.35
599	A100	30c multi	2.75	.40
600	A100	55c multi	3.25	1.00
601	A100	$1.50 multi	5.50	5.50
		Nos. 598-601 (4)	12.90	7.25

Christmas 1987.

Transportation and Communications Decade — A101

Designs: 18c, Telecommunications link. 30c, Express mail service. 60c, Guadalcanal Road Improvement Project. $2, Beechcraft Queen Air, Henderson Airfield control tower.

Perf. 14x13½

1987, Oct. 31   **Litho.**   **Unwmk.**
602	A101	18c multicolored	.30	.25
603	A101	30c multicolored	.55	.35
604	A101	60c multicolored	.70	.70
605	A101	$2 multicolored	3.00	3.00
		Nos. 602-605 (4)	4.55	4.30

Queen Victoria's Birdwing Butterfly — A102

Designs: No. 606a, Male. No. 606b, Larva. No. 606c, Pupa. No. 606d, Female.

1987, Nov. 25   **Wmk. 384**   **Perf. 14½**
606	A102	Strip of 4	20.00 20.00
a.-d.		45c any single	4.25 4.25

Intl. Fund for Agricultural Development (IFAD), 10th Anniv. — A103

Natl. colors and: No. 607, Student, Natl. Agricultural Training Institute (NATI) farm and emblem (left stamp). No. 608, Students in working in NATI field and emblem (right stamp). No. 609, Flatbed truck transporting produce and emblem (left stamp). No. 610, Canoes, seagulls and emblem (right stamp).

Wmk. 384

1988, Feb. 12   **Litho.**   **Perf. 14½**
607		50c multicolored	.70	.70
608		50c multicolored	.70	.70
a.	A103	Pair, #607-608	1.50	1.50
609		$1 multicolored	.80	.80
610		$1 multicolored	.80	.80
a.	A103	Pair, #609-610	1.75	1.75
		Nos. 607-610 (4)	3.00	3.00

EXPO '88, Brisbane, Apr. 30-Oct. 30 — A104

Designs: 22c, Yacht in dry dock. 80c, Canoe. $1.50, Huts.

Perf. 13½x14

1988, Apr. 30   **Unwmk.**
611	A104	22c multicolored	.25	.25
612	A104	80c multicolored	.75	.75
613	A104	$1.50 multicolored	1.25	1.25
a.		Souv. sheet of 3, #611-613	2.50	2.50
b.		As "a," surcharged $3.50 in margin ('90)	12.00	12.00
		Nos. 611-613 (3)	2.25	2.25

National Independence, 10th Anniv. — A105

22c, Capitana in Estrella Bay. 55c, Flag raising, 1893. 80c, Supreme Court. $1, Traditional celebration.

Perf. 13x13½

1988, July 7   **Litho.**   **Wmk. 373**
614	A105	22c multicolored	1.10	.25
615	A105	55c multicolored	1.90	.60
616	A105	$1 multicolored	1.60	1.40
617	A105	$1 multicolored	1.90	1.90
		Nos. 614-617 (4)	6.50	4.15

Australia Bicentennial — A106

Ships: 35c, M.V. Papuan Chief. 60c, M.V. Nimos. 70c, S.S. Malaita. $1.30, S.S. Makambo.

1988, July 30   **Wmk. 384**   **Perf. 14**
618	A106	35c multicolored	1.25	.35
619	A106	60c multicolored	1.60	.55
620	A106	70c multicolored	1.60	.85
621	A106	$1.30 multicolored	2.10	2.10
a.		Souvenir sheet of 4, #618-621	4.75	4.75
		Nos. 618-621 (4)	6.55	3.85

A107

Wmk. 384

1988, Aug. 5   **Litho.**   **Perf. 14½**
622	A107	22c Archery	.75	.25
623	A107	55c Weight lifting	1.00	.65
624	A107	70c Running	1.25	1.25
625	A107	80c Boxing	1.50	1.50
		Nos. 622-625 (4)	4.50	3.65

Souvenir Sheet
Wmk. 373
626	A107	$2 Olympic Stadium, horiz.	3.25 3.25

1988 Summer Olympics, Seoul.

Lloyds of London, 300th Anniv.
Common Design Type

Designs: 22c, King George V and Queen Mary at Lloyd's ground-breaking ceremony, 1925. 50c, Forthbank, horiz. 65c, Soltel Satellite Ground Station, horiz. $2, Empress of China.

1988, Oct. 31   **Perf. 14**
627	CD341	22c multicolored	.65	.25
628	CD341	50c multicolored	1.75	.45
629	CD341	65c multicolored	2.00	.75
630	CD341	$2 multicolored	3.50	3.00
		Nos. 627-630 (4)	7.90	4.45

Orchids — A108

No. 631, Bulbophyllum dennisii. No. 632, Calanthe langei. No. 633, Bulbophyllum blumei. No. 634, Grammatophyllum speciosum.

Perf. 13½x13

1989, Jan. 20   **Litho.**   **Wmk. 373**
631	A108	22c multicolored	1.25	.30
632	A108	35c multicolored	1.50	.50
633	A108	55c multicolored	2.00	1.25
634	A108	$2 multicolored	3.25	3.25
		Nos. 631-634 (4)	8.00	5.35

Intl. Red Cross, 125th Anniv. — A109

Perf. 14x14½

1989, May 16   **Wmk. 384**
635		35c Disabled children	.60	.60
636		35c Children's Center minibus	.60	.60
a.		Pair, #635-636	1.40	1.40
637		$1.50 Patient abed	2.40	2.40
638		$1.50 Physical therapy	2.40	2.40
a.		A109 Pair, #637-638	5.25	5.25
		Nos. 635-638 (4)	6.00	6.00

Sea Slugs A110

No. 639, Phyllidia varicosa. No. 640, Chromodoris bullocki. No. 641, Chromodoris leopardus. No. 642, Phidiana indica.

1989, June 30   **Wmk. 373**   **Perf. 14½**
639	A110	22c multicolored	1.25	.30
640	A110	70c multicolored	2.75	1.75
641	A110	80c multicolored	3.00	2.50
642	A110	$1.50 multicolored	4.00	4.00
		Nos. 639-642 (4)	11.00	8.55

Moon Landing, 20th Anniv.
Common Design Type

Apollo 16: 22c, Splashdown. 35c, Launch. 70c, Mission emblem. 80c, Ultraviolet color enhancement of Earth. $4, The Moon, as photographed during the Apollo 11 mission.

1989, July 20   **Wmk. 384**   **Perf. 14**
Size of Nos. 644-645: 29x29mm
643	CD342	22c multicolored	.75	.30
644	CD342	35c multicolored	1.25	.55
645	CD342	70c multicolored	2.00	2.00
646	CD342	80c multicolored	2.25	2.25
		Nos. 643-646 (4)	6.25	5.10

Souvenir Sheet
647	CD342	$4 multicolored	6.50 6.50

Blowing Soap Bubbles A111

Children's games — 5c, Five stones catch, vert. 73c, Coconut shell empire. $1, Seed wind sound, vert.
$3, Baseball, softball, vert.

1989, Nov. 17   **Wmk. 384**
648	A111	5c multicolored	.30	.55
649	A111	67c shown	2.00	2.00
650	A111	73c multicolored	2.00	2.00
651	A111	$1 multicolored	3.00	3.00
		Nos. 648-651 (4)	7.30	7.55

Souvenir Sheet
Wmk. 373
652	A111	$3 multicolored	9.50 9.50

World Stamp Expo '89.

Christmas — A112

1989, Nov. 30   **Wmk. 384**
653	A112	18c Butterfly, fishermen	.70	.30
654	A112	25c Nativity	.90	.35
655	A112	45c Hospital ward	1.60	.50
656	A112	$1.50 Tug of war	3.75	3.75
		Nos. 653-656 (4)	6.95	4.90

Personal Ornaments A113

1990, Feb. 14   Litho.   Wmk. 373
657	A113	5c shown	.40	1.00
658	A113	12c Necklace	.70	.45
659	A113	18c Islander, diff.	.75	.60
660	A113	$2 Head ornament	6.75	6.75
		Nos. 657-660 (4)	8.60	8.80

Cowrie Shells A114

1990, July 23
666	A114	4c Spindle cowrie	.50	1.00
667	A114	20c Map cowrie	1.25	.40
668	A114	35c Sieve cowrie	1.50	.50
669	A114	50c Egg cowrie	2.50	2.50
670	A114	$1 Prince cowrie	4.25	4.25
		Nos. 666-670 (5)	10.00	8.65

Queen Mother, 90th Birthday
Common Design Types

25c, Queen Mother, 1987. $5, Inspecting damage to Buckingham Palace, 1940.

1990, Aug. 4   Wmk. 384   Perf. 14x15
671	CD343	25c multicolored	1.25	.40

Perf. 14½
672	CD344	$5 brown & blk	5.25	6.00

First Postage Stamp, 150th Anniv. A115

Designs: 35c, Postman, mail van. 45c, Solomon Islands Post Office. 50c, Solomon Islands No. 1. 55c, Young philatelist. 60c, Solomon Islands No. 20, Penny Black.

1990, Oct. 15   Wmk. 373   Perf. 14
673	A115	35c multicolored	1.50	.50
674	A115	45c multicolored	1.50	.55
675	A115	50c multicolored	1.75	1.75
676	A115	55c multicolored	1.75	1.75
677	A115	60c multicolored	2.50	2.50
		Nos. 673-677 (5)	9.00	7.05

Birds A116

10c, Purple swamphen. 25c, Rufous brown pheasant dove. 30c, Superb fruit dove. 45c, Cardinal honeyeater. $2, Pigmy parrot.

1990, Dec. 5
678	A116	10c multi	1.00	1.00
679	A116	25c multi	1.75	.70
680	A116	30c multi	2.25	.75
681	A116	45c multi	2.50	.90
682	A116	$2 multi	5.50	5.50
		Nos. 678-682 (5)	13.00	8.85

Birdpex '90, 20th Intl. Ornithological Congress, New Zealand.

Crop Pests — A117

7c, Sweet potato weevil. 25c, Melon fly. 40c, Taro beetle. 90c, Cocoa weevil borer. $1.50, Rhinoceros beetle.

Perf. 14x13½
1991, Jan. 16   Litho.   Wmk. 373
683	A117	7c multi	.75	.50
684	A117	25c multi	1.25	.35
685	A117	40c multi	1.75	.65
686	A117	90c multi	2.75	2.75
687	A117	$1.50 multi	3.00	3.00
		Nos. 683-687 (5)	9.50	7.25

For No. 683 overprinted, see No. 884A.

Elizabeth & Philip, Birthdays
Common Design Types
Wmk. 384
1991, June 17   Litho.   Perf. 14½
688	CD346	90c multicolored	1.40	1.40
689	CD345	$2 multicolored	3.00	3.00
a.		Pair, #688-689 + label	4.50	4.50

No. 689a exists with two different labels.

Nutritional Foods — A118

1991, June 24   Wmk. 373   Perf. 14
690	A118	5c Coconut water	.25	.50
691	A118	75c Feed your child	1.75	1.75
692	A118	80c Mother's milk	2.00	2.00
693	A118	90c Local food	2.50	2.50
		Nos. 690-693 (4)	6.50	6.75

A 65c value, depicting healthy and unhealthy foods, was prepared but not issued. Value $325.

9th South Pacific Games — A119

Wmk. 384
1991, Aug. 8   Litho.   Perf. 14
694	A119	25c Volleyball	1.40	.35
695	A119	40c Judo	1.75	.75
696	A119	65c Squash	2.50	2.50
697	A119	90c Lawn bowling	2.75	2.75
		Nos. 694-697 (4)	8.40	6.35

Souvenir Sheet
698	A119	$2 Games emblem	7.75	7.75

Christmas — A120

Wmk. 373
1991, Oct. 28   Litho.   Perf. 14
699	A120	10c Food preparation	.45	.25
700	A120	25c Church service	.80	.25
701	A120	65c Feast	2.25	1.00
702	A120	$2 Cricket match	4.50	4.50
a.		Souvenir sheet of 4, #699-702	9.50	9.50
		Nos. 699-702 (4)	8.00	6.00

Phila Nippon '91 — A121

Tuna fishing: 5c, Yellowfin tuna. 30c, Boat for pole and line tuna fishing. 80c, Pole and line tuna fishing. $2, Arabushi processing. No. 707a, Food made from tuna, tori nanban. b, Aka miso soup.

Wmk. 384
1991, Nov. 16   Litho.   Perf. 14
703	A121	5c multicolored	.35	.25
704	A121	30c multicolored	1.05	.50
705	A121	80c multicolored	2.50	2.50
706	A121	$2 multicolored	4.50	4.50
		Nos. 703-706 (4)	8.40	7.75

Souvenir Sheet
707	A121	80c Sheet of 2, #a.-		
b.			3.75	3.75

No. 707 contains two 28x45mm stamps.

Queen Elizabeth II's Accession to the Throne, 40th Anniv.
Common Design Type
Wmk. 384 (5c, 60c), 373
1992, Feb. 6   Litho.   Perf. 14
708	CD349	5c multicolored	.35	.60
709	CD349	20c multicolored	.65	.25
710	CD349	40c multicolored	.95	.45
711	CD349	60c multicolored	1.00	1.00
712	CD349	$5 multicolored	5.00	5.00
		Nos. 708-712 (5)	7.95	7.30

Alvaro Mendana de Niera (1541-1595), Discoveries in the Solomon Islands — A122

Granada '92: 10c, Thousand Ships Bay. 65c, Route to the Solomon Islands. 80c, Alvaro Mendana de Niera. $1, Graciosa Bay settlement. $5, Sailing ships.

Perf. 15x14½
1992, Apr. 24   Litho.   Wmk. 373
713	A122	10c multicolored	.85	.45
714	A122	65c multicolored	1.50	.70
715	A122	80c multicolored	1.60	1.60
716	A122	$1 multicolored	2.25	2.25
717	A122	$5 multicolored	4.75	4.75
		Nos. 713-717 (5)	10.95	9.75

A123

Perf. 14x13½
1992, May 3   Litho.   Wmk. 373
718	A123	25c Early portrait	.75	.40
719	A123	70c Wearing USMC fatigues	1.50	1.50
720	A123	90c Wearing uniform, cap	1.50	1.50
a.		Booklet pane, 2 ea #718, 720	4.50	
721	A123	$2 Statue	2.25	2.25
a.		Booklet pane, 2 ea #719, 721	7.50	
		Nos. 718-721 (4)	6.00	5.65

Souvenir Sheet
722	A123	$4 In dress uniform	9.50	9.50
a.		Booklet pane of 1	7.50	
		Complete booklet, one each #720a, 721a, 722a	17.00	

Sergeant Major Jacob Vouza (1891-1984). One margin of Nos. 720a, 721a, and 722a is rouletted 8.

A124

World Columbian Stamp Expo '92, Chicago: 25c, Solomon Airlines domestic routes. 80c, Boeing 737-400 airplanes. $1.50, Solomon Airlines international routes. $5, Columbus and Santa Maria.

1992, May 22
723	A124	25c multicolored	1.00	.25
724	A124	80c multicolored	2.75	2.00
725	A124	$1.50 multicolored	3.75	3.75
726	A124	$5 multicolored	7.50	7.50
a.		Souvenir sheet of 4, #723-726	15.00	15.00
b.		As "a," ovptd. with Taipei '93 emblem in sheet margin	8.00	8.00
		Nos. 723-726 (4)	15.00	13.50

No. 726b issued Aug. 14, 1993.

Miniature Sheets

Battle of Guadalcanal, 50th Anniv. — A125

Scenes from battle of Guadalcanal: No. 727a, Japanese landing at Esperance. b, US landings. c, Australian Navy cruiser. d, US Navy post office. e, Royal New Zealand Air Force PBY Catalina.

No. 728a, US Marine Wildcat fighters. b, Henderson Field under construction and attack. c, Heavy cruiser USS Quincy. d, Australian Navy heavy cruiser Canberra. e, US Marines land on Guadalcanal. f, Japanese aircraft carrier Ryujo. g, Japanese Zeke fighters attack US positions. h, Japanese bombers attack American beachhead. i, Japanese destroyers of Tokyo Express. j, Japanese heavy cruiser Chokai.

Wmk. 384
1992, Aug. 7   Litho.   Perf. 14
727	A125	30c Sheet of 5, #a.-		
e.		+ label	5.00	5.00
728	A125	80c Sheet of 10, #a.-j. + label	20.00	20.00

See No. 889.

Orchids A126

15c, Dendrobium hybrid. 70c, Vanda "Amy Laycock". 95c, Dendrobium mirbelianum. $2.50, Dendrobium macrophyllum.

Perf. 14½x14
1992, Dec. 14   Litho.   Wmk. 373
729	A126	15c multicolored	.90	.30
730	A126	70c multicolored	1.75	1.25
731	A126	95c multicolored	2.25	2.25
732	A126	$2.50 multicolored	3.50	3.50
		Nos. 729-732 (4)	8.40	7.30

See Nos. 752-755.

Crabs A127

5c, Stalk-eyed ghost. 10c, Red-spotted. 25c, Flat. 30c, Land hermit. 40c, Grapsid. 45c, Red & white painted. 55c, Swift-footed. 60c, Spanner. 70c, Red hermit. 80c, Red-eyed. 90c,

Rathbun red. $1, Coconut. $1.10, Red-spotted white. $4, Ghost. $10, Mangrove fiddler.

Wmk. 373

1993, Jan. 15 Litho. *Perf. 13*

733	A127	5c multicolored	.25	.55
734	A127	10c multicolored	.25	.55
735	A127	25c multicolored	.25	.55
736	A127	30c multicolored	.25	.25
737	A127	40c multicolored	.30	.30
738	A127	45c multicolored	.30	.30
739	A127	55c multicolored	.35	.35
740	A127	60c multicolored	.40	.35
741	A127	70c multicolored	.50	.45
742	A127	80c multicolored	.55	.50
743	A127	90c multicolored	.60	.55
744	A127	$1 multicolored	.65	.60
745	A127	$1.10 multicolored	.70	.70
746	A127	$4 multicolored	2.25	*3.00*
a.		Souvenir sheet of 1, perf. 14	4.00	4.00
747	A127	$10 multicolored	6.25	6.25
		Nos. 733-747 (15)	13.85	15.25

No. 746a for Hong Kong '97. Issued: #733-747, 1/15/93; #746a, 2/3/97.

World War II, 50th Anniv. A128

Designs: 30c, US War Memorial, Skyline Ridge. 80c, Country flags, Guadalcanal. 95c, Major General Alexander A. Vandegrift, map. $4, WWII Scouts, Gizo Islands.

Wmk. 373

1993, Apr. 19 Litho. *Perf. 14*

748	A128	30c multicolored	.55	.35
749	A128	80c multicolored	1.75	1.40
750	A128	95c multicolored	2.00	1.75
751	A128	$4 multicolored	6.25	6.25
		Nos. 748-751 (4)	10.55	9.75

Orchid Type of 1992

Perf. 14½x14

1993 Litho. Wmk. 373

752	A126	20c like #729	.70	.40
753	A126	85c like #730	1.75	1.50
754	A126	$1.15 like #731	2.10	2.10
755	A126	$3 like #732	3.50	3.50
		Nos. 752-755 (4)	8.05	7.50

Nos. 752, 755 are inscribed "World Orchid Conference." Nos. 753-754 are inscribed "Indopex '93 Exhibition."
Issued: #752, 755, 4/24; #753-754, 4/29.

Sinking of PT 109, 50th Anniv. A129

Designs: 30c, PT 109 about to be rammed. 50c, Native, Lt. John F. Kennedy. 95c, Message for help written on coconut, natives in canoe. $1.10, Kennedy, Navy and Marine Corps Medal. $5, PT 109.

Wmk. 373

1993, July 30 Litho. *Perf. 13*

756	A129	30c multicolored	.75	.50
757	A129	50c multicolored	1.00	.70
758	A129	95c multicolored	1.25	1.25
759	A129	$1.10 multicolored	2.50	2.50
		Nos. 756-759 (4)	5.50	4.95

Souvenir Sheet

Perf. 13x13½

760	A129	$5 multicolored	8.50	8.50

Nicobar Pigeon — A130

50c, One on ground. 65c, Two on branches. 70c, One on branch. $1.10, One on berry branch. $3, Two in flight.

Wmk. 373

1993, Sept. 21 Litho. *Perf. 14*

761	A130	30c multi	1.25	1.00
762	A130	50c multi	1.60	1.25
763	A130	65c multi	2.10	1.75
764	A130	70c multi	3.00	2.50
765	A130	$1.10 multi	1.25	1.25
766	A130	$3 multi	2.25	2.25
		Nos. 761-766 (6)	11.45	10.00

World Wildlife Fund.

Dogs A131

30c, Dachshund. 80c, German shepherd. 95c, Dobermann pinscher. $1.10, Australian cattle dog.
$4, Boxer.

Wmk. 373

1994, Feb. 18 Litho. *Perf. 14½*

767	A131	30c multi	1.10	.40
768	A131	80c multi	1.75	1.75
769	A131	95c multi	2.00	2.00
770	A131	$1.10 multi	2.25	2.25
		Nos. 767-770 (4)	7.10	6.40

Souvenir Sheet

771	A131	$4 multi	11.00	11.00

Hong Kong '94.
No. 771 overprinted "19-25 Aug. Jakarta '95 Surcharge $2-00." was available only at the exhibition. Value, $14.

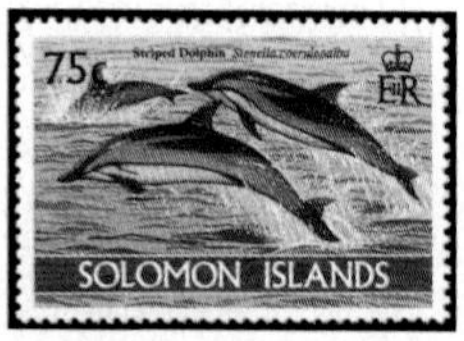

Dolphins A132

Wmk. 373

1994, May 9 Litho. *Perf. 14*

772	A132	75c Striped	1.10	.80
773	A132	85c Risso's	1.25	1.10
774	A132	$1.15 Common	1.75	1.75
775	A132	$2.50 Spinner	3.75	3.75
776	A132	$3 Bottlenose	4.25	4.25
		Nos. 772-776 (5)	12.10	11.65

Miniature Sheet

Butterflies — A133

Designs: a, Vindula sapor. b, Papilio aegeus. c, Graphium hicetaon. d, Graphium mendana. e, PHILAKOREA '94 emblem. f, Graphium meeki. g, Danaus schenkii. h, Papilio ptolychus. i, Phaedyma fissizonata.

Wmk. 373

1994, Aug. 16 Litho. *Perf. 13½*

777	A133	70c Sheet of 9, #a.-i.	8.50	8.50

For overprint see No. 842.

Intl. Year of the Family — A134

Designs: a, Girl writing letter in Brisbane, Australia, family reading letter on Santa Isabel, Solomon Islands. b, Boeing 737-400, Brisbane Intl. Airport, Australia. c, Boeing 737-400, Henderson Airfield, Guadalcanal, DHC 6-Twin Otter. d, Fera Airfield, Buala, Santa Isabel. e, Family.

1994, Aug. 18 *Perf. 13*

778	A134	$1.10 Strip of 5, #a.-e.	6.75	6.75
f.		Sheet of 1, #778	7.25	7.25

Volcanoes of the Solomon Islands A135

Designs: 30c, Cook Island Volcano erupting under sea, 1967. 70c, Kavachi Volcano erupting from sea, 1977. 80c, Kavachi Volcano forming temporary island, 1978. 90c, Tinakulu Volcano, permanent island.
No. 783: a, Map of Solomon Island volcanoes. b, Diagram illustrating formation of volcanic island archipelago.

Wmk. 373

1994, Oct. 24 Litho. *Perf. 14*

779	A135	30c multicolored	.85	.50
780	A135	70c multicolored	1.00	1.00
781	A135	80c multicolored	1.25	1.25
782	A135	90c multicolored	1.90	1.75
		Nos. 779-782 (4)	5.00	4.50

Souvenir Sheet

783	A135	$2 Sheet of 2, #a.-b.	5.50	5.50

La Perouse Expedition, 210th Anniv. A136

Designs: 30c, La Perouse, King Louis XVI. 80c, Map of Ile de La Perouse. 95c, L'Astrolabe. $1.10, La Boussole. $3, L'Astrolabe foundering on reef.

Wmk. 384

1994, Dec. 16 Litho. *Perf. 14*

784	A136	30c multicolored	.75	.35
785	A136	80c multicolored	1.50	1.50
786	A136	95c multicolored	2.00	2.00
787	A136	$1.10 multicolored	2.25	2.25
788	A136	$3 multicolored	3.50	3.50
		Nos. 784-788 (5)	10.00	9.60

Visit South Pacific Year A137

30c, Tourists watching traditional dance, land hermit crab. 50c, Dendrobium rennellii, milkweed butterfly. 95c, Diver, moorish idol, fish. $1.15, Boats at shore, grapsid crab.
$4, Flower, yellow-bibbed lorry.

Perf. 15x14½

1995, Feb. 17 Litho. Wmk. 373

789	A137	30c multicolored	.35	.35
790	A137	50c multicolored	.85	.85
791	A137	95c multicolored	.95	.95
792	A137	$1.15 multicolored	1.10	1.10
		Nos. 789-792 (4)	3.25	3.25

Souvenir Sheet

793	A137	$4 multicolored	9.00	9.00

FAO, 50th Anniv. A138

1995, Apr. 5 *Perf. 12*

794	A138	70c Banana	1.10	.90
795	A138	75c Paw paw	1.10	.90
796	A138	95c Pomelo	1.50	1.40
797	A138	$2 Star fruit	2.75	2.75
		Nos. 794-797 (4)	6.45	5.95

Souvenir Sheet

798	A138	$3 Mango	4.00	4.00

End of World War II, 50th Anniv.

Common Design Types

Admirals, aircraft carriers: 95c, Vice Adm. Chuichi Nagumo, Akagi. $1, Rear Adm. Frank J. Fletcher, USS Yorktown. $2, Vice Adm. Robert L. Ghormley, USS Wasp. $3, Vice Adm. William F. Halsey, USS Enterprise.
$5, Reverse of War Medal 1939-45.

1995, May 8 *Perf. 13½*

799	CD351	95c multicolored	1.75	1.75
800	CD351	$1 multicolored	1.75	1.75
801	CD351	$2 multicolored	3.25	3.25
802	CD351	$3 multicolored	4.25	4.25
		Nos. 799-802 (4)	11.00	11.00

Souvenir Sheet

Perf. 14

803	CD352	$5 multicolored	6.50	6.50

Orchids — A139

Designs: 45c, Calanthe triplicata. 75c, Dendrobium mohlianum. 85c, Flickingeria comata. $1.15, Dendrobium spectabile.
$4, Coelogyne asperata.

Wmk. 373

1995, Sept. 1 Litho. *Perf. 14*

804	A139	45c multicolored	1.75	.35
805	A139	75c multicolored	2.00	1.10
806	A139	85c multicolored	2.00	1.50
807	A139	$1.15 multicolored	2.50	2.50
		Nos. 804-807 (4)	8.25	5.45

Souvenir Sheet

808	A139	$4 multicolored	6.00	6.00

Singapore '95 (#808).

Christmas — A140

Designs: 90c, Start of canoe race. $1.05, Pan pipers, Christmas tree. $1.25, Picnic on beach. $1.45, Local church, nativity.

1995, Nov. 6 *Perf. 13x13½*

810	A140	90c multicolored	1.00	.80
811	A140	$1.05 multicolored	1.00	.85
812	A140	$1.25 multicolored	1.25	1.10
813	A140	$1.45 multicolored	1.75	1.50
		Nos. 810-813 (4)	5.00	4.25

Guglielmo Marconi (1847-1937), Radio, Cent. — A141

Designs: $1.05, Demonstration, Salisbury Plain, 1896. $1.20, Birth of maritime radio, 1900. $1.35, First ground air transmitter, Croydon, 1920. $1.45, Marconi visiting Japan on world tour, 1933-34.

Perf. 14½x14

1996, Feb. 28 Litho. Wmk. 373

814	A141	$1.05 multicolored	1.00	1.00
815	A141	$1.20 multicolored	1.25	1.25
816	A141	$1.35 multicolored	1.50	1.50
817	A141	$1.45 multicolored	1.75	1.75
		Nos. 814-817 (4)	5.50	5.50

Lories
A142

75c, Palm lorikeet. $1.05, Duchess lorikeet.
$1.20, Yellow-bibbed lory. $1.35, Cardinal lory.
$1.45, Meek's lorikeet.
$3, Rainbow lorikeet.

1996, Apr. 10   Litho.   Perf. 14
818 A142 75c multicolored   1.50 .60
819 A142 $1.05 multicolored   1.60 .80
820 A142 $1.20 multicolored   1.75 1.50
821 A142 $1.35 multicolored   2.50 2.50
822 A142 $1.45 multicolored   2.50 2.50
   Nos. 818-822 (5)   9.85 7.90

Souvenir Sheet
823 A142 $3 multicolored   5.75 5.75

CAPEX '96 — A143

Island scenes: 40c, Dug-out canoe. 90c,
Man, bicycle. $1.20, Mobile Post Office bus.
$1.45, "Tulagi Express."
$4, "Tepuke," traditional canoe from Temotu
Province.

Wmk. 384
1996, June 8   Litho.   Perf. 13
824 A143 40c multicolored   .55 .45
825 A143 90c multicolored   1.40 1.00
826 A143 $1.20 multicolored   1.50 1.50
827 A143 $1.45 multicolored   2.50 2.50
   Nos. 824-827 (4)   5.95 5.45

Souvenir Sheet
828 A143 $4 multicolored   4.25 4.25

1996 Summer Olympic Games, Atlanta — A144

Olympic posters: 90c, Tokyo, 1964. $1.20,
Los Angeles, 1932. $1.35, Paris, 1924. $2.50,
London, 1908.

Wmk. 384
1996, June 30   Litho.   Perf. 14
829 A144 90c multicolored   .70 .55
830 A144 $1.20 multicolored   .85 .85
831 A144 $1.35 multicolored   1.00 1.00
832 A144 $2.50 multicolored   1.60 1.60
   Nos. 829-832 (4)   4.15 4.00

First Christian Mission, 150th Anniv. — A145

Designs: 40c, Suiesi, Makira Bay, 1846-47.
65c, Original sketches by Rev. L. Verguet,
1846, Surimahe. $1.35, Bishop Epalle's grave,
Isabel, 1845. $1.45, Makira Mission, Jean
Claude Colin, Marist founder.

Wmk. 373
1996, Sept. 12   Litho.   Perf. 14
833 A145 40c multicolored   .40 .25
834 A145 65c multicolored   .50 .50
835 A145 $1.35 multicolored   .80 .75
836 A145 $1.45 multicolored   1.00 1.00
   Nos. 833-836 (4)   2.70 2.50

Souvenir Sheet

Taipei '96 — A146

1996, Oct. 21
837 A146 $1.50 Sandford's eagle 2.50 2.50

UNICEF, 50th Anniv. A147

Wmk. 373
1996, Nov. 21   Litho.   Perf. 14½
838 A147 40c Food   .35 .30
839 A147 $1.05 Recreation   .70 .70
840 A147 $1.35 Medicine   1.00 1.00
841 A147 $2.50 Education   1.50 1.50
   Nos. 838-841 (4)   3.55 3.50

For surcharge see No. B4.

No. 777 Ovptd. in Red with SINGPEX '97 Emblem
Wmk. 373
1997, Feb. 21   Litho.   Perf. 13½
842 A133 70c Sheet of 9, #a.-i. 9.00 9.00

Overprint is centered over entire sheet with
each stamp containing portion of SINGPEX
'97 emblem.
Overprint exists in black from a limited
printing.

Northern Common Cuscus A148

15c, In tree. 60c, Eating berries. $2.50, In
tree, climbing right. $3, Two in branches.

Wmk. 373
1997, Apr. 21   Litho.   Perf. 12
843 A148 15c multicolored   .25 .25
844 A148 60c multicolored   .30 .30
845 A148 $2.50 multicolored   1.10 1.10
846 A148 $3 multicolored   1.40 1.40
   Nos. 843-846 (4)   3.05 3.05

Whales — A149

a, Whale, calf, vert. b, Whale breaching.

Wmk. 373
1997, May 29   Litho.   Perf. 14½
847 A149 $2 Sheet of 2, #a.-b. 3.50 3.50
PACIFIC 97.

Queen Elizabeth II & Prince Philip,
50th Wedding Anniv. — A150

#848, Queen with two horses. #849, Prince.
#850, Prince on polo pony. #851, Queen.
#852, Queen, Prince at Royal Ascot.

1997, July 10   Perf. 13
848 $3 multicolored   2.25 2.25
849 $3 multicolored   2.25 2.25
 a. A150 Pair, #848-849   5.00 5.00
850 $3 multicolored   2.25 2.25
851 $3 multicolored   2.25 2.25
 a. A150 Pair, #850-851   5.00 5.00
   Nos. 848-851 (4)   9.00 9.00

Souvenir Sheet
852 A150 $3 multicolored   4.00 4.00

South Pacific Commission, 50th Anniv. — A151

Chelonia mydas: 50c, Laying eggs. 90c,
Young turtles entering water. $1.50, Group
swimming under water. $2, Two adults under
water.

Wmk. 384
1997, Sept. 29   Litho.   Perf. 14
853 A151 50c multicolored   .60 .40
854 A151 90c multicolored   .85 .75
855 A151 $1.50 multicolored   1.25 1.25
856 A151 $2 multicolored   1.40 1.40
   Nos. 853-856 (4)   4.10 3.80

Christmas A152

Designs: $1.10, Oni mako. $1.40, Ysabel
dancing women with bamboo sticks. $1.50,
Pan pipers from Small Malaita. $1.70, Western
bamboo band.
No. 861, vert.: a, Pachycephala pectoralis.
b, Papilio aegeus, graphium meeki.

Wmk. 373
1997, Nov. 24   Litho.   Perf. 13½
857 A152 $1.10 multicolored   .75 .75
858 A152 $1.40 multicolored   .90 .90
859 A152 $1.50 multicolored   1.00 1.00
860 A152 $1.70 multicolored   1.25 1.25
   Nos. 857-860 (4)   3.90 3.90

Souvenir Sheet of 2
Perf. 14
861 A152 $1.50 #a.-b.   4.00 4.00
China Stamp Exhibition, Bangkok '97 (#861).
Issued: #857-860, 11/24; #861, 12/5.

Game Fish — A153

50c, Black marlin. $1.20, Shortbill swordfish.
$1.40, Swordfish. $2, Indo-Pacific sailfish.

Perf. 14½
1998, Feb. 27   Litho.   Unwmk.
862 A153 50c multicolored   .85 .45
863 A153 $1.20 multicolored   1.40 1.10
864 A153 $1.40 multicolored   1.75 1.75
865 A153 $2 multicolored   2.00 2.00
 a. Souv. sheet of 1, wmk. triangles 2.50 2.50
   Nos. 862-865 (4)   6.00 5.30
Singpex '98 (#865a). No. 865a issued 7/23
and sold for $3.

Diana, Princess of Wales (1961-97)
Common Design Type

$2, Wearing white dress (without hat).
#867: a, Up close. b, Wearing white hat,
dress. c, Wearing evening dress, black background. d, Taking flowers from children.

Perf. 14½x14
1998, Mar. 31   Wmk. 373
866 CD355 $2 multicolored   .90 .90
   Complete booklet, 10 #866   9.00

Sheet of 4
867 CD355 $2.50 #a.-d.   6.00 6.00

No. 867 sold for $10 + 50c, with surtax from
international sales being donated to the Princess Diana Memorial Fund and surtax from
national sales being donated to designated
local charity.
For overprint see No. 1095; for surcharge
see No. B5.

Technical Cooperation Between Solomon Islands and Republic of China A154

Designs: 50c, Harvesting watermelons.
$1.50, Harvesting rice.
No. 870: a, 80c, Growing cucumbers. b,
$1.20, Growing tomatoes.

Wmk. 373
1998, May 29   Litho.   Perf. 13
868 A154 50c multicolored   .40 .40
869 A154 $1.50 multicolored   1.10 1.10

Souvenir Sheet
870 A154 Sheet of 2, #a.-b.   2.25 2.25

Melanesian Trade and Culture Show — A155

a, Group raising arms during traditional
dance. b, Men with bows and arrow. c, Man
smiling in front of water. d, Four men with
poles in traditional dance. e, Masked man
kneeling down with bow and arrow. f, Man in
traditional garb, flowers. g, Group carrying
poles. h, Man with spear and shield. i, Man in
traditional garb, sun over water.

1998, July 3   Perf. 13½
871 Sheet of 9   6.50 6.50
 a.-c. A155 50c any single   .40 .40
 d.-f. A155 $1.20 any single   .50 .50
 g.-i. A155 $1.50 any single   .65 .65

Souvenir Sheet

New Natl. Parliament Building — A156

1998, July 7
872 A156 $4 multicolored   3.75 3.75
Independence, 20th anniv.

Souvenir Sheet

Australia '99 World Stamp Expo — A157

Designs: a, HMS Endeavour, 1770. b, Los Reyes being careened at Guadalcanal, 1568.

1999, Mar. 19   **Perf. 13¼x13¾**
873 A157 $10 Sheet of 2, #a.-
     b.   13.00 13.00

PhilexFrance '99, World Philatelic Exhibition. A158

Marine Life: a, Beach. b, Great frigate bird. c, Coconut crab. d, Green turtle. e, Royal Spanish dancer nudibranch. f, Sun moon and stars butterflyfish. g, Striped Sweetlips. h, Saddle-back butterflyfish. i, Cuttlefish. j, Giant clam. k, Lionfish. l, Spiny lobster.

1999, July 2   **Perf. 13¼**
874 A158 $1 Sheet of 12, #a.-l.   9.00 9.00

1st Manned Moon Landing, 30th Anniv.
Common Design Type

Designs: 50c, Lift-off. $1.50, Lunar module above moon's surface. $2.50, Aldrin beside US flag. $3.40, Splashdown. $4, Earth as seen from moon.

Perf. 14x13¾

			Wmk. 384	
1999, July 20		**Litho.**		
875	CD357	50c multicolored	.50	.35
876	CD357	$1.50 multicolored	1.00	1.00
877	CD357	$2.50 multicolored	2.00	2.00
878	CD357	$3.40 multicolored	2.50	2.50
		Nos. 875-878 (4)	6.00	5.85

Souvenir Sheet
Perf. 14

879	CD357	$4 multicolored	4.00	4.00
a		Ovptd. in margin in red	4.50	4.50

No. 879 contains one circular stamp 40mm in diameter.
Issued 7/7/2000, overprint on No. 879a reads "WORLD STAMP EXPO - USA VALUE $5.00." Sold for $5.

Queen Mother's Century
Common Design Type

Queen Mother: $1, Inspecting bomb damage at Portsmouth, 1941. $1.50, At the Derby, 1983. $2.30, Receiving birthday wishes. $4.90, As colonel-in-chief of Royal Army Medical Corps. $3, With King George VI, Winston Churchill, V-E Day, 1945.

1999, Aug. 16   **Perf. 13½**
880	CD358	$1 multicolored	.90	.50
881	CD358	$1.50 multicolored	1.10	.95
882	CD358	$2.30 multicolored	1.50	1.50
883	CD358	$4.90 multicolored	2.50	2.50
		Nos. 880-883 (4)	6.00	5.45

Souvenir Sheet
884	CD358	$5 black	4.00	4.00

No. 683 overprinted "China '99" in red for international stamp exhibition, Beijing
1999, Aug. 21
884A	A117	7c Sweet potato weevil	1.75	1.75

Ferrari Racing Cars A159

1999, Sept. 27   **Wmk. 373**   **Perf. 14**
885	A159	$1 212E	.85	.55
886	A159	$1.50 250TR	1.00	.75
887	A159	$3.30 250LM	1.75	1.75
888	A159	$4.20 612 Can-Am	3.00	3.00
		Nos. 885-888 (4)	6.60	6.05

Guadalcanal Type of 1992

Designs: a, Flags at half staff. b, Cenotaph, Honiara. c, Solomon Peace Memorial Park. d, US War Memorial, Skyline Ridge. e, Reunion ship Ocean Pearl.

1999, Aug. 16   **Wmk. 384**
889	A125	30c Sheet of 5, #a.-e, + label	2.75	2.75
f.		Sheet of 10, #727a-727e, 889a-889e + label	8.50	8.50

Melanesian Mission, 150th Anniv. — A160

Christmas: a, $1, Bishop George Augustus Selwyndd. b, $1, Bishop John Coleridge Patteson. c, $3.30, Text. d, $1.50, Stained glass. e, $1.50, Southern Cross.

1999, Nov. 12   **Unwmk.**
890 A160 Strip of 5, #a.-e.   4.50 4.50
See Norfolk Islands #693.

Millennium A161

Designs: Nos. 891, 893a, $1 Munda lighthouse, war canoe. Nos. 892, 893b, $4, Tulagi lighthouse, security boat.

2000, Apr. 27   **Perf. 13½x13¼**
891	A161	$1 multi	1.50	1.00
892	A161	$4 multi	5.00	5.00

Souvenir Sheet
893	A161	Sheet of 2, #a.-b.	7.50	7.50

Nos. 893a, 893b have red violet margins.

Souvenir Sheet

Commonwealth Youth Minister's Meeting — A162

2000, May 22 **Litho.** **Perf. 13½x13¼**
894	A162	$6 multi	8.00	8.00

Year of the Dragon A163

Dragon head facing: $1, Front. $3.90, Left.

Perf. 11¾x11½
2000, Nov. 13   **Litho.**   **Unwmk.**
895-896	A163	Set of 2	3.50	3.50
896a		Souvenir sheet, #895-896	3.50	3.50

East Rennell Island World Heritage Site A164

Map and: 50c, Rennell Island. $3.40, Lake Tegano. $4, Rennell shrikebill. $4.90, Endemic orchid.

Perf. 11¾x11½
2000, Nov. 30   **Litho.**
897-900	A164	Set of 4	10.00 10.00

2000 Summer Olympics and Olymphilex, Sydney — A165

Runners in: $1, 100-meter race. $4.50, 1500-meter race.

2000, Dec. 11   **Perf. 14**
901-902	A165	Set of 2	5.50	5.50
a.		Souvenir sheet, #901-902	5.50	5.50

Birds A166

Designs: 5c, Yellow-throated white eye. 20c, Purple swamphen. 50c, Blyth's hornbill. 80c, Yellow-faced myna. 90c, Blue-faced parrotfinch. $1, Crested tern. $2, Rainbow lorikeet. $3, Eclectus parrot. $4, Dwarf kingfisher. $10, Beach thick-knee. $20, Brahminy kite. $50, Superb fruit dove.

	Wmk. 373		**Perf. 14¼x14½**	
2001				
903	A166	5c multi	.25	.25
904	A166	20c multi	.25	.25
905	A166	50c multi	.30	.30
906	A166	80c multi	.40	.40
907	A166	90c multi	.50	.50
908	A166	$1 multi	.60	.60
909	A166	$2 multi	1.00	1.00
910	A166	$3 multi	1.50	1.50
911	A166	$4 multi	2.00	2.00
912	A166	$10 multi	4.00	4.00

Size: 48x38mm
Perf. 13¾x13½
913	A166	$20 multi	8.75	8.75
913A	A166	$50 multi	25.00	25.00
		Nos. 903-913 (11)	19.55	19.55

Issued: Nos. 5c-$20, 2/1/01; $50, 6/1/01.

East Rennell Island Type of 2000 and

Hong Kong 2001 Stamp Exhibition A167

Snake color: $1.70, Yellow and brown. $2.30, Green and yellow.

2001, Feb. 1   **Litho.**   **Perf. 11¾x11½**
914-915	A167	Set of 2	3.75	3.75

Souvenir Sheet
916	A164	$5 Like #900	6.25	6.25

UN High Commissioner for Refugees, 50th Anniv. — A168

Designs: 50c, Refugees. $1, Food and medical supplies. $1.90, Shelter. $2.30, Education.

Perf. 14¼
2001, July 28   **Litho.**   **Unwmk.**
917-920	A168	Set of 4	4.75 4.75

Souvenir Sheet

New Year 2001 (Year of the Snake) — A168a

No. 920A: b, Red-banded tree snake. c, Whip snake. d, Pacific boa. e, Guppy's snake.

2001, Dec. 13   **Perf. 14½**
920A	A168a	$1 Sheet of 4, #b-e	4.50	4.50

Reef Fish A169

Designs: 70c, Amphiprion chrysopterus. 90c, Amphiprion perideraion. $1, Premnas biaculeatus. $1.50, Amphiprion melanopus. $2.10, Amphiprion clarkii. $4.50, Dascyllus trimaculatus.

Wmk. 373
2001, Dec. 27   **Litho.**   **Perf. 14**
921-926	A169	Set of 6	7.50	7.50
926a		Souvenir sheet, #921-926	8.50	8.50

Worldwide Fund for Nature (WWF) A170

Various depictions of gray cuscus: $1, $1.70, $2.30, $5.

2002, Jan. 31
927-930	A170	Set of 4	5.75	5.75
a.		Horiz. strip of 4	6.25	6.25

Reign Of Queen Elizabeth II, 50th Anniv. Issue
Common Design Type

Designs: Nos. 931, 935a, $1, Princess Elizabeth with baby carriage, 1933. Nos. 932, 935b, $1.90, Wearing sunglasses. Nos. 933, 935c, $2.10, In 1955. Nos. 934, 935d, $2.30, Wearing hat. No. 935e, $10, 1955 portrait by Annigoni (38x50mm).

Perf. 14¼x14½, 13¾ (#935e)
2002, Feb. 6   **Litho.**   **Wmk. 373**
With Gold Frames
931	CD360	$1 multicolored	.75	.75
932	CD360	$1.90 multicolored	1.60	1.60
933	CD360	$2.10 multicolored	1.75	1.75
934	CD360	$2.30 multicolored	1.90	1.90
		Nos. 931-934 (4)	6.00	6.00

Souvenir Sheet
Without Gold Frames
935	CD360	Sheet of 5, #a-e	10.00	10.00

Methodist Mission, Cent. A172

Designs: $1, Typical old school building, Western Solomons. $1.70, Mrs. J. F. Goldie and companions. $2.10, Tandanya, first mission schooner. $2.30, Rev. J. F. Goldie and Solomon Islands chiefs.
$5, Rev. Goldie and Sam Aqarao, vert.

2002, May 23 Unwmk. Perf. 14¼
937-940 A172 Set of 4 8.00 8.00
Souvenir Sheet
941 A172 $5 multi 4.00 4.00

United We Stand — A173

Perf. 13½x13¼
2002, June 17 Unwmk.
942 A173 $2.10 multi 3.50 3.50
Souvenir Sheet

New Year 2002 (Year of the Horse) — A173a

No. 942A: b, Horse. c, Horse, horiz.

Perf. 13½x13¾, 13¾x13½
2002, July 7 Litho.
942A A173a $4 Sheet of 2, #a-b 8.50 8.50
No. 942 was printed in sheets of 4.

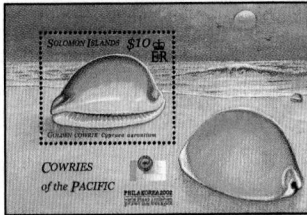

Cowrie Shells — A174

No. 943: a, $1, Sieve cowrie. b, $1, Kitten cowrie. c, $1, Stolid cowrie, eroded cowrie. d, $1.90, Tapering cowrie. e, $1.90, Tiger cowrie. f, $1.90, Lynx cowrie. g, $2.30, Map cowrie. h, $2.30, Pacific deer cowrie. i, $2.30, Tortoise cowrie.
$10, Golden cowrie.

Perf. 14¼x14½
2002, Aug. 2 Wmk. 373
943 A174 Sheet of 9, #a-i 15.00 15.00
Souvenir Sheet
944 A174 $10 multi 12.00 12.00
Phila Korea 2002 World Stamp Exhibition, Seoul.

Queen Mother Elizabeth (1900-2002)
Common Design Type

Designs: No. 945, $1, Without hat (sepia photograph). No. 946, $2.30, Wearing blue hat.
No. 947: a, $5, Wearing tiara (black and white photograph). b, $5, Wearing green blue hat.

Wmk. 373
2002, Aug. 5 Litho. Perf. 14¼
With Purple Frames
945 CD361 $1 multicolored 1.25 1.25
946 CD361 $2.30 multicolored 2.75 2.75
Souvenir Sheet
Without Purple Frames
Perf. 14½x14¼
947 CD361 Sheet of 2, #a-b 7.00 7.00

Battle of Guadalcanal, 60th Anniv. — A175

US servicemen: $1, No. 952d, Coast Guard signalman First Class Douglas Munro. $1.90, No. 952b, Marine Corps Capt. Joe Foss. $2.10, No. 952c, Marine Corps Platoon Sergeant Mitchell Paige. $2.30, No. 952a, Navy Rear Admiral Norman Scott.

2002, Aug. 7 Unwmk. Perf. 14
948-951 A175 Set of 4 8.00 8.00
Souvenir Sheet
952 A175 $5 Sheet of 4, #a-d 12.50 12.50

Christmas — A176

Paintings: $1, Christmas Night, by Lucas Cranach, the Elder. $2.10, Madonna and Child, by Giovanni Bellini. $2.30, Nativity, by Perugino, horiz. $5, Madonna and Child, by Simone Martini.

2002, Nov. 25 Litho. Perf. 14
953-956 A176 Set of 4 8.50 8.50

New Year 2003 (Year of the Ram) A177

Perf. 14¼x14½
2003, Apr. 15 Litho. Unwmk.
957 A177 $3 multi 3.50 3.50
Issued in sheets of 4.

U. S. Medals of Honor — A178

Designs: $1, Air Force Medal of Honor. $1.90 Navy Medal of Honor. $2.10, Army Medal of Honor. $2.30, Medal of Honor ribbon.

2003, June 6 Perf. 14
958-961 A178 Set of 4 9.00 9.00

Prince William, 21st Birthday — A179

No. 962: a, In gray suit. b, In red shirt. c, In black suit.
$15, In blue shirt.

2003, June 21
962 A179 $9 Sheet of 3, #a-c 16.00 16.00
Souvenir Sheet
963 A179 $15 multi 13.00 13.00

Solomon Islands — Republic of China Diplomatic Relations, 20th Anniv. A180

Designs: $1.50, Rice farmers. $2.10, Hospital.

2003, July 8 Perf. 14¼
964-965 A180 Set of 2 5.00 5.00

Coronation of Queen Elizabeth II, 50th Anniv. — A181

No. 966: a, Wearing tiara. b, Wearing green hat. c, Wearing blue hat.
$15, Wearing tiara, diff.

2003, June 2 Litho. Perf. 14
966 A181 $9 Sheet of 3, #a-c 16.00 16.00
Souvenir Sheet
967 A181 $15 multi 15.00 15.00

Powered Flight, Cent. — A182

No. 968: a, Boeing 747. b, Boeing 707. c, Lockheed Model 649. d, Boeing Model 247D. e, Fokker F.VII. f, Orville and Wilbur Wright.
$15, Concorde.

2003, Dec. 17
968 A182 $4 Sheet of 6, #a-f 16.00 16.00
Souvenir Sheet
969 A182 $15 multi 12.00 12.00

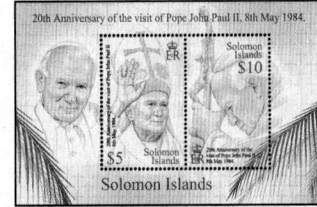

Visit of Pope John Paul II, 20th Anniv. — A183

No. 970: a, $5, Pope waving. b, $10, Pope with crucifix.

2004, Aug. 6 Litho. Perf. 14
970 A183 Sheet of 2, #a-b 8.00 8.00
For No. 970 overprinted, see No. 1025.

2004 Summer Olympics, Athens — A184

Designs: $1.50, Runner at starting blocks. $2, Runner in full stride. $2.20, Runner at finish line. $10, Solomon Islands flag, Olympic rings.

2004, Aug. 13 Perf. 14
971-974 A184 Set of 4 8.00 8.00

Orchids A185

No. 975: a, Calanthe triplicata. b, Dendrobium johnsoniae. c, Dendrobium capituliflorum. d, Spathoglottis plicata. e, Dendrobium mirbelianum. f, Dendrobium polysema. g, Paphiopedilum bougainvilleanum. h, Coelogyne asperata. i, Dendrobium macrophyllum. j, Dendrobium spectabile.

2004, Aug. 28 Perf. 13½
975 Block of 10 17.00 17.00
  a-e. A185 $2.60 Any single 1.00 1.00
  f-j. A185 $5 Any single 2.00 2.00

Pres. Ronald Reagan (1911-2004) — A186

2004, Sept. 30 Litho. Perf. 14
976 A186 $5 multi 9.00 9.00
Printed in sheets of 4.

Merchant Ships A187

Designs: $1.50, MV Bilikiki. $2.20, MV Spirit of Solomons. $3, SS Oceana. $20, RMS Queen Elizabeth 2.

2004, Oct. 11 Perf. 13¼
977-980 A187 Set of 4 12.00 12.00

FIFA (Fédération Internationale de Football Association), Cent. — A188

No. 981, $2.10: a, Player and ball. b, Players.
No. 982, $10: a, Players. b, Player and ball.

2004, Nov. 1   Perf. 14
Horiz. Pairs, #a-b
981-982 A188   Set of 2   11.00 11.00

Bird Life International — A189

No. 983, $2.10: a, Rufous-tailed waterhen. b, Buff-banded rail. c, Purple swamphen. d, Woodford's rail e, Roviana rail. f, Makira moorhen.
No. 984, $5: a, Solomon Islands hawk-owl (denomination at LR). b, White-throated eared nightjar (denomination at LR). c, Solomon Islands hawk-owl (denomination at LL). d, White-throated eared nightjar (denomination at UR). e, Marbled frogmouth. f, Fearful owl.
No. 985, $7.50: a, Beach kingfisher. b, Collared kingfisher. c, Ultramarine kingfisher. d, Moustached kingfisher. e, Little kingfisher. f, Variable kingfisher.

2004, Nov. 15   Perf. 13¾
Sheets of 6, #a-f
983-985 A189   Set of 3   40.00 40.00

Christmas — A190

Paintings: 10c, Adoration of the Magi, by Peter Paul Rubens. 50c, Madonna della Tenda, by Raphael, vert. $1.50, Madonna and Child, by Titian, vert. $2.60, Madonna by the Arch, by Albrecht Dürer, vert. $3, Holy Family, by Frans Floris. $10, Madonna and Child, by unknown artist.

2004, Dec. 8   Perf. 14
986-991 A190   Set of 6   8.00 8.00

Battle of Trafalgar, Bicent. — A191

No. 992, $1.90: a, Vice-Admiral Horatio Lord Nelson. b, HMS Victory. c, Sir Thomas Masterman Hardy. d, The first engagement. e, Breaking the line. f, The death of Nelson.
No. 993, $2.60: a, Lord Cuthbert Collingwood. b, Napoleon Bonaparte. c, Destruction of the Bucentaure. d, Race and chase, 1805. e, The Nelson Touch — Band of Brothers. f, The Nelson Touch.
No. 994, $5: a, Nelson and Hardy on deck. b, Nelson sends the signal "England expects." c, Attempted siege of HMS Victory. d, Neptune tows Victory to Gibraltar. e, Funeral procession on Thames. f, Nelson's Column.
No. 995, $10: a, Nelson's early years. b, The letters of Nelson. c, Siege of Calvi — Nelson loses the sight of his eye. d, Santa Cruz de Tenerife — Nelson loses his arm. e, The Battle of Cape St. Vincent. f, The Battle of the Nile.

2005, Jan. 3   Perf. 13¼
Sheets of 6, #a-f
992-995 A191   Set of 4   50.00 50.00

Baha'is in Solomon Islands, 50th Anniv. — A192

Designs: $1.50, Geometric design. $3, Globe, hands, laurel branches. $5, Alvin and Gertrude Blum, horiz.

2005, Mar. 21   Litho.   Perf. 14¼
996-998 A192   Set of 3   4.50 4.50

End of World War II, 60th Anniv. — A193

No. 999: a, $2.50, Japanese forces land at Tulagi. b, $2.50, USS Lexington under air attack during Battle of the Coral Sea. c, $2.50, Coastwatcher and Solomon Island scouts. d, $2.50, US forces land at Tulagi and Guadalcanal virtually unopposed. e, $2.50, HMAS Canberra sinking at Iron Bottom Sound. f, $5, Cactus Air Force in action over Henderson Airfield. g, $5, "Tokyo Express" nightly bombardments by Japanese warships. h, $5, P-38 Lightnings shoot down Admiral Yamamoto. i, $5, Lt. John F. Kennedy's PT-109 sank after collision with Japanese warship Amagiri. j, $5, Sgt. Maj. Vouza and medals.
No. 1000, RAN coastwatchers sending enemy intelligence reports by teleradio.

2005, Apr. 21   Perf. 13¾
999 A193   Sheet of 10, #a-j   16.00 16.00
Souvenir Sheet
1000 A193 $5 multi   3.50 3.50

Pacific Explorer 2005 World Stamp Expo, Sydney (#1000).

Europa Stamps, 50th Anniv. (in 2006) A194

No. 1001: a, Spain #1262. b, Netherlands #417.
No. 1002: a, Andorra (French) #174. b, Belgium #573.
No. 1003: a, Belgium #496. b, Spain #1567.
No. 1004: a, Austria #657. b, San Marino #701.
No. 1005: a, Netherlands #494. b, Norway #842.
No. 1006: a, Germany #749. b, Italy #750.

2005, May 16   Perf. 13½x13¾
1001	Horiz. pair	1.25	1.25
a.-b.	A194 $1 Either single	.55	.55
c.	Souvenir sheet, #1001	1.25	1.25
1002	Horiz. pair	2.50	2.50
a.-b.	A194 $2.10 Either single	1.10	1.10
c.	Souvenir sheet, #1002	2.50	2.50
1003	Horiz. pair	2.75	2.75
a.-b.	A194 $2.50 Either single	1.25	1.25
c.	Souvenir sheet, #1003	2.75	2.75
1004	Horiz. pair	4.75	4.75
a.-b.	A194 $5 Either single	2.00	2.00
c.	Souvenir sheet, #1004	4.75	4.75
1005	Horiz. pair	9.00	9.00
a.-b.	A194 $10 Either single	4.25	4.25
c.	Souvenir sheet, #1005	9.00	9.00
1006	Horiz. pair	16.00	16.00
a.-b.	A194 $15 Either single	7.50	7.50
c.	Souvenir sheet, #1006	16.00	16.00
	Nos. 1001-1006 (6)	36.25	36.25

Queen Elizabeth II's Royal Year — A195

No. 1007, $1: a, Order of the Garter. b, Trooping the Color.
No. 1008, $2.10: a, Royal Ascot. b, Garden party.
No. 1009, $2.50: a, Royal visits. b, State visits.
No. 1010, $5: a, State Opening of Parliament. b, Remembrance Day.
No. 1011, $10: a, Investitures. b, Christmas broadcast.
No. 1012, $15: a, Maundy service. b, Chelsea Flower Show.

2005, June 3   Perf. 14½
Horiz. Pairs, #a-b
1007-1012 A195   Set of 6   40.00 40.00

A196

A197

A198

Pope John Paul II (1920-2005) A199

Embossed on Metal
2005, July   Die Cut Perf. 12½
Self-Adhesive
1013	A196	$1.20 shown	.70	.70
1014	A196	$1.20 Pope, diff.	.70	.70
1015	A197	$2.60 shown	1.40	1.40
1016	A197	$2.60 Pope, diff.	1.40	1.40
1017	A198	$5 shown	2.75	2.75
1018	A198	$5 Pope, diff.	2.75	2.75
1019	A199	$10 shown	5.75	5.75
1020	A199	$10 Pope, diff.	5.75	5.75
		Nos. 1013-1020 (8)	21.20	21.20

BirdLife International — A200

No. 1021, $2.10: a, Finsch's pygmy parrot. b, Cardinal lory. c, Solomon's cockatoo. d, Eclectus parrot. e, Rainbow lory. f, Song parrot.
No. 1022, $5: a, Red-knobbed imperial pigeon. b, Yellow-bibbed fruit dove. c, Claret-

---

breasted fruit dove. d, Nicobar pigeon. e, Stephan's ground dove. f, Crested cuckoo dove.
No. 1023, $7.50: a, Pied goshawk. b, Imitator sparrowhawk. c, Buff-headed coucal. d, Black-faced pitta. e, Melanesian megapode. f, Blyth's hornbill.

2005, Sept. 1   Litho.   Perf. 14½x14¾
Sheets of 6, #a-f
1021-1023 A200   Set of 3   40.00 40.00

Rotary International, Cent. — A201

2005, Sept. 12   Perf. 14½
1024 A201 $2.50 multi   1.75 1.75

No. 970 Overprinted

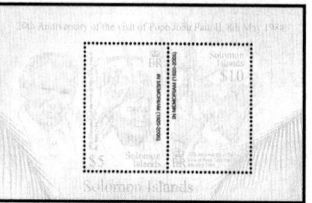

No. 1025: a, $5. b, $10.

2005, Oct. 3   Perf. 14
1025 A183   Sheet of 2, #a-b   7.00 7.00

Christmas — A202

Stories by Hans Christian Andersen (1805-75): $1, The Little Fir Tree. $2.10, The Nightingale. $2.50, The Emperor's New Clothes. $5, The Phoenix. $10, The Tinderbox. $15, The Red Shoes.

2005, Oct. 10
1026-1031 A202   Set of 6   19.00 19.00

Battle of Trafalgar, Bicent. — A203

Designs: $5, HMS Victory. $10, Ship in battle, horiz. $20, Admiral Horatio Nelson.

2005, Oct. 18   Perf. 13¼
1032-1034 A203   Set of 3   17.00 17.00

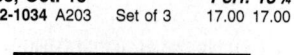

Worldwide Fund for Nature (WWF) — A204

Various views of prehensile-tailed skink: $1.50, $2.60, $3, $10.

2005, Dec. 7   **Perf. 14½**
1035-1038 A204 Set of 4   5.25 5.25
1038a   Sheet, 2 each # 1035-1038   11.50 11.50

Queen Elizabeth II, 80th Birthday A205

Queen Elizabeth II: $2.10, As young girl. $2.50, As woman. $5, Holding camera. $20, Wearing red hat.
No. 1043: a, $10, Like $2.50. b, $15, Like $5.

2006, Apr. 21   **Litho.**   **Perf. 14**
Stamps With White Frames
1039-1042 A205 Set of 4   14.00 14.00
Souvenir Sheet
Stamps Without Frames
1043 A205 Sheet of 2, #a-b   12.00 12.00

Anniversaries — A206

No. 1044, $2.20: a, Great Eastern. b, Isambard Kingdom Brunel (1806-59), engineer.
No. 1045, $2.50: a, Charles Darwin. b, Green turtle.
No. 1046, $5: a, Diving bell. b, Edmond Halley (1656-1742), astronomer.
No. 1047, $10: a, Locomotive "Rocket." b, George Stephenson (1781-1848), inventor.

2006, Apr. 30   **Perf. 14¾x14½**
Horiz. Pairs, #a-b
1044-1047 A206 Set of 4   22.50 22.50
Darwin's voyage on the Beagle, 175th anniv. (#1045).

Christopher Columbus (1451-1506), Explorer — A207

Designs: $1.90, Niña. $2.20, Pinta. $2.60, Santa Maria. $10, Arms of Columbus. $20, Columbus.

2006, May 22   **Perf. 13¼x13**
1048-1051 A207 Set of 4   9.50 9.50
Souvenir Sheet
1051A A207 $20 multi   12.00 12.00
Washington 2006 World Philatelic Exhibition.

2006 World Cup Soccer Championships, Germany — A208

Match scenes from: $4, 1954 West Germany finals victory. $5, 1966 England finals victory. $10, 1998 France finals victory. $20, 2006 Solomon Islands vs. Australia playoff.

2006, June 9   **Perf. 14**
1052-1055 A208 Set of 4   12.00 12.00

Victoria Cross, 150th Anniv. A209

Victoria Cross and: $1, Captured Russian gun used to cast the Victoria Cross. $2.20, Midshipman Charles Lucas, first recipient of Victoria Cross. $2.50, Queen Victoria awarding first Victoria Crosses. $5, Corporal Sukanaivalu, Fijian infantryman at Bougainville, 1944. $10, Corporal Rattey, Australian infantryman at Bougainville, 1945. $15, Private Partridge, Australian infantryman at Bougainville, 1945.

2006, June 26   **Perf. 14x14½**
1056-1061 A209 Set of 6   15.00 15.00

Prehistoric Animals — A210

Designs: 5c, Baryonyx. 10c, Diplodocus. $1.50, Pteranodon. $2.15, Argentinosaurus. $2.40, Centrosaurus. $3, Allosaurus. $10, Ankylosaurus. $20, Iguanodon.

2006, Aug. 14   **Perf. 13¼x13¾**
1062-1069 A210 Set of 8   17.00 17.00

Intl. Coconut Day — A210a

Designs: $1.50, First grade copra drier. $2.40, Standard copra drier. $3, Coconut oil expeller. $5, Coconuts, palm tree, ship, truck on dock, bird.

2006, Sept. 2   **Litho.**   **Perf. 14¼**
1069A-1069D A210a Set of 4   5.00 5.00

Cone Shells — A211

Designs: 5c, Conus marmoreus. 10c, Conus auratinus. 20c, Conus ferrugineus. 50c, Conus consors. 80c, Conus magdalenae. 90c, Conus sulcatus brettinghami. $1, Conus tmetus. $1.50, Conus aureus. $2, Conus corallinus. $3, Conus floccatus. $4, Conus punniculus. $10, Conus pohlianus. $20, Conus proximus. $50, Conus canonicus.

2006, Oct. 31   **Perf. 13x12½**
1070 A211 5c multi   .25 .30
1071 A211 10c multi   .25 .30
1072 A211 20c multi   .25 .30
1073 A211 50c multi   .40 .25
1074 A211 80c multi   .30 .25
1075 A211 90c multi   .50 .30
1076 A211 $1 multi   .75 .40
1077 A211 $1.50 multi   .90 .60
1078 A211 $2 multi   1.00 .75
1079 A211 $3 multi   1.00 1.25
1080 A211 $4 multi   1.25 1.75
1081 A211 $10 multi   3.50 3.50
1082 A211 $20 multi   6.75 6.75
1083 A211 $50 multi   17.50 17.50
Nos. 1070-1083 (14)   34.60 34.20

Tales of Beatrix Potter — A212

Designs: $1.50, The Tale of Peter Rabbit. $1.90, The Tale of Squirrel Nutkin. $2.15, The Tailor of Gloucester. $2.40, The Tale of Benjamin Bunny. $2.65, The Tale of Two Bad Mice. $5, The Tale of Mrs. Tiggy-Winkle.

2006, Dec. 4   **Perf. 13x13½**
1084-1089 A212 Set of 6   8.00 8.00
1089a   Miniature sheet, #1084-1089   8.00 8.00

Wedding of Queen Elizabeth II and Prince Philip, 60th Anniv. — A213

Designs: $2.10, Couple looking straight ahead. $2.50, Couple looking at each other. $5, Wedding ceremony. No. 1093, $20, Elizabeth with flowers. No. 1094, $20, Wedding party.

2007, Jan. 31   **Perf. 13¾**
1090-1093 A213 Set of 4   11.00 11.00
Souvenir Sheet
Perf. 14
1094 A213 $20 multi   7.00 7.00
No. 1094 contains one 42x56mm stamp.

No. 867 Overprinted "1997-2007" in Metallic Blue
Method, Perf. and Watermark As Before

2007, Aug. 3
1095 CD355 $2.50 Sheet of 4, #a-d   3.00 3.00
No. 1095 sold for $10.50 and is additionally overprinted "10th Anniversary / in Memorium" in sheet margin at upper left and upper right.

Princess Diana (1961-97) A214

Various photographs of Princess Diana: $2.10, $2.50, $5, $20.

Perf. 13x12½
2007, Dec. 8   **Litho.**   **Unwmk.**
1096-1099 A214 Set of 4   8.25 8.25

A215

Royal Air Force, 90th Anniv. — A216

Designs: No. 1100, $4, Sir Hugh Trenchard (1873-1956), founder of Royal Air Force. No. 1101, $4, Wing Commander Guy Gibson (1918-44), leader of Dambusters raid. No. 1102, $4, Sir Charles Portal (1893-1971), Marshal. No. 1103, $4, Sir William Sholto Douglas (1893-1969), Marshal. No. 1104, $4, Sir Hugh Dowding (1882-1970), Marshal. $20, Battle of Britain.

Perf. 14¼x14
2008, Apr. 30   **Wmk. 373**
1100-1104 A215 Set of 5   5.25 5.25
Souvenir Sheet
1105 A216 $20 multi   5.25 5.25

British Monarchs — A217

Designs: No. 1106, $2, William I (1027-87). No. 1107, $2, Henry II (1133-89). No. 1108, $2, Henry IV (1366-1413). No. 1109, $2, Henry VI (1421-71). No. 1110, $2, Richard III (1452-1485). No. 1111, $2, Elizabeth I (1533-1603). No. 1112, $2, James I (1566-1625). No. 1113, $2, Edward VII (1841-1910).

Perf. 13x12½
2008, July 15   **Unwmk.**
1106-1113 A217 Set of 8   4.25 4.25
See Nos. 1122-1129.

2008 Summer Olympics, Beijing A218

Designs: $2.15, Field hockey, bamboo. $3, Pole vault, dragon. $4, Table tennis, lantern. $5, Runner, fish.

2008, Aug. 8   **Perf. 13¼**
1114-1117 A218 Set of 4   3.75 3.75

Police A219

Inscriptions: $1.90, Restoration of law and order. $2.15, Freedom of movement. $2.40, Children relaxing. $2.65, Community policing, vert.

2008, Aug. 20   **Perf. 13¾**
1118-1121 A219 Set of 4   2.40 2.40

British Monarchs Type of 2008

Designs: No. 1122, $2, William II (c. 1056-1100). No. 1123, $2, Richard I (1157-99). No. 1124, $2, Edward III (1312-77). No. 1125, $2, Edward IV (1442-83). No. 1126, $2, Henry VIII (1491-1547). No. 1127, $2, Charles I (1600-49). No. 1128, $2, George I (1660-1727). No. 1129, $2, George V (1865-1936).

Perf. 13x12½

2009, Apr. 21   Litho.   Unwmk.
1122-1129   A217   Set of 8   4.00   4.00

Nos. 1122-1129 each were printed in sheets of 8 + central label.

Ships
A220

Alvaro de Mendaña de Neira (1541-95), Discoverer of Solomon Islands — A221

Designs: $3, Discovery. $4, HMS Bounty. $5, Mayflower. $6, USS North Carolina. $10, Boussole and Astrolabe. $20, USS Saratoga.

2009, May 25   Wmk. 406   Perf. 14
1130-1135   A220   Set of 6   12.50   12.50
Souvenir Sheet
1136   A221 $15 multi   4.00   4.00

Naval Aviation, Cent.
A222

Designs: $2, Grumman Hellcat. $2.50, Blackburn Skua. $3.50, Fairey Albacore. $10, Gloster Sea Gladiator. $20, Short 184 Seaplane.

2009, June 25
1137-1140   A222   Set of 4   4.75   4.75
Souvenir Sheet
1141   A222 $20 multi   5.25   5.25

Nos. 1137-1140 each were printed in sheets of 8 + central label.

Wedding of Prince William and Catherine Middleton — A227

No. 1163: a, Couple, hand visible, "L" in "Islands" over pale yellow background. b, Couple, hand not visible, first "S" in "Islands" over pale yellow background. c, As "a," "L" in "Islands" over gray background. d, As "b," first "S" in "Islands" over gray background.
No. 1164: a, Prince William. b, Catherine Middleton.

Perf. 13 Syncopated
2011, May 15   Litho.   Unwmk.
1163   A227 $7.50 Sheet of 4, #a-d   7.75   7.75
Souvenir Sheet
1164   A227 $15 Sheet of 2, #a-b   7.75   7.75

Miniature Sheets

A228

No. 1165 — Two images of Marilyn Monroe (1926-62), actress: a, $9, Wearing fur coat and hat, wearing yellow dress. b, $9, Kneeling on couch, with bare shoulders. c, $9, Wearing gown with thin straps, wearing pink dress and gloves. d, $9, Playing with hair, wearing black dress. e, $27, With hands near mouth, with man.
No. 1166 — 60th anniv. of reign of Queen Elizabeth II, with Queen: a, $9, With Nelson Mandela. b, $9, Trooping the Color. c, $9, In State Coach, 2002. d, $9, With royal family, 1983. e, $27, With Duke and Duchess of Cambridge.
No. 1167 — British royalty: a, $9, Princess Diana. b, $9, Prince Harry. c, $9, Duke and Duchess of Cambridge, child sitting in chair at left. d, $9, Duke and Duchess of Cambridge, with boy standing. e, $27, Princess Diana, diff.
No. 1168 — Bishop Desmond Tutu: a, $9, With South African Truth and Reconciliation Commission. b, $9, With Dalai Lama. c, $9, Embracing 1986 Nobel Peace Prize recipient Wole Soyinka. d, $9, With Mahatma Gandhi. e, $27, Receiving Presidential Medal of Freedom from Pres. Barack Obama.
No. 1169 — Solomon Islands Cathedrals: a, $9, Holy Cross Cathedral, Honiara, Pope John Paul II. b, $9, St. Peter's Cathedral, Gizo, Pope Benedict XVI. c, $9, Anglican St. Barnabas Provincial Cathedral, Honiara. d, $9, Anglican St. Barnabas Provincial Cathedral, Archbishop of Canterbury Rowan Williams and Pope Benedict XVI. e, $27, St. Augustine Cathedral, Auki, Pope John Paul II.
No. 1170 — Maritime history: a, $9, Two Solomon Islands canoes. b, $9, One Solomon Islands canoe. c, $9, Galleon. d, $9, Spanish galleon. e, $27, Alvaro de Mendaña de Neyra (1542-95), discoverer of Solomon Islands.
No. 1171 — Sinking of the Titanic, cent.: a, $9, Titanic hitting iceberg. b, $9, Titanic sinking, lifeboats in water. c, $9, Titanic wreckage underwater. d, $9, Submarine near Titanic wreckage. e, $27, Titanic sinking, lifeboats in water, diff.
No. 1172 — Lighthouses of Oceania and birds: a, $9, Kaipara North Head Lighthouse, New Zealand, Chlidonias albostriatus. b, $9, Cape Liptrap Lighthouse, Australia, Chroicocephalus scopulinus. c, $9, Maatsuyker Island Lighthouse, Australia, Chroicocephalus novaehollandiae. d, $9, Cape Campbell Lighthouse, New Zealand, Sterna anaethetus. e, $27, Cape Reinga Lighthouse, New Zealand, Gelochelidon nilotica.
No. 1173 — Solomon Islands volcanoes and minerals: a, $9, Simbo Island, Cerussite. b, $9, Kavachi, Mimetite with wulfenite. c, $9, Tinakula, Smithsonite. d, $9, Kana Keoki, Tsumcorite. e, $27, Tinakula, Mimetite with smithsonite.
No. 1174 — Lapita pottery and shells: a, $9, Pottery fragment, 1000 B.C., Trochus niloticus. b, $9, 3,000 year-old pottery shard, Conus gloriamus. c, $9, Pottery fragments, 1000 B.C., Lycina aurantium. d, $9, Shard of Lapita pottery with dentate stamping, Nautilus pompilius. e, $27, Lapita pottery ornament, Murex pecten.
No. 1175 — U.S. Medal of Honor and its recipients in Battle of Guadalcanal: a, $9, Lieutenant Colonel Harold William Bauer (1908-42). b, $9, First Lieutenant Jefferson Joseph DeBlanc (1921-2007). c, $9, Colonel Mitchell Paige (1918-2003). d, $9, Gunnery Sergeant John Basilone (1916-45). e, $27, General Alexander Archer Vandegrift (1887-1973).
No. 1176 — 2012 Summer Olympics, London: a, $9, Discus. b, $9, Judo. c, $9, Track cycling. d, $9, Running. e, $27, Rowing.
No. 1177 — Bats: a, $9, Myotis adversus, denomination in black. b, $9, Pipistrellus angulatus. c, $9, Myotis adversus, denomination in white. d, $9, Pteropus admiralitatum. e, $27, Saccolaimus saccolaimus.
No. 1178 — Dolphins: a, $9, Stenella longirostris. b, $9, Tursiops truncatus. c, $9, Stenella coruleoalba. d, $9, Sousa chinensis. e, $27, Stenella attenuata.
No. 1179 — Whales: a, $9, Two Balaenoptera edeni, name of animal at left. b, $9, Megaptera novaeangliae. c, $9, Mesoplodon densirostris. d, $9, Balaenoptera edeni, name of animal at LL. e, $27, Balaenoptera edeni, name of animal at R.
No. 1180 — Birds: a, $9, Rhipidura leucophrys. b, $9, Myzomela cardinalis. c, $9, Cinnyris jugularis. d, $9, Rhipidura rufifrons. e, $27, Pachycephala pectoralis.

No. 1181 — Birds of prey: a, $9, Aviceda subcristata. b, $9, Haliastur indus. c, $9, Haliastur sphenurus. d, $9, Haliaeetus leucogaster. e, $27, Circus approximans.
No. 1182 — Owls: a, $9, Two Tyto alba. b, $9, One Tyto alba. c, $9, Ninox jacquinoti. d, $9, Nesasio solomonensis. e, $27, Two Tyto alba, diff.
No. 1183 — Butterflies: a, $9, Papilio toboroi. b, $9, Ornithoptera victoriae. c, $9, Vindula sapor. d, $9, Graphium hicetaon. e, $27, Papilio aegeus aegeus.
No. 1184 — Reef fish: a, $9, Chaetodon meyeri. b, $9, Chaetodon ephippium. c, $9, Acanthurus lineatus. d, $9, Chaetodon ocellicaudus. e, $27, Heniochus acuminatus.
No. 1185 — Reptiles and amphibians: a, $9, Acrochordus granulatus. b, $9, Crocodylus porosus. c, $9, Corucia zebrata. d, $9, Ceratobatrachus guentheri. e, $27, Cyrtodactylus biordinis.
No. 1186 — Turtles: a, $9, Chelonia mydas. b, $9, Eretmochelys imbricata. c, $9, Caretta caretta. d, $9, Lepidochelys olivacea. e, $27, Dermochelys cariacea.
No. 1187 — Dinosaurs: a, $9, Dimorphodon. b, $9, Kentrosaurus. c, $9, Spinosaurus. d, $9, Liopleurodon. e, $27, Tyrannosaurus rex.
No. 1188 — Orchids: a, $9, Laelia harpophylla. b, $9, Cypripedium parviflorum. c, $9, Chysis bractescens. d, $9, Laelia anceps. e, $27, Cypripedium pubescens.

2012, June 5   Litho.   Perf. 13¼
Sheets of 5, #a-e
1165-1188   A228   Set of 24   435.00   435.00

SEMI-POSTAL STAMPS

> Catalogue values for unused stamps in this section are for Never Hinged items.

No. 452 Ovptd. in Red "+ 50c SURCHARGE / CYCLONE RELIEF FUND / 1982"
Perf. 13½x13
1982, May 3   Litho.   Wmk. 373
B1   CD331 $1 + 50c multi   2.25   2.25

Nos. 546 and 569 Srchd. "Cyclone Relief Fund 1986" and New Value in Scarlet
Perf. 14½x14
1986, Sept. 23   Litho.   Wmk. 384
B2   CD336 $1 + 50c multi   1.75   1.75

Souvenir Sheet
Perf. 13½
B3   Sheet of 2   7.50   7.50
   a.   A95 55c + 25c multi   2.25   2.25
   b.   A95 $1.65 + 75c multi   4.50   4.50

No. 840 Surcharged in Red

Wmk. 373
2003, Feb. 8   Litho.   Perf. 14½
B4   A147 $1.35 +$3 multi   7.00   7.00

World AIDS Day.

No. 866 Surcharged in Red

Perf. 14½x14
2003, Mar. 17   Wmk. 373
B5   CD355 $2 +$5 multi   7.25   7.25

Surtax for Cyclones Zoe and Beni Relief Fund.

No. 926 Surcharged in Red

Wmk. 373
2008, Oct. 23   Litho.   Perf. 14
B6   A169   Sheet of 6, #921-925, B6a   3.75   3.75
   a. $4.50+$3 multi   2.00   2.00

POSTAGE DUE STAMPS

D1

Perf. 12

		1940, Sept. 1	**Typo.**		**Wmk. 4**
J1	D1	1p emerald		4.50	8.00
J2	D1	2p dark red		4.75	8.00
J3	D1	3p chocolate		4.75	13.00
J4	D1	4p dark blue		7.25	13.00
J5	D1	5p deep green		8.00	27.50
J6	D1	6p brt red vio		8.00	20.00
J7	D1	1sh dull violet		10.00	32.50
J8	D1	1sh6p turq green		17.50	60.00

Nos. J1-J8 (8)   64.75   182.00
Set, never hinged   120.00

SOMALIA

sō-'mä-lē-ə

(Somali Democratic Republic)

(Italian Somaliland)

(Benadir)

LOCATION — Eastern Africa, bordering on the Indian Ocean and the Gulf of Aden
GOVT. — Probably none
AREA — 246,201 sq. mi.
POP. — 7,140,643 (1999 est.)
CAPITAL — Mogadishu

The former Italian colony which included the territory west of the Juba River became known as Oltre Giuba (Trans-Juba), was absorbed into Italian East Africa in 1936. Somalia stamps continued in use in Italian East Africa for several years. It was under British military administration from 1941-49. Italian trusteeship took effect in 1950, with a UN Advisory Council helping the administrator. On July 1, 1960, the former Italian colony merged with Somaliland Protectorate (British) to form the independent Republic of Somalia.

4 Besas = 1 Anna
16 Annas = 1 Rupee
100 Besas = 1 Rupee (1922)
100 Centesimi = 1 Lira (1905, 1925)
100 Centesimi = 1 Somalo (1950)
100 Centesimi = 1 Somali
Shilling (1961)

Catalogue values for unused stamps in this country are for Never Hinged items, beginning with Scott 170 in the regular postage section, Scott B52 in the semipostal section, Scott C17 in the airpost section, Scott CB11 in the airpost semi-postal section, Scott CE1 in the airpost special delivery section, Scott E8 in the special delivery section, Scott J55 in the postage due section, and Scott Q56 in the parcel post section.

Used values in italics are for postally used Italian Somalia stamps. CTO's or stamps with fake cancels sell for about the same as unused, hinged stamps.

Watermark

Wmk. 140 —
Crown

Italian Somaliland

Elephant — A1   Lion — A2

Wmk. 140

1903, Oct. 12   Typo.   Perf. 14

1	A1	1b brown	140.00	26.00
2	A1	2b blue green	1.60	15.00
3	A2	1a claret	1.60	19.00
4	A2	2a orange brown	2.00	37.50
5	A2	2½a blue	1.60	37.50

6	A2	5a orange	2.00	75.00
7	A2	10a lilac	2.00	75.00
		Nos. 1-7 (7)	150.80	285.00

For surcharges see Nos. 8-27, 40-50, 70-77.

Surcharged

1905, Dec. 29

8	A2	15c on 5a org	3,500.	1,300.
9	A2	40c on 10a lilac	1,100.	450.00

Surcharged

1906-07

10	A1	2c on 1b brown	6.50	19.00
11	A1	5c on 2b blue grn	6.50	14.00
a.		Double surcharge	350.00	
b.		Double surcharge, one invtd.		5,250.
c.		Pair, one without surcharge		5,000.

Surcharges on No. 11c are virtually on top of each other. Certificates are necessary.

Surcharged

12	A2	10c on 1a claret	6.50	14.00
13	A2	15c on 2a brn org ('06)	6.50	14.00
14	A2	25c on 2½a blue	16.00	14.00
15	A2	50c on 5a yellow	32.50	35.00

Surcharged

16	A2	1 l on 10a lilac	32.50	47.50
		Nos. 10-16 (7)	107.00	157.50

Nos. 15 and 16 With Bars Over Former Surcharge and

1916, Apr.

18	A2	5c on 50c on 5a yel	47.50	52.50
a.		Double surcharge, one invtd.	5,000.	
19	A2	20c on 1 l on 10a dl lil	9.50	35.00

No. 4 Surcharged

20	A2	20c on 2a org brn	24.00	16.00
		Nos. 18-20 (3)	81.00	103.50

Nos. 11-16 Surcharged

a   b

1922, Feb. 1

22	A1(a)	3b on 5c on 2b	13.00	24.00
23	A2(b)	6c on 10c on 1a	24.00	19.00
24	A2(b)	9b on 15c on 2a	24.00	24.00
25	A2(b)	15b on 25c on 2½a	24.00	18.00
a.		"15" at left omitted		300.00
26	A2(b)	30b on 50c on 5a	26.00	52.50
27	A2(b)	60b on 1 l on 10a	26.00	87.50
		Nos. 22-27 (6)	137.00	225.00

Victory Issue

Italy Nos. 136-139 Surcharged

1922, Apr.

28	A64	3b on 5c olive grn	2.00	7.25
29	A64	6b on 10c red	2.00	7.25
30	A64	9b on 15c slate grn	2.00	11.00
31	A64	15b on 25c ultra	2.00	11.00
		Nos. 28-31 (4)	8.00	36.50

Nos. 10-16 Surcharged with Bars and

c   d

1923, July 1

40	A1	1b brown	9.50	37.50
41	A1(c)	2b on 2c on 1b	9.50	37.50
42	A1(c)	3b on 2c on 1b	9.50	18.00
43	A1(d)	5b on 50c on 5a	9.50	19.00
44	A1(c)	6b on 5c on 2b	17.50	19.00
45	A2(d)	18b on 10c on 1a	17.50	19.00
46	A2(d)	20b on 15c on 2a	21.00	19.00
47	A2(d)	25b on 15c on 2a	21.00	19.00
48	A2(d)	30b on 25c on 2½a	24.00	24.00
49	A2(d)	60b on 1 l on 10a	24.00	52.50
50	A2(d)	1r on 1 l on 10a	65.00	65.00
		Nos. 40-50 (11)	228.00	329.50

No. 40 is No. 10 with bars over the 1907 surcharge.

Propagation of the Faith Issue
Italy Nos. 143-146 Surcharged

1923, Oct. 24   Wmk. 140

51	A68	6b on 20c ol grn & brn org	11.50	50.00
52	A68	13b on 30c cl & brn org	11.50	50.00
53	A68	20b on 50c vio & brn org	7.50	57.50
54	A68	30b on 1 l bl & brn org	7.50	87.50
		Nos. 51-54 (4)	38.00	245.00

Fascisti Issue

Italy Nos. 159-164 Surcharged in Red or Black

1923, Oct. 29   Unwmk.   Perf. 14

55	A69	3b on 10c dk grn (R)	15.00	19.00
56	A69	13b on 30c dk vio (R)	15.00	19.00
57	A69	20b on 50c brn car	15.00	26.00
		Wmk. 140		
58	A70	30b on 1 l blue	15.00	50.00
59	A70	1r on 2 l brown	15.00	60.00
60	A71	3r on 5 l blk & bl (R)	15.00	90.00
		Nos. 55-60 (6)	90.00	264.00

Manzoni Issue
Italy Nos. 165-170 Surcharged in Red

1924, Apr. 1

61	A72	6b on 10c brn red & blk	12.00	75.00
62	A72	9b on 15c bl grn & blk	12.00	75.00
63	A72	13b on 30c blk & sl	12.00	75.00
64	A72	20b on 50c org brn & blk	12.00	75.00

Surcharged in Red

65	A72	30b on 1 l bl & blk	72.50	450.00
66	A72	3r on 5 l vio & blk	475.00	3,000.
		Nos. 61-66 (6)	595.50	3,750.

Victor Emmanuel Issue

Italy Nos. 175-177 Overprinted

1925-26   Unwmk.   Perf. 13½, 11

67	A78	60c brown car	2.25	13.50
a.		Perf. 11	180.00	375.00
68	A78	1 l dk bl, perf. 11	3.00	19.00
a.		Perf. 13½	10.50	57.50
69	A78	1.25 l dk blue ('26)	2.25	30.00
a.		Perf. 11	1,050.	1,875.
		Nos. 67-69 (3)	7.50	62.50

Stamps of 1907-16 with Bars over Original Values

1926, Mar. 1   Wmk. 140   Perf. 14

70	A1	2c on 1b brown	27.50	55.00
71	A1	5c on 2b blue grn	19.00	27.50
72	A2	10c on 1a rose red	13.00	11.00
73	A2	15c on 2a org brn	13.00	14.50
74	A2	20c on 2a org brn	14.50	14.50
75	A2	25c on 2½a blue	14.50	19.00
76	A2	50c on 5a yellow	19.00	35.00
77	A2	1 l on 10a dull lil	27.50	47.50
		Nos. 70-77 (8)	148.00	224.00

Saint Francis of Assisi Issue

Italy Nos. 178-180 Overprinted

1926, Apr. 12			Perf. 14	
78	A79	20c gray green	2.40	13.50
79	A80	40c dark violet	2.40	13.50
80	A81	60c red brown	2.40	24.00

Italy Nos. 182 and Type of 1926 Overprinted in Red

Unwmk.			Perf. 11	
81	A82	1.25 l dark blue	2.40	35.00
		Perf. 14		
82	A83	5 l + 2.50 l ol grn	6.50	67.50
		Nos. 78-82 (5)	16.10	153.50

Italian Stamps of 1901-26 Overprinted

1926-30			Wmk. 140	
83	A43	2c org brn	7.50	6.50
84	A48	5c green	7.50	6.50
85	A48	10c claret	7.50	.40
86	A49	20c violet brown	11.00	2.40
87	A46	25c grn & pale grn	7.50	1.60
88	A49	30c gray ('30)	20.00	50.00
89	A49	60c brn org	9.00	12.00
a.		Double overprint		4,000.
90	A46	75c dk red & rose	160.00	50.00
91	A46	1 l brown & grn	9.00	.80
92	A46	1.25 l blue & ultra	19.00	2.40
93	A46	2 l dk grn & org	42.50	16.00
94	A46	2.50 l dk grn & org	42.50	24.00
95	A46	5 l blue & rose	90.00	57.50
96	A51	10 l gray grn & red	90.00	97.50
		Nos. 83-96 (14)	523.00	327.60

Volta Issue

Type of Italy, 1927, Overprinted

1927, Oct. 10				
97	A84	20c purple	7.00	40.00
98	A84	50c deep orange	12.00	30.00
a.		Double overprint	175.00	
99	A84	1.25 l brt blue	17.00	77.50
		Nos. 97-99 (3)	36.00	147.50

Italian Stamps of 1927-28 Overprinted in Black or Red

1928-30				
100	A86	7½c lt brown	34.00	75.00
a.		Double overprint	550.00	
101	A85	50c brn & sl (R)	34.00	10.00
102	A86	50c brt vio ('30)	60.00	90.00
		Perf. 11		
		Unwmk.		
103	A85	1.75 l deep brown	105.00	20.00
		Nos. 100-103 (4)	233.00	195.00

Monte Cassino Issue

Monte Cassino Issue of Italy Overprinted in Red or Blue

1929, Oct. 14		Wmk. 140	Perf. 14	
104	A96	20c dk green (R)	6.00	21.00
105	A96	25c red org (Bl)	6.00	21.00
106	A98	50c + 10c crim (Bl)	6.00	22.50
107	A98	75c + 15c ol brn (R)	6.00	22.50
108	A96	1.25 l + 25c dk vio (R)	13.50	42.50
109	A98	5 l + 1 l saph (R)	13.50	45.00

Overprinted in Red

Unwmk.				
110	A100	10 l + 2 l gray brn	13.50	67.50
		Nos. 104-110 (7)	64.50	242.00

Royal Wedding Issue

Type of Italian Royal Wedding Stamps of 1930 Overprinted

1930, Mar. 17			Wmk. 140	
111	A101	20c yellow green	3.00	9.00
112	A101	50c + 10c dp org	2.25	9.00
113	A101	1.25 l + 25c rose red	2.25	18.00
		Nos. 111-113 (3)	7.50	36.00

Ferrucci Issue

Types of Italian Stamps of 1930 Overprinted in Red or Blue

1930, July 26				
114	A102	20c violet (R)	6.00	6.00
115	A103	25c dk grn (R)	6.00	6.00
116	A103	50c black (R)	6.00	11.00
117	A103	1.25 l dp bl (R)	6.00	21.00
118	A104	5 l + 2 l dp car (bl)	13.50	45.00
		Nos. 114-118 (5)	37.50	89.00

Virgil Issue

Types of Italian Stamps of 1930 Overprinted in Red or Blue

1930, Dec. 4		Photo.	Wmk. 140	
119	A106	15c violet blue	1.20	11.00
120	A106	20c org brn	1.20	4.50
121	A106	25c dark green	1.20	4.50
122	A106	30c lt brown	1.20	4.50
123	A106	50c dull violet	1.20	4.50
124	A106	75c rose red	1.20	9.00
125	A106	1.25 l gray blue	1.20	11.00
		Engr.		
		Unwmk.		
126	A106	5 l + 1.50 l dk vio	4.50	45.00
127	A106	10 l + 2.50 l ol brn	4.50	67.50
		Nos. 119-127 (9)	17.40	161.50

Saint Anthony of Padua Issue

Types of Italian Stamps of 1931 Overprinted in Blue or Red

1931, May 7		Photo.	Wmk. 140	
129	A116	20c brown (Bl)	1.60	21.00
130	A116	25c green (R)	1.60	7.50
131	A118	30c gray brn (Bl)	1.60	7.50
132	A118	50c dull vio (Bl)	1.60	7.50
133	A120	1.25 l slate bl (R)	1.60	37.50

Overprinted in Red or Black

Engr.			Unwmk.	
134	A121	75c black (R)	1.60	21.00
135	A122	5 l + 2.50 l dk brn (Bk)	10.50	73.00
		Nos. 129-135 (7)	20.10	175.00

Italy Nos. 218, 221 Overprinted in Red

1931			Wmk. 140	
136	A94	25c dk green (R)	15.00	25.00
137	A95	50c purple (R)	15.00	4.50

Lighthouse at Cape Guardafui — A3

Tower at Mnara Ciromo — A4

Governor's Palace at Mogadishu — A5

Termite Nest — A6

Ostrich — A7

Hippopotamus — A8

Greater Kudu — A9

Lion — A10

1932		Wmk. 140 Photo.	Perf. 12	
138	A3	5c dp brn	12.00	15.00
139	A3	7½c violet	19.00	37.50
140	A3	10c gray black	26.00	.40
141	A3	15c olive green	9.50	1.20
142	A4	20c carmine	400.00	.40
143	A4	25c dp grn	9.50	.40
144	A4	30c dk brn	105.00	1.20
145	A5	35c dark blue	11.00	22.50
146	A5	50c violet	475.00	.40
147	A5	75c carmine	11.00	.80
148	A6	1.25 l dark blue	37.50	.80
149	A6	1.75 l red orange	26.00	.80
150	A6	2 l carmine	11.00	.40
151	A7	2.55 l indigo	60.00	135.00
152	A7	5 l carmine	34.00	15.00
153	A8	10 l violet	52.50	37.50
154	A9	20 l dark green	110.00	150.00
155	A10	25 l dark blue	110.00	290.00
		Nos. 138-155 (18)	1,519.	709.30
		Set, never hinged	3,750.	

1934-37			Perf. 14	
138a	A3	5c deep brown	3.75	.80
139a	A3	7½c violet	3.75	50.00
140a	A3	10c gray black	3.75	.40
141a	A3	15c olive green	3.75	2.40
142a	A4	20c carmine	3.75	.25
143a	A4	25c deep green	3.75	.40
144a	A4	30c dark brown	7.50	.40
145a	A5	35c dark blue	19.00	57.50
146a	A5	50c violet	50.00	.40
147a	A5	75c carmine	67.50	.40
148a	A6	1.25 l dark blue	135.00	1.20
149a	A6	1.75 l red orange	340.00	42.50
150a	A6	2 l carmine	82.50	.80
151a	A7	2.55 l indigo	375.00	975.00
152a	A7	5 l carmine	37.50	3.25
153a	A8	10 l violet	290.00	45.00
154a	A9	20 l dark green	15,000.	2,500.
155a	A10	25 l dark blue	950.00	825.00
		Nos. 138a-153a,155a (17)	2,376.	2,005.
		Set, never hinged	5,650.	

Nos. 146 and 150 with "POSTA AEREA" overprints were never issued in Somalia.

Eleven denominations in the foregoing series exist perf. 12x14, 14x12 or compound 12 and 14. See the *Scott Classic Specialized Catalogue of Stamps & Covers* for detailed listings.

Types of 1932 Issue Overprinted in Black or Red

1934, May			Perf. 14	
156	A3	10c brown (Bk)	21.00	50.00
157	A4	25c green	21.00	50.00
158	A5	50c dull vio (Bk)	21.00	50.00
159	A6	1.25 l blue	21.00	50.00
160	A7	5 l brown black	21.00	50.00
161	A8	10 l car rose (Bk)	21.00	97.50
162	A9	20 l dull blue	21.00	97.50
163	A10	25 l dark green	21.00	97.50
		Nos. 156-163 (8)	168.00	542.50
		Set, never hinged	375.00	

Duke of the Abruzzi (Luigi Amadeo, 1873-1933).

Mother and Child
A11

1934, Oct.				
164	A11	5c ol grn & brn	5.25	21.00
165	A11	10c yel brn & blk	5.25	21.00
166	A11	20c scarlet & blk	5.25	19.00
167	A11	50c dk violet & brn	5.25	19.00
168	A11	60c org brn & blk	5.25	26.00
169	A11	1.25 l dk blue & grn	5.25	45.00
		Nos. 164-169,C1-C6 (12)	63.00	302.00
		Nos. 164-169, never hinged	75.00	

Second Colonial Arts Exhibition, Naples.

Catalogue values for unused stamps in this section, from this point to the end of the section, are for Never Hinged items.

Somalia

Tower at Mnara Ciromo — A12

Governor's Palace, Mogadishu — A13

Design: 5c, 20c, 60c, Ostrich.

Wmk. 277

1950, Mar. 24		Photo.	Perf. 14	
170	A12	1c gray black	4.75	13.50
171	A12	5c carmine rose	.35	.25
172	A13	6c violet	2.40	4.00
173	A12	8c Prus green	2.40	4.00
174	A13	10c dark green	.35	.25
175	A12	20c blue green	.35	.25

176 A12 35c red 9.00 13.50
177 A13 55c brt blue 4.00 .80
178 A12 60c purple 4.00 .80
179 A12 65c brown 12.00 4.75
180 A13 1s deep orange 18.50 4.75
Nos. 170-180,E8-E9 (13) 91.60 81.35

Council in
Session
A14

1951, Oct. 4
181 A14 20c dk green & brn 3.25 3.25
182 A14 55c brown & violet 8.75 12.00
Nos. 181-182,C27A-C27B (4) 24.00 30.25

Meeting of First Territorial Council.

Fair Emblem,
Palm Tree and
Minaret — A16

1952, Sept. 14 Wmk. 277 Perf. 14
185 A16 25c red & dk brown 3.50 3.50
186 A16 55c blue & dk brown 3.50 4.00
Nos. 185-186,C28 (3) 11.00 11.50

1st Somali Fair, Mogadishu, Sept. 14-28.

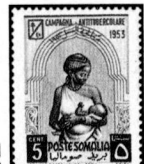

Mother and
Child — A17

Center in Dark Brown

1953, May 27
187 A17 5c rose violet .70 1.75
188 A17 25c rose .70 1.75
189 A17 50c blue 1.25 1.75
Nos. 187-189,C29 (4) 5.15 8.25

Anti-tuberculosis campaign.

Laborer at
Fair
Entrance
A18

1953, Sept. 28 Unwmk. Perf. 11½
190 A18 25c dk green & gray .50 .75
191 A18 60c blue & gray 1.25 1.75
Nos. 190-191,C30-C31 (4) 3.50 4.75

2nd Somali Fair, Mogadishu, 9/28-10/12.

Map and
Stamps
of 1903
A19

Perf. 13x13½
1953, Dec. 16 Engr. Wmk. 277
"Stamps" in Brown and Rose Carmine
192 A19 25c deep magenta .75 1.00
193 A19 35c dark green .75 1.00
194 A19 60c orange 1.00 1.75
Nos. 192-194,C32-C33 (5) 5.00 8.00

50th anniv. of the 1st Somali postage stamps.

Somalia
Brushwood
A20

Perf. 12½x13½
1954, June 1 Photo. Unwmk.
195 A20 25c dp blue & dk gray .90 1.50
196 A20 60c orange brn & brown .90 1.50
Nos. 195-196,C37-C38 (4) 4.50 6.00

Convention of Nov. 11, 1953, with the Sovereign Military Order of Malta, providing for the care of lepers.

Somali
Flag — A21

Perf. 13½x13
1954, Oct. 12 Litho. Wmk. 277
197 A21 25c brn, bl, red & yel .45 .50

Adoption of a Somali flag. See No. C39.

Adenium
Somalense — A22

Flowers: 5c, Haemanthus multiflorus martyn. 10c, Grinum scabrum. 25c, Poinciana elata. 60c, Calatropis procera. 1s, Pancratium. 1.20s, Sesamothamnus bussernus.

1955, Feb. Photo. Perf. 13
198 A22 1c bl, dp rose & dk ol brn .30 .30
199 A22 5c bl, rose lil & grn .30 .30
200 A22 10c lilac & green 1.00 .40
201 A22 25c vio brn, yel & grn 1.60 1.60
202 A22 60c blk, car & grn .30 .30
203 A22 1s red brn & grn .30 .75
204 A22 1.20s dk brn, yel & grn .65 1.25
Nos. 198-204,E10-E11 (9) 6.75 6.40

See #216-220. For overprint see #242.

Weaver at
Loom
A23

Design: 30c, Cattle fording stream.

Perf. 13½x14
1955, Sept. 24 Wmk. 303
205 A23 25c dark brown .70 .70
206 A23 30c dark green .70 .70
Nos. 205-206,C46-C47 (4) 3.40 3.90

3rd Somali Fair, Mogadishu, Sept. 1955.

Casting
Ballots — A24

1956, Apr. 30 Perf. 14
207 A24 5c brown & gray grn .35 .35
208 A24 10c brown & ol bis .35 .35
209 A24 25c brown & brn red .35 .35
Nos. 207-209,C48-C49 (5) 2.55 3.20

Opening of the territory's first democratically elected Legislative Assembly.

Arms of
Somalia — A25

Coat of Arms in Dull Yellow, Blue and Black

1957, May 6 Wmk. 303 Perf. 13½
210 A25 5c lt red brown .40 .50
211 A25 25c carmine .40 .50
212 A25 60c bluish violet .40 .75
Nos. 210-212,C50-C51 (5) 2.70 3.25

Issued in honor of the new coat of arms.

Dam at
Falcheiro
A26

10c, Juba River Bridge. 25c, Silos at Margherita.

1957, Sept. 28 Photo. Perf. 14
213 A26 5c brown & purple .25 .25
214 A26 10c bister & bl grn .25 .25
215 A26 25c carmine & blue .25 .70
Nos. 213-215,C52-C53 (5) 2.75 3.20

Fourth Somali Fair and Film Festival.

Flower Type of 1955

Flowers: 1c, Adenium Somalense. 10c, Grinum scabrum. 15c, Adansonia digitata. 25c, Poinciana elata. 50c, Gloriosa virescens.

1956-59 Wmk. 303 Photo. Perf. 13
216 A22 1c bl, dp rose & dk ol brn .50 .50
217 A22 10c lil, grn & yel ('59) .40 .40
218 A22 15c red, grn & yel ('58) .70 .60
219 A22 25c dull lil, grn & yel ('59) .40 .80
220 A22 50c bl, grn, red & yel ('58) .70 .70
Nos. 216-220 (5) 2.70 3.00

Fencer — A27

Soccer
Player
A28

Designs: 2c, Runner crossing finish line. 5c, Discus thrower. 6c, Motorcyclist. 10c, Archer. 25c, Boxers.

1958, Apr. 28 Wmk. 303 Perf. 14
221 A27 2c violet .25 .25
222 A28 4c green .25 .25
223 A27 5c vermilion .25 .25
224 A28 6c gray .25 .25
225 A27 8c violet blue .25 .25
226 A28 10c orange .25 .25
227 A28 25c dark green .25 .25
Nos. 221-227,C54-C56 (10) 2.50 2.80

Book and
Assembly
Palace — A29

1959, June 19
228 A29 5c green & ultra .25 .25
229 A29 25c ocher & ultra .25 .25
Nos. 228-229,C59-C60 (4) 2.00 2.50

Opening of Somalia's Constituent Assembly. See No. C60a.

White
Stork — A30

Birds: 10c, Saddle-billed stork. 15c, Sacred ibis. 25c, Pink-backed pelican.

1959, Sept. 4 Photo. Perf. 14
230 A30 5c yellow, blk & red .35 .25
231 A30 10c brown, red & yel .35 .25
232 A30 15c orange & black .35 .25
233 A30 25c dk car, blk & org .35 .25
Nos. 230-233,C61-C62 (6) 2.90 2.10

Incense
Bush — A31

Design: 60c, Girl burning incense.

1959, Sept. 28 Wmk. 303
234 A31 20c orange & black .25 .30
235 A31 60c blk, org & dk red .25 .30
Nos. 234-235,C63-C64 (4) 2.00 2.20

5th Somali Fair, Mogadishu.

Arms of
University
Institute — A32

Designs: 50c, Map of Africa and arms, horiz. 80c, Arms of University Institute.

1960, Jan. 14 Photo. Perf. 14
236 A32 5c brown & salmon .25 .25
237 A32 50c lt vio bl, brn & blk .25 .25
238 A32 80c brt red & blk .35 .35
Nos. 236-238,C65-C66 (5) 1.75 1.85

Opening of the University Institute of Somalia.

Globe and
Uprooted
Oak
Emblem
A33

Palm — A34

Design: 60c, Like 10c but with inscription and emblem rearranged.

1960, Apr. 7   **Perf. 14**
239 A33 10c yel brn, grn & blk .25 .25
240 A33 60c dp bister & blk .25 .25
241 A34 80c pink, grn & blk .25 .25
    Nos. 239-241,C67 (4) 1.65 2.00

World Refugee Year, 7/1/59-6/30/60.

Republic

No. 217 Overprinted

Somaliland
Independence
26 June 1960

Wmk. 303
1960, June 26   **Photo.**   **Perf. 13**
242 A22 10c lilac, grn & yel 19.00 24.00
    Nos. 242,C68-C69 (3) 88.00 96.50

Independence of British Somaliland, which became part of the Republic of Somalia.

Gazelle and Map of Africa — A36

25c, NYC skyline, UN Building and UN flag.

1960, July 1   **Perf. 14**
243 A36 5c lilac & brown .40 .40
244 A36 25c blue .45 .45
    Nos. 243-244,C70-C71 (4) 4.90 4.90

Somalia independence.

Boy Drawing Giraffe A37

1960, Nov. 24
245 A37 10c shown .30 .30
246 A37 15c Zebra .40 .40
247 A37 25c Black rhinoceros .45 .45
    Nos. 245-247,C72 (4) 4.90 4.90

Olympic Torch, Somalia Flag — A38

10c, Runners, flag and Olympic rings.

1960   **Wmk. 303**   **Perf. 14**
248 A38 5c green & blue .25 .25
249 A38 10c yellow & blue .25 .25
    Nos. 248-249,C73-C74 (4) 3.10 3.10

17th Olympic Games, Rome, 8/25-9/11.

Girl Harvesting Papaya — A39

Girl harvesting: 10c, Durrah (sorghum). 20c, Cotton. 25c, Sesame. 40c, Sugar cane. 50c, Bananas. 75c, Peanuts, horiz. 80c, Grapefruit, horiz.

1961, July 5   **Photo.**
250 A39 5c multicolored .25 .25
251 A39 10c multicolored .25 .25
252 A39 20c multicolored .25 .25
253 A39 25c multicolored .25 .25
254 A39 40c multicolored .30 .25
255 A39 50c multicolored .50 .40
256 A39 75c multicolored .80 .80
257 A39 80c multicolored 2.75 2.75
    Nos. 250-257 (8) 5.35 5.20

Shield, Bow and Quiver — A40

Design: 45c, Pottery and incense jug.

1961, Sept. 28
258 A40 25c blk, car & ocher .25 .25
259 A40 45c blk, bl grn & ocher .25 .25
    Nos. 258-259,C82-C83 (4) 3.15 3.15

6th Somali Fair, Mogadishu.

Pomacanthus Semicirculatus A41

Fish: 15c, Girl embroidering fish on cloth. 40c, Novaculichthys taeniourus.

1962, Apr. 26   **Photo.**
260 A41 15c brown, blk & pink .35 .35
261 A41 25c orange, blk & ultra .35 .35
262 A41 40c green, blk & rose .65 .65
    Nos. 260-262,C84 (4) 4.85 4.85

Mosquito Trapped by Sprays A42

Design: 25c, Man with spray gun and malaria eradication emblem, vert.

1962, Oct. 25   **Wmk. 303**   **Perf. 14**
263 A42 10c orange red & grn .45 .45
264 A42 25c rose lilac, brn & blk .45 .45
    Nos. 263-264,C85-C86 (4) 4.50 4.50

WHO drive to eradicate malaria.

Police Auxiliary Woman A43

10c, Army auxiliary woman. 25c, Radio police car. 75c, First aid army auxiliary, vert.

1963, May 15   **Wmk. 303**   **Perf. 14**
265 A43 5c multicolored .25 .25
266 A43 10c black & orange .25 .25
267 A43 25c multicolored .25 .25
268 A43 75c multicolored .55 .55
    Nos. 265-268,C87-C88 (6) 4.90 4.90

Women's auxiliary forces.

Carved Fork and Spoon and Wheat Emblem A44

1963, June 25   **Photo.**
269 A44 75c green & red brown .65 .65

FAO "Freedom from Hunger" campaign. See No. C89.

Pres. Aden Abdulla Osman — A45

1963, Sept. 15   **Wmk. 303**   **Perf. 14**
270 A45 25c bl, dk brn, org & lt bl .40 .40
    Nos. 270,C90-C91 (3) 2.40 2.40

3rd anniv. of independence.

Dunes Theater A46

55c, African Merchants' and Artisans' Exhibit.

1963, Sept. 28   **Photo.**
271 A46 25c blue green .40 .40
272 A46 55c carmine rose .80 .80
    Nos. 271-272,C92 (3) 3.20 3.20

7th Somali Fair, Mogadishu.

Somali Credit Bank Building A47

1964, May 16   **Wmk. 303**   **Perf. 14**
273 A47 60c indigo, red lil & yel .85 .85
    Nos. 273,C93-C94 (3) 5.35 5.35

10th anniv. of the Somali Credit Bank.

Running — A48

1964, Oct. 10   **Wmk. 303**   **Perf. 14**
274 A48 10c shown .25 .25
275 A48 25c High jump .25 .25
    Nos. 274-275,C95-C96 (4) 4.10 4.10

18th Olympic Games, Tokyo, Oct. 10-25. See also Nos. C95-C96.

DC-3 A49

Design: 20c, Passengers leaving DC-3.

1964, Nov. 8   **Photo.**   **Perf. 14**
276 A49 5c dk blue & lil rose .45 .45
277 A49 20c blue & orange .95 .95
    Nos. 276-277,C97-C98 (4) 9.55 9.55

Establishment of Somali Air Lines.

ITU Emblem and Map of Africa — A50

1965, May 17   **Wmk. 303**   **Perf. 14**
278 A50 25c dp blue & dp org .55 .30
    Nos. 278,C99-C100 (3) 3.50 2.35

ITU centenary.

Tanning Industry A51

25c, Meat industry; cannery, cattle. 35c, Fishing industry; cannery, fishing boats.

1965, Sept. 28   **Perf. 14**
279 A51 10c sepia & buff .25 .25
280 A51 25c sepia & pink .25 .25
281 A51 35c sepia & lt blue .25 .25
    Nos. 279-281,C101-C102 (5) 4.55 3.40

8th Somali Fair, Mogadishu.

Hottentot Fig and Gazelle A52

Designs: 60c, African tulip and giraffes. 1sh, Ninfea and flamingos. 1.30sh, Pervincia and ostriches. 1.80sh, Bignonia and zebras.

1965, Nov. 1   **Wmk. 303**   **Perf. 14**
Flowers in Natural Colors
282 A52 20c blk & brt bl .25 .25
283 A52 60c blk & dk gray .25 .25
284 A52 1sh blk, sl grn & ol grn .65 .65
285 A52 1.30sh blk & dp grn 1.50 1.50
286 A52 1.80sh blk & brt bl 3.00 3.00
    Nos. 282-286 (5) 5.65 5.65

Narina's Trogon A53

Birds: 35c, Bateleur eagle, vert. 50c, Vulture. 1.30sh, European roller. 2sh, Vulturine guinea fowl, vert.

1966, June 1   Photo.   Wmk. 303
287	A53	25c multicolored	.30	.30
288	A53	35c brt blue & multi	.30	.30
289	A53	50c multicolored	.40	.40
290	A53	1.30sh multicolored	2.00	2.00
291	A53	2sh multicolored	3.25	3.25
		Nos. 287-291 (5)	6.25	6.25

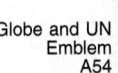

Globe and UN Emblem A54

UN emblem and: 1sh, Map of Africa. 1.50sh, Map of Somalia.

1966, Oct. 24   Litho.   Perf. 13x12½
292	A54	35c bl, pur & brt bl	.55	.25
293	A54	1sh brn, yel & brick red	.55	.25
294	A54	1.50sh grn, blk, bl & yel	1.00	.60
		Nos. 292-294 (3)	2.10	1.10

21st anniversary of United Nations.

Woman Sitting on Crocodile A55

Paintings: 1sh, Woman and warrior. 1.50sh, Boy leading camel. 2sh, Women pounding grain.

Wmk. 303
1966, Dec. 1   Photo.   Perf. 14
295	A55	25c multicolored	.25	.25
296	A55	1sh multicolored	.35	.25
297	A55	1.50sh multicolored	.60	.25
298	A55	2sh multicolored	1.60	.95
		Nos. 295-298 (4)	2.80	1.70

Somali art, exhibited in the Garesa Museum, Mogadishu.

UNESCO Emblem A56

1966, Dec. 20   Wmk. 303   Perf. 14
299	A56	35c blk, dk red & gray	.25	.25
300	A56	1sh blk, emer & yel	.25	.25
301	A56	1.80sh blk, ultra & red	1.75	1.75
		Nos. 299-301 (3)	2.25	2.25

UNESCO, 20th anniv.

Haggard's Oribi — A57

Gazelles: 60c, Long-snouted dik-dik. 1sh, Gerenuk. 1.80sh, Soemmering's gazelle.

1967, Feb. 20   Photo.   Perf. 14
302	A57	35c blk, ultra & bis	.25	.25
303	A57	60c blk, org & brn	.25	.25
304	A57	1sh blk, red & brn	.40	.40
305	A57	1.80sh blk, yel grn & brn	2.75	2.75
		Nos. 302-305 (4)	3.65	3.65

Dancers — A58

Designs: Various Folk Dances.

Unwmk.
1967, July 15   Litho.   Perf. 13
306	A58	25c multicolored	.25	.25
307	A58	50c multicolored	.25	.25
308	A58	1.30sh multicolored	.25	.25
309	A58	2sh multicolored	2.10	2.10
		Nos. 306-309 (4)	2.85	2.85

Boy Scout Giving Scout Sign — A59

Designs: 50c, Boy Scouts with flags. 1sh, Boy Scout cooking and tent. 1.80sh, Jamboree emblem.

1967, Aug. 15
310	A59	35c multicolored	.25	.25
311	A59	50c multicolored	.25	.25
312	A59	1sh multicolored	.55	.55
313	A59	1.80sh multicolored	2.10	2.10
		Nos. 310-313 (4)	3.15	3.15

12th Boy Scout World Jamboree, Farragut State Park, Idaho, Aug. 1-9.

Pres. Abdirascid Ali Scermarche and King Faisal — A60

Designs: 1sh, Clasped hands, flags of Somalia and Saudi Arabia.

Wmk. 303
1967, Sept. 21   Photo.   Perf. 14
314	A60	50c black & lt blue	.25	.25
315	A60	1sh multicolored	.55	.55
		Nos. 314-315,C103 (3)	2.55	2.55

Visit of King Faisal of Saudi Arabia.

Gaterin Gaterinus A61

Tropical Fish: 50c, Chaetodon semilarvatus. 1sh, Priacanthus hamrur. 1.80sh, Epinephelus summana.

1967, Nov. 15   Litho.   Perf. 14
316	A61	35c dk bl, yel & blk	.50	.50
317	A61	50c brt bl, ocher & blk	.50	.50
318	A61	1sh emer, org, brn & blk	1.50	1.50
319	A61	1.80sh pur, yel & blk	2.75	2.75
		Nos. 316-319 (4)	5.25	5.25

Physician Treating Infant — A62

WHO, 20th anniv.: 1sh, Physician examining boy, and nurse. 1.80sh, Physician and nurse treating patient.

Wmk. 303
1968, Mar. 20   Photo.   Perf. 14
320	A62	35c blk, scar, bl & brn	.30	.30
321	A62	1sh blk, grn & brn	.30	.30
322	A62	1.80sh blk, org & brn	1.60	1.60
		Nos. 320-322 (3)	2.20	2.20

Woman and Basket with Lemons A63

Waterbuck — A64

Designs: 10c, Oranges. 25c, Coconuts. 35c, Papayas. 40c, Limes. 50c, Grapefruit. 1sh, Bananas. 1.30sh, Cotton bolls. 1.80sh, Speke's gazelle. 2sh, Lesser kudu. 5sh, Hunter's hartebeest. 10sh, Clark's gazelle (dibatag).

1968   Litho.   Perf. 11½
323	A63	5c lt blue & multi	.25	.25
324	A63	10c yellow & multi	.25	.25
325	A63	25c lt lilac & multi	.25	.25
326	A63	35c salmon & multi	.25	.25
327	A63	40c buff & multi	.25	.25
328	A63	50c multicolored	.25	.25
329	A63	1sh lt blue & multi	.85	.85
330	A63	1.30sh gray & multi	2.50	2.50
331	A64	1.50sh lt blue & multi	.45	.45
332	A64	1.80sh multicolored	.45	.45
333	A64	2sh pink & multi	1.40	1.40
334	A64	5sh multicolored	2.75	2.75
335	A64	10sh multicolored	10.00	10.00
		Nos. 323-335 (13)	19.90	19.90

Issued: #323-330, 4/25; #331-335, 5/10.

Javelin — A65

Wmk. 303
1968, Oct. 12   Photo.   Perf. 14
336	A65	35c shown	.25	.25
337	A65	50c Running	.25	.25
338	A65	80c High jump	.25	.25
339	A65	1.50sh Basketball	1.90	1.20
a.		Souvenir sheet of 4, #336-339	6.75	6.75
		Nos. 336-339 (4)	2.65	1.95

19th Olympic Games, Mexico City, Oct. 12-27. No. 339a sold for 3.65sh.

Statuette — A66

Statuettes: 25c, Woman grinding grain. 35c, Woman potter. 2.80sh, Woman mat maker.

Perf. 11½x12
1968, Dec. 1   Litho.   Unwmk.
340	A66	25c rose lil, blk & brn	.25	.25
341	A66	35c brick red, blk & brn	.25	.25
342	A66	2.80sh green, blk & brn	1.90	1.20
		Nos. 340-342 (3)	2.40	1.70

Cornflower and Rhinoceros A67

80c, Sunflower & elephant. 1sh, Oleander & antelopes. 1.80sh, Chrysanthemums & storks.

Perf. 13x12½
1969, Mar. 25   Litho.   Unwmk.
343	A67	40c red & multi	.25	.25
344	A67	80c violet & multi	.25	.25
345	A67	1sh blue & multi	.65	.65
346	A67	1.80sh yellow & multi	3.00	3.00
		Nos. 343-346 (4)	4.15	4.15

ILO Emblem and Blacksmiths — A68

Designs: 1sh, Oxdrawn plow. 1.80sh, Drawing water from well.

Wmk. 303
1969, May 10   Photo.   Perf. 14
347	A68	25c dk red, dp bis & blk	.25	.25
348	A68	1sh car rose, brn & blk	.25	.25
349	A68	1.80sh multicolored	1.75	1.75
		Nos. 347-349 (3)	2.25	2.25

ILO, 50th anniversary.

Mahatma Gandhi — A69

Designs: 1.50sh, Gandhi, globe and hands releasing dove, horiz. 1.80sh, Gandhi seated.

Unwmk.
1969, Oct. 2   Photo.   Perf. 13
Size: 25x35½mm
350	A69	35c brown violet	.40	.40

Perf. 14½x14
Size: 37½x20mm
351	A69	1.50sh bister brn	.60	.60

Perf. 13
Size: 25x35½mm
352	A69	1.80sh olive gray	4.00	4.00
		Nos. 350-352 (3)	5.00	5.00

Mohandas K. Gandhi (1869-1948), leader in India's fight for independence.

1970
US Space Explorations. Set of seven. 60, 80c, 1, 1.50, 1.80, 2, 2.80sh. Souv. sheet, 14sh, Not officially issued - available Feb. 14. Values: set, $6; souvenir sheet, $32.50.

Nivprale
Vevanes
A70

Butterflies: 50c, Leschenault. 1.50sh,
Papilio (ornytoptera) aeacus. 2sh, Urania
riphaeus.

Perf. 12½x13
1970, Mar. 25   Litho.   Unwmk.
353 A70   25c multicolored   .30   .30
354 A70   50c multicolored   .30   .30
355 A70   1.50sh orange & multi   .80   .80
356 A70   2sh yellow & multi   3.00   3.00
Nos. 353-356 (4)   4.40   4.40

Somali Democratic Republic

Lenin Addressing
Crowd — A71

Designs: 25c, Lenin walking with children.
1.80sh, Lenin in his study, horiz.

Perf. 12x12½, 12½x12
1970, Apr. 22   Litho.   Unwmk.
357 A71   25c multicolored   .25   .25
358 A71   1sh multicolored   .45   .45
359 A71   1.80sh multicolored   2.10   2.10
Nos. 357-359 (3)   2.80   2.80

Lenin (1870-1924), Russian communist
leader.

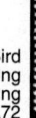

Bird
Feeding
Young
A72

35c, Monument & Battle of Dagahtur. 1sh,
Arms of Somalia, UN emblem, vert. 2.80sh,
Boy milking camel, & star, vert.

Perf. 14x13½, 13½x14
1970, July 28   Photo.   Wmk. 303
360 A72   25c blue & multi   .25   .25
361 A72   35c slate & multi   .25   .25
362 A72   1sh violet & multi   .55   .55
363 A72   2.80sh blue & multi   2.00   2.00
Nos. 360-363 (4)   3.05   3.05

10th anniversary of independence.

"Agriculture" — A73

40c, Soldier and flag. 1sh, Hand on open
book. 1.80sh, Grain, scales of justice and
dove.

Perf. 14x13½
1970, Oct. 21   Photo.   Wmk. 303
364 A73   35c green & multi   .25   .25
365 A73   40c ultra & blk   .40   .40
366 A73   1sh red brown & blk   .45   .45
367 A73   1.80sh multicolored   1.25   1.25
Nos. 364-367 (4)   2.35   2.35

First anniversary of Oct. 21st Revolution.

Snake
Strangling
Black Man,
Map of
South
Africa
A74

Design: 1.80sh, Concentration camp and
symbols of justice holding scales.

Perf. 14x13½
1971, June 20   Photo.   Wmk. 303
368 A74   1.30sh multicolored   .55   .55
369 A74   1.80sh gray, red & blk   2.10   2.10

Against racial discrimination in South Africa.

Waves
A75

Design: 2.80sh, Waves and globe.

1971, June 30
370 A75   25c black & blue   .40   .40
371 A75   2.80sh blk, grn & bl   2.10   2.10

3rd World Telecommunications Day, May 17.

Map of Africa and Telecommunications
System — A76

Design: 1.50sh, Map of Africa and telecommunications system, diff.

1971, July 25
372 A76   1sh blk, lt bl & grn   .55   .55
373 A76   1.50sh black & yellow   1.50   1.50

Pan-African Telecommunications system.

White
Rhinoceros
A77

Wild Animals: 1sh, Cheetahs. 1.30sh,
Zebras. 1.80sh, Lion attacking camel.

1971, Aug. 25
374 A77   35c ocher & multi   .40   .40
375 A77   1sh violet & multi   .95   .95
376 A77   1.30sh violet & multi   2.25   2.25
377 A77   1.80sh multicolored   4.50   4.50
Nos. 374-377 (4)   8.10   8.10

Headquarters, Mogadishu, Flag, Map
of Africa — A78

Design: 1.30sh, Desert Fort.

1971, Oct. 18
378 A78   1.30sh blk & red org   .85   .85
379 A78   1.50sh blk, blue & yel   1.75   1.75

East and Central African Summit Conf.

Revolution
Monument
A79

1sh, Field workers. 1.35sh, Building
workers.

1971, Oct. 21
380 A79   10c black & blue   .25   .25
381 A79   1sh blk, yel brn & grn   .55   .55
382 A79   1.35sh blk, dp brn & yel   1.75   1.75
Nos. 380-382 (3)   2.55   2.55

2nd anniversary of 1969 revolution.

Vaccination of Cow — A80

1.80sh, Veterinarian vaccinating cow.

Perf. 14x13½
1971, Nov. 28   Photo.   Wmk. 303
383 A80   40c blk, red & bl   .40   .25
384 A80   1.80sh lt green & multi   1.75   1.75

Rinderpest campaign.

Postal
Union
Emblem,
Dove and
Letter
A81

1972, Jan. 25   Unwmk.
385 A81   1.50sh multicolored   1.75   1.75

10th anniv. of APU. See No. C108.

Children
and
UNICEF
Emblem
A82

Design: 50c, Mother and child, vert.

1972, Mar. 30   Perf. 13x14, 14x13
386 A82   50c blk, bis brn & dk
brn   .25   .25
387 A82   2.80sh lt blue & multi   2.10   2.10

UNICEF, 25th anniv. (in 1971).

Camel
A83

Designs: 10c, Cattle and cargo ship. 20c,
Bull. 40c, Sheep. 1.70sh, Goat.

1972, Apr. 10   Perf. 14x13
388 A83   5c green & multi   .25   .25
389 A83   10c multicolored   .30   .30
390 A83   20c multicolored   .30   .30
391 A83   40c orange red & blk   .30   .30
392 A83   1.70sh dull grn & blk   3.75   3.75
Nos. 388-392 (5)   4.90   4.90

Hands
Holding
Infant
A84

1sh, Youth Corps emblem, marchers with
flags. 1.50sh, Woman, man, tent, tractor.

1972, Oct. 21   Photo.   Perf. 14x13½
393 A84   70c yellow & multi   .25   .25
394 A84   1sh red & multi   .40   .40
395 A84   1.50sh lt blue & multi   1.60   1.60
Nos. 393-395 (3)   2.25   2.25

3rd anniversary of October 21 Revolution.

Folk Dance
A85

Folk Dances: 40c, Man and woman, vert.
1sh, Group dance, vert. 2sh, Two men and a
woman.

1973   Photo.   Perf. 14x13½, 13½x14
396 A85   5c dull blue & multi   .25   .25
397 A85   40c brown & multi   .25   .25
398 A85   1sh yellow & multi   .55   .55
399 A85   2sh brick red & multi   1.90   1.90
Nos. 396-399 (4)   2.95   2.95

Hand
Writing
Somali
Script
A86

40c, Flame and "FAR SOMALI" inscription,
vert. 1sh, Woman and sunburst with Somali
script.

Perf. 13½x14, 14x13½
1973, Oct. 21   Photo.
400 A86   40c red & multi   .25   .25
401 A86   1sh blue & multi   .35   .35
402 A86   2sh yellow & multi   1.90   1.90
Nos. 400-402 (3)   2.50   2.50

Publicity for use of Somali script.

Map of Africa and
Emblem — A87

Map of Africa
with Target on
Somalia — A88

1974, June 12   Perf. 13½x14
403 A87   40c multicolored   .40   .40
404 A88   2sh multicolored   2.00   2.00

OAU Meeting, Mogadishu.

Hurdler
A89

1sh, Runners. 1.40sh, Netball, vert.

1974, Aug. 1   Perf. 14x13, 13x14
405	A89	50c black & orange	.25	.25
406	A89	1sh black & green	.40	.40
407	A89	1.40sh black & olive	2.00	2.00
		Nos. 405-407 (3)	2.65	2.65

Victory
Pioneers — A90

Pioneers Helping
Woman — A91

1974, Aug. 25   Photo.   Perf. 13x14
408	A90	40c multicolored	.25	.25
409	A91	2sh multicolored	1.90	1.90

Victory Pioneers, founded Aug. 24, 1972, to
defend Socialist Revolution.

Map of
Arab
Countries
A92

Flags of
Arab
Countries
A93

1974, Sept. 1   Perf. 14x13
410	A92	1.50sh multicolored	.95	.95
411	A93	1.70sh multicolored	3.00	3.00

Somalia's admission to the Arab League,
Feb. 14, 1974.

Tank
Tracks in
Desert
A94

Somalis Reading
Books — A95

Perf. 14x13½, 13½x14
1974, Oct. 21   Litho.
412	A94	40c multicolored	.25	.25
413	A95	2sh multicolored	1.75	1.75

5th anniversary of the Oct. 21st Revolution.

Carrier
Pigeons
A96

Design: 3sh, Postrider.

1975, Feb. 15   Litho.   Perf. 14x13½
414	A96	50c blue & multi	.25	.25
415	A96	3sh multicolored	1.75	1.75

UPU centenary (in 1974).

Africa
A97

Design: 1.50sh, Carrier pigeons.

1975, Apr. 10
416	A97	1sh multicolored	.30	.30
417	A97	1.50sh multicolored	1.60	1.60

African Postal Union.

Somali
Warrior — A98

Designs: Traditional costumes of Somali
men (1sh, 10sh) and women (40c, 50c, 5sh).

1975, Oct. 27   Photo.   Perf. 13½
418	A98	10c yellow & multi	.25	.25
419	A98	40c lt blue & multi	.25	.25
420	A98	50c multicolored	.25	.25
421	A98	1sh green & multi	.25	.25
422	A98	5sh claret & multi	2.40	.80
423	A98	10sh rose & multi	6.50	2.40
		Nos. 418-423 (6)	9.90	4.20

Monument — A99

IWY
Emblem
A100

1975, Dec. 10   Litho.   Perf. 13½x14
424	A99	50c blk & red org	.25	.25
425	A100	2.30sh blk, pink & mag	2.40	2.40

International Women's Year.

Abdulla
Hassan
Monument
A101

Abdulla Hassan
with
Warriors — A102

1.50sh, Abdulla Hassan speaking to his
men. 2.30sh, Attacking horsemen, horiz.

Perf. 14x13½, 13½x14
1976, Nov. 30   Photo.
426	A101	50c multicolored	.25	.25
427	A102	60c multicolored	.25	.25
428	A102	1.50sh multicolored	.85	.85
429	A102	2.30sh multicolored	2.50	2.50
		Nos. 426-429 (4)	3.85	3.85

Sayid Mohammed Abdulla Hassan (1864-
1920), poet and military leader.

Cypraea
Gracilis
A103

Sea Shells: 75c, Charonia bardayi. 1sh,
Chlamys townsendi. 2sh, Cymatium ranzanii.
2.75sh, Conus argillaceus. 2.90sh, Strombus
oldi.

1976, Dec. 15   Photo.   Perf. 14x13½
430	A103	50c blue & multi	.35	.35
431	A103	75c blue & multi	.35	.35
432	A103	1sh blue & multi	.50	.50
433	A103	2sh blue & multi	2.00	2.00
434	A103	2.75sh blue & multi	7.00	7.00
435	A103	2.90sh blue & multi	10.00	10.00
a.		Souvenir sheet of 6, #430-435	32.50	32.50
		Nos. 430-435 (6)	20.20	20.20

No. 435a sold for 11sh.

Benin Head and Hunters — A104

Benin Head and: 75c, Handicrafts. 2sh,
Dancers. 2.90sh, Musicians.

1977, Aug. 30   Photo.   Perf. 14x13½
436	A104	50c multicolored	.25	.25
437	A104	75c multicolored	.25	.25
438	A104	2sh multicolored	.95	.95
439	A104	2.90sh multicolored	3.00	3.00
		Nos. 436-439 (4)	4.45	4.45

2nd World Black and African Festival, FES-
TAC '77, Lagos, Nigeria, Jan. 15-Feb. 12.

Arms of
Somalia
A105

Designs: 75c, Somali flags, vert. 1.50sh,
Pres. Mohammed Siad Barre and globe. 2sh,
Arms over rising sun and flags, vert.

Perf. 13½x14, 14x13½
1977, Sept. 30   Photo.
440	A105	75c multicolored	.25	.25
441	A105	1sh multicolored	.80	.80
442	A105	1.50sh multicolored	1.10	1.10
443	A105	2sh multicolored	2.00	2.00
		Nos. 440-443 (4)	4.15	4.15

Somali Socialist Revolutionary Party, established July 1, 1976.

Licaon
Pictus
A106

Protected Animals: 75c, Bush baby. 1sh,
Somali ass. 1.50sh, Aardwolf. 2sh, Greater
kudu. 3sh, Giraffe.

1977, Nov. 25   Photo.   Perf. 14x13½
444	A106	50c multicolored	.40	.40
445	A106	75c multicolored	.40	.40
446	A106	1sh multicolored	1.25	1.25
447	A106	1.50sh multicolored	1.75	1.75
448	A106	2sh multicolored	3.00	3.00
449	A106	3sh multicolored	7.50	7.50
a.		Souvenir sheet of 6, #444-449	26.00	26.00
		Nos. 444-449 (6)	14.30	14.30

Leonardo
da Vinci's
Flying
Machine
A107

ICAO Emblem and: 1.50sh, Montgolfier's
balloon. 2sh, Wright brothers' plane. 2.90sh,
Somali Airlines turbojet.

1977, Dec. 23   Photo.   Perf. 14x13½
450	A107	1sh multicolored	.25	.25
451	A107	1.50sh multicolored	.55	.55
452	A107	2sh multicolored	1.20	1.20
453	A107	2.90sh multicolored	2.40	2.40
a.		Souvenir sheet of 4, #450-453	14.50	14.50
		Nos. 450-453 (4)	4.40	4.40

ICAO, 30th anniv. No. 453a sold for 10sh.

Dome of the
Rock — A108

Lithographed and Engraved
1978, Apr. 30   Perf. 13x14
454	A108	75c multicolored	.25	.25
455	A108	2sh multicolored	1.75	1.75

Palestinian fighters and their families.

Stadium and Soccer Player — A109

Designs: 4.90sh, Stadium and goalkeeper.
5.50sh, Stadium and player.

1978, Aug. 5   Litho.   Perf. 14x13½
456	A109	1.50sh multicolored	.80	.80
457	A109	4.90sh multicolored	2.40	2.40
458	A109	5.50sh multicolored	4.00	4.00
a.		Souvenir sheet of 3, #456-458	17.50	17.50
		Nos. 456-458 (3)	7.20	7.20

11th World Cup Soccer Championship,
Argentina, June 1-25. No. 458a sold for 14sh.

Acacia Tortilis — A110

Trees: 50c, Ficus sycomorus, vert. 75c, Terminalia catapa, vert. 2.90sh, Baobab.

1978, Sept. 5   Photo.   Perf. 14
459	A110	40c multicolored	.25	.25
460	A110	50c multicolored	.25	.25
461	A110	75c multicolored	.25	.25
462	A110	2.90sh multicolored	3.25	3.25
	Nos. 459-462 (4)		4.00	4.00

Forest conservation.

Hibiscus — A111

Flowers of Somalia: 1sh, Cassia baccarinii. 1.50sh, Kigelia somalensis. 2.30sh, Dichrostachys glomerata.

1978, Dec. 15   Photo.   Perf. 13½x14
463	A111	50c multicolored	.25	.25
464	A111	1sh multicolored	.55	.55
465	A111	1.50sh multicolored	1.60	1.60
466	A111	2.30sh multicolored	2.40	2.40
a.	Souv. sheet, #463-466, perf. 14		12.00	12.00
	Nos. 463-466 (4)		4.80	4.80

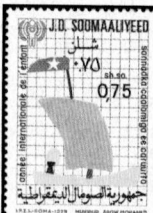

Huri and Siganus Rivulatus A112

Fishery Development: 80c, Sail huri, gaterin gaterinus. 2.30sh, Fishing boats, hypacanthus amia. 2.50sh, Motorized fishing boat, mackerel.

1979, Sept. 1   Photo.   Perf. 14x13½
467	A112	75c multicolored	.55	.55
468	A112	80c multicolored	.55	.55
469	A112	2.30sh multicolored	1.50	1.50
470	A112	2.50sh multicolored	3.50	3.50
	Nos. 467-470 (4)		6.10	6.10

Sailing, IYC Emblem — A113

IYC Emblem, Children's Drawings: 50c, 90c, Schoolboy. 1.50sh, 2.50sh, Houses. 3sh, 4sh, Bird and flower. 1sh, as 75c.

1979, Sept. 10   Photo.   Perf. 13½x14
471	A113	50c multicolored	.30	.30
472	A113	75c multicolored	.30	.30
473	A113	1.50sh multicolored	.80	.80
474	A113	3sh multicolored	2.50	2.50
	Nos. 471-474 (4)		3.90	3.90

Souvenir Sheet of 4
474A	A113	#b.-e.	10.00 10.00

Intl. Year of the Child. No. 474A contains 90c, 1sh, 2.50sh, 4sh stamps and sold for 10sh.

University Students, Outdoor Classrooms — A114

Flower and: 50c, Housing construction. 75c, Children's recreation. 1sh, Doctor examining child, woman and man carrying grain and fish. 2.40sh, Woman and children carrying produce over dam. 3sh, Dish antenna.

1979, Nov. 30   Litho.   Perf. 14x13½
475	A114	20c multicolored	.30	.30
476	A114	50c multicolored	.30	.30
477	A114	75c multicolored	.65	.65
478	A114	1sh multicolored	.65	.65
479	A114	2.40sh multicolored	1.90	1.90
480	A114	3sh multicolored	2.40	2.40
	Nos. 475-480 (6)		6.20	6.20

Oct. 21 revolution, 10th anniversary.

Barbopsis Devecchii A115

Freshwater Fish: 90c, Phreatichthys andruzzii. 1sh, Uegitglanis zammaranoi. 2.50sh, Pardi's catfish.

1979, Dec. 12
481	A115	50c multicolored	.70	.70
482	A115	90c multicolored	.70	.70
483	A115	1sh multicolored	2.10	2.10
484	A115	2.50sh multicolored	2.10	2.10
a.	Souvenir sheet of 4, #481-484		11.50	11.50
	Nos. 481-484 (4)		5.60	5.60

No. 484a sold for 10sh.

Taleh Fortress, Congress Emblem — A116

1980, June 1   Photo.   Perf. 14x13½
485	A116	2.25sh multicolored	1.10	1.10
486	A116	3.50sh multicolored	2.00	2.00

1st International Congress of Somalian Studies, Mogadishu, July 6-13.

View of Marka — A117

1sh, Gandershe. 2.30sh, Afgooye. 3.50sh, Muqdisho.

1980, July 1   Litho.   Perf. 14
487	A117	75c shown	.30	.30
488	A117	1sh multi + label	1.00	1.00
489	A117	2.30sh multi + label	1.00	1.00
490	A117	3.50sh multi + label	4.00	4.00
	Nos. 487-490 (4)		6.30	6.30

See Nos. 502-505, 527-530.

A118

1sh, Batis perkeo. 2.25sh, Rynchostruthus socotranus louisae. 5sh, Laniarius ruficeps.

1980, July 30   Photo.   Perf. 13½x14
491	A118	1sh multi	.65	.65
492	A118	2.25sh multi	1.60	1.60
493	A118	5sh multi	3.50	3.50
a.	Souvenir sheet of 3, #491-493		11.00	11.00
	Nos. 491-493 (3)		5.75	5.75

A119

Perf. 13½x14, 14x13½
1981, Oct. 16   Litho.
494	A119	75c Globe, grain	.30	.30
495	A119	3.25sh Emblem, horiz.	1.50	1.50
496	A119	5.50sh like No. 494	3.00	3.00
	Nos. 494-496 (3)		4.80	4.80

World Food Day.

13th World Telecommunications Day — A120

1sh, Shepherdess, sheep, dish antenna. 3sh, Emblems.

1981, Oct. 10   Perf. 13½x14
497	A120	1sh multicolored	.80	.80
498	A120	3sh multicolored	1.60	1.60
499	A120	4.60sh like No. 498	3.25	3.25
	Nos. 497-499 (3)		5.65	5.65

Hegira, 1500th Anniv. — A121

1981, Oct.   Photo.   Perf. 13½x14
500	A121	1.50sh multicolored	.55	.55
501	A121	3.80sh multicolored	1.90	1.90

View Type of 1980
1982, May 31   Litho.   Perf. 13½x14
502	A117	2.25sh Balcad	1.20	1.20
503	A117	4sh Jowhar	1.60	1.60
504	A117	5.50sh Golaleey	2.40	2.40
505	A117	8.30sh Muqdisho	2.75	2.75
	Nos. 502-505 (4)		7.95	7.95

Nos. 502-505 were each printed in sheets of 10 stamps and 5 labels showing regional map. Value for stamps with attached label: +25%.

1982 World Cup — A122

Designs: Various soccer players.

1982, June 13
506	A122	1sh multicolored	.55	.55
507	A122	1.50sh multicolored	1.25	1.25
508	A122	3.25sh multicolored	3.00	3.00
a.	Souvenir sheet of 3, #506-508		13.00	13.00
	Nos. 506-508 (3)		4.80	4.80

ITU Plenipotentiaries Conference, Nairobi, Sept. — A123

1982, Oct. 15   Photo.   Perf. 14x13½
509	A123	75c green & multi	.25	.25
510	A123	3.25sh orange & multi	1.40	1.40
511	A123	5.50sh blue & multi	3.50	3.50
	Nos. 509-511 (3)		5.15	5.15

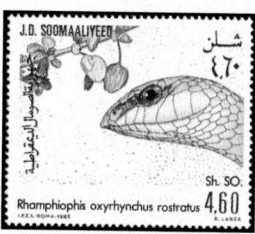

Local Snakes — A124

2.80sh, Bitis arietans. 3.20sh, Psammophis punctulatus. 4.60sh, Rhamphiophis oxyrhynchus. 8.60sh, Sphalerosophis josephscorteccii.

1982, Dec. 20   Photo.   Perf. 14
512	A124	2.80sh multicolored	1.60	1.60
513	A124	3.20sh multicolored	3.25	3.25
514	A124	4.60sh multicolored	4.75	4.75
	Nos. 512-514 (3)		9.60	9.60

Souvenir Sheet
515	A124	8.60sh multicolored	20.00 20.00

Somali Woman — A125

1982, Dec. 30   Perf. 14x13½
516	A125	1sh yel & multi	.30	.30
517	A125	5.20sh lilac & multi	1.75	1.75
518	A125	5.80sh org & multi	1.90	1.90
519	A125	6.40sh blue & multi	2.10	2.10
520	A125	9.40sh lt brn & multi	3.25	3.25
521	A125	25sh green & multi	8.00	8.00
	Nos. 516-521 (6)		17.30	17.30

A126

1983, July 20   **Perf. 13½x14**
522 A126 5.20sh multicolored   1.40 1.40
523 A126 6.40sh multicolored   2.40 2.40
World Communications Year.

2nd Intl. Congress of Somali Studies,
Hamburg — A127

Various views of Hamburg.

1983, Aug. 1   **Perf. 14**
524 A127 5.20sh multicolored   .85 .85
525 A127 6.40sh multicolored   3.25 3.25

Military
Uniforms — A128

Designs: a, Air Force. b, Women's Auxiliary
Corps. c, Border Police. d, People's Militia. e,
Army Infantry. f, Custodial Corps. g, Police. h,
Navy.

1983, Oct. 21   **Litho.**   **Perf. 13½x14**
526   Strip of 8   11.00 11.00
a.-h. A128 3.20sh, any single   1.20 1.20

View Type of 1980

1983
527 A117 2.80sh Barawe   .80 .80
528 A117 3.20sh Bur Hakaba   .80 .80
529 A117 5.50sh Baydhabo   1.60 1.60
530 A117 8.60sh Dooy Nuunaay   4.00 4.00
Nos. 527-530 (4)   7.20 7.20

Nos. 527-530 were each printed in sheets of
10 stamps and 5 decorative labels. Value for
stamps with attached label: +25%.

Sea Shells
A129

No. 531, Volutocorbis rosavittoriae. No. 532,
Phalium bituberculosum. No. 533, Conus
milneedwarsi.
No. 534, Cypraea broderipi.

1984, Feb. 15   **Litho.**   **Perf. 14x13½**
531 A129 2.80sh multicolored   .80 .80
532 A129 3.20sh multicolored   2.25 2.25
533 A129 5.50sh multicolored   5.75 5.75
Nos. 531-533 (3)   8.80 8.80

Souvenir Sheet
Perf. 14

534 A129 15sh multicolored   13.00 13.00

Olympics
1984 — A130

1984, Sept.   **Litho.**   **Perf. 13½x14**
535 A130 1.50sh Runners   .55 .55
536 A130 3sh Discus   1.20 1.20
537 A130 8sh Pole vaulting   3.50 3.50
a.   Souvenir sheet of 3, #535-537   8.00 8.00
Nos. 535-537 (3)   5.25 5.25

No. 537a sold for 15sh.

Riccione
Fair — A131

1984, Sept.   **Litho.**   **Perf. 13½x14**
538 A131 5.20sh multicolored   1.75 1.75
539 A131 6.40sh multicolored   4.25 4.25

Animals
A132

No. 540, Hystrix cristata. No. 541,
Ichneumia albicauda. No. 542, Mungos
mungo. No. 543, Mellivora capensis.

1984, Sept.   **Litho.**   **Perf. 14x13½**
540 A132 1sh multicolored   .35 .35
541 A132 1.50sh multicolored   .35 .35
542 A132 2sh multicolored   1.75 1.75
543 A132 4sh multicolored   3.00 3.00
a.   Souvenir sheet of 4, #540-
543   11.00 11.00
Nos. 540-543 (4)   5.45 5.45

No. 543a sold for 10sh.

Intl. Civil Aviation Org., 40th
Anniv. — A133

1984, Nov. 20   **Litho.**   **Perf. 14**
544 A133 3sh multicolored   1.20 1.20
545 A133 6.40sh multicolored   2.40 2.40

Souvenir Sheet

546   Sheet of 2   8.00 8.00
a.   A133 3sh like No. 544   1.20 1.20
b.   A133 6.40sh like No. 545   2.40 2.40

No. 546 contains 2 49½x46mm stamps.
Sold for 10sh.

Dove — A134

Constellations from the Book of Fixed Stars,
by Abd al-Rahman al-Sufi.

1985, Aug. 10   **Litho.**   **Perf. 13½x14**
547 A134 4.30sh shown   1.20 1.20
548 A134 11sh Bull   2.40 2.40
549 A134 12.50sh Rams   2.40 2.40
550 A134 13.80sh Archer   2.90 2.90
Nos. 547-550 (4)   8.90 8.90

Architecture — A135

1985, Sept.   **Litho.**   **Perf. 13½x14**
551 A135 2sh Ras Kiambone   .25 .25
552 A135 6.60sh Hannassa   .40 .40
553 A135 10sh Mnarani   1.20 1.20
554 A135 18.60sh as #551, diff.   4.75 4.75
Nos. 551-554 (4)   6.60 6.60

Nos. 551-554 were each printed in sheets of
10 stamps and 5 decorative labels. Value for
stamps with attached label: +10%.
See Nos. 572-575.

Lady
Somalia
Seated in
Posthorn
A136

1985, Oct.   **Perf. 14x14½**
555 A136 2sh multicolored   .95 .95
556 A136 20sh multicolored   4.00 4.00
a.   Souvenir sheet of 2, #555-
556, perf. 13½   9.50 9.50

ITALIA '85, Rome. No. 556a sold for 30sh.

Bats
A137

2.50sh, Triaenops persicus. 4.50sh, Cardi-
oderma cor. 16sh, Tadarida condylura. 18sh,
Coleura afra.

1985, Dec. 25   **Litho.**   **Perf. 14x13½**
557 A137 2.50sh multi   1.00 1.00
558 A137 4.50sh multi   1.40 1.40
559 A137 16sh multi   4.00 4.00
560 A137 18sh multi   5.25 5.25
Nos. 557-560 (4)   11.65 11.65

Souvenir Sheet

561   Sheet of 4   16.00 16.00
a.   A137 2.50sh like #552   1.00 1.00
b.   A137 4.50sh like #553   1.40 1.40
c.   A137 16sh like #554   4.00 4.00
d.   A137 18sh like #555   5.25 5.25

Nos. 561a-561d printed in continuous
design. No. 561 sold for 50sh.

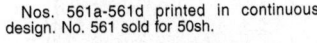

Economic Trade Agreement with
Kenya — A138

Design: Presidents Arap Moi and Barre, satellite communications.

1986, Feb. 15   **Perf. 14**
562 A138 9sh multi   1.75 1.75
563 A138 14.50sh multi   2.75 2.75

EUROFLORA
Flower Exhibition,
Genoa — A139

10sh, Flower arrangement. 15sh, Arrangement, diff.

1986, Apr. 25   **Perf. 13½x14**
564 A139 10sh multi   .80 .80
565 A139 15sh multi   2.40 2.40
a.   Souvenir sheet of 2, #564-565   5.25 5.25

No. 565a sold for 30sh.

3rd Intl. Congress
on Somali
Studies — A140

1986, May 26
566 A140 11.35sh multi   .80 .80
567 A140 20sh multi   2.40 2.40

1986 World Cup Soccer
Championships, Mexico — A141

Various soccer plays.

1986, June   **Perf. 14x13½**
568 A141 3.60sh multi   .55 .55
569 A141 4.80sh multi   .55 .55
570 A141 6.80sh multi   1.75 1.75
571 A141 22.60sh multi   2.40 2.40
a.   Souvenir sheet of 4, #568-
571   10.00 10.00
Nos. 568-571 (4)   5.25 5.25

No. 571a sold for 50sh.

Architecture Type of 1985

1986   **Litho.**   **Perf. 13½x14**
572 A135 10sh Bulaxaar   .40 .40
573 A135 15sh Saylac   .40 .40
574 A135 20sh Saylac, diff.   .80 .80
575 A135 31sh Jasiiradaha
Jawaay   4.75 4.75
Nos. 572-575 (4)   6.35 6.35

Nos. 572-575 were each printed in sheets of
10 stamps and 5 decorative labels. Value for
stamps with attached label: +10%.

Red Crescent — Red Cross
Rehabilitation Center,
Mogadishu — A143

1987, May 8   **Litho.**   **Perf. 13½x13**
576 A143 56sh multi   6.75 6.75

Souvenir Sheet

577 A143 56sh multi, diff.   8.75 8.75

No. 577 sold for 60sh. See Norway No. 908.

A144

1987, Sept. 27   Litho.   Perf. 13½x14
578 A144 20sh Running   2.10 2.10
579 A144 48sh Javelin   4.75 4.75
a.   Souvenir sheet of 2, #578-
        579   10.00 10.00
OLYMPHILEX '87, Rome. No. 579a sold for
75sh.

A145

1987, Oct. 5   Photo.   Perf. 13½x14½
580 A145 53sh multicolored   2.00 2.00
581 A145 72sh multicolored   3.25 3.25
Intl. Year of Shelter for the Homeless.

GEOSOM
'87 — A146

Maps: 10sh, 160,000,000 years ago. 20sh,
60,000,000 years ago. 40sh, 15,000,000 years
ago. 50sh, Today.

1987, Nov. 24   Litho.   Perf. 13½x14
582 A146 10sh multi   1.25 1.25
583 A146 20sh multi, diff.   2.40 2.40
584 A146 40sh multi, diff.   4.75 4.75
585 A146 50sh multi, diff.   6.50 6.50
a.   Souv. sheet of 2, #583, 585   37.50 37.50
        Nos. 582-585 (4)   14.90 14.90
Symposium on the Geology of Somalia,
Mogadishu, 11/24-12/1. #585a sold for 130sh.

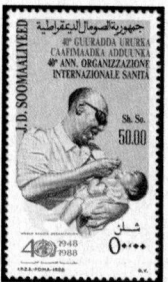

A147

1988, Dec. 31   Litho.   Perf. 13½x14
586 A147 50sh multicolored   .80   .80
587 A147 168sh multicolored   4.00 4.00
World Health Organization, 40th anniv.

Wildlife
A148

No. 588, Lepus somaliensis. No. 589,
Syncerus caffer. No. 590, Papio hamadryas.
No. 591, Hippopotamus amphibius.

Perf. 13½x14, 14x13½
1989, Oct. 20   Litho.
588 A148 75sh multicolored   .55   .55
589 A148 198sh multicolored   1.90 1.90
590 A148 200sh multicolored   3.25 3.25
591 A148 216sh multicolored   4.00 4.00
a.   Souvenir sheet of 2, #590-
        591   13.00 13.00
        Nos. 588-591 (4)   9.70 9.70
No. 591a contains 2 labels like #588-589.
Sold for 700sh.

Somali
Revolution,
20th Anniv.
A149

Flowers, children's games: 70sh, Kick ball.
100sh, Swinging. 150sh, Teeter-totter. 300sh,
Jumping rope, stick and hoop.

1989, Dec. 12   Litho.   Perf. 14x13½
592 A149 70sh multicolored   1.40 1.40
593 A149 100sh multicolored   2.00 2.00
594 A149 150sh multicolored   3.00 3.00
595 A149 300sh multicolored   5.00 5.00
        Nos. 592-595 (4)   11.40 11.40

A150

Liberation: Nos. 599-600, Dove breaking
chains, horiz.

1991   Litho.   Perf. 13½x14, 14x13½
596 A150 70sh lilac & multi   .65   .65
597 A150 100sh grn bl & multi   .90   .90
598 A150 150sh brt blue &
           multi   1.40 1.40
599 A150 150sh yellow & multi   1.40 1.40
600 A150 300sh yel grn & mul-
           ti   2.75 2.75
601 A150 300sh yel grn & mul-
           ti   2.75 2.00
        Nos. 596-601 (6)   9.85 9.10
Issued: Nos. 599-600, July 2; others, July 4.

No. 599 Ovptd. in Blue

1991   Litho.   Perf. 14x13½
602 A150 150sh yellow & multi   4.00 4.00

A151

Various minarets.

1991   Litho.   Perf. 14
603 A151 30sh multicolored   .30   .30
604 A151 40sh multicolored   .45   .45
605 A151 75sh multicolored   .75   .75
606 A151 150sh multicolored   2.25 2.25
        Nos. 603-606 (4)   3.75 3.75

Relief efforts have demonstrated the
breakdown of government services in
Somalia. It is unclear which faction has
control of the Postal Service, if any is
operating. The status of Scott Nos. 607-
638 will be reviewed once more information is available.

Gazelles
A152

500sh, Two Speke's. 700sh, One Speke's.
800sh, One Soemmering's. 1000sh, Two
Soemmering's.

Inscribed in Black
1992   **Perf. 14x13½**
607 A152 500sh multicolored   3.25
608 A152 700sh multicolored   4.50
609 A152 800sh multicolored   6.00
610 A152 1000sh multicolored   7.25
        Nos. 607-610 (4)   21.00
World Wildlife Fund.

Without WWF Emblem
Inscribed in red lilac
611 A152 100sh like #607   .85
612 A152 200sh like #608   1.75
613 A152 300sh like #609   2.40
614 A152 400sh like #610   3.50
Inscribed in black
615 A152 1500sh Baboons   10.00
616 A152 2500sh Hippopota-
           mus   17.50
617 A152 3000sh Giraffes   20.00
618 A152 5000sh Leopard   30.00
        Nos. 607-618 (12)   107.00
Nos. 607-618 are part of an expanding set.
Numbers may change.
For overprints see No. 629-632.

Nos. 607-610 Ovptd. in Orange

1992   Litho.   Perf. 14x13½
629 A152 500sh on #607   3.50
630 A152 700sh on #608   5.00
631 A152 800sh on #609   6.50
632 A152 1000sh on #610   9.00
        Nos. 629-632 (4)   24.00

Discovery
of America,
500th
Anniv.
A153

Designs: 100sh, Sighting land from crow's
nest. 200sh, Three men pointing from ship.
300sh, Columbus in his cabin. 400sh, Claiming land. 2000sh, Building fort in New World.
No. 638: a, 800sh, like #634. b, 900sh, like
#635. c, 1300sh, like #633.

1992
633 A153 100sh multicolored   .40
634 A153 200sh multicolored   1.00
635 A153 300sh multicolored   1.25
636 A153 400sh multicolored   1.50
637 A153 2000sh multicolored   8.00
        Nos. 633-637 (5)   12.15

Souvenir Sheet
638 A153 Sheet of 3, #a.-c.   12.00
Nos. 638a-638c do not have white border.
No. 638 exists imperf.

SEMI-POSTAL STAMPS

Italy Nos. B1-B3
Overprinted

Italy No. B4
Surcharged

1916   Wmk. 140   Perf. 14
B1   SP1   10c + 5c rose   16.00   45.00
B2   SP2   15c + 5c slate   67.50   57.50
B3   SP2   20c + 5c orange   16.00   52.50
B4   SP2   20c on 15c + 5c
           slate   67.50   95.00
        Nos. B1-B4 (4)   167.00 250.00

Holy Year Issue
Italy Nos. B20-B25 Surcharged in
Black or Red

1925, June 1   Perf. 12
B5   SP4   6b + 3b on 20c +
           10c   3.75   22.50
B6   SP4   13b + 6b on 30c +
           15c   3.75   24.00
B7   SP4   15b + 8b on 50c +
           25c   3.75   22.50
B8   SP4   18b + 9b on 60c +
           30c   3.75   30.00
B9   SP8   30b + 15b on 1 l
           +50c (R)   3.75   37.50
B10 SP8   1r + 50b on 5 l
           +2.50 l (R)   3.75   57.50
        Nos. B5-B10 (6)   22.50 194.00

Colonial Institute Issue

"Peace" Substituting
Spade for
Sword — SP10

1926, June 1   Typo.   Perf. 14
B11 SP10 5c + 5c brown   1.10   9.50
B12 SP10 10c + 5c olive grn   1.10   9.50
B13 SP10 20c + 5c blue grn   1.10   9.50
B14 SP10 40c + 5c brn red   1.10   9.50
B15 SP10 60c + 5c orange   1.10   9.50
B16 SP10 1 l + 5c blue   1.10   20.00
        Nos. B11-B16 (6)   6.60   67.50
The surtax was for the Italian Colonial
Institute.

Italian
Semi-Postal
Stamps of
1926
Overprinted

1927, Apr. 21   Unwmk.   Perf. 11½
B17 SP10 40c + 20c dk brn
           & blk   3.75   42.50
B18 SP10 60c + 30c brn
           red & ol
           brn   3.75   42.50
B19 SP10 1.25 l + 60c dp bl
           & blk   3.75   60.00

B20 SP10 5 l + 2.50 l dk grn & blk 6.00 92.50
Nos. B17-B20 (4) 17.25 237.50

The surtax was for the charitable work of the Voluntary Militia for Italian National Defense.

Allegory of Fascism and Victory — SP11

1928, Oct. 15 Wmk. 140 Perf. 14
B21 SP11 20c + 5c blue grn 3.25 13.50
B22 SP11 30c + 5c red 3.25 13.50
B23 SP11 50c + 10c purple 3.25 22.50
B24 SP11 1.25 l + 20c dk blue 4.00 30.00
Nos. B21-B24 (4) 13.75 79.50

46th anniv. of the Societa Africana d'Italia. The surtax aided that society.

Italian Semi-Postal Stamps of 1928 Overprinted

1929, Mar. 4 Unwmk. Perf. 11
B25 SP10 30c + 10c red & blk 4.50 26.00
B26 SP10 50c + 20c vio & blk 4.50 28.00
B27 SP10 1.25 l + 50c brn & bl 6.75 50.00
B28 SP10 5 l + 2 l ol grn & blk 6.75 97.50
Nos. B25-B28 (4) 22.50 201.50

The surtax was for the charitable work of the Voluntary Militia for Italian National Defense.

Italian Semi-Postal Stamps of 1926 Ovptd. in Black or Red

1930, Oct. 20 Perf. 14
B29 SP10 30c + 10c dk bl grn & blk (Bk) 35.00 60.00
B30 SP10 50c + 10c dk grn & vio (R) 35.00 97.50
B31 SP10 1.25 l + 30c ol brn & red brn (R) 35.00 97.50
B32 SP10 5 l + 1.50 l ind brn (R) 110.00 260.00
Nos. B29-B32 (4) 215.00 515.00

The surtax was for the charitable work of the Voluntary Militia for Italian National Defense.

Irrigation Canal SP14

1930, Nov. 27 Photo. Wmk. 140
B33 SP14 50c + 20c ol brn 4.00 24.00
B34 S414 1.25 l + 20c dp blue 4.00 24.00
B35 SP14 1.75 l + 20c green 4.00 26.00
B36 SP14 2.55 l + 50c purple 9.00 42.50
B37 SP14 5 l + 1 l dp car 9.00 65.00
Nos. B33-B37 (5) 30.00 181.50

25th anniv. of the Italian Colonial Agricultural Institute. The surtax was for the aid of that institution.

SP15

King Victor Emmanuel III — SP16

1935, Jan. 1
B38 SP15 5c + 5c blk brn 6.00 34.00
B39 SP15 7½c + 7½c vio 6.00 34.00
B40 SP15 15c + 10c ol blk 6.00 34.00
B41 SP15 20c + 10c rose red 6.00 34.00
B42 SP15 25c + 10c dp grn 6.00 34.00
B43 SP15 30c + 10c brn 6.00 34.00
B44 SP15 50c + 10c pur 6.00 34.00
B45 SP15 75c + 15c rose car 6.00 34.00
B46 SP15 1.25 l + 15c dp bl 6.00 34.00
B47 SP15 1.75 l + 25c red org 6.00 34.00
B48 SP15 2.75 l + 25c gray 37.50 135.00
B49 SP15 5 l + 1 l dp cl 37.50 135.00
B50 SP15 10 l + 1.80 l red brn 37.50 135.00
B51 SP16 25 l + 2.75 l brn & red 200.00 500.00
Nos. B38-B51 (14) 372.50 1,245.
Set, never hinged 850.00

Visit of King Victor Emmanuel III.

Catalogue values for unused stamps in this section, from this point to the end of the section, are for Never Hinged items.

Somalia

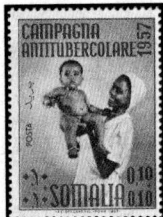

Nurse Holding Infant — SP17

1957, Nov. 30 Wmk. 303 Perf. 14
B52 SP17 10c + 10c red & brn .60 .60
B53 SP17 25c + 10c grn & brn .60 .60
Nos. B52-B53,CB11-CB12 (4) 2.90 3.10

The surtax was for the fight against tuberculosis.

Republic

Refugees SP18

1964, Dec. 12 Photo. Perf. 14
B54 SP18 25c + 10c vio bl & red .55 .30
Nos. B54,CB13-CB14 (3) 3.90 2.10

The surtax was to help refugees.

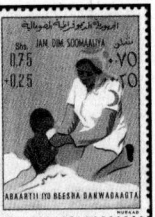

Red Cross Nurse Feeding Child — SP19

Famine Relief: 80c+20c, Nomad in parched land, horiz. 2.40sh+10c, Family with fish and produce. 2.90sh+10c, Physician and Aid Society emblem, horiz.

1976, Dec. 10 Perf. 13x14, 14x13
B55 SP19 75c + 25c multi .55 .55
B56 SP19 80c + 20c multi .55 .55
B57 SP19 2.40sh + 10c multi 1.75 1.75
B58 SP19 2.90sh + 10c multi 2.40 2.40
Nos. B55-B58 (4) 5.25 5.25

Refugees SP20

1981, Dec. 15 Photo. Perf. 13½x14
B59 SP20 2sh + 50c multi .85 .85
B60 SP20 6.80sh + 50c multi 4.00 4.00
a. Souvenir sheet of 2, #B59-B60 8.00 8.00

TB Bacillus Centenary — SP31

1982, Dec. 30 Photo. Perf. 14
B61 SP31 4.60sh + 60c multi 2.00 2.00
B62 SP31 5.80sh + 60c multi 2.50 2.50

AIR POST STAMPS

View of Coast AP1

Cheetahs AP2

Wmk. 140
1934, Oct. Photo. Perf. 14
C1 AP1 25c sl bl & red org 5.25 21.00
C2 AP1 50c dk grn & blk 5.25 19.00
C3 AP1 75c brn & red org 5.25 19.00
a. Imperf. 3,000.

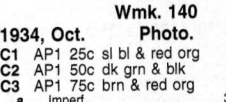

C4 AP2 80c org brn & blk 5.25 21.00
C5 AP2 1 l scar & blk 5.25 26.00
C6 AP2 2 l dk bl & brn 5.25 45.00
Nos. C1-C6 (6) 31.50 151.00
Set, never hinged 80.00

2nd Colonial Arts Exhibition, Naples. For overprint see No. CO1.

Banana Tree and Airplane AP3

Designs: 25c, 1.50 l, Banana tree and plane. 50c, 2 l, Plane over cotton field. 60c, 5 l, Plane over orchard. 75c, 10 l, Plane over field workers. 1 l, 3 l, Small girl watching plane.

1936 Photo.
C7 AP3 25c slate green 3.50 9.00
C8 AP3 50c brown 2.00 .25
C9 AP3 60c red orange 4.00 13.50
C10 AP3 75c orange brn 3.50 2.40
C11 AP3 1 l deep blue 2.00 .25
C12 AP3 1.50 l purple 3.50 .80
C13 AP3 2 l slate blue 7.50 1.20
C14 AP3 3 l copper red 26.00 15.00
C15 AP3 5 l yellow green 30.00 18.00
C16 AP3 10 l dp rose red 37.50 34.00
Nos. C7-C16 (10) 119.50 94.40
Set, never hinged 260.00

Catalogue values for unused stamps in this section, from this point to the end of the section, are for Never Hinged items.

Somalia

AP8

1950-51 Wmk. 277
C17 AP8 30c yellow brn 8.00 3.75
C18 AP8 45c dk carmine 8.00 3.75
C19 AP8 65c dk blue vio 8.00 3.75
C20 AP8 70c dull blue 8.00 6.50
C21 AP8 90c olive brn 8.00 6.50
C22 AP8 1s lilac rose 9.50 3.75
C23 AP8 1.35s violet 14.50 8.00
C24 AP8 1.50s blue green 14.50 9.50
C25 AP8 3s blue 67.50 37.50
C26 AP8 5s chocolate 67.50 37.50
C27 AP8 10s red org ('51) 135.00 24.00
Nos. C17-C27 (11) 348.50 144.50

Scene in Mogadishu AP8a

1951, Oct. 4
C27A AP8a 1s vio & Prus bl 3.25 1.50
C27B AP8a 1.50s ol grn & chnt brn 8.75 13.50

First Territorial Council meeting.

Plane, Palm Tree and Minaret — AP9

1952, Sept. 14
C28 AP9 1.20s ol bis & dp bl 4.00 4.00

1st Somali Fair, Mogadishu, Sept. 14-28.

Mother and Child — AP10

1953, May 27
C29 AP10 1.20s dk grn & dk brn 2.50 *3.00*
Somali anti-tuberculosis campaign.

Fair Entrance AP11

1953, Sept. 28   Unwmk.   Perf. 11½
C30 AP11 1.20s brn car & pink   .75 *1.00*
C31 AP11 1.50s yel brn & buff   1.00 *1.25*
2nd Somali Fair, Mogadishu, Sept. 28-Oct. 12, 1953.

Plane over Map and Stamps of 1903 AP12

Perf. 13x13½
1953, Dec. 16   Engr.   Wmk. 277
Early Stamps in Brn and Rose Car
C32 AP12 60c orange brown   1.25 *1.75*
C33 AP12 1s greenish black   2.25 *2.50*
1st Somali postage stamps, 50th anniv.

"UPU" among Constellations — AP13

Perf. 11½
1953, Dec. 16   Photo.   Unwmk.
C34 AP13 1.20s red & cream   .50 *1.30*
C35 AP13 1.50s brown & cream   1.00 *2.25*
C36 AP13 2s green & lt blue   1.00 *2.25*
Nos. C34-C36 (3)   2.50 *5.80*
UPU, 75th anniv. (in 1949).

Alexander Island Juba River — AP14

1954, June 1   Perf. 13½x12½
C37 AP14 1.20s dk grn & brn   1.10 *1.25*
C38 AP14 2s dk car & pur   1.60 *1.75*
See note after No. 196.

Somali Flag — AP15

Perf. 13½x13
1954, Oct. 12   Litho.   Wmk. 277
C39 AP15 1.20s multicolored   .45 *.55*
Adoption of Somali flag.

Haggard's Oribi — AP16

Designs: 45c, Phillip's dik-dik. 50c, Speke's gazelle. 75c, Gerenuk. 1.20s, Soemmering's gazelle. 1.50s, Waterbuck.

Wmk. 277
1955, Apr. 12   Photo.   Perf. 13½
Antelopes in Natural Colors
Size: 22x33mm
C40 AP16 35c gray grn & blk   .35 *.80*
C41 AP16 45c lilac & blk   5.50 *2.25*
C42 AP16 50c rose lil & blk   .40 *.80*
C43 AP16 75c red   3.75 *.80*
C44 AP16 1.20s dk gray grn   3.75 *5.00*
C45 AP16 1.50s bright blue   5.50 *7.50*
Nos. C40-C45 (6)   19.25 *17.15*
See Nos. C57-C58.

Caravan at Water Hole AP17

Design: 1.20s, Village well.

Perf. 13½x14
1955, Sept. 24   Wmk. 303
C46 AP17 45c brown & orange   .75 *1.25*
C47 AP17 1.20s sapphire & pink   1.25 *1.25*
3rd Somali Fair, Mogadishu, Sept. 1955.

Ballot Type of Regular Issue
1956, Apr. 30   Photo.   Perf. 14
C48 A24 60c brown & ultra   .75 *1.00*
C49 A24 1.20s brown & org   .75 *1.00*
Opening of the territory's first democratically elected Legislative Assembly.

Arms Type of Regular Issue
Coat of Arms in Dull Yellow, Blue and Black
1957, May 6   Wmk. 303   Perf. 13½
C50 A25 45c blue   .75 *.75*
C51 A25 1.20s bluish green   .75 *.75*
Issued in honor of the new coat of arms.

Type of Regular Issue, 1957 and

Oil Well — AP18

Design: 60c, Irrigation canal construction.

1957, Sept. 28   Perf. 14
C52 A26 60c blue & brown   1.00 *1.00*
C53 AP18 1.20s black & ver   1.00 *1.00*
Fourth Somali Fair and Film Festival.

Sport Type of Regular Issue
60c, Runner. 1.20s, Bicyclist. 1.50s, Basketball player.

1958, Apr. 28   Wmk. 303   Perf. 14
C54 A27 60c brown   .25 *.25*
C55 A27 1.20s blue   .25 *.40*
C56 A27 1.50s rose carmine   .25 *.40*
Nos. C54-C56 (3)   .75 *1.05*

Animal Type of 1955
3s, Lesser kudu. 5s, Hunter's hartebeest.
Size: 20½x36½mm

1958-59   Photo.
C57 AP16 3s ocher & sepia   2.00 *2.25*
C58 AP16 5s gray, blk & yel ('59) 2.00 *2.25*
See No. CE1.

Police Bugler AP19

1959, June 19   Photo.
C59 AP19 1.20s ocher & ultra   .75 *1.00*
C60 AP19 1.50s olive grn & ultra   .75 *1.00*
a.   Souv. sheet of 4, #228-229,
    C59-C60   6.00 *8.00*
Opening of the Constituent Assembly of Somalia.

Marabou AP20

1959, Sept. 4   Wmk. 303
C61 AP20 1.20s shown   .75 *.55*
C62 AP20 2s Great egret   .75 *.55*

Incense Shipment, 15th Century B.C. AP21

Design: 2s, Incense burner and view of Mogadishu harbor.

1959, Sept. 28   Perf. 14
C63 AP21 1.20s red & blk   .50 *.60*
C64 AP21 2s blue, blk & org   1.00 *1.00*
5th Somali Fair, Mogadishu.

University Institute and Arms AP22

Design: 1.20s, Front view of Institute.

1960, Jan. 14
C65 AP22 45c grn, blk & org
    brn   .35 *.35*
C66 AP22 1.20s blue, ultra & blk   .55 *.65*
Opening of the University Institute of Somalia.

Stork and Uprooted Oak Emblem — AP23

1960, Apr. 7   Wmk. 303   Perf. 14
C67 AP23 1.50s lt grn, bl & red   .90 *1.25*
World Refugee Year, 7/1/59-6/30/60.

Republic
#C42, C44 Overprinted Like #242
Wmk. 277
1960, June 26   Photo.   Perf. 13½
Antelopes in Natural Colors
C68 AP16 50c rose lil & blk   40.00 *40.00*
C69 AP16 1.20s dk gray grn   29.00 *32.50*
See note after No. 242.

Parliament and Italian Flag AP25

1.80s, Somali flag and assembly building.

1960, July 1   Wmk. 303   Perf. 14
C70 AP25 1s org red, grn &
    red   .80 *.80*
C71 AP25 1.80s red org, ultra &
    blk   3.25 *3.25*
Somalia's independence.

Animal Type of Regular Issue
1960, Nov. 24
C72 A37 3s Leopard   3.75 *3.75*

Olympic Games Type
45c, Runner, flag, Olympic rings. 1.80s, Long distance runner, flag, Olympic rings.

1960, Nov. 24
C73 A38 45c lilac & blue   .85 *.85*
C74 A38 1.80s org ver & bl   1.75 *1.75*
17th Olympic Games, Rome, 8/25-9/11.

Amauris Fenestrata and Jet Plane AP26

Various Butterflies.

1961, Sept. 9
C75 AP26 60c blue, brn &
    yel   .40 *.40*
C76 AP26 90c yel, blk & grn   .50 *.50*
C77 AP26 1s multicolored   2.40 *.35*
C78 AP26 1.80s org, blk & red   1.10 *1.10*
C79 AP26 3s multicolored   2.40 *2.40*
C80 AP26 5s ver, blk & brt
    bl   8.00 *3.50*
C81 AP26 10s multicolored   12.50 *6.50*
Nos. C75-C81 (7)   27.30 *14.75*

Wooden Headrest, Comb and Cap AP27

Design: 1.80sh, Camel, metal sculpture.

1961, Sept. 28   Wmk. 303   Perf. 14
C82 AP27 1sh blk, ultra &
    ocher   .40 *.40*
C83 AP27 1.80sh blk, yel & brn   2.25 *2.25*
6th Somali Fair, Mogadishu.

Fish Type
Fish: 2.70sh, Lutianus sebae.

1962, Apr. 26
C84 A41 2.70sh ultra, brn & rose
    brn   3.50 *3.50*

Mosquitoes and Malaria Eradication Emblem — AP28

Wmk. 303

1962, Oct. 25 **Photo.** *Perf. 14*
C85 AP28 1sh bis brn & blk .85 .85
C86 AP28 1.80sh lt green & blk 2.75 2.75

WHO drive to eradicate malaria.

Police Auxiliary Women — AP29

Women's Auxiliary Forces: 1.80sh, Army auxiliary women with flag.

1963, May 15 **Wmk. 303** *Perf. 14*
C87 AP29 1sh dk bl, yel & org .85 .85
C88 AP29 1.80sh multicolored 2.75 2.75

Freedom from Hunger Type

Design: 1sh, Sower and wheat.

1963, June 25
C89 A44 1sh dk brn, yel & bl 2.75 2.75

President Osman Type

1963, Sept. 15 **Wmk. 303** *Perf. 14*
C90 A45 1sh multicolored .70 .70
C91 A45 1.80sh multicolored 1.30 1.30

Somali Fair Type

Design: 1.80sh, Government Pavilion.

1963, Sept. 28 **Photo.**
C92 A46 1.80sh blue 2.00 2.00

Map of Somalia, Animals and Globe AP30

1.80sh, Somali Credit Bank emblem.

1964, May 16 **Wmk. 303** *Perf. 14*
C93 AP30 1sh multicolored 1.75 1.75
C94 AP30 1.80sh blk, bl & yel 2.75 2.75

10th anniversary of Somali Credit Bank.

Olympic Type

1964, Oct. 10 **Photo.**
C95 A48 90c Diving .85 .85
C96 A48 1.80sh Soccer 2.75 2.75
a. Souvenir sheet, #274-275, C95-C96 40.00

No. C96a sold for 3.55sh.

Elephants and DC-3 AP31

Design: 1.80sh, Plane over Mogadishu.

1964, Nov. 8 **Photo.** *Perf. 14*
C97 AP31 1sh brown & green 2.90 2.90
C98 AP31 1.80sh black & blue 5.25 5.25

Establishment of Somali Air Lines.

ITU Type

1965, May 17 **Wmk. 303** *Perf. 14*
C99 A50 1sh dp grn & blk .85 .65
C100 A50 1.80sh rose lil & brn 2.10 1.40

Somali Fair Type

Designs: 1.50sh, Sugar industry; harvesting sugar cane and refinery. 2sh, Dairy industry; bottling plant and milk cow.

1965, Sept. 28 **Photo.** *Perf. 14*
C101 A51 1.50sh sepia & pale bl 1.20 .55
C102 A51 2sh sepia & rose 2.50 2.10

Faisal Type

Design: 1.80sh, Ka'aba, Mecca, Pres. Abdirascid Ali Scermarche and King Faisal.

1967, Sept. 21 **Wmk. 303** *Perf. 14*
C103 A60 1.80sh blk, dp rose & org 1.75 1.75

Egret — AP32

Birds: 1sh, Southern carmine bee-eater. 1.30sh, Bruce's green pigeon. 1.80sh, Broad-tailed paradise whydah.

Perf. 11½

1968, Nov. 1 **Unwmk.** **Litho.**
C104 AP32 35c blue & multi .35 .25
C105 AP32 1sh grn & multi .45 .25
C106 AP32 1.30sh vio bl & multi 1.10 .95
C107 AP32 1.80sh yel & multi 2.75 2.50
Nos. C104-C107 (4) 4.65 3.95

Somali Democratic Republic
Postal Union Type

1.30sh, Postal Union emblem and letter.

Perf. 14x13½

1972, Jan. 25 **Photo.** **Unwmk.**
C108 A81 1.30sh multicolored 1.75 1.75

AIR POST SEMI-POSTAL STAMPS

King Victor Emmanuel III — SPAP1

Wmk. 140

1934, Nov. 5 **Photo.** *Perf. 14*
CB1 SPAP1 25c + 10c gray grn 9.00 26.00
CB2 SPAP1 50c + 10c brn 9.00 26.00
CB3 SPAP1 75c + 15c rose red 9.00 26.00
CB4 SPAP1 80c + 15c blk brn 9.00 26.00
CB5 SPAP1 1 l + 20c red 9.00 26.00
CB6 SPAP1 2 l + 20c brt bl 9.00 26.00
CB7 SPAP1 3 l + 25c pur 26.00 120.00
CB8 SPAP1 5 l + 25c org 26.00 120.00
CB9 SPAP1 10 l + 30c rose vio 26.00 120.00
CB10 SPAP1 25 l + 2 l dp grn 26.00 120.00
Nos. CB1-CB10 (10) 158.00 636.00
Set, never hinged 375.00

65th birthday of King Victor Emmanuel III; non-stop flight from Rome to Mogadishu. For overprint see No. CBO1.

Catalogue values for unused stamps in this section, from this point to the end of the section, are for Never Hinged items.

Somalia
Type of Semi-Postal Stamps, 1957
1957, Nov. 30 **Wmk. 303** *Perf. 14*
CB11 SP17 55c + 20c dk bl & brn .85 .95
CB12 SP17 1.20s + 20c vio & brn .85 .95

The surtax was for the fight against tuberculosis.

Type of Semi-Postal Issue, 1964

Designs: 75c+20c, Destroyed Somali village. 1.80sh+50c, Soldier aiding children, and map of Somalia, vert.

1964, Dec. 12 **Photo.** *Perf. 14*
CB13 SP18 75c + 20c blk, org red & brn .85 .40
CB14 SP18 1.80sh + 50c blk, ol bis & slate 2.50 1.40

AIR POST SPECIAL DELIVERY STAMP

Catalogue value for the stamp in this section is for a Never Hinged item.

Antelopes APSD1

Wmk. 303

1958, Oct. 4 **Photo.** *Perf. 14*
CE1 APSD1 1.70s org ver & blk 2.75 2.25

AIR POST OFFICIAL STAMP

No. C1 Overprinted

Wmk. 140

1934, Nov. 11 **Photo.** *Perf. 14*
CO1 AP1 25c sl bl & red org 2,800. 5,250.
Never hinged 4,900.

Forgeries of this overprint exist.

AIR POST SEMI-POSTAL OFFICIAL STAMP

Air Post Semi-Postal Stamps of 1934 Overprinted in Black

1934, Nov. 5 **Wmk. 140** *Perf. 14*
CBO1 SPAP1 25 l + 2 l cop red 2,950. 6,000.
Never hinged 5,250.

SPECIAL DELIVERY STAMPS

Italy No. E3 Surcharged

1923, July 16 **Wmk. 140** *Perf. 14*
E1 SD1 30b on 60c dl red 32.50 30.00

Italy, Type of 1908 Special Delivery Stamp Surcharged

E2 SD2 60b on 1.20 l bl & red 47.50 57.50

"Italia" SD3

1924, June **Engr.** **Unwmk.**
E3 SD3 30b dk red & brn 13.00 24.00
E4 SD3 60b dk blue & red 24.00 35.00

Nos. E3-E4 Surcharged in Black or Red

1926, Oct.
E5 SD3 70c on 30b (Bk) 15.00 21.00
E6 SD3 2.50 l on 60b (R) 17.00 29.00
a. Imperf., pair 1,200.

Same Surcharge on No. E3
1927 *Perf. 11*
E7 SD3 1.25 l on 30b 16.50 19.00
a. Perf. 14 300.00 975.00
b. Imperf., pair 1,050.

Catalogue values for unused stamps in this section, from this point to the end of the section, are for Never Hinged items.

Somalia

Bananas, Grant's Gazelles SD4

Wmk. 277

1950, Apr. 24 **Photo.** *Perf. 14*
E8 SD4 40c blue green 15.00 13.50
E9 SD4 80c violet 18.50 21.00

Gardenias SD5

Design: 1s, Eryrhina melanocantha.

1955, Feb. *Perf. 13*
E10 SD5 50c lilac & green .90 1.10
E11 SD5 1s bl, rose brn & grn 1.40 1.25

AUTHORIZED DELIVERY STAMP

Italy No. EY2 Overprinted in Black

1939 **Wmk. 140** ***Perf. 14***

EY1	AD2	10c brown	80.00	—

No. EY1 has yellowish gum. A 1941 printing in grayish brown, with white gum, was not issued. The overprint on the 1939 printing is located between the "OS" and "AN" of POSTE ITALIANE, while the overprint on the 1941 printing is centered. Value: unused, 80 cents; never hinged, $2.00.

POSTAGE DUE STAMPS

Values for Nos. J1-J41 are for examples with perforations touching or cutting into the design on at least one side. Examples with perforations clear of the design on all four sides are scarce and command considerable premiums.

Postage Due Stamps of Italy Overprinted

1906-08 **Wmk. 140** ***Perf. 14***

J1	D3	5c buff & mag	26.00	*52.50*
J2	D3	10c buff & mag	75.00	75.00
J3	D3	20c org & mag	52.50	*90.00*
J4	D3	30c buff & mag	52.50	*105.00*
J5	D3	40c buff & mag	375.00	105.00
J6	D3	50c buff & mag	82.50	*120.00*
J7	D3	60c buff & mag ('08)	75.00	*120.00*
J8	D3	1 l blue & mag	1,500.	550.00
J9	D3	2 l blue & mag	1,500.	550.00
J10	D3	5 l blue & mag	1,500.	550.00
J11	D3	10 l blue & mag	300.00	*500.00*
		Nos. J1-J11 (11)	5,538.	*2,817.*

Postage Due Stamps of Italy Overprinted at Top of Stamps

1909-19

J12	D3	5c buff & mag	9.50	*30.00*
J13	D3	10c buff & mag	9.50	*30.00*
J14	D3	20c buff & mag	20.00	*60.00*
J15	D3	30c buff & mag	60.00	*60.00*
J16	D3	40c buff & mag	60.00	*82.50*
J17	D3	50c buff & mag	60.00	*105.00*
J18	D3	60c buff & mag ('19)	82.50	*90.00*
J19	D3	1 l blue & mag	170.00	105.00
J20	D3	2 l blue & mag	240.00	*240.00*
J21	D3	5 l blue & mag	275.00	325.00
J22	D3	10 l blue & mag	55.00	*110.00*
		Nos. J12-J22 (11)	1,041.	*1,237.*

Same with Overprint at Bottom of Stamps

1920

J12a	D3	5c buff & magenta	150.00	225.00
b.		Double overprint	550.00	
J13a	D3	10c buff & magenta	150.00	225.00
J14a	D3	20c buff & magenta	210.00	150.00
J15a	D3	30c buff & magenta	210.00	150.00
J16a	D3	40c buff & magenta	210.00	225.00
J17a	D3	50c buff & magenta	210.00	210.00
J18a	D3	60c buff & magenta	210.00	210.00
J19a	D3	1 l blue & magenta	210.00	300.00
J20a	D3	2 l blue & magenta	210.00	300.00
J21a	D3	5 l blue & magenta	210.00	375.00
		Nos. J12a-J21a (10)	1,980.	2,370.

D4

1923, July 1

J23	D4	1b buff & black	3.00	*11.50*
J24	D4	2b buff & black	3.00	*11.50*
a.		Inverted numeral and ovpt.	550.00	
J25	D4	3b buff & black	3.00	*11.50*
J26	D4	5b buff & black	4.50	*11.50*
J27	D4	10b buff & black	4.50	*11.50*
J28	D4	20b buff & black	4.50	*11.50*
J29	D4	40b buff & black	4.50	*11.50*
J30	D4	1r blue & black	4.50	*62.50*
		Nos. J23-J30 (8)	31.50	*143.00*

Type of Postage Due Stamps of Italy Overprinted

1926, Mar. 1

J31	D3	5c buff & black	30.00	*37.50*
J32	D3	10c buff & black	30.00	26.00
J33	D3	20c buff & black	30.00	*45.00*
J34	D3	30c buff & black	30.00	26.00
J35	D3	40c buff & black	30.00	26.00
J36	D3	50c buff & black	45.00	26.00
J37	D3	60c buff & black	45.00	26.00
J38	D3	1 l blue & black	67.50	45.00
J39	D3	2 l blue & black	105.00	45.00
J40	D3	5 l blue & black	115.00	60.00
J41	D3	10 l blue & black	150.00	82.50
		Nos. J31-J41 (11)	677.50	445.00

Numerals and Ovpt. Invtd.

J32a	D3	10c	260.00
J33a	D3	20c	825.00
J34a	D3	30c	260.00
J35a	D3	40c	260.00
J36a	D3	50c	260.00
J37a	D3	60c	260.00

Postage Due Stamps of Italy, 1934, Overprinted in Black

1934, May 12

J42	D6	5c brown	1.50	*7.50*
J43	D6	10c blue	1.50	*7.50*
J44	D6	20c rose red	4.00	15.00
J45	D6	25c green	4.00	15.00
J46	D6	30c red orange	12.00	*19.00*
J47	D6	40c black brown	12.00	*26.00*
J48	D6	50c violet	20.00	9.00
J49	D6	60c black	20.00	*45.00*
J50	D7	1 l red orange	27.50	22.50
J51	D7	2 l green	50.00	45.00
J52	D7	5 l violet	52.50	*105.00*
J53	D7	10 l blue	52.50	*110.00*
J54	D7	20 l carmine	60.00	*170.00*
		Nos. J42-J54 (13)	317.50	*596.50*

Catalogue values for unused stamps in this section, from this point to the end of the section, are for Never Hinged items.

Somalia

D5

1950 **Wmk. 277** **Photo.** ***Perf. 14***

J55	D5	1c dark gray violet	4.50	4.50
J56	D5	2c deep blue	4.50	4.50
J57	D5	5c blue green	4.50	4.50
J58	D5	10c rose lilac	4.50	4.50
J59	D5	40c violet	16.50	16.50
J60	D5	1s dark brown	22.50	22.50
		Nos. J55-J60 (6)	57.00	57.00

PARCEL POST STAMPS

These stamps were used by affixing them to the way bill so that one half remained on it following the parcel, the other half staying on the receipt given the sender. Most used halves are right halves. Complete stamps were and are obtainable canceled, probably to order. Both unused and used values are for complete stamps.

Parcel Post Stamps of Italy, 1914-17, Overprinted

1917-19 **Wmk. 140** ***Perf. 13½***

Q1	PP2	5c brown	8.00	*67.50*
a.		Double overprint	500.00	—
Q2	PP2	10c blue	9.50	*45.00*
Q3	PP2	20c black ('19)	375.00	225.00
Q4	PP2	25c red	16.00	*80.00*
a.		Double overprint	—	—
Q5	PP2	50c orange	165.00	97.50
Q6	PP2	1 l lilac	52.50	*97.50*
Q7	PP2	2 l green	72.50	*97.50*
Q8	PP2	3 l bister	80.00	*170.00*
Q9	PP2	4 l slate	87.50	*170.00*
		Nos. Q1-Q9 (9)	866.00	*1,050.*

Halves Used

Q1	1.60
Q2	1.60
Q3	7.25
Q4	3.50
Q5	6.00
Q6	4.75
Q7	4.75
Q8	4.75
Q9	4.75

Nos. Q5-Q9 were overprinted in 1922 with a slightly different type in which the final "A" of SOMALIA is directly over the final "A" of ITALIANA. They were not regularly issued. Value for set: unused $1,600; never hinged $2,400.

Parcel Post Stamps of Italy, 1914-17, Overprinted

1923

Q10	PP2	25c red	75.00	*165.00*
Q11	PP2	50c orange	110.00	*165.00*
Q12	PP2	1 l violet	135.00	275.00
Q13	PP2	2 l green	135.00	275.00
Q14	PP2	3 l bister	210.00	275.00
Q15	PP2	4 l slate	210.00	275.00
		Nos. Q10-Q15 (6)	875.00	*1,430.*

Halves Used

Q10	4.75
Q11	4.75
Q12	3.00
Q13	3.00
Q14	4.75
Q15	5.50

Parcel Post Stamps of Italy, 1914-17, Surcharged

1923

Q16	PP2	3b on 5c brown	27.50	*37.50*
Q17	PP2	5b on 5c brown	27.50	*37.50*
Q18	PP2	10b on 10c blue	27.50	34.00
Q19	PP2	25b on 25c red	27.50	52.50
Q20	PP2	50b on 50c org	35.00	*75.00*
Q21	PP2	1r on 1 l lilac	47.50	75.00
Q22	PP2	2r on 2 l green	80.00	120.00
Q23	PP2	3r on 3 l bister	80.00	120.00
Q24	PP2	4r on 4 l slate	95.00	120.00
		Nos. Q16-Q24 (9)	447.50	671.50

Halves Used

Q16	1.60
Q17	1.60
Q18	1.60
Q19	3.25
Q20	3.25
Q21	3.25
Q22	3.25
Q23	3.25
Q24	3.25

No. Q16 has the numeral "3" at the left also.

Parcel Post Stamps of Italy, 1914-22 Overprinted

1926-31 **Red Overprint**

Q25	PP2	5c brown	34.00	*82.50*
Q26	PP2	10c blue	32.50	*82.50*
Q27	PP2	20c black	72.50	82.50
Q28	PP2	25c red	72.50	82.50
Q29	PP2	50c orange	72.50	82.50
Q30	PP2	1 l violet	97.50	82.50
Q31	PP2	2 l green	160.00	82.50
Q32	PP2	3 l yellow	30.00	*82.50*
Q33	PP2	4 l slate	30.00	*82.50*
Q34	PP2	10 l vio brn ('30)	55.00	*105.00*
Q35	PP2	12 l red brn '31)	55.00	*105.00*
Q36	PP2	15 l olive ('31)	55.00	*190.00*
Q37	PP2	20 l dull vio ('31)	55.00	*190.00*
		Nos. Q25-Q37 (13)	821.50	*1,332.*

Halves Used

Q25	2.00
Q26	2.00
Q27	3.25
Q28	3.25
Q29	3.25
Q30	3.25
Q31	3.25
Q32	3.25
Q33	3.25
Q34	4.00
Q35	4.00
Q36	4.00
Q37	4.00

Nos. Q25-Q31 come with two types of overprint: I — The first "I" and last "A" of ITALIANA extend slightly at both sides of SOMALIA. II — Only the "I" extends. These seven stamps with type I overprint were not regularly issued, and Nos. Q27-Q31 (type I) sell for less than with type II overprint.

Black Overprint

Q38	PP2	10 l violet brown	82.50	87.50
Q39	PP2	12 l red brown	55.00	87.50
Q40	PP2	15 l olive	55.00	87.50
Q41	PP2	20 l dull violet	55.00	87.50
		Nos. Q38-Q41 (4)	247.50	350.00

Halves Used

Q38	4.00
Q39	4.00
Q40	4.00
Q41	4.00

Same Overprint on Parcel Post Stamps of Italy, 1927-38

1928-39 **Black Overprint**

Q42	PP3	25c red, type I ('31)	45.00	*52.50*
		Never hinged	160.00	
Q43	PP3	30c ultra	6.00	*7.50*
Q43A	PP3	50c orange	*12,750.*	
Q44	PP3	60c red	6.00	*8.00*
Q45	PP3	1 l lilac brn, type II ('31)	40.00	*52.50*
Q46	PP3	2 l green, type II ('31)	40.00	*52.50*
Q47	PP3	3 l bister	15.00	*20.00*
Q48	PP3	4 l gray black	15.00	*20.00*
Q49	PP3	10 l rose lil ('34)	475.00	*675.00*
Q50	PP3	20 l lil brn ('34)	475.00	*750.00*
		Nos. Q42-Q43,Q44-Q50 (9)	1,117.	*1,638.*

Halves Used

Q42	8.75
Q43	.45
Q43A	160.00
Q44	.45
Q45	2.75
Q46	2.75
Q47	.80
Q48	.80
Q49	20.00
Q50	20.00

The 25c, 1 l and 2 l come with both types of overprint (see note below No. Q37). Both types were regularly issued. Values are for type I on 25c, type II on 1 l and 2 l.

Red Overprint

Q51	PP3	5c brown ('39)	16.00	
Q52	PP3	3 l bister ('30)	32.50	*80.00*
		Half stamp		2.00
Q53	PP3	4 l gray black ('30)	32.50	*80.00*
		Half stamp		2.00
		Nos. Q51-Q53 (3)	81.00	

Same Overprint in Black on Italy Nos. Q24-Q25

1940 ***Perf. 13***

Q54	PP3	5c brown	6.00	*13.50*
		Half stamp		.50
Q55	PP3	10c deep blue	7.50	*13.50*
		Half stamp		.50

Catalogue values for unused stamps in this section, from this point to the end of the section, are for Never Hinged items.

Somalia

PP1

1950 **Wmk. 277** **Photo.** ***Perf. 14***

Q56	PP1	1c cerise	9.50	*9.50*
Q57	PP1	3c dark gray violet	9.50	*9.50*
Q58	PP1	5c rose lilac	9.50	*9.50*
Q59	PP1	10c red orange	9.50	*9.50*
Q60	PP1	20c dark brown	9.50	*9.50*
Q61	PP1	50c blue green	24.00	*24.00*
Q62	PP1	1s violet	67.50	*67.50*
Q63	PP1	2s brown	82.50	*82.50*
Q64	PP1	3s blue	135.00	*135.00*
		Nos. Q56-Q64 (9)	356.50	*356.50*

Halves Used

Q56	.25
Q57	.25
Q58	.25
Q59	.25
Q60	.25
Q61	.25
Q62	1.60
Q63	2.00
Q64	3.25

SOMALI COAST

sō-'mä-lē 'kōst

(Djibouti)

LOCATION — Eastern Africa, bordering on the Gulf of Aden
GOVT. — French Overseas Territory
AREA — 8,500 sq. mi.
POP. — 86,000 (est. 1963)
CAPITAL — Djibouti (Jibuti)

The port of Obock, which issued postage stamps in 1892-1894, was included in the territory and began to use stamps of Somali Coast in 1902. See Obock in Vol. 4.

On Mar. 19, 1967, the territory changed its name to the French Territory of the Afars and Issas. The Republic of Djibouti was proclaimed June 27, 1977.

100 Centimes = 1 Franc

Catalogue values for unused stamps in this country are for Never Hinged items, beginning with Scott 224 in the regular postage section, Scott B13 in the semipostal section, Scott C1 in the airpost section, Scott CB1 in the airpost semi-postal section, and Scott J39 in the postage due section.

Obock Nos. 32-33, 35, 45 with Overprint or Surcharge Handstamped in Black, Blue or Red

Navigation and Commerce
A1   A2

A3

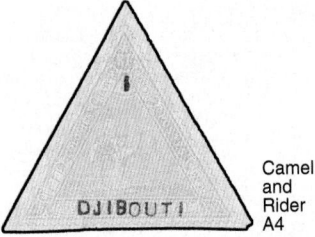

Camel and Rider
A4

1894   Unwmk.   Perf. 14x13½

1	A1	5c grn & red, *grnsh* (with bar)	165.00	140.00
a.		Without bar	1,250.	800.00
2	A2	25c on 2c brn & bl, *buff* (Bl & Bk)	350.00	225.00
a.		"25" omitted	1,000.	950.00
b.		"25" double	1,600.	
c.		"DJIBOUTI" omitted	1,000.	850.00
d.		"DJIBOUTI" inverted	1,100.	975.00
e.		"DJIBOUTI" double	1,600.	1,250.
3	A3	50c on 1c blk & red, *bl* (R & Bl)	350.00	250.00
a.		"5" instead of "50"	1,600.	1,150.
b.		"0" instead of "50"	1,600.	1,150.
c.		"DJIBOUTI" omitted	1,600.	1,250.

Imperf

4	A4	1fr on 5fr car	625.00	500.00
a.		"DJIBOUTI" omitted	4,500.	
b.		"DJIBOUTI" double	1,900.	1,650.
c.		"1" double	1,900.	1,650.
5	A4	5fr carmine	1,900.	1,350.

Counterfeits exist of Nos. 4-5.

View of Djibouti, Somali Warriors — A5

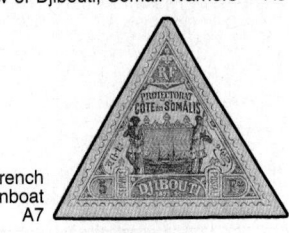

French Gunboat
A7

Crossing Desert (Size: 66mm wide, including simulated perfs.) — A8

Designs: 15c, 25c, 30c, 40c, 50c, 75c, Different views of Djibouti. 1fr, 2fr, Djibouti quay.

Imperf. (Simulated Perforations in Frame Color)

1894-1902   Typo.
Quadrille Lines Printed on Paper

6	A5	1c blk & claret	3.50	2.75
7	A5	2c claret & blk	3.50	3.50
8	A5	4c vio brn & bl	14.00	10.50
9	A5	5c bl grn & red	14.00	7.00
10	A5	5c grn & yel grn ('02)	10.50	7.75
11	A5	10c brown & grn	17.50	10.50
a.		Half used as 5c on cover		200.00
12	A5	15c violet & grn	17.50	10.50
13	A5	25c rose & blue	27.50	10.50
14	A5	30c gray brn & rose	25.00	10.50
a.		Half used as 15c on cover		600.00
15	A5	40c org & bl ('00)	52.50	35.00
a.		Half used as 20c on cover		950.00
16	A5	50c blue & rose	27.50	17.50
a.		Half used as 25c on cover		2,000.
17	A5	75c violet & org	50.00	35.00
18	A5	1fr ol grn & blk	25.00	21.00
19	A5	2fr gray brn & rose	90.00	70.00
a.		Half used as 1fr on cover		2,400.
20	A7	5fr rose & blue	180.00	140.00
21	A8	25fr rose & blue	1,000.	1,050.
22	A8	50fr blue & rose	600.00	675.00
		Nos. 6-20 (15)	558.00	392.00

High values are found with the overprint "S" (Specimen) erased and, usually, a cancellation added.
Values for bisects are for complete covers, newspapers or other printed matter.
For surcharges see Nos. 24-27B.

1899   Black Surcharge

23	A5	40c on 4c vio brn & bl	3,000.	32.50
a.		Double surcharge	5,500.	1,400.
b.		Pair, one without surcharge		4,250.
c.		Inverted surcharge		1,600.
d.		Double surcharge, both inverted		3,000.

Nos. 17-20 Surcharged

1902   Blue Surcharge

24	A5	0.05c on 75c	70.00	42.50
a.		Inverted surcharge	550.00	500.00
b.		Double surcharge	550.00	500.00
c.		Pair, one without surcharge	2,500.	
25	A5	0.10c on 1fr	80.00	62.50
a.		Inverted surcharge	510.00	400.00
b.		Double surcharge	510.00	400.00
26	A5	0.40c on 2fr	550.00	400.00
a.		Double surcharge	2,000.	1,850.

Black Surcharge

27	A7	0.75c on 5fr	525.00	450.00
a.		Inverted surcharge	2,600.	2,100.
b.		Double surcharge	2,600.	2,100.

Obock No. 57 Surcharged in Blue

27B	A7	0.05c on 75c gray lil & org	1,500.	1,050.

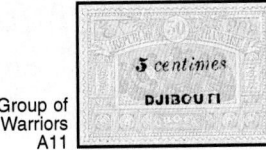

A10

Nos. 15-16 Surcharged in Black

28	A10	5c on 40c	10.50	7.00
a.		Double surcharge	130.00	130.00
29	A10	10c on 50c	27.50	27.50
a.		Inverted surcharge	510.00	500.00
b.		Double surcharge	600.00	

Stamps of Obock Surcharged

Group of Warriors
A11

Black Surcharge

30	A11	5c on 30c bis & yel grn	17.50	10.50
a.		Inverted surcharge	275.00	275.00
b.		Double surcharge	325.00	275.00
c.		Triple surcharge		1,500.

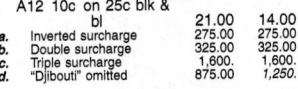

A12

Red Surcharge

31	A12	10c on 25c blk & bl	21.00	14.00
a.		Inverted surcharge	275.00	275.00
b.		Double surcharge	325.00	325.00
c.		Triple surcharge	1,600.	1,600.
d.		"Djibouti" omitted	875.00	1,250.

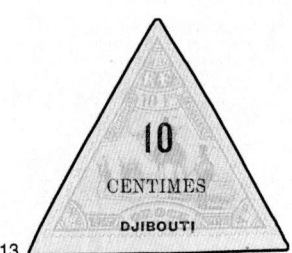

A13

Black Surcharge

32	A13	10c on 10fr org & red vio	40.00	32.50
a.		Double surcharge	250.00	200.00
b.		Double surch., one invtd.	2,200.	2,100.
c.		Triple surcharge	1,500.	1,500.
d.		"Djibouti" omitted	115.00	80.00

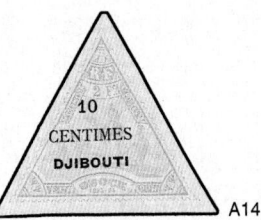

A14

Black Surcharge

33	A14	10c on 2fr dl vio & org	62.50	52.50
a.		Double surcharge	450.00	435.00
b.		Double surcharge, one inverted	2,200.	2,200.
c.		Triple surcharge, one inverted	2,700.	2,700.
d.		"DJIBOUTI" inverted	250.00	225.00
e.		Large "0" in "10"	160.00	125.00

Same Surcharge on Obock No. 53 in Red

33D	A7	10c on 25c blk & bl	32,500.	22,500.

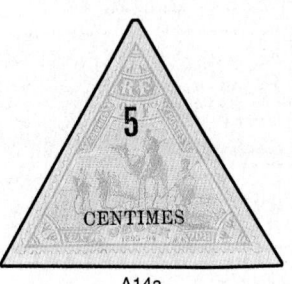

A14a

Black Surcharge on Obock Nos. 63-64

33E	A14a	5c on 25fr brn & bl	62.50	55.00
33F	A14a	10c on 50fr red vio & grn	80.00	60.00
g.		"01" instead of "10"	225.00	210.00
h.		"CENTIMES" inverted	2,750.	2,750.
i.		Double surcharge	2,750.	2,100.
k.		Double surcharge, one inverted	2,750.	2,250.

Tadjoura Mosque
A15

Somalis on Camel
A16

Warriors — A17

1902   Engr.   Perf. 11½

34	A15	1c brn vio & org	1.40	1.10
35	A15	2c yel brn & yel grn	2.10	1.40
36	A15	4c bl & carmine	3.50	2.10
37	A15	5c bl grn & yel grn	3.50	1.75
38	A15	10c car & red org	7.00	4.25
39	A15	15c brn org & bl	7.00	4.25
40	A15	20c vio & green	17.50	7.75
41	A16	25c blue	25.00	12.50
a.		25c indigo & blue ('03)	25.00	15.00
42	A16	30c red & black	12.50	5.00
43	A16	40c orange & blue	17.50	10.00
44	A16	50c grn & red org	45.00	37.50
45	A16	75c orange & vio	10.50	7.00
46	A17	1fr red org & vio	35.00	17.50
47	A17	2fr yel grn & car	42.50	32.50
a.		Without names of designer and engraver at bottom	140.00	140.00
48	A17	5fr orange & blue	35.00	27.50
		Nos. 34-48 (15)	265.00	172.10

1903

49	A15	1c brn vio & blk	1.40	1.10
50	A15	2c yel brn & blk	1.40	1.10
51	A15	4c lake & blk	2.10	2.10
a.		4c red & black	2.75	2.50
52	A15	5c bl grn & blk	4.25	3.50
53	A15	10c carmine & blk	8.50	3.50

54 A15 15c org brn & blk 25.00 10.50
a. 15c brown & black 21.00 10.50
55 A16 20c dl vio & blk 25.00 17.50
56 A16 25c ultra & blk 25.00 14.00
58 A16 40c orange & blk 10.50 10.50
a. 40c bister & black 22.50 22.50
59 A16 50c green & blk 25.00 17.50
60 A16 75c buff & blk 14.00 10.50
a. 75c brown orange & black 77.50 77.50
61 A17 1fr orange & blk 21.00 21.00
62 A17 2fr yel grn & blk 14.00 10.50
a. Without names of designer and engraver at bottom 50.00 50.00
63 A17 5fr red org & blk 25.00 21.00
a. 5fr ocher & black 35.00 32.50
Nos. 49-63 (14) 202.15 144.30

Imperforates, transposed colors and inverted centers exist in the 1902 and 1903 issues. Most of these were issued from Paris and some are said to have been fraudulently printed.

Tadjoura Mosque A18

Somalis on Camel — A19

Warriors — A20

1909 **Typo.** ***Perf. 14x13½***

64 A18 1c maroon & brn 1.10 1.10
65 A18 2c vio & ol gray 1.10 1.10
66 A18 4c ol gray & bl 1.40 1.10
67 A18 5c grn & gray grn 1.75 1.10
68 A18 10c car & ver 4.50 1.75
69 A18 20c blk & red brn 7.00 5.50
70 A19 25c bl & pale bl 5.00 4.00
71 A19 30c brn & scar 7.75 5.50
72 A19 35c vio & grn 10.50 7.00
73 A19 40c rose & vio 10.50 6.25
74 A19 45c brn & bl grn 10.50 6.25
75 A19 50c maroon & brn 10.50 7.00
76 A19 75c scarlet & grn 21.00 14.00
77 A20 1fr vio & brn 27.50 22.50
78 A20 2fr brn & rose 42.50 32.50
79 A20 5fr vio brn & bl grn 70.00 45.00
Nos. 64-79 (16) 232.60 161.65

Drummer A21

Somali Girl A22

Djibouti-Addis Ababa Railroad Bridge — A23

1915-33 ***Perf. 13½x14***

Chalky Paper

80 A21 1c brt vio & red brn .25 .30
81 A21 2c ocher & ind .25 .30
82 A21 4c dk brn & red .30 .30
83 A21 5c yel grn & grn 1.10 1.10
84 A21 5c org & dl red ('22) .70 .70
85 A22 10c car & dk red 2.10 1.10
86 A22 10c ap grn & grn ('22) 1.40 1.40
87 A22 10c ver & grn ('25) .35 .70
88 A22 15c brn vio & car ('18) 1.10 .70
89 A22 20c org & blk brn .35 .35
90 A22 20c dp grn & bl grn ('25) .35 .35
91 A22 20c dk grn & red ('27) .70 .70
92 A22 25c ultra & dl bl 1.10 .85
93 A22 25c blk & bl grn ('22) 1.40 1.40
94 A22 30c blk & bl grn 2.75 2.10
95 A22 30c rose & red brn ('22) 1.40 1.40
96 A22 30c vio & ol grn ('25) .35 .70
97 A22 30c grn & dl grn ('27) .70 .70
98 A22 35c lt grn & dl rose .70 .70
99 A22 40c bl & brn vio 1.10 .70
100 A22 45c red brn & dk bl 1.10 .70
101 A22 50c car rose & blk 10.50 7.00
102 A22 50c ultra & ind ('24) 1.40 1.40
103 A22 50c dk brn & red vio ('25) 1.10 .70
104 A22 60c ol grn & red vio ('25) .70 .70
105 A22 65c car rose & ol grn ('25) .70 .70
106 A22 75c dl vio & choc .70 .70
107 A22 75c ind & ultra ('25) .70 .70
108 A22 75c brt vio & ol brn ('27) 2.10 1.75
109 A22 85c vio brn & bl grn ('25) 1.10 1.10
110 A22 90c brn red & brt red ('30) 7.75 5.50
111 A23 1fr bis brn & red 2.10 1.40
112 A23 1.10fr lt brn & ultra ('28) 4.25 5.50
113 A23 1.25fr dk bl & blk brn ('33) 10.50 8.50
114 A23 1.50fr lt bl & dk bl ('30) 1.40 1.40
115 A23 1.75fr gray grn & lt red ('33) 9.00 5.50
116 A23 2fr bl vio & blk 3.50 2.75
117 A23 3fr red vio ('30) 10.50 8.50
118 A23 5fr rose red & blk 7.00 4.25
Nos. 80-118 (39) 94.55 75.30

No. 99 is on ordinary paper.

For surcharges and overprints see Nos. 119-134, 183-193.

Nos. 83, 92 Surcharged in Green or Blue

1922

119 A21 10c on 5c (G) .70 .70
a. Double surcharge 110.00
120 A22 50c on 25c (Bl) .70 .70

Type of 1915 Surcharged in Various Colors

1922

121 A22 0,01c on 15c vio & rose (Bk) .35 *.45*
122 A22 0,02c on 15c vio & rose (Bl) .35 *.65*
123 A22 0,04c on 15c vio & rose (G) .70 .70
124 A22 0,05c on 15c vio & rose (R) .70 .70
Nos. 121-124 (4) 2.10 2.50

Nos. 88, 99 and Type of 1915 Surcharged

1923-27

125 A22 60c on 75c ol grn & vio .70 .70
126 A22 65c on 15c ('25) 2.75 2.75
127 A22 85c on 40c ('25) 2.10 2.10
128 A22 90c on 75c brn red & red ('27) 5.50 5.50
Nos. 125-128 (4) 11.05 11.05

No. 118 and Type of 1915-17 Surcharged with New Value and Bars in Black or Red

1924-27

129 A23 25c on 5fr 1.40 1.40
130 A23 1.25fr on 1fr dk bl & ultra (R) ('26) 1.40 1.10
131 A23 1.50fr on 1fr lt bl & dk bl ('27) 1.40 1.40
132 A23 3fr on 5fr ver & red vio ('27) 7.00 7.00
133 A23 10fr on 5fr brn red & ol brn ('27) 10.50 10.50
134 A23 20fr on 5fr gray grn & lil rose ('27) 14.00 *17.50*
Nos. 129-134 (6) 35.70 38.90

Common Design Types pictured following the introduction.

Colonial Exposition Issue

Common Design Types

Engr., Name of Country Typo. in Black

1931 ***Perf. 12½***

135 CD70 40c deep green 5.50 5.50
136 CD71 50c violet 5.50 5.50
137 CD72 90c red orange 5.50 5.50
138 CD73 1.50fr dull blue 5.50 5.50
Nos. 135-138 (4) 22.00 22.00

Paris International Exposition Issue

Common Design Types

1937 **Engr.** ***Perf. 13***

139 CD74 20c deep violet 1.90 1.90
140 CD75 30c dark green 1.90 1.90
141 CD76 40c car rose 1.90 1.90
142 CD77 50c dk brn & bl 1.90 1.90
143 CD78 90c red 1.90 1.90
144 CD79 1.50fr ultra 2.10 2.10
Nos. 139-144 (6) 11.60 11.60

Colonial Arts Exhibition Issue

Souvenir Sheet

Common Design Type

1937 ***Imperf.***

145 CD75 3fr dull violet 14.00 *21.00*

Mosque of Djibouti — A24

Somali Warriors — A25

Governor Léonce Lagarde — A26

View of Djibouti — A27

1938-40 ***Perf. 12x12½, 12½***

146 A24 2c dull red vio .25 .25
147 A24 3c slate grn ('40) .25 .25
148 A24 4c dull red brn .25 .25
149 A24 5c carmine .25 .25
150 A24 10c blue gray .25 .25
151 A24 15c slate black .35 .30
152 A24 20c dark orange .35 .30
153 A25 25c dark brown .70 .70
154 A25 30c dark blue .35 .35
155 A25 35c olive grn 1.10 .70
156 A24 40c org brn ('40) .35 .35
157 A24 45c dull grn ('40) .35 .35
158 A25 50c red .70 .70
159 A25 55c dull red vio 1.10 .70
160 A25 60c black ('40) .70 .70
161 A25 65c orange brown 1.10 1.10
162 A25 70c lt violet ('40) 1.40 1.40
163 A26 80c gray blk 2.75 2.10
164 A25 90c rose vio ('39) 1.40 1.40
165 A26 1fr carmine 3.50 2.10
166 A26 1fr black ('40) .55 .55
167 A26 1.25fr magenta ('39) 1.10 1.10
168 A26 1.40fr pck bl ('40) 1.10 1.10
169 A26 1.50fr dull green 1.10 1.10
170 A26 1.60fr brn car ('40) 1.10 1.10
171 A26 1.75fr ultra 1.40 1.10
172 A26 2fr dk orange 1.10 1.10
173 A26 2.25fr ultra ('39) 1.75 1.75
174 A26 2.50fr org brn ('40) 1.75 1.75
175 A26 3fr dull violet 1.10 1.10
176 A27 5fr brn & pale cl 2.10 2.10
177 A27 10fr ind & pale bl 2.50 2.75
178 A27 20fr car lake & gray 2.50 2.75
Nos. 146-178 (33) 36.60 33.85

For types A24-A26 without "RF," see Nos. 237A-237C.

For overprints and surcharge see Nos. 194-223.

New York World's Fair Issue

Common Design Type

1939 **Engr.** ***Perf. 12½x12***

179 CD82 1.25fr car lake .70 1.40
180 CD82 2.25fr ultra .70 1.40

Mosque of Djibouti and Marshal Pétain — A28

1941, Nov. 10 **Engr.** ***Perf. 12x12½***

181 A28 1fr yellow brown .35
182 A28 2.50fr blue .35
Set, never hinged 1.40

Nos. 181-182 were issued by the Vichy government in France, but were not placed on sale in Somali Coast.

For surcharges, see Nos. B11-B12.

Nos. 80-82, 84, 88, 91, 97, 103, 105, 114-115 Overprinted in Black or Red

Perf. 13½x14, 14x13½

1943 **Unwmk.**

183 A21 1c brt vio & red brn 3.50 3.50
184 A21 2c ocher & ind 3.50 3.50
185 A21 4c dk brn & red 30.00 30.00
186 A21 5c yel grn & grn 3.50 3.50
187 A22 15c brn vio & car 10.50 10.50
188 A22 20c 3.50 3.50
189 A22 30c 3.50 3.50
190 A22 50c 3.50 3.50
191 A22 65c car rose & ol grn 3.50 3.50
192 A23 1.50fr lt bl & dk bl (R) 3.50 3.50
193 A23 1.75fr gray grn & lt red 14.00 14.00
Nos. 183-193 (11) 82.50 82.50
Set, never hinged 130.00

Stamps of 1938-40 Overprinted in Black or Red

On A24

On A25

On A26

On A27

1943 ***Perf. 12x12½, 12½***

194	A24	2c	dl red vio	5.50	5.50
195	A24	3c	sl grn (R)	5.50	5.50
196	A24	4c	dl red brn	5.50	5.50
197	A24	5c	carmine	5.50	5.50
198	A24	10c	bl gray (R)	1.40	1.40
199	A24	15c	sl blk (R)	5.50	5.50
200	A24	20c	dk org	5.50	5.50
201	A25	25c	dk brn (R)	5.50	5.50
202	A25	30c	dk bl (R)	1.20	1.20
203	A25	35c	olive (R)	5.50	5.50
204	A24	40c	brn org	1.20	1.20
205	A24	45c	dl grn	5.50	5.50
206	A25	55c	dl red vio (R)	5.50	5.50
207	A25	60c	blk (R)	1.40	1.40
208	A25	70c	lt vio (R)	1.20	1.20
a.			Inverted overprint	275.00	275.00
b.			Double overprint	325.00	325.00
209	A26	80c	gray blk (R)	2.10	2.10
210	A25	90c	rose vio (R)	1.20	1.20
211	A26	1.25fr	magenta	3.50	3.50
212	A26	1.40fr	pck bl (R)	2.10	2.10
213	A26	1.50fr	dl grn	3.50	3.50
214	A26	1.60fr	brn car	3.50	3.50
215	A26	1.75fr	ultra (R)	12.00	12.00
216	A26	2fr	dk org	1.60	1.60
217	A26	2.25fr	ultra (R)	3.50	3.50
218	A26	2.50fr	chestnut	2.10	2.10
219	A26	3fr	dl vio (R)	3.50	3.50
220	A27	5fr	brn & pale cl	17.50	17.50
221	A27	10fr	ind & pale bl	180.00	180.00
222	A27	20fr	car lake & gray	17.50	17.50

The space between overprint on Nos. 206 and 208 measures 10½mm.

No. 161 Surcharged in Black

223	A25	50c on 65c	org brn	1.60	1.60
			Nos. 194-223 (30)	316.60	316.60
			Set, never hinged	450.00	

Catalogue values for unused stamps in this section, from this point to the end of the section, are for Never Hinged items.

Locomotive and Palms — A29

1943 **Unwmk.** **Photo.** ***Perf. 14½x14***

224	A29	5c	royal blue	.70	.35
225	A29	10c	pink	.70	.35
226	A29	25c	emerald	.70	.70
227	A29	30c	gray blk	.70	.70
228	A29	40c	violet	.70	.70
229	A29	80c	red brn	.70	.70
230	A29	1fr	aqua	.70	.70
231	A29	1.50fr	scarlet	.70	.70
232	A29	2fr	brown	.70	.70
233	A29	2.50fr	ultra	1.40	1.10
234	A29	4fr	brt org	1.40	1.10
235	A29	5fr	dp rose lil	1.40	1.10
236	A29	10fr	lt ultra	2.10	1.75
237	A29	20fr	green	2.10	1.60
			Nos. 224-237 (14)	14.70	12.25

For surcharges see Nos. 240-247.

Types of 1938-40 Without "RF"

1944, Apr. 3 **Engr.** ***Perf. 12½***

237A	A24	40c	org brn	1.10
237B	A25	50c	red	1.40
237C	A26	1.50fr	dull green	2.10
			Nos. 237A-237C (3)	4.60

Nos. 237A-237C were issued by the Vichy government in France, but were not placed on sale in Somali Coast.

Eboue Issue
Common Design Type

1945 **Engr.** ***Perf. 13***

238	CD91	2fr	black	.70	.70
239	CD91	25fr	Prus grn	1.75	1.40

Nos. 238 and 239 exist imperforate.

Nos. 224, 226 and 233 Surcharged in Carmine or Black

1945 ***Perf. 14½x14***

240	A29	50c on 5c	(C)	.70	.70
a.			Inverted surcharge	310.00	
b.			Double surcharge	240.00	
241	A29	60c on 5c	(C)	.70	.70
a.			Inverted surcharge	225.00	
b.			Double surcharge	190.00	
242	A29	70c on 5c	(C)	.70	.70
a.			Inverted surcharge	225.00	
b.			Double surcharge, one inverted	325.00	
243	A29	1.20fr on 5c	(C)	.70	.70
a.			Double surcharge, one inverted	325.00	
244	A29	2.40fr on 25c		1.10	1.40
a.			Inverted surcharge	240.00	
b.			Double surcharge	225.00	
c.			Bars doubly surcharged	125.00	
245	A29	3fr on 25c		1.10	1.40
a.			Inverted surcharge	310.00	
b.			Double surcharge, one inverted	375.00	
246	A29	4.50fr on 25c		1.40	1.40
a.			Inverted surcharge	225.00	
247	A29	15fr on 2.50fr	(C)	2.10	2.10
a.			Surcharge bars omitted	180.00	
b.			Value doubly surcharged	240.00	
			Nos. 240-247 (8)	8.50	9.10

Danakil Tent — A30

Khor-Angar Outpost A31

Obock-Tadjouran Road — A32

Somali Woman A33

Somali Village A34

Djibouti Mosque A35

1947 **Unwmk.** **Photo.** ***Perf. 13***

248	A30	10c	vio bl & org	.35	.25
249	A30	30c	ol brn & org	.35	.25
250	A30	40c	dp plum & org	.35	.25
251	A31	50c	bl grn & org	.70	.30
252	A31	60c	choc & dp yel	.70	.30
253	A31	80c	vio bl & org	.70	.30
254	A32	1fr	bl & choc	.70	.30
255	A32	1.20fr	bl grn & ol grn	1.10	.80
256	A32	1.50fr	org & vio bl	.70	.30
257	A33	2fr	red lil & bl gray	.70	.55
258	A33	3fr	dp bl & brn org	1.40	.85
259	A33	3.60fr	car rose & cop red	2.10	1.75
260	A33	4fr	choc & bl gray	1.75	1.10
261	A34	5fr	org & choc	1.10	.70
262	A34	6fr	gray bl & int bl	1.75	.85
263	A34	10fr	gray bl & red lil	1.75	.90
264	A35	15fr	choc, gray bl & pink	2.10	1.10
265	A35	20fr	dk bl, gray bl & org	2.75	1.40
266	A35	25fr	vio brn, lil rose & gray bl	7.00	3.50
			Nos. 248-266 (19)	28.05	15.75

Military Medal Issue
Common Design Type

1952 **Engraved and Typographed**

267	CD101	15fr	blk, grn, yel & dk pur	9.00	8.00

Imperforates
Most stamps of Somali Coast from 1956 onward exist imperforate in issued and trial colors, and also in small presentation sheets in issued colors.

FIDES Issue
Common Design Type and

Lighthouse, Ras-Bir — A36

15fr, Loading ship and map, Djibouti.

1956 **Unwmk.** **Engr.** ***Perf. 13***

268	CD103	15fr	purple	2.10	1.40
269	A36	40fr	dp ultra & gray	3.25	1.75

Flower Issue
Common Design Type

Design: 10fr, Haemanthus, horiz.

1958 **Photo.** ***Perf. 12½x12***

270	CD104	10fr	grn, red & yel	4.25	1.40

Wart Hog — A37

40c, Cheetah. 50c, Gerenuk, vert.

1958 **Engr.** ***Perf. 13***

271	A37	30c	red brn & sepia	.70	.35
272	A37	40c	brn & olive	.70	.35
273	A37	50c	brn, grn & gray	1.10	.70
			Nos. 271-273,C21 (4)	12.50	6.40

Human Rights Issue
Common Design Type

1958, Dec. 10 **Unwmk.**

274	CD105	20fr	brt pur & dk bl	3.50	2.10

Universal Declaration of Human Rights, 10th anniv.

Parrotfish A38

Designs: Various Tropical Fish.

1959 **Engr.** ***Perf. 13***

275	A38	1fr	brt bl, brn & red org	.85	.55
276	A38	2fr	blk, lt bl, yel & grn	.85	.55
277	A38	3fr	vio & blk brn	.85	.55
278	A38	4fr	brt grnsh bl, org & lt brn	1.10	.70
279	A38	5fr	brt grnsh bl & blk	1.75	.90
280	A38	20fr	brt bl, dl red brn & rose	3.25	2.00
281	A38	25fr	red, grn & ultra	5.00	2.50
282	A38	60fr	bl & dk grn	11.00	5.00
			Nos. 275-282 (8)	24.65	12.75

No. 276 is vertical.

Flamingo — A39

Birds: 15fr, Bee-eater, horiz. 30fr, Sacred ibis, horiz. 75fr, Pink-backed pelican.

1960 **Unwmk.** ***Perf. 13***

283	A39	10fr	bluish grn, bis & cl	2.75	1.40
284	A39	15fr	rose lil, grn & yel	3.50	1.40
285	A39	30fr	bl, blk, org & brn	7.75	4.25
286	A39	75fr	grn, sl grn & yel	12.00	7.00
			Nos. 283-286 (4)	26.00	14.05

Dragon Tree — A40

Klipspringer — A41

Designs: 4fr, Cony. 6fr, Large flatfish. 25fr, Fennecs. 40fr, Griffon vulture.

1962, Mar. 24 **Engr.** ***Perf. 13***

287	A40	2fr	grn, yel, org & brn	2.10	1.40
288	A40	4fr	ocher & choc	2.10	1.40
289	A40	6fr	brn, mar, grn & yel	4.25	2.75
290	A40	25fr	red brn, ocher & grn	8.50	5.00
291	A40	40fr	dk bl, brn & gray	11.00	7.00
292	A41	50fr	bis, bl & lil	11.00	8.50
			Nos. 287-292 (6)	38.95	26.05

Meleagrina
Margaritifera
A42

Sea Shells: 10fr, Tridacna squamosa, horiz.
25fr, Strombus tricornis, horiz. 30fr, Trochus
dentatus.

Shells in Natural Colors

1962, Nov. 24		Photo.	
293	A42 8fr red & blk	1.75	.90
294	A42 10fr car rose & blk	1.75	1.10
295	A42 25fr dp bl & brn	3.75	1.60
296	A42 30fr rose lil & brn	3.75	2.00
	Nos. 293-296 (4)	11.00	5.60

See Nos. C28-C29.

Red Cross Centenary Issue
Common Design Type

1963, Sept. 2	Engr.	Perf. 13	
297	CD113 50fr org brn, gray & car	6.25	6.25

Astraea
Coral — A43

Design: 6fr, Organ-pipe coral.

1963, Nov. 30	Photo.	Perf. 13x13½	
298	A43 5fr multi	2.10	1.40
299	A43 6fr multi	2.10	1.40

See Nos. C26-C27, C30.

Human Rights Issue
Common Design Type

1963, Dec. 20	Engr.	Perf. 13	
300	CD117 70fr dk brn & ultra	8.50	8.50

Philatec Issue
Common Design Type

1964, Apr. 7	Unwmk.	Perf. 13	
301	CD118 80fr dp lil rose, grn & brn	7.75	7.75

Houri
(Somali
Sailboats)
A44

Design: 25fr, Sambouk (Somali sailboats).

1964, June 9		Engr.	
302	A44 15fr multi	1.75	1.10
303	A44 25fr multi	2.50	1.50

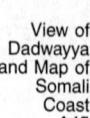 

View of
Dadwayya
and Map of
Somali
Coast
A45

Design: 20fr, View of Tadjourah and map of
Somali Coast.

1965, Oct. 20	Engr.	Perf. 13	
304	A45 6fr ultra, sl grn & red brn	1.00	.70
305	A45 20fr ultra, org brn & brt grn	1.00	1.00

Senna — A46

1966	Engr.	Perf. 13	
306	A46 5fr shown	1.40	1.00
307	A46 8fr Poinciana	1.40	1.00
308	A46 25fr Aloe	1.75	1.75
	Nos. 306-308,C41 (4)	9.55	7.00

Desert
Monitor
A47

1967, May 8	Engr.	Perf. 13	
309	A47 20fr red brn, ocher & sepia	7.00	4.25

Stamps of Somali Coast were replaced in
1967 by those of the French Territory of the
Afars and Issas.

SEMI-POSTAL STAMPS

Somali Girl — SP1

1915	Unwmk.	Perf. 13½x14	
Chalky Paper			
B1	SP1 10c + 5c car & dk red	9.00	8.50

Curie Issue
Common Design Type

1938	Engr.	Perf. 13	
B2	CD80 1.75fr + 50c brt ultra	7.75	7.75

French Revolution Issue
Common Design Type
**Photo., Name and Value Typo. in
Black**

1939			
B3	CD83 45c + 25c green	9.00	9.00
B4	CD83 70c + 30c brown	9.00	9.00
B5	CD83 90c + 35c red org	9.00	9.00
B6	CD83 1.25fr + 1fr rose pink	9.00	9.00
B7	CD83 2.25fr + 2fr blue	9.00	9.00
	Nos. B3-B7 (5)	45.00	45.00

Common Design Type and

Somali
Guard
SP2

Local Police — SP3

1941	Photo.	Perf. 13½	
B8	SP2 1fr + 1fr red		1.40
B9	CD86 1.50fr + 3fr maroon		1.40
B10	SP3 2.50fr + 1fr blue		1.40
	Nos. B8-B10 (3)		4.20
	Set, never hinged		5.25

Nos. B8-B10 were issued by the Vichy government in France, but were not placed on
sale in Somali Coast.

Nos. 181-182
Surcharged in Black
or Red

1944	Engr.	Perf. 12x12½	
B11	50c + 1.50fr on 2.50fr dp bl (R)		.35
B12	+ 2.50fr on 1fr yel brn		.35
	Set, never hinged		1.40

Colonial Development Fund.
Nos. B11-B12 were issued by the Vichy
government in France, but were not placed on
sale in Somali Coast.

> **Catalogue values for unused
> stamps in this section, from this
> point to the end of the section, are
> for Never Hinged items.**

Red Cross Issue
Common Design Type
Inscribed "Djibouti"

1944		Perf. 14½x14	
B13	CD90 5fr + 20fr emerald	1.75	2.00

The surtax was for the French Red Cross
and national relief.

Tropical Medicine Issue
Common Design Type

1950	Engr.	Perf. 13	
B14	CD100 10fr + 2fr red brn & red	7.75	6.25

The surtax was for charitable work.

Anti-Malaria Issue
Common Design Type

1962, Apr. 7	Unwmk.	Perf. 13	
B15	CD108 25fr + 5fr aqua	7.00	7.00

Infant, Sun,
Chest and
Skulls
SP4

1965, Dec. 10	Engr.	Perf. 13	
B16	SP4 25fr + 5fr ocher, sl & brt grn	2.75	2.50

Campaign against tuberculosis.

AIR POST STAMPS

> **Catalogue values for unused
> stamps in this section are for
> Never Hinged items.**

Inscribed "Djibouti"
Common Design Type

1941	Unwmk. Photo.	Perf. 14½x14	
C1	CD87 1fr dk orange	.70	.70
C2	CD87 1.50fr brt red	.70	.70
C3	CD87 5fr brown red	1.40	1.00
C4	CD87 10fr black	1.40	1.00
C5	CD87 25fr ultra	2.75	2.10
C6	CD87 50fr dark green	2.75	2.10
C7	CD87 100fr plum	4.25	3.50
	Nos. C1-C7 (7)	13.95	11.10

Obock & Djibouti — AP1

1943, June 21	Engr.	Perf. 13	
C7A	AP1 1.50fr red brown		1.00
C7B	AP1 4fr ultramarine		1.00

50th Ann. of transfer of capital from Obock
to Djibouti.
Nos. C7A-C7B were issued by the Vichy
government in France, but were not placed on
sale in Somali Coast.

Victory Issue
Common Design Type

1946		Perf. 12½	
C8	CD92 8fr deep blue	1.75	1.40

Chad to Rhine Issue
Common Design Types

1946			
C9	CD93 5fr gray black	2.40	1.60
C10	CD94 10fr dp orange	2.40	1.60
C11	CD95 15fr violet brn	2.40	1.60
C12	CD96 20fr brt violet	2.40	1.60
C13	CD97 25fr blue green	4.25	3.00
C14	CD98 50fr lt ultra	4.25	3.25
	Nos. C9-C14 (6)	18.10	12.65

Somali Gazing
Skyward —
AP1a

Frontier Post, Loyada — AP2

Governor's Mansion, Djibouti — AP3

Perf. 12½x13, 13x12½			
1947	Photo.	Unwmk.	
C15	AP1a 50fr gray bl & choc	6.25	1.40
C16	AP2 100fr multicolored	7.75	2.75
C17	AP3 200fr multicolored	10.50	4.25
	Nos. C15-C17 (3)	24.50	8.40

UPU Issue
Common Design Type

1949	Engr.	Perf. 13	
C18	CD99 30fr bl, dp bl, brn red & grn	14.00	10.50

Liberation Issue
Common Design Type

1954, June 6			
C19	CD102 15fr indigo & pur	10.50	8.50

Somali Woman and Map of Djibouti — AP4

1956, Feb. 20   Unwmk.
C20 AP4 500fr dk vio & rose
vio   60.00 50.00

Mountain Reedbucks — AP5

1958, July 7   Perf. 13
C21 AP5 100fr ultra, lt grn & dk
red brn   10.00 5.00

Albert Bernard, Flag and Troops — AP6

1960, Jan. 18
C22 AP6 55fr ultra, sepia & car   2.75 1.75
25th death anniv. of Administrator Albert Bernard at Moraito.

Great Bustard — AP7

1960, Oct. 24   Unwmk.   Perf. 13
C23 AP7 200fr brn, org & slate   22.50 15.00

Salt Dealers' Caravan at Assal Lake — AP8

1962, Jan. 6   Engr.   Perf. 13
C24 AP8 500fr dk bl, red brn,
pink & blk   25.00 15.00

Obock — AP9

1962, Mar. 11   Unwmk.   Perf. 13
C25 AP9 100fr blue & org brn   5.00 3.50
Centenary of the founding of Obock.

Rostellaria Magna — AP10

40fr, Millepore coral. 55fr, Brain coral. 100fr, Lambis bryonia (seashell). 200fr, Branch coral.

1962-63   Photo.   Perf. 13½x12½
C26 AP10 40fr multi ('63)   3.50 1.40
C27 AP10 55fr multi ('63)   5.00 3.50
C28 AP10 60fr multi   6.25 2.75
C29 AP10 100fr multi   10.00 5.00
C30 AP10 200fr multi ('63)   12.00 7.00
Nos. C26-C30 (5)   36.75 19.65

Telstar Issue
Common Design Type
1963, Feb. 9   Engr.   Perf. 13
C31 CD111 20fr dp claret & dk
grn   1.00 1.00

Zaroug (Somali Sailboats) — AP11

Designs: 50fr, Sambouk (boat) building. 300fr, Žeima sailboat.

1964-65   Engr.   Perf. 13
C32 AP11 50fr blue, ocher &
choc   4.25 2.10
C33 AP11 85fr dk Prus grn,
dk brn &
mag   5.50 2.75
C34 AP11 300fr ultra, lt brn &
bl grn ('65)   15.00 7.75
Nos. C32-C34 (3)   24.75 12.60

Discus Thrower — AP12

1964, Oct. 10   Engr.
C35 AP12 90fr rose lil, red brn
& blk   10.00 7.75
18th Olympic Games, Tokyo, Oct. 10-25.

ITU Issue
Common Design Type
1965, May 17
C36 CD120 95fr lil rose, brt bl
& lt brn   15.00 9.00

Camels in Ghoubet Kharab and Map of Somali Coast — AP13

1965   Engr.   Perf. 13
C37 AP13 45fr Abbe Lake   3.25 1.75
C38 AP13 65fr shown   4.00 1.75
Issue dates: 45fr, Oct. 20; 65fr, July 16.

French Satellite A-1 Issue
Common Design Type
Designs: 25fr, Diamant rocket and launching installations. 30fr, A-1 satellite.

1966, Jan. 28   Engr.   Perf. 13
C39 CD121 25fr redsh brn, ol brn
& dl red   3.25 3.25
C40 CD121 30fr ol brn, dl red &
redsh brn   3.25 3.25
a. Strip of 2, #C39-C40 + label 7.00 7.00
Each sheet contains 16 triptychs (2x8).

Stapelia — AP14

1966   Engr.   Perf. 13
C41 AP14 55fr sl grn, dl mag &
emer   5.00 3.25

Feather Starfish and Coral — AP15

Fish: 25fr, Regal angelfish. 40fr, Pomacanthops filamentosus. 50fr, Amphiprion ephippium. 70fr, Squirrelfish. 80fr, Surgeonfish. 100fr, Pterois lunulatus.

1966   Photo.   Perf. 13
C42 AP15 8fr multicolored   3.50 3.50
C43 AP15 25fr multicolored   5.50 5.50
C44 AP15 40fr multicolored   8.50 8.50
C45 AP15 50fr multicolored   9.00 9.00
C46 AP15 70fr multicolored   14.00 14.00
C47 AP15 80fr multicolored   15.00 15.00
C48 AP15 100fr multicolored   21.00 21.00
Nos. C42-C48 (7)   76.50 76.50

French Satellite D-1 Issue
Common Design Type
1966, June 10   Engr.   Perf. 13
C49 CD122 48fr dk brn, brt bl &
grn   4.25 2.75
Nos. C49 (1)   4.25 2.75

────────────

AIR POST SEMI-POSTAL STAMPS

| **Catalogue values for unused stamps in this section are for Never Hinged items.** |

SPAP1

Unwmk.
1942, June 22   Engr.   Perf. 13
CB1 SPAP1 1.50fr + 3.50fr grn   .70 6.25
CB2 SPAP1 2fr + 6fr brown   .70 6.25
Native children's welfare fund.
Nos. CB1-CB2 were issued by the Vichy government in France, but were not placed on sale in Somali Coast

Colonial Education Fund
Common Design Type
1942, June 22
CB3 CD86a 1.20fr + 1.80fr blue
& red   .70 6.25
Nos. CB3 (1)   .70
No. CB3 was issued by the Vichy government in France, but was not placed on sale in Somali Coast.

Pharaoh Sacrificing before Horus and Hathor — SPAP2

Unwmk.
1964, Aug. 28   Engr.   Perf. 13
CB4 SPAP2 25fr + 5fr multi   9.00 7.75
UNESCO world campaign to save historic monuments in Nubia.

────────────

POSTAGE DUE STAMPS

D1

1915   Unwmk.   Typo.   Perf. 14x13½
Chalky Paper
J1 D1 5c deep ultra   .35 .55
J2 D1 10c brown red   .55 .70
J3 D1 15c black   .85 1.20
J4 D1 20c purple   1.75 2.10
J5 D1 30c orange   1.75 2.10
J6 D1 50c maroon   2.75 3.25
J7 D1 60c green   4.25 5.00
J8 D1 1fr dark blue   5.25 6.25
Nos. J1-J8 (8)   17.50 21.15
See Nos. J11-J20.

Type of 1915 Issue
Surcharged

1927
J9 D1 2fr on 1fr light red   10.50 10.50
J10 D1 3fr on 1fr lilac rose   10.50 10.50

Type of 1915
1938   Engr.   Perf. 12½x13
J11 D1 5c light ultra   .25 .30
J12 D1 10c dark carmine   .25 .30
J13 D1 15c brown black   .30 .35
J14 D1 20c violet   .30 .35
J15 D1 30c orange yellow   1.10 1.20
J16 D1 50c brown   .65 .70
J17 D1 60c emerald   1.00 1.10
J18 D1 1fr indigo   2.00 2.00
J19 D1 2fr red   .90 1.00
J20 D1 3fr dark brown   1.25 1.40
Nos. J11-J20 (10)   8.00 8.70
Set, never hinged   11.50
Inscribed "Inst de Grav" below design.

Postage Due Stamps of 1915 Overprinted in Red or Black

1943   Unwmk.   Perf. 14x13½
J21 D1 5c ultra (R)   2.75 2.75
J22 D1 10c brown red   2.75 2.75
J23 D1 15c black (R)   2.75 2.75
J24 D1 20c purple   2.75 2.75
J25 D1 30c orange   2.75 2.75
J26 D1 50c maroon   2.75 2.75

J27 D1 60c green 2.75 2.75
J28 D1 1fr dark blue (R) 2.75 2.75
Nos. J21-J28 (8) 22.00 22.00
Set, never hinged 35.00

Postage Due Stamps of 1938 Overprinted in Red or Black

1943 ***Perf. 12 ½x13***
J29 d1 5c lt ultra (R) 2.10 2.10
J30 D1 10c dark car 2.10 2.10
J31 D1 15c brn blk (R) 2.10 2.10
J32 D1 20c violet 2.10 2.10
J33 d1 30c org yel 2.10 2.10
J34 D1 50c brown 2.10 2.10
J35 D1 60c emerald 2.10 2.10
J36 D1 1fr indigo (R) 2.10 2.10
J37 D1 2fr red 8.50 8.50
J38 D1 3fr dk brn (R) 10.00 10.00
Nos. J29-J38 (10) 35.30 35.30
Set, never hinged 55.00

For type D1 without "RF," see Nos. J38A-J38E.

Type D1 Without "RF"
Engraved, Values Typo

1944, Apr. 3
J38A D1 30c org yel .30
J38B D1 50c yel brn .30
J38C D1 60c grn .55
J38D D1 2fr red .65
J38E D1 3fr sepia 1.00
Nos. J38A-J38E (5) 2.80
Set, never hinged 4.25

Nos. J38A-J38E were issued by the Vichy government in France, but were not placed on sale in Somali Coast.

Catalogue values for unused stamps in this section, from this point to the end of the section, are for Never Hinged items.

D2

1947 **Photo.** ***Perf. 13½x13***
J39 D2 10c purple .35 .25
J40 D2 30c brown .35 .25
J41 D2 50c green .65 .50
J42 D2 1fr deep orange .65 .50
J43 D2 2fr lilac rose .90 .80
J44 D2 3fr dk org brn .90 .80
J45 D2 4fr blue 1.10 .90
J46 D2 5fr orange red 1.10 .90
J47 D2 10fr olive green 1.10 .90
J48 D2 20fr blue violet 2.75 2.00
Nos. J39-J48 (10) 9.85 7.80

SOMALILAND PROTECTORATE

sō-ˈmä-lē-ˌland

prə-ˈtek-t(ə-)rət

LOCATION — Eastern Africa, bordering on the Gulf of Aden
GOVT. — British Protectorate
AREA — 68,000 sq. mi.
POP. — 640,000 (estimated)
CAPITAL — Hargeisa

Formerly administered by the Indian Government, the territory was taken over by the British Foreign Office in 1898 and transferred to the Colonial Office in 1905.

Somaliland Protectorate became part of independent Somalia in 1960.

16 Annas = 1 Rupee
100 Cents = 1 Shilling (1951)

Catalogue values for unused stamps in this country are for Never Hinged items, beginning with Scott 108.

Stamps of India, 1882-1900, Overprinted at Top of Stamp

1903 **Wmk. 39** ***Perf. 14***
1 A17 ½a light green 3.00 5.00
2 A19 1a carmine rose 3.00 4.50
3 A21 2a violet 2.50 1.75
a. Double overprint 800.00
4 A28 2½a ultra 2.25 2.10
5 A22 3a brn org 3.50 4.00
6 A23 4a olive green 4.00 3.50
7 A25 8a red violet 4.25 6.00
8 A26 12a brown, *red* 4.50 9.00
a. Inverted overprint 1,200.
9 A29 1r car rose & grn 7.50 12.50
10 A30 2r yel brn & car rose 38.00 55.00
11 A30 3r grn & brn 36.00 67.50
12 A30 5r violet & blue 59.00 77.50

Wmk. Elephant's Head (38)
13 A14 6a bister 6.50 5.25
Nos. 1-13 (13) 174.00 253.60

Nos. 1-5 exist without the 2nd "I" of "BRITISH."

Same, but Overprinted at Bottom of Stamp

1903 **Wmk. 39**
14 A28 2½a ultra 6.50 8.50
15 A26 12a violet, *red* 13.00 14.00
16 A29 1r car rose & grn 9.00 17.50
17 A30 2r yel brn & car rose 130.00 200.00
18 A30 3r green & brn 140.00 200.00
a. Double overprint, both inverted, one albino 1,000.
19 A30 5r violet & blue 130.00 180.00

Wmk. 38
20 A14 6a bister 8.50 8.00
Nos. 14-20 (7) 437.00 628.00

Stamps of India, 1902-03, Ovptd.

1903 **Wmk. 39**
21 A33 ½a light green 3.25 .60
22 A34 1a car rose 1.40 .35
23 A35 2a violet 2.00 2.75
24 A37 3a brown orange 2.75 2.75
25 A38 4a olive green 1.60 4.50
26 A40 8a red violet 1.90 2.50
Nos. 21-26 (6) 12.90 13.45

The above overprints vary in length, also in the relative positions of the letters. Nos. 21-23 exist without the second "I" of "British."

A1

King Edward VII — A2

1904 **Wmk. 2** **Typo.**
27 A1 ½a dl grn & grn 2.25 4.50
28 A1 1a carmine & blk 19.00 3.50
29 A1 2a red vio & dull vio 2.25 2.40
30 A1 2½a ultramarine 9.50 4.00
31 A1 3a gray grn & vio brn 2.50 4.00
32 A1 4a black & gray grn 4.00 7.50
33 A1 6a vio & gray grn 9.50 18.00
34 A1 8a pale blue & blk 8.50 8.00
35 A1 12a ocher & blk 14.00 11.50

Wmk. Crown and C C (1)
36 A2 1r gray grn 18.00 47.50
37 A2 2r red vio & dull vio 60.00 90.00
38 A2 3r blk & gray grn 70.00 130.00
39 A2 5r carmine & blk 70.00 140.00
Nos. 27-39 (13) 289.50 470.90

1905 **Wmk. 3**
40 A1 ½a dl grn & grn 2.00 8.00
41 A1 1a carmine & blk 21.00 1.75
42 A1 2a red vio & dull vio 9.00 19.00
43 A1 2½a ultramarine 4.50 11.00
44 A1 3a gray grn & vio brn 2.50 16.00
45 A1 4a black & gray grn 5.00 20.00
46 A1 6a violet & gray grn 3.00 27.50
47 A1 8a pale blue & blk 8.00 11.00
48 A1 12a ocher & black 7.25 11.00
Nos. 40-48 (9) 62.25 125.25

Nos. 41, 42, 44-48 are on both ordinary and chalky paper.

1909
49 A1 ½a bluish green 45.00 40.00
50 A1 1a carmine 3.00 2.25

For overprints see Nos. O11-O16.

A3

King George V — A4

The ½, 1 and 2½a of type A3 are on ordinary paper, the other values of types A3 and A4 are on chalky paper.

1912-19
51 A3 ½a green .90 12.00
52 A3 1a carmine 3.00 .60
53 A3 2a red vio & dull vio 4.25 16.00
54 A3 2½a ultramarine 1.25 9.75
55 A3 3a gray grn & vio brn 2.75 10.00
56 A3 4a blk & grn ('13) 3.00 11.50
57 A3 6a violet & green 3.00 10.00
58 A3 8a lt blue & blk 4.25 17.50
59 A3 12a ocher & blk 4.00 24.00
60 A4 1r dull grn & grn 19.00 22.00
61 A4 2r red vio & dull vio ('19) 28.00 80.00
62 A4 3r blk & gray grn ('19) 85.00 175.00
63 A4 5r car & blk ('19) 90.00 250.00
Nos. 51-63 (13) 248.40 638.35

1921 **Wmk. 4**
64 A3 ½a blue green 3.75 16.00
65 A3 1a scarlet 4.25 .80
66 A3 2a vio & dull vio 5.00 1.10
67 A3 2½a ultramarine 1.25 9.50
68 A3 3a gray grn & vio brown 3.00 8.50
69 A3 4a black & grn 3.00 13.00
70 A3 6a violet & grn 2.00 15.00
71 A3 8a lt blue & blk 2.50 8.00
72 A3 12a ocher & blk 11.00 17.50
73 A4 1r dull grn & grn 10.00 55.00
74 A4 2r vio & dull vio 30.00 62.50
75 A4 3r blk & gray grn 42.50 125.00
76 A4 5r scarlet & blk 95.00 200.00
Nos. 64-76 (13) 213.25 531.90

Common Design Types
pictured following the introduction.

Silver Jubilee Issue
Common Design Type

1935, May 6 **Engr.** ***Perf. 11x12***
77 CD301 1a car & dk blue 2.75 4.00
78 CD301 2a black & ultra 3.25 4.25
79 CD301 3a ultra & brown 2.75 20.00
80 CD301 1r brown vio & ind 10.00 22.50
Nos. 77-80 (4) 18.75 50.75
Set, never hinged 34.00

Coronation Issue
Common Design Type

1937, May 13 ***Perf. 13½x14***
81 CD302 1a carmine .25 .40
82 CD302 2a black .35 2.00
83 CD302 3a bright ultra .50 1.00
Nos. 81-83 (3) 1.10 3.40
Set, never hinged 2.25

Blackhead Sheep — A5

Greater Kudu — A6

Map of Somaliland Protectorate A7

1938, May 10 **Wmk. 4** ***Perf. 12½***
84 A5 ½a green 1.25 5.75
Never hinged 2.50
85 A5 1a carmine .75 1.75
Never hinged 1.25
86 A5 2a deep claret 2.50 4.50
Never hinged 4.00
87 A5 3a ultra 10.00 17.50
Never hinged 17.50
88 A6 4a dark brown 4.00 12.00
Never hinged 6.00
89 A6 6a purple 9.00 13.00
Never hinged 15.00
90 A6 8a gray black 4.50 13.50
Never hinged 8.00
91 A6 12a orange 11.00 35.00
Never hinged 19.00
92 A7 1r green 9.00 85.00
Never hinged 15.00
93 A7 2r rose violet 16.00 85.00
Never hinged 27.50
94 A7 3r ultramarine 15.00 50.00
Never hinged 25.00
95 A7 5r black 20.00 50.00
Never hinged 32.50
a. Horiz. pair, imperf. btwn. 28,000.
Nos. 84-95 (12) 103.00 373.00
Set, never hinged 173.25

A8

A9

A10

1942, Apr. 22
96 A8 ½a green .25 .50
97 A8 1a carmine .25 .25
98 A8 2a deep claret .45 .25
99 A8 3a ultramarine 1.50 .25
100 A9 4a dark brown 1.75 .25
101 A9 6a purple 2.00 .25
102 A9 8a gray 2.75 .25
103 A9 12a orange 2.00 1.50
104 A10 1r green 2.25 2.75
105 A10 2r rose violet 3.75 9.50
106 A10 3r ultra 6.75 16.00
107 A10 5r black 11.00 11.00
Nos. 96-107 (12) 34.70 42.75
Set, never hinged 55.00

For surcharges see Nos. 116-126.

Catalogue values for unused stamps in this section, from this point to the end of the section, are for Never Hinged items.

Peace Issue
Common Design Type
Perf. 13¾x14

1946, Oct. 15 **Engr.** **Wmk. 4**
108 CD303 1a carmine .35 .25
Hinged .25
a. Perf. 13½ 19.00 65.00
Hinged 11.50
109 CD303 3a deep blue .35 .25
Hinged .25

Silver Wedding Issue
Common Design Types

1949, Jan. 28 **Photo.** ***Perf. 14x14½***
110 CD304 1a scarlet .40 .25
Hinged .25

Perf. 11½x11
Engraved; Name Typographed
111 CD305 5r gray black 8.00 8.50
Hinged 6.00

UPU Issue
Common Design Types
Surcharged in Black or Carmine with New Values in Annas
Engr.; Name Typo. on 3a, 6a

1949, Oct. 10   Perf. 13½, 11x11½

112	CD306	1a on 10c rose car	.40	.35
		Hinged		.25
113	CD307	3a on 30c ind (C)	2.00	4.50
		Hinged		1.25
114	CD308	6a on 50c rose vio	.55	3.25
		Hinged		.35
115	CD309	12a on 1sh red org	1.00	.60
		Hinged		.60
		Nos. 112-115 (4)	3.95	8.70

Nos. 96 and 98 to 107 Surcharged with New Value in Black or Carmine

1951, Apr. 2   Wmk. 4   Perf. 12½

116	A8	5c on ½a green	.40	2.25
117	A8	10c on 2a deep claret	.40	1.00
118	A8	15c on 3a ultramarine	1.75	2.25
119	A9	20c on 4a dark brown	2.50	.25
120	A9	30c on 6a purple	2.00	1.50
121	A9	50c on 8a gray	2.75	.25
122	A9	70c on 12a red	4.25	9.00
123	A10	1sh on 1r green	2.50	2.00
124	A10	2sh on 2r rose violet	5.75	25.00
125	A10	2sh on 3r ultra	15.00	10.00
126	A10	5sh on 5r black (C)	24.00	16.00
		Nos. 116-126 (11)	61.30	69.50

Coronation Issue
Common Design Type

1953, June 2   Engr.   Perf. 13½x13

127	CD312	15c dark green & blk	.40	.25

Camel Carrying Somali House — A11   Askari Militiaman — A12

Designs: 35c, 2sh, Rock Pigeon. 50c, 5sh, Martial eagle. 1sh, Blackhead sheep. 1sh30c, Tomb of Sheik Isaaq, Mait. 10sh, Taleh Fort.

1953-58   Engr.   Perf. 12½

128	A11	5c gray	.25	.60
129	A12	10c red orange	2.50	.60
130	A11	15c blue green	.70	.70
131	A11	20c rose red	.70	.40
132	A12	30c lt chocolate	2.50	.40
133	A11	35c blue	5.75	2.00
134	A11	50c lil rose & brn	6.50	.55
135	A11	1sh grnsh blue	1.25	.30
136	A11	1sh30c dark gray & ultra ('58)	24.00	3.75
137	A11	2sh violet & brn	27.50	7.50
138	A11	5sh emer & brn	35.00	11.00
139	A11	10sh rose lilac & brn	32.50	37.50
		Nos. 128-139 (12)	139.15	65.30

Nos. 131 and 135 Ovptd. "Opening of the Legislative Council 1957"

1957, May 21

140	A11	20c rose red	.25	.25
141	A11	1sh greenish blue	.35	.30

Nos. 131 and 136 Ovptd. "Legislative Council Unofficial Majority, 1960"

1960, Apr. 5

142	A11	20c rose red	.25	.25
143	A11	1sh30c dk gray & ultra	1.50	.30

Changes in the Legislative Council.

Three stamps of Somalia were overprinted "Somaliland Independence 26 June 1960" and issued in Hargeisa on that day. Somaliland Protectorate became part of Somalia on July 1, 1960. These three stamps are listed in Vol. 5 as Somalia Nos. 242, C68-C69.

Stamps of Somaliland Protectorate were replaced by those of Somalia in 1960.

OFFICIAL STAMPS

Official Stamps of India, 1883-1900, Overprinted

1903, June 1   Wmk. 39   Perf. 14

O1	A17	½a light green	8.50	55.00
O2	A19	1a carmine rose	20.00	12.50
O3	A21	2a violet	14.00	55.00
O4	A25	8a red violet	17.50	450.00
O5	A29	1r car rose & grn	20.00	750.00
		Nos. O1-O5 (5)	80.00	1,322.

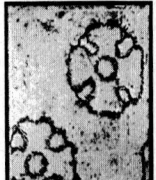

India Nos. 61-63, 68, 49 Overprinted

1903

O6	A33	½a green		.85
O7	A34	1a carmine rose		.85
O8	A35	2a violet		1.50
O9	A40	8a red violet		7.00
O10	A29	1r car rose & grn		22.50
		Nos. O6-O10 (5)		32.70

Nos. O6-O10 were not regularly issued, although used examples are known.

Regular Issue of 1904 Overprinted

1904   Wmk. Crown and C A (2)

O11	A1	½a gray green	9.50	55.00
O12	A1	1a carmine & blk	4.50	8.00
O13	A1	2a red vio & dull vio	300.00	70.00
O14	A1	8a pale blue & blk	80.00	150.00
		Nos. O11-O14 (4)	394.00	283.00

Wmk. Crown and C C (1)

O15	A2	1r gray green	275.00	1,100.

Same Overprint on No. 42

1905   Wmk. 3

O16	A1	2a red vio & dull vio	125.00	1,100.

The period after "M" may be found missing on Nos. O11-O14 and O16.

SOUTH AFRICA

sauth ˈa-fri-kə

LOCATION — Southern Africa
GOVT. — Republic
AREA — 472,730 sq. mi.
POP. — 43,426,386 (1999 est.)
CAPITAL — Pretoria (administrative); Cape Town (legislative); Bloemfontein (Judicial)

The union was formed on May 31, 1910, comprising the former British colonies of Cape of Good Hope, Natal, Transvaal and the Orange Free State, which became provinces. The union became a republic in 1961.

From Aug. 19, 1910, through December 31, 1937, the stamps of the provinces (Cape of Good Hope, Natal, Orange River Colony and Transvaal) were valid for postage throughout South Africa. They were demonetized effective Jan. 1, 1938.

For previous listings, see individual headings.

12 Pence = 1 Shilling
20 Shillings = 1 Pound
100 Cents = 1 Rand (1961)

Catalogue values for unused stamps in this country are for Never Hinged items, beginning with Scott 74 in the regular postage section, Scott B1 in the semipostal section, Scott J30 in the postage due section, and Scott O21 in the officials section.

Watermarks

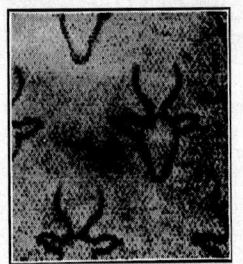

Wmk. 47 — Multiple Rosette    Wmk. 177 — Springbok's Head

Wmk. 201 — Multiple Springbok's Head

Wmk. 330 — Coat of Arms, Multiple

Wmk. 348 — RSA in Triangle, Multiple

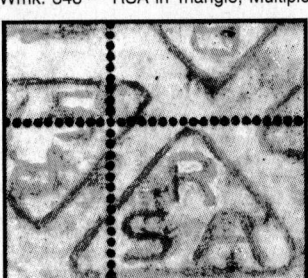

Wmk. 359 — RSA in Triangle, Tete Beche

Union of South Africa

George V — A1

1910   Engr.   Wmk. 47   Perf. 14

1	A1	2½p blue	3.25	1.75

Union Parliament opening, Nov. 4, 1910.

Type A2 stamps have very small margins at top and bottom. Values are for examples with perfs close to, or touching the frame.

George V — A2

1913-24   Typo.   Wmk. 177

2	A2	½p green	1.75	.30
a.		Double impression	15,000.	
e.		Printed on gummed side	1,500.	
3	A2	1p rose red	1.75	.25
d.		Printed on gummed side	925.00	
4	A2	1½p org brn ('20)	.80	.25
a.		Tête bêche pair	2.00	18.00
c.		Printed on gummed side	1,000.	
5	A2	2p dull violet	2.25	.25
d.		Printed on gummed side	1,000.	
6	A2	2½p ultra	5.50	1.60
7	A2	3p brn org & blk	13.00	.55
8	A2	3p ultra ('22)	4.75	1.75
9	A2	4p ol grn & org	11.00	.55
10	A2	6p violet & black	9.50	.70
11	A2	1sh orange	20.00	.90
12	A2	1sh3p violet ('20)	17.50	11.00
13	A2	2sh6p green & cl	70.00	5.50
14	A2	5sh blue & claret	140.00	9.00
15	A2	10sh ol grn & blue	350.00	14.50
16	A2	£1 red & dp grn ('16)	850.00	1,600.
a.		£1 lt red & gray green ('24)	1,100.	1,600.
		Nos. 2-16 (15)	1,497.	1,647.

The ½p, 1p and 1½p have the words "Revenue" and "Inkomst" on the stamps. On other stamps of this type these words are replaced by short vertical lines.

All values exist in many shades. No. 4a exists with and without gutter between.

Unwatermarked examples of the 1p are the result of misplaced watermarks.

Scott values watermarked stamps of South Africa in the normal upright position. Many issues exist with the watermark inverted, and some sideways. These varieties usually sell for a premium over the Scott values; however, in some instances the inverted watermarks sell for substantially less.

For overprint see No. O1.

Coil Stamps
Perf. 14 Horizontally

17	A2	½p green	9.25	1.90
18	A2	1p rose red ('14)	20.00	6.25
19	A2	1½p org brown ('20)	17.00	27.50
20	A2	2p dull violet ('21)	18.00	5.00
		Nos. 17-20 (4)	64.25	40.65

"Hope" — A3

Design: No. 22, inscribed SUIDAFRIKA.

1926   Engr.   Wmk. 201   Imperf.

21	A3	4p blue gray	2.00	1.40
22	A3	4p blue gray	2.00	1.40

Nos. 21 and 22 were privately rouletted and perforated, but such varieties were not officially made.

No. 21 (English inscription) was printed in a separate sheet from No. 22 (Afrikaans inscription).

English-Afrikaans Se-Tenant

Stamps with English inscriptions and with Afrikaans inscriptions were printed alternately in the same sheets, starting with No. 23. Major-number listings and values are for horizontal pairs (vertical pairs sell for about one-third less) of such stamps consisting of one English and one Afrikaans-inscribed stamp, unless otherwise described.

Values are for pairs with no fold marks between stamps and no perf separations.

Beware of pairs that have been rejoined.

Springbok A5

Jan van Riebeek's Ship, Drommedaris — A6

Orange Tree — A7

1926 Typo. *Perf. 14½x14*

23	A5	½p dk grn & blk, pair	3.00	4.00
	a.	Single, English	.25	.25
	b.	Single, Afrikaans	.25	.25
	c.	Tete beche pair ('27)	1,500.	
	d.	Center omitted	2,000.	
	e.	Booklet pane of 6	225.00	
	f.	As "e," perf. 14	350.00	
	g.	Missing "1" in "1/2" (Afrikaans only)	2,000.	
	h.	Perf 13½x14 ('27)	85.00	85.00
	i.	As "h," single, English		4.00
	j.	As "h," single, Afrikaans		4.00
24	A6	1p car & blk, pair	3.00	3.00
	a.	Single, English	.25	.25
	b.	Single, Afrikaans	.25	.25
	c.	Imperf., pair	1,350.	
	d.	Tete beche pair ('27)	1,750.	
	f.	Booklet pane of 6	200.00	
	g.	As "f," perf. 14	300.00	
	h.	Imperf on three sides, vert. pair	700.00	800.00
	i.	Perf 13½x14 ('27)	110.00	85.00
	j.	As "h," single, English		4.00
	k.	As "h," single, Afrikaans		4.00
25	A7	6p org & grn, pair	42.50	47.50
	a.	Single, English	3.00	2.25
	b.	Single, Afrikaans	3.00	2.25
		Nos. 23-25 (3)	48.50	54.50

Nos. 23c and 24d are from uncut sheets printed for the perf. 14 booklet panes of 1928, Nos. 23f and 24g.

See Nos. 33-35, 42, 45-50, 59-61, 98-99. For overprints see Nos. O2-O4, O6-O9, O12-O15, O18, O21-O25, O30-O32, O42-O45, O48.

Government Buildings, Pretoria — A8

"Groote Schuur," Rhodes's Home — A9

Native Kraal — A10

Gnu — A11

Trekking — A12

Ox Wagon — A13

Cape Town and Table Mountain — A14

Perf. 14, 14x13½

1927-28 Engr. Wmk. 201

26	A8	2p vio brn & gray, pair	14.00	30.00
	a.	Single, English	3.50	1.40
	b.	Single, Afrikaans	3.50	1.40
	c.	Perf. 14x13½, pair	45.00	47.50
	d.	As "c," single, English	6.00	.75
	e.	As "c," single, Afrikaans	6.00	.75
27	A9	3p red & blk, pair	24.00	37.50
	a.	Single, English	2.75	1.40
	b.	Single, Afrikaans	2.75	1.40
	c.	Perf. 14x13½, pair	80.00	82.50
	d.	As "c," single, English	6.50	2.75
	e.	As "c," single, Afrikaans	6.50	2.75
28	A10	4p brn, pair ('28)	32.50	67.50
	a.	Single, English	3.75	1.90
	b.	Single, Afrikaans	3.75	1.90
	c.	Perf. 14x13½, pair	67.50	82.50
	d.	As "c," single, English	5.00	2.75
	e.	As "c," single, Afrikaans	5.00	2.75
29	A11	1sh dp bl & bis brn, pair	47.50	87.50
	a.	Single, English	7.50	2.75
	b.	Single, Afrikaans	7.50	2.75
	c.	Perf. 14x13½, pair ('30)	75.00	90.00
	d.	As "c," single, English	7.50	2.00
	e.	As "c," single, Afrikaans	7.50	2.00
30	A12	2sh6p brn & bl grn, pair	150.00	500.00
	a.	Single, English	25.00	24.00
	b.	Single, Afrikaans	25.00	24.00
	c.	Perf. 14x13½, pair	475.00	700.00
	d.	As "c," single, English	37.50	37.50
	e.	As "c," single, Afrikaans	37.50	37.50
31	A13	5sh dp grn & blk, pair	300.00	900.00
	a.	Single, English	32.50	40.00
	b.	Single, Afrikaans	32.50	40.00
	c.	Perf. 14x13½, pair	525.00	1,100.
	d.	As "c," single, English	55.00	52.50
	e.	As "c," single, Afrikaans	55.00	52.50
32	A14	10sh ol brn & bl, pair	200.00	200.00
	a.	Single, English	25.00	16.00
	b.	Single, Afrikaans	25.00	16.00
	c.	Perf. 14x13½, pair	275.00	375.00
	d.	As "c," single, English	27.50	20.00
	e.	As "c," single, Afrikaans	27.50	20.00
	f.	Center inverted, single, English ('28)	20,000.	
	g.	Center inverted, single, Afrikaans ('28)	20,000.	
	h.	As "c," center inverted	60,000.	
		Nos. 26-32 (7)	768.00	1,822.

See Nos. 36-41, 43-44, 53-54, 58, 62-66. For overprints see Nos. O5, O10-O111, O16-O17, O19-O20, O28, O33-O35, O39, O41, O49-O53.

Types of 1926-28 Redrawn

No. 34

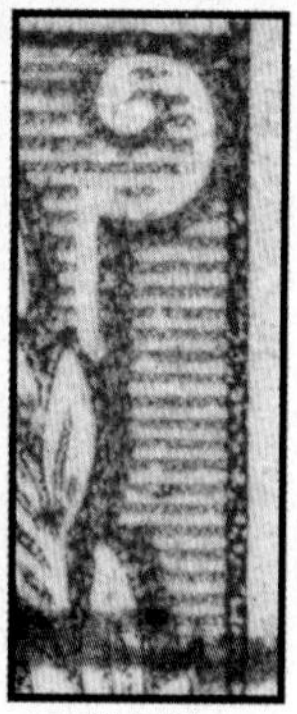
No. 35

"SUIDAFRIKA" (No Hyphen) on Afrikaans Stamps

The photogravure, unhyphenated stamps of 1930-45 are distinguished from the 1926-28 typographed or engraved stamps (also unhyphenated) by the following characteristics:

½p, 1p, 6p. Leg of "R" in AFRICA or AFRIKA ends in a straight line in the photogravure set; in a curved line in the typographed. No. 34, POSSEEL—INKOMSTE separated by ½mm; horiz. shading in side panels is close. No. 35, POSSEEL—INKOMSTE separated by 1mm; horiz. shading in side panels is wide.

2p. A memorial statue has been added just above and leftward of the "2" in value tablet on Nos. 36-37 (photogravure).

3p. Top frame on No. 38 consists of 3 heavy lines. On No. 27 it has 3 heavy and 2 very thin lines.

4p. On Nos. 40-41 the background in upper corners is solid. On No. 28 it consists of horizontal and vertical lines. No. 41 has pretzel-shaped scroll endings at bottom. On No. 40 these scroll endings enclose a solid mass of color.

1sh. No. 43 has no fine shading lines projecting from the curved top of the left inner frame, as No. 29 has. On No. 43 the shading of the last "A" of the country name partly covers the flower below it.

2sh6p. On No. 44 the shading below the country name is solid or shows signs of wear. On No. 30 it is composed of fine lines.

The engraved pictorials are much more finely executed and show details more clearly than the photogravure.

Perf. 15x14 (½p, 1p, 6p), 14

1930-45 Photo. Wmk. 201

33	A5	½p bl grn & blk, pair	6.00	3.50
	a.	Single, English	.25	.25
	b.	Single, Afrikaans	.25	.25
	c.	Tete-beche pair	1,450.	
	d.	As "c," gutter between	1,750.	
	e.	Booklet pane of 6	60.00	50.00
	f.	Vert. pair, monolingual	40.00	—
34	A6	1p car & blk, pair	5.50	3.50
	a.	Single, English	.25	.25
	b.	Single, Afrikaans	.25	.25
	c.	Center omitted	*4,500.*	
	d.	Frame omitted	*2,500.*	
	e.	Tete-beche pair	1,800.	
	f.	As "e," gutter between	1,500.	
	g.	Booklet pane of 6	40.00	20.00
35	A6	1p rose & blk, pair ('32)	60.00	4.50
	a.	Single, English	1.00	.25
	b.	Single, Afrikaans	1.00	.25
	c.	Center omitted	750.00	
36	A8	2p vio & gray, pair ('31)	28.00	24.00
	a.	Single, English	2.00	.40
	b.	Single, Afrikaans	2.00	.40
	c.	Frame omitted, single stamp (English)	*3,000.*	
	d.	Frame omitted, single stamp (Afrikaans)	*3,000.*	
	e.	Tete-beche pair	*6,500.*	
	f.	Booklet pane of 4	240.00	240.00
37	A8	2p vio & ind, pair ('38)	350.00	100.00
	a.	Single, English	16.00	7.25
	b.	Single, Afrikaans	16.00	7.25
38	A9	3p red & blk, pair ('31)	135.00	*100.00*
	a.	Single, English	7.25	6.75
	b.	Single, Afrikaans	7.25	6.75
39	A9	3p ultra & bl, pair ('33)	24.00	10.00
	a.	Single, English	2.00	.50
	b.	Single, Afrikaans	2.00	.50
	c.	Center omitted	30,000.	
	d.	Frame omitted	15,000.	
40	A10	4p redsh brn, pair ('32)	300.00	210.00
	a.	Single, English	25.00	11.00
	b.	Single, Afrikaans	25.00	11.00
41	A10	4p brn, pair ('36)	6.50	5.00
	a.	Single, English	.40	.35
	b.	Single, Afrikaans	.40	.35
42	A7	6p org & grn, pair ('31)	65.00	20.00
	a.	Single, English	1.75	.75
	b.	Single, Afrikaans	1.75	.75
43	A11	1sh dl bl & yel brn, pair	140.00	60.00
	a.	Single, English	9.00	2.00
	b.	Single, Afrikaans	9.00	2.00
	c.	1sh dp bl & brn, pair ('32)	72.50	32.50
	d.	As "c," single, English	5.25	.40
	e.	As "c," single, Afrikaans	5.25	.40
44	A12	2sh 6p brn & bl, pair ('45)	29.00	19.00
	a.	Single, English	1.75	.70
	b.	Single, Afrikaans	1.75	.70
	c.	2sh6p brn & sl grn ('36), pair	350.00	300.00
	d.	As "c," single, English	18.00	8.00
	e.	As "c," single, Afrikaans	18.00	8.00
	f.	2sh6p choc & dp grn ('37), pair	225.00	190.00
	g.	As "f," single, English	14.00	6.50
	h.	As "f," single, Afrikaans	14.00	6.50
	i.	2sh6p red brn & grn, pair ('32)	175.00	175.00
	j.	As "i," single, English	17.50	5.00
	k.	As "i," single, Afrikaans	17.50	5.00
		Nos. 33-44 (12)	1,149.	559.50

No. 34 unwatermarked, or watermarked multiple clover leaf, is a proof.

Types of 1926-28 with "SUID-AFRIKA" Hyphenated on Afrikaans Stamps, and

Gold Mine — A15

Government Buildings, Pretoria — A16

Government Buildings, Pretoria — A16a

Groote Schuur — A17

Groot Constantia — A18

½p. No. 45 shading in leaves and ornaments strengthened; 40 lines in center background. Size: 18½x22½mm.

No. 46 has 28 heavy horizontal shading lines in center background and similar thicker lines in frame. Top and bottom green bars are scored by a white horizontal line. Size: 18½x22½mm.

No. 47 is smaller, 18x22mm.

1p. No. 48, size 18½x22½mm.

No. 49, size 18x22mm.

No. 50. Size: 17½x21½mm.

2p. On Nos. 53-54, S's in SOUTH and POSTAGE are narrower than on Nos. 36-37.

5sh.On No. 64, Die I, U and A in SOUTH AFRICA have projections. Lines are contained within the design. Size 27x21¾mm.

5sh. On No. 65, Die I, dots are contained within the design, instead of lines. Size 27x21½mm.

5sh. On No. 66, Die II, U and A in SOUTH AFRICA have been redrawn to eliminate projections. Dots are contained within the design. Size 26¾x21½mm.

6p. Die I, "SUID-AFRIKA" 16½mm. Shading in leaves framing oval very faint and broken. Size: 18½x22½mm.

Die II, "SUID-AFRIKA" 17mm. Leaves strongly shaded. Heavy lines of shading in background of tree. Size: 18½x22½mm.

Die III, "question mark" scrolls below top panel are cleanly defined without intrusion of background shading. Size: 18x22mm.

Nos. 45-67 were printed in many shades. Some denominations in some printings were partly or wholly screened. Except for No. 47, the screened stamps were issued after 1947.

5sh. No. 65. Type I, letters "U" and "A" in SOUTH AFRICA have projections. Size: 27x21½mm.

No. 66. Type II, letters "U" and "A" redrawn to eliminate projections. Size: 26½x21½mm.

Perf. 15x14 (½p, 1p, 6p), 14

1933-54 Photo. Wmk. 201

45	A5	½p grn & gray, pair ('36)	6.00	2.25
a.		Single, English	.25	.25
b.		Single, Afrikaans	.25	.25
c.		Bklt. pane of 6, marginal ads	30.00	30.00
d.		Perf. 13½x14 (coil), pair	40.00	*70.00*
e.		As "d," single, English	1.75	1.25
f.		As "d," single, Afrikaans	1.75	1.25
46	A5	½p grn & gray, redrawn, pair ('37)	13.00	2.50
a.		Single, English	.25	.25
b.		Single, Afrikaans	.25	.25
c.		Booklet pane of 6	65.00	*45.00*
d.		Booklet pane of 2	17.50	*10.00*
e.		As "c," 4 blank margins	65.00	*45.00*
f.		Perf. 14½x14 (coil), pair	12.50	7.25
g.		As "f," single, English	2.25	.80
h.		As "f," single, Afrikaans	2.25	.80
47	A5	½p grn & gray, pair ('47)	3.00	5.50
a.		Single, English	.25	.25
b.		Single, Afrikaans	.25	.25
c.		Bklt. pane of 6, marginal ads	*18.00*	*16.00*
d.		As "c," no horiz. margins	18.00	*16.00*
48	A6	1p car & gray, pair ('34)	1.75	2.25
a.		Single, English	.25	.25
b.		Single, Afrikaans	.25	.25
c.		Booklet pane of 6	45.00	45.00
d.		Booklet pane of 2	3.50	*2.25*
e.		Perf. 13½x14 (coil), pair	85.00	125.00
f.		As "e," single, English	.70	.70
g.		As "e," single, Afrikaans	.70	.70
h.		Center omitted, pair	325.00	
j.		Bklt. pane of 6, marginal ads	32.50	32.50
k.		As "j," 4 blank margins	36.00	36.00
m.		Perf. 14½x14 (coil), pair	11.00	11.00
n.		As "m," single, English	1.40	1.40
p.		As "m," single, Afrikaans	1.40	1.40
q.		Pair, imperf.	200.00	
r.		Frame omitted	375.00	
49	A6	1p rose car & gray blk, pair ('40)	1.50	.30
a.		Single, English	.25	.25
b.		Single, Afrikaans	.25	.25
c.		Unwmkd., pair	325.00	325.00
d.		Booklet pane of 6	4.50	3.25
e.		Perf. 14½x14 (coil), pair	4.00	6.00
f.		As "e," single, English	1.40	.90
g.		As "e," single, Afrikaans	1.40	.90
h.		As "d," marginal ads	6.00	5.00
50	A6	1p car & blk, pair ('51)	1.50	4.00
a.		Single, English	.25	.25
b.		Single, Afrikaans	.25	.25
51	A15	1½p dk grn & gold, 27x21½mm, pair ('36)	7.00	3.50
a.		Single, English	.25	.25
b.		Single, Afrikaans	.25	.25
c.		Booklet pane of 4	30.00	15.00
d.		Center omitted, pair	1,000.	
52	A15	1½p sl grn & och, 22x18mm, pair ('41)	8.50	1.50
a.		Single, English	.25	.25
b.		Single, Afrikaans	.25	.25
c.		Center omitted, pair	25,000.	10,000.
d.		Booklet pane of 6	8.00	5.50
53	A16	2p bl vio & dl bl, pair ('38)	75.00	50.00
a.		Single, English	3.00	1.25
b.		Single, Afrikaans	3.00	1.25
54	A16	2p dl vio & gray, pair ('41)	65.00	*110.00*
a.		Single, English	1.00	1.75
b.		Single, Afrikaans	1.00	1.75
55	A16a	2p dp reddish vio & sl, 27x21½mm, pair ('45)	24.00	3.00
a.		Single, English	.50	.25
b.		Single, Afrikaans	.50	.25
56	A16a	2p pur & sl bl, 21½ x 17¼mm, pair ('50)	5.00	*21.00*
a.		Single, English	.25	.25
b.		Single, Afrikaans	.25	.25
c.		Booklet pane of 6 ('51)	15.00	*35.00*
57	A17	3p ultra, pair ('40)	15.00	3.50
a.		Single, English	.45	.25
b.		Single, Afrikaans	.45	.25
c.		3p bl, pair ('49)	3.75	*8.00*
d.		As "c," single, English	.25	.25
e.		As "c," single, Afrikaans	.25	.25
58	A10	4p choc brn, pair ('52)	4.50	*17.00*
a.		Single, English	.25	.70
b.		Single, Afrikaans	.25	.70
59	A7	6p org & bl grn, I, pair ('37)	70.00	47.50
a.		Single, English	3.75	1.10
b.		Single, Afrikaans	3.75	1.10
60	A7	6p org & grn, II, pair ('38)	42.00	3.00
a.		Single, English	1.50	.25
b.		Single, Afrikaans	1.50	.25
61	A7	6p red org & bl grn, III ('50), pair	3.75	1.50
a.		Single, English	.25	.25
b.		Single, Afrikaans	.25	.25
c.		6p org & grn, III, pair ('46)	20.00	1.90
d.		As "c," single, English	1.00	.25
e.		As "c," single, Afrikaans	1.00	.25
62	A11	1sh chlky bl & lt brn ('50), pair	11.00	*13.00*
a.		As "f," single, English	.55	.25
b.		As "f," single, Afrikaans	.55	.25
c.		1sh lt bl & ol brn, pair ('39)	55.00	18.00
d.		As "c," single, English	1.00	.25
e.		As "c," single, Afrikaans	1.00	.25
f.		1sh vio bl & brnsh blk, pair ('52)	16.00	*20.00*
g.		Single, English	.50	.30
h.		Single, Afrikaans	.50	.30
i.		As "c," frame omitted, vert. pair with normal)	13,000.	
63	A12	2sh6p brn & brt grn, pair ('49)	11.00	*30.00*
a.		Single, English	1.50	1.25
b.		Single, Afrikaans	1.50	1.25
64	A13	5sh grn & blk, I, pair	60.00	75.00
a.		Single, English	4.75	2.00
b.		Single, Afrikaans	4.75	2.00
64C	A13	5sh bl grn & blk, I, pair ('54)	42.50	21.00
d.		Single, English	1.00	.40
e.		Single, Afrikaans	1.00	.40
65	A13	5sh bl grn & blk, I, pair ('49)	42.50	*75.00*
a.		Single, English	3.75	3.50
b.		Single, Afrikaans	3.75	3.50
66	A13	5sh dp yel grn & blk, II, pair ('54)	50.00	*100.00*
a.		Single, English	4.50	4.50
b.		Single, Afrikaans	4.50	4.50
67	A18	10sh ol blk & bl, pair ('39)	50.00	17.50
a.		Single, English	3.00	1.00
b.		Single, Afrikaans	3.00	1.00
		Nos. 45-67 (23)	571.00	588.80

See Nos. 98-99. For overprints see Nos. O26-O27, O29, O36-O38, O40, O46-O47, O54.

George V and Springboks — A19

1935, May 1 Wmk. 201 ***Perf. 15x14***

68	A19	½p Prus grn & blk, pair	4.00	*12.00*
a.		Single, English top	.35	.35
b.		Single, Afrikaans top	.35	.35
69	A19	1p car rose & blk, pair	4.50	*8.00*
a.		Single, English top	.35	.25
b.		Single, Afrikaans top	.35	.25
70	A19	3p bl & dk bl, pair	16.00	*55.00*
a.		Single, English top	2.25	2.75
b.		Single, Afrikaans top	2.25	2.75
71	A19	6p org & grn, pair	32.50	*80.00*
a.		Single, English top	3.00	*3.75*
b.		Single, Afrikaans top	3.00	*3.75*
		Nos. 68-71 (4)	57.00	*155.00*
		Set, never hinged	100.00	

25th anniv. of the reign of George V.

English and Afrikaans inscriptions are transposed on alternate stamps. On the ½p, 3p and 6p with "SOUTH AFRICA" at top, "SILWER JUBILEUM" is at left of medallion, but on 1p with English at top, it is at the right.

Johannesburg International Philatelic Exhibition Issue

Souvenir Sheets

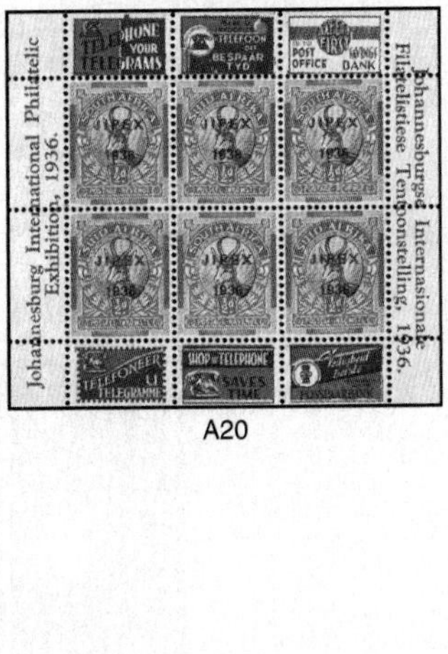

A20

A21

Black Overprint, "JIPEX 1936"

1936, Nov. 2 ***Perf. 15x14***

72	A20	Sheet of 6 (½p)	5.75	10.00
73	A21	Sheet of 6 (1p)	5.00	7.00
		Set, never hinged	25.00	

Sheets made by overprinting booklet panes Nos. 45c and 48j. Sheets exist with and without horizontal perforations through right margin. Sheet size: 81x72.

Catalogue values for unused stamps in this section, from this point to the end of the section, are for Never Hinged items.

George VI — A22

"KRONING SUID-AFRIKA" on alternate stamps.

1937, May 12 ***Perf. 14***

74	A22	½p grn & ol blk, pair	.80	1.10
a.		Single, English	.25	.25
b.		Single, Afrikaans	.25	.25
75	A22	1p car & ol blk, pair	.85	.90
a.		Single, English	.25	.25
b.		Single, Afrikaans	.25	.25
76	A22	1½p Prus grn & org, pair	.85	.80
a.		Single, English	.25	.25
b.		Single, Afrikaans	.25	.25
77	A22	3p bl & ultra, pair	1.75	*3.00*
a.		Single, English	.25	.25
b.		Single, Afrikaans	.25	.25
78	A22	1sh Prus bl & org brn, pair	5.00	5.00
a.		Single, English	.50	.25
b.		Single, Afrikaans	.50	.25
		Nos. 74-78 (5)	9.25	10.80

Coronation of George VI and Queen Elizabeth.

Wagon Wheel — A23

Voortrekker Family — A24

Alternate stamps inscribed "SOUTH AFRICA," "SUID-AFRIKA."

1938, Dec. 14 ***Perf. 15x14***

79	A23	1p rose & slate, pair	9.00	4.50
a.		Single, English	.30	.30
b.		Single, Afrikaans	.30	.30
80	A24	1½p red brn & Prus bl, pair	11.50	5.00
a.		Single, English	.30	.35
b.		Single, Afrikaans	.30	.35

Issued to commemorate the Voortrekkers.

Infantry A25

Nurse and Ambulance A26

Airman and Spitfires (Flight Lt. Robert Kershaw) A27

Sailor A28

Women's Services A29

Artillery — A30

Welder — A31

Tank Corps A32

Signal Corps — A33

Bilingual inscriptions on 2p and 1sh.

Perf. 14 (2p, 4p, 6p), 15x14

1941-43 Photo. Wmk. 201

81	A25	½p dp bl grn, pair	1.50	4.00
a.		Single, English	.25	.25
b.		Single, Afrikaans	.25	.25
82	A26	1p brt rose, pair	2.00	4.00
a.		Single, English	.25	.25
b.		Single, Afrikaans	.25	.25
83	A27	1½p Prus grn, pair ('42)	1.50	4.00
a.		Single, English	.25	.25
b.		Single, Afrikaans	.25	.25
84	A28	2p dk violet	1.00	.75
85	A29	3p dp blue, pair	18.50	40.00
a.		Single, English	1.75	.90
b.		Single, Afrikaans	1.75	.90
86	A30	4p org brn, pair	22.50	25.00
a.		Single, English	1.25	.25
b.		Single, Afrikaans	1.25	.25
c.		4p red brown, pair	37.50	42.50
d.		As "c," single, English	2.75	1.25
e.		As "c," single, Afrikaans	2.75	1.25
87	A31	6p brt red org, pair	11.75	14.00
a.		Single, English	.75	.25
b.		Single, Afrikaans	.75	.25
88	A32	1sh dark brown	2.25	1.00
89	A33	1sh3p dk ol brn, pair ('43)	13.00	11.00
a.		Single, English	.80	.30
b.		Single, Afrikaans	.80	.30
c.		1sh3p dark brown, pair	7.00	9.50
d.		As "c," single, English	.50	.25
e.		As "c," single, Afrikaans	.50	.25
		Nos. 81-89 (9)	74.00	103.75

Infantry A34

Nurse
A35

Airman — A36

Sailor — A37

Women's
Services — A38

Artillery — A39

Welder — A40

Tank
Corps — A41

Bilingual inscriptions on 4p and 1sh.

**Pairs: Perf. 14, Roul. 6½ btwn.
Strips of 3: Perf. 15x14, Roul. 6½ btwn.**

1942-43		Photo.	Wmk. 201	
90	A34	½p Horiz. strip of 3	2.00	1.50
a.		Single, English	.25	.25
b.		Single, Afrikaans	.25	.25
c.		As #90, imperf. between	1,300.	1,200.
91	A35	1p Horiz. strip of 3 ('43)	1.00	1.25
a.		Single, English	.25	.25
b.		Single, Afrikaans	.25	.25
c.		As #91, imperf. between	1,100.	1,100.
92	A36	1½p Horiz. pair	.70	2.50
a.		Single, English	.25	.25
b.		Single, Afrikaans	.25	.25
c.		As #92, roul. 13	4.50	4.50
d.		As #92, imperf. btwn.	325.00	400.00
93	A37	2p Horiz. pair ('43)	1.00	2.25
a.		Single, English	.25	.25
b.		Single, Afrikaans	.25	.25
c.		As #93, imperf. btwn.	1,200.	1,100.
94	A38	3p Vert strip of 3	8.00	18.00
a.		Single, English	.25	.25
b.		Single, Afrikaans	.25	.25
95	A39	4p Vert. strip of 3	18.00	11.00
a.		Single	.25	.25
96	A40	6p Horiz. pair	2.00	2.25
a.		Single, English	.25	.25
b.		Single, Afrikaans	.25	.25
97	A41	1sh Vert. pair	17.00	4.25
a.		Single	.25	.25
		Nos. 90-97 (8)	49.70	43.00

Because of the rouletting these are collected as pairs or strips of three, even on the bilingual stamps.

**Types of 1926 Redrawn
"SUID-AFRIKA" Hyphenated
Coil Stamps**

1943		Photo.		Perf. 15x14
98	A5	½p myrtle grn, vert. pair	4.00	7.00
a.		Single, English	.25	.25
b.		Single, Afrikaans	.25	.25
99	A6	1p rose pink, vert. pair	5.00	5.00
a.		Single, English	.25	.25
b.		Single, Afrikaans	.25	.25

"Victory" — A42

"Peace" — A43

Design: 3p, Profiles of couple ("Hope").

1945, Dec. 3		Photo.		Perf. 14
100	A42	1p rose pink & choc, pair	.35	1.25
a.		Single, English	.25	.25
b.		Single, Afrikaans	.25	.25
101	A43	2p vio & sl bl, pair	.35	1.25
a.		Single, English	.25	.25
b.		Single, Afrikaans	.25	.25
102	A43	3p ultra & dp ultra, pair	.50	1.50
a.		Single, English	.25	.25
b.		Single, Afrikaans	.25	.25
		Nos. 100-102 (3)	1.20	4.00

World War II victory of the Allies.

George VI — A44

King
George VI
and Queen
Elizabeth
A45

Princesses
Margaret
Rose and
Elizabeth
A46

Perf. 15x14

1947, Feb. 17			Wmk. 201	
103	A44	1p cer & gray, pair	.30	.40
a.		Single, English	.25	.25
b.		Single, Afrikaans	.25	.25
104	A45	2p purple, pair	.30	.60
a.		Single, English	.25	.25
b.		Single, Afrikaans	.25	.25
105	A46	3p dk blue, pair	.40	.75
a.		Single, English	.25	.25
b.		Single, Afrikaans	.25	.25
		Nos. 103-105 (3)	1.00	1.75

Visit of the British Royal Family, Mar.-Apr., 1947.

George VI,
Elizabeth — A47

1948, Apr. 26		Photo.		Perf. 14
106	A47	3p dp chlky bl & sil, pair	.90	1.25
a.		Single, English	.25	.25
b.		Single, Afrikaans	.25	.25

25th anniv. of the marriage of George VI and Queen Elizabeth.

Gold Mine — A48

**Vertical Pairs Perf. 14 all around,
Rouletted 6½ between**

1948, Apr.				
107	A48	1½p sl & och, vert. pair	1.60	2.50
a.		Single, English	.25	.25
b.		Single, Afrikaans	.25	.25

"Wanderer"
in Port
Natal
A49

1949, May 2		Photo.		Perf. 15x14
108	A49	1½p red brown, pair	.80	.80
a.		Single, English	.25	.25
b.		Single, Afrikaans	.25	.25

Mercury and
Globe — A50

1949, Oct. 1				Perf. 14x15
109	A50	½p dk green, pair	.50	1.00
a.		Single, English	.25	.25
b.		Single, Afrikaans	.25	.25
110	A50	1½p dk red, pair	.70	1.00
a.		Single, English	.25	.25
b.		Single, Afrikaans	.25	.25
111	A50	3p ultra, pair	1.00	1.00
a.		Single, English	.25	.25
b.		Single, Afrikaans	.25	.25
		Nos. 109-111 (3)	2.20	3.00

75th anniv. of the UPU.

Except for Nos. 216, 310-313, 518a, 669a this is the end of bi-lingual multiples in the postage section.

Voortrekkers en Route to Natal — A51

Voortrekker
Monument,
Pretoria
A52

Voortrekkers Looking Toward Natal,
and Open Bible — A53

1949, Dec. 1				Perf. 15x14
112	A51	1p magenta	.25	.25
113	A52	1½p dull green	.25	.25
114	A53	3p dark blue	.25	.25
		Nos. 112-114 (3)	.75	.75

Inauguration of the Voortrekker Monument at Pretoria.

Riebeeck's
Seal and
Dutch East
India
Company
Monogram
A54

Maria de la
Quellerie — A55

2p, van Riebeeck's Ships. 4½p, Jan van
Riebeeck. 1sh, Landing of van Riebeeck.

Perf. 15x14, 14x15

1952, Mar. 14			Wmk. 201	
115	A54	½p dk brn & red vio	.25	.25
116	A55	1p dark green	.25	.25
117	A54	2p dark purple	.25	.25
118	A55	4½p dark blue	.25	.25
119	A54	1sh brown	.55	.50
		Nos. 115-119 (5)	1.55	1.50

300th anniv. of the landing of Jan van
Riebeeck at the Cape of Good Hope.

**Nos. 116-117 Overprinted "SATISE"
(1p) and "SADIPU" (2p)**

1952, Mar. 26				
120	A55	1p dark green	.30	.55
121	A54	2p dark purple	.35	.70

South African Tercentenary Intl. Stamp
Exhib., Cape Town, Mar. 26-Apr. 5, 1952.

Coronation Issue

Queen
Elizabeth II — A97

1953, June 3				Perf. 14x15
192	A97	2p violet blue		.30 .25

Cape
Triangle of
1853
A98

1953, Sept. 1				Perf. 15x14
193	A98	1p red & dk brown		.25 .25
194	A98	4p blue & indigo		.25 .25

Cent. of the introduction of postage stamps
in South Africa.

Merino Ram and
Sheep — A99

1953, Oct. 1				Perf. 14
195	A99	4½p shown	.50	.25
196	A99	1sh3p Springbok	1.25	.25
197	A99	1sh6p Aloes	1.25	.40
		Nos. 195-197 (3)	3.00	.90

Arms of
Orange
Free State,
Pen and
Scroll
A100

1954, Feb. 23				Perf. 15x14
198	A100	2p red org & dk brown		.25 .25
199	A100	4½p gray & rose violet		.25 .25

Orange Free State centenary.

Wart Hog
A101

White
Rhinoceros
A102

Lion — A103

1954, Oct. 14   *Perf. 15x14*
200	A101	½p shown	.25	.25
201	A101	1p Gnu	.25	.25
202	A101	1 ½p Leopard	.25	.25
203	A101	2p Zebra	.25	.25

Perf. 14
204	A102	3p shown	.25	.25
205	A102	4p Elephant	.45	.25
206	A102	4 ½p Hippopotamus	.55	.80
207	A103	6p shown	.50	.25
208	A103	1sh Kudu	3.00	.55
209	A103	1sh3p Springbok	2.00	.35
210	A102	1sh6p Gemsbok	1.75	.50
211	A102	2sh6p Nyala	4.25	.30
212	A102	5sh Giraffe	10.50	1.60
213	A102	10sh Sable ante-lope	16.00	3.75
		Nos. 200-213 (14)	40.25	9.30

See Nos. 221-228, 241-244, 247, 250-253.

Paul Kruger — A104

Portrait: 6p, Martinus Wessels Pretorius.

Perf. 14x15
1955, Oct. 21   Photo.   Wmk. 201
214	A104	3p slate green	.30	.25
215	A104	6p brown violet	.60	.30

Centenary of Pretoria.

Andries Pretorius, Church of the Vow and Flag of Natalia — A105

Inscribed alternately in English and Afrikaans.

1955, Dec. 1   *Perf. 14*
216	A105	2p ultra & cer, pair	.80	4.00
a.		Single, English	.25	.25
b.		Single, Afrikaans	.25	.25

Union Covenant Celebrations, Pietermaritzburg, Dec. 13-18, 1955.

German Wagon and House — A106

1958, July 1   *Perf. 14*
218	A106	2p pale lilac & brown	.30	.30

Cent. of the arrival of German settlers.

Seal of Academy A107

1959, May 1   Photo.   *Perf. 15x14*
219	A107	3p brt blue & dk blue	.30	.30
a.		Dark blue omitted	2,250.	

50th anniv. of the South African Academy of Science and Art, Pretoria.

Globe Showing Antarctica and South Africa — A108

Perf. 14x15
1959, Nov. 16   Wmk. 330
220	A108	3p blue grn, brn & org	.30	.25

South African Natl. Antarctic Expedition.

Animal Types of 1954
1959-60   Wmk. 330   *Perf. 15x14*
221	A101	½p Wart hog ('60)	.35	3.00
222	A101	1p Gnu	.25	.25
a.		Redrawn	.40	.25

Perf. 14
223	A102	3p White rhino	.30	.25
224	A102	4p Elephant	.75	.30
225	A103	6p Lion	1.50	1.50
226	A102	1sh Kudu	4.50	.75
227	A102	2sh6p Nyala	4.50	3.00
228	A102	5sh Giraffe ('60)	12.00	25.00
		Nos. 221-228 (8)	24.15	34.05

On No. 222a, the numeral "1" is centered above "S." On No. 222, "1" is slightly to right of "S."

Prime Ministers Botha, Smuts, Hertzog, Malan, Strydom and Verwoerd A109

Flag and Notes from National Anthem — A110

Pushing Wheel Uphill A111

6p, Arms of the Union and of four provinces. 1sh6p, Official Union festival emblem.

Perf. 14x15, 15x14
1960   Photo.   Wmk. 330
235	A109	3p chocolate	.25	.25
236	A110	4p lt blue & red org	.25	.25
237	A110	6p yel grn, red & brn	.25	.25
238	A111	1sh yel, dk bl & blk	.50	.25
239	A111	1sh6p lt blue & blk	1.60	1.00
		Nos. 235-239 (5)	2.85	2.00

50th anniv. of the founding of the Union. See Nos. 245-246, 248-249.

Map, Old and New Locomotives — A112

1960, May 2   *Perf. 15x14*
240	A112	1sh3p dark blue	1.25	1.25

Centenary of railways in South Africa.

Types of 1954 and 1960

Designs: ½c, Wart hog. 1c, Gnu. 1 ½c, Leopard. 2c, Zebra. 2 ½c, Prime Ministers. 3 ½c, Flag and music notes. 5c, Lion. 7 ½c, Arms of Union and four provinces. 10c, Pushing wheel uphill. 12 ½c, Springbok. 20c, Gemsbok. 50c, Giraffe. 1r, Sable antelope.

Perf. 15x14, 14x15, 14 (A102, A103)
1961, Feb. 14   Photo.   Wmk. 330
241	A101	½c dk bluish grn	.25	.25
242	A101	1c rose brown	.25	.25
243	A101	1 ½c sepia	.25	.25
244	A101	2c purple	.25	.25
245	A109	2 ½c chocolate	.25	.25
246	A110	3 ½c lt bl & red org	.30	.25
247	A103	5c org & dk brn	.35	.25
248	A110	7 ½c yel grn, red & brn	.40	1.00
249	A111	10c yel, dk bl & blk	.50	.40
250	A103	12 ½c dull grn & dk brn	1.25	1.25
251	A102	20c pink & dk brn	2.50	2.50
252	A102	50c org yel & blk	5.50	8.25
253	A102	1r blue & black	15.00	15.00
		Nos. 241-253 (13)	27.05	30.15

Republic

Natal Pigmy Kingfisher A112a

Coral Tree Flower A112b

Pouring Gold A113

Groot Constantia A114

Designs: 1 ½c, Afrikander bull. 3c, Crimson-breasted shrike. 5c, Baobab tree. 7 ½c, Corn. 10c, Castle entrance, Cape Town. 12 ½c, Protea flower. 20c, Secretary bird. 50c, Cape Town, harbor. 1r, Bird of Paradise flower.

Two types of 2 ½c:

Type I — Lines of building faint.

Type II — Lines of building very strong; strong line between bottom of building and top of name panel.

Perf. 14x15, 15x14
1961, May 31   Photo.   Wmk. 330
254	A112a	½c blue, mag & brn	.25	.25
a.		Perf. 14x13 ½ ('63)	.25	.25
255	A112b	1c gray & red	.25	.25
256	A112a	1 ½c brown carmine	.25	.25

Perf. 14
257	A113	2c ultra & org	.25	.25
258	A114	2 ½c vio & grn (I)	.30	.25
a.		Type II	.40	.25
259	A113	3c pink, dk bl & red	.30	.25
260	A114	5c grnsh bl & yel	.35	.25
261	A114	7 ½c emerald & brn	.60	.25
a.		Brown omitted		
262	A114	10c emer & dk brn	.80	.25
263	A114	12 ½c dk grn, red & yel	2.25	.30
a.		Yellow omitted	1,000.	
264	A114	20c sal, sl bl & pink	3.75	.30
265	A113	50c ultra & blk	22.50	2.25
266	A113	1r blue, org & grn	15.00	2.25
		Nos. 254-266 (13)	46.85	7.35

1961-63   Unwmk.   *Perf. 15x14*
269	A112b	1c gray & red	.25	.25

Perf. 14
270	A113	2c ultra & org ('63)	8.00	.35
271	A114	2 ½c violet & grn (II)	.30	.25
272	A113	3c pink, dk bl & red	.60	.25
273	A114	5c grnsh blue & yel	.75	.25
274	A114	7 ½c emer & brn ('62)	1.10	.50
275	A114	10c green & dk brn	1.25	.70
276	A114	20c sal, sl bl & pink ('63)	14.00	4.50
277	A113	50c ultra & blk ('62)	18.00	4.75
		Nos. 269-277 (9)	44.25	11.80

See Nos. 289-298, 317-322, 324, 326-338, 340-342, 376-377, 379-382, 383-385 and designs A135-A136.

Boeing 707 and Bleriot Monoplane — A115

Perf. 14x15
1961, Dec. 1   Photo.   Wmk. 330
280	A115	3c blue & red	.40	.25

50th anniv. of South Africa's 1st air mail.

Folk Dancers — A116

1962, Mar. 1
281	A116	2 ½c lt brn, choc & red org	.35	.25

50th anniv. of folk dancing in South Africa.

"Chapman" Arriving in 1820 A117

Perf. 15x14
1962, Aug. 20   Photo.   Wmk. 330
282	A117	2 ½c dp plum & bl grn	.40	.25
283	A117	12 ½c choc & blue	3.00	1.60

Unveiling of the precinct stone of the British Settlers Monument at Grahamstown.

Red Disa Orchid, Castle Rock, Kirstenbosch Botanic Gardens — A118

1963, Mar. 14   *Perf. 14*
284	A118	2 ½c multicolored	.40	.25

50th anniv. of the Kirstenbosch Botanic Gardens, Cape Town.

Centenary Emblem and Nurse — A119

12 ½c, Centenary emblem and globe, horiz.

1963, Aug. 30   Wmk. 348   *Perf. 14*
285	A119	2 ½c rose claret, blk & red	.35	.25

Perf. 15x14

286 A119 12½c dk bl gray & red   3.50 1.60
   a.   Red Cross omitted   *1,600.*

Centenary of the International Red Cross.

Assembly Seat, Bunga Building, Umtata A120

Perf. 14½x14

1963, Dec. 11   **Wmk. 348**

287 A120 2½c dk brn & lt grn   .30 .25
   a.   Light green omitted   *1,600.*

Transkei Legislative Assembly, 1st meeting.

Types of 1961

Perf. 15x14, 14x15

1963-67   **Photo.**   **Wmk. 348**

Colors as Before

289 A112b   1c   .25 .25
290 A112a   1½c ('67)   2.25 1.00

Perf. 14

291 A113   2c ('64)   .25 .25
292 A114   2½c (II) ('64)   .50 .25
293 A114   5c ('66)   1.50 .25
294 A114   7½c ('66)   10.00 6.00
295 A114   10c ('64)   1.25 .25
296 A114   20c ('66)   1.50 .45
297 A113   50c ('66)   35.00 7.50
298 A113   1r ('64)   62.50 37.50
   Nos. 289-298 (10)   115.00 53.70

Rugby Board Emblem, Springbok and Ball — A121

Design: 12½c, Rugby player diving over goal line, horiz.

Perf. 14x15, 15x14

1964, May 8   **Photo.**   **Wmk. 348**

301 A121   2½c dk grn & brn   .50 .25
302 A121   12½c yel grn & blk   4.50 3.00

South African Rugby Board, 75th anniv.

John Calvin — A122

1964, July 10   **Perf. 14**

303 A122   2½c choc, brt car & vio   .35 .25

John Calvin (1509-64), French theologian and leader of the Reformation.

Nurse's Lamp — A123

Design: 12½c, Nurse holding lamp, horiz.

Perf. 14x15, 15x14

1964, Oct. 12   **Photo.**   **Wmk. 348**

304 A123   2½c gold & ultra   .50 .25
305 A123   12½c ultra & gold   3.50 3.50
   a.   Gold omitted   *1,500.*

South African Nursing Assoc., 50th anniv.

ITU Emblem and Satellites A124

Design: 12½c, ITU emblem, old and new communication equipment.

1965, May 17   **Perf. 15x14**

306 A124   2½c brt blue & org   .40 .25
307 A124   12½c green & claret   2.75 2.25
   Cent. of the ITU.

Pulpit, Groote Kerk, Cape Town — A125

Design: 12½c, Emblem of Dutch Reformed Church of South Africa, horiz.

Perf. 14x15, 15x14

1965, Oct. 21   **Photo.**   **Wmk. 348**

308 A125   2½c dp brown & yel   .25 .25
309 A125   12½c lt ultra, ocher & blk   1.25 1.10

Tercentenary of the Dutch Reformed Church in South Africa.

Diamond — A126

2½c, Flying bird, symbol of freedom & the future, horiz. 3c, Corn. 7½c, Table Mountain, horiz. Inscribed alternately in English & Afrikaans.

1966, May 31   **Perf. 14**

310 A126   1c blk, yel, dk & lt grn, pair   .50 .50
   a.   Single, English   .25 .25
   b.   Single, Afrikaans   .25 .25
311 A126   2½c dk bl, ultra & yel grn, pair   1.25 1.25
   a.   Single, English   .25 .25
   b.   Single, Afrikaans   .25 .25

Perf. 14x15, 15x14

312 A126   3c red brn, red & yel, pair   2.50 2.50
   a.   Single, English   .25 .25
   b.   Single, Afrikaans   .25 .25
313 A126   7½c ultra, vio bl, och & blk, pair   7.50 7.50
   a.   Single, English   .50 .40
   b.   Single, Afrikaans   .50 .40
   Nos. 310-313 (4)   11.75 11.75

5th anniversary of the Republic.

Nos. 310-313 with watermark 359 are reprints made for U.P.U. presentation booklets.

Hendrik F. Verwoerd and Union Buildings, Pretoria A127

Designs: 3c, Verwoerd's portrait, vert. 12½c, Verwoerd and map of South Africa.

Perf. 15x14, 14x15

1966, Dec. 6   **Photo.**   **Wmk. 348**

314 A127   2½c grnsh blue & blk   .25 .25
315 A127   3c yellow grn & blk   .25 .25
316 A127   12½c dull blue & blk   .75 .65
   Nos. 314-316 (3)   1.25 1.15

Dr. Verwoerd (1901-1966), Prime Minister.

Types of 1961 Redrawn and

Industry — A128

(Inscriptions in larger, bolder type)

½c, 1 ½c and 1r   REPUBLIEK VAN · REPUBLIC OF SUID-AFRIKA · SOUTH AFRICA

On the 1r, the "N" of "VAN" is over the final "A" of "AFRIKA." On Nos. 266 and 298, the "N" is over "KA."

REPUBLIC OF SOUTH AFRICA

REPUBLIEK VAN SUID-AFRIKA

1c, 7 ½c and 12 ½c

REPUBLIEK VAN SUID-AFRIKA

REPUBLIC OF SOUTH AFRICA

2 ½c, 5c, 10c and 20c

REPUBLIC OF SOUTH AFRICA · SUID-AFRIKA

2c, 3c and 50c (similar)

Perf. 14x15, 15x14

1964-68   **Photo.**   **Wmk. 348**

Colors as Before

317 A112a   ½c   .25 .25
   a.   Imperf., pair   400.00
318 A112b   1c   .40 .25

Perf. 14

319 A113   2c ('68)   .40 .25
320 A114   2½c   .45 .25
321 A113   3c   .75 .25
322 A114   12½c   2.75 .25
323 A128   15c ('67)   6.00 .25
324 A113   1r   19.00 3.00
   Nos. 317-324 (8)   30.00 4.75

See No. 339.

Redrawn Types of 1964-68

4c, Groot Constantia (like 2½c). 6c, Corn (like 7½c). 9c, Protea flower (like 12½c).

1967-71   **Photo.**   **Wmk. 359**

326 A112a   ½c   .25 .25
327 A112b   1c   .25 .25
328 A112a   1½c   .25 .25
329 A113   2c ('68)   2.00 .25
330 A114   2½c   .25 .25
331 A113   3c   .25 .25
332 A114   4c ('71)   .40 .25
333 A114   5c ('68)   .25 .25
334 A114   6c ('71)   1.10 .25
335 A114   7½c   1.90 .25
336 A114   9c ('71)   1.40 .25
337 A114   10c ('68)   4.25 .30
338 A114   12½c ('70)   3.50 .65
339 A128   15c ('69)   6.50 .50
340 A114   20c ('68)   8.00 .65
341 A113   50c ('68)   8.75 1.00
342 A113   1r ('68)   12.00 2.10
   Nos. 326-342 (17)   51.30 7.95

Luminescence

Starting in 1969, South Africa began to add phosphorescent "frames" to its definitive stamps.

In 1971, stamps began to appear with the phosphorescent element throughout the paper.

Phosphorescent commemoratives include Nos. 357, 359 et cetera.

Martin Luther — A129

Door of Wittenberg Church — A130

Perf. 14x15

1967, Oct. 31   **Litho.**   **Wmk. 348**

343 A129   2½c pink & black   .25 .25

Wmk. 359

344 A130   12½c black & orange   1.75 1.60

450th anniversary of the Reformation.

Pres. J. J. Fouché — A133

Design: 12½c, Full-face portrait.

Perf. 14x15

1968, Apr. 10   **Photo.**   **Wmk. 348**

345 A133   2½c lt rose brn & dk brn   .25 .25
346 A133   12½c grysh bl & vio bl   .45 .40

Wmk. 359

347 A133   12½c grysh bl & vio bl   .50 .40
   Nos. 345-347 (3)   1.20 1.05

Pres. Jacobus Johannes Fouché, inauguration.

James B. M. Hertzog Statue — A134

Designs: 2½c, Hertzog in 1902, with hat, horiz. 3c, Hertzog in 1924, horiz.

Perf. 13½x14, 14x13½

1968, Sept. 21   **Photo.**   **Wmk. 359**

348 A134   2½c dk brn, lem & blk   .25 .25

Wmk. 348

349 A134   3c multicolored   .25 .25
350 A134   12½c org brn, org & blk   1.50 1.40
   Nos. 348-350 (3)   2.00 1.90

Unveiling of a monument in Bloemfontein honoring James Barry Munnik Hertzog (1866-1942), Boer general, prime minister of South Africa (1924-39).

Natal Pigmy Kingfisher A135

Kaffir Boom Flower A136

1969   **Wmk. 359**   **Photo.**   **Perf. 14**

351 A135   ½c blue & multi   .25 .25
   a.   Perf. 14x14½ (coil)   1.50 .25
352 A136   1c grysh brown & multi   .25 .25

See Nos. 374-375.

Springbok, Torch and Rings — A137

1969, Mar. 15   Perf. 14x13½
353 A137 2½c olive, ind & red   .25 .25
354 A137 12½c bister, ind & red   .95 .85
South African Natl. Games, Bloemfontein, Mar. 15-Apr. 19.

Groote Schuur Hospital and Dr. Barnard A138

Hands Holding Heart A139

Perf. 13½x14
1969, July 7   Photo.   Wmk. 348
355 A138 2½c dp rose, pink & plum .25 .25

Perf. 15x14
Wmk. 359
356 A139 12½c dp bl & dp car   2.00 1.60

1st heart transplant operation (by Dr. Christiaan Barnard) and opening of the 47th South African Medical Cong., Pretoria.

Stagecoach of 1869 — A140

Transvaal No. 1 — A141

Perf. 13½x14, 14x13½
1969, Oct. 6   Photo.   Wmk. 359
357 A140 2½c ocher, Prus bl & yel   .35 .25
358 A141 12½c sal, grn & gold   3.25 2.25
Centenary of South African postage stamps.

Water Drop and Flower — A142

Design: 3c, Waves, horiz.

1970, Feb. 14   Perf. 14
359 A142 2½c brn, brt bl & grn   .25 .25
360 A142 3c pale gray, bl & ind   .50 .25
Issued to publicize the Water 70 campaign of the Department of Water Affairs.

Sower — A143

"BIBLIA" A144

1970, Aug. 24   Photo.   Perf. 14
361 A143 2½c multicolored   .30 .25

Photo; Gold Impressed
362 A144 12½c ultra, blk & gold   2.25 1.90
150th anniv. of the South African Bible Soc.

Strijdom Tower, Johannes G. Strijdom — A145

Map of Antarctica A146

Perf. 14x13½, 13½x14
1971, May 22   Photo.   Wmk. 359
363 A145 5c blue, yel & blk   .50 .25
364 A146 12½c brn bl, vio bl & red   2.25 2.25

Wmk. 330
365 A145 5c blue, yel & blk   2.25 1.00
Nos. 363-365 (3)   5.00 3.50

Intl. Stamp Exhib. (INTERSTEX), Cape Town, May 22-31. No. 364 also for the 10th anniv. of the Antarctic Treaty pledging peaceful uses of and scientific cooperation in Antarctica.

Landing of British Settlers, 1820, by Thomas Baines A147

Martinus Steyn, Paul Kruger, Unification Monument — A148

1971, May 31   Wmk. 359
366 A147 2c magenta & rose red   .25 .25
367 A148 4c blue green & blk   .30 .25
10th anniv. of the Republic of South Africa.

Hendrik Verwoerd Dam A149

1972, Mar. 4   Photo.   Perf. 14
Size: 37x22mm
368 A149 4c shown   .25 .25
369 A149 5c Aerial view of dam   .45 .25
Size: 57x22mm
370 A149 10c Dam, reservoir and Verwoerd   1.50 .90
Nos. 368-370 (3)   2.20 1.40

Inauguration of the Hendrik F. Verwoerd Dam of the Orange River Project.

Ram's Head and Wool Mark — A150

Lamb and Wool Mark — A151

1972, May 15   Wmk. 359   Perf. 14
371 A150 4c blue & multi   .25 .25
372 A151 15c dull bl & dk bl   1.75 .40
South African wool industry. Issued in sheets of 100 with advertisements in margin. See Nos. 378-378A, 382A.

Cats — A152

1972, Sept. 19   Wmk. 359
373 A152 5c multicolored   1.50 .40
Centenary of the SPCA.

Redrawn Types of 1964-69 and Types of 1972
Perf. 14x15 (½c), 14 (1c, #382A), 12½

1972-74   Photo.   Unwmk.
374 A135 ½c blue & multi   8.00 8.75
375 A136 1c grysh brn & red   .25 .25
376 A113 2c brt blue & org   .55 .25
377 A113 3c rose red & bluish black   .60 .70
378 A150 4c blue & multi   1.00 .25
378A A150 4c brown & multi   .45 .25
379 A114 5c grnsh bl & yel   1.25 .30
380 A114 6c emerald & brn   2.75 4.25
381 A114 9c dk grn, red & yel   2.50 .85
382 A114 10c emer & dk brn   2.75 .50
382A A151 15c dull bl & dk bl   3.00 4.00
383 A114 20c sal, sl bl & pink   3.00 .65
384 A113 50c ultra & black   7.75 2.00
385 A113 1r bl, org & grn   21.00 4.00
Nos. 374-385 (14)   54.85 27.00

Issued: 2c, 1972; 6c, 15c, 1974: others, 1973.

Pylon — A153

Designs: 4c, Electrical usage, pylon, power plant, horiz. 15c, Smokestacks.

1973, Feb. 1   Photo.   Perf. 12x12½
Size: 37½x20mm
386 A153 4c blue & multi   .25 .25

Arms of University A154

Old University, Cape Town A156

New University, Pretoria A155

Size: 20x27mm
Perf. 12½
387 A153 5c blue & black   .35 .25
388 A153 15c ocher & multi   3.75 1.50
Nos. 386-388 (3)   4.35 2.00
Electricity Supply Commission, 50th anniv.

1973, Apr. 2   Unwmk.   Perf. 12½
389 A154 4c blue & multi   .25 .25

Perf. 12x12½
Wmk. 359
390 A155 5c gold & multi   .35 .25

Unwmk.   Perf. 12½
391 A156 15c gold & blk   3.25 1.65
Cent. of the Univ. of South Africa (UNISA).

Woltemade, Sailor and Horse — A157

Designs: 5c, Sinking ship in storm. 15c, "De Jonge Thomas" sinking.

1973, June 2   Photo.   Perf. 12x12½
392 A157 4c brown red, ol & blk   .25 .25
393 A157 5c olive, blk & citron   .45 .25
394 A157 15c brown, blk & ocher   4.50 4.50
Nos. 392-394 (3)   6.20 5.00

Bicentenary of Wolraad Woltemade's heroism in saving 14 people from the ship "De Jonge Thomas" in Table Bay.

C. J. Langenhoven and Anthem — A158

4c, 5c, vert., Portrait and signature.

1973, Aug. 1   Perf. 12½
Size: 27x20mm
395 A158 4c orange, blk & ultra   .75 .25

Perf. 12½x12, 12x12½
Size: 21x38mm, 37x21mm
396 A158 5c orange, blk & ultra   .90 .25
397 A158 15c orange, blk & ultra   4.50 1.50
Nos. 395-397 (3)   6.15 2.00

Cornelis Jacob Langenhoven (1873-1932), lawyer, writer, who worked for recognition of Afrikaans language.

World Map and Communications Network — A159

Perf. 12½
1973, Oct. 1   Photo.   Unwmk.
398 A159 15c ultra & multi   .60   .50
a.   Wmk. 359   1.50 1.25
International Telecommunications Day.

Restored Houses,
Tulbagh — A160

Design: 5c, Church Street, Tulbagh.

1974, Mar. 14   Unwmk.   Perf. 12½
Size: 27x21mm
400 A160 4c Prus green & multi   .25   .25
Size: 57x20mm
401 A160 5c ocher & multi   .35   .25
Restoration of historic Church Street in
Tulbagh after 1969 earthquake.

Burgerspond — A161

1974, Apr. 7   Litho.   Perf. 12½x12
402 A161 9c multicolored   .55   .40
Centenary of the first official coin struck in
South Africa, 1874. The £1 gold coin shows
portrait of Pres. Thomas Francois Burger.

Prime Minister D. F.
Malan — A162

1974, May 22   Photo.   Unwmk.
403 A162 4c lt ultra & dk blue   .70   .35
Centenary of the birth of Daniel F. Malan
(1874-1959), prime minister of South Africa.

Congress
Emblem
A163

1974, June 13   Perf. 12x12½
404 A163 15c silver & dk blue   .70   .35
15th World Sugar Cong., Durban, 6/13-30.

"50"
A164

1974, July 13   Photo.   Unwmk.
405 A164 4c red & black   .40   .25
50th anniversary of radio in South Africa.

Cultural Center, Grahamstown — A165

1974, July 13   Perf. 12x12½
406 A165 5c red & black   .35   .25
Natl. Monument to British settlers of 1820.

Natal No. 78, Transvaal No. 145, Cape
of Good Hope No. 28 and Orange
River Colony No. 4 — A166

1974, Oct. 9   Photo.   Perf. 12½
407 A166 15c multicolored   .75   .65
Centenary of Universal Postal Union.

Wild   Cape
Iris — A167   Gannet — A168

Galjoen — A169

Bokmakierie (Shrike) — A170

Designs: 2c, Heather. 3c, Geranium. 4c,
Calla lily. 7c, Zebrafish. 9c, Angelfish. 10c,
Moorish idol. 14c, Roman fish. 15c, Greater
double-collared sunbird. 20c, Yellow-billed
hornbill. 25c, Barberton daisy. 50c, Blue
cranes. 1r, Bateleur eagles.

Photo. and Engr.
1974, Nov. 11   Unwmk.   Perf. 12½
408 A167 1c pink & multi   .25   .25
409 A167 2c yellow & multi   .25   .25
410 A167 3c multicolored   .25   .25
411 A167 4c multicolored   .25   .25
412 A168 5c dull blue & multi   .25   .25
413 A169 6c multicolored   .25   .25
414 A169 7c lilac & multi   .30   .25
415 A169 9c buff & multi   .35   .25
416 A169 10c lt blue & multi   .40   .25
417 A169 14c salmon & multi   .60   .25
418 A168 15c gray & multi   .60   .25
419 A168 20c yellow & multi   .80   .30
420 A167 25c dk brown & multi   1.10   .35
Perf. 12x12½
421 A170 30c gray & multi   4.50   .75
422 A170 50c citron & multi   4.00 1.00
423 A170 1r multicolored   7.50 2.00
       Nos. 408-423 (16)   21.65 7.15
The coils that follow are two colors while the
above sheet stamps are multicolored.

1974   Photo.   Perf. 12½
Coil Stamps
430 A167 1c pink & violet   .45   .40
431 A167 2c yellow & grn   .90   .45
432 A168 5c dull blue & blk   2.00   .75
433 A169 10c lt blue & indigo   5.00 5.00
       Nos. 430-433 (4)   8.35 6.60
See note on color that follows No. 423.

1975-76   Same Designs   Perf. 14
430a A167   1c   .55   .25
431a A167   2c ('76)   .45   .25
433a A169 10c ('76)   5.00 5.50
       Nos. 430a-433a (3)   6.00 6.00
No. 430a has black control number on back
of every fifth stamp.

Voortrekker Monument and
Encampment — A171

1974, Dec. 6   Unwmk.   Perf. 12½
438 A171 4c multicolored   .35   .25
Voortrekker Monument, 25th anniversary.

Sasolburg
Refinery
A172

Perf. 12x12½, 12½
1975, Feb. 26   Litho.
439 A172 15c red & multi   .75   .65
25th anniversary of South Africa Coal, Oil
and Gas Corp., Ltd. (SASOL).

Pres. Nicolaes
Diederichs — A173

Litho. and Engr.
1975, Apr. 19   Perf. 12½x12
440 A173 4c brown & gold   .25   .25
Litho.
441 A173 15c ultra & gold   .40   .40
Installation of Dr. Nicolaes Diederichs as
third State President.

Jan C.
Smuts — A174

1975, May 24   Litho. and Engr.
442 A174 4c black   .30   .25
Smuts (1870-1950), lawyer, gen., statesman.

Dutch East
Indiaman,
by Baines
A175

Designs: Paintings by John Thomas Baines.

1975, June 18   Photo.   Perf. 12x12½
443 A175 5c gold & multi   .25   .25
444 A175 9c gold & multi   .25   .25
445 A175 15c gold & multi   .30   .25
446 A175 30c gold & multi   .55   .55
a.   Souvenir sheet of 4   1.25 1.25
       Nos. 443-446 (4)   1.35 1.30
John Thomas Baines (1820-75), painter.
#446a contains 4 litho. stamps similar to #443-
446.

Gideon Malherbe
House,
Paarl — A176

Photo. and Engr.
1975, Aug. 14   Perf. 12½
447 A176 4c multicolored   .30   .25
Society of Real Afrikaners (Genootskap van
Regte Afrikaaners), cent.

Automatic Letter
Sorting — A177

1975, Sept. 11 Photo. Perf. 12½x12
448 A177 4c brt blue & multi   .30   .25
Postal automation.

Title Page, First   Afrikaans
Afrikaans   Monument,
Paper — A178   Paarl — A179

1975, Oct. 10   Litho.   Perf. 12½x12
449 A178 4c black & orange   .25   .25
450 A179 5c multicolored   .25   .25
Inauguration of Afrikaans Language
Monument.

Table Mountain — A180

1975, Nov. 13   Litho.   Perf. 12½
451 A180 15c shown   2.75 1.75
452 A180 15c Johannesburg   2.75 1.75
453 A180 15c Cape vineyards   2.75 1.75
454 A180 15c Lions, Kruger
                Natl. Park   2.75 1.75
a.   Block of 4, #451-454   11.00 11.00
Tourist publicity.

Satellites, Radar and Africa on
Globe — A181

1975, Dec. 3   Litho.   Perf. 12½
455 A181 15c dk vio blue & multi   .30   .25
Satellite communications.

Lawn Bowler — A182

No. 457, Cricket batsman. No. 458, Polo player. No. 459, Golfer (Gary Player).

1976   Photo.   Perf. 12½x12
456 A182 15c green & blk   .45   .25
457 A182 15c yellow grn & blk   .45   .25
458 A182 15c olive & blk   .45   .25
459 A182 15c brt green & blk   .45   .25
  a. Miniature sheet of 4, #456-459   2.00   1.90
    Nos. 456-459 (4)   1.80   1.00

3rd World Bowling Championships, Zoo Lake Club, Johannesburg, Feb. 1976 (No. 456); cent. of cricket in South Africa (No. 457); intl. polo (No. 458); Gary Player, South African golf champion (No. 459).
Issue dates: #456, Feb. 18. #457, Mar. 12. #458, Aug. 16. #459, 459a, Dec. 2.

No. 456 Overprinted in Gold

1976, Apr. 6   Photo.   Perf. 12½x12
460 A182 15c green & black   .45   .45

Victory of South Africa in 3rd World Bowling championships.

Picnic under Baobab Tree A183

Paintings by Erich Mayer: 10c, Wagons at Foot of Blauberg, Transvaal. 15c, Hartbeesspoort Dam, near Pretoria. 20c, Street in Doornfontein.

1976, Apr. 20   Photo.   Perf. 12x12½
461 A183 4c ocher & multi   .25   .25
462 A183 10c dk green & multi   .25   .25
463 A183 15c multicolored   .35   .30
464 A183 20c multicolored   .60   .55
  a. Souvenir sheet of 4, #461-464   1.75   1.75
    Nos. 461-464 (4)   1.45   1.35

Erich Mayer (1876-1960), painter. Artist's signature in horizontal gutter between 2 setenant pairs.

Wildlife Protection A184

1976, June 5   Litho.   Perf. 12x12½
465 A184 3c Cheetah   .25   .25
466 A184 10c Black rhinoceros   .30   .25
467 A184 15c Blesbok   .60   .35
468 A184 20c Zebra   .75   .50
    Nos. 465-468 (4)   1.90   1.35

All values exist on yellow toned paper. Value, twice that of stamps on white paper.

Emily Hobhouse, by Johan Hoekstra — A185

1976, June 8   Photo.   Perf. 12½x12
469 A185 4c multicolored   .30   .25

Emily Hobhouse (1860-1926), the "Angel of Mercy" during Anglo-Boer War.

S.S. Dunrobin Castle, 1876 A186

1976, Oct. 5   Litho.   Perf. 12x12½
470 A186 10c multicolored   .75   .30

Ocean Mail Service contract, centenary.

Family with Globe — A187

1976, Nov. 6   Photo.   Perf. 12½x12
471 A187 4c salmon & dull red   .30   .25

Family planning.

Wine Glasses — A188

1977, Feb. 14   Litho.   Perf. 12½x12
472 A188 15c multicolored   .50   .25
  a. Word "Die" omitted from left inscription   16.00   20.00

Quality of the Vintage Symposium, Cape Town, Feb. 14-21.

Jacob Daniel du Toit — A189

1977, Feb. 21   Photo.
473 A189 4c multicolored   .30   .25

Dr. Jacob Daniel du Toit (Totius; 1877-1953), theologian, educator, poet.

Transvaal Supreme Court A190

1977, May 18   Photo.   Perf. 12x12½
474 A190 4c red brown   .30   .25

Transvaal Supreme Court, centenary.

Sugarbush (Protea Repens) — A191

Photo. (1-5, 8, 10, 15, 20c); Litho. (others)
1977, May 27   Perf. 12½
475 A191 1c shown   .25   .25
476 A191 2c P. punctata   .25   .25
477 A191 3c P. nerilfolia   .25   .25
478 A191 4c P. longifolia   .25   .25
479 A191 5c P. cynaroides   .25   .25
480 A191 6c P. canaliculata   .25   .25
481 A191 7c P. lorea   .25   .25
482 A191 8c P. mundii   .25   .25
483 A191 9c P. roupelliae   .25   .25
484 A191 10c P. aristata   .25   .25
485 A191 15c P. eximia   .25   .25
486 A191 20c P. magnifica   .25   .25
487 A191 25c P. grandiceps   .30   .25
488 A191 30c P. amplexicaulis   .45   .25
489 A191 50c Leucospermum cordifolium   .60   .30
490 A191 1r Paranomus reflexus   1.60   .90
491 A191 2r Orothamnus zeyheri   3.50   1.75
    Nos. 475-491 (17)   9.45   6.45

Perf. 14
477a A191 3c Litho.   .25   .25
479a A191 5c   .25   .25
480a A191 6c   .25   .25
481a A191 7c   .25   .25
482a A191 8c   .25   .25
483a A191 9c   .25   .25
484a A191 10c   .25   .25
486a A191 20c Litho.   .85   .35
487a A191 25c   .65   .65
488a A191 30c   .80   .30
490a A191 1r   3.00   .95
491a A191 2r   5.75   1.75
    Nos. 477a-491a (13)   14.30   5.85

Perf. 14 Vertically
Photo.   Coil Stamps
492 A191 1c Silver tree   .30   .25
493 A191 2c Bottle brush   .30   .25
494 A191 5c Blushing bride   .30   .25
495 A191 10c Leucadendrom sessile   .30   .25
    Nos. 492-495 (4)   1.20   1.00

Some printings have control number on back of every fifth stamp.

Gymnastics — A192

1977, Aug. 15   Litho.   Perf. 12½x12
496 A192 15c multicolored   .40   .30

8th Intl. Cong. of Physical Education and Sports for Girls and Women, Cape Town, Aug. 14-20.

World Map and "M" A193

1977, Sept. 15   Litho.   Perf. 12x12½
497 A193 15c multicolored   .40   .30

Introduction of international metric system.

Nuclear Power Plant and Uranium Atom A194

1977, Oct. 8
498 A194 15c multicolored   .40   .30

Uranium development.

Flag of South Africa A195

1977, Nov. 11
499 A195 5c multicolored   .25   .25

50th anniversary of national flag.

Walvis Bay, 1878 — A196

1978, Mar. 10   Litho.   Perf. 12½
500 A196 15c multicolored   .55   .40

Centenary of Walvis Bay annexation.

Dr. Andrew Murray — A197

1978, May 9   Perf. 12½x12
501 A197 4c multicolored   .25   .25

Dr. Andrew Murray, pioneer theologian, 150th birth anniversary.

Railroad Rail and ISCOR Emblem — A198

1978, June 5   Litho.   Perf. 12
502 A198 15c multicolored   .45   .40

50th anniversary of ISCOR (Iron and Steel Industrial Corporation).

Saldanha Bay — A199

Design: No. 504, Richard's Bay.

1978, July 21   Litho.   Perf. 12½
503 A199 15c multicolored   .55   .55
504 A199 15c multicolored   .55   .55
  a. Pair, #503-504   1.10   1.10

Opening of new harbors on east and west coasts of South Africa.

Landscape by Volschenk — A200

Designs: Landscapes by J. E. A. Volschenk.

1978, Aug. 21
505 A200 10c multicolored   .25   .25
506 A200 15c multicolored   .25   .25
507 A200 20c multicolored   .35   .35

508 A200 25c multicolored   .45   .45
  a. Souvenir sheet of 4, #505-508   1.90 1.90
    Nos. 505-508 (4)   1.30 1.30
Jan Ernst Abraham Volschenk (1853-1936), first South African professional artist.

B. J. Vorster — A201

1978, Oct. 10   Litho.   Perf. 12½x12
509 A201 4c maroon & gold   .25   .25
  a. Perf. 14½x14   .75   .30

Perf. 14½x14
510 A201 15c violet & gold   .40   .30
Inauguration of Balthazar John Vorster as president of South Africa.

Golden Gate Highlands National Park — A202

Designs: 15c, Blyde River Canyon, Transvaal. 20c, Amphitheater, Natal National Park. 25c, Cango Caves, Cape Province.

1978, Nov. 13   Perf. 12½
511 A202 10c multicolored   .25   .25
512 A202 15c multicolored   .25   .25
513 A202 20c multicolored   .35   .35
514 A202 25c multicolored   .55   .55
  Nos. 511-514 (4)   1.40 1.40
Tourist publicity.

Tellurometer and Dr. I. R. Wadley — A203

1979, Feb. 12   Litho.   Perf. 12½
515 A203 15c multicolored   .30   .25
15th anniversary of the invention of the tellurometer (to measure radio distances).

South Africa No. C5 A204

1979, Mar. 30   Litho.   Perf. 14½x14
516 A204 15c multicolored   .35   .30
First stamp printed by South African Government Printer, 50th anniversary.

"Save Fuel" A205

Fuel Economy: No. 518, Language inscriptions reversed.

1979, Apr. 2   Photo.   Perf. 12x12½
517 A205 4c red & black   .25   .25
518 A205 4c red & black   .25   .25
  a. Pair, #517-518   .40   .40

Battle of Isandlwana, by Melton Prior — A206

15c, Battle of Ulundi, by Louis Creswicke. 20c, Battle of Rorke's Drift, by Lt. Col. Crealock.

1979, May 25   Litho.   Perf. 14x13½
519 A206 4c red & black   .25   .25
520 A206 15c red & black   .40   .35
521 A206 20c red & black   .50   .40
  a. Souv. sheet, #519-521 + label 3.00 3.00
    Nos. 519-521 (3)   1.15 1.00
Centenary of Zulu War.

"Health Care and Service" — A207

1979, June 19   Litho.   Perf. 12½x12
522 A207 4c multicolored   .25   .25
  a. Perf. 14¼x14   .30   .30
Health Year.

Boy and Girl Watching Candle — A208

1979, Sept. 13   Litho.   Perf. 14½x14
523 A208 4c multicolored   .25   .25
South African Christmas Stamp Fund, 50th anniversary.

Cape Town University, 150th Anniversary — A209

1979, Oct. 1   Litho.   Perf. 14x14½
524 A209 4c multicolored   .25   .25
  a. Perf. 12x12½   .30   .30

Gary Player Rose — A210

Roses: 15c, Prof. Chris Bernard. 20c, Southern Sun. 25c, Soaring Wings.

1979, Oct. 4   Litho.   Perf. 14½x14
525 A210 4c multicolored   .25   .25
526 A210 15c multicolored   .35   .30
527 A210 20c multicolored   .45   .40
528 A210 25c multicolored   .65   .55
  a. Souvenir sheet of 4, #525-528 2.25 2.25
    Nos. 525-528 (4)   1.70 1.50
Rosafari 1979, 4th World Rose Convention, Pretoria, October.

Stellenbosch University — A211

1979, Nov. 8
529 A211 4c shown   .25   .25
530 A211 15c Rhenish Church   .30   .25
Stellenbosch (oldest town in South Africa), 300th anniversary.

A212

1979, Dec. 18   Photo.   Perf. 12½x12
531 A212 4c multicolored   .25   .25
Federation of Afrikaans Cultural Societies, 50th anniv.

A213

Paintings by Pieter Wenning (1873-1921): 5c, Still Life with Sweet Peas. 25c, House in the Suburbs, Cape Town.

1980, May 6   Litho.   Perf. 14½x14
532 A213 5c multicolored   .25   .25
Size: 45x37mm
533 A213 25c multicolored   .40   .30
  a. Souvenir sheet of 2, #532-533 .90   .65

Great Star of Africa Diamond — A214

1980, May 12   Litho.   Perf. 14x14½
534 A214 15c shown   .65   .50
535 A214 20c Cullinan II diamond   .75   .65
World Diamond Congress.

A215

1980, Sept. 3   Litho.   Perf. 14½x14
536 A215 5c multicolored   .25   .25
Christian Louis Leipoldt (1880-1947), writer and physician.

A216

1980, Oct. 9   Litho.
537 A216 5c multicolored   .25   .25
University of Pretoria, 50th anniv.

Marine With Ships, by Willem van de Velde — A217

Paintings: 10c, Firetail and Trainer, by George Stubbs. 15c, Lavinia, by Thomas Gainsborough, vert. 20c, Landscape, by Pieter Post.

1980, Nov. 3   Perf. 14½x14
538 A217 5c multicolored   .25   .25
539 A217 10c multicolored   .25   .25
540 A217 15c multicolored   .25   .25
541 A217 20c multicolored   .30   .30
  a. Souvenir sheet of 4, #538-541 1.00 1.00
    Nos. 538-541 (4)   1.05 1.05
Natl. Gallery, 50th anniv.

P.J. Joubert, Paul Kruger, M.W. Pretorius (First Leaders of Triumvirate Government) — A218

Design: 10c, Monument, flag of South African Republic, 1880, vert.

1980, Dec. 15   Perf. 14x14½ 14½x14
542 A218 5c multicolored   .25   .25
543 A218 10c multicolored   .25   .25
Paardekraal Monument (built on site of founding of triumverate government) centennial.

British Troops in Battle of Amajuba — A219

1981, Feb. 27   Litho.   Perf. 14x14½
544 A219 5c Boer snipers, vert.   .25   .25
545 A219 15c shown   .35   .35
Battle of Amajuba centenary (led to independence of Orange Free State).

Scene from Verdi's Aida A220

1981, May 23   Litho.   Perf. 14½x14
546 A220 20c Raka ballet scene   .35   .30
547 A220 25c shown   .45   .35
  a. Souvenir sheet of 2, #546-547 1.25 1.00
Opening of State Theater, Pretoria.

Pres. Marais
Viljoen — A221

1981, May 30   **Perf. 14x14½**
       Size: 57x21mm
548 A221 5c Former presidents   .25   .25
549 A221 15c shown   .30   .25

Deaf Girl Learning to
Speak — A222

1981, June 12   **Perf. 14½x14**
550 A222 5c shown   .25   .25
551 A222 15c Man reading braille   .30   .25
       Institute for the Deaf and Blind, Worcester,
centenary.

Natl. Cancer Assn.
50th Anniv. — A223

1981, July 10
552 A223 5c multicolored   .25   .25

Calanthe
Natalensis — A224

1981, Sept. 11   **Litho.**
553 A224 5c shown   .25   .25
554 A224 15c Eulophia speciosa   .30   .25
555 A224 20c Disperis fanniniae   .40   .25
556 A224 25c Disa uniflora   .50   .35
a.   Souvenir sheet of 4, #553-556   2.00 1.90
       Nos. 553-556 (4)   1.45 1.10
10th World Orchid Conf., Durban, 9/11-17.

Voortrekker
Movement, 50th
Anniv. — A225

1981, Sept. 30   **Perf. 14x14½**
557 A225 5c multicolored   .25   .25

Scouting
Year — A226

1982, Feb. 22   Litho.   Perf. 14½x14
558 A226 15c Baden-Powell   .40   .25

TB Bacillus
Centenary — A227

1982, Mar. 24   **Litho.**
559 A227 20c multicolored   .40   .25

Return of Simonstown Naval Base,
25th Anniv. — A228

1982, Apr. 2   **Perf. 14½x14**
560 A228 8c Submarine   .25   .25
561 A228 15c Strike craft   .25   .25
562 A228 20c Mine sweeper   .25   .25
563 A228 25c Harbor patrol
       boats   .35   .25
a.   Souvenir sheet of 4, #560-563   2.75 2.25
       Nos. 560-563 (4)   1.10 1.00

Old Provost,
Grahamstown
A229

Design: 2c, Tuynhuys, Kaapstad (Cape
Town). 3c, Appelhof, Bloemfontein. 4c, Raad-
saal, Pretoria. 5c, Die Kasteel, Kaapstad. 6c,
Goewermentsgebou, Bloemfontein. 7c,
Drostdy, Graaf-Reinet. 8c, Leeuwenhof, Cape
Town. 9c, Libertas, Pretoria. 10c, City Hall,
Pietermaritzburg. 11c, City Hall, Kimberley.
12c, City Hall, Port Elizabeth. 14c, Johannes-
burg City Hall. 15c, Hotel Milner, Matjes-
fontein. 16c, Durban City Hall. 20c, Post
Office, Durban. 25c, Melrose House, Pretoria.
30c, Old Legislative Assembly Building, Pieter-
maritzburg. 50c, Raadsaal, Bloemfontein. 1r,
Houses of Parliament, Cape Town. 2r,
Uniegebou, Pretoria.
       Coils have different designs.

1982-87   **Litho.**   **Perf. 14x14½**
564 A229 1c brown ('84)   .25   .25
565 A229 2c apple green   .25   .25
566 A229 2c green   .75   .25
567 A229 2c slate grn ('85)   .25   .25
568 A229 3c purple ('85)   1.25   .25
569 A229 4c olive grn ('85)   .25   .25
570 A229 5c carmine   .25   .25
571 A229 6c brt green   .25   .25
572 A229 7c gray green   .25   .25
573 A229 8c blue   .25   .25
574 A229 8c intense bl ('83)   .25   .25
575 A229 9c brt rose lilac   .25   .25
576 A229 10c lt red brown   .25   .25
577 A229 10c violet brn ('83)   .30   .25
578 A229 11c cerise ('84)   .25   .25
579 A229 12c dp ultra ('85)   .35   .25
580 A229 14c rose brn ('86)   .50   .25
581 A229 16c red ('87)   .60   .25
582 A229 20c vermilion   .25   .25
583 A229 20c black ('85)   .60   .25
584 A229 25c bister   .25   .25

       Size: 45x27mm
       Perf. 14½x14
586 A229 30c brown ('86)   1.50   .25
587 A229 50c Prus blue ('86)   2.25   .25
588 A229 1r violet blue ('86)   2.50   .25
589 A229 2r cerise ('85)   5.00   .25
       Nos. 564-589 (25)   19.10 6.25
       For surcharge see No. B12.

       Engr.
590 A229 1c dark brown   .25   .25
591 A229 2c slate grn ('83)   .25   .25
592 A229 3c violet   .25   .25
593 A229 4c olive green   .25   .25
594 A229 5c dark lake ('83)   .25   .25
595 A229 6c green blk ('84)   .25   .35
596 A229 15c blue   .25   .25
597 A229 20c black ('83)   .50   .25

       Size: 45x27mm
       Perf. 14½x14
598 A229 30c violet brown   .45   .25
599 A229 50c Prus blue   .70   .25
600 A229 1r violet blue   1.50   .25
601 A229 2r rose carmine   3.00   .30
       Nos. 590-601 (12)   7.90 3.15
In some cases there are slight design differences from litho. stamp.

       Perf. 14 Horiz.
       Photo.   Coil Stamps
1c, Residence, Swellendam. 2c, City Hall,
East London. 5c, Rissik St. PO, Johannesburg. 10c, Morgenster, Somerset West.
602 A229 1c brown   .25   .25
603 A229 2c green   .40   .25
604 A229 5c dark red   .45   .25
605 A229 10c brown   .70   .25
       Nos. 602-605 (4)   1.80 1.00

Bradysaurus
A230

Prehistoric Animals (Karoo Fossils).

1982, Dec. 1   Litho.   Perf. 14x14½
606 A230 8c shown   .25   .25
607 A230 15c Lystrosaurus   .45   .25
608 A230 20c Euparkeria   .60   .25
609 A230 25c Thrinaxodon   .90   .35
a.   Souvenir sheet of 4, #606-609   1.75 1.75
       Nos. 606-609 (4)   2.20 1.10

Weather
Station,
Gough
Island
A231

20c, Marion Island station. 25c, Reading
instruments. 40c, Weather balloon, Antarctica.

1983, Jan. 19   **Litho.**
610 A231 8c shown   .25   .25
611 A231 20c multicolored   .30   .25
612 A231 25c multicolored   .40   .25
613 A231 40c multicolored   .60   .40
       Nos. 610-613 (4)   1.55 1.15

Steam Locomotives — A232

1983, Apr. 27   **Litho.**
614 A232 10c Class S2, 1952   .25   .25
615 A232 20c Class 16E, 1935   .45   .35
616 A232 25c Class 6H, 1901   .60   .45
617 A232 40c Class 15F, 1939   1.00   .70
       Nos. 614-617 (4)   2.30 1.75

Soccer — A233

       Perf. 14½x14 (10c, 25c), 14x14½
       (20c, 40c)
1983, July 20   **Litho.**
618 A233 10c Rugby, vert.   .25   .25
619 A233 20c shown   .25   .25
620 A233 25c Sailing, vert.   .35   .25
621 A233 40c Equestrian   .45   .30
       Nos. 618-621 (4)   1.30 1.05

Plettenberg Bay — A234

1983, Oct. 12   Litho.   Perf. 14½x14
622 A234 10c shown   .25   .25
623 A234 20c Durban Beach   .25   .25
624 A234 25c West Coast beach   .25   .25
625 A234 40c Clifton beach
       scene   .40   .30
a.   Souvenir sheet of 4, #622-625   1.50 1.40
       Nos. 622-625 (4)   1.15 1.05

English Writers of
South Africa — A235

Designs: 10c, Thomas Pringle (1789-1834).
20c, Pauline Smith (1882-1959). 25c, Olive
Schreiner (1855-1920). 40c, Percy FitzPatrick
(1862-1931).

1984, Feb. 24   Litho.   Perf. 14½x14
626 A235 10c multicolored   .25   .25
627 A235 20c multicolored   .25   .25
628 A235 25c multicolored   .25   .25
629 A235 40c multicolored   .45   .25
       Nos. 626-629 (4)   1.20 1.00

Manganese — A236

1984, June 8   Litho.   Perf. 14x14½
630 A236 11c shown   .30   .25
631 A236 20c Chromium   .55   .25
632 A236 25c Vanadium   .75   .25
633 A236 30c Titanium   .85   .30
       Nos. 630-633 (4)   2.45 1.05

Bloukrans
River
Bridge
A237

25c, Durban 4-level Bridge Interchange.
30c, Mfolozi Railroad Bridge. 45c, Gouritz
River Bridge.

1984, Aug. 24
634 A237 11c shown   .25   .25
635 A237 25c multicolored   .50   .25
636 A237 30c multicolored   .60   .25
637 A237 45c multicolored   .90   .40
       Nos. 634-637 (4)   2.25 1.15

New Constitution
A238

No. 638, Preamble (English). No. 639, Preamble (Africaans). No. 640, Symbolic pillars, anthem. No. 641, Arms.

1984, Sept. 3   Litho.   Perf. 14x14½
638	A238	11c multicolored	.35	.25
639	A238	11c multicolored	.35	.25
a.		Pair, #638-639	.70	.35
640	A238	25c multicolored	.75	.40
641	A238	30c multicolored	.85	.45
		Nos. 638-641 (4)	2.30	1.35

Military Medals — A239

1984, Nov. 9   Perf. 14½x14
642	A239	11c Pro Patria	.25	.25
643	A239	25c De Wet	.25	.25
644	A239	30c John Chard Decoration	.40	.25
645	A239	45c Honoris Crux	.55	.30
a.		Miniature sheet of 4, #642-645	1.25	1.10
		Nos. 642-645 (4)	1.45	1.05

Pres. Pieter Willem Botha (b. 1916) — A240

1984, Nov. 2   Litho.   Perf. 14x14½
646	A240	11c multicolored	.30	.25
647	A240	25c multicolored	.60	.30

Frans David Oerder, Painter (1867-1944) A241

11c, Reflections. 25c, Ladies in a Garden. 30c, Still-Life with Lobster. 50c, Still-Life with Marigolds.

1985, Feb. 22   Litho.   Perf. 14½x14
648	A241	11c multicolored	.25	.25
649	A241	25c multicolored	.25	.25
650	A241	30c multicolored	.30	.25
651	A241	50c multicolored	.45	.25
a.		Souvenir sheet of 4, #648-651	1.50	1.50
		Nos. 648-651 (4)	1.25	1.00

Cape Parliament Cent. A242

12c, Parliament. 25c, Speaker's chair. 30c, The National Convention, by Edward Roworth. 50c, South African arms.

1985, May 15   Litho.
652	A242	12c multicolored	.25	.25
653	A242	25c multicolored	.30	.25
654	A242	30c multicolored	.35	.25
655	A242	50c multicolored	.65	.30
		Nos. 652-655 (4)	1.55	1.05

Indigenous Flowers — A243

1985, Aug. 23   Litho.   Perf. 14½x14
656	A243	12c Freesia	.25	.25
657	A243	25c Nerine	.35	.25
658	A243	30c Ixia	.40	.25
659	A243	50c Gladiolus	.70	.45
		Nos. 656-659 (4)	1.70	1.20

Cape Silver — A244

1985, Nov. 5   Perf. 14½x14, 14x14½
660	A244	12c Sugar bowl, horiz.	.25	.25
661	A244	25c Tea pot, horiz.	.40	.25
662	A244	30c Goblet	.50	.25
663	A244	50c Coffee pot	.90	.35
		Nos. 660-663 (4)	2.05	1.10

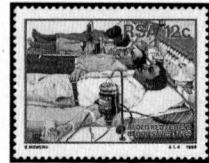

Blood Transfusion Services A245

1986, Feb. 20   Perf. 14½x14
664	A245	12c Blood donation	.30	.25
665	A245	20c Transfusion	.70	.25
666	A245	25c Surgery	.90	.25
667	A245	30c Emergency aid	1.10	.35
		Nos. 664-667 (4)	3.00	1.10

Republic of South Africa, 25th Anniv. A246

1986, May 30   Litho.   Perf. 14x14½
668	A246	14c Text in Afrikaans	.75	.25
669	A246	14c Text in English	.75	.25
a.		Pair, #668-669	2.00	2.00

Cultural Heritage — A247

Restoration projects: 14c, Drostdyhof, Free Street, Graaff-Reinet, 19th cent. 20c, Pilgrim's Rest, Eastern Transvaal, 1873. 25c, J.T. Strapp and Son importers, c. 1893, Bethlehem. 30c, Palmdene, c. 1897, Pietermaritzburg.

1986, Aug. 14   Perf. 14½x14
670	A247	14c multicolored	.40	.25
671	A247	20c multicolored	.60	.30
672	A247	25c multicolored	.70	.35
673	A247	30c multicolored	.85	.40
		Nos. 670-673 (4)	2.55	1.30

Johannesburg, Cent. — A248

Discovery of Gold in Roodepoort, Cent. — A249

14c, Johannesburg, 1886. 20c, Gold mine. 25c, Johannesburg, 1986. 30c, Gold.

1986, Sept. 25   Perf. 14x14½
674	A248	14c multicolored	.65	.25
675	A249	20c multicolored	.95	.35
676	A248	25c multicolored	1.10	.40
677	A249	30c multicolored	1.40	.50
a.		Souvenir sheet of 1	1.90	1.90
		Nos. 674-677 (4)	4.10	1.50

No. 677a for Johannesburg stamp exhibition. Sold for 50c.

Pearl Mountain — A250

20c, The Column, Drakensburg. 25c, Maltese Cross, Cedarberg. 30c, Bourke's Luck Potholes.

1986, Nov. 20   Litho.   Perf. 14x14½
678	A250	14c multicolored	.50	.50
679	A250	20c multicolored	.70	.70
680	A250	25c multicolored	.90	.90
681	A250	30c multicolored	1.10	1.10
		Nos. 678-681 (4)	3.20	3.20

Beetles — A251

No. 690, Chaetodera regalis. No. 691, Trichostetha fascicularis. No. 692, Julodis viridipes. No. 693, Ceroplesis militaris.

1987, Mar. 6   Litho.   Perf. 14x14½
690	A251	14c multicolored	.50	.50
691	A251	20c multicolored	.70	.70
692	A251	25c multicolored	.90	.90
693	A251	30c multicolored	1.10	1.10
		Nos. 690-693 (4)	3.20	3.20

Petroglyphs A252

16c, Eland, Sebaaieni Cave. 20c, Leaping lion, Clocolan. 25c, Black wildebeest, uMhlwazini Valley. 30c, San dance, Floukraal.

1987, June 4   Perf. 14½x14
694	A252	16c multi	.65	.65
695	A252	20c multi	.90	.90
696	A252	25c multi	1.10	1.10
697	A252	30c multi	1.40	1.40
		Nos. 694-697 (4)	4.05	4.05

Paarl, 300th Anniv. A253

1987, Sept. 3
698	A253	16c Oude Pastorie	.35	.35
699	A253	20c Winegrowing	.40	.40
700	A253	25c Wagon-building	.50	.50
701	A253	30c KWV Cathedral Cellar	1.10	1.10
		Nos. 698-701 (4)	2.35	2.35

A souvenir sheet of one, No. 701, has decorative margin picturing emblem of the natl. philatelic exhibition at Paarl, Sept. 16-19. Sold for 50c. Value $3.

Map, "The Bible" in 76 Languages — A254

Religious Paintings by Rembrandt A255

Designs: 30c, Belshazzar's Feast. 50c, St. Matthew and the Angel, vert.

Perf. 14x14½, 14½x14 (30c)
1987, Nov. 19
702	A254	16c shown	.35	.35
703	A255	30c shown	.65	.65
704	A255	50c multicolored	1.10	1.10
		Nos. 702-704 (3)	2.10	2.10

Bible Society of South Africa.
A 40c stamp was prepared and sent to post offices, but was not issued. Some were sold contrary to the withdrawal order, and used examples are known.
For surcharge see No. B13.

Discovery of the Cape of Good Hope by Bartolomeu Dias — A256

Designs: 16c, Dias, astrolabe, Cape of Good Hope. 30c, Kwaaihoek Memorial. 40c, Caravels, 1488. 50c, Martellus Map, c. 1489.

1988, Feb. 3   Perf. 14½x14
706	A256	16c multicolored	.55	.55
707	A256	30c multicolored	1.00	1.00
708	A256	40c multicolored	1.25	1.25
709	A256	50c multicolored	1.60	1.60
		Nos. 706-709 (4)	4.40	4.40

A souvenir sheet of one, No. 709, has decorative margin picturing emblem of the natl. philatelic exhibition held at Pietermaritzburg, Nov. 22-27. Sold for 70c. Value $3.50.
For surcharge see No. B14.

French Huguenot Settlement of the Cape, 300th Anniv. — A257

16c, Memorial, Franschhoek. 30c, Map of France. 40c, French-Dutch Bible, 1672. 50c, St. Bartholomew's Day Massacre, 1572.

1988, Apr. 13   Perf. 14x14½
710	A257	16c multicolored	.40	.40
711	A257	30c multicolored	.75	.75
712	A257	40c multicolored	1.10	1.10
713	A257	50c multicolored	1.50	1.50
		Nos. 710-713 (4)	3.75	3.75

For surcharges see Nos. B15-B18.

Lighthouses A258

1988, June 9   **Perf. 14½x14**
714 A258 16c Pelican Point, 1932   .65   .65
715 A258 30c Groenpunt, 1824   1.25 1.25
716 A258 40c Agulhas, 1849   1.60 1.60
717 A258 50c Umhlanga Rocks, 1954   2.00 2.00
  a.   Souvenir sheet of 4, #714-717   7.00 7.00
    Nos. 714-717 (4)   5.50 5.50

"Standardised Mail"
"STANDARD POSTAGE"
Stamps inscribed thus were sold for the amount shown in ( ) on date of issue.

Succulents
A259

1c, Huernia zebrina. 2c, Euphorbia symmetrica. 5c, Lithops dorotheae. 7c, Gibbaeum newbrownii. 10c, Didymaotus lapidiformis. 16c, Vanheerdea divergens. 18c, Faucaria tigrina. 20c, Conophytum mundum. 21c, Gasteria armstrongii. 25c, Cheiridopsis pecularis. 30c, Tavaresia barklyi. 35c, Dinteranthus wilmotianus. 40c, Frithia pulchra. (45c), Stapelia grandiflora. 50c, Lapidaria margaretae. 90c, Dioscorea elephantipes. 1r, Trichocaulon cactiforme. 2r, Crassula columnaris. 5r, Anacampseros albissima.
No. 754, Adromischus marianiae. No. 755, Titanopsis calcarea. No. 756, Dactylopsis digitata. No. 757, Pleiospilos bolusii.

1988-93   **Litho.**   **Perf. 14x14½**
735 A259 1c multi   .25 .25
736 A259 2c multi   .25 .25
737 A259 5c multi   .25 .25
738 A259 7c multi   .25 .25
739 A259 10c multi   .25 .25
740 A259 16c multi   .25 .25
741 A259 18c multi   .25 .25
742 A259 20c multi   .25 .25
743 A259 21c multi   .25 .25
744 A259 25c multi   .25 .25
745 A259 30c multi   .25 .25
  a.   Strip, 2 ea 1c, 2c, 5c, 7c, 30c   6.00
746 A259 35c multi   .35 .25
747 A259 40c multi   .40 .25
748 A259 (45c) multi   .40 .25
749 A259 50c multi   .50 .50
750 A259 90c multi   .80 .50
751 A259 1r multi   1.00 .70
752 A259 2r multi   2.00 1.00
753 A259 5r multi   7.50 3.00
    Nos. 735-753 (19)   15.70 9.20

Coil Stamps
Photo.
Perf. 14 Horiz.
754 A259 1c multi   1.75 1.75
755 A259 2c multi   .45 .45
756 A259 5c multi   .45 .45
757 A259 10c multi   .85 .85
    Nos. 754-757 (4)   3.50 3.50

Issued: 18c, 4/1/89; 5r, 3/1/90; 21c, 4/2/90; #748, 4/1/93; others, 9/1/88.

Map and Settlers — A260

Exodus, Tapestry by W.H. Coetzer Studio — A261

Crossing the Drakensburg, Tapestry by Coetzer Studio — A262

Church of the Vow, Pietermaritzburg — A263

Perf. 14x14½, 14½x14 (50c)
1988, Nov. 21   **Litho.**
758 A260 16c multicolored   .65 .40
759 A261 30c multicolored   1.10 .70
760 A262 40c multicolored   1.50 .95
761 A263 50c multicolored   1.75 1.25
    Nos. 758-761 (4)   5.00 3.30

The Great Trek, 150th anniv.

Discovery of a Living Specimen of the Coelacanth, 50th Anniv. A264

Designs: 16c, *Latimeria chalumnae.* 30c, J. L. B. Smith, Margaret Courtenay-Latimer. 40c, Smith Institute of Ichthyology, Grahamstown. 50c, Fish, GEO two-man research submarine.

1989, Feb. 9   **Perf. 14½x14**
762 A264 16c multicolored   .80 .80
763 A264 30c multicolored   1.40 1.40
764 A264 40c multicolored   2.00 2.00
765 A264 50c multicolored   2.50 2.50
  a.   Souvenir sheet of 1   7.00 7.00
  b.   Souvenir sheet of 2   1.25 1.25
    Nos. 762-765 (4)   6.70 6.70

No. 765a has decorative margin picturing emblem of the natl. philatelic exhibition WANDERERS 101, held Sept. 6-9. Sold for 1.50r. No. 765b was issued 6/97, sold for 1r and is inscribed for Old Mutual Environmental Education Center in sheet margin.

Soil Conservation Campaign of the Natl. Grazing Strategy — A265

1989, May 3   **Perf. 14x14½**
766 A265 18c Desertification   .50 .50
767 A265 30c Eroded gullies   .80 .80
768 A265 40c Barrage   1.10 1.10
769 A265 50c Verdant plain   1.40 1.40
    Nos. 766-769 (4)   3.80 3.80

Natl. Rugby Board, Cent. A266

Springboks, foreign team emblems, match scenes.

1989, June 22
770 A266 18c France, 1980   .60 .45
771 A266 30c Australia, 1963   1.10 .80
772 A266 40c New Zealand, 1937   1.50 1.10
773 A266 50c British Isles, 1896   1.90 1.40
    Nos. 770-773 (4)   5.10 3.75

Paintings by Jacob Hendrik Pierneef (1886-1957) A267

No. 774, Composition in Blue, 1928. No. 775, Zanzibar, 1926. No. 776, The Bushveld, 1949. No. 777, Cape Homestead, 1942.

1989, Aug. 3   **Perf. 14½x14**
774 A267 18c multicolored   .40 .25
775 A267 30c multicolored   .75 .30
776 A267 40c multicolored   1.10 .40
777 A267 50c multicolored   1.25 .50
  a.   Souvenir sheet of 4, #774-777   3.50 3.50
    Nos. 774-777 (4)   3.50 1.45

Election of Pres. Frederik Willem de Klerk, Aug. 15 — A268

1989, Sept. 20   **Perf. 14x14½**
778 A268 18c shown   .40 .25
779 A268 45c Portrait, diff.   1.00 .55

Fossil Fuels, Nuclear and Thermal Power A269

18c, SOEKOR gas project, Mossel Bay. 30c, SASOL coal conversion plant. 40c, Koeberg nuclear power plant. 50c, ESKOM thermal power station.

1989, Oct. 19
780 A269 18c multicolored   .45 .25
781 A269 30c multicolored   .80 .45
782 A269 40c multicolored   .95 .50
783 A269 50c multicolored   1.25 .60
    Nos. 780-783 (4)   3.45 1.80

Cooperation in Southern Africa — A270

Maps and: 18c, Cahora Bassa hydroelectric power project. 30c, Railway network. 40c, Lesotho Highlands water project. 50c, Veterinary care.

1990, Feb. 15   **Perf. 14½x14**
Size of 18c, 40c: 68x26mm
784 A270 18c multicolored   .65 .35
785 A270 30c multicolored   1.10 .60
786 A270 40c multicolored   1.25 .75
787 A270 50c multicolored   1.75 .85
  a.   Miniature sheet of 4, #784-787   4.75 4.75
    Nos. 784-787 (4)   4.75 2.55

Stamp Day — A271

Stamps on stamps: a, Great Britain #1. b, Cape of Good Hope #2. c, Natal #4. d, Orange River Colony #10. e, Transvaal #3.

1990, May 12   **Litho.**
788   Strip of 5   2.75 2.75
  a.-e.   A271 21c any single   .50 .50

Penny Black, 150th anniv.

Birds — A272

Designs: 21c, Tauraco corythaix. 35c, Cossypha natalensis. 40c, Mirafra africana. 50c, Telophorus zeylonus.

1990, Aug. 2   **Litho.**   **Perf. 14x14½**
789 A272 21c multicolored   .65 .40
790 A272 35c multicolored   1.00 .70
791 A272 40c multicolored   1.25 .90
792 A272 50c multicolored   1.50 .95
    Nos. 789-792 (4)   4.40 2.95

A souvenir sheet of 1 #792 was sold by the Philatelic Foundation of South Africa. Value $5.

Karoo Landscape, Near Britstown A273

Tourism: #794, Camps Bay, Cape Peninsula. #795, Giraffes, Kruger Natl. Park. #796, Boschendal homestead, Drakenstein.

1990, Nov. 1   **Litho.**   **Perf. 14½x14**
793 A273 50c multicolored   1.00 1.00
794 A273 50c multicolored   1.00 1.00
795 A273 50c multicolored   1.00 1.00
796 A273 50c multicolored   1.00 1.00
  a.   Block of 4, #793-796   4.25 4.25

A274

National Decorations: No. 797, Woltemade Cross for Bravery. No. 798, Order of the Southern Cross. No. 799, Order of the Star of South Africa. No. 800, Order for Meritorious Service. No. 801, Order of Good Hope.

1990, Dec. 6
797 A274 21c multicolored   .40 .30
798 A274 21c multicolored   .40 .30
799 A274 21c multicolored   .40 .30
800 A274 21c multicolored   .40 .30
801 A274 21c multicolored   .40 .30
  a.   Souv. sheet of 5, #797-801   2.50 2.50
  b.   Strip of 5, #797-801   2.00 2.00

A275

Animal Breeding: a, Boer horse. b, Bonsmara cattle. c, Dorper sheep. d, Ridgeback dog. e, Putterie racing pigeon.

1991, Feb. 21   **Litho.**
802   Strip of 5   3.75 3.00
  a.-e.   A275 21c Any single   .75 .60

Achievements — A276

Designs: 25c, First heart transplant, vert. 40c, Matimba power plant. 50c, Dolos breakwater blocks. 60c, Western Deep Levels Gold Mine, world's deepest mine, vert.

Perf. 14½x14 (25c, 60c), 14x14½ (40c, 50c, #806a)
1991, May 30   **Litho.**
803 A276 25c multicolored   .40 .25
804 A276 40c multicolored   .60 .30
805 A276 50c multicolored   .70 .35
806 A276 60c multicolored   .55 .40
  a.   Souvenir sheet of 1   3.75 3.75
    Nos. 803-806 (4)   2.25 1.30

30th anniv. of Republic of South Africa.

1st Registration of Nurses & Midwives, Cent. — A277

1991, Aug. 15 Litho. Perf. 14x14½
807 A277 60c multicolored .85 .85

Creation of South African Post Office Ltd. — A278

1991, Oct. 1 Litho.
808 27c Post office .40 .25
809 27c Telkom SA Ltd. .40 .25
a. A278 Pair, #808-809 1.00 1.00

South African Scientists A279

Designs: 27c, Sir Arnold Theiler (1867-1936), veterinarian. 45c, Sir Basil Schonland (1896-1972), physicist. 65c, Dr. Robert Broom (1866-1951), paleontologist. 85c, Dr. Alexander L. du Toit (1878-1948), geologist.

1991, Oct. 9 Perf. 14½x14
810 A279 27c multicolored .50 .25
811 A279 45c multicolored .80 .50
812 A279 65c multicolored 1.25 .65
813 A279 85c multicolored 1.50 .80
Nos. 810-813 (4) 4.05 2.20

Antarctic Treaty, 30th Anniv. A280

27c, SA Agulhas, penguins. 65c, Meteorological chart.

1991, Dec. 5 Litho.
814 A280 27c multicolored .85 .25
815 A280 65c multicolored 2.10 .95

Conservation — A281

1992, Feb. 6 Litho. Perf. 14x14½
816 A281 27c Prevent erosion .55 .25
817 A281 65c Water pollution 1.50 .90
818 A281 85c Air pollution 1.90 1.10
Nos. 816-818 (3) 3.95 2.25

A souvenir sheet of 1 #817 was sold by Intersapa. Value $5.

A282

Designs depicting history of postal stones: No. 819, Sailing ships at Table Bay. No. 820, Sailors going ashore at Aguada de Saldanha. No. 821, Sailors discovering postal stone near Versse River. No. 822, Finding letters under postal stones. No. 823, Reading news from other mariners.

1992, May 9 Litho. Perf. 14x14½
819 A282 35c multicolored .60 .50
820 A282 35c multicolored .60 .50
821 A282 35c multicolored .60 .50
822 A282 35c multicolored .60 .50
823 A282 35c multicolored .60 .50
a. Strip of 5, #819-823 3.25 3.25

Stamp Day.

A283

Antique Cape Furniture: No. 824, Queen Anne settee, c. 1750-70. No. 825, Stinkwood settee, c. 1800. No. 826, Canopy bed, c. 1800, vert. No. 827, Rocking cradle, 19th cent. No. 828, Waterbutt, c. 1800, vert. No. 829, Flemish style cabinet, c. 1700, vert. No. 830, Armoire, c. 1780-1790, vert. No. 831, Church chair, late 17th cent, vert. No. 832, Tub chair, c. 1770-1790, vert. No. 833, Bible desk, c. 1770, vert.

Perf. 14½x14, 14x14½
1992, July 9 Litho.
824 A283 35c multicolored .65 .55
825 A283 35c multicolored .65 .55
826 A283 35c multicolored .65 .55
827 A283 35c multicolored .65 .55
828 A283 35c multicolored .65 .55
829 A283 35c multicolored .65 .55
830 A283 35c multicolored .65 .55
831 A283 35c multicolored .65 .55
832 A283 35c multicolored .65 .55
833 A283 35c multicolored .65 .55
a. Miniature sheet of 10, #824-833 6.50 6.50

Sports A284

No. 834, Formula 1 Grand Prix. No. 835, Soccer. No. 836, Paris-le Cap Rally. No. 837, Track. No. 838, Rugby. No. 839, Cricket.

1992, July 24 Perf. 14x14½
834 A284 35c multicolored .40 .30
835 A284 35c multicolored .40 .30
836 A284 55c multicolored .65 .50
837 A284 70c multicolored .80 .65
838 A284 90c multicolored 1.00 .85
839 A284 1.05r multicolored 1.50 1.25
a. Souvenir sheet of 6, #834-839 4.75 4.75
Nos. 834-839 (6) 4.75 3.85

A285

1992, Oct. 8 Litho. Perf. 14½x14
840 A285 35c Women's Monument .35 .35
841 A285 70c Sekupu Player .90 .75
842 A285 90c The Hunter 1.25 .95
843 A285 1.05r Postman Lehman 1.50 .85
a. Souvenir sheet of 4, #840-843 4.00 4.00
Nos. 840-843 (4) 4.00 2.90

Sculptures by Anton van Wouw (1862-1945). No. 843a sold for 3.30r.

A286

South African Harbors.

1993, Jan. 28 Litho.
844 A286 35c Walvis Bay .35 .30
845 A286 55c East London .65 .45
846 A286 70c Port Elizabeth .85 .60
847 A286 90c Cape Town 1.00 .80
848 A286 1.05r Durban 1.25 .90
a. Souv. sheet, #844-848 + label 4.25 4.25
Nos. 844-848 (5) 4.10 3.05

No. 848a sold for 3.90r.

A287

Aircraft: a, Bristol Boxkite, 1907. b, Voisin, 1909. c, Bleriot XI, 1911. d, Paterson No. 2 biplane, 1913. e, Henri Farman F.27, 1915. f, BE2e, 1918. g, Vickers Vimy Silver Queen, 1920. h, SE-5a, 1921. i, Avro 504K, 1921. j, Armstrong-Whitworth Atalanta, 1930. k, DH66 Hercules, 1931. l, Westland Wapiti, 1931. m, Junkers F.13, 1932. n, Handley Page HP-42, 1933. o, Junkers Ju52/3m, 1934. p, Junkers Ju86, 1936. q, Hawker Hartbees, 1936. r, Short Empire flying boat Canopus, 1937. s, Miles Master II and Airspeed AS-10 Oxford, 1940. t, Harvard Mk IIa, 1942. u, Short Sunderland, 1945. v, Avro York, 1946. w, Douglas DC-7B, 1955. x, Sikorsky S-55C, 1956. y, Boeing 707-344, 1959.

Miniature Sheet of 25

1993, May 7 Litho. Perf. 14x14½
849 A287 45c #a.-y. 18.00 18.00

A souvenir sheet containing #849a, 849y was sold by the Philatelic Foundation of South Africa.

A288

Endangered Fauna: 1c, Heleophryne rosei. 2c, Bradypodion taeniabronchum. 5c, Cordylus giganteus. 10c, Psammobates geometricus. 20c, Atelerix frontalis. 40c, Bunolagus monticularis. (45c), Diceros bicornis. 50c, Cercopithecus mitis. 55c, Proteles cristatus. 60c, Lycaon pictus. 70c, Hippotragus equinus. 75c, Poecilogale albinucha. 80c, Otis kori. 85c, Serinus citrinipectus. 90c, Spheniscus demersus. 1r, Grus carunculatus. 2r, Hirundo atrocaerulea. 5r, Polemaetus bellicosus. 10r, Terathopius ecaudatus.

Inscriptions in Latin

1993-95 Litho. Perf. 14x14½
850 A288 1c multicolored .25 .25
851 A288 2c multicolored .25 .25
852 A288 5c multicolored .25 .25
853 A288 10c multicolored .25 .25
854 A288 20c multicolored .25 .25
a. Strip, 1c, 2 ea 2c, 20c 1.00
b. Strip, 20c, 2 ea 5c, 10c 1.00
c. Strip, 20c, 2 each 5c, 10c, perf. 14½ vert. 1.00
855 A288 40c multicolored .30 .25
856 A288 (45c) multicolored .35 .25
857 A288 50c multicolored .35 .25
a. Strip, #850, 852, 857, 2 #851, perf. 14½ vert. 1.10
858 A288 55c multicolored .35 .25
859 A288 60c multicolored .40 .25
860 A288 70c multicolored .45 .25
861 A288 75c multicolored .50 .25
862 A288 85c multicolored .60 .25
862A A288 85c multicolored .60 .30
863 A288 90c multicolored .65 .25
a. Booklet pane of 10 — —
Complete booklet, #863a — —
864 A288 1r multicolored .75 .25
865 A288 2r multicolored 1.75 .25
866 A288 5r multicolored 4.00 .50
867 A288 10r multicolored 7.50 1.50
Nos. 850-867 (19) 19.80 6.30

#857a exists with tab showing Reader's Digest emblem in either red or black; also in different order with emblem in blue.

Issued: No. #854b, 8/24/94; #854c, 10/94; #857a, 9/1/95; 85c, 10/2/95; #863a, 1995; others, 9/3/93.

See designs A336 and A343 (no frames).

Wildlife Type with English Inscriptions

Designs: 1c, Table Mountain ghost frog. 2c, Smith's dwarf chameleon. 10c, Geometric tortoise. 20c, Southern African hedgehog. 40c, Riverine rabbit. (45c), Black rhinoceros. 50c, Samango monkey. 60c, Cape hunting dog. 70c, Roan antelope. 90c, Jackass penguin. 1r,

Wattled crane. 2r, Blue swallow. 5r, Martial eagle. 20r, Fish Eagle.

Perf. 14x14¼, 14 Vert. on 1 or 2 sides (1c, 2c, 10c, 55c), 13x14½ (#867F)

1996-98 Litho.
867A A288 1c multicolored .25 .25
867B A288 2c multicolored .25 .25
867C A288 10c multicolored .25 .25
867D A288 20c multicolored .25 .25
867E A288 40c multicolored .25 .25
867F A288 (45c) multicolored .40 .25
n. Booklet pane of 10 3.00
Complete booklet, #867Fn 3.00
o. Souvenir sheet of 1 .55 .55
867G A288 50c multicolored .25 .25
867H A288 55c multicolored .60 .60
p. Strip of 5, 1c, 10c, 55c, 2 2c, perf 14 vert. 1.10
867I A288 70c multicolored .25 .25
867J A288 90c multicolored .45 .25
867K A288 1r multicolored .45 .25
867L A288 2r multicolored 1.00 .25
867M A288 5r multicolored 2.00 .90

Perf. 14x14¼ Syncopated
867Q A288 20c multicolored .25 .25
867R A288 (45c) multicolored .60 .45
867S A288 50c multicolored .50 .25
867T A288 60c multicolored .25 .25
w. With English inscription superimposed over Latin inscription — —
867U A288 1r multicolored 3.50 .40

Size: 34x25mm
Perf. 14¾ Syncopated
867V A288 20r multicolored 9.50 4.75

No. 867Fn is inscribed in sheet margin for ExpoScience Internationale '97, and sold for 1r.

No. 867Hp has tab showing Reader's Digest emblem and release date in either green or orange.

Issued: No. 867Hp, 8/1; No. 867F, 7/7/97. See Nos. C6A-C6E.

First Postal Services in South Africa, 190th Anniv. A289

Designs: 45c, Dragoons, Cape Town-False Bay Route. 65c, Ox train, Cape Town-Stellenbosch. 85c, Khoi-Khoin runners. 1.05r, Post riders, Cape Town-eastern districts.

1993, Oct. 8 Perf. 14x14½
868 A289 45c multicolored .55 .55
869 A289 65c multicolored .85 .75
870 A289 85c multicolored 1.00 .95
871 A289 1.05r multicolored 1.25 1.25
Nos. 868-871 (4) 3.65 3.50

Tourism A290

a, Namaqualand. b, North Beach, Durban. c, Lion. d, Apple Express. e, Oryx gazella.

1993, Nov. 12 Litho. Perf. 14½x14
872 Strip of 5 3.50 3.50
a.-e. A290 85c Any single .70 .70

Export Fruits A291

1994, Jan. 28 Litho. Perf. 14½x14
873 A291 85c Grapes .65 .55
874 A291 90c Apples .70 .60
875 A291 1.05r Plums .85 .70
876 A291 1.25r Oranges 1.10 .85
877 A291 1.40r Avocados 1.25 .95
Nos. 873-877 (5) 4.55 3.65

A souvenir sheet of 1 #873 was sold for 3r by the Philatelic Foundation of South Africa. Value $3.50.

Peace and Goodwill — A292

Childrens' drawings: 45c, Smiling faces, by Nicole Davies. 70c, Dove flying toward olive tree, by Robynne Lawrie. 95c, Three girls, dove, scattered cartridge cases, by Batami Nothmann. 1.15r, Faces surrounding "peace," by Karen Uys.

1994, Apr. 8   Litho.   Perf. 14½x14
878 A292 45c multicolored   .40   .40
879 A292 70c multicolored   .60   .55
880 A292 95c multicolored   .75   .80
881 A292 1.15r multicolored   .95   .85
a.   Souvenir sheet of 1   3.00 3.00
          Nos. 878-881 (4)   2.70 2.60

No. 881a was issued 8/97, sold for 1.15r and is inscribed "Chernobyl's Children, a decade later 1986-1996" in margin.

Inauguration of Pres. Nelson Mandela — A293

Perf. 14x14½, 14½x14
1994, May 10   Litho.
882 A293 45c shown   .70   .60
883 A293 70c Anthems, horiz.   1.10   .90
884 A293 95c Flag, horiz.   1.60 1.25
885 A293 1.15r Union Bldgs.,
             horiz.   2.00 1.50
          Nos. 882-885 (4)   5.40 4.25

Tugboats — A294

1994, May 13   Perf. 14½x14
886 A294 45c TS McEwen   .50   .40
887 A294 70c Sir William Hoy   .70   .65
888 A294 95c Sir Charles Elliott .95   .90
889 A294 1.15r Eland   1.25 1.00
890 A294 1.35r Pioneer   1.40 1.25
a.   Souvenir sheet of 5, #886-890 5.50 5.50
          Nos. 886-890 (5)   4.80 4.20

Our Family — A295

Children's paintings: a, Mother Hands Out Work (C1.5). b, My Friends and I at Play (C2.5). c, Family Life (C3.5). d, Sunday in Church (C4.5). e, I Visit My Brother in the Hospital (C5.5).

1994, July 10   Litho.   Perf. 14x14½
891   Strip of 5   2.50 2.50
a.-e.   A295 45c Any single   .50   .50

Stamp Day — A296

1994, Sept. 30   Litho.   Perf. 14
892 A296 50c Bulk mail   .40   .40
893 A296 70c Proof of delivery   .55   .55
894 A296 95c Registered mail   .75   .75
895 A296 1.15r Express delivery   .85   .85
          Nos. 892-895 (4)   2.55 2.55

Heather — A297

Designs: a, Erica tenuifolia. b, Erica urnaviridis. c, Erica decora. d, Erica aristata. e, Erica dichrus.

1994, Nov. 18   Litho.   Perf. 14
896   Strip of 5   4.50 4.50
a.-e.   A297 95c Any single   .90   .90

Tourism — A298

#897, Phacochoerus aethiopicus, Eastern, Transvaal Province. #898, Lost City, Sun City, North West Province. #899, Ceratotherium simum, KwaZulu/Natal Province. #900, Waterfront, Cape Town, Western Cape Province. #901, Adansonia digitata, Northern Transvaal Province. #902, Highland Route, Free State. #903, Augrabies Falls, Northern Cape Province. #904, Addo Elephant Natl. Park, Eastern Cape Province. #905, Union Buildings, Pretoria, Gauteng.

1995-97   Litho.   Perf. 14
897 A298 50c multicolored   .60   .60
898 A298 50c multicolored   .60   .60
899 A298 60c multicolored   .70   .70
900 A298 60c multicolored   .70   .70
901 A298 60c multicolored   .70   .70
a.   #901 + label, perf. 14 on one
          side   1.25 1.25
b.   Souvenir sheet of 1   3.50 3.50
902 A298 60c multicolored   .70   .70
903 A298 60c multicolored   .70   .70
904 A298 60c multicolored   .70   .70
905 A298 60c multicolored   .70   .70
a.   Strip of 5, #901-905   3.75 3.75
          Nos. 897-905 (9)   6.10 6.10

#901a sold for 70c; #901b for 1.10r on date of issue.
Issued: #897, 1/18; #898, 2/15; #899, 4/28; #900, 5/12; #901-905, 6/30; #901a, 2/97; #901b 8/97.

South African Airforce, 75th Anniv. — A299

DeHavilland DH-9 biplane, Cheetah D fighter.

1995, Feb. 1   Litho.   Perf. 14
906 A299 50c multicolored   1.75 1.75

First Trans-Africa Flight, 75th Anniv. — A300

Vickers Vimy bomber Silver Queen, map of route.

1995, Feb. 1
907 A300 95c multicolored   .55   .55

South Africa, 1995 Rugby World Cup Champions A301

Designs: No. 908, Shown. No. 909, Player running with ball, vert. No. 910, Player holding trophy, vert. No. 911, Like #908, World Champions. No. 912, Scrum, two players.

1995   Litho.   Perf. 14
908 A301 (60c) multicolored   .30   .30
a.   Perf. 14 horiz.   .30   .30
909 A301 (60c) multicolored   .30   .30
a.   Souvenir sheet of 1   1.25 1.25
b.   Perf. 14 vert.   .30   .30
c.   Booklet pane, 5 each #908a,
          909b   5.25
          Complete booklet, #909c 5.25
d.   Booklet pane, 10 #909b 5.25
          Complete booklet, #909d 5.25
910 A301 (60c) multicolored   .30   .30
911 A301 (60c) multicolored   .30   .30

Size: 68x26mm
912 A301 1.15r multicolored   .55   .55
          Nos. 908-912 (5)   1.75 1.75

Issued: #910-911, 6/28; others 5/25.

CSIR (Council for Scientific and Industrial Research), 50th Anniv. A302

1995, June 15
913 A302 (60c) Purifying water   .60   .60

Marine Science in South Africa, Cent. A303

1995, Aug. 25   Litho.   Perf. 14
914 A303 (60c) Dr. JDF Gilchrist .60   .60

Souvenir Sheet

Singapore '95 — A304

1995, Sept. 1
915 A304 (60c) multicolored   1.00 1.00

Masakhane Campaign A305

1995   Perf. 14x14¼
916 A305 (60c) multicolored   .60   .60
a.   Booklet pane of 10   6.00
          Complete booklet, No. 916a 6.00

Booklet Stamp
Size: 29x20mm
916B A305 (60c) multicolored   .60   .60
c.   Booklet pane of 10   6.00
          Complete booklet, #916c 6.00

Issued: #916, 9/16; #916B, 12/1.

Visit of Pope John Paul II — A306

1995, Sept. 16   Perf. 14
917 A306 (60c) multicolored   .90   .90

Mahatma Gandhi — A307

Designs: (60c), 1906 Photograph. 1.40r, Ghandhi in later years.

1995, Oct. 2
918 A307 (60c) blue   .85   .85
a.   Souvenir sheet of 1   1.25 1.25
919 A307 1.40r brown   1.90 1.90
a.   Souvenir sheet of 1   2.40 2.40

No. 918a is inscribed in sheet margin for 50th anniv. of Congress Alliance for Democratic South Africa. Issued July 1997.
Design on stamp in No. 919a extends to perforations.
See India Nos. 1534-1535.

World Post Day — A308

1995
920 A308 (60c) multicolored   .70   .70

Size: 65x60mm
Imperf
921 A308 5r multicolored   2.75 2.75
          Stampex '95.
Issued: (60c), 10/9; 5r, 10/19.

UN, 50th Anniv. A309

1995, Oct. 24   Litho.   Perf. 14
922 A309 (60c) multicolored   .50   .50

Souvenir Sheet

UNESCO, 50th Anniv. — A310

1995, Oct. 24
923 A310 (60c) multicolored   .50   .50

Shells — A311

1995, Nov. 24
924 A311 (60c) Afrivoluta priglei   .55   .55
925 A311 (60c) Lyria africana   .55   .55
926 A311 (60c) Marginella mosai-
          ca   .55   .55
927 A311 (60c) Conus pictus   .55   .55
928 A311 (60c) Gypreaea fultoni   .55   .55
  a.   Strip of 5, #924-928   2.75   2.75

— A312

1996 African Cup of Nations Soccer Championships: Nos. 929-933, Various soccer
plays, map of Africa. No. 934, Player in traditional uniform.

1996, Jan. 8   Litho.   Perf. 14
Color of "RSA"
929 A312 (60c) blue   .60   .60
930 A312 (60c) yellow   .60   .60
931 A312 (60c) red   .60   .60
932 A312 (60c) gray   .60   .60
933 A312 (60c) green   .60   .60
  a.   Strip of 5, Nos. 929-933   3.00   3.00
Souvenir Sheet
934 A312 (1.15r) multicolored   .70   .70

South African Victory
in African Nations
Soccer
Championship
A312a

1996, Feb. 8   Litho.   Perf. 14½x14
934A A312a (60c) multicolored   .70   .70

City of Bloemfontein, 150th
Anniv. — A313

1996, Mar. 28   Litho.   Perf. 14
935 A313 (60c) multicolored   .80   .80

Souvenir Sheet

New Year 1996 (Year of the Rat) —
A313a

1996, May 18   Litho.   Perf. 14
940D A313a 60c multicolored   1.00   1.00
CHINA '96.

Man in a Donkey Cart, by Gerard
Sekoto (1913-93) — A314

Paintings: #942, 2r, Song of the Pick. #943,
2r, Yellow Houses, Sophiatown, 1940, vert.

1996, June 1   Litho.   Perf. 14
941 A314 1r multicolored   .60   .60
942 A314 2r multicolored   1.25   1.25
Souvenir Sheet
943 A314 2r multicolored   1.50   1.50

Youth
Day — A315

1996, June 8
944 A315 (60c) multicolored   .50   .50

Comrades Marathon, 75th
Anniv. — A316

1996, June 8   Litho.   Perf. 14
945 A316 (60c) multicolored   .50   .50

Souvenir Sheet

Parliament Building, Toronto — A316a

1996, June 8   Litho.   Perf. 14
945A A316a 2r multicolored   1.50   1.50
CAPEX '96.

A317

1996 Summer Olympic Games, Atlanta: No.
946: a, Cycling. b, Swimming. c, Boxing. d,
Running. e, Pole vault.
1.40r, South African Olympic emblem.

1996, July 5   Litho.   Perf. 14½x14
946 A317 (70c) Strip of 5, #a.-e.   2.40   2.40
Perf. 14
947 A317 1.40r multicolored   .85   .85
No. 946 was issued in sheets of 10 stamps.

A318

Background color: a, Vermilion & multi. b,
Deep blue & multi. c, Deep yellow & multi. d,
Bright blue & multi. e, Red & multi.

1996, Aug. 1   Litho.   Perf. 14
948   Strip of 5   2.50   2.50
  a.-e. A318 (70c) any single   .50   .50
New Democratic Constitution.

South African Merchant Marine, 50th
Anniv. — A319

Paintings of ships, by Peter Bilas: No. 949:
a, Sea Pioneer. b, SA Winterberg.
No. 950: a, Langloof. b, SA Vaal.
2r, Constantia.

1996, Aug. 5   Litho.   Perf. 14
949 A319   Pair   1.25   1.25
  a.-b.   (70c) any single   .60   .60
950 A319   Pair   2.75   2.75
  a.-b.   1.40r any single   1.25   1.25
Souvenir Sheet
950C A319   2r multicolored   1.50   1.50
No. 950C contains one 72x30mm stamp.

A320

1996, Aug. 9   Litho.   Perf. 14
951 A320 70c multicolored   .50   .50
Natl. Women's Day.

A321

1996, Oct. 9
952 A321 70c multicolored   .50   .50
World Post Day.

Christmas — A322

1996, Oct. 9
953 A322 70c multicolored   .50   .50
No. 953 exists in a privately produced souvenir, sold at 2r for charitable purposes.

Souvenir Sheet

Bloemfontein, 150th Natl. Stamp
Show — A323

1996, Oct. 9   Litho.   Perf. 14½x14
954 A323 2r multicolored   1.50   1.50

South African Nobel
Laureates, Death
Cent. of Alfred
Nobel — A324

a, Max Theiler, medicine, 1951. b, Albert
Luthuli, peace, 1960. c, Alfred Nobel (1833-
96). d, Allan Cormack, medicine, 1979. e,
Aaron Klug, chemistry, 1982. f, Desmond
Tutu, peace, 1984. g, Nadine Gordimer, literature, 1991. h, Symbol for Nobel Prizes 1901-
96. i, Nelson R. Mandela, peace, 1993. j, F.W.
de Klerk, peace, 1993.

1996, Nov. 4
955 A324 (70c) Sheet of 10, #a.-
          j.   4.75   4.75
  k.   Souvenir sheet, #955c   .60   .60

First
Motor
Car in
South
Africa,
Cent.
A325

1997, Jan. 4   Litho.   Perf. 14
956 A325 (70c) multicolored   1.00   1.00

Souvenir Sheet

Hong Kong '97 — A326

Perf. 14 Syncopated
1997, Feb. 12   Litho.
957 A326 3r multicolored   2.50   2.50

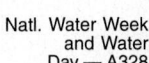

Natl. Water Week and Water Day — A328

Save water for: No. 959, Farming. No. 960, Gardening. No. 961, Health. No. 962, Housing. No. 963, For all.

Perf. 14 Syncopated on 2 or 3 Sides
1997, Mar. 22   **Litho.**

Booklet Stamps

959	A328 (70c) multicolored	.60	.60
960	A328 (70c) multicolored	.60	.60
961	A328 (70c) multicolored	.60	.60
962	A328 (70c) multicolored	.60	.60
963	A328 (70c) multicolored	.60	.60
a.	Booklet pane, 2 each #959-963	6.00	6.00
	Complete booklet	6.00	

Perf. 14x14¼ on 2 or 3 Sides
1997, Mar.   **Litho.**

Booklet Stamps

963B	A328 (70c) Like #959	.60	.60
963C	A328 (70c) Like #960	.60	.60
963D	A328 (70c) Like #961	.60	.60
963E	A328 (70c) Like #962	.60	.60
963F	A328 (70c) Like #963	.60	.60
g.	Bklt. pane, 2 ea #963B-963F	6.00	6.00
	Complete booklet, #963Fg	6.00	

South African Navy, 75th Anniv. — A329

Warships: No. 964, Strike craft SAS Kobie Coetsee. No. 965, Survey ship SAS Protea. No. 966, Mine counter-measures ship SAS Umkomaas. No. 967, Submarine Emily Hobhouse, anti-submarine frigate SAS President Pretorius.

1997, Apr. 1   **Perf. 14 Syncopated**

964	A329 (70c) multicolored	.60	.60
965	A329 (70c) multicolored	.60	.60
966	A329 (70c) multicolored	.60	.60
967	A329 (70c) multicolored	.60	.60
a.	Block of 4, #964-967	2.40	2.40

First Democratic Elections, 5th Anniv. — A330

People voting, signs saying: No. 968, "Election Day, 27, April, 1994." No. 969, "Polling Station." No. 970, "Register Here." No. 971, "Vote Here." No. 972, "Ballot Box."

Perf. 14 Syncopated
1997, Apr. 26   **Litho.**

968	A330 (70c) black & red	.50	.50
969	A330 (70c) black & red	.50	.50
970	A330 (70c) black & red	.50	.50
971	A330 (70c) black & red	.50	.50
972	A330 (70c) black & red	.50	.50
b.	Strip of 5, #968-972	2.50	2.50

Souvenir Sheet

New Year 1997 (Year of the Ox) — A330a

1997, May 2   **Litho.**   **Perf. 14**
972A   A330a 4.50r multicolored   2.25   2.25

SAPDA '97.

Cultural Artifacts — A331

1997, May 18   **Perf. 14**

973	A331 (70c) Zulu baskets	.50	.50
974	A331 (70c) S. Sotho figure	.50	.50
975	A331 (70c) S. Ndebele figure	.50	.50
976	A331 (70c) Venda door	.50	.50
977	A331 (70c) Tsonga medicine gourd	.50	.50
978	A331 (70c) Wooden pot, N. cape	.50	.50
979	A331 (70c) Khoi walking stick	.50	.50
980	A331 (70c) Tswana knife handle	.50	.50
981	A331 (70c) Xhosa pipe	.50	.50
982	A331 (70c) Swazi vessel	.50	.50
a.	Sheet of 10, #973-982	5.00	5.00

1997, Dec.   **Perf. 14x15**

973a	Zulu baskets	.60	.60
974a	S. Sotho figure	.60	.60
975a	S. Ndebele figure	.60	.60
976a	Venda door	.60	.60
977a	Tsonga medicine gourd	.60	.60
978a	Wooden pot, N. cape	.60	.60
979a	Khoi walking stick	.60	.60
980a	Tswana knife handle	.60	.60
981a	Xhosa pipe	.60	.60
982b	Swazi vessel	.60	.60
982c	Bklt. pane, 2 #973a-981a, 982b	6.00	
	Complete booklet, 2 #982c	12.00	

A332

Birds — No. 983, White-breasted cormorant. No. 984, Hammerkop. No. 985, Pied kingfisher. No. 986, Purple heron. No. 987, Black-headed heron. No. 988, Darter. No. 989, Green-backed heron. No. 990, White-faced duck. No. 991, Saddle-billed stork. No. 992, Water dikkop.

1997, June 5   **Perf. 14**

983	A332 (70c) multicolored	.50	.50
984	A332 (70c) multicolored	.50	.50
985	A332 (70c) multicolored	.50	.50
986	A332 (70c) multicolored	.50	.50
987	A332 (70c) multicolored	.50	.50
988	A332 (70c) multicolored	.50	.50
989	A332 (70c) multicolored	.50	.50
990	A332 (70c) multicolored	.50	.50
a.	Souvenir sheet of 1	1.25	1.25
991	A332 (70c) multicolored	.50	.50
992	A332 (70c) multicolored	.50	.50
a.	Sheet of 10, #983-992	5.00	5.00
b.	Booklet pane of 10, #983-992, perf. 14x14¾	5.00	5.00
	Complete booklet, 2 #992b	10.00	

Birds look bluer and browner on some stamps from No. 992b. No. 992a has Ilsapex 98 emblem in margin, which is not found on No. 992b.

No. 990a, issued 7/11/97, is inscribed in sheet margin for JUNASS '97, and sold for 2r.

Grocott's, Muirhead & Gowie Buildings, Grahamstown — A333

1997, May 29   **Litho.**   **Perf. 14**
993   A333 5r multicolored   1.90   1.90

PACIFIC 97.

Indigenous Cattle A335

Perf. 14½ Syncopated
1997, Aug. 10

999	A335 (70c) Nguni	.60	.60
1000	A335 (70c) Bonsmara	.60	.60
1001	A335 (70c) Afrikander	.60	.60
1002	A335 (70c) Drakensberger	.60	.60
a.	Block of 4, #999-1002	2.40	2.40

Antarctic Wildlife A336

1997, Aug. 27   **Litho.**   **Perf. 14**

1003	A336 (70c) Leopard seal	.50	.50
1004	A336 1.20r Antarctic skua	.85	.85
1005	A336 1.70r King penguin	1.25	1.25
	Nos. 1003-1005 (3)	2.60	2.60

Enoch Sontonga (1873-1905), Author of Africa's Natl. Anthem — A337

No. 1007, "Nkosi Sikelel iAfrika".

Perf. 14 Syncopated
1997, Sept. 24   **Litho.**

1006	A337 (70c) shown	.50	.50
1007	A337 (70c) multicolored	.50	.50
a.	Pair, #1006-1007	1.00	1.00

Heritage Day.

Souvenir Sheet

Cape Town '97 Natl. Stamp Show — A338

1997, Oct. 8   **Perf. 14**
1008   A338 4.50r multicolored   2.25   2.25

Souvenir Sheet

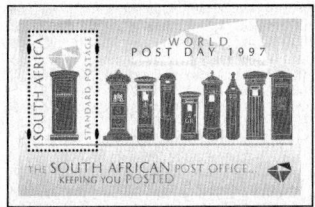

World Post Day — A339

1997, Oct. 9   **Perf. 14 Syncopated**
1009   A339 (70c) multicolored   .70   .70

No. 1009 sold for 1r on day of issue.

SANTA (South African Natl. Tuberculosis Assoc., 50th Anniv. — A340

Designs featuring former Christmas seals: No. 1010, Bethlehem. No. 1011, Candles on each side of Cross of Lorraine. No. 1012, Candles, angels, Cross. No. 1013, Cross, angel kneeling. No. 1014, Santa carrying Cross. No. 1015, Madonna and Child, Cross. No. 1016, Christmas trees. No. 1017, Magi. No. 1018, Bell, stained glass window. No. 1019, Native African kneeling, flag.

1997, Nov. 3   **Perf. 14 Syncopated**

1010	A340 (70c) multicolored	.50	.50
1011	A340 (70c) multicolored	.50	.50
1012	A340 (70c) multicolored	.50	.50
1013	A340 (70c) multicolored	.50	.50
1014	A340 (70c) multicolored	.50	.50
1015	A340 (70c) multicolored	.50	.50
1016	A340 (70c) multicolored	.50	.50
1017	A340 (70c) multicolored	.50	.50
1018	A340 (70c) multicolored	.50	.50
1019	A340 (70c) multicolored	.50	.50
a.	Sheet of 10, #1010-1019	5.00	5.00

Souvenir Sheet

New Year 1998 (Year of the Tiger) — A341

1998, Jan. 28   **Litho.**   **Perf. 14x14½**
1020   A341 5r multicolored   2.50   2.50

Natl. Sea Rescue Institute A342

1998, Feb. 11   **Perf. 14 Syncopated**
1021   A342 (70c) multicolored   .90   .90

Fauna (no frame) — A343

5c, Giant girdle-tailed lizard. 10c, Geometric tortoise. 20c, Southern African hedgehog. 30c, Spotted hyena. 40c, Riverine rabbit. 50c, Samango monkey. 60c, Cape hunting dog. 70c, Roan antelope. 80c, Kori bustard. 90c, Jackass penguin. 1r, Wattled crane. #1032, Impala. #1033, Waterbuck. #1034, Blue wildebeest. #1035, Eland. #1036, Kudu. #1037, Black rhinoceros. #1038, White rhinoceros. #1039, Buffalo. #1040, Lion. #1041, Leopard. #1042, African elephant. #1044, Giraffe. 1.50r, Tawny eagle, vert. 2r, Blue swallow. 2.30r, Cape vulture, vert. 5r, Martial eagle. 10r, Bateleur. 20r, Fish eagle.

Perf. 14x14¼, 14x14¼, 14¼x14
Syncopated (#1043), 14x14¼
Syncopated on 2 or 3 Sides
(#1036B-1036F, 1042B-1042F)

1998-2000			**Litho.**	
1021A	A343	5c multi	.25	.25
1022	A343	10c multi	.25	.25
1023	A343	20c multi	.25	.25
1024	A343	30c multi	.25	.25
1025	A343	40c multi	.25	.25
1026	A343	50c multi	.25	.25
1027	A343	60c multi	.25	.25
1028	A343	70c multi	.25	.25
1029	A343	80c multi	.35	.35
1030	A343	90c multi	.35	.35
1031	A343	1r multi	.35	.35
1032	A343	(1.10r) multi, vert.	.65	.65
1033	A343	(1.10r) multi, vert.	.65	.65
1034	A343	(1.10r) multi, vert.	.65	.65
1035	A343	(1.10r) multi, vert.	.65	.65
1036	A343	(1.10r) multi, vert.	.65	.65
a.		Strip of 5, #1032-1036	3.25	3.25
h.		Booklet pane, 2 each #1032-1036, "Standard" 5mm long	6.50	
		Booklet, #1036h	6.50	
1036B	A343	(1.10r) Like #1034	.40	.40
1036C	A343	(1.10r) Like #1035	.40	.40
1036D	A343	(1.10r) Like #1036	.40	.40
1036E	A343	(1.10r) Like #1032	.40	.40
1036F	A343	(1.10r) Like #1033	.40	.40
g.		Booklet pane, 2 each #1036B-1036F	4.00	
		Booklet, #1036Fg	4.00	
1037	A343	(1.10r) multi	.40	.40
a.		Booklet pane of 10	4.00	
		Complete bklt., #1037a	4.00	
1038	A343	(1.30r) multi	.50	.50
1039	A343	(1.30r) multi	.50	.50
1040	A343	(1.30r) multi	.50	.50
1041	A343	(1.30r) multi	.50	.50
1042	A343	(1.30r) multi	.50	.50
a.		Booklet pane, 2 ea #1038-1042	5.00	
		Complete bklt., #1042a	5.00	
1042B	A343	(1.30r) Like #1038	.50	.50
1042C	A343	(1.30r) Like #1039	.50	.50
1042D	A343	(1.30r) Like #1040	.50	.50
1042E	A343	(1.30r) Like #1041	.50	.50
1042F	A343	(1.30r) Like #1042	.50	.50
g.		Booklet pane, 2 each #1042B-1042F	5.00	
		Complete bklt., #1042Fg	5.00	
1043	A343	2r multi	.80	.80
1043A	A343	2r multi	.80	.80
1044	A343	3r multi	1.25	1.25
1045	A343	5r multi	2.25	2.25

Size: 20x38mm
Perf. 14¼x13¾

1045A	A343	1.50r multi	.60	.60
1045B	A343	2.30r multi	.90	.90

Size: 35x25mm
Perf. 14¼x14

1046	A343	10r multi	4.00	4.00
a.		Perf. 14¾	4.00	4.00

Perf. 14¾ Syncopated

1047	A343	20r multi	7.75	7.75
	Nos. 1021A-1047 (40)		32.05	32.05

Self-adhesive

1048	A343	(1.10r) like #1033	.65	.65
1049	A343	(1.10r) like #1032	.65	.65
1050	A343	(1.10r) like #1036	.65	.65
1051	A343	(1.10r) like #1035	.65	.65
1052	A343	(1.10r) like #1034	.65	.65
a.		Strip of 5, #1048-1052	3.25	
h.		Booklet, 2 each #1048-1052	6.50	

Booklet Stamps
Self-Adhesive

Serpentine Die Cut 11x11¼

1052B	A343	(1.30r) Like #1035	.45	.45
1052C	A343	(1.30r) Like #1036	.45	.45
1052D	A343	(1.30r) Like #1032	.45	.45
1052E	A343	(1.30r) Like #1034	.45	.45
1052F	A343	(1.30r) Like #1033	.45	.45
g.		Booklet pane, 2 each #1052B-1052F	4.50	

Nos. 1038-1042F are inscribed "Airmail Postcard."

"Standard" on Nos. 1032-1036, 1036a is 5½mm long.

Nos. 1042B-1042F are booklet stamps. No. 1052Fg is a complete booklet. Nos. 1036B-1036F were issued in a booklet.

Issued: #1037, 1/98; 10c, 40c, 50c, 70c, 90c, 1r, 1/16/98; #1038-1042, 4/98; #1036B-1036F, 5/18/98; 3r, 6/24/98; 20c, 6/25/98; #1032-1036, 1048-1052, 5/18/98; 10r, 20r, 9/21/98; #1046a, 10/28/98; #1043A, 1/9/99; #1052B-1052F, 12/99; 1.50r, 2.30r, 6/5/00; 5c, 7/4/00.

Souvenir Sheet

Leopard — A344

1998, May 1   **Perf. 14**
1053 A344 5r multicolored   2.50 2.50

SAPDA '98 Stamp Show, Johannesburg.

A345

1998, June 8
1054 A345 (1.10r) multicolored   .80 .80

1998 World Cup Soccer Championships, France. No. 1054 was issued in sheets of 10.

A346

Early South African History: #1055, Early stone age hand axe. #1056, Musuku. #1057, San rock engravings. #1058, Early iron age pots. #1059, Khoekhoe pot. #1060, Florisbad skull. #1061, San rock art. #1062, Mapungubwe gold. #1063, Lydenburg head. #1064, Taung child.

1998, June 28   **Perf. 14x14½**

1055	A346	(1.10r) multicolored	.55	.55
1056	A346	(1.10r) multicolored	.55	.55
1057	A346	(1.10r) multicolored	.55	.55
1058	A346	(1.10r) multicolored	.55	.55
1059	A346	(1.10r) multicolored	.55	.55
1060	A346	(1.10r) multicolored	.55	.55
1061	A346	(1.10r) multicolored	.55	.55
1062	A346	(1.10r) multicolored	.55	.55
1063	A346	(1.10r) multicolored	.55	.55
1064	A346	(1.10r) multicolored	.55	.55
a.		Sheet of 10, #1055-1064	5.50	5.50
		Booklet, 2 #1064a	11.00	

Raptors — A347

Designs: No. 1065, Pale chanting goshawk. No. 1066, Jackal buzzard. No. 1067, Lanner falcon. No. 1068, Bearded vulture. No. 1069, Black harrier. No. 1070, Cape vulture. No. 1071, Bateleur. No. 1072, Spotted eagle owl.

No. 1073, White-headed vulture. No. 1074, African fish eagle.

1998, Aug. 16   **Perf. 14x15**

1065	A347	(1.10r) multicolored	.65	.65
1066	A347	(1.10r) multicolored	.65	.65
1067	A347	(1.10r) multicolored	.65	.65
1068	A347	(1.10r) multicolored	.65	.65
1069	A347	(1.10r) multicolored	.65	.65
1070	A347	(1.10r) multicolored	.65	.65
1071	A347	(1.10r) multicolored	.65	.65
1072	A347	(1.10r) multicolored	.65	.65
1073	A347	(1.10r) multicolored	.65	.65
1074	A347	(1.10r) multicolored	.65	.65
a.		Sheet of 10, #1065-1074	6.50	6.50
b.		Booklet pane, #1065-1074	6.50	
		Complete booklet, 2 #1074b + 2 prepaid postcards	14.00	

Vert. and horiz. perforations extend to top, bottom and right edges of sheet on No. 1074a, but do not on No. 1074b.

Natl. Arbor Week A348

Trees: No. 1075, Baobab. No. 1076, Umbrella thorn. No. 1077, Shepherd's tree. No. 1078, Karee.

1998, Sept. 4   **Litho.**   **Perf. 13¾x14**

1075	A348	(1.10r) multicolored	.75	.75
1076	A348	(1.10r) multicolored	.75	.75
1077	A348	(1.10r) multicolored	.75	.75
1078	A348	(1.10r) multicolored	.75	.75
a.		Block of 4, #1075-1078	3.00	3.00

Christmas — A349

1998, Oct. 9   **Litho.**   **Perf. 14x15**

1079	A349	(1.10r)	Angel	.80	.80
1080	A349	(1.10r)	Bell	.80	.80
1081	A349	(1.10r)	Package	.80	.80
1082	A349	(1.10r)	Christmas tree	.80	.80
1083	A349	(1.10r)	Star	.80	.80
a.			Strip of 5, #1079-1083	4.00	4.00

Souvenir Sheet

World Post Day — A351

1998, Oct. 9   **Litho.**   **Perf. 14x14½**
1089 A351 5r multicolored   2.50 2.50

Souvenir Sheet

ILSAPEX 1998, Midrand, South Africa — A352

Designs of unissued stamps created for 1927 definitive series in colors of: a, Red and green. b, Green and black.

1998, Oct. 20 Litho.   **Perf. 14½x14¼**
1090 A352 5r Sheet of 2, #a.-b.   4.00 4.00

Souvenir Sheet

Whales — A354

1998, Oct. 23 Litho.   **Perf. 13½x14**
1095 A354 5r multicolored   3.00 3.00

See Namibia #919, Norfolk Island #665.

Souvenir Sheet

Clover SA Limited, 100th Anniv. — A354a

1998, Nov. 15 Litho.   **Perf. 14¼x14**
1095A A354a (1.10r) multicolored 2.25 2.25

Universal Declaration of Human Rights, 50th Anniv. — A355

1998, Dec. 9   **Perf. 14¼**
1096 A355 (1.10r) multicolored   1.00 1.00

UPU, 125th Anniv. — A356

Designs: No. 1097, Dennis Royal Mail vehicle, 1913. No. 1098, Ford V8 Mail van, 1935. No. 1099, Mobile post office, 1937. No. 1100, Trojan post office van, 1927.

1999, Feb. 15 Litho.   **Perf. 13¾x14**

1097	A356	(1.10r) multi	.75	.75
1098	A356	(1.10r) multi	.75	.75
1099	A356	(1.10r) multi	.75	.75
1100	A356	(1.10r) multi	.75	.75
a.		Block of 4, #1097-1100	3.00	3.00

New Year 1999 (Year of the Rabbit) — A357

1999, Feb. 16 Litho. Perf. 14x13½
1101 A357 5r multicolored 2.50 2.50

Ships of the Southern Oceans — A358

1999, Mar. 19 Litho. Perf. 13¾x14
1102 A358 (1.10r) Endeavour .75 .75
1103 A358 (1.10r) HMS Beagle .75 .75
1104 A358 (1.10r) Discovery .75 .75
1105 A358 (1.10r) Heemskerck .75 .75
   a. Block of 4, #1102-1105 3.00 3.00

Souvenir Sheet
Perf. 13¾
1106 A358 5r Lawhill, vert. 2.25 2.25
Australia 99 World Stamp Expo (No. 1106).

AIDS
Awareness — A359

Perf. 14¼x14 on 3 sides
1999, Apr. 1
1107 A359 (1.20r) purple & multi .60 .60
1108 A359 (1.20r) green & multi .60 .60
   a. Booklet pane, 5 each #1107-1108 6.00
     Complete booklet, #1108a 6.00

Souvenir Sheets

IBRA '99, Nuremberg, Germany — A360

1999, Apr. 27 Perf. 14¼x14
1109 A360 5r multi 3.00 3.00

SAPDA '99, Johannesburg — A361

1999, Apr. 30 Perf. 13¾
1110 A361 5r multi 2.75 2.75

A362

1999, May 1 Perf. 14x14¾
1111 A362 (1.20r) Nurse .70 .70
1112 A362 (1.20r) Washerwoman .70 .70
1113 A362 (1.20r) Lumberjack .70 .70
1114 A362 (1.20r) Tree planter .70 .70
1115 A362 (1.20r) Cook .70 .70
1116 A362 (1.20r) Fisherman .70 .70
1117 A362 (1.20r) Construction worker .70 .70
1118 A362 (1.20r) Miner .70 .70
1119 A362 (1.20r) Mailman .70 .70
1120 A362 (1.20r) Jackhammerer .70 .70
   a. Sheet of 10, #1111-1120 7.00 7.00
Labor Day.

A363

1999, June 16 Perf. 14x14¼
1121 A363 (1.20r) multi 1.00 1.00
Inauguration of Pres. Thabo Mbeki.

Souvenir Sheet

Order of St. John, 900th Anniv. — A364

1999, June 23 Perf. 14x14¾
1122 A364 2r multi 1.50 1.50

Standard Bank Arts Festival, 25th Anniv. — A365

1999, June 29 Perf. 14x14¼
1123 A365 (1.20r) shown .90 .90
1124 A365 (1.20r) Film .90 .90
1125 A365 (1.20r) Music .90 .90
1126 A365 (1.20r) Mask, diff. .90 .90
1127 A365 (1.20r) Painter .90 .90
   a. Strip of 5, #1123-1127 4.50 4.50

Traditional Wall Art — A366

1999, Aug. 8 Perf. 13¼x13¾
1128 A366 (1.20r) North Ndebele .80 .80
1129 A366 (1.20r) South Ndebele .80 .80
1130 A366 (1.20r) Swazi .80 .80
1131 A366 (1.20r) Venda .80 .80
1132 A366 (1.20r) South Sotho .80 .80
1133 A366 (1.20r) Xhosa .80 .80
1134 A366 (1.20r) North Sotho .80 .80
1135 A366 (1.20r) Tsonga .80 .80
1136 A366 (1.20r) Zulu .80 .80
1137 A366 (1.20r) Tswana .80 .80
   a. Sheet of 10, #1128-1137 8.00 8.00

Souvenir Sheet

China 1999 World Philatelic Exhibition — A367

1999, Aug. 21 Perf. 14x13¼
1138 A367 5r multi 3.00 3.00

Souvenir Sheet

JOPEX '99 — A368

1999, Sept. 8 Litho. Perf. 14¼x14½
1139 A368 5r Strelitzia flower 3.25 3.25

Migratory Animals — A369

1999, Oct. 4 Litho. Perf. 14x14¾
1140 A369 (1.20r) multi .80 .80
1141 A369 (1.20r) multi .80 .80
1142 A369 (1.20r) multi .80 .80
1143 A369 (1.20r) multi .80 .80
1144 A369 (1.20r) multi .80 .80
1145 A369 (1.20r) multi .80 .80
1146 A369 (1.20r) multi .80 .80
1147 A369 (1.20r) multi .80 .80
1148 A369 (1.20r) multi .80 .80

No. 1140, Barn swallow. No. 1141, Great white shark. No. 1142, Lesser kestrel. No. 1143, Common dolphin. No. 1144, European bee-eater. No. 1145, Loggerhead turtle. No. 1146, Curlew sandpiper. No. 1147, Wandering albatross. No. 1148, Springbok. No. 1149, Lesser flamingo.

1149 A369 (1.20r) multi .80 .80
   a. Sheet of 10, #1140-1149 8.00 8.00
     Complete booklet, 2 #1149a (stitched in) + 2 postal cards 20.00
     Complete booklet sold for 29r.

Boer War, Cent. A370

1999, Oct. 11 Litho. Perf. 13¾
1150 A370 (1.20r) Boer men, woman 1.25 1.25
1151 A370 (1.20r) Soldiers, ship 1.25 1.25
   a. Pair, #1150-1151 2.50 2.50
   b. Booklet pane, #1150-1151, perf. 13¼x13¾ ('02) 2.75 —
   Issued: No. 1151b, 5/31/02. See note after No. 1282.

Millennium — A371

2000, Jan. 1 Litho. Perf. 13¼x13¾
1152 A371 (1.20r) multi 1.10 1.10

Start of National Lottery A372

2000, Mar. 2 Litho. Perf. 13¼x13¾
1153 A372 (1.20r) multi 1.00 1.00

Family Day — A373

2000, Apr. 5 Litho. Perf. 13¼
1154 A373 (1.30r) multi 1.00 1.00

Souvenir Sheet

The Stamp Show 2000, London — A374

2000, May 20 Litho. Perf. 13¼
1155 A374 4.60r multi 2.75 2.75

Frogs and Toads — A375

No. 1156: a, Banded stream frog. b, Yellow-striped reed frog. c, Natal leaf-folding frog. d, Paradise toad. e, Table Mountain ghost frog. f, Banded rubber frog. g, Dwarf grass frog. h, Long-toed tree frog. i, Namaqua rain frog. j, Bubbling kassina.
4.60r, Forest tree frog.

Perf. 13¼x13¾

2000, June 23 **Litho.**

1156	Sheet of 10	7.00	7.00
a.-j.	A375 1.30r Any single	.70	.70

Souvenir Sheet

Perf. 13¼

1157	A375 4.60r multi	2.75	2.75

Junass 2000, Boksburg (No. 1157). No. 1157 contains one 48x30mm stamp.

Medicinal Plants — A376

No. 1158: a, Stalked bulbine. b, Wild dagga. c, Wild garlic. d, Pig's ear. e, Wild ginger.
No. 1159: a, Red paintbrush. b, Cancer bush. c, Yellow star flower. d, Bitter aloe. e, Sour fig.

2000, Aug. 1 ***Perf. 13¾x13¼***

1158	Horiz. strip of 5	2.50	2.50
a.-e.	A376 1.30r Any single	.50	.50
1159	Horiz. strip of 5	4.00	4.00
a.-e.	A376 2.30r Any single	.80	.80

2000 Summer Olympics, Sydney — A377

Olympic rings and: 1.30r, Flagbearer. 1.50r, Elena Meyer of South Africa and Derartu Tulu of Ethiopia. 2.20r, Joshua Thugwane. 2.30r, South African flag. 6.30r, Penny Heyns.

2000, Sept. 1 ***Perf. 13¼x13¾***

1160-1164	A377 Set of 5	5.00	5.00

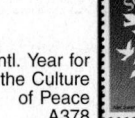

Intl. Year for the Culture of Peace A378

2000, Sept. 19 **Litho.** ***Perf. 13¼***

1165	A378 1.30r multi	.70	.70

World Heritage Sites — A379

Designs: No. 1166, 1.30r, Robben Island. No. 1167, 1.30r, Greater St. Lucia Wetland Park. No. 1168, 1.30r, Sterkfontein Fossil Hominid Complex.

2000, Sept. 22 ***Perf. 13¼x13¾***

1166-1168	A379 Set of 3	2.00	2.00

World Post Day — A380

2000 **Litho.** ***Perf. 13¼x13***

1169	A380 1.30r multi	.70	.70
a.	Perf. 13¾x13 + label	.75	.75

Issued: No. 1169, 10/9; No. 1169a, 11/8. No. 1169a was issued in sheets of 20 stamps + 20 different labels depicting characters on the MTN Gladiators 3 television show that sold for 35r.

Souvenir Sheet

Year of the Dragon — A381

2000, Oct. 9 **Litho.** ***Perf. 13½x13***

1170	A381 4.60r multi	2.10	2.10

Writers of the Boer War Era — A382

Medals and: 1.30r, Sol Plaatje, Johanna Brandt. 4.40r, Sir Arthur Conan Doyle, Sir Winston Churchill.

2000, Oct. 25 **Litho.** ***Perf. 13¼x13¾***

1171-1172	A382 Set of 2	2.75	2.75
a.	Booklet pane, #1171-1172	3.25	—

Issued: No. 1172a, 5/31/02. See note after No. 1282.

A383

Fish, Flowers, Butterflies and Birds — A384

Designs: 5c, Palette surgeonfish. 10c, Blue-banded surgeonfish. 20c, Royal angelfish. 30c, Emperor angelfish. 40c, Blackbar triggerfish. 50c, Coral rockcod. 60c, Powder-blue surgeonfish. 70c, Threadfin butterflyfish. 80c, Longhorn cowfish. 90c, Longnose butterflyfish. 1r, Coral beauty. Nos. 1184, 1199B, 1199G, 1200, 1205, 1210, 1215, 1219A, 1220, 1225, Botterblom, vert. Nos. 1185, 1199C, 1199H, 1201, 1206, 1211, 1216, 1219B, 1221, 1226, Blue marguerite, vert. Nos. 1186, 1199D, 1199I, 1202, 1207, 1212, 1217, 1219C, 1222, 1227, Karoo violet, vert. Nos. 1187, 1199E, 1199J, 1203, 1208, 1213, 1218, 1219D, 1223, 1228, Tree pelargonium, vert. Nos. 1188, 1199F, 1199K, 1204, 1209, 1214, 1219, 1219E, 1224, 1229, Black-eyed susy, vert. 1.40r, Gold-banded forester. 1.50r, Brenton blue. 1.60r, Yellow pansy butterfly. No. 1191, Silver-barred charaxes. No. 1231, Large-spotted acraea butterfly. 2r, Lilac-breasted roller, vert. 2.10r, Koppie charaxes butterfly. 2.30r, Citrus swallowtail. 2.50r, Common grass-yellow butterfly. 3r, Woodland kingfisher, vert. 5r, White-fronted bee-eater, vert. 6.30r, Green-banded swallowtail. 7r, Southern milkweed butterfly. 10r, African green pigeon, vert. 12.60r, False dotted-border. 14r, Lilac tip butterfly. 20r, Purple-crested lourie, vert.

Non-English country name inscriptions at top: Nos. 1199B, 1199F, 1199I, 1200, 1204, 1207, 1217, 1219A, 1219E, 1220, 1224, 1227, Afrika Borwa. Nos. 1199C, 1199J, 1201, 1208, 1218, 1219B, 1221, 1228, Ningizimu Afrika. Nos. 1199D, 1202, 1219C, 1222, Suid-Afrika. Nos. 1199E, 1203, 1219D, 1223, Afrika Tshipembe. Nos. 1199G, 1205, 1215, 1225, Afrika Dzonga. Nos. 1199H, 1206, 1216, 1226, Afrika Sewula. Nos. 1199K, 1209, 1219, 1229, Mzantsi Afrika.

Perf. 14½x14¾, 14¾x14½

2000, Nov. 15 **Litho.**

1173	A383	5c multi	.25	.25
a.	Perf. 13		.25	.25
1174	A383	10c multi	.25	.25
a.	Perf. 13		.25	.25
1175	A383	20c multi	.25	.25
a.	Perf. 13		.25	.25
b.	Perf. 14x13¾		.25	.25
1176	A383	30c multi	.25	.25
a.	Perf. 13		.25	.25
1177	A383	40c multi	.25	.25
a.	Perf. 13		.25	.25
1178	A383	50c multi	.25	.25
a.	Perf. 13		.25	.25
1179	A383	60c multi	.25	.25
a.	Perf. 13		.25	.25
1180	A383	70c multi	.25	.25
a.	Perf. 13		.25	.25
b.	Perf. 14x13¾		.25	.25
1181	A383	80c multi	.30	.30
a.	Perf. 13		.30	.30
1182	A383	90c multi	.35	.35
a.	Perf. 13		.30	.30
1183	A383	1r multi	.35	.35
a.	Perf. 13		.35	.35
1184	A383	1.30r multi	.50	.50
1185	A383	1.30r multi	.50	.50
1186	A383	1.30r multi	.50	.50
1187	A383	1.30r multi	.50	.50
1188	A383	1.30r multi	.50	.50
a.	Horiz. strip of 5, #1184-1188		2.50	2.50
1189	A383	1.40r multi	.55	.55
1190	A383	1.50r multi	.60	.60
1191	A383	1.90r multi	.70	.70
1192	A383	2r multi	.80	.80
a.	Perf. 13		.80	.80
1193	A383	2.30r multi	.85	.85
1194	A383	3r multi	1.10	1.10
a.	Perf. 13		1.10	1.10
1195	A383	5r multi	2.10	2.10
a.	Perf. 13		2.10	2.10
1196	A383	6.30r multi	2.75	2.75
1197	A383	10r multi	4.00	4.00
a.	Perf. 13 ('01)		4.00	4.00
1198	A383	12.60r multi	5.50	5.50
a.	Perf. 13 ('01)		6.00	6.00
1199	A383	20r multi	8.00	8.00
a.	Perf. 13		6.50	6.50
m.	Perf. 13¾x14		5.25	5.25

Issued: Nos. 1197a, 1199a, 10/1/01. No. 1179a, 10/1/01. Nos. 1178a, 1192a, 1194a, 1195a, 2002. No. 1173a, 4/2/03; No. 1174a, 5/22/03; Nos. 1175a, 1181a, 9/22/03; Nos. 1176a, 1182a, 1199a, 2/27/03; Nos. 1177a, 1180a, 1183a, 9/23/03. Nos. 1175b, 1180b, 2/24/10; No. 1199m, 2/1/10.

Coil Stamps

Self-Adhesive

Serpentine Die Cut 13¼x13½

2000, Nov. 1 **Litho.**

1199B	A384 1.30r multi	—	—
1199C	A384 1.30r multi	—	—
1199D	A384 1.30r multi	—	—
1199E	A384 1.30r multi	—	—
1199F	A384 1.30r multi	—	—
1199G	A384 1.30r multi	—	—
1199H	A384 1.30r multi	—	—
1199I	A384 1.30r multi	—	—
1199J	A384 1.30r multi	—	—
1199K	A384 1.30r multi	—	—

Booklet Stamps

Self-Adhesive

Die Cut Perf. 13x12½ on 2 or 3 Sides

2000, Nov. 15 **Litho.**

1200	A384 1.30r multi	.50	.50
1201	A384 1.30r multi	.50	.50
1202	A384 1.30r multi	.50	.50
1203	A384 1.30r multi	.50	.50
1204	A384 1.30r multi	.50	.50
1205	A384 1.30r multi	.50	.50
1206	A384 1.30r multi	.50	.50
1207	A384 1.30r multi	.50	.50
1208	A384 1.30r multi	.50	.50
1209	A384 1.30r multi	.50	.50
a.	Booklet, #1200-1209	5.00	

2001, May 16 **Litho.** ***Perf. 13***

1210	A383 1.40r multi	.55	.55
1211	A383 1.40r multi	.55	.55
1212	A383 1.40r multi	.55	.55
1213	A383 1.40r multi	.55	.55
1214	A383 1.40r multi	.55	.55
a.	Horiz. strip of 5, #1210-1214	2.75	2.75

"Standard Postage" in Thin Letters

Coil Stamps

Serpentine Die Cut 13½

Photo.

Self-Adhesive

1215	A384 (1.40r) multi	.55	.55
1216	A384 (1.40r) multi	.55	.55
1217	A384 (1.40r) multi	.55	.55
1218	A384 (1.40r) multi	.55	.55
1219	A384 (1.40r) multi	.55	.55
1219A	A384 (1.40r) multi	.55	.55
1219B	A384 (1.40r) multi	.55	.55
1219C	A384 (1.40r) multi	.55	.55
1219D	A384 (1.40r) multi	.55	.55
1219E	A384 (1.40r) multi	.55	.55
f.	Strip of 10, #1215-1219E	5.50	

Die Cut Perf. 13x12½ on 2 or 3 Sides

Photo.

Booklet Stamps

"Standard Postage" in Thin Letters

1220	A384 (1.40r) multi	.55	.55
1221	A384 (1.40r) multi	.55	.55
1222	A384 (1.40r) multi	.55	.55
1223	A384 (1.40r) multi	.55	.55
1224	A384 (1.40r) multi	.55	.55
1225	A384 (1.40r) multi	.55	.55
1226	A384 (1.40r) multi	.55	.55
1227	A384 (1.40r) multi	.55	.55
1228	A384 (1.40r) multi	.55	.55
1229	A384 (1.40r) multi	.55	.55
a.	Booklet, #1220-1229	5.50	
	Nos. 1173-1229 (66)	51.20	51.20

Designs: Nos. 1229B, 1229G, 1229M, 1229R, Botterblom, vert. Nos. 1229C, 1229H, 1229N, 1229S, Blue marguerite, vert. Nos. 1229D, 1229I, 1229O, 1229T, Karoo violet, vert. Nos. 1229E, 1229J, 1229P, 1229U, Tree pelargonium, vert. Nos. 1229F, 1229K, 1229Q, 1229V, Black-eyed susy, vert.

Non-English country name inscriptions at top: Nos. 1229B, 1229F, 1229I, 1229M, 1229Q, 1229T, Afrika Borwa. Nos. 1229C, 1229J, 1229N, 1229U, Ningizimu Afrika. Nos. 1229D, 1229O, Suid-Afrika. Nos. 1229E, 1229P, Afrika Tshipembe. Nos. 1229G, 1229R, Afrika Dzonga. Nos. 1229H, 1229S, Afrika Sewula. Nos. 1229K, 1229V, Mzantsi Afrika.

With "Standard Postage" in Thick Letters

Coil Stamps

Self-Adhesive

Serpentine Die Cut 13½x12¾

2001, May 30 **Litho.**

1229B	A384 (1.40r) multi	—	—
1229C	A384 (1.40r) multi	—	—
1229D	A384 (1.40r) multi	—	—
1229E	A384 (1.40r) multi	—	—
1229F	A384 (1.40r) multi	—	—
1229G	A384 (1.40r) multi	—	—
1229H	A384 (1.40r) multi	—	—
1229I	A384 (1.40r) multi	—	—
1229J	A384 (1.40r) multi	—	—
1229K	A384 (1.40r) multi	—	—

Booklet Stamps

Die Cut Perf. 13x12½ on 2 or 3 Sides

1229M	A384 (1.40r) multi	—	—
1229N	A384 (1.40r) multi	—	—
1229O	A384 (1.40r) multi	—	—
1229P	A384 (1.40r) multi	—	—
1229Q	A384 (1.40r) multi	—	—
1229R	A384 (1.40r) multi	—	—
1229S	A384 (1.40r) multi	—	—
1229T	A384 (1.40r) multi	—	—
1229U	A384 (1.40r) multi	—	—
1229V	A384 (1.40r) multi	—	—
w.	Booklet pane of 10, #1229M-1229V	—	—

Nos. 1215-1229 have "Standard Postage" in thin letters.

Type of 2000

2001, June 16 **Litho.** ***Perf. 13***

1230	A383 1.60r multi	.60	.60
1231	A383 1.90r multi	.75	.75
1232	A383 2.10r multi	.80	.80
1233	A383 2.50r multi	1.00	1.00
1234	A383 7r multi	2.75	2.75
1235	A383 14r multi	6.00	6.00
	Nos. 1230-1235 (6)	11.90	11.90

Myths and
Legends — A385

Designs: 1.30r, The Rain Bull. 1.50r, The
Treasure of the Grosvenor. 2.20r, Seven
Magic Birds. 2.30r, The Hole in the Wall. 6.30r,
Van Hunks and the Devil.

2001, Jan. 24   Litho.   Perf. 13¾
1236-1240 A385   Set of 5   4.50 4.50

Souvenir Sheet

Hong Kong 2001 Stamp
Exhibition — A386

2001, Feb. 1   Perf. 14½x14
1241 A386 4.60r Tree snake   2.75 2.75

Sports
Stars
A387

Designs: No. 1242, 1.40r, Ernie Els, golfer.
No. 1243, 1.40r, Terence Parkin, swimmer.
No. 1244, 1.40r, Hezekiel Sepeng, runner. No.
1245, 1.40r, Rosina Magola, netball player.
No. 1246, 1.40r, Francois Pienaar, rugby
player. No. 1247, 1.40r, Zanele Situ, javelin
thrower. No. 1248, 1.40r, Hestrie Cloete, high
jumper. No. 1249, 1.40r, Lucas Radebe, soccer player. No. 1250, 1.40r, Vuyani Bungu,
boxer. No. 1251, 1.40r, Jonty Rhodes, cricket
player.

2001, Feb. 28   Perf. 13¾x14
1242-1251 A387   Set of 10   6.00 6.00
1251a   Sheet of 15 #1251 +15 la-
    bels, perf. 14½x14   8.50

Labels on No. 1251a depict players from the
2000-01 South African World Cup Cricket
team.

Kgalagadi Transfrontier Park — A388

Designs: 1.40r, Gemsboks, flags of South
Africa and Botswana. 2.50r, Cheetahs. 2.90r,
Sociable weaver birds. 3.60r, Meerkats.

2001, May 12   Litho.   Perf. 13x13¼
1252-1255 A388   Set of 4   4.50 4.50
1254a   Souvenir sheet, #1253-1254   3.00 3.00

See Botswana Nos. 714-717.

Campaign Against Child
Abuse — A389

2001, May 16   Perf. 13¾
1256 A389 1.40r multi   .50 .50

Soweto Uprising,
25th
Anniv. — A390

2001, June 16   Litho.   Perf. 13¾
1257 A390 1.40r multi   .50 .50

Bats — A391

No. 1258: a, Cape horseshoe bat. b,
Welwitsch's hairy bat. c, Schreiber's long-fin-
gered bat. d, Wahlberg's epauletted fruit bat.
e, Short-eared trident bat. f, Common slit-
faced bat. g, Egyptian fruit bat. h, Egyptian
free-tailed bat, vert. i, De Winton's long-eared
bat. j, Large-eared free-tailed bat.

Serpentine Die Cut 11¼
2001, June 22   Self-Adhesive
1258 A391   Sheet of 10, #a-j   4.50 4.50
a.-j.   1.40r Any single   .45 .45

Boer War,
Cent. — A392

Designs: 1.40r, Rev. J. D. Kestell. 3r, Capt.
Thomas Crean.

2001, Aug. 1   Perf. 13¼
1259-1260 A392   Set of 2   2.00 2.00
a.   Booklet pane, #1259-1260, perf.
    13¼x13¾   2.25 —

Issued: No. 1260a, 5/31/02. See note after
No. 1282.

World Conference
Against Racism,
Durban — A393

No. 1262: a, Kgotlelelo le pharologantsho.
b, Kubeketelelana kanye nekwehlukana. c,
Verdraagsaamheid en diversiteit. d, U
kondelelana na u fhambana. e, Kutlwisiso ka
mefutafuta. f, Ku va ni mbilu yo leha ni
kuhambana-hambana. g, Ibekezelelwano

nehlukahlukano. h, Kgothlelelo le pharolo-
gano. i, Ukubekezelelana nokungafani. j,
Ukunyamezelana nokungafani.

2001, Aug. 1   Perf. 13¾x13½
1261 A393 2.10r shown   .75 .75
1262   Sheet of 10   6.00 6.00
a.-j.   A393 1.40r Any single   .60 .60

See Brazil No. 2809.

Musical Instruments — A394

Designs: 1.40r, Concertina. 1.90r, Trumpet.
2.50r, Electric guitar. 3r, African drum. 7r,
Cello.

Litho. with Foil Application
2001, Aug. 23   Perf. 13¼x14
1263-1267 A394   Set of 5   5.25 5.25

Christmas
A395

Designs: 2r, Tree. 3r, Angel.

2001, Oct. 1   Litho.   Perf. 13¼
1268-1269 A395   Set of 2   1.90 1.90

Frame — A396

2001, Oct. 1   Serpentine Die Cut
Self-Adhesive
1270 A396 (1.40r) multi   .60 .60
a.   Double-sided pane of 10 + 40
    labels   6.00

Volvo Round-the-
World Yacht
Race — A397

Designs: 1.40r, Yacht.
6r, Yacht, horiz.

2001, Oct. 23   Perf. 13
1271 A397 1.40r multi   .75 .75
Souvenir Sheet
Perf. 14x13¼
1272 A397   6r multi   1.25 1.25
No. 1272 contains one 40x30mm stamp.

2003 ICC Cricket
World Cup, South
Africa — A398

2001, Nov. 1   Perf. 14x13¾
1273 A398 (1.40r) multi   .85 .85

Souvenir Sheet

New Year 2002 (Year of the
Horse) — A399

2001, Nov. 2   Perf. 14x13¼
1274 A399 6r multi   2.25 2.25

Marine Life — A400

No. 1275: a, Hammerhead shark. b, Loggerhead turtle, vert. c, Clown triggerfish, vert. d,
Cape fur seal, vert. e, Bottlenosed dolphins. f,
Crowned seahorse, vert. g, Blue-spotted rib-
bontail ray, vert. h, Moorish idol. i, Common
octopus. j, Coral rock cod.

Serpentine Die Cut 12¾
2001, Nov. 2   Self-Adhesive
1275 A400   Sheet of 10   4.50 4.50
a.-j.   (1.40r) Any single   .45 .45

Johannesburg World Summit on
Sustainable Development — A401

Designs: Nos. 1276a, 1281c, Prosperity,
vert. Nos. 1276b, 1281a, People, vert. Nos.
1276c, 1281b, Planet, vert. (1.50r) Water,
sanitation and energy for all. No. 1278, Buildings, globe. No. 1279, Clean environment for
health. (3.30r), Food security for all.
Sizes: Nos. 1276a-1276c, 22x32mm, Nos.
1281a-1281c, 21x26mm.

Perf. 13¾x13¼, 13¼x13 (#1277, 1279, 1280), 13¼x13¾ (#1278)

2002　　　　　　　　　**Litho.**

1276	A401	(1.40r)	Strip of 3,		
			#a-c	1.40	1.40
1277	A401	(1.50r)	multi	.50	.50
1278	A401	(3r)	multi	.95	.95
1279	A401	(3r)	multi	.95	.95
1280	A401	(3.30r)	multi	1.00	1.00

Booklet Stamps
Self-Adhesive

Serpentine Die Cut on 2 or 3 Sides

1281	A401	(1.40r)	Strip of 3,		
			#a-c	1.40	1.40
d.		Booklet pane, 4 #1281a, 3			
		#1281b-1281c		4.50	4.50
		Nos. 1276-1281 (6)		6.20	6.20

Issued: Nos. 1276, 1278, 1281, 4/17. No. 1277, 1279, 1280, 8/25. No. 1279 is airmail.

Souvenir Sheet

End of Boer War, Cent. — A402

No. 1282: a, 1.50r, Army officer. b, 3.30r, Government official.

2002, May 31　　　　　*Perf. 13¼x13¾*

1282	A402	Sheet of 2, #a-b	1.50	1.50
c.		Booklet pane, #1282	1.90	—
		Complete booklet, #1151b,		
		1172a, 1260a, 1282c + 2		
		postal cards		10.50

No. 1282c has rouletting between margin of No. 1282 and the booklet pane margin. Complete booklet sold for 45r.

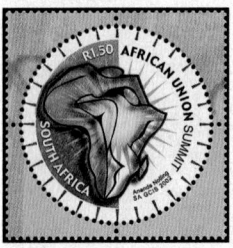

African Union Summit A403

2002, June 25　　　　　　*Perf. 13½*

1283	A403	1.50r multi	.90	.90

Values are for stamps with surrounding selvage.

Type of 2000

Designs: 1.80r, Emperor moth. 2.20r, Peach moth. 2.80r, Snouted tiger moth. 9r, False tiger moth. 16r, Moon moth.

2002, Sept. 20　　**Litho.**　　*Perf. 13*

1284	A383	1.80r multi	.55	.55
1285	A383	2.20r multi	.70	.70
1286	A383	2.80r multi	.85	.85
1287	A383	9r multi	2.75	2.75
1288	A383	16r multi	5.00	5.00
		Nos. 1284-1288 (5)	9.85	9.85

A404　　　　　　A405

A406　　　　　　A407

A408　　　　　　A409

ICC Cricket World Cup

2002　　　　　　　*Perf. 12½x12¾*

1289	A404	(1.50r) multi	.50	.50
1290	A405	(1.50r) multi	.50	.50
1291	A407	(1.50r) multi	.50	.50
1292	A409	(1.50r) multi	.50	.50
1293	A406	(1.50r) multi	.50	.50
1294	A408	(1.50r) multi	.50	.50
		Nos. 1289-1294 (6)	3.00	3.00

Issued: Nos. 1289, 1290, 9/23; 1292, 1294, 11/1; Nos. 1291, 1293, 12/21.

Souvenir Sheet

Steve Biko (1946-77), Anti-apartheid Leader — A410

2002, Oct. 9　　　　　*Perf. 14¾x14½*

1295	A410	4.75r multi	1.50	1.50

See note under No. 1321.

Souvenir Sheet

World Post Day — A411

2002, Oct. 9　　　　　*Perf. 13¼x13½*

1296	A411	4.75r multi	1.50	1.50

Christmas — A412

Stained glass patterns: 1.50r, 3r.

2002, Oct. 23　　　　　*Perf. 14x14¾*

1297-1298	A412	Set of 2	1.40	1.40

Souvenir Sheets

Sawfish — A413

Designs: No. 1299, 7r, Pristis pectinata. No. 1300, 7r, Pristis microdon.

2002, Oct. 23　　　　　　*Perf. 13¾*

1299-1300	A413	Set of 2	4.50	4.50

JUNASS Philatelic Exhibition (#1299); Algoapex Philatelic Exhibition (#1300).

Souvenir Sheet

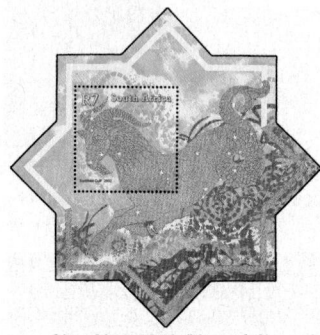

New Year 2003 (Year of the Ram) — A414

2002, Nov. 1　　　　　　*Perf. 14½*

1301	A414	7r multi	2.25	2.25

AIDS Prevention — A415

No. 1302 — AIDS prevention ribbon and: a, Man with sunglasses, male symbol. b, Woman with open mouth. c, Woman with sunglasses, female symbol. d, Hand holding candle, "Stop." e, Woman, candle. f, Hand holding candle, "Be safe." g, Candle, hand pointing at ribbon. h, Open hand. i, Face in droplet. j, Open hand, pills.

Serpentine Die Cut 11¾

2002, Nov. 29　　　**Self-Adhesive**

1302		Booklet of 10	5.25	5.25
a.-j.		A415 (1.50r) Any single	.50	.50

Souvenir Sheet

Solar Eclipse of Dec. 4, 2002 — A416

2002, Dec. 4　　　　　　*Perf. 14½*

1303	A416	4.75r multi	1.50	1.50

ICC Cricket World Cup — A417

No. 1304: a, Huts with windmill blades. b, Horseman. c, Cricket players with bats. d, Bus with people on roof. e, Mother and child. f, Double-decker bus.

2003, Feb. 28　　　　　*Perf. 14¼x13¾*

1304	A417	(1.50r) Sheet of 6, #a-		
		f	2.75	2.75

Souvenir Sheet

Tembisile (Chris) Hani (1942-93), African National Congress Leader — A418

2003, Apr. 27　　**Litho.**　　*Perf. 14¾*

1305	A418	(1.65r) multi	.60	.60

See note after No. 1321.

Life in Informal Settlements — A419

No. 1306: a, Women carrying water jugs on head. b, Man with guitar. c, Man with rake. d, Woman using sewing machine. e, Two children. f, Drink vendor. g, Shoemakers. h, Woman with green cap. i, Young woman with cap and tire. j, Woman with child.

2003, May 16　　　　　*Perf. 14x13¾*

1306	A419	(1.65r) Sheet of 10,		
		#a-j	5.25	5.25

Souvenir Sheet

Africa Day — A420

2003, May 25　　　　　　*Perf. 14¾*

1307	A420	11.70r multi	3.75	3.75

Souvenir Sheet

Oliver Reginald Tambo (1917-93), African National Congress President — A421

2003, May 29

1308	A421	(1.65r) multi	1.25	1.25

See note after No. 1321.

Ballroom Dancing — A422

Designs: 1.65r, Salsa. 2.20r, Rumba. 2.80r, Waltz. 3.30r, Foxtrot. 3.80r, Tango.

2003, July 23		**Perf. 13¼x13¾**	
1309-1313	A422	Set of 5	4.75 4.75

Dogs — A423

No. 1314: a, Africanis. b, Rhodesian Ridgeback. c, Boerboel. d, Basenji.

2003, Aug. 1		**Perf. 14½**	
1314	A423	(1.65r) Sheet of 4, #a-d	2.75 2.75

Type of 2000

Designs: No. 1315, Botterblom, vert. No. 1316, Blue marguerite, vert. No. 1317, Karoo violet, vert. No. 1318, Tree pelargonium, vert. No. 1319, Black-eyed susy, vert.

2003, Sept. 15	**Litho.**	**Perf. 13**	
1315	A383	(1.65r) multi	.60 .60
a.		(2.40r) Perf. 14x13¾	.65 .65
b.		(2.40r) Perf. 14¾x14½	.65 .65
1316	A383	(1.65r) multi	.60 .60
a.		(2.40r) Perf. 14x13¾	.65 .65
b.		(2.40r) Perf. 14¾x14½	.65 .65
1317	A383	(1.65r) multi	.60 .60
a.		(2.40r) Perf. 14x13¾	.65 .65
b.		(2.40r) Perf. 14¾x14½	.65 .65
1318	A383	(1.65r) multi	.60 .60
a.		(2.40r) Perf. 14x13¾	.65 .65
b.		(2.40r) Perf. 14¾x14½	.65 .65
1319	A383	(1.65r) multi	.60 .60
a.		Horiz. strip of 5, #1315-1319	3.00 3.00
b.		(2.40r) Perf. 14x13¾	.65 .65
c.		Horiz. strip of 5, #1315a, 1316a, 1317a, 1318a, 1319b	3.25 3.25
d.		(2.40r) Perf. 14¾x14½	.65 .65
e.		Horiz. strip of 5, #1315b, 1316b, 1317b, 1318b, 1319d	3.25 3.25

Issued: Nos. 1315a, 1316a, 1317a, 1318a, 1319b, 2/1/10; Nos. 1315b, 1316b, 1317b, 1318b, 1319d, 2/24/10.

Souvenir Sheet

Walter Max Ulyate Sisulu (1912-2003), African National Congress Deputy President — A424

2003, Sept. 24		**Perf. 14¾**	
1320	A424	11.70r multi	4.75 4.75

See note after No. 1321.

Souvenir Sheet

Robert Mangaliso Sobukwe (1924-1978), Pan Africanist Congress President — A425

2003, Sept. 24		**Perf. 14¾**	
1321	A425	11.70r multi	4.75 4.75

Nos. 1295, 1305, 1308, 1320 and 1321 were sold in, but unattached to, a commemorative booklet that sold for 60r.

Stamp of Fortune Television Show — A426

2003, Sept. 29		**Perf. 14¼x14**	
1322	A426	(1.65r) multi	.60 .60

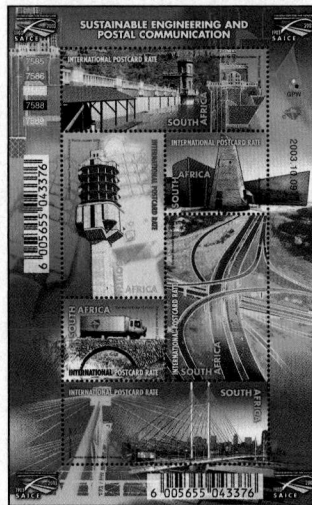

Engineering and Postal Communication — A427

No. 1323, (3.30r): a, Shongweni Dam (60x23mm). b, Kimberley Microwave Tower (30x47mm). c, Northern Cape Legislature Building (30x23mm). d, Durban Westville highway interchange (30x47mm). e, Postal truck on Community Bridge, Limpopo (30x23mm). f, Nelson Mandela Bridge, Johannesburg (60x23mm).

2003, Oct. 9		**Perf. 14x14¼**	
1323	A427	Sheet of 6, #a-f	8.00 8.00
g.		Like No. 1323, with PIARC World Road Congress inscription in margin	8.00 8.00

Souvenir Sheet

South Africa - India Diplomatic Relations, 10th Anniv. — A428

2003, Oct. 16		**Perf. 14¾**	
1324	A428	3.35r multi	1.40 1.40

Bid for Hosting 2010 World Cup Soccer Championships — A429

Emblem, soccer fan with painted face and: No. 1325, (3.80r), Map of Africa. No. 1326, (4.25r), Soccer players.

2003, Oct. 23			
1325-1326	A429	Set of 2	2.40 2.40

No. 1325 is airmail.

Cape of Good Hope Triangle Stamps, 150th Anniv. A430

2003, Oct. 23	**Litho.**	**Perf. 12½x12¾**	
1327	A430	(1.65r) blue	.60 .60

Printed in sheets of 4.

A431

Christmas — A432

No. 1328: a, Joseph, Mary on donkey. b, Angels. c, Magi. d, Madonna and Child. e, Dove.

2003, Nov. 3	**Litho.**	**Perf. 14x14¼**	
1328		Horiz. strip of 5	3.00 3.00
a.-e.		A431 (1.65r) Any single	.55 .55
		Perf. 14¾	
1329	A432	3.80r shown	1.50 1.50

Elephants — A433

No. 1330: a, African elephants. b, Asian elephant.

2003, Dec. 9		**Perf. 14¼x14**	
1330	A433	3.35r Horiz. pair, #a-b	3.25 3.25

South Africa — Thailand diplomatic relations, 10th anniv. See Thailand No. 2105.

Powered Flight, Cent. — A434

No. 1331: a, Paterson Biplane. b, "Silver Queen" Vickers Vimy. c, Wapiti. d, De Havilland DH-9. e, Junkers Ju52/53. f, Sikorsky S-55 helicopter. g, Boeing 707. h, Rooivalk helicopter. i, SUNSAT Microsatellite. j, Mark Shuttleworth, first African in space, and Space Station.

2003, Dec. 17		**Perf. 14¼x14**	
1331	A434	(1.65r) Sheet of 10, #a-j	7.00 7.00

New Year 2004 (Year of the Monkey) — A435

2004, Jan. 22		**Perf. 13¾**	
1332	A435	11.70r multi	4.50 4.50

Road Safety A436

No. 1333 — Inscriptions: a, Be visible. b, Don't drink and drive. c, Maintain your vehicle. d, Slow down. e, Don't drive when tired.

		Perf. 13¼x13¾	
2004, Mar. 24			**Litho.**
1333		Vert. strip of 5	3.00 3.00
a.-e.		A436 (1.70r) Any single	.60 .60

End of Apartheid, 10th Anniv. — A437

No. 1334: a, Dove, map of Africa. b, People voting. c, Women and child. d, Sports fans holding flag and trophies. e, Woman with handicrafts.

2004, Apr. 27	**Litho.**	**Perf. 13¼**	
1334		Vert. strip of 5	3.00 3.00
a.-e.		A437 (1.70r) Any single	.60 .60

Miniature Sheet

Legacy of Slaves — A438

No. 1335, (1.70r): a, Slave bell, Vergelegen, and slave lodge, Cape Town. b, Hidayat al-Islam, first book in Arabic-Afrikaans. c, Chair and cupboard. d, Traditional foods. e, Indian workers in sugar cane fields. f, Chinese mine workers.

2005, May 1			
1335	A438	Sheet of 6, #a-f	4.25 4.25

Souvenir Sheet

FIFA (Fédération Internationale de Football Association), Cent. — A439

2004, Apr. 30	**Litho.**	**Perf. 14¾**	
1336	A439	4.35r multi	2.00 2.00

Spiders — A440

No. 1337: a, Hedgehog spider. b, Golden orb-web spider, vert. c, Lynx spider, vert. d, Black button spider, vert. e, Ladybird spider. f, Flower crab spider. g, Rain spider, vert. h, Horn baboon spider. i, Trap door spider. j, Spotted crab spider.

Serpentine Die Cut 9½x9, 9x9½
2004, July 30
Self-Adhesive
1337	A440	Sheet of 10, #a-j	7.50 7.50
a.-j.		(1.70r) Any single	.75 .75

Volunteers — A441

No. 1338: a, Environmental helpers. b, Caring for the elderly. c, Education. d, Medical and ambulance services. e, Surf life saving. f, Helping abandoned pets. g, Caring for orphans. h, Fire fighters. i, Community gardens. j, Tape aids for the blind.

2004, Aug. 9   **Perf. 13½x13¾**
1338	A441	(1.70r) Sheet of 10, #a-j	7.00 7.00

Sports — A442

No. 1339: a, Archery. b, Track. c, Equestrian. d, Cycling. e, Rhythmic gymnastics. f, Canoeing. g, Soccer. h, Swimming. i, Boxing. j, Tennis.

2004, Aug. 13   **Perf. 13¾x13½**
1339	A442	(1.70r) Sheet of 10, #a-j	7.00 7.00

Christmas
A443

Icons: (1.70r), Madonna and Child. (4r), Jesus Christ, Pantocrator.

2004, Oct. 1
1340-1341	A443	Set of 2	2.00 2.00

No. 1341 is inscribed "International Airmail Letter."

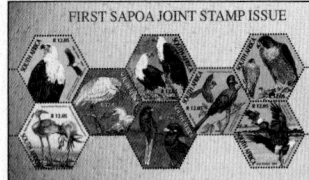

Birds — A444

No. 1342: a, African fish eagles, national bird of Namibia. b, African fish eagles, national bird of Zimbabwe. c, Peregrine falcons, national bird of Angola. d, Cattle egrets, national bird of Botswana. e, Purple-crested louries, national bird of Swaziland. f, Blue cranes, national bird of South Africa. g, Bartailed trogons. h, African fish eagles, national bird of Zambia.

2004, Oct. 9   **Perf. 14**
1342	A444	12.05r Sheet of 8, #a-h	32.50 32.50

See Botswana Nos. 792-793, Namibia No. 1052, Swaziland Nos. 727-735, Zambia No. 1033, and Zimbabwe No. 975.

Souvenir Sheet

Regular Air Mail Service in South Africa, 75th Anniv. — A445

Litho. with Hologram
2004, Oct. 9   **Perf. 13¾**
1343	A445	12.05r multi	4.25 4.25

South African Police Service, 10th Anniv. — A446

No. 1344: a, South African Police Service badge, South African flag. b, Fighting drugs. c, Police air wing. d, Fingerprint and forensic science. e, Special task force. f, Protecting women and children. g, Sector policing. h, The Dignified Blue. i, SAPS mounted unit. j, Dog unit.

Serpentine Die Cut 13½x13
2004, Nov. 23   **Litho.**
Self-Adhesive
1344	A446	Sheet of 10	7.00 7.00
a.-j.		(1.70r) Any single	.70 .70

South African
Large Telescope
A447

No. 1345: a, Exterior of building. b, Cutaway view of building. c, Building aperture, top

of telescope, Southern Cross constellation. d, Telescope. e, Building aperture, entire telescope.

2004, Dec. 1   **Perf. 13¾x13½**
1345		Horiz. strip of 5	8.00 8.00
a.-e.		A447 4r Any single	1.60 1.60

Souvenir Sheet

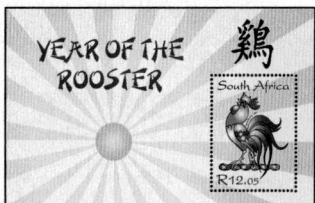

New Year 2005 (Year of the Rooster) — A448

2005, Feb. 9   **Perf. 14¾x14½**
1346	A448	12.05r multi	4.50 4.50

Souvenir Sheet

Freedom Charter, 50th Anniv. — A449

No. 1347: a, "Freedom Charter" in mirror image. b, "Freedom Charter" and "50."

Perf. 14¼x13¾
2005, June 24   **Litho.**
1347	A449	(1.77r) Sheet of 2, #a-b	1.40 1.40

Miniature Sheet

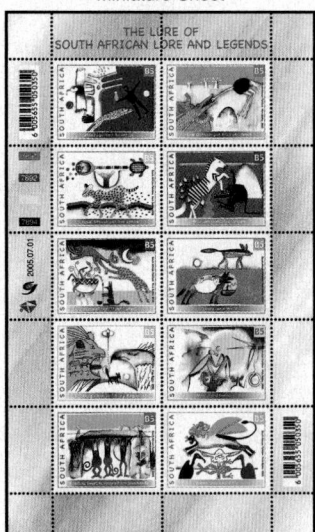

Legends — A450

No. 1348: a, Honeyguide's Revenge. b, How Ostrich Got His Long Neck. c, How Serval Got His Spots. d, How Zebra Got His Stripes. e, Jackal, the Tiger Eater. f, Jackal and Wolf. g, King Lion and King Eagle. h, Mantis and the Moon. i, Words as Sweet as Honey from Sankhambi. j, When Lion Could Fly.

2005, July 1
1348	A450	B5 Sheet of 10, #a-j	12.00 12.00

Nos. 1348a-11348j each sold for 3.75r on day of issue.

Miniature Sheet

Small Mammals — A451

No. 1349: a, Lesser bushbaby (24x60mm). b, Riverine rabbit (24x30mm). c, African wildcat (48x30mm). d, Yellow mongoose (24x60mm). e, Steenbok (48x30mm). f, Cape fox (24x30mm).

2005, July 15   **Perf. 14**
1349	A451	(1.77r) Sheet of 6, #a-f	4.25 4.25

Energy Sources — A452

2005, Sept. 26   **Perf. 14x14¼**
1350	A452	(1.77r) Wave	.70 .70
1351	A452	(3.65r) Wind	1.40 1.40
1352	A452	(4.25r) Sun	1.75 1.75
		Nos. 1350-1352 (3)	3.85 3.85

Inscription on No. 1350, Standard Postage; No. 1351, International Airmail Postcard; No. 1352, International Airmail Letter.

Christmas
A453

Wire and bead sculptures: (1.77r), Candle, Christmas tree, heart. (4.25r), Angel and dove.

2005, Oct. 3
1353	A453	(1.77r) multi	.70 .70
1354	A453	(4.25r) multi	1.60 1.60

Inscription on No. 1353, Standard Postage; No. 1354, International Airmail Letter.

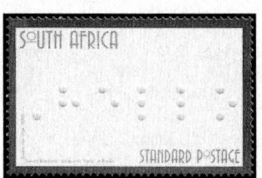

Prevention of Blindness — A454

Litho. & Embossed
2005, Oct. 13   **Perf. 14¼x14**
1355	A454	(1.77r) org brn & gray	.70 .70

Souvenir Sheet

New Year 2006 (Year of the Dog) — A455

No. 1356: a, Seeing-eye dog. b, Drug-sniffing dog and luggage. c, Bird-chasing dog at airport.

2006, Jan. 26   *Perf. 13¼x13*
1356 A455 B5 Sheet of 3, #a-c   4.25 4.25
Nos. 1356a-1356c each sold for 3.75r on day of issue.

Rock Art — A456

No. 1357: a, Detail of Linton Panel, Iziko South African Museum. b, Reedbuck, South African Museum of Rock Art (inscription at LR). c, San ritual specialist, South African Museum of Rock Art (inscription at LL). d, Rhinoceros, Wildebeest Kuil rock art site. e, Eland, Game Pass rock art site.

2006, Feb. 15
1357   Horiz. strip of 5   3.50 3.50
a.-e.   A456 (1.77r) Any single   .70   .70

Miniature Sheet

Rural Medical Outreach — A457

No. 1358: a, Helicopter and rescuer (24x60mm). b, Doctors clasping hands (24x30mm). c, Airplane, paramedics tending to man on stretcher, horiz. (48x30mm). d, Motorcycle ambulance, paramedic assisting man (24x30mm). e, Phelophepa Health Train, doctor examining woman, horiz. (72x30mm). f, Ambulance, attendants moving patient on gurney (24x30mm).

2006, May 2   Litho.   *Perf. 13¼*
1358 A457 (1.85r) Sheet of 6, #a-
         f   4.25 4.25

Chief Bhambatha Zondi, Leader of 1906 Rebellion — A458

2006, June 9   *Perf. 14x13½*
1359 A458 (1.85r) multi   .65   .65

Red Cross War Memorial Children's Hospital, 50th Anniv. — A459

Designs: (1.85r), Nurse and ill child. (4.40r), Hospital building, horiz.

Perf. 13¾x13½, 13½x13¾
2006, June 18
1360-1361 A459   Set of 2   2.25 2.25
Inscription on No. 1360 reads "Standard Postage;" on No. 1361, "International Letter."

Souvenir Sheet

Women's Anti-Apartheid March to the Union Building, Pretoria, 50th Anniv. — A460

2006, Aug. 9   *Perf. 14¾x14*
1362 A460 B5 multi   1.40 1.40
No. 1362 sold for 3.75r on day of issue.

Miniature Sheet

Clivia Flowers — A461

No. 1363, (1.85r): a, Clivia nobilis. b, Clivia miniata. c, Clivia gardenii. d, Clivia caulescens. e, Clivia mirabilis. f, Clivia robusta.

2006, Sept. 6   *Perf. 13x13¼*
1363 A461   Sheet of 6, #a-f   3.25 3.25

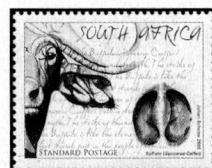

Animal, Text and Tracks A462

Animal, Herd and Tracks A463

No. 1364: a, Buffalo. b, Elephant. c, Blue wildebeest. d, Hippopotamus. e, Black rhinoceros. f, Giraffe. g, Spotted hyena. h, Leopard. i, Warthog. j, Zebra.

Litho. & Embossed

2006, Sept. 15   *Perf. 13¾x13¼*
1364   Sheet of 10   6.00 6.00
a.-e.   A462 (1.85r) Any single   .60   .60
f.-j.   A463 (1.85r) Any single   .60   .60

Christmas — A464

No. 1365: a, Antelope. b, Warthog. c, Zebra. d, Hippopotamus. e, Lion, as Santa, in sleigh. (4.40r), Lion as Santa.

2006, Oct. 2   Litho.   *Perf. 13½x13*
1365   Horiz. strip of 5   2.50 2.50
a.-e.   A464 (1.85r) Any single   .50   .50
1366 A464 (4.40r) multi   1.40 1.40
Inscriptions on Nos. 1365a-1365e read "Standard Postage;" on No. 1366, "International Airmail Letter."

World Post Day — A465

No. 1367 — Boy and slogan: a, "Start an Adventure." b, "Be Cool." c, "Learn More." d, "Have Fun." e, "Travel the World."

2006, Oct. 9   *Perf. 13x13¼*
1367   Horiz. strip of 5   2.50 2.50
a.-e.   A465 (1.85r) Any single   .50   .50

Owls — A466

No. 1368: a, Barn owl. b, Cape eagle owl. c, African barred owlet. d, Verreaux's eagle owl. e, Pel's fishing owl.

2007, Aug. 3   Litho.   *Perf. 14½*
1368   Horiz. strip of 5   6.50 6.50
a.-e.   A466 (4.64r) Any single   1.25 1.25

Souvenir Sheet

Scouting, Cent. — A467

No. 1369: a, Scout saluting. b, Scouting fleur-de-lis.

2007, Aug. 22
1369 A467 (3.90r) Sheet of 2,
              #a-b   2.25 2.25

Souvenir Sheet

New Year 2007 (Year of the Pig) — A468

Litho. & Embossed With Foil Application

2007, Sept. 7
1370 A468 (4.89r) green & gold   2.75 2.75

World Post Day — A469

2007, Oct. 9   Litho.   *Perf. 14x14¼*
1371 A469 (3.90r) multi   1.25 1.25
First telephone exchange in South Africa, 125th anniv.

Cheetah A470

Ostrich A471

2007, Oct. 19   *Perf. 14*
1372 A470 (3.90r) multi   1.25 1.25
1373 A471 (4.89r) multi   1.50 1.50
a.   Perf. 14¾x14½   1.60 1.60
Issued: No. 1373a, 9/3/09.

Miniature Sheet

Intl. Polar and Heliophysical Year — A472

No. 1374: a, King penguins (24x30mm). b, Scientists at SANAE IV Base, Antarctica (72x30mm). c, Wandering albatross (24x60mm). d, Adélie penguins (24x30mm). e, Killer whale (48x30mm). f, Weddell seal (24x30mm).

2007, Oct. 31
1374 A472 (1.93r) Sheet of 6,
              #a-f   3.50 3.50

Mills — A473

No. 1375: a, Mostert's Mill, Cape Town. b, La Cotte Watermill, Franschhoek. c, Witpoort Watermill, Stoffberg. d, Dwars Rivier Watermill, Cederberg. e, Colesberg Horse and Mill, Colesberg.

2007, Nov. 9   *Perf. 14½*
1375   Vert. strip of 5   7.00 7.00
a.-e.   A473 (4.64r) Any single   1.40 1.40

Union Castle Line Ships A474

No. 1376: a, Dane. b, Kildonan Castle. c, SA Vaal. d, Edinburgh Castle. e, Windsor Castle.

2007, Dec. 5
1376   Vert. strip of 5   6.25 6.25
a.-e.   A474 (4.01r) Any single   1.25 1.25

118th Inter-Parliamentary Union
Assembly, Cape Town — A475

2008, Apr. 13   Litho.   Perf. 13¾
1377 A475 (2.05r) multi   .55   .55

Diplomatic Relations Between South
Africa and People's Republic of
China — A476

No. 1378 — Flags of South Africa and People's Republic of China: a, Within circle of text.
b, Above text.

2008, Apr. 24
1378 A476   Sheet of 2   1.90   1.90
  a.   (2.05r) multi   .55   .55
  b.   (4.90r) multi   1.25   1.25

No. 1378a is inscribed "Standard Postage";
No. 1378b, "International Airmail Small Letter."

Miniature Sheet

Constitutional Court Buildings — A477

No. 1379: a, Part of building, looking up
from street level (56x26mm). b, Covered
entranceway (26x26mm). c, Plaza between
buildings (56x26mm). d, Chambers
(26x26mm). e, Rectangular and cylindrical
towers (86x26mm). f, Three-storied buildings
and plaza (26x26mm). g, Shadows on interior
column (26x26mm). h, Wall with multicolored
words (26x26mm). i, Curved wall (26x26mm).
j, Building and street (56x26mm).

2008, June 25   Perf. 14x13¼
1379 A477   Sheet of 10   5.25   5.25
  a.-j.   (2.05r) Any single   .50   .50

Nos. 1379a-1379j are each inscribed "Standard Postage."

Souvenir Sheets

A478

Pres. Nelson Mandela, 90th
Birthday — A479

2008, July 15   Perf. 13¼
1380 A478 (2.05r) multi   .60   .60
1381 A479 (4.90r) multi   1.40   1.40

No. 1381 is airmail.

Souvenir Sheet

Alma Ata Declaration on Primary
Health Care, 30th Anniv. — A480

2008, Sept. 6   Litho.   Perf. 13¼x14
1382 A480 (2.05r) multi   .50   .50

Souvenir Sheet

Onderstepoort, Cent. — A481

Litho. With Foil Application
2008, Oct. 8   Perf. 13¾x13¼
1383 A481 (2.05r) multi   .45   .45

World Post
Day — A482

No. 1384: a, Aberdeen Post Office. b, West
Bank Post Office, East London. c, Main Post
Office, Durban. d, Church Square Post Office,
Pretoria. e, Frankfort Post Office.

2008, Oct. 9   Litho.   Perf. 13¼x13¾
1384   Horiz. strip of 5   2.25   2.25
  a.-e.   A482 (2.05r) Any single   .45   .45

Nos. 1384a-1384e are each inscribed
"Standard Postage."

Miniature Sheets

A483

South African Airways, 75th
Anniv. — A484

No. 1385 — Captain's cap and uniform
insignia, with cap insignia at top: a, With
"S.A.A./S.A.L" in crest. b, With large crown
over winged springbok flying left. c, With coat
of arms above winged springbok flying left. d,
With coat of arms above winged springbok flying right. e, With winged springbok in red circle. f, With crest having colors of South African
flag.
No. 1386 — Airline emblem on tail of: a,
Junkers Ju53/3m. b, Douglas DC-4. c, Boeing
707. d, Boeing 747 (winged springbok). e,
Airbus A300. f, Boeing 747 (colors of South
African flag).

**Litho. & Embossed With Foil
Application**
2009, Jan. 30   Perf. 13¼
1385 A483   Sheet of 6   2.40   2.40
  a.-f.   (2.05r) Any single   .40   .40
Litho.
1386 A484   Sheet of 6   5.75   5.75
  a.-f.   (4.90r) Any single   .95   .95

Nos. 1385a-1385f are inscribed "Standard
Postage"; Nos. 1386a-1386f, "International
Airmail Small Letter."

Rose
Varieties
A485

Serpentine Die Cut
2009, Feb. 13   Litho.
Self-Adhesive
1387 A485 (2.05r) Johannesburg
                 Sun   .40   .40
1388 A485 (2.05r) Rina Hugo   .40   .40
1389 A485 (2.05r) Beauty From
                 Within   .40   .40
1390 A485 (2.05r) Bewitched   .40   .40
1391 A485 (2.05r) Cotlands Rose .40   .40
  a.   Miniature sheet, 2 each #1387-
      1391   4.00
    Nos. 1387-1391 (5)   2.00   2.00

Nos. 1387-1391 are each inscribed "Standard Postage."

Souvenir Sheet

Intl. Polar Year — A486

2009, Mar. 2   Perf. 13¼x13¾
1392 A486   Sheet of 2   1.40   1.40
  a.   (2.05r) Sooty albatrosses   .40   .40
  b.   (4.90r) Jellyfish   1.00   1.00

No. 1392a is inscribed "Standard Postage";
No. 1392b, "International Small Letter."

Pres.
Kgalema
Motlanthe
A487

2009, Mar. 19   Perf. 14½
1393 A487 (2.05r) multi   .45   .45

Occupational Health — A488

No. 1394 — Inscriptions: a, Ergonomics in
the office. b, Medical surveillance. c, Personal
protective equipment. d, Ensure a safe work
place. e, Training in the work place.

2009, Mar. 20   Perf. 13¾x13¼
1394   Vert. strip of 5   2.25   2.25
  a.-e.   A488 (2.05r) Any single   .45   .45

Miniature Sheet

Artwork in the Constitutional
Court — A489

No. 1395: a, The Benefit of the Doubt 2,
tapestry by Marlene Dumas (26x35mm). b,
Forgotten Family 1, by Penny Siopis
(52x35mm). c, Bass Player, by Dumile Feni
(26x35mm). d, Head, by William Kentridge
(26x35mm). e, Hotel with Landscape (Spy), by
Robert Hodgins (52x35mm). f, Hotlands, by
Andrew Verster (26x70mm). g, Discussion,
tapestry by Willie Bester (52x35mm). h, The
Smoker, by Gerard Sekoto (52x35mm). i,
Tethered Monkey, by Albert Adams
(26x35mm). j, Blue Dress 3, by Judith Mason
(26x35mm).

2009, June 5   Litho.   Perf. 14½
1395 A489   Sheet of 10   5.50   5.50
  a.-j.   (2.25r) Any single   .55   .55

Nos. 1395a-1395j are inscribed "Standard
Postage."

Artifacts From Mapungubwe
Archaeological Site — A490

No. 1396: a, Gold bowl. b, Spouted pots. c,
Gold rhinoceros. d, Terra cotta bowl. e, Gold
scepter.

2009, Sept. 23
1396   Horiz. strip of 5   7.50   7.50
  a.-e.   A490 (5.40r) Any single   1.50   1.50

Nos. 1396a-1396e are inscribed "International Small Letter."

Souvenir Sheets

South Africa No. 1 — A491

Show Emblem — A492

2009, Oct. 9   *Perf. 13¾*
1397   A491 (2.25r) multi   .60   .60
1398   A492 (5.40r) multi   1.50   1.50

Joburg 2010 Intl. Stamp Show, Johannesburg. No. 1397 is inscribed "Standard Postage," and No. 1398, "International Small Letter."

Souvenir Sheet

Solomon Kalushi Mahlangu (1956-79), Executed African National Congress Member — A493

2009, Oct. 15   *Perf. 13¼x13¾*
1399   A493 (2.25r) multi   .60   .60

No. 1399 is inscribed "Standard Postage."

Pres. Jacob Zuma A494

2009, Nov. 10   *Perf. 13¼*
1400   A494 (2.25r) multi   .60   .60

Miniature Sheet

Bridging the Digital Divide — A495

No. 1401: a, People, cellular phone, open letter (56x28mm triangle). b, City, cellular phones, envelope (28x28mm square). c, Envelope and letter (80x40mm triangle). d, Letter box and digital code (20x60mm rhomboid). e, Computer, boat, hot-air balloons, paper airplane (80x40mm triangle).

Litho. With Foil Application
2010, Jan. 18   *Perf. 13¾*
1401   A495   Sheet of 5 + label   5.50   5.50
   a.-e.   (4.05r) Any single   1.10   1.10

Nos. 1401a-1401e are inscribed "Southern Africa Small Letter."

Hand Signs for Calling Taxis A496

No. 1402: a, Randberg to Tembisa. b, Tembisa to Sebenza. c, Turffontein to Mulbarton. d, Gauteng to Johannesburg Central Business District. e, Germiston to Katlehong. f, Johannesburg to Sandton. g, Alexandra to Randburg. h, Emdeni to Highgate. i, Local to the area. j, Johannesburg to Phola Park.

2010, Jan. 29 Litho.   *Perf. 13¾x13¼*
1402   Sheet of 10   6.00   6.00
   a.-j.   A496 (2.25r) Any single   .60   .60

Nos. 1402a-1402j are inscribed "Standard Postage." Portions of the designs were applied by a thermographic process producing a shiny, raised effect. Sand grains were added to the thermographic ink.

Miniature Sheet

2010 World Cup Soccer Championships, South Africa — A497

No. 1403 — Soccer players, ball, 2010 World Cup mascot and flag of: a, Namibia. b, South Africa. c, Zimbabwe. d, Malawi. e, Swaziland. f, Botswana. g, Mauritius. h, Lesotho. i, Zambia.

2010, Apr. 9   *Perf. 13¾*
1403   A497   Sheet of 9   14.50   14.50
   a.-i.   5.75r Any single   1.60   1.60

See Botswana Nos. 896-905, Lesotho No. , Malawi No. 753, Mauritius No. , Namibia No. 1188, Swaziland Nos. 794-803, Zambia Nos. 1115-1118, and Zimbabwe Nos. 1112-1121.

Miniature Sheet

History of Constitution Hill — A498

No. 1404 — Photographs of Old Fort prison complex that housed famous political prisoners: a, Cellblock Number Four (48x40mm). b, Atrium of Women's Jail (24x40mm). c, Awaiting-Trial Block (48x40mm). d, Flogging frame in Cell 3 of Cellblock Number Four (48x40mm). e, Remaining stairwells of Awaiting-Trial Block (24x40mm). f, Cells in the Fort (24x40mm). g, Isolation cells in Cellblock Number Four (80x24mm). h, Guard house in front of isolation cells (24x40mm). i, Entrance to the Fort (48x40mm). j, Ramparts (96x40mm).

2010, May 28   *Perf. 13½*
1404   A498   Sheet of 10 + central label   6.75   6.75
   a.-j.   2.40r Any single   .60   .60

A499

2010 World Cup Soccer Championships, South Africa — A500

Zakumi, official mascot of 2010 World Cup Soccer Championships: No. 1405, Holding soccer ball. No. 1406, Dribbling soccer ball, ball at right. No. 1407, Holding flag of South Africa. No. 1408, Running with soccer ball. No. 1409, With arms raised.
Designs: No. 1410, Emblem of 2010 World Cup Soccer Championships. No. 1411, Official soccer ball. No. 1412, World Cup Trophy.

2010, June 11   *Die Cut*
Self-Adhesive
1405   A499   2.40r multi   .65   .65
1406   A499   2.40r multi   .65   .65
1407   A499   2.40r multi   .65   .65
1408   A499   2.40r multi   .65   .65
1409   A499   2.40r multi   .65   .65
   a.   Horiz. strip of 5, #1405-1409   3.25

Serpentine Die Cut
1410   A500   4.90r multi   1.25   1.25
1411   A500   4.90r multi   1.25   1.25
1412   A500   4.90r multi   1.25   1.25
   a.   Sheet of 6, 2 each #1410-1412   7.50
    Nos. 1405-1412 (8)   7.00   7.00

Miniature Sheet

South African Railways, 150th Anniv. — A501

No. 1413: a, Natal 0-4-0, 1860. b, Class NGC 16 Garratt 2-6-2+2-6-2, 1937. c, Class 24 2-8-4, 1948. d, Class 25 4-8-4, 1953. e, Class GMA/M Garratt 4-8-2+2-8-4, 1954. f, Class 35 Co-Co Diesel-electric locomotive, 1974. g, Class 9E Co-Co electric locomotive, 1978. h, Class 26 4-8-4, 1981. i, Class 19E Bo-Bo dual voltage electric locomotive, 2009. j, Gautrain Electrostar Bo-Bo, 2010.

2010, June 25   *Perf. 13½x12¾*
1413   A501   Sheet of 10   6.25   6.25
   a.-j.   2.40r Any single   .60   .60

Miniature Sheet

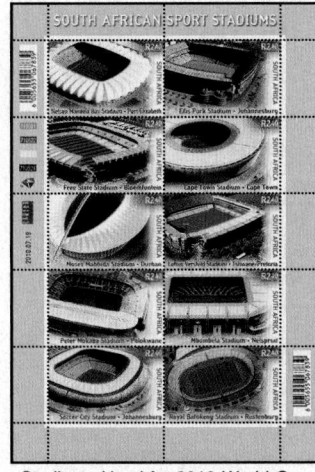

Stadiums Used for 2010 World Cup Soccer Championships — A502

No. 1414: a, Nelson Mandela Bay Stadium, Port Elizabeth. b, Ellis Park Stadium, Johannesburg. c, Free State Stadium, Bloemfontein. d, Cape Town Stadium, Cape Town. e, Moses Mabhida Stadium, Durban. f, Loftus Versfeld Stadium, Tshwane/Pretoria. g, Peter Mokaba Stadium, Polokwane. h, Mbombela Stadium, Nelspruit. i, Soccer City Stadium, Johannesburg. j, Royal Bafokeng Stadium, Rustenburg.

2010, July 19   *Perf. 13¼x13*
1414   A502   Sheet of 10   6.75   6.75
   a.-j.   2.40r Any single   .65   .65

Birds — A503

No. 1415: a, Blue korhaan. b, Buff-streaked chat. c, White-bellied korhaan. d, White-winged flufftail. e, Yellow-breasted pipit.

2010, Aug. 6   *Litho.*
1415   Horiz. strip of 5   8.00   8.00
   a.-e.   A503 5.75r Any single   1.60   1.60

See No. 1464.

Richtersveld UNESCO World Heritage Site — A504

No. 1416: a, Namaqua chameleon. b, Namaqua sandgrouse. c, Bastard quiver tree. d, Nama tribesman. e, Gray rhebok.

2010, Sept. 23   *Perf. 13¾x13¼*
1416   Horiz. strip of 5   3.50   3.50
   a.-e.   A504 2.40r Any single   .70   .70

Miniature Sheet

South African Stamps, Cent. — A505

No. 1417 — Stamps of South Africa with original denominations distorted: a, #1 (30x30mm). b, #43b (30x30mm). c, #C5

(30x30mm). d, #1385f (30x30mm). e, #402 (30x60mm). f, #284 (60x30mm). g, #362 (30x60mm). h, #1355 (60x30mm). i, #C87g (60x30mm). j, #980 (30x60mm). k, #C98i (30x30mm). l, #438 (90x30mm).

2010, Oct. 9   *Perf. 13¼*
1417   A505   Sheet of 12   8.50   8.50
a.-l.   (2.40r) Any single   .70   .70

World Post Day. Nos. 1417a-1417 are inscribed "Standard Postage."

Beadwork
A506

Designs: 5c, Ladybug. 10c, Bird. 20c, Llama. 30c, Cell phone. 40c, Hammerhead bird. 50c, Airplane. 60c, Angel. 70c, Nguni cow. 80c, Boxer. 90c, Zebra. 1r, Miner. 2r, Tsonga fertility figure. Nos. 1430, 1445, 1452, Zulu neckpiece, vert. Nos. 1431, 1446, 1453, Ndebele neckpiece, vert. Nos. 1432, 1447, 1454, Xhosa neckpiece, vert. Nos. 1433, 1448, 1455, Swazi necklace, vert. Nos. 1434, 1449, 1456, Tsonga love token pin, vert. 3r, Ndebele married woman's apron. (4.80r), Tsonga neckpiece. (4.90r), Zulu neckpiece, diff. 5r, Mfengu tobacco bag. (5.75r), Bhaca neckpiece. No. 1440, Bhaca neckpiece, diff. 10r, South Sotho ceremonial whisk. (16.90r), Bhaca neckpiece, diff. (19.35r), Vendan pin. 20r, Zulu neckpiece of lion's claws. Nos. 1451, 1458, Bhaca neckpiece, vert.

2010, Oct. 27   *Perf. 14½*
1418   A506   5c multi   .25   .25
1419   A506   10c multi   .25   .25
1420   A506   20c multi   .25   .25
1421   A506   30c multi   .25   .25
1422   A506   40c multi   .25   .25
1423   A506   50c multi   .25   .25
1424   A506   60c multi   .25   .25
1425   A506   70c multi   .25   .25
1426   A506   80c multi   .25   .25
1427   A506   90c multi   .25   .25
1428   A506   1r multi   .30   .30
1429   A506   2r multi   .60   .60
1430   A506   (2.40r) multi   .70   .70
1431   A506   (2.40r) multi   .70   .70
1432   A506   (2.40r) multi   .70   .70
1433   A506   (2.40r) multi   .70   .70
1434   A506   (2.40r) multi   .70   .70
a.   Horiz. strip of 5, #1430-1434   3.50   3.50
1435   A506   3r multi   .90   .90
1436   A506   (4.80r) multi   1.40   1.40
1437   A506   (4.90r) multi   1.50   1.50
1438   A506   5r multi   1.50   1.50
1439   A506   (5.75r) multi   1.75   1.75
1440   A506   (6r) multi   1.75   1.75
1441   A506   10r multi   3.00   3.00
1442   A506   (16.90r) multi   5.00   5.00
1443   A506   (19.35r) multi   5.75   5.75
1444   A506   20r multi   6.00   6.00
Nos. 1418-1444 (27)   35.45   35.45

Self-Adhesive
Size: 20x27mm
Serpentine Die Cut 13¼x12¾
1445   A506   (2.40r) multi   .70   .70
1446   A506   (2.40r) multi   .70   .70
1447   A506   (2.40r) multi   .70   .70
1448   A506   (2.40r) multi   .70   .70
1449   A506   (2.40r) multi   .70   .70
a.   Horiz. or vert. strip of 5, #1445-1449   3.50
1451   A506   (6r) multi   1.75   1.75
Nos. 1445-1451 (6)   5.25   5.25

Booklet Stamps
Die Cut Perf. 12½x12¼ on 2 or 3 Sides
1452   A506   (2.40r) multi   .70   .70
1453   A506   (2.40r) multi   .70   .70
1454   A506   (2.40r) multi   .70   .70
1455   A506   (2.40r) multi   .70   .70
1456   A506   (2.40r) multi   .70   .70
a.   Booklet pane of 10, 2 each #1452-1456   7.00
1457   A506   (4.80r) multi   1.40   1.40
a.   Booklet pane of 10   14.00
1458   A506   (6r) multi   1.75   1.75
a.   Booklet pane of 10   17.50
Nos. 1452-1458 (6)   5.25   5.25

Nos. 1430-1434, 1445-1449 and 1452-1456 are inscribed "Standard Postage." No. 1436 is inscribed "B5." No. 1437 is inscribed "Airmail Postcard." No. 1439 is inscribed "International Small Letter." Nos. 1440, 1451 and 1458 are inscribed "B4." No. 1457 is inscribed "B5." No. 1442 is inscribed "Registered letter small." No. 1443 is inscribed "Registered letter medium."

Nos. 1436, 1440, 1441, 1442, 1443 and 1444 each have two perforations below the line of horizontal perforations at top and two perforations above the line of horizontal perforations at bottom. Nos. 1445-1449 were printed in foldable sheets of 100 containing 20

of each stamp. No. 1451 was printed in a foldable sheet of 50.

Miniature Sheet

National Arms — A507

No. 1459 — Arms used from: a, 1910-30 (antelope standing on ribbon). b, 1930-32 (antelopes on wide grass field without flowers). c, 1932-2000 (antelopes on narrow grass field with flowers). d, 2000-present (bird at top).

2010, Oct. 29   *Litho.*   *Perf. 13½*
1459   A507   Sheet of 4   2.80   2.80
a.-d.   (2.40r) Any single   .70   .70

Nos. 1459a-1459d are each inscribed "Standard Postage."

Quiz of South African History A508

No. 1460 — Inscriptions: a, First SA film that won an Academy Award for best foreign language film of the year. b, Number of UNESCO World Heritage Sites in SA. c, Which SA invention has been to the moon? d, Which fish is known as a living fossil. e, Indian spiritual and political leader whose career started in SA. f, When were SA's gold and diamond deposits formed? g, Animal used by Dr. Chris Barnard in trials preceding the first heart transplant. h, Telescope strong enough to see candlelight on the moon. i, The largest bird in the world occurring in SA. j, Where in SA was gold first mined?

2010, Nov. 5   *Perf. 13¾x13¼*
1460   Sheet of 10   15.00   15.00
a.-j.   A508 4.90r Any single   1.50   1.50

Each stamp on sheet has a scratch-off panel that covers the answer to the question on that stamp. Unused values are for stamps with unscratched panels. Values for used stamps are for stamps with panels unscratched or scratched.

SumbandilaSAT — A509

No. 1461 — Inscriptions: a, Engineering SumbandilaSAT. b, SumbandilaSAT in orbit. c, 12m S-band antenna at Hartebeeshoek. d, Soyuz 2.1b on launch platform. e, Sumbandila-SAT, vert.

2011, Apr. 1   *Perf. 13¼*
1461   Sheet of 10, 2 each   7.50   7.50
a.-e.   A509 (2.50r) Any single   .75   .75

Nos. 1461a-1461e are each inscribed "Standard Postage."

Souvenir Sheet

South African Constitution, 15th Anniv. — A510

2011, May 23   *Perf. 13*
1462   A510   2.50r multi   .75   .75

African Musical Instruments A511

No. 1463: a, //Gwasi. b, Ramkie. c, Sansa. d, Drums. e, Bullroarer. f, Horns. g, Flute. h, Xylophone. i, Rattles. j, Bows.

2011, June 30   *Perf. 13¼*
1463   Sheet of 10   17.50   17.50
a.-j.   A511 6r Any single   1.75   1.75

Birds Type of 2010

No. 1464: a, Green twinspot. b, Olive bushshrike. c, Cape parrot. d, Knysna turaco. e, African crowned eagle.

2011, July 15   *Perf. 13¼x13¾*
1464   Horiz. strip of 5   8.75   8.75
a.-e.   A503 6r Any single   1.75   1.75

Miniature Sheet

Vegetables — A512

No. 1465: a, Spinach. b, Tomatoes. c, Beet. d, Carrots. e, Cabbage. f, Butternut squash.

2011, Aug. 12   *Perf. 13¼*
1465   A512   Sheet of 6   10.50   10.50
a.-f.   (6.25r) Any single   1.75   1.75

Nos. 1465a-1465f are each inscribed "B4."

Miniature Sheet

Emblems of South African National Rugby Team — A513

No. 1466 — Emblem used from: a, 1906-33. b, 1935-72. c, 1937-62. d, 1963-64. e, 1965-89. f, 1966-91. g, 1992-95. h, 1996-2003. i, 2004-08. j, 2009-11.

Litho. With Foil Application
2011, Aug. 19   *Perf. 14½*
1466   A513   Sheet of 10   16.00   16.00
a.-j.   (6r) Any single   1.60   1.60

Nos. 1466a-1466j are each inscribed "International Small Letter."

Miniature Sheet

Flora and Fauna of Cape Floral Region — A514

No. 1467: a, Cape ghost frog. b, Fish eagle, vert. c, Cape vulture. d, Cape clawless otter, vert. e, Caracal. f, Strelitzia. g, Cape sugar bird, vert. h, Cape aloe, vert. i, Erica, vert. j, King protea.

Serpentine Die Cut 20
2011, Sept. 23   *Litho.*
Self-Adhesive
1467   A514   Sheet of 10   12.50
a.-j.   (5r) Any single   1.25   1.25

Nos. 1467a-1467j are each inscribed "B5."

Souvenir Sheet

62nd Intl. Astronautical Congress, Cape Town — A515

2011, Oct. 3   *Perf. 13¾x13½*
1468   A515   (2.50r) multi   .65   .65

No. 1468 is inscribed "Standard Postage."

South African Historical Links With Indonesia A516

No. 1469: a, Bo-Kaap Museum, Cape Town. b, Ghoema drum maker. c, Toerang hat and Kaparang sandals. d, Minstrel group. e, Sheikh Yusuf (1626-99), establisher of Islam in South Africa.

2011, Oct. 15   *Perf. 13¾x13¼*
1469   Vert. strip of 5   3.25   3.25
a.-e.   A516 (2.50r) Any single   .65   .65

Nos. 1469a-1469e are each inscribed "Standard Postage." See Indonesia No. 2298.

Souvenir Sheets

A517

Arrival of Indians in South Africa,
150th Anniv. — A518

Designs: No. 1470, SS Truro.
No. 1471 — Indian indentured workers: a,
Cutting sugar cane. b, Arriving at Durban
harbor.

2011 **Perf. 14x14¼**
1470 A517 (2.50r) multi .65 .65
1471 A518 (2.50r) Sheet of 2, #a-
b 1.25 1.25

Issued: No. 1470, 10/21; No. 1471, 11/25.
Nos. 1470, 1471a and 1471b are each
inscribed "Standard Postage."

A519

Albert Luthuli (c.
1898-1967),
President of
African National
Congress — A520

Designs: No. 1472, Bronze sculpture of
Luthuli. No. 1473, Luthuli with beard. No.
1474, Luthuli without beard.

2011, Dec. 9 **Perf. 13¼x13¾**
1472 A519 (2.50r) copper & blk .65 .65
1473 A520 (2.50r) copper & blk .65 .65
1474 A520 (2.50r) copper & blk .65 .65
Nos. 1472-1474 (3) 1.95 1.95

Nos. 1472-1474 are each inscribed "Standard Postage," and were printed in sheets of
10 containing 2 No. 1472 and 4 each Nos.
1473-1474.

South African Native National
Congress, Cent. — A521

2012, Jan. 6 **Perf. 13¼x13¾**
1475 A521 (2.50r) multi .65 .65
No. 1475 is inscribed "Standard Postage."

Miniature Sheet

Paintings by George Pemba (1912-
2001) — A522

No. 1476: a, Mother's Child. b, Township
Granny. c, The Minister's New Convert. d, Portrait of Mr. Gluck. e, Xhosa Woman. f, Portrait.
g, Ting-Ting. h, Mr. Pemba's Mother. i, Family
Life. j, Portrait of Xolile Ndongeni.

2012, Apr. 2 Litho. Perf. 13¾x13¼
1476 A522 Sheet of 10 16.00 16.00
a.-j. (6.30r) Any single 1.60 1.60
Nos. 1476a-1476j are inscribed "International Small Letter."

Miniature Sheet

National Symbols — A523

No. 1477: a, National flag. b, National coat
of arms. c, Enoch Sontonga, composer of
national anthem, Nkosi Sikelel' i Afrika. d,
National tree (Real yellowwood). e, National
animal (Springbok). f, National fish (Galjoen).
g, National flower, (Giant protea). h, National
bird (Blue crane).

2012, Apr. 20 Serpentine Die Cut
Self-Adhesive
1477 A523 Sheet of 8 5.75
a.-h. (2.65r) Any single .70 .70
Nos. 1477a-1477h are inscribed "Standard
Postage."

Miniature Sheet

Commercial and Medicinal
Plants — A524

No. 1478: a, Freesias. b, Rooibos tea. c,
Baberton daisies. d, Honeybush tea. e, Cape
aloe. f, Gladiolus. g, African potato. h, King
protea. i, Marula. j, Buchu.

Die Cut Perf. 14½x14¾
2012, May 18 Self-Adhesive
1478 A524 Sheet of 10 6.50
a.-j. (2.65r) Any single .65 .65
Nos. 1478a-1478j are inscribed "Standard
Postage."

South Africa's Role in
Astronomy — A525

No. 1479 — Inscriptions: a, Celebrating
Astronomers in South Africa (56x37mm). b,
KAT7 (Karoo Array Telescope 7) (56x37mm).
c, Astronomical Culture in South Africa
(28x74mm). d, South African National Space

Agency (28x37mm). e, SunSat 1 (28x74mm).
f, Innes Telescope, The Johannesburg Observatory (56x37mm). g, SumbandilaSAT
(28x37mm). h, Southern African Large Telescope (SALT) (28x37mm). i, HartRAO
(Hartebeesthoek Radio Astronomy Observatory) (28x37mm). j, South African Astronomical Observatory (SAAO) (56x37mm). k, South
African Astronomical Observatory (SAAO),
1828 (56x37mm).

Litho. With Foil Application
2012, June 5 Perf. 14¼
1479 A525 Sheet of 11 7.25 7.25
a.-k. (2.65r) Any single .65 .65
Nos. 1479a-1479k are inscribed "Standard
Postage."

Souvenir Sheet

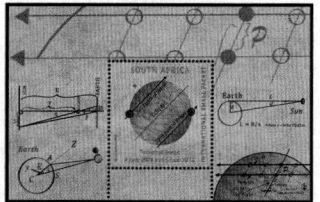

Transit of Venus — A526

2012, June 5 Perf. 14½
1480 A526 (27.40r) multi 6.75 6.75
No. 1480 is inscribed "International Small
Packet."

Souvenir Sheet

University of Cape Town Faculty of
Health Sciences, Cent. — A527

No. 1481 — Details from mosaic in Faculty
of Health Sciences Library: a, Head. b, Hands.

2012, June 6 Litho. Perf. 13¼x13¾
1481 A527 Sheet of 2 1.30 1.30
a.-b. (2.65r) Either single .65 .65
Nos. 1481a-1481b are each inscribed
"Standard Postage."

Souvenir Sheet

Krotoa (c. 1642-74), Translator for First
Dutch Settlers — A528

2012, Sept. 6 Perf. 14½
1482 A528 (2.65r) multi .65 .65
Arrival of Dutch at Cape of Good Hope,
360th anniv. No. 1482 is inscribed "Standard
Postage."

A529

A530

A531

A532

Ancient
Meteorite Strike
at Vredefort
Dome
UNESCO
World Heritage
Site — A533

Serpentine Die Cut 18
2012, Sept. 21 Self-Adhesive
1483 A529 (5.30r) multi 1.25 1.25
1484 A530 (5.30r) multi 1.25 1.25
1485 A531 (5.30r) multi 1.25 1.25
1486 A532 (5.30r) multi 1.25 1.25
1487 A533 (5.30r) multi 1.25 1.25
a. Horiz. strip of 5, #1483-1487 6.25
Nos. 1483-1487 (5) 6.25 6.25
Nos. 1483-1487 are each inscribed "B5."

Miniature Sheet

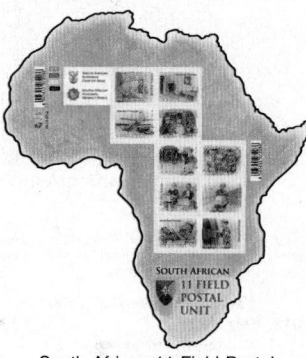

South African 11 Field Postal
Unit — A534

No. 1488: a, Customer giving parcel to window clerk. b, Parcel on conveyor belt. c, Parcels on forklift near airplane. d, Five soldiers
outside of field post office. e, Two soldiers with
parcels at field post office. f, Soldier inventory-
ing stack of parcels and mail bags. g, Soldiers
opening parcels. h, Soldier holding parcel and
letter. i, Soldier reading letter. j, Soldier placing
letter in mail box.

Serpentine Die Cut 12½
2012, Oct. 9 Self-Adhesive
1488 A534 Sheet of 10 6.50
a.-j. (2.65r) Any single .65 .65
Nos. 1488a-1488j each are inscribed "Standard Postage."

Miniature Sheet

Alexandra Township, Johannesburg,
Cent. — A535

No. 1489 — Art: a, Alex Under Siege, by
Kim Berman (40x30mm). b, Alexandra Scene,
by David Koloane (40x30mm). c, Evening
Township Scene, by Julian Motau (40x30mm).
d, Alex Youth Collaborating, by Sipho Gwala
(40x30mm). e, Alex from the Far East Bank,
by Joachim schönfeldt.

2012, Oct. 26 Perf. 13x13¼
1489 A535 Sheet of 5 8.00 8.00
a.-j. (6.60r) Any single 1.60 1.60
Nos. 1489a-1489e each are inscribed "B4."

Souvenir Sheet

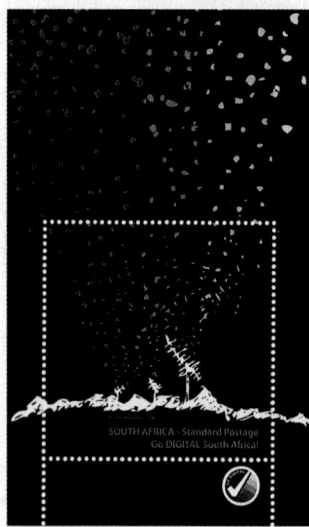

Go Digital — A536

2012, Nov. 23   *Perf. 13¼x13¾*
1490 A536 (2.65r) multi   .65 .65
    No. 1490 is inscribed "Standard Postage."

Souvenir Sheet

Rescue South Africa Disaster
Response Team — A537

No. 1491: a, Disaster Response Team
member, helicopter. b, Disaster Response
Team members carrying litter.

Serpentine Die Cut 14½
2013, Feb. 22   Litho.
Self-Adhesive
1491 A537   Sheet of 2   2.50
a.-b.   B5 Either single   1.25 1.25
    Nos. 1491a-1491b each sold for 5.30r on
day of issue.

Souvenir Sheet

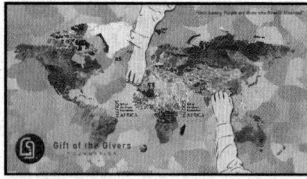

Gift of the Givers Foundation — A538

No. 1492: a, Hand, map of Europe and
Africa. b, Hand, map of Asia.

2013, Feb. 22   *Die Cut*
Self-Adhesive
1492 A538   Sheet of 2   2.50
a.-b.   B5 Either single   1.25 1.25
    Nos. 1492a-1492b each sold for 5.30r on
day of issue.

Miniature Sheet

International Year of Water
Cooperation — A539

No. 1493 — Inscriptions: a, Human consumption (hand holding glass under faucet). b,
Working for Water Program (worker cutting log
with chain saw). c, Industry (wind generators).
d, Agriculture (irrigator). e, Biodiversity (fish
and dragonfly).

2013, Mar. 22   *Die Cut*
Self-Adhesive
1493 A539   Sheet of 5   7.00
a.-e.   (6.30r) Any single   1.40 1.40
    Nos. 1493a-1493e are each inscribed "Inter-
national Small Letter." A rotatable cardboard
disc is attached to the center of the sheet of
stamps with a plastic grommet, allowing only
one stamp and one block of informative text to
be seen at a time. The unused value is for a
sheet with the covering disc attached.

Miniature Sheet

Butterflies and Moths — A540

No. 1494: a, Leto venus. b, Alaena mar-
garitacea. c, Charaxes marieps. d, Colotis
erone. e, Chrysoritis dicksoni. f,
Lepidochrysops lotana. g, Kedestes barberae
bunta. h, Erikssonia edgei. i, Trimenia
malagrida maryae. j, Aeropetes tulbaghia.

Die Cut Perf. 14¾x14¼
2013, May 10   **Self-Adhesive**
1494 A540   Sheet of 10   5.50
a.-j.   (2.80r) Any single   .55 .55
    Nos. 1494a-1494j are each inscribed "Stan-
dard Postage."

Souvenir Sheet

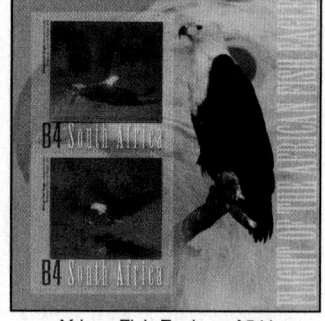

African Fish Eagle — A541

No. 1495 — Fish eagle facing: a, Right. b,
Left.

**Litho. With 3-Dimensional Plastic
Affixed**
Serpentine Die Cut 14½
2013, June 14   **Self-Adhesive**
1495 A541   Sheet of 2   2.80
a.-b.   B4 Either single   1.40 1.40
    Nos. 1495a-1495b each sold for 6.90r on
day of issue.

Miniature Sheet

Kirstenbosch National Botanical
Gardens, Cape Town, Cent. — A542

No. 1496: a, Silver tree (26x53mm). b, Natal
lily (29x38mm). c, Centenary gold strelitzia
amd bee (57x28mm triangular). d, Krantz
aloe, bird and ninepin (26x53mm). e, Ninepin
heath and bird (38x29mm). f, Silver restio
(40x40mm triangular). g, Albany cycad
(32x32mm). h, Welwitschia (57x28mm triangular). i, White gardenia (53x26mm). j, King
protea and bird (32x32mm).

**Litho., Sheet Margin Litho. With Foil
Application**
2013, July 1   *Serpentine Die Cut 27*
Self-Adhesive
1496 A542   Sheet of 10   6.00
a.-j.   (2.80r) Any single   .60 .60
    Nos. 1496a-1496j are each inscribed "Stan-
dard Postage."

Miniature Sheet

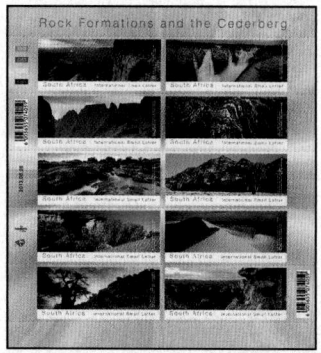

Rock Formations — A543

No. 1497: a, Igneous rock formation, Karoo
National Park. b, Igneous rock formation and
waterfall, Augrabies Falls National Park. c,
Igneous rock formation, Gray's Pass, Drakensberg. d, Metamorphic rock formation of
amphibolite in Sand River gneiss, Limpopo
Province. e, Metamorphic rock formations on
the Olifants River, Limpopo Province. f, Metamorphic rock formation, Ai-Ais Richtersveld
National Park. g, Sedimentary rock formation,
Golden Gate Highlands National Park. h, Sand
dunes (future sedimentary rock formation),

Addo Elephant National Park. i, Sedimentary
rock formation, Greater Mapungubwe Transfrontier Conservation Area. j, Table Mountain
sandstone, Cederberg Wilderness Area.

Serpentine Die Cut 13½
2013, Aug. 8   Litho.
Self-Adhesive
1497 A543   Sheet of 10   14.00
a.-j.   (6.60r) Any single   1.40 1.40
    Nos. 1497a-1497j are each inscribed "Inter-
national Small Letter."

Symbols of
South
African
Cultures
A544

No. 1498: a, Blombos ochre, earliest symbolic design in South Africa. b, N'wana, symbol of fertility. c, Amasumpa, headrest symbolic of wealth. d, Ukhamba, ceremonial beer
container symbolic of unity. e, Blombos shell
beads, oldest symbolic ornaments in South
Africa. f, Starburst engraving, symbol associated with womanhood. g, Rhinoceros engraving, symbol of rain and abundance. h,
Phalaphala, horn symbolic of communication.
i, Ngwenya symbol of royalty. j, Litshoba
mhlope, ritual whisk symbolic of divine
illumination.

Perf. 13¾x13¼
2013, Sept. 20   Litho.
1498   Sheet of 10   9.00 9.00
a.-j.   A544 (4.50r) Any single   .90 .90
    Nos. 1498a-1498j are each inscribed "DL
Fastmail."

Miniature Sheet

South African Post Office
Achievements — A545

No. 1499 — Inscriptions: a, eBusiness
boost communication. b, More people are
banking on us. c, Address expansion. d, Providing third-party services of other organizations. e, Steps to reduce our carbon footprint.

Serpentine Die Cut
2013, Oct. 9   Litho.
Self-Adhesive
1499 A545   Sheet of 5   3.00
a.-e.   (2.80r) Any single   .60 .60
    Nos. 1499a-1499e are each inscribed
"Standard Postage."

Souvenir Sheet

Diplomatic Relations Between South
Africa and Mexico, 20th
Anniv. — A546

2013, Oct. 25   Litho.   *Perf. 12½*
1500 A546 (6.90r) multi   1.40 1.40
    No. 1500 is inscribed "B4."

Rivonia Trial,
50th Anniv.
A547

Defendants: No. 1501, Ahmed Kathrada. No. 1502, Andrew Mlangeni. No. 1503, Arthur Goldreich (1929-2011). No. 1504, Denis Goldberg. No. 1505, Elias Motsoaledi (1924-94). No. 1506, Govan Mbeki (1910-2001). No. 1507, Harold Wolpe (1926-96). No. 1508, James Kantor (1927-75). No. 1509, Lionel Bernstein (1920-2002). No. 1510, Nelson Mandela (1918-2013). No. 1511, Raymond Mhlaba (1920-2005). No. 1512, Walter Sisulu (1912-2003).

Perf. 14¾x14½
2013, Nov. 26   Litho.
Booklet Panes of 1

1501	A547	(2.80r)	multi	.55	.55
1502	A547	(2.80r)	multi	.55	.55
1503	A547	(2.80r)	multi	.55	.55
1504	A547	(2.80r)	multi	.55	.55
1505	A547	(2.80r)	multi	.55	.55
1506	A547	(2.80r)	multi	.55	.55
1507	A547	(2.80r)	multi	.55	.55
1508	A547	(2.80r)	multi	.55	.55
1509	A547	(2.80r)	multi	.55	.55
1510	A547	(2.80r)	multi	.55	.55
1511	A547	(2.80r)	multi	.55	.55
1512	A547	(2.80r)	multi	.55	.55
a.	Complete booklet of 12, #1501-1512			6.75	
	Nos. 1501-1512 (12)			6.60	6.60

Nos. 1501-1512 were each inscribed "Standard Postage."

A548    A549

A550   A551

Details From
Keiskamma
Guernica — A552

Serpentine Die Cut 12¾x12¼ on 2 or 3 Sides
2013, Nov. 29   Litho.
Booklet Stamps
Self-Adhesive

1513	A548	(2.80r)	multi	.55	.55
1514	A549	(2.80r)	multi	.55	.55
1515	A550	(2.80r)	multi	.55	.55
1516	A551	(2.80r)	multi	.55	.55
1517	A552	(2.80r)	multi	.55	.55
a.	Booklet pane of 10, 2 each #1513-1517			5.50	
	Nos. 1513-1517 (5)			2.75	2.75

World AIDS Day, 25th anniv. Nos. 1513-1517 are each inscribed "Standard Postage."

Miniature Sheets

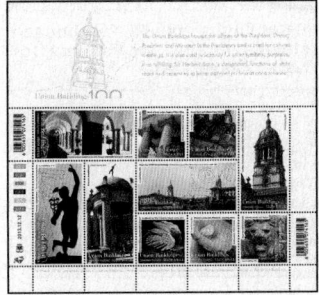

A553

Union Buildings, Pretoria,
Cent. — A554

No. 1518: a, Arcade around central court, with Tuscan colonnades and groin vault roof (60x30mm). b, Detail of Ionic order, loggia of West Wing (30x30mm). c, Tower Clock with Westminster chimes (30x30mm). d, Lantern, dome order and base of East Tower with Atlas sculpture, by Abraham Broadbent, on top (30x60mm). e, Hermes sculpture, by George Ness, Amphitheater (30x60mm). f, Rostrum, Amphitheater (30x60mm). g, Front view of the Union Buildings 60x30mm). h, Bronze sculpture of Southern Yellow-billed Hornbill, by Mike Edwards (30x30mm). i, Women's Memorial, iMbokodo (Grinding Stone), sculpture by Wilma Cruise (30x30mm). j, Carved stone lion's head, by Anton von Wouw (30x30mm).

No. 1519: a, Construction of building (60x30mm). b, Rostrum, Amphitheater (30x30mm). c, Construction of building, diff. (30x60mm). d, Aloe pretoriensis discovered on Meintjieskop (30x30mm). e, Carved keystone depicting cherub, by von Wouw (30x30mm). f, Construction of the Tower (30x60mm). g, Construction of building, diff. (30x30mm). h, Sir Herbert Baker (1862-1946), architect (30x30mm). i, Front view of buildings from the gardens (60x30mm). j, 1929 Armistice Day Service (30x30mm).

2013, Dec. 12   Litho.   **Perf. 13¼**

1518	A553	Sheet of 10	5.50	5.50
a.-j.	(2.80r) Any single		.55	.55
1519	A554	Sheet of 10	14.00	14.00
a.-j.	(6.90r) Any single		1.40	1.40

Nos. 1518a-1519j are each inscribed "Standard Postage." Nos. 1519a-1519j are each inscribed "B4."

This stamp, released Feb. 11, 2014, had a franking value of 2.80r, but was only made available in a folder that sold for 50r.

Miniature Sheet

Cape Town, 2014 World Design
Capital — A555

No. 1520 — Quotation from: a, Michael Elion. b, Mark Shuttleworth. c, Desmond Tutu. d, Nelson Mandela. e, Miriam Makeba.

Serpentine Die Cut 14½
2014, Feb. 28   Litho.
Self-Adhesive

1520	A555	Sheet of 5	4.75	
a.-e.	5r Any single		.95	.95

Miniature Sheet

Big Game Animals — A556

No. 1521: a, Leopard. b, Lion. c, Buffalos. d, Black rhinoceroses. e, Elephant.

Serpentine Die Cut 18
2014, May 9   Litho.
Self-Adhesive

1521	A556	Sheet of 5	7.00	
a.-e.	(7.20r) Any single		1.40	1.40

Nos. 1521a-1521e are each inscribed "B4."

Souvenir Sheet

Elephant, Fabric Art Embroidered by
Tunga Embroidery Studio — A557

Litho. & Silk-Screened
2014, May 30   **Perf. 13½x14**

1522	A557	(22.80r)	multi	4.25	4.25

No. 1522 is inscribed "Econoparcel."

Souvenir Sheet

Hamilton Naki (1926-2005),
Surgeon — A558

No. 1523: a, Naki, vert. b, Naki filling syringe, horiz.

Perf. 13½x13¼, 13¼x13½
2014, June 26   Litho.

1523	A558	Sheet of 2	6.00	6.00
a.-b.	(15.25r) Either single		3.00	3.00

Nos. 1523a-1523b are each inscribed "International Small Parcel."

Popular Musicians — A559

No. 1524: a, Brenda Fassie (1964-2004). b, Solomon Linda (1909-62). c, Bernoldus Niemand (1959-95). d, Spokes Mashiyane (1933-72). e, Miriam Makeba (1932-2008). f, Johannes Kerkorrel (1960-2002). g, Lucky Dube (1964-2007). h, Simon Nkabinde (1935-99). i, Taliep Petersen (1950-2006). j, Kippie Moeketsi (1925-83).

Serpentine Die Cut 11
2014, July 3   Litho.
Self-Adhesive

1524		Sheet of 10	6.00	
a.-j.	A559 (3r) Any single		.60	.60

Nos. 1524a-1524j are each inscribed "Standard Postage."

Miniature Sheet

World War I, Cent. — A560

No. 1525 — Inscriptions: a, German South West Africa Campaign. b, German East Africa Campaign. c, Palestine Campaign. d, S.S. Mendi. e, Delville Wood. f, Marrières Wood.

2014, July 28   Litho.   **Perf. 13¼**

1525	A560	Sheet of 6	11.50	11.50
a.-f.	10r Any single		1.90	1.90

Souvenir Sheet

Democratic Elections, 20th Anniv. — A561

2014, Aug. 15   Litho.   Perf. 12½
1526 A561 B5 multi   1.10 1.10
No. 1526 sold for 5.95r on day of issue.

Souvenir Sheet

Second Inauguration of Pres. Jacob Zuma — A562

2014, Aug. 15   Litho.   Perf. 12½
1527 A562 (3r) multi   .55 .55
No. 1527 is inscribed "Standard Postage."

Endangered Birds — A563

No. 1528: a, Damara tern. b, Taita falcon. c, Leach's storm petrel. d, White-winged flufftail. e, Tristan albatross.

2014, Sept. 1   Litho.   Perf. 12½
1528   Horiz. strip of 5   13.00 13.00
a.-e.   A563 (14r) Any single   2.60 2.60
Nos. 1528a-1528e are each inscribed "International Small Letter."

Miniature Sheet

Parks — A564

No. 1529: a, Addo Elephant National Park. b, Karoo National Park. c, Kruger National Park. c, Augrabies Falls National Park. d, Kgalagadi Transfrontier Park.

Serpentine Die Cut 11
2014, Sept. 17   Litho.
Self-Adhesive
1529 A564   Sheet of 5   5.50
a.-e.   B5 Any single   1.10 1.10
Nos. 1529a-1529e each sold for 5.95r on day of issue.

Miniature Sheet

Hands of Postal Workers — A565

No. 1530: a, Hands holding twine. b, Hands sorting mail. c, Hand touching letter on counter near bin of letters. d, Hand operating keyboard. e, Hand holding electronic scanner pointed at envelope.

Serpentine Die Cut 13½
2014, Oct. 9   Litho.
Self-Adhesive
1530 A565   Sheet of 5   8.75
a.-e.   10r Any single   1.75 1.75
The outer part of the sheet can be removed and the inner part with the stamps can be folded into a small box.

Ceramic
Vessels — A566

Vessels by: No. 1531, Unnamed artist from Mossel Bay. No. 1532, Ephraim Ziqubu. No. 1533, Clive Sithole. No. 1534, Clementina van der Walt. No. 1535, Mthandeni Mkhize and Matrinah Xaba. No. 1536, Unnamed artist from Melmoth. No. 1537, Unnamed artist from Lydenburg. No. 1538, Rebecca Matibe. No. 1539, Andile Dyalvane. No. 1540, Hyme Rabinowitz.

Die Cut Perf. 12¾x12½ on 2 or 3 Sides
2014, Nov. 13   Litho.
Booklet Stamps
Self-Adhesive
1531 A566 (3r) multi   .55 .55
1532 A566 (3r) multi   .55 .55
1533 A566 (3r) multi   .55 .55
1534 A566 (3r) multi   .55 .55
1535 A566 (3r) multi   .55 .55
1536 A566 (3r) multi   .55 .55
1537 A566 (3r) multi   .55 .55
1538 A566 (3r) multi   .55 .55
1539 A566 (3r) multi   .55 .55
1540 A566 (3r) multi   .55 .55
a.   Booklet pane of 10, #1531-
      1540   5.50
      Nos. 1531-1540 (10)   5.50 5.50
Nos. 1531-1540 are each inscribed "Standard Postage."

Souvenir Sheet

UNI Global Union World Congress, Cape Town — A567

2014, Dec. 5   Litho.   Perf. 13x13¼
1541 A567 5r multi   .85 .85

SEMI-POSTAL STAMPS

> Catalogue values for unused stamps in this section are for Never Hinged items.

English-Afrikaans Se-Tenant Stamps with English inscriptions and with Afrikaans inscriptions of Nos. B1-B11 were printed alternately in the same sheets. Major-number listings and values are for pairs consisting of one English and one Afrikaans-inscribed stamp.

Church of the Vow — SP1

Cradock's Pass — SP2

Voortrekker — SP3

Voortrekker Woman — SP4

1933-36 Photo. Wmk. 201 Perf. 14
B1 SP1 ½p + ½p grn & blk,
                pair ('36)   11.00 5.50
a.   Single, English   .55   .55
b.   Single, Afrikaans   .55   .55
B2 SP2 1p + ½p rose & blk,
                pair   7.25 3.75
a.   Single, English   .45   .35
b.   Single, Afrikaans   .45   .35
B3 SP3 2p + 1p dull vio &
                gray, pair   12.00 6.00
a.   Single, English   .55   .60
b.   Single, Afrikaans   .55   .60
B4 SP4 3p + 1½p dp blue &
                gray, pair   18.00 9.50
a.   Single, English   1.50 1.10
b.   Single, Afrikaans   1.50 1.10
      Nos. B1-B4 (4)   48.25 24.75
Issued to commemorate the Voortrekkers. Surtax went to the National Memorial Fund for a national Voortrekker monument.

Voortrekker Plowing — SP5

Crossing the Drakensberg — SP6

Signing Dingaan-Relief Treaty — SP7

Proposed Monument — SP8

1938, Dec. 14   Perf. 14
B5 SP5 ½p + ½p dl grn & ind,
                pair   7.00 6.75
a.   Single, English   1.00   .60
b.   Single, Afrikaans   1.00   .60
B6 SP6 1p + 1p rose & sl,
                pair   17.00 7.75
a.   Single, English   1.00   .70
b.   Single, Afrikaans   1.00   .70
Perf. 15x14
B7 SP7 1½p + ½p Prus grn
                & choc, pair   22.50 13.50
a.   Single, English   1.40 1.40
b.   Single, Afrikaans   1.40 1.40
B8 SP8 3p + 3p chlky bl,
                pair   26.00 16.00
a.   Single, English   1.75 2.00
b.   Single, Afrikaans   1.75 2.00
      Nos. B5-B8 (4)   72.50 44.00
Voortrekker centenary. Surtax went to the Natl. Memorial Fund for a Voortrekker monument.

"The Old Vicarage," Huguenot Museum — SP9

Rising Sun and Cross — SP10

Huguenot Dwelling, Drakenstein Mountain Valley — SP11

1939, July 17   Photo.   Perf. 14
B9 SP9 ½p + ½p Prus grn
                & gray brn, pair   11.00 8.00
a.   Single, English   1.00   .85
b.   Single, Afrikaans   1.00   .85
B10 SP10 1p + 1p rose car &
                Prus grn, pair   13.00 10.00
a.   Single, English   1.00 1.00
b.   Single, Afrikaans   1.00 1.00
Perf. 15x14
B11 SP11 1½p + 1½p, pair   27.50 15.00
a.   Single, English   1.60 1.60
b.   Single, Afrikaans   1.60 1.60
      Nos. B9-B11 (3)   51.50 33.00
250th anniv. of the landing of the Huguenots in South Africa. Surtax went to a fund to build a Huguenot memorial at Paarl.

No. 581 Surcharged in English or Afrikaans

a

b

1987, Nov. 16   Litho.   Perf. 14x14½

B12	Pair	1.00	1.00
a.	A229 16c +10c red	.50	.50
b.	A229(b) 16c +10c red	.50	.50

Surcharge for flood relief.

No. 702 Surcharged in English or Afrikaans

1987, Dec. 1

B13	Pair	1.00	1.00
a.	A254 16c +10c multicolored	.50	.50
b.	A254(b) 16c +10c multicolored	.50	.50

"+10c" is overprinted below text on Nos. B13a-B13b. Surcharge for flood relief.

No. 706 Surcharged in English or Afrikaans

1988, Mar. 1   Perf. 14½x14

B14	Pair	1.00	1.00
a.	A256 16c +10c multicolored	.50	.50
b.	A256(b) 16c +10c multicolored	.50	.50

Surcharge for flood relief.

Nos. 710-713 Surcharged in English or Afrikaans

c

d

1988, Apr. 13   Perf. 14x14½

B15	Pair	.85	.85
a.	A257(c) 16c +10c multicolored	.40	.40
b.	A257(d) 16c +10c multicolored	.40	.40
B16	Pair	1.60	1.60
a.	A257(c) 30c +10c multicolored	.80	.80
b.	A257(d) 30c +10c multicolored	.80	.80
B17	Pair	2.25	2.25
a.	A257(c) 40c +10c multicolored	1.10	1.10
b.	A257(d) 40c +10c multicolored	1.10	1.10
B18	Pair	2.75	2.75
a.	A257(c) 50c +10c multicolored	1.25	1.25
b.	A257(d) 50c +10c multicolored	1.25	1.25
	Nos. B12-B18 (7)	10.45	10.45

Surcharge for flood relief.
On Nos. B16a, B16b, the "+ 10" is in upper left corner.

AIR POST STAMPS

Mail Plane — AP1

Unwmk.

1925, Feb. 26   Litho.   Perf. 12

C1	AP1 1p red	4.50	10.00
C2	AP1 3p ultramarine	10.00	13.00
C3	AP1 6p violet	17.50	24.00
C4	AP1 9p gray green	29.00	32.50
	Nos. C1-C4 (4)	61.00	79.50
	Set, never hinged	150.00	

Forgeries exist.

Biplane in Flight — AP2

1929, Aug. 16   Typo.   Perf. 14x13½

C5	AP2 4p blue green	8.50	2.75
C6	AP2 1sh orange	27.50	21.00
	Set, never hinged	75.00	

> Catalogue values for unused stamps in this section, from this point to the end of the section, are for Never Hinged items.

"AIRMAIL POSTCARD"
"AIRMAIL POSTCARD RATE"

Stamps inscribed thus were sold for the amount shown in ( ) on date of issue.
See Nos. 1038-1042F for stamps included with postage sets.

Endangered Fauna Type of 1993

1996, May 8   Litho.   Perf. 14x14½

C6A	A288 (1r) White rhinoceros	.70	.70
C6B	A288 (1r) Buffalo	.70	.70
C6C	A288 (1r) Lion	.70	.70
f.	Souvenir sheet of 1 + label	.80	.80
C6D	A288 (1r) Leopard	.70	.70
C6E	A288 (1r) African elephant	.70	.70
g.	Strip of 5, #936-940	3.50	
h.	Sheet of 10, 2 each #936-940	7.00	
i.	Booklet pane of 5, #936-940 + 5 labels	4.00	
	Complete booklet, #940c	4.00	

No. C6Cf is inscribed in sheet margin for Coach House, and sold for 1r.
Issued: #C6Cf, 2/97; #C6Ei, 7/27/97.

Inauguaration of Blue Train — AP3

Designs: No. C7, Double-headed Class 6E 1, electric locomotives, Cape Town to Beaufort West. No. C8, Double-headed Class 6E 1 electric lovomotives, Hex River Valley. No. C9, 1960's Steam powered locomotives between Three Sisters and Huchinson. No. C10, Diesel locomotives, Modder River Bridge near Kimberly. No. C11, Diesel locomotives, Northern Transvaal.

1997, Aug. 1   Perf. 14 Syncopated

C7	AP3 (1r) multicolored	.70	.70
a.	Souv. sheet of 1, perf. 14	.70	.70
C8	AP3 (1r) multicolored	.70	.70
C9	AP3 (1r) multicolored	.70	.70
a.	Souvenir sheet of 1, perf. 14	.70	.70
C10	AP3 (1r) multicolored	.70	.70
C11	AP3 (1r) multicolored	.70	.70
a.	Strip of 5, #C7-C11	3.50	3.50

No. C7a is inscribed in sheet margin for The Cape Stamp Show and Harmers of London stamp auctioneers.
No. C9a was issued 11/97, sold for 1.30r and is inscribed for Eastgate Universal Stamps & Coins in sheet margin.

1998, Nov.   Litho.   Perf. 14¾x14
Booklet Stamps

C12	AP3 (1r) Like #C7	.70	.70
C13	AP3 (1r) Like #C8	.70	.70
C14	AP3 (1r) Like #C9	.70	.70
C15	AP3 (1r) Like #C10	.70	.70
C16	AP3 (1r) Like #C11	.70	.70
a.	Bklt. pane, 2 ea #C12-C16	7.00	
	Complete booklet, #C16a	7.00	
	Nos. C12-C16 (5)	3.50	3.50

Tourism AP4

Western Cape of South Africa: No. C7, Sandstone Cliffs. No. C8, Robben Island. No. C9, Pinehurst Homestead. No. C10, Waterfront, Capetown. No. C11, Boschendal Wine Estate.

1998, Sept. 28   Litho.   Perf. 14½x14
Booklet Stamps

C17	AP4 (1.30r) multicolored	.60	.60
C18	AP4 (1.30r) multicolored	.60	.60
C19	AP4 (1.30r) multicolored	.60	.60
C20	AP4 (1.30r) multicolored	.60	.60
C21	AP4 (1.30r) multicolored	.60	.60
a.	Bklt. pane, 2 ea #C17-C21 + label	6.00	
	Complete booklet, #C21a	6.00	
	Nos. C17-C21 (5)	3.00	3.00

Perf. 14¾x14 on 3 sides

1998, Sept. 28   Litho.

KwaZulu-Natal: No. C22, Drakensberge. No. C23, Zulu women and huts. No. C24, Rhinoceros and pelicans. No. C25, Rickshaw driver. No. C26, Indian dancers.

C22	AP4 (1.30r) multicolored	.60	.60
C23	AP4 (1.30r) multicolored	.60	.60
C24	AP4 (1.30r) multicolored	.60	.60
C25	AP4 (1.30r) multicolored	.60	.60
C26	AP4 (1.30r) multicolored	.60	.60
a.	Booklet pane, 2 ea #C22-C26	6.00	
	Complete booklet, #C26a	6.00	

Worldwide Fund for Nature AP5

No. C27, Cuvier's beaked whale. No. C28, Minke whale. No. C29, Bryde's whale. No. C30, Pygmy right whale.

1998, Oct. 23   Litho.   Perf. 14¾x14

C27	AP5 (1.30r) multicolored	1.00	1.00
C28	AP5 (1.30r) multicolored	1.00	1.00
C29	AP5 (1.30r) multicolored	1.00	1.00
C30	AP5 (1.30r) multicolored	1.00	1.00
a.	Block of 4, #C27-C30	4.00	4.00
b.	Booklet pane, 3 each #C27-C28, 2 each #C29-C30	10.00	
	Complete booklet	10.00	
	Complete booklet, 2 #C30b + 2 postal cards	30.00	

No. C30b exists with and without perfs running through side and bottom pane margins.

Tourism Type of 1998

Mpumalanga and Northern Province: No. C31, Blyde River Canyon. No. C32, Lone Creek Falls. No. C33, Ndebele women. No. C34, Pilgrim's Rest historical town. No. C35, Elephants, Thulamela, Kruger National Park.

1999, Aug.   Litho.   Perf. 14¾x14

C31	AP4 (1.30r) multi	.50	.50
C32	AP4 (1.30r) multi	.50	.50
C33	AP4 (1.30r) multi	.50	.50
C34	AP4 (1.30r) multi	.50	.50
C35	AP4 (1.30r) multi	.50	.50
a.	Booklet pane, 2 each #C31-C35	5.00	
	Complete booklet, #C35a	5.00	

Big Game Animals — AP6

Designs: Nos. C36, C45, Elephant. Nos. C37, C44, Lion. Nos. C38, C43, Rhinoceros. Nos. C39, C42, Leopard. Nos. C40, C41, Buffalo.

Perf. 14¾x14½ on 3 or 4 Sides

2001, Apr. 25   Litho.
Booklet Stamps

C36	AP6 (1.90r) multi	.70	.70
C37	AP6 (1.90r) multi	.70	.70
C38	AP6 (1.90r) multi	.70	.70
C39	AP6 (1.90r) multi	.70	.70
C40	AP6 (1.90r) multi	.70	.70
a.	Booklet pane, 2 each #C36-C40	7.00	
	Booklet, 2 #C40a + 2 postal cards	14.00	

Self-Adhesive
Size: 30x24mm
Serpentine Die Cut 12x11½ on 2 or 3 Sides

C41	AP6 (1.90r) multi	.70	.70
C42	AP6 (1.90r) multi	.70	.70
C43	AP6 (1.90r) multi	.70	.70
C44	AP6 (1.90r) multi	.70	.70
C45	AP6 (1.90r) multi	.70	.70
a.	Booklet, 2 each #C41-C45	7.00	

See Nos. C65-C69.

Tourism — AP7

Designs: No. C46, (2.10r), Cango Caves. No. C47, (2.10r), Table Mountain. No. C48, (2.10r), West Coast. No. C49, (2.10r), Snow-covered mountains near Elliot. No. C50, (2.10r), Augrabies Waterfall. No. C51, (2.10r), Stellenbosch vineyard country. No. C52, (2.10r), Flowers, Namaqualand. No. C53, (2.10r), Tsitsikamma Forest. No. C54, (2.10r), Cape Mountain zebras. No. C55, (2.10r), Richtersveld Desert.

2001, Sept. 6   Litho.   Perf. 13¼x13¾

C46-C55	AP7 Set of 10	7.00	7.00

Pres. Nelson Mandela — AP8

Various photographs. Color of country name and size of stamps: a, Lilac, 31x48mm. b, Red and lilac, 50x38mm. c, Orange, 31x48mm. d, Orange, 31x31mm. e, Orange, 38x50mm. f, White, 38x50mm. g, White, 50x38mm. h, White, 31x48mm. i, Lilac, 38x50mm. j, Red, 31x31mm.

2001, Nov. 26   Perf. 14¾x14, 13¾

C56	Booklet	9.00	
a.-j.	AP8 (2.10r) Any booklet pane	.90	.90

No. C56 sold for 45r and included two postal cards.

Shaka (1785-1828), Zulu King — AP9

2003, Sept. 24   Litho.   Perf. 13x13¼

C57	AP9 (3.30r) multi	1.10	1.10

Miniature Sheet

Flora and Fauna of Table Mountain — AP10

No. C58: a, Cape sugarbird, vert. b, Dark opal butterflies. c, King protea. d, Cape rock hyrax. e, Cuckoo wasp. f, Table Mountain ghost frog. g, Table Mountain cockroaches. h, Staavia dodii, vert. i, Spotted skaapsteker. j, Duvalia immaculata.

Serpentine Die Cut 9x9½, 9½x9

2004, Sept. 1   Litho.
Self-Adhesive

C58	AP10 Sheet of 10	17.50	17.50
a.-j.	(10r) Any single	1.75	1.75

World Post Day — AP11

2004, Sept. 23   *Perf. 14*
C59 AP11 (3.45r) multi   1.25 1.25

Rotary International, Cent. — AP12

No. C60: a, Doctor listening to boy's heartbeat, infant receiving oral vaccination. b, Child at computer, welder.

2005, Feb. 23   *Perf. 14¼x14*
C60   Horiz. pair   3.25 3.25
   a.-b.   AP12 (4r) Either single   1.50 1.50

Miniature Sheet

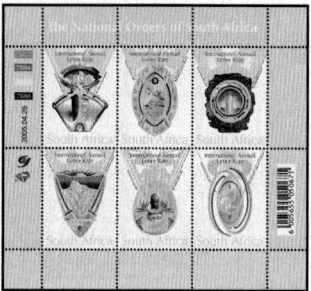

National Orders — AP13

No. C61: a, Order of Mapungubwe. b, Order of Merit for Bravery. c, Order of the Baobab. d, Order of Luthuli. e, Order of Ikhamanga. f, Order of the Companions of O. R. Tambo.

Litho. & Embossed with Foil Application
2005, Nov. 26   *Perf. 14¾x14¼*
C61 AP13 (4.25r) Sheet of 6, #a-f 9.00 9.00

Miniature Sheet

Art — AP14

No. C62: a, Boland Winter, by Eric Laubscher. b, Table Mountain, by Maggie Laubser. c, Fishermen Drawing Nets, by Walter Battis. d, Oh, South Africa, You've Turned My World Completely Upside Down, by Lallitha Jawahirlal. e, Untitled, by Lucky Sibiya. f, Untitled, by Sophie Masiza. g, Azibuye Emasisweni, by Trevor Makhoba. h, Kontantwinkel Riebeck-Wes, by John Kramer. i, Houses in the Hills, by Gladys Mgudlandlu. j, Sequence City, by Usha Seejarim.

2005, May 6   **Litho.**   *Perf. 14¼x14¾*
C62 AP14 (3.65r) Sheet of 10, #a-j   13.50 13.50

Intl. Year of Physics — AP15

2005, July 7   *Perf. 14½*
C63 AP15 (3.65r) multi   1.40 1.40

Miniature Sheet

"Hello" in Various Languages and Flag — AP16

No. C64: a, Hallo! b, Hi! c, Sawubona. d, Ndi Masiari! e, Lotjha!. f, Avuxeni. g, Dumela. h, Molo!

2005, Oct. 9
C64 AP16 (3.65r) Sheet of 8, #a-h   9.50 9.50

Big Game Animals Type of 2001
Serpentine Die Cut 12¼x12¾ on 2 or 3 Sides
2005, Oct. 10   **Self-Adhesive**
Booklet Stamps
Size: 30x24mm

C65 AP6 (3.65r) Buffalo   1.25 1.25
C66 AP6 (3.65r) Leopard   1.25 1.25
C67 AP6 (3.65r) Rhinoceros   1.25 1.25
C68 AP6 (3.65r) Lion   1.25 1.25
C69 AP6 (3.65r) Elephant   1.25 1.25
   a.   Booklet, 2 each # C65-C69   12.50

Big Game Animals — AP17

Serpentine Die Cut 12½x13½
2006, Feb. 24   **Self-Adhesive**
Booklet Stamps

C70 AP17 (3.65r) Lion   1.25 1.25
C71 AP17 (3.65r) Buffalo   1.25 1.25
C72 AP17 (3.65r) Elephant   1.25 1.25
C73 AP17 (3.65r) Rhinoceros   1.25 1.25
C74 AP17 (3.65r) Leopard   1.25 1.25
   a.   Booklet, 2 each #C70-C74   12.50

Cyclists — AP18

2006, Mar. 6   *Perf. 13¼x13¾*
C75 AP18 (4.25r) multi   1.50 1.50

Souvenir Sheet

2010 World Cup Soccer Championships, South Africa — AP19

2006, July 7   **Litho.**   *Perf. 14¾x14½*
C76 AP19 (4.40r) multi   1.40 1.40

Miniature Sheet

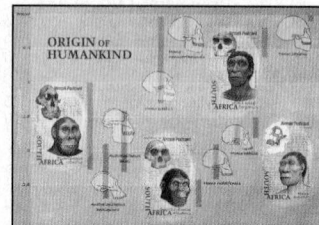

Origins of Humans — AP20

No. C77: a, Paranthropus robustus. b, Australopithecus africanus. c, Homo heidelbergensis. d, Homo ergaster.

Serpentine Die Cut 11½x11¾
2006, Nov. 10   **Self-Adhesive**
C77 AP20 (3.80r) Sheet of 4, #a-d   4.75 4.75

Big Game Animals — AP21

Serpentine Die Cut 13½x13¾ on 2 or 3 Sides
2007, Aug. 17   **Litho.**
Booklet Stamps
Self-Adhesive

C78 AP21 (4.01r) Elephant   1.10 1.10
C79 AP21 (4.01r) Leopard   1.10 1.10
C80 AP21 (4.01r) Buffalo   1.10 1.10
C81 AP21 (4.01r) Lion   1.10 1.10
C82 AP21 (4.01r) Rhinoceros   1.10 1.10
   a.   Booklet pane, 2 each #C78-C82   11.00
   Nos. C78-C82 (5)   5.50 5.50

Souvenir Sheet

24th UPU Congress, Nairobi — AP22

2007, Oct. 9   *Perf. 13¾*
C83 AP22 (4.64r) multi   1.40 1.40

Souvenir Sheet

2010 World Cup Soccer Championships, South Africa — AP23

2007, Nov. 23   *Perf. 13¼x13½*
C84 AP23 (4.64r) multi   1.40 1.40

Birds — AP24

No. C85: a, Southern ground hornbill. b, Kori bustard. c, Common ostrich. d, Blue crane. e, Bearded vulture.

2008, July 1   **Litho.**   *Perf. 13¼x13¾*
C85   Horiz. strip of 5   6.50 6.50
   a.-e.   AP24 (4.90r) Any single   1.25 1.25
   Nos. C85a-C85e are each inscribed "International Airmail Small Letter."

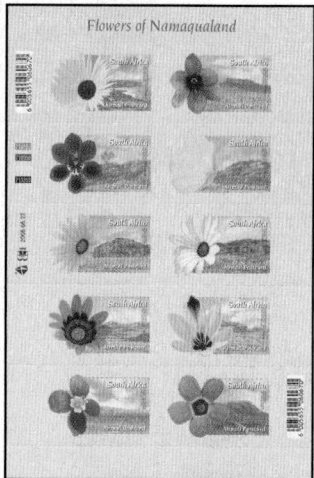

Intl. Congress of Entomology Conference, Durban — AP25

2008, July 4   *Perf. 13¾x13¼*
C86 AP25 (4.20r) multi   1.10 1.10

Miniature Sheet

Flowers — AP26

No. C87: a, Common bokbaaivygie. b, Bokkeveld pride. c, Springbok painted petals. d, White-eyed duiker-root. e, Namaqualand daisy. f, Satin boneseed. g, Karoo gazania. h, Harlequin hesperantha. i, Showy sunflax. j, Red-eye sorrel.

2008, Aug. 22   *Die Cut*
Self-Adhesive
C87 AP26   Sheet of 10   11.00
   a.-j.   (4.20r) Any single   1.10 1.10
   Nos. C87a-C87j are each inscribed "Airmail Postcard."

Souvenir Sheet

2010 World Cup Soccer Championships, South Africa — AP27

2008, Sept. 5   *Perf. 13¼x13¾*
C88 AP27 (3.70r) multi   .95 .95

Miniature Sheet

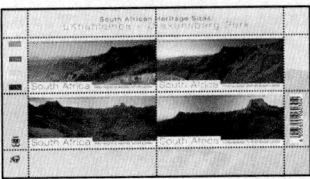

uKhahlamba-Drakensberg
Park — AP28

No. C89: a, View overlooking Eastern Buttress with Devils Tooth. b, View from the Sentinel overlooking the Eastern Buttress. c, Amphitheater from the Royal Natal National Park. d, View of the Sentinel and Amphitheater.

2008, Sept. 23   **Perf. 13¼x13¾**
C89   AP28   Sheet of 4   4.75   4.75
  a.-d.   (4.90r) Any single   1.10   1.10

Nos. C89a-C89d are each inscribed "International Airmail Small Letter."

Big Game
Animals — AP29

Booklet Stamps

***Serpentine Die Cut 12¼x12¾ on 2
or 3 Sides***

2008, Nov. 14   **Self-Adhesive**
C90   AP29   (4.20r)   Elephant   .80   .80
C91   AP29   (4.20r)   Lion   .80   .80
C92   AP29   (4.20r)   Leopard   .80   .80
C93   AP29   (4.20r)   Buffalo   .80   .80
C94   AP29   (4.20r)   Rhinoceros   .80   .80
  a.   Booklet pane of 10, 2 each
     #C90-C94   8.25
   Nos. C90-C94 (5)   4.00   4.00

Nos. C90-C94 are each inscribed "Airmail Postcard."

Souvenir Sheet

2010 World Cup Soccer
Championships, South Africa — AP30

Perf. 13¼x13¾
2009, June 14   **Litho.**
C95   AP30   (5.40r) multi   1.40   1.40

No. C95 is inscribed "International Airmail Small Letter."

Miniature Sheet

Gemstones — AP31

No. C96: a, Garnet. b, Sugilite. c, Rhodocrosite. d, Jasper.

Litho. With Foil Application
2009, July 10   **Perf. 13½**
C96   AP31   Sheet of 4   4.50   4.50
  a.-d.   (4.60r) Any single   1.10   1.10

Nos. C96a-C96d are inscribed "Airmail Postcard."

Birds — AP32

No. C97: a, Jackass penguins. b, Black oyster catchers. c, Common cape gannets. d, Cape cormorants. e, Black-backed sea gull.

2009, Aug. 3   **Litho.**   **Perf. 14¾x14½**
C97   Horiz. strip of 5   7.00   7.00
  a.-e.   AP32 (5.40r) Any single   1.40   1.40

Nos. C97a-C97e are inscribed "International Airmail Small Letter."

Miniature Sheet

Dinosaurs — AP33

No. C98: a, Afrovenator. b, Afrovenator skeleton. c, Ouranosaurus. d, Ouranosaurus skeleton. e, Heterodontosaurus, vert. f, Heterodontosaurus skeleton, vert. g, Jobaria, vert. h, Jobaria skeleton, vert. i, Suchomimus, vert. j, Suchomimus skeleton, vert.

Perf. 13¼x13, 13x13¼ (#C98e-C98j)
2009, Nov. 2
C98   AP33   Sheet of 10   12.50   12.50
  a.-j.   (4.60r) Any single   1.25   1.25

Nos. C98a-C98j are inscribed "International Airmail Postcard." The stamp designs, when viewed through red and blue glasses, become three-dimensional.

Miniature Sheet

Life of Fishermen — AP34

No. C99: a, Fish on net, boats ashore. b, Men pushing boat in shallow water. c, Sun, house, men near boat. d, Fishemen in boat on water. e, Fishermen, boat ashore near rocks. f, Fishing community. g, Men in boat, house. h, Boat ashore, fisherman with rod. i, Fish, houses, boat. j, Man hanging fish to dry.

2010, Feb. 19   **Perf. 13¼x13**
C99   AP34   Sheet of 10   14.00   14.00
  a.-j.   (5.40r) Any single   1.40   1.40

Nos. C99a-C99j are inscribed "International Airmail Small Letter."

Big Game
Animals — AP35

Booklet Stamps

***Die Cut Perf. 12¾x12½ on 2 or 3
Sides***

2010, May 5   **Self-Adhesive**
C100   AP35   (4.90r)   Elephant   1.40   1.40
C101   AP35   (4.90r)   Lion   1.40   1.40
C102   AP35   (4.90r)   Buffalo   1.40   1.40
C103   AP35   (4.90r)   Leopard   1.40   1.40

C104   AP35   (4.90r)   Rhinoceros   1.40   1.40
  a.   Booklet pane of 10, 2 each
     #C100-C104   14.00
    Nos. C100-C104 (5)   7.00   7.00

Nos. C100-C104 are inscribed "Airmail Postcard."

Cats — AP36

No. C105: a, African wild cat (60x60mm). b, Serval (30x30mm). c, Caracal (30x30mm). d, Black-footed cat (30x30mm). e, African golden cat (30x30mm).

2011, Feb. 4   **Perf. 13¼**
C105   AP36   Block of 5   6.25   6.25
  a.-e.   (4.30r) Any single   1.25   1.25

Nos. C105a-C015e are each inscribed "Africa Airmail." Perforations trace around the cat's head on No. C105a.

Souvenir Sheet

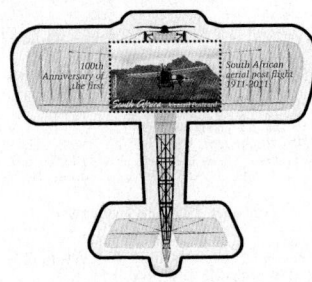

First South African Air Mail Flight,
Cent. — AP37

2011, Oct. 7   **Perf. 13x13¼**
C106   AP37   (5.10r)   multi   1.40   1.40

No. C106 is inscribed "Airmail Postcard."

Sunbirds — AP40

Designs: No. C113, White-bellied sunbird. No. C114, Dusky sunbird. No. C115, Neergaard's sunbird. No. C116, Plain-backed sunbird. No. C117, Collared sunbird.

2012, Aug. 10   **Perf. 13¼x13¾**
C113   AP40   (5.40r)   multi   1.40   1.40
C114   AP40   (5.40r)   multi   1.40   1.40
C115   AP40   (5.40r)   multi   1.40   1.40
C116   AP40   (5.40r)   multi   1.40   1.40
C117   AP40   (5.40r)   multi   1.40   1.40
  a.   Horiz. strip of 5, #C113-C117   7.00   7.00
    Nos. C113-C117 (5)   7.00   7.00

Nos. C113-C117 each are inscribed "International Airmail Small Letter."

Miniature Sheet

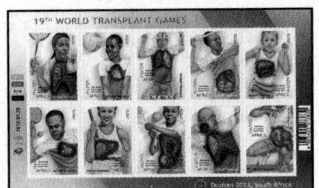

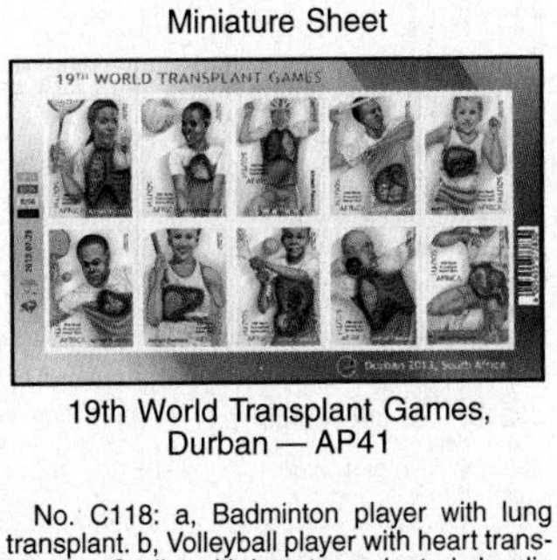

19th World Transplant Games,
Durban — AP41

No. C118: a, Badminton player with lung transplant. b, Volleyball player with heart transplant. c, Cyclist with lung transplant. d, Javelin thrower with kidney transplant. e, Runner with liver transplant. f, Table tennis player with heart transplant. g, Relay runner with liver transplant. h, tennis player with kidney transplant. i, Shot putter with lung transplant. j, Hurdler with kidney and pancreas transplant.

Die Cut Perf. 14¼x14¾
2013, July 29   **Litho.**
        Self-Adhesive
C118   AP41   Sheet of 10   11.00
  a.-j.   (5.70r) Any single   1.10   1.10

Nos. C118a-C118j are each inscribed "Airmail Postcard."

Big Game
Animals — AP42

***Die Cut Perf. 12¼x12¾ on 2 or 3
Sides***
2014, May 9   **Litho.**
    Booklet Stamps
     Self-Adhesive
C119   AP42   (6.05r)   Buffalo   1.10   1.10
C120   AP42   (6.05r)   Elephant   1.10   1.10
C121   AP42   (6.05r)   Leopard   1.10   1.10
C122   AP42   (6.05r)   Black rhi-
            noceros   1.10   1.10
C123   AP42   (6.05r)   Lion   1.10   1.10
  a.   Booklet pane of 10, 2 each
     #C119-C123   11.00
    Nos. C119-C123 (5)   5.50   5.50

Nos. C119-C123 are inscribed "Airmail Postcard."

Miniature Sheet

South African Aviation Corps,
Cent. — AP43

No. C124: a, Pilot's wings (52x26mm). b, Shoulder title (38x26mm). c, Henry Farman biplane (52x38mm). d, 1914-15 Star (38x38mm). e, Tunic detail (38x38mm).

Die Cut Perf. 12½
2015, Feb. 5   **Litho.**
     Self-Adhesive
C124   AP43   Sheet of 5   5.00
  a.-e.   (6.05r) Any single   1.00   1.00

Nos. C124a-C124e are each inscribed "Airmail Postcard."

REGISTRATION STAMPS

Miniature Sheet

Intl. Year of Biodiversity — R1

No. F1: a, Giant African mantis, Common lionfish. b, Black rhinoceros. c, Common chameleon, African reed frog. d, Lilac-breasted roller, Baobab tree.

Perf. 13¼x13¾
2010, Mar. 12   **Litho.**
F1   R1   Sheet of 4   18.00   18.00
  a.-d.   (15.85r) Any single   4.50   4.50

Nos. F1a-F1d are inscribed "Small Registered Letter."

Miniature Sheet

Port Elizabeth, Cent. — R2

No. F2: a, View of Algoa Bay From Lady Donkin's Pyramid, lithograph by George Dinsdale. b, The Donkin, photograph by Tim Hopwood. c, Port Elizabeth, painting by Ethel Sawyer. d, Coega harbor, photograph by Hopwood. e, Birth of Site and Service, watercolor by George Mnyaluza Milwa Pemba. f, Red Location Museum, photograph by Hopwood. g, Old Doll House Railway Station, photograph in Binnell Collection. h, Old Court House, photograph by Hopwood. i, Queen Street and North End, photograph in Port Elizabeth Museum. j, Nelson Mandela Bay Stadium, photograph by Hopwood.

Serpentine Die Cut 14½

2013, July 26

Self-Adhesive

F2 R2 Sheet of 10 40.00
a.-j. (19.60r) Any single 4.00 4.00

Nos. F2a-F2j each are inscribed "Registered Letter Small."

Miniature Sheet

Lighthouses — R3

No. F3: a, Cape Agulhas Lighthouse. b, Umhlanga Rocks Lighthouse. c, Bird Island Lighthouse. d, Green Point Lighthouse. e, Robben Island Lighthouse.

Serpentine Die Cut 14½

2014, Aug. 20 Litho.

Self-Adhesive

F3 R3 Sheet of 5 20.00
a.-e. (20.80r) Any single 4.00 4.00

Nos. F3a-F3e are each inscribed "Registered small letter."

POSTAGE DUE STAMPS

D1

Wmk. Springbok's Head (177)

1914-15 Typo. *Perf. 14*

J1 D1 ½p green & blk 2.50 4.25
J2 D1 1p red & blk 2.50 .25
J3 D1 2p vio & blk ('14) 7.50 .80
J4 D1 3p ultra & blk 2.50 .80
J5 D1 5p brown & blk 4.50 *30.00*
J6 D1 6p gray & blk 11.00 *30.00*
J7 D1 1sh black & red 77.50 *160.00*
Nos. J1-J7 (7) 108.00 *226.10*

1922 Unwmk. Litho. *Rouletted 7-8*

J8 D1 ½p blue grn & blk 1.60 *15.00*
J9 D1 1p dull red & blk 1.75 1.25
J10 D1 1½p yellow brn & blk 2.00 2.40
Nos. J8-J10 (3) 5.35 *18.65*

1922-26 *Perf. 14*

J11 D1 ½p blue grn & blk .85 1.75
J12 D1 1p rose & blk ('23) .90 .25
J13 D1 1½p yel brn & blk ('24) 1.60 1.25
J14 D1 2p vio & blk ('23) 1.40 .80
a. Imperf. pair 300.00 400.00
J15 D1 3p blue & blk ('26) 8.00 22.50
J16 D1 6p gray & blue ('23) 16.00 8.00
Nos. J11-J16 (6) 28.75 34.55

D2

1927-28 Typo.

J17 D2 ½p blue green & blk 1.00 3.50
J18 D2 1p rose & black 1.40 .80
J19 D2 2p violet & black 1.40 1.25
J20 D2 3p ultra & black 13.00 25.00
J21 D2 6p gray & black 24.00 20.00
Nos. J17-J21 (5) 40.80 50.55

Type of 1927-28 Redrawn

Perf. 15x14

1932-40 Photo. Wmk. 201

J22 D2 ½p blue grn & blk ('34) 2.75 1.75
J23 D2 1p rose car & blk ('34) 2.50 .95
J24 D2 2p blk violet & blk 15.00 2.50
a. 2p dark purple & black ('40) 32.50 .25
J25 D2 3p dp blue & blk 27.50 14.00
J26 D2 3p ultra & dk bl ('35) 8.00 .40
J27 D2 3p blue & dk bl ('40) 85.00 3.50
J28 D2 6p brn org & grn ('33) 25.00 6.00
J29 D2 6p red org & grn ('38) 15.00 3.50
Nos. J22-J29 (8) 180.75 32.60

The ½p No. J22 photogravure has larger but thinner numeral and the "d" is taller and thinner than on No. J17.

The 1p No. J23 photogravure has numeral with parallel sides. The "d" is taller and thicker than on No. J18.

On Nos. J25 and J27 the numeral is followed by a large "d" with thick lines and a large round period below it.

Nos. J22, J24 and J25 have frame in photogravure, value typographed.

Catalogue values for unused stamps in this section, from this point to the end of the section, are for Never Hinged items.

See "English-Afrikaans Se-tenant" note preceding No. 23.

D3

Horiz. strips of Three, Perf. 15x14 All Around, Rouletted 6½ Between

1943-44 Photo. Wmk. 201

J30 D3 ½p Prus green ('44) 15.00 *50.00*
a. Single .25 .25
J31 D3 1p brt carmine 11.00 5.50
a. Single .25 .25
J32 D3 2p dark purple 9.00 12.00
a. Single .25 .25
J33 D3 3p dark blue 55.00 85.00
a. Single .25 1.25
Nos. J30-J33 (4) 90.00 152.50

Catalogued as strips of 3 because of the perforations.

Type of 1932-38 Redrawn

Thick Numerals, Capital "D"

1948-49 *Perf. 15x14*

J34 D2 ½p blue green & blk 9.00 13.50
J35 D2 1p deep rose & blk 16.00 6.00
J36 D2 2p dk pur & blk ('49) 17.50 9.00
J37 D2 3p ultra & dk blue 16.00 17.50
J38 D2 6p dp org & grn ('49) 37.50 8.00
Nos. J34-J38 (5) 96.00 54.00

Redrawn Type of 1948-49

Hyphen between Suid-Afrika

1950-58 *Perf. 15x14*

J40 D2 1p car rose & blk 1.25 .45
J41 D2 2p dk pur & blk ('51) .85 .30
J42 D2 3p ultra & dk blue 6.25 2.50
J43 D2 4p emer & dk grn ('58) 14.50 15.00
J44 D2 6p dp org & grn ('52) 11.50 11.50
J45 D2 1sh brn red & dk brn ('58) 17.50 16.00
Nos. J40-J45 (6) 51.85 45.75

D4

Perf. 15x14

1961, Feb. 14 Photo. Wmk. 330

J46 D4 1c cerise & blk .25 2.50
J47 D4 2c purple & blk .25 2.50
J48 D4 4c brt & dk green 1.10 *6.00*
J49 D4 5c chalky bl & slate 2.00 *6.50*
J50 D4 6c vermilion & dk grn 8.00 *7.00*
J51 D4 10c maroon & dk brn 8.50 *10.00*
Nos. J46-J51 (6) 20.10 *34.50*

Republic

D5

Afrikaans Inscription on Top and Left Side

1961-69 *Perf. 15x14*

J52 D5 1c cerise & blk .50 .50
J53 D5 4c brt & dk green 4.25 3.00
J54 D5 6c vermilion & dk grn 8.50 7.25

English Inscription on Top and Left Side

J55 D5 1c cerise & blk ('62) .30 3.50
J56 D5 2c purple & blk .40 .40
J57 D5 4c brt & dk grn ('69) 12.00 17.00
J58 D5 5c chlky bl & dk bl 2.40 3.00
J59 D5 5c chlky bl & blk ('62) 2.75 11.00
J60 D5 10c maroon & dk brn 4.75 3.00
Nos. J52-J60 (9) 35.85 48.65

1967-70 Photo. Wmk. 359

Afrikaans Inscription on Top and Left Side

J61 D5 1c car rose & blk .25 .25
J62 D5 2c brt pur & blk .25 .25
a. Perf. 14 ('71) 25.00 25.00
J63 D5 4c lt grn & blk ('71) 27.50 25.00
a. 4c bright & dark green ('70) *110.00* *110.00*
J64 D5 5c dk blue & blk .85 .85
J65 D5 6c orange & dk grn 4.25 *9.75*
J66 D5 10c dk rose brn & blk 3.50 2.10

English Inscription on Top and Left Side

J67 D5 1c car rose & blk .25 .25
J68 D5 2c brt purple & blk .40 .40
a. Perf. 14 ('71) 25.00 25.00
J69 D5 4c lt grn & blk ('71) 27.50 25.00
a. 4c bright & dark green ('70) *35.00* *35.00*
b. As "a," perf. 14 ('71) *6.00* 6.00
J70 D5 5c dk blue & blk .85 .85
J71 D5 6c orange & dk grn 4.25 *9.75*
J72 D5 10c dk rose brn & blk 3.50 2.10
Nos. J61-J72 (12) 73.35 *76.55*

D6

1972, Mar. 22 *Perf. 14x13½*

J73 D6 1c brt yellow green .55 *1.75*
J74 D6 2c orange .80 *3.00*
J75 D6 4c dull purple 2.00 *3.00*
J76 D6 6c yellow 2.00 *5.50*
J77 D6 8c bright blue 3.50 *5.50*
J78 D6 10c rose red 6.00 *8.50*
Nos. J73-J78 (6) 14.85 *27.25*

On the 2c, 6c and 10c "TO PAY" in first row at left.

OFFICIAL STAMPS

Type A2 stamps have very small margins at top and bottom. Values are for examples with perfs close to, or touching the frame.

No. 5 Overprinted in Black, Periods in Overprint

1926 Wmk. 177 *Perf. 14*

O1 A2 2p dull violet 22.50 2.00

See "English-Afrikaans Se-tenant" note preceding No. 23.

On Nos. 23-25

Perf. 14½x14

Wmk. 201

O2 A5 ½p dk grn & blk, pair 8.00 *18.00*
a. Single, English .75 1.50
b. Single, Afrikaans .75 1.50
O3 A6 1p car & blk, pair 4.00 *8.50*
a. Single, English .25 .50
b. Single, Afrikaans .25 .50
O4 A7 6p org & grn, pair 550.00 80.00
a. Single, English 25.00 11.00
b. Single, Afrikaans 25.00 11.00

Nos. 26 and 25 Overprinted, No Periods in Overprint — b

(Reading Up)

1928-29 *Perf. 14, 14½x14*

Space between words 19mm

O5 A8 2p vio brn & gray, pair ('29) 7.50 *20.00*
a. Single, English .50 *1.50*
b. Single, Afrikaans .50 *1.50*
c. Space 17½mm, pair 6.00 *24.00*
d. As "c," single, English .50 *2.00*
e. As "c," single, Afrikaans .50 *2.00*

Space between words 11½mm

O6 A7 6p org & grn, pair 22.50 *47.50*
a. Single, English 2.75 *2.75*
b. Single, Afrikaans 2.75 *2.75*

#23-25 Ovptd. type "b" Reading Down

Space between words 13½-14mm

1929 *Perf. 14½x14*

O7 A5 ½p grn & blk, pair 2.50 *4.75*
a. Single, English .25 .35
b. Single, Afrikaans .25 .35
c. Period after "OFFISIEEL" on English stamp 5.00 5.00
d. Pair, "c" + normal ½p 45.00 45.00
e. Period after "OFFISIEEL." on Afrikaans stamp 5.00 5.00
f. Pair, "e" + normal ½p 55.00 65.00
O8 A6 1p car & blk, pair 3.00 *6.00*
a. Single, English .30 .50
b. Single, Afrikaans .30 .50
O9 A7 6p org & grn, pair 8.00 *40.00*
a. Single, English 1.25 *3.50*
b. Single, Afrikaans 1.25 *3.50*
c. Period after "OFFISIEEL." on English stamp 10.00 *10.00*
d. Pair, "c" + normal 6p 75.00 *150.00*
e. Period after "OFFISIEEL." on Afrikaans stamp 12.00 *12.00*
f. Pair, "e" + normal 6p 90.00 *160.00*
Nos. O7-O9 (3) 13.50 *50.75*

#29-30 Ovptd. type "b" Reading Down

Space between words 17½-19mm

1931 Engr. *Perf. 14, 14x13½*

O10 A11 1sh dp bl & bis brn, pair 40.00 *90.00*
a. Single, English 3.00 *10.00*
b. Single, Afrikaans 3.00 *10.00*
c. Period after "OFFICIAL." on Afrikaans stamp 50.00 50.00
d. Pair, "c" + normal 1sh 115.00 *240.00*

O11 A12 2sh6p brn & bl grn, pair | 65.00 | 150.00
a. Single, English | 10.00 | 19.00
b. Single, Afrikaans | 10.00 | 19.00
c. Period after "OFFICIAL." on Afrikaans stamp | 72.50 | 100.00
d. Pair, "c" + normal 2sh6p | 300.00 | 550.00

Regular Issues of 1930-45
Overprinted type "b" Reading Down
("SUIDAFRIKA" on Afrikaans stamps)
Perf. 15x14 (½p, 1p, 6p), 14
1930-47 Photo. Wmk. 201
Space between words 9½-12mm
(Various spacings occur in same setting)

O12 A5 ½p bl grn & blk (#33), pair ('31) | 2.25 | 5.00
a. Single, English | .25 | .40
b. Single, Afrikaans | .25 | .40
c. Period after "OFFISIEEL." on English stamp | 5.00 | 5.00
d. Pair, "c" + normal ½p | 37.50 | 60.00
e. Period after "OFFISIEEL." on Afrikaans stamp | 5.00 | 5.00
f. Pair, "e" + normal ½p | 27.50 | 50.00

Space between words 12½-13½mm

O13 A5 ½p bl grn & blk, pair (#33) | 3.00 | 4.00
a. Single, English | .25 | .50
b. Single, Afrikaans | .25 | .50
O14 A6 1p car & blk, pair (#34) | 6.00 | 6.00
a. Single, English | .50 | .60
b. Single, Afrikaans | .50 | .60
c. Period after "OFFISIEEL." on English stamp | 5.00 | 5.00
d. Pair, "c" + normal 1p | 50.00 | 75.00
e. Period after "OFFISIEEL." on Afrikaans stamp | 5.00 | 5.00
f. Pair, "e" + normal 1p | 35.00 | 55.00
O15 A6 1p rose & blk, pair (#35) ('33) | 15.00 | 9.00
a. Single, English | 1.00 | 1.00
b. Single, Afrikaans | 1.00 | 1.00
c. Double ovpt., pair | 275.00 | 400.00
d. As "c," English | — | —
e. As "c," Afrikaans | — | —

Space between words 20½-22mm

O16 A8 2p vio & gray, pair (#36) ('31) | 8.00 | 11.00
a. Single, English | .80 | 1.50
b. Single, Afrikaans | .80 | 1.50
O17 A8 2p vio & ind, pair (#37) | 150.00 | 100.00
a. Single, English | 10.00 | 10.00
b. Single, Afrikaans | 10.00 | 10.00

Space between words 12½-13½mm

O18 A7 6p org & grn, pair (#42) | 8.50 | 8.50
a. Single, English | .75 | 1.00
b. Single, Afrikaans | .75 | 1.00
c. Period after "OFFISIEEL." on English stamp | 7.00 | 7.00
d. Pair, "c" + normal 6p | 90.00 | 100.00
e. Period after "OFFISIEEL." on Afrikaans stamp | 5.50 | 5.50
f. Pair, "e" + normal 6p | 75.00 | 90.00

Space between words 21mm

O19 A11 1sh dp bl & brn, pair (#43c) ('32) | 60.00 | 90.00
a. Single, English | 7.50 | 7.50
b. Single, Afrikaans | 7.50 | 7.50
c. 1sh dk bl & yel brn (#43), 19mm, pair | 50.00 | 90.00
d. As "c," single, English | 8.50 | 7.50
e. As "c," single, Afrikaans | 8.50 | 7.50
f. As "c," spaced 21mm, pair | 42.50 | 65.00
g. As "f," single, English | 6.00 | 7.50
h. As "f," single, Afrikaans | 6.00 | 7.50

Space between words 17½-18½mm

O20 A12 2sh6p brn & sl grn (#44c) ('37), pair | 80.00 | 140.00
a. Single, English | 15.00 | 15.00
b. Single, Afrikaans | 15.00 | 15.00
c. Spaced 21mm, pair | 75.00 | 75.00
d. As "c," single, English | 4.50 | 8.00
e. As "c," single, Afrikaans | 4.50 | 8.00
f. 2sh6p red brn & grn, pair (#44i) ('33) | 50.00 | 90.00
g. As "f," single, English | 5.00 | 8.50
h. As "f," single, Afrikaans | 5.00 | 8.50
j. 2sh6p brn & bl, 19-20mm pair (#44) ('47) | 30.00 | 60.00
k. As "j," single, English | 3.00 | 5.00
m. As "j," single, Afrikaans | 3.00 | 5.00
Nos. O12-O20 (9) | 332.75 | 373.50

[box] Catalogue values for unused stamps in this section, from this point to the end of the section, are for Never Hinged items.

Regular Issue of 1933-54
Overprinted type "b" Reading Down
("SUID-AFRIKA" Hyphenated)
1935-50 Photo. Perf. 15x14, 14
Space between words given with each listing

O21 A5 ½p grn & gray (#45), 12½-13mm, pair ('36) | 7.00 | 30.00
a. Single, English | .25 | 1.75
b. Single, Afrikaans | .25 | 1.75
O22 A5 ½p grn & gray, (#46), 11½-13mm, pair ('38) | 12.00 | 12.50
a. Single, English | .50 | 1.25
b. Single, Afrikaans | .50 | 1.25
O23 A5 ½p grn & gray (#47), 11½mm, pair ('48) | 1.25 | 5.00
a. Single, English | .25 | .70
b. Single, Afrikaans | .25 | .70
O24 A6 1p car & gray (#48), 11-13mm, pair | 4.00 | 3.00
a. Single, English | .25 | .25
b. Single, Afrikaans | .25 | .25
O25 A6 1p rose car & gray blk (#49), 11½-12mm, pair ('41) | 1.00 | .50
a. Single, English | .25 | .25
b. Single, Afrikaans | .25 | .25
O26 A15 1½p dk grn & gold (#51), 19-21mm, pair ('37) | 30.00 | 25.00
a. Single, English | 2.25 | 1.75
b. Single, Afrikaans | 2.25 | 1.75
O27 A15 1½p sl grn & ocher (#52), 16mm, pair ('44) | 50.00 | 11.50
a. Single, English | 1.25 | 1.25
b. Single, Afrikaans | 1.25 | 1.25
c. Ovpt. spaced 14-14½mm, pair | 3.00 | 10.00
d. As "c," single, English | .25 | .80
e. As "c," single, Afrikaans | .25 | .80
O28 A8 2p bl vio & dl bl (#53), 20-21mm, pair ('39) | 150.00 | 40.00
a. Single, English | 7.50 | 2.50
b. Single, Afrikaans | 7.50 | 2.50
O29 A16 2p pur & sl (#55), 19-21mm, pair ('48) | 5.75 | 25.00
a. Single, English | .25 | 2.00
b. Single, Afrikaans | .25 | 2.00
O30 A7 6p org & bl grn, I (#59), 12-13mm, pair ('38) | 80.00 | 45.00
a. Single, English | 6.50 | 3.75
b. Single, Afrikaans | 6.50 | 3.75
O31 A7 6p org & grn, II (#60), 12-13mm, pair ('39) | 14.00 | 10.00
a. Single, English | 1.25 | 1.25
b. Single, Afrikaans | 1.25 | 1.25
O32 A7 6p org & grn III (#61), 11½-12mm, pair ('47) | 5.00 | 11.00
a. Single, English | .85 | 1.25
b. Single, Afrikaans | .85 | 1.25
O33 A11 1sh lt bl & ol brn (#62c), 19-21mm, pair ('40) | 80.00 | 50.00
a. Single, English | 4.50 | 2.50
b. Single, Afrikaans | 4.50 | 2.50
c. "OFFICIAL" on both sides | 3,000.
d. "OFFISIEEL" on both sides | 3,000.
e. 1sh chlky bl & lt brn (#62) ('50), pair | 11.00 | 30.00
f. As "e," single, English | 2.00 | 2.50
g. As "e," single, Afrikaans | 2.00 | 2.50
h. 1sh vio bl & brnsh blk (#62f), 18-19mm, pair | 65.00 | 27.50
j. As "h," single, English | 4.50 | 2.00
k. As "h," single, Afrikaans | 4.50 | 2.00
O34 A13 5sh grn & blk (#64) 19-20mm, pair | 65.00 | 160.00
a. Single, English | 3.50 | 13.50
b. Single, Afrikaans | 3.50 | 13.50
O35 A13 5sh bl grn & blk (#65), 20mm, pair | 40.00 | 110.00
a. Single, English | 3.50 | 12.50
b. Single, Afrikaans | 3.50 | 12.50
O36 A18 10sh ol blk & bl (#67), 19½-20mm, pair ('48) | 100.00 | 275.00
a. Single, English | 10.00 | 24.00
b. Single, Afrikaans | 10.00 | 24.00
Nos. O21-O36 (16) | 645.00 | 813.50

Nos. 52 and 56 Overprinted type "b" Reading Up
Space between words 16mm
1949-50 Size: 22x18mm Perf. 14
O37 A15 1½p sl grn & ocher, pair | 85.00 | 85.00
a. Single, English | 5.00 | 4.00

b. Single, Afrikaans | 5.00 | 4.00
Size: 21½x17½mm
O38 A16 2p pur & sl bl, pair ('50) | 3,250. | 3,750.
a. Single, English | 200. | 275.
b. Single, Afrikaans | 200. | 275.

Nos. 64, 67 Overprinted

c

Space between words 18-19mm
1940 Perf. 14
O39 A13 5sh grn & blk, pair | 125.00 | 140.00
a. Single, English | 12.00 | 12.50
b. Single, Afrikaans | 12.00 | 12.50
O40 A18 10sh ol brn & bl, pair | 500.00 | 525.00
a. Single, English | 32.50 | 37.50
b. Single, Afrikaans | 32.50 | 37.50

No. 54 Overprinted type "c" Reading Up
Space between words 19mm
1945 Perf. 14
O41 A8 2p dl vio & gray, pair | 11.00 | 32.50
a. Single, English | 1.00 | 2.25
b. Single, Afrikaans | 1.00 | 2.25

No. 47 Overprinted

1947 Perf. 15x14
O42 A5 ½p grn & gray, pair | 22.50 | 20.00
a. Single, English | 1.00 | 2.00
b. Single, Afrikaans | 1.00 | 2.00

Stamps of 1937-54 Overprinted

1950-54 Perf. 15x14, 14
Space between words 10mm
O43 A5 ½p grn & gray, pair (#47) | .90 | 1.50
a. Single, English | .25 | .25
b. Single, Afrikaans | .25 | .25
O44 A6 1p rose car & gray blk, pair (#49) | 1.00 | 6.00
a. Single, English | .25 | .25
b. Single, Afrikaans | .25 | .25
O45 A6 1p car & blk, pair (#50) | 1.00 | 3.50
a. Single, English | .25 | .25
b. Single, Afrikaans | .25 | .25

Space between words 14½mm
O46 A15 1½p sl grn & ocher, pair (#52) | 2.00 | 5.00
a. Single, English | .25 | .35
b. Single, Afrikaans | .25 | .35
O47 A16 2p pur & sl bl, pair (#56) | 1.00 | 2.00
a. Single, English | .25 | .25
b. Single, Afrikaans | .25 | .25
c. Ovpt. reading up, pair

Space between words 10mm
O48 A7 6p red org & bl grn, III, pair (#61c) | 2.00 | 4.00
a. Single, English | .35 | .35
b. Single, Afrikaans | .35 | .35

Space between words 19mm
O49 A11 1sh chlky bl & lt brn, pair (#62) | 6.75 | 18.00
a. Single, English | .50 | 2.00
b. Single, Afrikaans | .50 | 2.00
c. 1sh vio bl & brnsh blk (#62f), pair | 175.00 | 200.00
d. As "c," single, English | 12.50 | 17.50
e. As "c," single, Afrikaans | 12.50 | 17.50
O50 A12 2sh6p brn & brt grn, pair (#63) | 10.00 | 37.50
a. Single, English | 1.00 | 3.50
b. Single, Afrikaans | 1.00 | 3.50

O51 A13 5sh bl grn & blk, pair (#64) | 190.00 | 125.00
a. Single, English | 10.00 | 10.00
b. Single, Afrikaans | 10.00 | 10.00
O52 A13 5sh pale bl grn & blk, I, pair (#65) | 65.00 | 85.00
a. Single, English | 5.00 | 6.50
b. Single, Afrikaans | 5.00 | 6.50
O53 A13 5sh dp yel grn & blk, II, pair (#66) | 80.00 | 100.00
a. Single, English | 8.00 | 9.00
b. Single, Afrikaans | 8.00 | 9.00
O54 A18 10sh ol blk & bl, pair (#67) | 80.00 | 250.00
a. Single, English | 9.00 | 22.50
b. Single, Afrikaans | 9.00 | 22.50
Nos. O43-O54 (12) | 439.65 | 637.50

BOPHUTHATSWANA
ˌbō-ˌpü-tät-ˈswä-nə

LOCATION — Noncontiguous enclaves, Republic of South Africa
GOVT. — Self-governing tribal homeland
AREA — 27,340 sq. mi.
POP. — 1,660,000 (1985)
CAPITAL — Mmabatho

[box] Catalogue values for all unused stamps in this country are for Never Hinged items.

Independence from South Africa — A1

4c, Hands, dove released. 10c, Leopard (state emblem). 15c, Coat of arms. 20c, Flag.

Perf. 12½
1977, Dec. 6 Litho. Unwmk.
1 A1 4c multicolored | .60 | .60
2 A1 10c multicolored | 1.10 | .85
3 A1 15c multicolored | 2.40 | 1.75
4 A1 20c multicolored | 3.25 | 2.40
Nos. 1-4 (4) | 7.35 | 5.60

An imperf. souvenir sheet exists containing Nos. 1-4 printed in one color (blue). Not valid for postage.

Tribal Totems — A2

Designs: 1c, African buffalo (Malete, Hwaduba). 2c, Bush pig (Kolobeng). 3c, Chacma baboon (Hurutshe, Tlaro). 4c, Leopard (state emblem). 5c, Crocodile (Kwena-Fokeng). 6c, Savanna monkey (Kgatla). 7c, Lion (Taung). 8c, Spotted hyena (Phiring). 9c, Cape porcupine (Rokologadi). 10c, Aardvark (Tlokwa). 15c, Fish (Tlhaping). 20c, Hunting dog (Tlhalerwa). 25c, Common duiker (Mfatlha). 30c, African elephant (Tlhako, Tloung). 50c, Python (Nogeng). 1r, Hippopotamus (Kubung). 2r, Greater kudu (Rolong).

1977, Dec. 6
5 A2 1c multicolored | .25 | .25
6 A2 2c multicolored | .25 | .25
7 A2 3c multicolored | .25 | .25
8 A2 4c multicolored | 4.00 | 1.90
9 A2 5c on 4c multi | 1.10 | .60
10 A2 6c multicolored | .25 | .25
11 A2 7c multicolored | 1.00 | 1.00
12 A2 8c multicolored | .25 | .25
13 A2 9c multicolored | .25 | .25
14 A2 10c multicolored | .25 | .25
15 A2 15c multicolored | .35 | .25
16 A2 20c multicolored | .35 | .25
17 A2 25c multicolored | .40 | .25
18 A2 30c multicolored | .45 | .25
19 A2 50c multicolored | .65 | .40
20 A2 1r multicolored | 1.40 | 1.10
21 A2 2r multicolored | 2.50 | 2.50
Nos. 5-21 (17) | 14.05 | 10.25

No. 9 was printed as a 4c stamp. Grass was printed over the 4c at upper right and 5c printed at upper left. Copies exist without the surcharge. No. 9A does not have the 4c.

Perf. 14

5a	A2	1c	.55	.55
6a	A2	2c	.55	.55
7a	A2	3c	.55	.55
8a	A2	4c	.55	.55
9A	A2	5c multicolored	.55	.55
11a	A2	7c	.55	.55
12a	A2	8c	.60	.60
14a	A2	10c	.60	.60
		Nos. 5a-14a (8)	4.50	4.50

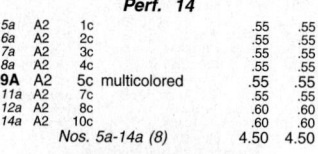

World Hypertension Month — A3

4c, Avoid kidney infections. 10c, Lower salt intake. 15c, Overeating is dangerous.

1978, Apr. 7   Perf. 12x12½

22	A3	4c multicolored	.55	.55
23	A3	10c multicolored	.95	.95
24	A3	15c multicolored	1.40	1.40
		Nos. 22-24 (3)	2.90	2.90

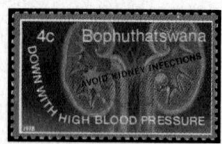

Road Safety A4

4c, Don't drink and drive. 10c, Keep children off roads. 15c, Pedestrians observe crossing signals. 20c, Observe stop signs.

1978, July 12

25	A4	4c multicolored	.55	.35
26	A4	10c multicolored	.80	.50
27	A4	15c multicolored	1.00	.60
28	A4	20c multicolored	1.60	.80
		Nos. 25-28 (4)	3.95	2.25

Cutting and Polishing Semi-precious Stones — A5

1978, Oct. 3

29	A5	4c Cutting slabs of travertine	.50	.25
30	A5	10c Polishing travertine	1.00	.70
31	A5	15c Sorting stones	1.60	1.00
32	A5	20c Factory at Taung	2.00	1.25
		Nos. 29-32 (4)	5.10	3.20

1st Airplane Flight, 75th Anniv. — A6

1978, Dec. 1   Perf. 12½

33	A6	10c Wright Flyer	1.50	1.50
34	A6	15c Orville and Wilbur Wright	2.00	2.00

Pres. Lucas M. Mangope — A7

1978, Dec. 6

35	A7	4c Profile	.40	.40
36	A7	15c Portrait	.85	.85

Sorghum Beer Production A8

1979, Feb. 28   Perf. 14x14½

37	A8	4c Drying germinated wheat	.30	.30
38	A8	15c Cooking ground grain	.80	.80
39	A8	20c Straining the liquid	1.00	1.00
40	A8	25c Drinking beer	1.40	1.40
		Nos. 37-40 (4)	3.50	3.50

Tate-Knoetze Boxing Match — A9

1979, June 2

41	A9	15c John Tate	.70	.70
42	A9	15c Kallie Knoetze	.70	.70
a.		Pair, #41-42	2.00	2.00

Intl. Children's Year — A10

Illustrations by local youths: 4c, Boy dazzled by sun, from a folk tale, by Hendrick Sebapo. 15c, Africans and animal silhouettes, by Daisy Morapedi. 20c, Man in profile and landscape, by Peter Tladi. 25c, Old man, boy and mule, by Sebapo.

1979, June 7   Perf. 14½x14

43	A10	4c multicolored	.25	.25
44	A10	15c multicolored	.25	.25
45	A10	20c multicolored	.40	.40
46	A10	25c multicolored	.50	.50
		Nos. 43-46 (4)	1.40	1.40

Platinum Industry A11

Designs: 4c, Pouring molten metal. 15c, Platinum in industrial use. 20c, Telecommunications satellite in orbit. 25c, Jewelry.

1979, Aug. 15   Perf. 14x14½

47	A11	4c multicolored	.25	.25
48	A11	15c multicolored	.25	.25
49	A11	20c multicolored	.35	.35
50	A11	25c multicolored	.55	.55
		Nos. 47-50 (4)	1.40	1.40

Agriculture A12

1979, Oct. 25

51	A12	5c Cattle	.25	.25
52	A12	15c Picking cotton	.25	.25
53	A12	20c Researcher in corn field	.40	.40
54	A12	25c Fish in net	.45	.45
		Nos. 51-54 (4)	1.35	1.35

Stop Smoking Campaign — A13

1980, Mar. 5   Perf. 14½x14

55	A13	5c multicolored	.65	.65

Edible Wild Fruit — A14

5c, Landolphia capensis. 10c, Vangueria infausta. 15c, Bequaertiodendron magalismontanum. 20c, Sclerocarya caffra.

1980, June 4

56	A14	5c multicolored	.25	.25
57	A14	10c multicolored	.40	.40
58	A14	15c multicolored	.60	.60
59	A14	20c multicolored	.80	.80
		Nos. 56-59 (4)	2.05	2.05

Birds — A15

1980, Sept. 10

60	A15	5c Pied babbler	.25	.25
61	A15	10c Carmine bee-eater	.40	.40
62	A15	15c Shaft-tailed whydah	.60	.60
63	A15	20c Meyer's parrot	.75	.75
		Nos. 60-63 (4)	2.00	2.00

Sun City Tourist Attractions A16

5c, Hotel, casino, country club. 10c, Golfer at Gary Player Country Club. 15c, Casino interior. 20c, Night club dancers.

1980, Dec. 5   Perf. 14x14½

64	A16	5c multicolored	.25	.25
65	A16	10c multicolored	.25	.25
66	A16	15c multicolored	.40	.40
67	A16	20c multicolored	.50	.50
		Nos. 64-67 (4)	1.40	1.40

Intl. Year for the Disabled — A17

1981, Jan. 30   Perf. 14½x14

68	A17	5c shown	.25	.25
69	A17	15c Blind boy	.25	.25
70	A17	20c Archer in wheelchair	.40	.40
71	A17	25c X-ray (tuberculosis)	.45	.45
		Nos. 68-71 (4)	1.35	1.35

Easter A18

Bible quotes and: 5c, Lamb, sunset. 15c, Bread. 20c, Man holding lamb. 25c, Wheat field.

1981, Apr. 1   Perf. 14x14½

72	A18	5c multicolored	.25	.25
73	A18	15c multicolored	.25	.25
74	A18	20c multicolored	.40	.40
75	A18	25c multicolored	.45	.45
		Nos. 72-75 (4)	1.35	1.35

Telephones — A19

5c, Siemens & Halske wall telephone, 1885. 15c, Ericsson table model, 1895. 20c, Hasler table model, 1900. 25c, Mix & Genest wall model, 1904.

1981, July 31   Perf. 14½x14

76	A19	5c multicolored	.25	.25
77	A19	15c multicolored	.30	.30
78	A19	20c multicolored	.35	.35
79	A19	25c multicolored	.45	.45
		Nos. 76-79 (4)	1.35	1.35

Grasses — A20

5c, Themeda triandra. 15c, Rhynchelytrum repens. 20c, Eragrostis capensis. 25c, Monocymbium ceresiiforme.

1981, Nov. 25

80	A20	5c multicolored	.25	.25
81	A20	10c multicolored	.30	.30
82	A20	20c multicolored	.35	.35
83	A20	25c multicolored	.45	.45
		Nos. 80-83 (4)	1.35	1.35

Boy Scouts, 75th Anniv. — A21

1982, Jan. 29

84	A21	5c Scout, 1982	.25	.25
85	A21	15c Mafeking Siege stamps	.35	.35
86	A21	20c Scout cadet, 1907	.45	.45
87	A21	25c Lord Baden-Powell	.55	.55
		Nos. 84-87 (4)	1.60	1.60

Easter — A22

1982, Apr. 1

88	A22	15c John 12:1	.25	.25
89	A22	20c Matthew 21:1-2	.25	.25
90	A22	25c Mark 11:5-6	.50	.50
91	A22	30c Matthew 21:7	.60	.60
		Nos. 88-91 (4)	1.60	1.60

Table Telephones — A23

1982, Sept. 3

92	A23	8c Ericsson, 1878	.25	.25
93	A23	15c Ericsson, 1885	.25	.25
94	A23	20c Ericsson, 1893	.30	.30

95 A23 25c Siemens & Halske,
1898 .35 .35
Nos. 92-95 (4) 1.15 1.15

Independence, 5th Anniv. — A24

8c, Old parliament building. 15c, New government offices. 20c, University, Mmabatho. 25c, Civic Center, Mmabatho.

1982, Dec. 6 *Perf. 14x14½*
96 A24 8c multicolored .25 .25
97 A24 15c multicolored .25 .25
98 A24 20c multicolored .30 .30
99 A24 25c multicolored .35 .35
Nos. 96-99 (4) 1.15 1.15

Pilanesberg Nature Reserve — A25

No. 100, Ceratotherium simum. No. 101, Equus burchelli. No. 102, Hippotragus niger. No. 103, Alcelaphus caama.

1983, Jan. 5
100 A25 8c multicolored .25 .25
101 A25 20c multicolored .45 .45
102 A25 25c multicolored .55 .55
103 A25 40c multicolored .80 .80
Nos. 100-103 (4) 2.05 2.05

Easter
A26

1983, Mar. 30 *Perf. 14½x14*
104 A26 8c Matthew 21:7 .25 .25
105 A26 20c Mark 11:7 .35 .35
106 A26 25c Matthew 21:8 .40 .40
107 A26 40c Mark 11:9 .65 .65
Nos. 104-107 (4) 1.65 1.65

Telephones — A27

10c, ATM table model, c. 1920. 20c, A/S Elektrisk wall model, c. 1900. 25c, Ericsson wall model, c. 1900. 40c, Ericsson wall model, c. 1900, diff.

1983, June 22
108 A27 10c multicolored .25 .25
109 A27 20c multicolored .35 .35
110 A27 25c multicolored .45 .45
111 A27 40c multicolored .70 .70
Nos. 108-111 (4) 1.75 1.75

Birds of the
Veld — A28

10c, Kori bustard. 20c, Black korhaan. 25c, Red-crested korhaan. 40c, Stanley bustard.

1983, Sept. 14
112 A28 10c multicolored .25 .25
113 A28 20c multicolored .45 .45
114 A28 30c multicolored .60 .60
115 A28 40c multicolored 1.00 1.00
Nos. 112-115 (4) 2.30 2.30

Grasses — A29

No. 116, Panicum maximum. No. 117, Hyparrhenia dregeana. No. 118, Cenchrus ciliaris. No. 119, Urochloa brachyura.

1984, Jan. 20
116 A29 10c multicolored .25 .25
117 A29 20c multicolored .30 .30
118 A29 25c multicolored .35 .35
119 A29 40c multicolored .50 .50
Nos. 116-119 (4) 1.40 1.40

Easter
A30

1984, Mar. 23 *Perf. 14½x14*
120 A30 10c Mark 11:11 .25 .25
121 A30 20c Mark 11:15 .30 .30
122 A30 25c Matthew 21:19 .40 .40
123 A30 40c Matthew 21:19, diff. .65 .65
Nos. 120-123 (4) 1.60 1.60

See Nos. 165-168, 173-176.

Mining
Industry
A31

1984, Apr. 2 *Perf. 14½x14*
124 A31 11c multicolored .70 .70

Telephones — A32

11c, Shuchhardt table model, c. 1905. 20c, Siemens wall model, c. 1925. 25c, Ericsson table model, c. 1900. 30c, Oki table model, c. 1930.

1984, July 20
125 A32 11c multicolored .25 .25
126 A32 20c multicolored .30 .30
127 A32 25c multicolored .40 .40
128 A32 30c multicolored .45 .45
Nos. 125-128 (4) 1.40 1.40

Lizards
A33

Designs: 11c, Yellow-throated plated lizard. 25c, Transvaal girdled lizard. 30c, Ocellated sand lizard. 45c, Bibron's thick-toed gecko.

1984, Sept. 25 *Perf. 14x14½*
129 A33 11c multicolored .25 .25
130 A33 25c multicolored .30 .30
131 A33 30c multicolored .35 .35
132 A33 45c multicolored .50 .50
Nos. 129-132 (4) 1.40 1.40

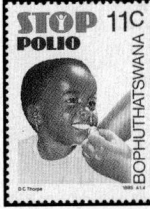

Child Health
Care — A34

1985, Jan. 25
133 A34 11c Stop Polio .25 .25
134 A34 25c Stop Measles .35 .35
135 A34 30c Stop Diphtheria .45 .45
136 A34 50c Stop Whooping
Cough .80 .80
Nos. 133-136 (4) 1.85 1.85

Mafeking,
Cent. — A35

Portraits: 11c, Montshiwa (1814-1896), chief of the Barolong booRatshidi. 25c, Sir Charles Warren (1840-1927), army commander who established the Crown Colony and laid out the town of Mafeking.

1985, Mar. 11
137 A35 11c multicolored .25 .25
138 A35 25c multicolored .60 .60

Industries
A36

Designs: 1c, Textile mill, Bophuthatswana. 2c, Sewing cloth sacks, Selosesha. 3c, Ceramic tile production line. 4c, Processing sheepskin. 5c, Manufacture of crossbows. 6c, Automobile parts. 7c, Hosiery factory, Babelegi. 8c, Specialized bicycle factory. 9c, Lawn mower assembly line. 10c, Dress factory, Thaba Nchu. 12c, Automobile upholstery factory. 14c, Milling industry, Mafeking. 15c, Manufacturing of plastic bags. 16c, Brickworks, Mmabatho. 18c, Manufacturing of cutlery. 20c, Men's clothing factory. 25c, Chromium plating baby carriage parts. 30c, Spray-painting metal beds. 50c, Milk processing plant. 1r, Printing works. 2r, Industrial complex, Babelegi.

1985-89 *Perf. 14½x14*
139 A36 1c multicolored .25 .25
140 A36 2c multicolored .25 .25
141 A36 3c multicolored .25 .25
142 A36 4c multicolored .25 .25
143 A36 5c multicolored .25 .25
144 A36 6c multicolored .25 .25
145 A36 7c multicolored .25 .25
146 A36 8c multicolored .25 .25
147 A36 9c multicolored .25 .25
148 A36 10c multicolored .25 .25
149 A36 12c multicolored .25 .25
150 A36 14c multicolored .30 .30
151 A36 15c multicolored .35 .35
152 A36 16c multicolored .35 .35
153 A36 18c multicolored .40 .40
154 A36 20c multicolored .45 .45
155 A36 25c multicolored .60 .60
156 A36 30c multicolored .70 .70
157 A36 50c multicolored 1.10 1.10
158 A36 1r multicolored 2.25 2.25
159 A36 2r multicolored 4.75 4.75
Nos. 139-159 (21) 14.00 14.00

Issued: 1c-10c, 15c, 20c, 25c, 30c-2r, 10/25/85; 12c, 4/1/85; 14c, 4/1/86; 16c, 4/1/87; 18c, 7/3/89.

Easter Type of 1984

1985, Apr. 2
165 A30 12c Matthew 21:14 .25 .25
166 A30 25c Matthew 21:14, diff. .30 .30
167 A30 30c Matthew 21:15 .35 .35
168 A30 50c Matthew 21:15-16 .55 .55
Nos. 165-168 (4) 1.45 1.45

Tree Conservation
A37

No. 169, Fourea saligna. No. 170, Boscia albitrunca. No. 171, Erythrina lysistemon. No. 172, Bequaertiodendron magalismontanum.

1985, July 4 *Perf. 14x14½*
169 A37 12c multicolored .25 .25
170 A37 25c multicolored .35 .35
171 A37 30c multicolored .40 .40
172 A37 50c multicolored .65 .65
Nos. 169-172 (4) 1.65 1.65

Easter Type of 1984

1986, Mar. 6 *Perf. 14½x14*
173 A30 12c John 12:2 .25 .25
174 A30 20c John 12:3 .35 .35
175 A30 25c John 12:3, diff. .45 .45
176 A30 30c Matthew 26:7 .60 .60
Nos. 173-176 (4) 1.65 1.65

Paintings of Thaba Nchu in the
Africana Museum,
Johannesburg — A38

14c, Wesleyan Mission Station and Residence of Moroka, Chief of the Barolong, 1834, by Charles Davidson Bell. 20c, James Archbell's Congregation, 1834, by Bell. 25c, Mission Station at Thaba Nchu, 1850, by Thomas Baines (1822-75).

1986, May 15 *Perf. 14x14½*
177 A38 14c multicolored .25 .25
178 A38 20c multicolored .30 .30
179 A38 25c multicolored .45 .45
Nos. 177-179 (3) 1.00 1.00

Incorporation of Thaba Nchu and Bophuthatswana, Oct. 1, 1983.
A souvenir sheet of one No. 179 has decorative margin continuing the painting and picturing the emblem of the philatelic exhibition held at Johannesburg, Oct. 6-11. Sold for 50c. Value $1.

Temisano
Development
Projects
A39

14c, Agricultural production. 20c, Community development. 25c, Vocational training. 30c, Secondary industries.

1986, Aug. 6 *Perf. 14½x14*
180 A39 14c multicolored .25 .25
181 A39 20c multicolored .30 .30
182 A39 25c multicolored .40 .40
183 A39 30c multicolored .45 .45
Nos. 180-183 (4) 1.40 1.40

BOP
Airways,
5th Anniv.
A40

14c, Airline personnel, aircraft. 20c, Passengers. 25c, Mmabatho Intl. Airport. 30c, Cessna Citation.

1986, Oct. 16　　Perf. 14x14½

184	A40	14c multicolored	.25	.25
185	A40	20c multicolored	.40	.40
186	A40	25c multicolored	.50	.50
187	A40	30c multicolored	.55	.55
		Nos. 184-187 (4)	1.70	1.70

Sports — A41

1987, Jan. 22

188	A41	14c Netball	.25	.25
189	A41	20c Tennis	.30	.30
190	A41	25c Soccer	.35	.35
191	A41	30c Running	.45	.45
		Nos. 188-191 (4)	1.35	1.35

Wildflowers — A42

No. 192, Berkheya zeyheri. No. 193, Plumbago auriculata. No. 194, Pterodiscus speciosus. No. 195, Gazania krebsiana.

1987, Apr. 23

192	A42	16c multicolored	.30	.30
193	A42	20c multicolored	.35	.35
194	A42	25c multicolored	.45	.45
195	A42	30c multicolored	.50	.50
		Nos. 192-195 (4)	1.60	1.60

A souvenir sheet of one No. 194 has decorative black and white inscribed margin picturing the emblem of the natl. philatelic exhibition held at Paarl, Sept. 16-19. Sold for 70c. Value $1.50.

Education — A43

Designs: 16c, E.M. Mokgoko Farmer Training Center, Ramatlabama. 20c, Main lecture block, University of Bophuthatswana, Mmabatho. 25c, Manpower Center. 30c, Hotel training school, Odi.

1987, Aug. 6　　Perf. 14½x14

196	A43	16c multicolored	.25	.25
197	A43	20c multicolored	.30	.30
198	A43	25c multicolored	.35	.35
199	A43	30c multicolored	.45	.45
		Nos. 196-199 (4)	1.35	1.35

Independence, 10th Anniv. — A44

Communications.

1987, Dec. 4

200	A44	16c Postal service	.25	.25
201	A44	30c Telephone	.30	.30
202	A44	40c Radio	.40	.40
203	A44	50c Television	.50	.50
		Nos. 200-203 (4)	1.45	1.45

Easter
A45

1988, Mar. 31

204	A45	16c John 12:12-14	.25	.25
205	A45	30c Mark 14:10-11	.30	.30
206	A45	40c John 13:5	.40	.40
207	A45	50c John 13:26	.45	.45
		Nos. 204-207 (4)	1.40	1.40

Natl. Parks Board Activities — A46

1988, June 23　　Perf. 14½x14

208	A46	16c Environmental education	.25	.25
209	A46	30c Conservation	.40	.40
210	A46	40c Catering	.50	.50
211	A46	50c Tourism	.65	.65
		Nos. 208-211 (4)	1.80	1.80

A souvenir sheet of one No. 211 has black and white decorative margin picturing the emblem of the natl. philatelic exhibition held at Pietermaritzburg, Nov. 22-27. Sold for 70c. Value $3.

Crops
A47

1988, Sept. 15　　Perf. 14½x14

212	A47	16c Sunflowers	.25	.25
213	A47	30c Peanuts	.40	.40
214	A47	40c Cotton	.55	.55
215	A47	50c Cabbages	.65	.65
		Nos. 212-215 (4)	1.85	1.85

Dams — A48

1988, Nov. 17

216	A48	16c Ngotwane	.30	.30
217	A48	30c Groothoek	.55	.55
218	A48	40c Sehujwane	.85	.85
219	A48	50c Molatedi	.90	.90
		Nos. 216-219 (4)	2.60	2.60

Easter
A49

1989, Mar. 9

220	A49	16c Mark 26:26	.30	.30
221	A49	30c Matthew 26:39	.55	.55
222	A49	40c Mark 14:45	.85	.85
223	A49	50c John 18:10	1.00	1.00
		Nos. 220-223 (4)	2.70	2.70

Children's
Art — A50

Designs: 18c, "Rooster," by Thembi Atong. 30c, "Thatched Hut in Rural Setting," by

Muhammad Mahri. 40c, "Modern World," by Tshepo Mashokwe. 50c, "Cityscape," by Miles Brown.

1989, May 11

224	A50	18c multicolored	.25	.25
225	A50	30c multicolored	.40	.40
226	A50	40c multicolored	.55	.55
227	A50	50c multicolored	.70	.70
		Nos. 224-227 (4)	1.90	1.90

Birds of
Prey — A51

1989, Sept. 1　　Perf. 14x14½

228	A51	18c Elanus caeruleus	.70	.70
229	A51	30c Melierax canorus	1.10	1.10
230	A51	40c Falco naumanni	1.50	1.50
231	A51	50c Circaetus gallicus	1.90	1.90
a.		Souvenir sheet of 1	4.75	4.75
		Nos. 228-231 (4)	5.20	5.20

No. 231a has multicolored decorative margin picturing emblem of the WANDERERS 101 natl. philatelic exhibition held Sept. 6-9. Sold for 1.50r.

Traditional
Thatched
Dwellings
A52

1989, Nov. 28　　Perf. 14½x14

232	A52	18c shown	.25	.25
233	A52	30c multi, diff.	.40	.40
234	A52	40c multi, diff.	.45	.45
235	A52	50c multi, diff.	.55	.55
		Nos. 232-235 (4)	1.65	1.65

Community
Services
A53

1990, Jan. 11

236	A53	18c Playground	.25	.25
237	A53	30c Immunization clinic	.35	.35
238	A53	40c Library	.50	.50
239	A53	50c Hospital	.60	.60
		Nos. 236-239 (4)	1.70	1.70

Wildlife
(Small
Mammals)
A54

21c, Dendromus mystacalis. 30c, Ictonyx striatus. 40c, Elephantulus myurus. 50c, Procavia capensis.

1990, Apr. 11　Litho.　Perf. 14½x14

240	A54	21c multicolored	.40	.40
241	A54	30c multicolored	.55	.55
242	A54	40c multicolored	.70	.70
243	A54	50c multicolored	.90	.90
a.		Souvenir sheet of 1	2.75	2.75
		Nos. 240-243 (4)	2.55	2.55

No. 243a has multicolored inscribed margin; text publicizes the natl. philatelic exhibition. Sold for 1.50r.

Sandgrouses — A55

1990, July 12　Litho.　Perf. 14x14½

244	A55	21c Pterocles burchelli	.75	.75
245	A55	35c Pterocles bicinctus	1.40	1.40
246	A55	40c Pterocles namaqua	1.50	1.50
247	A55	50c Pterocles gutturalis	1.90	1.90
		Nos. 244-247 (4)	5.55	5.55

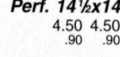

Bus Manufacturing — A56

a, Chassis welding. b, Mounting the engine. c, Body construction. d, Spray painting. e, Completed models and bare chassis.

1990, Aug. 3　　Perf. 14½x14

248		Strip of 5	4.50	4.50
a.-e.		A56 21c any single	.90	.90

Traditional
Activities — A57

1990, Oct. 4　　Perf. 14x14½

249	A57	21c Basketry	.40	.40
250	A57	35c Tanning	.60	.60
251	A57	40c Beer making	.70	.70
252	A57	50c Pottery making	1.00	1.00
		Nos. 249-252 (4)	2.70	2.70

Bophuthatswana Air Force, 10th
Anniv. — A58

Helicopters: a, Alouette III. b, BK117. Airplanes: c, Pilatus Trainer PC-7. d, Pilatus Porter PC-6. e, Casa 212.

1990, Dec. 12　　Perf. 14½x14

253		Strip of 5	6.00	6.00
a.-e.		A58 21c any single	1.40	1.40

Edible Wild
Fruit — A59

1991, Jan. 24　Litho.　Perf. 14x14½

254	A59	21c Annona senegalensis	.40	.40
255	A59	35c Strychnos pungens	.65	.65
256	A59	40c Ficus sycomorus	.85	.85
257	A59	50c Dovyalis caffra	1.00	1.00
		Nos. 254-257 (4)	2.90	2.90

Easter
A60

1991, Mar. 21　Litho.　Perf. 14½x14

258	A60	21c Mark 14:46	.45	.45
259	A60	35c Mark 14:53	.65	.65
260	A60	40c Mark 14:65	.85	.85
261	A60	50c Mark 14:67	.95	.95
		Nos. 258-261 (4)	2.90	2.90

Locomotives
A61

1991, July 4   **Litho.**
Size: 72x25mm (25c, 50c)
262 A61 25c Class 6A   .85   .85
263 A61 40c Class 7A   1.40   1.40
264 A61 50c Class 6Z   1.75   1.75
265 A61 60c Class 8   2.40   2.40
    Nos. 262-265 (4)   6.40   6.40

A souvenir sheet of 1 #265 was sold by the Philatelic Foundation of South Africa. Value $6.
See Nos. 291-294.

Maps of
Africa — A62

25c, Caneiro chart, 1502. 40c, Cantino chart, 1502. 50c, Contarini map, 1506. 60c, Waldseemuller map, 1507.

1991, Sept. 12   **Litho.**   *Perf. 14x14½*
266 A62 25c multicolored   .90   .90
267 A62 40c multicolored   1.50   1.50
268 A62 50c multicolored   1.90   1.90
269 A62 60c multicolored   2.50   2.50
    Nos. 266-269 (4)   6.80   6.80

Maps of
Africa
A63

27c, Fracanzano, 1508. 45c, Waldseemuller, 1513. 65c, Waldseemuller, 1516. 85c, Laurent Fries, 1522.

1992, Jan. 9   **Litho.**   *Perf. 14½x14*
270 A63 27c multicolored   .90   .90
271 A63 45c multicolored   1.50   1.50
272 A63 65c multicolored   1.90   1.90
273 A63 85c multicolored   2.50   2.50
    Nos. 270-273 (4)   6.80   6.80

Easter
A64

1992, Apr. 1   **Litho.**
274 A64 27c Mark 15:1   .25   .25
275 A64 45c Mark 15:15   .45   .45
276 A64 65c Mark 15:17-18   .60   .60
277 A64 85c Mark 15:19   .80   .80
    Nos. 274-277 (4)   2.10   2.10

Acacia
Trees — A65

1992, Sept. 17   **Litho.**
278 A65 35c Karroo   .30   .30
279 A65 70c Erioloba   .65   .65
280 A65 90c Tortilis   .75   .75
281 A65 1.05r Mellifera   .85   .85
    Nos. 278-281 (4)   2.55   2.55

A souvenir sheet of 1 #279 exists. Sold for 2.50r. Value $3.75.

Lost City Hotel
Complex, Sun
City — A66

a, View from lake. b, Palace. c, Porte cochere. d, Lobby of Palace. e, Tusk bar.

1992, Nov. 19   **Litho.**   *Perf. 14x14½*
282   Strip of 5   2.00   2.00
  a.-e. A66 35c any single   .50   .50

Chickens
A67

1993, Feb. 12   **Litho.**   *Perf. 14½x14*
283 A67 35c Light Sussex   .45   .45
284 A67 70c Rhode Island red   .90   .90
285 A67 90c Brown leghorn   1.25   1.25
286 A67 1.05r White leghorn   1.40   1.40
    Nos. 283-286 (4)   4.00   4.00

A souvenir sheet of 1 #284 exists. Sold for 3r. Value $5.

Easter
A68

1993, Mar. 5
287 A68 35c Luke 23:25   .60   .60
288 A68 70c John 19:17   1.25   1.25
289 A68 90c Mark 15:21   1.60   1.60
290 A68 1.05r Mark 15:23   1.90   1.90
    Nos. 287-290 (4)   5.35   5.35

Trains Type of 1991

Designs: 45c, Mafeking locomotive shed, c. 1933, RR classes 10, 8, & 12. 65c, Locomotive No. 5. 85c, 1934 Royal visit, White Train, SAR Class 16B. 1.05r, SAR class 19D.

1993, June 18   **Litho.**
Size: 72x25mm (45c, 85c)
291 A61 45c multicolored   .75   .75
292 A61 65c multicolored   1.10   1.10
293 A61 85c multicolored   1.40   1.40
294 A61 1.05r multicolored   1.75   1.75
  a.   Souvenir sheet of 4, #291-294   5.00   5.00
    Nos. 291-294 (4)   5.00   5.00

Maps of
Africa
A69

Name of cartographer, year published: 45c, Sebastian Munster, 1540. 65c, Jacopo Gastaldi, 1564. 85c, Gerardus Mercator the Younger, 1595. 1.05r, Abraham Ortelius, 1570.

1993, Aug. 20   **Litho.**
295 A69 45c multicolored   .60   .60
296 A69 65c multicolored   .90   .90
297 A69 85c multicolored   1.25   1.25
298 A69 1.05r multicolored   1.50   1.50
    Nos. 295-298 (4)   4.25   4.25

Easter
A70

1994, Mar. 25   **Litho.**   *Perf. 14½x14*
299 A70 35c Luke 22:33   .65   .65
300 A70 65c Luke 23:35-36   1.25   1.25
301 A70 85c Luke 23:36   1.60   1.60
302 A70 1.05r Luke 23:38   1.90   1.90
    Nos. 299-302 (4)   5.40   5.40

Bophuthatswana ceased to exist 4/27/94.

CISKEI

'sis-,kī

LOCATION — Enclave, Republic of South Africa
GOVT. — Self-governing tribal homeland
AREA — 5,592 sq. mi.
POP. — 1,000,000
CAPITAL — Bisho

> Catalogue values for all unused stamps in this country are for Never Hinged Items.

Independence
from South
Africa — A1

        Perf. 14x14½
1981, Dec. 4   **Litho.**   **Unwmk.**
1 A1 5c Pres. Sebe   .25   .25
2 A1 15c Coat of arms   .25   .25
3 A1 20c Flag   .30   .30
4 A1 25c Mace   .35   .35
    Nos. 1-4 (4)   1.15   1.15

An imperf. souvenir sheet exists containing Nos. 1-4 printed in one color (black). Not valid for postage.

Birds
A2   A3

1c, Tauraco corythaix. 2c, Motacilla capensis. 3c, Centropus superciliosus. 4c, Nectarinia famosa. 5c, Anthropoides paradisea. 6c, Onychognathus morio. 7c, Ceryle maxima. 8c, Bostrychia hagedash. 9c, Cuculus clamosus. 10c, Lybius torquatus. 11c, Oriolus larvatus. 12c, Alcedo cristata. 14c, Upupa epops. 15c, Haliaeetus vocifer. 16c, Batis capensis. 18c, Euplectes progne. 20c, Macronyx capensis. 21c, Aplopelia larvata. 25c, Burhinus capensis. 30c, Treron calva. 50c, Poicephalus robustus. 1r, Apaloderma narina. 2r, Bubo capensis.

1981-90   *Perf. 14½x14*
5 A2 1c multicolored   .25   .25
6 A2 2c multicolored   .25   .25
7 A2 3c multicolored   .25   .25
8 A2 4c multicolored   .25   .25
9 A2 5c multicolored   .25   .25
10 A2 6c multicolored   .25   .25
11 A2 7c multicolored   .25   .25
12 A2 8c multicolored   .25   .25
13 A2 9c multicolored   .25   .25
14 A2 10c multicolored   .25   .25
15 A2 11c multicolored   .55   .25
16 A2 12c multicolored   .55   .25
17 A2 14c multicolored   .65   .25
18 A2 15c multicolored   .25   .25
19 A2 16c multicolored   .65   .25
20 A3 18c multicolored   1.00   .25
21 A2 20c multicolored   .35   .25
22 A2 21c multicolored   3.25   .25
23 A2 25c multicolored   .40   .25
24 A2 30c multicolored   .55   .35
25 A2 50c multicolored   .90   .60

26 A2 1r multicolored   1.50   1.10
27 A2 2r multicolored   3.25   2.25
    Nos. 5-27 (23)   16.35   9.05

Issued: 11c, 4/4/82; 12c, 4/1/85; 14c, 4/1/86; 16c, 4/1/87; 18c, 7/3/89; 21c, 7/3/90; others, 12/4/81.

Nursing
A4

8c, Cecilia Makiwane, vert. 15c, Surgery, vert. 20c, Nurses pledge to serve. 25c, Hospital care.

1982, Apr. 30   *Perf. 14½x14, 14x14½*
34 A4 8c multicolored   .25   .25
35 A4 15c multicolored   .30   .30
36 A4 20c multicolored   .45   .45
37 A4 25c multicolored   .55   .55
    Nos. 34-37 (4)   1.55   1.55

Pineapple
Industry
A5

1982, Aug. 20   *Perf. 14x14½*
38 A5 8c Spraying   .25   .25
39 A5 15c Harvesting   .25   .25
40 A5 20c Transporting fruit to cannery   .25   .25
41 A5 30c Packing   .40   .40
    Nos. 38-41 (4)   1.15   1.15

Small
Mammals
A6

1982, Oct. 29
42 A6 8c Lepus capensis   .25   .25
43 A6 15c Vulpes chama   .35   .35
44 A6 20c Xerus inaurus   .40   .40
45 A6 25c Felis caracal   .45   .45
    Nos. 42-45 (4)   1.45   1.45

Trees — A7

1983, Feb. 2   *Perf. 14½x14*
46 A7 8c Cussonia spicata   .25   .25
47 A7 20c Curtisia dentata   .30   .30
48 A7 25c Calodendrum capense   .35   .35
49 A7 40c Podocarpus falcatus   .60   .60
    Nos. 46-49 (4)   1.50   1.50

1984, Jan. 6
50 A7 10c Rhus chirindensis   .25   .25
51 A7 20c Phoenix reclinata   .30   .30
52 A7 25c Ptaeroxylon obliquum   .35   .35
53 A7 40c Apodytes dimidiata   .60   .60
    Nos. 50-53 (4)   1.50   1.50

Sharks — A8

1983, Apr. 13   *Perf. 14x14½*
54 A8 8c Dusky   .25   .25
55 A8 20c Ragged-tooth   .35   .35

Size: 57x21mm
56 A8 25c Tiger   .40   .40
57 A8 30c Scalloped hammerhead   .50   .50
58 A8 40c Great white   .60   .60
    Nos. 54-58 (5)   2.10   2.10

Educational Institutions — A9

1983, July 6

59	A9	10c Lovedale	.25	.25
60	A9	20c Fort Hare	.25	.25
61	A9	25c Healdtown	.30	.30
62	A9	40c Lennox Sebe	.40	.40
		Nos. 59-62 (4)	1.20	1.20

Military Uniforms — A10

6th Foot, 1st Warwickshire Regiment, 1821-27 (No. 63): a, White drill uniform (D1.5). b, Light Company privates (D2.5). c, Grenadier Company sergeants (D3.5). d, Light Co. Officers (D4.5). e, Officer and field officer (D5.5).

Cape Mounted Rifles, 1827-35 (No. 64): a, Trooper and sergeant, 1830 (D1.5). b, Trooper and sergeant in full dress, 1835 (D2.5). c, Officers, 1830 (D3.5). d, Officers in full dress, 1827-34 (D4.5). e, Officers in full dress, 1834 (D5.5).

1983, Sept. 28   *Perf. 14½x14*

63		Strip of 5	2.25 2.25
a.-e.		A10 20c any single	.45 .45

1984, Oct. 26

64		Strip of 5	2.50 2.25
a.-e.		A10 25c any single	.50 .40

Sheets of 10 containing two strips of five.

Coastal Angling A11

Bait.

1984, Apr. 12   *Perf. 14x14½*

65	A11	11c Sand prawn	.25	.25
66	A11	20c Coral worm	.25	.25
67	A11	25c Bloodworm	.45	.45
68	A11	30c Red-bait	.55	.55
		Nos. 65-68 (4)	1.50	1.50

1985, Mar. 7

Game fish — 11c, Lithognathus lithognathus. 25c, Pachymetopon grande. 30c, Argyrosomus hololepidotus. 50c, Pomadasys commersonni.

69	A11	11c multicolored	.25	.25
70	A11	25c multicolored	.45	.30
71	A11	30c multicolored	.55	.35
72	A11	50c multicolored	.90	.60
		Nos. 69-72 (4)	2.15	1.50

Migratory Birds and Maps — A12

1984, Aug. 17   *Perf. 14½x14*

73	A12	11c Banded sand martin	.25	.25
74	A12	25c House martin	.45	.45
75	A12	30c Greater striped swallow	.50	.50
76	A12	45c European swallow	.75	.75
		Nos. 73-76 (4)	1.95	1.95

Brownies A13

1985, May 3

77	A13	12c shown	.25	.25
78	A13	25c Rangers planting saplings	.25	.25
79	A13	30c Guide color guard	.30	.30
80	A13	50c Camping	.55	.55
		Nos. 77-80 (4)	1.35	1.35

Intl. Year of the Child, 75th anniv. of the Girl Guide movement.

Small Businesses A14

1985, Aug. 8   *Perf. 14x14½*

81	A14	12c Furniture	.25	.25
82	A14	25c Dress making	.30	.30
83	A14	30c Welding	.40	.40
84	A14	50c Basketry	.70	.70
		Nos. 81-84 (4)	1.65	1.65

Troop Ships — A15

1985, Nov. 15   *Perf. 14½x14*

85	A15	12c Antelope	.25	.25
86	A15	25c Pilot	.40	.40
87	A15	30c Salisbury	.45	.45
88	A15	50c Olive Branch	.85	.85
		Nos. 85-88 (4)	1.95	1.95

Miniature Sheet

Halley's Comet — A16

Comet streaking through the solar system: a, A1.10. b, A2.10. c, A3.10. d, A4.10. e, A5.10. f, A6.10. g, A7.10. h, A8.10. i, A9.10. j, A10.10.

1986, Mar. 20

89		A16 Sheet of 10	8.00	8.00
a.-j.		12c any single	1.00	1.00

Military Uniforms — A17

98th Foot Regiment: 14c, Fifer in winter. 20c, Private in summer. 25c, Grenadier Company sergeant in summer. 30c, Sergeant-major in winter.

1986, June 12

90	A17	14c multicolored	.25	.25
91	A17	20c multicolored	.35	.35
92	A17	25c multicolored	.45	.45
93	A17	30c multicolored	.50	.50
a.		Souvenir sheet of 1	2.00	2.00
		Nos. 90-93 (4)	1.55	1.55

No. 93a for the natl. philatelic exhibition held at Johannesberg, Oct. 6-11. Sold for 50c.

Bicycle Factory, Dimbaza A18

1986, Sept. 18

94	A18	14c Welding frames	.25	.25
95	A18	20c Painting	.35	.35
96	A18	25c Spoke installation	.40	.40
97	A18	30c Assembly	.50	.50
		Nos. 94-97 (4)	1.50	1.50

Independence, 5th Anniv. — A19

14c, Pres. Sebe. 20c, Natl. shrine, Ntaba kaNdoda. 25c, Legislative Assembly, Bisho. 30c, Automatic telephone exchange, Bisho.

1986, Dec. 4   *Perf. 14x14½*

98	A19	14c multicolored	.25	.25
99	A19	20c multicolored	.30	.30
100	A19	25c multicolored	.35	.35
101	A19	30c multicolored	.45	.45
		Nos. 98-101 (4)	1.35	1.35

Edible Mushrooms A20

1987, Mar. 19

102	A20	14c Boletus edulis	.35	.35
103	A20	20c Macrolepiota zeyheri	.45	.45
a.		Souvenir sheet of 1	3.75	3.75
104	A20	25c Termitomyces	.50	.50
105	A20	30c Russula capensis	.65	.65
		Nos. 102-105 (4)	1.95	1.95

No. 103a has fawn and black decorative margin picturing emblem of the natl. philatelic exhibition held at Paarl, Sept. 16-19. Sold for 50c.

Nkone Cattle A21

1987, June 18   *Perf. 14½x14*

106	A21	16c Cow and calf	.25	.25
107	A21	20c Cow	.30	.30
108	A21	25c Bull	.35	.35
109	A21	30c Herd	.45	.45
		Nos. 106-109 (4)	1.35	1.35

Toys — A22

Perf. 14x14½, 14½x14

1987, Sept. 17

110	A22	16c Windmill, vert.	.25	.25
111	A22	20c Rag doll, vert.	.30	.30
112	A22	25c Clay horse	.35	.35
113	A22	30c Wire vehicle	.45	.45
		Nos. 110-113 (4)	1.35	1.35

Folklore A23

Legend of Sikulume: 16c, Seven birds. 20c, Sikulume escapes cannibals. 25c, Fights sea monster. 30c, Elopes and is pursued by bride's father.

1987, Nov. 6   *Perf. 14½x14*

114	A23	16c multicolored	.25	.25
115	A23	30c multicolored	.30	.30
116	A23	25c multicolored	.35	.35
117	A23	30c multicolored	.45	.45
		Nos. 114-117 (4)	1.35	1.35

See Nos. 122, 139-142, 147-150.

Endangered and Protected Plant Species — A24

16c, Clivia nobilis. 30c, Dierama pulcherrimum. 40c, Moraea reticulata. 50c, Crinum campanulatum.

1988, Mar. 17   *Perf. 14x14½*

118	A24	16c multicolored	.25	.25
119	A24	30c multicolored	.45	.45
120	A24	40c multicolored	.55	.55
121	A24	30c multicolored	.70	.70
a.		Souvenir sheet of 1	2.50	2.50
		Nos. 118-121 (4)	1.95	1.95

No. 121a margin pictures the emblem of the natl. philatelic exhibition held at Pietermaritzburg, Nov. 22-27. Sold for 1r.

Folklore Type of 1987
Miniature Sheet

Legend of Mbulukazi: a, Two wives (B1.10). b, Two doves appear to Numbakatali (B2.10). c, Birth of Mbulukazi and brother (B3.10). d, Mbulukazi and brother at river (B4.10). e, Chief's son announces marriage (B5.10). f, Chief's son presents wives Mbulukazi and Mahlunguluza with huts (B6.10). g, Mahlunguluza drowns Mbulukazi (B7.10). h, Ox tears down Mahlunguluza's hut (B8.10). i, Mbulukazi revived (B9.10). j, Chief's son embraces Mbulukazi, banishes Mahlunguluza (B10.10).

1988, Aug. 26
Size of Nos. 122a-122j: 36x20mm

122		Sheet of 10	2.50	2.50
a.-j.		A23 16c any single	.30	.30

Citrus Farming A25

1988, Sept. 29

123	A25	16c Nursery	.25	.25
124	A25	30c Grafting	.40	.40
125	A25	40c Picking fruit	.50	.50
126	A25	50c Grading	.65	.65
		Nos. 123-126 (4)	1.80	1.80

Poisonous Mushrooms A26

1988, Dec. 1

127	A26	16c Amanita phalloides	.75	.75
128	A26	30c Chlorophyllum molybdites	1.50	1.50

129 A26 40c Amanita muscaria 1.90 1.90
130 A26 50c Amanita pantherina 2.40 2.40
Nos. 127-130 (4) 6.55 6.55

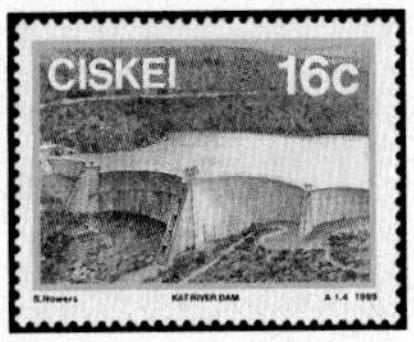

Dams — A27

1989, Mar. 2 ***Perf. 14½x14***
131 A27 16c Kat River .25 .25
132 A27 30c Cata .50 .50
133 A27 40c Binfield Park .60 .60
134 A27 50c Sandile .70 .70
Nos. 131-134 (4) 2.05 2.05

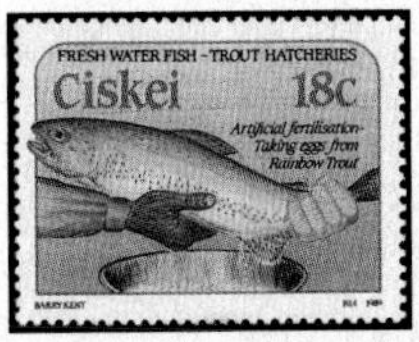

Trout Hatcheries A28

Artificial fertilization: 18c, Obtaining eggs from trout. 30c, Fertilized ova, alevins. 40c, Rainbow trout at 5 weeks. 40c, Adult male rainbow trout.

1989, June 8
135 A28 18c multicolored .30 .30
136 A28 30c multicolored .45 .45
137 A28 40c multicolored .65 .65
138 A28 50c multicolored .70 .70
a. Souvenir sheet of 1 4.00 4.00
Nos. 135-138 (4) 2.10 2.10

No. 138a margin pictures emblem of the natl. philatelic exhibition WANDERERS 101, held Sept. 6-9. Sold for 1.50r.

Folklore Type of 1987

Legend of the Little Jackal and the Lion: 18c, Lion and Jackal hunt large eland. 30c, Jackal and offspring climbing to lair. 40c, Lion roaring, jackal under rock. 50c, Lion falling.

1989, Sept. 21
139 A23 18c multicolored .25 .25
140 A23 30c multicolored .30 .30
141 A23 40c multicolored .40 .40
142 A23 50c multicolored .50 .50
Nos. 139-142 (4) 1.45 1.45

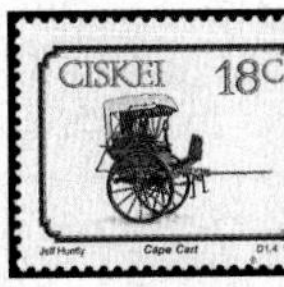

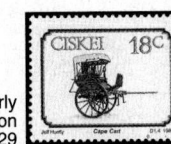

Early Transportation A29

1989, Dec. 7 ***Perf. 14x14½***
143 A29 18c Cape cart .25 .25
144 A29 30c Jubilee Spider .40 .40
145 A29 40c Transport wagon .45 .45
146 A29 50c Voortrekker wagon .60 .60
Nos. 143-146 (4) 1.70 1.70

Folklore Type of 1987

The Legend of Five Heads: 18c, Mpunzikazi presenting offering to Makanda Mahlanu, the 5-headed snake chief. 30c, Snake chief kills Mpunzikazi. 40c, Mpunzanyan presents offering to snake chief. 50c, Snake chief transformed into a man and marries Mpunzanyan.

1990, Mar. 15 ***Perf. 14½x14***
147 A23 18c multicolored .25 .25
148 A23 30c multicolored .30 .30
149 A23 40c multicolored .40 .40
150 A23 50c multicolored .55 .55
Nos. 147-150 (4) 1.50 1.50

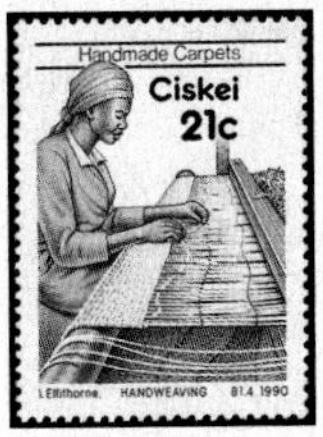

Handmade Carpets — A30

1990, June 14 Litho. ***Perf. 14x14½***
151 A30 21c Hand weaving .30 .30
152 A30 35c Spinning .45 .45
153 A30 40c Dyeing yarn .55 .55
154 A30 50c Hand weaving, diff. .65 .65
a. Souvenir sheet of 1 2.25 2.25
Nos. 151-154 (4) 1.95 1.95

No. 154a for the 150th anniv. of the Penny Black. Sold for 1.50r.

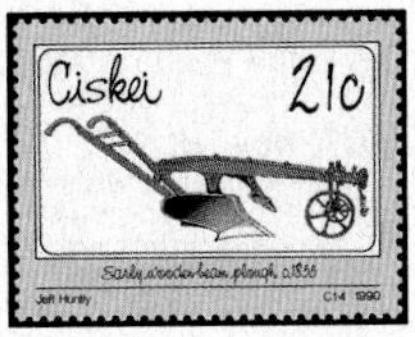

Plows — A31

21c, Wooden beam, c. 1855. 35c, Triple disc, c. 1895. 40c, Reversible disc, c. 1895. 50c, "Het Volk", c. 1910.

1990, Sept. 6 Litho. ***Perf. 14½x14***
155 A31 21c multicolored .25 .25
156 A31 35c multicolored .40 .40
157 A31 40c multicolored .50 .50
158 A31 50c multicolored .60 .60
Nos. 155-158 (4) 1.75 1.75

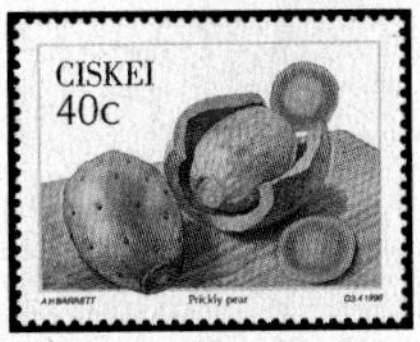

Prickly Pear — A32

1990, Nov. 29 **Litho.**
159 A32 21c Vendor .45 .45
160 A32 35c Prickly pear bush .70 .70
161 A32 40c shown .80 .80
162 A32 50c Flowering prickly pear 1.00 1.00
Nos. 159-162 (4) 2.95 2.95

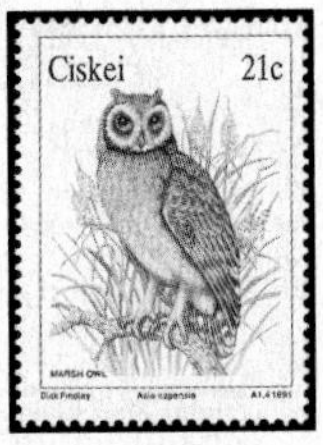

Owls — A33

1991, Feb. 2 Litho. ***Perf. 14x14½***
163 A33 21c Marsh owl .95 .95
164 A33 35c Scops owl 1.50 1.50
165 A33 40c Barn owl 1.90 1.90
166 A33 50c Wood owl 2.10 2.10
a. Miniature sheet of 1 7.00 7.00
Nos. 163-166 (4) 6.45 6.45

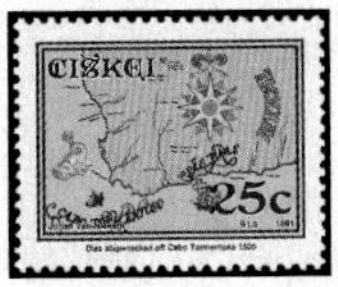

First Letter From South Africa — A34

Designs: a, Map showing location of Sao Bras (Mossel Bay), 1500. b, Storm-damaged ship off Cabo Tormentoso, 1500. c, Pedro d'Ataide lands at Sao Bras, 1501. d, D'Ataide leaves letter in boot, 1501. e, Joao da Nova finds letter, 1501.

1991, May 11 **Litho.**
167 A34 25c Strip of 5, #a.-e. 4.50 4.50

Inscriptions on #167a & 167b are reversed.

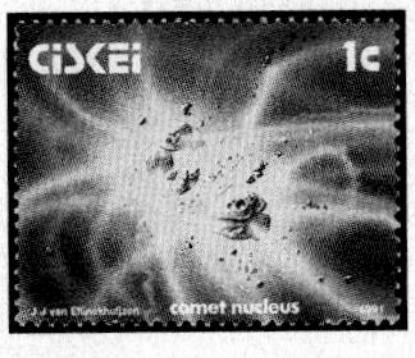

Solar System A35

1991, Aug. 1 Litho. ***Perf. 14½x14***
168 A35 1c Comet nucleus .25 .25
169 A35 2c Trojan asteroids .25 .25
170 A35 5c Meteoroid .25 .25
171 A35 7c Pluto .25 .25
172 A35 10c Neptune .25 .25
173 A35 20c Uranus .25 .25
174 A35 25c Saturn .30 .30
175 A35 30c Jupiter .35 .35
176 A35 35c Asteroid belt .40 .40
177 A35 40c Mars .50 .50
178 A35 50c Earth's moon .60 .60
179 A35 60c Earth .70 .70
180 A35 1r Venus 1.25 1.25
181 A35 2r Mercury 2.75 2.75
182 A35 5r Sun 6.50 6.50
a. Min. sheet of 15, #168-182 17.50 17.50
Nos. 168-182 (15) 14.85 14.85

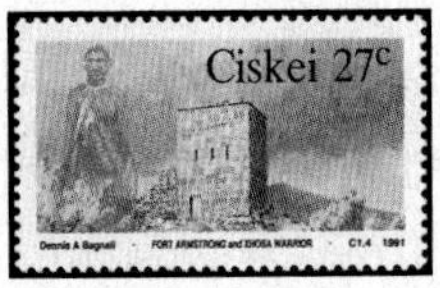

Frontier Forts A36

Designs: 27c, Xhosa warrior, Fort Armstrong. 45c, Sir George Grey, Keiskamma Hoek Post. 65c, Chief Sandile, Fort Hare. 85c, Cavalryman, Cavalry Barracks, Peddie.

1991, Nov. 7 Litho. ***Perf. 14x14½***
183 A36 27c multicolored .25 .25
184 A36 45c multicolored .35 .35
185 A36 65c multicolored .45 .45
186 A36 85c multicolored .70 .70
Nos. 183-186 (4) 1.75 1.75

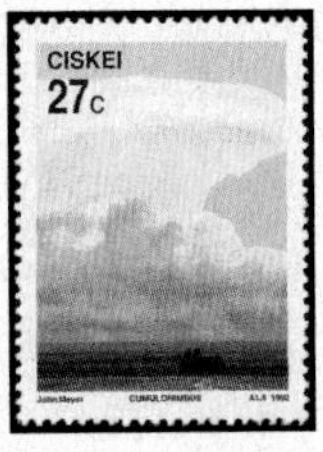

Cloud Formations — A37

1992, Mar. 19 **Litho.**
187 A37 27c Cumulonimbus .30 .30
188 A37 45c Altocumulus .60 .60
189 A37 65c Cirrus .75 .75
190 A37 85c Cumulus 1.10 1.10
Nos. 187-190 (4) 2.75 2.75

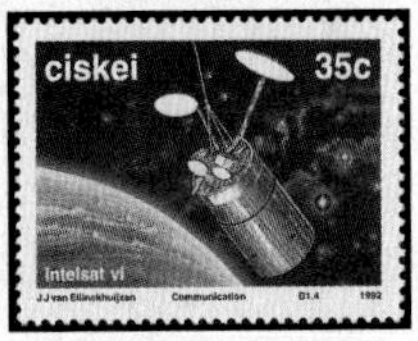

Satellites A38

1992, June 4 Litho. ***Perf. 14½x14***
191 A38 35c Intelsat VI .60 .60
192 A38 70c GPS Navstar 1.10 1.10
193 A38 90c Meteosat 1.40 1.40
194 A38 1.05r Landsat VI 1.60 1.60
Nos. 191-194 (4) 4.70 4.70

A souvenir sheet of one No. 192 exists. Sold for 2.50r. Value $2.50.

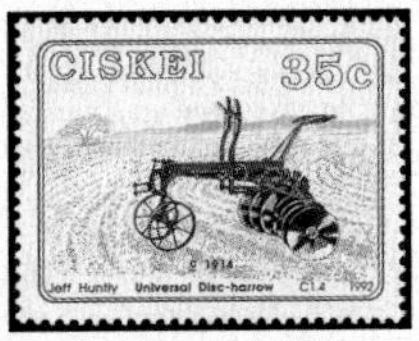

Farm Implements A39

35c, John Deere universal disc-harrow, c. 1914. 70c, John Deere clod crusher & pulverizer, c. 1914. 90c, Self-dump hay rake, c. 1910. 1.05r, McCormick hay tedder, c. 1900.

1992, Aug. 20 **Litho.**
195 A39 35c multicolored .60 .60
196 A39 70c multicolored 1.10 1.10
197 A39 90c multicolored 1.40 1.40
198 A39 1.05r multicolored 1.60 1.60
Nos. 195-198 (4) 4.70 4.70

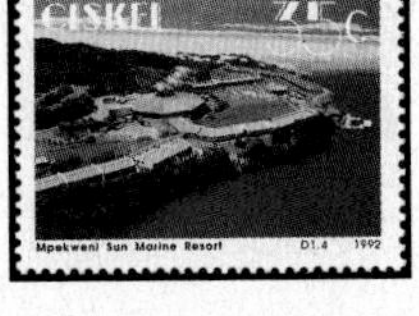

Hotels A40

Designs: 35c, Mpekweni Sun Marine Resort. 70c, Katberg Protea Hotel. 90c, Fish River Sun Hotel. 1.05r, Amatola Sun Hotel.

1992, Nov. 5 **Litho.**
199 A40 35c multicolored .60 .60
200 A40 70c multicolored 1.10 1.10
201 A40 90c multicolored 1.40 1.40
202 A40 1.05r multicolored 1.60 1.60
Nos. 199-202 (4) 4.70 4.70

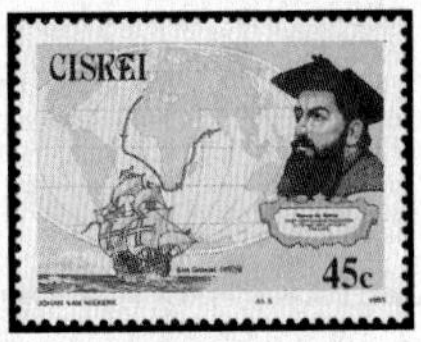

Famous Explorers A41

Map of voyage, sailing ship, and explorer: 45c, San Gabriel, 1497-98, Vasco da Gama. 65c, Endeavour, 1768-71, James Cook. 85c, Victoria, 1519, Ferdinand Magellan. 90c, Golden Hinde, 1577-80, Sir Francis Drake. 1.05r, Heemskerck, 1642, Abel Tasman.

1993, May 19 **Litho.**
203 A41 45c multicolored .70 .70
204 A41 65c multicolored 1.25 1.25
205 A41 85c multicolored 1.80 1.40
206 A41 90c multicolored 1.50 1.50
207 A41 1.05r multicolored 1.75 1.75
Nos. 203-207 (5) 7.00 6.60

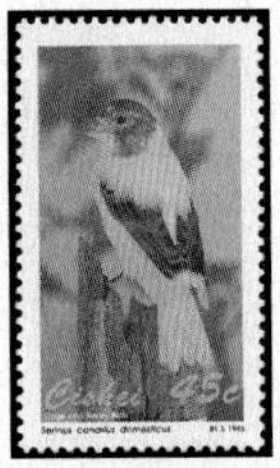

Small Cage Birds — A42

Designs: 45c, Serinus canarius domesticus. 65c, Melopsittacus undulatus. 85c, Agapornis roseicollis. 90c, Nymphicus hollandicus. 1.05r, Chloebia gouldiae.

1993, July 16 **Litho.**
208 A42 45c multicolored .60 .60
209 A42 65c multicolored 1.10 1.10
210 A42 85c multicolored 1.25 1.25
211 A42 90c multicolored 1.40 1.40
212 A42 1.05r multicolored 1.50 1.50
Nos. 208-212 (5) 5.85 5.85

A souvenir sheet of one No. 210 has inscription for National Philatelic Exhibition. Sold for 3r. Value $5.75.

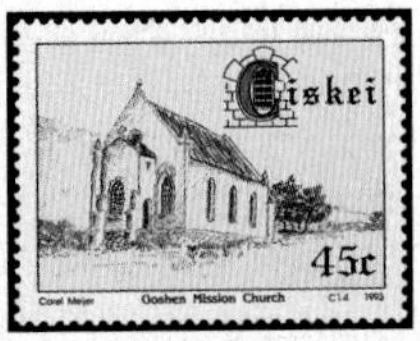

Churches A43

45c, Goshen Mission Church. 65c, Kamastone Mission Church. 85c, Richie Thompson Memorial Church. 1.05r, Bryce Ross Memorial Church.

1993, Sept. 17 **Litho.**
213 A43 45c black, buff & red .50 .50
214 A43 65c black, blue & red .70 .70
215 A43 85c black, tan & red .95 .95
216 A43 1.05r blk, lt yel & red 1.25 1.25
Nos. 213-216 (4) 3.40 3.40

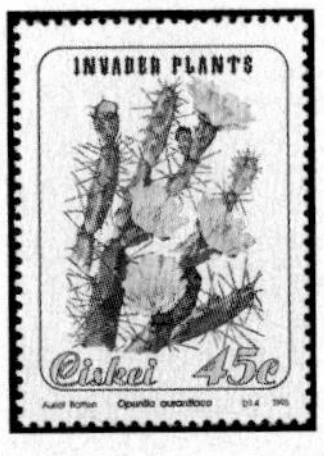

Invader Plants — A44

1993, Nov. 5 Litho. ***Perf. 14x14½***
217 A44 45c Opuntia aurantiaca .60 .60
218 A44 65c Datura stramonium .80 .80
219 A44 85c Sesbania punicea 1.10 1.10
220 A44 1.05r Nicotiana glauca 1.40 1.40
a. Souvenir sheet, #217-220 3.75 3.75
Nos. 217-220 (4) 3.90 3.90

Shipwrecks
A45

1994, Feb. 18   Litho.   Perf. 14½x14
221	A45	45c SS Losna, 1921	.85	.85
222	A45	65c Catherine, 1846	1.25	1.25
223	A45	85c Bennebroek, 1713	1.50	1.50
224	A45	1.05r Sao Joao Bapista, 1622	2.10	2.10
		Nos. 221-224 (4)	5.70	5.70

Roses
A46

45c, Herman Steyn. 70c, Esther Geldenhuys. 95c, Margaret Wasserfall. 1.15r, Prof. Fred Ziady.

1994, Apr. 15   Litho.   Perf. 14½x14
225	A46	45c multicolored	.45	.45
226	A46	70c multicolored	.75	.75
227	A46	95c multicolored	.90	.90
228	A46	1.15r multicolored	1.25	1.25
a.		Souvenir sheet of 4, #225-228	3.50	3.50
		Nos. 225-228 (4)	3.35	3.35

Ciskei ceased to exist April 27, 1994.

TRANSKEI

ˌtranˌt̪sˈki

LOCATION — Enclave, East Cape Province, Republic of South Africa
GOVT. — Self-governing tribal homeland
AREA — 16,910 sq. mi.
POP. — 2,876,122 (1985)
CAPITAL — Umtata

> Catalogue values for all unused stamps in this country are for Never Hinged items.

Independence from
South Africa — A1

4c, Paramount Chief K.D. Matanzima. 10c, Mace, flag. 15c, Matanzima, diff. 20c, Coat of arms.

Perf. 12½
			Unwmk.	
1	A1	4c multicolored	.40	.40
2	A1	10c multicolored	.90	.90
3	A1	15c multicolored	1.50	1.50
4	A1	20c multicolored	2.00	2.00
		Nos. 1-4 (4)	4.80	4.80

An imperf. souvenir sheet exists containing Nos. 1-4 printed in one color (black). Not valid for postage.

Lubisi
Dam — A2

2c, Soil cultivation. 3c, Threshing sorghum. 4c, Transkei matron. 5c, Grinding corn. 6c, Cutting Phormium tenax. 7c, Shepherd boy. 8c, Felling timber. 9c, Agricultural school. 10c, Picking tea. 15c, Wood gathering. 20c, Weaving industry. 25c, Improving cattle breeds. 30c, Sledge transportation. 50c, Map, coat of arms. 1r, Administrative Building, Umtata. 2r, The Bunga, flag.

1976, Oct. 26   Perf. 12x12½
5	A2	1c multicolored	.25	.25
6	A2	2c multicolored	.25	.25
7	A2	3c multicolored	.25	.25
8	A2	4c multicolored	2.75	.30
9	A2	5c multicolored	2.75	.30
10	A2	6c multicolored	.25	.25
11	A2	7c multicolored	.25	.25
12	A2	8c multicolored	.25	.25
13	A2	9c multicolored	.25	.25
14	A2	10c multicolored	.25	.25
15	A2	15c multicolored	.30	.25
16	A2	20c multicolored	.30	.25
17	A2	25c multicolored	.35	.25
18	A2	30c multicolored	.60	.50
19	A2	50c multicolored	.55	.50
20	A2	1r multicolored	1.25	1.25
21	A2	2r multicolored	2.00	1.90
		Nos. 5-21 (17)	12.85	7.50

Perf. 14
5a	A2	1c	.25	.25
6a	A2	2c	.25	.25
7a	A2	3c	.25	.25
8a	A2	4c	.25	.25
9a	A2	5c	.25	.25
10a	A2	6c	.25	.25
12a	A2	8c	.25	.25
13a	A2	9c	.25	.25
14a	A2	10c	.40	.40
15a	A2	15c	.50	.50
16a	A2	20c	.70	.70
17a	A2	25c	1.00	1.00
18a	A2	30c	1.25	1.25
19a	A2	50c	2.00	2.00
		Nos. 5a-19a (14)	7.85	7.85

Transkei Airways Inaugural Flight, Umtata-Johannesburg — A3

1977, Feb. 11
22	A3	4c Aircraft	.60	.60
23	A3	15c Aircraft, terminal	2.40	2.40

Artemesia affra — A4

Medicinal plants.

1977, May 16   Perf. 12½x12
24	A4	4c shown	.40	.40
25	A4	10c Bulbine natalensis	1.60	1.60
26	A4	15c Melianthus major	2.40	2.40
27	A4	20c Cotyledon orbiculata	3.25	3.25
		Nos. 24-27 (4)	7.65	7.65

1978, Sept. 25

Edible fruit.
28	A4	4c Carissa bispinosa	.25	.25
29	A4	10c Dovyalis caffra	.35	.35
30	A4	15c Harpephyllum caffrum	.50	.50
31	A4	20c Syzygium cordatum	.70	.70
		Nos. 28-31 (4)	1.80	1.80

1981, Apr. 15

Medicinal plants.
32	A4	4c Leonotis leonurus	.25	.25
33	A4	15c Euphorbia bupleurifolia	.25	.25
34	A4	20c Pelargonium reniforme	.35	.35
35	A4	25c Hibiscus trionum	.50	.50
		Nos. 32-35 (4)	1.35	1.35

Transkei Radio, 1st Anniv.
A5

1977, Oct. 26   Perf. 12x12½
36	A5	4c Disc jockey	.40	.40
37	A5	15c Announcer	1.00	1.00

"Help the Blind" — A6

1977, Nov. 18   Perf. 12½x12
38	A6	4c Basket weaver	.25	.25
39	A6	15c Reading Braille	.60	.60
40	A6	20c Spinning wool	.80	.80
		Nos. 38-40 (3)	1.65	1.65

1978, Nov. 30

"Care for Cripples."
41	A6	4c Leg brace on boy	.25	.25
42	A6	10c Man in wheelchair	.60	.60
43	A6	15c Nurse examining boy	.85	.85
		Nos. 41-43 (3)	1.70	1.70

Men's Pipes
A7

1978, Mar. 1   Perf. 12x12½
44	A7	4c shown	.40	.40
45	A7	10c multi, diff.	.60	.60
46	A7	15c multi, diff.	1.00	1.00
47	A7	20c Woman's and witch doctor's pipes	1.10	1.10
		Nos. 44-47 (4)	3.10	3.10

Weaving Industry
A8

1978, June 9
48	A8	4c Angora goat	.25	.25
49	A8	10c Spinning mohair	.60	.60
50	A8	15c Dyeing mohair	1.00	1.00
51	A8	20c Weaving mohair rug	1.25	1.25
		Nos. 48-51 (4)	3.10	3.10

Initiation Ceremony of Xhosa Men — A9

1979, Jan. 30   Perf. 12½
52	A9	4c Chi Cha youth	.40	.40
53	A9	10c Youths in seclusion	.60	.60
54	A9	15c Umtshilo dance	1.00	1.00
55	A9	20c Leaving the Sutu	1.10	1.10
		Nos. 52-55 (4)	3.10	3.10

Chief Matanzima — A10

1979, Feb. 20   Perf. 14½x14
56	A10	4c brn car & gold	.25	.25
57	A10	15c olive grn & gold	.40	.40

Inauguration of Matanzima, second state president.

Water Resources — A11

4c, Windmill. 10c, Woman filling water jar. 15c, Irrigation, Indwe River, horiz. 20c, Ncora dam, horiz.

1979, Mar. 13   Perf. 14½x14, 14x14½
58	A11	4c multicolored	.25	.25
59	A11	10c multicolored	.25	.25
60	A11	15c multicolored	.35	.35
61	A11	20c multicolored	.45	.45
		Nos. 58-61 (4)	1.30	1.30

Waterfalls — A12

1979, Sept. 4
62	A12	4c Magwa Falls	.25	.25
63	A12	10c Bawa Falls	.25	.25
64	A12	15c Waterfall Bluff, horiz.	.30	.30
65	A12	20c Tsitsa Falls, horiz.	.40	.40
		Nos. 62-65 (4)	1.20	1.20

Child Health Care — A13

5c, Pre-natal nourishment. 15c, Primary feeding. 20c, Immunization.

1979, Dec. 3   Perf. 14½x14
66	A13	5c multicolored	.25	.25
67	A13	15c multicolored	.45	.45
68	A13	20c multicolored	.65	.65
		Nos. 66-68 (3)	1.35	1.35

Fishing Flies — A14

a, Durham ranger. b, Colonel Bates. c, Black gnat. d, Zug bug. e, March brown.

1980, Jan. 15   Perf. 14x14½
69		Strip of 5	1.25	1.25
a.-e.		A14 5c any single	.25	.25

1981, Jan. 15

Designs: a, Kent's lightning. b, Wickham's fancy. c, Jock Scott. d, Green highlander. e, Tan nymph.
70		Strip of 5	1.50	1.50
a.-e.		A14 10c any single	.30	.30

1982, Jan. 6

a, Royal coachman. b, Light spruce. c, Montana nymph. d, Butcher. e, Blue charm.
71		Strip of 5	2.00	2.00
a.-e.		A14 10c any single	.40	.40

1983, Mar. 2

Designs: a, Alexandra. b, Kent's marbled sedge. c, White marabou. d, Mayfly nymph. e, Silver Wilkinson.
72		Strip of 5	2.00	2.00
a.-e.		A14 20c any single	.40	.40

1984, Feb. 10

Designs: a, Silver gray. b, Ginger quill. c, Hardy's favorite. d, March brown nymph. e, Kent's spectrum Mohawk.

73   Strip of 5   2.50 2.50
   a.-e. A14 20c any single   .50 .50

Rotary Intl., 75th Anniv. — A15

1980, Feb. 22   *Perf. 14½x14*
74 A15 15c blk, ultra & gold   .30 .30

Cycads — A16

5c, Encephalartos altensteinii. 10c, Encephalartos princeps. 15c, Encephalartos vilosus. 20c, Encephalartos friderici-guilielmi.

1980, Apr. 30
75 A16   5c multicolored   .25 .25
76 A16 10c multicolored   .25 .25
77 A16 15c multicolored   .30 .30
78 A16 20c multicolored   .45 .45
   Nos. 75-78 (4)   1.25 1.25

Birds — A17

1980, July 30
79 A17   5c Cuculus solitarius   .25 .25
80 A17 10c Batis capensis   .55 .55
81 A17 15c Balearica pavonina   .85 .85
82 A17 20c Ploceus ocularius   1.10 1.10
   Nos. 79-82 (4)   2.75 2.75

Tourism — A18

1980, Oct. 26
83 A18   5c Hole in the Wall   .25 .25
84 A18 10c Port St. Johns   .25 .25
85 A18 15c The Citadel   .40 .40
86 A18 20c The Archway   .45 .45
   Nos. 83-86 (4)   1.35 1.35

Xhosa Women's Headdresses — A19

1981, Aug. 28
87 A19   5c Eyamakhwenkwe   .25 .25
88 A19 15c Eyabafana   .25 .25
89 A19 20c Umfazana   .30 .30

90 A19 25c Ixhegokazi   .40 .40
   a.   Souvenir sheet of 4, #87-90   1.00 1.00
   Nos. 87-90 (4)   1.20 1.20

Independence, 5th Anniv. — A20

1981, Oct. 26   *Perf. 14x14½*
91 A20   5c State House   .30 .30
92 A20 15c University   .50 .50

Boy Scout Movement, 75th Anniv. — A21

1982, May 14   *Perf. 14½x14*
93 A21   8c Salute   .25 .25
94 A21 10c Planting tree   .25 .25
95 A21 20c Rafting   .30 .30
96 A21 25c Nature hike with dog   .40 .40
   Nos. 93-96 (4)   1.20 1.20

Great Medical Pioneers — A22

1982, Oct. 5
97 A22 15c Hippocrates   .25 .25
98 A22 20c Anton van Leeuwenhoek   .25 .25
99 A22 25c William Harvey   .30 .30
100 A22 30c Joseph Lister   .35 .35
   Nos. 97-100 (4)   1.15 1.15

1983, Aug. 17
101 A22 10c Edward Jenner   .25 .25
102 A22 20c Gregor Mendel   .25 .25
103 A22 25c Louis Pasteur   .30 .30
104 A22 40c Florence Nightingale   .40 .40
   Nos. 101-104 (4)   1.20 1.20

1984, Oct. 12
105 A22 11c Nicholas of Cusa   .25 .25
106 A22 25c William Morton   .25 .25
107 A22 30c Wilhelm Roentgen   .30 .30
108 A22 45c Karl Landsteiner   .45 .45
   Nos. 105-108 (4)   1.25 1.25

1985, Sept. 20
109 A22 12c Andreas Vesalius   .25 .25
110 A22 25c Marcello Malpighi   .30 .30
111 A22 30c Francois Magendie   .40 .40
112 A22 50c William Stewart Halsted   .60 .60
   Nos. 109-112 (4)   1.55 1.55
   Nos. 97-112 (16)   4.95 4.95

Umtata, Cent. A23

Architecture: 8c, City Hall. 15c, The Bunga. 20c, Botha Sigcau Building. 25c, Palace of Justice, Matanzima Building.

1982, Nov. 10   *Perf. 14x14½*
113 A23   8c multicolored   .25 .25
114 A23 15c multicolored   .25 .25
115 A23 20c multicolored   .25 .25
116 A23 25c multicolored   .30 .30
   Nos. 113-116 (4)   1.05 1.05

Wildcoast Holiday Resort, Mzamba A24

1983, May 25
117 A24 10c Hotel complex   .25 .25
118 A24 20c Beach scene   .30 .30
119 A24 25c Casino   .40 .40
120 A24 40c Carousel   .55 .55
   Nos. 117-120 (4)   1.50 1.50

Post Offices A25

1983, Nov. 9   *Perf. 14½x14*
121 A25 10c Lady Frere   .25 .25
122 A25 20c Idutywa   .25 .25
123 A25 25c Lusikisiki   .25 .25
124 A25 40c Cala   .35 .35
   Nos. 121-124 (4)   1.10 1.10

1984, May 11
125 A25 11c Umzimkulu   .25 .25
126 A25 20c Mount Fletcher   .25 .25
127 A25 25c Qumbu   .25 .25
128 A25 30c Umtata   .35 .35
   Nos. 125-128 (4)   1.10 1.10

Xhosa Lifestyle A26

1c, Amagqira. 2c, Horsemen. 3c, Mat maker. 4c, Xhosa dancers. 5c, Man, donkeys. 6c, Musicians. 7c, Fingo brides. 8c, Tasting beer. 9c, Thinning corn. 10c, Dance demonstration. 11c, Carrying water from the river. 12c, Meal preparation. 14c, Weeding. 15c, Stick fighting. 16c, Morning pasture. 20c, Abakhwetha dancers. 21c, Building initiation hut. 25c, Tribesmen singing. 30c, Matrons. 50c, Pipe maker. 1r, Intonjane women. 2r, Abakhwetha.

1984-90
129 A26   1c multicolored   .25 .25
130 A26   2c multicolored   .25 .25
131 A26   3c multicolored   .25 .25
132 A26   4c multicolored   .25 .25
133 A26   5c multicolored   .25 .25
134 A26   6c multicolored   .25 .25
135 A26   7c multicolored   .25 .25
136 A26   8c multicolored   .25 .25
137 A26   9c multicolored   .25 .25
138 A26 10c multicolored   .25 .25
139 A26 11c multicolored   .25 .25
140 A26 12c multicolored   .25 .25
141 A26 14c multicolored   .25 .25
142 A26 15c multicolored   .25 .25
143 A26 16c multicolored   .25 .25
144 A26 20c multicolored   .30 .30
145 A26 21c multicolored   .30 .30
146 A26 25c multicolored   .35 .35
147 A26 30c multicolored   .35 .35
148 A26 50c multicolored   .70 .70
149 A26   1r multicolored   1.40 1.40
150 A26   2r multicolored   3.00 3.00
   Nos. 129-150 (22)   10.15 10.15

Issued: 11c, 4/2/84; 12c, 4/1/85; 14c, 4/1/86; 16c, 4/1/87; 21c, 7/3/90; others, 7/6/84.

Soil Conservation A27

Designs: 11c, Erosion from over-grazing. 25c, Wall construction to collect sediment. 30c, Regeneration of vegetation. 50c, Cattle grazing on verdant plain.

1985, Feb. 7
155 A27 11c shown   .25 .25
156 A27 25c multicolored   .25 .25
157 A27 30c multicolored   .30 .30
158 A27 50c multicolored   .45 .45
   Nos. 155-158 (4)   1.25 1.25

Bridges A28

1985, Apr. 18
159 A28 12c Tsitsa   .25 .25
160 A28 25c White Kei   .30 .30
161 A28 30c Mitchell   .35 .35
162 A28 50c Umzimvubu   .55 .55
   Nos. 159-162 (4)   1.45 1.45

Match Industry — A29

1985, July 25   *Perf. 14½x14*
163 A29 12c Peeling logs   .25 .25
164 A29 25c Splint chopping   .25 .25
165 A29 30c VPO machine   .25 .25
166 A29 50c Filling boxes   .40 .40
   Nos. 163-166 (4)   1.15 1.15

Port St. Johns A30

Designs: 12c, Early street scene. 20c, Coaster Umzimvubu at the Old Jetty. 25c, Unloading corn from wagons at the Jetty. 30c, View of the town, 1890's.

1986, Feb. 6
167 A30 12c multicolored   .25 .25
168 A30 20c multicolored   .40 .40
169 A30 25c multicolored   .45 .45
170 A30 30c multicolored   .50 .50
   a.   Souvenir sheet of 4, #167-170   1.25 1.25
   Nos. 167-170 (4)   1.60 1.60

Aloes — A31

1986, May 1
171 A31 14c Aloe ferox   .25 .25
172 A31 20c Aloe arborescens   .30 .30
173 A31 25c Aloe maculata   .40 .40
174 A31 30c Aloe ecklonis   .50 .50
   a.   Souvenir sheet of 1   1.40 1.40
   Nos. 171-174 (4)   1.45 1.45

No. 174a margin pictures emblem of the natl. philatelic exhibition held at Johannesburg, Oct. 6-11. Sold for 50c.

Hydroelectric Power Stations A32

14c, First Falls, Umtata River. 20c, Second Falls, Umtata River. 25c, Ncora, Qumanco River. 30c, Collywobbles, Mbashe River.

1986, July 24
175 A32 14c shown   .25 .25
176 A32 20c multicolored   .25 .25
177 A32 25c multicolored   .30 .30
178 A32 30c multicolored   .40 .40
   Nos. 175-178 (4)   1.20 1.20

Independence, 10th Anniv. — A33

Designs: 14c, Prime Minister G. M. Matanzima. 20c, Technical College, Umtata. 25c, University of Transkei, Umtata. 30c, Palace of Justice, Umtata.

1986, Oct. 26
179	A33	14c multicolored	.25	.25
180	A33	20c multicolored	.25	.25
181	A33	25c multicolored	.30	.30
182	A33	30c multicolored	.35	.35
		Nos. 179-182 (4)	1.15	1.15

Transkei Airways, 10th Anniv. — A34

1987, Feb. 5
183	A34	14c shown	.25	.25
184	A34	20c Aircraft tail	.40	.40
185	A34	25c Nose, propellers	.50	.50
186	A34	30c Plane, control tower	.60	.60
		Nos. 183-186 (4)	1.75	1.75

Beadwork — A35

1987, May 22   *Perf. 14x14½*
187	A35	16c Pondo girl	.25	.25
188	A35	20c Bomvana woman	.30	.30
189	A35	25c Xessibe woman	.35	.35
a.		Souvenir sheet of 1	1.60	1.60
190	A35	30c Xhosa man	.65	.65
		Nos. 187-190 (4)	1.55	1.55

No. 189a has blue and black decorative margin picturing the emblem of the natl. philatelic exhibition held at Paarl, Sept. 16-19. Sold for 50c.

Spiders — A36

16c, Latrodectus indistinctus. 20c, Nephila pilipes fenestrata. 25c, Lycosidae. 30c, Argiope nigrovittata.

1987, Aug. 24
191	A36	16c multicolored	.25	.25
192	A36	20c multicolored	.35	.35
193	A36	25c multicolored	.40	.40
194	A36	30c multicolored	.50	.50
		Nos. 191-194 (4)	1.50	1.50

Domestic Animals A37

1987, Oct. 22
195	A37	16c Black pigs	.25	.25
196	A37	30c Goats	.30	.30
197	A37	40c Merino sheep	.40	.40
198	A37	50c Cattle	.50	.50
		Nos. 195-198 (4)	1.45	1.45

Seaweed — A38

1988, Feb. 18
199	A38	16c Plocamium corallorhiza	.25	.25
200	A38	30c Gelidium amanzil	.30	.30
201	A38	40c Ecklonia biruncinata	.40	.40
202	A38	50c Halimeda cuneata	.50	.50
		Nos. 199-202 (4)	1.45	1.45

Blanket Factory, Butterworth A39

1988, May 5   *Perf. 14½x14*
203	A39	16c Spinning machines	.25	.25
204	A39	30c Warping machine	.25	.25
205	A39	40c Weaving machine	.30	.30
206	A39	50c Raising the nap	.40	.40
		Nos. 203-206 (4)	1.20	1.20

Wreck of the *Grosvenor*, 1782 — A40

Designs: 16c, Ship, map. 30c, *The Wreck of the Grosvenor*, by R. Smirke. 40c, Dirk hilt, compass and coins salvaged. 50c, *African Hospitality*, by G. Morland.

1988, Aug. 4
207	A40	16c multicolored	.35	.35
208	A40	30c multicolored	.60	.60
209	A40	40c multicolored	.80	.80
210	A40	50c multicolored	1.00	1.00
a.		Souvenir sheet of 1	3.25	3.25
		Nos. 207-210 (4)	2.75	2.75

No. 210a margin pictures emblem of the natl. philatelic exhibition at Pietermaritzburg, Nov. 22-27. Sold for 1r.

Endangered Species A41

1988, Oct. 20
211	A41	16c Felis nigripes	.40	.40
212	A41	30c Philantomba monticola	.75	.75
213	A41	40c Ourebia ourebi	1.00	1.00
214	A41	50c Lycaon pictus	1.25	1.25
		Nos. 211-214 (4)	3.40	3.40

Locomotive, Trains and Bridges — A42

Designs: 16c, Class 14 CRB locomotive. 30c, CRB pulling train over Toleni-Halt Bridge. 40c, Train on the Great Kei River Bridge, vert. 50c, Train in the Kei Valley.

1989, Jan. 19   *Perf. 14x14½, 14½x14*
215	A42	16c multi	.30	.30
216	A42	30c multi	.55	.55
217	A42	40c multi	.85	.85
218	A42	50c multi, vert.	.95	.95
		Nos. 215-218 (4)	2.65	2.65

A souvenir sheet of one No. 218 has margin picturing the emblem of the natl. philatelic exhibition WANDERERS 101, held Sept. 6-9. Sold for 1.50r. Value $5.

Basketry A43

1989, Apr. 20   *Perf. 14½x14*
219	A43	18c shown	.25	.25
220	A43	30c multi, diff.	.35	.35
221	A43	40c multi, diff.	.40	.40
222	A43	50c multi, diff.	.55	.55
		Nos. 219-222 (4)	1.55	1.55

Mackerel A44

1989, July 20
223	A44	18c shown	.55	.55
224	A44	30c Squid	.90	.90
225	A44	40c Brown mussel	1.10	1.10
226	A44	50c Rock lobster	1.50	1.50
		Nos. 223-226 (4)	4.05	4.05

Trees A45

1989, Oct. 5   *Perf. 14x14½*
227	A45	18c Broom cluster fig	.50	.50
228	A45	30c Natal fig	.90	.90
229	A45	40c Broad-leaved coral	1.10	1.10
230	A45	50c Cabbage tree	1.50	1.50
		Nos. 227-230 (4)	4.00	4.00

Fossils A46

18c, Ginkgo koningensis. 30c, Pseudoctenis spatulata. 40c, Rissikia media. 50c, Taeniopteris anavolans.

1990, Jan. 18
231	A46	18c multicolored	.65	.65
232	A46	30c multicolored	1.25	1.25
233	A46	40c multicolored	1.60	1.60
234	A46	50c multicolored	2.25	2.25
		Nos. 231-234 (4)	5.75	5.75

Great Medical Pioneers — A47

1990, Mar. 29   *Perf. 14x14½*
235	A47	18c Aretaeus	.65	.65
236	A47	30c Claude Bernard	1.10	1.10
237	A47	40c Oscar Minkowski	1.50	1.50
238	A47	50c Frederick Banting	2.00	2.00
		Nos. 235-238 (4)	5.25	5.25

Diviners — A48

21c, Dancing to the Drum. 35c, Lecturing Imichetywa. 40c, Initiation ceremony. 50c, Induction ceremony.

1990, June 28   Litho.   *Perf. 14x14½*
239	A48	21c multicolored	.65	.65
240	A48	35c multicolored	1.10	1.10
241	A48	40c multicolored	1.25	1.25
242	A48	50c multicolored	1.50	1.50
a.		Souvenir sheet of 1	5.00	5.00
		Nos. 239-242 (4)	4.50	4.50

No. 242a for the 150th anniv. of the Penny Black. Sold for 1.50r.

Flowers — A49

21c, Cyrtanthus obliquus. 35c, Disa crassicornis. 40c, Sandersonia aurantiaca. 50c, Podranea ricasoliana.

1990, Sept. 20   Litho.   *Perf. 14x14½*
243	A49	21c multicolored	.70	.70
244	A49	35c multicolored	1.10	1.10
245	A49	40c multicolored	1.40	1.40
246	A49	50c multicolored	1.50	1.50
		Nos. 243-246 (4)	4.70	4.70

Parasitic Plants — A50

1991, Jan. 10   Litho.
247	A50	21c Harveya pulchra	.65	.65
248	A50	35c Harveya speciosa	1.10	1.10
249	A50	40c Alectra sessiliflora	1.25	1.25
250	A50	50c Hydnora africana	1.60	1.60
		Nos. 247-250 (4)	4.60	4.60

Dolphins A51

1991, Apr. 4   Litho.   *Perf. 14½x14*
251	A51	25c Delphinus delphis	.95	.95
252	A51	35c Tursiops truncatus	1.50	1.50
253	A51	50c Sousa plumbea	1.90	1.90
254	A51	60c Grampus griseus	2.25	2.25
		Nos. 251-254 (4)	6.60	6.60

Birds — A52

1991, June 20   Litho.
255	A52	25c Balearica regulorum	.80	.80
256	A52	40c Gyps coprotheres	1.25	1.25
257	A52	50c Grus carunculata	1.50	1.50

258 A52 60c Neophron
percnopterus 1.75 1.75
a. Souvenir sheet of 1 5.50 5.50
Nos. 255-258 (4) 5.30 5.30

Medical
Pioneers — A53

Developers of vaccines: 25c, Emil von Behring (1854-1917) and Shibasaburo Kitasato (1852-1931), diphtheria. 40c, Leon Albert Calmette (1863-1933) and Camille Guerin (1872-1961), tuberculosis. 50c, Jonas Salk (b. 1914), polio. 60c, John Franklin Enders (1897-1985), measles.

1991, Sept. 26 Litho. Perf. 14x14½
259 A53 25c multicolored .85 .85
260 A53 40c multicolored 1.50 1.50
261 A53 50c multicolored 1.75 1.75
262 A53 60c multicolored 2.40 2.40
Nos. 259-262 (4) 6.50 6.50

Orchids — A54

1992, Feb. 20 Litho.
263 A54 27c Eulophia speciosa .30 .30
264 A54 45c Satyrium sphaero-
carpum .50 .50
265 A54 65c Disa scullyi .75 .75
266 A54 85c Disa tysonii .95 .95
Nos. 263-266 (4) 2.50 2.50

Medical
Pioneers
A55

27c, Thomas Huckle Weller (b. 1915), developer of rubella vaccine. 45c, Ignaz Philipp Semmelweis (1818-65), diagnosed septicaemia. 65c, Sir James Young Simpson (1811-70), 1st to use chloroform in obstetrics. 85c, Rene Theophile Hyacinthe Laennec (1781-1826), inventor of stethoscope.

1992, Apr. 1 Litho. Perf. 14½x14
267 A55 27c multicolored .70 .70
268 A55 45c multicolored 1.25 1.25
269 A55 65c multicolored 1.75 1.75
270 A55 85c multicolored 2.25 2.25
Nos. 267-270 (4) 5.95 5.95

Waterfowl — A56

No. 271, Anas erythrorhyncha. No. 272, Anas hottentota. No. 273, Oxyura punctata. No. 274, Thalassornis leuconotus. No. 275, Anas sparsa. No. 276, Alopochen aegyptiacus. No. 277, Anas smithi. No. 278, Anas capensis.

1992, July 16 Litho. Perf. 14x14½
271 A56 35c multicolored .60 .60
272 A56 35c multicolored .60 .60
a. Pair, #271-272 1.25 1.25
273 A56 70c multicolored 1.25 1.25
274 A56 70c multicolored 1.25 1.25
a. Pair, #273-274 2.50 2.50
275 A56 90c multicolored 1.60 1.60
276 A56 90c multicolored 1.60 1.60
a. Pair, #275-276 3.25 3.25
277 A56 1.05r multicolored 1.60 1.60
278 A56 1.05r multicolored 1.60 1.60
a. Pair, #277-278 3.25 3.25
Nos. 271-278 (8) 10.10 10.10

A souvenir sheet of 1 #273 was sold by the Philatelic Foundation of South Africa. Value $5.

Fossils
A57

Designs: 35c, Pseudomelania sutherlandi. 70c, Gaudryceras denseplicatum. 90c, Neithea quinquecostata. 1.05r, Pugilina (Mayeria) acuticarinatus.

1992, Sept. 17 Litho. Perf. 14½x14
279 A57 35c multicolored .75 .75
280 A57 70c multicolored 1.50 1.50
281 A57 90c multicolored 2.00 2.00
282 A57 1.05r multicolored 2.25 2.25
Nos. 279-282 (4) 6.50 6.50

Dogs — A58

1993, Feb. 12 Litho.
283 A58 35c Papillon .55 .55
284 A58 70c Pekingese 1.10 1.10
285 A58 90c Chihuahua 1.50 1.50
286 A58 1.05r Dachshund 1.75 1.75
Nos. 283-286 (4) 4.90 4.90

A souvenir sheet of one No. 284 exists. Sold for 3r. Value $6.

Prehistoric
Animals
A59

1993, June 18 Litho.
287 A59 45c Fabrosaurus 1.00 1.00
288 A59 65c Diictodon 1.40 1.40
289 A59 85c Chasmatosaurus 1.75 1.75
290 A59 1.05r Rubidgea 2.25 2.25
Nos. 287-290 (4) 6.40 6.40

Medical
Pioneers
A60

Designs: 45c, Sir Alexander Fleming (1881-1955), discovered penicillin and Lord Howard Walter Florey (1898-1968), purified penicillin for general use. 65c, Alexis Carrel (1873-1944), developed Carrel-Dakin fluid and method to suture blood vessels. 85c, James Lind (1716-1794), recommended citrus fruit to combat scurvy. 1.05r, Santiago Ramon y Cajal (1852-1934), established neuron as basic unit of nervous structure.

1993, Aug. 20 Litho.
291 A60 45c multicolored 1.00 1.00
292 A60 65c multicolored 1.25 1.25
293 A60 85c multicolored 1.60 1.60
294 A60 1.05r multicolored 2.00 2.00
Nos. 291-294 (4) 5.85 5.85

Doves — A61

Designs: 45c, Streptopelia senegalensis. 65c, Turtur tympanistria. 85c, Turtur chalcospilos. 1.05r, Oena capensis.

1993, Oct. 15 Litho. Perf. 14x14½
295 A61 45c multicolored .90 .90
296 A61 65c multicolored 1.25 1.25
297 A61 85c multicolored 1.60 1.60
298 A61 1.05r multicolored 1.90 1.90
a. Souvenir sheet of 4, #295-298 5.50 5.50
Nos. 295-298 (4) 5.65 5.65

No. 298a sold for 3.50r.

Modern
Shipwrecks
A62

1994, Mar. 18 Litho. Perf. 14½x14
299 A62 45c Clan Lindsay,
1898 1.10 1.10
300 A62 65c Horizon, 1967 1.75 1.75
301 A62 85c Oceanos, 1991 2.40 2.40
302 A62 1.05r Forresbank, 1958 2.75 2.75
Nos. 299-302 (4) 8.00 8.00

A souvenir sheet of 1 #301 exists. Sold for 3r. Value $8.

Transkei ceased to exist April 27, 1994.

VENDA

'ven-də

LOCATION — Enclave, Republic of South Africa
GOVT. — Self-governing tribal homeland
AREA — 4,040 sq. mi.
POP. — 343,480 (1980)
CAPITAL — Thohoyandou

Catalogue values for all unused stamps in this country are for Never Hinged items.

Independence from South Africa — A1

Designs: 4c, Mace, flag. 15c, Administrative buildings. 20c, P.R. Mphephu, paramount chief and president. 25c, Coat of arms.

Perf. 14½x14
1979, Sept. 13 Litho. Unwmk.
1 A1 4c multicolored .35 .35
2 A1 15c multicolored .90 .90
3 A1 20c multicolored 1.25 1.25
4 A1 25c multicolored 1.60 1.60
Nos. 1-4 (4) 4.10 4.10

Flowers — A2

1c, Tecomaria capensis. 2c, Catophractes alexandri. 3c, Tricliceras longipedunculatum. 4c, Dissotis princeps. 5c, Gerbera jamesonii. 6c, Hibiscus mastersianus. 7c, Nymphaea caerulaea. 8c, Crinum lugardiae. 9c, Xerophyta retinervis. 10c, Hypoxis angustifolia. 11c, Combretum microphyllum. 12c, Clivia caulescens. 15c, Pycnostachys urticifolia. 20c, Zantedeschia jucunda. 25c, Leonotis mollis. 30c, Littonia modesta. 50c, Protea caffra. 1r, Adenium multiflorum. 2r, Strelitzia caudata.

1979-85 Perf. 12½, 14 (11c, 12c)
5 A2 1c multicolored .25 .25
6 A2 2c multicolored .25 .25
7 A2 3c multicolored .25 .25
8 A2 4c multicolored .25 .25
9 A2 5c multicolored 1.60 .60
10 A2 6c multicolored .25 .25
11 A2 7c multicolored .25 .25
12 A2 8c multicolored .30 .25
13 A2 9c multicolored .25 .25
14 A2 10c multicolored .25 .25
15 A2 11c multicolored .25 .25
16 A2 12c multicolored .35 .25
17 A2 15c multicolored .25 .25
18 A2 20c multicolored .25 .25
19 A2 25c multicolored 2.00 .75
20 A2 30c multicolored .35 .25
21 A2 50c multicolored .60 .25

22 A2 1r multicolored .80 .40
23 A2 2r multicolored 1.75 1.00
Nos. 5-23 (19) 10.50 6.50

Issue dates: 11c, Apr. 2, 1984; 12c, Apr. 1, 1985; others, Sept. 13, 1979.

Perf. 14
5a A2 1c .25 .25
6a A2 2c .25 .25
7a A2 3c .25 .25
9a A2 5c .25 .25
12a A2 8c .25 .25
14a A2 10c .40 .25
19a A2 25c 1.25 .60
21a A2 50c 2.75 1.25
Nos. 5a-21a (8) 5.65 3.35

Wood Carvings — A3

Designs: 5c, Man with cup. 10c, Woman with corn, bowl and spoon. 15c, King Nebuchadnezzar, horiz. 20c, Python killing woman, horiz.

1980, Feb. 13 Perf. 14½x14, 14x14½
24 A3 5c multicolored .25 .25
25 A3 10c multicolored .35 .35
26 A3 15c multicolored .50 .50
27 A3 20c multicolored .65 .65
Nos. 24-27 (4) 1.75 1.75

Tea
Cultivation
A4

1980, May 14 Perf. 14x14½
28 A4 5c Plants in nursery .25 .25
29 A4 10c Harvest .25 .25
30 A4 15c Withering .35 .35
31 A4 20c Cut, twist, curl unit .50 .50
Nos. 28-31 (4) 1.35 1.35

Banana
Industry
A5

1980, Aug. 13
32 A5 5c Plants .25 .25
33 A5 10c Cutting "hands" .25 .25
34 A5 15c Sorting .35 .35
35 A5 20c Packing .50 .50
Nos. 32-35 (4) 1.35 1.35

Butterflies — A6

1980, Nov. 13 Perf. 14½x14
36 A6 5c Precis tugela .25 .25
37 A6 10c Charaxes bohemani .25 .25
38 A6 15c Catacroptera cloanthe .50 .50
39 A6 20c Papilio dardanus .60 .60
Nos. 36-39 (4) 1.60 1.60

Sunbirds — A7

1981, Feb. 16

40	A7	5c Anthreptes collaris	.25	.25
41	A7	15c Nectarinia mariquensis	.35	.35
42	A7	20c Nectarinia talatala	.45	.45
43	A7	25c Nectarinia senegalensis	.55	.55
		Nos. 40-43 (4)	1.60	1.60

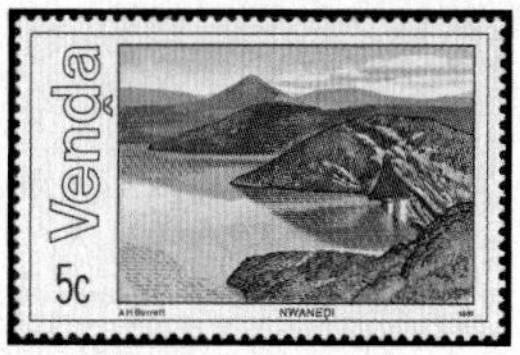

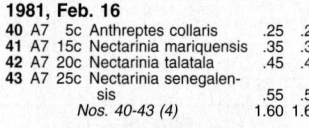

Nwanedi Dam — A8

1981, May 6

44	A8	5c shown	.25	.25
45	A8	15c Mahovhohovho Falls	.25	.25
46	A8	20c Phiphidi Falls	.30	.30
47	A8	25c Lake Fundudzi	.40	.40
		Nos. 44-47 (4)	1.20	1.20

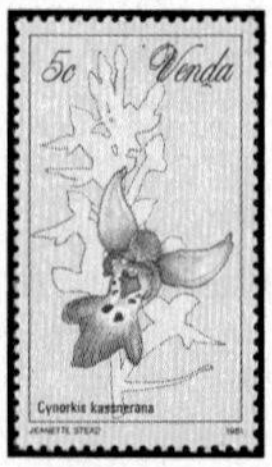

Orchids — A9

1981, Sept. 11

48	A9	5c Cynorkis kassnerana	.25	.25
49	A9	15c Eulophia fridericii	.25	.25
50	A9	20c Bonatea densiflora	.40	.40
51	A9	25c Mystacidium braybonIae	.45	.45
a.		Souvenir sheet of 4, #48-51	.90	.90
		Nos. 48-51 (4)	1.35	1.35

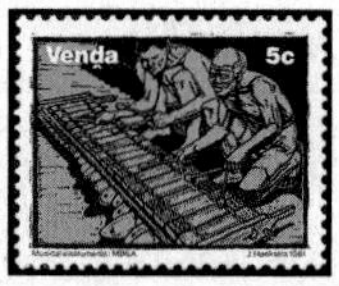

Musical Instruments A10

1981, Nov. 13 *Perf. 14x14½*

52	A10	5c Mbila	.25	.25
53	A10	15c Phalaphala	.25	.25
54	A10	20c Tshizambi	.25	.25
55	A10	25c Ngoma	.40	.40
		Nos. 52-55 (4)	1.15	1.15

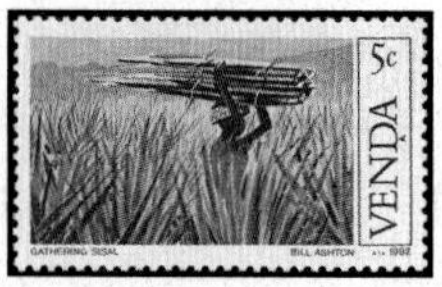

Sisal Cultivation A11

1982, Feb. 26

56	A11	5c Harvesting	.25	.25
57	A11	10c Drying	.25	.25
58	A11	20c Grading	.35	.35
59	A11	25c Baling	.45	.45
		Nos. 56-59 (4)	1.30	1.30

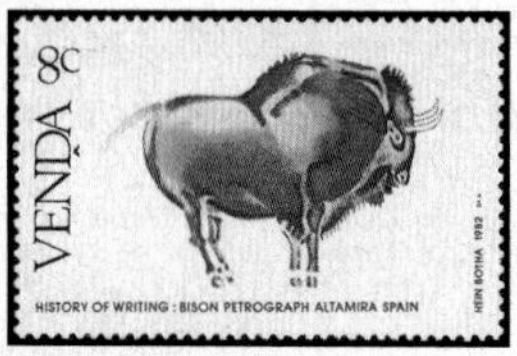

History of Writing — A12

Designs: 8c, Bison, petroglyph, Atlamira, Spain. 15c, Animal, petroglyph, eastern California. 20c, Pictographic script on a Sumerian tablet. 25c, Bushman burial stone, Humansdorp, South Africa.

1982, June 15 *Perf. 14½x14*

60	A12	8c multicolored	.25	.25
61	A12	15c multicolored	.25	.25
62	A12	20c multicolored	.35	.35
63	A12	25c multicolored	.45	.45
		Nos. 60-63 (4)	1.30	1.30

1983, May 11 **Size: 21x37mm**

10c, Indus Valley script, 3000 B.C. 20c, Sumerian cuneiform, 2000 B.C. 25c, Egyptian hieroglyphics, 1300 B.C. 40c, Chinese handscroll, A.D. 1100.

64	A12	10c multicolored	.25	.25
65	A12	20c multicolored	.30	.30
66	A12	25c multicolored	.35	.35
67	A12	40c multicolored	.40	.40
		Nos. 64-67 (4)	1.30	1.30

1984, Feb. 17 *Perf. 14x14½*
Size: 37½x20½mm

Designs: 10c, Evolution of the cuneiform sign. 20c, Evolution of the Chinese character. 25c, Development of Cretan hieroglyphics. 40c, Development of Egyptian hieroglyphics.

68	A12	10c multicolored	.25	.25
69	A12	20c multicolored	.30	.30
70	A12	25c multicolored	.35	.35
71	A12	40c multicolored	.60	.60
		Nos. 68-71 (4)	1.50	1.50

1985, Mar. 21 *Perf. 14½x14*
Size: 34x24½mm

Designs: 11c, Southern Arabic characters. 25c, Phoenician characters. 30c, Aramaic characters. 50c, Canaanite characters.

72	A12	11c multicolored	.25	.25
73	A12	25c multicolored	.30	.30
74	A12	30c multicolored	.35	.35
75	A12	50c multicolored	.60	.60
		Nos. 72-75 (4)	1.50	1.50

1986, Apr. 10 *Perf. 14x14½*
Size: 24½x34mm

76	A12	14c Etruscan	.25	.25
77	A12	20c Greek	.40	.40
78	A12	25c Roman	.45	.45
79	A12	30c Cyrillic	.55	.55
		Nos. 76-79 (4)	1.65	1.65

1988, Apr. 28 *Perf. 14½x14*
Size: 34x26mm

80	A12	16c Chinese	.25	.25
81	A12	30c Hindi	.30	.30
82	A12	40c Russian	.40	.40
83	A12	50c Arabic	.45	.45
		Nos. 80-83 (4)	1.40	1.40
		Nos. 60-83 (24)	8.40	8.40

See Nos. 209-212.

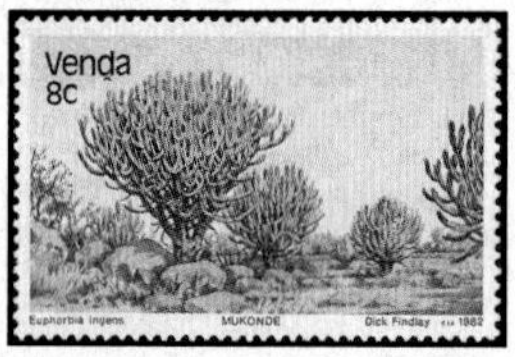

Trees A13

1982, Sept. 17

84	A13	8c Euphorbia ingens	.25	.25
85	A13	15c Pterocarpus angolensis	.25	.25
86	A13	20c Ficus ingens	.35	.35
87	A13	25c Adansonia digitata	.45	.45
		Nos. 84-87 (4)	1.30	1.30

1983, Aug. 3

88	A13	10c Gardenia spatulifolia	.25	.25
89	A13	20c Hyphaene natalensis	.30	.30
90	A13	25c Albizia adianthifolia	.30	.30
91	A13	40c Sesamothamnus lugardii	.55	.55
		Nos. 88-91 (4)	1.40	1.40

1984, June 21

92	A13	11c Afzelia quanzensis	.25	.25
93	A13	20c Peltophorum africanum	.30	.30
94	A13	25c Gyrocarpus americanus	.35	.35
95	A13	30c Acacia sieberana	.40	.40
		Nos. 92-95 (4)	1.30	1.30
		Nos. 84-95 (12)	3.85	3.85

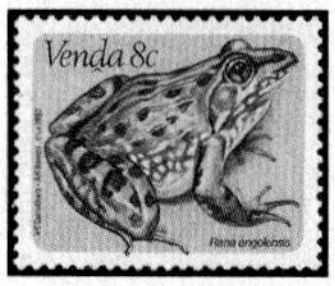

Frogs — A14

8c, Rana angolensis. 15c, Chiromantis xerampelina. 20c, Leptopelis. 25c, Ptychadena anchietae.

1982, Nov. 26 *Perf. 14x14½*

96	A14	8c multicolored	.25	.25
97	A14	15c multicolored	.30	.30
98	A14	20c multicolored	.35	.35
99	A14	25c multicolored	.45	.45
		Nos. 96-99 (4)	1.35	1.35

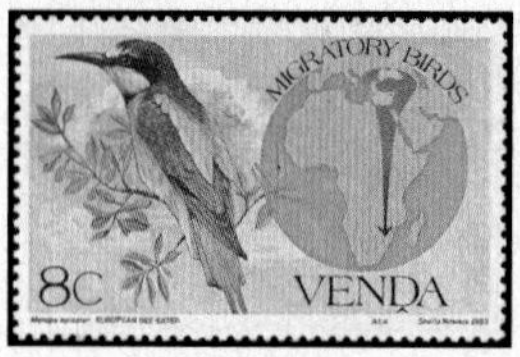

Migratory Birds and Maps — A15

1983, Feb. 16 *Perf. 14½x14*

100	A15	8c European bee-eater	.25	.25
101	A15	20c Steppe eagle	.40	.40
102	A15	25c Plum-colored starling	.50	.50
103	A15	40c White-bellied stork	.85	.85
		Nos. 100-103 (4)	2.00	2.00

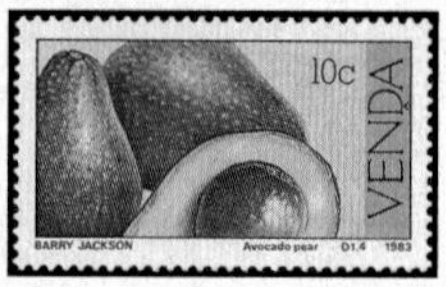

Subtropical Fruit A16

1983, Oct. 26 *Perf. 14x14½*

104	A16	10c Avocado	.25	.25
105	A16	20c Mango	.25	.25
106	A16	25c Papaya	.30	.30
107	A16	40c Litchi	.50	.50
		Nos. 104-107 (4)	1.30	1.30

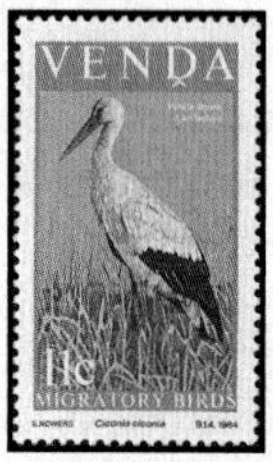

Migratory Birds — A17

1984, Apr. 26 *Perf. 14½x14*

108	A17	11c White stork	.30	.30
109	A17	20c Paradise flycatcher	.55	.55
110	A17	25c Yellow-billed kite	.65	.65
111	A17	30c Wood sandpiper	.85	.85
		Nos. 108-111 (4)	2.35	2.35

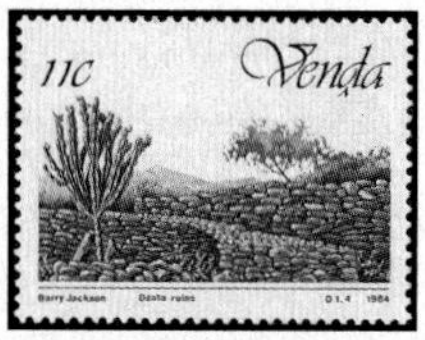

Independence, 5th Anniv. — A18

1984, Sept. 13 *Perf. 14½x14*

112	A18	11c Dzata Ruins	.25	.25
113	A18	25c Traditional hut	.25	.25
114	A18	30c Low-income housing	.30	.30
115	A18	45c Modern home	.45	.45
		Nos. 112-115 (4)	1.25	1.25

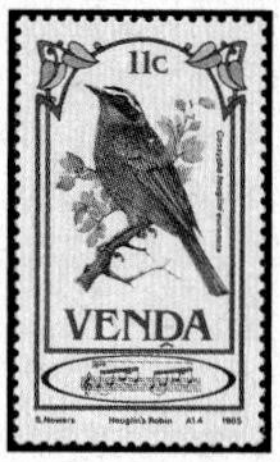

Songbirds — A19

1985, Jan. 10

116	A19	11c Heuglin's robin	.25	.25
117	A19	25c Black-collared barbet	.40	.40
118	A19	30c Black-headed oriole	.50	.50
119	A19	50c Kurrichane thrush	.85	.85
		Nos. 116-119 (4)	2.00	2.00

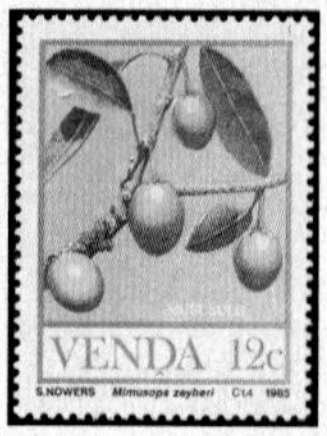

Food of the Veld — A20

1985, June 21 *Perf. 14x14½*

120	A20	12c Mimusops zeyheri	.25	.25
121	A20	25c Ziziphus mucronata	.25	.25
122	A20	30c Citrullus lanatus	.30	.30
123	A20	50c Berchemia discolor	.50	.50
		Nos. 120-123 (4)	1.30	1.30

See Nos. 173-176.

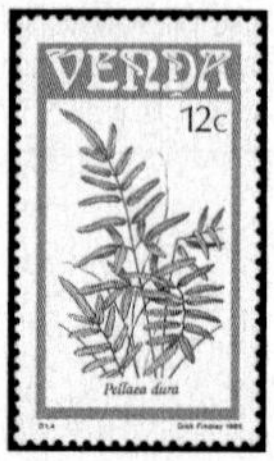

Ferns — A21

12c, Pellaea dura. 25c, Actiniopteris radiata. 30c, Adiantum hispidulum. 50c, Polypodium polypodioides.

1985, Sept. 5 *Perf. 14½x14*

124	A21	12c multicolored	.25	.25
125	A21	25c multicolored	.25	.25
126	A21	30c multicolored	.30	.30
127	A21	50c multicolored	.50	.50
		Nos. 124-127 (4)	1.30	1.30

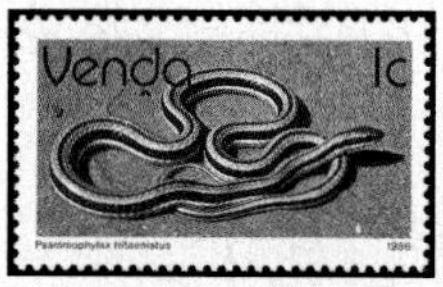

Reptiles A22

1c, Psammophylax tritaeniatus. 2c, Pseudaspis cana. 3c, Nucras taeniolata ornata. 4c, Bitis arietans. 5c, Mabuya capensis. 6c, Naja haje annulifera. 7c, Mabuya quinquetaeniata margaritifer. 8c, Philothamnus semivariegatus. 9c, Gerrhosaurus flavigularis. 10c, Prosymna sundevallii lineata. 14c, Platysaurus intermedius. 15c, Lacerta rupicola. 16c, Varanus niloticus. 18c, Dendroaspis polylepis. 20c, Afroedura transvaalica. 21c, Chamaeleo dilepsis. 25c, Elapsoidea sundevallii longicauda. 30c, Pachydactylus tigrinus. 50c, Mehelya capensis. 1r, Cordylus warreni depressus. 2r, Python sebae natalensis.

1986-90 *Perf. 14x14½*

128	A22	1c multicolored	.25	.25
129	A22	2c multicolored	.25	.25
130	A22	3c multicolored	.25	.25
131	A22	4c multicolored	.25	.25
132	A22	5c multicolored	.25	.25
133	A22	6c multicolored	.25	.25
134	A22	7c multicolored	.25	.25
135	A22	8c multicolored	.25	.25
136	A22	9c multicolored	.25	.25
137	A22	10c multicolored	.25	.25
138	A22	14c multicolored	.30	.30
139	A22	15c multicolored	.30	.30
140	A22	16c multicolored	.35	.35
141	A22	18c multicolored	.40	.40
142	A22	20c multicolored	.45	.45
143	A22	21c multicolored	.45	.45
144	A22	25c multicolored	.55	.55
145	A22	30c multicolored	.65	.65
146	A22	50c multicolored	1.10	1.10
147	A22	1r multicolored	2.25	2.25
148	A22	2r multicolored	4.50	4.50
		Nos. 128-148 (21)	13.80	13.80

Issued: 14c, 4/1/86; 16c, 4/1/87; 18c, 7/3/89; 21c, 8/3/90; others, 1/16/86.

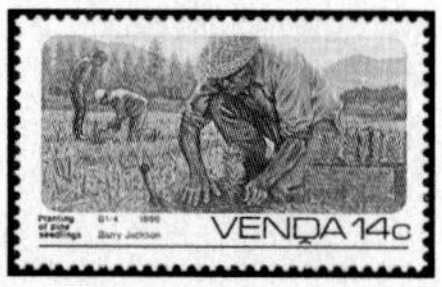

Forestry A23

Designs: 14c, Planting pine seedlings. 20c, Felling and extracting saw timber. 25c, Unloading timber at sawmill. 30c, Construction workers using pre-cut lumber.

1986, June 26   **Perf. 14x14½**
153 A23 14c multicolored   .25   .25
154 A23 20c multicolored   .40   .40
155 A23 25c multicolored   .45   .45
156 A23 30c multicolored   .55   .55
    Nos. 153-156 (4)   1.65   1.65

FIVA World Classic Car Rally — A24

1986, Sept. 4   **Perf. 14½x14**
157 A24 14c 1910 Maxwell   .25   .25
158 A24 20c 1929 Bentley 4½ l   .25   .25
159 A24 25c 1933 Plymouth
       Coupe   .35   .35
160 A24 30c 1958 Mercedes
       Cabriolet   .40   .40
  a.   Souvenir sheet of 1   1.40   1.40
    Nos. 157-160 (4)   1.25   1.25

No. 160a for the natl. philatelic exhibition held at Johannesburg, Oct. 6-11. Sold for 50c.

Waterfowl — A25

14c, Sarkidiornis melanotos. 20c, Dendrocygna viduata. 25c, Plectropterus gambensis. 30c, Alopochen aegyptiacus.

1987, Jan. 8   **Perf. 14x14½, 14½x14**
161 A25 14c multicolored   .90   .90
162 A25 20c multicolored   1.40   1.40
163 A25 25c multicolored   1.60   1.60
  a.   Souvenir sheet of 1   4.50   4.50
164 A25 30c multicolored   2.10   2.10
    Nos. 161-164 (4)   6.00   6.00

Nos. 163-164 are horiz. No. 163a margin pictures emblem of the natl. philatelic exhibition held at Paarl, Sept. 16-19. Sold for 50c.

Wood Carvings — A26

1987, Apr. 9   **Perf. 14½x14**
165 A26 16c Iron Master   .35   .35
166 A26 20c Distant Drums   .40   .40
167 A26 25c Sunrise   .55   .55
168 A26 30c Obedience   .70   .70
    Nos. 165-168 (4)   2.00   2.00

Freshwater Fish — A27

16c, Hydrocynus vittatus. 20c, Opsardium zambezense. 25c, Oreochromis mossambicus. 30c, Clarias gariepinus.

1987, July 2   **Perf. 14x14½**
169 A27 16c multicolored   .30   .30
170 A27 20c multicolored   .35   .35
171 A27 25c multicolored   .40   .40
172 A27 30c multicolored   .55   .55
    Nos. 169-172 (4)   1.60   1.60

Food of the Veld Type

1987, Oct. 2
173 A20 16c Grewia occidentalis   .25   .25
174 A20 30c Phoenix reclinata   .30   .30
175 A20 40c Halleria lucida   .45   .45
176 A20 50c Cucumis africanus   .55   .55
    Nos. 173-176 (4)   1.55   1.55

Coffee Industry A28

1988, Jan. 21   **Perf. 14½x14**
177 A28 16c Harvesting   .25   .25
178 A28 30c Weighing   .30   .30
179 A28 40c Sun drying   .40   .40
180 A28 50c Roasting   .50   .50
    Nos. 177-180 (4)   1.45   1.45

Nurse's Training College, Shayandima A29

1988, Aug. 18
181 A29 16c shown   .25   .25
182 A29 30c Microscopy   .30   .30
183 A29 40c Anatomy lecture   .40   .40
184 A29 50c Clinical training   .50   .50
    Nos. 181-184 (4)   1.45   1.45

Watercolors by Kenneth Thabo A30

1988, Oct. 6
185 A30 16c Fetching Water   .25   .25
186 A30 30c Grinding Maize   .30   .30
187 A30 40c Offering Food   .40   .40
188 A30 50c Kindling the Fire   .50   .50
  a.   Souvenir sheet of 1   1.90   1.90
    Nos. 185-188 (4)   1.45   1.45

No. 188a for the natl. philatelic exhibition held at Pietermaritzburg, Nov. 22-27. Sold for 1.50r.
See Nos. 193-196.

Traditional Kitchenware A31

1989, Jan. 5
189 A31 16c Ndongwana   .25   .25
190 A31 30c Ndilo   .30   .30
191 A31 40c Mufaro   .40   .40
192 A31 50c Muthatha   .50   .50
    Nos. 189-192 (4)   1.45   1.45

Art Type of 1988

Traditional dances: watercolors by Kenneth Thabo.

1989, Apr. 5
193 A30 18c Domba   .25   .25
194 A30 30c Tshinzerere   .30   .30
195 A30 40c Malende   .40   .40
196 A30 50c Malombo   .50   .50
    Nos. 193-196 (4)   1.45   1.45

Endangered Bird Species — A32

18c, Bucorvus leadbeateri. 30c, Torgos tracheliotus. 40c, Terathopius ecaudatus. 50c, Polemaetus bellicosus.

1989, June 27
197 A32 18c multicolored   .90   .90
198 A32 30c multicolored   1.25   1.25
199 A32 40c multicolored   1.60   1.60
200 A32 50c multicolored   2.25   2.25
  a.   Souvenir sheet of 1   4.00   4.00
    Nos. 197-200 (4)   6.00   6.00

No. 200a for the natl. philatelic exhibition WANDERERS 101, held Sept. 6-9. Sold for 1.50r.

Independence, 10th Anniv. — A33

18c, Pres. Ravele. 30c, Presidential office. 40c, Presidential residence. 50c, Thohoyandou Stadium.

1989, Sept. 13
201 A33 18c multicolored   .25   .25
202 A33 30c multicolored   .30   .30
203 A33 40c multicolored   .40   .40
204 A33 50c multicolored   .45   .45
    Nos. 201-204 (4)   1.40   1.40

Wildlife Conservation, Nwanedi Natl. Park — A34

1990, Mar. 1
205 A34 18c Panthera leo   .50   .50
206 A34 30c Equus burchelli   .90   .90
207 A34 40c Acinonyx jubatus   1.10   1.10
208 A34 50c Ceratotherium
       simum   1.25   1.25
  a.   Souvenir sheet of 1   4.00   4.00
    Nos. 205-208 (4)   3.75   3.75

No. 208a for the natl. philatelic exhibition. Sold for 1.50r.

History of Writing Type

Designs: 21c, Calligraphy. 30c, Musical notation, Beethoven's *Moonlight Sonata.* 40c, Computer characters. 50c, Black-and-white television picture transmitted across interstellar distances by the Arecibo radio telescope.

1990, May 23   **Litho.**   **Perf. 14½x14**
209 A12 21c multicolored   .25   .25
210 A12 30c multicolored   .35   .35
211 A12 40c multicolored   .45   .45
212 A12 50c multicolored   .65   .65
    Nos. 209-212 (4)   1.70   1.70

Aloe Plants — A35

1990, Aug. 23   **Litho.**   **Perf. 14½x14**
213 A35 21c Aloe globuligemma   .40   .40
214 A35 35c Aloe aculeata   .60   .60
215 A35 40c Aloe lutescens   .70   .70
216 A35 50c Aloe angelica   .85   .85
    Nos. 213-216 (4)   2.55   2.55

Butterflies — A36

1990, Nov. 15   **Perf. 14x14½**
217 A36 21c Pseudacraea bois-
       duvalii   .60   .60
218 A36 35c Papilio nireus   1.10   1.10
219 A36 40c Charaxes jasius   1.25   1.25
220 A36 50c Aeropetes tulbaghia   1.40   1.40
    Nos. 217-220 (4)   4.35   4.35

Birds A37

21c, Batis capensis. 35c, Cossypha natalensis. 40c, Anthreptes collaris. 50c, Phyllastrephus flavostriatus.

1991, Mar. 7   **Litho.**   **Perf. 14½x14**
221 A37 21c multicolored   .55   .55
222 A37 35c multicolored   .85   .85
223 A37 40c multicolored   1.00   1.00
224 A37 50c multicolored   1.25   1.25
    Nos. 221-224 (4)   3.65   3.65

A38

Chinese inventions.

1991, June 6   **Litho.**   **Perf. 14½x14**
225 A38 25c Paper made from
       pulp   .90   .90
226 A38 40c Magnetic compass   1.40   1.40
227 A38 50c Abacus   1.75   1.75
228 A38 60c Gunpowder   2.00   2.00
  a.   Souvenir sheet of 1   3.25   3.25
    Nos. 225-228 (4)   6.05   6.05

Hotels A39

1991, Aug. 29   **Litho.**
229 A39 25c Venda Sun   .50   .50
230 A39 40c Mphephu Resort   .90   .90
231 A39 50c Sagole Spa   1.10   1.10
232 A39 60c Luphephe-Nwanedi
       Resort   1.50   1.50
    Nos. 229-232 (4)   4.00   4.00

Trees A40

1991, Nov. 21   **Litho.**
233 A40 27c Acacia
       xanthophloea   .55   .55
234 A40 45c Faurea saligna   1.00   1.00
235 A40 65c Strelitzia caudata   1.40   1.40
236 A40 85c Kigelia africana   1.75   1.75
    Nos. 233-236 (4)   4.70   4.70

Clothing
Factory
A41

1992, Mar. 5   **Litho.**
237	A41	27c	Setting the web	.35	.35
238	A41	45c	Knitting a pattern	.80	.80
239	A41	65c	Using sewing ma- chine	1.10	1.10
240	A41	85c	Testing for flaws	1.40	1.40
		Nos. 237-240 (4)		3.65	3.65

Bees
A42

1992, May 21   **Litho.**
241	A42	35c	Honey bee	.80	.80
242	A42	70c	Carder bee	1.60	1.60
243	A42	90c	Leafcutter bee	1.75	1.75
244	A42	1.05r	Carpenter bee	2.25	2.25
		Nos. 241-244 (4)		6.40	6.40

A souvenir sheet of 1 #242 was sold by the Philatelic Foundation of South Africa. Value $3.75.

Inventions
A43

Designs: 35c, Plow, Egypt 1259 B.C. 70c, Wheel, Mesopotamia, 3200 B.C. 90c, Brickmaking, Egypt, 3000 B.C. 1.05r, Sailing ship, Egypt, 1600 B.C.

1992, Aug. 13
245	A43	35c	multicolored	.70	.70
246	A43	70c	multicolored	1.40	1.40
247	A43	90c	multicolored	1.50	1.50
248	A43	1.05r	multicolored	2.00	2.00
		Nos. 245-248 (4)		5.60	5.60

Crocodile
Farming
A44

1992, Oct. 15   **Litho.**
249	A44	35c	Emerging from water	.70	.70
250	A44	70c	Egg laying	1.40	1.40
251	A44	90c	Hatchlings	1.50	1.50
252	A44	1.05r	Maternal care	2.00	2.00
		Nos. 249-252 (4)		5.60	5.60

Domestic
Cats — A45

1993, Mar. 19   **Litho.**
253	A45	45c	Burmese	.90	.90
254	A45	65c	Tabby	1.75	1.75
255	A45	85c	Siamese	1.90	1.90
256	A45	1.05r	Persian	2.50	2.50
		Nos. 253-256 (4)		7.05	7.05

A souvenir sheet of one No. 254 has inscription for National Philatelic Exhibition. Sold for 3r. Value $6.50.

Herons
A46

Designs: 45c, Butorides striatus. 65c, Nycticorax nycticorax. 85c, Ardea purpurea. 1.05r, Ardea melanocephala.

1993, July 16   **Litho.**   *Perf. 14½x14*
257	A46	45c	multicolored	1.00	1.00
258	A46	65c	multicolored	1.50	1.50
259	A46	85c	multicolored	1.75	1.75
260	A46	1.05r	multicolored	2.25	2.25
a.		Souvenir sheet of 4, #257-260		6.50	6.50
		Nos. 257-260 (4)		6.50	6.50

Shoe
Factory — A47

45c, Punching out sole lining. 65c, Shaping heel. 85c, Joining upper to inner sole. 1.05r, Forming sole.

1993, Sept. 17   **Litho.**   *Perf. 14x14½*
261	A47	45c	multicolored	.45	.45
262	A47	65c	multicolored	.60	.60
263	A47	85c	multicolored	.70	.70
264	A47	1.05r	multicolored	1.00	1.00
		Nos. 261-264 (4)		2.75	2.75

Inventions
A48

1993, Nov. 5   **Litho.**   *Perf. 14x14½*
265	A48	45c	Axe	.60	.60
266	A48	65c	Armor	.90	.90
267	A48	85c	Arch	1.10	1.10
268	A48	1.05r	Aqueduct	1.40	1.40
		Nos. 265-268 (4)		4.00	4.00

Dogs
A49

1994, Jan. 14   **Litho.**   *Perf. 14½x14*
269	A49	45c	Cocker spaniel	1.00	1.00
270	A49	65c	Maltese	1.60	1.60
271	A49	85c	Scottish terrier	1.90	1.90
272	A49	1.05r	Miniature schnau- zer	2.50	2.50
		Nos. 269-272 (4)		7.00	7.00

A souvenir sheet of 1 #271 was sold for 3r by the Philatelic Foundation of Southern Africa and sold for 1.50r. Value $7.

Monkeys
A50

Designs: 45c, Cercopithecus aethiops. 65c, Galago moholi. 85c, Cercopithecus mitis. 1.05r, Otolemur crassicaudatus.

1994, Mar. 4   **Litho.**   *Perf. 14½x14*
273	A50	45c	multicolored	.90	.90
274	A50	65c	multicolored	1.40	1.40
275	A50	85c	multicolored	1.60	1.60
276	A50	1.05r	multicolored	2.10	2.10
a.		Souvenir sheet of 4, #273-276		6.00	6.00
		Nos. 273-276 (4)		6.00	6.00

Starlings
A51

45c, Lamprotornis nitens. 70c, Cinnyricinclus leucogaster. 95c, Onychognathus morio. 1.15r, Creatophora cinerea.

1994, Apr. 29   **Litho.**   *Perf. 14½x14*
277	A51	45c	multicolored	1.10	1.10
278	A51	70c	multicolored	1.75	1.75
279	A51	95c	multicolored	2.25	2.25
280	A51	1.15r	multicolored	2.75	2.75
		Nos. 277-280 (4)		7.85	7.85

Venda ceased to exist April 27, 1994. The Venda postal service continued to operate until 1996.

SOUTH ARABIA

sauth ə-'rā-bē-ə

LOCATION — Southern Arabia
GOVT. — Federation; British dependency
AREA — 61,890 sq. mi.
POP. — 771,000 (est. 1966)
CAPITAL — Al Ittihad

The Federation of South Arabia was established in 1959 and consists of 14 states including Aden colony and part of Aden protectorate. When the Federation became independent, Nov. 30, 1967, it became the People's Republic of Southern Yemen. See People's Democratic Republic of Yemen, Vol. 6.

100 Cents = 1 Shilling
1000 Fils = 1 Dinar (1965)

> **Catalogue values for all unused stamps in this country are for Never Hinged items.**

Common Design Types pictured following the introduction.

Red Cross Centenary Issue
Common Design Type
Wmk. 314

1963, Nov. 25   **Litho.**   *Perf. 13*
1	CD315	15c	black & red	.40	.40
2	CD315	1sh25c	ultra & red	.85	.85

Arms of
Federation of
South
Arabia — A1

Flag of Federation — A2

Perf. 14½x14
1965, Apr. 1   **Photo.**   **Unwmk.**
3	A1	5f	blue	.25	.25
4	A1	10f	light violet blue	.25	.25
5	A1	15f	blue green	.25	.25
6	A1	20f	green	.25	.25
7	A1	25f	orange brown	.25	.25
8	A1	30f	lemon	.30	.25
9	A1	35f	red brown	.30	.25
10	A1	50f	rose red	.30	.25
11	A1	65f	light yellow green	.35	.25
12	A1	75f	rose carmine	.40	.25

Perf. 14½
Flag in Black, Yellow, Green and Blue
13	A2	100f	reddish brown	.55	.25
14	A2	250f	dark blue	5.75	1.75
15	A2	500f	dark red	11.00	2.00
16	A2	1d	violet	18.00	18.00
		Nos. 3-16 (14)		38.20	24.50

For overprints, see People's Democratic Republic of Yemen.

Intl. Cooperation Year Issue
Common Design Type with Coat of Arms Replacing Queen's Portrait
Wmk. 314

1965, Oct. 24   **Litho.**   *Perf. 14½*
17	CD318	5f	blue grn & claret	.30	.25
18	CD318	65f	lt violet & green	.90	.25

Churchill Memorial Issue
Common Design Type with Coat of Arms Replacing Queen's Portrait
Design in Black, Gold and Carmine Rose
Unwmk.

1966, Jan. 24   **Photo.**   *Perf. 14*
19	CD319	5f	bright blue	.25	.25
20	CD319	10f	green	.55	.25
21	CD319	65f	brown	1.25	.50
22	CD319	125f	violet	1.75	1.50
		Nos. 19-22 (4)		3.80	2.50

World Cup Soccer Issue
Common Design Type with Coat of Arms Replacing Queen's Portrait

1966, July 1   **Litho.**   *Perf. 14*
23	CD321	10f	multicolored	.40	.25
24	CD321	50f	multicolored	1.50	.30

WHO Headquarters Issue
Common Design Type with Coat of Arms Replacing Queen's Portrait

1966, Sept. 20   **Litho.**   **Unwmk.**
25	CD322	10f	multicolored	.60	.25
26	CD322	75f	multicolored	1.50	.45

UNESCO Anniversary Issue
Common Design Type with Coat of Arms Replacing Queen's Portrait

1966, Dec. 15   **Litho.**   *Perf. 14*
27	CD323	10f	"Education"	.40	.30
28	CD323	65f	"Science"	1.50	1.25
29	CD323	125f	"Culture"	4.00	*1.50*
		Nos. 27-29 (3)		5.90	3.05

SOUTHERN NIGERIA

'sə-th̲ərn nī-'jir-ē-ə

LOCATION — In western Africa bordering on the Gulf of Guinea
GOVT. — British Crown Colony and Protectorate
AREA — 90,896 sq. mi.
POP. — 8,590,545
CAPITAL — Lagos

The Protectorate of Southern Nigeria, formed in 1900, absorbed in that year the Niger Coast Protectorate. In 1906 it united with Lagos and became the Colony and Protectorate of Southern Nigeria. An amalgamation was effected in 1914 between Northern and Southern Nigeria to form the Colony and Protectorate of Nigeria. See Nigeria, Northern Nigeria, Niger Coast Protectorate and Lagos.

12 Pence = 1 Shilling
20 Shillings = 1 Pound

Victoria — A1

Wmk. Crown and C A (2)

1901, Mar. Typo. *Perf. 14*

1	A1	½p yel grn & blk	2.00	*3.00*
a.		½p yel grn & sepia ('02)	2.50	*3.00*
2	A1	1p car rose & blk	2.00	2.00
a.		1p carmine rose & sepia ('02)	3.00	2.00
3	A1	2p org brn & blk	3.75	*6.00*
4	A1	4p ol grn & blk	3.25	*27.50*
5	A1	6p red vio & blk	4.25	*9.50*
6	A1	1sh blk & gray grn	9.75	*30.00*
7	A1	2sh6p brn & blk	57.50	*95.00*
8	A1	5sh yellow & blk	60.00	*120.00*
9	A1	10sh vio & blk, *yel*	150.00	*300.00*
		Nos. 1-9 (9)	292.50	593.00

Edward VII — A2

1903-04

10	A2	½p yel grn & blk	1.10	.35
11	A2	1p car rose & blk	1.50	.80
12	A2	2p org brn & blk	14.00	1.75
13	A2	2½p ultra & blk ('04)	2.25	1.50
14	A2	4p ol grn & blk	4.00	*6.25*
15	A2	6p red vio & blk	8.50	*9.25*
16	A2	1sh blk & gray grn	42.50	22.50
17	A2	2sh6p brown & blk	42.50	*75.00*
18	A2	5sh yellow & blk	90.00	*225.00*
19	A2	10sh vio & blk, *yel*	45.00	*150.00*
20	A2	£1 pur & gray grn	475.00	*1,000.*
		Nos. 10-20 (11)	726.35	1,492.

1904-07 Chalky Paper Wmk. 3

21	A2	½p yel grn & blk	.75	.25
22	A2	1p carmine & blk	14.00	.25
23	A2	2p org brn & blk	3.00	.50
24	A2	2½p ultra & blk	1.25	1.10
24A	A2	3p vio & org brn ('07)	11.00	1.50
25	A2	4p ol grn & blk ('05)	16.00	*29.00*
26	A2	6p red vio & blk	14.50	5.00
27	A2	1sh blk & gray grn	3.75	*4.00*
28	A2	2sh6p brn & blk ('05)	27.50	*21.00*
29	A2	5sh yellow & blk	57.50	*90.00*
30	A2	10sh vio & blk, *yel* ('08)	175.00	*225.00*
31	A2	£1 pur & gray grn ('05)	325.00	*400.00*
		Nos. 21-31 (12)	649.25	*777.60*

#23 and 24 are on ordinary paper, #24A and 25 on chalky, and the other values on both papers.

1907-10 Ordinary Paper

32	A2	½p green ('08)	2.25	.25
33	A2	1p carmine	1.00	.25
34	A2	2p gray	3.00	.80
35	A2	2½p ultra	7.50	4.25

Chalky Paper

36	A2	3p violet, *yel*	2.25	.35
37	A2	4p scar & blk, *yel*	2.50	.90
38	A2	6p red vio & dl vio	29.00	3.75
39	A2	1sh black, *green*	8.00	.50
40	A2	2sh6p car & blk, *bl*	17.50	2.50
41	A2	5sh scar & grn, *yel*	45.00	*55.00*
42	A2	10sh red & grn, *grn*	100.00	*140.00*
43	A2	£1 blk & vio, *red*	250.00	*300.00*
		Nos. 32-43 (12)	468.00	*508.55*

1910 Ordinary Paper Redrawn

44	A2	1p carmine	1.10	.25

In the redrawn stamp the "1" of "1d" is not as thick as in No. 33 but the "d" is taller and broader.

King George V — A3

1912

45	A3	½p green	3.00	.25
46	A3	1p carmine	3.00	.25
47	A3	2p gray	1.00	.95
48	A3	2½p ultra	5.75	3.25
49	A3	3p violet, *yel*	1.25	.35
50	A3	4p scar & blk, *yel*	1.60	*2.40*
51	A3	6p red vio & dl vio	3.00	1.50
52	A3	1sh black, *green*	3.50	1.00
53	A3	2sh6p red & blk, *bl*	10.00	*50.00*
54	A3	5sh red & grn, *yel*	26.00	*87.50*
55	A3	10sh red & grn, *grn*	60.00	110.00
56	A3	£1 blk & vio, *red*	225.00	*275.00*
		Nos. 45-56 (12)	343.10	532.45

Stamps of Southern Nigeria were replaced in 1914 by those of Nigeria.

SOUTHERN RHODESIA

'sə-th̲ərn rō-'dē-zh,ē-,ə

LOCATION — Southeastern Africa between Northern Rhodesia and Mozambique
GOVT. — British Colony
AREA — 150,333 sq. mi.
POP. — 4,010,000 (est. 1963)
CAPITAL — Salisbury

Prior to 1923 this territory was administered by the British South Africa Company. The colony was created in that year by the British Government at the request of the inhabitants. In 1953, Southern Rhodesia joined Northern Rhodesia and Nyasaland to form the Federation of Rhodesia and Nyasaland. When the Federation dissolved at the end of 1963, Southern Rhodesia again became an internally self-governing colony. See Rhodesia and Northern Rhodesia.

12 Pence = 1 Shilling
20 Shillings = 1 Pound

Catalogue values for unused stamps in this country are for Never Hinged items, beginning with Scott 56 in the regular postage section and Scott J1 in the postage due section.

King George V — A1

1924-30 Unwmk. Engr. *Perf. 14*

1	A1	½p dark green	5.00	.25
a.		Vert. pair, imperf. btwn.	1,200.	1,300.
b.		Horiz. pair, imperf. btwn.	1,200.	1,300.
c.		Horiz. pair, imperf. vert.	1,300.	
2	A1	1p scarlet	3.25	.25
a.		Horiz. pair, imperf. btwn.	950.00	1,100.
b.		Perf. 12½ (coil) ('30)	3.25	*92.50*
c.		Vert. pair, imperf. btwn.	1,700.	
d.		Vert. pair, imperf. horiz.	1,000.	
3	A1	1½p bister brown	4.00	.90
a.		Horiz. pair, imperf. btwn.	*15,000.*	
b.		Vert. pair, imperf. btwn.	*8,000.*	
4	A1	2p vio blk & blk	6.00	1.75
a.		Horiz. pair, imperf. btwn.	*17,000.*	
5	A1	3p deep blue	5.00	5.00
6	A1	4p org red & blk	5.00	*3.25*
7	A1	6p lilac & blk	4.50	*7.50*
a.		Horiz. pair, imperf. btwn.	*45,000.*	
8	A1	8p gray grn & blk	14.50	*55.00*
9	A1	10p rose red & bl	20.00	*57.50*
10	A1	1sh turq bl & blk	8.00	*11.00*
11	A1	1sh6p yellow & blk	22.50	*40.00*
12	A1	2sh brown & blk	20.00	20.00
13	A1	2sh6p blk brn & bl	37.50	70.00
14	A1	5sh bl grn & bl	85.00	*175.00*
		Nos. 1-14 (14)	240.25	447.40

Values for imperf between pairs are for stamps from the same pane. Stamps separated by wide margins are cross-gutter pairs and sell for much lower prices.

George V A2

Victoria Falls A3

1931-37 *Perf. 11½, 14 (1p)*

16	A2	½p dp green ('33)	2.00	.25
a.		Bklt. pane of 6 ('32)	*150.00*	
b.		Perf. 12	2.75	1.10
c.		Perf. 14 ('35)	2.25	1.00
17	A2	1p scarlet ('35)	1.25	.25
a.		Bklt. pane of 6 ('32)	*150.00*	
b.		Perf. 11½ ('33)	3.25	.25
c.		Perf. 12	2.50	.80
18	A2	1½p dp brown ('32)	3.00	.90
a.		Bklt. pane of 6 ('32)	*600.00*	
b.		Perf. 12 ('33)	62.50	*47.50*

Typo. *Perf. 14½x14*

19	A3	2p blk brn & blk	9.00	1.75
20	A3	3p dark blue	11.50	12.50

Perf. 12, 11½ (2sh6p)

Engr.

21	A2	4p org red & blk	1.50	1.75
a.		Perf. 14 ('37)	37.50	*70.00*
b.		Perf. 11½ ('35)	20.00	5.75
22	A2	6p rose lilac & blk	2.50	3.50
a.		Perf. 14 ('36)	8.00	1.50
b.		Perf. 11½ ('33)	17.50	1.75
23	A2	8p green & violet	2.00	*3.75*
a.		Perf. 11½ ('34)	20.00	*37.50*
24	A2	9p gray grn & ver ('34)	7.50	13.00
25	A2	10p car & ultra	8.50	2.75
a.		Perf. 11½ ('33)	7.50	*15.00*
26	A2	1sh turq bl & blk	2.25	3.00
a.		Perf. 11½ ('36)	140.00	70.00
b.		Perf. 14 ('37)	250.00	160.00
27	A2	1sh6p ocher & blk	12.00	*25.00*
a.		Perf. 11½ ('36)	75.00	*140.00*
28	A2	2sh dk brn & blk	27.50	8.00
a.		Perf. 11½ ('33)	42.50	35.00
29	A2	2sh6p ol brn & ultra ('33)	50.00	35.00
a.		Perf. 12	40.00	*47.50*
30	A2	5sh bl grn & ultra	50.00	57.50
		Nos. 16-30 (15)	190.50	168.90

Victoria Falls — A4

1932, May *Perf. 12½*

31	A4	2p dark brn & grn	8.50	1.50
32	A4	3p dark blue	8.50	2.25
a.		Vert. pair, imperf. horiz.	*15,000.*	*16,000.*
b.		Vert. pair, imperf. btwn.	*35,000.*	
		Set, never hinged	24.00	

See Nos. 37-37A.

Silver Jubilee Issue

Victoria Falls and George V A5

1935, May 6 *Perf. 11x12*

33	A5	1p car rose & olive	4.50	3.25
34	A5	2p blk brn & lt grn	8.00	8.50
35	A5	3p blue & violet	6.50	*11.00*
36	A5	6p dp violet & blk	11.00	*22.50*
		Nos. 33-36 (4)	30.00	*45.25*
		Set, never hinged	42.50	

25th anniv. of the reign of George V.

"Postage and Revenue" A6

1935-41 *Perf. 14*

37	A6	2p dk brn & grn ('41)	3.00	.25
b.		Perf. 12½	7.00	18.00
37A	A6	3p deep blue ('38)	4.00	1.25
		Set, never hinged	17.00	

Queen Elizabeth, George VI — A7

1937, May 12 *Perf. 12½*

38	A7	1p carmine & gray grn	.45	*1.00*
39	A7	2p brown & green	.45	*1.75*
40	A7	3p lt blue & violet	2.00	*9.50*
41	A7	6p red violet & blk	1.10	*4.00*
		Nos. 38-41 (4)	4.00	16.25
		Set, never hinged	7.50	

Coronation of George VI & Elizabeth.

King George VI — A8

1937, Nov. 25 *Perf. 14*

42	A8	½p yellow green	.40	.25
43	A8	1p red	.40	.25
44	A8	1½p red brown	.75	.35
45	A8	4p orange red	1.00	.25
46	A8	6p dark gray	1.00	.60
47	A8	8p blue green	1.50	4.00
48	A8	9p blue	1.25	1.10
49	A8	10p violet	1.75	*3.50*
50	A8	1sh green & blk	1.50	.25
51	A8	1sh6p ocher & blk	9.50	3.00
52	A8	2sh brown & blk	16.00	.70
53	A8	2sh6p violet & blue	8.00	8.00
54	A8	5sh green & blue	15.00	3.50
		Nos. 42-54 (13)	58.05	25.75
		Set, never hinged	85.00	

Catalogue values for unused stamps in this section, from this point to the end of the section, are for Never Hinged items.

Seal of British South Africa Co. — A9

Fort Salisbury, 1890 — A10

Cecil John Rhodes — A11

Pioneer Fort and Mail Coach A12

Rhodes Makes Peace, 1896 — A13

Victoria Falls Bridge — A14

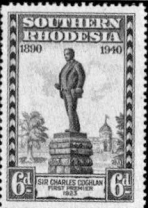

Sir Charles Coghlan — A15

Queen Victoria, George VI, Lobengula's Kraal and Government House A16

Unwmk.
1940, June 3　　Engr.　　Perf. 14

56	A9	½p dp grn & dull vio	.25	.65
57	A10	1p red & vio blue	.25	.25
58	A11	1½p cop brn & blk	.25	.80
59	A12	2p pur & brt grn	.50	.40
60	A13	3p dk blue & blk	.80	1.00
61	A14	4p brn & bl grn	2.00	3.00
62	A15	6p sepia & dull grn	1.50	3.00
63	A16	1sh dk bl & brt grn	1.50	2.00
		Nos. 56-63 (8)	7.05	11.10

50th anniv. of the founding of Southern Rhodesia by Cecil John Rhodes.

Pioneer — A17

1943, Nov. 1　　Photo.　　Wmk. 201

64	A17	2p Prus grn & choc	.35	.50

50th anniv. of Matabeleland under British control.

Princess Elizabeth and Princess Margaret Rose A18

King George VI and Queen Elizabeth A19

Unwmk.
1947, Apr. 1　　Engr.　　Perf. 14

65	A18	½p dk green & blk	.30	.60
66	A19	1p carmine & blk	.30	.60

Visit of the British Royal Family, Apr., 1947.

Victory Issue

Queen Elizabeth A20　　　George VI A21

Princess Elizabeth A22　　Princess Margaret Rose A23

1947, May 8

67	A20	1p deep carmine	.25	.25
68	A21	2p slate black	.25	.25
69	A22	3p deep blue	.60	.50
70	A23	6p red orange	.30	.75
		Nos. 67-70 (4)	1.40	1.75

Victory of the Allied Nations in WW II.

Common Design Types pictured following the introduction.

UPU Issue
Common Design Types
Engr.; Name Typo.
1949, Oct. 10　Wmk. 4　Perf. 11x11½

71	CD307	2p slate black	.70	.50
72	CD308	3p slate blue	1.25	1.75

75th anniv. of the UPU.

Queen Victoria and King George VI A24

Unwmk.
1950, Sept. 12　　Engr.　　Perf. 14

73	A24	2p choc & blue grn	.90	1.10

60th anniversary of Rhodesia.

Hospital, Doctor and Natives A25

Designs: 1p, African Scene. 2p, Native Houses, Modern City and Cecil Rhodes. 4½p, Dam and Natives. 1sh, Transportation.

1953, Apr. 15

74	A25	½p dk brown & blue	.25	.40
75	A25	1p blue grn & fawn	.25	.25
76	A25	2p vio & dk bl grn	.35	.25
77	A25	4½p dk bl & bl grn	1.50	1.75
78	A25	1sh chestnut & blk	3.25	1.75
		Nos. 74-78 (5)	5.60	5.40

#77 is inscribed Matabeleland Diamond Jubilee.

Type of Nyasaland Prot., 1953
1953, May 30　　　Perf. 14x13½

79	A17	6p purple	.35	.35

Nos. 74-79 were issued to commemorate the Central African Cecil Rhodes Centenary Exhibition.

Coronation Issue

Elizabeth II — A26

1953, June 1　　　　Perf. 12x12½

80	A26	2sh6p cerise	7.25	7.25

Sable Antelope A27　　　Rhodes' Grave A28

Flame Lily — A29

Designs: 1p, Tobacco planter. 3p, Farm Worker. 4½p, Victoria Falls. 6p, Baobab tree. 9p, Lion. 1sh, Zimbabwe ruins. 2sh, Birchenough Bridge. 2sh6p, Kariba Gorge. 5sh, Basket maker. 10sh, Balancing rocks. £1, Arms.

Perf. 14x13½, 13½x14
1953, Aug. 31
Portrait in Various Positions

81	A27	½p rose lake & dk ol grn	.35	.45
82	A27	1p choc & grn	.35	.25
83	A28	2p rose vio & org brn	.35	.25

Size: 28x22½mm

84	A29	3p car & sep	.70	1.50
85	A29	4p gray, brn, car & grn	3.50	.40
86	A29	4½p ultra & blk	3.00	4.50
87	A28	6p aqua & olive	4.50	1.50
88	A29	9p org brn & dp bl	4.50	4.25
89	A29	1sh grnsh bl & rose vio	1.75	.25
90	A29	2sh red & rose vio	16.00	7.00
91	A29	2sh6p org brn & ol grn	8.00	8.00
92	A28	5s dk grn & org brn	11.00	9.00

Size: 37x27mm

93	A29	10sh ol grn & red brn	19.00	27.50
94	A29	£1 dk gray & car	25.00	32.50
		Nos. 81-94 (14)	98.00	97.35

Ansellia Orchid — A30

1964, Feb. 19　　Photo.　　Perf. 14½
Size: 23x19mm

95	A30	½p Corn	.25	2.00
96	A30	1p Cape buffalo	.25	.25
a.		Purple omitted	3,500.	
97	A30	2p Tobacco	.60	.25
98	A30	3p Kudu	.25	.25
99	A30	4p Oranges	.30	.25

Perf. 13½x13
Size: 27x23mm

100	A30	6p Flame lily	.50	.25
101	A30	9p shown	2.75	1.25
102	A30	1sh Emeralds	3.75	.25
a.		Green omitted	4,500.	
103	A30	1sh3p Aloe	3.00	.25
104	A30	2sh Lake Kyle	2.50	2.50
105	A30	2sh6p Tiger fish	4.00	1.00
a.		Red omitted	4,750.	
b.		Ultra omitted	14,000.	

Perf. 14½x14
Size: 32x27mm

106	A30	5sh Cattle	4.00	2.75
107	A30	10sh Guinea fowl	11.50	8.50
108	A30	£1 Arms	14.00	18.00
		Nos. 95-108 (14)	47.65	37.75

#95-108 with overprint "Independence 11th November 1965" are listed as Rhodesia #208-221.

Stamps of Southern Rhodesia were replaced in 1965 by those of Rhodesia (formerly Southern Rhodesia).

POSTAGE DUE STAMPS

Catalogue values for unused stamps in this section are for Never Hinged items.

Great Britain Postage Due Stamps of 1938-51 Overprinted in Black

1951　　Wmk. 251　　Perf. 14x14½

J1	D1	½p emerald	3.75	17.50
J2	D1	1p violet blue	3.50	2.75
J3	D1	2p black brown	3.00	2.25
J4	D1	3p violet	3.25	3.00
J5	D1	4p brt blue	2.25	4.00
a.		4p slate green	275.00	600.00
J6	D1	1sh blue	3.00	4.50
		Nos. J1-J6 (6)	18.75	34.00

SOUTH GEORGIA

'sauth 'jor-jə

LOCATION — Island in South Atlantic Ocean, 1,100 mi. east of Tierra del Fuego
GOVT. — Dependency of Falkland Islands
AREA — 1,450 sq. mi.
POP. — Military and biological staff only.
CAPITAL — Grytviken Harbor (military garrison)

South Georgia remained a dependency of the Falkland Islands in 1962 when three other dependencies became Antarctic Territory, a separate colony. In 1985 South Georgia and the South Sandwich Islands became a separate colony. See Falkland Islands Dependencies Nos. 3L1-3L8.

12 Pence = 1 Shilling
20 Shillings = 1 Pound
100 Pence = 1 Pound (1971)

Catalogue values for all unused stamps in this country are for Never Hinged items.

Reindeer — A1

Sperm Whale — A2

Designs: 1p, South Sandwich Islands map. 2½p, Penguins. 3p, Fur seals. 4p, Finback whale and ship. 5½p, Elephant seals. 6p, Sooty albatross. 9p, Whaling ship. 1sh, Leopard seal. 2sh, Shackleton's cross. 2sh6p, Wandering albatross. 5sh, Elephant and fur seals. 10sh, Plankton and krill (shrimp). No. 15, Blue whale. No. 16, King penguins.

Wmk. 314 Upright

1963-69 Engr. *Perf. 15*

1	A1	½p	dull red	.55	*1.25*
a.			Perf. 14x15 ('67)	1.00	*1.60*
b.			Watermark sideways ('70)	1.60	*4.00*
2	A2	1p	violet blue	2.75	1.25
3	A2	2p	blue green	1.40	1.00
4	A1	2½p	black	6.00	2.50
5	A2	3p	olive	3.00	.35
6	A1	4p	green	5.50	.75
7	A1	5½p	dull violet	2.75	.40
8	A2	6p	orange	.80	.45
9	A1	9p	blue	7.50	1.75
10	A1	1sh	lilac	.90	.30
11	A1	2sh	cit & lt blue	27.50	7.00
12	A1	2sh6p	blue	25.00	4.50
13	A1	5sh	ocher	22.00	4.50
14	A2	10sh	rose claret	47.50	12.50
15	A1	£1	ultra	110.00	62.50
16	A2	£1	slate green	12.00	*17.50*
			Nos. 1-16 (16)	275.15	118.50
			Set, hinged	135.00	

Issued: No. 16, 12/1/69; others 7/10/63.

Nos. 1-14 Surcharged with New Value (Decimal Currency) and 3 Bars

Wmk. 314 Upright; Sideways on ½p

1971-72 *Perf. 15*

17	A1	½p	on ½p dull red	1.25	1.00
a.			Wmk. upright ('73)	4.00	3.50
18	A2	1p	on 1p vio blue	2.00	.90
a.			Wmk. sideways ('76)	.75	3.25
19	A1	1½p	on 5½p dull vio	1.50	1.50
20	A2	2p	on 2p blue grn	.90	.50
21	A1	2½p	on 2½p black	2.50	.70
22	A2	3p	on 3p olive	1.25	.75
23	A1	4p	on 4p green	1.25	.90
24	A2	5p	on 6p orange	2.25	.90
25	A1	6p	on 9p blue	1.75	.55
26	A1	7½p	on 1sh lilac	2.50	1.50
27	A1	10p	on 2sh cit & lt bl	35.00	13.00
28	A1	15p	on 2sh6p blue	13.00	9.00
29	A1	25p	on 5sh ocher	10.00	7.50
30	A2	50p	on 10sh rose claret, glazed paper ('72)	8.50	*15.00*
a.			Wmk. sideways ('76)	17.50	*30.00*
c.			Ordinary paper	40.00	20.00
			Nos. 17-30 (14)	83.65	53.70

Two types of surcharge are found on ½p, 1p, 1½p and 50p.

Issued: Nos. 17-29, 30c, 2/15/71. No. 30, 12/1/72. No. 30a, 3/9/76.

Wmk. 373 Sideways; Upright on 3p, 50p; Inverted on 1p, 5p

1977

17b	A1	½p	on ½p dull red	1.75	*2.00*
18b	A2	1p	on 1p vio blue	1.00	*2.00*
19b	A1	1½p	on 5½p dl vio	1.25	*2.00*
21b	A1	2½p	on 2½p black	14.00	3.25
22b	A2	3p	on 3p olive	7.00	3.25
23b	A1	4p	on 4p green	20.00	14.00
24b	A2	5p	on 6p orange	4.00	2.75
26b	A1	7½p	on 1sh lilac	2.00	*5.00*
27b	A1	10p	on 2sh cit & lt bl	1.50	*6.50*
28b	A1	15p	on 2sh6p blue	2.75	*5.50*
29b	A1	25p	on 5sh ocher	2.00	*6.00*
30b	A2	50p	on 10sh lil rose ('79)	2.00	*6.00*
			Nos. 17b-30b (12)	59.25	*58.25*

Ernest Shackleton and "Quest" — A3

1½p, "Endurance" in ice of Weddell Sea. 5p, Launching of sailboat "James Caird." 10p, Route of "James Caird" to South Georgia.

1972, Jan. 5 Litho. *Perf. 13½*

31	A3	1½p	vio bl, blk & yel	1.25	*1.50*
32	A3	5p	bl grn, blk & yel	1.50	*1.75*
33	A3	10p	lt blue & blk	1.75	*2.00*
34	A3	20p	multicolored	2.25	*2.25*
			Nos. 31-34 (4)	6.75	7.50

Sir Ernest Shackleton (1874-1922), explorer of Antarctica.

Common Design Types pictured following the introduction.

Silver Wedding Issue, 1972
Common Design Type

Design: Queen Elizabeth II, Prince Philip, elephant seal and king penguins.

1972, Nov. 20 Photo. *Perf. 14x14½*

35	CD324	5p	slate grn & multi	.50	.50
36	CD324	10p	violet & multi	.90	.90

Princess Anne's Wedding Issue
Common Design Type

1973, Dec. 1 Litho. *Perf. 14*

37	CD325	5p	citron & multi	.25	.25
38	CD325	15p	slate & multi	.50	.50

Churchill, Parliament and Big Ben — A4

Design: 25p, Churchill and battleship.

1974, Dec. 14 Litho. *Perf. 14½*

39	A4	15p	vio blue & multi	1.25	1.00
40	A4	25p	orange & multi	2.00	1.25
a.			Souvenir sheet of 2, #39-40	7.50	7.50

Sir Winston Churchill (1874-1965).

Capt. James Cook — A5

Cook's "Possession" — A6

Design: 16p, Possession Bay.

1975, Apr. 26 Wmk. 314

41	A5	2p	multicolored	2.25	1.25
42	A6	8p	multicolored	3.50	1.75
43	A6	16p	multicolored	3.75	2.50
			Nos. 41-43 (3)	9.50	5.50

Bicentenary of Capt. Cook's discovery of South Georgia.

"Discovery" and Biological Laboratory — A7

Designs: 8p, "William Scoresby" and Nansen-Pettersson water sampling bottles. 11p, "Discovery II" and plankton net. 25p, Biological station and krill (shrimp).

Wmk. 373

1976, Dec. 21 Litho. *Perf. 14*

44	A7	2p	multicolored	1.50	.65
45	A7	8p	multicolored	1.75	1.10
46	A7	11p	multicolored	2.00	1.25
47	A7	25p	multicolored	3.25	1.50
			Nos. 44-47 (4)	8.50	4.50

50th anniversary of the biological investigations of the "Discovery."

Queen with Regalia and Westminster Abbey — A8

6p, Prince Philip visiting Shackleton Memorial, 1957. 33p, Queen in procession after coronation.

1977, Feb. 7 *Perf. 13½x14*

48	A8	6p	multicolored	.25	.25
49	A8	11p	multicolored	.40	.30
50	A8	33p	multicolored	.90	.90
			Nos. 48-50 (3)	1.55	1.45

25th anniv. of the reign of Elizabeth II.

Elizabeth II Coronation Anniversary Issue
Common Design Types
Souvenir Sheet
Unwmk.

1978, June 2 Litho. *Perf. 15*

51		Sheet of 6	3.00	3.00
a.	CD326	25p Panther of Henry VI	.80	.65
b.	CD327	25p Elizabeth II	.80	.65
c.	CD328	25p Fur seal	.80	.65

No. 51 contains 2 se-tenant strips of Nos. 51a-51c, separated by horizontal gutter with commemorative and descriptive inscriptions and showing central part of coronation procession with coach.

Resolution A9

Cook's voyages: 6p, Map of South Georgia and South Sandwich Islands with Cook's route. 11p, King penguin, drawing by Forster. 25p, Cook after Flaxman/Wedgwood medallion.

1979, Feb. 14 Litho. *Perf. 11*

52	A9	3p	multicolored	1.50	1.00
53	A9	6p	multicolored	1.50	.90
54	A9	11p	multicolored	2.00	1.25

Lithographed; Embossed

55	A9	25p	multicolored	2.75	1.75
			Nos. 52-55 (4)	7.75	4.90

Capt. Cook's voyages.

SOUTH GEORGIA and SOUTH SANDWICH ISLANDS

Queen Elizabeth II 60th Birthday
Common Design Type

Designs: 10p, With King George and Queen Mary at christening of Prince Charles, 1948. 24p, Engagement of Prince Charles and Lady Diana, Buckingham Palace Music Room, 1981. 29p, Order of the British Empire, service at St. Paul's Cathedral, London, 1974. 45p, Banquet for Canadian Prime Minister Trudeau during the 1976 Olympics. 58p, Visiting Crown Agents' offices, 1983.

1986, Apr. 21 Wmk. 384 *Perf. 14½*

101	CD337	10p	multicolored	.40	.40
102	CD337	24p	multicolored	.60	.60
103	CD337	29p	multicolored	.70	.70
104	CD337	45p	multicolored	.85	.85
105	CD337	58p	multicolored	1.00	1.00
			Nos. 101-105 (5)	3.55	3.55

Wedding of Prince Andrew and Sarah Ferguson — A12

1986, Nov. 10 Litho. *Perf. 14½*

106	A12	17p	Couple at Ascot	.85	*1.10*
107	A12	22p	Wedding	.95	*1.40*
108	A12	29p	Andrew, helicopter	1.75	1.75
			Nos. 106-108 (3)	3.55	4.25

Birds A13

1p, Dominican gull. 2p, Blue-eyed cormorant. 3p, Wattled sheathbill. 4p, Brown skua. 5p, Cape pigeon. 6p, South Georgia diving petrel. 7p, South Georgia pipit. 8p, South Georgia pintail. 9p, Fairy prion. 10p, Chinstrap penguin. 20p, Macaroni penguin. 25p, Light-mantled sooty albatross. 50p, Southern giant petrel. £1, Wandering albatross. £3, King penguin.

1987, Apr. 24 Litho. Wmk. 384

109	A13	1p	multicolored	1.50	*1.75*
110	A13	2p	multicolored	1.75	*2.00*
111	A13	3p	multicolored	2.25	2.25
112	A13	4p	multicolored	2.00	2.25
113	A13	5p	multicolored	2.00	2.25
114	A13	6p	multicolored	2.00	2.25
115	A13	7p	multicolored	2.25	*2.25*
116	A13	8p	multicolored	2.25	*2.25*
117	A13	9p	multicolored	2.25	*2.25*
118	A13	10p	multicolored	2.50	*2.25*
119	A13	20p	multicolored	2.75	*2.50*
120	A13	25p	multicolored	2.75	*2.50*
121	A13	50p	multicolored	3.00	2.75

| 122 | A13 | £1 multicolored | 3.50 | 4.00 |
| 123 | A13 | £3 multicolored | 7.50 | 8.00 |

Nos. 109-123 (15) 40.25 41.50

3, 4, 7, 8, 20, 25, 50p and £3 vert.

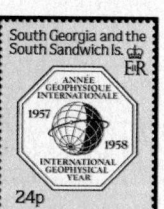

Intl. Geophysical
Year, 30th
Anniv. — A14

1987, Dec. 5   Litho.   Perf. 14½
124	A14 24p shown	.90	.65
125	A14 29p Grytviken Whaling Station	1.00	.75
126	A14 58p Glaciologist	1.75	1.25

Nos. 124-126 (3) 3.65 2.65

Sea Shells
A15

10p, Gaimardia trapesina. 24p, Margarella tropidophoroides. 29p, Trophon scotianus. 58p, Chlanidota densesculpta.

1988, Feb. 26   Wmk. 384   Perf. 14½
127	A15 10p multicolored	.75	.35
128	A15 24p multicolored	1.50	.65
129	A15 29p multicolored	1.75	.70
130	A15 58p multicolored	3.00	1.50

Nos. 127-130 (4) 7.00 3.20

Lloyds of London, 300th Anniv.
Common Design Type

10p, Queen Mother at the official opening of the Lloyds Building, Lime Street, 1957. 24p, Lindblad Explorer, horiz. 29p, Leith Harbor whaling station, horiz. 58p, Whale oil tanker Horatio on fire.

1988, Sept. 17   Perf. 14
131	CD341 10p multicolored	.80	.40
132	CD341 24p multicolored	1.25	.80
133	CD341 29p multicolored	1.75	.90
134	CD341 58p multicolored	2.50	1.60

Nos. 131-134 (4) 6.30 3.70

Glacier Formations — A16

1989, July 31
135	A16 10p Glacier headwall	.70	.50
136	A16 24p Accumulation area	1.10	.90
137	A16 29p Ablation area	1.25	1.00
138	A16 58p Calving front	2.50	1.50

Nos. 135-138 (4) 5.55 3.90

Combined
Services
Expedition,
1964-65
A17

10p, "Last ordeal" of the trek. 24p, Survey of Royal Bay. 29p, HMS *Protector.* 58p, 1st Ascent of Mt. Paget.

1989, Nov. 28   Perf. 14x14½
139	A17 10p multicolored	.70	.50
140	A17 24p multicolored	1.10	.90
141	A17 29p multicolored	1.25	1.00
142	A17 58p multicolored	2.50	1.50

Nos. 139-142 (4) 5.55 3.90

Queen Mother, 90th Birthday
Common Design Types

Designs: 26p, Queen Mother. £1, King, Queen & Air Raid Wardens, 1940.

Perf. 14x15
1990, Sept. 15   Wmk. 384
| 143 | CD343 26p multicolored | 1.00 | 1.00 |

Perf. 14½
| 144 | CD344 £1 blue & black | 4.75 | 4.75 |

Shipwrecks
A18

Wmk. 384
1990, Dec. 22   Litho.   Perf. 14
145	A18 12p Brutus	.65	.50
146	A18 26p Bayard	1.25	1.00
147	A18 31p Karrakatta	1.50	1.10
148	A18 62p Louise	2.75	2.00

Nos. 145-148 (4) 6.15 4.60

Elizabeth & Philip, Birthdays
Common Design Types

1991, July 2   Perf. 14½
149	CD345 31p multicolored	2.75	2.75
150	CD346 31p multicolored	2.75	2.75
a.	Pair, #149-150 + label	7.00	7.00

No. 150a exists with two different labels.

Elephant
Seals
A19

1991, Nov. 2   Wmk. 373   Perf. 14
151	A19 12p Two bulls	.85	.75
152	A19 26p One bull	1.50	1.50
153	A19 29p Using sand as sunscreen	1.75	1.75
154	A19 31p Bull, close up	1.75	1.75
155	A19 34p Harem on beach	2.00	2.00
156	A19 62p Cow and pup	3.25	2.50

Nos. 151-156 (6) 11.10 10.35

**Queen Elizabeth II's Accession to
the Throne, 40th Anniv.**
Common Design Type

1992, Feb. 6
157	CD349 7p multicolored	.50	.45
158	CD349 14p multicolored	.75	.70
159	CD349 29p multicolored	1.10	1.10
160	CD349 34p multicolored	1.25	1.25
161	CD349 68p multicolored	2.25	2.25

Nos. 157-161 (5) 5.85 5.75

South
Georgia
Teal
A20

1992, Mar. 22   Wmk. 384
162	A20 2p Adult, young	.75	.40
163	A20 6p Adult, nest of eggs	1.00	.70
164	A20 12p Four swimming	1.60	1.60
165	A20 20p Adult, two chicks	2.10	2.00

Nos. 162-165 (4) 5.45 4.70

World Wildlife Fund.

South
Georgia
Whaling
Museum
A21

Designs: 15p, Abandoned factory, Grytviken. 31p, Whaler's lighter, bones. 36p, King Edward Cove. 72p, Museum Building.

Wmk. 373
1993, June 29   Litho.   Perf. 13½
| 166-169 | A21 Set of 4 | 8.50 | 8.50 |

Macaroni
Penguins
A22

16p, Swimming underwater. 34p, Part of rookery. 39p, Two juveniles. 78p, Two adults.

Perf. 14x14½
1993, Dec. 10   Litho.   Wmk. 373
| 170-173 | A22 Set of 4 | 8.25 | 8.25 |

Ovptd. with Hong Kong '94 Emblem
1994, Feb. 18
| 174-177 | A22 Set of 4 | 8.25 | 8.25 |

Whales
and
Dolphins
A23

Designs: 1p, Hourglass dolphin. 2p, Southern right whale dolphin. 5p, Long-finned pilot whale. 8p, Southern bottlenose whale. 9p, Killer whale. 10p, Minke whale. 20p, Sei whale. 25p, Humpback whale. 50p, Southern right whale. £1, Sperm whale. £3, Fin whale. £5, Blue whale.

Wmk. 373
1994, Jan. 24   Litho.   Perf. 14
178	A23 1p multicolored	1.50	1.10
179	A23 2p multicolored	2.00	1.75
180	A23 5p multicolored	2.50	2.00
181	A23 8p multicolored	2.75	2.00
182	A23 9p multicolored	2.75	2.00
183	A23 10p multicolored	2.75	2.00
184	A23 20p multicolored	4.00	3.00
185	A23 25p multicolored	4.00	3.00
186	A23 50p multicolored	5.00	3.00
187	A23 £1 multicolored	6.25	3.75
188	A23 £3 multicolored	11.50	7.00
189	A23 £5 multicolored	18.50	11.00

Nos. 178-189 (12) 63.50 41.85

Native
Wildlife
A24

17p, Bull elephant seals. 35p, Fur seal, vert. 40p, Gray-headed albatrosses. 65p, King penguins, vert.

Wmk. 384
1994, Sept. 28   Litho.   Perf. 14
190	A24 17p multicolored	1.00	1.00
191	A24 35p multicolored	2.00	2.00
192	A24 40p multicolored	2.25	2.25
193	A24 65p multicolored	3.25	3.25

Nos. 190-193 (4) 8.50 8.50

Capt. C. A.
Larsen's
First Voyage
to South
Georgia
A25

1994, Dec. 1
194	A25 17p Map of Jason Harbor	.75	.75
195	A25 35p Castor, 1886	1.75	1.75
196	A25 40p Hertha, 1884	2.00	2.00
197	A25 65p Jason, 1881	3.25	3.25

Nos. 194-197 (4) 7.75 7.75

End of World War II, 50th Anniv.
Common Design Types

#198, HMS Queen of Bermuda moored at Leith Harbor. #199, 4-inch gun, Hansen Point, four men of Norwegian Defense Force. £1, Reverse of War Medal 1939-45.

Wmk. 384
1995, May 8   Litho.   Perf. 14
198	CD351 50p multicolored	3.50	3.50
199	CD351 50p multicolored	3.50	3.50
a.	Pair, #198-199	7.75	7.75

Souvenir Sheet
Wmk. 373
| 200 | CD352 £1 multicolored | 7.00 | 7.00 |

No. 199a is a continuous design.

Yachts — A26

Wmk. 373
1995, Nov. 16   Litho.   Perf. 14½
201	A26 35p Damien II	1.75	1.75
202	A26 40p Curlew	2.25	2.25
203	A26 76p Mischief	3.75	3.75

Nos. 201-203 (3) 7.75 7.75

Sir Ernest Shackleton's King Haakon
Bay-Stromness Trek, 80th
Anniv. — A27

Designs: 15p, Shackleton, Ridge 2493 Point of No Return. 20p, Frank Worsley, King Haakon Bay from Shackleton Gap. 30p, Map of Shackleton's route. 65p, Tom Crean, Manager's Villa, Stromness Whaling Station.

Wmk. 384
1996, May 20   Litho.   Perf. 14
204	A27 15p multicolored	.85	.85
205	A27 20p multicolored	1.50	1.50
206	A27 30p multicolored	2.00	2.00
207	A27 65p multicolored	3.75	3.75

Nos. 204-207 (4) 8.10 8.10

Chinstrap
Penguins — A28

Perf. 14½x14
1996, Nov. 8   Litho.   Wmk. 373
208	A28 17p Swimming	1.00	1.00
209	A28 35p Male, female	1.50	1.50
210	A28 40p Feeding chicks	2.00	2.00
211	A28 76p Feeding on krill	4.00	4.00
a.	Souvenir sheet of 1, perf. 14x14½	4.75	4.75

Nos. 208-211 (4) 8.50 8.50

Return of Hong Kong to China (#211a).

Queen Elizabeth and Prince Philip,
50th Wedding Anniv. — A29

#212, Queen. #213, Prince driving team of horses. #214, Queen looking at horses. #215, Prince. #216, Princess Anne on horseback, Queen. #217, Prince, child on horseback. £1.50, Queen, Prince in open carriage, horiz.

Perf. 14½x14
1997, July 10   Litho.   Wmk. 384
212	15p multicolored		.90	.90
213	15p multicolored		.90	.90
a.	A29 Pair, #212-213		2.25	2.25
214	17p multicolored		1.00	1.00
215	17p multicolored		1.00	1.00
a.	A29 Pair, #214-215		2.75	2.75
216	40p multicolored		2.50	2.50
217	40p multicolored		2.50	2.50
a.	A29 Pair, #216-217		6.00	6.00
	Nos. 212-217 (6)		8.80	8.80

Souvenir Sheet
218	A29	£1.50 multicolored	8.50	8.50

Flora and Fauna — A30

a, Reindeer. b, Antarctic tern. c, Gray-headed albatross. d, King penguin. e, Prickly burr. f, Fur seal.

Perf. 14½x14
1998, Mar. 16   Litho.   Wmk. 373
219	A30	35p Sheet of 6, #a.-f.	10.00	10.00

Diana, Princess of Wales (1961-97)
Common Design Type

Designs: a, Looking left. b, In white evening dress. c, In red dress. d, In white.

1998, Mar. 31
220	CD355	35p Sheet of 4, #a.-d.	5.25	5.25

No. 220 sold for £1.40 + 20p, with surtax and 50% of the profits from the issue being donated to the Princess Diana Memorial Fund.

Tourism
A31

Designs: 30p, MS Explorer. 35p, Wandering albatross. 40p, Elephant seal. 65p, Post Office, King Edward Point.

Wmk. 373
1998, Sept. 28   Litho.   Perf. 14½
221	A31	30p multicolored	2.50	1.50
222	A31	35p multicolored	2.75	1.75
223	A31	40p multicolored	3.00	2.00
224	A31	65p multicolored	3.75	3.25
	Nos. 221-224 (4)		12.00	8.50

Island
Views
A32

Designs: 9p, Grytviken and Sugartop Mountain. 17p, Old sealing ships, Grytviken. 35p, King Edward Point. 40p, Arrival at South Georgia. 65p, Church, Grytviken.

Wmk. 384
1999, Jan. 4   Litho.   Perf. 14
225	A32	9p multicolored	2.00	.85
226	A32	17p multicolored	2.75	1.25
227	A32	35p multicolored	4.00	1.75
228	A32	40p multicolored	4.25	1.75
229	A32	65p multicolored	5.25	2.00
	Nos. 225-229 (5)		18.25	7.60

Souvenir Sheet

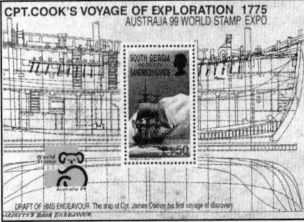

Capt. James Cook's Ship HMS
Resolution, 1773 — A33

1999, Mar. 5   Perf. 13½
230	A33	£1.50 multicolored	18.50	18.50

Australia '99, World Stamp Expo.

Queen Mother's Century
Common Design Type

Queen Mother: 25p, At air raid shelter, 1940. 30p, With Prince Edward, Lady Sarah Armstrong-Jones, Viscount Linley, 70th birthday. 35p, With Prince William, 94th birthday. 40p, As colonel-in-chief of Royal Anglian Regiment. £1, Funeral procession for Queen Victoria, portrait of Victoria.

Wmk. 384
1999, Aug. 18   Litho.   Perf. 13½
231	CD358	25p multicolored	3.00	2.75
232	CD358	30p black	3.25	3.50
233	CD358	35p multicolored	4.25	4.50
234	CD358	40p multicolored	4.75	4.50
	Nos. 231-234 (4)		15.25	14.75

Souvenir Sheet
235	CD358	£1 black	15.00	15.00

Birds — A34

Designs: 1p, Chinstrap penguin, vert. 2p, White chinned petrel. 5p, Gray backed storm petrel, vert. 10p, South Georgia pipit, vert. 11p, Gray headed albatross. 30p, Blue petrel, vert. 35p, Black browed albatross. 40p, South Georgia diving petrel. 50p, Macaroni penguin, vert. £1, Light mantled sooty albatross. £3, South Georgia pintail. £5, King penguin, vert.

Wmk. 384
1999, Nov. 15   Litho.   Perf. 14
236	A34	1p multicolored	1.00	1.40
237	A34	2p multicolored	1.25	1.40
238	A34	5p multicolored	1.50	1.50
239	A34	10p multicolored	1.75	1.75
240	A34	11p multicolored	1.90	1.90
241	A34	30p multicolored	2.75	3.00
242	A34	35p multicolored	3.00	3.00
243	A34	40p multicolored	3.25	3.00
244	A34	50p multicolored	3.75	3.75
245	A34	£1 multicolored	6.25	6.25
246	A34	£3 multicolored	14.00	15.00
247	A34	£5 multicolored	20.00	21.00
	Nos. 236-247 (12)		60.40	62.95

Millennium — A35

Perf. 14½x14¼
1999, Dec. 18   Litho.   Wmk. 384
248	A35	11p Sunrise	2.00	2.00
249	A35	11p Church	2.00	2.00
250	A35	11p Albatrosses	2.00	2.00
251	A35	35p Penguins	3.00	3.00
252	A35	35p Reindeer	3.00	3.00
253	A35	35p Sunset	3.00	3.00
	Nos. 248-253 (6)		15.00	15.00

Sir Ernest Shackleton (1874-1922),
Polar Explorer — A36

Designs: 35p, Voyage across Scotia Sea, 1916. 40p, Shackleton, Thomas Crean and Frank Worsley crossing South Georgia. 65p, Shackleton's grave.

2000, Feb. 20   Wmk. 373   Perf. 14
254	A36	35p multi	6.00	6.00
255	A36	40p multi	6.25	6.25
256	A36	65p multi	7.50	7.50
	Nos. 254-256 (3)		19.75	19.75

See British Antarctic Territory Nos. 285-287, Falkland Islands Nos. 758-760.

Prince William, 18th Birthday
Common Design Type

William: 25p, In suit, carrying bag, vert. 30p, With ski equipment, vert. 35p, Wearing suit and wearing sweater. 40p, In suit, waving. 50p, In beret, saluting.

Perf. 13¾x14¼, 14¼x13¾
2000, June 21   Litho.   Wmk. 373
Stamps With White Border
257	CD359	25p multi	2.75	2.75
258	CD359	30p multi	3.00	3.00
259	CD359	35p multi	3.25	3.25
260	CD359	40p multi	4.00	4.00
	Nos. 257-260 (4)		13.00	13.00

Souvenir Sheet
Stamps Without White Border
Perf. 14¼
261		Sheet of 5	16.00	16.00
a.	CD359	25p multi	2.25	2.25
b.	CD359	30p multi	2.50	2.50
c.	CD359	35p multi	2.75	2.75
d.	CD359	40p multi	3.00	3.00
e.	CD359	50p multi	3.25	3.25

King
Penguins — A37

#262, 37p, Penguins at sea. #263, 37p, Adult & creche. #264, 43p, Advertisement walk & courtship. #265, 43p, Nesting.

Perf. 13¾x14
2000, Oct. 16   Litho.   Wmk. 373
262-265	A37	Set of 4	20.00	20.00

Royal
Fleet
Auxiliary
Vessels
A38

Designs: No. 266, 37p, RFA Sir Percivale. No. 267, 37p, RFA Tidespring. No. 268, 43p, RFA Diligence. No. 269, 43p, RFA Gold Rover.

Wmk. 373
2001, May 28   Litho.   Perf. 14
266-269	A38	Set of 4	20.00	20.00

Marine
Life — A39

Designs: 33p, Icefish. No. 271, 37p, Spiny back crab. No. 272, 37p, Krill, vert. 43p, Toothfish, vert.

Wmk. 373
2001, Oct. 22   Litho.   Perf. 13¾
270-273	A39	Set of 4	20.00	20.00

Reign Of Queen Elizabeth II, 50th Anniv. Issue
Common Design Type

Designs: Nos. 274, 278a, 20p, With dog, 1952. Nos. 275, 278b, 37p, With Prince Philip, 1997. Nos. 276, 278c, 43p, Examining royal stamp collection, 1946. Nos. 277, 278d, 50p, Wearing blue hat, 1999. No. 278e, 50p, 1955 portrait by Annigoni (38x50mm).

Perf. 14¼x14½, 13¾ (#278e)
2002, Feb. 6   Litho.   Wmk. 373
With Gold Frames
274	CD360	20p multicolored	1.50	1.50
275	CD360	37p multicolored	3.00	3.00
276	CD360	43p multicolored	3.50	3.50
277	CD360	50p multicolored	4.00	4.00
	Nos. 274-277 (4)		12.00	12.00

Souvenir Sheet
Without Gold Frames
278	CD360	Sheet of 5, #a-e	16.50	16.50

World Record Animals — A40

No. 279: a, 10p, Fin whale. b, 10p, Blue whale. c, 20p, Sperm whale. d, 37p, Leopard seal with mouth open. e, 37p, Leopard seal on ice. f, 43p, Elephant seal. £1.50, Elephant seal, diff.

2002, Mar. 2   Litho.   Perf. 13¾
279	A40	Sheet of 6, #a-f	18.50	18.50

Souvenir Sheet
280	A40	£1.50 multi	18.50	18.50

Queen Mother Elizabeth (1900-2002)
Common Design Type

Designs: 22p, Wearing hat (black and white photograph). 40p, Wearing tiara. Nos. 283, 285a, 45p, Holding dog (black and white photograph). Nos. 284, 285b, 95p, Wearing white stole.

Perf. 14¼, 13¾x14¼ (#283-284)
2002, Aug. 5   Litho.   Wmk. 373
With Purple Frames
281	CD361	22p multicolored	1.25	1.25
282	CD361	40p multicolored	2.00	2.00
283	CD361	45p multicolored	2.50	2.50
284	CD361	95p multicolored	5.25	5.25
	Nos. 281-284 (4)		11.00	11.00

Souvenir Sheet
Without Purple Frames
Perf. 14½x14¼
285	CD361	Sheet of 2, #a-b	9.00	9.00

Antarctic Fur
Seals — A41

Designs: No. 286, 40p, Seal in water. No. 287, 40p, Two seals on ice. No. 288, 45p, Six seals. No. 289, 45p, One seal.

Wmk. 373
2002, Oct. 25   Litho.   Perf. 13¾
286-289	A41	Set of 4	21.00	21.00

Worldwide Fund for Nature (WWF) — A42

Gray-headed albatross: 40p, Adults at nesting ground. No. 291, 45p, Adult and chick (WWF emblem at LL). No. 292, 45p, Two adults (WWF emblem at UL). 70p, Bird's head.

Wmk. 373

2003, Jan. 7		**Litho.**	**Perf. 14**	
290-293	A42	Set of 4	10.00	10.00
293a		Strip of 4	11.00	11.00

Head of Queen Elizabeth II
Common Design Type
Wmk. 373

2003, June 2		**Litho.**	**Perf. 13¾**	
294	CD362	£2 multi	9.00	9.00

Prince William, 21st Birthday
Common Design Type

No. 295: a, Color photograph at right. b, Color photograph at left.

Wmk. 373

2003, June 21		**Litho.**	**Perf. 14¼**	
295		Horiz. pair	9.00	9.00
a.-b.		CD364 70p Either single	4.00	4.00

History of South Georgia — A43

No. 296: a, HMS Sappho visits Grytviken, 1906. b, Norwegian reindeer introduced, 1911. c, Largest blue whale landed, 1912. d, Shackleton's island crossing, 1916. e, Shackleton Memorial Cross, 1922. f, Discovery investigations, 1925. g, First powered flight over South Georgia, 1938. h, Operation Tabarin, 1943. i, Duke of Edinburgh visits, 1957. j, Bird Island Research Station, 1958. k, Mt. Paget climbed, 1964. l, Liberation of the island, 1982. m, Royal charter and crest, 1985. n, Museum inaugurated, 1992. o, Applied fishery research, 2001. p, Grytviken remedial work, 2003.

Wmk. 373

2004, Feb. 6		**Litho.**	**Perf. 13¼**	
296	A43	40p Sheet of 16, #a-p	40.00	40.00

Royal Navy Ships A44

Designs: 10p, HMS Ajax. 25p, HMS Amazon. 45p, HMS Dartmouth. 50p, HMS Penelope. 70p, HMS St. Austell Bay. £1, HMS Plymouth.

Wmk. 373

2004, Apr. 26		**Litho.**	**Perf. 14**	
297-302	A44	Set of 6	18.50	18.50

Merchant Ships A45

Designs: No. 303, 42p, RMS Queen Elizabeth 2. No. 304, 42p, MS Endeavour. 50p, MS Lindblad Explorer. 75p, SS Canberra.

Perf. 13¼x13½

2004, Nov. 10		**Litho.**		
303-306	A45	Set of 4	15.50	15.50

Animal Juveniles — A46

Designs: 1p, Skua. 2p, Reindeer. 3p, Antarctic prion, horiz. 5p, Humpback whale, horiz. 10p, Gentoo penguins. 25p, Antarctic fur seal. 50p, South Georgia pintail, horiz. 75p, Light-mantled sooty albatross. £1, Weddell seal, horiz. £2, King penguin, horiz. £3, Southern right whale, horiz. £5, Wandering albatross.

(42p), Elephant seal, horiz.

Perf. 13½x13¼, 13¼x13½

2004, Nov. 15			**Wmk. 373**	
307	A46	1p multi	.25	.25
308	A46	2p multi	.40	.40
309	A46	3p multi	.50	.50
310	A46	5p multi	.65	.65
311	A46	10p multi	.80	.80
312	A46	25p multi	1.10	1.10
313	A46	50p multi	2.40	2.40
314	A46	75p multi	3.50	3.50
315	A46	£1 multi	4.75	4.75
316	A46	£2 multi	8.50	8.50
317	A46	£3 multi	12.00	12.00
318	A46	£5 multi	19.00	19.00
		Nos. 307-318 (12)	53.85	53.85

Booklet Stamp
Self-Adhesive
Unwmk.
Serpentine Die Cut 12½

319	A46	(42p) multi	2.50	2.50
a.		Booklet pane of 4	10.00	
		Complete booklet, 2 #319a	20.00	

No. 319 is inscribed "Airmail Postcard."

Grytviken, Cent. — A47

Designs: 24p, Capt. Carl Anton Larsen, founder of Grytviken. 42p, Grytviken from Mount Hodges. 50p, Whale catcher Fortuna. £1, Ski jumper.

2004, Dec. 10	**Wmk. 373**	**Perf. 13¾**		
320-323	A47	Set of 4	11.50	11.50

Duncan Carse (1913-2004), Survey Expedition Leader — A48

Designs: No. 324, 50p, Carse. No. 325, 50p, Map of South Georgia, surveyors. 75p, Carse as radio broadcaster. £1, AMOW, Carse's hut, Undine South.

2005, Sept. 26	**Litho.**	**Perf. 13¾**		
324-327	A48	Set of 4	14.00	14.00

A49

A50

A51

A52

A53

Penguins A54

2005, Nov. 1			**Perf. 14**	
328	A49	45p multi	3.00	3.00
329	A50	45p multi	3.00	3.00
330	A51	45p multi	3.00	3.00
331	A52	45p multi	3.00	3.00
332	A53	45p multi	3.00	3.00
333	A54	45p multi	3.00	3.00
		Nos. 328-333 (6)	18.00	18.00

Queen Elizabeth II, 80th Birthday A55

Queen: No. 334, 50p, As child, with dog. Nos. 335, 338a, 50p, As young woman. Nos. 336, 338b, 75p, As older woman. £1, Wearing hat.

2006, Apr. 21		**Litho.**	**Perf. 14**	
With White Frames				
334-337	A55	Set of 4	11.00	11.00
Souvenir Sheet				
Without White Frames				
338	A55	Sheet of 2, #a-b	9.00	9.00

BirdLife International A56

Birds: 24p, Black-browed albatross. 45p, Southern giant petrel. 50p, White-chinned petrel. 75p, Wandering albatross.

No. 343: a, Black-browed albatross, diff. b, White-chinned petrel, diff.

Wmk. 373

2006, Oct. 18		**Litho.**	**Perf. 13¾**	
339-342	A56	Set of 4	12.00	12.00
Souvenir Sheet				
343	A56	£1 Sheet of 2, #a-b	13.00	13.00

Communications — A57

Designs: 25p, Mail drop from Royal Air Force Hercules plane. 50p, Radio/wireless room. 60p, MV Sigma. £1.05, SS Fleurus.

Perf. 14¼x14

2006, Nov. 30		**Litho.**	**Wmk. 373**	
344-347	A57	Set of 4	14.50	14.50

Mapping — A58

No. 348, 50p: a, Map of Neumayer Glacier, 1958. b, Map of Neumayer Glacier, 2003.
No. 349, 60p: a, Kern DKM1 theodolite and map. b, Landsat 7 satellite.

2007, Jan. 5			**Perf. 13¾**	
Horiz. Pairs, #a-b				
348-349	A58	Set of 2	14.50	14.50

Falkland Islands War, 25th Anniv. — A59

Designs: 25p, Ellerbeck Peak, Wasp helicopter. 50p, Stanley Peak, Wessex 3 helicopter. 60p, Sheridan Peak, Royal Marines Commandos. £1.05, Mills Peak, Royal Marines.

Perf. 12½x13

2007, Apr. 25		**Litho.**	**Wmk. 373**	
350-353	A59	Set of 4	14.50	14.50
353a		Souvenir sheet, #350-353	14.50	14.50

On No. 353a, the bottom perforations of Nos. 352-353 measure 13¼.

Scouting, Cent. — A60

Designs: 25p, Cover of Oct. 8, 1921 *Young Britain* magazine. 50p, Scouts James Marr and Norman Mooney raising flag on the Quest. 60p, Marr and Mooney with Sir Ernest Shackleton. 85p, Autographed postcard depicting Marr. £1.05, The Quest locked in ice.

Perf. 14¼

2007, Oct. 15		**Litho.**	**Unwmk.**	
354-358	A60	Set of 5	19.00	19.00

Intl. Polar Year A61

Designs: 50p, Zoological Building, Moltke Base. 60p, Meteorological Station, King Edward Point. 85p, Zooplankton. £1.05, Leopard seals.

2008, Jan. 25 Litho. Perf. 14¼x14
359-362 A61 Set of 4 16.00 16.00

Marine Stewardship Council — A62

Ships and marine life: 50p, Longliner, Patagonian toothfish. 60p, Trawler, Mackerel icefish. 85p, Krill trawler and refrigerator ship, Krill. £1.05, Fishery Patrol Vessel Pharos SG.

Perf. 14¼
2008, May 1 Litho. Unwmk.
363-366 A62 Set of 4 16.50 16.50

Worldwide Fund for Nature (WWF) — A63

Chinstrap penguins: No. 367, 55p, Three adults. No. 368, 55p, Two adults and a chick. 65p, Three adults in water. 90p, Two adults.

2008, July 10 Litho. Perf. 14
367-370 A63 Set of 4 13.00 13.00
370a Souvenir sheet of 4, #367-370 13.50 13.50

Falkland Islands Dependencies Letter Patent, Cent. — A64

Designs: 27p, H.M.S. Sappho. 65p, Magistrate's Residence, Grytviken. 90k, James Innes Wilson, 1909-1914 Magistrate. £1.10, S.S. Coronda.

2008, Nov. 30 Litho. Perf. 14
371-374 A64 Set of 4 14.50 14.50

Souvenir Sheet

Preservation of Polar Regions — A65

No. 375 — Antarctic ozone map of: a, September 2008. b, September 1979.

Serpentine Die Cut
2009, Apr. 2 Litho.
Self-Adhesive
375 A65 £1.10 Sheet of 2,
#a-b 11.50 11.50

Naval Aviation, Cent. A66

Royal Navy aircraft and ships: 27p, Supermarine Walrus, HMS Exeter. 65p, Westland Wasp HASI helicopter, HMS Plymouth. 90p, Westland Whirlwind HARI helicopter, HMS Protector. £1.10, Agusta Westland AW101 Merlin helicopter, HMS Lancaster.

2009, May 27 Litho. Perf. 14
376-379 A66 Set of 4 13.00 13.00

Ernest H. Shackleton (1874-1922), Explorer — A67

Designs: 1p, Shackleton at age 11. 2p, Shackleton at age 16. 5p, Shackleton on Discovery Expedition, 1902. 10p, Shackleton's wife, Emily, and children, Raymond, Cecily and Edward. 27p, Shackleton, Frank Wild, Dr. Eric Marshall and Jameson Adams aboard the Nimrod, 1909. 55p, Endurance trapped in ice. 65p, Launching the lifeboat James Caird, horiz. 90p, Shackleton, Frank Worsley and Tom Crean after crossing South Georgia, horiz. £1, Shackleton as Major. £2, Ship Quest. £3, Shackleton's grave, horiz. £5, Shackleton at desk, horiz.

2009, Aug. 14 Litho. Perf. 14
380 A67 1p multi .25 .25
381 A67 2p multi .30 .30
382 A67 5p multi .40 .40
383 A67 10p multi .50 .50
384 A67 27p multi 1.00 1.00
385 A67 55p multi 2.00 2.00
386 A67 65p multi 2.50 2.30
387 A67 90p multi 3.25 3.25
388 A67 £1 multi 3.50 3.50
389 A67 £2 multi 7.50 7.50
390 A67 £3 multi 11.00 11.00
391 A67 £5 multi 17.50 17.50
Nos. 380-391 (12) 49.70 49.50

Corals — A68

Designs: 55p, Thouarella sp. 65p, Paragorgia sp. 90p, Stylaster sp. £1.40, Thouarella sp., diff.

2009, Nov. 9 Litho. Perf. 13¼
392-395 A68 Set of 4 13.00 13.00

South Georgia Post Office, Cent. — A69

No. 396, 65p: a, SS Cachelote, first mail ship. b, Old postal hut.
No. 397, 90p: a, Post Office, 2009. b, FPV Pharos SG, current mail ship.

2009, Dec. 23 Litho. Perf. 14
Horiz. Pairs, #a-b
396-397 A69 Set of 2 12.00 12.00

Cephalopods A70

Designs: 27p, Galiteuthis glacialis. 65p, Psychroteuthis glacialis. 90p, Thaumeledone gunteri. £1.10, Stauroteuthis gilchristi.
£2, Mesonychoteuthis hamiltoni, Physeter macrocephalus.

2010, Apr. 7 Perf. 13¼
398-401 A70 Set of 4 9.25 9.25
Souvenir Sheet
402 A70 £2 multi 6.50 6.50
No. 402 contains one 51x51mm stamp.

Miniature Sheet

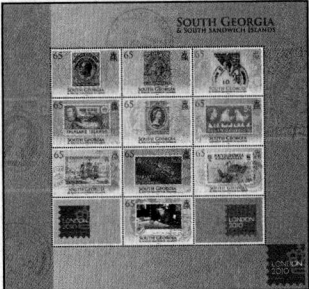

London 2010 Festival of Stamps — A71

No. 403: a, South Georgia essay depicting King George V. b, Falkland Islands #52. c, Bisect of Falkland Islands #56. d, Falkland Islands Dependencies #3L8. e, Falkland Islands Dependencies #1L18. f, South Georgia #13. g, South Georgia #42. h, Falkland Islands Dependencies #1LB1. i, South Georgia & South Sandwich Islands #165. j, South Georgia & South Sandwich Islands #391.

2010, Apr. 12 Perf. 14x14¾
403 A71 65p Sheet of 10, #a-j,
+ 2 labels 22.00 22.00

Shipwrecks and Hulks — A72

Designs: 60p, Bayard. 70p, Dias, Albatros. 95p, Karrakatta. £1.15, Petrel.

2010, June 25 Perf. 14x14¾
404-407 A72 Set of 4 12.00 12.00

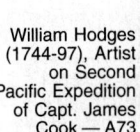 

William Hodges (1744-97), Artist on Second Pacific Expedition of Capt. James Cook — A73

Artwork by Hodges depicting: No. 408, 70p, The Resolution. No. 409, 70p, Monuments on Easter Island, horiz. 95p, Capt. Cook. £1.15, Possession Bay, South Georgia, horiz.

2010, Sept. 30 Perf. 13¾
408-411 A73 Set of 4 12.00 12.00

Flora — A74

Designs: 27p, Small fern. 70p, Water blinks. 95p, Antarctic pearlwort. £1.15, Adder's tongue.

2010, Dec. 15 Perf. 13x13¼
412-415 A74 Set of 4 13.00 13.00

Pets — A75

Designs: 45p, Vervet monkey. 60p, Anne-Marie Sorlle with puppies. 70p, Whalers with dog and fox. 95p, Nan Brown with penguin, Stugie. £1.15, Perce Blackborow and cat, Mrs. Chippy. £1.20, Sir Ernest Shackleton and puppy, Query.

2011, Feb. 15 Perf. 13¼
416-421 A75 Set of 6 18.50 18.50

Sir Alister Hardy (1896-1985), Marine Biologist — A76

Hardy and: 60p, Continuous plankton recorder type II. 70p, Microscope. 95p, Whaling Station, Grytviken. £1.15, RRS Discovery.

2011, Mar. 15 Perf. 13¼x13½
422-425 A76 Set of 4 11.50 11.50

Wedding of Prince William and
Catherine Middleton — A77

Couple: 70p, Laughing at rugby match. 95p,
In St. James's Palace. £1.15, At wedding
ceremony.
£2, Wedding portrait, vert.

2011, July 25　Litho.　Perf. 14
426-428 A77　Set of 3　　　9.50 9.50
Souvenir Sheet
Perf. 14¾x14
429　A77　£2 multi　　　　6.75 6.75
No. 429 contains one 32x48mm stamp.

Paintings of Petrels by John
Gale — A78

Designs: 60p, Southern Giant Petrel. 70p,
Snow Petrels. 95p, Cape Petrel. £1.15, South
Georgia Diving Petrels.

2011, Aug. 10　　　　Perf. 13½
430-433 A78　Set of 4　　　11.50 11.50

Filming in
South
Georgia
of *Frozen
Planet*
Television
Series
A79

Designs: 60p, Elephant seals. 70p, Wandering albatross on ground. 95p, Blonde fur seal
pup. £1.15, King penguin and juveniles. £2.50,
Wandering albatross in flight.

2011, Sept. 15　　　Perf. 13¼x13¾
434-437 A79　Set of 4　　　11.00 11.00
Souvenir Sheet
438　A79　£2.50 multi　　　8.00 8.00

Polar Explorers — A80

No. 439, 60p: a, Frank Wild (1873-1939),
expedition ship Discovery and Polar Medal. b,
Capt. Robert Falcon Scott (1868-1912) and
Discovery.
No. 440, 70p: a, Wild, members of Nimrod
expedition, British flag and Polar Medal. b,
Ernest Shackleton (1874-1922) and expedition
ship Nimrod.
No. 441, 95p: a, Wild, members of Aurora
expedition and Polar Medal. b, Douglas Maw-
son (1882-1958) and expedition ship Aurora.
No. 442, £1.15: a, Wild, members of Endur-
ance expedition and Polar Medal. c,
Shackleton and expedition ship Endurance.

2011, Nov. 23　　　　Perf. 14¼
Horiz. Pairs, #a-b
439-442 A80　Set of 4　　　21.50 21.50

Miniature Sheet

Marine Life — A81

No. 443: a, Ten-legged sea spider. b, Pink
cushion seastar. c, White-tipped nudibranch.
d, Branching sea cucumber. e, Giant Antarctic
isopod. f, South Georgia top shell.

2012, Jan. 1　　　　Perf. 13¼
443　A81 70p Sheet of 6, #a-f　13.50 13.50

Worldwide Fund for Nature
(WWF) — A82

Birds: Nos. 444, 448a, 60p, Imperial shags.
Nos. 445, 448b, 70p, Antarctic terns. Nos.
446, 448c, 95p, Southern skuas. Nos. 447,
448d, £1.15, Kelp gulls.
£3.50, Southern skua and chicks.

2012, Mar. 10　　　　Perf. 14
Stamps With White Frames
444-447 A82　Set of 4　　　11.00 11.00
Stamps Without White Frame
448　A82　Strip of 4, #a-d　11.00 11.00
Souvenir Sheet
449　A82　£3.50 multi　　11.50 11.50
No. 448 was printed in sheets of 16 containing four each Nos. 448a-448d.

Reign of Queen
Elizabeth II, 60th
Anniv. — A83

Photograph of Queen Elizabeth II from: 60p,
1952. 70p, 1977. 95p, 2002. £1.15, 2012.
£3, Queen Elizabeth II in 1957.

2012, May 28　Litho.　Perf. 13½
450-453 A83　Set of 4　　　10.50 10.50
Souvenir Sheet
454　A83　£3 multi　　　　9.25 9.25
No. 454 contains one 30x48mm stamp.

Blue Whales — A84

Blue whale: 65p, Underwater. 75p, At
water's surface. £1, Blowhole, with bird in
flight. £1.20, Flukes.

2012, Aug. 31　　　　Perf. 13¼
455-458 A84　Set of 4　　　11.50 11.50

Marine
Protected
Area — A85

Designs: No. 459, 65p, King penguins and
Fisheries Protection Vessel Pharos SG. No.
460, 65p, Elephant seals and cruise ship. No.
461, 75p, Adult gray-headed albatrosses in
flight, chick on scale. No. 462, 75p, Patagonian toothfish and fishing boats. £1, Antarctic
krill, lantern fish and squid. £1.20, Benthic
fauna.

2012, Nov. 9　　　　Perf. 13¾
459-464 A85　Set of 6　　　16.00 16.00

Mountains and Explorers — A86

No. 465, 65p: a, Stenhouse Peak. b, Com-
mander Joseph R. Stenhouse (1887-1941).
No. 466, 75p: a, Mount Carse. b, Verner
Duncan Carse (1913-2004).
No. 467, £1: a, Mount Paget and Allardyce
Range. b, Sir William Lamond Allardyce
(1861-1930).

2012, Dec. 11　　　　Perf. 14
Horiz. Pairs, #a-b
465-467 A86　Set of 3　　　16.00 16.00

Star Trails
A87

Star trails over: 65p, Harker Glacier. 75p,
Maiviken Hut. £1, Shipwrecks of the Albatros
and Dias. £1.20, Hope Point Memorial Cross.

2013, June 4　　　Perf. 13¼x13½
468-471 A87　Set of 4　　　11.50 11.50

Sir Rex Hunt (1926-2012), Governor of
Falkland Islands — A88

South Georgia and South Sandwich Islands
coat of arms and Hunt: 65p, At scene of helicopter crash. 75p, In front of Government
House, 1982. £1, Holding coins to commemorate the 25th anniv. of the liberation of the
Falkland Islands, 2007. £1.20, Wearing red
jacket.

2013, June 11　　　　Perf. 14
472-475 A88　Set of 4　　　11.50 11.50

Coronation of
Queen Elizabeth
II, 60th
Anniv. — A89

Queen Elizabeth II: 65p, Wearing tiara
before coronation. 75p, In carriage, wearing
crown after coronation. £1, On balcony of
Buckingham Palace. £1.20, Holding orb and
scepter.

2013, July 22　　　Perf. 13½x13¼
476-479 A89　Set of 4　　　11.00 11.00

Shallow
Marine
Surveys
Group
A90

Marine life: Nos. 480, 484a, 65p, Chiton.
Nos. 481, 484b, 75p, Anemone. Nos. 482,
484c, £1, Crocodile fish. Nos. 483, 484d,
£1.20, Brittle star.
No. 485a, £1, Starfish, vert.

2013, Aug. 29　　　Perf. 13¼x13½
Stamps With White Frames
480-483 A90　Set of 4　　　11.50 11.50
Stamps Without White Frames
484　A90　Strip of 4, #a-d　11.50 11.50
Souvenir Sheet
Perf. 13½x13¼
485　A90　Sheet of 3 (see
　　　footnote)　　　　　9.75 9.75
　a.　A90 £1 multi　　　　3.25 3.25
No. 485 contains No. 485a, Ascension No.
1104a and Falkland Islands No. 1107a. This
sheet was sold in Ascension, Falkland Islands
and South Georgia and the South Sandwich
Islands.

Habitat
Restoration
A91

Emblem of South Georgia Heritage Trust
and: 5p, RRS Ernest Shackleton. 30p, Bölkow
BO-105 helicopters. 65p, Workers loading bait
hoppers on helicopter. 75p, Rat eating bait.
£1, South Georgia pintails. £1.20, South Georgia pipit.

2013, Dec. 15　Litho.　Perf. 13¾
486-491 A91　Set of 6　　　13.00 13.00

Whalers
Church,
Grytviken,
Cent. — A92

Designs: 30p, Church under construction.
50p, Capt. Carl A. Larsen (1860-1924),
Antarctic explorer. 65p, People at church service. 75p, Church exterior. £1, Church and
helicopter. £1.20, Church at night.

2013, Dec. 24　Litho.　Perf. 13¼
492-497 A92　Set of 6　　　14.50 14.50

Royal
Christenings
A93

Photographs from christening of: 65p,
Queen Elizabeth II. 75p, Prince Charles. £1,
Prince William. £1.20, Prince George.

2014, June 23　Litho.　Perf. 13¼x13
498-501 A93　Set of 4　　　12.50 12.50

Reindeer
on South
Georgia
A94

Designs: 65p, Introduction of reindeer,
1911. 75p, Female reindeer, calf, penguin. £1,

Reindeer grazing. £1.20, Reindeer eradication.

2014, Oct. 14   Litho.   Perf. 14
502-505 A94 Set of 4   12.00 12.00

Frank Worsley (1872-1943), Member of Imperial Trans-Antarctic Expedition — A95

Designs: 65p, Worsley wearing captain's hat. 75p, Worsley and Reginald James observing stars. £1, Worsely and Lionel Greenstreet looking across King Edward Cove. £1.20, Worsley and expedition leader Ernest Shackleton onboard the ice-trapped ship Endurance.

2014, Nov. 5   Litho.   Perf. 14
506-509 A95 Set of 4   12.00 12.00

Tom Crean (1877-1938), Member of Imperial Trans-Antarctic Expedition — A96

Designs: 65p, Crean with pipe in mouth. 75p, Crean with sled dog pups. £1, Launch of the boat James Caird. £1.20, Crean and other crew members on the Endurance.

2014, Nov. 5   Litho.   Perf. 14
510-513 A96 Set of 4   12.00 12.00

Frank Hurley (1885-1962), Member of Imperial Trans-Antarctic Expedition — A97

Designs: 65p, Hurley and Alexander Macklin on the Endurance. 75p, Hurley and other crew near stove on Endurance. £1, Crew eating dinner on the Endurance, 1915. £1.20, Hurley and Dr. Leonard Hussey playing chess on the Endurance.

2014, Nov. 5   Litho.   Perf. 14
514-517 A97 Set of 4   12.00 12.00

Explorers, Scientists and Ships A98

Designs: 1p, Bill Tilman (1898-1977), explorer, and the Mischief. 2p, Alister Hardy (1896-1985), marine biologist, and the William Scoresby. 5p, Stanley Kemp (1882-1945), marine biologist, and the Discovery. 10p, Ernest Shackleton (1874-1922), polar explorer, and the Endurance. 50p, Robert Cushman Murphy (1887-1973), ornithologist, and the Daisy. 70p, Wilhelm Fichner (1877-1957), explorer, and the Deutschland. 80p, Otto Nordenskjöld (1869-1928), polar explorer, and the Antarctic. £1, Carl Anton Larsen (1860-1924), Antarctic explorer, and the Jason. £1.25, Karl Schrader (1852-1930), astronomer, and the Moltke. £2, James Weddell (1787-1834), explorer, and the Jane. £3, Fabian von Bellingshausen (1778-1852), explorer, and the Vostok. £5, James Cook (1728-79), explorer, and the Resolution.

2015, Jan. 5   Litho.   Perf. 14
518 A98 1p multi   .25 .25
519 A98 2p multi   .25 .25
520 A98 5p multi   .25 .25

521 A98 10p multi   .30 .30
522 A98 50p multi   1.50 1.50
523 A98 70p multi   2.10 2.10
524 A98 80p multi   2.40 2.40
525 A98 £1 multi   3.00 3.00
526 A98 £1.25 multi   3.75 3.75
527 A98 £2 multi   6.00 6.00
528 A98 £3 multi   9.00 9.00
529 A98 £5 multi   15.00 15.00
　Nos. 518-529 (12)   43.80 43.80

Albatrosses — A99

Designs: 70p, Black-browed albatross. 80p, Gray-headed albatross. £1, Light-mantled albatross. £1.25, Wandering albatross.

2015, Jan. 30   Litho.   Perf. 13¼
530-533 A99 Set of 4   11.50 11.50

SEMI-POSTAL STAMPS

Liberation of South Georgia, 10th Anniv. — SP1

Designs: 14p+6p, King Edward Point, Winter 1982. 29p+11p, Queen Elizabeth 2 in Cumberland Bay. 34p+16p, Royal Marines on South Sandwich Islands. 68p+32p, HMS Endurance and Wasp Helicopter.

Wmk. 384
1992, June 20   Litho.   Perf. 14
B1 SP1 14p +6p multicolored   1.00 1.00
B2 SP1 29p +11p multicolored   1.75 1.75
B3 SP1 34p +16p multicolored   2.00 2.00
B4 SP1 68p +32p multicolored   4.00 4.00
a.　Souvenir sheet of 4, #B1-B4   12.50 12.50
　Nos. B1-B4 (4)   8.75 8.75

Surtax for Soldiers', Sailors' and Airmen's Families Association.

AIR POST STAMPS

Penguins — AP1

Designs: No. C1, (60p), King penguins and chick. No. C2, (60p), Macaroni penguin. No. C3, (60p), Chinstrap penguins. No. C4, (60p), Gentoo penguin and juveniles.

2010, Oct. 25   Litho.   Perf. 13¾
C1-C4 AP1 Set of 4   8.00 8.00
C4a　Sheet of 8, 2 each #C1-C4   16.50 16.50

SOUTH KASAI

This part of a Congo province declared itself an autonomous state and in 1961 issued several series of stamps, some of which were overprints on Congo (ex-Belgian) stamps. Established nations did not recognize South Kasai as an independent state.

SOUTH MOLUCCAS
(Republik Maluku Selatan)

It appears that stamps of the so-called republic of South Moluccas were privately issued and had no postal use. Accordingly, they are not recognized as postage stamps.

SOUTH RUSSIA

sauth ˈrəsh-ə

LOCATION — An area in southern Russia bordering on the Caspian and Black Seas.

A provisional government set up and maintained by General Denikin in opposition to the Bolshevik forces in Russia following the downfall of the Empire. The stamps were used in the field postal service established for carrying on communication between the various armies united in the revolt. These armies included the Don Cossacks, the Kuban Cossacks, and also the neighboring southern Russian people in favor of the counter-revolution against the Bolsheviks.

100 Kopecks = 1 Ruble

Values for used stamps are for canceled to order examples. Postally used stamps sell for considerably more.

Watermark

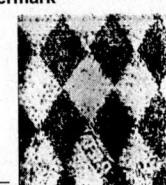

Wmk. 171 — Diamonds

Don Government (Novocherkassk) Rostov Issue

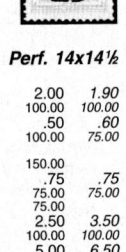

Russian Stamps of 1909-17 Surcharged

1918   Unwmk.   Perf. 14x14½
1 A14 25k on 1k dl org yel   2.00 1.90
a.　Inverted surcharge   100.00 100.00
2 A14 25k on 2k dl grn   .50 .60
a.　Inverted surcharge   100.00 75.00
b.　Double impression (surcharge normal)   150.00
3 A14 25k on 3k car   .75 .75
a.　Double surcharge   75.00 75.00
b.　Inverted surcharge   75.00
4 A15 25k on 4k car   2.50 3.50
a.　Inverted surcharge   100.00 100.00
5 A14 50k on 7k blue   5.00 6.50

Imperf
6 A14 25k on 1k orange   .60 1.25
a.　Double impression (surcharge normal)   150.00
7 A14 25k on 2k dull grn   7.50 12.50
8 A14 25k on 3k red   4.75 3.00
a.　Inverted surcharge   100.00
　Nos. 1-8 (8)   23.60 30.00

Counterfeits exist of Nos. 1-8.

Ermak, Cossack Leader — A1

Inscription on Back

1919   Perf. 11½
10 A1 20k green   50.00 85.00

This stamp was available for both postage and currency.

Novocherkassk Issue

25 1P. 1P.

Russian stamps with these surcharges are bogus.

Kuban Government Ekaterinodar Issues
Russian Stamps of 1909-17 Surcharged

-25　d   -70 к.　e

-1 p.　f   1 p.　g

-3 рубля　h   10 рублей　i

1918-20   Unwmk.   Perf. 14x14½
20 A14(d) 25k on 1k dl org yel   .50 1.75
a.　Inverted surcharge   75.00 27.50
b.　Dbl. surch., one inverted   75.00 25.00
21 A14(d) 50k on 2k dl grn   6.00 6.00
a.　Inverted surcharge   50.00 27.50
b.　Double surcharge   100.00 20.00
c.　Dbl. surcharge inverted   75.00 20.00
22 A14(e) 70k on 5k dk cl   2.00 5.50
23 A14(f) 1r on 3k car   5.00 5.00
a.　Inverted surcharge   50.00 20.00
b.　Double surcharge   50.00 15.00
c.　Pair, one without surch.   50.00 15.00
24 A14(g) 1r on 3k car   .65 1.00
a.　Inverted surcharge   50.00 20.00
b.　Double surcharge   100.00 20.00
c.　Pair, one without surcharge   100.00 20.00
25 A15(h) 3r on 4k rose   10.00 15.00
b.　Inverted surcharge   100.00 50.00
c.　Double surcharge   100.00 60.00
d.　Dbl. surcharge inverted   100.00 60.00
26 A15(i) 10r on 4k rose   15.00 5.00
a.　10r on 4k carmine   20.00 20.00
b.　Inverted surcharge   100.00 55.00
27 A11(i) 10r on 15k red brn & dp bl   1.25 2.00
a.　Surchd. on face & back   40.00 15.00
b.　Dbl. surch., one inverted   75.00 60.00
28 A14(i) 25r on 3k car   10.00 3.00
a.　Inverted surcharge   100.00 20.00
29 A14(i) 25r on 7k bl   25.00 50.00
a.　Inverted surcharge   100.00 100.00
30 A11(i) 25r on 14k bl & car   75.00 80.00
a.　Inverted surcharge   100.00 100.00
31 A11(i) 25r on 25k dl grn & dk vio   30.00 60.00
a.　Inverted surcharge   80.00 70.00
　Nos. 20-31 (12)   180.40 234.25

Imperf
35 A14(d) 25d on 1k org   5.00 2.50
36 A14(d) 50k on 2k gray grn   2.00 .60
a.　Inverted surcharge   50.00 25.00
b.　Double surcharge   50.00 25.00
c.　Pair, one without surch.   50.00 30.00

37	A14(e)	70k on 5k claret	2.50	*3.25*
38	A14(f)	1r on 3k red	1.40	*2.00*
a.		Inverted surcharge	40.00	*20.00*
b.		Double surcharge	30.00	*15.00*
c.		Pair, one without surch.	30.00	*15.00*
d.		Double surcharge, both inverted	100.00	
39	A14(g)	1r on 3k red	1.00	*1.00*
a.		Double surcharge	20.00	*20.00*
b.		Pair, one without surch.	20.00	*20.00*
c.		As "a," inverted	40.00	*45.00*
d.		Inverted surcharge	100.00	
40	A11(i)	10r on 15k red brn & dp bl	4.75	*5.50*
41	A14(i)	25r on 3k red	6.00	*10.00*
a.		Inverted surcharge	100.00	
		Nos. 35-41 (7)	22.65	*24.85*

No. 31 is said to exist imperf.

Russian Stamps of 1909-17 Surcharged

1919			**Perf. 14, 14½x15**	
45	A14	70k on 1k dl org yel	1.75	*1.00*
a.		Inverted surcharge	100.00	

Imperf
46	A14	70k on 1k orange	1.25	*2.40*
a.		Inverted surcharge	100.00	*20.00*
b.		Double surch., one inverted	100.00	*25.00*

The 1k postal savings stamp with this surcharge inverted is a proof. Value, $500. Counterfeits exist of Nos. 20-46.

On Russia Nos. AR1-AR3

A2

1919		**Wmk. 171**	**Perf. 14½x15**	
47	A2	10r on 1k red, *buff*	50.00	*60.00*
a.		Inverted surcharge	75.00	
48	A2	10r on 5k grn, *buff*	50.00	*60.00*
a.		Double surcharge	250.00	
49	A2	10r on 10k brn, *buff*	120.00	*150.00*
		Nos. 47-49 (3)	220.00	*270.00*

Counterfeits exist of Nos. 47-49.

Crimea

Russian Stamp of 1917 Surcharged

1919		**Unwmk.**	**Imperf.**	
51	A14	35k on 1k orange	2.00	*3.00*
a.		Comma, instead of period in surcharge	2.00	

A3

Paper with Buff Network; Inscription on Back

1919			**Imperf.**	
52	A3	50k brown	40.00	*85.00*

Available for both postage and currency.

Russia Nos. 77, 82, 123, 73, 119 Surcharged

Nos. 53-57   Nos. 58-59

1920			**Perf. 14x14½**	
53	A14	5r on 5k dk claret	1.25	*2.40*
a.		Inverted surcharge	100.00	
b.		Double surcharge	100.00	
54	A8	5r on 20k dl bl & dk car	1.25	*2.40*
a.		Inverted surcharge	100.00	
b.		Double surcharge	100.00	
c.		"5" omitted	75.00	

Imperf
55	A14	5r on 5k claret	1.25	*2.40*
a.		Double surcharge	25.00	

Same Surcharge on Stamp of Denikin Issue, No. 64
57	A5	5r on 35k lt bl	12.00	*14.00*
a.		Double surcharge	80.00	
		Nos. 53-57 (4)	15.75	*21.20*

1920			**Perf. 14x14½**	
58	A14	100r on 1k dl org yel	5.00	
a.		"10" in place of "100"	150.00	
b.		Inverted surcharge	150.00	
c.		Double surcharge	150.00	

Imperf
59	A14	100r on 1k orange	2.75	

Nos. 53-57 were issued at Sevastopol during the occupation by General Wrangel's army. Nos. 58-59 were prepared but not used.

Denikin Issue

A5   St. George — A6

1919		**Unwmk.**	**Imperf.**	
61	A5	5k orange	.30	*.25*
62	A5	10k green	.30	*.25*
63	A5	15k red	.30	*.35*
64	A5	35k light blue	.30	*.25*
65	A5	70k dark blue	.30	*.35*
a.		Tête bêche pair	90.00	
66	A6	1r brown & red	1.00	*.90*
67	A6	2r gray vio & yellow	1.75	*1.60*
68	A6	3r dl rose & green	1.10	*1.25*
69	A6	5r slate & violet	1.50	*1.40*
70	A6	7r gray grn & rose	2.50	*3.25*
71	A6	10r red & gray	2.25	*2.50*
		Nos. 61-71 (11)	11.60	*12.35*

Perf. 11½
68a	A6	3r dull rose & green	3.00	*10.00*
69a	A6	5r slate & violet	4.00	*10.00*
71a	A6	10r red & gray	3.00	*10.00*
		Nos. 68a-71a (3)	10.00	*30.00*

Nos. 61-71 were issued at Ekaterinodar and used in all parts of South Russia that were occupied by the People's Volunteer Army under Gen. Anton Ivanovich Denikin. The inscription on the stamps reads "United Russia."

Stamps of type A6 with rosettes instead of numerals in the small circles at the sides may be essays. Perforated examples of Nos. 61-67 and 70 are of private origin.

For surcharges see Russia, Offices in Turkish Empire Nos. 303-319.

SOUTH SUDAN

sauth sü-'dan

LOCATION — Central Africa, between Central Africa and Ethiopia
GOVT. — Republic
AREA — 239,285 sq. mi.
POP. — 10,625,176 (2012 estimate)
CAPITAL — Juba

South Sudan achieved independence from Sudan on July 9, 2011.

100 Piasters = 1 Pound

Catalogue values for all unused stamps in this country are for Never Hinged items.

Flag of South
Sudan — A1

John Garang
(1945-2005),
Leader of Sudan
People's
Liberation
Army — A2

2011, July 9		**Litho.**	**Perf. 12**	
1	A1	£1 multi	8.75	*8.75*
2	A2	£3.50 multi	30.00	*30.00*

A £2.50 stamp depicting the coat of arms was prepared and affixed to commercially-made first day covers that were canceled, but the stamp was apparently not sold in South Sudan.

A3

A4

Designs: £1, Shoe-billed storks. £2, Bearded vultures. £5, Saddle-billed storks. £10, Nile lechwe. £20, White-eared kob. £50, Arms of South Sudan.

Perf. 12¼x12 (A3), 14¾x14½ (A4)				
2012			**Litho.**	
3	A3	£1 multi	—	*—*
4	A4	£2 multi	—	*—*
5	A3	£5 multi	—	*—*
6	A4	£10 multi	—	*—*
7	A3	£20 multi	—	*—*
8	A3	£50 multi	—	*—*

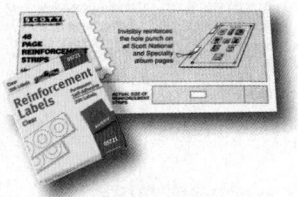

SOUTH WEST AFRICA

sauth 'west 'a-fri-kə

(Namibia)

LOCATION — Southwestern Africa between Angola, Botswana and South Africa, bordering on the Atlantic Ocean
GOVT. — Administered by the Republic of South Africa under a mandate of the League of Nations
AREA — 318,261 sq. mi.
POP. — 1,039,800 (1982)
CAPITAL — Windhoek

Formerly a German possession, South West Africa was occupied by South African forces in 1915 and by the Treaty of Versailles was mandated to the Union of South Africa. On March 20, 1990 it became Namibia.

12 Pence = 1 Shilling
20 Shillings = 1 Pound
100 Cents = 1 Rand (1961)

Catalogue values for unused stamps in this country are for Never Hinged items, beginning with Scott 125 in the regular postage section, Scott B1 in the semipostal section, Scott J86 in the postage due section, and Scott O13 in the officials section.

Watermarks

Watermarks 177, 201, 330, 348 and 359 can be found at the beginning of South Africa.

Major-number listings and values of Nos. 1-40 and 85-93 are for pairs with both overprints.

Stamps of South Africa, Nos. 2-3, 5 and 9-16, Overprinted in English or Afrikaans alternately throughout the sheets.

Setting I

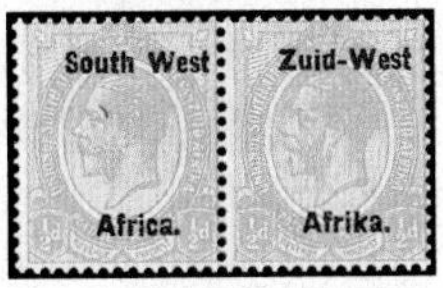

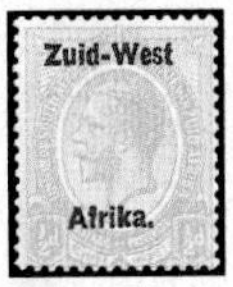

"South West" 14½mm wide
"Zuid-West" 13mm wide
Overprint Spaced 14mm

1923, Jan. 2 Wmk. 177 *Perf. 14*

1 A2 ½p green, pair 4.00 *10.50*
a. Single, Dutch 1.10 *1.10*
2 A2 1p red, pair 7.50 *10.50*
a. Single, Dutch 1.10 *1.10*
b. Inverted overprint, pair 550.00
c. As "b," single, English 125.00
d. As "b," single, Dutch 125.00
e. As #2, English "Af.rica" 175.00 275.00
f. Double overprint, pair 1,000.
g. As "f," single, English 500.00
h. As "f," single, Dutch 500.00
3 A2 2p dl vio, pair 9.00 *14.00*
a. Single, Dutch 1.75 *1.75*
b. Inverted overprint, pair 700.00 800.00
c. As "b," single, English 150.00
d. As "b," single, Dutch 150.00
4 A2 3p ultra, pair 11.00 *19.00*
a. Single, Dutch 3.25 *3.25*
5 A2 4p ol grn & org, pair 19.00 *52.50*
a. Single, Dutch 4.50 *4.50*
6 A2 6p vio & blk, pair 9.25 *50.00*
a. Single, Dutch 4.75 *4.75*
7 A2 1sh org, pair 27.50 *55.00*
a. Single, Dutch 5.75 *5.75*
b. As #7, without period after "Afrika" *7,500.*
8 A2 1sh3p violet, pair 45.00 *62.50*
a. Single, Dutch 6.50 *6.50*
b. Inverted overprint, pair 400.00
c. As "b," single, English 75.00
d. As "b," single, Dutch 75.00
9 A2 2sh6p grn & cl, pair 70.00 *150.00*
a. Single, Dutch 22.50 *22.50*
10 A2 5sh blue & cl, pair 200.00 *375.00*
a. Single, Dutch 57.50 *57.50*
11 A2 10sh ol grn & bl, pair 1,500. *2,900.*
a. Single, Dutch 475.00 *500.00*
12 A2 £1 red & dp grn, pair 800.00 *2,000.*
a. Single, Dutch 300.00 *300.00*
Nos. 1-12 (12) 2,702. *5,699.*

Most values exist with "t" of "West" partly or totally missing. Vertical displacement in overprinting accounts for the stamps with only one line of overprint.

The English overprint of Setting I is the same as that of Setting III. See Nos. 16a-27a.

Setting II

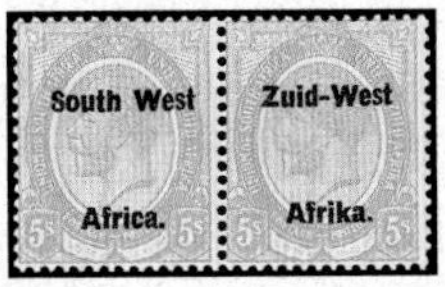

Words Same Width as Setting I
Overprint Spaced 9½-10mm

1923, Apr.

13 A2 5sh blue & cl, pair 160.00 *300.00*
a. Single, English 52.50 *52.50*
b. Single, Dutch 52.50 *52.50*
c. As #13, without period after "Afrika" 1,200. 1,400.
d. As "b," without period after "Afrika" 225.00 225.00
14 A2 10sh ol grn & bl, pair 575.00 *1,000.*
a. Single, English 160.00 *160.00*
b. Single, Dutch 160.00 *160.00*
c. As #14, without period after "Afrika" 2,600. *3,250.*
d. As "b," without period after "Afrika" 550.00 550.00
15 A2 £1 red & green, pair 1,150. *1,700.*
a. Single, English 225.00 *225.00*
b. Single, Dutch 225.00 *225.00*
c. As #15, without period after "Afrika" 6,000. 5,750.
d. As "b," without period after "Afrika" 1,000. 1,000.

Setting III

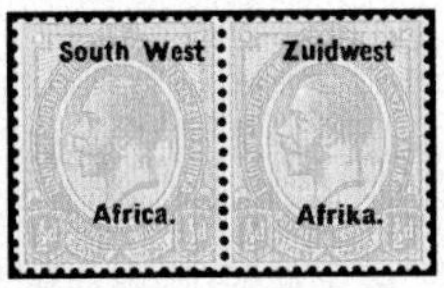

English as in Setting I
"Zuidwest" 11mm wide, No Hyphen
Overprint Spaced 14mm

1923-24

16 A2 ½p grn, pair ('24) 11.00 *40.00*
a. Single, English 1.10 *4.25*
b. Single, Dutch .75 *4.25*
17 A2 1p red, pair 6.25 *10.50*
a. Single, English 1.10 *1.60*
b. Single, Dutch .30 *1.60*
18 A2 2p dull vio, pair 11.00 *14.00*
a. Single, English .50 *1.50*
b. Single, Dutch .50 *1.50*
c. Dbl. ovpt., pair 1,200.
d. As "c," single, English 150.00
e. As "c," single, Dutch 150.00
19 A2 3p ultra, pair 6.00 *13.00*
a. Single, English .70 *1.50*
b. Single, Dutch .70 *1.50*
20 A2 4p ol grn & org, pair 7.00 *24.00*
a. Single, English .75 *3.25*
b. Single, Dutch .75 *3.25*
21 A2 6p vio & blk, pair 14.00 *47.50*
a. Single, English 1.00 *5.50*
b. Single, Dutch 1.00 *5.50*
22 A2 1sh orange, pair 16.00 *52.50*
a. Single, English 1.50 *5.75*
b. Single, Dutch 1.50 *5.75*
23 A2 1sh3p violet, pair 32.50 *52.50*
a. Single, English 2.25 *6.25*
b. Single, Dutch 2.25 *6.25*
24 A2 2sh6p grn & cl, pair 52.50 *92.50*
a. Single, English 7.00 *11.50*
b. Single, Dutch 7.00 *11.50*
25 A2 5sh blue & cl, pair 75.00 *150.00*
a. Single, English 11.00 *21.00*
b. Single, Dutch 11.00 *21.00*
26 A2 10sh ol grn & bl, pair 190.00 *300.00*
a. Single, English 35.00 *47.50*
b. Single, Dutch 35.00 *47.50*
27 A2 £1 red & grn, pair 350.00 *475.00*
a. Single, English 55.00 *70.00*
b. Single, Dutch 55.00 *70.00*
Nos. 16-27 (12) 771.25 *1,271.*

Setting IV

Type g (on left), Type h (on right)

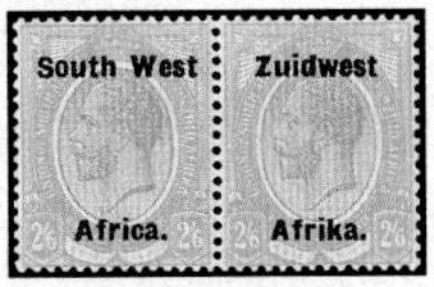

"South West" 16mm wide
"Zuidwest" 12mm wide
Overprint Spaced 14mm

1924, July

28 A2 2sh6p grn & cl, pair 92.50 *175.00*
a. Single, English 15.00 *32.50*
b. Single, Dutch 15.00 *32.50*

Setting VI

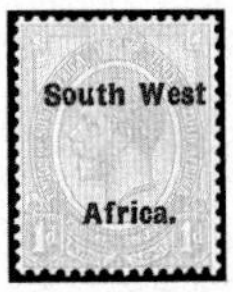

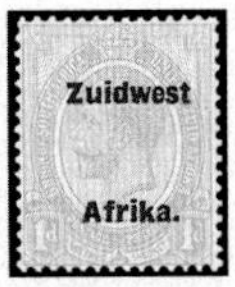

"South West" 16, 16½mm wide
"Zuidwest" 12½mm wide
Overprint Spaced 9½mm

1924, Dec.

29 A2 ½p green, pair 8.00 *45.00*
a. Single, English .50 *5.75*
b. Single, Dutch .50 *5.75*
30 A2 1p red, pair 4.25 *11.50*
a. Single, English .25 *1.60*
b. Single, Dutch .25 *1.60*
31 A2 2p dull vio, pair 5.75 *25.00*
a. Single, English .30 *2.00*
b. Single, Dutch .30 *2.00*
32 A2 3p ultra, pair 5.25 *32.50*
a. Single, English .50 *3.25*
b. Single, Dutch .50 *3.25*
33 A2 4p ol grn & org, pair 7.50 *52.50*
a. Single, English .70 *4.50*
b. Single, Dutch .70 *4.50*
34 A2 6p vio & blk, pair 10.50 *55.00*
a. Single, English .75 *5.75*
b. Single, Dutch .75 *5.75*
35 A2 1sh orange, pair 12.50 *55.00*
a. Single, English .90 *5.75*
b. Single, Dutch .90 *5.75*
36 A2 1sh3p violet, pair 17.50 *55.00*
a. Single, English 1.25 *5.75*
b. Single, Dutch 1.25 *5.75*
37 A2 2sh6p grn & cl, pair 37.50 *80.00*
a. Single, English 5.00 *11.50*
b. Single, Dutch 5.00 *11.50*
38 A2 5sh blue & cl, pair 52.50 *140.00*
a. Single, English 8.50 *16.00*
b. Single, Dutch 8.50 *16.00*
39 A2 10sh ol grn & bl, pair 95.00 *180.00*
a. Single, English 13.00 *22.50*
b. Single, Dutch 13.00 *22.50*
40 A2 £1 red & grn, pair 300.00 *475.00*
a. Single, English 50.00 *75.00*
b. Single, Dutch 50.00 *75.00*
Nos. 29-40 (12) 556.25 *1,206.*

Setting VII

South Africa Nos. 21-22 Overprinted

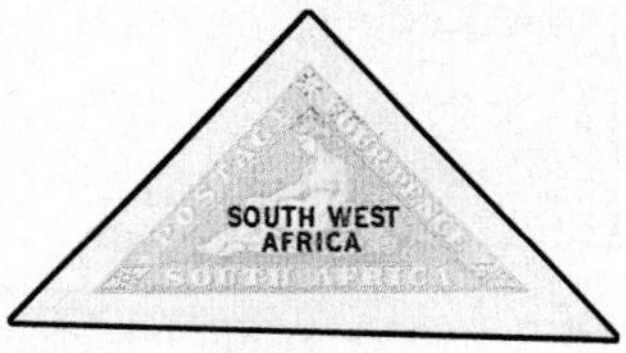

m

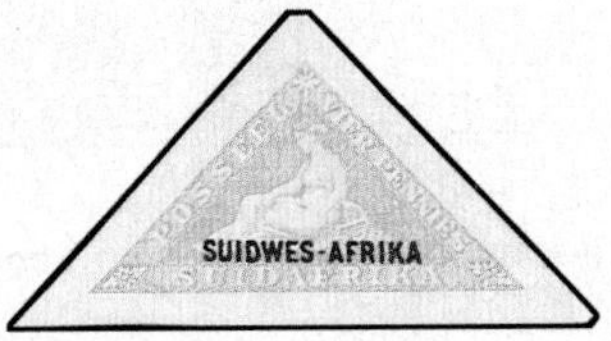

n

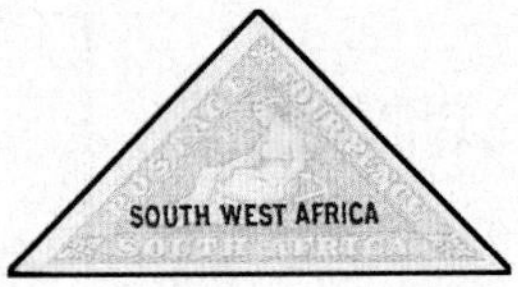

o

1926-27 Wmk. 201 *Imperf.*

81 A3 (m) 4p blue gray .85 *3.50*
82 A3 (n) 4p blue gray .85 *3.50*
83 A3 (o) 4p blue gray ('27) 7.00 *22.50*
Nos. 81-83 (3) 8.70 *29.50*

Nos. 81-83 were not officially perforated, but firms and individuals applied various forms of perforation and rouletting for their own convenience. Perf. 11 examples of Nos. 81-82 were made by John Meinert, Ltd., Windhoek, same values.

Setting VIII

South Africa Nos. 23-25 Overprinted Alternately with type "p" on English-inscribed Stamps and type "q" on Afrikaans-inscribed Stamps

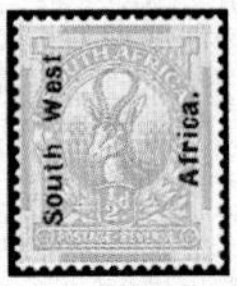

p

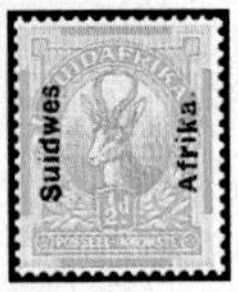

q

"South West" 16½mm wide
"Suidwes" 11mm wide
Overprint Spaced 11½mm

1926 Typo. *Perf. 14½x14*

85 A5 ½p dk grn & blk, pair 4.75 *12.00*
a. Single, English .75 *1.00*
b. Single, Afrikaans .75 *1.00*
c. Ovpt. "q" on English stamp .75 *1.00*
d. Ovpt. "p" on Afrikaans stamp .75 *1.00*
e. Pair, "c" + "d" ('27) 2.25 *9.00*
f. As "e," without period after "Africa" 175.00
86 A6 1p car & blk, pair 4.00 *8.00*
a. Single, English .50 *.80*
b. Single, Afrikaans .50 *.80*
c. Ovpt. "q" on English stamp .50 *.50*
d. Ovpt. "p" on Afrikaans stamp .50 *.50*
e. Pair, "c" + "d" ('27) 3.50 *3.50*
f. As "e," without period after "Africa" 350.00
87 A7 6p org & grn, pair 25.00 *55.00*
a. Single, English 7.00 *8.50*
b. Single, Afrikaans 7.00 *8.50*
c. Ovpt. "q" on English stamp 3.00 *3.50*
d. Ovpt. "p" on Afrikaans stamp 3.00 *3.50*
e. Pair, "c" + "d" ('27) 10.00 *35.00*
f. As "e," without period after "Africa" 210.00
Nos. 85-87 (3) 33.75 *75.00*

For overprints see Nos. O1-O3.

Setting IX

South Africa Nos. 26-27, 29-32 Overprinted in Blue with types "p" and "q" Spaced 16mm

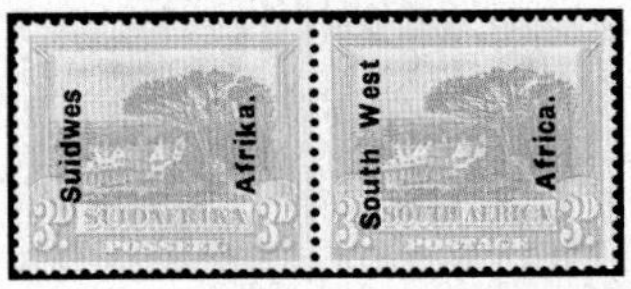

1927 Engr. *Perf. 14*

88 A8 2p vio brn & gray, pair 5.50 *17.50*
a. Single, English .60 *2.00*
b. Single, Afrikaans .60 *2.00*
89 A9 3p red & blk, pair 5.50 *32.50*
a. Single, English .75 *3.00*
b. Single, Afrikaans .75 *3.00*
90 A11 1sh dp bl & bis brn, pair 17.50 *37.50*
a. Single, English 1.75 *4.50*
b. Single, Afrikaans 1.75 *4.50*
91 A12 2sh6p brn & bl grn, pair 40.00 *110.00*
a. Single, English 8.00 *15.00*
b. Single, Afrikaans 8.00 *15.00*
92 A13 5sh dp grn & blk, pair 85.00 *225.00*
a. Single, English 17.50 *22.50*
b. Single, Afrikaans 17.50 *22.50*
93 A14 10sh ol brn & bl, pair 75.00 *180.00*
a. Single, English 12.00 *22.50*
b. Single, Afrikaans 12.00 *22.50*
Nos. 88-93 (6) 228.50 *602.50*

South Africa Nos. 12 and 16a Overprinted at Foot

1927   Typo.   Wmk. 177

94	A2 1sh3p violet	1.50	7.50
a.	Without period after "A"	110.00	
95	A2 £1 lt red & gray grn	110.00	190.00
a.	Without period after "A"	1,750.	2,600.

South Africa Nos. 23-25 Overprinted type "r" at Foot

1927   Wmk. 201   Perf. 14½x14

96	A5 ½p green & blk, pair	2.75	8.00
a.	Single, English	.25	.90
b.	Single, Afrikaans	.25	.90
c.	As #96, without period after "A" on one stamp	47.50	85.00
97	A6 1p car & blk, pair	1.50	3.75
a.	Single, English	.25	.65
b.	Single, Afrikaans	.25	.65
c.	As #97, without period after "A" on one stamp	47.50	85.00
d.	Ovpt. at top, pair ('30)	2.00	16.00
e.	As "d," single, English	.35	1.90
f.	As "d," single, Afrikaans	.35	1.90
98	A7 6p org & grn, pair	11.00	28.00
a.	Single, English	1.75	3.25
b.	Single, Afrikaans	1.75	3.25
c.	As #98, without period after "A" on one stamp	125.00	
	Nos. 96-98 (3)	15.25	39.75

For overprints see Nos. O5-O7.

South Africa Nos. 26-32 Overprinted type "r" at Top

1927-28   Engr.   Perf. 14

99	A8 2p vio brn & gray, pair	10.50	32.50
a.	Single, English	1.25	1.75
b.	Single, Afrikaans	1.25	1.75
c.	As #99, without period after "A" on one stamp	85.00	140.00
d.	Double ovpt., one inverted	800.00	1,050.
100	A9 3p red & blk, pair	7.00	26.00
a.	Single, English	1.00	3.75
b.	Single, Afrikaans	1.00	3.75
c.	As #100, without period after "A" on one stamp	92.50	150.00
101	A10 4p brn, pair ('28)	17.50	45.00
a.	Single, English	1.75	8.00
b.	Single, Afrikaans	1.75	8.00
c.	As #101, without period after "A" on one stamp	97.50	150.00
102	A11 1sh dp bl & bis brn, pair	22.50	55.00
a.	Single, English	1.75	5.75
b.	Single, Afrikaans	1.75	5.75
c.	As #102, without period after "A" on one stamp	1,500.	1,800.
103	A12 2sh6p brn & bl grn, pair	47.50	97.50
a.	Single, English	6.50	14.00
b.	Single, Afrikaans	6.50	14.00
c.	As #103, without period after "A" on one stamp	250.00	400.00
104	A13 5sh dp grn & blk, pair	70.00	140.00
a.	Single, English	9.50	21.00
b.	Single, Afrikaans	9.50	21.00
c.	As #104, without period after "A" on one stamp	325.00	475.00
105	A14 10sh ol brn & bl, pair	110.00	225.00
a.	Single, English	20.00	32.50
b.	Single, Afrikaans	20.00	32.50
c.	As #105, without period after "A" on one stamp	425.00	675.00
	Nos. 99-105 (7)	285.00	621.00

Nos. 99-102 exist perf 14x13½. Values about two times those shown. For overprint see No. O8.

South Africa Nos. 33-34 Overprinted type "r" at Foot

1930   Photo.   Perf. 15x14

106	A5 ½p bl grn & blk, pair	15.00	37.50
a.	Single, English	1.50	3.25
b.	Single, Afrikaans	1.50	3.25
107	A6 1p car rose & blk, pair	10.00	30.00
a.	Single, English	1.25	3.25
b.	Single, Afrikaans	1.25	3.25

Kori Bustard — A15

Cape Cross — A16

Mail Transport — A17

Bogenfels — A18

Windhoek — A19

Waterberg — A20

Lüderitz Bay — A21

Bush Scene — A22

Elands — A23

Zebras and Brindled Gnus — A24

Herero Houses — A25

Welwitschia Plant — A26

Okuwahakan Falls — A27

Perf. 14x13½

1931-37   Wmk. 201   Engr.

108	A15 ½p grn & blk, pair	3.25	3.00
a.	Single, English	.25	.25
b.	Single, Afrikaans	.25	.25
109	A16 1p red & ind, pair	2.75	3.00
a.	Single, English	.25	.25
b.	Single, Afrikaans	.25	.25
110	A17 1½p vio brn, pair ('37)	29.00	4.50
a.	Single, English	1.00	.35
b.	Single, Afrikaans	1.00	.35

111	A18 2p dk brn & dk bl, pair	.80	6.50
a.	Single, English	.25	.25
b.	Single, Afrikaans	.25	.25
112	A19 3p dp bl & gray blk, pair	.80	5.00
a.	Single, English	.25	.25
b.	Single, Afrikaans	.25	.25
113	A20 4p brn vio & grn, pair	2.10	8.00
a.	Single, English	.30	.25
b.	Single, Afrikaans	.30	.25
114	A21 6p ol brn & bl, pair	1.75	11.00
a.	Single, English	.30	.25
b.	Single, Afrikaans	.30	.25
115	A22 1sh bl & vio brn, pair	3.00	15.00
a.	Single, English	.50	.30
b.	Single, Afrikaans	.50	.30
116	A23 1sh3p ocher & pur, pair	8.75	12.50
a.	Single, English	.60	.60
b.	Single, Afrikaans	.60	.60
117	A24 2sh6p dk gray & rose, pair	27.50	27.50
a.	Single, English	2.75	2.00
b.	Single, Afrikaans	2.75	2.00
118	A25 5sh vio brn & ol grn, pair	19.00	45.00
a.	Single, English	3.50	3.25
b.	Single, Afrikaans	3.50	3.25
119	A26 10sh grn & brn, pair	52.50	57.50
a.	Single, English	9.50	7.00
b.	Single, Afrikaans	9.50	7.00
120	A27 20sh bl grn & mar, pair	85.00	95.00
a.	Single, English	12.50	12.50
b.	Single, Afrikaans	12.50	12.50
	Nos. 108-120 (13)	236.20	293.50

For overprints see Nos. O13-O27.

George V — A28

1935, May 6   Perf. 14x13½

121	A28 1p carmine & blk	1.25	.30
122	A28 2p dk brown & blk	1.25	.30
123	A28 3p blue & blk	8.00	22.50
124	A28 6p violet & blk	4.00	13.00
	Nos. 121-124 (4)	14.50	36.10
	Set, never hinged	30.00	

25th anniv. of the reign of George V.

Catalogue values for unused stamps in this section, from this point to the end of the section, are for Never Hinged items.

Coronation Issue
Inscribed alternately in English and Afrikaans

George VI — A29

1937, May 12   Engr.   Perf. 13½x14

125	A29 ½p emer & blk, pair	.45	.25
a.	Single, English	.25	.25
b.	Single, Afrikaans	.25	.25
126	A29 1p car & blk, pair	.45	.25
a.	Single, English	.25	.25
b.	Single, Afrikaans	.25	.25
127	A29 1½p org & blk, pair	.45	.25
a.	Single, English	.25	.25
b.	Single, Afrikaans	.25	.25
128	A29 2p dk brn & blk, pair	.45	.30
a.	Single, English	.25	.25
b.	Single, Afrikaans	.25	.25
129	A29 3p brt bl & blk, pair	.55	.30
a.	Single, English	.25	.25
b.	Single, Afrikaans	.25	.25
130	A29 4p dk vio & blk, pair	.55	.35
a.	Single, English	.25	.25
b.	Single, Afrikaans	.25	.25
131	A29 6p yel & blk, pair	.60	3.25
a.	Single, English	.25	.30
b.	Single, Afrikaans	.25	.30
132	A29 1sh gray & blk, pair	2.00	3.50
a.	Single, English	.25	.75
b.	Single, Afrikaans	.25	.75
	Nos. 125-132 (8)	5.50	8.45

George VI & Queen Elizabeth coronation.

Voortrekker Issue
South Africa Nos. 79-80 Overprinted type "r"

1938, Dec. 14   Photo.   Perf. 15x14

133	A23 1p rose & sl, pair	14.00	22.50
a.	Single, English	1.50	1.75
b.	Single, Afrikaans	1.50	1.75
134	A24 1½p red brn & Prus bl, pair	21.00	27.50
a.	Single, English	2.00	2.25
b.	Single, Afrikaans	2.00	2.25

Issued to commemorate the Voortrekkers.

South Africa Nos. 81-89 Overprinted — s

Perf. 14 (2p, 4p, 6p); 15x14

1941-43   Wmk. 201

135	A25 ½p dp blue grn, pair	1.75	2.75
a.	Single, English	.25	.25
b.	Single, Afrikaans	.25	.25
136	A26 1p brt rose, pair	2.00	3.75
a.	Single, English	.25	.25
b.	Single, Afrikaans	.25	.25
137	A27 1½p Prus grn, pair ('42)	3.00	4.00
a.	Single, English	.25	.25
b.	Single, Afrikaans	.25	.25
138	A28 2p dk violet	.60	1.75
a.	Single, English	1.00	1.25
b.	Single, Afrikaans	1.00	1.25
139	A29 3p dp blue, pair	24.50	26.00
a.	Single, English	1.00	1.25
b.	Single, Afrikaans	1.00	1.25
140	A30 4p brown, pair	7.50	20.00
a.	Single, English	.80	1.00
b.	Single, Afrikaans	.80	1.00
141	A31 6p brt red org, pair	8.00	9.00
a.	Single, English	.75	1.00
b.	Single, Afrikaans	.75	1.00
142	A32 1sh dk brown	1.60	2.00
143	A33 1sh3p dk ol brn, pair ('43)	15.00	24.50
a.	Single, English	1.25	1.50
b.	Single, Afrikaans	1.25	1.50
	Nos. 135-143 (9)	63.95	93.75

South Africa Nos. 90-97 Overprinted

t   u

Pairs or Strips of 3 Perf. 14 or 15x14 all around, Rouletted 6½ or 13 btwn.

1942-45   Wmk. 201

144	A34(t) ½p dp grn, horiz. strip of 3	.75	7.00
a.	Single, English	.25	.25
b.	Single, Afrikaans	.25	.25
c.	½p dp bl grn, horiz. strip of 3	4.25	7.50
d.	As "c," single, English	.25	.25
e.	As "c," single, Afrikaans	.25	.25
145	A35(t) 1p brt car, horiz. strip of 3	3.50	7.00
a.	Single, English	.25	.25
b.	Single, Afrikaans	.25	.25
c.	1p rose car, horiz. strip of 3	4.00	7.00
d.	As "c," single, English	.25	.25
e.	As "c," single, Afrikaans	.25	.25
146	A36(u) 1½p cop brn, horiz. pair	.75	1.75
a.	Single, English	.25	.25
b.	Single, Afrikaans	.25	.25
147	A37(t) 2p dk vio, horiz. pair	8.50	5.50
a.	Single, English	.25	.25
b.	Single, Afrikaans	.25	.25
148	A38(t) 3p dp bl, vert. strip of 3	4.00	22.50
a.	Single, English	.25	.65
b.	Single, Afrikaans	.25	.65
149	A39(t) 4p sl grn, vert. strip of 3	5.00	22.50
a.	Single	.30	.35
b.	As "c," single	55.00	60.00
c.	Invtd. ovpt., strip of 3	850.00	550.00
150	A40(t) 6p brt red org, horiz. pair	7.00	3.00
a.	Single, English	.30	.35
b.	Single, Afrikaans	.30	.35
c.	Inverted overprint, pair	650.00	
d.	As "c," single, English	60.00	60.00
e.	As "c," single, Afrikaans	60.00	60.00
151	A41(u) 1sh dk brn, vert. pair	15.00	29.00
a.	Single	1.25	2.00
b.	As "c," single	85.00	
c.	Inverted overprint, pair	700.00	375.00

152	A41(t)	1sh dk brn, vert. pair	5.00	6.50
a.		Single	.30	*.35*
b.		As "c," single	55.00	40.00
c.		Invtd. ovpt., vert. pair	600.00	350.00
		Nos. 144-152 (9)	49.50	104.75

Issue years: #144-145, 147-151, 1943; #152, 1944; #144c, 145c, 149c, 1945.

Peace Issue

South Africa Nos. 100-102 Overprinted Type "w"

1945, Dec. 3 Wmk. 201 ***Perf. 14***

153	A42	1p rose pink & choc, pair	.40	.75
a.		Single, English	.25	.25
b.		Single, Afrikaans	.25	.25
c.		Inverted overprint, pair	400.00	425.00
d.		As "c," single, English	40.00	
e.		As "c," single, Afrikaans	40.00	
154	A43	2p vio & sl bl, pair	.40	.75
a.		Single, English	.25	.25
b.		Single, Afrikaans	.25	.25
155	A43	3p ultra & dp ultra, pair	1.75	*2.00*
a.		Single, English	.30	.25
b.		Single, Afrikaans	.30	.25
		Nos. 153-155 (3)	2.55	3.50

WW II victory of the Allies.

Royal Visit Issue

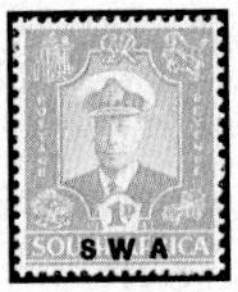

South Africa Nos. 103-105 Overprinted

1947, Feb. 17 ***Perf. 15x14***

156	A44	1p cerise & gray, pair	.30	.25
a.		Single, English	.25	.25
b.		Single, Afrikaans	.25	.25
157	A45	2p purple, pair	.30	.60
a.		Single, English	.25	.25
b.		Single, Afrikaans	.25	.25
158	A46	3p dk blue, pair	.40	.45
a.		Single, English	.25	.25
b.		Single, Afrikaans	.30	.25
		Nos. 156-158 (3)	1.00	1.30

Visit of the British Royal Family, Mar.-Apr., 1947.

South Africa No. 106 Overprinted

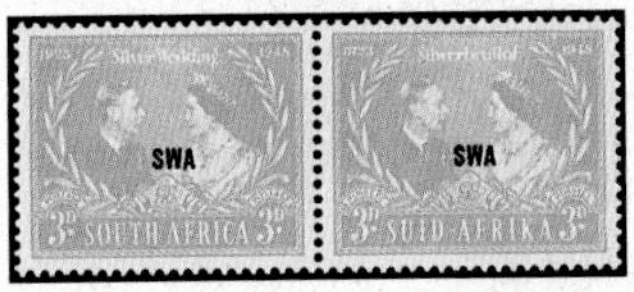

1948, Apr. 26 ***Perf. 14***

159	A47	3p dp chalky bl & sil, pair	1.25	.35
a.		Single, English	.25	.25
b.		Single, Afrikaans	.25	.25

25th anniv. of the marriage of George VI and Queen Elizabeth.

UPU Issue

South Africa Nos. 109-111 Overprinted type "w" 13mm wide

1949, Oct. 1 ***Perf. 14x15***

160	A50	½p dk green, pair	1.10	*2.25*
a.		Single, English	.25	*.30*
b.		Single, Afrikaans	.25	*.30*
161	A50	1½p dk red, pair	1.10	*1.75*
a.		Single, English	.25	.25
b.		Single, Afrikaans	.25	.25
162	A50	3p ultra, pair	1.75	*2.00*
a.		Single, English	.25	*.30*
b.		Single, Afrikaans	.25	*.30*
		Nos. 160-162 (3)	3.95	6.00

75th anniv. of the UPU.

This ends the bi-lingual multiples in the postage section.

Voortrekker Monument Issue

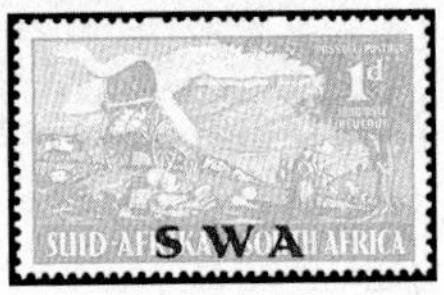

South Africa Nos. 112-114 Ovptd.

1949, Dec. 1 ***Perf. 15x14***

163	A51	1p magenta	.25	.25
164	A52	1½p dull green	.25	.25
165	A53	3p dark blue	.30	.30
		Nos. 163-165 (3)	.80	.80

Inauguration of the Voortrekker Monument at Pretoria.

South Africa Nos. 115-119 Overprinted

w

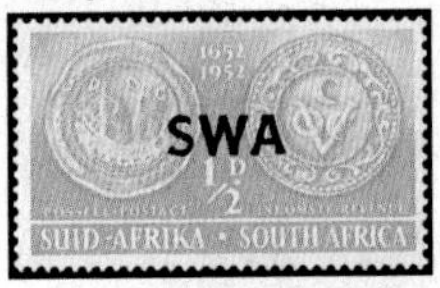

x

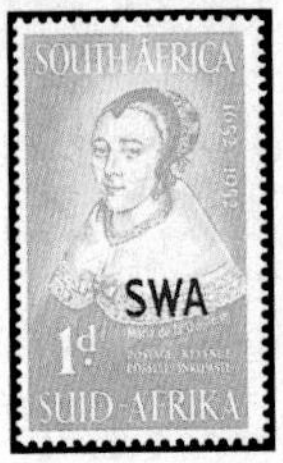

1952, Mar. 14 ***Perf. 15x14, 14x15***

166	A54(w)	½p dk brn & red vio	.40	*.50*
167	A55(x)	1p dark green	.40	.40
168	A54(w)	2p dark purple	.85	.40
169	A55(x)	4½p dark blue	.85	*2.00*
170	A54(w)	1sh brown	1.75	1.00
		Nos. 166-170 (5)	4.25	4.30

300th anniv. of the landing of Jan van Riebeeck at the Cape of Good Hope.

Coronation Issue

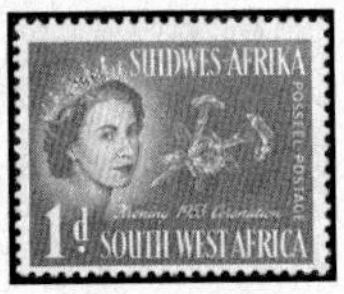

Queen Elizabeth II and Flowers — A54

Various flowers.

1953, June 2 Photo. ***Perf. 14***

244	A54	1p carmine rose	.55	.30
245	A54	2p dark green	.55	.30
246	A54	4p deep magenta	1.10	.65
247	A54	6p deep blue	1.10	1.00
248	A54	1sh chestnut brown	1.60	1.25
		Nos. 244-248 (5)	4.90	3.50

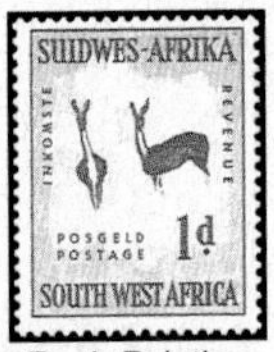

Rock Painting of Two Bucks — A55

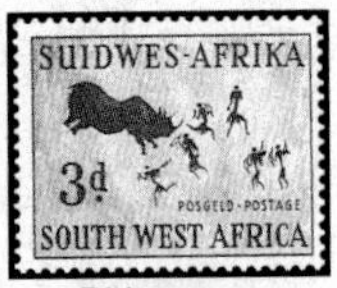

Rhinoceros Hunt — A56

Designs: 2p, "White Lady" (rock painting). 4p, Elephant and giraffe (rock painting). 4½p, Karakul lamb. 6p, Owambo blowing Kudu horn. 1sh, Ukuanjama woman. 1sh3p, Herero woman. 1sh6p, Ukuanjama girl. 2sh6p, Lioness. 5sh, Cape Oryx. 10sh, Elephant.

1954, Nov. 15 Wmk. 201 ***Perf. 14***

249	A55	1p rose brown	.55	.25
250	A55	2p dk brown	.55	.25
251	A56	3p brown vio	1.40	.25
252	A56	4p olive gray	1.75	.25
253	A55	4½p blue vio	1.10	.25
254	A55	6p gray green	1.50	.40
255	A55	1sh magenta	2.10	.50
256	A55	1sh3p rose pink	4.00	1.25
257	A55	1sh6p dull purple	4.50	1.10
258	A55	2sh6p yel brown	8.50	2.50
259	A55	5sh blue	19.00	6.00
260	A55	10sh dk green	37.50	16.00
		Nos. 249-260 (12)	82.45	29.00

1960 Wmk. 330 ***Perf. 14***

261	A55	1p rose brown	1.50	.60
262	A55	2p dark brown	1.75	.80
263	A56	3p brown vio	2.40	1.50
264	A56	4p olive gray	5.50	6.25
265	A55	1sh6p dull purple	26.00	21.00
		Nos. 261-265 (5)	37.15	30.15

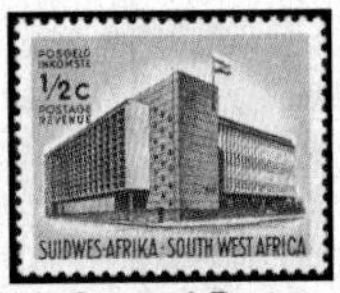

General Post Office, Windhoek — A57

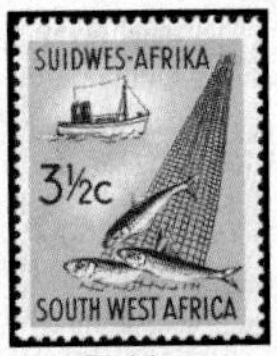

Fishing Industry — A58

Designs: 1c, Finger Rock, Asab. 1½c, Monument, Mounted Soldier. 2c, Quivertree (aloe dichotoma Masson). 2½c, Administrator's residence. 3c, Swakopmund Lighthouse and flamingoes. 5c, Flamingo. 7½c, Christchurch. 10c, Diamonds. 12½c, Fort Namutoni. 15c, Hardap Dam. 20c, Topaz. 50c, Tourmaline. 1r, Heliodor.

1961-63 Wmk. 330 Photo. ***Perf. 14***

266	A57	½c blue & brown	.70	.35
267	A58	1c pale lil & brn	.35	.30
268	A58	1½c sal & dk pur	.35	.30
269	A58	2c yel & green	1.00	*1.40*
270	A57	2½c lt bl & red brn	.75	.35
271	A58	3c dp rose & vio bl	5.50	1.25
272	A58	3½c blue grn & ind	1.00	.40
273	A58	5c bluish gray & red	8.00	2.10
274	A58	7½c yellow & brn	.90	.90
275	A58	10c brt blue & yel	1.75	.55
276	A57	12½c yellow & ind	2.75	2.75
277	A57	15c dp brn & blue	16.00	5.75
278	A58	20c sal, brn & blk	5.50	2.10
279	A58	50c org yel & Prus grn	7.75	5.50
280	A58	1r brt blue, mar & yel	10.00	*12.00*
		Nos. 266-280 (15)	62.30	36.00

Issued: 3c, 10/1/62; 15c, 3/16/63; others, 2/14/61.

1962-73 **Unwmk.**

281	A57	½c blue & brn	.60	*2.25*
282	A58	1½c sal & dk pur ('63)	6.75	.55
283	A58	2c yellow & grn	5.25	5.00
284	A57	2½c lt bl & red brn ('64)	9.00	7.00
285	A58	3c dp rose & vio bl ('73)	2.50	1.50
286	A58	3½c bl grn & ind ('66)	12.00	5.50
287	A58	5c bluish gray & red	7.75	3.25
		Nos. 281-287 (7)	43.85	25.05

See Nos. 304-308, 314-328.

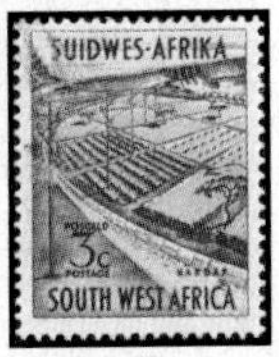

Hardap Dam and Development — A59

1963, Mar. 16 **Wmk. 330**

294	A59	3c sepia green	.90	.90

Opening of Hardap Dam near Mariental.

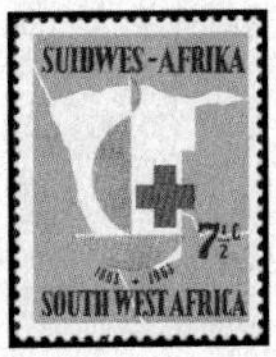

Centenary Emblem and S.W.A. Map — A60

Design: 15c, Emblem and globe.

1963, Aug. 30 Unwmk. ***Perf. 14***

295	A60	7½c blue, blk & red	5.75	5.00
296	A60	15c brn org, blk & red	12.00	8.00

Centenary of the International Red Cross.

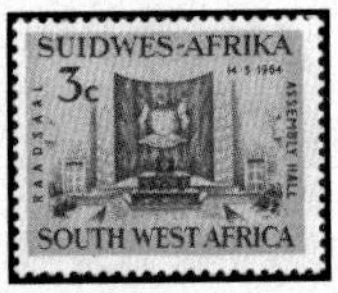

Assembly Hall — A61

1964, May 14 Photo. Wmk. 330

297	A61	3c salmon pink & vio bl	.90	.75

Issued to commemorate the opening of the new hall of the Legislative Assembly.

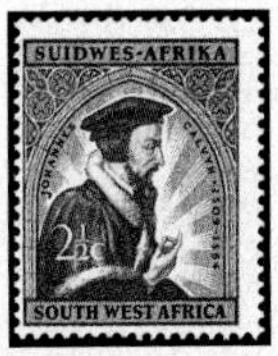

John Calvin — A62

1964, Oct. 1 Unwmk. ***Perf. 14***

298	A62	2½c magenta & gold	.50	.55
299	A62	15c green & gold	3.75	3.75

John Calvin (1509-64), French theologian and leader of the Reformation.

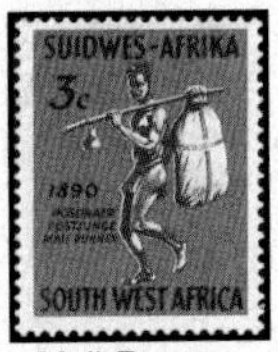

Mail Runner, 1890 — A63

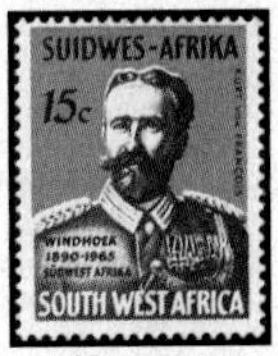

Kurt von François — A64

Wmk. 348

1965, Oct. 18 Photo. ***Perf. 14***

300	A63	3c red & deep brown	.55	.30
301	A64	15c green & deep brn	2.75	1.75

75th anniversary of Windhoek.

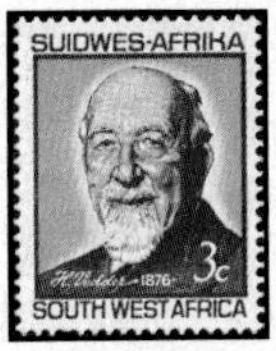

Dr. H. H. Vedder, Missionary, Educator and Senator, 90th Birthday — A65

1966, July 4 ***Perf. 14***

302	A65	3c black & salmon	.40	.30
303	A65	15c black & light blue	2.50	2.25

Types of 1961-62

1966-67 Wmk. 348 Photo. ***Perf. 14***

Chalky Paper

304	A57	½c lt blue & brn	*2.00*	*.50*
304A	A58	1c pale lil & brn	.75	.25
305	A58	2c brt yel & dp grn	.75	.25
306	A57	2½c gray blue & red brn	1.00	.25
307	A58	3½c pale grn & vio bl	4.25	2.00
308	A58	7½c brt yel & brn	4.00	.80
		Nos. 304-308 (6)	*12.75*	*4.05*

The watermark on Nos. 304, 305-308 is very faint, and these stamps can be distinguished by the shades and by the thick chalky paper. The watermark on No. 304A is clear.

Issued: 2c, 2½c, 1966; others, 1967.

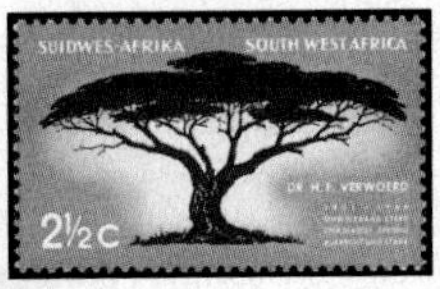

Camelthorn Tree — A66

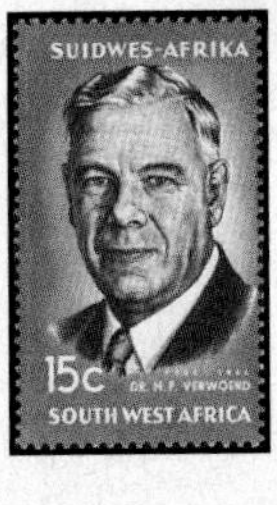

Verwoerd — A67

Design: 3c, Waves breaking against rock.

Perf. 14, 14x15 (15c)

1967, Jan. 6 Litho. Wmk. 348

309	A66 2½c green & black	.30	.25
310	A67 3c brt blue & brown	.40	.25
311	A67 15c rose lilac & black	2.75	2.50
	Nos. 309-311 (3)	3.45	3.00

Dr. Hendrik F. Verwoerd (1901-1966), Prime Minister of South Africa.

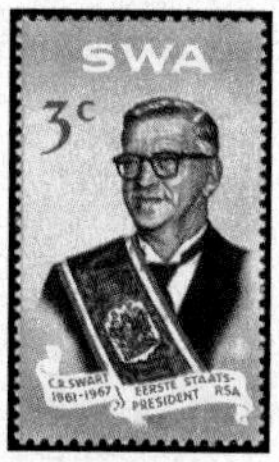

Swart — A68

15c, President and Mrs. C. R. Swart.

Perf. 14x15

1968, Jan. 2 Photo. Wmk. 359

312	Strip of 3	4.00	4.00
a.	A68 3c Single, English	.45	.30
b.	A68 3c Single, Afrikaans	.45	.30
c.	A68 3c Single, German	.45	.30
313	Strip of 3	11.00	11.00
a.	A68 15c Single, English	2.75	2.00
b.	A68 15c Single, Afrikaans	2.75	2.00
c.	A68 15c Single, German	2.75	2.00

Charles Robberts Swart, 1st president of South Africa, (1961-67).

Types of 1961-62

Designs: 4c, like 2½c. 6c, Christchurch. 9c, Fort Namutoni.

1968-72 Wmk. 359 Photo. *Perf. 14*

314	A57 ½c blue & brown	1.25	.25
315	A57 ½c blue & brn, redrawn ('70)	2.50	1.00
316	A58 1c pale lilac & brn ('70)	1.00	.25
317	A58 1½c salmon & dk pur	1.25	.35
318	A58 1½c sal & dk pur, redrawn ('71)	15.00	17.50
319	A58 2c yel & grn, redrawn ('70)	4.00	.35
320	A57 2½c lt bl & red brn ('70)	2.00	.30
321	A58 3c dp rose & vio bl ('70)	8.50	1.75
322	A57 4c lt bl & red brn ('71)	2.00	1.50
323	A58 5c bluish gray & red	4.25	.45
324	A58 6c yel & brn ('71)	8.75	7.50
325	A57 9c yel & ind ('71)	10.00	9.00
326	A58 10c brt bl & yel ('70)	18.00	2.50
327	A57 15c dp brn & bl ('72)	25.00	7.00
328	A58 20c org, brn & blk	19.00	2.00
	Nos. 314-328 (15)	122.50	51.70

Nos. 315, 318-319 are without inscription "Posgeld Incomste Postage Revenue" and the numerals have been enlarged. The ½c (#315), 2c and 10c were also issued as coils.

Water Type of South Africa, 1970

2½c, Water drop and flower. 3c, Waves, horiz.

1970, Feb. 14 *Perf. 14*

329	A142 2½c brown, brt bl & grn	.80	.50
330	A142 3c pale gray, bl & indigo	1.00	.60

Water '70 campaign of the South African Department of Water Affairs.

Bible Society Types of South Africa

Designs: 2½c, Sower, stained glass window. 12½c, "BIBLIA" and open book.

1970, Aug. 24 Photo. *Perf. 14*

331	A143 2½c multicolored	1.10	.55

Photo.; Gold Impressed

332	A144 12½c ultra, blk & gold	11.00	8.00

South African Bible Soc., 150th anniv.

Stamp Exhibition Types of South Africa

Perf. 14x13½, 13½x14

1971, May 31 Photo. Wmk. 359

333	A145 5c blue, yel & blk	4.00	3.25
334	A146 12½c grnsh bl, vio bl & red	47.50	27.50

Intl. Stamp Exhib. (INTERSTEX), Cape Town, May 22-31. No. 334 also for the 10th anniv. of the Antarctic Treaty pledging peaceful uses of and scientific cooperation in Antarctica.

Republic Anniversary Types of South Africa

1971, May 31 *Perf. 14*

335	A147 2c mag, rose red & buff	2.00	1.25
336	A148 4c blue green & black	4.25	1.50

10th anniv. of the Republic of South Africa.

Cat Type of South Africa

1972, Sept. 19 *Perf. 14*

337	A152 5c multicolored	3.75	2.75

Cent. of the SPCA.

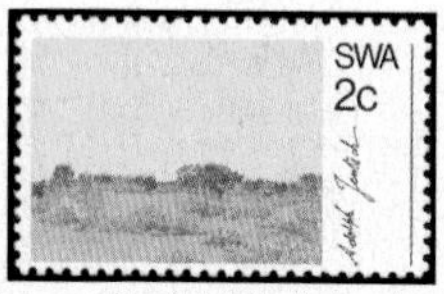

Landscape, by Adolph Jentsch — A69

Designs: Various landscapes by Adolph Jentsch (1888-1977). 10c, 15c, vert.

1973, Apr. 28 Litho. *Perf. 11½x12½*

338	A69 2c multicolored	.85	.85
339	A69 4c multicolored	1.40	1.40
340	A69 5c multicolored	1.75	1.75
341	A69 10c multicolored	3.00	3.00
342	A69 15c multicolored	5.00	5.00
	Nos. 338-342 (5)	12.00	12.00

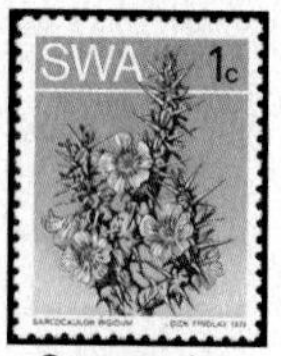

Sarcocaulon Rigidum A70

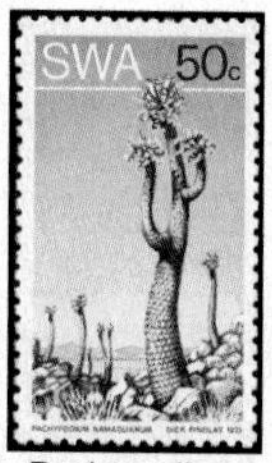

Pachypodium Namaqua-num A71

Designs: 1c-50c, Various succulent plants. 1r, Welwitschia. 30c, 1r, horiz.

1973, Sept. 1 Litho. *Perf. 12½*

Plants in Natural Colors

343	A70 1c light blue	.25	.25
344	A70 2c yellow	.25	.25
345	A70 3c salmon pink	.25	.25
346	A70 4c gray	.30	.25
347	A70 5c blue	.50	.25
348	A70 6c greenish gray	2.50	*3.00*
349	A70 7c bright yellow	1.50	*2.00*
350	A70 9c dull yellow	1.00	*1.75*
351	A70 10c blue green	.60	.25
352	A70 14c yellow green	2.00	*2.25*
353	A70 15c light brown	1.50	.50
354	A70 20c light olive	5.00	3.50
355	A70 25c orange	5.00	4.00

Perf. 12x12½, 12½x12

356	A71 30c dull yellow	1.25	1.00
357	A71 50c light green	1.75	1.50
358	A71 1r blue green	2.00	5.00
	Nos. 343-358 (16)	25.65	26.00

1979 Same Designs *Perf. 14*

344a	A70 2c	.70	.35
345a	A70 3c	.70	.35
347a	A70 5c	1.00	.50
351a	A70 10c	1.00	.50
356a	A70 30c	1.75	.75
357a	A70 50c	3.00	.90
	Nos. 344a-357a (6)	8.15	3.35

Coil Stamps

1973, Sept. 1 Photo. *Perf. 14*

359	A70 1c brt pink & black	1.00	.70
360	A70 2c yellow & black	.75	.60
361	A70 5c red & black	1.75	.80

1978 *Perf. 14 Vertically*

361A	A70 1c brt pink & black	5.00	4.00
362	A70 2c yellow & black	1.50	.50
362A	A70 5c red & black	1.50	.65
	Nos. 359-362A (6)	11.50	7.25

For overprints, see Nos. 423-428.

NOTE: coil stamps, Nos. 359-362A, are printed in two colors, sheet stamps are multicolored.

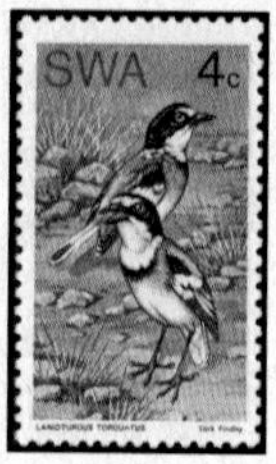

Chat-shrike — A72

Rare birds: 5c, Rosy-faced lovebirds. 10c, Damara rockjumper. 15c, Ruppell's parrot.

Perf. 12½x11½

1974, Feb. 13 Litho.

363	A72 4c shown	3.25	2.00
364	A72 5c multicolored	4.50	2.50
365	A72 10c multicolored	11.00	8.50
366	A72 15c multicolored	18.50	15.00
	Nos. 363-366 (4)	37.25	28.00

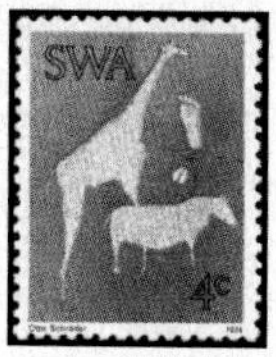

Rock Carvings, Twyfelfontein — A73

1974, Apr. 10 Litho. *Perf. 12½*

367	A73 4c Giraffe & horse	1.50	.85
368	A73 5c Elephant	2.25	1.10

Perf. 12x12½

Size: 37x21½mm

369	A73 15c Deer, horiz.	9.50	5.25
	Nos. 367-369 (3)	13.25	7.20

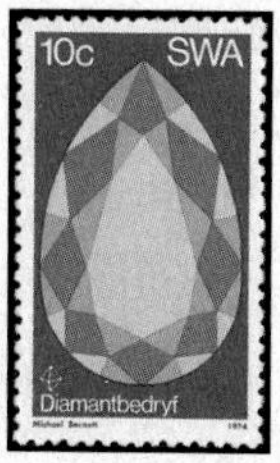

Mining — A74

1974, Sept. 30 *Perf. 12½x11½*

370	A74 10c Diamonds	5.50	3.75
371	A74 15c Diamond open pit mining	6.75	4.75

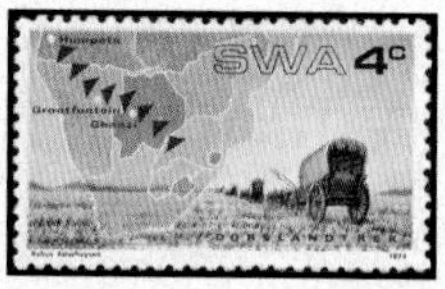

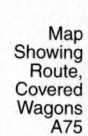

Map Showing Route, Covered Wagons A75

Perf. 11½x12

1974, Nov. 13 Unwmk.

372	A75 4c yellow & multi	1.10	.90

Centenary of "Thirstland Trek" from Transvaal through Kalahari Desert to Angola.

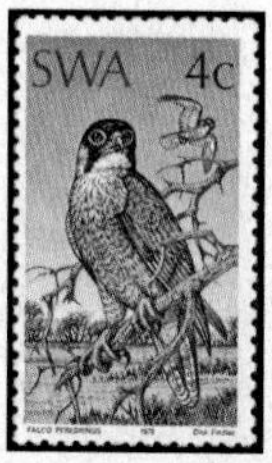

Peregrine Falcon — A76

Designs: Protected Birds of Prey.

1975, Mar. 19 *Perf. 12½x11½*

373	A76 4c shown	2.75	1.50
374	A76 5c Black eagle	3.25	1.75
375	A76 10c Martial eagle	7.00	4.50
376	A76 15c Egyptian vulture	9.50	7.50
	Nos. 373-376 (4)	22.50	15.25

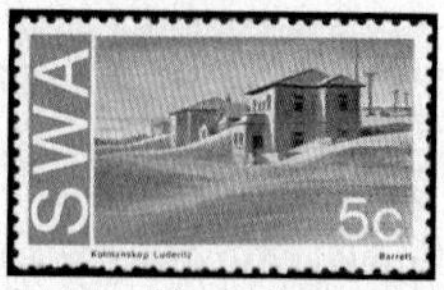

Kolmanskop, Ghost Diamond Mining Town — A77

Designs: 9c, German steam traction engine, 1896. 15c, Old Fort, Windhoek and statue of Colonial German trooper on horseback.

1975, July 23 Litho. *Perf. 12x12½*

377	A77 5c violet & multi	.30	.30
378	A77 9c ocher & multi	.70	.70
379	A77 15c yellow & multi	1.10	1.10
	Nos. 377-379 (3)	2.10	2.10

Historic monuments.

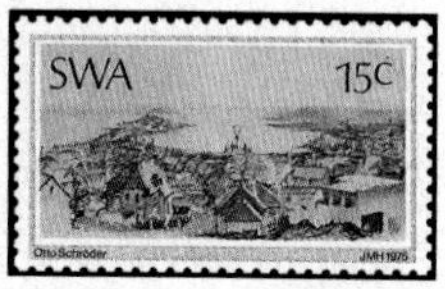

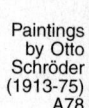

Paintings by Otto Schröder (1913-75) A78

1975, Oct. 15 Litho. *Perf. 12x12½*

380	A78 15c Luderitz	1.00	1.00
381	A78 15c Swakopmund	1.00	1.00
382	A78 15c Unloading freighters	1.00	1.00
383	A78 15c Ships at anchor, Walvis Bay	1.00	1.00
a.	Souvenir sheet of 4, #380-383	5.00	5.00
b.	Block of 4, #380-383	4.50	4.50

No. 383a has a horizontal gutter with black inscription on silver panel.

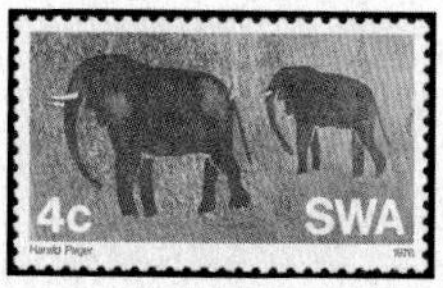

Elephants A79

Pre-historic Rock Paintings: 10c, Rhinoceros. 15c, Antelope and hunter. 20c, Hunter with bow and arrow.

1976, Mar. 12 Litho. *Perf. 12x12½*

384	A79 4c red brown & multi	.25	.25
385	A79 10c red brown & multi	.55	.55
386	A79 15c red brown & multi	.85	.85
387	A79 20c red brown & multi	1.40	1.40
a.	Souvenir sheet of 4, #384-387	3.75	3.75
	Nos. 384-387 (4)	3.05	3.05

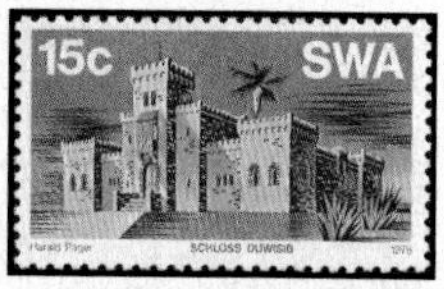

Schloss Duwisib A80

Castles Built by German Settlers: 10c, Schwerinsburg. 20c, Heynitzburg.

1976, May 14 Litho. *Perf. 12x12½*

388	A80 10c multicolored	.55	.55
389	A80 15c multicolored	.85	.85
390	A80 20c multicolored	1.10	1.10
	Nos. 388-390 (3)	2.50	2.50

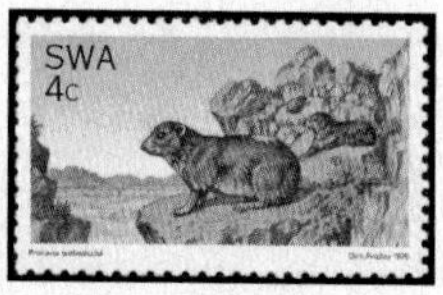

Nature Protection A81

1976, July 16 Litho. *Perf. 11½x12½*

391	A81 4c Daman	.40	.40
392	A81 10c Dik-diks	1.00	1.25
393	A81 15c Tree squirrel	1.50	1.50
	Nos. 391-393 (3)	2.90	3.15

Augustineum Training Institute,
Windhoek — A82

20c, Katutura State Hospital, Windhoek.

1976, Sept. 17 Litho. Perf. 12x12½
394 A82 15c ocher & black .55 .55
395 A82 20c citron & black .75 .75

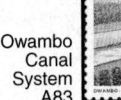

Owambo
Canal
System
A83

20c, Ruacana Dam and hydroelectric
station.

1976, Nov. 19 Litho. Perf. 12x12½
396 A83 15c multicolored .55 .55
397 A83 20c multicolored .75 .75

Water and electricity supply.

Sinking Ship off Namib Shore — A84

Designs: Namib Desert, various views.

1977, Mar. 29 Litho. Perf. 12½
398 A84 4c multicolored .25 .25
399 A84 10c multicolored .45 .45
400 A84 15c multicolored .70 .65
401 A84 20c multicolored 1.00 .95
Nos. 398-401 (4) 2.40 2.30

Owambo
Kraal
A85

Designs: 10c, Giant grain baskets. 15c,
Women pounding corn. 20c, Body painting.

1977, July 15 Litho. Perf. 12x12½
402 A85 4c multicolored .25 .25
403 A85 10c multicolored .35 .35
404 A85 15c multicolored .50 .50
405 A85 20c multicolored .80 .80
Nos. 402-405 (4) 1.90 1.90

Traditions of the Wambo people.

J. G. Strijdom Airport,
Windhoek — A86

1977, Aug. 22 Perf. 12½
406 A86 20c multicolored .55 .45

Drostdy,
Lüderitz,
1910
A87

Historic Houses: 10c, Woermannhaus,
Swakopmund, 1895. 15c, Neu-Heusis, Windhoek. 20c, Schmelenhaus, Bethanie, 1814.

1977, Nov. 4 Litho. Perf. 12x12½
407 A87 5c multicolored .25 .25
408 A87 10c multicolored .35 .35
409 A87 15c multicolored .55 .55
410 A87 20c multicolored .75 .75
a. Souvenir sheet of 4, #407-410 2.25 2.25
Nos. 407-410 (4) 1.90 1.90

Side-winding
Adder — A88

Small Animals of the Namib Desert: 10c,
Golden sand mole. 15c, Palmato gecko. 20c,
Namaqua chameleon.

1978, Feb. 6 Litho. Perf. 12½
411 A88 4c multicolored .25 .25
412 A88 10c multicolored .40 .40
413 A88 15c multicolored .60 .60
414 A88 20c multicolored .85 .85
Nos. 411-414 (4) 2.10 2.10

Bushman
Hunter
Disguised
as Ostrich
A89

Bushmen: 10c, Woman carrying ostrich
eggs on back. 15c, Making fire. 20c, Family
sitting in front of hut.

1978, Apr. 14 Litho. Perf. 12x12½
415 A89 4c brown, buff & blk .25 .25
416 A89 10c brown, buff & blk .30 .30
417 A89 15c brown, buff & blk .50 .50
418 A89 20c brown, buff & blk .65 .65
Nos. 415-418 (4) 1.70 1.70

Lutheran Church, Windhoek — A90

Designs: 10c, Lutheran Church,
Swakopmund. 15c, Rhenish Mission Church,
Otjimbingwe. 20c, Rhenish Mission Church,
Keetmanshoop.

1978, June 16 Litho. Perf. 12½
419 A90 4c ol bister & blk .25 .25
420 A90 10c bister & blk .30 .30
421 A90 15c pale red brn & blk .50 .50
422 A90 20c blue gray & blk .65 .65
a. Souvenir sheet of 4, #419-422 1.75 1.75
Nos. 419-422 (4) 1.70 1.70

**Type of 1973 Inscribed in English,
German or Afrikaans:**

a, UNIVERSAL / SUFFRAGE
b, ALLGEMEINES / WAHLRECHT
c, ALGEMENE / STEMREG

1978, Nov. 1 Litho. Perf. 12½
423 Strip of 3 .25 .25
a.-c. A70 4c any single .25 .25
424 Strip of 3 .30 .30
a.-c. A70 5c any single .25 .25
425 Strip of 3 .60 .60
a.-c. A70 10c any single .25 .25
426 Strip of 3 .90 .90
a.-c. A70 15c any single .25 .25
427 Strip of 3 1.20 1.20
a.-c. A70 20c any single .35 .35
428 Strip of 3 1.60 1.60
a.-c. A70 25c any single .50 .50
Nos. 423-428 (6) 4.85 4.85

General suffrage. Printed se-tenant with
inscriptions alternating horizontally and vertically in sheets of 30 (3x10).

Greater
Flamingoes
A91

Water Birds: 15c, White-breasted cormorants. 20c, Chestnut-banded plovers. 25c,
White pelicans.

1979, Apr. 5 Litho. Perf. 14x14½
429 A91 4c multicolored .25 .25
430 A91 15c multicolored .40 .40
431 A91 20c multicolored .55 .55
432 A91 25c multicolored .70 .70
Nos. 429-432 (4) 1.90 1.90

Silver
Topaz
A92

1979, Nov. 26 Litho. Perf. 14x14½
433 A92 4c shown .30 .30
434 A92 15c Aquamarine .50 .50
435 A92 20c Malachite .80 .80
436 A92 25c Amethyst .95 .95
Nos. 433-436 (4) 2.55 2.55

Killer
Whale — A93

5c, Humpback whale. 10c, Southern right
whale. 15c, Sperm whale, giant squid. 20c,
Fin whale. 25c, Blue whale, diver.

1980, Mar. 25 Litho. Perf. 14x14½
437 A93 4c shown .35 .30

Size: 37½x21mm
438 A93 5c multicolored .40 .30
439 A93 10c multicolored .75 .55

Size: 57½x21mm
440 A93 15c multicolored 1.25 .85
441 A93 20c multicolored 1.75 1.10

Size: 87½x21mm
442 A93 25c multicolored 1.90 1.25
a. Souvenir sheet of 6, #437-442 7.00 7.00
Nos. 437-442 (6) 6.40 4.35

Impala
A94

1980, June 25 Litho. Perf. 14½x14
443 A94 5c shown .25 .25
444 A94 10c Tsessebe .30 .30
445 A94 15c Roan antelope .40 .40
446 A94 20c Sable antelope .55 .55
Nos. 443-446 (4) 1.50 1.50

Cape Hunting
Dog — A95

1c, Black backed jackal. 3c, Hyena. 4c, Dorcas antelope. 5c, Oryx. 6c, Greater kudu. 7c,
Zebra, horiz. 8c, Porcupine, horiz. 9c, Honey
badger, horiz. 10c, Cheetah, horiz. 11c, Blue
wildebeest ('84). 12c, Syncerus caffer, horiz.
('85). 15c, Hippopotamus, horiz. 20c, Taurotragus oryx, horiz. 25c, Rhinoceros, horiz.
30c, Lion, horiz. 50c, Giraffe. 1r, Leopard. 2r,
Elephant.
No. 464, Suricate suricate. No. 465, Guenon. No. 466, South African chacma.

1980-85 Litho. Perf. 14½x14
447 A95 1c multicolored .25 .25
448 A95 2c multicolored .25 .25
449 A95 3c multicolored .25 .25
450 A95 4c multicolored .25 .25
451 A95 5c multicolored .25 .25
452 A95 6c multicolored .25 .25

Perf. 14x14¼14½
453 A95 7c multicolored .25 .25
454 A95 8c multicolored .25 .25
455 A95 9c multicolored .25 .25
456 A95 10c multicolored .25 .25
456A A95 11c multicolored .85 .35
456B A95 12c multicolored .55 .30
c. Booklet pane of 10 5.50

Perf. 14x14½
457 A95 15c multicolored .30 .30
458 A95 20c multicolored .45 .45
459 A95 25c multicolored .55 .55
460 A95 30c multicolored .65 .65

Perf. 14½x14
461 A95 50c multicolored 1.00 1.00
462 A95 1r multicolored 1.75 1.75
463 A95 2r multicolored 3.75 3.25
Nos. 447-463 (19) 12.35 11.10

Coil Stamps

1980, Oct. 1 Litho. Perf. 14 Vert.
464 A95 1c multicolored .40 .40
465 A95 2c multicolored .40 .40
466 A95 5c multicolored .40 .40
Nos. 464-466 (3) 1.20 1.20

See Nos. 556-557.

Von Bach Dam, Swakop River — A96

1980, Nov. 25 Litho. Perf. 14x14½
467 A96 5c shown .25 .25
468 A96 10c Swakoppoort Dam .25 .25
469 A96 15c Naute Dam .25 .25
470 A96 20c Hardap Dam .35 .35
Nos. 467-470 (4) 1.10 1.10

Water conservation in the desert.

Fish River Canyon — A97

Designs: Views of Fish River Canyon.

1981, Mar. 20 Litho. Perf. 14½x14
471 A97 5c multicolored .25 .25
472 A97 15c multicolored .25 .25
473 A97 20c multicolored .25 .25
474 A97 25c multicolored .30 .30
Nos. 471-474 (4) 1.05 1.05

Aloe Erinacea — A98

1981, Aug. 14
475 A98 5c shown .25 .25
476 A98 15c Aloe viridiflora .25 .25
477 A98 20c Aloe pearsonii .30 .30
478 A98 25c Aloe littoralis .30 .30
Nos. 475-478 (4) 1.10 1.10

Paul Weiss-Haus Building, 1909,
Luderitz — A99

Historic buildings in Luderitz: 15c, Deutsche
Afrika Bank, 1906. 20c, Schroederhaus, 1911.
25c, Imperial P.O., 1908.

1981, Oct. 16
479 A99 5c shown .25 .25
480 A99 15c multicolored .25 .25
481 A99 20c multicolored .30 .30
482 A99 25c multicolored .40 .40
a. Souvenir sheet of 4, #479-482 1.25 1.25
Nos. 479-482 (4) 1.20 1.20

Salt
Making
A100

5c, Salt pan. 15c, Dumping and washing.
20c, Stockpiling. 25c, Loading.

1981, Dec. 4　Litho.　Perf. 14x14½
483	A100	5c multicolored	.25	.25
484	A100	15c multicolored	.25	.25
485	A100	20c multicolored	.25	.25
486	A100	25c multicolored	.30	.30
		Nos. 483-486 (4)	1.05	1.05

Kalahari
Starred
Tortoise
A101

1982, Mar. 12
487	A101	5c shown	.25	.25
488	A101	15c Leopard tortoise	.25	.25
489	A101	20c Angulated tortoise	.45	.45
490	A101	25c Speckled padloper	.55	.55
		Nos. 487-490 (4)	1.50	1.50

Discoverers of South-West
Africa — A102

15c, Archbishop Olaus Magnus, sea monster. 20c, Bartolomeu Dias, ships, map. 25c, Caravel. 30c, Dias erecting cross, Angra das Voltas.

1982, May 28　Litho.　Perf. 14½x14
491	A102	15c multicolored	.25	.25
492	A102	20c multicolored	.40	.30
493	A102	25c multicolored	.65	.45
494	A102	30c multicolored	.70	.50
		Nos. 491-494 (4)	2.00	1.45

The
Needle,
Upper
Brandberg
A103

Mountain peaks: 6c, Brandberg. 15c, Omatako twin peaks. 25c, Spitzkuppe, Karakul sheep.

1982, Aug. 3　Litho.　Perf. 14x14½
495	A103	6c multicolored	.25	.25
496	A103	15c multicolored	.25	.25
497	A103	20c shown	.25	.25
498	A103	25c multicolored	.35	.35
		Nos. 495-498 (4)	1.10	1.10

Traditional
Headdress,
Herero
Tribe — A104

1982, Oct. 15　Litho.　Perf. 14x14½
499	A104	6c shown	.25	.25
500	A104	15c Himba	.25	.25
501	A104	20c Ngandjera	.30	.30
502	A104	25c Kwanyama	.40	.40
		Nos. 499-502 (4)	1.20	1.20

See Nos. 524-527.

Fort
Vogelsang
A105

Bethany Chief Joseph
Fredericks — A106

25c, Angra Pequena Bay. 30c, Explorer Heinrich Vogelsang. 40c, Adolf Luderitz (1834-1886).

Perf. 14x14½ (6c, 25c), 14½x14 (20c, 30-40c)

1983, Mar. 16
503	A105	6c shown	.25	.25
504	A106	20c shown	.25	.25
505	A106	25c multicolored	.35	.35
506	A106	30c multicolored	.40	.40
507	A106	40c multicolored	.60	.60
		Nos. 503-507 (5)	1.85	1.85

City of Luderitz centenary (1982).

Diamond
Field, 1908
A107

Ernest Oppenheimer
(1880-1957),
Diamond Industry
Leader — A108

Perf. 14x14½ (10-20c), 14½x14 (25-40c)

1983, June 8　　　　Litho.
508	A107	10c shown	.25	.25
509	A107	20c Field, diff.	.35	.35
510	A108	25c shown	.45	.45
511	A108	40c August Stauch, prospector	.75	.75
		Nos. 508-511 (4)	1.80	1.80

75th anniv. of discovery of diamonds at Luderitz.

Zebras Drinking, by J.J. van
Ellinckhuijzen (b. 1940) — A109

Paintings: 20c, Rossing Mountain, by Herman H.-J. Henckert (b. 1906). 25c, Stampeding Buffalo, by Fritz Krampe (1913-1966). 40c, Erongo Mountains, by Johann Blatt (1905-1973).

1983, Sept. 1　　　Perf. 14x14½
512	A109	10c multicolored	.25	.25
513	A109	20c multicolored	.30	.30
514	A109	25c multicolored	.40	.40
515	A109	40c multicolored	.65	.65
		Nos. 512-515 (4)	1.60	1.60

Lobster
Industry
A110

1983, Nov. 23　　　Perf. 13½x14
516	A110	10c Lobsters	.25	.25
517	A110	20c Dinghies	.30	.30
518	A110	25c Raising trap	.40	.40
519	A110	40c Packaging	.65	.65
		Nos. 516-519 (4)	1.60	1.60

Historic Buildings,
Swakopmund — A111

10c, Hohenzollern House. 20c, Railway Station. 25c, Imperial District Bureau. 30c, Ritterburg.

1984, Mar. 8　Litho.　Perf. 14x13½
520	A111	10c multicolored	.25	.25
521	A111	20c multicolored	.35	.35
522	A111	25c multicolored	.45	.45
523	A111	30c multicolored	.55	.55
		Nos. 520-523 (4)	1.60	1.60

Headdress Type of 1982

1984, May 25　　　　　　Litho.
524	A104	11c Kwambi	.25	.25
525	A104	20c Bushman	.35	.35
526	A104	25c Kwaluudhi	.45	.45
527	A104	30c Mbukushu	.55	.55
		Nos. 524-527 (4)	1.60	1.60

German Colonization
Centenary — A112

1984, Aug. 7　Litho.　Perf. 13½x14
528	A112	11c Map, flag	.40	.40
529	A112	25c Flag raising	.70	.70
530	A112	30c Land marker	.75	.75
531	A112	45c Corvettes Elisabeth & Leipzig	1.75	1.75
		Nos. 528-531 (4)	3.60	3.60

Spring
Flowers — A113

1984, Nov. 22　Litho.　Perf. 14½x14
532	A113	11c Sweet thorn	.25	.25
533	A113	25c Camel thorn	.45	.45
534	A113	30c Hook thorn	.55	.55
535	A113	45c Candle-pod acacia	.85	.85
		Nos. 532-535 (4)	2.10	2.10

Ostrich
A114

1985, Mar. 15
536	A114	11c Head of bird	.35	.35
537	A114	25c Female nesting	.70	.70
538	A114	30c Chick, eggs	.80	.80
539	A114	50c Male mating dance	1.25	1.25
		Nos. 536-539 (4)	3.10	3.10

Historic Buildings, 1900-1912,
Windhoek — A115

12c, Erkrath, Gathemann Buildings, Kaiser Street. 25c, Gymnasium. 30c, Supreme Court. 50c, Railway Station.

1985, June 6
540	A115	12c multicolored	.25	.25
541	A115	25c multicolored	.30	.30
542	A115	30c multicolored	.40	.40
543	A115	50c multicolored	.55	.55
		Nos. 540-543 (4)	1.50	1.50

600mm Narrow-gauge
Locomotives — A116

12c, Zwilling Schmalspur, 1898. 25c, Feldspur Side-Tank. 30c, 0-6-2 Side-Tank, 1904. 50c, Henschel hd Smalspoor, 1912.

1985, Aug. 2
544	A116	12c multicolored	.35	.35
545	A116	25c multicolored	.70	.70
546	A116	30c multicolored	.80	.80
547	A116	50c multicolored	1.50	1.50
		Nos. 544-547 (4)	3.35	3.35

Swakopmund-Tsumeb Railway line, 79th anniv.

Endemic
Musical
Instruments
A117

12c, Lidumu-dumu. 25c, Ngoma. 30c, Okambulum bumbwa. 50c, Gwashi.

1985, Oct. 17
548	A117	12c multicolored	.25	.25
549	A117	25c multicolored	.25	.25
550	A117	30c multicolored	.30	.30
551	A117	50c multicolored	.55	.55
		Nos. 548-551 (4)	1.35	1.35

Diogo Cao,
Portuguese
Explorer,
1486 Visit to
SWA
A118

1986, Jan. 24　　　Perf. 14½x14
552	A118	12c Erecting padroes on shore	.35	.35
553	A118	20c Cao coat of arms	.55	.55
554	A118	25c Caravel	.75	.75
555	A118	30c Portrait	.95	.95
		Nos. 552-555 (4)	2.60	2.60

Wildlife Type of 1980

1986-87　　Litho.　　Perf. 14x14½
556	A95	14c Caracal, horiz.	4.25	4.25
557	A95	16c Warthog, horiz.	2.50	2.50

Issue dates: 14c, Apr. 1; 16c, Apr. 1, 1987.

Rock
Formations
A119

Designs: 14c, Granite bornhardt, Erongo. 20c, Vingerklip, Outjo. 25c, Aeolian sandstone, Kuiseb River. 30c, Columnar dolerite, Twyfelfontein.

1986, Apr. 24　　　Perf. 14½x14
566	A119	14c multicolored	.30	.30
567	A119	20c multicolored	.50	.50
568	A119	25c multicolored	.65	.65
569	A119	30c multicolored	.95	.95
		Nos. 566-569 (4)	2.40	2.40

Karakul Wool (Swakara) Industry — A120

1986, July 10   **Perf. 14x14½**
570	A120	14c Model	.30 .30
571	A120	20c Hand loom	.45 .45
572	A120	25c Sheep	.65 .65
573	A120	30c Rams	.75 .75
a.		Souvenir sheet of 1	3.00 3.00
		Nos. 570-573 (4)	2.15 2.15

No. 573a margin pictures design of No. 570 and Johannesburg stamp exhib. emblem. Sold for 50c to benefit stamp exhib.

Caprivi Strip — A121

1986, Nov. 6   **Litho.**   **Perf. 14½x14**
574	A121	14c Lake Liambezi	.35 .35
575	A121	20c Stock and crop farming	.60 .60
576	A121	25c Settlement	.75 .75
577	A121	30c Map	1.20 1.20
		Nos. 574-577 (4)	2.90 2.90

Paintings by Thomas Baines (1820-1875) A122

Designs: 14c, *Rhenish Mission Church at Gababis,* 1863. 20c, *Outspan in October,* 1861. 25c, *Outspan Under Oomahaama Tree,* 1862. 30c, *Swa-Kop River S.W. Africa,* 1861.

1987, Feb. 19   **Litho.**   **Perf. 14½x14**
578	A122	14c multicolored	.45 .45
579	A122	20c multicolored	.75 .75
580	A122	25c multicolored	.85 .85
a.		Souvenir sheet of 1	3.25 3.25
581	A122	30c multicolored	1.00 1.00
		Nos. 578-581 (4)	3.05 3.05

No. 580a for the natl. philatelic exhibition at Paarl, Sept. 16-19. Sold for 50c.

Insects A123

16c, Garreta nitens. 20c, Alcimus stenurus. 25c, Anthophora caerulea. 30c, Hemiempusa capensis.

1987, May 7
582	A123	16c multicolored	.75 .75
583	A123	20c multicolored	.95 .95
584	A123	25c multicolored	1.25 1.25
585	A123	30c multicolored	1.40 1.40
		Nos. 582-585 (4)	4.35 4.35

Resorts — A124

16c, Okaukuejo, Etosha Natl. Park. 20c, Daan Viljoen Game Park. 25c, Ai-Ais Hot Springs. 30c, Hardap, Mariental.

1987, July 23
586	A124	16c multicolored	.40 .40
587	A124	20c multicolored	.55 .55
588	A124	25c multicolored	.65 .65
589	A124	30c multicolored	.80 .80
		Nos. 586-589 (4)	2.40 2.40

Shipwrecks A125

16c, Hope, 1804. 30c, Tilly, 1885. 40c, Eduard Bohlen, 1909. 50c, Dunedin Star, 1942.

1987, Oct. 15
590	A125	16c multicolored	.70 .70
591	A125	30c multicolored	1.20 1.20
592	A125	40c multicolored	1.60 1.60
593	A125	50c multicolored	2.10 2.10
		Nos. 590-593 (4)	5.60 5.60

Discovery of the Cape of Good Hope by Bartolomeu Dias, 500th Anniv. — A126

1988, Jan. 7   **Perf. 14x14½**
594	A126	16c shown	.40 .40
595	A126	30c Caravel	.70 .70
596	A126	40c The Cantino Map, 1502	1.00 1.00
597	A126	50c King John II	1.25 1.25
		Nos. 594-597 (4)	3.35 3.35

Historic Sites A127

16c, Sossusvlei Clay Pans. 30c, Sesriem Canyon. 40c, Hoaruseb clay castles. 50c, Hoba meteorite.

1988, Mar. 3   **Perf. 14½x14**
598	A127	16c multicolored	.35 .35
599	A127	30c multicolored	.60 .60
600	A127	40c multicolored	.85 .85
601	A127	50c multicolored	1.40 1.40
		Nos. 598-601 (4)	3.20 3.20

Postal Service, Cent. A128

16c, Otyimbingue P.O., 1888. 30c, Windhoek P.O., 1904. 40c, Mail runner, 1888. 50c, Camel post, 1904.

1988, July 7   **Perf. 14x14½**
602	A128	16c multicolored	.40 .40
603	A128	30c multicolored	.85 .85
604	A128	40c multicolored	1.20 1.20
605	A128	50c multicolored	1.40 1.40
a.		Souvenir sheet of 1	4.00 4.00
		Nos. 602-605 (4)	3.85 3.85

No. 605a for the natl. philatelic exhibition held at Windhoek, July 7-9. Sold for 1r.

Birds — A129

16c, Namibornis hereo. 30c, Ammomanes grayi. 40c, Eupodotis rueppellii. 50c, Tockus monteiri.

1988, Nov. 3
606	A129	16c multicolored	1.10 1.10
607	A129	30c multicolored	1.60 1.60
608	A129	40c multicolored	1.90 1.90
609	A129	50c multicolored	2.10 2.10
		Nos. 606-609 (4)	6.70 6.70

Missionaries and Mission Stations — A130

16c, Carl Hahn (1818-95) & Gross-Barmen Mission. 30c, Johann Kronlein (1826-92) & Berseba Mission. 40c, Franz Kleinschmidt (1812-64) & Rehoboth Mission. 50c, Johann Schmelen (1777-1848) & Bethanien Mission.

1989, Feb. 16
610	A130	16c multicolored	.40 .40
611	A130	30c multicolored	.75 .75
612	A130	40c multicolored	1.20 1.20
613	A130	50c multicolored	1.40 1.40
		Nos. 610-613 (4)	3.75 3.75

Aviation Industry, 75th Anniv. A131

Maps and aircraft — 18c, Beechcraft 1900. 30c, Ryan Navion, 1948. 40c, Junkers F13, 1930. 50c, Pfalz Otto biplane, 1914.

1989, May 18   **Perf. 14½x14**
614	A131	18c multicolored	.85 .85
615	A131	30c multicolored	1.20 1.20
616	A131	40c multicolored	1.60 1.60
617	A131	50c multicolored	2.10 2.10
a.		Souvenir sheet of 1	5.00 5.00
		Nos. 614-617 (4)	5.75 5.75

No. 617a has decorative bright blue and black inscribed margin picturing emblem of natl. philatelic exhibition WANDERERS 101, held Sept. 6-9. Sold for 1.50r.

Namib Desert Sand Dunes — A132

1989, Aug. 14   **Perf. 14x14½**
Size of 30c, 50c: 31x21½mm
618	A132	18c Barchan dunes	.25 .25
619	A132	30c Star dunes	.50 .50
620	A132	40c Transverse dunes	.75 .75
621	A132	50c Crescent dunes	.95 .95
		Nos. 618-621 (4)	2.45 2.45

Suffrage, UN Resolution 435 — A133

1989, Aug. 24
622	A133	18c dull org & gray vio	.25 .25
623	A133	35c green & blue	.50 .50
624	A133	45c yellow & purple	.80 .80
625	A133	60c golden brn & gray grn	1.20 1.20
		Nos. 622-625 (4)	2.75 2.75

Minerals — A134

Mines A135

No. 626, Gypsum. No. 627, Fluorite. No. 628, Mimetite. No. 629, Cuprite. No. 630, Azurite. No. 631, Boltwoodite. No. 632, Dioptase. No. 633, Alluvial diamond field, Oranjemund. No. 634, Lead, copper & zinc mine, Tsumeb. No. 635, Zinc mine, Rosh Pinah. No. 636, Diamonds. No. 637, Wulfenite. No. 638, Tin mine, Uis. No. 639, Uranium mine, Rossing. No. 640, Gold.

1989-90   **Perf. 14½x14**
626	A134	1c multicolored	.25 .25
627	A134	2c multicolored	.25 .25
628	A134	5c multicolored	.25 .25
629	A134	7c multicolored	.25 .25
630	A134	10c multicolored	.25 .25
631	A134	16c multicolored	.30 .30
631A	A134	18c see footnote	14.00 8.00
632	A134	20c multicolored	.30 .30
633	A135	25c multicolored	.35 .35
634	A135	30c multicolored	.40 .40
635	A135	35c multicolored	.50 .50
636	A135	40c multicolored	.55 .55
637	A134	45c multicolored	.65 .65
638	A135	50c multicolored	.70 .70
639	A135	1r multicolored	1.50 1.50
640	A135	2r multicolored	3.00 3.00
		Nos. 626-640 (16)	23.50 17.50

No. 631 has formula, K(H3O)(UO2)(SiO4); No. 631A, K2(UO2)2(SiO3)2(OH)2.5HO2O.
Issued: No. 631A, 10/25/90; others, 11/16/89.
This set remained in use until Namibia issued a definitive set Jan. 2, 1991.

Flora — A136

18c, Adenium boehmianum. 35c, Adansonia digitata. 45c, Kigelia africana. 60c, Harpagophytum procumbens.

1990, Feb. 1   **Perf. 14½x14**
641	A136	18c multicolored	.40 .40
642	A136	35c multicolored	.80 .80
643	A136	45c multicolored	1.00 1.00
644	A136	60c multicolored	1.25 1.25
a.		Souvenir sheet of 1	5.00 5.00
		Nos. 641-644 (4)	3.45 3.45

No. 644a margin publicizes the natl. phil. exhib. Sold for 1.50r.

SEMI-POSTAL STAMPS

> Catalogue values for unused stamps in this section are for Never Hinged items.

Voortrekker Monument Issue

South Africa Nos. B1-B4 Overprinted

1935-36 Wmk. 201 *Perf. 14*

B1 SP1 ½p + ½p grn & blk, pair 3.00 *7.00*
a. Single, English .40 *.85*
b. Single, Afrikaans .40 *.85*
B2 SP2 1p + ½p rose & blk, pair 4.00 4.00
a. Single, English .45 .45
b. Single, Afrikaans .45 .45
B3 SP3 2p + 1p dl vio & gray, pair 17.50 10.00
a. Single, English 1.75 1.25
b. Single, Afrikaans 1.75 1.25
B4 SP4 3p + 1½p dp bl & gray, pair 30.00 40.00
a. Single, English 3.25 *4.50*
b. Single, Afrikaans 3.25 *4.50*
Nos. B1-B4 (4) 54.50 61.00

Voortrekker Centenary Issue

South Africa Nos. B5-B8 Overprinted

1938, Dec. 14 *Perf. 14*

B5 SP5 ½p + ½p dl grn & indigo, pair 11.00 *25.00*
a. Single, English 1.00 *2.25*
b. Single, Afrikaans 1.00 *2.25*

Perf. 15x14

B6 SP6 1p + 1p rose & sl, pair 27.50 20.00
a. Single, English 1.50 1.50
b. Single, Afrikaans 1.50 1.50
B7 SP7 1½p + 1½p Prus grn & choc, pair 29.00 *35.00*
a. Single, English 2.00 *3.25*
b. Single, Afrikaans 2.00 *3.25*
B8 SP8 3p + 3p chlky bl, pair 55.00 *85.00*
a. Single, English 4.50 *8.50*
b. Single, Afrikaans 4.50 *8.50*
Nos. B5-B8 (4) 122.50 *165.00*

Same Overprint on South Africa Nos. B9-B11

1939, July 17 *Perf. 14*

B9 SP9 ½p + ½p Prus grn & gray brn, pair 14.00 *16.00*
a. Single, English 1.00 1.25
b. Single, Afrikaans 1.00 1.25
B10 SP10 1p + 1p rose car & Prus grn, pair 21.00 16.00
a. Single, English 1.25 1.25
b. Single, Afrikaans 1.25 1.25

Perf. 15x14

B11 SP11 1½p + 1½p rose vio, dk vio & Prus grn, pair 34.00 20.00
a. Single, English 2.00 1.75
b. Single, Afrikaans 2.00 1.75
Nos. B9-B11 (3) 69.00 52.00

250th anniv. of the landing of the Huguenots in South Africa. Surtax went to a fund to build a Huguenot memorial at Paarl.

AIR POST STAMPS

South Africa Nos. C5-C6 Overprinted

1930 Unwmk. *Perf. 14x13½*

C1 AP2 4p blue green 10.00 *32.50*
a. Without period after "A" 80.00 150.00
C2 AP2 1sh orange 16.00 *57.50*
a. Without period after "A" 500.00 *750.00*

Overprinted

C3 AP2 4p blue green 1.50 *7.00*
a. Double overprint 200.00
b. Inverted overprint 200.00
c. Small "I" in "AIR" 6.00
C4 AP2 1sh orange 4.25 *17.50*
a. Double overprint 575.00

Monoplane over Windhoek — AP3

Biplane over Windhoek — AP4

Wmk. 201

1931, Mar. 5 Engr. *Perf. 14*

C5 AP3 3p blue & dk brn, pair 40.00 *45.00*
a. Single, English 3.00 *3.00*
b. Single, Afrikaans 3.00 *3.00*
C6 AP4 10p brn vio & blk, pair 85.00 *85.00*
a. Single, English 7.00 *7.00*
b. Single, Afrikaans 7.00 *7.00*

POSTAGE DUE STAMPS

Postage Due Stamps of South Africa and Transvaal Overprinted like Regular Issues.

Setting I

On South Africa Nos. J11, J14

1923 Unwmk. *Perf. 14*

J1 D1 ½p blue grn & blk, pair 6.75 *30.00*
a. Single, English .75 *5.50*
b. Single, Dutch .75 *5.50*
c. As #J1, without period after "Afrika" 130.00
d. Inverted ovpt., pair 600.00
J2 D1 2p violet & blk, pair 4.00 *28.00*
a. Single, English .50 *5.00*
b. Single, Dutch .50 *5.00*
c. As #J2, without period after "Afrika" 170.00 170.00

On South Africa Nos. J9-J10

Rouletted 7-8

J3 D1 1p dull red & blk, pair 8.00 *30.00*
a. Single, English .90 *5.50*
b. Single, Dutch .90 *5.50*
c. As #J3, without period after "Afrika" 150.00 150.00
d. Pair, imperf. between 1,800.
J4 D1 1½p yel brn & blk, pair 1.50 *16.00*
a. Single, English .25 *2.75*
b. Single, Dutch .25 *2.75*
c. As #J4, without period after "Afrika" 110.00 110.00

On South Africa Nos. J3-J4, J6

Perf. 14

Wmk. 177

J5 D1 2p vio & blk, pair 42.50 *55.00*
a. Single, English 3.00 *10.00*
b. Single, Dutch 3.00 *10.00*
c. As #J5, without period after "Afrika" 275.00
d. "Wes" for "West" 325.00
J6 D1 3p ultra & blk, pair 21.00 *55.00*
a. Single, English 1.50 *10.00*
b. Single, Dutch 1.50 *10.00*
J7 D1 6p gray & blk, pair 40.00 *65.00*
a. Single, English 4.00 *13.00*
b. Single, Dutch 4.00 *13.00*
Nos. J5-J7 (3) 103.50 *175.00*

On Transvaal Nos. J5-J6

Wmk. Multiple Crown and C A (3)

J8 D1 5p vio & blk, pair 4.50 *55.00*
a. Single, English .75 *11.00*
b. Single, Dutch .75 *11.00*
c. As #J8, without period after "Afrika" 130.00 130.00
J9 D1 6p red brn & blk, pair 19.00 *55.00*
a. Single, Dutch 2.50 *11.00*
b. As #J9, without period after "Afrika" 275.00

For No. J9 single in English see No. J17a and note after No. 27.

The "t" of "West" may be found partly or entirely missing on Nos. J1, J3-J6, J8-J9.

Setting II

On South Africa No. J9

Rouletted

Unwmk.

J10 D1 1p dull red & blk, pair *14,000.*
a. Single, English 800.00 1,600.
b. Single, Dutch 800.00 1,600.

On South Africa Nos. J3-J4

Perf. 14

Wmk. 177

J11 D1 2p vio & blk, pair 19.00 *50.00*
a. Single, English 1.75 *9.00*
b. Single, Dutch 1.75 *9.00*
c. As #J11, without period after "Afrika" 275.00 250.00
J12 D1 3p ultra & blk, pair 8.50 *32.50*
a. Single, English 1.00 *5.50*
b. Single, Dutch 1.00 *5.50*
c. As #J12, without period after "Afrika" 130.00 *150.00*

On Transvaal No. J5

Wmk. Multiple Crown and C A (3)

J13 D1 5p vio & blk, pair 75.00 200.00
a. Single, English 15.00 *20.00*
b. Single, Dutch 15.00 *20.00*

Setting III

On South Africa Nos. J11, J12, J9

Unwmk.

J14 D1 ½p blue grn & blk, pair 17.50 *37.50*
a. Single, Dutch 1.50 *5.50*
J15 D1 1p rose & blk, pair 27.50 *37.50*
a. Single, English 1.50 *6.00*
b. Single, Dutch 1.50 *6.00*

Rouletted 7

J16 D1 1p dull red & blk, pair 9.50 *37.50*
a. Single, Dutch 1.00 *6.00*

For Nos. J14 and J16 singles in English see Nos. J1a and J3a and note after No. 27.

On Transvaal No. J6

Perf. 14

Wmk. 3

J17 D1 6p red brn & blk, pair 23.50 *100.00*
a. Single, English 2.50 *20.00*
b. Single, Dutch 2.50 *20.00*

See note below No. 27.

Setting IV

On South Africa Nos. J11-J12, J16

1924 Unwmk.

J18 D1 ½p blue grn & blk, pair 8.50 *35.00*
a. Single, English .75 *5.50*
b. Single, Dutch .75 *5.50*
J19 D1 1p rose & blk, pair 8.50 *32.50*
a. Single, English .60 *5.50*
b. Single, Dutch .60 *5.50*
J20 D1 6p gray & blk, pair 3.00 *45.00*
a. Single, English .30 *9.00*
b. Single, Dutch .30 *9.00*

On Transvaal No. J5

Wmk. Multiple Crown and C A (3)

J21 D1 5p vio & blk, pair 800.00 *1,200.*
a. Single, English 140.00 *175.00*
b. Single, Dutch 140.00 *175.00*

Setting V

i

j

"South West" 16mm wide
"Zuidwest" 12mm wide
Overprint Spaced 12mm

On South Africa Nos. J4, J11, J13

1924 Unwmk.

J22 D1 ½p green & blk, pair 3.50 *32.50*
a. Single, English .25 *6.50*
b. Single, Dutch .25 *6.50*
J23 D1 1½p yel brown & blk 5.75 *47.50*
a. Single, English .50 *7.50*
b. Single, Dutch .50 *7.50*

Wmk. Springbok's Head (177)

J24 D1 3p ultra & black, pair 16.00 *60.00*
a. Single, English 1.75 *11.00*
b. Single, Dutch 1.75 *11.00*

On Transvaal No. J5

Wmk. Multiple Crown and C A (3)

J25 D1 5p violet & blk, pair 3.00 *25.00*
a. Single, English .40 *7.50*
b. Single, Dutch .40 *7.50*

Setting VI

On South Africa Nos. J4, J11-J16

1924, Dec. Unwmk.

J26 D1 ½p blue grn & blk, pair 14.00 *40.00*
a. Single, English 1.00 *7.50*
b. Single, Dutch 1.00 *7.50*
J27 D1 1p rose & blk, pair 2.25 *14.00*
a. Single, English .25 *1.75*
b. Single, Dutch .25 *1.75*
c. As #J27, without period after "Africa" 100.00
J28 D1 1½p yel brn & blk, pair 5.00 *35.00*
a. Single, English .30 *6.50*
b. Single, Dutch .30 *6.50*
c. As #J28, without period after "Africa" 110.00
J29 D1 2p vio & blk, pair 3.00 *19.00*
a. Single, English .35 *3.50*
b. Single, Dutch .35 *3.50*
c. As #J29, without period after "Africa" 85.00
J30 D1 3p bl & blk, pair 5.25 *20.00*
a. Single, English .85 *3.75*
b. Single, Dutch .85 *3.75*
c. As #J30, without period after "Africa" 92.50
J31 D1 6p gray & blk, pair 16.00 *57.50*
a. Single, English 2.00 *14.00*
b. Single, Dutch 2.00 *14.00*
c. As #J31, without period after "Africa" 180.00
Nos. J26-J31 (6) 45.50 *185.50*

Wmk. Springbok's Head (177)

J32 D1 3p ultra & black, pair 10.00 *65.00*
a. Single, English 1.75 *11.00*
b. Single, Dutch 1.75 *11.00*

On Transvaal No. J5

Wmk. 3

J33 D1 5p violet & blk, pair 3.25 *22.50*
a. Single, English .25 *3.50*
b. Single, Dutch .25 *3.50*
c. As #J33, without period after "Africa" 92.50 *75.00*

Setting VIII

On South Africa Nos. J18, J13-J16

1927 Unwmk.

J34 D2 1p rose & black, pair 1.25 *13.00*
a. Single, English .25 *2.25*
b. Single, Afrikaans .25 *2.25*
c. As #J34, without period after "Africa" 10.50 *17.50*
J35 D1 1½p yel brn & blk, pair 1.25 *22.50*
a. Single, English .25 *3.50*
b. Single, Afrikaans .25 *3.50*
c. As #J35, without period after "Africa" 50.00 *60.00*
J36 D1 2p vio & blk, pair 6.00 *18.00*
a. Single, English .30 *3.25*
b. Single, Afrikaans .30 *3.25*
c. As #J36, without period after "Africa" 50.00 *60.00*
J37 D1 3p bl & blk, pair 16.00 *50.00*
a. Single, English 1.75 *11.00*
b. Single, Afrikaans 1.75 *11.00*
c. As #J37, without period after "Africa" 70.00 70.00
J38 D1 6p gray & blk, pair 12.00 *40.00*
a. Single, English 1.50 *8.50*
b. Single, Afrikaans 1.50 *8.50*
c. As #J38, without period after "Africa" 100.00 115.00
Nos. J34-J38 (5) 36.50 *143.50*

On Transvaal No. J5

Wmk. Multiple Crown and C A (3)

J39 D1 5p violet & blk, pair 22.50 *97.50*
a. Single, English 3.00 *22.50*
b. Single, Afrikaans 3.00 *22.50*

South Africa Nos. J15-J16 Overprinted

1928 Unwmk.

J79 D1 3p blue & black 1.65 *12.00*
a. Without period after "A" 42.50 45.00
J80 D1 6p gray & black 7.50 *32.50*
a. Without period after "A" 150.00

Same Overprint on South Africa Nos. J17-J21

J81 D2 ½p blue grn & blk .65 *9.50*
J82 D2 1p rose & black .65 *4.00*
a. Without period after "A" 45.00 *50.00*
J83 D2 2p violet & black .65 *5.00*
a. Without period after "A" 62.50
J84 D2 3p ultra & black 2.75 *30.00*
J85 D2 6p gray & black 1.75 *22.50*
a. Without period after "A" 62.50 *225.00*
Nos. J81-J85 (5) 6.45 *71.00*

Catalogue values for unused stamps in this section, from this point to the end of the section, are for Never Hinged items.

D3

Wmk. 201

1931, Feb. 23 Litho. Perf. 12
Size: 19x22mm

J86	D3	½p yel green & blk	2.00	8.50
J87	D3	1p rose & black	2.00	1.65
J88	D3	2p violet & black	2.50	3.25
J89	D3	3p blue & black	5.00	15.00
J90	D3	6p gray & black	17.50	30.00
		Nos. J86-J90 (5)	29.00	58.40

Cover values are for properly franked commercial items. Philatelic usages also exist and sell for less.

Photo. (Frame) & Typo. (Center)
1959 Perf. 14½x14
Size: 17x21mm

J91	D3	1p rose & black	2.25	15.00
J92	D3	2p violet & black	2.25	15.00
J93	D3	3p blue & black	2.25	15.00
		Nos. J91-J93 (3)	6.75	45.00

1960 Size: 17x21mm Wmk. 330

J94	D3	1p rose & black	3.75	4.50
J95	D3	3p blue & black	3.75	6.00

D4

1961, Feb. Photo. Perf. 14½x14

J96	D4	1c green & black	1.00	4.25
J97	D4	2c red & black	1.00	4.25
J98	D4	4c lilac & black	1.00	6.00
J99	D4	5c blue & black	1.75	5.25
J100	D4	6c emerald & black	2.00	7.50
J101	D4	10c yellow & black	4.50	11.00
		Nos. J96-J101 (6)	11.25	38.25

Type of South Africa, 1972
1972 Wmk. 359 Perf. 14x13½

J102	D6	1c bright green	1.10	5.00
J103	D6	8c violet blue	3.75	8.50

OFFICIAL STAMPS

Nos. 85-87 (Setting VIII) Overprinted at top with type "c" on English-inscribed Stamps and type "d" on Afrikaans-inscribed Stamps

Without Periods after Words
1927 Wmk. 201 Perf. 14½x14

O1	A5	½p dk grn & blk, pair	95.00	200.00
a.		Single, English	12.50	30.00
b.		Single, Afrikaans	12.50	30.00
O2	A6	1p car & blk, pair	95.00	200.00
a.		Single, English	12.50	30.00
b.		Single, Afrikaans	12.50	30.00
O3	A7	6p org & grn, pair	120.00	225.00
a.		Single, English	15.00	30.00
b.		Single, Afrikaans	15.00	30.00

South Africa No. 5 Overprinted As Nos. 85-87 plus "c" and "d"
Perf. 14
Wmk. 177

O4	A2	2p dull violet	225.00	375.00
a.		Single, English	35.00	45.00
b.		Single, Afrikaans	35.00	45.00

Nos. 96-98 Overprinted like Nos. J79-J85 at foot, Overprinted Types "c" and "d" at Top
1929 Wmk. 201 Perf. 14½x14

O5	A5	½p green & blk, pair	1.25	17.50
a.		Single, English	.25	2.75
b.		Single, Afrikaans	.25	2.75

O6	A6	1p car & blk, pair	2.00	23.00
a.		Single, English	.25	2.75
b.		Single, Afrikaans	.25	2.75
O7	A7	6p org & grn, pair	4.50	23.00
a.		Single, English	.75	3.75
b.		Single, Afrikaans	.75	3.75
		Nos. O5-O7 (3)	7.75	63.50

No. 99 Overprinted in Black

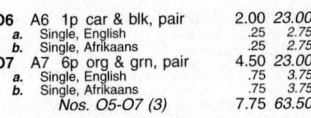

With Periods after Words
Perf. 14

O8	A8	2p vio brn & gray, pair	2.50	22.50
a.		Single, English	.35	3.75
b.		Single, Afrikaans	.35	3.75
c.		Without period after "OFFICIAL"	7.00	50.00
d.		Pair, "c" + normal 2p	17.00	95.00
e.		Without period after "OFFISIEEL"	7.00	50.00
f.		Pair, "e" + normal 2p	17.00	95.00
g.		Pair, "c" + "e"	22.00	95.00

In each sheet of 120 stamps there were 12 No. O8c and 10 No. O8e.

South Africa Nos. 23-25 Overprinted

Without Periods after Words
1929 Wmk. 201 Perf. 14½x14

O9	A5	½p green & blk, pair	.85	16.00
a.		Single, English	.25	2.75
b.		Single, Afrikaans	.25	2.75
O10	A6	1p car & blk, pair	1.25	17.50
a.		Single, English	.25	3.25
b.		Single, Afrikaans	.25	3.25
O11	A7	6p org & grn, pair	3.00	27.50
a.		Single, English	.40	6.50
b.		Single, Afrikaans	.40	6.50
		Nos. O9-O11 (3)	5.10	61.00

South Africa No. 26 Overprinted

With Periods after Words
Perf. 14

O12	A8	2p vio brn & gray, pair	1.50	22.00
a.		Single, English	.25	3.50
b.		Single, Afrikaans	.25	3.50
c.		Without period after "OFFICIAL"	3.75	45.00
d.		Pair, "c" + normal 2p	17.00	95.00
e.		Without period after "OFFISIEEL"	6.50	50.00
f.		Pair, "e" + normal 2p	17.00	95.00
g.		Pair, "c" + "e"	22.00	95.00

Catalogue values for unused stamps in this section, from this point to the end of the section, are for Never Hinged items.

Nos. 108-109, 111 and 114 Overprinted in Red

1931

O13	A15	½p green & blk, pair	15.00	22.00
a.		Single, English	1.25	3.75
b.		Single, Afrikaans	1.25	3.75
O14	A16	1p red & indigo, pair	1.50	19.00
a.		Single, English	.25	3.50
b.		Single, Afrikaans	.25	3.50
O15	A18	2p dk brn & dk bl, pair	3.75	11.00
a.		Single, English	.40	2.25
b.		Single, Afrikaans	.40	2.25
O16	A21	6p ol brn & bl, pair	5.75	15.00
a.		Single, English	.50	3.25
b.		Single, Afrikaans	.50	3.25
		Nos. O13-O16 (4)	26.00	67.00

No. 110 Overprinted in Red

1938, July 1 Wmk. 201

O17	A17	1½p violet brn, pair	36.50	50.00
a.		Single, English	3.50	6.00
b.		Single, Afrikaans	3.50	6.00

Nos. 108-111, 114 Ovptd. in Red

1945-50 Wmk. 201 Perf. 14x13½

O18	A15	½p grn & blk, pair	14.00	35.00
a.		Single, English	1.50	5.00
b.		Single, Afrikaans	1.50	5.00
O19	A16	1p red & ind, pair ('50)	14.00	20.00
a.		Single, English	.85	3.25
b.		Single, Afrikaans	.85	3.25
O20	A17	1½p vio brn, pair	40.00	55.00
a.		Single, English	5.00	7.00
b.		Single, Afrikaans	5.00	7.00
O21	A18	2p dk brn & dk bl, pair ('47)	675.00	875.00
a.		Single, English	100.00	100.00
b.		Single, Afrikaans	100.00	100.00
O22	A21	6p ol brn & bl, pair	30.00	70.00
a.		Single, English	2.00	8.00
b.		Single, Afrikaans	2.00	8.00
		Nos. O18-O20,O22 (4)	98.00	180.00

Nos. 108-111, 114 Ovptd. in Red

1951-52

O23	A15	½p grn & blk, pair ('52)	19.00	25.00
a.		Single, English	2.00	4.50
b.		Single, Afrikaans	2.00	4.50
O24	A16	1p red & ind, pair	6.00	22.50
a.		Single, English	.40	2.00
b.		Single, Afrikaans	.40	2.00
c.		Ovpt. transposed, pair	110.00	250.00
d.		As "c," single, English ovpt.	10.00	
e.		As "c," single, Afrikaans ovpt.	10.00	
O25	A17	1½p violet brn, pair	30.00	32.50
a.		Single, English	3.00	5.00
b.		Single, Afrikaans	3.00	5.00
c.		Ovpt. transposed, pair	80.00	95.00
d.		As "c," single, English ovpt.	7.50	
e.		As "c," single, Afrikaans ovpt.	7.50	
O26	A18	2p dk brn & dk bl, pair	4.00	26.00
a.		Single, English	.45	3.50
b.		Single, Afrikaans	.45	3.50
c.		Ovpt. transposed, pair	75.00	250.00
d.		As "c," single, English ovpt.	4.50	
e.		As "c," single, Afrikaans ovpt.	4.50	
O27	A21	6p ol brn & blue, pair	4.00	55.00
a.		Single, English	.50	7.50
b.		Single, Afrikaans	.50	7.50
c.		Ovpt. transposed, pair	28.00	170.00
d.		As "c," single, English ovpt.	4.00	
e.		As "c," single, Afrikaans ovpt.	4.00	
		Nos. O23-O27 (5)	63.00	161.00

"Overprint transposed" means English inscription on Afrikaans stamp, or vice versa. Use of official stamps ceased in Jan. 1955.

SPAIN

'spān

LOCATION — Southwestern Europe, Iberian Peninsula
GOVT. — Monarchy
AREA — 194,884 sq. mi.
POP. — 39,167,744 (1999 est.)
CAPITAL — Madrid

Spain was a monarchy until about 1931, when a republic was established. After the Civil War (1936-39), the Spanish State of Gen. Francisco Franco was recognized. The monarchy was restored in 1975.

32 Maravedis = 8 Cuartos = 1 Real
1000 Milesimas = 100 Centimos = 1 Escudo (1866)
100 Milesimas = 1 Real
4 Reales = 1 Peseta
100 Centimos = 1 Peseta (1872)
100 Cents = 1 Euro (2002)

Catalogue values for unused stamps in this country are for Never Hinged items, beginning with Scott 909 in the regular postage section, Scott B139 in the semi-postal section, Scott C159 in the airpost section, and Scott E21 in the special delivery section.

Watermarks

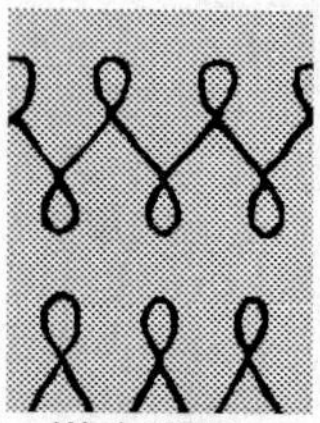

Wmk. 104 — Loops

Wmk. 105 — Crossed Lines

Wmk. 116 — Crosses and Circles

Wmk. 178 — Castle

Stamps punched with a small round hole have done telegraph service. In this condition most of them sell for 20 cents to $20.

Stamps of 1854 to 1882 canceled with three parallel horizontal bars or two thin lines are remainders. Most of these are valued through No. 101 and 174 through 254. In a few cases, the bar cancels are scarcer than regular used examples and sell for more. Where no special listing is present, and if available, they sell for about the same as regular used stamps.

For additional shades see the *Scott Classic Catalogue.*

Kingdom

Queen Isabella II
A1 A2

A2a

A2b

A2c

Type I

Type II

6 CUARTOS:
Type I — "T" and "O" of CUARTOS separated.
Type II — "T" and "O" joined.

Unwmk.

1850, Jan. 1 Litho. *Imperf.*

1	A1	6c blk, thin paper (II)	650.00	17.00
a.		Thick paper (II)	650.00	25.00
b.		Thick paper (I)	850.00	20.00
c.		Thin paper (I)	850.00	32.50
2	A2	12c lilac	3,000.	250.00
a.		Thin paper	*4,500.*	325.00
3	A2a	5r red	3,000.	250.00
4	A2b	6r blue	3,750.	800.00
5	A2c	10r green	5,850.	1,700.

Stamps of types A2, A3, A4, A6, A7a and A8 are inscribed "FRANCO" on the cuarto values and "CERTIFICADO," "CERTIFO" or "CERT DO" on the reales values.

A3

1851, Jan. 1 Thin Paper Typo.

6	A3	6c black	375.00	3.50
a.		Thick paper	825.00	20.00
7	A3	12c lilac	7,000.	200.00
8	A3	2r red	*24,000.*	*7,000.*
9	A3	5r rose	3,000.	225.00
a.		5r red brown (error)	*22,000.*	—
10	A3	6r blue	5,250.	750.00
a.		Cliche of 2r in plate of 6r	—	*125,000.*
11	A3	10r green	3,750.	500.00

A4

1852, Jan. 1 Thick Paper

12	A4	6c rose	400.00	3.50
a.		Thin paper	625.00	5.50
13	A4	12c lilac	2,600.	150.00
14	A4	2r pale red	*18,000.*	*4,500.*
15	A4	5r yellowish green	2,950.	125.00
16	A4	6r grnsh blue	*4,600.*	525.00

Arms of Madrid — A5

Isabella II — A6

1853, Jan. 1 Thin Paper

17	A5	1c bronze	3,000.	400.00
18	A5	3c bronze	*18,000.*	*7,000.*
19	A6	6c carmine rose	750.00	2.25
a.		Thick paper	975.00	16.00
b.		Thick bluish paper	1,300.	22.50
20	A6	12c reddish purple	2,750.	135.00
21	A6	2r vermilion	*15,000.*	*2,500.*
22	A6	5r lt green	2,500.	130.00
23	A6	6r deep blue	3,900.	450.00

Nos. 17-18 were issued for use on Madrid city mail only. *They were reprinted on this white paper in duller colors.*

A7

A7a

Coat of Arms of Spain — A8

1854 Thin White Paper

24	A7	2c green	2,650.	525.00
c.		Thick paper	3,650.	525.00
25	A7a	4c carmine	450.00	2.10
a.		Thick paper	675.00	17.50
26	A8	6c carmine	400.00	1.60
27	A7a	1r indigo	4,000.	350.00
		Bar cancellation		21.00
28	A8	2r scarlet	2,100.	120.00
		Bar cancellation		10.00
c.		Thick paper	—	250.00
29	A8	5r green	2,000.	110.00
		Bar cancellation		16.00
30	A8	6r blue	4,500.	325.00
		Bar cancellation		25.00

See boxed note on bar cancellation before No. 1.

Thick Bluish Paper

31	A7	2c green	*17,500.*	*2,100.*
b.		Thin paper	18,500.	2,400.
32	A7a	4c carmine	525.00	5.50
c.		Thin paper	600.00	17.50
32A	A8	6c carmine	1,050.	19.00
d.		Thin paper	—	100.00
33	A7a	1r pale blue	—	*7,500.*
a.		Thin paper	—	9,500.
34	A8	2r dull red	*7,500.*	700.00
a.		Thin paper	7,500.	700.00

Full margins = ¾mm.

The 2c with watermark 104 is a proof.

Isabella II — A9

Blue Paper

1855, Apr. 1 Wmk. 104

36	A9	2c green	*3,400.*	140.00
a.		2c yellow green	*4,000.*	175.00
		Bar cancellation, #36 or 36a		10.00
37	A9	4c brown red	300.00	1.00
a.		4c carmine	440.00	2.50
b.		4c lake	350.00	.90
		Bar cancellation, #37, 37a or 37b		2.50
		Bar cancellation		2.50
38	A9	1r green blue	1,300.	15.00
a.		1r blue	1,600.	20.00
		Bar cancellation, #38 or 38a		5.00
b.		Cliché of 2r in plate of 1r	*25,000.*	*3,250.*
		Bar cancellation, #38b		850.00
39	A9	2r reddish pur	900.00	15.00
a.		2r deep violet	1,450.	20.00
		Bar cancellation, #39, 39a or 39b		13.50

Rough Yellowish Paper

1856, Jan. 1 Wmk. 105

40	A9	2c green	*4,000.*	250.00
		Bar cancellation		15.00
41	A9	4c rose	13.50	2.25
		Bar cancellation		2.50
42	A9	1r grnsh blue	*5,500.*	200.00
a.		1r dull blue	*5,750.*	275.00
		Bar cancellation, #42 or 42a		8.50
43	A9	2r brown purple	600.00	25.00
a.		2r dark reddish purple	775.00	45.00
		Bar cancellation, #43, 43a		7.50

White Smooth Paper

1856, Apr. 11 Unwmk.

44	A9	2c blue green	700.00	42.50
a.		2c yellow green	825.00	50.00
		Bar cancellation, #44 or 44a		7.50
45	A9	4c rose	5.75	.35
a.		4c carmine ('59)	9.25	20.00
46	A9	1r blue	27.50	25.00
a.		1r pale greenish blue	40.00	32.50
		Bar cancellation, #46 or 46a		4.00
47	A9	2r brown lilac	90.00	29.00
a.		2r dull lilac	100.00	35.00
		Bar cancellation, #47 or 47a		10.00

Three types of No. 45.

1859

48	A9	12c dark orange	200.00	
		Bar cancellation		55.00
a.		Tete-beche pair (#48)	5,750.	
		Bar cancellation		150.00

Nos. 48-48b were never put in use. *Reprints exist.*

A10

1860-61 Tinted Paper

49	A10	2c green, *grn*	400.00	19.00
		Bar cancellation		2.50
50	A10	4c orange, *grn*	55.00	.80
51	A10	12c car, *buff*	350.00	14.00
		Bar cancellation		8.75
52	A10	19c brn, *buff* ('61)	2,500.	1,200.
53	A10	1r blue, *grn*	325.00	12.50
		Bar cancellation		4.50
54	A10	2r lilac, *lil*	400.00	11.00
		Bar cancellation		4.50

A11

1862, July 16

55	A11	2c dp bl, *yel*	37.50	11.00
56	A11	4c dk brn, *redsh buff*	2.40	.70
a.		4c brown, *white*	24.00	7.00
		Bar cancellation		2.50
57	A11	12c blue, *pnksh*	42.50	8.50
		Bar cancellation		3.25
58	A11	19c car, *lil*	200.00	225.00
a.		19c carmine, *white*	300.00	275.00
		Bar cancellation, #58 or 58a		175.00
59	A11	1r brown, *yel*	57.50	17.50
		Bar cancellation		3.50
60	A11	2r green, *pnksh*	37.50	11.00
		Bar cancellation		3.25
		Nos. 55-60 (6)	377.40	273.70

A12

1864, Jan. 1

61	A12	2c dk bl, *lil*	50.00	20.00
62	A12	4c rose, *redsh buff*	2.50	1.00
a.		4c carmine, *reddish buff*	22.50	7.50
		Bar cancellation, #62 or 62a		2.50
63	A12	12c green, *pnksh*	42.50	14.50
64	A12	19c violet, *pnksh*	210.00	190.00
65	A12	1r brown, *grn*	190.00	75.00
		Bar cancellation		5.00
66	A12	2r blue, *pnksh*	45.00	12.00
		Bar cancellation, #66 or 66a		5.00
		Nos. 61-66 (6)	540.00	312.50

A13

1865, Jan. 1 Litho. *Imperf.*

67	A13	2c rose	325.00	35.00
68	A13	4c blue	*2,750.*	
69	A13	12c blue & rose	425.00	19.00
		Bar cancellation		5.25
a.		Frame inverted	*13,500.*	800.00
		Bar cancellation		*100.00*
70	A13	19c brn & rose	1,300.	600.00
		Bar cancellation		100.00
71	A13	1r yellow grn	425.00	65.00
		Bar cancellation		17.50
72	A13	2r red lilac	425.00	35.00
		Bar cancellation		16.00

73	A13	2r rose	550.00	65.00
		Bar cancellation		17.50
a.		2r salmon	475.00	70.00
		Bar cancellation		12.50

No. 68 is without gum and was never put in use.

A majority of the perforated stamps from 1865 to about 1950 are rather poorly centered. The very fine examples that are valued will be fairly well centered. Poorly centered stamps sell for less. Stamps of some issues are almost always badly centered, and our values will be for examples with fine centering. Such issues will be noted.

1865, Jan. 1 *Perf. 14*

74	A13	2c rose red	600.00	130.00
		Bar cancellation		13.50
75	A13	4c blue	60.00	1.00
76	A13	12c bl & rose	750.00	60.00
		Bar cancellation		10.50
a.		Frame inverted	*20,000.*	*2,650.*
		As "a," bar cancel		50.00
77	A13	19c brn & rose	*4,000.*	*2,500.*
78	A13	1r yellow grn	2,000.	525.00
		Bar cancellation		26.50
79	A13	2r violet	1,700.	250.00
		Bar cancellation		24.00
80	A13	2r rose	1,400.	350.00
a.		2r salmon	1,400.	350.00
b.		2r dull orange	1,400.	350.00
		Bar cancellation, #80, 80a or 80b		35.00

Values for Nos. 74-80 are for stamps with perforations touching the frame on at least one side.

A14

1866, Jan. 1

81	A14	2c rose	250.00	32.50
		Bar cancellation		5.50
82	A14	4c blue	42.50	.80
83	A14	12c orange	260.00	12.75
a.		12c orange yellow	350.00	25.00
84	A14	19c brown	1,250.	525.00
		Bar cancellation		50.00
		Nos. 81-84 (4)	1,802.	571.05

A14a

1866

85	A14	10c green	300.00	27.50
		Bar cancellation		4.00
86	A14	20c lilac	200.00	21.00
		Bar cancellation		4.00
87	A14a	20c dull lilac	1,250.	75.00
		Bar cancellation		3.00
		Nos. 85-87 (3)	1,750.	123.50

For the Type A14a 20c in green, see Cuba No. 25.

A15

A15a

A15b

A15c

1867-68

88	A15	2c yell brn	450.00	47.50
89	A15a	4c blue	27.50	1.00
90	A15b	12c org yell	250.00	8.00
a.		12c dark orange	300.00	12.00
b.		12c red orange ('68)	925.00	40.00
91	A15c	19c rose	1,450.	425.00
		Bar cancellation		40.00

See Nos. 100-102. For overprints see Nos. 114a-115a, 124-128, 124a-128a, 124c-124c, 124e-126e.

A15d

A15e

92	A15d	10c blue green	275.00	24.50
		Bar cancellation		2.50
93	A15e	20c lilac	130.00	10.50
		Bar cancellation		2.50

For overprints see Nos. 116-117, 116a-117a, 116c-117c, 117d, 117e, 117f.

A16

A17

A18

94	A16	5m green	47.50	17.50
		Bar cancellation		2.50
95	A17	10m brown	47.50	17.50
a.		Tête bêche pair	*20,000.*	
96	A18	25m bl & rose	225.00	24.00
		Bar cancellation		5.00
a.		Frame inverted		*50,000.*
97	A18	50m bis brn	22.00	.80
		Bar cancellation		2.75
		Nos. 94-97 (4)	342.00	59.80

See No. 98. For overprints see Nos. 118-122, 118a-122a, 120c-122c, 122d, 120e, 122e, 119f, 122f.

A19

1868-69

98	A18	25m blue	275.00	14.50
		Bar cancellation		3.75
99	A19	50m violet	29.00	.60
		Bar cancellation		2.50
100	A15b	100m brown	550.00	75.00
		Bar cancellation		3.00
101	A15c	200m green	210.00	14.00
		Bar cancellation		3.00
102	A15c	19c brown	2,700.	525.00

For overprints see #123, 123a, 123c, 123e.

Provisional Government

Excellent counterfeits exist of the provisional and provincial overprints.

For Madrid

Regular Issues Handstamped in Black

HABILITADO
POR LA
NACION.

1868-69

116	A15d	10c green	40.00	16.00
117	A15e	20c lilac	40.00	12.00
118	A16	5m green	40.00	5.50
119	A17	10m brown	30.00	5.50
120	A18	25m bl & rose	50.00	14.50
g.		Frame inverted	*15,000.*	
121	A18	25m blue	70.00	12.00
g.		Double overprint (black & red)		75.00
122	A18	50m bis brn	10.00	5.00
123	A19	50m violet	10.00	5.00
124	A15b	100m brown	150.00	28.50
125	A15c	200m green	50.00	9.00
126	A15b	12c org yel (#90)	50.00	11.00
127	A15c	19c rose	600.00	140.00
128	A15c	19c brown	1,000.	165.00
		Nos. 116-128 (13)	2,140.	429.00

Nos. 116-128 exist with handstamp in blue, a few in red. These sell for more.

For Andalusian Provinces

Regular Issues Handstamped Vertically in Blue

HABILITADO
POR LA
NACION.

114a	A15	2c brown	87.50	36.00
115a	A15a	4c blue	60.00	25.00
116a	A15d	10c green	60.00	15.00
117a	A15e	20c lilac	40.00	16.00
118a	A16	5m green	40.00	8.25
119a	A17	10m brown	25.00	6.00
120a	A18	25m bl & rose	70.00	15.00
b.		Frame inverted	*22,000.*	
121a	A18	25m blue	70.00	15.50
122a	A18	50m bis brn	15.00	5.50
123a	A19	50m violet	15.00	5.50
124a	A15b	100m brown	140.00	32.50
125a	A15c	200m green	50.00	12.00
126a	A15b	12c org yel (#90)	50.00	13.50
127a	A15c	19c rose	600.00	210.00
128a	A15c	19c brown	1,200.	275.00
		Nos. 114a-128a (15)	2,522.	690.75

For Valladolid Province

Regular Issues Handstamped in Black

HABILITADO
POR LA
NACION

(Two types of overprint)

116c	A15d	10c green	60.00	16.50
117c	A15e	20c lilac	60.00	19.00
120c	A18	25m blue & rose	80.00	15.00
121c	A18	25m blue	80.00	21.00
122c	A18	50m bis brn	25.00	9.25
123c	A19	50m violet	25.00	7.75
124c	A15b	100m brown	150.00	38.00
125c	A15c	200m green	60.00	15.00
126c	A15b	12c orange	60.00	12.50
127c	A15c	19c rose	*600.00*	*175.00*
128c	A15c	19c brown	*1,300.*	*240.00*
		Nos. 116c-126c (9)	600.00	154.00

For Asturias Province Llanes (Oviedo)

Regular Issues Handstamped in Black

Habilitado por
la Junta
Revolucionaria

117d	A15e	20c lilac	210.00	125.00
122d	A18	50m bister brown	230.00	125.00

For Teruel Province

Regular Issues Handstamped in Black

HPN

117e	A15e	20c lilac	90.00	55.00
120e	A18	25m blue & rose	110.00	55.00
122e	A18	50m bister brown	85.00	32.50
123e	A19	50m violet	85.00	32.50
124e	A15b	100m brown	185.00	75.00
125e	A15c	200m green	135.00	45.00
126e	A15b	12c orange	110.00	60.00
		Nos. 117e-126e (7)	800.00	355.00

For Salamanca Province

Regular Issues Handstamped in Blue

HABILITADO
POR LA
NACION

117f	A15e	20c lilac	90.00	55.00
119f	A17	10m brown	80.00	42.00
122f	A18	50m bister brown	90.00	50.00
		Nos. 117f-122f (3)	260.00	147.00

Duke de la Torre Regency

"España" — A20

1870, Jan. 1 **Typo.**

159	A20	1m brn lil, *buff*	6.50	6.50
		Bar cancellation		2.00
b.		1m brown lilac, *pinkish buff*	7.00	7.75
161	A20	2m blk, *pinkish*	7.75	8.00
a.		2m black, *buff*	8.75	9.00
163	A20	4m bister brn	16.00	13.50
164	A20	10m rose	19.00	6.00
a.		10m carmine	21.00	7.50
165	A20	25m lilac	52.50	6.50
		Bar cancellation		2.00
a.		25m gray lilac	55.00	6.50
b.		25m aniline violet	85.00	8.25
166	A20	50m ultra	11.50	.35
a.		50m dull blue	125.00	5.00
167	A20	100m red brown	35.00	5.25
		Bar cancellation		1.40
a.		100m claret	35.00	6.25
b.		100m orange brown	35.00	5.50
168	A20	200m pale brown	32.50	5.25
		Bar cancellation		2.00
169	A20	400m green	350.00	25.00
		Bar cancellation		3.00
170	A20	1e600m dull lilac	1,700.	850.00
		Bar cancellation		27.50
171	A20	2e blue	1,400.	525.00
		Bar cancellation		27.50
172	A20	12c red brown	325.00	7.25
173	A20	19c yel grn	450.00	225.00

The 12c carmine rose and 12c blue on pink paper were not put in use. Value $2,000. and $4,000., respectively.

Kingdom

A21

1872, Oct. 1 *Imperf.*

174	A21	¼c ultra	2.25	2.25
a.		Complete 1c (block of 4 ¼c)	120.00	90.00
		Bar cancellation		5.00
b.		As "a," one cliche inverted	1,800.	*1,750.*

See No. 221A.

A22

King Amadeo

A23 A24

1872-73 *Perf. 14*

176	A22	2c gray lilac	20.00	8.00
a.		2c violet	32.50	18.00
b.		Imperf.		75.00
177	A22	5c green	150.00	62.50
a.		Imperf.	170.00	
178	A23	5c rose ('73)	27.50	5.75
179	A23	6c blue	160.00	39.00
180	A23	10c brown lilac	400.00	240.00
181	A23	10c ultra ('73)	8.50	.55
		Bar cancellation		3.50
182	A23	12c gray lilac	27.50	2.50
		Bar cancellation		3.50
183	A23	20c gray vio ('73)	140.00	80.00
		Bar cancellation		5.25
184	A23	25c brown	60.00	12.00
		Bar cancellation		2.75
185	A23	40c pale red brn	80.00	10.50
		Bar cancellation		2.75
186	A23	50c deep green	105.00	11.00
		Bar cancellation		2.75
187	A24	1p lilac	115.00	55.00
		Bar cancellation		4.00
188	A24	4p red brown	750.00	625.00
		Bar cancellation		12.00
189	A24	10p deep green	2,300.	2,400.
		Bar cancellation		250.00

First Republic

Mural Crown — A25

1873, July 1 *Imperf.*

190 A25 ¼c green 1.00 1.00
a. Complete 1c (block of 4 ¼c) 37.50 20.00
As "a," bar cancellation 2.50
d. As "a," ultra (error) 210.00 160.00

"España" — A26

1873, July 1 *Perf. 14*

191 A26 2c orange 13.50 6.00
192 A26 5c claret 30.00 6.00
Bar cancellation 3.00
193 A26 10c green 6.75 .35
Bar cancellation *2.00*
a. Tête bêche pair *32,500.*
194 A26 20c black 110.00 25.00
Bar cancellation 3.75
195 A26 25c dp brn 35.00 6.00
Bar cancellation 2.50
196 A26 40c brown vio 42.50 6.00
Bar cancellation 2.50
197 A26 50c ultra 21.00 6.75
Bar cancellation 2.50
198 A26 1p lilac 72.50 32.50
Bar cancellation 2.50
199 A26 4p red brown 800.00 475.00
Bar cancellation 12.50
200 A26 10p violet brn 2,100. 1,750.
Bar cancellation 24.00

Only one example of No. 193a is known, and it is in a block of six stamps.

"Justice" — A27

1874, July 1

201 A27 2c yellow 22.50 8.50
Bar cancellation 2.10
202 A27 5c violet 45.00 10.00
Bar cancellation 2.10
a. 5c red violet 32.50 10.00
203 A27 10c ultra 12.50 .40
a. Imperf. 13.50
204 A27 20c dark green 225.00 45.00
Bar cancellation 4.00
205 A27 25c red brown 50.00 6.75
Bar cancellation 2.10
a. 25c lilac (error) 325.00
As "a," bar cancellation 30.00
b. Imperf. 57.50
206 A27 40c violet 450.00 8.00
Bar cancellation 2.10
a. 40c brown (error) 250.00
b. Imperf. 190.00
207 A27 50c yellow 105.00 8.25
Bar cancellation 2.10
a. Imperf. 120.00
208 A27 1p yellow green 100.00 34.00
Bar cancellation 2.10
a. 1p emerald 92.50 47.50
b. Imperf. 175.00
209 A27 4p rose 800.00 410.00
Bar cancellation 8.00
a. 4p carmine 800.00 600.00
210 A27 10p black 3,200. 1,900.
Bar cancellation 10.50

Coat of Arms — A28

1874, Oct. 1

211 A28 10c red brown 25.00 .70
Bar cancellation 1.60
a. 10c brown 42.50 3.50
b. Imperf. 90.00

Kingdom

Nos. 212-221 are almost always badly centered and are often irregularly perforated. Values are for stamps with complete perforations and fine centering. Sound stamps with average centering are worth about 50% of these values. Stamps with very fine centering sell for more.

King Alfonso XII — A29

1875, Aug. 1

Blue Framed Numbers on Back, 1-100 on Each Sheet

212 A29 2c org brn 22.50 11.00
a. 2c chocolate brown 30.00 15.00
b. Imperf. 45.00 45.00
213 A29 5c lilac 95.00 13.00
a. Imperf. 95.00 87.50
214 A29 10c blue 8.25 .40
Bar cancellation 2.00
a. Imperf. 22.50 22.50
215 A29 20c brn org 300.00 125.00
216 A29 25c rose 72.50 8.00
Bar cancellation 2.00
217 A29 40c deep brown 125.00 37.50
Bar cancellation 4.50
a. Imperf. 140.00 140.00
218 A29 50c gray lilac 175.00 42.50
Bar cancellation 5.25
219 A29 1p black 225.00 80.00
Bar cancellation 3.00
220 A29 4p dark green 600.00 525.00
221 A29 10p ultra 1,800. 1,750.

1876, June 1 *Imperf.*

221A A21 ¼c green .25 .25
b. Complete 1c (block 4 ¼c) 1.10 .30
As "b," on cover 30.00
c. As "b," two ¼c sideways, one invtd. 110.00 110.00
d. As "b," both upper ¼c invtd. 140.00 140.00
e. As "b," upper left ¼c invtd. 1,000. 500.00
f. As "b," both lower ¼c invtd. 140.00 140.00

No. 221Ac has one stamp upright, one inverted, one facing right and one facing left.

Nos. 222-230 are almost always badly centered. Values are for stamps with fine centering, fresh color and, in the case of mint stamps, full original gum. Sound stamps with average centering are worth about 50% of these values. Stamps with very fine centering sell for more.

King Alfonso XII — A30

Type I

Type II

ONE PESETA:
Type I — Thin figures of value and "PESETA" in thick letters.
Type II — Thick figures of value and "PESETA" in thin letters.

Wmk. 178

1876, June 1 **Engr.** *Perf. 14*

222 A30 5c yellow brown 15.50 3.75
223 A30 10c blue 3.75 .45
Bar cancellation 50.00
224 A30 20c bronze green 19.00 13.00
225 A30 25c brown 8.50 5.50
226 A30 40c black brown 80.00 *100.00*
227 A30 50c green 15.00 6.75
228 A30 1p dp blue, I 20.00 9.00
a. 1p ultra, II 27.50 13.00
229 A30 4p brown violet 55.00 *57.50*
230 A30 10p vermilion 150.00 125.00
Nos. 222-230 (9) 366.75 320.95

Imperf

222a A30 5c 11.50
223a A30 10c 5.75
225a A30 25c 12.50
227a A30 50c 18.00
228b A30 1p 26.00
229a A30 4p 92.50
230a A30 10p 200.00

Two plates each were used for the 5c, 10c, 25c, 50c, 1p and 10p. The 1p plates are most easily distinguished.

The 20c value also exists imperf. Value $500.

King Alfonso XII — A31

Unwmk.

1878, July 1 **Typo.** *Perf. 14*

232 A31 2c mauve 32.50 11.00
a. Imperf. 60.00
233 A31 5c orange 45.00 14.00
234 A31 10c brown 8.25 .50
Bar cancellation 3.00
235 A31 20c black 175.00 125.00
a. Imperf. 275.00
236 A31 25c olive bister 25.00 2.75
Bar cancellation 6.25
237 A31 40c red brown 190.00 140.00
238 A31 50c blue green 120.00 11.00
Bar cancellation 2.00
239 A31 1p gray 100.00 21.00
Bar cancellation 2.00
240 A31 4p violet 225.00 125.00
241 A31 10p blue 450.00 350.00
a. Imperf. 475.00
Nos. 232-241 (10) 1,370. 800.25

A32

1879, May 1

242 A32 2c black 9.50 4.50
Bar cancellation 3.00
243 A32 5c gray green 15.00 1.10
Bar cancellation 3.00
244 A32 10c rose 15.00 .45
Bar cancellation 2.00
245 A32 20c red brown 175.00 15.00
Bar cancellation 2.00
246 A32 25c bluish gray 15.50 .45
Bar cancellation 2.00
247 A32 40c brown 29.00 5.50
Bar cancellation 2.00
248 A32 50c dull buff 130.00 5.00
Bar cancellation 2.00
a. 50c yellow 190.00 7.00
249 A32 1p brt rose 150.00 2.25
Bar cancellation 2.00
250 A32 4p lilac gray 750.00 32.50
Bar cancellation 3.00
251 A32 10p olive bister 2,200. *175.00*
Bar cancellation 6.25

A33

1882, Jan. 1

252 A33 15c salmon 10.50 .25
Bar cancellation 2.00
a. 15c reddish orange 35.00 .45
253 A33 30c red lilac 310.00 5.25
Bar cancellation 2.00
254 A33 75c gray lilac 210.00 4.75
Bar cancellation 2.00
a. Imperf. 300.00

Nos. 255-270 are usually poorly centered and often exhibit defective perforations. Values are for fine to very fine examples, well centered but not very fine, fresh and without perforation faults. Average examples sell for about half these values.

King Alfonso XIII — A34

1889-99

255 A34 2c blue green 6.00 .45
256 A34 2c black ('99) 35.00 7.25
257 A34 5c blue 12.50 .25
258 A34 5c blue grn ('99) 145.00 1.40
259 A34 10c yellow brown 16.50 .25
260 A34 10c red ('99) 240.00 4.50
261 A34 15c violet brown 4.75 .25
262 A34 20c yellow green 50.00 4.75
263 A34 25c blue 20.00 .25
264 A34 30c olive gray 82.50 5.25
265 A34 40c brown 87.50 3.00
266 A34 50c rose 80.00 2.10
267 A34 75c orange 210.00 4.25
268 A34 1p dark violet 55.00 .45
a. 1p carmine rose (error) 350.00
269 A34 4p carmine rose 650.00 47.50
270 A34 10p orange red 1,200. 110.00

The 15c yellow, type A34 is an official stamp listed as No. O9.
Several values exist imperf.

Nos. 272-286 are almost always badly centered. Values are for stamps with fine centering, fresh color and, if unused, full original gum. Sound stamps with average centering sell for about half these values. Very fine stamps sell more more.

King Alfonso XIII — A35

Control Number on Back

1901-05 **Engr.** **Unwmk.**

272 A35 2c bister brown 3.25 .25
273 A35 5c dark green 5.75 .25
274 A35 10c rose red 9.50 .25
275 A35 15c blue black 17.00 .25
276 A35 15c dull lilac ('02) 13.00 .25
277 A35 15c purple ('05) 6.25 .25
278 A35 20c grnsh black 32.50 2.75
279 A35 25c blue 6.25 .40
280 A35 30c deep green 42.50 .35
281 A35 40c olive bister 150.00 5.00
282 A35 40c rose ('05) 300.00 4.50
283 A35 50c slate blue 32.50 .55
b. 50c blue green (error) *2,250.* *1,100.*
284 A35 1p lake 30.00 .80
285 A35 4p dk violet 250.00 22.50
286 A35 10p brown orange 225.00 72.50
Nos. 272-286 (15) 1,123. 110.85
Set, never hinged 2,500.

There are numerous shades and unissued colors for this issue.

Imperf

272a A35 2c 57.50
273a A35 5c 25.00
274a A35 10c 25.00
275a A35 15c 110.00
276a A35 15c 22.50
277a A35 15c 17.00
278a A35 20c 90.00
279a A35 25c 17.00
280b A35 30c 110.00
282a A35 40c 300.00
283a A35 50c 125.00
284a A35 1p 57.50
285a A35 4p 200.00
286a A35 10p 190.00

The 15c in red brown (value $850), 30c blue ($950), 1p olive ($1,000), 1p blue green ($900) and 1p dark violet ($900) were prepared but not issued.

Nos. 287-296 are almost always badly centered. Values are for stamps with fine centering, fresh color and, if unused, full original gum. Sound stamps with average centering sell for about half these values. Very fine stamps sell for more.

Don Quixote Starts Forth A36

10c, Don Quixote attacks windmill. 15c, Meets country girls. 25c, Sancho Panza tossed in blanket. 30c, Don Quixote knighted. 40c, Tilting at sheep. 50c, On Wooden horse. 1p, Adventure with lions. 4p, In bullock cart, 10p, The Enchanted Lady.

Control Number on Back

1905, May 1 **Typo.**

287 A36 5c dark green 1.25 1.10
a. Imperf. 50.00
288 A36 10c orange red 2.50 1.75
289 A36 15c violet 2.50 1.75
a. Imperf. 80.00
290 A36 25c dark blue 7.00 3.50
291 A36 30c dk blue green 50.00 10.00
292 A36 40c bright rose 70.00 32.50
293 A36 50c slate 22.50 7.00
294 A36 1p rose red 200.00 90.00

295	A36	4p dk violet	110.00	90.00
296	A36	10p brown orange	160.00	135.00
		Nos. 287-296 (10)	625.75	372.60
		Set, never hinged	2,500.	

300th anniversary of the publication of Cervantes' "Don Quixote."

Counterfeits exist of Nos. 287-296.

For surcharges see Nos. 586-588, C91.

Six stamps picturing King Alfonso XIII and Queen Victoria Eugenia were put on sale Oct. 1, 1907, at the Madrid Industrial Exhibition. They were not valid for postage. Value, unused $40, mint never hinged $60.

The original labels were engraved and perf 11½. Examples printed by other methods or with other perfs are reprints. Value $2.

Alfonso XIII — A46

Blue Control Number on Back

Perf. 13x12½, 13, 13½x13, 14

1909-22 **Engr.**

297	A46	2c dark brown	.55	.55
a.		No control number	.55	.25
		Never hinged	2.00	
298	A46	5c green	2.00	.25
299	A46	10c carmine	3.00	.25
300	A46	15c violet	9.50	.25
301	A46	20c olive green	50.00	.90
302	A46	25c deep blue	4.75	.25
303	A46	30c blue green	9.75	.25
304	A46	40c rose	15.50	.65
305	A46	50c blue ('22)	11.50	.40
a.		50c slate blue	12.50	.40
		Never hinged	24.00	
306	A46	1p lake	32.50	.40
307	A46	4p deep violet	80.00	12.00
309	A46	10p orange	100.00	26.00
		Nos. 297-309 (12)	319.05	42.15
		Set, never hinged	1,200.	

Nos. 297-309 exist imperforate. Value $500.

The 5c exists in carmine; the 10c in yellow orange (value $400); the 15c in blue (value $400); the 4p in lake (value $1,000). The 5c and 15c are unissued trial colors, privately perforated and back-numbered. The 4p lake is known only with perfin "B.H.A." (Banco Hispano-Americano). 100 examples of the 4p exist, most poorly centered.

See Nos. 310, 315-317. For overprints see Nos. C1-C5, C58-C61.

Counterfeits exist.

Control Number on Back in Red or Orange

1917

310	A46	15c yellow ocher	3.50	.35
		Never hinged	6.00	
a.		Control number in blue	14.50	1.10

Control Number on Back in Blue

1918

313	A46	40c light red	82.50	5.75
		Never hinged	150.00	

A47

1920 **Typo.** ***Imperf.***

314	A47	1c blue green	.25	.25
		Never hinged	.30	

Perf. 13x12½,

Litho.

315	A46	2c bister	5.00	.25
316	A46	20c violet	42.50	.25
		Nos. 314-316 (3)	47.75	.75
		Set, Never Hinged	145.00	

Nos. 314-315 have no control number on back.

For overprints and surcharge see Nos. 358, 449, 457, 468, 10L1, 11LB1.

1921 **Engr.**

317	A46	20c violet	30.00	.25
		Never hinged	52.50	

Madrid Post Office — A48

1920, Oct. 1 **Typo.** ***Perf. 13½***

Center and Portrait in Black

318	A48	1c blue green	.25	*.25*
319	A48	2c olive bister	.25	*.25*

Control Number on Back

320	A48	5c green	1.00	*1.10*
321	A48	10c red	1.00	*1.10*
322	A48	15c yellow	1.60	1.40
323	A48	20c violet	1.90	1.75
324	A48	25c gray blue	3.00	3.00
325	A48	30c dark green	7.00	5.50
326	A48	40c rose	29.00	7.25
327	A48	50c brt blue	32.50	20.00
328	A48	1p brown red	32.50	16.50
329	A48	4p brown violet	100.00	70.00
330	A48	10p orange	200.00	145.00
		Nos. 318-330 (13)	410.00	273.10
		Set, never hinged	1,200.	

King Alfonso XIII
A49 A49a

Type I Type II

FIFTEEN CENTIMOS:
Type I — Narrow "5."
Type II — Wide "5."

Type I Type II

TWENTY FIVE CENTIMOS:
Type I — "25" is 2¾mm high. Vertical stroke of "5" is 1mm long.
Type II — "25" is 3mm high. Vertical stroke of "5" is 1½mm long.

Perf. 11 to 14, Compound

1922-26 **Engr.** **Unwmk.**

331	A49	2c olive green	.85	.25
a.		2c deep orange (error)	87.50	*210.00*
		Never hinged	*125.00*	

Control Number on Back

332	A49	5c red violet	4.00	.25
333	A49	5c claret	1.60	.25
334	A49	10c carmine	1.60	1.10
335	A49	10c yellow green	1.50	.25
a.		10c blue green ('23)	2.25	.25
		Never hinged	7.50	
336	A49	15c slate bl (I)	8.00	.25
a.		15c black green (II)	27.50	2.25
		Never hinged	65.00	
337	A49	20c violet	3.50	.25
		Never hinged	14.00	
338	A49	25c carmine (I)	3.50	.25
a.		25c rose red (II)	5.50	1.00
		Never hinged	15.00	
b.		25c lilac rose (error)	100.00	160.00
		Never hinged	*225.00*	
339	A49	30c black brn ('26)	15.00	.25
		Never hinged	42.50	
340	A49	40c deep blue	4.00	.25
341	A49	50c orange	19.50	.25
a.		50c orange red	77.50	1.90
		Never hinged	150.00	
342	A49a	1p blue black	18.00	.25
343	A49a	4p lake	85.00	4.00
344	A49a	10p brown	40.00	13.50
		Nos. 331-344 (14)	206.05	21.35
		Set, never hinged	650.00	

Nos. 331, 334, 336-344 exist imperf.

The 5c exists in vermilion (value $110); the 25c in dark blue (value $200). The 50c exists in red brown, the 4p in brown and 10p in lake; value, each $90. These five were not regularly issued.

For overprints see Nos. 359-370, 467.

"Santa Maria" and View of Seville A50

Herald of Barcelona — A51

Exposition Buildings — A52

King Alfonso XIII and View of Barcelona A53

1929, Feb. 15 ***Perf. 11***

345	A50	1c grnsh blue	2.50	2.50
346	A51	2c pale yel grn	.30	.30
347	A52	5c rose lake	.50	.50

Control Number on Back

348	A53	10c green	.50	.50
349	A50	15c Prus blue	.85	.85
350	A51	20c purple	.55	.55
351	A50	25c brt rose	.55	.55
352	A52	30c black brn	4.00	*4.75*
353	A53	40c dark blue	7.75	7.75
354	A51	50c deep orange	7.75	*4.75*
355	A52	1p blue black	11.50	*12.00*
356	A53	4p deep rose	25.00	25.00
357	A53	10p brown	65.00	*70.00*
		Nos. 345-357,E2 (14)	146.25	152.50
		Set, never hinged	300.00	

Perf. 14

345a	A50	1c greenish blue	.70	.70
348a	A53	10c green	20.00	37.50
349a	A50	15c Prus blue	22.50	22.50
350a	A51	20c purple	26.00	37.50
351a	A50	25c bright rose	32.50	37.50
352a	A52	30c black brown	32.50	37.50
353a	A53	40c dark blue	70.00	90.00
354a	A51	50c deep orange	32.50	37.50
355a	A52	1p blue black	32.50	37.50
356a	A53	4p deep rose	25.00	25.00
357a	A53	10p brown	110.00	140.00
		Nos. 345a-357a,E2a (12)	436.70	540.70
		Set, never hinged	725.00	

Seville and Barcelona Exhibitions.

Nos. 345-357 exist imperf. Value, set $2,500. See note after No. 432.

Nos. 314, 331, 333, 335-344 Overprinted in Red or Blue

Sociedad
de las Naciones
LV reunión
del Consejo
Madrid.

1929, June 10 ***Imperf.***

358	A47	1c blue green	.50	.80

Perf. 13½x12½

359	A49	2c olive green	.55	*1.00*
360	A49	5c claret (Bl)	.55	*1.00*
361	A49	10c yellow green	.55	*1.00*
362	A49	15c slate blue	.55	*1.00*
363	A49	20c violet	.55	*1.00*
364	A49	25c carmine (Bl)	.55	*1.00*
365	A49	30c black brown	2.25	*4.00*
366	A49	40c deep blue	2.25	*4.00*
367	A49	50c orange (Bl)	2.25	*4.00*
368	A49a	1p blue black	11.00	*19.00*
369	A49a	4p lake (Bl)	11.00	*21.00*
370	A49a	10p brown (Bl)	40.00	*70.00*
		Nos. 358-370,E4 (14)	84.55	*153.80*
		Set, never hinged	250.00	

55th assembly of League of Nations at Madrid June 10-16. The stamps were available for postal use only on those days.

Nos. 359-370 values are for off-center copies. Well centered stamps seel for about 4 times these values.

Exposition Building — A54

1930 **Litho.** ***Perf. 11***

371	A54	5c dk blue & salmon	6.25	5.00
372	A54	5c dk violet & blue	6.25	5.00
		Set, Never Hinged	22.50	

Barcelona Philatelic Congress and Exhibition. "C. F. y E. F." are the initials of "Congreso Filatelico y Exposicion Filatelica." For each admission ticket, costing 2.75 pesetas, the holder was allowed to buy one of each of these stamps.

A55

Locomotives A56

1930, May 10 ***Perf. 14***

373	A55	1c light blue	.95	*.95*
374	A55	2c apple green	.95	*.95*

Control Number on Back

375	A55	5c lake	1.10	*1.10*
376	A55	10c yellow green	1.10	*1.10*
377	A55	15c bluish gray	1.10	*1.10*
378	A55	20c purple	1.10	*1.10*
379	A55	25c brt rose	1.10	*1.00*
380	A55	30c olive gray	3.50	3.50
381	A55	40c dark blue	3.50	3.50
382	A55	50c dk orange	8.00	*8.00*
383	A56	1p dark gray	8.00	*8.00*
384	A56	4p deep rose	80.00	100.00
385	A56	10p bister brn	300.00	375.00
		Nos. 373-385,C12-C17,E6 (20)	565.90	*652.80*
		Set, never hinged	1,800.	

11th Intl. Railway Congress, Madrid, 1930.

These stamps were on sale May 10-21, 1930, exclusively at the Palace of the Senate in Madrid and at the Barcelona and Seville expositions.

Forgeries are plentiful.

Francisco de Goya at Age 80
("1746 1828") ("1828 1928")
A57 A59

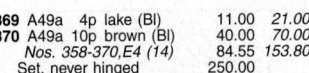

"La Maja Desnuda" — A58

1930, June 15   Litho.   Perf. 12½
Inscribed "Correos Espana"

386	A57	1c yellow	.25	.25
387	A57	2c bister brn	.25	.25
388	A57	5c lilac rose	.25	.25
389	A57	10c green	.25	.25

Engr.

390	A57	15c lt blue	.30	.25
391	A57	20c brown violet	.30	.25
392	A57	25c red	.30	.25
393	A57	30c brown	4.25	4.00
394	A57	40c dark blue	4.25	4.00
395	A57	50c vermilion	4.25	4.00
396	A57	1p black	5.00	4.75
397	A58	1p dark violet	1.25	.75
398	A58	4p slate gray	.90	.55
399	A58	10p red brown	12.50	7.00

Inscribed "1828 Goya 1928"
Litho.

400	A59	2c olive green	.25	.25
401	A59	5c gray violet	.25	.25

Engr.

402	A59	25c rose carmine	.40	.35
	Nos. 386-402,C18-C30,CE1,E7			
	(32)		49.40	41.90
	Set, never hinged		66.00	

To commemorate the death of Francisco de Goya y Lucientes, painter and engraver.
Nos. 386-399 were issued in connection with the Spanish-American Exposition at Seville.
Nos. 386-402 exist imperf. Value, set $300.
See note after No. 432.

King Alfonso XIII — A61

Two types of the 40c

Type I   Type II

1930   Perf. 11½, 12x11½

406	A61	2c red brown	.25	.25

Control Number on Back

407	A61	5c black brown	.70	.25
408	A61	10c green	3.25	.25
409	A61	15c slate green	11.00	.25
410	A61	20c dark violet	6.00	.70
411	A61	25c carmine	.70	.25
412	A61	30c brown lake	15.50	1.75
413	A61	40c dk blue (I)	21.00	1.10
a.		Type II	27.50	1.10
		Never hinged	60.00	
414	A61	50c orange	19.00	1.90
	Nos. 406-414 (9)		77.40	6.70
	Set, never hinged		240.00	

Nos. 406-414 exist imperf. Value for set, $350.
For overprints see #450-455, 458-466, 469-487.

Bow of "Santa Maria" — A63

Stern of "Santa Maria" — A64

"Santa Maria," "Niña," "Pinta" — A65

Columbus Leaving Palos — A66

Columbus Arriving in America — A67

1930, Sept. 29   Litho.   Perf. 12½

418	A63	1c olive gray	.25	.25
419	A64	2c olive green	.25	.25
420	A63	2c olive green	.25	.25
421	A64	5c red brown	.25	.25
422	A63	5c red brown	.25	.25
423	A64	10c blue green	.85	.70
424	A63	15c ultra	.85	.90
425	A64	20c violet	1.25	1.10

Engr.

426	A65	25c dark red	1.25	1.10
427	A66	30c bis brn, bl & blk brn	5.00	5.50
428	A65	40c ultra	4.50	5.00
429	A66	50c dk vio, bl & vio brn	6.50	5.75
430	A65	1p black	6.50	5.75
431	A67	4p blk & dk blue	8.00	6.50
432	A67	10p red brn & dk brn	25.00	25.00
	Nos. 418-432,E8 (16)		62.85	60.45
	Set, never hinged		135.00	

Christopher Columbus tribute.
Nos. 418 to 432 were privately produced. Their promoters presented a certain quantity of these labels to the Spanish Postal Authorities, who placed them on sale and allowed them to be used for three days, retaining the money obtained from the sale.
This note will also apply to Nos. 345-357, 386-402, 433-448, 557-571, B1-B105, C18-C57, C73-C87, CB1-CB5, CE1, E2, E7-E9, E15 and EB1.
Many so-called "errors" of color and perforation are known.
Nos. 418-432 exist imperf. Value, set $450. stamps.
See Nos. 2671, B194.

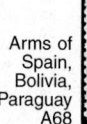

Arms of Spain, Bolivia, Paraguay — A68

Pavilion and Map of Central America — A69

Exhibition Pavilion of Ecuador — A70

Colombia Pavilion — A71

Dominican Republic Pavilion A72

Uruguay Pavilion A73

Argentina Pavilion A74

Chile Pavilion A75

Brazil Pavilion A76

Mexico Pavilion A77

Cuba Pavilion A78

Peru Pavilion A79

U.S. Pavilion A80

Exhibition Pavilion of Portugal — A81

King Alfonso XIII and Queen Victoria — A82

Unwmk.
1930, Oct. 10   Photo.   Perf. 14

433	A68	1c blue green	.25	.25
434	A69	2c bister brown	.25	.25
435	A70	5c olive brown	.25	.25
436	A71	10c dark green	.35	.35
437	A72	15c indigo	.35	.35
438	A73	20c violet	.35	.35
439	A74	25c car rose	.35	.35
440	A75	25c car rose	.35	.35
441	A76	30c rose lilac	1.75	1.75
442	A77	40c slate blue	1.00	1.00
443	A78	40c slate blue	1.00	1.00
444	A79	50c brown org	1.75	1.75
445	A80	1p ultra	2.50	2.50
446	A81	4p brown violet	30.00	27.50
447	A82	10p brown	2.10	2.10

Perf. 11, 14
Engr.

448	A82	10p dk reddish brn	47.50	47.50
	Nos. 433-448,C50-C57,E9			
	(25)		112.30	103.85
	Set, never hinged		325.00	

Spanish-American Union Exhibition, Seville.
The note after No. 432 will also apply to Nos. 433-448. All values exist imperforate. Value, set: hinged $250; never hinged $350.
Reprints of Nos. 433-448 have blurred colors, yellowish paper and an inferior, almost invisible gum. They sell for about one-tenth the value of originals.

Revolutionary Issues
Madrid Issue

Regular Issues of 1920-30 Overprinted in Black, Green or Red

1931   On No. 314   Imperf.

449	A47	1c blue green	.25	.25

On Nos. 406-411
Perf. 11½

450	A61	2c red brown (G)	.30	.25
451	A61	5c black brn (R)	.40	.40
452	A61	10c green	.70	.70
453	A61	15c slate grn (R)	1.40	1.50
454	A61	20c dk violet (R)	1.40	1.50
455	A61	25c carmine (G)	1.90	2.25
		Nos. 449-455,E10 (8)	11.35	11.85
		Set, never hinged	22.50	

The status of Nos. 449-455, E10 has been questioned.

First Barcelona Issue

Regular Issues of 1920-30 Overprinted in Black or Red

1931 **On No. 314** *Imperf.*

457	A47	1c blue green	.25	.25

On Nos. 406-414
Perf. 11½

458	A61	2c red brown	.25	.25
459	A61	5c black brown	.25	.25
460	A61	10c green	.55	.55
461	A61	15c slate grn (R)	.60	.60
462	A61	20c dk violet (R)	.60	.60
463	A61	25c carmine	.60	.60
464	A61	30c brown lake	4.50	4.50
465	A61	40c dk blue (R)	1.25	1.25
466	A61	50c orange	1.25	1.25

On Stamp of 1922-26

467	A49a	1p blue blk (R)	7.50	6.25
		Nos. 457-467,E11 (12)	23.10	21.85
		Set, never hinged	45.00	

Nos. 457-467 are known both with and without accent over "U."

The status of Nos. 457-467, E11 has been questioned.

Second Barcelona Issue

Regular Issues of 1920-30 Overprinted in Black or Red

On No. 314 *Imperf.*

468	A47	1c blue green	.25	.25

On Nos. 406-414
Perf. 11½

469	A61	2c red brown	.25	.25
470	A61	5c black brown (R)	.25	.25
471	A61	10c green	.25	.25
472	A61	15c slate grn (R)	1.40	1.25
473	A61	20c dark violet (R)	.40	.45
474	A61	25c carmine	.40	.45
475	A61	30c brown lake	5.75	5.75
476	A61	40c dark blue (R)	1.25	1.25
477	A61	50c orange	4.50	3.50
		Nos. 468-477 (10)	14.70	13.65
		Set, never hinged	27.50	

The status of Nos. 469-477, C58-C61 has been questioned.

General Issue of the Republic

Nos. 406-414, 342 Overprinted in Blue or Red

1931, May 27

478	A61	2c red brown	.25	.25
479	A61	5c black brn (R)	.25	.25
480	A61	10c green (R)	.30	.25
481	A61	15c slate grn (R)	3.50	.25
482	A61	20c dk violet (R)	1.50	1.00
483	A61	25c carmine	.50	.25
484	A61	30c brown lake	4.50	1.00
485	A61	40c dk blue (R)	4.50	.55
486	A61	50c orange	7.75	.55
487	A49a	1p blue blk (R)	57.50	1.00
		Nos. 478-487,E12 (11)	87.05	6.60
		Set, never hinged	230.00	

The setting contained 18 repetitions of "Republica Espanola" for each vertical row of 10 stamps. According to its sheet position, a stamp received different parts of the overprinted words.

Overprint position varieties include: reading down on 25c, 30c, 40c and 50c; double on 1p; double, both reading down, on 25c, 40c and 50c.

"Republica Espanola"
Stamps of various Spanish colonies overprinted "Republica Espanola" are listed with the colonies.

Fountain of Lions, The Alhambra, Granada
A84

Interior of Mosque, Córdoba — A85

Alcántara Bridge and Alcazar, Toledo
A86

Francisco García y Santos
A87

Puerta del Sol, Madrid, on April 14, 1931 as Republic Was Proclaimed
A88

Perf. 12½

1931, Oct. 10 **Unwmk.** **Engr.**

491	A84	5c violet brown	.25	.25
492	A85	10c blue green	.35	.35
493	A86	15c dark violet	.35	.35
494	A85	25c deep red	.35	.35
495	A87	30c olive green	.35	.35
496	A84	40c indigo	.90	.90
497	A85	50c orange red	.90	.90
498	A86	1p black	1.60	1.60
499	A88	4p red violet	8.00	8.00
500	A88	10p red brown	25.00	*25.00*
		Nos. 491-500,C62-C67,CO1-CO6,O20-O29 (32)	100.25	99.35
		Set, never hinged	170.00	

3rd Pan-American Postal Union Cong., Madrid.

Nos. 491-500 exist imperforate. Value, set: hinged $150; never hinged $250.

Symbolical of Montserrat Cut With a Saw — A89

Abbott Oliva and Monastery Workman — A90

"Black Virgin"
A91 A92

Montserrat Monastery — A93

1931, Dec. 9 *Perf. 11, 14*

501	A89	1c myrtle green	1.25	1.50
a.		Perf. 14	21.00	21.00
		Never hinged	40.00	
502	A89	2c red brown	.70	1.10
a.		Perf. 14	15.00	16.00
		Never hinged	30.00	

Control Number on Back

503	A89	5c black brown	.85	1.40
a.		Perf. 14	15.00	16.00
		Never hinged	30.00	
504	A89	10c yellow green	.95	1.40
a.		Perf. 14	15.00	19.00
		Never hinged	30.00	
505	A90	15c myrtle green	1.25	1.75
a.		Perf. 14	21.00	25.00
		Never hinged	40.00	
506	A91	20c dark violet	2.50	2.50
a.		Perf. 11	110.00	150.00
		Never hinged	*210.00*	
507	A92	25c lake	3.50	3.50
a.		Perf. 14	6.25	7.25
		Never hinged	12.50	
508	A91	30c deep red	35.00	32.50
a.		Perf. 14	45.00	45.00
		Never hinged	87.50	
509	A93	40c dull blue	20.00	18.00
a.		Perf. 11	150.00	175.00
		Never hinged	*310.00*	
510	A90	50c dark orange	45.00	40.00
a.		Perf. 14	70.00	80.00
		Never hinged	*140.00*	
511	A92	1p gray black	45.00	40.00
a.		Perf. 11	87.50	110.00
		Never hinged	*175.00*	
512	A93	4p lilac rose	425.00	400.00
a.		Perf. 14	575.00	900.00
		Never hinged	*1,000.*	
513	A92	10p deep brown	325.00	275.00
a.		Perf. 14	800.00	950.00
		Never hinged	*1,500.*	
		Nos. 501-511,C68-C72,E13 (17)	270.55	262.20
		Set, never hinged	410.00	
		Nos. 501-513,C68-C72,E13 (19)	978.00	903.65
		Set, never hinged	2,000.	

Commemorative of the building of the old Monastery at Montserrat, started in 1031, and of the image of the Black Virgin (said to have been carved by St. Luke) which was crowned by Pope Leo XIII in 1881.

Nos. 501-513 exist imperforate. Value, set $4,000.

For surcharges see Nos. 589, C92-C96.

Francisco Pi y Margall — A95

Joaquín Costa — A96

Nicolás Salmerón
A97

Pablo Iglesias
A99

Emilio Castelar — A100

1931-32 *Perf. 11½*

Control Number on Back

516	A95	5c brnsh black	3.00	.30
517	A96	10c yellow green	7.25	.30
518	A97	15c slate green	4.75	.25
520	A99	25c lake	22.50	.70
b.		Imperf.	175.00	
		Never hinged	225.00	
521	A99	30c carmine rose	7.25	.25
c.		Imperf.	82.50	
		Never hinged	125.00	
522	A100	40c dark blue	42.50	4.50
523	A97	50c orange	52.50	7.75
		Never hinged	165.00	
		Nos. 516-523 (7)	139.75	14.05
		Set, never hinged	425.00	

Without Control Number

516a	A95	5c brownish blk ('32)	4.50	.25
517a	A96	10c yel grn ('32)	4.00	.25
518a	A97	15c sl grn ('32)	.60	.25
520a	A99	25c lake	32.50	.25
521a	A99	30c carmine rose	1.90	.25
522a	A100	40c dark blue ('32)	.25	.25
523a	A97	50c orange ('32)	26.00	.50
		Nos. 516a-523a (7)	69.75	2.00
		Set, never hinged	150.00	

Without Control Number, Imperf.

516b	A95	5c	6.50
517b	A96	10c	11.00
518b	A97	15c	6.25
520c	A99	25c	*110.00*
521b	A99	30c	5.50
522b	A100	40c	14.00
523b	A97	50c	125.00
		Nos. 516b-523b (7)	278.25
		Set, Never Hinged	550.00

See Nos. 532, 538, 550, 579, 579a.

For overprints and surcharges see Nos. 7LC12-7LC13, 7LC15-7LC16, 7LC18, 7LE4, 8LB6, 8LB9-8LB10, 9LC17-9LC18, 10L7, 10L10-10L12, 10L16-10L18, 10L22-10L23, 11L7, 11L10-11L12, 11LB8, 12L4, 12L8, 12L11-12L12, 13L8, 14L6, 14L10-14L12, 14L18, 14L22-14L24.

Blasco Ibáñez
A103

Manuel Ruiz-Zorrilla
A104

Without Control Number

1931-34 *Perf. 11½*

526	A103	2c red brown ('32)	.25	.25
528	A103	5c chocolate ('34)	.25	.25
532	A95	20c dark violet	.25	.25
534	A104	25c lake ('34)	.45	.25
538	A100	60c apple green ('32)	.25	.25
		Nos. 526-538 (5)	1.45	1.25
		Set, never hinged	2.50	

Imperf

526a	A103	2c	14.00
528a	A103	5c	2.75
532a	A95	20c	6.25
534a	A104	25c	5.25
538a	A100	60c	6.25
		Nos. 526a-538a (5)	34.50
		Set, never hinged	70.00

For overprints and surcharges see Nos. 8LB3, 8LB7, 9LC3, 9LC8-9LC9, 9LC14, 10L6, 10L13, 11L4, 11L8, 11LB5, 11LB9, 12L5, 12L9, 13L5, 13L7, 14L3, 14L7, 14L15, 14L19.

Cliff Houses, Cuenca — A105

Alcázar of Segovia — A106

Gate of the Sun at Toledo — A107

1932-38 ***Perf. 10***

539	A105	1p gray black ('38)	.25	.25
540	A106	4p magenta ('38)	.30	.40
541	A107	10p deep brown ('38)	.65	.70
		Nos. 539-541 (3)	1.20	1.35
		Set, never hinged	2.75	

Imperf

539a	A105	1p	5.25	2.75
540a	A106	4p	9.00	6.50
541a	A107	10p	6.50	6.00
		Nos. 539a-541a (3)	20.75	15.25
		Set, never hinged	45.00	

Perf. 11½

539b	A105	1p	.25	.25
540b	A106	4p	.70	.85
541b	A107	10p	1.90	3.00
		Nos. 539b-541b (3)	2.85	4.10
		Set, never hinged	5.00	

For overprints and surcharge see Nos. 9LC19, 10L19, 13L9, 14L25, 14L27-14L28.

Numeral — A108

1933 **Unwmk.** **Typo.** ***Imperf.***

542	A108	1c blue green	.25	.25

Perf. 11½

543	A108	2c buff	.25	.25
a.		Perf. 13½x13	.65	.25
		Never hinged	1.40	
		Set, never hinged	.65	

See Nos. 592-597. For surcharges and overprints see Nos. 590-590A, 634A-634D, 8LB1-8LB2, 9LC1-9LC2, 9LC4-9LC7, 9LC11-9LC12, 9LC20, 9LC26, 10L2-10L4, 11L1-11L2, 11LB2-11LB3, 12L1-12L2, 13L1-13L3, 14L1, 14L13.

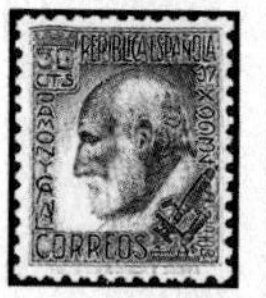
Santiago Ramón y Cajal — A109

1934 **Engr.** ***Perf. 11½x11***

545	A109	30c black brown	6.00	1.10
		Never hinged	16.00	
a.		Perf. 14	22.50	30.00
		Never hinged	42.50	
b.		Imperf.	32.50	
		Never hinged	55.00	

Type of 1931 and

Mariana Pineda A110

Concepción Arenal A111

Gumersindo de Azcarate A112

Gaspar Melchor de Jovellanos A113

1935

546	A110	10c green	.25	.25
b.		10c blue green ('36)	.25	.25
547	A111	15c slate	.25	.25
b.		15c yellow green ('36)	.25	.25
548	A112	30c carmine rose	7.25	.25
549	A113	30c rose red	.25	.25
550	A97	50c dark blue	1.00	.30
		Nos. 546-550 (5)	9.00	1.30
		Set, never hinged	22.00	

Imperf

546a	A110	10c	1.60	
547a	A111	15c	5.25	
548a	A112	30c	26.00	
549a	A113	30c	1.90	
550a	A97	50c	*225.00*	
		Nos. 546a-550a (5)	259.75	
		Set, never hinged	500.00	

Shades exist.

For overprints and surcharges see Nos. 7LE3, 8LB4-8LB5, 8LB8, 10L8-10L9, 10L14, 10L20-10L21, 11L5-11L6, 11L9, 11LB6-11LB7, 11LB10, 12L6-12L7, 12L10, 13L6, 14L4-14L5, 14L8, 14L16-14L17, 14L20.

Lope's Bookplate A116

Lope de Vega A117

Alcántara and Alcázar, Toledo A118

1935, Oct. 12 ***Perf. 11½x11, 11x11½***

552	A116	15c myrtle green	6.25	.30
553	A117	30c rose red	2.75	.30
554	A117	50c dark blue	12.00	3.00
555	A118	1p blue black	23.00	2.00
		Nos. 552-555 (4)	44.00	5.60
		Set, never hinged	100.00	

Imperf

552a	A116	15c	450.00	
553a	A117	30c	16.00	
554a	A117	50c	70.00	
555a	A118	1p	65.00	
		Nos. 552a-555a (4)	601.00	
		Set, never hinged	1,100.	

Perf. 14

553b	A117	30c	6.50	14.50
554b	A117	50c	29.00	45.00
555b	A118	1p	32.50	50.00
		Nos. 553b-555b (3)	68.00	109.50
		Set, never hinged	150.00	

Lope Felix de Vega Carpio (1562-1635), Spanish dramatist and poet.

For surcharge see No. 11LB11.

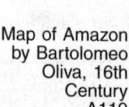

Map of Amazon by Bartolomeo Oliva, 16th Century A119

1935, Oct. 12 ***Perf. 11½***

556	A119	30c rose red	2.10	.95
		Never hinged	5.50	
a.		Perf. 14	26.00	
		Never hinged	54.00	
b.		Imperf.	37.50	
		Never hinged	72.50	

Proposed Iglesias Amazon Expedition.

Miguel Moya — A120

Torcuato Luca de Tena — A121

José Francos Rodríguez A122

Alejandro Lerroux A123

Nazareth School and Rotary Press — A124

1936, Feb. 14 **Photo.** ***Perf. 12½***

Size: 22x26mm

557	A120	1c crimson	.25	.25
558	A121	2c orange brown	.25	.25
559	A122	5c black brown	.25	.25
560	A123	10c emerald	.25	.25

Size: 24x28½mm

561	A120	15c blue green	.25	.25
562	A121	20c violet	.25	.25
563	A122	25c red violet	.25	.25
564	A123	30c crimson	.25	.25

Size: 25½x30½mm

565	A120	40c orange	.55	.40
566	A121	50c ultra	.25	.25
567	A122	60c olive green	.55	.40
568	A123	1p gray black	.55	.40
569	A124	2p lt blue	7.25	3.25
570	A124	4p lilac rose	7.25	6.50
571	A124	10p red brown	18.50	15.50
		Nos. 557-571,E15 (16)	37.15	29.00
		Set, never hinged	70.00	
		Nos. 557-571,C73-C87,E15 (31)	68.30	47.90
		Set, never hinged	130.00	

Madrid Press Association, 40th anniversary.

Nos. 557-571 exist imperf. Values about 7 times those of perf. stamps.

See note after No. 432. See Nos. C73-C87.

Arms of Madrid — A125

1936, Apr. 2 **Engr.** ***Imperf.***

572	A125	10c brown black	47.50	47.50
573	A125	15c dark green	47.50	47.50
		Set, never hinged	135.00	

1st National Philatelic Exhibition which opened in Madrid, Apr. 2, 1936.

For overprints see Nos. C88-C89.

"Republica Espanola" — A126

1936 **Litho.** ***Perf. 11½, 13½x13***

574	A126	2c orange brown	.25	.25
		Never hinged	.35	

For surcharges & overprints see #591, 9LC24, 10L5, 11L3, 11LB4, 12L3, 13L4, 14L2, 14L14.

Gregorio Fernández — A127

1936, Mar. 10 **Engr.** ***Perf. 11½***

576	A127	30c carmine	1.10	.85
		Never hinged	2.25	
a.		Perf. 14	9.00	8.25
		Never hinged	17.50	
b.		Imperf.	15.00	
		Never hinged	22.50	

Tercentenary of the death of Gregorio Fernandez, sculptor.

For overprints see Nos. 7LC20-7LC21.

Type of 1931 and

Pablo Iglesias
A128 A129

Velázquez A130

Fermín Salvoechea A131

1936-38 ***Perf. 11, 11½, 11½x11***

577	A128	30c rose red	.25	.25
578	A129	30c car rose	1.10	.50
579	A100	40c car rose ('37)	1.10	.50
580	A129	45c carmine ('37)	.25	.25
581	A130	50c dark blue	.25	.25
582	A131	60c indigo ('37)	.75	.90
583	A131	60c dp orange ('38)	6.00	5.00
		Nos. 577-583 (7)	9.70	7.65
		Set, never hinged	26.00	

Perf. 14

577a	A128	30c rose red	6.50	
578a	A129	30c carmine rose	6.75	
579a	A100	40c carmine rose	6.50	
580a	A129	45c carmine	6.00	
582a	A131	60c indigo	6.00	
583a	A131	60c deep orange	9.50	
		Nos. 577a-583a (6)	41.25	
		Set, never hinged	90.00	

Nos. 577-583 exist imperf. Value, set $70, never hinged $150.

For overprints see Nos. C90, 7LC17, 7LC22-7LC23, 10L15, 14L21.

Statue of Liberty, Spanish and US Flags — A132

1938, June 1 **Photo.** ***Perf. 11½***

585	A132	1p multicolored	16.50	17.50
		Never hinged	32.50	
a.		Imperf., pair	82.50	55.00
		Never hinged	110.00	
b.		Horiz. pair, imperf. vert.	62.50	82.50
		Never hinged	92.50	
c.		Souvenir sheet of 1	27.50	32.50
		Never hinged	44.00	
d.		As "c," imperf.	350.00	250.00
		Never hinged	600.00	

150th anniv. of the US Constitution.

For surcharge see No. C97.

No. 289 Surcharged in Black

14 ABRIL 1938
VII Aniversario
de la República
45 cts.

1938   *Perf. 14*
586 A36 45c on 15c violet   15.50 15.50
    Never hinged   19.00

7th anniversary of the Republic.
Values are for examples with perforations nearly touching the design on one or two sides.

No. 289 Surcharged in Black

a

FIESTA DEL
1ºMAYO
1938
TRABAJO
45
céntimos

b

Fiesta del Trabajo
1 MAYO
1938
1 Peseta

1938, May 1
587 A36 45c on 15c violet   3.00 3.00
588 A36 1p on 15c violet   5.25 5.25
    Set, never hinged   12.00

Issued to commemorate Labor Day.
Values are for examples with perforations nearly touching the design on one or two sides.

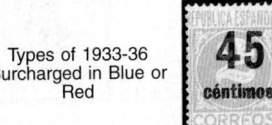

No. 507
Surcharged in
Black

2'50 PTAS.

1938, Nov. 10   *Perf. 11½*
589 A92 2.50p on 25c lake   .25 .25
    Never hinged   .25
  b.   Perf. 14   3.50 6.00
     Never hinged   6.00

Types of 1933-36
Surcharged in Blue or
Red

45
céntimos

1938   *Perf. 10, 11, 13½x13, 13x14*
590 A108 45c on 1c grn (R)   .40 .25
  b.   Imperf.   6.00 5.00
     Never hinged   10.00
590A A108 45c on 2c buff (Bl)   17.00 14.00
591 A126 45c on 2c org brn
      (Bl)   .25 .25
    Nos. 590-591 (3)   17.65 14.50
    Set, never hinged   29.00

Many overprint varieties exist.

Numeral Type of 1933
1938-39   *Litho.*   *Perf. 11½, 13*
White or Gray Paper
592 A108 5c gray brown   .25 .25
593 A108 10c yellow green   .25 .25
594 A108 15c slate green   .25 .25
595 A108 20c vio, gray paper   .25 .25
596 A108 25c red violet   .25 .25
597 A108 30c scarlet   .25 .25
    Nos. 592-597 (6)   1.50 1.50
    Set, never hinged   1.75

"Republic" — A133

1938   *Perf. 11½*
598 A133 40c rose red   .25 .25
599 A133 45c car rose   .25 .25
  a.   Printed on both sides   11.00 11.00
     Never hinged   27.50
600 A133 50c ultra   .25 .25
601 A133 60c dp ultra   .50 .30
    Nos. 598-601 (4)   1.05
    Set, never hinged   1.10

Nos. 598-601 exist imperf. Value for set $22.50

Machine
Gunners
A134

Infantry — A135

Perf. 11½x11, 11x11½, Imperf.
1938, Sept. 1   Photo.
602 A134 25c dark green   12.00 9.25
603 A135 45c red brown   12.00 9.25
    Set, never hinged   60.00

43rd Division of the Republican Army. Sold only at the Philatelic Agency and for foreign exchange.
Nos. 602-603 exist imperf. Value, set $60.

Blast Furnace
A136

Steel Mill and
Sculpture,
"Defenders of
Numantia"
A137

1938, Aug. 9   *Perf. 16*
604 A136   45c black   .25 .25
605 A137 1.25p dark blue   .25 .25
    Set, never hinged   2.00

Issued in honor of the workers of Sagunto.

Submarine — A137a

Designs: 1p, 15p, U-Boat D1. 2p, 6p, U-Boat A1. 4p, 10p, U-Boat B2.

1938, Aug. 11   *Perf. 16*
605A A137a 1p blue   5.50 5.50
605B A137a 2p red brown   10.00 10.00
605C A137a 4p red orange   12.00 12.00
605D A137a 6p deep blue   25.00 25.00
605E A137a 10p magenta   40.00 40.00
605F A137a 15p dp gray
        green   350.00 350.00
    Nos. 605A-605F (6)   442.50 442.50
    Set, never hinged   700.00

Souvenir Sheet
Perf. 10½
605G A137a Sheet of 3   500.00 500.00
    Never hinged   775.00
  a.   4p carmine & gray
      black   100.00 100.00
  b.   6p dull blue & gray
      black   100.00 100.00
  c.   15p green & gray black   100.00 100.00

Nos. 605A-605G were issued for use on a proposed submarine mail service between Barcelona and Mahon, Minorca. One voyage was made on this mail route, carrying 300 agency-prepared covers. The stamps were also valid for ordinary mail.

Nos. 605A-605G were sold only at the Philatelic Agency in Barcelona, for double their face value.

Nos. 605A-605G exist imperf. Value: set of 6 stamps, $775 unused, $1,000 never hinged; souvenir sheet, $2,250 unused, $2,900, never hinged.

Riflemen
A138

Machine
Gunners
A139

Bomb
Throwing — A140

1938, Nov. 25   Engr.   *Perf. 10*
606 A138 5c sepia   3.50 3.50
607 A138 10c dp violet   3.50 3.50
608 A138 25c blue green   3.50 3.50
609 A139 45c rose red   3.50 3.50
610 A139 60c dark blue   6.25 6.25
611 A139 1.20p black   125.00 125.00
612 A140 2p orange   37.50 37.50
613 A140 5p dark brown   200.00 200.00
614 A140 10p dk blue grn   40.00 40.00
    Nos. 606-614 (9)   422.75 422.75
    Set, never hinged   800.00

Honoring the Militia. Sold only at the Philatelic Agency and for foreign exchange. Exist imperf. Value unused $1,200, never hinged $1,800.

Spanish State

Arms of Spain — A141

1936   Litho.   *Imperf.*
Thin Transparent Paper
615 A141 30c blue   250.00
616 A141 30c pale green   250.00

Perf. 11
Thick Wove Paper
617 A141 30c dark blue   550.00 150.00
    Set, never hinged   1,500.

Issued in Granada during siege. After the city was liberated, these stamps were used throughout the province of Granada.
Well-centered copies of No. 617 are worth twice as much as the values above.
Many forgeries exist.

A143

Cathedral of
Burgos — A145

University of
Salamanca
A146

Cathedral del Pilar,
Zaragoza — A147

"La Giralda,"
Seville — A148

Xavier Castle,
Navarre — A149

Court of Lions,
Alhambra at
Granada
A150

Mosque,
Córdoba
A151

Alcántara Bridge
and Alcázar,
Toledo — A152

Soldier
Carrying
Flag — A153

Troops Landing
at Algeciras
A154

30

Type II

Two types of 30c:
Type I — Imprint 12mm long; "3" does not touch frame.
Type II — Imprint 8mm long; "3" touches frame.

1936   Unwmk.   Litho.   *Imperf.*
623 A143 1c green   6.00 4.50
Perf. 11½
624 A143 2c orange brown   .60 .45
625 A145 5c gray brown   .60 .55
626 A146 10c green   .60 .45
627 A147 15c dull green   .60 .45
628 A148 25c rose lake   .85 .45
629 A149 30c carmine (I)   .60 .45
  a.   Type II   .70 .55
     Never hinged   1.70
630 A150 50c deep blue   14.00 8.75
631 A151 60c yellow green   .95 .70

632 A152 1p black 5.25 3.75
633 A153 4p rose vio, red & yel 52.50 29.00
634 A154 10p light brown 52.50 29.00
Nos. 623-634 (12) 135.05 78.50
Set, never hinged 310.00

Nos. 624-634 exist imperf. Value, set $275. Numerous forgeries exist for Nos. 623-634.
Nos. 625-631, 633-634 were privately overprinted "VIA AEREA" and plane, supposedly for use in Ifni.
For surcharges see Nos. 9LC21, 9LC23.

Nos. 542-543 Surcharged in Two Lines

1936 ***Imperf., Perf. 11½***
634A A108 5c on 1c bl grn 2.25 3.00
634B A108 5c on 2c buff 2.25 3.00
634C A108 10c on 1c bl grn 2.25 3.00
634D A108 15c on 2c buff 2.25 3.00
Nos. 634A-634D (4) 9.00 12.00
Set, never hinged 15.00

Issued in the Balearic Islands to meet a shortage of these values. Nos. 634A and 634C are imperf., Nos. 634B and 634D are perf. 11½.

St. James of Compostela — A155

St. James Cathedral A156

Pórtico de la Gloria A157

Type I

Type II

Two types of 30c:
I — No dots in "1937."
II — Dot before and after "1937."

1937 ***Perf. 11½, 11x11½***
635 A155 15c violet brown .95 1.25
636 A156 30c rose red (I) 5.00 .55
a. Type II 17.50 14.00
Never hinged 37.50
637 A157 1p blue & orange 14.50 3.25
a. Center inverted 350.00 250.00
Never hinged 500.00
Nos. 635-637 (3) 20.45 5.05
Set, never hinged 60.00

Holy Year of Compostela. Nos. 635-637 exist imperf. Value for set $175.

"Estado Espanol"
A159 A160

"El Cid" — A161

Isabella I — A162

Two types of 5c, 30c and 10p:
5 Centimos: Type I Imprint 9½mm long. Type II Imprint 14mm long.
30 Centimos: Type I Imprint, "Hija De B. Fournier Burgos." Type II Imprint, "Fournier Burgos".
10 Pesetas: Type I "10" 2½mm high. Type II "10" 3mm high.

With Imprint

1936-40 ***Imperf.***
638 A159 1c green .25 .25
Perf. 11
640 A160 2c brown .25 .25
Perf. 11, 11½, 11½x11, 11½x10½
641 A161 5c brown (I) .45 .25
642 A161 5c brown (II) .25 .25
643 A161 10c green .25 .25
Perf. 11, 11x11½
644 A162 15c gray black .25 .25
645 A162 20c dark violet .40 .25
646 A162 25c brown lake .25 .25
647 A162 30c rose (I) .50 .25
648 A162 30c rose (II) 17.50 2.10
649 A162 40c orange 1.60 .25
650 A162 50c dark blue 1.60 .25
651 A162 60c yellow .30 .25
652 A162 1p blue 16.50 .50
653 A162 4p magenta 21.00 5.25
654 A161 10p dk bl (I) ('37) 75.00 40.00
655 A161 10p dp bl (II) ('40) 32.50 15.00
Nos. 638-655 (17) 168.85 65.85
Set, never hinged 375.00

No. 638 was privately perforated. See Nos. 662-667. For overprint and surcharges see Nos. E18, 9LC10, 9LC13, 9LC15-9LC16, 9LC22, 9LC25, 9LC27-9LC30, 9LC34-9LC53.

Ferdinand the Catholic — A163

1938 ***Perf. 10½, 11½x11***
Imprint: "Lit Fournier Vitoria"
656 A163 15c deep green 1.75 .25
657 A163 30c deep red 5.75 .25
Imprint: "Fournier Vitoria"
Perf. 10
658 A163 15c deep green 1.75 .25
659 A163 20c purple 13.00 1.40
660 A163 25c brown car .90 .25
661 A163 30c deep red 6.50 .25
Nos. 656-661 (6) 29.65 2.65
Set, never hinged 110.00

Nos. 656-661 exist imperf.; value for set, $150. Part-perf. varieties exist.
For overprints see Nos. C98-C99.

Type I

Type II

Two types of the 15 Centimos:
Type I — Medieval style numerals with diagonal line through "5."
Type II — Modern numerals. Narrower "5" without diagonal line.

Without Imprint

1938-50 ***Perf. 11, 13½***
662 A159 1c green, imperf. .25 .25
663 A160 2c brn (18½x22mm; '40) .25 .25
a. 2c bis brn (17½x21mm; '48) .25 .25
Never hinged .30
664 A161 5c gray brn ('39) .25 .25
a. Perf. 13½x13¼ ('49) .25 .25
665 A161 10c dk carmine .25 .25
a. 10c rose .35 .25
Never hinged .75
b. Perf. 13½x13¼ ('49) .25 .25
666 A161 15c dk green (I) .90 .25
666A A161 15c dk green (II) .60 .25
b. Perf 13½x13¼ ('50) .65 .25
667 A162 70c dk blue ('39) .75 .25
Nos. 662-667 (7) 3.25 1.75
Set, never hinged 4.85

Emblem of the Falange — A164

1938, July 17 ***Perf. 10***
668 A164 15c bl grn & lt grn 4.25 3.75
669 A164 25c rose red & rose 4.25 3.75
670 A164 30c bl & lt bl 2.25 2.50
671 A164 1p brown & yellow 90.00 80.00
Nos. 668-671 (4) 100.75 90.00
Set, never hinged 250.00

Second anniversary of the Civil War.
Nos. 678-681 exist imperforate, Value, set $725 hinged, $950 never hinged.

Isabella I — A165

1938-39 **Litho.** ***Perf. 10***
672 A165 20c brt violet ('39) .60 .25
673 A165 25c brown carmine 6.00 .60
674 A165 30c rose red .25 .25
675 A165 40c dull violet .30 .25
676 A165 50c indigo ('39) 27.50 2.50
677 A165 1p deep blue 9.00 .90
Nos. 672-677 (6) 43.65 4.75
Set, never hinged 120.00

Nos. 672-677 exist imperf. Value set, $225 hinged, $350 never hinged.

Gen. Francisco Franco — A166

Imprint: "Sanchez Toda"

1939-40 ***Perf. 10***
678 A166 20c brt violet .35 .25
679 A166 25c rose lake .35 .25
680 A166 30c rose carmine .30 .25
681 A166 40c slate green .25 .25
682 A166 45c vermilion ('40) 1.75 1.75
683 A166 50c indigo .30 .25
684 A166 60c orange 2.75 2.75
685 A166 70c blue .40 .25
686 A166 1p black 11.00 .25
687 A166 2p dark brown 15.00 1.25
688 A166 4p dark violet 85.00 17.50
689 A166 10p light brown 40.00 44.00
Nos. 678-689 (12) 157.45 69.00
Set, never hinged 250.00

#686-689 have value & "Pta." on 1 line while #702-705 have value & "Pta." on 2 lines.
Nos. 678-689 exist imperf. Value set, $525 hinged, $700 never hinged.

Without Imprint
Perf. 9½x10½

1939-47 **Litho.** **Unwmk.**
690 A166 5c dull brn vio .50 .25
691 A166 10c brown orange 2.25 .65
692 A166 15c lt green .55 .25
693 A166 20c brt violet ('40) .55 .25
694 A166 25c dp claret ('40) .55 .25
695 A166 30c blue ('40) .55 .25
697 A166 40c Prus grn ('40) .55 .25
a. 40c greenish black .65 .25
Never hinged 1.10
698 A166 45c ultra ('41) .55 .25
699 A166 50c indigo ('40) .50 .25
a. Perf. 11½ ('47) 32.50 3.00
Never hinged 55.00
700 A166 60c dull org ('40) .70 .25
701 A166 70c blue ('40) .85 .25
702 A166 1p gray blk ('40) 7.50 .25
703 A166 2p dull brn ('41) 8.75 .25
704 A166 4p dull rose ('40) 32.50 .25
705 A166 10p lt brown ('40) 160.00 2.75
Nos. 690-705 (15) 216.85 6.65
Set, never hinged 425.00

Perf. 13x13¼
1949-53 **Litho.** **Unwmk.**
693a A166 20c brt violet .25 .25
694a A166 25c dp claret .25 .25
695a A166 30c blue .25 .25
696 A166 35c aqua ('51) .25 .25
697b A166 40c Prus grn ('50) .25 .25
698a A166 45c ultra ('52) .25 .25
699b A166 50c indigo .25 .25
700a A166 60c dull org .25 .25
701a A166 70c blue ('53) 16.00 .25
702a A166 1p gray blk ('51) 8.25 .25
703a A166 2p dull brn ('50) 3.00 .25
704a A166 4p dull rose 5.00 .25
Nos. 693a-704a (12) 34.25 3.00
Set, never hinged 80.00

The 40c exists in three types, with variations in the value tablet: I. "CTS" does not touch bottom line. II. Light background in tablet. "CTS" touches bottom line. III. As type I, but with well defined lines of white and color around rectangle.
The 60c exists in two types: I. Top and left side of value tablet touch rest of design. II. Tablet separated from rest of design by white lines.
Five values exist with perf. 10: 5c, 10c, 45c, 4p and 10p.
Nos. 690-704 exist imperf. Values, set: mint, never hinged, $1,600; unused, $1,200.
The imperforate 10c dull claret, type A166, without imprint, is a postal tax stamp, RA14.

1944 **Redrawn**
706 A166 1p gray 50.00 .65
Never hinged 110.00

"PTS" instead of "PTA" as No. 702.
Nos. 690-704 and 706 exist imperforate. Value, set $925.

The value reads "PTAS" instead of "PTS"

1944 **Unwmk.** ***Perf. 9½x10½***
709 A166 10p brown 14.00 .30
Never hinged 20.00
a. Perf. 13 ('53) 1.10 .30

General Franco — A167

1942-48 **Engr.** ***Perf. 12½x13***
712 A167 40c chestnut .40 .25
713 A167 75c dk bl, perf. 9½x10½ ('46) 3.50 .40
714 A167 90c dk green ('48) .30 .25
a. Perf. 9½x10½ ('47) 1.40 .25
715 A167 1.35p purple ('48) .90 .25
a. Perf. 9½x10½ ('46) 2.00 .40
Nos. 712-715 (4) 5.10 1.15
Set, never hinged 8.50

St. John of the Cross — A168

1942 **Litho.** ***Perf. 9½x10½***
721 A168 20c violet .55 .25
722 A168 40c salmon 1.25 .60
723 A168 75c ultra 1.50 1.75
Nos. 721-723 (3) 3.30 2.60
Set, never hinged 5.25

St. John of the Cross (1542-1591).
Nos. 721-723 exist imperforate. Value, $65 hinged, $80 never hinged.

Holy Year Issues

Statue in St. James Cathedral A169

St. James of Compostela A170

Incense Burner — A171

Perf. 9½x10½
1943, Oct. **Litho.** **Unwmk.**
724 A169 20c deep blue .25 .25
725 A170 40c dk red brown .50 .25
726 A171 75c deep blue 2.10 2.10

Nos. 725 and 727 exist imperforate. Value, $550.

Carvings in St. James Cathedral
A172   A174

St. James — A173

1943-44 **Perf. 9½x10½, 10½x9½**
727 A172 20c rose red ('44) .25 .25
728 A173 40c dull green .50 .25
729 A174 75c dk blue ('44) 2.75 2.25

St. James' Casket   East Portal of
A175   Cathedral
          A176

St. James Cathedral — A177

1944
730 A175 20c red violet .25 .25
731 A176 40c dull brown .70 .25
732 A177 75c bright blue 30.00 32.00
Nos. 724-732 (9) 37.30 37.85
Set, never hinged 110.00

Millenium of Castile Issues

Arms of   Arms of
Soria — A178   Castile — A179

Arms of Avila   Fortress
A180   A181

Arms of Segovia
A182

Arms of Fernan González
A183

Arms of Burgos   Arms of
A185   Santander
          A186

1944 **Litho.** **Perf. 9½x10½**
733 A178 20c violet .30 .25
734 A179 40c dull brown 3.00 .50
735 A180 75c blue 3.00 3.00
736 A181 20c rose violet .25 .25
737 A182 40c dull brown 2.75 .50
738 A183 75c dull blue 2.60 2.75
739 A180 20c red violet .25 .25
740 A185 40c dull brown 2.10 .50
741 A186 75c blue 3.00 3.25
Nos. 733-741 (9) 17.25 11.25
Set, never hinged 32.50

Nos. 733, 738 and 741 exist imperforate. Value, $650. Value never hinged, $900.
No. 739 exists imperforate on grayish paper.

Francisco Gomez de Quevedo y Villegas (1580-1645), Writer — A187

1945, Sept. 8 **Engr.** **Perf. 10**
742 A187 40c dark brown .65 .55
Never hinged 1.10

Exists imperf. Value $80.

Type of Semi-Postal Stamp, 1940 Without Imprint at Lower Left and Right
1946, Jan. 1 **Litho.** **Perf. 11**
743 SP20 50c (40c + 10c) sl grn & rose vio 1.40 .25
Never hinged 2.40

No. 743 was used as an ordinary postage stamp of 50c denomination.
Exists imperf. Value $80.

Elio Antonio de   University of
Nebrija — A188   Salamanca and
          Signature of
          Francisco de
          Vitoria — A189

1946, Oct. 12 **Engr.** **Perf. 9½x10**
744 A188 50c deep plum .40 .30
745 A189 75c deep blue .50 .45
Nos. 744-745,C121 (3) 2.80 3.25
Set, never hinged 5.25

Stamp Day and the Day of the Race, Oct. 12, 1946.
Nos. 744-745 and C121 exist imperforate. Value set, $160 hinged, $240 never hinged.

Francisco de Goya — A190

1946, Oct 26
746 A190 25c deep plum .25 .25
747 A190 50c green .25 .25
748 A190 75c dark blue .60 .75
Nos. 746-748 (3) 1.25
Set, never hinged 1.00

Francisco de Goya, birth bicentenary.
Nos. 746-748 exist imperforate. Value set, $25 hinged, $32.50 never hinged.

Benito Jeronimo Feijoo y Montenegro — A191

1947, June 1 **Unwmk.**
749 A191 50c deep green .45 .35
Never hinged .65

No. 749 exists imperforate. Value, $35.

Don Quixote   "Don Quixote"
Reading   by Zuloaga
A192   A193

1947, Oct. 9 **Engr.** **Perf. 9½x10½**
750 A192 50c sepia .25 .25
751 A193 75c dark blue .40 .45
Nos. 750-751,C122 (3) 5.15 5.20
Set, never hinged 7.75

Stamp Day and the 400th anniv. of the birth of Miguel de Cervantes Saavedra.
Nos. 750-751 and C122 exist imperforate. Value set, $550 hinged, $650 never hinged.

General Franco
A194   A195

1948 **Litho.** **Perf. 12½x13**
752 A194 15c green .25 .25
753 A195 50c violet .80 .25
Set, never hinged 1.25

Nos. 752 and 753 exist imperforate. Value set, $400 hinged, $550 never hinged.
See Nos. 760-768, 780, 801-803. For surcharges see Nos. B137-B138.

Hernando   Mateo
Cortez — A196   Aleman — A197

1948, June 15 **Engr.** **Perf. 12½x13**
754 A196 35c black .25 .25
Perf. 9½x10½
755 A197 70c dk violet brn 1.40 2.00
a. Perf. 12½x13 25.00 25.00
Set, never hinged 2.25

No. 754 exists imperforate. Value set, $100 hinged, $125 never hinged.

Ferdinand III   Grandson of
(The   Adm. Ramon de
Saint) — A198   Bonifaz — A199

1948, Sept. 20 **Litho.** **Perf. 12½x13**
756 A198 25c rose violet .25 .25
757 A199 30c scarlet .25 .25
Set, never hinged .50

700th anniversary of the Spanish navy and of the capture of Seville by Ferdinand the Saint.

José de   Train Crossing
Salamanca y   Pancorbo
Mayol — A200   Viaduct — A201

Perf. 12½x13, 13x12½
1948, Oct. 9 **Unwmk.**
758 A200 50c brown .50 .25
759 A201 5p deep green 1.40 .25
Nos. 758-759,C125 (3) 3.40 2.00
Set, never hinged 6.00

Centenary of Spanish railroads.

Franco Types of 1948
1948-49 **Litho.** **Perf. 12½x13**
760 A194 5c brown .30 .25
761 A195 25c vermilion .30 .25
762 A195 35c blue green .30 .25
763 A195 40c red brown .65 .25
764 A195 45c car rose ('49) .40 .25
765 A194 50c bister 1.10 .25
766 A195 70c purple ('49) 1.90 .30
767 A195 75c dk vio blue 1.60 .30
768 A195 1p rose pink 5.00 .25
Nos. 760-768 (9) 11.55 2.35
Set, never hinged 17.50

Imperforates exist of Nos. 761 ($100), 762 ($300), 764 ($300) and 768 ($500).

Symbols of UPU
A202

1949, Oct. 9
769 A202 50c red brown .35 .25
770 A202 75c violet blue .35 .55
Nos. 769-770,C126 (3) .95 1.25
Set, never hinged 2.25

75th anniv. of the UPU.

St. John of God — A203

1950, Mar. 8 **Engr.** **Unwmk.**
771 A203 1p dark violet 7.00 4.50
Never hinged 12.50

400th anniversary of the death of St. John of God, humanitarian.

Pedro Calderon de la Barca — A204

Designs: 10c Lope de Vega. 15c, Tirso de Molina. 20c, Juan Ruiz de Alarcon, dramatist. 50c, St. Antonio Maria Claret y Clara.

1950-53   **Photo.**   **Perf. 12½**
772 A204   5c brown ('51)   .25   .25
773 A204   10c dp rose brn ('51)   .25   .25
773A A204   15c dk sl grn ('53)   .25   .25
774 A204   20c violet   .25   .25

Perf. 12½x13
Engr.
775 A204   50c dp bluish gray ('51)   2.50   1.50
Nos. 772-775 (5)   3.50   2.50
Set, never hinged   4.35

No. 774 exists imperforate. Value, $250.

Stamp of 1850 — A205

1950, Oct. 12   **Engr.**   **Imperf.**
776 A205   50c purple   4.00   4.00
777 A205   75c ultra   4.00   4.00
778 A205   10p dk slate grn   55.00   55.00
779 A205   15p red   55.00   55.00
Nos. 776-779,C127-C130 (8)   237.00   237.00
Set, never hinged   450.00

Centenary of Spain's stamps.

Franco Type of 1948

1950   **Litho.**   **Perf. 12½x13**
780 A195   45c red   .60   .25
Never hinged   .90

Queen Isabella I — A206

1951, Apr. 22   **Photo.**   **Perf. 12½**
781 A206   50c brown   .45   .45
782 A206   75c blue   .55   .55
783 A206   90c rose brown   .35   .35
784 A206   1.50p orange   6.00   6.00
785 A206   2.80p olive grn   13.00   13.00
Nos. 781-785 (5)   20.35   20.35
Set, never hinged   40.00

500th anniversary of the birth of Queen Isabella I. See Nos. C132-C136.

Ferdinand, the Catholic — A210

1952, May 10   **Photo.**   **Perf. 13**
787 A210   50c green   .40   .40
788 A210   75c indigo   1.50   1.50
789 A210   90c rose brown   .35   .35
790 A210   1.50p orange   5.00   5.00
791 A210   2.80p brown   9.00   9.00
Nos. 787-791 (5)   16.25   16.25
Set, never hinged   35.00

500th anniversary of the birth of Ferdinand the Catholic of Spain. See Nos. C139-C143.

Maria Michaela Dermaisiéres A211

1952, May 26   **Perf. 12½x13**
792 A211   90c claret   .25   .25
Never hinged   .30

35th International Eucharistic Congress, Barcelona, 1952. See No. C137.

Dr. Santiago Ramon y Cajal — A212

Portrait: 4.50p, Dr. Jaime Ferran y Clua.

1952, July 8   **Photo.**
793 A212   2p bright blue   10.00   .50
794 A212   4.50p red brown   .50   .80
Set, never hinged   25.00

Centenary of the births of Dr. Santiago Ramon y Cajal and Dr. Jaime Ferran y Clua.

University Seal — A213

Luis de Leon — A214

Cathedral of Salamanca A215

1953, Oct. 12   **Perf. 12½x13, 13x12½**
795 A213   50c deep magenta   .50   .35
796 A214   90c dark olive gray   1.60   1.60
797 A215   2p brown   11.00   3.50
Nos. 795-797 (3)   13.10   5.45
Set, never hinged   21.00

Stamp Day, 10/12/53, and 700th anniv. of the founding of the University of Salamanca.

The Magdalene — A216

1954, Jan. 10   **Perf. 12½x13**
798 A216   1.25p deep magenta   .25   .25
Never hinged   .30

José de Ribera, painter, 300th death anniv.

St. James of Compostela A217

St. James Cathedral A218

1954, Mar. 1
799 A217   50c dark brown   .25   .25
800 A218   3p blue   20.00   4.00
Set, never hinged   55.00

Holy year of Compostela, 1954.

Franco Types of 1948

1954   **Litho.**   **Perf. 12½x13**
801 A194   5c olive gray   .25   .25
802 A195   30c deep green   .25   .25
803 A194   80c dull car rose   1.50   .25
Nos. 801-803 (3)   2.00   .75
Set, never hinged   4.75

Virgin by Alonso Cano — A219

Virgins: 15c, Begoña. 25c, Of the Abandoned. 30c, Black. 50c, Of the Pillar. 60c, Covadonga. 80c, Kings'. 1p, Almudena. 2p, Africa. 3p, Guadalupe.

1954, July 18   **Photo.**   **Perf. 12½x13**
804 A219   10c dk car rose   .25   .25
805 A219   15c olive green   .25   .25
806 A219   25c purple   .25   .25
807 A219   30c brown   .25   .25
808 A219   50c brown olive   .50   .25
809 A219   60c gray   .25   .25
810 A219   80c grnsh gray   2.25   .25
811 A219   1p lilac gray   2.25   .25
812 A219   2p red brown   .70   .25
813 A219   3p bright blue   .60   .60
Nos. 804-813 (10)   7.55   2.85
Set, never hinged   11.00

Issued to publicize the Marian Year.

Marcelino Menendez y Pelayo — A220

1954, Oct. 12
814 A220   80c dk gray grn   5.25   .35
Never hinged   9.50

Stamp Day, October 12, 1954.

Gen. Franco — A221

Imprint: "F.N.M.T."

1954-56   **Perf. 12½x13**
815 A221   10c dk car lake   .25   .25
816 A221   15c bister   .25   .25
817 A221   20c dk ol grn ('55)   .25   .25
818 A221   25c blue violet   .25   .25
819 A221   30c brown   .25   .25
820 A221   40c rose vio ('55)   .25   .25
821 A221   50c dk brn olive   .25   .25
822 A221   60c dk vio brown   .25   .25
823 A221   70c dk green   .25   .25
824 A221   80c dk blue grn   .25   .25
825 A221   1p dp orange   .25   .25
826 A221   1.40p lil rose ('56)   .25   .25
827 A221   1.50p lt bl grn ('56)   .25   .25
828 A221   1.80p emerald ('56)   .25   .25
829 A221   2p red   12.00   1.25
830 A221   2p red lilac ('56)   .25   .25
831 A221   3p Prus blue   .25   .25
832 A221   5p dk red brn   .25   .25
833 A221   6p dk gray ('55)   .25   .25
834 A221   8p brt vio ('56)   .25   .25
835 A221   10p yel grn ('55)   .25   .25
Nos. 815-835 (21)   17.00   6.25
Set, never hinged   20.00

Coils: The 1.50p, No. 830, the 3p and the 6p were issued in coils in brighter tones (the 3p in 1974, others in 1973). Every fifth stamp has a black control number on the back.
See Nos. 937-938, 1852-1855.

St. Ignatius of Loyola — A222

St. Ignatius and Loyola Palace A223

Perf. 13x12½, 12½x13
1955, Oct. 12   **Photo.**   **Unwmk.**
836 A222   25c dull purple   .25   .25
837 A223   60c bister   .40   .30
838 A222   80c Prus green   1.65   .25
Nos. 836-838 (3)   2.30   .80
Set, never hinged   4.25

4th cent. of the death of St. Ignatius of Loyola, founder of the Jesuit Order, and Day of the Stamp.

Symbols of Telegraph and Radio Communi-cation A224

1955, Dec. 8   **Perf. 13x12½**
839 A224   15c dk olive bis   .30   .25
840 A224   80c Prus green   4.25   .25
841 A224   3p bright blue   8.00   1.25
Nos. 839-841 (3)   12.55   1.75
Set, never hinged   27.50

Spanish telegraph system centenary.

St. Vincent Ferrer — A225

1955, Dec. 20   **Perf. 13**
842 A225   15c olive bister   .35   .25
Never hinged   .60

Canonization of St. Vincent Ferrer, 5th cent.

"Holy Family" by El Greco — A226

1955, Dec. 24   **Perf. 13x12½**
843 A226   80c dark green   3.25   .65
Never hinged   6.00

Marching Soldiers and Dove — A227

1956, July 17   **Unwmk.**
844 A227   15c olive bis & brn   .25   .25
845 A227   50c lt ol grn & ol   .50   .30
846 A227   80c mag & grnsh blk   4.25   .25
847 A227   3p ultra & dp blue   4.25   1.40
Nos. 844-847 (4)   9.25   2.20
Set, never hinged   19.00

20th anniversary of Civil War.

Ciudad de Toledo
A228

1956, Aug. 3   **Perf. 12½x13**
848 A228 3p blue   3.25   2.00
    Never hinged   5.75

Issued to publicize the voyage of the S. S. Ciudad de Toledo to Central and South America carrying the First Floating (Industrial) Exposition.

Black Virgin of Montserrat — A229

Design: 60c, Monastery of Montserrat, mountains and crucifix.

1956, Sept. 11   **Perf. 13x12½**
849 A229 15c bister   .25   .25
850 A229 60c violet black   .25   .25
851 A229 80c blue green   .30   .40
    Nos. 849-851 (3)   .80   .90
    Set, never hinged   .85

75th anniv. of the coronation of the Black Virgin of Montserrat.

Archangel Gabriel by Fra Angelico — A230

1956, Oct. 12   **Engr.**
852 A230 80c dull green   .75   .35
    Never hinged   1.00

Stamp Day, Oct. 12.

Statistical Chart A231

1956, Nov. 3   **Perf. 12½x13**
853 A231 15c dk olive bis   .30   .30
854 A231 80c green   2.75   .60
855 A231 1p red orange   2.75   .60
    Nos. 853-855 (3)   5.80   1.50
    Set, never hinged   10.00

Centenary of Spanish Statistics.

Hermitage and Monument A232

1956, Dec. 4
856 A232 80c dull blue grn   2.00   .25
    Never hinged   5.50

20th anniversary of the nomination of Gen. Franco as chief of state and commander in chief of the army.

Hungarian Children — A233

1956, Dec. 17   **Perf. 13x12½**
857 A233 10c brown lake   .25   .25
858 A233 15c dk bister   .25   .25
859 A233 50c olive gray   .30   .25
860 A233 80c dk blue grn   2.00   .25
861 A233 1p red orange   2.25   .25
862 A233 3p brt blue   6.00   2.25
    Nos. 857-862 (6)   11.05   3.50
    Set, never hinged   19.00

Issued in sympathy to the children of Hungary.

St. Marguerite Alacoque's Vision of Jesus — A234

1957, Oct. 12   **Photo.**   **Unwmk.**
863 A234 15c dk olive bis   .25   .25
864 A234 60c violet blk   .25   .25
865 A234 80c dk blue grn   .30   .25
    Nos. 863-865 (3)   .80   .75
    Set, never hinged   .90

Centenary of the feast of the Sacred Heart of Jesus and for Stamp Day 1957.

Gonzalo de Cordoba — A235

1958, Feb. 28   **Engr.**   **Perf. 13x12½**
866 A235 1.80p yellow green   .25   .25
    Never hinged   .30

Issued in honor of El Gran Capitan, 15th century military leader.

"The Parasol," by Goya — A236

"Wife of the Bookseller of Carretas Street" — A237

Goya Paintings: 50c, Duke of Fernan-Nunez. 60c, The Crockery Seller. 70c, Isabel Cobos de Porcel. 80c, Goya by Vicente Lopez. 1p, "El Pelele" (Carnival Doll). 1.80p, Goya's grandson Marianito. 2p, The Vintage. 3p, The Drinker.

1958, Mar. 24   **Photo.**   **Perf. 13**
Gold Frame
867 A236 15c bister   .25   .25
868 A237 40c plum   .25   .25
869 A237 50c olive gray   .25   .25
870 A237 60c violet gray   .25   .25
871 A237 70c dp yellow grn   .25   .25
872 A237 80c dk slate grn   .25   .25
873 A237 1p orange red   .25   .25
874 A237 1.80p brt green   .25   .25
875 A237 2p red lilac   .30   .30
876 A236 3p brt blue   .50   .50
    Nos. 867-876 (10)   2.80   2.80
    Set, never hinged   3.00

Issued to honor Francisco Jose de Goya and for the "Day of the Stamp," Mar. 24.
See Nos. 1111-1114. For other art types see A240a, A246a, A257, A272, A285a, A300, A310, A324, A340-A341, A360, A371 and footnote following No. 1606.

Exhibition Emblem and Globe — A238

1958, June 7   **Perf. 13x12½**
877 A238 80c car, dk brn & gray   .25   .25
  a.   Souvenir sheet, imperf.   17.50   17.50
878 A238 3p car, vio blk & bl   .85   .85
  a.   Souvenir sheet, imperf.   17.50   17.50
    Set, never hinged   2.00
    #877a-878a never hinged   55.00

No. 877a sold for 2p, No. 878a for 5p. Universal and Intl. Exposition at Brussels.

Charles V — A239

Various Portraits of Charles V: 50c, 1.80p, with helmet. 70c, 2p, facing left. 80c, 3p, with beret.

1958, July 30   **Photo.**   **Perf. 13**
879 A239 15c buff & brown   .25   .25
880 A239 50c lt grn & ol brn   .25   .25
881 A239 70c gray, grn & blk   .25   .25
882 A239 80c pale brn & Prus grn   .25   .25
883 A239 1p bis & brick red   .25   .25
884 A239 1.80p pale grn & brt grn   .25   .25
885 A239 2p gray & lilac   .30   .30
886 A239 3p pale brn & brt bl   .75   .60
    Nos. 879-886 (8)   2.55   2.40
    Set, never hinged   3.25

400th anniv. of the death of Charles V (Carlos I of Spain.)

Escorial and Streamlined Train — A240

Designs: 60c, 2p, Railroad bridge at Despeñaperros, vert. 80c, 3p, Train and Castle de La Mota.

1958, Sept. 29   **Perf. 12½x13**
887 A240 15c dk olive bis   .25   .25
888 A240 60c dk purple   .25   .25
889 A240 80c dk blue grn   .25   .25
890 A240 1p red orange   .25   .25
891 A240 2p red lilac   .25   .25
892 A240 3p blue   .70   .40
    Nos. 887-892 (6)   1.95   1.65
    Set, never hinged   3.00

Intl. Railroad Cong., Madrid, Sept. 28-Oct. 7.

Velazquez Self-portrait A240a

Velazquez Paintings: 15c, The Drinkers, horiz. 40c, The Spinners. 50c, Surrender of Breda. 60c, The Little Princesses. 70c, Prince Balthazar. 1p, The Coronation of Our Lady. 1.80p, Aesop. 2p, Vulcan's Forge. 3p, Menippus.

1959, Mar. 24   **Photo.**   **Perf. 13**
Gold Frame
893 A240a 15c dk brown   .25   .25
894 A240a 40c rose violet   .25   .25
895 A240a 50c olive   .25   .25
896 A240a 60c black brown   .25   .25
897 A240a 70c dp yellow grn   .25   .25
898 A240a 80c dk slate grn   .25   .25
899 A240a 1p orange red   .25   .25
900 A240a 1.80p emerald   .25   .25
901 A240a 2p red lilac   .25   .25
902 A240a 3p brt blue   .35   .45
    Nos. 893-902 (10)   2.60   2.70
    Set, never hinged   2.75

Issued to honor Diego de Silva Velazquez (1599-1660) and for Stamp Day, Mar. 24.
For other art types see A236-A237, A246a, A257, A272, A285a, A300, A310, A324, A340-A341, A360, A371 and footnote following No. 1606.

Civil War Memorial — A241

1959, Apr. 1.   **Litho.**   **Unwmk.**
903 A241 80c yel grn & dk sl grn   .25   .25
    Never hinged   .30

Inauguration of the war memorial at the monastery of the Holy Cross in the Valley of the Fallen.

Louis XIV and Philip IV — A242

1959, Oct. 24   **Photo.**   **Perf. 13x12½**
904 A242 1p gold & rose brn   .25   .25
    Never hinged   .30

300th anniv. of the signing of the Treaty of the Pyrenees. Design shows the French-Spanish meeting at Isle des Faisans in 1659, as pictured in the Lebrun Tapestry, Versailles.

Monastery of Guadalupe A243

80c, Monastery, different view. 1p, Portals.

1959, Nov. 16   **Engr.**   **Perf. 12½x13**
905 A243 15c lt red brown   .25   .25
906 A243 80c slate   .25   .25
907 A243 1p rose red   .25   .25
    Nos. 905-907 (3)   .75   .75
    Set, never hinged   .80

Entrance of the Franciscan Brothers into Guadalupe monastery, 50th anniv.

Holy Family, by
Goya — A244

1959, Dec. 10   Photo.   Perf. 13x12½
908 A244 1p orange brown   .25 .25
Never hinged   .35

Catalogue values for unused
stamps in this section, from this
point to the end of the section, are
for Never Hinged items.

Lidian Bull
A245

Bullfighter, 19th
Century — A246

Designs: 20c, Rounding up bulls. 25c, Running with the bulls, Pamplona. 30c, Bull entering arena. 50c, Bullfighting with cape. 70c, Bullfighting with banderillas. 80c, 1p, 1.40p, 1.50p, Fighting with muleta, various poses. 1.80p, Mounted bullfighter placing banderillas.

Perf. 12½x13, 13x12½

			Unwmk.	
1960, Feb. 29		**Engr.**		
909	A245	15c sepia & bis	.25	.25
910	A245	20c vio & bl vio	.25	.25
911	A245	25c gray	.25	.25
912	A246	30c sepia & bister	.25	.25
913	A246	50c dull vio & sep	.25	.25
914	A246	70c sepia & sl grn	.25	.25
915	A246	80c blue grn & grn	.25	.25
916	A246	1p red & brn	.25	.25
917	A246	1.40p brown & lake	.25	.25
918	A246	1.50p grnsh bl & grn	.25	.25
919	A245	1.80p grn & dk grn	.25	.25
920	A246	5p brn & brn car	.55	.45
	Nos. 909-920,C159-C162 (16)		4.60	4.35

Murillo Self-
portrait
A246a

Murillo Paintings: 25c, The Good Shepherd. 40c, Rebecca and Eliezer. 50c, Virgin of the Rosary. 70c, Immaculate Conception. 80c, Children with Shell. 1.50p, Holy Family with a Bird, horiz. 2.50p, Children Playing Dice. 3p, Children Eating. 5p, Children counting Money.

1960, Mar. 24   Photo.
Gold Frame

921	A246a	25c dull violet	.25	.25
922	A246a	40c plum	.25	.25
923	A246a	50c olive gray	.25	.25
924	A246a	70c dp yel grn	.25	.25
925	A246a	80c deep green	.25	.25
926	A246a	1p violet brown	.25	.25
927	A246a	1.50p blue green	.25	.25
928	A246a	2.50p rose car	.25	.25
929	A246a	3p brt blue	1.25	.60
930	A246a	5p deep red brn	.35	.25
	Nos. 921-930 (10)		3.60	2.85

Issued to honor Bartolome Esteban Murillo (1617-1682) and for Stamp Day, Mar. 24.
For other art types see A236-A237, A240a, A257, A272, A285a, A300, A310, A324, A340-A341, A360, A371 and footnote following No. 1606.

Christ of
Lepanto — A247

80c, 2.50p, 10p, Holy Family Church, Barcelona.

1960, Mar. 27   Perf. 13x12½
931	A247	70c brn car & grn	1.60	1.25
932	A247	80c blk & ol grn	1.60	1.25
933	A247	1p cl & brt red	1.60	1.25
934	A247	2.50p brt vio & gray		
		vio	1.60	1.25
935	A247	5p sepia & bister	1.60	1.25
936	A247	10p sepia & bister	1.60	1.25
	Nos. 931-936,C163-C166 (10)		28.60	20.50

First International Congress of Philately, Barcelona, March 26-Apr. 5. Nos. 931-936 could be bought at the exhibition upon presentation of 5p entrance ticket.

Franco Type of 1954-56
Imprint: "F.N.M.T.-B"
1960, Mar. 31   Photo.   Perf. 13
937	A221	1p deep orange	1.40	.60
938	A221	5p dark red brown	1.40	.60

Printed and issued at the International Congress of Philately in Barcelona.

St. Juan de
Ribera — A248

1960, Aug. 16   Photo.   Perf. 13
939	A248	1p orange red	.25	.25
940	A248	2.50p lilac rose	.25	.25

Canonization of St. Juan de Ribera.

Common Design Types
pictured following the introduction.

Europa Issue, 1960
Common Design Type
1960, Sept. 19   Perf. 12½x13
Size: 38½x21½mm
941	CD3	1p sl grn & ol bis	.75	.25
942	CD3	5p choc & salmon	.75	.50

St. Vincent de
Paul — A249

1960, Sept. 27   Unwmk.   Perf. 13
943	A249	25c violet	.25	.25
944	A249	1p orange red	.40	.25

3rd centenary of the death of St. Vincent de Paul.

Pedro Menendez de
Aviles — A250

70c, 2.50p, Hernando de Soto. 80c, 3p, Ponce de Leon. 1p, 5p, Alvar Nunez Cabeza de Vaca.

1960, Oct. 12   Perf. 13x12½
945	A250	25c vio bl, *bl*	.25	.25
946	A250	70c slate grn, *pink*	.25	.25
947	A250	80c dk grn, *pale brn*	.25	.25
948	A250	1p org brn, *yel*	.25	.25
949	A250	2p dk car rose, *pink*	.30	.25
950	A250	2.50p lil rose, *buff*	.60	.25
951	A250	3p dk blue, *grnsh*	2.75	.50
952	A250	5p dk brown, *cit*	2.25	.85
	Nos. 945-952 (8)		6.90	2.85

Florida's discovery & colonization, 4th cent.

Runner — A251

Sports: 40c, 2p, Bicycling, horiz. 70c, 2.50p, Soccer, horiz. 80c, 3p, Athlete with rings. 1p, 5p, Hockey on roller skates, horiz.

Perf. 13x12½, 12½x13
1960, Oct. 31   Photo.
953	A251	25c dk vio, brn & blk	.25	.25
954	A251	40c purple, org & blk	.25	.25
955	A251	70c brt green & red	.25	.25
956	A251	80c dp grn, car & blk	.25	.25
957	A251	1p red org, brt grn		
		& blk	.55	.25
958	A251	1.50p Prus grn, brn &		
		blk	.40	.25
959	A251	2p red lil, emer &		
		blk	1.10	.25
960	A251	2.50p lil rose & green	.40	.25
961	A251	3p ultra, red & blk	.75	.25
962	A251	5p red brn, bl & blk	.75	.35
	Nos. 953-962,C167-C170 (14)		7.80	4.20

Isaac
Albeniz — A252

1960, Nov. 7   Perf. 13
963	A252	25c dark gray	.25	.25
964	A252	1p orange red	.25	.25

Isaac Albeniz, composer, birth centenary.

Courtyard
of Samos
Monastery
A253

1p, Fountain, vert. 5p, Facade, vert.

Perf. 12½x13, 13x12½
1960, Nov. 21   Engr.
965	A253	80c bl grn & Prus grn	.25	.25
966	A253	1p org brn & car rose	1.10	.25
967	A253	5p sepia & ocher	1.10	.45
	Nos. 965-967 (3)		2.45	.95

Issued in honor of the reconstructed Benedictine monastery at Samos, Lugo.

Adoration, by
Velazquez — A254

1960, Dec. 1   Photo.   Perf. 13x12½
968 A254 1p orange red   .30 .25

Flight into
Egypt by
Francisco
Bayeu
A255

1961, Jan. 23   Perf. 12½x13
969	A255	1p copper red	.25	.25
970	A255	5p dull red brown	.45	.30

World Refugee Year.

Leandro F. de
Moratin, by
Goya — A256

1961, Feb. 13   Perf. 13
971	A256	1p henna brown	.25	.25
972	A256	1.50p dk blue green	.25	.25

Leandro Fernandez de Moratin (1760-1828), poet and dramatist, 200th birth anniv.

St. Peter by El
Greco — A257

El Greco Paintings: 40c, Virgin Mary. 70c, Head of Christ. 80c, Knight with Hand on Chest. 1p, Self-portrait. 1.50p, Baptism of Christ. 2.50p, Holy Trinity. 3p, Burial of Count Orgaz. 5p, Christ Stripped of His Garments. 10p, St. Mauritius and the Theban Legion.

Gold Frame

1961, Mar. 24   Perf. 13
973	A257	25c violet black	.25	.25
974	A257	40c lilac	.25	.25
975	A257	70c green	.30	.25
976	A257	80c Prus green	.30	.25
977	A257	1p chocolate	2.50	.25
978	A257	1.50p grnsh blue	.30	.25
979	A257	2.50p dk car rose	.50	.25
980	A257	3p bright blue	1.25	.45
981	A257	5p black brown	3.50	1.40
982	A257	10p purple	.60	.30
	Nos. 973-982 (10)		9.75	3.90

El Greco and Stamp Day, March 24.
For other art types see A236-A237, A240a, A246a, A272, A285a, A300, A310, A324, A340-A341, A360, A371 and footnote following No. 1606.

Diego
Velazquez — A258

Velazquez Paintings: 1p, Duke de Olivares. 2.50p, Infanta Margarita. 10p, Detail from The Spinners, horiz.

Unwmk.
1961, Apr. 17   Engr.   Perf. 13
983	A258	80c dk blue & sl		
		grn	2.00	.75
a.		Souvenir sheet	8.00	8.50
984	A258	1p brn red &		
		choc	6.00	.75
a.		Souvenir sheet	8.50	8.50
985	A258	2.50p vio bl & bl	1.50	1.00
a.		Souvenir sheet	8.50	8.50
986	A258	10p grn & yel grn	7.00	2.50
a.		Souvenir sheet	8.50	8.50
	Nos. 983-986 (4)		16.50	5.00

300th anniversary (in 1960) of the death of Velazquez, painter.
Each souvenir sheet contains one imperf. stamp. The colors of the stamps have been changed: 80c, red brown & slate; 1p, blue & violet; 2.50p, green & blue; 10p, slate blue & greenish blue. The sheets were sold at a premium.

Canceled Stamp — A259

1961, May 6 Photo. *Perf. 13x12½*

987	A259	25c	gray & red	.25	.25
988	A259	1p	orange & blk	1.10	.25
989	A259	10p	olive grn & brn	1.10	.60
			Nos. 987-989 (3)	2.45	1.10

Issued for International Stamp Day.

Juan Vazquez de Mella — A260

1961, June 8 Unwmk. *Perf. 13*

990	A260	1p	henna brown	.45	.25
991	A260	2.30p	red lilac	.25	.25

Birth centenary of Juan Vazquez de Mella y Fanjul, politician and writer.

Flag, Angel and Peace Doves — A261

Designs: 80c, Ships and Strait of Gibraltar. 1p, Alcazar and horseman. 1.50p, Ruins and triumphal arch. 2p, Horseman over Ebro. 2.30p, Victory parade. 2.50p, Ship building. 3p, Steel industry. 5p, Map of Spanish irrigation dams and statue, horiz. 6p, Dama de Elche statue and power station. 8p, Mining development. 10p, General Franco.

1961, July 10

992	A261	70c	multicolored	.25	.25
993	A261	80c	multicolored	.25	.25
994	A261	1p	multicolored	.25	.25
995	A261	1.50p	gold, pink & brn	.25	.25
996	A261	2p	gold, gray & bl	.25	.25
997	A261	2.30p	multicolored	.25	.25
998	A261	2.50p	multicolored	.25	.25
999	A261	3p	gold, red & dk gray	.35	.25
1000	A261	5p	bl grn, ol gray & pink	2.25	1.10
1001	A261	6p	multicolored	1.10	.75
1002	A261	8p	gold, ol & sep	.70	.55
1003	A261	10p	gold, gray & grn	.70	.55
			Nos. 992-1003 (12)	6.85	4.95

25th anniversary of national uprising.

Christ, San Clemente, Tahull — A262

Designs: 25c, Bas-relief, Compostela Cathedral. 1p, Cloister of Silos. 2p, Virgin of Irache.

1961, July 24 Unwmk. *Perf. 13*

Gold Frame

1004	A262	25c	blue violet	.40	.25
1005	A262	1p	orange brown	.50	.25
1006	A262	2p	deep plum	.70	.25
1007	A262	3p	grnsh bl, sal & blk	.90	.40
			Nos. 1004-1007 (4)	2.50	1.15

Seventh Exposition of the Council of Europe dedicated to Romanesque art, Barcelona-Santiago de Compostela, July 10-Oct. 10.

Luis de Argote y Gongora — A263

1961, Aug. 10 Photo. *Perf. 13*

1008	A263	25c	violet black	.25	.25
1009	A263	1p	henna brown	.50	.25

400th anniversary of the birth of Luis de Argote y Gongora, poet.

Europa Issue

Common Design Type

1961, Sept. 18 *Perf. 12½x13*

Size: 37½x21½mm

1010	CD4	1p	brt vermilion	.25	.25
1011	CD4	5p	brown	*.45*	*.30*

Cathedral at Burgos — A264

1961, Oct. 1 *Perf. 13*

1012	A264	1p	gold & olive green	.25	.25

25th anniversary of the nomination of Gen. Francisco Franco as Head of State.

Builders of the New World

Sebastian de Belalcazar — A265

Portraits: 70c, 2.50p, Blas de Lezo. 80c, 3p, Rodrigo de Bastidas. 1p, 5p, Nuflo de Chaves.

1961, Oct. 12 Photo. *Perf. 13x12½*

1013	A265	25c	indigo, *grn*	.25	.25
1014	A265	70c	grn, *cream*	.25	.25
1015	A265	80c	sl grn, *pnksh*	.25	.25
1016	A265	1p	dk blue, *sal*	.60	.25
1017	A265	2p	dk car, *bluish*	3.75	.25
1018	A265	2.50p	lil, *pale lil*	.90	.45
1019	A265	3p	blue, *grysh*	1.90	.80
1020	A265	5p	brown, *yel*	2.00	.90
			Nos. 1013-1020 (8)	9.90	3.40

Issued to honor the discoverers and conquerors of Colombia and Bolivia.

See Nos. 1131-1138, 1187-1194, 1271-1278, 1316-1323, 1377-1384, 1489-1496, 1548, 1550, 1587-1588, 1632-1633.

Views of Escorial Monastery — A266

Designs: 70c, Patio of the Kings. 80c, Patio. 1p, Garden of the Monks and Escorial, horiz. 2.50p, Staircase. 5p, General view of Escorial, horiz. 6p, Main altar.

Perf. 13x12½, 12½x13

1961, Oct. 31 Engr. Unwmk.

1021	A266	70c	bl grn & ol grn	.25	.25
1022	A266	80c	Prus grn & ind	.25	.25
1023	A266	1p	ocher & dk red	.55	.25
1024	A266	2.50p	cl & dull vio	.55	.25
1025	A266	5p	bister & dk brn	1.60	.70
1026	A266	6p	sl bl & dull pur	2.25	1.50
			Nos. 1021-1026 (6)	5.45	3.20

Alfonso XII Monument, Retiro Park — A267

Designs: 1p, King Philip II. 2p, Town hall, horiz. 2.50p, Cibeles fountain, horiz. 3p, Alcala gate, horiz. 5p, Cervantes memorial, Plaza de Espagna.

Photogravure (25c, 2p, 5p)

Engraved (1p, 2.50p, 3p)

1961, Nov. 13 Unwmk. *Perf. 13*

1027	A267	25c	gray & dull pur	.25	.25
1028	A267	1p	bis brn & gray	.30	.25
1029	A267	2p	claret & gray	.30	.25
1030	A267	2.50p	black & lilac	.25	.25
1031	A267	3p	slate & ind	.60	.35
1032	A267	5p	Prus grn & beige	1.10	.55
			Nos. 1027-1032 (6)	2.80	1.90

400th anniv. of Madrid as capital of Spain.

Church of St. Mary, Naranco — A268

Designs: 1p, King Fruela I, founder of Oviedo. 2p, Cross of the Angels. 2.50p, King Alfonso II. 3p, King Alfonso III. 5p, Apostles from Oviedo Cathedral (sculpture).

1961, Nov. 27

1033	A268	25c	pur & gray grn	.25	.25
1034	A268	1p	bis brn & brn	.30	.25
1035	A268	2p	dk brn & pale pur	.65	.25
1036	A268	2.50p	claret & ind	.30	.25
1037	A268	3p	slate & indigo	.65	.45
1038	A268	5p	ol & ol grn	1.25	.55
			Nos. 1033-1038 (6)	3.40	2.00

1200th anniversary of the founding of Oviedo, capital of Asturia.

Nativity Sculptured by José Gines — A269

1961, Dec. 1 Photo. *Perf. 13x12½*

1039	A269	1p	dull purple	.30	.25

"La Cierva" Autogiro — A270

2p, Hydroplane "Plus Ultra.," horiz. 3p, "Jesus del Gran Poder," plane of Madrid-Manila flight, horiz. 5p, Bustard hunt by plane. 10p, Madonna of Loretto, patron saint of Spanish airmen.

1961, Dec. 11 Unwmk. *Perf. 13*

1040	A270	1p	indigo & blue	.25	.25
1041	A270	2p	grn, dl pur & blk	.25	.25
1042	A270	3p	blk & ol grn	1.25	.35
1043	A270	5p	dl pur, gray bl & blk	2.50	.90
1044	A270	10p	blk, lt bl & ol gray	1.25	.60
			Nos. 1040-1044 (5)	5.50	2.35

50th anniversary of Spanish aviation.

Provincial Arms Issue

Alava — A271

1962 Photo. *Perf. 13*

1045	A271	5p	Alava	.25	.25
1046	A271	5p	Albacete	.25	.25
1047	A271	5p	Alicante	.25	.25
1048	A271	5p	Almeria	.25	.25
1049	A271	5p	Avila	.25	.25
1050	A271	5p	Badajoz	.25	.25
1051	A271	5p	Baleares	.25	.25
1052	A271	5p	Barcelona	.25	.25
1053	A271	5p	Burgos	.65	.40
1054	A271	5p	Caceres	.35	.25
1055	A271	5p	Cadiz	.45	.35
1056	A271	5p	Castellon de la Plana	3.50	1.50
			Nos. 1045-1056 (12)	6.95	4.50

1963

1057	A271	5p	Ciudad Real	.45	.35
1058	A271	5p	Cordoba	3.50	1.25
1059	A271	5p	Coruña	.55	.35
1060	A271	5p	Cuenca	.55	.35
1061	A271	5p	Fernando Po	.80	.75
1062	A271	5p	Gerona	.25	.25
1063	A271	5p	Gran Canaria	.25	.25
1064	A271	5p	Granada	.25	.25
1065	A271	5p	Guadalajara	.55	.35
1066	A271	5p	Guipuzcoa	.25	.25
1067	A271	5p	Huelva	.25	.25
1068	A271	5p	Huesca	.25	.25
			Nos. 1057-1068 (12)	7.90	4.90

1964

1069	A271	5p	Ifni	.25	.25
1070	A271	5p	Jaen	.25	.25
1071	A271	5p	Leon	.25	.25
1072	A271	5p	Lerida	.25	.25
1073	A271	5p	Logrono	.25	.25
1074	A271	5p	Lugo	.25	.25
1075	A271	5p	Madrid	.25	.25
1076	A271	5p	Malaga	.25	.25
1077	A271	5p	Murcia	.25	.25
1078	A271	5p	Navarra	.25	.25
1079	A271	5p	Orense	.25	.25
1080	A271	5p	Oviedo	.25	.25
			Nos. 1069-1080 (12)	3.00	3.00

1965

1081	A271	5p	Palencia	.25	.25
1082	A271	5p	Pontevedra	.25	.25
1083	A271	5p	Rio Muni	.25	.25
1084	A271	5p	Sahara	.25	.25
1085	A271	5p	Salamanca	.25	.25
1086	A271	5p	Santander	.25	.25
1087	A271	5p	Segovia	.25	.25
1088	A271	5p	Seville	.25	.25
1089	A271	5p	Soria	.25	.25
1090	A271	5p	Tarragona	.25	.25
1091	A271	5p	Tenerife	.25	.25
1092	A271	5p	Teruel	.25	.25
			Nos. 1081-1092 (12)	3.00	3.00

Arms of Spain — A271a

1966

1093	A271	5p	Toledo	.25	.25
1094	A271	5p	Valencia	.25	.25
1094A	A271	5p	Valladolid	.25	.25
1094B	A271	5p	Vizcaya	.25	.25
1094C	A271	5p	Zamora	.25	.25
1094D	A271	5p	Zaragoza	.25	.25
1094E	A271	5p	Ceuta	.25	.25
1094F	A271	5p	Melilla	.25	.25
1094G	A271a	10p	Spain	.25	.25
			Nos. 1093-1094G (9)	2.25	2.25
			Nos. 1045-1094G (57)	20.95	15.35

Zurbaran Self-portrait
A272

Zurbaran Paintings: 25c, Martyr, horiz. 40c, Burial of St. Catherine. 70c, St. Casilda. 80c, Jesus crowning St. Joseph. 1.50p, St. Jerome. 2.50p, Virgin of Grace. 3p, The Apotheosis of St. Thomas Aquinas. 5p, The Virgin as a child. 10p, The Immaculate Virgin.

Unwmk.

1962, Mar. 24		Photo.	*Perf. 13*
		Gold Frame	
1095	A272	25c olive gray	.40 .25
1096	A272	40c purple	.40 .25
1097	A272	70c green	.50 .25
1098	A272	80c Prus green	.40 .25
1099	A272	1p chocolate	7.50 .25
1100	A272	1.50p brt blue grn	.90 .25
1101	A272	2.50p dk car rose	.90 .25
1102	A272	3p bright blue	1.00 .35
1103	A272	5p deep brown	2.50 .75
1104	A272	10p olive green	2.50 .75
		Nos. 1095-1104 (10)	17.00 3.60

Issued to honor Francisco de Zurbaran (1598-1664) and for Stamp Day, March 24.
For other art types see A236-A237, A240a, A246a, A257, A285a, A300, A310, A324, A340-A341, A360, A371 and footnote following No. 1606.

San Jose Convent, Avila A272a

St. Theresa (by Velázquez?) A273

Design: 1p, St. Theresa by Bernini.

1962, Apr. 10			*Perf. 13*
1105	A272a	25c bluish blk	.25 .25
1106	A272a	1p brown	.25 .25
			Perf. 13x12½
1107	A273	3p bright blue	1.25 .40
		Nos. 1105-1107 (3)	1.75 .90

4th centenary of St. Theresa's reform of the Carmelite order.

Mercury — A274

1962, May 7			
1108	A274	25c vio, rose & mag	.25 .25
1109	A274	1p brn, org & lt brn	.25 .25
1110	A274	10p dp grn, ol grn & brt grn	1.75 .80
		Nos. 1108-1110 (3)	2.25 1.30

International Stamp Day, May 7.

Painting Type of 1958

Rubens Paintings: 25c, Ferdinand of Austria. 1p, Self-portrait. 3p, Philip II. 10p, Duke of Lerma on horseback.

1962, May 28			*Perf. 13*
		Gold Frame	
		Size: 25x30mm	
1111	A237	25c violet black	.65 .30
1112	A237	1p chocolate	5.75 .30
1113	A237	3p blue	5.25 2.00

Perf. 13x12½			
		Size: 26x38mm	
1114	A237	10p slate green	4.00 2.75
		Nos. 1111-1114 (4)	15.65 5.35

St. Benedict — A275

Berruguete Sculptures: 80c, Apostle. 1p, St. Peter. 2p, St. Christopher carrying Christ Child. 3p, Ecce Homo (Christ). 10p, St. Sebastian.

1962, July 9			*Perf. 13x12½*
1115	A275	25c lt blue & plum	.25 .25
1116	A275	80c sal & ol gray	.35 .25
1117	A275	1p gray & red	.45 .25
1118	A275	2p gray & magenta	3.50 .25
1119	A275	3p brn pink & dk bl	1.50 .85
1120	A275	10p rose & brown	1.50 .50
		Nos. 1115-1120 (6)	7.55 2.35

Alonso Berruguete (1486-1561), architect, sculptor and painter.

El Cid, Statue by Cristobal — A276

2p, Equestrian statue by Anna Huntington. 3p, El Cid's treasure chest, horiz. 10p, Oath-taking ceremony at Santa Gadea, horiz.

Perf. 13x12½, 12½x13			
1962, July 30			*Engr.*
1121	A276	1p lt green & gray	.25 .25
1122	A276	2p brown & choc	1.40 .25
1123	A276	3p blue & sl grn	4.25 1.10
1124	A276	10p lt grn & sl grn	2.75 .60
		Nos. 1121-1124 (4)	8.65 2.20

El Cid Campeador (Rodrigo Diaz de Vivar, 1040-99), Spain's national hero.

Europa Issue

Bee and Honeycomb — A277

1962, Sept. 13		Photo.	*Perf. 12½x13*
1125	A277	1p deep rose	.25 .25
1126	A277	5p dull green	1.00 .40

Discus Thrower — A278

80c, Runner. 1p, Hurdler. 3p, Sprinter at start.

1962, Oct. 7			*Perf. 13x12½*
1127	A278	25c pale pink & vio blk	.25 .25
1128	A278	80c pale yel & dk grn	.25 .25
1129	A278	1p pale rose & brn	.25 .25
1130	A278	3p pale bl & dk bl	.25 .30
		Nos. 1127-1130 (4)	1.00 1.05

Second Spanish-American Games, Madrid, Oct. 7-12.

Builders of the New World
Portrait Type of 1961

Portraits: 25c, 2p, Alonso de Mendoza. 70c, 2.50p, Jiménez de Quesada. 80c, 3p, Juan de Garay. 1p, 5p, Pedro de la Gasca.

1962, Oct. 12			**Unwmk.**
1131	A265	25c rose lil, *gray*	.25 .25
1132	A265	70c grn, *pale pink*	1.00 .25
1133	A265	80c dk grn, *pale yel*	.70 .25
1134	A265	1p red brn, *gray*	1.40 .25
1135	A265	2p car, *lt bl*	3.25 .25
1136	A265	2.50p dk vio,*pnksh*	.70 .25
1137	A265	3p dp bl, *pale pink*	7.00 1.25
1138	A265	5p brn, *pale yel*	3.50 1.50
		Nos. 1131-1138 (8)	17.80 4.25

UPAE Emblem — A279

1962, Oct. 20		Engr.	*Perf. 13*
1139	A279	1p sepia & green	.25 .25

50th anniv. of the founding of the Postal Union of the Americas and Spain, UPAE.

The Annunciation, by Murillo — A280

Mysteries of the Rosary: 70c, The Visitation, Correa. 80c, Nativity, Murillo. 1p, The Presentation, Pedro de Campaña. 1.50p, The Finding in the Temple, (unknown painter). 2p, The Agony in the Garden, Gianquinto. 2.50p, The Scourging at the Pillar, Alonso Cano. 3p, The Crowning with Thorns, Tiepolo. 5p, Carrying of the Cross, El Greco. 8p, The Crucifixion, Murillo. 10p, The Resurrection, Murillo.

1962, Oct. 26			
1140	A280	25c lilac & brown	.25 .25
1141	A280	70c grn & dk bl grn	.25 .25
1142	A280	80c ol & dk bl grn	.25 .25
1143	A280	1p green & gray	4.00 .70
1144	A280	1.50p green & dk bl	.25 .25
1145	A280	2p brown & violet	1.10 .50
1146	A280	2.50p dk brn & rose claret	.40 .25
1147	A280	3p lilac & gray	.40 .25
1148	A280	5p brn & dk car	.60 .35
1149	A280	8p vio brn & blk	.60 .25
1150	A280	10p grn & yel grn	.95 .25
		Nos. 1140-1150,C171-C174 (15)	11.65 4.80

Holy Family by Pedro de Mena — A281

1962, Dec. 6		Photo.	*Perf. 13x12½*
1151	A281	1p olive gray	.35 .25

Malaria Eradication Emblem A282

1962, Dec. 21			*Perf. 12½x13*
1152	A282	1p blk, yel grn & yel	.25 .25

WHO drive to eradicate malaria.

Pope John XXIII and St. Peter's, Rome A283

1962, Dec. 29			**Engr.**
1153	A283	1p dp plum & blk	.25 .25

Vatican II, the 21st Ecumenical Council of the Roman Catholic Church. See No. 1199.

St. Paul, by El Greco — A284

1963, Jan. 25			*Perf. 13*
1154	A284	1p brn, blk & olive	.30 .25

St. Paul's visit to Spain, 1,900th anniv.

Courtyard, Poblet Monastery — A285

Designs: 1p, Royal sepulcher. 3p, View of monastery, horiz. 5p, Gothic arch.

Perf. 12½x13, 13x12½			
1963, Feb. 25			**Unwmk.**
1155	A285	25c choc & slate grn	.25 .25
1156	A285	1p org ver & rose car	.35 .25
1157	A285	3p vio bl & dk bl	1.10 .25
1158	A285	5p brown & ocher	2.40 .90
		Nos. 1155-1158 (4)	4.10 1.65

Issued in honor of the Cistercian monastery of Santa Maria de Poblet.

José de Ribera, Self-portrait A285a

Ribera Paintings: 25c, Archimedes. 40c, Jacob's Flock. 70c, Triumph of Bacchus. 80c, St. Christopher. 1.50p, St. Andrew. 2.50p, St. John the Baptist. 3p, St. Onofre. 5p, St. Peter. 10p, The Immaculate Virgin.

Unwmk.

1963, Mar. 24		Photo.	*Perf. 13*
		Gold Frame	
1159	A285a	25c violet	.35 .25
1160	A285a	40c red lilac	.40 .25
1161	A285a	70c green	1.00 .25
1162	A285a	80c dark green	1.00 .25
1163	A285a	1p brown	1.00 .25
1164	A285a	1.50p blue green	1.00 .25
1165	A285a	2.50p car rose	2.75 .25
1166	A285a	3p dark blue	3.00 .50
1167	A285a	5p olive	10.50 2.25
1168	A285a	10p dull red brn	4.00 1.40
		Nos. 1159-1168 (10)	25.00 5.90

Issued to honor José de Ribera (1588-1652) and for Stamp Day, Mar. 24.
For other art types see A236-A237, A240a, A246a, A257, A272, A300, A310, A324, A340-A341, A360, A371 and footnote following No. 1606.

Coach — A286

1963, May 3   **Perf. 13x12½**
1169 A286 1p multicolored   .25   .25

First Intl. Postal Conference, Paris, 1863.

Globe
A287

1963, May 8   **Perf. 12½x13**
1170 A287 25c multicolored   .25   .25
1171 A287   1p multicolored   .25   .25
1172 A287 10p multicolored   1.10   .65
    Nos. 1170-1172 (3)   1.60   1.15

Issued for International Stamp Day, 1963.

"Give us
this Day
our Daily
Bread..."
A288

1963, June 1   **Unwmk.**
1173 A288 1p multicolored   .25   .25

FAO "Freedom from Hunger" campaign.

"Pillars of
Hercules" and
Globes — A289

Designs: 80c, Fleet of Columbus. 1p, Columbus and compass rose.

1963, June 4   **Perf. 13**
1174 A289 25c multicolored   .25   .25
1175 A289 80c brn, lt grn & gold   .25   .25
1176 A289   1p sl grn, sepia & gold   .25   .25
    Nos. 1174-1176 (3)   .75   .75

Cong. of Institutions of Spanish Culture, June 5-15.

Seal of Council
of San
Sebastian
A290

80c, Burning of city, 1813. 1p, View, 1836.

1963, June 27   **Photo.**
1177 A290 25c vio, grn & blk   .25   .25
1178 A290 80c dk brn, gray & red   .25   .25
1179 A290   1p dk grn, grn & ol   .30   .25
    Nos. 1177-1179 (3)   .80   .75

Rebuilding of San Sebastian, 150th anniv.

Europa Issue

Our Lady of
Europe — A291

1963, Sept. 16   **Engr.**   **Perf. 13x12½**
1180 A291 1p bis brn & choc   .25   .25
1181 A291 5p bluish grn & blk   *.55*   *.40*

Arms of Order of
Mercy — A292

King James
I — A293

Designs: 1p, Our Lady of Mercy. 1.50p, St. Pedro Nolasco. 3p, St. Raimundo de Penafort.

1963, Sept. 24   **Photo.**   **Perf. 13**
1182 A292 25c blk, car rose &
    gold   .25   .25
         Engr.
1183 A293 80c sepia & green   .25   .25
1184 A293   1p gray vio & brn
    vio   .25   .25
1185 A293 1.50p dull bl & blk   .25   .25
1186 A293   3p gray & black   .25   .25
    Nos. 1182-1186 (5)   1.25   1.25

Coronation of Our Lady of Mercy, 75th anniv.

Builders of the New World
Portrait Type of 1961

25c, 2p, Father Junipero Serra. 70c, 2.50p, Vasco Nuñez de Balboa. 80c, 3p, José de Galvez. 1p, 5p, Diego Garcia de Paredes.

1963, Oct. 12   **Perf. 13x12½**
1187 A265 25c vio bl, *bl*   .25   .25
1188 A265 70c grn, *pale rose*   .25   .25
1189 A265 80c dk grn, *yel*   .50   .25
1190 A265   1p dk bl, *pale
    rose*   .60
1191 A265   2p magenta, *lt bl*   1.75   .25
1192 A265 2.50p vio blk, *dl rose*   1.10   .25
1193 A265   3p brt bl, *pink*   2.40   1.00
1194 A265   5p brown, *yel*   3.00   2.25
    Nos. 1187-1194 (8)   9.85   4.75

The Good
Samaritan — A294

1963, Oct. 28   **Unwmk.**
1195 A294 1p gold, pur & brt car   .25   .25

Centenary of International Red Cross.

Holy Family by
Alonso Berruguete
(1486-1561) — A295

1963, Dec. 2   **Photo.**   **Perf. 13x12½**
1196 A295 1p dark green   .25   .25

Christmas 1963. See No. 1279.

Father Raymond
Lully — A296

Portrait: 1.50p, Cardinal Luis Antonio de Belluga (1662-1743).

1963, Dec. 5   **Engr.**
1197 A296   1p dk violet & blk   .25   .25
1198 A296 1.50p sepia & dull vio   .25   .25
    Nos. 1197-1198,C175-C176 (4)   3.50   1.45

Papal Type of 1962

Design: 1p, Pope Paul VI and St. Peter's, Rome.

1963, Dec. 30   **Perf. 12½x13**
1199 A283 1p dk green & blk   .25   .25

Second session of Vatican II, the 21st Ecumenical Council of the Roman Catholic Church.

Alcazar,
Segovia
A297

Dragon Caves,
Majorca — A298

Tourism: 40c, Potes, Santander. 50c, Leon Cathedral. No. 1202, Crypt of San Isidro at Leon. No. 1203, Costa Brava. 80c, Christ of the Lanterns, Cordova. No. 1206, Court of Lions, Alhambra, Granada. No. 1208, Interior of La Mezquita, Cordova. 1.50p, View of Gerona.

1964   **Engr.**   **Perf. 13**
1200 A297 40c sepia & blue   .25   .25
1201 A298 50c gray & sepia   .25   .25
1202 A297 70c ind & dk bl grn   .25   .25
1203 A298 70c violet & brown   .25   .25
1204 A298 80c dp ultra & blk   .25   .25
1205 A297   1p vio bl & pur   .25   .25
1206 A297   1p rose red & dl
    pur   .25   .25
1207 A298   1p dk green & blk   .25   .25
1208 A298   1p brn vio & rose   .25   .25
1209 A297 1.50p gray grn, brn &
    blk   .25   .25
    Nos. 1200-1209 (10)   2.50   2.50

See Nos. 1280-1289.

Santa Maria de
Huerta
Monastery — A299

Designs: 1p, Great Hall. 5p, View of monastery with apse, horiz.

1964, Feb. 24   **Perf. 13x12½, 12½x13**
1212 A299 1p gray grn & grn   .25   .25
1213 A299 2p grnsh blue & sepia   .25   .25
1214 A299 5p dark blue   1.50   .75
    Nos. 1212-1214 (3)   2.00   1.25

Santa Maria Monastery, Huerta, 8th cent.

Joaquin Sorolla,
Self-portrait
A300

Sorolla Paintings: 25c, The Jug (woman and child). 40c, Oxen and Driver, horiz. 70c, Man and Woman from La Mancha. 80c, Fisher Woman of Valencia. 1p, Self-portrait. 1.50p, Round up, horiz. 2.50p, And People Still Say Fish Are Dear (fishermen tending to wounded man), horiz. 3p, Children at the Beach, horiz. 5p, Unloading the Boat. 10p, Man and Woman on Horseback, Valencia.

Gold Frame

1964, Mar. 24   **Photo.**   **Perf. 13**
1215 A300 25c violet   .25   .25
1216 A300 40c purple   .25   .25
1217 A300 70c dp yellow grn   .25   .25
1218 A300 80c bluish grn   .25   .25
1219 A300   1p brown   .25   .25
1220 A300 1.50p Prus blue   .25   .25
1221 A300 2.50p dk car rose   .25   .25
1222 A300   3p violet blue   .45   .45
1223 A300   5p chocolate   1.40   1.00
1224 A300 10p deep green   .65   .35
    Nos. 1215-1224 (10)   4.25   3.55

Issued to honor Joaquin Sorolla y Bastida (1863-1923) and for Stamp Day, March 24.
    For other art types see A236-A237, A240a, A246a, A257, A272, A285a, A310, A324, A340-A341, A360, A371 and footnote following No. 1606.

"Peace"
A301

"Sport" — A302

Designs: 40c, Radio and television. 50c, New apartments. 70c, Agriculture. 80c, Reforestation. 1p, Economic development. 1.50p, Modern architecture. 2p, Transportation. 2.50p, Hydroelectric development. 3p, Electrification. 5p, Scientific achievements. 6p, Buildings, tourism. 10p, Generalissimo Franco.

1964, Apr. 1
1225 A301 25c blk, emer &
    gold   .25   .25
1226 A302 30c blk, bl & sal
    pink   .25   .25
1227 A301 40c gold & blk   .25   .25
1228 A302 50c multicolored   .25   .25
1229 A301 70c multicolored   .25   .25
1230 A301 80c multicolored   .25   .25
1231 A302   1p multicolored   .25   .25
1232 A302 1.50p multicolored   .25   .25
1233 A301   2p multicolored   .25   .25
1234 A302 2.50p multicolored   .25   .25
1235 A301   3p gold, blk & red   .90   .90

1236	A302	5p gold, grn & red	.30	.30
1237	A301	6p multicolored	.45	.45
1238	A302	10p multicolored	.55	.55
		Nos. 1225-1238 (14)	4.70	4.70

Issued to commemorate 25 years of peace.

Bullfight and Unisphere — A303

Designs: 1p, Spanish pavilion, horiz. 2.50p, La Mota castle, Medina de Campo. 5p, Spanish dancer. 50p, Jai alai.

Perf. 12½x13, 13x12½

1964, Apr. 23   **Engr.**

1239	A303	1p bl grn & yel grn	.25	.25
1240	A303	1.50p carmine & brn	.25	.25
1241	A303	2.50p dk bl & sl grn	.25	.25
1242	A303	5p car & dk car rose	.30	.30
1243	A303	50p vio bl & dk bl	.85	.40
		Nos. 1239-1243 (5)	1.90	1.45

New York World's Fair, 1964-65.

Stamp of 1850 and Modern Stamps — A304

1964, May 6   **Perf. 13x12½**

1244	A304	25c dk car rose & dl pur	.25	.25
1245	A304	1p yel grn & dk bl	.25	.25
1246	A304	10p orange & rose red	.40	.35
		Nos. 1244-1246 (3)	.90	.85

Issued for International Stamp Day, 1964.

Virgin of Hope — A305

1964, May 31 **Photo.**   **Perf. 13x12½**

| 1247 | A305 | 1p dark green | .25 | .25 |

Canonical coronation of the Virgin of Hope (La Macarena) in St. Gil's Church, Seville, May 31.

Santa Maria — A306

Designs (ships): 15c, 13th cent. ship of King Alfonso X, from medieval manuscript, vert. 25c, Carrack, from 15th cent. engraving, vert. 50c, Galley. 70c, Galleon. 80c, Xebec. 1p, Warship, Santisima Trinidad, vert. 1.50p, 18th cent. corvette, Atrevida, vert. 2p, Steamer, Isabel II. 2.50p, Frigate, Numancia, Spain's 1st armored ship. 3p, Destroyer. 5p, Submarine of Isaac Peral. 6p, Cruiser, Baleares. 10p, Training ship, Juan Sebastian Elcano.

1964, July 16   **Perf. 13**

1248	A306	15c dp rose & vio blk	.25	.25
1249	A306	25c org yel & gray grn	.25	.25
1250	A306	40c ultra & dk bl	.25	.25

1251	A306	50c slate grn & dk bl	.25	.25
1252	A306	70c vio & dk bl	.25	.25
1253	A306	80c dl bl grn & ultra	.25	.25
1254	A306	1p org & vio brn	.25	.25
1255	A306	1.50p car & sepia	.25	.25
1256	A306	2p blk & slate grn	.75	.25
1257	A306	2.50p rose car & dl vio	.25	.25
1258	A306	3p sepia & indigo	.25	.25
1259	A306	5p dk bl, lt grn & vio	.90	.90
1260	A306	6p lt green & vio	.80	.80
1261	A306	10p org yel & rose red	.35	.25
		Nos. 1248-1261 (14)	5.30	4.70

Issued to honor the Spanish Navy.

Europa Issue
Common Design Type

1964, Sept. 14 **Photo.**   **Perf. 12½x13**
Size: 21½x39mm

| 1262 | CD7 | 1p bis, red & grn | *.30* | .25 |
| 1263 | CD7 | 5p brt bl, mag & grn | *1.00* | *.55* |

Madonna of Alcazar — A307

1964, Oct. 9 **Photo.**   **Perf. 13**

| 1264 | A307 | 25c bister & brn | .25 | .25 |
| 1265 | A307 | 1p gray & indigo | .25 | .25 |

Reconquest of Jerez de la Frontera, 700th anniv.

Gold Olympic Rings

Shot Put — A308

1964, Oct. 10

1266	A308	25c shown	.25	.25
1267	A308	80c Broad jump	.25	.25
1268	A308	1p Slalom	.25	.25
1269	A308	3p Judo	.25	.25
1270	A308	5p Discus	.25	.25
		Nos. 1266-1270 (5)	1.25	1.25

1964 Olympic Games.

Builders of the New World
Portrait Type of 1961

25c, 2p, Diego de Almagro. 70c, 2.50p, Francisco de Toledo. 80c, 3p, Archbishop Toribio de Mogrovejo. 1p, 5p, Francisco Pizarro.

1964, Oct. 12   **Perf. 13x12½**

1271	A265	25c pale grn & vio	.25	.25
1272	A265	70c pink & ol gray	.25	.25
1273	A265	80c buff & Prus grn	.30	.25
1274	A265	1p buff & gray vio	.30	.25
1275	A265	2p pale bl & ol gray	.30	.25
1276	A265	2.50p pale grn & cl	.25	.25
1277	A265	3p gray & dk bl	3.00	1.00
1278	A265	5p yellow & brown	1.75	1.25
		Nos. 1271-1278 (8)	6.40	3.75

Christmas Type of 1963

Nativity by Francisco de Zurbaran (1598-1664).

1964, Dec. 4   **Photo.**

| 1279 | A295 | 1p olive black | .25 | .25 |

Tourism Types of 1964

Designs: 25c, Columbus monument, Barcelona. 30s, Facade of Santa Maria, Burgos. 50c, Santa Maria la Blanca (medieval synagogue), Toledo. 70c, Bridge, Zamora. 80c, La Giralda (tower) and Cathedral of Seville. 1p, Boat and nets in Cudillero harbor. No. 1286, Cathedral of Burgos, interior. No. 1287, View of Mogrovejo, Santander. 3p, Bridge, Cambados, Pontevedra. 6p, Silk merchants' hall (Lonja), Valencia, interior.

1965   **Engr.**   **Perf. 13**

1280	A298	25c dk blue & blk	.25	.25
1281	A298	30c dull grn & sep	.25	.25
1282	A298	50c cl & rose car	.25	.25

1283	A297	70c vio bl & ind	.25	.25
1284	A298	80c rose cl & dk pur	.25	.25
1285	A298	1p dp cl, car & blk	.25	.25
1286	A298	2.50p brn vio & bis	.25	.25
1287	A297	2.50p dull bl & gray	.25	.25
1288	A298	3p rose car & dk brn	.25	.25
1289	A298	6p slate & black	.25	.25
		Nos. 1280-1289 (10)	2.50	2.50

Alfonso X, the Wise (1232-84) — A309

25c, Juan Donoso-Cortes (1809-53). 2.50p, Gaspar M. Jovellanos (1744-1810). 5p, St. Dominic de Guzman (1170-1221).

1965, Feb. 25 **Engr.**   **Perf. 13x12½**

1292	A309	25c slate bl & blk	.25	.25
1293	A309	70c blue & indigo	.25	.25
1294	A309	2.50p slate grn & sep	.25	.25
1295	A309	5p dull grn & sl grn	.25	.25
		Nos. 1292-1295 (4)	1.00	1.00

Julio Romero de Torres, Self-portrait A310

De Torres Paintings: 25c, Girl with Jar. 40c, "The Song" (girl with guitar). 70c, Madonna of the Lanterns. 80c, Girl with guitar. 1.50p, "The Poem of Cordova" (pensive woman). 2.50p, Martha and Mary. 3p, "The Poem of Cordova" (two women holding statue of angel). 5p, Girl with the Charcoal. 10p, Back of woman's head.

1965, Mar. 24 **Photo.**   **Perf. 13**
Gold Frame

1296	A310	25c dull purple	.25	.25
1297	A310	40c purple	.25	.25
1298	A310	70c olive green	.25	.25
1299	A310	80c slate green	.25	.25
1300	A310	1p dk red brn	.25	.25
1301	A310	1.50p blue green	.25	.25
1302	A310	2.50p lilac rose	.25	.25
1303	A310	3p dark blue	.35	.25
1304	A310	5p brown	.35	.25
1305	A310	10p slate green	.50	.30
		Nos. 1296-1305 (10)	2.95	2.55

Issued to honor Julio Romero de Torres (1880-1930) and for Stamp Day, March 24.

For other art types see A236-A237, A240a, A246a, A257, A272, A285a, A300, A324, A340-A341, A360, A371 and footnote following No. 1606.

Bull and Symbolic Stamps — A311

1965, May 6   **Perf. 13x12½**

1306	A311	25c multicolored	.25	.25
1307	A311	1p orange & multi	.25	.25
1308	A311	10p multicolored	.50	.30
		Nos. 1306-1308 (3)	1.00	.80

Issued for International Stamp Day, 1965.

ITU Emblem, Old and New Communication Equipment — A312

1965, May 17   **Perf. 12½x13**

| 1309 | A312 | 1p salmon, blk & red | .25 | .25 |

International Telecommunication Union, cent.

Pilgrim — A313

Design: 2p, Pilgrim (profile).

1965, July 25 **Photo.**   **Perf. 13**

| 1310 | A313 | 1p multicolored | .25 | .25 |
| 1311 | A313 | 2p multicolored | .25 | .25 |

Issued to commemorate the Holy Year of St. James of Compostela, patron saint of Spain.

Explorer, Royal Flag of Spain and Ships — A314

1965, Aug. 28   **Perf. 13x12½**

| 1312 | A314 | 3p red, blk & yel | .25 | .25 |

400th anniv. of the settlement of Florida, and the 1st permanent European settlement in the continental US, St. Augustine, Fla. See US No. 1271.

Europa Issue

St. Benedict — A315

1965, Sept. 27 **Engr.**   **Perf. 13x12½**

| 1313 | A315 | 1p yel grn & sl grn | .25 | .25 |
| 1314 | A315 | 5p lilac & violet | *.40* | *.25* |

Sports Palace, Madrid — A316

1965, Oct. 9 **Photo.**   **Perf. 13**

| 1315 | A316 | 1p gray, gold & dk brn | .25 | .25 |

Issued to commemorate the meeting of the International Olympic Committee in Madrid.

Builders of the New World
Portrait Type of 1961

25c, 2p, Don Fadrique de Toledo. 70c, 2.50p, Father José de Anchieta. 80c, 3p, Francisco de Orellana. 1p, 5p, St. Luis Beltran.

1965, Oct. 12 **Photo.**   **Perf. 13x12½**

| 1316 | A265 | 25c pale grn & dp pur | .25 | .25 |
| 1317 | A265 | 70c pink & brown | .25 | .25 |

1318	A265	80c	cream & Prus		
			grn	.25	.25
1319	A265	1p	buff & dk vio	.25	.25
1320	A265	2p	lt bl & dk ol grn	.25	.25
1321	A265	2.50p	lt blue & pur	.25	.25
1322	A265	3p	gray & dk bl	1.00	.35
1323	A265	5p	yellow & brn	1.00	.30
		Nos. 1316-1323 (8)		3.50	2.15

Chamber of Charles V, Yuste Monastery — A317

Yuste Monastery: 1p, Courtyard, horiz. 5p, View of monastery, horiz.

Perf. 12½x13, 13x12½

1965, Nov. 15   **Engr.**

1324	A317	1p	bl gray & blk	.25	.25
1325	A317	2p	red brn & brn blk	.25	.25
1326	A317	5p	grayish bl & grn	.25	.25
		Nos. 1324-1326 (3)		.75	.75

Monastery of Yuste, Estremadura.

Stamp of 1865 (No. 78) — A318

Designs: 1p, Stamp of 1865 (No. 77). 5p, Stamp of 1865 (No. 80).

1965, Nov. 22   **Perf. 13x12½**

1327	A318	80c	blk & yel grn	.25	.25
1328	A318	1p	plum, brn & rose	.25	.25
1329	A318	5p	sepia & org brn	.25	.25
		Nos. 1327-1329 (3)		.75	.75

Cent. of the 1st Spanish perforated postage stamps.

Nativity A319

1965, Dec. 1   **Photo.**   **Perf. 12½x13**

| 1330 | A319 | 1p | bright green | .25 | .25 |

Virgin of Peace, Antipolo — A320

Design: 3p, Father Andres de Urdaneta.

1965, Dec. 3   **Perf. 13x12½**

| 1331 | A320 | 1p | pale sal & ol brn | .25 | .25 |
| 1332 | A320 | 3p | gray & dp blue | .25 | .25 |

Christianization of the Philippines, 400th anniv.

Globe and Four Beasts of Apocalypse — A321

1965, Dec. 29   **Photo.**   **Perf. 13x12½**

| 1333 | A321 | 1p | grnsh bl, yel & brn | .25 | .25 |

Vatican II, the 21st Ecumenical Council of the Roman Catholic Church, 10/11/62-12/8/65.

Adm. Alvaro de Bazan (1526-88) — A322

2p, Daza de Valdes, scientist, 17th cent.

1966, Feb. 26   **Engr.**   **Perf. 13x12½**

| 1334 | A322 | 25c | dull blue & gray | .25 | .25 |
| 1335 | A322 | 2p | magenta & violet | .25 | .25 |

See Nos. C177-C178.

Exhibition Emblem; Type Block "P" — A323

1966, Mar. 4   **Photo.**   **Perf. 13**

| 1336 | A323 | 1p | red, grn & vio bl | .25 | .25 |

Graphic Arts and Advertising Packaging Exhibition "Graphispack," Barcelona, 3/4-13.

José Maria Sert, Self-portrait A324

Sert Paintings: 25c, The Magic Ball. 40c, Evocation of Toledo, horiz. 70c, Christ on the Cross. 80c, Parachutists. 1.50p, "Audacity." 2.50p, "Justice." 3p, Jacob Wrestling with the Angel. 5p, "The Five Continents." 10p, Sts. Peter and Paul.

1966, Mar. 24   **Gold Frame**

1337	A324	25c	dk purple	.25	.25
1338	A324	40c	dp magenta	.25	.25
1339	A324	70c	green	.25	.25
1340	A324	80c	dk ol grn	.25	.25
1341	A324	1p	claret brn	.25	.25
1342	A324	1.50p	dull blue	.25	.25
1343	A324	2.50p	dk red	.25	.25
1344	A324	3p	deep blue	.25	.25
1345	A324	5p	sepia	.25	.25
1346	A324	10p	grnsh blk	.25	.25
		Nos. 1337-1346 (10)		2.50	2.50

Issued to honor José Maria Sert (1876-1945) and for Stamp Day, Mar. 24.

For other art types see A236-A237, A240a, A246a, A257, A272, A285a, A300, A310, A340-A341, A360, A371 and footnote following No. 1606.

Santa Maria Church, Guernica — A325

Designs: 1p, Arms of Guernica and Luno. 3p, Tree of Guernica.

1966, Apr. 28   **Photo.**   **Perf. 13**

1347	A325	80c	bl, sepia & grn	.25	.25
1348	A325	1p	yel grn & multi	.25	.25
1349	A325	3p	bl, grn & vio brn	.25	.25
		Nos. 1347-1349 (3)		.75	.75

Founding of Guernica and Luno, 6th cent.

Cover with Stamp of 1850 (#1) A326

Designs (covers): 1p, 5r (#3). 10p, 10r (#5).

1966, May 6   **Perf. 12½x13**

1350	A326	25c	rose vio, blk &		
			red	.25	.25
1351	A326	1p	red brn, org & blk	.25	.25
1352	A326	10p	ol grn, grn & org	.25	.25
		Nos. 1350-1352 (3)		.75	.75

Issued for International Stamp Day, 1966.

Bohi Valley — A327

Torla, Huesca A328

Tourism: 40c, Portal of Sigena Monastery, Huesca. 50c, Santo Domingo Church, Soria. 80c, Torre del Oro, Seville. 1p, Palm and view, Pico de Teyde, Santa Cruz de Tenerife. 1.50p, Monastery of Guadalupe, Caceres. 2p, Alcala de Henares University. 3p, Seo Cathedral, Lerida. 10p, Courtyard of St. Gregorio, Valladolid.

1966   **Engr.**   **Perf. 13**

1353	A327	10c	gray grn & bl		
			grn	.25	.25
1354	A328	15c	gray grn & brn	.25	.25
1355	A327	40c	bis brn & brn	.25	.25
1356	A327	50c	car rose & dp		
			cl	.25	.25
1357	A327	80c	lilac & rose vio	.25	.25
1358	A327	1p	vio bl & bl grn	.25	.25
1359	A328	1.50p	dk bl & blk	.25	.25
1360	A328	2p	sl bl & sepia	.25	.25
1361	A328	3p	ultra & blk	.25	.25
1362	A327	10p	brt bl & grnsh		
			bl	.25	.25
		Nos. 1353-1362 (10)		2.50	2.50

Tree and Globe A329

1966, June 6   **Photo.**   **Perf. 12½x13**

| 1363 | A329 | 1p | brn & dk grn | .25 | .25 |

6th Intl. Forestry Cong., Madrid, June 6-18.

Navy Emblem — A330

1966, July 1   **Photo.**   **Perf. 13**

| 1364 | A330 | 1p | gray & dk bl | .25 | .25 |

Naval Week, Barcelona, July 1-8.

Guadamur Castle — A331

Castles: 25c, Alcazar, Segovia. 40c, La Mota. 50c, Olite. 70c, Monteagudo. 80c, Butron, vert. 1p, Manzanares. 3p, Almansa, vert.

1966, Aug. 13   **Engr.**   **Perf. 13**

1365	A331	10c	grysh bl & sep	.25	.25
1366	A331	25c	violet & purple	.25	.25
1367	A331	40c	grnsh bl & bl grn	.25	.25
1368	A331	50c	grnsh bl & ultra	.25	.25
1369	A331	70c	vio bl & ind	.25	.25
1370	A331	80c	vio & sl grn	.25	.25
1371	A331	1p	ol bis & gray	.25	.25
1372	A331	3p	rose & red lil	.25	.25
		Nos. 1365-1372 (8)		2.00	2.00

Don Quixote, Dulcinea and Aldonza Lorenzo — A332

1966, Sept. 5   **Photo.**   **Perf. 13**

| 1373 | A332 | 1.50p | sal, lt grn & blk | .25 | .25 |

4th World Congress of Psychiatry, Madrid.

Europa Issue

The Rape of Europa A333

1966, Sept. 28   **Photo.**   **Perf. 12½x13**

| 1374 | A333 | 1p | multicolored | .25 | .25 |
| 1375 | A333 | 5p | multicolored | .25 | .25 |

Don Quixote and Sancho Panza on Clavileno — A334

1966, Oct. 9   **Perf. 13x12½**

| 1376 | A334 | 1.50p | sl bl, red brn & | | |
| | | | dk brn | .25 | .25 |

17th Cong. of the Intl. Astronautical Federation.

Builders of the New World

Types of 1961 and

Title Page of "Dotrina Christiana" — A335

30c, Antonio de Mendoza. 1p, José A. Manso de Velasco. 1.20p, Coins of Lima, 1699. 1.50p, Manuel de Castro y Padilla. 3p, Portal of Oruro Convent, Bolivia. 3.50p, Manuel de Amat. 6p, Inca courier, El Chasqui.

1966, Oct. 12

1377 A265 30c pale pink & brn .25 .25
1378 A335 50c pale bis & brn .25 .25
1379 A265 1p gray & vio .25 .25
1380 A335 1.20p gray & slate .25 .25
1381 A265 1.50p pale grn & dp grn .25 .25
1382 A335 3p pale gray & dp bl .25 .25
1383 A265 3.50p pale lil & pur .25 .25
1384 A265 6p buff & sepia .25 .25
Nos. 1377-1384 (8) 2.00 2.00

Ramon del Valle Inclan — A336

Portraits: 3p, Carlos Arniches. 6p, Jacinto Benavente y Martinez.

1966, Nov. 7 Photo. *Perf. 13*

1385 A336 1.50p blk & green .25 .25
1386 A336 3p blk & gray vio .25 .25
1387 A336 6p blk & slate .25 .25
Nos. 1385-1387 (3) .75 .75

Issued to honor Spanish writers.
See design A355.

Carthusian Monastery, Jerez A337

St. Mary Carthusian Monastery: 1p, Portal, vert. 5p, Entrance gate.

Perf. 13x12½, 12½x13

1966, Nov. 24 Engr.

1388 A337 1p grnsh bl & sl bl .25 .25
1389 A337 2p green & yel grn .25 .25
1390 A337 5p lilac & claret .25 .25
Nos. 1388-1390 (3) .75 .75

Nativity, Sculpture by Pedro Duque Cornejo A338

1966, Dec. 5 Photo. *Perf. 12½x13*

1391 A338 1.50p multicolored .25 .25

Regional Costumes Issue

Woman from Alava — A339

1967 Photo. *Perf. 13*

1392 A339 6p shown .25 .25
1393 A339 6p Albacete .25 .25
1394 A339 6p Alicante .25 .25
1395 A339 6p Almeria .25 .25
1396 A339 6p Avila .25 .25
1397 A339 6p Badajoz .25 .25
1398 A339 6p Baleares .25 .25
1399 A339 6p Barcelona .25 .25
1400 A339 6p Burgos .25 .25
1401 A339 6p Caceres .25 .25
1402 A339 6p Cadiz .25 .25
1403 A339 6p Castellon de la Plana .25 .25
Nos. 1392-1403 (12) 3.00 3.00

1968

1404 A339 6p Ciudad Real .25 .25
1405 A339 6p Cordoba .25 .25
1406 A339 6p Coruna .25 .25
1407 A339 6p Cuenca .25 .25
1408 A339 6p Fernando Po .25 .25
1409 A339 6p Gerona .25 .25
1410 A339 6p Gran Canaria, Las Palmas .25 .25
1411 A339 6p Granada .25 .25
1412 A339 6p Guadalajara .25 .25
1413 A339 6p Guipuzcoa .25 .25
1414 A339 6p Huelva .25 .25
1415 A339 6p Huesca .25 .25
Nos. 1404-1415 (12) 3.00 3.00

1969

1416 A339 6p Ifni .25 .25
1417 A339 6p Jaen .25 .25
1418 A339 6p Leon .25 .25
1419 A339 6p Lerida .25 .25
1420 A339 6p Logroño .25 .25
1421 A339 6p Lugo .25 .25
1422 A339 6p Madrid .25 .25
1423 A339 6p Malaga .25 .25
1424 A339 6p Murcia .25 .25
1425 A339 6p Navarra .25 .25
1426 A339 6p Orense .25 .25
1427 A339 6p Oviedo .25 .25
Nos. 1416-1427 (12) 3.00 3.00

1970

1428 A339 6p Palencia .25 .25
1429 A339 6p Pontevedra .25 .25
1430 A339 6p Sahara .25 .25
1431 A339 6p Salamanca .25 .25
1432 A339 6p Santa Cruz de Tenerife .25 .25
1433 A339 6p Santander .25 .25
1434 A339 6p Segovia .25 .25
1435 A339 6p Seville .25 .25
1436 A339 6p Soria .25 .25
1437 A339 6p Tarragona .25 .25
1438 A339 6p Teruel .25 .25
1439 A339 6p Toledo .25 .25
Nos. 1428-1439 (12) 3.00 3.00

1971

1440 A339 6p Valencia .25 .25
1441 A339 8p Valladolid .25 .25
1442 A339 8p Vizcaya .25 .25
1443 A339 8p Zamora .25 .25
1444 A339 8p Zaragoza .25 .25
Nos. 1440-1444 (5) 1.25 1.25
Nos. 1392-1444 (53) 10.60 10.60

Archers A340

Ornament — A341

50c, Boar hunt. 1.20p, Bison. 1.50p, Hands. 2p, Warrior. 2.50p, Deer. 3.50p, Archers. 4p, Hunters & gazelle. 6p, Hunters & deer herd.

1967, Mar. 27 Photo. *Perf. 13*

Gold Frame

1449 A340 40c ocher & car rose .25 .25
1450 A340 50c gray & dk red .25 .25
1451 A341 1p ocher & org ver .25 .25
1452 A340 1.20p gray & rose brn .25 .25
1453 A340 1.50p gray & red .25 .25
1454 A341 2p lt brn & dk car rose .25 .25
1455 A341 2.50p sky bl & rose brn .25 .25
1456 A340 3.50p yellow & blk .25 .25
1457 A341 4p citron & red .25 .25
1458 A341 6p olive & red .25 .25
Nos. 1449-1458 (10) 2.50 2.50

Issued for Stamp Day, 1967. The designs are from paleolithic and mesolithic wall paintings found in Spanish caves.

For other art types see A236-A237, A240a, A246a, A257, A272, A285a, A300, A310, A324, A360, A371 and footnote following No. 1606.

Palma Cathedral and Conference Emblem — A342

1967, Mar. 28

1459 A342 1.50p brt blue grn .25 .25

Issued to publicize the Congress of the Interparliamentary Union, Palma de Mallorca.

W. K. Röntgen, X-ray Tube and Atom — A343

1967, Apr. 3 Photo. *Perf. 13*

1460 A343 1.50p green .25 .25

7th Cong. of Latin Radiologists and 1st Cong. of European Radiologists, Barcelona, Apr. 2-8.

Averroes (1120-1198), Physician and Philosopher — A344

Portraits: 3.50p, José de Acosta (1539-1600), Jesuit, historian, poet. 4p, Moses ben Maimonides (1135-1204), Jewish philosopher and physician. 25p, Andres Laguna, 16th century physician.

1967, Apr. 6 Engr. *Perf. 13x12½*

1461 A344 1.20p lil & dl vio .25 .25
1462 A344 3.50p mag & dl pur .25 .25
1463 A344 4p brn & sep .25 .25
1464 A344 25p dl bl & blk .25 .25
Nos. 1461-1464 (4) 1.00 1.00

Europa Issue

Common Design Type

1967, May 2 Photo. *Perf. 13*

Size: 25x31mm

1465 CD10 1.50p sl grn, red brn & dl red .25 .25
1466 CD10 6p vio, brt bl & brn .25 .25

Exhibition Building and Fountain, Valencia — A345

1967, May 3

1467 A345 1.50p gray grn .25 .25

International Fair at Valencia, 50th anniv.

Numeral Postmark No. 3 of 1850 — A346

Designs: 1.50p, No. 2, 12c stamp of 1850 with crowned M postmark of Madrid. 6p, No. 4, 6r stamp of 1850 with 1r postmark.

1967, May 6

1468 A346 40c brn org, dl bl & blk .25 .25
1469 A346 1.50p brn, grn & blk .25 .25
1470 A346 6p bl, red & blk .25 .25
Nos. 1468-1470 (3) .75 .75

Intl. Stamp Day, 1967. See #1527-1528.

Guardian Angel Over Indigent Sleeper — A347

1967, May 16 *Perf. 13*

1471 A347 1.50p bl, blk, brn & red .25 .25

Issued for National Caritas Day to honor Caritas, Catholic welfare organization.

Betanzos Church, Coruña — A348

International Tourist Year Emblem A349

Tourism: 1p, Tower of St. Miguel Church, Palencia. 1.50p, Human pyramid (Castellers). 2.50p, Columbus monument, Huelva. 5p, The Enchanted City, Cuenca. 6p,Church of Our Lady, Sanlucar, Cadiz.

1967, July 26 Engr. *Perf. 13*

1472 A348 10c ultra & blk .25 .25
1473 A348 1p dl bl & blk .25 .25
1474 A348 1.50p lt brn & blk .25 .25
1475 A348 2.50p grnsh bl & dk bl .25 .25
1476 A349 3.50p dl pur & dk bl .25 .25
1477 A348 5p yel grn & dk grn .25 .25
1478 A348 6p red lil & dl lil .25 .25
Nos. 1472-1478 (7) 1.75 1.75

Balsareny Castle — A350

Castles: 1p, Jarandilla. 1.50p, Almodovar. 2p, Ponferrada, vert. 2.50p, Peniscola. 5p, Coca. 6p, Loarre. 10p, Belmonte.

1967, Aug. 11 Engr.

1479 A350 50c gray & lt brn .25 .25
1480 A350 1p bl gray & dl pur .25 .25
1481 A350 1.50p bl gray & sage grn .25 .25
1482 A350 2p brick red & bis brn .25 .25
1483 A350 2.50p grnsh bl & sep .25 .25
1484 A350 5p rose vio & vio bl .25 .25
1485 A350 6p bis brn & gray brn .25 .25
1486 A350 10p aqua & slate .25 .25
Nos. 1479-1486 (8) 2.00 2.00

Globe, Snowflake
and Thermometer
A351

1967, Aug. 30   Photo.
1487 A351 1.50p bright blue   .25   .25
  12th Intl. Refrigeration Cong., Madrid, Sept.
4-8.

Galleon, Map of
Americas, Spain
and Philippines
A352

1967, Oct. 10   Photo.   Perf. 13
1488 A352 1.50p red lilac   .25   .25
  4th Congress of Spanish, Portuguese,
American & Philippine Municipalities, Barcelona, Oct. 6-12.

Builders of the New World
Types of 1961 and

Nootka
Settlement
A353

  Designs: 40c, Francisco de la Bodega. 50c,
Old map of Nootka coast, vert. 1p, Francisco
Antonio Mourelle. 1.50p, Esteban José Marti-
nez. 3p, Old maps of coast of Northern Cali-
fornia. 3.50p, Cayetano Valdes. 6p, Ships,
San Elias, Alaska.

1967, Oct. 12
1489 A265   40c pink & grnsh
                   gray   .25   .25
1490 A353   50c dk brn   .25   .25
1491 A265   1p pale bl & red lil .25 .25
1492 A353   1.20p dk ol grn   .25   .25
1493 A265   1.50p pale pink & bl
                   grn   .25   .25
1494 A353   3p buff & vio blk   .25   .25
1495 A265   3.50p pale pink & bl .25   .25
1496 A353   6p red brn, bluish .25   .25
      Nos. 1489-1496 (8)   2.00 2.00

  Issued to honor the explorers of the Northwest coast of North America.

Roman Statue and
Gate — A354

  Designs: 3.50p, Ancient plower with ox
team, horiz. 6p, Roman coins of Caceres.

1967, Oct. 31   Photo.   Perf. 13
1497 A354 1.50p multi   .25   .25
1498 A354 3.50p multi   .25   .25
1499 A354   6p multi   .25   .25
      Nos. 1497-1499 (3)   .75   .75
  Founding of Caceres by the Romans,
2000th anniv.

José Bethencourt
A355

  1.50p, Enrique Granados (composer).
3.50p, Ruben Dario (poet). 6p, St. Ildefonso.

1967, Nov. 15
1500 A355 1.20p gray & red brn   .25   .25
1501 A355 1.50p blk & grn   .25   .25
1502 A355 3.50p brn & pur   .25   .25
1503 A355   6p blk & slate   .25   .25
      Nos. 1500-1503 (4)   1.00 1.00
  Issued to honor famous Spanish men.
See design A336.

Santa Maria de
Veruela
Monastery — A356

  Designs: 3.50p, Aerial view of monastery,
horiz. 6p, Inside view, horiz.

1967, Nov. 24   Engr.   Perf. 13
1504 A356 1.50p ultra & ind   .25   .25
1505 A356 3.50p grn & blk   .25   .25
1506 A356   6p rose vio & bis
                 brn   .25   .25
      Nos. 1504-1506 (3)   .75   .75

St. José Receiving
Last Unction, by
Goya — A357

1967, Nov. 27   Photo.
1507 A357 1.50p multi   .25   .25
  200th anniversary of the canonization of St.
José de Calasanz (1556-1648), founder of the
first Christian Schools in Rome.

Nativity, by
Francisco
Salzillo — A358

1967, Dec. 5
1508 A358 1.50p multi   .25   .25
  Christmas, 1967.

Slalom
A359

  3.50p, Bobsled, vert. 6p, Ice hockey.

1968, Feb. 6   Photo.   Perf. 13
1509 A359 1.50p multi   .25   .25
1510 A359 3.50p multi   .25   .25
1511 A359   6p multi   .25   .25
      Nos. 1509-1511 (3)   .75   .75
  Issued to commemorate the 10th Winter
Olympic Games, Grenoble, France, Feb. 6-18.

Mariano Fortuny,
Self-portrait
A360

  Fortuny Paintings: 40c, The Vicariate, horiz.
50c, "Fantasy" (pianist). 1p, "Idyll" (piper and
sheep). 1.20p, The Print Collector, horiz. 2p,
Old Man in the Sun. 2.50p, Calabrian Man.
3.50p, Lady with Fan. 4p, Battle of Tetuan,
1860. 6p, Queen Christina in Carriage, horiz.

1968, Mar. 25   Photo.   Perf. 13
Gold Frame
1512 A360   40c dp red lil   .25   .25
1513 A360   50c dk bl grn   .25   .25
1514 A360   1p brown   .25   .25
1515 A360   1.20p dp vio   .25   .25
1516 A360   1.50p dp grn   .25   .25
1517 A360   2p org brn   .25   .25
1518 A360   2.50p car rose   .25   .25
1519 A360   3.50p dk red brn   .25   .25
1520 A360   4p dk ol   .25   .25
1521 A360   6p brt bl   .25   .25
      Nos. 1512-1521 (10)   2.50 2.50
  Issued to honor Mariano Fortuny y Carbo
(1838-74), and for Stamp Day.
  For other art types see A236-A237, A240a,
A246a, A257, A272, A285a, A300, A310,
A324, A340-A341, A371 and footnote following No. 1606.

Beatriz
Galindo
A361

  Famous Women: 1.50p, Agustina de Aragon. 3.50p, Maria Pacheco. 6p, Rosalia de
Castro.

1968, Apr. 8   Engr.   Perf. 12½x13
1522 A361 1.20p yel brn & blk
                  brn   .25   .25
1523 A361 1.50p bl grn & dk bl .25   .25
1524 A361 3.50p lt vio & dk vio .25   .25
1525 A361   6p gray bl & blk   .25   .25
      Nos. 1522-1525 (4)   1.00 1.00

Europa Issue
Common Design Type

1968, Apr. 29   Photo.   Perf. 13
Size: 38x22mm
1526 CD11 3.50p brt bl, gold &
                  brn   .25   .25

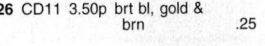

Spain No. 1 with
Galicia Puebla
Postmark — A362

  Stamp Day: 3.50p, Spain No. 4 with Serena
postmark.

1968, May 6   Photo.   Perf. 13
1527 A362 1.50p blk, bl & ocher .25   .25
1528 A362 3.50p bl, dk grn & blk .25   .25
  See Nos. 1568-1569, 1608, 1677, 1754.

Map of León and
Seal — A363

  Designs: 1.50p, Roman legionary. 3.50p,
Emperor Galba coin, horiz.

Perf. 13x12½, 12½x13
1968, June 15   Photo.
Size: 25x38½mm
1529 A363   1p lil, red brn & yel .25   .25
Size: 25x47½mm
1530 A363 1.50p brn, dk brn &
                  buff   .25   .25
Size: 37½x26mm
1531 A363 3.50p ocher & sl grn   .25   .25
      Nos. 1529-1531 (3)   .75   .75
  1900th anniversary of the founding of León
by the Roman Legion VII Gemina.

Human Rights
Emblem — A364

1968, June 25 Photo. Perf. 13x12½
1532 A364 3.50p bl, red & grn   .25   .25
  International Human Rights Year, 1968.

Benavente Palace,
Baeza — A365

  Tourism: 1.20p, View of Salamanca with
Tormes River Bridge, horiz. 1.50p, Statuary
group from St. Vincent's Church, Avila (The
Adoration of the Magi). 2p, Tomb of Martin
Vazquez de Arce, Cathedral of Sigüenza,
horiz. 3.50p, Portal of St. Mary's Church,
Sangüesa, Navarre.

1968, July 15   Engr.   Perf. 13
1533 A365   50c dp rose & brn   .25   .25
1534 A365   1.20p emer & sl grn   .25   .25
1535 A365   1.50p dp grn & ind   .25   .25
1536 A365   2p lil rose & blk   .25   .25
1537 A365   3.50p brt lil & rose lil .25 .25
      Nos. 1533-1537 (5)   1.25 1.25

Escalona
Castle,
Toledo — A366

  Castles: 1.20p, Fuensaldaña, Valladolid.
1.50p, Peñafiel, Valladolid. 2.50p, Vil-
lasobroso, Pontevedra. 6p, Frias, Burgos,
vert.

1968, July 29   Engr.   Perf. 13
1538 A366   40c dk bl & sepia   .25   .25
1539 A366   1.20p vio brn & vio
                   blk   .25   .25
1540 A366   1.50p ol & blk   .25   .25
1541 A366   2.50p ol grn & blk   .25   .25
1542 A366   6p vio bl & bl grn   .25   .25
      Nos. 1538-1542 (5)   1.25 1.25

Rifle
Shooting
A367

  Designs: 1.50p, Horse jumping. 3.50p,
Bicycling. 6p, Sailing, vert.

Perf. 12½x13, 13x12½
1968, Sept. 24   Photo.
1543 A367   1p multi   .25   .25
1544 A367   1.50p multi   .25   .25
1545 A367   3.50p multi   .25   .25
1546 A367   6p multi   .25   .25
      Nos. 1543-1546 (4)   1.00 1.00
  19th Olympic Games, Mexico City, 10/12-27.

Builders of the New World
Types of 1961 and

Map of Capuchin Missions along Orinoco River, 1732 — A368

1p, Diego de Losada. 1.50p, Losada family coat of arms. 3.50p, Diego de Henares. 6p, Map of Caracas, drawn by Diego de Henares, 1578, horiz.

1968, Oct. 12   Photo.   Perf. 13

1547	A368	40c grnsh bl, *bluish*	.25	.25
1548	A265	1p red lil, *gray*	.25	.25
1549	A368	1.50p sl, *pale rose*	.25	.25
1550	A265	3.50p dk bl, *pnksh*	.25	.25
1551	A368	6p dk ol bis	.25	.25
		Nos. 1547-1551 (5)	1.25	1.25

Christianization of Venezuela and the founding of Caracas.

St. Maria del Parral Monastery, Segovia — A369

3.50p, Monastery, inside view. 6p, Madonna & Child, statue from main altar.

1968, Nov. 25   Engr.   Perf. 13

1552	A369	1.50p gray bl & rose vio	.25	.25
1553	A369	3.50p brn & red brn	.25	.25
1554	A369	6p rose claret & brn	.25	.25
		Nos. 1552-1554 (3)	.75	.75

Nativity, by Federico Fiori da Urbino — A370

1968, Dec. 2   Photo.   Perf. 13x12½

| 1555 | A370 | 1.50p gold & multi | .25 | .25 |

Christmas, 1968.

Alonso Cano by Velázquez A371

Cano Paintings: 40c, St. Agnes. 50c, St. John. 1p, Jesus and Angel. 2p, Holy Family. 2.50p, Circumcision of Jesus. 3p, Jesus and the Samaritan Woman. 3.50p, Madonna and Child. 4p, Sts. John Capistrano and Bernardino, horiz. 5p, Vision of St. John the Baptist.

Gold Frame

1969, Mar. 24   Photo.   Perf. 13

1556	A371	40c deep plum	.25	.25
1557	A371	50c green	.25	.25
1558	A371	1p sepia	.25	.25
1559	A371	1.50p slate grn	.25	.25
1560	A371	2p red brown	.25	.25
1561	A371	2.50p dp red lil	.25	.25
1562	A371	3p ultra	.25	.25
1563	A371	3.50p dk rose brn	.25	.25

1564	A371	4p dull lilac	.25	.25
1565	A371	6p slate blue	.25	.25
		Nos. 1556-1565 (10)	2.50	2.50

Alonso Cano (1601-1667), and Stamp Day. For other art types see A236-A237, A240a, A246a, A257, A272, A285a, A300, A310, A324, A340-A341, A360 and footnote following No. 1606.

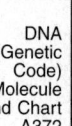 

DNA (Genetic Code) Molecule and Chart A372

1969, Apr. 7   Photo.   Perf. 13

| 1566 | A372 | 1.50p gray & multi | .25 | .25 |

Issued to publicize the 6th European Congress of Biochemistry, Madrid, Apr. 7-11.

Europa Issue
Common Design Type

1969, Apr. 28
Size: 38x22mm

| 1567 | CD12 | 3.50p multi | .25 | .25 |

Stamp Day Type of 1968

1.50p, Spain #6 with crowned M and "AL.3/1851" postmark. 3.50p, Spain #11 with Corvera postmark.

1969, May 6   Photo.   Perf. 13

| 1568 | A362 | 1.50p blk, red & grn | .25 | .25 |
| 1569 | A362 | 3.50p grn, bl & red | .25 | .25 |

Issued for Stamp Day, 1969.

Spectrum A373

1969, May 26

| 1570 | A373 | 1.50p blk & multi | .25 | .25 |

Issued to publicize the 15th International Spectroscopy Colloquium, Madrid, May 26-30.

World Map, Red Crescent, Cross, Lion and Sun Emblems A374

1969, May 30

| 1571 | A374 | 1.50p multi | .25 | .25 |

League of Red Cross Societies, 50th anniv.

Last Supper, Finial from Lugo Cathedral — A375

1969, June 4

| 1572 | A375 | 1.50p grn, brn & blk | .25 | .25 |

300th anniversary of the dedication of Galicia Province to the reign of Jesus.

Turegano Castle, Segovia A376

Castles: 1.50p, Villalonso, Zamora. 2.50p, Velez Blanco, Almeria. 3.50p, Castilnovo, Segovia. 6p, Torrelobaton, Valladolid.

1969, June 24   Engr.   Perf. 13

1573	A376	1p dl grn & sl	.25	.25
1574	A376	1.50p bluish lil & dk bl	.25	.25
1575	A376	2.50p bl vio & bluish lil	.25	.25
1576	A376	3.50p red brn & ol grn	.25	.25
1577	A376	6p gray grn & dl brn	.25	.25
		Nos. 1573-1577 (5)	1.25	1.25

Father Junipero Serra — A377

1969, July 16   Photo.   Perf. 13

| 1578 | A377 | 1.50p multi | .25 | .25 |

Bicentenary of San Diego, Calif.

Rock of Gibraltar — A378

2p, View of Gibraltar across the Bay of Algeciras.

1969, July 18

| 1579 | A378 | 1.50p bl grn | .25 | .25 |
| 1580 | A378 | 2p brt rose lil | .25 | .25 |

Dama de Elche — A379

Tourism: 1.50p, Alcañiz Castle, Teruel, horiz. 3p, Murcia Cathedral. 6p, St. Maria de la Redonda, Logrono.

1969, July 23   Engr.   Perf. 13

1581	A379	1.50p dl grn & blk	.25	.25
1582	A379	3p yel grn & bl grn	.25	.25
1583	A379	3.50p gray bl & dk bl	.25	.25
1584	A379	6p yel grn & vio blk	.25	.25
		Nos. 1581-1584 (4)	1.00	1.00

Builders of the New World
Types of 1961 and

Santo Domingo Church, Santiago, Chile — A380

1.50p, Casa de Moneda de Chile, horiz. 2p, Ambrosio O'Higgins. 3.50p, Pedro de Valdivia. 6p, First large bridge over Mapocho River, horiz.

1969, Oct. 12   Photo.   Perf. 13

1585	A380	40c lt bl & dk red brn	.25	.25
1586	A380	1.50p pale rose & dk vio	.25	.25
1587	A265	2p pale pink & ol	.25	.25
1588	A265	3.50p pale yel & dk Prus grn	.35	.30
1589	A380	6p pale yel & blk brn	.25	.25
		Nos. 1585-1589 (5)	1.35	1.30

Exploration and development of Chile. See Nos. 1630-1631, 1634.

Adoration of the Magi, by Juan Bautista Mayno — A381

Christmas: 2p, Nativity, bas-relief from altar of Cathedral of Gerona.

1969, Nov. 3

| 1590 | A381 | 1.50p multi | .25 | .25 |
| 1591 | A381 | 2p multi | .25 | .25 |

Tomb of Alfonso VIII and Wife, Las Huelgas Monastery, Burgos — A382

Designs: 1.50p, Las Huelgas Monastery. 6p, Inside view, vert.

1969, Nov. 22   Engr.

1592	A382	1.50p lt bl grn & indigo	.25	.25
1593	A382	3.50p ultra & vio bl	.40	.35
1594	A382	6p olive & yel grn	.25	.25
		Nos. 1592-1594 (3)	.90	.85

See Nos. 1639-1641.

St. Juan de Avila, by El Greco — A383

Design: 50p, Bishop Rodrigo Ximenez de Rada, Juan de Borgona mural.

1970, Feb. 25   Engr.   Perf. 13

| 1595 | A383 | 25p pale pur & ind | 4.00 | .25 |
| 1596 | A383 | 50p brn org & brn | 1.60 | .25 |

St. Stephen, by Luis de Morales — A384

Morales Paintings: 1p, Annunciation. 1.50p, Madonna and Child with St. John. 2p, Madonna and Child. 3p, Presentation at the Temple. 3.50p, St. Jerome. 4p, St. John de Ribera. 5p, Ecce Homo. 6p, Pieta. 10p, St. Francis of Assisi.

1970, Mar. 24   Photo.   Perf. 13

1597	A384	50c gold & multi	.25	.25
1598	A384	1p gold & multi	.25	.25
1599	A384	1.50p gold & multi	.25	.25
1600	A384	2p gold & multi	.25	.25
1601	A384	3p gold & multi	.25	.25
1602	A384	3.50p gold & multi	.25	.25
1603	A384	4p gold & multi	.25	.25
1604	A384	5p gold & multi	.25	.25
1605	A384	6p gold & multi	.25	.25
1606	A384	10p gold & multi	.25	.25
		Nos. 1597-1606 (10)	2.50	2.50

Issued to honor Luis de Morales, "El Divino" (1509-1586), and for Stamp Day.

For other art types see A397, A410, A431, A448, A473, A501, A522, A538, A558 and footnote following No. 876.

Europa Issue
Common Design Type
1970, May 4 Photo. *Perf. 13x12½*
Size: 37½x22mm
1607 CD13 3.50p brt bl & gold .25 .25

Stamp Day Type of 1968
Stamp Day: 2p, Spain No. 51 with "Ferro Carril de Langreo" postmark.
1970, May 4 *Perf. 13x12½*
1608 A362 2p dl red, grn & blk .25 .25

Barcelona Fair Building A385

1970, May 27 *Perf. 13*
1609 A385 15p multi .25 .25
Barcelona Trade Fair, 50th anniversary.

Miguel Primo de Rivera — A386

1970, June 6 Photo. *Perf. 13*
1610 A386 2p buff, brn & ol grn .25 .25
Gen. Miguel Primo de Rivera (1870-1930), Spanish dictator, 1923-1930.

Valencia de Don Juan Castle — A387

Castles: 1.20p, Monterrey. 3.50p, Mombeltran. 6p, Sadaba. 10p, Bellver.

1970, June 24 Engr.
1611 A387 1p blk & dl bl .35 .25
1612 A387 1.20p lt grnsh bl & vio .25 .25
1613 A387 3.50p pale grn & brn .25 .25
1614 A387 6p sep & dl pur .25 .25
1615 A387 10p fawn & sepia .80 .25
Nos. 1611-1615 (5) 1.90 1.25

Alcazaba Castle, Almeria A388

Tourism: 1p, Malaga Cathedral. 1.50p, St. Mary of the Assumption, Lequemo, vert. 2p, Cloister of St. Francis of Orense. 3.50p, Market (Lonja), Zaragoza, vert. 5p, The Gate of Vitoria, vert.

1970, July 23 Engr. *Perf. 13*
1616 A388 50c bluish gray & dl pur .25 .25
1617 A388 1p red brn & ocher .25 .25
1618 A388 1.50p bluish gray & sl bl .25 .25
1619 A388 2p sl & dk bl .40 .25
1620 A388 3.50p pur & vio bl .25 .25
1621 A388 5p gray grn & red brn .80 .25
Nos. 1616-1621 (6) 2.20 1.50

Tailor, from Book Published in Madrid, 1589 A389

1970, Aug. 18 Photo. *Perf. 13*
1622 A389 2p mag, brn & dl vio .25 .25
14th Intl. Tailoring Congress, Madrid.

Diver and Map of Europe A390

1970, Aug. 25
1623 A390 2p grn & brt bl .25 .25
12th European Championships in Swimming, Diving and Water Polo, Barcelona.

Concha Espina — A391

1p, Guillen de Castro. 1.50p, Juan Ramon Jimenez. 2p, Gustavo Adolfo Becquer. 2.50p, Miguel de Unamuno. 3.50p, José M. Gabriel y Galan.

1970, Sept. 21 Photo. *Perf. 13x12½*
1624 A391 50c brn, vio bl & pale rose .25 .25
1625 A391 1p sl grn, dp rose lil & gray .25 .25
1626 A391 1.50p dk bl, brt grn & gray .25 .25
1627 A391 2p grn, dk ol & buff .25 .25
1628 A391 2.50p pur, rose lake & buff .25 .25
1629 A391 3.50p brn, dk red & gray .25 .25
Nos. 1624-1629 (6) 1.50 1.50
Issued to honor Spanish writers.

Builders of the New World
Portrait Type of 1961 and Building Type of 1969
40c, Ecala House, Queretaro, Mexico. 1.50p, Mexico Cathedral, horiz. 2p, Vasco de Quiroga. 3.50p, Brother Juan de Zumarraga. 6p, Cathedral Towers, Morelia, Mexico.

1970, Oct. 12 Photo. *Perf. 13*
1630 A380 40c lt bl & ol gray .25 .25
1631 A380 1.50p lt bl & brn .25 .25
1632 A265 2p buff & dk vio .50 .25
1633 A265 3.50p pale grn & dk grn .25 .25
1634 A380 6p pale pink & Prus bl .25 .25
Nos. 1630-1634 (5) 1.50 1.25
Exploration and development of Mexico.

Map of Western Mediterranean — A392

1970, Oct. 20 Photo. *Perf. 13*
1635 A392 2p multi .25 .25
Geographical and Statistical Institute, cent.

Adoration of the Shepherds, by El Greco — A393

Christmas: 2p, Adoration of the Shepherds, by Murillo.

1970, Oct. 30
1636 A393 1.50p multi .25 .25
1637 A393 2p multi .25 .25

UN Emblem and Headquarters — A394

1970, Nov. 3
1638 A394 8p multi .25 .25
25th anniversary of the United Nations.

Monastery Type of 1969
Ripoll Monastery: 2p, Portal. 3.50p, View of monastery. 5p, Inside court.

1970, Nov. 12 Engr.
1639 A382 2p vio & pur .45 .25
1640 A382 3.50p org & mar .25 .25
1641 A382 5p Prus grn & yel grn .90 .25
Nos. 1639-1641 (3) 1.60 .75

Map with Main European Pilgrimage Routes — A395

Cathedral of St. David, Wales A396

#1643, Map of main pilgrimage routes. #1644, St. Bridget statue, Vadstena, Sweden. #1645, Santiago Cathedral. #1646, Tower of St. Jacques, Paris. #1647, Pilgrim before entering Santiago de Compostela. #1648, St. James statue, Pistoia, Italy. #1649, Lugo Cathedral. 2.50p, Villafranca del Bierzo church. #1652, Astorga Cathedral. 3.50p, San Marcos de León. #1654, Charlemagne, bas-relief, Aachen Cathedral, Germany. #1655, San Tirso de Sahagun. 5p, San Martín de Fromista. 6p, Bas-relief, King's Hospital, Burgos. 7p, Portal of Santo Domingo de la Calzada. 7.50p, Cloister, Najera. 8p, Puente de la Reina (Christ on the Cross and portal). 9p, Santa Maria de Eunate. 10p, Cross of Roncesvalles.

1971 Engr. *Perf. 13*
1642 A395 50c grnsh bl & sep .25 .25
1643 A396 50c bl & dl vio .25 .25
1644 A395 1p brn & sl grn .25 .25
1645 A395 1p grn & sl grn .25 .25
1646 A395 1.50p dl grn & dp plum .25 .25
1647 A396 1.50p vio bl & lil .25 .25
1648 A395 2p dk pur & blk .25 .25
1649 A395 2p sl grn & dk bl .80 .25
1650 A396 2.50p vio brn & dl vio .25 .25
1651 A395 3p ultra & dk bl .25 .25
1652 A395 3p dl red & rose lil .40 .25
1653 A396 3.50p dp org & gray grn .25 .25
1654 A396 4p ol grn .35 .25
1655 A396 4p grnsh bl & brn .25 .25
1656 A396 5p lt grn & blk .35 .25
1657 A395 6p lt ultra .25 .25
1658 A395 7p lil & dl vio .45 .25
1659 A396 7.50p car lake & dl vio .25 .25
1660 A395 8p grn & vio blk .25 .25
1661 A396 9p grn & vio .25 .25
1662 A395 10p grn & brn .40 .25
Nos. 1642-1662 (21) 6.50 5.25
Holy Year of Compostela, 1971.

Ignacio Zuloaga, Self-portrait A397

Zuloaga Paintings: 50c, "My Uncle Daniel." 1p, View of Segovia, horiz. 1.50p, Countess of Alba. 3p, Juan Belmonte. 4p, Countess of Noailles. 5p, Pablo Uranga. 8p, Cobblers' Houses at Lerma, horiz.

1971, Mar. 24 Photo. *Perf. 13*
1663 A397 50c gold & multi .25 .25
1664 A397 1p gold & multi .25 .25
1665 A397 1.50p gold & multi .25 .25
1666 A397 2p gold & multi .25 .25
1667 A397 3p gold & multi .25 .25
1668 A397 4p gold & multi .25 .25
1669 A397 5p gold & multi .25 .25
1670 A397 8p gold & multi .25 .25
Nos. 1663-1670 (8) 2.00 2.00
Ignacio Zuloaga (1870-1945). Stamp Day. For other art types see A384, A410, A431, A448, A473, A501, A522, A538, A558 and footnote following No. 876.

Amadeo Vives, Composer A398

2p, St. Teresa of Avila. 8p, Benito Perez Galdos, writer. 15p, Ramon Menendez Pidal, writer.

1971, Apr. 20
1671 A398 1p multicolored .25 .25
1672 A398 2p multicolored .25 .25
1673 A398 8p multicolored .25 .25
1674 A398 15p multicolored .25 .25
Nos. 1671-1674 (4) 1.00 1.00

Europa Issue
Common Design Type
1971, Apr. 29 Photo. *Perf. 13*
Size: 37x26mm
1675 CD14 2p lt bl, brn & vio bl .45 .25
1676 CD14 8p lt brn, dk brn & dk grn .30 .30

Stamp Day Type of 1968
Spain No. 1 with blue "A" cancellation.

1971, May 6
1677 A362 2p black, bl & olive .25 .25

Gymnast — A399

Design: 2p, Gymnast on bar.

1971, May 14
1678 A399 1p ocher & multi .25 .25
1679 A399 2p lt blue & multi .25 .25
9th European Gymnastic Championships for Men, Madrid, May 14-15.

Great
Bustard
A400

Designs: 2p, Pardine lynx. 3p, Brown bear.
5p, Red-legged partridge, vert. 8p. Spanish
ibex, vert.

1971, May 24
1680 A400 1p multicolored   .25 .25
1681 A400 2p multicolored   .25 .25
1682 A400 3p multicolored   .25 .25
1683 A400 5p multicolored   .35 .25
1684 A400 8p multicolored   .35 .35
        Nos. 1680-1684 (5)   1.45 1.35

Legionnaires — A401

2p, Legionnaires on dress parade. 5p,
Memorial service. 8p, Desert fighter and tank
column.

1971, June 21   Photo.   Perf. 13
1685 A401 1p multicolored   .25 .25
1686 A401 2p multicolored   .25 .25
1687 A401 3p multicolored   .25 .25
1688 A401 8p multicolored   .30 .30
        Nos. 1685-1688 (4)   1.05 1.05
50th anniversary of the Legion, a voluntary
military organization.

UNICEF Emblem,
Children of
Various
Races — A402

1971, Sept. 10
1689 A402 8p multicolored   .25 .25
        25th anniv. of UNICEF.

Don Juan of
Austria, Fleet
Commander
A403

Designs: 5p, Battle of Lepanto, horiz. 8p,
Holy League banner in Cathedral.

1971, Oct. 7   Engr.   Perf. 13
1690 A403 2p sepia & slate grn   .40 .25
1691 A403 5p chocolate   .75 .25
1692 A403 8p rose car & vio bl   .60 .60
        Nos. 1690-1692 (3)   1.75 1.10
400th anniversary of the Battle of Lepanto
against the Turks.

Hockey Players,
Hockey League
and Games
Emblems — A404

1971, Oct. 15   Photo.
1693 A404 5p multicolored   .50 .25
First World Hockey Cup, Barcelona, Oct. 15-
24.

De
Havilland
DH-9 over
Seville
A405

Design: 15p, Boeing 747 over Plaza de la
Cibeles, Madrid.

1971, Oct. 25
1694 A405 2p multicolored   .25 .25
1695 A405 15p multicolored   .25 .25
50th anniversary of Spanish air mail service.

Nativity, Avia
Altarpiece
A406

Christmas: 8p, Nativity, Sagas altarpiece.

1971, Nov. 4   Perf. 12½x13
1696 A406 2p multicolored   .25 .25
1697 A406 8p multicolored   .25 .25

Emilia Pardo
Bazan — A407

Portraits: 25p, José de Espronceda. 50p,
King Fernan Gonzalez.

1972, Jan. 27   Engr.   Perf. 13
1698 A407 15p brown & slate grn   .25 .25
1699 A407 25p lt grn & slate grn   .25 .25
1700 A407 50p claret & dp brn   .55 .25
        Nos. 1698-1700 (3)   1.05 .75
Honoring Emilia Pardo Bazan (1852-1921),
novelist (15p); José de Espronceda (1808-
1842), poet (25p); Fernan Gonzalez (910-
970), first King of Castile (50p).

Figure
Skating — A408

Design: 2p, Ski jump and Sapporo Olympic
emblem, horiz.

1972, Feb. 10   Photo.
1701 A408 2p gray & multi   .35 .25
1702 A408 15p blue & multi   .25 .25
11th Winter Olympic Games, Sapporo,
Japan, Feb. 3-13.

Don Quixote Title
Page, 1605 — A409

1972, Feb. 24   Engr.   Perf. 13x12½
1703 A409 2p brown & claret   .25 .25
International Book Year 1972.

A410

Gutierrez Solana Paintings: 1p, Clowns,
horiz. 2p, José Gutierrez Solana with wife and
child. 3p, Balladier. 4p, Fisherman. 5p, Mask
makers. 7p, The book collector. 10p, Merchant
marine captain. 15p, Afterdinner speaker,
horiz.

1972, Mar. 24   Photo.   Perf. 13
1704 A410 1p gold & multi   .25 .25
1705 A410 2p gold & multi   .35 .25
1706 A410 3p gold & multi   .40 .25
1707 A410 4p gold & multi   .25 .25
1708 A410 5p gold & multi   1.25 .35
1709 A410 7p gold & multi   .55 .25
1710 A410 10p gold & multi   .55 .25
1711 A410 15p gold & multi   .55 .25
        Nos. 1704-1711 (8)   4.15 2.10
José Gutierrez Solana (1886-1945). Stamp
Day 1972.
For other art types see A384, A397, A431,
A448, A473, A501, A522, A538, A558 and
footnote following No. 876.

A411

1972, Apr. 21
1712 A411 1p Fir   .25 .25
1713 A411 2p Strawberry tree   .35 .25
1714 A411 3p Cluster pine   .40 .25
1715 A411 5p Evergreen oak   .55 .25
1716 A411 8p Juniper   .35 .30
        Nos. 1712-1716 (5)   1.90 1.30

Europa Issue
Common Design Type and

Europeans
Interlocking
A412

1972, May 2
1717 A412 2p dull grn & ocher   1.40 .25
        Size: 25x38mm
1718 CD15 8p multicolored   .50 .40

Pre-stamp
Cordoba
Postmark
(1824-42)
A413

1972, May 6   Perf. 12½x13
1719 A413 2p dull yel, blk & car   .25 .25
        Stamp Day 1972.

Santa Catalina
Castle,
Jaen — A414

Castles: 1p, Sajazarra, Rioja, vert. 3p, Biar,
Alicante. 5p, San Servando, Toledo. 10p,
Pedraza, Segovia.

1972, June 22   Engr.   Perf. 13
1720 A414 1p dull bl grn & brn   .45 .35
1721 A414 2p gray olive & grn   .85 .25
1722 A414 3p rose car & red
                    brn   .85 .25
1723 A414 5p vio bl & dull grn   .85 .25
1724 A414 10p slate & lilac   2.50 .25
        Nos. 1720-1724 (5)   5.50 1.35

Weight Lifting,
Olympic
Emblems — A415

1972, Aug. 26   Photo.   Perf. 13
1725 A415 1p Olympic emblems,
                    fencing, horiz.   .25 .25
1726 A415 2p shown   .25 .25
1727 A415 5p Sculling   .25 .25
1728 A415 8p Pole vaulting   .25 .25
        Nos. 1725-1728 (4)   1.00 1.00
20th Olympic Games, Munich, 8/26-9/11.

Egyptian
Mongoose
A416

1972, Sept. 14
1729 A416 1p Aquatic mole, vert.   .25 .25
1730 A416 2p Chamois, vert.   .25 .25
1731 A416 3p Wolf, vert.   .25 .25
1732 A416 5p shown   .50 .25
1733 A416 7p Spotted genet   .40 .25
        Nos. 1729-1733 (5)   1.65 1.25

Brigadier M.A. de
Ustariz — A417

San Juan,
1870
A418

1972, Oct. 12   Photo.   Perf. 13

1734	A417	1p shown	.25	.25
1735	A418	2p shown	.25	.25
1736	A418	5p San Juan, 1625	.40	.25
1737	A418	8p Map of Plaza and Bay, 1792	.40	.30
		Nos. 1734-1737 (4)	1.30	1.05

450th anniversary of San Juan.

St. Tomas Monastery, Avila — A419

8p, Inside view. 15p, Cloister, horiz.

1972, Oct. 26   Engr.

1738	A419	2p Prus bl & gray grn	.80	.25
1739	A419	8p gray & claret	.65	.30
1740	A419	15p violet & red lil	.50	.25
		Nos. 1738-1740 (3)	1.95	.80

Teatro del Liceo, Barcelona A420

1972, Nov. 7   Perf. 12½x13

1741	A420	8p ultra & sepia	.25	.25

125th anniversary of the Gran Teatro del Liceo in Barcelona.

Annunciation — A421

Christmas: 8p, Angel and shepherds. Designs are from Romanesque murals in the Collegiate Basilica of San Isidro, Leon.

1972, Nov. 14   Photo.   Perf. 13

1742	A421	2p gold & multi	.25	.25
1743	A421	8p gold & multi	.25	.25

Juan de Herrera and Escorial A422

Great Spanish Architects: 10p, Juan de Villanueva and Prado. 15p, Ventura Rodriguez and Apollo Fountain.

1973, Jan. 29   Engr.   Perf. 12½x13

1744	A422	8p sepia & slate grn	.50	.25
1745	A422	10p blk brn & bluish blk	1.60	.30
1746	A422	15p brt green & indigo	.40	.25
		Nos. 1744-1746 (3)	2.50	.75

Myrica Faya — A423

Designs: Flora of Canary Islands.

1973, Mar. 21   Photo.   Perf. 13

1747	A423	1p Apollonias canariensis, horiz.	.25	.25
1748	A423	2p shown	.55	.25
1749	A423	4p Palms	.25	.25
1750	A423	5p Holly	.55	.25
1751	A423	15p Dracaena draco	.30	.25
		Nos. 1747-1751 (5)	1.90	1.25

Europa Issue
Common Design Type and

Europa, Roman Mosaic — A424

1973, Apr. 30   Photo.   Perf. 13

1752	A424	2p multicolored	.40	.25

Size: 37x26mm

1753	CD16	8p lt blue, blk & red	.35	.25

Stamp Day Type of 1968

Stamp Day: 2p, Spain No. 23 with red Madrid, 1853, cancellation.

1973, May 5

1754	A362	2p black, blue & red	.25	.25

Iznajar Dam on Genil River — A425

1973, June 9   Photo.   Perf. 12½x13

1755	A425	8p multicolored	.25	.25

11th Congress of the International Commission on High Dams, Madrid, June 11-15.

Oñate University, Guipuzcoa A426

Designs: 2p, Plaza del Campo and fountain, Lugo. 3p, Plaza de Llerena and fountain, Badajoz, vert. 5p, House of Columbus, Las Palmas. 8p, Windmills, La Mancha.

1973, June 11   Engr.   Perf. 13

1756	A426	1p gray & sepia	.25	.25
1757	A426	2p brt grn & sl grn	.55	.25
1758	A426	3p dk brn & org brn	.55	.25
1759	A426	5p dk gray & vio blk	1.40	.25
1760	A426	8p dk gray & car	.60	.25
		Nos. 1756-1760 (5)	3.35	1.25

Azure-winged Magpie — A427

Birds: 1p, Black-bellied sand grouse, horiz. 2p, Black stork, horiz. 7p, Imperial eagle, horiz. 15p, Red-crested pochard.

1973, July 3   Photo.   Perf. 13

1761	A427	1p multicolored	.25	.25
1762	A427	2p multicolored	.35	.25
1763	A427	5p multicolored	.50	.40
1764	A427	7p multicolored	.60	.25
1765	A427	15p multicolored	.25	.25
		Nos. 1761-1765 (5)	1.95	1.40

Knight, Holy Fraternity of Castile, 1488 — A428

Uniforms: 2p, Knight, Castile, 1493, horiz. 3p, Harquebusier, 1534. 7p, Mounted rifleman, 1560. 8p, Infantry sergeants, 1567.

1973, July 17

1766	A428	1p multicolored	.25	.25
1767	A428	2p multicolored	.50	.25
1768	A428	3p multicolored	.50	.25
1769	A428	7p multicolored	.40	.25
1770	A428	8p multicolored	.40	.25
		Nos. 1766-1770 (5)	2.05	1.25

See Nos. 1794-1798, 1824-1828, 1869-1873, 1902-1906, 1989-1993, 2020-2024, 2051-2055, 2078-2082.

Fish in Net A429

1973, Sept. 12   Photo.   Perf. 13

1771	A429	2p multicolored	.25	.25

6th Intl. Fishing Exhibition, Vigo, Sept. 12-19.

Conference Hall — A430

1973, Sept. 14

1772	A430	8p multicolored	.25	.25

Plenipotentiary Conf. of the Intl. Telecommunications Union, Torremolinos, Sept. 1973.

Vicente López, Self-portrait A431

Stamp Day (Paintings by Vicente López y Portana (1772-1850)): 1p, King Ferdinand VII. 3p, Señora de Carvallo. 4p, Marshal Castelldosrrius. 5p, Queen Isabella II. 7p, Francisco Goya. 10p, Maria Amalia de Sajonia. 15p, The organist Felix López.

1973, Sept. 29   Photo.   Perf. 13

1773	A431	1p gold & multi	.25	.25
1774	A431	2p gold & multi	.25	.25
1775	A431	3p gold & multi	.25	.25
1776	A431	4p gold & multi	.25	.25
1777	A431	5p gold & multi	.25	.25
1778	A431	7p gold & multi	.25	.25
1779	A431	10p gold & multi	.25	.25
1780	A431	15p gold & multi	.25	.25
		Nos. 1773-1780 (8)	2.00	2.00

For other art types see A384, A397, A410, A448, A473, A501, A522, A538, A558 and footnote following No. 876.

Leon Cathedral, Nicaragua A432

Designs: 2p, Subtiava Church. 5p, Portal of Governor's House, vert. 8p, Rio San Juan Castle.

1973, Oct. 12

1781	A432	1p multicolored	.25	.25
1782	A432	2p multicolored	.30	.25
1783	A432	5p multicolored	.50	.25
1784	A432	8p multicolored	.50	.25
		Nos. 1781-1784 (4)	1.55	1.00

Hispanic-American buildings in Nicaragua.

Pope Gregory XI and Pedro Fernandez Pecha — A433

1973, Oct. 26

1785	A433	2p multicolored	.25	.25

600th anniversary of the founding of the Order of the Hermites of St. Jerome by Pedro Fernandez Pecha.

St. Domingo de Silos Monastery — A434

Designs: 8p, Cloister walk, horiz. 15p, Three saints, sculpture.

Perf. 13x12½, 12½x13

1973, Oct. 26   Engr.

1786	A434	2p brn & rose mag	.45	.25
1787	A434	8p dk blue & purple	.25	.25
1788	A434	15p Prus grn & indigo	.25	.25
		Nos. 1786-1788 (3)	.95	.75

St. Domingo de Silos Monastery, Burgos.

Nativity, Column Capital, Silos Church — A435

Christmas: 8p, Adoration of the Kings, Butrera Church, horiz.

1973, Nov. 6   Photo.   Perf. 13

1789	A435	2p multicolored	.25	.25
1790	A435	8p multicolored	.25	.25

Map of Spain and Americas with Dates of First Printings A436

500 years of Spanish Printing: 7p, Teacher and Pupils, woodcut from "Libros de los Suenos," Valencia, 1474, vert. 15p, Title page from "Los Sinodales," Segovia, 1472.

1973, Dec. 11   Engr.   Perf. 13

1791	A436	1p ind & slate grn	.30	.25
1792	A436	7p violet bl & purple	.25	.25
1793	A436	15p purple & black	.25	.25
		Nos. 1791-1793 (3)	.80	.75

Uniform Type of 1973

Uniforms: 1p, Harquebusier on horseback, 1603. 2p, Harquebusiers, 1632. 3p, Cuirassier, 1635. 5p, Mounted drummer of the Dragoons, 1677. 9p, Two Musketeers, 1694.

1974, Jan. 5   **Photo.**   *Perf. 13*
1794 A428 1p multicolored   .25 .25
1795 A428 2p multicolored   .50 .25
1796 A428 3p multicolored   .70 .25
1797 A428 5p multicolored   .90 .25
1798 A428 9p multicolored   .25 .25
  Nos. 1794-1798 (5)   2.60 1.25

Nautical Chart of
Western Europe
and North
Africa — A437

1974, Jan. 26
1799 A437 2p multicolored   .25 .25
  50th anniv. of the Superior Geographical
Council of Spain. The chart is from a 14th
cent. Catalan atlas.

M. Biada
and Steam
Engine
A438

1974, Apr. 2   **Photo.**   *Perf. 13*
1800 A438 2p multicolored   .25 .25
  Barcelona-Mataro Railroad, 125th anniv.

Young
Collector,
Album,
Magnifier
A439

Exhibition Emblem — A440

  Design: 8p, Emblem, globe and arrows.

1974, Apr. 4   *Perf. 13*
1801 A439 2p lilac rose & multi   .25 .25
  Perf. 12½
1802 A440 5p buff, blk & dull bl   .35 .30
1803 A440 8p dull green & multi   .30 .25
  Nos. 1801-1803 (3)   .90 .80
  Espana 75, International Philatelic Exhibition, Madrid, Apr. 4-13, 1975.

Woman with
Offering — A441

  Europa: 8p, Woman from Baza, painted
sculpture.

1974, Apr. 29   **Photo.**   *Perf. 13*
1804 A441 2p multicolored   .45 .25
1805 A441 8p multicolored   .25 .25

No. 28 and
1854
Seville
Cancel
A442

1974, May 6
1806 A442 2p black, blue & red   .25 .25
  World Stamp Day.

Father
Jaime
Balmes
A443

  Designs: 10p, Father Pedro Poveda. 15p,
Jorge Juan y Santacilla.

1974, May 28   **Engr.**   *Perf. 13*
1807 A443 8p blue gray & sepia   .25 .25
1808 A443 10p red brn & dk brn   .60 .25
1809 A443 15p brown & slate   .25 .25
  Nos. 1807-1809 (3)   1.10 .75
  Famous Spaniards: Jaime Balmes (1810-
1848), mathematician; death centenary of
Pedro Poveda, pedagogue; Don Jorge Juan
(1712-1773), explorer and writer.

Templeto, by
Bramante,
Rome — A444

1974, June 4   **Photo.**
1810 A444 5p multicolored   .25 .25
  Cent. of the Spanish Academy of Fine Arts,
Rome.

Aqueduct,
Segovia
A445

  Designs: 2p, Tajo Bridge, Alcantara. 3p,
Marcus Valerius Martial lecturing. 4p, Triumphal Arch, Tarragona, vert. 5p, Theater,
Merida. 7p, Bishop Ossius of Cordoba preaching. 8p, Tribunal Arch, Talavera Forum, vert.
9p, Emperor Trajan, vert.

1974, June 25   **Engr.**
1811 A445 1p brown & black   .25 .25
1812 A445 2p gray grn & sepia   .30 .25
1813 A445 3p lt & dk brown   .25 .25
1814 A445 4p green & indigo   .25 .25
1815 A445 5p gray bl & choc   .25 .25
1816 A445 7p gray grn & lilac   .25 .25
1817 A445 8p dk brown & green   .25 .25
1818 A445 9p brt red lil & cl   .25 .25
  Nos. 1811-1818 (8)   2.05 2.00
  Roman architecture and history in Spain.

Greek
Tortoise
A446

  Reptiles: 2p, Common chameleon. 5p, Wall
gecko. 7p, Emerald lizard. 15p, Blunt-nosed
viper.

1974, July 3   **Photo.**
1819 A446 1p multicolored   .25 .25
1820 A446 2p multicolored   .30 .25
1821 A446 5p multicolored   .60 .50
1822 A446 7p multicolored   .40 .25
1823 A446 15p multicolored   .25 .25
  Nos. 1819-1823 (5)   1.80 1.50

Uniform Type of 1973

  Uniforms: 1p, Hussar and horse, 1705. 2p,
Artillery officers, 1710. 3p, Piper and drummer, Granada Regiment, 1734. 7p, Mounted
standard-bearer, Numancia Dragoons, 1737.
8p, Standard-bearer and soldier, Zamora Regiment, 1739.

1974, July 17
1824 A428 1p multicolored   .25 .25
1825 A428 2p multicolored   .40 .25
1826 A428 3p multicolored   .40 .25
1827 A428 7p multicolored   .30 .25
1828 A428 8p multicolored   .25 .25
  Nos. 1824-1828 (5)   1.60 1.25

Life Saving
A447

1974, Sept. 5   **Photo.**   *Perf. 13*
1829 A447 2p multicolored   .25 .25
  18th World Life Saving Championships, Barcelona, Sept. 1974.

Eduardo Rosales,
by Federico
Madrazo — A448

  Stamp Day (Eduardo Rosales, 1836-73,
Paintings): 1p, Tobias and the Angel. 3p, The
Last Will of Isabella the Catholic. 4p, Nena
(little girl). 5p, Presentation of John of Austria
to Charles I. 7p, The First Step. 10p, St. John
the Evangelist. 15p, St. Matthew.

1974, Sept. 29   **Photo.**   *Perf. 13*
1830 A448 1p gold & multi   .25 .25
1831 A448 2p gold & multi   .25 .25
1832 A448 3p gold & multi,
            horiz.   .25 .25
1833 A448 4p gold & multi   .25 .25
1834 A448 5p gold & multi,
            horiz.   .25 .25
1835 A448 7p gold & multi,
            horiz.   .25 .25
1836 A448 10p gold & multi   .30 .25
1837 A448 15p gold & multi   .25 .25
  Nos. 1830-1837 (8)   2.05 2.00
  For other art types see A384, A397, A410,
A431, A473, A501, A522, A538, A558 and
footnote following No. 876.

"International
Mail" — A449

UPU Monument,
Bern — A450

1974, Oct. 9
1838 A449 2p dark blue & multi   .25 .25
1839 A450 8p red & multi   .25 .25
  Centenary of Universal Postal Union.

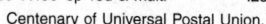

Sobremonte House, Cordoba,
Argentina — A451

Ruins of San
Ignacio de Mini,
18th
Century — A452

The Gaucho
Martin
Fierro — A453

  Design: 2p, Municipal Council Building,
Buenos Aires, 1829.

1974, Oct. 12
1840 A451 1p multicolored   .25 .25
1841 A451 2p multicolored   .40 .25
1842 A452 5p multicolored   .30 .25
1843 A453 10p multicolored   .25 .25
  Nos. 1840-1843 (4)   1.20 1.00
  Cultural ties with Latin America.

Nativity,
Valdavia
Church
A454

Adoration of the
Kings, Valcobero
Church — A455

1974   **Photo.**   *Perf. 13*
1844 A454 2p multicolored   .25 .25
1845 A455 3p lt blue & multi   .25 .25
1846 A455 8p olive & multi   .25 .25
  Nos. 1844-1846 (3)   .75 .75
  Christmas 1974.
  Issue dates: 2p, 8p, Nov. 4; 3p, Dec. 2.

Teucriun
Lanigerum
A456

  Flowers: 2p, Hypericum ericoides. 4p, Thy-
mus longiflorus. 5p, Anthyllis onobrychioides.
8p, Helianthemun paniculatum.

1974, Nov. 8
1847 A456 1p multicolored   .25 .25
1848 A456 2p multicolored   .25 .25
1849 A456 4p multicolored   .25 .25

1850	A456	5p multicolored	.25	.25
1851	A456	8p multicolored	.25	.25
		Nos. 1847-1851 (5)	1.25	1.25

**Franco Type of 1954-56
Imprint: "F.N.M.T."**

1974-75   Photo.   Perf. 12½x13

1852	A221	4p rose car ('75)	.25	.25
1853	A221	7p brt ultra	.25	.25
1854	A221	12p blue green	.25	.25
1855	A221	20p rose carmine	.25	.25
		Nos. 1852-1855 (4)	1.00	1.00

Leyre
Monastery
A457

8p, Column and bas-relief, vert. 15p, Crypt.

1974, Dec. 10   Engr.   Perf. 12½x13

1862	A457	2p slate grn & bl gray	.45	.25
1863	A457	8p carmine	.25	.25
1864	A457	15p grnsh black	.35	.25
		Nos. 1862-1864 (3)	1.05	.75

Leyre Monastery, Navarre.

Spain Nos. 1 and
1802 — A458

Mail
Coach,
1850
A459

Designs: 8p, Mail ship of Indian Service.
10p, Chapel of St. Mark.

Perf. 12½x13, 13x12½

1975, Jan. 2   Engr.

1865	A458	2p slate blue	.35	.30
1866	A459	3p olive & brown	.45	.40
1867	A459	8p lilac & slate bl	1.00	.50
1868	A458	10p brn & slate grn	.50	.40
		Nos. 1865-1868 (4)	2.30	1.60

125th anniversary of Spanish postage
stamps.

Uniform Type of 1973

1p, Sergeant and grenadier, Toledo Regiment, 1750. 2p, Royal Artillery, 1762. 3p, Queen's Regiment, 1763. 5p, Fusiliers, Vitoria Regiment, 1766. 10p, Dragoon, Sagunto Regiment, 1775.

1975, Jan. 7   Photo.   Perf. 13

1869	A428	1p multicolored	.25	.25
1870	A428	2p multicolored	.25	.25
1871	A428	3p multicolored	1.60	.50
1872	A428	5p multicolored	.50	.25
1873	A428	10p multicolored	1.40	.25
		Nos. 1869-1873 (5)	4.00	1.25

Antonio
Gaudi
A460

Designs: 10p, Antonio Palacios and Casa
Guell, Barcelona. 15p, Secundino Zuazo.

1975, Feb. 25   Engr.   Perf. 13

1874	A460	8p green & black	.25	.25
1875	A460	10p carmine & dp claret	.40	.25
1876	A460	15p brown & black	.25	.25
		Nos. 1874-1876 (3)	.90	.75

Contemporary Spanish architects.

Souvenir Sheets

Spanish Goldsmiths' Works — A461

Designs: 2p, Agate box, 9th cent. 3p, Votive crown of Recesvinto. 8p, Cover of Evangelistary, Roncesvalles Collegiate Church, 12th cent. 10p, Chalice of Infanta Donna Urraca, 11th cent. 12p, Processional monstrance, St. Domingo de Silos, 16th cent. 15p, Sword of Boabdil, 15th cent. 25p, Sword and head of Charles V (Carlos I of Spain). 50p, Earring and bracelet from Aliseda, 6th-4th centuries B.C. 3p, 10p, 12p, 25p vertical (No. 1878).

1975, Apr. 4   Engr.   Perf. 13

1877	A461	Sheet of 4	8.00	8.00
a.		2p gray & Prussian blue	2.00	2.00
b.		8p brown & Prus blue	2.00	2.00
c.		15p gray & dark carmine	2.00	2.00
d.		50p dark carmine & gray	2.00	2.00
1878	A461	Sheet of 4	8.00	8.00
a.		3p slate green & gray	2.00	2.00
b.		10p sepia & slate	2.00	2.00
c.		12p gray & bluish black	2.00	2.00
d.		25p sepia & bluish black	2.00	2.00

Espana 75 Intl. Phil. Exhib., Madrid, 4/4-13.

Pomegranates
A462

1975, Apr. 21   Photo.

1879	A462	1p Almonds, nuts and blossoms, horiz.	.25	.25
1880	A462	2p shown	.25	.25
1881	A462	3p Oranges	.25	.25
1882	A462	4p Chestnuts	.25	.25
1883	A462	5p Apples	.25	.25
		Nos. 1879-1883 (5)	1.25	1.25

Woman Gathering
Honey, Arana
Cave — A463

Europa: 12p, Horse, wall painting from Tito
Bustillo Cave, horiz.

1975, Apr. 28   Photo.   Perf. 13

| 1884 | A463 | 3p brown & multi | .25 | .25 |
| 1885 | A463 | 12p brown & multi | .35 | .25 |

Pre-stamp León
Cancellation
A464

1975, May 6   Perf. 12½x13

| 1886 | A464 | 3p multicolored | .25 | .25 |

World Stamp Day.

World Tourism Organization
Emblem — A465

1975, May 12   Photo.   Perf. 13

| 1887 | A465 | 3p dark blue | .25 | .25 |

First General Assembly of the World Tourism Organization, Madrid, May 1975.

Fair Emblem,
Agricultural
Symbols — A466

1975, May 14

| 1888 | A466 | 3p multicolored | .25 | .25 |

25th Agricultural Fair.

Equality
Between
Men and
Women
A467

1975, June 3

| 1889 | A467 | 3p multicolored | .25 | .25 |

International Women's Year.

Virgin of
Cabeza
Sanctuary
A468

1975, June 18   Photo.   Perf. 13

| 1890 | A468 | 3p multicolored | .25 | .25 |

Virgin of Cabeza Sanctuary, site of siege
during Civil War, 1937.

Cervantes'
Prison Cell,
Argamasilla de
Alba — A469

Tourism: 2p, Bridge of St. Martin, Toledo. 3p, Church of St. Peter, Tarrasa. 4p, Arch, Alhambra, Granada, vert. 5p, Street, Mijas, Malaga, vert. 7p, Church of St. Mary, Tarrasa, vert.

1975, June 25   Engr.   Perf. 13

1891	A469	1p purple & black	.25	.25
1892	A469	2p red brn & brn	.25	.25
1893	A469	3p slate & sepia	.25	.25
1894	A469	4p orange & claret	.25	.25
1895	A469	5p slate grn & indigo	.25	.25
1896	A469	7p violet bl & indigo	.40	.25
		Nos. 1891-1896 (6)	1.65	1.50

Salamander — A470

1975, July 9   Photo.   Perf. 13

1897	A470	1p shown	.25	.25
1898	A470	2p Newt	.25	.25
1899	A470	3p Tree toad	.25	.25
1900	A470	6p Midwife toad	.25	.25
1901	A470	7p Leaf frog	.25	.25
		Nos. 1897-1901 (5)	1.25	1.25

Uniform Type of 1973

1p, Cavalry officer, 1788. 2p, Fusilier, Asturias Regiment, 1789. 3p, Infantry Colonel, 1802. 4p, Artillery standard-bearer, 1803. 7p, Sapper, 1809.

1975, July 17

1902	A428	1p multicolored	.25	.25
1903	A428	2p multicolored	.50	.25
1904	A428	3p multicolored	.25	.25
1905	A428	4p multicolored	.25	.25
1906	A428	7p multicolored	.25	.25
		Nos. 1902-1906 (5)	1.50	1.25

Infant and
Children
Playing
A471

1975, Sept. 9   Photo.   Perf. 13

| 1907 | A471 | 3p multicolored | .25 | .25 |

"Defend Life."

Scroll and
Emblem
A472

1975, Sept. 25

| 1908 | A472 | 3p multicolored | .25 | .25 |

13th International Congress of Latin Notaries, Barcelona, Sept. 26-Oct. 4.

Blessing of
the Birds
A473

Scenes from Apocalypse: 2p, Angel at River of Life. 3p, Angel Guarding Gate of Paradise. 4p, Fox carrying cock. 6p, Daniel with wild bulls. 7p, The Last Judgment. 10p, Four horsemen of the Apocalypse. 12p, Bird holding snake.

1975, Sept. 29

1909	A473	1p gold & multi	.25	.25
1910	A473	2p gold & multi, vert.	.25	.25
1911	A473	3p gold & multi, vert.	.25	.25
1912	A473	4p gold & multi	.25	.25
1913	A473	6p gold & multi	.25	.25
1914	A473	7p gold & multi, vert.	.25	.25
1915	A473	10p gold & multi, vert.	.25	.25
1916	A473	12p gold & multi, vert.	.25	.25
		Nos. 1909-1916 (8)	2.00	2.00

Millenium Gerona Cathedral.

For other art types see A384, A397, A410, A431, A448, A501, A522, A538, A558 and footnote following No. 876.

Symbols of
Industry
A474

1975, Oct. 7   Engr.   Perf. 13

| 1917 | A474 | 3p violet & lilac | .25 | .25 |

Spanish industrialization.

Pioneers' Covered Wagon A475

Designs: 1p, El Cabildo, meeting house of 1st Uruguayan Government. 3p, Fort St. Theresa over River Plate. 8p, Montevideo Cathedral, vert.

1975, Oct. 12   **Photo.**
1918 A475 1p multicolored   .25 .25
1919 A475 2p multicolored   .25 .25
1920 A475 3p multicolored   .25 .25
1921 A475 8p multicolored   .25 .25
   Nos. 1918-1921 (4)   1.00 1.00

Cultural ties with Latin America; sesquicentennial of Uruguay's independence.

Ruined Columns, San Juan de la Peña — A476

3p, Monastery, horiz. 8p, Cloister, horiz.

Perf. 13x12½, 12½x13
1975, Oct. 28   **Engr.**
1922 A476 3p slate grn & brn   .30 .25
1923 A476 8p violet & brt lil   .25 .25
1924 A476 10p dp magenta &
       car   .25 .25
   Nos. 1922-1924 (3)   .80 .75

San Juan de la Pena Monastery.

Madonna, Mosaic, Navarra Cathedral — A477

Christmas: 12p, Flight into Egypt, carved capital, Navarra Cathedral, horiz.

1975, Nov. 4   **Photo.**   **Perf. 13**
1925 A477 3p multicolored   .25 .25
1926 A477 12p multicolored   .25 .25

King Juan Carlos I — A478

Queen Sofia and King — A479

Designs: No. 1928, Queen Sofia.

1975, Dec. 29   Photo.   Perf. 13x12½
1927 A478 3p multicolored   .25 .25
1928 A478 3p multicolored   .25 .25
     Perf. 12½
1929 A479 3p multicolored   .25 .25
1930 A479 12p multicolored   .25 .25
   Nos. 1927-1930 (4)   1.00 1.00

King Juan Carlos I, accession to the throne.

Pilgrim Virgin, Pontevedra A480

1976, Jan. 2   **Engr.**   **Perf. 13**
1931 A480 3p rose & brown   .25 .25

Holy Year of St. James of Compostela, patron saint of Spain.

Mountains and Center Emblem — A481

1976, Feb. 10   **Photo.**
1932 A481 6p multicolored   .25 .25

Catalunya Excursion Center, centenary.

Cosme Damian Churruca — A482

Navigators: 12p, Luis de Requesens. 50p, Juan Sebastian Elcano, horiz.

1976, Mar. 1   **Engr.**   **Perf. 13**
1933 A482 7p vio brn & grnsh
       blk   1.50 .25
1934 A482 12p lt blue & violet   .55 .25
1935 A482 50p dp brn & gray ol   .55 .25
   Nos. 1933-1935 (3)   2.30 .75

A. G. Bell, Radar and Telephone A483

1976, Mar. 10   **Photo.**
1936 A483 3p multicolored   .25 .25

Centenary of first telephone call by Alexander Graham Bell, March 10, 1876.

"Watch at Street Crossings" A484

Road Safety: 3p, "Don't pass when in doubt," vert. 5p, "Wear seat belts."

1976, Apr. 6   **Photo.**   **Perf. 13**
1937 A484 1p orange & multi   .25 .25
1938 A484 3p gray & multi   .35 .25
1939 A484 5p lilac & multi   .25 .25
   Nos. 1937-1939 (3)   .85 .75

St. George, Alcoy Cathedral A485

1976, Apr. 23
1940 A485 3p multicolored   .25 .25

7th centenary of the apparition of St. George in Alcoy.

Talavera Pottery A486

Europa: 12p, Lace making.

1976, May 3   **Photo.**   **Perf. 13**
1941 A486 3p multicolored   .65 .25
1942 A486 12p multicolored   .80 .30

17th Conference of European Postal and Telecommunications Administrations.

6r Stamp of 1851 with Coruna Cancel — A487

1976, May 6
1943 A487 3p blue, org & blk   .25 .25

World Stamp Day.

Coin of Caesar Augustus A488

7p, Map of Roman camp on banks of Ebro, and coin. 25p, Orpheus, mosaic from Roman era, vert.

1976, May 26   **Engr.**   **Perf. 13**
1944 A488 3p dk brn & mar   1.90 .25
1945 A488 7p dk brown & blue   1.00 .30
1946 A488 25p brown & black   .50 .25
   Nos. 1944-1946 (3)   3.40 .80

Founding of Saragossa, 2000th anniv.

Spanish-made Rifle, 1757 — A489

Designs (Bicentennial Emblem and): 3p, Bernardo de Galvez, Spanish governor. 5p, Dollar bank note, Richmond, 1861. 12p, Spanish capture of Pensacola from English.

1976, May 29
1947 A489 1p dk brn & vio bl   .25 .25
1948 A489 3p sl grn & dk brn   .90 .25
1949 A489 5p dk brn & sl grn   .40 .25
1950 A489 12p sl grn & dk brn   .40 .30
   Nos. 1947-1950 (4)   1.95 1.05

American Bicentennial.

Old Customs House, Cadiz A490

Customs Houses: 3p, Madrid. 7p, Barcelona.

1976, June 9
1951 A490 1p black & maroon   .25 .25
1952 A490 3p sepia & green   .55 .25
1953 A490 7p red brn & vio brn   1.10 .35
   Nos. 1951-1953 (3)   1.90 .85

Postal Savings Box with Symbols — A491

Railroad Post Office — A492

Rural Mailman in Winter A493

Postal Service: 10p, Automatic letter sorting machine.

1976, June 16   **Photo.**
1954 A491 1p multicolored   .25 .25
1955 A492 3p multicolored   .35 .25
1956 A493 6p multicolored   .25 .25
1957 A493 10p multicolored   .25 .25
   Nos. 1954-1957 (4)   1.10 1.00

King and Queen, Map of Americas A494

1976, June 25
1958 A494 12p multicolored   .25 .25

Visit of King Juan Carlos I and Queen Sofia to the Americas, June 1976.

San Marcos, León — A495

Tourism (Famous Hotels): 2p, Las Cañadas, Tenerife. 3p, Portal of R. R. Catolicos, Santiago, vert. 4p, Cruz de Tejeda, Las Palmas. 7p, Gredos, Avila. 12p, La Arruzafa, Cordoba.

1976, June 30   **Engr.**   **Perf. 13**
1959 A495 1p slate & sepia   .25 .25
1960 A495 2p green & indigo   .65 .25
1961 A495 3p brn & red brn   .45 .25
1962 A495 4p sepia & slate   .25 .25
1963 A495 7p slate & sepia   .85 .35
1964 A495 12p rose brn & pur   1.00 .25
   Nos. 1959-1964 (6)   3.45 1.60

Greco-Roman Wrestling — A496

Montreal Olympic Emblem and: 1p, Men's rowing, horiz. 2p, Boxing, horiz. 12p, Basketball.

1976, July 9   **Photo.**
1965	A496	1p multicolored	.25 .25
1966	A496	2p lilac & multi	.35 .25
1967	A496	3p multicolored	.25 .25
1968	A496	12p multicolored	.25 .25
	Nos. 1965-1968 (4)		1.10 1.00

21st Olympic Games, Montreal, Canada, July 17-Aug. 1.

King Juan Carlos I — A497

1976-77   **Photo.**   **Perf. 13**
1969	A497	10c orange ('77)	.25 .25
1970	A497	25c apple grn ('77)	.25 .25
1971	A497	30c dp blue ('77)	.25 .25
1972	A497	50c purple ('77)	.25 .25
1973	A497	1p emerald ('77)	.25 .25
1974	A497	1.50p scarlet	.25 .25
1975	A497	2p dp blue	.25 .25
1976	A497	3p dp green	.25 .25
1977	A497	4p blue grn ('77)	.25 .25
1978	A497	5p dp car rose	.25 .25
1979	A497	6p brt green ('77)	.25 .25
1980	A497	7p olive	.25 .25
1982	A497	8p brt blue ('77)	.25 .25
1983	A497	10p lilac rose ('77)	.25 .25
1984	A497	12p golden brown	.25 .25
1985	A497	15p vio blue ('77)	.30 .25
1986	A497	20p brt red lil ('77)	.35 .25
	Nos. 1969-1986 (17)		4.40 4.25

Nos. 1976, 1978-1980, 1982-1983 also issued as coils with number on back of every fifth stamp.

See Nos. 2185-2194, 2268-2270.

Nos. 1969-1970, 1972-1973, 1975-1983, 1985-1986, 2185-2194 and 2268-2270 also printed on prephosphored paper. Value, mint set of 27 values, $40.

Uniform Type of 1973

Uniforms: 1p, Trumpeter, Alcantara Regiment, 1815. 2p, Sapper, 1821. 3p, Engineer in dress uniform, 1825. 7p, Artillery infantry, 1828. 25p, Infantry riflemen, 1830.

1976, July 17
1989	A428	1p multicolored	.25 .25
1990	A428	2p multicolored	.80 .25
1991	A428	3p multicolored	.30 .25
1992	A428	7p multicolored	.25 .25
1993	A428	25p multicolored	.30 .25
	Nos. 1989-1993 (5)		1.90 1.25

Blood Donors — A498

1976, Sept. 7   **Engr.**   **Perf. 13**
1994	A498	3p carmine & black	.25 .25

Give blood, save a life!

Mosaic, Batitales — A499

Designs: 3p, Lugo city wall. 7p, Obverse and reverse of Roman 1st Legion coin.

1976, Sept. 22
1995	A499	1p black & purple	.25 .25
1996	A499	3p black & dp brn	.25 .25
1997	A499	7p green & magenta	.45 .25
	Nos. 1995-1997 (3)		.95 .75

2000th anniversary of Lugo City.

Parliament, Madrid A500

1976, Sept. 23
1998	A500	12p green & sepia	.25 .25

63rd Conference of Inter-parliamentary Union, Madrid.

Still Life, by L. E. Menendez — A501

Luis Eugenio Menendez Paintings: 2p, Peaches and jar. 3p, Pears, melon and barrel. 4p, Brace of pigeons and basket. 6p, Sea bream and oranges, horiz. 7p, Water melon and bread, horiz. 10p, Figs, bread and jug, horiz. 12p, Various fruits, horiz.

1976, Sept. 29   **Photo.**   **Perf. 13**
1999	A501	1p gold & multi	.25 .25
2000	A501	2p gold & multi	.25 .25
2001	A501	3p gold & multi	.25 .25
2002	A501	4p gold & multi	.25 .25
2003	A501	6p gold & multi	.25 .25
2004	A501	7p gold & multi	.30 .25
2005	A501	10p gold & multi	.25 .25
2006	A501	12p gold & multi	.30 .25
	Nos. 1999-2006 (8)		2.10 2.00

Luis Eugenio Menendez (1716-1780). Stamp Day 1976.

For other art types see A384, A397, A410, A431, A448, A473, A522, A538, A558 and footnote following No. 876.

St. Christopher Carrying Christ Child — A502

Christmas: 3p, Nativity, horiz. Both designs after painted wood carvings.

1976, Oct. 8
2007	A502	3p multicolored	.75 .25
2008	A502	12p multicolored	1.50 .50

Nicoya Church, Costa Rica — A503

Juan Vazquez de Coronado — A504

Designs: 3p, Orosi Mission, Costa Rica, horiz. 12p, Tomas de Acosta.

1976, Oct. 12
2009	A503	1p multicolored	.25 .25
2010	A504	2p multicolored	.25 .25
2011	A503	3p multicolored	.25 .25
2012	A504	12p multicolored	.25 .25
	Nos. 2009-2012 (4)		1.00 1.00

Spain's link with Costa Rica.

Map of South and Central America, Santa Maria, King and Queen A505

1976, Oct. 12
2013	A505	12p multicolored	.25 .25

Visit of King Juan Carlos I and Queen Sofia to Latin America.

St. Peter of Alcantara Monastery A506

Tomb of Peter of Alcantara A507

St. Peter of Alcantara A508

1976, Oct. 29   **Engr.**   **Perf. 13**
2014	A506	3p dp brown & sepia	.30 .25
2015	A507	7p dk purple & blk	.25 .25
2016	A508	20p brown & dk brown	.30 .25
	Nos. 2014-2016 (3)		.85 .75

St. Peter of Alcantara (1499-1562), Franciscan reformer.

Hand Releasing Doves A509

1976, Nov. 23   **Litho.**   **Perf. 13**
2017	A509	3p multicolored	.25 .25

11th Philatelic Exhibition of the National Association of the Handicapped.

Casals and Cello A510

Design: 5p, Manuel de Falla and Fire Dance from El Amor Brujo.

1976, Dec. 29   **Engr.**   **Perf. 13**
2018	A510	3p black & vio bl	.25 .25
2019	A510	5p slate grn & car	.25 .25

Birth centenaries of Pablo Casals (1876-1973), cellist and composer, and of Manuel de Falla (1876-1946), composer.

Uniform Type of 1973

Uniforms: 1p, Outrider, Calatrava Lancers, 1844. 2p, Sapper, 1850. 3p, Corporal, Light Infantry, 1860. 4p, Drum Major, 1861. 20p, Artillery Captain, Mounted, 1862.

1977, Jan. 5   **Photo.**   **Perf. 13**
2020	A428	1p multicolored	.25 .25
2021	A428	2p multicolored	.35 .25
2022	A428	3p multicolored	.25 .25
2023	A428	4p multicolored	.25 .25
2024	A428	20p multicolored	.25 .25
	Nos. 2020-2024 (5)		1.35 1.25

King James I A511

1977, Feb. 10   **Engr.**   **Perf. 13**
2025	A511	4p purple & ocher	.25 .25

James I, El Conquistador (1208-1276), King of Aragon, 700th death anniversary.

Jacinto Verdaguer — A512

Portraits: 7p, Miguel Servet. 12p, Pablo Sarasate. 50p, Francisco Tarrega.

1977, Feb. 22
2026	A512	5p purple & dk red	.25 .25
2027	A512	7p olive & slate grn	.25 .25
2028	A512	12p dk blue & bl grn	.25 .25
2029	A512	50p lt green & brown	.55 .25
	Nos. 2026-2029 (4)		1.30 1.00

Honoring Jacinto Verdaguer (1845-1902), Catalan poet; Miguel Servet (1511-1553), physician and theologian; Pablo Sarasate (1844-1908), violinist and composer; Francisco Tarrega (1854-1909), creator of modern Spanish guitar music.

Marquis de Penaflorida — A513

1977, Feb. 24   **Engr.**   **Perf. 13**
2030	A513	4p dull green & brn	.25 .25

Bicentenary of the Economic Society of the Friends of the Land (agricultural improvements).

Trout
A514

1977, Mar. 8   **Photo.**
2031 A514 1p Salmon, vert. .25 .25
2032 A514 2p shown .25 .25
2033 A514 3p Eel .25 .25
2034 A514 4p Carp .25 .25
2035 A514 6p Barbel .25 .25
Nos. 2031-2035 (5) 1.25 1.25

Slalom
A515

1977, Mar. 24   **Engr.**   *Perf. 13*
2036 A515 5p multicolored .25 .25
World Ski Championships, Granada, Sierra
Nevada, Mar. 24-27.

La Cuadra,
1900
A516

Spanish Pioneer Automobiles: 4p, Hispano
Suiza, 1916. 5p, Elizalde, 1915. 7p, Abadal,
1914.

1977, Apr. 23   **Photo.**   *Perf. 13*
2037 A516 2p multicolored .25 .25
2038 A516 4p multicolored .25 .25
2039 A516 5p multicolored .25 .25
2040 A516 7p multicolored .25 .25
Nos. 2037-2040 (4) 1.00 1.00

Ordesa
National
Park
A517

Europa: 3p, Tree in Doñana National Park.

1977, May 2   **Litho.**
2041 A517 3p multicolored .25 .25
2042 A517 12p multicolored .25 .25

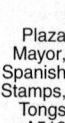 

Plaza
Mayor,
Spanish
Stamps,
Tongs
A518

1977, May 7   **Engr.**   *Perf. 13*
2043 A518 3p multicolored .25 .25
50th anniversary of Philatelic Market on
Plaza Mayor, Madrid.

Enrique de
Osso, St.
Theresa
and Book
A519

1977, June 7   **Photo.**
2044 A519 8p multicolored .25 .25
Centenary of the founding by Enrique de
Osso of the Society of St. Theresa of Jesus.

Toledo Gate,
Ciudad
Real — A520

Tourism: 2p, Roman aqueduct, Almuñecar.
3p, Cathedral, Jaen, vert. 4p, Ronda Gorge,
Malaga, vert. 7p, Ampudia Castle, Palencia.
12p, Bisagra Gate, Toledo.

1977, June 24   **Engr.**   *Perf. 13*
2045 A520 1p orange & brown .25 .25
2046 A520 2p sepia & slate .25 .25
2047 A520 3p violet & purple .25 .25
2048 A520 4p brt & dk green .25 .25
2049 A520 7p brown & black .25 .25
2050 A520 12p vio & org brn .25 .25
Nos. 2045-2050 (6) 1.50 1.50

Uniform Type of 1973

Uniforms: 1p, Military Administration official,
1875. 2p, Cavalry lancers, 1883. 3p, General
Staff Commander, 1884. 7p, Trumpeter, Divi-
sional Artillery, 1887. 25p, Medical Corps official, 1895.

1977, July 16   **Photo.**
2051 A428 1p multicolored .25 .25
2052 A428 2p multicolored .25 .25
2053 A428 3p multicolored .25 .25
2054 A428 7p multicolored .25 .25
2055 A428 25p multicolored .30 .25
Nos. 2051-2055 (5) 1.30 1.25

A521

St. Emilian Cuculatus and earliest known
Catalan manuscript.

1977, Sept. 9   **Engr.**   *Perf. 13*
2056 A521 5p violet, grn & brn .25 .25
Millennium of Catalan language.

A522

Federico Madrazo (1815-94) Portraits: 1p,
The Boy Florez. 2p, Duke of San Miguel. 3p,
Senora Coronado. 4p, Campoamor. 6p, Mar-
quesa de Montelo. 7p, Rivadeneyra. 10p,
Countess de Vilches. 15p, Senora Gomez de
Avellaneda.

1977, Sept. 29   **Photo.**   *Perf. 13*
2057 A522 1p gold & multi .25 .25
2058 A522 2p gold & multi .25 .25
2059 A522 3p gold & multi .25 .25
2060 A522 4p gold & multi .25 .25
2061 A522 6p gold & multi .25 .25
2062 A522 7p gold & multi .25 .25

2063 A522 10p gold & multi .25 .25
2064 A522 15p gold & multi .25 .25
Nos. 2057-2064 (8) 2.00 2.00
For other art types see A384, A397, A410,
A431, A448, A473, A501, A538, A558 and
footnote following No. 876.

Sailing Ship and Mail Routes, 18th
Century — A523

1977, Oct. 7   **Engr.**
2065 A523 15p black, brn & grn .30 .30
ESPAMER '77 Philatelic Exhibition, Barcelona, Oct. 7-13, and for the Bicentenary for
regular mail routes to the Indies (Central and
South America). No. 2065 issued in sheets of
8 stamps and 8 labels showing exhibition
emblem.

Church of
St. Francis,
Guatemala
City
A524

Designs (Guatemala City): 3p, Modern
buildings. 7p, Government Palace. 12p,
Columbus Square and monument.

1977, Oct. 12   **Photo.**   *Perf. 13*
2066 A524 1p multicolored .25 .25
2067 A524 3p multicolored .25 .25
2068 A524 7p multicolored .25 .25
2069 A524 12p multicolored .25 .25
Nos. 2066-2069 (4) 1.00 1.00
Spain's link with Guatemala.

San Pedro
Monastery,
Cardeña
A525

Designs: 7p, Cloister. 20p, Tomb of El Cid
and Dona Gimena.

1977, Oct. 28   **Engr.**
2070 A525 3p vio blue & slate .25 .25
2071 A525 7p brown & maroon .25 .25
2072 A525 20p green & slate .25 .25
Nos. 2070-2072 (3) .75 .75
San Pedro Monastery, Cardena, Burgos.

Adoration
of the
Kings
A526

Christmas: 12p, Flight into Egypt, vert.
Designs from Romanesque paintings in Jaca
Cathedral Museum.

1977, Nov. 3   **Photo.**
2073 A526 5p multicolored .25 .25
2074 A526 12p multicolored .25 .25

Old and
New Iberia
Planes
A527

1977, Nov. 3
2075 A527 12p multicolored .25 .25
IBERIA, Spanish Airlines, 50th anniversary.

Felipe de Borbon,
Prince of
Asturias — A528

1977, Dec. 22   **Photo.**   *Perf. 13*
2076 A528 5p multicolored .25 .25
Felipe de Borbon, Spanish crown prince.

Judo, Games
Emblem — A529

1977, Dec. 29
2077 A529 3p multicolored .25 .25
10th World Judo Championships, Taiwan.

Uniform Type of 1973

Uniforms: 1p, Flag bearer, 1908. 2p, Lieutenant Colonel, Hussar, 1909. 3p, Mounted
artillery lieutenant, 1912. 5p, Engineers' captain, 1921. 12p, Captain General, 1925.

1978, Jan. 5
2078 A428 1p multicolored .25 .25
2079 A428 2p multicolored .25 .25
2080 A428 3p multicolored .25 .25
2081 A428 5p multicolored .25 .25
2082 A428 12p multicolored .25 .25
Nos. 2078-2082 (5) 1.25 1.25

Hilarión
Eslava and
Score
A530

8p, José Clara and sculpture. 25p, Pio
Baroja and farm. 50p, Antonio Machado Ruiz
and castle.

1978, Feb. 20   **Engr.**   *Perf. 13*
2083 A530 5p black & dk pur .25 .25
2084 A530 8p blue grn & blk .25 .25
2085 A530 25p yel grn & blk .30 .25
2086 A530 50p dk pur & dk brn .55 .25
Nos. 2083-2086 (4) 1.35 1.00
Miguel Hilarión Eslava (1807-1878), composer; José Clara, sculptor; Pio Baroja (1872-
1956), author and physician; Antonio
Machado Ruiz (1875-1939), poet and
playwright.

Burial of Christ, by de Juni — A531

Detail from Burial of
Christ — A532

Designs: No. 2089, Juan de Juni. No. 2090,
Rape of Sabine Women, by Rubens. No.
2091, Rape (detail) and Rubens portrait. No.
2092, Rubens signature and palette. No.
2093, Judgment of Paris, by Titian. No. 2094,
Judgment and Titian portrait. No. 2095, Initial
"TF" and palette.

1978, Mar. 28   Engr.   Perf. 12½x13
2087	A532	3p multicolored	.25	.25
2088	A532	3p multicolored	.25	.25
2089	A532	3p multicolored	.25	.25
a.		Strip of 3, #2087-2089	.25	
2090	A532	5p multicolored	.25	.25
2091	A532	5p multicolored	.25	.25
2092	A532	5p multicolored	.25	.25
a.		Strip of 3, #2090-2092	.25	
2093	A532	8p multicolored	.25	.25
2094	A532	8p multicolored	.25	.25
2095	A532	8p multicolored	.25	.25
a.		Strip of 3, #2093-2095	.25	

Juan de Juni (1507-77), sculptor, (3p); Peter Paul Rubens (1577-1640), painter, (5p); Titian (1477-1576), painter, (8p).

Edelweiss in Pyrenees — A533

Designs: 5p, Fish and duck, wetlands. 7p, Forest, and forest destroyed by fire. 12p, Waves, oil rig, tanker and city. 20p, Sea gulls and seals, vert.

1978, Apr. 4   Photo.   Perf. 13
2096	A533	3p multicolored	.25	.25
2097	A533	5p multicolored	.25	.25
2098	A533	7p multicolored	.25	.25
2099	A533	12p multicolored	.25	.25
2100	A533	20p multicolored	.25	.25
		Nos. 2096-2100 (5)	1.25	1.25

Protection of the environment.

Palace of Charles V, Granada A534

Europa: 12p, The Lonja, Seville.

1978, May 2   Engr.   Perf. 13
2101	A534	5p dull grn & sl grn	.25	.25
2102	A534	12p dull grn & car rose	.25	.25

"España" — A535

1978, May 5   Photo.   Perf. 12½
2103	A535	12p multicolored	.25	.25

Spain's admission to the Council of Europe.

Symbols and Emblems of Postal Service A536

1978, June 27   Engr.   Perf. 13
2104	A536	5p slate green	.25	.25

Stamp Day.

Map of Las Palmas, 16th Century A537

5p, Hermitage of Columbus Church, vert. 12p, View of Las Palmas, 16th century.

1978, June 23   Photo.
2105	A537	3p multicolored	.25	.25
2106	A537	5p multicolored	.25	.25
2107	A537	12p multicolored	.25	.25
		Nos. 2105-2107 (3)	.75	.75

Founding of Las Palmas, 500th anniv.

Pablo Picasso, Self-portrait A538

Picasso Paintings: 3p, Señora Canals. 8p, Jaime Sabartes. 10p, End of the Act (actress). 12p, Science and Charity (woman patient, doctor, nurse and child), horiz. 15p, "Las Mennas" (blue period), horiz. 20p, The Sparrows. 25p, The Painter and his Model, horiz.

1978, Sept. 29   Photo.   Perf. 13
2108	A538	3p gold & multi	.25	.25
2109	A538	5p gold & multi	.25	.25
2110	A538	8p gold & multi	.25	.25
2111	A538	10p gold & multi	.25	.25
2112	A538	12p gold & multi	.25	.25
2113	A538	15p gold & multi	.25	.25
2114	A538	20p gold & multi	.25	.25
2115	A538	25p gold & multi	.30	.25
		Nos. 2108-2115 (8)	2.05	2.00

Pablo Picasso (1881-1973). Stamp Day 1978.

A 7p stamp like No. 2111 was not issued.
For other art types see A384, A397, A410, A431, A448, A473, A501, A522, A558 and footnote following No. 876.

José de San Martin A539

Design: 12p, Simon Bolivar.

1978, Oct. 12   Engr.   Perf. 13
2116	A539	7p sepia & car	.25	.25
2117	A539	12p violet & car	.25	.25

José de San Martin (1778-1850) and Simon Bolivar (1783-1830), South American liberators.

Flight into Egypt, Capital from St. Mary de Nieva A540

Christmas: 12p, Annunciation, capital from St. Mary de Nieva.

1978, Nov. 3   Photo.   Perf. 13
2118	A540	5p multicolored	.25	.25
2119	A540	12p multicolored	.25	.25

Mexican Calendar Stone A541

Designs (King Juan Carlos I, Queen Sofia and): No. 2121, Machu Picchu. No. 2122, Calchaqui jars from Tucuman and Angalgala.

1978
2120	A541	5p multicolored	.25	.25
2121	A541	5p multicolored	.25	.25
2122	A541	5p multicolored	.25	.25
		Nos. 2120-2122 (3)	.75	.75

Royal visits to Mexico, Peru and Argentina. Issued: #2120 (Mexico), Nov. 17; #2121 (Peru), Nov. 22; #2122 (Argentina), Nov. 26.

King Philip V — A542

Rulers of Spain: No. 2124, Louis I. 8p, Ferdinand VI. 10p, Carlos III. 12p, Carlos IV. 15p, Ferdinand VII. 20p, Isabella II. 25p, Alfonso XII. 50p, Alfonso XIII. 100p, Juan Carlos I.

1978, Nov. 22   Engr.   Perf. 13
2123	A542	5p dk blue & rose red	.25	.25
2124	A542	5p olive & dull grn	.25	.25
2125	A542	8p vio bl & red brn	.25	.25
2126	A542	10p blue grn & blk	.25	.25
2127	A542	12p brown & mar	.25	.25
2128	A542	15p black & indigo	.25	.25
2129	A542	20p olive & indigo	.25	.25
2130	A542	25p ultra & vio brn	.30	.25
2131	A542	50p vermilion & brn	.55	.25
2132	A542	100p ultra & vio blk	1.10	.35
		Nos. 2123-2132 (10)	3.70	2.60

Spanish Flag, Preamble to Constitution, Parliament — A543

1978, Dec.   Photo.   Perf. 13
2133	A543	5p multicolored	.25	.25

Proclamation of New Constitution.

Illuminated Pages from Bible and Codex — A544

1978, Dec. 27
2134	A544	5p multicolored	.25	.25

Millennium of the consecration of the Basilica of Santa Maria de Ripoll.

Car and Drop of Oil — A545

Designs: 8p, Insulated house and thermometer. 10p, Hand pulling plug.

1979, Jan. 24   Photo.   Perf. 13
2135	A545	5p multicolored	.25	.25
2136	A545	8p multicolored	.25	.25
2137	A545	10p multicolored	.25	.25
		Nos. 2135-2137 (3)	.75	.75

Energy conservation.

De La Salle, Students A546

1979, Feb. 14   Photo.   Perf. 13
2138	A546	5p multicolored	.25	.25

Institute of Christian Brothers, founded by Jean-Baptiste de la Salle, centenary.

Jorge Manrique — A547

Portraits: 8p, Fernan Caballero (pen name of Cecilia Böhl de Faber). 10p, Francisco Villaespesa. 20p, Gregorio Marañon.

1979, Feb. 28   Engr.
2139	A547	5p green & brown	.25	.25
2140	A547	8p dark red & blue	.25	.25
2141	A547	10p brown & purple	.25	.25
2142	A547	20p green & olive	.25	.25
		Nos. 2139-2142 (4)	1.00	1.00

Jorge Manrique, poet, 500th death anniversary; Fernan Caballero, Francisco Villaespesa, and Gregorio Marañon, writers, birth centenaries.

Running and Jumping A548

Sport for All: 8p, Children kicking ball and skipping rope, jogging and bicycling. 10p, Family jogging, and dog.

1979, Mar. 14   Photo.   Perf. 13
2143	A548	5p multicolored	.25	.25
2144	A548	8p multicolored	.25	.25
2145	A548	10p multicolored	.25	.25
		Nos. 2143-2145 (3)	.75	.75

Children in Library A549

1979, Apr. 27   Photo.   Perf. 13
2146	A549	5p multicolored	.25	.25

International Year of the Child.

Manuel Ysasi (1810-1855) Postal Reformer — A550

Europa: 5p, Mounted messenger and postilion, 1761 engraving, vert.

1979, Apr. 30   Engr.
2147	A550	5p brown & sepia	.25	.25
2148	A550	12p red brn & sl grn	.25	.25

Radar and Satellite A551

5p, Symbolic people and cables, vert.

1979, May 17   Photo.   Perf. 13
2149	A551	5p multicolored	.25	.25
2150	A551	8p multicolored	.25	.25

World Telecommunications Day, May 17.

Bulgaria No. 1, Sofia Opera House, Housing Development — A552

1979, May 18
2151 A552 12p multicolored .25 .25

Philaserdica '79, International Philatelic Exhibition, Sofia, Bulgaria, May 18-27.

Tank, Jet and Destroyer A553

1979, May 25
2152 A553 5p multicolored .25 .25

Armed Forces Day.

Messenger Handing Letter to King — A554

1979, June 15   **Litho. & Engr.**
2153 A554 5p multicolored .25 .25

Stamp Day 1979.

Daroca Gate, Zaragoza — A555

Architecture: 8p, Gerona Cathedral. 10p, Interior, Carthusian Monastery Church, Granada. 20p, Portal, Palace of the Marques de Dos Aguas, Valencia.

1979, June 27   **Engr.**
2154 A555 5p vio bl & lilac brn .25 .25
2155 A555 8p dk blue & sepia .25 .25
2156 A555 10p black & green .25 .25
2157 A555 20p brown & sepia .25 .25
    Nos. 2154-2157 (4) 1.00 1.00

Turkey Sponge A556

Fauna: 7p, Crayfish. 8p, Scorpion. 20p, Starfish. 25p, Sea anemone.

1979, July 11   **Photo.**   **Perf. 13**
2158 A556 5p multicolored .25 .25
2159 A556 7p multicolored .25 .25
2160 A556 8p multicolored .25 .25
2161 A556 20p multicolored .25 .25
2162 A556 25p multicolored .30 .25
    Nos. 2158-2162 (5) 1.30 1.25

Gen. Antonio Gutierrez and Battle A557

1979, Aug.   **Engr.**
2163 A557 5p multicolored .25 .25

Naval defense of Tenerife, 18th century.

A558

Juan de Juanes Paintings: 8p, Immaculate Conception. 10p, Holy Family. 15p, Ecce Homo. 20p, St. Stephen in the Synagogue. 25p, The Last Supper, horiz. 50p, Adoration of the Mystic Lamb, horiz.

1979, Sept. 28   **Photo.**   **Perf. 13x13½**
2164 A558 8p multicolored .25 .25
2165 A558 10p multicolored .25 .25
2166 A558 15p multicolored .25 .25
2167 A558 20p multicolored .25 .25
2168 A558 25p multicolored .30 .25
2169 A558 50p multicolored .55 .25
    Nos. 2164-2169 (6) 1.85 1.50

For other art types see A384, A397, A410, A431, A448, A473, A501, A522, A538 and footnote following No. 876.

A559

Zaragoza Cathedral, Mother and Child statue.

1979, Oct. 3   **Photo.**   **Perf. 13x13½**
2170 A559 5p multicolored .25 .25

8th Mariology and 15th International Marianist Congresses, Zaragoza, Oct. 3-12.

Felipe de Borbon, Hospital A560

1979, Oct.   **Perf. 13½x13**
2171 A560 5p multicolored .25 .25

Hospital of the Child Jesus, centenary.

St. Bartholomew College, Bogota — A561

Hispanidad 79: 12p, University of St. Mark, Lima, coat of arms.

1979, Oct. 12   **Engr.**   **Perf. 13**
2172 A561 7p multicolored .25 .25
2173 A561 12p multicolored .25 .25

Clasped Hands, Badge, Governor's Palace A562

Design: No. 2175, Statute book, vert.

Lithographed and Engraved
1979, Oct. 27   **Perf. 13**
2174 A562 8p multicolored .25 .25
2175 A562 8p multicolored .25 .25

Catalonian and Basque autonomy statute.

Type A54, Barcelona Coat of Arms A563

Photogravure and Engraved
1979, Nov. 6   **Perf. 13½x13**
2176 A563 5p multicolored .25 .25

Barcelona Philatelic Congress and Exhibition, 50th anniversary.

Nativity, Capital from St. Peter the Elder A564

Christmas 1979: 19p, Flight into Egypt, column from St. Peter the Elder, Huesca.

1979, Nov. 14   **Photo.**
2177 A564 8p multicolored .25 .25
2178 A564 19p multicolored .25 .25

Carlos I, Coat of Arms A565

Kings of the House of Austria (Hapsburg Dynasty): 20p, Philip II. 25p, Philip III. 50c, Philip IV. 100p, Carlos II.

1979, Nov. 22   **Engr.**   **Perf. 13**
2179 A565 15p sl grn & dk bl .25 .25
2180 A565 20p dk blue & mag .25 .25
2181 A565 25p violet & yel bis .30 .25
2182 A565 50p brown & sl grn .55 .25
2183 A565 100p magenta & brn 1.10 .30
    Nos. 2179-2183 (5) 2.45 1.30

2nd International Olive Oil Year — A566

1979, Dec. 4   **Photo.**   **Perf. 13½x13**
2184 A566 8p multicolored .25 .25

King Juan Carlos I Type of 1976
1980-84   **Photo.**   **Perf. 13**
2185 A497 13p dk red brn ('81) .25 .25
2186 A497 14p red orange ('82) .25 .25
2187 A497 16p sepia .30 .25
2188 A497 17p bluish gray ('84) .25 .25
2189 A497 19p orange .35 .25
2190 A497 30p dk green ('81) .40 .25
2191 A497 50p org ver ('81) .90 .25
2192 A497 60p blue ('81) .80 .25
2193 A497 75p brt yel grn ('81) 1.00 .30
2194 A497 85p gray ('81) 1.25 .45
    Nos. 2185-2194 (10) 5.75 2.75

No. 2186 and 2187 also issued as coil with number on back of every fifth stamp.

Train and People A567

1980, Feb. 20   **Engr.**   **Perf. 13½**
2200 A567 3p shown .25 .25
2201 A567 4p Bus .25 .25
2202 A567 5p Subway .25 .25
    Nos. 2200-2202 (3) .75 .75

Public transportation.

Steel Export A568

1980, Mar. 15   **Photo.**   **Perf. 13½x13**
2203 A568 5p shown .25 .25
2204 A568 8p Ships .25 .25
2205 A568 13p Shoes .25 .25
2206 A568 19p Machinery .25 .25
2207 A568 25p Technology .30 .25
    Nos. 2203-2207 (5) 1.30 1.25

Federico Garcia Lorca (1899-1936) — A569

Europa: 19p, José Ortega y Gasset (1883-1955), philosopher and statesman.

1980, Apr. 28   **Engr.**   **Perf. 13½**
2208 A569 8p violet & ol grn .25 .25
2209 A569 19p brown & dk grn .25 .25

Armed Forces Day A570

1980, May 24   **Photo.**   **Perf. 13½x13**
2210 A570 8p multicolored .25 .25

Soccer Players A571

1980, May 23
2211 A571 8p shown .25 .25
2212 A571 19p Soccer ball, flags .25 .25

World Soccer Cup 1982.

Bourbon Arms, Ministry of Finance A572

1980, June 9   **Engr.**   **Perf. 13½**
2213 A572 8p dark brown .25 .25

Public Finances in Bourbon Spain Exhibition.

Helen Keller, Sign Language A573

1980, June 27
2214 A573 19p dk yel grn & rose lake .25 .25

Helen Keller (1880-1968), deaf mute writer and lecturer.

Mounted Postman, 12th Century Panel, Barcelona — A574

Lithographed and Engraved
1980, June 28 *Perf. 13x12½*
2215 A574 8p multicolored .25 .25

Stamp Day.

King Alfonso and Count of Maceda at 1930 National Exhibition A575

1980, July 1 **Photo.** *Perf. 13½*
2216 A575 8p multicolored .25 .25

1st Natl. Stamp Exhibition, Barcelona, 50th anniv.

A576

Altar of the Virgin, La Palma Cathedral.

1980, July 12 **Engr.** *Perf. 13*
2217 A576 8p black & brown .25 .25

Appearance of the Virgin of the Snow at La Palma, 300th anniversary.

A577

1980, Aug. 9 **Engr.** *Perf. 13*
2218 A577 100p slate & sepia 1.10 .25

Ramon Perez de Ayala (1881-1962), novelist and diplomat.

Souvenir Sheet

La Atlantida Ruins, Mexican Bonampak Musicians — A578

Designs: b, Sun Gate, Tiahuanaco; Roman arch, Medinaceli. c, Alonso de Ercilla, Garcilaso de la Vega; title pages from La Arauca and Commentario Reales. d, Virgin of Quito, Virgin of Seafarers.

1980, Oct. 3 **Engr.** *Perf. 13*
2219 A578 Sheet of 4 + 2 labels 2.25 2.25
  a. 25p multicolored .30 .30
  b. 25p multicolored .30 .30
  c. 50p multicolored .55 .45
  d. 100p multicolored 1.10 .85
ESPAMER '80 Stamp Exhib., Madrid, Oct. 3-12.

400th Anniversary of Buenos Aires — A579

1980, Oct. 24
2220 A579 19p multicolored .25 .25

Miniature Sheet

The Creation, Tapestry, Gerona Cathedral — A580

1980, Nov. **Litho.** *Perf. 13½x13*
2221 A580 Sheet of 6 2.50 2.00
  a.-c. 25p, any single .25 .25
  d.-f. 50p, any single .55 .25

Conference Building, Flags of Participants A581

1980, Nov. 11 **Photo.** *Perf. 13½*
2222 A581 22p multicolored .25 .25

Holy Family Church of Santa Maria, Cuina — A582

Christmas 1980, 22p, Adoration of the Kings, portal, Church of Santa Maria, Cuina, horiz.

1980, Nov. 12
2223 A582 10p multicolored .25 .25
2224 A582 22p multicolored .25 .25

Pedro Vives and His Airplane A583

Designs: Aviation pioneers.

1980, Dec. 10
2225 A583 5p shown .25 .25
2226 A583 10p Benito Loygorri .25 .25
2227 A583 15p Alfonso De Orleans .25 .25
2228 A583 22p Alfredo Kindelan .25 .25
Nos. 2225-2228 (4) 1.00 1.00

Winter University Games A584

1981, Mar. 4 *Perf. 13½x13*
2229 A584 30p multicolored .35 .25

Picasso's Birth Centenary Emblem, by Joan Miro — A585

1981, Mar. 27 *Perf. 13*
2230 A585 100p multicolored 1.00 .25

Pablo Picasso (1881-1973).

Galician Autonomy — A586

1981, Mar. 27 **Photo.** *Perf. 13*
2231 A586 12p multicolored .25 .25

Homage to the Press A587

1981, Apr. 8 **Photo.** *Perf. 13½x13*
2232 A587 12p multicolored .25 .25

International Year of the Disabled — A588

1981, Apr. 29 **Litho.**
2233 A588 30p multicolored .35 .25

Soccer Players A589

1981, May 2 **Photo.**
2234 A589 12p Soccer players, diff., vert. .25 .25
2235 A589 30p shown .35 .25

1982 World Cup Soccer.

Europa Issue

La Jota Folkdance A590

1981, May 4 **Engr.**
2236 A590 12p shown .25 .25
2237 A590 30p Virgin of Rocio procession .35 .25

Armed Forces Day — A591

1981, May 29 **Photo.** *Perf. 13x13½*
2238 A591 12p multicolored .25 .25

Gabriel Miro (1879-1930), Writer — A592

Famous Men: 12p, Francisco de Quevedo (1580-1645), writer. 30p, St. Benedict (480-543), patron saint of Europe.

1981, June 17 **Engr.**
2239 A592 6p purple & dk grn .25 .25
2240 A592 12p brown & purple .25 .25
2241 A592 30p dk green & brown .35 .25
Nos. 2239-2241 (3) .85 .75

Mail Messenger, 14th Cent., Woodcut A593

Photogravure and Engraved
1981, June 19 *Perf. 12½x13*
2242 A593 12p multicolored .25 .25

Stamp Day.

Map of Balearic Islands, Diego Homem's Atlas, 1563 — A594

1981, July 8   Photo.   Perf. 13x12½
2243 A594 7p shown   .25 .25
2244 A594 12p Canary Islds.,
Prunes map, 1563 .25 .25

Kings Alfonso XII and Juan Carlos, Advocates Arms A595

1981, July 27   Engr.   Perf. 13½x13
2245 A595 50p multicolored   .55 .25

Chamber of Advocates of State (Public Prosecutor) centenary.

King Sancius VI of Navarre with City Charter, 12th Cent. Miniature A596

1981, Aug. 5   Photo.   Perf. 12½x13
2246 A596 12p multicolored   .25 .25

Vitoria, 800th anniv.

Exports A597

1981, Sept. 30   Photo.   Perf. 13½x13
2247 A597 6p Fruit   .25 .25
2248 A597 12p Wine   .25 .25
2249 A597 30p Vehicles   .35 .25
Nos. 2247-2249 (3)   .85 .75

Congress Palace, Buenos Aires A598

1981, Oct. 12   Engr.   Perf. 13½x13
2250 A598 12p dk bl & car rose   .25 .25

ESPAMER '81 Intl. Stamp Exhibition, Buenos Aires, Nov. 13-22.

World Food Day A599

1981, Oct. 16
2251 A599 30p multicolored   .35 .25

Souvenir Sheet

Guernica, by Pablo Picasso (1881-1973) — A600

1981, Oct. 25   Photo.
2252 A600 200p multicolored   2.25 2.25
Control number comes in two types.

A601

Christmas 1981: 12p, Adoration of the Kings, Cervera de Pisuerga, Palencia. 30p, Nativity, Paredes de Nava.

1981, Nov. 18   Litho.   Perf. 13
2253 A601 12p shown   .25 .25
2254 A601 30p multicolored   .35 .25

A602

King Juan Carlos I.

1981, Oct. 21   Engr.   Perf. 13x12½
2268 A602 100p brown   1.25 .25
2269 A602 200p dark green   2.60 .25
2270 A602 500p dark blue   6.25 .55
Nos. 2268-2270 (3)   10.10 1.05

Postal Museum, Madrid A603

1981, Nov. 30   Engr.   Perf. 13
2273 A603 7p Telegrapher   .25 .25
2274 A603 12p Coach   .25 .25

Souvenir Sheet
2275   Sheet of 4   1.90 1.90
c.   A603 50p Emblem   .55 .50
d.   A603 100p Cap, posthorn, pouch   1.10 1.00

No. 2275 also contains Nos. 2273, 2274.

Royal Mint Building, Seville A604

1981, Dec. 4   Engr.   Perf. 13
2276 A604 12p black & brown   .25 .25

Spanish Administration of the Bourbons in the Indies.

A605

12p, Iparraguirre (1820-81). 30p, Juan Ramon Jimenez (1881-1958), writer. 50p, Pedro Calderon (1600-81), playwright.

1981-82
2277 A605 12p black & dk bl   .25 .25
2278 A605 30p dk bl & dk grn   .35 .25
2279 A605 50p black & violet   .55 .25
Nos. 2277-2279 (3)   1.15 .75

Issued: 12p, 12/16; 30p, 50p, 3/10/82.

A606

1982, Feb. 24   Photo.
2280 A606 14p Poster by Joan Miro   .25 .25
2281 A606 33p Cup, emblem   .40 .25

Espana '82 World Cup Soccer.

Andres Bello (1782-1865), Writer — A607

1982, Mar. 10   Engr.
2282 A607 30p grn & dk grn   .35 .25

St. John of Compostelo — A608

1982, Mar. 31   Photo.   Perf. 13
2283 A608 14p multicolored   .25 .25

Holy Year of Compostelo.

A609-A610

Operetta composers and scenes from their works: #2284, Manuel Fernandez Caballero (1835-1906). #2285, Gigantes and Cabezudos. #2286, Amadeo Vives Roig (1871-1932). #2287, Dona Francisquita. #2288, Tomas Breton Hernandez (1850-1923). #2289, Verbena of Paloma.

Lithographed and Engraved
1982, Apr. 28   Perf. 13
2284 A609 3p multicolored   .25 .25
2285 A610 3p multicolored   .25 .25
a.   Pair, #2284-2285   .25 .25

2286 A609 6p multicolored   .25 .25
2287 A610 6p multicolored   .25 .25
a.   Pair, #2284-2285   .25 .25
2288 A609 8p multicolored   .25 .25
2289 A610 8p multicolored   .25 .25
a.   Pair, #2284-2285   .25 .25
See Nos. 2319-2324, 2378-2383.

Europa 1982 — A611

14p, Unification, 1512. 33p, Discovery of New World, 1492.

1982, May 3   Engr.   Perf. 12½
2290 A611 14p multicolored   .25 .25
2291 A611 33p multicolored   .40 .25

Armed Forces Day — A612

1982, May 28   Photo.   Perf. 13
2292 A612 14p multicolored   .25 .25

1982 World Cup A613

Designs: Soccer players.

1982, June 13   Perf. 13
2293 A613 14p multicolored   .25 .25
2294 A613 33p multicolored   .40 .25

Souvenir Sheets
2295   Sheets of 4, #2293-2294, 9p, 100p, each   1.75 1.75
a.   A613 9p Captains' handshake   .25 .25
b.   A613 100p Player holding cup   1.10 1.10

#2295 has two types of margin, each showing 7 arms of the 14 host cities. One sheet has 3 blue coats of arms, the other has 2.

Stamp Day — A614

1982, July 16   Litho.   Perf. 12½
2296 A614 14p Map, postal code   .25 .25

Organ Transplants A615

1982, July 28   Photo.   Perf. 13
2297 A615 14p Symbolic organs   .25 .25

Storks and Express Train — A616

Locomotive, 1850 — A617

Perf. 12½, 13 (A617)
1982, Sept. 27 Photo.
2298 A616 9p shown .25 .25
2299 A617 14p shown .25 .25
2300 A617 33p Santa Fe locomotive .40 .25
 Nos. 2298-2300 (3) .90 .75
23rd Intl. Railways Congress, Malaga.

ESPAMER '82 Intl. Stamp Exhibition, San Juan, Oct. 12-17 A618

1982, Oct. 12 Engr. **Perf. 13½x13**
2301 A618 33p dk blue & pur .40 .25

St. Teresa of Avila (1515-1582) — A619

33p, Statue by Gregorio Hernandez.

1982, Oct. 15
2302 A619 33p multicolored .40 .25

Visit of Pope John Paul II, Oct. 31-Nov. 9 — A620

1982, Oct. 31 Engr. **Perf. 12½**
2303 A620 14p multicolored .25 .25

Water Wheel, Alcantarilla A621

Landscapes and Monuments: 6p, Bank of Spain, 19th cent., horiz. 9p, Crucifixion. 14p,

St. Martin's Tower, Teruel. 33p, St. Andrew's Gate, Zamora.

1982, Nov. 5 **Perf. 13x12½, 12½x13**
2304 A621 4p gray & dk blue .25 .25
2305 A621 6p dk blue & gray .25 .25
2306 A621 9p brt blue & vio .25 .25
2307 A621 14p brt blue & vio .25 .25
2308 A621 33p claret & brown .40 .25
 Nos. 2304-2308 (5) 1.40 1.25

Christmas 1982 A622

14p, Nativity, wood carving, by Gil de Siloe. 33p, Flight into Egypt.

1982, Nov. 17 Photo. **Perf. 13½**
2309 A622 14p multicolored .25 .25
2310 A622 33p multicolored .40 .25

Pablo Gargallo, Sculptor, Birth Centenary A623

1982, Dec. 9 Engr. **Perf. 13**
2311 A623 14p blue & dk grn .25 .25

Salesian Fathers in Spain, Centenary A624

1982, Dec. 16 Photo. **Perf. 12½x13**
2312 A624 14p multicolored .25 .25

Arms of King Juan Carlos I A625

1983, Feb. 9 Photo. **Perf. 12½**
2313 A625 14p multicolored .25 .25

Andalusia Autonomy Statute A626

1983 Litho. **Perf. 13½**
2314 A626 14p shown .25 .25
2315 A626 14p Cantabria .25 .25
 Issued: #2314, Feb. 28; #2315, Mar. 15.

State Security Forces A627

1983, Mar. 23 Photo.
2316 A627 9p Natl. Police Force .25 .25
2317 A627 14p Civil Guard .25 .25
2318 A627 33p Superior Police Corps .40 .25

Operetta Type of 1982
 Designs: #2319, Scene from La Parranda. Francisco Alonso Lopez (1887-1948). #2320, Francisco Alonso Lopez (1887-1948). #2321, Jacinto Guerrero y Torres (1895-1951). #2322, Scene from La Rosa del Azafran. #2323, Jesus de Guridi Bidaola (1886-1961). #2324, Scene from El Caserio.

Lithographed and Engraved
1983, Apr. 22 **Perf. 13**
2319 A610 4p multicolored .25 .25
2320 A609 4p multicolored .25 .25
a. Pair, #2319-2320 .25 .25
2321 A609 6p multicolored .25 .25
2322 A610 6p multicolored .25 .25
a. Pair, #2321-2322 .25 .25
2323 A609 9p multicolored .25 .25
2324 A610 9p multicolored .25 .25
a. Pair, #2323-2324 .35 .35

Europa 1983 — A628

 Designs: 16p, Scene from Don Quixote, by Miguel Cervantes. 38p, L. Torres Quevaedo's Niagara Spanish aerocar.

1983, May 5 Engr. **Perf. 13x12½**
Granite Paper
2325 A628 16p dk grn & brn red .25 .25
2326 A628 38p brown .45 .25

Francisco Salzillo Alvarez (1707-83), Painter — A629

 Designs: 38p, Antonio Soler Ramos (1729-1783), composer. 50p, Joaquin Turina Perez (1882-1949), composer. 100p, St. Isidro Labrador (1082-1170), patron saint of Madrid.

1983, May 14 **Perf. 13**
2327 A629 16p purple & dk grn .25 .25
2328 A629 38p blue & brown .45 .25
2329 A629 50p bl grn & dk brn .55 .25
2330 A629 100p red brn & pur 1.10 .25
 Nos. 2327-2330 (4) 2.35 1.00

World Communications Year — A630

1983, May 17 Photo. **Perf. 13**
2331 A630 38p multicolored .45 .25

Rioja Autonomous Region — A631

Lithographed and Engraved
1983, May 25 **Perf. 13**
2332 A631 16p multicolored .25 .25

Armed Forces Day — A632

1983, May 26 Photo.
2333 A632 16p multicolored .25 .25

Intl. Canine Exhibition, Madrid, June 1984 A633

Lithographed and Engraved
1983, June 8 **Perf. 13½**
2334 A633 10p Pointer .25 .25
2335 A633 16p Mastiff .25 .25
2336 A633 26p Iberian hound .35 .25
2337 A633 38p Navarro pointer .50 .25
 Nos. 2334-2337 (4) 1.35 1.00

Discovery of Tungsten Bicentenary — A634

Scouting Year A635

400th Anniv. of University of Zaragoza A636

1983, June 22 Photo. **Perf. 13**
2338 A634 16p Elhuyar brothers .25 .25
2339 A635 38p multicolored .45 .25
2340 A636 50p multicolored .60 .25
 Nos. 2338-2340 (3) 1.30 .75

Murcia Autonomous Region — A637

Photogravure and Engraved
1983, July 8 **Perf. 13½**
2341 A637 16p Arms .25 .25

Asturias Autonomous Region — A638

14p, Victory Cross, Covadonga Basilica.

Lithographed and Engraved
1983, Sept. 8   **Perf. 13**
2342 A638 14p multicolored   .25 .25

Intl. Institute of Statistics, 44th Congress, Madrid, Sept. 12-22
A639

1983, Sept. 12   **Photo.**   **Perf. 13**
2343 A639 38p Institute building   .45 .25

Stamp Day — A640

Lithographed and Engraved
1983, Oct. 8   **Perf. 13x12½**
2344 A640 16p Roman mail cart   .35 .30

No. 2344 se-tenant with label publicizing ESPANA '84 Philatelic Exhibition, April 27-May 6, 1984.

Valencia Autonomy Statute, 1st Anniv. A641

1983, Oct. 10   **Perf. 13**
2345 A641 16p multicolored   .25 .25

View of Seville, 16th cent. — A642

1983, Oct. 12   **Engr.**   **Perf. 12½x13**
2346 A642 38p multicolored   .45 .25

Spanish-American trade in 17th century.

Stained-glass Windows A643

Designs: 10p, King, Leon Cathedral. 16p, Epiphany, Gerona Cathedral. 38p, Apostle Santiago, Royal Hospital Chapel, Santiago.

Lithographed and Engraved
1983, Oct. 28   **Perf. 12½x13**
2347 A643 10p multicolored   .25 .25
2348 A643 16p multicolored   .25 .25
2349 A643 38p multicolored   .45 .25
     Nos. 2347-2349 (3)   .95 .75

Church at Llivia, Gerona — A644

Designs: 6p, Temple, Santa Maria del Mar, Barcelona. 16p, Cathedral, Ceuta. 38p, Gate of the Santiago Bridge, Melilla. 50p, Charity Hospital, Seville.

1983, Nov. 9   **Engr.**   **Perf. 13x12½**
2350 A644 3p dk bl gray & grn   .25 .25
2351 A644 6p dark blue gray   .25 .25
2352 A644 16p red brn & dull vio   .25 .25
2353 A644 38p bis brn & rose   .45 .25
     car
2354 A644 50p brown & org red   .55 .25
     Nos. 2350-2354 (5)   1.75 1.25

Christmas 1983 — A645

16p, The Nativity, Tortosa. 38p, The Adoration, Vich.

1983, Nov. 23   **Photo.**   **Perf. 13x13½**
2355 A645 16p multicolored   .25 .25
2356 A645 38p multicolored   .45 .25

Indalecio Prieto (1883-1962), Patriot — A646

1983, Dec. 14   **Engr.**   **Perf. 13**
2357 A646 16p red brn & blk   .25 .25

Industrial Accident Prevention A647

7p, Construction worker. 10p, Fire. 16p, Electrical plug, pliers.

1984, Jan. 25   **Photo.**   **Perf. 13½**
2358 A647 7p multicolored   .25 .25
2359 A647 10p multicolored   .25 .25
2360 A647 16p multicolored   .25 .25
     Nos. 2358-2360 (3)   .75 .75

Extremadura Statute of Autonomy, First Anniv. — A648

Lithographed and Engraved
1984, Feb. 25   **Perf. 13**
2361 A648 16p multicolored   .25 .25

1500th Anniv. of City of Burgos A649

1984, Mar. 1   **Engr.**
2362 A649 16p multicolored   .25 .25

Carnivals A650

No. 2363, Santa Cruz de Tenerife. No. 2364, Valencia Fallas.

1984   **Photo.**   **Perf. 13½x13**
2363 A650 16p multicolored   .25 .25
2364 A650 16p multicolored   .25 .25
   Issued: #2363, Mar. 5; #2364, Mar. 16.

Man and the Biosphere A651

38p, da Vinci's Study of Man.

1984, Apr. 11
2365 A651 38p multicolored   .45 .25

Aragon Statute of Autonomy, 2nd Anniv. A652

Lithographed and Engraved
1984, Apr. 23   **Perf. 13x13½**
2366 A652 16p Map   .25 .25

Souvenir Sheet

Juan Carlos — A653

Espana '84 (Spanish Royal Family): b, Sofia of Greece. c, Cristina de Borbon. d, Prince of Asturias Felipe de Borbon. e, Elene de Borbon.

1984, Apr. 27   **Perf. 12½x13**
2367 A653   Sheet of 5   3.25 3.25
   a.-e.   38p, any single   .65 .65

Congress Emblem — A654

1984, May 3   **Engr.**   **Perf. 13x13½**
2368 A654 38p purple & red   .45 .25
   World Philatelic Federation, 53rd Congress, Madrid, May 7-9.

Europa (1959-84) A655

1984, May 5
2369 A655 16p orange   .25 .25
2370 A655 38p dark blue   .45 .25

Armed Forces Day A656

Design: 17p, Monument to Hunters Regiment of Caceres, by Mariano Benlliure.

1984, May 19   **Photo.**   **Perf. 13½x13**
2371 A656 17p multicolored   .25 .25

Canary Islds. Statute of Autonomy — A657

Lithographed and Engraved
1984, May 29   **Perf. 13**
2372 A657 16p Arms, map   .25 .25

Castilla-La Mancha Statute of Autonomy — A658

1984, May 31   **Perf. 13**
2373 A658 17p Arms   .25 .25

King Alfonso X (1252-84) A659

Design: 38p, Ignacio Barroquer (1884-1965), ophthalmologist

1984, June 20   **Engr.**   **Perf. 13**
2374 A659 16p multicolored   .25 .25
2375 A659 38p multicolored   .45 .25

Balearic Islands Statute of Autonomy — A660

1984, June 29 Litho. & Engr.
2376 A660 17p multicolored .25 .25

Feast of San Fermin of Pamplona A661

1984, July 5 Photo.
2377 A661 17p Bull runners .25 .25

Operetta Type of 1982

#2378, El Nino Judio. #2379, Pablo Luna (1880-1942). #2380, Ruperto Chapi (1851-1909). #2381, La Revoltosa. #2382, La Reina Mora. #2383, Jose Serrano (1873-1941).

Lithographed and Engraved
1984, July 20 Perf. 13
2378 A610 6p multicolored .25 .25
2379 A609 6p multicolored .25 .25
  a. Pair, #2378-2379 .25 .25
2380 A609 7p multicolored .25 .25
2381 A610 7p multicolored .25 .25
  a. Pair, #2380-2381 .25 .25
2382 A610 10p multicolored .25 .25
2383 A609 10p multicolored .25 .25
  a. Pair, #2382-2383 .30 .30

1984 Summer Olympics A662

Greek or Roman sculptures.

1984, July 27 Photo.
2384 A662 1p Chariot race .25 .25
2385 A662 2p Diving, vert. .25 .25
2386 A662 5p Wrestling .25 .25
2387 A662 8p Discus, vert. .25 .25
  Nos. 2384-2387 (4) 1.00 1.00

Navarra Statute of Autonomy A663

Lithographed and Engraved
1984, Aug. 16 Perf. 13
2388 A663 17p multicolored .25 .25

Intl. Bicycling Championship, Barcelona, Aug. 27-Sept. 2 — A664

1984, Aug. 27 Photo.
2389 A664 17p multicolored .25 .25

Castilla and Leon Statute of Autonomy A665

1984, Sept. 5 Litho. & Engr.
2390 A665 17p multicolored .25 .25

Jerez Vintage Feast — A666

17p, Women picking grapes.

1984, Sept. 20 Photo. Perf. 13
2391 A666 17p multicolored .25 .25

Journey to the Holy Land by Sister Egeria, 1600th Anniv. — A667

1984, Sept. 26
2392 A667 40p Map, Sister Egeria .45 .25

Stamp Day — A668

1984, Oct. 5 Litho. & Engr.
2393 A668 17p Arab postrider .25 .25

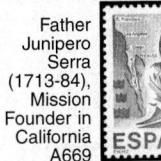

Father Junipero Serra (1713-84), Mission Founder in California A669

1984, Oct. 12 Engr. Perf. 13
2394 A669 40p Map, Serra, mission .45 .25

Christmas 1984 A670

17p, Nativity. 40p, Adoration of the Kings, vert.

1984, Nov. 21 Photo.
2395 A670 17p multicolored .25 .25
2396 A670 40p multicolored .45 .25

Madrid Autonomy Statue A671

1984, Nov. 28 Litho. & Engr.
2397 A671 17p Arms, buildings .25 .25

Andean Pact, 15th Anniv. A672

Condor, Flags of Bolivia, Colombia, Ecuador, Peru and Venezuela.

1985, Jan. 16 Photo. Perf. 13
2398 A672 17p multicolored .25 .25

The Virgin of Louvain, by Jan Gossaert (c. 1478-1536) A673

1985, Jan. 21 Perf. 13½
2399 A673 40p multicolored .45 .25

EUROPALIA '85. See Belgium No. 1185.

Santa Cruz College, Valladolid University, 500th Anniv. — A674

1985, Feb. 20 Litho. & Engr.
2400 A674 17p Main gateway .25 .25

OLYMPHILEX '85, Lausanne, Switz. — A675

1985, Mar. 18 Photo.
2401 A675 40p multicolored .45 .25

ESPAMER '85, Cuba A676

1985, Mar. 20 Engr.
2402 A676 40p Cathedral, Havana .45 .25

Fairs A677

No. 2403, Seville. No. 2404, Alcoy. No. 2405, Arriondas-Ribadesella. No. 2406, Toledo, vert.

Perf. 13½, 13½x14 (#2405)
1985 Photo.
2403 A677 17p multicolored .25 .25
2404 A677 17p multicolored .25 .25
2405 A677 17p multicolored .25 .25
2406 A677 18p multicolored .25 .25
  Nos. 2403-2406 (4) 1.00 1.00

Issued: #2403, Apr. 16; #2404, Apr. 22; #2405, Aug. 2; #2406, June 6.

Intl. Youth Year — A678

1985, Apr. 17 Engr. Perf. 13½
2407 A678 17p blk, hn brn & dk grn .25 .25

Europa '85 A680

Designs: 18p, Antonio de Cabezon (1510-1566), organist and composer, court Musician to Felipe II. 45p, Natl. Youth Orchestra.

1985, May 3 Engr.
2408 A680 18p dk bl, dk red & blk, buff .25 .25
2409 A680 45p ol grn, dk red & blk, buff .45 .25

Armed Forces Day A681

1985, May 24 Photo.
2410 A681 18p multicolored .25 .25

Natl. Flag Bicent. — A682

#2411, Arms of King Carlos III, text of 1785 Decree, sailing ship Santisima Trinidad. #2412, Natl. arms, Article No. 4 from 1978 Constitution, lion ornament from Chamber of Deputies Building.

Lithographed and Engraved
1985, May 28 Perf. 13x13½
2411 18p multicolored .25 .25
2412 18p multicolored .25 .25
  a. A682 Pair, #2411-2412 .50 .45

Intl. Environment Day — A683

1985, June 5   **Photo.**
2413 A683 17p multicolored   .25 .25

Juan Carlos — A684

1985-92   **Photo.**   **Perf. 14**
2414	A684	10c indigo	.25 .25
2415	A684	50c lt blue green	.25 .25
2416	A684	1p brt blue	.25 .25
2417	A684	2p dark green	.25 .25
2418	A684	3p chestnut brn	.25 .25
2419	A684	4p olive green	.25 .25
2420	A684	5p brt rose lilac	.25 .25
2421	A684	6p brown black	.25 .25
2422	A684	7p brt violet	.25 .25
2423	A684	7p apple grn	.25 .25
2424	A684	8p gray black	.25 .25
2425	A684	10p lake	.25 .25
2426	A684	12p red	.25 .25
2427	A684	13p Prus blue	.25 .25
2428	A684	15p emerald	.25 .25
2429	A684	17p yellow bis	.25 .25
2430	A684	18p grnsh bl	.25 .25
2431	A684	19p violet brn	.25 .25
a.		Booklet pane of 6	1.50
2432	A684	20p brt pink	.25 .25
2433	A684	25p olive green	.30 .25
2434	A684	27p deep rose lil	.35 .25
2435	A684	30p ultra	.35 .25
2436	A684	45p brt green	.50 .25
2437	A684	50p violet blue	.55 .25
2438	A684	55p black brown	.60 .25
2439	A684	60p dark orange	.65 .25
2440	A684	75p deep rose lil	.80 .30
		Nos. 2414-2440 (27)	8.85 6.80

Issued: 1p, 5p, 8p, 12p, 18p, 45p, 6/12; #2422, 17p, 7/16; #2423, 1/86; 2p, 3p, 4p, 10p, 4/3/86; 19p, 9/27/86; 6p, 20p, 30p, 1/26/87; 50p, 60p, 75p, 4/24/89; 10c, 50c, 13p, 15p, 5/16/89; 25p, 55p, 12/14/90; 27p, 2/92.

Astrophysical Observatory Opening, La Palma, Canary Islands — A685

1985, June 25   **Photo.**   **Perf. 14**
2441 A685 45p multicolored   .50 .25

European Music Year — A686

Designs: 12p, Ataulfo Argenta, conductor. 17p, Tomas Luis de Victoria, composer. 45p, Fernando Sor, composer.

Litho. & Engr.
1985, June 26   **Perf. 13**
2442 A686 12p multicolored   .25 .25
2443 A686 17p multicolored   .25 .25
2444 A686 45p multicolored   .50 .25
    Nos. 2442-2444 (3)   1.00 .75

Bernal Diaz del Castillo (1492-1585), Historian — A687

Famous men: 12p, Esteban Terradas (1883-1950), mathematician. 17p, Vicente Aleixandre (1898-1984), 1977 Nobel laureate in literature. 45p, Leon Felipe Camino (1884-1968), poet.

1985, July 24   **Engr.**   **Perf. 13½**
2445 A687   7p dk red, blk & dk
       grn, buff   .25 .25
2446 A687 12p brt ver, dk bl &
       blk, buff   .25 .25
2447 A687 17p blk, dk grn & dk
       red, buff   .25 .25
2448 A687 45p bis, blk & dk grn,
       buff   .55 .25
    Nos. 2445-2448 (4)   1.30 1.00

Monastic Mail Delivery, 1122 — A688

Lithographed and Engraved
1985, Sept. 27   **Perf. 13**
2449 A688 17p multicolored   .25 .25
    Stamp Day 1985.

12th Rhythmic Gymnastics World Championships, Valladolid — A689

1985, Oct. 9   **Photo.**   **Perf. 13x13½**
2450 A689 17p Ribbon exercise   .25 .25
2451 A689 45p Hoop exercise   .50 .25

Souvenir Sheet

Prado Museum, La Alcachofa Fountain — A690

Lithographed and Engraved
1985, Oct. 18   **Perf. 13**
2452 A690 17p multicolored   .50 .50
    EXFILNA '85, Madrid, Oct. 18-27.

Virgin and Child, Seville Cathedral A691

Stained glass windows: 12p, Monk, by Peter Boniface, Toledo Cathedral. 17p, King Henry II of Castile, Alcazar of Segovia.

1985, Oct. 24   **Perf. 12½x13**
2453 A691   7p multicolored   .25 .25
2454 A691 12p multicolored   .25 .25
2455 A691 17p multicolored   .25 .25
    Nos. 2453-2455 (3)   .75 .75

Christmas 1985 A692

14th-15th century paintings in the Episcopal Museum, Vich: 17p, Nativity, Guimera Altarpiece retable, 14th cent., by Ramon de Mur. 45p, Epiphany, from an embroidered frontal, 15th cent.

1985, Nov. 27   **Photo.**   **Perf. 13½**
2456 A692 17p multicolored   .25 .25
2457 A692 45p multicolored   .50 .25

Birds — A693

6p, Sylvia cantillans. 7p, Monticola saxatilis. 12p, Sturnus unicolor. 17p, Panurus biarmicus.

1985, Dec. 4   **Litho. & Engr.**
2458 A693   6p multicolored   .25 .25
2459 A693   7p multicolored   .25 .25
2460 A693 12p multicolored   .25 .25
2461 A693 17p multicolored   .35 .25
    Nos. 2458-2461 (4)   1.10 1.00
    Wildlife conservation.

Count of Penaflorida (1729-1785) — A694

1985, Dec. 11   **Engr.**   **Perf. 13½**
2462 A694 17p dark blue   .25 .25
Francisco Javier de Munibe e Idiaquez, founded Natl. Economic Society of Friends in 1765.

Government Palace, Madrid, and Accession Agreement Text — A695

17p, Map and flags of EEC countries. 30p, Hall of Columns, Royal Palace. 45p, Member flags.

1986, Jan 7.   **Litho.**   **Perf. 13½x13**
2463 A695   7p multicolored   .25 .25
2464 A695 17p multicolored   .25 .25
2465 A695 30p multicolored   .35 .25
2466 A695 45p multicolored   .60 .25
  a.   Bklt. pane of 4, #2463-2466   3.25
    Nos. 2463-2466 (4)   1.45 1.00

Admission of Spain and Portugal to European Economic Community. See Portugal Nos. 1661-1662.

Tourism — A696

Historic sites: 12p, Inner courtyard, La Lupiana Monastery, Guadalajara. 35p, Balcony of Europe, Nerja.

1986, Jan. 20   **Engr.**   **Perf. 13x12½**
2467 A696 12p dk rose, brn & gray
       brn   .25 .25
2468 A696 35p brt blue & sep   .45 .25

2nd World Conference on Merino Sheep — A697

1986, Jan. 27   **Photo.**   **Perf. 13½**
2469 A697 45p multicolored   .50 .25

Masquerade, 19th Cent., by F. Hohenleiter — A698

1986, Feb. 5
2470 A698 17p multicolored   .25 .25
    Cadiz Carnival.

Intl. Peace Year — A699

Lithographed and Engraved
1986, Feb. 12   **Perf. 13x13½**
2471 A699 45p multicolored   .50 .25

Festival of Religious Music, Cuenca A700

1986, Mar. 26   **Photo.**   **Perf. 13½**
2472 A700 17p multicolored   .25 .25

Chamber of Commerce, Cent. — A701

Painting detail: Swearing in of the Regent, Queen Maria Christina, Before the Spanish Parliament, 1886, by Francisco Jover and Joaquin Sorolla y Bastida, Senate Palace, Madrid.

1986, Apr. 9   Engr.   Perf. 13½
2473 A701 17p sage grn & grnsh blk   .25 .25

Emigration of Spaniards — A702

1986, Apr. 22   Photo.
2474 A702 45p multicolored   .50 .25

Europa 1986 — A703

Lithographed and Engraved
1986, May 5   Perf. 13x13½
2475 A703 17p Youth feeding birds .25 .25
2476 A703 45p Girl watering tree   .55 .25

Our Lady of the Dew Festival, Almonte A704

1986, May 14   Photo.   Perf. 13½x13
2477 A704 17p multicolored   .25 .25

Army Day A705

Captains-General Building, Canary Islands.

1986, May 16   Engr.   Perf. 13½
2478 A705 17p pale yel brn, sep & red   .25 .25

Rodrigo City Cathedral A706

Design: 35p, Calella Lighthouse.

1986, June 16   Perf. 12½x13½
2479 A706 12p blue & black   .25 .25
2480 A706 35p multicolored   .55 .25

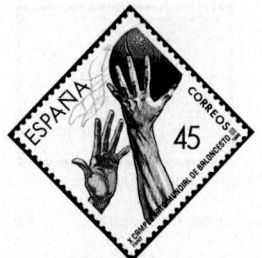

10th World Basketball Championships, July 5-20 — A707

1986, July 4   Photo.   Perf. 12½
2481 A707 45p multicolored   .50 .25

Famous Men — A708

Designs: 7p, Francisco Loscos Bernal (1823-1886), botanist. 11p, Salvador Espriu (1913-1985), author. 17p, Jose Martinez Ruiz (Azorin, 1873-1967), writer. 45p, Jose Vitoriano Gonzalez (Juan Gris, 1887-1927), painter.

1986, July 16   Engr.   Perf. 13
2482 A708 7p olive grn & bl   .25 .25
2483 A708 11p brt rose & blk   .25 .25
2484 A708 17p dk brn vio & blk   .25 .25
2485 A708 45p org, red vio & blk .50 .25
    Nos. 2482-2485 (4)   1.25 1.00

Mystery of the Virgin's Death Festival Elche — A709

17p, Angels carrying soul.

1986, Aug. 11 Photo. Perf. 13x13½
2486 A709 17p multicolored   .25 .25

5th World Swimming, Water Polo, Diving and Synchronized Swimming Championships — A710

1986, Aug. 13   Engr.   Perf. 13½
2487 A710 45p multicolored   .50 .25

10th World Pelota Championships — A711

1986, Sept. 12
2488 A711 17p multicolored   .25 .25

Stamp Day — A712

Messenger, The Husband's Return, Song 63, TI1 Codex, 1979 edition, Spanish Royal Academy.

1986, Sept. 27 Litho. Perf. 13x12½
2489 A712 17p multicolored   .25 .25

Souvenir Sheet

EXFILNA '86, Cordova, Oct. 9-18 — A713

1986, Oct. 7   Litho. & Engr.
2490 A713 17p Man, Cordova "Mosque"   .25 .25

Discovery of America, 500th Anniv. (in 1992) — A714

Men and text: 7p, Aristotle, text from De Cielo et Mundo. 12p, Seneca, text from Medea. 17p, San Isidoro, text from Etimologias. 30p, Pedro de Ailly, text from Imago Mundi. 35p, Mayan, prophesy from Libros de Chilam Balam. 45p, European, prophesy from Libros de Chilam Balam.

Lithographed and Engraved
1986, Oct. 15   Perf. 13x13½
2491 A714 7p multicolored   .25 .25
2492 A714 12p multicolored   .25 .25
2493 A714 17p multicolored   .25 .25
2494 A714 30p multicolored   .35 .25
2495 A714 35p multicolored   .40 .25
2496 A714 45p multicolored   .50 .25
  a.   Bklt. pane of 6, #2491-2496 1.90
    Nos. 2491-2496 (6)   2.00 1.50

Caspar de Portola y Rovira (1717-1786), Pioneer of California — A715

1986, Nov. 6   Perf. 13½
2497 A715 22p multicolored   .25 .25

Christmas A716

Wood carving details: 19p, The Holy Family, by Diego de Siloe (c. 1495-1563), Natl. Sculpture Museum, Valladolid, vert. 48p, Nativity, Toledo Cathedral altarpiece, by Felipe de Borgona (c. 1475-1543).

1986, Nov. 19   Photo.   Perf. 13½
2498 A716 19p multicolored   .25 .25
2499 A716 48p multicolored   .55 .25

Spanish-Islamic Cultural Heritage — A717

Famous men: 7p, Abd Al Rahman II (792-852), 4th independent emir of Cordoba. 12p, Ibn Hazm (994-1064), scholar. 17p, Al-Zarqali (1061-1100), astronomer. 45p, Alfonso VII, scholar, Toledo School of Translators.

1986, Dec. 3   Engr.
2500 A717 7p org red & dk red brn   .25 .25
2501 A717 12p brn blk & red org .25 .25
2502 A717 17p black & dk blue   .25 .25
2503 A717 45p green & black   .50 .25
    Nos. 2500-2503 (4)   1.25 1.00

Alfonso R. Castelao (1886-1950), Artist, Writer — A718

Lithographed and Engraved
1986, Dec. 11   Perf. 13x13½
2504 A718 32p El Buen Cura, 1917   .40 .25

Globe, Chateau de la Muette A719

1987, Jan. 14   Perf. 14
2505 A719 48p multicolored   .55 .25

Organization for Economic Cooperation and Development, OECD, 25th anniv.

EXPO '92, Seville A720

19p, Geometric shapes. 48p, Earth, Moon's surface.

1987, Jan. 21   Photo.
2506 A720 19p multicolored   .35 .25
2507 A720 48p multicolored   .95 .25

See Nos. 2540-2541, 2550-2551.

Portrait of Vitoria, by Vera Fajardo A721

1987, Feb. 11   Engr.
2508 A721 48p dark rose brown .55 .25

Francisco de Vitoria (c. 1486-1546), theologian, teacher and a founder of intl. law.

Marine Corps, 450th Anniv. A722

Design: 18th Cent. 74-gun man-of-war, period standard bearer, corps insignia.

1987, Feb. 25
2509 A722 19p multicolored .25 .25

Deusto University, Cent. — A723

1987, Feb. 26 Engr. Perf. 14x13½
2510 A723 19p blk, hn brn & dk grn .25 .25

UN Child Survival Campaign A724

1987, Mar. 4 Perf. 13½x14
2511 A724 19p red brown & blk .25 .25

Constitution of Cadiz, 175th Anniv. — A725

Nos. 2512a-2512c in a continuous design: The Promulgation of 1812, by Salvador Viniegra. No. 2512d, Anniv. emblem.

1987, Mar. 18 Litho. Perf. 13½
2512 Strip of 4 1.25 1.25
a.-d. A725 25p, any single .30 .25

Ceramicware A726

Designs: 7p, Pharmaceutical jar, 15th cent., Manises of Valencia. 14p, Abstract figurine, 20th cent., Sargadelos of Galicia. 19p, Neoclassical lidded urn, 18th cent., Buen Retiro of Madrid. 32p, Water jar, 20th cent., Salvatierra of Extremadura. 40p, Pitcher, 18th cent., Talavera of Toledo. 48p, Pitcher, 18th-19th cent., Granada of Andalucia.

Lithographed and Engraved
1987, Mar. 20 Perf. 12½x13
2513 Block of 6 + 3 labels 2.25 2.25
a. A726 7p multicolored .25 .25
b. A726 14p multicolored .25 .25
c. A726 19p multicolored .30 .25

d. A726 32p multicolored .45 .30
e. A726 40p multicolored .50 .30
f. A726 48p multicolored .60 .30
See No. 2552.

Passion Week in Zamora and Seville A727

Paintings: 19p, The Amanecer Procession, by Gallego Marquina, vert. 48p, Jesus Carrying the Cross, by Martinez Montanes, and the Gate of Forgiveness, Seville Cathedral.

1987, Apr. 13 Photo. Perf. 14x13½
2514 A727 19p multicolored .25 .25
2515 A727 48p multicolored .55 .25

Tourism A728

14p, Rock of Ifach, Calpe. 19p, Nave of Santa Marina d'Ozo Church, Pontevedra, before restoration. 40p, Sonanes Palace, Villacarriedo. 48p, Monastery of St. Joan de les Abadesses, Gerona, vert.

1987 Engr. Perf. 12½x13
2515A A728 14p dp bl & sage grn .25 .25
2516 A728 19p dp grn & grnsh blk .30 .25
2516A A728 40p dp claret .50 .25
2517 A728 48p black .60 .25
Nos. 2515A-2517 (4) 1.65 1.00
Issued: 19p, 48p, 4/21; 14p, 40p, 6/10.

Europa 1987 A729

Modern architecture: 19p, Bilbao Bank, Madrid, designed by Saenz de Oiza, vert. 48p, Natl. Museum of Roman Art, Merida, designed by Rafael Moneo.

Lithographed and Engraved
1987, May 4 Perf. 14x13½
2518 A729 19p multicolored .25 .25
2519 A729 48p multicolored .55 .25

Horse Fair, Jerez de La Frontera A730

1987, May 6 Photo. Perf. 13½x14
2520 A730 19p multicolored .25 .25

Ramon Carande (1887-1986), Historian — A731

1987, May 29 Engr.
2521 A731 40p blk & dk vio brn .45 .25

Postal Code Inauguration — A732

1987, June 1 Litho. Perf. 14
2522 A732 19p multicolored .25 .25

Eibar Weaponry School, 75th Anniv. A733

1987, July 2 Litho. Perf. 14
2523 A733 20p multicolored .25 .25

1992 Summer Olympics, Barcelona A734

1987, July 15 Photo.
2524 A734 32p Casa de Battlo masonry .50 .25
2525 A734 65p Athletes 1.00 .25

25th Folk Festival of the Pyrenees, Jaca — A735

1987, July 22
2526 A735 50p multicolored .55 .25

Monturiol and Submarine Designs A736

1987, Sept. 9 Engr. Perf. 13½x14
2527 A736 20p black brown .25 .25
Narcis Monturiol (d. 1887), builder of the submarine Ictineos.

Stamp Day — A737

Illuminated codex from *Constitutiones Jacobi II Regis Majoricum*, 14th cent., King Albert I Royal Library, Brussels.

Litho & Engr.
1987, Sept. 16 Perf. 13
2528 A737 20p multicolored .25 .25
Postal service of Mallorca under James II.

ESPAMER '87 — A738

Designs: 8p, Handstamped letter that traveled from La Coruna to Havana, Cuba, 18th cent. 12p, La Coruna Harbor, 19th cent., engraving. 20p, Illustration of Havana harbor from *Viaje Alrededor da La Isla de Cuba*, by Francisco Mialche, 18th cent. 50p, West Indies packets.

1987, Oct. 2 Litho. & Engr. Perf. 13
2529 A738 Sheet of 4 3.25 3.25
a. 8p blk, brt blue & red .30 .30
b. 12p brt blue, red & blk .45 .45
c. 20p blk, brt blue & red .75 .75
d. 50p blk, brt blue & red 1.75 1.75

No. 2529 printed se-tenant (rouletted between) with ESPAMER entrance ticket. Sold for 180p. Size: 150x83mm (including ticket).

Souvenir Sheet

EXFILNA '87, Gerona, Oct. 24-Nov. 1 — A739

Greek statue, Emporion, Olympic torchbearer.

1987, Oct. 24 Photo. Perf. 13x12½
2530 A739 20p multicolored .25 .25

Discovery of America, 500th Anniv. (in 1992) — A740

Ships and: 14p, Amerigo Vespucci (1454-1512), Italian navigator. 20p, Ferdinand and Isabella. 32p, Friar Juan Perez, Queen's confessor. 40p, Juan de la Cosa (c. 1460-1510), master of the Santa Maria, cartographer who made first map of the New World. 50p, Christopher Columbus. 65p, Vicente Yanez Pinzon (c. 1460-1523) and Martin Alonso Pinzon (c. 1441-1493), brothers, navigators and ship owners, accompanied Columbus on voyage.

Litho. & Engr.
1987, Oct. 30 Perf. 13
2531 A740 14p multicolored .25 .25
2532 A740 20p multicolored .25 .25
2533 A740 32p multicolored .40 .25
2534 A740 40p multicolored .45 .25
2535 A740 50p multicolored .55 .25
2536 A740 65p multicolored .75 .30
a. Bklt. pane of 6, #2531-2536 3.00
Nos. 2531-2536 (6) 2.65 1.55

Christmas — A741

1987, Nov. 17 Photo. Perf. 14x13½
2537 A741 20p Ornaments .30 .25
2538 A741 50p Zambomba, tambourine .60 .25

Self-portrait, Sculpture by Victorio Macho (1887-1966) A742

1987, Dec. 23 **Engr.**
2539 A742 50p brown black .55 .25

EXPO '92 Type of 1987

1987, Dec. 29 Photo. Perf. 13½x14
2540 A720 20p like No. 2506 .30 .25
2541 A720 50p like No. 2507 .55 .25

HRH Sofia and Juan Carlos, 50th Birth Annivs. — A743

1988, Jan. 5 Perf. 13x13½
2542 A743 20p Sofia .30 .25
2543 A743 20p Juan Carlos .30 .25
a. Pair, #2542-2543 + label .60 .50

Clara Campoamor (b. 1888), Suffragette — A744

1988, Feb. 12 Photo. Perf. 14
2544 A744 20p multicolored .25 .25

1988 Winter Olympics, Calgary — A745

1988, Feb. 15 Perf. 14
2545 A745 45p Speed skater .60 .25

Passion Week in Valladolid and Malaga — A746

Designs: 20p, Valladolid Cathedral and 17th cent. statue of Christ at the column by Gregorio Fernandez. 50p, Christ carrying the cross along Malaga procession route.

1988, Mar. 30 Photo. Perf. 14
2546 A746 20p multicolored .30 .25
2547 A746 50p multicolored .60 .25

Tourism A747

18p, Paella pan, ingredients. 45p, Covadonga Natl. Park.

1988, Apr. 7
2548 A747 18p multicolored .25 .25
2549 A747 45p multicolored .50 .25

EXPO '92 Type of 1987

Era of Discoveries: 8p, Road to globe, rays of light, vert. 45p, Compass rose, globe.

1988, Apr. 12
2550 A720 8p multicolored .25 .25
2551 A720 45p multicolored .50 .25

Art Type of 1987

Glassware: a, Chalice, Valencia, 18th cent. b, Cadalso de los Vidrios, Madrid, 18th cent. c, Candy dish, La Granja de San Ildefonso, 18th cent. d, Castril double-handled jar, Andalucia, 18th cent. e, Jug, Catalina, 17th cent. f, Bottle, Baleares, 20th cent.

Litho. & Engr.

1988, Apr. 13 Perf. 12½x13
2552 Block of 6 + 6 labels 1.75 1.75
a.-f. A726 20p any single .25 .25

Stamp Day 1988 — A748

Francis of Taxis, postmaster by royal appointment (1505) in charge of establishing communications between Spain, France, Germany, Rome, Naples.

1988, Apr. 29 Engr. Perf. 12½x13
2553 A748 20p dk violet & dk brn .25 .25

General Workers' Union (UGT), Cent. A749

Emblem and Pablo Iglesias, union pioneer.

1988, May 1 Photo. Perf. 14
2554 A749 20p multicolored .25 .25

Europa 1988 — A750

Transport and communication: 20p, Locomotive made in Spain and operated in Cuba, 1837. 50p, Spanish telegraph in the Philippines linking Plaza de Manila and Bagumbayan Camp, 1818.

1988, May 5 Engr. Perf. 13
2555 A750 20p black & dk red .25 .25
2556 A750 50p black & dk grn .50 .25

Jean Monnet (1888-1979), Economist A751

1988, May 9 Perf. 14x13½
2557 A751 45p blue black .50 .25

Universal Exposition, Barcelona, Cent. A752

1988, May 31 Photo. Perf. 13½x14
2558 A752 50p multicolored .55 .25

Intl. Music and Dance Festival, Granada — A753

1988, June 1 Perf. 14x13½
2559 A753 50p multicolored .55 .25

World Expo '88, Brisbane, Australia A754

1988, June 14 Perf. 13½x14
2560 A754 50p Bull .55 .25

Coronation of the Virgin of Hope — A755

1988, June 18 Perf. 14x13½
2561 A755 20p multicolored .25 .25

Holy Week in Malaga.

Souvenir Sheet

EXFILNA '88, June 25-July 3, Madrid — A756

1988, June 25 Perf. 13x12½
2562 A756 20p Ciudadela Fortress floor plan .25 .25

Tourism A757

18p, Cantabrian Coast storehouse. 45p, Dulzaina (wind instrument).

1988, July 11 Engr. Perf. 13½x14
2563 A757 18p multicolored .30 .25
2564 A757 45p multicolored .60 .25

28th World Roller Hockey Championships, La Coruna — A758

1988, Sept. 7 Photo. Perf. 13½x14
2565 A758 20p multicolored .25 .25

1st World Cong. of Spanish Regional Shelters — A759

1988, Sept. 9 Perf. 14
2566 A759 20p multicolored .25 .25

1988 Summer Olympics, Seoul — A760

1988, Sept. 10 Litho.
2567 A760 50p Yachting .55 .25

Catalonia Millennium — A761

1988, Sept. 21 Photo. Perf. 12½
2568 A761 20p multicolored .25 .25

1st Call to Session of the Leon Court, 800th Anniv. — A762

Illumination & seal of Alfonso IX, King of Leon.

1988, Sept. 26 Photo. Perf. 12½x13
2569 A762 20p multicolored .25 .25

Federation of Spanish Philatelic Societies, 25th Anniv. A763

1988, Sept. 27 Perf. 14x13½
2570 A763 20p multicolored .25 .25

1992 Summer Olympics, Barcelona A764

1988, Oct. 3　　Photo.　　Perf. 14
2571　A764　8p multicolored　　.25　.25
See Nos. B139-B141.

A765

Design: Castle in Valencia and royal seal of James I, 13th cent.

1988, Oct. 7　　　　Perf. 14x13½
2572　A765　20p multicolored　　.25　.25
Reconquest of Valencia by King James I, 750th anniv.

A766

1988, Oct. 10　　　　Perf. 13x13½
2573　A766　20p multicolored　　.25　.25
Civil Law, cent.

Discovery of America (in 1992), 500th Anniv. — A767

Conquerors, exporers and symbols: No. 2574, Hernando Cortez, conqueror of Mexico, and serpent Quetzalcoatl. No. 2575, Vasco Nunez de Balboa, discoverer of the Pacific Ocean, and sun setting over sea. No. 2576, Francisco Pizarro, conqueror of Peru, and llama. No. 2577, Portuguese navigator Ferdinand Magellan, Juan de Elcano (c. 1476-1526) and globe symbolizing circumnavigation of the world. No. 2578, Alvar Nunez Cabeza de Vaca (c. 1490-1560), explorer, and sunrise. No. 2579, Andres de Urdaneta (1498-1568), and symbol of the west-to-east route between the Philippines and America that he discovered.

1988, Oct. 13　　Engr.　　Perf. 13x13½
2574　A767　10p multicolored　　.25　.25
2575　A767　10p multicolored　　.25　.25
2576　A767　20p multicolored　　.25　.25
2577　A767　20p multicolored　　.25　.25
2578　A767　50p multicolored　　.55　.25
2579　A767　50p multicolored　　.55　.25
　　a.　Bklt. pane of 6, #2574-2579　2.25
　　Nos. 2574-2579 (6)　　2.10 1.50

Henry III of Castile, 1st Prince of Asturias — A768

1988, Oct. 26　　Photo.　　Perf. 13
2580　A768　20p multicolored　　.25　.25

1st Bestowal of the title Prince of Asturias, 600th anniv., guaranteeing that the throne would continue to be inherited according to primogeniture.

Christmas — A769

1988, Nov. 24　　Photo.　　Perf. 14
2581　A769　20p Snowflakes,
　　　　　　　horiz.　　　　.25　.25
2582　A769　50p Shepherd　　.55　.25

Sites and Cities Appearing on the UNESCO World Heritage List — A770

18p, Mosque de Cordoba, vert. 20p, Burgos Cathedral, vert. 45p, El Escorial Monastery. 50p, The Alhambra, Granada.

1988, Dec. 1　　Engr.　　Perf. 12½x13
2583　A770　18p multicolored　　.25　.25
2584　A770　20p multicolored　　.30　.25
2585　A770　45p multicolored　　.55　.25
2586　A770　50p multicolored　　.65　.25
　　Nos. 2583-2586 (4)　　1.75 1.00

Natl. Constitution, 10th Anniv. — A771

1988, Dec. 7　　Photo.　　Perf. 14
2587　A771　20p multicolored　　.25　.25

Souvenir Sheet

Charles III (1759-1788) and the Enlightenment — A772

1988, Dec. 14　　Engr.　　Perf. 13x12½
2588　A772　45p black & dk grn　　.55　.55

Natl. Organization for the Blind, 50th Anniv. — A773

1988, Dec. 27　　Photo.　　Perf. 14
2589　A773　20p multicolored　　.25　.25

Fr. Luis de Granada (1504-1588) A774

1988, Dec. 31
2590　A774　20p multicolored　　.25　.25

1992 Summer Olympics, Barcelona A775

1989, Jan. 3
2591　A775　20p multicolored　　.25　.25

Stamp Collecting — A776

1989, Jan. 3
2592　A776　20p multicolored　　.25　.25

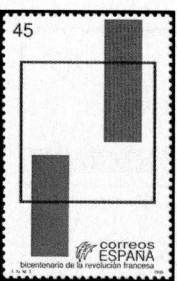

French Revolution, Bicent. — A777

1989, Jan. 24　　Photo.　　Perf. 13
2593　A777　45p multicolored　　.50　.25

Maria de Maeztu (b. 1882), Educator A778

1989, Feb. 7　　Photo.　　Perf. 14x13½
2594　A778　20p multicolored　　.25　.25

Postal Service, Cent. A779

Litho. & Engr.
1989, Mar. 11　　　　Perf. 13½x14
2595　A779　20p Uniform, 1889　　.25　.25

Stamp Day — A780

Design: Intl. postal treaty negotiated with France and Italy by Franz von Taxis, 1601.

1989, Apr. 4　　Engr.　　Perf. 13
2596　A780　20p black　　.25　.25

A781

1989, Apr. 22　　　　Perf. 14x13½
2597　A781　20p black　　.25　.25
Casa del Cordon, Burgos.

A782

Europa: Children's toys.

1989, May 5　　Photo.　　Perf. 13x13½
2598　A782　40p shown　　.40　.25
2599　A782　50p Top　　.50　.25

Spain's Presidency of the European Economic Community A783

1989, May 9　　　　Perf. 13½x14
2600　A783　45p multicolored　　.50　.25

Souvenir Sheet

Holy Family with St. Anne, by El Greco — A784

1989, May 20   Litho.   Perf. 14x13½
2601 A784 20p multicolored   .25 .25
EXFILNA '89. Exists imperf in different colors.

Gabriela Mistral (1889-1957), Chilean Poet Awarded 1945 Nobel Prize for Literature — A785

Litho. & Engr.
1989, June 1   Perf. 14x13½
2602 A785 50p multicolored   .60 .25

European Parliament 3rd Elections — A786

1989, June 12 Photo. Perf. 13x13½
2603 A786 45p multicolored   .50 .25

Lace A787

Lace produced in: a, Catalonia. b, Andalusia. c, Extremadura. d, Canary Isls. e, Castile-La Mancha. f, Galicia.

Litho. & Engr.
1989, June 20   Perf. 13x12½
2604   Block of 6 + 3 labels   1.40 1.40
a.-f. A787 20p any single   .25 .25
Three center labels printed in a continuous design and picture lace-making.

Pope John Paul II at the Intl. Catholic Youth Forum, Santiago — A788

1989, Aug. 19 Engr. Perf. 13x12½
2605 A788 50p myrtle grn, dk red brn & blk   .55 .25

Athletics World Cup, Barcelona A789

1989, Sept. 1   Photo.   Perf. 13½x14
2606 A789 50p multicolored   .55 .25

A790

Litho. & Engr.
1989, Sept. 19   Perf. 14x13½
2607 A790 50p multicolored   .55 .25
Charlie Chaplin (1889-1977), English comedian and actor.

Type A34 — A791

1989, Oct. 2   Photo.   Perf. 14x13½
2608 A791 50p gray, ver & blk   .55 .25
Cent. of the 1st Alfonso XIII issue.

A792

Fr. Andres Manjon (d. 1923), teacher.

1989, Oct. 13
2609 A792 20p multicolored   .25 .25
Founding of the Ave Maria Schools by Fr. Manjon, cent.

A793

UPAE emblem and "Irrigating Corn Field in November, 17th Cent.," an illustration from the *New Chronicle and Good Government,* by Guaman Poma de Ayala.

1989, Nov. 7   Litho. & Engr.
2610 A793 50p multicolored   .55 .25
America issue.

Christmas A794

Perf. 14x13½, 13½x14
1989, Nov. 29   Photo.
2611 A794 20p Star, "NAVIdAd 89," vert.   .25 .25
2612 A794 45p shown   .50 .25

Sites on the UNESCO World Heritage List — A795

No. 2613, Altamira Caverns. No. 2614, Santiago de Compostela. No. 2615, Roman aqueduct, Segovia. No. 2616, Guell Park and palace, Mila House.

Litho. & Engr.
1989, Dec. 5   Perf. 13x12½
2613 A795 20p multicolored   .25 .25
2614 A795 20p multicolored   .25 .25
2615 A795 20p multicolored   .25 .25
2616 A795 20p multicolored   .25 .25
Nos. 2613-2616 (4)   1.00 1.00

Souvenir Sheet

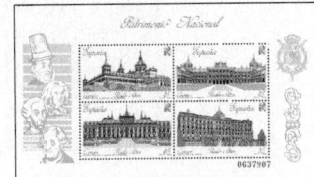

Sites on the World Heritage List — A796

Royal palaces: a, El Escorial. b, Aranjuez. c, Summer palace, La Granja, San Ildefonso. e, Madrid.

1989, Dec. 20 Engr. Perf. 13x13½
2617   Sheet of 4   2.00 2.00
a.-d. A796 45p any single   .30 .30

Illustration by Daniel Garcia Perez, Winner of the 2nd Youth Stamp Design Contest — A797

1990, Jan. 29 Photo. Perf. 14x13½
2618 A797 20p multicolored   .25 .25
1992 Summer Olympics, Barcelona.

A798

1990, Feb. 2
2619 A798 20p multicolored   .25 .25
World Cycle Cross Championship, Getzu.

A799

1990, Feb. 12   Engr.
2620 A799 20p dark purple   .25 .25
Victoria Kent (1897-1987), prisons directer, reformer.

Honorary Postman Rafael Alvarez Sereix and Cancel — A800

Litho. & Engr.
1990, Apr. 18   Perf. 13
2621 A800 20p sepia, buff & dull grn   .25 .25
Stamp Day.

Europa 1990 A801

Post offices.

Perf. 13½x14, 14x13½
1990, May 4   Photo.
2622 A801 20p Vitoria   .25 .25
2623 A801 50p Malaga, vert.   .50 .25

Intl. Telecommunications Union, 125th Anniv. — A802

1990, May 17   Perf. 13½x14
2624 A802 8p multicolored   .25 .25

Wrought Iron — A803

Designs: a, 15th Cent. door knocker. b, 16th cent. lyre-shaped door knocker. c, 17th Cent. pistol. d, 17th-18th Cent. door knocker. e, 19th Cent. lock. f, Fire iron.

Litho. & Engr.
1990, May 18   Perf. 12½
2625   Block of 6 + 3 labels   1.75 1.75
a.-f. A803 20p any single   .25 .25
Nos. 2625a-2625f printed se-tenant in a continuous design. Three labels continue the design and contain text or picture a forge.

Souvenir Sheet

Patio de La Infanta, Zaporta Palace, Zaragoza — A804

1990, May 25 Engr. Perf. 14x13½
2626 A804 20p red brown   .25 .25
EXFILNA '90.

Charity, by Lopez Alonso — A805

1990, June 19 Litho. Perf. 13½x13
2627 A805 8p multicolored   .25 .25
Daughters of Charity in Spain, bicentennial.

Jose Padilla, Composer, Birth Centenary — A806

1990, June 19 Photo. Perf. 13x12½
2628 A806 20p multicolored   .30 .25

Town of Estella, 900th Anniv. — A807

1990, June 19 Litho. & Engr.
2629 A807 45p multicolored   .60 .25

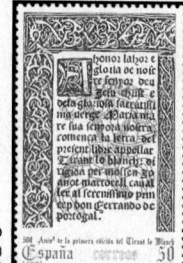

Novel, "Tirant lo Blanch," 500th Anniv. — A808

1990, June 19 Perf. 12½x13
2630 A808 50p multicolored   .65 .25

Souvenir Sheet

Crypt, Palencia Cathedral — A809

1990, June 22 Engr. Perf. 13½x14
2631 A809 20p red brown   .25 .25
Topical philatelic exposition.

A810

1990, Aug. 27 Photo. Perf. 14x13½
2632 A810 50p multicolored   .55 .25
17th Intl. Congress of Historical Sciences.

A811

America Issue: UPAE emblem and Carribean fauna.

Litho. & Engr.
1990, Nov. 14 Perf. 14
2633 A811 50p multicolored   .55 .25

Christmas: Scenes from the film "Cosmic Poem" by Jose Antonio Sistiaga.

1990, Nov. 22 Photo.
2634 A812 25p multicolored   .30 .25
2635 A812 45p multi, horiz.   .50 .25

A813

Tapestries in Monastery of San Lorenzo: a, The Crucifixion by Jan van Roome and Bernard van Orley. b, Flamenco Soldiers by Philip Wouvermans. c, Shipwreck of the Telemac by Miguel Angel Houasse. d, Flowers by Francisco Goya.

Litho. & Engr.
1990, Nov. 28 Perf. 13
2636   Sheet of 4   1.00 1.00
a.-d. A813 20p any single   .25   .25

European Tourism Year — A814

1990, Dec. 1 Photo. Perf. 14
2637 A814 45p multicolored   .50 .25

World Heritage List — A815

Designs: No. 2638, Church of San Vicente, Avila. No. 2639, Tower of San Pedro, Teruel, vert. No. 2640, Church of San Miguel de Lillo, Oviedo, vert. No. 2641, Tower of Bujaco, Caceres.

Litho. & Engr.
1990, Dec. 10 Perf. 13
2638 A815 20p multicolored   .30 .25
2639 A815 20p multicolored   .30 .25
2640 A815 20p multicolored   .30 .25
2641 A815 20p multicolored   .30 .25
Nos. 2638-2641 (4)   1.20 1.00

Natl. Orchestra of Spain A816

1990, Dec. 20 Photo. Perf. 13½x14
2642 A816 25p grn, yel grn & blk .30 .25

Maria Moliner (1900-1981), Spanish Linguist — A817

1991, Jan. 21 Photo. Perf. 14x13½
2643 A817 25p multicolored   .35 .25

Souvenir Sheet

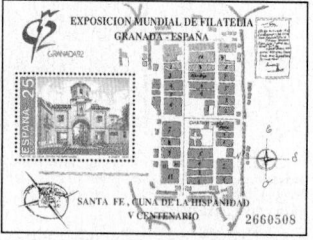

Santa Fe, 500th Anniv. — A818

Litho. & Engr.
1991, Apr. 19 Perf. 13½x14
2644 A818 25p brown & purple   .35 .35
World Philatelic Exhibition, Granada '92.

Child's Drawing — A819

1991, Apr. 12 Photo. Perf. 14x13½
2645 A819 25p Olympic rings, sailboats .35 .25

Juan de Tassis y Peralta (1582-1622), Postal Reformer A820

1991, Apr. 26 Engr. Perf. 12½
2646 A820 25p black   .35 .25
Stamp Day.

Souvenir Sheet

Porcelain and Ceramics — A821

a, Apothecary jar, 17th cent. b, Figurine, 18th cent. c, Vase, 19th cent. d, Plate, 19th cent.

1991, May 3 Litho. & Engr. Perf. 13
2647 A821 25p Sheet of 4, #a.-d. 1.50 1.50
a.-d. Any single   .30 .25
See No. 2692.

Europa A822

25p, INTA-NASA ground station. 45p, Olympus I satellite.

1991, May 28 Litho. Perf. 13½x14
2648 A822 25p multicolored   .35 .25
2649 A822 45p multicolored   .55 .25

St. John of the Cross (1651-1695), Mystic — A823

Anniversaries: No. 2651, Fr. Luis de Leon (1527-1591), Augustinian writer, vert. No. 2652, Abd Al Rahman III (891-961), Moslem caliph, vert. No. 2653, St. Ignatius of Loyola (1451-1556), founder of Society of Jesus, vert.

Perf. 13½x14, 14x13½

1991, June 6				**Litho.**
2650	A823	15p multicolored	.25	.25
2651	A823	15p multicolored	.25	.25
2652	A823	25p multicolored	.35	.25
2653	A823	25p multicolored	.35	.25
	Nos. 2650-2653 (4)		1.20	1.00

Antique Furniture A824

Designs: a, Wedge top armoire, 18th cent. b, Hutch cabinet, c. 19th cent. c, Ladder-back cane chair, c. 19th cent. d, Baby cradle, 19th cent. e, Round-top trunk, c. 19th cent. f, Ornate chest, c. 18th cent.

Litho. & Engr.

1991, Sept. 9		**Perf. 12½x13**	
2654		Block of 6 + 3 labels	1.90 1.90
a.-f.	A824 25p any single		.30 .25

Orfeo Catala (Catalan Choral Society), Cent. — A825

1991, Sept. 6		**Litho.**	**Perf. 14x13½**		
2655	A825	25p multicolored		.35	.25

Intl. Fishing Exposition, Vigo — A826

1991, Sept. 10				
2656	A826	55p multicolored	.65	.25

America Issue — A827

Litho. & Engr.

1991, Nov. 4			**Perf. 14x13½**	
2657	A827	55p Nocturlabe	.65	.25

Christmas — A828

25p, The Nativity, illustration from 17th cent. book. 45p, The Birth of Christ, 16th cent. icon.

1991, Nov. 22	**Photo.**	**Perf. 14x13½**		
2658	A828	25p multicolored	.35	.25
2659	A828	45p multicolored	.55	.25

Souvenir Sheet

The Meadowlands of St. Isidro by Goya — A829

1991, Dec. 12		**Perf. 13½x14**		
2660	A829	25p multicolored	.35	.35

EXFILNA '91, Madrid.

Sites on UNESCO World Heritage List — A830

#2661, Giralda bell tower, Seville Cathedral. #2662, Alcantara Gate, Toledo, vert. #2663, Casa de las Conchas, Salamanca, vert. #2664, Garajonay Natl. Park, Gomera, Canary Islands.

Perf. 12½x13, 13x12½

1991, Dec. 16			**Engr.**	
2661	A830	25p brown & blue	.40	.25
2662	A830	25p red brn & brn	.40	.25
2663	A830	25p red brn & blk	.40	.25
2664	A830	25p violet & dk grn	.40	.25
	Nos. 2661-2664 (4)		1.60	1.00

See Nos. 2756, 2830.

Carlos Ibanez de Ibero (1825-1891), Cartographer A831

Antarctic Treaty, Research Ship A52 — A832

1991, Dec. 27	**Litho.**	**Perf. 14x13½**		
2665	A831	25p multicolored	.35	.25
2666	A832	55p multicolored	.65	.25

Margarita Xirgu (1889-1969), Actress — A833

1992, Jan. 20		**Perf. 14**		
2667	A833	25p lake & gold	.35	.25

Child's Drawing A834

1992, Feb. 14		**Perf. 13½x14**		
2668	A834	25p multicolored	.35	.25

EXPO 92.

Pedro Rodriguez Campomanes (1723-1802), Historian, Postal Administrator — A835

1992, Feb. 21		**Perf. 13x12½**		
2669	A835	27p multicolored	.45	.25

Expo '92, Seville A836

1992, Feb. 28		**Perf. 13½x14**		
2670	A836	27p gray, blk & brn	.40	.25

Columbus Types of 1930
Souvenir Sheet

1992, Apr. 24	**Engr.**	**Perf. 14**		
2671		Sheet of 2	10.00	10.00
a.	A65 250p black		4.50	2.50
b.	A67 250p brown		4.50	2.50

Intl. Philatelic Exhibition, Granada '92.

Miniature Sheets

Expo '92, Seville — A837

#2672: a, Expo '92 World Trade Center. b, Aerial tram. c, Avenue 4. d, Barqueta Gate. e, Nature pavilion. f, Biosphere. g, Alamillo Bridge. h, Press center. i, 15th Century pavilion. j, Expo harbor. k, Tourist train. l, One day entrance ticket.

#2673: a, Cartuja Monastery. b, Arena. c, Monorail train. d, Europe Avenue. e, Discovery pavilion. f, Auditorium. g, Avenue 1. h, Plaza of the Future. i, Gate to Italy's exhibit. j, Terminal. k, Expo theater. l, Expo Mascot, Curro.

1992, Apr. 21	**Litho.**	**Perf. 13½x14**		
2672	A837	Sheet of 12 + 4 labels	5.00	5.00
a.-l.		17p any single	.40	.25

2673	A837	Sheet of 12 + 4 labels	8.50	8.50
a.-l.		27p any single	.60	.30

See No. B195.

1992 Paralympics, Barcelona — A838

1992, Apr. 22	**Photo.**	**Perf. 14**		
2674	A838	27p multicolored	.60	.25

Discovery of America, 500th Anniv. A839

Europa: 17p, Preparation Before Departing from Palos, by R. Espejo. 45p, Globe, ships, and buildings at La Rabida.

1992, May 5	**Photo.**	**Perf. 14**		
2675	A839	17p multicolored	.75	.25
2676	A839	45p multicolored	1.50	.25

Souvenir Sheets

Voyages of Columbus — A840

#2677, Columbus in sight of land. #2678, Landing of Columbus. #2679, Columbus soliciting aid from Isabella. #2680, Columbus welcomed at Barcelona. #2681, Columbus presenting natives. #2682, Columbus.

Borders on Nos. 2677-2682 are lithographed. Nos. 2677-2682 are similar in design to US Nos. 230-231, 234-235, 237, 245.

1992, May 22		**Perf. 14**		
2677	A840	60p blue	1.25	1.10
2678	A840	60p brown violet	1.25	1.10
2679	A840	60p chocolate	1.25	1.10
2680	A840	60p purple	1.25	1.10
2681	A840	60p black brown	1.25	1.10
2682	A840	60p black	1.25	1.10
	Nos. 2677-2682 (6)		7.50	6.60

See US Nos. 2624-2629, Italy Nos. 1883-1888 and Portugal Nos. 1918-1923.

1992 Winter & Summer Olympics, Albertville & Barcelona A841

1992, June 19	**Photo.**	**Perf. 14**		
2683	A841	45p multicolored	.60	.25

A842

1992, June 5	**Photo.**	**Perf. 14x13½**		
2684	A842	27p blue & yellow	.40	.25

World Environment Day.

A843

1992, Oct. 29   Litho.   Perf. 14x13½
2685 A843 17p multicolored   .25   .25
Juan Luis Vives (1492-1540), Philosopher.

Pamplona
Choir,
Cent.
A844

1992, Oct. 29   Perf. 13½x14
2686 A844 27p multicolored   .35   .25

Unified
Europe — A845

1992, Nov. 4   Photo.   Perf. 14x13½
2687 A845 45p multicolored   .60   .25

Christmas
A846

1992, Nov. 5   Perf. 13½x14
2688 A846 27p multicolored   .40   .25

1992
Special
Olympics,
Madrid
A847

1992, Sept. 7   Photo.   Perf. 13½x14
2689 A847 27p brown & blue   .35   .25

Souvenir Sheet

St. Paul's Church, Valladolid — A848

Litho. & Engr.
1992, Oct. 9   Perf. 14x13½
2690 A848 27p multicolored   .35   .35
Exfilna '92, Natl. Philatelic Exhibition,
Valladolid.

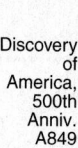 

Discovery
of
America,
500th
Anniv.
A849

1992, Oct. 15   Perf. 13½x14
2691 A849 60p dk brn, lt brn &
        bis   .75   .25

Natl. Heritage Type of 1991
Miniature Sheet

Codices: a, Veitia, 18th cent. b, Trujillo of
Peru, 18th cent. c, The Chess Book, 13th cent.
d, General History of New Spain, 16th cent.

Litho. & Engr.
1992, Dec. 10   Perf. 13
2692 A821 27p Sheet of 4, #a.-d. 1.75 1.40

Road Safety   Environmental
A850   Protection
                 A851

Health and
Sanitation — A852

1993   Photo.   Perf. 14x13½
2693 A850 17p green & red   .35   .25
2694 A851 28p green & blue   .40   .25
2695 A852 65p blue & green   .90   .25
    Nos. 2693-2695 (3)   1.65   .75
Issued: 17p, 4/20; 28p, 1/4; 65p, 2/12.

Maria Zambrano (1904-1991),
Writer — A854

1993, Jan. 18   Photo.   Perf. 14
2697 A854 45p buff, lil rose & brn .65 .25

Andres Segovia
(1893-1987),
Guitarist — A855

1993, Feb. 19   Engr.   Perf. 14x13½
2698 A855 65p black & brown   .90   .25

1908
Mailbox,
Madrid
Postal
Museum
A856

Litho. & Engr.
1993, Mar. 12   Perf. 13½x14
2699 A856 28p multicolored   .45   .25
Stamp Day.

Mushrooms — A857

No. 2700, Amanita caesarea. No. 2701,
Lepiota procera. No. 2702, Lactarius
sanguifluus. No. 2703, Russula cyanoxantha.

1993, Mar. 18   Photo.   Perf. 14
2700 A857 17p multicolored   .35   .25
2701 A857 17p multicolored   .35   .25
2702 A857 28p multicolored   .40   .25
2703 A857 28p multicolored   .40   .25
    Nos. 2700-2703 (4)   1.50 1.00
        See Nos. 2759-2762.

Souvenir Sheet

Holy Week Celebration — A858

1993, Apr. 2   Litho.   Perf. 14x13½
2704 A858 100p multicolored   1.40 1.40
Exfilna '93, Alcaniz. Margin of No. 2704 is
Litho. & Engr.

Fusees, by
Joan Miro
A859

Europa: 65p, La Bague d'Aurore, by Miro,
vert.

Perf. 13½x14, 14x13½
1993, May 5   Litho.
2705 A859 45p blue & black   .90   .25
Litho. & Engr.
2706 A859 65p multicolored   1.40   .25

Year of St.
James
A860

Designs: 17p, Transfer of St. James' body
by boat. 28p, Discovery of tomb of St. James.
45p, St. James on horseback.

1993, May 13   Photo.   Perf. 13½x14
2707 A860 17p multicolored   .35   .25
2708 A860 28p multicolored   .40   .25
2709 A860 45p multicolored   .60   .25
    Nos. 2707-2709 (3)   1.35   .75

World Telecommunications
Day — A861

1993, May 17
2710 A861 28p multicolored   .40   .25

Compostela '93 — A862

Stylized designs: 28p, Pilgrims paying homage to Saint James. 100p, Pilgrim under star

---

tree while on way to Santiago de Camposte-
la, vert.

1993, May 18   Photo.   Perf. 13½x14
2711 A862 28p multicolored   .45   .25
Souvenir Sheet
Perf. 14x13½
2712 A862 100p multicolored   3.00 1.75

World
Environment
Day — A863

1993, June 4   Litho.   Perf. 14x13½
2713 A863 28p multicolored   .40   .25

King Juan Carlos — A864a
A864

1993-98   Photo.   Perf. 14x13½
A864 Gold and:
2714 A864   1p prussian bl   .25   .25
2715 A864   2p green   .25   .25
2716 A864 10p magenta   .25   .25
2717 A864 15p green   .25   .25
2718 A864 16p brn lake   .25   .25
2719 A864 17p yel org   .25   .25
2720 A864 18p grn bl   .25   .25
2721 A864 19p brown   .25   .25
2722 A864 20p lil rose   .25   .25
2723 A864 21p dark grn   .25   .25
2724 A864 28p vio brn   .35   .25
2725 A864 29p olive   .40   .25
2726 A864 30p ultramarine   .40   .25
2727 A864 32p green   .45   .25
2728 A864 35p red   .40   .25
2729 A864 45p bluish grn   .55   .25
2730 A864 55p sepia   3.00   .50
  a.   Block of 4, #2714, 2720,
        2725, 2730 + 2 labels   3.00   .50
2731 A864 60p org brn   1.00   .50
  a.   Block of 4, #2716, 2721,
        2726, 2731 + 2 labels   2.50 1.25
2732 A864 65p red org   .70   .25
  a.   Block of 4, #2719, 2724,
        2729, 2732 + 2 labels   2.50 2.00
2733 A864 70p vermilion   .90   .45

Engr.
2734 A864a 100p brown   2.50   .30
2735 A864a 200p green   6.25   .60
2736 A864a 300p maroon   11.00   .90
2737 A864a 500p blue   17.50 1.50
2738 A864a 1000p vio blk   35.00 4.00
    Nos. 2714-2738 (25)   82.90 13.00

Issued: 17p, 28p, 45p, 65p, 5/21/93; 1p,
18p, 29p, 1/31/94; 55p, 5/27/94; 19p, 30p,
1/3/95; 10p, 60p, 6/5/95; 1000p, 11/24/95;
100p, 200p, 300p, 500p, 12/12/96; 21p, 32p,
1/27/97; 2p, 16p, 5/19/97; 15p, 3/6/98; 35p,
2/13/98; 70p, 1/30/98. 20p, 11/20/00.

Don Juan de
Borbon (1913-
1993), Count of
Barcelona — A865

1993, June 20   Photo.   Perf. 14x13½
2744 A865 28p multicolored   .35   .25

Igualada-Martorell Railway,
Cent. — A866

1993, July 4   Engr.   Perf. 13½x14
2745 A866 45p black & green   .60   .25

Natl. Mint
(F.N.M.T.),
Cent.
A867

1993, Sept. 13
2746 A867 65p dark blue   .90   .25

Explorers
A868

Designs: 45p, Alejandro Malaspina (1754-
1809), Italian explorer of South America. 65p,
Jose Celestino Mutis (1732-1808), Spanish
naturalist in the Americas, vert.

Perf. 13½x14, 14x13½
1993, Sept 20   **Litho.**
2747 A868 45p multicolored   .60   .25
2748 A868 65p multicolored   .90   .25

Ciconia
Nigra
A869

Endangered birds: No. 2750, Gypaetus
barbatus (Quebrantahuesos).

Litho. & Engr.
1993, Oct. 11   Perf. 13½x14
2749 A869 65p pink & black   .90   .25
2750 A869 65p orange & black   .90   .25

Child's
Painting — A870

1993, Oct. 2   Litho.   Perf. 14x13½
2751 A870 45p multicolored   .60   .25

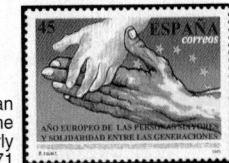

European
Year of the
Elderly
A871

1993, Oct. 29   Photo.   Perf. 14
2752 A871 45p multicolored   .60   .25

A872

Christmas — A873

Perf. 13½x14, 14x13½
1993, Nov. 23   **Photo.**
2753 A872 17p multicolored   .25   .25
Litho., Photo. & Engr.
2754 A873 28p multicolored   .40   .25

Jorge Guillen
(1893-1984),
Poet — A874

1993, Nov. 29   Engr.   Perf. 14x13½
2755 A874 28p green   .40   .25

UNESCO World Heritage Type of 1991

Design: 50p, Monastery of Santa Maria of
Poblet, Tarragona.

1993, Dec. 3   Engr.   Perf. 13x12½
2756 A830 50p multicolored   .65   .25

Spanish
Film
Industry
A875

29p, Luis Bunuel (1900-83), director. 55p,
Segundo de Chomon (1871-1929), film
pioneer.

1994, Jan. 28   Photo.   Perf. 14
2757 A875 29p multicolored   .40   .25
2758 A875 55p multicolored   .75   .25

Mushroom Type of 1993
1994, Feb. 18   Photo.   Perf. 14
2759 A857 18p Boletus satanas   .25   .25
2760 A857 18p Boletus edulis   .25   .25
2761 A857 29p Amanita phal-   .35   .25
            loides
2762 A857 29p Lactarius delici-   .35   .25
            osus
      Nos. 2759-2762 (4)   1.20 1.00

Minerals — A876

a, Cinnabar. b, Sphalerite. c, Pyrite. d,
Galena.

1994, Feb. 25
2763 A876 29p Block of 4, #a.-d.,
            + 2 labels   2.75 2.00

Barrister's
Mailbox
A877

Litho. & Engr.
1994, Mar. 9   Perf. 13½x14
2764 A877 29p light & dark brn   .40   .25
      Stamp Day.

ILO, 75th
Anniv.
A878

1994, Apr. 7   Photo.   Perf. 13½x14
2765 A878 65p multicolored   .85   .25

Art of
Salvador
Dali (1904-
89)
A879

Paintings: #2766, Retrato de Gala. #2767,
Poesia de America. #2768, El Gran Mas-
turbador. #2769, Port Alguer. #2770, Self portrait. #2771, Cesta del Pan. #2772, El Enigma
Sin Fin. #2173, Galatea de las Esferas.

1994, Apr. 22   Perf. 13½x14, 14x13½
2766 A879 18p multi   .25   .25
2767 A879 18p multi, vert.   .25   .25
2768 A879 29p multi   .40   .25
2769 A879 29p multi, vert.   .40   .25
2770 A879 55p multi, vert.   .80   .25
2771 A879 55p multi, vert.   .80   .25
2772 A879 65p multi   1.00 .25
2773 A879 65p multi, vert.   1.00 .25
      Nos. 2766-2773 (8)   4.90 2.00

Josep Pla (1897-1981), Writer — A880

1994, Apr. 23   Engr.   Perf. 13½x14
2774 A880 65p dark grn & lake   .85   .25

A881

Painting: Martyrdom of St. Andrew, by
Rubens.

1994, Apr. 29   Photo.   Perf. 14
2775 A881 55p multicolored   .70   .25
Carlos de Amberes Foundation, 400th anniv.

A882

A883

1994, May 3   **Photo.**
2776 A882 18p multicolored   .25   .25
Litho., Photo. & Engr.
2777 A883 29p multicolored   .40   .25
Santa Cruz de Tenerife, 400th anniv.
(#2776). Complutense University of Madrid,
700th Anniv. (#2777).

Europa
A884

Designs: 55p, Severo Ochoa (1905-93),
1959 Nobel Laureate in Medicine. 65p, Miguel
Angel Catalan (1894-1957), physicist.

1994, May 5   Litho. & Engr.
2778 A884 55p multicolored   .65   .25
2779 A884 65p multicolored   .80   .25

Spanish
Literature
A885

Novels by Camilo Jose Cela: 18p, The Family of Pascual Duarte. 29p, Journey to Alcarria.

1994, May 11   **Photo.**
2780 A885 18p multicolored   .25   .25
2781 A885 29p multicolored   .55   .25

King Sancho
Ramirez, 900th
Death
Anniv. — A886

Treaty of Tordesillas, 500th
Anniv. — A887

Design: 55p, Natl. Archives, Simancas.

Litho. & Engr.
1994, June 7   **Perf. 14**
2782 A886 18p multicolored   .25   .25
2783 A887 29p multicolored   .35   .25
2784 A887 55p multicolored   .70   .25
      Nos. 2782-2784 (3)   1.30 .75

Souvenir Sheet

Cathedral of St. Anne, Las Palmas,
Grand Canary Island — A888

1994, July 1   **Perf. 13½x14**
2785 A888 100p multicolored   2.00 1.50
Exfilna '94, Natl. Philatelic Exhibition, Grand
Canary Island.

Yachts — A889

1994, July 15   Photo.   Perf. 14x13½
2786 A889 16p Giralda   .25 .25
2787 A889 29p Saltillo   .35 .25

Roman City of Augusta Emerita
(Merida), Badajoz — A890

Litho. & Engr.
1994, Sept. 8   **Perf. 13**
2788 A890 55p lake, brn & buff   .80 .25
UNESCO World Heritage list.

Museum of Cards,
Alava — A891

Antique cards: 18p, Horse of Spades. 29p,
Jack of Diamonds. 55p, King of Hearts. 65p,
War god, Mars, of Diamonds.

1994, Sept. 20 Photo.   Perf. 14x13½
2789 A891 18p multicolored   .25 .25
2790 A891 29p multicolored   .35 .25
2791 A891 55p multicolored   .70 .25
2792 A891 65p multicolored   .90 .25
    Nos. 2789-2792 (4)   2.20 1.00

Postal Transportation — A892

1994, Oct. 11   Litho.   Perf. 13½
2793 A892 65p DC-8   .90 .25

Public Transit — A893

Civil Guard
A894

1994, Oct. 17   Photo.   Perf. 14x13½
2794 A893 18p multicolored   .25 .25
                Perf. 13½x14
2795 A894 29p multicolored   .40 .25

Western
European
Union
A895

1994, Oct. 21   **Perf. 13½x14**
2796 A895 55p multicolored   .75 .25

Olympic
Venues
A896

Designs: a, Track. b, Skiing. c, Equestrian.
d, Wrestling. e, Archery. f, Cycling. g, Soccer.
h, Field hockey. i, Swimming. j, Sailing.

1994, Oct. 27
2797   Block of 10 + 10 labels   6.00 5.00
    a.-j. A896 29p any single   .50 .40
Labels inscribed with names of Spanish
gold medalists and Intl. Olympic Committee
cent.
See Nos. 2822, 2850.

Christmas — A897

1994, Nov. 18   **Perf. 14x13½**
2798 A897 29p multicolored   .40 .25

Spanish
Motion
Pictures
A898

Designs: 30p, Belle Epoque, by Fernando
Trueba. 60p Volver A Empezar (Begin the
Beguine), by Jose Luis Garci.

1995, Jan. 20   Photo.   Perf. 14
2799 A898 30p multicolored   .40 .25
2800 A898 60p multicolored   .85 .25

City of
Logrono,
900th
Anniv.
A899

1995, Jan. 25
2801 A899 30p multicolored   .40 .25

Souvenir Sheet

SIERRA NEVADA '95,
Granada — A900

1995, Jan. 30
2802 A900 130p White star flow-
               er   1.75 1.75
World Alpine Skiing Championships.

Mushrooms — A901

19p, Coprinus comatus. 30p, Dermocybe
cinnamomea.

1995, Feb. 9   Photo.   Perf. 13½x14
2803 A901 19p multicolored   .25 .25
2804 A901 30p multicolored   .40 .25

Minerals — A902

Designs: a, Dolomite. b, Technical School
for Mining Engineers, Madrid. c, Aragonite.

1995, Feb. 24
2805   A902   Strip of 3   1.25 1.25
    a.-c.   30p any single   .40 .25

Stamp Day
A903

1995, Mar. 9   **Engr.**
2806 A903 30p Bronze lion's
               head   .40 .25

Alejandro Goicoechea Omar, TALGO
Train — A904

Design: 60p, Young Omar, early train.

1995, Mar. 17   Photo.   Perf. 14
2807 A904 30p multicolored   .40 .25
2808 A904 60p multicolored   .85 .25

A905

1995, Apr. 6
2809 A905 60p multicolored   .85 .25
Nature conservation in Europe.

A906

18th Century Sailing Ships: 19p, San Juan
Nepomuceno. 30p, San Telmo.

Litho. & Engr.
1995, Apr. 7   **Perf. 14**
2810 A906 19p multicolored   .30 .25
    a.   Miniature sheet of 4   1.20 1.20
2811 A906 30p multicolored   .70 .25
    a.   Miniature sheet of 4   2.80 2.80
    See also Nos. 2847-2848.

Lebaniego Celebration Year — A907

60p, Mountains, St. Toribio Monastery.

1995, Apr. 21   Photo.   Perf. 12½
2812 A907 30p multicolored   .40 .25
2813 A907 60p multicolored   .85 .25

Spanish
Literature
A908

Designs: 19p, El Nino Yuntero, by Miguel
Hernandez (1910-42). 30p, Juanita la Larga,
by Juan Valera (1824-1905), vert.

Litho. & Engr.
1995, Apr. 27   **Perf. 14**
2814 A908 19p multicolored   .25 .25
                Engr.
2815 A908 30p green & blue   .40 .25

Jose Marti
(1853-95),
Cuban
Writer
A909

1995, Apr. 28   **Photo.**
2816 A909 60p multicolored   .85 .25

Spanish Cartoon Characters A910

1995, May 4   Photo.   Perf. 14
2817 A910 30p Captain Trueno   .45   .25
2818 A910 60p Carpanta, vert.   .90   .25
See Nos. 2854-2855.

Europa A911

1995, May 5
2819 A911 60p multicolored   .90   .25

Motion Pictures, Cent. A912

19p, Auguste and Louis Lumiere, early camera.

1995, May 12   Engr.   Perf. 14
2820 A912 19p brownish black   .25   .25

Press Assoc. of Madrid, Cent. A913

1995, May 12   Litho.
2821 A913 30p multicolored   .45   .25

Olympic Venue Type of 1994

Designs: a, Track. b, Basketball. c, Boxing. d, Soccer. e, Gymnastics. f, Equestrian. g, Field hockey. h, Canoeing. i, Polo. j, Two-man rowing. k, Tennis. l, Shooting. m, Sailing. n, Water polo.

1995, June 2   Photo.   Perf. 14
2822   Block of 14 + 6 labels   6.25 6.25
a.-n.   A896 30p any single   .45   .25
Labels are inscribed with names of Spanish silver medallists.

UN, 50th Anniv. A914

FAO, 50th Anniv. — A915

World Tourism Organization, 20th Anniv. — A916

1995, June 26
2823 A914 60p multicolored   .90   .25
2824 A915 60p multicolored   .90   .25
2825 A916 60p multicolored   .90   .25
Nos. 2823-2825 (3)   2.70   .75

A917

1995, July 1
2826 A917 60p multicolored   .90   .25
Spanish Presidentcy of the European Community Council of Ministers.

A918

1995, Sept. 4   Photo.   Perf. 14
2827 A918 60p multicolored   .90   .25
4th World Conference on Women, Beijing.

Souvenir Sheet

17th Intl. Conference of Cartography, Barcelona — A919

1995, Sept. 5
2828 A919 130p multicolored   2.75 2.25

Santiago de Compostela University, 500th Anniv. — A920

1995, Sept. 15
2829 A920 30p multicolored   .45   .25

UNESCO World Heritage Type of 1991 and

A921

#2830, Royal Monastery of Santa Maria de Guadalupe, vert. #2831, Map of Santiago de Compostela's 9th cent. route through northern Spain.

1995, Sept. 29   Engr.   Perf. 12½
2830 A830 60p dark brown   1.00   .25

Photo. & Engr.
2831 A921 60p multicolored   1.00   .25

Ecological Protection System, Lagunas Manchegas — A922

Ducks: 60p, Anade real, pato colorado.

1995, Oct. 11   Photo.   Perf. 14
2832 A922 60p multicolored   .90   .25
America Issue.

Souvenir Sheet

EXFILNA '95, Nat. Philatelic Exhibition, Malaga — A923

Litho. & Engr.
1995, Oct. 6   Perf. 14x13½
2833 A923 130p dark green   2.00 2.00

Archaeology — A924

#2834, Cave of Menga, Antequera, Malaga. #2835, Ruins of Torralba, Minorca.

1995, Oct. 20   Photo.
2834 A924 30p multicolored   .50   .25
2835 A924 30p multicolored   .50   .25

Souvenir Sheet

The Contemporary Poets, by Antonio Maria Esquivel (1806-57) — A925

Group of poets: a, Seated at left. b, One reading from paper. c, Four standing. d, Standing, seated at right.

1995, Oct. 27
2836 A925   Sheet of 4   3.25 3.25
a.   19p multicolored   .30   .25
b.   30p multicolored   .55   .45
c.-d.   60p any single   1.25   .90

Christmas A926

Design: 30p, Capital sculpture of "Adoration of the Magi," Collegiate Church of San Martin de Elines, Cantabria.

1995, Nov. 17   Photo.   Perf. 14
2837 A926 30p multicolored   .45   .25

Espamer '96, Aviation & Space Philatelic Exhibitions, Seville — A927

#2838, Sevilla-Plaza de Armas Railway Station. #2839, Lorenzo Galindez de Carvajal, Master Courier, King Fernando's Court, vert.

1995, Dec. 20   Photo.   Perf. 13
2838 A927 60p multicolored   .90   .25
2839 A927 60p multicolored   .90   .25

Spanish Motion Pictures, Cent. A928

Designs: 30p, Scene from first Spanish motion picture, "Salida de los Fieles del Pilar de Zaragoza." 60p, Poster for 1952 motion picture, "Bienvenido, Mister Marshall."

1996, Jan. 30   Photo.   Perf. 14
2840 A928 30p multicolored   .45   .25
2841 A928 60p multicolored   .90   .25

Spanish Mining — A929

Designs: 30p, Miner's lamp from Museum of Mining and Industry, mine shaft. 60p, Fluorite.

1996, Feb. 7
2842 A929 30p multicolored   .45   .25
2843 A929 60p multicolored   .90   .25

Madrid-Irun Visual Telegraph Line, 150th Anniv. — A930

1996, Mar. 8   Engr.   Perf. 14
2844 A930 60p lake & gray grn   .90   .25
Stamp Day.

Barcelona, 10th Anniv. of Urban Transformation — A931

1996, Mar. 22
2845 A931 30p multicolored .45 .25

Endangered Wildlife — A932

1996, Mar. 27 Photo.
2846 A932 30p Ursus arctos .45 .25

18th Cent. Sailing Ship Type of 1995
Designs: 30p, King Phillip. 60p, Catalán.

Litho. & Engr.
1996, Apr. 19 Perf. 14x13½
2847 A906 30p multicolored .50 .25
a. Miniature sheet of 4 2.50 2.50
2848 A906 60p multicolored 1.00 .25
a. Miniature sheet of 4 4.50 4.50

Nos. 2847-2848 printed in miniature sheets of 4.

Madrid Bar Assoc., 400th Anniv. A933

1996, Apr. 23 Photo. Perf. 14
2849 A933 19p multicolored .30 .25

Olympic Venue Type of 1994
Symbols of Olympic venues, bronze ribbon: a, like #2797a. b, like #2822c. c, like #2797b. d, like #2797h. e, like #2797i. f, like #2822h. g, like #2822k. h, like #2822 l. i, like #2797j.

1996, Apr. 26 Photo. Perf. 14
2850 Block of 9 + 6 labels 5.00 4.50
a.-i. A896 30p Any single .50 .25

Labels are inscribed with names of Spanish bronze medalists.

Souvenir Sheets

A934

Royal Family — A935

Espamer '96 Philatelic Exhibition, World Aviation and Space Exposition: No. 2851a, Map of Seville-Larache Air Route, 1921. b, Zeppelin cover, Seville, 1930. c, Rocket launch. d, Hispano HA 200 SAETA aircraft.

1996, May 4
2851 Sheet of 4 7.00 6.50
a.-d. A934 100p any single 1.60 1.40
2852 A935 400p multicolored 7.00 6.50

Carmen Amaya, Flamenco Dancer — A936

1996, May 6 Perf. 14x13½
2853 A936 60p multicolored .90 .25

Europa.

Cartoon Characters Type of 1995
1996, May 10 Perf. 14x13½, 13½x14
2854 A910 19p El Jabato, vert. .35 .25
2855 A910 30p El Reporter Tribulete .65 .25

Paintings by Francisco de Goya Y Lucientes (1746-1828) — A937

19p, Gen. Don Antonio Ricardos, vert. 30p, Dairymaid of Bordeaux, vert. 60p, Boys with a Mastiff. 130p, The 3rd of May, 1808.

1996, May 31 Photo. Perf. 14x13½
2856 A937 19p multicolored .35 .25
2857 A937 30p multicolored .60 .25

Perf. 13½x14
2858 A937 60p multicolored 1.10 .25
2859 A937 130p multicolored 2.00 .40
Nos. 2856-2859 (4) 4.05 1.15

Philatelic Service, 50th Anniv. A938

1996, June 4 Perf. 13½x14
2860 A938 30p multicolored .65 .25

Popular Personalities — A939

Designs: 19p, José Monge Cruz, singer, vert. 30p, Lola Flores, movie star.

Perf. 14x13½, 13½x14
1996, June 14
2861 A939 19p multicolored .25 .25
2862 A939 30p multicolored .45 .25

Lanuza Central Market, Zaragoza A940

1996, July 5 Photo. Perf. 13½x14
2863 A940 30p multicolored .65 .25

19th Intl. Congress of Architects, Barcelona.

Gerardo Diego (1896-1987), Poet — A941

Joaquín Costa (1846-1911), Lawyer, Teacher — A942

1996, Sept. 13 Engr.
2864 A941 19p red, black & vio .30 .25

Litho. & Engr.
2865 A942 30p multicolored .60 .25

UNICEF, 50th Anniv. — A943

1996, Sept. 13 Photo.
2866 A943 60p blue, black & red 1.00 .25

Archaeological Finds — A944

Designs: No. 2867, Naveta Des Tudons, tomb, 2000-1500BC. No. 2868, Cabezo de Alcala, reamains of Roman temple, 54-49BC.

1996, Sept. 27 Photo.
2867 A944 30p multicolored .50 .25
2868 A944 30p multicolored .50 .25

Souvenir Sheet

Exfilna '96, Natl. Philatelic Exhibition, Vitoria-Gasteiz — A945

Painting of Vitoria-Gasteiz, capital of Alava Province, by Ignacio Diaz Ruiz de Olano (1860-1937).

1996, Oct. 11 Engr. Perf. 14x13½
2869 A945 130p rose carmine 2.25 2.00

Sheet margin is litho.

America Issue — A946

Traditional costume of Charro Region, Salamanca.

1996, Oct. 15 Photo. Perf. 14
2870 A946 60p multicolored .85 .25

Sites on UNESCO World Heritage List — A947

Designs: 19p, Albaicin, old Muslim quarter, Granada, vert. 30p, Gateway to Tiberiades Square, statue of Maimonides. 60p, Deer, De Donana Natl. Park, Huelva province, vert.

Perf. 12½x13, 13x12½
1996, Oct. 25 Engr.
2871 A947 19p dark blue violet .35 .25
2872 A947 30p deep claret .55 .25
2873 A947 60p dark blue 1.10 .25
Nos. 2871-2873 (3) 2.00 .75

Spanish Literature A948

Designs: 30p, "La Regenta," by Leopoldo Garcia-Alas Ureña (1852-1901), vert. 60p, Don Juan Tenorio, by José Zorrilla Moral (1817-93).

Perf. 14x13½, 13½x14
1996, Nov. 13 Engr.
2874 A948 30p bl, dep mag & dp vio .40 .25
2875 A948 60p dp blue & dp brn .80 .25

Christmas — A949

Birth of Christ, by Fernando Gallego.

1996, Nov. 22 Photo. Perf. 14
2876 A949 30p multicolored .40 .25

Souvenir Sheet

Official Map of Spain and Its Provinces — A950

1996, Dec. 5
2877 A950 130p multicolored 2.25 2.00

A951

Endangered species.

1997, Jan. 30   Photo.   Perf. 14x13½
2878 A951 32p Genetta genetta   .45   .25
See Nos. 2928, 2978-2980.

A952

1997, Feb. 28   Photo.   Perf. 14x13½
2879 A952 32p multicolored   .40   .25
Juvenia '97, Natl. Juvenile Philatelic Exhibition.

Stamp Day A953

1997, Mar. 7   Engr.   Perf. 14
2880 A953 65p Antique letter box 1.00   .25

Spanish Motion Pictures — A954

1997, Mar. 12   Photo.
2881 A954 21p "Trip to Nowhere"   .25   .25
2882 A954 32p "The South"   .40   .25

World Day of Water — A955

1997, Mar. 22   Perf. 14x13½
2883 A955 65p multicolored   .80   .25

19th Cent. Sailing Ships — A956

1997, Apr. 16   Litho. & Engr.
2884 A956 21p Frigate Asturias   .40   .25
a.   Miniature sheet of 4   1.50   1.50

2885 A956 32p Spanish Brigantine   .60   .25
a.   Miniature sheet of 4   3.00   3.00

Bilbao School of Engineering, Cent., — A957

194p, Atocha Station, High-Speed Spanish Train (AVE), 5th Anniv.

1997, Apr. 22   Photo.   Perf. 14x13½
2886 A957 32p multicolored   .75   .25
2887 A957 194p multicolored   3.00   .70

Dr. Josep Trueta (1897-1977), Orthopedic Surgeon — A958

1997, Apr. 30   Perf. 14
2888 A958 32p multicolored   .40   .25

Stories and Legends — A959

Europa: Princess, Prince, gnome, castle.

1997, May 5   Photo.   Perf. 14x13½
2889 A959 65p multicolored   1.25   .25

Fictional Characters A960

Designs: 21p, "El Lazarillo de Tormes," vert. 32p, "El Séneca," by José María Pemán.

1997, May 8   Engr.   Perf. 14
2890 A960 21p green & black   .30   .25
2891 A960 32p black & blue   .60   .25

Anxel Fole (1903-86), Poet, Writer A961

1997, May 17   Photo.
2892 A961 65p multicolored   1.00   .25

Comics A962

21p, The Ulysses Family. 32p, The Masked Warrior.

1997, May 30
2893 A962 21p multicolored   .30   .25
2894 A962 32p multicolored   .65   .25

Popular Personalities — A963

32p, Manuel Rodríguez Sánchez (Manolete) (1917-47), bullfighter. 65p, Charlie Rivel (Josep Andreu i Lasserre) (1896-1983), circus clown.

1997, June 5   Photo.   Perf. 14
2895 A963 32p multicolored   .50   .25
2896 A963 65p multicolored   1.25   .25

A964

"The Age of Man" Cultural Exhibition: a, 21p, Painting, "The Annunciation," from Church of Nuestra Señora de la Peña, Agreda. b, 32p, Cathedral of El Burgo de Osma. c, 65p, Miniature from Codex titled "Commentary on the Apocalypse," by Beatus of Liebana, 786AD. d, 140p, Statue of Santo Domingo de Silos.

1997, June 13   Perf. 13
2897 A964 Sheet of 4, #a.-d.   4.50 4.00

A965

1997, June 24   Perf. 14
2898 A965 65p multicolored   .80   .25
30th European Men's Basketball Championships.

NATO Summit, Madrid — A966

1997, July 8   Perf. 13
2899 A966 65p multicolored   1.25   .25

A967

Design: Natl. monument to honor grape harvesting, Requena.

1997, July 11   Litho.   Perf. 14
2900 A967 32p multicolored   .40   .25

A968

Anniversaries: 21p, Don Antonio Canovas del Castillo (1828-97), politician. 32p, Roman colony of Elche, 2000th anniv. 65p, Naval defense of Tenerife, bicent., horiz.

1997, July 24   Photo.
2901 A968 21p multicolored   .25   .25
2902 A968 32p multicolored   .40   .25
2903 A968 65p multicolored   .80   .25
Nos. 2901-2903 (3)   1.45   .75

Peace in Basque Region — A969

1997, July 30   Photo.   Perf. 14
2904 A969 32p multicolored   .35   .25

Spanish Artists — A970

Designs: 32p, Mariano Benlliure Gil (1862-1947), sculptor. 65p, Photograph of Remero Vasco, by José Ortiz Echagüe (1886-1980).

1997, Sept. 12
2905 A970 32p multicolored   .50   .25
2906 A970 65p black & beige   1.00   .25

VIGO '97, World Exposition on Fisheries A971

1997, Sept. 17   Litho.
2907 A971 32p multicolored   .35   .25

Anniversaries — A972

21p, City of Melilla, 500th anniv., vert. 32p, Declaration of St. Pascual Baylon as patron saint of World Eucharistic Congress, cent., vert. 65p, Ausias March (1397-1459), writer.

1997, Sept. 24   **Photo.**
2908 A972 21p multicolored .25 .25
2909 A972 32p multicolored .50 .25

Engr.
2910 A972 65p multicolored 1.00 .25
Nos. 2908-2910 (3) 1.75 .75

Sites on UNESCO World Heritage List — A973

Churches in Oviedo: 21p, San Julian de los Prados. 32p, Santa Cristina de Lena.

1997, Sept. 26   **Engr.**   **Perf. 13**
2911 A973 21p multicolored .50 .25
2912 A973 32p multicolored .75 .25

29th Intl. Congress of Transport and Communications Museums, Madrid — A974

1997, Oct. 1   **Litho.**   **Perf. 14x13½**
2913 A974 140p multicolored 2.00 .65

Souvenir Sheet

Monument to Don Pelayo, Revillagigedo Palace, Gijón — A975

1997, Oct. 4   **Litho. & Engr.**   **Perf. 14**
2914 A975 140p multicolored 2.50 2.00

Exfilna '97, Natl. Stamp Exhibition, Gijón, Asturias

Opening of Royal Theater, Madrid — A976

Designs: 21p, Miguel Fleta (1897-1938), opera singer. 32p, Outside view of theater.

1997, Oct. 11   **Engr.**   **Perf. 14x13½**
2915 A976 21p violet brown .25 .25
2916 A976 32p gray brown .40 .25

America Issue — A977

1997, Oct. 10   **Photo.**
2917 A977 65p Postman .80 .30

Foundation of St. Cristobal de La Laguna, 500th Anniv. — A978

1997, Oct. 17   **Litho. & Engr.**
2918 A978 32p multicolored .40 .25

6th World Conference on Down Syndrome, Madrid — A979

1997, Oct. 23   **Photo.**   **Perf. 13½x14**
2919 A979 65p blue & yellow .80 .30

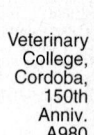

Veterinary College, Cordoba, 150th Anniv. — A980

1997, Nov. 14   **Engr.**   **Perf. 14**
2920 A980 21p green & blue .25 .25

Christmas — A981

Painting, Adoration of the Kings, by Pedro Berruguete.

1997, Nov. 20   **Photo.**
2921 A981 32p multicolored .40 .25

Jewish Heritage in Spain A982

Designs: 21p, Porta Nova, Ourense. No. 2923, Women's Gallery, Cordoba Synagogue. No. 2924, Jewish quarter, Caceres, 15th cent. 65p, Jewish Museum, Girona.

1997, Nov. 28   **Engr.**   **Perf. 13½x14**
2922 A982 21p black & brown .30 .25
2923 A982 32p black & violet .50 .25
2924 A982 32p black & brown .50 .25
2925 A982 65p black & violet 1.00 .30
   a. Strip of 4, #2922-2925 3.00 1.25

See Nos. 2969-2972.

Spanish Sports Accomplishments — A983

1997, Dec. 5   **Photo.**
2926 A983 32p multicolored 1.25 .25

XACOBEO 99 — A984

1998, Jan. 12   **Photo.**   **Perf. 14x13½**
2927 A984 35p blk, org & gray .60 .25

Endangered Fauna — A985

1998, Feb. 5
2928 A985 35p Lynx pardina .90 .25

Bilbao Athletic Club, Cent. A986

1998, Feb. 10   **Perf. 13½x14**
2929 A986 35p multicolored .45 .25

Comic Book Characters A987

Designs: 35p, Mortadelo and Filemón, by Ibáñez, vert. 70p, Zipi & Zape, by Escobar.

Perf. 14x13½, 13½x14
1998, Feb. 26   **Photo.**
2930 A987 35p multicolored .50 .25
2931 A987 70p multicolored 1.10 .45
See Nos. 2998-2999.

Gredos State Hotel A988

1998, Mar. 12   **Photo.**   **Perf. 13½x14**
2932 A988 35p multicolored .45 .25

Self-Government Statutes for Melilla and Ceuta — A989

1998, Mar. 16   **Perf. 13½x14, 14x13½**
2933 A989 150p Melilla 1.90 1.00
2934 A989 150p Ceuta, vert. 1.90 1.00

"Generation of '98" Authors — A990

Design: Azorín (José Martínez Ruiz) (1873-1967), Pío Baroja (1872-1956), Miguel de Unamuno (1864-1936), Ramiro de Maetzu (1874-1936), Antonio Machado (1875-1939), Ramon Valle Inclán (1866-1936).

1998, Apr. 3   **Photo.**   **Perf. 14**
2935 A990 70p multicolored 1.10 .45

A991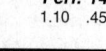

Design: Pedro Abarca de Bolea, Count of Aranda (1719-98), soldier, politician.

1998, Apr. 17
2936 A991 35p multicolored .45 .25

A992

Literary characters from: 35p, Fernando de Rojas' "Le Celestina." 70p, Benito Perez Galdos' "Fortunata and Jacinta."

1998, Apr. 29   **Engr.**   **Perf. 14x13½**
2937 A992 35p multicolored .55 .25
2938 A992 70p multicolored 1.10 .45

Ships A993

1998, Apr. 30   **Litho.**   **Perf. 14**
2939 A993 35p Embarcación real .45 .25
2940 A993 70p Jabeque tajo .90 .45

Popular Festivals — A994

1998, May 5   **Photo.**
2941 A994 70p Bonfire of St. John .90 .45

Europa.

College of Medicine, Madrid, Cent. A995

Dr. D. Carlos Jiménez Díaz (1898-1967).

1998, May 18 **Perf. 13½x14**
2942 A995 35p multicolored .45 .25

Popular Personalities — A996

35p, Félix Rodríguez de la Fuente (b. 1928), wildlife activist. 70p, Alfonso Aragón Bermúdez ("Fofó") (1923-76), circus comic, vert.

1998, May 28 **Perf. 13½x14, 14x13½**
2943 A996 35p multicolored .55 .25
2944 A996 70p multicolored 1.10 .45

King Philip II (1527-98) — A997

1998, June 1 **Photo.** **Perf. 14x13½**
2945 A997 35p multicolored .45 .25

Fedrico Garcia Lorca (1898-1936), Poet, Dramatist — A998

1998, June 2 **Litho. & Engr.**
2946 A998 35p multicolored .85 .25

Spanish Stamp Engravers A999

35p, Antonio Manso (1934-93), Spain #2129. 70p, J.L.L. Sánchez Toda (1901-), Spain #546.

1998, June 5 **Perf. 14**
2947 A999 35p multicolored .45 .25
2948 A999 70p multicolored .90 .45

Philippine Independence, Cent. — A1000

Design: Spanish flag, Basilica of Cebu, Holy Child of Cebu, Philippine flag.

1998, June 12 **Photo.** **Perf. 13½x14**
2949 A1000 70p multicolored .95 .50
See Philippines No. 2539.

Sculpture, "Foster Brothers," by Aniceto Marinas (1866-1953) A1000a

1998, July 10 **Photo.** **Perf. 14**
2949A A1000a 35p multi .50 .25

Expo '98, Lisbon A1001

1998, Sept. 4
2950 A1001 70p multicolored 1.00 .50

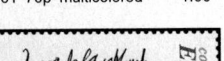

Letter Writing — A1002

Scenes from "Don Quixote" — #2951: a, "En un lugas de la Mancha." b, "Llenósele la fantasía." c, "Armado caballero." d, "La del alba sería." e, "Le molió como cibera." f, "El donoso escrutinio." g, "Has de saber, amigo Sancho." h, "Los gigantes." i, "Viole bajar y subir con tanta gracia." j, "El escuadrón de ovejas." k, "Los galeotes." l, "Los cueros."
No. 2952: a, "El encantamiento." b, "Oh princesa del toboso." c, "El caballero de los espejos." d, "El leon." e, "La cueva de montesinos." f, "Clavileño." g, "Sancho gobernador." h, "Doña Rodríguez." i, "Compañero mío." j, "Parecioles espaciosísimo." k, "El caballero de la blanca luna." l, "La vuelta a casa."

1998, Sept. 25 **Perf. 13**
2951 Sheet of 12 4.50 4.50
a.-l. A1002 20p any single .30 .25
2952 Sheet of 12 4.50 4.50
a.-l. A1002 20p any single .30 .25
See #3016, 3053-3954, 3121, 3175.

20th Intl. Conference on Data Protection, Santiago de Compostela — A1003

1998, Sept. 16 **Litho.** **Perf. 14**
2953 A1003 70p multicolored .90 .45

Souvenir Sheet

EXFILNA '98 Natl. Philatelic Exhibition — A1004

Litho. & Engr.
1998, Sept. 18 **Perf. 14**
2954 A1004 150p Cathedral of Barcelona 2.75 2.25

UNESCO World Heritage Sites — A1005

Designs: 35p, Walled city of Cuenca. 70p, Silk Exchange, Valencia.

1998, Sept. 19 **Engr.** **Perf. 13**
2955 A1005 35p blue & brown .60 .25
2956 A1005 70p red & brown 1.40 .45

Angel Ganivet (1865-98), Writer A1006

1998, Oct. 6 **Engr.** **Perf. 14**
2957 A1006 35p brown & purple .50 .25

The Giralda of Seville, 800th Anniv. — A1007

1998, Oct. 6
2958 A1007 70p multicolored 1.00 .50

A1008

1998, Oct. 8 **Engr.** **Perf. 14**
2959 A1008 35p brn & yel grn .50 .25
Aga Khan Architecture Award, Alhambra of Granada.

Stamp Day A1009

1998, Oct. 9 **Photo.**
2960 A1009 70p multicolored 1.00 .50

María Guerrero (1867-1928), Theater Actress — A1010

1998, Oct. 13
2961 A1010 70p multicolored 1.00 .50
America Issue.

Spanish Railroads, 150th Anniv. A1011

1998, Oct. 28 **Engr.**
2962 A1011 35p multicolored .50 .25

Juan Carlos I Antarctic Base A1012

1998, Nov. 6 **Photo.**
2963 A1012 35p multicolored .50 .25

A1013

Christmas (Works of art): 35p, Chestnut Seller, by Rafael Seco. 70p, Marriage of the Virgin and St. Joseph, Cathedral of Oviedo.

1998, Nov. 13
2964 A1013 35p multicolored .50 .25
2965 A1013 70p multicolored 1.00 .50

Souvenir Sheet

A1014

The Cathedral of San Salvador, Zaragoza (Details from Altarpiece: a, Holding cross, angel. b, Holy family.

1998, Nov. 11   Photo.   Perf. 14
2966 A1014 35p Sheet of 2, a.-b. 1.50 1.25

Founding of New Mexico, 400th Anniv. A1015

Designs: 35p, Expedition of Juan de Oñate. 70p, Early map of Nueva Espana (Mexico) and Nuevo Mexico.

1998, Nov. 20
2967 A1015 35p multicolored   .50 .25
2968 A1015 70p multicolored   1.00 .50

Jewish Heritage in Spain Type of 1997

Designs: No. 2969, Bust of Benjamin de Tudela, Tudela Commune, Navarre. No. 2970, Residence, Hervás Community, Cáceres. No. 2971, Courtyard, Corpus Christi Church, Segovia. No. 2972, Santa Maria la Blanca Synagogue, Toledo.

1998, Nov. 23   Engr.
2969 A982 35p dp blue & dp ol   .60 .25
2970 A982 35p dp blue & dp cl   .60 .25
2971 A982 70p dp blue & dp ol   1.10 .50
2972 A982 70p dp blue & dp cl   1.10 .50
 a.   Strip of 4, #2969-2972   4.00 4.00

Nos. 2969, 2971 have Star of David. Nos. 2970, 2972 have menorah.

UNESCO Biosphere Reserve, Minorca A1016

1998, Dec. 2   Photo.
2973 A1016 35p multicolored   .50 .25

Spanish Olympic Academy, 30th Anniv. A1017

1998, Dec. 9
2974 A1017 70p Bust of Plato, amphora   1.00 .50

Universal Declaration of Human Rights, 50th Anniv. A1018   A1019

Designs: 35p, Angel Sanz Briz (1910-80), Spanish ambassador. 70p, Fingerprints.

1998, Dec. 10
2975 A1018 35p multicolored   .50 .25
2976 A1019 70p multicolored   1.00 .50

Carthusian Horses — A1020

Designs: a, 100p, Mare standing with colt. b, 185p, Two with heads together. c, 35p, Adult standing in grass. d, 150p, Adult standing in flowers. e, 20p, Colt lying down, mare eating grass. f, 70p, Head of adult, silhouette.

1998, Dec. 29
2977 A1020   Block of 6, #a.-f.   25.00 25.00

España 2000, Intl. Philatelic Exhibition.
Issued in sheets of two blocks, the lower one in a different order. Two of the devices shown on the coat of arms appear on each block at the intersection of the perfs. On the top block the crown is on a.-b., d.-e., while the "H" is on b.-c., e.-f. On the bottom block the location of these devices is reversed, giving all the stamps in the sheet a slightly different design.
See #3019, 3052.

Gallotia simonyi machadoi A1020a

Pandion haliaetus A1020b

Puffinus puffinus — A1020c

1999, Jan. 28   Photo.   Perf. 14
2978 A1020a   35p multicolored   .50 .25
2979 A1020b   70p multicolored   1.00 .50
2980 A1020c   100p multicolored   1.40 .70
 Nos. 2978-2980 (3)   2.90 1.45

Endangered fauna.

Xacobeo '99 A1021

Designs: 35p, Stone cross of Paradela, vert. 70p, Sculpture of St. James, door on Church of St. James, Sangüesa. 100p, Stone cross, Cizur Bridge, Pamplona, vert. 185p, Jurisdictional stone pillar, Boadilla del Camino, vert.

Litho. & Engr.
1999, Feb. 22   Perf. 13¾
2981 A1021   35p multicolored   .60 .25
2982 A1021   70p multicolored   1.25 .45
2983 A1021   100p multicolored   1.50 .65
2984 A1021   185p multicolored   2.75 1.10
 Nos. 2981-2984 (4)   6.10 2.45

Barcelona Soccer Club, Cent. — A1022

1999, Mar. 11   Photo.   Perf. 14
2985 A1022 35p multicolored   .45 .25

Juvenia '99, Natl. Junior Philatelic Exhibition A1023

1999, Mar. 12   Litho.   Perf. 14
2986 A1023 35p multicolored   .50 .25

Spanish Police Force, 175th Anniv. A1024

1999, Mar. 26
2987 A1024 35p multicolored   .50 .25

Souvenir Sheet

Palace of Alfonso I el Batallador, Zaragoza — A1025

Litho. & Engr.
1999, Apr. 9   Perf. 14x13½
2988 A1025 185p multicolored   3.00 2.75

Exfilna '99, Zaragoza.

Spanish Amateur Radio Union, 50th Anniv. A1026

1999, Apr. 16   Photo.   Perf. 14
2989 A1026 70p multicolored   .95 .50

7th World Track & Field Championships, Seville — A1027

1999, Apr. 30   Photo.   Perf. 14x13½
2990 A1027 70p multicolored   .90 .45

Monfragüe Nature Park A1028

Litho. & Engr.
1999, May 5   Perf. 13½x14
2991 A1028 70p multicolored   .90 .45

Europa.

Barcelona Subway System, 75th Anniv. A1029

1999, May 7   Photo.   Perf. 14
2992 A1029 70p multicolored   .90 .45

Spanish Art — A1030

Designs: 35p, Portrait of King Solomon. 70p, Artifact from cathedral, Palencia.

1999, May 14
2993 A1030 35p multicolored   .50 .25
2994 A1030 70p multicolored   1.00 .45

Introduction of the Euro — A1031

Design: a, European Union flag.
Maps: b, Germany. c, Austria. d, Belgium e, Spain. f, Finland. g, France. h, Netherlands. i, Ireland. j, Italy. k, Luxembourg. l, Portugal.

1999, May 28   Perf. 13½x14
2995 A1031 166p Sheet of 12,
  #a.-l.   35.00 30.00

Denomination is shown in both pesetas and euros. Each stamp shows the equivilent of 1 euro in the currency of the represented country.

Royal Recreation Club of Huelva A1032

1999, June 7
2996 A1032 35p multicolored   .45 .25

Souvenir Sheet

Palma '99, Natl. Topical Philatelic Exhibition — A1033

1999, June 18   Perf. 14x13½
2997 A1033 185p multicolored   3.00 3.00

Comic Book Character Type of 1998

35p, Dona Urraca, by Jorge, vert. 70p, El Coyote, by José Mallorquí Figuerola, vert.

1999, June 11   **Photo.**   *Perf. 13¾*
2998 A987 35p multicolored   .50   .25
2999 A987 70p multicolored   1.00   .45

Defense of Las Palmas de Gran Canaria, 400th Anniv. — A1034

1999, June 25   **Litho. & Engr.**
3000 A1034 70p multicolored   .90   .45

A1035

1999, July 2   **Photo.**   *Perf. 13¾*
3001 A1035 35p multicolored   .45   .25

San Pedro de Villanueva Benedictine Monastery.

Village of Balmaseda, 800th Anniv. — A1036

1999, July 12
3002 A1036 35p multicolored   .45   .25

Carlos Buigas (b. 1898), Graphic Designer A1037

1999, July 12
3003 A1037 70p multicolored   .90   .45

General Society of Authors and Editors, Cent. — A1038

1999, July 12
3004 A1038 70p multicolored   .90   .45

Spanish Mining Institute, 150th Anniv. A1039

1999, July 12
3005 A1039 150p multicolored   1.90   .95

El Cid (Rodrigo Diaz de Vivar) (1040-99) A1040

1999, July 16   **Photo.**   *Perf. 13¾*
3006 A1040 35p multicolored   .45   .25

Paintings by Jose Vela Zanetti (1913-99) A1041

70p, "Winter." 150p, "The Harvest."

1999, Sept. 10   **Photo.**   *Perf. 13¾*
3007 A1041 70p multi   1.25   .45
3008 A1041 150p multi, vert.   2.25   .95

Diego Velazquez (1599-1660), Painter — A1042

Paintings: 35p, Sebastián de Morra. 70p, Sibyl.

1999, Sept. 24
3009 A1042 35p multicolored   .45   .25
3010 A1042 70p multicolored   .90   .45

Intl. Year of Older Persons A1043

1999, Sept. 30
3011 A1043 35p multicolored   .45   .25

Oix Castle, Lower Pyrenees A1044

1999, Oct. 1   **Engr.**   *Perf. 13½x14*
3012 A1044 70p blue & vio brn   .90   .45

World Heritage Sites — A1045

Designs: 35p, San Millán de Yuso Monastery. 70p, San Millán de Suso Monastery.

1999, Oct. 8   *Perf. 13x12½*
3013 A1045 35p multicolored   .75   .25
3014 A1045 70p multicolored   1.50   .45

UPU, 125th Anniv. A1046

1999, Oct. 9   **Photo.**   *Perf. 13¾*
3015 A1046 70p multicolored   .90   .45

Letter Writing Type of 1998

Designs: a, "Cumplimos 150 años." b, "Recorremos el mundo." c, "Llegamos juntos." d, "Escríbeme." e, "Ama la lectura." f, "Vive la naturaleza." g, "Te mostramos el patrimonio." h, "Te acercamos a la pintura." i, "Jugamos contigo." j, "Sentimos la musica." k, "Y además nos coleccionan." l, "Os esperamos."

1999, Oct. 13   **Photo.**   *Perf. 13x12½*
3016   Sheet of 12   4.50   4.50
   a.-l. A1002 20p any single   .30   .25

America Issue, A New Millennium Without Arms — A1047

1999, Oct. 15   *Perf. 13¾*
3017 A1047 70p multicolored   .90   .45

Intl. Congress of Money Museums, Madrid — A1048

1999, Oct. 18   **Engr.**   *Perf. 13x12½*
3018 A1048 70p blue & brown   .90   .45

Carthusian Horse Type of 1998

Designs: a, 185p, White horse, six men. b, 70p, Espana Intl. Philatelic Exhibition emblem. c, 100p, Two white horses. d, 150p, Two white horses, one with leg raised. e, 35p, Emblem, exhibition dates. f, 20p, Horse, handler.

1999, Nov. 3   **Photo.**   *Perf. 13¾*
3019 A1020 Block of 6, #a.-f.   14.00   14.00
   See footnote following No. 2977.

Christmas A1049

35p, Adoration of the Magi, Toledo Cathedral retable. 70p, Child, statue, candles.

1999, Nov. 5
3020 A1049 35p multi, vert.   .60   .25
3021 A1049 70p multi   1.25   .45

Spanish Postage Stamps, 150th Anniv. A1050

a, King Juan Carlos, altered 12c design A2. b, King, altered 6c design A1. c, King, altered 5r design A2. d, King, altered 6r design A2. e, 150th anniv. emblem, altered 6c design A1. f, King, altered 10r design A2. g, King, coat of arms.

Litho. & Engr.

2000, Jan. 3   *Perf. 13¾x14*
3022   Sheet of 12   7.00   6.50
   a.-g. A1050 35p any single   .60   .25

#3022 contains 2 ea #3022a-3022d, 3022f, 1 ea #3022e, 3022g.

Endangered Butterflies — A1051

Designs: 35p, Parnassius apollo. 70p, Agriades zullichi.

2000, Jan. 31   **Photo.**   *Perf. 13¾*
3023 A1051 35p multi   .60   .25
3024 A1051 70p multi   1.25   .45

First Printing at Montserrat Monastery, 500th Anniv. — A1052

2000, Feb. 4   **Photo.**   *Perf. 13¾*
3025 A1052 35p multi   .45   .25

Holy Roman Emperor Charles V (1500-58) A1053

2000, Feb. 24   *Perf. 12¾x13*
3026 A1053 35p shown   .60   .25
3027 A1053 70p At age 40   1.25   .45

Souvenir Sheet
Perf. 13¼x12¾
3028 A1053 150p In armor   2.75   1.75

No. 3028 contains one 40x49mm stamp. See Belgium Nos. 1791-1793.

"Age of Man" Exhibition, Astorga — A1054

Designs: 70p, Carving of the Virgin Mary. 100p, Cross, Arab perfume bottle.

2000, Mar. 24   **Photo.**   *Perf. 14x13¾*
3029 A1054 70p multi   .75   .40
3030 A1054 100p multi   1.10   .55

Ferdinand of Aragon Inn, Sos A1055

2000, Apr. 7   *Perf. 13¾x14*
3031 A1055 35p multi   .60   .25

University Anniversaries — A1056

35p, Lleida, 700th anniv. 70p, Valencia, 500th anniv. (in 1999).

2000, Apr. 12 Engr. Perf. 13¾x14
3032 A1056 35p red lil & brown .50 .25
3033 A1056 70p blue & choc 1.00 .40

A1057

2000, Apr. 28 Photo. Perf. 14x13¾
3034 A1057 35p multi .60 .25

Royal Barcelona Sports Club, soccer team, cent.

A1058

2000, May 4
3035 A1058 35p multi .60 .25

María de las Mercedes de Borbón y Orleáns (1910-2000), mother of King Juan Carlos.

Europa Issue
Common Design Type
2000, May 9
3036 CD17 70p multi .75 .40

Royal Academy of Medicine, Seville, 300th Anniv. A1060

Julio Rey Pastor (1888-1962), Mathematician — A1061

Pharmacy College of Granada, 150th Anniv. — A1062

Valencia, City of Arts and Sciences A1063

2000, May 25 Perf. 13¾x14, 14x13¾
3037 A1060 35p multi .60 .25
3038 A1061 70p multi 1.00 .40
3039 A1062 100p multi 1.50 .55
3040 A1063 185p multi 3.00 1.00
  Nos. 3037-3040 (4) 6.10 2.20

Intl. Mathematics Year (No. 3038).

Comic Strips A1064

Designs: 35p, Las Hermanas Gilda, by Manuel Vázquez. 70p, Roberto Alcázar y Pedrín, by Eduardo Vañó, vert.

2000, May 26 Perf. 13¾x14, 14x13¾
3041 A1064 35p multi .60 .25
3042 A1064 70p multi 1.25 .40

Guggenheim Museum, Bilbao — A1065

2000, June 2 Photo. Perf. 13¾x14
3043 A1065 70p multi 1.00 .40

Bilbao, 700th anniv.

Angel From Prayer in the Garden, Sculpture by Francisco Salzillo (1707-73) A1066

2000, June 9 Photo. Perf. 14x13¼
3044 A1066 70p multi 1.10 .40

Souvenir Sheet

Fountains of San Francisco, Aviles — A1067

Litho. & Engr.
2000, June 16 Perf. 14x13¾
3045 A1067 185p multi 3.50 2.50

Exfilna 2000 Philatelic Exhibition, Aviles.

Trees A1068

Designs: 70p, Pinus sylvestris. 150p, Quercus ilex (encina).

Perf. 12¾x12½
2000, June 19 Photo.
3046-3047 A1068 Set of 2 3.50 1.10

Local Festivals A1069

Designs: 35p, Fire Walking Festival, San Pedro Manrique. 70p, Chivalry Festival of San Juan, Ciudadela.

2000, June 23 Perf. 13¾x14
3048-3049 A1069 Set of 2 1.60 .55

Josemaria Escrivá de Balaguer (1902-75), Founder of Opus Dei. A1070

Litho. & Engr.
2000, June 26 Perf. 13¾x14
3050 A1070 70p black & orange 1.10 .40

Souvenir Sheet

World Map of Juan de la Cosa, 500th Anniv. — A1071

2000, July 14 Photo. Perf. 13¾x14
3051 A1071 150p multi 2.50 1.50

Carthusian Horses Type of 1998

No. 3052: a, 20p, Head of horse, five horses. b, 35p, White horse, sun partially obscured by clouds. c, 70p, Horse's head, two horses galloping. d, 100p, Heads of two horses. e, 150p, Horse's head, horse in lilac. f, 185p, Horse with bridle.

2000, July 28
3052 A1020 Block of 6, #a-f 13.00 13.00
  See note following No. 2977.

Letter Writing Type of 1998

No. 3053: a, Atapuerca Man, 800,000 B.C. b, Cave paintings of Altamira, 12,000 B.C. c, Phoenecians, 1100 B.C. d, Tartessians, 800 B.C. e, Iberians and Celts, 500 B.C. f, Lady of Elche, Iberian statue, 480 B.C. g, Carthaginians, 237 B.C. h, Roman Spain, 197 B.C. i, Viriathus, Lusitanian war leader against Romans, 147 B.C. j, Siege of Numantia, 133 B.C. k, Segovia aqueduct, A.D. 50. l Vandals, Suebis, and Alanis, 409.
No. 3054: a, Visigoths, 415. b, Conversion of Recared to Catholicism, 589. c, Arabs, 711. d, Victory over Arabs by Asturian King, Pelayo, 722. e, Discovery of alleged tomb of St. James, 813. f, Collapse of the caliphate, 1031. g, Death of El Cid, 1099. h, Alfonso VIII's victory at Las Navas de Tolosa, 1212. i, Alfonso X (the Wise) becomes King, 1252. j, Trastámara Dynasty, 1369. k, Spanish Inquisition, 1478. l, Union of Aragon and Castile, 1479.

2000, Sept. 22 Perf. 13x12¾
3053 Sheet of 12 2.50 2.50
  a.-l. A1002 20p Any single .25 .25
3054 Sheet of 12 2.50 2.50
  a.-l. A1002 20p Any single .25 .25

World Heritage Sites — A1072

Designs: 35p, Las Médulas. 70p, Pyrénées — Mt. Perdido, vert. 150p, Catalan Music Palace, Barcelona.

Perf. 13x12¾(35p), 12¾
2000, Sept. 21 Litho. (35p), Engr.
3055-3057 A1072 Set of 3 2.75 1.40

Souvenir Sheets

España 2000 Intl. Philatelic Exhibition — A1073

Designs: No. 3058, Hand of Julio Iglesias, singer. No. 3059, Signature of Alejandro Sanz, singer. No. 3060, Signature of Antonio Banderas, movie star. No. 3061, Mannequin, signature of Jesús del Pozo, fashion designer. No. 3062, Signature of Miguel Induráin, cyclist. No. 3063, Soccer ball, signature of Raúl González, soccer player. No. 3064, Hands of Joaquín Cortés, dancer. No. 3065, Feet of Sara Baras, dancer. No. 3066, Emblem of TVE 1 television network. No. 3067, Radio and antenna. No. 3068, Newspaper mastheads.
  Illustration reduced.

Perf. 13 (round stamps), 13¾x14
2000 Photo.
3058-3068 A1073 200p Set of 11 35.00 35.00

150th anniv. of Spanish stamps, #3066. Nos. 3060-3061, 3064-3068 each contain one 41x28mm rectangular stamp.
  Exist imperf. Value $65.
  Issued: #3058-3059, 10/6; #3060, 10/7; #3061, 10/8; #3062-3063, 10/9; #3064-3065, 10/10; #3066, 10/11; #3067, 10/12; #3068, 10/13.

Alfredo Kraus (1927-99), Operatic Tenor — A1074

2000, Oct. 27 Perf. 14x13¾
3069 A1074 70p multi 1.00 .40

America Issue, Fight Against AIDS — A1075

2000, Oct. 19 Photo. Perf. 14x13¾
3070 A1075 70p multi 1.00 .40

Christmas
A1076

Designs: 35p, Nativity scene. 70p, Birth of Christ, by Conrad von Soest.

2000, Nov. 9   **Perf. 12¾**
3071-3072 A1076 Set of 2   1.50 .55
See Germany No. B878-B879.

Santa María la Real Church, Aranda de Duero — A1077

2000, Nov. 10 Engr.   **Perf. 14x13¾**
3073 A1077 35p brown   .50 .25

Spanish Literature
A1078

Designs: 35p, Entre Naranjos, by Vicente Blasco Ibáñez. 70p, La Venganza de Don Mendo, by Pedro Muñoz Seca. 100p, El Alcalde Zalamea, by Pedro Calderón de la Barca.

Photo., Engr. (100p)
2000, Nov. 17   **Perf. 13¾x14**
3074-3076 A1078 Set of 3   3.25 1.50

Commercial Agents College, 75th Anniv. — A1079

2001, Jan. 8 Photo.   **Perf. 14x13¾**
3077 A1079 40p multi   .60 .25

Fire Fighters — A1080

2001, Jan. 19
3078 A1080 75p multi   1.10 .45

Infantry College, Toledo, 150th Anniv.
A1081

2001, Feb. 16   **Perf. 13¾x14**
3079 A1081 120p multi   2.00 .65

Intl. Campaign Against Domestic Violence — A1082

2001, Feb. 22   **Perf. 14x13¾**
3080 A1082 155p multi   2.25 .85

First Spanish Mail Box, Mayorga
A1083

2001, Mar. 2 Engr.   **Perf. 13¾x14**
3081 A1083 155p black   2.25 .85
Stamp Day.

Juvenia 2001, Natl. Youth Philatelic Exhibition
A1084

2001, Mar. 9   **Photo.**
3082 A1084 120p multi   1.75 .70

Placencia Inn — A1084a

2001, Mar. 16   **Perf. 14x13¾**
3083 A1084a 40p multicolored   .60 .25

Famous People
A1085

Designs: 40p, Joaquín Rodrigo (1901-99), musician. 75p, Rafael Alberti (1902-99), writer.

2001, Mar. 22 Engr.   **Perf. 13¾x14**
3084-3085 A1085 Set of 2   1.75 .60

Castles
A1086

Designs: 40p, Zuda, Tortosa, vert. 75p, Cid, Jadraque. 155p, San Fernando, Figueres. 260p, Montesquiu, Montesquiu.

2001, Apr. 20   **Perf. 14x13¾, 13¾x14**
3086-3089 A1086 Set of 4   8.00 3.00

Book Day — A1087

2001, Apr. 23 Photo.   **Perf. 14x13¾**
3090 A1087 40p multi   .60 .25

Souvenir Sheet

First Flights, 75th Anniv. — A1088

No. 3091: a, 40p, Spain-Argentina. b, 75p, Spain-Philippines. c, 155p, Spain-Equatorial Guinea. d, 260p, Commemorative flight.

2001, Apr. 26   **Perf. 13¾x14**
3091 A1088   Sheet of 4, #a-d   8.00 3.00

Grand Theater, Liceu — A1089

2001, Apr. 27   **Perf. 14x13¾**
3092 A1089 120p multi   1.75 .65

King Juan Carlos — A1091

2001   **Photo.**   **Perf. 12¾x13¼**
3093 A1091   5p sil & lil rose   .25 .25
3094 A1091   40p sil & yel grn   .60 .25
3095 A1091   75p sil & bl vio   1.10 .40
3096 A1091   100p sil & lt red brn   1.50 .55
   Nos. 3093-3096 (4)   3.45 1.45

Issued: 40p, 5/4; 5p, 75p, 6/28; 100p, 7/15. See also Nos. 3133-3140, 3271-3274, 3337-3343, 3387-3391.

Europa — A1092

2001, May 9 Photo.   **Perf. 14x13¾**
3097 A1092 75p multi   .80 .40

Architecture
A1093

Designs: 40p, San Martiño Church, Noia. 75p, Santa Maria Cathedral, Tui. 155p, Villaconcha dovecote, Frechilla.

Engr., Photo. (75p)
2001, May 17   **Perf. 14x13¾**
3098-3100 A1093 Set of 3   4.00 1.50

Luarca Harbor
A1094

2001, May 26 Photo.   **Perf. 13¾x14**
3101 A1094 40p multi   .60 .25

Cardinal Rodrigo de Castro (1523-1600) — A1095

2001, June 1
3102 A1095 40p multi   .60 .25

Leopoldo Alas, "Clarín," (1852-1901), Writer — A1096

2001, June 13
3103 A1096 75p multi   1.10 .40

Trees
A1097

Designs: 40p, Olive. 75p, Beech.

2001, June 22   **Perf. 12¾**
3104-3105 A1097 Set of 2   1.75 .60

King's Soccer Cup, 25th Anniv.
A1098

2001, July 6 Litho.   **Perf. 13¾x14**
3106 A1098 40p multi   .60 .25
Issued in sheets of 8 + 4 labels.

Local Festivals
A1099

Designs: 40p, Cipotegato, Tarazona. 120p, Giants of Pí, Barcelona, vert.

Perf. 13¾x14, 14x13¾
2001, July 10   **Photo.**
3107-3108 A1099 Set of 2   2.40 .80

Baltasar Gracian (1601-58), Writer A1100

2001, July 13   *Perf. 13¾x14*
3109 A1100 120p multi   1.75 .60

"Age of Man" Exhibition — A1101

Designs: 120p, Our Lady of La Calva. 155p, Cathedral dome, Zamora.

2001, July 20   Engr.   *Perf. 14x13¾*
3110-3111 A1101   Set of 2   4.00 1.50

Grandparent's Day — A1102

Siervas de Jesús de la Caridad A1103

Perf. 14x13¾, 13¾x14
2001, July 26   Photo.
3112 A1102 40p multi   .60 .25
3113 A1103 75p multi   1.10 .40

Salamanca, European City of Culture — A1104

2001, Sept. 5   Photo.   *Perf. 13x13¼*
3114 A1104 75p multi   1.10 .40

Covadonga Basilica, Cent. of Consecration — A1105

2001, Sept. 7   *Perf. 13¾x14*
3115 A1105 40p multi   .60 .25

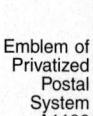 

Emblem of Privatized Postal System A1106

2001, Sept. 15
3116 A1106 40p multi   .60 .25

Souvenir Sheet

Exfilna 2001 Natl. Philatelic Exhibition, Vigo — A1107

Engr. (Litho. Margin)
2001, Sept. 21
3117 A1107 260p multi   4.00 4.00

St. Dominic of Silos (c. 1000-73) — A1108

Litho. & Engr.
2001, Oct. 4   *Perf. 14x13¾*
3118 A1108 40p multi   .60 .25
   a.   Souvenir sheet of 1 with margin like stamp design   .60 .60
   b.   Souvenir sheet of 1 with margin differing   .60 .60

Year of Dialogue Among Civilizations A1109

2001, Oct. 9   Photo.
3119 A1109 120p multi   1.75 .70
Stamp Day.

Posidonia Oceanica, Ses Salines Nature Reserve A1110

2001, Oct. 15   *Perf. 13¾x14*
3120 A1110 155p multi   2.25 .85
America issue — UNESCO World Heritage Sites.

Letter Writing Type of 1998
No. 3121: a, Christopher Columbus, 1492. b, Treaty of Tordesillas, 1494. c, Election of King Charles I as Holy Roman Emperor Charles V, 1519. d, Conquest of Mexico by Hernán Cortés, 1519. e, Circumnavigation by Juan Sebastián Elcano, 1522. f, Campaign against Incas by Francisco Pizarro, 1532. g, Ascension to throne of King Philip II, 1556. h, Start of construction of El Escorial Monastery, 1563. i, Battle of Lepanto, 1571. j, Saints John of the Cross, Teresa of Jesus and painter El Greco, 1580. k, First play by Lope de Vega, 1593. l, Ascension to throne of King Philip III, 1598.

2001, Oct. 19   *Perf. 13x12½*
3121   Sheet of 12   5.25 5.25
   a.-l.   A1002 25p Any single   .40 .25

Souvenir Sheet

Bullfighter Curro Romero — A1111

2001, Oct. 25   *Perf. 14x13¾*
3122 A1111 260p multi   4.00 4.00

Christmas A1112

Designs: 40p, Virgin With Child, by Alfredo Roldan. 75p, Adoration of the Shepherds, by José Ribera.

2001, Nov. 8   *Perf. 12¾*
3123-3124 A1112   Set of 2   1.75 .60
   a.   Souvenir sheet, # 3123-3124, Germany #B895-B896, litho., perf. 13¼   5.50 5.50
See Germany No. B896a.

Score of "El Sombrero de Tres Picos," by Manuel de Falla (1876-1946) — A1113

2001, Nov. 14   Photo.   *Perf. 13¾x14*
3125 A1113 75p multi   1.10 .40

Comic Strips A1114

Designs: 40p, Cartoon by Josep Coll i Coll. 75p, Rompetechos, by Francisco Ibañez.

2001, Nov. 20
3126-3127 A1114   Set of 2   1.75 .60

Carlos Cano (1946-2000), Singer — A1115

2001, Nov. 23   *Perf. 14x13¾*
3128 A1115 40p black   .60 .25

Intl. Volunteer Day for Economic and Social Development A1116

2001, Nov. 27
3129 A1116 120p multi   1.75 .70

World Heritage Sites — A1117

No. 3130: a, Catalan Romanesque Churches of the Vall de Boí. b, The Mystery of Elx (Elche). c, Hospital de Sant Pau, Barcelona. d, San Cristóbal de La Laguna. e, Archaeological Site of Atapuerca. f, Palmeral de Elche. g, Monuments of Oviedo. h, Roman Walls of Lugo. i, Rock Art of the Mediterranean Basin. j, Ibiza, Biodiversity and Culture. k, Archaeological Ensemble of Tarraco. l, University and Historic Precinct of Alcalá de Henares.

2001, Nov. 30   *Perf. 12¾*
3130   Sheet of 12   7.00 7.00
   a.-l.   A1117 40p Any single   .60 .25

Souvenir Sheet

Ministry of Development, 150th Anniv. — A1118

No. 3131 — Maps showing: a, 40p, Automated postal centers. b, 75p, Ports. c, 120p, High-speed train lines. d, 155p, Airports. e, 260p, Highways.

2001, Dec. 11
3131 A1118   Sheet of 5, #a-e, + label   11.00 10.00

Souvenir Sheet

King Juan Carlos, 25th Anniv. of Reign — A1119

No. 3132: a, 40p, Crown Prince Felipe. b, 40p, Princess Elena (patterned dress). c, 40p, Royal arms. d, 40p, Princess Cristina (black dress). e, 75p, King Juan Carlos. f, 75p, Queen Sofia. g, 260p, Royal palace, Madrid (49x28mm).

2001, Dec. 14   *Perf. 12¾x13¼*
3132 A1119   Sheet of 7, #a-g   10.00 10.00

100 Cents = 1 Euro (€)
King Juan Carlos Type of 2001 With Euro Denominations Only
2002, Jan. 2   Photo.   *Perf. 13½x14*
3133 A1091   1c sil & black   .25 .25
3134 A1091   5c sil & brt blue   .25 .25
3135 A1091   10c sil & gray blue   .25 .25
3136 A1091   25c sil & claret   .60 .25
3137 A1091   50c sil & gray   1.25 .35

3138 A1091 75c sil & red lil   1.90 .55
Perf. 12¾x13¼
3139 A1091 €1 sil & green   2.50 .75
3140 A1091 €2 sil & ver   5.00 1.50
Nos. 3133-3140 (8)   12.00 4.15

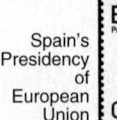

Spain's Presidency of European Union
A1120

Color of star at UR: 25c, Orange. 50c, White.

2002, Jan. 2   Photo.   Perf. 13¾x14
3141-3142 A1120   Set of 2   1.90 .65

Trees
A1121

Designs: 50c, Savin (sabina). 75c, Elm (olmo).

2002, Jan. 25   Perf. 12¾
3143-3144 A1121   Set of 2   3.00 1.10

A1122   A1123
A1124   A1125
A1126   A1127

A1128   A1129

Flowers
A1128   A1129
Die Cut Perf. 13
2002, Feb. 20   Litho.
Self-Adhesive
3145   Booklet of 8   5.50
  a. A1122 25c multi   .60 .25
  b. A1123 25c multi   .60 .25
  c. A1124 25c multi   .60 .25
  d. A1125 25c multi   .60 .25
  e. A1126 25c multi   .60 .25
  f. A1127 25c multi   .60 .25
  g. A1128 25c multi   .60 .25
  h. A1129 25c multi   .60 .25

España 2002 Youth Philatelic Exhibition, Salamanca
A1130

Designs: 50c, Exhibition emblem. €1.80, Emblem and New Cathedral, vert.

2002, Feb. 22   Photo.   Perf. 13¾x14
3146 A1130   50c multi   1.25 .45
Souvenir Sheet
Perf. 14x13¾
3147 A1130   €1.80 multi   5.00 4.50
See No. 3183.

Father Francisco Piquer, Founder of Pawn Brokerage
A1131

2002, Feb. 25   Litho.   Perf. 14x13¾
3148 A1131 25c multi   .60 .25
Caja Madrid Savings Bank, 300th anniv.

Real Madrid Soccer Team, Cent.
A1132

2002, Feb. 25   Perf. 13¾x14
3149 A1132 75c yel & gray   1.90 .65

Souvenir Sheet

Tarazona Town Hall Portico — A1133

2002, Feb. 26
3150 A1133 €2.10 multi   5.25 5.25
Philaiberia '02, Tarazona.

Alejandro Mon (1801-82), Politician — A1134

2002, Feb. 27   Perf. 14x13¾
3151 A1134 25c multi   .60 .25

Retirement of Peseta Currency — A1135

2002, Feb. 28   Litho.
3152 A1135 25c multi   .60 .25

Sil Canyons, Ribiera Sacra — A1136

Cabo de Gata Natl. Park
A1137

2002, Mar. 8   Perf. 14x13¾, 13¾x14
3153 A1136 75c multi   2.00 .65
3154 A1137 €2.10 multi   5.50 2.75

Zaragoza Military Academy, 75th Anniv. — A1138

2002, Mar. 15   Perf. 14x13¾
3155 A1138 25c multi   .60 .25

Real Unión Soccer Team, Cent. — A1139

2002, Mar. 22
3156 A1139 50c multi   1.25 .45

Stamp Day
A1140

2002, Mar. 25   Perf. 13¾x14
3157 A1140 25c multi   .60 .25

Castle Type of 2001
Designs: 25c, Banyeres de Mariola. 50c, Soutomaior. 75c, Catalorao.

2002, Apr. 8   Engr.   Perf. 13¾x14
3158-3160 A1086   Set of 3   3.75 1.40

Tudela, 1200th Anniv.
A1141

2002, Apr. 12   Photo.
3161 A1141 75c multi   1.90 .70

Monastery of Sant Cugat, 1000th Anniv.
A1142

2002, Apr. 12
3162 A1142 €1.80 multi   4.50 2.25

Luis Cernuda (1902-63), Poet
A1143

2002, May 8
3163 A1143 50c multi   .90 .45

Dr. Federico Rubio (1827-1902) — A1144

2002, May 8
3164 A1144 50c multi   1.25 .45

Europa
A1145

2002, May 9
3165 A1145 50c multi   1.25 .45

Reincorporation of Menorca to Spanish Crown, Bicent. — A1146

2002, May 10
3166 A1146 50c multi   1.25 .45

World Equestrian Games — A1147

No. 3167: a, Carriage driving. b, Endurance (Raid). c, Dressage (Doma). d, Reining. e, Vaulting (Volteo). f, Jumping (Saltos). g, Three-day event (Completo).

2002, May 11   Perf. 12¾x13¼
3167   Sheet of 7 + 2 labels   9.50 9.50
  a.-e. A1147 25c Any single   .60 .25
  f. A1147 75c multi   1.90 .70
  g. A1147 €1.80 multi   4.50 2.25

Dolores Peinado (1819-94), Character From Folk Song "La Dolores" A1148

2002, May 31   **Perf. 13¾x14**
3168 A1148 50c multi   1.25 .50

Souvenir Sheet

Exfilna 2002 Natl. Philatelic Exhibition, Salamanca — A1149

No. 3169 — Plaza Mayor, Salamanca: a, 25c, West facade. b, 25c, City Hall. c, 25c, Royal Pavilion. d, €1.80, Aerial view.

Engr. (#a-c), Litho. (#d, margin)
2002, July 7   **Perf. 13¾x14**
3169 A1149 Sheet of 4, #a-d 6.25 6.25

Iberian Airlines, 75th Anniv. A1150

Airplanes: 25c, Rohrbach R-VIII Roland. 50c, Boeing 747.

2002, June 10 Photo.   Perf. 13¾x14
3170-3171 A1150 Set of 2 1.90 .75

Wine Producing Regions — A1151

Grapes and map of: 25c, Rias Baixas region. 50c, Rioja region. 75c, Manzanilla — Sanlúcar de Barrameda region.

2002   **Perf. 14x13¼**
3172-3174 A1151 Set of 3 3.75 1.50
Issued: 25c, 7/27; 50c, 75c, 9/20.

Letter Writing Type of 1998

No. 3175: a, Publication of *Don Quixote*, by Miguel de Cervantes, 1605. b, Accession to throne of King Philip IV and rise in power of Conde-Duque de Olivares, 1621. c, Rivalry of poets Francisco de Quevedo and Luis de Góngora, 1620. d, Painting of "Las Meninas" by Diego Velázquez, 1656. e, Accession to throne of King Charles II, 1665. f, Accession to throne of King Philip V, 1701. g, Accesstion to throne of King Ferdinand VI, 1746. h, Accession to throne of King Charles III, 1759. i, Squillaci Riots, 1766. j, Gaspar Melchor de Jovellanos, 1787. k, Accession to throne of King Charles IV, 1788. l, Appointment of Manuel de Godoy as prime minister, 1792.

2002, Sept. 27   **Perf. 12¾**
3175   Sheet of 12   4.50 4.50
a.-l.   A1002 10c Any single .30 .25

Expiatory Temple of the Holy Family, by Architect Antonio Gaudí (1852-1926) A1152

2002, Sept. 27 Litho.   Perf. 14x13¾
3176 A1152 50c blue & black 1.25 .50

A1153

A1154

A1155

A1156

A1157

A1158

A1159

Paintings With Musical Instruments by Goyo Domínguez A1160

2002, Sept. 30   Die Cut Perf. 13
Self-Adhesive

3177   Booklet pane of 8   5.00
a.   A1153 25c multi   .60 .25
b.   A1154 25c multi   .60 .25
c.   A1155 25c multi   .60 .25
d.   A1156 25c multi   .60 .25
e.   A1157 25c multi   .60 .25
f.   A1158 25c multi   .60 .25
g.   A1159 25c multi   .60 .25
h.   A1160 25c multi   .60 .25

America Issue — Youth, Education and Literacy A1161

2002, Oct. 14 Photo.   Perf. 13¾x14
3178 A1161 75c multi   1.90 .75

Almanzor (Muhammad ibn Abu Amir al-Mansur, c. 938-1002), Caliph of Córdoba — A1162

2002, Oct. 25
3179 A1162 75c multi   1.90 .75

Dijous Bó Fair, Mallorca — A1163

2002, Nov. 4   **Perf. 14x13¾**
3180 A1163 75c multi   1.90 .75

UNESCO World Heritage Sites — A1164

No. 3181 — Architectural details of: a, Aranjuez. b, Santa Maria Church, Calatayud. c, San Martin Church, Teruel. d, Santa Maria Church, Tobed. e, Santa Tecla Church, Cervera de la Cañada. f, San Pablo Church, Zaragoza.

2002, Nov. 8
3181 A1164 Sheet of 7, #a-
          d, f, 2 #e, + 5
          labels   19.00 19.00
a.-b.   25c Either single .60 .25
c.   50c multi   1.25 .50
d.   75c multi   1.90 .75
e.   €1.80 multi   4.50 2.25
f.   €2.10 multi   5.25 2.75

The two examples of No. 3181e are tete-beche in the sheet.

Alcañiz Inn — A1164a

2002, Nov. 15   **Perf. 13¾x14**
3182 A1164a 25c multicolored .60 .25

España 2002 Youth Philatelic Exhibition, Salamanca — A1165

Designs: No. 3183a, 50c, Like #3146. Nos. 3183b, 3190, 75c, Character from comic Strip "El Capitan Alatriste," by Arturo Pérez-Reverte. Nos. 3183c, 3185, 75c, Television and names of television shows. Nos. 3183d, 3189, 75c, Hand and compact disc. Nos. 3183e, 3187, 75c, Radio, musical notes and logos of Spanish radio stations. Nos. 3183f, 3188, 75c, Skier, race car, soccer ball, bicyclist and names of Spanish sports stars. Nos. 3183g, 3186, 75c, Photojournalist. Nos. 3183h, 3184, 75c, Clapboard and names of Spanish film personalities. No. 3183i, €1.80, Like #3147, vert.

2002   Litho.   Die Cut Perf. 13
Self-Adhesive (#3183)

3183 A1165 Sheet of 9   19.00 19.00
a.   50c multi   1.25 .50
b.-h.   75c Any single   1.90 .75
i.   €1.80 multi   4.50 2.25
Souvenir Sheets
Perf. 13¾x14
3184-3190 A1165 Set of 7 11.50 11.50

Issued: No. 3183, 11/17; No. 3184, 11/18; No. 3185, 11/19; No. 3186, 11/20; No. 3187, 11/21; No. 3188, 11/22; No. 3189, 11/23; No. 3190, 11/24.

No. 3183 exists with at least three different pictures on backing paper.

San Jorge Church, Alcoy — A1166

Litho. & Engr.
2002, Nov. 25   **Perf. 14x13¾**
3191 A1166 75c multi   1.90 .75

Compludo Forge, León A1167

2002, Nov. 27   **Perf. 13¾x14**
3192 A1167 50c multi   1.25 .50

Souvenir Sheet

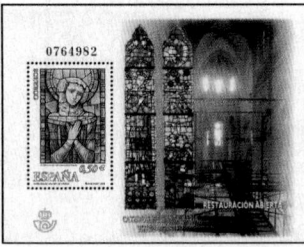

Stained Glass Window, Santa Maria Cathedral, Vitoria-Gasteiz — A1168

2002, Nov. 27   **Perf. 14x13¾**
3193 A1168 50c multi   1.50 1.00

Crucifix, Hío — A1169

2002, Nov. 29
3194 A1169 25c multi   .60 .25

Christmas A1170

Designs: 25c, Adoration of the Magi, from church altarpiece, Calzadilla de los Barros. 50c, Maternity, by Goyo Dominguez.

2002, Nov. 29   **Photo.**
3195-3196 A1170 Set of 2   1.90 .75

Opening of Somport Tunnel A1171

2003, Jan. 17 Photo. Perf. 13¾x14
3197 A1171 51c multi   1.10 .55

Traditional Dress from Ansó Valley — A1172

2003, Jan. 20   Perf. 14x13¾
3198 A1172 76c multi   1.75 .85

World Leprosy Day, 50th Anniv. — A1173

2003, Jan. 21
3199 A1173 26c multi   .55 .30

Pedro Rodríguez de Campomanes (1723-1802), Jurist — A1174

2003, Feb. 14
3200 A1174 26c multi   .55 .30

Juvenia 2003 Natl. Youth Philatelic Exhibition, Benissa A1175

2003, Feb. 21   Perf. 13¾x14
3201 A1175 51c multi   1.10 .55

Práxedes Mateo Sagasta (1825-1903), Politician — A1176

2003, Mar. 11
3202 A1176 26c multi   .55 .30

ABC Newspaper, Cent. A1177

2003, Mar. 17
3203 A1177 €2.15 multi   4.50 2.25

Nobel Prize Winners For Physiology or Medicine From Spain — A1178

No. 3204: a, Santiago Ramón y Cajal, 1906. b, Severo Ochoa, 1959.

Litho. & Engr.
2003, Mar. 20   Perf. 13x12¾
3204 A1178 Horiz. pair   3.25 3.25
  a.   51c multi   1.25 .55
  b.   76c multi   1.90 .80

See Sweden No. 2460.

School of Civil Engineering, Madrid, Bicent. — A1179

Designs: 26c, Tui Bridge. No. 3206: a, Estrecho de Puentes Dam. b, El Musel Port.

2003, Mar. 21 Photo. Perf. 13¾x14
3205 A1179 26c multi   .55 .30
Souvenir Sheet
3206   Sheet of 3, #3205,
        3206a, 3206b   4.00 2.00
  a.   A1179 51c multi   1.25 .55
  b.   A1179 76c multi   1.75 .80

La Verdad Newspaper, Cent. A1180

2003, Mar. 26
3207 A1180 26c multi   .55 .30

Paintings by Chico Montilla A1181

No. 3208: a, La Hoz de Priego. b, Fields of Gold. c, Desfiladero de los Tornos. d, Campos de Pastrana. e, Campos de Armilla. f, Nenúfar. g, De qué Color es el Vento? h, Flores Tempranas.

Die Cut Perf. 13
2003, Mar. 28   Litho.
Self-Adhesive
3208   Booklet pane of 8   4.50
  a.-h. A1181 26c Any single   .55 .30

Ramón José Sender (1901-82), Writer A1182

Litho. & Engr.
2003, Mar. 31   Perf. 13½x14
3209 A1182 €2.15 multi   4.75 2.40

Rural Schools A1183

2003, Apr. 3 Photo. Perf. 13¾x14
3210 A1183 26c multi   .55 .30

Souvenir Sheet

EXFILNA 2003 Natl. Philatelic Exhibition, Granada — A1184

Litho. (margin) & Engr. (stamp)
2003, Apr. 7
3211 A1184 €2.15 multi   4.75 2.40

Aviles, 1000th Anniv. A1185

2003, Apr. 11   Photo.
3212 A1185 51c multi   1.10 .55

Stamp Day A1186

2003, Apr. 11
3213 A1186 €1.85 multi   4.00 2.00

Europa A1187

2003, Apr. 24
3214 A1187 76c multi   1.75 .85

Atlético de Madrid Soccer Team, Cent. — A1188

2003, Apr. 25   Perf. 14x13¾
3215 A1188 26c red & blue   .60 .30

Roman Theater, Zaragoza A1189

2003, May 5   Perf. 13¾x14
3216 A1189 €1.85 multi   4.25 2.10

European Year of the Disabled A1190

2003, May 8   Photo. & Embossed
3217 A1190 76c multi   1.75 .85

Castles A1191

Designs: 26c, San Felipe Castle, Ferrol. 51c, Cuellar Castle, Segovia. 76c, Montilla Castle, Córdoba.

2003, May 17 Engr. Perf. 13¾x14
3218-3220 A1191 Set of 3   3.75 1.90

Battles of Ceriñola and Garellano, 500th anniv. (No. 3220).

World Swimming Championships,
Barcelona — A1192

2003, May 23 Photo. *Perf. 14x13¾*
3221 A1192   Sheet of 5 + la-
              bel   13.00 6.50
   a. 26c Breaststroke   .60   .30
   b. 51c Diving   1.25   .60
   c. 76c Synchronized swimming 1.75   .85
   d. €1.85 Freestyle   4.25 2.10
   e. €2.15 Water polo   5.00 2.50

Max Aub (1903-
72),
Writer — A1193

2003, June 2   Engr.
3222 A1193 76c black & red   1.75   .85

Sabadell Soccer
Team,
Cent. — A1194

2003, June 4   Photo.
3223 A1194 76c multi   1.75   .85

Juan Bravo Murillo
(1803-73), Prime
Minister — A1195

2003, June 9
3224 A1195 51c multi   1.25   .60

Diario de Cadiz
Newspaper, 136th
Anniv. — A1196

2003, June 16
3225 A1196 26c multi   .60   .30

Royal Automobile Club of Spain,
Cent. — A1197

2003, June 27   *Perf. 13¾x14*
3226 A1197   Sheet of 4   7.75 4.00
   a. 26c 1967 Dodge Dart Bar-
       reiros   .60   .30
   b. 51c 1957-73 Seat 600   1.10   .55
   c. 76c 1907 Hispano-Suiza 20/30
       HP   1.75   .85
   d. €1.85 1953 Pegaso Z-102
       Berlinetta   4.25 2.10

Chilean Postage
Stamps, 150th
Anniv. — A1198

2003, July 1   Photo. *Perf. 14x13¾*
3227 A1198 76c Chile Type A1 1.75   .85

El Diario
Montañés
Newspaper,
Cent. — A1199

2003, July 4
3228 A1199 26c multi   .60   .30

Santa Catalina Inn, Jaén — A1200

2003, July 9   *Perf. 13x13¼*
3229 A1200 76c multi + label 1.75   .85

Diario de Navarra Newspaper,
Cent. — A1201

2003, July 11   *Perf. 13¾x14*
3230 A1201 26c multi   .60   .30

Seu Vella,
Lleida,
800th
Anniv.
A1202

2003, July 22 Engr. *Perf. 13¾x14*
3231 A1202 €1.85 pur & brn blk 4.25 2.10

El Adelanto de
Salamanca
Newspaper, 120th
Anniv. — A1203

2003, July 24 Photo. *Perf. 14x13¾*
3232 A1203 26c multi   .60   .30

A1204   A1205

A1206   A1207

A1208   A1209

Paintings by Alfredo Roldán
A1210   A1211
Die Cut Perf. 13

2003, July 28   Litho.
              Self-Adhesive
3233   Booklet pane of 8   5.00
   a. A1204 A multi   .60   .30
   b. A1205 A multi   .60   .30
   c. A1206 A multi   .60   .30
   d. A1207 A multi   .60   .30
   e. A1208 A multi   .60   .30
   f. A1209 A multi   .60   .30
   g. A1210 A multi   .60   .30
   h. A1211 A multi   .60   .30

Nos. 3233a-3233g each sold for 26c on day
of issue.

El Correo Gallego Newspaper, 125th
Anniv. — A1212

2003, Aug. 1   Photo. *Perf. 13¾x14*
3234 A1212 26c multi   .60   .30

El Comercio de Gijón Newspaper,
125th Anniv. — A1213

2003, Sept. 2
3235 A1213 26c multi   .60   .30

Holy Cross of
Caravaca
A1214

2003, Sept. 4   *Perf. 14x13¾*
3236 A1214 76c multi   1.75   .85
       Holy Year 2003.

World Sailing Championships, Gulf of
Cádiz — A1215

2003, Sept. 9   *Perf. 13¾x14*
3237 A1215 76c multi   1.75   .85

Wine of Penedés
Region — A1216

Wine of Montilla-
Moriles
Region — A1217

Wine of
Valdepeñas
Region — A1218

Wine of Bierzo
Region — A1219

2003

3238	A1216	26c multi	.60 .30
3239	A1217	51c multi	1.25 .60
3240	A1218	76c multi	1.75 .90
3241	A1219	€1.85 multi	4.50 2.25
		Nos. 3238-3241 (4)	8.10 4.05

Perf. 14x13¾

Issued: 26c, 10/30; others, 9/22.

Academy of Military Engineering, Bicent. — A1220

2003, Sept. 24   **Perf. 13¾x14**
3242 A1220 51c multi   1.25 .60

Souvenir Sheet

Santa María Cathedral, León, 700th Anniv — A1221

2003, Sept. 26   **Litho. & Engr.**
3243 A1221 76c multi   2.00 1.00

Souvenir Sheet

Royal Geographical Society, Cent. — A1222

2003, Oct. 1
3244 A1222 €1.85 multi   4.75 2.50

Trees — A1223

Designs: 26c, Ficus macrophylla. 51c, Quercus rober.

2003, Oct. 3   Photo.   Perf. 14x13¾
3245-3246 A1223 Set of 2   1.90 .95

School of Aeronautical Engineering, Madrid, 75th Anniv. — A1224

2003, Oct. 6   **Perf. 13¾x14**
3247 A1224 51c multi   1.25 .60

America Issue - Rail Transport A1225

2003, Oct. 14
3248 A1225 76c multi   1.75 .90

El Viejo y el Pájaro, by Luis Seoane (1910-79) A1226

2003, Oct. 17   **Perf. 14x13¾**
3249 A1226 €1.85 multi   4.50 2.25

El Correo de Andalucia Newspaper, Cent. — A1227

Faro de Vigo Newspaper, 150th Anniv. — A1228

La Voz de Galicia Newspaper, 121st Anniv. — A1229

2003, Nov. 3   **Perf. 13¾x14**
3250 A1227 26c multi   .60 .30
3251 A1228 26c multi   .60 .30
3252 A1229 26c multi   .60 .30
      Nos. 3250-3252 (3)   1.80 .90

Camilo José Cela (1916-2002), 1989 Nobel Laureate in Literature A1230

2003, Nov. 10   **Perf. 14x13¾**
3253 A1230 26c multi   .65 .30

Parade of the Magi — A1231

Nativity, by Raquel Fariñas — A1232

2003, Nov. 10
3254 A1231 26c multi   .65 .30
3255 A1232 51c multi   1.25 .60
      Christmas.

España 2004 Intl. Philatelic Exhibition A1233

Designs: 76c, Exhibition emblem. €1.85, Exhibition venue, Valencia.

2003, Nov. 14   **Perf. 13¾x14**
3256 A1233 76c multi   1.90 .95

Souvenir Sheet
3257 A1233 €1.85 multi   4.50 2.25

Organos de Montoro A1234

2003, Nov. 17
3258 A1234 51c multi   1.25 .60

Souvenir Sheet

Completion of National Geological Map — A1235

2003, Nov. 24
3259 A1235 26c multi   .65 .30

Souvenir Sheets

Constitution, 25th Anniv. — A1236

Various photos or paintings with inscriptions in lower left corner of: No. 3260, 26c, RCM-FNMT. No. 3261, 26c, Miguel Torner. No. 3262, 26c, R. Seco. No. 3263, 26c, Araceli

Alarcón. No. 3264, 26c, Galicia. No. 3265, 26c, Fesanpe. No. 3266, 26c, J. Carrero. No. 3267, 26c, J. Carrero, vert. No. 3268, 26c, Goyo Domínguez, vert. No. 3269, 26c, Juan Bautista Nieto, vert.

2003, Dec. 5   **Perf. 13¾x14, 14x13¾**
3260-3269 A1236 Set of 10   6.50 3.25

Powered Flight, Cent. A1237

2003, Dec. 17   Engr.   Perf. 13¾x14
3270 A1237 76c blue & brown   1.90 .95

King Juan Carlos Type of 2001 With Euro Denominations Only

2004, Jan. 2   Photo.   Perf. 12¾x13¼
3271	A1091	2c sil & brt pink	.25 .25
3272	A1091	27c sil & blue	.70 .35
a.		Sheet of 4 + label	2.80 2.80
3273	A1091	52c sil & bister brn	1.25 .65
3274	A1091	77c sil & dull grn	1.90 .95
		Nos. 3271-3274 (4)	4.10 2.20

No. 3272a issued 5/25.

Roman Art of Jaca — A1238

No. 3275: a, Grate. b, Huesca Cathedral Bible page. c, Painting of two apostles. d, Cloister, Monastery of San Juan de la Peña. e, Coins. f, Capital, Church of Santiago de Jaca. g, Detail of sarcophagus of Doña Sancha. h, Wooden carved crucifix.

Serpentine Die Cut 13
2004, Jan. 16   **Litho.**
Self-Adhesive
3275   Booklet pane of 8   5.75
a.-h. A1238 A Any single   .70 .35

Nos. 3275a-3275h each sold for 27c on day of issue.

Souvenir Sheets

Paintings of Women Reading by Fabio Hurtado (1960-) — A1239

No. 3276: a, 27c, Woman reading book in rowboat. b, 52c, Woman with head on hand reading book. c, 77c, Woman reading newspaper.
No. 3277: a, 27c, Woman with legs crossed reading book. b, 52c, Woman on back reading book. c, 77c, Woman with black hat reading book.

2004, Jan. 23   Photo.   Perf. 13¾x14
Sheets of 3, #a-c, + label
3276-3277 A1239 Set of 2   8.00 4.50

Campaign Against Cancer A1240

2004, Feb. 2
3278 A1240 27c multi   .70 .35

"La Terrona" Oak Tree, Zarza de Montánchez A1241

2004, Feb. 6   *Perf. 14x13¾*
3279 A1241 52c multi   1.40   .70

World Rowing Championships, Banyoles — A1242

2004, Feb. 9   *Perf. 13¾x14*
3280 A1242 77c multi   1.90   .95

School Letter Writing Campaign — A1243

No. 3281 — Scenes from comic strip Trazo de Tiza, by Miguelanxo Prado: a, Woman on cliff. b, Sailboat. c, Woman near injured gull. d, Aerial view of lighthouse.

2004, Feb. 10
3281 A1243 27c Sheet of 4, #a-
    d, + 12 labels   2.75 1.40

Souvenir Sheet

Santa María de Carracedo Monastery, Bierzo — A1244

2004, Mar. 8   *Perf. 14x13¾*
3282 A1244 €1.90 multi   4.75 2.40

36th Chess Olympiad A1245

2004, Mar. 18   *Perf. 13¾x14*
3283 A1245 77c multi   1.90   .95

Clocks — A1246

No. 3284: a, 27c, Clock with Muse Calliope, 19th cent. b, 52c, Clock with Cupid, 18th cent. c, 77c, Clock with Empress María Luisa, child and harp, 19th cent. d, €1.90, Clock with Venus and Cupid, 18th cent.

     Perf. 13¼x12¾
2004, Mar. 31   Litho. & Engr.
3284 A1246   Sheet of 4, #a-d   8.50 4.25

Diario de Burgos Newspaper, 113th Anniv. — A1247

2004, Apr. 1   Photo.   *Perf. 14x13¾*
3285 A1247 27c multi   .65   .35

March 11, 2004 Terrorist Attacks — A1248

2004, Apr. 2   Litho.   *Perf. 14x13¾*
3286 A1248 27c black & gray   .65   .35

Booklet Stamp
Self-Adhesive
Size: 22x33mm
Serpentine Die Cut 13
3287 A1248   A black & gray   .65   .35
   a.   Booklet pane of 8   5.25
No. 3287 sold for 27c on day of issue.

Egg Painting Festival, Pola de Siero A1249

2004, Apr. 5   Photo.   *Perf. 13¾*
3288 A1249 27c multi   .65   .35

Miniature Sheet

Paintings of Shawls, by Soledad Fernández — A1250

2004, Apr. 7   *Perf. 14x13¾*
3289 A1250   Sheet of 4   8.50 8.50
  a.   27c Shawl, shell   .65   .35
  b.   52c Shawl, hands   1.25   .65
  c.   77c Shawl, flowers   1.90   .95
  d.   €1.90 Shawl on chair   4.50 2.25

Department of Technical Engineering of Public Works, 150th Anniv. — A1251

2004, Apr. 15   *Perf. 13¾x14*
3290 A1251 52c multi   1.25   .60

Cable Inglés Loading Pier, Almadrabillas, Cent. — A1252

2004, Apr. 27
3291 A1252 52c multi   1.25   .60

Europa — A1253

2004, Apr. 29   *Perf. 14x13¾*
3292 A1253 77c multi   1.90   .95

Expansion of the European Union A1254

2004, May 3   *Perf. 13¾x14*
3293 A1254 52c multi   1.25   .60

Self-Portrait with the Neck of Rafael, by Salvador Dali (1904-89) — A1255

2004, May 11   Photo.
3294 A1255 77c multi   1.90   .95

FIFA (Fédération Internationale de Football Association), Cent. — A1256

2004, May 21
3295 A1256 77c multi   1.90   .95

Wedding of Prince Felipe and Letizia Ortiz Rocasolano — A1257

2004, May 22
3296 A1257 27c multi   .65   .30

España 2004 Intl. Philatelic Exhibition — A1258

No. 3297 — Music: a, Vicente Martín y Soler (1754-1806), opera composer. b, Band instruments.

2004, May 23   Photo.   *Perf. 13¾x14*
3297 A1258   Horiz. pair + cen-
    tral label   1.90 1.90
  a.   27c multi   .65   .30
  b.   52c multi   1.25   .60

Miniature Sheet

España 2004 Intl. Philatelic Exhibition — A1259

No. 3298 — Royalty: a, Prince Felipe and Letizia Ortiz Rocasolano. b, Prince Felipe. c, King Juan Carlos and Queen Sofia.

Litho., Litho. & Engr. (#3298c)
2004, May 24   *Perf. 13¾x14*
3298 A1259   Sheet of 3 + 3
    labels   17.00 17.00
  a.   27c multi   .65   .30
  b.   77c multi   1.90   .95
  c.   €6 multi   14.00 7.00

España 2004 Intl. Philatelic Exhibition — A1260

No. 3299 — Festival of the Bulls, Valencia: a, Running of the bulls. b, Bullfighter.

2004, May 26 **Photo.** *Perf. 13¾x14*
3299 A1260 Horiz. pair + central label 2.50 2.50
a. 27c multi .60 .30
b. 77c multi 1.90 .95

Miniature Sheet

España 2004 Intl. Philatelic Exhibition — A1261

No. 3300 — Sports: a, Tennis. b, Motorcycle racing. c, Golf.

2004, May 27 *Perf. 12¾x13*
3300 A1261 Sheet of 3 + 3 labels 7.00 7.00
a. 35c multi .85 .40
b. 52c multi 1.25 .65
c. €1.90 multi 4.50 2.25

España 2004 Intl. Philatelic Exhibition — A1262

No. 3301 — The Sea: a, Yacht Bravo España. b, Valencia skyline.

2004, May 28 **Photo.** *Perf. 13¾x14*
3301 A1262 Horiz. pair + central label 3.25 3.25
a. 52c multi 1.25 .65
b. 77c multi 1.90 .95

Diario de Valencia Newspaper, 214th Anniv. — A1263

2004, May 29
3302 A1263 27c multi .65 .30

Jacobean Holy Year — A1264

2004, June 11 *Perf. 14x13¾*
3303 A1264 52c multi 1.25 .65

Lerma Inn A1265

2004, July 18 *Perf. 13¾x14*
3304 A1265 52c multi 1.25 .65

Castles A1266

Designs: 27c, Granadilla Fortress, Granadilla. 52c, Aguas Mansas Castle, Agoncillo.

77c, Mota Fortress, Alcalá la Real. €1.90, Villafuerte de Esgueva Castle, Villafuerte de Esgueva, vert.

2004 **Engr.** *Perf. 13¾x14, 14x13¾*
3305-3308 A1266 Set of 4 8.50 4.25

Issued: 27c, 77c, 7/1; 52c, €1.90, 7/19.

Anchor Museum, Salinas — A1267

2004, July 16 **Photo.** *Perf. 14x13¾*
3309 A1267 €1.90 multi 4.75 2.40

Ceramics in Paintings by Antonio Miguel González — A1268

No. 3310: a, Jar with two handles and lid, oranges. b, Goblet, amphora and jar. c, Pitcher with handle at top, bread, garlic. d, Decorated pitcher with side handle. e, Pitcher with handle at top, pentagonal dodecahedron, bread, tomatoes. f, Vase. g, Pitcher with side handle, plate of pears, grapes. h, Jar with flower design and lid.

Serpentine Die Cut 13
2004, July 22 **Litho.**
Self-Adhesive
3310 Booklet pane of 8 5.25
a.-h. A1268 A Any single .65 .35

Nos. 3310a-3310h sold for 27c on day of issue.

Círculo Oscense Building, Huesca, Cent. A1269

2004, July 23 **Photo.** *Perf. 13¾x14*
3311 A1269 52c multi 1.25 .65

Our Lady of the Snows Festival, Vitoria-Gasteiz, 50th Anniv. — A1270

2004, July 30 *Perf. 14x13¾*
3312 A1270 27c multi .65 .30

Ribeiro Wine Grapes — A1271

Wine of Malaga — A1272

2004, Sept. 1 *Perf. 14x13¾*
3313 A1271 27c multi .70 .35
3314 A1272 52c multi 1.25 .65

First Philippines Stamp, 150th Anniv. — A1273

2004, Sept. 6 *Perf. 13¾x14*
3315 A1273 77c Philippines #1 1.90 .95

Heraldo de Aragón Newspaper, 109th Anniv. — A1274

2004, Sept. 20 *Perf. 14x13¾*
3316 A1274 27c multi .70 .35

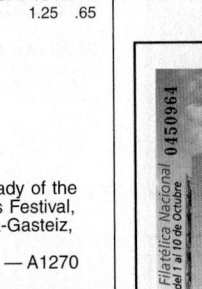

Nautical Astronomy, 250th Anniv. — A1275

2004, Sept. 24 *Perf. 13¾x14*
3317 A1275 €1.90 multi 4.75 2.40

Souvenir Sheet

EXFILNA 2004 National Philatelic Exhibition, Valladolid — A1276

Litho. & Engr.
2004, Oct. 1 *Perf. 14x13¾*
3318 A1276 €1.90 multi 4.75 4.75

Buildings in China and Spain — A1277

Designs: 52c, Park Guell, Barcelona. 77c, Jinmao Tower, Shanghai.

2004, Oct. 8 **Photo.**
3319-3320 A1277 Set of 2 3.25 1.60

See People's Republic of China Nos. 3406-3407.

America Issue — Environmental Protection — A1278

2004, Oct. 14 *Perf. 13¾x14*
3321 A1278 77c multi 2.00 1.00

CERN (European Organization for Nuclear Research), 50th Anniv. — A1279

2004, Oct. 19
3322 A1279 €1.90 multi 5.00 2.50

Nature — A1280

Designs: 27c, Cíes Islands. 52c, Ebro Delta Natural Park, horiz. 77c, Taburiente Caldera National Park, horiz.

2004, Oct. 21 *Perf. 14x13¾, 13¾x14*
3323-3325 A1280 Set of 3 4.25 2.10

Taburiente Caldera National Park, 50th anniv. (#3325).

First Registered Letter, 400th Anniv. — A1281

2004, Oct. 22 *Perf. 13¾x14*
3326 A1281 77c multi 2.00 1.00

Stamp Day.

Ebre Observatory, Cent. — A1282

2004, Nov. 5
3327 A1282 €1.90 multi   5.00 2.50

Start of Reign of Alfonso I, King of Aragon, 900th Anniv. — A1283

Litho. & Engr.
2004, Nov. 12   **Perf. 14x13¾**
3328 A1283 €1.90 multi   5.00 2.50

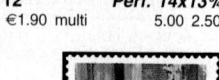

Christmas A1284

Designs: 27c, Birth of Christ, 18th cent. Neapolitan nativity scene. 52c, Nativity, by Juan Manuel Cossío.

2004, Nov. 17   **Photo.**
3329-3330 A1284   Set of 2   2.25 1.10

Queen Isabella I (1451-1504) A1285

2004, Nov. 26
3331 A1285 €2.19 multi   6.00 3.00

Royal Expedition for Smallpox Vaccination in Latin America and Philippines, Bicent. — A1286

2004, Nov. 30   Engr.   Perf. 13¾x14
3332 A1286 77c brown   2.10 1.10

Souvenir Sheet

Stained Glass, Toledo Cathedral — A1287

Litho. & Engr.
2004, Dec. 3   **Perf. 14x13¾**
3333 A1287 €1.90 multi   5.25 5.25

Arms of the Prince of Asturias A1288

2004, Dec. 23   Photo.   Perf. 13¾x14
3334 A1288 27c multi   .75 .40
Best wishes for Prince Felipe's marriage to Letizia Ortiz Rocasolano on May 22, 2004.

A1289   A1290

A1291   A1292

A1293   A1294

A1295   A1296

Paintings of Circus Performers by Manolo Elices

2005, Jan. 3   Litho.   Die Cut Perf. 13
Self-Adhesive
3335   Booklet pane of 8   6.00
   a. A1289 A multi   .75 .35
   b. A1290 A multi   .75 .35
   c. A1291 A multi   .75 .35
   d. A1292 A multi   .75 .35
   e. A1293 A multi   .75 .35
   f. A1294 A multi   .75 .35
   g. A1295 A multi   .75 .35
   h. A1296 A multi   .75 .35
Nos. 3335a-3335h each sold for 28c on day of issue.

Signing of European Union Constitutional Treaty — A1297

2005, Jan. 12   Photo.   Perf. 13¾x14
3336 A1297 28c multi   .75 .35

King Juan Carlos Type of 2001 With Euro Denominations Only
Perf. 12¾x13¼
2005, Jan. 14   **Photo.**
3337 A1091 28c sil & ol grn   .75 .35
3338 A1091 35c sil & orange   .90 .45
3339 A1091 40c sil & blue gray   1.00 .50
3340 A1091 53c sil & dull pur   1.40 .70
3341 A1091 78c sil & red   2.00 1.00
3342 A1091 €1.95 sil & yel brn   5.00 2.50
3343 A1091 €2.21 sil & ol brn   5.75 2.75
   Nos. 3337-3343 (7)   16.80 8.25

Ahuehuete Tree, Retiro Park, Madrid — A1298

2005, Jan. 17   Photo.   Perf. 14x13¾
3344 A1298 78c multi   2.00 1.00

Road Safety A1299

Blood Donation A1300

2005, Jan. 26   **Perf. 13¾x14**
3345 A1299 28c multi   .75 .35
3346 A1300 53c multi   1.40 .70

University of Seville, 500th Anniv. — A1301

2005, Feb. 3   Engr.   Perf. 14x13¾
3347 A1301 28c brn & claret   .75 .35

First Royal Spanish Pharmacopoeia, 500th Anniv. — A1302

2005, Feb. 3   **Litho. & Engr.**
3348 A1302 28c multi   .75 .35

Miniature Sheet

Children's Songs and Stories — A1303

No. 3349: a, Al Levantar una Lancha. b, Aquí te Espero. c, Estaba la Pájara Pinta. d, Cuatro Esquinitas. e, El Patio de mi Casa. f, Pero Mira Cómo Beben. g, Los Pollitos Cantan. h, Para Entrar en Clase.

2005, Feb. 14   **Photo.**
3349 A1303   Sheet of 8   11.00 11.00
  a.-c.   28c Any single   .75 .40
  d.-f.   53c Any single   1.40 .70
  g.-h.   78c Either single   2.10 1.10

Juvenia 2005 Youth Stamp Exhibition, Tordera — A1304

2005, Feb. 25   **Perf. 14x13¾**
3350 A1304 28c multi   .75 .35

Sevilla FC (Seville Soccer Team), Cent. A1305

Real Sporting de Gijón Soccer Team, Cent. — A1306

15th Mediterranean Games, Almería — A1307

2005, Mar. 1   **Perf. 13¾x14**
3351 A1305 35c red   .95 .45

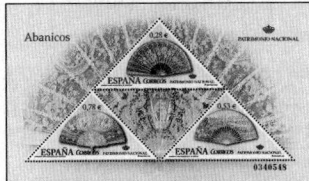

Perf. 14x13¾

3352	A1306	40c multi	1.10	.55
3353	A1307	78c multi	2.10	1.10
		Nos. 3351-3353 (3)	4.15	2.10

Europa
A1308

2005, Apr. 15   **Perf. 13¾x14**

3354	A1308	53c multi	1.40	.70

Juan Valera
(1824-1905),
Writer and
Diplomat
A1309

2005, Apr. 18   **Engr.**   **Perf. 14x13¾**

3355	A1309	€2.21 vio brn & blue	5.75	2.75

Souvenir Sheet

Publication of Don Quixote, 400th
Anniv. — A1310

Various scenes from book.

2005, Apr. 22

3356	A1310	Sheet of 4	10.00	10.00
a.		28c black	.75	.35
b.		53c black	1.40	.70
c.		78c black	2.00	1.00
d.		€2.21 black	5.75	2.75

Telegraphy in Spain, 150th
Anniv. — A1311

2005, Apr. 26   **Photo.**   **Perf. 13¾x14**

3357	A1311	28c multi	.75	.35

Intl. Year of
Physics — A1312

Die Cut Perf. 13¼

2005, Apr. 28   **Litho.**
Self-Adhesive

3358	A1312	28c multi	.75	.35

Souvenir Sheet

Fans — A1313

No. 3359 — Fan depicting: a, Flowers. b,
Madrid street scene. c, Nymphs.

2005, May 9   **Photo.**   **Perf. 13¾**

3359	A1313	Sheet of 3 + label	4.00	4.00
a.		28c multi	.70	.35
b.		53c multi	1.40	.70
c.		78c multi	1.90	.95

Diario Palentino
Newspaper, 124th
Anniv. — A1314

Ultima Hora Newspaper, 112th
Anniv. — A1315

Diario de Ibiza Newspaper, 112th
Anniv. — A1316

2005, May 16   **Perf. 14x13¾**

3360	A1314	78c multi	1.90	.95

Perf. 13¾x14

3361	A1315	€1.95 multi	4.75	2.40
3362	A1316	€2.21 multi	5.50	2.75
		Nos. 3360-3362 (3)	12.15	6.10

Inn,
Oropesa
A1317

2005, June 13   **Engr.**   **Perf. 13¾x14**

3363	A1317	€1.95 brown	4.75	2.40

Souvenir Sheet

EXFILNA 2005, Alicante — A1318

Litho. & Engr.

2005, June 20   **Perf. 14x13¾**

3364	A1318	€2.21 multi	5.50	2.75

Castles
A1319

Designs: 78c, Alcaudete Castle. €1.95,
Valderrobres Castle. €2.21, Molina de Aragón
Castle.

2005, July 4   **Engr.**   **Perf. 13¾x14**

3365-3367	A1319	Set of 3	12.00	6.00

Fingerprint Registration for
Newborns — A1320

2005, July 11   **Photo.**

3368	A1320	28c multi	.70	.35

Stamp
Day — A1321

Die Cut Perf. 13

2005, Sept. 1   **Litho.**
Self-Adhesive

3369	A1321	28c multi	.70	.35

Nuestra
Señora de
la
Asuncion
Church,
Pont de
Suert
A1322

2005, Sept. 7   **Photo.**   **Perf. 13¾x14**

3370	A1322	28c multi	.70	.35

Lunnispark
Building
A1323

Lucho
A1324

Lupita in
Bed — A1325

Die Cut Perf. 13

2005, Sept. 16   **Litho.**
Self-Adhesive

3371		Booklet pane of 8	5.75	
a.	A1323	28c shown	.70	.35
b.	A1324	28c shown	.70	.35
c.	A1324	28c Green building	.70	.35
d.	A1324	28c Lulila	.70	.35
e.	A1324	28c Lupita	.70	.35
f.	A1325	28c shown	.70	.35
g.	A1324	28c Lublú	.70	.35
h.	A1323	28c Orange building	.70	.35

Los Lunnis children's television show.

World Cycling Championships,
Madrid — A1326

2005, Sept. 20   **Photo.**   **Perf. 13¾x14**

3372	A1326	78c multi	1.90	.95

España
2006
World
Philatelic
Exhibition,
Malaga
A1327

2005   **Photo.**   **Perf. 13¾x14**

3373	A1327	53c multi	1.40	.70

Gardens
A1328

No. 3374: a, Gardens of La Granja de San
Ildefonso, Segovia. b, Bagh-e-Shahzadeh
Garden, Kerman, Iran.

2005, Oct. 10

3374		Horiz. pair + central la- bel	7.25	3.75
a.	A1328	78c multi	1.90	.95
b.	A1328	€2.21 multi	5.25	2.60

See Iran No. 2912.

15th Iberoamerican Summit,
Salamanca — A1329

2005, Oct. 13
3375 A1329 78c multi 1.90 .95

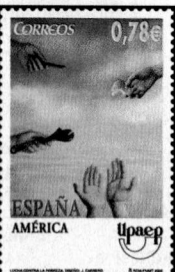

America Issue,
Fight Against
Poverty
A1330

2005, Oct. 14 *Perf. 12¾*
3376 A1330 78c multi 1.90 .95

La Orotava, 500th
Anniv. — A1331

2005, Oct. 20 *Perf. 14x13¾*
3377 A1331 €2.21 multi 5.50 2.75

Colonial Postage Stamps for Cuba and
Philippines, 150th Anniv. — A1332

2005, Oct. 20 *Perf. 13¾x14*
3378 A1332 €2.21 multi 5.50 2.75

Prince of Asturias Awards, 25th
Anniv. — A1333

2005, Oct. 20 *Perf. 13¼x13*
3379 A1333 28c multi + label .70 .35
Printed in sheets of 8 stamps + 8 different
labels.

Miniature Sheet

Scenes from Television Show "Al Filo
de lo Imposible" — A1334

No. 3380: a, Underwater cave explorers. b,
Hot-air balloon with man on rope outside of
gondola. c, Man pulling sled. d, Kayaker. e,
Climber on snowy mountain. f, Rock climber.

2005, Oct. 24 *Perf. 14x13¾*
3380 A1334 Sheet of 6 + 6 labels 4.25 2.10
a.-f. 28c Any single .70 .35
See No. 3398.

A1335

Christmas
A1336

2005, Oct. 31
3381 A1335 28c multi .70 .35
3382 A1336 53c multi 1.25 .65

Souvenir Sheet

Stained Glass Window, Avila
Cathedral — A1337

2005, Nov. 2 *Litho. & Engr.*
3383 A1337 €2.21 multi 5.25 2.60

Euromediterranean Summit,
Barcelona — A1338

2005, Nov. 3 Photo. *Perf. 13¾x14*
3384 A1338 53c multi 1.25 .65

Queen Juana of
Castile (1479-
1555)
A1339

2005, Nov. 4 *Perf. 14x13¾*
3385 A1339 28c multi .70 .35
Parliament of Toro, 500th anniv.

Toys — A1340

No. 3386: a, Marionettes. b, Tops. c, Toy
car. d, Toy truck. e, Doll. f, Container of marbles. g, Toy horse and cart. h, Toy motorcycle.

2006, Jan. 2 Litho. *Die Cut Perf. 13*
Self-Adhesive
3386 Booklet pane of 8 5.50
a.-h. A1340 A Any single .65 .35
Nos. 3386a-3386h each sold for 28c on day
of issue.

**King Juan Carlos Type of 2001 With
Euro Denominations Only**

2006		**Photo.**	*Perf.*	*12¾x13¼*
3387	A1091	29c sil & brown	.70	.35
3388	A1091	57c sil & org	1.40	.70
3389	A1091	€2.26 sil & pur	5.50	2.75
3390	A1091	€2.33 sil & claret	5.50	2.75
3391	A1091	€2.39 sil & dull grn	5.75	2.75
	Nos. 3387-3391 (5)		18.85	9.30

Issued: 29c, 57c, 2/1; €2.26, 1/5; €2.33,
€2.39, 2/13.

Carnation — A1341

Die Cut Perf. 13
2006, Jan. 20 *Litho.*
Self-Adhesive
3392 A1341 28c multi .70 .35
No. 3392 was printed in sheets of 10, which
were bound in booklets of 10 sheets.

Bank of Spain,
150th
Anniv. — A1342

2006, Jan. 27 Engr. *Perf. 14x13¾*
3393 A1342 78c brown & black 1.90 .95

Cypress Tree, La
Anunciada
Convent,
Villafranca del
Bierzo — A1343

2006, Jan. 30 *Photo.*
3394 A1343 53c multi 1.40 .70

Sparrow — A1344

Die Cut Perf. 13
2006, Feb. 1 Self-Adhesive Litho.
3395 A1344 A multi .70 .35
No. 3395 sold for 29p on day of issue, and
was printed in sheets of 10 which were bound
in booklets of 10 sheets.

Intl. Year of Deserts and
Desertification — A1345

2006, Feb. 6 Photo. *Perf. 13¾x14*
3396 A1345 29c multi .70 .35

Woman
Suffrage,
75th Anniv.
A1346

2006, Mar. 8
3397 A1346 29c blue & sepia .70 .35

**"Al Filo de lo Imposible" Type of
2005**

No. 3398: a, Cyclists. b, Man in desert. c,
Parachutist. d, Kayakers. e, Rafters. f, Waterfall rock climbers.

2006, Mar. 22 *Perf. 14x13¾*
3398 A1334 Sheet of 6 + 6 labels 12.00 6.00
a. 29c multi .70 .35
b. 38c multi .95 .45
c. 41c multi 1.00 .50
d. 57c multi 1.40 .70
e. 78c multi 1.90 .95
f. €2.39 multi 6.00 3.00

Goldfinch
A1347

Strelitzia Flower
A1348

2006, Apr. 1 Litho. *Die Cut Perf. 13*
3399 A1347 29c multi .70 .35
3400 A1348 38c multi .95 .45

Nos. 3399-3400 were each printed in sheets of 10, which were bound in booklets of 10 sheets.

Civic
Values — A1349

Designs: No. 3401, 29c, Water conservation. No. 3402, 29c, Man with "No Drugs" balloons. 38c, Social Security and Labor inspectors, cent., horiz. 57c, Fight against human trafficking, horiz.

Perf. 14x13¾, 13¾x14
2006, Apr. 4 Photo.
3401-3404 A1349 Set of 4 3.75 1.90

Diario de Pontevedra Newspaper,
117th Anniv. — A1350

Diario de Léon
Newspaper,
Cent. — A1351

Diario de Avila
Newspaper, 108th
Anniv. — A1352

El Norte de
Castilla
Newspaper, 150th
Anniv. — A1353

Levante-El Mercantil Valenciano
Newspaper, 134th Anniv. — A1354

2006, Apr. 20 *Perf. 13¾x14, 14x13¾*
3405 A1350 41c multi 1.10 .55
3406 A1351 41c multi 1.10 .55
3407 A1352 41c multi 1.10 .55
3408 A1353 41c red & blk 1.10 .55
3409 A1354 41c multi 1.10 .55
 Nos. 3405-3409 (5) 5.50 2.75

Souvenir Sheet

Christopher Columbus (1451-1506),
Explorer — A1355

2006, Apr. 24 *Perf. 14x13¾*
3410 A1355 €2.39 multi 6.25 3.00

Coronation of
Santa Maria de
Los Remedios
Icon,
Cent. — A1356

2006, Apr. 27
3411 A1356 €2.33 multi 6.00 3.00

Souvenir Sheet

Exfilna 2006 Philatelic Exhibition,
Algeciras — A1357

Litho. & Engr.
2006, May 5 *Perf. 13¾x14*
3412 A1357 €2.39 multi 6.25 3.00

Inauguration of Taxis Family Postal
System in Spain, 500th
Anniv. — A1358

2006, May 9 Photo.
3413 A1358 29c multi .75 .35

Internet
Day
A1359

25th Intl.
Mathematics
Conference,
Madrid — A1360

Die Cut Perf. 13
2006, May 17 Litho.
3414 A1359 29c multi .75 .35
3515 A1360 57c multi 1.50 .75

Socialist
Youth In
Spain,
Cent.
A1361

2006, May 23 Photo. *Perf. 13¾x14*
3416 A1361 78c multi 2.00 1.00

Souvenir Sheet

España 06 Intl. Philatelic Exhibition,
Málaga — A1362

2006, May 29
3417 A1362 78c multi 2.00 1.00

San Pedro and
San Marcial
Festivals,
Irún — A1363

2006, June 5 *Perf. 14x13¾*
3418 A1363 29c multi .75 .35

Architecture
A1364

Designs: 29c, Casa Battló, Barcelona. 38c, Vapor Aymerich, Amt y Jover, Terrassa. 41c, Depósitos del Sol Library, Albacete. 57c, Campos Eliseos Theater, Bilbao. 78c, Alfredo Kraus Auditorium, Las Palmas, horiz. €2.33, Bus station, Casar de Cáceres, horiz.

Engr., Photo. (41c, 78c, €2.33)
2006, June 8 *Perf. 14x13¾, 13¾x14*
3419-3424 A1364 Set of 6 12.00 6.00

Al-Idrisi (c. 1100-
65), Geographer
A1365

2006, June 15 Photo. *Perf. 14x13¾*
3425 A1365 78c multi 2.00 1.00

Greenfinch
A1366

Iris
A1367

2006, July 5 Litho. *Die Cut Perf. 13*
Self-Adhesive
3426 A1366 29c multi .75 .35
3427 A1367 41c multi 1.10 .55

Nos. 3426-3427 were each printed in sheets of 10 which were bound in booklets of 10 sheets.

Sanlúcar
de
Barrameda
Horse
Race
A1368

2006, July 6 Photo. *Perf. 13¾x14*
3428 A1368 €2.33 multi 6.00 3.00

Archaeology
A1369

Designs: 29c, Los Millares archaeological site. 57c, Art on vase from L'Alcudia archaeological site, horiz. 78c Moixent Warrior, bronze sculpture.

2006, July 6 *Perf. 14x13¾, 13¾x14*
3429-3431 A1369 Set of 3 4.25 2.10

Earth
Sciences
A1370

Designs: No. 3432, 29c, Derived cartography. No. 3433, 29c, Vulcanology and seismology.

2006, July 13 *Perf. 13¾x14*
3432-3433 A1370 Set of 2 1.50 .75

Benavides Thursday Market, Orbigo, 700th Anniv. A1371

Aragon-Cataluña Canal, Cent. — A1372

2006, July 20
3434 A1371 38c multi 1.00 .50
3435 A1372 38c multi 1.00 .50

Diplomatic Relations Between Spain and Israel, 20th Anniv. A1373

2006, Sept. 1
3436 A1373 78c multi 2.00 1.00

Castles A1374

Designs: 29c, Baños de la Encina Castle. €2.39, Torroella de Montgri.

2006, Sept. 8 **Engr.**
3437-3438 A1374 Set of 2 6.75 3.50

A1375

Europa — A1376

2006, Sept. 12 Photo. Perf. 14x13¾
3439 A1375 29c multi .75 .35
3440 A1376 57c multi 1.50 .75

Bridges Between Spain and Portugal — A1377

No. 3441: a, Ayamonte International Bridge (Vila Real de Santo António). b, Alcántara Bridge.

2006, Sept. 14 **Perf. 13x13¼**
3441 Horiz. pair 2.25 1.10
a. A1377 29c multi .75 .35
b. A1377 57c multi 1.50 .75
See Portugal Nos. 2855-2856.

Rioja Grape Harvest Festival A1378

2006, Sept. 21 **Perf. 13¾x14**
3442 A1378 29c multi .75 .35

Real Club Deportivo La Coruna Soccer Team, Cent. A1379

2006, Sept. 25
3443 A1379 57c multi 1.50 .75

Souvenir Sheet

Victory of Spanish Team at 2006 World Basketball Championships — A1380

2006, Oct. 2 Photo. Perf. 13¾x14
3444 A1380 29c multi .75 .35

Swallow A1381

Poinsettia A1382

2006, Oct. 4 Litho. Die Cut Perf. 13
Self-Adhesive
3445 A1381 29c multi .75 .35
3446 A1382 29c multi .75 .35

Souvenir Sheets

España 06 World Philatelic Exhibition, Malaga — A1383

Exhibition emblem and: No. 3447, €2.33, Emblem of Vitorio & Lucchino, fashion designers. No. 3448, €2.33, Silhouette of hat and hand (cinema), vert. No. 3449, €2.33, Musical notes and staff. No. 3450, €2.33, Guitarist, vert. No. 3451, €2.33, Hand (flamenco dancing). No. 3452, €2.33, Tennis racquet and

basketball, vert. No. 3453, €2.33, Pablo Picasso (1881-1973), artist.

2006 Photo. Perf. 13¾x14, 14x13¾
3447-3453 A1383 Set of 7 42.00 21.00
Issued: No. 3447, 10/8; No. 3448, 10/9; Nos. 3449-3450, 10/10; No. 3451, 10/11; No. 3452, 10/12; No. 3453, 10/13.

America Issue, Energy Conservation — A1384

2006, Oct. 14 **Perf. 13¾**
3454 A1384 78c multi 2.00 1.00

Appointment of First Spanish Postmen, 250th Anniv. — A1385

Die Cut Perf. 13
2006, Oct. 25 **Litho.**
Self-Adhesive
3455 A1385 29c multi .75 .35
Stamp Day.

Ramón Rubial (1906-99), Politician A1386

2006, Oct. 27 Engr. Perf. 14x13¾
3456 A1386 57c multi 1.50 .75

A1387

Christmas A1388

Die Cut Perf. 13
2006, Nov. 2 Self-Adhesive Litho.
3457 A1387 29c multi .75 .35
3458 A1388 57c multi 1.50 .75

Souvenir Sheet

Stained Glass Window, School of Architecture, Polytechnic University of Madrid — A1389

Litho. & Engr.
2006, Nov. 3 **Perf. 14x13¾**
3459 A1389 €2.39 multi 6.25 3.25

St. Francis Xavier (1506-52) A1390

2006, Nov. 7 **Perf. 13¾x14**
3460 A1390 29c multi .80 .40

Television Broadcasting in Spain, 50th Anniv. — A1391

2006, Nov. 8 **Photo.**
3461 A1391 29c multi .80 .40

La Vanguardia Newspaper, 125th Anniv. — A1392

2006, Nov. 9 **Perf. 14x13¾**
3462 A1392 29c multi .80 .40

Pío Baroja (1872-1956), Writer — A1393

2006, Nov. 23
3463 A1393 29c multi .80 .40

Revision of Spanish Coat of Arms, 25th Anniv. — A1394

2006, Nov. 23
3464 A1394 29c multi .80 .40

A1395

Historical
Memory
Year
A1396

2006, Nov. 30   **Perf. 13¾x14**
3465 A1395 29c multi   .80 .40
3466 A1396 29c multi   .80 .40

Toys — A1397

No. 3467: a, Tricycle. b, Bus. c, Train. d,
Bowling game. e, Baby carriage. f, Seaplane.
g, Printing kit. h, Firetruck.

2007, Jan. 2 Litho. Die Cut Perf. 13
Self-Adhesive
3467   Booklet pane of 8   6.50
a.-h. A1397 A Any single   .80 .40
   Nos. 3467a-3467h each sold for 30c on day
of issue.

King Juan
Carlos — A1398

Perf. 12¾x13¼
2007, Jan. 13   **Photo.**
Color of Portrait
3468 A1398 30c blue   .80 .40
3469 A1398 58c olive grn   1.50 .75
3470 A1398 €2.43 org brn   6.25 3.25
3471 A1398 €2.49 rose pink   6.50 3.25
   Nos. 3468-3471 (4)   15.05 7.65

   See Nos. 3532-3539, 3615-3618, 3688-
3691, 3774-3777.

Hoopoe
A1399

Red Rose
A1400

Die Cut Perf. 13
2007, Jan. 20   **Litho.**
Self-Adhesive
3472 A1399 30c multi   .80 .40
3473 A1400 39c multi   1.00 .50
   Nos. 3472-3473 each were printed in sheets
of 10, which were bound in booklets of 10
sheets.

Teacher
and Pupils
A1401

2007, Jan. 23   **Self-Adhesive**
3474 A1401 58c multi   1.50 .75

Las Provincias Newspaper, 140th
Anniv. (in 2006) — A1402

2007, Jan. 31 Photo. Perf. 13¾x14
3475 A1402 42c multi   1.10 .55

Stylized
Periodic
Table of
Elements
A1403

Gregorian
Calendar, 425th
Anniv. — A1404

Die Cut Perf. 13
2007, Feb. 2 Self-Adhesive Litho.
3476 A1403 30c multi   .80 .40
3477 A1404 42c multi   1.10 .55

Institute of
Catalan
Studies,
Cent.
A1405

2007, Feb. 5 Photo. Perf. 13¾x14
3478 A1405 30c multi   .80 .40

2007 America's Cup Challenger
Races — A1406

2007, Feb. 8
3479 A1406 30c multi   .80 .40

Earth and
Space
Sciences
A1407

   Designs: 30c, Map (cartography). 78c,
Yebes Astronomical Center radio telescope.

Die Cut Perf. 13
2007, Feb. 16   **Litho.**
Self-Adhesive
3480-3481 A1407 Set of 2   3.00 1.50

Fuentepiña Pine Tree — A1408

2007, Mar. 5 Photo. Perf. 13¾x14
3482 A1408 78c multi   2.10 1.10

Mosaic
from
Roman
Villa,
Pedrosa
de la
Vega
A1409

Roman
Baths,
Campo
Valdés
A1410

2007, Mar. 8
3483 A1409 30c multi   .80 .40
3484 A1410 30c multi   .80 .40

European
Economic
Community, 50th
Anniv. — A1411

2007, Mar. 23   **Perf. 14x13¾**
3485 A1411 58c multi   1.60 .80

Canary
A1412

Violet
A1413

2007, Apr. 2 Litho. Die Cut Perf. 13
Self-Adhesive
3486 A1412 30c multi   .80 .40
3487 A1413 42c multi   1.25 .60

Souvenir Sheet

Madrid Movement, 25th
Anniv. — A1414

2007, Apr. 13 Photo. Perf. 13¾x14
3488 A1414 30c multi   .85 .40

Souvenir Sheet

Mallorca Cathedral — A1415

Engr., Litho. Margin
2007, Apr. 16
3489 A1415 €2.43 blue   6.75 3.25
   Exfilna 2007 National Philatelic Exhibition,
Palma de Mallorca.

Europa — A1416

2007, Apr. 23 Photo. Perf. 14x13¾
3490 A1416 58c multi   1.60 .80
   Scouting, cent.

Architecture
A1417

   Designs: 30c, Valleacerón Chapel,
Almadenejos. 39c, El Capricho, Comillas. 42c,
Santa Caterina Market, Barcelona. 58c, Viz-
caya Bridge, Las Arenas, horiz. 78c, Barajas
Airport, Madrid. €2.49, Casa Lis, Salamanca,
horiz.

Photo., Engr. (39c, 58c)
2007, Apr. 26 Perf. 14x13¾, 13¾x14
3491-3496 A1417 Set of 6   13.50 6.75

Juvenia 2007 Natl. Youth Philatelic Exhibition, Calahorra A1418

2007, Apr. 28 Photo. Perf. 13¾x14
3497 A1418 30c multi .85 .40

Stamp Day — A1419

2007, May 7 Litho. Die Cut Perf. 13
Self-Adhesive
3498 A1419 30c multi .80 .40

Song of the Cid, 800th Anniv. A1420

2007, May 9 Die Cut Perf. 13
Self-Adhesive
3499 A1420 30c multi .80 .40

Law of the Court of Auditors, 25th Anniv. — A1421

2007, May 12 Photo. Perf. 14x13¾
3500 A1421 30c multi .80 .40

Civic Values — A1422

Designs: 30c, Racial integration. 39c, No school violence. 58c, Organ donation. 78c, Equality of the sexes.

2007, May 16
3501-3504 A1422 Set of 4 5.50 2.75

Mushrooms A1423

Designs: 30c, Tricholoma equestre. 78c, Amanita muscaria.

2007, June 1
3505-3506 A1423 Set of 2 3.00 1.50

Carmen Conde (1907-96), Writer A1424

Rosa Chacel (1898-1994), Writer — A1425

2007, June 4 Engr. Perf. 13¾x14
3507 A1424 €2.49 red & blk 6.75 3.50
3508 A1425 €2.49 org & blk 6.75 3.50

Real Betis Balompié Soccer Team, Cent. A1426

2007, June 14 Photo. Perf. 13¾x14
3509 A1426 78c multi 2.10 1.10

Canonical Coronation of Blessed Mary of the O — A1427

2007, June 16 Perf. 14x13¾
3510 A1427 30c multi .85 .40

Nightingale A1428   Hyacinth A1429

2007, July 2 Litho. Die Cut Perf. 13
Self-Adhesive
3511 A1428 30c multi .85 .40
3512 A1429 30c multi .85 .40

Spanish Armed Forces Peace Missions — A1430

2007, July 4 Photo. Perf. 13x13¼
3513 A1430 30c multi .85 .40

Expo Zaragoza 2008 A1431

2007, July 5 Litho. Die Cut Perf. 13
Self-Adhesive
3514 A1431 58c multi 1.60 .80

Miniature Sheet

Scenes From Television Show "Al Filo de lo Imposible" — A1432

No. 3515: a, Diver under ice shelf. b, Skier. c, People pulling sleds. d, Sailboat in Antarctic waters. e, Kayaker in fjord. f, Iditarod dog sled team.

2007, July 12 Photo. Perf. 14x13¾
3515 A1432 Sheet of 6 + 6
labels 13.50 13.50
a. 30c multi .85 .40
b. 39c multi 1.00 .50
c. 42c multi 1.10 .55
d. 58c multi 1.60 .80
e. 78c multi 2.10 1.10
f. €2.43 multi 6.75 3.25

Nature Parks A1433

Designs: No. 3516, 30c, Albufera Nature Park. No. 3517, 30c, Lagunas de Ruidera Nature Park.

2007, July 19 Perf. 13¾x14
3516-3517 A1433 Set of 2 1.75 .85

Miniature Sheet

Lighthouses — A1434

No. 3518: a, Punta del Hidalgo Lighthouse, Tenerife. b, Cabo Mayor Lighthouse, Cantabria. c, Punta Almina Lighthouse, Ceuta. d, Melilla Lighthouse, Melilla. e, Cabo de Palos Lighthouse, Murcia. f, Gorliz Lighthouse, Vizcaya.

2007, Sept. 6
3518 A1434 Sheet of 6 + 6
labels 13.50 13.50
a. 30c multi .85 .40
b. 39c multi 1.00 .50
c. 42c multi 1.10 .55
d. 58c multi 1.60 .80
e. 78c multi 2.10 1.10
f. €2.43 multi 6.75 3.25

Castles A1435

Designs: No. 3519, €2.49, Almenar Castle. No. 3520, €2.49, Villena Castle.

2007, Sept. 10 Engr. Perf. 13¾x14
3519-3520 A1435 Set of 2 14.00 7.00

Souvenir Sheet

Statues of Asclepius, Greek God of Medicine — A1436

No. 3521: a, Statue from Museum of Ampurias, Spain. b, Statue from National Archaeological Museum, Athens.

2007, Sept. 13 Photo. Perf. 12¾x13
3521 A1436 Sheet of 2 2.50 2.50
a. 30c multi .85 .40
b. 58c multi 1.60 .80

See Greece No. 2319.

Dupont Lark — A1437   Daisy — A1438

2007, Oct. 1 Litho. Die Cut Perf. 13
Self-Adhesive
3522 A1437 30c multi .85 .40
3523 A1438 30c multi .85 .40

El Adelantado de Segovia Newspaper, 106th Anniv. — A1439

2007, Oct. 4 Photo. Perf. 13¾x14
3524 A1439 78c multi 2.25 1.10

America Issue, Education For All A1440

2007, Oct. 11
3525 A1440 78c multi 2.25 1.10

Miniature Sheet

Women's Clothing by Balenciaga In Costume Museum, Madrid — A1441

No. 3526: a, Ivory chantilly lace and taffeta dress, 1948-50. b, Red silk satin two-piece party dress, 1960. c, Red morning coat and dress, 1960s. d, Yellow linen dress.

2007, Oct. 18 Photo. Perf. 13¼x13
3526 A1441 Sheet of 4 6.25 6.25
  a. 39c multi 1.10 .55
  b. 42c multi 1.25 .60
  c. 58c multi 1.60 .80
  d. 78c multi 2.25 1.10

Altarpiece Sculpture Depicting Epiphany, by Damián Forment A1442

Children in Envelope A1443

Die Cut Perf. 13
2007, Oct. 31 Litho.
Self-Adhesive
3527 A1442 30c multi .90 .45
3528 A1443 58c multi 1.75 .85
Christmas.

Self-Portraits A1444

Self-portraits of: 39c, Pedro Berruguete. 42c, Mariano Salvador Maella.

2007, Nov. 5 Photo. Perf. 14x13¾
3529-3530 A1444 Set of 2 2.40 1.25

Souvenir Sheet

Stained-Glass Window by Alberto Martorell — A1445

Litho. & Engr.
2007, Nov. 9 Perf. 13¾x14
3531 A1445 €2.43 multi 7.25 3.75

King Juan Carlos Type of 2007
2008, Jan. 2 Photo. Perf. 12¾x13¼
Color of Portrait
3532 A1398 1c black .25 .25
3533 A1398 2c lilac rose .25 .25
3534 A1398 5c blue .25 .25
3535 A1398 10c greenish blue .30 .25
3536 A1398 31c brown .90 .45
3537 A1398 60c violet blue 1.75 .90
3538 A1398 78c rose 2.40 1.25
3539 A1398 €2.60 slate green 7.75 3.50
  Nos. 3532-3539 (8) 13.85 7.10

Toys — A1446

No. 3540: a, Steamship with wheels. b, Bean bag target with clown's face. c, Three sand pails. d, Stagecoach. e, Wafer container. f, Diabolo. g, Building blocks. h, Submarine.

2008, Jan. 2 Litho. Die Cut Perf. 13
Self-Adhesive
3540 Booklet pane of 8 7.50
  a.-h. A1446 A Any single .90 .45
Nos. 3540a-3540h each sold for 31c on day of issue.

Green Woodpecker A1447

Camellia A1448

2008, Jan. 10 Die Cut Perf. 13
Self-Adhesive
3541 A1447 31c multi .90 .45
3542 A1448 60c multi 1.75 .90

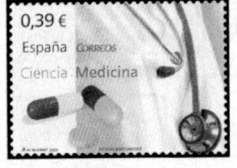

Sciences A1449

Designs: 39c, Medicine. 43c, Meteorology.

2008, Jan. 17 Litho.
Self-Adhesive
3543-3544 A1449 Set of 2 2.40 1.25
See also Nos. 3613-3614.

La Voz de Avilés Newspaper, Cent. — A1450

2008, Jan. 30 Photo. Perf. 13¾x14
3545 A1450 31c multi .95 .45

International Years — A1451

Designs: 78c, Intl. Polar Year. €2.60, Intl. Year of Planet Earth.

Die Cut Perf. 13
2008, Feb. 4 Litho.
Self-Adhesive
3546-3547 A1451 Set of 2 10.50 5.25

Hand and Phone Number for Abused Women's Hotline A1452

2008, Feb. 11 Die Cut Perf. 13
Self-Adhesive
3548 A1452 31c multi .95 .45

Black Poplar of Horcajuelo A1453

2008, Feb. 18 Photo. Perf. 14x13¾
3549 A1453 €2.44 multi 7.50 3.75

Expo Zaragoza 2008 A1454

Die Cut Perf. 13
2008, Feb. 22 Litho.
Self-Adhesive
3550 A1454 31c multi .95 .45

Civic Values A1455

Designs: 31c, Fight against child exploitation. 39c, Intergenerational solidarity. 43c, Cultural diversity.

2008, Feb. 29 Photo. Perf. 13¾x14
3551-3553 A1455 Set of 3 3.50 1.75

Archaeology — A1456

Designs: No. 3554, 31c, Bicha of Balazote. No. 3555, 31c, Funerary urn of Apophis I.

2008, Mar. 3
3554-3555 A1456 Set of 2 1.90 .95

Landscapes — A1457

Designs: No. 3556, 31c, Hoces del Río Duratón Nature Park. No. 3557, 31c, Montes de Toledo.

2008, Mar. 10
3556-3557 A1457 Set of 2 2.00 1.00

Maritime Rescue Craft A1458

Die Cut Perf. 13
2008, Mar. 12 Litho.
Self-Adhesive
3558 A1458 31c multi 1.00 .50

University of Oviedo, 400th Anniv. A1459

2008, Mar. 14 Photo. Perf. 13¾x14
3559 A1459 31c multi 1.00 .50

European Parliament, 50th Anniv. — A1460

2008, Mar. 19
3560 A1460 60c multi 1.90 .95

Common Kestrel — A1461

Tulips — A1462

2008, Apr. 1 Litho. Die Cut Perf. 13
Self-Adhesive
3561 A1461 31c multi 1.00 .50
3562 A1462 43c multi 1.40 .70

Palacio de Longoria, Madrid A1463

Casa Vicens, Barcelona A1464

Agbar Tower, Barcelona A1465

Tenerife Auditorium, Tenerife — A1466

Torrespaña, Madrid — A1467

Montjuic Communications Tower, Barcelona A1468

2008, Apr. 2   Engr.   Perf. 13¾x14
3563 A1463 31c multi   1.00 .50
Perf. 14x13¾
3564 A1464 31c multi   1.00 .50
Photo.
3565 A1465 31c multi   1.00 .50
Perf. 13¾x14
3566 A1466 31c multi   1.00 .50

Perf. 13¼x13
3567 A1467 31c multi   1.00 .50
3568 A1468 31c multi   1.00 .50
      Nos. 3563-3568 (6)   6.00 3.00

Traditional Sports and Games A1469

Designs: No. 3569, Court handball (Pelota Valenciana). No. 3570, Handball (Pelota Vasca), vert. No. 3571, Stone carrying (Levantamiento de piedras), vert. No. 3572, Bar throwing (Lanzamiento de barra), vert. No. 3573, Sling hurling (Tiro con honda), vert.
No. 3574, Rowing race (regatas de traineras). No. 3575, Human tower (castillos humanos), vert.
No. 3576 — Bowling: a, Bolo leonés. b, Bolo palma. c, Bolo asturiano.
No. 3577, vert. — Martial arts: a, Stick fighting (palo canario). b, Wrestling (lucha leonesa). c, Wrestling (lucha canaria).
No. 3578 — Throwing games: a, Chito. b, Chave. c, Calva.

2008 Photo.   Perf. 13¾x14, 14x13¾
3569 A1469 43c multi + label   1.40 .70
3570 A1469 43c multi + label   1.40 .70
3571 A1469 43c multi + label   1.40 .70
3572 A1469 43c multi + label   1.40 .70
3573 A1469 43c multi + label   1.40 .70
3574 A1469 43c multi + label   1.40 .70
3575 A1469 43c multi + label   1.25 .60
      Nos. 3569-3575 (7)   9.65 4.80
Miniature Sheets
3576   Sheet of 3 + 3 labels 4.25 2.10
a.-c. A1469 43c Any single   1.40 .70
3577   Sheet of 3 + 5 labels 4.25 2.10
a.-c. A1469 43c Any single   1.40 .70
3578   Sheet of 3 + 3 labels 3.50 1.75
a.-c. A1469 43c Any single   1.10 .55

Issued: Nos. 3569-3570, 4/16; No. 3571, 5/16; Nos. 3572-3573, 5/30. Nos. 3574, 3577, 7/16; No. 3575, 10/9; No. 3576, 6/5; No. 3578, 10/27.

Souvenir Sheet

Europa — A1470

2008, Apr. 23   Perf. 13¼x12¾
3579 A1470 60c multi   1.90 .95

Souvenir Sheet

Cross of Victory, San Salvador Cathedral, Oviedo — A1471

2008. Apr. 28   Perf. 14x13¾
3580 A1471 €2.44 multi   7.50 3.75
   Exfilna 2008 (National Philatelic Exhibition), Oviedo.

Royal Decree of the Maritime Post — A1472

2008, May 5 Litho. Die Cut Perf. 13
Self-Adhesive
3581 A1472 39c black & brown   1.25 .60
   Stamp Day.

El Progreso Newspaper, Lugo, Cent. — A1473

2008, May 9 Photo. Perf. 13¾x14
3582 A1473 31c multi   1.00 .50

Joan Oró (1923-2004), Biochemist A1474

Zenobia Camprubí (1887-1956), Literary Translator A1475

María Lejárraga (1874-1974), Writer — A1476

Design: No. 3586, Carmen Martín Gaite (1925-2000), writer.

2008, June 2   Engr.   Perf. 14x13¾
3583 A1474 31c black   1.00 .50
3584 A1475 31c ver & black   1.00 .50
3585 A1476 31c black & ver   1.00 .50
3586 A1476 31c black & ver   1.00 .50
      Nos. 3583-3586 (4)   4.00 2.00

Souvenir Sheets

Francisco de Goya Monument, Zaragoza — A1477

Model of Expo Zaragoza Grounds — A1478

Engr. (Litho. Margin)
2008   Perf. 14x13¾
3587 A1477 €2.60 Prus blue   8.00 4.00
Photo.
Perf. 13¾x14
3588 A1478 Sheet of 3   11.50 5.75
a.   31c Expo buildings   1.00 .50
b.   78c Buildings, diff.   2.40 1.25
c.   €2.60 Bridge Pavilion   8.00 4.00

Issued: No. 3587, 6/13; No. 3588, 7/4.

European Bee-eater A1479

Dahlia A1480

2008, July 1 Litho. Die Cut Perf. 13
Self-Adhesive
3589 A1479 31c multi   1.00 .50
3590 A1480 60c multi   1.90 .95

2008 Summer Olympics, Beijing A1481

2008, July 8   Perf. 13¾x14
3591 A1481 31c multi   1.00 .50

Souvenir Sheet

Spain, UEFA 2008 Soccer
Champions — A1482

2008, July 24   **Photo.**
3592 A1482 €1 multi   3.25 1.60

Souvenir Sheets

Tapestries — A1483

Tapestries of works by Francisco de Goya:
60c, The Swing. €2.60, The Blind Man and
the Guitar.

2008, July 29   **Perf. 12¾**
3593-3594 A1483   Set of 2   10.00 5.00

Miniature Sheet

Lighthouses — A1484

No. 3595: a, Barbaria Lighthouse, Isla de
Formantera. b, Irta Lighthouse, Castelón. c,
Pechiguera Lighthouse, Isla de Lanzarote. d,
Silleiro Lighthouse, Pontevedra. e, Tor-
redembarra Lighthouse, Tarragona. f, Punta
Orchilla Lighthouse, Isla de la Hierro.

2008, Sept. 2   **Photo.**   **Perf. 14x13¾**
3595 A1484   Sheet of 6   10.50 5.25
   a.-f.   60c Any single   1.75 .85

Self-Portraits
A1485

Self-portrait of: No. 3596, 31c, Antonio
Maria Esquivel (1806-57). No. 3597, 43c,
Darío de Regoyos (1857-1913).

2008, Sept. 8
3596-3597 A1485   Set of 2   2.10 1.10

Royal Spanish
Tennis Federation,
Cent. — A1486

2008, Sept. 19   **Litho.**
3598 A1486 31c red & orange   .90 .45

Jay   Daffodil
A1487   A1488

2008, Oct. 1   **Die Cut Perf. 13**
Self-Adhesive
3599 A1487 31c multi   .90 .45
3600 A1488 31c multi   .90 .45

Mushrooms — A1489

Designs: No. 3601, 31c, Lepista nuda. No.
3602, 31c, Boletus regius.

2008, Oct. 10   **Photo.**   **Perf. 13¾x14**
3601-3602 A1489   Set of 2   1.75 .85

America
Issue,
National
Day
A1490

2008, Oct. 13
3603 A1490 78c multi   2.00 1.00

Castles
A1491

Designs: No. 3604, €2.60, Maqueda Castle,
Toledo. No. 3605, €2.60, La Calahorra Castle,
Granada.

2008, Oct. 16   **Engr.**
3604-3605 A1491   Set of 2   13.50 6.75

Miniature Sheet

Women's Clothing by Pedro Rodriguez
In Costume Museum, Madrid — A1492

No. 3606: a, Red ball gown, 1968-70. b,
Strapless dress, c. 1947. c, V-neck chiffon
dress, 1960s. d, Pink crepe dress with
embroidery.

Photo. & Embossed
2008, Oct. 23   **Perf. 13¼x13**
3606 A1492   Sheet of 4   3.25 1.60
   a.-d.   31c Any single   .80 .40

Creche
Figures
A1493

Maternity, by J.
Carrero — A1494

Die Cut Perf. 13
2008, Nov. 3   **Litho.**
Self-Adhesive
3607 A1493 31c multi   .80 .40
3608 A1494 60c multi   1.60 .80

Souvenir Sheet

Dancers — A1495

No. 3609: a, Flamenco dancer, Spain. b,
Irish dancer, Ireland.

2008, Nov. 7   **Photo.**   **Perf. 13¼x13**
3609 A1495   Sheet of 2   3.50 1.75
   a.   60c multi   1.50 .75
   b.   78c multi   2.00 1.00

See Ireland Nos. 1809-1810.

Souvenir Sheet

Stained-Glass Window, by Dragant de
Burdeos — A1496

Photo., Litho. & Engr.
2008, Nov. 14   **Perf. 13¾x14**
3610 A1496 €2.60 multi   6.75 3.50

Symbols of
Nation and
Autonomous
Communities
A1497

No. 3611: a, Flag of Spain. b, Flag and map
of Asturias. c, Flag and map of Galicia. d, Flag
and map of Cantabria. e, Arms of Spain. f,
Flag and map of Cataluña. g, Flag and map of
Basque Country (Euzkadi). h, Flag and map of
Andalusia.

2009, Jan. 2   **Litho.**   **Die Cut Perf. 13**
Self-Adhesive
3611   Booklet pane of 8   7.25
   a.-h.   A1497 A Any single   .90 .45

On day of issue, Nos. 3611a-3611h each
sold for 32c.
See Nos. 3682, 3762.

Fan and
Manila
Shawl
A1498

2009, Jan. 2   **Die Cut Perf. 13**
Self-Adhesive
3612 A1498 B multi   1.75 .85

Sold for 62c on day of issue.

Sciences Type of 2008
Designs: 39c, Botany. 43c, Genetics.

2009, Jan. 12   **Die Cut Perf. 13**
Self-Adhesive
3613-3614 A1449   Set of 2   2.25 1.10

King Juan Carlos Type of 2007
Perf. 12¾x13¼
2009, Jan. 14   **Photo.**
Color of Portrait
3615 A1398   32c red   .85 .40
3616 A1398   62c gray   1.60 .80
3617 A1398 €2.47 olive green   6.50 3.25
3618 A1398 €2.70 blue   7.00 3.50
   Nos. 3615-3618 (4)   15.95 7.95

La Rioja Newspaper, 120th
Anniv. — A1499

2009, Jan. 15   **Photo.**   **Perf. 13¾x14**
3619 A1499 32c multi   .85 .40

Great Tit
A1500

Hydrangea
A1501

Die Cut Perf. 13

2009, Jan. 20   **Litho.**

Self-Adhesive

3620	A1500	32c multi	.85	.40
3621	A1501	62c multi	1.60	.80

Archaeology — A1502

Roman mosaics: No. 3622, €2.70, Oceanus, from Carranque archaeological site, Toledo. No. 3623, €2.70, Oriens, from Casa del Mitreo, Mérida.

2009, Feb. 10   **Photo.**   **Perf. 13¾x14**

3622-3623	A1502	Set of 2	14.00	7.00

Civic
Values
A1503

Designs: 32c, Planting for the Planet. 62c, Balancing of work and family life. 78c, Reduction of carbon dioxide output.

2009, Feb. 17   **Litho.**

3624-3626	A1503	Set of 3	4.50	2.25

Renewable
Energy — A1504

Designs: 32c, Hydroelectric energy. 43c, Wind energy. 62c, Solar energy. 78c, Geothermal energy.

2009, Feb. 20   **Photo.**   **Perf. 13**

3627-3630	A1504	Set of 4	5.50	2.75

Millennium
Development
Goals — A1505

2009, Mar. 2

3631	A1505	32c multi	.85	.40

Nature
Parks
A1506

Designs: No. 3632, 43c, Cañón Río Lobos Nature Park. No. 3633, 43c, Izki Nature Park.

2009, Mar. 9   **Perf. 13¾x14**

3632-3633	A1506	Set of 2	2.40	1.25

Gladiolus
A1507

Capercaillie
A1508

2009, Apr. 1 Litho.   **Die Cut Perf. 13**

Self-Adhesive

3634	A1507	32c multi	.90	.45
3635	A1508	43c multi	1.25	.60

Council of
Europe,
60th Anniv.
A1509

2009, Apr. 6   **Perf. 13¾x14**

3636	A1509	62c multi	1.75	.85

Miniature Sheet

Lighthouses — A1510

No. 3637: a, Porto Colom Lighthouse, Mallorca. b, Higuera Lighthouse, Huelva. c, Igeldo Lighthouse, Guipúzcoa. d, Arinaga Lighthouse, Grand Canary Island. e, Tower of Hercules Lighthouse, La Coruña. f, Torrox Lighthouse, Málaga.

2009, Apr. 15   **Photo.**   **Perf. 14x13¾**

3637	A1510	Sheet of 6	10.50	5.25
a.-f.		62c Any single	1.75	.85

Europa
A1511

2009, Apr. 23   **Litho.**   **Perf. 13¾x14**

3638	A1511	62c multi	1.75	.85

Intl. Year of Astronomy.

Traditional Dances — A1512

Designs: No. 3639, Isa. No. 3640, Mateixa. No. 3641, Bolero. No. 3642, Rueda (75x29mm). No. 3643, Aurresku, vert. (29x75mm). No. 3644, Muñeira, vert. No. 3645, Fandango, vert. No. 3646, Candil, vert. No. 3648, La Sardana. No. 3647, Seguidillas, vert.

No. 3649, Sevillanas, vert. (29x41mm). No. 3650, La Jota, vert. (29x41mm).

2009   **Photo.**   **Perf. 13x12¾**

3639	A1512	43c multi	1.25	.60
3640	A1512	43c multi	1.25	.60
3641	A1512	43c multi + label	1.25	.60

Perf. 12¾x13¼

3642	A1512	43c multi	1.25	.60

Perf. 13¼x12¾

3643	A1512	43c multi	1.25	.60

Perf. 12¾x13

3644	A1512	43c multi + label	1.25	.60
3645	A1512	43c multi + label	1.25	.60
3646	A1512	43c multi + label	1.25	.60
3647	A1512	43c multi + label	1.25	.60

Perf. 13x12¾

3648	A1512	43c multi + label	1.25	.60
	Nos. 3639-3648 (10)		12.50	6.00

Souvenir Sheet

Perf. 14x13¾

3649	A1512	43c multi	1.25	.60
3650	A1512	43c multi	1.25	.60

Issued: Nos. 3639, 3649, 4/27; Nos. 3640-3641, 5/14; Nos. 3642-3643, 6/4; Nos. 3644-3645, 7/22; Nos. 3646-3647, 9/14. Nos. 3648, 3650, 10/15.

King Alfonso VI of
León and Castile
(c. 1040-1109)
A1513

2009, May 7   **Photo.**   **Perf. 14x13¾**

3651	A1513	39c multi	1.10 .55

St. Dominic de la
Calzada (1019-
1109)
A1514

2009, May 7

3652	A1514	62c multi	1.75 .85

Souvenir Sheet

Stained-Glass Window of Spanish
National Mint Paper Factory,
Burgos — A1515

2009, May 29   **Litho. & Engr.**

3653	A1515	€2.70 multi	7.75 3.75

Miniature Sheet

Women's Clothing Designed by
Manuel Piña (1944-94) — A1516

No. 3654: a, Linen dress and hat. b, Knitted wool suit. c, Linen dress with hoops. d, Silk wedding dress.

Photo. & Embossed

2009, June 15   **Perf. 13¼x13**

3654	A1516	Sheet of 4	3.75	1.90
a.-d.		32c Any single	.90	.45

Graellsia
Isabelae
A1517

Geranium
A1518

2009, July 1 Litho.   **Die Cut Perf. 13**

Self-Adhesive

3655	A1517	32c multi	.90	.45
3656	A1518	62c multi	1.75	.85

Souvenir Sheet

Tapestries — A1519

No. 3657 — Tapestries of sports scenes taken from painting: a, By Francisco de Goya (El Juego de Pelota a Pala). b, By Antonio González Velázquez (Juego de Bolos).

2009, July 6   **Photo.**   **Perf. 12¾**

3657	A1519	Sheet of 2	9.75	5.00
a.		78c multi	2.25	1.10
b.		€2.70 multi	7.50	3.75

Souvenir Sheet

Introduction of the Euro, 10th Anniv. — A1520

Litho. & Engr.

2009, July 10   *Perf. 14x13¾*
3658 A1520 €1 multi   2.75 1.40

Traffic Safety — A1521

2009, July 14   Photo.   *Perf. 13x13¼*
3659 A1521 32c multi   .90 .45

Famous Men — A1522

Designs: No. 3660, 32c, Claudio Moyano (1809-90), explorer. No. 3661, 32c, Charles Darwin (1809-82), naturalist. No. 3662, 32c, Louis Braille (1809-52), educator of the blind.

Engr., Litho. & Engr. (#3662)

2009, July 15   *Perf. 14x13¾*
3660-3662 A1522 Set of 3   2.75 1.40

Braille dots on No. 3662 were applied by a thermographic process.

First Powered Flight in Spain, Cent. A1523

2009, Sept. 5   Photo.   *Perf. 13¾x14*
3663 A1523 32c multi   .95 .45

Real Sociedad Soccer Team, Cent. A1524

2009, Sept. 7   **Litho.**
3664 A1524 32c multi   .95 .45

Canal of Castile A1525

Los Tilos Bridge, La Palma Island A1526

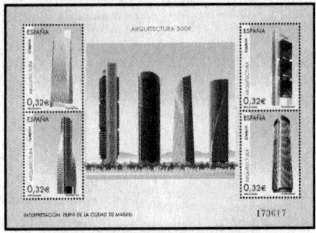

Four Towers Business Area, Madrid — A1527

No. 3667: a, Crystal Tower (with white area above top floors). b, Caja Madrid Tower (3 separate blocks in rectangular frame). c, Space Tower (with helical sides). d, Sacyr Vallehermoso Tower (with black area above top floors).

2009, Sept. 9   Photo.   *Perf. 13¾x14*
3665 A1525 32c multi   .95 .45
3666 A1526 32c multi   .95 .45

Souvenir Sheet
Perf. 14x13¾

3667 A1527   Sheet of 4   4.00 2.00
a.-d.   32c Any single   .95 .45

Arévalo Castle, Avila A1528

Javier Castle, Navarre A1529

2009, Sept. 21   Engr.   *Perf. 13¾x14*
3668 A1528 €2.70 brn & blk   8.00 4.00
3669 A1529 €2.70 black   8.00 4.00

Hyphoraia Dejeani A1530

Pansies — A1531

2009, Oct. 1   Litho.   *Die Cut Perf. 13*
Self-Adhesive
3670 A1530 32c multi   .95 .45
3671 A1531 32c multi   .95 .45

Souvenir Sheet

Isla de los Faisanes, Engraving by Adam Perelle — A1532

2009, Oct. 6   Photo.   *Perf. 13¾x14*
3672 A1532 €2.47 multi   7.50 3.75

Exfilna 2009 Stamp Exhibition, Irún.

America Issue, Spanish Playing Cards A1533

2009, Oct. 8
3673 A1533 78c multi   2.40 1.25

Royal Spanish Soccer Federation, Cent. — A1534

2009, Oct. 14   Litho.   *Perf. 14x13¾*
3674 A1534 32c multi   .95 .50

Mushrooms — A1535

Designs: No. 3675, 32c, Cantharellus cibarius. No. 3676, 32c, Boletus pinophilus.

2009, Oct. 16   Photo.   *Perf. 13¾x14*
3675-3676 A1535 Set of 2   1.90 .95

Compare with Type A1489.

Souvenir Sheet

Paintings by Diego Velázquez — A1536

No. 3677: a, The Royal Family of Felipe IV. b, The Infanta Margarita Teresa in a Blue Dress.

2009, Oct. 29   *Perf. 14x13¾*
3677 A1536 Sheet of 2   4.25 2.10
a.   62c multi   1.90 .95
b.   78c multi   2.25 1.10

See Austria No. 2228.

A1537

A1538

Christmas A1539

No. 3678 — Details from Adoration of the Shepherds and Landscape with Lady in Red, by J. Carrero: a, Holy Family. b, Adoration of the Shepherds.
32c, Maternity, by Carrero. 62c, The Coming of the Three Wise Men, by Carrero.

Perf. 13¼x12¾
2009, Oct. 31   **Litho. & Engr.**
3678 A1537   Sheet of 2   15.00 7.50
a.-b.   €2.47 Either single   7.50 3.75

Litho.
Self-Adhesive
Die Cut Perf. 13
3679 A1538 32c multi   .95 .50
3680 A1539 62c multi   1.90 .95

Juvenia 2009 Youth Philately Exhibition, Mieres — A1540

2009, Nov. 6   Litho.   *Perf. 14x13¾*
3681 A1540 39c multi   1.25 .60

Symbols of Nation and Autonomous Communities Type of 2009

No. 3682 — a, Arms and building of the Congress of Deputies. b, Flag and map of La Rioja. c, Flag and map of Castilla-La Mancha. d, Flag and map of Valencia. e, Arms and building of the Senate. f, Flag and map of the Canary Islands. g, Flag and map of Murcia. h, Flag and map of Aragon.

2010, Jan. 2   *Die Cut Perf. 13*
Self-Adhesive
3682   Booklet pane of 8   7.75
a.-h.   A1497 A Any single   .95 .45

On day of issue, Nos. 3682a-3682h each sold for 34c.

Tourism
A1541

2010, Jan. 2 Self-Adhesive Litho.
3683 A1541 B multi   1.90 .95

No. 3683 sold for 64c on day of issue.

Butterflies
A1542

Designs: No. 3684, Artimelia latreillei. No. 3685, Euphydryas aurinia. No. 3686, Zygaena rhadamanthus. No. 3687, Zerynthia rumina.

2010 Litho. Die Cut Perf. 13
Self-Adhesive
3684 A1542 34c multi   .95 .45
3685 A1542 34c multi   .95 .45
3686 A1542 64c multi   1.90 .95
3687 A1542 64c multi   1.75 .85
  Nos. 3684-3687 (4)   5.55 2.70

Issued: Nos. 3684, 3686, 1/20; Nos. 3685, 3687, 4/1.

King Juan Carlos Type of 2007
2010, Feb. 5 Photo. Perf. 12¾x13¼
Color of Portrait
3688 A1398   34c dark blue   .95 .45
3689 A1398   45c olive green 1.25 .60
3690 A1398   64c bister   1.75 .85
3691 A1398   €2.75 brt rose lil 7.50 3.75
  Nos. 3688-3691 (4)   11.45 5.65

Civic
Values
A1543

Designs: €1, Trash recycling. €2, Responsible consumption of goods (jar with lock).

2010, Feb. 11 Litho. Perf. 13¾x14
3692-3693 A1543 Set of 2   8.25 4.00

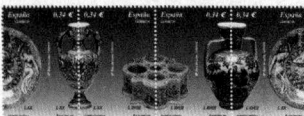

Ceramics — A1544

No. 3694 — Items from Ruiz de Luna Museum, Talavera: a, Plate from 1970 at left, amphora from 20th cent. at right. b, Amphora at left, inkwell from 18th cent. at right. c, Inkwell at left, pitcher from 18th cent. at right. d, Pitcher at left, plate at right.

Perf. 13¼x13¾
2010, Feb. 18 Photo.
3694 A1544 Horiz. strip of 4 3.75 1.90
  a.-d. 34c Any single   .90 .45

Spanish Presidency of the European Union — A1545

Background color: 34c, Red. 64c, Gray.

Die Cut Perf. 13
2010, Feb. 22 Litho.
Self-Adhesive
3695-3696 A1545 Set of 2   2.75 1.40

Musical Instruments
A1546

Design: No. 3697, Trumpet (trompeta). No. 3698, Euphonium (bombardino). 45c, Tenor saxophone. 64c, French horn.

2010 Litho. Die Cut Perf. 13
Self-Adhesive
3697 A1546 34c multi   .95 .45
3698 A1546 34c multi   .95 .45
3699 A1546 45c multi   1.25 .60
3700 A1546 64c multi   1.60 .80
  Nos. 3697-3700 (4)   4.75 2.30

Issued: No. 3697, 4/9; No. 3698, 10/5; No. 3699, 2/24; No. 3700, 7/1.

Constituent
Assembly,
Bicent. — A1547

2010, Mar. 1 Litho. Perf. 14x13¾
3701 A1547 34c multi   .95 .45

Souvenir Sheet

Cathedrals of Plasencia — A1548

2010, Mar. 4   Litho. & Engr.
3702 A1548 €2.75 brown & blue 7.50 3.75

Goya Award, Poster for Film "Celda 211"
A1549

2010, Mar. 9 Litho. Perf. 13¾x14
3703 A1549 34c multi   .95 .45

Seven Goya Awards, Poster for Film "Agora"
A1550

2010, Apr. 5 Litho. Perf. 13¾x13¼
3704 A1550 34c multi   .95 .45

Latin American Independence, Bicent. — A1551

2010, Apr. 7   Photo.
3705 A1551 €2.49 multi   6.75 3.50

UNESCO World Heritage Sites — A1552

Designs: No. 3706, 45c, Patio of Casa de las Torres, Ubeda. No. 3707, 45c, Jabalquinto Palace, Baeza.

2010, Apr. 15   Perf. 12¾
3706-3707 A1552 Set of 2   2.40 1.25

Urban Planners
A1553

Designs: No. 3708, 34c, Carlos María de Castro (1810-93), and map of Madrid. No. 3709, 34c, Ildefonso Cerdá (1815-76), and map of Barcelona.

2010 Photo. Perf. 13¾x13¼
3708-3709 A1553 Set of 2   1.90 .95

Issued: No. 3708, 4/20; No. 3709, 10/14.

Gran Via, Madrid, Cent. — A1554

2010, Apr. 21 Litho. Perf. 13¼x13¾
3710 A1554 34c blue & yellow .90 .45

Souvenir Sheet

Spanish Pavilion at Expo 2010, Shanghai — A1555

Perf. 13¾x13¼
2010, Apr. 21   Photo.
3711 A1555 €2.49 multi   6.75 3.50

Levante U. D. Soccer Team, Cent. (in 2009)
A1556

2010, Apr. 23
3712 A1556 34c multi   .90 .45

El Correo Newspaper, Bilbao, Cent. — A1557

2010, Apr. 30   Perf. 13¼x13¾
3713 A1557 34c multi   .90 .45

Europa
A1558

2010, May 6   Perf. 13¾x13¼
3714 A1558 64c multi   1.75 .85

Souvenir Sheet

Kingdom of León, 1100th Anniv. — A1559

Photo. & Embossed With Foil Application
Perf. 13x12¼x12¼x13x12¾
Syncopated
2010, May 6
3715 A1559 €2.49 multi   6.50 3.25

Compostela Jubilee Year — A1560

Die Cut Perf. 13
2010, May 13   Litho.
Self-Adhesive
3716 A1560 34c multi   .85 .40

Parks — A1561

Flora or fauna and scenery from: No. 3717, 45c, Sierras de Cazoria, Segura y Las Villas Nature Park. No. 3718, 45c, Doñana National

Park. No. 3719, 45c, Garajonay National Park. No. 3720, 45c, Picos de Europa National Park. No. 3721, 45c, Monfragüe National Park. No. 3722, 45c, Sierra Nevada National Park. No. 3723, 45c, Ordesa y Monte Perdido National Park. No. 3724, 45c, Lago de Sanabria Nature Park. No. 3725, 45c, Teide National Park. No. 3726, 45c, Cabrera Archipelago National Park. No. 3727, 45c, Aigüestortes y Lago de San Mauricio National Park. No. 3728, 45c, Cabo de Gata Nijar Nature Park.

2010   Photo.   Perf. 13¼x13¾
3717-3728 A1561 Set of 12   14.50 7.25

Issued: Nos. 3717-3719, 5/20; Nos. 3720-3722, 7/19; Nos. 3723-3725, 9/15; Nos. 3726-3728, 10/2.

2010 Ibero-American Athletics Championships, San Fernando A1562

2010 European Athletics Championships, Barcelona A1563

2010 World Cup Soccer Championships, South Africa — A1564

2010, June 4
3729 A1562 34c multi   .85   .40
3730 A1563 64c multi   1.60   .80
3731 A1564 78c multi   1.90   .95
   Nos. 3729-3731 (3)   4.35 2.15

Gregorio Marañón (1887-1960), Founder of Institute of Medical Pathology — A1565

Julián Arcas (1832-82), Guitarist — A1566

2010, June 11   Perf. 13¾x13¼
3732 A1565 34c multi   .85   .40

Perf. 13¼x13¾
3733 A1566 34c pur & orange   .85   .40

Entry Into European Community, 25th Anniv. — A1567

Die Cut Perf. 13
2010, June 12   Litho.
3734 A1567 34c multi   .85   .45

Souvenir Sheet

Oscar Niemeyer International Cultural Center, Asturias — A1568

2010, June 19   Perf. 13¾x13¼
3735 A1568 €2.49 multi   6.25 3.25

Filatem 2010 Thematic Philatelic Exhibition, Asturias.

José Luis López Vázquez (1922-2009), Actor — A1569

2010, July 6 Photo. Perf. 13¼x13¾
3736 A1569 45c multi   1.25   .60

Souvenir Sheet

Zenobia and Emperor Aurelian, tapestry by Gerard Peemas — A1570

2010, July 12
3737 A1570 78c multi   2.10 1.10

Souvenir Sheet

Segovia Cathedral — A1571

Litho. & Engr.
2010, July 15   Perf. 14x13¾
3738 A1571 €2.75 blue & brn 7.25 3.75

Renewable Energy — A1572

Designs: No. 3739, 78c, Biomass energy. No. 3740, 78c, Tidal energy (mareomotriz). No. 3741, 78c, Wave energy (undimotriz).

2010, Sept. 3 Photo. Perf. 13¼x13
3739-3741 A1572 Set of 3   6.00 3.00

World Alzheimer's Disease Day — A1573

2010, Sept. 9   Perf. 13¾x13¼
3742 A1573 34c multi   .90   .45

Cádiz Soccer Team, Cent. A1574

2010, Sept. 10
3743 A1574 34c multi   .90   .45

Roman Walls of Lugo UNESCO World Heritage Site — A1575

Mosque-Cathedral of Cordoba UNESCO World Heritage Site — A1576

2010, Sept. 17 Photo. Perf. 13x12¾
3744 A1575 34c multi   .95   .45
Souvenir Sheet
Litho. & Engr.
Perf.
3745 A1576 €2 multi   5.50 2.75

Miniature Sheet

Lighthouses — A1577

No. 3746: a, Avilés Lighthouse, San Juan de Nieva, Asturias. b, Ciutadella de Menorca Lighthouse, Menorca Island. c, Cabo de Huertas Lighthouse, Alicante. d, Punta de la Polacra Lighthouse, Nijar, Almería. e, San Cibrao Lighthouse, Cervo, Lugo. f, Punta Cumplida Lighthouse, Barlovento, La Palma Island.

Perf. 13¼x13¾
2010, Sept. 20   Photo.
3746 A1577 Sheet of 6   10.50 5.25
  a.-f. 64c Any single   1.75   .85

Famous Men — A1578

Designs: No. 3747, 34c, Francisco Ayala (1906-2009), writer. No. 3748, 34c, Gonzalo Torrente Ballester (1910-99), writer. No. 3749, 34c, Vicente Ferrer (1920-2009), humanitarian.

Litho. & Engr.
2010, Oct. 8   Perf. 14x13¾
3747-3749 A1578 Set of 3   3.00 1.50

America Issue, Spanish Arms — A1579

Perf. 13¼x13¾
2010, Oct. 11   Photo.
3750 A1579 78c multi   2.25 1.10

People, Flags of Bicentennial Group Countries — A1580

2010, Oct. 11   **Perf. 13¾x13¼**
3751 A1580 78c multi   2.25 1.10

The Bicentennial Group countries are Spain and nine Ibero-American countries (Argentina, Bolivia, Chile, Colombia, Ecuador, El Salvador, Mexico, Paraguay, and Venezuela) that achieved their independence from Spain 200 years ago.

El Día Newspaper, Santa Cruz de Tenerife, Cent. — A1581

2010, Oct. 15
3752 A1581 34c multi   1.00 .50

Miniature Sheet

Women's Clothing Designed by Manuel Pertegaz — A1582

No. 3753: a, Silk wedding dress. b, Taffeta suit and skirt. c, Taffeta cocktail dress with floral print. d, Black lace and white satin cocktail dress.

Photo. & Embossed
2010, Oct. 15   **Perf. 13¼x13**
3753 A1582 Sheet of 4   4.00 2.00
a.-d.   34c Any single   1.00 .50

Souvenir Sheet

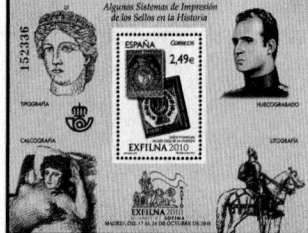

Spain #18 and Cliché — A1583

2010, Oct. 18 Litho.   **Perf. 13¼x13¾**
3754 A1583 €2.49 multi   7.00 3.50
Exfilna 2010 National Philatelic Exhibition, Madrid.

Souvenir Sheet

Religious Buildings in Spain and Turkey — A1584

No. 3755: a, Santa María de la Mayor Collegiate Church, Toro, Spain. b, Ortaköy Mosque, Istanbul, Turkey.

Perf. 13¾x13¼
2010, Oct. 18   Photo.
3755 A1584   Sheet of 2   3.50 1.75
a.-b.   64c Either single   1.75 .85
See Turkey No. 3240.

Souvenir Sheet

Victory of Spanish Team at 2010 World Cup Soccer Championships — A1585

Photo. & Embossed With Foil Application
2010, Oct. 21   **Perf. 13¼x13¾**
3756 A1585 €2 multi   5.75 3.00

Christmas A1586

Designs: 34c, Mother holding baby. 64c, Columns, arms holding baby.

Die Cut Perf. 13
2010, Nov. 3   Litho.
Self-Adhesive
3757-3758 A1586 Set of 2   2.75 1.40

Souvenir Sheet

Sculpture From San Salvador Monastery, Oña — A1587

2010, Nov. 5 Photo.   **Perf. 13¼x13¾**
3759 A1587 78c multi   2.25 1.10
San Salvador Monastery, 1000th anniv.

Souvenir Sheet

Bilbao Cathedral — A1588

Litho. & Engr.
2010, Nov. 8   **Perf. 14x13¾**
3760 A1588 €2.75 multi   7.50 3.75

Tourism A1589

2011, Jan. 3 Litho.   **Die Cut Perf. 13**
Self-Adhesive
3761 A1589 B multi   1.75 .85
No. 3761 sold for 65c on day of issue.

Symbols of Nation and Autonomous Communities Type of 2009

No. 3762: a, Constitutional Court Building. b, Flag and map of Ceuta. c, Flag and map of Extremadura. d, Flag and map of Melilla. e, Flag and map of Balearic Islands. f, Flag and map of Madrid. g, Flag and map of Castilla y León. h, Flag and map of Navarra.

2011, Jan. 3   **Die Cut Perf. 13**
Self-Adhesive
3762   A1497   Booklet pane of 8   7.50
a.-h.   A1497 A Any single   .90 .45
On day of issue, Nos. 3762a-3762h each sold for 35c.

Butterflies A1590

Designs: No. 3763, 65c, Melanargia ines. No. 3764, 65c, Charaxes jasius. No. 3765,

65c, Papilio machaon. No. 3766, 65c, Argynnis adippe.

2011, Jan. 12   Litho.
Self-Adhesive
3763-3766 A1590 Set of 4   7.00 3.50

St. Sebastian Festival, El Pont de Suert, 425th Anniv. — A1591

2011, Jan. 20   **Perf. 14x13¾**
3767 A1591 35c multi   .95 .45

2010 Malaspina Oceanographic Expedition — A1592

2011, Jan. 20   **Die Cut Perf. 13**
Self-Adhesive
3768 A1592 50c multi   1.40 .70

Stringed Instruments A1593

Designs: No. 3769, 35c, Guitar. No. 3770, 35c, Violin. No. 3771, 35c, Lute. No. 3772, 35c, Mandolin.

2011, Jan. 24   Litho.
Self-Adhesive
3769-3772 A1593 Set of 4   3.75 1.90

Almería Railway Station A1594

2011, Jan. 27   **Perf. 13¾x14**
3773 A1594 35c multi   .95 .50

King Juan Carlos Type of 2007
2011, Feb. 4 Photo. Perf. 12¾x13¼
Color of Portrait
3774 A1398   35c lilac   .95 .50
3775 A1398   50c bright blue   1.40 .70
3776 A1398   80c brt blue grn   2.25 1.10
3777 A1398   €2.84 blue violet   7.75 4.00
    Nos. 3774-3777 (4)   12.35 6.30

Marie Curie (1867-1934), Chemist — A1595

Litho. & Engr.
2011, Feb. 7   **Perf. 13¾x14**
3778 A1595 35c multi   .95 .45
Intl. Year of Chemistry.

Property Act, 150th Anniv. A1596

2011, Feb. 8 Litho.
3779 A1596 65c multi 1.75 .90

Civic Values A1597

Designs: No. 3780, 35c, Respect on the Internet. No. 3781, 35c, Protect people with disabilities. No. 3782, 35c, Clean up and dispose of dog droppings. No. 3783, 35c, Use safety belts.

2011, Feb. 18 *Die Cut Perf. 13*
Self-Adhesive
3780-3783 A1597 Set of 4 4.00 2.00

Souvenir Sheet

Sigüenza Cathedral — A1598

2011, Mar. 4 *Perf. 13¾x14*
3784 A1598 €2.84 multi 8.00 4.00

Intl. Women's Day A1599

Die Cut Perf. 13
2011, Mar. 8 **Self-Adhesive** **Litho.**
3785 A1599 80c multi 2.25 1.10

Europa — A1600

2011, Apr. 4 **Photo.** *Perf. 13¼x13¾*
3786 A1600 65c multi 1.90 .95
Intl. Year of Forests.

Jubilee Year of the Holy Cross of Canjáyar A1601

2011, Apr. 11 **Litho.** *Perf. 14x13¾*
3787 A1601 65c multi 1.90 .95

Miniature Sheet

Lighthouses — A1602

No. 3788: a, Calella Lighthouse, Barcelona. b, Chipiona Lighthouse, Cádiz. c, Punta La Entallada Lighthouse, Fuerteventura Island. d, Cap Sant Sebastià Lighthoue, Girona. e, Castell de Ferro Lighthouse, Granada. f, Valencia Lighthouse, Valencia.

Perf. 13¼x13¾
2011, Apr. 11 **Photo.**
3788 A1602 Sheet of 6 11.50 5.75
a.-f. 65c Any single 1.90 .95

Juvenia 2011 National Youth Philatelic Exhibition, Santa Fe — A1603

2011, Apr. 12 **Litho.** *Perf. 14x13¾*
3789 A1603 65c multi 1.90 .95

Movie Poster for *Pa Negre*, Winner of 2010 Goya Award for Best Film A1604

Goya Award — A1605

2011, Apr. 26 **Litho.** *Perf. 13¾x14*
3790 A1604 35c multi 1.00 .50
Souvenir Sheet
Photo.
Perf. 13¾x13¼
3791 A1605 €2.84 multi 8.25 4.25
Goya Awards, 25th anniv.

Souvenir Sheet

Alhambra of Granada UNESCO World Heritage Site — A1606

2011, May 12 **Litho. & Engr.** **Perf.**
3792 A1606 €2 multi 5.75 3.00

Souvenir Sheet

Dido Bids Farewell to Aeneas, 17th Cent. Tapestry — A1607

Perf. 13¼x13¾
2011, May 16 **Photo.**
3793 A1607 €2.84 multi 8.25 4.25

Miniature Sheet

Military Aviation in Spain, Cent. — A1608

No. 3794: a, Aerospatiale SA-332 Super Puma helicopter (41x29mm). r. b, Two CASA-101 Aviojets (41x29mm). c, Lockheed C-130 Hercules (41x29mm). d, Eurofighter EF-2000 Typhoon (123x29mm).

2011, May 31 *Perf. 13¾x13¼*
3794 A1608 Sheet of 4 7.75 4.00
a.-d. 65c Any single 1.90 .95

Conversion of Abandoned Railroad Lines to Greenways — A1609

2011, June 13 **Litho.** *Perf. 13¾x14*
3795 A1609 35c multi 1.00 .50

Corps of Architects of the Treasury, 105th Anniv. A1610

2011, June 17
3796 A1610 80c multi 2.25 1.10

World Youth Day — A1611

2011, July 1 *Perf. 14x13¾*
3797 A1611 80c multi 2.25 1.10
See Vatican City No. 1472.

Souvenir Sheet

Albarracín Cathedral — A1612

2011, July 15 **Litho. & Engr.**
3798 A1612 €2.84 blue & green 8.25 4.25

Film Personalities A1613

Designs: No. 3799, 80c, Luis García Berlanga (1921-2010), director. No. 3800, 80c, Rafael Azcona (1926-2008), screenwriter.

2011, July 22 **Litho.**
3799-3800 A1613 Set of 2 4.75 2.40

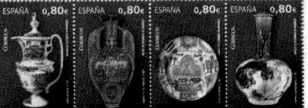

Ceramics From Manises — A1614

No. 3801: a, Pitcher with lid and handle. b, Vase. c, Plate. d, Bottle.

Perf. 13¼x13¾
2011, Sept. 5 **Photo.**
3801 A1614 Horiz. strip of 4 9.00 4.50
a.-d. 80c Any single 2.25 1.10

Miniature Sheet

Art by Antoni Tàpies (1923-2012) — A1615

No. 3802 — Unnamed works depicting: a, Face and flags on blue background. b, Horizontal line across brown area. c, Chair on gray background. d, Abstract on red background.

2011, Sept. 12
3802 A1615 Sheet of 4   9.00 4.50
a.-d.   80c Any single   2.25 1.10

Miniature Sheets

Spanish National Soccer Team — A1616

No. 3803 — Soccer players from 1900-70 with Spanish text in black capitals: a, Pichichi (41x56mm). b, Zamora Parando (41x56mm). c, El Gol de Zarra (41x56mm). d, Una Excelente Delantera (82x28mm). e, El Gol de Marcelino (82x28mm).

No. 3804 — Soccer players from 1970-2010 with Spanish text in black capitals: a, Celebración del Gol Clasificatorio para Argentina 78 (41x56mm). b, Mundial España 82 (41x56mm). c, Victoria de la Selección en los Juegos Olímpicos 92 (82x28mm). d, El Gol de Torres en la Eurocopa 2008 (41x56mm). e, El Gol de Iniesta en el Mundial 2010 (82x28mm).

2011, Sept. 19   **Perf. 13¼x13¼**
3803 A1616 Sheet of 5 + label   11.50 5.50
a.-e.   80c Any single   2.25 1.10
3804 A1616 Sheet of 5 + label   11.50 5.50
a.-e.   80c Any single   2.25 1.10

Souvenir Sheet

Exfilna 2011 National Philatelic Exposition, Valladolid — A1617

2011, Oct. 1   **Litho.**   **Perf. 13¾x14**
3805 A1617 €2.84 multi   7.75 4.00

Awarding of 2010 Nobel Prize in Literature to Mario Vargas Llosa — A1618

Litho. (Litho & Engr. Label)
2011, Oct. 3   **Perf. 14x13¾**
3806 A1618 80c multi   2.25 1.10

Miguel Delibes (1920-2010), Writer — A1619

Gaspar Melchor de Jovellanos (1744-1811), Statesman and Writer — A1620

Luis Rosales (1910-92), Poet A1621

Miguel Servet (1511-53), Physician and Theologian — A1622

Litho. & Engr.
2011, Oct. 3   **Perf. 14x13¾**
3807 A1619 80c multi   2.25 1.10
  Perf. 13¾x14
3808 A1620 80c multi   2.25 1.10
  Litho.
3809 A1621 80c multi   2.25 1.10
3810 A1622 80c multi   2.25 1.10
  Nos. 3807-3810 (4)   9.00 4.40

America Issue, Mailbox — A1623

  Perf. 13¼x13¾
2011, Oct. 11   **Photo.**
3811 A1623 80c multi   2.25 1.10

Miniature Sheet

Women's Clothing Designed by Elio Berhanyer — A1624

No. 3812: a, Black and white strapless ball gown. b, Green and white striped dress. c, Coat and dress. d, Black and white polka dot ball gown.

Photo. & Embossed
2011, Oct. 20   **Perf. 13¼x13**
3812 A1624 Sheet of 4   9.00 4.50
a.-d.   80c Any single   2.25 1.10

Holy Family with Baby Jesus, Sculpture by Luisa Roldán A1625

Holy Family — A1626

Die Cut Perf. 13
2011, Nov. 3   **Self-Adhesive**   **Litho.**
3813 A1625 35c multi   1.00 .50
3814 A1626 65c multi   1.90 .95
  Christmas.

National Library, 300th Anniv. A1627

2011, Nov. 4   **Perf. 13¾x14**
3815 A1627 80c multi   2.25 1.10

Barcelona Boat Show, 50th Anniv. — A1628

2011, Nov. 5   **Perf. 14x13¾**
3816 A1628 80c multi   2.25 1.10

Souvenir Sheet

Tarazona Cathedral — A1629

2011, Nov. 8   **Litho. & Engr.**
3817 A1629 €2.84 blue & green 7.75 4.00

Year of Russia in Spain and Year of Spain in Russia A1630

2011, Nov. 10   **Litho.**   **Perf. 13¾x14**
3818 A1630 80c multi   2.25 1.10

Arches and Gates A1631

No. 3819: a, Macarena Arch, Seville. b, Alcalá Gate, Madrid. c, Santa María Arch, Burgos. d, Serrano Gate, Valencia. e, Triumphal Arch, Barcelona. f, Palmas Gate, Badajoz. g, Bisagra Gate, Toledo. h, Bará Arch, Tarragona.

2012, Jan. 2   **Die Cut Perf. 13**
  Self-Adhesive
3819   Booklet pane of 8   7.75
a.-h. A1631 A Any single   .95 .45
  Nos. 3819a-3819h each sold for 36c on day of issue.

Tourism A1632

2012, Jan. 2   **Litho.**
  Self-Adhesive
3820 A1632 B multi   1.90 .95
  No. 3820 sold for 70c on day of issue.

Lorca Tourist Attractions A1633

Designs: No. 3821, 36c, Virgin of the Orchards Sanctuary (Santuario de la Virgen de las Huertas). No. 3822, 36c, Castle (Castillo). No. 3823, 36c, Town Hall (Ayuntamiento). No. 3824, 36c, Guevara Palace (Palacio de Guevara). No. 3825, 36c, St. Patrick's Collegiate Church (Colegiata de San Patricio).

2012, Jan. 2   **Die Cut Perf. 13**
  Self-Adhesive
3821-3825 A1633 Set of 5   4.75 2.40

Civic Values A1634

Designs: 36c, No pollution. 51c, Follow speed limits. 70c, Avoid distractions while driving.

2012, Jan. 9 Self-Adhesive Litho.
3826-3828 A1634 Set of 3 4.25 2.10

Intl. Year of Sustainable Energy for All — A1635

2012, Feb. 27 Die Cut Perf. 13
Self-Adhesive
3829 A1635 70c multi 1.90 .95

King Juan Carlos — A1636

Perf. 12¾x13¼
2012, Feb. 27 Photo.
Color of Portrait
3830 A1636 36c red .95 .50
3831 A1636 51c green 1.40 .70
3832 A1636 85c blue 2.25 1.10
3833 A1636 €2.90 dk rose brn 7.75 4.00
  Nos. 3830-3833 (4) 12.35 6.30
    See Nos. 3887-3890.

Tourism A1637

Die Cut Perf. 13
2012, Feb. 28 Litho.
Self-Adhesive
3834 A1637 70c multi 1.90 .95

Military Anniversaries A1638

Designs: No. 3835, 85c, Battle of Navas de Tolosa, 800th anniv. No. 3836, 85c, Conquest of Navarre, 500th anniv.

2012, Feb. 29 Perf. 14x13¾
3835-3836 A1638 Set of 2 4.50 2.25

Souvenir Sheet

Matron and Warrior in Boat, Tapestry by Gerard Peemans — A1639

2012, Mar. 8 Photo. Perf. 13¼x13¾
3837 A1639 €2.90 multi 7.75 4.00

Royal and Military Order of San Fernando, 200th Anniv. — A1640

2012, Mar. 12 Litho. Perf. 14x13¾
3838 A1640 85c multi 2.25 1.10

1812 Constitution, Bicent. A1641

2012, Mar. 16 Photo. Perf. 12¾
3839 A1641 36c multi .95 .45

Souvenir Sheet

Spanish Coin Depicting Burgos Cathedral — A1642

2012, Mar. 16 Litho. & Engr. Perf.
3840 A1642 €2 multi 5.25 2.60
  Burgos Cathedral UNESCO World Heritage Site.

Stringed Instruments A1643

No. 3841: a, Harp. b, Balalaika. c, Banjo. d, Sitar. e, Rabel (rebec).

2012, Apr. 2 Litho. Die Cut Perf. 13
Self-Adhesive
3841 Horiz. strip of 5 4.75
  a.-e. A1643 36c Any single .95 .45

Europa — A1644

2012, Apr. 4 Perf. 14x13¾
3842 A1644 70c multi 1.90 .95

Severiano Ballesteros (1957-2011), Golfer — A1645

José Hierro (1922-2002), Poet — A1646

Manuel Garcia Matos (1912-74), Musicologist — A1647

2012, Apr. 11 Perf. 13¾x14
3843 A1645 70c multi 1.90 .95
3844 A1646 70c multi 1.90 .95
3845 A1647 70c multi 1.90 .95
  Nos. 3843-3845 (3) 5.70 2.85

Souvenir Sheet

Seville Cathedral — A1648

2012, Apr. 17
3846 A1648 €2.90 multi 7.75 3.75

Actors — A1649

No Habrá Paz para los Malvados, Winner of 2012 Goya Award for Best Film A1650

Designs: No. 3847, Fernando Rey (1917-94). No. 3848, Francisco Rabal (1926-2001).

2012, Apr. 26 Perf. 14x13¾
3847 A1649 36c multi .95 .45
3848 A1649 36c multi .95 .45
Perf. 13¾x14
3849 A1650 70c multi 1.90 .95
  Nos. 3847-3849 (3) 3.80 1.85

Souvenir Sheet

Toledo Cathedral — A1651

Litho. & Engr.
2012, May 21 Perf. 13¾x14
3850 A1651 €2.90 blue & brown 7.25 3.75

Notary Law, 150th Anniv. A1652

2012, May 28 Litho.
3851 A1652 85c multi 2.25 1.10

Antonio Mingote (1919-2012), Cartoonist A1653

2012, May 30 Perf. 14x13¾
3852 A1653 36c multi .90 .45

Miniature Sheet

Coches de época

Automobiles — A1654

No. 3853: a, 1934 Citröen C-11. b, 1956 Renault Dauphine. c, 1957 SEAT 600. d, 1961 Simca 1000.

2012, May 30   **Perf. 13¾x14**
3853   A1654   Sheet of 4   9.00   4.50
a.-d.   85c Any single   2.25   1.10

Armory School, Eibar, Cent. A1655

2012, June 7
3854   A1655   85c multi   2.10   1.10

Pendones de León

Banners of Léon — A1656

       Perf. 13¼x13¾
2012, June 12   **Photo.**
3855   A1656   85c multi   2.10   1.10

Souvenir Sheet

CATEDRAL DE SANTIAGO DE COMPOSTELA

Statue of St. James, Santiago de Compostela Cathedral — A1657

2012, June 14   **Litho.**   **Perf. 14x13¾**
3856   A1657   €2.90 multi   7.25   3.75

CUERPO DE ABOGADOS DEL ESTADO

Emblem of State Lawyers Corps — A1658

2012, June 18
3857   A1658   85c multi   2.10   1.10

Spanish Olympic Committee, Cent. — A1659

Spanish Olympic Committee emblem and: No. 3858, 85c, Lucius Minicius Natalis, charioteer and first Spanish champion in ancient Olympics. No. 3859, 85c, Gonzalo de Figueroa y Torres (1861-1921), founder of Spanish Olympic Committee. No. 3860, 85c, Juan Antonio Samaranch (1920-2010), International Olympic Committee President.

2012, July 2   **Litho.**   **Perf. 13¾x14**
3858-3860   A1659   Set of 3   6.25   3.25

Sciences — A1660

Noi. 3861: a, Geology. b, Paleontonlogy.

2012, July 11   **Perf. 14x13¾**
3861   A1660   Horiz. pair   1.80   .90
a.-b.   36c Either single   .90   .45

Souvenir Sheet

CATEDRAL DE OVIEDO   178649

Oviedo Cathedral — A1661

2012, July 13   **Litho. & Engr.**
3862   A1661   €2.90 multi   7.25   3.75

Churches — A1662

No. 3863: a, Episcopal Palace, Astorga, Spain. b, Church of the Savior on Spilled Blood, St. Petersburg, Russia.

2012, July 17   **Litho.**
3863   A1662   Horiz. pair   4.25   2.10
a.-b.   85c Either single   2.10   1.10

See Russia No. 7376.

Miniature Sheet

ARTE CONTEMPORÁNEO

MANOLO VALDÉS   190699

Art by Manolo Valdés — A1663

No. 3864: a, Profil con Fondo Azul (Profile with Blue Background), painting. b, La Infanta Margarita, sculpture. c, Reina Mariana XII (Queen Mariana XII), sculpture. d, Vivienne III, painting.

2012, July 18   **Perf. 14x13¾**
3864   A1663   Sheet of 4   5.00   2.50
a.-d.   51c Any single   1.25   .60

Mushrooms — A1664

Designs: No. 3865, 51c, Entoloma lividum. No. 3866, 51c, Calocybe gambosa. No. 3867, 51c, Amanita verna.

2012, Sept. 6   **Perf. 13¾x14**
3865-3867   A1664   Set of 3   4.00   2.00

Souvenir Sheet

CATEDRAL DE PALMA DE MALLORCA   142199

Palma de Mallorca Cathedral — A1665

2012, Sept. 10   **Litho.**
3868   A1665   €2.90 multi   7.50   3.75

Old Alcaudete Train Station and Olive Oil Greenway, Jaen A1666

2012, Sept. 12   **Perf. 13¾x14**
3869   A1666   70c multi   1.90   .95

Miniature Sheet

Women's Clothing Designed by Pedro del Hierro — A1667

No. 3870: a, Red violet satin dress. b, Sequined lace dress with floral pattern. c, Pink and black party dress. d, Dress with white lace and pink bodice.

Photo. & Embossed
2012, Sept. 17   **Perf. 13¼x13**
3870   A1667   Sheet of 4   9.00   4.50
a.-d.   85c Any single   2.25   1.10

Souvenir Sheet

Lady of Calahorra — A1668

2012, Oct. 5   Litho.   Perf. 14x13¾
3871 A1668 €2.90 multi   7.50 3.75
    Exfilna 2012 National Philatelic Exhibition,
Calahorra.

Souvenir Sheet

Barcelona Cathedral — A1669

2012, Oct. 9   Litho. & Engr.
3872 A1669 €2.90 brown   7.50 3.75

Castilla y León Museum of
Contemporary Art, Léon — A1670

National
Museum of
Roman
Art, Mérida
A1671

Queen
Sofia
National
Museum of
Art, Madrid
A1672

Museum of
Art and
Popular
Costumes,
Seville
A1673

2012, Oct. 11   Litho.   Perf. 13¾x14
3873 A1670 51c multi   1.40 .70
3874 A1671 51c multi   1.40 .70
3875 A1672 51c multi   1.40 .70
3876 A1673 51c multi   1.40 .70
    Nos. 3873-3876 (4)   5.60 2.80

Colonial
Postal
Shelter in
Andes
Mountains
A1674

2012, Oct. 16
3877 A1674 85c multi   2.25 1.10

Mammals — A1675

    No. 3878: a, Red deer (denomination at
LR). b, Ibex (denomination at LL).

2012, Oct. 19   Perf. 12¾
3878 A1675 Horiz. pair   4.50 2.25
a.-b.   85c Either single 2.25 1.10
    See Romania Nos. 5395-5396.

Adoration
of the
Magi,
Mural in
Chapel of
St. Martin,
Salamanca
A1676

Madonna and
Child — A1677

2012, Nov. 5   Die Cut Perf. 13
                Self-Adhesive
3879 A1676 36c multi   .95 .45
3880 A1677 70c multi   1.75 .90
        Christmas.

Souvenir Sheet

Spain, Champions of 2012 UEFA
European Soccer
Tournament — A1678

2012, Nov. 6   Perf.
3881 A1678 €1 multi   2.60 1.40

America Issue,
Legend of the
Lovers of
Teruel — A1679

2012, Nov. 8   Perf. 14x13¾
3882 A1679 85c multi   2.25 1.10

Civil Administrators — A1680

State Comptrollers and
Auditors — A1681

2012, Nov. 12   Perf. 13¾x14
3883 A1680 85c multi   2.25 1.10
3884 A1681 85c multi   2.25 1.10

Souvenir Sheet

White Virgin and Child, León
Cathedral — A1682

**   Litho. & Engr.**
2012, Nov. 15   Perf. 14x13¾
3885 A1682 €2.90 brown   7.50 3.75

22nd Ibero-American Summit,
Cádiz — A1683

2012, Nov. 16   Litho.   Perf. 13¾x14
3886 A1683 36c multi   .95 .45

King Juan Carlos Type of 2012
2013, Jan. 2   Photo.   Perf. 12¾x13¼
            Color of Portrait
3887 A1636 37c Prus bl   1.00 .50
3888 A1636 52c orange   1.40 .70
3889 A1636 75c yel green   2.00 1.00
3890 A1636 90c brown   2.40 1.25
    Nos. 3887-3890 (4)   6.80 3.45

Tourism
A1684

2013, Jan. 2   Litho.   Die Cut Perf. 13
            Self-Adhesive
3891 A1684 75c multi   2.00 1.00

Arches and
Gates
A1685

    No. 3892: a, Alcázar Gate, Avila. b, Roman
Arch of Cáparra, Cáceres. c, Roman Arch of
Medinaceli. d, Capuchin Arch, Andújar. e,
Arch of the Giants, Antequera. f, Toledo Gate,
Madrid. g, Castilla Gate, Tolosa. h, Roman
Arch of Cavanes, Castellón.

2013, Jan. 2   Die Cut Perf. 13
            Self-Adhesive
3892   Booklet pane of 8   8.00
a.-h. A1685 A Any single   1.00 .50
    Nos. 3892a-3892h each sold for 37c on day
of issue.

International Year
of Water
Cooperation
A1686

2013, Jan. 3   Litho.
            Self-Adhesive
3893 A1686 90c multi   2.50 1.25

Setting of
Boundary Stones
Between Spain
and France, 500th
Anniv. — A1687

2013, Jan. 8   Perf. 14x13¾
3894 A1687 52c multi   1.40 .70

2013 Men's World Handball
Championships, Spain — A1688

2013, Jan. 11   Perf. 13¾x14
3895 A1688 90c multi   2.50 1.25

Map of Western Hemisphere, Laws of Burgos, and Christopher Columbus — A1689

2013, Jan. 15
3896 A1689 52c multi   1.40 .70
Laws of Burgos regulating treatment of Indians and colonizers, 500th anniv.

International Equal Pay Day — A1690

2013, Feb. 22   Die Cut Perf. 13
Self-Adhesive
3897 A1690 52c multi   1.40 .70

Percussion Instruments A1691

No. 3898: a, Tambor (drum). b, Pandereta (tambourine). c, Castañuelas (castanets). d, Platillos (cymbals). e, Timbales (timpani).

2013, Feb. 22   Litho.
Self-Adhesive
3898   Horiz. strip of 5   5.00
a.-e. A1691 37c Any single   1.00 .50

Kingdom of Granada, 1000th Anniv. A1692

2013, Feb. 26   Perf. 13¾x14
3899 A1692 37c multi   1.00 .50

Miniature Sheet

Art of Antonio López — A1693

No. 3900: a, Gran Vía, 1974-81. b, Sink and Mirror, 1967. c, New Refrigerator, 1991-94. d, House of Antonio López Torres, 1972-80.

2013, Mar. 11   Photo.   Perf. 12¾
3900 A1693   Sheet of 4   5.75 3.00
a.-d.   52c Any single   1.40 .70

Miniature Sheet

Automobiles — A1694

No. 3901: a, 1962 Mercedes-Benz 190. b, 1948 Citroen 2CV. c, 1938 Volkswagen Beetle. d, 1963 SEAT 1500.

2013, Mar. 15   Litho.   Perf. 13¾x14
3901 A1694   Sheet of 4   9.75 5.00
a.-d.   90c Any single   2.40 1.25

Souvenir Sheet

Spanish Coin Depicting San Lorenzo de El Escorial Royal Monastery — A1695

2013, Mar. 21   Litho. & Engr.   Perf.
3902 A1695   €3.10 multi   8.00 4.00
San Lorenzo de El Escorial Royal Monastery UNESCO World Heritage Site.

Souvenir Sheet

Film Personalities — A1696

No. 3903: a, Rafael Gil (1913-86), director. b, Fernando Fernán Gómez (1921-2007), actor and director. c, Tony Leblanc (1922-2012), actor.

2013, Apr. 8   Photo.   Perf. 13¾x13¼
3903 A1696   Sheet of 3   4.25 2.10
a.-c.   52c Any single   1.40 .70

Europa A1697

2013, Apr. 23   Litho.
3904 A1697 75c multi   2.00 1.00

Wedding of Odotano and Zenobia, Tapestry by Workshop of Gerard Peemans — A1698

Photo. & Engr.
2013, Apr. 25   Perf. 13¼x13¾
3905 A1698 €3.10 multi   8.25 4.25

Spanish Federation of Philatelic Societies, 50th Anniv. A1699

2013, Apr. 29   Litho.   Perf. 13¾x13¼
3906 A1699 37c multi   1.00 .50

A1700

Bridges — A1701

Designs: No. 3907, Besalú Bridge. No. 3908, Los Santos Bridge.

2013, May 4   Photo.   Perf. 13¼x13¾
3907 A1700 €2 multi   5.50 2.75
Souvenir Sheet
Litho.
Perf. 12¾x13¼
3908 A1701 €2 multi   5.50 2.75
See Nos. 3916-3919, 3929-3932, 3936-3937.

Aviation in the Canary Islands, Cent. A1702

2013, May 7   Litho.   Perf. 13¾x13¼
3909 A1702 52c multi   1.40 .70

Baskonia Sports Club and Baskonia Mendi Taldea, Cent. — A1703

2013, May 7   Perf. 13¼x13¾
3910 A1703 52c multi   1.40 .70

Marian Jubilee Year — A1704

2013, May 21
3911 A1704 90c multi   2.40 1.25

Miniature Sheet

Endangered Marine Life — A1705

No. 3912: a, Ballena Vasca (Basque whale). b, Atún rojo (Bluefin tuna). c, Foca monje (Mediterranean monk seal). d, Lamprea marina (Sea lamprey).

2013, June 3   Perf. 13¾x13¼
3912 A1705   Sheet of 4   4.00 2.00
a.-d.   37c Any single   1.00 .50

Barcelona-Sarriá Railway, 150th Anniv. — A1706

2013, June 11   Litho.
3913 A1706 52c multi   1.40 .70

Public Treasury Inspection Service Seal A1707

2013, June 11
3914 A1707 52c multi   1.40 .70

Emilio Aragón (1929-2012), Miliki the Clown — A1708

2013, June 12   Perf. 13¼x13¾
3915 A1708 37c multi   1.00 .50

Bridges Type of 2013

Designs: No. 3916, Piedra Bridge, Logroño.
No. 3917, Tajo Bridge, Ronda, vert. No. 3918,
Sancho el Mayor Bridge, Navarra. No. 3919,
Puentecillas Bridge, Palencia.

**Perf. 13¼x13¾, 13¼x12¾ (#3917),
12¾x13¼ (#3919)**

2013		Photo. (#3916, 3918), Litho.		
3916	A1700	€1 multi	2.75	1.40
3917	A1701	€1 multi	2.75	1.40
3918	A1700	€1 multi	2.60	1.40
3919	A1701	€2 multi	5.25	2.60
	Nos. 3916-3919 (4)		13.35	6.80

Issued: Nos. 3916-3917, 6/18; Nos. 3918-3919, 6/20.

Day of
Victims of
Terrorism
A1709

Perf. 13¾x13¼

2013, June 27			Litho.	
3920	A1709	37c multi	1.00	.50

Friar Rosendo Salvado y Rotea (1814-1900), Missionary — A1710

St. Telmo (1190-1246) and Tui Cathedral A1711

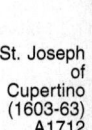

St. Joseph
of
Cupertino
(1603-63)
A1712

Perf. 13¾x13¼, 14x13¾ (#3922)

2013, July 4				
3921	A1710	90c multi	2.40	1.25
3922	A1711	90c multi	2.40	1.25
3923	A1712	90c multi	2.40	1.25
	Nos. 3921-3923 (3)		7.20	3.75

Souvenir Sheet

Victory of Spanish Men's Handball
Team in 2013 World
Championships — A1713

2013, July 9		**Perf. 13¾x13¼**		
3924	A1713	€1 multi	2.60	1.25

Era Querimònia,
700th
Anniv. — A1714

2013, July 11		**Perf. 13¼x13¾**		
3925	A1714	52c multi	1.40	.70

Miniature Sheet

Women's Dresses by Paco
Rabanne — A1715

No. 3926 — Mannequins wearing items
from Rabanne's collection of unwearable
dresses: a, Silver and plastic ankle-length
dress. b, Yellow and blue dress made of zippers. c, See-through dress of red diamonds. d,
Dress made of large golden disks.

2013, Sept. 12		Photo.	**Perf. 13x12¾**	
3926	A1715	Sheet of 4	5.75	3.00
a.-d		52c Any single	1.40	.70

Miniature Sheet

Civic Values for Children — A1716

No. 3927: a, Fellowship (compañerismo). b,
Respect (respeto). c, Sportsmanship
(deportes). d, Road safety (seguridad vial),
vert.

Perf. 13¾x13¼, 13¼x13¾

2013, Sept. 18				
3927	A1716	Sheet of 4	4.00	2.00
a.-d.		37c Any single	1.00	.50

Souvenir Sheet

Painting of King Fernando I, San Isidro
Basilica, León — A1717

Perf. 12¾x13¼

2013, Sept. 20			Litho.	
3928	A1717	€3.10 multi	8.50	4.25

Exfilna (National Philatelic Exhibition) 2013,
León.

Bridges Type of 2013

Designs: €1, Dragon Bridge, Alcalá de
Guadaíra. No. 3930, Carlos Fernández
Casado Bridge, León, vert.
No. 3931, Iron Bridge (Puente del Pilar),
Stone Bridge, Basilica of Our Lady of Pilar,
vert. €3.10, Roman Bridge, Mérida.

Perf. 12¾x13¼

2013, Sept. 25			Litho.	
3929	A1701	€1 multi	2.75	1.40

Perf. 13¾x13¼

| 3930 | A1700 | €2 multi | 5.50 | 2.75 |

Souvenir Sheets

| 3931 | A1700 | €2 multi | 5.50 | 2.75 |

Engr.

Perf. 13¼x13¾

| 3932 | A1700 | €3.10 blue & brn | 8.50 | 4.25 |

Campaign Against
Discrimination — A1718

2013, Oct. 3		Litho.	**Die Cut Perf. 13**	
3933	A1718	37c multi	1.00	.50

America issue.

State
Lotteries,
250th
Anniv.
A1719

2013, Oct. 5		Litho.	**Perf. 13¾x13¼**	
3934	A1719	37c multi	1.00	.50

Mushrooms — A1720

No. 3935: a, Agaricus xanthodermus. b,
Amanita pantherina. c, Marasmius oreades.

2013, Oct. 8		Litho.	**Perf. 13¾x13¼**	
3935		Horiz. strip of 3	3.00	1.50
a.-c.	A1720	37c Any single	1.00	.50

Bridges Type of 2013
Souvenir Sheets

Designs: No. 3936, Frías Bridge, Burgos,
vert. No. 3937, Toledo Bridge, Madrid, vert.

Litho. & Engr.

2013, Oct. 9			**Perf. 13¾**	
3936	A1700	€3.10 blue & brn	8.50	4.25
3937	A1700	€3.10 blue & brn	8.50	4.25

Juvenia
2013
National
Youth
Philatelic
Exhibition,
Alicante
A1721

2013, Oct. 14		Litho.	**Perf. 13¾x14**	
3938	A1721	75c multi	2.00	1.00

Intl. Red Cross, 150th Anniv. — A1722

2013, Oct. 28		Photo.	**Perf. 12¾**	
3939	A1722	90c multi	2.40	1.25

No. 3939 was printed in sheets of 6 + central label. See Belgium No. 2665.

Souvenir Sheet

75th Birthdays of King Juan Carlos
and Queen Sofia — A1723

Engr. (Sheet Margin Litho. & Engr.)

2013, Nov. 5			**Perf. 13¾x14**	
3940	A1723	€3 black	8.00	4.00

The Nursing
Virgin, by Alonso
Cano — A1724

Die Cut Perf. 13
2013, Nov. 6   **Litho.**
Self-Adhesive
3941 A1724 A multi   1.00   .50
Christmas. No. 3941 sold for 37c on day of
issue.

Puerta del Sol
Clock, Madrid and
Twelve
Grapes — A1725

Die Cut Perf. 13
2013, Nov. 6   **Litho.**
Self-Adhesive
3942 A1725 B multi   2.00 1.00
New Year 2014. No. 3942 sold for 75c on
day of issue.

Sports For
All
A1726

No. 3943: a, Long-distance races. b, Bicycle
touring. c, Hiking.

Perf. 13¾x13¼
2013, Nov. 12   **Litho.**
3943   Horiz. strip of 3   3.00 1.50
a.-c. A1726 37c Any single   1.00   .50

Diplomatic Relations Between Spain
and Japan, 400th Anniv. — A1727

No. 3944: a, Potted geraniums on decorative shelf. b, Lespedeza thunbergii.

Perf. 13¼x13¾
2013, Nov. 14   **Litho.**
3944 A1727   Horiz. pair   5.00 2.50
a.-b.   90c Either single 2.50 1.25

Souvenir Sheet

Adolfo Suárez Gonzalez (1932-2014),
Prime Minister — A1728

Litho. & Engr.
2013, Nov. 15   Perf. 13¾x14
3945 A1728 €3.10 multi   8.50 4.25

Tourism
A1729

2014, Jan. 2 Litho. Die Cut Perf. 13
Self-Adhesive
3946 A1729 76c multi   2.10 1.10

Arches and
Gates — A1730

No. 3947: a, Malena Arch, Tarancón. b,
Finca Miralles Gate, Barcelona. c, San Ginés
Gate, Miranda del Castañar. d, Villalar Arch,
Baeza. e, Estrella Arch, Cáceres. f, San
Benito Arch, Sahagún. g, Bridge Gate Cor-
doba. h, San Lorenzo Gate, Laredo.

2014, Jan. 2 Litho. Die Cut Perf. 13
Self-Adhesive
3947   Booklet pane of 8   8.00
a.-h. A1730 A Any single   1.00   .50
Nos. 3947a-3947h each sold for 37c on day
of issue.

Royal
Spanish
Academy,
300th
Anniv.
A1731

2014, Jan. 3 Litho. Die Cut Perf. 13
Self-Adhesive
3948 A1731 38c multi   1.10   .55

European Organization for Nuclear
Research (CERN), 60th
Anniv. — A1732

2014, Jan. 3 Litho. Die Cut Perf. 13
Self-Adhesive
3949 A1732 54c multi   1.50   .75

Arrival in
Florida of
Juan Ponce
de Léon,
500th
Anniv. (in
2013)
A1733

2014, Jan. 3 Litho. Die Cut Perf. 13
Self-Adhesive
3950 A1733 92c multi   2.50 1.25

Father Junípero Serra (1713-84),
Founder of Missions in California
A1734

2014, Jan. 20 Litho. Perf. 13¾x13¼
3951 A1734 92c multi   2.50 1.25

Statue of Pedro Cieza de Léon (c.
1520-54), Conquistador and Chronicler
of Peruvian History — A1735

2014, Jan. 20 Litho. Perf. 13¾x13¼
3952 A1735 92c multi   2.50 1.25

Reflection of Food and Wine on
Spoon — A1736

2014, Jan. 23 Litho. Perf. 13¼x13¾
3953 A1736 54c multi   1.50   .75
Selection of Burgos as 2013 Spanish Culinary Capital.

Real
Racing
Club de
Santander
Soccer
Team,
Cent.
A1737

2014, Jan. 28 Litho. Perf. 13¾x13¼
3954 A1737 54c multi   1.50   .75

Royal Trust Housing Foundation of
Seville, Cent. — A1738

2014, Jan. 28 Litho. Perf. 13¾x13¼
3955 A1738 54c multi   1.50   .75

Collectible
Items — A1739

No. 3956: a, Lottery tickets. b, Picture post-
cards. c, Stickers. d, Minerals. e, Watches. f,
Toy soldiers. g, Coins and currency. h,
Stamps.

Die Cut Perf. 13
2014, Feb. 3   **Litho.**
Self-Adhesive
3956   Booklet pane of 8   8.75
a.   A1739 1c multi   .25   .25
b.   A1739 2c multi   .25   .25
c.   A1739 5c multi   .25   .25
d.   A1739 10c multi   .25   .25
e.   A1739 25c multi   .70   .35
f.   A1739 50c multi   1.40   .70
g.-h. A1739 €1 Either single 2.75 1.40

Rural Architecture — A1740

No. 3957: a, Windmills, La Mancha. b,
Granary, Asturias. c, House near water,
Barranca.

2014, Feb. 6 Litho. Perf. 12¾x13¼
3957 A1740   Vert. strip of 3   4.50 2.25
a.-c.   54c Any single   1.50   .75

Telgraph
College,
Cent.
A1741

Perf. 13¾x13¼
2014, Feb. 12   **Litho.**
3958 A1741 54c multi   1.50   .75

Pilgrimage to Compostela of St.
Francis of Assisi, 800th
Anniv. — A1742

Perf. 13¾x13¼
2014, Feb. 14   **Litho.**
3959 A1742 54c multi   1.50   .75

Blas de Lezo y Olavarrieta (1689-
1741), Admiral — A1743

Perf. 13¾x13¼
2014, Feb. 14   **Litho.**
3960 A1743 54c multi   1.50   .75

Kingdom
of Badjoz,
1000th
Anniv.
A1744

Perf. 13¾x13¼
2014, Feb. 14   **Litho.**
3961 A1744 54c multi   1.50   .75

Launch of Submarine Designed By Isaac Peral, 125th Anniv. — A1745

Perf. 13¼x13¾
2014, Feb. 18   **Litho.**
3962 A1745 54c multi   1.50 .75

Souvenir Sheet

Exfilna 2014 National Philatelic Exhibition, Torremolinos — A1746

Litho. & Engr.
2014, Feb. 27   **Perf. 14x13¾**
3963 A1746 €3.16 multi   8.75 4.50

State Society for Industrial Participation Foundation, 50th Anniv. — A1747

Perf. 13¾x13¼
2014, Mar. 10   **Litho.**
3964 A1747 38c multi   1.10 .55

Museums — A1748

Designs: No. 3965, Guadalajara Museum, decorated plaster fragment, decorated bowl, Roman sculpture. No. 3966, Museum of Spanish Abstract Art, Cuenca, painting by Fernando Zóbel.

Perf. 12¾x13¼
2014, Mar. 12   **Litho.**
3965 A1748 54c multi   1.50 .75
3966 A1748 54c multi   1.50 .75

QR Code and Smiling Face A1749

Die Cut Perf. 13
2014, Mar. 14   **Litho.**
Self-Adhesive
3967 A1749 A multi   1.00 .50
No. 3967 sold for 37c on day of issue.

Souvenir Sheet

2-Euro Coin Depicting Park Güell UNESCO World Heritage Site, Barcelona — A1750

2014, Mar. 24   **Litho. & Engr.**   **Perf.**
3968 A1750 €3.16 multi   8.75 4.50

Establishment of Marca España Commission — A1751

Perf. 13¾x13¼
2014, Mar. 25   **Litho.**
3969 A1751 92c multi   2.60 1.25

Marca España A1752

Designs: No. 3970, Worker wearing air filter in factory, "E." No. 3971, Pechon Beach, "S." No. 3972, Court of the Lions, Alhambra, Granada, "P." No. 3973, Las Meninas, by Diego Velázquez, "A." No. 3974, *Don Quixote*, by Miguel de Cervantes, *The Time of the Hero*, by Mario Vargas Llosa, "N." No. 3975, Electron microoscope, "A."

Litho. & Embossed
2014   **Perf. 13¾x13¼**
3970 A1752 €1 multi + label   2.75 1.40
3971 A1752 €1 multi + label   2.75 1.40
3972 A1752 €1 multi + label   2.75 1.40
3973 A1752 €1 multi + label   2.75 1.40
3974 A1752 €1 multi + label   2.75 1.40
3975 A1752 €1 multi + label   2.75 1.40
    Nos. 3970-3975 (6)   16.50 8.40

Issued: No. 3970, 4/14; No. 3971, 4/30; No. 3972, 5/5; No. 3973, 5/22; No. 3974, 6/5; No. 3975, 6/13.

Paco de Lucía (1947-2014), Guitarist — A1753

Die Cut Perf. 13
2014, Apr. 23   **Litho.**
Self-Adhesive
3976 A1753 B multi   2.10 1.10
Europa. No. 3976 sold for 76c on day of issue.

Souvenir Sheets

A1754

Spanish Cuisine — A1755

No. 3977: a, Tangerine and blossom. b, Iberian ham.
No. 3978: a, 350/ Ajo Blanco, dish by Ferran Adrià. b, Traditional Ajo Blanco (garlic and almond soup with grapes).

2014, Apr. 24   Litho.   Perf. 13¾x13¼
3977 A1754   Sheet of 2   17.50 8.75
a.-b.   €3.15 Either single   8.75 4.25

Perf.
3978 A1755   Sheet of 2   17.50 8.75
a.-b.   €3.15 Either single   8.75 4.25

Gum on No. 3977 is tangerine flavored. Gum on No. 3978 is almond flavored.

Ages of Man Eucharistic Religious Art Exhibiton, Aranda de Duero — A1756

Litho. With Foil Application
2014, May 6   **Perf. 13¼x13½**
3979 A1756 76c multi   2.10 1.10

Souvenir Sheet

UNESCO Intangible Cultural Heritage — A1757

No. 3980: a, Patio Festival, Cordoba. b, Cante de las Minas Flamenco Festival, La Unión.

2014, May 8   Photo.   Perf. 13¾x13
3980 A1757   Sheet of 2   11.00 5.50
a.-b.   €2 Either single   5.50 2.75

Biscayne (Basque Country) Soccer Federation, Cent. A1758

2014, May 16   Litho.   Perf. 13¾x13¼
3981 A1758 76c multi   2.10 1.10

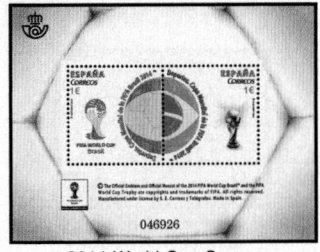

2014 World Cup Soccer Championships, Brazil — A1759

No. 3982: a, Emblem of 2014 World Cup tournament, half of soccer ball with colors of Spanish flag. b, Half of soccer ball showing Brazilian flag, World Cup.

2014, June 12   **Litho.**   **Perf. 12¾**
3982 A1759   Sheet of 2   5.50 2.80
a.-b.   €1 Either single   2.75 1.40

Souvenir Sheet

Toledo UNESCO World Heritage Sites — A1760

No. 3983: a, Toledo Cathedral. b, Alcázar, horiz.

Perf. 13¾x13¼, 13¼x13¾ (#3983b)
2014, June 19   **Litho. & Engr.**
3983 A1760   Sheet of 2   5.50 2.80
a.-b.   €1 Either single   2.75 1.40

Souvenir Sheet

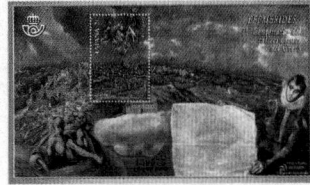

View and Plan of Toledo, by El Greco — A1761

Photo. & Engr.
2014, June 19   **Perf. 13¼x13¾**
3984 A1761 €2 multi   5.50 2.75

Stylized Ears of Corn and Emblem of Corps of Agricultural Engineers — A1762

Arches and Emblem of Corps of Civil Engineers A1763

Perf. 13¾x13¼
2014, June 20 Litho.
3985 A1762 54c multi 1.50 .75
3986 A1763 54c multi 1.50 .75

National Organization of the Blind, 75th Anniv. — A1764

EFE News Agency, 75th Anniv. A1765

Spanish Air Force, 75th Anniv. A1766

Perf. 13¾x13¼
2014, June 27 Litho.
3987 A1764 38c multi 1.10 .55
3988 A1765 38c multi 1.10 .55
3989 A1766 38c multi 1.10 .55
Nos. 3987-3989 (3) 3.30 1.65

Souvenir Sheet

Ca Va, by Miquel Barcelo — A1767

2014, July 8 Litho. Perf. 13¾x13¼
3990 A1767 €3.15 multi 8.50 4.25

Movie Stars — A1768

No. 3991: a, Manolo Escobar (1931-2012). b, Sara Montiel (1928-2013). c, Alfredo Landa (1933-2013).

2014, July 11 Litho. Perf. 12½x12¾
3991 Vert. strip of 3 6.00 3.00
a.-c. A1768 76c Any single 2.00 1.00
Nos. 3991a-3991c each have film sprocket holes punched in the design.

Souvenir Sheet

Harley-Davidson Motorcycles — A1769

No. 3992: a, 1927 Harley-Davidson 350, front wheel of 1929 Harley-Davidson 1200J (41x58mm). b, Gas tank of 1929 Harley-Davidson 1200J (41x29mm). c, Harley-Davidson 1200J (41x29mm).

2014, July 17 Litho. Perf. 12½x13¼
3992 A1769 Sheet of 3 7.50 3.75
a.-c. 92c Any single 2.50 1.25

Brotherhood of the White Virgin, 400th Anniv. — A1770

2014, July 31 Litho. Perf. 13¼x13¾
3993 A1770 76c multi 2.00 1.00

2014 Intl. Sailing Federation World Championships, Santander A1771

2014, Sept. 1 Litho. Perf. 13¼x13¾
3994 A1771 92c multi 2.40 1.25

Royal and Military Order of San Hermenegildo, Bicent. — A1772

Center for Advanced Studies in National Defense, 50th Anniv. — A1773

Perf. 13¾x13¼
2014, Sept. 10 Litho.
3995 A1772 76c multi 2.00 1.00
Perf. 13¼x13¾
3996 A1773 76c multi 2.00 1.00

Souvenir Sheet

The Death of Dido Tapestry, c. 1660 — A1774

Engr., Litho. Sheet Margin
2014, Sept. 18 Perf. 13¼x13¾
3997 A1774 €3.15 gray green 8.00 4.00

Saint John Paul II (1920-2005) — A1775

2014, Sept. 25 Litho. Perf. 13¾x14
3998 A1775 92c multi 2.40 1.25

Arms of León, San Isisdro Basilica, Parliamentary Seating Arrangement — A1776

2014, Oct. 1 Litho. Perf. 13¾x13¼
3999 A1776 76c multi 2.00 1.00
León, site of first democratic parliament in Europe, 1188.

Taula of Torretrencada A1777

2014, Oct. 1 Litho. Perf. 14x14¼
4000 A1777 92c multi 2.40 1.25

Faces, Map of North and South America A1778

2014, Oct. 9 Litho. Perf. 13¾x13¼
4001 A1778 92c multi 2.40 1.25
America issue.

Souvenir Sheet

Cartoons by Forges — A1779

2014, Oct. 9 Litho. Perf. 13¼x13¾
4002 A1779 €3.15 black + 8 labels 8.00 4.00

Souvenir Sheet

King Felipe VI's Accession to the Throne — A1780

No. 4003: a, King Felipe VI. b, King Felipe VI and Queen Letizia.

Litho., Sheet Margin Litho. & Silk-Screened
2014, Oct. 12 Perf. 13¾x13¼
4003 A1780 Sheet of 2 5.00 2.50
a.-b. €1 Either single 2.50 1.25

Irun Railroad Station A1781

2014, Oct. 17 Litho. Perf. 13¾x13¼
4004 A1781 76c multi 1.90 .95

Peseta Currency — A1783

No. 4006: a, Back of 1953 one-peseta banknote (58x41mm). b, Obverse of 1944 one-peseta coin (41x41mm).

Litho. (#4006a), Litho & Embossed with Foil Application (#4006b)
2014, Nov. 4 Perf. 13¼x13¾
4006 A1783 Horiz. pair 10.00 5.00
a.-b. €2 Either single 5.00 2.50

Souvenir Sheet

Publication of Children's Book *Platero y yo*, by Juan Ramón Jiménez, Cent. — A1784

Litho. & Engr. With Foil Application
2014, Nov. 7   Perf. 13¾x13¼
4007 A1784 €3.15 multi   8.00 4.00

A1785

Christmas
A1786

Litho. With Foil Application
2014, Nov. 11   Die Cut Perf. 13
Self-Adhesive
4008 A1785 A multi   .95 .45
Litho.
Serpentine Die Cut 10
4009 A1786 B multi   1.90 .95
a.   Tete-beche pair   3.80

On day of issue No. 4008 sold for 38c and No. 4009 sold for 76c. Parts of the design of No. 4009 were printed with thermographic ink which changes color when warmed. No. 4009 was printed in sheets of 6.

Gates
A1787

No. 4010: a, Moon Gate, Cordoba. b, Chain Gate, Brihuega. c, St. Mary's Gate, Hondarribia. d, St. Peter's Gate, Peñíscola.

2015, Jan. 2 Litho. Die Cut Perf. 13
Booklet Stamps
Self-Adhesive
4010 Block of 4   4.00
a.-d. A1787 A Any single   1.00 .50
e.   Booklet pane of 8, 2 each
          #4010a-4010d   8.00

On day of issue, Nos. 4010a-4010d each sold for 42c.

A1788

Tourism
A1789

Litho. & Embossed
2015, Jan. 2   Die Cut Perf. 13
Self-Adhesive
4011 A1788 90c multi   2.25 1.10
4012 A1789 €1 multi   2.40 1.25

St. Teresa of Avila (1515-82)
A1790

Litho. & Embossed
2015, Jan. 5   Die Cut Perf. 13
Self-Adhesive
4013 A1790 A multi   .95 .50

No. 4013 sold for 42c on day of issue.

Spanish National Research Council, 75th Anniv. (in 2014)
A1791

Litho. & Embossed
2015, Jan. 5   Die Cut Perf. 13
Self-Adhesive
4014 A1791 A2 multi   1.25 .60

No. 4014 sold for 55c on day of issue.

Evocative Self-Portrait, by Pablo Picasso (1881-1973)
A1792

Litho. & Embossed
2015, Jan. 5   Die Cut Perf. 13
Self-Adhesive
4015 A1792 C multi   2.25 1.10

Exhibition of early Picasso works, A Coruña. No. 4015 sold for €1 on day of issue.

National Transplant Organization, 25th Anniv.
A1793

Litho. & Embossed
2015, Jan. 16   Die Cut Perf. 13
Self-Adhesive
4016 A1793 B multi   2.10 1.10

No. 4016 sold for 90c on day of issue.

A1794

Winning Designs in Stamp Design Contest
A1795

Litho. & Embossed
2015, Jan. 19   Die Cut Perf. 13
Self-Adhesive
4017 A1794 42c multi   .95 .50
4018 A1795 55c multi   1.25 .60

Intl. Year of Light (No. 4017).

King Felipe VI
A1796   A1797

2015, Jan. 19 Litho. Perf. 12¾x13¼
Color of Portrait
4019 A1796 1c org brn   .25 .25
4020 A1796 4c brown   .25 .25
4021 A1796 10c blue green   .25 1.10
4022 A1796 €1 rose lake   2.25 1.10
4023 A1796 €2 blue   4.50 2.25

Engr. & Embossed With Foil Application
Die Cut Perf. 13
Self-Adhesive
4024 A1797 €5 black & gold   11.50 5.75
Nos. 4019-4024 (6)   19.00 9.85
Nos. 4019-4023 have a punched out "ñ."

Souvenir Sheet

Culinary Capitals of 2014 and 2015 — A1798

No. 4025: a, Tapas bar from Vitoria, 2014 Culinary Capital. b, Local foods from Caceres, 2015 Culinary Capital.

2015, Jan. 28 Litho. Perf. 13¼x13¾
4025 A1798 Sheet of 2   4.25 2.25
a.-b.   90c Either single   2.10 1.10

Nos. 4025a-4025b have a punched out "ñ."

Button and Badge Collecting
A1799

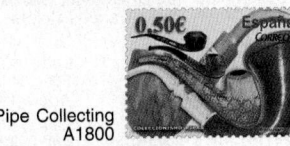

Pipe Collecting
A1800

Coin Collecting
A1801

Stamp Collecting
A1802

2015, Feb. 3   Litho.
Booklet Stamps
Self-Adhesive
4026 Block of 4   8.50
a.   A1799 25c multi   .55 .30
b.   A1800 50c multi   1.10 .55
c.   A1801 €1 multi   2.25 1.10
d.   A1802 €2 multi   4.50 2.25
e.   Booklet pane of 8, 2 each
          #4026a-4026d   17.00

Royal Artillery College, 250th Anniv. (in 2014)
A1803

General Juan Prim (1814-70)
A1804

Military Health Services, 500th Anniv.
A1805

2015, Feb. 6 Litho. Perf. 13¾x13¼
4027 A1803 90c multi   2.00 1.00
Perf. 13¼x13¾
4028 A1804 90c multi   2.00 1.00
4029 A1805 90c multi   2.00 1.00
Nos. 4027-4029 (3)   6.00 3.00

Nos. 4027-4029 have a punched out "ñ."

Royal Soccer Federation of Andalusia, Cent. — A1806

Perf. 13¼x13¾
2015, Feb. 19   Litho.
4030 A1806 90c multi   2.00 1.00

No. 4030 has a punched out "ñ."

Submarine Force, Cent.
A1807

Perf. 13¾x13¼
2015, Feb. 20   Litho.
4031 A1807 90c multi   2.00 1.00

No. 4031 has a punched out "ñ."

First International Congress on Bullfighting as a Cultural Heritage — A1808

Perf. 13¼x13¾
2015, Feb. 20   Litho.
4032 A1808 €1 multi   2.25 1.10

No. 4032 has a punched out "ñ."

Museums — A1809

Designs: No. 4033, 55c, National Archaeological Museum, Madrid. No. 4034, 55c, Thyssen-Bornemisza Museum, Madrid. No. 4035, 55c, Lázaro Galdiano Museum, Madrid.

2015, Mar. 3   Litho.   Perf. 13x13¼
4033-4035 A1809   Set of 3   3.75 1.90
Nos. 4033-4035 have punched out "ñ."

Souvenir Sheet

Exfilna 2015, National Philatelic Exhibition, Avilés — A1810

No. 4036: a, Building in color. b, Building in shades of gray and black.

Litho. (#4036a), Litho. & Engr. (#4036b)
2015, Mar. 13   Perf. 13¼x13¾
4036 A1810   Sheet of 2   6.50 3.25
a.   42c multi   .95 .45
b.   €2.42 multi   5.50 2.75
Nos. 4036a-4036b have a punched out "ñ."

Lace — A1811

No. 4037: a, Flag of Croatia, lace from Lepoglava, Croatia. b, Flag colors of Spain, lace from Seville.

Perf. 13¼x13¾
2015, Mar. 31   Litho.
4037 A1811   Horiz. pair   4.50 2.25
a.-b.   €1 Either single   2.25 1.10
Nos. 4037a-4037b have numerous punched out holes. See Croatia No.

SEMI-POSTAL STAMPS

Red Cross Issue

Princesses María Cristina and Beatrice SP1

Queen as a Nurse — SP2    Queen Victoria Eugénia — SP3

Prince of Asturias — SP4   King Alfonso XIII — SP5

Perf. 12½
1926, Sept. 15   Unwmk.   Engr.
B1 SP1   1c black   2.50 2.25
B2 SP2   2c ultra   2.50 2.25
B3 SP3   5c violet brn   5.50 4.00
B4 SP4   10c green   4.50 4.00
B5 SP1   15c indigo   1.75 1.50
B6 SP4   20c dull violet   1.75 1.50
a.   20c violet brown (error)   600.00 375.00
B7 SP5   25c rose red   .30 .30
B8 SP1   30c blue green   42.50 40.00
B9 SP3   40c dark blue   24.00 21.00
B10 SP2   50c red orange   24.00 21.00
B11 SP4   1p slate   1.75 1.10
B12 SP3   4p magenta   1.40 .80
B13 SP5   10p brown   1.40 1.10
Nos. B1-B13,EB1 (14)   122.60 109.55
Set, never hinged   260.00

The 20c was printed in violet brown for use in the colonies (Cape Juby, Spanish Guinea, Spanish Morocco and Spanish Sahara). No. B6a, the missing overprint error, is listed here because it is not known to which colony it belongs.
For overprints see Nos. B19-B46.

Airplane and Map of Madrid-Manila Flight — SP6

1926, Sept. 15
B14 SP6   15c dp ultra & org   .40 .40
B15 SP6   20c car & yel grn   .40 .40
B16 SP6   30c dk brn & ultra   .40 .40
B17 SP6   40c dk grn & brn org   .40 .40
B18 SP6   4p magenta & yel   100.00 100.00
Nos. B14-B18,CB1-CB5 (10)   109.10 109.10
Set, never hinged   250.00

Madrid to Manila flight of Captains Eduardo G. Gallarza and Joaquim Loriga y Taboada.
Nos. B1-B18, CB1-CB5 and EB1 were used for regular postage on Sept. 15, 16, 17, 1926. Subsequently the unsold stamps were given to the Spanish Red Cross Society, by which they were sold uncanceled but they then had no franking power.
For overprints see Nos. B47-B53.

Coronation Silver Jubilee Issue
Red Cross Stamps of 1926 Overprinted "ALFONSO XIII," Dates and Ornaments in Various Colors

1927, May 27
B19 SP1   1c black (R)   6.00 6.00
B20 SP2   2c ultra (Bl)   11.00 11.00
B21 SP3   5c vio brn (R)   2.75 2.75
a.   Double overprint   37.50
B22 SP4   10c green (Bl)   75.00 75.00
B23 SP1   15c indigo (R)   2.25 2.25
B24 SP4   20c dull vio (Bl)   4.00 4.00
B25 SP5   25c rose red (R)   .50 .50
B26 SP1   30c blue grn (Bl)   1.00 1.00
B27 SP3   40c dk blue (R)   1.00 1.00
B28 SP2   50c red org (Bl)   1.00 1.00
B29 SP4   1p slate (R)   2.25 2.25
B30 SP3   4p magenta (Bl)   11.00 11.00
B31 SP5   10p brown (G)   42.50 42.50
Nos. B19-B31 (13)   160.25 160.25
Set, never hinged   375.00

Same with Additional Surcharges of New Values
B32 SP2   3c on 2c (G)   9.50 9.50
B33 SP2   4c on 2c (Bk)   9.50 9.50
B34 SP5   10c on 25c (Bk)   .55 .55
B35 SP5   25c on 25c (Bl)   .55 .55
B36 SP2   55c on 2c (R)   1.00 1.00
B37 SP4   55c on 10c (Bk)   55.00 55.00
B38 SP4   55c on 20c (Bk)   55.00 55.00
B39 SP1   75c on 15c (R)   .70 .70
B40 SP1   75c on 30c (R)   140.00 140.00
B41 SP3   80c on 5c (R)   52.50 50.00
B42 SP3   2p on 40c (R)   1.00 1.00
B43 SP4   2p on 1p (R)   1.00 1.00
B44 SP2   5p on 50c (G)   1.90 1.90

B45 SP3   5p on 4p (Bk)   3.25 3.25
B46 SP5   10p on 10p (G)   27.50 27.50
Nos. B32-B46 (15)   358.95 356.45
Set, never hinged   800.00

Nos. B14-B18 Overprinted

B47 SP6   15c (Br)   .50 .40
a.   Double overprint   30.00
B48 SP6   20c (Bl)   .50 .40
a.   Brown overprint (error)   65.00
b.   Inverted overprint   30.00
B50 SP6   30c (R)   .50 .40
a.   Blue overprint (error)   65.00
b.   Double overprint   30.00
B52 SP6   40c (R)   .50 .40
a.   Inverted overprint   30.00
b.   Double ovpt. (Bl + Br)   95.00
B53 SP6   4p (Bl)   100.00 95.00
Nos. B47-B53 were available for ordinary postage.

Semi-Postal Special Delivery Stamp Overprinted "ALFONSO XIII," Dates and Ornaments in Violet
B54 SPSD1   20c   5.50 5.50
Nos. B47-B54 (6)   107.50 102.10

Nos. CB1-CB5 Overprinted in Various Colors

B55 SPAP1   5c (R)   2.25 1.60
a.   Inverted overprint   30.00
B56 SPAP1   10c (R)   2.50 2.25
a.   Inverted overprint   30.00
B57 SPAP1   25c (Bl)   .40 .40
B58 SPAP1   50c (Bl)   .40 .40
a.   Double ovpt., one invtd.   72.50
B59 SPAP1   1p (R)   3.00 2.50
a.   Inverted overprint   95.00

Same with Additional Surcharges of New Values
B60 SPAP1   75c on 5c (R)   5.00 3.25
a.   Inverted surcharge   30.00
B61 SPAP1   75c on 10c (R)   22.50 13.00
a.   Inverted surcharge   30.00
B62 SPAP1   75c on 25c (Bl)   47.50 27.50
a.   Double surcharge   55.00
B63 SPAP1   75c on 50c (Bl)   18.00 13.00
Nos. B55-B63 (9)   101.55 63.90
Set, never hinged   300.00

Nos. B54-B63 were available for postage.

Stamps of Spanish Offices in Morocco and Spanish Colonies, 1926 (Spain Types SP3,SP5) Surcharged in Various Colors

On Spanish Morocco
B64 SP3   55c on 4p bis (Bl)   25.00 21.00
B65 SP5   80c on 10p vio (Br)   25.00 21.00

On Spanish Tangier
B66 SP5   1p on 10p vio (Br)   135.00 110.00
B67 SP3   4p bis (G)   45.00 40.00

On Cape Juby
B68 SP3   5p on 4p bis (R)   85.00 70.00
B69 SP5   10p on 10p vio (R)   45.00 40.00

On Spanish Guinea
B70 SP5   1p on 10p vio (Bl)   25.00 21.00
B71 SP3   2p on 4p bis (R)   25.00 21.00

On Spanish Sahara
B72 SP5   80c on 10p vio (R)   40.00 32.50
B73 SP3   2p on 4p bis (R)   25.00 21.00
Nos. B64-B73 (10)   475.00 397.50
Set, never hinged   1,300.

Nos. B64-B73 were available for postage in Spain only.
Nos. B19-B73 were for the 25th year of the reign of King Alfonso XIII.
Counterfeits of Nos. B64-B73 abound.

Catacombs Restoration Issues

Pope Pius XI and King Alfonso XIII SP7

1928, Dec. 23   Engr.   Perf. 12½
Santiago Issue
B74 SP7   2c violet & blk   .30 .30
B75 SP7   2c lake & blk   .35 .35
B76 SP7   3c bl blk & vio   .30 .30
B77 SP7   3c dl bl & vio   .35 .35
B78 SP7   5c ol grn & vio   .65 .65
B79 SP7   10c yel grn & blk   1.25 1.25
B80 SP7   15c bl grn & vio   3.25 3.25
B81 SP7   25c dp rose & vio   3.25 3.25
B82 SP7   40c ultra & blk   .30 .30
B83 SP7   55c ol brn & vio   .30 .30
B84 SP7   80c red & blk   .30 .30
B85 SP7   1p gray blk & vio   .30 .30
B86 SP7   2p red brn & blk   4.25 4.25
B87 SP7   3p pale rose & vio   4.25 4.25
B88 SP7   4p vio brn & blk   4.25 4.25
B89 SP7   5p grnsh blk & vio   4.25 4.25

Toledo Issue
B90 SP7   2c bl blk & car   .30 .30
B91 SP7   2c ultra & car   .35 .35
B92 SP7   3c bis brn & ultra   .30 .30
B93 SP7   3c ol grn & ultra   .35 .35
B94 SP7   5c red vio & car   .65 .65
B95 SP7   10c yel grn & ultra   1.25 1.25
B96 SP7   15c slate bl & car   3.25 3.25
B97 SP7   25c red brn & ultra   3.25 3.25
B98 SP7   40c ultra & car   .30 .30
B99 SP7   55c dk brn & ultra   .30 .30
B100 SP7   80c black & car   .30 .30
B101 SP7   1p yellow & car   .30 .30
B102 SP7   2p dk gray & ultra   4.25 4.25
B103 SP7   3p violet & car   4.25 4.25
B104 SP7   4p vio brn & car   4.25 4.25
B105 SP7   5p bister & ultra   4.25 4.25
Nos. B74-B105 (32)   55.80 55.80
Set, never hinged   140.00

Nos. B74-B105 replaced regular stamps from Dec. 23, 1928 to Jan. 6, 1929. The proceeds from their sale were given to a fund to restore the catacombs of Saint Damasus and Saint Praetextatus at Rome.
Nos. B74-B105 exist imperf. Value set, $325 hinged, $400 never hinged.

Issues of the Republic

SP13

1938, Apr. 15   Perf. 11½
B106 SP13   45c + 2p bl & grnsh bl   .90 .75
a.   Imperf., pair   17.50 14.50
b.   Souv. sheet of 1   26.00 26.00
c.   Souv. sheet of 1, imperf.   725.00 650.00
Never hinged   1,000.

Surtax for the defenders of Madrid.
For overprint and surcharge see Nos. B108, CB6.

Nurse and Orderly Carrying Wounded Soldier — SP14

1938, June 1   Engr.   Perf. 10
B107 SP14   45c + 5p cop red   .55 .55
a.   Imperf., pair   220.00

For surcharge see No. CB7.

No. B106 Overprinted in Black

1938, Nov. 7   **Perf. 11½**

B108 SP13 45c + 2p   3.25   3.25
Never hinged   5.00

Defense of Madrid, 2nd anniversary.
A similar but larger overprint was applied to cover blocks of four. Value, $15 hinged, $30 never hinged.

Values for souvenir sheets of 1937-38 are for examples with some faults. Undamaged sheets are very hard to find.

Spanish State
Souvenir Sheets

Alcazar, Toledo SP15

Design: No. B108C, A patio of Alcazar after Civil War fighting.

1937   **Unwmk.**   **Photo.**   **Perf. 11½**
Control Numbers on Back

B108A SP15 2p org brn   22.00   22.00
   b.   Imperf.   450.00   450.00
B108C SP15 2p dark green   22.00   22.00
   d.   Imperf.   450.00   450.00
   Never hinged   95.00
   Set, never hinged   125.00
   Set, B108Ab, B108Cd,
   never hinged   1,300.

Nos. B108A-B108C sold for 4p each.

SP16

Designs: 20c, Covadonga Cathedral. 30c, Palma Cathedral, Majorca. 50c, Alcazar of Segovia. 1p, Leon Cathedral.

1938   **Unwmk.**   **Photo.**   **Perf. 12½**
Control Numbers on Back

B108E SP16   Sheet of 4   42.50   42.50
   f.   20c dull violet   5.00   5.00
   g.   30c rose red   5.00   5.00
   h.   50c bright blue   5.00   5.00
   i.   1p greenish gray   5.00   5.00
   j.   Imperf. sheet   72.50   65.00
   Never hinged   125.00

Each sheet sold for 4p.

SP17

Designs, alternating in sheet: Flag bearer. Battleship "Admiral Cervera." Soldiers in trenches. Moorish guard.

1938, July 1   **Unwmk.**   **Perf. 13**
Control Numbers on Back

B108K SP17   Sheet of 20   40.00   40.00
   Never hinged   52.50
   l.   Imperf. sheet   185.00   185.00
   Never hinged   240.00

Sheet measures 175x132mm. Consists of five vertical rows of four 2c violet, 3c deep blue, 5c olive gray, 10c deep green and 30c red orange, with each denomination appearing in two different designs. Marginal inscription: "Homenaje al Ejercito y a la Marina" (Honoring the Army and Navy). Sold for 4p, or double face value.

Souvenir Sheets

Don Juan of Austria — SP18

Battle of Lepanto SP19

Perf. 12½
1938, Dec. 15   **Unwmk.**   **Engr.**
Control Numbers on Back

B108M SP18 30c dk car   22.50   22.50
B108N SP19 50c blue black   22.50   22.50
   Nos. B108M-B108N (2)   45.00   45.00
   Set, never hinged   77.50

Imperf

B108O SP18 30c black vio   400.00   *550.00*
B108P SP19 50c dk sl grn   400.00   *550.00*
   Nos. B108O-B108P (2)   800.00   *1,100.*
   Set, never hinged   1,300.

Victory over the Turks in the Battle of Lepanto, 1571.
Nos. B108M-B108P contain one stamp. The dates "1571-1938" appear in the lower sheet margin. Size: 89x74mm. Sold for 10p a pair.

LOCAL CHARITY STAMPS

Hundreds of different charity stamps were issued by local organizations and cities during the Civil War, 1936-39. Some had limited franking value, but most were simply charity labels. They are of three kinds: 1. Local semipostals. 2. Obligatory surtax stamps. 3. Propaganda or charity labels.

Ruins of Belchite SP20

Miracle of Calanda — SP21

Designs: 10c+5c, 70c+20c, Ruins of Belchite. 15c+10c, 80c+20c, The Rosary. 20c+10c, 1.50p+50c, El Pilar Cathedral. 25c+10c, 1p+30c, Mother Raffols praying. 40c+10c, 2.50p+50c, The Little Chamber. 45c+15c, 1.40p+40c, Oath of the Besieged. 10p+4p, The Apparition.

Perf. 10½, 11½x10½, 11½
1940, Jan. 29   **Litho.**   **Unwmk.**
Design SP20

B109   10c + 5c dp bl & vio
   brn   .25   .25
B110   15c + 10c rose vio &
   dk grn   .25   .25

B111   20c + 10c vio & dp bl   .25   .25
B112   25c + 10c dp rose &
   vio brn   .25
B113   40c + 10c sl grn &
   rose vio   .25
B114   45c + 15c vio & dp
   rose   .30
B115   70c + 20c multi   .30   .30
B116   80c + 20c dp rose &
   vio   .40
B117   1p + 30c dk sl grn &
   pur   .40   .40
B118   1.40p + 40c pur &
   gray blk   40.00   40.00
B119   1.50p + 50c lt bl &
   brn vio   .50   .50
B120   2.50p + 50c choc & bl   .50   .50

Design SP21

B121   4p + 1p rose lil &
   sl grn   12.00   12.00
B122   10p + 4p ultra &
   chnt   190.00   190.00
   Nos. B109-B122, CB8-
   CB17, EB2 (25)   464.70   464.60
   Set, never hinged   950.00

19th centenary of the Virgin of the Pillar. The surtax was used to help restore the Cathedral at Zaragoza, damaged during the Civil War.
No. B121 exists in violet & slate green, No. B122 in ultramarine & brown violet. Value, $42.50 each.
Nos. B109-B122 exist imperf. Value, $750.
See No. 743, CB8-CB17.

General Franco — SP23

1940, Dec. 23   **Unwmk.**   **Perf. 10**

B123 SP23 20c + 5c dk grn &
   red   .65   .65
B124 SP23 40c + 10c dk bl & red   .90   .40
   Set, never hinged   3.50

The surtax was for the tuberculosis fund. See Nos. RA15, RAC1.

Stamps of 10c denomination, types SP23 to SP28, are postal tax issues.

Knight and Lorraine Cross — SP24

1941, Dec. 23

B125 SP24 20c + 5c bl vio & red   .50   .30
B126 SP24 40c + 10c sl grn &
   red   .50   .25
   Set, never hinged   1.40

The surtax was used to fight tuberculosis. See Nos. RA16, RAC2.

Cross of Lorraine — SP25

1942, Dec. 23   **Litho.**

B127 SP25 20c + 5c pale brn &
   rose red   1.40   1.25
B128 SP25 40c + 10c lt bluish
   grn & rose red   .80   .45
   Set, never hinged   4.00

The surtax was used to fight tuberculosis. See Nos. RA17, RAC3.

Cross of Lorraine — SP26

1943, Dec. 23   **Photo.**   **Perf. 11½**

B129 SP26 20c + 5c dl sl grn
   & dl red   3.25   1.40
B130 SP26 40c + 10c brt bl &
   dl red   2.00   1.10
   Set, never hinged   12.00

The surtax was used to fight tuberculosis. See Nos. RA18, RAC4.

Dragon Slaying — SP27

Perf. 9½x10
1944, Dec. 23   **Litho.**   **Unwmk.**

B131 SP27 20c + 5c sl grn &
   red   .25   .25
B132 SP27 40c + 10c dl vio &
   red   .50   .50
B133 SP27 80c + 10c ultra &
   rose   7.75   7.75
   Nos. B131-B133 (3)   8.50   8.50
   Set, never hinged   16.00

The surtax was used to fight tuberculosis. See Nos. RA19, RAC5.

St. George Slaying the Dragon — SP28

Lorraine Cross in Red

1945, Dec. 23

B134 SP28 20c + 5c dl gray
   grn   .25   .25
B135 SP28 40c + 10c vio   .30   .25
B136 SP28 80c + 10c ultra   8.00   7.50
   Nos. B134-B136 (3)   8.55   8.00
   Set, never hinged   14.00

The surtax was used to fight tuberculosis. See Nos. RA20, RAC6.

Nos. 753 and 768 Surcharged in Blue

1950, Oct. 23

B137 A195 50c + 10c   32.50   32.50
   a.   "Caudillo" 14¾mm wide   95.00   97.50
B138 A195 1p + 10c   32.50   32.50
   a.   "Caudillo" 14¾mm wide   95.00   97.50
   Set, never hinged   120.00
   #B137a-B138a, never hinged   300.00

Visit of General Franco to Canary Islands. First printing, brighter colors and pale blue surcharge, was issued in Canary Islands. Value, $200 hinged, $300 never hinged, $200 used. Second printing was issued in Madrid Feb. 22, 1951. See No. CB18.

> Catalogue values for unused stamps in this section, from this point to the end of the section, are for Never Hinged items.

1992 Summer Olympics, Barcelona SP29

1988, Oct. 3   Photo.   Perf. 14
B139 SP29 20p +5p Track and
field   .35   .35
B140 SP29 45p +5p Badminton   .60   .60
B141 SP29 50p +5p Basketball   .70   .70
    Nos. B139-B141 (3)   1.65 1.65

See Nos. B146-B152, B163-B168, B177-B179, B184-B186, B191-B193.

EXPO '92, Seville — SP30

Globes and sites of previous exhibitions: No. B142, Crystal Palace, London, 1851. No. B143, Eiffel Tower, Paris, 1889. No. B144, "The Atom," Brussels, 1958. No. B145, Monument, Osaka, 1970.

1989, Feb. 9   Photo.   Perf. 14x13½
B142 SP30 8p +5p multi   .25   .25
B143 SP30 8p +5p multi   .25   .25
B144 SP30 20p +5p multi   .30   .30
B145 SP30 20p +5p multi   .30   .30
    Nos. B142-B145 (4)   1.10 1.10

Summer Olympics Type of 1988
1989, Mar. 7   Photo.   Perf. 14
B146 SP29 8p +5p Handball   .25   .25
B147 SP29 18p +5p Boxing   .35   .35
B148 SP29 20p +5p Cycling   .35   .35
B149 SP29 45p +5p Equestrian   .60   .60
    Nos. B146-B149 (4)   1.55 1.55

1989, Oct. 3   Photo.   Perf. 13½x14
B150 SP29 18p +5p Fencing   .65   .65
B151 SP29 20p +5p Soccer   .65   .65
B152 SP29 45p +5p Pommel
horse   1.25 1.25
    Nos. B150-B152 (3)   2.55 2.55

500th Anniv. Emblem and Produce or Fauna Indigenous to the Americas — SP31

1989, Oct. 16   Litho.   Perf. 13x13½
B153 SP31 8p +5p Cocoa   .25   .25
B154 SP31 8p +5p Corn   .25   .25
B155 SP31 20p +5p Tomato   .30   .30
B156 SP31 20p +5p Horse   .30   .30
B157 SP31 50p +5p Potato   .60   .60
B158 SP31 50p +5p Turkey   .60   .60
a.   Bkt. pane of 6, #B153-B158   2.25
    Nos. B153-B158 (6)   2.30 2.30

Discovery of America, 500th anniv.

EXPO '92, Seville SP32

Curro, the character trademark, and symbols of development in Spain.

1990, Feb. 22   Photo.   Perf. 14
B159 SP32 8p +5p multi   .25   .25
B160 SP32 20p +5p multi, diff.   .30   .30
B161 SP32 45p +5p multi, diff.   .60   .60
B162 SP32 50p +5p multi, diff.   .70   .70
    Nos. B159-B162 (4)   1.85 1.85

Summer Olympics Type of 1988
1990, Mar. 7   Photo.   Perf. 13½x14
B163 SP29 18p +5p Weight lifting   .30   .30
B164 SP29 20p +5p Field hockey   .30   .30
B165 SP29 45p +5p Judo   .55   .55
    Nos. B163-B165 (3)   1.15 1.15

1990, Oct. 3   Photo.   Perf. 13½x14
B166 SP29 8p +5p Wrestling   .25   .25
B167 SP29 18p +5p Swimming   .40   .40
B168 SP29 20p +5p Baseball   .50   .50
    Nos. B166-B168 (3)   1.15 1.15

Discovery of America, 500th Anniv. (in 1992) — SP33

Drawings of sailing ships.

1990, Oct. 15   Litho.   Perf. 13
B169 SP33 8p +5p "Viajes-A"   .25   .25
B170 SP33 8p +5p "Viajes-B"   .25   .25
B171 SP33 20p +5p "Viajes-C"   .30   .30
B172 SP33 20p +5p "Viajes-D"   .30   .30
a.   Bkt. pane of 4, #B169-B172   1.00
    Nos. B169-B172 (4)   1.10 1.10

Expo '92, Seville SP34

Designs: 15p+5p, La Cartuja, Monastery of Santa Maria de las Cuevas. 25p+5p, Amphitheater. 45p+5p, La Cartuja Bridge. 55p+5p, La Barqueta Bridge.

Litho. & Engr.
1991, Feb. 12   Perf. 14
B173 SP34 15p +5p multi   .30   .30
B174 SP34 25p +5p multi   .40   .40
B175 SP34 45p +5p multi   .65   .65
B176 SP34 55p +5p multi   .80   .80
    Nos. B173-B176 (4)   2.15 2.15

Summer Olympics Type of 1988
1991, Mar. 7   Litho.   Perf. 13½x14
B177 SP29 15p + 5p Five athletes   .30   .30
B178 SP29 25p + 5p Kayaking   .40   .40
B179 SP29 45p + 5p Rowing   .65   .65
    Nos. B177-B179 (3)   1.35 1.35

Madrid, European City of Culture, 1992 SP35

Designs: 15p+5p, Fountain of Apollo. 25p+5p, Statue of Alvaro de Bazan. 45p+5p, Bank of Spain. 55p+5p, St. Isidore's Institute.

1991, July 29   Photo.   Perf. 13½x14
B180 SP35 15p + 5p multi   .30   .30
B181 SP35 25p + 5p multi   .40   .40
B182 SP35 45p + 5p multi   .60   .60
B183 SP35 55p + 5p multi   .75   .75
    Nos. B180-B183 (4)   2.05 2.05

Summer Olympics Type of 1988
1991, Oct. 3   Litho.   Perf. 14
B184 SP29 15p +5p Tennis   .45   .45
B185 SP29 25p +5p Table tennis   .60   .60
B186 SP29 55p +5p Shooting   1.25 1.25
    Nos. B184-B186 (3)   2.30 2.30

Discovery of America, 500th Anniv., 1992 — SP36

15p+5p, Garcilaso Gomez Suarez de Figueroa, the Inca, poet. 25p+5p, Pope Alexander VI. 45p+5p, Luis de Santangel, banker. 55p+5p, Friar Toribio de Paredes, monk.

1991, Oct. 15   Photo.   Perf. 13x13½
B187 SP36 15p +5p multi   .30   .30
B188 SP36 25p +5p multi   .40   .40
B189 SP36 45p +5p multi   .60   .60
B190 SP36 55p +5p multi   .75   .75
a.   Bkt. pane of 4, #B187-B190   2.00
    Nos. B187-B190 (4)   2.05 2.05

Summer Olympics Type of 1988
1992, Mar. 6   Photo.   Perf. 13½x14
B191 SP29 15p +5p Archery   .40   .40
B192 SP29 25p +5p Sailing   .55   .55
B193 SP29 55p +5p Volleyball   1.10 1.10
    Nos. B191-B193 (3)   2.05 2.05

Columbus Type of 1930
Souvenir Sheet
1992, Mar. 31   Engr.   Perf. 14
B194   Sheet of 3   1.00 1.00
a.   A65 17p +5p dark red   .30   .30
b.   A65 17p +5p ultramarine   .30   .30
c.   A65 17p +5p black   .30   .30

Discovery of America, 500th anniv.

Expo '92 Type
Design: No. B195, Seville, 16th cent.

1992, Apr. 21   Litho.   Perf. 13½x14
Souvenir Sheet
B195 A837 17p +5p multi   .35   .35

1992 Summer Olympics, Barcelona — SP37

No. B196, Mascot COBI. No. B197, Hand holding torch, horiz. No. B198, "25 Jul".

Perf. 14x13½, 13½x14
1992, July 16   Photo.
B196 SP37 17p +5p multi   .40   .40
B197 SP37 17p +5p multi   .40   .40
B198 SP37 17p +5p multi   .40   .40
    Nos. B196-B198 (3)   1.20 1.20

1992 Summer Olympics, Barcelona SP38

Designs: a, Olympic Stadium. b, San Jordi Sports Palace. c, INEF Sports University.

1992, July 25   Perf. 13½x14
B199 SP38 27p +5p Triptych,
#a.-c.   1.40 1.40

1992 Summer Olympics, Barcelona SP39   SP40

#B200, Olympic mascot as stamp collector. #B201, Sagrada Family Church, Barcelona.

1992, July 29   Photo.   Perf. 14x13½
B200 SP39 17p +5p multi   .35   .35
B201 SP40 17p +5p multi   .35   .35

Olymphilex '92 (#B201).

Madrid, European City of Culture — SP41

#B202, Municipal Museum. #B203, Royal Theater. #B204, The Prado Museum. #B205, Queen Sofia Natl. Center for the Arts.

1992, Nov. 24   Photo.   Perf. 14x13½
B202 SP41 17p +5p multi   .35   .30
B203 SP41 17p +5p multi   .35   .30
B204 SP41 17p +5p multi   .35   .30
B205 SP41 17p +5p multi   .35   .30
    Nos. B202-B205 (4)   1.40 1.20

AIR POST STAMPS

Regular Issue of 1909-10 Overprinted in Red or Black

Perf. 13x12½, 14
1920, Apr. 4   Unwmk.
C1 A46 5c green (R)   1.50   1.00
a.   Imperf., pair   105.00   105.00
b.   Double overprint   35.00   35.00
c.   Inverted overprint   90.00   90.00
d.   Double ovpt., one invtd.   35.00   35.00
e.   Triple overprint   35.00   35.00
C2 A46 10c car (Bk)   1.75   1.25
a.   Imperf., pair   105.00   105.00
b.   Double overprint   35.00   35.00
d.   Double ovpt., one invtd.   35.00   35.00
C3 A46 25c dp blue (R)   3.25   1.75
a.   Inverted overprint   90.00   90.00
b.   Double overprint   35.00   35.00
C4 A46 50c sl blue (R)   13.00   6.00
a.   Imperf., pair   105.00   105.00
C5 A46 1p lake (Bk)   42.50   22.50
a.   Imperf., pair   385.00   385.00
    Nos. C1-C5 (5)   62.00   32.50
Set, never hinged   170.00

Dangerous counterfeits are plentiful.
A 30c green was authorized, but not issued. Value: hinged $550; never hinged $900.
For overprints see Nos. C58-C61.

"Spirit of St. Louis" over Coast of Europe — AP1

Seville-Barcelona Exposition Issue
Control Numbers on Back
1929, Feb. 15   Engr.   Perf. 11
C6 AP1 5c brown   6.00   5.00
C7 AP1 10c rose   6.00   5.00
C8 AP1 25c dark blue   7.00   5.50
C9 AP1 50c purple   8.00   5.75
C10 AP1 1p green   37.50   25.00
C11 AP1 4p black   25.00   20.00
    Nos. C6-C11 (6)   89.50   66.25
Set, never hinged   300.00

Nos. C6 to C11 exist imperforate. Value set, $800.

The so-called errors of color of Nos. C10, C18-C21, C23-C24, C28-C31, C37, C40, C42, C44, C46, C48, C50, C52, C55, C62-C67 are believed to have been irregularly produced.

Plane and
Congress
Seal — AP2

Railway Congress Issue
Control Numbers on Back

1930, May 10		**Litho.**	**Perf. 14**	
C12	AP2	5c bister brn	6.00	7.50
C13	AP2	10c rose	6.00	7.50
C14	AP2	25c dark blue	6.00	7.50
C15	AP2	50c purple	17.50	15.00
a.		Vert. pair, imperf. between	300.00	
		Never hinged	600.00	
C16	AP2	1p yellow green	35.00	30.00
C17	AP2	4p black	35.00	30.00
		Nos. C12-C17 (6)	92.25	92.25
		Set, never hinged	400.00	

The note after No. 385 will apply here also.
Dangerous counterfeits exist.

Goya Issue

Fantasy of
Flight
AP3

Asmodeus and
Cleofas — AP4

Fantasy of
Flight
AP5

Fantasy of
Flight — AP6

1930, June 15		**Engr.**	**Perf. 12½**	
C18	AP3	5c brn red & yel	.25	.25
C19	AP3	15c blk & red org	.25	.25
C20	AP3	25c brn car & dp red	.25	.25
C21	AP4	5c ol grn & grnsh bl	.25	.25
C22	AP4	10c sl grn & yel grn	.25	.25
C23	AP4	20c ultra & rose red	.25	.25
C24	AP4	40c vio bl & lt bl	.30	.30
C25	AP5	30c brown & vio	.30	.30
C26	AP5	50c ver & grn	.30	.30
C27	AP5	4p brn car & blk	2.00	2.00
C28	AP6	1p vio brn & vio	.30	.30
C29	AP6	4p bl blk & sl grn	2.00	2.00
C30	AP6	10p blk brn & bis brn	7.00	7.00
		Nos. C18-C30,CE1 (14)	13.95	13.95
		Set, never hinged	18.75	

Nos. C18-C30 exist imperf. Value for set, $150.

Christopher Columbus Issue

La Rábida Monastery — AP7

Martín Alonso
Pinzón — AP8

Vicente Yanez
Pinzón — AP9

Columbus in His Cabin — AP10

1930, Sept. 29			**Litho.**	
C31	AP7	5c lt red brn	.25	.25
C32	AP7	5c olive bister	.25	.25
C33	AP7	10c blue green	.25	.25
C34	AP7	15c dark violet	.25	.25
C35	AP7	20c ultra	.25	.25
		Engr.		
C36	AP8	25c carmine rose	.25	.25
C37	AP9	30c dp red brn	2.00	2.00
C38	AP8	40c indigo	2.00	2.00
C39	AP9	50c orange	2.00	2.00
C40	AP8	1p dull violet	2.00	2.00
C41	AP10	4p olive green	2.00	2.00
C42	AP10	10p light brown	11.00	12.00
		Nos. C31-C42 (12)	22.50	23.50
		Set, never hinged	35.00	

Nos. C31-C42 exist imperf. Value for set, $190.

Spanish-American Issue

AP11

Columbus
AP12

Columbus
and Pinzón
Brothers
AP13

1930, Sept. 29				**Litho.**
C43	AP11	5c lt red	.25	.25
C44	AP11	10c dull green	.25	.25
		Engr.		
C45	AP12	25c scarlet	.25	.25
C46	AP12	50c slate gray	2.50	2.10
C47	AP12	1p fawn	2.50	2.10
C48	AP13	4p slate blue	2.50	2.10
C49	AP13	10p brown violet	11.00	10.00
		Nos. C43-C49 (7)	19.25	17.05
		Set, never hinged	35.00	

Nos. C43-C49 exist imperf. Value for set, $250.

Spanish-American Exhibition Issue

Santos-Dumont and First Flight of His
Airplane — AP14

Teodoro
Fels and
His
Airplane
AP15

Dagoberto Godoy and Pass over
Andes — AP16

Sacadura
Cabral
and Gago
Coutinho
and Their
Airplane
AP17

Sidar of Mexico
and Map of
South
America — AP18

Ignacio Jiménez
and Francisco
Iglesias — AP19

Charles A.
Lindbergh,
Statue of
Liberty,
Spirit of
St. Louis
and Cat
AP20

Santa
Maria,
Plane and
Torre del
Oro,
Seville
AP21

1930, Oct. 10			**Photo.**	**Perf. 14**
C50	AP14	5c gray black	.90	.55
C51	AP15	10c dk olive grn	.90	.55
C52	AP16	25c ultra	.90	.55
C53	AP17	50c blue gray	1.90	1.40
C54	AP18	50c black	1.90	1.40
C55	AP19	1p car lake	4.00	3.00
a.		1p brown violet	75.00	75.00
		Never hinged	175.00	
C56	AP20	1p deep green	4.00	3.00
C57	AP21	4p slate blue	7.25	5.50
		Nos. C50-C57 (8)	21.75	15.95
		Set, never hinged	90.00	

Exist imperf. Value, set $110.
Note after No. 432 also applies to Nos. C31-C57.

Reprints of Nos. C50-C57 have blurred impressions, yellowish paper. Value: one-tenth of originals. Examples of No. C56 exist with portrait of Lindbergh inverted, doubled with one inverted and missing.

Nos. C1-C4
Overprinted in Red or
Black

1931			**Perf. 13x12½**	
C58	A46	5c green (R)	12.50	11.50
C59	A46	10c carmine (Bk)	12.50	11.50
C60	A46	25c deep blue (R)	17.50	16.50
C61	A46	50c slate blue (R)	35.00	26.00
		Nos. C58-C61 (4)	77.50	65.50
		Set, never hinged	160.00	

Counterfeits of overprint exist.
The status of Nos. C58-C61 has been questioned.

Plane
and
Royal
Palace,
Madrid
AP22

Madrid
Post
Office
and
Cibeles
Fountain
AP23

Plane
over
Calle de
Alcalá,
Madrid
AP24

1931, Oct. 10			**Engr.**	**Perf. 12**
C62	AP22	5c brown violet	.25	.30
C63	AP22	10c deep green	.25	.30
C64	AP22	25c dull red	.25	.30
C65	AP23	50c deep blue	.45	.50
C66	AP23	1p deep violet	.65	.60
C67	AP24	4p black	9.00	9.00
		Nos. C62-C67 (6)	10.85	11.00
		Set, never hinged	15.00	

3rd Pan-American Postal Union Congress, Madrid.
Exist imperf. Value, set $45.
For overprints see Nos. CO1-CO6.

Montserrat Issue

Plane over
Montserrat
Pass — AP25

1931, Dec. 9   *Perf. 11½*
Control Number on Back
C68 AP25 5c black brown   .50   .50
C69 AP25 10c yellow green   2.00   2.00
C70 AP25 25c deep rose   7.00   7.50
C71 AP25 50c orange   22.50 30.00
C72 AP25 1p gray black   15.00 20.00
  Nos. C68-C72 (5)   74.05 74.05
  Set, never hinged   100.00

                                   Perf. 14
C68a AP25 5c   7.50   14.50
C69a AP25 10c   40.00 45.00
C70a AP25 25c   72.50 72.50
C71a AP25 50c   72.50 72.50
C72f AP25 1p   72.50 72.50
  Nos. C68a-C72f (5)   265.00 277.00
  Set, never hinged   275.00

900th anniv. of Montserrat Monastery.
Nos. C68-C72 exist imperf. Value set, $525.

Autogiro over
Seville — AP26

1935-39   *Perf. 11½*
C72A AP26 2p gray blue   22.50 4.50
  g. Imperf., pair   450.00

            Re-engraved
C72B AP26 2p dk blue ('38)   .75   .25
  c. Imperf., pair   20.00
  d. Perf. 10 ('39)   1.50   1.10
  Set, #C72A-C72B, never
    hinged   45.00

The sky has heavy horizontal lines of shad-
ing. Entire design is more heavily shaded than
No. C72A.
No. C72B exists privately perforated 14.
Value, $9 unused, $9 used.
For overprints see Nos. 7LC14, 7LC19,
14L26.

Eagle and Newspapers — AP27

Press Building,
Madrid — AP28

Don Quixote and Sancho Panza Flying
on the Wooden Horse — AP29

Design: 15c, 30c, 50c, 1p, Autogiro over
House of Nazareth.

1936, Mar. 11   Photo.   *Perf. 12½*
C73 AP27 1c rose car   .25   .25
C74 AP28 2c dark brown   .25   .25
C75 AP27 5c black brown   .25   .25
C76 AP28 10c dk yellow grn   .25   .25
C77 AP28 15c Prus blue   .25   .25
C78 AP27 20c violet   .25   .25
C79 AP28 25c magenta   .25   .25
C80 AP28 30c red orange   .25   .25
C81 AP27 40c orange   .50   .25
C82 AP28 50c light blue   .30   .25
C83 AP28 60c olive green   .65   .40
C84 AP28 1p brnsh black   .65   .45
C85 AP29 2p brt ultra   5.75   2.25
C86 AP29 4p lilac rose   5.75   2.75
C87 AP29 10p violet brown   16.00 11.00
  Nos. C73-C87 (15)   31.20 18.85
  Set, never hinged   46.75

Madrid Press Association, 40th anniv.
Exist imperf. Value, set $250 hinged, and
$325 never hinged.
See note after No. 432.

Types of Regular
Postage of 1936
Overprinted in
Blue or Red

1936   *Imperf.*
C88 A125 10c dk red (Bl)   100.00 100.00
C89 A125 15c dk blue (R)   100.00 100.00
  Set, never hinged   450.00

1st National Philatelic Exhibition which
opened in Madrid, Apr. 2, 1936.

No. 577 Overprinted in
Black

1936, Aug. 1   *Perf. 11½*
C90 A128 30c rose red   3.00   3.75
        Never hinged   7.75
  b. Imperf., pair   140.00

Issued in commemoration of the flight of
aviators Antonio Arnaiz and Juan Calvo from
Manila to Spain.
Counterfeit overprints exist.
Exists privately perforated 14. Value, $50
unused, $50 used.

No. 288 Surcharged in Black

1938, Apr. 13   *Perf. 14*
C91 A36 2.50p on 10c   90.00 80.00
        Never hinged   175.00

7th anniversary of the Republic.
Values are for examples with perforations
nearly touching the design on one or two
sides.

No. 507
Surcharged in
Various Colors

1938, Aug.   *Perf. 11½*
C92 A92 50c on 25c (Bk)   29.00 29.00
C93 A92 1p on 25c (G)   2.25   1.50
C94 A92 1.25p on 25c (R)   2.25   1.50
C95 A92 1.50p on 25c (Bl)   2.25   1.50
C96 A92 2p on 25c (Bk &
          R)   40.00 34.00
  Nos. C92-C96 (5)   75.75 67.50
  Set, never hinged   150.00

No. 585 Surcharged

1938, June 1   *Perf. 11*
C97 A132 5p on 1p multi   275.   275.
        Never hinged   500.
  a. Imperf., pair   600.   550.
  b. Inverted surcharge   350.   350.
  c. Souvenir sheet   1,500. 1,500.
        Never hinged   2,500.
  d. As "c," imperf.   6,500. 6,500.
  e. As "c," inverted
        surcharge   6,000. 6,000.

Counterfeit surcharges exist.

Type of 1938-39
Overprinted in Red or
Carmine

1938, May   *Perf. 10, 10½*
C98 A163 50c indigo (R)   .70   .55
C99 A163 1p dk blue (C)   3.00   .70
  Set, never hinged   4.50

Exist imperf. Value, each $100.
Examples without overprint are proofs.

Juan de
la Cierva
and his
Autogiro
over
Madrid
AP30

1939, Jan. Unwmk. Litho.   *Perf. 11*
C100 AP30 20c red orange   .60   .40
C101 AP30 25c dk carmine   .45   .25
C102 AP30 35c brt violet   .65   .40
C103 AP30 50c dk brown   .65   .25
C105 AP30 1p blue   .65   .25
C107 AP30 2p green   3.25   1.75
C108 AP30 4p dull blue   5.00   2.75
  Nos. C100-C108 (7)   11.25 6.05
  Set, never hinged   19.00

Exist imperf. Value, set $325.

1941-47   *Perf. 10*
C109 AP30 20c dk red orange   .25   .25
C110 AP30 25c redsh brown   .25   .25
C111 AP30 35c lilac rose   1.60   .50
C112 AP30 50c brown   .45   .25
C113 AP30 1p chalky blue   1.40   .25
C114 AP30 2p lt gray grn   1.60   .25
C115 AP30 4p gray blue   5.00   .30
C116 AP30 10p brt purple ('47) 3.75   .65
  Nos. C109-C116 (8)   14.30 2.70
  Set, never hinged   26.00

Issued in honor of Juan de la Cierva (1895-
1936), inventor of the autogiro.
Nos. C109-C115 exist imperf. Value, set
$300.
The overprint "EXPOSICION NACIONAL
DE FILATELIA 1948 SAN SEBASTIAN" multiple, in parallel horizontal lines, on Nos. C109
to C113 and other airmail stamps, was privately applied.

Correo Aéreo   **Correo
                           Aéreo**

Nos. 625-634, 660, 676 and 677 with
either of these overprints have not been
established as issues of the Spanish
government.

Mariano
Pardo de
Figueroa
(Dr.
Thebussem)
AP31

1944, Oct. 12   Engr.   *Perf. 10*
C117 AP31 5p brt ultra   15.00 13.00
        Never hinged   23.00

"Stamp Day" and "Day of the Race," Oct. 12,
1944. Valid for franking air mail correspondence one day only.

Mail
Coach,
Plane and
Count of
St. Louis
AP32

1945, Oct. 12   Unwmk.
C118 AP32 10p yellow green   17.50 *19.00*
        Never hinged   25.00

"Stamp Day" and "Day of the Race," Oct. 12,
1945, and to honor Luis José Sartorius, Count
of St. Louis, who issued the decree for Spain's
1st postage stamps. No. C118 was valid for
franking air mail correspondence one day
only.
C118 exists imperf. Value, $1,000.

Maj.
Joaquin
Garcia
Morato
AP33

1945, Nov. 27
C119 AP33 10p deep claret   13.50 5.50
        Never hinged   35.00

C119 exists imperf. Value, $500 hinged,
$800 never hinged.

Capt. Carlos Haya
Gonzalez — AP34

1945, Dec. 14
C120 AP34 4p red   5.50   4.50
        Never hinged   12.50

No. C120 exists imperf. Values: $500
hinged; $750 never hinged.

Bartolomé de las
Casas — AP35

1946, Oct. 12   *Perf. 11½x11*
C121 AP35 5.50p green   1.90   2.50
        Never hinged   3.00

Stamp Day and Day of the Race. Exists
imperf. Value $16.

Don Quixote
and Sancho
Panza Astride
Clavileno
AP36

1947, Oct. 9 — Perf. 10

C122	AP36	5.50p purple	4.50	4.50
		Never hinged		6.75

Stamp Day and the 400th anniversary of the birth of Miguel de Cervantes Saavedra. C122 exists imperf. Value, $1,200.

Manuel de Falla — AP37

Ignacio Zuloaga — AP38

1947, Dec. 1 — Perf. 9½x10½
Control Number on Back

C123	AP37	25p dk vio brn	20.00	15.00
C124	AP38	50p dk carmine	100.00	40.00
		Set, never hinged		225.00

Counterfeits exist.
For overprint see No. CB18.
No. C124 exists imperf. Value, $1,200.

Train and Plane — AP39

1948, Oct. 9 — Litho. Perf. 13x12½

C125	AP39	2p scarlet	1.50	1.50
		Never hinged		2.25

Cent. of Spanish railroads and Stamp Day.

UPU Type of Regular Issue with Pedestal and Propeller Added

1949, Oct. 9 — Perf. 12½x13

C126	A202	4p dk olive green	.25	.45
		Never hinged		.40

Stamp Day and the 75th anniv. of the UPU.

Stamp of 1850 — AP40

1950, Oct. 12 — Engr. Imperf.

C127	AP40	1p rose brn	4.50	4.50
C128	AP40	2.50p brown org	4.50	4.50
C129	AP40	20p dark blue	55.00	55.00
C130	AP40	25p green	55.00	55.00
		Nos. C127-C130 (4)	169.00	188.00
		Set, never hinged		225.00

Centenary of Spanish postage stamps.

Map of Western Hemisphere — AP41

1951, Apr. 16 — Photo. Perf. 12½

C131	AP41	1p blue	4.50	2.25
		Never hinged		6.25

6th Congress of the Postal Union of the Americas and Spain.

Isabella I AP42

1951, Oct. 12 — Engr. Perf. 13

C132	AP42	60c dk gray grn	6.50	.40
C133	AP42	90c orange	.80	.55
C134	AP42	1.30p plum	5.00	4.00
C135	AP42	1.90p sepia	4.50	4.00
C136	AP42	2.30p dk blue	2.75	2.75
		Nos. C132-C136 (5)	19.55	11.70
		Set, never hinged		27.50

Stamp Day and 500th anniv. of the birth of Queen Isabella I.

"The Eucharist" by Tiepolo — AP43

1952, May 26 — Photo. Perf. 12½x13

C137	AP43	1p gray green	3.00	.60
		Never hinged		3.50

35th International Encharistic Congress, Barcelona, 1952.

St. Francis Xavier — AP44

1952, July 3 — Engr.

C138	AP44	2p deep blue	30.00	14.00
		Never hinged		75.00

400th anniv. of the death of St. Francis Xavier.

Ferdinand the Catholic and Columbus Presenting Natives AP45

1952, Oct. 12

C139	AP45	60c dull green	.25	.25
C140	AP45	90c orange	.25	.25
C141	AP45	1.30p plum	.45	.30
C142	AP45	1.90p sepia	2.00	2.00
C143	AP45	2.30p deep blue	10.00	9.50
		Nos. C139-C143 (5)	12.95	12.30
		Set, never hinged		17.50

500th anniversary of the birth of Ferdinand the Catholic and to publicize Stamp Day.

Joaquin Sorolla y Bastida — AP46

1953, Oct. 9 — Perf. 13x12½

C144	AP46	50p dark violet	250.00	22.50
		Never hinged		500.00

Issued to honor Joaquin Sorolla y Bastida (1863-1923), impressionist painter.

Miguel Lopez de Legazpi — AP47

1953, Nov. 5

C145	AP47	25p gray black	50.00	27.50
		Never hinged		100.00

Spanish-Philippine Postal Convention of 1951.

Leonardo Torres Quevedo (1852-1939), Mathematician and Inventor — AP48

1955, Sept. 6 — Engr. Unwmk.

C146	AP48	50p bluish gray & blk	5.00	.90
		Never hinged		11.00

35th International Encharistic Congress, Barcelona, 1952.

Plane and Caravel AP49

1955-56 — Photo. Perf. 12½x13

C147	AP49	20c gray grn ('56)	.25	.25
C148	AP49	25c gray violet	.25	.25
C149	AP49	50c ol gray ('56)	.25	.25
C150	AP49	1p red orange	.25	.25
C151	AP49	1.10p emer ('56)	.25	.25
C152	AP49	1.40p rose car	.25	.25
C153	AP49	3p brt blue ('56)	.25	.25
C154	AP49	4.80p yellow	.25	.25
C155	AP49	5p redsh brown	1.50	.25
C156	AP49	7p lilac ('56)	.45	.25
C157	AP49	10p lt ol grn ('56)	.50	.25
		Nos. C147-C157 (11)	4.00	2.75
		Set, never hinged		4.00

Mariano Fortuny y Carbo (1838-1874), Painter — AP50

1956, Jan. 10 — Engr. Perf. 13x12½

C158	AP50	25p grnsh black	14.00	.90
		Never hinged		30.00

Catalogue values for unused stamps in this section, from this point to the end of the section, are for Never Hinged items.

Bullfight Type of Regular Issue

25c, Small town arena. 50c, Fighting with cape. 1p, Dedication of the bull. 5p, Bull ring.

1960, Feb. 29 — Engr. Unwmk.
Perf. 13x12½, 12½x13

C159	A246	25c brn car & dl lil	.25	.25
C160	A245	50c blue	.25	.25
C161	A246	1p red & dull red	.25	.25
C162	A245	5p red lilac & vio	.55	.40
		Nos. C159-C162 (4)	1.15	1.00

Jai Alai AP51

1960, Mar. 27 — Photo. Perf. 12½x13

C163	AP51	1p brt red & dk brn	4.75	3.25
C164	AP51	5p dull brn & mag	4.75	3.25
C165	AP51	6p vio blk & mag	4.75	3.25
C166	AP51	10p grn, mag & dk brn	4.75	3.25
		Nos. C163-C166 (4)	19.00	13.00

1st Intl. Cong. of Philately, Barcelona, Mar. 26-Apr. 5. Nos. C163-C166 could be bought at the exhibition upon presentation of 5p entrance ticket.

Sport Type of Regular Issue

Sports: 1.25p, 6p, Steeplechase, horiz. 1.50p, 10p, Basque ball game.

1960, Oct. 31 — Perf. 12½x13, 13x12½ Unwmk.

C167	A251	1.25p choc & car	.30	.25
C168	A251	1.50p pur, brn & blk	.30	.25
C169	A251	6p vio blk & car	.95	.55
C170	A251	10p ol grn, red & blk	1.25	.55
		Nos. C167-C170 (4)	2.80	1.50

Rosary Type of Regular Issue

Mysteries of the Rosary: 25c, The Ascension, Bayeu. 1p, The Descent of the Holy Ghost, El Greco. 5p, The Assumption, Mateo Cerezo. 10p, The Coronation of the Virgin Mary, El Greco.

1962, Oct. 26 — Engr. Perf. 13

C171	A280	25c vio & dl gray vio	.25	.25
C172	A280	1p olive & brown	.35	.25
C173	A280	5p brn & rose cl	.60	.25
C174	A280	10p bluish grn & yel grn	1.40	.50
		Nos. C171-C174 (4)	2.60	1.15

Recaredo I, Visigothic King, 586-601 — AP52

Portrait: 50p, Francisco Cardinal Jimenez de Cisneros (1436-1517).

1963, Dec. 5 — Engr. Perf. 13x12½

C175	AP52	25p dull purple	1.10	.40
C176	AP52	50p green & black	1.90	.55

1966, Feb. 26

Portraits: 25p, Seneca (4 B.C.-65 A.D.). 50p, Pope St. Damasus I (304?-384).

C177	AP52	25p yel grn & dk grn	1.75	.25
C178	AP52	50p sky bl & gray bl	2.75	.55

Plaza de Espana, Seville AP53

20p, Rande River Bridge, Pontevedra.

1981, Nov. 26 — Engr. Perf. 13

C179	AP53	13p shown	.25	.25
C180	AP53	20p multicolored	.25	.25

St. Thomas, by El Greco — AP54

13p, Sts. Andrew and Francis.

1982, July 7 — Photo. Perf. 13

C181	AP54	13p multicolored	.25	.25
C182	AP54	20p shown	.25	.25

Bowling AP55

1983, Apr. 13   Photo.   Perf. 13
C183 AP55 13p Bicycling, vert. .25 .25
C184 AP55 20p shown .25 .25

AIR POST SEMI-POSTAL STAMPS

Red Cross Issue

Ramon Franco's Plane Plus Ultra SPAP1

1926, Sept. 15   Engr.   Unwmk.

Perf. 12½, 13

CB1 SPAP1 5c black & vio 1.40 1.40
CB2 SPAP1 10c ultra & blk 3.00 3.00
CB3 SPAP1 25c carmine & blk .30 .30
CB4 SPAP1 50c red org & blk .30 .30
CB5 SPAP1 1p black & green 2.50 2.50
Nos. CB1-CB5 (5) 7.50 7.50
Set, never hinged 10.00

For overprints and surcharges see Nos. B55-B63.

No. B106 Surcharged in Black

1938, Apr. 15   Perf. 11½
CB6 SP13 45c + 2p + 5p 250. 225.
   Never hinged 650.
a. Imperf., pair 1,150. 900.
b. Souvenir sheet of 1 3,000. 4,500.
   Never hinged 6,000.
c. Souvenir sheet, imperf. 6,000. 6,000.
d. Souv. sheet, surch. invtd. 6,500. 5,750.

The surtax was used to benefit the defenders of Madrid.
This issue has been extensively counterfeited.

No. B107 Surcharged

1938, June 1   Perf. 10
CB7 SP14 45c + 5p + 3p 10.00 9.75
   Never hinged 17.50

Monument SPAP2

Dome Fresco by Goya, Cathedral of Zaragoza SPAP3

#CB9, CB14, Caravel Santa Maria. #CB10, CB12, The Ascension. #CB13, The Coronation. #CB17, Bombardment of Cathedral of Zaragoza.

Perf. 10½, 11½x10½, 11½

1940, Jan. 29   Litho.   Unwmk.
Bicolored

CB8 SPAP2 25c + 5c .40 .40
CB9 SPAP2 50c + 5c .40 .40
CB10 SPAP2 65c + 15c .40 .40
CB11 SPAP2 70c + 15c .40 .40
CB12 SPAP2 90c + 20c .40 .40
CB13 SPAP2 1.20p + 30c .40 .40
CB14 SPAP2 1.40p + 40c .50 .50
CB15 SPAP2 2p + 50c .75 .75
CB16 SPAP3 4p + 1p sl grn & rose lil 15.00 15.00
CB17 SPAP3 10p + 4p chnt & ultra 200.00 200.00
Nos. CB8-CB17 (10) 218.65 218.65
Set, never hinged 550.00

19th centenary of the Pillar Virgin. The surtax was used to help restore the Cathedral at Zaragoza, damaged during the Civil War.
No. CB16 exists in slate green & violet, No. CB17 in red violet & ultramarine. Value, $32.50 each.
Nos. CB8-CB17 exist imperf. Value, set $400.

No. C123 Surcharged in Black

1950-51   Perf. 9½x10½
Control Number on Back

CB18 AP37 25p + 10c 250.00 250.00
   Never hinged 500.00
a. Without control number 2,500. 1,500.
   Without control number, never hinged 4,800.

Visit of Gen. Franco to the Canary Islands, Oct., 1950.
The control number was printed on the gum, and regummed examples of No. CB18 are frequently offered as No. CB18a.
Counterfeit surcharges exist.
Issued: #CB18a, 10/23/50; #CB18 2/22/51.

AIR POST SPECIAL DELIVERY STAMP

Goya Commemorative Issue

Type of Air Post Stamp of 1930 Overprinted

1930   Unwmk.   Perf. 12½
CE1 AP4 20c bl blk & lt brn (Bk) .25 .25
   Never hinged .25
a. Blue overprint 15.00 7.75
   Never hinged 21.00
b. Overprint omitted 15.00 22.50
   Never hinged 25.00

See note after No. 432.

AIR POST OFFICIAL STAMPS

Pan-American Postal Union Congress Issue
Types of Air Post Stamps of 1931 Overprinted in Red or Blue

1931   Unwmk.   Perf. 12
CO1 AP22 5c red brown (R) .25 .25
CO2 AP22 10c blue grn (Bl) .25 .25
CO3 AP22 25c rose (Bl) .25 .25
CO4 AP23 50c lt blue (R) .25 .25
CO5 AP23 1p violet (R) .25 .25
CO6 AP24 4p gray blk (R) 3.50 3.50
Nos. CO1-CO6 (6) 4.75 4.75
Set, never hinged 7.00

Shades exist.
Nos. CO1-CO6 exist imperf. Value, set $22.50

SPECIAL DELIVERY STAMPS

Pegasus and Coat of Arms — SD1

1905-25   Unwmk.   Typo.   Perf. 14
Control Number on Back

E1 SD1 20c deep red 45.00 .30
   Never hinged 100.00
a. 20c rose red, litho. ('25) 38.00 .30
   Never hinged 70.00
b. Imperf., pair 300.00
c. As "a," imperf., pair 300.00

Gazelle SD2

1929   Engr.   Perf. 11
Control Number on Back

E2 SD2 20c dull red 19.50 22.50
   Never hinged 37.50
a. Perf. 14 32.50 37.50
   Never hinged 60.00

Seville and Barcelona Exhibitions. See note after No. 432.

Pegasus — SD3

1929-32   Perf. 13½x12½, 11½
Control Number on Back

E3 SD3 20c red 21.00 4.00
   Never hinged 40.00
a. Imperf., pair 400.00
b. Without control number, perf. 11½ ('32) 60.00 1.50
   Never hinged 97.50
c. As "b," imperf., pair 950.00

No. E3 Overprinted like Nos. 358-370

E4 SD3 20c red (Bl) 12.00 25.00
   Never hinged 30.00

League of Nations 55th assembly.
For overprints see Nos. E5, E10-E12.

No. E3 Overprinted in Blue

1930   Perf. 13½x12½, 11½
E5 SD3 20c red 13.50 .75
   Never hinged 40.00

Railway Congress Issue

Electric Locomotive — SD4

1930, May 10   Litho.   Perf. 14
Control Number on Back

E6 SD4 20c brown orange 50.00 50.00
   Never hinged 105.00

See note after No. 385.

Goya Issue

Type of Regular Issue of 1930 Overprinted

1930   Perf. 12½
E7 A57 20c lilac rose .25 .30
   Never hinged .45

Christopher Columbus Issue

Type of Regular Issue of 1930 Overprinted

1930 Sept. 29
E8 A64 20c brown violet 1.90 1.90
   Never hinged 3.00

See note after No. 432.

Spanish-American Exhibition Issue

View of Seville Exhibition — SD5

1930, Oct. 10   Photo.   Perf. 14
E9 SD5 20c orange .45 .30
   .60

See note after No. 432.

Madrid Issue

No. E5 Overprinted in Green

1931   Perf. 11½
E10 SD3 20c red 5.00 5.00
   Never hinged 8.00

The status of No. E10 has been questioned.

Barcelona Issue

No. E3 Overprinted

E11 SD3 20c red   5.50 5.50
   Never hinged   12.00

No. E11 also exists with accent over "U."
The status of No. E11 has been questioned.

No. E3 Overprinted in Blue

E12 SD3 20c red   6.50 1.25
   Never hinged   21.00

Montserrat Issue

Pegasus — SD6

1931   Engr.   Perf. 11
Control Number on Back
E13 SD6 20c vermilion   25.00 25.00
   Never hinged   38.00
   a.   Perf. 14   55.00 60.00

SD7

1934   Perf. 10
E14 SD7 20c vermilion   .25 .25
   Never hinged   .20
   a.   Imperf., pair   32.50

For overprints see #10LE1, 11LE1-11LE4, 14LE1.

Newsboy — SD8

1936   Photo.   Perf. 12½
E15 SD8 20c rose carmine   .25 .30
   Never hinged   .50

40th anniversary of the Madrid Press Association.
See note after No. 432.

Pegasus SD9

Spanish State

1937-38   Unwmk.   Litho.   Perf. 11
With imprint "Hija. deB Fournier-Burgos"
E16 SD9 20c violet brn   7.75 4.50
   Never hinged   11.00
   a.   Imperf., pair   77.50

Without Imprint
E17 SD9 20c dk vio brn ('38)   1.50 .30
   Never hinged   3.00
   a.   Imperf., pair   50.00

No. 645 Overprinted in Black

1937
E18 A162 20c dark violet   11.00 11.00
   Never hinged   14.50

Pegasus SD10

1939-42   Perf. 10½
Imprint: "SANCHEZ TODA"
E19 SD10 25c carmine   4.50 .70
   Never hinged   6.25
   a.   Imperf., pair   50.00

Without Imprint
Perf. 10
E20 SD10 25c carmine ('42)   .25 .25
   Never hinged   .30
   a.   Imperf., pair   8.50

> Catalogue values for unused stamps in this section, from this point to the end of the section, are for Never Hinged items.

"Flight" SD11

Centaur — SD12

Perf. 12½x13, 13x12½
1956, Feb. 12   Photo.   Unwmk.
E21 SD11 2p scarlet   .25 .25
E22 SD12 4p black & magenta   .25 .25
1965-66
E23 SD11   3p dp car   .25 .25
E24 SD11   5p dp org ('66)   .25 .25
E25 SD12 6.50p dk vio & rose brn ('66)   .25 .25
   Nos. E21-E25 (5)   1.25 1.25

Chariot SD13

Mail Circling Globe — SD14

1971, June 1   Photo.   Perf. 13
E26 SD13 10p red & yel grn   .25 .25
E27 SD14 15p red, bl & blk   .25 .25

Communications — SD15

1993, Apr. 20   Photo.   Perf. 14x13½
E28 SD15 180p red & yellow   2.50 .35

SEMI-POSTAL SPECIAL DELIVERY STAMPS

Red Cross Issue

Royal Family Group SPSD1

1926   Unwmk.   Engr.   Perf. 12½, 13
EB1 SPSD1 20c red vio & vio brn   8.75 8.75
   Never hinged   17.00

See notes after Nos. 432 and B18.
For overprint see No. B54.

Motorcyclist and Zaragoza Cathedral SPSD2

1940   Litho.   Perf. 11½
EB2 SPSD2 25c + 5c rose red & buff   .40 .30

19th cent. of the Pillar Virgin. The surtax was used to help restore the Cathedral at Zaragoza, damaged during the Civil War.

DELIVERY TAX STAMPS

D1

1931   Unwmk.   Litho.   Perf. 11½
ER1 D1 5c black   7.25 .25
   Never hinged   12.00

For overprints see Nos. ER2-ER3, 7LE5-7LE6.

No. ER1 Overprinted in Red

1931
ER2 D1 5c black   1.25 1.40
   Never hinged   2.25

No. ER2 also exists with accent over "U."

No. ER1 Overprinted in Red

ER3 D1 5c black   3.00 3.00
   Never hinged   5.50

These stamps were originally issued for Postage Due purpose but were later used as regular postage stamps.

WAR TAX STAMPS

These stamps did not pay postage but represented a fiscal tax on mail matter in addition to the postal fees. Their use was obligatory.

Coat of Arms — WT1

Unwmk.
1874, Jan. 1   Typo.   Perf. 14
MR1 WT1 5c black   11.00 .95
   a.   Imperf., pair   14.00
MR2 WT1 10c pale blue   12.00 1.60
   a.   Imperf., pair   62.50

Coat of Arms — WT2

1875, Jan. 1
MR3 WT2 5c green   6.00 .60
   a.   Imperf., pair   27.50
MR4 WT2 10c lilac   12.00 2.75
   a.   Imperf., pair   55.00

King Alfonso XII — WT3

1876, June 1
MR5 WT3 5c pale green   7.50 1.00
MR6 WT3 10c blue   7.50 1.00
   a.   Cliche of 5c in plate of 10c   125.00
MR7 WT3 25c black   50.00 17.00
MR8 WT3 1p lilac   475.00 110.00
MR9 WT3 5p rose   900.00 300.00

Nos. MR5-MR9 exist imperforate. Value, $1,100.

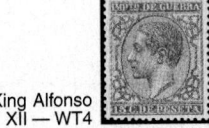

King Alfonso XII — WT4

1877, Sept. 1
MR10 WT4 15c claret   27.50 1.00
   a.   Imperf., pair   100.00
MR11 WT4 50c yellow   900.00 110.00

WT5

1879
MR12 WT5 5c blue   65.00
MR13 WT5 10c rose   37.50
MR14 WT5 15c violet   25.00
MR15 WT5 25c brown   40.00
MR16 WT5 50c olive green   25.00

MR17	WT5	1p bister	40.00	
MR18	WT5	5p gray	150.00	
	Nos. MR12-MR18 (7)		382.50	

Nos. MR12-MR18 were never placed in use.
Nos. MR17 and MR18 exist imperforate.
Value, $225.

WT6

Inscribed "1897 A 1898"

1897			**Perf. 14**	
MR19	WT6	5c green	3.25	2.10
MR20	WT6	10c green	3.25	2.10
MR21	WT6	15c green	750.00	250.00
MR22	WT6	20c green	8.25	3.25

Nos. MR19-MR22 exist imperf. Value for set $825.

Inscribed

1898				
MR23	WT6	5c black	2.25	1.75
MR24	WT6	10c black	2.25	1.75
MR25	WT6	15c black	50.00	9.50
MR26	WT6	20c black	3.50	3.00
	Nos. MR23-MR26 (4)		58.00	16.00

Nos. MR23-MR26 exist imperf. Value about $275 a pair.

King Alfonso
XIII — WT7

1898				
MR27	WT7	5c black	9.00	.60
a.	Imperf., pair		85.00	

OFFICIAL STAMPS

Coat of Arms — O1

		Unwmk.		
1854, July 1		**Typo.**		**Imperf.**
O1	O1	½o blk, *yellow*	2.10	2.75
O2	O1	1o blk, *rose*	2.75	3.25
a.	1o black, *blue*		29.00	
O3	O1	4o blk, *green*	7.50	9.25
O4	O1	1 l blk, *blue*	52.50	60.00
	Nos. O1-O4 (4)		64.85	75.25

Coat of Arms — O2

1855-63				
O5	O2	½o blk, *yellow*	1.50	1.75
a.	½o black, *straw* ('63)		1.75	1.90
O6	O2	1o blk, *rose*	1.50	1.75
a.	1o black, *salmon rose*		3.25	1.90
O7	O2	4o blk, *green*	3.25	1.90
a.	4o black, *yellow green*		8.75	1.90
O8	O2	1 l blk, *gray blue*	14.50	17.50
	Nos. O5-O8 (4)		20.75	22.90

The "value indication" on Nos. O1-O8 actually is the weight of the mail in onzas (ounces, "o") and libras (pounds, "l") for which they are valid.

Type of Regular Issue of 1889

1895				**Perf. 14**
O9	A34	15c yellow	11.00	6.00
a.	Imperf., pair		250.00	

Coat of Arms — O5

1896-98				
O10	O5	rose	5.25	1.75
a.	Imperf., pair		87.50	
O11	O5	dk blue ('98)	19.00	6.00

Cervantes Issue

Chamber of
Deputies
O6

Statue of
Cervantes — O7

Cervantes — O9

National
Library
O8

1916, Apr. 22		**Engr.**	**Perf. 12**	
	For the Senate			
O12	O6	green & blk	1.10	.90
O13	O7	brown & blk	1.10	.90
O14	O8	carmine & blk	1.10	.90
O15	O9	brown & blk	1.10	.90
	For the Chamber of Deputies			
O16	O6	violet & blk	1.10	.90
O17	O7	carmine & blk	1.10	.90
O18	O8	green & blk	1.10	.90
O19	O9	violet & blk	1.10	.90
	Nos. O12-O19 (8)		8.80	7.20

Exist imperf. Value set of pairs, $110.
Exist with centers inverted. Value for set, $87.50

Pan-American Postal Union Congress Issue

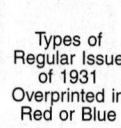

Types of
Regular Issue
of 1931
Overprinted in
Red or Blue

1931				**Perf. 12½**
O20	A84	5c dk brown (R)	.50	.25
O21	A85	10c brt green (Bl)	.50	.25
O22	A86	15c dull violet (R)	.50	.25
O23	A85	25c deep rose (Bl)	.50	.25
O24	A87	30c olive green (Bl)	.50	.25
O25	A84	40c ultra (R)	.70	.60
O26	A85	50c deep orange (Bl)	.70	.60
O27	A86	1p blue black (R)	.70	.60
O28	A88	4p magenta (Bl)	14.00	14.00
O29	A88	10p lt brown (R)	25.00	25.00
	Nos. O20-O29 (10)		43.60	42.05
	Set, never hinged		70.00	

Nos. O22-O29 exist imperf. Values about 3 times those quoted.

Mail
Coach
O30

Decorative
Mailbox
Opening
O10

Mail
Pouch
O11

Bicycle for
Mail
Delivery
O12

1999		**Photo.**	**Perf. 13¾x14**	
O30	O9	multi	—	
O31	O10	multi	—	
O32	O11	multi	—	
O33	O12	multi	—	
a.	Horiz. strip, #O30-O33		—	

For use by the Philatelic Service to any address. Not normally available unused.

POSTAL TAX STAMPS

PT5

		Perf. 10½x11½		
1937, Dec. 23				**Litho.**
RA11	PT5	10c blk, pale bl & red	8.00	5.00
	Never hinged		21.00	
a.	Imperf. pair		80.00	
	Never hinged		120.00	

The tax was for the tuberculosis fund.

PT6

1938, Dec. 23			**Perf. 11½**	
RA12	PT6	10c multicolored	4.50	1.75
	Never hinged		10.00	
a.	Imperf. pair		45.00	
	Never hinged		55.00	

The tax was for the tuberculosis fund.

"Spain"
Holding
Wreath of
Peace
over
Marching
Soldiers
PT7

1939, July 18			**Perf. 11**	
RA13	PT7	10c blue	.25	.25
	Never hinged		.25	
a.	Imperf. pair		65.00	
	Never hinged		82.50	

Type of Regular Issue, 1939
Without Imprint

		Unwmk.		
1939, Dec. 23		**Litho.**		**Imperf.**
RA14	A166	10c dull claret	.25	.25
	Never hinged		.25	

Tuberculosis Fund Issue
Types of Corresponding Semi-Postal Stamps

1940, Dec. 23			**Perf. 10**	
RA15	SP23	10c violet & red	.25	.25
	Never hinged		.25	

1941, Dec. 23				
RA16	SP24	10c black & red	.25	.25
	Never hinged		.25	

1942, Dec. 23				
RA17	SP25	10c dl sal & rose red	.25	.25
	Never hinged		.25	

1943, Dec. 23		**Photo.**	**Perf. 11**	
RA18	SP26	10c purple & dl red	.30	.25
	Never hinged		.50	

		Perf. 9½x10		
1944, Dec. 23		**Litho.**	**Unwmk.**	
RA19	SP27	10c salmon & rose	.25	.25
	Never hinged		.25	

1945, Dec. 23				
RA20	SP28	10c salmon & car	.25	.25
	Never hinged		.25	

Mother and
Child — PT8

1946, Dec. 22		**Litho.**	**Perf. 9½x10½**	
RA21	PT8	5c violet & red	.25	.25
RA22	PT8	10c green & red	.25	.25
	Set, never hinged		.40	

See No. RAC7.

Lorraine Cross
PT9

Tuberculosis
Sanatorium
PT10

		Perf. 9½x10½		
1947, Dec. 22			**Unwmk.**	
RA23	PT9	5c dk brown & red	.25	.25
RA24	PT10	10c vio bl & red	.25	.25
	Set, never hinged		.40	

See No. RAC8.

Aesculapius — PT11

Photogravure; Cross Engraved

1948, Dec. 22		**Unwmk.**	**Perf. 12½**	
RA25	PT11	5c brown & car	.25	.25
RA26	PT11	10c dp green & car	.25	.25
	Set, never hinged		.40	

The tax on Nos. RA15-RA26 was used to fight tuberculosis. See Nos. RAB1, RAC9.

"El Cid" — PT11a

1949, Feb. 1 Litho. Perf. 10½x9½
RA27 PT11a 5c violet .25 .25
  Never hinged .25

The tax aided displaced children. Valid for ordinary postage after Dec. 24, 1949.

Tuberculosis Fund Issues

Galleon and Lorraine Cross — PT12

Photogravure; Cross Engraved
1949, Dec. 22 Perf. 12½
RA28 PT12 5c violet & red .25 .25
RA29 PT12 10c yel grn & red .25 .25
  Set, never hinged .40

See Nos. RAB2, RAC10.

Pine Branch and Candle — PT13

1950, Dec. 22 Cross in Carmine
RA30 PT13 5c rose violet .25 .25
RA31 PT13 10c deep green .25 .25
  Set, never hinged .35

See Nos. RAB3, RAC11.

Children at Seashore — PT14

1951, Oct. 1 Cross in Carmine
RA32 PT14 5c rose brown .25 .25
RA33 PT14 10c dull green .35 .25
  Set, never hinged .75

See No. RAC12.

Nurse and Baby — PT15

1953, Oct. 1 Cross in Carmine
RA34 PT15 5c carmine lake .30 .25
RA35 PT15 10c gray blue .80 .25
  Set, never hinged 2.25

The tax on RA28-RA35 was used to fight tuberculosis. See No. RAC13.

POSTAL TAX SEMI-POSTAL STAMPS

Types of Corresponding Postal Tax Stamps

Photogravure; Cross Engraved
1948 Unwmk. Perf. 12½
RAB1 PT11 50c + 10c red brn & car .80 .75
  Never hinged 1.25

1949
RAB2 PT12 50c + 10c dk ol bis & red .50 .25
  Never hinged .80

1950
RAB3 PT13 50c + 10c brn & car 1.25 1.25
  Never hinged 2.25

The surtax on Nos. RAB1-RAB3 was used to fight tuberculosis. Combines domestic letter rate and tax obligatory Dec. 22-Jan. 3.

POSTAL TAX AIR POST STAMPS

Tuberculosis Fund Issues
Franco Type of Semi-Postal Stamps
Unwmk.
1940, Dec. 23 Litho. Perf. 10
RAC1 SP23 10c bright pink & red .90 .90
  Never hinged 2.50

Knight and Lorraine Cross — PTAP2

1941, Dec. 23
RAC2 PTAP2 10c blue & red .25 .25
  Never hinged .50

Lorraine Cross and Doves PTAP3

1942, Dec. 23
RAC3 PTAP3 10c dl sal & rose .80 .50
  Never hinged 1.25

Cross of Lorraine — PTAP4

1943, Dec. 23 Photo. Perf. 11
RAC4 PTAP4 10c vio & dl red .90 1.00
  Never hinged 1.60

Tuberculosis Sanatorium PTAP5

1944, Dec. 23 Litho. Perf. 10x9½
RAC5 PTAP5 25c salmon & rose 3.75 3.75
  Never hinged 5.50

Lorraine Cross and Eagle — PTAP6

1945, Dec. 23 Perf. 10
RAC6 PTAP6 25c red & car 1.40 1.25
  Never hinged 1.75

Eagle — PTAP7

1946, Dec. 22
RAC7 PTAP7 25c red & car .25 .25
  Never hinged .40

Tuberculosis Sanatorium PTAP8

1947, Dec. 22 Perf. 11½
RAC8 PTAP8 25c red vio .25 .25
  Never hinged .40

Plane over Sanatorium PTAP9

Photogravure; Cross Engraved
1948, Dec. 22 Perf. 12½
RAC9 PTAP9 25c ultra & car .30 .25
  Never hinged .60

Bell and Lorraine Cross — PTAP10

1949, Dec. 22
RAC10 PTAP10 25c maroon & red .25 .25
  Never hinged .25

Dove and Flowers — PTAP11

1950, Dec. 22
RAC11 PTAP11 25c dk bl & car .30 .30
  Never hinged .60

Mother and Child — PTAP12

1951, Oct. 1
RAC12 PTAP12 25c brn & car .50 .25
  Never hinged .80

Tobias and Archangel PTAP13

1953, Oct. 1
RAC13 PTAP13 25c brn & car 3.50 5.50
  Never hinged 6.50

FRANCHISE STAMPS

F1

1869 Unwmk. Litho. Imperf.
S1 F1 blue 52.50 38.00
  a. Tête bêche pair 135.00 120.00

The franchise of No. S1 was granted to Diego Castell to use in distributing his publications on Spanish postal history.

F2

1881
S2 F2 black, buff 36.00 15.50

The franchise of No. S2 was granted to Antonio Fernandez Duro for his book, "Reseña histórico-descriptiva de los sellos correos de España."

Reprints of No. S2 have been made on carmine, blue, gray, fawn and yellow paper.

CARLIST STAMPS

From the beginning of the Civil War (April 21, 1872) until separate stamps were issued on July 1, 1873, stamps of France were used on all mail from the provinces under Carlist rule.

King Carlos VII — A1 / Tilde on N — A1a

1873, July 1 Unwmk. Litho. Imperf.
X1 A1 1r blue 650.00
X2 A1a 1r blue 550.00 350.00

These stamps were reprinted three times in 1881 and once in 1887. The originals have 23 white lines and dots in the lower right spandrel. They are thin and of even width and spacing. The first reprint has 17 to 20 lines in the spandrel, most of them thick and of irregular width and length. The second and third reprints have 21 very thin lines, the second from the bottom being almost invisible. In the fourth reprint the lower right spandrel is an almost solid spot of color.

Originals of type A1 have the curved line above "ESPAÑA" broken at the left of the "E." All reprints of this type have the curved line continuous.

The reprints exist in various shades of blue, rose, red, violet and black.

King Carlos VII
A2   A3

A4

1874
X3 A2 1r violet 325.00 325.00
X4 A3 16m rose 5.50 72.50
X5 A4 ½r rose 150.00 100.00

Nos. X3 and X6-X7 were for use in the Basque Provinces and Navarra; No. X4 in Catalonia, and No. X5 in Valencia.

Two types of No. X5, alternating in each sheet.

No. X4 with favor cancellation (lozenge of dots) sells for same price as unused.

A5

1875   **White Paper**
X6   A5   50c green   8.00   82.50
   a.   50c blue green   25.00   100.00
   b.   Bluish paper   50.00
X7   A5   1r brown   8.00   82.50
   a.   Bluish paper   50.00
   Set, #X6-X7, never hinged   24.00

Fake cancellations exist on Nos. X1-X7.

REVOLUTIONARY OVERPRINTS

Issued by the Nationalist (Revolutionary) Forces

Many districts or cities made use of the stamps of the Republic overprinted in various forms. Most such overprinting was authorized by military or postal officials but some were without official sanction. These overprints were applied in patriotic celebration and partly as a protection from the use of unoverprinted stamps seized or stolen by soldiers.

BURGOS AIR POST STAMPS

Revenue Stamps Overprinted in Red, Blue or Black

RAP1

1936, Dec. 1   **Unwmk.**   *Perf. 11½*
Control Number on Face of Stamp
7LC1   RAP1   25c gray grn & blk (R)   47.50   47.50
   a.   Blue overprint   47.50   47.50
7LC2   RAP1   1.50p bl & blk (R)   6.00   6.00
7LC3   RAP1   3p rose & blk (Bl)   6.00   6.00
   Nos. 7LC1-7LC3 (3)   59.50   59.50
   Set, never hinged   105.00

RAP2   RAP4

Perf. 13½
Blue Control Number on Back
7LC4   RAP2   15c green (R)   3.75   3.75
7LC5   RAP2   25c blue (R)   27.50   27.50
   Set, never hinged   45.00

Perf. 11½
Without Control Number
Overprint in Black
7LC6   RAP4   1.50p dk blue   6.50   6.50
7LC7   RAP4   3p carmine   6.50   6.50
   Set, never hinged   21.00

RAP5   RAP6

Overprint in Black
Perf. 13½, 11½
7LC8   RAP5   1.20p green   25.00   25.00
   Never hinged   37.50

Perf. 14
Control Number on Back
7LC9   RAP6   1.20p green   25.00   25.00
7LC10   RAP6   2.40p green   25.00   25.00
   Set #7LC9-7LC10, never hinged   70.00

No. 7LC9 is inscribed "CLASE 8a."

RAP7

1937   **Unwmk.**   *Perf. 11½*
Control Number on Back
7LC11   RAP7   25c ultra (R)   225.00   225.00

Stamps of Spain, 1931-36, Overprinted in Red or Black (10p)

Perf. 11, 11½, 11x11½
1937   **Unwmk.**
Overprint 13mm high
7LC12   A100   40c blue   1.10   1.10
   a.   Ovpt. 15mm high   1.10   1.10
7LC13   A97   50c dark blue   1.40   1.40
   a.   Ovpt. 15mm high   1.40   1.40
7LC14   A130   50c dark blue   1.75   1.75
   a.   Ovpt. 15mm high   1.75   1.75
7LC15   A100   60c apple green   2.50   2.50
   a.   Ovpt. 15mm high   2.50   2.50
7LC16   AP26   2p gray blue   32.50   32.50
   a.   Ovpt. 15mm high   32.50   32.50
7LC17   A49a   10p brown   82.50   82.50
   a.   Ovpt. 15mm high   82.50   82.50
   Nos. 7LC12-7LC17 (6)   121.75   121.75

Issue dates: Nos. 7LC12-7LC17, 4/1. Nos. 7LC12a-7LC17a, 5/1.

Spain Nos. 576, 578 and 541b overprinted in Blue or Black

Nos. 7LC18, 7LC19   Nos. 7LC20, 7LC21

Perfs as on Basic Stamps
1937, May
7LC18   A127   30c carmine (Bk)   1.40   1.40
7LC19   A127   30c carmine (Bl)   .70   .70
7LC20   A129   30c car rose (Bk)   1.40   1.40
7LC21   A129   30c car rose (Bl)   .70   .70
7LC22   A107   10p dp brn (Bk)   11.00   11.00
   Nos. 7LC18-7LC22 (5)   15.20   15.20

Spain Nos. 539b and 540b, the 1p and 4p values, were prepared with this overprint in January, 1938, but were not issued. Value, each $4.50.

BURGOS ISSUE SPECIAL DELIVERY STAMPS

Pair of Spain No. 546 Overprinted in Black

1936   **Unwmk.**   *Perf. 11½x11*
7LE3   A110   20c (10c+10c) emer   4.50   4.50
   Never hinged   9.00
   a.   Overprint inverted   14.00

Type of Regular Stamp of 1931 Overprinted in Red

7LE4   A95   20c dark violet   10.00   10.00

Type of Delivery Tax Stamp of 1931 Overprinted in Red on Block of 4

Perf. 11½
7LE5   D1   20c black   8.75   8.00
   Never hinged   13.50

Same Overprinted in Red on Block of 4

7LE6   D1   20c black   30.00   25.00
   Never hinged   50.00

SD1

1936   **Unwmk.**   *Perf. 11½*
7LE7   SD1   20c green & blk   7.25   5.50
7LE8   SD1   20c green & red   7.25   5.50
   Set, never hinged   25.00

Nos. 7LE7-7LE8 exist with control number on back. Value $42.50 each.

CADIZ ISSUE SEMI-POSTAL STAMPS

Stamps of Spain, 1931-36, Surcharged in Black or Red

1936   **Unwmk.**   *Imperf.*
8LB1   A108   1c + 5c blue grn   .25   .25
Perf. 11½x11, 11½
8LB2   A108   2c + 5c orange brn   .25   .25
8LB3   A103   5c + 5c choc (R)   .45   .45
8LB4   A110   10c + 5c green   .45   .45
8LB5   A111   15c + 5c Prus grn (R)   2.75   2.75

8LB6   A95   20c + 5c dk vio (R)   3.25   3.25
8LB7   A104   25c + 5c lake   2.50   2.50
8LB8   A113   30c + 5c rose red   1.40   1.40
8LB9   A100   40c + 5c dk blue (R)   3.25   3.25
8LB10   A97   50c + 5c dk blue (R)   6.50   6.50
   Nos. 8LB1-8LB10 (10)   21.05   21.05

CANARY ISLANDS AIR POST STAMPS

Issued for Use via the Lufthansa Service

Stamps of Spain, 1932-34, Surcharged in Blue

1936, Oct. 27   **Unwmk.**   *Imperf.*
9LC1   A108   50c on 1c bl grn   27.50   17.50
Perf. 11½x11
9LC2   A108   80c on 2c buff   14.50   6.50
9LC3   A103   1.25p on 5c choc   30.00   17.50
   Nos. 9LC1-9LC3 (3)   72.00   41.50
   Set, never hinged   82.50

The date July 18, 1936, in the overprints of Nos. 9LC1-9LC22 marks the beginning of the Franco insurrection.

Spain Nos. 542, 543, 528 and 641 Surcharged in Black, Red or Green

The surcharge on Nos. 9LC4 and 9LC6 exists in two types: Type I, 2½-3mm space between numerals and "Cts.". Type II, 1½-2mm space between numerals and "Cts."

1936-37   *Imperf.*
9LC4   A108   50c on 1c bl grn (I)   4.50   2.75
   a.   Overprint type II   11.00   7.75
9LC5   A108   50c on 1c bl grn (R) ('37)   4.50   2.75
Perf. 11, 11½x11
9LC6   A108   80c on 2c buff (I)   2.25   1.60
   a.   Overprint type II   5.50   3.25
9LC7   A108   80c on 2c buff (G) ('37)   3.25   1.60
9LC8   A103   1.25 Pts on 5c choc (R)   6.25   4.50
9LC9   A103   Pts 1.25 on 5c choc (R) ('37)   17.00   11.00
9LC10   A161   1.25p on 5c brn (G) ('37)   3.25   1.40
   Nos. 9LC4-9LC10 (7)   41.00   25.60
   Set, never hinged   65.00

Issued: Nos. 9LC4, 9LC6, 11/28/36; No. 9LC8, 1/7/37; Nos. 9LC4a, 9LC6a, 9LC9, 2/12/37; Nos. 9LC5, 9LC7, 9LC10, 3/2/37.

Spain Nos. 542, 543 and 641 Surcharged in Blue

The surcharge on Nos. 9LC11-9LC13 exists in two types: Type I, 18mm tall. Type II, 20mm tall.

1937, Mar. 31   *Imperf.*
9LC11   A108   50c on 1c bl grn (I)   11.00   5.50
   a.   Overprint type II   4.50   2.25
Perf. 11
9LC12   A108   80c on 2c buff (I)   11.00   4.50
   a.   Overprint type II   2.75   1.10
9LC13   A161   1.25p on 5c brown (I)   3.25   1.10
   Nos. 9LC11-9LC13 (3)   25.25   11.10
   Set, never hinged   40.00

Type II overprints issued 4/17/37.

Stamps of Spain, 1931-1936, Surcharged in Blue or Red (#9LC17, 9LC19)

The surcharge on Nos. 9LC15 and 9LC18 exists in two types: Type I, 2mm space between "+" and denomination. Type II, "+" abuts surcharged denomination. Other values are Type I.

1937

9LC14 A104 25c + 50c lake 55.00 10.00
9LC15 A162 30c + 80c rose 19.50 7.75
a. Overprint type II 19.50 7.75
9LC16 A162 30c + 1.25p rose 25.00 8.25
9LC17 A97 50c + 1.25p dp bl 32.50 11.00
9LC18 A100 60c + 80c ap grn 25.00 8.75
a. Overprint type II 27.50 10.00
9LC19 A105 1p + 1.25p bl blk 80.00 22.50
Nos. 9LC14-9LC19 (6) 237.00 68.25
Set, never hinged 350.00

The surcharge represents the airmail rate and the basic stamp the postage rate.

Issued: 9LC15a, 9LC18a, 4/15. 9LC14-9LC19, 5/5.

Spain Nos. 542, 624 and 641 Surcharged in Black

1937, May 25 Unwmk. *Imperf.*

9LC20 A108 50c on 1c bl grn 7.75 4.50

Perf. 11½, 11½x11

9LC21 A143 80c on 2c org brn 6.50 2.25
9LC22 A161 1.25p on 5c gray brn 6.50 2.25
Nos. 9LC20-9LC22 (3) 20.75 9.00
Set, never hinged 30.00

Stamps and Type of Spain, 1933-36, Surcharged in Black

1937, July *Perf. 13½x13, 11, 11½*

9LC23 A143 50c on 2c org brn 3.50 2.25
9LC24 A126 80c on 2c org brn 300.00 180.00
9LC25 A161 80c on 5c gray brn 3.50 2.25
9LC26 A108 1.25p on 1c bl grn 4.25 2.25
9LC27 A161 2.50p on 10c grn 16.00 8.75

Spain Nos. 647, 650 and 652 Surcharged in Black or Red

Perf. 11

9LC28 A162 30c + 80c rose 3.00 1.40
9LC29 A162 50c + 1.25p dk bl (R) 10.50 5.00
9LC30 A162 1p + 1.25p bl (R) 16.00 8.75
Nos. 9LC23-9LC30 (8) 356.75 210.65
Set, never hinged 550.00

See note after No. 9LC19.

AP1

Perf. 14x13½

1937, July 16 Wmk. 116

Surcharge in Various Colors

9LC31 AP1 50c on 5c ultra (Br) 2.75 2.50
9LC32 AP1 80c on 5c ultra (G) 1.90 1.75
9LC33 AP1 1.25p on 5c ultra (V) 2.25 2.25
Nos. 9LC31-9LC33 (3) 6.90 6.50
Set, never hinged 10.00

Spain Nos. 641, 643 and 640 Surcharged in Green or Orange

1937, Oct. 29 Unwmk. *Perf. 11*

9LC34 A161 50c on 5c (G) 9.25 3.75
9LC35 A161 80c on 10c (O) 5.75 2.75
9LC36 A160 1.25p on 2c (G) 10.50 7.25
Nos. 9LC34-9LC36 (3) 25.50 13.75
Set, never hinged 40.00

Spain Nos. 638, 640 and 643 Surcharged in Red, Blue or Violet

1937, Dec. 23 *Imperf.*

9LC37 A159 50c on 1c (R) 10.50 4.50

Perf. 11, 11x11½

9LC38 A160 80c on 2c (Bl) 4.25 2.75
9LC39 A161 1.25p on 10c (V) 9.25 3.50
Nos. 9LC37-9LC39 (3) 24.00 10.75
Set, never hinged 37.50

Spain Nos. 647, 650 to 652 Surcharged in Black, Green or Brown

1937, Dec. 29

9LC40 A162 30c + 30c rose 4.50 3.75
9LC41 A162 50c + 2.50p dk bl (G) 29.00 21.00
9LC42 A162 60c + 2.30p yel (G) 29.00 21.00
9LC43 A162 1p + 5p bl (Br) 35.00 21.00
Nos. 9LC40-9LC43 (4) 97.50 66.75
Set, never hinged 110.00

See note after No. 9LC19.

Stamps of Spain, 1936, Surcharged in Black, Green, Blue or Red

No. 9LC44

No. 9LC46

1938, Feb. 2 *Perf. 11, 11½, 11x11½*

9LC44 A160 50c on 2c brn 5.00 3.75
9LC45 A161 80c on 5c brn (G) 3.75 3.25
9LC46 A162 30c + 80c rose (Bl) 4.50 2.50
9LC47 A161 1.25p on 10c grn (Bl) 4.50 3.25
9LC48 A162 50c + 1.25p dk bl (R) 4.50 2.75
Nos. 9LC44-9LC48 (5) 22.25 15.50
Set, never hinged 27.50

Spain Nos. 645, 646 and 649 Surcharged in Brown, Green or Violet

1938, Feb. 14

9LC51 A162 2.50p on 20c (Br) 50.00 25.00
9LC52 A162 5p on 25c (G) 50.00 25.00
9LC53 A162 10p on 40c (V) 50.00 25.00
Nos. 9LC51-9LC53 (3) 150.00 75.00
Set, never hinged 175.00

MALAGA ISSUE

Stamps of 1920-36 Overprinted in Black or Red

1937 Unwmk. *Imperf.*

10L1 A47 1c blue green .25 .25
10L2 A108 1c blue green .25 .25
10L3 A108 1c lt green (R) .25 .25

Perf. 13½, 13½x13, 11, 11½x11

10L4 A108 2c orange brn 14.50 14.50
10L5 A126 2c orange brn .25 .25
10L6 A103 5c chocolate (R) .25 .25
10L7 A96 10c yellow green 12.00 12.00
10L8 A110 10c emerald .30 .30
10L9 A111 15c Prus grn (R) .55 .55
10L10 A97 15c blue grn (R) .55 .55
10L11 A95 20c dk violet (R) .50 .50
10L12 A99 25c lake 1.50 1.50
10L13 A104 25c lake .50 .50
10L14 A113 30c carmine .50 .50
10L15 A129 30c carmine rose 2.50 2.50
10L16 A100 40c blue (R) .45 .45
10L17 A97 50c dk blue (R) 2.50 2.50
10L18 A100 60c apple green 1.40 1.40
10L19 A105 1p black (R) 2.75 2.75
Nos. 10L1-10L19 (19) 41.75 41.75

Stamps of 1932-35 Overprinted in Red or Black in panes of 25, reading down. "8.2.37" and "!Arriba Espana!" form the lower half of all overprints. The upper half varies.

Overprint a (1st and 2nd rows): "MALAGA AGRADECIDA A TRANQUILLO-BIANCHI"

Overprint b (3rd row): "MALAGA A SU SALVADOR QUEIPO DE LLANO"

Overprint c (4th and 5th rows): "MALAGA A SU CAUDILLO FRANCO"

Values are for vertical strips of 3 containing examples of each overprint type.

1937 *Perf. 11½*

10L20 A111 15c Prus grn (R) 5.50 5.50
a. 15c single stamp, ovpt. a .85 .85
b. 15c single stamp, ovpt. b 1.60 1.60
c. 15c single stamp, ovpt. c .85 .85
10L21 A113 30c rose red (Bk) 5.50 5.50
a. 30c single stamp, ovpt. a .85 .85
b. 30c single stamp, ovpt. b 1.60 1.60
c. 30c single stamp, ovpt. c .85 .85
10L22 A97 50c dk blue (R) 8.75 8.75
a. 50c single stamp, ovpt. a 1.60 1.60
b. 50c single stamp, ovpt. b 3.25 3.25
c. 50c single stamp, ovpt. c 1.60 1.60
10L23 A100 60c apple grn (Bk) 11.00 11.00
a. 60c single stamp, ovpt. a 1.60 1.60
b. 60c single stamp, ovpt. b 3.25 3.25
c. 60c single stamp, ovpt. c 1.60 1.60
Nos. 10L20-10L23 (4) 30.75 30.75

SPECIAL DELIVERY STAMP

Overprinted like Nos. 10L1-10L19 on Type of Special Delivery Stamp of 1934

1937 *Perf. 10*

10LE1 SD7 20c rose red (Bk) .45 .45

ORENSE ISSUE

Stamps of 1931-36 Overprinted in Red, Blue or Black

1936 *Imperf.*

11L1 A108 1c blue grn (Bl) .45 .45
a. Red overprint 1.10 1.10

Perf. 11½, 13½x13

11L2 A108 2c org brn (Bk) 3.50 3.25
11L3 A126 2c org brn (Bk) .65 .65
11L4 A103 5c brown (R) 1.50 1.50
11L5 A110 10c lt green (Bl) 2.25 2.25
a. Red overprint 11.00 11.00
11L6 A111 15c Prus grn (R) 3.25 3.25
11L7 A95 20c violet (Bl) 3.25 3.25
11L8 A104 25c lake (Bk) 3.75 3.75
11L9 A113 30c rose red (Bl) 2.75 2.75
a. Black overprint 5.50 5.50
11L10 A100 40c blue (R) 3.75 3.75
a. Imperf, pair 50.00
11L11 A97 50c dark blue (R) 6.50 6.50
11L12 A100 60c apple grn (Bk) 4.75 4.75
a. Red overprint 17.00 17.00
b. As "a," Imperf, pair 50.00
Nos. 11L1-11L12 (12) 36.35 36.10

SEMI-POSTAL STAMPS

Stamps of Spain, 1931-36, Surcharged in Blue on front and on back of stamp

1936-37 Unwmk. *Imperf.*

11LB1 A47 1c + 5c bl grn 2.25 2.25
11LB2 A108 1c + 5c grn .40 .40

Perf. 13½x13, 11½, 11½x11

11LB3 A108 2c + 5c org brn .45 .45
11LB4 A126 2c + 5c red brn .45 .45
11LB5 A103 5c + 5c choc .65 .65
11LB6 A110 10c + 5c emer .65 .65
11LB7 A111 15c + 5c Prus grn .95 .95
11LB8 A95 20c + 5c vio .65 .65
11LB9 A104 25c + 5c lake .95 .95
11LB10 A113 30c + 5c rose red 2.75 2.75
11LB11 A117 30c + 5c rose red 42.50 42.50
11LB12 A100 60c + 5c apl grn 250.00 190.00
Nos. 11LB1-11LB12 (12) 302.65 242.65

SPECIAL DELIVERY STAMPS

Type of Special Delivery Stamp of 1934 Overprinted "!VIVA ESPANA!" in Blue or Black

1936 *Perf. 10*

11LE1 SD7 20c rose red (Bl) 1.90 1.90
11LE2 SD7 20c rose red (Bk) 4.25 4.25

Same with Surcharge "+ 5 cts."

11LE3 SD7 20c + 5c rose red 1.00 1.00

Same Surcharge, Overprint Repeated at Right

11LE4 SD7 20c + 5c rose red 1.10 1.10
Nos. 11LE1-11LE4 (4) 8.25 8.25

SAN SEBASTIAN ISSUE

For Use in Province of Guipuzcoa

Stamps of 1931-36 Overprinted in Red or Blue

1937 Unwmk. *Imperf.*

12L1 A108 1c bl grn (R) .65 .65

Perf. 11, 13½

12L2 A108 2c buff (Bl) 1.00 1.50
12L3 A126 2c org brn (Bl) 2.10 2.10
12L4 A95 5c chocolate (R) 5.00 5.00
12L5 A103 5c chocolate (R) 1.75 1.75
12L6 A110 10c emerald (R) 1.75 1.75
12L7 A111 15c Prus grn (R) 2.10 2.10
12L8 A95 20c dk violet (R) 2.75 2.75
12L9 A104 25c car lake (Bl) 2.75 2.75
12L10 A113 30c rose red (Bl) 2.75 2.75
12L11 A100 40c blue (R) 5.50 5.50
12L12 A97 50c dark blue (R) 5.50 5.50
Nos. 12L1-12L12 (12) 33.60 34.10

SANTA CRUZ DE TENERIFE ISSUE

Stamps of Spain, 1931-36 Overprinted in Black or Red

1936		Unwmk.		Imperf.
13L1	A108	1c bl grn (R)	.75	.75
13L2	A108	1c bl grn (Bk)	2.75	2.75

Perf. 11, 13½

13L3	A108	2c buff (Bk)	5.50	5.50
13L4	A126	2c org brn (Bk)	.95	.95
13L5	A103	5c choc (R)	3.00	3.00
13L6	A110	10c green (R)	3.00	3.00
13L7	A104	25c lake (Bk)	11.00	11.00
13L8	A100	40c dk blue (R)	3.25	3.25
13L9	A107	10p dp brn (Bk)	300.00	225.00
		Nos. 13L1-13L9 (9)	330.20	255.20

Many forgeries of #13L9 exist.

SEVILLE ISSUE

Stamps of Spain, 1931-36, Overprinted in Black or Red

1936				Imperf.
14L1	A108	1c blue grn (Bk)	.30	.30

Perf. 13½x13, 11, 11½x11

14L2	A126	2c org brn (Bk)	.35	.35
14L3	A103	5c chocolate (R)	.45	.45
14L4	A110	10c emerald (Bk)	.55	.55
14L5	A111	15c Prus grn (R)	1.40	1.40
14L6	A95	20c violet (R)	1.40	1.40
14L7	A104	25c lake (Bk)	1.40	1.40
14L8	A113	30c carmine (Bk)	1.40	1.40
14L9	A128	30c rose red (Bk)	8.25	8.25
14L10	A100	40c blue (R)	5.50	5.50
14L11	A97	50c dk blue (R)	5.50	5.50
14L12	A100	60c apple grn (Bk)	6.75	6.75
		Nos. 14L1-14L12 (12)	33.25	33.25

Stamps of Spain, 1931-36, Handstamped in Black

				Imperf
14L13	A108	1c blue grn	.30	.30

Perf. 13½x13, 11, 11x11½, 11½x11

14L14	A126	2c orange brn	.45	.45
14L15	A103	5c chocolate	.45	.45
14L16	A110	10c emerald	.45	.45
14L17	A111	15c Prus green	.55	.55
14L18	A95	20c violet	.55	.55
14L19	A104	25c lake	.55	.55
14L20	A113	30c carmine	.55	.55
14L21	A128	30c rose red	3.00	3.00
14L22	A100	40c blue	1.10	1.10
14L23	A97	50c dk blue	3.00	3.00
14L24	A100	60c apple grn	1.00	1.00
14L25	A105	1p black	3.00	3.00
14L26	AP26	2p gray blue	13.50	13.50
14L27	A106	4p magenta	7.25	7.25
14L28	A107	10p deep brown	10.50	10.50
		Nos. 14L13-14L28,14LE1 (17)	47.95	47.95

The date "Julio-1936" in the overprints of Nos. 14L1-14L28 and 14LE1 marks the beginning of the Franco insurrection.

SPECIAL DELIVERY STAMP

Overprinted like Nos. 14L13-14L25 on Type of Special Delivery Stamp of 1934

1936			Perf. 10
14LE1	SD7	20c rose red	1.75 1.75

SPANISH GUINEA

'spa-nish 'gi-nē

LOCATION — In western Africa, bordering on the Gulf of Guinea
GOVT. — Spanish Colony
AREA — 10,852 sq. mi.
POP. — 212,000 (est. 1957)
CAPITAL — Santa Isabel

Spanish Guinea 1-84 were issued for and used only in the continental area later called Rio Muni. From 1909 to 1960, Spanish Guinea also included Fernando Po, Elobey, Annobon and Corisco.

Fernando Po and Rio Muni united in 1968 to become the Republic of Equatorial Guinea.

100 Centimos = 1 Peseta

Catalogue values for unused stamps in this country are for Never Hinged items, beginning with Scott 319 in the regular postage section, Scott B13 in the semi-postal section, and Scott C13 in the airpost section.

King Alfonso XIII — A1

Blue Control Numbers on Back

1902	Unwmk.	Typo.	Perf. 14	
1	A1	5c dark green	12.50	6.25
2	A1	10c indigo	12.50	6.25
3	A1	25c claret	92.50	47.50
4	A1	50c deep brown	92.50	47.50
5	A1	75c violet	92.50	47.50
6	A1	1p carmine rose	140.00	47.50
7	A1	2p olive green	180.00	100.00
8	A1	5p dull red	275.00	175.00
		Nos. 1-8 (8)	897.50	477.50
		Set, never hinged	1,800.	

Exists imperf, value set $3,500.

Revenue Stamps Surcharged

Blue or Black Control Numbers on Back

1903		Imperf.	
8A	10c on 25c blk (R)	550.00	240.00
8B	10c on 50c org (Bl)	140.00	40.00
8D	10c on 1p 25c car (Bk)	750.00	400.00
8F	10c on 2p cl (Bk)	800.00	600.00
g.	Blue surcharge	1,450.	800.00
8H	10c on 2p 50c red brn (Bl)	1,100.	725.00
8J	10c on 5p ol blk (R)	1,500.	525.00

Nos. 8A-8J are surcharged on stamps inscribed "Posesiones Espanolas de Africa Occidental" and "1903," with arms at left.

This surcharge was also applied to revenue stamps of 10, 15, 25, 50, 75 and 100 pesetas and in other colors.

See Nos. 98-101C.

King Alfonso XIII — A2

Blue Control Numbers on Back

1903		Typo.	Perf. 14	
9	A2	¼c black	1.50	.85
10	A2	½c blue green	1.50	.85
11	A2	1c claret	1.50	.70
12	A2	2c dark olive	1.50	.70
13	A2	3c dark brown	1.50	.70
14	A2	4c vermilion	1.50	.70
15	A2	5c black brown	1.50	.70
16	A2	10c red brown	2.50	.85
17	A2	15c dark blue	8.50	6.25
18	A2	25c orange buff	8.50	6.25
19	A2	50c carmine lake	16.00	14.00
20	A2	75c violet	21.00	14.00
21	A2	1p blue green	35.00	22.00
22	A2	2p dark green	35.00	22.00
23	A2	3p scarlet	95.00	28.50
24	A2	4p dull blue	110.00	50.00
25	A2	5p dark violet	210.00	72.50
26	A2	10p carmine rose	300.00	100.00
		Nos. 9-26 (18)	852.00	341.55
		Set, never hinged	1,700.	

Blue Control Numbers on Back

1905		Same, Dated "1905"		
27	A2	1c black	.30	.25
28	A2	2c blue grn	.30	.25
29	A2	3c claret	.30	.25
30	A2	4c bronze grn	.30	.25
31	A2	5c dark brown	.30	.25
32	A2	10c red	1.60	.85
33	A2	15c black brown	4.50	2.75
34	A2	25c chocolate	4.50	2.75
35	A2	50c dark blue	9.75	6.25
36	A2	75c orange buff	11.00	6.25
37	A2	1p carmine rose	11.00	6.25
38	A2	2p violet	26.00	13.00
39	A2	3p blue green	67.50	27.50
40	A2	4p dark green	67.50	39.00
40A	A2	5p vermilion	110.00	42.00
41	A2	10p dull blue	200.00	130.00
		Nos. 27-41 (16)	514.85	277.85
		Set, never hinged	950.00	

Stamps of Elobey, 1905, Overprinted in Violet or Blue

1906				
42	A1	1c rose	4.00	2.25
43	A1	2c deep violet	4.00	2.25
44	A1	3c black	4.00	2.25
45	A1	4c orange red	4.00	2.25
46	A1	5c deep green	4.00	2.25
47	A1	10c blue green	9.25	5.25
48	A1	15c violet	16.00	9.00
49	A1	25c rose lake	16.00	9.00
50	A1	50c orange buff	22.50	13.00
51	A1	75c dark blue	26.00	15.00
52	A1	1p red brown	47.50	25.00
53	A1	2p black brown	67.50	37.50
54	A1	3p vermilion	97.50	55.00
55	A1	4p dark brown	475.00	250.00
56	A1	5p bronze green	475.00	250.00
57	A1	10p claret	*2,000.*	*1,100.*
		Nos. 42-54 (13)	322.25	180.00

King Alfonso XIII — A3

Blue Control Numbers on Back

1907			Typo.	
58	A3	1c dark green	.75	.25
59	A3	2c dull blue	.75	.25
60	A3	3c violet	.75	.25
61	A3	4c yellow grn	.75	.25
62	A3	5c carmine lake	.75	.25
63	A3	10c orange	4.00	1.25
64	A3	15c brown	3.00	.80
65	A3	25c dark blue	3.00	.80
66	A3	50c black brown	3.00	.80
67	A3	75c blue green	3.00	.80
68	A3	1p red	6.00	1.40
69	A3	2p dark brown	9.00	6.25
70	A3	3p olive gray	9.00	6.25
71	A3	4p maroon	13.00	6.25
72	A3	5p green	13.50	9.50
73	A3	10p red violet	20.00	12.00
		Nos. 58-73 (16)	90.25	47.35
		Set, never hinged	210.00	

Issue of 1907 Surcharged in Black or Red

1908-09				
74	A3	05c on 1c dk grn (R)	3.00	1.50
75	A3	05c on 2c blue (R)	3.00	1.50
76	A3	05c on 3c violet	3.00	1.50
77	A3	05c on 4c yel grn	3.00	1.50
78	A3	05c on 10c orange	3.00	1.50
a.		Red surcharge	5.25	2.75
84	A3	15c on 10c orange	14.00	9.00
		Nos. 74-84 (6)	29.00	16.50

Many stamps of this issue are found with the surcharge inverted, sideways, double and in both black and red. Other stamps of the 1907 issue are known with this surcharge but are not believed to have been put in use. Value, each $17.

King Alfonso XIII — A4

Blue Control Numbers on Back

1909		Typo.	Perf. 14½	
85	A4	1c orange brown	.25	.25
86	A4	2c rose	.25	.25
87	A4	5c dark green	1.40	.25
88	A4	10c vermilion	.40	.25
89	A4	15c dark brown	.40	.25
90	A4	20c violet	.65	.35
91	A4	25c dull blue	.65	.35
92	A4	30c chocolate	.85	.30
93	A4	40c lake	.50	.30
94	A4	50c dark violet	.50	.30
95	A4	1p blue green	13.50	7.00
96	A4	4p orange	3.50	4.25
97	A4	10p red	3.50	4.25
		Nos. 85-97 (13)	26.35	18.35
		Set, never hinged	50.00	

For overprints see Nos. 102-114.

Revenue Stamps Surcharged in Black

1909 — Imperf.

With or Without Control Numbers on Back

98	10c on 50c bl grn	87.50	57.50
a.	Red or violet surcharge	110.00	80.00
99	10c on 1p 25c vio	150.00	80.00
100	10c on 2p dk brn	600.00	350.00
100A	10c on 5p dk vio	600.00	350.00
101	10c on 25p red brn	*800.00*	*575.00*
101A	10c on 50p brn lil	*2,750.*	*1,600.*
101B	10c on 75p car	*2,750.*	*1,600.*
101C	10c on 100p org	*2,750.*	*1,600.*

For additional revenue stamps surcharged for postal use see Rio de Oro Nos. 44-45.

Stamps of 1909 Overprinted with Handstamp in Black, Blue, Green or Red

1911				
102	A4	1c orange brn (Bl)	.40	.35
103	A4	2c rose (G)	.40	.35
104	A4	5c dk green (R)	2.00	.35
105	A4	10c vermilion	1.15	.45
106	A4	15c dk brown (R)	2.00	.75
107	A4	20c violet	2.50	1.15
108	A4	25c dull blue (R)	3.00	2.40
109	A4	30c choc (Bl)	3.75	3.50
110	A4	40c lake (Bl)	4.00	3.50
111	A4	50c dark violet	6.75	5.00
112	A4	1p blue grn (R)	55.00	40.00
113	A4	4p orange (R)	29.00	23.00
114	A4	10p red (G)	37.50	*40.00*
		Nos. 102-114 (13)	147.45	120.80
		Set, never hinged	300.00	

The date "1911" is missing from the overprint on the first stamp in each row, or ten times in each sheet of 100 stamps. This variety occurs on all stamps of the series. Value, set $550.

King Alfonso XIII — A5

Blue Control Numbers on Back

1912		Typo.	Perf. 13½	
115	A5	1c black	.30	.30
116	A5	2c dark brown	.30	.30
117	A5	5c deep green	.30	.30
118	A5	10c red	.30	.30
119	A5	15c claret	.30	.30
120	A5	20c red	.30	.30
121	A5	25c dull blue	.30	.30
122	A5	30c lake	3.50	2.00
123	A5	40c car rose	2.10	1.00
124	A5	50c brown org	2.00	.35
125	A5	1p dark violet	2.25	1.25
126	A5	4p lilac	5.00	2.50
127	A5	10p blue green	10.50	9.50
		Nos. 115-127 (13)	27.45	18.70
		Set, never hinged	50.00	

For overprints and surcharges see Nos. 141-157.

King Alfonso XIII — A6

Blue Control Numbers on Back

1914			Perf. 13	
128	A6	1c dull violet	.35	.30
129	A6	2c car rose	.35	.30
130	A6	5c deep green	.35	.30
131	A6	10c vermilion	.35	.30
132	A6	15c dark violet	.35	.30
133	A6	20c dark brown	1.05	.55
134	A6	25c dark blue	.45	.35
135	A6	30c brown orange	1.60	.55
136	A6	40c blue green	1.60	.55
137	A6	50c dp claret	.75	.35
138	A6	1p vermilion	2.00	*2.25*
139	A6	4p maroon	7.00	4.50
140	A6	10p olive black	7.75	*8.50*
		Nos. 128-140 (13)	23.95	19.10
		Set, never hinged	60.00	

Stamps with these or similar overprints are unauthorized and fraudulent.

Stamps of 1912 Overprinted

1917			Perf. 13½	
141	A5	1c black	125.00	85.00
142	A5	2c dark brown	125.00	85.00
143	A5	5c deep green	.40	.35
144	A5	10c red	.40	.35
145	A5	15c claret	.40	.35
146	A5	20c red	.40	.35
147	A5	25c dull blue	.40	.35
148	A5	30c lake	.40	.35
149	A5	40c carmine rose	.75	.40
150	A5	50c brown orange	.40	.35
151	A5	1p dark violet	.75	.40
152	A5	4p lilac	8.25	4.00
153	A5	10p blue green	8.25	4.00
		Nos. 141-153 (13)	270.80	181.25
		Set, never hinged	550.00	

Nos. 143-153 exist with overprint double, inverted, in dark blue, reading "9117" and in pairs one without overprint.

HTADO.
1917
15 Cénts.

Stamps of 1917 Surcharged

1918

154 A5 5c on 40c car rose 36.00 14.50
155 A5 10c on 4p lilac 36.00 14.50
156 A5 15c on 20c red 65.00 25.00
157 A5 25c on 10p bl grn 65.00 25.00
a. "52" for "25" *500.00 425.00*
Nos. 154-157 (4) 202.00 79.00
Set, never hinged 345.00

The varieties "Gents" and "Censt" occur on Nos. 154-157. Values 50 percent more.

King Alfonso XIII
A7 A8

1919 **Typo.** ***Perf. 13***

Blue Control Numbers on Back

158 A7 1c lilac 1.00 .30
159 A7 2c rose 1.00 .30
160 A7 5c vermilion 1.00 .30
161 A7 10c violet 1.75 .30
162 A7 15c brown 1.75 .55
163 A7 20c blue 1.75 .80
164 A7 25c green 1.75 .80
a. 25c blue (error) 62.50
165 A7 30c orange 2.25 .80
166 A7 40c orange 4.50 .80
167 A7 50c red 4.50 .80
168 A7 1p light green 4.50 2.75
169 A7 4p claret 10.00 *10.50*
170 A7 10p brown 20.00 19.00
Nos. 158-170 (13) 55.75 38.00
Set, never hinged 90.00

1920

Blue Control Numbers on Back

171 A8 1c brown .35 .30
172 A8 2c dull rose .35 .30
173 A8 5c gray green .35 .30
174 A8 10c dull rose .35 .30
175 A8 15c orange .35 .30
176 A8 20c yellow .35 .35
177 A8 25c dull blue 1.15 .35
178 A8 30c greenish blue 42.50 25.00
179 A8 40c lt brown 2.00 .35
180 A8 50c lilac 2.40 .35
181 A8 1p light red 2.40 .35
182 A8 4p bright rose 6.50 6.25
183 A8 10p gray lilac 10.00 *12.50*
Nos. 171-183 (13) 69.05 47.00
Set, never hinged 120.00

A9

1922

Blue Control Numbers on Back

184 A9 1c dark brown .70 .25
185 A9 2c claret .70 .25
186 A9 5c blue green .70 .25
187 A9 10c pale red 4.75 1.15
188 A9 15c orange .70 .30
189 A9 20c lilac 3.00 1.05
190 A9 25c dark blue 4.75 1.40
191 A9 30c violet 4.50 1.50
192 A9 40c turq blue 3.25 .75
193 A9 50c deep rose 3.25 .75
194 A9 1p myrtle green 3.25 .75
195 A9 4p red brown 13.00 13.00
196 A9 10p yellow 26.00 25.00
Nos. 184-196 (13) 68.55 46.40
Set, never hinged 130.00

Nipa House — A10

1924

Blue Control Numbers on Back

197 A10 5c choc & bl .25 .25
198 A10 10c gray grn & bl .25 .25
199 A10 15c rose & blk .25 .25
200 A10 20c violet & blk .25 .25
201 A10 25c org red & blk .40 .25
202 A10 30c orange & blk .40 .25
203 A10 40c dl bl & blk .40 .25
204 A10 50c claret & blk .40 .25
205 A10 60c red brn & blk .40 .25
206 A10 1p dk vio & blk 1.60 .25
a. Center inverted 600.00 140.00
207 A10 4p brt bl & blk 3.75 2.25
208 A10 10p bl grn & blk 8.75 4.50
Nos. 197-208 (12) 17.10 9.25
Set, never hinged 25.00

Seville-Barcelona Issue of Spain, 1929, Overprinted in Red or Blue

1929 ***Perf. 11***

209 A52 5c rose lake .35 .40
210 A53 10c green (R) .35 .40
211 A50 15c Prus bl (R) .35 .40
212 A51 20c purple (R) .35 .40
213 A50 25c brt rose .35 .40
214 A52 30c black brn .35 .40
215 A53 40c dk blue (R) .70 .65
216 A51 50c dp orange .70 .65
217 A52 1p blue blk (R) 11.50 6.00
218 A53 4p deep rose 22.00 11.50
219 A53 10p brown 42.50 23.00
Nos. 209-219 (11) 79.50 44.20
Set, never hinged 160.00

Porter A11 · Drummers A12

King Alfonso XIII and Queen Victoria — A13

1931 **Engr.** ***Perf. 14***

220 A11 1c blue green .30 .25
221 A11 2c red brown .30 .25

Blue Control Numbers on Back

222 A11 5c brown black .30 .25
223 A11 10c light green .30 .25
224 A11 15c dark green .30 .25
225 A11 20c deep violet .30 .25
226 A12 25c carmine .30 .25
227 A12 30c lake .40 .25
228 A12 40c dark blue .90 .65
229 A12 50c red orange 1.75 1.25
230 A13 80c blue violet 3.25 1.90
231 A13 1p black 5.75 5.25
232 A13 4p violet rose 37.50 20.00
233 A13 5p dark brown 17.50 14.00
Nos. 220-233 (14) 69.15 45.05
Set, never hinged 175.00

Exist imperf. Value for set, $300.

See Nos. 262-271. For overprints and surcharges see Nos. 234-277, 282-283, 298.

REPUBLICA
ESPAÑOLA

Stamps of 1931 Overprinted

1931

234 A11 1c blue green .30 .30
235 A11 2c red brown .30 .30
236 A11 5c brown black .30 .30
237 A11 10c light green .30 .30
238 A11 15c dark green .30 .30
239 A11 20c deep violet .30 .30
240 A12 25c carmine .30 .30
241 A12 30c lake .30 .30
242 A12 40c dark blue 2.25 .65
243 A12 50c red orange 14.50 7.75
244 A13 80c blue violet 4.50 2.50
245 A13 1p black 14.50 5.00
246 A13 4p violet rose 25.00 14.50
247 A13 5p dark brown 25.00 14.50
Nos. 234-247 (14) 88.15 47.30
Set, never hinged 200.00

República
Española

Stamps of 1931 Overprinted in Red or Blue

1933

248 A11 1c blue grn (R) .30 .25
249 A11 2c red brown (Bl) .30 .25
250 A11 5c brown blk (R) .30 .25
251 A11 10c lt green (Bl) .30 .25
252 A11 15c dk green (R) .30 .25
253 A11 20c dp violet (R) .30 .25
254 A12 25c carmine (Bl) .30 .25
255 A12 30c lake (Bl) .30 .25
256 A12 40c dk blue (R) 3.50 .95
257 A12 50c red orange (Bl) 22.00 4.75
258 A13 80c blue vio (R) 7.25 4.25
259 A13 1p black (R) 25.00 4.50
260 A13 4p violet rose (Bl) 47.50 20.00
261 A13 5p dk brown (Bl) 47.50 20.00
Nos. 248-261 (14) 155.15 56.45
Set, never hinged 250.00

Types of 1931
Without Control Number

1934-35 **Engr.** ***Perf. 10***

262 A11 1c blue green ('35) 11.50 .25
263 A11 2c red brown ('35) 11.50 .25
264 A11 5c black brn 2.25 .25
265 A11 10c light green 2.25 .25
266 A11 15c dark green 3.50 .25
267 A12 30c rose red 4.50 .35
268 A12 50c indigo ('35) 9.75 1.10
Nos. 262-268 (7) 45.25 2.70
Set, never hinged 70.00

Types of 1931

1941 **Litho.** **Unwmk.**

269 A11 5c olive gray 2.40 .25
270 A11 20c violet 2.40 .25
271 A12 40c gray green .95 .25
Nos. 269-271 (3) 5.75 .75
Set, never hinged 7.00

HABILITADO
.30 Cts

Stamps of 1931-33 Surcharged in Black

1936-37 ***Perf. 10, 14***

272 A12 30c on 40c (#228) 5.50 3.50
273 A12 30c on 40c (#242) 22.00 5.25
274 A12 30c on 40c (#256) 80.00 25.00
Nos. 272-274 (3) 107.50 33.75
Set, never hinged 170.00

The surcharge on Nos. 272-274 exists in two types, differing in the "3" which is scarcer in italic.

1
peseta.

No. 268 Surcharged in Red

275 A12 1p on 50c indigo 30.00
276 A12 4p on 50c indigo 90.00
277 A12 5p on 50c indigo 55.00
Nos. 275-277 (3) 175.00

Nos. 275-277 were not issued.

Territorios
Españoles del
Golfo de Guinea

Stamps of Spain, 1936, Overprinted in Black or Carmine

1938 ***Perf. 11***

278 A161 10c gray green 1.75 .55
279 A162 15c gray black (C) 1.75 .55
280 A162 20c dark violet 4.25 1.75
281 A162 25c brown lake 4.25 1.75
Nos. 278-281 (4) 12.00 4.60
Set, never hinged 16.00

Nos. 278-281 exist imperf. Value $175.

Habilitado
40 cts.

Stamps of 1931-33, Surcharged in Black

1939

282 A13 40c on 80c (#244) 12.00 8.00
283 A13 40c on 80c (#258) 12.00 5.00
Set, never hinged 32.50

A14 · A15

Revenue Stamps Surcharged in Black

1940-41 ***Perf. 11½***

284 A14 5c on 35c pale grn 6.00 2.10
285 A14 25c on 60c org brn 6.25 2.50
286 A14 50c on 75c blk brn 8.75 2.75
Nos. 284-286 (3) 21.00 7.35

Red Surcharge

287 A15 10c on 75c blk brn 8.75 2.75
288 A15 15c on 1.50p lt vio 6.25 2.50
289 A15 25c on 60c org brn 11.00 3.50
Nos. 287-289 (3) 26.00 8.75

A16 · A17

Black or Carmine Surcharge
Perf. 11

290 A16 1p on 17p deep red 52.50 15.50
291 A17 1p on 40p yel grn (C) 12.50 4.00

See No. C1

A18 · A19

Black Surcharge
Perf. 11, 13x12½

292 A18 5c carmine 5.25 1.40
293 A19 1p yellow 87.50 32.50

A20

Black Surcharge

294 A20 1p on 15c gray grn 9.50 3.25

General Francisco
Franco — A21

1940 Perf. 11½, 13½
295 A21 5c olive brown 3.75 .50
296 A21 40c blue 5.50 .50
297 A21 50c green 6.75 .50
a. 50c greenish gray 40.00 9.00
Nos. 295-297 (3) 16.00 1.50
Set, never hinged 75.00

Nos. 295-297 exist imperf. Values $50.

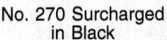

No. 270 Surcharged
in Black

1942
298 A11 3p on 20c vio 10.00 1.40

Spain, Nos. 702 and
704 Overprinted in
Carmine or Black

1942 Perf. 9½x10½
299 A166 1p gray blk (C) .55 .25
300 A166 4p dl rose (Bk) 7.50 .75

The overprint on No. 299 exists in two types:
Spacing between lines of 2mm, and spacing of
3mm. The 3mm spacing sells for about twice
as much.
For surcharges and overprint see #302-303,
C3.

Spain, No. 703
Overprinted in
Carmine

1943
301 A166 2p dull brown .85 .25

Nos. 299 and 301
Surcharged in Green

1949 Unwmk. Perf. 9½x10½
302 A166 5c (cinco) on 1p gray
blk .25 .25
303 A166 15c on 2p dl brn .25 .25

The two types of No. 299, described in footnote, also exist on No. 302.

Men Poling
Canoe
A22

1949, Oct. 9 Litho. Perf. 12½x13
304 A22 4p dk vio .85 .65
Never hinged 1.25

UPU, 75th anniversary.

San Carlos
Bay — A23

Designs: Various Views

1949-50 Perf. 12½x13
305 A23 2c brown .25 .25
306 A23 5c rose vio .25 .25
307 A23 10c Prussian bl .25 .25
308 A23 15c dp ol gray .25 .25
309 A23 25c red brown .25 .25
309A A23 30c brt yel ('50) .25 .25
310 A23 40c olive gray .30 .25
311 A23 45c rose lake .30 .25
312 A23 50c brn orange .30 .25
312A A23 75c ultra ('50) .30 .25
313 A23 90c dl bl grn .35 .25
314 A23 1p gray 1.10 .25
315 A23 1.35p violet 4.00 1.10
316 A23 2p sepia 11.00 2.25
317 A23 5p lilac rose 14.00 5.75
318 A23 10p light brn 60.00 23.00
Nos. 305-318 (16) 93.15 35.10
Set, never hinged 180.00

> **Catalogue values for unused
> stamps in this section, from this
> point to the end of the section, are
> for Never Hinged items.**

Surveyor
A24

1951, Dec. 5
319 A24 50c orange .40 .25
320 A24 5p indigo 7.50 1.25

Intl. Conference of West Africans, 1951.

Drummer
A25

1952, Mar. 10
321 A25 5c red brown .25 .25
322 A25 50c olive gray .40 .25
323 A25 5p violet 2.40 .25
Nos. 321-323 (3) 3.05 .75

Musician
A26

Design: 60c, Musician facing right.

1953, July 1 Photo.
324 A26 15c sepia .25 .25
325 A26 60c brown .30 .25
Nos. 324-325, B25-B26 (4) 1.10 1.00

Woman and
Dove
A27

Drummer
A28

1953, Sept. 5 Perf. 13x12½
326 A27 5c orange .25 .25
327 A27 10c brt lilac rose .25 .25
328 A27 60c brown .25 .25
329 A28 1p dull purple 1.60 .35
330 A28 1.90p greenish blk 2.50 .35
Nos. 326-330 (5) 4.85 1.35

Tragocephala
Nobilis — A29

Butterfly: 60c, Papilio antimachus.

1953, Nov. 23
331 A29 15c dark green .35 .25
332 A29 60c brown .45 .25
Nos. 331-332, B27-B28 (4) 1.35 1.00

Colonial Stamp Day.

Hunter
A30

Design: 60c, Hunter and elephant.

1954, June 10 Perf. 12½x13
333 A30 15c dark gray green .35 .25
334 A30 60c dark brown .50 .25
Nos. 333-334, B29-B30 (4) 1.40 1.00

Swimming
Turtle
A31

1954, Nov. 23
335 A31 15c shown .30 .25
336 A31 60c Shark .75 .25
Nos. 335-336, B31-B32 (4) 1.65 1.00

Colonial Stamp Day.

Manuel
Iradier y
Bulfy, Birth
Cent. (in
1954)
A32

1955, Jan. 18
337 A32 60c orange brown .50 .25
338 A32 1p dark violet 3.25 .30

Priest Saying
Mass — A33

1955, June 1 Photo. Perf. 13x12½
339 A33 50c olive gray .30 .25
Nos. 339, B33-B34 (3) .95 .75

Centenary of the establishment of an Apostolic Prefecture at Fernando Po.

Palace of
Pardo
A34

1955, July 18 Perf. 12½x13
340 A34 5c ol brn .30 .25
341 A34 15c brn lake .30 .25
342 A34 80c Prus grn .35 .25
Nos. 340-342 (3) .95 .75

Treaty of Pardo, 1778.

Red-eared
Guenons — A35

1955, Nov. 23 Perf. 13x12½
343 A35 70c gray grn & bl .60 .25
Nos. 343, B35-B36 (3) 1.15 .75

Colonial Stamp Day.

Orchid — A36

Flower: 50c, Strophantus Kombe.

1956, June 1 Unwmk.
344 A36 20c bluish green .25 .25
345 A36 50c brown .30 .25
Nos. 344-345, B37-B38 (4) 1.10 1.00

See Nos. 360-361, B53-B54.

Arms of Santa
Isabel — A37

1956, Nov. 23 Perf. 13x12½
346 A37 70c light olive green .25 .25
Nos. 346, B39-B40 (3) .75 .75

Colonial Stamp Day.

African Gray
Parrot — A38

1957, June 1 Photo.
347 A38 70c olive green .40 .25
Nos. 347, B41-B42 (3) .95 .75

Elephants
A39

Design: 70c, Elephant, vert.

Perf. 12½x13, 13x12½
1957, Nov. 23
348 A39 20c blue green .35 .25
349 A39 70c emerald .45 .25
Nos. 348-349, B43-B44 (4) 1.45 1.00

Colonial Stamp Day.

Boxing
A40

Basketball — A41

Various Sports: 15c, 2.30p, Jumping. 80c, 3p, Runner at finish line.

1958, Apr. 10　Photo.　Unwmk.
350　A40　5c violet brn　.25　.25
351　A41　10c orange brn　.25　.25
352　A40　15c brown　.25　.25
353　A41　80c green　.25　.25
354　A40　1p orange red　.25　.25
355　A41　2p rose lilac　.35　.25
356　A40　2.30p dl violet　.40　.25
357　A41　3p brt blue　.45　.25
　　Nos. 350-357 (8)　2.45　2.00

Preaching
Missionary — A42

Design: 70c, Crucifix and missal.

1958, June 1　Perf. 13x12½
358　A42　20c blue green　.30　.25
359　A42　70c green　.30　.25
　　Nos. 358-359,B48-B49 (4)　1.25　1.00
Catholic missions in Spanish Guinea, 75th anniv.

Type of 1956 Inscribed: "Pro-Infancia 1959"

1959, June 1　Perf. 13x12½
360　A36　20c Castor bean　.25　.25
361　A36　70c Digitalis　.30　.25
　　Nos. 360-361,B53-B54 (4)　1.10　1.00
Promoting child welfare.
Stamps of Spanish Guinea were succeeded by those of Fernando Po and Rio Muni in 1960.

SEMI-POSTAL STAMPS

Red Cross Issue

Types of Semi-Postal Stamps of Spain, 1926, Ovptd. in Black or Blue

1926　Unwmk.　Perf. 12½, 13
B1　SP3　5c black brown　11.00　7.00
B2　SP4　10c dark green　11.00　7.00
B3　SP1　15c dark vio (Bl)　2.50　1.75
B4　SP4　20c violet brown　2.50　1.75
B5　SP5　25c deep carmine　2.50　1.75
B6　SP1　30c olive green　2.50　1.75
B7　SP3　40c ultra　.55　.25
B8　SP2　50c red brown　.55　.25
B9　SP5　60c myrtle green　.55　.25
B10　SP4　1p vermilion　.55　.25

B11　SP3　4p bister　2.25　1.50
B12　SP5　10p light violet　7.50　5.00
　　Nos. B1-B12 (12)　43.95　28.50
　　Set, never hinged　60.00
　　See Spain No. B6a for No. B4 without overprint. For surcharges see Spain Nos. B70-B71.

> Catalogue values for unused stamps in this section, from this point to the end of the section, are for Never Hinged items.

Allegory — SP1

1950, Dec. 1　Photo.　Perf. 13x12½
B13　SP1　50c + 10c ultra　.35　.30
B14　SP1　1p + 25c dk grn　12.00　4.00
B15　SP1　6.50p + 1.65p dp org　3.00　2.00
　　Nos. B13-B15 (3)　15.35　6.30
The surtax was to help the native population.

Leopard — SP2

1951, Nov. 23
B16　SP2　5c + 5c brown　.25　.25
B17　SP2　10c + 5c red orange　.25　.25
B18　SP2　60c + 15c olive brn　.35　.25
　　Nos. B16-B18 (3)　.85　.75
Colonial Stamp Day, Nov. 23.

Love Lily — SP3

1952, June 1
B19　SP3　5c + 5c brown　.25　.25
B20　SP3　50c + 10c gray　.25　.25
B21　SP3　2p + 30c blue　1.50　1.00
　　Nos. B19-B21 (3)　2.00　1.50
The surtax was to help the native population.

Brown-cheeked
Hornbill — SP4

1952, Nov. 23　Perf. 12½
B22　SP4　5c + 5c brown　.25　.25
B23　SP4　10c + 5c brown car　.25　.25
B24　SP4　60c + 15c dk green　.45　.30
　　Nos. B22-B24 (3)　.95　.80
Colonial Stamp Day, Nov. 23.

Music Type of Regular Issue
1953, July 1　Perf. 12½x13
B25　A26　5c + 5c like #324　.25　.25
B26　A26　10c + 5c like #325　.30　.25
The surtax was to help the native population.

Insect Type of Regular Issue
1953, Nov. 23　Perf. 13x12½
B27　A29　5c + 5c like #331　.25　.25
B28　A29　10c + 5c like #332　.30　.25

Hunter Type of Regular Issue
1954, June 10　Perf. 12½x13
B29　A30　5c + 5c like #333　.25　.25
B30　A30　10c + 5c like #334　.30　.25
The surtax was to help the native population.

Type of Regular Issue
1954, Nov. 23
B31　A31　5c + 5c like #335　.30　.25
B32　A31　10c + 5c like #336　.30　.25

Type of Regular Issue and

Baptism — SP5

Perf. 13x12½
1955, June 1　Photo.　Unwmk.
B33　A33　10c + 5c like #339　.30　.25
B34　SP5　25c + 10c shown　.35　.25

Type of Regular Issue and

Red-eared
Guenons
SP6

Perf. 13x12½, 12½x13
1955, Nov. 23
B35　A35　5c + 5c like #343　.25　.25
B36　SP6　15c + 5c shown　.30　.25

Flower Type of Regular Issue
1956, June 1　Perf. 13x12½
B37　A36　5c + 5c like #344　.25　.25
B38　A36　15c + 5c like #345　.30　.25
The tax was for native welfare work.

Type of Regular Issue and

Drummers
and Arms
of Bata
SP7

Perf. 13x12½, 12½x13
1956, Nov. 23
B39　A37　5c + 5c like #346　.25　.25
B40　SP7　15c + 5c shown　.25　.25

Type of Regular Issue and

African
Gray
Parrot
SP8

Perf. 13x12½, 12½x13
1957, June 1　Photo.　Unwmk.
B41　A38　5c + 5c like #347　.25　.25
B42　SP8　15c + 5c shown　.30　.25
The surtax was for child welfare.

Type of Regular Issue, 1957
Perf. 12½x13, 13x12½
1957, Nov. 23
B43　A39　10c + 5c like #348　.30　.25
B44　A39　15c + 5c like #349　.35　.25

Pigeons
and Arms
of Valencia
and Santa
Isabel
SP9

1958, Mar. 6　Perf. 12½x13
B45　SP9　10c + 5c org brn　.25　.25
B46　SP9　15c + 10c bister　.25　.25
B47　SP9　50c + 10c ol gray　.25　.25
　　Nos. B45-B47 (3)　.75　.75
The surtax was to aid the victims of the Valencia flood, Oct., 1957.

Type of Regular Issue, 1958
1958, June 1　Photo.　Perf. 13x12½
B48　A42　10c + 5c like #358　.30　.25
B49　A42　15c + 5c like #359　.35　.25
The surtax was to help the native population.

Butterflies — SP10

Stamp Day: Various butterflies.

1958, Nov. 23　Unwmk.
B50　SP10　10c + 5c brown red　.35　.25
B51　SP10　25c + 10c brt pur　.35　.25
B52　SP10　50c + 10c gray olive　.40　.25
　　Nos. B50-B52 (3)　1.10　.75

Type of Regular Issue 1956
Inscribed: "Pro-Infancia 1959"
1959, June 1　Photo.　Perf. 13x12½
B53　A36　10c + 5c like #361　.25　.25
B54　A36　15c + 5c like #360　.30　.25
The surtax was for child welfare.

Early
Bicycle — SP11

Designs: 20c+5c, Bicycle race. 50c+20c, Bicyclist winning race.

1959, Nov. 23
B55　SP11　10c + 5c lt rose brn　.25　.25
B56　SP11　20c + 5c turq blue　.25　.25
B57　SP11　50c + 20c olive gray　.30　.25
　　Nos. B55-B57 (3)　.80　.75
Stamp Day.

AIR POST STAMPS

AP1

Type I — "Correo Aereo," 20½mm.
Type II — "Correo Aereo," 22mm.
Revenue Stamp Surcharged

1941   Unwmk.   Perf. 11

C1   AP1 1p on 17p dp red, I   35.00   8.00
  a.   Type II   45.00 11.00

Spain No. C113 Overprinted in Red

1942, June 23

C2   AP30 1p chalky blue   1.90   .35

No. 300 Overprinted
in Green

The overprint exists in two types: Type I —
The numeral 1's are lower case L's. Type II —
The numeral 1's are actual ones.

1948, Jan. 15   Perf. 10½x9½

C3   A166 4p dull rose   9.00   2.75
       Never hinged   15.00

Count of Argelejo and Frigate Catalina
at Fernando Po, 1778
AP2

1949, Nov. 23 Photo. Perf. 12½x13

C4   AP2 5p dark slate green   1.00   .75
       Never hinged   1.50

Stamp Day, Nov. 23, 1949.

Manuel Iradier and
Native
Products — AP3

1950, Nov. 23   Unwmk.   Perf. 12½

C5   AP3 5p dk brn   2.50   1.00
       Never hinged   3.50

Stamp Day, Nov. 23, 1950.

Benito
Rapids
AP4

Various views.

1951, Mar. 1   Litho.   Perf. 12½x13

C6   AP4 25c ocher   .25   .25
C7   AP4 50c lilac rose   .25   .25
C8   AP4 1p green   .25   .25
C9   AP4 2p bright blue   .25   .25
C10 AP4 3.25p rose lilac   .50   .25
C11 AP4 5p gray brown   4.00   1.75
C12 AP4 10p rose red   15.50   6.25
       Nos. C6-C12 (7)   21.00   9.25
       Set, never hinged   50.00

> **Catalogue values for unused
> stamps in this section, from this
> point to the end of the section, are
> for Never Hinged items.**

Woman Holding
Dove — AP5

1951, Apr. 22   Engr.   Perf. 10

C13 AP5 5p dark blue   21.00   2.75

500th birth anniv. of Queen Isabella I.

Ferdinand the
Catholic — AP6

1952, July 18 Photo. Perf. 13x12½

C14 AP6 5p red brown   25.00   6.00

500th birth anniv. of Ferdinand the Catholic
of Spain.

Soccer
Players — AP7

1955-56   Unwmk.

C15 AP7 25c blue vio ('56)   .30   .25
C16 AP7 50c olive ('56)   .30   .25
C17 AP7 1.50p brown ('56)   1.05   .25
C18 AP7 4p rose car ('56)   3.25   .45
C19 AP7 10p yellow grn   1.75   .45
       Nos. C15-C19 (5)   6.65   1.65

Planes and Arm
Holding
Spear — AP8

1957, Sept. 19   Perf. 13x12½

C20 AP8 25p bister & sepia   15.00   .95

30th anniv. of the Atlantida Squadron flight
to Spanish Guinea.

SPECIAL DELIVERY STAMP

View of
Fernando
Po — SD1

Perf. 12½x13

1951, Mar. 1   Litho.   Unwmk.

E1   SD1 25c rose carmine   .35   .25
       Never hinged   .50

SPANISH MOROCCO

'spa-nish mə-'rä-ₐkō

LOCATION — Northwest coast of Africa
GOVT. — Spanish Protectorate
AREA — 17,398 sq. mi. (approx.)
POP. — 1,010,117 (1950)
CAPITAL — Tetuán

Spanish authority in northern
Morocco was established after Spain's
invasion of the area in 1859. Spanish
Morocco was a Spanish Protectorate
until 1956 when it, along with the
French and Tangier zones of Morocco,
became the independent country,
Morocco.

100 Centimos = 1 Peseta

> **Catalogue values for unused
> stamps in this country are for
> Never Hinged items, beginning
> with Scott 280 in the regular post-
> age section, Scott B27 in the semi-
> postal section, Scott C24 in the
> airpost section, and Scott E11 in
> special delivery section.**

Unoverprinted Spanish stamps were
used in Spanish Morocco from 1860
until the appearance of separate issues
for the territory in 1903. Spain No. E1
was used as a regular postage stamp in
April 1914.

Spanish Offices in Morocco

Spain No. 221A
Overprinted in Carmine

1903-09   Unwmk.   Imperf.

1   A21 ¼c blue green   .55   .25
  a.   Complete 1c (block 4 ¼c) 2.25   1.50

See Nos. 26, 39, 52, Tetuan 1, 7.

Stamps of Spain
Overprinted in Carmine
or Blue — a

**On Stamps of 1900
Perf. 14**

2   A35 2c bister brown   1.75   1.40
3   A35 5c green   2.10   .80
4   A35 10c rose red (Bl)   2.25   .35
5   A35 15c brt violet   3.25   .80
6   A35 20c grnsh black   13.00   3.50
7   A35 25c blue   1.00   .85
8   A35 30c blue green   7.50   3.50
9   A35 40c rose (Bl)   13.00   6.00
10   A35 50c slate grn   7.75   5.75
11   A35 1p lake (Bl)   16.00   8.00
12   A35 4p dull violet   42.50 14.00
13   A35 10p brown org (Bl)   42.50 35.00
       Nos. 1-13 (13)   153.15 80.20
       Set, never hinged   375.00

Many varieties of overprint exist. Nos. 7-13
exist imperf. Value, $500.
See Tetuan Nos. 2-6, 8-15.

On Stamps of 1909-10

1909-10   Perf. 13x12½, 14

14   A46 2c dark brown   .75   .25
15   A46 5c green   3.75   .30
16   A46 10c carmine (Bl)   4.25   .30
17   A46 15c violet   10.50   .65
18   A46 20c olive green   26.00   1.25
19   A46 25c deep blue   95.00
20   A46 30c blue green   8.50   .65
21   A46 40c rose (Bl)   8.50   .65
22   A46 50c slate blue   14.50 14.00
23   A46 1p lake (Bl)   34.50 29.00
24   A46 4p deep violet   95.00
25   A46 10p orange (Bl)   95.00
       Nos. 14-18,20-23 (9)   111.25 47.05
       Set, never hinged   200.00
       Nos. 14-25 (12)   396.25

The stamps overprinted "Correo Espanol
Marruecos" were used in all Morocco until the
year 1914. After the issue of special stamps
for the Protectorate the "Correo Espanol"
stamps were continued in use solely in the city
of Tangier.

Many varieties of overprint exist.
Nos. 19, 24 and 25 were not regularly
issued.
See Nos. 27-38, 40-51, 53-67, 75-76, 78.

Spanish Morocco

Spain No. 221A
Overprinted in Carmine

1914   Imperf.

26   A21 ¼c green   .25   .25
  a.   Complete 1c (block 4 ¼c) 1.25   .90

Stamps of Spain 1909-
10 Overprinted in
Carmine or Blue

Perf. 13x12½, 14

27   A46 2c dark brown (C)   .35   .25
28   A46 5c green (C)   .35   .25
29   A46 10c carmine (Bl)   .35   .25
30   A46 15c violet (C)   1.50   .90
31   A46 20c olive grn (C)   3.00   1.90
32   A46 25c deep blue (C)   3.00   1.50
33   A46 30c blue grn (C)   5.75   2.75
34   A46 40c rose (Bl)   13.00   3.75
35   A46 50c slate blue (C)   6.50   2.75
36   A46 1p lake (Bl)   6.50   3.75
37   A46 4p dp violet (C)   33.00 24.00
38   A46 10p orange (Bl)   50.00 32.00
       Nos. 26-38,E1 (14)   129.30 76.90
       Set, never hinged   350.00

Many varieties of overprint exist, including
inverted.
#27-38 exist imperf. Value for set, $525.

Stamps of Spain 1876
and 1909-10
Overprinted in Red or
Blue

1915   Imperf.

39   A21 ¼c blue grn (R)   .25   .25
  a.   Complete 1c (block 4 ¼c) 1.50   1.50

Perf. 13x12½, 14

40   A46 2c dk brown (R)   .30   .30
41   A46 5c green (R)   .35   .35
42   A46 10c carmine (Bl)   .35   .35
43   A46 15c violet (R)   .35   .35
44   A46 20c olive grn (R)   1.25   .35
45   A46 25c deep blue (R)   1.25   .55
46   A46 30c blue grn (R)   1.40   .60
47   A46 40c rose (R)   3.75   .55
48   A46 50c slate blue (R)   6.25   .55
49   A46 1p lake (Bl)   6.25   .60
50   A46 4p deep violet (R)   42.50 26.00
51   A46 10p orange (Bl)   60.00 29.00
       Nos. 39-51,E2 (14)   127.25 61.45
       Set, never hinged   350.00

One stamp in the setting on Nos. 39-51 has
the first "R" of "PROTECTORADO" inverted.
Many other varieties of overprint exist, including double and inverted.
Nos. 40-51 exist imperf. Value, set $650.

Stamps of Spain 1877
and 1909-10
Overprinted in Red or
Blue — b

1916-18   Imperf.

52   A21 ¼c blue grn (R)   1.25   .25
  a.   Complete 1c (block 4 ¼c) 2.00   1.40

Perf. 13x12½, 14

53   A46 2c dk brn (R)   1.25   .25
54   A46 5c green (R)   5.50   .25
55   A46 10c carmine (Bl)   6.00   .25
56   A46 15c violet (R)   140.00
57   A46 20c olive grn (R)   140.00
58   A46 25c dp blue (R)   21.00   3.25
59   A46 30c blue grn (R)   27.50 22.00
60   A46 40c rose (R)   28.50   .50
61   A46 50c slate blue (R)   13.50   .25
62   A46 1p lake (Bl)   33.00   2.40
63   A46 4p dp violet (R)   55.00 32.50
64   A46 10p orange (Bl)   110.00 72.50
       Nos. 52-55,58-64 (11) 302.50 134.40
       Set, never hinged   440.00
       Nos. 52-64 (13)   582.50
       Set, never hinged   1,100.

Nos. 56-57 were not regularly issued.
Varieties of overprint, including double and
inverted, exist for several denominations.
The 5c exists in olive brown. Value $525.

Same Overprint on Spain No. 310

1920
65	A46	15c ocher (Bl)	5.50	.30

Exists imperf.; also with overprint inverted.

Nos. 44, 46 Perforated through the middle and each half Surcharged "10 céntimos" in Red

1920
66	A46	10c on half of 20c	5.00	1.90
67	A46	15c on half of 30c	11.00	7.25

No. E1 Divided and Surcharged in Black

68	SD1	10c on half of 20c	12.00	7.75
a.		"10/cts." surcharge added	160.00	50.00
		Nos. 66-68 (3)	28.00	16.90

Values of Nos. 66-68 are for pairs, both halves of the stamp. Varieties were probably made deliberately.

"Justice" — A1

Revenue Stamps Perforated through the Middle and each half Surcharged in Red or Green

1920   *Perf. 11½*
69	A1	5c on 5p lt bl	11.50	2.40
70	A1	5c on 10p green	.50	.25
71	A1	10c on 25p dk grn	15.50	8.00
a.		Inverted surcharge	13.50	12.00
72	A1	10c on 50p indigo	.55	.40
73	A1	15c on 100p red (G)	.55	.40
74	A1	5c on 500p cl (G)	15.50	8.00
		Nos. 69-74 (6)	29.10	11.70
		Set, never hinged	55.00	

Values of Nos. 69-74 are for pairs, both halves of the stamp.

Stamps of Spain 1917-20 Overprinted Type "a" in Blue or Red

1921-24   *Perf. 13*
75	A46	15c ocher (Bl)	1.50	.25
76	A46	20c violet (R)	2.25	.25

Stamps of Spain 1920-21 Overprinted Type "b" in Red

Imperf
77	A47	1c blue green	1.50	.25

Engr.   *Perf. 13*
78	A46	20c violet	11.00	.25

See No. 92.

Stamps of Spain, 1922 Overprinted Type "a" in Red or Blue

1923-28   *Perf. 13½x12½*
79	A49	2c olive green (R)	4.25	.25
80	A49	5c red violet (Bl)	4.25	.25
81	A49	10c yellow green (R)	5.00	.25
82	A49	20c violet (R)	7.00	1.10
		Nos. 79-82 (4)	20.50	1.85

Same Overprinted Type "b"

1923-25
83	A49	2c olive green (R)	.75	.25
84	A49	5c red violet (Bl)	.75	.25
85	A49	10c yellow grn (R)	3.00	.25
86	A49	15c blue (R)	3.00	.25
87	A49	20c violet (R)	6.50	.25
88	A49	25c carmine (Bl)	13.00	1.50
89	A49	40c deep blue (R)	13.50	5.00
90	A49	50c orange (Bl)	35.00	8.50
91	A49a	1p blue black (R)	55.00	5.00
		Nos. 83-91,E3 (10)	142.50	31.00
		Set, never hinged	350.00	

Spain No. 314 Overprinted Type "a" in Red

1927   *Imperf.*
92	A47	1c blue green	.25	.25

Mosque of Alcazarquivir A2   Moorish Gateway at Larache A3

Well at Alhucemas A4

View of Xauen — A5

View of Tetuan — A6

1928-32   *Engr.*   *Perf. 14, 14½*
93	A2	1c red ("Cs")	.25	.25
94	A2	1c car rose ("Ct") ('32)	.50	.40
95	A2	2c dark violet	.30	.25
96	A2	5c deep blue	.35	.25
97	A2	10c dark green	.35	.25
98	A2	15c orange brown	.75	.35
99	A3	20c olive green	.75	.35
100	A3	25c copper red	.80	.35
102	A3	30c black brown	2.60	.40
103	A3	40c dull blue	3.25	.40
104	A3	50c brown violet	6.75	.40
105	A4	1p yellow green	8.25	.45
106	A5	2.50p red violet	32.50	10.00
107	A6	4p ultra	24.00	7.50
		Nos. 93-107,E4 (15)	86.40	23.20
		Set, never hinged	225.00	

For surcharges see Nos. 164-167.

Seville-Barcelona Issue of Spain, 1929, Ovptd. in Red or Blue

1929   *Perf. 11, 14*
108	A50	1c greenish blue	.40	.30
109	A51	2c pale yel grn	.40	.30
110	A52	5c rose lake (Bl)	.40	.30
111	A53	10c green	.40	.30
112	A50	15c Prussian blue	.40	.30
113	A51	20c purple	.40	.30
114	A50	25c bright rose (Bl)	.40	.30
115	A52	30c black brown (bl)	1.00	.75
116	A50	40c dark blue	1.00	.75
117	A51	50c deep orange (Bl)	1.00	.75
118	A52	1p blue black	8.00	5.75
119	A53	4p deep rose (Bl)	18.00	12.50
120	A53	10p brown (Bl)	40.00	29.00
		Nos. 108-120 (13)	71.80	51.60
		Set, never hinged	115.00	

See Nos. L1-L11.

Stamps of Spain, 1922-31, Overprinted Type "a" in Black, Blue or Red

1929-34   *Perf. 11½, 13x12½*
121	A49	5c claret (Bk)	3.50	.25
122	A61	10c green (R)	3.00	.45
123	A61	15c slate grn (R)	110.00	1.10
124	A61	20c violet (R)	3.00	.50
125	A61	30c brown lake (Bl)	3.25	1.10
126	A61	40c dark blue (R)	12.00	5.50
127	A49	50c orange (Bl)	30.00	5.25
128	A49a	1p brown (Bl)	5.00	5.75
		Nos. 121-128 (8)	167.75	19.90
		Set, never hinged	300.00	

Stamps of Spain, 1922-26, overprinted diagonally as above, and with no control number, or with "A000,000" on back, were not issued but were presented to the delegates at the 1929 UPU Congress in London. Value of complete set of 16, $3,250.

Stamps of Spain 1931-32, Overprinted in Black

1933-34   *Imperf.*
130	A108	1c blue green	.25	.25

Perf. 11½
131	A108	2c buff	.25	.25
132	A95	5c brnsh black	.25	.25
133	A96	10c yellow green	.25	.25
134	A97	15c slate green	.25	.25
135	A95	20c dark violet	.30	.25
136	A104	25c lake	.30	.25
137	A99	30c carmine rose	60.00	6.00
138	A100	40c dark blue	.65	.25
139	A97	50c orange	1.25	.30
140	A100	60c apple green	1.25	.30
141	A105	1p blue black	1.25	.50
142	A106	4p magenta	2.75	2.50
143	A107	10p deep brown	3.50	5.50
		Nos. 130-143,E7 (15)	74.00	17.35
		Set, never hinged	130.00	

Street Scene in Tangier — A7

View of Xauen A8

Gate in Town Wall, Arzila — A9

Street Scene in Tangier A10

Mosque of Alcazarquivir A11

Caliph and His Guard A12

View of Tangier A13

Green Control Numbers Printed on Gum

1933-35   *Photo.*   *Perf. 14, 13½*
144	A7	1c brt rose	.35	.25
145	A8	2c green ('35)	.35	.25
146	A9	5c magenta ('35)	.35	.25
147	A10	10c dark green	.45	.25
148	A11	15c yellow ('35)	3.00	.30
149	A7	20c slate green	1.25	.30
150	A12	25c crimson ('35)	29.00	.30
151	A10	30c red brown	8.00	.35
152	A13	40c deep blue	12.50	.35
153	A13	50c red orange	42.50	5.00
154	A8	1p slate blk ('35)	18.00	.35
155	A9	2.50p brown ('35)	32.50	5.00
156	A11	4p yel grn ('35)	42.50	5.00
157	A12	5p blue ('35)	42.50	5.25
		Nos. 144-157,E5 (15)	234.40	23.45
		Set, never hinged	400.00	

For surcharge see No. CB1.

Mosque — A14

Landscape A15

Green Control Numbers Printed on Gum

1935
158	A14	25c violet	1.25	.25
159	A15	30c crimson	16.50	.25
160	A14	40c orange	8.50	.25
161	A15	50c bright blue	8.50	.30
162	A14	60c dk blue green	8.50	.35
163	A15	2p brown lake	42.50	6.00
		Nos. 158-163 (6)	85.75	7.40
		Set, never hinged	160.00	

See No. 174.

Regular Issue and Special Delivery Stamp of 1928, Surcharged in Blue, Green or Red with New Values and Ornaments

1936
164	A6	1c on 4p ultra (Bl)	.35	.25
165	A5	2c on 2.50p red vio (G)	.35	.25
166	A3	5c on 25c cop red (R)	.35	.25
167	A4	10c on 1p yel grn (G)	10.00	4.00
168	SD2	15c on 20c blk (Bl)	7.75	2.10
		Nos. 164-168 (5)	18.80	6.85
		Set, never hinged	24.50	

Caliph and Viziers — A16

View of Bokoia A17

View of Alcazarquivir — A18

Sidi Saida Mosque A19

Caliph and Procession A20

Without Control Numbers

1937		Photo.	Perf. 13½	
169	A16	1c green	.30	.25
170	A17	2c red violet	.30	.25
171	A18	5c orange	.30	.25
172	A16	15c violet	.30	.25
173	A19	30c red	.85	.25
a.		Souvenir sheet of 4, #170-173	22.00	12.00
174	A14	1p ultra	7.50	.30
a.		Souv. sheet of 4, #169-171, 174	22.00	12.00
175	A20	10p brown	60.00	17.50
		Nos. 169-175 (7)	69.55	19.05
		Set, never hinged	150.00	

Nos. 173a, 174a for 1st year of the Spanish Civil War.

Nos. 173a, 174a were privately overprinted "TANGER" in black on each stamp in the sheet for "use" in the International City of Tangier, and "GUINEA" for "use" in Spanish Guinea.

Harkeno Rifleman — A21

Troops Marching A22

Designs: 2c, Legionnaires. 5c, Cavalryman leading his mount. 10c, Moroccan phalanx. 15c, Legion flag-bearer. 20c, Colonial soldier. 25c, Ifni sharpshooters. 30c, Mounted trumpeters. 40c, Cape Juby Dromedary Corps. 50c, Regular infantry. 60c, Caliphate guards. 1p, Orderly on guard. 2p, Sentry. 2.50p, Regular cavalry. 4p, Orderly.

1937			Perf. 13½	
176	A21	1c dull blue	.35	.25
177	A21	2c orange brn	.35	.25
178	A21	5c cerise	.35	.25
179	A21	10c emerald	.35	.25
180	A21	15c brt blue	.35	.25
181	A21	20c red brown	.35	.25
182	A21	25c magenta	.35	.30
183	A21	30c red orange	.35	.30
184	A21	40c orange	.35	.35
185	A21	50c ultra	.35	.35
186	A21	60c yellow grn	.35	.35
187	A21	1p blue violet	.35	.35
188	A21	2p Prus blue	11.50	5.00
189	A21	2.50p gray black	11.50	5.00
190	A21	4p dark brown	11.50	5.00
191	A22	10p black	11.50	5.00
		Nos. 176-191,E6 (17)	50.45	23.75
		Set, never hinged	120.00	

First Year of Spanish Civil War.
Exists imperf. Value, set $250.
For overprints see Nos. 214-229.

Spanish Quarter — A25

Designs: 10c, Moroccan quarter. 15c, Street scene, Larache. 20c, Tetuan.

1939		Unwmk. Photo.	Perf. 13½	
194	A25	5c orange	.30	.25
195	A25	10c brt blue grn	.30	.25
196	A25	15c golden brown	.50	.30
197	A25	20c brt ultra	.50	.30
		Nos. 194-197 (4)	1.60	1.10

Postman — A26

Mail Box — A27

Landscape A28

Street Scene, Alcazarquivir A29

View of Xauen — A30

Sentry Guarding Palace at Sat — A31

The Chieftain — A32

Market Place, Larache — A33

Tetuán — A34

Ancient Gateway at Xauen — A35

Scene in Alcazarquivir A36

Post Office A37

Spanish War Veterans — A38

Victory Flag Bearers — A39

Cavalry — A40

Day of Court — A41

1940		Unwmk. Photo.	Perf. 11½x11	
198	A26	1c dark brown	.35	.30
199	A27	2c olive grn	.35	.30
200	A28	5c dk blue	.35	.30
201	A29	10c dk red lilac	.35	.30
202	A30	15c dk green	.45	.35
203	A31	20c purple	.35	.35
204	A32	25c black brown	.35	.35
205	A33	30c brt green	.35	.35
206	A34	40c slate green	2.75	.35
207	A35	45c orange ver	1.10	.35
208	A36	50c brown orange	1.10	.35
209	A37	70c sapphire	1.10	.35
210	A38	1p indigo & brn	3.25	.35
211	A39	2.50p choc & dk grn	18.00	4.75
212	A40	5p dk cerise & sep	3.50	.45
213	A41	10p dk ol grn & brn org	32.50	8.00
		Nos. 198-213,E8 (17)	67.05	17.90
		Set, never hinged	120.00	

"ZONA" printed in black on back.
Exists imperf. Value, set $325.

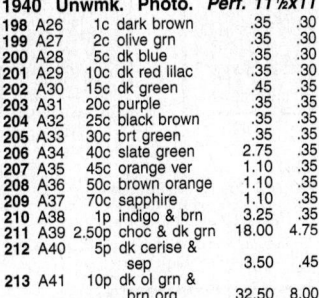

Stamps of 1937 Overprinted in Various Colors

1940		Unwmk.	Perf. 13½	
214	A21	1c dull blue (Bk)	.95	.70
215	A21	2c org brn (Bk)	.95	.70
216	A21	5c cerise (Bk)	.95	.70
217	A21	10c emerald (Bk)	.95	.70
218	A21	15c brt blue (Bk)	.95	.70
219	A21	20c red brn (Bk)	.95	.70
220	A21	25c mag (Bk)	.95	.70
221	A21	30c red org (V)	.95	.70
222	A21	40c orange (V)	1.60	1.40
223	A21	50c ultra (Bk)	1.60	1.40
224	A21	60c yel grn (Bk)	1.60	1.40
225	A21	1p blue vio (V)	1.60	1.40
226	A21	2p Prus bl (Bl)	50.00	50.00
227	A21	2.50p gray blk (V)	50.00	50.00
228	A21	4p dk brn (Bl)	50.00	50.00
229	A22	10p black (R)	50.00	50.00
		Nos. 214-229,E10 (17)	226.00	220.70
		Set, never hinged	500.00	

4th anniversary of Spanish Civil War.

Larache A42

Alcazarquivir A43

Market Place, Larache — A44

Tangier
A45   A46

1941		Unwmk. Photo.	Perf. 10½	
230	A42	5c dk brn & brn	.25	.25
231	A43	10c dp rose & ver	.25	.25
232	A44	15c sl grn & yel grn	.25	.25
233	A45	20c vio bl & dp bl	.55	.25
234	A46	40c dp plum & claret	1.50	.25
		Nos. 230-234 (5)	2.80	1.25
		Set, never hinged	5.00	

Exists imperf. Value, set $150.

1943			Perf. 12x12½	
234A	A43	5c dark blue	.25	.25
235	A44	40c dull violet brn	100.00	.25

Plowing A47

Harvesting A48

Returning from Work A49

Transporting Wheat — A50

Vegetable Garden A51

Picking Oranges A52

Goat Herd — A53

1944   Unwmk.   Photo.   Perf. 12½

236	A47	1c choc & lt bl	.25	.25
237	A48	2c sl grn & lt grn	.25	.25
238	A49	5c choc & grnsh blk	.25	.25
239	A50	10c brt ultra & red org	.25	.25
240	A51	15c sl grn & lt grn	.25	.25
241	A52	20c dp cl & blk	.25	.25
242	A53	25c lt bl & choc	.25	.25
243	A47	30c yel grn & brt ultra	.25	.25
244	A48	40c choc & red vio	.25	.25
245	A49	50c brt ultra & red brn	.65	.25
246	A50	75c yel grn & brt ultra	.90	.25
247	A51	1p brt ultra & choc	.90	.25
248	A52	2.50p blk & brt ultra	7.75	1.75
249	A53	10p sal & gray blk	11.50	3.75
		Nos. 236-249 (14)	23.95	8.50
		Set, never hinged	50.00	

Exists imperf. Value, set $125.

Potters A54

Dyers A55

Blacksmiths A56

Cobblers A57

Weavers A58

Metal Workers A59

1946   Unwmk.   Litho.   Perf. 10½x10

250	A54	1c purple & brn	.25	.25
251	A55	2c dk Prus grn & vio blk	.25	.25
252	A54	10c dp org & vio bl	.25	.25
253	A55	15c dk bl & bl grn	.25	.25
254	A54	25c yel grn & ultra	.25	.25
255	A56	40c dk bl & brn, perf. 12½	.25	.25
256	A55	45c black & rose	.50	.25
257	A57	1p dk Prus grn & dp bl	.60	.25

258	A58	2.50p dp org & gray	1.75	.65
259	A59	10p dk bl & gray	3.00	1.50
		Nos. 250-259 (10)	7.35	4.15
		Set, never hinged	15.00	

Control letter "Z" in circle in black on back. Exists imperf. Value, set $85.

A60

Sanitorium — A61

1946, Sept. 1   Perf. 11½x10½, 10½

260	A60	10c crim & bl grn	.25	.25
261	A61	25c crimson & brn	.25	.25
		Nos. 260-261,B14-B16 (5)	1.80	1.25

Issued to aid anti-tuberculosis work.

A62

A63

1947   Perf. 10

262	A62	10c carmine & blue	.25	.25
263	A63	25c red & chocolate	.25	.25
		Nos. 262-263,B17-B19 (5)	1.90	1.55

Issued to aid anti-tuberculosis work.

Commerce by Railroad A64

Commerce by Truck A65

Urban Market A66

Country Market A67

Caravan A68

Maritime Commerce A69

1948   Litho.   Perf. 10, 10x10½

264	A64	2c purple & brn	.25	.25
265	A65	5c dp cl & vio	.25	.25
266	A66	15c brt ultra & bl grn	.25	.25
267	A67	25c blk & Prus grn	.25	.25
268	A65	35c brt ultra & gray blk	.25	.25
269	A68	50c red & violet	.25	.25
270	A66	70c dk gray grn & ultra	.25	.25
271	A67	90c cer & dk gray grn	.25	.25
272	A68	1p brt ultra & vio	.60	.25
273	A64	2.50p vio brn & sl grn	1.50	.45
274	A69	10p blk & dp ultra	2.75	1.25
		Nos. 264-274 (11)	6.85	3.95
		Set, never hinged	11.00	

Exists imperf. Value, set $120.

Emblem of Tuberculosis Association — A70

Design: 25c, Plane over sanatorium.

1948, Oct. 1   Perf. 10

275	A70	10c car & green	.25	.25
276	A70	25c car & grnsh gray	1.75	.65
		Nos. 275-276,B20-B23 (6)	29.85	10.15

See No. B39.
Exists imperf. Value, set $75.

Emblem of Tuberculosis Association — A71

10c, Road of Health. 25c, Minaret and Palm.

1949

Black Control Number on Back

277	A71	5c car & green	.25	.25
278	A71	10c car & dk vio	.25	.25
279	A71	25c car & black	.90	.30
		Nos. 277-279,B25-B26 (5)	3.35	1.50

> **Catalogue values for unused stamps in this section, from this point to the end of the section, are for Never Hinged items.**

Mail Transport, 1890 — A72

Designs: 5c, 50c, 90c, Mail transport, 1890. 10c, 45c, 1p, Mail transport, 1906. 15c, 1.50p, Mail transport, 1913. 35c, 75c, 5p, Mail transport, 1914. 10p, Mail transport, 1918.

1950   Litho.   Perf. 10½

Black Control Number on Back

280	A72	5c choc & vio bl	.25	.25
281	A72	10c deep bl & sep	.25	.25
282	A72	15c grnsh blk & emer	.25	.25
283	A72	35c pur & gray blk	.25	.25
284	A72	45c dp car & rose lil	.25	.25

285	A72	50c emer & dk brn	.25	.25
286	A72	75c dk vio bl & bl	.25	.25
287	A72	90c grnsh blk & rose car	.25	.25
288	A72	1p blk brn & gray	.25	.25
289	A72	1.50p carmine & blue	1.00	.25
290	A72	5p black & vio brn	1.75	.25
291	A72	10p purple & blue	40.00	10.00
		Nos. 280-291,E11 (13)	77.50	22.75

UPU, 75th anniv. (in 1949).
Nos. 280-291 exist imperf. Value $500.

Herald — A73

Frame and Device in Carmine

1950   Unwmk.   Perf. 10
Black Control Number on Back

292	A73	5c gray black	.25	.25
293	A73	10c Old fort	.25	.25
294	A73	25c Sanatorium	1.00	.50
		Nos. 292-294,B27-B28 (5)	3.15	1.85

Boar Hunt A74

10c, 1p, Hunters and hounds. 50c, Boar hunt. 5p, Fishermen. 10p, Moorish fishing boat.

1950, Dec. 30   Perf. 10½x10
Black Control Number on Back

295	A74	5c dk brn & rose vio	.25	.25
296	A74	10c carmine & gray	.25	.25
297	A74	50c green & sepia	.25	.25
298	A74	1p bl vio & claret	.45	.25
299	A74	5p dp claret & bl vio	.70	.25
300	A74	10p grnsh blk & dp cl	2.25	.40
		Nos. 295-300 (6)	4.15	1.65

Nos. 295-300 exist imperf. Value, set $100.

Emblem — A75

10c, Patients expressing gratitude. 25c, Plane in the Clouds.

Dated "1951"
Frame and Device in Carmine
Black Control Number on Back

1951		Litho.	Perf. 12	
301	A75	5c green	.25	.25
302	A75	10c blue violet	.25	.25
303	A75	25c gray black	.85	.30
		Nos. 301-303,B29-B32 (7)	15.00	5.65

Issued to aid anti-tuberculosis work.

Armed Attack A76

Designs: 10c, Horses on parade. 15c, Holiday procession. 20c, Road to market. 25c, "Brother-hoods." 35c, "Offering." 45c, Soldiers. 50c, On the rooftop. 75c, Teahouse. 90c, Wedding. 1p, Pilgrimage. 5p, Storyteller. 10p, Market corner.

Black Control Number on Back

1952			Perf. 11	
304	A76	5c dk blue & brn	.25	.25
305	A76	10c dk brn & lil rose	.25	.25

306	A76	15c black & emer	.25	.25
307	A76	20c ol grn & red vio	.25	.25
308	A76	25c red & lt blue	.25	.25
309	A76	35c olive & orange	.25	.25
310	A76	45c red & rose red	.25	.25
311	A76	50c rose car & gray grn	.25	.25
312	A76	75c purple & ultra	.25	.25
313	A76	90c dk bl & rose vio	.25	.25
314	A76	1p dk bl & red brn	.25	.25
315	A76	5p red & blue	1.25	.25
316	A76	10p dk grn & gray blk	1.75	.40
		Nos. 304-316,E12 (14)	6.00	3.65

Nos. 304-316 exist imperf. Value, set $200.

Worship — A77

10c, Distributing alms. 25c, Prickly pear.

Black Control Number on Back

1952, Oct. 1   Dated "1952"

317	A77	5c car & dk ol grn	.25	.25
318	A77	10c car & dk brown	.25	.25
319	A77	25c car & dp blue	.35	.25
		Nos. 317-319,B33-B37 (8)	10.45	4.35

Nos. 317-319, B33-B37 exist imperf. Value, set of 8 $400.

Semi-Postal Types of 1948-49 Dated "1953"

1953   Litho.   Perf. 10

Black Control Number on Back

320	SP7	5c shown	.25	.25
321	SP9	10c like #B26	.25	.25
322	SP7	25c like #B23	.85	.35
		Nos. 320-322,B38-B42 (8)	18.45	6.50

Issued to aid anti-tuberculosis work.
Nos. 320-322, B38-B42 exist imperf. Value, set of 8 $200.

A78

1953, Nov. 15

Black Control Number on Back

323	A78	5c red	.25	.25
324	A78	10c gray green	.25	.25

Nos. 323-324 exist imperf. Value, set $100.

Mountain
Women — A79

50c and 2.50p, Water carrier. 90c and 2p, Mountaineers and donkey. 1p and 4.50p, Moorish women and child. 10p, Mounted dignitary.

1953, Dec. 15   Photo.

Black Control Number on Back

334	A79	35c grn & rose vio	.25	.25
335	A79	50c red & green	.25	.25
336	A79	90c dk bl & org	.25	.25
337	A79	1p dk brn & grn	.25	.25
338	A79	1.25p dk grn & car rose	.25	.25
339	A79	2p dk rose vio & bl	.25	.25
340	A79	2.50p black & orange	.85	.25
341	A79	4.50p brt car rose & dk grn	7.50	.35
342	A79	10p green & black	9.00	.65
		Nos. 334-342,E13 (10)	19.25	3.00

25th anniv. of Spanish Morocco's first definitive postage stamps.

Nos. 334-342, E13 exist imperf. Value, set of 10 $200.

Zauia — A80

10c, "The Family." 25c, Plane, Spanish coast.

1954, Nov. 1   Dated "1954"

Black Control Number on Back

343	A80	5c car & bl grn	.25	.25
344	A80	10c car & dk brn	.25	.25
345	A80	25c car & blue	.25	.25
		Nos. 343-345,B43-B45 (6)	8.55	4.90

Nos. 343-345, B43-B45 exist imperf. Value, set of 6 $300.

Queen's
Gate — A81

1955   Litho.   Perf. 11

Black Control Number on Back

Frames in Black

346	A81	15c shown	.25	.25
347	A81	25c Saida	.25	.25
348	A81	80c like #346	.25	.25
349	A81	1p like #347	.25	.25
350	A81	15p Ceuta	3.00	.65
		Nos. 346-350,E14 (6)	4.25	1.90

Honor Guard — A82

Designs: 25c, 80c, 3p, Caliph Moulay Hassan ben el-Medi. 30c, 1p, 5p, Caliph and procession. 15p, Coat of arms.

Perf. 13x12½

1955, Nov. 8   Photo.   Unwmk.

351	A82	15c ol brn & ol	.25	.25
352	A82	25c lil & dp rose	.25	.25
353	A82	30c brn blk & Prus grn	.25	.25
354	A82	70c Prus grn & yel grn	.25	.25
355	A82	80c ol & ol brn	.25	.25
356	A82	1p dk bl & redsh brn	.25	.25
357	A82	1.80p black & bl vio	.25	.25
358	A82	3p blue & gray	.25	.25
359	A82	5p dk grn & brn	1.25	.45

Engr.

360	A82	15p red brn & yel grn	2.75	1.65
		Nos. 351-360 (10)	6.00	4.10

30th anniv. of accession to throne by Caliph Moulay Hassan ben el-Medi ben Ismail.
Nos. 351-360 exist imperf. Value, set $750.
Succeeding issues, released under the Kingdom, are listed under Morocco.

SEMI-POSTAL STAMPS

Types of
Semi-Postal
Stamps of
Spain, 1926,
Ovptd. in
Black or Blue

1926   Unwmk.   Perf. 12½, 13

B1	SP1	1c orange	8.50	5.50
B2	SP2	2c rose	12.00	10.00
B3	SP3	5c black brn	4.50	3.50
B4	SP4	10c dark grn	4.50	3.50
B5	SP1	15c dk violet (Bl)	.80	.65
B6	SP4	20c violet brn	.80	.65
B7	SP5	25c deep carmine	.80	.65
B8	SP3	30c olive grn	.80	.65
B9	SP3	40c ultra	.25	.25
B10	SP2	50c red brown	.25	.25
B11	SP4	1p vermilion	.25	.25
B12	SP3	4p bister	.80	.65
B13	SP5	10p light violet	3.50	2.75
		Nos. B1-B13,EB1 (14)	40.50	31.65
		Set, never hinged	70.00	

See Spain No. B6a for No. B6 without overprint. For surcharges see Spain Nos. B64-B65.

Tuberculosis Fund Issues

SP1   SP2

SP3

Perf. 10½, 11½x10½

1946, Sept. 1   Litho.   Unwmk.

B14	SP1	25c + 5c crim & rose vio	.25	.25
B15	SP2	50c + 10c crim & blue	.30	.25
B16	SP3	90c + 10c crim & gray brn	.75	.25
		Nos. B14-B16 (3)	1.25	.65

Medical
Center — SP4   Nurse and
Children — SP5

"Protection" — SP6

1947   Perf. 10

B17	SP4	25c + 5c red & violet	.25	.25
B18	SP5	50c + 10c red & blue	.35	.25
B19	SP6	90c + 10c red & sepia	.80	.55
		Nos. B17-B19 (3)	1.35	.95

Herald — SP7

Designs: No. B21, Protection. No. B22, Sun bath. No. B23, Plane over Ben Karrich.

1948, Oct. 1

B20	SP7	50c + 10c car & dk vio	.35	.25
B21	SP7	90c + 10c car & dk gray	1.50	.50
B22	SP7	2.50p + 50c car & brn	10.00	3.25
B23	SP7	5p + 1p car & vio bl	16.00	5.25
		Nos. B20-B23 (4)	27.85	9.25

See Nos. 320, 322.

Moulay Hassan ben
el-Medi ben
Ismail — SP8

1949, May 15

B24	SP8	50c + 10c lilac rose	1.10	.45

Wedding of the Caliph at Tetuan, June 5.

Tuberculosis Fund Issues

Flag — SP9

Design: No. B26, Fight with dragon.

Black Control Numbers on Back

1949

B25	SP9	50c + 10 car & brown	.35	.30
B26	SP9	90c + 10 car & grnsh gray	1.60	.40

See No. 321.

> **Catalogue values for unused stamps in this section, from this point to the end of the section, are for Never Hinged items.**

Crowd at Fountain of
Life — SP10

90c+10c, Mohammedan hermit's tomb.

Black Control Numbers on Back

1950, Oct. 1   Litho.   Perf. 10

Frame and Cross in Carmine

B27	SP10	50 + 10c dk brown	.40	.30
B28	SP10	90 + 10c dk green	1.25	.55

Warrior — SP11

Designs: 90c+10c, Fort. 1p+5p, Port of Salvation. 1.10p+25c, Road to market.

Black Control Numbers on Back

1951	Unwmk.	Perf. 12	
B29	SP11	50c + 10c car & brn		
B30	SP11	90c + 10c car & bl	.25	.25
B31	SP11	1p + 5p car & gray	.40	.25
B32	SP11	1.10p + 25c car & gray	8.25	2.75
			4.75	1.60
	Nos. B29-B32 (4)		13.60	4.80

See No. B40.

Pilgrimage — SP12

Designs: 60c+25c, Palmettos. 90c+10c, Fort. 1.10p+25c, Agave. 5p+2p, Warrior.

Black Control Numbers on Back

1952			Perf. 11	
B33	SP12	50 + 10c car & gray	.25	.25
B34	SP12	60 + 25c car & dk grn	.80	.40
B35	SP12	90 + 10c car & vio brn	.80	.40
B36	SP12	1.10p + 25c car & pur	2.25	.80
B37	SP12	5p + 2p car & gray	5.50	1.75
	Nos. B33-B37 (5)		9.55	3.55

Armed Horseman in Action — SP13

#B39, As #276. #B42, Plane & clouds.

Black Control Numbers on Back

1953			Perf. 10	
B38	SP13	50c + 10c car & vio	.30	.25
B39	A70	60c + 25c car & brn	2.50	.80
B40	SP11	90c + 10c car & blk	.80	.35
B41	SP13	1.10p + 25c car & vio brn	4.00	1.25
B42	A73	5p + 2p car & bl	9.50	3.00
	Nos. B38-B42 (5)		17.10	5.60

Stork — SP14

50c+10c, Father & Child. 5p+2p, Tomb.

Black Control Numbers on Back

1954		Photo.	
B43	SP14	5c + 5c car & rose vio	.25	.25
B44	SP14	50c + 10c car & gray grn	.80	.40
B45	SP14	5p + 2p car & gray	6.75	3.50
	Nos. B43-B45 (3)		7.75	4.10

AIR POST STAMPS

Mosque de Baja and Plane — AP1

View of Tetuán and Plane AP2

10c, Stork of Alcazar. 25c, Shore scene, plane. 40c, Desert tribesmen watching plane. 75c, View of shoreline at Larache. 1p, Arab mailman, plane above. 1.50p, Arab farmers, stork. 2p, Plane at twilight. 3p, Shadow of plane over city.

1938		Unwmk. Photo.	Perf. 13½	
C1	AP1	5c red brown	.25	.25
C2	AP1	10c emerald	.25	.25
C3	AP1	25c crimson	.25	.25
C4	AP1	40c dull blue	2.00	.50
C5	AP2	50c cerise	.25	.25
C6	AP2	75c ultra	.25	.25
C7	AP1	1p dark brown	.25	.25
C8	AP1	1.50p purple	.65	.35
C9	AP1	2p brown lake	.40	.25
C10	AP1	3p gray black	1.75	.25
	Nos. C1-C10 (10)		6.30	2.85
	Set, Never Hinged		11.00	

Nos. C1-C10 exist imperf. Value of set, $100. For surcharge see No. C32.

Landscape, Ketama — AP3

Mosque, Tangier — AP4

Velez — AP5

Sanjurjo — AP6

Strait of Gibraltar — AP7

1942			Perf. 12½	
C11	AP3	5c deep blue	.25	.25
C12	AP4	10c orange brn	.25	.25
C13	AP5	15c grnsh black	.25	.25

C14	AP6	90c dark rose	.25	.25
C15	AP7	5p black	1.50	.85
	Nos. C11-C15 (5)		2.50	1.85
	Set, never hinged		3.25	

Exist imperf. Value, set $55.

Strait of Gibraltar — AP8

Designs: 5c, 1.75p, Strait of Gibraltar. 10c, 3p, Market day. 30c, 4p, Kebira Fortress. 6.50p, Airmail arrival. 8p, Horseman.

1949		Litho.	Perf. 10	
C16	AP8	5c vio brn & brt grn	.25	.25
C17	AP8	10c blk & rose lilac	.25	.25
C18	AP8	30c dk vio bl & grnsh gray	.25	.25
C19	AP8	1.75p car & bl vio	.25	.25
C20	AP8	3p dk blue & gray	.25	.25
C21	AP8	4p grnsh blk & car rose	.30	.25
C22	AP8	6.50p brt grn & brn	.95	.25
C23	AP8	8p rose lil & bl vio	1.60	.40
	Nos. C16-C23 (8)		4.10	2.15
	Set, never hinged		5.50	

Exist imperf. Value, set $80.

> **Catalogue values for unused stamps in this section, from this point to the end of the section, are for Never Hinged items.**

Road to Tetuan — AP9

Designs: 4p, Arrival of mail from Spain. 8p, Greeting plane. 16p, Shadow of plane.

1952			Perf. 11	
	Black Frames and Inscriptions			
	Black Control Numbers on Back			
C24	AP9	2p brt blue	.25	.25
C25	AP9	4p scarlet	.30	.25
C26	AP9	8p dk olive green	.45	.25
C27	AP9	16p violet brown	2.25	.95
	Nos. C24-C27 (4)		3.25	1.70

Part of the proceeds was used toward the establishment of a postal museum at Tetuan.

Plane over Boat — AP10

Designs: 60c, Mosques, Sidi Saidi. 1.10p, Plowing. 4.50p, Fortress, Xauen.

1953			Perf. 10	
C28	AP10	35c dp bl & car rose	.25	.25
C29	AP10	60c dk car & sl grn	.25	.25
C30	AP10	1.10p dp blue & blk	.30	.25
C31	AP10	4.50p dk car & dk brn	1.25	.40
	Nos. C28-C31 (4)		2.05	1.15

Exist imperf. Value, set $125.

No. C6 Surcharged in Black

Type I

Type II

1953			Perf. 13½	
C32	AP2	50c on 75c ultra (I)	.50	.25
a.		50c on 75c ultra (II)	.50	.25
b.		Vert. gutter pair, types I and II	2.75	

Sheets of 2 panes, 25 stamps each, with gutter between. Upper pane surcharged type I, lower type II.

AIR POST SEMI-POSTAL STAMPS

No. 150 Surcharged in Black

1936		Unwmk.	Perf. 14	
CB1	A12	25c + 2p on 25c	14.00	5.75
		Never hinged	50.00	
a.		Bars at right omitted	57.50	42.50
b.		Blue surcharge	45.00	15.00

25c was for postage, 2p for air post.

Nos. C1-C10 surcharged "Lucha Antituberculosa," a Lorraine cross and surtax are stated to be bogus.

Crowd at Palace — SPAP1

1949, May 15		Unwmk.	Perf. 10	
CB2	SPAP1	1p + 10c gray black	.75	.35

Wedding of the Caliph at Tetuan, June 5.

SPECIAL DELIVERY STAMPS

Special Delivery Stamp of Spain Overprinted in Blue

1914		Unwmk.	Perf. 14	
E1	SD1	20c red	5.75	2.60

Special Delivery Stamp of Spain Overprinted in Blue

1915				
E2	SD1	20c red	3.00	1.60

For bisected surcharge see No. 68.

Special Delivery Stamp of Spain Overprinted in Blue

1923
E3 SD1 20c red   12.00 9.75

Mounted Courier SD2

1928   **Engr.**   **Perf. 14, 14½**
E4 SD2 20c black   5.00 1.60

For surcharge see No. 168.

Moorish Postman — SD3

1935   **Photo.**   **Perf. 14**
Green Control Number on Back
E5 SD3 20c vermilion   1.15 .25

See No. E9.

Mounted Courier — SD4

1937   **Perf. 13½**
E6 SD4 20c bright carmine   .25 .25

1st Year of the Spanish Civil War.
For surcharge see No. E10.

Spain No. E14 Overprinted in Black

1938   **Perf. 10**
E7 SD7 20c vermilion   1.50 .25

Arab Postman — SD5

1940   **Photo.**   **Perf. 11½x11**
E8 SD5 25c scarlet   .85 .35

"ZONA" printed on back in black.

Type of 1935

1940   **Litho.**   **Perf. 10**
E9 SD3 20c black brown   2.60

No. E9 was prepared but not issued.
Exists imperf. Value, $10.

No. E6 Surcharged with New Value, Bars and

1940   **Perf. 13½**
E10 SD4 25c on 20c brt car   12.00 9.50

4th anniversary of Spanish Civil War.

> **Catalogue values for unused stamps in this section, from this point to the end of the section, are for Never Hinged items.**

Airmail 1935 — SD6

1950   **Unwmk.**   **Litho.**   **Perf. 10½**
E11 SD6 25c carmine & gray   32.50 10.00

UPU, 75th anniv. (in 1949).

Moorish Postrider SD7

1952   **Perf. 11**
Black Control Number on Back
E12 SD7 25c car & rose car   .25 .25

Rider with Special Delivery Mail — SD8

1953   **Photo.**   **Perf. 10**
Black Control Number on Back
E13 SD8 25c dk bl & car rose   .40 .25

25th anniv. of Spanish Morocco's first definitive postage stamps.

Gate of Tangier — SD9

1955   **Litho.**   **Perf. 11**
Black Control Number on Back
E14 SD9 2p violet & black   .25 .25

SEMI-POSTAL SPECIAL DELIVERY STAMP

Type of Semi-Postal Special Delivery Stamp of Spain, 1926, Overprinted like #B1-B13

1926   **Unwmk.**   **Perf. 12½, 13**
EB1 SPSD1 20c ultra & black   2.75 2.40

POSTAL TAX STAMPS

General Francisco Franco — PT1

1937-39 Unwmk. Photo.   **Perf. 12½**
RA1 PT1 10c sepia   .50 .25
 a.   Sheet of 4, imperf.   4.50 1.75
RA2 PT1 10c copper brn ('38)   .50 .25
 a.   Sheet of 4, imperf.   4.50 1.75
RA3 PT1 10c blue ('39)   .50 .25
 a.   Sheet of 4, imperf.   4.50 1.75
  Nos. RA1-RA3 (3)   1.50 .75
Set, never hinged   3.50
Set, RA1a-RA3a   13.50

The tax was used for the disabled soldiers in North Africa.

Soldiers PT2

1941   **Litho.**   **Perf. 13½**
RA4 PT2 10c brt grn   4.00 .25
RA5 PT2 10c rose pink   4.00 .25
RA6 PT2 10c henna brn   4.00 .25
RA7 PT2 10c ultra   4.00 .25
  Nos. RA4-RA7 (4)   16.00 1.00
Set, never hinged   25.00

The tax was used for the disabled soldiers in North Africa.
Exist imperf. Value, set $60.

General Francisco Franco — PT3

1943   **Photo.**   **Perf. 10**
RA8 PT3 10c chalky blue   9.00 .25
RA9 PT3 10c slate blue   9.00 .25
RA10 PT3 10c dl gray brn   9.00 .25
RA11 PT3 10c blue violet   9.00 .25
  Nos. RA8-RA11 (4)   36.00 1.00
Set, never hinged   52.50

Exists imperf. Value, set $125.

1944   **Perf. 12**
RA12 PT3 10c dp mag & brn   6.00 .25
RA13 PT3 10c dp org & dk grn   6.00 .25
Set, never hinged   16.00

Exists imperf. Value, set $45.00.

1946   **Litho.**
RA14 PT3 10c ultra & brown   6.75 .25
RA15 PT3 10c gray blk & rose lil   6.75 .25
Set, never hinged   17.50

Exists imperf. Value, set $100.

TANGIER

For the International City of Tangier
Seville-Barcelona Issue of Spain, 1929, Ovptd. in Blue or Red

1929   **Perf. 11**
L1 A52 5c rose lake   .30 .30
L2 A53 10c green (R)   .30 .30
L3 A50 15c Prus blue (R)   .30 .30
L4 A51 20c purple (R)   .30 .30
L5 A50 25c brt rose   .30 .30
L6 A52 30c black brn   .30 .30
L7 A53 40c dk blue (R)   .75 .75
L8 A51 50c deep org   .75 .75
L9 A52 1p blue blk (R)   7.75 7.75
L10 A53 4p deep rose   21.00 21.00
L11 A53 10p brown   30.00 30.00
  Nos. L1-L11 (11)   62.05 62.05
Set, never hinged   105.00

> **Overprints of 1937-39**
> The following overprints on stamps of Spain exist in black or in red:
> "TANGER" vertically on Nos. 517-518, 522-523, 528, 532, 534, 539-543, 549.
> "Correo Espanol Tanger" horizontally or vertically in three lines on Nos. 540, 592-597 (gray paper), 598-601.
> "Tanger" horizontally on Nos. 539-541, 592-601.
> "Correo Tanger" horizontally in two lines on five consular stamps.

Woman — A1

Man — A3

Palm Tree — A2

Old map of Tangier — A4

Tangier Street — A5

Moroccan Women — A6

Head of Moor — A7

Perf. 9½x10½, 12½x13 (1c, 2c, 10c, 20c)

1948-51   **Photo.**   **Unwmk.**
L12 A1 1c blue grn ('51)   .25 .25
L13 A1 2c red org ('51)   .25 .25

Engr.
L14 A2 5c vio brn ('49)   .25 .25
L15 A3 10c deep blue ('51)   .25 .25
L16 A3 20c gray ('51)   .25 .25
L17 A2 25c green ('51)   .25 .25
L18 A4 30c dk slate grn   .35 .25

L19	A5	45c car rose	.35	.25
L20	A6	50c dp claret	.35	.25
L21	A7	75c deep blue	.70	.25
L22	A7	90c green	.60	.25
L23	A4	1.35p org ver	2.10	.35
L24	A6	2p purple	3.75	.35
L25	A5	10p dk grnsh bl ('49)	4.25	.65
		Nos. L12-L25,LE1 (15)	14.80	4.45
		Set, never hinged	25.00	

Nos. L18-L25, LE1 exist imperf. Value, set $400.

TANGIER SEMI-POSTAL STAMPS

Types of
Semi-Postal
Stamps of
Spain, 1926,
Overprinted

1926			*Perf. 12½, 13*	
LB1	SP1	1c orange	7.50	8.00
LB2	SP2	2c rose	7.50	8.00
LB3	SP3	5c black brn	3.75	3.75
LB4	SP4	10c dk green	3.75	3.75
LB5	SP4	15c dk violet	1.25	1.60
LB6	SP4	20c violet brn	1.25	1.60
LB7	SP5	25c dp carmine	1.25	1.60
LB8	SP3	30c olive grn	1.25	1.60
LB9	SP3	40c ultra	.35	.35
LB10	SP2	50c red brn	.35	.35
LB11	SP4	1p vermilion	.75	.75
LB12	SP3	4p bister	.75	.75
LB13	SP5	10p lt violet	3.25	3.25
		Nos. LB1-LB13,LEB1 (14)	35.95	38.35
		Set, never hinged	65.00	

For overprints & surcharges see Spain Nos. B66-B67.

TANGIER AIR POST STAMPS

Overprints of 1939
The following overprints on stamps of Spain exist in black or in red:
"Correo Aereo Tanger" in two lines on Nos. 539-541, 596 (gray paper), 600, C72B.
"Via Aerea Tanger" in three lines on Nos. 539-540, 592-597 (gray paper), 599, 601, E14.
"Correo Aereo Tanger" in three lines on four consular stamps.
"Correo Espanol Tanger" in three lines on No. C72B.
"Tanger" on No. C72B.

Plane over
Shore — AP1

Twin-Engine
Plane — AP2

Passenger Plane
in Flight — AP3

		Perf. 11x11½, 11½		
1949-50		**Engr.**		**Unwmk.**
LC1	AP1	20c violet brn ('50)	.25	.25
LC2	AP2	25c bright red	.25	.25
LC3	AP3	35c dull green	.25	.25
LC4	AP1	1p violet ('50)	.80	.25
LC5	AP2	2p deep blue	1.50	.25
LC6	AP3	10p brown violet	2.75	1.00
		Nos. LC1-LC6 (6)	5.80	2.25
		Set, never hinged	9.50	

Nos. LC1, LC4-LC6 exist imperf. Value $100 each.

TANGIER SPECIAL DELIVERY STAMP

Arab
Postrider — SD1

1949	**Unwmk.**	**Engr.**	**Perf. 13**	
LE1	SD1	25c red	.85	.35
		Never hinged	1.40	

TANGIER SEMI-POSTAL SPECIAL DELIVERY STAMP

Types of Semi-Postal Special Delivery Stamp of Spain, 1926, Overprinted like #LB1-LB13

1926		**Unwmk.**	**Perf. 12½, 13**	
LEB1	SPSD1	20c ultra & black	3.00	3.00
		Never hinged	5.00	

TETUAN

Stamps of Spanish
Offices in Morocco,
1903-09, Handstamped
in Black, Blue or Violet

1908		**Unwmk.**	**Imperf.**	
1	A21	¼c blue green	13.00	10.00
		Perf. 14		
2	A35	2c bister brown	175.00	60.00
3	A35	5c green	165.00	35.00
4	A35	10c rose red	165.00	35.00
5	A35	20c grnsh black	325.00	125.00
6	A35	25c blue	125.00	35.00
		Nos. 1-6 (6)	968.00	300.00

Same Handstamp On Stamps of Spain, 1876 and 1900-05, in Black, Blue or Violet

1908			**Imperf.**	
7	A21	¼c deep green	7.50	3.25
		Perf. 14		
8	A35	2c bister brn	55.00	13.00
9	A35	5c dark green	70.00	22.50
10	A35	10c rose red	77.50	22.50
11	A35	15c purple	77.50	25.00
12	A35	20c grnsh black	175.00	110.00
13	A35	25c blue	95.00	35.00
14	A35	30c blue green	200.00	60.00
15	A35	40c olive bister	250.00	110.00
		Nos. 7-15 (9)	1,007.	401.25

Counterfeits of this overprint are plentiful.

SPANISH SAHARA

'spa-nish sə-'har-ə

(Spanish Western Sahara)

LOCATION — Northwest Africa, bordering on the Atlantic Ocean.
GOVT. — Spanish possession
AREA — 102,703 sq. mi.
POP. — 76,425 (1970)
CAPITAL — Aaiún

Spanish Sahara was a subdivision of Spanish West Africa. It included the colony of Rio de Oro and the territory of Saguiet el Hamra. Spanish Sahara was formerly known as Spanish Western Sahara, which superseded the older title of Rio de Oro.

In 1976, Spanish Sahara was divided between Morocco and Mauritania.

100 Centimos = 1 Peseta

> **Catalogue values for unused stamps in this country are for Never Hinged items, beginning with Scott 51 in the regular postage section, Scott B13 in the semipostal section, Scott C8 in the airpost section, and Scott E1 in the special delivery section.**

Tuareg and
Camel — A1

1924		**Unwmk.**	**Typo.**	**Perf. 13**
		Control Number on Back		
1	A1	5c blue green	3.00	.90
2	A1	10c gray green	3.00	.90
3	A1	15c turq blue	3.00	.90
4	A1	20c dark violet	3.00	1.25
5	A1	25c red	3.00	1.25
6	A1	30c red brown	3.00	1.25
7	A1	40c dark blue	3.00	1.25
8	A1	50c orange	3.00	1.25
9	A1	60c violet	3.00	1.25
10	A1	1p rose	16.00	6.50
11	A1	4p chocolate	70.00	33.00
12	A1	10p claret	170.00	105.00
		Nos. 1-12 (12)	283.00	154.70
		Set, never hinged	450.00	

Nos. 1-12 were for use in La Aguera & Rio de Oro.
An unissued set of 10, similar to Nos. 3-12, exists perf. 10 or imperf, and no control number except on 50c. The set also exists perf 14. Value, $200.
Nos. 1-12 also exist perf 14. Value, unused $300.
For overprints see Nos. 24-35.

Seville-Barcelona
Issue of Spain,
1929 Overprinted
in Blue or Red

1929			**Perf. 11**	
13	A52	5c rose lake	.30	.30
14	A53	10c green (R)	.30	.30
15	A50	15c Prus blue (R)	.30	.30
16	A51	20c purple (R)	.40	.30
17	A50	25c bright rose	.40	.30
18	A52	30c black brown	.40	.30
19	A53	40c dark blue (R)	.90	.45
20	A53	50c deep orange	.90	.45
21	A52	1p blue black (R)	3.50	1.90
22	A53	4p deep rose	27.50	17.50
23	A53	10p brown	52.50	35.00
		Nos. 13-23 (11)	87.40	57.10
		Set, never hinged	125.00	

Stamps of 1924
Overprinted in Red or
Blue

1931			**Perf. 13**	
24	A1	5c blue grn (R)	.95	.65
25	A1	10c gray grn (R)	.95	.65
26	A1	15c turq blue (R)	.95	.65
27	A1	20c dark violet (R)	.95	.65
28	A1	25c red	.95	.65
29	A1	30c red brown	.95	.65
30	A1	40c dark blue (R)	4.50	.90
31	A1	50c orange	4.50	2.25
32	A1	60c violet	4.50	2.25
33	A1	1p rose	4.50	2.25
34	A1	4p chocolate	45.00	22.00
35	A1	10p claret	92.50	50.00
		Nos. 24-35 (12)	161.20	83.55
		Set, never hinged	240.00	

The stamps of the 1931 issue exist with the overprint reading upward, downward, or horizontally. Some values also exist with double overprint, double overprint, one inverted and diagonal overprint.

Stamps of Spain,
1936-40, Overprinted
in Carmine or Blue

1941-46		**Unwmk.**	**Imperf.**	
36	A159	1c green	2.25	1.50
		Perf. 10 to 11		
37	A160	2c org brn (Bl)	2.25	1.50
38	A161	5c gray brown	.70	.45
39	A161	10c dk car (Bl)	2.25	1.50
40	A161	15c dark green	.70	.45
41	A166	20c bright violet	.70	.45
42	A166	25c deep claret	1.75	.90
43	A166	30c light blue	1.75	1.10
44	A166	40c Prus grn	.70	.45
45	A166	50c indigo	20.00	1.50
46	A166	70c blue	13.50	1.90
47	A166	1p gray black	26.50	2.75
48	A166	2p dull brown	150.00	75.00
49	A166	4p dull rose (Bl)	425.00	225.00
50	A166	10p lt brown	1,250.	325.00
		Nos. 36-50 (15)	1,898.	639.20
		Set, never hinged	3,000.	

The stamps of this issue are normally poorly centered and are valued thus.
Counterfeit overprints exist.

> **Catalogue values for unused stamps in this section, from this point to the end of the section, are for Never Hinged items.**

Dorcas
Gazelles — A2

Designs: 2c, 20c, 45c, 3p, Caravan. 5c, 75c, 10p, Camel troops.

1943		**Unwmk.**	**Perf. 12½**	
51	A2	1c brown & lil rose	.35	.30
52	A2	2c yel grn & sl bl	.35	.30
53	A2	5c magenta & vio	.40	.30
54	A2	15c slate grn & grn	.40	.30
55	A2	20c violet & red brn	.45	.30
56	A2	40c rose vio & vio	.45	.30
57	A2	45c brn vio & red	.60	.35
58	A2	75c indigo & blue	.60	.35
59	A2	1p red & brown	2.00	1.25
60	A2	3p bl vio & sl grn	4.50	2.00
61	A2	10p black brn & blk	80.00	32.50
		Nos. 51-61,E1 (12)	91.85	39.20

Nos. 51-61, El exist imperf. Value for set, $150.

Gen.
Franco and
Desert
Scene
A5

1951		**Photo.**	**Perf. 12½x13**	
62	A5	50c deep orange	.25	.25
63	A5	1p chocolate	.35	.30
64	A5	5p blue green	30.00	12.00
		Nos. 62-64 (3)	30.60	12.55

Visit of Gen. Francisco Franco, 1950.

Allegorical Figure
and Globe — A6

1953, Mar. 2   **Perf. 13x12½**
65	A6	5c red orange	.25	.25
66	A6	35c dk slate green	.25	.25
67	A6	60c brown	.35	.25
		Nos. 65-67 (3)	.85	.75

75th anniv. of the founding of the Royal Geographical Society.

Woman Musician — A7

Design: 60c, Man musician.

1953, June 1
68	A7	15c olive gray	.25	.25
69	A7	60c brown	.25	.25
		Nos. 68-69,B25-B26 (4)	1.00	1.00

Orange Scorpionfish — A8

Fish: 60c, Banded sargo.

1953, Nov. 23   **Perf. 12½x13**
70	A8	15c dk olive green	.25	.25
71	A8	60c orange	.40	.25
		Nos. 70-71,B27-B28 (4)	1.15	1.00

Colonial Stamp Day.

Hurdlers A9

Runner — A10

1954, June 1   **Perf. 12½x13, 13x12½**
72	A9	15c gray green	.25	.25
73	A10	60c brown	.30	.25
		Nos. 72-73,B29-B30 (4)	1.05	1.00

Atlantic Flyingfish A11

1954, Nov. 23   **Perf. 12½x13**
74	A11	15c shown	.25	.25
75	A11	60c Gilthead	.40	.25
		Nos. 74-75,B31-B32 (4)	1.15	1.00

Colonial Stamp Day.

Emilio Bonelli A12

1955, June 1   **Photo.**   **Unwmk.**
76	A12	50c olive gray	.25	.25
		Nos. 76,B33-B34 (3)	.75	.75

Birth cent. of Emilio Bonelli, explorer.

Scimitar-horned Oryx — A13

1955, Nov. 23
77	A13	70c green	.25	.25
		Nos. 77,B35-B36 (3)	.75	.75

Colonial Stamp Day.

Antirrhinum Romosissimum A14

Design: 50c, Sesiviun portulacastrum.

1956, June 1   **Perf. 13x12½**
78	A14	20c bluish green	.25	.25
79	A14	60c brown	.35	.25
		Nos. 78-79,B37-B38 (4)	1.10	1.00

Arms of Aaiun and Camel Rider A15

1956, Nov. 23   **Perf. 12½x13**
80	A15	70c olive grn & sepia	.25	.25
		Nos. 80,B39-B40 (3)	.75	.75

Colonial Stamp Day.

Dromedaries — A16

15c, 80c, Ostrich. 50c, 1.80p, Mountain gazelle.

1957, Apr. 10   **Perf. 13x12½**
81	A16	5c purple	.25	.25
82	A16	15c bister	.25	.25
83	A16	50c dark olive	.25	.25
84	A16	70c yellow green	.70	.25
85	A16	80c blue green	.75	.25
86	A16	1.80p lilac rose	.75	.25
		Nos. 81-86 (6)	2.95	1.50

Golden Eagle — A17

1957, June 1   **Photo.**   **Unwmk.**
87	A17	70c dark green	.25	.25
		Nos. 87,B41-B42 (3)	.75	.75

Striped Hyena — A18

Design: 70c, Striped Hyena, horiz.

Perf. 13x12½, 12½x13

1957, Nov. 23
88	A18	20c slate green	.25	.25
89	A18	70c yellowish green	.25	.25
		Nos. 88-89,B43-B44 (4)	1.00	1.00

Stamp Day.

Don Quixote and the Lion A19

Cervantes — A20

1958, June 1   **Perf. 12½x13, 13x12½**
90	A19	20c bister brn & grn	.25	.25
91	A20	70c dk grn & yel grn	.30	.25
		Nos. 90-91,B48-B49 (4)	1.05	1.00

Cervantes Type of 1958

Designs: 20c, Actor as "Peribanez," by Lope de Vega. 70c, Lope de Vega.

1959, June   **Photo.**   **Perf. 13x12½**
92	A20	20c lt green & brn	.25	.25
93	A20	70c yel grn & slate grn	.30	.25
		Nos. 92-93,B53-B54 (4)	1.05	1.00

Promoting child welfare.

Gray Heron — A21

Birds: 50c, 1.50p, 5p, Sparrowhawk. 75c, 2p, 10p, Sea gull.

1959, Oct. 15   **Perf. 13x12½**
94	A21	25c dull violet	.25	.25
95	A21	50c dark olive	.25	.25
96	A21	75c dark brown	.25	.25
97	A21	1p red orange	.30	.25
98	A21	1.50p brt green	.35	.25
99	A21	2p brt red lilac	1.00	.30
100	A21	3p blue	1.05	.30
101	A21	5p red brown	1.90	.35
102	A21	10p olive green	11.00	4.75
		Nos. 94-102 (9)	16.35	6.95

Scene from "The Pilferer Don Pablos" by Quevedo — A22

Francisco Gomez de Quevedo A23

1960, June   **Perf. 13x12½, 12½x13**
103	A22	35c slate green	.25	.25
104	A23	80c Prussian green	.25	.25
		Nos. 103-104,B58-B59 (4)	1.00	1.00

Francisco Gomez de Quevedo, writer.

Houbara Bustard — A24

Design: 50c, 1p, 2p, 5p, Doves.

1961, Apr. 18   **Photo.**   **Perf. 13x12½**
105	A24	25c blue violet	.25	.25
106	A24	50c olive gray	.25	.25
107	A24	75c brown violet	.25	.25
108	A24	1p orange ver	.25	.25
109	A24	1.50p blue green	.25	.25
110	A24	2p magenta	.80	.25
111	A24	3p dark blue	.95	.25
112	A24	5p red brown	1.10	.35
113	A24	10p olive	3.00	1.50
		Nos. 105-113 (9)	7.10	3.60

Map of Spanish Sahara — A25

Gen. Franco and Camel Rider A26

Design: 70c, Chapel of Aaiun.

1961, Oct. 1   **Perf. 13x12½, 12½x13**
114	A25	25c gray violet	.25	.25
115	A26	50c olive brown	.25	.25
116	A25	70c brt green	.25	.25
117	A26	1p red orange	.25	.25
		Nos. 114-117 (4)	1.00	1.00

25th anniv. of the nomination of Gen. Francisco Franco as Chief of State.

Neurada Procumbres — A27

50c, 1.50p, 10p, Anabasis articulata, flower. 70c, 2p, Euphorbia resinifera, cactus.

1962, Feb. 26   **Perf. 13x12½**
118	A27	25c black violet	.25	.25
119	A27	50c dark brown	.25	.25
120	A27	70c brt green	.25	.25
121	A27	1p orange ver	.30	.25
122	A27	1.50p blue green	.40	.25
123	A27	2p red lilac	1.25	.25
124	A27	3p slate	2.00	.30
125	A27	10p olive	4.75	1.50
		Nos. 118-125 (8)	9.45	3.30

Clock Fish — A28

Design: 50c, Avia fish, horiz.

Perf. 13x12½, 12½x13

1962, July 10   **Photo.**
126   A28   25c violet black   .25   .25
127   A28   50c dark green   .25   .25
128   A28   1p orange brown   .30   .25
      Nos. 126-128 (3)   .80   .75

Goats
A29

Stamp Day: 35c, Sheep.

1962, Nov. 23   **Perf. 12½x13**
129   A29   15c yellow green   .25   .25
130   A29   35c magenta   .25   .25
131   A29   1p orange brown   .25   .25
      Nos. 129-131 (3)   .75   .75

Seville Cathedral
Tower — A30

1963, Jan. 29   **Perf. 13x12½**
132   A30   50c olive   .25   .25
133   A30   1p brown orange   .25   .25
      Issued to help Seville flood victims.

Camel Riders — A31

Design: 50c, Tuareg and camel.

1963, June 1   **Unwmk.**
134   A31   25c deep violet   .25   .25
135   A31   50c gray   .25   .25
136   A31   1p orange red   .25   .25
      Nos. 134-136 (3)   .75   .75
      Issued for child welfare.

Hands Releasing
Dove and
Arms — A32

1963, July 12
137   A32   50c Prussian green   .25   .25
138   A32   1p orange brown   .25   .25
      Issued for Barcelona flood relief.

John Dory
A33

Fish: 50c, Plain bonito, vert.

Perf. 12½x13, 13x12½

1964, Mar. 6   **Photo.**
139   A33   25c purple   .25   .25
140   A33   50c olive green   .25   .25
141   A33   1p brown red   .45   .25
      Nos. 139-141 (3)   .95   .75
      Issued for Stamp Day 1963.

Moth and
Flowers
A34

Design: 50c, Two moths, vert.

Perf. 12½x13, 13x12½

1964, June 1   **Unwmk.**
142   A34   25c dull violet   .25   .25
143   A34   50c brown black   .25   .25
144   A34   1p orange red   .45   .25
      Nos. 142-144 (3)   .95   .75
      Issued for child welfare.

Camel Rider and
Microphone — A35

Designs: 50c, 1.50p, 3p, Boy with flute and
camels. 70c, 2p, 10p, Woman with drum.

1964, Sept.   Photo.   Perf. 13x12½
145   A35   25c dull purple   .25   .25
146   A35   50c olive   .25   .25
147   A35   70c green   .25   .25
148   A35   1p dull red brn   .30   .25
149   A35   1.50p bright green   .30   .25
150   A35   2p Prus green   .35   .30
151   A35   3p dark blue   .40   .30
152   A35   10p carmine lake   1.50   .70
      Nos. 145-152 (8)   3.60 2.55

Squirrel — A36

Stamp Day: 1p, Squirrel's head, horiz.

1964, Nov. 23   **Unwmk.**
153   A36   50c olive gray   .25   .25
154   A36   1p brown carmine   .25   .25
155   A36   1.50p green   .25   .25
      Nos. 153-155 (3)   .75   .75

Tuareg
Girl — A37   Wellhead and
                   Camel
                   Rider — A38

25 Years of Peace: 1p, Physician examining
patient, horiz.

Perf. 13x12½, 12½x13

1965, Feb. 22   **Photo.**
156   A37   50c black brown   .25   .25
157   A38   1p dark red   .25   .25
158   A38   1.50p deep blue   .25   .25
      Nos. 156-158 (3)   .75   .75

Anthia Sexmaculata — A39

1p, 3p, Blepharopsis mendica, vert.

Perf. 12½x13, 13x12½

1965, June 1   Photo.   Unwmk.
159   A39   50c slate blue   .25   .25
160   A39   1p blue green   .30   .25
161   A39   1.50p brown   .35   .30
162   A39   3p dark blue   1.40   .60
      Nos. 159-162 (4)   2.30 1.40
      Issued for child welfare.

Basketball   Arms and
A40   Camels
                      A41

1965, Nov. 23   **Perf. 13x12½**
163   A40   50c rose claret   .25   .25
164   A41   1p deep magenta   .25   .25
165   A40   1.50p slate blue   .25   .25
      Nos. 163-165 (3)   .75   .75
      Issued for Stamp Day.

Ship "Rio
de Oro"
A42

Design: 1.50p, S.S. Fuerte Ventura.

1966, June 1   Photo.   Perf. 12½x13
166   A42   50c olive   .25   .25
167   A42   1p dark red brown   .25   .25
168   A42   1.50p blue green   .30   .25
      Nos. 166-168 (3)   .80   .75
      Issued for child welfare.

Ocean
Sunfish — A43

Designs: 10c, 1.50p, Bigeye tuna, horiz.

1966, Nov. 23   Photo.   Perf. 13
169   A43   10c bl gray & cit   .25   .25
170   A43   40c slate & pink   .25   .25
171   A43   1.50p brown & olive   .30   .25
172   A43   4p rose vio & gray   .45   .25
      Nos. 169-172 (4)   1.25 1.00
      Issued for Stamp Day.

A44

Designs: 40c, 4p, Flower and leaves.

1967, June 1   Photo.   Perf. 13
173   A44   10c blk, ocher & gray
                   grn   .25   .25
174   A44   40c emerald & lilac   .25   .25
175   A44   1.50p dk grn & yel grn .25   .25
176   A44   4p brt blue & org   .30   .25
      Nos. 173-176 (4)   1.05 1.00
      Issued for child welfare.

Aaiun
Harbor
A45

Design: 4p, Villa Cisneros Harbor.

1967, Sept. 28 Photo. Perf. 12½x13
177   A45   1.50p brt bl & red brn   .25   .25
178   A45   4p brt bl & bis brn   .25   .25
      Modernization of harbor installations.

Ruddy
Sheldrake
A46

Stamp Day: 1.50p, Flamingo, vert. 3.50p,
Rufous bush robin.

1967, Nov. 23   Photo.   Perf. 13
179   A46   1p bister brn & grn   .25   .25
180   A46   1.50p brt rose & gray   .30   .25
181   A46   3.50p brn red & sep   .45   .25
      Nos. 179-181 (3)   1.00   .75

Zodiac Issue

Scorpio — A47

1.50p, Aries. 2.50p, Virgo.

1968, Apr. 25   Photo.   Perf. 13
182   A47   1p brt mag, *lt yel*   .25   .25
183   A47   1.50p brown, *pink*   .25   .25
184   A47   2.50p dk vio, *yel*   .40   .25
      Nos. 182-184 (3)   .90   .75
      Issued for child welfare.

Mailman — A48

Stamp Day: 1p, Post horn, pigeon, letter and
Spain No. 1. 1.50p, Letter, canceller and various stamps of Spain and Ifni.

1968, Nov.   Photo.   Perf. 13x12½
185   A48   1p dp lil rose & dk bl .25   .25
186   A48   1.50p green & sl grn   .30   .25
187   A48   2.50p dp org & dk bl   .45   .25
      Nos. 185-187 (3)   1.00   .75

Dorcas Gazelle — A49

Designs: 1.50p, Doe and fawn. 2.50p, Gazelle and camel. 6p, Leaping gazelle.

1969, June 1   Photo.   Perf. 13
188 A49   1p gldn brn & blk   .25 .25
189 A49 1.50p gldn brn & blk   .30 .25
190 A49 2.50p gldn brn & blk   .35 .30
191 A49   6p gldn brn & blk   .55 .35
Nos. 188-191 (4)   1.45 1.15

Child welfare. See Nos. 196-199, 209-212.

Woman Playing Drum — A50

Stamp Day: 1.50p, Man with flute. 2p, Drum and camel rider, horiz. 25p, Flute, horiz.

1969, Nov. 23   Photo.   Perf. 13
192 A50 50c brn red & lt ol   .25 .25
193 A50 1.50p dk bl grn & grnsh
              gray   .25 .25
194 A50   2p indigo & bis brn   .30 .25
195 A50 25p brn & lt bl grn   1.00 .30
Nos. 192-195 (4)   1.80 1.05

Animal Type of 1969

Fennec: 50c, Sitting. 2p, Running. 2.50p, Head. 6p, Vixen and pups.

1970, June 1   Photo.   Perf. 13
196 A49 50c dp bister & blk   .25 .25
197 A49   2p org brn & blk   .25 .25
198 A49 2.50p dp bister & blk   .30 .25
199 A49   6p dp bister & blk   .50 .25
Nos. 196-199 (4)   1.30 1.00

Issued for child welfare.

Grammodes Boisdeffrei — A51

Designs: 1p, like 50c. 2p, 5p, Danaus chrysippus. 8p, Celerio euphorbiae.

1970, Nov. 23   Photo.   Perf. 12½
200 A51 50c red & multi   .25 .25
201 A51   1p carmine & multi   .30 .25
202 A51   2p green & multi   .35 .25
203 A51   5p Prus bl & multi   .45 .30
204 A51   8p dk blue & multi   .75 .40
Nos. 200-204 (5)   2.10 1.45

Issued for Stamp Day. See Nos. 233-234.

Gazelle, Arms of   Smara
Aaiun — A52   Mosque — A53

Designs: 2p, Inn, horiz. 5p, Assembly building, Aaiun, horiz.

Perf. 12½x13, 13x12½
1971, June 1   Photo.
205 A52   1p multicolored   .25 .25
206 A53   2p gray grn & ol   .25 .25
207 A53   5p lt bl & lt red brn   .30 .25
208 A53 25p lt bl & grnsh gray   .90 .35
Nos. 205-208 (4)   1.70 1.10

Issued for child welfare.

Animal Type of 1969

Birds: 1.50p, 2p, Trumpeter bullfinch. 5p, Cream-colored courser. 24p, Lanner (falcon).

1971, Nov. 23   Photo.   Perf. 12½
209 A49 1.50p black & multi   .25 .25
210 A49   2p blue & multi   .25 .25
211 A49   5p green & multi   .30 .25
212 A49 24p black & multi   .85 .35
Nos. 209-212 (4)   1.65 1.10

Stamp Day.

Saharan
Woman — A55

1.50p, 2p, Saharan man. 8p, 10p, Man's head. 12p, Woman. 15p, Soldier. 24p, Dancer.

1972, Feb. 18   Photo.   Perf. 13
213 A55   1p blue, pink & brn   .25 .25
214 A55 1.50p brn, lil & blk   .25 .25
215 A55   2p green, buff & sep   .25 .25
216 A55   5p grn, pur & vio brn   .25 .25
217 A55   8p black, lt grn & vio   .30 .25
218 A55 10p blk, gray & Prus bl   .35 .30
219 A55 12p multicolored   .40 .35
220 A55 15p multicolored   .50 .45
221 A55 24p multicolored   1.00 .60
Nos. 213-221 (9)   3.55 2.95

Tuareg
Woman — A56

1972, June 1   Photo.   Perf. 13
222 A56   8p shown   .30 .25
223 A56 12p Tuareg man   .40 .25

Child welfare.

Mother and
Child — A57

1972, Nov. 23   Photo.   Perf. 13
224 A57   4p shown   .25 .25
225 A57 15p Saharan man   .45 .25

Stamp Day. See No. 229.

Dunes
A58

Design: 7p, Old Market and Gate, Aaiun.

1973, June 1   Photo.   Perf. 13
226 A58   2p multicolored   .25 .25
227 A58   7p multicolored   .30 .25

Child welfare.

Type of 1972 and

View of
Villa
Cisneros
A59

1973, Nov. 23   Photo.   Perf. 13
228 A59   2p shown   .25 .25
229 A57   7p Tuareg man   .30 .25

Stamp Day.

UPU Monument,
Bern — A60

1974, May   Photo.   Perf. 13
230 A60 15p multicolored   .55 .25

Centenary of the Universal Postal Union.

Gate, Smara
Mosque — A61

2p, Court and Minaret, Villa Cisneros Mosque.

1974, May
231 A61   1p multicolored   .25 .25
232 A61   2p multicolored   .25 .25

Child welfare.

Animal Type of 1970

1974, Nov.   Photo.   Perf. 13
233 A51   2p Desert eagle owl   .25 .25
234 A51   5p Lappet-faced vulture .25 .25

Stamp Day.

Espana 75
Emblem, Spain
No. 1084 — A63

1975, Apr. 4   Photo.   Perf. 13
235 A63   8p olive, blk & bl   .25 .25

Espana 75 Intl. Phil. Exhib., Madrid, 4/4-13.

Children
A64

1975   Photo.   Perf. 13
236 A64 1.50p shown   .25 .25
237 A64   3p Children's village   .25 .25

Child welfare.

Old Man — A65

1975, Nov. 7   Photo.   Perf. 13
238 A65   3p blk, lt grn & mar   .25 .25

SEMI-POSTAL STAMPS

Red Cross Issue

Types of Semi-Postal Stamps of Spain, 1926, Overprinted

1926   Unwmk.   Perf. 12½, 13
B1 SP3   5c black brown   8.75 8.75
B2 SP4 10c dark green   8.75 8.75
B3 SP1 15c dark violet   2.75 2.75
B4 SP4 20c violet brown   2.75 2.75
B5 SP5 25c deep carmine   2.75 2.75
B6 SP1 30c olive green   2.75 2.75
B7 SP3 40c ultra   .25   .25
B8 SP2 50c red brown   .25   .25
B9 SP5 60c myrtle green   .25   .25
B10 SP4   1p vermilion   .25   .25
B11 SP3   4p bister   2.75 2.10
B12 SP5 10p light violet   7.25 6.00
Nos. B1-B12 (12)   39.50 37.60
Set, never hinged   57.50

See Spain No. B6a for No. B4 without overprint. For surcharges see Spain Nos. B72-B73.

Catalogue values for unused stamps in this section, from this point to the end of the section, are for Never Hinged items.

Shepherd and Lamb — SP1

1950, Oct. 20　Photo.　*Perf. 13x12½*
B13	SP1	50c + 10c brown	.40 .25
B14	SP1	1p + 25c rose brn	16.50 7.25
B15	SP1	6.50p + 1.65p dk gray grn	8.50 2.25
		Nos. B13-B15 (3)	25.40 9.75

The surtax was for child welfare.

Dromedary and Calf — SP2

1951, Nov. 23
B16	SP2	5c + 5c brown	.25 .25
B17	SP2	10c + 5 red org	.25 .25
B18	SP2	60c + 15c olive brn	.50 .30
		Nos. B16-B18 (3)	1.00 .80

Colonial Stamp Day, Nov. 23.

Child and Protector — SP3

1952, June 1
B19	SP3	5c + 5c brown	.30 .25
B20	SP3	50c + 10c gray	.35 .35
B21	SP3	2p + 30c blue	1.75 1.25
		Nos. B19-B21 (3)	2.40 1.85

The surtax was for child welfare.

Ostrich — SP4

1952, Nov. 23　*Perf. 12½*
B22	SP4	5c + 5c brn	.25 .25
B23	SP4	10c + 5c brn car	.35 .25
B24	SP4	60c + 15c dk grn	.45 .30
		Nos. B22-B24 (3)	1.05 .80

Colonial Stamp Day, Nov. 23.

Musician Type of Regular Issue

1953, June 1　*Perf. 13x12½*
B25	A7	5c + 5c like #68	.25 .25
B26	A7	10c + 5c like #69	.25 .25

The surtax was for child welfare.

Fish Type of Regular Issue

1953, Nov. 23　*Perf. 12½x13*
B27	A8	5c + 5c like #70	.25 .25
B28	A8	10c + 5c like #71	.25 .25

Athlete Types of Regular Issue

1954, June 1　*Perf. 12½x13, 13x12½*
B29	A9	5c + 5c brn org	.25 .25
B30	A10	10c + 5c purple	.25 .25

The surtax was to help the native population.

Fish Type of Regular Issue

1954, Nov. 23
B31	A11	5c + 5c like #74	.25 .25
B32	A11	10c + 5c like #75	.25 .25

Type of Regular Issue and

Emilio Bonelli SP5

1955, June 1　Photo.　Unwmk.
B33	A12	15c + 5c red vio	.25 .25
B34	SP5	25c + 10c violet	.25 .25

The surtax was for child welfare.

Antelope Type of Regular Issue

15c+5c, Head of scimitar-horned oryx.

1955, Nov. 23　*Perf. 12½x13*
B35	A13	5c + 5c org brn	.25 .25
B36	A13	15c + 5c olive bister	.25 .25

Flower Type of Regular Issue

1956, June 1　*Perf. 13x12½*
B37	A14	5c + 5c like #78	.25 .25
B38	A14	15c + 5c like #79	.25 .25

The tax was for the children.

Aaiun Type of Regular Issue and

Arms of Villa Cisneros and Man — SP6

Perf. 12½x13, 13x12½
1956, Nov. 23　　Unwmk.
B39	A15	5c + 5c pur & blk	.25 .25
B40	SP6	15c + 5c bis & grn	.25 .25

Eagle Type of Regular Issue

15c+5c, Lesser spotted eagle in flight.

1957, June 1　*Perf. 13x12½*
B41	A17	5c + 5c red brown	.25 .25
B42	A17	15c + 5c golden brn	.25 .25

The surtax was for child welfare.

Hyena Type of Regular Issue
Perf. 13x12½, 12½x13
1957, Nov. 23
B43	A18	10c + 5c like #88	.25 .25
B44	A18	15c + 5c like #89	.25 .25

Stork and Arms of Valencia and Aaiun SP7

1958, Mar. 6　Photo.　*Perf. 12½x13*
B45	SP7	10c + 5c org brn	.25 .25
B46	SP7	15c + 10c bister	.25 .25
B47	SP7	50c + 10c brn olive	.25 .25
		Nos. B45-B47 (3)	.75 .75

The surtax was to aid the victims of the Valencia flood, Oct. 1957.

Cervantes Type of Regular Issue

15c+5c, Don Quixote & Sancho Panza.

1958, June 1　*Perf. 13x12½*
B48	A20	10c + 5c hn brn & chnt brn	.25 .25
B49	A20	15c + 5c dp org & slate grn	.25 .25

The surtax was for child welfare.

Hoopoe Lark — SP8

25c+10c, Hoopoe larks, horiz. 50c+10c, Bird.

Perf. 13x12½, 12½x13
1958, Nov. 23　Photo.　Unwmk.
B50	SP8	10c + 5c brn red	.25 .25
B51	SP8	25c + 10c brt pur	.25 .25
B52	SP8	50c + 10c olive	.30 .25
		Nos. B50-B52 (3)	.80 .75

Cervantes Type of Regular Issue

10c+5c, Lope de Vega. 15c+5c, Actress from "Star of Seville," by Lope de Vega.

1959, June　*Perf. 13x12½*
B53	A20	10c + 5c org brn & ol gray	.25 .25
B54	A20	15c + 5c dp ocher & choc	.25 .25

The surtax was for child welfare.

Mailman — SP9

Stamp Day: 20c+5c, Mailman. 50c+20c, Mailman on camel.

1959, Nov. 23　　Photo.
B55	SP9	10c + 5c rose & brn	.25 .25
B56	SP9	20c + 5c lt grn & brn	.25 .25
B57	SP9	50c + 20c ol gray & slate	.25 .25
		Nos. B55-B57 (3)	.75 .75

Quevedo Type of Regular Issue

Designs: 10c+5c, Francisco Gomez de Quevedo. 15c+5c, Winged wheel and hourglass, symbolic of "Hora de Todas."

1960, June 1　*Perf. 12½x13, 13x12½*
B58	A23	10c + 5c maroon	.25 .25
B59	A22	15c + 5c bister brown	.25 .25

The surtax was for child welfare.

Leopard — SP10

Stamp Day: 20c+5c, Desert fox. 30c+10c, Eagle and leopard. 50c+20c, Sand fox.

1960, Nov. 23　Photo.　*Perf. 13x12½*
B60	SP10	10c + 5c rose lilac	.25 .25
B61	SP10	20c + 5c dk slate grn	.25 .25
B62	SP10	30c + 10c chocolate	.30 .25
B63	SP10	50c + 20c olive gray	.40 .30
		Nos. B60-B63 (4)	1.20 1.05

Animal Type of 1961 inscribed: "Pro-Infancia 1961"

Designs: Various Mountain Gazelles.

1961, June 21　　Unwmk.
B64	SP10	10c + 5c rose brn	.25 .25
B65	SP10	25c + 10c gray vio	.25 .25
B66	SP10	80c + 20c dk grn	.35 .25
		Nos. B64-B66 (3)	.85 .75

The surtax was for child welfare.

Alonso Fernandez de Lugo — SP11

Stamp Day: #B68, B70, Diego de Herrera.

1961, Nov. 23　　*Perf. 13x12½*
B67	SP11	10c + 5c org red	.25 .25
B68	SP11	25c + 10c dk pur	.25 .25
B69	SP11	30c + 10c dk red brn	.25 .25
B70	SP11	1p + 10c red org	.35 .25
		Nos. B67-B70 (4)	1.10 1.00

AIR POST STAMPS

In 1942, seven air post stamps of Spain, Nos. C100-C108, were overprinted "SAHARA ESPANOL", but satisfactory information regarding their status is not available.

Catalogue values for unused stamps in this section are for Never Hinged items.

Ostriches — AP1　　Desert Scene — AP2

1943　　Unwmk.　Litho.　*Perf. 12½*
C8	AP1	5c cer & vio brn	.25 .25
C9	AP2	25c yel grn & ol grn	.25 .25
C10	AP1	50c ind & turq grn	.25 .25
C11	AP2	1p pur & grnsh bl	.30 .25
C12	AP1	1.40p gray grn & bl	.35 .25
C13	AP2	2p mag & org brn	2.50 1.40
C14	AP1	5p brown & purple	3.25 1.40
C15	AP2	6p brt bl & gray grn	62.50 25.00
		Nos. C8-C15 (8)	69.65 29.05

Nos. C8-C15 exist imperf. Value of set $125.

Diego Garcia de Herrera AP3

1950, Nov. 23　　Photo.
C16	AP3	5p rose violet	2.75 1.10

Stamp Day.

Woman Holding Dove — AP4

1951, Apr. 22　Engr.　*Perf. 10*
C17	AP4	5p deep green	25.00 7.25

500th birth anniv. of Queen Isabella I. No. C17 is valued in the grade of fine.

Helmet and Trappings — AP5

1952, July 18   Photo.   Perf. 13x12½
C18 AP5 5p brown   27.50 6.50
500th birth anniv. of Ferdinand the Catholic, of Spain.

Plane and Camel Rider — AP6

1961, May 16   Unwmk.
C19 AP6 25p gray brown   3.00 1.00

SPECIAL DELIVERY STAMPS

Catalogue value for unused stamps in this section are for Never Hinged items.

Type A2 Inscribed "URGENTE"
1943   Unwmk.   Perf. 12½
E1 A2 25c Camel troops   1.75   .95

Messenger on Motorcycle — SD1

**   Unwmk.**
1971, Sept. 6   Photo.   Perf. 13
E2 SD1 10p bright rose & olive   .85 .40

SPANISH WEST AFRICA

'spa-nish 'west 'a-fri-kə

LOCATION — Northwest Africa bordering on the Atlantic Ocean
GOVT. — Spanish administration
AREA — 117,000 sq. mi.
POP. — 95,000 (1950)
CAPITAL — Sidi Ifni

Spanish West Africa was the major political division of Spanish areas in northwest Africa. It included Spanish Sahara (Rio de Oro and Saguiet el Hamra) Ifni and, for administrative purposes, Southern Morocco. Separate stamp issues have been used for Rio de Oro, Ifni and La Aguera.

Catalogue values for all unused stamps in this country are for Never Hinged items.

Native — A1

**   Perf. 13x12½**
1949, Oct.   Litho.   Unwmk.
1   A1 4p dark gray green   3.00 1.10
UPU, 75th anniversary.

Nomad Camp A2

5c, 30c, 75c, 2p, Tinzgarrentz Oasis. 10c, 40c, 90c, 5p, Desert well. 15c, 45c, 1p, Caravan.

1950, June 5   Perf. 12½x13
2   A2   2c brown   .40   .25
3   A2   5c rose violet   .40   .25
4   A2 10c Prussian blue   .40   .25
5   A2 15c dp ol gray   .40   .25
6   A2 25c red brown   .40   .25
7   A2 30c bright yellow   .40   .25
8   A2 40c olive gray   .40   .25
9   A2 45c rose lake   .40   .25
10   A2 50c brown orange   .40   .25
11   A2 75c ultramarine   .40   .25
12   A2 90c dull blue grn   .50   .25
13   A2   1p gray   .50   .50
14   A2   1.35p violet   1.25 1.00
15   A2   2p sepia   2.50 1.25
16   A2   5p lilac rose   25.00 10.00
17   A2 10p light brown   50.00 25.00
     Nos. 2-17 (16)   83.75 40.25

AIR POST STAMPS

Isabella the Catholic, Queen of Castile — AP1

**   Perf. 13x12½**
1949, Nov. 23   Photo.   Unwmk.
C1   AP1 5p yellow brown   2.25 1.00
Stamp Day, Nov. 23, 1949.

Desert Camp AP2

Designs: Various Desert Scenes.

1951, Mar. 1   Litho.   Perf. 12½x13
C2   AP2 25c ocher   .45   .25
C3   AP2 50c lilac rose   .45   .25
C4   AP2   1p green   .45   .25
C5   AP2   2p bright blue   1.25   .30
C6   AP2 3.25p rose lilac 2.25 1.00
C7   AP2   5p gray brown   20.00 16.00
C8   AP2 10p rose red   42.50 22.50
     Nos. C2-C8 (7)   67.35 29.55

SPECIAL DELIVERY STAMP

Tilimenzo Pass and Franco SD1

**   Perf. 12½x13**
1951, Mar. 1   Litho.   Unwmk.
E1   SD1 25c rose carmine   .45   .30

SRI LANKA

„srē 'läŋ-kə"

LOCATION — Indian Ocean south of India
GOVT. — Democratic Socialist Republic
AREA — 26,244 sq. mi.
POP. — 19,144,875 (1999 est.)
CAPITAL — Colombo

Sri Lanka was named Ceylon until May 22, 1972. Issues inscribed "Ceylon" are listed under that name in Volume 2.

100 Cents = 1 Rupee

Catalogue values for all unused stamps in this country are for Never Hinged items.

Watermark

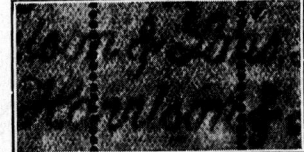

Wmk. 385 — CARTOR

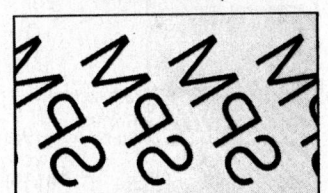

Wmk. 233 — "Harrison & Sons, London" in Script

Wmk. 388 — Multiple "SPM"

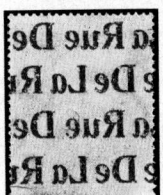

Wmk. 408

Lotus and Sunrise over Adam's Peak — A162

1972, May 22   Litho.   Perf. 13½x13
470 A162 15c blue & multi   .85   .60
Inauguration of Ceylon as Republic of Sri Lanka.

A162a

Overprinted "1972" in Red
1972, May 26   Perf. 14x13½
471 A162a 5c orange brn & multi .45 .60
World Fellowship of Buddhists, Sri Lanka, May 22-28.
Supposedly not issued without overprint, copies sell for 25-cents.

Book Year Emblem, Oil Lamp — A163

1972, Sept. 8   Photo.   Perf. 13
472 A163 20c yellow & dk brn   .40   .50
International Book Year 1972.

Imperial Angelfish A164

Tropical Fish: 3c, Green chromide. 30c, Skipjack bonito. 2r, Black ruby barbs.

**   Perf. 14x13½**
1972, Oct. 12   Litho.   Unwmk.
473 A164   2c ultra & multi   .25 1.25
474 A164   3c dp org & multi   .25 1.25
475 A164 30c brt grn & multi 2.25   .40
476 A164   2r dp green & multi 6.50 6.00
     Nos. 473-476 (4)   9.25 8.90
3rd Session of Indian Ocean Fisheries Commission, Colombo, Oct. 9-14.

Bandaranaike Memorial Hall — A165

1973, May 17   Litho.   Perf. 14
477 A165 15c lt ultra & vio blue   .40 .40
Opening of Bandaranaike Memorial International Conference Hall.

Women Holding Lotus A166

Rock and Temple Paintings: 35c, King giving away his children, Degaldoruwa Temple, near Kandy, 18th cent. 50c, Prince and gravedigger, Polonaruwa, 12th cent. 90c, Holy man holding lotus, Polonaruwa, 12th cent. Design of 1.55r is from Sigiriya, 5th cent.

1973, Sept. 3   **Perf. 13½x14**
478 A166 35c lt gray & multi   .45   .25
479 A166 50c gray & multi   .60   .25
480 A166 90c slate & multi   .85   .85
481 A166 1.55r brown & multi   1.00 1.75
  a. Souvenir sheet of 4, #478-481   5.25 5.25
                                      2.90 3.10

For surcharges see Nos. 538-540.

Bandaranaike Conference Hall — A167

1974, Sept. 6   Litho.   Perf. 14
482 A167 85c multicolored   .50   .50

20th Commonwealth Parliamentary Conference, Sri Lanka, Sept. 1-15.

S.W.R.D. Bandaranaike A168

1974, Sept. 25   Photo.   Perf. 14½
486 A168 15c ultra & multi   .40   .40

For surcharge see No. 541.

"UPU," "100" and UPU Emblem A170

1974, Oct. 9   Litho.   Perf. 13
490 A170 50c multicolored   1.75 1.25

Parliament, Colombo A171

1975, Apr. 1   Litho.   Perf. 13½
491 A171 1r multicolored   .40   .40

Interparliamentary Union, Spring Meeting at Bandaranaike Memorial International Conference Hall, Sri Lanka, Mar. 31-Apr. 5.

Ponnambalam Ramanathan A172

1975, Sept. 4   Litho.   Perf. 13½
492 A172 75c multicolored   .45   .70

Sir Ponnambalam Ramanathan (1851-1930), lawyer and educator.

D. J. Wimalasurendra A173

1975, Sept. 17
493 A173 75c ultra & blue blk   .45   .70

Devapura Jayasena Wimalasurendra (1874-1953), engineer and irrigation specialist.

Map, Mrs. Bandaranaike, Dove — A174

1975, Dec. 22   Litho.   Perf. 13½
494 A174 1.15r blue & multi   3.75 1.90

International Women's Year 1975.
For surcharge, see No. 1579.

Rhododendron Zeylanicum A175

Flowers: 50c, Exacum trinerve. 75c, Daffodil orchid. 10r, Wormia triquetra.

1976, Jan. 1   Litho.   Perf. 13
495 A175 25c blue & multi   .25   .25
496 A175 50c ocher & multi   .25   .25
497 A175 75c black & multi   .25   .25
498 A175 10r black & multi   4.00 4.50
  a. Souvenir sheet of 4, #495-
      498   20.00 20.00
      Nos. 495-498 (4)   4.75 5.25

Mahaveli-ganga Sluice — A176

1976, Jan. 8   Litho.   Perf. 13x12½
499 A176 85c lt blue, lt grn & lil   .45 1.00

Mahaveli-ganga River diversion.

Radar Station — A177

1976, May 6   Litho.   Perf. 14
500 A177 1r blue & multi   1.00 1.25

Opening of Satellite Earth Station, Padukka.

Prince Siddhartha as White Elephant and Sleeping Queen — A178

Birth of Buddha: 10c, King consulting astrologers. 1.50r, King entertaining astrologers at banquet. 2r, Queen taken in procession to her parents. 2.25r, Flag bearers, musicians in procession. 5r, Queen giving birth to Prince Siddhartha, the Buddha. Designs taken from 18th cent. wall paintings in Dambawa Vihara Temple.

1976, May 7   Litho.   Perf. 13½
501 A178 5c blue & multi   .25   .75
502 A178 10c blue & multi   .25   .75
503 A178 1.50r blue & multi   .85 1.00
504 A178 2r blue & multi   .85 1.00
505 A178 2.25r blue & multi   1.75 2.00
506 A178 5r blue & multi   4.00 5.00
  a. Souvenir sheet of 6, #501-
      506   14.00 14.00
      Nos. 501-506 (6)   7.95 10.50

Blue Sapphire A179

Gems of Sri Lanka: 1.15r, Cat's-eye. 2r, Star sapphire. 5r, Ruby.

1976, June 16   Perf. 12x12½
507 A179 60c multicolored   6.50   .40
508 A179 1.15r multicolored   10.50 2.40
509 A179 2r multicolored   12.00 5.00
510 A179 5r multicolored   16.00 16.00
  a. Souv. sheet of 4, #507-510   65.00 45.00
      Nos. 507-510 (4)   45.00 23.80

Prime Minister Sirimavo Bandaranaike A180

1976, Aug. 3   Photo.   Perf. 14¼x14½
511 A180 1.15r pink & multi   .40   .40
512 A180 2r pink & multi   .70   .70

5th Summit Conference of Non-aligned Countries, Colombo, Aug. 9-19.
For surcharges, see Nos. 1347-1348.

Statue of Liberty — A181

1976, Nov. 29   Litho.   Perf. 14
513 A181 2.25r lt blue & indigo   .85 1.25

American Bicentennial.

A. G. Bell, Telephone and Telephone Line — A182

1976, Dec. 21   Litho.   Perf. 13x13½
514 A182 1r orange & multi   .90   .35

Centenary of first telephone call by Alexander Graham Bell, Mar. 10, 1876.

Maitreya Bodhisattva — A183

Bronze Statues: 1r, Sundara Murti Swami, 11th century. 5r, Goddess Tara.

1977, Jan. 1   Litho.   Perf. 12½x13
515 A183 50c multicolored   .45   .45
516 A183 1r multicolored   .45   .45
517 A183 5r multicolored   4.00 4.50
      Nos. 515-517 (3)   4.90 5.40

Colombo Museum, centenary.

Kandyan Crown, 1737-1815 A184

2r, Kandyan throne and footstool, 1693-1815.

1977, Jan. 18
518 A184 1r multicolored   .60   .60
519 A184 2r multicolored   1.90 2.50

Rahula Thero — A185

No. 521, Ponnambalam Arunachalam.

1977   Litho.   Perf. 13½
520 A185 1r multicolored   1.10 1.10
521 A185 1r multicolored   .70   .70

Sri Rahula Thero, 15th cent. poet and scholar, and Sir Ponnambalam Arunachalam (1851-1930), 1st president of Ceylon University Assoc., member of Congress.
Issue dates: #520, Feb. 23; #521, Mar. 10.

Brass Lamps — A186

Handicrafts: 25c, Jewelry box and jewelry. 50c, Caparisoned ivory elephant. 5r, Sinhala wooden mask.

1977, Apr. 7   Perf. 13
522 A186 20c multicolored   .25   .25
523 A186 25c multicolored   .25   .25
524 A186 50c multicolored   .45   .45
525 A186 5r multicolored   2.50 2.75
  a. Souvenir sheet of 4, #522-525 5.75 5.75
      Nos. 522-525 (4)   3.45 3.70

Mohammed Cassim Siddi Lebbe — A187

1977, June 11   Litho.   Perf. 13
526 A187 1r multicolored   .50   .80

Lebbe (1838-98), lawyer, educator and Moslem journalist.

Girl Guide
A188

1977, Dec. 13   Litho.   Perf. 15
527 A188 75c multicolored   1.25 .50
60th anniversary of Sri Lanka Girl Guides.

Parliament and
Wheel of
Life — A189

1978, Feb. 4   Photo.   Perf. 12x12½
528 A189 15c green & gold   .40 .25
J.R. Jayewardene, first elected president, assumption of office.
See Nos. 559, 611-611A, 847. For surcharges see Nos. 542, 572, 698A-698B.

Runners — A190

1978, Apr. 27   Litho.   Perf. 15
529 A190 15c multicolored   .40 .60
National Youth Service Council.
For surcharge see No. 543.

Bodhisattva
in Royal
Attire in
Lotus
Position
A191

Vesak Festival: 50c, Bodhisattva without royal attire cutting off his hair with sword. Both designs from rock carvings in Borobudur Temple, Java.

1978, May 16   Perf. 13
530 A191 15c multicolored   1.10 1.10
531 A191 50c multicolored   1.50 1.50

Veera Puran Appu
and his Flag — A192

1978, Aug. 8   Litho.   Perf. 13
532 A192 15c multicolored   .40 .30
Veera Puran Appu (1848-1908), revolutionist, 130th birth anniversary.

Birdwing
Butterfly — A193

Butterflies: 50c, Tamil lacewing. 5r, Blue oakleaf. 10r, Blue mormon.

1978, Nov. 28   Litho.   Perf. 14x13½
534 A193 25c multicolored   .90 .25
535 A193 50c multicolored   1.50 .25
536 A193 5r multicolored   2.75 1.75
537 A193 10r multicolored   2.75 2.75
  a. Souvenir sheet of 4, #534-537   20.00 16.00
  Nos. 534-537 (4)   7.90 5.00

Nos. 478,
480-481
Surcharged

1978   Litho.   Perf. 13½x14
538 A166 5c on 90c multi   10.50 10.50
539 A166 10c on 35c multi   3.50   3.50
540 A166 1r on 1.55r multi   7.00   7.00
  Nos. 538-540 (3)   21.00 21.00

Nos. 486, 528
Surcharged

No. 529 Surcharged
In Black on Pink
Panel

Perf. 14½, 12x12½, 15
1979, Jan.   Litho.; Engr.
541 A168 25c on 15c multi   7.00 7.00
542 A189 25c on 15c multi   7.00 7.00
543 A190 25c on 15c multi   7.00 7.00
  Nos. 541-543 (3)   21.00 21.00

**Ceylon No. 390 Overprinted
Vertically "SRI LANKA" in Green
and Surcharged in Black**
1979, Mar. 22   Photo.   Perf. 11½
Granite Paper
544 A118 15c on 10c brt green   4.50 3.00

Arrival of Sacred
Tooth — A194

Wall Paintings from Kelaniya Temple: 25c, Prince Danta and Princess Hema Mala bringing Sacred Tooth from Kalinga, 4th century A.D. 1r, Princess Theri Sanghamitta bringing, by ship, the bodhi tree branch, 3rd century B.C. 10r, King Kirti offering fan of authority to supreme patriarch, 18th century.

1979, May 3   Litho.   Perf. 13½
546 A194 25c multicolored   .25 .25
547 A194 1r multicolored   .25 .25
548 A194 10r multicolored   2.00 2.00
  a. Souvenir sheet of 3, #546-548   4.25 4.25
  Nos. 546-548 (3)   2.50 2.50
2523rd Vesak Festival, May 11.

Wrestlers — A195

Design: 50r, Dancer. Woodcarvings from Embekke Temple.

1979, May 18   Litho.   Perf. 14
549 A195 20r multicolored   1.75 1.25
550 A195 50r multicolored   4.25 3.50

Piyadasa
Sirisena — A196

1979, May 22   Perf. 13x13½
551 A196 1.25r deep green   .60 .60
Piyadasa Sirisena (1875-1946), patriot, journalist, novelist and poet.

Dudley S.
Senanayake — A197

1979, June 19   Photo.
552 A197 1.25r deep green   .40 .40
27th death anniversary of Prime Minister Dudley S. Senanayake.

Mother
Feeding Child,
IYC Emblem
A198

Designs: 3r, Faces and IYC emblem. 5r, Children with rope and ball, IYC emblem.

1979, July 31   Litho.   Perf. 12½
553 A198 5c multicolored   .25 .25
554 A198 3r multicolored   .40 .90
555 A198 5r multicolored   .45 1.10
  Nos. 553-555 (3)   1.10 2.25
International Year of the Child.

Ceylon No. 2,
Rowland
Hill — A199

1979, Aug. 27   Litho.   Perf. 13½
556 A199 3r multicolored   .60 1.00
Sir Rowland Hill (1795-1879), originator of penny postage.

Airlanka
Emblem — A200

1979, Sept. 1   Litho.   Perf. 12½
557 A200 3r red, dk grn & blk   1.25 1.60
Airlanka National Airline, inaugural flight, Colombo-Bangkok.

Coconut
Palm — A201

1979, Oct. 9   Litho.   Perf. 13½
558 A201 2r multicolored   1.50 1.50
Asian and Pacific Coconut Community, 10th anniversary.

No. 528 Redrawn Without Date
1979, Oct. 9   Photo.   Perf. 13
Size: 20x24mm
559 A189 25c green & gold   .65 .25

Family in
Cogwheel,
Parliament
A202

1979, Oct.   Litho.   Perf. 13½
560 A202 2r multicolored   1.25 1.50
Intl. Conf. of Parliamentarians on Population & Development, Colombo, Aug. 28-Sept. 1.

Swami Vipulananda
(1892-1947),
Philosopher &
Theologian — A203

1979, Nov. 18   Perf. 12½
561 A203 1.25r multicolored   .40 .50

Text and
Crescent
A204

1979, Nov. 22
562 A204 3.75r multicolored   .60 1.50
Hegira (pilgrimage year).

Institute
Emblem — A205

1979, Nov. 29   Perf. 13
563 A205 15c multicolored   .40 .60
Ayurveda Medical Institute, 50th anniversary.

Blue Magpie — A206

15c, Lorikeet. 75c, Arrenga. 1r, Spurfowl. 5r, Yellow-fronted barbet. 10r, Yellow-eared bulbul.

1979, Dec. 13   Litho.   Perf. 14
564 A206 10c shown .25 .25
565 A206 15c multicolored .25 .25
566 A206 75c multicolored .25 .25
567 A206 1r multicolored .25 .25
568 A206 5r multicolored 1.50 1.50
569 A206 10r multicolored 1.90 1.90
a. Souvenir sheet of 6, #564-
569 11.00 11.00
Nos. 564-569 (6) 4.40 4.40

For surcharges, see Nos. 1062B, 1512.

Rotary Emblem, Map of Sri Lanka A207

1979, Dec. 27   Litho.   Perf. 14½
570 A207 1.50r multicolored 1.10 1.50
Rotary International, 75th anniversary.

A. Ratnayake, Educator and Pres. of Senate — A208

1980, Jan. 7   Photo.   Perf. 14x13½
571 A208 1.25r slate green .40 .40

No. 559 Surcharged

1980, Mar. 17   Photo.   Perf. 13
572 A189 35c on 25c multi .50 .40
One position has ".33" instead of ".35."

Leaf, Wheel, Fan (Buddhist Symbols) A209

1980, Mar. 25   Photo.   Perf. 13½x14
573 A209 10c Steeple .50 1.25
574 A209 35c shown .50 .40
All Ceylon Buddhist Cong., 60th anniv.

Col. Henry Olcott, Buddhist Emblem — A210

1980, May 17   Litho.   Perf. 14
575 A210 2r multicolored 1.25 1.50
Col. Henry S. Olcott (1832-1907), American theosophist and Buddhist lecturer, centenary of arrival in Sri Lanka.

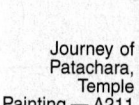 

Journey of Patachara, Temple Painting — A211

Vesak Festival (Paintings, life of Buddha): 1.60r, Patachara crossing river.

1980, May 23   Perf. 13½x14
576 A211 35c multicolored .40 .40
577 A211 1.60r multicolored 1.90 2.10

George E. De Silva — A212

1980, June 8   Perf. 13x13½
578 A212 1.60r multicolored .50 .50
George E. de Silva (1879-1950), politician.

Siva Temples, Polonnaruwa — A213

No. 580, Cave Temples, Dambulla. No. 581, Sacred Tooth Temple, Kandy. No. 582, Abhayagiri Hill. No. 583, Jetavanarama Hill. No. 584, Sigiri.

1980, Aug. 25   Litho.   Perf. 13½
579 A213 35c shown .25 .40
580 A213 35c multicolored .25 .40
581 A213 35c multicolored .25 .40
582 A213 1.60r multicolored .80 1.25
583 A213 1.60r multicolored .80 1.25
584 A213 1.60r multicolored .80 1.25
a. Souvenir sheet of 6, #579-584 4.00 4.00
Nos. 579-584 (6) 3.15 4.95

UNESCO "Cultural Triangle" Project.

Department of Cooperative Development, 50th Anniversary A214

1980, Oct. 1   Litho.   Perf. 13½
585 A214 20c multicolored .40 .50

Women's Movement Emblem A215

1980, Oct. 16   Photo.   Perf. 14x13½
586 A215 35c multicolored .40 .50
Mahila Samiti (Rural Women's Movement), 50th anniversary.

Nativity — A216

1980, Nov. 20   Litho.   Perf. 13½
587 A216 35c shown .30 .30
588 A216 3.75r Three kings .80 .90
a. Souvenir sheet of 2, #587-588 2.00 2.00
Christmas 1980/Year of the family.

Colombo Public Library Opening A217

1980, Dec. 17   Perf. 12x12½
589 A217 35c multicolored .40 .40

Peacock Banner A218

Designs: Ancient flags.

1980, Dec. 18   Perf. 13
590 A218 10c shown .25 .25
591 A218 25c Elephant banner .25 .25
592 A218 1.60r Sinhalese royal flag .25 .25
593 A218 20r Kings Civil Standard 1.75 2.10
a. Souvenir sheet of 4, #590-593 2.50 2.50
Nos. 590-593 (4) 2.50 2.85

Examples of No. 593a overprinted in the margin for the 2010 National Stamp Fair, Colombo sold for 600r.
For surcharge on No. 592, see No. 1550.

Fishing Cat — A219

No. 595, Golden palm cat. No. 596, Mouse deer. No. 597, Rusty-spotted cat.

1981, Feb. 10   Litho.   Perf. 14
594 A219 2.50r on 1.60r shown .55 .25
595 A219 3r on 1.50r multi .55 .25
596 A219 4r on 2r multi .55 .45
597 A219 5r on 3.75r multi .85 .60
a. Souvenir sheet of 4, #594-597 3.00 3.00
Nos. 594-597 (4) 2.50 1.55

See Nos. 728-730A, 928. For surcharge see No. 731.

Population and Housing Census — A220

1981, Mar. 2   Litho.   Perf. 12½x12
598 A220 50c multicolored 1.00 1.25

Ceylon Light Infantry Centenary A221

1981, Apr. 1   Litho.   Perf. 12
599 A221 2r multicolored 1.60 1.60

The Death of Buddha, Carved Panel, 1st Cent. — A222

1981, May 5   Perf. 13x13½
600 A222 35c shown .25 .25
601 A222 50c Silk banner .25 .25
602 A222 7r Statuette 2.00 3.25
a. Souvenir sheet of 3, #600-602 5.75 5.75
Nos. 600-602 (3) 2.50 3.75

Vesak Festival.

St. John Baptist de la Salle A223

1981, May 15   Litho.   Perf. 12½x12
603 A223 2r multicolored 2.25 2.25
De la Salle Brothers Order, 300th anniv.

Polwatte Sri Buddadatta A224

Famous Men: No. 605, Mohottiwatte Gunananda, Buddhist leader. No. 606, Gnanapra Kasar, Catholic missionary. No. 607, Al-Haj T.B. Jayah, Muslim teacher. No. 608, James Peiris. No. 609, N.M. Perera, founded first Marxist Party in Sri Lanka, 1935.

1981   Photo.   Perf. 12
604 A224 50c olive bister .75 1.00
605 A224 50c dull red brown .75 1.00
606 A224 50c lilac .75 1.00
607 A224 50c gray green .75 1.00
608 A224 50c brown .75 1.00
609 A224 50c crimson rose .75 1.00
Nos. 604-609 (6) 4.50 6.00

Issued: #604-606, 5/22; #607, 5/31; #609, 6/6; #608, 12/20.
See #623-624, 640-642, 646, 672-676, 713-717.

Intl. Year of the Disabled — A225

1981, June 19   Litho.   Perf. 12x12½
610 A225 2r multicolored 1.50 1.75

No. 528 Redrawn with Denomination in Upper Right Corner

1981-83 Photo. *Perf. 13*
Size: 20x24mm

611 A189 50c green & gold 3.00 .25
611A A189 60c green & gold 11.00 1.75

Issued: 50c, June 6; 60c, Dec. 30, 1983.
For surcharges see Nos. 698A-698B.

Hand Putting Ballot in Box A226

Perf. 12½x12, 12x12½

1981, July 7 Litho.
612 A226 50c shown .30 .30
613 A226 7r Ballot box on map, vert. 2.40 3.00

Universal Franchise, 50th anniv.

Rhys Davids (Society Founder) A227

1981, July 14 *Perf. 12½x12*
614 A227 35c multicolored 1.25 .65

All Ceylon Buddhist Students' Federation, 25th Anniv. A228

1981, July 21 Litho. *Perf. 13½*
615 A228 2r multicolored 1.50 1.50

Family Planning — A229

1981, Sept. 25
616 A229 50c multicolored 1.50 1.50

7th World Acupuncture Cong. — A230

1981, Oct. 20 Litho. *Perf. 12x12½*
617 A230 2r multicolored 4.25 4.25

Visit of Queen Elizabeth II, Oct. A231

Designs: Flags of Gt. Britain and Sri Lanka.

1981, Oct. 21 *Perf. 14*
618 A231 50c multicolored .75 .75
619 A231 5r multicolored 2.25 2.25
a. Souvenir sheet of 2, #618-619 3.50 4.00

Forest Conservation A232

1981, Nov. 27 *Perf. 13½x13*
620 A232 35c Forest .25 .25
621 A232 50c Tree planting .30 .30
622 A232 5r Jack tree 2.50 2.75
a. Souvenir sheet of 3, #620-622, perf. 14x13 2.75 3.75
Nos. 620-622 (3) 3.05 3.30

Famous Men Type of 1981

Designs: No. 623, F.R. Senanayaka (1882-1926), lawyer and politician. No. 624, Philip Gunawardhane, politician, 10th death anniv.

1982 Litho. *Perf. 14*
623 A224 50c brown 1.00 1.00
624 A224 50c bright rose 1.00 1.00

Issue dates: #623, Jan. 1; #624, Jan. 11.

Dept. of Inland Revenue, 50th Anniv. — A233

1982, Feb. 9 Litho. *Perf. 14*
625 A233 50c multicolored 1.00 1.00

Natl. Television Inauguration A234

1982, Feb. 15
626 A234 2.50r multicolored 3.75 3.75

Sesquicentennial of Cricket Introduction and Centenary of Sri Lanka vs. England Match — A235

1982, Feb. 17
627 A235 2.50r multicolored 9.00 9.00

Osbeckia Wightiana A236

2r, Mesua nagassarium. 7r, Rhodomyrtus tomentosa. 20r, Phaius tancarvilleae.

1982, Apr. 1 *Perf. 12*
628 A236 35c shown .25 .25
629 A236 2r multicolored .35 .25
630 A236 7r multicolored .80 .85

---

631 A236 20r multicolored 2.25 2.25
a. Souvenir sheet of 4, #628-631 10.50 10.50
Nos. 628-631 (4) 3.65 3.60

Examples of No. 631a overprinted in the margin for the 2010 National Stamp Fair, Colombo sold for 750r.

Food and Nutrition Planning A237

1982, Apr. 6 Litho. *Perf. 13*
632 A237 50c multicolored 2.40 2.40

World Hindu Conference A238

1982, Apr. 21 *Perf. 14x14½*
633 A238 50c multicolored 1.60 1.60

Vesak Festival 1982 A239

Scenes from Jataka Story (Pre-incarnation of Buddha), Cloth Painting, 3rd cent. B.C., Hanguranketa Temple (King Vessantara and): 35c, Giving away white elephant. 50c, Royal Family in Vankagiri Forest. 2.50r, Giving away his children to a Brahmin. 5r, Royal family in chariot.

1982, Apr. 23 *Perf. 14*
634 A239 35c multicolored .80 .25
635 A239 50c multicolored .95 .25
636 A239 2.50r multicolored 3.25 2.75
637 A239 5r multicolored 4.25 4.25
a. Souvenir sheet of 4, #634-637 13.50 13.50
Nos. 634-637 (4) 9.25 7.50

New Parliament Building Opening A240

1982, Apr. 29
638 A240 50c multicolored 1.40 1.40

Scouting Year A241

1982, May 24 Litho. *Perf. 12½x12*
639 A241 50c multicolored 2.50 2.25

Famous Men Type of 1981

1982 *Perf. 12x12½*
640 A224 50c C.W.W. Kannan-gara 1.50 1.50
641 A224 50c G.P. Malalasekara 1.50 1.50
642 A224 50c John Kotelawala 1.50 1.50
Nos. 640-642 (3) 4.50 4.50

Issued: #640, 5/22; #641, 5/26; #642, 6/8.

World Buddhist Leaders Conference — A242

1982, June 10 *Perf. 12½x12*
643 A242 50c multicolored 1.50 1.50

World Environment Day — A243

1982, June 5
644 A243 50c multicolored 2.50 2.10

YMCA Centenary — A244

1982, June 24 Photo. *Perf. 11½*
645 A244 2.50r multicolored 5.00 5.00

Famous Men Type of 1981
1982, June 14 Litho. *Perf. 12x12½*
646 A224 50c Waitialingam Duraiswamy 1.50 1.50

Weliwita Saranankara Sangharaja A245

1982, July 5
647 A245 50c orange & black 1.50 1.50

25th Anniv. of Sasana Sevaka Samithiya A246

1982, Aug. 8
648 A246 50c multicolored 2.25 2.25

TB Bacillus Centenary A247

1982, Sept. 21
649 A247 50c Koch, microscope, bacillus 3.00 2.50

Eye Donation
Society — A248

1982, Nov. 16　Litho.　Perf. 12x12½
650 A248 2.50r Emblems, map　　4.50 4.75

125th Anniv. of Ceylon Postage
Stamps — A249

1982, Dec. 1　Litho.　Perf. 13½
651 A249　50c Ceylon #5, 302　　.65 .65
652 A249 2.50r Ceylon #12, #611 2.50 2.50
　a.　Souv. sheet of #651-652, perf. 12　4.00 4.00
　　　Natl. Stamp Exhibition.
　Examples of No. 652a overprinted in the
margin for the 2010 National Stamp Fair,
Colombo sold for 350r.

Sir Oliver
Goonetilleke
A250

1982, Dec. 17　Litho.　Perf. 12x12½
653 A250 50c black & brown　　.80 1.10

25th Anniv.
of Sarvodaya
Social
Movement
A251

1983, Jan. 1　　　　Perf. 13½
654 A251 50c multicolored　　1.50 1.50

55th Anniv.
of Amateur
Radio
Society
A252

1983, Jan. 17
655 A252 2.50r multicolored　　4.50 4.50

Customs
Cooperation
Council and First
Intl. Customs
Day — A253

1983, Jan. 26　Litho.　Perf. 12
656 A253 50c orange & multi　　.80 .80
657 A253　5r green & multi　　5.25 6.00

Bottlenose
Dolphin
A254

1983, Feb. 22　　　　Perf. 14½x14
658 A254　50c shown　　　1.00 .25
659 A254　2r Dugongs　　1.60 1.00
660 A254 2.50r Humpback
　　　　　　whale　　　4.75 2.50
661 A254　10r Great sperm
　　　　　　whale　　10.50 8.75
　　Nos. 658-661 (4)　　17.85 12.50

Ceylon
Shipping
Corp.
A255

1983, Mar. 1　　　　Perf. 12x12½
662 A255　50c Container ship　.40 .25
663 A255 2.50r Liner services
　　　　　　map　　　　1.50 .90
664 A255　5r Conventional ship 2.25 2.10
665 A255　20r Oil tanker　　3.50 5.50
　　Nos. 662-665 (4)　　7.65 8.75

Intl. Women's
Day — A256

1983, Mar. 8　　　　Perf. 13½
666 A256 50c Woman, flag　　.40 .25
667 A256　5r Woman, map　1.50 2.25

Commonwealth Day — A257

1983, Mar. 14
668 A257　50c Waterfall　　　.25 .25
669 A257 2.50r Tea picking　　.25 .25
670 A257　5r Harvesting　　.35 .50
671 A257　20r Cultural pageant 1.40 1.75
　　Nos. 668-671 (4)　　2.25 2.75

Famous Men Type of 1981
　No. 672, Henry W. Amarasuriya. No. 673,
Charles A. Lorenz. No. 674, Simon G. Perera.
No. 675, Nordeen H.M. Abdul Cader. No. 676,
C.W. Tamotherampillai.

1983　　　Litho.　　　Perf. 12
672 A224 50c multicolored　　.45 .75

Size: 29x40mm
673 A224 50c multicolored　　.45 .75
674 A224 50c multicolored　　.45 .75
675 A224 50c multicolored　　.45 .75
676 A224 50c multicolored　1.25 1.25
　　Nos. 672-676 (5)　　3.05 4.25
　No. 676 shows Tamotherampillai looking
towards the right of the stamp. A version that
was to be issued May 22, showed someone
labeled C. W. Tamotherampillai looking
straight ahead.
　Issued: No. 676, Oct. 1; others, May 22.

25th Anniv.
of Lions
Club
A258

1983, May 7　Litho.　　Perf. 14
677 A258 2.50r multicolored　　4.25 2.75

Vesak Festival
1983 — A259

Various Colombo murals.

1983, May 13　　　Perf. 12½x12
678 A259 35c multicolored　　.25 .25
679 A259 50c multicolored　　.25 .25
680 A259　5r multicolored　1.10 1.10
681 A259　10r multicolored　1.90 1.90
　a.　Souvenir sheet of 4, #678-681　3.75 4.25
　　Nos. 678-681 (4)　　3.50 3.50

125th Anniv. of Telecommunication
Service — A260

1983, May 17　　　Perf. 12x12½
682 A260　2r shown　　　1.00 .80
683 A260　10r World Communica-
　　　　　　tions Year　3.00 4.25

Gam Udawa Village Re-awakening
Movement — A261

1983, June 23　Litho.　Perf. 12x12½
684 A261 50c Family　　　.25 .30
685 A261　5r Village　　.75 1.75

Cattle
Transport
A262

1983, Aug. 1　Litho.　　Perf. 12
686 A262 35c shown　　　.30 .30
687 A262　2r Train　　3.25 3.25
688 A262 2.50r Cattle cart　1.75 1.75
689 A262　5r Model T Ford　3.50 3.50
　　Nos. 686-689 (4)　　8.80 8.80

Sir Tikiri Banda
Panabokke, 20th
Death
Anniv. — A263

1983, Sept. 2　Litho.　Perf. 13½x14
690 A263 50c dark red　　1.50 1.50

Ceylon
Wood
Pigeon
A264

1983, Dec. 1　Litho.　Perf. 14½
691 A264 25c shown　　　1.20 1.20
692 A264 35c Ceylon white-eye　1.20 1.20
693 A264　2r Dusky-blue fly-
　　　　　　catcher　　1.75 1.75
694 A264 20r Ceylon coucal　2.75 2.75
　a.　Souvenir sheet of 4, #691-694　7.00 7.00
　　Nos. 691-694 (4)　　6.90 6.90
　Examples of No. 694a overprinted in the
margin for the 2010 National Stamp Fair,
Colombo sold for 650r.
　See No. 877. For surcharge see No. 780A.

Christmas, Stone
Carvings — A265

1983, Dec. 5　Litho.　Perf. 12½x13
695 A265 50c multicolored　　.25 .25
696 A265　5r ultra & bister　.50 1.75
　a.　Souv. sheet, #695-696+label　1.10 2.25

A266

1983, Nov. 25　Litho.　Perf. 14x15
697 A266 50c brown　　　2.25 2.25
　Rev. Pelene Thero (1878-1955), Buddhist
leader.

A267

1983　　　Litho.　　Perf. 13½
698 A267 50c Ahamed Orabi Al-
　　　　　　Misri　　　1.50 1.50

No. 611 Surcharged
in Black

No. 611A Surcharged
in Green

1983-85　　Photo.　　Perf. 13
698A A189 60c on 50c ('83)　17.00 4.00

Size: 20x24mm
698B A189 75c on 60c (G) ('85)　1.00 .40
　Ovpt. on No. 698A also exists with two bars.
Value, $20.
　Issue dates: both Dec. 1.

World
Food Day
(Oct. 16)
A268

1984, Jan. 2   **Perf. 12½x12**
699 A268 3r Rice paddy   .70 1.75

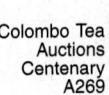

Colombo Tea
Auctions
Centenary
A269

1984, Jan. 31
700 A269 1r Auction House   .25   .25
701 A269 2r Emblem   .50   .50
702 A269 5r Tea picker   1.25 1.75
703 A269 10r Auction   2.50 3.50
          Nos. 700-703 (4)   4.50 6.00

Mahapola
Anniversary
(Educational
System) — A270

1984, Feb. 10   **Perf. 12**
704 A270 60c Students   .25   .25
705 A270 1r Classroom   .25   .25
706 A270 5.50r Student in library,
          lab   .35 1.50
707 A270 6r Emblem   .40 1.50
          Nos. 704-707 (4)   1.25 3.50

Vesak
Festival
1984
A271

Wooden Casket Paintings, Temple Godapi-
tiya Rajamaha Vihara, Akuressa: Scenes from
Daham Sonda Jathaka legend.

1984, Apr. 27   Litho.   Perf. 14
708 A271 35c multicolored   .25   .25
709 A271 60c multicolored   .80   .70
710 A271 5r multicolored   2.75 2.75
711 A271 10r multicolored   3.25 3.25
a.   Souv. sheet of 4, #708-711, perf.
          13x13½   4.50 4.50
          Nos. 708-711 (4)   7.05 6.95

Lions Club Intl.,
District
306A — A272

1984, May 5   Litho.   Perf. 14x14½
712 A272 60c multicolored   2.10 1.50

Famous Men Type of 1981

Designs: No. 713, K. Balasingham, lawyer.
No. 714, Mohamed Macan Markar (1879-
1952), Muslim politician. No. 715, W. Arthur
de Silva (d. 1942), industrialist. No. 716, Tissa
Mahanayake Thero (1826-1907), Buddhist
educator. No. 717, G.P. Wickremarachchi,
medical pioneer.

1984, May 22   Litho.   Perf. 12x12½
713 A224 60c brown   .45   .80
714 A224 60c green   .45   .80
715 A224 60c orange red   .45   .80
716 A224 60c bister   .45   .80
717 A224 60c yellow green   .45   .80
          Nos. 713-717 (5)   2.25 4.00

Public
Service
Mutual
Provident
Assoc.
Centenary
A273

1984, June 16   **Perf. 13x13½**
718 A273 4.60r Emblem   1.00 2.00

Village Re-
awakening
Movement
A274

1984, June 23   **Perf. 12x12½**
719 A274 60c "One Million Hous-
          es"   .60   .80

Asia-Pacific Broadcasting Union, 20th
Anniv. — A275

1984, June 30   **Perf. 12½x12**
720 A275 7r Map   3.00 3.25

For surcharge see No. 776.

Cultural
Pageant
A276

Procession: a, Drummers, elephant. b,
Torch bearers, 3 elephants (green or red
masks). c, Torch bearers, 3 elephants (orange
or yellow masks). d, Dancers. Continuous
design.

1984, Aug. 11   Litho.   Perf. 12½x12
721   Strip of 4   7.00 7.00
a.-d.   A276 4.60r any single   1.50 1.50
e.   Souvenir sheet of 4   7.50 7.50

Orchid Circle of
Sri Lanka, 50th
Anniversary
A277

60c, Vanda memoria. 4.60r, Acanthephip-
pium bicolor. 5r, Vanda Tessellata. 10r,
Anoectochillus setaceus.

1984, Aug. 31   **Perf. 14**
722 A277 60c multi   1.60 1.60
723 A277 4.60r multi   3.25 3.25
724 A277 5r multi   2.25 2.25
725 A277 10r multi   7.00 7.00
a.   Souvenir sheet of 4, #722-
          725   13.00 13.00
          Nos. 722-725 (4)   14.10 14.10

Wildlife Type of 1981

2.50r, Felis viverrina. 3r, Paradoxurus
zeylonensis. 4r, Tragulus meminna. 5r, Felis
rubiginosa.

1982-89   Litho.   Perf. 14
728 A219 2.50r multicolored   .40   .30
729 A219 3r multicolored   5.50 5.50

730 A219 4r multicolored   .40   .40
730A A219 5r multi, ('89)   .50   .40
          Nos. 728-730A (4)   6.80 6.60
No. 729 has brown inscriptions. See No.
928 for black inscriptions.
No. 728 is unwatermarked.
Issued: 2.50r, 6/1/83; 3r, 6/21/83; 4r,
11/16/82; 5r, 12/1/89.

No. 728 Surcharged in Brown
1985, Dec. 1   Litho.   Perf. 14
731 A219 5.75r on 2.50r multi   5.25 2.75

The
Observer
Newspaper,
150th
Anniv.
A280

1984, Aug. 31   Litho.   Perf. 13x13½
732 A280 4.60r Publisher, Colom-
          bo   3.50 4.00

Natl. School
Games — A281

1984, Oct. 5   **Perf. 13½x13**
733 A281 60c blue, gray & blk   2.75 2.25

D. S. Senanayake (1884-1952), Prime
Minister — A282

35c, Irrigated field. 60c, Statue. 4.60r, Reservoir. 6r, Parliament House, Colombo.

1984, Oct. 20   **Perf. 14½x14**
734 A282 35c multicolored   .25   .25
735 A282 60c multicolored   .25   .25
736 A282 4.60r multicolored   .45   .55
737 A282 6r multicolored   .65   .75
          Nos. 734-737 (4)   1.60 1.80

World Food
Program — A284

1984, Dec. 10   Litho.   Perf. 13x13½
738 A284 7r Globe, Sri Lankans
          working field   2.40 1.60

Baari Arabic College,
Weligama,
Cent. — A285

1984, Dec. 24   **Perf. 13x12½**
739 A285 4.60r dull bl grn & blk   2.25 2.75

Intl. Youth
Year — A286

1985, Jan. 1   **Perf. 12½x13**
740 A286 4.60r multicolored   .80   .60
741 A286 20r multicolored   3.00 3.50

For surcharge see No. 790.

World Religion
Day — A287

Design: Emblems of World religions.

1985, Jan. 20   **Perf. 12**
742 A287 4.60r multicolored   3.50 3.50

Royal College,
Colombo, 150th
Anniv. — A288

1985, Jan. 29   **Perf. 13x12½**
743 A288 60c College crest   .25   .30
744 A288 7r Campus   3.00 3.75

Mahapola
Scholarship
Program for
Development &
Education, 5th
Anniv. — A289

60c, Diplomas, freighter, office buildings.

1985, Feb. 7   **Perf. 14**
745 A289 60c multicolored   1.40 1.75

Wariyapola Sri
Sumangala Thero,
Leader of the 1818
Great Uva
Rebellion — A290

1985, Mar. 2   **Perf. 13x13½**
746 A290 60c brown & yellow   1.10 1.25

Victoria
Project
A291

Perf. 12½x12, 12x12½
1985, Apr. 12   **Litho.**
747 A291 60c Victoria Dam   1.25 1.25
748 A291 7r Dam, map, vert.   7.50 7.50

Vesak Festival
1985 — A292

Designs: 35c, Frontispiece of the Buddhist
Annual golden jubilee issue. 60c, Women wor-
shiping at temple, Vesak Poya Holiday cent.

6r, Bauddha Mandiraya, Colombo. 9r, Buddhist flag cent.

1985, Apr. 26   **Perf. 13x12½**
749	A292	35c multicolored	.25 .25
750	A292	60c multicolored	.25 .25
751	A292	6r multicolored	.85 .85
752	A292	9r multicolored	1.75 1.75
a.		Souvenir sheet of 4, #749-752	7.25 7.25
		Nos. 749-752 (4)	3.10 3.10

Natl. Heroes — A293

No. 753, Waskaduwe Sri Subhuthi Thero (1835-1917), Pali scholar, philologist responsible for the Sinhala dictionary. No. 754, Rev. Fr. Peter A. Pillai (1904-64), educational & social reformer. No. 755, Dr. Senarath Paranavitane (c. 1900-72), epigraphist. No. 756, A.M. Wapche Marikar (1829-1925), educational reformer, architect.

1985, May 22   **Perf. 13x12½**
Pale Yellow Orange and
753	A293	60c tan	.45 .70
754	A293	60c brt rose lilac	.45 .70
755	A293	60c brown	.45 .70
756	A293	60c emerald	.45 .70
		Nos. 753-756 (4)	1.80 2.80

Gam Udawa — Yovur Udanaya Village Reformation Movement A294

1985, June 23   **Perf. 13½x13**
757	A294	60c multicolored	1.60 1.60

Colombo Young Poets Assoc., 50th Anniv. — A295

1985, June 25   **Perf. 14**
758	A295	60c Emblem	1.75 1.75

Kothmale Project Commission — A296

60c, Dam, lake. 6r, Hydro-electric power station.

1985, Aug. 24
759	A296	60c multicolored	1.00 1.00
760	A296	6r multicolored	5.00 5.00

A297

Child Survival: 35c, Mother breastfeeding. 60c, Infant, oral inoculant. 6r, Weighing toddler. 9r, Infant, intravenous inoculant.

1985, Sept. 1   **Wmk. 385**   **Perf. 13½**
761	A297	35c multicolored	.45 .25
762	A297	60c multicolored	.65 .40
763	A297	6r multicolored	2.50 2.75

764	A297	9r multicolored	3.25 3.50
a.		Souvenir sheet of 4, #761-764	7.50 7.50
		Nos. 761-764 (4)	6.85 6.90

A298

1985, Sept. 2   **Unwmk.**   **Perf. 14**
765	A298	7r Womb, infant	5.50 5.50

10th Asian & Oceanic Congress of Obstetrics & Gynecology.

World Tourism Org., 10th Anniv. A299

1r, Conch shell horn. 6r, Parliament complex. 7r, Tea plantation. 10r, Buddhist monastery, Ruwanveliseya.

1985, Sept. 27   **Litho.**   **Perf. 14**
766	A299	1r multicolored	.55 .25
767	A299	6r multicolored	1.50 1.50
768	A299	7r multicolored	2.25 2.25
769	A299	10r multicolored	2.75 2.75
a.		Souv. sheet of 4, #766-769, perf. 13½	9.00 9.00
		Nos. 766-769 (4)	7.05 6.75

Land Development Ordinance, 50th Anniv. — A300

1985, Oct. 15   **Perf. 14x15**
770	A300	4.60r Deeds presentation	3.50 3.75

Sinhal Translation, Koran — A301

1985, Oct. 17   **Wmk. 385**   **Perf. 13½**
771	A301	60c violet & gold	3.25 2.50

Christmas — A302

60c, Our Lady of Matara. 9r, Our Lady of Madhu.

1985, Nov. 5   **Perf. 12**
772	A302	60c multicolored	.40 .25
773	A302	9r multicolored	2.00 2.25
a.		Souvenir sheet of 2, #772-773	9.25 10.00

SAARC 1st Summit, Dec. 7-8 A303

1985, Dec. 8   **Perf. 14½x14**
774	A303	60c shown	6.00 7.00
775	A303	5.50r Flags on UN emblem	6.00 6.00

No. 720 Surcharged in Intense Blue

1986, Jan. 20   **Perf. 12½x12**
776	A275	1r on 7r Map	12.00 4.50

Viceroy Special Train A304

1986, Feb. 2   **Perf. 12½x13**
777	A304	1r multicolored	1.75 1.50

Colombo-Kandy line inauguration.

Students A305

1986, Feb. 14   **Perf. 14**
778	A305	75c multicolored	.80 1.10

Mahapola Scholarship Program for development and education, 6th anniv.

Don Richard Wijewardene (1886-1950), Newspaper Publisher — A306

1986, Feb. 23   **Perf. 14x15**
779	A306	75c sage grn & brn	.40 1.00

Welitara Gnanatillake Mahanayake Thero (1858-1941), Scientist — A307

1986, Feb. 26   **Wmk. 385**   **Perf. 13½**
780	A307	75c multicolored	1.00 1.10

No. 692 Surcharged
1986, Mar. 10   **Litho.**   **Perf. 14½**
780A	A264	7r on 35c	8.00 1.50

Natl. Red Cross Society, 50th Anniv. A308

1986, Mar. 31   **Perf. 12½x13**
781	A308	75c multicolored	3.25 2.50

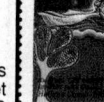

Halley's Comet A309

50c, Comet is not an omen. 75c, Constellations. 6.50r, Trajectory diagrams. 8.50r, Edmond Halley.

1986, Apr. 5   **Perf. 12½**
782	A309	50c multicolored	.25 .25
783	A309	75c multicolored	.25 .25
784	A309	6.50r multicolored	.40 1.25
785	A309	8.50r multicolored	.55 2.00
a.		Souvenir sheet of 4, #782-785, perf. 12½x13	8.50 10.50
		Nos. 782-785 (4)	1.45 3.75

Sinhalese and Tamil New Year — A310

Designs: 50c, Woman lighting lamp. 75c, Woman, holiday foods. 6.50r, Women celebrating around table. 8.50r, Food preparation, feast, anointment ritual.

1986, Apr. 10
786	A310	50c multicolored	.25 .25
787	A310	75c multicolored	.25 .25
788	A310	6.50r multicolored	.50 1.75
789	A310	8.50r multicolored	.80 2.00
a.		Souvenir sheet of 4, #786-789, perf. 13x12½	5.00 5.50
		Nos. 786-789 (4)	1.80 4.25

No. 740 Surcharged
1986, Apr. 29   **Perf. 12½x13**
790	A286	1r on 4.60r multi	9.00 4.50

Vesak Festival A311

Jathaka Story frescoes from the house Samudragiri Vihara, Mirissa, recounting the life of Siddhartha (583-463 B.C.): 50c, King Kurudhamma Jathakaya gives elephant to the brahman. 75c, Vasavarthi heaven. 5r, Sujatha's milk rice offering. 10d, Thapassu and Bhalluka's parched corn and honey offering.

1986, May 16
791	A311	50c multicolored	.25 .25
792	A311	75c multicolored	.25 .25
793	A311	5d multicolored	.60 2.00
794	A311	10d multicolored	.70 3.00
		Nos. 791-794 (4)	1.80 5.50

Natl. Heroes — A312

No. 795, Kalukondayave Sri Prajnasekhara Mahanayaka Thero (1895-1977), theologian. No. 796, Brahmachari Walisinghe Harischandra (1876-1913), historian, social reformer. No. 797, Martin Wickramasinghe (1890-1970), author. No. 798, Ganapathipillai Gangaser Ponnambalam (1901-72), diplomat. No. 799, Aboobucker Mohammed Abdul Azeez (1911-73), scholar.

1986, May 22   **Perf. 13x12½**
795	A312	75c multicolored	.25 .70
796	A312	75c multicolored	.25 .70
797	A312	75c multicolored	.25 .70

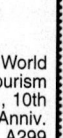

798 A312 75c multicolored .25 .70
799 A312 75c multicolored .25 .70
Nos. 795-799 (5) 1.25 3.50

Natl. Cooperative Movement, 75th Anniv. — A313

1986, June 23
800 A313 1r multicolored 1.60 2.00

Gam Udawa, Intl. Year of Housing A314

1986, June 23 *Perf. 13½x13*
801 A314 75c multicolored 2.10 2.10

Arthur V. Dias — A315

1986, July 31 *Perf. 14x15*
802 A315 1r multicolored 2.50 2.50

World Wildlife Fund A316

Elephants: a, Adult with tusks. b, Adult, calf. c, Adult. d, Family in river.

1986, Aug. 5 *Perf. 15x14*
803 Strip of 4 70.00 40.00
a.-d. A316 5r any single 15.00 10.00

2nd Indo-Pacific Congress on Legal Medicine and Forensic Sciences — A317

1986, Aug. 14 *Perf. 13½x13*
804 A317 8.50r multicolored 4.00 4.00

Submarine Cable — A318

1986, Sept. 8 *Perf. 13½x14*
805 A318 5.75r Handset, map 7.75 4.75
South-East Asia, Middle East, Western Europe Submarine Cable System.

Dag Hammarskjold Award — A320

1986, Sept. 20 *Litho.* *Perf. 13x12½*
808 A320 2r multicolored 1.90 1.50

Second Natl. School Games, Sept. 22-27 — A321

1986, Sept. 22 *Perf. 12*
809 A321 1r multicolored 4.75 2.40

Natl. Surveyor's Institute, 60th Anniv. — A322

1986, Sept. 27 *Perf. 13½x13*
810 A322 75c multicolored 1.00 1.25

Ananda College, Cent. A323

College crest and: 75c, College. 5r, Athletic field. 5.75r, Founders Migettuwatte Gunananda, Hikkaduwe Sumangala and Col. H.S. Olcott, Buddhist flag and College, 1886, 1986. 6r, Crest on flag.

1986, Nov. 1 *Perf. 12*
811 A323 75c multicolored .25 .25
812 A323 5r multicolored .50 .80
813 A323 5.75r multicolored .55 .80
814 A323 6r multicolored .65 1.00
Nos. 811-814 (4) 1.95 2.85

Wildlife Conservation — A324

35c, Mangrove habitat. 50c, Rhizophora apiculata. 75c, Germinating flower. 6r, Fiddler crab.

1986, Nov. 11
815 A324 35c multicolored 1.25 1.25
816 A324 50c multicolored 1.40 1.40
817 A324 75c multicolored 1.50 1.50
818 A324 6r multicolored 11.00 11.00
Nos. 815-818 (4) 15.15 15.15
Preservation of mangrove habitats.
For surcharges on Nos. 815 and 818, see Nos. 1513 and 1516.

Intl. Year of Shelter for the Homeless A325

1987, Jan. 1 *Litho.* *Perf. 13x13½*
819 A325 75c multicolored 3.00 .95

A.I. Thero, 19th Cent. Theologian A326

1987, Jan. 29 *Perf. 12*
820 A326 5.75r multicolored 4.50 1.25

Proctor John De Silva (b. 1854), Lawyer and Playwright A327

1987, Jan. 31
821 A327 5.75r multicolored 1.10 1.10

Mahapola Educational Plan, 7th Anniv. — A328

1987, Feb. 6
822 A328 75c multicolored 1.25 1.25

Dr. R.L. Brohier, Historian — A329

1987, Feb. 14
823 A329 5.75r multicolored 3.75 1.75

Sri Lanka Tire Corp., 25th Anniv. A330

1987, Mar. 23 *Perf. 14*
824 A330 5.75r multicolored .80 .80

Sri Lanka Medical Assoc., Cent. A331

1987, Mar. 24 *Perf. 13x13½*
825 A331 5.75r multicolored 3.25 3.50

Farmers' Pension and Social Security Plan — A332

1987, Mar. 29 *Perf. 14*
826 A332 75c multicolored 1.60 1.60

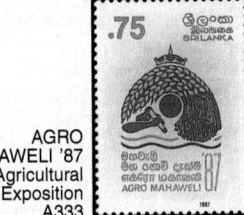

AGRO MAHAWELI '87 Agricultural Exposition A333

1987, Apr. 2 *Perf. 12*
827 A333 75c multicolored .60 .60

Child Immunization Program — A334

1987, Apr. 7 *Perf. 13½*
828 A334 1r multicolored 4.25 1.50
World Health Day.

Sinhalese and Tamil New Year — A335

1987, Apr. 9 *Perf. 12*
829 A335 75c Three girls, swing .25 .25
830 A335 5r Lamp, women .80 .80

Vesak Festival Lanterns A336

1987, May 4 *Perf. 12*
831 A336 50c Lotus .25 .25
832 A336 75c Octagonal .25 .25
833 A336 5r Star .45 .45
834 A336 10r Gok .65 .65
a. Souvenir sheet of 4, #831-834 1.75 1.75
Nos. 831-834 (4) 1.60 1.60

Natl. Olympic Committee, 50th
Anniv. — A337

1987, May 8   *Perf. 13½*
835 A337 10r multicolored   3.75 1.60

Birds
A338

50c, Layard's parakeet. 1r, Legge's
flowerpecker. 5r, Sri Lanka white-headed starling. 10r, Sri Lanka rufous babbler.

1987, May 18   *Perf. 14*
836 A338 50c multicolored   .70 .25
837 A338 1r multicolored   1.10 .25
  a.   Dated "1989"   1.10
838 A338 5r multicolored   1.60 1.75
839 A338 10r multicolored   2.10 2.25
  a.   Souvenir sheet of 4, #836-839   9.75 9.75
  b.   As #839, dated "1990"   2.25 2.25
       Nos. 836-839 (4)   5.50 4.50

Natl.
Heroes — A339

#840, Heenatiyana Sri Dhammaloka Thero,
20th cent. theologian. #841, P. de S.
Kularatne, educator. #842, M.C. Abdul
Rahuman, politician.

1987, May 22   *Perf. 12*
840 A339 75c multicolored   .60 .40
841 A339 75c multicolored   .60 .40
842 A339 75c multicolored   .60 .40
       Nos. 840-842 (3)   1.80 1.20

Gam
Udawa
A340

1987, June 23
843 A340 75c multicolored   .50 .50
     Village reformation movement.

Natl.
Forestry
Agency,
Cent.
A341

75c, Mesua nagassarium. 5r, Elephants in
forest.

1987, June 25
844 A341 75c multicolored   .30 .30
845 A341 5r multicolored   2.00 2.00

Founder
H.S. Olcott
and
College
A342

1987, June 30
846 A342 75c multicolored   4.00 .55
     Dharmaraja College, cent.

**No. 528 Redrawn with Denomination
in Upper Right Corner**
1987, July 1   **Photo.**   *Perf. 13x13½*
       Size: 20x24mm
847 A189 75c green & gold   .40 .25

Youth
Services
Emblem
A343

1987, July 15   **Litho.**   *Perf. 12*
848 A343 75c multicolored   .40 .40
     Natl. Youth Services Act, 20th anniv.

Mahaweli
Games — A344

1987, Sept. 5   **Litho.**   *Perf. 12*
849 A344 75c multicolored   5.25 2.75

Ceylon Bible
Society, 175th
Anniv. — A345

1987, Oct. 2
850 A345 5.75r multicolored   .80 .80

Kandy Friend-in-Need Society, 150th
Anniv. — A346

1987, Nov. 4   *Perf. 13½x13*
851 A346 75c multicolored   .40 .40

Christmas
1987 — A347

1987, Nov. 25   **Litho.**   *Perf. 12*
852 A347 75c Mother and Child   .25 .25
853 A347 10r Infant, star, dove   .50 .50
  a.   Souvenir sheet of 2, #852-853   1.60 1.60

Sir Ernest de Silva
(1887-1957),
Banker,
Philatelist — A348

1987, Nov. 25   *Perf. 13x13½*
854 A348 75c multicolored   .40 .40

1st Convocation
Ceremony at
Buddhist and Pali
University — A349

1987, Dec. 14   *Perf. 12*
855 A349 75c yel, lake & org yel   .40 .40

Missionary Work
of Fr. Joseph Vaz
(1651-1711),
300th
Anniv. — A350

1987, Dec. 15
856 A350 75c multicolored   .40 .40

Buddhist
Publication Soc.,
Kandy, 30th
Anniv. — A351

Design: Wheel of Life, dagaba (temple
cupola) and Bo (Tree of Life) leaf.

1988, Jan. 1   **Litho.**   *Perf. 12*
857 A351 75c multicolored   .50 .50

Mahapola
Dharmayatra,
5th Anniv.
A352

1988, Jan. 4   *Perf. 13½x13*
858 A352 75c multicolored   .60 .60

Ceylon Arts Soc.,
Cent. — A353

1988, Jan. 8   *Perf. 12*
859 A353 75c multicolored   1.00 .90

Opening of
the Natl.
Youth Center,
Maharagama
A354

1988, Jan. 31   *Perf. 13½x13*
860 A354 1r multicolored   5.50 .80

Natl.
Independence,
40th
Anniv. — A355

1988, Feb. 4   *Perf. 12*
861 A355 75c shown   .25 .25
862 A355 8.50r Heraldic lion, "40"   1.10 1.10

Mahapola
Movement, 8th
Anniv. — A356

75c, Youth Education Services.

1988, Feb. 11
863 A356 75c multicolored   .40 .40

Transportation Board, 30th
Anniv. — A357

1988, Feb. 19
864 A357 5.75r multicolored   .80 .80

Weligama Sri
Sumangala Maha
Nayake Thero
(1825-1905),
Buddhist Monk,
Sanskrit
Scholar — A358

1988, Mar. 13
865 A358 75c multicolored   .40 .40

Artillery
Regiment,
Cent.
A359

1988, Apr. 20
866 A359 5.75r multicolored   4.25 1.25

Chevalier I.X. Pereira (1888-1951), Politician — A360

1988, Apr. 26   Litho.   Perf. 12
867 A360 5.75r multicolored   .50   .50

Vesak Festival A361

Paintings in Suriyagoda Sri Narendraramaya Viharaya temple, Kandy District: 50c, Buddha inviting deities and brahmas to be born into the world as Buddhists. 75c, Buddha walking seven steps on seven lotus flowers, followers paying homage.

1988, May 13   Perf. 12½x12
868 A361 50c multicolored   .40   .40
869 A361 75c multicolored   .40   .40
  a.   Souvenir sheet of 2, #868-869   2.40   2.40

Natl. Heroes — A362

Designs: No. 870, Rev.-Father Ferdinand Bonnel (1873-1945), Jesuit priest who founded St. Michael's College, Batticaloa. No. 871, Sir Razik Fareed (1893-1984), political and social reformer. No. 872, W.F. Gunawardhana (b. 1861), founder of the Oriental Studies Soc. No. 873, Edward Alexander Nugawela (1898-1972), politician. No. 874, Sir Edwin Arthur Lewis Wijeyewardene (b 1887), first Ceylonese chief justice, attorney general.

1988, May 22   Perf. 12x12½
870 A362 75c multicolored   .25   .25
871 A362 75c multicolored   .25   .25
872 A362 75c multicolored   .25   .25
873 A362 75c multicolored   .25   .25
874 A362 75c multicolored   .25   .25
  Nos. 870-874 (5)   1.25   1.25

Gam Udawa, 10th Anniv. A363

1988, June 23   Litho.   Perf. 12
875 A363 75c multicolored   .60   .30

Village reformation movement.

Maliyadeva College, Cent. — A364

1988, June 30   Perf. 13½x13
876 A364 75c multicolored   .60   .30

Bird Type of 1983
1988, Sept. 28   Litho.   Perf. 14½
877 A264 7r like No. 692   1.00   1.00

Mohamed J.M. Lafir (1929-1980), World Amateur Billiards Champion — A365

1988, July 5   Litho.   Perf. 12½x12
878 A365 5.75r multicolored   1.00   .60

Australia Bicentennial — A366

1988, July 19   Litho.   Perf. 12
879 A366 8.50r multicolored   1.00   .75

A367

1988, Aug. 11   Perf. 12x12½
880 A367 75c multicolored   .50   .30

Gunaratna Maha Nayake Thero (1752-1832), Buddhist and Sinhalese language scholar.

A368

1988, Sept. 3   Perf. 12
881 A368 75c multicolored   .50   .30

Mahaweli games.

1988 Summer Olympics, Seoul — A369

75c, Running. 1r, Swimming. 5.75r, Boxing. 8.50r, Handshake, map, emblems.

1988, Sept. 6   Perf. 12x12½
882 A369 75c multicolored   .25   .25
883 A369 1r multicolored   .25   .25
884 A369 5.75r multicolored   .55   .55
885 A369 8.50r multicolored   .95   .95
  a.   Souvenir sheet of 4, #882-885   2.25   2.25
  Nos. 882-885 (4)   2.00   2.00

WHO, 40th Anniv. — A370

1988, Sept. 12   Perf. 12
886 A370 75c multicolored   .50   .50

3rd Natl. School Games, Sept. 20-25 A371

1988, Sept. 20
887 A371 1r multicolored   4.25   .60

Mahatma Gandhi — A372

1988, Oct. 2   Perf. 12
888 A372 75c multicolored   3.50   1.00

Transportation and Communication Decade, 1978-88 — A373

Modes of transportation and: 75c, Globe. 5.75r, Communication tower.

1988, Oct. 24   Litho.   Perf. 12½x12
889 A373 75c multicolored   .75   .25
890 A373 5.75r multicolored   4.00   2.40

For surcharge, see No. 1580.

Randenigala Project — A374

75c, Woman, dam, power station. 5.75r, Hydrelectric dam.

1988, Oct. 31   Perf. 12
891 A374 75c multicolored   .35   .35
892 A374 5.75r multicolored   1.05   1.05

Some stamps were distributed at the time the set was originally planned to be issued in 1986.

Opening of Gramodaya Folk Art Center — A375

1988, Nov. 17   Litho.   Perf. 13½
893 A375 75c multicolored   .50   .50

Christmas — A376

8.50r, Shepherds see star.

1988, Nov. 25   Perf. 12x12½
894 A376 75c shown   .25   .25
895 A376 8.50r multicolored   1.00   1.00
  a.   Souvenir sheet of 2, #894-895   3.00   3.00

E.W. Adikaram (1905-85), Educator — A377

1988, Dec. 28   Perf. 12
896 A377 75c multicolored   .50   .50

Waterfalls — A378

1989, Aug. 11   Litho.   Perf. 12
897 A378 75c Dunhinda   .30   .30
898 A378 1r Rawana   .30   .30
899 A378 5.75r Laxapana   1.25   1.25
900 A378 8.50r Diyaluma   1.75   1.75
  Nos. 897-900 (4)   3.60   3.60

Free Distribution of School Text Books, 10th Anniv. A379

1989, Jan. 23   Litho.   Perf. 13½x13
901 A379 75c multicolored   .40   .40

Poets — A380

No. 902, Wimalaratne Kumaragama. No. 903, G.H. Perera. No. 904, Sagara Palansuriya. No. 905, P.B. Alwis Perera.

1989, Jan. 27   *Perf. 13*
902 A380 75c multicolored .25 .25
903 A380 75c multicolored .25 .25
904 A380 75c multicolored .25 .25
905 A380 75c multicolored .25 .25
    Nos. 902-905 (4) 1.00 1.00

Mahapola Educational Plan, 8th Anniv. — A381

1989, Feb.   *Perf. 13½*
906 A381 75c multicolored .40 .25

Chamber of Commerce, 150th Anniv. — A382

1989, Mar. 25   *Litho.*   *Perf. 12*
907 A382 75c multicolored .40 .25

AGRO Mahaweli A383

1989, Sept. 2   *Litho.*   *Perf. 12*
908 A383 75c multicolored .65 .30

Famous Men A384

No. 909, Simon Casie Chitty. No. 910, Parawahera Sri Vajiragnana Thero. No. 911, Fr. Maurice Le Goc. No. 912, Hemapala Munidasa. No. 913, Ananda Samarakoon.

1989, May 22
909 A384 75c multicolored .35 .35
910 A384 75c multicolored .35 .35
911 A384 75c multicolored .35 .35
912 A384 75c multicolored .35 .35
913 A384 75c multicolored .35 .35
    Nos. 909-913 (5) 1.75 1.75
    Nos. 910-913 vert.

Hartley College, 150th Anniv. (in 1988) — A385

1989, June 5
914 A385 75c multicolored .40 .25

Vesak Festival A386

Various paintings in Medawala Viharaya, Harispattuwa.

1989, May 15   *Litho.*   *Perf. 12½x12*
915 A386 50c multicolored .25 .25
916 A386 75c multicolored .25 .25
917 A386 5r multicolored .55 .40
918 A386 5.75r multicolored .65 .50
a.   Souvenir sheet of 4, #915-918 2.10 2.10
    Nos. 915-918 (4) 1.70 1.40

For surcharge see No. 953A.

Pres. Premadasa's Declaration Establishing the Ministry of Buddha Sasana — A387

1989, June 18   *Litho.*   *Perf. 12½x12*
919 A387 75c multicolored .40 .40

Gam Udawa, 11th Anniv. A388

1989, June 23
920 A388 75c multicolored .50 .40

Village reformation movement.

French Revolution, Bicent. A389

1989, Aug. 26   *Litho.*   *Perf. 13½x13*
921 A389 8.50r rose & deep blue 1.75 1.75

Bank of Ceylon, 50th Anniv. A390

75c, Old, new headquarters. 5r, Emblem, flowers.

1989, Aug. 31
922 A390 75c multicolored .25 .25
923 A390 5r multicolored .80 .65

Jana Saviya Grants A391

1989, June 23   *Litho.*   *Perf. 12x11½*
924 A391 75c multicolored .70 .70

Development program to eliminate poverty and improve the standard of living through education and by providing food, health care, shelter and clothing.
See No. 953. For surcharge see No. 955.

Baptist Mission, 177th Anniv. A392

1989, Aug. 19   *Perf. 12½x12*
925 A392 5.75r James Chater,
    church, 1812 1.00 1.00

For surcharge, see No. 1405.

State Literary Festival — A393

1989, Sept. 22   *Perf. 12x11½*
926 A393 75c multicolored .50 .40

Wilhelm Geiger — A394

1989, Sept. 30   *Perf. 13x13½*
927 A394 75c multicolored .50 .40

Wilhelm Geiger (1856-1943), German philologist who studied Sinhalese.

Wildlife Type of 1981

1989, Oct. 11   *Perf. 14*
928 A219 3r like No. 595 4.00 .40

No. 928 has black inscriptions and is dated "1989." See No. 729 for brown inscriptions.

Famous Lawyers — A395

No. 929, H.V. Perera (1890-1969). No. 930, Sir Ivor Jennings (1903-1965).

1989, Oct. 16   *Perf. 12x11½*
929 A395 75c multicolored .25 .25
930 A395 75c multicolored .25 .25

Sir Cyril de Zoysa — A396

1989, Oct. 26   *Perf. 13x13½*
931 A396 75c multicolored .50 .40

Sir Cyril de Zoysa (1896-1978), key figure in the Buddhist cultural reformation.

Asia-Pacific Telecommunity, 10th Anniv. — A397

1989, Nov. 1   *Perf. 12x12½*
932 A397 5.75r multicolored .90 .60

For surcharge, see No. 1574.

Sri Sucharitha Viyaparaya Oratory Children's Soc., 50th Anniv. A398

1989, Nov. 9   *Perf. 13*
933 A398 75c multicolored .60 .60

1st Moon Landing, 20th Anniv. — A399

75c, Apollo 11 liftoff, crew. 1r, Astronaut descending ladder. 2r, Astronaut on lunar surface. 5.75r, Lunar surface, view of Earth.

1989, Nov. 10   *Perf. 12x12½*
934 A399 75c multicolored .25 .25
935 A399 1r multicolored .25 .25
936 A399 2r multicolored .45 .40
937 A399 5.75r multicolored 1.25 .70
a.   Souvenir sheet of 4, #934-937 3.25 3.25
    Nos. 934-937 (4) 2.20 1.60

For No. 937 surcharged, see No. 1515.

Christmas — A400

75c, Adoration of the Shepherds. 8.50r, Adoration of the Magi.

1989, Nov. 21   *Perf. 13½*
938 A400 75c multicolored .25 .25
939 A400 8.50r multicolored .80 .80
a.   Souvenir sheet of 2, #938-939 2.25 2.25

Devananda Nayake Thero — A401

1989, Nov. 25   *Perf. 12x11½*
940 A401 75c multicolored .50 .50

Devananda Nayake Thero (1921-1983), religious scholar, educator, reformer.

Rev. William Ault, College and Crest A402

1989, Nov. 29   *Perf. 11½x12*
941 A402 75c multicolored .50 .40

Batticaloa Methodist Central College, 175th anniv.

Nuwara Eliya Golf Club, Cent. A403

1989, Dec. 8   **Perf. 14x13½**
942 A403 75c shown   4.50   .50
943 A403 8.50r Course, golf
            house   12.00 9.50

Raja — A404

1989, Dec. 12   **Perf. 13x13½**
944 A404 75c multicolored   7.50 1.25
Raja (1913-1988), the royal tusker of the Sri Dalada Maligawa that carried the relic casket in the Kandy Esala Procession.

Gampaha Wickamarachchi Ayurveda Medical College, 60th Anniv. — A405

1989, Dec. 14   **Perf. 13½x13**
945 A405 75c Founder, institute   .70   .40

Udunuwara Sri Sarananda Mahanayake Thero (1867-1947), Educator — A406

1989, Dec. 20   **Perf. 12x12½**
946 A406 75c multicolored   .50   .35

Railway Dept., 125th Anniv. A407

75c, Train, viaduct. 2r, Train, light signal, Maradana Station. 3r, Steam locomotive, semaphore signal. 7r, 1st train in Sri Lanka.

1989, Dec. 27   **Perf. 11½x12, 13 (3r)**
947 A407 75c multicolored   1.00   .30
948 A407 2r multicolored   2.40   .50
949 A407 3r multicolored   2.40   .85
950 A407 7r multicolored   4.75 2.00
      Nos. 947-950 (4)   10.55 3.65

A408

1989, Dec. 28   **Perf. 13x13½**
951 A408 75c multicolored   2.25   .35
Thomas Cooray (1901-88), 1st native Sri Lankan Cardinal.

A409

1990, Jan. 14   **Perf. 12x12½**
952 A409 1r multicolored   3.25   .35
Justin Wijayawardena (1904-82), educator, politician.

Jana Saviya Grants Type of 1989
1990, Jan. 31   Litho.   Perf. 12x11½
953 A391 1r multicolored   .75   .40

No. 918 Surcharged

1990, Feb. 16   Litho.   Perf. 12½x12
953A A386 25c on 5.75r multi   1.40   .30

Induruwe Uttarananda Mahanayake Thero — A411

1990, Mar. 15   Litho.   Perf. 12
954 A411 1r multicolored   2.25 1.40

No. 924 Surcharged

1990, Mar. 22   Litho.   Perf. 12x11½
955 A391 1r on 75c multi   3.00 1.75

Silver Jubilee of Laksala A413

Traditional handicrafts.

1990, Apr. 2   Litho.   Perf. 12
956 A413 1r Drums   .40   .25
957 A413 2r Silverware   .55   .25
958 A413 3r Lacquerware   .90   .30
959 A413 8r Dumbara mats   2.40 2.75
      Nos. 956-959 (4)   4.25 3.55

Vesak Festival A414

Various paintings in Wewurukannala Buduraja Maha Viharaya.

1990, May 2   **Perf. 12½x12**
960 A414 75c multicolored   .25   .25
961 A414 1r multicolored   .25   .25
962 A414 2r multicolored   .30   .30
963 A414 8r multicolored   1.10 1.10
a.   Souvenir sheet of 4, #960-963   2.25 2.25
      Nos. 960-963 (4)   1.90 1.90

A415

1990, May 22   **Perf. 12**
964 A415 1r Rev. T.M.F. Long   .60   .35

Size: 25x39mm
Perf. 12x12½
965 A416 1r D.P.A. Wijewardene   .60   .35
966 A416 1r L.T.P. Manjusri   .60   .35
967 A416 1r M.D. Ratnasuriya   .60   .35
      Nos. 964-967 (4)   2.40 1.40

Famous Men — A416

Gam Udawa Program, 12th Anniv. A417

1990, June 23   **Perf. 12½x12**
968 A417 1r multicolored   2.50   .60

Dept. of Archaeology, Cent. — A418

1r, Gold reliquary from Delivala Temple, c. 200 B.C. 2r, Statuette of Ganesha (the Elephant God) from Polonnaruwa. 3r, Terrace of the Bodhi-tree at Isurumuni Vihara. 8r, Stone seat with inscription of King Nissankamalle, 12th cent. A.D.

1990, July 7   **Perf. 12**
969 A418 1r black & orange   .40   .25
970 A418 2r black & gray   .70   .25
971 A418 3r black, yel grn & gold   1.00   .40
972 A418 8r black & gold   2.40 1.50
      Nos. 969-972 (4)   4.50 2.40

Sri Lanka Tennis Assoc., 75th Anniv. — A419

No. 973, Player ready to volley. No. 974, Player receiving volley. No. 975, Men players. No. 976, Women players.

1990, Aug. 14   **Perf. 13½**
973   1r multicolored   1.00 1.00
974   1r multicolored   1.00 1.00
a.   A419 Pair, #973-974   2.25 2.25

975   8r multicolored   3.50 3.50
976   8r multicolored   3.50 3.50
a.   A419 Pair, #975-976   7.75 7.75
      Nos. 973-976 (4)   9.00 9.00

Fish — A420

25c, Spotted loach. 2r, Ornate paradise fish. 8r, Mountain labeo. 20r,

1990, Sept. 14   **Perf. 11½**
977 A420 25c multicolored   .30   .30
978 A420 2r multicolored   .45   .45
979 A420 8r multicolored   1.25 1.25
980 A420 20r multicolored   2.50 2.50
a.   Souvenir sheet of 4, #977-980   5.50 5.50
      Nos. 977-980 (4)   4.50 4.50

For No. 979 surcharged, see No. 1303A.

A421

1r, Letter box, 1904. 2r, Mail runner, 1815. 5r, Mail coach, 1832. 10r, Nuwara-Eliya Post Office, 1894.

1990, Dec. 26   **Perf. 12**
981 A421 1r multicolored   .85   .60
982 A421 2r multicolored   1.60   .85
983 A421 5r multicolored   3.25 2.75
984 A421 10r multicolored   4.25 4.25
      Nos. 981-984 (4)   9.95 8.45

Sri Lanka Postal Service, 175th anniv.

A422

1990, Oct. 28   Litho.   Perf. 12
985 A422 1r multicolored   6.25 1.75
Rukmani Devi (1923-78), actress.

Christmas A423

1r, Mary, Joseph at inn. 10r, Adoration of the Magi.

1990, Nov. 28   **Perf. 13**
986 A423 1r multicolored   .75   .45
987 A423 10r multicolored   5.25 4.75
a.   Souv. sheet of 2, #986-987, perf.
      12   7.00 7.00

World AIDS Day A424

1990, Nov. 30
988 A424 1r multicolored 1.50 .25
989 A424 8r AIDS Virus 5.50 4.00

A425

1990, Dec. 8 *Perf. 12*
990 A425 1r multicolored 3.50 1.60

Dharmapala College, 50th anniv.

A426

1990, Dec. 14 **Litho.** *Perf. 12*
991 A426 1r olive green & brown 4.25 1.50

Peri Sunderam (b. 1890), political & social reformer.

Ceylon Institute of Chemistry, 50th anniv. — A427

1991, Jan. 25 **Litho.** *Perf. 12*
992 A427 1r multicolored 4.25 1.50

Vesak Festival A428

Various scenes from Buddha's life.

1991, May 17 **Litho.** *Perf. 12*
993 A428 75c multicolored .45 .25
994 A428 1r multicolored .45 .25
995 A428 2r multicolored .85 .40
996 A428 11r multicolored 3.75 3.25
  a. Souvenir sheet of 4, #993-996 6.50 6.50
  Nos. 993-996 (4) 5.50 4.15

A429

1991, May 31 *Perf. 12*
997 A429 1r multicolored 2.00 1.10

Mahabodhi Society, cent.

A430

Famous men — No. 998, Narada Thero. No. 999, Sir Muttu Coomaraswamy. No. 1000, Dr. Andreas Nell. No. 1001, W.A. Silva.

1991, May 22 **Litho.** *Perf. 12x12½*
998 A430 1r multicolored .75 .65
999 A430 1r multicolored .75 .65
1000 A430 1r multicolored .75 .65
1001 A430 1r multicolored .75 .65
  Nos. 998-1001 (4) 3.00 2.60

Gam Udawa, 13th Anniv. A431

1991, June 23 **Litho.** *Perf. 12½*
1002 A431 1r multicolored 3.25 .90

Henpitagedera Gnanaseeha Nayake Thero (1909-1981), Religious Leader — A432

1991, Aug. 1
1003 A432 1r multicolored 2.50 .95

Colombo Plan, 40th Anniv. A433

1991, July 1 **Litho.** *Perf. 12*
1004 A433 1r multicolored 3.75 1.40

Survey Dept., 190th Anniv. A434

1991, Aug. 2 *Perf. 12½*
1005 A434 1r multicolored 3.50 1.25

Police Service, 125th Anniv. A435

1991, Sept. 3 **Litho.** *Perf. 12½*
1006 A435 1r multicolored 1.75 .70

6th SAARC Summit A436

8r, Flags encircling building.

1991, Dec. 21 **Litho.** *Perf. 12½*
1007 A436 1r shown .25 .25
1008 A436 8r multicolored .70 1.25

Kingswood College, Cent. — A437

1991, Oct. 26 *Perf. 12½x12*
1009 A437 1r multicolored 1.00 .50

Christmas — A439

1991, Nov. 19 **Litho.** *Perf. 12½*
1014 A439 1r The Annunciation .40 .25
1015 A439 10r Nativity scene 1.50 2.00
  a. Sheet of 2, #1014-1015 2.50 2.50

A440

Telecommunications: 1r, Early telephone network. 2r, Switchboard operations. 8r, Satellite transmitters, cable network. 10r, Telephone, fiber optic cable, computer, cordless telephone, FAX machine.

1991, Nov. 23
1016 A440 1r multicolored .25 .25
1017 A440 2r multicolored .30 .25
1018 A440 8r multicolored .90 1.10
1019 A440 10r multicolored .90 1.10
  Nos. 1016-1019 (4) 2.35 2.70

5th South Asian Federation Games A441

1r, Mascot. 2r, Emblem. 4r, Stadium, Colombo. 11r, Globe and flags.

1991, Dec. 22 *Perf. 14*
1020 A441 1r multicolored .30 .25
1021 A441 2r multicolored .60 .25
1022 A441 4r multicolored 1.10 1.25
1023 A441 11r multicolored 2.50 3.50
  Nos. 1020-1023 (4) 4.50 5.25

Year of Exports A442

1992, Jan. 13 **Litho.** *Perf. 11½x12*
1024 A442 1r multicolored 3.00 1.00

Mahinda College, Cent. A443

1992, Mar. 2 **Litho.** *Perf. 11½x12*
1025 A443 1r multicolored .40 .40

General Ranjan Wijeratne (1931-1991) A444

1992, Mar. 2 **Litho.** *Perf. 12x12½*
1026 A444 1r multicolored .60 .25

Tea Production, 125th Anniv. A445

Field of tea and: 1r, Tea picker. 2r, Family, cup and glass of tea. 5r, Package of tea. 10r, James Taylor.

1992, Feb. 12 *Perf. 13½*
1027 A445 1r multicolored .70 .25
1028 A445 2r multicolored 1.40 .30
1029 A445 5r multicolored 3.25 2.50
1030 A445 10r multicolored 4.75 4.00
  Nos. 1027-1030 (4) 10.10 7.05

Newstead College, 175th Anniv. (in 1991) A446

1992, Mar. 13 **Litho.** *Perf. 11½x12*
1031 A446 1r multicolored .40 .40

Dated 1991.

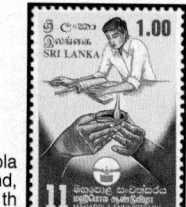
Mahapola Scholarship Fund, 11th Anniv. — A447

1992, Mar. 30 *Perf. 12*
1032 A447 1r multicolored .40 .40

Vesak Festival A448

Mural paintings from Kottimbulwala Rajamaha Vihara: 75c, Dukula and Parika retiring to forest. 1r, Sama and parents living in forest. 8r, Sama directing blind parents to hermitage. 11r, Sama's parents approach wounded son.

1992, May 5 **Litho.** *Perf. 11½x12*
1033 A448 75c multicolored .25 .25
1034 A448 1r multicolored .35 .25
1035 A448 8r multicolored 1.75 1.75

1036	A448	11r multicolored	2.50	2.50
a.		Souvenir sheet, #1033-1036	5.50	5.50
		Nos. 1033-1036 (4)	4.85	4.75

A449

National Heroes: No. 1037, Wadeebhasinha Dewamottawe Amarawansa Thero. No. 1038, R. A. Mirando. No. 1039, Gate Mudaliyar N. Canaganayagam. No. 1040, I.L.M. Abdul Azeez.

1992, May 22   Perf. 14

1037	A449	1r multicolored	.25	.25
1038	A449	1r multicolored	.25	.25
1039	A449	1r multicolored	.25	.25
1040	A449	1r multicolored	.25	.25
		Nos. 1037-1040 (4)	1.00	1.00

A450

1992, June 14   Litho.   Perf. 12x12½

1041	A450	1r multicolored	.70	.45

Introduction of Buddhism on Sri Lanka by Anubudu Mihindu Jayanthi, 2300th anniv.

Gam Udawa, 14th Anniv. A451

1992, June 23   Perf. 12

1042	A451	1r multicolored	.90	.45

Postal Excellence Service Awards A452

Designs: 1r, Award presentation, postal work. 10r, Award of excellence medals, No. 1043 canceled on envelope.

1992, July 11   Litho.   Perf. 14

1043	A452	1r multicolored	.75	.75
1044	A452	10r multicolored	4.50	4.50

A453

Masks of Sri Lanka.

1992, Aug. 19   Litho.   Perf. 13

1045	A453	1r Narilata	.40	.25
1046	A453	2r Mudali	.50	.40
1047	A453	5r Queen	1.00	.75
1048	A453	10r King	1.75	1.75
a.		Souvenir sheet, #1045-1048	4.50	4.50
		Nos. 1045-1048 (4)	3.65	3.15

A454

1992, Sept. 15   Litho.   Perf. 14

1049	A454	1r Running	.35	.25
1050	A454	11r Rifle shooting	2.50	2.50
1051	A454	13r Swimming	3.00	3.00
1052	A454	15r Weight lifting	3.25	3.25
a.		Souvenir sheet, #1049-1052	11.00	11.00
		Nos. 1049-1052 (4)	9.10	9.00

1992 Summer Olympics, Barcelona.

Cricket in Sri Lanka, 160th Anniv. A455

1992, Sept. 8   Litho.   Perf. 13

1053	A455	5r multicolored	5.50	3.25

Vijaya Kumaratunga, Entertainer and Political Leader, Birth Anniv. — A456

1992, Oct. 9

1054	A456	1r multicolored	.80	.50

Al-Bahjathul Ibraheemiyyah Arabic College, Cent. — A457

1992, Oct. 24   Perf. 12

1055	A457	1r multicolored	.60	.50

A458

1992, Oct. 25   Litho.   Perf. 12x11½

1056	A458	1r multicolored	2.25	.75

Dutch Reformed Church in Sri Lanka, 350th anniv.

Christmas A459

1992, Nov. 17   Litho.   Perf. 12x11½

1057	A459	1r Holy Family	.50	.25
1058	A459	9r Church, family	2.50	2.50
a.		Souvenir sheet, #1057-1058	3.50	3.50

Discovery of America, 500th Anniv. A460

Designs: 1r, Ships at sea, Aug. 1492. 11r, First landing in the Americas, Oct. 1492. 13r, Santa Maria aground, Dec. 1492. 15r, Return to Spain, Apr. 1493.

1992, Dec. 1   Perf. 14

1059	A460	1r multicolored	1.00	.35
1060	A460	11r multicolored	2.00	2.00
1061	A460	13r multicolored	2.75	2.75
1062	A460	15r multicolored	3.00	3.00
a.		Souvenir sheet, #1059-1062	9.50	9.50
		Nos. 1059-1062 (4)	8.75	8.10

No. 564 Surcharged

1992, Dec. 1   Litho.   Perf. 14

1062B	A206	2r on 10c multi	8.25	1.00

Dambagasare Sri Sumedhankara Maha Nayake Thero (1892-1984), Buddhist Monk — A461

1992, Dec. 10   Litho.   Perf. 12

1063	A461	1r multicolored	.40	.40

University Education in Sri Lanka A462

1992, Dec. 12   Litho.   Perf. 12

1064	A462	1r multicolored	.40	.40

No. 1064 was not available until Dec. 1993.

University of Colombo, 50th Anniv. (in 1992) A463

1993, Mar. 23   Litho.   Perf. 13

1065	A463	1r multicolored	1.10	.35

Zahira College, Cent. A464

1993, Apr. 7

1066	A464	1r multicolored	1.25	.40

Vesak Festival — A465

Designs based on verses from the Dhammapada (sermons of Buddha): 75c, Magandiya being presented to Buddha. 1r, Kisa Gotami carrying dead child. 3r, Patachara, dead family members. 10r, Conversion of Angulimala, the murderer.

1993, Apr. 30   Perf. 12x12½

1067	A465	75c multicolored	.25	.25
1068	A465	1r multicolored	.35	.35
1069	A465	3r multicolored	.75	.75
1070	A465	10r multicolored	1.50	1.50
a.		Souvenir sheet, #1067-1070	3.50	3.50
		Nos. 1067-1070 (4)	2.85	2.85

A466

1r, Guide, tent, emblem. 5r, Activities, map.

1993, May 10   Perf. 12

1071	A466	1r multicolored	.80	.35
1072	A466	5r multicolored	2.40	2.10

Girl Guides in Sri Lanka, 75th Anniv. (in 1992).

A467

National Heroes: No. 1073, Yagirala Sri Pagnananda Maha Nayaka Thero. No. 1074, C.P. De Silva. No. 1075, Wilmot A. Perera. No. 1076, N.D.H. Abdul Caffoor.

1993, May 22   Perf. 14

1073	A467	1r multicolored	.45	.50
1074	A467	1r multicolored	.45	.50
1075	A467	1r multicolored	.45	.50
1076	A467	1r multicolored	.45	.50
		Nos. 1073-1076 (4)	1.80	2.00

Gam Udawa, 15th Anniv. A468

1993, June 23   Litho.   Perf. 12½

1077	A468	1r multicolored	1.90	.50

Co-operative Consumer Service, 50th Anniv. — A469

1993, July 3   Perf. 13

1078	A469	1r multicolored	2.25	.50

Birds
A470

Designs: 3r, Ashy-headed laughing thrush. 4r, Ceylon brown-capped babbler. 5r, Red-faced malkoha. 10r, Ceylon hill-mynah.

1993, July 14   **Perf. 12½x12**
1079	A470	3r multicolored	.60	.60
1080	A470	4r multicolored	.60	.60
1081	A470	5r multicolored	1.00	1.00
1082	A470	10r multicolored	2.00	2.00
a.		Souvenir sheet, #1079-1082	5.00	5.00
		Nos. 1079-1082 (4)	4.20	4.20

Talawila Church, 150th Anniv.
A471

1993, July 26   **Perf. 13**
1083	A471	1r multicolored	1.50	.50

Postal Excellence Service Awards — A472

1993, Aug. 22
1084	A472	1r multicolored	1.50	.50

Technical Education in Sri Lanka, Cent.
A473

1993, Dec. 17
1085	A473	1r multicolored	1.50	.50

Musaeus College, Cent. — A474

1993, Nov. 15
1086	A474	1r multicolored	2.75	.50

Christmas
A475

Designs: 1r, Presentation of infant Jesus in Temple of Jerusalem. 17r, Boy Jesus in Temple.

1993, Nov. 30   **Litho.**   **Perf. 14x13½**
1087	A475	1r multicolored	.30	.25
1088	A475	17r multicolored	1.60	1.60
a.		Souvenir sheet, #1087-1088	2.25	2.25

Youth and Health — A476

1993, Dec. 16   **Perf. 14**
1089	A476	1r multicolored	.80	.40

Old Boy's Assoc., Trinity College, Kandy, Cent. — A478

1994, Feb. 11   **Litho.**   **Perf. 12½**
1091	A478	1r multicolored	.50	.45

St. Thomas College, Matara, 150th Anniv.
A479

1994, Mar. 10   **Litho.**   **Perf. 13**
1092	A479	1r multicolored	.50	.45

St. Joseph's College, 125th Anniv.
A480

1994, Apr. 4   **Litho.**   **Perf. 12½**
1093	A480	1r multicolored	.60	.35

Siyambalangamuwe Sri Gunaratana Thero — A481

1994, Apr. 2   **Litho.**   **Perf. 13**
1094	A481	1r multicolored	2.50	.45

ILO, 75th Anniv. — A482

1994, May 12
1095	A482	1r multicolored	1.75	.45

Vesak Festival
A483

Designs show actions by Bodhisatva in four of ten perfections: 1r, Dana, displaying generosity. 2r, Sila, morality. 5r, Nekkhamma, ascetic surrounded by worshippers. 17r, Panna, wisdom dispensed by Bodhisatva to others.

1994, May 7   **Litho.**   **Perf. 12½**
1096	A483	1r multicolored	.25	.25
1097	A483	2r multicolored	1.25	1.25
1098	A483	5r multicolored	1.25	1.25
1099	A483	17r multicolored	2.25	2.25
a.		Souvenir sheet, #1096-1099	5.50	5.50
		Nos. 1096-1099 (4)	5.00	5.00

Famous People
A484

Designs: No. 1100, Pres. Ranasinghe Premadasa. No. 1101, Ven. Mihiripanne Dhammaratana Thero. No. 1102, E. Periyathambipillai, poet. No. 1103, Dr. Colvin R. De Silva, politician.

1994, May 22   **Litho.**   **Perf. 14**
1100	A484	1r multicolored	.35	.40
1101	A484	1r multicolored	.35	.40
1102	A484	1r multicolored	.35	.40
1103	A484	1r multicolored	.35	.40
		Nos. 1100-1103 (4)	1.40	1.60

World Conference of Intl. Federation of Social Workers, Colombo
A485

1994, July 9   **Litho.**   **Perf. 12½**
1104	A485	8r blue, lt blue & blk	4.25	4.25

Bellanwila Sri Somaratana Nayake Thero — A486

1994, Aug. 2   **Litho.**   **Perf. 12½**
1105	A486	1r multicolored	2.60	.40

Infotel Lanka '94
A487

1994, Sept. 8
1106	A487	10r multicolored	3.25	3.25

Intl. Year of Indigenous People — A488

Designs: 1r, Veddah man making bow. 17r, Veddah man seated by rock art paintings.

1994, Sept. 12   **Litho.**   **Perf. 12**
1107	A488	1r multicolored	.55	.50
1108	A488	17r multicolored	5.00	5.00

Natl. Wildlife & Nature Protection Society, Cent.
A489

1r, Emblem. 2r, Rhino-horned lizard. 10r, Giant squirrel. 17r, Sloth bear.

1994, Nov. 24   **Litho.**   **Perf. 12½**
1109	A489	1r multicolored	.50	.25
1110	A489	2r multicolored	.90	.90
1111	A489	10r multicolored	2.50	2.50
1112	A489	17r multicolored	3.75	3.75
a.		Souvenir sheet, #1109-1112	8.00	8.00
		Nos. 1109-1112 (4)	7.65	7.40

Gam Udawa, 16th Anniv.
A490

1994, Sept.   **Litho.**   **Perf. 13**
1113	A490	1r multicolored	1.00	.25

A491

1994, Oct. 11   **Litho.**   **Perf. 12½**
1114	A491	1r multicolored	2.75	.90

Double entry bookkeeping, 500th anniv.

A492

1995, Feb. 22   **Perf. 14**
1115	A492	1r Water lily	1.25	.25

Richmond College Old Boys Assoc., Cent.
A493

1994   **Perf. 12½**
1116	A493	1r multicolored	.40	.25

ICAO, 50th Anniv.
A494

1994, Dec. 7   **Litho.**   **Perf. 13**
1117	A494	10r multicolored	4.75	3.00

Christmas
A495

Designs: 1r, Nativity. 17r, Jesus growing up, at home with Joseph and Mary.

1994, Dec. 8   Litho.   *Perf. 13*
1118 A495 1r multicolored   .30   .25
1119 A495 17r multicolored   3.75 3.75
  a. Souvenir sheet, #1118-1119   4.50 4.50

Assoc. for Advancement of Science, 50th Anniv. — A496

1994, Dec. 19   Litho.   *Perf. 13*
1120 A496 1r multicolored   3.25   .60

Orchid Circle of Ceylon, 60th Anniv. — A498

Orchids: 50c, Dendrobium maccarthiae. 1r, Cottonia peduncularis. 5r, Bulbophyllum wightii. 17r, Habenaria crinifera.

1994, Dec. 27   Litho.   *Perf. 13*
1122 A498 50c multicolored   .35   .25
1123 A498 1r multicolored   .50   .40
1124 A498 5r multicolored   .90   .90
1125 A498 17r multicolored   1.75 3.00
  a. Souvenir sheet, #1122-1125   6.00 6.00
  Nos. 1122-1125 (4)   3.50 4.55

Visit of Pope John Paul II, Beatification of Fr. Joseph Vaz — A499

1995, Jan. 20
1126 A499 1r multicolored   5.00 1.00

St. Joseph's College, Colombo, Cent. A500

1995, Mar. 2   Litho.   *Perf. 13*
1127 A500 1r multicolored   1.60   .50

Royal Asiatic Society of Sri Lanka, 150th Anniv. — A501

1995, Apr. 4
1128 A501 1r multicolored   3.50   .90

Sirimavo Bandaranaike, World's First Woman Prime Minister — A502

1995, Apr. 17   Litho.   *Perf. 12*
1129 A502 2r multicolored   2.25 1.10

A503

Vesak Festival (Designs show actions by a Bodhisatva in four of ten perfections): 1r, Endeavor, standing on shore. 2r, Forebearance, one holding another. 10r, Veracity, two people listening to truths. 17r, Resolution, man holding hoe.

1995, May 5   *Perf. 12x12½*
1130 A503 1r multicolored   .35   .25
1131 A503 2r multicolored   .45   .25
1132 A503 10r multicolored   1.40 1.10
1133 A503 17r multicolored   2.50 2.25
  a. Souvenir sheet, #1130-1133   5.50 5.50
  Nos. 1130-1133 (4)   4.70 3.85

M. C. Abdul Cader — A504

1995, June 3   *Perf. 11*
1134 A504 2r multicolored   2.50 1.25

St. Aloysius College, Galle, Cent. A506

1995, June 21   Litho.   *Perf. 12½x12*
1136 A506 2r multicolored   2.50 1.25

T.B. Ilangaratna (1913-92), Politician A507

1995, July 7   Litho.   *Perf. 13*
1137 A507 2r multicolored   2.50 1.25

Dhamma School, Cent. A508

1995, Aug. 3
1138 A508 2r multicolored   2.50 1.25

General Post Office, Colombo, Cent. A509

1995, Aug. 22   Litho.   *Perf. 13½*
1139 A509 1r multicolored   1.75   .45

Help the Elderly — A510

1995, Oct. 1   Litho.   *Perf. 14x13½*
1140 A510 2r multicolored   2.50 1.10

41st Commonwealth Parliamentary Conference — A511

1995, Oct. 9   Litho.   *Perf. 14x13½*
1141 A511 2r multicolored   2.50 1.10

UN, 50th Anniv. — A512

1995, Oct. 24   *Perf. 13½x14*
1142 A512 2r multicolored   2.50 1.10

World Thrift Day — A513

1995, Oct. 15
1143 A513 2r multicolored   2.50 1.10

A515

1995, Dec. 8
1146 A515 2r multicolored   3.50 1.25

SAARC, 10th anniv.

A516

50c, Little Basses. 75c, Great Basses. 2r, Devinuwara. 20r, Galle.

1996, Jan. 22   Litho.   *Perf. 12*
1147 A516 50c multicolored   .75   .50
1148 A516 75c multicolored   .75   .50
1149 A516 2r multicolored   1.75 1.00
1149A A516 2.50r like #1149   .75   .50
1150 A516 20r multicolored   5.00 2.75
  a. Souv. sheet, #1147-1149,
        1150   10.00 10.00
  Nos. 1147-1150 (5)   9.00 5.25

Lighthouses of Sri Lanka. Examples of No. 1150a overprinted in the margin for the 2010 National Stamp Fair, Colombo sold for 500r.
For surcharges see Nos. 1191-1193, 1282A.

Vincent High School, Batticaloa, 175th Anniv. — A517

1996, Jan. 17   Litho.   *Perf. 13*
1151 A517 2r multicolored   2.50 1.10

Handicrafts A518

25c, Traditional sesath. 8.50r, Pottery. 10.50r, Mats. 17r,

1996, Mar. 13   *Perf. 12*
1152 A518 25c multicolored   .25   .25
1153 A518 8.50r multicolored   .50   .45
1154 A518 10.50r multicolored   .80   .70
1155 A518 17r multicolored   1.10 1.10
  a. Souvenir sheet, #1152-1155 4.25 4.25
  Nos. 1152-1155 (4)   2.65 2.50

For surcharges see Nos. 1189-1190, 1548, 1575.

Christmas A514

Designs: 2r, Arms of Colombo and Kurunegla, Persian cross from Anuradhapura, Christian church. 20r, Clasping arms, nativity scene.

1995, Nov. 10   Litho.   *Perf. 13*
1144 A514 2r multicolored   .50   .25
1145 A514 20r multicolored   3.00 2.40
  a. Souvenir sheet, #1144-1145 4.00 4.00

A519

1996, Mar. 21
1156 A519 2r multicolored   3.00 1.10

Chundikuli Girls' College, Jaffna, cent.

A520

Vesak Festival: 1r, Capa cradling her son, teasing her husband. 2r, Dantika, mahout, elephant. 5r, Subha holding her eye in her hand, man of low morals. 10r, Punna explaining purification by water to Brahmin.

1996, Apr. 30   Litho.   Perf. 12
1157 A520 1r multicolored   .25   .25
1158 A520 2r multicolored   .50   .50
1159 A520 5r multicolored   .65   .65
1160 A520 10r multicolored   1.25 1.25
   a.   Souvenir sheet, #1157-1160   3.00 3.00
        Nos. 1157-1160 (4)   2.65 2.65

1996 Summer Olympic Games, Atlanta A521

1996, July 22   Litho.   Perf. 13½
1161 A521 1r Diving, vert.   .30   .25
1162 A521 2r Volleyball, vert.   1.25   .55
1163 A521 5r Shooting   1.50 1.50
1164 A521 17r Running   3.00 3.00
        Nos. 1161-1164 (4)   6.05 5.30

Sri Lanka, 1996 World Cup Cricket Champions — A522

1996, Aug. 18
1165 A522 2r Bowler   .55   .55
1166 A522 10.50r Wicketkeeper   1.10 1.10
1167 A522 17r Batsman   1.60 1.60
1168 A522 20r Trophy   1.75 1.75
   a.   Souvenir sheet, #1165-1168   5.50 5.50
        Nos. 1165-1168 (4)   5.00 5.00

No. 1168a contains two se-tenant pairs.

Jaffna Central College, 180th Anniv. A523

1996, Sept. 7   Litho.   Perf. 13½
1169 A523 2r multicolored   2.75 1.10

A524

1996, Nov. 4   Litho.   Perf. 13½x14
1170 A524 2r multicolored   3.00 1.25

UNESCO, 50th anniv.

A525

Christmas (Scenes of parables from murals, Trinity College Chapel): 2r, Washing of the feet. 17r, Good Samaritan.

1996, Dec. 2   Perf. 13½x13
1171 A525 2r multicolored   .35   .25
1172 A525 17r multicolored   1.90 1.60
   a.   Souvenir sheet, #1171-1172   2.25 2.25

UNICEF, 50th Anniv. — A526

1996, Dec. 12   Litho.   Perf. 13½x14
1173 A526 5r multicolored   1.10   .90

Swami Vivekananda A527

1997, Jan. 15   Perf. 13½x13
1174 A527 2.50r multicolored   1.50   .90

Personalities A528

Designs: No. 1175, Lt. Gen. Denzil Kobbekaduwa. No. 1176, Ven. Welivitiye Serata Thero. No. 1177, Dr. S.A. Wickremasinghe.

1997, Apr. 4   Litho.   Perf. 13½x13
1175 A528 2r multicolored   .60   .60
1176 A528 2r multicolored   .60   .60
1177 A528 2r multicolored   .60   .60
        Nos. 1175-1177 (3)   1.80 1.80

Vesak Festival — A529

Cemeteries, monuments to the dead: 1r, Thuparama. 2.50r, Ruwanvalisaya. 3r, Abhayagiri Dagaba. 17r, Jetavana Dagaba.

1997, May 7   Perf. 12x12½
1178 A529 1r multicolored   .25   .25
1179 A529 2.50r multicolored   .25   .25
1180 A529 3r multicolored   .25   .25
1181 A529 17r multicolored   1.25 1.25
   a.   Souvenir Sheet of 4, #1178-
        1181   2.75 2.75
        Nos. 1178-1181 (4)   2.00 2.00

D.J. Kumarage, Birth Cent. — A530

1997, Apr. 4   Litho.   Perf. 13½x14
1182 A530 2.50r multicolored   1.75   .90

Medicinal Herbs — A531

2.40r, Munronia pinnata. 14r, Rauvolfia serpentina.

1997, July 22   Litho.   Perf. 13½x14
1183 A531 2.50r multicolored   .30   .25
1184 A531 14r multicolored   1.50 1.50

Tourism A532

1997, Sept. 11   Perf. 12
1185 A532 20r multicolored   3.50 3.00

St. Servatius College, Matara, Cent. A533

1997, Nov. 1   Perf. 12½x12
1186 A533 2.50r multicolored   .90   .30

Mahagama Sekera — A534

1997, Apr. 4   Litho.   Perf. 13½x13
1187 A534 2r multicolored   .85   .40

Asterisks obliterate portions of Mahagama Sekera's name.

Sri Jayawardenapura Vidalaya, Kotte, 175th Anniv. — A535

1997, Jan. 28   Perf. 12½
1188 A535 2.50r multicolored   .60   .30

Nos. 1153-1154 Srchd.

1997, May 6   Litho.   Perf. 12
1189 A518 1r on 8.50r, #1153   8.00 1.00
1190 A518 11r on 10.50r, #1154
        (a)   6.50 6.50
   a.   Surcharge type b   6.50 6.50

Surcharge Type a on #1190 is 2½mm high. Type b surcharge is 3mm high.

No. 1149 Surcharged

c   d

e

1997, Feb. 12   Litho.   Perf. 12
1191 A516(c) 2.50r on 2r   6.00 6.00
1192 A516(d) 2.50r on 2r   6.00 6.00
1193 A516(e) 2.50r on 2r   6.00 6.00
        Nos. 1191-1193 (3)   18.00 18.00

A number has been reserved additional surcharge on No. 1149.

Reptiles A537

2.50r, Lyre head lizard. 5r, Boie's roughside. 17r, Common Lanka skink. 20r, Great forest gecko.

1997, Oct. 18   Litho.   Perf. 12

1195	A537	2.50r multicolored	.30	.30
1196	A537	5r multicolored	.45	.45
1197	A537	17r multicolored	.85	.85
1198	A537	20r multicolored	.95	.95
a.		Souvenir sheet, #1195-1198	3.00	3.00
		Nos. 1195-1198 (4)	2.55	2.55

A538

Christmas: 2.50r, Holy Family. 20r, Adoration of the Magi.

1997, Nov. 20   Perf. 12½x13

1199	A538	2.50r multicolored	.30	.25
1200	A538	20r multicolored	1.50	.90
a.		Souvenir sheet, #1199-1200	1.90	1.90

A539

Personalities: #1201, Hegoda Sri Indasara Thero (1932-87), religious leader. #1202, Abdul Aziz (d. 1990), politician. #1203, Subramaniam Vithiananthan (b. 1924), teacher, writer. #1204, Vivienne Goonewardene (1916-96), politician.

1997, Nov. 11   Litho.   Perf. 12½

1201	A539	2.50r multicolored	.30	.30
1202	A539	2.50r multicolored	.30	.30
1203	A539	2.50r multicolored	.30	.30
1204	A539	2.50r multicolored	.30	.30
a.		Block of 4, #1201-1204	1.40	1.40

Young Men's Buddhist Assoc., Colombo, Cent. A540

1998, Jan. 1   Litho.   Perf. 12½

1205	A540	2.50r multicolored	.70	.35

Traditional Jewelry and Crafts — A541

Designs: 2.50r, Chunam box. 5r, Necklace of agate. 10r, Bangle and hairpin. 17r, Sigiri earrings.

1998, Apr. 24   Litho.   Perf. 13½

1206	A541	2.50r multicolored	.45	.25
1207	A541	5r multicolored	.70	.30
1208	A541	10r multicolored	1.25	1.25
1209	A541	17r multicolored	2.00	2.00
a.		Souvenir sheet, #1206-1209	5.00	5.00
		Nos. 1206-1209 (4)	4.40	3.80

Independence, 50th Anniv. — A542

Natl. flag and: 2r, People holding up arms, letters and symbols. No. 1211, Ceylon #300. No. 1212, People standing, images of industry and technology. 5r, People playing musical instruments, book, pen, television, musical instruments. 10r, People holding up items, symbols of religion, government.

Perf. 13, 13½ (#1211)

1998, Feb. 4   Litho.

1210	A542	2r multicolored	.60	.25
1211	A542	2.50r multicolored	.85	.60
1212	A542	2.50r multicolored	.85	.60
1213	A542	5r multicolored	.85	.70
1214	A542	10r multicolored	1.75	1.50
		Nos. 1210-1214 (5)	4.90	3.65

No. 1211 is 28x38mm.

William Gopallawa, 1st President A543

1998   Litho.   Perf. 13½

1215	A543	2.50r multicolored	.60	.25

5th Natl. Scout Jamboree A544

Designs: 2.50r, Scouts holding flag, emblem, campground. 17r, Campground, flag, emblems, scout saluting.

1998, Feb. 18

1216	A544	2.50r multicolored	1.25	1.00
1217	A544	17r multicolored	3.50	2.75

World Health Organization, 50th Anniv. — A545

1998, Apr. 7   Litho.   Perf. 13x12½

1218	A545	2.50r multicolored	.80	.25

St. John's College, Jaffna, 175th Anniv. — A546

1998, May 7   Litho.   Perf. 14½x14

1219	A546	2.50r multicolored	.40	.25

Elephas Maximus Ceylonensis — A547

Designs: 2.50r, Wading in lake. 10r, Female, calf. 17r, Three standing in plains. 50r, Large bull.

1998, May 28   Perf. 13

1220	A547	2.50r multicolored	1.00	.70
1221	A547	10r multicolored	1.50	1.10
1222	A547	17r multicolored	2.10	1.40
1223	A547	50r multicolored	3.50	2.75
a.		Souvenir sheet, #1220-1223	9.00	9.00
		Nos. 1220-1223 (4)	8.10	5.95

Vesak Festival — A548

Kelaniya Rajamaha Vihara paintings: 1r, Waterfalls, tree. 2.50r, Procession of people, elephant with rider. 4r, Looking at mother with newborn baby. 17r, Presenting child for ceremony, laying stone.

1998, Apr. 30   Litho.   Perf. 12½

1224	A548	1r multicolored	.40	.25
1225	A548	2.50r multicolored	.40	.25
1226	A548	4r multicolored	.75	.35
1227	A548	17r multicolored	1.75	1.00
a.		Souvenir sheet, #1224-1227	2.75	2.75
		Nos. 1224-1227 (4)	3.30	1.85

SAARC Summit, Colombo — A549

1998   Litho.   Perf. 14½x14

1228	A549	2.50r multicolored	1.10	.35

1998, Year of Information Technology A550

1998   Litho.   Perf. 13½

1229	A550	2.50r multicolored	.90	.25

Personalities A551

#1230, Ven. Pannakitti Nayake Thero. #1231, Sir Nicholas Attygalle. #1232, Dr. Samuel Fisk Green. #1233, Prof. Ediriweera Sarachchandra.

1998   Perf. 13

1230	A551	2.50r multicolored	.50	.35
1231	A551	2.50r multicolored	.50	.35
1232	A551	2.50r multicolored	.50	.35
1233	A551	2.50r multicolored	.50	.35
		Nos. 1230-1233 (4)	2.00	1.40

Meteorological Dept., 50th Anniv. — A552

1998   Litho.   Perf. 14x13½

1234	A552	2.50r multicolored	1.75	.55

26th Forum of South Asia, Africa & Middle East Lions Clubs Intl. — A553

1998, Nov. 20   Litho.   Perf. 14x14½

1235	A553	2.50r multicolored	3.00	1.25

Christmas A554

1998, Dec. 10   Perf. 13½x14

1236	A554	2.50r Nativity	.35	.25
1237	A554	20r Annunciation	1.60	1.50
a.		Souvenir sheet, #1236-1237	2.00	2.00

A555

S.W.R.D. Bandaranaike, Birth Cent.: No. 1238, Wearing white scarf. No. 1239, Wearing blue scarf.

1999, Jan. 8   Litho.   Perf. 12

1238	A555	3.50r multicolored	1.00	1.00
1239	A555	3.50r multicolored	1.00	1.00
a.		Souvenir sheet, #1238-1239, perf. 12½	2.25	2.25

Kandyan Dancer — A556

1999, Feb. 3   Photo.   Perf. 12

1240	A556	1r brown	.25	.25
1241	A556	2r green blue	.25	.25
1242	A556	3r plum	.25	.25
1243	A556	3.50r blue	.25	.25
1244	A556	4r dark red	.25	.25

Size: 21x26mm

1245	A556	5r green	.25	.25
1246	A556	10r violet	.35	.30
1247	A556	13.50r bright red	.45	.40
1248	A556	17r blue green	.55	.45
1249	A556	20r olive bister	.65	.55
		Nos. 1240-1249 (10)	3.50	3.20

Telecommunications, 50th Anniv. — A557

Portraits of Sir Arthur C. Clarke, diagrams of Orbital Concept: a, Rocket launch, satellites, space shuttle. b, Satellites, earth from outer space, space capsule.

1999, Feb. 10   Litho.   Perf. 12
1250 A557 3.50r Pair, #a.-b.   2.25 2.25
          Dated 1998.

Salvation Army, 116th Anniv. A558

1999, Apr. 28   Litho.   Perf. 11¾x12
1251 A558 3.50r multicolored   1.00 .70

British Council, 50th Anniv. — A559

1999, May 20   Perf. 12
1252 A559 3.50r multicolored   .80 .45

Sumithrayo Organization Suicide Hot Line, 25th Anniv. — A560

1999, June 14   Perf. 12½
1253 A560 3.50r multicolored   1.00 .50

Vesak Festival — A561

Designs: 2r, Flowers. 3.50r, Leaf, wheel. 13.50r, Nut, flower. 17r, Young people with traditional lanterns.

Unwmk.
1999, May 25   Litho.   Perf. 12
1254 A561   2r multicolored   .25 .25
1255 A561 3.50r multicolored   .25 .25
1256 A561 13.50r multicolored   .80 .80
1257 A561   17r multicolored   1.00 1.00
      Nos. 1254-1257 (4)   2.30 2.30
          Souvenir Sheet
              Wmk. 388
              Perf. 12½
1258   Sheet of 4   2.75 2.75
  a. A561 2r like #1254   .25 .25
  b. A561 3.50r like #1255   .25 .25
  c. A561 13.50r like #1256   .80 .80
  d. A561 17r like #1257   1.00 1.00

Independent Television Network, 20th Anniv. — A562

1999, June 5   Unwmk.   Perf. 12¾
1259 A562 3.50r multicolored   .70 .40

Vidyodaya Pirivena, 125th Anniv. A563

Perf. 12¾
1999, Sept. 17   Litho.   Unwmk.
1260 A563 3.50r multicolored   .60 .30

Sri Lankan Cinema, 50th Anniv. — A564

3.50r, Handaya, 1979. 4r, Nidhanaya, 1972. 10r, Gam Peraliya, 1963. 17r, Kadawunu Poronduwa, 1947.

1999, Sept. 17   Litho.   Perf. 12¾
1261 A564 3.50r multicolored   .25 .25
1262 A564   4r multicolored   .35 .30
1263 A564   10r multicolored   .55 .40
1264 A564   17r multicolored   1.50 1.25
  a.   Souvenir sheet, #1261-1264   3.00 3.00
      Nos. 1261-1264 (4)   2.65 2.20

Bhakthi Prabodanaya Magazine, Cent. — A565

1999, Sept.   Litho.   Perf. 12x12¼
1265 A565 3.50r multicolored   .60 .30

Hector Kobbekaduwa, Politician — A566

Perf. 12¾x12½
1999, Sept. 19   Wmk. 388   Litho.
1266 A566 3.50r multicolored   .60 .30

National Army, 50th Anniv. — A567

1999, Oct. 10   Unwmk.   Perf. 12¾
1267 A567 3.50r multicolored   .80 .40

Convention on the Rights of the Child, 10th Anniv. — A568

1999, Nov. 20   Perf. 12¾x12½
1268 A568 3.50r multicolored   1.25 .70

A569

1999, Nov. 26   Perf. 12¾
1269 A569 3.50r multicolored   .60 .30
Balangoda Ananda Maitreya Mahanyake Thero (b. 1895), Buddhist priest.

A570

Paintings — 3.50r, By David Paynter. 4r, By Justin Daraniyagala. 17r, By Ivan Peries. 20r, By Solias Mendis.

1999, Dec. 12   Perf. 12¾
1270 A570 3.50r multicolored   .40 .25
1271 A570   4r multicolored   .40 .25
1272 A570   17r multicolored   .80 .80
1273 A570   20r multicolored   1.25 1.25
  a.   Souvenir sheet of 4, #1270-
       1273   4.00 4.00
      Nos. 1270-1273 (4)   2.85 2.55

Athletic Accomplishments — A571

Designs: 1r, Kumar Anandan's swim across Palk Strait. 3.50r, World champions in cricket. 13.50r, International fame in track and field.

1999   Perf. 12¾
1274 A571   1r multicolored   .35 .25
1275 A571 3.50r multicolored   .80 .75
1276 A571 13.50r multicolored   1.60 2.00
      Nos. 1274-1276 (3)   2.75 3.00

Natl. Commission for UNESCO, 50th Anniv. — A572

Perf. 12¾x12½
1999, Nov. 16   Litho.   Wmk. 388
1277 A572 13.50r multicolored   3.50 2.75

Christmas A573

1999, Nov. 30   Perf. 12½x12¾
1278 A573 3.50r shown   .30 .25
1279 A573 20r Magi   1.10 .80
  a.   Souvenir sheet, #1278-1279   2.50 2.50

Famous People — A574

Designs: No. 1280, Dr. Pandithamani S. Kanapathipillai, Tamil scholar. No. 1281, Sunil Santha, musician. No. 1282, Dr. Al Haj Badi-udin Mahmud, Education minister.

1999, Dec. 3   Perf. 12¾x12½
1280 A574 3.50r multi   1.25 .70
1281 A574 3.50r multi   2.00 .90
1282 A574 3.50r multi   1.25 .70
      Nos. 1280-1282 (3)   4.50 2.30

No. 1149A Surcharged

1999, Dec. 3   Litho.   Perf. 12
1282A A516 2r on 2.50r multi   11.00 1.40

Butterflies — A575

Designs: 3.50r, Striped albatross. 13.50r, Ceylon tiger. 17r, Three-spot grass yellow. 20r, Great orange tip.

Perf. 12x11¾
1999, Dec. 30   Unwmk.
Granite Paper
1283 A575 3.50r multi   .50 .30
1284 A575 13.50r multi   1.10 .85
1285 A575   17r multi   1.50 1.25
1286 A575   20r multi   1.75 1.40
  a.   Souvenir sheet, #1283-1286   5.00 5.00
      Nos. 1283-1286 (4)   4.85 3.80

Corals
A576

1999, Dec. 30   *Perf. 11¾x12*
Granite Paper
1287	A576	3.50r Boulder	.35	.40
1288	A576	13.50r Blue-tipped	1.50	1.10
1289	A576	14r Brain-boulder	1.50	1.10
1290	A576	22r Elkhorn	1.75	1.40
a.		Souvenir sheet, #1287-1290	5.75	5.75
		Nos. 1287-1290 (4)	5.10	4.00

For surcharge, see No. 1581.

Auditor General's Department,
Bicent. — A576a

Perf. 12½x12¾
1999, Dec.	**Litho.**	**Unwmk.**
1290B	A576a 3.50r multi	.80 .60

Year 2000 — A577

Satellite and: 10r, Birds, religious symbols. No. 1292, Scales, girl, Red Cross, computer. No. 1293, airplane, satellite dish, man at computer. No. 1294, Hands, symbols of women's equality, crippled and blind.

2000, Jan. 1   *Perf. 11¾*
Granite Paper
1291	A577	10r multi	.30	.30
1292	A577	100r multi	4.25	4.25
1293	A577	100r multi	4.25	4.25
1294	A577	100r multi	4.25	4.25
a.		Souvenir sheet, #1291-1294	13.50	13.50
		Nos. 1291-1294 (4)	13.05	13.05

Kurunagala Diocese, 50th Anniv. A578

Unwmk.
2000, Feb. 2	**Litho.**	*Perf. 12*
1295	A578 13.50r multi	1.50 1.75

Wesley College, Colombo, 125th Anniv. A579

2000, Mar. 2   *Perf. 11¾x12*
1296 A579 3.50r multi   .60 .30

Panadura Pinwatte Saddharmakara Vidyayathana Pirivena, Cent. — A580

2000, Mar. 12
1297 A580 3.50r multi   .60 .30

Vesak Festival — A581

2r, Arrival of Jaya Sri Maha Bodhi sapling. 3.50r, King Devanampiyatissa carrying sapling on his head. 10r, Venerating sapling. 13.50r, Royal tree planting, Anuradhapura.

2000, Apr. 28   **Litho.**   *Perf. 12¾x12½*
1298-1301	A581	Set of 4	2.50 2.00
1301a		Souvenir sheet, #1298-1301	4.50 4.50

Sri Lanka Bar Association, 25th Anniv. (in 1999) — A582

2000, June 10   *Perf. 12*
1302 A582 3.50r multi   .60 .30

Co-operative Wholesale Establishment, 50th Anniv. — A583

2000, July 1   *Perf. 12¾*
1303 A583 3.50r multi   .60 .30

No. 979 Surcharged

2000, July 21   **Litho.**   *Perf. 11½*
1303A A420 50c on 8r multi   7.50 3.25

St. Patrick's College, Jaffna, 150th Anniv. A584

2000, July 21
1304 A584 3.50r multi   1.25 .70

Survey Dept., 200th Anniv. A585

2000, Aug. 2
1305 A585 3.50r multi   .65 .30

Central Bank of Sri Lanka, 50th Anniv. — A586

2000, Aug. 27   *Perf. 13¼*
1306 A586 3.50r multi   .60 .30

Dr. Maria Montessori (1870-1952), Educator — A587

2000, Aug. 31   *Perf. 11¾*
1307 A587 3.50r multi   .65 .30

2000 Summer Olympics, Sydney — A588

Sydney Olympic Games emblem and: a, Hurdler, map. b, Shooter, runners. c, Runners. d, Hurdlers, swimmer.

2000, Sept. 7
1308	A588	10r Horiz. strip of 4, #a-d	3.00 3.00
e.		Souvenir sheet, #1308	3.75 3.75

All Ceylon Young Men's Muslim Association Conference, 50th Anniv. — A589

2000, Sept. 16
1309 A589 3.50r multi   .60 .30

Hotel Industry, 25th Anniv. A590

2000, Sept. 18   *Perf. 12¾*
1310 A590 10r multi   3.00 1.75

Immigration and Emigration Dept., 50th Anniv. A591

2000, Oct. 2   *Perf. 11¾*
1311 A591 3.50r multi   1.00 .70

Traditional Dancer — A592

Perf. 13½x13 Syncopated
2000, Oct. 5			**Litho.**
1312	A592	50r multi	1.75 1.75
1313	A592	100r multi	3.50 3.50
1314	A592	200r multi	6.75 6.75
		Nos. 1312-1314 (3)	12.00 12.00

All-Ceylon Buddhist Congress Natl. Awards Ceremony A593

2000, Aug. 27   **Litho.**   *Perf. 12¾*
1315 A593 3.50r multi   1.00 .70

Saumiyamoorthy Thondaman, Government Minister — A594

2000, Oct. 30
1316 A594 3.50r multi   .70 .40

Famous People — A595

Designs: No. 1317, 3.50r, Most Ven. Baddegama Siri Piyaratana Nayake Thero, educator. No. 1318, 3.50r, Aluthgamage Simon de Silva (1874-1920), writer. No. 1319, 3.50r, Desigar Ramanujam (1907-68), politician.

Perf. 12x12¼ (#1317), 12¾x12½
2000, Nov. 14
1317-1319 A595 Set of 3   1.25 1.00

Christmas A596

Designs: 2r, Joseph, Mary, donkey. 17r, Holy family.

2000, Nov. 23   *Perf. 12¾x12½*
1320-1321 A596   Set of 2   2.25 1.75
1321a   Souvenir sheet, #1320-
     1321, perf. 12   2.50 2.50

Lalith Athulathmudali (1936-93),
Politician — A597

2000, Nov. 30   *Perf. 12½x12¾*
1322 A597 3.50r multi   .60 .30

Medicina
Alternativa
Medical
Society,
38th Anniv.
A598

2000, Dec. 1   *Perf. 12¾*
1323 A598 13.50r multi   2.25 1.50

Ladies' College,
Cent. — A599

2000, Dec. 7
1324 A599 3.50r multi   .75 .30

Navy, 50th
Anniv.
A600

2000, Dec. 9
1325 A600 3.50r multi   1.00 .50

Peliyagoda Vidyalankara Pirivena,
125th Anniv. — A601

2000, Dec. 30   *Perf. 12x12¼*
1326 A601 3.50r multi   .60 .30

Bishop's
College,
125th
Anniv.
A602

2001, Jan. 19   Litho.
1327 A602 3.50r multi   .60 .30

St.
Thomas'
College,
150th
Anniv.
A603

2001, Feb. 3   *Perf. 12¾*
1328 A603 3.50r multi   .60 .30

Lanka
Mahila
Samiti
Women's
Training
Society,
70th Anniv.
A604

2001, Feb. 15
1329 A604 3.50r multi   .60 .30

Air Force,
50th Anniv.
A605

2001, Mar. 9
1330 A605 3.50r multi   1.20 .50

St.
Lawrence's
School,
Cent.
A606

2001, Mar. 15
1331 A606 3.50r multi   .60 .30

Bernard Soysa
(1914-97),
Politician — A607

2001, Mar. 20   *Perf. 12¾*
1332 A607 3.50r multi   .60 .30

Vesak
Festival — A608

Designs: 2r, Sri Nagadeepa Chaithya,
Jaffna. 3.50r, Muthiyangana Chaithya,
Badulla. 13.50r, Kirivehera, Kataragama. 17r,
Sri Dalada Maligawa, Kandy.

2001, Apr. 7 Litho.   *Perf. 13½x13¾*
1333 A608   2r multi   .25 .25
   a.   Perf. 14¼   .25 .25
     Perf. 14¼
1334 A608   3.50r multi   .25 .25
   a.   Perf. 13½x13¾   .25 .25
1335 A608   13.50r multi   .90 .90
1336 A608   17r multi   1.25 1.25
   a.   Souvenir sheet, #1333a, 1334-
     1336   2.75 2.75

Hansa Jataka, by George Keyt (1901-
93) — A609

2001, Apr. 24   *Perf. 13¼*
1337 A609 13.50r multi   1.60 2.00

Coins
A610

Designs: 3.50r, Kahavanu gold coin, 9th
cent. 13.50r, Vijayabahu I silver coin, 1055-
1111. 17r, Sethu copper coin, 13th-14th cent.
20r, Buddha Jayanthi 5r commemorative silver
coin, 1957.

Perf. 13¾x13½, 14¼ (17r)

2001, June 18
1338 A610   3.50r multi   .25 .25
1339 A610   13.50r multi   .90 .90
1340 A610   17r multi   1.25 1.25
   a.   Perf. 13¾x13½x14¼x13½   1.25 1.25
1341 A610   20r multi   1.60 1.60
   a.   Perf. 13¾x13½x14¼x13½   1.60 1.60
   b.   Souvenir sheet, #1338-1339,
     1340a, 1341a   4.50 4.50

Colombo Plan, 50th
Anniv. — A611

2001, July 2   *Perf. 13½x13¾*
1342 A611 10r multi   1.00 1.00

US-Sri
Lankan
Diplomatic
Relations,
150th
Anniv.
A612

2001, July 3   *Perf. 12¾*
1343 A612 10r multi   1.25 1.00

Lance
Corporal
Gamini
Kularatne
(1966-91),
Military
Hero — A613

2001, July 14   *Perf. 13¾x13½*
1344 A613 3.50r multi   .60 .30

Prince and
Princess of
Wales
College,
Moratuwa,
125th Anniv.
A614

2001, Sept. 14   *Perf. 13¼*
1345 A614 3.50r multi   .60 .30

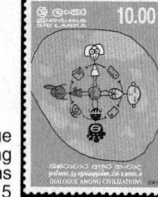

Year of Dialogue
Among
Civilizations
A615

2001, Oct. 9   *Perf. 13x13½*
1346 A615 10r multi   1.30 1.00

No. 511
Surcharged

2001, July 9 Photo.   *Perf. 14¼x14½*
1347 A180 5r on 1.15r multi   5.00 4.00
1348 A180 10r on 1.15r multi   7.00 5.00

An additional surcharge was released in this
set. The editors would like to examine it.

13th Meeting of
Parties to the
Montreal
Protocol — A616

2001, Oct. 18 Litho.   *Perf. 13x13¼*
1349 A616 13.50r multi   .75 1.10

Ramakrishna Mission Students' Home,
Batticaloa, 75th Anniv. — A617

2001, Oct. 19   *Perf. 12¾*
1350 A617 3.50r multi   .60 .30

Drummer — A618

Drummer from: 1r, 2r, 3r, 3.50r, Daul. 4r, 5r,
10r, Kandy. 13.50r, 17r, 20r, Low country.

2001, Nov. 8 Litho.   *Perf. 12½x13¼*
1351 A618   1r rose   .25 .25
1352 A618   2r emerald   .25 .25
1353 A618   3r fawn   .25 .25
1354 A618   3.50r dark blue   .25 .25

     Size: 23x28mm
     Perf. 13¼x12½

1355 A618   4r pink   .35 .25
1356 A618   5r orange   .35 .25
1357 A618   10r violet   .75 .30
1358 A618   13.50r dull purple   1.00 .45
1359 A618   17r yel orange   1.25 .50
1360 A618   20r Prus blue   1.50 .60
   Nos. 1351-1360 (10)   6.20 3.35

See Nos. 1389A, 1410. For surcharges, see
Nos. 1409, 1514, 1549, 1582.

S.W.R.D. Bandaranaike Natl. Memorial Foundation, 25th Anniv. — A619

2001, Nov. 27   **Perf. 13¾x13¼**
1361 A619 3.50r multi   .60 .30

Christmas A620

Designs: 3.50r, Jesus and children. 17r, The Annunciation.

2001, Nov. 28   **Perf. 13**
1362-1363 A620 Set of 2   1.00 .75
1363a   Souvenir sheet, #1362-1363   1.25 1.25

Frogs A621

Designs: 3.50r, Conical wart pygmy tree frog. 13.50r, Sharp-snout saddle tree frog. 17r, Round-snout pygmy tree frog. 20r, Sri Lanka wood frog.

2001, Dec. 3   **Perf. 13¼x13**
1364-1367 A621 Set of 4   3.50 2.75
1367a   Souvenir sheet, #1364-1367   3.75 3.75

St. Bridget's Convent, Cent. A622

2002, Feb. 1
1368 A622 3.50r multi   .60 .30

Ceylon Government Gazette, 200th Anniv. — A623

2002, Mar. 15 Litho.   **Perf. 13¾x14**
1369 A623 3.50r multi   .60 .30

D. S. Senanayake (1884-1952), Prime Minister — A624

2002, Mar. 22   **Perf. 14x13¾**
1370 A624 3.50r multi   .60 .30

Gamini Dissanayake (1942-94), Assassinated Government Minister — A625

2002, Mar. 27   **Perf. 13¾x14**
1371 A625 3.50r multi   .60 .30

Lester James Peries (b. 1919), Film Director A626

2002, Apr. 5   **Perf. 13¼x13**
1372 A626 3.50r multi   .60 .30

Natural Beauty of Sri Lanka — A627

Designs: 5r, Sinharaja Forest Reserve. 10r, Horton Plains National Park. 13.50r, Knuckles Range. 20r, Rumassala Cliff and Bonavista Coral Reef.

2002, Apr. 10   **Perf. 13x13¼**
1373-1376 A627 Set of 4   2.00 2.00

Pres. Ranasinghe Premadasa (1924-93) A628

2002, Apr. 29   **Perf. 13¾x14**
1377 A628 4.50r multi   .60 .25

Sri Lanka - Japan Diplomatic Relations, 50th Anniv. — A629

2002, Apr. 29   **Perf. 14x13¾**
1378 A629 16.50r multi   1.00 .75

Vesak Festival A630

Dambulla Raja Maha Vihara rock paintings: 3r, Queen Mahamaya's dream. 4.50r, Birth of Prince Siddhartha. 16.50r, Siddhartha's exhibition of archery talents. 23r, Ordination of Prince Siddhartha.

2002, May 17   **Perf. 13¾x14**
1379-1382 A630 Set of 4   2.00 1.50
1382a   Souvenir sheet, #1379-1382   2.25 2.25

Most Venerable Madihe Pannasiha Maha Nayaka Thera, Religious Leader, 90th Birthday — A631

2002, June 23   **Perf. 14x13¾**
1383 A631 4.50r multi   .60 .25

Sri Lanka Oriental Studies Society, Cent. A632

2002, July 24   **Perf. 13¾x14**
1384 A632 4.50r multi   .75 .25

Rifai Thareeq Association, 125th Anniv. — A633

2002, July 26
1385 A633 4.50r multi   .75 .25

14th Asian Track and Field Championships, Colombo — A634

Designs: 4.50r, Discus thrower. 16.50r, Sprinter. 23r, Hurdler. 26r, Long jumper.

2002, Aug. 8
1386-1389 A634 Set of 4   3.00 3.00

Daul Drummer Type of 2001
Perf. 12½x13¼
2002, Aug. 16   **Litho.**
1389A A618 4.50r blue violet   —
For surcharge, see No. 1785.

National Museum, 125th Anniv. — A635

No. 1390: a, Carved lion (sitting). b, Carved lion (standing with head turned).

2002, Aug. 27
1390 A635 4.50r Horiz. pair, #a-b   2.00 2.00

Woman's Hand Holding Flower — A636

2002, Aug. 28   **Perf. 14x13¾**
1391 A636 10r multi   1.10 .65
Tourism promotion.

Dr. A. C. S. Hameed (1929-99), Government Minister — A637

2002, Sept. 3
1392 A637 4.50r multi   .70 .25

Freemasons' Hall, Colombo, Cent. — A638

2002, Sept. 5   **Perf. 13¾x14**
1393 A638 4.50r multi   .90 .50

Holy Cross College, Kalutara, Cent. A639

2002, Sept. 13
1394 A639 4.50r multi   .70 .25

German Dharmaduta Society, 50th Anniv. — A640

2002, Sept. 21   **Perf. 14x13¾**
1395 A640 4.50r multi   1.00 .25

Intl. Children's Day — A641

2002, Oct. 1
1396 A641 4.50r multi   .70 .25

Dr. M. C. M. Kaleel (1899-1995), Government Minister — A642

2002, Oct. 18
1397 A642 4.50r green   .70 .25

Uduppiddy American Mission College, 150th Anniv. A643

2002, Oct. 19 **Litho.** **Perf. 13¾x14**
1398 A643 4.50r multi 1.50 1.50

Dr. Wijayananda Dahanayake (1902-97), Prime Minister — A644

2002, Oct. 22 **Litho.** **Perf. 14x13¾**
1399 A644 4.50r brown .70 .25

Sri Lanka - Netherlands Relations, 400th Anniv. — A645

2002, Nov. 22 **Perf. 13¾x14**
1400 A645 16.50r multi 1.50 1.00

Christmas — A646

Designs: 4.50r, Madonna and Child. 26r, Holy Family.

2002, Dec. 15 **Perf. 13x13¼**
1401-1402 A646 Set of 2 2.00 1.60
1402a Souvenir sheet, #1401-1402 2.00 2.00

Sri Lanka - China Rubber and Rice Pact, 50th Anniv. A647

2002, Dec. 20 **Perf. 13¾x14**
1403 A647 4.50r multi .75 .25

Kopay Christian College, 150th Anniv. A648

2002, Dec. 28
1404 A648 4.50r multi .70 .25

No. 925 Srchd.

2002 ? **Litho.** **Perf. 12½x12**
1405 A392 25c on 5.75r multi

No. 1354 Surcharged

2002 ? **Litho.** **Perf. 12½x13¼**
1406 A618 4.50r on 3.50r dk bl —— ——

Teachers' College, Maharagama, Cent. — A649

2003, Jan. 21 **Perf. 13¾x14**
1407 A649 4.50r multi .70 .25

Holy Family Convent, Bambalapitiya, Cent. — A650

2003, Feb. 3 **Perf. 14x13¾**
1408 A650 4.50r multi .80 .25

Drummer Type of 2001 and

No. 1359 Surcharged

Drummer from: 16.50r, Low country.

Perf. 13¼x12½
2003, Feb. 17 **Litho.**
1409 A618 50c on 5r org yel .50 .35
1410 A618 16.50r purple 1.30 .90

M. D. Banda (1914-74), Government Minister — A651

2003, Mar. 14 **Perf. 13¾x14**
1411 A651 4.50r multi .80 .25

Balagalle Saraswati Maha Pirivena, Cent. A652

2003, Apr. 3
1412 A652 4.50r multi .80 .25

D. B. Welagedara, Politician — A653

2003, Apr. 22 **Perf. 14x13¾**
1413 A653 4.50r multi .80 .25

Vesak Festival — A654

Designs: 2.50r, Paying obeisance to parents. 3r, Dhamma school. 4.50r, Going on alms round. 23r, Meditation.

2003, Apr. 26
1414-1417 A654 Set of 4 2.00 1.50
1417a Souvenir sheet, #1414-1417 2.25 2.25

Dagoba Construction Features — A655

Designs: 4.50r, Stupa. 16.50r, Guard stone, horiz. (58x28mm). 50r, Moonstone, horiz.

2003, Apr. 28 **Perf. 13x13¼, 13¼x13**
1418-1420 A655 Set of 3 3.50 2.50
1420a Souvenir sheet, #1418-1420 4.00 4.00

Second World Hindu Conference, Colombo — A656

2003, May 2 **Perf. 14x13¾**
1421 A656 4.50r multi .90 .25

International Nursing Day — A657

2003, May 12 **Perf. 13¾x14**
1422 A657 4.50r multi .90 .25

Sirimavo Bandaranaike Memorial Exhibition Center — A658

2003, May 17 **Perf. 13¼x12**
1423 A658 4.50r multi .90 .25

Al-Haj H. S. Ismail (1901-73), Parliament Speaker — A659

2003, May 18 **Perf. 14x13¾**
1424 A659 4.50r multi .65 .25

Board of Investment, 25th Anniv. — A660

2003, May 21 **Perf. 13¾x12**
1425 A660 4.50r multi .65 .25

World Biodiversity Day — A661

Designs: 4r, Pidurutalagal Mountain Range. 4.50r, Seven Maidens Mountain Range. 16.50r, Kirigalpoththa Mountain. 23r, Ritigala Mountain.

2003, May 22 **Perf. 13¾x12**
1426-1429 A661 Set of 4 3.00 1.75

Saralankara College, Gonapinuwala, Cent. — A662

2003, June 6 **Perf. 13¾x14**
1430 A662 4.50r multi .65 .25

A663

First Arab settlement, Beruwala: 4.50r, Masjidul Abrar. 23r, Masjidul Abrar, horiz. (57x22mm).

Perf. 14x13¾, 13¼x12 (23r)
2003, June 8
1431-1432 A663 Set of 2 1.50 1.10

A664

2003, June 23 **Perf. 14x13¾**
1433 A664 4.50r multi .65 .25

Anti-narcotics Week.

Syamopali Maha Nikaya, 250th Anniv. A665

Designs: No. 1434, 4.50r, Asgiri Maha Viharaya. No. 1435, 4.50r, Malwathu Maha Viharaya.

2003, July 13   *Perf. 13¾x14*
1434-1435 A665   Set of 2   1.10 .75

Lanka Philex Intl. Stamp Exhibition, Colombo — A666

2003, July 31   *Perf. 13¼x12*
1436 A666 16.50r multi   1.25 .75
   a.   Souvenir sheet of 1   2.25 2.25

Dr. Ananda Tissa de Alwis, Government Minister — A667

2003, Aug. 21   *Perf. 13¾x14*
1437 A667 4.50r multi   .70 .35

Panadura Controversy, 130th Anniv. — A668

2003, Aug. 24   *Perf. 14x13¾*
1438 A668 4.50r multi   .70 .35

Venerable Haldanduwana Dhammarakkitha Thero — A669

2003, Sept. 3   *Litho.*
1439 A669 4.50r multi   .70 .35

Ragama Walpola Poson Maha Perahara, 75th Anniv. A670

2003, Sept. 10   *Perf. 13¾x14*
1440 A670 4.50r multi   .90 .45

M. H. M. Ashraff (1948-2000), Government Minister — A671

2003, Sept. 18   *Perf. 14x13¾*
1441 A671 4.50r multi   .75 .35

Sisters of the Holy Angels, Cent. A672

2003, Sept. 27   *Perf. 13¾x14*
1442 A672 4.50r multi   .75 .35

Birds — A673

No. 1443: a, Black-necked stork. b, Purple swamphen. c, Gray heron. d, White-throated kingfisher. e, Black-crowned night heron. f, Scarlet minivet. g, White-rumped shama. h, Malabar trogon. i, Asian paradise flycatcher. j, Little green bee-eater. k, Brown wood owl. l, Crested serpent eagle. m, Crested goshawk. n, Jungle owlet. o, Rufous-bellied eagle. p, Black-headed munia. q, Pompadour green pigeon. r, Plum-headed parakeet. s, Coppersmith barbet. t, Emerald dove. u, Blue-faced malkoha. v, Scimitar babbler. w, Painted francolin. x, Red-backed woodpecker. y, Malabar pied hornbill.

2003, Sept. 27   *Perf. 14x13¾*
1443 A673 4.50r Sheet of 25, #a-y   19.50 19.50

World Habitat Day — A674

2003, Oct. 6   *Perf. 13*
1444 A674 4.50r multi   .70 .25

World Post Day — A675

2003, Oct. 9   *Perf. 14x13¾*
1445 A675 23r multi   2.25 1.50

Blue Sapphire — A676

2003, Oct. 21   *Perf. 12x13½*
1446 A676 4.50r multi   .70 .25
See also No. 1497.

Ponificate of Pope John Paul II, 25th Anniv. — A677

2003, Oct. 22   *Perf. 13*
1447 A677 4.50r multi   1.75 .40

Deepavali Festival — A678

2003, Oct. 23
1448 A678 4.50r multi   .70 .25

Pinnawala Elephant Orphanage A679

Designs: 4.50r, Two adult and two young elephants. 16.50r, Elephants and caretaker. 23r, Two adult elephants. 26r, Elephants in water.

2003, July 13   *Litho.*   *Perf. 13½x13*
1449-1452 A679   Set of 4   5.50 3.50
  1452a   Souvenir sheet, #1449-1452   6.00 6.00

For surcharge, see No. 1576.

Waterfalls — A680

Designs: 2.50r, Ramboda. 4.50r, Saint Clair. 23r, Bopath Ella. 50r, Devon.

2003, Nov. 11   *Perf. 14x13¾*
1453-1456 A680   Set of 4   4.00 2.75

Ukku Banda Wanninayake (1905-73), Finance Minister — A681

2003, Nov. 23   *Perf. 13*
1457 A681 4.50r multi   .65 .25

Christmas A682

Designs: 4.50r, Church. 16.50r, Shepherds and angel, vert.

2003, Nov. 30
1458-1459 A682   Set of 2   .80 .70

Pandith W. D. Amaradeva, Musician, 76th Birthday — A683

2003, Dec. 5
1460 A683 4.50r multi   1.00 .35

Gangarama Seemamalakaya — A684

2003, Dec. 20
1461 A684 4.50r multi   .65 .25

Daham Pahana, Sri Pushparamaya, Malegoda — A685

2003, Dec. 31
1462 A685 4.50r multi   .65 .25

Shazuliyathul Fassiya Tharika — A686

2004, Jan. 6
1463 A686 18r multi   1.00 .70

Chavakachcheri Hindu College, Cent. — A687

2004, Jan. 30
1464 A687 4.50r multi   *Perf. 12x13½*
     1.00   .25

Royal-Thomian Cricket Match, 125th Anniv. — A688

2004, Jan. 30   *Perf. 13*
1465 A688 4.50r multi   1.10   .40

Pres. Dingiri Banda Wijetunga A689

2004, Feb. 15   *Litho.*   *Perf. 13*
1466 A689 4.50r multi   .75   .25

Planters Association of Ceylon, 150th Anniv. — A690

2004, Feb. 17   *Perf. 13¾x14*
1467 A690 4.50r multi   .75   .40

Kalashuri Most Venerable Mapalagama Vipulasara Thero, Religious Leader — A691

Maithripala Senanayeke A692

Cathiravelu Sittampalam (1898-1964), First Posts and Telecommunications Minister — A693

M. G. Mendis, Communist Leader — A694

2004, Feb. 28   *Perf. 13x13¼*
1468 A691 3.50r multi   .50   .25
1469 A692 3.50r multi   .50   .25
1470 A693 3.50r multi   .50   .25
1471 A694 3.50r multi   .50   .25
     Nos. 1468-1471 (4)   2.00 1.00

Nos. 1468-1471 are dated 2002. They were made available then, but not issued.

75th Ananda-Nalanda Cricket Match — A695

2004, Mar. 7   *Perf. 12x13¼*
1472 A695 4.50r multi   1.20   .50

St. Anthony's College, Kandy, 150th Anniv. — A696

2004, Mar. 12   *Perf. 13½x12*
1473 A696 4.50r multi   .65   .25

Vesak Festival — A697

Various scenes of Sittara painting on wooden casket (with white borders on top and bottom): 4r, 4.50r, 16.50r, 20r.
26r, Scene of Sittara painting (no white borders).

2004, Apr. 30
1474-1477 A697   Set of 4   2.00 2.00
     Souvenir Sheet
1478 A697 26r multi   1.50 1.50

Gongalegoda Banda (1809-49), Leader of 1848 Rebellion — A698

2004, May 22   *Perf. 14x13¾*
1479 A698 4.50r multi   .65   .25

World Blood Donor Day — A699

2004, June 15   *Perf. 13*
1480 A699 4.50r multi   .75   .25

2004 Summer Olympics, Athens — A700

Designs: 4.50r, Swimming. 16.50r, Women's track. 17r, Shooting. 20r, Men's track.

2004, Aug. 6   *Litho.*
1481-1484 A700   Set of 4   2.40 2.40

Sri Siddhartha Buddharakkhita, 18th Cent. Religious Leader — A701

2004, Aug. 16
1485 A701 4.50r brown   .65   .25

Robert Gunawardena, Communist Leader — A702

2004, Aug. 23   *Perf. 14x13¾*
1486 A702 4.50r multi   .65   .25

Pres. Junius Richard Jayewardene (1906-96) A703

2004, Sept. 27   *Perf. 13*
1487 A703 4.50r multi   .65   .25

Intl. Day of Peace — A704

2004, Sept. 21
1488 A704 4.50r multi   .65   .25

Sri Chandrarathna Manawasinghe, Writer — A705

2004, Oct. 6   *Perf. 12x13¼*
1489 A705 4.50r multi   .65   .25

Government Service Buddhist Association, 50th Anniv. — A706

2004, Oct. 7   *Perf. 13*
1490 A706 4.50r multi   .65   .25

World Post Day — A707

2004, Oct. 9   *Perf. 12x13½*
1491 A707 4.50r multi   1.00   .25

Raddelle Sri Pannaloka Anunayaka Thero, Religious Leader — A708

2004, Oct. 20   *Perf. 13*
1492 A708 4.50r multi   .65   .25

Christmas
A709

2004, Nov. 27   *Perf. 14x13¾*
1493 A709 5r multi   .65 .25

Fathers Jacome Gonsalves and
Edmond Peiris — A710

2004, Nov. 27   *Perf. 13¼x12*
1494 A710 20r multi   .90 .90

Information and Communication
Technology Week — A711

2004, Nov. 29   *Perf. 13¾x14*
1495 A711 5r multi   .90 .25

De Soysa Hospital for Women,
Colombo, 125th Anniv.
A712

2004, Dec. 11   *Perf. 13½x14*
1496 A712 5r multi   .65 .25

Blue Sapphire Type of 2003

2004, Dec. 14 Litho.   *Perf. 12x13½*
1497 A676 5r multi   1.00 .25

Most Venerable
Talalle Siri
Dhammananda
Maha Nayaka
Thero,
Educator — A713

2005, Mar. 13   *Perf. 14x13¾*
1498 A713 5r multi   .65 .25

Most Venerable
Hammalawa
Saddhatissa
Nayaka Maha
Thero (1914-90),
Monk — A714

2005, Mar. 22
1499 A714 5r multi   .65 .25

T. B. Tennakoon,
Politician — A715

2005, Mar. 25
1500 A715 5r multi   .65 .25

D. A.
Rajapaksa
(1905-67),
Politician
A716

2005, Mar. 25   *Perf. 13¾x14*
1501 A716 5r multi   .65 .25

Vesak
Festival — A717

Designs: 4.50r, Ambulatory meditation. 5r,
Spiritual bliss through Buddhism. 10r, Meditation in standing posture. 50r, Sedentary
meditation.

2005, May 12   *Perf. 14x13¾*
1502-1505 A717   Set of 4   3.00 3.00
1505a   Sheet, #1502-1505   3.25 3.25
Compare with Type A723.

Rev.
Marcelline
Jayakody
(1902-98)
A718

2005, June 3   *Perf. 13*
1506 A718 20r multi   1.25 1.25

Rana Viru
Day — A719

2005, June 7   *Perf. 14x13¾*
1507 A719 50r multi   1.50 1.50

Deshamanya M.
A. Bakeer Markar
(1917-96),
Parliament
Speaker — A720

2005, July 20
1508 A720 5r multi   .60 .25

Most Venerable
Matara Kithalagama
Sri Seelalankara
Nayaka
Thero — A721

2005, July 21
1509 A721 25r multi   .70 .70

South Asia Tourism Year — A722

2005, July 29   *Perf. 13*
1510 A722 100r multi   3.00 3.00

Kalutara
Bodhi
Trust
A723

2005, Aug. 6   *Perf. 13¾x14*
1511 A723 5r multi   .50 .25

Nos. 564, 815,
818, 937 and 1352
Surcharged

Methods and Perfs As Before
2005
1512 A206 50c on 10c #564   1.25 1.25
1513 A324 50c on 35c #815   1.25 1.25
1514 A618 50c on 2r #1352   1.25 1.25
1515 A399 50c on 5.75r #937   1.25 1.25
1516 A324 50c on 6r #818   1.25 1.25
   Nos. 1512-1516 (5)   6.25 6.25
Issued: No. 1514, 9/16; others, 3/21.

Postal Headquarters — A725

2005, Sept. 12 Litho.   *Perf. 13½x14*
1518 A725 5r multi   .40 .25

Ampitiya
National
Seminary
A726

2005, Oct. 1
1519 A726 10r multi   .40 .25

World
Post Day
A727

2005, Oct. 9
1520 A727 5r multi   .40 .25

General Sir John Kotelawala Defense
Academy, 25th Anniv. — A728

2005, Oct. 11 Litho.   *Perf. 13*
1521 A728 5r multi   .50 .25

Christmas
A729

Cross of Blessed Joseph Vaz, Madonna and
Child and: 5r, Angel. 30r, Star of Bethlehem.

2005, Dec. 3   *Perf. 13¾x14*
1522-1523 A729   Set of 2   1.10 1.10
1523a   Souvenir sheet, #1522-1523   1.20 1.20

Admission to the
UN, 50th
Anniv. — A730

2005, Dec. 13 Litho.   *Perf. 14x13½*
1524 A730 20r multi   .90 .90

Amarapura
Maha
Nikaya,
Bicent.
A731

2005, Dec. 20   **Perf. 13½x14**
1525 A731 10r multi   .50 .50

Ancient Sri Lanka — A732

Designs: 5r, Minhagalkanda and stone tools. 20r, Extinct animals in Ratnapura gem gravels and rhinoceros and hippopotamus bone fragments. 25r, Kuruwita, Batadombalena and human skull from Bellan-bandi Palassa. 30r, Agriculture on the Horton Plains, fossilized barley pollen grain.

2005, Dec. 21   **Perf. 13¼x12**
1526-1529 A732   Set of 4   2.75 2.75

Damage
From Dec.
26, 2004
Tsunami
A733

Designs: 5r, Damaged Kalmunai Post Office, vehicles. 20r, Train derailed near Telwatte. 30r, Giant wave breaking along coast. 33r, Lighthouse and tsunami wave.

2005, Dec. 26   **Litho.**   **Perf. 13¾x14**
1530-1533 A733   Set of 4   1.75 1.75
1533a   Souvenir sheet, #1530-1533   1.75 1.75

Animals of Wilpattu National
Park — A734

Designs: 5r, Barking deer. 10r, White-bellied sea eagle. 20r, Sloth bear. 50r, Leopard.

2006, Jan. 4   **Litho.**   **Perf. 13½x12**
1534 A734 5r multi   .60 .60
   a.   Souvenir sheet of 1   .60 .60
1535 A734 10r multi   .60 .60
   a.   Souvenir sheet of 1   .60 .60
1536 A734 20r multi   .95 .95
   a.   Souvenir sheet of 1   .95 .95
1537 A734 50r multi   2.40 2.40
   a.   Souvenir sheet of 1   2.40 2.40
    Nos. 1534-1537 (4)   4.55 4.55

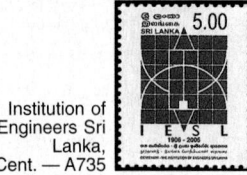

Institution of
Engineers Sri
Lanka,
Cent. — A735

2006, Jan. 6   **Litho.**   **Perf. 12x13¼**
1538 A735 5r black & blue   .35 .25

Europa Stamps,
50th Anniv. — A736

Sri Lanka flag and: 100r, Ceylon #336. 500r, Ship, maps of Europe and Sri Lanka.

2006, Feb. 2   **Perf. 12¾x13¼**
1539-1540 A736   Set of 2   13.50 13.50
1540a   Souvenir sheet, #1539-1540   13.50 13.50

Most Venerable
Madithiyawala
Vijithasena
Anunayake
Thero — A737

2006, Mar. 5   **Litho.**   **Perf. 14x13¾**
1541 A737 17r multi   .75 .75

100th Kingswood-Dharmaraja Cricket
Match — A738

2006, Mar. 24   **Perf. 13¾x14**
1542 A738 4.50r multi   .50 .50

Vesak — A739

No. 1543: a, Wall painting depicting a plea to the Master to descend from heaven, Tivamka Image House, Polonnaruva (1/50). b, Bas-relief of Queen Mahamaya on her way to visit her parents, Jetavana Vihara, Anuradhapura (2/50). c, Wall painting depicting birth of Prince Siddhartha, Shailabimbarama Vihara, Dodanduwa (3/50). d, Wall painting of royal teacher Asita visiting Prince Siddhartha, Purwarama Viharaya, Kataluva (4/50). e, Bas-relief of Great Renunciation, Girihandu Vihara, Ambalantota (5/50). f, Rock painting depicting defeat of evils by the Master, Hindagala Vihara, Hindagala (6/50). g, Rock painting depicting first sermon of Dhammachakka, Rangiri Dambulu Vihara, Dambulla (7/50). h, Wall painting depicting conversion of Alavaka, Sapugoda Vihara, Beruvala (8/50). i, Wall painting depicting funeral pyre of the Master, Veheragalla Samudragiri Vihara, Mirissa (9/50). j, Tapassu and Bhalluka arriving in Sri Lanka with relics of the Master, Girihandu Seya, Tiriyaya (10/50). k, Wall painting depicting perfection of generosity, Bodhirukkharama Vihara, Eluvapitiya (11/50). l, Rock painting depicting perfection of wisdom, Kaballelena Vihara, Wariyapola (12/50). m, Wall painting depicting perfection of reunification, Degaldoruwa Vihara, Kandy (13/50). n, Wall painting depicting perfection of equanimity, Paramakanda Vihara, Anamaduwa (14/50). o, Wall painting depicting perfection of loving kindness, Sunandarama Vihara, Ambalangoda (15/50). p, Recitation of Chullahastpadopama Sutta by Arhat Mahinda, Stupa, Mihintale (16/50). q, Establishment of Buddhism in Sri Lanka, Rajagiri Lena, Mihintale (17/50). r, Sri Maha Bodhi entering city, Sri Maha Bodhi, Anuradhapura (18/50). s, Writing Dhamma on ola leaves, Alu Vihara, Matale (19/50). t, Arrival of tooth relic of the Master, Lankapattana, Trincomalee (20/50). u, Practice of aranyaka, Situlpavuva Vihara (21/50). v, Symbols of three traditions, Lovamahapaya, Abhayagiri Vihara, Vajra symbol and lotus (22/50). w, Emergence of katikavatas, Vatadage, Polonnaruva (23/50). x, Buddhist discourse between Sri Lanka and Southeast Asia, Tooth Relic Temple, Kandy (24/50). y, Translation of the Tripitaka into Sinhala, Buddhajayanti Vihara, Colombo (25/50). z, Vesak festival scene, Deepaduttarama Vihara, Kotahena (26/50). aa, Serving of food to Buddhist clergy, Refectory at Abhayagiriya, Anuradhapura (27/50). ab, Chanting Paritta, Nishshanka Lata Mandapa, Polonnaruva (28/50). ac, Combination with village, temple tank and stupa, Tissamaharama Stupa (29/50). ad, Veneration of Bodhi tree, Bodhighara, Nillakgama (30/50). ae, Hatthikuchchi Vihara, Galgamuva,

Padhanaghara, Anuradhapura (31/50). af, Ritual performance for tooth relic, Atadage, Polonnaruva (32/50). ag, Perahara, Subodharma Vihara, Karagampitiya (33/50). ah, Wall painting of a street market, Mulgirigala Vihara, local coin (34/50). ai, Sanctity of the temple, Namal Uyana, Ranava (35/50). aj, Ruvanvalisaya and Thuparama Stupas, Anuradhapura (36/50). ak, Kirivehera Stupa, Kataragama, Seruvila Stupa (37/50). al, Mahiyangana and Nagadipa Stupas, Jaffna (38/50). am, Kelaniya Stupa and Samantakuta (39/50). an, Mutiyangana Stupa, Badulla, and Deeghavapi Stupa (40/50). ao, Painted stupa, Hanguranketa Raja Maha Vihara, ancient stupas at Kandarodai, Jaffna (41/50). ap, Facade of Mihintale Stupa, bas-relief of Bahiravas (42/50). aq, Twin pond, Anuradhapura, Punkalasa lotus pond, Polonnaruva (43/50). ar, Moonstone, Mangul Maha Vihara, Lahugala (44/50). as, Bodhisattva Avalokiteshvara, Muhudumaha Vihara, Potuvil (45/50). at, Nalanda Gedige, Naula, Satmahal Prasada, Polonnaruva (46/50). au, Bas-relief of Vimana, Lankatilaka Vihara, Polonnaruva (47/50). av, Thuparama Image House, Polonnaruva, Tampita Vihara, Menikkadawara (48/50). aw, Wall painting depicting Buddhist cosmos, Omalpe Vihara, Kolonne (49/50). ax, Depiction of time in the motif of Makara, Madanvala Vihara, Hanguranketa (50/50).

2006, May 5   **Litho.**   **Perf. 13¼x12**
1543   Sheet of 50   21.00 21.00
   a.-j.   A739 2.50r Any single   .25 .25
   k.-t.   A739 4.50r Any single   .30 .30
   u.-ad.   A739 5r Any single   .30 .30
   ae.-an.   A739 10r Any single   .50 .50
   ao.-ax.   A739 17r Any single   .75 .75

Sinhala Bauddhaya Newspaper,
Cent. — A740

2006, May 7   **Perf. 13¾x14**
1544 A740 5r multi   .40 .25

Natl. Cadet Corps,
125th
Anniv. — A741

2006, May 18   **Perf. 12x13¼**
1545 A741 2r multi   .40 .25

Kotte Sri Kalyani Samagridharma
Maha Sanga Sabha, 150th
Anniv. — A742

2006, June 25   **Perf. 13¾x14**
1546 A742 4.50r multi   .40 .25

Sri Lanka
Ramanna Maha
Nikaya — A743

2006, June 29   **Perf. 14x13¾**
1547 A743 4.50r multi   .40 .25

**Nos. 592, 1154, and 1353
Surcharged**

Methods and Perfs As Before
2006
1548 A518 10r on 10.50r #1154   1.00 1.00
1549 A618 20r on 3r #1353   1.50 1.50
1550 A218 50r on 1.60r #592   3.50 3.50
    Nos. 1548-1550 (3)   6.00 6.00

Size, location and style of surcharges vary.

St. Vincent Boys
Home, Maggona,
125th
Anniv. — A744

2006, July 15   **Litho.**   **Perf. 14x13¾**
1551 A744 10r multi   .50 .50

Lakshman
Kadiragamar
(1932-2005),
Foreign
Minister — A745

2006, Aug. 10
1552 A745 10r multi   .50 .50

St. John Dal Bastone Church,
Talangama, 125th Anniv. — A746

2006, Aug. 13   **Perf. 13¾x14**
1553 A746 5r multi   .40 .25

St. John Ambulance, Cent. — A747

2006, Aug. 15
1554 A747 5r multi   .50 .30

Tenth
South
Asian
Games
A748

Designs: 10r, High jump. 100r, Cycling.

2006, Aug. 17
1555-1556 A748   Set of 2   4.00 4.00

St. Joseph's Church, Wennappuwa, 125th Anniv. — A749

2006, Aug. 23
1557 A749 2r multi .35 .25

Senaka Bibile (1920-77), Pharmacologist A750

2006, Sept. 29 *Perf. 12x13½*
1558 A750 10r multi .50 .50

World Children's Day A751

2006, Oct. 1 *Perf. 13¾x14*
1559 A751 5r multi .35 .25

Flowers — A752

Designs: No. 1560, Indian laburnum. No. 1561, Sacred lotus. No. 1562, Foxtail orchid. No. 1563, Orange jessamine.

2006, Oct. 2 *Perf. 14x13¾*
1560 A752 4.50r multi .30 .30
1561 A752 4.50r multi .30 .30
1562 A752 50r multi 1.25 1.25
  a. Miniature sheet of 8, 4 each
    #1560, 1562 7.25 7.25
1563 A752 50r multi 1.25 1.25
  a. Miniature sheet of 8, 4 each
    #1561, 1563 7.25 7.25
    Nos. 1560-1563 (4) 3.10 3.10

World Post Day A753

2006, Oct. 9 *Perf. 13¾x14*
1564 A753 40r multi 1.50 1.50

Christmas A754

2006, Nov. 13 *Perf. 14x13¾*
1565 A754 5r multi .35 .25

St. Anthony's Shrine, Wahakotte A755

2006, Nov. 13 *Perf. 13¾x14*
1566 A755 20r multi .60 .60

Rugby in Sri Lanka, 125th Anniv. (in 2003) — A756

2006, Dec. 8 *Perf. 13*
1567 A756 4.50r multi .75 .30

D. M. Rajapaksa, Politician — A757

2006, Dec. 14 *Perf. 14x13¾*
1568 A757 5r multi .35 .25

Vee Bissakara Govijana Chaityaya, Ambuluwawa A758

Biodiversity Complex, Ambuluwawa — A759

2006, Dec. 18 *Perf. 12x13½*
1569 A758 5r multi .35 .25
                 Perf. 13¾x14
1570 A759 25r multi .75 .75

Kande Viharaya A760

2007, Jan. 6 *Perf. 13¾x14*
1571 A760 5r multi .35 .25

Ceylon Nos. 351, 352, 397, 403, and Sri Lanka Nos. 494, 890, 932, 1153, 1290, 1355, and 1452 Srchd.

Methods and Perfs As Before
2007
1572 A86 50c on 35c Ceylon
      #351 .75 .75
1573 A124 50c on 60c Ceylon
      #403 .75 .75
1574 A397 50c on 5.75r #932 .75 .75
1575 A518 50c on 8.50l #1153 .75 .75
1576 A679 50c on 26r #1452 .75 .75
1577 A91 4.50r on 50c Ceylon
      #352 1.00 .75
1578 A122 4.50r on 50c Ceylon
      #397 1.00 .75
1579 A174 4.50r on 1.15r #494 1.00 .75
1580 A373 4.50r on 5.75r #890 1.00 .75
1581 A576 4.50r on 22r #1290 1.00 .75
1582 A618 5r on 4r #1355 1.00 .75
    Nos. 1572-1582 (11) 9.75 8.25
Issued: Nos. 1572-1576, 1582, 2/13; Nos. 1577-1581, 1/29.

Diplomatic Relations Between Sri Lanka and People's Republic of China, 50th Anniv. — A761

2007, Feb. 7 *Litho. Perf. 13¼x12*
1583 A761 50r multi 2.50 2.50

ICC Cricket World Cup — A762

Flags of participating nations, Sri Lanka Cricket emblem and: 5r, Batsman and players. 50r, Players, Sri Lanka flag.

2007, Feb. 23 *Perf. 13*
1584-1585 A762 Set of 2 1.50 1.50

I. M. R. A. Iriyagolle (1907-73), Education and Cultural Affairs Minister — A763

2007, Mar. 20 *Litho. Perf. 14x13¾*
1586 A763 5r multi .35 .30

First Ceylon Postage Stamps, 150th Anniv. A764

Designs: 5r, Steamship, Ceylon #2. 10r, Mail runner, Ceylon #6, 10, 11. 20r, Mail canoe, Ceylon #3, 4. 45r, Mail coach, Ceylon #15.

2007, Apr. 1 *Litho. Perf. 13¾x14*
1587-1590 A764 Set of 4 2.25 2.25
1590a   Souvenir sheet, #1587-1590 2.50 2.50

Wall Paintings of Thelapatta Jataka — A765

No. 1591, 5r: a, House at right. b, House at center.
No. 1592, 20r: a, Flag bearer at right. b, King on throne at right.

2007, Apr. 20 *Litho. Perf. 13¾x14*
Horiz. Pairs, #a-b
1591-1592 A765 Set of 2 3.00 3.00
1592c   Souvenir sheet, #1591-1592, perf. 13¾x13¼ 3.00 3.00

Sri Lankan Cricket Team, Runners-up in 2007 ICC Cricket World Cup — A766

Designs: No. 1593, 15r, Team, stadium. No. 1594, 15r, Players on field, faces of players.

2007, Apr. 30 *Perf. 13¾x14*
1593-1594 A766 Set of 2 2.75 2.75

Shells A767

Designs: 5r, Textile cone. 12r, Aquatile hairy triton. 15r, Rose-branched murex. 45r, Trapezium horse conch.

2007, May 22 *Litho. Perf. 13¾x14*
1595-1598 A767 Set of 4 5.50 5.50
1598a   Souvenir sheet, #1595-1598 5.75 5.75

Scouting, Cent. — A768

2007, May 26 *Perf. 13½x12*
1599 A768 5r multi .35 .25

Sri Sangamitta Balika Maha Vidyalaya, Cent. — A769

2007, June 17 *Perf. 12x13¼*
1600 A769 5r multi .35 .25

Sri Lanka-Japan Friendship Society, 50th Anniv. — A770

2007, June 26   Litho.   Perf. 13¼x12
1601 A770 15r multi   1.10 1.10

Ceylon Baithulmal Fund, 50th Anniv. — A771

2007, July 3   Litho.   Perf. 12x13¼
1602 A771 5r multi   .35 .25

Prisons Day — A772

2007, July 16   Perf. 14x13¾
1603 A772 5r multi   .40 .25

Jabbar Central College, Galagedara, 104th Anniv. — A773

2007, July 27   Perf. 13¼x12
1604 A773 5r multi   .35 .25

First Sri Lankan Buddhist Mission to Germany, 50th Anniv. — A774

2007, Aug. 22   Perf. 13
1605 A774 5r multi   .35 .25

Diplomatic Relations Between Sri Lanka and Nepal, 50th Anniv. — A775

2007, Sept. 1   Litho.   Perf. 13
1606 A775 15r multi   1.10 1.10

Shrine of Our Lady of Matara, Cent. A776

2007, Sept. 9   Litho.   Perf. 13
1607 A776 5r multi   .35 .25

World Tourism Day A777

2007, Sept. 27
1608 A777 5r multi   .40 .25

Lions International in Sri Lanka, 50th Anniv. — A778

2007, Oct. 6   Perf. 12x13¼
1609 A778 5r multi   .40 .25

World Post Day — A779

2007, Oct. 9   Perf. 13¼x12
1610 A779 5r multi   .50 .25

Constellations — A780

2007, Oct. 9   Litho.   Perf. 13x12¾
Size: 20x25mm
1611 A780 50c Aries   .35 .35
1612 A780 1r Taurus   .35 .35
1613 A780 2r Gemini   .35 .35
1614 A780 3r Cancer   .35 .35
1615 A780 4r Leo   .35 .35
1616 A780 4.50r Virgo   .35 .35
1617 A780 5r Libra   .35 .35
1618 A780 10r Scorpius   .35 .35
1619 A780 12r Sagittarius   .35 .35
1620 A780 15r Capricornus   .40 .40
1621 A780 20r Aquarius   .45 .45
1622 A780 25r Pisces   .60 .60
  a. Sheet of 12, #1611-1622 2.50 2.50
Size: 25x30mm
Perf. 12x13½
1623 A780 30r Centaurus   .70 .70
1624 A780 35r Ursa Major   .80 .80
1625 A780 40r Ophiuchus   .90 .90
1626 A780 45r Orion   1.05 1.05
  a. Sheet of 4, #1623-1626   3.75 3.75
      Nos. 1611-1626 (16)   8.05 8.05

National Farmer's Day — A781

2007, Oct. 16   Litho.   Perf. 13
1627 A781 5r multi   .35 .25

Fauna of Udawalawe National Park A782

Designs: 5r, Water buffalos. 15r, Herd of elephants. 40r, Ruddy mongoose. 45r, Common langurs.

2007, Oct. 31   Perf. 13
1628-1631 A782 Set of 4   3.00 3.00
  1630a Souvenir sheet, #1629-
         1630, perf. 13¾x14   3.00 3.00
  1631a Souvenir sheet, #1628,
         1631, perf. 13¾x14   3.00 3.00

Leslie Goonewardene (1909-83), Governmental Minister — A783

2007, Nov. 6   Litho.   Perf. 13
1632 A783 5r multi   .70 .70

Commonwealth Games Federation General Assembly, Colombo — A784

Emblem and: 5r, Man blowing into conch shell. 45r, Winged figures.

2007, Nov. 7   Litho.   Perf. 13
1633-1634 A784 Set of 2   1.50 1.50

St. Henry's College, Ilavalai, Cent. A785

2007, Nov. 10
1635 A785 5r multi   .35 .25

Christmas A786

2007, Nov. 18
1636 A786 5r multi   .35 .25

St. James' Church, Mutwal A787

2007, Nov. 18
1637 A787 30r multi   .75 .75

Muthiah Muralidaran, Cricket Player — A788

2007, Dec. 3   Perf. 13¾
Granite Paper
1638 A788 5r multi   .50 .30
  a. Sheet of 12 + 3 labels   6.00 6.00
Values are for stamps with surrounding selvage.

Children's Stories — A789

No. 1639 — Scenes from the Race Between the Hare and Tortoise: a, Hare and tortoise before race (green panels). b, Hare sleeping (pink panels). c, Hare leaping (blue panels).

2007, Dec. 9   Perf. 12x13¼
1639 A789 Horiz. strip of 3   .75 .75
  a.-c.   5r Any single   .25 .25

St. Mary's Church, Maggona, 150th Anniv. A790

2007, Dec. 9   Perf. 13
1640 A790 5r multi   .35 .25

Intl. Anti-Corruption Day — A791

2007, Dec. 10   Litho.
Granite Paper
1641 A791 5r multi   .35 .25

Global Knowledge to the Village — A792

2008, Jan. 4   Perf. 13¼x12
1642 A792 5r multi   .40 .25
Opening of 500th Nenasala Center.

Most Venerable Halgasthota Sri Devananda Mahanayaka Thero — A793

2008, Jan. 30   Perf. 14x13¾
1643 A793 5r multi   .35 .25

Independence,
60th
Anniv. — A794

2008, Feb. 4   *Perf. 12x13¼*
1644 A794 5r multi   .35 .25

Deshamanya N. U. Jayawardena
(1908-2002), Governor of Central
Bank — A795

2008, Feb. 25   *Perf. 13½x14*
1645 A795 5r multi   .35 .25

7th
Commonwealth
Youth Ministers
Meeting,
Colombo — A796

Perf. 13¼x12¾ Syncopated
2008, Apr. 26
1646 A796 5r multi   .35 .25

St. Mary's
Convent,
Matara,
Cent.
A797

Perf. 12¾x13¼ Syncopated
2008, Apr. 29
1647 A797 5r multi   .35 .25

Ancient Sri
Lanka — A798

Designs: 5r, Megalithic cist, bead necklace,
Ibbankatuwa, 600-400 B.C. 10r, Basawakku-
lama Veva (reservoir), 3rd cent. B.C. 12r,
Inscribed Vallipuram gold plate, 1st cent. 15r,
Alakolavela iron furnace, 1st-2nd cent. 30r,
Gajalakshmi coin, 1st cent. B.C.-A.D. 4th
cent., punch mark coin, 3rd cent. B.C.-A.D. 4th
cent. 40r, Sigiri painting, 5th cent.

2008, Apr. 30   *Perf. 12x13¼*
1648-1653 A798 Set of 6   3.50 3.50

Vesak
A799

Various Dahamsonda Jataka wall paintings
from Reswehere Raja Maha Vihara,
Kudakatnoruwa: 4.50r, 5r, 15r, 40r.

2008, May 9   *Perf. 13¾x14*
1654-1657 A799 Set of 4   2.50 2.50
1657a   Souvenir sheet, #1654-1657,
    perf. 13¾x13½   3.00 3.00

2008 Summer Olympics,
Beijing — A800

Designs: 5r, Shooting. 15r, Javelin. 40r,
Boxing. 45r, Running.

2008, July 23   *Perf. 12¾x13*
1658-1661 A800 Set of 4   3.25 3.25
1658a   Tete-beche pair   .40 .40
1659a   Tete-beche pair   1.00 1.00
1660a   Tete-beche pair   2.50 2.50
1661a   Tete-beche pair   3.00 3.00

15th South Asian Association for
Regional Cooperation Summit,
Colombo — A801

2008, Aug. 2   *Perf. 13*
Granite Paper
1662 A801 15r multi   .75 .75

Takiko Yoshida,
Philantropist
A802

Perf. 13¼x12¾ Syncopated
2008, Aug. 16
1663 A802 5r multi   .35 .25

Employees'
Provident Fund,
50th
Anniv. — A803

2008, Sept. 11   *Perf. 14x13¾*
1664 A803 5r multi   .35 .25

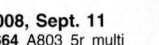

Ancient Sri Lanka — A804

Designs: 5r, Gold ingot, coin and mold, 8th-
10th cents. 10r, Medirigiriya Vatadage ruins
and conjectural drawing of structure, 7th cent.
15r, Urinal stone from Western monastery,
Anuradhapura, cross section of sanitary system, 7th-8th cents. 20r, Jewelry, 6th-9th cents.
30r, Bodhisattva Vajrapani, Avalokithesvara,
and sculpture of royal family, Isurumuniya, 8th-
9th cents.

2008, Sept. 16   *Perf. 13¼x12*
1665-1669 A804 Set of 5   3.00 3.00

Lion — A805

Perf. 12½ Syncopated
2008, Sept. 24   **Photo. & Engr.**
Granite Paper
Color of Denomination
1670 A805   50r red violet   1.05 1.05
1671 A805   70r blue   1.60 1.60
1672 A805   100r olive green   2.10 2.10
1673 A805   500r orange   10.00 10.00
1674 A805   1000r purple   21.00 21.00
1675 A805   2000r blue green   42.50 42.50
  Nos. 1670-1675 (6)   78.25 78.25

World Post
Day
A806

2008, Oct. 9   **Litho.**   *Perf. 13½x14*
1676 A806 5r multi   .35 .25

Dutch
Burgher
Union of
Ceylon,
Cent.
A807

2008, Oct. 22
1677 A807 5r multi   .35 .25

Anton Jayasuriya
(1930-2005),
Acupuncturist
A808

Perf. 13¼x12¾ Syncopated
2008, Nov. 7
1678 A808 5r multi   .35 .25

Pieter Keuneman
(1917-97),
Politician — A809

2008, Dec. 1
1679 A809 5r multi   .35 .25

The Two Men and the Bear — A810

Perf. 12¾x13¼ Syncopated
2008, Dec. 5
1680 A810 5r multi   .35 .25

Most Venerable
Weweldeniye
Medhalankara
Mahanayake
Mahathero
A811

Perf. 13¼x12¾ Syncopated
2008, Dec. 7
1681 A811 5r multi   .35 .25

Christmas
A812

Perf. 12¾x13¼ Syncopated
2008, Dec. 9
1682 A812 5r multi   .35 .25

St. Mary's
Cathedral,
Kaluwella
A813

Perf. 13¼x12¾ Syncopated
2008, Dec. 9
1683 A813 30r multi   .75 .75

Universal
Declaration
of Human
Rights,
60th Anniv.
A814

2008, Dec. 10   *Perf. 13¾x14*
1684 A814 5r multi   .40 .25

Sri Lanka Transport Board, 50th Anniv. — A815

2008, Dec. 30   *Perf. 13¼x12*
1685 A815 5r multi   .35   .25

Madu Ganga Wetlands A816

Designs: 5r, Lumnitzera littorea flowers, river. 25r, Mangroves and river.

2009, Feb. 2   Litho.   *Perf. 13¾x14*
1686-1687 A816   Set of 2   .80   .80

Year of English and Information Technology A817

2009, Feb. 13   *Perf. 14x13¾*
1688 A817 5r multi   .35   .25

University of Sri Jayewardenepura, Nugegoda, 50th Anniv. — A818

2009, Feb. 18   *Perf. 13¾x14*
1689 A818 5r multi   .35   .25

F. R. Jayasuriya (1909-84), Economics Professor at Kelaniya University — A819

2009, Feb. 25   *Perf. 14x13¾*
1690 A819 5r multi   .35   .25

A. P. de Zoysa (1890-1968), Buddhist Scholar — A820

2009, Mar. 5   *Perf. 13¾x14*
1691 A820 5r multi   .35   .25

Moors Sports Club (Cricket Team), Cent. A821

Perf. 12¾x13¼ Syncopated
2009, Mar. 5
1692 A821 5r multi   .35   .25

Sri Lanka Railway Running Shed, Dematagoda, Cent. — A822

2009, Mar. 9   Litho.
1693 A822 5r multi   .35   .25

Mahmoud Shamsuddeen Kariapper, Politician — A823

2009, Mar. 13   *Perf. 12x13¼*
1694 A823 5r multi   .35   .25

University of Vocational Technology A824

Perf. 13¼x12¾ Syncopated
2009, Mar. 31
1695 A824 5r multi   .35   .25

Natural Rubber Research and Development in Sri Lanka, Cent. — A825

Perf. 12¾x13¼ Syncopated
2009, Apr. 2
1696 A825 5r multi   .35   .25

Jeyaraj Fernandopulle (1953-2008), Politician — A826

Perf. 13¼x12¾ Syncopated
2009, Apr. 7
1697 A826 5r multi   .35   .25

Leprosy Hospital, Hendala, 300th Anniv. (in 2008) A827

2009, Apr. 23   *Perf. 13¾x14*
1698 A827 5r multi   .35   .25

Sri Sumangala College, Panadura, Cent. A828

Perf. 12¾x13¼ Syncopated
2009, Apr. 23
1699 A828 5r multi   .35   .25

Handupelpola Sri Punnaratana Nayaka Maha Thero, Politician — A829

Perf. 13¼x12¾ Syncopated
2009, May 2
1700 A829 5r multi   .35   .25

Most Venerable Welithara Sri Gnanawimala Tissa Mahanayake Thero (1766-1833), Religious Leader — A830

2009, May 5
1701 A830 5r multi   .35   .25

Vesak Festival A831

Designs 4r, Visit to the temple. 5r, Meditation.

2009, May 5   *Perf. 13¾x14*
1702 A831 4r multi   .45   .45
Perf. 12¾x13¼ Syncopated
1703 A831 5r multi   .55   .55

Nimal S. de Silva, President of 2009-10 World Health Assembly A832

2009, June 8   *Perf. 13¾x14*
1704 A832 5r multi   .35   .25

Polonnaruwa Era — A833

Designs: 5r, Galpotha inscription of King Nissankamalla, obverse and reverse of coin of Queen Leelawathi. 10r, Siva Temple and adornments.15r, Parakrama Samudra Reservoir and statue of King Parakramabahu or of a sage. 25r, Palace of King Parakramabahu and Audience Hall of King Nissankamalla. 30r, Ancient hospital, medical trough, surgical instrument and grinding stone. 40r, Scupltures of Siva, Uma, and Saiva Saint Karaikkal Ammaiyar.

Perf. 12¾x13¼ Syncopated
2009, June 23
1705-1710 A833   Set of 6   3.25   3.25

Mahmood Hasarath, Educator — A834

2009, July 25   *Perf. 14x13¾*
1711 A834 5r slate blue   .35   .25

Hameed Al Husseinie College Colombo, 125th Anniv. A835

2009, July 30   *Perf. 13¾x14*
1712 A835 5r multi   .35   .25

University of Kelaniya, 50th Anniv. — A836

2009, July 31   *Perf. 13¼x12*
1713 A836 5r multi   .35   .25

Bank of Ceylon, 70th Anniv. — A837

2009, Aug. 3   *Perf. 14x13¾*
1714 A837 5r multi   .35   .25

Retirement of Colombo Archbishop Oswald Gomis — A838

2009, Aug. 10   Litho.
1715 A838 15r multi   .60   .60

Sri Lanka Customs, 200th Anniv. A839

Perf. 12¾x13¼ Syncopated
2009, Aug. 25
1716 A839 15r multi   .70 .70

Sree Narayana Gurudev (1856-1924), Religious Leader — A840

2009, Sept. 4   **Perf. 14x13¾**
1717 A840 5r multi   .35 .25

Sivali Central College, Ratnapura, Cent. — A841

2009, Sept. 25   **Perf. 13¼x12**
1718 A841 15r multi   .70 .70

World Post Day — A842

2009, Oct. 9   **Perf. 14x13¾**
1719 A842 15r multi   .80 .80

Sri Lanka Army, 60th Anniv. A843

2009, Oct. 10   **Perf. 13**
1720 A843 15r multi   .70 .70

Humane Eradication of Rabies — A844

2009, Nov. 5   **Perf. 14x13¾**
1721 A844 15r multi   .70 .70

A845

Christmas A846

2009, Nov. 8   **Perf. 14x13¾**
1722 A845 5r multi   .35 .25
   a.   Souvenir sheet of 2   .50 .50
       Perf. 13¾x14
1723 A846 15r multi   .65 .65
   a.   Souvenir sheet of 2   1.00 1.00
No. 1722a sold for 20r; No. 1723a for 40r.

Diplomatic Relations Between Sri Lanka and Cuba, 50th Anniv. — A847

2009, Nov. 9   **Perf. 12x13¼**
1724 A847 5r multi   .45 .25

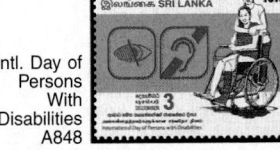

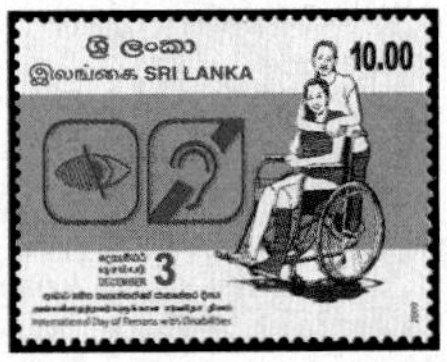

Intl. Day of Persons With Disabilities A848

2009, Dec. 3   **Perf. 13¾x14**
1725 A848 10r multi   .50 .50

Voet Lights Society, 110th Anniv. A849

2009, Dec. 4
1726 A849 15r multi   .60 .60

Peduru Hewage William de Silva (1908-88), Politician — A850

Perf. 13¼x12¾ Syncopated
2009, Dec. 15   **Litho.**
1727 A850 10r multi   .50 .50

Dr. Hudson Silva (1929-99), Founder of Intl. Eye Bank — A851

2009, Dec. 21   **Perf. 14x13¾**
1728 A851 10r multi   .50 .50

D. M. Dasanayake (1953-2008), Politician — A852

2010, Jan. 8   **Perf. 14x13¾**
1729 A852 10r multi   .50 .50

Thurstan College, Colombo, 60th Anniv. — A853

2010, Jan. 11   **Perf. 13¼x12**
1730 A853 10r multi   .50 .50

Ceylon-German Technical Training Institute, 50th Anniv. — A855

2010, Feb. 15   **Litho.**   **Perf. 13¾x14**
1733 A855 10r multi   .50 .50

Government Officers' Benefit Association, Cent. (in 2009) — A856

2010, Feb. 24
1734 A856 5r multi   .35 .25

Rotary International in Sri Lanka, 80th Anniv. (in 2009) — A857

2010, Mar. 18   **Perf. 14x13¾**
1735 A857 10r multi   .50 .50

M. J. C. Fernando (1885-1939), Buddhist Leader — A858

2010, Mar. 27   **Perf. 13¾x14**
1736 A858 10r multi   .50 .50

Buddhist Flag, 125th Anniv. — A859

2010, Apr. 28   **Perf. 14x13¾**
1737 A859 5r multi   .35 .25

Vesak Festival — A860

Designs: 4r, Arrival of Lord Buddha at Mahiyanganaya. 5r, Mahiyangana Stupa. 10r, Mirisawetiya Stupa, Anuradhapura, horiz. 30r, Jetawana Stupa, Anuradhapura, horiz.

2010, May 24   **Perf. 14x13¾, 13¾x14**
1738-1741 A860   Set of 4   2.00 2.00
 1741a   Souvenir sheet of 4,   2.00 2.00
       #1738-1741

St. Anthony's Shrine, Kochchikade, 175th Anniv. — A861

2010, June 12   **Perf. 14x13¾**
1742 A861 5r multi   .35 .25

Sri Kalyaniwansa Nikaya Buddhist Order, 200th Anniv. — A862

2010, June 17   **Perf. 13¾x14**
1743 A862 10r multi   .50 .50

Mahajana College, Tellippalai, Cent. A863

2010, June 18   **Litho.**
1744 A863 10r multi   .50 .50

Pepiliyana Sunethra Mahadevi Piriven Rajamaha Viharaya, 600th Anniv. — A864

2010, June 20   *Perf. 13¼x12*
1745 A864 5r multi   .35 .25

Victory and Peace — A865

2010, July 6   *Perf. 14x13¾*
1746 A865 5r multi   .35 .25

Postal History — A866

No. 1747: a, National Postal Museum. b, Philatelic Exhibition Center.

2010, July 6   *Perf. 13¾x14*
1747 A866 5r Horiz. pair, #a-b   .50 .50
A souvenir sheet containing Nos. 1747a-1747b sold for 60r.

Anuradhapura Teaching Hospital, 50th Anniv. — A867

2010, July 10
1748 A867 5r multi   .35 .25

Royal College, Colombo, 175th Anniv. A868

2010, July 16   **Litho.**
1749 A868 10r multi   .50 .50

Kokuvil Hindu College, Cent. A869

2010, July 22
1750 A869 10r multi   .50 .50

M. P. De Zoysa, Politician, Cent. of Birth — A870

2010, Aug. 9   *Perf. 14x13¾*
1751 A870 10r multi   .50 .50

2010 Youth Olympics, Singapore — A871

Perf. 12¾x13¼ Syncopated
2010, Aug. 12
1752 A871 10r multi   .50 .50

World Indigenous People's Day — A872

No. 1753: a, Indigenous people. b, Art by indigenous people.

2010, Aug. 25   *Perf. 13¾x14*
1753 A872 5r Horiz. pair, #a-b   .50 .50
A souvenir sheet containing Nos. 1753a-1753b sold for 60r.

Central Bank of Sri Lanka, 60th Anniv. — A873

2010, Aug. 27   *Perf. 13¼x12*
1754 A873 10r multi   .50 .50

Beaches — A874

Designs: 15r, Pasikudah Beach. 25r, Trincomalee Beach. 40r, Arugam Bay Beach.

2010, Sept. 7   *Perf. 13¼*
1755-1757 A874   Set of 3   2.50 2.50
Souvenir sheets of 1 of Nos. 1755-1757 each sold for 100r.

Horton Plains National Park — A875

Designs: 5r, Sri Lanka whistling thrush. 15r, Sambur, horiz. 25r, Rhinohorn lizard, horiz. 40r, Purple-faced leaf monkey.

2010, Sept. 7   *Perf. 13¼*
1758-1761 A875   Set of 4   3.00 3.00
Four souvenir sheets each containing one of Nos. 1758 -1761 sold for 15r, 25r, 35r and 50r, respectively.

University of Peradeniya Faculty of Engineering, 60th Anniv. — A876

2010, Sept. 9   **Litho.**   *Perf. 13¾x14*
1762 A876 15r multi   .60 .60

Vienna Convention for Ozone Layer Protection, 25th Anniv. — A877

2010, Sept. 16   *Perf. 14x13¾*
1763 A877 5r multi   .35 .25

St. Michael's Church, Koralawella, 150th Anniv. — A878

2010, Sept. 29
1764 A878 5r multi   .35 .25

World Children's Day — A879

2010, Oct. 3   *Perf. 13*
1765 A879 5r multi   .35 .25

Children's Story, "The Story of How the Tortoise Flew" — A880

2010, Oct. 3   *Perf. 13¾x14*
1766 A880 5r multi   .35 .25

World Post Day A881

2010, Oct. 9   **Litho.**
1767 A881 5r multi   .35 .25

Rankot Viharaya, Panadura, 200th Anniv. A882

2010, Oct. 10
1768 A882 5r multi   .35 .25

Diocese of Colombo Diocesan Council, 125th Anniv. A883

2010, Oct. 14
1769 A883 5r multi   .35 .25

Louis Braille (1809-52), Educator of the Blind A884

2010, Oct. 15
1770 A884 5r multi   .35 .25

World Fellowship of Buddhists, 60th
Anniv. — A885

2010, Nov. 14   Litho.   Perf. 13½x12
1771 A885 5r multi   .25   .25

Magam Ruhunupura Rajapaksa
Port — A886

2010, Nov. 18   Perf. 13¾x14
1772 A886 5r multi   .25   .25

Christmas
A887

Designs: 5r, People around Christmas tree.
15r, St. Mary's Church, Kegalle.

2010, Nov. 28
1773-1774 A887 Set of 2   .35   .35
1774a   Souvenir sheet of 2,
           #1773-1774   .65   .65

No. 1774a sold for 35r.

Sri Lanka
Navy, 60th
Anniv.
A888

2010, Dec. 9   Perf. 13
1775 A888 5r multi   .25   .25

Holy Emmanuel
Church,
Moratuwa, 150th
Anniv. — A889

2010, Dec. 27   Perf. 14x13¾
1776 A889 5r multi   .25   .25

Labugama Reservoir, 125th
Anniv. — A890

2011, Jan. 18   Perf. 13½x12
1777 A890 5r multi   .25   .25

Dr. P. R.
Anthonis (1911-
2009), University
of Colombo
Chancellor
A891

2011, Jan. 21   Perf. 14x13¾
1778 A891 5r multi   .25   .25

Intl. Year of
Chemistry
A892

2011, Jan. 30   Perf. 12x13½
1779 A892 5r multi   .25   .25

Trains
A893

No. 1780: a, Viceroy Special steam locomotive BB 240. b, Viceroy Special locomotive B2
213. c, Sentinel Camel steam rail car V2 331.
d, Narrow gauge steam locomotive JI 220.
45r, Viceroy Special steam train B1 251.

Perf. 12¾x13½ Syncopated
2011, Feb. 2   Granite Paper
1780   Horiz. strip of 4   .40   .40
a.-d.   A893 5r Any single   .25   .25
Souvenir Sheet
Perf. 13¾x14
1781 A893 45r multi   1.10 1.10

Viceroy Special steam train, 25th anniv. No.
1781 contains one 123x30mm stamp and sold
for 60r.

St. Mary's
Church,
Dehiwala,
175th
Anniv.
A894

2011, Feb. 6   Perf. 13¾x14
1782 A894 5r multi   .25   .25

Southlands College, Galle, 125th
Anniv. — A895

2011, Feb. 18   Perf. 13½x12
1783 A895 5r multi   .25   .25

Sri Lanka
Air Force,
60th Anniv.
A896

2011, Mar. 2   Perf. 13¾x14
1784 A896 5r multi   .25   .25

No. 1389A Surcharged

Method and Perf As Before
2011, Apr. 1
1785 A618 15r on 4.50r #1389A   .30   .30

First Man in
Space, 50th
Anniv.
A897

2011, Apr. 26   Litho.   Perf. 13¾
1787 A897 5r multi   .25   .25
  Values are for stamp with surrounding
selvage.

Sambuddhatva Jayanthi
(Enlightenment of Buddha) Festival,
2600th Anniv. — A898

No. 1788 — Inscriptions at bottom: a, Buddhism is a universal doctrine. b, Let us practice Buddhist principles. c, Let us take care of
our parents and respect them. d, Let us help
the sick. e, Person who practices Buddhism
illuminates the entire world. f, Let us build an
antinarcotic society.

2011, Apr. 29   Perf. 13½x12
Granite Paper
1788 A898 5r Block of 6, #a-f   .55   .55

Rabindranath
Tagore (1861-
1941),
Poet — A899

2011, May 7   Perf. 14x13¾
1789 A899 5r multi   .25   .25

Vesak Festival — A900

No. 1790 — Map of India and Sri Lanka,
Sambuddhatva Jayanthi Festival 2600th anni-
versary emblem and Buddhist temples at: a,
Lumbini, Nepal. b, Buddhagaya, India. c,
Baranesa Isipathanarama, India. d, Kusinara,
India.

2011, May 14   Perf. 14x13¾
1790 A900 5r Block of 4, #a-d   .40   .40
  e.   Souvenir sheet, #1790a-1790d   .65 .65
    No. 1790e sold for 35r.

Bridges — A901

No. 1791: a, Ancient stone bridge,
Mahakanadarawa. b, Suspension bridge,
Peradeniya.
No. 1792: a, Wooden bridge, Bogoda. b,
Steel arch bridge, Ruwanwella.

2011, May 27   Perf. 13½x12
1791 A901 10r Vert. pair, #a-b   .40   .40
1792 A901 15r Vert. pair, #a-b   .55   .55
  c.   Souvenir sheet of 2, #1791a,
          1792a, perf. 13½   .75   .75
  d.   Souvenir sheet of 2, #1791b,
          1792b, perf. 13½   .75   .75

Nos. 1792c and 1792d each sold for 40r.

People's
Bank,
50th
Anniv.
A902

Perf. 12¾x13½ Syncopated
2011, July 1
1793 A902 5r multi   .25   .25

Radampala Sri Sumangala Central
College, Cent. — A903

2011, July 15   Perf. 13¾x14
1794 A903 5r multi   .25   .25

Non-aligned Movement, 50th Anniv. — A904

Perf. 13½x12¾ Syncopated
2011, July 21
1795 A904 5r multi .25 .25

World Tourism Day A905

Designs: No. 1796, 5r, Buddhist stupa ("Heritage" at left). No. 1797, 5r, Sigiriya Rock ("Heritage" at right). No. 1798, 5r, Dancers and drummers. No. 1799, 5r, Sri Lankan women and flag. No. 1800, 15r, Woman bathing under floating flowers. No. 1801, 15r, Waterfall. 30r, Elephants. 35r, Leopard. 40r, Sailboat near shore. 45r, Whitewater rafters.

2011, Sept. 27 **Litho.** **Perf. 13**
1796-1805 A905 Set of 10 3.75 3.75
1805a Souvenir sheet of 10,
#1796-1805, + 2 central
labels 3.75 3.75

World Children's Day — A906

Perf. 13½x12¾ Syncopated
2011, Oct. 1
1806 A906 5r multi .25 .25

World Post Day A907

Perf. 12¾x13½ Syncopated
2011, Oct. 9
1807 A907 5r multi .25 .25

First South Asian Beach Games, Hambantota — A908

2011, Oct. 11 **Perf. 13¾x14**
1808 A908 5r multi .25 .25

Dudley Senanayake (1911-73), Prime Minister — A909

Perf. 13½x12¾ Syncopated
2011, Oct. 14
1809 A909 5r black & brown .25 .25

Telephone and Number for Government Information Center — A910

Perf. 12¾x13½ Syncopated
2011, Oct. 17
1810 A910 5r multi .25 .25

Old Automobiles — A911

Designs: No. 1811, 5r, 1928 Austin 12. No. 1812, 5r, 1934 Rolls Royce 20/25. No. 1813, 5r, 1937 Jaguar SS 100. No. 1814, 5r, 1949 Morris Minor.

Perf. 12¾x13¼ Syncopated
2011, Oct. 28
1811-1814 A911 Set of 4 .40 .40

Christmas A912

Designs: 5r, Shrine of Our Lady of Lourdes, Kalaoya. 20r, Holy Family, dove with flags of Sri Lanka and Vatican City on wings.

Perf. 13¼x12¾ Syncopated
2011, Nov. 27
1815-1816 A912 Set of 2 .45 .45
1816a Souvenir sheet of 2,
#1815-1816, perf.
14x13¾ .80 .80

No. 1816a sold for 45r.

Most Venerable Kotagama Wachissara Thero, Religious Figure — A913

Perf. 13¼x12¾ Syncopated
2011, Nov. 28
1817 A913 5r multi .25 .25

World AIDS Day — A914

2011, Dec. 1 **Litho.**
1818 A914 5r multi .25 .25

Sri Lankan Film Personalities A915

Designs: No. 1819, 5r, Eddy Jayamanna (1915-81), comedian. No. 1820, 5r, Sandaya Kumari, actress. No. 1821, 5r, Titus Thotawatta (1929-2011), director. 10r, Joe Abewickrama (1927-2011), actor. 15r, Malini Fonseka, actress. 20r, Gamini Fonseka (1936-2004), actor.

2012, Jan. 21 **Perf. 14x13¾**
1819-1824 A915 Set of 6 1.10 1.10
1824a Souvenir sheet of 6,
#1819-1824, imperf. 1.10 1.10

Sri Lankan Branch of Institute of Chartered Ship Brokers, 25th Anniv. — A916

Perf. 12¾x13¼ Syncopated
2012, Feb. 9
1825 A916 5r black & brown .25 .25

Scouting in Sri Lanka, Cent. A917

2012, Feb. 22 **Perf. 13**
1826 A917 5r multi .25 .25
a. Souvenir sheet of 4 #1826, imperf. .35 .35

Peonies — A918

No. 1827: a, Denomination at LL. b, Denomination at LR.

2012, Mar. 10 Litho. Perf. 13¾x14
1827 A918 30r Horiz. pair, #a-b .95 .95

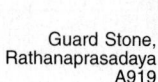

Guard Stone, Rathanaprasadaya A919

Perf. 13 Syncopated
2012, Mar. 10 **Litho.**
1828 A919 50r mar & multi 1.25 1.25
1829 A919 100r bl vio & multi 2.50 2.50

Sustainable Energy For All — A920

2012, Mar. 20 **Perf. 13¼x12**
1830 A920 5r multi .25 .25

Asian-Pacific Postal Union, 50th Anniv. — A921

2012, Apr. 1 **Perf. 13¾x14**
1831 A921 5r multi .25 .25

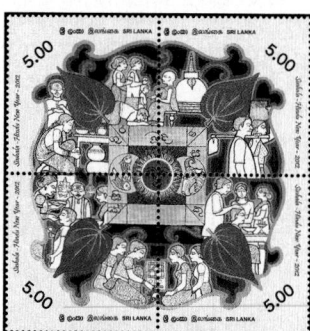

Sinhala (Hindu New Year) — A922

No. 1832 — People and leaves with denomination at: a, UL. b, UR. c, LL. d, LR.

2012, Apr. 10 **Perf. 13**
Granite Paper
1832 A922 5r Block of 4, #a-d .35 .35

Sapugaskanda Petroleum Refinery — A923

2012, Apr. 30 **Perf. 13¾x14**
1833 A923 5r multi .25 .25
Ceylon Petroleum Corporation, 50th anniv.

Sambuddhatva Jayantiya (Enlightenment of Buddha), 2600th Anniv. — A924

2012, May 3 **Perf. 13¼x12**
1834 A924 5r multi .25 .25

Vesak Festival A925

Leaves, religious symbols and emblems, with denomination at: 5r, Left. 12r, Right.

2012, May 6   *Perf. 13¾x14*
1835-1836	A925	Set of 2	.30	.30
1836a		Souvenir sheet of 2, #1835-1836	.30	.30

Professor Walpola Sri Rahula Thero (1907-97), Buddhist Historian — A926

2012, May 15   *Perf. 14x13¾*
1837	A926	5r multi	.25	.25

St. Philip Neri's Church, Udammita South, 225th Anniv. — A927

2012, May 26   *Litho.*
1838	A927	5r multi	.25	.25

Kusuma Gunawardena (1912-85), Abettor in Jail Break of Anti-Colonial Leaders — A928

2012, May 28   *Perf. 14x13¾*
1839	A928	5r multi	.25	.25

Asgiri Maha Viharaya, 700th Anniv. A929

2012, June 12   *Perf. 13¾x14*
1840	A929	5r multi	.25	.25

Ceylon School for the Deaf and Blind, Cent. — A930

Perf. 12¾x13¼ Syncopated
2012, June 17   *Litho. & Embossed*
1841	A930	5r multi	.25	.25

Terra Cotta Figure, Sigiriya — A931

Perf. 13½x12¾ Syncopated
2012, July 16   *Litho.*
1842	A931	5r multi	.25	.25

Natl. Archaeology Week.

Department of Agriculture, Cent. — A932

2012, July 22   *Perf. 13¼x12*
1843	A932	5r multi	.25	.25

2012 Summer Olympics, London — A933

Big Ben and: 5r, Running. 15r, Swimming. 25r, Shooting. 75r, Badminton.

Perf. 13½x12¾ Syncopated
2012, July 23
1844-1847	A933	Set of 4	1.90	1.90
1847a		Souvenir sheet of 4, #1844-1847, perf. 14x13¾	1.90	1.90

58th Commonwealth Parliamentary Conference, Colombo — A934

Perf. 12¾x13½ Syncopated
2012, Sept. 11
1848	A934	5r multi	.25	.25

Colonial Buildings — A935

Designs: No. 1849, 15r, Galle Face Hotel, Colombo. No. 1850, 15r, National Museum. No. 1851, 15r, Colombo Municipal Council Building. No. 1852, 15r, Old Parliament Building.

2012, Sept. 11   *Perf. 13¼x12*
1849-1852	A935	Set of 4	.90	.90
1850a		Souvenir sheet of 2, #1849-1850, perf. 13¼	.45	.45
1852a		Souvenir sheet of 2, #1851-1852, perf. 13¼	.45	.45

World Children's Day A936

2012, Oct. 1   *Litho.*   *Perf. 13*
1853	A936	5r multi	.25	.25

World Post Day — A937

2012, Oct. 6   *Perf. 12x13¼*
1854	A937	5r multi	.25	.25

Flowers A938

Designs: No. 1855, 5r, Exacum trinevirum. No. 1856, 5r, Plumeria rubra. No. 1857, 5r, Hibiscus rosa-sinensis. No. 1858, 5r, Helianthus annuus.

2012, Oct. 7   *Perf. 13¾x14*
1855-1858	A938	Set of 4	.30	.30
1858a		Souvenir sheet of 4, #1855-1858	.30	.30

2012 World Post Day Stamp Exhibition (#1858a).

World Health Organization Service in Sri Lanka, 60th Anniv. — A939

2012, Oct. 16   *Perf. 14x13¾*
1859	A939	12r multi	.25	.25

Sri Lanka Insurance, 50th Anniv. A940

Perf. 12¾x13½ Syncopated
2012, Oct. 31
1860	A940	5r multi	.25	.25

Christmas A941

Designs: 5r, Holy Family, doves and children. 25r, Flight into Egypt, man pulling woman and children in cart.

Perf. 12¾x13½ Syncopated
2012, Dec. 2
1861-1862	A941	Set of 2	.50	.50
1862a		Souvenir sheet of 2, #1861-1862, perf. 13¾x14	.50	.50

Aviation in Sri Lanka, Cent. A942

Designs: 5r, Blériot monoplane. 12r, Air Ceylon jet. 15r, Sri Lankan Airlines jet. 25r, Mihin Lanka Airlines jet.

Perf. 12¾x13¼ Syncopated
2012, Dec. 7
1863-1866	A942	Set of 4	.90	.90
1866a		Souvenir sheet of 4, #1863-1866, perf. 13¾x14	.90	.90

Moonstones, Guard Stones and Balustrades — A943

Designs: 50c, Vishnu Dewala moonstone, Kandy. 1r, Watadage moonstone, Polonnaruwa. 2r, Rajamaha Vihara moonstone, Beligala. 3r, Abayagiri Vihara moonstone, Anuradhapura. 4r, Jethawana Vihara guard stone, Anuradhapura, vert. 4.50r, Rajamaha Vihara guard stone, Arattana, vert. 5r, Tissamaharamaya guard stone, vert. 10r, Abayagiri Rathnaprasadaya guard stone, Anuradhapura, vert. 12r, Abayagiri Stupa guard stone, Anuradhapura, vert. 15r, Dematamal Vihara guard stone, Buttala, vert. 20r, Mahavihara balustrade, Anuradhapura. 25r, Lankathilaka Image House balustrade, Polonnaruwa. 30r, Jethawanarama Vihara balustrade, Anuradhapura. 40r, Mahavihara balustrade, Anuradhapura, diff. 55r, Mahavihara balustrade, Anuradhapura, diff. 75r, Yapahuwa balustrade.

2012, Dec. 12   *Perf. 13 Syncopated*
Granite Paper
1867	A943	50c multi	.25	.25
1868	A943	1r multi	.25	.25
1869	A943	2r multi	.25	.25
1870	A943	3r multi	.25	.25
1871	A943	4r multi	.25	.25
1872	A943	4.50r multi	.25	.25
1873	A943	5r multi	.25	.25
1874	A943	10r multi	.25	.25
1875	A943	12r multi	.25	.25
1876	A943	15r multi	.25	.25
1877	A943	20r multi	.30	.30
1878	A943	25r multi	.40	.40
1879	A943	30r multi	.50	.50
1880	A943	40r multi	.65	.65
1881	A943	55r multi	.90	.90
1882	A943	75r multi	1.25	1.25
	Nos. 1867-1882 (16)		6.50	6.50

Diplomatic Relations Between Sri Lanka and Japan, 60th Anniv. A944

Designs: 5r, Lotus flowers. 65r, Cherry blossoms.

Perf. 12¾x13½ Syncopated
2013, Jan. 18
1883-1884	A944	Set of 2	1.10	1.10
1884a		Souvenir sheet of 2, #1883-1884, perf. 13¾x14	1.10	1.10

Rajans International Scout Centennial Gathering, Kandy — A945

Perf. 12¾x13¼ Syncopated
2013, Feb. 18
1885 A945 25r multi .40 .40

Opening of Mattala Rajapaksa International Airport — A946

2013, Mar. 18
1886 A946 5r black .25 .25

Sri Lanka Peace Pada Yatra (Peace March) — A947

2013, Apr. 5 **Perf. 13¼x12**
1887 A947 5r multi .25 .25

Dharmasoka College, Ambalangoda, Cent. — A948

Perf. 12¾x13¼ Syncopated
2013, May 4
1888 A948 5r multi .25 .25

Vesak Festival A949

Encounters of Prince Siddhartha with: 4r, Old man. 5r, Diseased man. 15r, Decaying corpse. 50r, Ascetic.

Perf. 12¾x13¼ Syncopated
2013, May 18
1889-1892 A949 Set of 4 1.25 1.25
1892a Souvenir sheet of 4, #1889-1892, perf. 13½x14 1.25 1.25

Dambegoda Bodhisattva Statue — A950

2013, May 25 **Perf. 12x13¼**
1893 A950 5r multi .25 .25

Swami Vivekananda (1863-1902), Lecturer on Hinduism in Western Countries — A951

Perf. 13¼x12½ Syncopated
2013, June 7
1894 A951 25r multi .40 .40

Christ Church Girls' College, Baddegama, 125th Anniv. — A952

Perf. 12¾x13½ Syncopated
2013, July 5 Litho.
1895 A952 5r multi .25 .25

Wildlife in Yala National Park A953

Designs: 5r, Hawksbill turtle. 15r, Swamp crocodile. 25r, Elephant, vert. 30r, Black-necked stork, vert. 40r, Wild boar. 50r, Spotted deer.

Perf. 13¾x14, 14x13¾
2013, July 28 Litho.
1896 A953 5r multi .25 .25
1897 A953 15r multi .25 .25
1898 A953 25r multi .40 .40
1899 A953 30r multi .45 .45
 a. Souvenir sheet of 2, #1898-1899 .85 .85
 b. As "a," with Thailand 2013 World Stamp Exhibition emblem in sheet margin .85 .85
1900 A953 40r multi .60 .60
 a. Souvenir sheet of 2, #1897, 1900 .85 .85
 b. As "a," with Thailand 2013 World Stamp Exhibition emblem in sheet margin .85 .85
1901 A953 50r multi .75 .75
 a. Souvenir sheet of 2, #1896, 1901 .85 .85
 b. As "a," with Thailand 2013 World Stamp Exhibition emblem in sheet margin .85 .85
 Nos. 1896-1901 (6) 2.70 2.70

Father Tissa Balasuriya (1924-2013), Founder of Center for Society and Religion — A954

Perf. 13½x12¾ Syncopated
2013, Aug. 29 Litho.
1902 A954 5r multi .25 .25

World Children's Day — A955

No. 1903 — The Umbrella Thief, by Sybil Wettasinghe, with word balloon at left beginning with: a, "In the village of Kirimama. . ." b, "What are you looking for?" c, "Ha. . .ha. . !"

Perf. 12¾x13½ Syncopated
2013, Oct. 1 Litho.
1903 A955 Horiz. strip of 3 .25 .25
 a.-c. 5r Any single .25 .25

World Post Day A956

2013, Oct. 9 Litho. **Perf. 12x13½**
1904 A956 5r multi .25 .25

Sigiriya UNESCO World Heritage Site A957

Stilt Fishermen A958

2013, Oct. 9 Litho. Perf. 13½x14
Granite Paper
1905 A957 15r multi .40 .40
1906 A958 15r multi .40 .40

The right parts of Nos. 1905-1906 could be personalized. The generic image depicting the emblem of Sri Lanka Post is shown.

Opening of Colombo-Katunayake Expressway — A959

Perf. 13½x12¾ Syncopated
2013, Oct. 27 Litho.
1907 A959 5r multi .25 .25

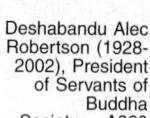

Father Tissa Balasuriya (1924-2013)...

Deshabandu Alec Robertson (1928-2002), President of Servants of Buddha Society — A960

Perf. 13½x12¾ Syncopated
2013, Oct. 30 Litho.
1908 A960 5r multi .25 .25

Dr. Premasiri Khemadasa (1937-2008), Composer A961

Perf. 13½x12¾ Syncopated
2013, Nov. 1 Litho.
1909 A961 5r multi .25 .25

Excise Department, Cent. — A962

Perf. 12¾x13½ Syncopated
2013, Nov. 6 Litho.
1910 A962 5r multi .25 .25

Commonwealth Heads of Government Meeting, Colombo — A963

Emblem, girl with flowers with background colors of: 5r, Red and purple. 25r, Blue and green.

2013, Nov. 14 Litho. Perf. 13½x14
1911-1912 A963 Set of 2 .45 .45
1912a Souvenir sheet of 2, #1911-1912 .45 .45

Dr. Tissa Abeysekara (1939-2009), Film Maker — A964

Perf. 12¾x13¼ Syncopated
2013, Nov. 27 Litho.
1913 A964 5r multi .25 .25

Christmas A965

Designs: 5r, People in circle around Holy Family. 30r, People, Madonna and child.

2013, Dec. 1   **Litho.**   *Perf. 14x13½*
1914-1915 A965   Set of 2   .55 .55
1915a   Souvenir sheet of 2,   .55 .55
    #1914-1915

All Ceylon Moor's Association, Cent. — A966

Perf. 12¾x13½ Syncopated
2013, Dec. 2   **Litho.**
1916 A966   5r blk & red   .25 .25

Dharmadasa Walpola (1927-83), Singer — A967

Perf. 13½x12¾ Syncopated
2013, Dec. 19   **Litho.**
1917 A967   5r multi   .25 .25

Venerable Baddegama Wimalawansa Nayaka Thero (1913-93), Buddhist Monk and Writer — A968

Perf. 13½x12¾ Syncopated
2013, Dec. 21   **Litho.**
1918 A968   5r multi   .25 .25

Sri Lanka Administrative Service, 50th Anniv. — A969

Perf. 13½x12¾ Syncopated
2013, Dec. 23   **Litho.**
1919 A969   5r multi   .25 .25

Thai Pongal Farmer's Festival A970

Designs: 5r, Farmer with ox-drawn plow. 25r, Man and woman cooking pongal.

2014, Jan. 12   **Litho.**   *Perf. 13½x14*
1920-1921 A970   Set of 2   .45 .45
1921a   Souvenir sheet of 2,   .45 .45
    #1920-1921

Deyata Kirula Exhibition, Kuliyapitiya A971

Perf. 13½x12¾ Syncopated
2014, Feb. 21   **Litho.**
1922 A971   5r multi   .25 .25

Sri Lankan Railway Civil Engineering Projects — A972

Designs: No. 1923, 5r, Nine Arch Viaduct, Gotuwala. No. 1924, 5r, Spiral railway, Demodara.

2014, Feb. 28   **Litho.**   *Perf. 13*
                 Granite Paper
1923-1924 A972   Set of 2   .25 .25

Mountain Hourglass Tree Frog — A973

Perf. 13½x12¾ Syncopated
2014, Mar. 3   **Litho.**
1925 A973   5r multi   .25 .25

World Wildlife Day.

H. Sri Nissanka (1898-1954), Jurist — A974

Perf. 13¼x12¾ Syncopated
2014, Apr. 4   **Litho.**
1926 A974   5r multi   .25 .25

Ceylon Fertilizer Company, Cent. A975

Perf. 12¾x13¼ Syncopated
2014, Apr. 4   **Litho.**
1927 A975   5r multi   .25 .25

Ho Chi Minh (1890-1969), President of North Viet Nam — A976

2014, Apr. 28   **Litho.**   *Perf. 12x13¼*
1928 A976   5r multi   .25 .25

World Conference on Youth, Colombo — A977

Perf. 12¾x13¼ Syncopated
2014, May 7   **Litho.**
1929 A977   5r multi   .25 .25

Vesak Festival — A978

Prince Siddhartha on the eve of renunciation: 5r, Sees the repulsive sight of sleeping dancers. 10r, Looking at his wife, Yasodhara, and son, Rahula. 15r, Crossing the River Anoma. 20r, Cutting off his hair.

2014, May 12   **Litho.**   *Perf. 14x13½*
1930-1933 A978   Set of 4   .80 .80
1933a   Souvenir sheet of 4,   .80 .80
    #1930-1933

Carey College, Cent. A979

Perf. 12¾x13¼ Syncopated
2014, May 29   **Litho.**
1934 A979   5r multi   .25 .25

World Environment Day — A980

Perf. 13¼x12¾ Syncopated
2014, June 5   **Litho.**
1935 A980   5r multi   .25 .25

Arrival of Methodist Missionaries in Sri Lanka, 200th Anniv. — A981

2014, June 29   **Litho.**   *Perf. 13*
1936 A981   5r multi   .25 .25

Pigeon Island Marine National Park A982

Designs: 7r, Rock pigeons. 10r, Sperm whale. 15r, Blacktip reef shark. 25r, Blackwedged butterflyfish. 35r, Scaly rock crab. 50r, Knotted fan coral.

2014, Aug. 22   **Litho.**   *Perf. 13½x14*
                 Granite Paper
1937-1942 A982   Set of 6   2.25 2.25
1942a   Souvenir sheet of 6,   2.25 2.25
    #1937-1942

Dr. R. L. Spittel (1881-1969), Surgeon — A983

Perf. 13¼x12¾ Syncopated
2014, Sept. 3   **Litho.**
1943 A983   10r multi   .25 .25

Asian-Pacific Postal Union Executive Council Meeting, Colombo — A984

Designs: 7r, Executive Council Meeting emblem. 10r, Executive Council Meeting Emblem, Asian-Pacific Postal Union Emblem, arms of Sri Lanka, map of Sri Lanka, emblem of Sri Lanka Post. 35r, Executive Council Meeting emblem, mail box, men and women. 50r, Executive Council Meeting emblem, map and flags of Asian-Pacific Postal Union members.

2014, Sept. 15   **Litho.**   *Perf. 13½x14*
1944-1947 A984   Set of 4   1.60 1.60
1947a   Souvenir sheet of 4,   1.60 1.60
    #1944-1947

Anagarika Dharmapala (1864-1933), Buddhist Missionary — A985

2014, Sept. 17 Litho. Perf. 13x12¾
1948 A985 10r multi   .25   .25

World Children's Day — A986

Perf. 13¼x12¾ Syncopated
2014, Oct. 1   Litho.
Granite Paper
1949 A986 10r multi   .25   .25

World Post Day A987

Perf. 12¾x13¼ Syncopated
2014, Oct. 9   Litho.
Granite Paper
1950 A987 10r multi   .25   .25

Dr. Ray Wijewardene (1924-2010), Engineer and Inventor — A988

2014, Oct. 31 Litho. Perf. 12x13¼
Granite Paper
1951 A988 10r multi   .25   .25

Christmas — A989

No. 1952 — Winning art in stamp design contest depicting Nativity scenes with Christmas tree and denomination at: a, Right. b, Left.

2014, Nov. 30 Litho. Perf. 13½x14
Granite Paper
1952 A989 10r Horiz. pair, #a-b   .30   .30
  c. Souvenir sheet of 2, #1952a-
    1952b   .30   .30

Sri Lanka Standards Institution, 50th Anniv. — A990

2014, Dec. 3 Litho. Perf. 12x13¼
Granite Paper
1953 A990 10r multi   .25   .25

Solar System — A991

Designs: 7r, Sun. 8r, Mercury. 10r, Venus. 12r, Earth. 15r, Moon. 20r, Mars. 25r, Jupiter. 30r, Saturn. 35r, Uranus. 40r, Neptune.

2014, Dec. 5 Litho. Perf. 12x13¼
Granite Paper
1954-1963 A991 Set of 10   3.25 3.25
1963a   Souvenir sheet of 10,
    #1954-1963, perf.
    13¼x12   3.25 3.25
1963b   As "a," with "National
    Stamp Exhibition 2014"
    inscription in sheet mar-
    gin, perf. 13¼x12   3.25 3.25

Visit of Pope Francis to Sri Lanka A992

Pope Francis and: 10r, St. Peter's Basilica. 75r, Holding cross.

2015, Jan. 13 Litho. Perf. 13½x14
Granite Paper
1964-1965 A992 Set of 2   1.40 1.40
1965a   Souvenir sheet of 2,
    #1964-1965   1.40 1.40

POSTAL-FISCAL STAMPS

The editors believe that six additional revenue stamps were authorized for postal use during 1979-98 and would like to examine them.

National Coat of Arms With Sinhalese Characters at Left and Right — PF1

Perf. 13x12
1979, May 28   Engr.   Wmk. 233
AR2 PF1 20r dark green   —
AR3 PF1 50r violet   —

Nos. AR2 and AR3 were issued in 1974 for revenue purposes, and were usable on mail starting on May 28, 1979.

Coat of Arms Type of 1979
Perf. 13x12
1983, Oct. 14   Engr.   Wmk. 233
AR4 PF1 100r carmine   26.00 32.00

National Coat of Arms — PF2

1984   Engr.   Perf. 14½x14
AR6 PF2 50r vermilion   2.00 2.00
AR7 PF2 100r deep claret   3.75 3.75

A lithographed 500r value exists but was not authorized for postal use.

Arms Type of 1984
Perf. 14½x14¼
1998, Dec. 16   Engr.   Wmk. 408
AR9 PF2 100r chocolate   —

An additional stamp was issued in this set. The editors would like to examine it.

National Coat of Arms — PF3

Granite Paper
Color of Denomination
Perf. 12½ Syncopated
2002, May 28   Litho. & Engr.
AR10 PF3 50r brown   —

Stamps of type PF3 with denominations of 500r and 1000r were not valid for postage. An additional stamp was issued in this set. The editors would like to examine it.

National Coat of Arms — PF4

Granite Paper
Color of Denomination
Perf. 12¾x12½ Syncopated
2007, Nov. 23   Photo. & Engr.
AR13 PF4 50r blue   1.15 1.15
AR14 PF4 100r gray green   2.50 2.50
AR15 PF4 200r lilac   5.00 5.00
  Nos. AR13-AR15 (3)   8.65 8.65

STELLALAND

ˈste-lə-ˌland

LOCATION — South Africa
GOVT. — Republic
AREA — 5,000 sq. mi. (approx.)
CAPITAL — Vryburg

This short-lived republic was set up by the Boers in an effort to annex territory ruled by the Bechuana chiefs. Great Britain refused to recognize it and in 1885 sent an expeditionary force which ended the political career of the country.
Stellaland was annexed by Great Britain in 1885 and became a part of British Bechuanaland.

12 Pence = 1 Shilling

Coat of Arms — A1

1884, Feb. Unwmk. Litho. Perf. 12
1 A1 1p red   225.00 375.00
  a. Horiz. pair, imperf. be-
    tween   4,250.
  b. Vert. pair, imperf. be-
    tween   4,600.
2 A1 3p orange   37.50 375.00
  a. Horiz. pair, imperf. vert. 1,400.
  b. Vert. pair, imperf. be-
    tween   2,200.
  c. Horiz. pair, imperf. be-
    tween   925.00
3 A1 4p gray   32.50 400.00
  a. Horiz. pair, imperf. be-
    tween   850.00
  b. Vert. pair, imperf. be-
    tween   2,400.
4 A1 6p lilac   35.00 400.00
  a. Horiz. pair, imperf. be-
    tween   1,750.
  b. Vert. pair, imperf. be-
    tween   2,000.
5 A1 1sh green   85.00 850.00
  Nos. 1-5 (5)   415.00 2,400.
Imperf. varieties are believed to be proofs.

No. 3 Handstamped in Blackish Violet

1885
6   A1 2p on 4p gray   4,000.
The status of No. 6 has long been questioned.

STRAITS SETTLEMENTS

'strāts 'se-təl-mənts

LOCATION — Malay Peninsula in southeastern Asia
GOVT. — British Colony
AREA — 1,356 sq. mi.
POP. — 1,435,895 (estimated)
CAPITAL — Singapore

The colony comprised the settlements of Malacca, Singapore and Penang, which were incorporated under one government in 1826 and the administration transferred from India to the Secretary of State for the Colonies in 1867.

The colony was dissolved in 1946 when Singapore became a separate crown colony. Malacca and Penang were incorporated into the Malayan Union, which became the Federation of Malaya in 1948.

Stamps of India were used in Malacca, Penang and Singapore, 1854-67.

See Malaya for stamps of the Federated Malay States, the Federation of Malaya, Johore, Kedah, Kelantan, Malacca, Negri Sembilan, Pahang, Penang, Perak, Perlis, Selangor, Sungei Ujong and Trengganu.

100 Cents = 1 Dollar

Stamps of India Surcharged in Red, Blue, Black Violet or Green

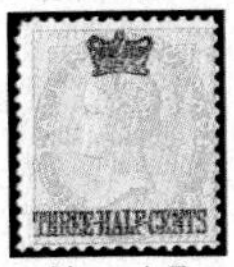
Nos. 1-7

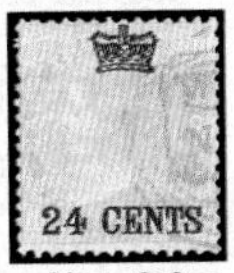
Nos. 8-9

1867, Sept. 1 Wmk. 38 *Perf. 14*

1	A7	1½c on ½a bl (R)	130.00	*200.00*
2	A7	2c on 1a brn (R)	200.00	100.00
3	A7	3c on 1a brn (Bl)	190.00	100.00
4	A7	4c on 1a brn (Bk)	300.00	275.00
5	A7	6c on 2a yel (V)	850.00	250.00
6	A7	8c on 2a yel (G)	325.00	42.50
7	A9	12c on 4a grn (R)	1,350.	325.00
a.		Double surcharge	4,500.	
8	A7	24c on 8a rose (Bl)	700.00	110.00
9	A7	32c on 2a yel (Bk)	475.00	120.00

Manuscript Surcharge, Pen Bar Across "THREE HALF" of No. 1

9A A7 2(c) on 1½c on ½a *20,000. 6,500.*

Values for Nos. 1-9A are for stamps with perforations touching the frame line on one or two sides. Used values for Nos. 1-9 are for stamps with company chops in addition to postal cancellations. Examples with postal cancels only sell for somewhat higher prices. For detailed listings, see the Scott Classic Specialized catalogue.

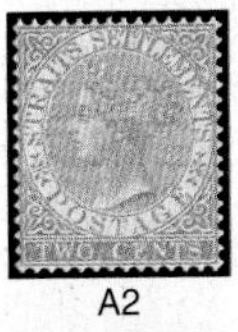
A2

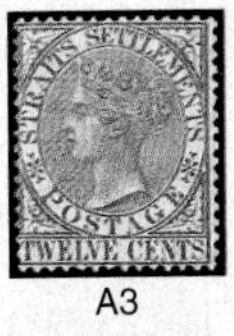
A3

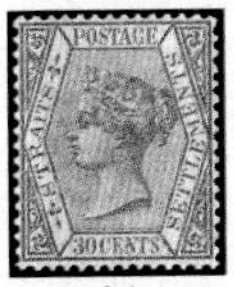
A4

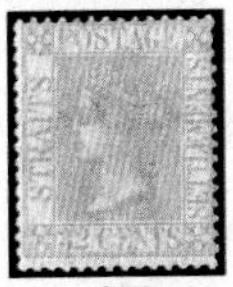
A5

1867-72 Typo. Wmk. 1 *Perf. 14*

10	A2	2c bister brown	52.50	7.50
11	A2	4c rose	87.50	13.50
12	A2	6c violet	150.00	22.50
13	A3	8c yellow	260.00	18.00
a.		8c orange	260.00	20.00
14	A3	12c blue	210.00	12.50
15	A3	24c green	190.00	8.00
16	A4	30c claret ('72)	425.00	17.50
17	A5	32c pale red	675.00	70.00
18	A5	96c olive gray	425.00	55.00
		Nos. 10-18 (9)	2,475.	224.50

Corner ornaments of types A2, A3 and A5 differ for each value.

See Nos. 19, 40-44, 48-50, 52-57. For surcharges see Nos. 20-35, 58-59, 61-66, 73-82, 91. For overprints see Malaya, Johore No. 1, Perak Nos. 1, O1-O2, Selangor Nos. 1-2, Sungei Ujong Nos. 2-3.

See the *Scott Classic Catalogue* for other shades.

Stamps of Straits Settlements, 1867-82, overprinted "B" are listed under Bangkok.

1871 *Perf. 12½*

19 A5 96c olive gray 2,750. 275.00

Stamps of 1867-72 Surcharged

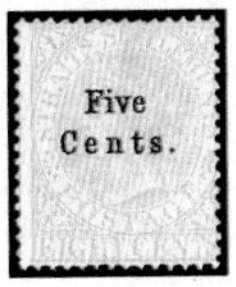

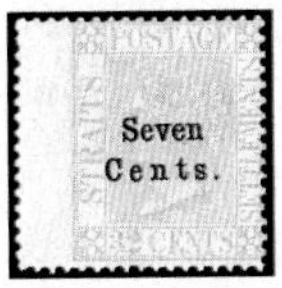

1879, May *Perf. 14*

20	A3	5c on 8c yellow	150.00	*190.00*
a.		No period after "CENTS"	1,100.	*1,300.*
21	A5	7c on 32c pale red	180.00	*200.00*
a.		No period after "CENTS"	1,800.	*2,200.*

No. 16 Surcharged

e

f

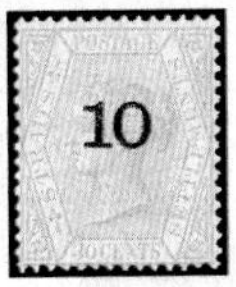
g

k

m

10 10
j h

1880

22	A4(e)	10c on 30c	325.00	55.00
23	A4(f)	10c on 30c	850.00	130.00
24	A4(g)	10c on 30c	325.00	55.00
25	A4(h)	10c on 30c	—	24,000.
25A	A4(j)	10c on 30c	8,000.	1,100.
25B	A4(k)	10c on 30c	8,000.	1,100.
25C	A4(m)	10c on 30c	8,000.	1,100.

Surcharges e & f and g, h, j & m are virtually identical. These must have an expert certificate identifying them. Values can be suspect because of misidentifications.

Unused examples are valued without gum.

With Additional Surcharge

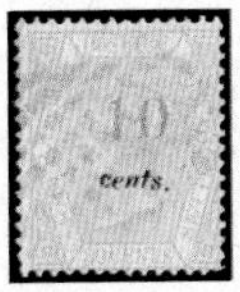

26	A4(e)	10c on 30c	600.	100.
27	A4(f)	10c on 30c	11,000.	1,100.
27A	A4(g)	10c on 30c	6,500.	650.
28	A4(h)	10c on 30c	*20,000.*	2,250.
28A	A4(j)	10c on 30c	*20,000.*	2,250.
28B	A4(k)	10c on 30c	*20,000.*	2,250.
28C	A4(m)	10c on 30c	*20,000.*	2,250.

Unused examples are valued without gum.

No. 13 Surcharged

n

5
cents.
o

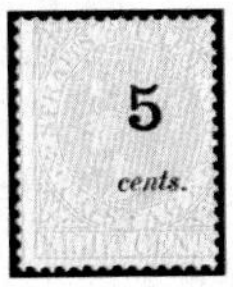
p

1880

29	A3(n)	5c on 8c yellow	180.00	*225.00*
30	A3(o)	5c on 8c yellow	700.00	*850.00*
31	A3(p)	5c on 8c yellow	190.00	*250.00*

No. 11 Surcharged

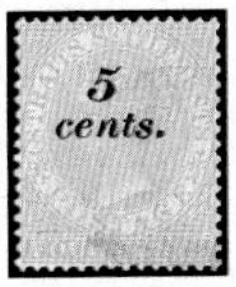

1882, Jan.

32 A2 5c on 4c rose 375.00 *400.00*

Nos. 12, 14a, 16 Surcharged

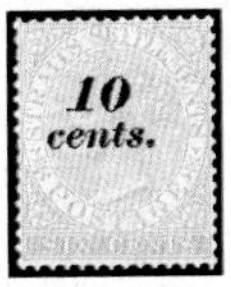

1880-81

33	A2	10c on 6c violet ('81)	90.00	7.50
a.		Double surcharge	—	3,250.
34	A3	10c on 12c blue ('81)	70.00	12.00
35	A4	10c on 30c claret	500.00	100.00
		Nos. 33-35 (3)	660.00	119.50

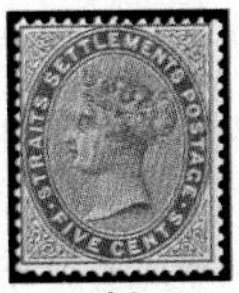
A6

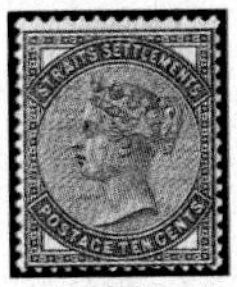
A7

1882, Jan. Typo. *Perf. 14*

38	A6	5c violet brown	120.00	*140.00*
39	A7	10c slate	500.00	80.00

See Nos. 45-47, 51. For surcharges see Nos. 60, 67-72, 89-92.

1882-99 Wmk. Crown and C A (2)

40	A2	2c bister brown	350.00	52.50
41	A2	2c car rose ('83)	13.00	1.00
a.		2c rose	47.50	4.75
42	A2	4c rose	150.00	10.50
43	A2	4c car rose ('99)	13.00	1.40
44	A2	4c bister brn ('83)	52.50	4.25
45	A6	5c ultra ('83)	19.00	1.10
46	A6	5c brown ('94)	14.00	1.10
47	A6	5c magenta ('99)	2.75	*2.40*
48	A2	6c violet	2.75	*11.00*
49	A3	8c orange	4.75	1.10
50	A3	8c ultra ('94)	5.25	.60
51	A7	10c slate	12.00	1.50
52	A3	12c vio brn ('83)	80.00	17.00
53	A3	12c claret ('94)	26.00	*12.00*
54	A3	24c blue grn ('83)	9.00	*6.00*
a.		24c yellow green ('84)	85.00	11.00
55	A4	30c claret ('91)	20.00	21.00
56	A5	32c red org ('87)	14.00	4.50
57	A5	96c olive gray ('88)	80.00	80.00
		Nos. 40-57 (18)	868.00	228.95

For overprints see Malaya, Perak Nos. O3-O9, Selangor Nos. 3-4, Sungei Ujong Nos. 6-7, 11.

Preceding Issues Surcharged

Surcharged Vertically

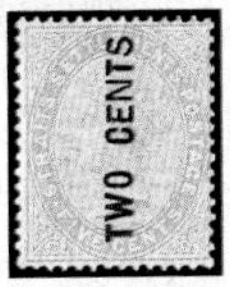

1883-84 Wmk. 2, 1

58	A3	2c on 8c orange	175.00	90.00
a.		Double surcharge	*3,750.*	*1,275.*
59	A5	2c on 32c pale red	900.00	900.00
a.		Double surcharge		
60	A6	2c on 5c ultra ('84)	175.00	180.00
a.		Pair, one without surcharge		
b.		Double surcharge		
		Nos. 58-60 (3)	1,250.	1,170.

Five types of surcharge on No. 58, two types on No. 59 and three types on No. 60.

Surcharged in Black

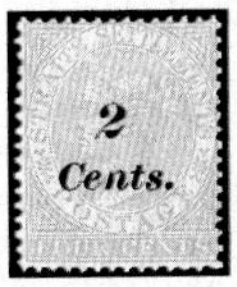

1883 Wmk. 2

61	A2	2c on 4c rose	90.00	*100.00*
b.		"s" of "Cents." inverted	1,700.	1,900.

Wmk. 1

62	A3	2c on 12c blue	425.00	180.00
a.		"s" of "Cents." inverted	7,000.	3,750.

Surcharged in Black or Blue

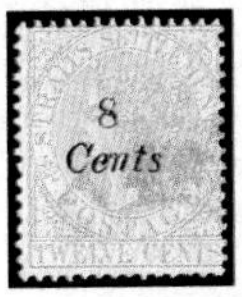

1884

63 A3 8c on 12c blue 950.00 175.00

Wmk. 2

64 A3 8c on 12c vio brn 600.00 175.00

With Additional Surcharge Handstamped in Red

65	A3	8c on 8c on 12c vio brn (R + Bk)	475.00	500.00
66	A3	8c on 8c on 12c vio brn (R + Bl)	10,000.	

Surcharged in Black or Red

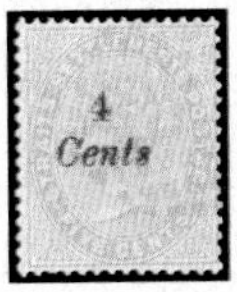

1884

67	A6	4c on 5c ultra (Bk)	3,500.	*4,250.*
68	A6	4c on 5c ultra (R)	160.00	125.00

No. 68 Surcharged in Red

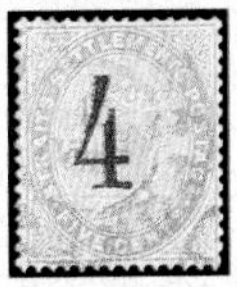

69 A6 4c on 4c on 5c ultra *37,500.*

No. 69 may be a trial printing. "Usage" seems to been restricted to less than 10 letters known sent from the Postmaster General to his wife.

Surcharged in Black

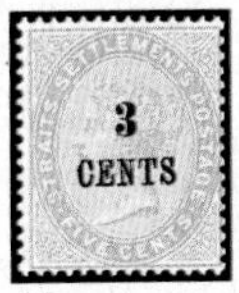

1885-87

70	A6	3c on 5c ultra	160.00	*250.00*
a.		Double surcharge	3,500.	

Surcharged in Black

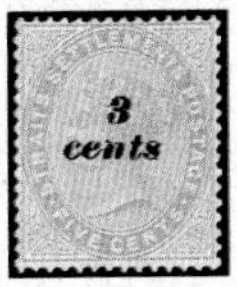

71 A6 3c on 5c vio brn ('86) 275.00 *290.00*

Surcharged **2 Cents.**

72 A6 2c on 5c ultra ('87) 42.50 90.00
a. Double surcharge 1,700. 1,600.
b. "C" omitted 4,500.

In the surcharged issues of 1883 to 1887, Nos. 59, 62, 63 and 71 are on stamps watermarked Crown and C C, the others are watermarked Crown and C A.

Surcharged  **THREE CENTS**

1885-94 Wmk. Crown and C A (2)
73 A5 3c on 32c magenta 2.25 1.10
74 A5 3c on 32c rose ('94) 2.75 .85
a. Without surcharge 4,500.

No. 74a value is for a stamp with perfs touching frame line.

Surcharged  **10 CENTS**

1891
75 A3 10c on 24c green 7.00 1.40
a. Narrow "0" in "10" 32.50 37.50

Surcharged  **THIRTY CENTS**

76 A5 30c on 32c red orange 14.00 4.25

Surcharged  **ONE CENT**

1892
77 A2 1c on 2c rose 2.25 4.25
78 A2 1c on 4c bister brn 7.00 6.25
a. Double surcharge 1,800.
79 A2 1c on 6c violet 1.75 9.50
a. Dbl. surch., one invtd. 2,150. 1,900.
80 A3 1c on 8c orange 1.25 3.25
81 A3 1c on 12c vio brown 5.75 10.50
Nos. 77-81 (5) 18.00 33.75

Surcharged  **ONE CENT**

82 A3 1c on 8c gray green 1.10 1.75

Queen Victoria — A13

1892-99 Typo.
83 A13 1c gray green 7.50 .80
84 A13 3c car rose ('95) 13.00 .55
85 A13 3c brown ('99) 14.00 .70
86 A13 25c dk vio & grn 37.50 7.50
87 A13 50c ol grn & car 25.00 3.00
88 A13 $5 org & car ('98) 500.00 275.00
Nos. 83-88 (6) 597.00 287.55

Denomination of $5, is in color on plain tablet.

Stamps of 1883-94 Surcharged 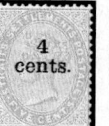 **4 cents.**

1899
89 A6 4c on 5c ultra 9.50 24.00
a. Double surcharge — 3,750.
90 A6 4c on 5c brown 3.25 5.25
91 A3 4c on 8c brt blue 2.25 1.40
a. 4c on 8c ultra 2.75 3.25
b. Double surcharge 1,600. 1,500.
Nos. 89-91 (3) 15.00 30.65

Type of 1882 Issue Surcharged  **FOUR CENTS**

92 A6 4c on 5c rose 1.10 .40
a. Without surcharge 40,000.

King Edward VII — A14

Numerals of 5c, 8c, 10c, 30c, $1 and $5, type A14, are in color on plain tablet.

1902 Wmk. 2 Typo.
93 A14 1c green 3.00 4.00
94 A14 3c vio & org 3.75 .25
95 A14 4c violet, red 5.00 .35
96 A14 5c violet 6.00 2.00
97 A14 8c violet, blue 4.75 .30
98 A14 10c vio & blk, yel 29.00 1.60
99 A14 25c violet & grn 16.00 9.00
100 A14 30c gray & car rose 22.00 8.50
101 A14 50c grn & car rose 22.50 22.50
102 A14 $1 green & blk 25.00 80.00
103 A14 $2 violet & blk 80.00 80.00
104 A14 $5 grn & brn org 215.00 180.00
104A A14 $100 dl vio & grn, yel 16,000.
Nos. 93-104 (12) 432.00 388.50

High values of the 1902 and 1904 issues with revenue cancellations are of minimal value. No. 104A is inscribed "Postage & Revenue" but the limit of weight probably precluded its use postally.
See Nos. 113, 115-128B, 133.

A15

A16

A17 A18

1903-04
105 A15 1c gray green 3.50 8.50
106 A16 3c dull violet 12.00 4.75
107 A17 4c violet, red 11.00 .35
108 A18 8c violet, blue 52.50 1.50
Nos. 105-108 (4) 79.00 15.10

See Nos. 109-112, 114, 129-132, 134.

1904-11 Chalky Paper Wmk. 3
109 A15 1c gray green 5.25 .25
110 A16 3c dull violet 3.00 .35
111 A17 4c violet, red 24.00 .80
112 A17 4c dull vio ('08) 6.50 .25
113 A14 5c violet ('06) 24.00 2.75
114 A18 8c violet, bl 52.50 1.60

115 A14 10c vio & blk, yel 9.00 .85
116 A14 10c vio, yel ('08) 15.00 1.10
117 A14 25c vio & grn 60.00 40.00
118 A14 25c violet ('09) 22.50 9.00
119 A14 30c gray & car rose 55.00 3.25
120 A14 30c vio & org ('09) 60.00 4.50
121 A14 50c grn & car rose 65.00 22.00
122 A14 50c blk, grn ('10) 9.50 5.25
123 A14 $1 green & blk 75.00 37.50
124 A14 $1 blk & red, bl ('11) 16.00 6.50
125 A14 $2 violet & blk 120.00 95.00
Revenue cancel 15.00
126 A14 $2 grn & red, yel ('09) 27.50 25.00
127 A14 $5 grn & brn org 325.00 210.00
128 A14 $5 grn & red, grn ('10) 150.00 80.00
Revenue cancel 6.50
128A A14 $25 green & blk 2,750. 2,750.
Revenue cancel 55.00
128B A14 $100 dl vio & grn, yel 17,500.
Revenue cancel 200.00
Nos. 109-128 (20) 1,124. 545.95

Nos. 125, 128A and 128B are on chalky paper, the other values are on both ordinary and chalky. The note about No. 104A will apply to No. 128B.

1906-11 Ordinary Paper
129 A15 1c blue grn ('10) 25.00 1.25
130 A16 3c carmine ('08) 7.50 .25
131 A17 4c carmine ('07) 8.50 3.00
132 A17 4c lake ('11) 3.50 .95
133 A14 5c orange ('09) 3.00 2.75
134 A18 8c ultra ('06) 4.50 .45
Nos. 129-134 (6) 52.00 8.85

Stamps of Labuan 1902-03, Overprinted or Surcharged in Red or Black

a b

c

Perf. 12½ to 16 and Compound

1907 Unwmk.
134A A38(a) 1c violet & blk 75.00 190.00
135 A38(a) 2c grn & blk 425.00 500.00
136 A38(a) 3c brn & blk 25.00 95.00
137 A38(c) 4c on 12c yel & blk 3.00 10.00
a. No period after "CENTS" 650.00 —
138 A38(c) 4c on 16c org brn & grn (Bk) 9.00 11.00
a. With additional name in red 700.00 800.00
139 A38(c) 4c on 18c bis & blk 3.00 10.00
a. No period after "CENTS" 425.00 525.00
b. "FOUR CENTS." & bar double 12,000.
140 A38(a) 8c org & blk 5.25 9.00
141 A38(b) 10c sl bl & brn 9.50 12.00
a. No period after "Settle-ments" 650.00
142 A38(a) 25c grnsh bl & grn 35.00 47.50
143 A38(a) 50c gray lil & vio 25.00 75.00
144 A38(a) $1 org & red brn 50.00 125.00
Nos. 134A-144 (11) 664.75 1,084.

A19

1908-11 Typo. Wmk. 3 Perf. 14
Chalky Paper
145 A19 $25 bl & vio, bl ('11) 3,000. 2,150.
146 A19 $500 violet & org 135,000.
Revenue cancel 400.

No. 146 is inscribed "Postage-Revenue" but was probably used only for revenue. Excellent forgeries of No. 146 exist.

A20

1910 Chalky Paper
147 A20 21c maroon & vio 7.00 40.00
148 A20 45c black, green 3.75 4.50

King George V
A21 A22

A23 A24

A25 A26

Die I (Type A24)

For description of dies I and II see front section of the Catalogue.
The 25c, 50c and $2 denominations of type A24 show the numeral on horizontally-lined tablet.

1912-18 Chalky Paper Wmk. 3
149 A21 1c green 12.00 1.60
150 A21 1c black ('18) 3.00 1.90
151 A25 2c dp green ('18) 2.25 .55
152 A22 3c scarlet 2.75 .25
a. 3c carmine 3.50 1.35
153 A23 4c gray violet 2.75 .65
154 A23 4c scarlet ('18) 3.00 .25
a. Booklet pane of 1
b. Booklet pane of 12
c. 4c carmine ('18) 2.00 .25
155 A24 5c orange 2.25 1.10
156 A25 6c claret ('18) 2.25 .55
157 A25 8c ultra 3.75 .85
158 A24 10c violet, yel 1.60 1.10
159 A24 10c ultra ('18) 10.00 1.60
160 A26 21c maroon & vio 12.00 13.00
161 A24 25c vio & red vio 17.00 15.00
162 A24 30c vio & org ('14) 8.50 5.25
163 A26 45c blk, bl grn, ol back ('14) 7.50 27.50
a. 45c black, emerald ('17) 4.00 13.75
164 A24 50c black, grn ('14) 6.50 4.50
a. 50c black, bl grn, olive back 25.00 10.00
b. 50c black, emerald 13.00 10.50
c. Die II 3.25 4.50
165 A24 $1 blk & red, bl ('14) 17.00 16.00
166 A24 $2 grn & red, yel ('15) 17.00 52.50
167 A24 $5 grn & red, grn ('15) 120.00 85.00
a. $5 grn & red, bl grn, ol back 190.00 115.00
b. $5 grn & red, emer ('15) 240.00 140.00
c. Die II 125.00 90.00
Nos. 149-167 (19) 251.10 229.15

The 1c, 3c, 5c and 8c are on ordinary paper.

Surface-colored Paper
168 A24 10c violet, yel 1.75 1.25
169 A26 45c black, grn ('14) 7.50 19.00
170 A24 $2 grn & red, yel ('14) 16.00 52.50
171 A24 $5 grn & red, grn 120.00 60.00
Nos. 168-171 (4) 145.25 132.75

See Nos. 179-201. For surcharges see Nos. B1-B2.

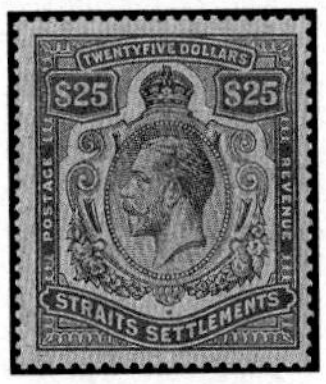

A27

1915

172	A27	$25 bl & vio, *bl*	2,150.	650.00
		Revenue cancel		5.75
173	A27	$100 red & blk, *bl*	*8,500.*	
		Revenue cancel		*90.00*
174	A27	$500 org & dl vio	*90,000.*	
		Revenue cancel		*200.00*

Although Nos. 173 and 174 were available for postage, it is probable that they were used only for fiscal purposes.

See Nos. 202-204, AR1.

Die II (Type A24)

1921-32 Ordinary Paper Wmk. 4

179	A21	1c black	.65	.25
180	A25	2c green	.65	.25
181	A25	2c brown	8.00	3.75
182	A22	3c green	1.75	.90
183	A23	4c scarlet	2.25	*5.00*
184	A23	4c dp violet ('25)	.70	.25
185	A23	4c orange ('29)	1.10	.25
186	A24	5c orange ('23)	2.75	1.50
a.		Die I	3.75	.25
187	A24	5c dk brown ('32)	3.25	.25
a.		Die I ('32)	5.75	.25
188	A25	6c claret	2.50	.25
189	A25	6c scarlet ('27)	3.00	.25
a.		6c rose red ('25)	30.00	11.00
190	A24	10c ultra (I)	2.00	4.25

Chalky Paper

191	A24	10c vio, *yel* ('27)	3.25	.35
a.		Die I ('25)	3.00	*14.00*
192	A25	12c ultra	1.35	.25
193	A26	21c mar & vio	7.00	*60.00*
194	A24	25c vio & red vio	5.75	2.00
a.		Die I	35.00	90.00
195	A24	30c violet & org	2.25	1.50
a.		Die I	29.00	*60.00*
196	A26	35c org & vio	14.00	7.00
197	A26	35c vio & car ('31)	11.50	8.00
198	A24	50c blk, *emer*	2.00	.45
199	A24	$1 blk & red, *bl*	7.00	1.40
200	A24	$2 grn & red, *yel*	11.50	9.25
201	A24	$5 grn & red, *grn*	100.00	37.50
202	A27	$25 bl & vio, *bl*	1,200.	200.00
203	A27	$100 red & blk, *bl*	8,000.	2,750.
204	A27	$500 org & dl vio	*65,000.*	
		Nos. 179-201 (23)	194.20	144.85

No. 192 is on ordinary paper.

Nos. 203 and 204 were probably used only for fiscal purposes.

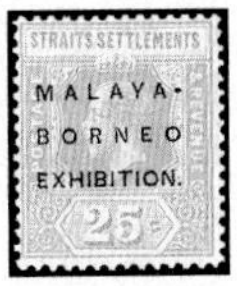

Stamps of 1912-21 Overprinted in Black

1922 Wmk. 3

151d	A25	2c deep green	40.00	*95.00*
154d	A23	4c scarlet	10.00	*26.00*
155d	A24	5c orange	8.00	*22.50*
157d	A25	8c ultra	2.25	*10.00*
161d	A24	25c vio & red vio	4.25	*47.50*
163d	A26	45c blk, *bl grn*, ol back	3.75	*42.50*
165d	A24	$1 blk & red, *bl*	475.00	*1,500.*
166d	A24	$2 grn & red, *yel*	30.00	*160.00*
167d	A24	$5 grn & red, *grn*	425.00	*750.00*

Wmk. 4

179d	A21	1c black	3.50	*22.50*
180d	A25	2c green	2.75	*16.00*
183d	A23	4c scarlet	4.00	*52.50*
186d	A24	5c orange (II)	3.25	*52.50*
190d	A24	10c ultra	2.75	*29.00*
199d	A24	$1 blk & red, *bl*	22.50	*160.00*
		Nos. 151d-199d (15)	1,037.	*2,986.*

Industrial fair at Singapore, Mar. 31-Apr. 15, 1922.

Common Design Types

pictured following the introduction.

Silver Jubilee Issue

Common Design Type

1935, May 6 Engr. *Perf. 11x12*

213	CD301	5c black & ultra	3.50	.35
214	CD301	8c indigo & green	3.75	*3.50*
215	CD301	12c ultra & brown	3.75	8.50
216	CD301	25c brn vio & ind	4.00	*12.75*
		Nos. 213-216 (4)	15.00	*25.10*
		Set, never hinged	25.00	

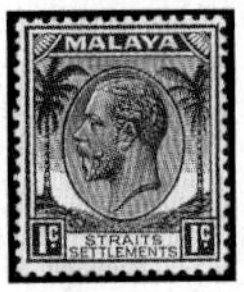

George V — A28

1936-37 Typo. *Perf. 14*

Chalky Paper

217	A28	1c black ('37)	1.60	.25
218	A28	2c green	1.60	.80
220	A28	4c orange brn	2.40	.80
221	A28	5c brown	1.10	.35
222	A28	6c rose red	1.35	1.25
223	A28	8c gray	3.75	.80
224	A28	10c dull vio	2.40	.70
225	A28	12c ultra	2.25	3.00
226	A28	25c rose red & vio	1.60	.60
227	A28	30c org & dk vio	1.40	3.50
229	A28	40c dk vio & car	1.40	2.75
230	A28	50c blk, *emerald*	4.75	1.40
232	A28	$1 red & blk, *blue*	20.00	1.90
233	A28	$2 rose red & gray grn	57.50	11.50
234	A28	$5 grn & red, *grn* ('37)	140.00	11.50
		Nos. 217-234 (15)	243.10	41.10
		Set, never hinged	325.00	

Coronation Issue

Common Design Type

1937, May 12 Engr. *Perf. 13½x14*

235	CD302	4c deep orange	.65	.25
236	CD302	8c gray black	.80	.25
237	CD302	12c bright ultra	1.80	1.10
		Nos. 235-237 (3)	3.25	1.60
		Set, never hinged	6.00	

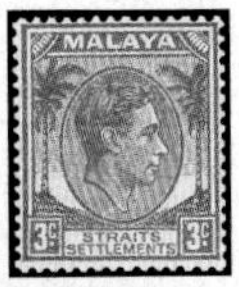

George VI — A29

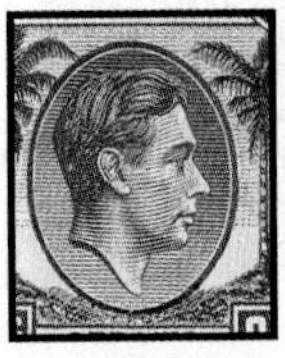

Die I

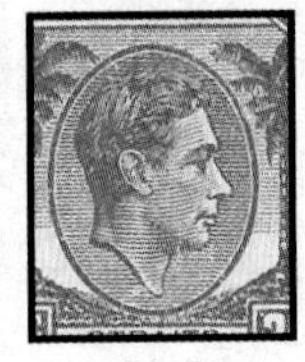

Die II

Two Dies

Die I. Printed in two operations. Lines of background touch outside of central oval. Foliage of palms touches outer frame line. Palm frond in front of King's eye has two points.

Die II. Printed from a single plate. Lines of background separated from central oval by a white line. Foliage of palms does not touch outer frame line. Palm frond in front of King's eye has one point.

1937-41 Typo. *Perf. 14*

238	A29	1c black (I)	6.00	.25
239	A29	2c green (I)	11.00	.25
c.		Die II ('38)	35.00	.45
239A	A29	2c brn org ('41) (II)	1.25	*20.00*
239B	A29	3c green ('41) (II)	5.00	4.25
240	A29	4c brown org (I)	13.50	.25
a.		Die II ('38)	50.00	.25
241	A29	5c brown (I)	12.00	.35
a.		Die II ('39)	20.00	.25
242	A29	6c rose red ('38) (I)	5.50	.65
243	A29	8c gray ('38) (I)	19.00	.25
244	A29	10c dull vio (I)	6.00	.25
245	A29	12c ultra ('38) (I)	6.00	.35
245A	A29	15c ultra ('41) (II)	5.00	*10.50*
246	A29	25c rose red & vio (I)	25.00	1.10
247	A29	30c org & vio (I)	11.00	2.00
248	A29	40c dk vio & rose red (I)	10.00	2.50
249	A29	50c blk, *emer* ('38) (I)	10.00	.45
250	A29	$1 red & blk, *bl* ('38) (I)	15.00	.40
251	A29	$2 rose red & gray grn ('38) (I)	30.00	12.50
252	A29	$5 grn & red, *grn* ('38) (I)	15.00	7.50
		Nos. 238-252 (18)	206.25	63.80
		Set, never hinged	375.00	

For overprints see Nos. 256-271, N1-N29 and Malaya, Malacca Nos. N1-N14, Penang Nos. N1-N26.

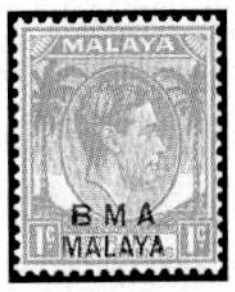

Stamps and Type of 1937-41 Overprinted in Red or Black

1945-48

256	A29	1c black (R)	.25	.25
257	A29	2c brown org (II)	.25	.25
a.		Die I ('46)	7.50	*3.75*
258	A29	3c green	.25	.25
259	A29	5c brown	.75	.60
260	A29	6c gray	.25	.25
261	A29	8c rose red	.25	.25
262	A29	10c dull vio (I)	.30	.25
a.		10c claret (II) ('48)	*10.00*	1.25
263	A29	12c ultra	1.75	*3.25*
264	A29	15c ultra (Bk)	2.25	*4.75*
265	A29	15c ultra (R)	.25	.25
266	A29	25c rose red & vio	1.40	.25
a.		Double overprint	400.00	
267	A29	50c blk, *emer* (R)	.60	.25
268	A29	$1 rose red & blk	2.00	.25
269	A29	$2 rose red & gray grn	2.50	.65
270	A29	$5 grn & red, *grn*	72.50	72.50
271	A29	$5 brn org & vio	3.75	2.75
		Nos. 256-271 (16)	89.30	87.00
		Set, never hinged	140.00	

The letters "B M A" are initials of "British Military Administration".

An 8c gray with BMA overprint was prepared but not issued. Value $5.

The 6c gray, 8c rose red and $5 brown orange & violet exist without BMA overprint, but were issued only with it.

No. 262a does not exist without overprint. No. 262 exists in at least three shades.

POSTAL-FISCAL STAMP

Type of 1915 with head George VI Inscribed "REVENUE" at each side

1938

AR1	A27	$25 Blue & purple, *blue*	4,250.	600.00

Although documentation authorizing its postal use has not been found, No. AR1 was frequently used as a postage stamp throughout 1941.

SEMI-POSTAL STAMPS

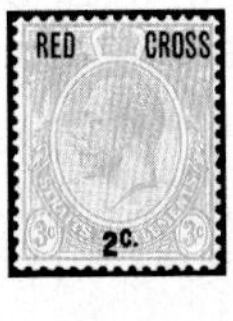

Nos. 152-153 Surcharged

1917 Wmk. 3 *Perf. 14*

B1	A22	3c + 2c scarlet	3.00	*32.50*
a.		No period after "C"	475.00	*900.00*
B2	A23	4c + 2c gray violet	4.00	*35.00*
a.		No period after "C"	525.00	*900.00*

POSTAGE DUE STAMPS

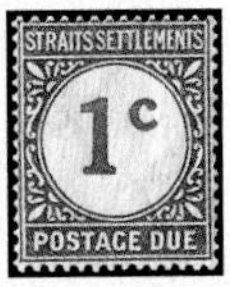

D1

1924-26 Typo. Wmk. 4 *Perf. 14*

J1	D1	1c violet	8.50	*5.50*
J2	D1	2c black	3.50	1.25
J3	D1	4c green ('26)	2.25	*5.00*
J4	D1	8c red	4.75	.60
J5	D1	10c orange	6.50	.90
J6	D1	12c ultramarine	7.50	.75
		Nos. J1-J6 (6)	33.00	*14.00*
		Set never hinged	55.00	

OCCUPATION STAMPS

Issued Under Japanese Occupation

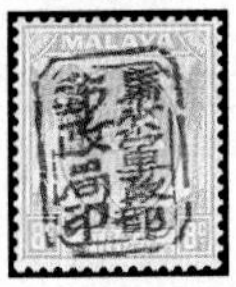

Nos. 238, 239A-B, 243 and 245A Hstmpd. in Red

1942, Mar. 16 Wmk. 4 *Perf. 14*

N1	A29	1c black	22.50	22.50
N2	A29	2c brown orange	16.00	16.00
N3	A29	3c green	70.00	*85.00*
N4	A29	8c gray	27.50	22.50
N5	A29	15c ultra	21.00	20.00
		Nos. N1-N5 (5)	157.00	166.00
		Set, never hinged	200.00	

Other denominations with this handstamp are believed to be proofs.

The handstamp reads: "Seal of Post Office of Malayan Military Department."

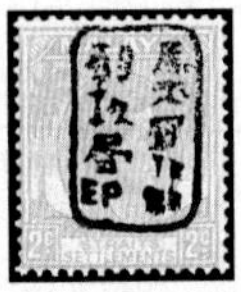

Stamps of 1937-41, Handstamped in Red, Black, Violet or Brown

1942, Apr. 3

N6	A29	1c black	4.00	4.00
N6A	A29	2c green (V)	3,750.	2,750.
N7	A29	2c brown org	3.50	3.50
N8	A29	3c green	3.50	3.50
N9	A29	5c brown	30.00	32.50
N10	A29	8c gray	8.50	8.50
N11	A29	10c dull violet	70.00	50.00
N12	A29	12c ultra	100.00	160.00
N13	A29	15c ultra	4.50	4.00
N14	A29	30c orange & vio	4,250.	4,250.
N15	A29	40c dk vio & rose red	150.00	125.00
N16	A29	50c blk, *emerald*	80.00	60.00
N17	A29	$1 red & blk, *bl*	105.00	80.00
N18	A29	$2 rose red & gray grn	180.00	225.00
N19	A29	$5 grn & red, *grn*	240.00	300.00

Nos. N6-N7, N9, N11-N12, N15-N19 with red handstamp were used in Sumatra. The 2c green with red handstamp was not regularly issued.

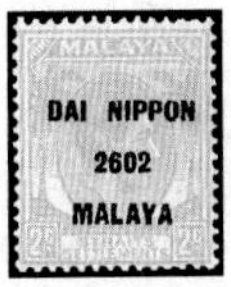

Straits Settlements Nos. 239A, 239B, 243 and 245A Ovptd. in Black

1942

N20	A29	2c brown orange	4.00	1.00
a.		Inverted overprint	17.50	27.50
b.		Dbl. ovpt., one invtd.	60.00	70.00
N21	A29	3c green	62.50	*75.00*
N22	A29	8c gray	11.00	4.75
a.		Inverted overprint	22.50	45.00
N23	A29	15c ultra	26.00	16.00
		Nos. N20-N23 (4)	103.50	96.75
		Set never hinged	165.00	

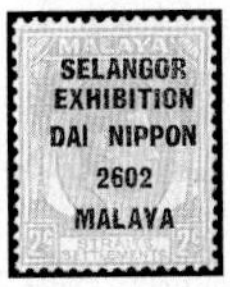

Straits Settlements Nos. 239A and 243 Overprinted in Black

1942, Nov. 3

N24	A29	2c brown orange	14.00	*25.00*
a.		Inverted overprint	375.00	425.00
N25	A29	8c gray	15.00	*25.00*
a.		Inverted overprint	375.00	425.00

Agricultural-Horticultural Exhibition held at Kuala Lumpur, Selangor, Nov. 1-2, 1942. Sold only at a temporary post office at the exhibition.

Straits Settlements Nos. 243, 245 and 248 Ovptd. in Black or Red

1943

N26	A29	8c gray (Bk)	1.60	1.00
a.		Inverted overprint	60.00	75.00
N27	A29	8c gray (R)	2.75	4.00
N28	A29	12c ultramarine	2.00	16.00
N29	A29	40c dk vio & rose red	4.25	8.00
		Nos. N26-N29 (4)	10.60	29.00
		Set never hinged	17.00	

The Japanese characters read: "Japanese Postal Service."

SUDAN

sü-'dan

LOCATION — Northeastern Africa, south of Egypt
GOVT. — Republic
AREA — 967,500 sq. mi.
POP. — 27,953,000 (1997 est.)
CAPITAL — Khartoum

10 Milliemes = 1 Piaster
100 Piasters = 1 Pound
Dinar (1992)
100 Qirsh = 1 Pound (2007)

Catalogue values for unused stamps in this country are for Never Hinged items, beginning with Scott 79 in the regular postage section, Scott C35 in the air post section, Scott CO1 in the air post official section, Scott J12 in the postage due section, and Scott O28 in the officials section.

Watermarks

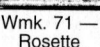

Wmk. 71 — Rosette

Wmk. 179 — Multiple Crescent and Star

Wmk. 214 — Multiple S G

Wmk. 334 — Rectangles

Wmk. 345 — Rhinoceros

Egyptian Stamps of 1884-93 Overprinted in Black

1897, Mar. 1   Wmk. 119   Perf. 14

1	A18	1m brown	4.25	2.50
a.		Inverted overprint	325.00	
2	A19	2m green	3.00	2.75
3	A20	3m orange	2.25	2.10
4	A22	5m carmine rose	3.00	2.00
a.		Inverted overprint	325.00	275.00
5	A14	1p ultra	10.00	2.50
6	A15	2p orange brown	85.00	19.00
7	A16	5p gray	87.50	22.50
a.		Double overprint	6,000.	
8	A23	10p violet	55.00	60.00
		Nos. 1-8 (8)	250.00	113.35

Counterfeits of Nos. 1-8 are plentiful.

Camel Post — A1

1898, Mar. 1   Typo.   Wmk. 71

9	A1	1m rose & brn	2.25	3.00
10	A1	2m brown & grn	4.00	3.00
11	A1	3m green & vio	4.50	2.75
12	A1	5m black & rose	4.00	2.00
13	A1	1p yel brn & ultra	16.00	4.75
14	A1	2p ultra & blk	45.00	4.00
15	A1	5p grn & org brn	50.00	21.00
16	A1	10p dp vio & blk	40.00	6.00
		Nos. 9-16 (8)	165.75	43.50

See Nos. 17-27, 43-50. For overprints see Nos. C3, MO1-MO15, O1-O9, O17-O24. For surcharges see Nos. 28, 62, C16.

1902-21   Wmk. 179

17	A1	1m car rose & brn ('05)	1.60	.90
18	A1	2m brown & grn	2.25	.25
19	A1	3m grn & vio ('03)	3.00	.35
20	A1	4m ol brn & bl ('07)	2.00	3.50
21	A1	4m brn & red ('07)	2.00	1.00
22	A1	5m blk & rose red ('03)	2.50	.25
23	A1	1p brn & ultra ('03)	3.00	.40
24	A1	2p ultra & blk ('08)	37.50	2.50
25	A1	2p org & vio brn, chalky paper ('21)	9.00	11.00
26	A1	5p grn & org brn ('08)	35.00	.45
27	A1	10p dp vio & blk ('11)	35.00	4.75
		Nos. 17-27 (11)	132.85	25.35

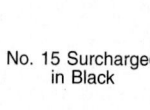

No. 15 Surcharged in Black

1903, Sept.   Wmk. 71

28	A1	5m on 5p	10.00	12.00
a.		Inverted surcharge	325.00	275.00

A2

1921-22   Typo.   Wmk. 179

29	A2	1m orange & blk ('22)	1.25	5.25
30	A2	2m dk brn & org ('22)	11.00	13.50
31	A2	3m green & vio ('22)	3.00	11.00
32	A2	4m brown & grn ('22)	8.00	9.00
33	A2	5m blk & ol brn ('22)	3.00	.25
34	A2	10m black & car ('22)	6.00	.25
35	A2	15m org brn & ultra	4.00	1.25
		Nos. 29-35 (7)	36.25	40.50

See Nos. 36-42. For overprints see Nos. C1-C2, O10-O16.
For surcharges see Nos. 60-61.

1927-40   Wmk. 214

36	A2	1m org yel & blk	1.00	.30
37	A2	2m dk brn & org	1.00	.30
38	A2	3m green & violet	1.00	.30
39	A2	4m brown & green	.90	.30
40	A2	5m blk & ol brn	.75	.30
a.		Booklet pane of 4		
41	A2	10m black & car	2.00	.35
42a	A2	15m org brn & ultra	4.00	.25
43	A1	2p orange & vio brn	4.50	.35
44	A1	3p dk bl & red brn ('40)	8.50	.35
45	A1	4p blk & ultra ('36)	4.75	.35
46	A1	5p dk grn & org brn	1.75	.35
47	A1	6p blk & pale bl ('36)	13.00	3.00
48	A1	8p blk & pck brn ('36)	13.00	5.00
49	A1	10p dp vio & blk	9.00	.40
50a	A1	20p bl & lt blue	9.00	.25
		Nos. 36-50a (15)	52.00	7.85

Charles George Gordon — A3

Gordon Memorial College A4

Memorial Service at Khartoum — A5

1935, Jan. 1   Engr.   Perf. 13½x14

51	A3	5m deep green	.75	.25
52	A3	10m brown	1.50	.30
53	A3	13m ultra	1.75	13.50
54	A3	15m carmine	3.00	.30
55	A4	2p deep blue	2.75	.25
56	A4	3p orange	3.00	.50
57	A4	10p dull violet	11.00	10.00
58	A5	20p black	32.50	72.50
59	A5	50p red brown	125.00	155.00
		Nos. 51-59 (9)	181.25	252.60
		Set, never hinged	325.00	

50th anniv. of the death of Gen. Charles George ("Chinese") Gordon (1833-85).

No. 41 Surcharged in Black

Wmk. Multiple S G (214)

1940, Feb. 25   Typo.   Perf. 14

60	A2	5m on 10m black & car	1.50	1.50

Nos. 40 and 48 Surcharged in Black

a   b

1940-41

61	A2(a)	4½p on 5m ('41)	65.00	12.00
62	A1(b)	4½p on 8p	57.50	14.00

Sudan Landscape A6

Perf. 13½, 14x13½

1941   Litho.   Unwmk.

Size: 21½x17½mm

63	A6	1m org & sl bl	2.50	6.00
64	A6	2m chocolate & org	2.50	6.00
65	A6	3m grn & rose vio	2.75	.25
66	A6	4m choc & bl grn	.60	.90
67	A6	5m indigo & ol bis	.25	.25
68	A6	10m indigo & rose pink	12.00	4.50
69	A6	15m chestnut & ultra	1.00	.25

Size: 29x25mm

71	A6	2p orange & claret	4.50	.90
72	A6	3p dk blue & fawn	.85	.25
73	A6	4p blk & brt ultra	2.75	.25
74	A6	5p dk grn & brn org	5.00	13.50
75	A6	6p ind & turq bl	15.00	1.25
76	A6	8p black & green	15.00	1.00
77	A6	10p rose vio & gray	57.50	1.10
78	A6	20p dk & lt blue	50.00	45.00
		Nos. 63-78 (15)	172.20	81.40
		Set, never hinged	300.00	

Catalogue values for unused stamps in this section, from this point to the end of the section, are for Never Hinged items.

Types of 1898-1940 with Changed Arabic Wording Below Camel

A7   A8

Wmk. 214

1948, Jan. 1   Typo.   Perf. 14

79	A7	1m dk org & blk	.45	5.50
80	A7	2m choc & org	1.00	5.00
81	A7	3m grn & rose lil	.40	7.50
82	A7	4m choc & sl grn	.65	2.00
83	A7	5m black & ol brn	9.75	2.75
84	A7	10m black & car	6.50	.25
a.		Center inverted		52,500.
85	A7	15m org brn & ultra	6.00	.25
86	A8	2p org yel & vio brn	10.00	3.00
87	A8	3p dk bl & red brn	8.50	.40
88	A8	4p black & ultra	4.50	2.00
89	A8	5p dk grn & org	4.50	6.00
90	A8	6p blk & pale bl	5.00	3.50
91	A8	8p blk & pck grn	6.25	5.00
92	A8	10p dp rose lil & blk	13.50	5.00
93	A8	20p dk blue & blue	5.25	.75
a.		Perf. 13	60.00	210.00
94	A8	50p ultra & car	8.25	2.75
		Nos. 79-94 (16)	90.50	51.65

Arabic inscription, types A7 and A8: "Berid es-Sudan"; types A1 and A2: "Postai-Sudaniye."

For overprints see Nos. O28-O43.

Stamp of 1898 — A9

1948, Oct. 1 *Perf. 12½x13*

95 A9 2p dull blue & gray blk .50 .25

50th anniv. of Sudan's 1st postage stamp.

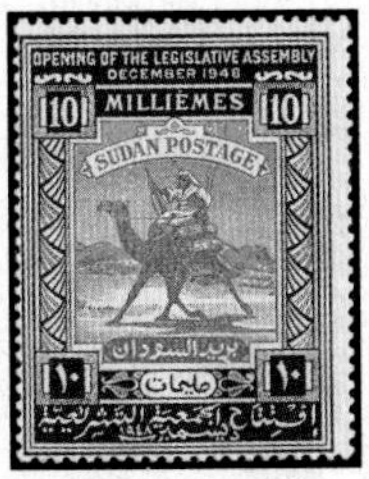

A10

1948, Dec. 19 *Perf. 13*

96 A10 10m black & carmine .75 .25
97 A10 5p dk green & orange 1.50 1.50

Legislative Assembly opening, Dec., 1948.

Nubian Ibex — A11

Cotton Picking — A12

Camel Post — A13

Designs: 2m, Shoebill. 3m, Giraffe. 4m, Baggara girl. 5m, Shilluk warrior. 10m, Hadendowa. 15m, Sudan policeman. 3p, Ambatch canoe. 3½p, Nuba wrestlers. 4p, Weaving. 5p, Saluka farming. 6p, Gum tapping. 8p, Darfur chief. 10p, Stack laboratory. 20p, Nile lechwe.

1951, Sept. 1 **Typo.** *Perf. 14*

Center in Black (#98-104)

98 A11 1m orange 3.50 1.75
99 A11 2m ultra 3.25 1.50
100 A11 3m dark green 9.75 5.00
101 A11 4m emerald 3.00 *5.50*
102 A11 5m plum 2.75 .25
103 A11 10m light blue .40 .25
104 A11 15m dp orange brn 7.00 .25

Perf. 13

105 A12 2p lt bl & dk bl .35 .25
106 A12 3p vio blue & brn 11.00 .25
107 A12 3½p brown & bl grn 3.00 .25
108 A12 4p blk & dp bl 3.75 .25
109 A12 5p emer & org brn 1.00 .25
110 A12 6p black & blue 8.50 2.75
111 A12 8p brown & dp bl 14.00 4.75
112 A12 10p green & black 1.75 1.50
113 A12 20p blk & bl grn 10.00 3.75
114 A13 50p blk & car 17.50 4.00
Nos. 98-114 (17) 100.50 32.50

See #159. For overprints see #O44-O61, O75.

Camel Post — A14

1954, Jan. 9 *Perf. 12½x13*

115 A14 15m emerald & brn org .55 *1.00*
116 A14 3p black & blue .65 *3.00*
117 A14 5p red violet & blk .80 *1.75*
Nos. 115-117 (3) 2.00 5.75

Self-government in the Sudan.

A quantity of these sets inscribed "1953" was sold in London. They were not valid for postage. Value, set $25.

Independent Republic

Map of Sudan and Sun — A15

Wmk. 214

1956, Sept. 15 **Engr.** *Perf. 14*

118 A15 15m rose lilac & org .40 .40
119 A15 3p dk blue & org .60 .60
120 A15 5p green & org .60 .60
Nos. 118-120 (3) 1.60 1.60

Independence Day, Jan. 1, 1956.

Rhinoceros Carrying Globe — A16

1958, Aug. 2 **Center in Orange**

121 A16 15m plum .50 .25
122 A16 3p blue .75 .35
123 A16 5p green 1.10 .75
Nos. 121-123 (3) 2.35 1.35

APU Cong., Khartoum, Aug. 2, 1958.

Soldier, Farmer and Map of Nile — A17

Lithographed and Engraved

1959, Nov. 17 **Unwmk.** *Perf. 14*

124 A17 15m brown, yel & ultra .30 .25
125 A17 3p multicolored .70 .40
126 A17 55m multicolored .80 .60
Nos. 124-126 (3) 1.80 1.25

Sudanese army revolution, 1st anniv.

Arab League Center A17a

Perf. 13x13½

1960, Mar. 22 **Photo.** **Wmk. 328**

127 A17a 15m dull green & blk .60 .40

Opening of the Arab League Center and the Arab Postal Museum in Cairo.

Uprooted Oak Emblem, Refugee Man and Child — A18

Wmk. 214

1960, Apr. 7 **Litho.** *Perf. 14*

128 A18 15m black, buff & ultra .25 .25
129 A18 55m black, beige & org .75 .50

World Refugee Year, 7/1/59-6/30/60.

Soccer Player — A19

1960, Aug. 25 **Wmk. 214** *Perf. 14*

130 A19 15m ultra, blk & yel .30 .25
131 A19 3p yellow, blk & grn .65 .40
132 A19 55m emerald, blk & yel .75 .50
Nos. 130-132 (3) 1.70 1.15

17th Olympic Games, Rome, 8/25-9/11.

Forest — A20

1960, Sept. 6

133 A20 15m multicolored .30 .25
134 A20 3p multicolored .65 .25
135 A20 55m multicolored .75 .50
Nos. 133-135 (3) 1.70 1.00

5th World Forestry Cong., Seattle, WA, Aug. 29-Sept. 10.

King Tirhaqah, 689-663 B.C. — A21

Unwmk.

1961, Mar. 1 **Engr.** *Perf. 14*

136 A21 15m yellow grn & brown .30 .25
137 A21 3p salmon & violet .60 .50
138 A21 55m lt blue & red brown 1.10 .70
Nos. 136-138 (3) 2.00 1.45

Save historic monuments in Nubia.

An imperf. souvenir sheet exists, not sold at post offices, containing one each of Nos. 136-138. Size: 154x97mm. The sheet was not issued for postal purposes and cancellation requests are declined. Value $9.

Girl with Book — A22

1961, Nov. 17 **Litho.** **Wmk. 214**

139 A22 15m violet, claret & pink .30 .25
140 A22 3p orange, blk & blue .65 .40
141 A22 55m gray grn, blk & och .90 .65
Nos. 139-141 (3) 1.85 1.30

50 years of girls' education in the Sudan.

Malaria Eradication Emblem — A23

1962, Apr. 7 **Unwmk.** *Perf. 14*

142 A23 15m black, pur & blue .55 .25
143 A23 55m dk brown & green 1.10 .65

WHO drive to eradicate malaria.

Arab League Building, Cairo — A24

1962, Apr. 22 **Photo.** *Perf. 13½x13*

144 A24 15m deep orange .30 .25
145 A24 55m blue green .70 .50

Arab League Week, Mar. 22-28.

Type of 1951 and

Palace of the Republic, Khartoum — A25

Cotton Picker — A26

Designs: 15m, Straw cover. 35m, 4p, Wild animals. 55m, 6p, Cattle. 8p, Date palms. 10p, Sailboat. 20p, Bohein Temple, 1500 B.C. 50p, Sennar Dam. £1, Camel Post (A13 redrawn).

Perf. 14½x14, 14x14½

1962, Oct. 1 **Litho.** **Wmk. 345**

Size: 23x19mm, 19x23mm

146 A25 5m blue .25 .25
147 A26 10m blue & lilac .25 .25
148 A25 15m multicolored .25 .25
149 A25 2p lt purple .25 .25
150 A26 3p bl grn, red brn & brn .40 .25
151 A26 35m yel grn, brn & org brn .75 .25
152 A26 4p red, lt bl & lil .75 .25
153 A25 55m gray & yel ol .75 .30
154 A25 6p brown & lt blue .90 .30
155 A25 8p green .90 .30

Perf. 14x14½, 13x13½, 14x13½, 13½x14

Size: 24½x30mm, 30x24½mm

156 A26 10p lt bl, red brn & blk 1.00 .50
157 A25 20p gray ol & yel grn 2.50 1.10
158 A25 50p dk gray, ol & bl 6.00 1.75

Engr.

159 A13 £1 green & brn org 12.00 6.50
b. Wmk 334 — —
Nos. 146-159 (14) 26.95 12.50

The frame of No. 159 has been altered with Arabic inscription on top and English at bottom.

See Nos. 420, 427-428. For surcharge and overprints see Nos. 430, O62-O74, O92, O99-O100.

1975-79 **Unwmk.**

Perfs, Sizes and Printing Methods as Before

146a A25 5m ('76) .25 .25
147a A26 10m ('76) .25 .25
148a A25 15m .25 .25
149a A25 2p .25 .25
150a A26 3p ('76) .30 .25
151a A26 35m .50 .25
152a A26 4p .50 .25
153a A25 55m ('79) .50 .25
154a A25 6p .60 .25
155a A25 8p ('77) .75 .25
156a A26 10p 1.00 .40
157a A25 20p 2.00 .90
158a A25 50p 5.50 1.25
159a A13 £1 — *6.00*
Nos. 146a-158a (13) 12.65 5.05

For surcharges, see Nos. 368A-368D.

Corn and Millet — A27

1963, Mar. 21   Litho.   Wmk. 345
160 A27 15m. emer, gray & brn   .30 .25
161 A27 55m violet, lt & dk blue   .70 .40

FAO "Freedom from Hunger" campaign.

Centenary Emblem and Medals — A28

1963, Oct. 1   Perf. 14
162 A28 15m blk, red, gray & gold   .50 .25
163 A28 55m grn, gray, red & gold   1.00 .50

Centenary of the International Red Cross.

Melchior — A29

Designs: 30m, St. Joseph seated, with cross and manuscript, horiz. 55m, Archangel with cross. Designs from frescoes in excavated Faras Church.

1964, Mar. 8   Litho.   Perf. 14
164 A29 15m multicolored   .40 .25
165 A29 30m red brn, blk & brn   .55 .30
166 A29 55m red brn, blk & brn   1.25 .65
    Nos. 164-166 (3)   2.20 1.20

UNESCO world campaign to save historic monuments in Nubia.

Khashm El Girba Dam — A30

New York World's Fair, 1964-65: 3p, Pavilion. 55m, Illustrated map of Sudan, vert.

Perf. 14x14½, 14½x14
1964, Apr. 22   Wmk. 345
167 A30 15m lt vio bl & vio brn   .25 .25
168 A30 3p multicolored   .30 .30
169 A30 55m multicolored   .80 .35
    Nos. 167-169 (3)   1.35 .90

Eleanor Roosevelt and People Breaking Chains — A31

1964, Dec. 10   Perf. 14
170 A31 15m grnsh blue & blk   .25 .25
171 A31 3p violet & black   .40 .25
172 A31 55m orange brn & blk   .65 .65
    Nos. 170-172 (3)   1.30 1.15

Eleanor Roosevelt (1884-1962), on the 16th anniv. of the Universal Declaration of Human Rights.

Arab Postal Union Emblem — A32

1964, Dec. 30   Litho.
173 A32 15m brick red, blk & gold   .25 .25
174 A32 3p gray green, blk & gold   .40 .40
175 A32 55m violet, blk & gold   .85 .50
    Nos. 173-175 (3)   1.50 1.05

10th anniv. of the Permanent Office of the Arab Postal Union.

ITU Emblem, Old and New Communication Equipment — A33

1965, May 17   Wmk. 345   Perf. 13½
176 A33 15m brown & gold   .30 .25
177 A33 3p black & gold   .65 .30
178 A33 55m green & gold   2.25 .60
    Nos. 176-178 (3)   3.20 1.15

Cent. of the ITU.

"Gurashi" and Revolutionists — A34

1965, Nov. 10   Litho.   Perf. 12
179 A34 15m deep ocher & black   .30 .25
180 A34 3p bright red & black   .40 .25
181 A34 55m dark gray & black   .85 .50
    Nos. 179-181 (3)   1.55 1.00

1st anniv. of the October 21st Revolution and to honor "Gurashi," one of its heroes.

ICY Emblem — A35

Perf. 14½x14
1965, Dec. 10   Litho.   Wmk. 345
182 A35 15m violet & blk   .45 .25
183 A35 3p yellow green & blk   .55 .30
184 A35 55m vermilion & blk   1.75 .55
    Nos. 182-184 (3)   2.75 1.10

International Cooperation Year, 1965.

El Siddig el Mahdi — A36

1966, Jan. 1   Perf. 13
185 A36 15m lt blue & vio blue   .50 .25
186 A36 3p orange & brown   .75 .30
187 A36 55m gray & red brown   1.75 .90
    Nos. 185-187 (3)   3.00 1.45

El Siddig el Mahdi (1911-61), imam of Ansar region and political leader.

Mubarak Zaroug A37

1966, Jan. 1   Litho.
188 A37 15m pink & lt olive grn   .50 .25
189 A37 3p brt yel grn & dk grn   .75 .50
190 A37 55m org brn & dk brn   1.40 .85
    Nos. 188-190 (3)   2.65 1.60

Issued in memory of Mubarak Zaroug (1917-65), lawyer and political leader.

WHO Headquarters, Geneva — A38

1966, June 11 Photo. Perf. 11½x11
191 A38 15m blue   .30 .25
192 A38 3p magenta   .40 .30
193 A38 55m brown   1.25 .60
    Nos. 191-193 (3)   1.95 1.05

Inauguration of WHO Headquarters, Geneva.

Map of Sudan and Crests of Upper Nile, Blue Nile and Kassala Provinces — A39

Designs: 3p, Map of Sudan and crests of Equatoria, Kordofan and Khartoum Provinces. 55m, Map of Sudan and crests of Bahr El Gazal, Darfur and Northern Provinces.

1967, Apr. 1   Litho.   Perf. 14
194 A39 15m org, pur & lt bl grn   .25 .25
195 A39 3p dp org, vio & lt bl   .50 .35
196 A39 55m yel, dp clar & yel grn   1.10 .60
    Nos. 194-196 (3)   1.85 1.20

Month of the South.

Giraffe and ITY Emblem — A40

Perf. 12½x13
1967, Aug. 15   Litho.   Wmk. 345
197 A40 15m multicolored   .40 .25
198 A40 3p multicolored   1.00 .35
199 A40 55m multicolored   2.25 .60
    Nos. 197-199 (3)   3.65 1.20

International Tourist Year 1967.

Clasped Hands and Arab League Emblem — A41

Perf. 11x11½
1967, Aug. 29   Photo.   Unwmk.
200 A41 15m orange & ultra   .30 .25
201 A41 3p brown org & emer   .35 .35
202 A41 55m lemon & violet   .60 .40
    Nos. 200-202 (3)   1.25 1.00

Arab League Summit Conference.

Emblem of Palestine Liberation Organization — A42

1967, Aug. 29   Perf. 11½x11
203 A42 15m olive, car & yel   .50 .30
204 A42 3p green, car & yel   1.25 .40
205 A42 55m brt green, car & yel   1.50 .50
    Nos. 203-205 (3)   3.25 1.20

Palestine Liberation Organization.

Abdullahi el Fadil el Mahdi A43

Perf. 11½x11
1968, Feb. 15   Photo.   Unwmk.
206 A43 15m ultra & brt purple   .40 .25
207 A43 3p dp ultra & brt grn   .55 .30
208 A43 55m orange & green   1.20 .55
    Nos. 206-208 (3)   2.15 1.10

Issued in memory of Abdullahi el Fadil el Mahdi (1892-1966), political leader.

Mohammed Nur el Din — A44

1968, Feb. 15
209 A44 15m sl blue & apple grn   .40 .25
210 A44 3p blue & olive   .55 .30
211 A44 55m blue & violet blue   1.20 .50
    Nos. 209-211 (3)   2.15 1.05

Issued in memory of Mohammed Nur el Din (1898-1964), political leader.

Ahmed Yousif Hashim A45

Perf. 11½x11
1968, Mar. 5   Photo.   Unwmk.
212 A45 15m green & brown   .40 .25
213 A45 3p brt blue & sepia   .55 .30
214 A45 55m indigo & violet   1.20 .60
    Nos. 212-214 (3)   2.15 1.05

Ahmed Yousif Hashim (1906-1958), journalist.

Mohammed Ahmed el Mardi (1905-1966), Political Leader — A46

Perf. 11x11½

1968, Mar. 5   **Photo.**   **Unwmk.**
215	A46	15m Prus bl & vio bl	.50	.30
216	A46	3p ultra, och & dl rose	.75	.50
217	A46	55m dk blue & brown	1.40	.60
	Nos. 215-217 (3)		2.65	1.40

DC-3
A47

20th anniv. of Sudan Airways: 2p, De Havilland Dove. 3p, Fokker Friendship. 55m, De Havilland Comet 4C.

1968, Dec. 15   **Litho.**   **Perf. 13½x13**
218	A47	15m multicolored	.50	.25
219	A47	2p multicolored	1.00	.25
220	A47	3p multicolored	1.25	.30
221	A47	55m multicolored	1.75	.50
	Nos. 218-221 (4)		4.50	1.30

African Development Bank Emblem
(right) — A48

Wmk. Rectangles (334)

1969, Dec. 20   **Photo.**   **Perf. 13**
222	A48	2p black, gray & gold	.35	.25
223	A48	4p dark red & gold	.50	.30
224	A48	65m green & gold	1.00	.35
	Nos. 222-224 (3)		1.85	.90

5th anniv. of the African Development Bank.

ILO Emblem
A49

Unwmk.

1969, Dec. 27   **Litho.**   **Perf. 14**
225	A49	2p blue, blk & pink	.35	.25
226	A49	4p yellow, blk & silver	.45	.30
227	A49	65m green, blk & lilac	.90	.35
	Nos. 225-227 (3)		1.70	.90

50th anniv. of the ILO.

Citizens
A50

1970, May 25   **Perf. 11½x11**
228	A50	2p multicolored		
228A	A50	4p multicolored		
228B	A50	65m multicolored		
	Set, 228-228B	90.00	—

First anniv. of May 25th Revolution.
This set was withdrawn on day of issue; 1721 sets of the 2p, 4p and 65m stamps in same design were sold through the Philatelic service. A few copies of No. 228 were sold at Post offices. Nos. 229-231 were issued in October to replace this set.

Citizens
A51

1970, Oct. 21   **Photo.**   **Perf. 11½x11**
229	A51	2p brown, olive & red	.35	.25
230	A51	4p lt blue, olive & red	.55	.30
231	A51	65m olive, dk blue & red	.90	.40
	Nos. 229-231 (3)		1.80	.95

1st anniv. of the May 25th Revolution.

Map and
Flags of
UAR, Libya,
Sudan
A52

1971, Jan. 2   **Unwmk.**   **Perf. 11½**
| 232 | A52 | 2p lt green, car & blk | .50 | .25 |

Signing of the Charter of Tripoli affirming the unity of UAR, Libya and the Sudan, Dec. 27, 1970.

Education Year
Emblem — A53

1971, May 2   **Photo.**   **Perf. 11x11½**
233	A53	2p blue, blk & brn	.30	.25
234	A53	4p carmine, blk & brn	.45	.30
235	A53	65m vio brn, blk & brn	.85	.40
	Nos. 233-235 (3)		1.60	.95

International Education Year.

Emblem — A54

1971, Nov. 10   **Perf. 11x11½**
236	A54	2p yellow, grn & blk	.35	.25
237	A54	4p blue, grn & blk	.75	.35
238	A54	10½p gray, grn & blk	2.00	.55
	Nos. 236-238 (3)		3.10	1.15

2nd anniversary of May 25th Revolution.

Arab League and
Sudanese
Emblems — A55

1972, Feb. 10   **Photo.**   **Perf. 11x11½**
239	A55	2p yellow, grn & blk	.40	.25
240	A55	4p orange, bl & blk	.70	.30
241	A55	65m maroon, brn & blk	1.75	.55
	Nos. 239-241 (3)		2.85	1.10

25th anniv. (in 1971) of the Arab League.

UN Emblem — A56

1972, Mar. 12   **Photo.**   **Perf. 11x11½**
242	A56	2p emer, rose red & org	.40	.25
243	A56	4p ultra, rose red & org	.70	.30
244	A56	10½p blk, rose red & org	1.75	.55
	Nos. 242-244 (3)		2.85	1.10

25th anniv. (in 1970) of the UN.

Emblems
and
Measure
A57

1972, Apr. 22   **Photo.**   **Perf. 11½x11**
245	A57	2p multicolored	.40	.25
246	A57	4p lt blue & multi	.70	.30
247	A57	10½p pink & multi	1.75	.55
	Nos. 245-247 (3)		2.85	1.10

World Standards Day, Oct. 14, 1970.

Pres.
Nimeiry
and Arms
of Sudan
A58

1972, May 2   **Litho.**   **Perf. 13x13½**
248	A58	2p vio bl, blk & gold	.40	.25
249	A58	4p dp org, blk & gold	.70	.30
250	A58	10½p ol grn, blk & gold	1.75	.55
	Nos. 248-250 (3)		2.85	1.05

Election of Gaafar al-Nimeiry as President, Oct. 1971.

Arms of
Sudan
and
Congress
Emblem
A59

1972, Oct. 15   **Photo.**   **Perf. 11½x11**
251	A59	2p blue & multi	.30	.25
252	A59	4p multicolored	.60	.35
253	A59	10½p lt olive & multi	1.75	.45
	Nos. 251-253 (3)		2.65	1.05

Founding Congress of the Sudanese Socialist Union.

Letter and
African
Postal
Union
Emblem
A60

1972, Dec. 16
254	A60	2p yellow & multi	.30	.25
255	A60	4p multicolored	.55	.30
256	A60	10½p blue & multi	1.75	.45
	Nos. 254-256 (3)		2.60	1.00

10th anniv. (in 1971) of the APU.

Emblems of
Sudanese
Provinces
A61

Designs: 4p, Governing Council of Sudan. 10½p, Nat'l Coat of Arms and Unity emblem, vert.

1973, Jan. 1   **Litho.**   **Perf. 13**
257	A61	2p gold & multi	.30	.25
258	A61	4p dk red brn & blk	.40	.25
259	A61	10½p silver, org & grn	2.00	.40
	Nos. 257-259 (3)		2.70	.90

National Unity Day, March 3, 1972.

Emperor Haile
Selassie — A62

1973, June 25   **Unwmk.**   **Perf. 13**
260	A62	2p tan & multi	.60	.30
261	A62	4p silver & multi	1.00	.40
262	A62	10½p gold & multi	2.00	.60
	Nos. 260-262 (3)		3.60	1.30

80th birthday of Haile Selassie, Emperor of Ethiopia.

Nasser
and
Crowd
A63

1973, July 15   **Photo.**   **Perf. 11½x11**
263	A63	2p black	.50	.25
264	A63	4p pale green & blk	.75	.25
265	A63	10½p lilac & blk	1.75	.45
	Nos. 263-265 (3)		3.00	.95

Gamal Abdel Nasser (1918-70), President of Egypt.

UN and FAO Emblems, Portal and
Map of Resettlement Project — A64

1973, Dec. 30   **Litho.**   **Perf. 13**
266	A64	2p multicolored	.30	.25
267	A64	4p multicolored	.60	.25
268	A64	10½p multicolored	2.25	.50
	Nos. 266-268 (3)		3.15	1.00

World Food Program, 10th anniversary.

Scout Emblem,
Knotted Rope
and Stave — A65

1974, Jan. 15
269	A65	2p multicolored	.60	.25
270	A65	4p multicolored	.75	.35
271	A65	10½p multicolored	2.10	.65
	Nos. 269-271 (3)		3.45	1.25

24th World Boy Scout Conference.

INTERPOL
Emblem
A66

1974, Feb. 16   **Litho.**   **Perf. 13x13½**
272	A66	2p orange & multi	.70	.25
273	A66	4p gray & multi	1.00	.25
274	A66	10½p lt blue & multi	1.75	.50
	Nos. 272-274 (3)		3.45	1.00

50th anniv. of Intl. Criminal Police Organ.

K.S.M. Building A67

1974, July 1   Litho.   Perf. 13x13½
275 A67   2p lilac rose & multi   .50   .25
276 A67   4p lt green & multi   .75   .25
277 A67   10½p vermilion & multi   2.50   .55
  Nos. 275-277 (3)   3.75   1.05

50th anniversary of the Faculty of Medicine, University of Khartoum.

African Postal Union and UPU Emblems — A68

4p, Letters, Arab Postal Union and UPU emblems. 10½p, Letters, UPU and African Postal Union emblems.

1974, Sept. 9   Litho.   Perf. 13½
278 A68   2p multicolored   .25   .25
279 A68   4p lt blue & multi   .40   .30
280 A68   10½p lilac & multi   1.25   .45
  Nos. 278-280 (3)   1.90   1.00

Centenary of Universal Postal Union.

Ali Abdel Latif, Abdel Fadil Elmaz, Revolutionary Flag and Nile — A69

1975, July 26   Litho.   Perf. 14x13½
281 A69   2½p green & vio blue   .25   .25
282 A69   4p rose & vio blue   .40   .25
283 A69   10½p sepia & vio blue   1.00   .50
  Nos. 281-283 (3)   1.65   1.00

50th anniversary of 1924 revolution. Portraits show political and military leaders of the revolution.

ADB Emblem with Map of Africa A70

1975, July 26
284 A70   2½p multicolored   .25   .25
285 A70   4p multicolored   .40   .25
286 A70   10½p multicolored   1.00   .50
  Nos. 284-286 (3)   1.65   1.00

African Development Bank, 10th anniv.

Radar Station and Camel Rider — A71

1976, Feb. 2   Litho.   Perf. 13½x14
287 A71   2½p lt green & multi   .25   .25
288 A71   4p lilac & multi   .40   .25
289 A71   10½p vio blue & multi   1.25   .50
  Nos. 287-289 (3)   1.90   1.00

Umm Haraz Satellite Station.

IWY Emblem, Flag and Woman A72

1976, May 10   Litho.   Perf. 14x13½
290 A72   2½p multicolored   .25   .25
291 A72   4p multicolored   .35   .25
292 A72   10½p dk blue & multi   .90   .50
  Nos. 290-292 (3)   1.50   1.00

International Women's Year 1975.

Arms of Sudan, Olympic Rings, Track — A73

1976, July 17   Litho.   Perf. 13½x14
293 A73   2½p green & multi   .35   .25
294 A73   4p green & multi   .50   .30
295 A73   10½p green & multi   1.25   .60
  Nos. 293-295 (3)   2.10   1.15

21st Olympic Games, Montreal, Canada, July 17-Aug. 1.

Education, Engineering, Forestry, Agriculture and Defense — A74

1977, July 20   Litho.   Perf. 13½x14
296 A74   2½p multicolored   .25   .25
297 A74   4p multicolored   .25   .35
298 A74   10½p multicolored   .85   .35
  Nos. 296-298 (3)   1.35   .95

5th anniversary of national unity.

Archbishop Capucci — A75

1977, Oct. 22   Photo.   Perf. 11x11½
299 A75   2½p black   .75   .25
300 A75   4p black & green   1.00   .35
301 A75   10½p black & red   2.00   .60
  Nos. 299-301 (3)   3.75   1.20

Palestinian Archbishop Hilarion Capucci, jailed by Israel in 1974.

Fair Emblem, Sudanese Flag A76

Perf. 11½x 11
1978, Jan. 19   Photo.   Wmk. 342
302 A76   3p multicolored   .25   .25
303 A76   4p multicolored   .40   .25
304 A76   10½p multicolored   .65   .40
  Nos. 302-304 (3)   1.30   .90

International Khartoum Fair, Jan. 19-27.

APU Emblem A77

1978, Mar. 8   Litho.   Perf. 14x13½
305 A77   3p black, car & sil   .25   .25
306 A77   4p dk green, blk & sil   .30   .25
307 A77   10½p ultra, blk & sil   .75   .40
  Nos. 305-307 (3)   1.30   .90

APU, 25th anniv. (in 1977).

Jinnah and Sudanese Flag A78

1978, May 6   Litho.   Perf. 13
308 A78   3p multicolored   .25   .25
309 A78   4p multicolored   .40   .25
310 A78   10½p multicolored   .70   .40
  Nos. 308-310 (3)   1.35   .90

Mohammed Ali Jinnah (1876-1948), first Governor General of Pakistan.

Desert A79

1978, May 6   Perf. 14x13½
311 A79   3p multicolored   .25   .25
312 A79   4p multicolored   .45   .25
313 A79   10½p multicolored   1.25   .65
  Nos. 311-313 (3)   1.95   1.15

UN Desertification Conference.

Lion God Apedemek, African Unity Emblems — A80

1978, July 18   Litho.   Perf. 13½x14
314 A80   3p multicolored   .25   .25
315 A80   4p multicolored   .50   .25
316 A80   10½p multicolored   1.10   .40
  Nos. 314-316 (3)   1.85   .90

15th African Summit Conference, Khartoum, July 18-21.

A81

1979, Oct. 1   Litho.   Perf. 13½x14
317 A81   3½p multicolored   .25   .25
318 A81   6p multicolored   .40   .25
319 A81   13p multicolored   .85   .45
  Nos. 317-319 (3)   1.50   .95

May Revolution, 10th Anniversary.

A82

1980, Jan. 19   Litho.   Perf. 13½x14
320 A82   4½p orange & black   .25   .25
321 A82   8p olive green & blk   .40   .35
322 A82   15½p blue & black   .85   .50
  Nos. 320-322 (3)   1.50   1.10

UNESCO emblem, children holding globe.

IYC Emblem, Hands Protecting Child A83

1980, Mar. 15   Perf. 14x13½
323 A83   4½p multicolored   .30   .25
324 A83   8p multicolored   .40   .40
325 A83   15½p multicolored   1.50   .50
  Nos. 323-325 (3)   2.20   1.15

International Year of the Child (1979).

25th Anniv. of Independence — A84

1982, Mar. 4   Photo.   Perf. 11½
326 A84   60m multicolored   .50   .25
327 A84   120m multicolored   1.00   .30
328 A84   250m multicolored   1.75   .75
  Nos. 326-328 (3)   3.25   1.30

World Food Day, Oct. 16, 1981 A85

1983, Jan. 15   Photo.   Perf. 11½
329 A85   60m Emblem on map, reaching hands   .35   .25
330 A85   120m Produce   .60   .30
331 A85   250m Map, grain   1.25   .60
  Nos. 329-331 (3)   2.20   1.15

A86

1984, Feb. 20   Litho.   Perf. 13½
332 A86 10p pink & silver   .25   .25
333 A86 25p lt blue & silver   .55   .40
334 A86 40p green & silver   1.00   .75
   Nos. 332-334 (3)   1.80   1.40
25th Anniv. of Economic Commission for Africa (1983).

A87

1984, June 16   Litho.   Perf. 14
335 A87 10p multicolored   .30   .25
336 A87 25p multicolored   .70   .50
337 A87 40p multicolored   1.25   .65
   Nos. 335-337 (3)   2.25   1.40
Cent. of Shaykan Battle, Kordofan (1983).

Olympic Week
A88

1984, Dec. 1   Litho.   Perf. 14
338 A88 10p multicolored   .40   .25
339 A88 25p multicolored   .75   .50
340 A88 40p multicolored   1.40   .65
   Nos. 338-340 (3)   2.55   1.30

Sudan-Egypt Integration Charter, 2nd Anniv. — A89

1985, Mar. 16   Photo.   Perf. 13½x13
341 A89 10p multicolored   .35   .25
342 A89 25p multicolored   .70   .50
343 A89 40p multicolored   1.40   .65
   Nos. 341-343 (3)   2.45   1.40

Bakht Erruda, Teacher Training Institute — A90

1985, Apr. 1
344 A90 10p multicolored   .30   .25
345 A90 25p multicolored   .70   .50
346 A90 40p multicolored   1.10   .65
   Nos. 344-346 (3)   2.10   1.40

April 6 Uprising, 1st Anniv. A91

1986, Apr. 1   Litho.   Perf. 14
347 A91 5p multicolored   .25   .25
348 A91 25p multicolored   .65   .35
349 A91 40p multicolored   1.25   .65
   Nos. 347-349 (3)   2.15   1.25

World Food Day 1986
A92

Perf. 13x13½, 13½x13 (30p), 14 (50p)
1988, Jan. 1   Litho.
350 A92 25p Net fishermen   .45   .25
351 A92 30p Two fish, vert.   .40   .25
352 A92 50p Globe   .65   .45
353 A92 75p Stylized fish on wave 1.00 .60
354 A92 300p Fish in sea   3.50   1.75
   Nos. 350-354 (5)   6.00   3.30

Souvenir Sheet
Imperf
354A A92 75p like 25p   2.75   2.75

Child Survival — A93

Perf. 14, Imperf. (No. 357)
1988, Mar. 15   Litho.
355 A93 50p Breast-feeding, vert. .50   .30
356 A93 75p Oral rehydration   1.00   .40
357 A93 75p like 50p, vert.   1.75   1.75
358 A93 100p Oral vaccine   1.40   .60
359 A93 150p Growth monitoring   2.10   .90
   Nos. 355-359 (5)   6.75   3.95
No. 357 issued without gum. Size: 63x84mm.

Red Crescent in Sudan, 30th Anniv. (in 1987) — A94

Designs: 100p, Crescent, candle. 150p, Crescent, stylized figure of a man.

1988, Oct. 31   Litho.   Perf. 14
360 A94 40p org yel, blk & dk red .50   .30
361 A94 100p blk, blue grn & dk red 1.25 .60
362 A94 150p blk, brt blue & dk red 1.75 .90
   Nos. 360-362 (3)   3.50   1.80
Nos. 361-362 horiz.

World Food Day, Oct. 16, 1987, and the Small Farmer — A95

FAO emblem and: 40p, Early farming tools, horiz. 100p, Ox-drawn plow. 150p, Crude public water supply.

1988, Oct. 31   Perf. 13x13½, 13½x13
363 A95 40p multicolored   .40   .30
364 A95 100p shown   1.20   .60
365 A95 150p multicolored   1.60   .90
   Nos. 363-365 (3)   3.20   1.80

Khartoum Bank, 75th Anniv. A96

Designs: 40p, Anniv. emblem. 100p, Spheres, emblem, medallion on ribbon. 150p, Text, emblem.

1988, Oct. 31   Perf. 14
366 A96 40p multicolored   .50   .30
367 A96 100p multicolored   1.20   .60
368 A96 150p multicolored   1.60   .90
   Nos. 366-368 (3)   3.30   1.80

Nos. 156a, 157a, O72a, O73c Handstamp Surcharged in Various Colors

Methods and Perfs As Before
1988 ?   Unwmk.
368A A26 £5 on 10p #156a   —   —
368B A25 £5 on 20p #157a   —   —
368C A26 £10 on 10p #156a   —   —
368D A25 £10 on 20p #157a   —   —

On Official Stamps
368E A26 £5 on 10p #O72a   —   —
368F A25 £5 on 20p #O73a   —   —
368G A26 £10 on 10p #O72a   —   —
368H A25 £10 on 20p #O73c   —   —

The illustration shown is that of the £10 surcharge. The £5 surcharge has an oval representing "5" at the right side. Surcharge colors are known in blue, black, red and blends of these colors.

Declaration of Palestinian State, 1st Anniv. — A97

Nos. 370, 372, 374, Crowd of demonstrators.

1989, Dec. 10   Litho.   Perf. 14
369 A97 100p yellow grn & multi 1.75   .50
370 A97 100p buff & multi   2.00   .50
371 A97 150p lt vio & multi   2.50   1.00
372 A97 150p lt blue & multi   2.75   1.00
373 A97 200p pink & multi   3.50   1.25
374 A97 200p lt green & multi   3.50   1.25
   Nos. 369-374 (6)   16.00   5.50
Palestinian Uprising (Nos. 370, 372, 374).

African Development Bank, 25th Anniv. — A99

1989, Dec. 28   Perf. 13x13½
375 A99 100p yel grn, blk & sil 1.50   .50
376 A99 150p blue, blk & sil   2.50   .75
377 A99 200p plum, blk & sil   3.25   1.00
   Nos. 375-377 (3)   7.25   2.25

Independence, 33rd Anniv. (in 1989) — A100

1990, Jan. 22   Litho.   Perf. 13½x13
378 A100 50p blue & yellow   .50   .25
379 A100 100p deep claret & yel 1.25   .40
380 A100 150p brt rose & yel   1.75   .60
381 A100 200p dp rose lil & yel 2.50   .90
   Nos. 378-381 (4)   6.00   2.15

Mammals A101

25p, Leopard. 50p, Elephant. 75p, Giraffe, vert. 100p, White rhinoceros. 125p, Addax, vert.

1990, Feb. 20   Perf. 13x13½
382 A101 25p multicolored   .80   .25
383 A101 50p multicolored   1.25   .50

Perf. 14
384 A101 75p multicolored   2.00   .75
385 A101 100p multicolored   2.50   1.00
386 A101 125p multicolored   3.50   1.25
   Nos. 382-386 (5)   10.05   3.75
No. 385 inscribed "Rino."

Birds — A102

25p, Zande hornbill. 50p, Marabou stork. 75p, Buff-crested bustard. 100p, Saddle-bill. 150p, Bald-headed ibis.

1990, Mar. 25   Perf. 13½x13
387 A102 25p multicolored   .75   .25
388 A102 50p multicolored   1.40   .50
389 A102 75p multicolored   2.00   .80
390 A102 100p multicolored   2.75   1.00

Perf. 14
391 A102 150p multicolored   3.50   1.25
   Nos. 387-391 (5)   10.40   3.80

Traditional Dances A103

Perf. 13x13½, 13½x13
1990, May 10   Litho.
392 A103 25p Mardoum   .45   .30
393 A103 50p Zandi, vert.   1.00   .40
394 A103 75p Kambala, vert.   1.50   .60
395 A103 100p Nubian, vert.   1.75   .75
396 A103 125p Sword   2.25   .95
   Nos. 392-396 (5)   6.95   3.00

Natl. Salvation Revolution, 1st Anniv. — A104

1991, Apr. 14 Litho. Perf. 13

399	A104	150p multicolored	1.25	.75
400	A104	200p multicolored	1.75	1.00
401	A104	250p multicolored	2.00	1.25
402	A104	£5 multicolored	3.75	2.50
403	A104	£10 multicolored	7.50	4.75
		Nos. 399-403 (5)	16.25	10.25

For surcharge see No. 438.

Shoebill
A105

Camel Postman
A109

Designs: 50p, Sunflower. 75p, Gum arabic. 100p, Cotton. 125p, Crowned crane. 150p, Kenana Sugar Company, horiz. (30x24mm). 175p, Secretary bird (24x30mm). £2, Atbara cement factory, horiz. (30x24mm). 250p, Statue of King Taharqa (26x37mm). £3, Republican Palace (26x37mm). £4, Hug jar (24x30mm). No. 415, Gabana coffee pot (24x30mm). £8, Pterois volitans, horiz. (36x27mm). £10, Animal wealth, horiz. (36x27mm). £15, Nubian ibex.

1991, July 1 Litho. Perf. 13½x13

404	A105	25p shown	.25	.25
405	A105	50p multi	.40	.25
406	A105	75p multi	.60	.40
407	A105	100p multi	.80	.50
408	A105	125p multi	1.00	.55

Perf. 14x14½, 13½x14

409	A105	150p multi	1.25	.75
410	A105	175p multi	1.50	.85
411	A105	£2 multi	2.00	.95

Perf. 14

412	A105	250p multi	2.50	1.25
413	A105	£3 multi	3.00	1.50

Perf. 13½x14

414	A105	£4 multi	3.50	2.00
415	A105	£5 multi	4.25	2.40

Litho. & Engr.
Perf. 14
Wmk. 334

416	A109	£8 multi	6.00	4.00
417	A109	£10 multi	7.50	4.75
418	A109	£15 multi	11.00	7.00
419	A109	£20 shown	16.00	9.50
		Nos. 404-419 (16)	61.55	36.90

For surcharges on No. 416, see Nos. 605-606.

Types of 1962

Designs: 25p, Cattle. £5, Bohein temple. £10, Sailboat.

Perf. 14½x14
1990-92 Litho. Unwmk.

420	A25	25p multi ('92)	.25	.25

Perf. 14x13½

427	A25	£5 multi	14.50	10.00

Perf. 13½x14

428	A26	£10 multi	24.00	15.00

See Nos. O76-O100. For surcharges see Nos. 430, 436-453, O104-O111.

No. 156a
Handstamp
Surcharged in Blue
Violet

1990, Sept. Perf. 13½x14

430	A26	£1 on 10p #156a	65.00	8.50

Surcharge on No. 430 is often incomplete.

Pan-African Rinderpest Campaign
A114

Perf. 13½x13
1991, July 27 Litho. Unwmk.

431	A114	£1 black & brt grn	1.25	.50
432	A114	£2 dp violet & emer	2.50	1.75
433	A114	£5 org & blue grn	6.50	2.50
		Nos. 431-433 (3)	10.25	4.75

Nos. 404-409, 411-414, 416 Surcharged in Black, Blue Violet or Red

c

d

e

f

g

h

i

j

1992?-97
Perfs. & Printing Methods as Before

436	A105(c)	1d on 100p #407		
		(Blk)	5.00	2.50
437	A105(c)	2d on £2 #411		
		(BV)	9.00	4.75
438	A105(c)	2.50d on 25p #404		
		(BV)	12.50	5.75
438A	A25(d)	2.50d on 25p #420		
		(Blk)	2.50	1.75
439	A105(c)	3d on £3 #413		
		(BV)	15.00	7.00
440	A105(c)	4d on £4 #414		
		(Blk)	17.50	9.50

441	A105(e)	5d on 50p #405		
		(Blk)	2.75	.90
443	A105(d)	7.50d on 75p #406		
		(Blk)	7.50	5.00
446	A105(d)	1.50d on 150p #409		
		(Blk)	1.50	1.00
447	A105(f)	15d on 150p #409		
		(Blk)	4.00	—
448	A105(g)	25d on 75p #406		
		(Blk)		—
449	A105(h)	25d on 250p #412		
		(R)	7.00	4.00
451	A105(i)	35d on £8 #416		
		(Blk)	8.00	5.00
a.	Inverted surcharge			
452	A105(j)	100d on 125p #408		
		(Blk)	5.75	5.75
453	A105(j)	100d on 125p #408		
		(R)	50.00	—
		Nos. 436-453 (15)	148.00	52.90

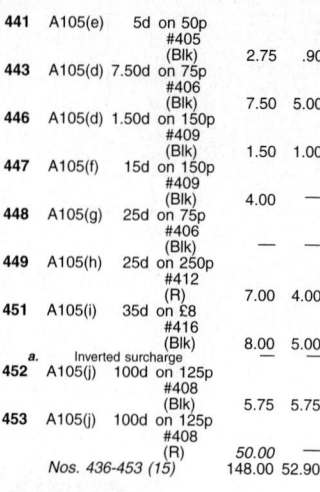

Intl. Human Rights Day — A115

Designs: £5, Chain links, rainbow of colors, horiz. 750p, Trellis, rose, inscription.

1993, Dec. 20 Litho. Perf. 14

454	A115	£4 multicolored	1.00	.65
455	A115	£5 multicolored	1.25	.90
456	A115	750p multicolored	1.75	1.25
		Nos. 454-456 (3)	4.00	2.80

Fung Sultanate, 5th Cent. — A116

Designs: £5, Inscription on tablet. 750p, Inscription in circle, helmet, horiz.

1993, Dec. 20

457	A116	£4 multicolored	1.00	.65
458	A116	£5 multicolored	1.25	.90
459	A116	750p multicolored	1.75	1.25
		Nos. 457-459 (3)	4.00	2.80

Wild Ass — A117

1994, July 15 Litho. Perf. 14½

460	A117	4d With young	1.00	.50
461	A117	8d Standing	1.50	1.00
462	A117	10d Running	1.75	1.25
463	A117	15d Up close	2.50	2.00
		Nos. 460-463 (4)	6.75	4.75

A118

1994, Aug. 1 Litho. Perf. 14

464	A118	5d vermilion & multi	.50	.40
465	A118	7d green & multi	1.00	.55
466	A118	15d gray & multi	2.00	1.10
		Nos. 464-466 (3)	3.50	2.05

Intl. Olympic Committee, cent.

ICAO, 50th
Anniv. — A119

1994, Dec. 7 Litho. Perf. 13½

467	A119	5d lilac & multi	.35	.25
468	A119	7d brown & multi	.60	.45
469	A119	15d blue & multi	1.25	.95
		Nos. 467-469 (3)	2.20	1.65

A120

1994 World Cup Soccer Championships, US: 4d, Goalie, green vest. 5d, Like 4d, blue vest. 7d, Player about to kick ball, green shirt. 8d, Like 7d, brown shirt. 10d, Player, long-sleeved shirt. 15d, Player, yellow shirt. 20d, Player, magenta & blue background. 25d, Player, white shirt & pants. 35d, Like 20d, blue & green background. 75d, Goalie, orange shirt, horiz. 100d, Player kicking ball, horiz.

1995, July 15 Litho. Perf. 14

470	A120	4d multicolored	.40	.25
471	A120	5d multicolored	.40	.25
472	A120	7d multicolored	.60	.35
473	A120	8d multicolored	.70	.35
474	A120	10d multicolored	.85	.50
475	A120	15d multicolored	1.00	.50
476	A120	20d multicolored	1.75	1.00
477	A120	25d multicolored	2.00	1.25
478	A120	35d multicolored	3.00	1.50
		Nos. 470-478 (9)	10.70	5.95

Souvenir Sheets

479	A120	75d multicolored	7.50	7.50
480	A120	100d multicolored	11.50	11.50

A121

1995, Dec. 16 Litho. Perf. 13½

481	A121	15d apple grn & blk	1.50	1.00
482	A121	25d blue & black	2.75	1.50
483	A121	30d purple & black	3.25	2.00
		Nos. 481-483 (3)	7.50	4.50

Arab League, 50th anniv.

A122

1996, May 4 Litho. Perf. 13½

484	A122	15d orange & multi	1.50	1.00
485	A122	25d apple grn & multi	2.75	1.50
486	A122	30d purple & multi	3.50	2.00
		Nos. 484-486 (3)	7.75	4.50

Common Market for East and South Africa (COMESA).

Abdel Rahman el Mahdi, (1885-1959) — A123

1997, Jan. 22 Photo. Perf. 13½

487	A123	25d black & violet	2.00	1.75
488	A123	35d black & red brown	3.25	2.00
489	A123	50d black & brown	4.25	3.00
		Nos. 487-489 (3)	9.50	6.75

Waiting For
Peace — A124

1997, June 1   Photo.   Perf. 13½x13
490 A124 5d multicolored   .75   .40

A125

1997, Oct. 15   Photo.   Perf. 13½
491 A125 25d lilac & multi   2.00   1.75
492 A125 35d apple grn &
                multi   3.00   2.75
493 A125 50d grn, blk & sil   4.00   3.50
    Nos. 491-493 (3)   9.00   8.00

Police Commanders, Arab Security Conference, 25th anniv.

A126

Al-Shaykh Qaribulla's Mosque: Various views of mosque.

1997, Nov. 1
494 A126 25d blue & multi   1.50   1.25
495 A126 35d yellow & multi   2.50   1.75
496 A126 50d buff & multi, vert. 3.50 2.50
    Nos. 494-496 (3)   7.50   5.50

A127

1998, Jan. 18   Litho.   Perf. 13½
497 A127 25d multicolored   1.75   1.25
498 A127 35d violet & multi   2.75   2.25
499 A127 50d multicolored   3.50   2.75
    Nos. 497-499 (3)   8.00   6.25

Pan African Postal Union, 18th anniv.

Sudanese
Archeology
A128

No. 500, Kerma pottery, 2500 BC. No. 501, Fresco, Faras church, 11th cent. No. 502, Close-up of fresco, Faras Church, 11th cent. 60d, C Group pottery, 2000 BC. No. 504, Meroe pottery, 4000 BC. No. 505, Tomb of Natakamani Meroitic king, 1st cent. BC, vert. 100d, C Group pottery, 2000 BC, diff.

1998, Jan. 25   Perf. 13½x13, 13x13½
500 A128 50d multicolored   2.25   2.00
501 A128 50d multicolored   2.25   2.00
502 A128 50d multicolored   2.25   2.00
503 A128 60d multicolored   2.50   2.25
504 A128 75d multicolored   3.25   2.50
505 A128 75d multicolored   3.25   2.50
506 A128 100d multicolored   4.25   3.50
    Nos. 500-506 (7)   20.00 16.75

Ruins, Camel
Post
Rider — A129

1998, Mar. 1   Perf. 13x13½
507 A129 100d multicolored   7.00   6.00

First Sudanese Postage Stamp, cent.

A130

1999, May 15   Litho.   Perf. 13¼x13½
508 A130 75d multicolored   4.50   3.75
509 A130 100d green & multi   6.00   5.50
510 A130 150d blue & multi   9.00   8.00
    Nos. 508-510 (3)   19.50 17.25

Battle of Kerreri, cent.

American Bombing of Elshifa
Pharmaceuticals Factory, Aug. 20,
1998 — A131

75d, Bomb damage. 100d, Company emblem, falling bombs. 150d, Casualties.

Perf. 13¾x13½, 13¾x13¼
1999, July 1   Litho.
511 A131 75d multi   4.50   3.75
512 A131 100d multi, vert.   6.00   5.50
513 A131 150d multi   9.00   8.00
    Nos. 511-513 (3)   19.50 17.25

A132

A133

Perf. 13¼x13½, 13½x13¼
1999, Oct. 20   Litho.
514 A132 75d shown   4.50   3.75
515 A133 100d shown   6.00   5.50
516 A132 150d 7 people   9.00   8.00
    Nos. 514-516 (3)   19.50 17.25

Intl. Year of the Elderly.

SOS Children's Villages, 50th
Anniv. — A134

1999, Oct. 31   Perf. 13½x13¼
517 A134 75d brn & multi   4.50   3.75
518 A134 100d grn & multi   6.00   5.50
519 A134 150d blue & multi   9.00   8.00
    Nos. 517-519 (3)   19.50 17.25

UPU, 125th Anniv.
(in 1999) — A134a

2000, Mar. 1   Litho.   Perf. 13½x13¼
Denomination   Color
519A A134a 75d red   5.00   4.50
519B A134a 100d violet   6.00   5.25
519C A134a 150d black   10.00   8.00
    Nos. 519A-519C (3)   21.00 17.75

Common Market
for Eastern and
Southern Africa
Free Trade
Area — A135

Panel color: 100d, White. 150d, Pink. 200d, Yellow.

2000, Oct. 31   Litho.   Perf. 13¼x13¾
520-522 A135   Set of 3   27.50 27.50

UN High
Commissioner for
Refugees, 50th
Anniv. — A136

Frame color: 100d, Green. 150d, Red. 200d, Violet.

Perf. 13¼x13½
2001, Aug. 15   Litho.
523-525 A136   Set of 3   27.50 27.50

Al-Zubair
Prize for
Innovation
and
Scientific
Excellence
A137

Frame color: 100d, Yellow. 150d, Red. 200d, Green.

2002, Feb. 14   Perf. 13¼
526-528 A137   Set of 3   30.00 30.00

Association for the
Promotion of
Scientific
Innovation — A138

Frame color: 100d, Black. 150d, Red. 200d, Green.

2002, Feb. 14
529-531 A138   Set of 3   30.00 30.00

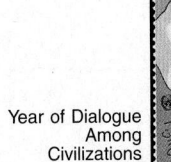
Year of Dialogue
Among
Civilizations
A139

Country name in: 100d, Red. 150d, Orange. 200d, Black.

2002, Jan. 28   Litho.   Perf. 13¼x13¾
532-534 A139   Set of 3   32.50 32.50

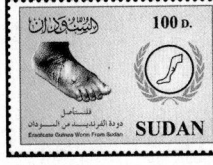
Guinea
Worm
Eradication
Campaign
A140

Designs: 100d, Infested foot, campaign emblem. 150d, Campaign emblem. 200d, Child, campaign emblem.

2002, Mar. 3   Litho.   Perf. 13¼
535-537 A140   Set of 3   27.50 27.50

Palestinian Intifada — A141

Country name in: 100d, Green. 150d, Red. 200d, Black.

Perf. 13½x13¼
2002, Feb. 14   Litho.
538-540 A141   Set of 3   30.00 30.00

Sudanese postal officials have declared as illegal the following items:
Sheets of six stamps depicting Pope John Paul II (2 different)
Miniature sheet of two stamps depicting Pope John Paul II (2 different).

Association of African Banknote and
Security Document Printers 11th
Annual Conference — A142

Conference emblem and: 100d, Association emblem, circular design. 150d, Banknote rosettes. 200d, Archaeological ruins.

2003, May 10   Litho.   Perf. 13½x13¼
541-543 A142   Set of 3   37.50 37.50

Mango — A143

Nile Perch — A144

Cattle — A145

Soldiers — A146

Muhammad
Ahmad (Al-
Mahdi, 1844-85),
Religious
Leader — A147

Butterflyfish — A148

Temple of Amun
Ra — A149
Baobab
Tree — A150

Doum Palm
Tree — A151

Sheep — A152

Grapefruit
A153

Oil Rigs
A154

Tomb of Sheikh El-
Mursi
A155

Camel Postman
A156

Perf. 13½x13¼, 13¼x13½
2003, July 15
544	A143	50d multi	.75	.75
545	A144	50d multi	.75	.75
546	A145	75d multi	1.25	1.25
547	A146	100d multi	1.50	1.50
548	A147	100d multi	1.50	1.50
549	A148	125d multi	2.00	2.00
550	A149	150d multi	2.25	2.25
551	A150	150d multi	2.25	2.25
552	A151	150d multi	2.25	2.25
553	A152	150d multi	2.25	2.25
554	A153	200d multi	3.00	3.00
555	A154	200d multi	3.00	3.00
556	A155	200d multi	4.50	4.50
557	A156	500d multi	7.50	7.50

a. Souvenir sheet, #544-557, im-
perf.   35.00   35.00
Nos. 544-557 (14)   34.75   34.75
For surcharges, see Nos. 638-639.

Parliament, 50th Anniv. — A157

Panel colors: 100d, Lilac. 200d, Yellow
orange. 250d, Pink.

2004, Jan. 5   **Perf. 13½x13¼**
558-560 A157   Set of 3   9.25 9.25

General Secretariat for Council of
Ministers, 50th Anniv. — A158

Panel colors: 100d, Light blue. 200d, Yellow.
250d, Pink.

2004, Jan. 8
561-563 A158   Set of 3   9.25 9.25

Rural Women's Innovation — A159

Panel colors: 100d, Light blue. 200d, Yellow.
250d, Lilac.

2004, Jan. 26
564-566 A159   Set of 3   9.25 9.25

Armed Forces,
50th
Anniv. — A160

Background color: 100d, Orange. 200d,
Red. 250d, Purple.

Perf. 13¼x13½
2004, Aug. 14   **Litho.**
567-569 A160   Set of 3   12.00 12.00

Peace — A161

Background color: 200d, Dark blue. 300d,
Green and yellow, 400d, Light blue.

2005, Jan. 9   **Perf. 13½x13¼**
570-572 A161   Set of 3   15.50 15.50

7th Conference of Sudanese Women's
General Union — A162

Panel color: 200d, White. 300d, Lilac. 400d,
Light blue.

Perf. 13½x13¼
2005, June 29   **Litho.**
573-575 A162   Set of 3   14.00 14.00

Merowe Dam Project — A163

Background color: 200d, Light blue. 300d,
Light green. 400d, Lilac.

2005, June 30
576-578 A163   Set of 3   13.00 13.00

World Summit on the Information
Society, Tunis — A164

Background color: 200d, Yellow green.
300d, Blue. 400d, Yellow orange.

2005, Sept. 24
579-581 A164   Set of 3   13.00 13.00

Merowe Dam
Housing
Rehabilitation
Projects — A165

Denomination in: 200d, Black. 300d, Green.
400d, Red.

2005, Oct. 1 Litho. Perf. 13¼x13¾
582-584 A165   Set of 3   12.50 12.50

Merowe Dam Archaeology
Project — A166

Map and clay pot: 200d, Shown. 300d, With
blue panel. 400d, With peach panel.

2005, Dec. 20   **Perf. 13¾x13¼**
585-587 A166   Set of 3   12.50 12.50

A167

A168

Independence, 50th Anniv. — A169

Perf. 13¼x13¾, 13¾x13¼
2006, Jan. 15
588	A167	200d multi	3.25	3.25
589	A168	300d multi	4.75	4.75
590	A169	400d multi	6.25	6.25

a. Souvenir sheet, #588-590, imperf.   35.00   35.00
Nos. 588-590 (3)   14.25   14.25

OPEC Intl. Development Fund, 30th
Anniv. — A170

Background color: 200d, Red. 300d, Green.
400d, Blue.

2006, Oct. 12 Litho. Perf. 13¾x13½
591-593 A170   Set of 3   11.50 11.50

100 qirsh = 1 pound

African Soccer Confederation, 50th
Anniv. — A171

Background colors: £2, Pink. £3.50, Pale
yellow. £4.50, White.

Perf. 13¾x13½
2007, Feb. 11   **Litho.**
594-596 A171   Set of 3   14.00 14.00

10th Meeting of
Regional African
Satellite
Communications
Organization
A172

Background colors: £1, Lilac. £2, Light
green. £3.50, Yellow. £4.50, Blue.

2007   **Perf. 13½x13¾**
597-600 A172   Set of 4   15.00 15.00

24th Universal Postal Union Congress,
Nairobi — A173

Panel color: £1, Lilac. £2, Brown. £3.50,
Blue. £4.50, Ocher.

2008   **Perf. 13¾x13½**
601-604 A173   Set of 4   15.00 15.00

Due to political unrest in Kenya, the UPU
Congress was moved to Geneva, Switzerland.

No. 416
Srchd. in
Black or
Red

Methods, Perfs and Watermarks As Before

2008
605	A109	£2 on £8 #416 (Bk)	12.00	12.00
606	A109	£2 on £8 #416 (R)	7.00	7.00

Comprehensive Peace Agreement, 3rd Anniv. — A174

Panel color in: £1, Blue. £2, Black. £3.50, Green. £4.50, Brown.

Perf. 13¾x13½

2008, Jan. 22   Litho.   Unwmk.
607-610	A174	Set of 4	17.50 17.50

Population and Housing Census — A175

Background colors: £1, Blue. £2, Yellow. £3.50, Lilac. £4.50, Green.

2008, Jan. 22   Litho.   Perf. 13¾x13½
611-614	A175	Set of 4	17.00 17.00

Arab Postal Day — A176

Emblem and: £2, Camel caravan. £3.50, World map, pigeon.

2008, Aug. 3
615-616	A176	Set of 2	8.75 8.75

Diplomatic Relations Between Sudan and People's Republic of China, 50th Anniv. — A177

Background color: £2.50, Pink. £5, Pale green. £6, Gray.

Perf. 13¾x13½

2009, Feb. 19   Litho.
617-619	A177	Set of 3	17.50 17.50

Merowe Dam Transmission Lines — A178

Background color: £2.50, Purple. £5, Green. £6, Blue.

2009
620-622	A178	Set of 3	15.50 15.50

Inauguration of Merowe Dam — A179

Panel color: £2.50, Pink. £5, Light blue. £6, Buff.

2009
623-625	A179	Set of 3	15.50 15.50

Completion of Merowe Dam — A180

Frame color: £3, Blue. £5.50, Orange brown. £7, Green.

2010, Apr. 7
626-628	A180	Set of 3	18.00 18.00

Solidarity — A181

Color of country name: £3, Green. £5.50, Yellow. £7, Orange brown.

2010, Sept. 7   Perf. 13½x13¾
629-631	A181	Set of 3	15.50 15.50

Sudan Radio — A182

Background color: £3, Green. £5.50, Blue. £7, Red.

2010, Sept. 26   Perf. 13¾x13½
632-634	A182	Set of 3	15.50 15.50

Sudan E-Government A183

Frame color: £3, Red. £5.50, Blue. £7, Blue green.

2011, July 27   Litho.   Perf. 13½x13¾
635-637	A183	Set of 3	15.50 15.50

No. 547 Surcharged in Black

No. 548 Surcharged in Black

Methods and Perfs As Before
2012
638	A146	£7 on 100d #547	5.75 5.75
639	A147	£7 on 100d #548	5.75 5.75

Arab Postal Day — A184

Denomination color: £3, Blue. £5.50, Red. £7, Black.

2012   Litho.   Perf. 13¾x13½
640-642	A184	Set of 3	10.50 10.50

Roseires Dam Heightening Project — A185

Color of top panel: £2, White. £3, Green. £5.50, Red. £7, Black.

2013
643-646	A185	Set of 4	12.00 12.00

AIR POST STAMPS

Nos. 40-41, 43 Overprinted in Black

Nos. C1-C2

No. C3

1931   Wmk. 214   Perf. 11½x12½, 14
C1	A2	5m blk & olive brown	1.00	1.00
C2	A2	10m blk & carmine	1.75	4.00
C3	A1	2p org & vio brown	2.50	3.50
		Nos. C1-C3 (3)	5.25	8.50

Statue of Gen. C. G. Gordon AP3

1931-35   Engr.   Perf. 14
C4	AP3	3m dk brn & grn ('33)	3.50	7.25
C5	AP3	5m grn & blk	1.50	.25
C6	AP3	10m car rose & blk	1.50	.25
C7	AP3	15m dk brn & brn	.75	.25
C8	AP3	2p org & blk	.65	.25
C9	AP3	2½p bl & red vio ('33)	4.75	.25
C10	AP3	3p gray & blk	1.00	.25
C11	AP3	3½p dl vio & blk	2.25	.90
C12	AP3	4½p gray & brn	12.50	16.50
C13	AP3	5p ultra & blk	1.75	.35
C14	AP3	7½p pck grn & dk grn ('35)	12.00	6.00
C15	AP3	10p pck bl & sep ('35)	11.50	2.00
		Nos. C4-C15 (12)	53.65	34.50

See Nos. C23-C30. For surcharges see Nos. C17-C22, C31-C34.

No. 43 Surcharged in Black

1932, July 18   Typo.
C16	A1	2½p on 2p	2.50 4.00

Nos. C6, C4-C5, C12 Surcharged

1935   Engr.   Perf. 14
C17	AP3	15m on 10m	.60	.25
a.		Double surcharge	950.00	1,100.
b.		Arabic characters omitted	750.00	
C18	AP3	2½p on 3m	1.25	6.00
a.		"½" 2¼mm high instead of 3mm	4.50	20.00
b.		Second Arabic character of surcharge omitted	65.00	125.00
C19	AP3	2½p on 5m	.85	1.75
a.		"½" 2¼mm high instead of 3mm	4.75	9.00
b.		Second Arabic character of surcharge omitted	40.00	60.00
c.		Inverted surcharge	1,000.	1,200.
d.		As "a," inverted	2,500.	20,000.
e.		As "b," inverted	1,500.	1,600.
f.		Pair, C19c and C19d	37,500.	
C20	AP3	3p on 4½p	2.50	18.50
C21	AP3	7½p on 4½p	9.00	52.50
a.		"7¼" instead of "7½"		
C22	AP3	10p on 4½p	9.00	52.50
		Nos. C17-C22 (6)	23.20	131.50

Type of 1931-35
1936-37   Perf. 11½x12½
C23	AP3	15m dk brn & brn ('37)	4.75	.25
C24	AP3	2p org & blk ('37)	5.25	18.00
C25	AP3	2½p bl & red vio	3.00	.25
C26	AP3	3p gray & blk ('37)	1.00	.40
C27	AP3	3½p dl vio & blk ('37)	2.50	15.00
C28	AP3	5p ultra & blk ('37)	4.25	.40
C29	AP3	7½p pck grn & dk grn ('37)	4.75	11.00
C30	AP3	10p pck bl & sep ('37)	7.00	27.50
		Nos. C23-C30 (8)	32.50	72.80

Nos. C25, C11, C14 and C15 Srchd. as in 1935

1938   Wmk. 214   Perf. 11½x12½, 14
C31	AP3	5m on 2½p	3.50	.25
C32	AP3	3p on 3½p	42.50	60.00
a.		On No. C27	700.00	750.00
C33	AP3	3p on 7½p	7.50	7.25
a.		On No. C29	700.00	750.00
C34	AP3	5p on 10p	1.75	5.50
a.		On No. C30	700.00	750.00
		Nos. C31-C34 (4)	55.25	73.00

Catalogue values for unused stamps in this section, from this point to the end of the section, are for Never Hinged items.

Bridge Over Blue Nile, Khartoum AP4

Designs: 2½p, Kassala Jebel. 3p, Water wheel. 3½p, Port Sudan. 4p, Gordon Memorial College. 4½p, Nile post boat. 6p, Suakin. 20p, General Post Office, Khartoum.

1950, July 1 Engr. *Perf. 12*

C35 AP4 2p dk bl grn & blk 5.75 1.75
C36 AP4 2½p red org & bl 1.00 1.50
C37 AP4 3p dp bl & plum 4.50 1.50
C38 AP4 3½p chnt & choc 4.50 *5.00*
C39 AP4 4p bl & brn 1.75 *3.50*
C40 AP4 4½p ultra & blk 3.00 *5.00*
C41 AP4 6p car & blk 3.50 *4.00*
C42 AP4 20p plum & blk 3.00 *6.75*
Nos. C35-C42 (8) 27.00 *29.00*

For overprints see Nos. CO1-CO8.

AIR POST OFFICIAL STAMPS

Catalogue values for unused stamps in this section are for Never Hinged items.

Nos. C35 to C42 Overprinted in Carmine or Black

1950, July 1 Wmk. 214 *Perf. 12*

CO1 AP4 2p dk bl grn & blk (C) 18.50 3.75
CO2 AP4 2½p red org & bl 1.75 *2.00*
CO3 AP4 3p dp bl & plum 1.00 *1.25*
CO4 AP4 3½p chnt & choc 1.00 *10.00*
CO5 AP4 4p bl & brn 1.00 *9.50*
CO6 AP4 4½p ultra & blk (C) 5.00 *21.00*
CO7 AP4 6p car & blk (C) 1.25 *5.50*
CO8 AP4 20p plum & blk (C) 5.50 *15.00*
Nos. CO1-CO8 (8) 35.00 68.00

POSTAGE DUE STAMPS

Postage Due Stamps of Egypt, 1889, Overprinted in Black

1897 Wmk. 119 *Perf. 14*

J1 D3 2m green 2.50 *6.00*
J2 D3 4m maroon 2.50 *6.00*
J3 D3 1p ultra 14.00 *5.00*
J4 D3 2p orange 14.00 *10.00*
Nos. J1-J4 (4) 33.00 27.00

Steamboat on Nile River — D1

1901 Typo. Wmk. 179

J5 D1 2m orange brn & blk 1.00 .85
J6 D1 4m blue green & brn 3.25 1.25
J7 D1 10m bl vio & bl grn 8.00 5.00
J8 D1 20m car rose & ultra 4.75 4.75
Nos. J5-J8 (4) 17.00 11.85

1927-30 Wmk. Multiple S G (214)

J9 D1 2m org brn & blk ('30) 4.50 3.00
J10 D1 4m blue grn & brn 1.75 1.00
J11 D1 10m violet & blue grn 2.75 *2.00*
Nos. J9-J11 (3) 9.00 6.00

Catalogue values for unused stamps in this section, from this point to the end of the section, are for Never Hinged items.

Redrawn

Bottom inscription altered — D2

1948, Jan. 1

J12 D2 2m dp orange & blk 2.75 *50.00*
J13 D2 4m blue grn & choc 4.50 *37.50*
J14 D2 10m rose lil & bl grn 26.50 *19.00*
a. Wmk. 345 ('71?)
J15 D2 20m brt car rose & ultra 28.50 *30.00*
a. Wmk. 345 ('73)
Nos. J12-J15 (4) 62.25 *136.50*

ARMY OFFICIAL STAMPS

Regular Issues of 1898 and 1902-08 Overprinted in Black

Nos. MO1, MO3 and MO2, MO4

1905 Wmk. 71 *Perf. 14*

MO1 A1 1m rose & brown 190.00 *200.00*
a. "OFFICIAL" 4,750. 3,250.
b. Pair, #MO1 and #MO2 4,500.
MO2 A1 1m rose & brown 3,000. *3,000.*

Wmk. 179

MO3 A1 1m car rose & brn 6.50 3.00
a. "OFFICIAL" 80.00 47.50
b. Inverted overprint 70.00 60.00
c. Horizontal overprint 450.00
MO4 A1 1m car rose & brn 60.00 30.00
a. Inverted overprint 350.00 375.00

Regular Issues of 1902-11 Overprinted in Black

1906-11

MO5 A1 1m car rose & brn 2.50 .30
a. "Army" and "Service" 14mm apart 550.00 400.00
b. Inverted overprint 650.00 *700.00*
c. Pair, one without ovpt. *7,000.*
d. Double overprint 1,750.
e. "Service" omitted *4,500.*
MO6 A1 2m brn & grn 22.50 1.25
a. Pair, one without ovpt. 4,000.
b. "Army" omitted 4,200. *4,200.*
MO7 A1 3m grn & vio 22.50 .50
a. Inverted overprint 2,200.
MO8 A1 5m blk & rose red 3.50 .25
a. Inverted overprint 375.00
b. Double overprint 325.00 250.00
c. Double ovpt., one invtd. 1,500. 550.00
MO9 A1 1p yel brn & ultra 22.50 .40
a. "Army" omitted 3,250. 3,250.
MO10 A1 2p ultra & blk ('09) 85.00 15.00
a. Double overprint 3,400.
MO11 A1 5p grn & org brn ('08) 175.00 75.00
MO12 A1 10p dp vio & blk ('11) 625.00 *750.00*
Nos. MO5-MO12 (8) 958.50 842.70

Same Overprint On Regular Issue of 1898

Wmk. 71

MO13 A1 2p ultra & blk 90.00 11.50
a. Inverted overprint
MO14 A1 5p grn & org brn 130.00 *250.00*
MO15 A1 10p dp vio & blk 175.00 475.00

There are two types of this overprint which may be distinguished by the size and shape of the "y."

OFFICIAL STAMPS

Regular Issue of 1898 Overprinted in Black

1902-06 Wmk. 71 *Perf. 14*

O1 A1 1m rose & brown 3.50 *11.00*
Never hinged 7.00
a. Inverted overprint 325.00 *450.00*
b. Round periods 8.00 *45.00*
c. Double overprint 650.00
d. Oval "O" in overprint 90.00
e. As "d," inverted overprint 5,500.
O2 A1 10p dp vio & blk ('06) 16.00 *27.50*
Never hinged 32.50

Same Ovpt. on Stamps of 1902-11

1903-12 Wmk. 179

O3 A1 1m car rose & brn ('04) .60 .25
Never hinged 1.20
a. Double overprint
O4 A1 3m grn & vio ('04) 3.25 .25
Never hinged 6.50
a. Double overprint
O5 A1 5m blk & rose red 3.25 .25
Never hinged 6.50
O6 A1 1p yel brn & ultra 6.00 .25
Never hinged 12.00
O7 A1 2p ultra & blk 30.00 .25
Never hinged 60.00
O8 A1 5p grn & org brn 2.75 .40
Never hinged 5.50
O9 A1 10p dp vio & blk 5.25 70.00
Never hinged 11.00
Nos. O3-O9 (7) 51.10 71.65

Regular Issue of 1927-40 Overprinted in Black

Perf. 14, 13½x 14

1936-46 Wmk. 214

O10 A2 1m dk org & int blk ('46) 2.25 *12.50*
O11 A2 2m dk brn & dk org ('45) 2.25 *8.00*
O12 A2 3m green & vio ('37) 2.00 .25
O13 A2 4m brown & green 3.25 *4.00*
O14 A2 5m blk & ol brn ('40) 3.00 .25
O15 A2 10m blk & car ('46) .90 .25
O16 A2 15m org brn & ultra ('37) 7.50 .35

Regular Issue of 1927-40 Overprinted in Black

O17 A1 2p org & vio brn ('37) 11.50 .25
O18 A1 3p dk bl & red brn ('46) 5.25 3.00
O19 A1 4p blk & ultra ('46) 22.00 5.50
O20 A1 5p dk grn & org brn 8.50 *9.00*
O21 A1 6p blk & pale bl ('46) 6.00 7.00
O22 A1 8p blk & pck grn ('46) 4.00 *22.50*
O23 A1 10p dp vio & blk ('37) 37.50 6.50
O24 A1 20p bl & lt bl ('46) 25.00 *32.50*
Nos. O10-O24 (15) 140.90 111.85

Catalogue values for unused stamps in this section, from this point to the end of the section, are for Never Hinged items.

Nos. 79-85 Overprinted Like #O10-O16

1948, Jan. 1

O28 A7 1m dk org & blk .50 *4.50*
O29 A7 2m choc & org 2.00 .25
O30 A7 3m grn & rose lil 5.00 *10.00*
O31 A7 4m choc & sl grn 4.75 *6.00*
O32 A7 5m blk & ol brn 4.75 .25
O33 A7 10m blk & car 4.25 1.00
O34 A7 15m org brn & ultra 5.00 .25

Nos. 86-94 Overprinted Like Nos. O17-O24

O35 A8 2p org yel & vio brn 5.00 .25
O36 A8 3p dk bl & red brn 6.00 .25
O37 A8 4p blk & ultra 4.25 .25
a. Perf. 13 13.00 *18.00*
O38 A8 5p dk grn & org 6.50 .25
O39 A8 6p blk & pale bl 4.25 .25
O40 A8 8p blk & pck grn 4.25 *6.50*
O41 A8 10p dp rose lil & blk 7.75 .25
O42 A8 20p dk bl & bl 5.75 1.00
a. Perf. 13
O43 A8 50p ultra & car 82.50 70.00
Nos. O28-O43 (16) 152.50 101.25

Nos. 98-104 Overprinted Liked Nos. O10-O16 in Red

1951, Sept. 1 Wmk. 214 *Perf. 14*

Center in Black

O44 A11 1m orange .75 *5.00*
O45 A11 2m ultra .75 *2.00*
O46 A11 3m dk grn 12.00 *18.00*
O47 A11 4m emerald .25 6.00
O48 A11 5m plum .25 .25
O49 A11 10m light blue .25 .25
O50 A11 15m dp org brn 1.00 .25

Nos. 105-114 Overprinted Like Nos. O17-O24 in Black or Red

Perf. 13

O51 A12 2p lt bl & dk bl .25 .25
a. Inverted overprint 1,100.
O52 A12 3p vio bl & brn 22.50 .25
O53 A12 3½p brn & bl grn .85 .40
O54 A12 4p blk & dp bl 5.00 .25
O55 A12 5p emer & org brn .90 .25
O56 A12 6p blk & bl 1.10 *4.50*
O57 A12 8p brn & dp bl 1.50 .35
O58 A12 10p grn & blk (R) 1.75 .35
O59 A12 20p blk & bl grn 2.75 1.25
a. Inverted overprint 3,500.
O60 A13 50p blk & car 8.50 4.00
Nos. O44-O60 (17) 60.35 43.60

No. 112 Overprinted Like Nos.O17-O24 in Black

1958

O61 A12 10p green & black 22.50 3.75

Nos. 146-159 Overprinted

Perf. 14½x14, 14x14½

1962, Oct. 1 Litho. Wmk. 345

Size: 23x19mm, 19x23mm

O62 A25 5m blue .30 .25
O63 A26 10m blue & lilac .30 .25
O64 A25 15m yel, vio, org & brn .30 .25
O65 A25 2p lt pur .35 .25
O66 A26 3p bl grn, red brn & brn .60 .25
O67 A26 35m yel grn, brn & org brn .75 .25
O68 A26 4p red, lt bl & lil .90 .30
O69 A25 55m gray & yel ol 1.20 .50
O70 A25 6p brn & lt bl 1.20 .50
O71 A25 8p green 1.50 .60

Size: 24½x30mm, 30x24½mm

O72 A26 10p lt bl, red brn & blk 1.90 .65
O73 A25 20p gray ol & yel grn 3.75 1.40
a. Perf. 13½x12½ 3.75 1.10
b. Perf. 13½x14 8.00 1.90
O74 A25 50p dk gray, ol & bl 8.25 3.50
a. Perf. 13½x14 8.25 3.25

Engr.

O75 A13 £1 grn & brn org 21.00 12.50
Nos. O62-O75 (14) 42.30 21.45

The overprint measures 12x4½mm on Nos. O62-O71; 16x6mm on Nos. O72-O75.

Same Perfs., Sizes and Printing Methods as Before

1975-79 Unwmk.

O62a A25 5m .25 .25
O63a A26 10m ('76) .25 .25
O64a A25 15m .25 .25
O65a A25 2p .25 .25
O66a A26 3p .35 .25
O67a A26 35m .40 .25
O68a A26 4p .45 .25
O69a A25 55m .75 .45
O70a A25 6p ('76) .80 .45
O71a A25 8p 1.10 .55
O72a A26 10p 1.50 .70
O73c A25 20p 2.50 1.25
O74b A25 50p 2.50 1.25
O75a A13 £1 ('79) 19.00 12.50
Nos. O62a-O75a (14) 30.35 18.90

For surcharges, see Nos. 368E-368H.

Nos. 404-419
Overprinted

Perf. 13½x13

1991, July 1   Litho.   Unwmk.

O76	A105	25p on #404	.30	.25
O77	A105	50p on #405	.30	.25
O78	A105	75p on #406	.50	.25
O79	A105	100p on #407	.60	.35
O80	A105	125p on #408	.70	.40

Size: 30x24mm
Perf. 14x14½, 13½x14

O81	A105	150p on #409	.80	.45
O82	A105	175p on #410	.95	.55
O83	A105	£2 on #411	1.20	.65

Size: 26x37mm
Perf. 14

O84	A105	250p on #412	1.40	.75
O85	A105	£3 on #413	1.60	.95

Size: 24x30mm
Perf. 13½x14

O86	A105	£4 on #414	2.25	1.25
O87	A105	£5 on #415	2.75	1.50

Size: 36x27mm
Perf. 14
Wmk. 334

O88	A105	£8 on #416	4.50	2.75
O89	A105	£10 on #417	5.50	3.75
O90	A105	£15 on #418	8.00	5.75
O91	A105	£20 on #419	11.00	7.50
		Nos. O76-O91 (16)	42.35	27.35

For surcharges see Nos. O104-O111.

Nos. 420, 427-428
Overprinted

1992   Litho.   Unwmk.   Perf. 14½

O92	A25	25p on #420	.35	.25

Perf. 14x13½, 13½x14

O99	A25	£5 on #427	3.00	1.75
O100	A25	£10 on #428	6.00	3.50
		Nos. O92-O100 (3)	9.35	5.50

Nos. O79,
O81, O83,
O85-O87
Srchd. in Blue
Violet or Black

Perf. 13½x13

1993?   Litho.   Unwmk.

O104	A105	1d on 100p #O79	1.25	.65

Perf. 13½x14

O105	A105	1.50d on 150p #O81	1.75	1.00
O107	A105	2d on £2 #O83	2.25	1.25

Perf. 14

O109	A105	3d on £3 #O85	3.25	2.00

Perf. 14½x14

O110	A105	4d on £4 #O86	4.25	2.75

Perf. 13½x14

O111	A105	5d on £5 #O87 (Blk)	5.50	3.25

Perf. 14
Size: 36x27mm

O112	A109	35d on £8 #O88	15.50	14.50
		Nos. O104-O112 (7)	33.75	25.40

Coat of Arms — O1

2003   Litho.   Perf. 13½x13¼

O113	O1	50d multi	.60	.50
O114	O1	100d multi	1.10	.95
O115	O1	225d multi	2.25	1.90
O116	O1	300d multi	3.75	3.00
		Nos. O113-O116 (4)	7.70	6.35

SURINAM

'sur-ə-ˌnam

(Dutch Guiana)

LOCATION — On the northeast coast of South America, bordering on the Atlantic Ocean
GOVT. — Republic
AREA — 63,234 sq. mi.
POP. — 431,156 (1999 est.)
CAPITAL — Paramaribo

The Dutch colony of Surinam became an integral part of the Kingdom of the Netherlands under the Constitution of 1954. It became an independent state November 25, 1975.

100 Cents = 1 Gulden (Florin)
100 Cents = 1 Dollar (2004)

Catalogue values for unused stamps in this country are for Never Hinged items, beginning with Scott 168 in the regular postage section, Scott B34 in the semi-postal section, Scott C23 in the airpost section, Scott CB1 in the airpost semi-postal section, and Scott J33 in the postage due section.

Watermark

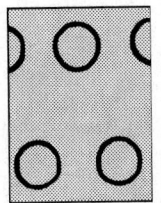

Wmk. 202 —
Circles

Early issues of Surinam were sent to the colony without gum. Many of these were subsequently gummed locally.

King William III — A1

Perf. 11½, 11½x12, 12½x12, 13½, 14
1873-89   Typo.   Unwmk.
Without Gum

1	A1	1c lil gray ('85)	2.50	3.00
2	A1	2c yellow ('85)	1.75	1.75
3	A1	2½c rose	1.75	1.75
4	A1	3c green	21.00	18.50
5	A1	5c dull violet	20.00	7.00
6	A1	10c bister	4.00	2.75
7	A1	12½c sl bl ('85)	21.00	8.25
8	A1	15c gray ('89)	25.00	8.25
9	A1	20c green ('89)	37.50	35.00
10	A1	25c grnsh blue	85.00	10.00
11	A1	25c ultra	300.00	25.00
12	A1	30c red brn ('88)	35.00	37.50
13	A1	40c dk brn ('89)	32.50	32.50
14	A1	50c brown org	32.50	21.00
15	A1	1g red brn & gray ('89)	52.50	52.50
16	A1	2.50g grn & org ('79)	80.00	70.00
		Nos. 1-16 (16)	752.00	334.75

Perf. 14, Small Holes

3b	A1	2½c rose	12.00	14.00
4b	A1	3c green	22.00	29.00
5b	A1	5c dull violet	22.00	18.00
6b	A1	10c bister	21.00	25.00

11b	A1	25c ultra	300.00	72.50
14b	A1	50c brown org	57.50	50.00
		Nos. 3b-14b (6)	434.50	208.50

The paper of Nos. 3-6, 11 and 14 sometimes has an accidental bluish tinge of varying strength. During its manufacture a chemical whitener (bluing agent) was added in varying quantities. No particular printing was made on bluish paper.

"Small hole" varieties have the spaces between the holes wider than the diameter of the holes.

Nos. 1-16 and 3b-14b exist with gum.
For surcharges see Nos. 23, 31-35, 39-42.

Numeral of Value — A2

1890   Perf. 11½x11, 12½
Without Gum

17	A2	1c gray	1.90	1.40
18	A2	2c yellow brn	3.00	2.50
19	A2	2½c carmine	2.50	2.00
20	A2	3c green	5.75	4.00
21	A2	5c ultra	27.50	1.50
		Nos. 17-21 (5)	40.65	11.40

Nos. 17-21 exist with gum.
For surcharges see Nos. 63-64.

A3

1892, Aug. 11   Perf. 10½
Without Gum

22	A3	2½c black & org	1.90	1.25
a.	First and fifth vertical words have fancy "F"		27.50	17.50
b.	Imperf.		2.50	
c.	As "a," imperf.		32.50	

No. 14 Surcharged in
Black

1892, Aug. 1   Perf. 14
Without Gum

23	A1	2½c on 50c	250.00	12.00
a.	Perf. 12½x12	375.00	12.00
b.	Perf. 11½x12	425.00	17.50
c.	Double surcharge	375.00	275.00
d.	Perf. 14, small holes	275.00	12.00

Nos. 23-23c were issued without gum.

Queen
Wilhelmina — A5

1892-93   Typo.   Perf. 12½
Without Gum

25	A5	10c bister	42.50	3.25
26	A5	12½c rose lilac	50.00	5.75
27	A5	15c gray	4.00	2.75
28	A5	20c green	4.50	3.25
29	A5	25c blue	10.00	5.75
30	A5	30c red brown	5.75	5.00
		Nos. 25-30 (6)	116.75	25.75

Nos. 25-30 exist with gum.
For surcharges see Nos. 65-66.

Nos. 7-12 Surcharged

1898   Perf. 11½x12, 12½x12, 13½
Without Gum

31	A1	10c on 12½c sl bl	27.50	4.00
32	A1	10c on 15c gray	65.00	55.00
33	A1	10c on 20c green	5.25	5.00
34	A1	10c on 25c grnsh bl	11.00	6.25
c.	Perf. 11½x12	12.00	12.00
34A	A1	10c on 25c ultra	575.00	500.00
b.	Perf. 11½x12	675.00	600.00
35	A1	10c on 30c red brn	4.25	4.25
a.	Double surcharge	325.00	

Dangerous counterfeits exist.

Netherlands Nos. 80, 83-84
Surcharged

No. 36   Nos. 37-38

1900, Jan. 8   Perf. 12½
Without Gum

36	A11	50c on 50c	27.50	9.00

Engr.
Perf. 11½x11

37	A12	100c on 1g dk grn	25.00	14.00
38	A12	2.50g on 2½g brn lil	25.00	12.50
		Nos. 36-38 (3)	77.50	35.50

For surcharge see No. 67.

Nos. 13-16 Surcharged

Perf. 11½, 11½x12, 12½x12, 14

1900 **Typo.**

Without Gum

39	A1	25c on 40c	5.00	3.50
40	A1	25c on 50c	5.00	3.50
a.		Perf. 14, small holes	130.00	*140.00*
b.		Perf. 11½x12	3.75	3.75
41	A1	50c on 1g	40.00	35.00
42	A1	50c on 2.50g	150.00	*175.00*
		Nos. 39-42 (4)	200.00	217.00

Counterfeits of No. 42 exist.

A9

Queen Wilhelmina
A10 A11

1902-08 **Typo.** *Perf. 12½*

Without Gum

44	A9	½c violet	1.00	.90
45	A9	1c olive grn	2.10	1.25
46	A9	2c yellow brn	11.50	4.50
47	A9	2½c blue grn	5.00	.45
48	A9	3c orange	8.25	5.25
49	A9	5c red	8.25	.45
50	A9	7½c gray ('08)	18.00	8.25
51	A10	10c slate	12.00	.95
52	A10	12½c deep blue	4.50	.45
53	A10	15c dp brown	30.00	10.50
54	A10	20c olive grn	27.50	5.25
55	A10	22½c brn & ol grn	24.00	13.00
56	A10	25c violet	20.00	1.25
57	A10	30c orange brn	47.50	15.00
58	A10	50c lake brown	37.50	9.25

Engr.

Perf. 11

59	A11	1g violet	60.00	20.00
60	A11	2½g slate blue	60.00	65.00
		Nos. 44-60 (17)	377.10	161.70

Nos. 44-60 exist with gum.

A12

1909 **Typeset** *Serrate Roulette 13½*

Without Gum

61	A12	5c red	13.50	11.50
a.		Tête bêche pair	190.00	175.00

Perf. 11½x10½

62	A12	5c red	14.50	12.00
a.		Tête bêche pair	140.00	140.00

Nos. 17-18, 29-30, 38 Surcharged in Red

Nos. 63-64

Nos. 65-66

No. 67

1911, July 15 **Typo.** *Perf. 12½*

Without Gum

63	A2	½c on 1c	1.75	1.10
64	A2	½c on 2c	12.25	9.00
65	A5	15c on 25c	75.00	57.50
66	A5	20c on 30c	14.00	9.50

Engr.

Perf. 11½x11

67	A12	30c on 2.50g on 2½g	125.00	110.00
		Nos. 63-67 (5)	228.00	187.10

A13

1912, July **Typeset** *Perf. 11½*

Without Gum

70	A13	½c lilac	.95	.95
a.		Horiz. pair, imperf. btwn.	200.00	
71	A13	2½c dk green	.95	.95
72	A13	5c pale red	8.75	8.75
a.		Vert. pair, imperf. btwn.	240.00	
73	A13	12½c deep blue	11.00	11.00
		Nos. 70-73 (4)	21.65	21.65

Numeral of Value — A14

Queen Wilhelmina
A15 A16

1913-31 **Typo.** *Perf. 12½*

74	A14	½c violet	.40	.25
75	A14	1c olive green	.40	.25
76	A14	1½c bl, perf 11 ½ ('21)	.40	.25
a.		Perf. 12½ ('32)	1.10	.85
77	A14	2c yellow brn	1.60	1.10
78	A14	2½c green	.95	.25
79	A14	3c yellow	.80	.65
80	A14	3c green ('26)	3.25	2.50
81	A14	4c chlky bl ('26)	8.25	5.00
82	A14	5c rose	1.60	.25
83	A14	5c green ('22)	2.00	1.00
84	A14	5c lilac ('26)	1.60	.25
85	A14	6c bister ('26)	2.75	2.50
86	A14	6c red org ('31)	2.25	.50
87	A14	7½c drab	1.00	.40
a.		Perf. 11x11½	1.40	.65
88	A14	7½c orange ('27)	1.40	.40
89	A14	7½c yellow ('31)	9.25	9.25
90	A14	10c violet ('22)	5.00	5.00
91	A14	10c rose ('26)	4.00	.55
92	A15	10c car rose	1.40	.65
93	A15	12½c blue	1.90	.65
94	A15	12½c red ('22)	2.00	2.25
95	A15	15c olive grn	.55	.70
96	A15	15c lt blue ('26)	7.75	4.75
97	A15	20c green	3.50	3.25
98	A15	20c blue ('22)	2.40	2.00
99	A15	20c ol grn ('26)	3.50	2.75
100	A15	22½c orange	2.50	2.50
101	A15	25c red violet	4.00	.40
102	A15	30c slate	5.00	1.10
103	A15	32½c vio & org ('22)	15.00	17.50
104	A15	35c sl & red ('26)	5.00	5.00

Perf. 11, 11½, 11½x11, 12½

Engr.

105	A16	50c green	4.00	.85
a.		Perf. 12½ ('32)	14.00	1.60
106	A16	1g brown	5.50	.50
a.		Perf. 12½ ('32)	15.00	1.00
107	A16	1½g dp vio ('26)	35.00	35.00
108	A16	2½g carmine ('23)	30.00	26.00
a.		Perf. 11½x11	35.00	32.50
		Nos. 74-108 (35)	175.90	136.20

Nos. 74, 75, 77-79, 82, 87, 105, 106 and 108 were issued both with and without gum.

Early printings of Nos. 74-104 had water soluble ink.

For surcharges see Nos. 116-120, 139.

Queen Wilhelmina — A17

1923, Oct. 5 *Perf. 11, 11x11½, 11½*

109	A17	5c green	1.10	.70
110	A17	10c car rose	1.75	1.50
111	A17	20c indigo	3.50	3.00
112	A17	50c brown org	19.00	19.00
113	A17	1g brown vio	26.00	17.00
114	A17	2½g gray blk	75.00	*200.00*
115	A17	5g brown	100.00	*240.00*
		Nos. 109-115 (7)	226.35	*481.20*

25th anniv. of the assumption of the government of the Netherlands by Queen Wilhelmina, at age 18.

Values for Nos. 114-115 used are for stamps with postmarks clearly dated before July 15, 1924.

Nos. 83, 93-94, 98 Surcharged in Black or Red

j

k

m

1925, Dec. 19 **Typo.** *Perf. 12½*

116	A14	3c on 5c green	1.10	1.10
117	A15	10c on 12½c red	2.25	2.25
118	A15	15c on 12½c blue (R)	1.60	1.60
119	A15	15c on 20c blue	1.60	1.60
		Nos. 116-119 (4)	6.55	6.55

No. 100 Surcharged in Blue

1926, Jan. 1

120	A15	12½c on 22½c org	27.50	27.50

Postage Due Stamps Nos. J14 and J29 Surcharged in Blue or Black

o

p

121	D2(o)	12½c on 40c (Bl)	3.25	3.25
122	D2(p)	12½c on 40c (Bk)	30.00	30.00
		Nos. 120-122 (3)	60.75	60.75

No. 121 issued without gum.

Queen Wilhelmina — A21

1927-30 **Engr.** *Perf. 11½*

123	A21	10c carmine	1.00	.40
124	A21	12½c red orange	1.75	1.90
125	A21	15c dark blue	2.00	.60
126	A21	20c indigo	2.00	.80
127	A21	21c dk brown ('30)	19.00	19.00
128	A21	22½c brown ('28)	8.00	9.75
129	A21	25c dk violet	3.00	.70
130	A21	30c dk green	3.00	1.10
131	A21	35c black brown	3.00	3.00
		Nos. 123-131 (9)	42.75	37.25

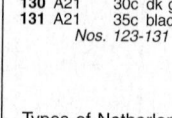

Types of Netherlands Marine Insurance Stamps Inscribed "SURINAME" and Surcharged

1927, Oct. 26

132	MI1	3c on 15c dk grn	.65	.65
133	MI1	10c on 60c car rose	.65	.65
134	MI1	12½c on 75c gray brn	.65	.65
135	MI2	15c on 1.50 dk blue	2.75	2.75
136	MI2	25c on 2.25g org brn	7.25	7.25
137	MI3	30c on 4½g black	9.00	7.25
138	MI3	50c on 7½g red	7.25	7.25
		Nos. 132-138 (7)	28.20	26.45

Nos. 135-137 have "FRANKEERZEGEL" in small capitals in one line. Nos. 135 and 136 have a heavy bar across the top of the stamp.

No. 88 Surcharged

1930, Mar. 1 **Typo.** *Perf. 12½*

139	A14	6c on 7½c orange	1.90	1.00

Prince William I (Portrait by Van Key) — A22

1933, Apr. 24 **Photo.**

141	A22	6c deep orange	6.75	1.90

400th birth anniv. of Prince William I, Count of Nassau and Prince of Orange, frequently referred to as William the Silent.

Van Walbeeck's Ship
A23

Queen Wilhelmina
A24

1936-41 **Litho.** *Perf. 13½x12½*

142	A23	½c yellow brn	.30	.30
143	A23	1c lt yellow grn	.40	.25
144	A23	1½c brt blue	.55	.40
145	A23	2c black brown	.60	.25
146	A23	2½c green	.25	.25
a.		Perf. 13 ('41)	9.00	3.25
147	A23	3c dark ultra	.60	.40
148	A23	4c orange	.60	.75
149	A23	5c gray	.60	.25
150	A23	6c red	2.50	2.00
151	A23	7½c red violet	.25	.25
a.		7½c plum, perf. 13 ('41)	3.00	.25

Engr.

Perf. 14, 12½

Size: 20x30mm

152	A24	10c vermilion	.85	.25
a.		Perf. 12½ ('39)	60.00	11.50
153	A24	12½c dull green	3.50	1.25
154	A24	15c dark blue	1.25	.60
155	A24	20c yellow org	2.10	.60
156	A24	21c dk gray	3.25	3.00
a.		Perf. 12½ ('39)	3.75	3.75
157	A24	25c brown lake	2.40	1.00
158	A24	30c brown vio	3.75	1.00
159	A24	35c olive brown	4.00	4.00

Perf. 12½x14

Size: 22x33mm

160 A24	50c	dull yel grn	4.00	2.00
161 A24	1g	dull blue	8.25	3.00
162 A24	1.50g	black brown	22.50	18.00
163 A24	2.50g	rose lake	13.50	9.50
		Nos. 142-163 (22)	76.00	49.30

For surcharges see Nos. 181-183, B37-B40.

Queen Wilhelmina — A25

Perf. 12½x12

1938, Aug. 30 Photo. Wmk. 202

164 A25	2c	dull purple	.50	.30
165 A25	7½c	red orange	1.50	1.25
166 A25	15c	royal blue	3.00	3.00
		Nos. 164-166 (3)	5.00	4.55

Reign of Queen Wilhelmina, 40th anniv.

Catalogue values for unused stamps in this section, from this point to the end of the section, are for Never Hinged items.

Van Walbeeck's Ship — A26

1941 Unwmk. Typo. *Perf. 12*

168 A26	1c	lt yellow grn	1.00	.25
169 A26	2c	black brown	2.50	2.50

Type A26 is similar to type A23 except for the white side frame lines which extend to the base.

For surcharges see No. 180.

Queen Wilhelmina — A27

1941-46 Photo. *Perf. 13½x12½*

Size: 18x22½mm

174 A27	12½c	royal blue ('46)	1.50	.25

Perf. 12½

175 A27	15c	ultra	22.50	8.25

Royal Family — A28

1943, Nov. 2 Engr. *Perf. 13½x13*

176 A28	2½c	deep orange	.25	.35
177 A28	7½c	red	.25	.25
178 A28	15c	black	2.75	2.25
179 A28	40c	deep blue	3.25	2.75
		Nos. 176-179 (4)	6.50	5.60

Birth of Princess Margriet Francisca of the Netherlands.

Nos. 168, 151, 152 Surcharged with New Values and Bars in Black

1945 Unwmk. *Perf. 13, 14, 12*

180 A26	½c on 1c		.25	.25
181 A23	2½c on 7½c		3.50	3.00
182 A24	5c on 10c		1.25	.70
183 A24	7½c on 10c		1.50	.70
a.	Double surcharge		225.00	190.00
	Nos. 180-183 (4)		6.50	4.65

Bauxite Mine, Moengo A29

Queen Wilhelmina
A30 A31

Designs: 1½c, Bush Negroes on Cottica River near Moengo. 2c, Waterfall in interior. 2½c, Road scene, Coronie District. 3c, Surinam River near Berg en Dahl Plantation. 4c, Government Square, Paramaribo. 5c, Mining gold. 6c, Street in Paramaribo. 7½c, Sugar cane train.

1945, Nov. 5 Engr. *Perf. 12*

184 A29	1c	rose carmine	.25	.25
185 A29	1½c	rose lake	1.25	1.25
186 A29	2c	violet	.55	.40
187 A29	2½c	olive brn	.55	.40
188 A29	3c	dull green	1.25	.70
189 A29	4c	brown	1.25	.75
190 A29	5c	blue	1.25	.25
191 A29	6c	olive	2.25	1.60
192 A29	7½c	deep orange	.80	.35
193 A30	10c	blue	1.60	.25
194 A30	15c	brown	2.00	.25
195 A30	20c	dull green	3.25	.25
196 A30	22½c	gray	3.75	.90
197 A30	25c	carmine	10.00	4.50
198 A30	30c	olive green	10.00	.55
199 A30	35c	brt blue grn	17.00	7.25
200 A30	40c	rose lake	9.75	.25
201 A30	50c	red orange	9.75	.25
202 A30	60c	violet	9.75	.80
203 A31	1g	red brown	12.00	.35
204 A31	1.50g	lilac	10.00	.80
205 A31	2.50g	olive brn	20.00	.95
206 A31	5g	rose carmine	45.00	12.50
207 A31	10g	red orange	77.50	19.00
		Nos. 184-207 (24)	250.75	54.80

For surcharges see #240, B41-B46, CB2-CB3.

Nos. 151 and 152 Surcharged with New Value and Bar in Blue or Black

1947 *Perf. 13½x12½, 14*

209 A23	1½(c) on 7½c (Bl)		.25	*.25*
a.	Double surcharge		200.00	
210 A24	2½c on 10c (Bk)		1.75	.50

Numeral A32

Queen Wilhelmina A33

Perf. 12½x13½

1948, July 21 Unwmk. Photo.

211 A32	1c	dark red	.25	.25
212 A32	1½c	plum	.25	.25
213 A32	2c	purple	.25	.25
214 A32	2½c	olive grn	1.50	.25
215 A32	3c	dark green	.25	.25
216 A32	4c	red brown	.25	.25

Perf. 13½x12½

217 A33	5c	deep blue	.40	.25
218 A33	6c	dark olive	1.00	.75
219 A33	7½c	scarlet	.40	.25
220 A33	10c	blue	.60	.25
221 A33	12½c	dark blue	1.25	1.25
222 A33	15c	henna brown	1.75	.45
223 A33	17½c	dk vio brn	1.90	1.50
224 A33	20c	dk blue grn	1.60	.25
225 A33	22½c	slate blue	1.60	.75
226 A33	25c	crimson	1.60	.35
227 A33	27½c	car lake	1.60	.25
228 A33	30c	olive green	1.90	.25
229 A33	37½c	olive brn	3.25	2.25
230 A33	40c	lilac rose	2.25	.35
231 A33	50c	red orange	2.25	.35
232 A33	60c	purple	2.50	.45
233 A33	70c	black	3.00	.75
		Nos. 211-233 (23)	31.60	12.20

See Nos. 241-242.

Wilhelmina — A34

1948, Aug. 30 Engr. *Perf. 12½x14*

234 A34	7½c	vermilion	1.10	1.10
235 A34	12½c	deep blue	1.10	1.10

Reign of Queen Wilhelmina, 50th anniv.

Juliana — A35

Perf. 14x13

1948, Sept. 10 Wmk. 202 Photo.

236 A35	7½c	deep orange	3.50	3.50
237 A35	12½c	ultra	3.50	3.50

Investiture of Queen Juliana, Sept. 6, 1948.

For surcharges see Nos. B53-B54.

Post Horns Entwined — A36

1949, Oct. 1 Unwmk. *Perf. 11½x12*

238 A36	7½c	brown red	7.00	3.75
239 A36	27½c	dull blue	7.00	2.75

UPU, 75th anniversary.

No. 192 Surcharged with New Value, Square and Bar in Black

1950, Aug. 9 *Perf. 12*

240 A29	1c on 7½c dp org		.60	.60

Numeral Type of 1948

1951, Apr. 5 *Perf. 12½x13½*

241 A32	5c	deep blue	1.75	.25
242 A32	7½c	deep orange	4.25	2.25

A37

Queen Juliana — A38

1951, Apr. 5 *Perf. 13½x13*

243 A37	10c	blue	.45	.25
244 A37	15c	henna brn	1.00	.25
245 A37	20c	dk blue grn	2.40	.25
246 A37	25c	crimson	1.50	.40
247 A37	27½c	carmine lake	1.50	.25
248 A37	30c	olive green	1.50	.40
249 A37	35c	olive brown	1.90	1.60
250 A37	40c	lilac rose	2.10	.40
251 A37	50c	red orange	2.50	.45

Engr.

Perf. 12½x12

252 A38	1g	red brown	27.50	.50
		Nos. 243-252 (10)	42.35	4.75

For surcharge see No. 271.

Shooting Fish A39

Fisherman A40

Designs: 5c, Bauxite mining. 6c, Log raft. 7½c, Plowing with Water Buffalo. 10c, Woman picking fruit. 12½c, Armored catfish. 15c, Macaw. 17½c, Armadillo. 20c, Poling canoe. 25c, Common iguana.

1953-55 Photo. *Perf. 14x13, 13x14*

253 A39	2c	olive green	.25	.25
254 A40	2½c	blue green	.30	.25
255 A40	5c	gray	.50	.25
256 A40	6c	bright blue	2.50	1.75
257 A40	7½c	purple	.25	.25
258 A40	10c	bright red	.25	.25
259 A40	12½c	dk gray blue	3.25	2.10
260 A40	15c	crimson	1.10	.25
261 A40	17½c	red brown	5.00	3.00
262 A40	20c	Prus green	.90	.25
263 A40	25c	olive green	4.50	1.25
a.	Min. sheet of 4, #259-261, 263		90.00	90.00
		Nos. 253-263 (11)	18.80	9.85

Issued: 2c, 7½c, 10c, 20c, 5/9/53; #263a, 2/14/55;.others, 12/1/54.

Queen Juliana — A41

1954, Dec. 15 *Perf. 13½*

264 A41	7½c	dark red brown	.90	.90

Charter of the Kingdom, adopted Dec. 15, 1954.

See Netherlands No. 366, Netherlands Antilles No. 232.

Harvesting Bananas — A46

Designs: 7½c, Pounding rice. 10c, Preparing cassava. 15c, Fishing.

1955, May 12 *Perf. 14x13*

265 A46	2c	dark green	2.10	2.10
266 A46	7½c	dull yellow	3.25	3.00
267 A46	10c	orange brown	3.25	3.00
268 A46	15c	ultra	3.25	3.00
		Nos. 265-268 (4)	11.85	11.10

4th anniv. of the establishment of the Caribbean Tourist Assoc.

Globe and Mercury's Rod — A47

1955, Sept. 19 Unwmk. *Perf. 13x12*

269 A47	5c	bright ultra	.50	.45

Paramaribo Trade Fair, Oct. 1955.

Flags and Map of Caribbean — A48

1956, Dec. 6 Litho. *Perf. 13x14*

270 A48	10c	lt blue & red	.40	.35

10th anniv. of Caribbean Commission.

No. 247 Surcharged

1958, Nov. 11 Photo.   Perf. 13½x13
271 A37 8c on 27½c car lake   .25   .25

Queen Juliana — A49

Perf. 12½x12
1959, Oct. 15   Unwmk.   Litho.
272 A49   1g magenta   2.00   .25
273 A49   1.50g olive bister   3.25   .80
274 A49   2.50g dk carmine   4.75   .50
275 A49   5g dull blue   9.00   .50
     Nos. 272-275 (4)   19.00 2.05

Symbolic
Flowers — A50

1959, Dec. 15 Photo.   Perf. 12½x13
276 A50 20c multicolored   3.75 2.75
5th anniv. of the constitution. Flowers in design symbolize Netherlands, Surinam and Netherlands Antilles.

Charles Lindbergh's Plane — A51

10c, De Snip plane. 15c, Cessna 170B. 20c, Super Constellation. 40c, Boeing 707 Jet.

1960, Mar. 12   Perf. 12½
277 A51   8c chalky blue   1.25   1.40
278 A51 10c bright green   1.75   2.00
279 A51 15c rose red   1.75   2.00
280 A51 20c pale violet   2.00   2.40
281 A51 40c light brown   3.00   3.25
     Nos. 277-281 (5)   9.75 11.05
Inauguration of Zanderij Airport, Mar. 12. Nos. 277-281 show 25 years of Surinam's civil aviation.

Flag of Surinam and
Map — A52

Arms of
Surinam — A53

1960, July 1   Litho.   Perf. 12½x13
282 A52 10c multicolored   .70   .70
Perf. 13x12½
283 A53 15c multicolored   .70   .70
Day of Freedom, July 1.

Bananas — A54

1961, Mar. 1   Litho.   Perf. 13½
284 A54   1c shown   .25   .25
285 A54   2c Citrus fruit .25   .25
286 A54   3c Cacao   .25   .25
287 A54   4c Sugar cane   .25   .25
288 A54   5c Coffee   .25   .25
289 A54   6c Coconuts   .25   .25
290 A54   8c Rice   .25   .25
     Nos. 284-290 (7)   1.75 1.75

Finance
Building — A55

Buildings: 15c, Court of Justice. 20c, Concordia Lodge (Masons). 25c, Neve Shalom Synagogue, Paramaribo, horiz. 30c, Old Dutch lock in New Amsterdam. 35c, Government office, horiz. 40c, Governor's palace, horiz. 50c, Legislative Council, horiz. 60c, Old Dutch Reformed Church, horiz. 70c, Zeelandia Fortress, horiz.

1961   Perf. 13½x14, 14x13½
291 A55 10c multi   .25   .25
292 A55 15c multi   .25   .25
293 A55 20c multi   .30   .30
294 A55 25c multi   .65   .65
295 A55 30c multi   1.75   1.75
296 A55 35c multi   1.75   1.75
297 A55 40c multi   .90   .90
298 A55 50c multi   .90   .90
299 A55 60c multi   1.00   1.00
300 A55 70c multi   1.10   1.10
     Nos. 291-300 (10) 8.85 8.85
Issued: 10c, 20c, 25c, 50c, 70c, 4/1; others, 5/15.

Dag
Hammarskjold
(1905-1961)
A56

1962, Jan. 2   Litho.   Perf. 11½, 12½
301 A56 10c brt blue & blk   .30   .30
302 A56 20c lilac & blk   .30   .30
Dag Hammarskjold, Secretary General of the United Nations, 1953-61.
Sheets of both perfs. exist either with or without extension of perforations through the margins.

A56a

1962, Feb. 1   Photo.   Perf. 14x13
303 A56a 20c olive green   .50   .50
Silver wedding anniversary of Queen Juliana and Prince Bernhard.

A57

Malaria eradication emblem.

1962, May 2   Litho.   Perf. 13x14
304 A57   8c bright red   .30   .30
305 A57 10c blue   .30   .30
WHO drive to eradicate malaria.

Stoelmans Guesthouse — A58

Design: 15c, Torarica Hotel.

1962, July 4   Perf. 14x13½
306 A58 10c multicolored   .50   .50
307 A58 15c multicolored   .50   .50
Opening of the Torarica Hotel in Paramaribo and Stoelmans Guesthouse on Stoelman Island.

Deaconess Residence and Recreation
Area — A59

Design: 20c, Deaconess Hospital.

1962, Nov. 30
308 A59 10c multicolored   .50   .50
309 A59 20c multicolored   .50   .50

Hands
Holding
Wheat
Emblem
A60

20c, Farmer harvesting & wheat emblem, vert.

Perf. 14x13, 13x14
1963, Mar. 21   Photo.
310 A60 10c deep carmine   .30   .30
311 A60 20c dark blue   .30   .30
FAO "Freedom from Hunger" campaign.

Broken
Chain — A61

1963, June 28 Litho.   Perf. 14x13
312 A61 10c red & blk   .30   .30
313 A61 20c green & blk   .30   .30
Centenary of emancipation of the slaves.

Prince William of
Orange Landing
at Scheveningen
A61a

1963, Nov. 21 Photo.   Perf. 13½x14
Size: 26x26mm
314 A61a 10c dull bl, blk & brn   .30   .30
Founding of the Kingdom of the Netherlands, 150th anniv.

Faja Lobbi
Wreath — A62

1964, Dec. 15 Litho.   Perf. 12½x13
315 A62 25c multicolored   .40   .40
Charter of the Kingdom of the Netherlands, 10th anniv.

Abraham Lincoln
(1809-1865) — A63

1965, Apr. 14 Litho.   Perf. 12½x13
316 A63 25c olive bister & brn   .30   .30

ICY Emblem
A64

1965, May 26   Perf. 13x12½
317 A64 10c orange & blue   .30   .30
318 A64 15c red & violet bl .30   .30
International Cooperation Year.

Bauxite
Mine,
Moengo
A65

Designs: 15c, Alum Pottery Works, Paranam. 20c, Hydroelectric plant, Afobaka. 25c, Aluminum smeltery, Paranam.

1965, Oct. 9   Photo.   Unwmk.
319 A65 10c ocher   .55   .55
320 A65 15c dark green   .55   .55
321 A65 20c dark blue   .55   .55
322 A65 25c carmine   .55   .55
     Nos. 319-322 (4)   2.20 2.20
Opening of the Brokopondo Power Station.

Red-breasted
Blackbird — A66

2c, Great kiskadee. 3c, Silver-beaked tanager. 4c, Ruddy ground dove. 5c, Blue-gray tanager. 6c, Glittering-throated emerald (hummingbird). 8c, Turquoise tanager. 10c, Pale-breasted robin.

1966, Feb. 16 Litho.   Perf. 13x14
323 A66   1c brt grn, blk & red   .50   .50
324 A66   2c lt ultra, yel & brn .50   .50
325 A66   3c multi   .50   .50
326 A66   4c lt ol grn, red brn &
           blk   .50   .50
327 A66   5c org, ultra & blk   .50   .50
328 A66   6c multi   .50   .50
329 A66   8c gray, vio bl & blk   .50   .50
330 A66 10c multi   .50   .50
     Nos. 323-330 (8)   4.00 4.00

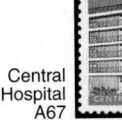

Central Hospital A67

Design: 15c, Hospital, side view.

1966, Mar. 9   Litho.   Perf. 13x12½
331 A67 10c multi   .60   .60
332 A67 15c multi   .60   .60

Opening of Central Hospital, Paramaribo.

Father Petrus Donders — A68

Designs: 10c, Church and parsonage, Batavia. 15c, Msgr. Joannes B. Swinkels. 25c, Cathedral, Paramaribo.

1966, Mar. 26   Photo.   Perf. 12½x13
333 A68   4c org brn & blk   .25   .25
334 A68 10c rose brn & blk   .25   .25
335 A68 15c yel brn & blk   .25   .25
336 A68 25c lt vio & blk   .25   .25
    Nos. 333-336 (4)   1.00   1.00

Centenary of the Redemptorist Mission in Surinam (Congregation of the Most Holy Redeemer).

100-Year-Old Tree — A69

1966, May 9   Litho.   Perf. 13x12½
337 A69 25c grn, dp org & blk   .60   .60
338 A69 30c red org, grn & blk   .60   .60

Centenary of the Surinam Parliament.

Television Transmitter, Eye and Globe — A70

1966, Oct. 20   Litho.   Perf. 12½x13
339 A70 25c dk bl & ver   .60   .60
340 A70 30c brn & ver   .60   .60

Inauguration of television service.

Bauxite Industry, 1916 — A71

Design: 25c, Bauxite industry, 1966.

1966, Dec. 19   Litho.   Perf. 13x12½
341 A71 20c yel, org & blk   .60   .60
342 A71 25c org, bl & blk   .60   .60

50th anniversary of bauxite industry.

Central Bank, Paramaribo A72

Design: 25c, Central Bank, different view.

1967, Apr. 1   Litho.   Perf. 13x12½
343 A72 10c dp yel & blk   .30   .30
344 A72 25c lil & blk   .30   .30

Central Bank of Surinam, 10th anniv.

Amelia Earhart, Lockheed Electra and Paramaribo A73

1967, June 3   Photo.   Perf. 13x12½
345 A73 20c yel & dk car   .40   .40
346 A73 25c yel & grn   .40   .40

30th anniv. of Amelia Earhart's visit to Surinam, June 3-4, 1937.

Siva Nataraja, God of Dance, and Ballerina's Foot — A74

Design: 25c, Drummer's mask "Bashi Lele," and scroll of violin.

1967, June 21   Litho.   Perf. 12½x13
347 A74 10c yel grn & bl   .30   .30
348 A74 25c yel grn & brn   .30   .30

20th anniv. of the Surinam Cultural Center Foundation.

New Amsterdam, 1660 (New York City) — A75

Designs after 17th Century Engravings: 10c, Fort Zeelandia, Paramaribo, 1670. 25c, Breda Castle, Netherlands, 1667.

1967, July 31   Litho.   Perf. 13½x13
349 A75 10c yel, blk & bl   .40   .40
350 A75 20c red brn, yel & blk   .40   .40
351 A75 25c bl grn, yel & blk   .40   .40
    Nos. 349-351 (3)   1.20   1.20

300th anniv. of the Treaty of Breda between Britain, France and the Netherlands.

WHO Emblem A76

1968, Apr. 7   Litho.   Perf. 13x12½
352 A76 10c magenta & dk bl   .25   .25
353 A76 25c bl & dk pur   .50   .50

WHO, 20th anniversary.

Chandelier and Christian Symbols A77

15c, like 10c, reversed. Brass chandelier from the Reformed Church, Paramaribo.

1968, May 29   Litho.   Perf. 13x12½
354 A77 10c dark blue   .25   .25
355 A77 25c dp yel grn   .50   .50

Reformed Church of Paramaribo, 300th anniv.

Missionary Store, 1768 — A78

Designs: 25c, Main Church and store, Paramaribo, 1868. 30c, C. Kersten & Co., 1968.

1968, June 29   Litho.   Perf. 13x12½
356 A78 10c yel & blk   .30   .30
357 A78 25c lt grnsh bl & blk   .30   .30
358 A78 30c lilac rose & blk   .90   .90
    Nos. 356-358 (3)

200th anniv. of C. Kersten & Co., which is partially owned by the Evangelical Brotherhood Missionary Society.

Joden Savanne Synagogue — A79

Designs: 20c, Map of Joden Savanne and Surinam River. 30c, Gravestone, 1733. The Hebrew inscriptions are quotations from the Bible: 20c, Joshua 24:2; 25c, Isaiah 56:7; 30c, Genesis 31:52.

1968, Aug. 28   Perf. 12½x13
359 A79 20c multi   .35   .35
360 A79 25c multi   .50   .50
361 A79 30c multi   .50   .50
    Nos. 359-361 (3)   1.35   1.35

Founding of the first synagogue in the Western Hemisphere in 1685 in Joden Savanne, Surinam.

Spectacled Caiman A80

20c, Squirrel monkey, vert. 25c, Armadillo.

Perf. 13x12½, 12½x13
1969, Aug. 20   Litho.
362 A80 10c grn & multi   .90   .75
363 A80 20c bl gray & multi   .90   .75
364 A80 25c vio & multi   .90   .75
    Nos. 362-364 (3)   2.70   2.25

Mahatma Gandhi — A81

1969, Oct. 2   Litho.   Perf. 12½x13
365 A81 25c red & blk   1.00   1.00

Mohandas K. Gandhi (1869-1948), leader in India's fight for independence.

ILO Emblem A82

1969, Oct. 29   Litho.   Perf. 13x12½
366 A82 10c brt bl grn & blk   .25   .25
367 A82 25c red & blk   .40   .40

ILO, 50th anniversary.

Queen Juliana and Rising Sun — A82a

1969, Dec. 15   Photo.   Perf. 14x13
368 A82a 25c blue & multi   .50   .50

15th anniv. of the Charter of the Kingdom of the Netherlands. Phosphorescent paper.

"1950-1970" A83

1970, Apr. 3   Litho.   Perf. 13x12½
369 A83 10c brn, grn & org   .25   .25
370 A83 25c emer, dk bl & org   .40   .40

20th anniv. of secondary education in Surinam.

Inauguration of UPU Headquarters, Bern — A84

Design: 25c, UPU Headquarters, sideview and UPU emblem.

1970, May 20   Litho.   Perf. 13x12½
371 A84 10c sky bl & dk pur   .25   .25
372 A84 25c red & blk   .50   .50

"UNO" — A85

1970, June 26   Litho.   Perf. 12½x13
373 A85 10c ocher & yel   .25   .25
374 A85 25c dp bl & ultra   .50   .50

25th anniversary of the United Nations.

Plane over Paramaribo — A86

Designs: 20c, Plane over map of Totness, 25c, Plane over Nieuw-Nickerie.

1970, July 15
375 A86 10c bl, vio bl & gray   .40   .40
376 A86 20c yel, red & gray   .40   .40
377 A86 25c pink, dk red & gray .40   .40
    Nos. 375-377 (3)   1.20   1.20

40th anniv. of domestic airmail service.

Plan of Soccer Field and Ball — A87

Plan of soccer field with ball in different positions.

1970, Oct. 1
378 A87 4c yel, red brn & blk .25 .25
379 A87 10c pale lem, red brn & blk .25 .25
380 A87 15c lt yel grn, red brn & blk .25 .25
381 A87 25c lt grn, red brn & blk .65 .65
Nos. 378-381 (4) 1.40 1.40

50th anniv. of the Soccer Assoc. of Surinam.

Cocoi Heron
A88

Birds in Flight: 20c, Flamingo. 25c, Scarlet macaw.

1971, Feb. 14 Litho. Perf. 13x12½
382 A88 15c gray & multi .75 .75
383 A88 20c ultra & multi .75 .75
384 A88 25c pale grn & multi .75 .75
Nos. 382-384 (3) 2.25 2.25

25th anniversary of regular air service between the Netherlands, Surinam and Netherlands Antilles.

Morse Key — A89

Designs: 20c, Telephone. 25c, Lunar landing module, telescope.

1971, May 17 Photo. Perf. 12½x13
385 A89 15c light green & multi .45 .40
386 A89 20c blue & multi .55 .55
387 A89 25c lilac & multi .75 .60
Nos. 385-387 (3) 1.75 1.55

3rd World Telecommunications Day.

Prince Bernhard, Fokker F27, Boeing 747B — A89a

1971, June 29 Photo. Perf. 13x14
388 A89a 25c multi .60 .50

60th birthday of Prince Bernhard.

Map of Surinam, Population Chart — A90

Design: 30c, Map of Surinam and individual representing population.

1971, July 31 Litho. Perf. 12½x13
389 A90 15c gray bl, blk & ver .25 .25
390 A90 30c ver, gray bl & blk .50 .50

50th anniv. of the first census; introduction of civil registration in Surinam.

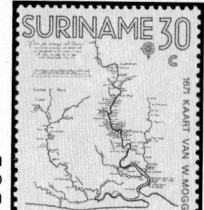

William Mogge's Map of Surinam
A91

1971, Oct. 27 Perf. 11½x11
391 A91 30c dull yel & dk brn .80 .85

300th anniv. of the first map of Surinam.

Map of Albina — A92

August Kappler — A93

20c, View of Albina from Maroni River.

1971, Dec. 13 Perf. 13x12½, 12½x13
392 A92 15c sapphire & blk .55 .55
393 A92 20c brt grn & blk .60 .60
394 A93 25c yel & blk .60 .60
Nos. 392-394 (3) 1.75 1.75

125th anniv. of the founding of Albina by August Kappler (1815-1887).

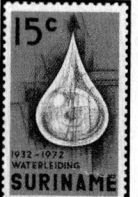

Drop of Water — A94

Design: 30c, Faucet and water tower.

1972, Feb. 2 Perf. 12½x13
395 A94 15c vio & blk .60 .60
396 A94 30c bl & blk .75 .75

Surinam water works, 40th anniversary.

Air Mail Envelope
A95

1972, Aug. 2 Litho. Perf. 13x12½
397 A95 15c red & blue .25 .25
398 A95 30c blue & red .50 .50

Arrival of the 1st airmail in Surinam, carried by Capt. Dutertre from French Guiana, 50th anniv.

Giant Tree — A96

Designs: 20c, Wood transport by air lift. 30c, Hands tending seedling.

1972, Dec. 20 Photo. Perf. 12½x13
399 A96 15c yel & dk brn .25 .25
400 A96 20c bl & dp brn .25 .25
401 A96 30c brt grn & dp brn .95 .95
Nos. 399-401 (3) 1.45 1.45

Surinam Forestry Commission, 25th anniv.

Hindu Woman in Rice Field — A97

25c, J. F. A. Cateau van Rosevelt with map of Surinam, ship "Lalla Rookh." 30c, Symbolic bird, flower, sun, flag, factories.

1973, June 5 Litho. Perf. 13½x14
402 A97 15c purple & yel .45 .45
403 A97 25c maroon & gray .45 .25
404 A97 30c yel & light blue .50 .50
Nos. 402-404 (3) 1.40 1.20

1st immigrants from India, cent.

Queen Juliana, Surinam and House of Orange Colors
A97a

Engr. & Photo.
1973, Sept. 4 Perf. 12½x12
405 A97a 30c sil, blk & org .80 .80

25th anniversary of reign of Queen Juliana.

INTERPOL Emblem — A98

Design: 30c, INTERPOL emblem, Surinam visa handstamp.

1973, Nov. 7 Litho. Perf. 14x14½
406 A98 15c vio bl & multi .25 .25
407 A98 30c lt bl, lil & blk .80 .80

50th anniv. of Intl. Criminal Police Org.

Mailman — A99

15c, Pigeons carrying Letters. 30c, Map of Surinam, plane, ship, train and truck.

1973, Dec. 12 Litho. Perf. 12½x13
408 A99 15c lt yel grn & bl .25 .25
409 A99 25c sal, blk & bl .35 .35
410 A99 30c ver & multi .60 .60
Nos. 408-410 (3) 1.20 1.20

Centenary of stamps of Surinam.

Patient and Blood Transfusion
A100

30c, Cross section of tissue and oscilloscope.

1974, June 1 Litho. Perf. 14½x14
411 A100 15c red brn & multi .25 .25
412 A100 30c lemon & multi .50 .50

75th anniversary of the Medical College.

Crop Dusting
A101

1974, July 17 Litho. Perf. 13½
413 A101 15c shown .25 .25
414 A101 30c Fertilizer plant .50 .50

Foundation for Development of Mechanical Agriculture in Surinam, 25th anniv.

Old Title Page — A102

1974, July 31 Perf. 14x14½
415 A102 15c multicolored .25 .25
416 A102 30c multicolored .50 .50

"Weekly Wednesday Surinam Newspaper," bicent. 1st editor was Beeldsnijder Matroos.

Paramaribo Main Post Office
A103

Design: 30c, Post Office, different view.

1974, Sept. 11 Litho. Perf. 14½x14
417 A103 15c brown & blk .25 .25
418 A103 30c blue & blk .70 .70

Centenary of Universal Postal Union.

Gold Panner
A104

Design: 30c, Modern excavator.

1975, Feb. 5 Litho. Perf. 13x12½
419 A104 15c brown & olive bis .25 .25
420 A104 30c vermilion & maroon .80 .80

Centenary of prospecting policy granting concessions for winning of raw materials.

Symbolic Design
A105

1975, June 25 Litho. Perf. 13x12½
421 A105 15c green & multi .55 .55
422 A105 25c blue & multi .60 .60
423 A105 30c red & multi .60 .60
Nos. 421-423 (3) 1.75 1.75

Cent. of Intl. Meter Convention, Paris, 1875.

Hands Holding Saw — A106

Designs: 50c, Book with notes and letter "a." 75c, Hands holding ball.

1975, Nov. 25   Litho.   *Perf. 13½x14*
424 A106 25c yellow, red & brn .60 .60
425 A106 50c yellow, red & pur 1.40 1.40
426 A106 75c dk bl, org & emer 2.00 2.00
  Nos. 424-426 (3) 4.00 4.00

Independence. Sheets of 10 (5x2) with ornamental margins.

Oncidium Lanceanum A107

Central Bank, Paramaribo A109

Orchids: 2c, Epidendrum stenopetalum. 3c, Brassia lanceana. 4c, Epidendrum ibaguense. 5c, Epidendrum fragrans.

1975-76   Litho.   *Perf. 14½x13½*
427 A107 1c multicolored .35 .35
428 A107 2c multicolored .35 .35
429 A107 3c multicolored .35 .35
430 A107 4c multicolored .35 .35
431 A107 5c multicolored .35 .35
  Perf. 14x13½
436 A109 1g rose lil & blk 1.75 .35
437 A109 1½g brn, dp org & blk 3.00 .35
438 A109 2½g red brn, org red & blk 4.50 .35
439 A109 5g grn, yel grn & blk 8.50 .35
440 A109 10g dk vio bl & blk 19.00 .95
  Nos. 427-431,436-440 (10) 38.50 4.10

Issued: #436-439, Nov. 25, 1975; #427-431, Feb. 18, 1976; #440, May 5, 1976.
For surcharges see Nos. 772-774, 810.

Flag of Surinam — A110

Design: 35c, Coat of Arms.

1976, Mar. 3   *Perf. 14x13½*
445 A110 25c emerald & multi .65 .65
446 A110 35c red orange & multi .85 .85

Sheets of 12 (6x2) with ornamental margins.

Pomacanthus Semiculatus — A111

Fish: 2c, Adioryx diadema. 3c, Pogonoculius zebra. 4c, Balistes vetula. 5c, Myripristis jacobus.

1976, June 2   Litho.   *Perf. 12½x13*
447 A111 1c multicolored .25 .25
448 A111 2c multicolored .25 .25
449 A111 3c multicolored .25 .25
450 A111 4c multicolored .25 .25
451 A111 5c multicolored .25 .25
  Nos. 447-451,C55-C57 (8) 6.75 4.10

See #471-475, 504-508, C72-C74, C85-C87.

19th Century Switchboard and Telephone — A112

35c, Satellite, globe and 1976 telephone.

1976, Aug. 5   Litho.   *Perf. 13½x14*
452 A112 20c yellow & multi .45 .45
453 A112 35c ultra & multi .90 .90

Centenary of first telephone call by Alexander Graham Bell, Mar. 10, 1876.

The Story of Anansi Tori, by A. Baag — A113

Designs: 30c, "Surinam Now" (young people), by R. Chang. 35c, Lamentation, by Nola Hatterman, vert. 50c, Chess Players, by Q. Jan Telting.

Perf. 13½x14, 14x13½
1976, Sept. 29   Photo.
454 A113 20c multicolored .40 .40
455 A113 30c multicolored .70 .60
456 A113 35c multicolored .90 .70
457 A113 50c multicolored 1.25 1.25
  Nos. 454-457 (4) 3.25 2.95

Paintings by Surinam artists.

Franklin's Divided Snake Poster, 1754 — A114

1976, Nov. 10   Litho.   *Perf. 13½x14*
458 A114 20c green & blk .65 .65
459 A114 60c orange & blk 2.10 2.10

American Bicentennial.

Ionopsis Utricularioides A115

Orchids: 30c, Rodiguezia secunda. 35c, Oncidium pusillum. 55c, Sobralia sessilis. 60c, Octomeria surinamensis.

1977, Jan. 19   Litho.   *Perf. 14½x13½*
460 A115 20c vermilion & multi .45 .25
461 A115 30c ultra & multi .65 .25
462 A115 35c magenta & multi .65 .50
463 A115 55c rose lil & multi 1.25 .90
464 A115 60c green & multi 1.25 1.00
  Nos. 460-464 (5) 4.25 2.90

Surinam Costume A116

Various Surinamese women's costumes.

1977, Mar. 2   Litho.   *Perf. 14x13½*
465 A116 10c brt blue & multi .35 .35
466 A116 15c green & multi .35 .35
467 A116 35c violet & multi .45 .45
468 A116 60c orange & multi 1.00 1.00
469 A116 75c ultra & multi 1.25 1.25
470 A116 1g yellow & multi 1.60 1.60
  Nos. 465-470 (6) 5.00 5.00

Fish Type of 1976

Tropical Fish: 1c, Liopropoma carmabi. 2c, Holacanthus ciliaris. 3c, Opistognathus aurifrons. 4c, Anisotremus virginicus. 5c, Gramma loreto.

1977, June 8   Litho.   *Perf. 13x13½*
471 A111 1c multicolored .25 .25
472 A111 2c multicolored .25 .25
473 A111 3c multicolored .25 .25
474 A111 4c multicolored .25 .25
475 A111 5c multicolored .25 .25
  Nos. 471-475,C72-C74 (8) 6.50 5.05

Edison's Phonograph, 1877 — A117

Design: 60c, Modern turntable.

1977, Aug. 24   Litho.   *Perf. 13½x14*
476 A117 20c multicolored .35 .35
477 A117 60c multicolored .85 .85

Invention of the phonograph, cent.

Packet Curacao, 1827 A118

Designs: 15c, Helvoetsluis Harbor and postmark, 1827. 30c, Sea chart and technical details of packet Curacao. 35c, Logbook and compass rose. 60c, Map of Paramaribo harbor and 1852 postmark. 95c, Modern liner Stuyvesant.

1977, Sept. 28   Litho.   *Perf. 14x13½*
478 A118 5c grnsh bl & dk bl .25 .25
479 A118 15c orange & mar .25 .25
480 A118 30c lt brn & blk .25 .25
481 A118 35c olive & blk .25 .25
482 A118 60c lilac & blk .30 .30
483 A118 95c yel grn & dk grn .70 .70
  Nos. 478-483 (6) 2.00 2.00

Regular steamer connection between the Netherlands and Surinam, 150th anniversary.

Passiflora Quadrangularis A119

Flowers: 30c, Centropogon surinamensis. 55c, Gloxinia perennis. 60c, Hydrocleis nymphoides. 75c, Clusia grandiflora.

1978, Feb. 8   Litho.   *Perf. 13x14*
484 A119 20c multicolored .60 .60
485 A119 30c multicolored .60 .60
486 A119 55c multicolored .95 .75

487 A119 60c multicolored 1.10 .95
488 A119 75c multicolored 1.25 1.10
  Nos. 484-488 (5) 4.50 4.00

Javanese Costume — A120

People of Surinam, Costumes: 20c, Forest black. 35c, Chinese. 60c, Creole. 75c, Aborigine Indian. 1g, Hindustani.

1978, Mar. 1   Litho.   *Perf. 13x14*
489 A120 10c multicolored .35 .35
490 A120 20c multicolored .35 .35
491 A120 35c multicolored .35 .35
492 A120 60c multicolored .55 .55
493 A120 75c multicolored .65 .65
494 A120 1g multicolored 1.00 1.00
  Nos. 489-494 (6) 3.25 3.25

Air Post Stamps of 1972 Surcharged

1977, Nov. 15   Litho.   *Perf. 13½x14*
495 AP6 1c on 25c #C44 .25 .25
496 AP6 4c on 15c #C42 .25 .25
497 AP6 4c on 30c #C45 .25 .25
498 AP6 5c on 40c #C47 .35 .25
499 AP6 10c on 75c #C54 .45 .25
  Nos. 495-499 (5) 1.55 1.25

"Luchtpost" obliterated with 2 bars.

Old Municipal Church A121

Johannes King — A122

Designs: 55c, New Municipal Church. 60c, Johannes Raillard.

1978, May 31   Litho.   *Perf. 14x13*
500 A121 10c blue, blk & gray .30 .30
501 A122 20c gray & blk .30 .30
502 A121 55c rose lil & blk .50 .50
503 A122 60c orange & blk .55 .55
  Nos. 500-503 (4) 1.65 1.65

Evangelical Brothers Community Church, Paramaribo, bicentenary.

Fish Type of 1976

Tropical Fish: 1c, Nannacara Anomala. 2c, Leporinus fasciatus. 3c, Pristella riddlei. 4c, Nannostomus beckfordi. 5c, Rivulus agilae.

1978, June 21   *Perf. 12½x13½*
504 A111 1c multicolored .25 .25
505 A111 2c multicolored .25 .25
506 A111 3c multicolored .25 .25
507 A111 4c multicolored .25 .25
508 A111 5c multicolored .25 .25
  Nos. 504-508,C85-C87 (8) 6.10 4.45

Souvenir Sheet

Commewijne River Development — A124

Development: 60c, Map of Surinam and dam. 95c, Planes and world map.

1978, Oct. 18   Litho.   Perf. 14x13
509   Sheet of 3   2.75 2.75
a.   A124 20c multi   .25   .25
b.   A124 60c multi   .35   .35
c.   A124 95c multi   .50   .50

Coconuts — A125

1978-85   Litho.   Perf. 13½x13
510   A125 5c shown   .25   .25
a.   Bklt. pane, 4 #510, 3 #511, 5
      #515 ('80)   2.00
511   A125 10c Oranges   .25   .25
512   A125 15c Papayas   .25   .25
a.   Bklt. pane, 5 #512, 6 #514 +
      label ('79)   2.00
513   A125 20c Bananas   .25   .25
514   A125 25c Soursop   .25   .25
514A A125 30c Cocoa beans
      ('85)   .85   .85
b.   Bklt. pane, 5 #514A, 1 #513 +
      label ('85)   3.25 3.25
515   A125 35c Watermelon   .55   .55
      Nos. 510-515 (7)   2.65 2.65

Wright Brothers' Flyer 1 — A126

Designs: 20c, Daedalus and Icarus, vert. 95c, DC 8. 125c, Concorde.

Perf. 13x14, 14x13
1978, Dec. 13   Litho.
516   A126 20c multicolored   .40   .40
517   A126 60c multicolored   .95   .95
518   A126 95c multicolored   1.40 1.40
519   A126 125c multicolored   1.75 1.75
      Nos. 516-519 (4)   4.50 4.50

75th anniversary of 1st powered flight.

Rodriguezia Candida — A127

Flowers: 20c, Stanhopea grandiflora. 35c, Scuticaria steelei. 60c, Bollea violacea.

1979, Feb. 7   Litho.   Perf. 13x14
520   A127 10c multicolored   .45   .45
521   A127 15c multicolored   .45   .45
522   A127 35c multicolored   .85   .60
523   A127 60c multicolored   1.10   .90
      Nos. 520-523 (4)   2.85 2.40

Javanese Dancer — A128

Dancing Costumes: 10c, Forest Negro. 15c, Chinese. 20c, Creole. 25c, Aborigine Indian. 35c, Hindustani.

1979, Feb. 28
524   A128 5c multicolored   .25   .25
525   A128 10c multicolored   .25   .25
526   A128 15c multicolored   .25   .25
527   A128 20c multicolored   .25   .25
528   A128 25c multicolored   .25   .25
529   A128 35c multicolored   .70   .70
      Nos. 524-529 (6)   1.95 1.95

Equetus Pulchellus A129

Tropical Fish: 2c, Apogon binotatus. 3c, Anisotremus virginicus. 5c, Bodianus rufus. 35c, Microspathodon chrysurus.

1979, May 30   Photo.   Perf. 14x13
530   A129 1c multicolored   .25   .25
531   A129 2c multicolored   .25   .25
532   A129 3c multicolored   .25   .25
533   A129 5c multicolored   .25   .25
534   A129 35c multicolored   .45   .30
      Nos. 530-534,C89-C91 (8)   5.20 3.90

See Nos. 557-561, C92-C94.

Javanese Wooden Head — A130

Folkart: 35c, Head ornament, Indian. 60c, Horse's head, Javanese.

1979, Aug. 29   Litho.   Perf. 14x13
535   A130 20c multicolored   .30   .30
536   A130 35c multicolored   .50   .50
537   A130 60c multicolored   .85   .85
      Nos. 535-537 (3)   1.65 1.65

Sir Rowland Hill — A131

1979, Oct. 3   Litho.   Perf. 13x14
538   A131 1g yellow & olive   1.50 1.00

Sir Rowland Hill (1795-1879), originator of penny postage.

SOS Emblem, House A132

Design: 60c, SOS emblem and buildings.

1979, Oct. 3   Litho.   Perf. 13x14
539   A132 20c multicolored   .35   .35
540   A132 60c multicolored   .80   .80

Intl. Year of the Child; SOS Children's Villages, 30th anniv.

Javanese Girl's Costume — A133

1980, Feb. 6   Photo.   Perf. 13x14
541   A133 10c Javanese girl   .40   .40
542   A133 15c Forest Black boy   .40   .40
543   A133 25c Chinese girl   .40   .40
544   A133 60c Creole girl   .95   .65
545   A133 90c Indian girl   1.10   .95
546   A133 1g Hindustani boy   1.25 1.00
      Nos. 541-546 (6)   4.50 3.80

Rotary Intl., 75th Anniversary A134

20c, Handshake, Rotary emblem, vert.

Perf. 13x14, 14x13
1980, Feb. 23   Litho.
547   A134 20c ultra & yellow   .30   .30
548   A134 60c ultra & yellow   .85   .65

Rowland Hill — A135

1980, May 6   Litho.   Perf. 13x14
549   A135 50c Mailcoach   .50   .50
550   A135 1g shown   1.25 1.25
a.   Souvenir sheet   1.40 1.40
551   A135 2g People mailing let-
      ters   2.75 2.75
      Nos. 549-551 (3)   4.50 4.50

London 1980 Intl. Stamp Exhibition, May 6-14. No. 550a contains No. 550 in changed colors. Blue and black margin shows designs of Nos. 549, 551, London 1980 emblem. (No. 550 in lilac rose and multicolored; stamps of No. 550a in light green and multicolored).

Weight Lifting — A136

1980, June 17
552   A136 20c shown   .25   .25
553   A136 30c Diving   .45   .45
554   A136 50c Gymnast   .55   .55
555   A136 75c Basketball   1.00 1.00
556   A136 150c Running   2.00 2.00
a.   Souvenir sheet of 3, #554-556   3.75 3.75
      Nos. 552-556 (5)   4.25 4.25

22nd Summer Olympic Games, Moscow, July 19-Aug. 3.

Fish Type of 1979

Tropical Fish: 10c, Osteoglossum bicirrhosum. 15c, Colossoma species. 25c, Hemigrammus pulcher. 30c, Petitella georgiae. 45c, Copeina guttata.

1980, Sept. 10   Photo.   Perf. 14x13
557   A129 10c multicolored   .25   .25
558   A129 15c multicolored   .25   .25
559   A129 25c multicolored   .25   .25
560   A129 30c multicolored   .25   .25
561   A129 45c multicolored   .70   .70
      Nos. 557-561,C92-C94 (8)   5.70 4.75

Souvenir Sheet

Open Hands (Reflection) — A137

1980, Nov. 19   Litho.   Perf. 13x14
562   Sheet of 3   5.00 5.00
a.   A137 50c shown   .50   .50
b.   A137 1g Shaking hands (coopera-
      tion)   .90   .90
c.   A137 2g Victory sign   1.75 1.75

5th anniv. of independence.

Passiflora Laurifolia — A138

Designs: Flower paintings by Maria Sibylle Merian (1647-1717) — 30c, Aphelandra pectinata. 60c, Caesalpinia pulcherrima. 75c, Hibiscus mutabilis. 1.25g, Hippeastrum puniceum.

1981, Jan. 14   Litho.   Perf. 13x14
563   A138 20c shown   .30   .30
564   A138 30c multicolored   .40   .40
565   A138 60c multicolored   .90   .90
566   A138 75c multicolored   1.00 1.00
567   A138 1.25g multicolored   1.90 1.90
      Nos. 563-567 (5)   4.50 4.50

Renovation of the Economic Order A139

1981, Feb. 25   Perf. 14x13
568   A139 30c shown   .25   .25
569   A139 60c Educational Order   .70   .70
570   A139 75c Social Order   .80   .80
571   A139 1g Political Order   1.10 1.10
a.   Souvenir sheet of 2, #569, 571   3.00 3.00
      Nos. 568-571 (4)   2.85 2.85

Government renovation.

Miniature Sheet

Youths — A140

1981, Apr. 29   Litho.   Perf. 14x13½
572   A140   Sheet of 2   2.75 2.75
a.   1g shown   .95   .95
b.   1.50g Youths, diff.   .95   .95

Youth and its future. Entire sheet in continuous design.

Souvenir Sheet

No. 424, Exhibition Hall — A141

1981, May 22   Litho.   Perf. 13½x14
573   Sheet of 3   5.00 5.00
a.   A141 50c shown   .55   .60
b.   A141 1g Penny Black   1.10 1.10
c.   A141 2g Austria #5   2.10 2.25

WIPA '81 Intl. Philatelic Exhibition, Vienna, May 22-31.

Leptodactylus Pentadactylus A142

40c, Phyllomedusa hypochondrialis. 60c, Hyla boans.

1981, June 24   Photo.   Perf. 14x13
574   A142 40c multicolored   .75   .35
575   A142 50c shown   .95   .50
576   A142 60c multicolored   1.10   .65
      Nos. 574-576,C95-C97 (6)   9.00 4.80

Child Wearing Earphones A143

100c, Child reading Braille. 150c, Woman in wheelchair.

1981, Sept. 16   Litho.   *Perf. 14x13*
580 A143   50c shown   .60 .60
581 A143   100c multicolored   1.50 1.50
582 A143   150c multicolored   2.40 2.40
  Nos. 580-582 (3)   4.50 4.50
Intl. Year of the Disabled.

Planter's House on Parakreek River — A144

Designs: Illustrations from Voyage to Surinam, by P.I. Benoit — 30c, Sarameca St., Paramaribo. 75c, Negro Hamlet, Paramaribo. 1g, Fish Market, Paramaribo. 1.25g, Blaauwe Berg Cascade.

1981, Oct. 21   Photo.   *Perf. 14x13*
583 A144   20c shown   .25 .25
584 A144   30c multicolored   .40 .40
585 A144   75c multicolored   1.00 1.00
586 A144   1g multicolored   1.40 1.40
  a. Miniature sheet of 1, perf
      13½x13   1.60 1.60
587 A144   1.25g multicolored   2.00 2.00
  Nos. 583-587 (5)   5.05 5.05

Research and Peaceful Uses of Space A145

1982, Jan. 13   Litho.
588 A145   35c Satellites   .60 .60
589 A145   65c Columbia space
      shuttle   1.25 1.25
590 A145   1g Apollo-Soyuz   1.75 1.75
  Nos. 588-590 (3)   3.60 3.60

Caretta Caretta A146

10c, Chelonia mydas. 20c, Dermochelys coriacea. 25c, Eretmochelys imbricata. 35c, Lepidochelys olivacea.

1982, Feb. 17   Photo.   *Perf. 14x13*
591 A146   5c multicolored   .35 .35
592 A146   10c multicolored   .35 .35
593 A146   20c multicolored   .45 .45
594 A146   25c multicolored   .60 .60
595 A146   35c multicolored   .80 .80
  Nos. 591-595,C98-C100 (8)   7.05 5.50

25th Anniv. of Lions Intl. in Surinam A147

1982, May 7   Litho.
596 A147   35c multicolored   .65 .65
597 A147   70c multicolored   1.25 1.25

A148

1982, May 18   Litho.   *Perf. 13x14*
598 A148   35c Helping the sick   1.10 1.10
599 A148   65c Birthplace, map   2.10 2.10
  a. Souvenir sheet   2.00 2.00

Beatification of Father Petrus Donders, May 23.

A149

1982, June 9   Litho.   *Perf. 13x14*
600 A149   50c Stamp designing   .75 .75
601 A149   100c Printing   1.50 1.50
602 A149   150c Collecting   2.25 2.25
  a. Souvenir sheet of 3, #600-602   5.00 5.00
  Nos. 600-602 (3)   4.50 4.50

PHILEXFRANCE '82 Stamp Exhibition, Paris, June 11-21. Nos. 600-602 in continuous design.

TB Bacillus Centenary A150

1982, Sept. 15   Litho.   *Perf. 14x13*
603 A150   35c Text   .40 .40
604 A150   65c Microscope   1.10 1.10
605 A150   150c Bacillus   3.00 3.00
  Nos. 603-605 (3)   4.50 4.50

Marienburg Sugar Co. Centenary A151

1982, Oct. 20
606 A151   35c Mill   .50 .50
607 A151   65c Gathering cane   .90 .90
608 A151   100c Rail transport   1.60 1.60
609 A151   150c Gears   2.50 2.50
  Nos. 606-609 (4)   5.50 5.50

A152

EBG Missionaries, 250th Anniv. in Caribbean: 35c, Municipal Church, horiz. 65c, St. Thomas Monastery, horiz. 150c, Johan Leonhardt Dober (1706-1766).

Perf. 14x13, 13x14
1982, Dec. 13   Litho.
610 A152   35c multicolored   .50 .50
611 A152   65c multicolored   .95 .95
612 A152   150c multicolored   2.50 2.50
  Nos. 610-612 (3)   3.95 3.95

Inga Edulis — A153

Flower Paintings by Maria Sibylle Merian (1647-1717) — 1c, Erythrina fusca, horiz. 2c, Ipomoea acuminata, horiz. 3c, Heliconia psittacorum, horiz. 5c, Ipomoea, horiz. 10c, Herba non denominata, horiz. 15c, Anacardium occidentale, horiz. 25c, Abelmoschus moschatus. 30c, Argemone mexicana. 35c, Costus arabicus. 45c, Muellera frutescens. 65c, Punica granatum.

1983, Jan. 12
613 A153   1c multicolored   .25 .25
614 A153   2c multicolored   .25 .25
615 A153   3c multicolored   .25 .25
616 A153   5c multicolored   .25 .25
617 A153   10c multicolored   .25 .25
618 A153   15c multicolored   .45 .45

619 A153   20c shown   .55 .55
620 A153   25c multicolored   .80 .80
621 A153   30c multicolored   1.00 1.00
622 A153   35c multicolored   1.10 1.10
623 A153   45c multicolored   1.25 1.25
624 A153   65c multicolored   2.10 2.10
  Nos. 613-624 (12)   8.50 8.50

Scouting Year — A154

1983, Feb. 22   Litho.   *Perf. 13x14*
625 A154   40c Anniv. emblem   1.00 1.00
626 A154   65c Baden-Powell   1.50 1.50
627 A154   70c Tent, campfire   1.60 1.60
628 A154   80c Ax in log   1.75 1.75
  Nos. 625-628 (4)   5.85 5.85

500th Birth Anniv. of Raphael — A155

Crayon sketches.

1983, Apr. 13   Photo.
629 A155   5c multicolored   .30 .30
630 A155   10c multicolored   .30 .30
631 A155   40c multicolored   .80 .80
632 A155   65c multicolored   1.25 1.25
633 A155   70c multicolored   1.25 1.25
634 A155   80c multicolored   1.50 1.50
  Nos. 629-634 (6)   5.40 5.40

1982 Coins and Banknotes A156

1983, June 1   Litho.   *Perf. 14x13*
635 A156   5c 1-cent coin   .25 .25
636 A156   10c 5-cent coin   .25 .25
637 A156   40c 10-cent coin   .65 .65
638 A156   65c 25-cent coin   1.10 1.10
639 A156   70c 1g note   1.25 1.25
640 A156   80c 2.50g note   1.50 1.50
  Nos. 635-640 (6)   5.00 5.00

For surcharge & overprints see Nos. 751, J59-J60.

25th Anniv. of Dept. of Construction — A157

1983, June 15   Litho.   *Perf. 13x14*
641 A157   25c Map   .55 .55
642 A157   50c Map, bulldozers   1.25 1.25

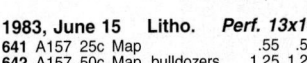

Local Butterflies A158

Drawings by Maria Sibylle Merian (1647-1717) — 1c, Papile anchisiades esper, vert. 2c, Urania leilus, vert. 3c, Morpho deidamia, vert. 5c, Thysania aguippina, vert. 10c, Morpho sp., vert. 15c, Metamorpha dido, vert. 20c, Morpho menelaus. 25c, Manduca rustica. 30c, Rothschildia sp. 35c, Catopsilia ebule. 45c, Pailio androgeos. 65c, Eumorpha vitis.

Perf. 13x14, 14x13
1983, Sept. 14   Litho.
643 A158   1c multicolored   .25 .25
644 A158   2c multicolored   .25 .25
645 A158   3c multicolored   .25 .25
646 A158   5c multicolored   .25 .25
647 A158   10c multicolored   .30 .25
648 A158   15c multicolored   .45 .30
649 A158   20c multicolored   .60 .40
650 A158   25c multicolored   1.00 .65
651 A158   30c multicolored   1.25 .65
652 A158   35c multicolored   1.50 .95
653 A158   45c multicolored   1.90 1.25
654 A148   65c multicolored   3.00 1.90
  Nos. 643-654 (12)   11.00 7.35

Manned Ballooning, 200th Anniv. — A159

Designs: 5c, 1783, sheep, cock and duck. 10c, first manned flight, d'Arlandes and Pilatre de Rozier. 40c, first hydrogen balloon, Jacques Charles. 65c, 1870, Paris flight, minister Gambetta. 70c, Double Eagle II, transatlantic flight. 80c, Intl. Balloon Festival, Albuquerque.

1983, Oct. 19   Litho.   *Perf. 13x14*
655 A159   5c multicolored   .25 .25
656 A159   10c multicolored   .25 .25
657 A159   40c multicolored   .95 .95
658 A159   65c multicolored   1.40 1.40
659 A159   70c multicolored   1.50 1.50
660 A159   80c multicolored   2.00 2.00
  Nos. 655-660 (6)   6.35 6.35

Martin Luther, 500th Birth Anniv. — A160

1983, Dec. 7   Litho.
661 A160   25c Portrait   .50 .50
662 A160   50c Engraving   1.25 1.10

Local Flowers — A161

5c, Catasetum discolor. 10c, Menadenium labiosum. 40c, Comparettia falcata. 50c, Rodriquezia decora. 70c, Oncidium papilio. 75c, Epidendrum porpax.

1984, Jan. 11   Litho.
663 A161   5c multicolored   .25 .25
664 A161   10c multicolored   .25 .25
665 A161   40c multicolored   .95 .95
666 A161   50c multicolored   1.40 1.25
667 A161   70c multicolored   1.60 1.40
668 A161   75c multicolored   1.90 1.50
  Nos. 663-668 (6)   6.35 5.60

Local Seashells — A162

40c, Arca zebra. 65c, Trachycardium egmontianum. 70c, Tellina radiata. 80c, Vermicularia knorrii

1984, Feb. 22 — Litho.

669	A162	40c multicolored	.95 .65
670	A162	65c multicolored	1.60 1.10
671	A162	70c multicolored	1.60 1.10
672	A162	80c multicolored	2.00 1.25
	Nos. 669-672 (4)		6.15 4.10

Intl. Civil Aviation Org., 40th Anniv. A163

35c, Sea plane. 65c, Surinam Airways jet.

1984, May 16 — Litho. Perf. 14x13

673	A163	35c multicolored	.65 .65
674	A163	65c multicolored	1.50 1.50

A164

Greek Art and Artifacts: Ancient Games.

1984, June 13 — Perf. 13x14

675	A164	2c Running	.25 .25
676	A164	3c Javelin, discus, long jump	.25 .25
677	A164	5c Massage	.25 .25
678	A164	10c Ointment massage	.25 .25
679	A164	15c Wrestling	.25 .25
680	A164	20c Boxing	.25 .25
681	A164	30c Horse racing	.75 .75
682	A164	35c Chariot racing	.85 .85
683	A164	45c Temple of Olympia	1.00 1.00
684	A164	50c Crypt entrance	1.10 1.10
685	A164	65c Olympia Stadium	1.90 1.90
686	A164	75c Zeus (bust)	1.90 1.90
a.	Min. sheet of 3, #675, 682, 686		3.25 3.25
	Nos. 675-686 (12)		9.00 9.00

1984 Summer Olympics.
For overprint see No. 843.

A165

1984, Sept. 18 — Litho. Perf. 13x14

687	A165	50c Ball, net	1.25 1.10
688	A165	90c Ball in net	2.00 1.90

Intl. Council of Military Sports basketball championship.

World Chess Championship, Moscow — A166

1984, Oct. 10 — Litho. Perf. 14x13

689	A166	10c Red Square	.40 .40
690	A166	15c Knight, king, pawn	.40 .40
691	A166	30c Kasparov	.70 .70
692	A166	50c Board	1.25 1.25
693	A166	75c Karpov	1.90 1.90
a.	Souv. sheet of 3 (30c, 50c, 75c), perf 13½x13		6.00 6.00
694	A166	90c Game	2.25 2.25
	Nos. 689-694 (6)		6.90 6.90

For overprints see Nos. 742, 796.

World Food Day, Oct. 16 — A167

1984, Oct. 10

695	A167	50c Children receiving milk	1.25 1.25
696	A167	90c Food	2.00 2.00

A168

Cacti.

1985, Jan. 9 — Litho. Perf. 13x14

697	A168	5c Leaf	.25 .25
698	A168	10c Melon	.25 .25
699	A168	30c Pillar	.95 .95
700	A168	50c Fig	1.40 1.40
701	A168	75c Nightqueen	2.25 2.25
702	A168	90c Segment	2.40 2.40
	Nos. 697-702 (6)		7.50 7.50

A169

Independence, 5th Anniv.: 5c, Star, red stripe from national flag. 30c, Unified labor. 50c, Perpetual flowering plant. 75c, Growth of agriculture. 90c, Peace dove and plant.

1985, Feb. 22

703	A169	5c multicolored	.25 .25
704	A169	30c multicolored	.60 .60
705	A169	50c multicolored	1.00 1.00
a.	Min. sheet of 3, 2 #703, #705		3.00
706	A169	75c multicolored	1.60 1.60
707	A169	90c multicolored	2.10 2.10
	Nos. 703-707 (5)		5.55 5.55

Chamber of Commerce and Industry, 75th Anniv. A170

1985, Apr. 17 — Litho. Perf. 14x13

708	A170	50c Chamber emblem	.75 .75
709	A170	90c Chamber, factories	1.75 1.75

UN Emblem, Natl. Coat of Arms — A171

1985, Apr. 29 — Litho. Perf. 13x14

710	A171	50c multicolored	.85 .85
711	A171	90c multicolored	1.90 1.90

UN, 40th anniv.

Trains — A172

No. 712, Surinam No. 192. No. 713, Monaco, No. J50. No. 714, Steam locomotive "Dam". No. 715, Diesel locomotive. No. 716, Steam locomotive "No. 3737". No. 717, Netherlands locomotive "IC III". No. 718, Stephenson's locomotive "Rocket". No. 719, French Railways high-speed TGV. No. 720, Stephenson's locomotive "Adler". No. 721, French Railways commuter train. No. 722, Locomotive "General". No. 723, Japanese bullet train "Shinkansen".

1985, June 5 — Litho. Perf. 13½

712	A172	5c multicolored	.25 .25
713	A172	5c multicolored	.25 .25
a.	Pair, #712-713		.40 .40
714	A172	10c multicolored	.25 .25
715	A172	10c multicolored	.25 .25
a.	Pair, #714-715		.60 .60
716	A172	20c multicolored	.50 .50
717	A172	20c multicolored	.50 .50
a.	Pair, #716-717		1.00 1.00
718	A172	30c multicolored	.85 .85
719	A172	30c multicolored	.85 .85
a.	Pair, #716-717		1.60 1.60
720	A172	50c multicolored	1.25 1.25
721	A172	50c multicolored	1.25 1.25
a.	Pair, #720-721		2.75 2.75
722	A172	75c multicolored	2.00 2.00
723	A172	75c multicolored	2.00 2.00
a.	Pair, #722-723		4.00 4.00
	Nos. 712-723 (12)		10.20 10.20

For surcharges see Nos. 749-750, 808-809, 928-929.

Birds — A173

10c, Toucan. 1g, American purple fowl. 1.50g, Tiger bird. 2.50g, Red ibis. 5g, Guyana red cockerel. 10g, Harpy eagle. 15g, Parrot. 25g, Owl. 1300g, Rose lepelaar. 1780g, Toucan. 2225g, Hummingbird. 2995g, Hoatzin.

1985-95 — Litho. Perf. 14x13

724	A173	10c multi	.25 .25
725	A173	1g multi	1.75 1.75
a.	Miniature sheet of 1		6.00 6.00
726	A173	1.50g multi	3.25 3.25
727	A173	2.50g multi	5.00 5.00
728	A173	5g multi	10.00 10.00
729	A173	10g multi	16.00 16.00
730	A173	15g multi	22.50 22.50
731	A173	25g multi	35.00 35.00
732	A173	1300g multi	37.50 37.50
733	A173	1780g multi	9.25 9.25
734	A173	2225g multi	11.50 11.50
735	A173	2995g multi	16.00 16.00
	Nos. 724-735 (12)		168.00 168.00

Nos. 724, 730 inscribed 1990.
Issued: 1g, 1.50g, 2.50g, 8/21; #725a, 5g, 1/2/86; 10g, 10/1/86; 10c, 15g, 1/30/91; 25g, 1/20/93; 1300g, 3/31/94; 1780g, 2225g, 2995g, 9/6/95.
See #1040, 1053-1055, 1108-1111, 1136-1138, 1160, 1194-1195, 1220-1221. For surcharges & overprint see #963-964, J63.

Mailboxes — A174

1985, Oct. 2 — Litho. Perf. 13x14

736	A174	15c Germany, 1900	.35 .35
737	A174	30c France, 1900	.55 .55
738	A174	50c England, 1932	.95 .95
739	A174	90c Netherlands, 1850	1.90 1.90
	Nos. 736-739 (4)		3.75 3.75

Natl. Independence, 10th Anniv. — A175

1985, Nov. 22

740	A175	50c Agriculture	1.25 1.25
741	A175	90c Industry	2.00 2.00
a.	Miniature sheet of 2, #740-741		3.25 3.25

No. 691 Ovptd. in Red

1985, Nov. 22 — Litho. Perf. 14x13

742	A166	30c multi	3.25 3.25

Orchids, World Wildlife Fund — A177

5c, Epidendrum ciliare. 15c, Cycnoches chlorochilon. 30c, Epidendrum anceps. 50c, Epidendrum vespa.

1986, Feb. 19 — Litho. Perf. 14x13

743	A177	5c multicolored	3.00 3.00
744	A177	15c multicolored	7.50 7.50
745	A177	30c multicolored	15.00 15.00
746	A177	50c multicolored	24.00 24.00
	Nos. 743-746 (4)		49.50 49.50

Halley's Comet A178

Designs: 50c, The Bayeux Tapestry, c. 1092, France. 110c, Halley's Comet.

1986, Mar. 5 — Litho. Perf. 14x13

747	A178	50c multi	1.00 1.00
748	A178	110c multi	2.00 2.00

Nos. 720-721 Surcharged in Red

1986, May 28 — Litho. Perf. 13½

749	A172	15c on 50c #720	2.50 2.50
750	A172	15c on 50c #721	2.50 2.50
a.	Pair, #749-750		6.00 6.00

No. 639 Surcharged

1986, June 25 — Litho. Perf. 14x13

751	A156	30c on 70c multi	2.75 2.75

Finance Building, Paramaribo, 150th anniv.

Surinam Shipping Co., 50th Anniv. A179

50c, Emblem. 110c, Freighter Saramacca.

1986, Sept. 1 — Litho. Perf. 14x13

752	A179	50c multicolored	.70 .70
753	A179	110c multicolored	2.00 2.00

Monkeys A180

1987, Jan. 7 — Litho.

755	A180	35c Alouatta	.60 .60
756	A180	60c Aotus	1.00 1.00
757	A180	110c Saimiri	2.00 2.00
758	A180	120c Cacajao	2.25 2.25
	Nos. 755-758 (4)		5.85 5.85

Esperanto, Cent. — A181

1987, Feb. 4 Litho.
759 A181 60c shown 1.00 1.00
760 A181 110 World map, doves 1.90 1.90
761 A181 120c L.L. Zamenhof 2.10 2.10
Nos. 759-761 (3) 5.00 5.00

10th Pan-American Games, Indianapolis, July 23 — A182

1987, June 3 Litho. Perf. 13x14
763 A182 90c Soccer 1.50 1.50
764 A182 110c Swimming 1.75 1.75
765 A182 150c Basketball 2.25 2.25
Nos. 763-765 (3) 5.50 5.50

Forestry Commission, 40th Anniv. — A183

1987, July 21 Litho. Perf. 13x14
766 A183 90c Emblem 1.50 1.50
767 A183 120c Logging 2.00 2.00
768 A183 150c Parrot in virgin forest 2.75 2.75
Nos. 766-768 (3) 6.25 6.25

Intl. Year of Shelter for the Homeless A184

1987, Sept. 2 Litho. Perf. 14x13
769 A184 90c Distressed boy, encampment 1.40 1.40
770 A184 120c Man, ghetto 2.10 2.10

Founders Catherine and William Booth — A185

1987, Sept. 2 Perf. 14x13
771 A185 150c multi 2.25 2.25
Salvation Army in the Caribbean, cent.

Nos. 436-438 Surcharged

1986, Dec. 29 Litho. Perf. 13½x13
772 A109 35c on 1g 2.75 2.75
773 A109 50c on 1.50g 4.25 4.25
774 A109 60c on 2.50g 5.50 5.50
Nos. 772-774 (3) 12.50 12.50

Fruits — A186

1987, Oct. 14 Litho. Perf. 13x13½
775 A186 10c Bananas .25 .25
776 A186 15c Cacao .25 .25
777 A186 20c Pineapple .25 .25
778 A186 25c Papaya .50 .50
779 A186 35c Oranges .75 .75
Nos. 775-779 (5) 2.00 2.00

Aircraft and Aircraft on Stamps — A187

1987, Oct. 14 Litho. Perf. 13½
784 A187 25c Degen, 1808 .25 .25
785 A187 25c Ultra Light .25 .25
a. Pair, #784-785 .90 .90
786 A187 35c J.C.H. El-lehammer, 1906 .55 .55
787 A187 35c Concorde jet .55 .55
a. Pair, #786-787 1.25 1.25
788 A187 60c Fokker F7, 1924 .90 .90
789 A187 60c Fokker F28 jet .90 .90
a. Pair, #788-789 2.10 2.10
790 A187 90c Spin Fokker, 1910 1.40 1.40
791 A187 90c DC-10 1.40 1.40
a. Pair, #790-791 3.00 3.00
792 A187 110c Orion, 1932 1.75 1.75
793 A187 110c Boeing 747 1.75 1.75
a. Pair, #792-793 3.75 3.75
794 A187 120c No. 346 1.90 1.90
795 A187 120c No. 518 1.90 1.90
a. Pair, #794-795 4.00 4.00
Nos. 784-795 (12) 13.50 13.50

No. 693a Overprinted "3e match sevilla 1987" on Stamps in 3 or 4 Lines and with Bar and "sevilla 1987" in Sheet Margin

1987, Nov. 2 Litho. Perf. 13½x13
Souvenir Sheet
796 Sheet of 3 32.50
a. A166 30c Kasparov 3.50
b. A166 50c Board 6.00
c. A166 75c Karpov 9.00

Alligators and Crocodiles A188

50c, Gavialis gangeticus. 60c, Crocodylus niloticus. 90c, Melanosuchus niger. 110c, Mississippi alligator.

1988, Jan. 20 Litho. Perf. 14x13
797 A188 50c multicolored .80 .80
798 A188 60c multicolored 1.10 1.10
799 A188 90c multicolored 1.50 1.50
800 A188 110c multicolored 2.10 2.10
Nos. 797-800 (4) 5.50 5.50

Traditional Wedding Costumes — A189

1988, Feb. 24 Litho. Perf. 13x14
801 A189 35c Javanese .50 .50
802 A189 60c Bushman .95 .95
803 A189 80c Chinese 1.10 1.10
804 A189 110c Creole 1.60 1.60
805 A189 120c Indian 1.75 1.75
806 A189 130c Hindustan 2.10 2.10
Nos. 801-806 (6) 8.00 8.00

Nos. 722-723 and 440 Surcharged in Black or Silver

No. 808

No. 810

Perf. 13½x13, 13½
1988, Mar. 23 Litho.
808 A172 60c on 75c #722 5.50
809 A172 60c on 75c #723 5.50
a. Pair, #808-809 11.00
810 A109 125c on 10g #440 (S) 12.00
Nos. 808-810 (3) 23.00

1988 Summer Olympics, Seoul — A190

1988, May 4 Litho. Perf. 13x14
812 A190 90c Relay 1.10 1.10
813 A190 110c Soccer 1.75 1.75
814 A190 120c Pole vault 1.90 1.90
a. Souvenir sheet of 3, #812-814 5.00 5.00
815 A190 250c Women's tennis 4.25 4.25
Nos. 812-815 (4) 9.00 9.00

Abolition of Slavery, 125th Anniv. — A191

50c, Abaisa Monument. 110c, Kwakoe Monument. 120c, Home of Anton de Kom.

1988, June 29 Litho.
816 A191 50c multicolored .65 .65
817 A191 110c multicolored 1.75 1.75
818 A191 120c multicolored 2.10 2.10
Nos. 816-818 (3) 4.50 4.50

See Netherlands Antilles Nos. 597-598.

Intl. Fund for Agricultural Development (IFAD), 10th Anniv. A192

1988, Sept. 21 Perf. 14x13
819 A192 105c Crop harvest 1.75 1.75
820 A192 110c Net fishing 1.75 1.75
821 A192 125c Agricultural research 2.25 2.25
Nos. 819-821 (3) 5.75 5.75

FILACEPT '88, The Netherlands, Oct. 18-23 — A193

1988, Oct. 18 Litho. Perf. 13x14
822 A193 120c Egypt #49 1.50 1.50
823 A193 150c Netherlands #334 2.25 2.25
824 A193 250c Surinam #238 3.50 3.50
Nos. 822-824 (3) 7.25 7.25

Souvenir Sheet
Same Types, Colors Changed (120c, 150c)
825 Sheet of 3 10.00 10.00
a. A193 120c Egypt Type A23 (4m green) 1.10 1.10
b. A193 150c Netherlands Type A81 (10c red brown) 1.40 1.40
c. A193 250c Surinam No. 239 2.40 2.40

Stylized Butterfly Stroke A194

1988, Nov. 1 Litho. Perf. 14x13
826 A194 110c multi 1.60 1.60
Anthony Nesty, swimmer and 1st Olympic gold medalist from Surinam.

Otters A195

1989, Jan. 18 Litho. Perf. 14x13
827 A195 10c Otter .25 .25
828 A195 20c Two on land .25 .25
829 A195 25c Two crossing log .50 .50
830 A195 30c Fishing .60 .60
Nos. 827-830,C107 (5) 4.60 4.60

Classic and Modern Automobiles — A196

No. 831, 1930 Mercedes Tourenwagen. No. 832, 1985 Mercedes-Benz 300E. No. 833, 1897 Daimler. No. 834, 1986 Jaguar Sovereign. No. 835, 1898 Renault Voiturette. No. 836, 1989 Renault 25TX. No. 837, 1927 Volvo Jacob. No. 838, 1989 Volvo 440. No. 839, Left half of Monaco #484. No. 840, Right half of Monaco #484. No. 841, 1936 Toyota AA. No. 842, 1988 Toyota Corolla sedan.

1989, June 7 Litho. Perf. 13½
831 A196 25c multi .60 .60
832 A196 25c multi .60 .60
a. Pair, #831-832 1.00 1.00
833 A196 60c multi 1.25 1.25
834 A196 60c multi 1.25 1.25
a. Pair, #833-834 2.50 2.50
835 A196 90c multi 2.00 2.00
836 A196 90c multi 2.00 2.00
a. Pair, #835-836 3.75 3.75
837 A196 105c multi 2.25 2.25
838 A196 105c multi 2.25 2.25
a. Pair, #837-838 4.50 4.50
839 A196 110c multi 2.40 2.40
840 A196 110c multi 2.40 2.40
a. Pair, #839-840 5.00 5.00
841 A196 120c multi 2.75 2.75
842 A196 120c multi 2.75 2.75
a. Pair, #841-842 5.75 5.75
Nos. 831-842 (12) 22.50 22.50

No. 686a Ovptd. "PHILEXFRANCE 7t/m 17 juli 1989" on Margin, with Exhibition Emblem on Stamps in Gold

1989, July 7 Litho. Perf. 13x14
Miniature Sheet
843 Sheet of 3 6.25 6.25
a. A164 2c on No. 675 .25 .25
b. A164 35c on No. 682 .40 .40
c. A164 75c on No. 686 .95 .95
PHILEXFRANCE '89.

Photography, 150th Anniv. A197

1989, Sept. 6 Litho. *Perf. 14x13*

844 A197 60c Joseph Niepce 1.00 1.00
845 A197 110c Daguerreotype camera 1.90 1.90
846 A197 120c Louis Daguerre 2.10 2.10
Nos. 844-846 (3) 5.00 5.00

America Issue — A198

UPAE emblem and pre-Columbian amulets — 60c, Amazon or Jade Stones. 110c, Bisque fertility statue.

1989, Oct. 12 Litho. *Perf. 13x14*

847 A198 60c multicolored 10.00 10.00
848 A198 110c multicolored 10.00 10.00

The White House, Washington, DC, and Stamps on Stamps A199

Perf. 13x14, 14x13

1989, Nov. 17 Litho.

849 A199 110c No. 445, vert. 2.00 2.00
850 A199 150c US No. 990 2.50 2.50
851 A199 250c No. 459 4.00 4.00
a. Souv. sheet, #849-851, perf 13x14, 14 8.75 8.75
Nos. 849-851 (3) 8.50 8.50

World Stamp Expo '89 and 20th UPU Congress, Washington, DC.

UNESCO Intl. Literacy Year — A200

1990, Jan. 19 Photo. *Perf. 13x14*

852 A200 60c shown 1.10 1.10
853 A200 110c Emblems 2.10 2.10
854 A200 120c Emblems, youth reading 2.25 2.25
Nos. 852-854 (3) 5.45 5.45

Arya Dewaker Temple, 60th Anniv. — A201

1990, Feb. 14 Litho.

855 A201 60c dk red brn, blk & red 1.10 1.10
856 A201 110c vio blue & blk 2.10 2.10
857 A201 200c emer grn & blk 3.50 3.50
Nos. 855-857 (3) 6.70 6.70

A202

110c, Surinam #C1. 200c, Great Britain #1. 250c, Great Britain #208.

1990, May 4

858 A202 110c multicolored 1.75 1.75
859 A202 200c multicolored 3.00 3.00
860 A202 250c multicolored 4.25 4.25
a. Souvenir sheet of 3, #858-860 11.00 11.00
Nos. 858-860 (3) 9.00 9.00

Penny Black, 150th anniv. Stamps World London '90.

A203

60c, Couple carrying baskets. 110c, Woman carrying bundle. 120c, Man carrying baskets.

1990, Aug. 9

861 A203 60c multicolored 1.00 1.00
862 A203 110c multicolored 1.90 1.90
863 A203 120c multicolored 2.10 2.10
Nos. 861-863 (3) 5.00 5.00

Javanese Immigration, cent.

Flowers — A204

No. 864, Punica granatum. No. 865, Passiflora laurifolia. No. 866, Hippeastrum puniceum. No. 867, Ipomaea batatas. No. 868, Hibiscus syriacus. No. 869, Jasminum officinale. No. 870, Musa serapionis. No. 871, Hibiscus mutabilis. No. 872, Plumiria rubra. No. 873, Hibiscus diversifolius. No. 874, Bixa orellana. Nol. 875, Ceasalpinia pulcherima.

1990, Sept. 5 *Perf. 13½*

864 A204 25c multicolored .45 .45
865 A204 25c multicolored .45 .45
a. Pair, #864-865 .80 .80
866 A204 35c multicolored .55 .55
867 A204 35c multicolored .55 .55
a. Pair, #866-867 1.10 1.10
868 A204 60c multicolored 1.00 1.00
869 A204 60c multicolored 1.00 1.00
a. Pair, #868-869 2.10 2.10
870 A204 105c multicolored 1.75 1.75
871 A204 105c multicolored 1.75 1.75
a. Pair, #870-871 3.50 3.50
872 A204 110c multicolored 1.75 1.75
873 A204 110c multicolored 1.75 1.75
a. Pair, #872-873 3.50 3.50
874 A204 120c multicolored 2.00 2.00
875 A204 120c multicolored 2.00 2.00
a. Pair, #874-875 4.00 4.00
Nos. 864-875 (12) 15.00 15.00

America Issue — A205

1990, Oct. 10 Litho. *Perf. 14x13*

876 A205 60c bluish grn & blk 4.75 4.75
877 A205 110c brn & blk 8.75 8.75

Organization of American States, Cent. — A206

1990, Oct. 10

878 A206 110c multicolored 1.60 1.60

Independence, 15th Anniv. — A207

1990, Nov. 21 Litho. *Perf. 13x14*

879 A207 10c shown .25 .25
880 A207 60c Passion flower .95 .95
881 A207 110c Dove with olive branch 2.10 2.10
Nos. 879-881 (3) 3.30 3.30

Architecture A208

Buildings: 35c, Waterfront warehouse. 60c, Upper class residence. 75c, Labor inspection building. 105c, Plantation supervisor's residence. 110c, Ministry of Labor. 200c, Small residences.

1991, May 15 Litho. *Perf. 14x13*

882 A208 35c multicolored .80 .80
883 A208 60c multicolored 1.10 1.10
884 A208 75c multicolored 1.50 1.50
885 A208 105c multicolored 2.10 2.10
886 A208 110c multicolored 2.25 2.25
887 A208 200c multicolored 4.00 4.00
Nos. 882-887 (6) 11.75 11.75

Nos. 714-715, 720-721 Surcharged

Methods and Perfs as Before

1991

888 A172 2c on 10c #714 1.00 1.00
889 A172 2c on 10c #715 1.00 1.00
a. Pair, #888-889 2.25 2.25
890 A172 3c on 50c #720 1.00 1.00
891 A172 3c on 50c #721 1.00 1.00
a. Pair, #890-891 2.25 2.25
Nos. 888-891 (4) 4.00 4.00

Puma Concolor A209

Various pictures of pumas.

Perf. 13x14, 14x13

1991, Sept. 12 Litho.

892 A209 10c multi, vert. .25 .25
893 A209 20c multi, vert. .25 .25
894 A209 25c multi, vert. .40 .40
895 A209 30c multi, vert. .50 .50
896 A209 125c multi 1.90 1.90
897 A209 500c multi 6.75 6.75
Nos. 892-897 (6) 10.05 10.05

Nos. 896-897 are airmail.

Discovery of America, 500th Anniv. (in 1991) — A210

Diagram showing Columbus' route: 60c, Western Atlantic and Caribbean Sea. 110c, Eastern Atlantic.

1991, Oct. 11 *Perf. 13x14*

898 60c lt bl, red & blk 2.50 2.50
899 110c lt bl, red & blk 5.50 5.50
a. A210 Pair, #898-899 11.00 11.00

UPAEP. No. 899a has continous design.

Snakes — A211

#900, Corallus enydris. #901, Corallus caninus. #902, Lachesis muta. #903, Boa constrictor. #904, Micrurus surinamensis. #905, Crotalus durissus. #906, Eunectes murinus. #907, Clelia cloelia. #908, Epicrates cenchris. #909, Chironius carinatus. #910, Oxybelis argentieus. #911, Spilotes pullatus.

1991, Nov. 14 *Perf. 13½*

900 A211 25c multicolored .30 .30
901 A211 25c multicolored .30 .30
a. Pair, #900-901 .80 .80
902 A211 35c multicolored .55 .55
903 A211 35c multicolored .55 .55
a. Pair, #902-903 1.10 1.10
904 A211 60c multicolored .90 .90
905 A211 60c multicolored .90 .90
a. Pair, #904-905 2.10 2.10
906 A211 75c multicolored 1.25 1.25
907 A211 75c multicolored 1.25 1.25
a. Pair, #906-907 2.50 2.50
908 A211 110c multicolored 1.75 1.75
909 A211 110c multicolored 1.75 1.75
a. Pair, #908-909 3.75 3.75
910 A211 200c multicolored 3.25 3.25
911 A211 200c multicolored 3.25 3.25
a. Pair, #910-911 6.75 6.75
Nos. 900-911 (12) 16.00 16.00

Orchids — A212

Designs: 50c, Cycnoches haagii. 60c, Lycaste cristata. 75c, Galeandra dives, horiz. 125c, Vanilla mexicana. 150c, Cyrtopodium glutiniferum. 250c, Gongora quinquenervis.

1992, Feb. 12 *Perf. 13x14, 14x13*

912 A212 50c multicolored .65 .65
913 A212 60c multicolored .85 .85
914 A212 75c multicolored 1.00 1.00
915 A212 125c multicolored 2.00 2.00
916 A212 150c multicolored 2.50 2.50
917 A212 250c multicolored 4.00 4.00
Nos. 912-917 (6) 11.00 11.00

Souvenir Sheet

A213

Designs: a, 75c, #847. b, 125c, #848. c, 150c, #898. d. 250c, #899.

1992, Mar. 24   Litho.   Perf. 13x13½
918 A213 Sheet of 4, #a.-d.   11.00 11.00
Granada '92, Intl. Philatelic Exibition.

1992 Summer Olympics, Barcelona — A214

1992, Apr. 8   Litho.   Perf. 13x14
919 A214 35c Basketball   .55   .55
920 A214 60c Volleyball   .95   .95
921 A214 75c Running   1.10   1.10
922 A214 125c Soccer   1.90   1.90
923 A214 150c Cycling   2.25   2.25
924 A214 250c Swimming   4.25   4.25
  a.   Souvenir sheet of 3, #921, 922, 924, perf 13x13½   7.50   7.50
  Nos. 919-924 (6)   11.00 11.00

YWCA, 50th Anniv. A215

1992, June 12   Litho.   Perf. 14x13
925 A215 60c red brown & multi 1.00 1.00
926 A215 250c purple & multi   4.00 4.00

Expulsion of Jews from Spain, 500th Anniv. A216

1992, Aug. 17
927 A216 250c multicolored   4.00 4.00

Nos. 712-713 Surcharged

1992, Aug. 17   Perf. 13½
928 A172 1c on 5c multi   1.75 1.75
929 A172 1c on 5c multi   1.75 1.75
  a.   Pair, #928-929   4.25 4.25

A217

1992, Sept. 15   Perf. 13x14
930 A217 60c green & multi   1.00 1.00
931 A217 250c pink & multi   4.00 4.00
Jan E. Matzeliger (1852-1889), inventor of shoe lasting machine.

A218

1992, Oct. 12
932 A218 60c blue grn & multi   1.50 1.50
933 A218 250c dp org & multi   6.00 6.00
Discovery of America, 500th anniv.

Christmas — A219

Various abstract designs.

1992, Nov. 15
934 A219 10c multicolored   .50   .50
935 A219 60c multicolored   1.00   1.00
936 A219 250c multicolored   3.50   3.50
937 A219 400c multicolored   6.00   6.00
  Nos. 934-937 (4)   11.00 11.00

Medicinal Plants A220

Designs: 50c, Costus arabicus, vert. 75c, Quassia amara, vert. 125c, Combretum rotundifolium. 500c, Bixa orellana.

Perf. 13x14, 14x13
1993, Feb. 3   Litho.
938 A220 50c multicolored   .85   .85
939 A220 75c multicolored   1.40   1.40
940 A220 125c multicolored   2.25   2.25
941 A220 500c multicolored   9.00   9.00
  Nos. 938-941 (4)   13.50 13.50

Beetles and Grasshoppers — A221

Designs: No. 942, Macrodontia cervicornis. No. 943, Acrididae. No. 944, Curculionidae. No. 945, Acrididae, diff. No. 946, Euchroma gigantea. No. 947, Tettigonidae. No. 948, Tettigonidae. No. 949, Phanaeus festivus. No. 950, Gryllidae. No. 951, Phanaeus lancifer. No. 952, Tettigonidae. No. 953, Batus barbicornis.

1993, June 30   Litho.   Perf. 13½
942 A221 25c multicolored   .40   .40
943 A221 25c multicolored   .40   .40
  a.   Pair, #942-943   .90   .90
944 A221 35c multicolored   .50   .50
945 A221 35c multicolored   .50   .50
  a.   Pair, #944-945   1.60   1.60
946 A221 50c multicolored   .70   .70
947 A221 50c multicolored   .70   .70
  a.   Pair, #946-947   2.00   2.00
948 A221 100c multicolored   1.40   1.40
949 A221 100c multicolored   1.40   1.40
  a.   Pair, #948-949   3.75   3.75
950 A221 175c multicolored   2.75   2.75
951 A221 175c multicolored   2.75   2.75
  a.   Pair, #950-951   6.75   6.75
952 A221 220c multicolored   3.25   3.25
953 A221 220c multicolored   3.25   3.25
  a.   Pair, #952-953   8.50   8.00
  Nos. 942-953 (12)   18.00 18.00

A222

#956b, 250c, like #955. #956c, 500c, like #956.

1993, July 30   Perf. 13x14
954 A222 50c Brazil No. 3   .75   .75
955 A222 250c Brazil No. 2   3.75   3.75
956 A222 500c Brazil No. 1   8.00   8.00
  Nos. 954-956 (3)   12.50 12.50

Souvenir Sheet
956A A222 Sheet of 2, #b.-c.   10.00 10.00
1st Brazilian postage stamps, 150th Anniv. Brasiliana '93 (#956A).
Nos. 956b-956c have purple border.

A223

America issue: Paleosuchus palpebrosus.

1993, Oct. 12   Perf. 14x13
957 A223 50g brown & multi   3.75 3.75
958 A223 100g green & multi   8.00 8.00

Christmas Angels — A224

25g, African angel with drum. 45g, Asian angel holding lamp. 50g, Oriental angel holding lantern. 150g, American Indian angel holding wand.

1993, Nov. 15   Litho.   Perf. 13x14
959 A224 25g multicolored   1.00   1.00
960 A224 45g multicolored   1.75   1.75
961 A224 50g multicolored   2.00   2.00
962 A224 150g multicolored   6.25   6.25
  Nos. 959-962 (4)   11.00 11.00

The foreign exchange rate of the Surinam florin was allowed to float freely against foreign currencies on Oct. 19, 1994. The florin's value against the dollar has fluctuated dramatically. Stamps may sell for values significantly different from those quoted in the Scott listings.

Nos. 729-730 Surcharged

1993   Litho.   Perf. 14x13
963 A173 5g on 10g Harpy eagle *1.90   .25*
964 A173 5g on 15g Parrot   *1.90 1.90*
Surcharges differ slightly. Issued: #963, 12/16. #964, 12/28.

Traditional Musical Instruments — A225

25g, Indian drum. 50g, Bosland Creooise drum. 75g, Tambourine. 100g, Hindu drum.

1994, Feb. 16   Litho.   Perf. 13x14
965 A225 25g multicolored   1.50   1.50
966 A225 50g multicolored   3.00   3.00
967 A225 75g multicolored   5.00   5.00
968 A225 100g multicolored   6.50   6.50
  Nos. 965-968 (4)   16.00 16.00

Environmental Protection A226

1994, June 8   Litho.   Perf. 14x13
969 A226 50g Smoke stacks   .75   .75
970 A226 350g Dying fish   6.25   6.25

Intl. Olympic Committee, Cent. — A227

1994, July 4   Litho.   Perf. 14x13
971 A227 250g multicolored   7.75 7.75

1994 World Cup Soccer Championships, U.S. — A228

1994, July 4   Perf. 13x14
972 A228 100g Goalkeeper's hands   1.25   1.25
973 A228 250g Soccer shoe   4.25   4.25
974 A228 300g Goal   6.50   6.50
  a.   Souvenir sheet of 2, #973-974   13.50 13.50
  Nos. 972-974 (3)   12.00 12.00

Butterflies — A229

No. 975, Dulcedo. No. 976, Ithomia. No. 977, Danaus. No. 978, Danaus, diff. No. 979, Echenais. No. 980, Bithijs. No. 981, Junonia evarette. No. 982, Anartia jatrophae. No. 983, Heliconius. No. 984, Heliconius erato. No. 985, Eurytides. No. 986, Parides.

1994, Sept. 7   Perf. 13½
975 A229 25g multicolored   *.45   .45*
976 A229 25g multicolored   *.45   .45*
  a.   Pair, #975-976   *.90   .90*
977 A229 30g multicolored   *.50   .50*
978 A229 30g multicolored   *.50   .50*
  a.   Pair, #977-978   *1.00   1.00*
979 A229 45g multicolored   *.75   .75*
980 A229 45g multicolored   *.75   .75*
  a.   Pair #979-980   *1.50   1.50*
981 A229 75g multicolored   *1.25   1.25*
982 A229 75g multicolored   *1.25   1.25*
  a.   Pair, #981-982   *2.50   2.50*
983 A229 250g multicolored   *4.00   4.00*
984 A229 250g multicolored   *4.00   4.00*
  a.   Pair, #983-984   *8.25   8.25*
985 A229 300g multicolored   *5.00   5.00*
986 A229 300g multicolored   *5.00   5.00*
  a.   Pair, #985-986   *10.00 10.00*
  Nos. 975-986 (12)   23.90 23.90

For surcharges see #1088-1091.

FEPAPOST '94 — A230

1994, Oct. 1   Litho.   Perf. 14x13
987 A230 250g Netherlands #B148   *3.50   3.50*
988 A230 300g #168   *4.00   4.00*
  a.   Souvenir sheet of 2, #987-988, perf. 13½x13   *7.50   7.50*

Post vehicles: 50g, Airplane, canoe. 400g, Van, donkey cart.

America Issue A231

1994, Oct. 12   **Litho.**   **Perf. 13½**
989 A231 50g multicolored   1.40 1.40
990 A231 400g multicolored   12.00 12.00

A232

Christmas: (A), Angel in sky. 250g, Mother reading to children. 625g, Woman kneeling in prayer.

1994, Nov. 22   **Perf. 13x14**
991 A232 (A) multicolored   .60 .60
992 A232 250g multicolored   1.90 1.90
993 A232 625g multicolored   5.00 5.00
  a.   Souvenir sheet, #992-993   9.00 9.00
    Nos. 991-993 (3)   7.50 7.50

No. 991 sold for 37g on day of issue.

A233

1995, Jan. 31
994 A233 375g shown   3.25 3.25
995 A233 650g Volleyballs   5.25 5.50
  a.   Souvenir sheet, #994-995   9.00 9.00

Volleyball, cent.

Medicinal Plants — A234

Designs: No. 998, Stachytarpheta jamaicense. No. 999, Ruellia tuberosa. No. 1000, Peperomia pellucida. No. 1001, Ocimum sanctum. No. 1002, Phyllanthus amarus. No. 1003, Portulaca oleracea. No. 1004, Wulffia baccata. No. 1005, Sesamum indicum. No. 1006, Ascelepias curassavica. No. 1007, Heliotropium indicum. No. 1008, Wedelia trilobata. No. 1009, Lantana camara.

1995, Mar. 31   **Litho.**   **Perf. 13½**
998 A234 30g multicolored   .35 .35
999 A234 30g multicolored   .35 .35
  a.   Pair, #998-999   .50 .50
1000 A234 50g multicolored   .50 .50
1001 A234 50g multicolored   .50 .50
  a.   Pair, #1000-1001   .80 .80
1002 A234 75g multicolored   .75 .75
1003 A234 75g multicolored   .75 .75
  a.   Pair, #1002-1003   1.40 1.40
1004 A234 250g multicolored   2.40 2.40
1005 A234 250g multicolored   2.40 2.40
  a.   Pair, #1004-1005   4.75 4.75
1006 A234 500g multicolored   4.75 4.75
1007 A234 500g multicolored   4.75 4.75
  a.   Pair, #1006-1007   9.50 9.50
1008 A234 600g multicolored   5.75 5.75
1009 A234 600g multicolored   5.75 5.75
  a.   Pair, #1008-1009   12.00 12.00
    Nos. 998-1009 (12)   29.00 29.00

World Wildlife Fund — A235

25g, Herpailurus yaguarondi. 30g, same up close. 50g, Leopardus tigrinus. 100g, same up close. 1000g, Leopardus wiedi. 1200g, same up close.

1995, May 31   **Perf. 14x13**
1010 A235 25g multicolored   .90 .40
1011 A235 30g multicolored   .90 .40
1012 A235 50g multicolored   .90 .40
1013 A235 100g multicolored   2.25 1.25
1014 A235 1000g multicolored   5.75 5.75
1015 A235 1200g multicolored   7.00 7.00
    Nos. 1010-1015 (6)   17.70 15.20

Nos. 1014-1015 are airmail and do not contain WWF emblem.

UN, 50th Anniv. — A236

1995, June 26   **Litho.**   **Perf. 13x14**
1016 A236 135g green & multi   .75 .75
1017 A236 740g blue & multi   5.00 5.00

Surinam Police Force, Cent. — A237

1995, June 21   **Perf. 14x13**
1018 A237 875g multicolored   6.00 6.00

Nilom Junior Chamber, 25th Anniv. A238

1995, Sept. 6   **Litho.**   **Perf. 14x13**
1019 A238 700g multicolored   3.75 3.75

Environmental Protection A239

1995, Oct. 12
1020 A239 135f multicolored   1.00 1.00
1021 A239 1500f multicolored   11.50 11.50

America issue.

A240

Christmas: 70g, Shepherds, star. 135g, Flight into Egypt. 295g, Magi. 1000g, Nativity, horiz.

1995, Nov. 15   **Perf. 13x14, 14x13**
1022 A240 70g multicolored   .35 .35
1023 A240 135g multicolored   .75 .75
1024 A240 295g multicolored   1.50 1.50
1025 A240 1000g multicolored   6.25 6.25
  a.   Souvenir sheet of 1   5.50 5.50
    Nos. 1022-1025 (4)   8.85 8.85

For surcharges see Nos. 1065A-1065B.

A241

Paintings of Jesters, by Corneille.

1995, Dec. 5   **Perf. 13x14**
1026 A241 135f With bird   1.00 1.00
1027 A241 615f With cat   4.75 4.75

Orchids — A242

No. 1028, Cyrtopodium cristatum. No. 1029, Epidendrum cristatum. No. 1030, Otostylis lepida. No. 1031, Cochleanthes guianensis. No. 1032, Rudolfiella aurantiaca. No. 1033, Catasetum longifolium. No. 1034, Maxillaria splendens. No. 1035, Encyclia granitica. No. 1036, Catasetum macrocarpum. No. 1037, Brassia caudata. No. 1038, Vanilla grandiflora. No. 1039, Maxillaria rufescens.

1996, Feb. 29   **Litho.**   **Perf. 13½**
1028 A242 10g multicolored   .25 .25
1029 A242 10g multicolored   .25 .25
  a.   Pair, #1028-1029   .30 .30
1030 A242 75g multicolored   .50 .50
1031 A242 75g multicolored   .50 .50
  a.   Pair, #1030-1031   1.00 1.00
1032 A242 135g multicolored   .85 .85
1033 A242 135g multicolored   .85 .85
  a.   Pair, #1032-1033   1.75 1.75
1034 A242 250g multicolored   1.60 1.60
1035 A242 250g multicolored   1.60 1.60
  a.   Pair, #1034-1035   3.50 3.50
1036 A242 300g multicolored   2.00 2.00
1037 A242 300g multicolored   2.00 2.00
  a.   Pair, #1036-1037   4.50 4.50
1038 A242 750g multicolored   4.75 4.75
1039 A242 750g multicolored   4.75 4.75
  a.   Pair, #1038-1039   11.00 11.00
    Nos. 1028-1039 (12)   19.90 19.90

Bird Type of 1985

1996, Apr. 16   **Litho.**   **Perf. 14x13**
1040 A173 2000f Kraagpapegaai   14.00 14.00

Ecotourism A243

Designs: No. 1041, Traditional huts. No. 1042, Butterfly in rain forest. No. 1043, Two natives. No. 1044, Native woman.

Perf. 13½x13 on 3 Sides
1996, Apr. 30   **Litho.**

Booklet Stamps
1041 A243 70g multicolored   1.50 1.50
1042 A243 70g multicolored   1.50 1.50
1043 A243 135g multicolored   3.00 3.00
1044 A243 135g multicolored   3.00 3.00
  a.   Booklet pane of 4, #1041-1044   9.00
    Complete booklet, #1044a   10.00

Radio, Cent. — A244

135g, First wireless radio communication device, vert. 615g, Guglielmo Marconi.

Perf. 13x14, 14x13
1996, May 17   **Litho.**
1045 A244 135g multicolored   1.00 1.00
1046 A244 615g multicolored   5.00 5.00

1996 Summer Olympic Games, Atlanta — A245

Olymphilex '96, Atlanta — A245a

Stamp on stamp: b, 135f, #678. c, 865f, #683.

1996, June 27   **Litho.**   **Perf. 13x14**
1047 A245 70g Basketball   .50 .50
1048 A245 135g Athletics   .95 .95
1049 A245 195g Badminton   1.40 1.40
1050 A245 200g Swimming   1.60 1.60
1051 A245 900g Cycling   7.00 7.00
1052 A245 1000g Hurdles   7.50 7.50
    Nos. 1047-1052 (6)   18.95 18.95

Souvenir Sheet
1052A A245a Sheet of 2, #b.-c.   9.00 9.00

Bird Type of 1985

Designs: 75f, Fisman. 160f, Fremusu-aka. 1765f, Roodpoot honingzuiger.

1996, Oct. 2   **Litho.**   **Perf. 14x13**
1053 A173 75f multicolored   .45 .45
1054 A173 160f multicolored   1.00 1.00
1055 A173 1765f multicolored   11.00 11.00
    Nos. 1053-1055 (3)   12.45 12.45

A246

Women's Traditional Costumes: Various styles.

1996, Oct. 9   **Litho.**   **Perf. 13x14**
1056 135f multicolored   1.25 1.25
1057 990f multicolored   7.75 7.75
  a.   A246 Pair, #1056-1057   10.00 10.00

America issue.

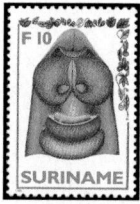

A247

Christmas: Various stylized designs of Madonna and Child.

1996, Oct. 30   **Litho.**   **Perf. 13x14**
1058 A247 10f multicolored   .25 .25
1059 A247 70f multicolored   .50 .50
1060 A247 135f multicolored   .90 .90
1061 A247 285f multicolored   2.40 2.40
1062 A247 750f multicolored   6.00 6.00
  a.   Souvenir sheet, #1062   6.25 6.25
    Nos. 1058-1062 (5)   10.05 10.05

A248

Youth Care: Paintings, by Jan Telting: 135f, Brown dog, child. 865f, White dog, child.

1996, Dec. 4   Litho.   Perf. 13x14
1063 A248 135f multicolored   1.00 1.00
1064 A248 865f multicolored   8.00 8.00

A249

City of Albina, 150th Anniv.: August Kappler (1815-87), founder.

1996, Dec. 13
1065 A249 875f multicolored   7.25 7.25

Nos. 1024, 1025
Surcharged in Black
or Silver

Methods and perfs as before
1996, Dec. 16
1065A A240 (125g) on 295g   2.40 2.40
1065B A240 (125g) on 1000g
                            (S)   2.40 2.40

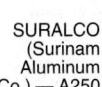

SURALCO
(Surinam
Aluminum
Co.) — A250

10f, Opening of aluminum smelter, Paranam, 1965. 70f, Drilling blasting holes for ore exploration, Moengo, 1947. 130f, Workers' housing, Moengo, 1919. 150f, Dust-free loading of alumina, Paranam dock, 1995. 160f, Constructing dam, power station, 1960. 730f, Schooner Moengo, 1922.

Perf. 13½x14 on 2 or 3 Sides
1996, Dec. 18   Booklet Stamps
1066 A250   10f multicolored   .25 .25
1067 A250   70f multicolored   .70 .70
1068 A250 130f multicolored   1.25 1.25
1069 A250 150f multicolored   1.40 1.40
1070 A250 160f multicolored   1.60 1.60
1071 A250 730f multicolored   7.25 7.25
  a. Booklet pane, #1066-1071 +
       label   12.50
     Complete booklet, #1071a   14.00

Heinrich von
Stephan (1831-
97) — A251

1997, Jan. 31   Litho.   Perf. 13x14
1072 A251 275f brown & multi   2.75 2.75
1073 A251 475f dk blue & multi   4.00 4.00

Fauna — A252

#1074, Cebus nigrivittatus. #1075, Cebus apella. #1076, Saguinus midas. #1077, Ateles paniscus. #1078, Ateles geoffroyi panamensis. #1079, Ateles geoffroyi frontatus. #1080, Cacajao calvus. #1081, Lagothrix flavicauda. #1082, Saguinus bicolor. #1083, Saguinus oedipus. #1084, Alouatta seniculus. #1085, Saimiri sciureus.

1997, Feb. 12   Litho.   Perf. 13½
1074 A252   25f multicolored   .25 .25
1075 A252   25f multicolored   .25 .25
  a.   Pair, #1074-1075   .40 .40
1076 A252   75f multicolored   .55 .55
1077 A252   75f multicolored   .55 .55
  a.   Pair, #1076-1077   1.25 1.25
1078 A252 100f multicolored   .75 .75
1079 A252 100f multicolored   .75 .75
  a.   Pair, #1078-1079   1.60 1.60
1080 A252 275f multicolored   2.00 2.00
1081 A252 275f multicolored   2.00 2.00
  a.   Pair, #1080-1081   4.50 4.50
1082 A252 300f multicolored   2.50 2.50
1083 A252 300f multicolored   2.50 2.50
  a.   Pair, #1082-1083   5.25 5.25
1084 A252 725f multicolored   5.25 5.25
1085 A252 725f multicolored   5.25 5.25
  a.   Pair, #1084-1085   12.00 12.00
     Nos. 1074-1085 (12)   22.60 22.60

Retracing and Completion of Amelia
Earhart's Trans-Global Flight by Linda
Finch — A253

1997, Mar. 30   Litho.   Perf. 14x13
1086 A253 275f multicolored   2.50 2.50

Surinam
Museum, 50th
Anniv.
A254

1997, Apr. 3
1087 A254 625f multicolored   4.75 4.75

**Nos. 983-986 Surcharged in Black
or Silver**

1996-97   Litho.   Perf. 13½
1088 A229   50f on 250g #983   1.40 1.40
1089 A229   50f on 250g #984   1.40 1.40
  a.   Pair, #1088-1089   6.75 6.75
1090 A229 100f on 300g #985
                            (S)   2.75 2.75
1091 A229 100f on 300g #986
                            (S)   2.75 2.75
  a.   Pair, #1090-1091   9.00 9.00
     Nos. 1088-1091 (4)   8.30 8.30

Issued; #1089a, 11/1; #1091a, 1/1/97.

Orchids — A255

Designs: 25f, Selenipedium steyermarkii. 50f, Phragmipedium schlimii. 75f, Criosantes

arietina. 200f, Cypripedium margaritaceum. 775f, Paphiopedilum gratrixianum.

1997, Apr. 3   Litho.   Perf. 13x14
1092 A255   25f multicolored   .25 .25
1093 A255   50f multicolored   .45 .45
1094 A255   75f multicolored   .60 .60
1095 A255 200f multicolored   1.75 1.75
1096 A255 775f multicolored   6.75 6.75
     Nos. 1092-1096 (5)   9.80 9.80

Souvenir Sheet

PACIFIC 97, San Francisco — A256

1997, May 29   Litho.   Perf. 13½x13
1097 A256 675f #458-459   5.00 5.00

A257

Mosques: 50f, Great Mosque, Isfahan, Iran. 125f, Dome of the Rock, Jerusalem. 175f, Madrasa of Ulugh beg, Samarkand. 225f, Taj Mahal, Agra, India. 275f, Kaiser St. Mosque, Paramaribo. 325f, Sülcjamiye, Istanbul.

1997, July 7   Perf. 13x14
Background Color
1098 A257   50f pink   .35 .35
1099 A257 125f olive   .90 .90
1100 A257 175f blue   1.25 1.25
1101 A257 225f purple   1.60 1.60
1102 A257 275f green   2.10 2.10
1103 A257 325f brown   2.50 2.50
  a.   Souvenir sheet of 1   2.75 2.75
     Nos. 1098-1103 (6)   8.70 8.70

A258

State Oil Co. Refinery, Saramacca: 50f, Pumping station. 125f, Derrick, butterfly. #1106, Storage tanks. #1107, Gauge, testing mechanism.

Booklet Stamps
Perf. 13x13½ on 3 Sides
1997, Aug. 16   Litho.
1104 A258   50f multicolored   .55 .55
1105 A258 125f multicolored   1.60 1.60
1106 A258 275f multicolored   3.75 3.75
1107 A258 275f multicolored   3.75 3.75
  a.   Booklet pane, #1104-1107   11.00
     Complete booklet, #1107a   12.50

Bird Type of 1985
1997, Sept. 17   Litho.   Perf. 14x13
1108 A173   50f Krabu-
                 owrukuku   .50 .50
1109 A173 125f Mangrodoifi   1.50 1.50
1110 A173 275f Peprefowru   2.00 2.00
1111 A173 3150f Kroonvink   25.00 25.00
     Nos. 1108-1111 (4)   29.00 29.00

A259

Child Care: 50f, Right side of boy's face. 100f, Left side of boy's face. 175f, Right side of girl's face. 225f, Left side of girl's face. 350f, 675f, Boy's face upside down, girl's face.

1997, Dec. 4   Litho.   Perf. 13x14
1112 A259   50f multicolored   .40 .40
1113 A259 100f multicolored   .75 .75
1114 A259 175f multicolored   1.25 1.25
1115 A259 225f multicolored   1.75 1.75
1116 A259 350f multicolored   2.75 2.75
     Nos. 1112-1116 (5)   6.90 6.90

Souvenir Sheet
1117 A259 675f multicolored   5.00 5.00

A260

Christmas: 125f, Madonna and Child. 225f, Children looking at baby. 450f, Angel. 675f, Children singing, horiz.

1997, Dec. 4
1118 A260 125f multicolored   1.00 1.00
1119 A260 225f multicolored   1.75 1.75
1120 A260 450f multicolored   3.50 3.50
     Nos. 1118-1120 (3)   6.25 6.25

Souvenir Sheet
1121 A260 675f multicolored   5.00 5.00

America Issue — A261

Designs: 170f, Postal worker, motorcycle. 230f, Postal worker carrying package.

1997, Dec. 10   Litho.   Perf. 13x14
1122   170f multicolored   1.00 1.00
1123   230f multicolored   1.40 1.40
  a. A261 Pair, #1122-1123   4.50 4.50

Moths & Butterflies — A262

1998, Jan. 26   Perf. 13½
1124 A262   50f Alcandor   .30 .30
1125 A262   50f Achilles   .30 .30
  a.   Pair, #1124-1125   .85 .85
1126 A262   75f Alphenor   .45 .45
1127 A262   75f Ceres   .45 .45
  a.   Pair, #1126-1127   1.50 1.50
1128 A262 100f Cecropia   .60 .60
1129 A262 100f Helenor   .60 .60
  a.   Pair, #1128-1129   1.90 1.90
1130 A262 175f Promothea   1.00 1.00
1131 A262 175f Cassiae   1.00 1.00
  a.   Pair, #1130-1131   3.25 3.25
1132 A262 275f Ino   2.10 2.10
1133 A262 275f Phidippus   2.10 2.10
  a.   Pair, #1132-1133   6.00 6.00
1134 A262 725f Palamedes   5.50 5.50
1135 A262 725f Helenor, diff.   5.50 5.50
  a.   Pair, #1134-1135   15.00 15.00
     Nos. 1124-1135 (12)   19.90 19.90

Bird Type of 1985

1998, Mar. 12   **Perf. 14x13, 13x14**
1136	A173	50f Marjrietje	.40	.40
1137	A173	225f Aka	2.10	2.10
1138	A173	2425f Timmerman, vert.	22.50	22.50
		Nos. 1136-1138 (3)	25.00	25.00

Hindustani Immigration, 125th Anniv.
A263

Designs: 175f, Painting showing first immigrants from boat, "Lala Rooch." 200f, Statue of Baba and Mai, first immigrants from India.

1998, June 4   **Perf. 14x13**
| 1139 | A263 | 175f multicolored | 1.60 | 1.60 |
| 1140 | A263 | 200f multicolored | 2.10 | 2.10 |

Temples
A264

Designs: 50f, Sri Lanka. 75f, Golden Pagoda, Burma, vert. 275f, Swayambhunath, Nepal, vert. 325f, Borobudur, Indonesia. 400f, Wat Phra Kaew, Thailand, vert. 450f, Peking Temple, China, vert.

675f, Statue, Borobudur, Indonesia, vert.

    Perf. 13½x12½, 12½x13½
1998, June 4
1141	A264	50f multicolored	.40	.40
1142	A264	75f multicolored	.60	.60
1143	A264	275f multicolored	2.25	2.25
1144	A264	325f multicolored	2.75	2.75
1145	A264	400f multicolored	3.00	3.00
1146	A264	450f multicolored	3.75	3.75
		Nos. 1141-1146 (6)	12.75	12.75

Souvenir Sheet
| 1147 | A264 | 675f multicolored | 6.50 | 6.50 |

No. 1147 is a continuous design.

Ferry Boat and Surinam Flag
A265

1998, Oct. 31   **Perf. 13½x14**
| 1148 | A265 | 275f blue & multi | 2.25 | 2.25 |
| 1149 | A265 | 400f sepia & multi | 3.25 | 3.25 |

See Guyana Nos. 3360A-3360B.

America Issue — A266

Outstanding women: 400f, Sophie Redmond (1907-55). 1000f, Grace Ruth Schneiders-Howard (1869-1968).

1998, Oct. 8   **Litho.**   **Perf. 13x14**
| 1150 | A266 | 400f multicolored | 3.75 | 3.75 |
| 1151 | A266 | 1000f multicolored | 8.25 | 8.25 |

World Stamp Exhibition, The Hague, Netherlands
A267

Designs: 400f, #245, portions of #174, #141. 800f, #174, portions of #245, #141. 2400f, #141, portions of #245, #174.

1998, Oct.   **Litho.**   **Perf. 14x13**
| 1152 | A267 | 400f multicolored | 3.00 | 3.00 |
| 1153 | A267 | 800f multicolored | 5.75 | 5.75 |

Souvenir Sheet
| 1154 | A267 | 2400f multicolored | 20.00 | 20.00 |

A268

Christmas: Various nativity scenes.

1998, Nov. 1   **Perf. 13x14**
1155	A268	50f multicolored	.40	.40
1156	A268	325f multicolored	1.60	1.60
1157	A268	400f multicolored	2.00	2.00
1158	A268	1225f multicolored	7.00	7.00
		Nos. 1155-1158 (4)	11.00	11.00

Souvenir Sheet
| 1159 | A268 | 1400f multicolored | 8.00 | 8.00 |

Bird Type of 1985

1998, Nov. 16   **Litho.**   **Perf. 14x13**
| 1160 | A173 | 3800f Butarides striatus | 16.00 | 16.00 |

A269

400f, Mother, child, foods. 1000f, Mother, child, flower.

1998, Dec. 4   **Litho.**   **Perf. 13x14**
| 1161 | A269 | 400f multicolored | 2.10 | 2.10 |
| 1162 | A269 | 1000f multicolored | 5.50 | 5.50 |

World Health Organization, 50th anniv.

Child Care — A270

1998, Dec. 4   **Litho.**   **Perf. 14x13**
1163	A270	375f shown	2.00	2.00
1164	A270	400f Flying kite, diff.	2.00	2.00
1165	A270	1225f Holding kite	7.00	7.00
		Nos. 1163-1165 (3)	11.00	11.00

Heliconia — A271

#1166, Caribaea kawauchi. #1167, Pastazae. #1168, Rostrata. #1169, Sexy pink. #1170, Collinsiana. #1171, Wagneriana. #1172, Bihai-nappi. #1173, Jaded forest. #1174, Golden torch. #1175, Latispatha-red yellow gyro. #1176, Sexy pink, diff. #1177, Nappi yellow.

1999, Jan. 27   **Litho.**   **Perf. 13½**
1166	A271	50f multicolored	.25	.25
1167	A271	50f multicolored	.25	.25
a.		Pair, #1166-1167	.30	.30
1168	A271	200f multicolored	.65	.65
1169	A271	200f multicolored	.65	.65
a.		Pair, #1168-1169	1.50	1.50
1170	A271	300f multicolored	1.00	1.00
1171	A271	300f multicolored	1.00	1.00
a.		Pair, #1170-1171	2.50	2.50
1172	A271	400f multicolored	1.25	1.25
1173	A271	400f multicolored	1.25	1.25
a.		Pair, #1172-1173	3.25	3.25
1174	A271	750f multicolored	2.50	2.50
1175	A271	750f multicolored	2.50	2.50
a.		Pair, #1174-1175	6.50	6.50

1176	A271	1300f multicolored	4.25	4.25
1177	A271	1300f multicolored	4.25	4.25
a.		Pair, #1176-1177	11.00	11.00
		Nos. 1166-1177 (12)	19.80	19.80

Old Plantation Houses
A272

1999, Mar. 17   **Litho.**   **Perf. 14x13**
1178	A272	75f Katwijk	.30	.30
1179	A272	300f Sorgvliet	1.25	1.25
1180	A272	400f Peperpot	1.50	1.50
1181	A272	2225f Spieringshoek	8.75	8.75
		Nos. 1178-1181 (4)	11.80	11.80

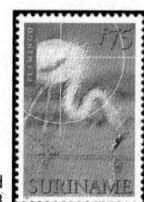

Endangered Species — A273

1999, June 30   **Litho.**   **Perf. 13x14**
1182	A273	75f Flamingo	.25	.25
1183	A273	375f Orangutan	.75	.75
1184	A273	450f Elephant	.90	.90
1185	A273	500f Whale	.95	.95
1186	A273	850f Frog	1.60	1.60
1187	A273	900f Rhinoceros	1.75	1.75
1188	A273	1600f Giant panda	3.00	3.00
1189	A273	7250f Tiger	14.00	14.00
		Nos. 1182-1189 (8)	23.20	23.20

Coppename Bridge
A274

1999, June 30   **Perf. 14x13**
| 1190 | A274 | 850f black & green | 1.60 | 1.60 |
| 1191 | A274 | 2250f black & blue | 4.25 | 4.25 |

A275   A276

1999, July 9   **Perf. 13x14**
1192	A275	850f multicolored	1.40	1.40
1193	A276	2650f multicolored	4.25	4.25
a.		Souvenir sheet, #1192-1193, perf. 13x13½	5.75	5.75

Surinam Conservation Foundation, 30th anniv. (No. 1192), Central Surinam Nature Preserve, 1st anniv. (No. 1193).

Bird Type of 1985-95

1999, Aug. 21   **Perf. 14x13**
| 1194 | A173 | 1000f Blauwtje | 1.90 | 1.90 |
| 1195 | A173 | 5500f Kepanki | 8.75 | 8.75 |

A277

1999, Oct. 9   **Perf. 13x14**
| 1196 | A277 | 950f Earth | 1.75 | 1.75 |
| 1197 | A277 | 1000f Saturn | 1.90 | 1.90 |

UPU, 125th anniv.

A278

1999, Oct. 9
1198		1000f Gun	1.75	1.75
1199		2250f Flower	3.50	3.50
a.	A278	Pair, #1198-1199	6.00	6.00

America issue, A New Millennium Without Arms.

Christmas — A279

1999, Nov. 3   **Perf. 13x14**
1200	A279	500f Star, stable	.80	.80
1201	A279	850f Christmas tree	1.40	1.40
1202	A279	900f Angel	1.50	1.50
1203	A279	1000f Candle	1.60	1.60
		Nos. 1200-1203 (4)	5.30	5.30

Souvenir Sheet
| 1204 | A279 | 2275f Mother and child | 4.25 | 4.25 |

Children's Pictures
A280

1999, Dec. 3   **Litho.**   **Perf. 14x13**
1205	A280	1100f multi	1.75	1.75
1206	A280	1400f multi, diff.	2.25	2.25
1207	A280	1600f multi, diff.	2.50	2.50
a.		Souvenir sheet of 1	2.75	2.75
		Nos. 1205-1207 (3)	6.50	6.50

Children's Drawings
A281

2000, Jan. 3   **Litho.**   **Perf. 14x13**
| 1208 | A281 | 1000f By Tahirih van Kanten | 2.00 | 2.00 |
| 1209 | A281 | 2500f By Tirsa Braaf | 5.50 | 5.50 |

See No. 1224.

Traffic Signs — A282

2000   **Perf. 13x14**
1210	A282	2000f Turn right	4.00	4.00
1211	A282	2000f No passing	4.00	4.00
1212	A282	2000f Sharp turns	4.00	4.00
1213	A282	2000f Traffic circle	4.00	4.00
		Nos. 1210-1213 (4)	16.00	16.00

Issued: #1210, 1/3; #1211, 4/3; #1212, 5/18. #1213, 9/29.

See Nos. 1246-1248, 1267-1268, 1275-1278, 1311-1312.

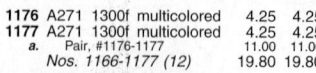

Fruits
A283

No. 1214, 50f: a, Citrullus vulgaris. b, Carica papaya.
No. 1215, 175f: a, Mangifera indica. b, Garcinia mangostana.
No. 1216, 200f: a, Musa nana. b, Citrus paradisi.
No. 1217, 250f: a, Punika granatum. b, Ananas comosus.
No. 1218, 325f: a, Cocos nucifera. b, Passiflora quadrangularis.
No. 1219, 5000f: a, Citrus sinensis. b, Persea gratissima.

2000, Feb. 29   Litho.   Perf. 13¼
Pairs, #a-b
1214-1219 A283 Set of 6   20.00 20.00
No. 1219 is airmail.

Bird Type of 1985
Designs: 1100f, Dendrocygna autumnalis. 4425f, Ceryle torquata.

2000, Apr. 3   Perf. 14x13
1220 A173 1100f multi   1.75 1.75
1221 A173 4425f multi   7.50 7.50

Surinam
River Bridge
A284

Lettering in: 1100f, Red. 1700f, Blue.

2000, May 18
1222-1223 A284 Set of 2   4.75 4.75

Children's Drawings Type
Souvenir Sheet
2000   Perf. 13¼x13
1224 A281 3575f #1208, 1209   6.50 6.50
World Stamp Expo 2000, Anaheim, Stampin' the Future children's stamp design contest.

2000
Summer
Olympic,
Sydney
A285

No. 1225, 1100f: a, Soccer. b, Track and field.
No. 1226, 3900f: a, Tennis. b, Swimming.
No. 1227: a, Soccer, diff. b, Swimming, diff.

2000, Aug. 8   Litho.   Perf. 13¼
Pairs, #a-b
1225-1226 A285 Set of 2   18.00 18.00
Souvenir Sheet
1227 A285 2500f Sheet of 2, #a-b   8.25 8.25

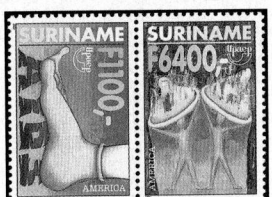

America Issue, Fight Against
AIDS — A286

No. 1228: a, 1100f, Foot with condom stamping out AIDS, horiz. b, 6400f, People holding condoms.

2000   Perf. 13x14
1228 A286 Pair, #a-b   13.50 13.50

25th Anniv. of
International
Agencies Ltd. as
Philatelic and
Numismatic
Agent — A287

Designs: 125f, Paper money. 5900f, Stamps.

2000, Nov. 24
1229-1230 A287 Set of 2   7.00 7.00
1230a   Souvenir sheet, #1229-1230   7.25 7.25

Children — A288

Child: 1100f, Walking. 3900f, Breastfeeding. 2000f, With umbilical cord, horiz.

2000, Dec. 5   Perf. 13x14
1231-1232 A288 Set of 2   6.00 6.00
Souvenir Sheet
Perf. 14x13
1233 A288 2000f multi   2.75 2.75

Fight Against
Poverty
A289

Country name in: 1100f, Green. 4900f, Red.

2000   Perf. 14x13
1234-1235 A289 Set of 2   6.00 6.00

Christmas — A290

Designs: 1100f, Star of Bethlehem. 3900f, Madonna and Child.
3000f, Magi with gifts, horiz.

2000   Perf. 13x14
1236-1237 A290 Set of 2   6.75 6.75
Souvenir Sheet
Perf. 14x13
1238 A290 3000f multi   4.25 4.25

No. 945a
Surcharged

Methods and Perfs as Before
2000 (?)
1238A   Pair   2.50 2.50
b. A221 1000f on 25c No. 942   .95 .95
c. A221 1000f on 25c No. 943   .95 .95
1239   Pair   6.75 6.75
a. A221 3100f on 35c No. 944   2.50 2.50
b. A221 3100f on 35c No. 945   2.50 2.50

Birds
A291

No. 1240, 50f: a, Rood zwart vink tagara. b, Tyarman.
No. 1241, 175f: a, Sabaku. b, Kolibrie.
No. 1242, 200f: a, Aka. b, Timmerman.
No. 1243, 250f: a, Paarskeel cotinga. b, Zwarte kraag donfowru.
No. 1244, 825f: a, Kees. b, Stonkuyake.
No. 1245, 7500f: a, Guyanese rood cotinga. b, Butabuta.

2001, Jan. 31   Litho.   Perf. 13¼
Pairs, #a-b
1240-1245 A291 Set of 6   18.00 18.00
No. 1245 is airmail.

Traffic Signs Type of 2000
2001   Litho.   Perf. 13x14
1246 A282 2000f No parking   4.50 4.50
1247 A282 4000f Drawbridge   5.00 5.00
1248 A282 4000f Tractor, No entry   5.00 5.00
Issued: 2000f, 3/8; No. 1247, 4/25; No. 1248, 9/12.

UN Women's Human
Rights
Campaign — A292

Designs: 1400f, Female and male symbols. 4600f, Woman.

2001, Mar. 15   Litho.   Perf. 13x14
1249-1250 A292 Set of 2   6.00 6.00

Youth
Philately — A293

Children's art by: 650f, Bhoelai Surender Kumar. 5350f, Sharon Cameron.

2001, Apr. 25
1251-1252 A293 Set of 2   6.00 6.00

Bird Type of 1985
Designs: 4500f, Charadrius collaris. 9000f, Bubo virginianus.

2001, May 10   Perf. 14x13
1253 A173 4500f multi   5.25 5.25
1254 A173 9000f multi   10.50 10.50

Fruit — A294

Designs: 150f, Sapotille. 200f, Noni vrucht. 800fr, Baby bananas. 1200f, Mope. 1700f, Pommerak.

2001, July 20   Litho.   Perf. 12¾x13½
1255-1259 A294 Set of 5   5.25 5.25

America Issue — A295

Paramaribo buildings: Nos. 1260a, 1261a, 1700f, Bishop's house. Nos. 1260b, 1261b, 7300f, Presidential palace.

2001, Sept. 12   Litho.   Perf. 14x13
Country Name in Red
1260 A295 Pair, #a-b   10.50 10.50
Souvenir Sheet
Country Name in Green
Perf. 13¼x13
1261 A295 Sheet of 2, #a-b   10.50 10.50

Stamp Day — A296

Designs: No. 1262a, 3750f, #648 (green background). No. 1262b, 5250f, #29 (red background).
No. 1263a, 3750f, #648 (red background). No. 1263b, 5250f, #29 (orange background).

2001, Oct. 19   Perf. 13x14
1262 A296 Pair, #a-b   10.50 10.50
Souvenir Sheet
Perf. 13x13¼
1263 A296 Sheet of 2, #a-b   10.50 10.50

Christmas
A297

Children's
Sports — A298

2001, Nov. 2   Perf. 13¼
1264 A297 1700f blue & multi   2.25 2.25
Perf. 14x13
1265 A298 5000f red & multi   6.25 6.25
Souvenir Sheet
Perf. 13¼x13
1266   Sheet of 2   8.50 8.50
a. A297 1700f green & multi   2.10 2.10
b. A298 5000f blue & multi   6.25 6.25

No. 947a
Surcharged
in Gold

2001, Dec. 7   Litho.   Perf. 13½
1266C   Pair   6.75 6.75
d. A221 2500f on 50c No. 946   3.25 3.25
e. A221 2500f on 50c No. 947   3.25 3.25

Traffic Signs Type of 2000
2001-02   Perf. 13x14
1267 A282 4000f Pedestrian crossing   5.00 5.00
1268 A282 4000f Yield   5.00 5.00
Issued: No. 1267, 12/7/01; No. 1268, 2/13/02.

Parrots
A299

No. 1269, 150f: a, Deroptyus acciptrinus. b, Amazona achrocephala.
No. 1270, 200f: a, Ara manilata. b, Amazona dufresniana.
No. 1271, 800f: a, Ara severa. b, Pionites melanocephala.
No. 1272, 1200f: a, Ara nobilis. b, Pionus fiscus.
No. 1273, 1700f: a, Ara chloroptera. b, Pionopsitta caicca.
No. 1274, 5325f: a, Ara macao. b, Amazona farinosa.

2002, Jan. 9　　　　　Perf. 13¼
Pairs, #a-b
1269-1274 A299　Set of 6　17.50 17.50
No. 1274 is airmail.

Traffic Signs Type of 2000

No. 1275, U turn. No. 1276, Pedestrian path. No. 1277, Train crossing without barriers. No. 1278, Motorcycles.

2002-03　Litho.　Perf. 13x14
1275 A282 4000f multicolored　3.75 3.75
Perf. 12¾x14
1276 A282 4000f multicolored　4.50 4.50
1277 A282 4000f multicolored　4.50 4.50
1278 A282 4000f multicolored　4.50 4.50
Nos. 1275-1278 (4)　17.25 17.25
Issued: No. 1275, 4/17/02; No. 1276, 6/19/02; No. 1277, 9/20/02; No. 1278, 2/13/03.

Costumes — A300

Costumes of: Nos. 1279a, 1279c, 1279e, 1279g, 1279i, 1279k, Various men. Nos. 1279b, 1279d, 1279f, 1279h, 1279j, 1279l, Various women.

2002, May 15　　Perf. 12¾x13¼
1279　Horiz. strip of 12　17.00 17.00
a.-b.　A300 150f Either single　.25 .25
c.-d.　A300 200f Either single　.25 .25
e.-f.　A300 800f Either single　.75 .75
g.-h.　A300 1200f Either single　1.10 1.10
i.-j.　A300 1700f Either single　1.60 1.60
k.-l.　A300 4950f Either single　4.50 4.50

Birds — A301

5000f, Royal flycatcher. 8500f, Swampufowru.

2002, June 19　　Perf. 12¾x14
1280 A301 5000f multicolored　5.75 5.75
1281 A301 8500f multicolored　10.00 10.00

Amphilex 2002 Intl. Stamp Exhibition, Amsterdam — A302

No. 1282: a, 1700f, Netherlands #244 (yellow background). b, 6800f, Netherlands #103 (maroon background).
No. 1283: a, 1700f, Like No. 1282a (maroon background). b, 6800f, Like No. 1282b (yellow background).

2002, Aug. 30　　Perf. 13¼x12¾
1282 A302　Horiz. pair, #a-b　8.75 8.75
Souvenir Sheet
1283 A302　Sheet of 2, #a-b　8.75 8.75

No. 1230a Overprinted in Gold
Souvenir Sheet

2002, Aug. 30　Litho.　Perf. 13x14
1284 A287　Sheet of 2　9.50 9.50
a.　250f on 125f #1229　.45 .45
b.　5900f #1230 overprinted　9.25 9.25

America Issue - Youth, Education and Literacy — A303

No. 1285 — Letters, numbers and: a, 1700f, Stylized head and question mark. b, 7300f, "X" in signature box.

2002, Sept. 20　　Perf. 13¼x12¾
1285 A303　Horiz. pair, #a-b　11.00 11.00

Christmas
A304

Designs: No. 1286, 1700f, Unclothed Santa Claus and clothing (light blue background). No. 1287, 5000f, Christmas tree, decorations and gifts (green background).
No. 1288: a, 1700f, Like No. 1286 (yellow background). b, 5000f, Like No. 1287 (blue background).

2002, Nov. 6
1286-1287 A304　Set of 2　7.00 7.00
Souvenir Sheet
1288 A304　Sheet of 2, #a-b　7.00 7.00

Nos. 949a, 953a Surcharged Like
No. 1266C in Gold or Silver
2002 ?　Litho.　Perf. 13½
1289　Pair　4.75 4.75
a.　A221 2500f on 100c #948　2.25 2.25
b.　A221 2500f on 100c #949　2.25 2.25
1290　Pair　9.00 9.00
a.　A221 3750f on 220c #952 (S)　4.50 4.50
b.　A221 3750f on 220c #953 (S)　4.50 4.50

Birds — A305

No. 1291: a, Falco deiroleucus. b, Lophornis ornatus. c, Touit purpurata. d, Thanlurania furcata. e, Myrmeciza ferruginea. f, Pteroglossus aracari. g, Cotinga cotinga. h, Granatellus pelzelni. i, Euphonia musica. j, Pitangus lictor. k, Cacicus haemorrhous. l, Columba speciosa.

2003, Jan. 9　　Perf. 13¼x14
1291　Block of 12　21.00 21.00
a.-b.　A305 150f Either single　.25 .25
c.-d.　A305 200f Either single　.25 .25
e.-f.　A305 800f Either single　.90 .90
g.-h.　A305 1200f Either single　1.25 1.25
i.-j.　A305 1700f Either single　1.90 1.90
k.-l.　A305 4950f Either single　5.50 5.50

No. 951a Surcharged in Silver Like
No. 1266C
2002, Dec. 30　Litho.　Perf. 13½
1292　Pair　5.00 5.00
a.　A221 2750f on 175c #950　2.50 2.50
b.　A221 2750f on 175c #951　2.50 2.50

Dolls — A306

No. 1293: a, A. M. 352/1030. b, S&H 1079, 1892. c, Jumeau, 1895 (denomination in white). d, Jumeau, 1895 (denomination in red). e, A. M. 390, 1900. f, Minerva, 1900. g, K&R 126, 1905. h, K&R, 1905. i, Handwerck, 1905. j, SFBJ, 1907. k, A. M. 980, 1920. l, K&R, 1910.

2003, May 12　　Perf. 13½x14
1293　Block of 12　12.50 12.50
a.-l.　A306 1000f Any single　1.00 1.00

A307

Designs: 150f, Izaak Enschedé. 800f, Old building of Johann Enschedé Printers, horiz. 1700f, Surinam #7. 3850f, First Surinam banknote printed by Enschedé, horiz. 7500f, Like 150f.

Perf. 12¾x13½, 13½x12¾
2003, June 3
1294-1297 A307　Set of 4　5.25 5.25
Souvenir Sheet
1298 A307 7500f multi　7.50 7.50
Johann Enschedé and Sons, printers, 300th anniv.

A308

Birds: 5400f, Anthracothorax viridigula. 6600f, Campephilus melanoleucos.

2003, Sept. 3　　Perf. 12¾x14
1299 A308　5400f multi　6.25 6.25
1300 A308　6600f multi　7.25 7.25

Traffic Signs Type of 2000
2003, Sept. 3　Litho.　Perf. 12¾x14
1301 A282 4000f 10% grade　4.50 4.50

America Issue - Flora and Fauna — A309

No. 1302: a, 1700f, Faya lobi. b, 8500f, Puma.

2003, Sept. 20　Litho.　Perf. 14x12¾
1302 A309　Horiz. pair, #a-b　8.25 8.25
a.　Souvenir sheet, #1302　8.25 8.25

Nos. 889a, 929a Surcharged

Methods and Perfs as Before
2003
1303　Pair　7.50 7.50
a.　A172 3500f on 1c on 5c #928　3.75 3.75
b.　A172 3500f on 1c on 5c #929　3.75 3.75
1304　Pair　7.50 7.50
a.　A172 3500f on 2c on 10c #888　3.75 3.75
b.　A172 3500f on 2c on 10c #889　3.75 3.75
Issued: No. 1303, 11/1; No. 1304, 12/1.

Christmas — A310

Designs: 1700f, Children, dog, toy horse. 5300f, Woman holding candle.

2003, Nov. 6　Litho.　Perf. 12¾x14
1306 A310 1700f multi　1.40 1.40
1307 A310 5300f multi　4.25 4.25
a.　Horiz. pair, #1306-1307 + central label　7.50 7.50
b.　Souvenir sheet, #1306-1307　7.50 7.50

Powered Flight, Cent.
A311

Designs: 1700f, Santos-Dumont 14bis, first European flight, 1906. 5300f, Replica of 1903 aircraft by Richard Pearse, New Zealand.

2003, Dec. 13　　Perf. 14x12¾
1308 A311 1700f multi　2.00 2.00
1309 A311 5300f multi　5.50 5.50
a.　Souvenir sheet, #1308-1309　7.50 7.50

The Surinam dollar replaced the florin in January 2004 at an exchange rate of 1000 florins to 1 dollar. Nos. 1310-1313, though issued after the introduction of the new currency, have denominations expressed in florins.

Butterflies
A312

No. 1310: a, Anartia amathea. b, Vanessa carye. c, Papilio demetrius. d, Precis octavia. e, Papilio blumei. f, Papilio aritodemus ponceanus. g, Zerynthia rumina. h, Parides gundlachianus. i, Ornithoptera priamus. j, Lyropteryx apollonia. k, Agrias narcissus. l, Elzunia bonplandii.

2004, Jan. 12　　Perf. 12¾x14
1310　Block of 12　22.00 22.00
a.-b.　A312 150f Either single　.25 .25
c.-d.　A312 200f Either single　.25 .25
e.-f.　A312 800f Either single　.65 .65
g.-h.　A312 1200f Either single　.95 .95
i.-j.　A312 1700f Either single　1.40 1.40
k.-l.　A312 L Either single　7.50 7.50
Nos. 1310k-1310l sold for 9500f on day of issue.

Traffic Signs Type of 2000

No. 1311, Horse and rider crossing. No. 1312, Large vehicles prohibited.

2004　Litho.　Perf. 12¾x14
1311 A282 4000f multi　7.75 7.75

1312 A282 4000f multi 7.75 7.75
a. Souvenir sheet, #1278, 1301, 1311, 1312 16.50 16.50

Issued: Nos. 1311-1312, 3/31; No. 1312a, 10/1.

Mailboxes of the World — A313

No. 1313: a, Indonesia. b, Brazil. c, Macao. d, Germany. e, Uruguay. f, Republic of Korea. g, Oman. h, Mexico. i, Australia. j, Switzerland. k, Hong Kong. l, United States.

2004, May 6

1313 Block of 12 25.00 25.00
a.-b. A313 150f Either single .25 .25
c.-d. A313 200f Either single .25 .25
e.-f. A313 800f Either single .65 .65
g.-h. A313 1200f Either single .95 .95
i.-j. A313 1700f Either single 1.40 1.40
k.-l. A313 K Either single 9.00 9.00

Nos. 1313k-1313l each sold for 11,500f ($11.50) on day of issue.

Greek Amphorae — A314

No. 1314 — Inscriptions: a, Athena en Poseidon. b, Wedren. c, Athena Promachus, 363/62 v. C. d, Hippodamia ontvoerd door Pelops, 415 v. C. e, Winnaar muziekconcours, 440-430 v. C. f, Wedren 485-470 v. C. g, Vaashals: speer-en discuswerpers. h, Wedren vier paarden. i, Heracles met leeuw van Nemea, 520 v. C. j, Amfoor, 566 v. C. k, Winnaar muziekconcours (no handles). l, Winnaar muziekconcours (with handles).

No. 1315 — Portions of an amphora: a, $2, Left. b, $3, Center. c, $5, Right.

2004, July 1

1314 Block of 12 28.00 28.00
a.-b. A314 5c Either single .25 .25
c.-d. A314 15c Either single .25 .25
e.-f. A314 20c Either single .25 .25
g.-h. A314 45c Either single .35 .35
i.-j. A314 80c Either single .60 .60
k.-l. A314 M Either single 12.50 12.50

Souvenir Sheet

1315 A314 Sheet of 3, #a-c 8.00 8.00

2004 Summer Olympics, Athens (No. 1315). Nos. 1314k-1314l each sold for $16 on day of issue, and are airmail.

America Issue - Birds — A315

Designs: $1.70, Duck. $12, Parrots.

2004, Sept. 16 *Perf. 14x12¾*

1316-1317 A315 Set of 2 11.00 11.00
1317a Souvenir sheet, #1316-1317 12.00 12.00

Birds — A316

No. 1318: a, Chloroceryle inda. b, Brotogeris chrysopterus. c, Buteo magnirostris. d, Buteo albicaudatus. e, Calliphlox amethystina (facing left). f, Calliphlox amethystina (facing right). g, Harpagus diodon. h, Aratinga pertinax. i, Chlorocersyle amazona. j, Galbula galbula. k, Buteogallus aequinoctialis. l, Polyborus plancus.

2004, Oct. 21 *Perf. 12¾x14*

1318 Block of 12 28.00 28.00
a.-b. A316 5c Either single .25 .25
c.-d. A316 15c Either single .25 .25
e.-f. A316 20c Either single .25 .25
g.-h. A316 45c Either single .35 .35
i.-j. A316 80c Either single .60 .60
k.-l. A316 M Either single 12.50 12.50

Nos. 1318k-1318l each sold for $16 on day of issue, and are airmail.
See Nos. 1329, 1350.

Child Care A317

Christmas A318

2004, Nov. 18 Litho. *Perf. 12¾x14*

1319 A317 $1.70 multi 1.40 1.40
1320 A318 $7.70 multi 6.25 6.25
a. Souvenir sheet, #1319-1320 7.75 7.75

Teddy Bears — A319

No. 1321: a, Bing, 1919. b, Steiff "Teddy Clown," 1926. c, Steiff "Teddy Girl," 1905. d, Steiff, 1905. e, Steif "Elliot," 1907. f, Ideal "Aloysius," 1907. g, Steiff, 1936. h, Steif "Zotty," 1951. i, Steiff, 1910. j, Steiff "Titanic," 1912. k, Steiff "Berlin," 1985. l, Aux Nations, 1903.

No. 1322: a, Blue mohair, 1938-52. b, Musical bear, 1937. c, Red mohair, 1908. d, Shaggy beige mohair, 1908. e, Ally bear, 1916. f, National bear, 1917. g, Cowboy, 1940s. h, Coronation bear, 1953. i, Tumbling bear, 1920-30s. j, Messenger bear, 1923. k, Bear on a tricycle, 1958. l, Michi Takahashi, 1999.

2004-05 Litho. *Perf. 12¾x14*

1321 Block of 12 21.00 21.00
a.-b. A319 5c Either single .25 .25
c.-d. A319 15c Either single .25 .25
e.-f. A319 20c Either single .25 .25
g.-h. A319 45c Either single .35 .35
i.-j. A319 80c Either single .65 .65
k.-l. A319 K Either single 9.00 9.00
1322 Block of 12 30.00 30.00
a.-b. A319 5c Either single .25 .25
c.-d. A319 15c Either single .25 .25
e.-f. A319 20c Either single .25 .25
g.-h. A319 45c Either single .35 .35
i.-j. A319 80c Either single .65 .65
k.-l. A319 N Either single 13.50 13.50

Issued: No. 1321, 2004; No. 1322, 3/1/05. Nos. 1321k-1321l each sold for $11.50 on day of issue, and are airmail. Nos. 1322k-1322l each sold for $17 on day of issue, and are airmail.

Butterflies — A320

No. 1323: a, Papilio chikae. b, Iphiclides podalirius. c, Paraphnaeus. d, Morpho didius. e, Delias eucharis. f, Parides sesostris. g, Baronia brevicornis. h, Graphium agamemnon. i, Papilio palinurus. j, Ornithoptera meridionalis. k, Battus bhilenor. l, Eurytides bellerophon.

2005, Jan. 5

1323 Block of 12 30.00 30.00
a.-b. A320 5c Either single .25 .25
c.-d. A320 15c Either single .25 .25
e.-f. A320 20c Either single .25 .25
g.-h. A320 45c Either single .35 .35
i.-j. A320 80c Either single .60 .60
k.-l. A320 N Either single 13.50 13.50

Nos. 1323k-1323l each sold for $17 on day of issue, and are airmail.

Ships A321

No. 1324: a, Louis Roux, Altana. b, Fanerom Eni. c, Nafsika. d, Aristeidis Glykas. e, G. D'Esposito. f, G. D'Esposito, diff.

2005, May 4 Litho. *Perf. 14x12¾*

1324 Block of 6 17.00 17.00
a. A321 5c multi .25 .25
b. A321 15c multi .25 .25
c. A321 20c multi .25 .25
d. A321 80c multi .60 .60
e. A321 $1.70 multi 1.40 1.40
f. A321 P multi 14.00 14.00

No. 1324f is airmail and sold for $18 on day of issue.

Orchids — A322

No. 1325: a, Vanda hybrid. b, Phalaenopsis hybrid, dark pink flowers. c, Dendrobium hybrid, pink flowers. d, Dendrobium hybrid, dark red flowers with foliage in background. e, Vanda hybrid, diff. f, Peristeria elata. g, Spathoglottis hybrid. h, Dendrobium hybrid, yellow orange flowers. i, Vanda sanderiana. j, Phalaenopsis hybrid, peach flowers. k, Phalaenopsis hybrid, pink flowers. l, Phalaenopsis hybrid, white flowers.

2005, June 29 *Perf. 12¾x14*

1325 Block of 12 27.50 27.50
a.-b. A322 5c Either single .25 .25
c.-d. A322 15c Either single .25 .25
e.-f. A322 20c Either single .25 .25
g.-h. A322 45c Either single .40 .40
i.-j. A322 80c Either single .70 .70
k.-l. A322 Q Either single 10.00 10.00

Nos. 1325k and 1325 l are airmail and each sold for $12.50 on day of issue. See No. 1337.

America Issue, Fight Against Poverty A323

Designs: $1.70, Teacher and children. $14.50, Farmer, oxen and plow.
$14, Teacher and children, diff.

Perf. 14x12¾, 12¾x14

2005, Sept. 14

1326-1327 A323 Set of 2 13.00 13.00

Souvenir Sheet

Perf. 12¾x13¼

1328 A323 $14 multi 11.50 11.50

Birds Type of 2004

No. 1329: a, Porphyrula flavirostris. b, Asio clamator. c, Herpetotheres cashinnans. d, Jacana jacana. e, Touit batavica. f, Dendrocygna autumnalis. g, Coccyzus minor. h, Busarellus nigricollis. i, Lophostrix cristata. j, Otus choliba. k, Chrysolampis mosquitus. l, Pyrrhula picta.

2005, Oct. 19 *Perf. 12¾x14*

1329 Block of 12 35.00 35.00
a.-b. A316 5c Either single .25 .25
c.-d. A316 15c Either single .25 .25
e.-f. A316 20c Either single .25 .25
g.-h. A316 80c Either single .65 .65
i.-j. A316 $1.80 Either single 1.40 1.40
k.-l. A316 P Either single 14.50 14.50

Nos. 1329k and 1329 l are airmail and each sold for $18 on day of issue.

Children — A324

Designs (country name in red): 80c, Girl jumping rope. $9.50, Boy on swing.
No. 1332 — Country name in white: a, Girl jumping rope, diff. b, Boy on swing, diff.

2005, Nov. 16 *Perf. 12¾x13¼*

1330-1331 A324 Set of 2 8.50 8.50

Souvenir Sheet

1332 A324 $5 Sheet of 2, #a-b 8.50 8.50

No. 891a Surcharged

Methods and Perfs as Before

2005, Dec. 1

1333 Pair 6.50 6.50
a. A172 $3.50 on 3c on 50c #891a 3.00 3.00
b. A172 $3.50 on 3c on 50c #891b 3.00 3.00

Europa Stamps, 50th Anniv. — A325

Designs: $1, Netherlands #379. $2, Netherlands #369. $9, Netherlands #375.

2006, Jan. 4 Litho. *Perf. 12¾x13¼*

1334-1336 A325 Set of 3 8.75 8.75
1336a Souvenir sheet, #1334-1336 8.75 8.75

Orchids Type of 2005

No. 1337: a, Dendrobium hybrid, yellow flowers. b, Dendrobium hybrid, white flowers. c, Phalaenopsis hybrid, light purple flowers. d, Phalaenopsis hybrid, pink flowers. e, Vanda hybrid, white flowers. f, Vanda hybrid, purple flowers. g, Dendrobium hybrid, purple and white flowers. h, Arachnis hybrid. i, Vanda hybrid, light orange flowers. j, Vanda hybrid, speckled purple flowers. k, Complex hybrid, orange flowers. l, Vanda hybrid, purple and white flowers.

2006, Feb. 15 *Perf. 12¾x14*

1337 Block of 12 28.00 28.00
a.-b. A322 5c Either single .25 .25
c.-d. A322 15c Either single .25 .25
e.-f. A322 20c Either single .25 .25
g.-h. A322 45c Either single .35 .35
i.-j. A322 80c Either single .60 .60
k.-l. A322 Q Either single 12.50 12.50

Nos. 1337k and 1337 l are airmail and each sold for $17.50 on day of issue.

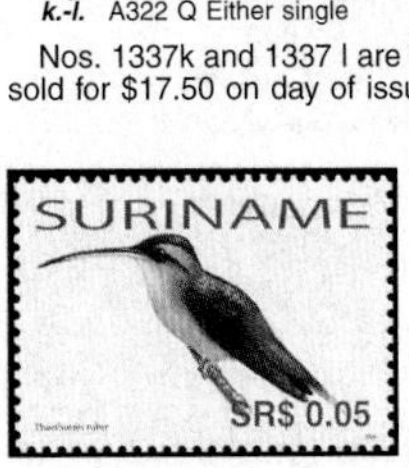

Birds — A326

No. 1338: a, Phaethornis ruber. b, Threnetes leucurus. c, Podager nacunda. d, Columbina passerina. e, Leptotila rufaxilla. f, Claravis pretiosa. g, Campylopterus largipennis. h, Otus choliba. i, Porzana albicollis. j, Amazilia fimbriata. k, Ciccata virgata. l, Nyctidromus albicollis.

2006, May 15 Litho. *Perf. 14x12¾*

1338 Block of 12 28.00 28.00
a.-b. A326 5c Either single .25 .25
c.-d. A326 15c Either single .25 .25
e.-f. A326 20c Either single .25 .25

g.-h. A326 45c Either single .30 .30
i.-j. A326 80c Either single .55 .55
k.-l. A326 Q Either single 12.50 12.50

Nos. 1338k-1338l each sold for $17.50, and are airmail.

Nobel Laureates — A327

No. 1339: a, Aung San Suu Kyi, Peace, 1991. b, Milton Friedman, Economics, 1976. c, Marie Curie, Chemistry, 1911. d, Johannes Diderik van der Waals, Physics, 1910. e, Selma Lagerlöf, Literature, 1909. f, Gary S. Becker, Economics, 1992.

2006, June 26   *Perf. 12¾x13¼*
1339   Block of 6   8.50 8.50
a. A327 20c multi .25 .25
b. A327 $1.20 multi .85 .85
c. A327 $1.70 multi 1.25 1.25
d. A327 $2 multi 1.40 1.40
e. A327 $3 multi 2.25 2.25
f. A327 $3.50 multi 2.50 2.50

America Issue, Energy Conservation A328

Designs: 80c, Solar-powered airplane. $16.20, Windmill.
No. 1342: a, $3.50, Glider. b, $12.50, Windmills.

2006, Sept. 15   *Perf. 14*
1340-1341 A328   Set of 2   12.50 12.50
Souvenir Sheet
1342 A328   Sheet of 2, #a-b   12.00 12.00

Fish — A329

No. 1343: a, Crown betta. b, Barbus barilioides. c, Macropodus opercularis. d, Xiphophorus maculatus. e, Acanthurus lineatus. f, Carassius auratus.

2006, Oct. 15   *Perf. 13¼x12¾*
1343   Block of 6   14.50 14.50
a. A329 $1.20 multi .85 .85
b. A329 $1.70 multi 1.25 1.25
c. A329 $2 multi 1.40 1.40
d. A329 $3 multi 2.25 2.25
e. A329 $3.50 multi 2.50 2.50
f. A329 $8.60 multi 6.25 6.25

Child Care — A330

Christmas A331

2006, Nov. 6   *Perf. 14*
1344 A330 $4 shown   3.00 3.00
1345 A331 $9.20 shown   6.75 6.75
Souvenir Sheet
1346   Sheet of 2   5.00 5.00
a. A330 80c Children with ball .60 .60
b. A331 $6 Stained glass, diff. 4.25 4.25

No. 447 Surcharged in Brown

Methods and Perfs As Before
2006, Dec. 1
1347 A111 $3.25 on 1c #447 2.40 2.40
1348 A111 $3.75 on 1c #447 2.75 2.75

Primates — A332

No. 1349: a, Hylobates lar. b, Leontopithecus rosalia. c, Saguinus imperator. d, Callithrix geoffroyi. e, Callithrix argentata. f, Pygathrix nemaeus nemaeus. g, Saimiri sciureus. h, Douc langur. i, Cercopithecus neglectus. j, Alouatta caraya. k, Verreaux sitaka. l, Pan troglodytes.

2006, Dec. 13   *Perf. 12¾x13¼*
1349   Block of 12   24.00 24.00
a. A332 R multi .25 .25
b. A332 20c multi .25 .25
c. A332 45c multi .35 .35
d. A332 80c multi .60 .60
e. A332 $1.20 multi .90 .90
f. A332 $1.70 multi 1.25 1.25
g. A332 $2 multi 1.40 1.40
h. A332 $3 multi 2.25 2.25
i. A332 $3.50 multi 2.50 2.50
j. A332 $4 multi 3.00 3.00
k. A332 $5 multi 3.75 3.75
l. A332 $10 multi 7.25 7.25

No. 1349a sold for 15c on day of issue.

Bird Type of 2004
2006, Dec. 20   *Perf. 12¾x14*
1350 A316 $10 Phaethornis superciliosus 7.25 7.25

Printed in sheets of 2 + label.

Orchids — A333

No. 1351: a, Cattleya labiata. b, Vuylstekeara. c, Cymbidium. d, Odontoglossum pestcatorei. e, Odontocidium f, Odontioda. g, Vanda. h, Cattleya. i, Paphiopedilum insigne. j, Phalaenopsis. k, Thunia. l, Oncidium.

2007, Jan. 3   *Perf. 12¾x13¼*
1351   Block of 12   24.00 24.00
a. A333 S multi .25 .25
b. A333 20c multi .25 .25
c. A333 45c multi .35 .35
d. A333 80c multi .60 .60
e. A333 $1.20 multi .90 .90
f. A333 $1.70 multi 1.25 1.25
g. A333 $2 multi 1.40 1.40
h. A333 $3 multi 2.25 2.25
i. A333 $3.50 multi 2.50 2.50
j. A333 $4 multi 3.00 3.00
k. A333 $5 multi 3.75 3.75
l. A333 $10 multi 7.25 7.25

No. 1351a sold for 10c on day of issue.

Butterflies A334

No. 1352: a, Great spangled fritillary. b, Peacock pansy. c, Viceroy. d, Unidentified taxco. e, Tropical buckeye. f, Limenitis popul.

2007, Feb. 14   *Perf. 14*
1352   Block of 6   9.00 9.00
a. A334 T multi .25 .25
b. A334 $1.20 multi .85 .85
c. A334 $1.70 multi 1.25 1.25
d. A334 $2 multi 1.40 1.40
e. A334 $3 multi 2.25 2.25
f. A334 $4 multi 3.00 3.00

No. 1352a sold for 5c on day of issue. See No. 1366.

Reptiles A335

No. 1353: a, Terapene carolina. b, Cuora flavomarginata. c, Chelonia mydas. d, Testudo hermanni. e, Uromastyx acanthinura. f, Physignathus cocincinus. g, Iguana iguana. h, Amblyrhynchus cristatus. i, Chamaeleo jacksoni. j, Crocodylus niloticus. k, Caiman crocodilus. l, Varanus komodensis.

2007, Mar. 21   *Perf. 13¼x12¾*   Litho.
1353   Block of 12   24.00 24.00
a. A335 S multi .25 .25
b. A335 20c multi .25 .25
c. A335 45c multi .30 .30
d. A335 80c multi .60 .60
e. A335 $1.20 multi .90 .90
f. A335 $1.70 multi 1.25 1.25
g. A335 $2 multi 1.50 1.50
h. A335 $3 multi 2.25 2.25
i. A335 $3.50 multi 2.60 2.60
j. A335 $4 multi 3.00 3.00
k. A335 $5 multi 3.75 3.75
l. A335 $10 multi 7.25 7.25

No. 1353a sold for 10c on day of issue.

Parrots — A336

No. 1354: a, Callocephalon fimbriatum. b, Cacatua ophthalmica. c, Cacatua galerita. d, Cacatua sulphure amazone. e, Calyporhychus magunificus. f, Cacatua sulphure amazone, diff. g, Eolophus rosicapillus. h, Cacatua sulphure amazone, diff. i, Parrot (inscribed "Pan troglodytes" in error).

2007, Apr. 26   *Perf. 14*
1354   Block of 9   11.50 11.50
a. A336 T multi .25 .25
b. A336 25c multi .25 .25
c. A336 55c multi .40 .40
d. A336 80c multi .60 .60
e. A336 $1.10 multi .80 .80
f. A336 $1.20 multi .90 .90
g. A336 $2 multi 1.50 1.50
h. A336 $4 multi 3.00 3.00
i. A336 $5 multi 3.75 3.75

No. 1354a sold for 5c on day of issue.

Birds — A337

No. 1355: a, Agamia agami. b, Botaurus pinnatus. c, Rallus maculatus. d, Melanerpes cruentatus. e, Piculus chrysochloros. f, Paroaria gularis. g, Gyanicterus cyanicterus. h, Tersina viridis. i, Sicalis floreola.

2007, May 23   *Perf. 12¾x13¼*
1355   Block of 9   18.00 18.00
a. A337 T multi .25 .25
b. A337 20c multi .25 .25
c. A337 45c multi .35 .35
d. A337 80c multi .60 .60
e. A337 $1.20 multi .90 .90
f. A337 $2 multi 1.50 1.50
g. A337 $4 multi 3.00 3.00
h. A337 $5 multi 3.75 3.75
i. A337 $10 multi 7.25 7.25

No. 1355a sold for 5c on day of issue. See Nos. 1373, 1388.

Fish — A338

No. 1356: a, Brachydanio rerio. b, Pterois miles. c, Pomacanthus annularis. d, Balsitoides conspicillum. e, Plectorhynchus orientalis. f, Chaetodon auriga.

2007, June 27   *Perf. 13¼x12¾*   Litho.
1356   Block of 6   15.00 15.00
a. A338 $1.20 multi .90 .90
b. A338 $1.70 multi 1.25 1.25
c. A338 $2 multi 1.50 1.50
d. A338 $3 multi 2.25 2.25
e. A338 $3.50 multi 2.60 2.60
f. A338 $8.60 multi 6.25 6.25

Ferrari Automobiles A339

No. 1357: a, 1947 125 S. b, 1962 250 GTO. c, 1984 GTO. d, 1999 F399. e, 1983 Mondial Cabriolet. f, 1994 F 333 SP. g, 1971 365 GT4 BB. h, 2006 FXX.

2007, July 11   *Perf. 14*
1357   Block of 8 + label   9.75 9.75
a. A339 10c multi .25 .25
b. A339 20c multi .25 .25
c. A339 50c multi .35 .35
d. A339 $1 multi .75 .75
e. A339 $1.60 multi 1.10 1.10
f. A339 $1.75 multi 1.25 1.25
g. A339 $2.25 multi 2.25 2.25
h. A339 $5 multi 3.50 3.50

No. 1357 was issued in sheets containing two blocks, one of which had the label in the lower right corner, and the other with the label in the upper left corner.

Primates — A340

No. 1358: a, Pan troglodytes. b, Cercopithecus neglectus. c, Nasalis larvatus. d, Macaca fascicularis. e, Mandrillus sphinx. f, Rhinopithecus roxellana.

2007, Aug. 15   Litho.   *Perf. 14*
1358   Block of 6   15.00 15.00
a. A340 $1.20 multi .90 .90
b. A340 $1.70 multi 1.25 1.25
c. A340 $2 multi 1.50 1.50
d. A340 $3 multi 2.25 2.25
e. A340 $3.50 multi 2.60 2.60
f. A340 $8.60 multi 6.25 6.25

America Issue, Education A341

Designs: 80c, Children in classroom. $16.20, Children in classroom, diff.
No. 1361: a, $7, Boy at blackboard. b, $9, Two children.

2007, Sept. 19
1359-1360 A341   Set of 2   12.50 12.50
Souvenir Sheet
1361 A341   Sheet of 2, #a-b   12.00 12.00

Christmas — A342

Designs: $4, Four children at desks. $6, Holy Family.
No. 1364: a, 80c, Children, words and letters. b, $9.20, Holy Family, sheep.

2007, Nov. 7

1362-1363	A342	Set of 2	7.25	7.25

Souvenir Sheet

1364	A342	Sheet of 2, #a-b	7.25	7.25

Frogs
A343

No. 1365: a, Agalychnis callidryas. b, Dendrobates pumilio. c, Sphaeramia nematoptera. d, Hoffmanni. e, Sphaeramia nematoptera, diff. f, Dendrobates histrionicus.

2007, Dec. 12   Litho.   Perf. 14x12¾

1365		Block of 6	11.00	11.00
a.	A343	T multi	.25	.25
b.	A343	$1.20 multi	.85	.85
c.	A343	$1.70 multi	1.25	1.25
d.	A343	$2 multi	1.40	1.40
e.	A343	$3 multi	2.25	2.25
f.	A343	$7 multi	5.00	5.00

On day of issue, No. 1365a sold for 5c.

Butterflies Type of 2007

No. 1366: a, Anthocharis bella. b, Satyr angelwing. c, Red lacewing. d, Inachis io. e, Purple sapphire. f, Pearly crescentspot. g, Monarch. h, Marpesia berania. i, Darkmuseum swallowtail. j, Byasa alcinous. k, Brown peacock. l, Brown and orange Mexican.

2008, Jan. 2   Litho.   Perf. 14

1366		Block of 12	24.00	24.00
a.	A334	T multi	.25	.25
b.	A334	25c multi	.25	.25
c.	A334	45c multi	.30	.30
d.	A334	80c multi	.60	.60
e.	A334	$1.20 multi	.90	.90
f.	A334	$1.70 multi	1.25	1.25
g.	A334	$2 multi	1.50	1.50
h.	A334	$3 multi	2.25	2.25
i.	A334	$3.50 multi	2.60	2.60
j.	A334	$4 multi	3.00	3.00
k.	A334	$5 multi	3.75	3.75
l.	A334	$10 multi	7.25	7.25

No. 1366a sold for 5c on day of issue.

Fish — A344

No. 1367: a, Sphaeramia nematoptera. b, Neophrynichthys latus. c, Cheilodipterus isostigmus.

2008, Feb. 13

1367	A344	Horiz. strip of 3	8.75	8.75
a.		$1.20 multi	.90	.90
b.		$3 multi	2.25	2.25
c.		$7.80 multi	5.50	5.50

Children in Native Costumes — A345

Children in various costumes.

2008, Mar. 19   Litho.   Perf. 14

1368	A345	Block of 12	24.00	24.00
a.		T multi	.25	.25
b.		25c multi	.25	.25
c.		45c multi	.35	.35
d.		80c multi	.60	.60
e.		$1.20 multi	.90	.90
f.		$1.70 multi	1.25	1.25
g.		$2 multi	1.50	1.50
h.		$3 multi	2.25	2.25
i.		$3.50 multi	2.60	2.60
j.		$4 multi	3.00	3.00
k.		$5 multi	3.75	3.75
l.		$10 multi	7.25	7.25

No. 1368a sold for 5c on day of issue.

2008 Summer Olympics, Beijing — A346

No. 1369: a, Archery. b, Weight lifting. c, Basketball. d, Runner crossing finish line.

2008, Apr. 9   Litho.   Perf. 14

1369		Horiz. strip of 4	5.25	5.25
a.	A346	$1 multi	.75	.75
b.	A346	$1.50 multi	1.10	1.10
c.	A346	$2 multi	1.50	1.50
d.	A346	$2.50 multi	1.90	1.90

Stamp Passion Philatelic Exhibition, the Netherlands
A347

No. 1370: a, Netherlands #104. b, Surinam #120. c, Netherlands #43. d, Netherlands #103. e, Netherlands #B85. f, Netherlands #C9. g, Netherlands #J27. h, Netherlands #O25. i, Surinam #B10. j, Surinam #C14. k, Netherlands #160. l, Netherlands #96.

2008, Apr. 9   Litho.   Perf. 14

1370		Block of 12	37.50	37.50
a.	A347	$1 multi	.75	.75
b.	A347	$1.50 multi	1.10	1.10
c.	A347	$2 multi	1.50	1.50
d.	A347	$2.50 multi	1.90	1.90
e.	A347	$3 multi	2.25	2.25
f.	A347	$3.50 multi	2.60	2.60
g.	A347	$4 multi	3.00	3.00
h.	A347	$5 multi	3.75	3.75
i.	A347	$5.50 multi	4.00	4.00
j.	A347	$6 multi	4.50	4.50
k.	A347	$7 multi	5.25	5.25
l.	A347	$9 multi	6.75	6.75

Images of some stamps are distorted.

Buildings — A348

No. 1371: a, F.H.R. Lim A Postraat 34A. b, Combékerk. c, Waterkant 10. d, Waterkant 14. e, Waterkant 12. f, Officierswoning 6. g, Grote Combéweg 33. h, Officierswoning 5. i, Officierswoning 9.

2008, Apr. 23

1371		Block of 9	16.50	16.50
a.	A348	V multi	.25	.25
b.	A348	40c multi	.30	.30
c.	A348	50c multi	.35	.35
d.	A348	80c multi	.60	.60
e.	A348	$1.20 multi	.90	.90
f.	A348	$2 multi	1.50	1.50
g.	A348	$4 multi	3.00	3.00
h.	A348	$5 multi	3.75	3.75
i.	A348	$8 multi	5.75	5.75

No. 1371a sold for 15c on day of issue.

Snakes
A349

No. 1372: a, Candoia carinata. b, Viper. c, Yellow Chondropython viridis. d, Red juvenile Chondropython viridis. e, Eyelash viper. f, Green mamba. g, Emerald tree boa. h, Tiger rat snake.

2008, May 21

1372		Block of 8 + label	33.00	33.00
a.	A349	$1 multi	.75	.75
b.	A349	$1.50 multi	1.10	1.10
c.	A349	$2 multi	1.50	1.50
d.	A349	$3 multi	2.25	2.25
e.	A349	$5 multi	3.75	3.75
f.	A349	$7.50 multi	5.25	5.25
g.	A349	$10 multi	7.25	7.25
h.	A349	$15 multi	11.00	11.00

Bird Type of 2007

No. 1373: a, Ceryle torquata. b, Tangara velia. c, Florisuga mellivora. d, Psarocollus viridis. e, Pionus fuscus. f, Chloroceryle aenea. g, Caryothraustes canadensis. h, Campephilus rubricollis.

Perf. 13¼x13¾

2008, Aug. 15   Litho.

Size: 16x21mm

1373		Horiz. strip of 8	8.00	8.00
a.	A337	30c multi	.25	.25
b.	A337	45c multi	.30	.30
c.	A337	50c multi	.35	.35
d.	A337	75c multi	.55	.55
e.	A337	90c multi	.65	.65
f.	A337	$1.40 multi	1.00	1.00
g.	A337	$2.50 multi	1.90	1.90
h.	A337	$4 multi	3.00	3.00
i.		Souvenir sheet, 2 each #1373e, 1373f + central label	6.75	6.75

America Issue, Festivals — A350

No. 1374: a, Two Carifesta participants. b, Surinam flag at Carifesta.
No. 1375: a, $7, Woman in Carnaval costume. b, $15, Woman wearing Carnaval hat.

2008, Sept. 17   Litho.   Perf. 14

1374	A350	Horiz. pair + central label	16.00	16.00
a.		$9 multi	6.75	6.75
b.		$12.50 multi	9.25	9.25

Souvenir Sheet

1375	A350	Sheet of 2, #a-b	16.50	16.50

Birds — A351

No. 1376: a, Ceryle rudis. b, Copsychus saularis. c, Dicaeum cruetatum. d, Garrulax perspicillatus. e, Halcyon smyrnensis. f, Leiothrix lutea.

2008, Oct. 15

1376		Block of 6	11.50	11.50
a.	A351	V multi	.25	.25
b.	A351	$1.10 multi	.80	.80
c.	A351	$1.80 multi	1.40	1.40
d.	A351	$3 multi	2.25	2.25
e.	A351	$4 multi	3.00	3.00
f.	A351	$5 multi	3.75	3.75

No. 1376a sold for 15c on day of issue. Bird names are misspelled on Nos. 1376c and 1376e.

Children and Adults — A352

No. 1377: a, Woman swinging girl by arms. b, Boy in soap box derby car.

No. 1378: a, $5, Woman and girl with cut flowers. b, $7, Woman and girl painting birdhouse.

2008, Nov. 5

1377	A352	Horiz. pair + central label	9.00	9.00
a.		80c multi	.60	.60
b.		$11.20 multi	8.25	8.25

Souvenir Sheet

1378	A352	Sheet of 2, #a-b	9.00	9.00

Flowers
A353

No. 1379: a, Ixora Nora Grant White. b, Ixora Bonnie Lynn. c, Ixora coccinea. d, Ixora Dwarf Pink. e, Ixora Dwarf Orange. f, Ixora Maui Pink.

2008, Dec. 10

1379		Block of 6	15.00	15.00
a.	A353	$1.10 multi	.80	.80
b.	A353	$1.80 multi	1.40	1.40
c.	A353	$2 multi	1.50	1.50
d.	A353	$3 multi	2.25	2.25
e.	A353	X multi	3.75	3.75
f.	A353	$7 multi	5.25	5.25

No. 1379e sold for $5.10 on day of issue.

Souvenir Sheet

Streptopelia Orientalis — A354

2009, Jan. 7   Litho.   Perf. 14

1380	A354	$9.50 multi	7.00	7.00

Frogs
A355

Designs: $1, Ceratophrys cornuta. $2, Bufo marinus. $2.50, Eleutherodactylus counouspeus. $3.50, Gastrotheca monticola. $5, Leptodactylus pentadactylus. $6, Pipa pipa. $7, Pseudis paradoxa.

2009, Feb. 15   Litho.   Perf. 14

1381-1387	A355	Set of 7	20.00	20.00

Nos. 1381-1387 were printed in a sheet containing 2 of each stamp + a central label.

Birds Type of 2007

No. 1388: a, Tinamus major. b, Crypturellus erythropus. c, Crypturellus variegatus. d, Crypturellus cinereus. e, Aburria pipile. f, Bucco capensis. g, Crypturellus soui. h, Ortalis motmot. i, Penelope marail. j, Chelidoptera tenebrosa.

2009, Mar. 18   Litho.   Perf. 14

1388		Block of 10	33.00	33.00
a.	A337	Z multi	.90	.90
b.	A337	$1.50 multi	1.10	1.10
c.	A337	$2.50 multi	1.75	1.75
d.	A337	$3 multi	2.25	2.25
e.	A337	$3.50 multi	2.50	2.50
f.	A337	$4 multi	3.00	3.00
g.	A337	$5 multi	3.50	3.50
h.	A337	$5.50 multi	4.00	4.00
i.	A337	$7 multi	5.25	5.25
j.	A337	$12 multi	8.75	8.75

No. 1388a sold for $1.25 on day of issue.

Electricity, 200th
Anniv. — A356

No. 1389: a, Sir Humphry Davy (1778-
1829), chemist. b, Diagram of light bulb. c,
Thomas Alva Edison (1847-1931), inventor.

2009, Mar. 21   Litho.   Perf. 14
1389		Vert. strip of 3	11.00 11.00
a.	A356	$2 blk & red	1.50 1.50
b.	A356	$5 blk & red	3.75 3.75
c.	A356	$8 blk & red	5.75 5.75

Mailboxes From
Around the
World — A357

2009, May 27   Litho.   Perf. 14
1390		Block of 10	29.00 29.00
a.	A357	Z Argentina	.90 .90
b.	A357	$2 Canada	1.50 1.50
c.	A357	$2.50 China	1.75 1.75
d.	A357	$3 India	2.25 2.25
e.	A357	$3.25 Ireland	2.40 2.40
f.	A357	$3.75 Russia	2.75 2.75
g.	A357	$5 Turkey	3.50 3.50
h.	A357	$5.50 Venezuela	4.00 4.00
i.	A357	$6.50 Yemen	4.50 4.50
j.	A357	$7 Great Britain	5.25 5.25

No. 1390a sold for $1.25 on day of issue.

Fish — A358

No. 1391: a, Cephalopholis miniata. b,
Epinephelus fasciatus. c, Pomacanthus
xanthocephalus. d, Anampses meleagrides. e,
Chaetodon bennetti. f, Cephalopholis argus. g,
Chaetodon xanthocephalus. h, Scarus
frenatus. i, Priacanthus hamrur. j,
Cephalopholis polleni. k, Pomacanthus
semicirculatus. l, Ostracion cubicus.

2009, July 8
1391		Block of 12	33.50 33.50
a.	A358	Z multi	.90 .90
b.	A358	$1.25 multi	.90 .90
c.	A358	$1.50 multi	1.10 1.10
d.	A358	$2 multi	1.50 1.50
e.	A358	$2.50 multi	1.75 1.75
f.	A358	$3 multi	2.25 2.25
g.	A358	$3.50 multi	2.50 2.50
h.	A358	$4 multi	3.00 3.00
i.	A358	$5.75 multi	4.25 4.25
j.	A358	$6 multi	4.50 4.50
k.	A358	$7 multi	5.25 5.25
l.	A358	$7.50 multi	5.50 5.50

No. 1391a sold for $1.25 on day of issue.

Children at Play — A359

No. 1392: a, $8, Knikkeren (marbles). b,
$15, Hoepelen (hoop rolling).
No. 1393: a, $10, Hoelahoep (hula hoop). b,
$12, Vijfsteentje (five girls in circle).

2009, Sept. 16
1392	A359	Horiz. pair, #a-b	17.00 17.00

Souvenir Sheet
1393	A359	Sheet of 2, #a-b	16.00 16.00

Miniature Sheet

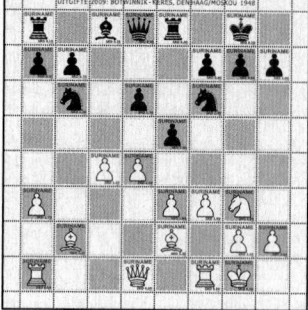

Chess Board — A360

No. 1394: a, 10c, Black rook. b, 20c, Black
bishop. c, 30c, Black queen. d, 40c, Black
rook. e, 50c, Black king. f, 60c, Black pawn. g,
70c, Black pawn. h, 80c, Black pawn. i, 90c,
Black pawn. j, $1, Black pawn. k, $1.10, Black
knight. l, $1.20, Black pawn. m, $1.30, Black
knight. n, $1.40, Black pawn. o, $1.50, White
pawn. p, $1.60, White pawn. q, $1.70, White
pawn. r, $1.80, White pawn. s, $1.90, White
pawn. t, $2, White knight. u, $2.10, White
bishop. v, $2.20, White bishop. w, $2.50,
White pawn. x, $3, White pawn. y, $4.50,
White rook. z, $4.80, White queen. aa, $4.90,
White rook. ab, $5, White king.

2009, Oct. 21   Litho.   Perf. 14
1394	A360	Sheet of 28, #a-ab, + 36 labels	37.00 37.00

No. 1394 shows position of pieces of 1948
match between Paul Keres and Mikhail Botvinnik. Compare with No. 1428.

Endangered Primates — A361

No. 1395: a, $1, Aotus trivirgatus. b, $1.50,
Alouatta palliata. c, $2, Cacajao calvus. d,
$2.50, Lagothrix lagotricha. e, $3, Pithecia
pithecia. f, $5, Callithrix mauesi. g, $7,
Alouatta seniculus. h, $8, Gorilla. i, $9,
Cercopithecus diana.

2009, Nov. 4
1395	A361	Block of 9, #a-i	29.00 29.00

Flowers — A362

No. 1396: a, Pulsatilla vernalis. b,
Crisanthemum maximum. c, Abronia villosa. d,
Aquilegia caerulea. e, Zinnia elegans. f, Bougainvillea glabra. g, Daffodil. h, Victoria cruziana. i, Rosa palustris. j, Nymphaea.

2009, Dec. 9   Perf. 14
1396		Block of 10	30.00 30.00
a.	A362	Z multi	.90 .90
b.	A362	$2 multi	1.50 1.50
c.	A362	$2.50 multi	1.90 1.90
d.	A362	$3 multi	2.25 2.25
e.	A362	$3.25 multi	2.40 2.40
f.	A362	$3.75 multi	2.75 2.75
g.	A362	$5 multi	3.75 3.75
h.	A362	$5.50 multi	4.00 4.00
i.	A362	$6.50 multi	4.75 4.75
j.	A362	$7 multi	5.25 5.25

No. 1396a sold for $1.25 on day of issue.

Miniature Sheet

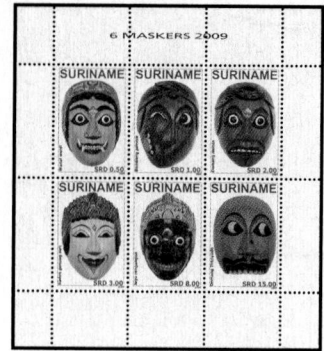

Masks — A363

No. 1397: a, 50c, Wadal werdi. b, $1,
Bambang painem. c, $2, Demang mones. d,
$3, Raden gunung sari. e, $8, Joyo ren-
gangon. f, $15, Demang tirtoyudo.

2009, Dec. 30   Perf. 12¾x13¼
1397	A363	Sheet of 6, #a-f	22.00 22.00

Shells — A364

No. 1398: a, Cardita megastropha. b,
Frangum unedo. c, Galeodea echinophora. d,
Architectonica maxima. e, Opeatostoma
pseudodon. f, Haliotis queketti. g, Cymatium
hepaticum. h, Clanculus pharaonius. i, Harpa
harpa. j, Hydatina nobilis.

2010, Jan. 20   Perf. 14
1398		Block of 10	30.00 30.00
a.	A364	$1 multi	.75 .75
b.	A364	$1.50 multi	1.10 1.10
c.	A364	$2 multi	1.50 1.50
d.	A364	$2.50 multi	1.90 1.90
e.	A364	$3 multi	2.25 2.25
f.	A364	$4 multi	3.00 3.00
g.	A364	$5 multi	3.75 3.75
h.	A364	$6 multi	4.50 4.50
i.	A364	$7 multi	5.25 5.25
j.	A364	$8 multi	6.00 6.00

No. 1398 was printed in a sheet containing
two irregular blocks of 10 + a central label.

Souvenir Sheet

Mushrooms — A365

No. 1399: a, $2, Amanita muscaria. b, $5,
Boletus edulis. c, $8, Agaricus xanthoderma.

2010, Feb. 24   Perf. 13¼x12¾
1399	A365	Sheet of 3, #a-c	11.00 11.00

Cuckoo
Clocks
A366

No. 1400 — Clock from: a, $1.50, 1760. b,
$2.50, 1890. c, $3.50, 1900. d, $4.50, 1910. e,
$5, 1920. f, $8, 1950.

2010, Mar. 25   Perf. 14
1400	A366	Block of 6, #a-f	18.50 18.50

Butterflies — A367

No. 1401: a, Maniola jurtina. b, Melanargia
galathea. c, Argynnis adippe. d, Apatura iris.
e, Lasiommata megera. f, Pararge aegeria. g,
Argynnis paphia. h, Vanessa atalanta. i,
Limenitis camilla. j, Polyomnatus bellargus. k,
Argynnis aglaja. l, Pyronia tithonus.
$12, Apatura ilia, horiz.

2010, Apr. 28
1401	A367	Block of 12	32.00 32.00
a.		70c multi	.50 .50
b.		$1.25 multi	.90 .90
c.		$1.75 multi	1.25 1.25
d.		$2.50 multi	1.90 1.90
e.		$2.75 multi	2.00 2.00
f.		$3 multi	2.25 2.25
g.		$3.75 multi	2.75 2.75
h.		$4.25 multi	3.00 3.00
i.		$4.50 multi	3.25 3.25
j.		$5 multi	3.75 3.75
k.		$6 multi	4.50 4.50
l.		$7 multi	5.25 5.25

Souvenir Sheet
Perf. 13¼x12¾
1402	A367	$12 multi	8.75 8.75

No. 1402 contains one 34x23mm stamp.

Birds — A368

No. 1403: a, Tangara chilensis. b, Lepto-
pogon amaurocephalus. c, Xolmis cinerea. d,
Tangara cayana. e, Conopophaga aurita. f,
Megarhynchus pitangua. g, Tangara mexicana. h, Picumnus exilis. i, Hirundinea ferruginea. j, Galbula albirostris. k, Tyrannopsis
sulphurea. l, Tangara varia.

2010, May 26   Perf. 14
1403		Block of 12	37.00 37.00
a.	A368	50c multi	.35 .35
b.	A368	$1 multi	.75 .75
c.	A368	$1.50 multi	1.10 1.10
d.	A368	$2 multi	1.50 1.50
e.	A368	$2.50 multi	1.90 1.90
f.	A368	$3 multi	2.25 2.25
g.	A368	$3.50 multi	2.60 2.60
h.	A368	$4 multi	3.00 3.00
i.	A368	$5 multi	3.75 3.75
j.	A368	$7 multi	5.25 5.25
k.	A368	$9 multi	6.50 6.50
l.	A368	$11 multi	8.00 8.00

Orchids
A369

No. 1404: a, Laeliocattleya. b, Coelogyne
mooreana. c, Phalaenopsis. d, Calanthe. e,
Maxillaria fucata. f, Cymbidium erythrostylum.
g, Cymbidium beaumont. h, Cattleya portia. i,
Miltoniopsis portelet. j, Sophrolaeliacattleya
marion. k, Dendrobium thwaitesii. l,
Ascocenda vernon.

2010, July 7
1404		Block of 12	34.00 34.00
a.	A369	A multi	.35 .35
b.	A369	55c multi	.40 .40
c.	A369	$1 multi	.75 .75
d.	A369	$1.50 multi	1.10 1.10
e.	A369	$2 multi	1.50 1.50
f.	A369	$2.50 multi	1.90 1.90
g.	A369	$3 multi	2.25 2.25
h.	A369	$4.50 multi	3.25 3.25
i.	A369	$5 multi	3.75 3.75

j.	A369 $6.50 multi	4.75	4.75
k.	A369 $7 multi	5.25	5.25
l.	A369 $11 multi	8.00	8.00

No. 1404a sold for 45c on day of issue.

America Issue, National
Symbols — A370

No. 1406: a, $11, Presidential Palace. b,
$13, National anthem.

2010, Sept. 15

1405	A370	Horiz. pair	20.50	20.50
a.	$13 National flag		9.50	9.50
b.	$15 National arms		11.00	11.00

Souvenir Sheet

1406	A370	Sheet of 2, #a-b	17.50	17.50

Primates — A371

No. 1407: a, A, Theropithecus gelada. b,
55c, Gorilla beringei. c, $1, Cercopithecus nic-
titans. d, $1.50, Microcebus myoxinus. e, $2,
Macaca silenus. f, $2.50, Lemur catta. g, $3,
Propithecus verrauxi. h, $4, Galago crassi-
caudatus. i, $4.50, Cacajao melanocephalus.
j, $5, Pan paniscus. k, $6.50, Lagothrix cana. l,
$9, Capucinus albifrons.

2010, Oct. 20 Litho. Perf. 12¾x13¼

1407	A371	Block of 12, #a-l	29.00	29.00

No. 1407a sold for 45c on day of issue.

Fish — A372

No. 1408: a, Amphiprion ocellaris. b,
Pomacentrus caeruleus. c, Barbus tetrazona.
d, Betta smaragdina. e, Calisa lalia. f,
Geophagus brasiliensis. g, Astronotus ocellatus. h, Microgeophagus ramirezi.

2010, Dec. 1 Litho. Perf. 13¼x12¾

1408		Block of 8	33.00	33.00
a.	A372 A multi		.35	.35
b.	A372 $1.55 multi		1.10	1.10
c.	A372 $3 multi		2.25	2.25
d.	A372 $5 multi		3.75	3.75
e.	A372 $7 multi		5.25	5.25
f.	A372 $8 multi		5.75	5.75
g.	A372 $9 multi		6.50	6.50
h.	A372 $11 multi		8.00	8.00

No. 1408a sold for 45c on day of issue.

Masks — A373

No. 1409: a, Begawan wiro sekti. b, Dewi
kilisuci. c, Kartolo. d, Bilung. e, Panji
amerdadu. f, Betara kalla.

2010, Dec. 29 Perf. 14

1409		Block of 6	22.00	22.00
a.	A373 50c multi		.35	.35
b.	A373 $1.50 multi		1.10	1.10
c.	A373 $3.50 multi		2.60	2.60
d.	A373 $6 multi		4.50	4.50
e.	A373 $8 multi		5.75	5.75
f.	A373 $10 multi		7.25	7.25

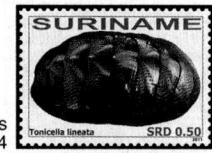

Shells
A374

Designs: 50c, Tonicella lineata. $1, Chione
paphia. $3.50, Callanaitis disjecta. $5, Angaria
tyria. $8, Epitonium pallasi. $9, Strombus
pipus. $13, Haliotis marmorata.

2011, Jan. 19 Perf. 13¼x12¾

1410-1416	A374	Set of 7	29.00	29.00

Nos. 1410-1416 were printed in a sheet
containing 2 of each stamp + a central label.

Mushrooms — A375

No. 1417: a, $8, Russula paludosa. b, $10,
Phaeolepiota aurea.

2011, Feb. 16 Perf. 14

1417	A375	Horiz. pair, #a-b	11.00	11.00

No. 1417 was printed in sheets containing
two pairs + two labels.

Postal Union of the Americas, Spain
and Portugal (UPAEP), Cent. — A376

No. 1418 — Arc of circles containing flags of
member nations: a, $5. b, $7. c, $9. d, $11.

2011, Mar. 16

1418	A376	Block of 4, #a-d	19.50	19.50

Maastricht
Paper Money
Fair — A377

No. 1419: a, Malaysia 100-ringit note. b,
Vanuatu 500-vatu note. c, Nepal 500-rupee
note. d, Samoa 20-tala note. e, Oman 1-rial
note. f, French Polynesia 10,000-franc note. g,
Gibraltar 1-pound note. h, Bhutan 1-ngultrum
note. i, Tonga 5-pa'anga note. j, Argentina
1,000,000-peso note. k, Surinam #751. l, Iceland 5000-kronur note.

2011, Apr. 4 Perf. 13½x12¾

1419		Block of 12	31.00	31.00
a.	A377 A multi		.30	.30
b.	A377 55c multi		.35	.35
c.	A377 $1 multi		.60	.60
d.	A377 $2.50 multi		1.50	1.50
e.	A377 $3 multi		1.90	1.90
f.	A377 $3.50 multi		2.10	2.10
g.	A377 $4 multi		2.50	2.50
h.	A377 $5 multi		3.00	3.00
i.	A377 $6 multi		3.75	3.75
j.	A377 $7 multi		4.25	4.25
k.	A377 $8 multi		5.00	5.00
l.	A377 $9 multi		5.50	5.50

No. 1419a sold for 45c on day of issue.

Peonies — A378

No. 1420: a, Red peony, denomination at
LR reading across. b, White peony, denomination at LL reading across. c, Pink peonies,
denomination at LL reading up. d, Red and
white peonies, denomination at LR reading
down.
$7, Pink peony.

2011, Apr. 20 Perf. 14

1420	A378	$2 Sheet of 4, #a-d	5.00	5.00

Souvenir Sheet

1421	A378	$7 multi	4.25	4.25

Birds — A379

No. 1422: a, Suiriri suiriri. b, Pitangus
sulphuratus. c, Pipra serena. d, Schiffornis
turdinus. e, Euphonia violacea. f, Ochthoeca
littoralis. g, Amazona farinosa. h,
Anthracothorax nigricollis. i, Psophia
crepitans. j, Euphonia plumbea. k, Piprites
chloris. l, Neopipo cinnamomea.

2011, May 25

1422		Block of 12	32.00	32.00
a.	A379 A multi		.30	.30
b.	A379 55c multi		.35	.35
c.	A379 $1 multi		.65	.65
d.	A379 $2.25 multi		1.40	1.40
e.	A379 $3.25 multi		2.00	2.00
f.	A379 $3.50 multi		2.25	2.25
g.	A379 $4.25 multi		2.75	2.75
h.	A379 $4.75 multi		3.00	3.00
i.	A379 $6 multi		3.75	3.75
j.	A379 $7 multi		4.50	4.50
k.	A379 $8 multi		5.00	5.00
l.	A379 $9 multi		5.50	5.50

Orchids — A380

No. 1423: a, Pink Phalaenopsis hybrid,
bright green background. b, Dendrobium
mousmee. c, Dendrobium densiflorum. d, Laelia purpurata. e, Encyclia vitellina. f, Miltoniopsis rozel. g, Yellow Cymbidium hybrid. h, Dendrobium hybrid. i, Ascocenda. j, Red
Cymbidium hybrid. k, Laeliocattleya hybrid. l,
Pink Phalaenopsis hybrid, olive green
background.

2011, June 29

1423		Block of 12	26.00	26.00
a.	A380 A multi		.30	.30
b.	A380 55c multi		.35	.35
c.	A380 $1 multi		.65	.65
d.	A380 $1.50 multi		.95	.95
e.	A380 $2 multi		1.25	1.25
f.	A380 $2.50 multi		1.60	1.60
g.	A380 $3 multi		1.90	1.90
h.	A380 $4 multi		2.50	2.50
i.	A380 $4.25 multi		2.75	2.75
j.	A380 $5.50 multi		3.50	3.50
k.	A380 $7 multi		4.50	4.50
l.	A380 $8 multi		5.00	5.00

No. 1423a sold for 45c on day of issue.

Primates — A381

No. 1424: a, A, Papio hamadryas. b, $2.55,
Saguinus oedipus. c, $4, Cebus apella. d, $6,
Erythrocebus patas. e, $8, Macaca nemes-
trina. f, $9, Chlorocebus pygerythrus.

2011, Aug. 10 Perf. 12¾x13¼

1424	A381	Block of 6, #a-f	18.50	18.50

No. 1424a sold for 45c on day of issue.

Azaleas
A382

No. 1425: a, Country name at UL, denomination adjacent to vignette. b, Country name
adjacent to vignette, denomination at LR.

2011, Sept. 14 Perf. 14¼x13¾

1425	A382	$1.50 Vert. pair, #a-b	1.90	1.90

America Issue, Mailboxes — A383

No. 1426: a, $11, Mailbox on black pedestal
near wall. b, $15, Rectangular mailbox.
No. 1427: a, $11, Mailbox on black pedestal.
b, $13, Top of mailbox.

2011, Sept. 14 Perf. 14

1426	A383	Horiz. pair, #a-b	17.00	17.00

Souvenir Sheet

1427	A383	Sheet of 2, #a-b	15.00	15.00

Miniature Sheet

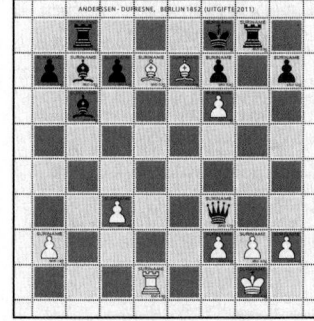

Chess Board — A384

No. 1428: a, 10c, Black rook. b, 20c, Black
king. c, 30c, Black rook. d, 40c, Black pawn. e,
50c, Black bishop. f, 60c, Black pawn. g, 70c,
White bishop. h, 80c, White bishop. i, 90c,
Black pawn. j, $1, Black pawn. k, $1.20, Black
bishop. l, $1.40, White pawn. m, $1.60, White
pawn. n, $1.75, Black queen. o, $1.90, White
pawn. p, $2.15, White pawn. q, $3, White

pawn. r, $4.50, White pawn. s, $5, White rook. t, $6, White king.

2011, Oct. 26

1428	A384	Sheet of 20, #a-t,		
		+ 44 labels	21.00	21.00

No. 1428 shows position of pieces at end of 1852 match between Adolf Anderssen and Jean Dufresne. Compare with No. 1394.

Masks — A385

No. 1429: a, $1, Botu terong. b, $2, Demang mundu. c, $3, Emban dawala. d, $7, Jarodeh. e, $8, Kelono baron sakeber. f, $9, Maheso suro.

2011, Dec. 7   **Perf. 14**

1429	A385	Block of 6, #a-f	18.50	18.50

Butterflies A386

No. 1430: a. Memphis aureola. b, Delias bagoe. c, Ornithoptera tithonus. d, Ogyris genoveva gela. e, Parnassius apollo. f, Dismorphia cordillera. g, Bhutannitis mansfieldi. h, Anthene definita. i, Papilio demoleus. j, Parides orellana. k, Papilio pelaus atkinsi. l. Mellicta britomartis.

2012, Jan. 18

1430		Block of 12	32.00	32.00
a.	A386 B multi		.35	.35
b.	A386 75c multi		.45	.45
c.	A386 90c multi		.55	.55
d.	A386 $1.25 multi		.75	.75
e.	A386 $1.55 multi		.95	.95
f.	A386 $3.50 multi		2.25	2.25
g.	A386 $4.50 multi		2.75	2.75
h.	A386 $5 multi		3.25	3.25
i.	A386 $6 multi		3.75	3.75
j.	A386 $8 multi		5.00	5.00
k.	A386 $8.50 multi		5.25	5.25
l.	A386 $9.50 multi		6.00	6.00

No. 1430a sold for 55c on day of issue.

New Year 2012 (Year of the Dragon) — A387

No. 1431 — Dragon and flower: a, $2. b, $3.

2012, Jan. 25   **Perf. 13¾**

1431	A387	Pair, #a-b	3.25	3.25

No. 1431 printed in sheets containing 2 pairs.

Churches — A388

No. 1432: a, $1, Martin Luther Church. b, $3, Seventh Day Adventist Church Center. c, $5, Christian and Alliance Missionary Church of Surinam. d, $6, Interior of Saints Peter and Paul Cathedral. e, $7, Exterior of Saints Peter

and Paul Cathedral, vert. f, $8, Steeple of Saints Peter and Paul Cathedral, vert.

2012, Feb. 15   **Perf. 14**

1432	A388	Block of 6, #a-f	18.50	18.50

Flowers A389

Designs: $1, Allamanda. $2, Anemone. $3, Amaryllis. $4, Wedelia. $5.50, Thunbergia. $7.50, Crossandra. $8, Dahlia. $9, Heliconia.

2012, Mar. 21

1433	A389	$1 multi	.60	.60
1434	A389	$2 multi	1.25	1.25
1435	A389	$3 multi	1.90	1.90
1436	A389	$4 multi	2.50	2.50
1437	A389	$5.50 multi	3.50	3.50
1438	A389	$7.50 multi	4.75	4.75
1439	A389	$8 multi	5.00	5.00
1440	A389	$9 multi	5.50	5.50
		Nos. 1433-1440 (8)	25.00	25.00

Nos. 1433-1440 were printed in sheets of 14 containing two of each stamp + 2 labels.

Birds — A390

No. 1441: a, Rostrhamus sociabilis. b, Thamnophilus murinus. c, Xiphorhynchus guttatus. d, Odontophorus gujanensis. e, Dryocopus lineatus. f, Bucco tamatia. g, Celeus undatus. h, Phaethornis longuemareus. i, Glaucis hirsuta. j, Elanus leucurus. k, Heliothryx aurita. l, Nonnula rubecula.

2012, May 23

1441		Block of 12	31.00	31.00
a.	A390 B multi		.35	.35
b.	A390 $1 multi		.65	.65
c.	A390 $1.45 multi		.90	.90
d.	A390 $2 multi		1.25	1.25
e.	A390 $2.50 multi		1.50	1.50
f.	A390 $3 multi		1.90	1.90
g.	A390 $3.50 multi		2.25	2.25
h.	A390 $4 multi		2.50	2.50
i.	A390 $5 multi		3.00	3.00
j.	A390 $7 multi		4.25	4.25
k.	A390 $9 multi		5.50	5.50
l.	A390 $11 multi		6.75	6.75

No. 1441a sold for 55c on day of issue.

Miniature Sheet

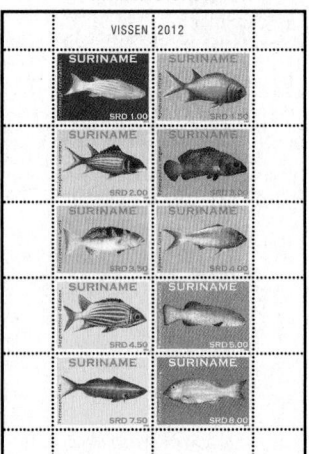

Fish — A391

No. 1442: a, $1, Crenimugil crenilabrus. b, $1.50, Myripristis vittata. c, $2, Neoniphon sammara. d, $3, Epinephelus ongus. e, $3.50, Plectropomus laevis. f, $4, Aphareus furca. g, $4.50, Sargocentron diadema. h, $5, Plectropomus areolatus. i, $7.50, Pterocaesio tile. j, $8, Lethrinus obsoletus.

2012, June 20

1442	A391	Sheet of 12, #a-l	25.00	25.00

2012 Summer Olympics, London A392

No. 1443: a, Badminton. b, Cycling. c, Diving. d, Equestrian. e, Gymnastics. f, Hammer throw. g, Javelin. h, Long jump. i, Relay race. j, Rowing. k, Swimming. l, Tennis.
No. 1444, vert.: a, Volleyball. b, Running. c, Hurdles.

2012, Aug. 15

1443		Block of 12	25.00	25.00
a.	A392 50c multi		.30	.30
b.	A392 $1 multi		.60	.60
c.	A392 $1.50 multi		.95	.95
d.	A392 $2 multi		1.25	1.25
e.	A392 $2.50 multi		1.50	1.50
f.	A392 $3 multi		1.90	1.90
g.	A392 $3.50 multi		2.25	2.25
h.	A392 $4 multi		2.50	2.50
i.	A392 $4.50 multi		2.75	2.75
j.	A392 $5 multi		3.25	3.25
k.	A392 $5.50 multi		3.50	3.50
l.	A392 $7 multi		4.25	4.25

Souvenir Sheet

1444		Sheet of 3	6.50	6.50
a.	A392 $2 multi		1.25	1.25
b.	A392 $3 multi		1.90	1.90
c.	A392 $5 multi		3.25	3.25

America Issue — A393

No. 1445: a, $13, Maluana. b, $15, Malohkoh.
No. 1446: a, $11, Maluana, diff. b, $13, Malohkoh, diff.

2012, Sept. 19

1445	A393	Horiz. pair, #a-b	17.00	17.00

Souvenir Sheet

1446	A393	Sheet of 2, #a-b	15.00	15.00

Lighthouses — A394

No. 1447: a, $1, Cabo Raper Lighthouse, Chile. b, $3, Punta Huacho Lighthouse, Peru. c, $5, Piedra Diamante Lighthouse, Argentina. d, $6, Manta Lighthouse, Ecuador. e, $7, Sao Joao Lighthouse, Brazil. f, $8, Santa Marta Lighthouse, Colombia.

2012, Oct. 24   **Perf. 14**

1447	A394	Block of 6, #a-f	18.50	18.50

Masks — A395

No. 1448: a, $1.50, Brojonoto. b, $2.50, Kelono sewandono. c, $4, Dewi walang wati. d, $6, Panji amiluhur. e, $8, Panji banyaksasi. f, 10, Rasonto.

2012, Dec. 5   **Litho.**

1448	A395	Block of 6, #a-f	19.50	19.50

Butterflies A396

No. 1449: a, Graphium antheus. b, Atrophaneura luchti. c, Pandemos pasiphae.

2013, Jan. 13

1449		Sheet of 3	3.75	3.75
a.	A396 $1 multi		.60	.60
b.	A396 $2 multi		1.25	1.25
c.	A396 $3 multi		1.90	1.90

Birds — A397

No. 1450: a, Aratinga aurea. b, Polytmus guainumbi. c, Terenotriccus erythrurus. d, Synallaxis albescens. e, Zonotrichia capensis. f, Synallaxis macconnelli. g, Thraupis palmarum. h, Certhiaxis gutturata. i, Tapera naevia. j, Automolus rubiginosus. k, Euscarthmus rufomarginatus. l, Thraupis episcopus.

2013, Feb. 20

1450		Sheet of 12	34.00	34.00
a.	A397 B multi		.35	.35
b.	A397 $1.45 multi		.90	.90
c.	A397 $1.75 multi		1.10	1.10
d.	A397 $2.25 multi		1.40	1.40
e.	A397 $2.75 multi		1.75	1.75
f.	A397 $3.25 multi		2.00	2.00
g.	A397 $3.75 multi		2.25	2.25
h.	A397 $4.25 multi		2.60	2.60
i.	A397 $5.50 multi		3.50	3.50
j.	A397 $7.50 multi		4.50	4.50
k.	A397 $9.50 multi		5.75	5.75
l.	A397 $12.50 multi		7.75	7.75

No. 1450a sold for 55c on day of issue.

Miniature Sheet

Flowers — A398

No. 1451: a, B, Agapanthus africanus. b, $1.35, Anthurium andraeanum. c, $1.85, Aquilegia vulgaris. d, $2.25, Ferocactus wislizenii. e, $2.50, Crocus vernus. f, $3.50, Gazania rigens. g, $3.75, Leucospermum, h, $4.25,

Saguaro cactus. i, $5.50, Sempervivum grandiflorum. j, $7.50, Telopea speciosissima. k, $10.50, Tulipa gesneriana. l, $11.50, Zantedeschia aethiopica.

2013, Mar. 13
1451 A398   Sheet of 12, #a-l   34.00 34.00
No. 1451a sold for 55c on day of issue.

Fish — A399

No. 1452: a, Cephalopholiss fulva. b, Epinephelus guttatus. c, Hypoplectrus puella. d, Hypoplectrus unicolor. e, Liopropoma carmabi. f, Serranus annularis. g, Serranus tabacarius. h, Petrometopon cruentatum. i, Mycteroperca venenosa. j, Serranus baldwini.

2013, May 15
1452   Sheet of 10   31.00 31.00
 a. A399 B multi   .30   .30
 b. A399 $1.45 multi   .85   .85
 c. A399 $2.50 multi   1.50   1.50
 d. A399 $3.50 multi   2.10   2.10
 e. A399 $4.50 multi   2.75   2.75
 f. A399 $5.50 multi   3.50   3.50
 g. A399 $6.50 multi   4.00   4.00
 h. A399 $7.50 multi   4.75   4.75
 i. A399 $8.50 multi   5.25   5.25
 j. A399 $9.50 multi   6.00   6.00
No. 1452a sold for 55c on day of issue.

Miniature Sheet

Thailand 2013 World Stamp Exhibition, Bangkok — A400

No. 1453: a, $2.50, Grand Palace, Bangkok. b, $4.50, Saints Peter and Paul Cathedral, Paramaribo. c, $5.50, Lophura diardi. d, $7.50, Ramphastos vitellinus. e, $9, Dendrobium. f, $11, Ixora.

2013, June 19
1453 A400   Sheet of 6, #a-f   25.00 25.00

Miniature Sheet

Fruit — A401

No. 1454: a, $1.75, Annona muricata. b, $2.25, Theobroma cacao. c, $4.75, Averrhoa carambola. d, $5.25, Chrysophyllum cainito. e, $6.75, Carica papaya. f, $8.25, Citrullus lanatus. g, $9.75, Persea americana. h, $11.25, Syzygium malaccense.

2013, Aug. 14   Litho.   Perf. 14
1454 A401   Sheet of 8, #a-h,
     + label   31.00 31.00

Souvenir Sheets

A402

America Issue — A403

No. 1455: a, $13, Anti-discrimination marchers. b, $15, Anti-discrimination poster with hand.
No. 1456: a, $15, Anti-discrimination monument and flowers. b, $17, Anti-discrimination parade banner.

2013, Sept. 18   Litho.   Perf. 14
1455 A402   Sheet of 2, #a-b   17.00 17.00
1456 A403   Sheet of 2, #a-b   19.50 19.50

Miniature Sheet

Monuments in Paramaribo — A404

No. 1457: a, $7, Mama Sranan Monument. b, $9, Statenmonument. c, $11, Helstone Mounument. d, $13, Monument to the Fallen.

2013, Oct. 23   Litho.   Perf. 14
1457 A404   Sheet of 4, #a-d   25.00 25.00

Unity — A405

No. 1458: a, $1.25, Ceiba pentandra. b, $1.75, Wan Bon, poem by Robin Dobru Raveles.

2013, Nov. 10   Litho.   Perf. 14
1458 A405   Vert. pair, #a-b, +
     central label   1.90 1.90

Masks — A406

No. 1459 — Inscriptions: a, $1, Dewi sekartaji. b, $2.50, Klono garudo lelono. c, $3.50, Kollo tekik salagonjo. d, $7.50, Kraeng sengkollo. e, $9.50, Panji amisani. f, $11, Patih dandang mangkurat.

2013, Dec. 4   Litho.   Perf. 14
1459 A406   Block of 6, #a-f   21.50 21.50

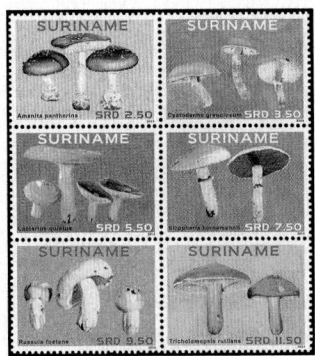
Mushrooms — A407

No. 1460: a, $2.50: a, Amanita pantherina. b, $3.50, Cystoderma granulosum. c, $5.50, Lactarius quietus. d, $7.50, Stropharia hornemannii. e, $9.50, Russula foetens. f, $11.50, Tricholomopsis rutilans.

2014, Jan. 15   Litho.   Perf. 14
1460 A407   Block of 6, #a-f   25.00 25.00

Birds — A408

No. 1461: a, Hylophilus muscicapinus. b, Euphonia plumbea. c, Columbina talpacoti. d, Lophotriccus vitiosus. e, Myrmotherula brachyra. f, Icterus nigrogularis. g, Passerina cyanoides. h, Pipra erythrocephala. i, Pithys albifrons. j, Xenops menutus. k, Terenura spodioptila. l, Scierurus mexicanus.

2014, Feb. 19   Litho.   Perf. 14
1461   Block of 12   37.50 37.50
 a. A408 B multi   .35   .35
 b. A408 $1.45 multi   .90   .90
 c. A408 $2 multi   1.25   1.25
 d. A408 $2.50 multi   1.50   1.50
 e. A408 $3.50 multi   2.10   2.10
 f. A408 $4.50 multi   2.75   2.75
 g. A408 $5.50 multi   3.50   3.50
 h. A408 $6 multi   3.75   3.75
 i. A408 $7 multi   4.25   4.25
 j. A408 $8 multi   5.00   5.00
 k. A408 $9 multi   5.50   5.50
 l. A408 $10 multi   6.25   6.25
No. 1461a sold for 55c on day of issue.

Flowers
A409

Designs: B, Dendrobium nobile. $1.45, Hemerocallis fulva. $2, Laeliocattleya. $2.50, Lycaste cruenta. $3.50, Ophrys apifera. $4.50, Paphiopedilum. $5, Phalaenopsis fuscata. $5.50, Sophrolaeliocattleya. $7, Vanda arcuata. $8, Vanda bensonii.

2014, Mar. 12   Litho.   Perf. 14
1462 A409   B multi   .35   .35
1463 A409 $1.45 multi   .90   .90
1464 A409 $2 multi   1.25   1.25
1465 A409 $2.50 multi   1.60   1.60
1466 A409 $3.50 multi   2.10   2.10
1467 A409 $4.50 multi   2.75   2.75
1468 A409 $5 multi   3.25   3.25
1469 A409 $5.50 multi   3.50   3.50
1470 A409 $7 multi   4.25   4.25
1471 A409 $8 multi   5.00   5.00
  Nos. 1462-1471 (10)   24.95 24.95
Nos. 1462-1471 were printed in sheets of 20, containing 2 of each stamp + central label.

50th Wandelmars Day — A410

No. 1472 — Wandelmars parade participants: a, $2, Three women. b, $4, Two women, vert.

2014, Apr. 1   Litho.   Perf. 14
1472 A410   Pair, #a-b   3.75 3.75

Butterflies
A411

No. 1473: a, Araschnia levana. b, Automeris moloneyi. c, Cercyonis pegala. d, Euchloe ausonides. e, Hypanartia lethe. f, Speyeria cybele. g, Lasaia sula. h, Lycaena epixanthe. i, Mythris rhodope. j, Parthenos sylvia. k, Sallya amulia. l, Vanessa gonerilla.

2014, May 14   Litho.   Perf. 14
1473   Block of 12   37.50 37.50
 a. A411 B multi   .35   .35
 b. A411 $1.45 multi   .90   .90
 c. A411 $2 multi   1.25   1.25
 d. A411 $2.50 multi   1.60   1.60
 e. A411 $3.50 multi   2.10   2.10
 f. A411 $4.50 multi   2.75   2.75
 g. A411 $5.50 multi   3.50   3.50
 h. A411 $6 multi   3.75   3.75
 i. A411 $7 multi   4.25   4.25
 j. A411 $8 multi   5.00   5.00
 k. A411 $9 multi   5.50   5.50
 l. A411 $10 multi   6.25   6.25
No. 1473a sold for 55c on day of issue.

2014 World Cup Soccer Championships, Brazil — A412

No. 1474 — Soccer ball and: a, Two players. b, One player. c, One player, diff. d, One player, diff.

2014, June 11   Litho.   Perf. 14
1474   Block of 4   12.50 12.50
 a. A412 $2 multi   1.25   1.25
 b. A412 $4 multi   2.50   2.50
 c. A412 $6 multi   3.75   3.75
 d. A412 $8 multi   5.00   5.00

Fish — A413

No. 1475: a, Chaetodon capistratus. b, Chaetodon striatus. c, Gramma loreto. d, Holacanthus isabelita. e, Halichoeres bivittatus. f, Holacanthus ciliaris. g, Lachnolaimus maximus. h, Mulloidichthys martinicus. i, Pempheris schomburgki. j, Pomacanthus arcuatus. k, Scarus croicensis. l, Pseudupeneus maculatus.

2014, July 16   **Litho.**   **Perf. 14**
1475		Block of 12	34.00	34.00
a.	A413	B multi	.35	.35
b.	A413	$1.45 multi	.90	.90
c.	A413	$2 multi	1.25	1.25
d.	A413	$2.50 multi	1.50	1.50
e.	A413	$3.50 multi	2.10	2.10
f.	A413	$4.50 multi	2.75	2.75
g.	A413	$5 multi	3.00	3.00
h.	A413	$5.50 multi	3.50	3.50
i.	A413	$6 multi	3.75	3.75
j.	A413	$7 multi	4.25	4.25
k.	A413	$8 multi	5.00	5.00
l.	A413	$9 multi	5.50	5.50

No. 1475a sold for 55c on day of issue.

A414

Airplanes — A415

No. 1476: a, $1.25, Walden III, U.S., 1909. b, $2.50, Chiribiri No. 5, Italy, 1912. c, $2.75, Fokker T-2, Netherlands, 1921. d, $3.50, Fokker F. VIIa-3m, Netherlands, 1925. e, $4.75, Potez 25A-2, France, 1925. f, $5.25, Albatros L73, Germany, 1926. g, $5.50, Douglas M-4, U.S., 1927. h, $6.50, Junkers G24, Germany, 1927.

No. 1477 — Flowers and part of Surinam Airways jet: a, $8, Tail section. b, $9, Fuselage, rear door, landing gear. c, $11, Fuselage, front door.

2014, July 17   **Litho.**   **Perf. 14**
1476	A414	Sheet of 8, #a-h, + central label	19.50	19.50

Souvenir Sheet

1477	A415	Sheet of 3, #a-c	17.00	17.00

Panama Canal, Cent. — A416

No. 1478: a, $2.50, Ship. b, $3.50, Ship, diff. c, $5.50, Ship, diff. d, $6.50, Ship near locks. e, $8, Ship, diff. f, $9, Locks.

2014, Oct. 22   **Litho.**   **Perf. 14**
1478	A416	Block of 6, #a-f	21.50	21.50

Masks — A417

No. 1479: a, $2.50, Dewi ragil kuning. b, $3.50, Patih gajah meto. c, $5.50, Kollo marko mamang. d, $7.50, Panji kudonowarongso. e, $9.50, Patih talang segoro. f, $11.50, Panji amiseno.

2014, Dec. 3   **Litho.**   **Perf. 14**
1479	A417	Block of 6, #a-f	24.50	24.50

Souvenir Sheet

Birds — A418

No. 1480: a, $13, Mimus saturninus. b, $16, Colinus cristatus.

2014, Dec. 31   **Litho.**   **Perf. 14**
1480	A418	Sheet of 2, #a-b	18.00	18.00

Butterflies A419

No. 1481: a, Agrias claudina sardanapalus. b, Phoebis sennae. c, Hemithea aestivaria. d, Palaeochrysophanus hippothoe. e, Thecla betulae. f, Antheraea polyphemus. g, Geometra papilionaria. h, Limenitis lorquini. i, Eacles imperialis. j, Boloria thore. k, Callithea leprieuri. l, Automeris io.

2015, Jan. 14   **Litho.**   **Perf. 14**
1481		Block of 12	37.00	37.00
a.	A419	$2.25 multi	1.40	1.40
b.	A419	$2.75 multi	1.75	1.75
c.	A419	$3.25 multi	2.00	2.00
d.	A419	$3.75 multi	2.25	2.25
e.	A419	$4.25 multi	2.60	2.60
f.	A419	$4.75 multi	3.00	3.00
g.	A419	$5.25 multi	3.25	3.25
h.	A419	$5.75 multi	3.50	3.50
i.	A419	$6.25 multi	3.75	3.75
j.	A419	$6.75 multi	4.25	4.25
k.	A419	$7.25 multi	4.50	4.50
l.	A419	$7.75 multi	4.75	4.75

Miniature Sheet

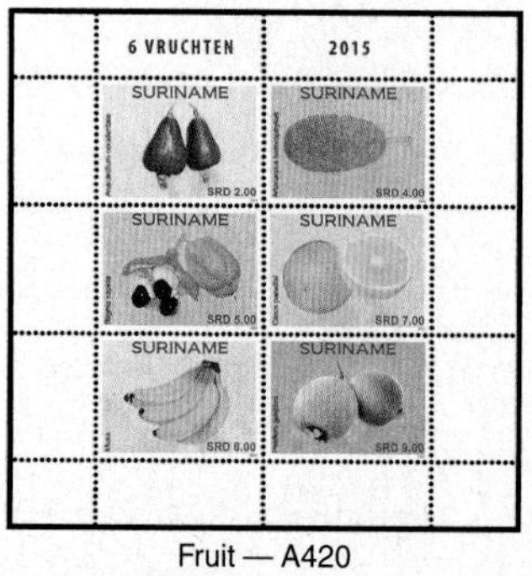

Fruit — A420

No. 1482: a, $2, Anacardium occidentale (cashews). b, $4, Artocarpus heterophyllus (jackfruit). c, $5, Blighia sapida (ackee). d, $7, Citrus paradisi (grapefruit). e, $8, Musa (bananas). f, $9, Psidium guajava (guava).

2015, Feb. 11   **Litho.**   **Perf. 14**
1482	A420	Sheet of 6, #a-f	21.50	21.50

Miniature Sheet

Birds — A421

No. 1483: a, $2.25, Daptrius ater. b, $2.75, Circus buffoni. c, $3.25, Buteogallus meridionalis. d, $3.75, Buteogallus urubitinga. e, $4.25, Dendrocygna autumnalis. f, $4.75, Ciccaba huhula. g, $5.25, Harpagus bidentatus. h, $5.75, Micrastur mirandollei. i, $6.25, Nyctibius griseus. j, $6.75, Spizaetus melanoleucus. k, $7.25, Ictinia plumbea. l, $7.75, Asturina nitida.

2015, Mar. 18   **Litho.**   **Perf. 14**
1483	A421	Sheet of 12, #a-l	37.00	37.00

SEMI-POSTAL STAMPS

SP1

SP2

Green Cross — SP3

Perf. 12½
1927, Aug. 1   **Unwmk.**   **Photo.**
B1	SP1	2c (+ 2c) bl blk & grn	1.10	1.00
B2	SP2	5c (+ 3c) vio & grn	1.10	1.00
B3	SP3	10c (+ 3c) ver & grn	2.00	1.75
		Nos. B1-B3 (3)	4.20	3.75
		Set, never hinged	10.50	

Surtax was given to the Green Cross Society, which promotes public health services.

Nurse and Patient — SP4

1928, Dec. 1   **Perf. 11½**
B4	SP4	1½c (+ 1½c) ultra	4.50	4.50
B5	SP4	2c (+ 2c) bl grn	4.50	4.50
B6	SP4	5c (+ 3c) vio	4.50	4.50
B7	SP4	7½c (+ 2½c) ver	4.50	4.50
		Nos. B4-B7 (4)	18.00	18.00
		Set, never hinged	67.50	

The surtax on these stamps was for a fund to combat indigenous diseases.

Good Samaritan — SP5

1929, Dec. 1   **Perf. 12½**
B8	SP5	1½c (+ 1½c) grn	6.75	6.75
B9	SP5	2c (+ 2c) scar	6.75	6.75
B10	SP5	5c (+ 3c) ultra	6.75	6.75
B11	SP5	6c (+ 4c) blk	6.75	6.75
		Nos. B8-B11 (4)	27.00	27.00
		Set, never hinged	72.50	

Surtax for the Green Cross Society.

Surinam Mother and Child — SP6

1931, Dec. 14
B12	SP6	1½c (+ 1½c) blk	4.75	4.75
B13	SP6	2c (+ 2c) car rose	4.75	4.75
B14	SP6	5c (+ 3c) ultra	4.75	4.75
B15	SP6	6c (+ 4c) dp grn	4.75	4.75
		Nos. B12-B15 (4)	19.00	19.00
		Set, never hinged	45.00	

The surtax was for Child Welfare Societies.

Designs Symbolical of the Creed of the Moravians
SP7   SP8

1935, Aug. 1   **Perf. 13x14**
B16	SP7	1c (+ ½c) dk brn	6.00	6.00
B17	SP7	2c (+ 1c) dp ultra	6.00	6.00
B18	SP8	3c (+ 1½c) grn	7.50	7.50
B19	SP8	4c (+ 2c) red org	7.50	7.50
B20	SP8	5c (+ 2½c) blk brn	9.00	9.00
B21	SP8	10c (+ 5c) car	9.00	9.00
		Nos. B16-B21 (6)	45.00	45.00
		Set, never hinged	90.00	

200th anniv. of the founding of the Moravian Mission in Surinam.

Surinam Child — SP9

1936, Dec. 14   **Perf. 12½**
B22	SP9	2c (+ 1c) dk grn	2.75	2.75
B23	SP9	3c (+ 1½c) dk bl	2.75	2.75
B24	SP9	5c (+ 2½c) brn blk	4.00	4.00
B25	SP9	10c (+ 5c) lake	4.00	4.00
		Nos. B22-B25 (4)	13.50	13.50
		Set, never hinged	26.50	

Surtax for baby food and the Green Cross Society.

"Emancipation"
SP10

Surinam Girl
SP11

1938, June 1   Litho.   Perf. 12½x12
B26 SP10 2½c (+ 2c) dk bl grn   2.40 1.90
Photo.
B27 SP11   3c (+ 2c) vio blk   2.40 1.90
B28 SP11   5c (+ 3c) dk brn   2.60 2.25
B29 SP11 7½c (+ 5c) indigo   2.60 2.25
Nos. B26-B29 (4)   10.00 8.30
Set, never hinged   20.00

75th anniv. of the abolition of slavery in Surinam. Surtax to Slavery Remembrance
Committee.

Creole
Woman — SP12

Javanese
Woman — SP13

Hindustani
Woman — SP14

American Indian
Woman — SP15

1940, Jan. 8   Engr.   Perf. 13x14
B30 SP12 2½c (+ 2c) dk grn   3.00 3.00
B31 SP13   3c (+ 2c) red org   3.00 3.00
B32 SP14   5c (+ 3c) dp bl   3.00 3.00
B33 SP15 7½c (+ 5c) henna
brn   3.00 3.00
Nos. B30-B33 (4)   12.00 12.00
Set, never hinged   25.00

Surtax to leper care and baby food.

> **Catalogue values for unused
> stamps in this section, from this
> point to the end of the section, are
> for Never Hinged items.**

Netherlands Coat of
Arms and Inscription,
"Netherlands Shall Rise
Again" — SP16

1941, Aug. 30   Litho.   Perf. 12½
B34 SP16 7½c + 7½c dp org,
ultra & blk   3.75 3.00
B35 SP16 15c + 15c scar, ul-
tra & blk   3.75 3.00
B36 SP16 1g + 1g gray & ul-
tra   26.00 22.50
Nos. B34-B36 (3)   33.50 28.50

The surtax was used to buy fighters for
Dutch pilots in the Royal Air Force of Great
Britain.

**Nos. 145, 169, 146, 151 Surcharged
in Red**

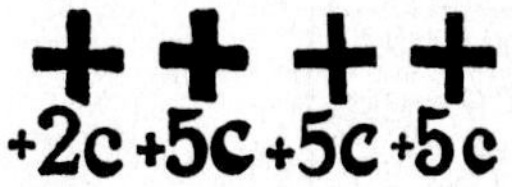

II   III   IV   V
1942, Jan. 2
B37 A23   2c + 2c blk brn, I   2.50 2.50
a.   Type II   2.50 2.50
B38 A26   2c + 2c blk brn, I   67.50 67.50
a.   Type II   67.50 67.50
B39 A23 2½c + 2c green, I   2.50 2.50
a.   Type II   2.50 2.50
B40 A23 7½c + 5c red vio, III   2.50 2.50
a.   Type IV   8.00 8.00
b.   Type V   20.00 20.00
Nos. B37-B40,CB1 (5)   77.50 77.50

The surtax was for the Red Cross.
In type III, the "c" may be "large," as illustrated, or "small," as in type II. Value is the
same.
The distinctive feature of type IV is the
pointed ending of the lower part of the "5."

**Types of Regular Issue of 1945
Surcharged in Black**

Unwmk.
1945, July 23   Engr.   Perf. 12
B41 A29 7½c + 5c dp org   3.75 2.50
B42 A30 15c + 10c brn   3.00 2.50
B43 A30 20c + 15c dl grn   3.00 2.50
B44 A30 22½c + 20c gray   3.00 2.50
B45 A30 40c + 35c rose lake   3.00 2.50
B46 A30 60c + 50c vio   3.00 2.50
Nos. B41-B46 (6)   18.75 15.00

Surtax for the National Welfare Fund.

Star — SP17

1947, Dec. 16   Photo.   Perf. 13½x13
B47 SP17 7½c + 12½c red
org   2.75 2.25
B48 SP17 12½c + 37½c blue   2.75 2.25
Nos. B47-B48,CB4-CB5 (4)   10.00 8.00

The surtax was used to combat leprosy.

Marie Curie — SP18

7½c+22½c, 27½c+12½c, Wm. Roentgen.

1950, May 15   Perf. 14x13
B49 SP18 7½c + 7½c   17.50 10.50
B50 SP18 7½c + 22½c   17.50 10.50
B51 SP18 27½c + 12½c   17.50 10.50
B52 SP18 27½c + 97½c   17.50 10.50
Nos. B49-B52 (4)   70.00 42.00

The surtax was used to combat cancer.

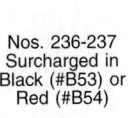

Nos. 236-237
Surcharged in
Black (#B53) or
Red (#B54)

1953, Feb. 18   Wmk. 202
B53 A35 12½c + 7½c on 7½c   2.75 2.75
B54 A35 20c + 10c on 12½c   2.75 2.75

The surtax was for flood relief in the
Netherlands.

Stadium, Paramaribo — SP19

1953, Aug. 29   Unwmk.   Perf. 13½
B55 SP19 10c + 5c claret   11.50 8.25
B56 SP19 15c + 7½c brn   11.50 8.25
B57 SP19 30c + 15c dk grn   11.50 8.25
Nos. B55-B57 (3)   34.50 24.75

Opening of the new stadium.

Surinam
Children — SP20

1954, Nov. 1   Perf. 13x14
B58 SP20 7½c + 3c sepia   6.00 4.75
B59 SP20 10c + 5c bl grn   6.00 4.75
B60 SP20 15c + 7½c red brn   6.00 4.75
B61 SP20 30c + 15c blue   6.00 4.75
Nos. B58-B61 (4)   24.00 19.00

Surtax for the youth center of the Moravian
Church.

Doves — SP21

1955, May 5   Perf. 14x13
B62 SP21 7½c + 3½c brt red   2.75 3.00
B63 SP21 15c + 8c ultra   2.75 3.00

The Netherlands' liberation, 10th anniv.

Queen Juliana
and Prince
Bernhard
SP22

1955, Oct. 27   Unwmk.
B64 SP22 7½c + 2½c dk olive   .55 .55

Royal visit to Surinam, 1955. Surtax for the
Royal present.

Theater,
1837 — SP23

Designs: 10c+5c, Theater and car, circa
1920. 15c+7½c, Theater and car, circa 1958.
20c+10c, Theater interior.

1958, Feb. 15   Litho.   Perf. 13x12½
B65 SP23 7½c + 3c lt bl & blk   .45 .45
B66 SP23 10c + 5c rose lil & blk   .45 .45
B67 SP23 15c + 7½c lt grn & blk   .45 .45
B68 SP23 20c + 10c org & blk   .45 .45
Nos. B65-B68 (4)   1.80 1.80

120th anniv. of the "Thalia" theatrical society.

Carved Eating
Utensils and
Map of South
America
SP24

Native Art (Map of So. America and):
10c+5c, Feather headgear. 15c+7c, Clay pottery. 20c+10c, Carved wooden stool.

1960, Jan. 15
B69 SP24   8c + 4c multi   .90 .90
B70 SP24 10c + 5c salmon, red
& bl   .90 .90
B71 SP24 15c + 7c red org, grn
& sepia   .90 .90
B72 SP24 20c + 10c lt bl, ultra &
bis   .90 .90
Nos. B69-B72 (4)   3.60 3.60

SP25

Design: Uprooted Oak emblem of WRY.

1960, Apr. 7   Perf. 13x14
B73 SP25   8c + 4c choc & grn   .25 .25
B74 SP25 10c + 5c vio bl & ol grn   .25 .25

World Refugee Year, July 1, 1959-June 30,
1960. The surtax was for aid to refugees.

SP26

1960, Aug. 10   Litho.   Perf. 14x13
B75 SP26   8c + 4c Shot put   .55 .55
B76 SP26 10c + 5c Basketball   .55 .55
B77 SP26 15c + 7c Runner   .85 .85
B78 SP26 20c + 10c Swimmer   .85 .85
B79 SP26 40c + 20c Soccer   .85 .85
Nos. B75-B79 (5)   3.65 3.65

17th Olympic Games, Rome, 8/25-9/11.
Surtax for Olympic Committee.

Girl
Scout
Signaling
SP27

Designs: 10c+3c, Scout Saluting, vert.
15c+4c, Brownies around toadstool. 20c+5c,
Scouts around campfire, vert. 25c+6c, Scouts
cooking outdoors.

Perf. 14x13, 13x14
1961, Aug. 19   Litho.
Multicolored Designs
B80 SP27   8c + 2c blue   .30 .30
B81 SP27 10c + 3c lilac   .35 .35
B82 SP27 15c + 4c yellow   .35 .35
B83 SP27 20c + 5c brn red   .40 .40
B84 SP27 25c + 6c aqua   .40 .40
Nos. B80-B84 (5)   1.80 1.80

Caribbean Girl Scout Jamborette.
Surtax for various charities.

Hibiscus
SP28

Flowers: 10c+5c, Caesalpinia pulcherrima.
15c+6c, Heliconia psittacorum. 20c+10c,
Lochnera rosea. 25c+12c, Ixora macrothyrsa.

1962, Mar. 7　Photo.　Perf. 14x13
Cross in Red

B85	SP28	8c + 4c dk ol & scar	.32 .30
B86	SP28	10c + 5c dk bl & org	.32 .30
B87	SP28	15c + 6c multi	.32 .30
B88	SP28	20c + 10c multi	.32 .30
B89	SP28	25c + 12c dk bl grn, red & yel	.32 .30
		Nos. B85-B89 (5)	1.60 1.50

The surtax was for the Red Cross.

Hands Protecting Duck — SP29

1962, Dec. 15　Litho.　Perf. 13x14

B90	SP29	2c + 1c shown	.25 .25
B91	SP29	8c + 2c Dog	.25 .25
B92	SP29	10c + 3c Donkey	.25 .25
B93	SP29	20c + 4c Horse	.25 .25
		Nos. B90-B93 (4)	1.00 1.00

The surtax was for the Organization for Animal Protection.

American Indian Girl — SP30

Girls: 10c+4c, Negro. 15c+10c, East Indian. 20c+10c, Indonesian. 40c+20c, Caucasian.

1963, Oct. 30　Photo.　Unwmk.

B94	SP30	8c + 3c Prus grn	.25 .25
B95	SP30	10c + 4c red brn	.25 .25
a.		Min. sheet, 2 each #B94-B95	1.25 1.25
B96	SP30	15c + 10c dp blue	.25 .25
B97	SP30	20c + 10c brn red	.25 .25
B98	SP30	40c + 20c red vio	.35 .35
		Nos. B94-B98 (5)	1.35 1.35

The surtax was for Child Welfare.

X-15 SP31

Designs: 8c+4c, Flag of the Aeronautical and Astronautical Foundation. 10c+5c, 20c+10c, Agena B Ranger rocket.

1964, Apr. 15　　　　Perf. 13x12½

B99	SP31	3c + 2c blk & rose lake	.25 .25
B100	SP31	8c + 4c blk, ultra & lt ultra	.25 .25
B101	SP31	10c + 5c blk & grn	.25 .25
B102	SP31	15c + 7c blk & yel brn	.25 .25
B103	SP31	20c + 10c blk & vio	.25 .25
		Nos. B99-B103 (5)	1.25 1.25

Surtax for the Aeronautical and Astronautical Foundation of Surinam.

Stylized Campfire amid Trees — SP32

1964, July 29　Litho.　Perf. 13x14

B104	SP32	3c + 1c brn ol, yel bis & lem	.25 .25
B105	SP32	8c + 4c bluish blk, vio bl & yel bis	.25 .25
B106	SP32	10c + 5c dk red, red & yel bis	.25 .25

B107	SP32	20c + 10c grnsh blk, ol grn & yel bis	.25 .25
		Nos. B104-B107 (4)	1.00 1.00

Jamborette at Paramaribo, Aug. 20-30, marking the 40th anniv. of the Surinam Boy Scout Association. Surtax for various charities.

Girls Skipping Rope — SP33

10c+4c, Children on swings. 15c+9c, Girl on scooter. 20c+10c, Boy rolling hoop.

1964, Nov. 30　Photo.　Perf. 14x13

B108	SP33	8c + 3c dk blue	.25 .25
B109	SP33	10c + 4c red	.25 .25
a.		Min. sheet, 2 each #B108-B109	.55 .55
B110	SP33	15c + 9c olive grn	.25 .25
B111	SP33	20c + 10c magenta	.25 .25
		Nos. B108-B111 (4)	1.00 1.00

Issued for Child Welfare.

Mother and Child — SP34

Designs: 4c+2c, Pregnant woman. 15c+7c, Child. 25c+12c, Old man.

1965, Feb. 27　Photo.　Perf. 13x14

B112	SP34	4c + 2c green	.25 .25
B113	SP34	10c + 5c brn & grn	.25 .25
B114	SP34	15c + 7c Prus bl & grn	.25 .25
B115	SP34	25c + 12c brt pur & grn	.25 .25
		Nos. B112-B115 (4)	1.00 1.00

50th anniv. of the Green Cross Assoc. which promotes public health services.

Girl with Leopard and Spider SP35

Designs: 10c+5c, Boy with monkey and spider. 15c+7c, Girl with tortoise and spider. 25c+10c, Boy with rabbit and spider.

Perf. 13x12½

1965, Nov. 26　Litho.　Unwmk.

B116	SP35	4c + 4c lt grn & blk	.25 .25
B117	SP35	10c + 5c ocher & blk	.25 .25
B118	SP35	15c + 7c dp org & blk	.25 .25
a.		Min. sheet, 2 each #B116, B118	.55 .55
B119	SP35	25c + 10c lt ultra & blk	.25 .25
		Nos. B116-B119 (4)	1.00 1.00

Issued for Child Welfare.

"Help them to a safe haven" SP35a

1966, Jan. 31　Photo.　Perf. 14x13

B120	SP35a	10c + 5c blk & grn	.25 .25
B121	SP35a	25c + 10c blk & rose brn	.25 .25
a.		Min. sheet of 3, 2 #B120, B121	.45 .45

The surtax was for the Intergovernmental Committee for European Migration (ICEM). The message on the stamps was given and signed by Queen Juliana.

Mary Magdalene, Disciples and "Round Table" Emblem — SP36

Mary Magdalene (John 20:18), and Service Club Emblems: 15c+8c, Toastmasters Intl. 20c+10c, Junior Chamber, Surinam. 25c+12c, Rotary Intl. 30c+15c, Lions Intl.

1966, Apr. 13　Photo.　Perf. 12½x13

B122	SP36	10c + 5c dp crim, blk & gold	.25 .25
B123	SP36	15c + 8c dp vio, blk & bl	.25 .25
B124	SP36	20c + 10c yel org, blk & ultra	.25 .25
B125	SP36	25c + 12c grn, blk & gold	.25 .25
B126	SP36	30c + 15c ultra, blk & gold	.25 .25
		Nos. B122-B126 (5)	1.25 1.25

Easter charities.

"New Year's Eve" Boys with Bamboo Gun — SP37

Designs: 15c+8c, "The End of Lent," boys pouring paint over each other. 20c+10c, "Liberation Day," parading children. 25c+12c, "Queen's Birthday," children on hobbyhorses. 30c+15c, "Christmas," Children decorating room with star.

1966, Nov. 25　Litho.　Perf. 12½x13

B127	SP37	10c + 5c multi	.25 .25
B128	SP37	15c + 8c multi	.25 .25
B129	SP37	20c + 10c multi	.25 .25
a.		Min. sheet of 3, 2 #B127, B129	.35 .35
B130	SP37	25c + 12c multi	.25 .25
B131	SP37	30c + 15c multi	.25 .25
		Nos. B127-B131 (5)	1.25 1.25

Child welfare.

Good Samaritan Giving His Coat — SP38

The Good Samaritan: 15c+8c, Dressing the wounds. 20c+10c, Feeding the poor man. 25c+12c, Poor man riding Samaritan's horse. 30c+15c, Samaritan taking poor man to the inn.

1967, Mar. 22

B132	SP38	10c + 5c yellow & blk	.25 .25
B133	SP38	15c + 8c lt blue & blk	.25 .25
B134	SP38	20c + 10c buff & blk	.25 .25
B135	SP38	25c + 12c pale rose & blk	.25 .25
B136	SP38	30c + 15c grn & blk	.25 .25
		Nos. B132-B136 (5)	1.25 1.25

Easter charities.

Children Stilt-walking — SP39

Children's Games: 15c+8c, Boys playing with marbles. 20c+10c, Girl playing dibs (five

stones). 25c+12c, Boy making kite. 30c+15c, Girls play-cooking.

1967, Nov. 21　Litho.　Perf. 12½x13

B137	SP39	10c + 5c multi	.25 .25
B138	SP39	15c + 8c multi	.25 .25
B139	SP39	20c + 10c multi	.25 .25
a.		Min. sheet, #B139, 2 #B137	.45 .45
B140	SP39	25c + 12c multi	.25 .25
B141	SP39	30c + 15c multi	.25 .25
		Nos. B137-B141 (5)	1.25 1.25

Child welfare.

Cross, Ash Wednesday — SP40

Easter Symbols: 15c+8c, Palms, Palm Sunday. 20c+10c, Bread and Wine, Maundy Thursday. 25c+12c, Cross, Good Friday. 30c+15c, Chrismon, Easter Sunday.

1968, Mar. 27　Litho.　Perf. 12½x13

B142	SP40	10c + 5c lilac & gray	.25 .25
B143	SP40	15c + 8c brick red & grn	.25 .25
B144	SP40	20c + 10c yellow & dk grn	.25 .25
B145	SP40	25c + 12c gray & blk	.25 .25
B146	SP40	30c + 15c brt yel & brn	.25 .25
		Nos. B142-B146 (5)	1.25 1.25

Easter charities.

Hopscotch — SP41

15c+8c, Balancing pyramid. 20c+10c, Handball. 25c+12c, Handicraft. 30c+15c, Tug-of-war.

1968, Nov. 22　Litho.　Perf. 12½x13

B147	SP41	10c + 5c fawn & blk	.25 .25
B148	SP41	15c + 8c lt ultra & blk	.25 .25
B149	SP41	20c + 10c pink & blk	.25 .25
a.		Min. sheet, #B149, 2 #B147	.50 .50
B150	SP41	25c + 12c yel grn & blk	.25 .25
B151	SP41	30c + 15c bluish lil & blk	.30 .30
		Nos. B147-B151 (5)	1.30 1.30

Child welfare.

Globe with Map of South America — SP42

1969, Apr. 2　Litho.　Perf. 12½x13

B152	SP42	10c + 5c bl & lt bl	.25 .25
B153	SP42	15c + 8c sl grn & yel	.25 .25
B154	SP42	20c + 10c sl grn & gray grn	.25 .25
B155	SP42	25c + 12c brn & bis	.25 .25
B156	SP42	30c + 15c vio & gray	.25 .25
		Nos. B152-B156 (5)	1.25 1.25

Easter charities.

Pillow Fight — SP43

15c+8c, Eating contest. 20c+10c, Pole climbing. 25c+12c, Sack race. 30c+15c, Obstacle race.

1969, Nov. 21   Litho.   Perf. 12½x13
B157	SP43	10c + 5c lt ultra & mag	.25	.25
B158	SP43	15c + 8c yel & brn	.25	.25
B159	SP43	20c + 10c gray & dp bl	.25	.25
a.		Min. sheet, #B159, 2 B157	.80	.80
B160	SP43	25c + 12c pink & brt bl	.25	.25
B161	SP43	30c + 15c emer & brn	.25	.25
		Nos. B157-B161 (5)	1.25	1.25

Child welfare.

Butterfly — SP44

Designs: 10c+5c, Flower. 20c+10c, Flying bird. 25c+12c, Sun. 30c+15c, Star.

1970, Mar. 25   Litho.   Perf. 12½x13
B162	SP44	10c + 5c multi	.50	.50
B163	SP44	15c + 8c multi	.50	.50
B164	SP44	20c + 10c multi	.50	.50
B165	SP44	25c + 12c multi	.50	.50
B166	SP44	30c + 15c multi	.50	.50
		Nos. B162-B166 (5)	2.50	2.50

Easter.

Ludwig van Beethoven, 1786 — SP45

Various Portraits of Beethoven: 15c+8c, In 1804. 20c+10c, In 1812. 25c+12c, In 1814. 30c+15c, In 1827 (death mask).

Portrait and Inscription in Gray and Ocher

1970, Nov. 25   Litho.   Perf. 12½x13
B167	SP45	10c + 5c green	.50	.50
B168	SP45	15c + 8c scarlet	.50	.50
B169	SP45	20c + 10c blue	.50	.50
a.		Min. sheet, #B169, 2 #B167	1.60	1.60
B170	SP45	25c + 12c red org	.50	.50
B171	SP45	30c + 15c purple	.50	.50
		Nos. B167-B171 (5)	2.50	2.50

Ludwig van Beethoven (1770-1827), composer. The surtax was for child welfare.

Donkey and Palm — SP46

Easter: 15c+8c, Cock. 20c+10c, Lamb of God. 25c+12c, Cross and Crown of Thorns. 30c+15c, Sun.

1971, Apr. 7   Litho.   Perf. 12½x13
B172	SP46	10c + 5c multi	.50	.50
B173	SP46	15c + 8c blue & multi	.50	.50
B174	SP46	20c + 10c	.50	.50

B175	SP46	25c + 12c multi	.50	.50
B176	SP46	30c + 15c multi	.50	.50
		Nos. B172-B176 (5)	2.50	2.50

Easter charities.

Leapfrog, by Peter Brueghel — SP47

Children's Games, by Peter Brueghel: 15c+8c, Girl strewing flowers. 20c+10c, Spinning the hoop. 25c+12c, Ball players. 30c+15c, Stilt walker.

1971, Nov. 24   Photo.   Perf. 13x14
B177	SP47	10c + 5c multi	.60	.60
B178	SP47	15c + 8c multi	.60	.60
B179	SP47	20c + 10c multi	.60	.60
a.		Min. sheet, #B179, 2 #B177	2.00	2.00
B180	SP47	25c + 12c multi	.60	.60
B181	SP47	30c + 15c multi	.60	.60
		Nos. B177-B181 (5)	3.00	3.00

Child welfare.

Easter Candle — SP48

Easter: 15c+8c, Christ teaching Apostles, and crosses. 20c+10c, Cup and folded hands. 25c+12c, Fish in net. 30c+15c, Judas' bag of silver.

1972, Mar. 29   Litho.   Perf. 12½x13
B182	SP48	10c + 5c multi	.45	.45
B183	SP48	15c + 8c multi	.45	.45
B184	SP48	20c + 10c multi	.45	.45
B185	SP48	25c + 12c multi	.45	.45
B186	SP48	30c + 15c multi	.45	.45
		Nos. B182-B186 (5)	2.25	2.25

Easter charities.

Toys — SP49

Designs: 15c+8c, Abacus and clock. 20c+10c, Pythagorean theorem. 25c+12c, Model of molecule. 30c+15c, Monkey wrench and drill. Each design represents a different stage of education.

1972, Nov. 29   Litho.   Perf. 12½x13
B187	SP49	10c + 5c multi	.50	.50
B188	SP49	15c + 8c multi	.50	.50
B189	SP49	20c + 10c multi	.50	.50
a.		Min. sheet, #B189, 2 #B187	1.50	1.50
B190	SP49	25c + 12c multi	.50	.50
B191	SP49	30c + 15c multi	.50	.50
		Nos. B187-B191 (5)	2.50	2.50

Child welfare.

Jesus Calming the Waves — SP50

Easter: 15c+8c, The washing of the feet. 20c+10c, Jesus carrying Cross. 25c+12c,

Cross and "ELI, ELI, LAMA SABACHTHANI?" 30c+15c, on the road to Emmaus.

1973, Apr. 4   Litho.   Perf. 12½x13
B192	SP50	10c + 5c multi	.45	.45
B193	SP50	15c + 8c multi	.45	.45
B194	SP50	20c + 10c multi	.45	.45
B195	SP50	25c + 12c multi	.45	.45
B196	SP50	30c + 15c multi	.45	.45
		Nos. B192-B196 (5)	2.25	2.25

Easter charities.

Red Cross and Florence Nightingale SP51

1973, Oct. 3   Litho.   Perf. 14½x14
B197	SP51	30c + 10c multi	.90	.90

30th anniversary of Surinam Red Cross.

Flower — SP52

1973, Nov. 28   Litho.   Perf. 14x14½
B198	SP52	10c + 5c shown	.25	.25
B199	SP52	15c + 8c Tree	.45	.45
B200	SP52	20c + 10c Dog	.40	.40
a.		Min. sheet, #B200, 2 #B198	1.25	1.25
B201	SP52	25c + 12c House	.60	.60
B202	SP52	30c + 15c Girl	.60	.60
		Nos. B198-B202 (5)	2.30	2.30

Child welfare.

Bitterwood — SP53

Tropical Flowers: 15c+8c, Passion flower. 20c+10c, Wild angelica. 25c+12c, Candlestick senna. 30c+15c, Blood flower.

1974, Apr. 3   Litho.   Perf. 14x14½
B203	SP53	10c + 5c multi	.45	.45
B204	SP53	15c + 8c multi	.45	.45
B205	SP53	20c + 10c multi	.45	.45
B206	SP53	25c + 12c multi	.45	.45
B207	SP53	30c + 15c multi	.45	.45
		Nos. B203-B207 (5)	2.25	2.25

Easter charities.

Boy Scout, Tent and Trees — SP54

Designs: 15c+8c, 5th Caribbean Jamboree emblem. 20c+10c, Scouts and emblem.

1974, Aug. 21   Litho.   Perf. 14x14½
B208	SP54	10c + 5c multi	.40	.40
B209	SP54	15c + 8c multi	.40	.40
B210	SP54	20c + 10c multi	.40	.40
		Nos. B208-B210 (3)	1.20	1.20

50th anniversary of Surinam Boy Scouts.

Fruit — SP55

Designs: 15c+8c, Children, birds and nest (security). 20c+10c, Flower, mother and child (protection). 25c+12c, Child and corn (good food). 30c+15c, Dancing children (child care).

1974, Nov. 27   Litho.   Perf. 14½x14
B211	SP55	10c + 5c multi	.25	.25
B212	SP55	15c + 8c multi	.35	.35
B213	SP55	20c + 10c multi	.35	.35
a.		Min. sheet, #B213, 2 #B211	1.00	1.00
B214	SP55	25c + 12c multi	.55	.55
B215	SP55	30c + 15c multi	.60	.60
		Nos. B211-B215 (5)	2.10	2.10

Child welfare.

The Good Shepherd — SP56

Designs: 20c+10c, Peter's denial. 30c+15c, The Women at the Tomb. 35c+20c, Jesus showing His wounds to Thomas.

1975, Mar. 26   Litho.   Perf. 12½x13
B216	SP56	15c + 5c yel grn & grn	.45	.45
B217	SP56	20c + 10c org & dk bl	.60	.60
B218	SP56	30c + 15c yel & red	.60	.60
B219	SP56	35c + 20c bl & pur	.60	.60
		Nos. B216-B219 (4)	2.25	2.25

Easter charities.

Woman and IWY Emblem — SP57

1975, May 14   Litho.   Perf. 12½x13
B220	SP57	15c + 5c multi	.65	.65
B221	SP57	30c + 15c multi	.65	.65

International Women's Year.

Carib Indian Water Jug — SP58

Designs: 20c+10c, 35c+20c, Indian arrow head, diff. 30c+15c, Wayana board with animal figures.

1975, Nov. 12   Litho.   Perf. 12½x13
B222	SP58	15c + 5c multi	.25	.25
B223	SP58	20c + 10c multi	.55	.55
a.		Min. sheet, #B223, 2 #B222	1.50	1.50
B224	SP58	30c + 15c multi	.90	.90
B225	SP58	35c + 20c multi	.90	.90
		Nos. B222-B225 (4)	2.60	2.60

Child welfare.

Feeding the Hungry — SP59

Paintings: 25c+15c, Visiting the Sick. 30c+15c, Clothing the Naked. 35c+15c, Burying the Dead. 50c+25c, Giving Water to the Thirsty. Designs after panels in Alkmaar Church, 1504.

Perf. 14½x13½

1976, Apr. 14   **Photo.**
B226	SP59 20c + 10c multi	.70	.70
B227	SP59 25c + 15c multi	.85	.85
B228	SP59 30c + 15c multi	1.25	1.25
a.	Souv. sheet, #B228, 2 #B226	3.50	3.50
B229	SP59 35c + 15c multi	1.25	1.25
B230	SP59 50c + 25c multi	1.75	1.75
	Nos. B226-B230 (5)	5.80	5.80

Easter.

Pekingese and Boy's Head — SP60

25c+10c, German shepherd. 30c+15c, Dachshund. 35c+15c, Retriever. 50c+25c, Terrier.

1976   **Litho.**   **Perf. 13½**
B231	SP60 20c + 10c multi	.90	.60
B232	SP60 25c + 10c multi	1.25	.80
B233	SP60 30c + 15c multi	1.50	.95
a.	Min. sheet, #B233, 2 #B231	8.00	6.50
B234	SP60 35c + 15c multi	1.50	1.00
B235	SP60 50c + 25c multi	2.40	1.50
	Nos. B231-B235 (5)	7.55	4.85

Surtax was for child welfare.

St. Veronica's Veil — SP61   Descent from the Cross — SP62

Easter: Religious scenes, side panels, front and back, from triptych by Jan Mostaert (1473-1555).

1977, Apr. 6   **Litho.**   **Perf. 13½x14**
B236	SP61 20c + 10c multi	.25	.25
B237	SP61 25c + 15c multi	.50	.50
B238	SP61 30c + 15c multi	.55	.55
B239	SP61 35c + 15c multi	.65	.65
B240	SP62 50c + 25c multi	.80	.80
	Nos. B236-B240 (5)	2.75	2.75

Dog and Girl's Head — SP63

Child's Head and: 25c+15c, Monkey. 30c+15c, Rabbit. 35c+15c, Cat. 50c+25c, Parrot.

1977, Nov. 23   **Litho.**   **Perf. 13x14**
B241	SP63 20c + 10c multi	.50	.50
B242	SP63 25c + 15c multi	.60	.60
B243	SP63 30c + 15c multi	.70	.70
a.	Min. sheet, #B243, 2 #B241	1.75	1.75
B244	SP63 35c + 15c multi	.85	.85
B245	SP63 50c + 25c multi	1.25	1.25
	Nos. B241-B245 (5)	3.90	3.90

Surtax was for child welfare.

Crosses, Luke 23:43 — SP64

Easter: 25c+15c, Serpent and Cross, John 3:14. 30c+15c, Lamb and blood, Exodus 12:13. 35c+15c, Passover plate, chalice and bread. 60c+30c, Cross and solar eclipse.

1978, Mar. 22   **Litho.**   **Perf. 12½x14**
B246	SP64 20c + 10c multi	.25	.25
B247	SP64 25c + 15c multi	.35	.35
B248	SP64 30c + 15c multi	.40	.40
B249	SP64 35c + 15c multi	.45	.45
B250	SP64 60c + 30c multi	.90	.90
	Nos. B246-B250 (5)	2.35	2.35

Child's Head and White Cat — SP65

Child's head and cats in various positions.

1978, Nov. 22   **Litho.**   **Perf. 14x13**
B251	SP65 20c + 10c multi	.30	.30
B252	SP65 25c + 15c multi	.50	.35
B253	SP65 30c + 15c multi	.55	.40
a.	Min. sheet, #B253, 2 #B251	1.65	1.65
B254	SP65 35c + 15c multi	.60	.50
B255	SP65 60c + 30c multi	1.00	.80
	Nos. B251-B255 (5)	2.95	2.35

Surtax was for child welfare.

Church, Cross and Chalice — SP66

Easter: Cross, chalice and various churches.

1979, Apr. 11   **Litho.**   **Perf. 13x14**
B256	SP66 20c + 10c multi	.25	.25
B257	SP66 30c + 15c multi	.40	.40
B258	SP66 35c + 15c multi	.55	.55
B259	SP66 40c + 20c multi	.65	.65
B260	SP66 60c + 30c multi	.95	.95
	Nos. B256-B260 (5)	2.80	2.80

Boy, Bird, Red Cross, Blood Transfusion Bottle — SP67

1979, Nov. 21   **Litho.**   **Perf. 13x14**
B261	SP67 20c + 10c multi	.25	.25
B262	SP67 30c + 15c multi	.40	.40
B263	SP67 35c + 15c multi	.55	.55
a.	Min. sheet, #B263, 2 #B261	2.25	2.25
B264	SP67 40c + 20c multi	.65	.65
B265	SP67 60c + 30c multi	.95	.95
	Nos. B261-B265 (5)	2.80	2.80

Surtax was for child welfare.

Cross — SP68

Easter: Various symbols.

1980, Mar. 26   **Litho.**   **Perf. 13x14**
B266	SP68 20c + 10c multi	.30	.30
B267	SP68 30c + 15c multi	.45	.45
B268	SP68 40c + 20c multi	.55	.55
B269	SP68 50c + 25c multi	.80	.80
B270	SP68 60c + 30c multi	.90	.90
	Nos. B266-B270 (5)	3.00	3.00

Anansi — SP69

Characters from Anansi and His Creditors: No. B272, Ba Tigri. No. B273, Kakafowroe. No. B274, Ontiman. No. B275, Mat Kalaka.

1980, Nov. 5   **Litho.**   **Perf. 13x14**
B271	SP69 20c + 10c shown	.30	.30
B272	SP69 25c + 15c multi	.45	.45
B273	SP69 30c + 15c multi	.50	.50
B274	SP69 35c + 15c multi	.55	.55
B275	SP69 60c + 30c multi	.95	.95
a.	Min. sheet, #B275, 2 #B271	1.75	1.75
	Nos. B271-B275 (5)	2.75	2.75

Surtax was for child welfare.

Woman Reading SP70

No. B277, Gardening. No. B278, With grandchildren.

1980, Dec. 10   **Perf. 14x13**
B276	SP70 25c + 10c shown	.40	.40
B277	SP70 50c + 15c multi	.70	.70
B278	SP70 75c + 20c multi	1.00	1.00
	Nos. B276-B278 (3)	2.10	2.10

Surtax was for the elderly.

Crucifixion — SP71

Easter: Scenes from the Passion of Christ.

1981, Apr. 8   **Litho.**   **Perf. 13x14**
B279	SP71 20c + 10c multi	.25	.25
B280	SP71 30c + 15c multi	.40	.40
B281	SP71 50c + 25c multi	.85	.85
B282	SP71 60c + 30c multi	.90	.90
B283	SP71 75c + 35c multi	1.10	1.10
	Nos. B279-B283 (5)	3.50	3.50

Surtax was for the elderly.

Indian Girl — SP72

1981, Nov. 26   **Litho.**
B284	SP72 20c + 10c shown	.25	.25
B285	SP72 30c + 15c Black	.45	.45
B286	SP72 50c + 25c Hindustani	.75	.75
B287	SP72 60c + 30c Javanese	.80	.80
B288	SP72 75c + 35c Chinese	.90	.90
a.	Souv. sheet, #B288, 2 #B285	3.00	3.00
	Nos. B284-B288 (5)	3.15	3.15

Surtax was for child welfare.

Easter — SP73

Designs: Stained-glass windows, Sts. Peter and Paul Church, Paramaribo.

1982, Apr. 7   **Litho.**   **Perf. 13x14**
B289	SP73 20c + 10c multi	.35	.35
B290	SP73 35c + 15c multi	.65	.65
B291	SP73 50c + 25c multi	1.00	1.00
B292	SP73 65c + 30c multi	1.00	1.00
B293	SP73 75c + 35c multi	1.25	1.25
	Nos. B289-B293 (5)	4.25	4.25

Man Pushing Wheelbarrow SP74

Children's Drawings of City Cleaning Activities.

1982, Nov. 17   **Litho.**
B294	SP74 20c + 10c multi	.35	.35
B295	SP74 35c + 15c multi	.65	.65
B296	SP74 50c + 25c multi	1.25	1.25
B297	SP74 65c + 30c multi	1.25	1.25
B298	SP74 75c + 35c multi	1.50	1.50
a.	Souv. sheet, #B298, 2 #B295	3.50	3.50
	Nos. B294-B298 (5)	5.00	5.00

Surtax was for child welfare.

Easter — SP75

Mosaic Symbols.

1983, Mar. 23   **Litho.**   **Perf. 13x14**
B299	SP75 10c + 5c Dove	.25	.25
B300	SP75 15c + 5c Bread	.35	.35
B301	SP75 25c + 10c Fish	.80	.80
B302	SP75 50c + 25c Eye	1.75	1.75
B303	SP75 65c + 30c Wine cup	1.90	1.90
	Nos. B299-B303 (5)	5.05	5.05

Pitcher — SP76

1983, Nov. 16   **Litho.**   **Perf. 13x14**
B304	SP76 10c + 5c shown	.35	.35
B305	SP76 15c + 5c Headdress	.35	.35
B306	SP76 25c + 10c Medicine rattle	.60	.60
B307	SP76 50c + 25c Sieve	1.75	1.75
B308	SP76 65c + 30c Basket	1.90	1.90
a.	Min. sheet, #B305, B306, B308	3.50	3.50
	Nos. B304-B308 (5)	4.95	4.95

Pillow Fight — SP43

15c+8c, Eating contest. 20c+10c, Pole climbing. 25c+12c, Sack race. 30c+15c, Obstacle race.

1969, Nov. 21   Litho.   Perf. 12½x13
B157 SP43 10c + 5c lt ultra &
            mag   .25   .25
B158 SP43 15c + 8c yel & brn   .25   .25
B159 SP43 20c + 10c gray & dp
            bl   .25   .25
 a.   Min. sheet, #B159, 2 B157   .80   .80
B160 SP43 25c + 12c pink & brt
            bl   .25   .25
B161 SP43 30c + 15c emer &
            brn   .25   .25
     Nos. B157-B161 (5)   1.25 1.25
         Child welfare.

Butterfly — SP44

Designs: 10c+5c, Flower. 20c+10c, Flying bird. 25c+12c, Sun. 30c+15c, Star.

1970, Mar. 25   Litho.   Perf. 12½x13
B162 SP44 10c + 5c multi   .50   .50
B163 SP44 15c + 8c multi   .50   .50
B164 SP44 20c + 10c multi   .50   .50
B165 SP44 25c + 12c multi   .50   .50
B166 SP44 30c + 15c multi   .50   .50
     Nos. B162-B166 (5)   2.50 2.50
            Easter.

Ludwig van Beethoven, 1786 — SP45

Various Portraits of Beethoven: 15c+8c, In 1804. 20c+10c, In 1812. 25c+12c, In 1814. 30c+15c, In 1827 (death mask).

Portrait and Inscription in Gray and Ocher

1970, Nov. 25   Litho.   Perf. 12½x13
B167 SP45 10c + 5c green   .50   .50
B168 SP45 15c + 8c scarlet   .50   .50
B169 SP45 20c + 10c blue   .50   .50
 a.   Min. sheet, #B169, 2 #B167 1.60 1.60
B170 SP45 25c + 12c red org   .50   .50
B171 SP45 30c + 15c purple   .50   .50
     Nos. B167-B171 (5)   2.50 2.50
Ludwig van Beethoven (1770-1827), composer. The surtax was for child welfare.

Donkey and Palm — SP46

Easter: 15c+8c, Cock. 20c+10c, Lamb of God. 25c+12c, Cross and Crown of Thorns. 30c+15c, Sun.

1971, Apr. 7   Litho.   Perf. 12½x13
B172 SP46 10c + 5c multi   .50   .50
B173 SP46 15c + 8c blue & multi   .50   .50
B174 SP46 20c + 10c multi   .50   .50

B175 SP46 25c + 12c multi   .50   .50
B176 SP46 30c + 15c multi   .50   .50
     Nos. B172-B176 (5)   2.50 2.50
        Easter charities.

Leapfrog, by Peter Brueghel — SP47

Children's Games, by Peter Brueghel: 15c+8c, Girl strewing flowers. 20c+10c, Spinning the hoop. 25c+12c, Ball players. 30c+15c, Stilt walker.

1971, Nov. 24   Photo.   Perf. 13x14
B177 SP47 10c + 5c multi   .60   .60
B178 SP47 15c + 8c multi   .60   .60
B179 SP47 20c + 10c multi   .60   .60
 a.   Min. sheet, #B179, 2 #B177 2.00 2.00
B180 SP47 25c + 12c multi   .60   .60
B181 SP47 30c + 15c multi   .60   .60
     Nos. B177-B181 (5)   3.00 3.00
         Child welfare.

Easter Candle — SP48

Easter: 15c+8c, Christ teaching Apostles, and crosses. 20c+10c, Cup and folded hands. 25c+12c, Fish in net. 30c+15c, Judas' bag of silver.

1972, Mar. 29   Litho.   Perf. 12½x13
B182 SP48 10c + 5c multi   .45   .45
B183 SP48 15c + 8c multi   .45   .45
B184 SP48 20c + 10c multi   .45   .45
B185 SP48 25c + 12c multi   .45   .45
B186 SP48 30c + 15c multi   .45   .45
     Nos. B182-B186 (5)   2.25 2.25
        Easter charities.

Toys — SP49

Designs: 15c+8c, Abacus and clock. 20c+10c, Pythagorean theorem. 25c+12c, Model of molecule. 30c+15c, Monkey wrench and drill. Each design represents a different stage of education.

1972, Nov. 29   Litho.   Perf. 12½x13
B187 SP49 10c + 5c multi   .50   .50
B188 SP49 15c + 8c multi   .50   .50
B189 SP49 20c + 10c multi   .50   .50
 a.   Min. sheet, #B189, 2 #B187 1.50 1.50
B190 SP49 25c + 12c multi   .50   .50
B191 SP49 30c + 15c multi   .50   .50
     Nos. B187-B191 (5)   2.50 2.50
         Child welfare.

Jesus Calming the Waves — SP50

Easter: 15c+8c, The washing of the feet. 20c+10c, Jesus carrying Cross. 25c+12c,

Cross and "ELI, ELI, LAMA SABACHTHANI?" 30c+15c, on the road to Emmaus.

1973, Apr. 4   Litho.   Perf. 12½x13
B192 SP50 10c + 5c multi   .45   .45
B193 SP50 15c + 8c multi   .45   .45
B194 SP50 20c + 10c multi   .45   .45
B195 SP50 25c + 12c multi   .45   .45
B196 SP50 30c + 15c multi   .45   .45
     Nos. B192-B196 (5)   2.25 2.25
        Easter charities.

Red Cross and Florence Nightingale SP51

1973, Oct. 3   Litho.   Perf. 14½x14
B197 SP51 30c + 10c multi   .90   .90
30th anniversary of Surinam Red Cross.

Flower — SP52

1973, Nov. 28   Litho.   Perf. 14x14½
B198 SP52 10c + 5c shown   .25   .25
B199 SP52 15c + 8c Tree   .45   .45
B200 SP52 20c + 10c Dog   .40   .40
 a.   Min. sheet, #B200, 2 #B198 1.25 1.25
B201 SP52 25c + 12c House   .60   .60
B202 SP52 30c + 15c Girl   .60   .60
     Nos. B198-B202 (5)   2.30 2.30
         Child welfare.

Bitterwood — SP53

Tropical Flowers: 15c+8c, Passion flower. 20c+10c, Wild angelica. 25c+12c, Candlestick senna. 30c+15c, Blood flower.

1974, Apr. 3   Litho.   Perf. 14x14½
B203 SP53 10c + 5c multi   .45   .45
B204 SP53 15c + 8c multi   .45   .45
B205 SP53 20c + 10c multi   .45   .45
B206 SP53 25c + 12c multi   .45   .45
B207 SP53 30c + 15c multi   .45   .45
     Nos. B203-B207 (5)   2.25 2.25
        Easter charities.

Boy Scout, Tent and Trees — SP54

Designs: 15c+8c, 5th Caribbean Jamboree emblem. 20c+10c, Scouts and emblem.

1974, Aug. 21   Litho.   Perf. 14x14½
B208 SP54 10c + 5c multi   .40   .40
B209 SP54 10c + 8c multi   .40   .40
B210 SP54 20c + 10c multi   .40   .40
     Nos. B208-B210 (3)   1.20 1.20
50th anniversary of Surinam Boy Scouts.

Fruit — SP55

Designs: 15c+8c, Children, birds and nest (security). 20c+10c, Flower, mother and child (protection). 25c+12c, Child and corn (good food). 30c+15c, Dancing children (child care).

1974, Nov. 27   Litho.   Perf. 14½x14
B211 SP55 10c + 5c multi   .25   .25
B212 SP55 15c + 8c multi   .35   .35
B213 SP55 20c + 10c multi   .35   .35
 a.   Min. sheet, #B213, 2 #B211 1.00 1.00
B214 SP55 25c + 12c multi   .55   .55
B215 SP55 30c + 15c multi   .60   .60
     Nos. B211-B215 (5)   2.10 2.10
         Child welfare.

The Good Shepherd — SP56

Designs: 20c+10c, Peter's denial. 30c+15c, The Women at the Tomb. 35c+20c, Jesus showing His wounds to Thomas.

1975, Mar. 26   Litho.   Perf. 12½x13
B216 SP56 15c + 5c yel grn &
            grn   .45   .45
B217 SP56 20c + 10c org & dk bl   .60   .60
B218 SP56 30c + 15c yel & red   .60   .60
B219 SP56 35c + 20c bl & pur   .60   .60
     Nos. B216-B219 (4)   2.25 2.25
        Easter charities.

Woman and IWY Emblem — SP57

1975, May 14   Litho.   Perf. 12½x13
B220 SP57 15c + 5c multi   .65   .65
B221 SP57 30c + 15c multi   .65   .65
     International Women's Year.

Carib Indian Water Jug — SP58

Designs: 20c+10c, 35c+20c, Indian arrow head, diff. 30c+15c, Wayana board with animal figures.

1975, Nov. 12   Litho.   Perf. 12½x13
B222 SP58 15c + 5c multi   .25   .25
B223 SP58 20c + 10c multi   .55   .55
 a.   Min. sheet, #B223, 2 #B222 1.50 1.50
B224 SP58 30c + 15c multi   .90   .90
B225 SP58 35c + 20c multi   .90   .90
     Nos. B222-B225 (4)   2.60 2.60
         Child welfare.

Feeding the Hungry — SP59

Paintings: 25c+15c, Visiting the Sick. 30c+15c, Clothing the Naked. 35c+15c, Burying the Dead. 50c+25c, Giving Water to the Thirsty. Designs after panels in Alkmaar Church, 1504.

Perf. 14½x13½

1976, Apr. 14   **Photo.**
B226	SP59 20c + 10c multi	.70	.70
B227	SP59 25c + 15c multi	.85	.85
B228	SP59 30c + 15c multi	1.25	1.25
a.	Souv. sheet, #B228, 2 #B226	3.50	3.50
B229	SP59 35c + 15c multi	1.25	1.25
B230	SP59 50c + 25c multi	1.75	1.75
	Nos. B226-B230 (5)	5.80	5.80

Easter.

Pekingese and Boy's Head — SP60

25c+10c, German shepherd. 30c+15c, Dachshund. 35c+15c, Retriever. 50c+25c, Terrier.

1976   **Litho.**   **Perf. 13½**
B231	SP60 20c + 10c multi	.90	.60
B232	SP60 25c + 10c multi	1.25	.80
B233	SP60 30c + 15c multi	1.50	.95
a.	Min. sheet, #B233, 2 #B231	8.00	6.50
B234	SP60 35c + 15c multi	1.50	1.00
B235	SP60 50c + 25c multi	2.40	1.50
	Nos. B231-B235 (5)	7.55	4.85

Surtax was for child welfare.

St. Veronica's Veil — SP61   Descent from the Cross — SP62

Easter: Religious scenes, side panels, front and back, from triptych by Jan Mostaert (1473-1555).

1977, Apr. 6   **Litho.**   **Perf. 13½x14**
B236	SP61 20c + 10c multi	.25	.25
B237	SP61 25c + 15c multi	.50	.50
B238	SP61 30c + 15c multi	.55	.55
B239	SP62 35c + 15c multi	.65	.65
B240	SP61 50c + 25c multi	.80	.80
	Nos. B236-B240 (5)	2.75	2.75

Dog and Girl's Head — SP63

Child's Head and: 25c+15c, Monkey. 30c+15c, Rabbit. 35c+15c, Cat. 50c+25c, Parrot.

1977, Nov. 23   **Litho.**   **Perf. 13x14**
B241	SP63 20c + 10c multi	.50	.50
B242	SP63 25c + 15c multi	.60	.60
B243	SP63 30c + 15c multi	.70	.70
a.	Min. sheet, #B243, 2 #B241	1.75	1.75
B244	SP63 35c + 15c multi	.85	.85
B245	SP63 50c + 25c multi	1.25	1.25
	Nos. B241-B245 (5)	3.90	3.90

Surtax was for child welfare.

Crosses, Luke 23:43 — SP64

Easter: 25c+15c, Serpent and Cross, John 3:14. 30c+15c, Lamb and blood, Exodus 12:13. 35c+15c, Passover plate, chalice and bread. 60c+30c, Cross and solar eclipse.

1978, Mar. 22   **Litho.**   **Perf. 12½x14**
B246	SP64 20c + 10c multi	.25	.25
B247	SP64 25c + 15c multi	.35	.35
B248	SP64 30c + 15c multi	.40	.40
B249	SP64 35c + 15c multi	.45	.45
B250	SP64 60c + 30c multi	.90	.90
	Nos. B246-B250 (5)	2.35	2.35

Child's Head and White Cat — SP65

Child's head and cats in various positions.

1978, Nov. 22   **Litho.**   **Perf. 14x13**
B251	SP65 20c + 10c multi	.30	.30
B252	SP65 25c + 15c multi	.50	.35
B253	SP65 30c + 15c multi	.55	.40
a.	Min. sheet, #B253, 2 #B251	1.65	1.65
B254	SP65 35c + 15c multi	.60	.50
B255	SP65 60c + 30c multi	1.00	.80
	Nos. B251-B255 (5)	2.95	2.35

Surtax was for child welfare.

Church, Cross and Chalice — SP66

Easter: Cross, chalice and various churches.

1979, Apr. 11   **Litho.**   **Perf. 13x14**
B256	SP66 20c + 10c multi	.25	.25
B257	SP66 30c + 15c multi	.40	.40
B258	SP66 35c + 15c multi	.55	.55
B259	SP66 40c + 20c multi	.65	.65
B260	SP66 60c + 30c multi	.95	.95
	Nos. B256-B260 (5)	2.80	2.80

Boy, Bird, Red Cross, Blood Transfusion Bottle — SP67

1979, Nov. 21   **Litho.**   **Perf. 13x14**
B261	SP67 20c + 10c multi	.25	.25
B262	SP67 30c + 15c multi	.40	.40
B263	SP67 35c + 15c multi	.55	.55
a.	Min. sheet, #B263, 2 #B261	2.25	2.25
B264	SP67 40c + 20c multi	.65	.65
B265	SP67 60c + 30c multi	.95	.95
	Nos. B261-B265 (5)	2.80	2.80

Surtax was for child welfare.

Cross — SP68

Easter: Various symbols.

1980, Mar. 26   **Litho.**   **Perf. 13x14**
B266	SP68 20c + 10c multi	.30	.30
B267	SP68 30c + 15c multi	.45	.45
B268	SP68 40c + 20c multi	.55	.55
B269	SP68 50c + 25c multi	.80	.80
B270	SP68 60c + 30c multi	.90	.90
	Nos. B266-B270 (5)	3.00	3.00

Anansi — SP69

Characters from Anansi and His Creditors: No. B272, Ba Tigri. No. B273, Kakafowroe. No. B274, Ontiman. No. B275, Mat Kalaka.

1980, Nov. 5   **Litho.**   **Perf. 13x14**
B271	SP69 20c + 10c shown	.30	.30
B272	SP69 25c + 15c multi	.45	.45
B273	SP69 30c + 15c multi	.50	.50
B274	SP69 35c + 15c multi	.55	.55
B275	SP69 60c + 30c multi	.95	.95
a.	Min. sheet, #B275, 2 #B271	1.75	1.75
	Nos. B271-B275 (5)	2.75	2.75

Surtax was for child welfare.

Woman Reading SP70

No. B277, Gardening. No. B278, With grandchildren.

1980, Dec. 10   **Perf. 14x13**
B276	SP70 25c + 10c shown	.40	.40
B277	SP70 50c + 15c multi	.70	.70
B278	SP70 75c + 20c multi	1.00	1.00
	Nos. B276-B278 (3)	2.10	2.10

Surtax was for the elderly.

Crucifixion — SP71

Easter: Scenes from the Passion of Christ.

1981, Apr. 8   **Litho.**   **Perf. 13x14**
B279	SP71 20c + 10c multi	.25	.25
B280	SP71 30c + 15c multi	.40	.40
B281	SP71 50c + 25c multi	.85	.85
B282	SP71 60c + 30c multi	.90	.90
B283	SP71 75c + 35c multi	1.10	1.10
	Nos. B279-B283 (5)	3.50	3.50

Surtax was for the elderly.

Indian Girl — SP72

1981, Nov. 26   **Litho.**
B284	SP72 20c + 10c shown	.25	.25
B285	SP72 30c + 15c Black	.45	.45
B286	SP72 50c + 25c Hindustani	.75	.75
B287	SP72 60c + 30c Javanese	.80	.80
B288	SP72 75c + 35c Chinese	.90	.90
a.	Souv. sheet, #B288, 2 #B285	3.00	3.00
	Nos. B284-B288 (5)	3.15	3.15

Surtax was for child welfare.

Easter — SP73

Designs: Stained-glass windows, Sts. Peter and Paul Church, Paramaribo.

1982, Apr. 7   **Litho.**   **Perf. 13x14**
B289	SP73 20c + 10c multi	.35	.35
B290	SP73 35c + 15c multi	.65	.65
B291	SP73 50c + 25c multi	1.00	1.00
B292	SP73 65c + 30c multi	1.00	1.00
B293	SP73 75c + 35c multi	1.25	1.25
	Nos. B289-B293 (5)	4.25	4.25

Man Pushing Wheelbarrow SP74

Children's Drawings of City Cleaning Activities.

1982, Nov. 17   **Litho.**
B294	SP74 20c + 10c multi	.35	.35
B295	SP74 35c + 15c multi	.65	.65
B296	SP74 50c + 25c multi	1.25	1.25
B297	SP74 65c + 25c multi	1.25	1.25
B298	SP74 75c + 35c multi	1.50	1.50
a.	Souv. sheet, #B298, 2 #B295	3.50	3.50
	Nos. B294-B298 (5)	5.00	5.00

Surtax was for child welfare.

Easter — SP75

Mosaic Symbols.

1983, Mar. 23   **Litho.**   **Perf. 13x14**
B299	SP75 10c + 5c Dove	.25	.25
B300	SP75 15c + 5c Bread	.35	.35
B301	SP75 25c + 10c Fish	.80	.80
B302	SP75 50c + 25c Eye	1.75	1.75
B303	SP75 65c + 30c Wine cup	1.90	1.90
	Nos. B299-B303 (5)	5.05	5.05

Pitcher — SP76

1983, Nov. 16   **Litho.**   **Perf. 13x14**
B304	SP76 10c + 5c shown	.35	.35
B305	SP76 15c + 5c Headdress	.35	.35
B306	SP76 25c + 10c Medicine rattle	.60	.60
B307	SP76 50c + 25c Sieve	1.75	1.75
B308	SP76 65c + 30c Basket	1.90	1.90
a.	Min. sheet, #B305, B306, B308	3.50	3.50
	Nos. B304-B308 (5)	4.95	4.95

Easter — SP77

1984, Apr. 4   Litho.   Perf. 13x14
B309 SP77 10c + 5c Cross, rose   .30   .30
B310 SP77 15c + 15c Cemetery   .30   .30
B311 SP77 25c + 10c Candles   .55   .55
B312 SP77 50c + 25c Cross,
                 crown of thorns   1.50 1.50
B313 SP77 65c + 30c Candle   1.75 1.50
       Nos. B309-B313 (5)   4.40 4.15

SP78

Boy Scouts in Surinam, 60th Anniv.:
30c+10c, 8th Caribbean Jamboree emblem.
35c+10c, Salute. 50c+10c, Gardening.
90c+10c, Campfire in map of Surinam. Surtax
was for Boy Scouts.

1984, Aug. 15   Litho.   Perf. 13x14
B314 SP78 30c + 10c multi   .90   .90
B315 SP78 35c + 10c multi   1.10 1.10
B316 SP78 50c + 10c multi   1.40 1.40
B317 SP78 90c + 10c multi   2.25 2.25
       Nos. B314-B317 (4)   5.65 5.65

Children's
Games — SP79

No. B318, Kites. No. B319, Kites, diff. No.
B320, Pingi-pingi-kasi. No. B321, Cricket. No.
B322, Peroen, peroen.

1984, Nov. 14   Litho.   Perf. 13x14
B318 SP79 5c + 5c multi   .30   .30
B319 SP79 10c + 5c multi   .30   .30
B320 SP79 30c + 10c multi   .70   .70
B321 SP79 50c + 25c multi   1.40 1.40
   a.   Souv. sheet of 3, #B319-B321 2.50 2.50
B322 SP79 90c + 30c multi   2.10 2.10
       Nos. B318-B322 (5)   4.80 4.80

Surtax was for child welfare.

Easter — SP80

1985, Mar. 27   Litho.   Perf. 12½x14
B323 SP80 5c + 5c multi   .30   .30
B324 SP80 10c + 5c multi   .30   .30
B325 SP80 30c + 15c multi   .80   .80
B326 SP80 50c + 25c multi   1.25 1.25
B327 SP80 90c + 30c multi   2.10 2.10
       Nos. B323-B327 (5)   4.75 4.75

Surtax for child welfare.

Map,
Emblem — SP81

1985, Oct. 22   Litho.   Perf. 13x14
B328 SP81 30c + 10c shown   .75   .75
B329 SP81 50c + 10c Crucifix,
                 missionaries   1.10 1.10
B330 SP81 90c + 20c Scroll   1.90 1.90
       Nos. B328-B330 (3)   3.75 3.75

Evangelical Brotherhood Mission in Surinam, 250th anniv. Surtax for mission medical
and social work.

Literacy — SP82

5c+5c, Boy reading. 10c+5c, Learning
alphabet. 30c+10c, Writing. 50c+25c, Girl
reading. 90c+30c, Studying.

1985, Nov. 6
B331 SP82 5c + 5c multi   .35   .35
B332 SP82 10c + 5c multi   .35   .35
B333 SP82 30c + 10c multi   .60   .60
B334 SP82 50c + 25c multi   1.25 1.25
   a.   Min. sheet of 3, #B332-B334 2.50 2.50
B335 SP82 90c + 30c multi   2.25 2.25
       Nos. B331-B335 (5)   4.80 4.80

Surtax for child welfare.

Easter — SP83

1986, Mar. 19   Litho.   Perf. 13x14
B336 SP83 5c + 5c multi   .25   .25
B337 SP83 10c + 5c multi   .25   .25
B338 SP83 30c + 15c multi   .65   .65
B339 SP83 50c + 25c multi   1.10 1.10
B340 SP83 90c + 30c multi   1.60 1.60
       Nos. B336-B340 (5)   3.85 3.85

Sts. Peter and Paul
Cathedral,
Cent. — SP84

1986, May 28   Litho.
B341 SP84 30c + 10c Exterior   .55   .55
B342 SP84 50c + 10c Saints,
                 bas-relief   .80   .80
B343 SP84 110c + 30c Baptismal
                 font   2.00 2.00
       Nos. B341-B343 (3)   3.35 3.35

Ancient Order
of Foresters
Court Charity,
Cent. — SP85

50c+20c, Foresters emblem. 110c+30c,
Court building.

1986, July 29   Litho.   Perf. 14x13
B344 SP85 50c + 20c multi   .90   .90
B345 SP85 110c + 30c multi   2.00 2.00

Youth
Activities
SP86

1986, Nov. 5   Litho.   Perf. 14x13
B346 SP86 5c + 5c Hopscotch   .30   .30
B347 SP86 10c + 5c Ballet   .30   .30
B348 SP86 30c + 10c Mobile li-
                 brary   .60   .60
B349 SP86 50c + 25c Crafts   1.10 1.10
   a.   Min. sheet of 3, #B347-B349 2.75 2.75
B350 SP86 110c + 30c Educa-
                 tion   2.40 2.40
       Nos. B346-B350 (5)   4.70 4.70

Surtax for Children's Charities.

Easter — SP87

Stations of the cross — 5c+5c, Crucifixion.
10c+5c, Christ on cross. 35c+15c, Descent
from cross. 60c+30c, Funeral procession.
110c+50c, Entombment.

1987, Apr. 8   Litho.   Perf. 13x14
B351 SP87 5c + 5c multi   .25   .25
B352 SP87 10c + 5c multi   .25   .25
B353 SP87 35c + 15c multi   .60   .60
B354 SP87 60c + 30c multi   1.10 1.10
B355 SP87 110c + 50c multi   1.90 1.90
       Nos. B351-B355 (5)   4.10 4.10

Surtax for annual Easter Charity programs.

Natl. Girl Guides
Movement, 40th
Anniv. — SP88

Designs: 15c+10c, Mushroom, Brownie's
emblem. 60c+10c, Clover, Guides' emblem.
110c+10c, Campfire, Rangers' emblem.
120c+10c, Ivy, Captain's emblem.

1987, May 7   Litho.
B356 SP88 15c + 10c multi   .50   .50
B357 SP88 60c + 10c multi   1.10 1.10
B358 SP88 110c + 10c multi   2.00 2.00
B359 SP88 120c + 10c multi   2.25 2.25
       Nos. B356-B359 (4)   5.85 5.85

Surtax for the Surinam Girl Guides.

Caribbean
Manari — SP89

50c+25c, Herring bone. 60c+30c, Tortoise-
back. 110c+50c, Whirlpool (squares).

1987, Nov. 4   Litho.   Perf. 13x14
B360 SP89 50c + 25c multi   .95   .95
B361 SP89 60c + 30c multi   1.00 1.00
B362 SP89 110c + 50c multi   1.90 1.90
   a.   Min. sheet of 2, #B360, B362 2.75 2.75
       Nos. B360-B362 (3)   3.85 3.85

Surtax to benefit child welfare organizations.

Easter — SP90

1988, Mar. 23   Perf. 13x13½
B363 SP90 50c + 25c multi   .80   .80
B364 SP90 60c + 30c multi   1.10 1.10
B365 SP90 110c + 50c multi   2.00 2.00
       Nos. B363-B365 (3)   3.90 3.90

Surtax for annual Easter Charity programs.

Intl. Red Cross and
Red Crescent
Organizations, 125th
Annivs. — SP91

#B367, Anniv. & blood donation emblems.

1988, Oct. 26   Litho.   Perf. 13x14
B366 SP91 60c + 30c multi   1.75 1.75
B367 SP91 120c + 60c multi   2.75 2.75

Children's
Drawings
SP92

50c+25c, Man and animal. 60c+30c, Children and nature. 110c+50c, Stop drugs.

1988, Dec. 5   Litho.   Perf. 14x13
B368 SP92 50c + 25c multi   1.00 1.00
B369 SP92 60c + 30c multi   1.10 1.10
B370 SP92 110c + 50c multi   2.25 2.25
   a.   Souv. sheet of 3, #B368,
         B370, perf 13½x13   4.25 4.25
       Nos. B368-B370 (3)   4.35 4.35

Surtax to benefit children's charities.

Easter 1989 — SP93

Details from Hungarian altarpieces:
60c+30c, Scenes of the Passion, by M.S.,
1506. 105c+50c, Crucifixion, by Tamas of
Koszvar, 1427. 110c+55c, Miracles, by Tamas
of Koszvar, 1427.

1989, Mar. 21   Litho.   Perf. 13½
       Size: No. B372, 28½x36½mm
B371 SP93 60c + 30c multi   1.10 1.10
B372 SP93 105c + 50c multi   2.00 2.00
B373 SP93 110c + 55c multi   2.25 2.25
       Nos. B371-B373 (3)   5.35 5.35

Surtax for annual East Charity programs.

Children's
Drawings
SP94

No. B374, Helping each other. No. B375,
Child and nature. No. B376, In the school bus.

1989, Dec. 6   Litho.   Perf. 14x13
B374 SP94 60c + 30c multi   1.40 1.40
B375 SP94 105c + 50c multi   2.40 2.40
B376 SP94 110c + 55c multi   2.50 2.50
   a.   Souv. sheet of 2, #B374, B376 3.75 3.75
       Nos. B374-B376 (3)   6.30 6.30

Surtax for children's charities.

Easter — SP95

Designs: No. B377, Mother holding Christ
child. No. B378, Christ, follower. No. B379,
Mary holding martyred Christ.

1990, Mar. 28 Litho. *Perf. 13x14*

B377 SP95 60c +30c multi 1.00 1.00
B378 SP95 105c +50c multi 1.75 1.75
B379 SP95 110c +55c multi 1.90 1.90
Nos. B377-B379 (3) 4.65 4.65

Children's Drawings SP96

60c+30c, Children, hammock. 105c+50c, Child, animal, palm tree. 110c+55c, Child, bird in tree.

1990, Dec. 4 Litho. *Perf. 14x13*

B380 SP96 60c +30c multi 1.25 1.25
B381 SP96 105c +50c multi 2.00 2.00
B382 SP96 110c +55c multi 2.25 2.25
a. Souv. sheet of 2, #B380, B382, perf. 13½x13 4.00 4.00
Nos. B380-B382 (3) 5.50 5.50

SP97

Easter: 60c+30c, Christ carrying cross. 105c+50c, The Crucifixion. 110c+55c, Woman cradling Christ's body.

1991, Mar. 20 Litho. *Perf. 13x14*

B383 SP97 60c +30c multi 1.25 1.25
B384 SP97 105c +50c multi 1.50 1.50
B385 SP97 110c +55c multi 2.25 2.25
a. Souv. sheet of 2, #B383, B385 4.25 4.25
Nos. B383-B385 (3) 5.00 5.00

SP98

Children's Drawings: 60c+30c, Child in wheelchair. 105c+50c, Child beside trees. 110c+55c, Children playing outdoors.

1991, Dec. 4 Litho. *Perf. 13x14*

B386 SP98 60c +30c multi 1.25 1.25
B387 SP98 105c +50c multi 2.25 2.25
B388 SP98 110c +55c multi 2.50 2.50
a. Souv. sheet of 2, #B386, B388 3.50 3.50
Nos. B386-B388 (3) 6.00 6.00

SP99

Easter: 60c+30c, Crucifixion. 105c+50c, Taking away body of Christ. 110c+55c, Resurrection.

1992, Mar. 18

B389 SP99 60c +30c multi 1.00 1.00
B390 SP99 105c +50c multi 2.00 2.00
B391 SP99 110c +55c multi 2.25 2.25
Nos. B389-B391 (3) 5.25 5.25

SP100

Children's Drawings: 60c + 30c, Child as tree. 105c + 50c, Face as tree. 110c, + 55c, Boy and girl hanging from tree.

1992, Dec. 3 Litho. *Perf. 13x14*

B392 SP100 60c +30c multi 1.00 1.00
B393 SP100 105c +50c multi 1.90 1.90
B394 SP100 110c +55c multi 2.10 2.10
a. Souv. sheet, #B392, B394 3.50 3.50
Nos. B392-B394 (3) 5.00 5.00

Surtax for Child Welfare.

SP101

Easter: 60c+30c, Message from Christ. 110c+50c, Crucifixion. 125c+60c, Resurrection.

1993, Mar. 31 Litho. *Perf. 13x14*

B395 SP101 60c +30c multi 1.25 1.25
B396 SP101 110c +50c multi 2.25 2.25
B397 SP101 125c +60c multi 2.50 2.50
Nos. B395-B397 (3) 6.00 6.00

SP102

Children Playing Hopscotch: 25c+10c, 2 children. 35c+10c, 3 children. 50c+25c, 8 children. 75c+25c, 7 children.

1993, Dec. 3

B398 SP102 25c +10c grn & multi 1.10 1.10
B399 SP102 35c +10c bl & multi 1.40 1.40
B400 SP102 50c +25c grn & multi 2.25 2.25
a. Souvenir sheet of 2, #B399-B400 4.50 4.50
B401 SP102 75c +25c bl & multi 3.00 3.00
Nos. B398-B401 (4) 7.75 7.75

Surtax for Child Welfare.

Stamps in No. B400a do not have the 1993 date in lower left corner.

AIR POST STAMPS

Allegory of Flight — AP1

Perf. 12½

1930, Sept. 3 Unwmk. Engr.

C1 AP1 10c dull red 3.75 .50
C2 AP1 15c ultra 3.75 .75
C3 AP1 20c dull green .25 .25
C4 AP1 40c orange .25 .35
C5 AP1 60c brown violet .55 .40
C6 AP1 1g gray black 1.60 1.75
C7 AP1 1½g deep brown 1.75 1.90
Nos. C1-C7 (7) 11.90 5.90

Nos. C1-C7 Overprinted in Black or Red

1931, Aug. 8

C8 AP1 10c red (Bk) 19.00 15.00
a. Double overprint 425.00
C9 AP1 15c ultra (Bk) 19.00 15.00
C10 AP1 20c dull grn (R) 19.00 15.00
C11 AP1 40c orange (Bk) 29.00 22.50
a. Double overprint 425.00
C12 AP1 60c brn vio (R) 62.50 52.50
C13 AP1 1g gray blk (R) 72.50 65.00
C14 AP1 1½g deep brn (Bk) 72.50 67.50
Nos. C8-C14 (7) 293.50 252.50

The variety with period omitted after "Do" occurs twice on each sheet.

Warning: The red overprint may dissolve in water.

Type of 1930
Thick Paper

1941, Sept. 25 Litho. *Perf. 13*

C15 AP1 20c lt green 1.25 .90
C16 AP1 40c lt orange 7.50 5.25
C17 AP1 2½g yellow 7.50 12.50
C18 AP1 5g blue green 300.00 350.00
C19 AP1 10g lt bister 17.50 52.50
Nos. C15-C19 (5) 333.75 421.15

The lines of shading on Nos. C15 and C16 are not as heavy as on Nos. C3 and C4. For surcharges see Nos. C24-C25.

Type of 1930
Redrawn

1941 Engr. *Perf. 12*

C20 AP1 10c light red 1.50 .35
C21 AP1 60c dl brn vio .85 .45
C22 AP1 1g black 19.00 22.50
Nos. C20-C22 (3) 21.35 23.30

Redrawn stamps have three horizontal lines through post horn and many minor variations. For surcharges see Nos. C23, CB1.

Catalogue values for unused stamps in this section, from this point to the end of the section, are for Never Hinged items.

Nos. C21, C17, C19 Surcharged with New Values and Bars in Carmine

1945, Mar. 12 *Perf. 13, 12*

C23 AP1 22½c on 60c .45 .70
a. Inverted surcharge 250.00 250.00
C24 AP1 1g on 2½g 15.00 15.00
C25 AP1 5g on 10g 22.50 22.50
Nos. C23-C25 (3) 37.95 38.20

Women of Netherlands and Surinam — AP2

Perf. 12x12½

1949, May 10 Photo. Unwmk.

C26 AP2 27½c henna brown 7.50 3.50

Valid only on first flight of Paramaribo-Amsterdam service.

Globe and Winged Post Horn — AP3

1954, Sept. 25 *Perf. 13½x12½*

C27 AP3 15c dp ultra & ultra 1.75 1.50

Establishment of airmail service in Surinam, 25th anniv.

Redstone Mercury Rocket and Comdr. Alan B. Shepard, Jr. — AP4

15c, Cosmonaut Gagarin in capsule and globe.

1961, July 3 Litho. *Perf. 12*

C28 AP4 15c multicolored .85 .85
C29 AP4 20c multicolored .85 .85

"Man in Space," Major Yuri A. Gagarin, USSR, and Comdr. Alan B. Shepard, Jr., US.

Printed in sheets of 12 (4x3) with ornamental borders and inscriptions. Two printings differ in shades and selvage perforations.

Water Tower — AP5

Designs: 15c, 65c, Brewery. 20c, Boat on lake. 25c, 75c, Wood industry. 30c, Bauxite mine. 35c, 50c, Poelepantje bridge. 40c, Ship in harbor. 45c, Wharf.

1965, July 31 Photo. *Perf. 14x13½*
Size: 25x18mm

C30 AP5 10c olive grn .25 .25
C31 AP5 15c ocher .25 .25
C32 AP5 20c slate grn .25 .25
C33 AP5 25c violet blue .25 .25
C34 AP5 30c blue green .25 .25
C35 AP5 35c red orange .35 .35
C36 AP5 40c orange .35 .35
C37 AP5 45c dk carmine .35 .35
C38 AP5 50c vermilion .35 .35
C39 AP5 55c emerald .35 .35
C40 AP5 65c bister .45 .45
C41 AP5 75c blue .45 .45
Nos. C30-C41 (12) 3.90 3.90

See Nos. C75-C82.

Eucyane Bicolor — AP6

1972, July 26 Litho. *Perf. 13½x14*

C42 AP6 15c shown .25 .25
C43 AP6 20c Helicopis cupido .35 .25
C44 AP6 25c Papilio thoas thoas .35 .25
C45 AP6 30c Urania leilus .40 .25
C46 AP6 35c Stalachtis calliope .40 .50
C47 AP6 40c Stalachtis phlegia .45 .40
C48 AP6 45c Victorina steneles .60 .25
C49 AP6 50c Papilio neophilus .65 .25
C50 AP6 55c Anartia amathea .80 .85
C51 AP6 60c Adelpha cytherea .85 1.25
C52 AP6 65c Heliconius doris metharmina .85 .85
C53 AP6 70c Nessaea obrinus 1.00 1.00
C54 AP6 75c Ageronia feronia 1.00 .80
Nos. C42-C54 (13) 7.95 7.15

Surinam butterflies. Valid for regular postage also. For surcharges, see Nos. 495-499.

#C42, C45 exist perf 14 with redrawn design.

Fish Type of 1976

Fish: 35c, Chaetodon unimaculatus. 60c, Centropyge loriculus. 95c, Caetodon collare.

1976, June 2 Litho. *Perf. 12½x13*

C55 A111 35c multicolored 1.00 .55
C56 A111 60c multicolored 1.75 .90
C57 A111 95c multicolored 2.75 1.40
Nos. C55-C57 (3) 5.50 2.85

Black-headed Sugarbird AP7

Birds of Surinam: 20c, Leistes militaris. 30c, Paradise tangara. 40c, Whippoorwill. 45c, Hemitraupis flavicollis. 50c, White-tailed gold-throated hummingbird. 55c, Saberwing. 60c, Blackcap parrot, vert. 65c, Toucan, vert. 70c, Manakin, vert. 75c, Collared parrot, vert. 80c, Cayenne cotinga, vert. 85c, Trogon, vert. 95c, Black-striped tropical tree owl, vert.

1977 Litho. *Perf. 14x13, 13x14*

C58 AP7 20c multi .25 .25
C59 AP7 25c multi .35 .25
C60 AP7 30c multi .40 .25
a. Min. sheet of 4, 2 each #C59-C60, perf. 13½x14 3.75 2.00
C61 AP7 40c multi .70 .40
C62 AP7 45c multi .70 .40
C63 AP7 50c multi .80 .50
C64 AP7 55c multi .95 .55
C65 AP7 60c multi 1.00 .65
C66 AP7 65c multi 1.10 .70
C67 AP7 70c multi 1.25 .70
C68 AP7 75c multi 1.25 .80
C69 AP7 80c multi 1.25 .80
C70 AP7 85c multi 1.40 .95
C71 AP7 95c multi 1.75 1.10
Nos. C58-C71 (14) 13.15 8.30

A souv. sheet of 4 with same stamps and perf. as No. C60a has marginal inscription "Amphilex 77" with magnifier over No. 424.

Sold in folder at phil. exhib. in Amsterdam May 26-June 5, 1977. Value $5.75.
Issued: 25c, 30c, 50c, 60c, 75c, 80c, 95c, Apr. 27; #C60a, May 26; others, Aug. 24.
See Nos. C88, C101. For surcharges and overprints see Nos. C102-C105, C108-C111, J58, J62.

Tropical Fish Type of 1976

60c, Chaetodon striatus. 90c, Bodianus pulchellus. 120c, Centropyge argi.

1977, June 8 Litho. ***Perf. 13x13½***

C72 A111 60c multi 1.00 .80
C73 A111 90c multi 1.75 1.10
C74 A111 120c multi 2.50 1.90
Nos. C72-C74 (3) 5.25 3.80

Type of 1965 Redrawn

Designs: 5c, Brewery. 10c, Water tower. 20c, Boat on lake. 25c, Wood industry. 30c, Bauxite mine. 35c, Poelepantje bridge. 40c, Ship in harbor. 60c, Wharf.

1976-78 Photo. ***Perf. 12½x13½***
Size: 22x18mm

C75 AP5 5c ocher .25 .25
a. Bklt. pane, 4 #C75, 3 #C82 + label 2.50
C76 AP5 10c olive green .55 .55
a. Bklt. pane, 1 #C76, 4 #C80 + label 2.75
C77 AP5 20c slate green .25 .25
a. Bklt. pane, 2 ea #C77-C79 2.75
b. Bklt. pane, 6 #C77, 2 #C81 2.50
C78 AP5 25c vio bl .55 .55
C79 AP5 30c bl grn .65 .65
C80 AP5 35c red org .55 .55
C81 AP5 40c org .90 .90
C82 AP5 60c dk car .75 .75
Nos. C75-C82 (8) 4.45 4.45

Nos. C75-C82 issued in booklets only. Nos. C75a and C77b have inscribed selvage the size of 4 stamps; Nos. C76a and C77a the size of 6 stamps.
Issued: 10c-35c, 12/8; 5c, 40c, 60c, #C77b, 1/11/78.

Tropical Fish Type of 1976

60c, Astyanax species. 90c, Corydoras wotroi. 120c, Gasteropelecus sternicla.

1978, June 21 Litho. ***Perf. 13x13½***

C85 A111 60c multi 1.00 .95
C86 A111 90c multi 1.60 1.00
C87 A111 120c multi 2.25 1.25
Nos. C85-C87 (3) 4.85 3.20

Bird Type of 1977

Design: 5g, Crested curassow, vert.

1979, Jan. 10 Engr. ***Perf. 13x13½***

C88 AP7 5g violet 6.00 3.00

Tropical Fish Type of 1979

60c, Cantherinus macrocerus. 90c, Holocenthrus rufus. 120c, Holacanthus tricolor.

1979, May 30 Photo. ***Perf. 14x13***

C89 A129 60c multi .75 .30
C90 A129 90c multi 1.25 .90
C91 A129 120c multi 1.75 1.40
Nos. C89-C91 (3) 3.75 2.60

Tropical Fish Type of 1979

60c, Symphysodon discus. 75c, Aeqidens curviceps. 90c, Catoprion mento.

1980, Sept. 10 Photo. ***Perf. 14x13***

C92 A129 60c multi 1.00 .80
C93 A129 75c multi 1.50 1.00
C94 A129 90c multi 1.50 1.25
Nos. C92-C94 (3) 4.00 3.05

Frog Type of 1981

75c, Phyllomedusa burmeisteri, vert. 1g, Dendrobates tinctorius, vert. 1.25g, Bufo guttatus, vert.

1981, June 24 ***Perf. 13x14***

C95 A142 75c multi 1.60 .80
C96 A142 1g multi 2.10 1.10
C97 A142 1.25g multi 2.50 1.40
Nos. C95-C97 (3) 6.20 3.30

Turtle Type of 1982

65c, Platemys platycephala. 75c, Phrynops gibba. 125c, Rhinoclemys punctularia.

1982, Feb. 17 Photo. ***Perf. 14x13***

C98 A146 65c multi 1.00 .65
C99 A146 75c multi 1.25 .80
C100 A146 125c multi 2.25 1.50
Nos. C98-C100 (3) 4.50 2.95

Bird Type of 1977

1985, Jan. 9 Litho. ***Perf. 13x14***

C101 AP7 90c Venezuelan Amazon, vert. 5.25 5.25

For overprint see No. J61.

No. C60 Surcharged in Brown

1986, Oct. 1 Litho. ***Perf. 14x13***

C102 AP7 15c on 30c multi *4.50 4.50*

Nos. C70-C71 and C67 Surcharged

1987, Mar. Litho. ***Perf. 13x14***

C103 AP7 10c on 85c No. C70 *2.00 2.00*
C104 AP7 10c on 95c No. C71 *2.00 2.00*
C105 AP7 25c on 70c No. C67 *6.00 6.00*
Nos. C103-C105 (3) *10.00 10.00*

Otter Type of 1989

1989, Jan. 18 Litho. ***Perf. 13x14***

C107 A195 185c Otters, vert. 3.00 3.00

No. C63 Surcharged

1993, Jan. 20 Litho. ***Perf. 14x13***

C108 AP7 35c on 50c multi .40 .40

Nos. C62, C64-C65 Surcharged

1994, Apr. 11 ***Perf. 14x13, 13x14***

C109 AP7 ( ) on 60c #C65 .25 .25
C110 AP7 ( ) on 45c #C62 1.00 1.00
C111 AP7 ( ) on 55c #C64 1.50 1.50
Nos. C109-C111 (3) 2.75 2.75

The face value of Nos. C109-C111 fluctuates with postal rate changes. Face values on day of issue were: No. C109, 2.50f; No. C110, 10f; No. C111, 25f. No. C109 paid the additional 5 grams letter rate to the Netherlands. No. C110 paid the basic rate to North and South America and the Caribbean. No. C111 paid the basic 10-gram letter rate to the Netherlands.
Size and location of surcharge varies.

AIR POST SEMI-POSTAL STAMPS

Catalogue values for unused stamps in this section are for Never Hinged items.

No. C20 Srchd. in Red

Unwmk.

1942, Jan. 2 Engr. ***Perf. 12***

CB1 AP1 10c + 5c lt red, III 2.50 2.50
a. Type IV 4.25 5.25
b. Type V 11.50 14.00

The surtax was for the Red Cross.
See note on types III and IV below No. B40.

Nos. 193 and 194 Surcharged in Carmine

1946, Feb. 24 ***Perf. 12***

CB2 A30 10c + 40c blue 1.00 1.00
CB3 A30 15c + 60c brown 1.00 1.00

The surtax was for the Red Cross.

Star Type of Semi-Postals

Perf. 13½x12½

1947, Dec. 16 Photo.

CB4 SP17 22½c + 27½c gray 2.25 1.75
CB5 SP17 27½c + 47½c grn 2.25 1.75

POSTAGE DUE STAMPS

D1

D2

Type I — 34 loops. "T" of "BETALEN" over center of loop; top branch of "E" of "TE" shorter than lower branch.
Type II — 33 loops. "T" of "BETALEN" over space between two loops.
Type III — 32 loops. "T" of "BETALEN" slightly to the left of center of loop; top branch of first "E" of "BETALEN" shorter than lower branch.
Type IV — 37 loops and letters of "PORT" larger than in the other 3 types.

Value in Black

Perf. 12½x12

1886-88 Typo. Unwmk.

Type III

J1 D1 2½c lilac 3.00 3.00
J2 D1 5c lilac 9.00 9.00
J3 D1 10c lilac 100.00 65.00
J4 D1 20c lilac 9.00 9.00
J5 D1 25c lilac 12.50 12.50
J6 D1 30c lilac ('88) 2.50 2.50
J7 D1 40c lilac 6.00 6.00
J8 D1 50c lilac ('88) 3.00 3.00
Nos. J1-J8 (8) 145.00 110.00

Type I

J1a D1 2½c 6.00 6.00
J2a D1 5c 11.00 11.00
J3a D1 10c 125.00 90.00
J4a D1 20c 22.50 22.50
J5a D1 25c 19.00 19.00
J6a D1 30c 22.50 22.50
J7a D1 40c 12.50 12.50
J8a D1 50c 4.00 4.00
Nos. J1a-J8a (8) 222.50 187.50

Type II

J1b D1 2½c 5.00 5.00
J2b D1 5c 10.00 10.00
J3b D1 10c 1,250. 1,250.
J4b D1 20c 9.00 9.00
J5b D1 25c 300.00 300.00
J6b D1 30c 75.00 75.00
J7b D1 40c 350.00 350.00
J8b D1 50c 5.00 5.00

Type IV

J3c D1 10c 350.00 250.00
J5c D1 25c 160.00 150.00
J7c D1 40c 150.00 150.00
Nos. J3c-J7c (3) 660.00 550.00

Nos. J1-J16 were issued without gum. For surcharges, see Nos. J15-J16.

1892-96 Value in Black ***Perf. 12½***

Type III

J9 D2 2½c lilac .40 .40
J10 D2 5c lilac 1.25 1.00
J11 D2 10c lilac 24.00 22.50
J12 D2 20c lilac 2.50 2.25
J13 D2 25c lilac 10.00 10.00

Type I

J9a D2 2½c .40 .40
J10a D2 5c 2.00 2.00
J11a D2 10c 24.00 20.00
J12a D2 20c 5.00 5.00
J13a D2 25c 13.00 12.50
J14 D2 40c ('96) 3.25 4.50

Type II

J9b D2 2½c .80 .80
J10b D2 5c 3.00 3.00
J11b D2 10c 40.00 42.50
J12b D2 20c 90.00 90.00
J13b D2 25c 100.00 100.00

For surcharges, see Nos. 121-122.

Stamps of 1888 Surcharged in Red

1911, July 15

J15 D1 10c on 30c lil (III) 80.00 80.00
a. 10c on 30c lilac (I) 200.00 225.00
b. 10c on 30c lilac (II) *1,800. 1,800.*
J16 D1 10c on 50c lil (III) 110.00 110.00
a. 10c on 50c lilac (I) 115.00 115.00
b. 10c on 50c lilac (II) 115.00 115.00

D3

Type I
Value in Color of Stamp

1913-31 ***Perf. 12½, 13½x12½***

J17 D2 ½c lilac ('30) .25 .25
J18 D2 1c lilac ('31) .25 .35
J19 D2 2c lilac ('31) .25 .25
J20 D2 2½c lilac .25 .25
J21 D2 5c lilac .25 .25
J22 D2 10c lilac .25 .25
J23 D2 12c lilac ('31) .25 .25
J24 D2 12½c lilac ('22) .25 .25
J25 D2 15c lilac ('26) .55 .45
J26 D2 20c lilac .85 .45
J27 D2 25c lilac .45 .25
J28 D2 30c lilac ('26) .45 .60
J29 D2 40c lilac 14.50 14.00
J30 D2 50c lilac ('26) 1.25 1.25
J31 D2 75c lilac ('26) 1.50 1.50
J32 D3 1g lilac ('26) 1.75 1.50
Nos. J17-J32 (16) 23.30 22.10

Catalogue values for unused stamps in this section, from this point to the end of the section, are for Never Hinged items.

D4

1945 Litho. ***Perf. 12***

J33 D4 1c light brown violet .25 .30
J34 D4 5c light brown violet 3.00 2.50
J35 D4 25c light brown violet 7.00 .50
Nos. J33-J35 (3) 10.25 3.30

D5

Perf. 13½x12½

1950 Unwmk. Photo.

J36 D5 1c purple 3.00 2.50
J37 D5 2c purple 4.50 2.25
J38 D5 2½c purple 3.75 2.50
J39 D5 5c purple 5.50 .50
J40 D5 10c purple 3.00 .50
J41 D5 15c purple 7.50 3.25
J42 D5 20c purple 2.50 4.50
J43 D5 25c purple 15.00 .25
J44 D5 50c purple 25.00 1.90
J45 D5 75c purple 62.50 50.00
J46 D5 1g purple 22.50 9.25
Nos. J36-J46 (11) 154.75 77.40

D6

1956

J47	D6	1c purple	.25	.25
J48	D6	2c purple	.50	.45
J49	D6	2½c purple	.50	.45
J50	D6	5c purple	.50	.45
J51	D6	10c purple	.50	.45
J52	D6	15c purple	.70	.70
J53	D6	20c purple	.70	.70
J54	D6	25c purple	.80	.40
J55	D6	50c purple	2.10	.50
J56	D6	75c purple	2.75	1.60
J57	D6	1g purple	4.00	1.25
		Nos. J47-J57 (11)	13.30	7.20

For surcharges, see Nos. J64-J69.

Stamps of 1977-1985 Overprinted

Perf. 13x14, 14x13

1987, July **Litho.**

J58	AP7	65c No. C66	3.00	3.00
J59	A156	65c No. 638	3.00	3.00
J60	A156	80c No. 640	3.75	3.75
J61	AP7	90c No. C101	4.25	4.25
J62	AP7	95c No. C71	5.00	5.00
J63	A173	1g No. 725	5.25	5.25
		Nos. J58-J63 (6)	24.25	24.25

Nos. J47, J50, J55 and J57 Surcharged

Methods and Perfs. As Before

2007, Dec. 3

J64	D6	$1 on 1c #J47	.75	.75
J65	D6	$1.50 on 1g #J57	1.10	1.10
J66	D6	$2 on 5c #J50	1.50	1.50
J67	D6	$3 on 50c #J55	2.25	2.25
J68	D6	$3.50 on 1g #J57	2.60	2.60
J69	D6	$4 on 1g #J57	3.00	3.00
		Nos. J64-J69 (6)	11.20	11.20

SWAZILAND

ˈswə-zē-ˌland

LOCATION — Southeast Africa bordered by the Transvaal and Zululand in South Africa and by Mozambique
GOVT. — Constitutional monarchy
AREA — 6,705 sq. mi.
POP. — 985,335 (1999 est.)
CAPITAL — Mbabane

An independent state in the 19th century, Swaziland was administered by Transvaal from 1894 to 1906, when the administration was transferred to the British High Commissioner for South Africa. In 1934 Swaziland and Bechuanaland Protectorate came under the administration of the British High Commissioner for Basutoland. The issuing of individual postage stamps had been resumed in 1933. Internal self-government was introduced in 1967. Independence was proclaimed September 6, 1968.

12 Pence = 1 Shilling
20 Shillings = 1 Pound
100 Cents = 1 Rand (1961)
100 Cents = 1 Emalangeni (1975)

Catalogue values for unused stamps in this country are for Never Hinged items, beginning with Scott 38 in the regular postage section and Scott J1 in the postage due section.

Coat of Arms — A1

Black Overprint

1889 Unwmk. ***Perf. 12½, 12½x12***

1	A1	½p gray	10.50	*25.00*
a.		Inverted overprint	1,250.	750.00
b.		"Swazielan"	1,800.	1,000.
c.		As "b," inverted overprint		7,500.
2	A1	1p rose	25.00	25.00
a.		Inverted overprint	800.00	*750.00*
3	A1	2p olive bister	32.50	18.00
a.		Inverted overprint	950.00	750.00
b.		"Swazielan"	550.00	475.00
c.		Perf. 12½x12	100.00	37.50
d.		As "c," "Swazielan"	1,250.	725.00
e.		As "d," inverted overprint		1,400.
f.		As "b," inverted overprint	7,500.	5,000.
g.		Double overprint	2,600.	
4	A1	6p gray blue	42.50	*60.00*
5	A1	1sh green	18.00	*16.00*
a.		Inverted overprint	1,100.	525.00
6	A1	2sh6p yellow	325.00	*450.00*
7	A1	5sh slate	175.00	*300.00*
a.		Inverted overprint	*1,900.*	*3,000.*
b.		"Swazielan"	*5,250.*	
c.		As "b," inverted overprint	*5,750.*	
8	A1	10sh lt brown	*6,500.*	*4,000.*

1892 **Red Overprint**

9	A1	½p gray	8.50	19.00
a.		Inverted overprint	575.00	
b.		Double overprint	525.00	*525.00*
c.		Pair, one without overprint		2,000.

Beware of counterfeits.
Reprints have a period after "Swazieland."

Stamps of Swaziland were replaced by those of Transvaal in 1895. Swaziland issues were resumed in 1933.

George V — A2

Perf. 14

1933, Jan. 2 Engr. Wmk. 4

10	A2	½p green	.40	*.35*
11	A2	1p carmine	.40	.25
12	A2	2p lt brown	.40	.50
13	A2	3p ultra	.55	*3.50*
14	A2	4p orange	3.50	*3.75*
15	A2	6p rose violet	1.60	*1.10*
16	A2	1sh olive green	1.75	*3.25*
17	A2	2sh6p violet	16.00	*25.00*
18	A2	5sh gray	37.50	*57.50*
19	A2	10sh black brown	135.00	*175.00*
		Nos. 10-19 (10)	197.10	*270.20*
		Set, never hinged	500.00	

Common Design Types pictured following the introduction.

Silver Jubilee Issue
Common Design Type

1935, May 4 ***Perf. 11x12***

20	CD301	1p carmine & blue	.55	*1.75*
21	CD301	2p black & ultra	2.00	*3.50*
22	CD301	3p ultra & brown	1.00	*8.00*
23	CD301	6p brown, vio & ind	3.25	*5.00*
		Nos. 20-23 (4)	6.80	18.25
		Set, never hinged	11.00	

Coronation Issue
Common Design Type

1937, May 12 ***Perf. 11x11½***

24	CD302	1p dark carmine	.35	*.95*
25	CD302	2p brown	.35	*.25*
26	CD302	3p deep ultra	.35	.55
		Nos. 24-26 (3)	1.05	1.75
		Set, never hinged	1.75	

George VI — A3

1938, Apr. 1 ***Perf. 13, 13x13½***

27	A3	½p green	.25	*1.25*
28	A3	1p rose carmine	.60	*1.25*
29	A3	1½p light blue	.30	*.85*
a.		Perf. 14 ('42)	1.60	1.25
30	A3	2p brown	.30	*.45*
31	A3	3p ultra	4.50	1.75
32	A3	4p red orange	.60	*1.40*
33	A3	6p rose violet	2.75	1.50
34	A3	1sh olive green	.75	.75
35	A3	2sh6p dark violet	12.50	4.00
36	A3	5sh gray	25.00	19.00
37	A3	10sh black brown	5.50	*7.00*
		Nos. 27-37 (11)	53.05	39.20
		Set, never hinged	85.00	

Catalogue values for unused stamps in this section, from this point to the end of the section, are for Never Hinged items.

Peace Issue

South Africa, Nos. 100-102 Overprinted

Basic stamps inscribed alternately in English and Afrikaans.

1945, Dec. 3 Wmk. 201 ***Perf. 14***

38	A42	1p rose pink & choc, pair	.80	*1.25*
a.		Single, English	.25	.25
b.		Single, Afrikaans	.25	.25
39	A43	2p vio & sl blue, pair	.80	*1.25*
a.		Single, English	.25	.25
b.		Single, Afrikaans	.25	.25
40	A43	3p ultra & dp ultra, pair	.80	*3.00*
a.		Single, English	.25	.25
b.		Single, Afrikaans	.25	.25
		Nos. 38-40 (3)	2.40	*5.50*

World War II victory of the Allies.

Royal Visit Issue
Type of Basutoland, 1947
Perf. 12½

1947, Feb. 17 Wmk. 4 Engr.

44	A3	1p red	.25	.25
45	A4	2p green	.25	.25
46	A5	3p ultramarine	.25	.25
47	A6	1sh dark violet	.25	.25
		Nos. 44-47 (4)	1.00	1.00

Visit of the British Royal Family, 3/25/47.

Silver Wedding Issue
Common Design Types

1948, Dec. 1 Photo. ***Perf. 14x14½***

48	CD304	1½p bright ultra	.30	.25

Perf. 11½x11

Engraved; Name Typographed

49	CD305	10sh violet brown	40.00	*47.50*

UPU Issue
Common Design Types
Engr.; Name Typo. on 3p, 6p
Perf. 13½, 11x11½

1949, Oct. 10 **Wmk. 4**

50	CD306	1½p blue	.30	.25
51	CD307	3p indigo	1.60	2.00
52	CD308	6p red lilac	.40	1.75
53	CD309	1sh olive	.50	.65
		Nos. 50-53 (4)	2.80	4.65

Coronation Issue
Common Design Type

1953, June 3 Engr. ***Perf. 13½x13***

54	CD312	2p yellow brown & blk	.30	.25

Asbestos Mine — A4

Married Woman — A5

1p, 2sh 6p, Highveld view. 3p, 1sh 3p, Courting couple. 4½p, 5sh, Warrior. 6p, £1, Kudu. 1sh, Asbestos mine. 10sh, Married woman.

Perf. 13x13½, 13½x13

1956, July 2 Engr. Wmk. 4
Center in Black, except Nos. 63-64

55	A4	½p orange	.40	.25
56	A4	1p emerald	.25	.25
57	A5	2p redsh brown	.40	.25
58	A5	3p rose red	.30	.25
59	A5	4½p ultra	.85	.25
60	A5	6p magenta	2.75	.25
61	A4	1sh gray olive	.40	.25
62	A5	1sh3p brown	4.50	*6.00*
63	A4	2sh6p car & brt grn	3.25	3.25
64	A5	5sh blue gray & vio	12.00	8.00
65	A5	10sh dull violet	25.00	20.00
66	A5	£1 turquoise	60.00	42.50
		Nos. 55-66 (12)	110.10	81.50

Nos. 55-61 and 63-66 Surcharged with New Value

I I II

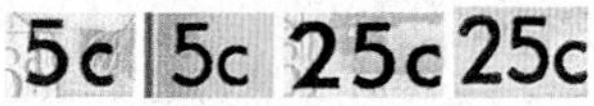

I II I II

I II III

I II III

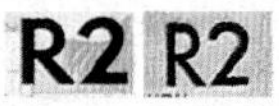

I II

1961

67	A4	½c on ½p	3.50	6.50
a.		Inverted surcharge	1,300.	
68	A4	1c on 1p	.25	.25
a.		"1c" at center	35.00	
b.		Double surcharge	1,500.	
69	A5	2c on 2p	.25	.25
70	A5	2½c on 2p	.25	.25
71	A5	2½c on 3p (I)	.25	.25
a.		Type II	.25	.25
72	A5	3½c on 2p	.25	.25
73	A5	4c on 4½p (II)	.25	.25
a.		Type I	.25	.25
74	A5	5c on 6p (II)	.25	.25
a.		Type I	.25	.25
75	A4	10c on 1sh	40.00	11.00
a.		Double surcharge	1,600.	
76	A4	25c on 2sh6p (I)	.40	1.50
a.		Type II, "25c" centered	1.60	1.00
b.		Type II, "25c" at lower left	450.00	*600.00*
77	A5	50c on 5sh (I)	.45	*1.50*
a.		Type II	9.50	3.00
b.		Type III	725.00	*850.00*
78	A5	1r on 10sh (I)	1.75	1.50
a.		Type II	4.00	*6.00*
b.		Type III	85.00	*120.00*
79	A5	2r on £1 (II, "R2" at middle left)	20.00	18.00
a.		Type I	15.00	19.00
b.		Type II, "R2" at center bottom	95.00	*180.00*
		Nos. 67-79 (13)	67.85	41.75

The type II "25c" surcharge is nearly centered in the sky on No. 76a, and is at lower left touching the value tablet on No. 76b.

Surcharge types are numbered chronologically.

For surcharges see Nos. J3-J6.

Types of 1956

½c, 10c, Asbestos mine. 1c, 25c, Highveld view. 2c, 1r, Married woman. 2½c, 12½c, Courting couple. 4c, 50c, Warrior. 5c, 2r, Kudu.

Perf. 13x13½, 13½x13

1961 Engr. Wmk. 4

Center in Black, except Nos. 88-89

80	A4	½c orange	.25	*1.25*
81	A4	1c emerald	.25	.25
82	A5	2c redsh brown	.25	*2.75*
83	A5	2½c rose red	.25	.25
84	A5	4c ultra	.25	*1.50*
85	A5	5c magenta	1.25	.25
86	A4	10c gray olive	.25	.25
87	A5	12½c brown	1.75	.70
88	A4	25c car & brt green	4.75	*6.50*
89	A5	50c blue gray & vio	5.50	3.00
90	A5	1r dull violet	14.00	*16.00*
91	A5	2r turquoise	22.50	16.00
		Nos. 80-91 (12)	51.25	48.70

Swazi Shields — A6

Designs: 1c, Battle axe. 2c, Forestry. 2½c, Ceremonial headdress. 3½c, Musical instrument. 4c, Irrigation. 5c, Widow bird. 7½c, Rock paintings. 10c, Secretary bird. 12½c, Pink arum lily. 15c, Married woman. 20c, Malaria control. 25c, Swazi warrior. 50c, Ground hornbill, horiz. 1r, Aloes. 2r, Msinsi (flame tree), horiz.

Perf. 12½x14, 14x12½

1962, Apr. 24 Photo. Wmk. 314

92	A6	½c ocher, blk & brn	.25	.25
93	A6	1c gray & orange	.25	*.25*
94	A6	2c lt yel grn, dk grn & blk	.25	*1.25*
95	A6	2½c vermilion & blk	.25	.25
96	A6	3½c gray & emerald	.25	*.70*
97	A6	4c aqua & black	.25	.25
98	A6	5c orange red & blk	1.50	.25
99	A6	7½c dull ocher & brn	2.00	.40
100	A6	10c lt blue & black	4.00	.25
101	A6	12½c lt olive & dp car	2.25	*3.50*
102	A6	15c red lilac & blk	1.75	1.25
103	A6	20c emerald & blk	.50	*1.50*
104	A6	25c ultra & blk	.60	*1.25*
105	A6	50c rose red & dk brn	18.00	7.00
106	A6	1r bister & emer	3.25	2.50
107	A6	2r ultra & scar	22.50	15.00
		Nos. 92-107 (16)	57.85	35.85

For surcharge & overprints see #138, 143-159.

Freedom from Hunger Issue

Common Design Type

1963, June 4 ***Perf. 14x14½***

108	CD314	15c lilac	.50	.50

Red Cross Centenary Issue

Common Design Type

1963, Sept. 2 Litho. ***Perf. 13***

109	CD315	2½c black & red	.30	.30
110	CD315	15c ultra & red	.80	.80

Train and Railroad Map — A7

Perf. 11½x12

1964, Nov. 5 Engr. Wmk. 314

111	A7	2½c purple & brt grn	.60	.25
112	A7	3½c dk olive & blue	.65	*1.10*
113	A7	15c dk brown & orange	.80	.70
114	A7	25c dk blue & yellow	1.00	.80
		Nos. 111-114 (4)	3.05	2.85

Opening of the Swaziland Railroad linking Ka Dake with Lourenco Marques.

ITU Issue

Common Design Type

Perf. 11x11½

1965, May 17 Litho. Wmk. 314

115	CD317	2½c blue & bister	.25	.25
116	CD317	15c red lil & rose red	.50	.50

Intl. Cooperation Year Issue

Common Design Type

1965, Oct. 25 ***Perf. 14½***

117	CD318	½c bl grn & claret	.25	.25
118	CD318	15c lt violet & grn	.50	.50

Churchill Memorial Issue

Common Design Type

1966, Jan. 24 Photo. ***Perf. 14***

Design in Black, Gold and Carmine Rose

119	CD319	½c brt blue	.25	.50
120	CD319	2½c green	.25	*.90*
121	CD319	15c brown	.50	.25
122	CD319	25c violet	.70	*.90*
		Nos. 119-122 (4)	1.70	2.55

UNESCO Anniversary Issue

Common Design Type

1966, Dec. 1 Litho. ***Perf. 14***

123	CD323	2½c "Education"	.25	.25
124	CD323	7½c "Science"	.40	.40
125	CD323	15c "Culture"	.80	.80
		Nos. 123-125 (3)	1.45	1.45

King Sobhuza II and Map of Swaziland A8

Design: 7½c, 25c, King Sobhuza II, vert.

Perf. 14½x14, 14x14½

1967, Apr. 25 Photo. Wmk. 314

126	A8	2½c multicolored	.25	.25
127	A8	7½c multicolored	.25	.25
128	A8	15c multicolored	.25	.25
129	A8	25c multicolored	.30	.30
		Nos. 126-129 (4)	1.05	1.05

Attainment of internal self-government.

King Sobhuza II, University Buildings and Graduates — A9

Perf. 14x14½

1967, Sept. 1 Photo. Unwmk.

130	A9	2½c yel, sepia & dp bl	.25	.25
131	A9	7½c blue, sepia & dp bl	.25	.25
132	A9	15c dl rose, sepia & dp bl	.25	.25
133	A9	25c lt vio, sepia & dp bl	.30	.30
		Nos. 130-133 (4)	1.05	1.05

1st conferment of degrees by the University of Botswana, Lesotho and Swaziland at Roma, Lesotho.

Swazi Reed Dance (Umhlanga) — A10

Designs: 3c, 15c, Feast of the First Fruits, Incwala (bull, sun and king), horiz.

Perf. 14½x14, 14x14½

1968, Jan. 5 Photo. Wmk. 314

134	A10	3c red, blk & silver	.25	.25
135	A10	10c brown, blk, org & sil	.25	.25
136	A10	15c red, blk & gold	.25	.25
137	A10	25c brown, blk, org & gold	.30	.30
		Nos. 134-137 (4)	1.05	1.05

No. 98 Surcharged with New Value

1968, May 1 ***Perf. 12½x14***

138	A6	3c on 5c org red & blk	.75	.45

Independent Kingdom

Plowing and King Sobhuza II A11

Designs: 4½c, Cable lift carrying asbestos. 17½c, Worker cutting sugar cane. 25c, Iron ore mining and map showing Swaziland railroad.

Perf. 14x12½

1968, Sept. 6 Photo. Wmk. 314

139	A11	3c gold & multi	.25	.25
140	A11	4½c gold & multi	.25	.25
141	A11	17½c gold & multi	.25	.25
142	A11	25c slate & gold	.30	.30
a.		Strip of 4, #139-142	4.00	4.00
		Nos. 139-142 (4)	1.05	1.05

Swaziland's independence.

Nos. 139-142 printed in sheets of 50. No. 142a printed in sheets of 20 (4x5).

Nos. 92-107 Overprinted; No. 96 Surcharged

1968, Sept. 6 ***Perf. 12½x14, 14x12½***

143	A6	½c ocher, blk & brn	.25	.25
144	A6	1c gray & orange	.25	.25
145	A6	2c multicolored	.25	.25
146	A6	2½c vermilion & blk	1.25	*2.25*
147	A6	3c on 2½c #146	.25	.25
148	A6	3½c gray & emerald	.25	.25
149	A6	4c aqua & black	.25	.25
150	A6	5c org red & blk	4.75	.25
151	A6	7½c dull ocher & brn	.75	.25
152	A6	10c lt blue & blk	5.00	.25
153	A6	12½c lt olive & dp car	.45	*.90*
154	A6	15c red lilac & blk	.45	*1.25*
155	A6	20c emerald & blk	1.25	*2.00*
156	A6	25c ultra & blk	.55	*1.10*
157	A6	50c rose red & dk brn	8.50	5.00
a.		Wmk. sideways	3.75	*10.00*
158	A6	1r bister & emerald	3.25	*5.00*
159	A6	2r ultra & scarlet	6.50	*11.50*
a.		Wmk. sideways	8.50	5.50
		Nos. 143-159 (17)	34.20	31.25

Caracal (African Lynx) — A12

Waterbuck — A12a

1c, Cape porcupine. 2c, Crocodile. 3c, Lion. 3½c, African elephants. 5c, Bush pig. 7½c, Impalas. 10c, Chacma baboon. 12½c, Ratel (honey badger). 15c, Leopard. 20c, Blue wildebeest (brindled gnu). 25c, White (square-lipped) rhinoceros. 50c, Burchell's zebra. 2r, Giraffe.

Perf. 13x12½, 12½x13

1969, Aug. 1 Litho. Wmk. 314

Size: 30½x21½mm

160	A12	½c multicolored	.25	.25
161	A12	1c multicolored	.25	.25
162	A12	2c multicolored	.25	.25
a.		Perf. 12½x12 ('75)	3.25	*5.00*

Size: 35x25mm

163	A12	3c multicolored	.90	.25
a.		Wmk. upright ('75)	5.00	5.00
164	A12	3½c multicolored	1.00	.25

Size: 30½x21½mm, 21½x30½mm

165	A12	5c multicolored	.35	.25
166	A12	7½c multicolored	.45	.25
167	A12	10c multicolored	.65	.25
168	A12	12½c multicolored	.75	*4.00*
169	A12	15c multicolored	1.25	.90
170	A12	20c multicolored	1.00	.75
171	A12	25c multicolored	1.50	*2.00*
172	A12	50c multicolored	1.75	*3.25*
173	A12a	1r multicolored	4.50	*6.50*
174	A12a	2r multicolored	9.50	*11.50*
		Nos. 160-174 (15)	24.35	30.90

See #228-229. For surcharges see #259-260.

King Sobhuza II and Flags — A13

Designs: 7½c, 25c, UN emblem, UN Headquarters, NY, and King Sobhuza II.

1969, Sept. 24 Litho. ***Perf. 13½***

175	A13	3c dp blue & multi	.25	.25
176	A13	7½c pink & multi	.25	.25
177	A13	12½c yellow & multi	.25	.25
178	A13	25c lt blue & multi	.35	.35
		Nos. 175-178 (4)	1.10	1.10

1st anniv. of admission to the UN.

Walking Racer, Shield and King — A14

Designs: 7½c, Runner. 12½c, Hurdler. 25c, Parade of Swaziland team with flag bearer.

Perf. 14x14½

1970, July 16 Litho. Wmk. 314

179	A14	3c red org & multi	.25	.25
180	A14	7½c yellow & multi	.25	.25
181	A14	12½c lt blue & multi	.30	.30
182	A14	25c multicolored	.40	.40
		Nos. 179-182 (4)	1.20	1.20

Issued to publicize the 9th Commonwealth Games, Edinburgh, July 16-25.

Bauhinia Galpinii and King — A15

Flowers of Swaziland: 10c, Crocosmia aurea. 15c, Gloriosa superba. 25c, Watsonia densiflora.

Perf. 14x14½

1971, Feb. 1 Litho. Wmk. 314

183	A15	3c bister & multi	.30	.35
184	A15	10c pale salmon & multi	.35	.35
185	A15	15c pale green & multi	.55	.55
186	A15	25c multicolored	1.00	1.00
		Nos. 183-186 (4)	2.20	2.25

King Sobhuza II — A16

Designs (King Sobhuza II): 3½c, In 1971. 7½c, In tribal costume at gathering of chiefs (Incwala). 25c, Opening Swazi parliament.

1971, Dec. 22
187	A16	3c blue & multi	.25	.25
188	A16	3½c gold, blk, bl & brn	.25	.25
189	A16	7½c gold & multi	.25	.25
190	A16	25c lilac & multi	.25	.25
		Nos. 187-190 (4)	1.00	1.00

50th anniv. of the reign of Sobhuza II.

UNICEF Emblem, King Sobhuza II — A17

1972, Apr. 17   **Perf. 14½x14**
191	A17	15c violet & black	.25	.25
192	A17	25c olive & black	.35	.60

25th anniv. (in 1971) of UNICEF.

Traditional Reed Dancers — A18

     Perf. 13½x14
1972, Sept. 11   **Wmk. 314**
193	A18	3½c shown	.25	.25
194	A18	7½c Swazi beehive hut	.25	.25
195	A18	15c Ezulwini Valley	.35	.35
196	A18	25c Usutu River fishing	.70	.70
		Nos. 193-196 (4)	1.55	1.55

Tourist publicity.

Mosquito Control A19

7½c, Anti-malaria vaccination.

1973, May 21   **Litho.**   **Perf. 14½**
197	A19	3½c shown	.25	.25
198	A19	7½c multicolored	.60	.50

25th anniv. of WHO.

Mpaka Coal Mines — A20

7½c, Oxen pulling plow. 15c, Weir over Komati River. 25c, Experimental rice plantation.

     Perf. 13½x14
1973, June 21   **Wmk. 314**
199	A20	3½c multicolored	.55	.25
200	A20	7½c multicolored	.30	.25
201	A20	15c multicolored	.35	.25
202	A20	25c multicolored	.50	.50
		Nos. 199-202 (4)	1.70	1.25

Development of natural resources.

Swaziland Coat of Arms — A21

10c, King Sobhuza II in dress uniform. 15c, Parliament. 25c, National Somhlolo Stadium.

1973, Sept. 7   **Litho.**   **Perf. 14**
203	A21	3c brick red & black	.25	.25
204	A21	10c dull orange & multi	.25	.25
205	A21	15c blue & multi	.35	.50
206	A21	25c yellow & multi	.40	1.00
		Nos. 203-206 (4)	1.25	2.00

5th anniversary of independence.

Botswana, Lesotho, Swaziland Flags and Cap — A22

12½c, Kwaluseni Campus. 15c, Map of Africa & location of Botswana, Lesotho & Swaziland. 25c, Shield of University.

1974, Mar. 29   **Perf. 14**
207	A22	7½c orange & multi	.25	.25
208	A22	12½c emerald & multi	.30	.25
209	A22	15c yellow & multi	.35	.30
210	A22	25c ultra & multi	.40	.40
		Nos. 207-210 (4)	1.30	1.20

10th anniversary of the University of Botswana, Lesotho and Swaziland.

Sobhuza as Student at Lovedale College, South Africa — A23

1974, July 22   **Litho.**   **Perf. 13x11**
211	A23	3c shown	.25	.25
212	A23	9c Sobhuza as middle-aged man	.25	.25
213	A23	50c As old man	.70	.60
		Nos. 211-213 (3)	1.20	1.10

75th birthday of King Sobhuza II.

Mail Carried by Overhead Cable A24

4c, Post Office, Lobamba. 10c, Mbabane temporary P.O., 1902. 25c, Mule-drawn mail coach.

1974, Oct. 9   **Perf. 14**
214	A24	4c multicolored	.25	.25
215	A24	10c multicolored	.25	.25
216	A24	15c shown	.30	.30
217	A24	25c multicolored	.40	.40
		Nos. 214-217 (4)	1.20	1.20

Centenary of Universal Postal Union.

Animal Type of 1969
"E" instead of "R"

Designs as before.

1975, Jan. 2   **Litho.**   **Perf. 12½x13**
228	A12a	1e multicolored	1.00	1.00
229	A12a	2e multicolored	2.50	6.00

Girl's Umcwasho Ceremony — A26

Swazi youth: 10c, Butimba, hunting ceremony. 15c, Lusekwane, ceremony of preparation, horiz. 25c, Gcina Regiment marching with flags.

1975, Mar. 20   **Wmk. 314**   **Perf. 14**
232	A26	3c lt green & multi	.25	.25
233	A26	10c lt violet & multi	.25	.25
234	A26	15c brown org & multi	.40	.40
235	A26	25c yellow & multi	.50	.50
		Nos. 232-235 (4)	1.40	1.40

Matsapa Airport Control Tower A27

5c, Fire brigade car and staff. 15c, Douglas C-47 Dakota. 25c, Hawker Siddeley 748.

1975, Aug. 18   **Litho.**   **Perf. 14½**
236	A27	4c multicolored	.40	.25
237	A27	5c multicolored	.70	.25
238	A27	15c multicolored	1.50	1.50
239	A27	25c multicolored	2.50	2.50
		Nos. 236-239 (4)	5.10	4.50

10th anniversary of internal air service.

Women in Service — A28

4c, Elephant with IWY emblem, horiz. 5c, Queen Labotsibeni, grandmother of King Sobhuza II, horiz. 15c, Handicrafts women.

     Wmk. 373
1975, Dec. 22   **Litho.**   **Perf. 14**
240	A28	4c ultra, blk & gray	.25	.25
241	A28	5c bister & multi	.25	.25
242	A28	15c multicolored	.35	.35
243	A28	25c multicolored	.40	.70
		Nos. 240-243 (4)	1.25	1.55

International Women's Year 1975.

Green Pigeon — A29

Birds: 1c, Black-headed oriole, horiz. 3c, Melba finch, horiz. 4c, Plum-colored starling. 5c, Black-headed heron. 6c, Stonechat. 7c, Chorister robin. 10c, Gorgeous bush shrike. 15c, Black-collared barbet. 20c, Gray heron. 25c, Giant kingfisher. 30c, Black eagle. 50c, Red bishop. 1e, Pin-tailed whydah. 2e, Lilac-breasted roller, horiz.

1976, Jan. 2   **Wmk. 373**   **Perf. 14**
244	A29	1c orange & multi	.75	2.00
245	A29	2c lilac & multi	.85	2.00
246	A29	3c yel grn & multi	1.25	.90
247	A29	4c gray blue & multi	.90	.30
248	A29	5c orange & multi	1.00	1.60
249	A29	6c orange & multi	1.75	2.00
250	A29	7c orange & multi	1.50	2.00
251	A29	10c slate & multi	1.60	1.50
252	A29	15c lt green & multi	2.50	.90
253	A29	20c ocher & multi	3.50	2.25
254	A29	25c orange & multi	4.00	2.25
255	A29	30c orange & multi	4.00	2.50
256	A29	50c sepia & multi	1.50	1.50
257	A29	1e vermilion & multi	2.50	3.50
258	A29	2e lt blue & multi	4.50	6.50
		Nos. 244-258 (15)	32.10	31.70

Nos. 166 and 168 Surcharged in Ultra or Brown

1976   **Wmk. 314**   **Perf. 13x12½**
259	A12	3c on 7½c multi (U)	1.00	1.25
260	A12	6c on 12½c multi (B)	1.75	1.75

Denomination at lower left on No. 260.

Blindness from Malnutrition — A30

Designs (WHO Emblem and): 10c, Retina, "Operation prevents blindness." 20c, Blind eye, "Blindness from trachoma." 25c, Medicine and syringe, "Medicine and rehabilitation."

     Wmk. 373
1976, June 15   **Litho.**   **Perf. 14**
261	A30	5c multicolored	.25	.25
262	A30	10c multicolored	.35	.25
263	A30	20c multicolored	.55	.55
264	A30	25c multicolored	.60	.60
		Nos. 261-264 (4)	1.75	1.65

World Health Day: Foresight prevents blindness.

Marathon Runner — A31

Designs (Olympic Rings and): 6c, Boxing. 20c, Soccer. 25c, Olympic torch and flame.

1976, July 17   **Litho.**   **Wmk. 373**
265	A31	5c lt blue & multi	.25	.25
266	A31	6c olive & multi	.25	.25
267	A31	20c lt violet & multi	.45	.45
268	A31	25c dull orange & multi	.60	.60
		Nos. 265-268 (4)	1.55	1.55

21st Olympic Games, Montreal, Canada, July 17-Aug. 1.

Soccer — A32

Designs: 5c, Player heading ball. 20c, Goalkeeper catching ball. 25c, Player kicking ball.

1976, Sept. 13   **Litho.**   **Perf. 14½**
269	A32	4c blue & multi	.25	.25
270	A32	5c olive & multi	.25	.25
271	A32	20c red & multi	.40	.40
272	A32	25c multicolored	.50	.50
		Nos. 269-272 (4)	1.40	1.40

FIFA membership for Swaziland in 1976 (Federation Internationale de Football Associations).

A. G. Bell and 1976 Telephone — A33

Designs (A. G. Bell and Telephone): 5c, 1895. 10c, 1876. 15c, 1877. 20c, 1905.

1976, Nov. 22   **Perf. 14**
273	A33	4c multicolored	.25	.25
274	A33	5c multicolored	.25	.25
275	A33	10c multicolored	.25	.25

276 A33 15c multicolored .25 .25
277 A33 20c multicolored .30 .30
Nos. 273-277 (5) 1.30 1.30

Centenary of first telephone call by Alexander Graham Bell, Mar. 10, 1876.

Elizabeth II and Sobhuza II — A34

Designs: 25c, Queen's coach at Admiralty Arch. 50c, Queen seated in coach.

1977, Feb. 7 Perf. 13½
278 A34 20c silver & multi .25 .25
279 A34 25c silver & multi .25 .25
280 A34 50c silver & multi .30 .30
Nos. 278-280 (3) .80 .80

25th anniv. of the reign of Elizabeth II.

Matsapa College A35

10c, Men's & Women's uniforms & jeep. 20c, Police badge. 25c, Dog handler & dog.

1977, May 2 Litho. Perf. 14
281 A35 5c multi .35 .35
282 A35 10c multi .50 .30
283 A35 20c multi, vert. .70 .70
284 A35 25c multi 1.25 1.25
Nos. 281-284 (4) 2.80 2.60

50 years of police training in Swaziland.

Various Animals A36

Rock Paintings: 10c, 20c, Groups of men. 15c, Cattle and herdsman.

Perf. 14x14½
1977, Aug. 8 Wmk. 373
285 A36 5c multicolored .30 .25
286 A36 10c multicolored .35 .30
287 A36 15c multicolored .55 .45
288 A36 20c multicolored .70 .55
a. Souvenir sheet of 4, #285-288 3.50 3.50
Nos. 285-288 (4) 1.90 1.55

Rock paintings from Highveld area, c. 1700-1850.

Evergreens, Timber, Map of Highveld — A37

Designs: 10c, Pineapple and map of Middleveld. 15c, Map of Lowveld, orange and lemon. 20c, Map of Lubombo and grazing cattle. No. 293, Map of Swaziland and produce, vert.: UL, Evergreens; UR, Orange and lemon; LL, Pineapple; LR, Cattle.

1977, Oct. 17 Litho. Perf. 13½
289 A37 5c multicolored .25 .25
290 A37 10c multicolored .65 .65
291 A37 15c multicolored .90 .90
292 A37 20c multicolored 1.30 1.30
Nos. 289-292 (4) 3.10 3.10

Souvenir Sheet

293 Sheet of 4 2.50 2.50
a.-d. A37 25c single stamp .65 .65

Nos. 293a-293d are vertical.

Cussonia Spicata Thunb. — A38

Trees: 10c, Sclerocarya birrea. 20c, Pterocarpus angolensis. 25c, Erythrina lysistemon.

1978, Jan. 12 Litho. Wmk. 373
294 A38 5c multicolored .25 .25
295 A38 10c multicolored .35 .25
296 A38 20c multicolored .45 .45
297 A38 25c multicolored .65 1.00
Nos. 294-297 (4) 1.70 1.95

Rural Electrification, Lobamba — A39

Hydroelectric Power: 10c, Edwaleni Power Station. 20c, Switchgear, Maguduza Power Station. 25c, Hydroturbine hall, Edwaleni.

1978, Mar. 6 Litho. Perf. 13½
298 A39 5c black & ocher .25 .25
299 A39 10c black & yel grn .25 .25
300 A39 20c black & blue .30 .30
301 A39 25c black & rose mag .35 .35
Nos. 298-301 (4) 1.15 1.15

Elizabeth II Coronation Anniversary Issue
Souvenir Sheet
Common Design Types

1978, Apr. 21 Unwmk. Perf. 15
302 Sheet of 6 1.75 1.75
a. CD326 25c Queen's lion .35 .35
b. CD327 25c Elizabeth II .35 .35
c. CD328 25c African Elephant .35 .35

No. 302 contains 2 se-tenant strips of Nos. 302a-302c, separated by horizontal gutter with commemorative and descriptive inscriptions and showing central part of coronation procession with coach.

Clay Pots A40

Handicrafts: 10c, Basketwork. 20c, Wooden utensils. 30c, Wooden pot with lid.

Wmk. 373
1978, June 26 Litho. Perf. 13½
303 A40 5c multicolored .25 .25
304 A40 10c multicolored .25 .25
305 A40 20c multicolored .25 .25
306 A40 30c multicolored .25 .25
Nos. 303-306 (4) 1.00 1.00

See Nos. 317-320.

Defense Force A41

Designs: 6c, King's Regiment. 10c, Tinkabi tractor and ox-drawn plow. 15c, Laying water pipe. 25c, Adult literacy class. 50c, Fire engine and ambulance.

1978, Sept. 6 Litho. Perf. 14
307 A41 4c multicolored .25 .25
308 A41 6c multicolored .25 .25
309 A41 10c multicolored .25 .25
310 A41 15c multicolored .35 .25
311 A41 25c multicolored .50 .40
312 A41 50c multicolored 1.50 .50
Nos. 307-312 (6) 3.10 1.90

10th anniversary of independence.

Angel Appearing to the Shepherds — A42

Christmas: 10c, Adoration of the Kings. 15c, Angel warning Joseph in a dream. 25c, Flight into Egypt.

1978, Dec. 12 Litho. Perf. 14
313 A42 5c multicolored .25 .25
314 A42 10c multicolored .25 .25
315 A42 15c multicolored .25 .25
316 A42 25c multicolored .25 .25
Nos. 313-316 (4) 1.00 1.00

Handicrafts Type of 1978

1979, Jan. 10 Perf. 13½
317 A40 5c Sisal bowls .25 .25
318 A40 15c Clay pots .30 .30
319 A40 20c Basketwork .35 .35
320 A40 30c Hide shield .40 .40
Nos. 317-320 (4) 1.30 1.30

Prospecting at Phophonyane A43

15c, Early 3-stamp battery mill. 25c, Cyanide tanks at Piggs Peak. 50c, Pouring off molten gold.

Wmk. 373
1979, Mar. 27 Litho. Perf. 14
321 A43 5c blue & gold .35 .30
322 A43 15c brown & gold .65 .30
323 A43 25c green & gold .75 .55
324 A43 50c red & gold 1.25 1.25
Nos. 321-324 (4) 3.00 2.40

Centenary of discovery of gold in Swaziland.

Girls at Piano, 1892, by Renoir A44

Paintings by Renoir: 15c, Madame Charpentier and her Children, 1878. 25c, Girls Picking Flowers, 1889. 50c, Girl with Watering Can, 1876.

1979, May 8 Perf. 13½
325 A44 5c multicolored .25 .25
326 A44 15c multicolored .25 .25
327 A44 25c multicolored .40 .40
328 A44 50c multicolored .75 .75
a. Souvenir sheet of 4, #325-328 2.25 2.25
Nos. 325-328 (4) 1.65 1.65

International Year of the Child.

Swaziland No. 40 and Rowland Hill — A45

Rowland Hill and: 20c, Swaziland #18. 25c, Swaziland #142. 50c, Swaziland #60.

1979, July 17 Litho. Perf. 14½
329 A45 10c multicolored .25 .25
330 A45 20c multicolored .25 .25
331 A45 25c multicolored .35 .35
Nos. 329-331 (3) .85 .85

Souvenir Sheet

332 A45 50c multicolored 1.10 1.10

Sir Rowland Hill (1795-1879), originator of penny postage.

5c Cupro-Nickel Coin — A46

Coins: 10c, King Sobhuza II and sugar cane. 20c, King and elephant head. 50c, Coat of arms. 1e, Mother and son.

Perf. 13½x14
1979, Sept. 6 Litho. Wmk. 373
333 A46 5c multicolored .25 .25
334 A46 10c multicolored .25 .25
335 A46 20c multicolored .35 .35
336 A46 50c multicolored .50 .50
337 A46 1e multicolored 1.00 1.00
Nos. 333-337 (5) 2.35 2.25

Big Bend Post Office A47

15c, Mount Ntondozi microwave station, vert. 20c, Swaziland #53. 50c, Swaziland #217.

1979, Nov. 22
338 A47 5c multicolored .25 .25
339 A47 15c multicolored .25 .25
340 A47 20c multicolored .25 .25
341 A47 50c multicolored .30 .30
Nos. 338-341 (4) 1.05 1.05

25th anniv. of Post and Telecommunications service (5c, 15c); 10th anniv. of UPU membership (20c, 50c).

Rotary International, 75th Anniversary A48

Wmk. 373
1980, Feb. 23 Litho. Perf. 14
342 A48 5c shown .25 .25
343 A48 15c Hospital equipment .40 .40
344 A48 50c Rotary principles .75 .75
345 A48 1e Headquarters, Evanston, IL 1.60 1.60
Nos. 342-345 (4) 3.00 3.00

Flowers A49

Designs: 1c, Brunsvigia radulosa, vert. 2c, Aloe suprafoliata, vert. 3c, Haemanthus magificus, vert. 4c, Aloe marlothii, vert. 5c, Dicoma zeyheri, vert. 6c, Aloe kniphofioides, vert. 7c, Cyrtanthus bicolor, vert. 10c, Eucomis autumnalis. 15c, Leucospermum gerrardii. 20c, Haemanthus multiflorus. 30c, Acridocarpus natalitius. 50c, Adenium swazicum. 1e, Protea simplex, vert. 2e, Calodendrum capense, vert. 5e, Gladiolus ecklonii, vert.

1980, Apr. 28 Unwmk. Perf. 13½
Without Year Inscription
346 A49 1c multicolored .25 .25
347 A49 2c multicolored .25 .25
348 A49 3c multicolored .25 .25
a. Perf. 12 3.50 3.50
349 A49 4c multicolored .25 .25
350 A49 5c multicolored .25 .25
a. Perf. 12 4.00 2.50
351 A49 6c multicolored .25 .25
352 A49 7c multicolored .25 .25
353 A49 10c multicolored .25 .25
354 A49 15c multicolored .25 .25

355	A49 20c multicolored	.30 .30
356	A49 30c multicolored	.40 .40
357	A49 50c multicolored	.40 .40

Size: 22x37½mm

358	A49 1e multicolored	1.00 1.00
359	A49 2e multicolored	2.50 2.50
360	A49 5e multicolored	5.00 5.00
	Nos. 346-360 (15)	11.85 11.85

1983   Inscribed "1983"   Perf. 12

346a	A49 1c	1.00 .75
347a	A49 2c	1.00 .75
349a	A49 4c	1.25 1.25
b.	As "a," without date inscription below design	—
351a	A49 6c	2.00 1.00
353a	A49 10c	2.50 2.50
355a	A49 20c	2.75 1.75
	Nos. 346a-355a (6)	10.50 7.00

For surcharges see Nos. 465-470.

Mail Runner, London 1980 Emblem — A50

1980, May 6   Wmk. 373   Perf. 14

361	A50 10c shown	.25 .25
362	A50 20c Mail truck	.30 .25
363	A50 25c Mail sorting	.35 .30
364	A50 50c Mail ropeway	.70 .70
	Nos. 361-364 (4)	1.60 1.50

London 80 Intl. Stamp Exhib., May 6-14.

Yellow Fish — A51

1980, Aug. 25   Litho.   Perf. 14

365	A51 5c shown	.40 .25
366	A51 10c Silver barbel	.40 .25
367	A51 15c Tigerfish	.70 .30
368	A51 30c Squeaker fish	.90 .50
369	A51 1e Bream	1.75 1.75
	Nos. 365-369 (5)	4.15 3.05

Oribi Antelope — A52

1980, Oct. 1   Litho.   Perf. 14

370	A52 5c shown	.30 .25
371	A52 10c Nile crocodile, vert.	.65 .25
372	A52 50c Pangolin	1.00 1.00
373	A52 1e Leopard, vert.	2.25 2.25
	Nos. 370-373 (4)	4.20 3.75

Bus — A53

1981, Jan. 5   Litho.   Perf. 14½

374	A53 5c shown	.25 .25
375	A53 25c Jet	.40 .25
376	A53 30c Truck	.50 .35
377	A53 1e Train	1.25 1.25
	Nos. 374-377 (4)	2.40 2.10

Mantenga Falls — A54

15c, Mananga Yacht Club. 30c, White rhinoceri, Mlilwane Game Sanctuary. 1e, Gambling.

1981, Apr. 16   Litho.   Perf. 14

378	A54 5c shown	.30 .30
379	A54 15c multicolored	.35 .35
380	A54 30c multicolored	.75 .50
381	A54 1e multicolored	1.00 1.00
	Nos. 378-381 (4)	2.40 2.15

Royal Wedding Issue
Common Design Type
Wmk. 373

1981, July 21   Litho.   Perf. 14

382	CD331 10c Bouquet	.25 .25
383	CD331 25c Charles	.30 .25
384	CD331 1e Couple	.75 .75
	Nos. 382-384 (3)	1.30 1.25

Installation of King Sobhuza II, 1921 — A55

60th Anniv. of King Sobhuza II's Reign (King and): 10c, Visit of Royal Family, 1947. 15c, Coronation of Queen Elizabeth II, 1953. 25c, Independence ceremony, 1968. 30c, Early portrait. 1e, Parliament buildings.

Wmk. 373

1981, Aug. 24   Litho.   Perf. 14½

385	A55 5c multicolored	.25 .25
386	A55 10c multicolored	.25 .25
387	A55 15c multicolored	.25 .25
388	A55 25c multicolored	.35 .35
389	A55 30c multicolored	.40 .40
390	A55 1e multicolored	1.00 1.00
	Nos. 385-390 (6)	2.50 2.50

Duke of Edinburgh's Awards, 25th Anniv. — A56

1981, Nov. 5   Litho.   Perf. 14

391	A56 5c Basketball	.25 .25
392	A56 20c Compass reading	.25 .35
393	A56 50c Square	.50 .90
394	A56 1e Duke of Edinburgh	1.10 1.10
	Nos. 391-394 (4)	2.10 2.60

Intl. Year of the Disabled — A57

1981, Dec. 7   Perf. 14x14½, 14½x14

395	A57 5c Men learning carpentry, horiz.	.35 .25
396	A57 15c Boy learning Braille	.60 .40
397	A57 25c Carpentry, diff.	.90 .65
398	A57 1e Driving, horiz.	2.50 2.50
	Nos. 395-398 (4)	4.35 3.80

Papilio Demodocus — A58

1982, Jan. 6   Litho.   Perf. 14

399	A58 5c shown	.75 .30
400	A58 10c Charaxes candiope	.75 .30
401	A58 50c Papilio nireus	2.00 1.50
402	A58 1e Eurema desjardinsii	5.00 2.50
	Nos. 399-402 (4)	8.50 4.60

Non-smoker, Flowers — A59

10c, Smoker, non-smoker.

1982, Apr. 27   Litho.   Perf. 14

403	A59 5c multicolored	.65 .65
404	A59 10c multicolored	.80 .80

First Intl. Conference on Smoking and Health, Apr. 25-29

A60

a, Female fishing owl. b, Pair. c, Owl in nest, egg. d, Adult and young owls. e, Male.

Perf. 13½x13

1982, June 16   Litho.   Wmk. 373

405	Strip of 5, multi	110.00 80.00
a.-e.	A60 35c, any single	14.00 7.50

Princess Diana Issue
Common Design Type

1982, July 1   Perf. 14½

406	CD333 5c Arms	.25 .30
407	CD333 20c Diana	.85 .30
408	CD333 50c Wedding	1.00 .40
409	CD333 1e Portrait	1.75 1.25
	Nos. 406-409 (4)	3.85 2.25

Sugar Industry — A61

1982, Sept. 1   Litho.

410	A61 5c Planting sugar cane	.25 .25
411	A61 20c Harvesting cane	.35 .25
412	A61 30c Mhlume Mills	.50 .35
413	A61 1e Rail transport	1.75 1.75
	Nos. 410-413 (4)	2.85 2.60

Baphalali Red Cross Society — A62

1982, Nov. 9   Perf. 14

414	A62 5c Immunization	.25 .25
415	A62 20c Red Cross Juniors	.35 .35
416	A62 50c Disaster relief	.85 .85
417	A62 1e Red Cross founder Henry Dunant	1.90 1.90
	Nos. 414-417 (4)	3.35 3.35

Scouting Year — A63

Perf. 14½x14

1982, Dec. 6   Litho.   Wmk. 373

418	A63 5c Reciting promise	.25 .25
419	A63 10c Hiking	.25 .25
420	A63 25c Community development	.40 .40
421	A63 75c Baden-Powell	1.60 1.60
	Nos. 418-421 (4)	2.50 2.50

Souvenir Sheet

422	A63 1e Emblem	2.75 2.75

A64

6c, Satellite view. 10c, King Sobhuza II, flag. 50c, Beehive huts, horiz. 1e, Spraying sugar crop, horiz.

1983, Mar. 14   Litho.   Perf. 14

423	A64 6c multicolored	.25 .25
424	A64 10c multicolored	.25 .25
425	A64 50c multicolored	.60 .60
426	A64 1e multicolored	1.60 1.60
	Nos. 423-426 (4)	2.70 2.70

Commonwealth Day.

Bearded Vulture — A65

Designs: a, Male. b, Pair. c, Nest, egg. d, Female at nest. e, Adult, fledgeling.

Perf. 13½x13

1983, May 16   Litho.   Wmk. 373

427	Strip of 5	22.50 20.00
a.-e.	A65 35c, any single	3.25 2.75

Souvenir Sheets

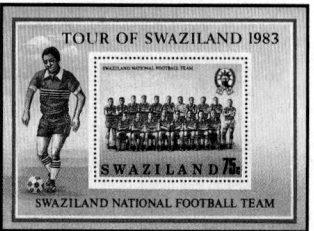

Soccer Tour of Swaziland 1983 — A66

1983, Aug. 20   Litho.   Perf. 14x13½

428	A66 75c Natl. team	1.25 1.25
429	A66 75c Tottenham Hotspur	1.25 1.25
430	A66 75c Manchester United	1.25 1.25
	Nos. 428-430 (3)	3.75 3.75

Manned Flight Bicentenary — A67

5c, Montgolfiere, 1783, vert. 10c, Wright brothers' plane. 25c, Royal Swazi Fokker Fellowship. 50c, Bell X-1 jet. 1e, Columbia space shuttle take-off, vert.

1983, Sept. 22   Litho.   Perf. 14

431	A67 5c multicolored	.25 .25
432	A67 10c multicolored	.25 .25
433	A67 25c multicolored	.45 .45
434	A67 50c multicolored	.75 .75
	Nos. 431-434 (4)	1.70 1.70

Souvenir Sheet

435	A67 1e multicolored	2.50 2.50

Alfred
Nobel,
100th Birth
Anniv.
A68

1983, Oct. 21
436 A68 6c Albert Schweitzer   2.75 1.00
437 A68 10c Dag Ham-
        marskjold   1.25   .50
438 A68 50c Albert Einstein   5.00 2.75
439 A68 1e shown   6.25 6.00
  Nos. 436-439 (4)   15.25 10.25

World
Food
Program
A69

1983, Nov. 29
440 A69 6c Maize   .25 .25
441 A69 10c Rice   .40 .40
442 A69 50c Cattle 1.25 1.25
443 A69 1e Tractor 2.10 2.10
  Nos. 440-443 (4)   4.00 4.00

Women's
College
A70

Wmk. 373
1984, Mar. 12   Litho.   Perf. 14
444 A70 5c shown   .25 .25
445 A70 15c Technical training
        school   .30 .30
446 A70 50c University .60 .60
447 A70 1e Primary school 1.10 1.10
  Nos. 444-447 (4)   2.25 2.25

Bald Ibis — A71

Designs: a, Male. b, Male, female. c, Nest,
egg. d, Female at nest. e, Adult, fledgeling.

1984, May 18   Litho.   Perf. 13½x13
448   Strip of 5   25.00 25.00
  a.-e. A71 35c, any single 3.75 3.00

1984 UPU Congress — A72

Mail Coaches.

1984, June 15   Litho.   Perf. 14½
449 A72 7c Mule-drawn coach   .45 .25
450 A72 15c Oxen-drawn post
        wagon   .55 .30
451 A72 50c Mule-drawn, diff. 1.25 1.00
452 A72 1e Bristol-London   1.90 1.90
  Nos. 449-452 (4)   4.15 3.45

1984
Summer
Olympics
A73

1984, July 28   Perf. 14
453 A73 7c Running   .25 .25
454 A73 10c Swimming .25 .25
455 A73 50c Shooting .80 .80
456 A73 1e Boxing   1.40 1.40
  a. Souvenir sheet of 4, #453-456 4.75 4.75
  Nos. 453-456 (4)   2.70 2.70

Local Fungi
A74

10c, Suillus bovinus. 15c, Langermannia
gigantea, vert. 50c, Coriolus versicolor, vert.
1e, Boletus edulis.

1984, Sept. 19   Litho.   Perf. 14
457 A74 10c multicolored 2.25 .40
458 A74 15c multicolored 3.00 .65
459 A74 50c multicolored 3.25 2.50
460 A74 1e multicolored   4.50 4.50
  Nos. 457-460 (4)   13.00 8.05

20th Anniv.
of Swazi
Railways
A75

10c, Opening ceremony. 25c, Type 15A
locomotive, Siweni Exchange Yard. 30c,
Container loading, Matsapha Station. 1e, No.
268, Alto Tunnel.

1984, Nov. 5   Litho.   Wmk. 373
461 A75 10c multicolored .40 .25
462 A75 25c multicolored .75 .60
463 A75 30c multicolored .85 .75
464 A75 1e multicolored 2.50 2.25
  a. Souvenir sheet of 4, #461-464 6.25 6.25
  Nos. 461-464 (4)   4.50 3.85

**Nos. 346a, 346-349, 351-352
Surcharged**
1984, Dec. 15   Litho.   Perf. 12
465 A49 10c on 4c #349a   3.00 3.00
  a. Perf. 13½ (#349)   35.00 35.00
  b. On No. 349b (perf. 12, without
      date inscription below de-
      sign)   45.00 45.00
Perf. 13½, 12 (#469)
466 A49 15c on 7c #352   .90 .30
467 A49 20c on 3c #348   .90 .40
  a. Perf 12   —
468 A49 25c on 6c #351   .90 .40
469 A49 30c on 1c #346a 1.00 .60
470 A49 30c on 2c #347   2.75 1.50
  Nos. 465-470 (6)   9.45 6.20

Rotary Intl.,
80th Anniv.
A76

10c, Rotary emblem, world map. 15c, Training scholarships. 50c, Two children. 1e, Nurse,
children.

1985, Feb. 23   Wmk. 373   Perf. 14
471 A76 10c multicolored .90 .45
472 A76 15c multicolored 1.50 .45
473 A76 50c multicolored 2.00 2.00
474 A76 1e multicolored 3.75 3.75
  Nos. 471-474 (4)   8.15 6.65

Life Cycle of the
Ground
Hornbill — A77

Audubon birth bicentenary.

1985, May 15   Wmk. 373
475   Strip of 5   16.00 16.00
  a.-e. A77 25c, any single 2.25 2.25

Queen Mother 85th Birthday
Common Design Type

10c, Visit to South Africa, 1947. 15c, With
Elizabeth II and Margaret. 50c, 75th birthday
celebration. 1e, Holding Prince Henry. 2e,
Greeting Prince Andrew.

Perf. 14½x14
1985, June 7   Litho.   Wmk. 384
476 CD336 10c multicolored .50 .25
477 CD336 15c multicolored .50 .25
478 CD336 50c multicolored 1.25 1.25
479 CD336 1e multicolored 1.75 1.75
  Nos. 476-479 (4)   4.00 3.50
Souvenir Sheet
480 CD336 2e multicolored 4.00 4.00

Classic Automobiles — A78

Wmk. 373
1985, Sept. 16   Litho.   Perf. 14
481 A78 10c Buick Tourer   .85 .40
482 A78 15c Four-cylinder Rover .90 .50
483 A78 50c De Dion Bouton 2.00 1.75
484 A78 1e Ford Model-T   3.25 3.25
  Nos. 481-484 (4)   7.00 5.90

Intl. Youth
Year
A79

1985, Dec. 2
485 A79 10c Bridge-building .25 .25
486 A79 20c Girl Guides camping .25 .25
487 A79 50c Recreation   .75 .65
488 A79 1e Guides collecting
        branches   1.40 1.40
  Nos. 485-488 (4)   2.65 2.55

Girl Guide Movement, 20c, 1e. IYY, 10c,
50c.

Halley's
Comet
A80

1986, Feb. 27   Wmk. 384   Perf. 14½
489 A80 1.50e multicolored 4.50 4.50

Queen Elizabeth II 60th Birthday
Common Design Type

10c, Princess Anne's christening, 1950.
30c, Wedding of Prince Charles and Lady
Diana, 1981. 45c, With George VI, the Dutch-
ess of York and Sobhuza II at Nhlangano,
1947. 1e, At Windsor Polo Ground, 1984. 2e,
Visiting Crown Agents' offices, 1983.

1986, Apr. 21   Perf. 14x14½
490 CD337 10c scar, blk & sil .25 .25
491 CD337 30c ultra & multi   .25 .25
492 CD337 45c green, blk & sil .30 .30
493 CD337 1e violet & multi   .50 .50
494 CD337 2e rose vio & multi 1.00 1.00
  Nos. 490-494 (5)   2.30 2.30

For overprints see Nos. 527-530.

Coronation of
Crown Prince
Makhosetive
A81

10c, Portrait, vert. 20c, Prince and King
Sobhuza II at an Incwala ceremony. 25c,
Prince at primary school. 30c, At school in
England. 40c, Escorted from Matsapha Airport
by Guard of Honor. 2e, Dancing the Simemo.

1986, Apr. 25   Perf. 14½
495 A81 10c multicolored .50 .50
496 A81 20c multicolored .75 .55
497 A81 25c multicolored .85 .60
498 A81 30c multicolored 1.10 .70
499 A81 40c multicolored 2.50 2.00
500 A81 2e multicolored 5.25 5.25
  Nos. 495-500 (6)   10.95 9.60

Assoc. of Round
Tables in Central
Africa, 50th
Anniv. — A82

Club emblems.

Wmk. 384
1986, Oct. 4   Litho.   Perf. 14
501 A82 15c Orbis   .40 .25
502 A82 25c Ehlanzeni 51 .50 .45
503 A82 55c Mbabane 30 1.10 .90
504 A82 70c Bulembu 54 1.25 1.25
505 A82 2e Manzini 44   2.75 2.75
  Nos. 501-505 (5)   6.00 5.60

Butterflies — A83

10c, Yellow pansy. 15c, Guineafowl. 20c,
Red forest charaxes. 25c, Paradise skipper.
30c, Broad-bordered acraea. 35c, Veined
swallowtail. 45c, Large striped swordtail. 50c,
Eyed pansy. 55c, Zebra white. 70c, Gaudy
commodore. 1e, Common dotted border. 5e,
Queen purple tip. 10e, Natal barred blue.

Unwmk.
1987, Mar. 17   Litho.   Perf. 14
506 A83 10c multicolored .55 .50
507 A83 15c multicolored .65 .50
508 A83 20c multicolored .65 .30
509 A83 25c multicolored .65 .60
510 A83 30c multicolored .65 .50
511 A83 35c multicolored .65 .50
512 A83 45c multicolored .70 .65
513 A83 50c multicolored .75 .50
514 A83 55c multicolored .75 .50
515 A83 70c multicolored 1.00 1.25
516 A83 1e multicolored 1.50 3.00
517 A83 5e multicolored 3.50 2.00
518 A83 10e multicolored 5.00 5.00
  Nos. 506-518 (13)   17.00 15.80

See Nos. 600-611. For surcharges see Nos.
574-577. Compare with design A101.

White
Rhinoceros
A84

1987, July 1   Wmk. 384   Perf. 14½
519 A84 15c Two adults   3.00 1.25
520 A84 25c Adult, calf   4.50 2.00
521 A84 45c Adult walking 7.75 3.50
522 A84 70c Adult in mud 9.50 6.25
  Nos. 519-522 (4)   24.75 13.00

World Wildlife Fund.

Flowers — A85

1987, Oct. 19 Litho. *Perf. 14½*
523	A85	15c	Blue moon	1.50	.75
524	A85	35c	Danse de feu	2.25	1.00
525	A85	55c	Odin	2.50	2.00
526	A85	2e	Lilium davidii	7.75	7.75
		Nos. 523-526 (4)		14.00	11.50

Nos. 491-494 Ovptd. "40TH WEDDING ANNIVERSARY" in Silver

Perf. 14x14½

1987, Dec. 9 Litho. Wmk. 384
527	CD337	30c	ultra & multi	.40	.30
528	CD337	45c	green, blk & sil	.50	.45
529	CD337	1e	violet & multi	1.00	1.00
530	CD337	2e	rose vio & multi	1.25	1.25
		Nos. 527-530 (4)		3.15	3.00

Insects A86

15c, Zabalius aridus. 55c, Callidea bohemani. 1e, Phymateus viridipes. 2e, Nomadacris septemfasciata.

Wmk. 384

1988, Mar. 14 Litho. *Perf. 14*
531	A86	15c	multicolored	1.75	.75
532	A86	55c	multicolored	3.25	1.25
533	A86	1e	multicolored	5.75	5.75
534	A86	2e	multicolored	9.00	9.00
		Nos. 531-534 (4)		19.75	16.30

1988 Summer Olympics, Seoul A87

1988, Aug. 22 Litho. Wmk. 384
535	A87	15c	Flag-bearer, stadium	1.25	.45
536	A87	35c	Tae kwon do	1.75	.95
537	A87	1e	Boxing	2.50	2.50
538	A87	2e	Tennis	4.50	4.50
		Nos. 535-538 (4)		10.00	8.40

Intl. Tennis Federation, 75th anniv. (2e).

Small Mammals A88

Wmk. 384

1989, Jan. 16 Litho. *Perf. 14*
539	A88	35c	Green monkey	2.10	.40
540	A88	55c	Rock dassie	2.75	.95
541	A88	1e	Zorilla	4.75	4.75
542	A88	2e	African wildcat	7.75	7.75
		Nos. 539-542 (4)		17.35	13.85

Intl. Red Cross and Red Crescent Organizations, 125th Annivs. — A89

Wmk. 373

1989, Sept. 21 Litho. *Perf. 12*
543	A89	15c	David Hynd	.35	.25
544	A89	60c	First aid	.90	.60
545	A89	1e	Sigombeni Clinic	1.50	1.50
546	A89	2e	Relief work	2.25	2.25
		Nos. 543-546 (4)		5.00	4.60

21st Birthday of King Mswati III A90

King Mswati III: 15c, With Prince of Wales, 1987. 60c, With Pope John Paul II, 1988. 1e, Introduction to the nation while crown prince. 2e, With queen mother.

Perf. 14½x14

1989, Nov. 15 Unwmk.
547	A90	15c	multicolored	.25	.25
548	A90	60c	multicolored	.55	.55
549	A90	1e	multicolored	.95	.95
550	A90	2e	multicolored	1.50	1.50
		Nos. 547-550 (4)		3.25	3.25

African Development Bank, 25th Anniv. — A91

15c, Manzini-Mahamba Road. 60c, Mbabane microwave radio link. 1e, Mbabane Government Hospital. 2e, Ezulwini Power Switching Station.

Perf. 14x14½

1989, Dec. 18 Wmk. 384
551	A91	15c	multicolored	.40	.25
552	A91	60c	multicolored	.70	.50
553	A91	1e	multicolored	1.25	1.25
554	A91	2e	multicolored	2.00	2.00
		Nos. 551-554 (4)		4.35	4.00

Stamp World London '90 — A92

Wmk. 384

1990, May 3 Litho. *Perf. 12½*
555	A92	15c	Intl. priority mail	.35	.30
556	A92	60c	Facsimile service	.80	.65
557	A92	1e	Post office	1.25	1.25
558	A92	2e	Ezulwini Earth Satellite Station	2.50	2.50
		Nos. 555-558 (4)		4.90	4.70

Souvenir Sheet
559	A92	2e	Mail runner	9.00	9.00

150th anniv. of the Penny Black.

Queen Mother, 90th Birthday
Common Design Types

75c, Queen Mother. 4e, King, Queen visiting Hatfield House.

1990, Aug. 4 Wmk. 384 *Perf. 14x15*
565	CD343	75c	multicolored	.60	.60

Perf. 14½
566	CD344	4e	multicolored	3.75	3.75

Intl. Literacy Year A94

Wmk. 373

1990, Sept. 21 Litho. *Perf. 14*
567	A94	15c	shown	.25	.25
568	A94	75c	Outdoor class	.65	.65
569	A94	1e	Modern instruction	.80	.80
570	A94	2e	Receiving diploma	1.25	1.25
		Nos. 567-570 (4)		2.95	2.95

UN Development Program, 40th Anniv. — A95

Perf. 13½x14

1990, Dec. 10 Litho. Wmk. 373
571	A95	60c	Rural water supply	.75	.75
572	A95	1e	Seed production	1.10	1.10
573	A95	2e	Low cost housing	2.00	2.00
		Nos. 571-573 (3)		3.85	3.85

Nos. 509-510, 512, 514 Surcharged

Unwmk.

1990, Dec. 17 Litho. *Perf. 14*
574	A83	10c on 25c	multi	.35	.35
575	A83	15c on 30c	multi	.75	.75
575A	A83	15c on 45c	multi	55.00	55.00
576	A83	20c on 45c	multi	.75	.75
577	A83	40c on 55c	multi	1.00	1.00

National Heritage A96

No. 578, Lobamba Hot Spring. No. 579, Sibebe Rock. No. 580, Jolobela Falls. No. 581, Mantjolo Sacred Pool.
No. 581A, Usushwana River.

Perf. 14x14½

1991, Feb. 11 Wmk. 233
578	A96	15c	multicolored	.75	.35
579	A96	60c	multicolored	1.75	.85
580	A96	1e	multicolored	2.25	2.25
581	A96	2e	multicolored	3.25	3.25
		Nos. 578-581 (4)		8.00	6.70

Souvenir Sheet
Perf. 14
581A	A96	2e	multicolored	8.75	8.75

Coronation of King Mswati III, 5th Anniv. A97

15c, King making radio address. 75c, Butimba royal hunt. 1e, King, schoolmates, 1986. 2e, King opening parliament.

Perf. 14x13½

1991, Apr. 24 Litho. Wmk. 373
582	A97	15c	multicolored	.35	.25
583	A97	75c	multicolored	1.25	.95
584	A97	1e	multicolored	1.25	1.25
585	A97	2e	multicolored	2.75	2.75
		Nos. 582-585 (4)		5.60	5.20

Elizabeth & Philip, Birthdays
Common Design Types

Wmk. 384

1991, June 17 Litho. *Perf. 14½*
586	CD346	1e	multicolored	1.50	1.50
587	CD345	2e	multicolored	2.40	2.40
a.		Pair, #586-587 + label		4.25	4.25

Flowers — A98

15c, Xerophyta retinervis. 75c, Bauhinia galpinii. 1e, Dombeya rotundifolia. 2e, Kigelia africana.

1991, Sept. 30 Wmk. 373 *Perf. 14*
588	A98	15c	multicolored	.70	.40
589	A98	75c	multicolored	1.60	1.25
590	A98	1e	multicolored	2.00	2.00
591	A98	2e	multicolored	3.25	3.00
		Nos. 588-591 (4)		7.55	6.65

Christmas — A99

20c, Santa Claus, children. 70c, Carolers. 1e, Priest reading Bible. 2e, Nativity Scene.

Wmk. 373

1991, Dec. 18 Litho. *Perf. 13½*
592	A99	20c	multicolored	.30	.25
593	A99	70c	multicolored	.85	.75
594	A99	1e	multicolored	1.10	1.10
595	A99	2e	multicolored	2.25	2.25
		Nos. 592-595 (4)		4.50	4.35

Reptiles A100

20c, Lubombo flat lizard. 70c, Natal hinged tortoise. 1e, Swazi thick-toed gecko. 2e, Nile monitor.

1992, Feb. 25
596	A100	20c	multicolored	1.25	.25
597	A100	70c	multicolored	2.75	1.50
598	A100	1e	multicolored	3.50	3.50
599	A100	2e	multicolored	4.75	4.75
		Nos. 596-599 (4)		12.25	10.00

Butterflies A101

1992-2000 Litho. *Perf. 14*
600	A101	5c	Red tip	.25	.25
601	A101	10c	like #506	.25	.25
602	A101	15c	like #507	.25	.25
603	A101	20c	like #508	.25	.25
604	A101	25c	like #509	.25	.25
605	A101	30c	like #510	.30	.25
606	A101	35c	like #511	.35	.30
607	A101	45c	like #512	.40	.35
608	A101	50c	like #513	.45	.40
609	A101	55c	like #514	.50	.45
610	A101	70c	like #515	.55	.55
611	A101	1e	like #516	1.00	1.00
612	A101	5e	Like #517	20.00	7.00
613	A101	10e	Like #518	20.00	9.00
		Nos. 600-611 (12)		4.80	4.55

Issued: Nos. 600-611, 8/26/92. No. 612, 2000.
Nos. 600-611 dated 1991. Nos. 612 and 613 dated 2000.
Nos. 600-612 have different portrait of King Mswati III from Nos. 506-517.

A102

Designs: 20c, Missionaries with royal family. 1e, Pioneer missionaries.

1992, Dec. 16 Litho. *Perf. 13½x14*
614	A102	20c	multicolored	.65	.55
615	A102	1e	multicolored	2.75	2.75

Evangelical Alliance Mission in Swaziland, cent.

20c, Calabashes. 70c, Contemporary pottery for cooking. 1e, Wooden bowls. 2e, Quern for grinding seeds.

Cooking Utensils — A103

1993, Mar. 18   Litho.   Perf. 13½x14
616 A103 20c multicolored .65 .25
617 A103 70c multicolored 1.50 .95
618 A103 1e multicolored 2.10 2.10
619 A103 2e multicolored 3.00 3.00
Nos. 616-619 (4) 7.25 6.30

Independence, 25th Anniv. — A104

King Mswati, 25th Birthday: 25c, King Mswati as baby with mother. 40c, King Mswati III addressing PTA meeting. 1e, King Sobhuza II receiving Instrument of Independence, 1968. 2e, King Mswati III delivering first speech on Coronation Day, 1986.

1993, Sept. 6   Litho.   Perf. 13½x14
620 A104 25c multicolored .25 .25
621 A104 40c multicolored .35 .25
622 A104 1e multicolored .90 .90
623 A104 2e multicolored 1.75 1.75
Nos. 620-623 (4) 3.25 3.15

Common Waxbill — A105

1993, Nov. 25   Perf. 13½
624 A105 25c Male & female .55 .30
625 A105 40c Nest & eggs .85 .35
626 A105 1e Incubating 1.90 1.90
627 A105 2e Feeding nestlings 3.25 3.25
Nos. 624-627 (4) 6.55 5.80

US Peace Corps, 25th Anniv. — A106

1994, Feb. 22   Litho.   Perf. 13½
628 A106 25c Education .40 .25
629 A106 40c Rural services .55 .25
630 A106 1e Swazi culture 2.00 2.00
631 A106 2e People to people 2.25 2.25
Nos. 628-631 (4) 5.20 4.75

Mushrooms — A107

1994, Sept. 15   Perf. 13½x14
632 A107 30c Horse mushroom 1.40 .60
633 A107 40c Penny bun bolete 1.40 .60
634 A107 1e RusulLa verdigris 3.00 2.00
635 A107 2e Honey fungus 4.00 4.00
Nos. 632-635 (4) 9.80 7.20

ICAO, 50th Anniv. A108

1994, Nov. 30   Litho.   Perf. 14
636 A108 30c Natl. airline .50 .25
637 A108 40c Control tower .55 .30
638 A108 1e Air rescue service 1.25 1.25
639 A108 2e Air traffic control 2.00 2.00
Nos. 636-639 (4) 4.30 3.80

Traditional Handicrafts — A109

1995, Apr. 7   Litho.   Perf. 13½
640 A109 35c Wooden bowls .65 .40
641 A109 50c Chicken nests .85 .60
642 A109 1e Leather crafts 1.75 1.75
643 A109 2e Wood carvings 3.25 3.25
Nos. 640-643 (4) 6.50 6.00

A110

FAO, 50th anniv.: 35c, Corn harvest. 50c, Planting vegetables. 1e, Herd of cattle. 2e, Sorghum harvest.

1995, June 5   Litho.   Perf. 13½
644 A110 35c multicolored .25 .25
645 A110 50c multicolored .45 .45
646 A110 1e multicolored .80 .80
647 A110 2e multicolored 1.60 1.60
Nos. 644-647 (4) 3.10 3.10

Lourie A111

1995, Sept. 27   Litho.   Perf. 13½x13
648 A111 35c Knysna lourie .65 .30
649 A111 50c Lourie in flight .85 .50
650 A111 1e Purple crested lourie 1.25 1.25
651 A111 2e Gray lourie 1.75 1.75
Nos. 648-651 (4) 4.50 3.80

Reptiles A112

1996, Jan. 17   Litho.   Perf. 13½x13
652 A112 35c Chameleon .70 .30
653 A112 50c Rock monitor .90 .50
654 A112 1e African python 1.50 1.50
655 A112 2e Tree agama 2.25 2.25
Nos. 652-655 (4) 5.35 4.55

Trees — A113

1996, Apr. 23   Litho.   Perf. 13
656 A113 40c Waterberry .40 .25
657 A113 60c Sycamore fig .50 .40
658 A113 1e Stem fruit .90 .90
659 A113 2e Wild medlar 1.25 1.25
Nos. 656-659 (4) 3.05 2.80

Local Landmarks A114

Designs: 40c, First church, Mahamba Methodist. 60c, Colonial Secretariat, Mbabane. 1e, King Sobhuza II Memorial Monument. 2e, First High Court Building, Hlatikulu.

1996, Aug. 26   Litho.   Perf. 13½x13
660 A114 40c multicolored .60 .30
661 A114 60c multicolored .75 .50
662 A114 1e multicolored 1.40 1.40
663 A114 2e multicolored 2.25 2.25
Nos. 660-663 (4) 5.00 4.45

UNICEF, 50th Anniv. A115

Designs: 40c, Basic education for all. 60c, Universal child immunization, vert. 1e, No more polio, vert. 2e, Children first, vert.

1996, Dec. 31   Litho.   Perf. 13½x14
664 A115 40c multicolored .30 .30

Perf. 14x13½
665 A115 60c multicolored .60 .60
666 A115 1e multicolored .80 .80
667 A115 2e multicolored 1.40 1.40
Nos. 664-667 (4) 3.10 3.10

Wild Animals A116

50c, Klipspringer, vert. 70c, Gray duiker, vert. 1e, Antbear. 2e, Cape clawless otter.

Perf. 14x13½, 13½x14
1997, Sept. 22   Litho.
668 A116 50c multicolored .50 .40
669 A116 70c multicolored .60 .50
670 A116 1e multicolored 1.00 1.00
671 A116 2e multicolored 1.75 1.75
Nos. 668-671 (4) 3.85 3.65

Traditional Costumes — A117

1997, Dec. 1   Litho.   Perf. 13x13½
672 A117 50c Umgaco .30 .30
673 A117 70c Sigeja .55 .55
674 A117 1e Umdada .85 .85
675 A117 2e Ligcebesha 1.75 1.75
Nos. 672-675 (4) 3.45 3.45

Toads and Frogs A118

1998, June 1   Litho.   Perf. 14
676 A118 55c Olive toad .45 .25
677 A118 75c African bullfrog .60 .35
678 A118 1e Water lily frog 1.10 1.10
679 A118 2e Bushveld rain frog 2.00 2.00
Nos. 676-679 (4) 4.15 3.70

Independence, 30th Anniv., King Mswati III, 30th Birthday — A119

55c, King Sobhuza II Memorial Park. 75c, King Mswati III taking oath. 1e, King Mswati III delivering 1st speech. 2e, King Sobhuza II receiving instrument of independence.

Perf. 13½x14, 14x13½
1998, Sept. 3   Litho.
680 A119 55c multicolored .45 .30
681 A119 75c multicolored .80 .75
682 A119 1e multicolored 1.25 1.10
683 A119 2e multicolored 1.75 1.75
Nos. 680-683 (4) 4.25 3.90

Traditional Utensils — A120

1999, May 17   Litho.   Perf. 13¾x13¼
684 A120 60c Grinding stone .50 .30
685 A120 75c Stirring sticks .60 .45
686 A120 80c Clay pot .60 .50
687 A120 95c Swazi spoons .70 .60
688 A120 1.75e Beer cup 1.25 1.25
689 A120 2.40e Mortar and pestle 1.75 1.75
Nos. 684-689 (6) 5.40 4.85

UPU, 125th Anniv. A121

60c, Internet service, vert. 80c, Cellular phone service, vert. 1e, Intl. mail exchange. 2.40e, Training school.

Perf. 13¾x13½
1999, Oct. 9   Litho.   Unwmk.
690 A121 60c multicolored .40 .30
691 A121 80c multicolored .55 .40

Perf. 13½x13¾
692 A121 1e multicolored 2.00 1.50
693 A121 2.40e multicolored 3.00 3.00
Nos. 690-693 (4) 5.95 5.20

Wildlife A122

Designs: 65c, Lion, vert. 90c, Leopard. 1.50e, Rhinoceros. 2.50e, Buffalo, vert.

Perf. 13½x13¼, 13¼x13½

2000. July 3		Litho.	Unwmk.	
694	A122	65c multi	.65	.30
695	A122	90c multi	.90	.40
696	A122	1.50e multi	3.00	2.25
697	A122	2.50e multi	2.50	2.50
	Nos. 694-697 (4)		7.05	5.45

Worldwide Fund for Nature (WWF) — A123

Designs: 65c, Oribi with young. 90c, Oribi. 1.50e, Klipspringers. 2.50e, Klipspringers, diff.

Wmk. 373

2001, Feb. 1		Litho.		Perf. 14	
698-701	A123	Set of 4		4.50	4.50
701a		Sheet, 4 each #698-701		19.00	19.00

Environmental Protection — A124

Designs: 70c, Fighting forest fires. 95c, Tree planting. 2.05e Construction of Maguga Dam. 2.80e, Building embankment.

2001, July 30		Litho.		Perf. 14	
702-705	A124	Set of 4		5.25	5.25

Reign Of Queen Elizabeth II, 50th Anniv. Issue
Common Design Type

Designs: Nos. 706, 710a, 70c, Princess Elizabeth, Princess Anne, Princes Philip and Charles, 1947. Nos. 707, 710b, 95c, Wearing purple hat. Nos. 708, 710c, 2.05e, Wearing crown. Nos. 709, 710d, 2.80e, Wearing yellow hat, 2001. No. 710e, 22.50e, 1955 portrait by Annigoni (38x50mm).

Perf. 14¼x14½, 13¾ (#710e)

2002, Feb. 6		Litho.	Wmk. 373	
With Gold Frames				
706	CD360	70c multicolored	.50	.50
707	CD360	95c multicolored	.75	.75
708	CD360	2.05e multicolored	1.50	1.50
709	CD360	2.80e multicolored	2.00	2.00
	Nos. 706-709 (4)		4.75	4.75

Souvenir Sheet
Without Gold Frames

710	CD360	Sheet of 5, #a-e	8.00	8.00

Tourism A125

Designs: 75c, Swazi chalets. 1e, King Mswati III facing lions, vert. 2.05e, Crocodile. 2.80e, Ostriches.

Perf. 13¼x13¾, 13¾x13¼

2002, Dec. 23		Litho.		
711-714	A125	Set of 4	4.75	4.75

Musical Instruments — A126

Designs: 80c, Mouth organ, vert. 1.05e, Rattles. 2.35e, Kudu horn trumpet. 2.80e, Chordphone, vert.

2003, Aug. 12		Litho.		Perf. 14	
715-718	A126	Set of 4		3.75	3.75

AIDS Prevention — A127

Designs: 85c, Community home-based care. 1.10e, Know your HIV status. 2.45e, Testing blood samples, vert. 3.35e, Unsterilized instruments can transmit HIV and AIDS, vert.

Perf. 13¼x13¾, 13¾x13¼

2004, Mar. 9		Litho.		
719-722	A127	Set of 4	4.75	4.75

Global 2003 Smart Partnership International Dialogue, Ezulwini — A128

Designs: 85c, King Mswati III, Swaziland flag, map of Africa. 1.10e, Map of Africa, Swaziland flag, Smart Partnership International Movement emblems, horiz. 2.45e, Sharing ideas. 3.35e, Man, woman at microphone.

Perf. 13¾x13¼, 13¼x13¾

2004, June 14		Litho.		
723-726	A128	Set of 4	3.75	3.75

Birds A129

Designs: 85c, Purple-crested louries, national bird of Swaziland. 1.10e, Blue cranes, national bird of South Africa. 1.35e, Cattle egrets, national bird of Botswana. 1.90e, African fish eagles, national bird of Zimbabwe. 2e, African fish eagles, national bird of Namibia. 2.45e, Bar-tailed trogons. 3e, African fish eagles, national bird of Zambia. 3.35e, Peregrine falcons, national bird of Angola.

No. 735: a, Cattle egrets, national bird of Botswana. b, African fish eagles, national bird of Namibia. c, Bar-tailed trogons. d, African fish eagles, national bird of Zambia. e, Peregrine falcons, national bird of Angola.

2004, Oct. 11		Litho.		Perf. 14	
727-734	A129	Set of 8		12.00	12.00
735		Sheet of 8, #727, 728, 730, #735a-735e		17.50	17.50
a.-b.		A129 1.90e Either single		2.00	2.00
c.		A129 2.25e multi		2.50	2.50
d.-e.		A129 2.30e Either single		2.50	2.50

See Botswana Nos. 792-793, Namibia No. 1052, South Africa No. 1342, Zambia No. 1033, and Zimbabwe No. 975.

Road Safety Council A130

Inscriptions: 85c, Stop Killing Them In Traffic. 1.10e, Avoid Accidents. 2.45e, Safe Crossing. 3.35e, No Overloading.

2005, Jan. 25		Litho.	Perf. 13¼x13¾		
736-739	A130	Set of 4		2.75	2.75

Snakes A131

Designs: 85c, Black mamba. 1.10e, Python. 2.45e, Boomslang. 3.35e, Puff adder.

2005, Apr. 5		Litho.	Perf. 13¼x13¾		
740-743	A131	Set of 4		4.00	4.00

Pope John Paul II (1920-2005) A132

2005, Aug. 18		Litho.		Perf. 14	
744	A132	4.50e multi		1.50	1.50

Locusts A133

Designs: 85c, Schistocerca solitaria. 1.10e, Red locust. 2.45e, Southern Africa desert locust. 3.35e, African migratory locust.

2005, Oct. 11		Litho.	Perf. 13¼x13¾		
745-748	A133	Set of 4		6.75	6.75

Queen Mothers — A134

Designs: 85c, Ntombi Tfwala. 1.10e, Dzeliwe Shongwe. 2e, Lomawa Ndwandwe. 2.45e, Labotsibeni Mdluli. 3.35e, Tibati Nkambule.

2006, Jan. 10			Perf. 13¾x13¼		
749-753	A134	Set of 5		9.00	9.00

Postal History A135

Designs: 90c, Manzini District Office and Post Office, 1920s. 1.15e, Ox wagon. 2e, Bremersdorp Post Office, 1893. 2.55e, Mail runner, vert. 3.50e, Mbabane Temporary Post Office, 1902.

Perf. 13¾

2006, May 8		Litho.	Unwmk.	
754-758	A135	Set of 5	9.00	9.00

Waterfalls — A136

Designs: 90c, Mgubudla Falls. 1.15e, Phophonyane Falls. 1.40e, Mantenga Falls, horiz. 2e, Malolotja Falls. 2.55e, Mabhudlweni Falls. 3.50e, Manzamnyama Falls.

2006, Sept. 26					
759-764	A136	Set of 6		11.50	11.50

Trees A137

Designs: 70c, Common cabbage tree. 85c, Broom cluster fig. 90c, Scented thorn. 1.05e, Natal mahogany. 1.15e, Marula. 1.40e, Stem fruit tree. 2e, Fever tree. 2.40e, Large-leaved coral tree. 2.55e, African teak. 3.50e, Red ivory. 5e, Common coral tree. 10e, Jacket-plum. 20e, Sausage tree.

2007, Jan. 23		Litho.	Perf. 13¼x13¾		
765	A137	70c multi		.35	.25
766	A137	85c multi		.35	.25
767	A137	90c multi		.40	.25
768	A137	1.05e multi		.50	.30
769	A137	1.15e multi		.55	.35
770	A137	1.40e multi		.60	.40
771	A137	2e multi		.70	.45
772	A137	2.40e multi		.80	.50
773	A137	2.55e multi		1.25	.80
774	A137	3.50e multi		1.50	1.25
775	A137	5e multi		2.00	2.00
776	A137	10e multi		4.00	4.00
777	A137	20e multi		7.50	7.50
	Nos. 765-777 (13)			20.50	18.30

Community-based Tourism — A138

Designs: 1e, Rock art at Nsangwini Rock Art Center. 1.20e, Mahamba Gorge Lodge. 2.70e, Shewula Mountain Camp. 3.70e, Khopo Camp, Ngwempisi Hiking Trails.

2008, Jan. 22		Litho.	Perf. 13½x13¾		
778-781	A138	Set of 4		7.25	7.25

Decorations and Jewelry for Warriors — A139

Designs: 1e, Shoulder strap. 2.70e, Beaded necklace, horiz. 3.70e, Anklets, horiz.

Perf. 13¾x13¼, 13¼x13¾

2008, May 27			Litho.		
782-784	A139	Set of 3		6.50	6.50

Independence, 40th Anniv. and 40th Birthday of King Mswati III — A140

Designs: 1e, Transportation infrastructure. 1.05e, King Mswati III receives constitution, vert. 1.30e, Maguga Dam. 1.60e, Maidens at reed dance, vert. 2.15e, First lilangeni currency. 2.40e, Health and social welfare. 2.75e, Information and communications technology. 2.90e, King Mswati III's 40th birthday. 3.95e, King Sobhuza at Independence ceremony, 1968, vert.

Perf. 13¼x13¾, 13¾x13¼

2008, Oct. 28			Litho.		
785-793	A140	Set of 9		9.50	9.50

2010 World Cup Soccer
Championships, South Africa — A141

Soccer players, ball, 2010 World Cup mascot and flag of: Nos. 794, 803a, 1e, Zimbabwe. Nos. 795, 803b, 1.25e, South Africa. Nos. 796, 803c, 1.50e, Mauritius. Nos. 797, 803d, 1.90e, Namibia. Nos. 798, 803e, 2.50e, Zambia. Nos. 799, 803f, 3.40e, Swaziland. Nos. 800, 803g, 3.80e, Malawi. Nos. 801, 803h, 4.60e, Botswana. Nos. 802, 803i, 4.90e, Lesotho.

On Plain Paper With Olive Brown Background

2010, Apr. 9   **Perf. 13½**
794-802 A141   Set of 9   9.00   9.00
On Gold-faced Paper
803 A141   Sheet of 9, #a-i   18.00 18.00
No. 803 sold for 45e.
See Botswana Nos. 896-905, Lesotho No. , Malawi No. 753, Mauritius No. , Namibia No. 1188, South Africa No. 1403, Zambia Nos. 1115-1118, and Zimbabwe Nos. 1112-1121.

Locusts
A142

Designs: No. 804, A, Southern African desert locust. No. 805, B, Schistocerca solitaria. No. 806, C, African migratory locust. No. 807, D, Red locust.

2012, Apr. 2   **Perf. 13¼x13¾**
804-807 A142   Set of 4   4.00 4.00
On day of issue, Nos. 804-807 sold for 1.35e, 1.70e, 3.30e and 4.90e, respectively.

Towards 2022 First World Vision A143

Designs: I, First national soccer team, 1968. II, National clinical laboratory services. III, Free primary education. IV, Lubovane Dam. V, Emergency preparedness and response. VI, Sikhuphe International Airport Air Traffic Control Tower and Fire Station.

2013, Sept. 4   **Litho.**   **Perf. 14¼x14**
808-813 A143   Set of 6   4.00 4.00
On day of issue, Nos. 808-813 sold for 1.45e, 2.10e, 2.90e, 3.50e, 3.90e and 5.25e respectively.

POSTAGE DUE STAMPS

Catalogue values for unused stamps in this section are for Never Hinged items.

D1

1933   **Typo.**   **Wmk. 4**   **Perf. 14**
J1   D1 1p carmine rose   4.00   17.50
   a.   Wmk. 4a (error)   275.00
J2   D1 2p violet   12.00   35.00
    Value, Nos. J1-J2 hinged $6.

No. 57 Surcharged

      I   II

1961   **Engr.**   **Perf. 13½x13**
J3   A5   (2d) on 2p, type I   8.00   12.00
   a.   Type II   .40
J4   A5   1c on 2p, type I   2.50   4.00
   a.   Type II   1.50   3.00
J5   A5   2c on 2p, type I   2.50   4.00
   a.   Type II   1.10   2.00
J6   A5   5c on 2p, type I   2.50   4.00
   a.   Type II   2.00   3.00
    Nos. J3-J6 (4)   15.50 24.00
    Nos. J3a-J6a (4)   5.00
    Nos. J4a-J6a (3)   4.35

No. J3a was surcharged after decimal currency was introduced.

Type of 1933

D2

1961   **Typo.**   **Perf. 14**
J7   D1 1c carmine rose   .25   1.00
J8   D1 2c violet   .30   1.25
J9   D1 5c green   .75   2.00
    Nos. J7-J9 (3)   1.30   4.25

          Wmk. 314
1971, Feb. 1   **Litho.**   **Perf. 11½**
J10   D2 1c carmine rose   .80   4.00
J11   D2 2c dull purple   1.25   4.50
J12   D2 5c green   2.00   6.00
    Nos. J10-J12 (3)   4.05 14.50

1977, Jan. 17   **Wmk. 373**
J10a   D2 1c carmine rose   .80   4.50
J11a   D2 2c dull purple   1.25   5.00
J12a   D2 5c green   2.00   6.50
    Nos. J10a-J12a (3)   4.05 16.00

1978-91   **Perf. 15x14**
    Size: 17½x21mm
J13   D2 1c carmine lake   .60   1.25
J14   D2 2c purple   .60   .80
J15   D2 5c green   .50   .80
J16   D2 10c sky blue   .50   .80
J17   D2 25c brown   .70   1.00
    Nos. J13-J17 (5)   2.90   4.65

Nos. J14-J15 reissued dated 1991.
Issued: 1c-5c, 4/20; 10c-25c, 7/17/91.

SWEDEN

'swē-dən

LOCATION — Northern Europe, occupying the eastern half of the Scandinavian Peninsula
GOVT. — Constitutional Monarchy
AREA — 173,341 sq. mi.
POP. — 9,182,927 (2007 est.)
CAPITAL — Stockholm

48 skilling banco = 1 riksdaler banco (until 1858)
100 öre = 1 riksdaler (1858 to 1874)
100 öre = 1 krona (since 1874)

Catalogue values for unused stamps in this country are for Never Hinged items, beginning with Scott 358 in the regular postage section, and Scott B37 in the semi-postal section.

Watermarks

Wmk. 180 — Crown

Wmk. 307 — Crown and 1955

Wmk. 181 — Wavy Lines

Values for unused stamps are for examples with original gum as defined in the catalogue introduction except Nos. 1-5, excluding reprints, and LX1 which are valued without gum.

Coat of Arms — A1

1855 Unwmk. Typo. *Perf. 14*

1	A1	3s blue green	*10,000.*	*5,000.*
a.		3s orange (error)		*3,000,000.*
2	A1	4s lt blue	1,600.	110.00
3	A1	6s gray	*10,000.*	1,600.
f.		Imperf.		—
4	A1	8s red org	5,500.	650.00
h.		Imperf.		5,750.
5	A1	24s dull red	*8,750.*	2,200.

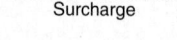

Nos. 1-5 were reprinted from new blocks in 1868 (twice), 1871 (No. 1 only) and 1885. The 1868 and 1871 printings were perf 14, and the 1885 printing was perf 13. These later printings were made after Nos. 1-5 were withdrawn, but before being demonetized. The post office did not distinguish between these and earlier printings, although most saw little, if any, postal use. See the Scott Specialized Catalogue of Stamps and Covers 1840-1940 for detailed listings.

Coat of Arms — A2

1858-62 *Perf. 14*

6	A2	5o green	210.00	20.00
a.		5o deep green	575.00	250.00
7	A2	9o violet	425.00	275.00
a.		9o red lilac	625.00	325.00
8	A2	12o blue	225.00	2.00
9	A2	12o ultra ('61)	450.00	12.50
10	A2	24o orange	500.00	30.00
a.		24o yellow	750.00	60.00
11	A2	30o brown	500.00	30.00
a.		30o dark red brown	750.00	87.50
12	A2	50o rose	600.00	110.00
a.		50o carmine	750.00	110.00
		Nos. 6-12 (7)	2,910.	479.50

Nos. 6 and 8 exist with double impressions. No. 8 is known printed on both sides. No. 11 exists imperf.

Nos. 6-8, 10-12 were reprinted in 1885, perf. 13. See the Scott Specialized Catalogue of Stamps and Covers 1840-1940 for detailed listings. Also reprinted in 1963, perf. 13½, with lines in stamp color crossing denominations, and affixed to book page. Value $12.50 each.

Lion and Arms
A3 A4

1862-69

13	A3	3o bister brown	275.00	14.00
a.		Printed on both sides		*3,700.*
14	A4	17o red violet ('66)	800.00	160.00
15	A4	17o gray ('69)	850.00	*800.00*
16	A4	20o vermilion ('66)	300.00	20.00
		Nos. 13-16 (4)	2,225.	994.00

Nos. 13-15 were reprinted in 1885, perf. 13. See the Scott Specialized Catalogue of Stamps and Covers 1840-1940 for detailed listings.

Numeral of Value — A5

Coat of Arms — A6

1872-77 *Perf. 14*

17	A5	3o bister brown	80.00	8.00
18	A5	4o gray ('76)	500.00	150.00
19	A5	5o blue green	400.00	5.00
a.		5o emerald	500.00	25.00
20	A5	6o violet	400.00	40.00
a.		6o dark violet	1,250.	300.00
21	A5	6o gray ('74)	1,100.	95.00
22	A5	12o blue	225.00	1.00
23	A5	20o vermilion	1,000.	9.00
a.		20o pale org ('75)	3,500.	50.00
b.		Double impression, dull yel & ver ('76)	3,500.	55.00
24	A5	24o orange	950.00	42.50
a.		24o yellow	950.00	42.50
25	A5	30o pale brown	825.00	11.00
a.		30o black brown	875.00	14.00
26	A5	50o rose	875.00	50.00
a.		50o carmine	900.00	50.00
27	A6	1rd bister & blue	1,150.	95.00
a.		1rd bister & ultra	1,150.	95.00
		Nos. 17-27 (11)	7,505.	506.50

1877-79 *Perf. 13*

28	A5	3o yellow brown	125.00	6.00
29	A5	4o gray ('79)	225.00	3.50
30	A5	5o dark green	140.00	1.00
31	A5	6o lilac	175.00	5.00
a.		6o red lilac	375.00	14.00
32	A5	12o blue	35.00	1.00
33	A5	20o vermilion	275.00	1.00
a.		"TRETIO" instead of "TJUGO" ('79)	12,000.	7,500.
34	A5	24o orange ('78)	75.00	30.00
a.		24o lemon yellow ('83)	625.00	55.00
35	A5	30o pale brown	450.00	2.00
a.		30o black brown	875.00	3.00
36	A5	50o carmine ('78)	325.00	9.00
37	A6	1rd bister & blue	2,400.	500.00
38	A6	1k bis & bl ('78)	625.00	20.00
		Nos. 28-36,38 (10)	2,450.	78.50

Imperf., Pairs

28a	A5	3o	1,000.	
29a	A5	4o	1,000.	
30a	A5	5o	1,000.	
31b	A5	6o	1,000.	
32a	A5	12o	1,000.	
33b	A5	20o	1,000.	
34b	A5	24o	1,000.	
35b	A5	30o	1,000.	*4,000.*
36a	A5	50o	1,000.	
38a	A6	1k	1,000.	

See Nos. 40-44, 46-49. For surcharges see Nos. B1-B10, B22-B31.

No. 37 has been reprinted in yellow brown and dark blue; perforated 13. Value, $325.

King Oscar II — A7

1885 Typo.

39	A7	10o dull rose	225.00	1.00
a.		Imperf., pair	*2,500.*	

Numeral Type with Post Horn on Back

1886-91

40	A5	2o orange ('91)	2.50	*8.00*
a.		Period before "FRIMARKE"	12.00	*22.50*
b.		Imperf., pair	725.00	
41	A5	3o yellow brn ('87)	15.00	*25.00*
42	A5	4o gray	30.00	2.00
43	A5	5o green	62.50	1.00
44	A5	6o red lilac ('88)	30.00	*62.50*
a.		6o violet	35.00	*62.50*
45	A7	10o pink	87.50	.50
a.		10o rose	87.50	.25
b.		Imperf.		3,250.
46	A5	20o vermilion	125.00	1.00
47	A5	30o pale brown	210.00	2.00
48	A5	50o rose	190.00	5.00
49	A6	1k bister & dk bl	100.00	3.00
a.		Imperf., pair	700.00	
		Nos. 40-49 (10)	852.50	110.00

Nos. 32, 34 with Blue Surcharge

1889, Oct. 1

50	A5	10o on 12o blue	3.75	*4.00*
51	A5	10o on 24o orange	11.00	*40.00*

A9

King Oscar II
A10 A11

Wmk. 180

1891-1904 Typo. *Perf. 13*

52	A9	1o brown & ultra ('92)	1.40	.65
53	A9	2o blue & yellow org	3.25	.40
54	A9	3o brn & org ('92)	.60	1.75
55	A9	4o car & ultra ('92)	4.75	.50

Engr.

56	A10	5o yellow green	2.75	.30
a.		5o blue green	11.50	.30
d.		5o brown (error)	*7,500.*	—
e.		Booklet pane of 6	140.00	
57	A10	8o red vio ('03)	3.25	1.25
58	A10	10o carmine	4.50	.30
c.		Booklet pane of 6	240.00	
59	A10	15o red brn ('96)	27.50	.50
60	A10	20o blue	28.00	.40
61	A10	25o red org ('96)	37.50	.50
62	A10	30o brown	55.00	.40
63	A10	50o slate	125.00	.85
64	A10	50o ol gray ('04)	100.00	.85
65	A11	1k car & sl ('00)	175.00	2.25
		Nos. 52-65 (14)	568.50	10.90

Imperf., Pairs

52a	A9	1o	87.50
53a	A9	2o	*325.00*
54a	A9	3o	*325.00*
55a	A9	4o	325.00
56b	A10	5o No. 56	85.00
c.		No. 56a	300.00
57a	A10	8o	500.00
58a	A10	10o	52.50
59a	A10	15o	500.00
60a	A10	20o	150.00
61a	A10	25o	600.00
62a	A10	30o	600.00
63a	A10	50o	650.00
64a	A10	50o	500.00
65a	A11	1k	625.00

No. 56d may be a color proof.

A booklet pane of 6 invalid stamps similar to No. 56 but with engraved lines through the denominations was released in 2004 to commemorate the 100th anniversary of the first Swedish booklet. This booklet pane is unwatermarked.

See Nos. 75-76.

Stockholm Post Office — A12

1903, Oct. 26

66	A12	5k blue	240.00	27.50
a.		Imperf., pair	3,000.	

Opening of the new General Post Office at Stockholm.

For surcharge see No. B11.

Arms — A13

Gustaf V — A14

Perf. 13, 13x13½

1910-14 Typo. Wmk. 180

67	A13	1o black ('11)	.65	*1.50*
68	A13	2o orange	1.75	*4.00*
69	A13	4o violet	2.50	1.10

Engr.

70	A14	5o green ('11)	14.00	*29.00*
71	A14	10o carmine	10.00	.50
72	A14	1k black, *yel* ('11)	95.00	.50
73	A14	5k claret, *yel* ('14)	2.00	*3.00*
		Nos. 67-73 (7)	125.90	*39.60*

See #77-98. For surcharges see #99-104, Q1-Q2.

1911 Unwmk.

75	A10	20o blue	22.50	15.00
76	A10	25o red orange	27.50	4.00

1910-19

77	A14	5o green ('11)	3.00	.30
a.		Booklet pane of 10	225.00	
b.		Booklet pane of 4	125.00	
78	A14	7o gray grn ('18)	.30	.30
a.		Booklet pane of 10	8.75	
79	A14	8o mag ('12)	.30	.30
80	A14	10o car ('10)	2.50	.30
a.		Booklet pane of 10	225.00	
b.		Booklet pane of 4	125.00	
81	A14	12o rose lake ('18)	.30	.30
a.		Booklet pane of 10	8.75	
82	A14	15o red brn ('11)	6.50	.30
a.		Booklet pane of 10	325.00	
83	A14	20o dp bl ('11)	9.50	.30
a.		Booklet pane of 10	350.00	
84	A14	25o org red ('11)	.30	.30
85	A14	27o pale bl ('18)	.40	.90
86	A14	30o clar brn ('11)	20.00	.30
87	A14	35o dk vio ('11)	17.00	.30
88	A14	40o ol grn ('17)	25.00	.30
89	A14	50o gray ('12)	50.00	.30
90	A14	55o pale bl ('18)	*2,100.*	*6,500.*
91	A14	65o pale ol grn ('18)	.65	2.00
92	A14	80o black ('18)	*2,100.*	*6,500.*
93	A14	90o gray grn ('18)	.60	.65
94	A14	1k blk, *yel* ('19)	92.50	.30
		Nos. 77-89,91,93-94 (16)	228.85	7.45

Excellent forgeries of Nos. 90 and 92 exist.

1911-19 Typo. Wmk. 181 *Perf. 13*

95	A13	1o black	.30	.30
96	A13	2o orange	.30	.30
97	A13	3o pale brown ('19)	.30	.30
98	A13	4o pale violet	.30	.30
		Nos. 95-98 (4)	1.20	1.20

Remainders of Nos. 95-98 received various private overprints, mostly as publicity for stamp exhibitions. They were not postally valid.

Unwatermarked Stamps with Watermarks

Stamps of these and later issues through the UPU Congress issue of 1924, are frequently found with watermark showing parts of the words "Kungl Postverket" in double-lined capitals. This watermark is normally located in the margins of the sheets of unwatermarked paper or paper watermarked wavy lines or crown.

Nos. 80, 84, 91, 90, 92 Surcharged

a

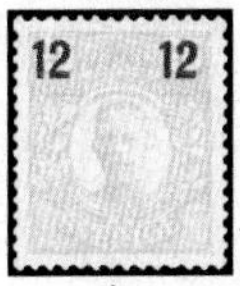

b

1918 Unwmk.

99	A14(a)	7o on 10o	.30	*.40*
100	A14(b)	12o on 25o	1.90	.40
a.		Inverted surcharge	625.00	1,200.
101	A14(a)	12o on 65o	.85	*1.40*
102	A14(a)	27o on 55o	.75	*1.60*
103	A14(a)	27o on 65o	1.40	*3.50*
104	A14(a)	27o on 80o	.85	*1.60*
		Nos. 99-104 (6)	6.05	8.90

Arms
A15

Heraldic Lion Supporting Arms of Sweden
A16

Two types each of 5o green, 5o copper red and 10o violet, type A16.

Perf. 10 Vertically

1920-25 Engr. Unwmk.

115	A15	3o copper red	.30	*.40*
116	A16	5o green ('25)	4.00	.40
117	A16	5o cop red ('21)	5.00	.40
118	A16	10o green ('21)	21.00	.40
a.		Tête bêche pair	*1,650.*	*3,250.*
119	A16	10o violet ('25)	5.25	.40
120	A16	25o orange ('21)	13.00	.40
121	A16	30o brown	.45	.45

Wmk. 181

122	A16	5o green	2.50	1.30
123	A16	5o cop red ('21)	8.25	1.00
124	A16	10o green ('21)	2.50	1.30
125	A16	30o brown	8.25	18.00
		Nos. 115-125 (11)	70.50	24.45

Coil Stamps

Unless part of a booklet pane any stamp perforated only horizontally or vertically is a coil stamp.

1920-26 Unwmk. *Perf. 10*

126	A16	5o green	4.00	1.00
a.		Booklet pane of 10	80.00	
127	A16	10o green ('21)	11.50	3.50
a.		Booklet pane of 10	225.00	
128	A16	10o violet ('25)	6.50	.85
a.		Booklet pane of 10	180.00	
129	A16	30o brown	32.50	4.00

Wmk. 181

130	A16	5o green	11.50	30.00
131	A16	10o green ('21)	45.00	*100.00*
a.		Booklet pane of 10	425.00	

Perf. 13 Vertically

Unwmk.

132	A16	5o green ('25)	4.00	1.50
133	A16	5o cop red ('21)	325.00	160.00
134	A16	10o violet ('26)	25.00	37.50

Wmk. 181

135	A16	5o green ('25)	2.00	*8.00*
136	A16	5o cop red ('22)	2.00	7.00
137	A16	10o green ('24)	9.00	*40.00*
138	A16	10o violet ('25)	8.00	*25.00*
		Nos. 126-138 (13)	486.00	418.35

The paper used for the earlier printings of types A16, A17, A18, A18a and A20 is usually tinted by the color of the stamp. Printings of 1934 and later are on white paper in slightly different shades.

King Gustaf V — A17

1920-21 Unwmk. *Perf. 10 Vertically*

139	A17	10o rose	30.00	.40
140	A17	15o claret	.30	.45
141	A17	20o blue	35.00	.50

Perf. 10

142	A17	10o rose	12.50	6.00
143	A17	20o blue ('21)	29.00	11.00
a.		Booklet pane of 10	550.00	
		Nos. 139-143 (5)	106.80	18.35

Wmk. 181

144	A17	20o blue	*4,000.*	

A18

Crown and Post Horn — A18a

See note after No. 138 regarding paper.
There are 2 types of the 35, 40, 45 and 60o.

1920-34 Unwmk. *Perf. 10 Vert.*

145	A18	35o yellow ('22)	42.50	.75
146	A18	40o olive green	32.50	.75
147	A18	45o brown ('22)	1.25	.55
148	A18	60o claret	19.00	.40
149	A18	70o red brn ('22)	.60	2.50
150	A18	80o deep green	.40	.40
151	A18	85o myr grn ('29)	4.50	.45
152	A18	90o lt blue ('25)	60.00	.30
153	A18a	1kr dp org ('21)	7.75	.40
154	A18	110o ultra	.50	.40
155	A18	115o red brn ('29)	9.00	.45
156	A18	120o gray blk ('25)	60.00	.60
157	A18	120o lil rose ('33)	14.00	.60
158	A18	140o gray black	.90	.30
159	A18	145o brt grn ('30)	8.50	.55

Wmk. 181

160	A18	35o yellow ('23)	50.00	7.50
161	A18	60o red violet	80.00	*150.00*
162	A18	80o blue green	8.25	15.00
163	A18	110o ultra	3.50	4.50
		Nos. 145-163 (19)	403.15	186.40

The value for #147 is for the 2nd type, issued in 1925.

Gustavus Adolphus — A19

Perf. 10 Vertically

1920, July 28 Unwmk.

164	A19	20o deep blue	2.25	.40

Wmk. 181

165	A19	20o blue	160.00	35.00

Unwmk.

Perf. 10

166	A19	20o blue	6.25	2.25
a.		Booklet pane of 10	130.00	
		Nos. 164-166 (3)	168.50	37.65

Tercentenary of Swedish post which first ran between Stockholm and Hamburg.

King Gustaf V — A20

See note after No. 138 regarding paper.
There are two types each of the 15o rose and 40o olive green.

1921-36 Unwmk. *Perf. 10 Vert.*

167	A20	15o vio ('22)	17.00	.40
168	A20	15o rose ('28)	5.50	.45
169	A20	15o brn ('36)	4.75	.45
170	A20	20o violet	.25	.30
171	A20	20o rose ('22)	22.50	.60
172	A20	20o org ('25)	.25	.45
174	A20	25o rose red ('22)	.55	1.50
175	A20	25o dk bl ('25)	17.00	.40
176	A20	25o ultra ('34)	17.00	.80
177	A20	25o yel org ('36)	27.50	.45
178	A20	30o blue ('23)	19.00	.45
179	A20	30o brn ('25)	20.00	.35
180	A20	30o lt ultra ('36)	6.00	.70
181	A20	35o red vio ('30)	24.00	.45
182	A20	40o blue	.45	.70
183	A20	40o ol grn ('29)	40.00	2.00
184	A20	45o brn ('29)	5.00	.90
185	A20	50o gray	1.75	1.00
186	A20	85o myr grn ('25)	17.00	2.00
187	A20	115o brn red ('25)	11.00	2.00
188	A20	145o apl grn ('25)	8.25	2.00
		Nos. 167-188 (21)	264.75	18.35

Wmk. 181

189	A20	15o vio ('22)	3,500.	1,050.
189A	A20	20o violet		*4,750.*

1922-36 Unwmk. *Perf. 10*

190	A20	15o violet	17.50	.70
a.		Booklet pane of 10	400.00	
191	A20	15o rose red ('25)	22.50	.90
a.		Booklet pane of 10	600.00	
192	A20	15o brown ('36)	5.75	1.25
a.		Booklet pane of 10	175.00	
193	A20	20o violet ('22)	.50	*1.50*
a.		Booklet pane of 10	10.00	
		Nos. 190-193 (4)	46.25	4.35

Gustavus Vasa — A21

1921, June *Perf. 10 Vertically*

194	A21	20o violet	14.00	*30.00*
195	A21	110o ultra	55.00	8.00
196	A21	140o gray black	30.00	8.00
		Nos. 194-196 (3)	99.00	46.00

400th anniversary of Gustavus Vasa's war of independence from the Danes.

Universal Postal Union Congress

Composite View of Stockholm's Skyline A22

King Gustaf V — A23

1924, July 4 Unwmk. *Perf. 10*

197	A22	5o red brown	1.60	*3.25*
198	A22	10o green	1.60	*3.25*
199	A22	15o dk violet	1.60	*2.50*
200	A22	20o rose red	12.50	*21.00*
201	A22	25o dp orange	15.00	*21.00*
202	A22	30o deep blue	15.00	*21.00*
a.		30o greenish blue	87.50	125.00

203 A22 35o black 20.00 *28.00*
204 A22 40o olive green 29.00 *32.50*
205 A22 45o deep brown 32.50 32.50
206 A22 50o gray 32.50 32.50
207 A22 60o violet brn 47.50 *55.00*
208 A22 80o myrtle grn 37.50 37.50
209 A23 1k green 57.50 *87.50*
210 A23 2k rose red 125.00 *250.00*
211 A23 5k deep blue 250.00 *450.00*

Wmk. 181

212 A22 10o green 26.00 *65.00*
Nos. 197-212 (16) 704.80 *1,142.*
Set, never hinged 1,400.

Postrider Watching Airplane A24

Carrier Pigeon and Globe — A25

1924, Aug. 16 Engr. Unwmk.

213 A24 5o red brown 2.75 4.50
214 A24 10o green 2.75 5.75
215 A24 15o dk violet 3.00 3.00
216 A24 20o rose red 21.00 32.50
217 A24 25o deep orange 26.00 32.50
218 A24 30o deep blue 26.00 32.50
a. 30o greenish blue 90.00 52.50
219 A24 35o black 32.50 47.50
220 A24 40o olive green 32.50 32.50
221 A24 45o deep brown 37.50 35.00
222 A24 50o gray 50.00 62.50
223 A24 60o violet brown 50.00 77.50
224 A24 80o myrtle green 37.50 37.50
225 A25 1k green 75.00 87.50
226 A25 2k rose red 110.00 75.00
227 A25 5k deep blue 225.00 225.00

Wmk. 181

228 A24 10o green 35.00 *65.00*
Nos. 213-228 (16) 766.50 855.75
Set, never hinged 1,600.

Universal Postal Union issue.

Royal Palace at Stockholm A26

1931, Nov. 26 Unwmk. *Perf. 10*

229 A26 5k dark green 90.00 12.50
Never hinged 300.00
a. Booklet pane of 10 3,100.

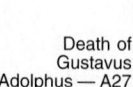

Death of Gustavus Adolphus — A27

1932, Nov. 1

230 A27 10o dark violet 2.50 5.50
a. Booklet pane of 10 40.00
231 A27 15o dark red 4.50 2.00
a. Booklet pane of 10 110.00

Perf. 10 Vertically

232 A27 10o dark violet 1.90 .40
233 A27 15o dark red 2.50 .40
234 A27 25o dark blue 6.00 .95
235 A27 90o dark green 20.00 2.25
Nos. 230-235 (6) 37.40 11.50
Set, never hinged 85.00

300th anniv. of the death of King Gustavus Adolphus II who was killed on the battlefield of Lützen, Nov. 6, 1632.

Catching Sunlight in Bowl — A28

1933, Dec. 6 *Perf. 10*

236 A28 5o green 2.50 2.00
a. Booklet pane of 10 60.00

There are two types of No. 236.

Perf. 10 Vertically

237 A28 5o green 2.50 .40

Perf. 13 Vertically

238 A28 5o green 3.50 7.25
Nos. 236-238 (3) 8.50 9.65
Set, never hinged 17.50

50th anniv. of the Swedish Postal Savings Bank.

The Old Law Courts — A29

The "Four Estates" and Arms of Engelbrekt A34

Designs: 10o, Stock exchange. 15o, Parish church (Storkyrkan). 25o, House of the Nobility. 35o, House of Parliament.

1935, Jan. 10 *Perf. 10*

239 A29 5o green 2.25 1.40
a. Booklet pane of 10 55.00
240 A29 10o dull violet 4.25 *5.75*
a. Booklet pane of 10 60.00
241 A29 15o carmine 4.75 1.10
a. Booklet pane of 10 125.00

Perf. 10 Vertically

242 A29 5o green 1.25 .40
243 A29 10o dull violet 5.75 .40
244 A29 15o carmine 2.25 .40
245 A29 25o ultra 6.00 .60
246 A29 35o deep claret 12.00 2.25
247 A34 60o deep claret 17.50 2.50
Nos. 239-247 (9) 56.00 14.80
Set, never hinged 125.00

500th anniv. of the Swedish Parliament.

Chancellor Axel Oxenstierna A35

Post Runner — A36

Mounted Courier — A37

Old Sailing Packet — A38

Mail Paddle Steamship A39

Mail Coach — A40

1855 Stamp Model — A41

Mail Train — A42

Postmaster General A. W. Roos — A43

Mail Truck and Trailer — A44

Modern Swedish Liner — A45

Junkers Plane with Pontoons — A46

1936, Feb. 20 Engr. *Perf. 10*

248 A35 5o green 1.75 .85
a. Booklet pane of 18 72.50
249 A36 10o dk violet 2.10 3.00
a. Booklet pane of 18 95.00
250 A37 15o dk carmine 3.00 .55
a. Booklet pane of 18 250.00

Perf. 10 Vertically

251 A35 5o green 1.75 .25
252 A36 10o dk violet 1.75 .25
253 A37 15o dk carmine 3.25 .25
254 A38 20o lt blue 8.25 5.00
255 A39 25o lt ultra 5.25 .50
256 A40 30o yellow brn 16.00 3.25
257 A41 35o plum 5.50 1.25
258 A42 40o olive grn 5.75 2.75
259 A43 45o myrtle grn 7.75 1.50
260 A44 50o gray 20.00 2.75
261 A45 60o maroon 25.00 .70
262 A46 1k deep blue 8.25 8.50
Nos. 248-262 (15) 115.35 31.35
Set, never hinged 320.00

300th anniv. of the Swedish Postal Service. See Nos. 946-950, B55-B56.

Airplane over Bromma Airport A47

Design Size: 33.25mm x 25.5mm

1936, May 23 *Perf. 10 Vert.*

263 A47 50o ultra 4.00 8.50
Never hinged 10.50

Opening of Bromma Airport near Stockholm.

Swedish Booklets

Before 1940, booklets were handmade and usually held two panes of 10 stamps (2x5). About every third booklet contained one row of stamps with straight edges at right or left side. Se-tenant pairs may be obtained with one stamp perforated on 4 sides and one perforated on 3 sides.

Starting in 1940, booklet stamps have one or more straight edges.

Some combination booklets containing multiple face-different stamps may exist with different configurations of those stamps. The most common configuration has been valued.

Emanuel Swedenborg — A48

1938, Jan. 29 *Perf. 12½*

264 A48 10o violet 1.00 .35
a. Perf. on 3 sides 8.00 4.00
Never hinged 17.00
b. Booklet pane of 10 30.00

Perf. 12½ Vertically

266 A48 10o violet .90 .25
267 A48 100o green 2.00 1.40
Nos. 264-267 (3) 3.90 2.00
Set, never hinged 14.00

250th anniv. of the birth of Swedenborg, scientist, philosopher and religious writer.

Johann Printz and Indian Chief — A49

"Kalmar Nyckel" Sailing from Gothenburg A50

Symbolizing the Settlement of New Sweden — A51

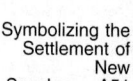

Holy Trinity Church, Wilmington, Del. — A52

Queen Christina — A53

1938, Apr. 8 *Perf. 12½ Vert.*

268 A49 5o green .40 .30
269 A50 15o brown .50 .30
270 A51 20o red .90 .70
271 A52 30o ultra 2.00 .85
272 A53 60o brown lake 2.50 .35

Perf. 12½

273 A49 5o green 1.00 1.00
a. Perf. on 3 sides 5.00 *7.50*
Never hinged 17.00
b. Booklet pane of 18 67.50
274 A50 15o brown 1.50 .70
a. Perf. on 3 sides 10.00 4.75
Never hinged 29.00
b. Booklet pane of 18 115.00
Nos. 268-274 (7) 8.80 4.20
Set, never hinged 39.00

Tercentenary of the Swedish settlement at Wilmington, Del. See No. B54.

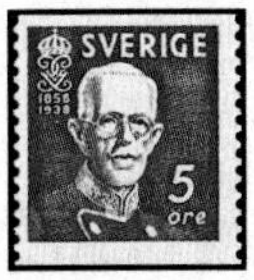

King Gustaf V — A54

1938, June 16 *Perf. 12½ Vert.*
275 A54 5o green .40 .30
276 A54 15(o) brown .45 .30
277 A54 30(o) ultra 5.00 .75

Perf. 12½

278 A54 5o green .85 .40
a. Perf. on 3 sides 5.00 5.50
Never hinged 22.50
b. Booklet pane of 10 45.00
279 A54 15(o) brown 1.00 .40
a. Perf. on 3 sides 7.00 1.40
Never hinged 35.00
b. Booklet pane of 10 37.50
Nos. 275-279 (5) 7.70 2.15
Set, never hinged 37.00

80th birthday of King Gustaf V.

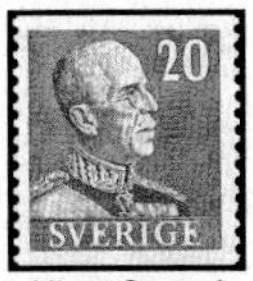

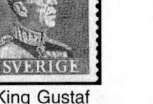

King Gustaf V — A55

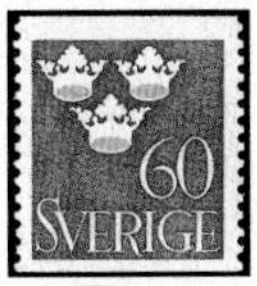

Three Crowns — A56

1939 *Perf. 12½ Vertically*
280 A55 10o violet .40 .40
281 A55 20o carmine 1.00 .60
282 A56 60o lake .40 .30
283 A56 85o dk green .30 .30
284 A56 90o peacock blue .30 .30
285 A56 1k orange .30 .30
286 A56 1.15k henna brn .30 .30
287 A56 1.20k brt rose vio .80 .30
288 A56 1.45k lt yel grn .85 .80

Perf. 12½

289 A55 10o violet 1.00 4.00
a. Perf. on 3 sides 25.00 65.00
Never hinged 80.00
b. Bklt. pane of 10, perf. on 4 sides 30.00
Nos. 280-289 (10) 5.65 7.60
Set, never hinged 20.00

See Nos. 394-398, 416-417, 425-426, 431, 439-441, 473, 588-591, 656-664.

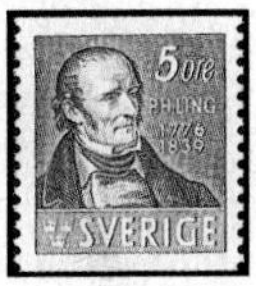

Per Henrik Ling — A57

1939, Feb. 25 *Perf. 12½ Vert.*
290 A57 5o green .25 .25
291 A57 25(o) brown .40 .40

Perf. 12½

292 A57 5o green .40 .40
a. Perf. on 3 sides 6.00 6.00
Never hinged 29.00
b. Booklet pane of 10 37.50
Nos. 290-292 (3) 1.05 1.05
Set, never hinged 4.00

Centenary of the death of P. H. Ling, father of Swedish gymnastics.

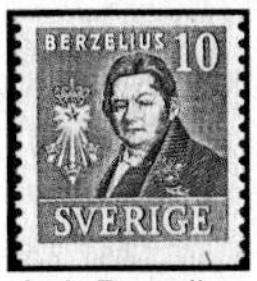

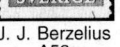

J. J. Berzelius A58

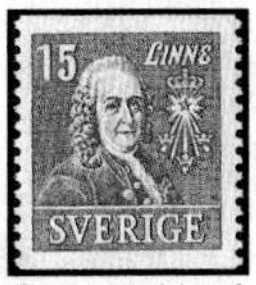

Carl von Linné A59

Perf. 12½ Vertically

1939, June 2 **Engr.**
293 A58 10o violet 1.00 .40
294 A59 15o fawn .25 .30
295 A58 30o ultra 6.00 .45
296 A59 50o gray 6.50 1.00

Perf. 12½

297 A58 10o violet .90 .65
a. Perf. on 3 sides 25.00 19.00
Never hinged 135.00
b. Booklet pane of 10 65.00
298 A59 15o fawn 1.00 .50
a. Perf. on 3 sides 5.00 .45
Never hinged 20.00
b. Booklet pane of 10 100.00
c. As "a," bklt. pane of 20 450.00
Nos. 293-298 (6) 15.65 3.30
Set, never hinged 70.00

200th anniv. of the founding of the Royal Academy of Science at Stockholm.

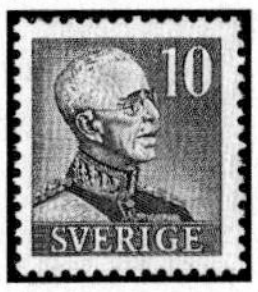

King Gustaf V — A60

Type A55 Re-engraved

1939-46 *Perf. 12½*
299 A60 5o dp green ('46) .30 .30
b. Perf. on 3 sides ('41) .30 .30
Never hinged .50
c. As "b," bklt. pane of 20 12.00
300 A60 10(o) violet ('46) .30 .30
a. Bklt. pane of 10, perf. on 4 sides 55.00
Never hinged .50
c. Perf. on 3 sides 2.00 .30
i. As "c," booklet pane of 20 50.00
300D A60 15(o) chestnut ('46) .30 .30
f. Perf. on 3 sides ('45) .30 .30
Never hinged .65
j. As "f," booklet pane of 20 7.75
300G A60 20(o) red ('42) .30 .25
h. Booklet pane of 20 6.50
Nos. 299-300G (4) 1.20 1.15
Set, never hinged 1.50

No. 300 differs slightly from the original due to deeper engraving. No. 300G was issued only in booklets; all examples have one straight edge.

Nos. 299, 300, 300D exist in booklet panes of 20 made from sheets of stamps. These can be collected as booklets.

1940-42 *Perf. 12½ Vertically*
301 A60 5o dp green ('41) .25 .30
302 A60 10(o) violet .25 .30
302A A60 15(o) chestnut ('42) .25 .30
303 A60 20(o) red .25 .30
304 A60 25(o) orange .40 .30
305 A60 30(o) ultra .40 .30
306 A60 35(o) red vio ('41) .40 .30
307 A60 40(o) olive grn .40 .30
308 A60 45(o) dk brown .40 .30
309 A60 50(o) gray blk ('41) 2.75 .30
Nos. 301-309 (10) 5.75 3.00
Set, never hinged 13.00

Numerals measure 4½mm high. Less shading around head gives a lighter effect. Horizontal lines only as background for "SVERIGE."

See Nos. 391-393, 399.

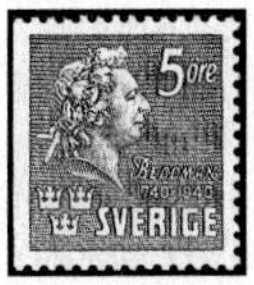

Carl Michael Bellman — A61

1940, Feb. 4 **Engr.** *Perf. 12½ Vert.*
310 A61 5o green .25 .25
311 A61 35(o) rose red .40 .40

Perf. 12½

312 A61 5o green .50 *.60*
a. Perf. on 3 sides 2.25 .75
Never hinged 21.00
b. Booklet pane of 10 50.00
c. As "a," bklt. pane of 20 425.00
Nos. 310-312 (3) 1.15 1.25
Set, never hinged 3.75

Bellman (1740-95), lyric poet.

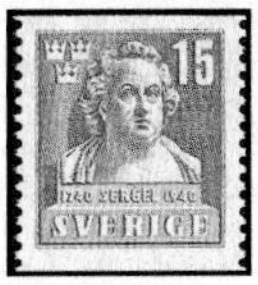

Tobias Sergel — A62

1940, Sept. 5 *Perf. 12½ on 3 Sides*
313 A62 15o lt brown 3.00 .50
a. Booklet pane of 20 275.00

Perf. 12½ Vertically

314 A62 15o lt brown .75 .40
315 A62 50o gray black 5.00 1.40
Nos. 313-315 (3) 8.75 2.30
Set, never hinged 70.00

Bicentenary of birth of Johan Tobias von Sergel (1740-1814), sculptor.

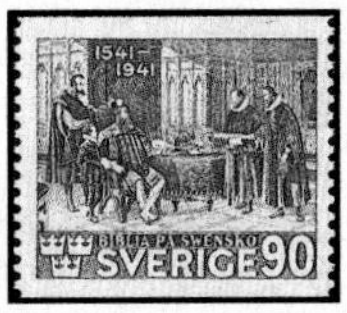

Reformers Presenting Bible to Gustavus Vasa — A63

1941, May 11 *Perf. 12½ on 3 Sides*
316 A63 15o brown 2.75 .45
a. Booklet pane of 18 90.00

Perf. 12½ Vertically

317 A63 15o brown .30 .25
318 A63 90o ultra 19.00 .95
Nos. 316-318 (3) 22.05 1.65
Set, never hinged 50.00

400th anniv. of the 1st authorized version of the Bible in Swedish.

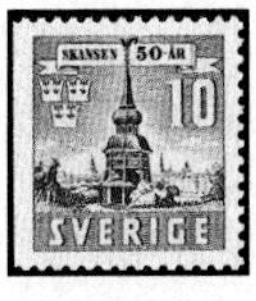

View of Skansen — A64

1941, June 18 *Perf. 12½ on 3 Sides*
319 A64 10o violet 2.50 .65
a. Booklet pane of 20 85.00

Perf. 12½ Vertically

320 A64 10o violet 3.00 .25
321 A64 60o red lilac 8.00 .60
Nos. 319-321 (3) 13.50 1.50
Set, never hinged 35.00

50th anniv. of Skansen, an open air extension of the Nordic Museum.

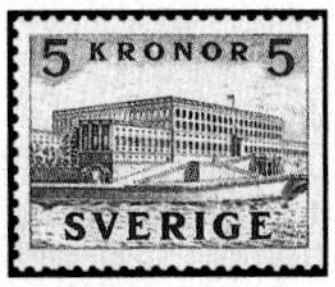

Royal Palace at Stockholm — A65

1941 *Perf. 12½ on 3 Sides*
322 A65 5k blue 1.50 .25
Never hinged 2.50
a. Perf. on 4 sides 25.00 1.00
Never hinged 70.00
b. Bklt. pane of 20, perf. 3 sides 50.00
c. Bklt. pane of 10, perf. 4 sides 575.00

For coil stamp see No. 537.

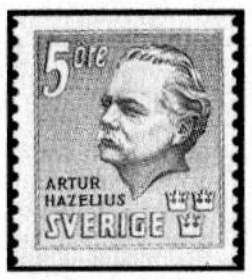

Artur Hazelius — A66

1941, Aug. 30 *Perf. 12½ on 3 Sides*
323 A66 5o lt green 2.50 .55
a. Booklet pane of 20 100.00

Perf. 12½ Vertically

324 A66 5o lt green .25 .25
325 A66 1k lt orange 7.00 4.00
Nos. 323-325 (3) 9.75 4.80
Set, never hinged 28.00

Issued to honor Artur Hazelius, founder of Skansen, Nordic museum.

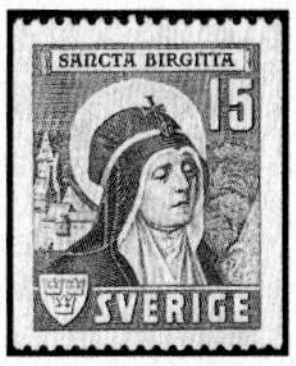

St. Bridget of Sweden — A67

Perf. 12½ on 3 Sides

1941, Oct. 7 **Engr.**
326 A67 15o deep brown 1.90 .40
a. Booklet pane of 18 60.00

Perf. 12½ Horiz.

327 A67 15o deep brown .25 .25
328 A67 1.20k red vio 21.00 10.50
Nos. 326-328 (3) 23.15 11.15
Set, never hinged 65.00

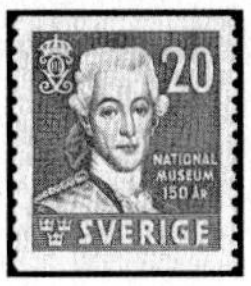

King Gustavus III — A68

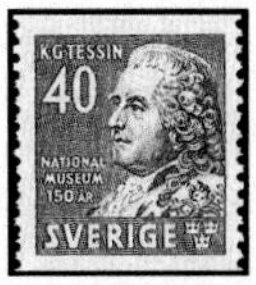

K. G. Tessin, Architect — A69

1942, June 29 *Perf. 12½ on 3 Sides*
329 A68 20o red 1.25 .45
a. Booklet pane of 20 45.00

Perf. 12½ Vertically

330 A68 20o red .60 .25
331 A69 40o olive green 14.00 1.25
Nos. 329-331 (3) 15.85 1.95
Set, never hinged 40.00

Sesquicentennial of the Swedish National Museum, Stockholm.

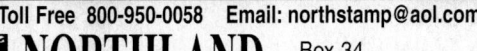

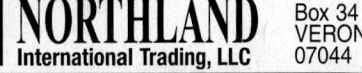

Torsten Rudenschold and Nils Mansson — A70

1942, July 1   *Perf. 12½ Horiz.*
332 A70 10o magenta   .25 .40
   a. Booklet pane of 10   3.50

Perf. 12½ Vertically
333 A70 10o magenta   .25 .35
334 A70 90o light blue   2.50 6.00
   Nos. 332-334 (3)   3.00 6.75
   Set, never hinged   5.00

Swedish Public School System, 100th anniv.

Carl Wilhelm Scheele — A71

1942, Dec. 9   *Perf. 12½ on 3 Sides*
335 A71 5o green   1.50 1.00
   a. Booklet pane of 20   55.00

Perf. 12½ Vertically
336 A71 5o green   .25 .25
337 A71 60o deep magenta   7.00 .60
   Nos. 335-337 (3)   8.75 1.85
   Set, never hinged   17.50

200th anniv. of the birth of Carl Wilhelm Scheele, chemist.

King Gustaf V — A72

Perf. 12½ Horizontally
1943, June 16
338 A72 20o red   .60 .45
339 A72 30o ultra   .90 2.50
340 A72 60o brt red vio   1.10 3.25

Perf. 12½ on 3 Sides
341 A72 20o red   4.50 1.10
   a. Booklet pane of 20   160.00
   Nos. 338-341 (4)   7.10 7.30
   Set, never hinged   16.00

85th birthday of King Gustaf V, June 16.

Rifle Federation Emblem — A73

1943, July 22   *Perf. 12½ Vert.*
342 A73 10o rose violet   .25 .25
343 A73 90o dp ultra   3.75 .45

Perf. 12½ on 3 Sides
344 A73 10o rose violet   .40 .40
   a. Booklet pane of 20   12.50
   Nos. 342-344 (3)   4.40 1.10
   Set, never hinged   11.00

50th anniversary of the Swedish Voluntary Rifle Associations.

Oscar Montelius — A74

1943, Sept. 9 Engr.   *Perf. 12½ Vert.*
345 A74 5o green   .25 .25
346 A74 1.20k brt red vio   6.00 2.50

Perf. 12½ on 3 Sides
347 A74 5o green   .55 .40
   a. Booklet pane of 20   19.00
   Nos. 345-347 (3)   6.80 3.15
   Set, never hinged   11.50

Montelius (1843-1921), archaeologist.

Johan Mansson's Chart of Baltic, 1644 — A75

Perf. 12½ on 3 Sides
1944, Apr. 15   Engr.   Unwmk.
348 A75 5o green   .60 .80
   a. Booklet pane of 20   25.00

Perf. 12½ Vertically
349 A75 5o green   .25 .25
350 A75 60o lake   4.25 .80
   Nos. 348-350 (3)   5.10 1.85
   Set, never hinged   12.00

1st Swedish Marine Chart, tercentenary.

"The Lion of Smaland"   Clas Fleming
A76   A77

30o, "Kung Karl." 40o,Stern of "Amphion," Flagship of Gustavus III. 90o, "Gustaf V."

1944, Oct. 13   *Perf. 12½ Vert.*
351 A76 10o purple   .35 .35
352 A77 20o red   .30 .25
353 A76 30o blue   .50 .80
354 A76 40o olive green   .60 1.25
355 A76 90o gray black   6.50 2.25

Perf. 12½ on 3 Sides
356 A76 10o purple   .60 2.00
   a. Booklet pane of 20   24.00
357 A77 20o red   2.25 .35
   a. Booklet pane of 20   90.00
   Nos. 351-357 (7)   11.10 7.25
   Set, never hinged   30.00

Issued to honor the Swedish Fleet and mark the tercentenary of the Swedish naval victory at Femern, 1644.
See Nos. B53, B57-B58.

> Catalogue values for unused stamps in this section, from this point to the end of the section, are for Never Hinged items.

Red Cross — A81

1945, Feb. 27   *Perf. 12½ Vert.*
358 A81 20o red   .60 .25

Perf. 12½ on 3 Sides
359 A81 20o red   3.00 .40
   a. Booklet pane of 20   65.00

Swedish Red Cross Society, 80th anniv.

Torch and Quill Pen — A82

1945, May 29   *Perf. 12½ Vert.*
360 A82 5o green   .25 .25
361 A82 60o carmine rose   7.00 .45

Perf. 12½ on 3 Sides
362 A82 5o green   .35 .45
   a. Booklet pane of 20   7.75
   Nos. 360-362 (3)   7.60 1.15

Tercentenary of Swedish press.

Rydberg — A83

1945, Sept. 21   *Perf. 12½ Vert.*
363 A83 20o red   .35 .25
364 A83 90o blue   7.00 .45

Perf. 12½ on 3 Sides
365 A83 20o red   1.50 .45
   a. Booklet pane of 20   32.50
   Nos. 363-365 (3)   8.85 1.15

Viktor Rydberg (1828-95), author.

Oak Tree — A84

1945, Oct. 27   *Perf. 12½ Vert.*
366 A84 10o violet   .25 .35
367 A84 40o olive   1.60 1.25

Perf. 12½ on 3 Sides
368 A84 10o violet   .40 .70
   a. Booklet pane of 20   10.00
   Nos. 366-368 (3)   2.25 2.30

125th anniv. of the Savings Bank movement.

Angel and Lund   View of Lund
Cathedral   Cathedral
A85   A86

Perf. 12½ Vertically
1946, May 28   Unwmk.
369 A85 15o orange brn   .70 .55
370 A86 20o red   .30 .25
371 A85 90o ultra   9.25 .85

Perf. 12½ on 3 Sides
372 A85 15o orange brn   .95 1.10
   a. Booklet pane of 20   19.00
373 A86 20o red   2.25 .45
   a. Booklet pane of 20   45.00
   Nos. 369-373 (5)   13.45 3.20

Lund Cathedral, 800th anniversary.

Mare and Colt — A87

1946, June 8   *Perf. 12½ Vert.*
374 A87 5o green   .25 .25
375 A87 60o carmine rose   8.25 .40

Perf. 12½ on 3 Sides
376 A87 5o green   .30 .45
   a. Booklet pane of 20   6.50
   Nos. 374-376 (3)   8.80 1.10

Centenary of Swedish agricultural shows.

Esaias Tegner — A88

Perf. 12½ Vertically
1946, Nov. 2   Engr.   Unwmk.
377 A88 10o deep violet   .25 .25
378 A88 40o dk olive grn   1.40 .45

Perf. 12½ on 3 Sides
379 A88 10o dp violet   .30 .25
   a. Booklet pane of 20   6.00
   Nos. 377-379 (3)   1.95 .95

Esaias Tegner (1782-1846), poet.

Nobel — A89

1946, Dec. 10   *Perf. 12½ Vert.*
380 A89 20o red   .80 .25
381 A89 30o ultra   2.25 .60

Perf. 12½ on 3 Sides
382 A89 20o red   1.90 .55
   a. Booklet pane of 20   40.00
   Nos. 380-382 (3)   4.95 1.40

50th anniversary of the death of Alfred Nobel, inventor and philanthropist.

Geijer — A90

1947, Apr. 23   *Perf. 12½ Vert.*
383 A90 5o dk yellow grn   .25 .25
384 A90 90o ultra   5.00 .25

Perf. 12½ on 3 Sides
385 A90 5o dk yellow grn   .30 .45
   a. Booklet pane of 20   7.00
   Nos. 383-385 (3)   5.55 .95

Centenary of the death of Erik Gustaf Geijer, historian, philosopher and poet.

King Gustaf V — A91

1947, Dec. 8 Engr.   *Perf. 12½ Horiz.*
386 A91 10o deep violet   .25 .25
387 A91 20o red   .25 .25
388 A91 60o red violet   1.40 1.40

Perf. 12½ on 3 Sides
389 A91 10o deep violet   .25 .30
   a. Booklet pane of 20   4.00
390 A91 20o red   .40 .40
   a. Booklet pane of 20   8.00
   Nos. 386-390 (5)   2.55 2.60

40th anniv. of the reign of King Gustaf V.

King and 3-Crown Types of 1939
1948   Unwmk.   *Perf. 12½ Vertically*
391 A60   5o orange   .25 .25
392 A60   10o green   .30 .25
393 A60   25o violet   1.50 .25
394 A56   55o orange brown   1.40 .25
395 A56   80o olive green   .80 .25
396 A56   1.10k violet   7.00 .25
397 A56   1.40k dk blue green   .80 .25
398 A56   1.75k brt grnsh blue   12.50 6.75

Perf. 12½ on 3 Sides
399 A60   10o green   .25 .25
   a. Booklet pane of 20   6.00
   Nos. 391-399 (9)   24.80 8.75

Plowman, Early and Modern Buildings — A92

1948, Apr. 26   *Perf. 12½ Vert.*
400 A92 15o orange brown   .25 .25
401 A92 30o ultra   .50 .55
402 A92 1k orange   1.50 1.25

Perf. 12½ on 3 Sides
403 A92 15o orange brown   .40 .50
   a. Booklet pane of 20   8.50
   Nos. 400-403 (4)   2.65 2.55

Centenary of the Swedish pioneers' settlement in the United States.

August Strindberg — A93

1949, Jan. 22   *Perf. 12½ Vert.*
404 A93 20o red   .45 .25
405 A93 30o blue   .80 .75
406 A93 80o olive green   2.75 .45

Perf. 12½ on 3 Sides

407 A93 20o red .80 .35
a. Booklet pane of 20 16.00
Nos. 404-407 (4) 4.80 1.80

Birth centenary of August Strindberg (1849-1912), author and playwright.

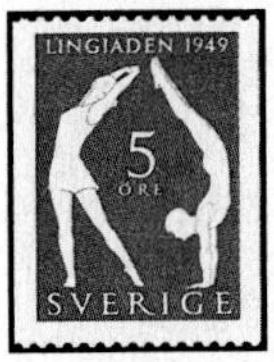

Girl and Boy Gymnasts — A94

Perf. 12½ Horiz.

1949, July 27 **Engr.**

408 A94 5o ultra .30 *.45*
409 A94 15o brown .35 .25

Perf. 12½ on 3 Sides

410 A94 15o brown .45 .65
a. Booklet pane of 20 9.00
Nos. 408-410 (3) 1.10 1.35

2nd Lingiad or World Gymnastics Festival, Stockholm, July-August 1949.

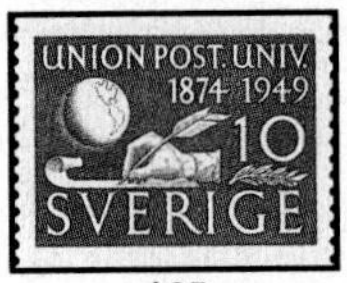

A95

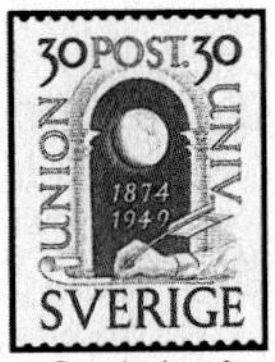

Symbols of UPU — A96

1949, Oct. 9 ***Perf. 12½ Vert.***

411 A95 10o green .25 .25
412 A95 20o red .30 .25

Perf. 12½ Horizontally

413 A96 30o lt blue .40 .65

Perf. 12½ on 3 sides

414 A95 10o green .25 .25
a. Booklet pane of 20 3.50
415 A95 20o red .25 .25
a. Booklet pane of 20 4.00
Nos. 411-415 (5) 1.45 1.65

75th anniv. of the formation of the UPU.

Three-Crown Type of 1939

Perf. 12½ Vertically

1949, Nov. 11 **Unwmk.**

416 A56 65o lt yellow grn .75 .30
417 A56 70o peacock blue 4.00 1.25

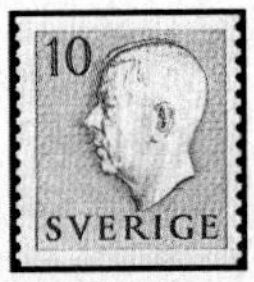

Gustaf VI Adolf (Letters in color) — A97

Without Imprint

1951, June 6 ***Perf. 12½ Vert.***

418 A97 10o dull green .25 .25
419 A97 15o chestnut brown .35 .25
420 A97 20o carmine rose .35 .25
421 A97 25o gray .65 .25
422 A97 30o ultra .45 .25

Perf. 12½ on 3 sides

423 A97 10o dull green .40 .25
a. Booklet pane of 20 8.00
424 A97 25o gray .50 .25
a. Booklet pane of 20 12.00
Nos. 418-424 (7) 2.95 1.75

See Nos. 435-438, 442-443, 456-461, 502, 505-509, 515-517.

Three-Crown Type of 1939

1951, June 1 ***Perf. 12½ Vert.***

425 A56 85o orange brown 5.75 1.60
426 A56 1.70k red 1.25 .25

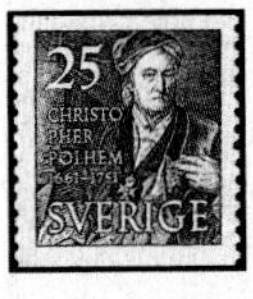

Christopher Polhem — A98

1951, Aug. 30 ***Perf. 12½ Vert.***

427 A98 25o gray 1.40 .25
428 A98 45o brown .55 .40

Perf. 12½ on 3 sides

429 A98 25o gray .45 .30
a. Booklet pane of 20 9.00
Nos. 427-429 (3) 2.40 .95

200th anniversary of the death of Christopher Polhem, engineer and technician.

Three Crown Type of 1939 and

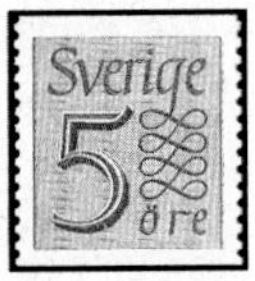

Numeral (Lettering in color) — A99

1951, Nov. **Engr.** ***Perf. 12½ Vert.***

430 A99 5o rose carmine .25 .25
431 A56 1.50k red violet 1.60 1.25

For other stamps similar to type A99, see type A115a, Nos. 503-504, 513-514, 570, 580, 666-667.

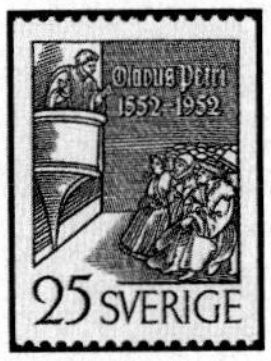

Olaus Petri Preaching — A100

1952, Apr. 19 ***Perf. 12½ Horiz.***

432 A100 25o gray black .45 .25
433 A100 1.40k brown 3.00 .80

Perf. 12½ on 3 sides

434 A100 25o gray black 2.00 2.60
a. Booklet pane of 20 50.00
Nos. 432-434 (3) 5.45 3.65

Olaus Petri (1493-1552), Lutheran clergyman, historian and Bible translator.

King and 3-Crown Types of 1951 and 1939

1952 ***Perf. 12½ Vertically***

Without Imprint

435 A97 20o gray .30 .25
436 A97 25o car rose 1.25 .25
437 A97 30o dk brown .50 .40
438 A97 40o blue 1.00 .40
439 A56 50o gray 1.75 .25
440 A56 75o orange brown 2.75 .80
441 A56 2k red violet .90 .25

Perf. 12½ on 3 sides

442 A97 20o gray .55 .60
a. Booklet pane of 20 15.00
443 A97 25o carmine rose 1.25 .40
a. Booklet pane of 20 27.50
Nos. 435-443 (9) 10.25 3.60

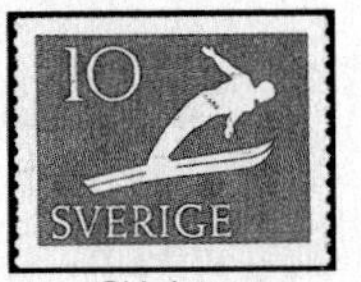

Ski Jump A101

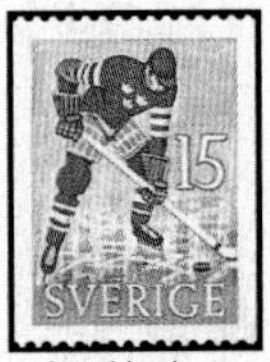

Ice Hockey A102

40o, Woman throwing slingball. 1.40kr, Wrestlers.

Perf. 12½ Vert. (V), Horiz. (H)

1953, May 27

444 A101 10o green (V) .50 .25
445 A102 15o brown (H) .75 *1.10*
446 A102 40o deep blue (H) 1.50 *1.60*
447 A101 1.40k red violet (V) 4.50 1.25

Perf. 12½ on 3 sides

448 A101 10o green .75 1.10
a. Booklet pane of 20 17.50
Nos. 444-448 (5) 8.00 5.30

50th anniv. of Swedish Athletic Association.

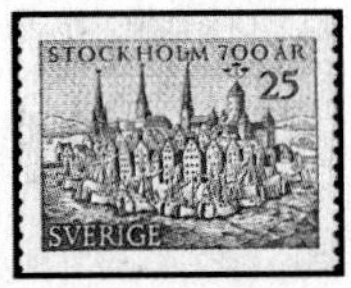

Old Stockholm A103

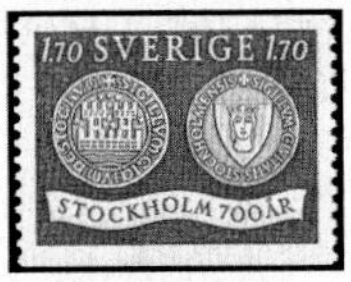

Original and Present Seals of Stockholm A104

1953, June 17 ***Perf. 12½ Vert.***

449 A103 25o blue .40 .25
450 A104 1.70k red 2.75 .75

Perf. 12½ on 3 sides

451 A103 25o blue .80 .30
a. Booklet pane of 20 17.50
Nos. 449-451 (3) 3.95 1.30

700th anniv. of the founding of Stockholm.

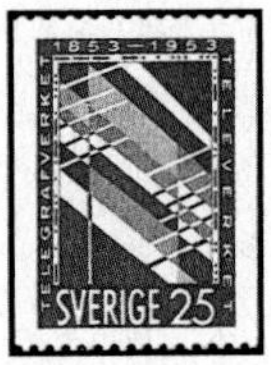

"Telephone" — A105

1953, Nov. 2 ***Perf. 12½ Horiz.***

452 A105 25o shown .30 .25
453 A105 40o "Radio" 1.50 *1.60*
454 A105 60o "Telegraph" 3.00 2.75

Perf. 12½ on 3 sides

455 A105 25o shown .85 .50
a. Booklet pane of 20 20.00
Nos. 452-455 (4) 5.65 5.10

Centenary of the foundation of the Swedish Telegraph Service.

King Type of 1951

1954 ***Perf. 12½ Vertically***

Without Imprint

456 A97 10o dark brown .25 .25
457 A97 25o ultra .25 .25
458 A97 30o red 9.00 .25
459 A97 40o olive green .60 .25

Perf. 12½ on 3 sides

460 A97 10o dark brown .25 .25
a. Booklet pane of 10 9.00
b. Booklet pane of 20 7.50
461 A97 25o ultra .25 .25
a. Booklet pane of 4 10.00 11.00
b. Booklet pane of 8 100.00 —
c. Booklet pane of 20 10.00 —
Nos. 456-461 (6) 10.60 1.50

The booklet pane of 4 contains two copies of No. 461 which are perforated on two adjoining sides.

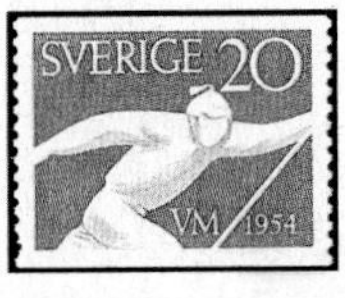

Skier — A106

1954, Feb. 13 ***Perf. 12½ Vert.***

462 A106 20o shown .50 .45
463 A106 1k Girl skier 8.50 1.25

Perf. 12½ on 3 sides

464 A106 20o shown 1.25 *1.90*
a. Booklet pane of 20 35.00
Nos. 462-464 (3) 10.25 3.60

World Ski Championship Matches, 1954.

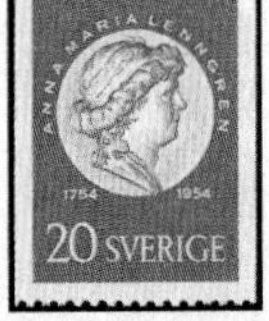

Anna Maria Lenngren — A107

1954, June 18 ***Perf. 12½ Horiz.***

465 A107 20o gray .30 .30
466 A107 65o dark brown 5.50 3.75

Perf. 12½ on 3 sides

467 A107 20o gray 1.25 1.90
a. Booklet pane of 20 35.00
Nos. 465-467 (3) 7.05 5.95

200th anniversary of the birth of Anna Maria Lenngren, author.

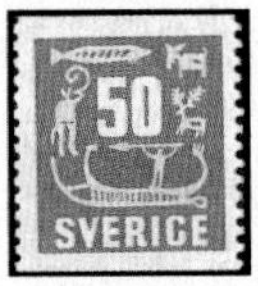

Rock Carvings — A108

1954, Nov. 8 ***Perf. 12½ Vert.***

468 A108 50o gray .30 .25
469 A108 60o dp carmine .50 .25
470 A108 65o dk olive grn 1.25 .25
471 A108 75o dk brown 2.00 .25
472 A108 90o dk blue .60 .25
Nos. 468-472 (5) 4.65 1.25

See Nos. 510-512, 655.

Three-Crown Type of 1939

1954, Dec. 10 ***Perf. 12½ Vert.***

473 A56 2.10k dp ultra 7.50 .50

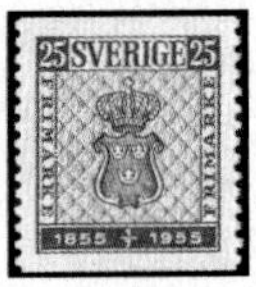

Coat of Arms — A109

1955, May 16 ***Perf. 12½ Vert.***

474 A109 25o blue .25 .25
475 A109 40o green 1.25 .35

Perf. 12½ on 3 sides

476 A109 25o blue .25 .25
a. Booklet pane of 4 9.00 8.50
b. Booklet pane of 20 4.00 —
Nos. 474-476 (3) 1.75 .85

Centenary of Sweden's 1st postage stamps.

The booklet pane of 4 contains two copies of No. 476 which are perforated on two adjoining sides.

Crown and Flag — A110

Perf. 12½

1955, June 6 **Unwmk.** **Litho.**

477 A110 10o green, bl & yel .25 .30
478 A110 15o lake, bl & yel .30 .40

National Flag Day.

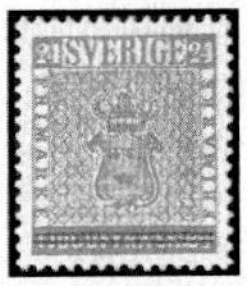

A111

Wmk. 307

1955, July 1 **Typo.** ***Perf. 13***

479 A111 3o yellow green 2.25 *5.00*
480 A111 4o blue 2.25 *5.00*
481 A111 6o gray 2.25 *5.00*
482 A111 8o orange yellow 2.25 *5.00*
483 A111 24o salmon 2.25 *5.00*
Nos. 479-483 (5) 11.25 25.00

Cent. of the 1st Swedish postage stamps. Nos. 479-483 were printed in sheets of nine. They were sold in complete sets at the Stockholmia Philatelic Exhibition, July 1-10, 1955. A set cost 45 ore (face value) plus 2k (entrance fee).

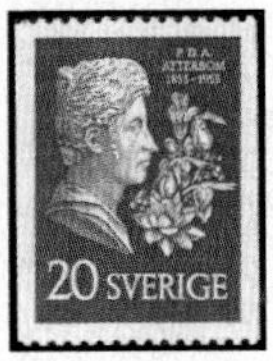

Per Atterbom — A112

Perf. 12½ Horizontally

1955, July 21 **Engr.** **Unwmk.**

484 A112 20o dark blue .40 .30
485 A112 1.40k sepia 4.00 .80

Perf. 12½ on 3 sides

486 A112 20o dark blue 1.25 *1.40*
a. Booklet pane of 20 35.00
Nos. 484-486 (3) 5.65 2.50

Cent. of the death of Per Daniel Amadeus Atterbom, poet.

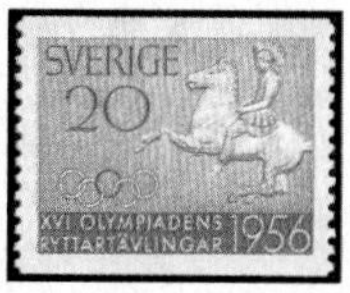

Greek Horseman A113

1956, Apr. 16 ***Perf. 12½ Vert.***

487 A113 20o carmine .85 .60
488 A113 25o ultra .85 .25
489 A113 40o gray green 4.00 2.10

Perf. 12½ on 3 sides

490 A113 20o carmine .40 *.70*
a. Booklet pane of 20 10.00
491 A113 25o ultra .40 .25
a. Booklet pane of 20 10.00
Nos. 487-491 (5) 6.50 3.90

Issued to publicize the Olympic Equestrian Competitions, Stockholm, June 10-17, 1956.

Northern Countries Issue

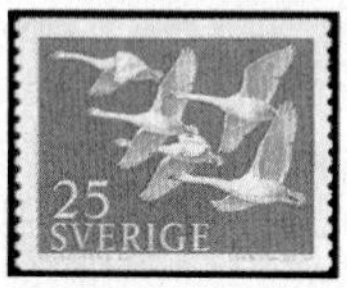

Whooper Swans — A113a

Perf. 12½ Vertically

1956, Oct. 30 **Engr.** **Unwmk.**

492 A113a 25o rose red .25 .25
493 A113a 40o ultra .75 .65

See footnote after Norway No. 354.

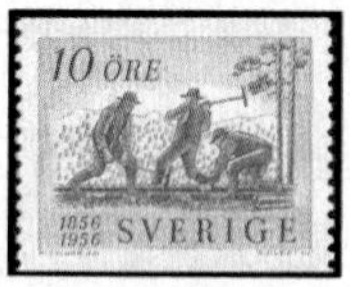

Railroad Builders — A114

Designs: 25o, First Swedish locomotive and passenger car. 40o, Express train crossing Arsta bridge.

1956, Dec. 1 ***Perf. 12½ Vert.***

494 A114 10o olive green .60 .25
495 A114 25o ultra .25 .25
496 A114 40o orange 3.00 *3.00*

Perf. 12½ on 3 sides

497 A114 10o olive green .45 .45
a. Booklet pane of 20 11.00
498 A114 25o ultra .75 .45
a. Booklet pane of 20 18.00
Nos. 494-498 (5) 5.05 4.40

Centenary of Swedish railroads.

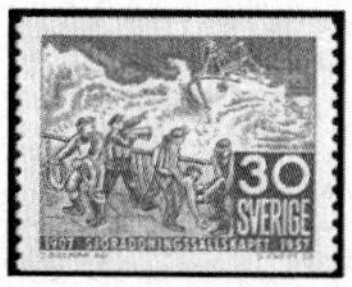

Ship in Distress and Lifeboat — A115

Perf. 12½ Vertically

1957, June 1 **Engr.** **Unwmk.**

499 A115 30o blue 3.75 .25
500 A115 1.40k deep rose 6.00 1.25

Perf. 12½ on 3 sides

501 A115 30o blue 1.60 1.50
a. Booklet pane of 20 45.00
Nos. 499-501 (3) 11.35 3.00

Swedish Life Saving Society, 50th anniv.

King Type of 1951

1957, June 1 ***Perf. 12½ Vert.***

Without Imprint

502 A97 25o dark brown 1.10 *1.75*

Re-engraved Types of 1951 & 1954 with Imprint, and

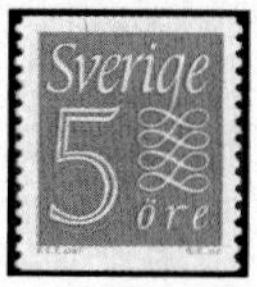

Numeral (Letters in white) — A115a

1957-64 ***Perf. 12½ Vertically***

503 A115a 5o red ('61) .25 .25
a. 5o dark red .25 .25
504 A115a 10o blue ('61) .25 .25
a. 10o dark blue .30 .25
505 A97 15o dark red .30 .25
506 A97 20o gray .25 .25
507 A97 25o brown .60 .25
508 A97 30o blue .45 .25
509 A97 40o olive green 1.25 .25
510 A108 55o vermilion 1.25 .25
511 A108 70o orange .60 .25
512 A108 80o yellow green .80 .25

Perf. 12½ on 3 sides

513 A115a 5o red ('61) .25 .25
a. Bklt. pane of 20 ('64) 2.00
Complete booklet, #513a 2.00
b. 5o dark red 5.00 1.00
c. Bklt. pane, 5 #513b, 5 #515 22.50
514 A115a 10o blue ('61) .25 .25
a. 10o dark blue 20.00 2.50
b. Bklt. pane, #514a, 3 #517 37.50 18.00
515 A97 15o dark red .60 .25
a. Bklt. pane of 20 12.00
516 A97 20o gray 1.00 .60
a. Bklt. pane of 20 30.00
517 A97 30o blue .75 .25
a. Bklt. pane of 20 35.00
Nos. 503-517 (15) 8.85 4.10

In the redrawn Numeral type A99, "Sverige, ore" and the "g" tail flourishes are white instead of in color.

Booklet pane including #513 is listed as #581b.

The booklet pane of 4, No. 514b, contains two copies of No. 517 which are imperf. on two adjoining sides. No. 514a was issued only in booklet pane No. 514b.

See Nos. 570, 580, 580a, 581b, 584b, 586b-586c, 666-667, 668a, 669b-669c.

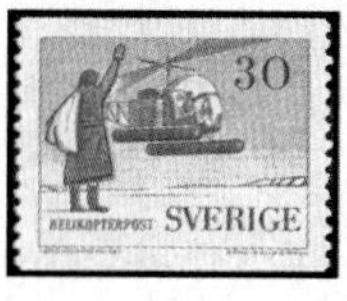

Helicopter Mail Service — A116

Perf. 12½ Vertically

1958, Feb. 10 **Engr.** **Unwmk.**

518 A116 30o blue .40 .25
519 A116 1.40k brown 4.50 1.00

Perf. 12½ on 3 sides

520 A116 30o blue .80 .55
a. Booklet pane of 20 20.00
Nos. 518-520 (3) 5.70 1.80

10th anniversary of helicopter mail service to the Stockholm archipelago, Feb. 10.

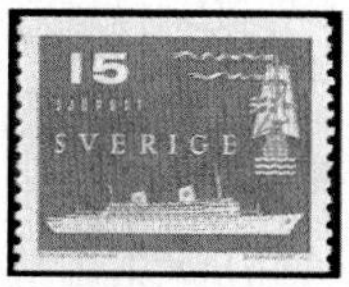

Modern and 17th Century Vessels — A117

1958, Feb. 10 ***Perf. 12½ Vert.***

521 A117 15o dark red .40 .25
522 A117 40o gray olive 4.25 3.25

Perf. 12½ on 3 sides

523 A117 15o dark red .50 .60
a. Booklet pane of 20 12.00
Nos. 521-523 (3) 5.15 4.10

3 centuries of transatlantic mail service.

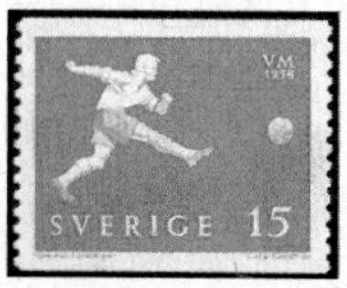

Soccer Player — A118

1958, May 8 ***Perf. 12½ Vert.***

524 A118 15o vermilion .85 .25
525 A118 20o yellow green .50 .25
526 A118 1.20k dark blue 1.90 1.10

Perf. 12½ on 3 sides

527 A118 15o vermilion .55 .45
a. Booklet pane of 20 9.00
528 A118 20o yellow green .50 *.65*
a. Booklet pane of 20 12.00
Nos. 524-528 (5) 4.30 2.70

Issued to publicize the 6th World Soccer Championships, Stockholm, June 8-29.

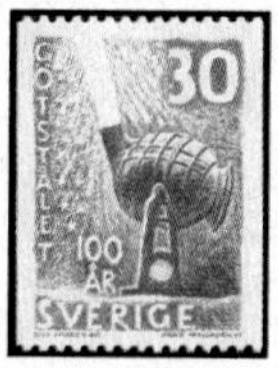

Bessemer Converter — A119

Perf. 12½ Horizontally

1958, July 18 **Engr.** **Unwmk.**

529 A119 30o gray blue .35 .25
530 A119 1.70k dull red brown 3.00 .95

Perf. 12½ on 3 sides

531 A119 30o gray blue .65 .55
a. Booklet pane of 20 15.00
Nos. 529-531 (3) 4.00 1.75

Centenary of the first successful Bessemer blow in Sweden, July 18, 1858.

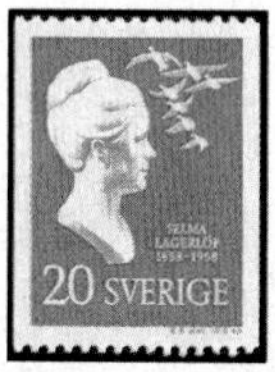

Selma Lagerlof — A120

1958, Nov. 20 ***Perf. 12½ Horiz.***

532 A120 20o dark red .30 .30
533 A120 30o blue .40 .25
534 A120 80o olive green .75 .90

Perf. 12½ on 3 Sides

535 A120 20o dark red .50 .75
a. Booklet pane of 20 13.00
536 A120 30o blue .50 .60
a. Booklet pane of 20 16.00
Nos. 532-536 (5) 2.45 2.80

Selma Lagerlof, writer, birth cent.

Palace Type of 1941

1958, Sept. 17 ***Perf. 12½ Vert.***

537 A65 5k blue 2.75 .25

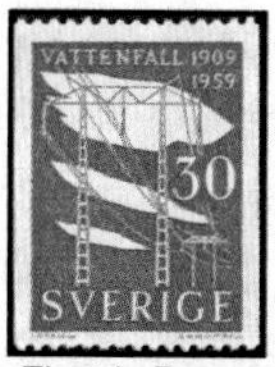

Electric Power Line — A121

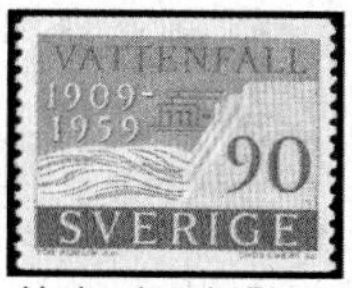

Hydroelectric Plant and Dam — A122

Perf. 12½ Horiz. (H), Vert. (V)

1959, Jan. 20 **Unwmk.**

538 A121 30o ultra (H) .45 .25
539 A122 90o carmine rose (V) 3.25 2.40

Perf. 12½ on 3 sides

540 A121 30o ultra .50 .50
a. Booklet pane of 20 14.00
Nos. 538-540 (3) 4.20 3.15

50th anniv. of the establishment of the State Power Board.

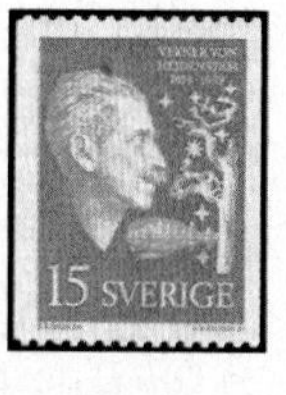

Verner von Heidenstam — A123

Perf. 12½ Horizontally

1959, July 6 **Engr.** **Unwmk.**

541 A123 15o rose carmine 1.00 .35
542 A123 1k slate 3.00 .90

Perf. 12½ on 3 Sides

543 A123 15o rose carmine .50 .95
a. Booklet pane of 20 13.00
Nos. 541-543 (3) 4.50 2.20

Verner von Heidenstam, poet, birth cent.

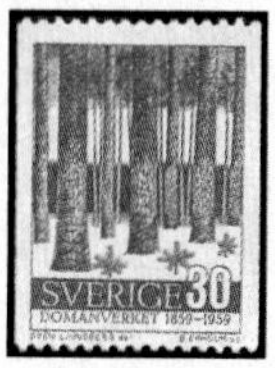

Forest — A124

Design: 1.40k, Felling tree.

1959, Sept. 4 ***Perf. 12½ Horiz.***

544 A124 30o green 1.50 .25
545 A124 1.40k brown red 3.50 .60

Perf. 12½ on 3 sides

546 A124 30o green 1.10 *1.10*
a. Booklet pane of 20 29.00
Nos. 544-546 (3) 6.10 1.95

Administration of crown lands and forests, cent.

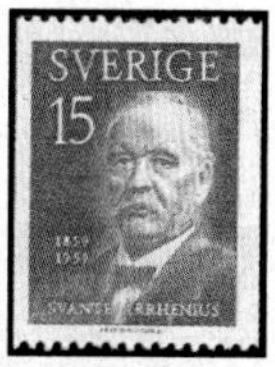

Svante Arrhenius — A125

Perf. 12½ Horizontally

1959, Dec. 10 **Engr.** **Unwmk.**

547 A125 15o dull red brown .25 .25
548 A125 1.70k dark blue 3.50 .45

Perf. 12½ on 3 sides

549 A125 15o dull red brown .45 .60
a. Booklet pane of 20 10.00
Nos. 547-549 (3) 4.20 1.30

Arrhenius (1859-1927), chemist and physicist.

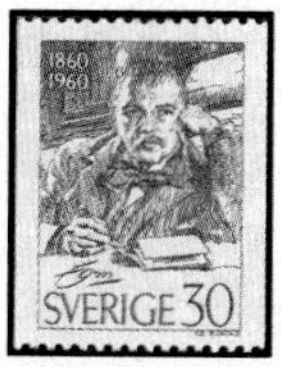

Anders Zorn — A126

1960, Feb. 18 ***Perf. 12½ Horiz.***

550 A126 30o gray .35 .25
551 A126 80o sepia 3.50 2.25

Perf. 12½ on 3 sides

552 A126 30o gray 1.60 .60
a. Booklet pane of 20 35.00
Nos. 550-552 (3) 5.45 3.10

Zorn (1860-1920), painter and sculptor.

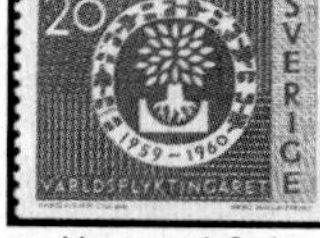

Uprooted Oak Emblem A127

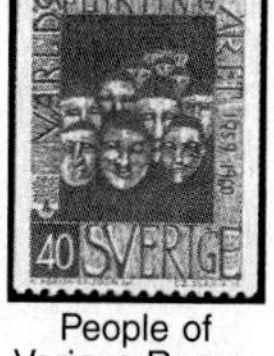

People of Various Races, WRY Emblem A128

Perf. 12½ Vert. (V), Horiz. (H)

1960, Apr. 7 **Engr.** **Unwmk.**

553 A127 20o red brown (V) .25 .25
554 A128 40o purple (H) .30 .30

Perf. 12½ on 3 sides

555 A127 20o red brown .50 .60
a. Booklet pane of 20 12.00
Nos. 553-555 (3) 1.05 1.15

World Refugee Year, 7/1/59-6/30/60.

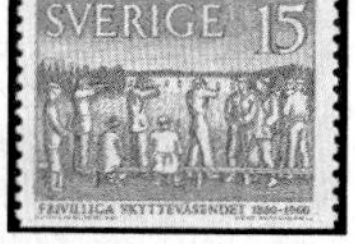

Target Shooting A129

Design: 90o, Parade of riflemen.

1960, June 30   *Perf. 12½ Vert.*

556 A129 15o rose carmine   .30 .25
557 A129 90o grnsh blue   2.50 2.00

Perf. 12½ on 3 sides

558 A129 15o rose carmine   .35 *.50*
   a.   Booklet pane of 20   9.00
    Nos. 556-558 (3)   3.15 2.75

Centenary of the founding of the Voluntary Shooting Organization.

Gustaf Froding — A130

1960, Aug. 22   *Perf. 12½ Horiz.*

559 A130 30o red brown   .30 .25
560 A130 1.40k slate green   2.60 .45

Perf. 12½ on 3 sides

561 A130 30o red brown   .45 .35
   a.   Booklet pane of 20   10.00
    Complete booklet, #561a   16.00
    Nos. 559-561 (3)   3.35 1.05

Gustaf Froding (1860-1911), poet.

Common Design Types pictured following the introduction.

Europa Issue, 1960
Common Design Type

1960, Sept. 19   *Perf. 12½ Vert.*
Size: 27x21mm

562 CD3 40o blue   .25 .25
563 CD3 1k red   *.80* .30

Hjalmar Branting (1860-1925), Labor Party Leader and Prime Minister — A131

1960, Nov. 23   Engr.

Perf. 12½ Horiz.
564 A131 15o rose carmine   .25 .25
565 A131 1.70k slate blue   3.00 .65

Perf. 12½ on 3 sides

566 A131 15o rose carmine   .45 .35
   a.   Booklet pane of 20   4.50
    Nos. 564-566 (3)   3.70 1.25

SAS Issue

DC-8 Airliner — A131a

1961, Feb. 24   Unwmk.
Perf. 12½ Vertically
567 A131a 40o blue   .30 .35

Perf. 12½ on 3 sides

568 A131a 40o blue   1.00 *1.25*
   a.   Booklet pane of 10   10.00

Scandinavian Airlines System, SAS, 10th anniv.

Numeral Type of 1957, Three-Crown Type of 1939 and

 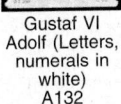 

Gustaf VI Adolf (Letters, numerals in white) A132

Rune Stone, Oland, 11th Century A133

1961-65   *Perf. 12½ Vert.*

570 A115a 15o green ('62)   .30 .25
571 A132 15o red   .35 .25
572 A132 20o gray   .35 .25
573 A132 25o brown   .65 .25
574 A132 30o ultra   1.50 .25
575 A132 30o lilac ('62)   .55 .25
576 A132 35o lilac   .55 .25
577 A132 35o ultra ('62)   1.10 .25
578 A132 40o emerald   1.00 .25
579 A132 50o gray grn ('62)   .65 .25

Perf. 12½ on 3 sides

580 A115a 15o grn ('65)   .30 .30
   a.   Bklt. pane, 2 each #514, 580, 583   2.25
    Complete booklet, #580a   2.25
581 A132 15o red   .25 .25
   a.   Bklt. pane of 20   5.00
    Complete booklet, #581a   6.75
   b.   Bklt. pane, 5 #513, 5 #581   2.50
    Complete booklet, #581b   2.50
582 A132 20o gray   1.25 .85
   a.   Bklt. pane of 20   27.50
    Complete booklet, #582a   27.50
583 A132 25o brown ('62)   .35 .25
   a.   Bklt. pane of 20   15.00
   b.   Bklt. pane of 4   2.25
    Complete booklet, #583b   2.25
584 A132 30o ultra   .65 .25
   a.   Bklt. pane of 20   15.00
    Complete booklet, #584a   16.00
   b.   Bklt. pane, #514 + 3 #584   4.00
    Complete booklet, #584b   4.00
585 A132 30o lilac ('64)   .65 .50
   a.   Bklt. pane of 20   14.00
    Complete booklet, #585a   22.00
586 A132 35o ultra ('62)   .55 .25
   a.   Bklt. pane of 20   12.50
   b.   Bklt. pane, 3 #514, 2 #586 + blank label   5.00 3.50
    Complete booklet, #586b   5.00
   c.   As "b," inscribed label   3.50 1.50

Perf. 12½ Vertically

588 A56 1.05k Prus grn ('62)   1.10 .40
589 A56 1.50k brown ('62)   .80 .30
590 A56 2.15k dk sl grn ('62)   4.00 .80
591 A56 2.50k emerald   1.50 .25

Perf. 12½ on 3 sides

592 A133 10k dl red brn   20.00 .65
   a.   Bklt. pane of 10 ('68)   250.00
   b.   Bklt. pane of 20   850.00
    Nos. 570-592 (22)   38.40 7.55

Booklet panes of 4, 5 or 6 (Nos. 580a, 583b, 584b, 586b, 586c) contain two stamps which are imperf. on two adjoining sides.

Combination panes (Nos. 580a, 581b, 584b, 586b, 586c) come in different arrangements of the denominations.

The label of No. 586c is inscribed "ett brev / betyder / sa / mycket" ("a letter means so much"). The label inscription "nord 63 / 5-13 oktober / GÖTEBORG" was privately applied to No. 586b by the Gothenburg Philatelic Society to raise funds for Nord 63 Philatelic Exhibition in Gothenburg. The pane was sold for the equivalent of $1 US, 5 times face value.

See Nos. 648-654A, 666a, 668-672F.

K.-G. Pilo, Self-portrait — A134

1961, Apr. 17   *Perf. 12½ Horiz.*

594 A134 30o brown   .35 .25
595 A134 1.40k Prus blue   3.50 1.30

Perf. 12½ on 3 sides

596 A134 30o brown   1.10 .45
   a.   Booklet pane of 20   30.00
    Complete booklet, #596a   30.00
    Nos. 594-596 (3)   4.95 2.00

Karl-Gustaf Pilo (1711-1793), painter. Self-portrait from "The Coronation of Gustavus III."

Jonas Alstromer A135

1961, June 2   *Perf. 12½ Vert.*

597 A135 15o dull claret   .25 .25
598 A135 90o grnsh blue   1.60 *2.25*

Perf. 12½ on 3 sides

599 A135 15o dull claret   .25 *.40*
   a.   Booklet pane of 20   7.00
    Nos. 597-599 (3)   2.10 2.90

200th anniversary of the birth of Jonas Alstromer, pioneer of agriculture and industry.

17th Century Printer and Student in Library — A136

Perf. 12½ Vert.

1961, Sept. 22   Engr.

600 A136 20o dark red   .30 .30
601 A136 1k blue   7.00 1.60

Perf. 12½ on 3 sides

602 A136 20o dark red   .30 .55
   a.   Booklet pane of 20   9.00
    Nos. 600-602 (3)   7.60 2.45

300th anniversary of the regulation requiring copies of all Swedish printed works to be deposited in the Royal Library.

Roentgen, Prudhomme, von Behring, van't Hoff — A137

1961, Dec. 9   *Perf. 12½ Vertically*

603 A137 20o vermilion   .25 .25
604 A137 40o blue   .25 .25
605 A137 50o green   .50 .25

Perf. 12½ on 3 sides

606 A137 20o vermilion   .25 .25
   a.   Booklet pane of 20   6.00
    Nos. 603-606 (4)   1.25 1.00

Winners of the 1901 Nobel Prize; Wilhelm K. Roentgen, Rene Sully Prudhomme, Emil von Behring, Jacob van't Hoff.

See Nos. 617-619, 637-639, 673-676, 689-692, 710-713, 769-772, 804-807.

A138

Footsteps and postmen's badges.

1962, Jan. 29   Engr.   *Perf. 12½ Vert.*

607 A138 30o lilac   .40 .25
608 A138 1.70k rose red   3.50 .65

Perf. 12½ on 3 sides

609 A138 30o lilac   .50 .50
   a.   Booklet pane of 20   11.00
    Complete booklet, #609a   13.50
    Nos. 607-609 (3)   4.40 1.40

Local mail delivery service in Sweden, cent.

A139

Voting Tool (Budkavle), Codex of Law and Gavel

1962, Mar. 21   *Perf. 12½ Horiz.*

610 A139 30o dark blue   .35 .25
611 A139 2k red   4.50 .35

Perf. 12½ on 3 sides

612 A139 30o dark blue   .40 .45
   a.   Booklet pane of 20   10.50
    Complete booklet, #612a   16.00
    Nos. 610-612 (3)   5.25 1.05

Centenary of the municipal reform laws.

St. George, Great Church, Stockholm A140

Skokloster Castle A141

Perf. 12½ Horiz. (H), Vert. (V)

1962, Sept. 24

613 A140 20o rose lake (H)   .25 .25
614 A141 50o dk slate grn (V)   .55 .35

Perf. 12½ on 3 sides

615 A140 20o rose lake   .25 .30
   a.   Booklet pane of 20   6.00
    Complete booklet, #615a   8.00
616 A141 50o dk slate grn   1.00 *1.25*
   a.   Booklet pane of 10   10.00
    Complete booklet, #616a   13.50
    Nos. 613-616 (4)   2.05 2.15

Nobel Prize Winners Type of 1961

Designs: 25o, Theodor Mommsen and Sir Ronald Ross. 50o, Hermann Emil Fischer, Pieter Zeeman and Hendrik Antoon Lorentz.

1962, Dec. 10   *Perf. 12½ Vert.*

617 A137 25o dark red   .30 *.30*
618 A137 50o blue   .40 *.40*

Perf. 12½ on 3 sides

619 A137 25o dark red   .40 .65
   a.   Booklet pane of 20   10.00
    Complete booklet, #619a   10.00
    Nos. 617-619 (3)   1.10 1.35

Winners of the 1902 Nobel Prize.

Ice Hockey — A143

1963, Feb. 15   *Perf. 12½ Horiz.*

620 A143 25o green   .40 .30
621 A143 1.70k violet bl   3.00 .85

Perf. 12½ on 3 sides

622 A143 25o green   .35 .65
   a.   Booklet pane of 20   7.00
    Nos. 620-622 (3)   3.75 1.80

1963 Ice Hockey World Championships.

Wheat Emblem and Stylized Hands — A144

1963, Mar. 21   *Perf. 12½ Vertically*

623 A144 35o lilac rose   .35 .25
624 A144 50o violet   .30 .35

Perf. 12½ on 3 sides

625 A144 35o lilac rose   .30 .40
   a.   Booklet pane of 20   6.00
    Complete booklet, #625a   10.00
    Nos. 623-625 (3)   .95 1.00

FAO "Freedom from Hunger" campaign.

Engineering and Industry Symbols — A145

1963, May 27   *Perf. 12½ Vertically*

626 A145 50o gray   .50 .35
627 A145 1.05k orange   3.25 3.00

Perf. 12½ on 3 sides

628 A145 50o gray   2.60 2.75
   a.   Booklet pane of 10   27.50
    Complete booklet, #628a   35.00
    Nos. 626-628 (3)   6.35 6.10

Gregoire François Du Reitz — A146

1963, Sept. 16   Engr.   Unwmk.

629 A146 25o brown   .40 .45
630 A146 35o dark blue   .30 .25
631 A146 2k dark red   4.00 .55

Perf. 12½ on 3 sides

632 A146 25o brown   .65 .75
   a.   Booklet pane of 20   16.00
    Complete booklet, #632a   19.00

633 A146 35o dark blue .40 .30
   a. Booklet pane of 20   10.00
      Complete booklet, #633a   16.00
      Nos. 629-633 (5)   5.75 2.30

300th anniversary of the Swedish Board of Health. Dr. Du Rietz (1607-1682) was first president of the "Collegium Medicorum," fore-runner of the Board of Health.

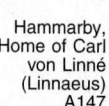

Hammarby, Home of Carl von Linné (Linnaeus) A147

1963, Oct. 25   *Perf. 12½ Vert.*
634 A147 20o orange red .30 .25
635 A147 50o yellow grn .30 .25
   Perf. 12½ on 3 sides
636 A147 20o orange red .30 .35
   a. Booklet pane of 20   6.00
      Nos. 634-636 (3)   .90 .85

Nobel Prize Winners Type of 1961

Designs: 25o, Svante Arrhenius, Niels Finsen, Bjornstjerne Bjornson. 50o, Antoine Henri Becquerel, Pierre and Marie Curie.

   Perf. 12½ Vertically
1963, Dec. 10   Engr.   Unwmk.
637 A137 25o gray olive .75 .70
638 A137 50o chocolate .40 .50
   Perf. 12½ on 3 sides
639 A137 25o gray olive .75 1.10
   a. Booklet pane of 20   16.00
      Complete booklet, #639a   22.50
      Nos. 637-639 (3)   1.90 2.30

Winners of the 1903 Nobel Prize.

A149

"The Assumption of Elijah."

1964, Feb. 3   *Perf. 12½ Horiz.*
640 A149 35o lt ultra .65 .25
641 A149 1.05k dull red 3.75 3.75
   Perf. 12½ on 3 sides
642 A149 35o lt ultra .45 .35
   a. Booklet pane of 20   10.00
      Complete booklet, #642a   13.50
      Nos. 640-642 (3)   4.85 4.35

Erik Axel Karlfeldt (1864-1931), poet.

A150

Seal of Archbishop Stephen.

1964, June 12   *Perf. 12½ Horiz.*
643 A150 40o slate green .30 .30
644 A150 60o orange brown .30 .35
   Perf. 12½ Vertically
645 A150 40o slate green .30 .30
   a. Booklet pane of 10   3.50
      Complete booklet, #645a   4.00
646 A150 60o orange brown .35 .55
   a. Booklet pane of 10   4.00
      Complete booklet, #646a   6.50
      Nos. 643-646 (4)   1.25 1.50

800th anniv. of the Archbishopric of Uppsala.

Types of Regular Issues, 1939-61, and

Post Horns — A151   Ship Grave, Skane (Bronze Age) — A152

1964-71   Engr.   *Perf. 12½ Vert.*
647 A151 20o sl bl & org yel ('65) .25 .25
648 A132 35o gray .60 .25
649 A132 40o ultra .60 .25
650 A132 45o orange .60 .25
651 A132 45o violet bl ('67) .60 .25
652 A132 50o green ('68) .55 .25
652A A132 55o dk red ('69) .40 .25
653 A132 60o rose car .65 .65
653A A132 65o dull grn ('71) .80 .25
654 A132 70o lil rose ('67) .50 .25
654A A132 85o dp cl ('71) .80 .30
655 A108 95o violet 3.00 4.00
656 A56 1.20k lt blue 3.50 3.50
657 A56 1.80k dk blue ('67) 1.25 .50
658 A56 1.85k blue ('67) 3.00 1.00
659 A56 2k dp car ('69) .75 .25
660 A56 2.30k choc ('65) 5.50 .25
661 A56 2.55k red 2.10 2.60
662 A56 2.80k red ('67) 1.40 .25
663 A56 2.85k orange ('65) 2.75 4.00
664 A56 3k brt ultra 1.40 .25
665 A152 3.50k grnsh gray ('66) 1.50 .25
   Perf. 12½ on 3 Sides
666 A115a 10o brown .25 .25
   a. Bklt. pane, 2 each #666, 667, 583   3.00
      Complete booklet, #666a   3.00
667 A115a 15o brown   .80
668 A132 30o rose red ('66) .85 .85
   a. Bklt. pane, 2 each #513, 580, 668   1.40
      Complete booklet, #668a   2.50
   b. Perf. on 3 sides 1.10 1.10

No. 668 is perf. on 2 adjoining sides.

669 A132 40o ultra .25 .25
   a. Bklt. pane of 20   16.00
      Complete booklet, #669a   27.00
   b. Bklt. pane, 2 ea #514, 669 1.50
      Complete booklet, #669b   2.50
   c. Bklt. pane, 2 each #513-514, 580, 668b-669   4.00
      Complete booklet, #669c   8.00
670 A132 45o org ('67) .65 .25
   a. Bklt. pane of 20   14.00
671 A132 45o vio bl ('67) .70 .25
   a. Bklt. pane of 20   14.00
      Complete booklet, #671a   22.50
672 A132 50o green ('69) .50 .60
   a. Bklt. pane of 10   5.00
672B A132 55o dk red ('69) .50 .25
   c. Bklt. pane of 10   5.00
672D A132 65o dull grn ('71) .85 .50
   e. Bklt. pane of 10   9.00
672F A132 85o dp cl ('71) .90 1.25
   g. Bklt. pane of 10   9.50
      Nos. 647-672F (32)   38.45 25.30

Some combination booklet panes of 4, 6 or 10 contain two stamps which are imperf. on two adjoining sides. Combination panes come in different arrangements of the denominations.

Fluorescent Paper

Starting in 1967, fluorescent paper was used in printing both definitive and commemorative issues. Its use was gradually eliminated starting in 1976. Numerous definitives and a few commemoratives were printed on both ordinary and fluorescent paper.

Nobel Prize Winners Type of 1961

30o, José Echegaray y Eizaguirre, Frédéric Mistral and John William Strutt, Lord Rayleigh. 40o, Sir William Ramsey and Ivan Petrovich Pavlov.

   Perf. 12½ Vertically
1964, Dec. 10   Engr.
673 A137 30o blue .45 .45
674 A137 40o red .70 .25
   Perf. 12½ on 3 Sides
675 A137 30o blue .45 .75
   a. Booklet pane of 20   12.00
      Complete booklet, #675a   12.00
676 A137 40o red .75 .35
   a. Booklet pane of 20   18.00
      Nos. 673-676 (4)   2.35 1.80

Winners of the 1904 Nobel Prize.

Visby Town Wall — A154

1965, Apr. 5   *Perf. 12½ Horiz.*
677 A154 30o dk car rose .30 .25
678 A154 2k brt ultra 4.25 .35
   Perf. 12½ on 3 Sides
679 A154 30o dk car rose .40 .35
   a. Booklet pane of 20   9.00
      Nos. 677-679 (3)   4.95 .95

Antenna — A155

1965, May 17   *Perf. 12½ Horiz.*
680 A155 60o lilac .45 .45
681 A155 1.40k bluish blk 2.25 1.90
   Perf. 12½ on 3 Sides
682 A155 60o lilac 1.10 1.60
   a. Booklet pane of 10   12.50
      Complete booklet, #682a   13.50
      Nos. 680-682 (3)   3.80 3.95

Centenary of the ITU.

Prince Eugen — A156

1965, July 5   *Perf. 12½ Horiz.*
683 A156 40o black .25 .25
684 A156 1k brown 2.10 .35
   Perf. 12½ on 3 Sides
685 A156 40o black .25 .25
   a. Booklet pane of 20   7.00
      Complete booklet, #685a   8.00
      Nos. 683-685 (3)   2.60 .85

Prince Eugen (1865-1947), painter and patron of the arts.

Fredrika Bremer (1801-65), Novelist — A157

   Perf. 12½ Vertically
1965, Oct. 25   Engr.
686 A157 25o violet .25 .25
687 A157 3k gray green 4.00 .35
   Perf. 12½ on 3 Sides
688 A157 25o violet .25 .25
   a. Booklet pane of 20   5.00
      Complete booklet, #688a   10.50
      Nos. 686-688 (3)   4.50 .85

Nobel Prize Winners Type of 1961

30o, Philipp von Lenard, Adolf von Baeyer. 40o, Robert Koch, Henryk Sienkiewicz.

   Perf. 12½ Vertically
1965, Dec. 10   Unwmk.
689 A137 30o ultra .35 .45
690 A137 40o dark red .40 .25
   Perf. 12½ on 3 Sides
691 A137 30o ultra .45 .75
   a. Booklet pane of 20   11.00
      Complete booklet, #691a   13.50
692 A137 40o dark red .85 .30
   a. Booklet pane of 20   19.00
      Complete booklet, #692a   22.00
      Nos. 689-692 (4)   2.05 1.75

Winners of the 1905 Nobel Prize.

Nathan Soderblom — A158

1966, Jan. 15   *Perf. 12½ Horiz.*
693 A158 60o brown .35 .25
694 A158 80o green .85 .25
   Perf. 12½ on 3 Sides
695 A158 60o brown .75 .90
   a. Booklet pane of 10   8.00
      Complete booklet, #695a   10.50
      Nos. 693-695 (3)   1.95 1.40

Nathan Soderblom (1866-1931), Protestant theologian, who worked for the union of Christian churches and received 1930 Nobel Peace Prize.

Speed Skater — A159

   Perf. 12½ on 3 Sides
1966, Feb. 18   Engr.
696 A159 5o rose red .25 .25
697 A159 25o slate green .25 .25
698 A159 40o dark blue .35 .70
   a. Bklt. pane, 4 ea #696-697, 2 #698   2.25
      Complete booklet, #698a   2.50
      Nos. 696-698 (3)   .85 1.20

World Speed Skating Championships for Men, Gothenburg, Feb. 18-20, and 75th anniversary of World Skating Championships.

National Museum, Staircase, 1866 — A160

1966, Mar. 26   *Perf. 12½ Vert.*
699 A160 30o violet .25 .25
   a. Booklet pane of 10   2.50
      Complete booklet, #699a   2.50
700 A160 2.30k olive green 1.40 1.75
   a. Booklet pane of 10   13.00
      Complete booklet, #700a   25.00

National Gallery, Blasieholmen, Stockholm, cent. The design is from an 1866 woodcut showing the inauguration of the Museum.

Baron Louis Gerhard De Geer — A161

1966, May 12   *Perf. 12½ Vertically*
701 A161 40o dark blue .25 .25
702 A161 3k brown carmine 3.75 .65
   Perf. 12½ on 3 Sides
703 A161 40o dark blue .25 .35
   a. Booklet pane of 20   8.00
      Nos. 701-703 (3)   4.25 1.25

Cent. of the reform of the Representative Assembly under the leadership of Minister of Justice (1858-70) Baron Louis Gerhard De Geer (1818-96).

Stage, Drottningholm Court Theater — A162

Perf. 12½ on 3 Sides

1966, June 15   Engr.

Salmon Paper

704 A162	5o vermilion	.25	.25
705 A162	25o olive bister	.25	.25
706 A162	40o dark purple	.40	.65
a.	Bklt. pane, 4 ea #704-705, 2 #706	2.00	
	Complete booklet, #706a	2.25	
	Nos. 704-706 (3)	.90	1.15

Drottningholm Court Theater, 200th anniv.

Almqvist and Wild Rose — A163

Perf. 12½ Horizontally

1966, Sept. 26   Engr.

707 A163	25o magenta	.25	.25
708 A163	1k green	2.25	.30

Perf. 12½ on 3 Sides

709 A163	25o magenta	.25	.25
a.	Booklet pane of 20	4.75	
	Complete booklet, #709a	8.00	
	Nos. 707-709 (3)	2.75	.80

Carl Jonas Love Almqvist (1793-1866), writer and poet.

Nobel Prize Winner Type of 1961

Designs: 30o, Joseph John Thomson and Giosue Carducci. 40o, Henri Moissan, Camillo Golgi and Santiago Ramon y Cajal.

Perf. 12½ Vertically

1966, Dec. 10   Engr.

710 A137	30o rose lake	.55	.25
711 A137	40o dark green	.50	.25

Perf. 12½ on 3 Sides

712 A137	30o rose lake	.55	.45
a.	Booklet pane of 20	11.00	
	Complete booklet, #712a	13.50	
713 A137	40o dark green	.55	.45
a.	Booklet pane of 20	12.00	
	Complete booklet, #713a	13.50	
	Nos. 710-713 (4)	2.15	1.40

Winners of the 1906 Nobel Prize.

Field Ball Player — A164

1967, Jan. 12   *Perf. 12½ Horiz.*

714 A164	45o dk violet blue	.25	.25
715 A164	2.70k dp rose lilac	2.75	1.50

Perf. 12½ on 3 Sides

716 A164	45o dk violet blue	.25	.30
a.	Booklet pane of 20	6.00	
	Complete booklet, #716a	8.00	
	Nos. 714-716 (3)	3.25	2.05

World Field Ball Championships, Jan. 12-21.

EFTA Emblem — A165

1967, Feb. 15   *Perf. 12½ Horiz.*

717 A165	70o orange	.45	.40

Perf. 12½ on 3 Sides

718 A165	70o orange	1.10	1.25
a.	Booklet pane of 10	15.00	
	Complete booklet, #718a	19.00	

European Free Trade Association. Tariffs were abolished Dec. 31, 1966, among EFTA members: Austria, Denmark, Finland, Great Britain, Norway, Portugal, Sweden, Switzerland.

"The Fjeld," by Sixten Lundbohm A166

Lion Fortress, Gothenburg A167

Uppsala Cathedral A168

Gripsholm Castle A169

1967   Engr.   *Perf. 12½ Vert.*

719 A166	35o dl bl & blk brn	.25	.25

Perf. 12½ Horiz.

720 A167	3.70k violet	2.10	.25
721 A168	4.50k dull red	2.40	.25

Perf. 12½ Vert.

722 A169	7k vio bl & rose red	3.25	.55

Perf. 12½ on 3 Sides

723 A166	35o dl bl & blk brn	.25	.25
a.	Booklet pane of 10	2.50	
	Complete booklet, #723a	4.00	
	Nos. 719-723 (5)	8.25	1.55

Issued: #719, 721, 723, 3/15; #720, 2/15; #722, 4/11.

Table Tennis — A170

1967, Apr. 11   *Perf. 12½ Horiz.*

724 A170	35o bright magenta	.30	.25
725 A170	90o greenish blue	1.30	.50

Perf. 12½ on 3 Sides

726 A170	35o bright magenta	.35	.40
a.	Booklet pane of 20	7.00	
	Complete booklet, #726a	10.00	
	Nos. 724-726 (3)	1.95	1.15

World Table Tennis Championships, Stockholm.

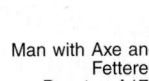

Man with Axe and Fettered Beast — A171

Designs: 15o, Man fighting two bears. 30o, Warrior disguised as wolf pursuing enemy. 35o, Two warriors with swords and lances. The designs are taken from 6th century bronze plates (1¾in. x 2½in.) used to decorate helmets; now in Swedish Museum of National Antiquities.

Perf. 12½ on 3 Sides

1967, May 17   Engr.

727 A171	10o dk brown & dp bl	.25	.25
728 A171	15o dp blue & dk brn	.25	.25
729 A171	30o brt pink & dk brn	.25	.25
730 A171	35o dk brown & brt pink	.25	.25
a.	Bklt. pane, 4 #727, 2 ea #728-730	2.10	2.75
	Nos. 727-730 (4)	1.00	1.00

Double Mortise Corner — A172

Lithographed and Photogravure

1967, June 16   *Perf. 12½*

731 A172	10o olive & multi	.25	.25
732 A172	35o dk blue multi	.30	.30
a.	Bklt. pane, 6 #731, 4 #732	1.75	2.00

Issued to honor generations of Finnish settlers in Sweden.

Right-hand Driving as Seen Through Windshield — A173

1967, Sept. 2   Engr.   *Perf. 12½ Vert.*

733 A173	35o dp bl, ocher & blk	.30	.35
734 A173	45o yel grn, ocher & blk	.35	.45

Perf. 12½ Horiz.

735 A173	35o dp bl, ocher & blk	.30	.45
a.	Booklet pane of 10	3.00	
736 A173	45o yel grn, ocher & blk	.25	.25
a.	Booklet pane of 10	2.50	
	Nos. 733-736 (4)	1.20	1.50

Issued to publicize the introduction of right-hand driving in Sweden, Sept. 3, 1967.

Postrider A174

The Prodigal Son, 13th cent., Rada Church A174a

Griffin A174b

Rocky Isles in Bloom, by Harald Lindberg A175

Dalsland Canal — A176

Log roller — A176a

Gothenburg Harbor — A176b

Horse-drawn timber sled — A176c

Nils Holgersson Riding Wild Goose — A176d

Windmills, Ölana Island — A176e

Steamer Storskar and Royal Palace, Stockholm A176f

Elk — A177   Roe deer — A177a

Dancing cranes — A177b

Mail Coach, by Eigil Schwab — A177c 751A

Illustration from Lapponia, by Johannes Schefferus — A177d

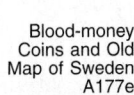

Blood-money Coins and Old Map of Sweden A177e

Great Seal, 1439 (St. Erik with Banner and Shield) — A177f

10o, Merchant vessel in Oresund, 1661. 20o, St. Stephen as a boy tending horses, medallion from Dädesio Church. #742, Lion, from Grodinge tapestry, 15th cent. 2.55k, Seal of Magnus Ladulas, 1285 (King Magnus Birgersson on throne with lily scepter and orb). 3k, Seal of Duke Erik Magnusson, 1306 (Duke on horseback with standard of Folkunga dynasty). 6k, Gustavus Vasa's silver daler.

1967-72   *Perf. 12½ Horiz. or Vert.*

737 A174	5o red & blk	.25	.25
738 A174	10o blue & blk	.25	.25
739 A174a	15o sl grn, grnsh ('71)	.25	.25
740 A174	20o sep, buff ('70)	.25	.25
741 A174b	25o bis & blk ('71)	.25	.25
742 A174b	25o blk & bis ('71)	.25	.25
a.	Pair, #741-742	.40	.50
743 A175	30o ultra & ver	.25	.25
744 A176	40o blk, dk grn & ultra ('68)	.30	.25

745 A176a 45o bl & brn blk ('70) .30 .25
746 A176b 55o bl & vio, vert. ('71) .40 .25
747 A176c 60o black brn ('71) .30 .25
747A A176d 65o brt blue ('71) .30 .25
748 A176e 75o slate grn ('71) .30 .25
749 A176f 80o blue & blk ('71) .40 .25
750 A177 90o sep & bl gray .55 .25
750A A177a 95o sepia ('72) .40 .25
751 A177b 1k slate grn ('68) .55 .25
751A A177c 1.20k multi ('71) .65 .25
751B A177d 1.40k lt bl & red ('72) .75 .25
752 A177f 2.55k brt blue ('70) 1.25 .65
753 A177f 3k dk gray bl ('70) 1.25 .25
754 A177e 4k black ('71) 1.60 .25
755 A177f 5k Prus grn ('70) 2.00 .25
755A A177e 6k indigo ('72) 3.00 .25

Perf. 12½ on 3 Sides, 12½ Horiz. (#761)

756 A174 5o red & blk .25 .25
a. Booklet pane of 20 .75
757 A174 10o bl & blk ('69) .25 .25
a. Booklet pane of 20 2.10
758 A175 30o ultra & ver .30 .30
a. Booklet pane of 10 3.25
759 A176 40o blk, dk grn & ultra ('68) .25 .30
a. Booklet pane of 10 2.75
760 A176a 45o bl & brn blk ('70) .25 .25
a. Booklet pane of 10 2.75
761 A176b 55o bl & vio ('71) .35 .25
a. Booklet pane of 10 3.50
762 A176d 65o brt blue ('71) .40 .40
a. Booklet pane of 10 4.00
763 A176e 75o slate grn ('72) .50 .25
a. Booklet pane of 10 5.50
764 A177 90o sepia & bl gray 1.00 1.00
a. Booklet pane of 10 10.00
Nos. 737-764 (33) 19.60 9.65

King Gustaf VI Adolf — A178

Perf. 12½ Horiz.

1967, Nov. 11 **Engr.**
765 A178 45o lt ultra .30 .25
766 A178 70o green .30 .30

Perf. 12½ on 3 Sides

767 A178 45o lt ultra .25 .25
a. Booklet pane of 20 4.50
768 A178 70o green .65 .95
a. Booklet pane of 10 6.50
Nos. 765-768 (4) 1.50 1.75

85th birthday of King Gustaf VI Adolf.

Nobel Prize Winners Type of 1961

35o, Eduard Buchner (Chemistry), Albert A. Michelson (Physics). 45o, Charles L. A. Laveran (Medicine), Rudyard Kipling (Literature).

1967, Dec. 9 ***Perf. 12½ Vert.***
769 A137 35o vermilion .65 .50
770 A137 45o dark blue .55 .25

Perf. 12½ on 3 Sides

771 A142 35o vermilion .70 .95
a. Booklet pane of 10 7.50
772 A142 45o dark blue .45 .50
a. Booklet pane of 10 6.50
Nos. 769-772 (4) 2.35 2.20

Winners of the 1907 Nobel Prize.

Franz Berwald, Violin and His Music — A179

1968, Apr. 3 ***Perf. 12½ Horiz.***
773 A179 35o black & red .35 .25
774 A179 2k blk, vio bl & org yel 3.00 .80

Perf. 12½ on 3 Sides

775 A179 35o black & red .45 .60
a. Booklet pane of 10 4.50
Nos. 773-775 (3) 3.80 1.65

Franz Berwald (1796-1868), composer. Design includes opening bar of overture to his opera, "The Queen of Golconda."

National Bank Seal — A180

Perf. 12½ Vertically

1968, May 15 **Engr.**
776 A180 45o dull blue .25 .25
777 A180 70o black, *pink* .30 .35

Perf. 12½ on 3 Sides

778 A180 45o dull blue .35 .50
a. Booklet pane of 10 4.00
779 A180 70o black, *pink* .55 .85
a. Booklet pane of 10 6.50
Nos. 776-779 (4) 1.45 1.95

300th anniv. of the National Bank of Sweden. Nos. 777, 779 are on non-fluorescent paper.

Seal of Lund University A181

1968, June 4 ***Perf. 12½ on 3 sides***
780 A181 10o deep blue .25 .25
781 A181 35o red .30 .50
a. Bklt. pane, 6 #780, 4 #781 2.25 2.75

300th anniversary of University of Lund.

Butterfly Orchid — A182

Nordic Wild Flowers: No. 783, Wood anemone. No. 784, Dog rose. No. 785, Prune Cherry. No. 786, Lily of the valley.

1968, June 4
782 A182 45o slate green .90 .55
783 A182 45o gray green .90 .55
784 A182 45o sl grn & rose car .90 .55
785 A182 45o gray green .90 .55
786 A182 45o slate green .90 .55
a. Bklt. pane, 2 each #782-786 11.00
Nos. 782-786 (5) 4.50 2.75

World Council of Churches' Emblem — A183

1968, July 4 ***Perf. 12½ Horiz.***
787 A183 70o plum .55 .60
788 A183 90o Prus green 1.00 .50

Perf. 12½ on 3 Sides

789 A183 70o plum .65 .95
a. Booklet pane of 10 7.50
Nos. 787-789 (3) 2.20 2.05

4th General Assembly of the World Council of Churches, Uppsala, July 4-19.

Electron Orbits — A184

Perf. 12½ Horizontally

1968, Aug. 9 **Engr.**
790 A184 45o rose carmine .55 .25
791 A184 2k dark blue 2.90 .40

Perf. 12½ on 3 Sides

792 A184 45o rose carmine .50 .45
a. Booklet pane of 10 5.00
Nos. 790-792 (3) 3.95 1.10

Establishment of the 1st 3 People's Colleges, cent.

"Orienteer" Finding Way through Forest — A185

Perf. 12½ Horizontally

1968, Sept. 5 **Engr.**
793 A185 40o violet & red brn .35 .40
794 A185 2.80k green & violet 3.00 3.00

Perf. 12½ on 3 Sides

795 A185 40o violet & red brn .40 .65
a. Booklet pane of 10 5.00
Nos. 793-795 (3) 3.75 4.05

Issued to publicize the World Championships in Orienteering, Linkoping, Sept. 28-29.

"Fingerkrok" by Axel Petersson A186

Perf. 12½ on 3 Sides

1968, Oct. 28 **Engr.**
796 A186 5o green .25 .25
797 A186 25o sepia 1.40 1.10
798 A186 45o blk brn & red brn .25 .25
a. Bklt. pane, 3 #796, 2 #797, 3 #798 3.00
Nos. 796-798 (3) 1.90 1.60

Axel Petersson, called "Doderhultarn" (1868-1925), sculptor.

Black-backed Gull — A187

Designs: No. 799, Varying hare. No. 801, Red fox. No. 802, Hooded crows harassing golden eagle. No. 803, Weasel.

Perf. 12½ on 3 Sides

1968, Nov. 9 **Engr.**
799 A187 30o blue .65 .80
800 A187 30o black .65 .80
801 A187 30o dark brown .65 .80
802 A187 30o black .65 .80
803 A187 30o blue .65 .80
a. Bklt. pane, 2 each #799-803 6.50
Nos. 799-803 (5) 3.25 4.00

See Nos. 873-877.

Nobel Prize Winners Type of 1961

35o, Elie Metchnikoff, Paul Ehrlich, Ernest Rutherford. 45o, Gabriel Lippmann, Rudolf Eucken.

1968, Dec. 10 ***Perf. 12½ Vertically***
804 A137 35o maroon .55 .50
805 A137 45o dark green .50 .25

Perf. 12½ on 3 Sides

806 A137 35o maroon .50 1.15
a. Booklet pane of 10 6.00
807 A137 45o dark green .45 .50
a. Booklet pane of 10 5.00
Nos. 804-807 (4) 2.00 2.40

Nordic Cooperation Issue

Five Ancient Ships — A187a

1969, Feb. 28 **Engr.** ***Perf. 12½ Vert.***
808 A187a 45o dark gray .35 .35
809 A187a 70o blue .55 .90

Perf. 12½ on 3 Sides

810 A187a 45o dark gray .50 .85
a. Booklet pane of 10 11.00
Nos. 808-810 (3) 1.40 2.10

50th anniv. of the Nordic Society and centenary of postal cooperation among the northern countries. The design is taken from a coin found at the site of Birka, an ancient Swedish town. See also Denmark Nos. 454-455, Finland No. 481, Iceland Nos. 404-405 and Norway Nos. 523-524.

Worker, by Albin Amelin — A188

Perf. 12½ Horiz.

1969, Mar. 31 **Engr.**
811 A188 55o dk carmine rose .45 .25
812 A188 70o dk blue .70 .65

Perf. 12½ on 3 Sides

813 A188 55o dk carmine rose .35 .25
a. Booklet pane of 10 4.00
Nos. 811-813 (3) 1.50 1.15

50th anniv. of the ILO.

Europa Issue, 1969

Common Design Type

1969, Apr. 28 **Photo.** ***Perf. 14 Vert.***

Size: 27x22mm

814 CD12 70o orange & multi 1.50 .45
815 CD12 1k vio blue & multi 1.00 .40

Perf. 14 on 3 Sides

816 CD12 70o orange & multi 1.50 2.00
a. Booklet pane of 10 17.50
Nos. 814-816 (3) 4.00 2.85

Not fluorescent.

Albert Engstrom with Owl, Self-portrait A189

1969, May 12 **Engr.** ***Perf. 12½ Vert.***
817 A189 35o black brown .30 .25
818 A189 55o blue gray .30 .25

Perf. 12½ on 3 Sides

819 A189 35o black brown .35 .55
a. Booklet pane of 10 3.50
820 A189 55o blue gray .30 .30
a. Booklet pane of 10 3.00
Nos. 817-820 (4) 1.25 1.35

Albert Engstrom (1869-1940), cartoonist.

Souvenir Sheet

Paintings by Ivan Agueli — A190

1969, June 6 **Litho.** ***Perf. 13½***
821 A190 Sheet of 6 2.50 4.25
a. 45o Landscape .40 .45
b. 45o Still life .40 .45
c. 45o Near East town .40 .45
d. 55o Young woman .40 .45
e. 55o Sunny landscape .40 .45
f. 55o Street at night .40 .45

Ivan Agueli (1869-1917), painter. Size: #821a-821c, 35x28mm. #821d-821e, 28x44mm. #821f, 48x44mm. Not fluorescent.

Tjorn Bridges — A191

Designs: 15o, 30o, Various bridges.

Size: 20x19mm

Perf. 12½ on 3 Sides

1969, Sept. 3 Bluish Paper Engr.
822 A191 15o deep blue   1.10 .45
823 A191 30o dk grn & blk   1.10 .45

Size: 41x19mm
824 A191 55o blk & dp bl   1.10 .45
  a. Bklt. pane, 2 each #822-824 8.00
      Nos. 822-824 (3)   3.30 1.35

Tjorn highway bridges connecting the Islands of Orust and Tjorn in the Gothenburg Archipelago with the mainland.

Man's Head, Woodcarving — A192

Warship Wasa, 1628 — A193

Designs: No. 826, Crowned lion. No. 827, Great Swedish coat of arms. No. 828, Lion, front view. No. 829, Man's head (different from No. 825).

1969, Sept. 3 *Perf. 12½ on 3 Sides*
825 A192 55o dark red   .40 .25
826 A192 55o brown   .40 .25
827 A193 55o dark blue   .60 .70
828 A192 55o brown   .40 .25
829 A192 55o dark red   .40 .25
830 A193 55o dark blue   .60 .70
  a. Bklt. pane, #827 & #830, 2 each
      #825-826, 828-829   5.50
      Nos. 825-830 (6)   2.80 2.40

Salvaging in 1961 of the warship Wasa, sunk on her maiden voyage, Aug. 10, 1628.

Soderberg A194

Bo Bergman A195

Perf. 12½ Horiz.

1969, Oct. 13   Engr.
831 A194 45o brown, *buff*   .40 .30

Perf. 12½ Vert.
832 A195 55o green, *grnsh*   .40 .25

Perf. 12½ on 3 Sides
833 A194 45o brown, *buff*   .50 .85
  a. Booklet pane of 10   5.00
      Complete booklet, #833a   6.50
834 A195 55o green, *grnsh*   .25 .40
  a. Booklet pane of 10   4.00
      Complete booklet, #834a   6.75
      Nos. 831-834 (4)   1.55 1.80

Hjalmar Soderberg (1869-1941), writer; Bo Bergman (1869-1967), poet.

Lever Light, Lightship, Landsort and Svenska Lighthouses — A196

Perf. 12½ Vert.

1969, Nov. 17   Photo.
835 A196 30o gray, blk & pink   .25 .25
836 A196 55o lt bl, blk & brn   .35 .25

300th anniversary of Swedish lighthouses.

Pelle's New Suit — A197

The Adventures of Nils — A198

Swedish Fairy Tales: No. 839, Pippi Longstocking (little girl, horse and monkey). No. 840, Vill-Vallareman (boy blowing horn). No. 841, Kattresan (child riding on back of cat).

Perf. 12½ on 3 Sides

1969, Nov. 17   Engr.
837 A197 35o org, red & dk
           brn   1.60 1.60
838 A198 35o dark brown   1.60 1.60
839 A197 35o org, red & dk
           brn   1.60 1.60
840 A198 35o dark brown   1.60 1.60
841 A197 35o org, red & dk
           brn   1.60 1.60
  a. Bklt. pane, 2 each #837-841 20.00 22.50
      Nos. 837-841 (5)   8.00 8.00

Issued for use in Christmas cards.

Dr. Emil T. Kocher and Wilhelm Ostwald — A199

55o, Selma Lagerlof, open book. 70o, Guglielmo Marconi, Carl Ferdinand Braun.

1969, Dec. 10   *Perf. 12½ Vert.*
842 A199 45o dull green   .75 .35
843 A199 55o blk, *pale sal*   .60 .25
844 A199 70o black   .75 1.25

Perf. 12½ on 3 Sides
845 A199 45o dull green   .45 .55
  a. Booklet pane of 10   5.00
846 A199 55o blk, *pale sal*   .40 .30
  a. Booklet pane of 10   4.50
      Nos. 842-846 (5)   2.95 2.70

Winners of the 1909 Nobel Prize.

Weather Vane, Soderala Church A200

Door with Iron Fittings, Bjorksta Church, Vastmanland A201

Swedish Art Forgings: 10o, like 5o, facing right. 30o, Memorial cross, Ekshärad churchyard, Varmland.

Perf. 12½ on 3 sides

1970, Feb. 9   Engr.
847 A200 5o slate grn & brn   .30 .25
848 A200 10o slate grn & brn   .30 .25
849 A200 30o blk & slate grn   .30 .25

Perf. 12½ Vert.
850 A201 55o brn & slate grn   .30 .25
  a. Bklt. pane, 2 each #847-850 2.00 3.75
      Complete booklet, #850a   3.00
      Nos. 847-850 (4)   1.20 1.00

Ljusman River Rapids A202

1970, May 11 Engr.   *Perf. 12½ Vert.*
851 A202 55o black & multi   .30 .25
852 A202 70o black & multi   .65 .60

European Nature Conservation Year, 1970.

Skiing — A203

"Around the Arctic Circle": No. 853, View of Kiruna. No. 855, Boat on mountain lake in Stora Sjofellet National Park. No. 856, Reindeer herd and herdsman. No. 857, Rocket probe under northern lights.

Perf. 12½ Horiz.

1970, June 5   Engr.
853 A203 45o sepia   .50 .85
854 A203 45o violet blue   .50 .85
855 A203 45o dull green   .50 .85
856 A203 45o sepia   .50 .85
857 A203 45o violet blue   .50 .85
  a. Bklt. pane, 2 each #853-857 5.50
      Nos. 853-857 (5)   2.50 4.25

China Palace, Drottningholm Park, 1769 — A204

Perf. 12½ Vert.

1970, Aug. 28   Photo.
858 A204 2k yel, grn & pink   1.50 .25

Glimmingehus, Skane Province, 15th Century — A205

Perf. 12½ Horiz.

1970, Aug. 28   Engr.
859 A205 55o gray green   .30 .25

Perf. 12½ on 3 Sides
860 A205 55o gray green   .35 .35
  a. Booklet pane of 10   2.50

Timber Industry A206

Miner A208

Shipping Industry — A207

Designs: No. 863, Heavy industry (propeller). No. 864, Hydroelectric power (dam and diesel). No. 865, Mining (freight train and mine). No. 866, Technical research.

Perf. 12½ on 3 sides

1970, Sept. 28   Engr.
861 A206 70o indigo & lt brn   2.00 2.50
862 A207 70o ind, lt brn & dp
           plum   2.00 2.50
863 A206 70o ind & dp plum   2.00 2.50
864 A206 70o ind & dp plum   2.00 2.50
865 A207 70o ind & dp plum   2.00 2.50
866 A206 70o dp plum & lt brn 2.00 2.50
  a. Booklet pane of 6, #861-866 12.00 20.00
867 A208 1k black, *buff*   .40 .35
  a. Booklet pane of 10   4.00

Perf. 12½ Vertically
868 A208 1k black, *buff*   .75 .30
      Nos. 861-868 (8)   13.15 15.65

Swedish trade and industry.

"Love, Not War" A209

Design: 70o, Four-leaf clovers symbolizing efforts for equality and brotherhood.

Engraved and Lithographed

1970, Oct. 24   *Perf. 12½ Horiz.*
869 A209 55o rose red, yel & blk .25 .40
  a. Booklet pane of 4   1.00
870 A209 70o emerald, yel & blk   .40 .55
  a. Booklet pane of 4   1.25

Perf. 12½ Vert.
871 A209 55o rose red, yel & blk .35 .30
872 A209 70o emerald, yel & blk   .30 .35
      Nos. 869-872 (4)   1.30 1.60

25th anniversary of the United Nations.

Bird Type of 1968

Birds: No. 873, Blackbird. No. 874, Great titmouse. No. 875, Bullfinch. No. 876, Greenfinch. No. 877, Blue titmouse.

Perf. 12½ on 3 Sides

1970, Nov. 20   Photo.
873 A187 30o blue grn & multi   .85 1.00
874 A187 30o bister & multi   .85 1.00
875 A187 30o blue & multi   .85 1.00
876 A187 30o pink & multi   .85 1.00
877 A187 30o org yel & multi   .85 1.00
  a. Bklt. pane, 2 each #873-877 8.00 14.00
      Nos. 873-877 (5)   4.25 5.00

Paul Johann Ludwig Heyse — A210

Designs: 55o, Otto Wallach and Johannes Diderik van der Waals. 70o, Albrecht Kossel.

Perf. 12½ Horiz.

1970, Dec. 10   Engr.
878 A210 45o violet   .80 .40
879 A210 55o slate blue   .50 .30
880 A210 70o gray   1.10 1.10

Perf. 12½ on 3 Sides
881 A210 45o violet   .60 1.10
  a. Booklet pane of 10   6.50
882 A210 55o slate blue   .65 .35
  a. Booklet pane of 10   6.50
      Nos. 878-882 (5)   3.65 3.25

Winners of the 1910 Nobel Prize.

Kerstin Hesselgren — A211

Perf. 12½ Horiz.

1971, Feb. 19   Engr.
883 A211 45o dp claret, *gray* .45 .40
884 A211 1k dp brn, *buff*   .65 .25

Perf. 12½ on 3 Sides
885 A211 45o dp claret, *gray* .30 .85
  a. Booklet pane of 10   3.25
      Nos. 883-885 (3)   1.40 1.50

50th anniv. of woman suffrage; Kerstin Hesselgren, was 1st woman member of Swedish Upper House.

Terns in Flight — A212

1971, Mar. 26   *Perf. 13½ Vert.*
886 A212 40o dark red   .40 .35
887 A212 55o violet blue   .80 .25

Perf. 12½ on 3 Sides

888 A212 55o violet blue .40 .25
a. Booklet pane of 10 4.50
Nos. 886-888 (3) 1.60 .85

Joint northern campaign for the benefit of refugees.

Abstract Music, by Ingvar Lidholm — A213

Perf. 12½ Horiz.

1971, Aug. 27 **Engr.**

889 A213 55o deep lilac .40 .25
890 A213 85o green .45 .30

Perf. 12½ on 3 Sides

891 A213 55o deep lilac .30 *.30*
a. Booklet pane of 10 3.00
Nos. 889-891 (3) 1.15 .85

The Three Kings, Grotlingbo Church — A214

Flight into Egypt, Stanga Church A215

Designs: 10o, Adam and Eve, Gammelgarn Church. 55o, Saint on horseback and Samson with the lion, Hogrän Church.

Perf. 12½ on 3 Sides

1971, Sept. 28 **Engr.**

892 A214 5o violet & brn .60 .45
893 A214 10o violet & sl grn .60 .45

Perf. 12½ Horiz.

894 A215 55o slate grn & brn .60 .40
895 A215 65o brown & vio blk .30 .25
a. Bklt. pane, #892-894, 2 #895 2.50 *4.50*
Nos. 892-895 (4) 2.10 1.55

Art of medieval stonemasons in Gotland.

Toddler and Automobile Wheel — A216

1971, Oct. 20 ***Perf. 12½ Vert.***

896 A216 35o black & red .25 *.30*
897 A216 65o dp blue & multi .60 .25

Perf. 12½ on 3 Sides

898 A216 65o dp blue & multi .40 .35
a. Booklet pane of 10 5.75
Nos. 896-898 (3) 1.25 .90

Publicity for road safety.

King Gustavus Vasa's Sword, c. 1500 — A217

Swedish Crown Regalia: No. 900, Scepter. No. 901, Crown. No. 902, Orb (Scepter, crown and orb were made in 1561 for Erik XIV). No. 903, Karl IX's anointing horn, 1606.

Perf. 12½ on 3 Sides

1971, Oct. 20 **Engr.**

899 A217 65o lt blue & multi .50 .40
900 A217 65o lt ol grn & multi .50 .40
901 A217 65o dk blue & multi .50 .40
902 A217 65o lt ol grn & multi .50 .40
903 A217 65o lt blue & multi .50 .40
a. Bklt. pane, 2 each #899-903 5.50 *10.00*
Nos. 899-903 (5) 2.50 2.00

Christmas Elf and Goat Bringing Gifts — A218

Christmas Customs (Old Prints): No. 905, Christmas market. No. 906, Dancing children and father playing fiddle. No. 907, Ice-skating on frozen waterways in Stockholm. No. 908, Sleigh ride to church.

1971, Nov. 10

904 A218 35o deep carmine 1.25 1.25
905 A218 35o violet blue 1.25 1.25
906 A218 35o violet brown 1.25 1.25
907 A218 35o violet blue 1.25 1.25
908 A218 35o slate green 1.25 1.25
a. Bklt. pane, 2 each #904-908 12.50 *16.00*
Nos. 904-908 (5) 6.25 6.25

Maurice Maeterlinck — A219

Designs: 65o, Wilhelm Wien and Allvar Gullstrand. 85o, Marie Sklodovska Curie.

1971, Dec. 10 ***Perf. 12½ Horiz.***

909 A219 55o orange .65 .55
910 A219 65o green .65 .25
911 A219 85o dk carmine .65 .60

Perf. 12½ on 3 Sides

912 A219 55o orange .60 *.80*
a. Booklet pane of 10 6.00
913 A219 65o green .65 .40
a. Booklet pane of 10 6.50
Nos. 909-913 (5) 3.20 2.60

Winners of the 1911 Nobel Prize.

Women Athletes — A220

1972, Feb. 23 ***Perf. 12½ on 3 Sides***

914 A220 55o Fencing .75 *.75*
915 A220 55o Diving .75 *.75*
916 A220 55o Gymnastics .75 *.75*
917 A220 55o Tennis .75 *.75*
918 A220 55o Figure skating .75 *.75*
a. Bklt. pane, 2 each #914-918 7.75 *12.00*
Nos. 914-918 (5) 3.75 3.75

Lars Johan Hierta, by Christian Eriksson — A221

Frans Michael Franzen, by Soderberg and Hultstrom — A222

Hugo Alfven, by Carl Milles — A223

Georg Stiernhielm, by David K. Ehrenstrahl — A224

Photo., Perf 12½ Horiz. (35, 85o); Engr., Perf. 12½ Vert. (50, 65o)

1972 Feb. 23

919 A221 35o multicolored .30 *.25*
920 A222 50o violet .40 .25
921 A223 65o bluish black .40 .25
922 A224 85o multicolored .50 *.55*
Nos. 919-922 (4) 1.60 1.30

Hierta (1801-72), journalist. Franzen (1772-1847), poet. Alfven (1872-1960), composer. Stiernhielm (1598-1672), poet, writer, scientist.

Lifting Molten Glass A225

Swedish Glassmaking: No. 924, Glass blower. No. 925, Decorating vase. No. 926, Annealing vase. No. 927, Polishing jug.

Perf. 12½ Horiz.

1972, Mar. 22 **Engr.**

923 A225 65o black .80 .90
924 A225 65o violet blue .80 .90
925 A225 65o carmine .80 .90
926 A225 65o black .80 .90
927 A225 65o violet blue .80 .90
a. Bklt. pane, 2 each #923-927 8.00
Nos. 923-927 (5) 4.00 4.50

Horses and Ruin of Borgholm Castle — A226

Designs: No. 929, Oland Island Bridge. No. 930, Kalmar Castle. No. 931, Salmon fishing. No. 932, Schooner Falken, Karlskrona.

1972, May 8 ***Perf. 12½ Horiz.***

928 A226 55o chocolate .65 *.85*
929 A226 55o dk violet blue .65 *.85*
930 A226 55o chocolate .65 *.85*
931 A226 55o blue green .65 *.85*
932 A226 55o dk violet blue .65 *.85*
a. Bklt. pane, 2 each #928-932 6.00
Nos. 928-932 (5) 3.25 4.25

Tourist attractions in Southeast Sweden.

"Only one Earth" Environment Emblem — A227

"Spring," Bror Hjorth — A228

1972, June 5 **Engr.** ***Perf. 12½ Vert.***

933 A227 65o blue & carmine .30 .25

Perf. 12½ Horiz.

934 A227 65o blue & carmine .30 .30
a. Booklet pane of 10 3.00
Complete booklet, #934a 6.00

Perf. 12½ Vert.

935 A228 85o brown & multi .45 .30
a. Booklet pane of 4 1.80
Complete booklet, #935a 7.50
Nos. 933-935 (3) 1.05 .85

UN Conference on Human Environment, Stockholm, June 5-16.

Junkers JU52 — A229

Historic Planes: 5o, Junkers F13. 25o, Friedrichshafen FF49. 75o, Douglas DC-3.

1972, Sept. 8 ***Perf. 12½ on 3 Sides***

Size: 20x19mm

936 A229 5o lilac .25 .25

Size: 44x19mm

937 A229 15o blue .45 .50
938 A229 25o blue .45 .50
939 A229 75o gray green .30 .30
a. Bklt. pane, #937-938, 2 ea #936, 939 1.60 *3.00*
Complete booklet, #939a 3.00
Nos. 936-939 (4) 1.45 1.55

Stockholm from the South, by Johan Fredrik Martin — A230

Amphion Figurehead, by Per Ljung — A231

Lady with Veil, by Alexander Roslin — A232

#941, Anchor Forge, by Pehr Hillestrom. #943, Quadriga, by Johan Tobias von Sergel. #945, (Queen) Sofia Magdalena, by Carl Gustaf Pilo.

1972, Oct. 7 **Engr.** ***Perf. 12½ Horiz.***

940 A230 75o greenish black .40 *.60*
941 A230 75o dark brown .40 *.60*

Perf. 12½ on 3 Sides

942 A231 75o dark carmine .45 *.55*
943 A231 75o dark carmine .45 *.55*

Perf. 12½ on 2 Sides

944 A232 75o dk brn, blk & dk car .45 *.60*
945 A232 75o dk brn, blk & dk car .45 *.60*
a. Booklet pane of 6, #940-945 2.75 *4.75*
Complete booklet, #945a 5.00

18th century Swedish art.

Types of 1936

Imprint: "1972"

1972, Oct. 7 ***Perf. 12½ on 3 Sides***

946 A36 10o dark carmine .35 *.50*
947 A37 15o yellow green .35 *.50*
948 A42 40o deep blue .35 *.50*
949 A44 50o deep claret .35 *.50*
950 A45 60o deep blue .35 *.50*
a. Bklt. pane, 2 each #946-950 3.00 *7.00*
Nos. 946-950 (5) 1.75 2.50

Olle Hjortzberg (1872-1959), stamp designer. Booklet sold for 5k of which 1.50k was for Stockholmia 74, Intl. Phil. Exhib., Sept. 21-29, 1973.

Santa Claus — A233

St. Lucia Singers A234

Perf. 14 on 3 Sides

1972, Nov. 6   **Photo.**
951 A233 45o Candles .35 .25
952 A233 45o shown .35 .25
  a.   Bklt. pane, 5 each #951-952 3.50

Perf. 12½ Vert.

953 A234 75o gray & multi .55 .25
    Nos. 951-953 (3) 1.25 .75

Christmas 1972 (children's drawings).

Horse — A235

Viking Ship — A236

Willows, by Peter A. Persson A237

Trosa, by Reinhold Ljunggren A238

Spring Birches, by Oskar Bergman A239

King Gustaf VI Adolf — A240

Perf. 12½ Horiz. or Vert.

1972-73   **Engr.**
954 A235 5o maroon ('73) .25 .25
955 A236 10o dk blue ('73) .25 .25
956 A237 40o sepia ('73) .25 .25
957 A238 50o blk & brn ('73) .30 .25
958 A239 55o yel grn ('73) .35 .25
959 A240 75o indigo .40 .25
960 A240 1k dp carmine .65 .25

1973   **Perf. 12½ on 3 Sides**
961 A235 5o maroon .25 .25
  a.   Booklet pane of 20 .50
962 A236 10o dark blue .25 .25
  a.   Booklet pane of 20 .60
    Complete booklet, #962a 1.00
963 A240 75o indigo .40 .25
  a.   Booklet pane of 10 4.00
    Nos. 954-963 (10) 3.35 2.50

King Gustaf VI Adolf — A245

Chinese Objects — A246

Designs: No. 983, King opening Parliament. No. 984, Etruscan vase and dish. No. 985, King with flowers.

1972, Nov. 11   **Perf. 12½ Vert.**
981 A245 75o violet blue 1.25 2.75
982 A246 75o slate green 1.25 2.75
983 A245 75o maroon 1.25 2.75
984 A246 75o violet blue 1.25 2.75

985 A245 75o slate green 1.25 2.75
  a.   Bklt. pane of 5, #981-985 5.75 15.00
    Complete booklet, #985a 8.00

90th birthday of King Gustaf VI Adolf. Booklet sold for 4.75k of which 1k was for the King Gustaf VI Adolf Foundation for Swedish Cultural Activities.

Paul Sabatier and Victor Grignard — A247

Dr. Alexis Carrel — A248

75o, Nils Gustaf Dalen. 1k, Gerhart Hauptmann.

1972, Dec. 8   **Engr.**   **Perf. 12½ Vert.**
986 A247 60o olive bister .60 .40

Perf. 12½ Horiz.

987 A248 65o dark blue .70 .40
988 A248 75o violet .90 .25
989 A248 1k redsh brown 1.10 .30
    Nos. 986-989 (4) 3.30 1.35

Winners of the 1912 Nobel Prize.

Mail Coach, 1923 — A249

Design: 70o, Postal autobus, 1972.

Perf. 12½ on 3 Sides

1973, Jan. 18   **Engr.**
990 A249 60o black, *yellow* .30 .25
  a.   Booklet pane of 10 3.00

Perf. 12½ Vert.

991 A249 70o blue, orange & grn .45 .25

Tintomara, by Lars Johan Werle — A250

Orpheus and Eurydice, by Christoph W. Gluck — A251

1973, Jan. 18   **Perf. 12½ Horiz.**
992 A250 75o green .55 .25

Booklet Stamp

993 A251 1k red lilac .55 .35
  a.   Booklet pane of 5 3.00

Bicentenary of the Royal Theater in Stockholm. The 75o shows a stage setting by Bo-Ruben Hedwall for Tintomara, a new opera, performed for the bicentenary celebration. The 1k shows painting by Pehr Hillestrom of Orpheus and Eurydice, which was first opera performed in Royal Theater.

Vaasa Ski Race, Dalecarlia — A252

Designs: No. 995, "Going to Church in Mora" (church boats), by Anders Zorn. No. 996, Church stables, Rättvik. No. 997, Falun copper mine. No. 998, Midsummer Dance, by Bengt Nordenberg.

1973, Mar. 2   **Perf. 12½ Horiz.**
994 A252 65o slate green .40 .40
995 A252 65o slate green .40 .40
996 A252 65o black .40 .40
997 A252 65o slate green .40 .40
998 A252 65o claret .40 .40
  a.   Bklt. pane, 2 each #994-998 4.00
    Nos. 994-998 (5) 2.00 2.00

Tourist attractions in Dalecarlia.

Worker, Confederation Emblem — A253

1973, Apr. 26   **Perf. 12½ Vert.**
999 A253 75o dark carmine .40 .25
1000 A253 1.40k slate blue .75 .25

75th anniversary of the Swedish Confederation of Trade Unions (LO).

Observer Reading Temperature A254

Design: No. 1002, Clouds, photographed by US weather satellite.

1973, May 24   **Engr.**   **Perf. 12½ Vert.**
1001 A254 65o slate green .75 .65
1002 A254 65o black & ultra .75 .65
  a.   Pair, #1001-1002 1.50 2.50

Cent. of the Swedish Weather Organization and of Intl. Meteorological Cooperation.

Nordic Cooperation Issue

Nordic House, Reykjavik A254a

1973, June 26   **Perf. 12½ Vert.**
1003 A254a 75o multicolored .45 .25
1004 A254a 1k multicolored .65 .25

A century of postal cooperation among Denmark, Finland, Iceland, Norway and Sweden and in connection with the Nordic Postal Conference, Reykjavik, Iceland.

Carl Peter Thunberg (1743-1828) — A255

Swedish Explorers: No. 1006, Anders Sparrman (1748-1820) and Polynesian double canoe. No. 1007, Nils Adolf Erik Nordenskjold (1832-1901) and ship in pack ice. No. 1008, Salomon August Andrée (1854-1897) and balloon on snow field. No. 1009, Sven Hedin (1865-1952) and camel riders.

1973, Sept. 22   **Perf. 12½ Horiz.**
1005 A255 1k sl grn, bl & brn .95 1.10
1006 A255 1k bl, sl grn & brn .95 1.10
1007 A255 1k bl, sl grn & brn .95 1.10
1008 A255 1k black & multi .95 1.10
1009 A255 1k black & multi .95 1.10
  a.   Bklt. pane of 5, #1005-1009 5.00 8.25
    Complete booklet, #1009a 8.50

Plower with Ox Team A256

Designs: No. 1011, Woman working flax brake. No. 1012, Farm couple planting potatoes. No. 1013, Women baking bread. No. 1014, Man with horse-drawn sower.

1973, Oct. 24   **Perf. 12½ Horiz.**
1010 A256 75o grnsh black 1.00 .45
1011 A256 75o red brown 1.00 .45
1012 A256 75o grnsh black 1.00 .45
1013 A256 75o plum 1.00 .45
1014 A256 75o red brown 1.00 .45
  a.   Bklt. pane, 2 ea #1010-1014 10.00
    Nos. 1010-1014 (5) 5.00 2.25

Centenary of Nordic Museum, Stockholm.

Gray Seal — A257

Protected Animals: 20o, Peregrine falcon. 25o, Lynx. 55o, Otter. 65o, Wolf. 75o, White-tailed sea eagle.

1973, Oct. 24   **Perf. 12½ on 3 Sides**
1015 A257 10o slate green .25 .25
1016 A257 20o violet .25 .25
1017 A257 25o Prus green .25 .25
1018 A257 55o Prus green .25 .25
1019 A257 65o violet .25 .25
1020 A257 75o slate green .35 .35
  a.   Bklt. pane, 2 each #1015-1020 2.50 3.00
    Nos. 1015-1020 (6) 1.60 1.60

King Gustaf VI Adolf — A258

1973, Oct. 24   **Perf. 12½ Vert.**
1021 A258 75o dk violet blue .30 .25
1022 A258 1k purple .50 .25

King Gustaf VI Adolf (1882-1973).

The Three Kings A259

Charles XIV John — A260

No. 1024, Merry country dance. No. 1026, Basket with stylized Dalecarlian gourd plant.

Perf. 14 Horiz.

1973, Nov. 12   **Photo.**
1023 A259 45o multicolored .35 .30
1024 A259 45o multicolored .35 .30
  a.   Bklt. pane, 5 each #1023-1024 3.50

Coil Stamps

1025 A260 45o multicolored 1.40 .25
1026 A260 75o multicolored 1.40 .25
  a.   Pair, #1025-1026 3.00 5.00
    Nos. 1023-1026 (4) 3.50 1.10

Christmas 1973. Designs are from Swedish peasant paintings.

The Goosegirl, by Josephson — A261

Perf. 12½ Horiz.

1973, Nov. 12   **Engr.**
1027 A261 10k multicolored 4.50 .35

Ernst Josephson (1851-1906), painter.

Alfred Werner and
Heike Kamerlingh-
Onnes
A262

Charles Robert
Richet
A263

Design: 1.40k, Rabindranath Tagore.

1973, Dec. 10 Engr. *Perf. 12½ Vert.*
1028 A262 75o dark violet   .55 .25

Perf. 12½ Horiz.
1029 A262 1k dark brown   .55 .30
1030 A263 1.40k green   .65 .25
    Nos. 1028-1030 (3)   1.75 .80
Winners of 1913 Nobel Prize.

Ski Jump
A264

Skiing: No. 1032, Cross-country race. No.
1033, Relay race. No. 1034, Slalom. No. 1035,
Women's cross-country race.

Perf. 12½ Horiz.
1974, Jan. 23   Engr.
1031 A264 65o slate green   .55 .65
1032 A264 65o violet blue   .55 .65
1033 A264 65o slate green   .55 .65
1034 A264 65o dk carmine   .55 .65
1035 A264 65o violet blue   .55 .65
  a. Bklt. pane, 2 each #1031-
     1035   11.00
    Nos. 1031-1035 (5)   2.75 3.25

Drawing
of First
Industrial
Digester
A265

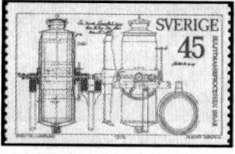

Hans Järta and Quotation from
1809 — A266

Samuel
Owen
and 19th
Century
Factory
A267

1974, Mar. 5 Engr. *Perf. 12½ Vert.*
1036 A265 45o sepia   .25 .25
1037 A266 60o green   .30 .30
1038 A267 75o dull red   .45 .25
    Nos. 1036-1038 (3)   1.00 .80
Centenary of sulphite pulp process (45o);
Hans Järta (1774-1847), statesman responsible for the Instrument of Government Act of
1809 (60o); Samuel Owen (1774-1854),
English-born industrialist who introduced new
production methods (75o).

Stora Sjofallet
(Great
Falls) — A268

Street in
Ystad — A269

1974, Apr. 2   *Perf. 12½ Horiz.*
1039 A268 35o blue grn & blk   .45 .25

Perf. 12½ on 3 Sides
1040 A269 75o dull claret   .30 .25
  a. Booklet of 10   3.00
    Complete booklet, #1040a   6.75

UPU
Type
of
1924
A270

1974   Engr. *Perf. 12½ on 3 Sides*
1041 A270 20o green   .30 .35
1042 A270 25o ultra   .30 .35
1043 A270 30o dark brown   .30 .35
1044 A270 35o dark red   .30 .35
  a. Bklt. pane, 2 each #1041-1044 2.50 3.50
    Complete booklet, #1044a   3.25
    Nos. 1041-1044 (4)   1.20 1.40

Miniature Sheets
Perf. 12½
1045   Sheet of 4   2.00 3.50
  a. A270 20o ocher, single stamp .40 .75
1046   Sheet of 4   2.00 3.50
  a. A270 25o dk vio, single stamp .40 .75
1047   Sheet of 4   2.00 3.50
  a. A270 30o dk red, single stamp .40 .75
1048   Sheet of 4   2.00 3.50
  a. A270 35o yel grn, single stamp .40 .75

Stockholmia 74 philatelic exhibition, Stockholm, Sept. 21-29. Booklet sold for 3k with
surtax going toward financing the exhibition.
Nos. 1045-1048 sold during exhibition in
folder with 5k entrance ticket.
  Issued: #1041-1044, 4/2; #1045-1048, 9/21.

"Man in Storm," by
Bror
Marklund — A271

Europa: 1k, Sculpture by Picasso, Lake
Vanern, Kristinehamm.

Perf. 12½ Horiz.
1974, Apr. 29   Engr.
1049 A271 75o violet brown   1.10 .30
1050 A271 1k slate green   1.25 .30

King Carl XVI
Gustaf — A272

1974-78   Engr. *Perf. 12½ Vert.*
1068 A272 75o slate grn   .40 .25
1069 A272 90o brt blue ('75)   .35 .25
1070 A272 1k maroon   .45 .25
1071 A272 1.10k rose red ('75)   .40 .25
1072 A272 1.30k green ('76)   .50 .25
1073 A272 1.40k violet bl ('77)   .75 .25
1074 A272 1.50k red lilac ('80)   .60 .25
1075 A272 1.70k orange ('78)   .85 .25
1076 A272 2k dk brown ('80)   .85 .25

Perf. 12½ on 3 Sides
1077 A272 75o slate green   .30 .25
  a. Booklet pane of 10   3.00
    Complete booklet, #1077a   6.75
1078 A272 90o brt blue ('75)   .30 .25
  a. Booklet pane of 10   3.00
    Complete booklet, #1078a   8.00
1079 A272 1k maroon ('76)   .40 .25
  a. Booklet pane of 10   4.00
    Complete booklet, #1079a   8.00
1080 A272 1.10k rose red ('77)   .40 .25
  a. Booklet pane of 10   4.00
    Complete booklet, #1080a   8.00
1081 A272 1.30k green ('78)   .50 .25
  a. Booklet pane of 10   5.00
    Complete booklet, #1081a   9.00
1082 A272 1.50k red lilac ('80)   .60 .25
  a. Booklet pane of 10   6.00
    Complete booklet, #1082a   10.00
    Nos. 1068-1082 (15)   7.65 3.75

A273

Central Post
Office,
Stockholm
A274

Mailman, Northernmost Rural Delivery
Route — A275

Perf. 12½ on 3 Sides
1974, June 7   Engr.
1084 A273 75o violet brown   .70 .40
1085 A274 75o violet brown   .70 .40
  a. Bklt. pane, 5 ea #1084-1085 7.00
    Complete booklet, #1085a   8.00

Perf. 12½ Vert.
1086 A275 1k slate green   .65 .25
    Nos. 1084-1086 (3)   2.05 1.05
Centenary of Universal Postal Union.

Regatta
A276

Scenes from Sweden's West Coast: No.
1088, Vinga Lighthouse. No. 1089, Varberg
Fortress. No. 1090, Seine fishing. No. 1091,
Fishing village Mollosund.

1974, June 7   *Perf. 12½ Horiz.*
1087 A276 65o crimson   .55 .55
1088 A276 65o blue   .55 .55
1089 A276 65o dk olive green   .55 .55
1090 A276 65o slate green   .55 .55
1091 A276 65o brown   .55 .55
  a. Bklt. pane, 2 each #1087-
     1091   4.50
    Complete booklet, #1091a   10.00
    Nos. 1087-1091 (5)   2.75 2.75

Mr. Simmons, by
Axel Fridell — A277

Perf. 12½ on 3 Sides
1974, Aug. 28   Engr.
1092 A277 45o black   .25 .25
  a. Booklet pane of 10   2.50
    Complete booklet, #1092a   4.00

Perf. 12½ Horiz.
1093 A277 1.40k deep claret   .75 .25
Swedish Publicists' Club, centenary.

Swedish Textile &
Clothing
Industries — A278

No. 1094, Thread and spool. No. 1095,
Sewing machines (abstract).

1974, Aug. 28   *Perf. 12½ Horiz.*
1094   85o deep violet   .40 .30
1095   85o black & org   .40 .30
  a. A278 Pair, #1094-1095   1.00 .90

Tugs in Stockholm Harbor — A279

No. 1096, Tanker. No. 1097, Liner "Snow
Storm." No. 1098, Ice breakers Tor and Atle.
No. 1099, Skane Train Ferry, Trelleborg-
Sassnitz.

1974, Nov. 16   *Perf. 12½ Horiz.*
1096 A279 1k dark blue   .80 .90
1097 A279 1k dark blue   .80 .90
1098 A279 1k dark blue   .80 .90
1099 A279 1k dark blue   .80 .90
1100 A279 1k dark blue   .80 .90
  a. Bklt. pane of 5, #1096-1100 4.00 7.00
    Complete booklet, #1100a   6.75
Swedish shipping industry.

Miniature Sheet

Quilt from Skepptuna Church — A280

Deer, Quilt from Hog
Church — A281

Designs are from woolen quilts, 15th-16th
centuries. Motifs shown on No. 1101 are stylized deer, griffins, lions, unicorn and horses.

1974, Nov. 16   Photo.   *Perf. 14*
1101 A280   Sheet of 10   9.50 13.00
  a.-j. 45o, single stamp   .95 1.00

Perf. 13 Horiz.
1102 A281 75o bl blk, red & yel   .45 .25

Max von
Laue — A282

Designs: 70o, Theodore William Richards.
1k, Robert Bárány.

1974, Dec. 10 Engr. *Perf. 12½ Vert.*
1103 A282 65o rose red .35 .25
1104 A282 70o slate .45 .30
1105 A282 1k indigo .95 .25
  Nos. 1103-1105 (3) 1.75 .80
  Winners of 1914 Nobel Prize.

A283

No. 1106, Sven Jerring's children's program. No. 1107, Televising parliamentary debate.

1974, Dec. 10 *Perf. 12½ Vert.*
1106 75o dk blue & brn .65 .25
1107 75o brown & dk bl .65 .25
  a. Pair, #1106-1107 1.25 *2.00*
  Swedish Broadcasting Corp., 50th anniv.

Account Holder's Envelope A285

Photogravure and Engraved
1975, Jan. 21 *Perf. 14 Vert.*
1108 A285 1.40k ocher & blk .65 .35
  Swedish Postal Giro Office, 50th anniv.

Male and Female Architects, New Parliament A286

Jenny Lind (1820-87), by J. O. Sodermark A287

1975, Mar. 25 Engr. *Perf. 12½ Vert.*
1109 A286 75o slate green .40 .25
  Perf. 12½ Horiz.
1110 A287 1k claret .60 .25
  Perf. 12½ on 3 Sides
1111 A286 75o slate green .35 .25
  a. Booklet pane of 10 3.50
    Complete booklet, #1111a 5.50
  Nos. 1109-1111 (3) 1.35 .75
  International Women's Year 1975.

Horseman, Helmet Decoration A288

"Gold Men" A289

Designs: 15o, Scabbard and hilt. 20o, Shield buckle. 55o, Iron helmet.

1975, Mar. 25 *Perf. 12½ on 3 sides*
1112 A288 10o dull red .25 .25
1113 A288 15o slate green .25 .25
1114 A288 20o violet .25 .25
1115 A288 55o violet brown .25 .25
  a. Bklt. pane, 2 each #1112-1115 .75 *1.60*
    Complete booklet, #1115a 2.00
  Perf. 12½ Horiz.
1116 A289 25o deep yellow .25 .25
  Nos. 1112-1116 (5) 1.25 1.25
  Treasures from tombs of the Vendel period (550-800 A.D.), and "gold men" (25o) from Eketorp II excavations (400-700 A.D.).

Europa Issue

New Year's Eve at Skansen, by Eric Hallstrom — A290

Inferno, by August Strindberg — A291

Perf. 12½ Vert.
1975, Apr. 28 Photo.
1117 A290 90o multi .75 .25
  Perf. 14¼ Horiz.
1118 A291 1.10k multi .75 .25

Capercaillie A292

Rok Stone, 9th Century A293

1975, May 20 Engr. *Perf. 12½ Vert.*
1119 A292 170o indigo .70 .25
  Perf. 12½ Horiz.
1120 A293 2k deep claret .85 .25

Metric Tape Measure — A294

Folke Filbyter Statue, by Milles — A296

Hernqvist by Per Krafft the Younger — A295

1975, May 20 *Perf. 12½ Vert.*
1121 A294 55o deep blue .35 .30
1122 A295 70o yel brn & dk brn .40 .30
  Perf. 12½ Horiz.
1123 A296 75o violet .40 .25
  Nos. 1121-1123 (3) 1.15 .85
  Cent. of Intl. Meter Convention, Paris, 1875; bicent. of Swedish veterinary medicine, founded by Peter Hernqvist (1726-1808); Carl Milles (1875-1955), sculptor.

Officers' Mess, Rommehed, 1798 — A297

No. 1124, Skelleftea Church Village, 17th cent. No. 1125, Foundry and furnace, Engelsberg, 18th cent. No. 1126, Gunpowder Tower, Visby. No. 1127, Falun Mine pithead gear, 1852.

1975, June 13 *Perf. 12½ Horiz.*
1124 A297 75o black .50 .75
1125 A297 75o dk carmine .50 .75
1126 A297 75o black .50 .75
1127 A297 75o dk carmine .50 .75
1128 A297 75o violet blue .50 .75
  a. Bklt. pane, 2 each #1124-1128 5.50
    Complete booklet, #1128a 8.00
  Nos. 1124-1128 (5) 2.50 3.75
  European Architectural Heritage Year 1975.

Rescue at Sea: Helicopter over Ice-covered Tanker — A298

Designs: No. 1129, Fire fighters: firemen fighting fire. No. 1130, Customs narcotics service: trained dogs checking cargo. No. 1131, Police: Officer talking to boy on bridge. No. 1132, Hospital Service: patient arriving by ambulance.

1975, Aug. 27 *Perf. 12½ Horiz.*
1129 A298 90o dk car rose .65 .45
1130 A298 90o dk bl .65 .45
1131 A298 90o dk car rose .65 .45
1132 A298 90o dk bl .65 .45
1133 A298 90o green .65 .45
  a. Bklt. pane, 2 each #1129-1133 6.50
    Complete booklet, #1133a 10.00
  Nos. 1129-1133 (5) 3.25 2.25
  Public service organizations watching, guarding, helping.

"Fryckstad" A299

"Gotland" A300

Design: 90o, "Prins August."

1975, Aug. 27 *Perf. 12½ on 3 Sides*
  Size: 20x19mm
1134 A299 5o green .25 .25
1135 A300 5o dark blue .25 .25
  Size: 45x19mm
1136 A299 90o slate green .55 .25
  a. Bklt. pane, 2 each #1134-1136 1.75 *2.50*
    Complete booklet, #1136a 3.25
  Nos. 1134-1136 (3) 1.05 .75

Scouts — A302

1975, Oct. 11 Photo. *Perf. 14 Vert.*
1137 90o Around campfire .50 .25
1138 90o In canoes .50 .25
  a. Pair, #1137-1138 1.25 *2.00*
  Nordjamb 75, 14th World Boy Scout Jamboree, Lillehammer, Norway, July 29-Aug. 7.

Hedgehog A303

Old Man Playing Key Fiddle — A304

Romeo and Juliet Ballet — A305

1975, Oct. 11 Engr. *Perf. 12½ Vert.*
1139 A303 55o black .30 .25
1140 A304 75o dk red .55 .25
  Perf. 12½ Horiz.
1141 A305 7k blue green 3.25 .25
  Perf. 12½ on 3 Sides
1142 A303 55o black .25 .25
  a. Booklet pane of 10 2.50
    Complete booklet, #1142a 5.50
  Nos. 1139-1142 (4) 4.35 1.00
  See No. 2642c.

Virgin Mary, 12th Cent. Statue — A306

Chariot of the Sun, from 12th Cent. Altar — A307

Mourning Mary, c. 1280 — A308

Jesse at Foot of Genealogical Tree, c. 1510 — A309

Christmas: #1145, Nativity, from 12th cent. gilt-copper altar. #1148, like #1147.

1975, Nov. 11 Photo.
  Perf. 14 Horiz.
1143 A306 55o multi .30 .25
  Perf. 12½ on 3 Sides
1144 A307 55o gold & multi .35 .30
1145 A307 55o gold & multi .35 .30
  a. Bklt. pane, 5 each #1144-1145 3.00
    Complete booklet, #1145a 5.50
  Perf. 12½ Horiz.
  Engr.
1146 A308 90o brown .50 .25
  Perf. 12½ on 3 Sides
1147 A309 90o red .60 .30
1148 A309 90o blue .60 .30
  a. Bklt. pane, 5 ea #1147-1148 6.00
    Complete booklet, #1148a 9.00
  Nos. 1143-1148 (6) 2.70 1.70

No. 1145a was issued with top row of 5 either No. 1144 or No. 1145.

William H. and William L. Bragg — A310

Designs: 90o, Richard Willstätter. 1.10k, Romain Rolland.

1975, Dec. 10 Engr. *Perf. 12½ Vert.*
1149 A310 75o claret .40 *.45*
1150 A310 90o violet blue .45 .25
1151 A310 1.10k slate green .55 .35
  Nos. 1149-1151 (3) 1.40 1.05
  Winners of 1915 Nobel Prize.

Cave of the Winds, by Eric Grate — A311

1976, Jan. 27   **Perf. 12½ Vert.**
1152 A311 1.90k slate green   .90 .25

The sculpture by Eric Grate (b. 1896) stands in front of the Town Hall of Vasteras.

Razor-billed Auks and Black Guillemot A312

Bobbin Lace Maker from Vadstena A313

1976, Mar. 10   Engr.   Perf. 12½ Vert.
1153 A312 85o dark blue   .55 .25

Perf. 12½ Horiz.
1154 A313 1k claret brn   .45 .30

Perf. 12½ on 3 Sides
1155 A312 85o dk bl   .30 .30
   a.   Booklet pane of 10   3.00
      Complete booklet, #1155a   8.00
1156 A313 1k claret brn   .40 .30
   a.   Booklet pane of 10   4.00
      Complete booklet, #1156a   6.75
      Nos. 1153-1156 (4)   1.70 1.15

Old and New Telephones, Relays — A314

1976, Mar. 10   **Perf. 12½ Vert.**
1157 A314 1.30k brt violet   .75 .25
1158 A314 3.40k red   1.35 .55

Centenary of first telephone call by Alexander Graham Bell, March 10, 1876.

Europa Issue

Lapp Elk Horn Spoon — A315

Tile Stove — A316

Perf. 14½ Horiz.
1976, May 3   **Photo.**
1159 A315 1k multi   .65 .25
1160 A316 1.30k multi   .65 .45

Wheat and Cornflower Seeds — A317

Viable and Nonviable Seedlings A318

1976, May 3   Engr.   Perf. 12½ Vert.
1161 A317 65o brown   .30 .25
1162 A318 65o choc & grn   .30 .25
   a.   Pair, #1161-1162   .90 .90

Swedish seed testing centenary.

King Carl XVI Gustaf and Queen Silvia — A319

Perf. 12½ Vert.
1976, June 19   **Engr.**
1163 A319 1k rose car   .30 .25
1164 A319 1.30k slate grn   .40 .25

Perf. 12½ on 3 Sides
1165 A319 1k rose car   .30 .25
   a.   Booklet pane of 10   3.00
      Complete booklet, #1165a   8.00
      Nos. 1163-1165 (3)   1.00 .75

Wedding of King Carl XVI Gustaf and Silvia Sommerlath.

View from Ringkallen, by Helmer Osslund — A320

Views in Angermanland Province: No. 1167, Tugboat pulling timber. No. 1168, Hay-drying racks. No. 1169, Granvagsnipan slope, Angerman River. No. 1170, Seine fishing.

1976, June 19   **Perf. 12½ Horiz.**
1166 A320 85o slate grn   .40 .40
1167 A320 85o vio bl   .40 .40
1168 A320 85o dp brn   .40 .40
1169 A320 85o vio bl   .40 .40
1170 A320 85o brn red   .40 .40
   a.   Bklt. pane, 2 each #1166-1170   4.50
      Complete booklet, #1170a   8.00
      Nos. 1166-1170 (5)   2.00 2.00

Roman Cross and Ship's Wheel — A321

1976, June 19   **Perf. 12½ Horiz.**
1171 A321 85o brt bl & bl   .55 .40

Swedish Seamen's Church, centenary.

Torgny Segerstedt and 1917 Page of Gothenburg Journal — A322

1976, June 19   **Perf. 12½ Vert.**
1172 A322 1.90k brn & blk   .80 .30

Torgny Segerstedt (1876-1945), editor in chief of the Gothenburg Journal of Commerce and Shipping, birth centenary.

Coiled Snake, Bronze Buckle — A323

Pilgrim's Badge, Adoration of the Magi — A324

Drinking Horn, 14th Century — A325

Chimney Sweep — A326

Girl's Head, by Bror Hjorth, 1922 — A327

Perf. 12½ Horiz., Vert. (30o)
1976, Sept. 8   **Engr.**
1173 A323 15o bister   .25 .25
1174 A324 20o green   .25 .25
1175 A325 30o dk rose brn   .25 .25
1176 A326 90o indigo   .40 .25
1177 A327 9k yel grn & sl grn   3.50 .25
      Nos. 1173-1177 (5)   4.65 1.25

Inventors A328

#1178, John Ericsson (1803-1889), ship propeller and "Monitor". #1179, Helge Palmcrantz (1842-80) & reaper. #1180, Lars Magnus Ericsson (1846-1926) & switchboard. #1181, Sven Wingquist (1876-1953) & ball bearing. #1182, Gustaf de Laval (1845-1913) & milk separator.

1976, Oct. 9   Engr.   Perf. 12½ Horiz.
1178 A328 1.30k multi   .60 .60
1179 A328 1.30k multi   .60 .60
1180 A328 1.30k multi   .60 .60
1181 A328 1.30k multi   .60 .60
1182 A328 1.30k multi   .60 .60
   a.   Bklt. pane of 5, #1178-1182   3.75 6.00

Swedish inventors and their technological inventions.

Hands and Cogwheels A329

1976, Oct. 9   **Perf. 12½ Vert.**
1183 A329 85o org & dk vio   .40 .25
1184 A329 1k yel grn & brn   .55 .25

Industrial safety.

Verner von Heidenstam, Lake Vattern — A330

1976, Nov. 17   **Perf. 12½ Vert.**
1185 A330 1k yellow green   .40 .25
1186 A330 1.30k blue   .55 .45

Verner von Heidenstam (1859-1940), Swedish poet, 1916 Nobel Prize winner.

Archangel Michael A331

Virgin Mary Visiting St. Elizabeth A332

Christmas: No. 1189, like No. 1187. No. 1190, St. Nicholas saving 3 children. No. 1191, like No. 1188. No. 1192, Illuminated page, prayer to Virgin Mary. 65o stamps are from Flemish prayer book, c. 1500. 1k stamps are from Austrian prayer book, late 15th century.

Perf. 12½ Horiz.
1976, Nov. 17   **Photo.**
1187 A331 65o blue & multi   .30 .25
1188 A332 1k gold & multi   .30 .25

Perf. 12½ on 3 Sides
1189 A331 65o blue & multi   .25 .40
1190 A331 65o blue & multi   .25 .40
   a.   Bklt. pane, 5 each #1189-1190   2.50
      Complete booklet, #1190a   4.00

Perf. 12½ Vert.
1191 A332 1k gold & multi   .30 .25
1192 A332 1k gold & multi   .30 .25
   a.   Bklt. pane, 5 each #1191-1192   3.00
      Complete booklet, #1192a   8.00
      Nos. 1187-1192 (6)   1.70 1.80

Five Water Lilies — A333

Photogravure and Engraved
1977, Feb. 2   **Perf. 12½ Horiz.**
1193 A333 1k brt grn & multi   .55 .25
1194 A333 1.30k ultra & multi   .65 .55

Nordic countries cooperation for protection of the environment and 25th Session of Nordic Council, Helsinki, Feb. 19.

Tailor — A334

1977, Feb. 24   **Perf. 12½ Vert.**
1195 A334 2.10k red brn   .95 .25

Longdistance Skating — A335

Perf. 12½ Horiz.
1977, Mar. 24   **Engr.**
1196 A335 95o shown   .45 .55
1197 A335 95o Swimming   .45 .55
1198 A335 95o Bicycling   .45 .55
1199 A335 95o Jogging   .45 .55
1200 A335 95o Badminton   .45 .55
   a.   Bklt. pane, 2 each #1196-1200   4.50
      Complete booklet, #1200a   8.00
      Nos. 1196-1200 (5)   2.25 2.75

Physical fitness.

Politeness, by "OA,"
1905 — A336

1977, Mar. 24   Perf. 12½ on 3 Sides
1201 A336 75o black   .35   .25
  a.   Booklet pane of 10   3.50
       Complete booklet, #1201a   6.75

Perf. 12½ Horiz.
1202 A336 3.80k red   2.00   .45

Oskar Andersson (1877-1906), cartoonist.

Calle
Schewen
A337

No. 1204, Seagull. No. 1205, Dancers and
accordionist. No. 1206, Fishermen in boat. No.
1207, Tree on shore at sunset.
  Designs are illustrations for poem The Calle
Schewen Waltz, by Evert Taube, and include
bars of music of this song.

1977, May 2 Engr. Perf. 12½ Horiz.
1203 A337 95o slate grn   .45   .45
1204 A337 95o vio bl   .45   .45
1205 A337 95o grn & blk   .45   .45
1206 A337 95o dark blue   .45   .45
1207 A337 95o red   .45   .45
  a.   Bklt. pane, 2 each #1203-1207   4.50
       Complete booklet, #1207a   9.00
       Nos. 1203-1207 (5)   2.25 2.25

Tourist publicity for Roslagen (archipelago)
and to honor Evert Taube (1890-1976), poet.

Gustavianum,
Uppsala
University
A338

1977, May 2   Photo.   Perf. 14 Vert.
1208 A338 1.10k multi   .55   .25

Perf. 14 on 3 Sides
1209 A338 1.10k multi   .35   .25
  a.   Booklet pane of 10   8.00
       Complete booklet, #1209a

Uppsala University, 500th anniversary.

Europa Issue

Forest in
Snow
A339

Rapadalen Valley — A340

1977, May 2   Perf. 14 Vert.
1210 A339 1.10k multi   1.10   .30
1211 A340 1.40k multi   1.10   .65

Owl — A341

Cast-iron Stove
Decoration — A342

Gotland
Ponies
A343

1977, Sept. 8 Engr. Perf. 12½ Vert.
1212 A341 45o dk slate grn   .50   .40

Perf. 12½ Horiz.
1213 A342 70o dk vio bl   .45   .25

Booklet Stamp
1214 A343 1.40k brown   .55   .35
  a.   Booklet pane of 5   2.75
       Complete booklet, #1214a   5.00
       Nos. 1212-1214 (3)   1.50 1.00

Wild
Berries — A344

Perf. 14 on 3 Sides
1977, Sept. 8   Photo.
1215 A344 75o Blackberry   .40   .40
1216 A344 75o Cranberry   .40   .40
1217 A344 75o Raspberry   .40   .40
1218 A344 75o Whortleberry   .40   .40
1219 A344 75o Alpine strawberry   .40   .40
  a.   Bklt. pane, 2 each #1215-1219   4.00 6.50
       Complete booklet, #1219a   8.00
       Nos. 1215-1219 (5)   2.00 2.00

Horse-drawn Trolley — A345

Designs: Public transportation.

1977, Oct. 8 Engr. Perf. 12½ Horiz.
1220 A345 1.10k shown   .75   .90
1221 A345 1.10k Electric trolley   .75   .90
1222 A345 1.10k Ferry   .75   .90
1223 A345 1.10k Tandem bus   .75   .90
1224 A345 1.10k Subway   .75   .90
  a.   Bklt. pane of 5, #1220-1224   3.75 6.50
       Complete booklet, #1224a   4.50

Putting up
Sheaf for the
Birds — A346

Preparing Dried
Soaked
Fish — A347

Traditional Christmas Preparations: No.
1227, Children baking ginger snaps. No. 1228,
Bringing in Yule tree. No. 1229, Making straw
goat. No. 1230, Candle dipping.

Perf. 12½ Horiz.
1977, Nov. 17   Engr.
1225 A346 75o violet   .35   .25
1226 A347 1.10k yel grn   .55   .25

Perf. 12½ on 3 Sides
1227 A346 75o ocher   .35   .25
1228 A346 75o slate grn   .35   .25
  a.   Bklt. pane, 5 each #1227-1228   2.50
       Complete booklet, #1228a   5.50
1229 A347 1.10k dk red   .40   .25
1230 A347 1.10k dk bl   .40   .25
  a.   Bklt. pane, 5 each #1229-1230   4.00
       Complete booklet, #1230a   8.00
       Nos. 1225-1230 (6)   2.40 1.50

Christmas 1977.

Henrik
Pontoppidan,
Karl Adolph
Gjellerup
A348

Design: 1.40k, Charles Glover Barkla.

1977, Nov. 17   Perf. 12½ Vert.
1231 A348 1.10k red brn   .60   .30
1232 A348 1.40k yel grn   .65   .65

  1917 Nobel Prize winners: Henrik Pontoppidan (1857-1943) and Karl Adolph Gjellerup
(1857-1919), Danish writers; Charles Glover
Barkla (1877-1944), English X-ray pioneer.

Space Without
Affiliation, by Arne
Jones — A349

1978, Jan. 25   Perf. 12½ Horiz.
1233 A349 2.50k vio bl   1.00   .25

Brown Bear — A350

1978, Apr. 11   Perf. 12½ Horiz.
1234 A350 1.15k dark brown   .50   .25

Europa Issue

Örebro
Castle — A351

Arch and
Stairs — A352

1978, Apr. 11   Perf. 12½ Vert.
1235 A351 1.30k slate green   1.35   .35

Perf. 12½ Horiz.
1236 A352 1.70k dull red   1.75   .65

Pentecostal
Preacher and
Congregation
A353

  Free Churches: No. 1238, Swedish Missionary Society. No. 1239, Evangelical
National Missionary Society. No. 1240, Baptist Society. No. 1241, Salvation Army.

1978, Apr. 11   Perf. 12½ on 3 sides
1237 A353 90o purple   .50   .50
1238 A353 90o slate   .50   .50
1239 A353 90o violet   .50   .50
1240 A353 90o slate   .50   .50
1241 A353 90o purple   .50   .50
  a.   Bklt. pane, 2 each #1237-1241   5.00 7.50
       Complete booklet, #1241a   8.00
       Nos. 1237-1241 (5)   2.50 2.50

Independent Christian Associations.

Brosarp Hills — A354

Grindstone
Production
A355

Red Limestone
Cliff — A356

Designs: No. 1243, Avocets. No. 1245,
Linnaea borealis (Linné's favorite flower.) No.
1247, Linné with Lapp drum, wearing Lapp
clothes and Dutch doctor's hat.

Perf. 12½ Horiz.
1978, May 23   Engr.
1242 A354 1.30k gray green   .65   .50
1243 A354 1.30k violet blue   .65   .50

Perf. 12½ on 3 Sides
1244 A355 1.30k violet brown   .65   .60
1245 A355 1.30k brown red   .65   .60

Perf. 12½ on 2 Sides
1246 A356 1.30k violet blue   .65   .60
1247 A356 1.30k violet blue   .65   .60
  a.   Bklt. pane of 6, #1242-1247   4.25 5.50
       Complete booklet, #1247a   8.00

Travels of Carl von Linné (1707-1778),
botanist.

Cranes, Lake Hornborgasjon — A357

Designs: No. 1248, Gliding School,
Alleberg. No. 1250, Skara Church, Lacko
Island. No. 1251, Ancient rock tomb, Luttra.
No. 1252, Cloth merchants, sculpture by Nils
Sjogren.

1978, May 23   Perf. 12½ Horiz.
1248 A357 1.15k dull green   .55   .45
1249 A357 1.15k maroon   .55   .45
1250 A357 1.15k violet blue   .55   .45
1251 A357 1.15k dk gray grn   .55   .45
1252 A357 1.15k brn & gray grn   .55   .45
  a.   Bklt. pane, 2 each #1284-
       1252   5.50
       Complete booklet, #1252a   10.00
       Nos. 1248-1252 (5)   2.75 2.25

Tourist publicity for Vastergotland.

Laurel and
Scroll — A358

1978, May 23   Perf. 12½ Vert.
1253 A358 2.50k gray & sl grn   1.00   .25

Stockholm University, centenary.

Homecoming, by Carl Kylberg — A359

Nude, by Karl Isakson
A360

Self-portrait, by Ivar Arosenius
A361

1978, Sept. 5 Engr. Perf. 12½ Vert.
1254 A359 90o multicolored .40 .40

Perf. 12½ Horiz.
1255 A360 1.15k multi .55 .30
1256 A361 4.50k multi 1.75 .50
    Nos. 1254-1256 (3) 2.70 1.20

Swedish painters: Carl Kylberg (1878-1952); Karl Isakson (1878-1922); Ivar Arosenius (1878-1909).

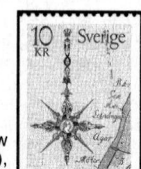
North Arrow (Compass Rose), Map, 1769 — A362

1978, Sept. 5 Perf. 12½ Horiz.
1257 A362 10k lilac 3.75 .25

Coronation Coach, 1699 — A363

1978, Oct. 7 Engr. Perf. 12½ Horiz.
1258 A363 1.70k dk red, yel .80 .45
  a. Booklet pane of 5 4.00
    Complete booklet, #1258a 8.00

Orange Russula — A364

Edible mushrooms — No. 1260, Lycoperdon perlatum. No. 1261, Macrolepiota procera. No. 1262, Cantharellus cibarius. No. 1263, Boletus edulis. No. 1264, Ramaria botrytis.

1978, Oct. 7 Perf. 12½ on 3 Sides
1259 A364 1.15k shown .60 .60
1260 A364 1.15k multicolored .60 .60
1261 A364 1.15k multicolored .60 .60
1262 A364 1.15k multicolored .60 .60
1263 A364 1.15k multicolored .60 .60
1264 A364 1.15k multicolored .60 .60
  a. Bklt. pane of 6, #1259-1264 4.00 7.50
    Complete booklet, #1264a 6.75

Toy Ferris Wheel — A365

Teddy Bear — A365a

Dalecarlian Wooden Horse — A365b

Doll — A365c

Spinning Tops — A366

Rider Drawing Water Cart — A366a

Perf. 12½ Horiz.
1978, Nov. 14 Engr.
1265 A365 90o dk red & grn .45 .25
1266 A365a 1.30k brt ultra .65 .25

Perf. 12½ on 3 Sides
Photo.
1267 A365b 90o multicolored .35 .25
1268 A365c 90o multicolored .35 .25
  a. Bklt. pane, 5 each #1267-1268 3.50
    Complete booklet, #1268a 8.00
1269 A366 1.30k multicolored .55 .25
1270 A366a 1.30k multicolored .55 .25
  a. Bklt. pane, 5 each #1269-1270 5.50
    Complete booklet, #1270a 9.00
    Nos. 1265-1270 (6) 2.90 1.50

Christmas 1978.

Fritz Haber — A367

Design: 1.70k, Max Planck.

1978, Nov. 14 Engr. Perf. 12½ Vert.
1271 A367 1.30k dark brown .65 .50
1272 A367 1.70k dark violet bl .85 .65

1918 Nobel Prize winners: Fritz Haber (1868-1934), German chemist; Max Planck (1858-1947), German physicist.
See #1310-1312, 1341-1344, 1387-1389.

Bandy — A368

1979, Jan. 25 Engr. Perf. 12½ Vert.
1273 A368 1.05k violet blue .45 .40
1274 A368 2.50k orange 1.10 .60

Child Wearing Gas Mask in Heavy Traffic — A369

1979, Mar. 13 Perf. 12½ Vert.
1275 A369 1.70k dark blue 1.00 1.00

International Year of the Child.

Drill-weave Tapestry, c. 1855-1860 — A370

1979, Mar. 13 Perf. 12½ Horiz.
1276 A370 4k gray & red 1.65 .25

Carrier Pigeon, Hand with Quill — A371

Perf. 14x14½ on 3 Sides
1979, Apr. 2 Photo.
1277 A371 (1k) ultra & yel 1.50 .25
  a. Booklet pane of 20 30.00
    Complete booklet, #1277a 52.50
    Price of booklet 20k.

DISCOUNT BOOKLETS

Every Swedish household received during Apr. 1979, 2 coupons for the purchase of 2 discount booklets, #1277a. The stamps were for use on post cards and letters within Sweden. The stamps are inscribed "INRIKES POST."

The program continued with numerous changes. The inscription changed to "PRIVATPOST" in 1981, the same year that denominations were added. At some point the stamps could also be used to Denmark, Norway, Finland and Iceland. In 1991 the discount value of the stamps ended July, 1.

The last stamps inscribed "PRIVAT POST" were issued in 1993.

Mail Service by Boat, Grisslehamn to Echero A372

Europa: 1.70k, Hand on telegraph.

1979, May 7 Engr. Perf. 12½ Vert.
1278 A372 1.30k slate grn & blk 2.25 .50
1279 A372 1.70k ocher & blk 2.25 1.00

Woodcutter, Winter — A373

Designs: No. 1281, Sowing, spring. No. 1282, Grazing cattle, summer. No. 1283, Harvester, summer. No. 1284, Plowing, autumn.

1979, May 7 Perf. 12½ Horiz.
1280 A373 1.30k multicolored .55 .45
1281 A373 1.30k sl grn & dk brn .55 .45
1282 A373 1.30k dk brn & sl grn .55 .45
1283 A373 1.30k sl grn & ocher .55 .45
1284 A373 1.30k multicolored .55 .45
  a. Bklt. pane, 2 each #1280-1284 5.75
    Complete booklet, #1284a 9.00
    Nos. 1280-1284 (5) 2.75 2.25

Tourist Steamer Juno — A374

Roller Bridge, Hajstorp — A375

Sailing Ship — A376

Gota Canal: No. 1286, Borenshult Lock. No. 1288, Hand-drawn gate. No. 1290, Rowboat in Forsvik lock.

1979, May 7 Perf. 12½ Horiz.
1285 A374 1.15k violet blue .55 .75
1286 A374 1.15k slate green .55 .75

Perf. 12½ on 3 Sides
1287 A375 1.15k dull purple .55 .85
1288 A375 1.15k carmine .55 .85

Perf. 12½ on 2 Sides
1289 A376 1.15k violet blue .55 .85
1290 A376 1.15k slate green .55 .85
  a. Bklt. pane of 6, #1285-1290 3.50 5.75
    Complete booklet, #1290a 6.00
    Nos. 1285-1290 (6) 3.30 4.90

Strikers and Sawmill A377

Temperance Movement Banner — A378

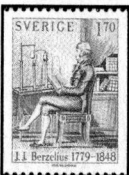
Jons Jacob Berzelius A379

Johan Olof Wallin A380

1979, Sept. 6 Engr. Perf. 12½ Vert.
1291 A377 90o car & dp brn .55 .35

Perf. 12½ Horiz.
Litho.
1292 A378 1.30k multi .55 .30
Engr.
1293 A379 1.70k brown & grn .75 .40
1294 A380 4.50k slate blue 1.75 .50
    Nos. 1291-1294 (4) 3.60 1.55

Centenaries of Sundsvall strike and Swedish Temperance Movement; birth bicentennials of Jons Jacob Berzelius (1779-1848), physician and chemist; Johan Olof Wallin (1779-1839), Archbishop and poet.

Dragonfly A381

Green Spotted Toad A383

Pike
A382

1979, Sept. 6   *Perf. 12½ Horiz.*
1295 A381 60o violet   .40 .40

Perf. 12½ Vert.
1296 A382 65o gray   .50 .35
1297 A383 80o olive green   .50 .55
   Nos. 1295-1297 (3)   1.40 1.30

Souvenir Sheet

Swedish Rococo — A384

Designs: 90o, Potpourri pot. 1.15k, Portrait, by Johan Henrik Scheffel. 1.30k, Silver coffeepot. 1.70k, Bust of Carl Johan Cronstedt.

Engraved and Photogravure
1979, Oct. 6   *Perf. 12x12½*
1298 A384   Sheet of 4   2.40 3.25
a.-d.   Any single   .50 .60

No. 1298 sold for 6k; surtax was for philately.

Herrings, Age Determination — A386

Sea Research: No. 1300, Acoustic survey of sea bottom. No. 1301, Water bloom of algae in Baltic Sea. No. 1302, Computer map of herring distribution in South Baltic Sea. No. 1303, Research ship Argos.

1979, Oct. 6   Engr.   *Perf. 12½ Horiz.*
1299 A386 1.70k multicolored   1.00 1.00
1300 A386 1.70k sepia   1.00 1.00
1301 A386 1.70k multicolored   1.00 1.00
1302 A386 1.70k sepia   1.00 1.00
1303 A386 1.70k multicolored   1.00 1.00
a.   Bkt. pane of 5, #1299-1303   4.50 6.50
  Complete booklet, #1303a   8.00

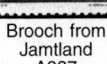
Brooch from Jamtland A387   Ljusdal Costume A388

Christmas (Costumes and Jewelry from): No. 1305, Pendant, Smaland. No. 1307, Osteraker. No. 1308, Goinge. No. 1309, Mora.

Perf. 12½ Horiz.
1979, Nov. 15   Engr.
1304 A387 90o dk Prus blue   .40 .30
1305 A387 1.30k dull red   .40 .25

Perf. 12½ on 3 Sides
Photo.
Size: 22x27mm
1306 A388 90o multicolored   .30 .30
1307 A388 90o multicolored   .30 .30
a.   Bkt. pane, 5 each #1306-1307   3.00
  Complete booklet, #1307a   6.75

Perf. 12½ Vert.
Size: 26x44mm
1308 A388 1.30k multicolored   .45 .25
1309 A388 1.30k multicolored   .45 .25
a.   Bkt. pane, 5 each #1308-1309   4.50
  Complete booklet, #1309a   9.00
  Nos. 1304-1309 (6)   2.30 1.65

Nobel Prize Winner Type of 1978

1919 Winners: 1.30k, Jules Bordet (1870-1961), Belgian bacteriologist. 1.70k, Johannes Stark (1874-1957), German physicist. 2.50k, Carl Spitteler (1845-1924), Swiss poet.

1979, Nov. 15   Engr.   *Perf. 12½ Vert.*
1310 A367 1.30k lilac   .70 .35
1311 A367 1.70k ultra   .90 1.00
1312 A367 2.50k olive green   1.25 .45
  Nos. 1310-1312 (3)   2.85 1.80

Wind Power — A389

Renewable Energy Sources: No. 1314, Biodegradable material. No. 1315, Solar energy. No. 1316, Geothermal energy. No. 1317, Hydro power.

1980, Jan. 29   *Perf. 12½ on 3 sides*
1313 A389 1.15k dark blue   .75 .85
1314 A389 1.15k dk grn & bis   .75 .85
1315 A389 1.15k yellow orange   .75 .85
1316 A389 1.15k dark green   .75 .85
1317 A389 1.15k dk bl & dk grn   .75 .85
a.   Bkt. pane, 2 each #1313-1317   7.50 12.50
  Complete booklet, #1317a   9.00
  Nos. 1313-1317 (5)   3.75 4.25

Crown Princess Victoria and King Gustaf — A390

1980, Feb. 26   *Perf. 12½ on 3 sides*
1318 A390 1.30k brt blue   .40 .25
a.   Booklet pane of 10   4.00
  Complete booklet, #1318a   9.00

Perf. 12½ Vert.
1319 A390 1.30k brt blue   .55 .25
1320 A390 1.70k carmine rose   .75 .40
  Nos. 1318-1320 (3)   1.70 .90

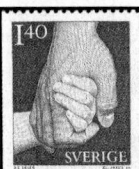
Child Holding Adult's Hand — A391   Hand Holding Cane — A392

1980, Apr. 22   *Perf. 12½ Horiz.*
1321 A391 1.40k red brown   .65 .25
1322 A392 1.60k slate green   .75 .25

Parents' insurance system; care for the elderly.

Squirrel — A393

Perf. 15 on 3 Sides
1980, May 12   **Photo.**
1323 A393 (1k) ultra & yellow   1.50 .25
a.   Booklet pane of 20   30.00
  Complete booklet, #1323a   52.50

See note after No. 1277.

Elise Ottesen-Jensen (1886-1973), Journalist A394

Europa: 1.70k, Joe Hill (1879-1915), member of American Workers' Movement and poet.

1980, June 4   Engr.   *Perf. 12½ Vert.*
1324 A394 1.30k green   1.10 .25
1325 A394 1.70k red   1.30 1.10

Banga Farm, Alfta, Halsingland Province — A395

Tourism (Halsingland Province): No. 1327, Iron Works, Iggesund. No. 1328, Blaxas Ridge, Forsa. No. 1329, Tybling farm, Tyby. No. 1330, Sunds Canal, Hudiksvall.

1980, June 4   *Perf. 12½ Horiz.*
1326 A395 1.15k red   .75 .75
1327 A395 1.15k dark blue   .75 .75
1328 A395 1.15k dark green   .65 .75
1329 A395 1.15k chocolate   .75 .75
1330 A395 1.15k dark green   .75 .75
a.   Bkt. pane, 2 each #1326-1330   7.50
  Complete booklet, #1330a   11.00
  Nos. 1326-1330 (5)   3.65 3.75

Chair, Scania, 1831 — A396   Cradle, North Bothnia, 19th Century — A397

Perf. 12½ Horiz.
1980, Sept. 9   **Engr.**
1331 A396 1.50k grnsh blue   .65 .25
Perf. 12½ Vert.
1332 A397 2k dk red brown   .95 .45
  Norden 80.

Scene from "Diagonal Symphony," 1924 — A398

1980, Sept. 9   *Perf. 12½ Horiz.*
1333 A398 3k dark blue   1.10 .30

Viking Eggeling (1880-1925), artist and film maker.

Souvenir Sheet

Swedish Automobile History — A399

90o, Gustaf Erikson's carriage. 1.15k, Vabis, 1909. 1.30k, Thulin, 1923. 1.40k, Scania, 1903. 1.50k, Tidaholm, 1917. 1.70k, Volvo, 1927.

Photogravure and Engraved
1980, Oct. 11   *Perf. 12½*
1334 A399   Sheet of 6   4.00 6.50
a.-f.   Any single   .65 .75

No. 1334 sold for 9k.

Bamse the Bear — A401

Farmer Kronblom — A402

Christmas 1980 (Comic Strip Characters): No. 1336, Mandel Karlsson, vert. No. 1337, Adamson, vert.

1980, Oct. 11   Engr.   *Perf. 12½ Vert.*
1335 A401 1.15k multicolored   .45 .30
Perf. 12½ on 3 sides
Photo.
1336 A401 1.15k multicolored   .50 .40
a.   Booklet pane of 10   5.00
Perf. 12½ Horiz.
  Complete booklet, #1336a   9.00
Engr.
1337 A401 1.50k black   .70 .25
Photo.
1338 A402 1.50k multicolored   .50 .25
a.   Booklet pane of 10   5.00
  Complete booklet, #1338a   10.50
  Nos. 1335-1338 (4)   2.15 1.20

Angel Blowing Horn — A403

Perf. on 3 Sides
1980, Nov. 18   **Engr.**
1339 A403 1.25k multicolored   .50 .25
a.   Booklet pane of 12   6.00

Christmas 1980.

Necken, by Ernst Josephson — A404

1980, Nov. 18   *Perf. 12½ Horiz.*
1340 A404 8k multicolored   3.25 .25

Nobel Prize Winner Type of 1978

1920 Winners: #1341, Knut Hamsun (1859-1953), Norwegian writer. #1342, August Krogh (1874-1949), Danish Physiologist, #1343, Charles-Edouard Guillaume (1861-1938), French physicist. #1344, Walther Nernst (1864-1941), German chemist.

1980, Nov. 18   *Perf. 13 on 3 Sides*
1341 A367 1.40k dk blue gray   .65 .40
1342 A367 1.40k red   .65 .40
a.   Bkt. pane, 5 each #1341-1342   6.50
  Complete booklet, #1342a   10.50
1343 A367 2k green   .85 .55
1344 A367 2k brown   .85 .55
a.   Bkt. pane, 5 each #1343-1344   8.50
  Complete booklet, #1344a   16.00
  Nos. 1341-1344 (4)   3.00 1.90

Ernst Wigforss (1881-1977), Politician & Writer — A405

1981, Jan. 29   Engr.   *Perf. 12½ Vert.*
1345 A405 5k rose carmine   2.25 .35

Freya (Fertility Goddess) — A406

Norse Mythological Characters: 10o, Thor (thunder god). 15o, Heimdall (rainbow god). 50o, Frey (god of peace, fertility, weather). 1k, Odin.

1981, Jan. 29   Perf. 12½ on 3 Sides
1346	A406	10o blue black	.25	.25
1347	A406	15o dk carmine	.25	.25
1348	A406	50o dk carmine	.30	.25
1349	A406	75o deep green	.30	.25
1350	A406	1k blue black	.35	.25
a.		Bkt. pane, 2 each #1346-1350	2.75	
		Complete booklet, #1350a	3.75	
		Nos. 1346-1350 (5)	1.45	1.25

Gyrfalcon
A407

1981, Feb. 26   Engr.   Perf. 12½ Vert.
1351	A407	50k multicolored	13.50	.75
a.		Booklet pane of 4	55.00	
		Complete booklet, #1351a	125.00	

Troll Chasing
Boy — A408

Europa: 2k, Lady of the Woods.

1981, Apr. 28   Engr.
1352	A408	1.50k dk blue & red	1.40	.50
1353	A408	2k dk green & red	1.40	.60

Intl. Year of the
Disabled — A409

1981, Apr. 28
1354	A409	1.50k dk green	.65	.30
1355	A409	3.50k purple	1.60	.70

Arms of Oster-gotland
Province — A410

Perf. 14½ on 3 Sides
1981, May 18   Photo.
1356	A410	1.40k shown	1.50	.25
1357	A410	1.40k Jamtland	1.50	.25
1358	A410	1.40k Dalarna	1.50	.25
1359	A410	1.40k Bohuslan	1.50	.25
a.		Bkt. pane, 5 each #1356-1359	30.00	
		Nos. 1356-1359 (4)	6.00	1.00

See note after No. 1277. See Nos. 1403-1406, 1456-1459, 1492-1495, 1534-1537, 1592-1595.

Sail Boat,
Bohuslan
A411

Perf. 12½ on 3 Sides
1981, May 26   Engr.
1360	A411	1.65k shown	.75	.75
1361	A411	1.65k Blekinge	.75	.75
1362	A411	1.65k Norrbotten	.75	.75
1363	A411	1.65k Halsingland	.75	.75
1364	A411	1.65k Gotland	.75	.75

1365	A411	1.65k Skane	.75	.75
a.		Bkt. pane of 6, #1360-1365	5.50	8.00
		Complete booklet, #1365a	8.00	

King Carl XVI
Gustaf
A412

Queen Silvia
A413

1981-84   Perf. 12½ Vert.
1366	A412	1.65k dark green	.65	.25
1367	A413	1.75k dark blue	.85	.50
1368	A412	1.80k dark blue ('83)	.85	.25
1369	A412	1.90k red ('84)	1.00	.25
1370	A412	2.40k violet brn	1.00	.75
1371	A413	2.40k grnsh black ('84)	1.00	1.00
1372	A412	2.70k brt lilac ('83)	1.25	1.10
1373	A413	3.20k red ('83)	1.40	1.25
		Nos. 1366-1373 (8)	8.00	5.35

Day and Night — A414

Perf. 12½ on 3 Sides
1981, Sept. 9   Engr.
1376	A414	1.65k dark blue	.50	.25
a.		Booklet pane of 10	5.00	
		Complete booklet, #1376a	10.50	

Scene from Par
Lagerkvist's
Autobiography
Guest of
Reality — A415

1981, Sept. 9   Perf. 12½ Horiz.
1377	A415	1.50k dark green	.75	.25

Conductor Sixten Ehrling and Opera
Singer Birgit Nilsson — A416

Bjorn Borg, Tennis
Player — A417

Designs: No. 1378, Electric locomotive. No. 1379, Trucks. No. 1381, Oil rig. No. 1383, Ingemar Stenmark, skier.

Perf. 12½ on 2 (Type A416) or 3 (Type A417) sides
1981, Sept. 9
1378	A416	2.40k rose carmine	1.25	1.00
1379	A416	2.40k red	1.25	1.00
1380	A416	2.40k rose lilac	1.25	1.00
1381	A416	2.40k deep violet	1.25	1.00
1382	A417	2.40k dark blue	1.25	1.00
1383	A417	2.40k dark blue	1.25	1.00
a.		Bkt. pane of 6, #1378-1383	7.50	12.00
		Complete booklet, #1383a	10.50	

Baker's
Sign — A418

1981, Sept. 9   Perf. 12½ Vert.
1384	A418	2.30k shown	3.00	.25
1385	A418	2.30k Pewter shop sign	3.00	.25
a.		Pair, #1384-1385	3.50	1.90

A419

Swedish Films: a, Olof Ahs in The Coachman. b, Ingrid Bergman and Gosta Ekman in Intermezzo. c, Greta Garbo in The Gosta Berling Saga. d, Stig Jarrel and Alf Kjellin in Persecution. e, Kari Sylwan and Harriet Andersson in Cries and Whispers.

Photogravure and Engraved
1981, Oct. 10   Perf. 13½
1386	A419	Sheet of 5	6.00	6.00
a.-e.		Any single	.90	.90
		No. 1386 sold for 10k.		

Nobel Prize Winner Type of 1978

1921 Winners: 1.35k, Albert Einstein (1879-1955), German physicist. 1.65k, Anatole France (1844-1924), French writer. 2.70k, Frederick Soddy (1877-1956), British chemist.

1981, Nov. 24   Engr.   Perf. 12½ Vert.
1387	A367	1.35k red	.90	.40
1388	A367	1.65k green	1.10	.30
1389	A367	2.70k blue	1.25	1.00
		Nos. 1387-1389 (3)	3.25	1.70

Christmas
1981 — A421

Designs: Wooden birds.

1981, Nov. 24   Perf. 12½ on 3 Sides
1390	A421	1.40k red	.80	.25
1391	A421	1.40k green	.80	.25
a.		Bkt. pane, 5 each #1390-1391	7.50	
		Complete booklet, #1391a	9.50	

Knight on
Horseback,
by John
Bauer
A422

John Bauer (1882-1918), Fairytale Illustrator: No. 1393, "What a Miserable Little Paleface, said the Troll Mother." No. 1394, Marsh Princess. No. 1395, Now the Dusk of the Night is already Upon Us.

Perf. 12x12½ on 3 sides
1982, Feb. 16   Engr.
1392	A422	1.65k multicolored	1.00	.75
1393	A422	1.65k multicolored	1.00	.75
1394	A422	1.65k multicolored	1.00	.75
1395	A422	1.65k multicolored	1.00	.75
a.		Bkt. pane of 4, #1392-1395	4.25	4.75
		Complete booklet, #1395a	6.00	

Impossible
Figures — A423

Designs: Geometric figures.

1982, Feb. 16   Perf. 12½ Horiz.
1396	A423	25o violet brown	.25	.25
1397	A423	50o brown olive	.25	.25
1398	A423	75o dark blue	.30	.25
		Nos. 1396-1398 (3)	.80	.75

Newspaper
Distributor, by
Svenolov Ehren
A424

Graziella, by
Carl Larsson
A425

1982, Feb. 16
1399	A424	1.35k deep violet	.70	.25
1400	A425	5k violet brown	1.90	.25

Europa Issue

Land
Reform,
19th
Cent.
A426

Anders Celsius
(1701-1744),
Inventor of
Temperature
Scale — A427

1982, Apr. 26   Engr.   Perf. 12½ Vert.
1401	A426	1.65k dk olive grn	3.00	.25

Perf. 12½ on 3 Sides
1402	A427	2.40k dark green	1.40	.80
a.		Booklet pane of 6	8.50	
		Complete booklet, #1402a	10.00	

Provincial Arms Type of 1981
Perf. 14 on 3 Sides
1982, Apr. 26   Photo.
1403	A410	1.40k Dalsland	2.00	.25
1404	A410	1.40k Oland	2.00	.25
1405	A410	1.40k Vastmandland	2.00	.25
1406	A410	1.40k Halsingland	2.00	.25
a.		Bkt. pane, 5 each #1403-1406	40.00	
		Complete booklet, #1406a	55.00	
		Nos. 1403-1406 (4)	8.00	1.00

See note after No. 1277.

Elin Wagner (1882-
1949), Writer — A428

Perf. 12½ Horiz.
1982, June 3   Engr.
1407	A428	1.35k Sketch by Siri Derkert	1.00	.50

Burgher
House — A429

Embroidered Lace
Ribbon, 19th
Cent. — A430

1982, June 3   Perf. 12½ Vert.
1408	A429	1.65k brown	1.00	.25

Perf. 12½ Horiz.
1409	A430	2.70k bister	1.40	1.10

Cent. of Museum of Cultural History, Lund.

1982 Intl.
Buoyage
System
A431

Designs: Various buoy signals.

1982, June 3   *Perf. 13 Horiz.*
1410 A431 1.65k shown 1.00 .55
1411 A431 1.65k Ferry 1.00 .55
1412 A431 1.65k Six sailboats 1.00 .55
1413 A431 1.65k One-globed
buoy 1.00 .55
1414 A431 1.65k Two-globed
buoy 1.00 .55
a. Bklt. pane, 2 each #1410-1414 7.50
Nos. 1410-1414 (5) 5.00 2.75

Vietnamese Workers in
Sweden — A432

Living Together: Swedish emigration and
immigration.

1982, Aug. 26 Engr.   *Perf. 13 Horiz.*
1415 A432 1.65k Leaving Swe-
den, 1880 1.00 .55
1416 A432 1.65k shown 1.00 .55
1417 A432 1.65k Local voting
right 1.00 .55
1418 A432 1.65k Girls 1.00 .55
a. Bklt. pane, 2 each #1415-
1418 8.50
Complete booklet, #1418a 11.00
Nos. 1415-1418 (4) 4.00 2.20

Wild Orchids — A433

Wild Orchids: 1.65k (No. 1419a), Orchis
mascula. 1.65k (No. 1419d), Cypripedium
calcéolus. 2.40k, Epipactis palustris. 2.70k,
Dactylorhiza sambucina.

Photogravure and Engraved
1982, Oct. 9   *Perf. 12x13*
1419 A433 Sheet of 4 5.00 6.00
a.-d. Any single 1.10 1.30

Sold for 10k for benefit of stamp collecting.

Christmas
1982 — A434

Stained-glass Windows, Church at Lye, Got-
land, 14th cent. — No. 1420, Angel. No. 1421,
Child in the Temple. No. 1422, Adoration of the
Kings. No. 1423, Tidings to the Shepherds.
No. 1424, Birth of Christ.

Perf. 13 on 3 Sides
1982, Nov. 24   Photo.
1420 A434 1.40k multi .65 .40
1421 A434 1.40k multi .65 .40
1422 A434 1.40k multi .65 .40
1423 A434 1.40k multi .65 .40
1424 A434 1.40k multi .65 .40
a. Bklt. pane, 2 each #1420-
1424 6.50 7.50
Complete booklet, #1424a 10.50
Nos. 1420-1424 (5) 3.25 2.00

Signature, Atomic Model — A435

Nobel Prizewinners in Physics (Quantum
Mechanics). Various Atomic Models: No.
1425, Niels Bohr, Denmark, 1922. No. 1426,
Erwin Schrodinger, Austria, 1933. No. 1427,
Louis de Broglie, France, 1929. No. 1428, Paul
Dirac, England, 1933. No. 1429, Werner
Heisenberg, Germany, 1932.

1982, Nov. 24 Engr.   *Perf. 13 Horiz.*
1425 A435 2.40k multi 1.25 1.10
1426 A435 2.40k multi 1.25 1.10
1427 A435 2.40k multi 1.25 1.10
1428 A435 2.40k multi 1.25 1.10
1429 A435 2.40k multi 1.25 1.10
a. Bklt. pane of 5, #1425-1429 6.75 8.00
Complete booklet, #1429a 9.00
Nos. 1425-1429 (5) 6.25 5.50

Fruit
A436

Games
A436a

Crown and
Posthorn
A436b

King Carl XVI
Gustaf
A436c

Queen Silvia
A436d

Games
A436e

5o, Horse chestnut. 10o, Norway maple.
15o, Dogrose. 20o, Sloe. 50o, Fox and
cheese. 60o, Dominoes. 70o, Ludo. 80o, Chinese checkers. 90o, Backgammon. 3k, Chess.

1983-85 Engr.   *Perf. 12½ Vert.*
1430 A436 5o brown .25 .25
1431 A436 10o green .25 .25
1432 A436 15o red .25 .25
1433 A436 20o blue .25 .25
1434 A436a 50o brt blue .30 .25
1435 A436a 60o green .30 .30
1436 A436a 70o yellow .30 .30
1437 A436a 80o red .40 .30
1438 A436a 90o mauve .45 .40
1439 A436b 1.60k deep blue .75 .25
1440 A436c 2k black .80 .25
1441 A436b 2.50k bister 1.10 .45
1442 A436c 2.70k dull red brn 1.10 1.00

Perf. 12½ Horiz.
1443 A436e 3k purple 1.40 .25

Perf. 12½ Vert.
1444 A436d 3.20k brt blue 1.50 1.60
1445 A436b 4k dp car 1.50 .25
Nos. 1430-1445 (16) 10.90 6.60

Issued: #1430-1433, 2/10/83; #1434-1438,
1443, 10/12/85; #1439-1442, 1444-1445,
1/24/85.
See Nos. 1567-1580, 1783.

Peace Movement
Centenary
A437

1983, Feb. 10
1446 A437 1.35k blue .55 .35

Nils Ferlin (1898-
1961),
Poet — A438

1983, Feb. 10
1447 A438 6k dk grn 2.50 .25

500th
Anniv. of
Printing
in
Sweden
A439

No. 1448, Lead type. No. 1449, Dialogus
Creaturarum, 1483. No. 1450, Carolus XII
Bible, 1703. No. 1451, ABC Books, 1760s. No.
1452, Laser photo composition.

1983, Feb. 10   *Perf. 13 Horiz.*
1448 A439 1.65k multi 1.00 .45
1449 A439 1.65k multi 1.00 .45
1450 A439 1.65k multi 1.00 .45
1451 A439 1.65k multi 1.00 .45
1452 A439 1.65k multi 1.00 .45
a. Bklt. pane, 2 each #1448-
1452 12.00
Complete booklet, #1452a 14.00
Nos. 1448-1452 (5) 5.00 2.25

Sweden-US Relations
Bicentenary — A440

2.70k, Ben Franklin, Swedish Arms.

1983, Mar. 24
1453 A440 2.70k multi 1.25 .65
a. Booklet pane of 5 6.25
Complete booklet, #1453a 6.75
See US No. 2036.

Nordic
Cooperation
Issue — A441

Perf. 12½ Horiz.
1983, Mar. 24   Engr.
Size: 21x27mm
1454 A441 1.65k Bicycling .75 .35

Perf. 13 Vert.
1455 A441 2.40k Sailing 1.25 .85

Provincial Arms Type of 1981
1983, Apr. 25 Photo.   *Perf. 14½x14*
1456 A410 1.60k Vastergotland 2.00 .25
1457 A410 1.60k Medelpad 2.00 .25
1458 A410 1.60k Gotland 2.00 .25
1459 A410 1.60k Gastrikland 2.00 .25
a. Bklt. pane, 5 each #1456-
1459 42.50
Complete booklet, #1459a 55.00
Nos. 1456-1459 (4) 8.00 1.00
See note after No. 1277.

Europa — A442

1.65k, Swedish Ballet Co. 2.70k, Sliding-jaw
wrench.

Perf. 12½ Horiz.
1983, Apr. 25   Engr.
1460 A442 1.65k multi 1.50 .50
1461 A442 2.70k multi 1.50 1.50

A443

Designs: 1k, 3k, 10-ore King Oscar II definitive essays, 1884. 2k, No. 39. 4k, No. 58.

1983, May 25   *Perf. 12½*
1462 A443 1k blue .90 .50
1463 A443 2k red .95 .55
1464 A443 3k blue 1.10 .85
1465 A443 4k green 1.25 1.00
a. Bklt. pane of 4, #1462-1465 4.75 5.25
Complete booklet, #1465a 6.75

STOCKHOLMIA Intl. Stamp Exhibition, Aug.
28-Sept. 7, 1986.

Red
Cross — A444

Greater
Karlso — A445

1983, Aug. 24   *Perf. 12½ Horiz.*
1466 A444 1.50k red .75 .25
1467 A445 1.60k dk blue .75 .25

Planorbis
Snail — A446

Arctic
Fox — A447

1983, Aug. 24   *Perf. 12½ on 3 Sides*
1468 A446 1.80k green .65 .25
a. Booklet pane of 10 6.50
Complete booklet, #1468a 10.50

Perf. 12½ Horiz.
1469 A447 2.10k grnsh blk 1.00 .55

See Nos. 1488-1489, 1526-1527, 1623-
1626, 1678-1680, 1762-1763.

Hjalmar Bergman
(1883-1931),
Writer — A448

No. 1470, Portrait. No. 1471, Jac the Clown
illustration by Nisse Skoog.

1983, Aug. 24   *Perf. 13 Horiz.*
1470 A448 1.80k multi .75 .25
1471 A448 1.80k multi .75 .25
a. Pair, #1470-1471 1.50 1.25

View of Helgeandsholmen, Stockholm,
by Franz Hogenberg, 1580 — A449

1983, Aug. 24   *Perf. 12½ Vert.*
1472 A449 2.70k dl pur & dk bl 1.25 .70

A450

Photogravure and Engraved

1983, Oct. 1 ***Perf. 13½***

1473 A450 Sheet of 5 5.25 *7.00*
a. 1.80k Wilhelm Stenhammar, pianist .95 .75
b. 1.80k Aniara (opera) .95 .75
c. 1.80k Lars Gullin, jazz saxophonist .95 .75
d. 1.80k ABBA, pop music group .95 .75
e. 2.70k Hins Anders, violinist 1.20 1.20

Sold for 11.50k.

Christmas 1983 — A452

Postcard designs: No. 1474, Christmas Gnomes around the tree. No. 1475, on straw goats. No. 1476, Folk children, Christmas porridge and gingerbread. No. 1477, Gnomes carrying Christmas gifts on a pole.

Perf. 12½x14 on 3 sides

1983, Nov. 22 **Photo.**

1474 A452 1.60k multi .65 .30
1475 A452 1.60k multi .65 .30
1476 A452 1.60k multi .65 .30
1477 A452 1.60k multi .65 .30
a. Bklt. pane, 3 each #1474-1477 7.50
Complete booklet, #1477a 15.00
Nos. 1474-1477 (4) 2.60 1.20

Chemistry, Nobel Prize Winners — A453

Designs: No. 1478, Arne Tiselius (1902-1971), Electrophoresis Studies. No. 1479, George De Hevesy (1885-1966), Radioactive isotope tracers. No. 1480 Svante Arrhenius (1859-1927), Theory of Electrolytic Dissociation. No. 1481, Theodor Svedberg (1884-1971), Colloid Studies. No. 1482, Hans Von Euler-Chelpin (1873-1964). Enzyme and Vitamin Structures.

Photogravure and Engraved

1983, Nov. 22 ***Perf. 12½ Horiz.***

1478 A453 2.70k slate 1.25 1.10
1479 A453 2.70k dp bl vio 1.25 1.10
1480 A453 2.70k red lilac 1.25 1.10
1481 A453 2.70k blue blk 1.25 1.10
1482 A453 2.70k grnsh blk 1.25 1.10
a. Bklt. pane of 5, #1478-1482 6.50 *8.50*

Postal Savings Centenary — A454

Design: 100o, Three crowns.

1984, Feb. 9 **Engr.** ***Perf. 12½ Vert.***

1483 A454 100o orange .45 .35
1484 A454 1.60k purple .65 .55
1485 A454 1.80k pink .95 .25
Nos. 1483-1485 (3) 2.05 1.15

Europa 1984 A455

Symbolic bridge of communications exchange.

1984, Feb. 9 ***Perf. 12½ Horiz.***

1486 A455 1.80k red 1.00 .25
a. Booklet pane of 10 10.00
Complete booklet, #1486a 14.00

Perf. 13 Vert.

1487 A455 2.70k dp ultra 2.75 1.50

Conservation Type of 1983 and

Angelica — A457

1984, Mar. 27 ***Perf. 12½ on 3 Sides***

1488 A447 1.90k Lemmings .60 .25
1489 A447 1.90k Musk ox .60 .25
a. Bklt. pane, 5 each #1488-1489 6.00
Complete booklet, #1489a 10.50

Perf. 12½ Horiz.

1490 A457 2k shown 1.00 .25
1491 A457 2.25k Alpine birch 1.10 1.00
Nos. 1488-1491 (4) 3.30 1.75

Provincial Arms Type of 1981

1984, Apr. 24 **Photo.** ***Perf. 14½x14***

1492 A410 1.60k Sodermanland 2.00 .25
1493 A410 1.60k Blekinge 2.00 .25
1494 A410 1.60k Vasterbotten 2.00 .25
1495 A410 1.60k Skane 2.00 .25
a. Bklt. pane, 5 ea #1492-1495 40.00
Complete booklet, #1495a 55.00
Nos. 1492-1495 (4) 8.00 1.00

See note after No. 1277.

A458

Swedish Patent System Centenary: No. 1496, Paraffin stove, F.W. Lindqvist, 1892. No. 1497, Industrial robot ASEA-IRB 6. No. 1498, Fan suction vacuum cleaner, Axel Wennergren, 1912. No. 1499, Inboard-outboard motor, AQ-200, No. 1500, SLIC integrated electronic circuit. No. 1501, Tetrahedron container, 1948, 1951.

Perf. 12½ on 3 Sides

1984, June 6 **Engr.**

1496 A458 2.70k red 1.25 1.25
1497 A458 2.70k sepia 1.25 1.25
1498 A458 2.70k green 1.25 1.25
1499 A458 2.70k green 1.25 1.25
1500 A458 2.70k sepia 1.25 1.25
1501 A458 2.70k blue 1.25 1.25
a. Bklt. pane of 6, #1496-1501 7.75 9.50
Complete booklet, #1501a 9.25

A459

Stockholmia '86 (Famous Letters): 1k, Erik XIV's marriage proposal to Queen Elizabeth I, 1561. 2k, Erik Dahlbergh to Sten Bielke, 1684. 3k, Feather letter, 1834. 4k, August Strindberg to Harriet Bosse, 1905.

Lithographed and Engraved

1984, June 6 ***Perf. 12½***

1502 A459 1k multi .90 .60
1503 A459 2k multi .95 .65
1504 A459 3k multi 1.10 .85
1505 A459 4k multi 1.25 1.10
a. Bklt. pane of 4, #1502-1505 4.75 *6.00*
Complete booklet, #1505a 6.75

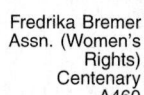

Fredrika Bremer Assn. (Women's Rights) Centenary A460

Perf. 12½ Vert.

1984, Aug. 28 **Engr.**

1506 A460 1.50k pink .70 .50
1507 A460 6.50k red 2.50 1.10

Medieval Towns A461

Engravings by E. Dahlbergh or M. Karl.

1984, Aug. 28 ***Perf. 12½x13***

1508 A461 1.90k Jonkoping 1.00 1.10
1509 A461 1.90k Karlstad 1.00 1.10
1510 A461 1.90k Gavle 1.00 1.10
1511 A461 1.90k Sigtuna 1.00 1.10
1512 A461 1.90k Norrkoping 1.00 1.10
1513 A461 1.90k Vadstena 1.00 1.10
a. Bklt. pane of 6, #1508-1513 6.25 *8.25*
Complete booklet, #1513a 8.00

Viking Satellite, 1985 A462

1984, Oct. 13 ***Perf. 12½ Vert.***

1514 A462 1.90k Satellite 1.00 .50
1515 A462 3.20k Receiving station 1.75 1.75

Souvenir Sheet

Swedish Aviation History — A463

Designs: a, Thulin D Two-Seater, 1915. b, SAAB-90 Scandia, 1946. c, Carl Gustaf Cederstrom (1867-1918, "The Flying Baron"), Bleriot, 1910. d, Tomten, 1927. e, Carl Nyberg's Flugan, 1900.

1984, Oct. 13 ***Perf. 12½***

1516 A463 Sheet of 5 5.75 5.75
a.-d. 1.90k, any single .90 .85
e. 2.70k, multi 1.10 1.00

Sold for 12k.

Christmas 1984 — A465

Birds — No. 1517, Coccothraustes coccothraustes. No. 1518, Bombycilla garrulus. No. 1519, Dendrocopos major. No. 1520, Sitta europaea.

Lithographed and Engraved

1984, Nov. 29 ***Perf. 12½ on 3 Sides***

1517 A465 1.60k multi 1.00 .35
1518 A465 1.60k multi 1.00 .35
1519 A465 1.60k multi 1.00 .35
1520 A465 1.60k multi 1.00 .35
a. Bklt. pane, 3 each #1517-1520 12.00
Complete booklet, #1520a 15.00
Nos. 1517-1520 (4) 4.00 1.40

Inner Ear A466

Nobel Prize Winners in Physiology or Medicine: No. 1521, Georg von Bekesy, 1961, hearing. No. 1522, John Eccles, Alan Hodgkin & Andrew Huxley, 1963, Nerve cell activation. No. 1523, Julius Axelrod, Bernard Katz & Ulf von Euler, 1970, nerve cell storage and release. No. 1524, Roger Sperry, 1981, brain functions. No. 1525, David Hubel, Torsten Wiesel, 1981, Visual information processing.

Perf. 12½ Horiz.

1984, Nov. 29 **Engr.**

1521 A466 2.70k shown 1.25 1.25
1522 A466 2.70k Nerve, arrows 1.25 1.25
1523 A466 2.70k Nerve (front, side) 1.25 1.25
1524 A466 2.70k Brain halves 1.25 1.25
1525 A466 2.70k Eye 1.25 1.25
a. Bklt. pane of 5, #1521-1525 7.00 *8.00*
Complete booklet, #1525a 9.00

Conservation Type of 1983 and

A467

No. 1526, Muscardinus avellanarius. No. 1527, Salvelinus salvelinus. No. 1528, Nigritella nigra. No. 1529, Nymphaea alba.

Perf. 13 on 3 Sides

1985, Mar. 14 **Engr.**

1526 A447 2k multicolored 1.25 .30
1527 A447 2k multicolored 1.25 .30
a. Bklt. pane, 5 each #1526-1527 13.00
Complete booklet, #1527a 14.00

World Wildlife Fund.

Perf. 12½ Horiz.

1528 A467 2.20k multi .75 .40
1529 A467 3.50k multi 1.75 .65
Nos. 1526-1529 (4) 5.00 1.65

World Table Tennis Championships A468

2.70k, Jan-Ove Waldner, Sweden. 3.20k, Cai Zhenhua, China.

1985, Mar. 14 ***Perf. 12½ Vert.***

1530 A468 2.70k blue 1.50 .90
1531 A468 3.20k mauve 1.90 1.20

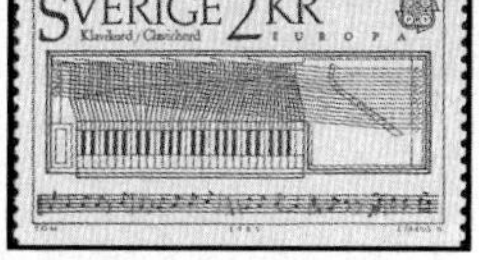

Clavichord — A469

Key Harp — A470

1985, Apr. 24 ***Perf. 13 Vert.***

1532 A469 2k bluish blk, *buff* 3.75 .50

Perf. 13 on 3 Sides

1533 A470 2.70k dl red brn, *buff* .90 .75
a. Booklet pane of 6 5.50

Europa 1985.

Provincial Arms Type of 1981
Perf. 14½x14 on 3 Sides
1985, Apr. 24 | | Photo.
1534 A410 1.80k Narke	1.50	.25
1535 A410 1.80k Angermanland	1.50	.25
1536 A410 1.80k Varmland	1.50	.25
1537 A410 1.80k Smaland	1.50	.25
a. Bklt. pane, 5 ea #1534-1537	30.00	
Complete booklet, #1537a	52.50	
Nos. 1534-1537 (4)	6.00	1.00

See note after No. 1277.

St. Cnut's Land Grant to Lund Cathedral, 900th Anniv. — A471

Seal of St. Cnut and: No. 1538, Lund Cathedral. No. 1539, City of Helsingdorg.

Perf. 12½ on 3 Sides
1985, May 21 | | Engr.
1538 A471 2k bluish blk & blk	.75	.25
1539 A471 2k blk & dk red	.75	.25
a. Bklt. pane, 5 each, #1538-1539	8.50	
Complete booklet, #1539a	13.00	

See Denmark Nos. 777-778.

Stockholmia '86 — A472

Paintings of old Stockholm: No. 1540, A View of Slussen, by Sigrid Hjerten (1919). No. 1541, Skeppsholmen, Winter, by Gosta Adrian-Nilsson (1919). No. 1542, A Summer's Night by the Riddarholmen, by Hilding Linnqvist (1945). No. 1543, Klara Church Tower, by Otte Skold (1927).

Lithographed and Engraved
1985, May 21 | | Perf. 12½
1540 A472 2k multi	1.10	1.10
1541 A472 2k multi	1.10	1.10
1542 A472 3k multi	1.25	1.25
1543 A472 4k multi	1.40	1.25
a. Bklt. pane of 4, #1540-1543	5.50	7.50
Complete booklet, #1543a	6.75	

Swedish Touring Club Cent. — A473

#1544, Touring Club Syl Station (c. 1920). #1545, Af Chapman Hostel, Stockholm.

1985, May 21 Engr. | **Perf. 12½ Vert.**
1544 2k blk & dp bl	.75	.45

Size: 58x23mm
1545 2k dp bl & blk	.75	.60
a. A473 Pair, #1544-1545	1.75	1.75

Trade Signs — A474

No. 1546, Music Shop, Slottsgatan. No. 1547, Furrier, Stockholm. No. 1548, Coppersmith, Landskrona. No. 1549, Haberdasher, Stockholm. No. 1550, Shoemaker, Norrkoping.

Perf. 12½ on 3 Sides
1985, Aug. 28 | | Engr.
1546 A474 10o multicolored	.25	.25
1547 A474 20o multicolored	.25	.25
1548 A474 20o multicolored	.25	.25
1549 A474 50o multicolored	.30	.25

1550 A474 2k multicolored	.70	.25
a. Bklt. pane, #1546-1549, 2 #1550	2.00	3.00
Complete booklet, #1550a	3.25	
Nos. 1546-1550 (5)	1.75	1.25

The Dying Spartan Hero, Otryades, 1779, by Johan Tobias Sergel — A475

Baron Carl Frederik Adelcrantz, Academy Pres., 1754, by Alexander Roslin (1718-1793) — A476

1985, Aug. 28 | | Perf. 12½ Vert.
1551 A475 2k slate blue	1.00	.30

Perf. 12½ Horiz.
1552 A476 7k dk red brn	4.00	.70

Royal Academy of Fine Arts, 250th anniv.

Intl. Youth Year — A477

Children's drawings: 2k, Participation, by Marina Karlsson. 2.70k, Development, by Madeleine Andersson. 3.20k, Peace, by Charlotta Ankar.

Lithographed and Engraved
1985, Oct. 12 | | Perf. 12½x13
1553 A477 Sheet of 3	4.25	5.25
a. 2k multi	1.25	.80
b. 2.70k multi	1.25	1.10
c. 3.20k multi	1.50	1.30

Sold for 10k.

Prime Minister Per Albin Hansson (1885-1946) — A478

Birger Sjoberg (1885-1929), Journalist, Novelist, Poet — A479

1985, Oct. 12 Engr. Perf. 12½ Vert.
1556 A478 1.60k black & red	.65	.65

Perf. 12½ Horiz.
1557 A479 4k dk blue grn	1.65	.45

Christmas 1985 — A480

15th cent. religious paintings by Albertus Pictor — No. 1558, Annunciation. No. 1559, Birth of Christ. No. 1560, Adoration of the Magi. No. 1561, Mary as the Apocalyptic Virgin.

Perf. 13x12½ on 3 Sides
1985, Nov. 21 | | Engr.
1558 A480 1.80k multicolored	.85	.50
1559 A480 1.80k multicolored	.85	.50
1560 A480 1.80k multicolored	.85	.50
1561 A480 1.80k multicolored	.85	.50
a. Bklt. pane, 3 each #1558-1561	10.50	
Complete booklet, #1561a	16.00	
Nos. 1558-1561 (4)	3.40	2.00

Nobel Laureates in Literature — A481

Authors: No. 1562, William Faulkner (1897-1962), 1949, Southern United States. No. 1563, Halldor Kiljan Laxness (b.1902), 1955, Iceland. No. 1564, Miguel Angel Asturias (1899-1974), 1967, Guatemala. No. 1565, Yasunari Kawabata (1899-1972), 1968, Japan. No. 1566, Patrick White (b. 1912), 1973, Australia.

Lithographed and Engraved
1985, Nov. 21 | | Perf. 13 Horiz.
1562 A481 2.70k myr grn	1.25	.95
1563 A481 2.70k dp brn, chlky bl & myr grn	1.25	.95
1564 A481 2.70k myr grn & tan	1.25	.95
1565 A481 2.70k chlky bl & myr grn	1.25	.95
1566 A481 2.70k chlky bl & ocher	1.25	.95
a. Bklt. pane of 5, #1562-1566	7.50	6.25
Complete booklet, #1566a	9.00	

Types of 1983-85
Engr., Litho. (1.80k, 3.20k, 6k)
1986-89 | | Perf. 12½ Vert.
1567 A436b 1.70k dk violet	.75	.25
1568 A436b 1.80k brt violet	.85	.25
1569 A436c 2.10k dk blue	1.00	.25
1570 A436c 2.20k int blue	1.00	.25
1571 A436c 2.30k dk ol grn	1.00	.25
1572 A436c 2.80k emerald	1.10	.80
1573 A436c 2.90k dk green	1.40	.60
1574 A436c 3.10k dk brown	1.40	.65
1575 A436b 3.20k yellow brn	1.40	.85
1576 A436c 3.30k dk rose brn	1.40	1.00
1577 A436d 3.40k dk red	1.50	.55
1578 A436d 3.60k green	1.75	.60
1579 A436d 3.90k violet blue	1.75	1.50
1580 A436b 6k blue green	2.00	.35
Nos. 1567-1580 (14)	18.30	8.15

Issued: 2.10, 2.90, 3.40k, 1/23'; 1.70, 2.80k, 2/20; 1.80, 3.10, 3.20, 3.60, 6k, 1/27/87; 2.20k, 1/29/88; 2.30, 3.30, 3.90k, 4/20/89.
See No. 1796.

Waterbirds A484

Perf. 13 on 2 or 3 Sides
1986, Jan. 23 | | Engr.
1582 A484 2.10k Eider	.75	.25
1583 A484 2.10k Smaspov	.75	.25
a. Bklt. pane, 5 each #1582-1583	7.50	
Complete booklet, #1583a	12.50	
1584 A484 2.30k Storlom	.85	.35
Nos. 1582-1584 (3)	2.35	.85

STOCKHOLMIA '86 — A485

Lithographed and Engraved
1986, Jan. 23 | | Perf. 13
1585 A485 2k #33a, cancel	.95	.95
1586 A485 2k Stamp engraver	.95	.95
1587 A485 3k #268, 271, US #836	1.25	1.10

1588 A485 4k Boy soaking stamps	1.50	1.40
a. Bklt. pane of 4, #1585-1588	4.75	6.50
Complete booklet, #1588a	6.75	

See US Nos. 2198-2201a.

Swedish PO, 350th Anniv. — A486

Lithographed and Engraved
1986, Feb. 20 | | Perf. 13x12½
1589 A486 2.10k org yel & dk bl	.75	.25
a. Bklt pane of 8	6.00	
Complete booklet, #1589a	12.00	

Sundial — A487

No. 1591, Motto of the Swedish Academy.

1986, Feb. 20 Engr. Perf. 13 Horiz.
1590 A487 1.70k dk bl & lake, gray	.75	.60
1591 A487 1.70k grn & dk red, gray	.75	.60
a. Pair, #1590-1591	1.60	1.50

Royal Swedish Academy of Letters, History and Antiquities, and Swedish Academy, bicents.

Provincial Arms Type of 1981
Perf. 15x14½ on 3 Sides
1986, Apr. 23 | | Photo.
1592 A410 1.90k Harjedalen	2.00	.25
1593 A410 1.90k Uppland	2.00	.25
1594 A410 1.90k Halland	2.00	.25
1595 A410 1.90k Lapland	2.00	.25
a. Bklt. pane, 5 each #1592-1595	40.00	
Complete booklet, #1595a	57.50	
Nos. 1592-1595 (4)	8.00	1.00

See note after No. 1277.

King Carl XVI Gustaf — A488   Royal Cipher — A489

40th birthday: No. 1598, King presenting Nobel Prize for literature to Czeslaw Milosz, 1980. No. 1600, Royal family at Soldien palace

Lithographed and Engraved
1986, Apr. 23 | | Perf. 12 on 3 Sides
1596 A488 2.10k grnsh blk & pale grn	1.25	.40
1597 A489 2.10k dk bl, pink & gold	1.25	.40
1598 A488 2.10k dk bl & pale bl	1.25	.40
1599 A489 2.10k dk bl, pale grn & gold	1.25	.40
1600 A488 2.10k blk & pale pink	1.25	.40
a. Bklt. pane, 2 each #1596-1600	13.00	11.00
Complete booklet, #1600a	16.00	
Nos. 1596-1600 (5)	6.25	2.00

Olof Palme (1927-1986), Prime Minister — A490

Perf. 13 on 3 Sides

1986, Apr. 11			Engr.	
1601	A490	2.10k dk lilac rose	1.10	1.10
1602	A490	2.90k grnsh black	1.25	1.25
a.		Bklt. pane, 5 ea #1601-1602	13.00	
		Complete booklet, #1602a	20.00	

Nordic
Cooperation
Issue — A491

Sister towns.

1986, May 27		Engr.	Perf. 13 Vert.	
1603	A491	2.10k Uppsala	.85	.30
1604	A491	2.90k Eskilstuna	1.25	.90

Europa
1986 — A492

1986, May 27			Perf. 13 Horiz.	
1605	A492	2.10k Automotive pollutants	2.10	.50

Perf. 13 on 3 Sides

1606	A492	2.90k Industrial pollutants	1.10	1.25
a.		Booklet pane of 6	6.75	
		Complete booklet, #1606a	12.50	

STOCKHOLMIA
'86 — A493

Designs: No. 1607, Mail handling terminal, Tomteboda, 1986. No. 1608, Railroad mail car, 19th cent. No. 1609, Post Office, 18th cent. No. 1610, Postman, 17th cent.

Lithographed and Engraved

1986, Aug. 29			Perf. 13	
1607	A493	2.10k multi	3.00	3.00
1608	A493	2.10k multi	3.00	3.00
1609	A493	2.90k multi	3.00	3.00
1610	A493	2.90k multi	3.00	3.00
a.		Bklt. pane of 4, #1607-1610	12.00	16.00
		Complete booklet, #1610a	16.00	

Bklt. sold for 40k, including 30k ticket to STOCKHOLMIA '86.

Souvenir Sheet

World Class Athletes in Track and Field — A494

Designs: a, Ann-Louise Skoglund, 400-meter hurdle, 1982. b, Dag Wennlund, 1986, and Eric Lemming, c. 1900, javelin. c, Standing high jumper and Patrik Sjoberg, high jump, 1985. d, Anders Garderud, 300-meter steeplechase record-holder.

1986, Oct. 18		Engr.	Perf. 12½	
1611	A494	Sheet of 4	5.25	7.00
a.-d.		2.10k, any single	1.25	1.25

No. 1611 sold for 11k to benefit philatelic organizations.

Intl. Peace
Year — A495

Amnesty Intl.,
25th
Anniv. — A496

1986, Oct. 18			Perf. 13 Vert.	
1612	A495	3.40k bluish blk & emer grn	2.25	2.25
1613	A496	3.40k dk red & bluish blk	2.25	2.25
a.		Pair, #1612-1613	4.50	5.00

Christmas — A497

Winter village scenes.

Perf. 13x12½ on 3 Sides

1986, Nov. 25		Litho. & Engr.	
1614	1.90k Postal van	1.00	.35
1615	1.90k Postman on bicycle	1.00	.35
1616	1.90k Children, sled	1.00	.35
1617	1.90k Child mailing letter	1.00	.35
a.	A497 Block of 4, #1614-1617	4.00	4.00
b.	Bklt. pane of 12, 3 #1617a	12.00	—
	Complete booklet, #1617b	19.00	

Nobel Peace Prize Laureates — A498

#1618, Bertha von Suttner, 1905. #1619, Carl von Ossietzky, 1935. #1620, Albert Luthuli, 1960. #1621, Martin Luther King, Jr., 1964. #1622, Mother Teresa, 1979.

1986, Nov. 25		Engr.	Perf. 13 Horiz.	
1618	A498	2.90k brt bl, blk & hn brn	1.50	1.50
1619	A498	2.90k blk & hn brn	1.50	1.50
1620	A498	2.90k brt bl, blk & brn blk	1.50	1.50
1621	A498	2.90k brn blk & hn brn	1.50	1.50
1622	A498	2.90k blk, brt bl & hn brn	1.50	1.50
a.		Bklt. pane of 5, #1618-1622	9.00	9.50
		Complete booklet, #1622a	12.50	

Conservation Type of 1983

No. 1623, Parnassius mnemosyne. No. 1624, Gentianella campestris. No. 1625, Osmoderma eremita. No. 1626, Arnica montana.

Perf. 13 on 3 Sides

1987, Mar. 10			Engr.	
1623	A447	2.10k multicolored	1.00	.25
1624	A447	2.10k multicolored	1.00	.30
a.		Booklet pane, 5 ea #1623-1624	10.00	
		Complete booklet, #1624a	16.00	

Perf. 13 Horiz.

1625	A447	2.50k multicolored	1.10	.25
1626	A447	4.20k multicolored	1.75	.30
		Nos. 1623-1626 (4)	4.85	1.30

Swedish
Aviation
Industry
A500

1987, Mar. 10			Perf. 13 Vert.	
1627	A500	25k Saab SF340	12.00	.40

Europa
1987 — A501

Nos. 1628-1629, City Library, Asplund. No. 1630, Lewerentz Marcus Church.

1987, May 14		Engr.	Perf. 13 Vert.	
1628	A501	2.10k int blk & grn	3.50	.35

Perf. 13 on 3 Sides

1629	A501	3.10k emer grn & red brn	1.10	1.10
1630	A501	3.10k emer grn & sep	1.10	1.10
a.		Bklt. pane, 3 each #1629-1630	7.00	
		Nos. 1628-1630 (3)	5.70	2.55

Illustrations from
Children's Novels by
Astrid Lindgren (b.
1907) — A502

No. 1631, Karlsson Pa Taket. No. 1632, Barnen and Bullerbyn. No. 1633, Madicken. No. 1634, Mio, Min Mio. No. 1635, Nils Karlsson-Pyssling. No. 1636, Emil and Lonneberga. No. 1637, Ronja Rovardotter. No. 1638, Pippi Longstocking. No. 1639, Broderna Lejonhjarta. No. 1640, Lotta Pa Brakmakargatan.

Perf. 13x12½ on 3 Sides

1987, May 14		Litho. & Engr.	
1631	A502	1.90k multi	2.00	.25
1632	A502	1.90k multi	2.00	.25
1633	A502	1.90k multi	2.00	.25
1634	A502	1.90k multi	2.00	.25
1635	A502	1.90k multi	2.00	.25
1636	A502	1.90k multi	2.00	.25
1637	A502	1.90k multi	2.00	.25
1638	A502	1.90k multi	2.00	.25
1639	A502	1.90k multi	2.00	.25
1640	A502	1.90k multi	2.00	.25
a.		Bklt. pane, 2 ea #1631-1640	40.00	
		Nos. 1631-1640 (10)	20.00	2.50

See note after No. 1277.

Medieval
Towns — A503

No. 1641, 2.10k, Hans Brask, Bishop of Linkoping, 16th cent. No. 1642, 2.10k, Nykopingshus Castle.

1987, May 14		Engr.	Perf. 12½ Vert.	
1641	A503	blk, dk vio & yel bis	1.00	.55
1642	A503	dk vio, blk & yel bis	1.00	.55
a.		Pair, #1641-1642	2.25	2.00

Swedes
in the
Service
of
Mankind
A504

Designs: No. 1643, Raoul Wallenberg, Swedish diplomat in Budapest during World War II. No. 1644, Dag Hammarskjold (1905-1961), UN secretary-general. No. 1645, Folke Bernadotte af Wisborg (1895-1948), organizer of the Red Cross operation that saved thousands from Nazi death camps.

Perf. 12½ Horiz.

1987, Aug. 10			Engr.	
1643	A504	3.10k blue	1.40	1.10
1644	A504	3.10k green	1.40	1.10
1645	A504	3.10k brown violet	1.40	1.10
a.		Bklt. pane, 2 each #1643-1645	8.50	
		Complete booklet, #1645a	12.50	
		Nos. 1643-1645 (3)	4.20	3.30

Gripsholm
Castle, 450th
Anniv. — A505

Paintings from the Royal Castle Collection, Gripsholm: No. 1646, King Gustav I Vasa (d. 1560), artist unknown. No. 1647, Blue Tiger, 1673, favorite horse of King Charles XI, by D.K. Ehrenstrahl. No. 1648, Hedvig Charlotta Nordenflycht (1718-1763), poet, by Kopia J.H. Scheffel. No. 1649, Gripsholm Castle Outer Courtyard, 17th Cent., 19th cent. lithograph by C.J. Billmark.

1987, Aug. 10			Perf. 13 Vert.	
1646	A505	2.10k multi	1.00	.40
1647	A505	2.10k multi	1.00	.40
1648	A505	2.10k multi	1.00	.40
1649	A505	2.10k multi	1.00	.40
a.		Bklt. pane of 8, 2 strips of #1646-1649 with gutter btwn.	8.50	
		Complete booklet, #1649a	13.00	
		Nos. 1646-1649 (4)	4.00	1.60

Botanical
Gardens
A506

Designs: No. 1650, Victoria cruziana (water lily), Victoria House, Bergian Garden, c. 1790, Stockholm University. No. 1651, Layout of baroque palace garden, by Carl Harleman (1700-1753), Uppsala University. No. 1652, White anemones, rock garden, Gothenberg Botanical Gardens, 1923. No. 1653, Tulip tree blossoms, Academy Garden, c. 1860, Lund University.

1987, Oct. 10		Engr.	Perf. 13 Vert.	
1650	A506	2.10k multi	1.00	.55
1651	A506	2.10k multi	1.00	.55
1652	A506	2.10k multi	1.00	.55
1653	A506	2.10k multi	1.00	.55
a.		Bklt. pane, 2 each #1650-1653 with gutter between	8.25	
		Nos. 1650-1653 (4)	4.00	2.20

The Circus in
Sweden,
Bicent. — A507

Litho. & Engr.

1987, Oct. 10			Perf. 13	
1654	A507	2.10k Juggler, clown	1.25	1.00
1655	A507	2.10k High wire	1.25	1.00
1656	A507	2.10k Equestrian	1.25	1.00
a.		Bklt. pane of 3, #1654-1656	3.75	4.00
		Complete booklet, 2 #1656a	13.00	

Stamp Day. Sold for 8k.

Christmas
A508

Customs: No. 1657, Putting porridge in the stable for the gray Christmas elf. No. 1658, Watering horses at a north-running stream on Boxing Day. No. 1659, Sled-race home from church on Christmas Day. No. 1660, Hanging out sheaves of wheat to foretell a good harvest.

1987, Nov. 25   **Perf. 13 on 3 Sides**   **Litho.**
1657	A508	2k multi	1.00	.30
1658	A508	2k multi	1.00	.30
1659	A508	2k multi	1.00	.30
1660	A508	2k multi	1.00	.30
a.		Bklt. pane, 3 each #1657-1660	12.50	
		Complete booklet, #1660a	16.00	
		Nos. 1657-1660 (4)	4.00	1.20

Nobel Prize Winners in Physics A509

Space and diagram or formula: No. 1661, Antony Hewish, Great Britain, 1974. No. 1662, Subrahmanyan Chandrasekhar, US, 1983. No. 1663, William Fowler, US, 1983. No. 1664, Arno Penzias and Robert Wilson, US, 1978. No. 1665, Martin Ryle, Great Britain, 1974.

1987, Nov. 25   **Engr.**   **Perf. 13**
1661	A509	2.90k dark blue	1.50	1.50
1662	A509	2.90k blk	1.50	1.50
1663	A509	2.90k dark blue	1.50	1.50
1664	A509	2.90k dark blue	1.50	1.50
1665	A509	2.90k blk	1.50	1.50
a.		Bklt. pane of 5, #1661-1665	8.00	10.00
		Complete booklet, #1665a	9.50	

Inland Boats A510

No. 1666, Skiff, Lake Hjalmaren. No. 1667, Village boat, Lake Vattern. No. 1668, Rowboat, Byske. No. 1669, Flat-bottomed rowboat, Asnen. No. 1670, Ice boat, Lake Vanern. No. 1671, Church boat, Lake Locknesjon.

1988, Jan. 29   **Engr.**   **Perf. 13**
1666	A510	3.10k multi	1.50	1.25
1667	A510	3.10k multi	1.50	1.25
1668	A510	3.10k multi	1.50	1.25
1669	A510	3.10k multi	1.50	1.25
1670	A510	3.10k multi	1.50	1.25
1671	A510	3.10k multi	1.50	1.25
a.		Bklt. pane of 6, #1666-1671	9.00	9.50
		Complete booklet, #1671a	12.00	

A511

A512

Settling of New Sweden, 350th Anniv. — A513

Designs: No. 1672, 17th Cent. European settlers negotiating with American Indians, map of New Sweden, the Swedish ships *Kalmar Nyckel* and *Fogel Grip*, based on an 18th cent. illustration from a Swedish book about the American Colonies. No. 1673, Bishop Hill and painter Olof Krans. No. 1674, Carl Sandburg (1878-1967), author, and Jenny Lind (1820-1867), opera singer known as the "Swedish Nightingale." No. 1675, Charles Lindbergh (1902-1974), and *The Spirit of St. Louis.* No. 1676, American astronaut with Swedish Hasselblad camera on the Moon. No. 1677, Swedish players in National Hockey League.

Litho. & Engr., Engr. (#1674-1675)
1988, Mar. 29   **Perf. 13x12½ Horiz.**
| 1672 | A511 | 3.60k multi | 1.60 | 1.60 |
| 1673 | A511 | 3.60k multi | 1.60 | 1.60 |

Perf. 13x12½ on 3 Sides
| 1674 | A512 | 3.60k brn | 1.60 | 1.60 |
| 1675 | A512 | 3.60k dk bl & brn | 1.60 | 1.60 |

Perf. 13x12½ on 2
1676	A513	3.60k dk bl & yel	1.60	1.60
1677	A513	3.60k dk red, dk bl & blk	1.60	1.60
a.		Bklt. pane of 6, #1672-1677	10.50	12.50
		Complete booklet, #1677a	14.00	

See US No. C117 and Finland No. 768.

Conservation Type of 1983

Species Inhabiting Coastal Waters — No. 1678, Haliaetus albicilla. No. 1679, Halichoerus grypus. No. 1680, Anguilla anguilla.

Perf. 13 on 3 Sides
1988, Mar. 29   **Engr.**
1678	A447	2.20k multicolored	1.00	.30
1679	A447	2.20k multicolored	1.00	.30
a.		Bklt. pane, 5 #1678, 5 #1679	10.00	
		Complete booklet, #1679a	20.00	

Perf. 13 Horiz.
| 1680 | A447 | 4.40k multicolored | 2.10 | .35 |
| | | *Nos. 1678-1680 (3)* | 4.10 | .95 |

Midsummer Celebration — A515

No. 1681, Wildflowers in meadow. No. 1682, Rowing. No. 1683, Children making wreaths. No. 1684, Raising maypole. No. 1685, Fiddlers. No. 1686, Ferry. No. 1687, Dancing. No. 1688, Accordion player. No. 1689, Maypole, residence. No. 1690, Bouquet of flowers.

Perf. 12½ on 3 Sides
1988, May 17   **Litho. & Engr.**
1681	A515	2k multicolored	2.00	.25
1682	A515	2k multicolored	2.00	.25
1683	A515	2k multicolored	2.00	.25
1684	A515	2k multicolored	2.00	.25
1685	A515	2k multicolored	2.00	.25
1686	A515	2k multicolored	2.00	.25
1687	A515	2k multicolored	2.00	.25
1688	A515	2k multicolored	2.00	.25
1689	A515	2k multicolored	2.00	.25
1690	A515	2k multicolored	2.00	.25
a.		Bklt. pane, 2 ea #1681-1690	40.00	
		Complete booklet, #1690a	60.00	
		Nos. 1681-1690 (10)	20.00	2.50

See note after No. 1277.

Skara Township Millennium A516

Design: Detail from Creation, a Skara Cathedral stained-glass window by Bo Beskow, 20th cent.

1988, May 17   **Perf. 13 Horiz.**
| 1691 | A516 | 2.20k multi | .90 | .40 |

Stora Mining Co., 700th Anniv. — A517

1988, May 17   **Engr.**
| 1692 | A517 | 4.40k Mine, 18th cent. | 1.65 | 1.25 |

Royal Dramatic Theater, Stockholm, Founded by King Gustav III in 1788 — A518

Design: Scene fron *The Queen's Diamond Ornament,* about the murder of King Gustav III at the Royal Opera in 1792.

1988, May 17
| 1693 | A518 | 8k grn, red & blk | 3.00 | 2.00 |

Self-portrait, 1923, by Nils Dardel (1888-1943) A519

Paintings: No. 1695, *Old Age Home in Autumn,* c. 1930, by Vera Nilsson (1888-1979). No. 1696, *Self-portrait,* 1912, by Isaac Grunewald (1899-1979). No. 1697, *Visit of an Eccentric Lady,* 1921, by Dardel. No. 1698, *Soap Bubbles,* 1927, by Nilsson. No. 1699, *The Fair,* 1915, by Grunewald.

Perf. 13 on 3 Sides
1988, Aug. 25   **Litho. & Engr.**
Size: 33x35mm (Nos. 1695, 1698)
1694	A519	2.20k shown	.95	.90
1695	A519	2.20k multi	.95	.90
1696	A519	2.20k multi	.95	.90
1697	A519	2.20k multi	.95	.90
1698	A519	2.20k multi	.95	.90
1699	A519	2.20k multi	.95	.90
a.		Bklt. pane of 6, #1694-1699	5.75	7.50

Europa — A520

Transport and communication — No. 1700, X2 high-speed train. No. 1701, X2 high-speed train, diff. No. 1702, Steam locomotive, 1887.

1988, Aug. 25   Engr.   Perf. 13 Vert.
| 1700 | A520 | 2.20k multi | 2.75 | .90 |

Perf. 13 on 3 Sides
1701	A520	3.10k multi	1.25	1.25
1702	A520	3.10k multi	1.25	1.25
a.		Bklt. pane, 3 each #1701-1702	7.50	
		Complete booklet, #1702a	12.50	
		Nos. 1700-1702 (3)	5.25	3.40

Common Swift — A521

1988, Aug. 25   **Perf. 12½ Vert.**
| 1703 | A521 | 20k brt vio & dk vio | 6.50 | .35 |

Dan Andersson (1888-1920), Poet, and Manuscript A522

Forest and Pond, Finnmarken — A523

1988, Oct. 8   Engr.   Perf. 13 Vert.
1704	A522	2.20k vio, dk bl & dk bl grn	1.10	.45
1705	A523	2.20k vio, dk bl & dk bl grn	1.10	.75
a.		Pair, #1704-1705	2.40	1.75

Soccer — A524

Match scenes: No. 1706, Dribble (Torbjorn Nilsson representing local club matches). No. 1707, Heading the ball (Ralf Edstrom of the national league). No. 1708, Kick (Pia Sundhage, women's soccer).

1988, Oct. 8   Litho. & Engr.   Perf. 13
1706	A524	2.20k multi	1.25	1.00
1707	A524	2.20k multi	1.25	1.00
1708	A524	2.20k multi	1.25	1.00
a.		Bklt. pane of 3, #1706-1708	3.75	4.25
		Complete booklet, 2 #1708a	12.50	

No. 1708a sold for 8.50k; surtax benefited stamp collecting.

Nobel Laureates in Chemistry A525

Designs: No. 1709, Willard F. Libby, US, 1960, carbon-14 method of dating artifacts. No. 1710, Karl Ziegler, West Germany, and Guilio Natta, Italy, 1963, catalysts. No. 1711, Aaron Klug, South Africa, 1982, electron microscopy. No. 1712, Ilya Prigogine, Belgium, 1977, proof that molecular order can occur spontaneously out of chaos.

1988, Nov. 29   **Perf. 12½ Vert.**
1709	A525	3.10k multi	1.40	1.25
1710	A525	3.10k multi	1.40	1.25
1711	A525	3.10k multi	1.40	1.25
1712	A525	3.10k multi	1.40	1.25
a.		Bklt. pane, 2 each #1709-1712	12.00	
		Complete booklet, #1712a	16.00	
		Nos. 1709-1712 (4)	5.60	5.00

Christmas — A526

Story of Christ's birth according to Luke (2:7-20): No. 1713, Angels appear to inform shepherds of Christ's birth. No. 1714, Star of Bethlehem, angel, horse. No. 1715, Birds singing. No. 1716, Magi offering gifts. No. 1717, Holy family. No. 1718, Shepherds with palm offering.

Perf. 12½x13 on 3 Sides

1988, Nov. 29

1713 A526 2k multi 1.00 .75
1714 A526 2k multi 1.00 .75
1715 A526 2k multi 1.00 .75
1716 A526 2k multi 1.00 .75
1717 A526 2k multi 1.00 .75
1718 A526 2k multi 1.00 .75
a. Bklt. pane, 2 each #1713-1718 12.00
Complete booklet, #1718a 16.00
Nos. 1713-1718 (6) 6.00 4.50

Nos. 1713 and 1716, 1714 and 1717, 1715 and 1718 have continuous designs.

Lighthouses A527

Designs: 1.90k, Twin masonry lighthouses, 1832, and concrete lighthouse, 1946, Nidingen, Kattegat Is. 2.70k, Soderarm, Uppland, 1839. 3.80k, Sydostbrotten, Gulf of Bothnia, 1963. 3.90k, Sandhammaren, Skane, c. 1860.

1989, Jan. 31 Engr. ***Perf. 13 Vert.***

1719 A527 1.90k multi 1.00 .50
1720 A527 2.70k multi 1.50 1.00
1721 A527 3.80k multi 1.75 1.50
1722 A527 3.90k multi 2.25 1.75
Nos. 1719-1722 (4) 6.50 4.75

Endangered Species — A528

No. 1723, Gulo gulo. No. 1724, Strix uralensis. No. 1725, Dendrocopos minor. No. 1726, Calidris alpina schinzii. No. 1727, Hyla arborea. No. 1728, Ficedula parva.

1989, Jan. 31 ***Perf. 13 on 3 Sides***

1723 A528 2.30k multicolored 1.00 .25
1724 A528 2.30k multicolored 1.00 .25
a. Bklt. pane, 5 each #1723-1724 8.50
Complete booklet, #1724a 16.00

Perf. 13 Horiz.

1725 A528 2.40k multicolored 1.00 .40
1726 A528 2.60k multicolored 1.50 .85
1727 A528 3.30k multicolored 1.50 1.10
1728 A528 4.60k multicolored 2.25 .50
Nos. 1723-1728 (6) 8.25 3.35

Opening of The Globe Arena, Stockholm — A529

Perf. 13 Horiz.

1989, Apr. 14 Litho. & Engr.

1729 A529 2.30k Exterior 1.25 .55
1730 A529 2.30k Ice hockey 1.25 .55
1731 A529 2.30k Gymnastics 1.25 .55
1732 A529 2.30k Concert 1.25 .55
a. Bklt. pane of 4, #1729-1732 5.00
Complete booklet, 2 #1732a separated by gutter 14.00

Nordic Cooperation Issue — A530

Folk costumes.

Perf. 13 Horiz.

1989, Apr. 20 Litho. & Engr.

1733 A530 2.30k Woman's wool waist 1.10 .40
1734 A530 3.30k Belt pouch 1.60 1.10

Natl. Labor Movement, Cent. — A531

1989, May 17 Engr. ***Perf. 13 Horiz.***

1735 A531 2.30k dk red & blk 1.10 .75

Europa 1989 — A532

Children's games: 2.30k, No. 1738, Sailing toy boats. No. 1737, Kick-sledding.

1989, May 17 ***Perf. 13 Vert.***

1736 A532 2.30k car lake 3.25 .75

Perf. 13

1737 A532 3.30k greenish blue 1.10 1.25
1738 A532 3.30k lilac 1.10 1.25
a. Bklt. pane, 3 #1737, 3 #1738 6.60
Complete booklet, #1738a 12.50
Nos. 1736-1738 (3) 5.45 3.25

Summer — A533

Perf. 13 on 3 Sides

1989, May 17 Litho.

1739 A533 2.10k Sailing 2.00 .35
1740 A533 2.10k Beach ball 2.00 .35
1741 A533 2.10k Cycling 2.00 .35
1742 A533 2.10k Canoeing 2.00 .35
1743 A533 2.10k Angling 2.00 .35
1744 A533 2.10k Camping 2.00 .35
1745 A533 2.10k Croquet 2.00 .35
1746 A533 2.10k Badminton 2.00 .35
1747 A533 2.10k Gardening 2.00 .35
1748 A533 2.10k Sand sculpture 2.00 .35
a. Bklt. pane, 2 ea #1739-1748 40.00
Complete booklet, #1748a 70.00
Nos. 1739-1748 (10) 20.00 3.50

See note after No. 1277.

Polar Exploration A534

Swedish polar techniques used in the Arctic (Nos. 1749-1751) and Antarctic: No. 1749, Aircraft, temperature experiment. No. 1750, Settlement, Arctic pass. No. 1751, Icebreaker, experiment. No. 1752, Penguins, tall ship and longboat. No. 1753, Antarctic transports, helicopter. No. 1754, Surveying, albatross.

Perf. 13 on 3 Sides

1989, Aug. 22 Litho. & Engr.

Size: 40x43mm (Nos. 1750, 1753)

1749 A534 3.30k multi 2.00 2.00
1750 A534 3.30k multi 2.00 2.00
1751 A534 3.30k multi 2.00 2.00
1752 A534 3.30k multi 2.00 2.00
1753 A534 3.30k multi 2.00 2.00
1754 A534 3.30k multi 2.00 2.00
a. Bklt. pane of 6, #1749-1754 13.00 *14.00*

Smaland Businesses A535

Perf. 12½x12 on 3 Sides

1989, Aug. 22 Engr.

1755 A535 2.30k Furniture 1.25 1.25
1756 A535 2.30k Assembly equipment 1.25 1.25
1757 A535 2.30k Sewing machines 1.25 1.25
1758 A535 2.30k Glassware 1.25 1.25
1759 A535 2.30k Metal springs 1.25 1.25
1760 A535 2.30k Matchsticks 1.25 1.25
a. Bklt. pane of 6, #1755-1760 8.00 *10.50*
Complete booklet, #1760a 9.25

Eagle Owl, *Bubo bubo* A536

1989, Aug. 22 ***Perf. 13 Vert.***

1761 A536 30k vio, blk & grn blk 10.00 .40

A536a

Birds and Coastline, Bla Jungfrun Natl. Park — A537

No. 1762, Rhododendron lapponicum. No. 1763, Calypso bulbosa.

Perf. 13x12½ on 3 Sides

1989, Sept. 12 Engr.

1762 A536a 2.40k multicolored .90 .25
1763 A536a 2.40k multicolored .90 .25
a. Bklt. pane, 5 ea #1762-1763 9.00
Complete booklet, #1763a 16.00

Perf. 12½ Vert.

1764 A537 4.30k dark blue, blk & brn vio 2.10 1.50
Nos. 1762-1764 (3) 3.90 2.00

See Nos. 1776-1780.

Swedish Kennel Club, Cent. — A538

a, Large spitz. b, Fox hound. c, Small spitz.

1989, Oct. 7 Litho. ***Perf. 13x12½***

1765 A538 Bklt. pane of 3 3.50 *4.50*
a.-c. 2.40k any single 1.10 1.00
Complete booklet, 2 #1765 12.50

Sold for 9.50k.

Christmas — A539

Holiday symbols: No. 1766, Top of Christmas tree, wreath. No. 1767, Candelabrum, foods. No. 1768, Star, poinsettia plant, grot pot. No. 1769, Bottom of tree, straw goat, gifts. No. 1770, Gifts, television, girl. No. 1771, Boy, grandfather, girl opening gift.

Perf. 12½x13 on 3 Sides

1989, Nov. 24 Litho.

1766 A539 2.10k multi 1.25 .50
1767 A539 2.10k multi 1.25 .50
1768 A539 2.10k multi 1.25 .50
1769 A539 2.10k multi 1.25 .50
1770 A539 2.10k multi 1.25 .50
1771 A539 2.10k multi 1.25 .50
a. Bklt. pane, 2 each #1766-1771 15.00
Complete booklet, #1771a 20.00
Nos. 1766-1771 (6) 7.50 3.00

Nobel Laureates in Physiology A540

Genetics: No. 1772, Thomas Morgan (1866-1945), US, 1933, chromosomal study of fruit flies to determine laws and mechanism of heredity. No. 1773, James Watson, US, and Francis Crick with Maurice Wilkins, Great Britain, 1962, molecular structure of DNA. No. 1774, Werner Arber, Switzerland, Daniel Nathans and Hamilton Smith, US, 1978, enzymatic cutting of nucleotides to create gene hybrids. No. 1775, Barbara McClintock, botanist, US, 1983, corn color studies that led to theory of gene jumping.

Perf. 12½ Vert.

1989, Nov. 24 Litho. & Engr.

1772 A540 3.60k multi 1.50 1.10
1773 A540 3.60k multi 1.50 1.10
1774 A540 3.60k multi 1.50 1.10
1775 A540 3.60k multi 1.50 1.10
a. Bklt. pane, 2 each #1772-1775 with gutter between 12.00
Complete booklet, #1775a 16.00
Nos. 1772-1775 (4) 6.00 4.40

Natl. Parks Type of 1989

Designs: No. 1776, Campground, sailboat on lake, Angso Park. No. 1777, Hiking, Pieljekaise Park. 3.70k, Three whooper swans over wetlands, Muddus Park. 4.10k, Deer, lake, Padjelanta Park. 4.80k, Bears, forest, Sanfjallet Park.

Perf. 13 on 3 Sides

1990, Jan. 26 Engr.

1776 A537 2.50k multicolored .95 .25
1777 A537 2.50k multicolored .95 .25
a. Bklt. pane, 5 each #1776-1777 9.50
Complete booklet, #1777a 16.00

Perf. 13 Vert.

1778 A537 3.70k multicolored 2.00 .30
1779 A537 4.10k multicolored 2.50 2.00
1780 A537 4.80k multicolored 2.50 1.75
Nos. 1776-1780 (5) 8.90 4.55

King and Queen Types of 1985-86 and

Queen Silvia — A541

King Carl XVI Gustaf — A542

King Carl XVI Gustav
A543

Queen Silvia
A544

King Carl XVI Gustaf — A545

Perf. 12½ Vert., Horiz. (A541, A542, A545)

1990-97				**Engr.**	
1783	A436c	2.50k	deep claret	1.00	.25
1784	A542	2.80k	dk blue	1.10	.25
1785	A542	2.90k	deep green	1.30	.25
1786	A542	3.20k	violet	1.50	.25
1787	A543	3.70k	dark red brown	1.50	.25
1788	A543	3.85k	black	1.75	.30
1789	A436d	4.60k	bright org	2.00	1.75
1790	A541	5k	deep rose vio	2.00	.40
1791	A545	(5k)	deep blue	2.10	.30
1792	A541	6k	deep claret	2.25	.60
1793	A544	6k	dark green	2.75	1.25
1794	A541	6.50k	purple	3.50	2.00
1795	A544	7.50k	purple	3.10	1.65
1796	A544	8k	brown red	3.10	1.00
	Nos. 1783-1796 (14)			28.95	10.50

Issued: 2.50k, 4.60k, 1/26; 5k, 3/20/91; 2.80k, 11/20/91; 2.90k, #1792, 1/2/93; 3.20k, 1/17/94; 6.50k, 3/18/94; 3.70k, #1793, 1/2/95; 3.85k, 7.50k, 1/2/96; (5k), 8k, 2/28/97.

No. 1791 is inscribed "BREV."

Viking Heritage
A546

Designs: No. 1801, Viking head of carved bone, dragon carving from a molding found in Birka. No. 1802, Three viking longships. No. 1803, Viking town. No. 1804, Bronze statue of pagan fertility god, silver filigree cross. No. 1805, Bishop's crosier, southern Russian carved statue of a deer. No. 1806, Viking longship (stern). No. 1807, Viking longship (bow), horsemen, woman, warrior, wolf. No. 1808, Sword hilts.

Perf. 12x13 on 3 Sides

1990, Mar. 28				**Litho. & Engr.**	
1801	A546	2.50k	multicolored	1.10	.85
1802	A546	2.50k	multicolored	1.10	.85
1803	A546	2.50k	multicolored	1.10	.85
1804	A546	2.50k	multicolored	1.10	.85
1805	A546	2.50k	multicolored	1.10	.85
1806	A546	2.50k	multicolored	1.10	.85
1807	A546	2.50k	multicolored	1.10	.85
1808	A546	2.50k	multicolored	1.10	.85
a.	Bklt. pane of 8, #1801-1808			9.00	*10.00*
	Complete booklet, #1808a			12.50	

Nos. 1802-1803, 1806-1807 printed in a continuous design.

Swedish Industrial Safety, Cent. — A547

1990, Mar. 28	**Engr.**		***Perf. 13 Horiz.***		
1809	A547	2.50k	Lumberjack	1.10	.30

Europa 1990 — A548

Post offices — No. 1810, Postal Museum, 1720. No. 1811, Sollebrunn, 1985. No. 1812, Vasteras, 1956.

1990, Mar. 28			***Perf. 13 Vert.***		
1810	A548	2.50k	multi	4.00	.45

Perf. 13 on 3 Sides

1811	A548	3.80k	multi	2.00	1.10
1812	A548	3.80k	multi	2.00	1.10
a.	Bklt. pane, 3 each #1811-1812			12.00	
	Complete booklet, #1812a			14.00	
	Nos. 1810-1812 (3)			8.00	2.65

World Equestrian Games, Stockholm
A549

No. 1813, Endurance riding. No. 1814, Combined training. No. 1815, Show jumping. No. 1816, Dressage. No. 1817, Volting. No. 1818, Four-in-hand.

Litho. & Engr.

1990, May 15			***Perf. 12½x13***		
1813	A549	3.80k	multicolored	1.60	1.40
1814	A549	3.80k	multicolored	1.60	1.40
1815	A549	3.80k	multicolored	1.60	1.40
1816	A549	3.80k	multicolored	1.60	1.40
1817	A549	3.80k	multicolored	1.60	1.40
1818	A549	3.80k	multicolored	1.60	1.40
a.	Bklt. pane of 6, #1813-1818			10.00	*11.50*
	Complete booklet, #1818a			16.00	

Apiculture — A550

#1819, Worker bee collecting nectar. #1820, Bee, bilberry flower. #1821, Worker bee. #1822, Apiary hive. #1823, Two bees in honeycomb. #1824, Drone, 7 cells, blue green panel. #1825, Queen bee, 7 cells, yellow panel. #1826, Swarm hanging from tree. #1827, Beekeeper. #1828, Honey.

1990, May 15				**Litho.**	
1819	A550	2.30k	multicolored	2.00	.40
1820	A550	2.30k	multicolored	2.00	.40
1821	A550	2.30k	multicolored	2.00	.40
1822	A550	2.30k	multicolored	2.00	.40
1823	A550	2.30k	multicolored	2.00	.40
1824	A550	2.30k	multicolored	2.00	.40
1825	A550	2.30k	multicolored	2.00	.40
1826	A550	2.30k	multicolored	2.00	.40
1827	A550	2.30k	multicolored	2.00	.40
1828	A550	2.30k	multicolored	2.00	.40
a.	Bklt. pane, 2 ea #1819-1828			40.00	
	Complete booklet, #1828a			70.00	
	Nos. 1819-1828 (10)			20.00	4.00

See note after No. 1277.

Wasa Nautical Museum — A551

Man-of-war *Wasa:* 2.50k, Bow. 4.60k, Stern.

1990, May 15	**Engr.**		***Perf. 13 Vert.***		
1829	A551	2.50k	org & blk	1.10	.45
1830	A551	4.60k	dk bl & org	2.00	1.50

Dearest Brothers, Sisters and Friends — A552

Proud City
A553

Allusions to poetry verses of Carl Michael Bellman (No. 1833) and Evert Taube: No. 1833, Fredmen in the gutter. No. 1834, Happy baker in San Remo. No. 1835, At sea. No. 1836, Violava.

Perf. 13 on 3 Sides

1990, Aug. 8				**Litho. & Engr.**	
1831	A552	2.50k	multicolored	1.75	1.50
1832	A553	2.50k	multicolored	1.75	1.50
1833	A552	2.50k	multicolored	1.75	1.50
1834	A552	2.50k	multicolored	1.75	1.50
1835	A553	2.50k	multicolored	1.75	1.50
1836	A552	2.50k	multicolored	1.75	1.50
a.	Bklt. pane of 6, #1831-1836			7.50	*12.00*

Paper Production
A554

#1837, Paper production c. 1600. #1838, Watermark. #1839, Newspaper mastheads. #1840, Modern paper production.

1990, Aug. 8			***Perf. 12½ Vert.***		
1837	A554	2.50k	multicolored	1.10	.45
1838	A554	2.50k	multicolored	1.10	.45
1839	A554	2.50k	multicolored	1.10	.45
1840	A554	2.50k	multicolored	1.10	.45
a.	Bklt. pane, 2 each #1837-1840 with gutter between			9.00	
	Complete booklet, #1840a			14.00	
	Nos. 1837-1840 (4)			4.40	1.80

Ovedskloster Palace — A555

1990, Aug. 8	**Engr.**		***Perf. 13 Vert.***		
1841	A555	40k	multicolored	11.00	.30

See Nos. 1874-1877.

Photography
A556

No. 1842, Bellows camera. No. 1843, August Strindberg. No. 1844, 35mm camera.

Litho. & Engr.

1990, Oct. 6			***Perf. 12½***		
1842	A556	2.50k	multi	1.10	1.25
1843	A556	2.50k	multi	1.10	1.25
1844	A556	2.50k	multi	1.10	1.25
a.	Bklt. pane of 3, #1842-1844			3.30	*5.00*
	Complete booklet, 2 #1844a			12.50	

Stamp Day. Booklet of two panes sold for 20k. Surtax benefited stamp collecting.

Clouds — A557

1990, Oct. 6	**Engr.**		***Perf. 12½ Horiz.***		
1845	A557	4.50k	Cumulus	2.00	.45
1846	A557	4.70k	Cumulonimbus	2.25	1.25
1847	A557	4.90k	Cirrus	2.50	1.25
1848	A557	5.20k	Alto cumulus	2.75	1.50
	Nos. 1845-1848 (4)			9.50	4.45

A558

1990, Oct. 6			***Perf. 12½ Vert.***		
1849	A558	2.50k	shown	1.20	.50
1850	A558	2.50k	Women bathing	1.20	.50
a.	Pair, #1849-1850			2.50	2.25

Moa Martinson (1890-1964), author.

Nobel Laureates in Literature — A559

No. 1851, Par Lagerkvist, 1951. No. 1852, Ernest Hemingway, 1954. No. 1853, Albert Camus, 1957. No. 1854, Boris Pasternak, 1958.

Perf. 13 on 2 Sides

1990, Nov. 27				**Engr.**	
1851	A559	3.80k	multicolored	1.50	1.40
1852	A559	3.80k	multicolored	1.50	1.40
1853	A559	3.80k	multicolored	1.50	1.40
1854	A559	3.80k	multicolored	1.50	1.40
a.	Bklt. pane, 2 each #1851-1854 with gutter between			13.00	
	Complete booklet, #1854a			18.50	
	Nos. 1851-1854 (4)			6.00	5.60

See Nos. 1914-1917.

Christmas — A560

Flowers — No. 1855, Schlumbergera x buckleyi. No. 1856, Helleborus niger. No. 1857, Rhododendron simsii. No. 1858, Hippeastrum x hortorum. No. 1859, Hyacinthus orientalis. No. 1860, Euphorbia pulcherrima.

Perf. 13 on 3 Sides

1990, Nov. 27				**Litho.**	
1855	A560	2.30k	multi	1.00	.55
1856	A560	2.30k	multi	1.00	.55
1857	A560	2.30k	multi	1.00	.55
1858	A560	2.30k	multi	1.00	.55
1859	A560	2.30k	multi	1.00	.55
1860	A560	2.30k	multi	1.00	.55
a.	Bklt. pane, 2 each #1855-1860			12.00	
	Complete booklet, #1860a			16.00	
	Nos. 1855-1860 (6)			6.00	3.30

Carta Marina by Olaus Magnus, 1572 — A561

Scandanavia by A. Bureas and J. Blaeus, 1662 — A562

Maps: No. 1863, Celestial globe by Anders Akerman, 1759. No. 1864, Contour map, 1938. No. 1865, Stockholm, 1989. No. 1866, Bedrock Map, Geological Survey, 1984.

Perf. 13 on 3 Sides

1991, Jan. 30 Litho. & Engr.

1861 A561 5k multicolored 2.40 1.75
1862 A562 5k multicolored 2.40 1.75
1863 A561 5k multicolored 2.40 1.75
1864 A561 5k multicolored 2.40 1.75
1865 A562 5k multicolored 2.40 1.75
1866 A561 5k multicolored 2.40 1.75
a. Bklt. pane of 6, #1861-1866 15.00 *18.00*

Fish — A563

No. 1868, Siluris glanis, diff. No. 1869, Cobitis taenia. No. 1870, Gobio gobio. No. 1871, Noemacheilus barbatulus. No. 1872, Leucaspius delineatus.

Perf. 13 on 3 Sides

1991, Jan. 30 Engr.

1867 A563 2.50k shown 1.25 .35
1868 A563 2.50k multi 1.25 .35
b. Bklt. pane, 5 each #1867-1868 13.50
Complete booklet, #1868b 16.00

Perf. 13 Vert.

1869 A563 5k multi 1.75 .25
1870 A563 5.40k multi 2.75 3.00
1871 A563 5.50k multi 2.40 .25
1872 A563 5.60k multi 2.40 1.75
Nos. 1867-1872 (6) 11.80 5.95

Palace Type of 1990

Designs: 10k, Stromsholm Castle. 20k, Karlberg Castle. 25k, Drottningholm Palace.

1991-92 Engr. *Perf. 13 Vert.*

1874 A555 10k blk & olive brn 4.00 .25
1876 A555 20k multicolored 7.00 .75

Size: 58x23mm

1877 A555 25k multicolored 9.00 .75
Nos. 1874-1877 (3) 20.00 1.75

Issued: 10k, 4/27; 25k, 3/20; 20k, 5/21/92.

A564

No. 1883, Seglora church. No. 1884, Flag above park. No. 1885, Wedding. No. 1886, Animals.

Perf. 12½x13 on 3 Sides

1991, May 15 Litho.

1883 A564 2.40k multi .95 .25
1884 A564 2.40k multi .95 .25
1885 A564 2.40k multi .95 .25
1886 A564 2.40k multi .95 .25
b. Bklt. pane, 5 ea #1883-1886 19.00
Complete booklet, #1886b 27.00
Nos. 1883-1886 (4) 3.80 1.00

Skansen Park, Stockholm, 100th anniv.

See note after No. 1277. Complete booklet of 20 stamps sold for 46k.

Kolmarden Zoological Park, Ostergotland A565

Perf. 12½ Horiz.

1991, May 15 Engr.

1887 A565 2.50k Polar bears 1.10 .25
1888 A565 4k Dolphin show 1.75 1.10

Norden '91.

A566

Public Parks, cent.: #1890, Dancing in park.

1991, May 15 *Perf. 13 Vert.*

1889 A566 2.50k dark blue 1.10 .50
1890 A566 2.50k dark blue 1.10 .50
a. Pair, #1889-1890 2.25 2.25

Europa — A567

Litho. & Engr.

1991, May 15 *Perf. 13*

1891 A567 4k Hermes space plane *1.75 1.75*
1892 A567 4k Freja satellite *1.75 1.75*
1893 A567 4k Tele-X satellite *1.75 1.75*
a. Bklt. pane of 3, #1891-1893 *5.50 8.50*

Olympic Champions A568

Designs: No. 1894, Magda Julin, figure skating, Antwerp, 1920. No. 1895, Toini Gustaffson, cross country skiing, Grenoble, 1968. No. 1896, Agneta Andersson, Anna Olsson, two-person kayak, Los Angeles, 1984. No. 1897, Ulrika Knape, diving, Munich, 1972.

Perf. 12x13 on 3 Sides

1991, Aug. 27 Litho. & Engr.

1894 A568 2.50k multicolored 1.10 .70
1895 A568 2.50k multicolored 1.10 .70
1896 A568 2.50k multicolored 1.10 .70
1897 A568 2.50k multicolored 1.10 .70
a. Bklt. pane, 2 each #1894-1897 9.00
Complete booklet, #1897a 14.00
Nos. 1894-1897 (4) 4.40 2.80

See Nos. 1937-1940, 1953-1956.

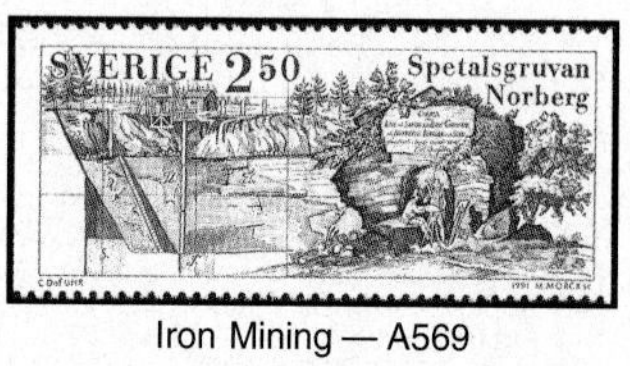

Iron Mining — A569

#1898, Spetal Mine, Norberg. #1899, Forsmark Mill. #1900, Ironworks forge. #1901, Forge welding. #1902, Dannemora Mine. #1903, Blast furnace, Pershyttan.

Perf. 13 on 2 or 3 Sides

1991, Aug. 27 Engr.

1898 A569 2.50k multicolored 1.25 .85
1899 A569 2.50k multicolored 1.25 .85

Size: 31x26mm

1900 A569 2.50k multicolored 1.25 *1.10*
1901 A569 2.50k multicolored 1.25 *1.10*

Size: 31x40mm

1902 A569 2.50k multicolored 1.25 *1.10*
1903 A569 2.50k multicolored 1.25 *1.10*
a. Bklt. pane of 6, #1898-1903 7.50 6.75
Complete booklet, #1903a 9.50

Coronation of King Gustavus III, by Carl Gustaf Pilo — A570

Details from painting: No. 1904, King Gustavus III. No. 1905, Gustavus with crown held above head. No. 1906, Chancellor Arvid Horn, Archbishop Mattias Beronius holding crown above Gustavus III.

1991, Oct. 5 Engr. *Perf. 13*

1904 A570 10k blue 4.00 3.50
1905 A570 10k violet 4.00 3.50

Size: 76x44mm

1906 A570 10k greenish black 5.00 5.00
a. Bklt. pane of 3, #1904-1906 13.00 13.00

Czeslaw Slania, engraver, 70th birthday. No. 1906a sold for 35k to benefit stamp collecting.

Rock Musicians A571

1991, Oct. 5 Litho. & Engr.

1907 A571 2.50k Lena Philipsson 1.75 1.00
1908 A571 2.50k Roxette 1.75 1.00
1909 A571 2.50k Jerry Williams 1.75 1.00
a. Bklt. pane of 3, #1907-1909 7.50 *5.00*

A572

Christmas: No. 1910, Boy with star, girl with snacks. No. 1911, Family dancing around Christmas tree. No. 1912, Cat beside tree. No. 1913, Child beside bed.

Perf. 12½x13 on 3 Sides

1991, Nov. 20 Litho.

1910 A572 2.30k multicolored .95 .45
1911 A572 2.30k multicolored .95 .45
1912 A572 2.30k multicolored .95 .45
1913 A572 2.30k multicolored .95 .45
b. Bklt. pane, 3 ea #1910-1913 12.00
Complete booklet, #1913b 22.50
Nos. 1910-1913 (4) 3.80 1.80

Nobel Laureates Type of 1990

Nobel Peace Prize Winners: No. 1914, Jean Henri Dunant, founder of Red Cross. No. 1915, Albert Schweitzer, physician and theologian. No. 1916, Alva Myrdal, disarmament negotiator. No. 1917, Andrei Sakharov, physicist.

1991, Nov. 20 Engr. *Perf. 13 Horiz.*

1914 A559 4k carmine 1.60 1.60
1915 A559 4k dk green 1.60 1.60
1916 A559 4k dk ultra 1.60 1.60
1917 A559 4k dk violet 1.60 1.60
a. Bklt. pane, 2 each #1914-1917 with gutter between 13.00
Complete booklet, #1917a 17.50
Nos. 1914-1917 (4) 6.40 6.40

A573

1992, Jan. 30 Engr. *Perf. 13 Horiz.*

1918 A573 2.30k red, grn & blk 1.10 .35

Outdoor Life Assoc., cent.

A574

A575

Wild Animals: No. 1920, Capreolus capreolus. No. 1921, Capreolus capreolus (with fawn). No. 1922, Ursus arctos (2 cubs). No. 1923, Ursus arctos (adult). No. 1924, Mustela erminea. No. 1925, Lutra lutra. No. 1926, Erinaeceus eropaeus. No. 1929, Mustela putorius. No. 1930, Castor fiber. No. 1932, Canis lupus. No. 1933, Sciurus vulgaris. No. 1934, Alces alces. No. 1935, Vulpes vulpes. No. 1936, Lynx lynx. No. 1936A, Lynx lynx.

Perf. 13 on 3 Sides

1992-2009 Engr.

1920 A574 2.80k multi 1.00 .25
1921 A574 2.80k multi 1.00 .25
b. Bklt. pane, 5 ea #1920-1921 10.00
Complete booklet, #1921b 16.00
1922 A574 2.90k multi 1.10 .30
1923 A574 2.90k multi 1.10 .30
b. Bklt. pane, 5 ea #1922-1923 11.00
Complete booklet, #1923b 16.00
1924 A574 3.85k multi 1.00 .25
1925 A574 3.85k multi 1.00 .25
a. Bklt. pane, 5 ea #1924-1925 16.00
Complete booklet, 1 #1925a 16.00

Perf. 13 Vert. (A574), Horiz. (A575)

1926 A574 1k multi .40 .30
1927 A574 2.80k like #1921 1.00 .25
1928 A574 2.90k like #1922 1.25 .25
1929 A574 3k multi 1.25 .45
1930 A575 3.20k multi 1.50 1.25
1931 A574 3.85k like #1924 1.50 .35
1932 A574 5.80k multi 2.75 .40
1933 A575 6k multi 2.50 .50
1934 A575 7k multi 3.50 .50
1935 A574 7.70k multi 3.00 .60
1936 A575 12k multi 3.75 .85

Perf. 12 Horiz. Syncopated

1936A A575 12k multi 3.25 3.25
Nos. 1920-1936 (17) 28.60 7.30

Issued: #1920-1921, 1930, 6k, 7k, Jan. 30; #1922-1923, 1928-1929, 1932, 1936, Jan. 28, 1993; 1k, 3.20k, 3.85k, 7.70k, 1/2/96. No. 1936A, 1/1/2009.

See Nos. 2207-2209, 2238.

Olympic Champions Type of 1991

No. 1937, Gunde Svan, cross-country skiing, Sarajevo, 1984. No. 1938, Thomas Wassberg, cross-country skiing, Lake Placid, 1980. No. 1939, Tomas Gustafson, speed skating, Sarajevo, 1984. No. 1940, Ingemar Stenmark, slalom skiing, Lake Placid, 1980.

Perf. 12x13 on 3 Sides

1992, Jan. 30 Litho. & Engr.

1937 A568 2.80k multicolored 1.25 .75
1938 A568 2.80k multicolored 1.25 .75
1939 A568 2.80k multicolored 1.25 .75
1940 A568 2.80k multicolored 1.25 .75
a. Bklt. pane, 2 each #1937-1940 10.50
Complete booklet, 1 #1940a 17.50
Nos. 1937-1940 (4) 5.00 3.00

European Soccer Championships, Sweden — A576

1992, Mar. 26 Engr. *Perf. 13 Vert.*

1941 A576 2.80k shown 1.25 .35
1942 A576 2.80k Two players 1.25 .35
a. Pair, #1941-1942 2.50 1.50

Sweden
No. 1a
A577

Litho. & Engr.

1992, Mar. 26		Perf. 13	
1943	A577 2.80k No. 1	3.50	3.00
1944	A577 4.50k No. 1	3.50	3.00
1945	A577 5.50k shown	3.00	1.60
a.	Bklt. pane, #1943-1944, 2 #1945	13.00	11.00
	Complete booklet, 1 #1945a	19.00	
	Nos. 1943-1945 (3)	10.00	7.60

No. 1945a sold for 25k. Surtax benefited stamp collecting.

Sailing Ships — A578

1992, Mar. 26			
1946	A578 4.50k Sprengtporten, 1785	2.10	1.50
1947	A578 4.50k Superb, 1855	2.10	1.50
1948	A578 4.50k Big T	2.10	1.50
a.	Bklt. pane of 3, #1946-1948	6.50	6.50

Europa. Discovery Race, Spain-Florida (No. 1948).

Children's Drawings A579

Perf. 13x12½ on 3 Sides

1992, May 21		Litho.	
1949	A579 2.50k Rabbit	1.25	.25
1950	A579 2.50k Horses	1.25	.25
1951	A579 2.50k Cat	1.25	.25
1952	A579 2.50k Elephant	1.25	.25
a.	Bklt. pane, 5 ea #1949-1952	25.00	
	Complete booklet, 1 #1952a	32.50	
	Nos. 1949-1952 (4)	5.00	1.00

See note after No. 1277.

Olympic Champions Type of 1991

Designs: No. 1953, Gunnar Larsson, swimming, 1972. No. 1954, Bernt Johansson, cycling, 1976. No. 1955, Anders Garderud, steeplechase, 1976. No. 1956, Gert Fredriksson, kayaking, 1948-1956.

Perf. 12x13 on 3 Sides

1992, May 21		Litho. & Engr.	
1953	A568 5.50k multicolored	2.50	2.50
1954	A568 5.50k multicolored	2.50	2.50
1955	A568 5.50k multicolored	2.50	2.50
1956	A568 5.50k multicolored	2.50	2.50
a.	Bklt. pane, 2 ea #1953-1956	21.00	
	Complete booklet, 1 #1956a	27.50	
	Nos. 1953-1956 (4)	10.00	10.00

Greetings Stamps — A580

No. 1957, Hand with flower. No. 1958, Cheese. No. 1959, Baby. No. 1960, Hand holding pen.

Perf. 13x12 on 3 Sides

1992, Aug. 14		Litho.	
1957	A580 2.80k multi	1.10	.85
1958	A580 2.80k multi	1.10	.85
1959	A580 2.80k multi	1.10	.85

1960	A580 2.80k multi	1.10	.85
b.	Bklt. pane, 2 each #1957-1960	9.00	
	Complete booklet, 1 #1960b	13.00	
	Nos. 1957-1960 (4)	4.40	3.40

88th Inter-Parliamentary Union Conference, Stockholm — A581

Swedish Patent and Registration Office, Cent. — A582

#1961, Riksdag building. #1962, First automatic lighthouse, Gustaf Dalen's sun valve.

Perf. 12½ Vert.

1992, Aug. 27		Engr.	
1961	A581 2.80k violet, tan	1.25	.25

Perf. 13 Horiz.

1962	A582 2.80k blue & black	1.25	.35

Kitchen Maid, by Rembrandt A583

The Triumph of Venus, by Francois Boucher A584

Paintings: No. 1965, Portrait of a Girl, by Albrecht Durer. No. 1966, Rorstrand Vase, by Erik Wahlberg. No. 1967, Motif from the Seine/The Tree and the River Bend III, by Carl Fredrik Hill. No. 1968, Sergel in his Studio, by Carl Larsson.

Perf. 12½ on 3 Sides

1992, Aug. 27		Litho. & Engr.	
1963	A583 5.50k multicolored	3.00	3.00
1964	A584 5.50k multicolored	3.00	3.00
1965	A583 5.50k multicolored	3.00	3.00
1966	A584 5.50k multicolored	3.00	3.00
1967	A583 5.50k multicolored	3.00	3.00
1968	A583 5.50k multicolored	3.00	3.00
a.	Bklt. pane of 6, #1963-1968	18.50	20.00

National Museum of Fine Arts, 200th anniv.

Prehistoric Animals — A585

No. 1969, Plateosaurus. No. 1970, Thoracosaurus scanicus. No. 1971, Coelodonta antiquitatis. No. 1972, Mammuthus primigenius.

Perf. 13x12½ on 3 Sides

1992, Oct. 3		Litho. & Engr.	
1969	A585 2.80k multi	1.25	.90
1970	A585 2.80k multi	1.25	.90
1971	A585 2.80k multi	1.25	.90

1972	A585 2.80k multi	1.25	.90
a.	Bklt. pane, 2 ea #1969-1972	10.40	
	Complete booklet, 1 #1972a	14.00	
	Nos. 1969-1972 (4)	5.00	3.60

No. 1972a sold for 27k to benefit stamp collecting.

1950 Automobiles — A586

1992, Oct. 3		Engr.	Perf. 12½ Vert.
1973	4k Saab 92	1.75	1.50
1974	4k Volvo P 831	1.75	1.50
a.	A586 Pair, #1973-1974	3.75	3.50

Birds of the Baltic Shores — A587

No. 1975, Pandion haliaetus. No. 1976, Limosa limosa. No. 1977, Mergus merganser. No. 1978, Tadorna tadorna.

Perf. 13

1992, Oct. 3		Litho. & Engr.	
1975	A587 4.50k multi	2.50	1.25
1976	A587 4.50k multi	2.50	1.25
1977	A587 4.50k multi	2.50	1.25
1978	A587 4.50k multi	2.50	1.25
a.	Bklt. pane of 4, #1975-1978	10.00	7.50
	Complete booklet, 2 #1978a with vertical gutter	27.50	

See Estonia Nos. 231-234, Latvia Nos. 332-335, and Lithuania Nos. 427-430.

A588   A589
A590   A591
Christmas

Icons: No. 1979, Joachim and Anna, 16th cent. No. 1980, Madonna and Child, 14th cent. No. 1981, Archangel Gabriel, 12th cent. No. 1982, St. Nicholas, 16th cent.

Perf. 12½x13 on 3 Sides

1992, Nov. 27		Litho. & Engr.	
1979	A588 2.30k multicolored	1.25	.50
1980	A589 2.30k multicolored	1.25	.50
1981	A590 2.30k multicolored	1.25	.50
1982	A591 2.30k multicolored	1.25	.50
a.	Bklt. pane, 3 ea #1979-1982	15.00	
	Complete booklet, #1982a	19.00	
	Nos. 1979-1982 (4)	5.00	2.00

See Russia Nos. 6103-6106.

Derek Walcott, Nobel Laureate in Literature, 1992 — A592

1992, Nov. 27		Engr.	Perf. 12½ Vert.
1983	A592 5.50k Text	2.25	1.60
1984	A592 5.50k Portrait	2.25	1.60
a.	Pair, #1983-1984	5.00	5.00

1993 Sports Championships — A593

Perf. 12½x13 on 3 Sides

1993, Jan. 28		Litho. & Engr.	
1985	A593 6k Gliding	2.40	1.90
1986	A593 6k Wrestling	2.40	1.90
1987	A593 6k Table tennis	2.40	1.90
1988	A593 6k Bowling	2.40	1.90
1989	A593 6k Team handball	2.40	1.90
1990	A593 6k Cross-country skiing	2.40	1.90
a.	Booklet pane, #1985-1990	14.50	13.50
	Complete booklet, #1990a	20.00	

World Gliding Championships, Borlange (#1985). World Wrestling Championships, Stockholm (#1986). World Table Tennis Championships, Gothenburg (#1987). European Bowling Championships, Malmo (#1988). World Team Handball Championships, Gothenburg (#1989). World Cross-Country Skiing Championships, Falun (#1990).

Uppsala Convocation, 400th Anniversary A594

Litho. & Engr.

1993, Mar. 25		Perf. 13 Vert.	
1991	A594 2.90k Stone carving	1.25	.45
1992	A594 2.90k Uppsala Cathedral	1.25	.45
a.	Pair, #1991-1992	2.50	2.00

A595

Tourist Attractions in Gothenburg: No. 1993, Roller coaster Liseberg Loop, Liseburg Amusement Park. No. 1994, Fountain of Poseidon, by Carl Milles.

1993, Mar. 25			
1993	A595 3.50k multicolored	1.75	1.40
1994	A595 3.50k multicolored	1.75	1.40
a.	Pair, #1993-1994	4.00	3.25

Fruit
A596   A596a

No. 1995, Ribes uva crispa. No. 1996, Pyrus communis. No. 1997, Victoria plum. No. 1998, Opal plum. No. 2001, Ribes nigrum. No. 2002, Rubus idaeus. No. 2004, Prunus avium. No. 2005, James Grieve apple. No. 2008, Fragaria ananassa.

Perf. 12½ on 3 Sides

1993-95		Engr.	
1995	A596 2.40k multi	1.10	.75
1996	A596 2.40k multi	1.10	.75
b.	Bklt. pane, 5 ea #1996-1996	11.00	
	Complete booklet, #1996b	14.00	
1997	A596 2.80k multi	1.25	.60
1998	A596 2.80k multi	1.25	.60
b.	Bklt. pane, 5 ea #1997-1998	12.50	
	Complete booklet, #1998b	16.00	
2001	A596a 3.35k multi	1.40	.60
2002	A596a 3.35k multi	1.40	.60
a.	Bklt. pane, 5 ea #2001-2002	13.50	
	Complete booklet, #2002a	13.50	

Perf. 12½ Vert.

2004	A596 2.40k multi	1.00	.75
2005	A596 2.80k multi	1.40	.50

Perf. 12½ Horiz.

2008 A596a 3.35k multi 1.40 .60
Nos. 1995-2008 (9) 11.30 5.75

Issued: #1995-1996, 2004, 3/25/93; #1997-1998, 2005, 1/17/94; #2000-2001, 2008, 1/2/95.

This is an expanding set. Numbers may change.

Oxe-eye
Daisy — A597

Poppy — A598

Buttercup
A599

Bluebell
A600

Perf. 12½x13 on 3 Sides

1993, May 21 Litho.

2013 A597 2.60k multicolored .95 .35
2014 A598 2.60k multicolored .95 .35
2015 A599 2.60k multicolored .95 .35
2016 A600 2.60k multicolored .95 .35
b. Bklt. pane, 5 ea #2013-2016 19.00
Complete booklet, #2016b 40.00
Nos. 2013-2016 (4) 3.80 1.40

See note after No. 1277.

Contemporary
Art — A601

Europa: No. 2017, Oguasark, by Olle Baertling (1911-81). No. 2018, Ade-Lidic-Nander II, by Oyvind Fahlstrom (1928-76), horiz. No. 2019, The Cubist Chair, by Otto G. Carlsund (1897-1948).

Litho. & Engr.

1993, May 21 Perf. 13

2017 A601 5k multicolored 2.10 1.90
2018 A601 5k multicolored 2.10 1.90
2019 A601 5k multicolored 2.10 1.90
a. Booklet pane of 3, #2017-2019 6.50 7.50

Butterflies — A602

No. 2020, Papilio machaon. No. 2021, Nymphalis antiopa. No. 2022, Colias palaeno. No. 2023, Euphydryas maturna.

1993, May 21 Perf. 12½ Horiz.

2020 A602 6k multicolored 2.25 2.10
2021 A602 6k multicolored 2.25 2.10
2022 A602 6k multicolored 2.25 2.10
2023 A602 6k multicolored 2.25 2.10
a. Booklet pane, 2 each #2020-2023 with gutter between 19.00
Complete booklet, #2023a 27.50
Nos. 2020-2023 (4) 9.00 8.40

 A603  A604

 A605 A606

Greetings

Perf. 13 on 3 Sides

1993, Aug. 6 Litho.

2024 A603 2.90k multicolored 1.00 .40
2025 A604 2.90k multicolored 1.25 .75
2026 A605 2.90k multicolored 1.00 .40
2027 A606 2.90k multicolored 1.25 .75
b. Booklet pane, 3 each #2024, 2026, 2 each #2025, 2027 11.00
Complete booklet, #2027b 16.00
Nos. 2024-2027 (4) 4.50 2.30

Sea
Birds
A607

Perf. 12½ Horiz.

1993, Aug. 26 Engr.

2028 A607 5k Mergus serrator 2.50 2.00
2029 A607 5k Melanitta fusca 2.50 2.00
2030 A607 5k Aythya fuligula 2.50 2.00
2031 A607 5k Somateria mollissima 2.50 2.00
a. Booklet pane, 2 each #2028-2031 with gutter between 20.00
Complete booklet, #2031a 27.50
Nos. 2028-2031 (4) 10.00 8.00

A608

No. 2032, Modern echo sounding. No. 2033, 1643 Method.

1993, Oct. 2 Engr. Perf. 13 Vert.

2032 2.90k multi 1.20 .35
2033 2.90k multi 1.20 .35
a. A608 Pair, #2032-2033 2.90 1.75

Hydrographic survey.

A609

1993, Oct. 2 Engr. Perf. 13

2034 A609 8k King holding flag 5.00 2.75
2035 A609 10k King 5.00 3.50
2036 A609 10k Queen Silvia 5.00 3.50

Size: 75x43mm

2037 A609 12k Royal family 5.50 5.25
a. Booklet pane, #2034-2037 21.00 15.00
Nos. 2034-2037 (4) 20.50 15.00

Reign of King Carl XVI Gustaf, 20th anniv.

Christmas — A610

Perf. 12½ on 3 Sides

1993, Nov. 25 Engr.

2038 A610 2.40k Plaited heart .95 .40
2039 A610 2.40k Straw goat .95 .40
b. Bklt. pane, 5 each #2038-2039 9.50
Complete booklet, #2039b 16.00

Toni Morrison,
Nobel laureate in
Literature,
1993 — A611

#2041, Stockholm City Hall.

1993, Nov. 25 Engr. Perf. 12½ Vert.

2040 A611 6k red brown & brown 3.00 1.75
2041 A611 6k multicolored 3.00 1.75
a. Pair, #2040-2041 6.50 4.25

European
Economic Assoc.
Agreement
A612

1994, Jan. 17 Perf. 12½ Vert.

2042 A612 5k Mother Svea 2.25 .65

Domestic
Animals — A613

No. 2047, North Sweden horse, vert. No. 2048, Two horses, vert. No. 2049, Red polled cattle, vert. No. 2050, Goat, vert. No. 2054, Swedish dwarf poultry. No. 2055, Gotland sheep. No. 2059, Mountain cow. No. 2060, Scanian goose. No. 2060A, Yellow duck.

1994-95 Engr. Perf. 13 on 3 Sides

2047 A613 3.20k multicolored 1.25 .40
2048 A613 3.20k multicolored 1.25 .40
a. Bklt. pane, 5 ea #2047-2048 12.50
2049 A613 3.70k multicolored 1.40 .40
2050 A613 3.70k multicolored 1.40 .40
a. Bklt. pane, 5 ea #2049-2050 14.00
Complete booklet, #2050a 14.00

Perf. 13 Vert.

2054 A613 3.10k multicolored 1.40 .45
2055 A613 3.20k multicolored 1.50 .30
2059 A613 6.40k multicolored 3.00 .60
2060 A613 7.40k multicolored 3.00 .60
2060A A613 7.50k multicolored 3.50 2.25
Nos. 2047-2060A (9) 17.70 5.80

Issued: #2047-2048, 2055, 2059, 1/17/94; #2049-2050, 2054, 1/2/95; 2060-2060A, 3/17/95.

This is an expanding set. Numbers may change.

Cats — A614

Litho. & Engr.

1994, Mar. 18 Perf. 13

2061 A614 4.50k Siamese 2.00 1.75
2062 A614 4.50k Persian 2.00 1.75
2063 A614 4.50k European 2.00 1.75
2064 A614 4.50k Abyssinian 2.00 1.75
a. Booklet pane of 4, #2061-2064 8.00 9.00

Roman De La
Rose — A615

Swedish,
French
Flags
A616

Swedish-French cultural relations: No. 2067, House of the Nobility, designed by Simon and Jean de la Vallee. No. 2068, Household Chores, by Hillestrom. No. 2069, Banquet for Gustavus III at the Trianon, 1784, by Lafrensen. No. 2070, Charles XIV John, by Gerard.

Litho. & Engr., Litho. (#2066)

1994, Mar. 18 Perf. 13 on 3 Sides

2065 A616 5k multicolored 2.25 2.25
2066 A616 5k multicolored 2.25 2.25
2067 A615 5k multicolored 2.25 2.25
2068 A615 5k multicolored 2.25 2.25
2069 A616 5k multicolored 2.25 2.25
2070 A615 5k multicolored 2.25 2.25
a. Booklet pane of 6, #2065-2070 14.00 15.50

See France Nos. 2410-2415.

Roses — A617

No. 2071, Nyponros rosa dumalis. No. 2072, Rosa alba maxima. No. 2073, Tuscany superb. No. 2074, Peace. No. 2075, Quatre saisons.

Perf. 12½x13 on 3 Sides

1994, May 11 Litho.

2071 A617 3.20k multicolored 1.10 .45
2072 A617 3.20k multicolored 1.10 .45
2073 A617 3.20k multicolored 1.10 .45
2074 A617 3.20k multicolored 1.10 .45
2075 A617 3.20k multicolored 1.10 .45
a. Bklt. pane, 2 ea #2071-2075 11.00
Nos. 2071-2075 (5) 5.50 2.25

Swedish
Design — A618

#2076, Vase with Irises, by Gunnar Wennerberg, 1897. #2077, Table and Chair, by Carl Malmsten; Wallpaper, by Uno Ahren, 1917. #2078, Cabinet, 1940s, and textile, 1920s, by Josef Franck. #2079, Fireworks Bowl, by Edward Hald, 1921. #2080, Silver water jug, by Wiwen Nilsson, 1941. #2081, Towel, by Astrid Sampe; Plate, by Stig Lindberg; Fork and Spoon, by Sigurd Persson, 1955.

Perf. 12½ on 3 Sides

1994, May 11 Litho. & Engr.

2076 A618 6.50k multicolored 2.50 2.50
2077 A618 6.50k multicolored 2.50 2.50
2078 A618 6.50k multicolored 2.50 2.50
2079 A618 6.50k multicolored 2.50 2.50

2080	A618	6.50k multicolored	2.50	2.50
2081	A618	6.50k multicolored	2.50	2.50
a.		Bklt. pane, #2076-2081	15.50	18.50

1994 World Cup Soccer
Championships, US — A619

1994, May 11 Engr. Perf. 12½ Vert.

2082	A619	3.20k red & blue	1.60	.50

First
Manned
Moon
Landing,
25th
Anniv.
A620

1994, May 11

2083	A620	6.50k multicolored	2.50	2.25

Greetings
A621

Perf. 12½ on 3 Sides

1994, Aug. 5 Litho.

2084	A621	3.20k Cat	1.10	.40
2085	A621	3.20k Snail	1.10	.40
2086	A621	3.20k Frog	1.20	.70
2087	A621	3.20k Dog	1.20	.70
a.		Booklet pane, 3 each #2084-2085, 2 each #2086-2087	11.50	
		Nos. 2084-2087 (4)	4.60	2.20

Swedish
Explorers
A622

Europa: No. 2088, Erland Nordenskiold
(1877-1932), explored South America. No.
2089, Eric Von Rosen (1879-1948), explored
Africa. No. 2090, Sten Bergman (1895-1975),
explored Asia and the Pacific.

Litho. & Engr.

1994, Aug. 26 Perf. 12½

2088	A622	5.50k multicolored	2.50	2.00
2089	A622	5.50k multicolored	2.50	2.00
2090	A622	5.50k multicolored	2.50	2.00
a.		Booklet pane of 3, #2088-2090	7.50	8.75

Finland-Sweden
Track and Field
Meet — A623

#2091, Seppo Raty, Finland, javelin. #2092,
Patrick Sjoberg, Sweden, high jump.

1994, Aug. 26 Perf. 12½ on 3 Sides

2091	A623	4.50k multicolored	2.00	2.00
2092	A623	4.50k multicolored	2.00	2.00
a.		Bklt. pane, 2 ea #2091-2092	8.50	8.50

See Finland Nos. 942-943.

Johan Helmich
Roman (1694-
1758),
Composer
A624

No. 2094, Opera House, Gothenburg.

Perf. 12½ Vert.

1994, Aug. 26 Engr.

2093	A624	3.20k multicolored	1.25	.25
2094	A624	3.20k multicolored	1.25	.25

Yes & No
Stamps — A625

1994, Oct. 1 Litho. Perf. 12½ Vert.

2095	A625	3.20k Ja	1.25	.60
2096	A625	3.20k Nej	1.25	.60

See Nos. 2107-2108.

World Wildlife
Fund — A626

#2097, Sterna caspia. #2098, Haliaeetus
albicilla. #2099, Dendrocopos leucotos.
#2100, Anser erythropus.

Litho. & Engr.

1994, Oct. 1 Perf. 12½

2097	A626	5.50k multicolored	3.00	2.00
2098	A626	5.50k multicolored	3.00	2.00
2099	A626	5.50k multicolored	3.00	2.00
2100	A626	5.50k multicolored	3.00	2.00
a.		Booklet pane of 4, #2097-2100	12.00	10.00

Frans G. Bengtsson (1894-1954),
Writer — A627

1994, Oct. 1 Engr. Perf. 12½ Vert.

2101	A627	6.40k multicolored	3.00	2.00

Nobel Laureates
in Literature
A628

Designs: 4.50k, Erik Axel Karlfeldt (1864-
1931). 5.50k, Eyvind Johnson (1900-76).
6.50k, Harry Martinson (1904-78).

1994, Nov. 11

2102	A628	4.50k multicolored	1.90	1.00
2103	A628	5.50k multicolored	2.25	1.25
2104	A628	6.50k multicolored	2.75	1.40
		Nos. 2102-2104 (3)	6.90	3.65

Christmas — A629

Scenes from medieval altar pieces: No.
2105, Annunciation. No. 2106, Flight to Egypt.

Perf. 12½x13 on 3 Sides

1994, Nov. 11 Litho. & Engr.

2105	A629	2.80k multicolored	1.25	.40
2106	A629	2.80k multicolored	1.25	.40
a.		Bklt. pane, 5 ea #2105-2106	12.50	

Yes & No Type of 1994

1995, Jan. 2 Litho. Perf. 12½ Vert.

2107	A625	3.70k Ja	1.40	.40
2108	A625	3.70k Nej	1.40	.40

Houses
A630

Designs: No. 2109, Country cottage. No.
2110, Soldier's log house. No. 2111, Farmhouse courtyard. No. 2112, Timbered farmhouse. No. 2113, Manor house.

Perf. 14 Horiz.

1995, Mar. 17 Litho. & Engr.

2109	A630	3.70k multicolored	2.00	.65
2110	A630	3.70k multicolored	2.00	.65
2111	A630	3.70k multicolored	2.00	.65
2112	A630	3.70k multicolored	2.00	.65
2113	A630	3.70k multicolored	2.00	.65
a.		Booklet pane of 5, #2109-2113	10.00	8.00
		Complete booklet, #2113a	11.50	

1995 Ice Hockey World
Championships — A631

1995 World
Track & Field
Championships
A632

Litho. & Engr.

1995, Mar. 17 Perf. 13 Vert.

2114	A631	3.70k multicolored	3.00	1.25

Perf. 13 Horiz.

2115	A632	3.70k multicolored	2.00	.75

See No. 2702.

A633

Wood
Sculptures, by
Bror
Hjorth — A634

Europa: Nos. 2116, 2118, Walt Whitman,
Christ, Socrates. Nos. 2117, 2119, Patrice
Lumumba, Albert Schweitzer, children
dancing.

1995, Mar. 17 Litho. Perf. 13

2116	A633	5k multicolored	2.25	1.75
2117	A634	5k multicolored	2.25	1.75
2118	A633	6k multicolored	2.50	2.00
2119	A634	6k multicolored	2.50	2.00
a.		Bklt. pane of 4, #2116-2119	9.50	10.00
		Complete booklet, 2 #2119a	19.00	

Swedish
Membership in
European
Union — A635

1995, Mar. 17 Perf. 13 Vert.

2120	A635	6k multicolored	3.00	1.10

Rock Speedwell
A636

Cloudberry
A637

Mountain
Heath — A638

Alpine
Arnica — A639

Perf. 13 on 3 Sides

1995, May 12 Litho.

2121	A636	3.70k multicolored	1.25	.45
2122	A637	3.70k multicolored	1.50	.60
2123	A638	3.70k multicolored	1.25	.45
2124	A639	3.70k multicolored	1.50	.60
a.		Booklet pane, 3 each #2121, 2123, 2 each #2122, 2124	13.50	
		Complete booklet, #2124a	13.50	
		Nos. 2121-2124 (4)	5.50	2.10

Tourist
Attractions — A640

No. 2125, Canal boat Wilhelm Tham on
Gota Canal. No. 2126, Sail boat anchored on
Lake Vattern.

1995, May 12 Engr.

2125	A640	5k dark green	2.10	1.75
2126	A640	5k dark violet	2.10	1.75
a.		Bklt. pane, 2 ea #2125-2126	8.50	
		Complete booklet, #2126a	8.50	

Trams
A641

#2127, Gothenburg, c. 1900. #2128, Norr-
koping, 1905. #2129, Helsingborg, 1921.
#2130, Kiruna, 1958. #2131, Stockholm, 1967.

1995, May 12 Perf. 13 Horiz.

2127	A641	7.50k rose claret	3.25	3.00
2128	A641	7.50k dp brown vio	3.25	3.00
2129	A641	7.50k dk green	3.25	3.00
2130	A641	7.50k dk gray violet	3.25	3.00
2131	A641	7.50k dk violet blue	3.25	3.00
a.		Bklt. pane of 5, #2127-2131	17.50	18.50
		Complete booklet, #2131a	17.50	

UN, 50th
Anniv.
A642

1995, Aug. 3 Engr. Perf. 13 Vert.

2132	A642	3.70k multicolored	2.00	.45

Greetings
A643

Children's drawings: No. 2133, "The Ball is
Yours," by M. Angesjo. No. 2134, Happy man,
by E. Sandstrom. No. 2135, Teddy Bear saying "I miss you," by L. Nordenhem. No. 2136,
Mussel saying "Hello," by C. Stenbom.

1995, Aug. 3 Litho. *Perf. 13x12½*

2133	A643 3.70k multicolored	1.40	.55
2134	A643 3.70k multicolored	1.40	.55
2135	A643 3.70k multicolored	1.75	1.00
2136	A643 3.70k multicolored	1.75	1.00
a.	Booklet pane, 3 each #2133-2134, 2 each #2135-2136	15.50	
	Complete booklet, #2136a	15.50	
	Nos. 2133-2136 (4)	6.30	3.10

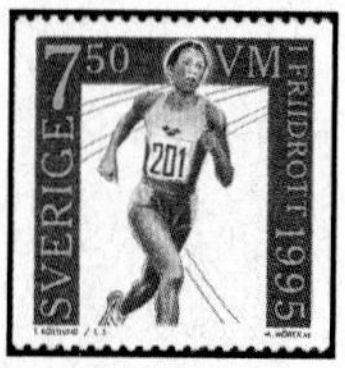

1995 IAAF World Track & Field Championships, Gothenburg
A644

Perf. 13 Horiz.

1995, Aug. 3 Litho. & Engr.

2137 A644 7.50k Maria Akraka 3.00 2.25

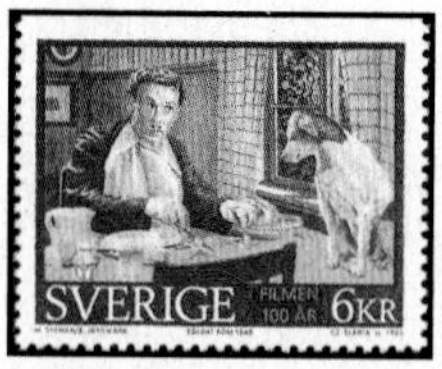

Motion Picture, Cent.
A645

Scenes from films: No. 2138, Soldier Bom, 1948. No. 2139, Sir Arne's Treasure, 1919. No. 2140, Wild Strawberries, 1957. No. 2141, House of Angels, 1992. No. 2142, One Summer of Happiness, 1951. No. 2143, The Apple War, 1971.

Litho. & Engr.

1995, Oct. 7 *Perf. 12½x13*

Booklet Stamps

2138 A645 6k multicolored	3.00	2.50
2139 A645 6k multicolored	3.00	2.50
2140 A645 6k multicolored	3.00	2.50
2141 A645 6k multicolored	3.00	2.50
2142 A645 6k multicolored	3.00	2.50
2143 A645 6k multicolored	3.00	2.50
a. Booklet pane, #2138-2143	18.00	*18.00*
Complete booklet, #2143a	19.00	

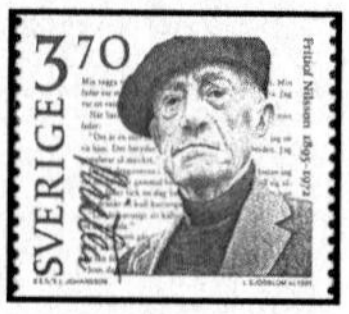

Fritiof Nilsson (1895-1972), Writer — A646

Litho. & Engr.

1995, Oct. 27 *Perf. 13 Vert.*

2144 A646 3.70k blue & claret 1.75 .40

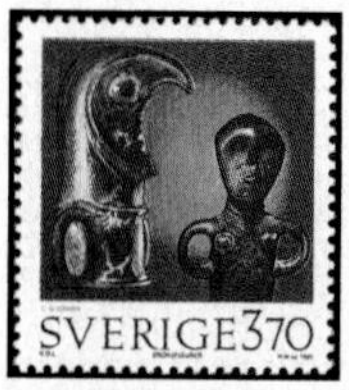

Ancient Artifacts — A647

Designs: No. 2145, Bronze cult figures of man with beak, nude woman, Bronze Age. No. 2146, Detail of gold collar, Great Migration period. No. 2147, Bracteate pendant picturing figure on horse, Great Migration period. No. 2148, Circular bronze cult object, Bronze Age.

1995, Oct. 27 *Perf. 13*

2145 A647 3.70k multicolored	1.50	1.25
2146 A647 3.70k multicolored	1.50	1.25
2147 A647 3.70k multicolored	1.50	1.25
2148 A647 3.70k multicolored	1.50	1.25
a. Booklet pane of 4, #2145-2148	6.00	*7.50*
Complete booklet, 2 #2148a	12.00	

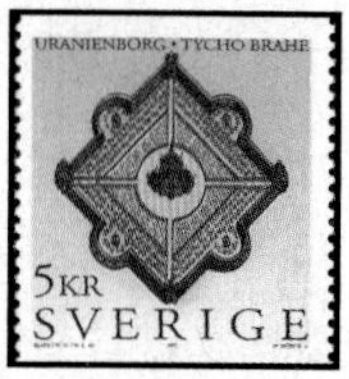

A648

Tycho Brache (1546-1601), Astronomer: 5k, Uranienborg Observatory, Ven Island. 6k, Sextant.

Litho. & Engr.

1995, Oct. 27 *Perf. 13 Vert.*

2149 A648 5k multicolored	1.90	1.25
2150 A648 6k multicolored	2.50	2.00

See Denmark Nos. 1035-1036.

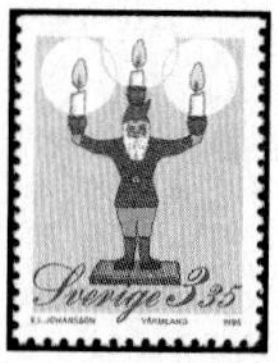

A649

Christmas candlesticks.

Perf. 12½x13 on 3 Sides

1995, Nov. 9 Litho.

2151 A649 3.35k Santa	1.10	.45
2152 A649 3.35k Apple	1.50	.80
2153 A649 3.35k Wrought iron	1.10	.45
2154 A649 3.35k Red wooden	1.50	.80
a. Booklet pane, 3 ea #2151, 2153, 2 ea #2152, 2154	12.50	
Complete booklet, No. 2151a	12.50	
Nos. 2151-2154 (4)	5.20	2.50

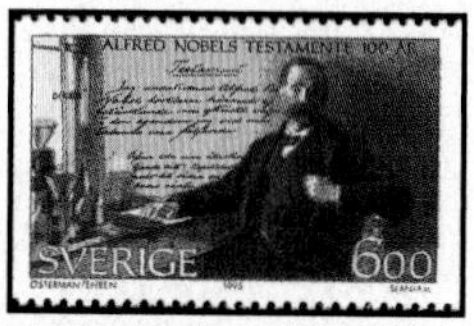

Nobel Prize Fund Established, Cent. — A650

Designs: No. 2155, Alfred Nobel, last will and testament. No. 2156, Nobel's home, 59 Avenue de Malakoff, Paris. No. 2157, Björkborn Laboratory, Karlkoga. No. 2158, Wilhelm Röntgen receiving the first physics prize, 1901.

Photo. & Engr.

1995, Nov. 9 *Perf. 13 Horiz.*

2155 A650 6k multicolored	2.75	2.50
2156 A650 6k multicolored	2.75	2.50
2157 A650 6k multicolored	2.75	2.50
2158 A650 6k multicolored	2.75	2.50
a. Booklet pane, #2155-2158	11.00	*12.00*
Complete booklet, No. 2158a	11.00	

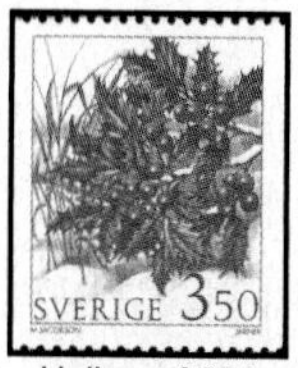

Holly — A651

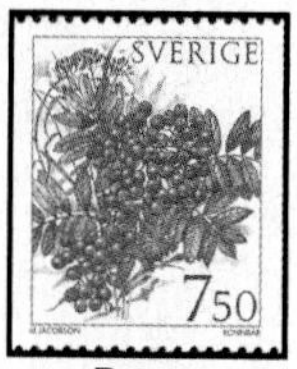

Rowan Berries — A652

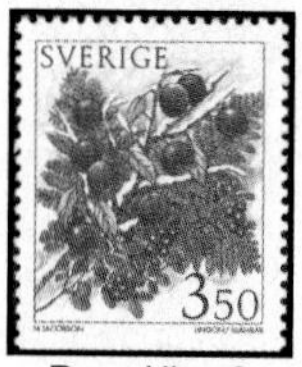

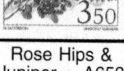

Rose Hips & Juniper — A653

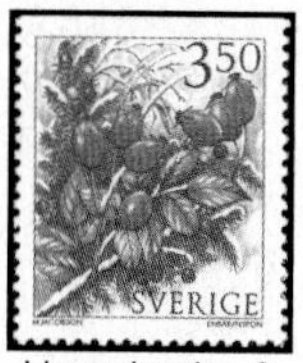

Lingonberries & Sloe — A654

1996, Jan. 2 Litho. *Perf. 13 Horiz.*

2159 A651 3.50k multicolored	1.50	.75
2160 A652 7.50k multicolored	3.25	1.60

Perf. 13 on 3 Sides

2161 A653 3.50k multicolored	1.25	.55
2162 A654 3.50k multicolored	1.25	.55
a. Bklt. pane, 5 ea, #2161-2162	12.50	
Complete booklet, #2162a	12.50	
Nos. 2159-2162 (4)	7.25	3.45

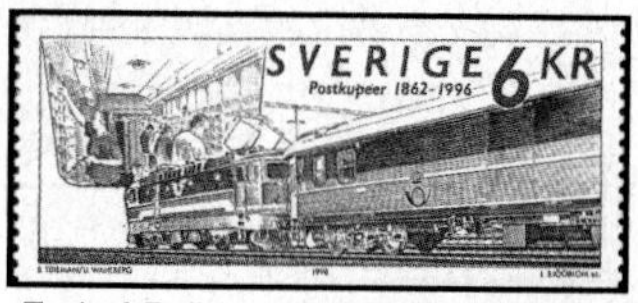

End of Railway Mail Sorting — A655

1996, Mar. 29 Engr. *Perf. 13 Vert.*

2163 A655 6k multicolored 3.00 1.25

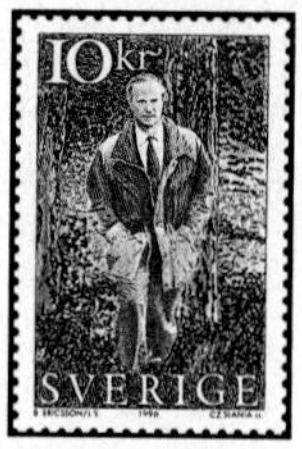

King Carl XVI Gustaf, 50th Birthday — A656

King Carl XVI Gustaf: No. 2164, In forest. No. 2165, In front of portrait of King Charles XIV John. No. 2166, In carriage with King Albert of Belgium, 1994. 20kr, With family.

Litho. & Engr.

1996, Apr. 19 *Perf. 13x12½*

2164 A656 10k multicolored	5.00	5.00
2165 A656 10k multicolored	5.00	5.00
2166 A656 10k multicolored	5.00	5.00

Size: 80x48mm

2167 A656 20k multicolored	10.00	6.50
a. Booklet pane, #2164-2167	25.00	25.00

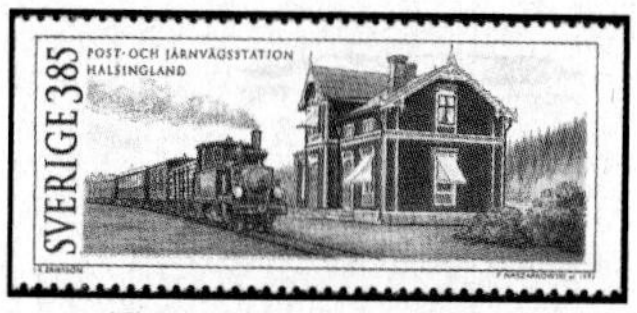

Historic Buildings — A657

Designs: No. 2168, Railway station, Halsingland. No. 2169, Motala Assembly Hall, Ostergotland. No. 2170, Parish storehouse, Smaland. No. 2171, Half-timbered barn, Vasterbotten. No. 2172, Sheep shelter, Gotland. No. 2173, Old Town Hall, Lidkoping.

Perf. 13 on 2 or 3 Sides

1996, Apr. 19

2168 A657 3.85k multicolored	1.50	.75
2169 A657 3.85k multicolored	1.50	.75

Size: 28x29mm

2170 A657 3.85k multicolored	1.50	1.00
2171 A657 3.85k multicolored	1.50	1.00

Size: 28x38mm

2172 A657 3.85k multicolored	1.50	1.00
2173 A657 3.85k multicolored	1.50	1.00
a. Booklet pane of 6, #2168-2173	9.00	*11.00*

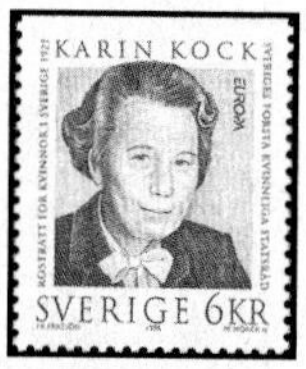

Famous Women — A658

Europa: No. 2174, Karin Kock (1891-1976), economist. No. 2175, Astrid Lindgren (b. 1907), creator of Pippi Longstocking.

Perf. 13 on 3 Sides

1996, May 3 Engr.

2174 A658 6k multicolored	*3.25*	2.25
2175 A658 6k multicolored	*3.25*	2.25
a. Bklt. pane, 2 ea #2174-2175	*9.00*	
Complete booklet, #2175a	*9.00*	

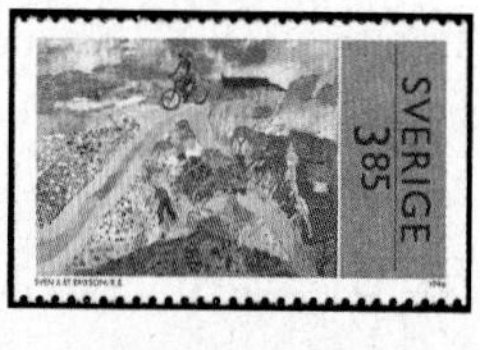

Summer Scenes
A659

Paintings by: No. 2176, Sven X:Et Erixson (1899-1970). No. 2177, Roland Svensson (b. 1910). No. 2178, Eric Hallström (1893-1946), No. 2179, Thage Nordholm (1927-90). No. 2180, Ragnar Sandberg (1902-72).

Perf. 13 on 2 Sides

1996, May 24 Litho.

2176 A659 3.85k multicolored	1.50	.40
2177 A659 3.85k multicolored	1.50	.40
2178 A659 3.85k multicolored	1.50	.40
2179 A659 3.85k multicolored	1.50	.40
2180 A659 3.85k multicolored	1.50	.40
a. Bklt. pane, 2 ea #2176-2180	15.00	
Complete booklet, #2180a	15.00	
Nos. 2176-2180 (5)	7.50	2.00

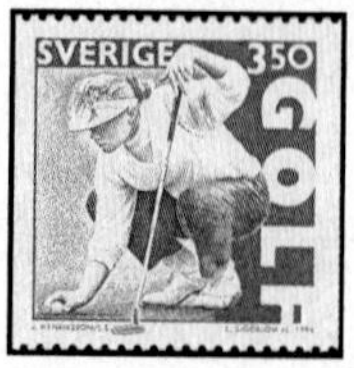

Golf — A660

1996, Aug. 23 Engr. *Perf. 13 Horiz.*

2181 A660 3.50k dark green, *buff* 2.25 1.25

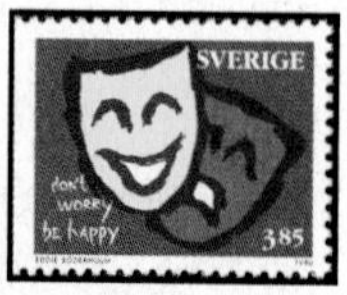

Greetings Stamps — A661

Designs: No. 2182, Masks of comedy, tragedy, "don't worry, be happy." No. 2183, Hearts, "Var Glad (Be happy)," vert. No. 2184, Posthorn. No. 2185, Hearts, person, "Minns du mig? (Do you remember me?)."

Perf. 13x12½ on 3 Sides

1996, Aug. 23 Litho.

2182 A661 3.85k multicolored	1.40	.40
2183 A661 3.85k multicolored	1.40	.40
2184 A661 3.85k multicolored	1.60	.75
2185 A661 3.85k multicolored	1.60	.75
a. Booklet pane, 3 each #2182-2183, 2 each #2184-2185	15.00	
Complete booklet, #2185a	15.00	
Nos. 2182-2185 (4)	6.00	2.30

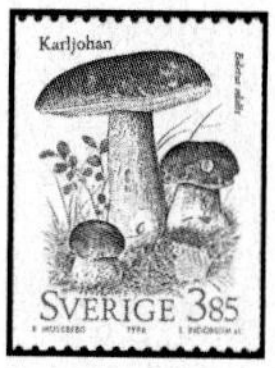

Mushrooms — A662

3.85k, Boletus edulis. #2187, Russula integra. #2188, Cantharellus cibarius. #2189, Craterellus cornucopioides. #2190, Coprinus comatus.

Perf. 13 Horiz.

1996, Aug. 23 Litho. & Engr.

2186 A662 3.85k multicolored 1.75 .45

Perf. 12½x13 on 3 Sides

2187 A662 5k multicolored	1.75	1.25
2188 A662 5k multicolored	1.75	1.25
2189 A662 5k multicolored	1.75	1.25
2190 A662 5k multicolored	1.75	1.25
a. Booklet pane of 4, #2187-2190	7.00	*8.50*
Complete booklet, #2190a	7.00	
Nos. 2186-2190 (5)	8.75	5.45

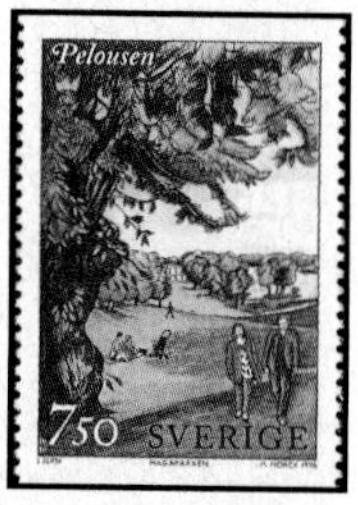

Ecopark, Stockholm
A663

Designs: No. 2191, Pelousen, grassy area, Haga Park. No. 2192, Copper tents, Haga Park. No. 2193, Rosendals Palace, roe deer. No. 2194, Isbladskarret, marsh birds.

Litho. & Engr.

1996, Aug. 23 *Perf. 12½Vert.*

2191 A663 7.50k multicolored	3.00	3.00
2192 A663 7.50k multicolored	3.00	3.00
2193 A663 7.50k multicolored	3.00	3.00

2194 A663 7.50k multicolored 3.00 3.00
a. Booklet pane of 4, #2191-2194 12.50 *15.50*
Complete booklet, #2194a 12.50

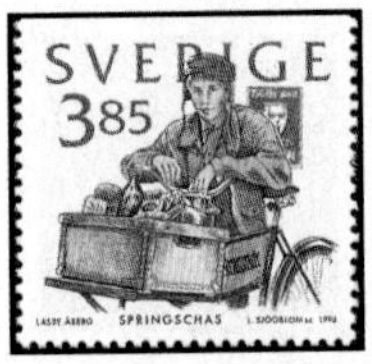

Four Decades A664

Designs: No. 2195, Errand boy, 1930's. No. 2196, Flower child, 1960's. No. 2197, Zoot-suiter, 1940's. No. 2198, Biker, 1950's.

Perf. 12½x13 on 3 Sides

1996, Oct. 5 **Litho. & Engr.**
2195 A664 3.85k multicolored 1.75 .65
2196 A664 3.85k multicolored 2.25 1.50
2197 A664 3.85k multicolored 1.75 .65
2198 A664 3.85k multicolored 2.25 1.50
a. Bklt. pane, 3 ea #2195, 2197, 2 ea #2196, 2198 17.50
Complete booklet, #2198a 17.50
Nos. 2195-2198 (4) 8.00 4.30

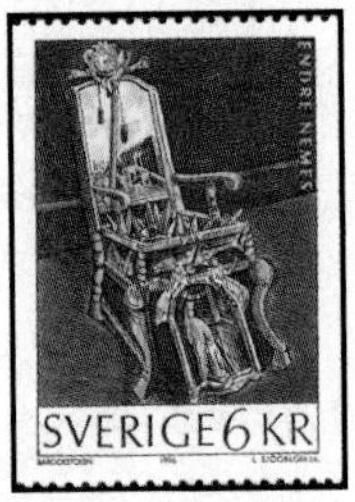

The Baroque Chair, by Endre Nemes — A665

1996, Oct. 5 ***Perf. 12½ Horiz.***
2199 A665 6k multicolored 3.00 1.60

See Czech Republic #2995, Slovakia #255.

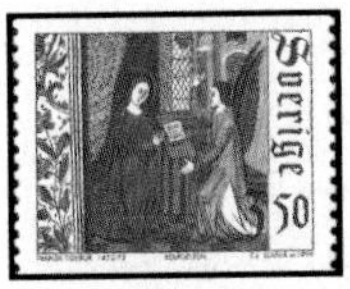

Christmas A666

Illustrations from Book of Hours (15th cent.): No. 2200, The Annunciation. No. 2201, The Birth. No. 2202, Adoration of the Magi.

Perf. 12½ Vert.

1996, Nov. 8 **Litho. & Engr.**
2200 A666 3.50k multicolored 1.75 1.00

Perf. 12½x13 on 3 Sides

2201 A666 3.50k multicolored 1.10 .45
2202 A666 3.50k multicolored 1.10 .45
a. Bklt. pane, 5 ea #2201-2202 11.00
Complete booklet, #2202a 11.00
Nos. 2200-2202 (3) 3.95 1.90

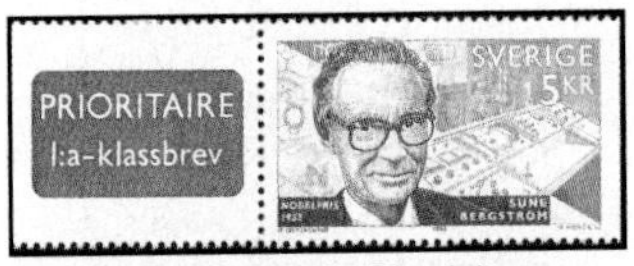

Nobel Laureates in Physiology or Medicine — A667

#2203, Sune Bergström (b. 1916), medical chemist. #2204, Bengt Samuelsson (b. 1934), medical chemist. #2205, Hugo Theorell (1903-82), biochemist. #2206, Ragnar Granit (1900-91), neurophysiologist.

Perf. 13x12½ on 3 Sides

1996, Nov. 8 **Engr.**
2203 A667 5k bl, grn & blk + label 2.00 1.50
2204 A667 5k grn, bl & blk + label 2.00 1.50
2205 A667 5k bl, grn & blk + label 2.75 2.25
2206 A667 5k grn & blk + label 2.75 2.25
a. Booklet pane, 3 each #2203-#2204, 2 each #2205-2206 23.00
Complete booklet, #2206a 23.00
Nos. 2203-2206 (4) 9.50 7.50

Wild Animal Types of 1992

1997, Jan. 2 **Engr.** ***Perf. 13 Vert.***
2207 A574 3.20k Gulo gulo 1.25 1.10
2208 A574 3.50k Nyclea scandiaca 1.25 .70

Perf. 13 Horiz.

2209 A575 7.70k Ciconia ciconia 4.25 4.25
Nos. 2207-2209 (3) 6.75 6.05

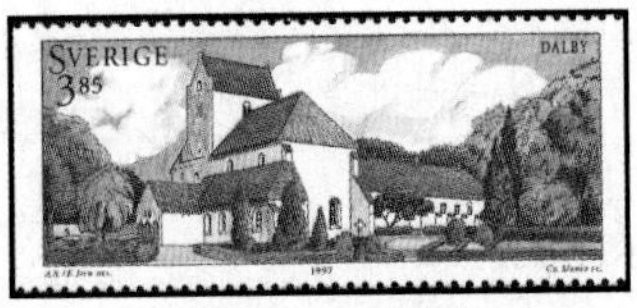

Churches — A668

Perf. 13 Horiz.

1997, Jan. 2 **Litho. & Engr.**
2210 A668 3.85k Dalby 1.60 1.60
2211 A668 3.85k Vendel 1.60 1.60

Size: 27x23mm

Perf. 13x12½ on 2 or 3 Sides

2212 A668 3.85k Hagby 1.60 *1.60*
2213 A668 3.85k Overtornea 1.60 *1.60*

Size: 27x37mm

2214 A668 3.85k Varnhem 1.60 *1.60*
2215 A668 3.85k Ostra Amtervik 1.60 *1.60*
a. Booklet pane of 6, #2210-2215 9.50 *12.50*
Complete booklet, #2215a 9.50

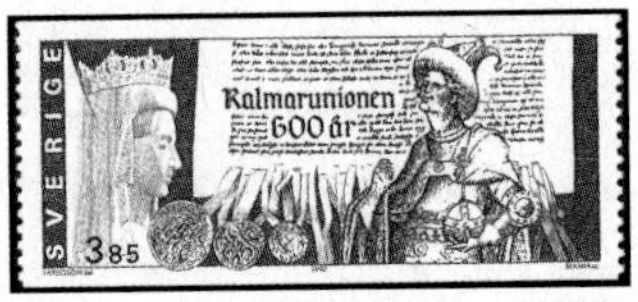

Kalmar Union, 600th Anniv. — A669

Design: Queen Margareta, Erik of Pomerania, coronation document.

1997, Jan. 2 **Engr.** ***Perf. 12½ Vert.***
2216 A669 3.85k dark blue 1.75 .50

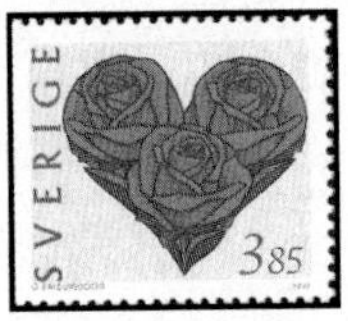

Love Stamps — A670

Perf. 13x12½ on 3 Sides

1997, Jan. 2 **Litho.**
2217 A670 3.85k gray & multi 1.75 .75
2218 A670 3.85k yellow & multi 1.75 .75
a. Bklt. pane, 5 ea #2217-2218 17.50
Complete booklet, #2218a 17.50

Stamps that follow, with denominations in parenthesis, are inscribed "Brev," "Ekonomibrev," "Foreningsbrev," etc.

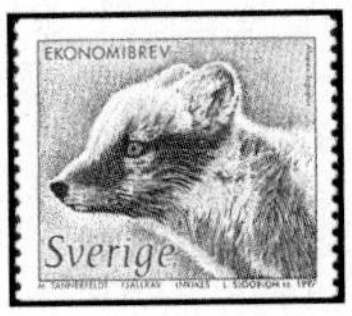

Wild Animals — A671

No. 2219, Alopex lagopus. No. 2220, Equus przewalskii. No. 2221, Panthera unica, adult. No. 2222, same, cubs.

Perf. 13 on 2 Sides

1997, Feb. 28 **Engr.**
2219 A671 (4.50k) multi 1.60 .55
2220 A671 (5k) multi 2.50 .35

Perf. 13 on 3 Sides

2221 A671 (5k) multi 2.00 .35
2222 A671 (5k) multi 2.00 .35
a. Bklt. pane, 3 ea #2221-2222 12.00
Complete booklet, #2222a 12.00
Complete booklet, 1 ea #2221-2222 10.00
Nos. 2219-2222 (4) 8.10 1.60

No. 2220 is 28x21mm.

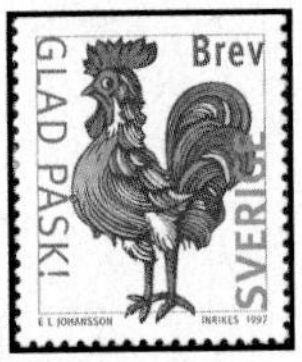

Easter Stamps — A672

Perf. 13x12½ on 3 Sides

1997, Feb. 28 **Litho.**
2223 A672 (5k) Rooster 3.00 .55
2224 A672 (5k) Daffodils 3.00 .55
a. Bklt. pane, 3 ea #2223-2224 18.00
Complete booklet, #2224a 19.00

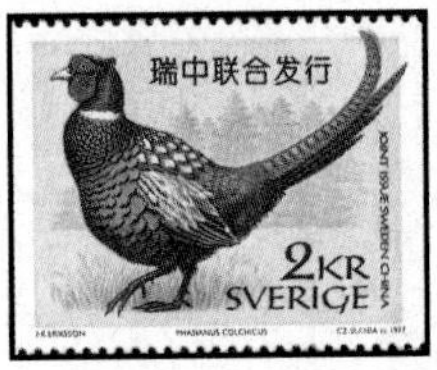

Pheasants A673

Designs: No. 2225, Phasianus colchicus. No. 2226, Chrysolophus amherstiae.

Perf. 12½ Horiz.

1997, May 9 **Litho. & Engr.**
2225 A673 2k multicolored 1.00 .60
2226 A673 2k multicolored 1.00 .60
a. Pair, #2225-2226 2.25 *1.40*

See China (PRC) Nos. 2763-2764.

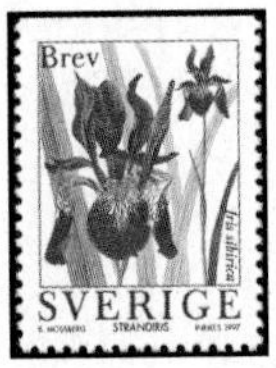

Garden Flowers — A674

#2227, Iris sibirica. #2228, Lonicera periclymenum. #2229, Aquilegia vulgaris. #2230, Hemerocallis flava. #2231, Viola x wittrokiana.

1997, May 9 **Litho.** ***Perf. 12½x13***
2227 A674 (5k) multicolored 2.10 .45
2228 A674 (5k) multicolored 2.10 .45
2229 A674 (5k) multicolored 2.10 .45
2230 A674 (5k) multicolored 2.10 .45
2231 A674 (5k) multicolored 2.10 .45
a. Bklt. pane, 2 ea #2227-2231 21.00
Complete booklet, #2231a 21.00
Nos. 2227-2231 (5) 10.50 2.25

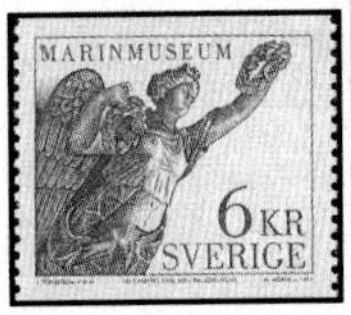

A675

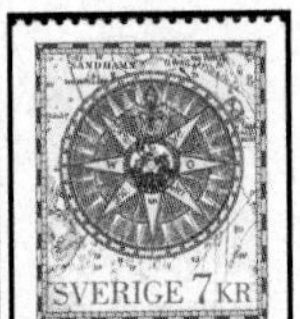

A676

6k, Ship's figurehead, 18th cent., Naval Museum, Karlskrona. 7k, Compass rose, 18th cent. atlas. 8k, Compass rose, 1568 atlas.

Perf. 12½ Vert.

1997, May 9 **Litho. & Engr.**
2232 A675 6k multicolored 2.50 1.20

Litho.

Perf. 12½ Horiz.

2233 A676 7k multicolored 2.50 1.50
2234 A676 8k multicolored 3.00 1.90
Nos. 2232-2234 (3) 8.00 4.60

18th Intl. Cartographic Conf. (#2233-2234).

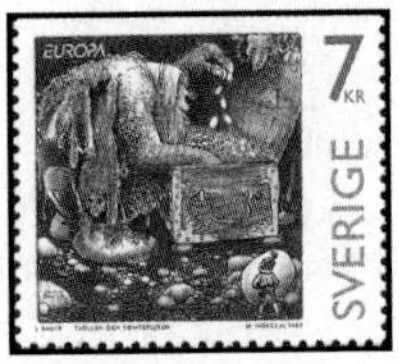

Gnomes and Trolls — A677

Illustrations from "Among Trolls and Sprites," by John Bauer: No. 2235, Troll looking through treasure chest, gnome. No. 2236, Trolls looking at girl seated on rock. No. 2237, Troll talking with boy.

Litho. & Engr.

1997, May 9 ***Perf. 12x13***
2235 A677 7k multicolored *2.75* 2.00
2236 A677 7k multicolored *2.75* 2.00
2237 A677 7k multicolored *2.75* 2.00
a. Bklt. pane, 2 ea, #2235-2237 *16.50*
Complete booklet, #2237a *16.50*
Nos. 2235-2237 (3) 8.25 6.00

Europa.

Wild Animal Type of 1992

No. 2238, Ailurus fulgens, vert.

Perf. 12½ Horiz.

1997, Aug. 21 **Engr.**
2238 A575 (3.50k) multi 2.00 1.50

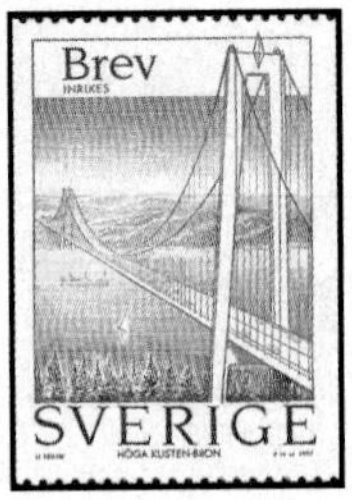

Construction of High Coast Bridge — A678

1997, Aug. 21
2239 A678 (5k) multicolored 2.50 .75

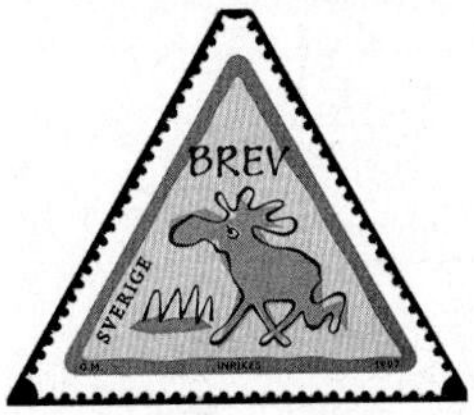

Swedish Elk A679

Designs: No. 2240, Elk as fantasy character. No. 2241, Bar code elk. No. 2242, Swedish elk, yellow bars. No. 2243, Forest elk, green background. No. 2244, Road sign elk, black silhouette against yellow. No. 2245, Old Norse elks, adult & calf.

1997, Aug. 21 **Litho.** ***Perf. 13***
2240 A679 (5k) multicolored 2.50 1.00
2241 A679 (5k) multicolored 2.50 1.00
2242 A679 (5k) multicolored 2.50 1.00
2243 A679 (5k) multicolored 2.50 1.00
2244 A679 (5k) multicolored 2.50 1.00
2245 A679 (5k) multicolored 2.50 1.00
a. Booklet pane, #2240-2245 15.00 *15.00*
Complete booklet, #2245a 15.00

Perforations at each corner of Nos. 2240-2245 end in a large hole within the pane or semi-circles at the edges of the pane, giving the corners of each stamp a slightly concave appearance.

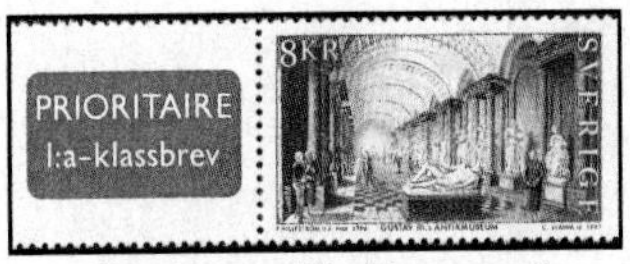

King Gustav III's Museum of Antiquities, Stockholm Palace — A680

Perf. 13x12½ on 3 Sides

1997, Aug. 21 **Engr.**
2246 A680 8k Muses Gallery 3.50 2.75
2247 A680 8k Endymion 3.50 2.75
a. Booklet pane, 2 each #2246-2247 + 4 labels 14.00
Complete booklet, #2247a 14.00

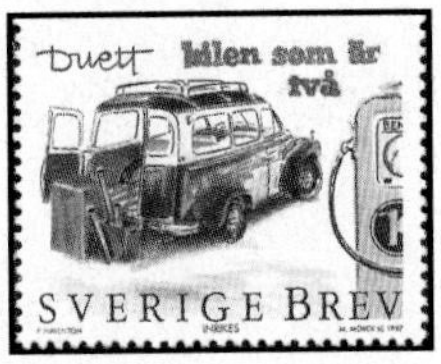

Classic Cars A681

#2248, 1958 Volvo Duett. #2249, 1955 Chevrolet Bel-Air. #2250, 1959 Porsche 356A Coupé. #2251, 1952, Citroen B11. #2252, 1963 Saab 96. #2253, 1961 E-Type Jaguar.

Perf. 12½x13 on 3 Sides

1997, Oct. 4 Litho. & Engr.

Booklet Stamps

2248 A681 (5k) multicolored 2.50 2.50
2249 A681 (5k) multicolored 2.50 2.50
2250 A681 (5k) multicolored 2.50 2.50
2251 A681 (5k) multicolored 2.50 2.50
2252 A681 (5k) multicolored 2.50 2.50
2253 A681 (5k) multicolored 2.50 2.50
a. Booklet pane, #2248-2253 15.00 *18.00*
Complete booklet, #2253a 15.00

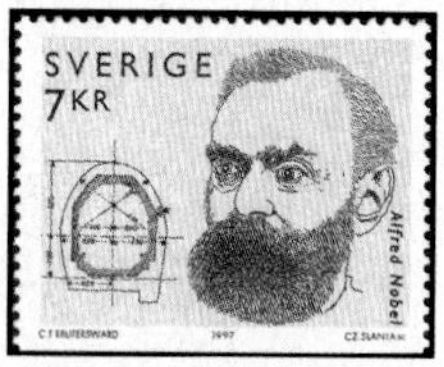

Alfred Nobel (1833-1896), Founder of Nobel Prize — A682

Design: No. 2255, Paul Karrer (1889-1971), winner of Nobel prize for chemistry, 1937.

Perf. 12½x13 on 3 Sides

1997, Nov. 13 Litho. & Engr.

2254 A682 7k lt pink & black 3.00 2.50
2255 A682 7k gray & black 3.00 2.50
a. Bklt. pane, 2 ea #2254-2255 12.00 *14.50*
Complete booklet, #2255a 12.00

See Switzerland Nos. 1004-1005.

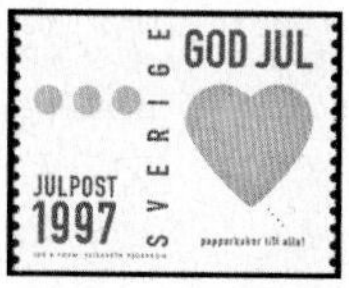

Christmas Gingerbread A683

Perf. 12½ Vert.

1997, Nov. 20 Litho.

2256 A683 (3.50k) Heart 1.75 1.50

Perf. 12½ on 3 Sides

2257 A683 (3.50k) Animals 1.50 1.00
2258 A683 (3.50k) People 1.50 1.00
a. Bklt. pane, 5 ea #2257-2258 15.00
Complete booklet, #2258a 15.00

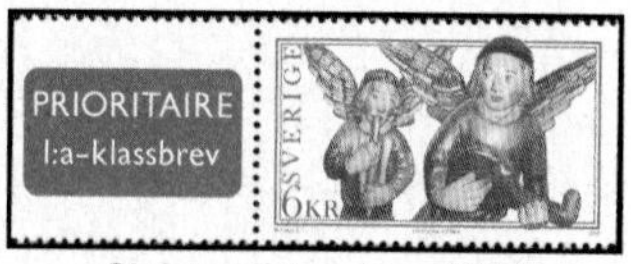

Christmas Angels — A684

Angels from altarpiece, Litslena Church: No. 2259, Playing horn, mandolin. No. 2260, Playing pipes, harp.

1997, Nov. 20 ***Perf. 13x12½***

2259 A684 6k multicolored 3.00 2.00
2260 A684 6k multicolored 3.00 2.00
a. Booklet pane, 5 each #2259-2260 + 10 labels 22.50
Complete booklet, #2260a 22.50

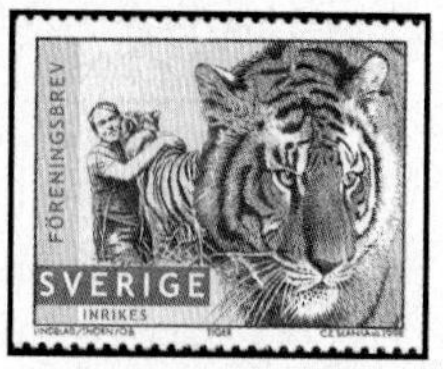

Photographer Jan Lindblad (1932-87) and His Tigers — A685

Perf. 12½ Horiz.

1998, Jan. 15 Litho. & Engr.

2261 A685 (3.50k) shown 2.00 1.25
2262 A685 (3.50k) Two tigers on rock 2.00 1.25
a. Pair, #2261-2262 4.25 3.50

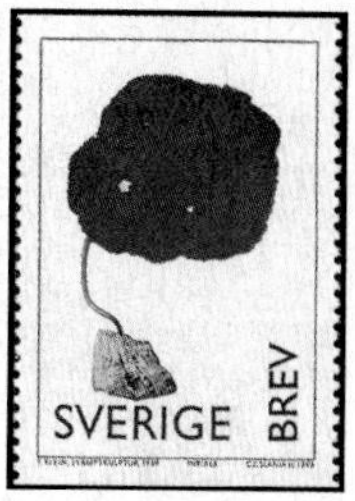

New Modern Museum of Art, Stockholm A686

#2263, Fungus Sculpture, by Yves Klein. #2264, Skeppsholmen, by Göran Gidenstam. #2265, Monogram, by Robert Rauschenberg.

1998, Jan. 15 ***Perf. 12½ Vert.***

2263 A686 (5k) multicolored 2.25 .65
2264 A686 (5k) multicolored 2.25 .65
2265 A686 (5k) multicolored 2.25 .65
a. Booklet pane of 3, #2263-2265 6.75 7.00
Complete booklet, 2 #2265a 13.50

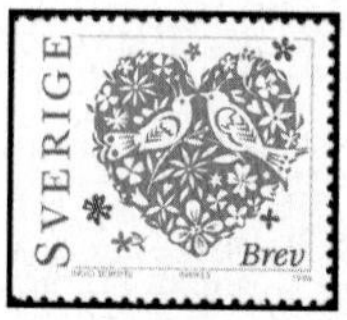

Valentine's Day — A687

Perf. 13 (on 3 Sides)

1998, Jan. 15 Litho.

2266 A687 (5k) dp grn & org red 2.00 .70
2267 A687 (5k) dp blue & rose red 2.00 .70
a. Bklt. pane, 3 ea #2266-2267 12.00
Complete booklet, #2267a 12.00

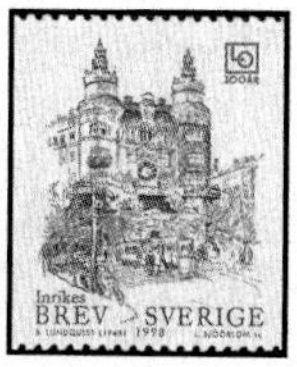

Swedish Confederation of Trade Unions, Cent. — A688

Perf. 12½ Horiz.

1998, Mar. 19 Engr.

2268 A688 (5k) multicolored 2.10 .50

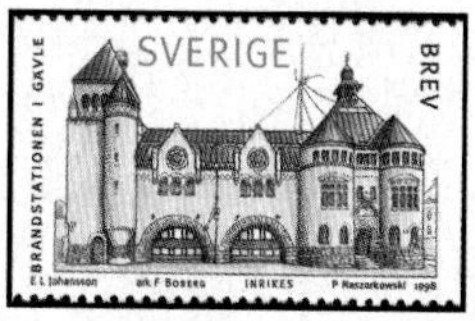

Public Buildings A689

#2269, Fire station, Gävle. #2270, Shoe shop, Askersund. #2271, Fish halls, Gothenburg. #2272, Rödalvarm (Red Mill) Cinema, Halmstad. #2273, Town Hotel, Eksjö.

1998, Mar. 19 ***Perf. 12½ Horiz.***

2269 A689 (5k) multicolored 2.00 .60
2270 A689 (5k) multicolored 2.00 .60
2271 A689 (5k) multicolored 2.00 .60
2272 A689 (5k) multicolored 2.00 .60
2273 A689 (5k) multicolored 2.00 .60
a. Booklet pane, #2269-2273 10.00
Complete booklet, #2273a 10.00

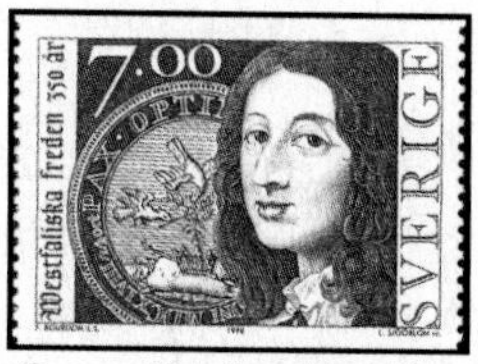

Queen Christina, Medallion Commemorating the Peace of Westphalia, 1648 — A690

1998, Mar. 19 Engr. ***Perf. 12½ Vert.***

2274 A690 7k rose brn & dp grn 3.25 2.00

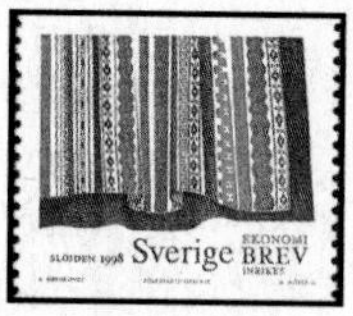

Handicrafts A691

Designs: (4.50k), Apron from costume, Dalecarlia. (5k), Wrought iron ornamental designs. No. 2277, Lovikka mitten. No. 2278, Boxes made from wood shavings.

1998, Mar. 19 ***Perf. 13 Vert.***

2275 A691 (4.50k) multicolored 2.00 1.25
2276 A691 (5k) multicolored 2.00 .40

Perf. 12½ on 3 Sides

2277 A691 8k multicolored 3.50 4.00
2278 A691 8k multicolored 3.50 4.00
a. Bklt. pane, 2 ea #2277-2278 14.00
Complete booklet, #2278a + 4 labels 14.00

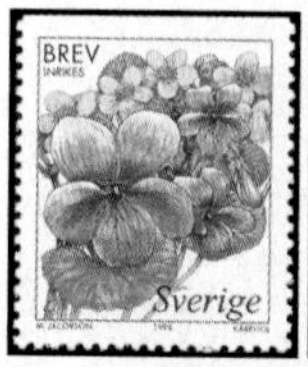
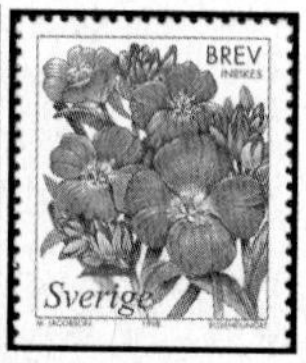

Wetland Flowers
A692 A693

Perf. 13 on 3 Sides

1998, May 14 Litho.

2279 A692 (5k) Marsh violet 2.25 .35
2280 A693 (5k) Great willow-herb 2.25 .35
a. Bklt pane, 5 ea #2279-2280 22.50
Complete booklet, #2280a 22.50

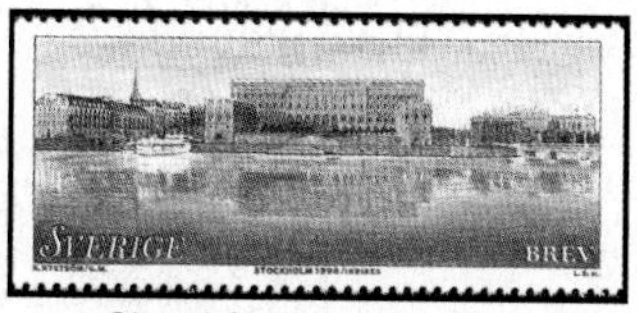

City of Stockholm — A694

Designs: Nos. 2281, 2287, Stockholm Palace. Nos. 2282, 2288, Skerry boats. No. 2283, Opera House, cent. No. 2284, Sail boats. No. 2285, Langholmen Beach, vert. No. 2286, Fireworks over City Hall, vert.

Perf. 13 on 2 or 3 Sides

1998, May 14 Litho. & Engr.

2281 A694 (5k) multicolored 2.10 1.25
2282 A694 (5k) multicolored 2.10 1.25

Size: 27x22mm

2283 A694 (5k) multicolored 2.25 1.60
2284 A694 (5k) multicolored 2.25 1.60

Size: 27x36mm

2285 A694 (5k) multicolored 2.25 1.60
2286 A694 (5k) multicolored 2.25 1.60
a. Booklet pane, #2281-2286 13.00 *14.50*
Complete booklet, #2286a 13.00 *14.50*

Size: 58x23mm

2287 A694 7k multicolored 2.50 2.50
2288 A694 7k multicolored 2.50 2.50
a. Bklt. pane, 2 ea #2287-2288 10.50
Complete booklet, #2288a 10.50

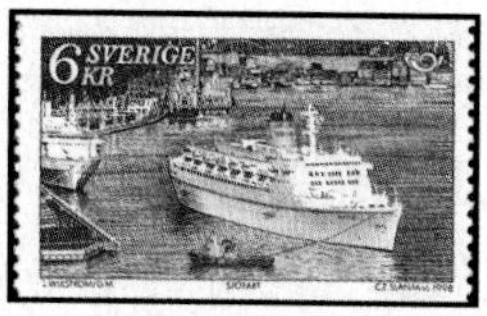

Cruise Ship Albatros in Stockholm Harbor — A695

1998, May 14 ***Perf. 13 Vert.***

Coil Stamp

2289 A695 6k multicolored 3.00 2.25

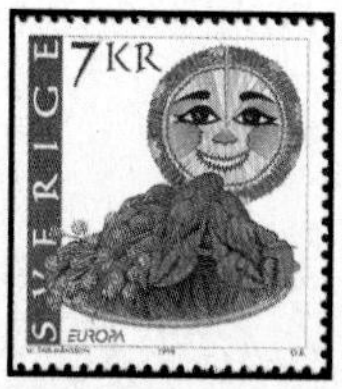

Festivals and Holidays — A696

Europa: No. 2290, Crayfish party, paper moon. No. 2291, Dancing around maypole, Midsummer in June.

Perf. 13 on 3 Sides

1998, May 14 Litho.

2290 A696 7k multicolored *2.75* 2.75
2291 A696 7k multicolored *2.75* 2.75
a. Bklt. pane, 2 ea #2289-2290 *11.00 13.00*
Complete booklet, #2291a + 4 labels *11.00 13.00*

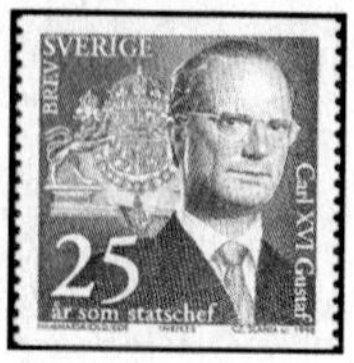

King Carl XVI Gustaf, 25th Anniv. of Accession to the Throne — A697

1998, May 14 Engr. ***Perf. 13 Vert.***

2292 A697 (5k) multicolored 2.25 .50

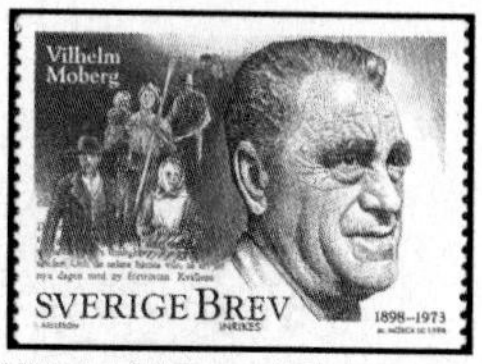

Vilhelm Moberg (1898-1973), Writer — A698

Litho. & Engr.

1998, Aug. 20 ***Perf. 13 Vert.***

Coil Stamp

2293 A698 (5k) multicolored 2.50 .80

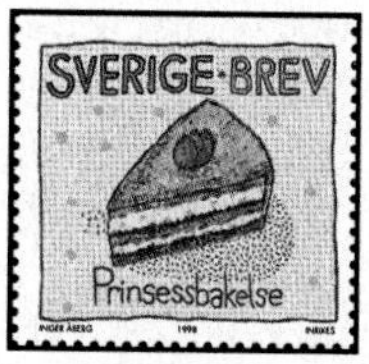

Pastries A699

Designs: No. 2294, Princess cake. No. 2295, Gustav Adolf pastry. No. 2296, Napoleon pastry. No. 2297, Mocha cake. No. 2298, National pastry. No. 2299, Lent bun (semla).

Perf. 13 on 3 Sides

1998, Aug. 20 Litho.

2294 A699 (5k) multicolored 2.25 1.25
2295 A699 (5k) multicolored 2.25 1.25
2296 A699 (5k) multicolored 2.25 1.25
2297 A699 (5k) multicolored 2.25 1.25
2298 A699 (5k) multicolored 2.25 1.25
2299 A699 (5k) multicolored 2.25 1.25
a. Booklet pane, #2294-2299 13.50 *14.50*
Complete booklet, #2299a 13.50

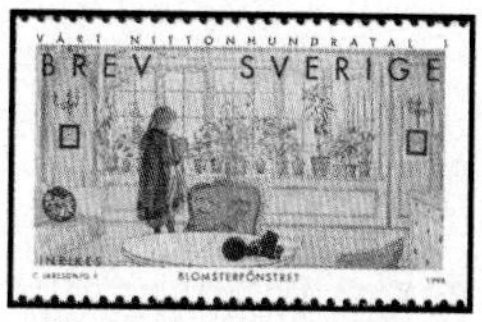

The Millennium — A700

Swedish developments during 1900's: No. 2300, Painting, "Flowers on the Window Sill," by Carl Larsson. No. 2301, Stockholm Stadium, poster for 1912 Olympic Games. No. 2302, Power plant, Porjus, Lapland. No. 2303, Inventions; zippers, ball bearings, vacuum cleaners, refrigerators. No. 2304, Johnson (shipping) Line. No. 2305, AB Radiotjänst, 1924. No. 2306, Jazz music, Charleston dance. No. 2307, Ellen Key, Kerstin Hesselgren, pioneers for women's rights. No. 2308, Arne Borg, swimmer, Gillis Grafström, figure skater, world champions. No. 2309, Ernst Rolf, entertainer, 1920's.

Perf. 12½ Horiz.

1998, Oct. 3 Litho. & Engr.

2300 A700 (5k) multicolored 2.50 2.50
2301 A700 (5k) multicolored 2.50 2.50
2302 A700 (5k) multicolored 2.50 2.50
2303 A700 (5k) multicolored 2.50 2.50
2304 A700 (5k) multicolored 2.50 2.50
2305 A700 (5k) multicolored 2.50 2.50
2306 A700 (5k) multicolored 2.50 2.50
2307 A700 (5k) multicolored 2.50 2.50
2308 A700 (5k) multicolored 2.50 2.50

2309	A700	(5k) multicolored	2.50	2.50
a.		Booklet pane, #2300-2309	25.00	30.00
		Complete booklet, #2309a	25.00	

See Nos. 2327-2336, 2379-2388.

Nobel Laureates
A701

Perf. 13x12½ on 3 Sides

1998, Oct. 3 — Engr.

2310	A701	6k Nadine Gordimer, 1991	2.25	2.00
2311	A701	6k Sigrid Undset, 1928	2.25	2.00
a.		Bklt. pane, 2 ea #2310-2311	9.00	
		Complete booklet, #2311a + 4 labels	9.00	

Sigismund (1566-1632), King of Sweden and Poland — A702

Perf. 12½ Horiz.

1998, Oct. 3 — Litho. & Engr.

2312	A702	7k multicolored	3.00	2.50

See Poland No. 3421.

A703

Perf. 12½ Horiz.

1998, Nov. 19 — Litho.

2313	A703	(4k) Hyacinth	2.00	1.25

Perf. 12½ on 3 Sides

2314	A703	(4k) Mistletoe	1.60	.50
2315	A703	(4k) Amaryllis	1.60	.50
a.		Bklt. pane, 5 ea #2314-2315	16.00	
		Complete booklet, #2315a	16.00	
2316	A703	6k Wreath	2.75	2.00
2317	A703	6k Azalea	2.75	2.00
a.		Bklt. pane, 5 ea #2316--2317	27.50	
		Complete booklet, #2317a	27.50	
		Nos. 2313-2317 (5)	10.70	6.25

Christmas.

A704

1999, Jan. 14 — Litho. Perf. 13 Vert.

2318	A704	(5k) multicolored	2.10	.40

Swedish Cooperative Union, cent.

A705

Swedish Coins: No. 2319, Gustav Vasa Daler. No. 2320, Carl XIV John Riksdaler.

1999, Jan. 14 — Engr. Perf. 12½ Vert.

2319	A705	(4.50k) dark green	1.60	1.00
2320	A705	(5k) dark blue	2.00	.40

A706

Easter Eggs: No. 2321, Sugar egg. No. 2322, Egg filled with marzipan chicks.

Perf. 12½ on 3 Sides

1999, Jan. 14 — Litho. Panel Color

2321	A706	(5k) green	2.25	1.00
2322	A706	(5k) red	2.25	1.00
a.		Bklt. pane, 3 ea #2321-2322	13.50	
		Complete booklet, #2322a	13.50	

"Little Sister Rabbit," by Ulf Nilsson — A707

Rabbits: No. 2323, Preparing meal over fireplace. No. 2324, Feeding Little Sister. No. 2325, Dancing to music. No. 2326, Hopping through thicket.

Perf. 12½ Vert.

1999, Jan. 14 — Litho. & Engr.

2323	A707	(5k) multicolored	2.00	1.00
2324	A707	(5k) multicolored	2.00	1.00
2325	A707	(5k) multicolored	2.00	1.00
2326	A707	(5k) multicolored	2.00	1.00
a.		Booklet pane, #2323-2326	8.00	7.50
		Complete booklet, #2326a	8.00	

The Millennium Type of 1998

Sweden in years 1939-1969: No. 2327, Scene from Bergman's film "Smiles of a Summer Night," 1955. No. 2328, Vällingby Centre. No. 2329, Silhouette of soldier, singer Ulla Bilquist. No. 2330, Cobra telephone, three-point seat belt, ASEA high voltage cables and breakers, Tetra Pak's milk carton. No. 2331, Scandinavian Airlines System formed, DC-4 over New York City, 1946. No. 2332, "Hyland's Corner," Carl-Gustaf Lindstedt, Prime Minister Tage Erlander on television. No. 2333, Protests of the 60's, Hep Stars band. No. 2334, Volvo Amazon car, family picnic. No. 2335, Ingemar Johansson, heavy-weight boxing champion, 1959, Mora-Nisse Karlsson, skiing champion, Gunder Hägg, running champion, 1941-45. No. 2336, Jazz singer Alice Babs, opera singer Jussi Björling.

Perf. 12½ Horiz.

1999, Mar. 11 — Litho.

2327	A700	(5k) multicolored	2.10	1.25
2328	A700	(5k) multicolored	2.10	1.25
2329	A700	(5k) multicolored	2.10	1.25
2330	A700	(5k) multicolored	2.10	1.25
2331	A700	(5k) multicolored	2.10	1.25
2332	A700	(5k) multicolored	2.10	1.25
2333	A700	(5k) multicolored	2.10	1.25
2334	A700	(5k) multicolored	2.10	1.25
2335	A700	(5k) multicolored	2.10	1.25
2336	A700	(5k) multicolored	2.10	1.25
a.		Booklet pane, #2327-2336	21.00	21.00
		Complete booklet, #2336a	21.00	

Construction of the Oresund Bridge — A708

(5k), Swan Pontoon Crane. 6k, Building bridge.

1999, Mar. 11 — **Perf. 12½ Vert.**

2337	A708	(5k) multicolored	2.50	.40
2338	A708	6k multicolored	3.00	2.00

Swedish Ships A709

Perf. 12½x13 on 3 Sides

1999, Mar. 11 — Litho. & Engr.

2339	A709	8k East Indiaman	3.50	3.00
2340	A709	8k Mary Anne	3.00	3.00
2341	A709	8k Beatrice	3.00	3.00
2342	A709	8k SS Austalic	3.00	3.00
a.		Booklet pane, #2339-2342	14.00	15.00
		Complete booklet, #2342a + 4 labels	15.00	

Australia '99 World Stamp Expo.

Pyramid Orchid — A710

Lady's Slipper — A711

Marsh Helleborine A712

Green-Winged Ordhid A713

Perf. 12½ on 3 Sides

1999, May 20 — Litho.

2343	A710	(5k) multicolored	2.10	.40
2344	A711	(5k) multicolored	2.50	.75
2345	A712	(5k) multicolored	2.10	.40
2346	A713	(5k) multicolored	2.50	.75
a.		Booklet pane, 3 each #2343, 2345, 2 each #2344 and #2346	22.50	
		Complete booklet, #2346a	22.50	
		Nos. 2343-2346 (4)	9.20	2.30

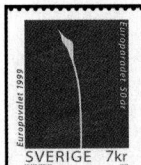

Council of Europe, 50th Anniv. — A714

1999, May 20 — **Perf. 12½ Horiz.**

2347	A714	7k multicolored	3.00	2.50

Europa — A715

No. 2348, Tyresta Natl. Park. No. 2349, Gotska Sandön Natl. Park.

Perf. 12½x13 on 3 Sides

1999, May 20

2348	A715	7k multicolored	2.50	2.00
2349	A715	7k multicolored	2.50	2.00
a.		Bklt. pane, 2 ea #2348-2349	10.00	11.00
		Complete bklt., #2349a+4 labels	10.00	

Post Bike — A716

Racing Bike — A717

Town Bike — A718

Messenger Bike — A719

Engr., Litho. (#2351)

1999, May 20 — **Perf. 12½ Horiz.**

2350	A716	(3.50k) multicolored	2.00	1.75

Perf. 12½ Vert.

2351	A717	(5k) multicolored	2.00	.90
2352	A718	6k multicolored	2.25	1.50
2353	A719	8k multicolored	2.75	2.25
		Nos. 2350-2353 (4)	9.00	6.40

Signs of the Zodiac A720

No. 2354: a, Aquarius. b, Pisces. c, Aries. d, Taurus. e, Gemini. f, Cancer.
No. 2355: a, Leo. b, Virgo. c, Libra. d, Scorpio. e, Sagittarius. f, Capricorn.

Litho. & Engr.

1999, Aug. 12 — **Perf. 13**

2354		Booklet pane of 6	15.00	12.00
a.-f.		A720 (5k) any single	2.50	1.75
2355		Booklet pane of 6	15.00	12.00
a.-f.		A720 (5k) any single	2.50	.75
		Complete booklet, #2354-2355	30.00	

Perforations at each corner of Nos. 2354a-2354f, 2355a-2355f end in a large hole within the pane or semi-circles at the edges of the pane, giving the corners of each stamp a slightly concave appearance.

Butterflies A721

a, Inachis io. b, Junonia orithya wallacei. c, Hypolimnas bolina. d, Vanessa atalanta.

1999, Aug. 12 — **Perf. 12½x13**

2356		Booklet pane of 4	10.00	10.50
a.-d.		A721 6k any single	2.50	1.75
		Complete bklt., #2356 + 4 labels	10.00	

See Singapore Nos. 903-907.

Nobel Laureates in Peace — A722

#2357, Auguste Beernaert (1829-1912).
#2358, Henri La Fontaine (1854-1943).

Perf. 13x12½ on 3 sides

1999, Sept. 30		Litho. & Engr.	
2357	A722 7k gold & blue	2.75	2.25
2358	A722 7k gold & red	2.75	2.25
a.	Bklt. pane, 2 ea #2357-2358	11.00	
	Complete booklet, #2358a + 4 labels	11.00	

See Belgium Nos. 1749-1750.

Dance Bands A723

Designs: a, Thorleifs. b, Arvingarna. c, Lotta Engbergs. d, Sten & Stanley.

1999, Oct. 2		Litho. & Engr.	Perf. 12¾
2359	Booklet pane of 4	13.00	13.00
a.-d.	A723 (5k) any single	3.25	2.25
	Complete booklet, 2 #2359	26.00	

A724

Christmas A725

Stained glass: No. 2360, Nativity, Klinte Church. No. 2361, Nativity, Hablingbro Church. No. 2362, Three kings, Hablingbro Church.
Madonna and child icons from: No. 2363, Bälinge Church. No. 2364, Skänninge Church.

Perf. 12½ Vert.

1999, Nov. 18			Litho.
2360	A724 (4.50k) multicolored	1.75	1.25

Perf. 12¾ on 3 sides

2361	A724 (4.50k) multicolored	1.50	.60
2362	A724 (4.50k) multicolored	1.50	.60
a.	Bklt. pane, 5 ea #2361-2362	15.00	
	Complete booklet, # 2362a	15.00	

Litho. & Engr.

2363	A725 6k multicolored	2.25	2.00
2364	A725 6k multicolored	2.25	2.00
a.	Booklet pane, 5 each #2363-2364 + 10 labels	22.50	
	Complete booklet, # 2364a	22.50	
	Nos. 2360-2364 (5)	9.25	6.45

Millennium — A726

Sun rays touching Heligholmen Island: No. 2365, Island rocks. No. 2366, Island map.

Perf. 12¾ Horiz.

1999, Dec. 27		Litho. & Engr.	
2365	A726 5k multicolored	2.25	1.75
2366	A726 5k multicolored	2.25	1.75
a.	Bklt. pane, 2 ea #2365-2366	9.00	
	Complete booklet, 2 #2366a	18.00	

New Year 2000 (Year of the Dragon) A727

Dragon from children's book "The Dragon with Red Eyes," by Astrid Lindgren: No. 2367, In flight (shown). No. 2368, With basket. No. 2369, In flight, diff.

Perf. 12¾ Horiz.

2000, Jan. 13			Litho.
2367	A727 (5k) multi	2.25	1.10
2368	A727 (5k) multi	2.25	1.10
2369	A727 (5k) multi	2.25	1.10
a.	Bklt. pane, 2 ea #2367-2369	13.50	
	Complete booklet, #2369a	13.50	

A728

Love.

2000, Jan. 13		**Perf. 12¾ on 3 sides**	
2370	A728 (5k) shown	3.00	1.25
2371	A728 (5k) Heart, diff.	3.00	1.25
a.	Bklt. pane, 3 ea #2370-2371	12.00	
	Complete booklet, #2371a	14.00	

A729

Watch of King Karl XII, 1701: (4.50k), Works. (5k), Face.

2000, Jan. 13	Engr.	**Perf. 12½ Vert.**	
2372	A729 (4.50k) blue	1.60	1.25
2373	A729 (5k) claret brown	2.25	.45

Souvenir Sheet

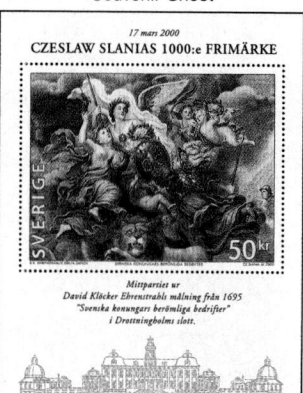

Detail of "Great Deeds by Swedish Kings," by David Ehrenstrahl — A730

Litho. & Engr.

2000, Mar. 17		**Perf. 12¾**	
2374	A730 50k multi	11.50	14.50

Czeslaw Slania's 1000th postage stamp.

Forests — A731

Designs: (3.80k), People in forest. No. 2376, Elk in forest. No. 2377, Bird in forest. 6k, Birch forest.

Perf. 12¾ Vert.

2000, Mar. 17			Litho.
2375	A731 (3.80k) multi	2.00	1.75
2376	A731 (5k) multi	1.90	.55
2377	A731 (5k) multi	1.90	.55
a.	Pair, #2376-2377	3.75	3.50
2378	A731 6k multi	2.50	2.00
	Nos. 2375-2378 (4)	8.30	4.85

Millennium Type of 1998

Sweden in the years 1970-99: No. 2379, Art in Stockholm subway stations. No. 2380, Swedish UN forces, postal clerk. No. 2381, Computer, mouse and mobile phone. No. 2382, Cullberg Ballet, Svenska Ord repertory company. No. 2383, Jönköping railway station. No. 2384, Youth with spiked hair, musical group ABBA. No. 2385, European Union flag, map of member countries. No. 2386, Scene from film, "The Apple War." No. 2387, Skiers Pernilla Wiberg, Ingemar Stenmark, tennis player Björn Borg. No. 2388, Photo of child in womb, taken by Lennart Nilsson.

Perf. 12¾ Horiz.

2000, Mar. 17			Litho.
2379	A700 (5k) multi	2.00	1.40
2380	A700 (5k) multi	2.00	1.40
2381	A700 (5k) multi	2.00	1.40
2382	A700 (5k) multi	2.00	1.40
2383	A700 (5k) multi	2.00	1.40
2384	A700 (5k) multi	2.00	1.40
2385	A700 (5k) multi	2.00	1.40
2386	A700 (5k) multi	2.00	1.40
2387	A700 (5k) multi	2.00	1.40
2388	A700 (5k) multi	2.00	1.40
a.	Booklet pane, #2379-2388	20.00	20.00
	Complete booklet, #2388a	20.00	

Art by Philip von Schantz (1928-98) — A732

Designs: No. 2389, A Peck of Apples. No. 2390, A Bowl of Blueberries.

Perf. 12¾ on 3 sides

2000, May 9			Litho.
2389	A732 (5k) multi	2.00	.60
2390	A732 (5k) multi	2.00	.60
a.	Bklt. pane, 5 ea #2389-2390	20.00	
	Complete booklet, #2390a	20.00	

A733

Oresund Bridge, Sweden-Denmark — A734

2000, May 9	Engr.	**Perf. 12½ Vert.**	
2391	A733 (5k) blue & ultra	2.25	.75

Litho.

Perf. 12¾ Horiz.

2392	A734 6k shown	2.50	1.75
2393	A734 6k Map	2.50	1.75
a.	Booklet pane, 2 each #2392-2393, + 4 etiquettes	10.00	
	Complete booklet, #2393a	10.00	

See Denmark Nos. 1187-1188.

Europa Issue
Common Design Type

2000, May 9 Litho.	**Perf. 12¾ Horiz.**	
2394	CD17 7k multi	3.00	2.25

2000 Summer Olympics, Sydney — A735

No. 2395: a, Hurdler Ludmila Engquist. b, Archer Magnus Petersson. c, Windsurfer Fredrik Palm. d, Beach volleyball player Lena Malm.

Perf. 12¾x12½ on 3 sides

2000, Aug. 17			Litho.
2395	A735 Booklet pane of 4	11.00	12.50
a.-d.	8k Any single	2.75	2.25
	Booklet, #2395 + 4 etiquettes	11.00	

Sky Conditions A736

No. 2396: a, Clouds and sun. b, Clouds and lightning. c, Clouds and rainstorm. d, Aurora borealis. e, Rainbow. f, Cumulus clouds.

2000, Aug. 17 Die Cut Perf. 9¾x10
Self-Adhesive

2396	Booklet of 6	12.00	
a.-f.	A736 (5k) Any single	2.00	1.25

King Carl XVI Gustaf — A737

Design: 8k, Queen Silvia.

Perf. 12¾ Vert.

2000, Aug. 17			Engr.
2397	A737 (5k) blue	2.25	.50
2398	A737 8k red	2.75	2.00

See Nos. 2466-2467.

Nobel Laureates for Literature — A738

a, Wislawa Szymborska. b, Nelly Sachs.

Perf. 12¾x12½ on 3 sides

2000, Oct. 7			Engr.
2399	A738 Pair	5.00	5.00
a.-b.	7k Any single	2.50	2.40
c.	Booklet pane, 2 #2399	10.00	
	Booklet, #2399c + 4 etiquettes	10.00	

Toys — A739

No. 2400: a, Doll, tea set, teddy bear. b, Marbles, tin soldier, yo-yo, jump rope. c, Pine cone cow, doll, horse-drawn wagon. d, Cars and policeman. e, Model train, mechanical men. f, Lego car, robot, Furbee.

Perf. 12¾ on 3 sides

2000, Oct. 7   **Litho. & Engr.**
2400   Booklet of 6   13.50 15.00
a.-f. A739 (5k) Any single   2.25   2.25

Christmas Songs — A740

Christmas Snowflakes — A741

Designs: No. 2401, Hey, Santas.
No. 2402, vert.: a, It's Christmas Again (four children, tree). b, Three Gingerbread Men. c, The Fox Runs Over the Ice. d, Christmas Has Come to Our House (three children, candles).
No. 2403: a, White background. b, Blue background.

Perf. 12¾ Vert.

2000, Nov. 16   **Litho.**
2401   A740 (4.30k) multi   1.50   1.00
         Perf. 12¾ on 3 sides
2402   Block of 4   6.00   5.50
a.-d. A740 (4.30k) Any single   1.50   .70
e.   Booklet pane, 3 ea #2402a,
         2402c, 2 ea #2402b, 2402d 15.00
         Booklet, #2402e   15.00
2403   A741 Pair   4.50   5.50
a.-b. 6k Any single   2.25   2.25
c.   Booklet pane, 5 #2403 + 10
         etiquettes   22.50
         Booklet, #2403c   22.50
         Nos. 2401-2403 (3)   12.00 12.00

Rock Carvings, Tanum World Heritage Site — A742

Swedish World Heritage Site A743

Designs: (4.50k), Rock carvings of animals and people. (5k), Rock carvings of ships.
No. 2406: a, Gammelstad Church Village. b, Karlskrona Naval Port. c, Theater, Drottningholm Palace. d, Engelsberg Ironworks.

2001, Jan. 31 Engr.   *Perf. 12½ Vert.*
2404 A742 (4.50k) blue, *gray*   2.00 1.25
2405 A742   (5k) red, *gray*   2.00   .45
                           Litho.
         Perf. 12½x12¾ on 3 sides
2406   Booklet pane of 4   8.00 10.00
a.-d. A743 6k Any single   2.00   2.00
         Booklet, #2406 + 4 etiquettes 8.00

New Year 2001 (Year of the Snake) — A744

No. 2407: a, Snake with tongue extended. b, Snake curled up.

Perf. 12¾ on 3 sides

2001, Jan. 31   **Litho.**
2407 A744 Pair   4.00   2.75
a.-b. (5k) Any single   2.00   1.00
c.   Booklet pane, 3 #2407   12.00
         Booklet, #2407c   12.00

Dogs — A745

No. 2408: a, Golden retriever. b, German shepherd. c, Labrador retriever. d, Dachshund.

2001, Jan. 31   *Perf. 12¾ Vert.*
2408 A745 Booklet of 4   8.00   7.50
a.-d. (5k) Any single   2.00   1.00

Birds — A746

Designs: (3.80k), Vanellus vanellus. (5k), Pica pica. 6k, Larus argentatus. 7k, Aegithalos caudatus.

2001, Mar. 22 Engr.   *Perf. 12¾ Vert.*
2409 A746 (3.80k) multi   1.75   1.25
2410 A746   (5k) multi   1.90   .50
2411 A746   6k multi   2.00   1.50
2412 A746   7k multi   2.25   1.75
         Nos. 2409-2412 (4)   7.90   5.00

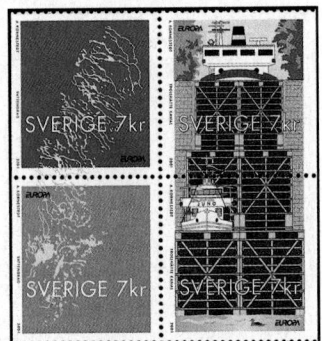

Europa — A747

No. 2413: a, Waterways of northern Sweden. b, Large ship in Trollhätte Canal, trees. c, Waterways of southern Sweden. d, Ship "Juno" in Trollhätte Canal, duck.

Perf. 12¾ on 3 Sides

2001, Mar. 22   **Litho.**
2413 A747 Booklet pane of
              4   11.00 12.00
a.-d. 7k Any single   2.75   2.25
         Booklet, #2413 + 4 eti-
           quettes   11.00

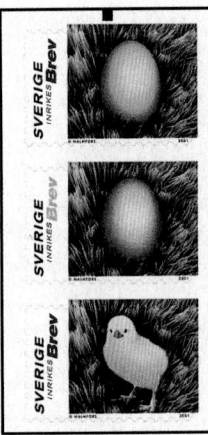

Easter A748

No. 2414: a, Orange egg. b, Purple egg. c, Chick.

2001, Mar. 22   Die Cut Perf. 9¾x10
              Self-Adhesive
2414 A748 Booklet pane of 3   6.00   6.00
a.-c. (5k) Any single   1.90   1.60
         Booklet, 2 #2414   12.00

Nobel Prize, Cent. A749

No. 2415: a, Alfred Nobel, Peace medal, obverse of Physics, Chemistry, Physiology or Medicine, Literature medal. b, Reverse of Physiology or Medicine medal. c, Reverse of medal for Physics or Chemistry. d, Reverse of Literature medal.

Perf. 12¾x13½ on 3 Sides

2001, Mar. 22   **Litho. & Engr.**
2415   Vert. strip of 4   10.00 12.50
a.-d. A749 8k Any single   2.50   2.50
e.   Booklet pane, #2415 + 4 eti-
         quettes + 4 blank labels 10.00
         Booklet, #2415e   10.00

See United States No. 3504.

Ivar Lo-Johansson (1901-90), Writer — A750

No. 2416: a, Portrait. b, Lo-Johansson, truck.

2001, May 17 Engr.   *Perf. 12¾ Vert.*
2416 A750 Pair   3.75   3.50
a.-b. (5k) Any single   1.90   .90

Peonies — A751

No. 2417: a, Fernleaf peony (two flowers, one bud). b, Chinese peony "Mons Jules Elie." c, Herbaceous peony (yellow). d, Common peony (flower and bud). e, Tree peony.

Perf. 12¾ on 3 Sides

2001, May 17   **Litho.**
2417   Horiz. strip of 5   9.25   6.00
a.-e. A751 (5k) Any single   1.90   1.10
f.   Booklet pane, 2 #2417   19.00
         Booklet, #2417f   19.00

Nobel Prize, Cent. — A752

Past winners: a, Doctors Without Borders. b, Red Cross.

Perf. 12¾ Vert.

2001, Aug. 16   **Litho.**
2418 A752 Horiz. pair   6.00   6.50
a.-b. 8k Any single   3.00   3.00

Daniel Solander (1733-82), Botanist on Endeavour A753

No. 2419: a, Barringtonia calyptrata and Solander. b, Cochlospermum gillivraei and Endeavour.

Perf. 12½x12¾ on 3 Sides

2001, Aug. 16   **Litho. & Engr.**
2419   Vert. pair   5.00   5.50
a.-b. 8k Any single   2.50   2.25
c.   Booklet pane, 2 #2419   10.00
         Booklet, #2419c + 4 eti-
           quettes   10.00

See Australia Nos. 1996-1997.

Fish A754

Designs: a, Perca fluviatilis. b, Abramis brama. c, Triglopsis quadricornis.

Die Cut Perf. 13½ Horiz.

2001, Aug. 16   **Litho. & Engr.**
              Self-Adhesive
2420   Booklet pane of 3   6.00   5.50
a.-c. A754 (5k) Any single   2.00   1.20
d.   Booklet, 2 #2420   12.00

Souvenir Sheet

Aviation — A755

No. 2421: a, Lilienthal glider, 1895. b, Royal Swedish Aero Club. c, Saab J-29, 1962. d, Friedrichshafen FF49. e, Trike ultralight, 1999. f, Douglas DC-3, 1938.

Perf. 12½x12¾

2001, Oct. 6   **Litho. & Engr.**
2421 A755 Sheet of 6   18.00 13.50
a.-f. 5k Any single   2.00   1.75

Stamp Design Contest Winners — A756

No. 2422: a, Rollerblader, by Emilie Kilström, Kikebo School, Oskarshamn. b, The Letter, by Thomas Fröhling.

Perf. 12¾ on 3 Sides

2001, Oct. 6			Litho.	
2422	A756	Horiz. pair	4.00	4.50
a.-b.		(5k) Any single	2.00	1.50
c.		Booklet pane, 3 #2422	12.00	
		Booklet, #2422c	12.00	

A757

Christmas — A758

Designs: No. 2423, Christmas tree.
No. 2424 — Tree ornaments (26x20mm): a, Star. b, Cracker. c, Angel. d, Heart e, Cone.
No. 2425 — Crumpled paper art by Yrjö Edelmann: a, Straw goat. b, Christmas tree.

Perf. 12¾ Vert.

2001, Nov. 21			Litho.	
2423	A757	(4.50k) multi	1.90	1.25

Self-Adhesive
Die Cut Perf. 10¾x11¼

2424		Vert. strip of 5	8.25	8.25
a.-e.		A757 (4.50k) Any single	1.60	.80
		Booklet, 2 #2424	16.50	

Water-Activated Gum
Perf. 12¾ on 3 Sides

2425	A758	Horiz. pair	4.50	5.25
a.-b.		6k Any single	2.25	2.25
c.		Booklet pane, 5 #2425 + 10 etiquettes	22.50	
		Booklet, #2425c	22.50	
		Nos. 2423-2425 (3)	14.65	

World Ice Hockey Championships A759

2002, Jan. 24	Litho.	Perf. 12¾ Vert.		
2426	A759	(5k) multi	2.00	1.10

Pandion Haliaetus A760

2002, Jan. 24			Engr.	
2427	A760	10k multi	2.25	1.25

New Year 2002 (Year of the Horse) — A761

No. 2428 — The Stones Family, by Bertil Almqvist: a, Boy and girl on horse. b, Girl on, and boy leading horse, dog running.

Perf. 12¾ on 3 Sides

2002, Jan. 24			Litho.	
2428	A761	Horiz. pair	4.00	2.50
a.-b.		(5k) Any single	2.00	1.00
c.		Booklet pane, 5 #2428	20.00	—
		Booklet, #2428c	20.00	

Love and Miss Terrified, by Joanna Rubin Dranger A762

No. 2429: a, "Det tror. . ." b, "Men jag. . ." c, "Anej!!!"

Die Cut Perf. 13¾ Horiz.

2002, Jan. 24			Litho.	
		Self-Adhesive		
2429	A762	Booklet pane of 3	6.00	5.00
a.-c.		(5k) Any single	2.00	1.25
d.		Booklet, 2 #2429	12.00	

Antarctic Expedition of Otto Nordenskjöld, Cent. — A763

No. 2430: a, Scientists, ship, gull. b, Ship, penguin.

Litho. & Engr., Litho. (#2430b)

2002, Jan. 24			Perf. 12¾ Horiz.	
2430	A763	Vert. pair	6.00	6.25
a.-b.		10k Any single	3.00	2.75
c.		Booklet pane, 2 #2430	12.00	—
		Booklet, #2430c + 4 etiquettes	12.00	

Astrid Lindgren (1907-2002), Children's Book Writer — A764

Designs: a, Pippi Langstrump (Pippi Longstocking). b, Karlsson pa Taket. c, Bröderna Lejonhjärta, vert. d, Lindgren (24x29mm). e, Emil i Lönneberga, vert. f, Lotta pa Brakmakargatan. g, Madicken.

2002, Mar. 5	Litho.	Perf. 13x13¼		
2431	A764	Booklet pane of 7	14.00	17.50
a.-g.		5k Any single	2.00	2.50
		Booklet, #2431	14.00	

Stockholm, 750th Anniv. — A765

Painting of Stockholm, 1535: (5k), Town and Lake Mälaren. 10k, Close-up view of Cathedral and palace.

2002, Mar. 21	Engr.	Perf. 12¾ Vert.		
2432	A765	(5k) shown	1.75	1.10

Size: 28x28mm

2433	A765	10k claret	3.00	2.25

A766

Swedish World Heritage Sites A767

Artifacts from Birka archaeological site: (3.80k), Cross. (4.50k), Runic stone. (5k), Man's face.
No. 2437 — Scenes from Visby: a, Town and ring wall. b, Wall towers. c, Burmeister building, flowers. d, Square, walls of St. Catherine's Church.

2002, Mar. 21	Engr.	Perf. 12½ Vert.		
2434	A766	(3.80k) purple	1.40	1.10
2435	A766	(4.50k) blue	1.75	.75
2436	A766	(5k) brn & claret	1.75	.75
		Nos. 2434-2436 (3)	4.90	2.60

Litho. & Engr.
Perf. 12½x12¾ on 3 Sides

2437		Booklet pane of 4	7.25	8.00
a.-d.		A767 (5k) Any single	1.75	1.40
		Booklet, #2437	7.25	

Kristianstad Sculptures — A768

No. 2438: a, Structure by Takashi Naraha. b, Sprung From, by Pal Svensson.

2002, Mar. 23			Litho. & Engr.	
			Perf. 12¾ Vert.	
2438	A768	Horiz. pair	5.50	5.50
a.-b.		8k Any single	2.75	2.50

Europa — A769

No. 2439: a, Charlie Rivel (1896-1983), clown. b, Clowns Without Borders (boy and clown). c, Cirkus Cirkör (performer with balloon). d, Cirkus Scott (woman on elephant).

Perf. 12¾ on 3 Sides

2002, May 2			Litho.	
2439	A769	Booklet pane of 4	11.00	12.50
a.-d.		8k Any single	2.75	3.00
		Booklet, #2439 + 4 etiquettes	11.00	

Art From Sweden and New Zealand A770

No. 2440: a, Rain Forest, glass vase blown by Ola Höglund, Sweden. b, Maori basket, by Willa Rogers, New Zealand.

Perf. 12½x12¾ on 3 Sides

2002, May 2			Litho. & Engr.	
2440	A770	Vert. pair	10.00	12.00
a.-b.		10k Any single	5.00	4.50
c.		Booklet pane, 2 #2440	20.00	—
		Booklet, #2440c + 4 etiquettes	20.00	

See New Zealand Nos. 1780, 1786.

A771

Summer in Bohuslän — A772

Designs: No. 2441, Waterfront building.
No. 2442: a, Lighthouse and gull. b, Lighthouse and three birds. c, Bridge, sailboat, waterfront buildings. d, Boat with outboard motor.

2002, May 10	Engr.	Perf. 12¾ Vert.		
2441	A771	(5k) multi	1.75	1.00

Litho.
Self-Adhesive
Serpentine Die Cut 6¾

2442	A772	Block of 4	7.00	7.50
a.-d.		(5k) Any single	1.75	1.00
e.		Booklet, #2442c-2442d, 2 #2442	17.50	

Grönköpings Veckoblad Satirical Newspaper, Cent. — A773

No. 2443: a, Newspaper and fictitious Postmaster of Grönköping. b, Fictitious police chief and criminal.

Perf. 12¾ Vert.

2002, Aug. 29			Litho. & Engr.	
2443	A773	Pair	4.00	3.75
a.-b.		(5k) Either single	2.00	1.75

Chefs
A774

No. 2444: a, Charles Emil Hagdahl (1809-97) and Cajsa Warg (1703-69). b, Marit "Hiram" Huldt, cook with cauldron and bird, flowers. c, Tore Wretman and medal. d, Leif Mannerström, fish and lobster. e, Gert Klötzke and Swedish Culinary Team. f, Christer Lingström, poultry, peas and apples.

Perf. 12½x12¾ on 3 Sides

2002, Aug. 29			Litho.
2444	A774	Booklet pane of 6	10.50 10.50
a.-f.	A774 (5k) Any single		1.75 1.25
	Booklet, #2444		10.50

Royal Palaces
A775

No. 2445: a, Sweden. b, Thailand.

Perf. 12½x13 on 3 Sides

2002, Oct. 5			Litho. & Engr.
2445	A775	Vert. pair	8.00 8.00
a.-b.	5k Either single		4.00 3.50
c.	Booklet pane 2 #2445		16.00 —
	Booklet, #2445c		16.00

See Thailand Nos. 2040-2041.

Motorcycle Racers — A776

No. 2446: a, Hakan Carlqvist. b, Sten Lundin. c, Anders Eriksson. d, Ulf Karlsson.
No. 2447: a, Ove Fundin. b, Tony Rickardsson. c, Peter Linden. d, Varg-Olle Nygren.

2002, Oct. 5		Litho.	Perf. 12¾
2446	A776	Booklet pane of 4	6.50 9.00
a.-d.	5k Any single		1.60 2.00

Litho. & Engr.

2447	A776	Booklet pane of 4	6.50 9.00
a.-d.	5k Any single		1.60 2.00
	Booklet, #2446-2447		13.00

Animated Film
Karl-Bertil Jonsson's Christmas
A777

Designs: No. 2448, Man with arm on Karl-Bertil's shoulder.
No. 2449: a, Karl-Bertil and mail sack of Christmas parcels. b, Karl-Bertil asleep with Robin Hood hat. c, Karl-Bertil giving parcel to poor man. d, Karl-Bertil with man, woman and child.

Perf. 12¾ Vert.

2002, Nov. 21			Litho.
2448	A777	(4.50k) multi	1.50 1.50

Self-Adhesive

Serpentine Die Cut 6½x6 on 3 Sides

2449		Block of 4	5.50 6.50
a.-d.	A777 (4.50k) Any single		1.40 1.00
e.	Booklet pane, 3 #2449a-2449b, 2 #2449c-2449d		14.00

Churches — A778

No. 2450: a, Kiruna Church. b, Habo Church. c, Sundborn Church. d, Tensta Bell Tower.

2002, Nov. 21		**Perf. 12¾ on 3 Sides**	
2450	A778	Block of 4	11.00 11.00
a.-d.	8k Any single		2.50 2.25
e.	Booklet pane, 3 #2450a-2450b, 2 #2450c-2450d		27.50 —
	Booklet, #2450e		27.50

St. Bridget (1303-73) — A779

2003, Jan. 20	Engr.	**Perf. 12¾ Vert.**	
2451	A779	(5.50k) red & brown	1.90 1.25

Swedish Sports Federation, Cent. — A780

No. 2452: a, Woman and child. b, Wheelchair racer. c, Snowboarder and sign language. d, Girl running.

Serpentine Die Cut 8½

2003, Jan. 20			Litho.
		Self-Adhesive	
2452		Booklet pane, 3 each #2452a, 2452c, 2 each #2452b, 2452d	17.50
a.-d.	A780 (5.50k) Any single		1.75 1.25

Europa — A781

Posters by: a, Anders Beckman, 1935. b, Georg Magnusson, 1930. c, Owe Gustafson, 1984. d, Carina Länk, 1993.

Perf. 12¾x12½ on 3 Sides

2003, Jan. 20			
2453	A781	Booklet pane of 4	11.00 12.50
a.-d.	10k Any single		2.75 2.50
	Booklet, #2453 + 4 etiquettes		11.00

Knots — A782

Various knots.

2003, Jan. 20	Engr.	**Perf. 12½ Vert.**	
2454	A782	(4.80k) green	1.40 1.75
2455	A782	(5k) blue	1.50 1.00
2456	A782	(5.50k) red	1.75 .65
	Nos. 2454-2456 (3)		4.65 3.40

Regional Houses — A783

Perf. 12¼ Vert. Syncopated

2003, Mar. 20			Engr.
2457	A783	2k Närke	.75 .55
2458	A783	4k Bohuslän	1.25 1.10
2459	A783	5k Medelpad	1.50 1.40
	Nos. 2457-2459 (3)		3.50 3.05

Nobel Prize Winners For Physiology or Medicine From Spain — A784

No. 2460: a, Santiago Ramón y Cajal, 1906. b, Severo Ochoa, 1959.

Perf. 12 Vert. Syncopated

2003, Mar. 20			Litho. & Engr.
2460	A784	Horiz. pair	5.50 6.00
a.-b.	10k Either single		2.75 2.75

See Spain No. 3204.

Flowers — A785

No. 2461: a, Hepatica nobilis. b, Primula veris. c, Tussilago farfara.

Die Cut Perf. 9¾x10

2003, Mar. 20			Litho.
		Self-Adhesive	
2461		Booklet pane of 3	4.50 5.50
a.-c.	A785 (5.50k) Any single		1.50 1.25
	Booklet, 2 #2461		9.00

Oland Moorland, UNESCO World Heritage Site
A786

No. 2462: a, Windmills. b, Megaliths and windmill. c, Cow and linear village. d, Sheep and lighthouse.

Perf. 12¾ Horiz.

2003, Mar. 20			Litho. & Engr.
2462		Booklet pane of 4	7.75 7.00
a.-d.	A786 (5.50k) Any single		1.90 1.50
	Booklet, #2462		7.75

A787

Garden Pavilions
A788

Designs: No. 2463, 1820s pavilion, by Frederik Blom.
No. 2464: a, Pavilion of Emanuel Swedenborg. b, Pavilion of Ebba Brahe. c, Västana farm pavilion, Borensberg. d, Godegard pavilion.

Perf. 12½ Vert. Syncopated

2003, May 16			Engr.
2463	A787	(5.50k) multi	1.75 1.40

Litho.

Self-Adhesive

Serpentine Die Cut 6½ on 3 Sides

2464		Block of 4	7.00 7.50
a.-d.	A788 (5.50k) Any single		1.75 1.25
e.	Booklet pane, 3 #2464a-2464b, 2 #2464c-2464d		17.50

Souvenir Sheet

St. Bridget (1303-73) — A789

Litho. & Engr.

2003, May 31			Perf. 13
2465	A789	40k multi	10.50 12.50

No. 2465 exists with and without numbers printed in LL and LR corners of the margin.

Royalty Type of 2000

Designs: (5.50k), King Carl XVI Gustaf. 10k, Queen Silvia.

Perf. 13 Vert. Syncopated

2003, Aug. 21			Engr.
2466	A737	(5.50k) red brown	2.00 .75
2467	A737	10k purple	3.50 2.00

Harvest Time — A790

No. 2468: a, Tree, radicchio, parsnip, cucumber, beet, onion. b, Pitchfork, artichoke,

pear, gourd, raspberries, apple, plum, pumpkin, eggplant. c, Trowel, garlic, peas, cabbage, tomato, potato, turnip, carrots. d, Strawberries, sunflower, cherries, plums, apple, pear.

Serpentine Die Cut 6½ on 3 Sides
2003, Aug. 21　　　　　　　　Litho.
Self-Adhesive

2468	A790	Block of 4	7.25	7.50
a.-d.		(5.50k) Any single	1.75	1.25
e.		Booklet pane, 3 each #2468a-2468b, 2 each #2468c-2468d	18.00	

Birds — A791

No. 2469: a, Recurvirostra avosetta. b, Podiceps auritus. c, Gavia arctica. d, Podiceps cristatus.

Perf. 12½x12¾ on 3 Sides
2003, Oct. 4　　　　　Litho. & Engr.

2469	A791	Booklet pane of 4	12.00	13.50
a.-d.		10k Any single	3.00	2.75
		Complete booklet, #2469 + 4 etiquettes	12.00	

See Hong Kong Nos. 1052-1055.

Building of East Indiaman "Götheborg" — A792

No. 2470: a, Figurehead (19x23mm). b, Ship under construction (19x23mm). c, Side view of ship, horiz. (23x40mm). d, Ship at sea (39x50mm).

2003, Oct. 4　　　　Perf. 12½x12¾

2470	A792	Booklet pane of 4	19.00	25.00
a.-b.		5.50k Either single	2.50	2.50
c.		10k multi	3.50	4.00
d.		30k multi	10.00	12.00
		Complete booklet, #2470 + label	19.00	

Christmas at Sundborn, by Carl Larsson — A793

No. 2471: a, Martina med Frukostbrickan. b, Kerstis Slädfärd.

Perf. 12¾ on 3 Sides
2003, Nov. 10　　　　　　　Litho.

2471	A793	Horiz. pair	5.25	6.00
a.-b.		9k Either single	2.50	2.25
c.		Booklet pane, 5 #2471 +10 etiquettes	26.50	
		Complete booklet, #2471c	26.50	

Christmas Paintings by Carl Larsson — A794

Designs: No. 2472, Aftonvarden.
No. 2473, vert.: a, Esbjörn pa Skidor. b, Brita med Julljus. c, Farfar och Esbjörn. d, Garden och Brygghuset.

Perf. 12¾ Vert. Syncopated
2003, Nov. 10

2472	A794	(5k) multi	1.50	1.40

Serpentine Die Cut 6½x6 on 3 Sides
Self-Adhesive

2473	A794	Block of 4	6.50	7.50
a.-d.		(5k) Any single	1.60	1.40
e.		Booklet pane, #2473b, 2473d, 2 #2473	16.00	

Anna Lindh (1957-2003), Murdered Minister of Foreign Affairs — A795

Perf. 12¾ on 3 Sides
2003, Nov. 11　　　　　　　Engr.

2474	A795	Pair	5.25	5.50
a.		(5.50k) claret	2.00	1.60
b.		10k blue	3.00	2.75
c.		Booklet pane, 2 each #2474a-2474b	10.00	
		Complete booklet, #2474c	10.00	

No. 2474c sold for 35k, 4k of which went to the Anna Lindh Memorial Fund.

Woodworking Tools — A796

Designs: (4.80k), Brace and bit. (5k), Saw. (5.50k), Plane.

Perf. 12 Vert. Syncopated
2004, Jan. 26　　　　　　　Engr.

2475	A796	(4.80k) green	1.40	1.40
2476	A796	(5k) blue	1.40	1.00
2477	A796	(5.50k) claret	1.60	.60
		Nos. 2475-2477 (3)	4.40	3.00

Flowers A797

No. 2478: a, Tulip. b, Lily. c, Hibiscus. d, Amaryllis. e, Calla lily.

Perf. 12¾ Horiz.
2004, Jan. 26　　　　　　　Litho.

2478		Vert. strip of 5	7.75	7.75
a.-e.		A797 (5.50k) Any single	1.50	1.25
f.		Booklet pane, 2 #2478	15.50	—
		Complete booklet, #2478f	15.50	

Europa A798

No. 2479 — Views of Lapland: a, Mountain with purple sky. b, Tents near lake.

Perf. 12¾x13½ on 3 Sides
2004, Jan. 26

2479	A798	Pair	5.75	6.50
a.-b.		10k Either single	2.75	2.75
c.		Booklet pane, 2 #2479	11.50	—
		Complete booklet, #2479c + 4 etiquettes	11.50	

Souvenir Sheet

Norse Mythology — A799

No. 2480 — Return to Valhalla: a, Return of a warrior (denomination at LR). b, Welcoming Valkyrie (denomination at UR).

Litho. & Engr.
2004, Mar. 26　　　　　　Perf. 12¾

2480	A799	Sheet of 2	5.75	7.00
a.-b.		10k Either single	2.75	3.00

Falun, UNESCO World Heritage Site — A800

No. 2481: a, Excavation pit, red mine shaft entrance building. b, Yellow green and green copper weighing building, red, white and purple mining operations building. c, Gray mine entrance building. d, Miners and houses.

Perf. 12½x12¾ on 3 Sides
2004, Mar. 26　　　　　　　Litho.

2481	A800	Block of 4	9.50	8.50
a.-d.		(5.50k) Any single	1.75	1.75
e.		Booklet pane, #2481b, 2481d, 2 each #2481a, 2481c	9.50	—
		Complete booklet, #2481e	9.50	

Swedish Soccer Association, Cent. — A801

No. 2482: a, Nils Liedholm. b, Hanna Ljungberg. c, Fredrik Ljungberg. d, Henrik Larsson. e, Victoria Svensson. f, Thomas Ravelli.

Serpentine Die Cut 7x6¼ on 3 Sides
2004, Mar. 26
Self-Adhesive

2482		Booklet pane of 6	10.50	13.00
a.-f.		A801 (5.50k) Any single	1.75	1.75

Sunset Scenes — A802

No. 2483: a, Fisherman. b, Lighthouse.

Perf. 12½ Vert. Syncopated
2004, May 13　　　　　　　Engr.

2483	A802	Horiz. pair	3.50	3.00
a.-b.		(5.50k) Either single	1.75	1.25

Stockholm Archipelago A803

No. 2484: a, Sailboat, red house, Gillöga. b, Rowboat, houses, Langviksskär. c, Ferry, Stora Nassa. d, Sailboat, lighthouse, Nämdöfjärden.

Serpentine Die Cut 6¾ on 3 Sides
2004, May 13　　　　　　　Litho.
Self-Adhesive

2484		Block of 4	7.00	7.50
a.-d.		A803 (5.50k) Any single	1.75	1.50
e.		Booklet pane, 3 #2484a-2484b, 2 #2484c-2484d	15.00	

Cottages A804

Designs: 3k, Blacksmith's cottage, Uppland. 6k, Dalsland cottage. 8k, Stone cottage, Gotland.

Perf. 12¾ Vert. Syncopated
2004, Aug. 19　　　　　　　Engr.

2485	A804	3k multi	.80	.60
2486	A804	6k multi	1.60	.90
2487	A804	8k multi	2.10	1.50
		Nos. 2485-2487 (3)	4.50	3.00

Birds — A805

Designs: (5k), Streptopelia decaocto. (5.50k), Swedish tumbler. 10k, Columba palumbus.

2004, Aug. 19

2488	A805	(5k) multi	1.40	1.25
2489	A805	(5.50k) multi	1.50	.60
2490	A805	10k multi	2.75	2.50
		Nos. 2488-2490 (3)	5.65	4.35

Forest Larder — A806

No. 2491: a, Mushrooms, lingonberries. b, Wild strawberries, butterfly, basket of blueberries. c, Juniper berries, basket of mushrooms. d, Cloudberries, cranberries.

Serpentine Die Cut 6½ on 3 Sides
2004, Aug. 19　　　　　　　Litho.
Self-Adhesive

2491	A806	Block of 4	7.25	6.00
a.-d.		(5.50k) Any single	1.75	1.25
e.		Booklet pane, 3 each #2491a-2491b, 2 each #2491c-2491d	15.00	

Nobel Prize Winners for Literature from Ireland — A807

No. 2492: a, William Butler Yeats, 1923. b, George Bernard Shaw, 1925. c, Samuel Beckett, 1969. d, Seamus Heaney, 1995.

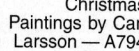

Perf. 12½x13½ on 3 Sides

2004, Oct. 1 **Litho. & Engr.**

2492	A807	Booklet pane of 4	11.00	12.50
a.-d.		10k Any single	2.75	2.75
		Complete booklet, #2492 + 4 etiquettes	11.00	

See Ireland Nos. 1576-1579.

Rock Music, 50th Anniv. — A808

No. 2493: a, Jerry Williams (29x39mm). b, Elvis Presley (36x39mm). c, Eva Dahlgren (29x39mm). d, Ulf Lundell (36x39mm). e, Tomas Ledin (29x39mm). f, Pugh Rogefeldt (29x39mm). g, Sahara Hotnights (36x33mm). h, Louise Hoffsten (29x33mm).

Litho., Litho. & Engr. (#2493b, 2493d)

2004, Oct. 2 **Perf. 12x12¾**

2493	A808	Booklet pane of 8 + 2 labels	14.00	16.50
a.-h.		5.50k Any single	1.75	1.75
		Complete booklet, #2493	14.00	
i.		Sheet of 9 #2493b	20.00	

Labels and margins of Nos. 2493 and 2493i have perforations reading "Rock 54-04." No. 2493i sold for 55k.

Regional Houses Type of 2003 and

Log Cabin — A809

Scanian Farm House — A810

Designs: 1k, Miner's house. 9k, Blekinge cottage.

Perf. 12 Vert. Syncopated

2004, Nov. 11 **Engr.**

2494	A809	50o multi	.30	.25

Perf. 12¼ Vert. Syncopated

2495	A783	1k multi	.35	.30
2496	A810	7k multi	2.00	1.25
2497	A810	9k multi	2.75	2.00
		Nos. 2494-2497 (4)	5.40	3.80

Birds — A811

No. 2498: a, Parus major. b, Emberiza citrinella. c, Pinicola enucleator. d, Pyrrhula pyrrhula.

Perf. 12¾ on 3 Sides

2004, Nov. 11 **Litho.**

2498	A811	Booklet pane of 4	12.00	13.00
a.-d.		10k Any single	3.00	2.75
		Complete booklet, #2498 + 4 etiquettes	12.00	

Christmas A812

Designs: No. 2499, Gnomes playing leap frog.
No. 2500: a, Three gnomes. b, Gnome with Christmas tree. c, Two gnomes with chair on skis. d, Gnome, birds at mail box.

Perf. 12¼ Vert. Syncopated

2004, Nov. 11

2499	A812	(5k) multi	1.50	1.50

Self-Adhesive

Serpentine Die Cut 6¼x6 on 3 Sides

2500		Block of 4	6.00	6.75
a.-d.	A812	(5k) Any single	1.50	1.50
e.		Booklet pane, 3 each #2500a-2500b, 2 each #2500c-2500d	15.00	

King Carl XVI Gustaf — A813

Queen Silvia — A814

Perf. 12½ Vert. Syncopated

2005, Jan. 27 **Engr.**

2501	A813	(5.50k) multi	1.60	1.00
2502	A814	10k multi	3.00	2.50

See No. 2560.

High Coast, UNESCO World Heritage Site — A815

No. 2503: a, Högbonden Lighthouse, birds on rocks. b, Cliffs and eagles, Storön Nature Reserve. c, Fishing boat at dock, Ulvön. d, Lakes near Häggvik.

Perf. 12¾x13½ on 3 Sides

2005, Jan. 27 **Litho. & Engr.**

2503	A815	Booklet pane of 4	12.00	14.00
a.-d.		10k Any single	3.00	3.00
		Complete booklet, #2503 + 4 etiquettes	12.00	

Swedish Design A816

No. 2504: a, Glassware, by Ingegerd Raman. b, Turn-o-matic number ticket machine, by A/E Design. c, Speedway 9000 welding helmet, by Carl-Göran Crafoord and Hakan Bergkvist. d, Camilla chair and Pilaster shelving unit, by John Kandell. e, Women's watch, by Vivianna Torun Bülow-Hübe. f, Streamliner toy car, by Ulf Hanses.

Die Cut Perf. 12½ Horiz.

2005, Jan. 27 **Self-Adhesive**

2504		Booklet pane of 6	10.00	10.00
a.-f.	A816	(5.50k) Any single	1.75	1.25

Oriolus Oriolus A817

Perf. 12½ Vert. Syncopated

2005, Mar. 10 **Litho. & Engr.**

2505	A817	11k multi	3.25	2.50

Dag Hammarskjold (1905-61), UN Secretary General — A818

No. 2506: a, Hammarskjold. b, United Nations flag.

2005, Mar. 10 **Engr.**

2506	A818	Horiz. pair	3.25	3.25
a.-b.		(5.50k) Either single	1.60	1.60

Europa A819

No. 2507: a, Lemon, star anise, elderberry marmalade. b, Apples, rosemary, Jerusalem artichokes. c, Chives, goat cheese, beets.

Perf. 12¾ Horiz.

2005, Mar. 10 **Litho.**

2507	A819	Vert. strip of 3	5.00	5.00
a.-c.		(5.50k) Any single	1.75	1.00
d.		Booklet pane, 2 #2507	10.00	—
		Complete booklet, #2507d	10.00	

Spring Flowers A820

No. 2508: a, Convallaria majalis. b, Gagea lutea. c, Pulsatilla vulgaris. d, Anemone nemorosa.

Serpentine Die Cut 10 on 3 Sides

2005, Mar. 10 **Self-Adhesive**

2508		Block of 4	6.50	6.50
a.-d.	A820	(5.50k) Any single	1.60	1.10
e.		Booklet pane, 3 each #2508a-2508b, 2 each #2508c-2508d	16.00	12.50
f.		As "a," serpentine die cut 6¾ on 3 sides	12.50	6.00
g.		As "b," serpentine die cut 6¾ on 3 sides	12.50	6.00
h.		As "c," serpentine die cut 6¾ on 3 sides	12.50	9.00
i.		As "d," serpentine die cut 6¾ on 3 sides	12.50	9.00
j.		Booklet pane, 3 each #2508f-2508g, 2 each #2508h-2508i	125.00	

Nos. 2508f-2508i issued 9/6.

Mother Svea A821

Perf. 12½ Vert. Syncopated

2005, May 26 **Litho. & Engr.**

2509	A821	15k multi	4.00	4.00

Tumba Bruk, manufacturer of Swedish banknotes, 250th anniv.

A822

Allotment Gardens — A823

No. 2510, Woman digging in garden.
No. 2511: a, Girl near shrub, man tending vegetable garden. b, Woman at table. c, Man tending garden, woman with basket of vegetables. d, Man watering garden.

Perf. 12¾ Vert. Syncopated

2005, May 26 **Litho.**

2510	A822	(5.50k) multi	1.50	1.50

Self-Adhesive

Serpentine Die Cut 10 on 3 Sides

2511	A823	Block of 4	6.00	7.50
a.-d.		(5.50k) Any single	1.50	1.50
e.		Complete booklet, 3 each #2511a, 2511c, 2 each #2511b, 2511d	15.00	

A824

Swedish Postage Stamps, 150th Anniv. — A825

No. 2512 — Details from stamps: a, #944 (1972). b, #430 (1951). c, #250 (1936). d, #1490 (1984).
No. 2513: a, Count Pehr Ambjörn Sparre, #2, printing press. b, Woman reading letter, cover. c, Airplane, train. d, Mailman in van at mailbox.

2005, May 26 **Litho.** **Perf. 12¾**

2512	A824	Booklet pane of 4	6.00	8.50
a.-d.		(5.50k) Any single	1.50	1.50

Litho. & Engr.

2513	A825	Booklet pane of 4		6.00	8.50
a.-d.		(5.50k) Any single		1.50	1.50
e.		Miniature sheet, 9 #2513a		20.00	—
		Complete booklet, #2512-2513		12.00	

No. 2513e sold for 55k.

Souvenir Sheet

Dissolution of Union of Sweden and Norway, Cent. — A826

No. 2514 — Svinesund Bridge: a, View of roadway with cars. b, View from valley.

Perf. 12½x12¾

2005, May 27 — Litho. & Engr.

2514	A826	Sheet of 2		6.50	7.00
a.-b.		10k Either single		3.25	3.25

See Norway Nos. 1430-1431.

Varberg Radio Station World Heritage Site — A827

Skogskyrkogarden Cemetery World Heritage Site — A828

Perf. 12½ Vert. Syncopated

2005, Sept. 23 — Engr.

2515	A827	(4.80k) grn & violet	1.40	1.40
2516	A828	(5k) multi	1.60	.50

Greta Garbo (1905-90), Actress — A829

No. 2517: a, Portrait. b, Caricature and "Greta."

Perf. 12¾x12½ on 3 Sides

2005, Sept. 23 — Litho. & Engr.

2517	A829	Pair		5.50	6.50
a.-b.		10k Either single		2.75	2.75
c.		Booklet pane, 2 each #2517a-2517b		11.00	—
		Complete booklet, #2517c + 4 etiquettes		11.00	
d.		Souvenir sheet of 4 #2517a, perf. 12¾x12½		115.00	135.00

No. 2517d sold for 45k and has a lithographed sheet margin. Single stamps from #2517d are perforated on all four sides.
See United States No. 3943.

Juvenile Wild Animals — A830

No. 2518: a, Lynx. b, Bear. c, Wolf. d, Fox.

Serpentine Die Cut 10 on 3 Sides

2005, Sept. 23 — Litho.

Self-Adhesive

2518	A830	Block of 4		6.00	
a.-d.		(5.50k) Any single		1.60	1.60
e.		Complete booklet, 3 each #2518a-2518b, 2 each #2518c-2518d		16.00	

A831

Mopeds — A832

No. 2519: a, Man, woman, Fram moped. b, Husqvarna moped. c, Kuli moped engine and wheel. d, Two men sitting on mopeds.
No. 2520: a, Man repairing hoisted moped. b, Three-wheeled platform scooter. c, Zundapp moped engine. d, Man riding moped.

Litho., Litho. & Engr. (#2519b, 2519c, 2520b, 2520c)

2005, Sept. 24 — Perf. 12¾

2519	A831	Booklet pane of 4		6.00	7.50
a.-d.		5.50k Any single		1.50	1.50
e.		Sheet of 9 #2519d		25.00	25.00
2520	A832	Booklet pane of 4		6.00	7.50
a.-d.		5.50k Any single		1.50	1.50
		Complete booklet, #2519-2520		12.00	

No. 2519e sold for 55k.

Christmas A833

Illustrations from Christmas in a Noisy Village, by Astrid Lindgren: No. 2521, Dog, child on skis.
No. 2522: a, Children near fence. b, Dog, children with sled. c, Girl wrapping gifts. d, Children looking at Christmas tree.

Perf. 12¾ Vert. Syncopated

2005, Nov. 10 — Litho.

2521	A833	(5k) multi	1.25	1.25

Self-Adhesive
Serpentine Die Cut 10 on 3 Sides

2522		Block of 4		6.50	6.50
a.-d.	A833	(5k) Any single		1.50	1.25
e.		Booklet pane, 3 each #2522a-2522b, 2 each #2522c-2522d		12.50	

Angel Musicians, Sculptures by Carl Milles — A834

No. 2523: a, Angel with horn facing right. b, Angel with horn facing left. c, Angel with flute facing right. d, Angel with flute facing forward.

Perf. 12¾ on 3 Sides

2005, Nov. 10 — Litho. & Engr.

2523	A834	Booklet pane of 4		10.00	13.00
a.-d.		10k Any single		2.50	2.50
		Complete booklet, #2523 + 4 etiquettes		10.00	

Swedish Railroads, 150th Anniv. — A835

Designs: 10k, X40 train.
No. 2525: a, Mallet steam locomotive (green). b, Gasoline-powered Rail bus (tan). c, SJ Class D electric locomotive (orange). d, R steam locomotive (black). e, RC electric locomotive (red).

Perf. 12½ Vert. Syncopated

2006, Jan. 26 — Litho.

2524	A835	10k multi	2.50	2.50

Litho. & Engr.
Booklet Stamps
Perf. 12½ Horiz.

2525		Vert. strip of 5		8.00	8.00
a.-e.	A835	(5.50k) Any single		1.60	1.50
f.		Booklet pane, 2 #2525		16.00	
		Complete booklet, #2525f		16.00	

Hearts — A836

No. 2526: a, Tattooed heart. b, Red heart. c, Heart-shaped leaf. d, Heart carved in tree trunk.

Serpentine Die Cut 10 on 3 Sides

2006, Jan. 26 — Litho.

Self-Adhesive

2526	A836	Block of 4, #a-d		6.00	5.00
a.-d.		(5.50k) Any single		1.50	1.40
e.		Booklet pane, 2 each #2526c-2526d, 3 each #2526a-2526b		15.00	

Souvenir Sheet

Norse Mythology — A837

No. 2527: a, Skogsraet, reindeer, goats and bird. b, Näcken, horse and violin.

Litho. & Engr.

2006, Mar. 29 — Perf. 12¾

2527	A837	Sheet of 2		5.25	7.00
a.-b.		10k Either single		2.50	3.00

Souvenir Sheet

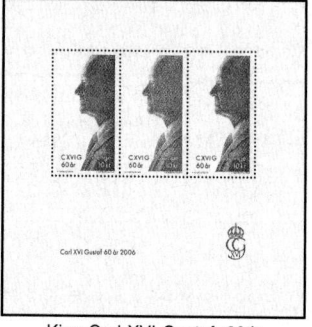

King Carl XVI Gustaf, 60th Birthday — A838

2006, Mar. 29 — Engr. Perf. 13x12¾

2528	A838	Sheet, 2 #2528a, 1 #2528b		8.00	10.00
a.		10k black		3.00	4.00
b.		10k blue		2.60	2.60

Coffee — A839

No. 2529: a, Coffee cups stacked on coffeemaker. b, Glass of cappucino. c, Espresso machine and cup, sugar dispenser and spoon. d, Steamed milk dispenser and measuring cup.

Serpentine Die Cut 10 on 3 Sides

2006, Mar. 29 — Litho.

Self-Adhesive

2529	A839	Block of 4		6.25	7.00
a.-d.		(5.50k) Any single		1.60	1.25
e.		Booklet pane, 3 each #2529a-2529b, 2 each #2529c-2529d		15.50	

Suomenlinna (Sveaborg) Fortress, Helsinki, Finland — A840

No. 2530: a, Ship without oars, flagpole at fortress. b, Ship with oars facing fortress. c, Ship with oars, windmill.

Litho. & Engr.
2006, May 4   **Perf. 12¾**

2530	A840	Booklet pane of 3	8.25	9.00
a.-c.		10k Any single	2.75	3.25
		Complete booklet, #2530	8.25	

See Finland No. 1266.

Track and Field Athletes — A841

Designs: (4.80k), Stefan Holm, high jump. 10k, Christian Olsson, triple jump.

No. 2533: a, Carolina Klüft, heptathlon. b, Kajsa Bergqvist, high jump.

Perf. 13¼ Vert. Syncopated
2006, May 4   **Litho.**

2531	A841	(4.80k) grn & multi	1.40	1.40
2532	A841	10k gray & multi	3.00	2.75
2533		Horiz. pair	3.00	3.00
a.-b.		A841 (5.50k) Either single	1.50	1.00
		Nos. 2531-2533 (3)	7.40	7.15

Europa A842

No. 2534 — Children's art by: a, Alexandros Terzis. b, Linda Wong.

Perf. 12¾x12½ on 3 Sides
2006, May 4

2534	A842	Pair	5.50	6.50
a.-b.		10k Either single	2.75	2.75
c.		Booklet pane, 2 each #2534a-2534b	11.00	
		Complete booklet, #2534c + 4 etiquettes	11.00	

Summer by the Lake — A843

No. 2536: a, Elk and immigrant women's picnic. b, Father and daughter fishing. c, Dog watching swimmers. d, Frog and boaters.

Perf. 12¼ Vert. Syncopated
2006, May 4

2535	A843	(5.50k) shown	1.50	1.50

Self-Adhesive
Size: 34x24mm
Serpentine Die Cut 10 on 3 Sides

2536		Block of 4	6.00	7.00
a.-d.		A843 (5.50k) Any single	1.50	1.00
e.		Booklet pane, 3 each #2536a-2536b, 2 each #2536c-2536d	15.00	

Famous Men — A844

Designs: (4.80k,) Carl Michael Bellman (1740-95), poet. (5k), Joseph Martin Kraus (1756-92), composer. (5.50k), Wolfgang Amadeus Mozart (1756-91), composer.

2006, Sept. 7   **Engr.**   **Perf. 12¾**

2537	A844	(5.50k) multi	3.00	3.00

Coil Stamps
Perf. 12½ Vert. Syncopated

2538	A844	(4.80k) multi	1.40	1.40
2539	A844	(5k) multi	1.40	1.40
2540	A844	(5.50k) multi	1.50	1.50
		Nos. 2537-2540 (4)	7.30	7.30

No. 2537 was issued in a sheet of 6 stamps that sold for 38k.

Hanseatic League, 650th Anniv. — A845

Designs: No. 2541, Hanseatic cog, 1380. No. 2542, Building and ships, Visby. No. 2543, City seal, shopper and salesman, Stockholm.

Perf. 12½x13½ on 3 Sides
2006, Sept. 7   **Litho. & Engr.**

2541	A845	10k multi	2.75	2.75
2542	A845	10k multi	2.75	2.75
2543	A845	10k multi	2.75	2.75
a.		Booklet pane, #2542-2543, 2 #2541	11.00	—
		Complete booklet, #2543a	11.00	

Souvenir Sheets

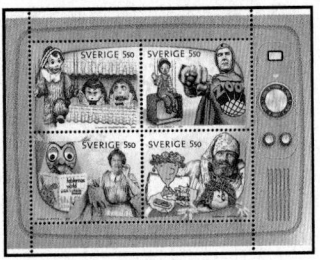

A846

Characters from Swedish Children's Television Shows — A847

No. 2544: a, Andy Pandy (marionette), Humle and Dumle (puppets). b, Anita on Television, Captain Zoom. c, Fablernas Värld (owl), Teskedsgumman (woman). d, Kalles Klätterträd (cartoon), Beppe Wolgers Godnattstunden (man in pajamas).

No. 2545: a, Trazan and Banarne, pink elephant. b, Pippi Longstockings, bear. c, Dinosaur, characters from Tjet och Allram Eest. d, Loophole, Bananas in Pajamas.

Litho. & Engr.
2006, Sept. 30   **Perf. 12½x13**

2544	A846	Sheet of 4	6.00	6.00
a.-d.		5.50k Any single	1.50	1.50

2545	A847	Sheet of 4	6.00	6.00
a.-d.		5.50k Any single	1.50	1.50
e.		Booklet pane, #2544-2545	12.00	
		Complete booklet, #2545e	12.00	
f.		Sheet of 9 #2545a	40.00	40.00

No. 2545e has a row of rouletting separating No. 2544 from No. 2545, and has a wider margin where the pane is attached to the booklet cover.

Winter Scenes in Art — A848

No. 2546: a, Bourdelle's Heracles in Snow, by Prince Eugen. b, Lelle-Kalle, by Sven Ljundberg. c, Modification of a Winter Landscape by W. O. Petersen, by Philip von Schantz. d, Rime Frost on Ice, by Gustaf Adolf Fjaestad.

Perf. 12¾ on 3 Sides
2006, Nov. 9   **Litho.**

2546	A848	Booklet pane of 4	12.00	—
a.-d.		10k Any single	3.00	3.00
		Complete booklet, #2546 + 4 etiquettes	12.00	

Christmas A849

Designs: No. 2547, Santa Claus, New Year's ornament, candles.

No. 2548: a, Star ornament. b, Spherical and New Year's ornaments. c, Bird at feeder, poinsettia. d, Candles.

Perf. 12½ Vert. Syncopated
2006, Nov. 9

2547	A849	(5k) multi	1.50	1.50

Self-Adhesive
Size: 25x25mm
Serpentine Die Cut 10 on 3 Sides

2548		Block of 4	6.00	
a.-d.		A849 (5k) Any single	1.50	1.50
e.		Booklet pane, 3 each #2548a-2548b, 2 each #2548c-2548d	15.00	

Linnaea Borealis — A850

Enneandria and Carl von Linné (1707-78), Creator of Linnaean Taxonomic System — A851

Perf. 12½ Vert. Syncopated
2007, Jan. 25   **Engr.**

2549	A850	(5.50k) multi	1.60	1.60

Litho. & Engr.

2550	A851	11k multi	3.25	3.25

Spring — A852

No. 2551: a, Birds, heart, musical notes. b, Sun, cloud, person. c, Flower, heart, person. d, Bird, sun, musical notes.

Serpentine Die Cut 10 on 3 Sides
2007, Jan. 25   **Litho.**

2551	A852	Block of 4	6.25	
a.-d.		(5.50k) Any single	1.50	1.50
e.		Booklet pane, 3 each #2551a-2551b, 2 each #2551c-2551d	15.50	

Souvenir Sheet

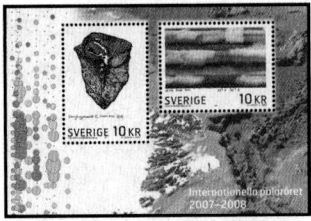

Intl. Polar Year — A853

No. 2552: a, Stenfragment I, etching by Svenerik Jakobsson. b, Arctic Ocean 2001 88 Degrees North, 145 Degrees East, by Johan Petterson.

Perf. 13, 12¾x13¼ (#2552b)
2007, Jan. 25   **Litho. & Engr.**

2552	A853	Sheet of 2	5.75	6.25
a.-b.		10k Either single	2.75	3.00

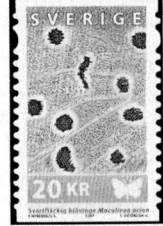

Wing of Maculinea Arion Butterfly — A854

Serpentine Die Cut 9 Vert. Syncopated
2007, Mar. 22   **Litho. & Engr.**
Self-Adhesive

2553	A854	20k multi	5.75	5.75

Printed in sheets of 40.

Swedish Sea Rescue Society, Cent. — A855

Designs: (4.80k), Rowboat, rescuer on jetski. (5k), Helicopter rescue. (5.50k), Nautical chart, rescue boat.

Litho. & Engr., Engr. (#2554, 2557)
2007, Mar. 22   **Perf. 13x12¾**

2554	A855	(5.50k) multi	1.90	1.90

Perf. 12½ Vert. Syncopated

2555	A855	(4.80k) multi	1.40	1.40
2556	A855	(5k) multi	1.40	1.40
2557	A855	(5.50k) multi	1.60	1.60
		Nos. 2554-2557 (4)	6.30	6.30

No. 2554 was printed in sheets of 6 that sold for 38k. Value, $15.

Europa
A856

No. 2558: a, "Jamboree", globe and airplane. b, Scouts.

Perf. 13½x12¾ on 3 Sides

2007, Mar. 22			Litho.
2558	A856	Horiz. or vert. pair	3.25 3.25
a.-b.		(5.50k) Either single	1.60 1.60
c.		Booklet pane, 2 each #2558a-2558b	6.50 —

Scouting, cent.

Swedish
Inventions — A857

No. 2559: a, Wall anchor for screws, by Oswald Thorsman. b, Allergy globe for flowers, by Elisabeth Gagnemyhr. c, Cooling food cover, by Birgitta Folcker-Sundell. d, Adjustable wrench, by Johan Petter Johansson.

Serpentine Die Cut 9 Horiz.

2007, Mar. 22			
2559		Horiz. strip or block of 4	5.75
a.-d.	A857	(5k) Any single	1.40 1.40
e.		Booklet paneof 20, 5 each #2559a-2559d	29.00

Queen Silvia Type of 2005
Perf. 12½ Vert. Syncopated

2007, May 10			Engr.
2560	A814	11k grn & blue	3.25 3.25

Souvenir Sheet

Botanical Illustrations by Georg Dionys Ehret — A858

No. 2561: a, Musa x paradisiaca. b, Podophyllum peltatum.

Litho. & Engr.

2007, May 10			Perf. 13
2561	A858	Sheet of 2	6.50 6.50
a.-b.		11k Either single	3.25 3.25

Exists with serial number in margin.

Children
Fishing — A859

Designs: No. 2562, Boy fishing in pail.
No. 2563: a, Boy on dock. b, Child kissing fish. c, Girls holding caught fish. d, Boys with fishing pole and caught fish.

Perf. 12½ Vert. Syncopated

2007, May 10		Litho.
2562	A859 (5.50k) multi	1.60 1.60

Size: 34x24mm
Self-Adhesive
Booklet Stamps
Serpentine Die Cut 10 on 3 Sides

2563		Block of 4	6.50
a.-d.	A859	(5.50k) Any single	1.60 1.60
e.		Booklet pane, 3 each #2563a-2563b, 2 each #2563c-2563d	16.00

Landscapes — A860

No. 2564: a, Rape field and house, Skane. b, Duck on lake, Muddus National Park. c, Elk in forest, Svealfallen. d, Hay field and Kallsjön Lake, Jämtland.

Perf. 12¾x13½

2007, May 10			Litho. & Engr.
2564	A860	Booklet pane of 4	13.00 —
a.-d.		11k Any single	3.25 3.25
		Complete booklet, #2564 + 4 etiquettes	13.00

Wing of Papilio
Machaon
A861

Serpentine Die Cut 9¼ Vert. Syncopated

2007, Sept. 27		Litho. & Engr.
		Self-Adhesive
2565	A861 50k multi	15.50 15.50

Chocolate
A862

Designs: No. 2566, Chocolate candy.
No. 2567: a, Chocolate bonbon with whipped cream and cherry. b, Chocolate-dipped strawberry. c, Cacao pod. d, Cup of cocoa.

Perf. 12½ Vert. Syncopated

2007, Sept. 27	Coil Stamp	Litho.
2566	A862 (5.50k) multi	1.75 1.75

Self-Adhesive
Booklet Stamps
Serpentine Die Cut 10 on 3 Sides
Size: 25x26mm

2567		Block of 4	7.00
a.-d.	A862	(5.50k) Any single	1.75 1.75
e.		Booklet pane of 10, 3 each #2567a-2567b, 2 each #2567c-2567d	17.50

Swedish
Fashion — A863

No. 2568 — Clothing designs by: a, Lars Wallin. b, Ann-Sofie Back. c, Katja of Sweden.

d, Behnaz Aram. e, Gunilla Pontén. f, Carin Rodebjer. g, Rohdi Heintz. h, Nakkna.

2007, Sept. 29			Litho. & Engr. Perf. 12½x13
2568		Booklet pane of 8	14.00 —
a.-h.		A863 5.50k Any single	1.75 1.75
		Complete booklet, #2568	14.00
i.		Miniature sheet, 4 each #2568a, 2568g	20.00 —

No. 2568i sold for 49k.

Sami Culture
A864

Designs: No. 2569, Reindeer from ceremonial drum, country name in red. No. 2570, Silver button, country name in green. No. 2571, Glass dish, country name in blue.

2007, Nov. 8		Perf. 12¾x13
2569	A864 11k multi	4.00 4.00

Booklet Stamps
Perf. 12¾x13 on 3 Sides

2570	A864 11k multi	3.50 3.50
2571	A864 11k multi	3.50 3.50
a.	Booklet pane of 6, 2 each #2569-2571	21.00
	Complete booklet, #2571a	21.00
	Nos. 2569-2571 (3)	11.00 11.00

No. 2569 was printed in sheets of 4 that sold for 49k. Examples of No. 2569 from booklet pane are perforated on 3 sides like Nos. 2570-2571. No. 2571a sold for 66k.

Souvenir Sheet

Astrid Lindgren (1907-2002),
Writer — A865

Litho. & Engr.

2007, Nov. 8		Perf. 12¾
2572	A865 11k multi	10.00 10.00

See Germany No. 2462.

Christmas
A866

Scenes from children's stories by Astrid Lindgren: No. 2573, Pippi Longstocking rolling gingerbread dough on floor.
No. 2574: a, Houses in winter. b, Children in snowball fight. c, Lotta and father roping Christmas tree to sled. d, Children and horse-drawn sleigh.

Perf. 12½ Vert. Syncopated

2007, Nov. 8	Coil Stamp	Litho.
2573	A866 (5k) multi	1.60 1.60

Self-Adhesive
Booklet Stamps
Serpentine Die Cut 10 on 3 Sides

2574		Block of 4	6.50
a.-d.	A866	(5k) Any single	1.60 1.60
e.		Booklet pane of 10, 3 each #2574a-2574b, 2 each #2574c-2574d	16.00

Olof von Dalin (1708-63),
Historian — A867

No. 2575: a, Illuminated letter "D." b, Illustration from first edition of The Swedish Argus.

Perf. 13¼ Vert. Syncopated

2008, Jan. 24			Engr.
2575	A867	Horiz. pair	7.00 7.00
a.-b.		11k Either single	3.50 3.50

Ingmar Bergman
(1918-2007), Film
Director — A868

Scene From "Fanny and
Alexander" — A869

Perf. 13 Vert. Syncopated

2008, Jan. 24		Engr.
2576	A868 (5.50k) indigo	1.75 1.75

Souvenir Sheet
Litho. & Engr.
Perf. 12¾x13¼

2577	A869 11k multi	4.00 4.00

A book containing an imperf example of No. 2577, an imperf example of the litho portions of No. 2577 and an imperf example of the engraved portions of No. 2577 sold for 299k.

A870

Insects — A871

Designs: (4.80k), Bombus hypnorum (bee). (5k), Formica rufa (ants). (5.50k), Coccinella (ladybug).

2008, Jan. 24		Litho.	Perf. 13½
2578	A870 (5.50k) multi		2.00 2.00

Coil Stamps
Engr.
Perf. 12½ Vert. Syncopated
Size: 27x21mm

2579	A871 (4.80k) multi	1.50 1.50

Size: 28x24mm

2580	A871 (5k) multi	1.60 1.60

Litho.
Perf. 13¼ Vert. Syncopated
Size: 27x28mm

2581	A870 (5.50k) multi	1.75 1.75
	Nos. 2578-2581 (4)	6.85 6.85

Coil Stamp
Perf. 13¼ Horiz. Syncopated
2581A A870 (5.50k) multi   1.75 1.75

No. 2578 was printed in a sheet of 6 that sold for 38k. Value, $15.

Dogs — A872

No. 2582: a, Lagotto Romagnolo (light green background). b, Saluki (pink background). c, Pug (yellow background). d, Great Dane (light blue background).

Serpentine Die Cut 10 on 3 Sides
2008, Jan. 24   Litho.
2582 A872 Block of 4   7.00
a.-d.   (5.50k) Any single   1.75 1.75
e.   Booklet pane of 10, 3 each #
     2582a, 2582c, 2 each
     #2582b, 2582d   17.50

Trees — A873

No. 2583: a, Juniperus communis tree. b, Juniperus communis berries.
No. 2584: a, Betula pendula tree. b, Betula pendula catkins.

Perf. 12 Vert. Syncopated
2008, Mar. 27   Litho.
2583 A873 Horiz. pair   .70   .70
a.-b.   1k Either single   .35   .35
2584 A873 Horiz. pair   1.40 1.40
a.-b.   2k Either single   .70   .70

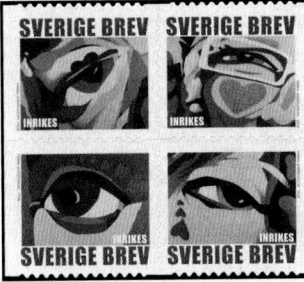

Eyes and Hearts — A874

No. 2585: a, Eye with heart-shaped pupil. b, Eye with heart on cheek. c, Eye with hearts as eyebrow. d, Eye with hearts as teardrops.

Serpentine Die Cut 10 on 3 Sides
2008, Mar. 27   Self-Adhesive
2585 A874 Block of 4   7.50
a.-d.   (5.50k) Any single   1.75 1.75
e.   Booklet pane of 10, 3 each
     #2585a-2585b, 2 each
     #2585c-2585d   19.00

Europa — A875

No. 2586: a, Semicolon. b, Comma.

Perf. 12¾ on 3 Sides
2008, Mar. 27   Litho. & Engr.
2586 A875 Pair   7.50 7.50
a.-b.   11k Either single   3.75 3.75
c.   Booklet pane of 4, 2 each
     #2586a-2586b   15.00
     Complete booklet, #2586c +
     4 etiquettes   15.00

Souvenir Sheet

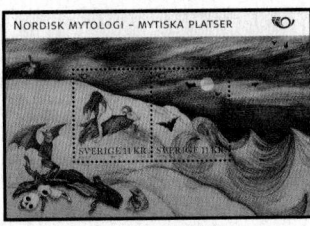

Blakulla — A876

No. 2587: a, Woman riding backwards on ram. b, Bats.

2008, Mar. 27   Perf. 12¾
2587 A876 Sheet of 2   7.50 7.50
a.-b.   11k Either single   3.75 3.75

Butterfly Wings — A877

Wings of: 5k, Argynnis aglaja. 10k, Parnassius apollo.

Serpentine Die Cut 9¼ Vert. Syncopated
2008, May 15   Litho. & Engr.
Self-Adhesive
2588 A877 5k multi   1.75 1.25
Size: 24x34mm
2589 A877 10k multi   3.50 2.50

Food Served Outdoors A878

Designs: No. 2590, Plate of crawfish, glasses of wine.
No. 2591: a, Strawberry cake, potatoes, cheese, pickled herring in sour cream and chives. b, Fish on grill. c, Coffee and pastries. d, Ham, bread, watermelon, wine.

Perf. 12¾ Vert. Syncopated
2008, May 15 Coil Stamp   Litho.
2590 A878 (5.50k) multi   1.90 1.90
Booklet Stamps
Self-Adhesive
Size: 34x23mm
Serpentine Die Cut 10 on 3 Sides
2591   Block of 4   7.75
a.-d.   (5.50k) Any single 1.90 1.90
e.   Booklet pane of 10, 3 each
     #2591a-2591b, 2 each
     #2591c-2591d   19.00

Sailing Ships A879

Designs: No. 2592, Tre Kronor af Stockholm.
No. 2593: a, Training ship Gunilla. b, Like #2592. c, Gratitude. d, Gladan and Falken.

Perf. 12½x12¾
2008, May 15   Litho. & Engr.
2592 A879 11k multi   4.25 4.25

Perf. 12½x12¾ on 3 Sides
2593   Booklet pane of 4 15.00 —
a.-d.   A879 11k Any single 3.75 3.75
     Complete booklet, #2593 + 4
     etiquettes   15.00

No. 2592 was printed in sheets of 4 that sold for 49k. Value, $17.50.

Organic Fruits and Vegetables A880

Designs: No. 2594, Apples. 11k, Carrots. No. 2596, vert.: a, Beets. b, Cabbages. c, Pumpkin. d, Potatoes.

Perf. 12½ Vert. Syncopated
2008, Sept. 25   Litho.
Coil Stamps
2594 A880 (5.50k) multi   1.75 1.75
Size: 27x21mm
2595 A880 11k multi   3.50 3.50
Booklet Stamps
Self-Adhesive
Serpentine Die Cut 10 on 3 Sides
Size: 23x27mm
2596   Block of 4   7.00
a.-d.   A880 (5.50k) Any single 1.75 1.75
e.   Booklet pane of 10, 3 each
     #2596a, 2596c, 2 each
     #2596b, 2596d   17.50

A881

Comic Strips — A882

No. 2597: a, Assar, by Ulf Lundkvist. b, Ensamma Mamman, by Cecilia Torudd. c, Arne Anka, by Charlie Christensen. d, Rocky, by Martin Kellerman.
No. 2598: a, Nameless Gloomy Girl, by Nina Hemmingsson. b, Hälge, by Lars Mortimer. c, Socker-Conny, by Joakim Pirinen. d, Swedish Manga, by Åsa Ekström.

2008, Sept. 25   Litho. & Engr.
                              Perf. 12½x13
2597 A881 Sheet of 4   7.00 7.00
a.-d.   5.50k Any single   1.75 1.75
2598 A882 Sheet of 4   7.00 7.00
a.-d.   5.50k Any single   1.75 1.75
e.   Booklet pane, #2597-2598 14.00
     Complete booklet, #2598e 14.00 —
f.   Miniature sheet of 9, 5
     #2597a, 4 #2598b   16.50 16.50

No. 2598e has a row of rouletting separating No. 2597 from No. 2598, and has a wider margin where the pane is attached to the booklet cover. No. 2598f sold for 54.50k.

Souvenir Sheet

Dario Fo, 1997 Nobel Laureate for Literature — A883

No. 2599: a, Fo (31x39mm). b, Illustration on Fo's Nobel diploma (34x50mm).

Litho. & Engr.
2008, Nov. 13   Perf. 12¾
2599 A883 Sheet of 2   5.25 5.25
a.-b.   11k Either single   2.60 2.60

Winter Activities — A884

No. 2600: a, Child sledding. b, Snowball lantern and house. c, Children making snowman.

2008, Nov. 13   Perf. 12¾ on 3 Sides
Booklet Stamps
2600 A884 Horiz. strip of 3 8.00 8.00
a.-c.   11k Any single   2.60 2.60
d.   Booklet pane of 6, 2 each
     #2600a-2600c   16.00 —
     Complete booklet, #2600d +
     6 etiquettes   16.00

A885

Christmas — A886

No. 2602 — Various wreaths with background color of: a, Green. b, Gray. c, Blue. d, Brown.

Perf. 12¾ Vert. Syncopated
2008, Nov. 13 Coil Stamp   Litho.
2601 A885 (5k) multi   1.25 1.25
Booklet Stamps
Self-Adhesive
2602 A886 Block of 4   5.00
a.-d.   (5k) Any single   1.25 1.25
e.   Complete booklet, 3 each
     #2602a-2602b, 2 each
     #2602c-2602d   12.50

A887

Greetings — A888

No. 2604: a, Swans. b, Skaters making hearts in ice. c, White hearts. d, Hearts as flowers.

Perf. 12¾ Vert. Syncopated
2009, Jan. 29   Litho. & Engr.
Coil Stamp
2603 A887 (6k) red & pink   1.50 1.50
Booklet Stamps
Self-Adhesive
Serpentine Die Cut 10 on 3 Sides
2604 A888 Block of 4   6.00
  a.-d. (6k) Any single   1.50 1.50
  e. Booklet pane of 10, 3 each
      #2604a-2604b, 2 each
      #2604c-2604d   15.00

Die cuts and rouletting are found on face of Nos. 2604a-2604d to prevent reuse of stamps.

Europa — A889

No. 2605: a, Polarimeter. b, Star chart of Crab Nebula, balloon.

Perf. 12¾ on 3 Sides
2009, Jan. 29   Litho.
Booklet Stamps
2605 A889 Horiz. or vert. pair 6.00 6.00
  a.-b. 12k Either single   3.00 3.00
  c. Booklet pane of 4, 2 each
      #2605a-2605b   12.00   —
      Complete booklet, #2605c +
      4 etiquettes   12.00

A small star-shaped hole is punched into No. 2605b.

Automobiles — A890

Designs: Nos. 2606, 2608e, Ford Mustang convertible. 12k, Volvo Amazon and trailer.
No. 2608: a, Volkswagen 1200. b, Volvo PV 444. c, Cadillac Coupe de Ville. d, Citroen DS 19.

Litho. & Engr.
2009, Jan. 29   Perf. 12¾
2606 A890 (6k) multi   1.75 1.75
Coil Stamp
Engr.
Perf. 12¾ Vert. Syncopated
2607 A890 12k multi   3.00 3.00
Booklet Stamps
Perf. 12¾ Horiz.
2608 Vert. strip of 5   7.50 7.50
  a.-e. A890 (6k) Any single   1.50 1.50
  f. Booklet pane of 10, 2 each
      #2608a-2608e   15.00   —
      Complete booklet, #2608f 15.00

No. 2606 was printed in sheets of 6 that sold for 41k. Value, $15.

A891

A892

Birds — A893

Designs: (5k), Pandion haliaetus. (5.50k), Accipiter nisus.
No. 2611: a, Haliaeetus albicilla. b, Asio flammeus.

Perf. 12¾ Vert. Syncopated
2009, Mar. 26   Engr.
Coil Stamps
2609 A891 (5k) multi   1.25 1.25
2610 A892 (5.50k) multi   1.40 1.40
Perf. 13¼ Vert. Syncopated
2611 A893 Horiz. pair   3.00 3.00
  a.-b. (6k) Either single   1.50 1.50
      Nos. 2609-2611 (3)   5.65 5.65

Creation of the Grand Duchy of Finland, Bicent. — A894

No. 2612 — Text and date: a, 1809. b, 2009.

Perf. 13¼ Vert. Syncopated
2009, Mar. 26   Litho.
Coil Stamps
2612 A894 Horiz. pair   6.00 6.00
  a.-b. 12k Either single   3.00 3.00

Souvenir Sheet

Wheel of Life, by Albertus Pictor (c. 1440-1509) — A895

No. 2613: a, Musician, man riding wheel. b, Man at top of wheel. c, Man falling off wheel, corpse.

Litho. & Engr.
2009, Mar. 26   Perf. 12¾x13
2613 A895 Sheet of 3   9.00 9.00
  a.-c. 12k Any single   3.00 3.00

Bananas — A896

No. 2614 — Clay figures: a, Young banana with love letter. b, Banana mother and child. c, Banana holding gift. d, Young banana giving flower to old banana.

Serpentine Die Cut 10 on 3 Sides
2009, Mar. 26   Litho.
Booklet Stamps
Self-Adhesive
2614 A896 Block of 4   6.00
  a.-d. (6k) Any single   1.50 1.50
  e. Booklet pane of 10, 3 each
      #2614a-2614b, 2 each
      #2614c-2614d   15.00

Queen Silvia Type of 2005
Perf. 12½ Vert. Syncopated
2009, May 14   Coil Stamp   Engr.
2615 A814 12k multi   3.00 3.00

Architecture — A897

Designs: No. 2616, Turning Torso, Malmö.
No. 2617: a, Kaknäs Tower, Stockholm. b, Lugnet ski jump, Falun. c, Balder roller coaster, Gothenburg. d, Like #2616.

2009, May 14 Engr. Perf. 12½x12¾
2616 A897 12k dark blue   3.25 3.25
Booklet Stamps
Perf. 12½x12¾ on 3 Sides
2617 Booklet pane of 4   12.00 12.00
  a.-d. A897 12k Any single   3.00 3.00
  e. Complete booklet, #2617 + 4
      etiquettes   12.00

No. 2616 was printed in a sheet of 4 stamps that sold for 53k.

Flora and Fauna A898

Designs: No. 2618, Sand star, Kosterhavet Park.
No. 2619: a, Globeflowers, Abisko National Park. b, Tree frog, Stenshuvud National Park. c, Dormouse, Garphyttan National Park. d, Cranberries, Store Mosse National Park.

Perf. 12¼ Vert. Syncopated
2009, May 14   Coil Stamp   Litho.
2618 A898 (6k) multi   1.50 1.50
Booklet Stamps
Self-Adhesive
Size: 37x26mm
Serpentine Die Cut 10 on 3 Sides
2619 Block of 4   6.00
  a.-d. A898 (6k) Any single   1.50 1.50
  e. Booklet pane of 10, 3 each
      #2619a-2619b, 2 each
      #2619c-2619d   15.00

Souvenir Sheet

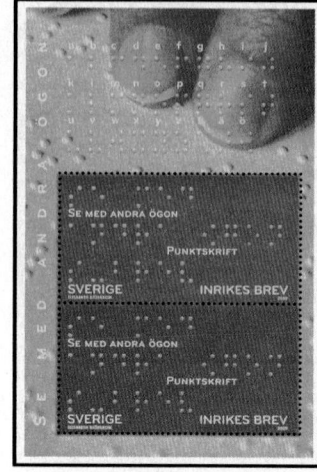

Braille Text — A899

No. 2620 — Text in Swedish and Braille with background color of: a, Red violet. b, Purple.

2009, May 14 Litho. Perf. 12¾x12½
2620 A899 Sheet of 2   3.00 3.00
  a.-b. (6k) Either single   1.50 1.50

Louis Braille (1809-52), educator of the blind. Braille dots were applied by a thermographic process.

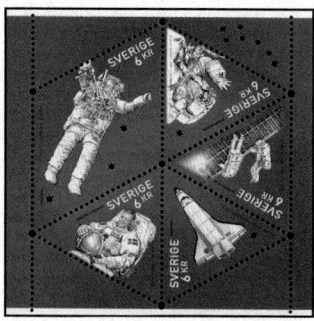

Christer Fugelsang, First Swede in Space — A900

No. 2621: a, Fugelsang waving (39x33mm). b, Fugelsang and Astronaut Robert Curbeam repairing solar panel (39x33mm). c, Space Shuttle Discovery (39x33mm). d, Fugelsang with helmet on lap (39x33mm). e, Fugelsang on space walk (39x66mm).

Litho. & Engr.
2009, Sept. 24   Perf. 12¾
2621 A900 Block of 5   8.75 8.75
  a.-e. 6k Any single   1.75 1.75
  f. Booklet pane, 2 #2621   17.50   —
      Complete booklet, #2621f 17.50
  g. Sheet of 9 #2621d   17.00 17.00

Star-shaped holes are punched into Nos. 2621a, 2621c and 2621e. No. 2621g sold for 59k.

A901

A902

Spices — A903

Designs: No. 2622, Anethum graveolens (dill). 12k, Allium schoenoprasum (chives).
No. 2624: a, Ocimum basilicum (basil). b, Capsicum (chili peppers). c, Rosmarinus officinalis (rosemary). d, Allium sativum (garlic).

Perf. 12½ Vert. Syncopated
2009, Sept. 24   Coil Stamps   Engr.
2622 A901 (6k) multi   1.75 1.75
2623 A902 12k multi   3.50 3.50

Booklet Stamps
Litho.
Serpentine Die Cut 10 on 3 Sides
2624 A903 Block of 4   7.00
a.-d.   (6k) Any single   1.75 1.75
e.   Booklet pane of 10, 3 each
         #2624a-2624b, 2 each
         #2624c-2624d   17.50

White Animals A910

No. 2625: a, Lagopus muta. b, Mustela erminea. c, Lepus timidus.

Perf. 12¾ on 3 Sides
2009, Nov. 19   **Engr.**
Booklet Stamps
2625   Horiz. strip of 3   10.50 10.50
a.-c. A910 12k Any single   3.50   3.50
d.   Booklet pane of 6, 2 each
       #2625a-2625c, + 6 eti-
       quettes   21.00
       Complete booklet, #2625d 21.00

A911

Christmas — A912

No. 2627 — Various wrapped gifts including: a, Lamp and bottle. b, Large ball and saw. c, Teddy bear and rolling pin. d, Toy train and flower.

Perf. 13¼ Vert. Syncopated
2009, Nov. 19   Coil Stamp   Litho.
2626 A911 (5.50k) multi   1.60 1.60

Booklet Stamps
Self-Adhesive
Serpentine Die Cut 10 on 3 Sides
2627 A912 Block of 4   6.40
a.-d.   (5.50k) Any single   1.60 1.60
e.   Booklet pane of 10, 3 each
         #2627a-2627b, 2 each
         #2627c-2627d   16.00

A913

Castles and Palaces — A914

Designs: Nos. 2628, 2629d, Läckö Castle. No. 2629a, Vadstena Castle. No. 2629b, Ulriksdal Palace. No. 2629c, Tjolöholm Castle. No. 2629e, Sofiero Palace.

2010, Jan. 28 Engr. Perf. 12¾x12½
2628 A913 12k blue & green   3.75 3.75

Booklet Stamps
Self-Adhesive
Serpentine Die Cut 10 Horiz. (A914),
Serpentine Die Cut 10 on 3 Sides
(A913)
2629   Booklet pane of 5 + 5
          etiquettes   16.50
a.-c. A914 12k Any single   3.25 3.25
d.-e. A913 12k Either single   3.25 3.25

No. 2628 was printed in sheets of 4 that sold for 53k. Value, $15.

Europa — A915

No. 2630 — Illustrations from children's books: a, Maja's Alphabet, by Lena Andersson. b, Children of the Forest, by Elsa Beskow.

Perf. 13¼ Vert. Syncopated
2010, Jan. 28   Litho. & Engr.
Coil Stamps
2630 A915 Horiz. pair   6.50 6.50
a.-b.   12k Either single   3.25 3.25

Black Cats — A916

No. 2631 — Cat: a, Drinking from saucer. b, Playing with ball. c, Arching back. d, Stretching.

Serpentine Die Cut 10
2010, Jan. 28   **Litho.**
Booklet Stamps
Self-Adhesive
2631 A916 Block of 4   6.40
a.-d.   (6k) Any single   1.60 1.60
e.   Booklet pane of 10, 3 each
         #2631a-2631b, 2 each
         #2631c-2631d   16.00

King Carl XVI Gustaf — A917

Queen Silvia — A918

Perf. 13¼ Vert. Syncopated
2010, Mar. 24   Coil Stamps   Engr.
2632 A917 (6k) dark green   1.75 1.75
2633 A918 12k dark brown   3.50 3.50

Wedding Rings — A919

Celebrations — A920

No. 2635: a, Cake. b, Birds. c, Hands and hearts. d, Champagne bottle and glasses.

Perf. 13¼ Vert. Syncopated
2010, Mar. 24   Coil Stamp   Litho.
2634 A919 (6k) multi   1.75 1.75

Booklet Stamps
Self-Adhesive
Serpentine Die Cut 10 on 3 Sides
2635 A920 Block of 4   7.00
a.-d.   (6k) Any single   1.75 1.75
e.   Booklet pane of 10, 3 each
         #2635a-2635b, 2 each
         #2635c-2635d   17.50

Souvenir Sheet

Life on the Coast — A921

No. 2636: a, Mytilus edulis. b, Fishing boat SD141 Emelie.

Litho. & Engr.
2010, Mar. 24   Perf. 13x12½
2636 A921 Sheet of 2   7.00 7.00
a.-b.   12k Either single   3.50 3.50

Karolinska Institutet, Bicent. — A922

No. 2637 — Electron microscope photographs by Lennart Nilsson of: a, Silicon (blue crystals) b, Selenium (red violet crystals).

Perf. 13¼ Vert. Syncopated
2010, May 13   **Engr.**
Coil Stamps
2637 A922 Horiz. pair   3.00 3.00
a.-b.   (5.50k) Any single   1.50 1.50

Sea Mammals — A923

No. 2638: a, Phocoena phocoena. b, Enhydra lutris. c, Balaenoptera musculus. d, Pusa hispida.

Perf. 13x12¾ on 3 Sides
2010, May 13   Litho. & Engr.
Booklet Stamps
2638 A923 Block of 4   13.00 13.00
a.-d.   12k Any single   3.25   3.25
e.   Booklet pane, #2638a-
         2638d + 4 etiquettes 13.00
       Complete booklet, #2638e 13.00

See Canada No. 2387.

A924

Pansies — A925

No. 2640 — Flower color: a, Yellow and red, green petal showing. b, Blue violet. c, Red. d, Purple and red.

Perf. 12½ Vert. Syncopated
2010, May 13   **Litho.**
Coil Stamp
2639 A924 (6k) multi   1.60 1.60

Booklet Stamps
Self-Adhesive
Serpentine Die Cut 10 on 3 Sides
2640 A925 Block of 4   6.40
a.-d.   (6k) Any single   1.60 1.60
e.   Booklet pane of 10, 3 each
         #2640a-2640b, 2 each
         #2640c-2640d   16.00

Souvenir Sheet

Wedding of Crown Princess Victoria and Daniel Westling — A926

No. 2641: a, Crown Princess Victoria (27x36mm). b, Royal monogram of Crown Princess Victoria (27x36mm). c, Crown Princess Victoria and Daniel Westling (54x40mm).

Perf. 13¼x12¾

2010, May 13	Litho. & Engr.
2641 A926 Sheet of 3	5.00 5.00
a.-c. 6k Any single	1.60 1.60

Souvenir Sheet

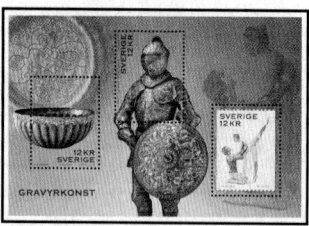

Art of Engraving — A927

No. 2642: a, Viking era silver bowl, engraved by Martin Mörck. b, Armor of King Erik XIV, engraved by Lars Sjööblom. c, Sweden Type A305, engraved by Czeslaw Slania.

Litho. & Engr.

2010, Aug. 26	Perf. 12¾
2642 A927 Sheet of 3	10.50 10.50
a.-c. 12k Any single	3.50 3.50

See Ireland No. 1895.

A928

A929

Swedish Foods — A930

Designs: No. 2643, Waffles and cloudberries. 12k, Crispbread and Västerbotten cheese.

No. 2645: a, Girl eating peppermint stick. b, Hand holding gravlax (marinated salmon). c, Man cutting pyramid cake. d, Man sniffing can of fermented herring.

Perf. 12½ Vert. Syncopated

2010, Aug. 26	Engr.

Coil Stamps

2643 A928 (6k) bis & org	1.75 1.75

Perf. 12¾ Vert. Syncopated

2644 A929 12k brn & bis	3.50 3.50

Booklet Stamps
Litho.
Serpentine Die Cut 10 on 3 Sides
Self-Adhesive

2645 A930 Block of 4	7.00
a.-d. (6k) Any single	1.75 1.75
e. Booklet pane of 10, 3 each #2645a-2645b, 2 each #2645c-2645d	17.50

Crime Novelists — A931

No. 2646: a, Maj Sjöwall, Per Wahlöö (1926-75), helicopter and handcuffs (66x27mm). b, Henning Mankell, dead body, handcuffs, gavel (66x27mm). c, Liza Marklund and police car (66x27mm). d, Hakan Nesser and pistol (33x30mm). e, Stieg Larsson (1954-2004) and laptop computer (33x30mm).

Litho. & Engr.

2010, Aug. 26	Perf. 13x12¾
2646 A931 Block of 5	8.75 8.75
a.-e. 6k Any single	1.75 1.75
f. Booklet pane, 2 #2646	17.50
Complete booklet, #2646f	17.50
g. Sheet of 9 #2646d	16.50 16.50

Nos. 2646a-2646c each have two holes and Nos. 2646d-2646e each have one hole drilled through stamp. No. 2646g sold for 59k.

A932

A933

A934

A935

Snowflakes
A936

Perf. 12¾x12½

2010, Nov. 18	Litho. & Engr.
2647 A932 12k multi	4.00 4.00

Self-Adhesive
Serpentine Die Cut 10 on 3 Sides, Serpentine Die Cut 10 Horiz. (A933)

2648 Booklet pane of 5 + 5 etiquettes	17.50
a. A933 12k multi	3.50 3.50
b. A934 12k multi	3.50 3.50
c. A932 12k multi	3.50 3.50
d. A935 12k multi	3.50 3.50
e. A936 12k multi	3.50 3.50

No. 2647 was printed in a sheet of 4 that sold for 53k. Value, $16.

Christmas — A937

No. 2649 — "J" as: a, Candy cane. b, Santa Claus. c, Christmas light. d, Stocking.

Serpentine Die Cut 10 on 3 Sides

2010, Nov. 18	Litho.

Booklet Stamps
Self-Adhesive

2649 A937 Block of 4	6.40
a.-d. (5.50k) Any single	1.60 1.60
e. Booklet pane of 10, 3 each #2649a, 2649c, 2 each #2649b, 2649d	16.00

Fossils — A938

Fossils of: 30k, Molluscs. 40k, Cuttlefish.

Serpentine Die Cut 9 Horiz.

2011, Jan. 27	Litho. & Engr.

Self-Adhesive

2650 A938 30k multi	9.25 9.25

Serpentine Die Cut 9 Vert.
Size: 28x28mm

2651 A938 40k multi	12.50 12.50

Bicycles and Tricycles A939

No. 2652: a, Tricycle and air pump. b, Bicycle and helmet. c, Bicycle and chain guard. d, Bicycle and chain ring. e, Tricycle and horn.

2011, Jan. 27	Perf. 12¾ Horiz.

Booklet Stamps

2652 Vert. strip of 5	9.50 9.50
a.-e. A939 (6k) Any single	1.90 1.90
f. Booklet pane, 2 #2652	19.00 —
Complete booklet, #2652f	19.00

A940

Flag of Sweden — A941

No. 2654: a, Flag on flagpole. b, People waving flags. c, Flag on person's forehead. d, Flag on vehicle.

2011, Jan. 27 Litho. Perf. 12½ Vert.

Coil Stamp

2653 A940 (6k) multi	1.90 1.90

Booklet Stamps
Self-Adhesive
Serpentine Die Cut 10 on 3 Sides

2654 A941 Block of 4	7.60
a.-d. (6k) Any single	1.90 1.90
e. Booklet pane of 10, 3 each #2654a-2654b, 2 each #2654c-2654d	19.00

Compare types A940 and A1015.

Hands and Curved Lines — A942

No. 2655 — Hands and lines in: a, Red. b, Blue.

Perf. 13¼ Vert. Syncopated

2011, Mar. 24	Litho. & Engr.

Coil Stamps

2655 A942 Horiz. pair, #a-b	3.25 3.25
a.-b. (5k) Either single	1.60 1.60

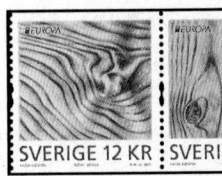

Europa — A943

No. 2655 — Wood of: a, Betula. b, Pica abies.

2011, Mar. 24   Coil Stamps
2656   A943   Horiz. pair, #a-b   8.00   8.00
a.-b.   12k Either single   4.00   4.00

Intl. Year of Forests.

A944

Renewable Energy — A945

No. 2658: a, Clouds, solar panels. b, Field, wind turbine. c, Trees, bioenergy tank. d, Underwater scene, wave energy converter.

Perf. 13 Vert. Syncopated
2011, Mar. 24   Coil Stamp   Litho.
2657   A944   (6k) multi   2.00   2.00

Booklet Stamps
Self-Adhesive
Serpentine Die Cut 10 on 3 Sides
2658   A945   Block of 4   8.00
a.-d.   (6k) Any single   2.00   2.00
e.   Booklet pane of 10, 3 each
       #2658a-2658b, 2 each
       #2658c-2658d   20.00

Scenes From Industrial Towns — A946

Buildings or workers in: Nos. 2659, 2660e, Mackmyra. No. 2660a, Forsvik, horiz. (58x29mm). No. 2660b, Glasriket. No. 2660c, Avesta. No. 2660d, Jonsered.

2011, Mar. 24   Engr.   Perf. 12¾x12½
2659   A946   12k dk brn & brn   4.25   4.25

Self-Adhesive
Serpentine Die Cut10 on 2 or 3 Sides
2660   Booklet pane of 5 + 5
           etiquettes   20.00
a.-e.   A946 12k Any single   4.00   4.00

No. 2659 was printed in sheets of 4 that sold for 53k.

Souvenir Sheet

Struve Geodetic Arc UNESCO World Heritage Site — A947

No. 2661: a, Theodolite. b, Wilhelm Struve (1793-1864), astronomer.

2011, May 6   Litho. & Engr.   Perf. 13
2661   A947   Sheet of 2   8.00   8.00
a.-b.   12k Either single   4.00   4.00

Water Lilies — A948

No. 2662: a, Four red water lilies, one white water lily, dragonfly. b, Four white water lilies, three yellow water lilies, dragonfly. c, Yellow water lily. d, White water lily.

Perf. 12¾ on 3 Sides
2011, May 12   Litho.
Booklet Stamps
2662   A948   Block of 4   15.00 15.00
a.-d.   12k Any single   3.75   3.75
e.   Booklet pane, #2662a-
       2662d + 4 etiquettes   15.00
       Complete booklet, #2662e   15.00

Banana Split A949

Ice Cream — A950

No. 2664: a, Ice cream bar. b, Vanilla ice cream cone. c, Sundae with cherries. d, Chocolate-coated ice cream cone.

Perf. 12½ Vert. Syncopated
2011, May 12   Litho.   Coil Stamp
2663   A949   (6k) multi   1.90   1.90

Booklet Stamps
Self-Adhesive
Serpentine Die Cut 10 on 3 Sides
2664   A950   Block of 4   7.60
a.-d.   (6k) Any single   1.90   1.90
e.   Booklet pane of 10, 3 each
       #2664a-2664b, 2 each
       #2664c-2664d   19.00

Equestrian Sports — A951

Designs: Nos. 2665, 2666a, Harness racing (Stig H. Johannson driving Victory Tilly). No. 2666b, Show jumping (Malin Baryard-Johnsson on Butterfly Flip). No. 2666c, Pony racing (Ebba Stigenberg on Norrskenets Grim). No. 2666d, Dressage (Jan Brink on Briar). No. 2666e, Eventing (Hannes Melin on Gaston KLG).

Perf. 12¾x12½
2011, Aug. 25   Litho. & Engr.
2665   A951   6k multi   2.00   2.00

Booklet Stamps
Perf. 12¾ Horiz.
2666   Vert. strip of 5   9.50   9.50
a.-e.   A951 6k Any single   1.90   1.90
f.   Booklet pane, 2 #2666   19.00   —
       Complete booklet, #2666f   19.00

No. 2665 was printed in sheets of 9 that sold for 59k.

Poppy, Rye and Barley Seed Capsules A952

Conifer Cones A953

A954

A955

A956

Seed Capsules A957

Perf. 12¼ Vert. Syncopated
2011, Aug. 25   Engr.
Coil Stamps
2667   A952   (6k) multi   1.90   1.90
2668   A953   12k multi   3.75   3.75

Booklet Stamps
Self-Adhesive
Litho.
Serpentine Die Cut 10 on 3 Sides
2669   Block of 4   7.75
a.   A954 (6k) multi   1.90   1.90
b.   A955 (6k) multi   1.90   1.90
c.   A956 (6k) multi   1.90   1.90
d.   A957 (6k) multi   1.90   1.90
e.   Booklet pane of 10, 3 each
       #2669a-2669b, 2 each
       #2669c-2669d   19.00

Winter Clothing — A958

Designs: Nos. 2670, 2671e, Mittens. No. 2671a, Socks, horiz. (62x32mm). No. 2671b, Hats (31x39mm). No. 2671c, Scarf (31x39mm). No. 2671d, Sweater (31x39mm).

Perf. 12¾x12½
2011, Nov. 17   Litho. & Engr.
2670   A958   12k multi   4.00   4.00

Booklet Stamps
Self-Adhesive
Serpentine Die Cut 10 on 2 or 3 Sides
2671   Booklet pane of 5 + 5
           etiquettes   19.00
a.-e.   A958 12k Any single   3.75   3.75

No. 2670 was printed in a sheet of 4 that sold for 53k. Value, $16.

Souvenir Sheet

Intl. Year of Chemistry — A959

No. 2672: a, Marie Curie (1867-1934), 1911 Nobel laureate for Chemistry (40x55mm). b, Nobel medal and radium, horiz. (36x28mm).

Perf. 13x12¾ (#2672a), 12¾ (#2672b)
2011, Nov. 17
2672   A959   Sheet of 2   7.50   7.50
a.-b.   12k Either single   3.75   3.75

See Poland No. 4024.

Christmas Cactus — A960

Poinsettia
A961

Amaryllis
A962

Hellebore
A963

Serpentine Die Cut 10 on 3 Sides
2011, Nov. 17   **Litho.**
Booklet Stamps

2673	Block of 4	7.00	
a.	A960 (5.50k) multi	1.75	1.75
b.	A961 (5.50k) multi	1.75	1.75
c.	A962 (5.50k) multi	1.75	1.75
d.	A963 (5.50k) multi	1.75	1.75
e.	Booklet pane of 10, 3 each #2673a-2673b, 2 each #2673c-2673d	17.50	

Christmas.

Europa — A964

No. 2674 — Tourist attractions: a, Dalarna. b, Ericsson Globe Arena, Stockholm.

Perf. 12½ Vert. Syncopated
2012, Jan. 12   **Engr.**
Coil Stamps

2674	A964	Horiz. pair	7.50	7.50
a.		12k green	3.75	3.75
b.		12k blue	3.75	3.75

A965

Octahedrons
A966   A967

Perf. 12½ Vert. Syncopated
2012, Jan. 12   **Coil Stamp**

2675	A965 (5.50k) green	1.75	1.75

Booklet Stamps
Self-Adhesive
Serpentine Die Cut 9 Horiz.

2676	Block or horiz. strip of 4	7.00	
a.	A966 (5.50k) blue	1.75	1.75
b.	A967 (5.50k) red	1.75	1.75
c.	A967 (5.50k) blue	1.75	1.75
d.	A966 (5.50k) red	1.75	1.75
e.	Booklet pane of 20, 5 each #2676a-2676d	35.00	

Lill-Babs Performing at People's Park
A968

Entrance to People's Park, Borlänge — A969

Entrance to People's Park, Björneborg
A970

Dance Floor at People's Park, Árvika
A971

Chocolate Wheel at People's Park, Kolsnäs
A972

2012, Jan. 12   Perf. 12¾

2677	A968 (6k) claret	2.00	2.00

Coil Stamp
Perf. 12½ Vert. Syncopated

2678	A969 (6k) purple	1.90	1.90

Booklet Stamps
Self-Adhesive
Serpentine Die Cut 10 on 3 Sides

2679	Block of 4	7.75	
a.	A970 (6k) red	1.90	1.90
b.	A971 (6k) blue	1.90	1.90
c.	A968 (6k) blue	1.90	1.90
d.	A972 (6k) red	1.90	1.90
e.	Booklet pane of 10, 3 each #2679a-2679b, 2 each #2679c-2679d	19.00	

No. 2677 was printed in a sheet of six that sold for 41k. Value, $15.

Fishing Pole With Ambassadeur Reel — A973

Salmon Fly — A974

Hi-Lo Wobbler and Toby Spoon Spinner Lures
A975

Coil Stamps
Die Cut Perf. 11¾x11½
2012, Mar. 21   **Self-Adhesive**

2680	A973 5k multi	1.50	1.50

Die Cut Perf. 11¾

2681	A974 10k multi	3.00	3.00
2682	A975 20k multi	6.00	6.00
	Nos. 2680-2682 (3)	10.50	10.50

Art Photography
A976

Designs: (6k), 2680, by Dawid.
No. 2684: a, Dreamer in the Blue House, by Sune Jonsson (man with open book, 58x29mm). b, At Home, by Gunnar Smoliansky (plant cutting in glass, 27x36mm). c, Agneta, Finland, by Denise Grünstein (woman swimming, 27x36mm). d, Attempting to Deal With Time and Space, by Annika von Hausswolff (person squeezing balloon, 27x36mm). e, Paris, by Christer Strömholm (people kissing, 27x36mm).

Perf. 12¼ Vert. Syncopated
2012, Mar. 21   **Coil Stamp**   **Litho.**

2683	A976 (6k) shown	1.90	1.90

Serpentine Die Cut 10 Horiz.,
Serpentine Die Cut 10 on 3 Sides
(#2684b-2684d)

2684	Booklet pane of 5 + 5 etiquettes	19.00	
a.-e.	A976 12k Any single	3.75	3.75

Poultry Breeds — A977

No. 2685: a, Hedemora hens (Hedemorahöna). b, Old Swedish dwarf hens (Gammalsvensk dvärghöna). c, Swedish spotted hens (Skansk blommehöna). d, Orust hens (Orusthöna).

Booklet Stamps
Serpentine Die Cut 10 on 3 Sides
2012, Mar. 21   **Self-Adhesive**

2685	A977 Block of 4	7.75	
a.-d.	(6k) Any single	1.90	1.90
e.	Booklet pane of 10, 3 each #2685a-2685b, 2 each #2685c-2685d	19.00	

Souvenir Sheet

Life on the Coast — A978

No. 2686: a, Häradskär Lighthouse, Arkö 833 pilot boat. b, Dash 8Q-300 surveillance airplane.

Litho. & Engr.
2012, Mar. 21   **Perf. 12¾**

2686	A978 Sheet of 2	7.50	7.50
a.-b	12k Either single	3.75	3.75

Type Fonts — A979

No. 2687: a, Berling Antiqua. b, Indigo Antiqua. c, Sispos. d, Satura. e, Traffic.

Serpentine Die Cut 9 Horiz.
2012, May 10   **Engr.**
Self-Adhesive

2687	Vert. strip of 5	17.50	
a.-e.	A979 12k Any single	3.50	3.50

A980

Olympic Gold Medalists — A981

Designs: 12k, Eric Lemming (1880-1930), javelin gold medalist, 1912 Olympics.
No. 2689: a, Ragnar Skanaker, pistol shooting gold medalist, 1972 Olympics. b, Carolina Klüft, heptathlon gold medalist, 2004 Olympics.

Litho. & Engr. (12k), Litho.
2012, May 10   **Perf. 12¾**

2688	A980 12k multi	4.00	4.00

Coil Stamps
Perf. 13¼ Vert. Syncopated

2689	A981 Horiz. pair	3.50	3.50
a.-b.	(6k) Either single	1.75	1.75

Perf. 12¾ Vert. Syncopated

2690	A980 12k multi	3.50	3.50

No. 2688 was printed in sheets of 4 that sold for 53k. Value, $16.

Flowers — A982

Designs: No. 2691: Cowslip, hairy violet, mountain everlasting, meadow saxifrage.
No. 2692: a, Cowslip (gullviva). b, Hairy violet (buskviol). c, Mountain everlasting (kattfot). d, Meadow saxifrage (mandelblomma).

Perf. 13¼ Vert. Syncopated
2012, May 10   **Litho.**   **Coil Stamp**

2691	A982 (6k) multi	1.75	1.75

Booklet Stamps
Self-Adhesive
Serpentine Die Cut 10 on 3 Sides

2692	Block of 4	7.00	
a.-d.	A982 (6k) Any single	1.75	1.75
e.	Booklet pane of 10, 3 each #2692a-2692b, 2 each #2692c-2692d	17.50	

Souvenir Sheet

Raoul Wallenberg (1912-47), Diplomat — A983

Litho. & Engr.
2012, May 10   **Perf. 12¾**

2693	A983 12k multi	3.50	3.50

Textile
Art
A984

Details from: Nos. 2694, 2695d, Peace in the Valley — At Last, by Teresa Oscarsson. No. 2695a, June Flowers, by Märta Maas-Fjetterström. No. 2695b, Hommage à Tuskaft, by Laris Strunke. No. 2695c, Oomph, by Viola Grasten. No. 2695e, Signs in an Archive, by Lennart Rohde.

2012, Aug. 16   **Perf. 12¾**
2694   A984   (6k) multi   2.10   2.10

Booklet Stamps
Perf. 12¾ Horiz.
2695   Vert. strip of 5   9.50   9.50
   a.-e.   A984 (6k) Any single   1.90   1.90
   f.   Booklet pane of 10, 2 each
     #2695a-2695e   19.00   —
     Complete booklet, #2695f   19.00

No. 2694 was printed in a sheet of six that sold for 41k. Value, $15.

Youths Writing — A985

No. 2696: a, Girl with pen and letter. b, Boy writing letter under desk lamp. c, Girl writing letter on computer. d, Girl with letter and envelopes.

Serpentine Die Cut 10 on 3 Sides
2012, Aug. 16   **Litho.**
Booklet Stamps
Self-Adhesive
2696   A985   Block of 4   7.75
   a.-d.   (6k) Any single   1.90   1.90
   e.   Booklet pane of 10, 3 each
     #2696a, 2696c, 2 each
     #2696b, 2696d   19.00

Souvenir Sheet

The Masked Ball, Opera by Daniel Auber — A986

No. 2697: a, Auber (1782-1871). b, King Gustav III of Sweden (1746-92), main character in opera.

Litho. & Engr.
2012, Nov. 9   **Perf. 12¾**
2697   A986   Sheet of 2   7.50   7.50
   a.-b.   12k Either single   3.75   3.75

See France No. 4298.

Christmas — A987

No. 2698 — Christmas tree and ornaments: a, Small orange ball, large red ball with star. b, Star with ribbon, small red ball. c, Candle and heart. d, Candle and angel.

Serpentine Die Cut 10 on 3 Sides
2012, Nov. 12   **Litho.**
Booklet Stamps
Self-Adhesive
2698   A987   Block of 4   7.00
   a.-d.   (5.50k) Any single   1.75   1.75
   e.   Booklet pane of 10, 3 each
     #2698a-2698b, 2 each
     #2698c-2698d   17.50

Sverige Brev   Water and Horizon — A988

Sverige Brev   Hearts in Nature — A989

No. 2700: a, Heart on rock. b, Three heart-shaped leaves and moss. c, Hear-shaped water droplet on leaf. d, Tulip petals.

Perf. 13 Vert. Syncopated
2013, Jan. 10   **Coil Stamp**
2699   A988   (6k) multi   1.90   1.90
Booklet Stamps
Self-Adhesive
2700   A989   Block of 4   7.60
   a.-d.   (6k) Any single   1.90   1.90
   e.   Booklet pane of 10, 3 each
     #2700a-2700b, 2 each
     #2700c-2700d   19.00

Insects — A990

No. 2701: a, Lygaeus equestris. b, Bryodema tuberculata. c, Melolontha melolontha. d, Aeshna serrata.

Die Cut Perf. 11¾x11½
2013, Jan. 10   **Engr.**
Coil Stamps
Self-Adhesive
2701   Vert. strip of 4   16.00
   a.-d.   A990 12k Any single   4.00   4.00

See No. 2727.

Ice Hockey Type of 1995 and

Ice Hockey Players — A991

No. 2703: a, Henrik Lundqvist. b, Jörgen Jönsson. c, Börje Salming. d, Nicklas Lidström.

Litho. & Engr.
2013, Mar. 13   **Perf. 12¾**
2702   A631   6k multi   2.00   2.00
Booklet Stamps
Self-Adhesive
Litho.
Serpentine Die Cut 10 on 3 Sides
2703   A991   Block of 4   7.60
   a.-d.   (6k) Any single   1.90   1.90
   e.   Booklet pane of 10, 2 each
     #2703a,-2703b, 3 each
     #2703c-2703d   19.00

No. 2702 was printed in sheets of 9 that sold for 59k. Value, $18.

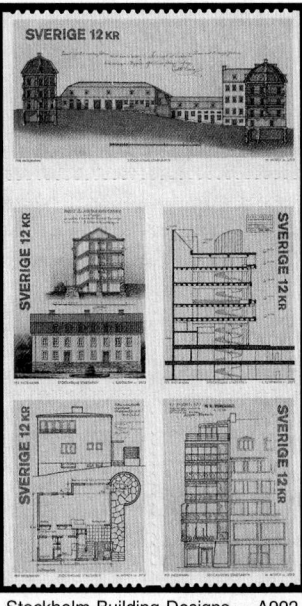

Stockholm Building Designs — A992

No. 2704 — Building blueprint drawings from Stockholm city archives: a, Spice merchant's building, 1795 (58x28mm). b, Three-story Gröna Garden worker's house, by J. F. Abom, 1854 (27x36mm). c, Kulturhuset (with spiral staircase), by Peter Celsing, 1970 (27x36mm). d, House in Bromma, by Edvin Engström, 1935 (27x36mm). e, Bredenberg's Department Store, by Gunnar Asplund, 1934 (27x36mm).

Serpentine Die Cut 10 on 2 or 3 Sides
2013, Mar. 14   **Litho. & Engr.**
Booklet Stamps
Self-Adhesive
2704   A992   Booklet pane of 5
     + 5 etiquettes   19.00
   a.-e.   12k Any single   3.75   3.75

Souvenir Sheet

Europa — A993

No. 2705 — Postal worker and mail vehicle: a, Electric bicycle. b, Club Car electric vehicle, horiz.

Perf. 12½x13¼
2013, Mar. 14   **Litho. & Engr.**
2705   A993   Sheet of 2   7.50   7.50
   a.-b.   12k Either single   3.75   3.75

Measuring Devices — A994

Designs: 30k, Aneroid barometer. 40k, Sundial. 50k, Compass.

Die Cut Perf. 11½ Syncopated
2013   **Self-Adhesive**   **Engr.**
Coil Stamps
2706   A994   30k blk & red   9.25   9.25
Die Cut Perf. 11¾ Syncopated
Size: 27x28mm
2707   A994   40k blk & blue   12.50   12.50
Size: 34x28mm
2708   A994   50k blk & blue   15.50   15.50
   Nos. 2706-2708 (3)   37.25   37.25

Issued: 30k, 40k, 5/8; 50k, 3/14.

A995

Cookies — A996

No. 2710 — Background color: a, Blue. b, Green. c, Red lilac. d, Orange brown.

Perf. 12½ Vert. Syncopated
2013, May 8   **Coil Stamp**   **Litho.**
2709   A995   (6k) multi   1.90   1.90
Booklet Stamps
Self-Adhesive
Serpentine Die Cut 10 on 3 Sides
2710   A996   Block of 4   7.60
   a.-d.   (6k) Any single   1.90   1.90
   e.   Booklet pane of 10, 3 each
     #2710a-2710b, 2 each
     #2710c-2710d   19.00

Baby Animals A997

Designs: Nos. 2711, 2712b, Lambs. No. 2712a, Calves. No. 2712c, Ducklings. No. 2712d, Kids. No. 2712e, Piglets.

Litho. & Engr.

2013, Aug. 22   *Perf. 12¾*
2711 A997 (6k) multi   2.00 2.00

Booklet Stamps
Perf. 12¾ Horiz.
2712   Vert. strip of 5   9.50 9.50
a.-e.   A997 (6k) Any single   1.90 1.90
f.   Booklet pane of 10, 2 each
   #2712a-2712e   19.00 —
   Complete booklet, #2712f   19.00

No. 2711 was printed in sheets of nine that sold for 59k. Value, $18.

Dahlias — A998

No. 2713: a, Decorative dahlia (orange red flower, country name at left). b, Ball dahlias (purple flowers, country name at right). c, Ruffle dahlia (pinkish violet flower and bud, country name at left). d, Waterlily dahlia (red flowers and bud, country name at right).

Serpentine Die Cut 10 on 3 Sides
2013, Aug. 22   *Litho.*

Booklet Stamps
Self-Adhesive
2713 A998   Block of 4   7.75
a.-d.   (6k) Any single   1.90 1.90
e.   Booklet pane of 10, 3 each
   #2713a-2713b, 2 each
   #2713c-2713d   19.00

Souvenir Sheet

Reign of King Carl XVI Gustav, 40th Anniv. — A999

No. 2714: a, Monogram of King Carl XVI Gustav (27½x36mm). b, King Carl XVI Gustav (27½x36mm). c, King Carl XVI Gustav, Crown Princess Victoria and Princess Estelle (55x41mm).

Litho. & Engr.
2013, Aug. 22   *Perf. 13x12¾*
2714 A999   Sheet of 3   5.75 5.75
a.-c.   6k Any single   1.90 1.90

Souvenir Sheet

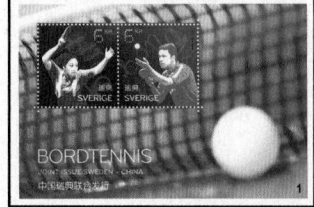

Table Tennis — A1000

No. 2715 — Players: a, Woman. b, Man.

2013, Sept. 27   *Litho.*   *Perf. 12¾*
2715 A1000   Sheet of 2   3.80 3.80
a.-b.   6k Either single   1.90 1.90

See People's Republic of China Nos. 4152-4153. A souvenir sheet containing Nos. 2715a and 2715b but having a different sheet margin was produced in limited quantities and sold only at the 2013 China International Collection Expo.

Top of 18th Century Tile Stove Made at Rörstrand Porcelain Factory — A1001

19th Century Tile Stove Made at Akerlindska Tile Factory — A1002

18th Century Tile Stove Made at Marieberg Porcelain Factory — A1003

19th Century White Tile Stove — A1004

Door of 18th Century Tile Stove — A1005

Serpentine Die Cut 10 on 2 or 3 Sides
2013, Nov. 14   *Litho. & Engr.*
Self-Adhesive
2716   Booklet pane of 5 + 5
     etiquettes   19.00
a.   A1001 12k multi   3.75 3.75
b.   A1002 12k multi   3.75 3.75
c.   A1003 12k multi   3.75 3.75
d.   A1004 12k multi   3.75 3.75
e.   A1005 12k multi   3.75 3.75

Souvenir Sheet

Awarding of 2011 Nobel Prize for Literature to Tomas Tranströmer — A1006

No. 2717: a, Tranströmer (31x39mm). b, Musical score from a sonata by Franz Schubert (34x50mm).

Litho. & Engr.
2013, Nov. 14   *Perf. 13x12¾*
2717 A1006   Sheet of 2   7.50 7.50
a.-b.   12k Either single   3.75 3.75

A1007

Christmas — A1008

No. 2718, Reindeer on hill. No. 2719: a, Two birds carrying heart on string. b, Foxes and Christmas tree. c, Hibernating bears and gift boxes. d, Squirrel and gingerbread man cookie.

Die Cut Perf. 11¾x11½
2013, Nov. 14   Coil Stamp   *Litho.*
Self-Adhesive
2718 A1007 (5.50k) multi   1.75 1.75

Booklet Stamps
Serpentine Die Cut 10 on 3 Sides
2719 A1008   Block of 4   7.00
a.-d.   (5.50k) Any single   1.75 1.75
e.   Booklet pane of 10, 3 each
   #2719a-2719b, 2 each
   #2719c-2719d   17.50

Bildmuseet, Umea, Sweden A1009

National Library, Riga, Latvia A1010

Die Cut Perf. 13x13½ Syncopated
2014, Jan. 16   *Litho.*
Coil Stamps
Self-Adhesive
2720 A1009 12k multi   3.75 3.75
2721 A1010 12k multi   3.75 3.75

Selecetion of Umea and Riga as European Capitals of Culture. See Latvia Nos. 857-858.

Sporting Events A1011

Designs: Nos. 2722, 2723a, Vasaloppet 90-kilometer cross-country skiing race. No. 2723b, Lidingöloppet 30-kilometer race. No. 2723c, Vansbrosimningen 3-kilometer swimming race. No. 2723d, Vatternrundan 300-kilometer bicycle race. No. 2723e, Engelbrektsloppet 60-kilometer cross-country skiing race.

Litho. & Engr.
2014, Jan. 16   *Perf. 13x13½*
2722 A1011 (6k) multi   2.00 2.00

Booklet Stamps
Die Cut Perf. 13x13½ Syncopated
2723   Vert. strip of 5   9.50
a.-e.   A1011 (6k) Any single   1.90 1.90
f.   Booklet pane of 10, 2 each
   #2723a-2723e   19.00

No. 2722 was printed in sheets of 9 that sold for 59k. Value, $18.

Souvenir Sheet

Icebreakers — A1012

No. 2724: a, Icebreaker Atle. b, Icebreaker Ymer, vert.

Perf. 12¾x13, 13x12¾
2014, Mar. 17   *Litho. & Engr.*
2724 A1012   Sheet of 2   7.50 7.50
a.-b.   12k Either single   3.75 3.75

Carl Michael Bellman (1740-95), Composer — A1013

Die Cut Perf. 13¼ Syncopated
2014, Mar. 27   *Litho. & Engr.*
Coil Stamp
Self-Adhesive
2725 A1013 100k multi   31.00 31.00

Zlatan Ibrahimovic, Soccer Player A1014

No. 2726 — Ibrahimovic: a, Scissor kicking, "Zlatan" at left. b, With soccer ball. c, Making leaping kick, "Zlatan" at upper right. d, With arms extended. e, In blue shirt, smiling.

Die Cut Perf. 13x13¼ Syncopated
2014, Mar. 27   *Litho.*
Booklet Stamps
Self-Adhesive
2726   Vert. strip of 5   9.50
a.-e.   A1014 (6k) Any single   1.90 1.90
f.   Booklet pane of 10, 2 each
   #2726a-2726e   19.00

Insects Type of 2013
Die Cut Perf. 11¾x11½
2014, Apr. 1   Coil Stamp   *Engr.*
Self-Adhesive
2727 A990 14k Aeshna serrata   4.25 4.25

Flag of Sweden A1015

Die Cut Perf. 13x13¼ Syncopated
2014, May 8   Coil Stamp   *Litho.*
Self-Adhesive
2728 A1015 (7k) multi   2.25 2.25

Compare types A1015 and A940.

Summer
Greetings — A1016

No. 2729: a, Flowers in paper airplane, ribbon. b, Gift box, trumpet under parachute, piece of candy and ladybug under balloons. c, Piece of candy under balloon, flower in bottle. d, Candles on cake, flowers, ribbon. e, Bouquet of flowers, ribbon.

Die Cut Perf. 13½ Syncopated
2014, May 8 **Litho.**
Booklet Stamps
Self-Adhesive

2729		Vert. strip of 5	11.25	
a.-e.	A1016 (7k) Any single		2.25	2.25
f.	Booklet pane of 10, 2 each #2729a-2729e		22.50	

Church
Art
A1017

Designs: No. 2730, 2731a, Skara Missal, baptismal font from Ottum Church. No. 2731b, Angel from Brahe Church, Visingsö, organ from Askeryd Church. No. 2731c, Room in monastery, Stockholm, candle holder from Torsaker Church. No. 2731d, Movement and face of clock in tower or German Church, Stockholm. No. 2731e, Baptismal font and candles from St. Peter's Church, Klippan.

Litho. & Engr.
2014, May 8 **Perf. 12¾**
| 2730 | A1017 (7k) multi | 2.40 | 2.40 |

Booklet Stamps
Perf. 12¾ Horiz.
2731		Vert. strip of 5	11.25	11.25
a.-e.	A1017 (7k) Any single		2.25	2.25
f.	Booklet pane of 10, 2 each #2731a-2731e		22.50	—
	Complete booklet, #2731f		22.50	

No. 2730 was printed in sheets of 9 that sold for 68k. Value, $22.50.

Souvenir Sheet

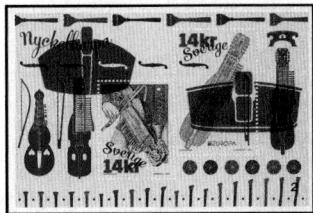

Europa — A1018

No. 2732: a, Musician playing nyckelharpa (31x39mm). b, Nyckelharpa and bow (34x50mm).

Litho. & Engr.
2014, May 8 **Perf. 13x12¾**
| 2732 | A1018 | Sheet of 2 | 8.50 | 8.50 |
| a.-b. | 14k Either single | | 4.25 | 4.25 |

A1019

A1020

A1021

A1022

A1023

A1024

Berries and
Leaves
A1025

Die Cut Perf. 13¾ Syncopated
2014, Aug. 21 **Engr.**
Coil Stamps
Self-Adhesive
| 2733 | A1019 (6.50k) multi | 1.90 | 1.90 |

Die Cut Perf. 13¼x13½ Syncopated
| 2734 | A1020 (7k) multi | 2.00 | 2.00 |

Booklet Stamps
2735		Vert. strip of 5	10.00	
a.	A1021 (7k) multi		2.00	2.00
b.	A1022 (7k) multi		2.00	2.00
c.	A1023 (7k) multi		2.00	2.00
d.	A1024 (7k) multi		2.00	2.00
e.	A1025 (7k) multi		2.00	2.00
f.	Booklet pane of 10, 2 each #2735a-2735e		20.00	

Chairs
A1026

No. 2736: a, Hug chair, designed by Anna von Schewen, 2002. b, Lilla Aland chair, designed by Carl Malmsten, 1940. c, Lamino chair, designed by Yngve Ekström, 1956. d, Cinema chair, designed by Gunilla Allard, 1993. e, Aluminiumfatöljen chair, designed by Mats Theselius, 1990.

Die Cut Perf. 13¼x13½ Syncopated
2014, Aug. 21 **Litho. & Engr.**
Self-Adhesive
| 2736 | | Booklet pane of 5 + 5 etiquettes | 20.00 | |
| a.-e. | A1026 14k Any single | | 4.00 | 4.00 |

Souvenir Sheet

Alice Tegnér (1864-1943), Composer
of Children's Songs — A1027

No. 2737: a, Tegnér. b, Children in ring, horiz.

Litho. & Engr.
2014, Nov. 13 **Perf. 12¾x13**
| 2737 | A1027 | Sheet of 2 | 7.50 | 7.50 |
| a.-b. | 14k Either single | | 3.75 | 3.75 |

A1028

Christmas — A1029

Designs: No. 2738, Mugs of mulled wine. No. 2739: a, Gingerbread house. b, Orange spiked with cloves. c, Lussebulle bun. d, Candy apple on stick. e, Marzipan pig.

Die Cut Perf. 13¼x13½ Syncopated
2014, Nov. 13 **Litho.**
Coil Stamp
Self-Adhesive
| 2738 | A1028 (6.50k) multi | 1.75 | 1.75 |

Booklet Stamps
2739		Vert. strip of 5	8.75	
a.-e.	A1029 (6.50k) Any single		1.75	1.75
f.	Booklet pane of 10, 2 each #2739a-2739e		17.50	

King Carl XVI
Gustaf — A1030

Queen
Silvia — A1031

Die Cut Perf. 13¾ Syncopated
2015, Jan. 15 **Coil Stamps** **Litho.**
Self-Adhesive
| 2740 | A1030 (7k) multi | 1.75 | 1.75 |
| 2741 | A1031 14k multi | 3.50 | 3.50 |

Popular Music
A1032

No. 2742: a, Avicii, record producer and disc jockey. b, Robyn, singer. c, Max Martin, songwriter and producer. d, First Aid Kit, folk singers. e, Seinabo Sey, singer and songwriter.

Die Cut Perf. 13¼x13½ Syncopated
2015, Jan. 15 **Litho.**
Booklet Stamps
Self-Adhesive
2742		Vert. strip of 5	8.75	
a.-e.	A1032 (7k) Any single		1.75	1.75
f.	Booklet pane of 10, 2 each #2742a-2742e		17.50	

Paintings by Prince
Eugen of Sweden
(1865-1947)
A1033

No. 2743: a, Molnet (Cloud), 1896. b, Det Gamla Slottet (The Old Castle), 1893. c, Hagastämningar, 1898. d, Oljekvarnen (Mill, Autumn Evening), 1908. e, Lyckans Tempel, 1892.

Die Cut Perf. 13¾ Syncopated
2015, Jan. 15 **Litho.**
Self-Adhesive
| 2743 | | Booklet pane of 5, #a-e, + 5 etiquettes | 17.50 | |
| a.-e. | A1033 14k Any single | | 3.50 | 3.50 |

A1034

A1035

A1036

A1037

A1038

A1039

Bees
A1040

Die Cut Perf. 13¾ Syncopated
2015, Mar. 26 **Coil Stamps** **Litho.**
Self-Adhesive
2744		Horiz. pair, #a-b	3.25	
a.	A1034 (6.50k) multi		1.60	1.60
b.	A1035 (6.50k) multi		1.60	1.60

Booklet Stamps
Die Cut Perf. 13¼x13½ Syncopated
2745		Vert. strip of 5, #a-e	8.75	
a.	A1036 (7k) multi		1.75	1.75
b.	A1037 (7k) multi		1.75	1.75
c.	A1038 (7k) multi		1.75	1.75
d.	A1039 (7k) multi		1.75	1.75
e.	A1040 (7k) multi		1.75	1.75
f.	Booklet pane of 10, 2 each #2745a-2745e		17.50	

Viking
Artifacts
A1041

Artifact and location where found: Nos. 2746, 2747c, Fitting for horse's bridle, Broa. No. 2747a, Three gold figurines, Lunda. No. 2747b, Silver jewelry, Aska. No. 2747d, Bronze Buddha, Helgö. No. 2747e, Gilded figurine depicting flying man. Uppakra.

Litho. & Engr.
2015, Mar. 26 **Perf. 12¾**
| 2746 | A1041 (7k) multi | 1.90 | 1.90 |
Booklet Stamps
Perf. 12¾ Horiz.
2747		Vert. strip of 5	8.75	8.75
a.-e.	A1041 (7k) Any single		1.75	1.75
f.	Booklet pane of 10, 2 each #2747a-2747e		17.50	—
	Complete booklet, #2747f		17.50	

No. 2746 was printed in sheets of 9 that sold for 73k.

Souvenir Sheet

Europa — A1042

No. 2748 — Old toys: a, Skoglund & Olson cast iron airplane, 1920s. b. Metal horse on cart, 1910s, Brio wooden donkey, 1950s.

2015, Mar. 26   **Litho. & Engr.**   **Perf. 13**
2748   A1042   Sheet of 2   7.00   7.00
    a.-b.   14k Either single   3.50   3.50

A1043

Decorated Farmhouses of Hälsingland UNESCO World Heritage Site — A1044

Designs: 1k, Wall decoration, Bortom farmhouse. 2k, Peony wallpaper, Bommars farmhouse. 5k, Room in Bommars farmhouse, and wall decoration, Gästgivars farmhouse. 10k, Doorway, Bortom farmhouse, and wall decoration, Gästgivars farmhouse. 20k, Jon-Lars farmhouse, decoration from Kristofers farmhouse.

Die Cut Perf. 13¾x13¼ Syncopated
2015, May 7   **Coil Stamps**   **Litho.**
Self-Adhesive
2749   A1043   1k multi   .25   .25
2750   A1043   2k multi   .50   .50

Engr.
Die Cut Perf. 13¼x13¾ Syncopated
2751   A1044   5k blue & brn   1.25   1.25
2752   A1044   10k red brn & bl   2.40   2.40
2753   A1044   20k blue & green   4.75   4.75
    Nos. 2749-2753 (5)   *9.15 9.15*

A1045

SVERIGE BREV   Magnolias — A1050

Die Cut Perf. 13¼x13¾ Syncopated
2015, May 7   **Coil Stamp**   **Litho.**
Self-Adhesive
2754   A1045   (7k) multi   1.75   1.75

Booklet Stamps
Die Cut Perf. 13¾x13¼ Syncopated
2755   Horiz. strip of 5, #a-e   8.75   8.75
   a.   A1046 (7k) multi   1.75   1.75
   b.   A1047 (7k) multi   1.75   1.75
   c.   A1048 (7k) multi   1.75   1.75
   d.   A1049 (7k) multi   1.75   1.75
   e.   A1050 (7k) multi   1.75   1.75
   f.   Booklet pane of 10, 2 each
      #2755a-2755e   17.50

SEMI-POSTAL STAMPS

Type of 1872-91 Issues Surcharged in Dark Blue

Perf. 13x13½
1916, Dec. 21   **Wmk. 181**
B1   A5   5o + 5o on 2o org   4.75   7.25
B2   A5   5o + 5o on 3o yel brn   4.75   7.25
B3   A5   5o + 5o on 4o gray   4.75   7.25
B4   A5   5o + 5o on 5o grn   4.75   7.25
B5   A5   5o + 5o on 6o lilac   4.75   7.25
B6   A5   10o + 10o on 12o pale
      bl   4.75   7.25
B7   A5   10o + 10o on 20o red
      org   4.75   7.25
B8   A5   10o + 10o on 24o yel   4.75   7.25
B9   A5   10o + 10o on 30o brn   4.75   7.25
B10   A5   10o + 10o on 50o rose
      red   4.75   7.25
    Nos. B1-B10 (10)   *47.50 72.50*

The surtax on Nos. B1-B31 was for the militia. See note after No. B21.
For surcharges see Nos. B22-B31.

No. 66 Surcharged in Dark Blue

1916, Dec. 21   **Wmk. 180**   **Perf. 13**
B11   A12   10o + 4.90k on 5k   150.00   375.00

Nos. J12-J22 Surcharged in Dark Blue

1916, Dec. 21   **Unwmk.**   **Perf. 13**
B12   D1   5o + 5o on 1o   25.00   18.00
B13   D1   5o + 5o on 3o   5.00   7.00
B14   D1   5o + 5o on 5o   18.00   7.00
B15   D1   5o + 10o on 6o   5.00   8.00
B16   D1   5o + 15o on 12o   42.50   32.50
B17   D1   10o + 20o on 20o   15.00   25.00
B18   D1   10o + 40o on 24o   55.00   100.00
B19   D1   10o + 20o on 30o   6.50   6.00
B20   D1   10o + 40o on 50o   20.00   42.50
B21   D1   10o + 90o on 1kr   150.00   375.00
    Nos. B12-B21 (10)   *342.00 621.00*

The surtax on Nos. B12-B21 is indicated not in figures, but in words at bottom of surcharge: Fem, 5; Tio, 10; Femton, 15; Tjugo, 20; Fyrtio, 40; Nittio, 90.

Nos. B1-B10 Surcharged

1918, Dec. 18   **Wmk. 181**
B22   A5   7o + 3o on #B1   8.00   9.00
B23   A5   7o + 3o on #B2   2.75   1.25
B24   A5   7o + 3o on #B3   2.75   1.25
B25   A5   7o + 3o on #B4   2.75   1.25
B26   A5   7o + 3o on #B5   2.75   1.25
B27   A5   12o + 8o on #B6   2.75   1.25
B28   A5   12o + 8o on #B7   2.75   1.25
B29   A5   12o + 8o on #B8   2.75   1.25
B30   A5   12o + 8o on #B9   2.75   1.25
B31   A5   12o + 8o on #B10   2.75   1.25
    Nos. B22-B31 (10)   *32.75 20.25*

The 12o+8o surcharge exists on Nos. B1-B5 and the 7o+3o surcharge exists on Nos. B6-B10. Value, each $72.50.
Nos. B24, B26, B28 and B30 exist with surcharge inverted. Value unused, each $140.

King Gustaf V — SP1

Unwmk.
1928, June 16   **Engr.**   **Perf. 10**
B32   SP1   5o (+ 5o) yel grn   2.75   6.00
B33   SP1   10o (+ 5o) dk vio   2.75   6.00
B34   SP1   15o (+ 5o) car   2.75   4.50
    Complete booklet, pane of 8
    ea. #B32, B33, B34   275.00
B35   SP1   20o (+ 5o) org   4.75   2.75
B36   SP1   25o (+ 5o) dk bl   4.75   3.25
    Nos. B32-B36 (5)   *17.75 22.50*
    Set, never hinged   27.50

70th birthday of King Gustaf V. The surtax was used for anti-cancer work.

> **Catalogue values for unused stamps in this section, from this point to the end of the section, are for Never Hinged items.**

King Gustaf V — SP2

1948, June 16   **Perf. 12½ Vertically**
B37   SP2   10o + 10o green   .55   .60
B38   SP2   20o + 10o red   .80   .75
B39   SP2   30o + 10o ultra   .55   .60

Perf. 12½ on 3 Sides
B40   SP2   10o + 10o green   .65   .70
   a.   Booklet pane of 20   10.00
B41   SP2   20o + 10o red   .80   .90
   a.   Booklet pane of 20   12.00
    Nos. B37-B41 (5)   *3.35 3.55*

90th anniv. of the birth of King Gustaf V. The surtax provided aid for Swedish youth.

King Gustaf VI Adolf — SP3

1952, Nov. 11   **Perf. 12½ Horiz.**
B42   SP3   10o + 10o green   .35   .40
B43   SP3   25o + 10o car rose   .35   .40
B44   SP3   40o + 10o ultra   .65   .60

Perf. 12½ on 3 Sides
B45   SP3   10o + 10o green   .35   .40
   a.   Booklet pane of 20   6.50
B46   SP3   25o + 10o car rose   .35   .40
   a.   Booklet pane of 20   7.00
    Nos. B42-B46 (5)   *2.05 2.20*

70th birthday of King Gustaf VI Adolf. The surtax was used to promote Swedish culture.

Henri Dunant — SP4

1959, May 8   **Perf. 12½ Horizontally**
B47   SP4   30o + 10o red   .50   .75

Perf. 12½ on 3 Sides
B48   SP4   30o + 10o red   1.00   1.25
   a.   Booklet pane of 20   18.00

Centenary of the Red Cross idea. The surtax went to the Swedish Red Cross.

King Gustav VI Adolf — SP5

Perf. 12½ Vertically
1962, Nov. 10   **Engr.**   **Unwmk.**
Size: 58x24mm
B49   SP5   20o + 10o brown   .30   .30
B50   SP5   35o + 10o blue   .30   .30

Perf. 12½ Horizontally
B51   SP5   20o + 10o brown   .30   .40
   a.   Booklet pane of 10   3.00
B52   SP5   35o + 10o blue   .30   .40
   a.   Booklet pane of 10   3.00
    Nos. B49-B52 (4)   *1.20 1.40*

80th birthday of King Gustav VI Adolf. The surtax went to the King Gustav VI Adolf 80th anniv. Foundation for Swedish Cultural Activities.

Ship Types of Regular Issues
Imprint: "1966"

Designs (Ships): 10o, "The Lion of Smaland." 15o, "Kalmar Nyckel." 20o, Old Sailing Packet. 25o, Mail Paddle Steamship. 30o, "Kung Karl." 40o, Stern of "Amphion."

1966, Nov. 15   **Perf. 12½ on 3 Sides**
B53   A76   10o vermilion   .30   .45
B54   A50   15o vermilion   .30   .45
B55   A38   20o slate grn   .30   .45
B56   A39   25o ultra   .25   .25
B57   A76   30o vermilion   .30   .55
B58   A76   40o vermilion   .30   .55
   a.   Bklt. pane. #B53-B54, B57-B58,
     2 #B55, 4 #B56   2.75
    Nos. B53-B58 (6)   *1.75 2.70*

The booklet sold for 3.50k and the surtax of 1.15k went to the National Cancer Fund.

Save the Children Sweden — SP6

No. B59 — Three children, birds with tree at center and: a, Right. b, Left.

Serpentine Die Cut 10 on 3 Sides
2011, Mar. 24   **Litho.**
Booklet Stamps
Self-Adhesive
B59   SP6   Horiz. pair   4.50
   a.-b.   (6k+1k) Either single   2.25   2.25
   c.   Booklet pane of 10, 5 each
     #B59a-B59b   22.50

Surtax for Save the Children Sweden.

Swedish Cancer Society — SP7

No. B60: a, Silhouette of man. b, Abstract design.

Booklet Stamps

2012, Jan. 12 **Self-Adhesive**
B60 SP7 Horiz. pair 4.25
a.-b. (6k+1k) Either single 2.10 2.10
c. Booklet pane of 10, 5 each 21.50
 #B60a-B60b

Surtax for Swedish Cancer Society.

SOS Children's Villages — SP8

No. B61: a, Woman and three children. b, Woman and child.

Booklet Stamps
2013, Jan. 10 **Self-Adhesive**
B61 SP8 Horiz. pair 4.50
a.-b. (6k+1k) Either single 2.25 2.25
c. Booklet pane of 10, 5 each 22.50
 #B61a-B61b

Surtax for SOS Children's Villages in Cambodia and Ukraine.

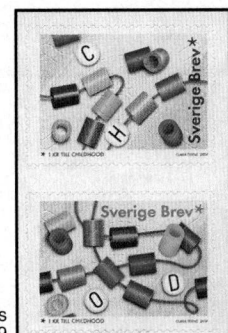

Beads
SP9

No. B62 — Beads with letters: a, "C" and "H." b, "O" and "D."

Die Cut Perf. 13x13½ Syncopated
2014, Jan. 16 **Litho.**
Booklet Stamps
Self-Adhesive
B62 SP9 Vert. pair 4.50 4.50
a.-b. (6k+1k) Either single 2.25 2.25
c. Booklet pane of 10, 6 #B62a, 22.50
 4 #B62b

Surtax for World Childhood Foundation.

Worldwide Fund for Nature (WWF) — SP10

No. B63 — Sun, bird and: a, Deer. b, Farmhouses and wind generator.

Die Cut Perf. 13¾x13¼ Syncopated
2015, May 7 **Self-Adhesive Litho.**
Booklet Stamps
B63 Horiz. pair, #a-b 3.80
a.-b. SP10 (7k)+1k Either single 1.90 1.90
c. Booklet pane of 10, 6 #B63a, 4 19.00
 #B63b

Surtax for Worldwide Fund for Nature.

AIR POST STAMPS

Official Stamps Surcharged in Dark Blue

1920, Sept. 17 **Wmk. 181** **Perf. 13**
C1 O3 10o on 3o brn 2.25 7.75
a. Inverted surcharge 375.00 1,350.
C2 O3 20o on 2o org 3.50 11.00
a. Inverted surcharge 375.00 1,100.

C3 O3 50o on 4o vio 19.00 25.00
a. Inverted surcharge 375.00 1,350.
Nos. C1-C3 (3) 24.75 43.75
Set, never hinged 62.50

Wmk. 180
C4 O3 20o on 2o org 3,250.
C5 O3 50o on 4o vio 190.00 600.00

Airplane over Stockholm AP2

Perf. 10 Vertically
1930, May 9 **Engr.** **Unwmk.**
C6 AP2 10o deep blue .25 .60
C7 AP2 50o dark violet .65 1.75
Set, never hinged 1.50

Flying Swans — AP3

1942-53 **Perf. 12½ on 3 Sides**
C8 AP3 20k brt ultra ('53) 4.50 .65
 Never hinged 7.00
a. Bklt. pane of 20 ('53) 725.00
b. Bklt. pane of 10 ('68) 65.00
c. Perf. on 4 sides 50.00 13.50
 Never hinged 140.00
d. As "c," bklt. pane of 10 1,350.

Issued: #C8c, May 4, 1942; #C8, July 7.

POSTAGE DUE STAMPS

D1

1874 **Unwmk.** **Typo.** **Perf. 14**
J1 D1 1o black 75.00 40.00
J2 D1 3o rose 75.00 40.00
J3 D1 5o brown 75.00 35.00
J4 D1 6o yellow 150.00 95.00
J5 D1 12o pale red 7.75 6.00
J6 D1 20o blue 80.00 37.50
J7 D1 24o violet 625.00 375.00
J8 D1 24o gray 75.00 52.50
J9 D1 30o dk grn 87.50 40.00
J10 D1 50o brown 275.00 60.00
J11 D1 1k blue & bister 300.00 70.00
Nos. J1-J11 (11) 1,825. 856.00

1877-86 **Perf. 13**
J12 D1 1o black ('80) 2.75 4.00
J13 D1 3o rose 6.25 7.25
J14 D1 5o brown 4.50 4.50
J15 D1 6o yellow 4.50 4.50
a. Printed on both sides 1,600.
J16 D1 12o pale red ('82) 14.50 17.00
J17 D1 20o pale blue ('78) 5.25 4.50
J18 D1 24o red lilac ('86) 26.00 29.00
a. 24o violet ('84) 26.00 29.00
J19 D1 24o gray lil ('82) 190.00 240.00
J20 D1 30o yellow green 6.50 4.50
J21 D1 50o yellow brown 10.50 5.75
J22 D1 1k blue & bister 30.00 17.50
Nos. J12-J22 (11) 300.75 338.50

Nos. J12-J17, J19-J22 exist imperf. Value, pairs, each $400.
For surcharges see Nos. B12-B21.

STAMPS FOR CITY POSTAGE

S1

1856-62 **Typo.** **Unwmk.** **Perf. 14**
LX1 S1 1sk (3o) blk ('58) 1,100. 550.00
LX2 S1 3sk (3o) bis brn ('62) 600.00 575.00

From 1856 to 1858 No. LX1 was sold at 1sk, from 1858 to 1862 at 3o. The paper of the 1sk black is thin while the paper of the 3o black is medium thick.

No. LX1 was reprinted three times with perf. 14, once with perf. 13. No. LX2 was reprinted once with each perforation. Value of lowest cost Perf. 14 reprints, $250 each. See the Scott Specialized Catalogue of Stamps and Covers 1840-1940 for detailed listings.

OFFICIAL STAMPS

O1

1874-77 **Unwmk.** **Typo.** **Perf. 14**
O1 O1 3o bister 90.00 42.50
O2 O1 4o gray ('77) 300.00 75.00
O3 O1 5o yel green 140.00 52.50
O4 O1 6o lilac 275.00 65.00
O5 O1 6o gray 525.00 175.00
O6 O1 12o blue 200.00 3.00
O7 O1 20o pale red 1,050. 90.00
O8 O1 24o yellow 1,050. 20.00
a. 24o orange 1,050. 22.50
O9 O1 30o pale brn 425.00 37.50
O10 O1 50o rose 600.00 125.00
O11 O1 1k bl & bis 1,700. 65.00
Nos. O1-O11 (11) 6,355. 750.50

Imperf., Pairs
O1a O1 3o 1,500.
O2a O1 4o 1,500.
O3a O1 5o 1,500.
O4a O1 6o 1,500.
O6a O1 12o 1,500.
O7a O1 20o 1,500.
O8b O1 24o 1,500.
O9a O1 30o 1,500.
O10a O1 50o 1,500.
O11a O1 1k 2,500.

1881-95 **Perf. 13**
O12 O1 2o org ('91) 1.40 2.00
O13 O1 3o bis brn 1.40 2.25
O14 O1 4o gray blk ('93) 2.50 .70
a. 4o gray ('82) 20.00 2.75
O15 O1 5o grn ('84) 5.25 .60
O16 O1 6o red lil ('82) 40.00 60.00
a. 6o lilac ('81) 45.00 65.00
O17 O1 10o car ('95) 3.00 .25
b. 10o rose ('85) 45.00 1.25
O18 O1 12o blue 57.50 22.50
O19 O1 20o ver ('82) 200.00 2.50
O20 O1 20o dk bl ('91) 5.75 .60
O21 O1 24o yellow 72.50 25.00
a. 24o orange 65.00 25.00
O22 O1 30o brown 26.00 .70
O23 O1 50o pale rose 140.00 25.00
O24 O1 50o pale gray ('93) 18.00 3.00
O25 O1 1k dk bl & yel brn 9.00 3.00
Nos. O12-O25 (14) 582.30 148.10

Imperf., Pairs
O12a O1 2o 400.00
O17a O1 10o No. O17 400.00
c. No. O17b 400.00
O20a O1 20o 50.00
O24a O1 50o 400.00

Surcharged in Dark Blue

1889
O26 O1 10o on 12o blue 13.00 18.00
a. Inverted surcharge 2,100. 5,000.
b. Perf. 14 5,500. 5,500.
O27 O1 10o on 24o yel 16.00 25.00
a. Inverted surcharge 7,000. 5,500.
b. Perf. 14 5,500. 5,500.

O3

1910-12 **Wmk. 180** **Typo.**
O28 O3 1o black .30 .10
O29 O3 2o orange 1.40 4.50
O30 O3 4o pale violet 1.75 4.00
O31 O3 5o green .50 1.10

O32 O3 8o claret .40 1.10
O33 O3 10o red 11.00 .70
O34 O3 15o red brown .80 .80
O35 O3 25o deep blue 7.00 1.75
O36 O3 25o red orange 7.00 2.50
O37 O3 30o chocolate 7.00 3.50
O38 O3 50o gray 7.00 3.50
O39 O3 1k black, yellow 7.75 7.75
O40 O3 5k claret, yellow 10.00 4.00
Nos. O28-O40 (13) 61.90 35.65

1910-19 **Wmk. Wavy Lines (181)**
O41 O3 1o black 2.00 3.75
O42 O3 2o orange .30 .40
O43 O3 3o pale brown .40 1.00
O44 O3 4o pale violet .30 .40
O45 O3 5o green .30 .40
O46 O3 7o gray green .40 1.25
O47 O3 8o rose 18.00 27.50
O48 O3 10o red .30 .25
O49 O3 12o rose red .30 .40
O50 O3 15o org brown .30 .30
O51 O3 20o deep blue .45 .30
O52 O3 25o orange .80 .50
O53 O3 30o chocolate .55 .55
O54 O3 35o dark violet .85 1.00
O55 O3 50o gray 3.25 2.25
Nos. O41-O55 (15) 28.50 40.25

For surcharges see Nos. C1-C5.

Use of official stamps ceased on July 1, 1920.

PARCEL POST STAMPS

Regular Issue of 1914 Surcharged

1917 **Wmk. 180** **Perf. 13**
Q1 A14 1.98k on 5k claret, yel 1.40 6.00
Q2 A14 2.12k on 5k claret, yel 1.40 6.00

SWITZERLAND

'swit-sər-lənd

(Helvetia)

LOCATION — Central Europe, between France, Germany and Italy
GOVT. — Republic
AREA — 15,943 sq. mi.
POP. — 7,062,400 (1998 est.)
CAPITAL — Bern

100 Rappen or Centimes = 1 Franc

Catalogue values for unused stamps in this country are for Never Hinged items, beginning with Scott 365 in the regular postage section, Scott B272 in the semi-postal section, Scott C46 in the airpost section, Scott CB1 in the airpost semi-postal section, and Scott 3O94, 4O40, 5O26, 7O31, 8O1, 9O1, 10O1, 11O1, 12O1 in the official sections.

Watermarks

Type I   Type II

Wmk. 182 —   Wmk. 183 —
Cross in Oval   Swiss Cross

Watermark 182 is not a true watermark, having been impressed after the paper was manufactured. There are two types: I- width just under 9mm; heighth just under 11mm; double oval lines nearly 1mm apart; cross has short, thick arms. II- width just under 8½mm; double oval lines very close together; cross has longer, thinner arms than Type I.

CANTONAL ADMINISTRATION

Unused values of Nos. 1L1-3L1 are for stamps without gum.
Counterfeit and repaired copies of Nos. 1L1-3L1 abound.

Zurich

A1   A2
Numerals of Value

1843   Unwmk.   Litho.   Imperf.
Red Vertical Lines
1L1 A1 4r black   20,000. 16,500.
1L2 A2 6r black   7,000. 1,750.

1846   Red Horizontal Lines
1L3 A1 4r black   17,500. 22,000.
1L4 A2 6r black   2,150. 1,650.

Five varieties of each value.

Reprints of the Zurich stamps show signs of wear and lack the red lines. Values 4r, $7,000; 6r, $2,350.

Coat of Arms — A3

1850   Unwmk.   Imperf.
1L5 A3 2½r black & red   6,000. 3,500.

No. 1L5 has separation designs in the margins between stamps as shown. Values are for stamps showing part of the separation design on all four sides.

Geneva

Coat of Arms — A4

1843   Unwmk.   Litho.   Imperf.
2L1 A4 10c blk, *yel grn*   62,500. 40,000.
a.   Either half   23,500. 9,250.
b.   Stamp composed of right
      half at left & left half at
      right   77,500. 60,000.

 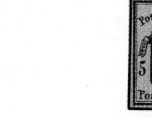

A5   A6

1845-48
2L2 A5 5c blk, *yel grn*   3,200. 1,675.
2L3 A6 5c blk, *yel grn* ('46)   2,200. 1,750.
2L4 A6 5c blk, *dk grn* ('48)   4,500. 2,750.

A7

1849-50
2L5 A7 4c black & red   40,000. 20,000.
2L6 A7 5c blk & red ('50)   2,750. 1,750.

Coat of Arms — A8

1851
2L7 A8 5c black & red   9,000. 3,800.

ENVELOPE STAMP USED AS ADHESIVE

E1

1847   Unwmk.   Imperf.
2LU1 E1 5c yel grn, see foot-
          note   23,500.

Value is for cut-out stamp used on folded letters. This use was authorized and is known from Feb. 19, 1847. Value of unused envelope cut-out, $550. Value of used cut-out off cover, $3,000.

Basel

Dove of Basel — A9

Typo. & Embossed
1845   Unwmk.   Imperf.
3L1 A1 2½r blk, crim &
          bl   14,000. 13,500.

FEDERAL ADMINISTRATION

Due to its tendency to damage the paper and/or the color of the stamps, the gum on Nos. 1-40 very often is removed. Unused values for Nos. 1-40 are for stamps without gum. Stamps with original gum sell for about the same prices.

A10   A11

1850   Unwmk.   Litho.   Imperf.
Full Black Frame Around Cross
1 A10 2½r black & red   3,000. 1,500.
2 A11 2½r black & red   2,500. 1,400.
Without Frame Around Cross
3 A10 2½r black & red   6,000. 2,750.
4 A11 2½r blk & red   52,500. 25,000.

Forty types of each.

A12   A13

1850
Full Black Frame Around Cross
5 A12 5r dk bl, blk &
        red   5,250. 1,250.
a.   5r dk grayish bl, blk &
     red   5,750. 1,250.
6 A13 10r yel, blk &
        red   115,000.

No. 6 used, with only parts of frame around cross showing, value $175 to $900.

Without Frame Around Cross
7 A12 5r lt bl, blk & red   1,750.   450.
a.   5r dp bl, blk & red   1,550.   450.
b.   5r pur bl, blk & red   —   5,500.
c.   5r grnsh bl, blk & red   2,000.   450.

---

8 A13 10r yel, blk & red   1,000.   125.
a.   10r buff, blk & red   1,275.   225.
b.   10r org yel, blk & red   1,250.   250.
d.   Half used as 5r on cover, 5r
     rate   16,000.

Beware of examples of Nos. 7-8 with faked frame added.

1851
Full Blue Frame Around Cross
9 A12 5r light blue & red   210,000.

No. 9 used, with only parts of frame around cross showing, value $180 to $3,750.

Without Frame Around Cross
10 A12 5r lt blue & red   650.   125.00

Beware of examples of No. 10 with faked frame added.

Forty types of each.

A14   A15

A16

1852
Vermilion Frame Around Cross
11 A14 15r vermilion   15,000.   700.
12 A15 15r vermilion   2,500.   125.
13 A16 15c vermilion   14,000. 1,000.

Ten types of each.

On October 1st, 1854, all stamps of the preceding issues were declared obsolete.

The Sitting Helvetia type (Scott Nos. 14-40) are valued with three margins clear of frame lines, with the fourth margin touching or lightly cutting into the frame line. Stamps with four margins clear of all frame lines are rare and command sustantial premiums.

Helvetia — A17

1854   Embossed.   Unwmk.
Thin Paper, Fine Impressions
Emerald Silk Threads
14 A17 5r orange brn   7,500. 1,700.
15 A17 5r red brown   625.   160.00
16 A17 10r blue   825.   80.00
17 A17 15r car rose   1,200.   175.00
a.   15r pale rose   1,350.   190.00
18 A17 40r pale yel grn   9,500. 1,300.
19 A17 40r yellow grn   1,250.   325.00

1854-55

Emerald Silk Threads
Medium Thick Paper
Fine Impressions

20	A17	5r pale yel brn	650.00	160.00
21	A17	10r blue	1,600.	125.00
22	A17	15r rose	925.00	110.00
23	A17	20r pale orange	1,400.	190.00

1855-57

Colored ( ) Silk Threads
Medium Thick Paper
Fine to Rough Impressions

24	A17	5r yel brn (yel)	550.00	115.00
25	A17	5r dk brn (blk)	325.00	40.00
26	A17	10r mlky bl (red)	1,000.	200.00
27	A17	10r blue (car)	300.00	50.00
a.		Thin paper	5,000.	475.00
28	A17	15r rose (bl)	550.00	75.00
29	A17	40r yel grn (mar)	1,000.	110.00
30	A17	1fr lav (blk)	1,400.	1,000.
31	A17	1fr lav (yel)	1,350.	1,000.
a.		Thin paper	*19,000.*	7,500.

1857

Thin (Emergency) Paper
Rough Impressions
Green Silk Threads

32	A17	5r pale gray brn	4,500.	1,000.
32A	A17	10r blue	6,500.	950.
33	A17	15r pale dl rose	3,250.	350.
34	A17	20r pale dl org	3,400.	275.

1858-62

Thick Ordinary Paper
Rough Impressions
Green Silk Threads

35	A17	2r gray	275.00	*575.00*
a.		One and one-half used as 3r on newspaper or wrapper		*15,000.*
c.		Half used as 1r on cover		
36	A17	5r brown	225.00	24.00
a.		5r black brown	275.00	47.50
b.		5r gray brown	240.00	27.50
c.		Half used as 2r on cover		*1,550.*
37	A17	10r blue	240.00	27.50
a.		Half used as 5r on cover		*7,250.*
b.		10r pale blue	260.00	27.50
c.		10r dark blue	250.00	24.00
d.		10r greenish blue	310.00	45.00
38	A17	15r dark rose	375.00	65.00
a.		15r pale rose	400.00	72.50
39	A17	20r dk org	475.00	75.00
a.		Half used as 10r on cover		*17,500.*
b.		20r yel orange	500.00	80.00
40	A17	40r grn (to dp grn)	450.00	100.00
a.		Half used as 20r on cover		*27,500.*
b.		40r yellow green	475.00	100.00
		Nos. 35-40 (6)	2,040.	866.50

Helvetia — A18

Double transfer errors, Nos. 43c, 44a, 55b, 60a, 61a, 61b, 67b, have the design impressed twice. These do not refer to the "embossed" watermark.

1862-64 Wmk. 182 *Perf. 11½*

White Wove Paper

41	A18	2c gray	125.00	4.75
42	A18	3c black	14.50	*115.00*
43	A18	5c dark brown	3.50	1.00
a.		5c bister brown	115.00	4.00
b.		5c gray brown	110.00	32.50
c.		Dbl. transfer, one invtd.	4,250.	500.00
d.		Dbl. transfer of lower left "5"		1,500.
44	A18	10c blue	625.00	1.00
a.		Dbl. transfer, one invtd.		*9,000.*
45	A18	20c orange	2.50	2.75
a.		20c yellow orange	400.00	4.00
46	A18	30c vermilion	1,500.	47.50
47	A18	40c green	1,400.	65.00
48	A18	60c bronze	1,400.	180.00
50	A18	1fr gold	25.00	*120.00*
a.		1fr yellowish bronze ('64)	1,600.	550.00

1867-78

52	A18	2c bister brown	3.25	1.80
a.		2c red brown	700.00	275.00
53	A18	10c carmine	4.75	1.00
54	A18	15c lemon	3.25	*45.00*
55	A18	25c blue green	1.60	*4.00*
a.		25c yellow green	60.00	40.00
b.		Dbl. transfer, one invtd.		600.00
56	A18	30c ultra	475.00	9.50
a.		30c blue	*2,200.*	275.00
58	A18	40c gray	1.60	*160.00*
59	A18	50c violet	55.00	55.00
		Nos. 52-59 (7)	544.45	*276.30*

1881 Granite Paper

60	A18	2c bister	.80	*22.50*
a.		Dbl. transfer, one invtd.	300.00	
61	A18	5c brown	.45	*10.00*
a.		Dbl. transfer, one invtd.	40.00	*450.00*
b.		Double transfer of lower left "5"		*1,250.*
62	A18	10c rose	8.00	*10.00*
63	A18	15c lemon	10.00	*450.00*
64	A18	20c orange	.80	*135.00*
65	A18	25c green	.60	*100.00*
66	A18	40c gray	1.00	*3,400.*
67	A18	50c deep violet	16.00	*475.00*
b.		Dbl. transfer, one invtd.	325.00	*4,500.*
68	A18	1fr gold	20.00	*1,100.*

The granite paper contains fragments of blue and red silk threads.

Forged or backdated cancellations are found frequently on Nos. 42, 50, 54, 58 and 60-68.

All stamps of the preceding issues were declared obsolete on October 1st, 1883. Some of the remainders of Nos. 41-68 were overprinted "AUSSER KURS" (Obsolete) diagonally in black.

Numeral — A19

Wmk. 182 (Type II)

1882-89 Typo. *Perf. 11½*

Granite Paper

69	A19	2c bister	2.50	1.25
70	A19	3c gray brown	3.25	*16.00*
a.		3c gray	65.00	72.50
71	A19	5c maroon	25.00	.80
a.		Tête bêche pair	—	
72	A19	5c deep grn ('99)	12.00	.80
73	A19	10c red	9.75	.80
74	A19	12c ultra	12.00	1.25
a.		12c dull blue	400.00	45.00
76	A19	15c lilac ('89)	80.00	4.00
		Nos. 69-76 (7)	144.50	*24.90*
		Set, never hinged	291.00	

Wmk. 182 (Type I)

69a	A19	2c olive brown	40.00	6.00
70b	A19	3c gray	65.00	75.00
71b	A19	5c brownish lilac	97.50	3.25
73a	A19	10c carmine	115.00	2.00
73b	A19	10c light rose	700.00	12.50
74c	A19	12c ultramarine	165.00	6.50
75	A19	15c yellow	200.00	40.00
75a	A19	15c yellow-orange	*20,000.*	*5,750.*
76b	A19	15c dull purple	500.00	32.50

Wmk. 182 (Type II)

1882 White Paper

77	A19	2c olive brown	525.00	450.00
78	A19	5c brownish lilac	1,425.	120.00
79	A19	10c pale rose	2,850.	77.50
80	A19	12c grayish ultra	300.00	32.50
81	A19	15c yellow	400.00	*400.00*

Nos. 77-81 were the first stamps issued in the Numeral series.

See Nos. 113-118.

Helvetia (Large numerals) A20

Helvetia (Small numerals) A21

Wmk. 182 (Type I)

1882-1904 Engr. *Perf. 11½ - 11¾*

82	A20	20c orange	200.00	6.25
83	A20	25c green	105.00	3.25
95b	A20	30c brown	—	*22,500.*
84	A20	40c gray	160.00	50.00
86	A20	50c blue	160.00	25.00
87	A20	1fr claret	275.00	7.00
88	A20	3fr yel brn ('91)	240.00	22.50

Wmk. 182 (Type II)

85	A21	40c gray ('04)	47.50	27.50
88d	A20	3fr yellow brown ('04)		*4,250.*

1888 Wmk. 182 (Type I) *Perf. 9½*

89	A20	20c orange	1,000.	125.00
90	A20	25c yellow grn	160.00	20.00
91	A20	40c gray	950.00	700.00
92	A20	50c blue	1,350.	375.00
93	A20	1fr claret	975.00	100.00

Values for Nos. 89-93 are for well-centered stamps with slightly uneven perforations. Stamps missing perforations sell for much less.

Wmk. 182 (Type I)

1891-1903 *Perf. 11½x11*

82c	A20	20c orange	*600.00*	8.25
83b	A20	25c green	*275.00*	6.00
95b	A20	30c red brown ('92)	*500.00*	52.50
84c	A20	40c gray	*1,100.*	135.00
86b	A20	50c blue	*450.00*	27.50
87c	A20	1fr claret	*825.00*	22.50
88c	A20	1fr claret		*17,500.*

Wmk. 182 (Type II)

82a	A20	20c orange	75.00	2.00
83a	A20	25c green	12.50	1.60
94	A20	25c blue ('99)	14.00	2.40
95	A20	30c red brn ('92)	40.00	2.40
84a	A20	40c gray	85.00	6.25
86a	A20	50c blue	50.00	14.00
96	A20	50c green ('99)	55.00	27.50
87a	A20	1fr claret	47.50	4.75
97	A20	1fr carmine ('03)	100.00	10.00
88a	A20	3fr yellow brown	175.00	30.00

Wmk. 182 (Type II)

1901-03 *Perf. 11½x12*

82b	A20	20c orange	32.50	2.00
94a	A20	25c blue	15.50	1.35
95a	A20	30c red brown	47.50	2.25
84b	A20	40c gray	100.00	40.00
96a	A20	50c green	77.50	8.00
87b	A20	1fr claret	*2,200.*	310.00
97a	A20	1fr carmine ('03)	475.00	42.50
88b	A20	3fr yellow brown	240.00	24.00

Numerous retouches and plate flaws exist on all values of this issue.

Nos. 82-88 are ½mm taller (paper size) than Nos. 82b-88b.

See Nos. 105-112, 119-125.

UPU Allegory — A22

1900 *Perf. 11½*

98	A22	5c gray green	40.00	2.00
99	A22	10c carmine rose	12.50	2.00
100	A22	25c blue	32.00	35.00
		Nos. 98-100 (3)	84.50	39.00

Re-engraved

101	A22	5c gray green	4.00	1.75
102	A22	10c carmine rose	57.50	47.50
103	A22	25c blue	800.00	*12,500.*

Universal Postal Union, 25th anniv.

The impression of the re-engraved stamps is much clearer, especially the horizontally lined background. The figures of value are lined instead of being solid.

Helvetia Types of 1882-1904

1905 Wmk. 183 *Perf. 11½x11*

White Paper

105	A20	20c orange	4.75	2.40
106	A20	25c blue	6.25	*10.00*
107	A20	30c brown	6.25	2.40
108a	A21	40c gray	115.00	*190.00*
109	A20	50c green	40.00	9.25
110	A20	1fr carmine	100.00	4.00
111	A20	3fr yellow brn	250.00	145.00

Some clichés in the plates of the 20c, 25c, 30c, 50c and 3fr have been retouched.

1906 Re-engraved *Perf. 11½x11*

112	A20	25c pale blue	7.75	2.75

In the re-engraved stamp the stars are larger and the background below "FRANCO" is of horiz. or horiz. and vert. crossed lines, instead of horiz. and curved lines.

1906 *Perf. 11½*

112a	A20	25c pale blue	110.00	9.50
108	A21	40c gray	35.00	14.00

1907 *Perf. 11½x12*

105a	A20	20c orange	8.00	8.00
109a	A20	50c green	47.50	16.00
110a	A20	1fr carmine	125.00	12.00
111a	A20	3fr yellow brown	310.00	225.00

Numeral Type of 1882-99

1905 Typo. *Perf. 11½*

Granite Paper

113	A19	2c dull bister	5.50	2.40
114	A19	3c gray brown	5.50	*80.00*
115	A19	5c green	5.50	.80
116	A19	10c scarlet	5.50	.80
117	A19	12c ultra	7.00	2.25
118	A19	15c brown vio	80.00	17.00
		Nos. 113-118 (6)	109.00	*103.25*

Helvetia Types of 1882-1904

1907 Engr. *Perf. 11½x12*

Granite Paper

119	A20	20c orange	4.00	4.00
120	A20	25c blue	12.50	*14.00*
121	A20	30c red brown	7.75	*20.00*
122	A21	40c gray	32.50	*57.50*
a.		Helvetia without diadem	375.00	*1,350.*
123	A20	50c gray green	8.50	*15.50*
124	A20	1fr carmine	32.50	7.75
125a	A20	3fr yellow brown		*14,500.*

There are retouches and plate flaws on all values.

Perf. 11½x11

120a	A20	25c deep blue	12.00	7.75
121a	A20	30c red brown	250.00	*475.00*
122b	A21	40c gray		*17,500.*
124a	A20	1fr carmine	*16,000.*	*6,500.*
125	A20	3fr yel brn	130.00	80.00

William Tell's Son — A23

Helvetia

A24 A25

1907-25 Typo. *Perf. 11½*
Granite Paper

126	A23	2c pale bister	.30	.55
127	A23	3c lilac brn	.25	*10.00*
128	A23	5c yellow grn	2.25	.50
129	A24	10c rose red	1.50	.50
130	A24	12c ocher	.30	*3.50*
131	A24	15c red vio	3.00	*13.00*
132	A25	20c red & yel ('08)	2.25	1.00
133	A25	25c dp blue ('08)	1.90	.65
a.		Tête bêche pair	17.00	*55.00*
134	A25	30c yel brn & pale grn ('08)	1.60	.50
135	A25	35c yel grn & yel ('08)	1.90	1.40
136	A25	40c red vio & yel ('08)	12.50	1.00
a.		Designer's name in full on the rock ('08)	6.00	*82.50*
137	A25	40c deep blue ('22)	1.75	.50
a.		40c light blue ('21)	5.50	1.90
138	A25	40c red vio & grn ('25)	25.00	.50
139	A25	50c dp grn & pale grn ('08)	11.00	.50
140	A25	60c brn org & buff ('18)	9.25	.65
141	A25	70c dk brn & buff ('08)	55.00	17.00
142	A25	70c vio & buff ('24)	14.50	2.25
143	A25	80c slate & buff ('15)	9.75	1.10
144	A25	1fr dp cl & pale grn ('08)	7.00	.55
145	A25	3fr bis & yel ('08)	275.00	2.10
		Nos. 126-145 (20)	436.00	*57.75*

No. 136 has two leaves and "CL" below sword hilt. No. 136a has three leaves and designer's full name below hilt.

For surcharges and overprints see Nos. 189, 199, O10-O13, O15, 1O6-1O8, 1O14-1O16, 2O18-2O26, 3O14-3O22.

1933 With Grilled Gum

135a	A25	35c yel grn & yel	1.40	*12.50*
138a	A25	40c red vio & grn	32.50	1.50
139a	A25	50c dp grn & pale grn	9.00	1.50
140a	A25	60c brn org & buff	12.00	1.50
142a	A25	70c vio & buff	17.50	3.75
143a	A25	80c slate & buff	13.00	4.25
144a	A25	1fr dp cl & pale grn	19.00	6.50
		Nos. 135a-144a (7)	104.40	31.50

"Grilled" Gum

In 1930-44 many Swiss stamps were treated with a light grilling process, applied with the gumming to counteract the tendency to curl. It resembles a faint grill of vertical and horizontal ribs covering the entire back of the stamp, and can be seen after the gum has been removed. Listings of the grilled gum varieties begin with No. 135a.

William Tell's Son — A26

Bow-string in front of stock

1909 *Perf. 11½, 12*
Granite Paper

146	A26	2c bister	.25	1.40
a.		Tête bêche pair	3.25	*17.50*
147	A26	3c dark violet	.25	*14.00*
148	A26	5c green	3.75	.25
a.		Tête bêche pair	14.00	*50.00*
		Nos. 146-148 (3)	4.25	*15.65*

See Nos. 149-163. For surcharges and overprints see Nos. 186, 193-195, 207-208, 1O1-1O3, 1O9-1O11, 2O1-2O7, 3O1-3O5.

First Redrawing

Bow-string behind stock. Thin loop above crossbow. Letters of "HELVETIA" without serifs.

1910-17 Granite Paper

149	A26	2c bister ('10)	8.75	8.00
150	A26	3c dk violet ('10)	.25	.25
a.		Tête bêche pair	2.75	2.75
b.		Booklet pane of 6	12.50	
151	A26	3c brown org ('17)	.25	.25
a.		Tête bêche pair	8.25	11.00
152	A26	5c green ('10)	21.00	6.50
a.		Tête bêche pair	92.50	175.00
		Nos. 149-152 (4)	30.25	15.00

Second Redrawing

Bow-string behind stock. Thick loop above crossbow. Letters of "HELVETIA" have serifs.

7½ CENTIMES:

Type I — Top of "7" is ½mm thick. The "1" of "½" has only traces of serifs. The two base plates of the statue are of even thickness.

Type II — Top of "7" is 1mm thick. The "1" of "½" has distinct serifs. The upper base plate is thinner than the lower.

1911-30 Granite Paper

153	A26	2c bister ('11)	.25	.25
a.		Tête bêche pair	3.25	1.60
154	A26	2½c claret ('18)	.25	*1.10*
155	A26	2½c ol, *buff* ('28)	.55	*2.10*
156	A26	3c ultra, *buff* ('30)	2.75	*6.00*
157	A26	5c green ('11)	1.75	.25
a.		Tête bêche pair	5.50	*10.00*
158	A26	5c org, *buff* ('21)	.25	.25
a.		Bklt. pane of 6 (5 #158, 168)	14.00	*47.50*
159	A26	5c gray vio, *buff* ('24)	.25	.25
a.		Bklt. pane of 6 (5 #159, 168)	6.50	*19.00*
160	A26	5c red vio, *buff* ('27)	.25	.25
a.		Bklt. pane 6 (5 #160, 168)	30.00	*65.00*
161	A26	5c dk grn, *buff* ('30)	.30	.25
a.		Bklt. pane 6 (5 #161, 169)	27.50	*70.00*
162	A26	7½c gray (I) ('18)	1.10	.25
a.		Tête bêche pair	13.00	*45.00*
c.		7½c slate (II)	4.50	2.75
163	A26	7½c dp grn, *buff* (I) ('28)	.30	*3.25*
		Nos. 153-163 (11)	8.00	*14.20*

1933 With Grilled Gum

156a	A26	3c ultra, *buff*	4.75	*17.50*
161b	A26	5c dark green, *buff*	.55	*5.00*

Helvetia — A27

1909 Granite Paper

164	A27	10c carmine	.60	.40
a.		Tête bêche pair	2.25	*6.00*
165	A27	12c bister brn	.85	.40
166	A27	15c red violet	26.00	1.10
		Nos. 164-166 (3)	27.45	1.90

For surcharge see No. 187.

William Tell — A28

TEN CENTIMES:

Type I — Bust 16½mm high. "HELVETIA" 15½mm wide. Cross bar of "H" at middle of the letter.

Type II — Bust 15mm high. "HELVETIA" 15mm wide. Cross bar of "H" above middle of the letter.

1914-30 Granite Paper *Perf. 11½*

167	A28	10c red, *buff* (type II)	.75	.25
a.		10c red, *buff* (type I)	2.50	*26.00*
b.		Tête bêche pair (II)	3.25	4.25
d.		Bklt. pane 6 (5 #167, 172)	50.00	*160.00*
168	A28	10c grn, *buff* (type II) ('21)	.25	.25
a.		Tête bêche pair	1.10	1.40
168C	A28	10c bl grn, *buff* (type II) ('28)	.25	.25
d.		Tête bêche pair	2.50	2.50
169	A28	10c vio, *buff* (type II) ('30)	2.25	.25
a.		Tête bêche pair	9.25	1.40
170	A28	12c brn, *buff*	.25	*3.25*
171	A28	13c ol grn, *buff* ('15)	1.40	.50
172	A28	15c vio, *buff*	3.50	.25
b.		15c dk vio, *buff*	32.50	4.25
c.		Tête bêche pair	87.50	125.00
173	A28	15c brn red, *buff* ('28)	2.50	2.75
174	A28	20c red vio, *buff* ('21)	3.25	.25
a.		Tête bêche pair	6.50	7.50
175	A28	20c ver, *buff* ('24)	1.00	.50
a.		Tête bêche pair	5.75	9.25
176	A28	20c car, *buff* ('25)	.25	.25
a.		Tête bêche pair	2.50	.55
177	A28	25c ver, *buff* ('21)	2.25	1.60
178	A28	25c car, *buff* ('22)	1.10	.85
179	A28	25c brn, *buff* ('25)	3.25	1.25
180	A28	30c dp bl, *buff* ('24)	9.25	.50
		Nos. 167-180 (15)	31.50	12.95

1932-33 With Grilled Gum

169c	A28	10c violet, *buff*	4.50	1.50
173a	A28	15c brn red, *buff* ('33)	50.00	*52.50*
176c	A28	20c carmine, *buff*	7.25	1.50
179a	A28	25c brown, *buff* ('33)	125.00	35.00
180a	A28	30c deep blue, *buff*	72.50	2.50
		Nos. 169c-180a (5)	259.25	93.00

For surcharges and overprints see Nos. 188, 196-198, 1O4-1O5, 1O12-1O13, 2O8-2O17, 3O6-3O13.

The Mythen A29

The Rütli — A30

The Jungfrau A31

1914-30 Engr. Granite Paper

181	A29	3fr dk green	650.00	6.50
182	A29	3fr red ('18)	87.50	1.40
183	A30	5fr dp ultra	35.00	3.00
184	A31	10fr dull violet	100.00	3.25
185	A31	10fr gray grn ('30)	225.00	37.50
		Nos. 181-185 (5)	1,097.	51.65

See No. 206. For overprints see Nos. 2O27-2O30, 3O23-3O26.

Stamps of 1909-14 Surcharged

a

b

c

1915

186	A26(a)	1c on 2c bister	.25	1.25
187	A27(b)	13c on 12c bis brn	.25	*9.25*
188	A28(c)	13c on 12c brn, *buff*	.30	.90
		Nos. 186-188 (3)	.80	*11.40*

No. 141 Surcharged

189	A25	80c on 70c	25.00	17.50

Significant of Peace A32

"Peace" A33

"Dawn of Peace" A34

Perf. 11½

1919, Aug. 1 Typo. Unwmk.

190	A32	7½c olive drab & blk	.80	*2.25*
191	A33	10c red & yel	1.10	*8.75*
192	A34	15c violet & yel	1.90	2.75
		Nos. 190-192 (3)	3.80	13.75

Commemorating Peace after World War I.

Nos. 151, 149, 162, 171-172, 133 Surcharged in Black, Red or Dark Blue

a

b

c

1921 Wmk. 183

193	A26(a)	2½c on 3c (Bl)	.25	1.10
a.		Tête bêche pair	1.10	*3.25*
b.		Inverted surcharge	800.00	*1,550.*
c.		Double surcharge	*550.00*	*775.00*
194	A26(a)	5c on 2c (R)	.25	*4.50*
a.		Double surcharge	*450.00*	*450.00*
195	A26(a)	5c on 7½c (R)	.25	.55
a.		Tête bêche pair	6.50	*55.00*
b.		Double surcharge	*550.00*	*550.00*
c.		5c on 7½c slate (II)	*2,200.*	*4,500.*
196	A28(b)	10c on 13c (R)	.25	*2.25*
a.		Double surcharge	*550.00*	*550.00*
197	A28(c)	20c on 15c (Bk)	.55	2.75
a.		Tête bêche pair	2.50	*55.00*
b.		Double surcharge	*875.00*	*875.00*
198	A28(c)	20c on 15c (Bl)	2.25	5.50
b.		Double surcharge	*875.00*	*875.00*
199	A25(c)	20c on 25c dp bl (R)	.25	.55
a.		Tête bêche pair	1.50	4.50
		Nos. 193-199 (7)	4.05	*17.20*

A36

1924 Typo. *Perf. 11½*
Granite Paper, Surface Colored

200	A36	90c grn & red, *grn*	15.00	2.75
201	A36	1.20fr brn rose & red, *rose*	5.25	5.25
202	A36	1.50fr bl & red, *bl*	37.50	6.50
203	A36	2fr gray blk & red, *gray*	47.50	6.75
		Nos. 200-203 (4)	105.25	21.25
		Set, never hinged	325.00	

1933 With Grilled Gum

200a	A36	90c	17.50	3.25
201a	A36	1.20fr	47.50	5.50
202a	A36	1.50fr	32.50	6.50
203a	A36	2fr	27.50	8.25
		Nos. 200a-203a (4)	125.00	23.50
		Set, never hinged	325.00	

For overprints see Nos. O16-O18, 2O31-2O34, 3O27-3O30.

1940 With Smooth Gum
Ordinary Paper

200b	A36	90c	16.00	*80.00*
201b	A36	1.20fr	16.00	*80.00*
202b	A36	1.50fr	16.00	*650.00*
		Nos. 200b-202b (3)	48.00	810.00
		Set, never hinged	120.00	

Building in Bern, Location of 1st
UPU Congress, 1874
A37   A38

1924, Oct. 9   Engr.   Wmk. 183
Granite Paper

204	A37	20c vermilion	.55	1.60
205	A38	30c dull blue	1.10	6.25
	Set, never hinged		3.25	

50th anniv. of the UPU.

Type of 1914 Issue

The
Rütli — A39

1928   Re-engraved   Perf. 11½

206	A39	5fr blue	110.00	9.75
	Never hinged		300.00	
a.	Imperf., pair, never hinged		10,000.	

In the re-engraved stamp the picture is clearer and lighter than on No. 183. "HELVE-TIA" is in smaller letters. The names at foot of the stamp are "Grasset-J. Sprenger" instead of "E. GRASSET-A. BURKHARD."
For overprints see Nos. 2O35, 3O31.

Nos. 155 and 163
Surcharged

1930, June   Perf. 11½

207	A26	3c on 2½c ol grn, *buff*	.25	2.75
208	A26	5c on 7½c dp grn, *buff*	.25	8.00
	Set, never hinged		1.10	

The Mythen
A40

1931   Engr.   Granite Paper

| 209 | A40 | 3fr orange brown | 65.00 | 5.25 |
| | Never hinged | | 150.00 | |

For overprints see Nos. 2O56, 3O47.

Dove on Broken
Sword — A41

"Peace"
A42

1932, Feb. 2   Typo.   Perf. 11½
Granite Paper

210	A41	5c peacock blue	.25	.25
211	A41	10c orange	.25	.25
212	A41	20c cerise	.25	.25
213	A41	30c ultra	2.25	1.60
214	A41	60c olive brown	17.50	8.75

Unwmk.
Photo.

215	A42	1fr olive gray & bl	17.50	8.75
	Nos. 210-215 (6)		38.00	19.85
	Set, never hinged		95.00	

Intl. Disarmament Conf., Geneva, Feb. 1932.
For overprints see #2O36-2O41, 3O32-3O37.

Louis   Alfred
Favre — A43   Escher — A44

Design: 30c, Emil Welti.

Wmk. 183
1932, May 31   Engr.   Perf. 11½
Granite Paper

216	A43	10c red brown	.25	.25
217	A44	20c vermilion	.25	.25
218	A44	30c deep ultra	.55	2.10
	Nos. 216-218 (3)		1.05	2.60
	Set, never hinged		3.00	

Completion of the St. Gotthard tunnel, 50th anniv.
Nos. 216-218 exist imperforate.

Staubbach   Mt. Pilatus
Falls   A47
A46

Chillon   Rhone
Castle   Glacier
A48   A49

St. Gotthard   Via Mala
Railroad   Gorge
A50   A51

Rhine Falls — A52

1934, July 2   Typo.   Perf. 11½
Granite Paper

219	A46	3c olive	.25	3.00
220	A47	5c emerald	.25	.25
221	A48	10c brt violet	.40	.25
222	A49	15c orange	.50	3.25
223	A50	20c red	.60	.60
224	A51	25c brown	7.75	8.25
225	A52	30c ultra	25.00	2.10
	Nos. 219-225 (7)		34.75	17.70
	Set, never hinged		100.00	

Tête bêche Pairs

220a	A47	5c		1.60	1.60
221a	A48	10c		1.50	.85
222a	A49	15c		1.75	3.00
223a	A50	20c		3.50	2.25

1934, Sept. 29   Souvenir Sheet

| 226 | Sheet of 4 | 500.00 | 550.00 |
| | Never hinged | 825.00 | |

No. 226 was issued in connection with the Swiss National Philatelic Exhibition at Zurich, Sept. 29 to Oct. 7, 1934. It contains one each of Nos. 220-223. Size: 62x72mm.
For overprints see Nos. 2O42-2O46, 3O48.

Staubbach
Falls
A53

Chillon
Castle
A55

St. Gotthard   Via Mala
Railroad   Gorge
A57   A58

Rhine   Balsthal
Falls — A59   Pass — A60

Alpine Lake of
Säntis — A61

Type I   Type II

Two types of 10c red violet:
I — Shading inside "0" of 10 has only vertical lines.
II — Shading in "0" includes two diagonal lines.

1936-42   Unwmk.   Engr.   Perf. 11½

227	A53	3c olive	.25	.25
228	A54	5c blue green	.25	.25
229	A55	10c red vio (II)	.85	.25
b.	Type I		.85	.25
230	A55	10c dk red brn ('39)	.25	.25
230B	A55	10c org brn ('42)	.25	.25
231	A56	15c orange	.40	1.10
232	A57	20c carmine	4.75	.25
233	A58	25c lt brown	.50	1.10
234	A59	30c ultra	.90	.25
235	A60	35c yellow grn	1.10	1.25
236	A61	40c gray	6.00	.25
	Nos. 227-236 (11)		15.50	5.45
	Set, never hinged		37.50	

Two types of the 20c. See Nos. 316-321.
For overprints see Nos. O1-O4, O6-O9, O19-O19-O22, O24-O27, 2O47-2O55, 2O68-2O68A, 2O70-2O73, 2O75-2O78, 3O38-3O46, 3O60-3O60A, 3O62-3O65, 3O67-3O70, 4O1-4O4, 4O6-4O9, 4O23-4O24, 4O27-4O28, 5O1-5O2, 5O5.

Tête bêche Pairs

228a	A54	5c blue green	.45	.30
229a	A55	10c red violet (II)	4.50	5.50
230a	A55	10c dark red brown	1.75	1.10
230d	A55	10c orange brown	.50	.60
232a	A57	20c carmine	25.00	35.00

1936-40   With Grilled Gum

227a	A53	3c olive	.65	6.25
228d	A54	5c blue green	.30	.25
229c	A55	10c red violet (II)	.30	.25
e.	Type I		1.00	.25
230e	A55	10c dk red brn ('40)	1.90	25.00
231a	A56	15c orange	.30	1.10
232c	A57	20c carmine	6.75	5.00
233a	A58	25c light brown	1.00	5.00
234a	A59	30c ultra	.95	.25

235a	A60	35c yellow green	1.40	3.25
236a	A61	40c gray	9.25	.50
	Nos. 227a-236a (10)		22.80	42.10
	Set, never hinged		47.50	

Mobile
Post Office
A62

1937, Sept. 5   Photo.
Granite Paper

| 237 | A62 | 10c black & yellow | .25 | .50 |
| | Never hinged | | .55 | |

No. 237 was sold exclusively by the traveling post office. It exists on two kinds of granite paper, black and red fibers or blue and red fibers. See No. 307 for type A62 redrawn.

View of
Labor
Building
from Lake
Geneva
A63

Palace of
League of
Nations
A64

Main
Building,
Palace of
League of
Nations
A65

Labor
Building
and Albert
Thomas
Monument
A66

1938, May 2   Perf. 11½
Granite Paper

238	A63	20c red & buff	.25	.25
239	A64	30c blue & lt blue	.45	.25
240	A65	60c brown & buff	1.75	2.25
241	A66	1fr black & buff	7.50	17.00
	Nos. 238-241 (4)		9.95	19.75
	Set, never hinged		25.00	

Opening of Assembly Hall of the Palace of the League of Nations.
For overprints see Nos. 2O57-2O64, 3O49-3O56.

Souvenir Sheet

A67

Engraved and Typographed

1938, Sept. 17 Unwmk. *Perf. 11½*

Granite Paper

242 A67	Sheet of 3	37.50	32.50
	Never hinged	70.00	
a.	AP4 10c on 65c gray bl & dp bl	19.00	*25.00*
b.	A68 20c red	1.10	*2.50*

Natl. Phil. Exhib. at Aarau, Sept. 17-25, and 25th anniv. of Swiss air mail. No. 242 contains 2 No. 243, but on granite paper, and a 10c on 65c similar to No. C22 but redrawn, with wing tips 1½mm from side frame lines; overall size 37x20½mm; no watermark.

On No. C22, wing tips touch frame lines; size is 36x21½mm; Wmk. 183.

Lake Lugano — A68

First Federal Pact, 1291 A69

Diet of Stans, 1481 A70

Citizens Voting A71

1938, Sept. 17 Engr. *Perf. 11½*

243 A68	20c red	.25	.25
a.	"c,"tête bêche pair	.50	*.85*
c.	Grilled gum	.40	*.40*
d.	As "c," tête bêche pair	1.40	*15.00*

Granite Paper

244 A69	3fr brn car, *grnsh*	11.00	8.75
245 A70	5fr slate bl, *grnsh*	7.50	6.00
246 A71	10fr grn, *grnsh*	47.50	35.00
	Nos. 243-246 (4)	66.25	50.00
	Set, never hinged	190.00	

No. 243 is printed on ordinary paper. Nos. 244-246 are on granite surface-colored paper. The greenish surface coating has faded on most examples.

For type A68 in orange brown, see No. 318.

See Nos. 242b, 284-286. For overprints see Nos. O5, O23, 2O65-2O67, 2O69, 2O74, 2O88-2O90, 3O57-3O59, 3O61, 3O66, 3O80-3O82, 4O5, 4O19-4O21, O4O25, 5O3, 5O23-5O25, 7O18-7O20.

Deputation of Trades and Professions — A72

Swiss Family A73

Alpine Scenery A74

Engr., Photo. (30c)

1939, Feb. 1 *Perf. 11½*

Inscribed in French

247 A72	10c dl pur & red	.25	.25
248 A73	20c lake & red	.50	.25
249 A74	30c dp blue & red	2.50	*3.00*

Inscribed in German

250 A72	10c dl pur & red	.25	.25
251 A73	20c lake & red	.40	.25
252 A74	30c dp blue & red	2.50	*8.25*

Inscribed in Italian

253 A72	10c dl pur & red	.25	.25
254 A73	20c lake & red	1.90	.25
255 A74	30c dp blue & red	2.50	*9.25*
	Nos. 247-255 (9)	11.05	*22.00*
	Set, never hinged	35.00	

National Exposition of 1939, Zurich.

Tree and Crossbow — A75

1939, May 6 Photo. *Perf. 11½*

Granite Paper

Inscribed in French

256 A75	5c deep green	.55	*1.60*
257 A75	10c gray brown	.55	*1.90*
258 A75	20c brt carmine	1.10	*1.60*
259 A75	30c violet blue	3.00	*8.00*

Inscribed in German

260 A75	5c deep green	.55	*2.50*
261 A75	10c gray brown	.55	*2.50*
262 A75	20c brt carmine	1.10	*3.50*
263 A75	30c violet blue	8.75	*9.50*

Inscribed in Italian

264 A75	5c deep green	.85	*4.50*
265 A75	10c gray brown	.55	*3.50*
266 A75	20c brt carmine	1.10	*4.25*
267 A75	30c violet blue	3.25	*11.00*
	Nos. 256-267 (12)	21.90	*54.35*
	Set, never hinged	32.50	

National Exposition of 1939.

The 5c, 10c and 20c stamps in the three languages exist se-tenant in coils. On the 10c coil stamp, the inscription "COURVOISIER S.A." beneath is design is smaller, with the "A" just left of the point on the "V" of "HELVETIA". On the sheet stamp, the "A" is just right of the "V". Value about three times that of the sheet stamp.

1939 With Grilled Gum

256a A75	5c	deep green	.75	*2.25*
257a A75	10c	gray brown	.75	*2.25*
258a A75	20c	bright carmine	1.90	*3.00*
260a A75	5c	deep green	.75	*1.60*
262a A75	20c	bright carmine	1.90	1.60
264a A75	5c	deep green	1.10	*3.75*
265a A75	10c	gray brown	1.00	*3.00*
266a A75	20c	bright carmine	1.90	*3.25*
		Nos. 256a-266a (8)	10.05	*20.70*

View of Geneva A76

Perf. 11½

1939, Aug. 22 Photo. Unwmk.

Granite Paper

268 A76	20c red, car & buff	.25	.25
269 A76	30c blue, car & gray	.30	*2.75*
	Set, never hinged	1.40	

75th anniv. of the founding of the Intl. Red Cross Society.

"The Three Swiss" — A77

William Tell — A78

Fighting Soldier — A79

Dying Warrior — A80

Standard Bearer — A81

Ludwig Pfyffer — A82

Jürg Jenatsch — A83

Francois de Reynold — A84

Joachim Forrer — A85

1941-59 Engr. *Perf. 11½*

Granite Paper

270 A77	50c dp pur, *grnsh*	4.25	.25
271 A78	60c red brn, *buff*	5.50	.25
272 A79	70c rose vio, *pale lil*	2.75	1.00
273 A80	80c blk, *pale gray*	1.10	.25
a.	80c black, *pale lilac* ('58)	.80	.50
274 A81	90c dk red, *pale rose*	1.00	.25
a.	90c dark red, *buff* ('59)	1.00	*1.25*
275 A82	1fr dk grn, *grnsh*	1.00	.25
276 A83	1.20fr red vio, *pale gray*	1.10	.25
a.	1.20fr red vio, *pale lil* ('58)	1.90	.75
277 A84	1.50fr dk bl, *buff*	1.50	.25
278 A85	2fr mar, *pale rose*	2.25	.25
a.	2fr maroon, *buff* ('59)	2.25	.50
	Nos. 270-278 (9)	20.45	3.00
	Set, never hinged	47.50	

For overprints see Nos. O28-O36, 2O79-2O87, 3O71-3O79, 4O10-4O18, 5O17-5O22, 6O6-6O8, 7O12-7O17.

Farmer Plowing A86

1941, Mar. 21 Photo.

Granite Paper

279 A86	10c brown & buff	.25	*.50*
	Never hinged	.25	

Natl. Agriculture Development Plan of 1941.

Masons, Knight and Bern Coat of Arms A87

1941, Sept. 6 Granite Paper

280 A87	10c multicolored	.25	*.75*
	Never hinged	.25	

750th anniversary of Bern.

"In order to Endure, Reclaim Used Materials" Inscribed in French A88

1942, Mar. 21 Unwmk. *Perf. 11½*

281 A88	10c shown	.35	*.50*
282 A88	10c German	.40	*1.00*
283 A88	10c Italian	6.25	4.00
	Nos. 281-283 (3)	7.00	5.50
	Set, never hinged	14.00	
	Sheet of 25	90.00	*550.00*

Printed in sheets of 25, containing 8 No. 281, 12 No. 282 and 5 No. 283.

Types of 1938

1955 Engr.

Cream-surfaced Granite Paper

284 A69	3fr brown car	7.00	.75
285 A70	5fr slate blue	5.00	.80
286 A71	10fr green	7.00	3.00
	Nos. 284-286 (3)	19.00	4.55
	Set, never hinged	27.50	

1942 Cream paper

284a A69	3fr	22.50	.50
285a A70	5fr	10.00	.50
286a A71	10fr	32.50	2.00
	Nos. 284a-286a (3)	65.00	3.00
	Set, never hinged	160.00	

The 1955 set is on cream-surfaced granite paper with white back, and blue and red fibers. The 1942 set is on colored-through cream paper with black and red fibers.

Zurich Stamps of 1843 A91

1943, Feb. 26

287 A91	10c blk & salmon	.25	.25
	Never hinged	.25	

Centenary of postage stamps of Switzerland. See Nos. B130-B131.

Apollo Statue — A94

1944, Mar. 21 Photo.

Granite Paper

290 A94	10c org yel & gray blk	.25	*1.00*
291 A94	20c cer & gray blk	.30	*1.00*
292 A94	30c lt bl & gray blk	.60	*6.00*
	Nos. 290-292 (3)	1.15	*8.00*
	Set, never hinged	2.50	

Olympic Jubilee.

Numeral of Value — A95

Olive Branch A96

Field of Crocus A97

Aged Couple A98

Designs: 60c, Keys of peace. 80c, Horn of plenty. 1fr, Dove of peace. 2fr, Plowing. 5fr, Clasped hands.

1945, May 9   Unwmk.   Perf. 12
Granite Paper

293	A95	5c gray & green	.25	.50
294	A95	10c gray & brown	.25	.25
295	A95	20c gray & car rose	.35	.25
296	A95	30c gray & ultra	.70	3.00
297	A95	40c gray & orange	2.00	10.00
298	A96	50c dark red	2.75	19.00
299	A96	60c dull gray	2.75	6.75
300	A96	80c slate green	6.25	85.00
301	A96	1fr blue	8.75	95.00
302	A96	2fr red brown	22.50	160.00

Engr.

303	A97	3fr dk sl grn, buff	30.00	65.00
304	A98	5fr brn lake, buff	100.00	325.00
305	A98	10fr rose vio, buff	110.00	125.00
		Nos. 293-305,B145 (14)	286.85	895.50
		Set, never hinged	525.00	

End of war in Europe.

Johann Heinrich Pestalozzi — A104

1946, Jan. 12   Engr.   Perf. 11½
306	A104	10c rose violet	.25	.25
		Never hinged		.25

200th anniversary of the birth of J. H. Pestalozzi, educational reformer.
For overprint see No. 4O22.

Mobile P.O. Type of 1937
Redrawn

1946, July 6   Photo.
Granite Paper
307	A62	10c black & yellow	1.10	.25
		Never hinged		3.00

The designer's and printer's names are larger on the redrawn stamp. There are many minor differences in the two designs. Sizes: 1937, 37½x21mm. 1946, 38x22½mm.

First Swiss Steam Locomotive — A105

Modern Steam Locomotive — A106

Electric Gotthard Express A107

Electric Trains Passing on Bridge A108

1947, Aug. 6   Photo.   Perf. 11½
Granite Paper
308	A105	5c dk grn, blk & yel	.40	.50
309	A106	10c dk brn, gray & blk	.40	.50
310	A107	20c dk red & red	.35	.50
311	A108	30c dk bl & bl gray	.90	1.75
		Nos. 308-311 (4)	2.05	3.25
		Set, never hinged	5.00	

Centenary of the opening of the first Swiss railroad, between Zurich and Baden.

Johann Rudolf Wettstein A109

Castle at Neuchatel A110

"Helvetia" A111

Symbol of Swiss Federal State A112

1948, Feb. 27   Granite Paper
312	A109	5c dp grn	.25	.50
313	A110	10c gray blk	.25	.25
314	A111	20c dk red	.30	.25
315	A112	30c dk bl & red	.45	1.25
		Nos. 312-315 (4)	1.25	2.25
		Set, never hinged	2.00	

Tercentenary of the acknowledgement of independence of the Swiss Confederation, and the centenaries of the Neuchatel Revolution and the Swiss Federal State.
See Nos. B178a and B178b for 10c and 20c denominations, type A109.

Types of 1936-42 and

Grisons National Park — A113

1948, Mar. 1   Engr.
316	A54	5c chocolate	.25	.25
a.		Tête bêche pair	1.25	1.25
317	A55	10c green	.25	.25
a.		Tête bêche pair	1.25	1.50
318	A68	20c org brn	.30	.25
a.		Tête bêche pair	1.65	2.25
319	A113	25c carmine	1.50	1.50
320	A59	30c grnsh bl	6.25	4.00
321	A61	40c ultra	11.00	.75
		Nos. 316-321 (6)	19.55	7.00
		Set, never hinged	42.50	

For overprints see Nos. 4O26, 5O4.

Figures Encircling Globe A114

Designs: 25c, Globe and inscribed ribbon. 40c, Globe and pigeons.

Perf. 11½
1949, May 16   Photo.   Unwmk.
322	A114	10c green	.25	.25
323	A114	25c dark red	.40	6.25
324	A114	40c brt blue	.60	4.00
		Nos. 322-324 (3)	1.25	10.50
		Set, never hinged	2.00	

75th anniv. of the UPU.

Post Horn A115

Horse Drawn Mail Coach A116

Design: 30c, Post bus with trailer.

1949, May 16
325	A115	5c gray, yel & pink	.25	.50
326	A116	20c pur, gray & yel	.25	.30
327	A116	30c dk org brn, gray & yel	.45	6.75
		Nos. 325-327 (3)	.95	7.55
		Set, never hinged	1.50	

Centenary of the establishment of the Federal Post in Switzerland.

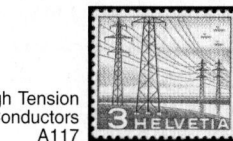

High Tension Conductors A117

Viaducts — A118

Mountain Railway — A119

Rotary Snow Plow — A120

Reservoir, Grimsel — A121

Lake Dam — A122

Dam and Power Station — A123

Alpine Postal Road — A124

Harbor of the Rhine — A125

Suspension Railway — A126

Railway Viaduct — A127

Triangulation Point — A128

Two types of 20c:
Type I — Three solid lines above curved rock.
Type II — Two solid lines above rock.

Perf. 12x11½
1949, Aug. 1   Engr.   Unwmk.
328	A117	3c gray	1.50	4.00
329	A118	5c orange	.25	.25
a.		Tête bêche pair	.90	.25
330	A119	10c yel grn	.25	.25
a.		Tête bêche pair	.60	.25
331	A120	15c aqua	.25	.50
332	A121	20c brown car (II)	.30	.25
a.		Tête bêche pair	1.75	.75
c.		Type I	2,000.	67.50
		Type I, never hinged	3,750.	
333	A122	25c red	.25	.25
334	A123	30c olive	.25	.25
335	A124	35c red brown	.45	.60
336	A125	40c deep blue	1.40	.25
337	A126	50c slate gray	1.40	.25
338	A127	60c blue green	4.00	.50
339	A128	70c purple	1.10	.30
		Nos. 328-339 (12)	11.40	7.65
		Set, never hinged	22.50	

For use in vending machines, some printings of the 5c, 10c, 20c (II), 25c, 30c and 40c carry a control number on the back of every fifth stamp. The number was applied on top of the gum.
For overprints see Nos. O37-O47, 3O83-3O93, 4O29-4O39, 5O6-5O16, 6O1-6O5, 7O1-7O11.

Symbolical of the Telegraph — A129

10c, Telephone. 20c, Radio. 40c, Television.

1952, Feb. 1   Photo.   Perf. 11½
340	A129	5c org & yel	.25	.50
341	A129	10c brt grn & pink	.30	.25
342	A129	20c dp red lil & gray bl	.45	.25
343	A129	40c dp bl & lt bl	1.40	4.75
		Nos. 340-343 (4)	2.40	5.75
		Set, never hinged	5.25	

"A century of telecommunications."

Zurich Airport and Tail of Plane A130

1953, Aug. 29
344	A130	40c blue, red & gray	3.25	10.50
		Never hinged		5.50

Opening of Zurich-Kloten airport.

Alpine Post Bus, Winter Background — A131

Design: 20c, Same, summer background.

1953, Oct. 8

345 A131 10c dk grn, grn & yel .25 .25
346 A131 20c dk red, red brn & yel .30 .25
Set, never hinged 1.00

Sold only on Swiss alpine post buses.

Symbols of Agriculture, Forestry and Horticulture — A132

Map and Nautical Emblems — A133

20c, Winged spoon. 40c, Football and map.

1954, Mar. 15 ***Perf. 11½***

347 A132 10c multicolored .25 .25
348 A132 20c multicolored .40 .25
349 A133 25c red, dk ol grn & gray 1.00 *3.00*
350 A132 40c bl, yel & brn 1.60 *3.50*
Nos. 347-350 (4) 3.25 *7.00*
Set, never hinged 6.00

Nos. 347-348 were issued to publicize exhibitions at Lucerne and Bern; No. 349, fifty years of navigation on the Rhine; No. 350, the 1954 World Soccer Championships in Switzerland.

Lausanne Cathedral A134

Alphorn Blower — A135

Designs: 10c, Vaud costume hat. 40c, Automobile steering wheel.

1955, Feb. 15 ***Perf. 11½***

351 A134 5c multi .25 *.60*
352 A134 10c grn, yel & red .25 *.50*
a. Souvenir sheet of 2 60.00 *80.00*
Never hinged 90.00
353 A135 20c red & sepia .55 .50
354 A134 40c bl, pink & gray 1.25 *2.10*
Nos. 351-354 (4) 2.30 *3.70*
Set, never hinged 5.50

No. 352a contains 10c and 20c multicolored, imperf. stamps of Cathedral type A134. Size: 104x52mm.

National Philatelic Exhibition (5c, #352a), Winegrowers' Festival (10c), Alpine Herdsman and Costume Festival (20c) and 25th Intl. Automobile Show (40c).

First Swiss Post Bus — A136

10c, North Gate of Simplon Tunnel and Stockalper Palace. 20c, Children crossing street and road signs. 40c, Planes and emblem of Swissair, vert.

1956, Mar. 1 **Photo.**

Granite Paper

355 A136 5c ol gray, blk & yel .25 *.50*
356 A136 10c brt grn, gray & red .25 .25
357 A136 20c multi .45 *.50*
358 A136 40c blue & red 1.00 *1.40*
Nos. 355-358 (4) 1.95 *2.65*
Set, never hinged 4.50

50th anniv. of the Swiss Motor Coach Service (#355); 50th anniv. of the opening of Simplon Tunnel (#356); Accident prevention (#357); 25th anniv. of the founding of Swissair (#358).

Inking Device, Printing Machine A137

Type I

10c, Train on southern ramp of Gotthard Railroad. 20c, Shield of civil defense and coat of arms. 40c, Munatius Plancus and view of Basel.

Two types of 10c:
I — "Black" bottom line on train.
II — Brown bottom line.

1957, Feb. 27 ***Perf. 11½***

Granite Paper

359 A137 5c multicolored .25 .25
360 A137 10c lt bl grn, dk grn & red brn (I) 1.10 .25
a. Type II 1.00 .50
361 A137 20c red org & gray .25 *.50*
362 A137 40c multi .75 *1.25*
Nos. 359-362 (4) 2.35 *2.25*
Set, never hinged 4.50

Intl. Exhibition for Graphic Arts, Lausanne, June 1-16, 1957 (#359). 75th anniv. of St. Gotthard railroad (#360). Civil defense (#361). 2000th anniv. of Basel (#362).

Rope and Symbol of European Unity — A138

1957, July 15 **Engr.** ***Perf. 11½***

363 A138 25c lt red .50 .35
364 A138 40c blue .80 .35
Set, never hinged *4.50*

Issued to emphasize European unity.

Catalogue values for unused stamps in this section, from this point to the end of the section, are for Never Hinged items.

Nyon Castle and Corinthian Capital A139

Designs: 10c, Woman's head and ribbons in Swiss colors. 20c, Crossbow emblem. 40c, Salvation Army hat.

1958, Mar. 5 **Photo.** **Unwmk.**

Granite Paper

365 A139 5c ol bis & dl pur .25 .25
366 A139 10c grn, dk grn & red .25 .25
367 A139 20c ver, lil & car .50 .25
368 A139 40c multicolored 1.40 1.25
Nos. 365-368 (4) 2.40 2.00

2000th anniv. of Nyon (#365). Saffa Exhibition, Zurich, July 17-Sept. 15 (#366). 25th anniv. of Swiss manufacturing emblem (#367). 75th anniv. of the Salvation Army in Switzerland (#368).

Symbol of Nuclear Fission A140

1958, Aug. 25 ***Perf. 11½***

Granite Paper

369 A140 40c blue, yel & red .60 .60

2nd UN Atomic Conf. for peaceful uses of atomic power, Geneva, Sept. 1958.

"Transportation" — A141

Designs: 10c, Fasces and post horn. 20c, Owl, rabbit and fish. 50c, Jean Calvin, Theodore de Beze and University of Geneva.

1959, Mar. 9 **Photo.** **Unwmk.**

Granite Paper

370 A141 5c multicolored .25 .25
371 A141 10c emer, yel & lt gray .30 .25
a. Souvenir sheet of 2, imperf. 14.00 14.00
372 A141 20c multicolored .60 .25
373 A141 50c multicolored 1.25 .75
Nos. 370-373 (4) 2.40 1.50

Opening of the Swiss House of Transport and Communications (5c). Natl. Phil. Exhib., St. Gall, Aug. 21-30 (10c and #371a). Protection of animals (20c). 400th anniv. of the University of Geneva (50c).

No. 371a contains a 10c green, gold and light gray and a 20c deep carmine. Sold for 2fr; the money went for the St. Gall Phil. Exhib.

Chain Symbolizing European Unity — A142

1959, June 22 **Engr.** ***Perf. 11½***

374 A142 30c brick red *1.60* .30
375 A142 50c lt ultra *2.75* .45

Issued to emphasize European Unity.

Overprinted "REUNION DES PTT D'EUROPE 1959" in Ultramarine or Red

1959, June 22

376 A142 30c brick red *37.50 6.50*
377 A142 50c lt ultra *37.50 6.50*

European Conference of PTT Administrations, Montreux, June 22-July 31. Nos. 376-377 were on sale only during the conference at a special P. O. in Montreux.

"Cancer Control" A143

Designs: 20c, Founding charter and scepter of University of Basel. 50c, Uprooted Oak Emblem. 75c, Swissair Jet DC-8.

1960, Apr. 7 **Photo.** ***Perf. 11½***

Granite Paper

378 A143 10c brt grn & red .55 .25
379 A143 20c car rose, gray blk & yel .55 .25
380 A143 50c ultra & yel .75 1.25
381 A143 75c lt bl, gray & red 3.50 4.00
Nos. 378-381 (4) 5.35 5.75

50th anniv. of the Swiss League for Cancer Control (10c). 500th anniv. of the University of Basel (20c). World Refugee Year, July 1, 1959-June 30, 1960 (50c). Swissair's entry into the jet age (75c).

Messenger, Fribourg A144

Cathedral, Lausanne A145

Designs: 10c, Messenger, Schwyz. 15c, Messenger and pack animal. 20c, Postilion on horseback. 30c, Grossmünster (church), Zürich. 35c, 1.30fr, Woodcutters' Guildhall, Biel. 40c, Cathedral, Geneva. 50c, Spalen Gate, Basel. 60c, Clock Tower, Berne. 70c, 2.80fr, Sts. Peter and Stephen Church, Bellinzona (tower omitted on 2.80fr). 75c, Bridge and water tower, Lucerne. 80c, Cathedral, St. Gallen. 90c, Munot tower, Schaffhausen. 1fr, Townhall, Fribourg. 1.20fr, Basel gate, Solothurn. 1.50fr, Reding house, Schwyz. 1.70fr, 2fr, 2.20fr, Church, Einsiedeln.

Two types of 5c, 10c, 20c, 50c:
5 Centimes:
Type I — Four lines on pike at left of hand.
Type II — Three lines.
10 Centimes:
Type I — Dot on pike below head.
Type II — No dot.
20 Centimes:
Type I — Ten dots on horiz. harness strip.
Type II — Nine dots.
50 Centimes:
Type I — 3 shading lines at right above arch.
Type II — 2 shading lines.

1960-63 **Engr.** ***Perf. 11½***

1.30fr, 1.70fr, 2.20fr, 2.80fr on Granite Paper, Red and Blue Fibers

382 A144 5c lt ultra (I) .25 .25
c. Tête bêche pair .25 .25
383 A144 10c blue grn (I) .25 .25
c. Tête bêche pair .40 .25
384 A144 15c lt red brn .25 .25
385 A144 20c rose pink (I) .30 .25
c. Tête bêche pair .90 .45
386 A145 25c emerald .35 .25
387 A145 30c vermilion .45 .25
388 A145 35c orange red .50 .30
389 A145 40c lilac .60 .25
390 A145 50c lt vio bl (I) .75 .25
c. Tête bêche pair 2.75 2.75
391 A145 60c rose red .90 .25
392 A145 70c orange 1.10 .40
393 A145 75c lt blue 1.20 .25
394 A145 80c dp claret 1.25 .25
395 A145 90c olive green 1.30 .25
396 A144 1fr dull orange 1.50 .25
397 A144 1.20fr dull red 1.75 .30
397A A145 1.30fr red brn, *pink* ('63) 1.90 .25
398 A144 1.50fr brt green 2.25 .50
398A A144 1.70fr rose lil, *pink* ('63) 2.50 .25
399 A144 2fr brt blue 3.25 .50
399A A144 2.20fr bl grn, *grn* ('63) 3.25 .50
399B A145 2.80fr org, *buff* ('63) 3.75 .40
Nos. 382-399B (22) 29.60 6.65

See Nos. 440-455.

1963-76

Violet Fibers, Fluorescent Paper

382d A144 5c lt ultra (I) .25 .25
g. Tête bêche pair ('68) .25 .25
383d A144 10c bl grn (I) .25 .25
e. Bklt. pane of 2 + 2 labels ('68) .65 .65
g. Tête bêche pair ('68) .35 .25
384a A144 15c lt red brn .55 .55
385d A144 20c rose pink (I) .30 .25
g. Tête bêche pair ('68) .70 .45
386a A145 25c emerald .35 .25
387a A145 30c vermilion .35 .25
c. Tête bêche pair ('68) 1.00 .75
389a A145 40c lilac ('67) .55 .35
c. Tête bêche pair ('76) 1.25 1.10
390d A145 50c lt vio bl (I) .75 .25
391a A145 60c rose red ('67) .80 .30
393a A145 75c lt blue ('68) 1.25 .45
394a A145 80c dp claret 1.00 .25
395a A145 90c olive grn ('67) 1.00 .25
396a A144 1fr dull org ('67) 2.00 .25
397b A144 1.20fr dl red ('68) 3.00 1.75
398b A144 1.50fr brt green ('68) 3.00 1.75
Nos. 382d-398b (15) 15.40 7.40

Coil Stamps

1960 **White Paper**

382b A144 5c lt ultra (II) 1.40 1.40
383b A144 10c blue grn (II) .85 .85
385b A144 20c rose pink (II) .85 .85
390b A145 50c lt vio bl (II) 4.00 4.00
Nos. 382b-390b (4) 7.10 7.10

The coil stamps were printed in sheets (available to collectors) and pasted into coils. Every fifth stamp has a control number on the back.

Other denominations issued in coils on white paper are: 40c, 60c, 90c, 1fr, 1.30fr, 1.70fr, 2.20fr and 2.80fr.

Denominations issued in coils on granite paper (red & blue fibers) are: 1.30fr, 1.70fr, 2.20fr and 2.80fr.

Violet Fibers, Fluorescent Paper

1965-68 Coil Stamps

382e	A144	5c lt ultra (II)	1.25	1.25
383h	A144	10c blue grn (II)	.60	.30
385e	A144	20c rose pink (II)	.60	.30
390e	A145	50c lt vio bl (II)	4.00	4.00
		Nos. 382e-390e (4)	6.45	5.85

Other denominations issued in coils on violet-fiber paper are: 40c, 60c, 90c and 1fr.

Common Design Types pictured following the introduction.

Europa Issue
Common Design Type

1960, Sept. 19 Unwmk. *Perf. 11½*
Size: 33x23mm

400	CD3	30c vermilion	.50	.25
401	CD3	50c ultra	.75	.40

Wall under Construction and Globe — A146

Designs: 10c, Symbolic sun (HYSPA Emblem). 20c, Ice hockey stick and puck. 50c, Wiring diagram on map of Switzerland.

1961, Feb. 20 Photo. *Perf. 11½*
Granite Paper

402	A146	5c gray, brick red & grnsh bl	.35	.25
403	A146	10c aqua & yel	.35	.25
404	A146	20c multicolored	1.50	.60
405	A146	50c ultra, gray & car rose	1.25	1.00
		Nos. 402-405 (4)	3.45	2.10

Development aid to new nations (5c). HYSPA 1961, Health and Sports Exhibition, Bern, May 18-July 17 (10c). Intl. Ice Hockey Championships, Lausanne and Geneva, Mar. 2-12 (20c). Fully automatic Swiss telephone service (50c).

St. Matthew and Angel — A147

Evangelists: 5fr, St. Mark and winged lion. 10fr, St. Luke and winged ox. 20fr, St. John and eagle.

Perf. 11½
1961, Sept. 18 Unwmk. Engr.
Granite Paper

406	A147	3fr rose carmine	4.00	.25
407	A147	5fr dark blue	6.50	.25
408	A147	10fr dark brown	8.25	.45
409	A147	20fr red	20.00	3.00
		Nos. 406-409 (4)	38.75	3.95

Designs are after 15th century wood carvings from St. Oswald's church, Zug.

Europa Issue
Common Design Type

1961, Sept. 18 Size: 26x21mm

410	CD4	30c vermilion	.50	.25
411	CD4	50c blue	.75	.35

Trans-Europe Express A148

10c, Rower. 20c, Jungfrau railroad station and Mönch. 50c, WHO Anti-malaria emblem.

1962, Mar. 19 Photo. *Perf. 11½*

412	A148	5c multicolored	.50	.25
413	A148	10c brt grn, lem & lil	.45	.25
414	A148	20c rose lil, pale bl & bis	.90	.25
415	A148	50c ultra, lt grn & rose lil	.90	.60
		Nos. 412-415 (4)	2.75	1.35

Introduction of Swiss electric TEE trains (5c). Rowing world championship, Lucerne, Sept. 6-9 (10c). 50th anniv. of the railroad station on the Jungfrau mountain (20c). WHO Anti-Malaria campaign (50c).

Europa Issue
Common Design Type

1962, Sept. 17 Unwmk. *Perf. 11½*
Size: 33x23mm

416	CD5	30c orange, yel & brn	.65	.40
417	CD5	50c ultra, lt grn & brn	1.00	.60

Boy Scout — A149

Designs: 10c, Swiss Alpine Club emblem. 20c, Luegelkinn viaduct. 30c, Wheat Emblem. No. 426, 428a, Red Cross Jubilee Emblem. No. 427, Post Office Building, Paris, 1863.

1963, Mar. 21 Photo.

422	A149	5c gray, dk red & brn	.55	.25
423	A149	10c dk grn, gray & red	.40	.25
424	A149	20c dk car, brn & gray	1.10	.25
425	A149	30c yel grn, yel & org	1.60	1.60
426	A149	50c blue, sil & red	.85	.80
427	A149	50c ultra, pink, yel & gray	.90	.75
		Nos. 422-427 (6)	5.40	3.90

Souvenir Sheet
Imperf

428		Sheet of 4	7.00	6.00
a.		A149 50c bl, lt bl, sil & red	1.75	1.25

50 years of Swiss Boy Scouts (5c). Cent. of Swiss Alpine Club (10c). 50 years Lötschberg Railroad (20c). FAO "Freedom from Hunger" campaign (30c). Red Cross Cent. (#426, 428). 1st Intl. Postal Conf., Paris 1863 (#427).

No. 428 sold for 3fr.

Europa Issue
Common Design Type

1963, Sept. 16 Unwmk. *Perf. 11½*
Granite Paper
Size: 26x21mm

429	CD6	50c ultra & ocher	.90	.60

EXPO Emblem A150

50c, EXPO emblem on globe & moon ("Outlook"). 75c, EXPO emblem on globe ("Insight").

1963, Sept. 16 Unwmk. *Perf. 11½*
Granite Paper

430	A150	10c brt grn & dk grn	.30	.25
431	A150	20c red & maroon	.35	.25
432	A150	50c ultra & red	.65	.40
433	A150	75c purple & red	1.00	.45
		Nos. 430-433 (4)	2.30	1.35

Issued to publicize the Swiss National Exhibition, Lausanne, Apr. 30-Oct. 25, 1964.

Road Tunnel Through Great St. Bernard A151

10c, Symbolic water god & waves. 20c, Soldiers of 1864 & 1964. 50c, Standards of Swiss Confederation & Geneva.

1964, Mar. 9 Photo.
Granite Paper

434	A151	5c ol, ultra & red	.25	.25
435	A151	10c Prus bl & grn	.25	.25
436	A151	20c red, ultra, blk & sal	.45	.25
437	A151	50c ultra, red, yel & blk	1.15	.65
		Nos. 434-437 (4)	2.10	1.40

1st Trans-Alpine Automobile route from Switzerland to Italy (5c). "Pro Aqua" water conservation campaign (10c). Centenary of the Swiss Noncommissioned Officers' Association (20c). Sesqui. of union of Geneva with Swiss Confederation (50c).

Europa Issue
Common Design Type

1964, Sept. 14 Engr. *Perf. 11½*
Size: 21x26mm
Violet Fibers, Fluorescent Paper

438	CD7	20c vermilion	*.45*	.25
439	CD7	50c ultra	*1.15*	.25

Type of Regular Issue, 1960-63

Designs: 5c, Lenzburg. 10c, Freuler Mansion, Näfels. 15c, St. Mauritius Church, Appenzell. 20c, Planta House, Samedan. 30c, Gabled houses, Gais. 50c, Castle and Abbey Church, Neuchâtel. 70c, Lussy House, Wolfenschiessen. 1fr, Santa Croce Church, Riva San Vitale. 1.20fr, Abbey Church, Payerne. 1.30fr, Church of St. Pierre de Clages. 1.50fr, La Porte de France, Porrentruy. 1.70fr, Frauenfeld Castle. 2fr, A Pro Castle, Seedorf. 2.20fr, Thomas Tower and Gate. Liestal. 2.50fr, St. Oswald's Church, Zug. 3.50fr, Benedictine Abbey, Engelberg.

1964-68 Engr. *Perf. 11½*
Violet Fibers, Fluorescent Paper

440	A144	5c car rose ('68)	.25	.25
441	A144	10c violet bl ('68)	.25	.25
b.		Tête bêche pair	.55	.55
c.		Booklet pane of 2 + 2 labels	.70	
442	A144	15c brown red ('68)	.35	.25
b.		Tête bêche pair	.80	.80
443	A144	20c blue grn ('68)	.45	.25
b.		Tête bêche pair	1.10	1.10
444	A144	30c vermilion ('68)	.70	.25
b.		Tête bêche pair	1.60	1.60
445	A144	50c ultra ('68)	1.15	.25
446	A145	70c brown ('67)	1.60	.25
447	A145	1fr dk green ('68)	2.25	.25
448	A145	1.20fr brown red ('68)	2.75	.25
449	A145	1.30fr violet bl ('66)	3.00	.75
450	A145	1.50fr green ('68)	3.50	.40
451	A145	1.70fr brown org ('66)	4.00	1.25
452	A145	2fr orange ('67)	4.50	.40
453	A145	2.20fr green	5.00	.80
454	A145	2.50fr Prus grn ('67)	5.75	.55
455	A145	3.50fr purple ('67)	8.00	.60
		Nos. 440-455 (16)	43.50	7.00

The 15c was issued in coils in 1972 (?) with control number on the back of every fifth stamp.

Nurse and Patient A152

Seated Helvetia, 1854 — A153

Women's Army Auxiliary A154

Intercontinental Communications Map — A155

1965, Mar. 8 Photo. *Perf. 11½*
Violet Fibers, Fluorescent Paper

462	A152	5c lt ultra & red	.25	.25
463	A153	10c emer, brn & blk	.25	.25
464	A154	20c red & multi	.45	.25

Granite Paper, Red and Blue Fibers

465	A155	50c dl bl grn & mar	1.15	.50
		Nos. 462-465 (4)	2.10	1.25

Nursing and auxiliary medical professions (5c). Natl. Postage Stamp Exhibition, NABRA, Bern, Aug. 27-Sept. 5, 1965 (10c). 20th anniv. of Women's Army Auxiliary Corps (20c). Cent. of ITU (50c).

See No. B344.

Swiss Arms, Cantonal Emblems of Valais, Neuchatel, Geneva A156

1965, June 1 Unwmk. *Perf. 11½*
Granite Paper, Red and Blue Fibers

466	A156	20c multicolored	.45	.25

150th anniversary of the entry of the cantons of Valais, Neuchatel and Geneva in the Swiss Confederation.

Matterhorn A157

30c, like 10c but inscribed in French "Cervin."

1965, June 1 Photo.
Granite Paper, Red and Blue Fibers

467	A157	10c grn, slate & dk red	.25	.25

Violet Fibers, Fluorescent Paper

468	A157	30c dk red, grn & slate	.70	.40

Year of the Alps; the cent. of the 1st winter-time visitors to the Alps and cent. of the 1st ascent of the Matterhorn. Nos. 467-468 on sale only at Swiss Alpine post buses.

Europa Issue
Common Design Type

1965, Sept. 14 Unwmk. *Perf. 11½*
Violet Fibers, Fluorescent Paper

469	CD8	50c bl, dk bl & grn	1.15	.25

Figure Skating A159

1965, Sept. 14 Photo.
Violet Fibers, Fluorescent Paper

470	A159	5c grn, dl bl & blk	.25	.25

Issued to publicize the World Figure Skating Championships, Davos, Feb. 22-27, 1966.

ITU Emblem and Atom Diagram A160

Cent. of the ITU: 30c, Symbol of communications, waves.

1965, Sept. 14
Violet Fibers, Fluorescent Paper

471	A160	10c ultra & multi	.25	.25

Granite Paper, Red and Blue Fibers

472	A160	30c org, red & gray	.70	.40

Violet Fibers, Fluorescent Paper
Paper from No. 473 onward is fluorescent and has violet fibers, unless otherwise noted.

European Kingfisher A161

Mercury's Helmet and Laurel A162

Flags of 13 Member Nations and Nuclear Fission A163

1966, Feb. 21   **Photo.**
473 A161 10c emer & multi   .25 .25
474 A162 20c dp mag, red & brt grn   .45 .25
475 A163 50c slate blue & multi   1.15 .40
    Nos. 473-475 (3)   1.85 .90

Intl. Cong. for Conservation "Pro Natura," Lucerne (10c). 50th anniv. of Swiss Trade Fair, Basel, Apr. 16-26 (20c). European Organization for Nuclear Research, CERN (50c).

Emblem of Society of Swiss Abroad — A164

1966, June 1   **Photo.**   **Perf. 11½**
476 A164 20c ultra & ver   .45 .25

50th anniv. of the Society of Swiss Abroad.

Europa Issue
Common Design Type
1966, Sept. 26   **Engr.**   **Perf. 11½**
          Size: 21x26mm
477 CD9 20c vermilion   .45 .25
478 CD9 50c ultra   1.15 .35

Finsteraarhorn — A165

1966, Sept. 26   **Photo.**
479 A165 10c lt grnsh bl, dk bl & dk red   .30 .25

Automobile Wheels and White Cane — A166

Flags of EFTA Members A167

1967, Mar. 13   **Photo.**   **Perf. 11½**
480 A166 10c bl grn, blk & yel   .25 .25
481 A167 20c multicolored   .45 .25

No. 480 issued to publicize the white cane as a distinguishing mark for blind pedestrians. No. 481 publicizes the European Free Trade Association, EFTA. See note after Norway No. 501.

Europa Issue
Common Design Type
1967, Mar. 13   **Engr.**
482 CD10 30c blue gray   .70 .25

Cogwheel and Swiss Emblem A169

Hourglass and Sun — A170

San Bernardino, from North — A171

Railroad Wheel A172

1967, Sept. 18   **Photo.**   **Perf. 11½**
483 A169 10c multicolored   .25 .25
484 A170 20c red, yel & blk   .45 .25
485 A171 30c multicolored   .70 .25
486 A172 50c multicolored   1.15 .50
    Nos. 483-486 (4)   2.55 1.25

50th anniv. of Swiss Week (10c). 50th anniv. of the Foundation for the Aged (20c). Opening of the San Bernardino Road Tunnel (30c). 75th anniv. of the Central Office for Intl. Railroad Transportation (50c).

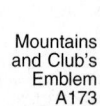 

Mountains and Club's Emblem A173

Golden Key with CEPT Emblem A174

Rook and Chessboard A175

Aircraft Tail and Satellites A176

1968, Mar. 14   **Photo.**   **Perf. 11½**
487 A173 10c grn, lt ultra & red   .25 .25
488 A174 20c Prus bl, yel & brn   .45 .25
489 A175 30c dk ol bis & vio bl   .70 .25
490 A176 50c dk blue & red   1.15 .35
    Nos. 487-490 (4)   2.55 1.10

50th anniv. of the Swiss Women's Alpine Club (10c). A unified Europe through postal cooperation (20c). 18th Chess Olympics, Lugano, Oct. 17-Nov. 6 (30c). Inauguration of the new Geneva-Cointrin Air Terminal (50c).

Worker's Protective Helmet A177

Double Geneva and Zurich Stamps of 1843 — A178

Map Showing Systematic Planning A179

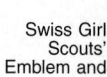 

Flag of Rhine Navigation Committee A180

1968, Sept. 12   **Photo.**   **Perf. 11½**
491 A177 10c bl grn & yel   .25 .25
492 A178 20c dp car, blk & yel grn   .45 .25
493 A179 30c multicolored   .70 .25
494 A180 50c bl, yel & blk   1.15 .50
    Nos. 491-494 (4)   2.55 1.25

50th anniv. of the Swiss Accident Insurance comp., SUVA (10c). 125th anniv. of 1st Swiss postage stamps (20c). 25th anniv. of the Swiss Society for Territorial Planning (30c). Cent. of the Rhine Navigation Act (50c).

Swiss Girl Scouts' Emblem and Camp — A181

Pegasus Constellation A182

Comptoir Suisse Emblem and Beaulieu Building, Lausanne A183

Swissair DC-8 and DH-3 — A185

Gymnaestrada Emblem (Man in Circle) — A184

1969, Feb. 12   **Photo.**   **Perf. 11½**
495 A181 10c multicolored   .25 .25
496 A182 20c dark blue   .45 .25
497 A183 30c red, ocher, grn & gray   .70 .25

498 A184 50c vio bl, bl, red, grn & sil   1.15 .50
499 A185 2fr bl, dk bl & red   4.50 2.00
    Nos. 495-499 (5)   7.05 3.25

50th anniv. of Swiss Girl Scouts (10c). Opening of 1st Swiss Planetarium, Lucerne, July 1 (20c). 50th anniv. of the Comptoir Suisse (trade fair, 30c). 5th Gymnaestrada (gymnastic meet), Basel, July 1-5 (50c). 50th anniv. of Swiss airmail service (2fr).

Europa Issue
Common Design Type
1969, Apr. 28   **Size: 32½x23mm**
500 CD12 30c brn org & multi   .70 .25
501 CD12 50c chlky bl & multi   1.15 .35

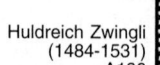 

Huldreich Zwingli (1484-1531) — A186

Famous Swiss: 20c, Gen. Henri Guisan (1874-1960). 30c, Francesco Borromini, architect (1599-1667). 50c, Othmar Schoeck, musician (1886-1957). 80c, Germaine de Stael, writer (1766-1817).

1969, Sept. 18   **Engr.**   **Perf. 11½**
502 A186 10c brt purple   .25 .25
503 A186 20c green   .45 .25
504 A186 30c deep carmine   .70 .25
505 A186 50c deep blue   1.15 .60
506 A186 80c red brown   1.90 1.00
    Nos. 502-506 (5)   4.45 2.35

Kreuzberge, Alpstein Mountains A187

Children Crossing Street — A188

Steelworker A189

1969, Sept. 18   **Photo.**
507 A187 20c blue & multi   .45 .25
508 A188 30c car & multi   .70 .25
509 A189 50c violet & multi   1.15 .45
    Nos. 507-509 (3)   2.30 .95

No. 508 publicizes the traffic safety campaign; No. 509 for 50th anniv. of the ILO.

Telex Tape — A190

Fireman Rescuing Child — A191

Pro Infirmis Emblem A192

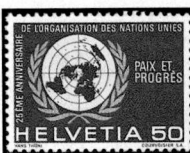

United Nations Emblem A193

New UPU Headquarters A194

1970, Feb. 26   **Photo.**   **Perf. 11½**
510 A190 20c dk grn, yel & blk   .45   .25
511 A191 30c dk car & multi   .70   .25
512 A192 30c red & multi   .70   .25
513 A193 50c dk bl, lt grnsh bl & sil   1.15   .35
514 A194 80c dk pur, sep & tan   1.90   .70
    Nos. 510-514 (5)   4.90 1.80

75th anniv. of the Swiss Telegraph Agency (20c). Cent. of the Swiss Firemen's Assoc. (No. 511). 50th anniv. of the Pro Infirmis Foundation (No. 512). UN, 25th anniv. (50c). New Headquarters of the UPU in Bern (80c).

Europa Issue
Common Design Type
1970, May 4   **Engr.**   **Perf. 11½**
     Size: 21x26mm
515 CD13 30c vermilion   .70   .25
516 CD13 50c brt blue   1.15   .35

Soccer A195

Census Form — A196

Piz Palu, Grisons A197

"Nature Conservation" A198

1970, Sept. 17   **Photo.**   **Perf. 11½**
517 A195 10c green & multi   .40   .25
518 A196 20c dk grn & multi   .45   .25
519 A197 30c slate bl & multi   .70   .25
520 A198 50c dk bl & multi   1.15   .65
    Nos. 517-520 (4)   2.70 1.40

75th anniv. of Swiss Soccer Association (10c). Federal Census of 1970 (20c). Swiss Alps (30c). Nature Conservation Year (50c).

Numeral — A199

Coil Stamps
1970, Sept. 17   **Engr.**   **Perf. 11½**
521 A199 10c brown lake   .25   .25
522 A199 20c olive grn   .45   .25
523 A199 50c ultra   1.15   .60
    Nos. 521-523 (3)   1.85 1.10

Control number in stamp's color on back of every fifth stamp. Nos. 521-523 were regularly issued only in coils, but exist in sheets of 50.

Gymnastic Trio — A200

Rose — A201

Switzerland No. 8 — A202

Rising Spiral — A203

Intelsat 4 Satellite A204

Adaptation of 1850 Design — A205

Design: No. 525, Runners (men).

1971, Mar. 11   **Photo.**   **Perf. 11½**
524 A200 10c ol, brn & bl   .25   .30
525 A200 10c gray, brn & yel   .25   .30
   a.   Pair, #524-525   .50   .30
526 A201 20c dk grn & multi   .45   .25
527 A202 30c dp car & multi   .70   .30
528 A203 50c dk bl & bis   1.15   .60
529 A204 80c multicolored   1.90 1.00
    Nos. 524-529 (6)   4.70 2.75

Souvenir Sheet
Typo.
Imperf
530 A205 2fr blue & multi   5.40 3.00

New article on gymnastics and sports in Swiss Constitution (10c); Intl. Child Welfare Org. (20c); NABA Natl. Postage Stamp Exhibition, Basel, June 4-13 (30c, 2fr); 2nd decade of development aid (50c); Intl. Space Communications Conf., Geneva, June-July, 1971 (80c).
    #525a printed checkerwise. #530 sold for 3fr.

Europa Issue
Common Design Type
1971, May 3   **Engr.**   **Perf. 11½**
     Size: 26x21mm
531 CD14 30c rose car & org   .70   .25
532 CD14 50c blue & org   1.15   .40

Europa Issue
Common Design Type
1972, May 2   **Size: 21x26mm**
544 CD15 30c multicolored   .70   .25
545 CD15 40c multicolored   .95   .35

Les Diablerets, Vaud — A206

Telecommunications Symbols — A207

1971, Sept. 23   **Photo.**   **Perf. 11½**
533 A206 30c rose lil & bl gray   .70   .30
534 A207 40c ultra, yel & brt pink   .95   .55

No. 534 for the 50th anniv. of Radio-Suisse, which is also in charge of air traffic control.

Alexandre Yersin (1863-1943) Bacteriologist A208

Physicians: 20c, Auguste Forel (1848-1931), psychiatrist. 30c, Jules Gonin (1870-1935), ophthalmologist. 40c, Robert Koch (1843-1910), German bacteriologist. 80c, Frederick G. Banting (1891-1941), Canadian physiologist.

1971, Sept. 23   **Engr.**
535 A208 10c gray olive   .25   .25
536 A208 20c bluish green   .45   .25
537 A208 30c carmine rose   .70   .25
538 A208 40c dark blue   .95   .55
539 A208 80c brt purple   1.90   .90
    Nos. 535-539 (5)   4.25 2.20

Wrench, Road Sign, Club Emblems A209

Electronic Switch Panel — A210

Boy's Head and Radio Waves A211

Symbolic Tree — A212

1972, Feb. 17   **Photo.**   **Perf. 11½**
540 A209 10c multicolored   .25   .25
541 A210 20c olive & multi   .45   .25
542 A211 30c orange & maroon   .70   .30
543 A212 40c blue, grn & pur   .95   .60
    Nos. 540-543 (4)   2.35 1.40

75th anniv. of the touring and automobile clubs of Switzerland (10c). 125th anniv. of Swiss railroads (20c). 50th anniv. of Swiss radio (30c). 50th annual congress of Swiss citizens living abroad, Bern, Aug. 25-27 (40c).

Alberto Giacometti (1901-66), Painter and Sculptor — A213

Portraits and Signatures: 20c, Charles Ferdinand Ramuz (1878-1947), writer. 30c, Le Corbusier (Charles Edouard Jeanneret; 1887-1965) architect. 40c, Albert Einstein (1879-1955), physicist. 80c, Arthur Honegger (1892-1955), composer.

Engraved & Photogravure
1972, Sept. 21   **Perf. 11½**
546 A213 10c ocher & blk   .25   .25
547 A213 20c lt olive & blk   .45   .25
548 A213 30c pink & blk   .70   .25
549 A213 40c lt blue & blk   .95   .60
550 A213 80c lil rose & blk   1.90   .75
    Nos. 546-550 (5)   4.25 2.10

Civil Defense Emblem A214

Spannörter, Swiss Alps — A215

Red Cross Rescue Helicopter A216

Clean Air, Fire, Earth and Water — A217

1972, Sept. 21   **Photo.**
551 A214 10c org, bl & yel   .25   .25
552 A215 20c bl grn & multi   .45   .30
553 A216 30c lilac, red & indigo   .75   .25
554 A217 40c lt blue & multi   .95   .60
    Nos. 551-554 (4)   2.40 1.40

Earth Satellite Station, Leuk, World Map — A218

Quill Pen and Arrows in Circle — A219

INTERPOL Emblem A220

1973, Feb. 15 **Photo.** **Perf. 11½**
555 A218 15c gray, yel & bl .35 .25
556 A219 30c multicolored .70 .25
557 A220 40c dp bl, lt bl & gray .95 .50
Nos. 555-557 (3) 2.00 1.00

Opening of the satellite station at Leuk; Swiss Association of Commercial Employees, cent. (30c); International Criminal Police Organization (INTERPOL), 50th anniv.

Sottoceneri A221

Sign of Inn "Zur Sonne," Toggenburg A222

Villages: 10c, Graubunden. 15c, Central Switzerland. 25c, Jura. 30c, Simme Valley. 35c, Central Switzerland (2 buildings). 40c, Vaud. 50c, Valais. 60c, Engadine. 70c, Sopraceneri. 80c, Eastern Switzerland.
Designs: 1fr, Rose window, Lausanne Cathedral. 1.10fr, Gallus Portal, Basel Cathedral. 1.20fr, Romanesque capital (eagle), St. Jean Baptiste Church, Grandson. 1.50fr, Ceiling medallion (bird feeding nestlings), Stein am Rhein Convent. 1.70fr, Romanesque capital (St. George and dragon), St. Jean Baptiste, Grandson. 1.80fr, Gargoyle, Bern Cathedral. 2fr, Bay window, Schaffhausen. 2.50fr, Cock weather vane, St. Ursus Cathedral, Solothurn. 3fr, Font, St. Maurice Church, Saanen. 3.50fr, Astronomical clock, Bern clock tower.

1973-80 **Engr.** **Perf. 11½**
Fluorescent, No Violet Fibers
558 A221 5c dl yel & dk bl .25 .25
559 A221 10c rose lil & ol grn .25 .25
560 A221 15c org & vio bl .35 .25
561 A221 25c emer & vio bl .60 .25
562 A221 30c brick red & dk bl .70 .25
563 A221 35c red org & brt vio ('75) .80 .25
564 A221 40c brt bl & blk .95 .25
565 A221 50c ol grn & org 1.15 .25
566 A221 60c yel brn & gray 1.40 .25
567 A221 70c sep & dk grn 1.60 .25
568 A221 80c brt grn & brick red 1.90 .25

Violet Fibers, Fluorescent Paper
569 A222 1fr pur ('74) 2.25 .25
a. Without fibers, fluorescent paper ('78) 2.25 1.50
570 A222 1.10fr Prus bl ('75) 2.50 .40
571 A222 1.20fr rose red ('74) 2.75 1.25
572 A222 1.30fr ocher 3.00 .90
573 A222 1.50fr grn ('74) 3.50 1.25
574 A222 1.70fr gray 4.00 .60
575 A222 1.80fr dp org 4.25 .60
576 A222 2fr ultra ('74) 4.75 .40
a. Without fibers, fluorescent paper ('78) 4.75 3.50
577 A222 2.50fr gldn brn ('75) 5.75 .60
578 A222 3fr dk car ('79) 7.00 1.00
579 A222 3.50fr ol grn ('80) 8.00 1.25
Nos. 558-579 (22) 57.70 11.25

No. 577 exists without tagging. Value, $60 unused, $30 used.

Europa Issue
Common Design Type
1973, Apr. 30 **Engr. and Photo.**
Size: 38x28mm
580 CD16 25c brown & yel .60 .25
581 CD16 40c ultra & yel .95 .35

"Man and Time" — A223

Skier and Championship Emblem A224

Child — A225

1973, Aug. 30 **Photo.** **Perf. 11½**
582 A223 15c multicolored .35 .25
583 A224 30c pink & multi .70 .25
584 A225 40c blue vio & blk .95 .50
Nos. 582-584 (3) 2.00 1.00

Opening of the Intl. Clock Museum, La Chaux-de-Fonds, 1974 (15c); Intl. Alpine Skiing Championships, St. Moritz, Feb. 2-10, 1974 (30c); "Terre des hommes" children's aid program (40c).

Souvenir Sheet

Medieval Postal Couriers — A226

1974, Jan. 29 **Photo.** **Perf. 11½**
585 A226 Sheet of 4 5.50 5.50
a. 30c Basel (with staff) 1.10 1.10
b. 30c Zug (without staff) 1.10 1.10
c. 60c Uri 1.40 1.10
d. 80c Schwyz 1.90 1.10

Cent. of UPU and for INTERNABA 74 Intl. Phil. Exhib., Basel, June 7-16. No. 585 sold for 3fr.

Pine and Cabin on Globe — A227

Gymnast and Hurdlers A228

Target and Pistol — A229

1974, Jan. 29
586 A227 15c lt green & multi .35 .25
587 A228 30c red & multi .70 .25
588 A229 40c blue & multi .95 .30
Nos. 586-588 (3) 2.00 .80

50th anniv. of Swiss Youth Hostels (15c); Cent. of Swiss Workers' Gymnast and Sports Association (SATUS) (30c); World Marksmanship Championships, Thun and Bern, Sept. 1974 (40c).

Old Houses, Parliament RR Station, Bern — A230

Eugéne Borel — A231

Designs: No. 590, Castle, Town Hall, Chauderon Center, Lausanne. 40c, Heinrich von Stephan. 80c, Montgomery Blair.

1974, Mar. 28 **Photo.** **Perf. 11½**
589 A230 30c orange & multi .70 .25
590 A230 30c scarlet & multi .70 .25
a. Pair, #589-590 1.40 .25

Engr.
591 A231 30c rose & blk .70 .25
592 A231 40c gray & blk .95 .50
593 A231 80c lt yel grn & blk 1.90 .75
Nos. 589-593 (5) 4.95 2.00

Cent. of the UPU. Nos. 589-590 publicize the Cent. Cong., Lausanne, May 22-July 5; Nos. 591-593 honor the founders of the UPU.

"Continuity," by Max Bill — A232

Europa: 40c, "Amazon," bronze sculpture by Carl Burckhardt.

1974, Mar. 28 **Photo.**
594 A232 30c red & black .70 .25
595 A232 40c ultra & sepia .95 .35

Oath of Allegiance, by Werner Witschi — A233

Sports Foundation Emblem A234

Conveyor Belts, Paths of Mail Transport and Delivery A235

1974, Sept. 19 **Photo.** **Perf. 11½**
596 A233 15c lil, ol & dk ol .35 .25
597 A234 30c silver & multi .70 .25
598 A235 30c plum & multi .70 .25
Nos. 596-598 (3) 1.75 .75

Centenary of Swiss Constitution (15c); Swiss Sports Foundation (No. 597); 125th anniversary of Swiss Federal Post (No. 598).

Standard Meter, Krypton Spectrum A236

Women of Four Races A237

Red Cross Flag, Barbed Wire — A238

"Ville de Lucerne" Dirigible A239

1975, Feb. 13 **Photo.** **Perf. 11½**
599 A236 15c grn, org & ultra .35 .25
600 A237 30c brown & multi .70 .25
601 A238 60c ultra, blk & red 1.40 .40
602 A239 90c blue & multi 2.10 1.00
Nos. 599-602 (4) 4.55 1.90

Cent. of Intl. Meter Convention, Paris, 1875 (15c); Intl. Women's Year 1975 (30c); 2nd Session of Diplomatic Conf. on Humanitarian Intl. Law, Geneva, Feb. 1975 (60c); Aviation and Space Travel exhibition in Museum of Transport and Communications, Lucerne (90c).

Mönch, by Ferdinand Hodler — A240

Vineyard Worker, by Maurice Barraud — A241

Europa: 50c, Still Life with Guitar, by René Auberjonois.

1975, Apr. 28 **Photo.** **Perf. 12x11½**
603 A240 30c gray & multi .70 .25
604 A241 50c multicolored 1.15 .50
605 A241 60c bl gray & multi 1.40 .80
Nos. 603-605 (3) 3.25 1.55

Man Pulling Wheel Chair Upstairs A242

"The Helping Hand" A243

Architectural Heritage Year Emblem A244

Beat Fischer von Reichenbach A245

1975, Sept. 11 | | **Photo.**
606 A242 15c lilac, blk & grn .35 .25
607 A243 30c red, blk & car .70 .25
608 A244 50c yel brn & mar 1.15 .60
609 A245 60c blue & multi 1.40 .75
Nos. 606-609 (4) 3.60 1.85

Special building features for the handicapped (15c); interdenominational telephone pastoral counseling (30c); European Architectural Heritage Year 1975 (50c); Fischer Post, Bern, tercentenary (60c).

Forest
A246

Fruits and Vegetables
A247

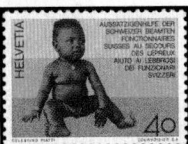
Black Infant — A248

Telephones of 1876 and 1976 — A249

1976, Feb. 12 **Photo.** **Perf. 11½**
Fluorescent, No Violet Fibers
610 A246 20c green & multi .50 .25
611 A247 40c car & multi .95 .25
612 A248 40c lil rose & multi .95 .25

Engr.
Violet Fibers, Fluorescent Paper
613 A249 80c lt bl & dk bl 1.90 1.00
Nos. 610-613 (4) 4.30 1.75

Centenary of Federal forest laws (20c); healthy nutrition to combat alcoholism (No. 611); fight against leprosy (No. 612); telephone centenary (80c).

Cotton and Gold Lace, St. Gall — A250

Pocket Watch, 18th Century — A251

1976, May 3 **Engr.** **Perf. 11½**
614 A250 40c red brn & multi .95 .25
615 A251 80c black & multi .95 .90

Europa. Both 40c and 80c are on fluorescent paper, the 80c having violet fibers.

Fawn, Frog and Swallow
A252

"Conserve Energy"
A253

St. Gotthard Mountains
A254

Skater
A255

1976, Sept. 16 **Photo.** **Perf. 11½**
Fluorescent, No Violet Fibers
616 A252 20c multicolored .75 .30
617 A253 40c multicolored .95 .25
618 A254 40c multicolored .95 .30
619 A255 80c multicolored 1.90 .90
Nos. 616-619 (4) 4.55 1.75

Wildlife protection (20c); energy conservation (No. 617); Pizzo Lucendro to Pizzo Rotondo, seen from Altanca (No. 618); World Men's Skating Championships, Davos, Feb. 5-6, 1977 (80c).

Oskar Bider, Bleriot Monoplane
A256

Swiss Aviation Pioneers: 80c, Eduard Spelterini and balloon gondola. 100c, Armand Dufaux and Dufaux plane. 150c, Walter Mittelholzer and Dornier hydroplane.

1977, Jan. 27 **Engr.** **Perf. 11½**
620 A256 40c multicolored .95 .65
621 A256 80c multicolored 1.90 1.25
622 A256 100c multicolored 2.25 1.00
623 A256 150c multicolored 3.50 1.75
Nos. 620-623 (4) 8.60 4.65

Blue Cross — A257

Festival Emblem
A258

Balloons Carrying Letters
A259

1977, Jan. 27 | | **Photo.**
624 A257 20c gray, bl & blk .45 .25
625 A258 40c red, gold & brn .95 .25
626 A259 80c lt bl & multi 1.90 1.00
Nos. 624-626 (3) 3.30 1.50

Blue Cross Society (care of alcoholics and fight against alcoholism), centenary (20c); Vintage Festival, Vevey, July 30-Aug. 14 (40c); JUPHILEX 77 Youth Philatelic Exhibition, Bern, Apr. 7-11 (80c).

Fluorescent Paper
From No. 624 onward the paper lacks violet fibers but is fluorescent, unless otherwise noted.

St. Ursanne on Doubs River — A260

Europa: 80c, Sils-Baselgia on Inn River.

1977, May 2 **Engr.** **Perf. 11½**
627 A260 40c multicolored .95 .25
628 A260 80c multicolored 1.90 .70

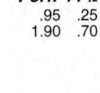

Worker and Factories
A261

Ionic Column and Shield
A262

Swiss Cross, Arrow and Butterfly
A263

1977, Aug. 25 **Photo.** **Perf. 11½**
629 A261 20c multicolored .45 .25
630 A262 40c multicolored .95 .40
631 A263 80c multicolored 1.90 1.00
Nos. 629-631 (3) 3.30 1.65

Federal Factories Act, centenary (20c); protection of cultural monuments (40c); Swiss hiking trails (80c).

Star Singer, Bergün — A264

Folk Customs: 10c, Horse race, Zürich. 20c, New Year's Eve costumes, Herisau. 25c, Chesslete, Solothurn. 30c, Rollelibutzen, Altstatten. 35c, Cutting off the goose, Sursee. 40c, Herald reading proclamation and men scaling wall, Geneva. 45c, Klausjagen, Kussnacht. 50c, Masked men, Laupen. 60c, Schnabelgeissen, Ottenbach. 70c, Procession (horse and masked men), Mendrisio. 80c, Griffins, Basel. 90c, Masked men, Lotschental.

1977-84 **Engr.** **Perf. 11½**
632 A264 5c blue grn .25 .25
 a. Bkt. pane of 4 ('84) .45
633 A264 10c dark red .25 .25
 a. Bkt. pane of 2 + 2 labels ('79) .45
 b. Bkt. pane of 4 ('84) .95
634 A264 20c orange .45 .25
 a. Booklet pane of 4 ('79) 1.90
635 A264 25c brown .60 .25
636 A264 30c brt green .70 .25
637 A264 35c olive .80 .25
 a. Bkt. pane of 4 ('84) 3.25
638 A264 40c brown lake .95 .25
 a. Booklet pane of 4 ('79) 3.75
 b. Violet fibers, fluorescent paper ('78) .95 .25
639 A264 45c gray blue 1.00 .30
640 A264 50c red brown 1.15 .25
 a. Bkt. pane of 2+2 labels ('84) 2.25
 b. Bkt. pane of 4 ('84) 4.50
641 A264 60c gray brown 1.40 .45
642 A264 70c purple 1.60 .30
643 A264 80c steel blue 1.90 .75
644 A264 90c deep brown 2.10 .90
Nos. 632-644 (13) 13.15 4.70

Issue dates: 30c, Nov. 25, 1982; 25c, 60c, Sept. 11, 1984; others, Aug. 25, 1977.

Arms of Vaud Canton
A265

Old Lucerne
A266

Title Page of "Melusine"
A267

Stylized Lens and Bellows
A268

Steamers on Swiss Lakes — A269

1978, Mar. 9 **Photo.** **Perf. 11½**
652 A265 20c multicolored .45 .25
653 A266 40c multicolored .95 .25
654 A267 70c multicolored 1.60 .80
655 A268 80c multicolored 1.90 1.00
Nos. 652-655 (4) 4.90 2.30

Miniature Sheet
656 A269 Sheet of 8 9.50 9.50
 a. 20c La Suisse, 1910 .45 .30
 b. 20c Il Verbano, 1906 .45 .30
 c. 40c MS Gotthard, 1970 .95 .85
 d. 40c Ville de Neuchatel, 1972 .95 .85
 e. 40c MS Romanshorn, 1958 .95 .85
 f. 40c Le Winkelried, 1871 .95 .85
 g. 70c DS Loetschberg, 1914 1.60 .90
 h. 80c DS Waedenswil, 1895 1.90 1.25

LEMANEX 78 Philatelic Exhibition, Lausanne, May 26-June 4 (#652); Founding of Lucerne, 800th anniv. (#653); printing in Geneva, 500th anniv. (#654); 2nd Intl. Triennial Photography Exhibition, Fribourg, June 17-Oct. 22 (#655).
Size of No. 656: 134x129mm. Sold for 5fr.

Stockalper Palace, Brig — A270

Europa: 80c, Diet Hall, Bern.

1978, May 2 **Engr.** **Perf. 11½**
657 A270 40c multicolored .95 .30
658 A270 80c multicolored 1.90 .75

Machinist
A271

#660, Chemical worker (French inscription).
#661, Construction worker (Italian inscription).

1978, Sept. 14 **Photo.** **Perf. 11½**
659 A271 40c multicolored .95 .45
660 A271 40c multicolored .95 .45
661 A271 40c multicolored .95 .45
 a. Strip of 3, #659-661 2.75 2.75

Industrial safety.

Joseph Bovet (1879-1951), Composer — A272

Portraits: 40c, Henri Dunant (1828-1910), founder of Red Cross. 70c, Carl Gustave Jung (1875-1961), psychologist. 80c, Auguste Piccard (1884-1962), physicist and balloonist.

1978, Sept. 14   **Engr.**
662 A272 20c dull green   .45   .25
663 A272 40c rose lake   .95   .25
664 A272 70c gray   1.60   .75
665 A272 80c blue gray   1.90   .90
   Nos. 662-665 (4)   4.90 2.15

Arms of Switzerland and Jura — A273

1978, Sept. 25   **Photo.**   *Perf. 11½*
666 A273 40c buff, red & blk   .95   .35

Admission of Jura as 23rd Canton.

Rainer Maria Rilke (1875-1926), Poet, Muzot Castle — A274

Designs: 40c, Paul Klee (1879-1940), painter and "heroic roses." 70c, Hermann Hesse (1877-1962), writer, and vines. 80c, Thomas Mann (1875-1955), writer, and Lubeck buildings.

1979, Feb. 21   **Engr.**   *Perf. 11½*
667 A274 20c gray green   .45   .25
668 A274 40c red   .95   .30
669 A274 70c brown   1.60   .70
670 A274 80c gray blue   1.90 1.00
   Nos. 667-670 (4)   4.90 2.25

O. H. Ammann, Verrazano-Narrows Bridge, NY — A275

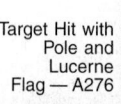

Target Hit with Pole and Lucerne Flag — A276

Hot Air Balloon A277

Airport, Swissair and Air France Jets — A278

1979, Feb. 21   **Photo.**
671 A275 20c multicolored   .45   .25
672 A276 40c multicolored   .95   .25
673 A277 70c multicolored   1.60   .70
674 A278 80c multicolored   1.90 1.00
   Nos. 671-674 (4)   4.90 2.20

Othmar H. Ammann (1879-1965), engineer, bridge builder in US; 50th Federal Riflemen's Festival, Lucerne, July 7-22; World Esperanto Congress, Lucerne; new runway at Basel-Mulhouse Intl. Airport.

Letter Box, 1845, Spalentor, Basel — A279

Europa: 80c, Microwave radio relay station on Jungfraujoch.

1979, Apr. 30   **Engr.**   *Perf. 11½*
675 A279 40c multicolored   .95   .35
676 A279 80c multicolored   1.90   .90

Helvetian Gold Quarter Stater, 2nd Century B.C. — A280

Three-stage Launcher Ariane — A283

Child and Dove — A281

Morse Key and Satellite A282

1979, Sept. 6   **Photo.**
677 A280 20c multicolored   .45   .25
678 A281 40c multicolored   .95   .25
679 A282 70c multicolored   1.60   .70
680 A283 80c multicolored   1.90   .90
   Nos. 677-680 (4)   4.90 2.10

Centenary of Swiss Numismatic Society; International Year of the Child; Union of Swiss Radio Amateurs, 50th anniv.; European Space Agency (ESA).

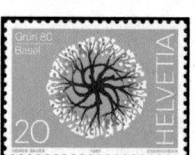

Tree in Bloom A284

Hand Carved Milk Bucket A285

Winterthur Town Hall — A286

"Pic-Pic," 1930 — A287

1980, Feb. 21   **Photo.**
681 A284 20c multicolored   .45   .25
682 A285 40c multicolored   .95   .25
683 A286 70c multicolored   1.60   .80
684 A287 80c multicolored   1.90 1.00
   Nos. 681-684 (4)   4.90 2.30

Green '80, Swiss Horticultural & Gardening Expo., Basel, 4/12-9/9/12; Swiss Arts Crafts Centers, 50th anniv.; Soc. for Swiss Art History, cent.; 50th Intl. Automobile Show, Geneva, 3/16.

Johann Konrad Kern (1808-1888), Politician A288

Europa: 80c, Gustav Adolf Hasler (1830-1900), communications pioneer.

1980, Apr. 28   **Lith. & Engr.**
         Granite Paper
685 A288 40c multicolored   .95   .25
686 A288 80c multicolored   1.90   .90

Postal Giro System A289

Postal Bus System A290

Security Printing Plant, 50th Anniversary A291

Swiss Telephone Service Centenary A292

Photo., Photo. & Engr. (70c)
1980, Sept. 5   *Perf. 12*
687 A289 20c multicolored   .45   .25
688 A290 40c multicolored   .95   .25
689 A291 70c multicolored   1.60   .75
690 A292 80c multicolored   1.90 1.10
   Nos. 687-690 (4)   4.90 2.35

Swiss Meteorological Office Centenary A293

Swiss Trade Union Federation Centenary A294

Opening of St. Gotthard Tunnel for Year-round Traffic — A295

1980, Sept. 5   **Photo.**
691 A293 20c multicolored   .35   .25
692 A294 40c multicolored   .55   .25
693 A295 80c multicolored   1.25 1.00
   Nos. 691-693 (3)   2.15 1.50

Granary, Kiesen, 17th Century A296

International Year of the Disabled A297

The Parish Clerk, by Albert Anker — A298

Theodolite and Rod — A299

DC-9 (50th Anniversary of Swissair) A300

1981, Mar. 9   **Photo.**   *Perf. 11½*
694 A296 20c multicolored   .45   .25
695 A297 40c multicolored   .95   .25
696 A298 70c multicolored   1.60   .80
697 A299 80c multicolored   1.90   .90
698 A300 110c multicolored   2.50 1.10
   Nos. 694-698 (5)   7.40 3.30

Ballenberg Open-air Museum of Rural Architecture, Furnishing and Crafts; Albert Anker (1831-1910), artist (70c); 16th Congress of the International Federation of Surveyors, Montreux, Aug. (80c).

Europa Issue

Couple Dancing in Native Costumes — A301

1981, May 4   **Photo.**   *Perf. 11½*
699 A301 40c shown   .95   .35
700 A301 80c Stone putting   1.90 1.00

Seal of Fribourg A302

1981, Sept. 3   **Photo. & Engr.**
701 A302 40c shown   .95   .25
702 A302 40c Seal of Solothurn   .95   .25
703 A302 80c Old Town Hall, Stans   1.90 1.00
   Nos. 701-703 (3)   3.80 1.50

Diet of Stans, 500th anniv., and entry of Fribourg & Solothurn into the Swiss Confederation.

Voltage Regulator A303

Crossbow Quality Emblem A304

Youths A305

Flower Mosaic, St. Peter's Cathedral, Geneva A306

1981, Sept. 3   **Photo.**
704	A303	20c multi	.45	.25
705	A304	40c multi	.95	.30
706	A305	70c multi	1.60	.75
707	A306	1.10fr multi	2.50	1.25
	Nos. 704-707 (4)		5.50	2.55

Technorama Industrial Fair, Winterthur; Crossbow Quality Emblem, 50th anniv.; Swiss Youth Assoc., 50th anniv.; restoration of St. Peter's Cathedral.

Gotthard Railway Centenary A307

Designs: Locomotives.

1982, Feb. 18   **Photo.**
708	A307	40c Steam	.95	.30
709	A307	40c Electric	.95	.30
a.	Pair, #708-709 + central label		1.90	.60

Swiss Hoteliers' Assoc. Centenary A308

Federal Gymnastic Society Sesquicentennial — A309

Intl. Gas Union, 50th Anniv. Convention, Lausanne A310

Bern Museum of Natural History Sesquicentennial — A311

Society of Chemical Industries Centenary A312

1982, Feb. 18
710	A308	20c multicolored	.45	.25
711	A309	40c multicolored	.95	.30
712	A310	70c multicolored	1.60	.75
713	A311	80c multicolored	1.90	1.00
714	A312	110c multicolored	2.50	1.10
	Nos. 710-714 (5)		7.40	3.40

Europa 1982 — A313

1982, May 3   **Photo.**   *Perf. 11½*
715	A313	40c Oath of Eternal Fealty	.45	.30
716	A313	80c Pact of 1291	1.90	1.00

Virgo, Schwarzee above Zermatt — A314

Signs of the Zodiac and City Views — 1fr, Aquarius, Old Bern. 1.10fr, Pisces, Nax near Sion. 1.20fr, Aries, Graustock. 1.40fr, Gemini, Bischofszell. 1.50fr, Taurus, Basel Cathedral. 1.60fr, Gemini, Schonengrund. 1.70fr, Cancer, Wetterhorn, Grindelwald. 1.80fr, Leo, Areuse Gorge, Neuchatel. No. 724, 2fr, Virgo, Jungfrau Monch Eiger Mts. 2.50fr, Libra, Fechy. 3fr, Scorpio, Corippo. 4fr, Sagittarius, Glarus. 4.50fr, Capricorn, Schuls.

Photogravure and Engraved
1982-86   *Perf. 11½*
717	A314	1fr multi	2.25	.30
718	A314	1.10fr multi	2.50	.30
719	A314	1.20fr multi	2.75	.30
719A	A314	1.40fr multi	3.25	1.40
720	A314	1.50fr multi	3.50	.30
721	A314	1.60fr multi	3.75	1.10
722	A314	1.70fr multi	4.00	.30
723	A314	1.80fr multi	4.25	1.00
724	A314	2fr multi	4.50	2.25
725	A314	2fr shown	4.50	.30
726	A314	2.50fr multi	5.75	.80
727	A314	3fr multi	7.00	1.25
728	A314	4fr multi	9.25	1.50
728A	A314	4.50fr multi	10.50	2.00
	Nos. 717-728A (14)		67.75	13.10

Issued: #717-719, 720-721, 8/23/82; #719A, 2/11/86; #722-724, 2/17/83; #725, 11/24/83; #726-727, 2/19/85; #728-728A, 2/21/84.

Zurich Tram Centenary A315

Centenary of Salvation Army in Switzerland A316

World Dressage Championship, Lausanne, Aug. 25-29 — A317

Intl. Water Supply Assoc., 14th World Congress, Zurich, Sept. 6-10 — A318

1982, Aug. 23   **Photo.**
729	A315	20c multicolored	.45	.25
730	A316	40c multicolored	.95	.25
731	A317	70c multicolored	1.60	.90
732	A318	80c multicolored	1.90	1.00
	Nos. 729-732 (4)		4.90	2.40

Fishing and Pisciculture Fed. Centenary A319

Zurich University Sesquicentennial — A320

Journalists' Fed. Centenary A321

Machine Manufacturers' Assoc. Centenary — A322

20c, Perch. 70c, Computer printouts. 80c, Micrometer, cycloidal computer pattern.

1983, Feb. 17   **Photo.**
     Granite Paper
733	A319	20c multicolored	.45	.25
734	A320	40c multicolored	.95	.30
735	A321	70c multicolored	1.60	.90
736	A322	80c multicolored	1.90	1.00
	Nos. 733-736 (4)		4.90	2.45

Europa 1983 — A323

Photogravure and Engraved
1983, May 3   *Perf. 11½*
737	A323	40c Celestial globe, 1594	.95	.25
738	A323	80c Cog railway, 1871	1.90	1.00

Basel Seal, 1832-1848 — A324

1983, May 26   **Photo.**
739	A324	40c multicolored	.95	.35

Basel Canton sesquicentennial (land division).

Octodurus Martigny Bimillenium A325

Swiss Kennel Club Centenary A326

Bicycle and Motorcycle Federation Centenary A327

World Communications Year — A328

1983, Aug. 22   **Photo.**
740	A325	20c multicolored	.45	.25
741	A326	40c multicolored	.95	.25
742	A327	70c multicolored	1.60	.90
743	A328	80c multicolored	1.90	.90
	Nos. 740-743 (4)		4.90	2.30

NABA-ZURI'84 Natl. Stamp Show, Zurich, June 22-July 1 — A329

1100th Anniv. of Saint Imier — A330

Upper City, Lausanne A331

1984, Feb. 21   **Photo.**
744	A329	25c multicolored	.60	.25
745	A330	50c multicolored	1.15	.35
746	A331	80c multicolored	1.90	1.10
	Nos. 744-746 (3)		3.65	1.70

Selection of Lausanne as permanent headquarters for the Intl. Olympic Committee (80c).

Europa (1959-1984) A332

1984, May 2   **Photo.**   *Perf. 11½*
747	A332	50c lilac rose	1.15	.50
748	A332	80c ultra	1.90	1.00

Souvenir Sheet

Panoramic View of Zurich — A333

1984, May 24
749	A333	Sheet of 4	5.50	5.50
a.-d.		50c any single	4.50	1.20

NABA-ZURI '84 Stamp Show. Sold for 3fr.

Fire Prevention A334

1984, Sept. 11   **Photo.**
750	A334	50c Flames, match	.70	.35

Railway Staff Association, Cent. — A335

Rheto-Roman Culture Bimillennium A336

Lake Geneva Rescue Soc., Cent. — A337

Intl. Congress on Large Dams, Lausanne A338

35c, Conductor's hat, paraphernalia. 50c, Engraved artifact, Chur. 70c, Rescuing drowning victim. 80c, Grande Dixence Dam, Canton Valais.

1985, Feb. 19   **Photo.**   **Perf. 12x11½**
751	A335	35c multicolored	.80	.25
752	A336	50c multicolored	1.15	.25
753	A337	70c multicolored	1.60	.90
754	A338	80c multicolored	1.90	1.10
		Nos. 751-754 (4)	5.45	2.50

Europa 1985 — A339

Designs: 50c, Ernest Ansermet (1883-1969), composer, conductor. 80c, Frank Martin (1890-1974), composer.

1985, May 7   **Photo.**   **Perf. 11½x12**
755	A339	50c multicolored	1.15	.25
756	A339	80c multicolored	1.90	1.00

Swiss Master Bakers and Confectioners Federation, Bern, Cent. — A340

Swiss Radio Intl., 50th Anniv. A341

Postal, Telegraph & Telephone Intl. Congress, Sept. 16-21, Interlaken A342

1985, Sept. 10   **Photo.**   **Perf. 12x11½**
757	A340	50c Baker	1.15	.25
758	A341	70c multi	1.60	.75
759	A342	80c PTTI 75th anniv.	1.90	.90
		Nos. 757-759 (3)	4.65	1.90

Swiss Worker's Relief Org., 50th Anniv. A343

Battle of Sempach, 600th Anniv. A344

Roman Chur Bimillennium A345

Vindonissa Bimillennium A346

Zurich Bimillennium A347

1986, Feb. 11   **Photo.**   **Perf. 12**
772	A343	35c Knot	.80	.40
773	A344	50c Military map, 1698	1.15	.25
774	A345	80c Mercury statue	1.90	.90
775	A346	90c Gallic head	2.10	1.00
776	A347	1.10fr Augustus coin	2.50	1.25
		Nos. 772-776 (5)	8.45	3.80

Europa 1986 — A348

1986, Apr. 22   **Photo.**   **Perf. 13½**
777	A348	50c Woman	1.15	.30
778	A348	90c Man	2.10	1.25

Mail Handling — A349

5c, Franz mail van, 1911. 10c, Parcel sorting. 20c, Mule post. 25c, Letter-facing, canceling. 30c, Mail coach, 1735-1960. 35c, Counter service. 45c, Packet steamer, 1837-40. 50c, Postman, 1986. 60c, Loading airmail, 1986. 75c, 17th Cent. courier. 80c, Postman, ca. 1900. 90c, Railroad mail car.

Photo. & Engr.

1986-89   **Perf. 13½x13**
779	A349	5c multicolored	.25	.25
780	A349	10c multicolored	.25	.25
781	A349	20c multicolored	.45	.25
782	A349	25c multicolored	.60	.25
783	A349	30c multicolored	.70	.90
784	A349	35c multicolored	.80	.40
785	A349	45c multicolored	1.00	.45
786	A349	50c multicolored	1.15	.35
a.		Bklt. pane of 10 ('88)	11.50	
787	A349	60c multicolored	1.40	.45
788	A349	70c multicolored	1.75	.75
789	A349	80c multicolored	1.90	.80
790	A349	90c multicolored	2.10	1.00
		Nos. 779-790 (12)	12.35	6.10

Issued: 5c, 10c, 25c, 35c, 80c, 90c, 9/9/86; 20c, 30c, 45c, 50c, 60c, 3/10/87; 75c, 3/7/89. For surcharge see No. B535.

Intl. Peace Year — A351

Swiss Winter Relief Fund, 50th Anniv. A352

Berne Convention for the Protection of Literary and Artistic Copyrights, Cent. — A353

25th Intl. Red Cross Conference, Geneva, Oct. 23-31 A354

1986, Sept. 9   **Photo.**   **Perf. 12x11½**
799	A351	35c multicolored	.80	.30
800	A352	50c multicolored	1.15	.25
801	A353	80c multicolored	1.90	1.00
802	A354	90c multicolored	2.10	1.10
		Nos. 799-802 (4)	5.95	2.65

Mobile P.O., 50th Anniv. A355

Lausanne University, 450th Anniv. A356

Swiss Engineers & Architects Assoc., Sesquicent. A357

Cointrin Airport-Geneva, Rail Link Opening, June 1, 1987 — A358

Baden Hot Springs, 2000th Anniv. A359

1987, Mar. 10   **Photo.**
803	A355	35c multicolored	.80	.35
804	A356	50c multicolored	1.15	.25
805	A357	80c multicolored	1.90	1.00
806	A358	90c multicolored	2.10	1.25
807	A359	1.10fr multicolored	2.50	1.50
		Nos. 803-807 (5)	8.45	4.35

Europa 1987 — A360

Sculpture: 50fr, Scarabaeus, 1979, by Bernard Luginbuhl. 90fr, Carnival Fountain, 1977, by Jean Tinguely, Basel Theater.

1987, May 26   **Photo.**   **Perf. 11½**
808	A360	50c multicolored	1.15	.30
809	A360	90c multicolored	2.10	1.25

Swiss Master Butchers' Federation, Cent. — A361

Stamp Day, 50th Anniv. A362

Swiss Dairy Assoc., Cent. — A363

1987, Sept. 4   **Photo.**   **Perf. 12x11½**
810	A361	35c multicolored	.80	.40
811	A362	50c multicolored	1.15	.40
812	A363	90c Cheesemaker	2.10	1.00
		Nos. 810-812 (3)	4.05	1.80

Tourism Industry, Bicent. — A364

Switzerland's four language regions: 50c, Clock Tower, Zug, German. 80c, Church of San Carlo, Blenio Valley, Italian. 90c, Witches' Tower, Sion Castle, French. 140c, Jorgenberg Castle ruins, Waltensburg/Vuorz, Surselva, Rhaeto-Romansh.

1987, Sept. 4   **Perf. 11½**
813	A364	50c multicolored	1.15	.40
814	A364	80c multicolored	1.90	.75
815	A364	90c multicolored	2.10	1.00
816	A364	140c multicolored	3.25	1.50
a.		Souvenir sheet of 4, #813-816	9.75	9.75
		Nos. 813-816 (4)	8.40	3.65

Swiss Women's Benevolent Soc., Cent. — A365

Swiss Hairdressers Assoc., Cent. — A366

Battle of Naefels, 600th Anniv. A367

European Campaign to Protect Undeveloped and Developing Lands A368

Intl. Music Festival, Lucerne, 50th Anniv. A369

50c, Banner of St. Fridolin, medieval manuscript. 90c, Girl playing a shawm.

1988, Mar. 8   Photo.   Perf. 12x11½
817	A365 25c multicolored	.60	.25
818	A366 35c multicolored	.80	.40
819	A367 50c multicolored	1.15	.25
820	A368 80c multicolored	1.90	.90
821	A369 90c multicolored	2.10	1.25
	Nos. 817-821 (5)	6.55	3.05

Europa 1988 — A370

50c, Arrows (transport). 90c, Circuitry (communication).

1988, May 24   Photo.   Perf. 11½
| 822 | A370 50c multicolored | 1.15 | .40 |
| 823 | A370 90c multicolored | 2.10 | 1.25 |

Swiss Accident Prevention Office, 50th Anniv. A371

Assoc. of Metalworkers and Watchmakers, Cent. — A372

Federal Topography Office, 150th Anniv. A373

Intl. Red Cross Museum, Geneva A374

80c, Triangulation pyramid, theodolite, map.

1988, Sept. 13   Photo.   Perf. 12x11½
824	A371 35c multicolored	.80	.40
825	A372 50c multicolored	1.15	.25
826	A373 80c multicolored	1.90	.90
827	A374 90c multicolored	2.10	1.10
	Nos. 824-827 (4)	5.95	2.65

Metamecanique, by Jean Tinguely — A375

1988, Nov. 25   Photo.   Perf. 13x12½
| 828 | A375 90c multicolored | 2.10 | 3.00 |

See France No. 2137.

Military Post, Cent. — A376

Delemont Municipal Charter, 700th Anniv. A377

Public Transport Assoc., Cent. — A378

Rhaetian Railway, Cent. — A379

Great St. Bernard Pass Bimillennium A380

25c, Army postman. 35c, Fontaine du Sauvage & the Porte au Loup, Delemont. 50c, Eye, modes of transportation. 80c, Train, viaduct. 90c, St. Bernard dog, statue of saint, hospice on summit.

1989, Mar. 2   Photo.   Perf. 12x11½
829	A376 25c multicolored	.60	.25
830	A377 35c multicolored	.80	.40
831	A378 50c multicolored	1.15	.25
832	A379 80c multicolored	1.90	1.00
833	A380 90c multicolored	2.10	1.10
	Nos. 829-833 (5)	6.55	3.00

Europa — A381

Children's games: 50c, Hopscotch. 90c, Blindman's buff.

1989, May 23   Perf. 11½
| 834 | A381 50c multicolored | 1.15 | .50 |
| 835 | A381 90c multicolored | 2.10 | 1.25 |

Industry — A382

2.75fr, Bricklayer. 2.80fr, Cook. 3fr, Cabinet maker. 3.60fr, Pharmacist. 3.75fr, Fisherman. 4fr, Wine grower. 5fr, Cheesemaker. 5.50fr, Dressmaker.

Engr., Litho. & Eng. (2.80, 3, 3.60, 4, 5fr)

1989-94   Perf. 13x13½
842	A382 2.75fr multi	6.25	2.25
843	A382 2.80fr multi	6.50	2.40
844	A382 3fr multi	7.00	1.75
845	A382 3.60fr multi	8.25	3.00
846	A382 3.75fr multi	8.75	3.50
847	A382 4fr multi	9.25	3.00
848	A382 5fr multi	11.50	4.00
849	A382 5.50fr multi	12.50	4.00
	Nos. 842-849 (8)	70.00	23.90

Issued: 2.75fr, 5.50fr, 8/29/89; 3.75fr, 3/6/90; 2.80fr, 3.60fr, 1/24/92; 5fr, 9/7/93; 4fr, 3/15/94; 3fr, 7/5/94.

Swiss Electricians' Assoc., Cent. — A383

Swiss Travel Fund, 50th Anniv. A384

Fribourg University, Cent. — A385

Opening of the Natl. Sound-Recording Archives, 1st Anniv. — A386

Interparliamentary Union, Cent. — A387

80c, "Wisdom" and "Science".

1989, Aug. 25   Photo.   Perf. 11½
851	A383 35c multicolored	.80	.45
852	A384 50c multicolored	1.15	.25
853	A385 80c multicolored	1.90	.80
854	A386 90c multicolored	2.10	1.00
855	A387 140c multicolored	3.25	1.25
	Nos. 851-855 (5)	9.20	3.75

Union of Swiss Philatelic Societies, Cent. — A388

Urban Railway System, Zurich A389

Assistance for Mountain Communities, 50th Anniv. A390

1990 World Ice Hockey Championships — A391

1990, Mar. 6
856	A388 25c No. 71, & type of		
	A20	.60	.25
857	A389 35c Locomotives	.80	.40
858	A390 50c Mountain farmer	1.15	.30
859	A391 90c Athletes	2.10	1.00
	Nos. 856-859 (4)	4.65	1.95

Europa 1990 — A393

Post offices.

Litho. & Engr.

1990, May 22   Perf. 13½
| 861 | A393 50c Lucerne | 1.15 | .25 |
| 862 | A393 90c Geneva | 2.10 | 1.25 |

Conrad Ferdinand Meyer (1825-1898), Writer — A394

Designs: 50c, Angelika Kaufmann (1741-1807), painter. 80c, Blaise Cendrars (1887-1961), journalist. 90c, Frank Buchser (1828-1890), artist.

1990, Sept. 5   Litho.
863	A394 35c green & blk	.80	.40
864	A394 50c blue & blk	1.15	.30
865	A394 80c yellow & blk	1.90	.80
866	A394 90c vermilion & blk	2.10	1.10
	Nos. 863-866 (4)	5.95	2.60

Swiss Confederation, 700th Anniv. in 1991 — A395

1990, Sept. 5   Photo.   Perf. 11½
| 867 | A395 50c shown | 1.15 | .40 |
| 868 | A395 90c multi, diff. | 2.10 | 1.25 |

Natl. Census
A396

1990, Nov. 20
869 A396 50c multicolored   1.15 .40

Animals — A397

1990-95   Litho. & Engr.   Perf. 13
870	A397	10c Cow	.30	.25
871	A397	50c House cats	1.15	.30
872	A397	70c Rabbit	1.60	.65
a.		Booklet pane of 10	16.00	
		Complete booklet, #872a	16.00	
873	A397	80c Barn owls	1.90	.60
874	A397	100c Horses	2.25	.80
875	A397	110c Geese	2.50	.60
876	A397	120c Dog	2.75	1.00
877	A397	140c Sheep	3.25	.75
878	A397	150c Goats	3.50	.75
879	A397	160c Turkey	3.75	1.25
880	A397	170c Donkey	4.00	.90
881	A397	200c Chickens	4.50	1.75
		Nos. 870-881 (12)	31.45	9.60

Issued: 50c, 3/6/90; 70c, 80c, 1/15/91; 10c, 160c, 1/24/92; 100c, 120c, 3/16/93; 150c, 200c, 7/5/94; #872a, 110c, 140c, 170c, 11/28/95.

Swiss Confederation, 700th
Anniv. — A398

Swiss
Parliament,
US Capitol
A399

1991, Feb. 22   Photo.   Perf. 12
884	A398	50c "700 jahre"	1.15	.25
885	A398	50c "700 onns"	1.15	.25
886	A398	50c "700 ans"	1.15	.25
887	A398	50c "700 anni"	1.15	.25
a.		Block of 4, #884-887	4.75	1.00
888	A399	1.60fr multicolored	3.75	.80
		Nos. 884-888 (5)	8.35	1.80

See US No. 2532.

Bern, 800th
Anniv. — A400

1991, Feb. 22   Perf. 11½
889 A400 80c multicolored   1.90 .60

Europa — A401

1991, May 14   Litho.   Perf. 11½
| 890 | A401 | 50c Ariane payload fairing | 1.15 | .25 |
| 891 | A401 | 90c Giotto probe | 1.75 | 1.00 |

Union of
Postal,
Telephone
and Telegraph
Officials,
Cent. — A402

1991, Sept. 10   Photo.   Perf. 11½
892 A402 80c multicolored   1.90 .70

Bridges
A403

Designs: 50c, Stone bridge near Lavertezzo. 70c, Wooden "New Bridge" near Bremgarten. 80c, Railway bridge between Koblenz and Felsenau. 90c, Ganter Bridge, Simplon Pass.

1991, Sept. 10
893	A403	50c multicolored	1.15	.25
894	A403	70c multicolored	1.60	.55
895	A403	80c multicolored	1.90	.75
896	A403	90c multicolored	2.10	.90
		Nos. 893-896 (4)	6.75	2.45

Mountain
Lakes — A404   A404a

A404b

Design: 50c, Lago Moesola. 60c, Lac de Tanay. 80c, Melchsee.

Litho., Litho. & Engr. (60c, #908)
1991-95   Perf. 13½x13
904	A404	50c shown	1.15	.25
905	A404	60c blue & multi	1.40	.25
a.		Booklet pane of 10	14.00	
907	A404	80c red & multi	1.90	.50
908	A404a	80c reddish orange	1.90	.40
909	A404b	90c multicolored	2.10	.75
a.		Booklet pane of 10	21.00	
		Complete booklet, #909a	21.00	
		Nos. 904-909 (5)	8.45	2.15

Issued: 50c, #907, 12/16/91; 60c, #908, 1/19/93; 90c, 11/28/95.
See No. 1102.

Bird Over
Rhine
River — A405

Faces of
Parents,
Child — A406

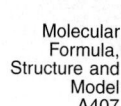 

Molecular
Formula,
Structure and
Model
A407

1992, Mar. 24   Photo.   Perf. 11½
911	A405	50c multicolored	1.15	.25
912	A406	80c multicolored	1.90	.60
913	A407	90c multicolored	2.10	1.00
		Nos. 911-913 (3)	5.15	1.85

Intl. Rhine Regulation, cent. (No. 911), Pro Familia Switzerland, 50th anniv. (No. 912), Intl. Chemical Nomenclature Conf., Geneva, cent. (No. 913).

A408

Europa: 90c, Columbus, map of voyage.

1992, Mar. 24
| 914 | A408 | 50c multicolored | 1.15 | .50 |
| 915 | A408 | 90c multicolored | 2.10 | 1.10 |

Discovery of America, 500th anniv.

A409

1992, May 22   Photo.   Perf. 12
916 A409 90c multicolored   2.10 .90

Protect the Alps.
See Austria No. 1571.

Comic Strips
A410

1992, May 22   Perf. 11½
917	A410	50c Cosey	1.15	.30
918	A410	80c Zep	1.90	.60
919	A410	90c Aloys	2.10	1.00
		Nos. 917-919 (3)	5.15	1.90

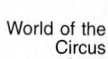

World of the
Circus
A411

50c, Clowns on trapeze. 70c, Sea lion, clown. 80c, Clown, elephant. 90c, Lipizzaner, harlequin.

1992, Aug. 25   Photo.   Perf. 12x11½
920	A411	50c multicolored	1.15	.30
921	A411	70c multicolored	1.60	.60
922	A411	80c multicolored	1.90	.60
923	A411	90c multicolored	2.10	1.00
		Nos. 920-923 (4)	6.75	2.50

Central Office
for Intl.
Carriage by
Rail, Cent. (in
1993) — A412

1992, Nov. 24   Photo.   Perf. 11½
924 A412 90c multicolored   2.10 .75

First Swiss Postage
Stamps, 150th
Anniv. — A413

Designs: 60c, Zurich Types A1, A2, Geneva Type A1. 80c, Stylized canceled stamp. 100c, Stylized stamps on album page.

1993, Mar. 16   Photo.   Perf. 11½
925	A413	60c multicolored	1.40	.50
926	A413	80c multicolored	1.90	.60
927	A413	100c multicolored	2.25	1.00
		Nos. 925-927 (3)	5.55	2.10

Paracelsus
(1493-1541),
Physician
A414

Opening of
Olympic
Museum,
Lausanne
A415

Intl.
Metalworkers'
Federation,
Cent. — A416

1993, Mar. 16   Photo.   Perf. 11½
928	A414	60c blue & sepia	1.40	.35
929	A415	80c multicolored	1.90	.75
930	A416	180c multicolored	4.25	1.75
		Nos. 928-930 (3)	7.55	2.85

Lake
Constance
Steamer
Hohentwiel
A417

1993, May 5   Photo.   Perf. 11½x12
931 A417 60c multicolored   1.40 .50

See Austria No. 1598, Germany No. 1786.

Contemporary
Architecture
A418

Europa: 60c, Media House, Villeurbanne, France. 80c, House, Breganzona, Switzerland.

Litho. & Engr.
1993, May 5   Perf. 13½
| 932 | A418 | 60c multicolored | 1.40 | .40 |
| 933 | A418 | 80c red & black | 1.90 | .90 |

Works of
Art by
Swiss
Women
A419

Designs: 60c, Work No. 095, by Emma Kunz. 80c, Grande Cantatrice Lilas Goergens, by Aloise Corbaz. 100c, Under the Rain Cloud, by Meret Oppenheim. 120c, Four

Spaces in Horizontal Bands, by Sophie Taeuber-Arp.

1993, Sept. 7   Photo.   Perf. 11½
934 A419 60c multicolored   1.40 .40
Size: 33x33½mm
935 A419 80c multicolored   1.90 .75
936 A419 100c multicolored   2.25 1.00
937 A419 120c multicolored   2.75 1.25
   Nos. 934-937 (4)   8.30 3.40

Swiss Sports School, 50th Anniv. A420

Jakob Bernoulli (1654-1705), Mathematician A421

Swiss Telecom PTT Participation in Unisource A422

ICAO, 50th Anniv. A423

1994, Mar. 15   Photo.   Perf. 11½
938 A420 60c multicolored   1.40 .40
939 A421 80c multicolored   1.90 .45
940 A422 100c multicolored   2.25 .85
941 A423 180c multicolored   4.25 1.25
   Nos. 938-941 (4)   9.80 2.95
   Intl. Congress of Mathematicians, Zurich (#939).

"Books and the Press" Exhibition, Geneva A424

1994, Mar. 15
942 A424 60c Early manuscripts 1.40 .40
943 A424 80c Letterpress   1.90 .75
944 A424 100c Electronic pub-
       lishing   2.25 1.00
   Nos. 942-944 (3)   5.55 2.15

1994 World Cup Soccer Championships, U.S. — A425

1994, Mar. 15
945 A425 80c multicolored   1.90 .65

Research Vehicles of August & Jacques Piccard — A426

   Europa: 60c, Bathyscaphe Trieste. 100c, Stratospheric balloon.

Georges Simenon (1903-89), Writer A427

1994, May 17   Photo.   Perf. 12
946 A426 60c multicolored   1.40 .50
947 A426 100c multicolored   2.25 1.00

Litho. & Engr.
1994, Oct. 15   Perf. 13
948 A427 100c multicolored   2.25 .90
   See Belgium No. 1567, France No. 2443.

A428

1994, Oct. 15   Photo.   Perf. 11½
949 A428 60c multicolored   1.40 .35
   Campaign to stop AIDS.

A429

Endangered species.

1995, Mar. 7   Photo.   Perf. 11½
950 A429 60c European beaver 1.40 .30
951 A429 80c Map butterfly   1.90 .50
952 A429 100c Green tree frog 2.25 .75
953 A429 120c Litte owl   2.75 .90
   Nos. 950-953 (4)   8.30 2.45

Swiss Wrestling Assoc., Cent. — A430

Swiss Assoc. of Producers & Distributors of Electricity, Cent. — A431

Swiss News Agency, Cent. — A432

UN, 50th Anniv. A433

1995, Mar. 7
954 A430 60c blue & black   1.40 .55
955 A431 60c multicolored   1.40 .55
956 A432 80c multicolored   1.90 1.50
957 A433 180c multicolored   4.25 1.75
   Nos. 954-957 (4)   8.95 4.35

Peace & Freedom A434

   Europa: 60c, Dove, faces. 100c, Zeus disguised as bull, abducting Europa, daughter of King of Phoenicia.

Litho., Engr. & Embossed
1995, May 16   Perf. 13
958 A434 60c lt blue & dk blue 1.40 .40
959 A434 100c orange & brown 2.25 .85

Switzerland-Liechtenstein Postal Relationship A435

Litho. & Engr.
1995, Sept. 5   Perf. 13½
960 A435 60c multicolored   1.40 .50
   See Liechtenstein No. 1055.
   No. 960 and Liechtenstein No. 1055 are identical. This issue was valid for postage in both countries.

Motion Pictures, Cent. — A436

   Scenes from motion pictures: 60c, La Vocation d'Andre Carrel. 80c, Anna Goldin-The Last Witch. 150c, Pipilotti's Mistakes-Absolution.

1995, Sept. 5   Photo.   Perf. 11½
961 A436 60c multicolored   1.40 .40
962 A436 80c multicolored   1.90 .70
963 A436 150c multicolored   3.50 1.25
   Nos. 961-963 (3)   6.80 2.35

Telecom '95, Geneva — A437

1995, Sept. 5
964 A437 180c multicolored   4.25 1.00

Swiss Charities, Solidarity Chain, 50th Anniv. A438

Touring Club, Cent. — A439

Federal Music Festival, Interlaken A440

Swiss Natl. Assoc. Pro Filia, Cent. — A441

Jean Piaget (1896-1980), Psychologist A442

1996, Mar. 12   Photo.   Perf. 11½
965 A438 70c multicolored   1.60 .50
966 A439 70c multicolored   1.60 .50
967 A440 90c multicolored   2.10 .60
968 A441 90c multicolored   2.10 .60
969 A442 180c multicolored   4.25 2.00
   Nos. 965-969 (5)   11.65 4.20

Famous Women — A443

   Europa: 70c, S. Corinna Bille (1912-79), author. 110c, Iris von Roten-Meyer (1917-90), writer, painter.

Litho. & Engr.
1996, May 14   Perf. 13½
970 A443 70c multicolored   1.60 .50
971 A443 110c multicolored   2.50 1.10

Modern Olympic Games, Cent. — A444

1996, May 14   Litho.   Perf. 13½
972 A444 180c multicolored   4.25 1.50

Guinness Record Stamp — A445

   Design: Aerial view of 11,000 gymnasts arranged as No. 909, making record as world's largest living postage stamp.

1996, June 27   Litho.   Perf. 13½x13
973 A445 90c multicolored   2.10 .80

Greeting Stamps A446

   Various ornate or floral patterns.

Serpentine Die Cut 7 Vert.
1996, Sept. 10   Typo.
Self-Adhesive
Booklet Stamps
974 A446 90c yellow & black 2.10 1.00
975 A446 90c blue & multi   2.10 1.00
976 A446 90c red & multi   2.10 1.00
977 A446 90c green & multi   2.10 1.00
   a. Booklet pane of 4, #974-977   8.25
       Complete booklet, 2 #977a   16.50

Music Boxes and Automata
A447

Designs: 70c, Ring with mechanical figures, musical movement, by Isaac-Daniel Piguet. 90c, Basso-piccolo mandolin cylinder music box, by Eduard Jaccard. 110c, Station automaton, by Paillard and Co. 180c, Kalliope disk music box.

1996, Sept. 10   Photo.   Perf. 11½

978	A447	70c multicolored	1.60	.40
979	A447	90c multicolored	2.10	.60
980	A447	110c multicolored	2.50	1.00
981	A447	180c multicolored	4.25	1.50
		Nos. 978-981 (4)	10.45	3.50

Stamp Design Competition Winners — A448

Designs: 70c, Golden cow. 90c, Smiling creature. 110c, Leaves. 180c, Dove.

1996, Nov. 26   Photo.   Perf. 11½

982	A448	70c blue & bister	1.60	.55
983	A448	90c multicolored	2.10	.80
984	A448	110c multicolored	2.50	1.00
985	A448	180c multicolored	4.25	1.75
		Nos. 982-985 (4)	10.45	4.10

"Globi" as Postman
A449

1997, Mar. 11   Litho.   Perf. 13x13½

986	A449	70c multicolored	1.60	.45

Swiss Railways, 150th Anniv.
A450

Designs: 70c, Locomotive 2000, 1990's. 90c, Red Arrow, 1930's. 140c, Pullman coach, 1920's-30's. 170c, Limmat steam locomotive, 1800's.

1997, Mar. 11   Photo.   Perf. 11½

987	A450	70c multicolored	1.60	.40
988	A450	90c multicolored	2.10	.55
989	A450	140c multicolored	3.25	1.25
990	A450	170c multicolored	4.00	1.75
		Nos. 987-990 (4)	10.95	3.95

Gallo-Roman Art — A451

Archaeological finds: 70c, Venus of Octodurus. 90c, Bronze bust of Bacchus. 110c, Ceramic fragment depicting Victoria. 180c, Mosaic theatrical mask.

1997, Mar. 11

991	A451	70c multicolored	1.60	.40
992	A451	90c multicolored	2.10	.50
993	A451	110c multicolored	2.50	.80
994	A451	180c multicolored	4.25	1.25
		Nos. 991-994 (4)	10.45	2.95

Swiss Air's North Atlantic Service, 50th Anniv. — A452

1997, Mar. 11   Litho.   Perf. 13½

995	A452	180c multicolored	4.25	1.10

Swiss Farmers' Union, Cent. — A453

1997, May 13   Litho.   Perf. 13½

996	A453	70c shown	1.60	.35
997	A453	90c Street map	2.10	.65

Swiss Municipalities' Union, cent. (#997).

Stories and Legends — A454

Europa: Devil and Billy Goat from legend of the "Devil's Bridge."

1997, May 13   Litho. & Engr.

998	A454	90c multicolored	2.10	1.10

King of Thailand's Visit to Switzerland, Cent. — A455

King Chulalongkorn (Rama V), Pres. Adolf Deucher.

1997, Sept. 12   Litho.   Perf. 13½

999	A455	90c multicolored	2.10	.75

Energy 2000 — A456

1997, Sept. 12   Photo.   Perf. 11½

1000	A456	70c Air (clouds)	1.60	.35
1001	A456	90c Fire	2.10	.65
1002	A456	110c Water	2.50	.95
1003	A456	180c Earth	4.25	1.50
		Nos. 1000-1003 (4)	10.45	3.45

Paul Karrer (1889-1971), Winner of Nobel Prize for Chemistry, 1937 — A457

Design: 110c, Alfred Nobel (1833-96), founder of Nobel Prize.

Litho. & Engr.

1997, Nov. 13   Perf. 13

1004	A457	90c gray & blk	2.10	.50
1005	A457	110c lt gray brn & blk	2.50	.75

Nos. 1004-1005 each issued in sheets of 8. See Sweden Nos. 2254-2255.

Swiss Postal Service A458

Various people from different generations, cultures. Each stamp inscribed in one of Switzerland's four national languages with message to keep in touch.

1997, Nov. 20   Litho.   Perf. 13
Color of Denomination

1006	A458	70c blue	1.60	.40
1007	A458	70c yellow	1.60	.40
1008	A458	70c green	1.60	.40
1009	A458	70c red	1.60	.40
a.		Strip of 4, #1006-1009	6.50	6.50

Division of Swiss PTT — A459

1998, Jan. 7   Litho.   Perf. 13½

1010	A459	90c Swisscom	2.10	.40
1011	A459	90c Swiss Post	2.10	.40

Confederation, 150th Anniv. and Helvetic Republic, Bicent. — A460

Stylized design, proclamation in one of four languages, location of denomination: No. 1012, German, LL. No. 1013, Romansch, LR. No. 1014, French, UL. No. 1015, Italian, UR.

1998, Mar. 10   Photo.   Perf. 11½

1012	A460	90c multicolored	2.10	1.00
1013	A460	90c multicolored	2.10	1.00
1014	A460	90c multicolored	2.10	1.00
1015	A460	90c multicolored	2.10	1.00
a.		Block of 4, #1012-1015	8.50	5.00

Printed in continuous design.

Swiss Old Age and Survivors' Insurance, 50th Anniv. A461

Opening of Natl. Museum, Prangins Castle A462

St. Gallen University, Cent. — A463

1998, Mar. 10

1016	A461	70c multicolored	1.60	.40
1017	A462	70c multicolored	1.60	.40
1018	A463	90c multicolored	2.10	.80
		Nos. 1016-1018 (3)	5.30	1.60

View of Switzerland A464

Designs: 10c, Simplon Pass. 20c, Snow-covered winter scene. 50c, Fence posts along country road. 70c, Hobbyhorses, posts. 90c, Stream, route marker. 110c, Lake, shoreline.

1998, Mar. 10   Litho.   Perf. 13x13½

1019	A464	10c multicolored	.25	.25
1020	A464	20c multicolored	.45	.25
1021	A464	50c multicolored	1.15	.30
1022	A464	70c multicolored	1.60	.30
1023	A464	90c multicolored	2.10	.30
1024	A464	110c multicolored	2.50	.75
		Nos. 1019-1024 (6)	8.05	2.15

See Nos. 1027-1029.

Sion, Candidate for 2006 Winter Olympic Games — A465

1998, Feb. 12   Litho.   Perf. 13½

1025	A465	90c multicolored	2.10	.75

National Day — A466

1998, May 12

1026	A466	90c multicolored	2.10	1.10

Europa.

View of Switzerland Type of 1998

140c, City of Zug. 170c, Olive grove, Castagnola. 180c, Road, mountains outside Reutigen.

1998, Sept. 8   Litho.   Perf. 13

1027	A464	140c multicolored	3.25	.50
1028	A464	170c multicolored	4.00	.60
1029	A464	180c multicolored	4.25	.75
		Nos. 1027-1029 (3)	11.50	1.85

Youth Sports — A467

Die Cut x Serpentine Die Cut

1998, Sept. 8   Photo.
Self-Adhesive
Booklet Stamps

1030	A467	70c Roller blading	1.60	.50
1031	A467	70c Snow boarding	1.60	.50
1032	A467	70c Mountain biking	1.60	.50
1033	A467	70c Street basketball	1.60	.50
1034	A467	70c Beach volleyball	1.60	.50
a.		Booklet pane, #1030-1034 + label	8.00	
		Complete booklet, 2 #1034a	16.00	

Universal Declaration of Human Rights, 50th Anniv. — A468

1998, Nov. 25   Litho.   Perf. 13½

1035	A468	70c multicolored	1.60	.50

Christmas A469

1998, Nov. 25

1036	A469	90c multicolored	2.10	.75

Bridge 24, Slender West Lake, Yangzhou A470

Chillon Castle, Lake Geneva A470A

Photo. & Engr.
1998, Nov. 25   **Perf. 13½**
1037 A470 20c multicolored   .45 .25
Photo.
1038 A470A 70c multicolored   1.60 .55
  a. Sheet of 4 each, #1038-
       1039   15.00 15.00

Souvenir Sheet
Perf. 11½
1039 A470A 90c Castle,
       Bridge 24   2.10 1.50

No. 1039 contains one 53x45mm stamp. See China (PRC) Nos. 2920-2921.
No. 1039 exists with China 1999 World Philatelic Exhibition emblem and a hologram in margin. These were sold for 3.50fr only canceled on cover.

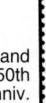

Switzerland Post, 150th Anniv. A471

1999, Jan. 21   Photo.   Perf. 12
1040 A471 90c multicolored   2.10 .75

Pingu the Penguin as Postman A472

1999, Mar. 9   Litho.   Perf. 13½
1041 A472 70c Carrying package 1.60 .50
1042 A472 90c In delivery cart 2.10 .65

See Nos. 1064-1065 for redrawn designs.

Comic Book, "Les Amours de Monsieur Vieux Bois," by Rodolphe Töpffer (1799-1846) — A473

Vieux Bois: No. 1043, Waving out of window, lady walking away. No. 1044, Down on knees, lady. No. 1045, In air after knocking over furniture. No. 1046, Pulling lady up to lift her over wall. No. 1047, Standing with his lady to be married.

Booklet Stamps
Die Cut x Serpentine Die Cut
1999, Mar. 9   **Self-Adhesive**
1043 A473 90c multicolored   2.10 .55
1044 A473 90c multicolored   2.10 .55
1045 A473 90c multicolored   2.10 .55
1046 A473 90c multicolored   2.10 .55
1047 A473 90c multicolored   2.10 .55
  a. Booklet pane, #1043-1047 +
       label   10.50
       Complete booklet, 2 #1047a 21.00

First Non-stop Balloon Flight Around World by Bertrand Piccard and Brian Jones — A473a

1999, Mar. 24   Litho.   Perf. 13½
1047B A473a 90c multicolored 2.10 .55

UPU, 125th Anniv. — A474

1999, May 5   Photo.   Perf. 12
1048 A474 20c shown   .45 .25
1049 A474 70c UPU emblem   1.60 .65
  a. Pair, #1048-1049   2.10 1.25

No. 1049 is 56x30mm. Issued in sheets of 8 stamps.

SOS Children's Village, Wabern, 50th Anniv. — A475

1999, May 5   Litho.   Perf. 13½
1050 A475 70c multicolored   1.60 .45

Vintners Festival, Vevey — A476

1999, May 5
1051 A476 90c multicolored   2.10 .55
       Complete booklet, 10 #1051 21.00

Council of Europe, 50th Anniv. — A477

1999, May 5   Photo.   Perf. 11½
1052 A477 90c multicolored   2.10 .55

Swiss National Park — A478

1999, May 5   Litho.   Perf. 13½
1053 A478 90c Horns of an ibex 2.10 1.10
       Europa.

Geneva Convention, 50th Anniv. — A479

1999, May 5
1054 A479 110c multicolored   2.50 .85

Field Marshal Aleksandr Suvorov's Alpine Campaign, 200th Anniv. A481

Designs: 70c, Suvorov and soldiers, monument at Schöllenen Gorge. 110c, Suvorov's vanguard by Lake Klöntal.

1999, Sept. 24   Photo.   Perf. 11¾
1056 A481 70c multicolored   1.60 .50
1057 A481 110c multicolored   2.50 .70

Nos. 1056-1057 each issued in sheets of 8 stamps.
See Russia Nos. 6534-6535.

Rights of the Child — A482

1999, Sept. 24   Litho.   Perf. 13½
1058 A482 70c multicolored   1.60 .45

Carl Lutz (1895-1975), Diplomat, Rescuer of Jews — A483

1999, Sept. 24
1059 A483 90c multicolored   2.10 .55

Christian Friedrich Schönbein (1799-1868), Discoverer of Ozone — A484

1999, Sept. 24
1060 A484 1.10fr multicolored   2.50 .60

Midday in the Alps, by Giovanni Segantini (1858-99) A485

1999, Sept. 24
1061 A485 180c multicolored   4.25 1.25

Christmas — A486

Perf. 13½x13¼
1999, Nov. 23   Litho.
1062 A486 90c multicolored   2.10 .75

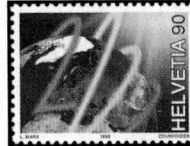

Millennium A487

Perf. 11¾x11½
1999, Nov. 23   Photo.
1063 A487 90c multicolored   1.40 .55

No. 1063 was printed in sheets of 8 stamps and 8 se-tenant labels with text or blank. Swiss Post offered to print photos or artwork sent in by customers on the blank labels. Personalized sheets sold for 14fr per sheet.

Pingu The Penguin Type of 1999
Redrawn to Omit Strings on Packages
1999, Dec. 6   Litho.   Perf. 13¼x13½
1064 A472 70c Like #1041 1.60 .55
1065 A472 90c Like #1042 2.10 .70

Intl. Cycling Union, Cent. — A488

2000, Mar. 7   Litho.   Perf. 13¼x13½
1066 A488 70c multicolored   1.60 .40

Swiss Souvenirs — A489

Souvenirs in snow domes: 10c, Alphorn. 20c, Fondue pot. 30c, Wine pitchers. 50c, Figurine of ibex. 60c, Neuchâtel "Pendule" wall clock. 70c, St. Bernard dog.

2000, Mar. 7   Litho.   Perf. 13x13¼
1067 A489 10c multicolored   .25 .25
1068 A489 20c multicolored   .45 .25
1069 A489 30c multicolored   .70 .35
1070 A489 50c multicolored   1.15 .45
1071 A489 60c multicolored   1.40 .50
1072 A489 70c multicolored   1.10 .60
       Nos. 1067-1072 (6)   5.05 2.40
       See No. 1101.

National Council of Women, Cent. A490

2000, May 10   Litho.   Perf. 13¼
1073 A490 70c multi   1.60 .55

Europa Issue
Common Design Type
2000, May 10
1074 CD17 90c multi   2.10 .75

Embroidery — A491

Embroidered
2000, June 21   Imperf.
Self-Adhesive
1075 A491 5fr multi   16.00 16.00
  a. Sheet of 4   225.00 225.00

A492

Designs: 120c, Payerne Church, violin. 130c, Church of St. Saphorin, waiter's tray. 180c, Vals hot springs, bather.

2000, June 21 Litho. Perf. 13x13¼
1076 A492 120c multi ... 2.75 .75
1077 A492 130c multi ... 3.00 .80
1078 A492 180c multi ... 4.25 1.00
Nos. 1076-1078 (3) ... 10.00 2.55
See Nos. 1089-1092, 1103-1105.

2000 Census — A493

2000, Sept. 15 Perf. 13¼x13½
1079 A493 70c multi ... 1.60 .55

A Perfect World, by Sandra Dobler A494

My Town, by Stephanie Aerschmann A495

Stampin' the Future children's stamp design contest winners: No. 1080, Alien From Outer Space, by Yannik Kehrli. No. 1081, Looks Below the Sun, by Charlotte Bättig.

Booklet Stamps
Serpentine Die Cut 5¾ Vert.
2000, June 15 Self-Adhesive
1080 A494 70c multi ... 1.60 .60
1081 A494 70c multi ... 1.60 .60
1082 A494 70c shown ... 1.60 .60
1083 A495 70c shown ... 1.60 .60
a. Booklet pane, #1080-1083 ... 6.50
Booklet, 2 #1083a ... 13.00

The booklet, which was sold unfolded, has rouletting between panes.

2000 Summer Olympics, Sydney A496

2000, Sept. 15 Photo. Die Cut
Booklet Stamps
Self-Adhesive
1084 A496 90c Swimmer ... 2.10 .60
1085 A496 90c Cyclist ... 2.10 .60
1086 A496 90c Runner ... 2.10 .60
a. Booklet pane, #1084-1086 ... 6.50
Booklet, #1086a ... 6.50

No. 1086a is separated from booklet cover by rouletting. The booklet was sold folded. See Nos. 1201-1202.

Stamp Day — A497

Perf. 13¼x13½
2000, Nov. 21 Litho.
1087 A497 70c multi ... 1.60 .40

Christmas — A498

2000, Nov. 21 Photo. Perf. 11½
Granite Paper
1088 A498 90c multi ... 2.10 .50
See No. 1197c.

Type of 2000
Designs: 200c, Mountain, hiker. 220c, Postbus, children. 300c, Cyclist, bridge and church, Biasca. 400c, Airplane at airport, tourist with suitcase.

2000-01 Litho. Perf. 13x13¼
1089 A492 200c multi ... 4.50 2.00
1090 A492 220c multi ... 5.00 2.25
1091 A492 300c multi ... 7.00 3.00
1092 A492 400c multi ... 9.25 3.75

Issued: 200c, 300c, 11/21/00. 220c, 400c, 3/13/01.

Alice Rivaz (1901-98), Writer — A499

Perf. 13¼x13½
2001, Mar. 13 Litho. & Engr.
1093 A499 70c multi ... 1.60 .40

Aero Club, Cent. A500

2001, Mar. 13 Litho. Perf. 13¼
1094 A500 90c multi ... 2.10 .55

Congratulations A501

2001, Mar. 13 Perf. 13¼x13½
1095 A501 90c multi ... 2.10 .60

Caritas, Cent. — A502

2001, Mar. 13
1096 A502 110c multi ... 2.50 .75

UN High Commissioner for Refugees, 50th Anniv. — A503

2001, Mar. 13
1097 A503 130c multi ... 3.00 1.00

Vela Museum, Ligornetto A504

2001, May 9
1098 A504 70c multi ... 1.60 .50

Europa — A505

2001, May 9
1099 A505 90c multi ... 2.10 .60

Chocosuisse, Cent. — A506

2001, May 9 Photo. Perf. 11½
Granite Paper
1100 A506 90c multi ... 2.10 .50
No. 1100 has a scratch-and-sniff coating with a chocolate aroma.

Swiss Souvenirs Type of 2000
Serpentine Die Cut 5¾ Horiz.
2001, May 9 Self-Adhesive Litho.
1101 A489 70c Like #1072 ... 1.60 .40
a. Booklet of 12 ... 19.50

No. 1101 was issued in coil rolls of 100 with backing paper wider than the stamp and the stamps spaced. Also issued in booklets with different backing paper with stamps adjoining. Used examples of each variety are identical.

Type of 1995
Serpentine Die Cut 5¾ Vert.
2001, May 9 Self-Adhesive Typo.
1102 A404b 90c multi ... 2.10 .45
a. Booklet of 12 ... 25.00

Type of 2000
Designs: 90c, Farm house, Willisau, people feeding horse. 100c, Boat on Lake Geneva, woman at water's edge. 110c, Kleine Matterhorn Glacier, skier.

2001, Sept. 20 Litho. Perf. 13x13¼
1103 A492 90c multi ... 2.10 .50
1104 A492 100c multi ... 2.25 .50
1105 A492 110c multi ... 2.50 .60
Nos. 1103-1105 (3) ... 6.85 1.60

The Birth of Venus, by Arnold Böcklin (1827-1901) A507

2001, Sept. 20 Perf. 13½
1106 A507 180c multi ... 4.25 2.00

Souvenir Sheet

Flowers — A508

70c, Melastoma malabathricum. 90c, Saraca cauliflora. 110c, Leontopodium alpinum. 130c, Gentiana clusii.

2001, Sept. 20 Perf. 13¼x12¾
1107 A508 Sheet of 4 ... 11.00 11.00
a. 70c multicolored ... 1.60 .80
b. 90c multicolored ... 2.10 .90
c. 110c multicolored ... 2.50 1.25
d. 130c multicolored ... 3.00 1.50
See Singapore Nos. 984-988.

Illustrations from Children's Book, "The Rainbow Fish," by Marcus Pfister — A509

2001, Sept. 20 Photo. Perf. 12¾x14
1108 A509 70c Fish, coral ... 1.60 .40
1109 A509 90c Fish, starfish ... 2.10 .50

Stamp Day Stamp Design Competition Winner — A510

Perf. 13¼x13½
2001, Nov. 20 Litho.
1110 A510 70c multi ... 1.60 .45

Christmas — A511

2001, Nov. 20 Perf. 11½
Granite Paper
1111 A511 90c multi ... 2.10 .60
See No. 1197a.

Geneva Escalade, 400th Anniv. — A512

Perf. 13¼x13½
2002, Mar. 12 Litho.
1112 A512 70c multi ... 1.60 .40

Federal Parliament Building, Cent. — A513

2002, Mar. 12
1113 A513 90c multi ... 2.10 .50

Rega Air Rescue Foundation A514

Litho. with Hologram Affixed
2002, Mar. 12 Perf. 13x13¾
1114 A514 180c multi ... 4.25 2.00

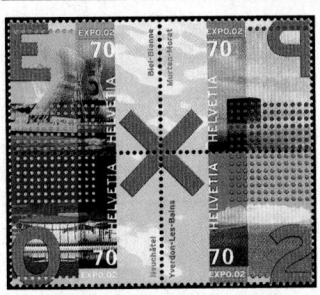

Expo.02, Switzerland — A515

No. 1115: a, "E." b, Backwards "P." c, "0." d, "2."

2002, Mar. 12 Photo. *Perf. 14x13¼*
Granite Paper
1115 A515 Block of 4 .... 6.50 4.50
a.-d. 70c Any single .... 1.60 .80

Swiss Railways, Cent. — A516

Designs: 70c, RABDe 500 Inter-city tilting train. 90c, Inter-city 2000 double-deck train. 120c, Seetal line railcar. 130c, Re 460 locomotive.

2002, Mar. 12 *Perf. 12¾x14*
1116 A516 70c multi .... 1.60 .40
1117 A516 90c multi .... 2.10 .70
1118 A516 120c multi .... 2.75 .75
1119 A516 130c multi 3.00 1.00
Nos. 1116-1119 (4) 9.45 2.85

Souvenir Sheet

Arteplage Mobile du Jura — A517

2002, May 15 Photo. *Perf. 14*
1120 A517 90c multi 2.10 1.25
Expo.02, Switzerland.

Europa
A518

2002, May 15 Litho. *Perf. 13¼*
1121 A518 70c Clown .... 1.60 .40
1122 A518 90c Clown, diff. .... 2.10 .50

Teddy Bears, Cent. — A519

No. 1123 — Teddy bear from: a, France, 1925 (round, with tan frame, 26mm diameter). b, Switzerland, 1950s (square with cut in corners, 25x25mm). c, Germany, 1904 (oval, 23x33mm). d, Switzerland, 2002 (rectangular, 26x23mm). e, England, c. 1920 (round, with blue and red frame, 26mm diameter).

2002, May 15 *Die Cut*
Self-Adhesive
1123 A519 Booklet pane of 5 10.50
a.-e. 90c Any single 2.10 1.00
f. Booklet, 2 #1123 .... 21.00

Cessation of Production at Swiss Post Stamp Printers A520

Litho. & Engr.
2002, Sept. 17 *Perf. 13¼*
1124 A520 70c multi .... 1.60 .40

Ladybug — A521

Serpentine Die Cut 12¼ Vert.
2002, Sept. 17 Litho.
Self-Adhesive
1125 A521 90c multi + label .... 2.10 .55
a. Booklet pane of 10 .... 21.00

Insects — A522

Designs: 10c, Anax imperator. 20c, Mesoacidalia aglaja. 50c, Rosalia alpina. 100c, Graphosoma lineatum.

Perf. 13¾x14¼
2002, Sept. 17 Litho.
1126 A522 10c multi .... .25 .25
1127 A522 20c multi .... .45 .25
1128 A522 50c multi .... 1.15 .25
1129 A522 100c multi .... 2.25 .30
Nos. 1126-1129 (4) 4.10 1.05

Minerals — A523

Designs: 200c, Quartz crystal. 500c, Titanite.

2002-05 Litho. *Perf. 13¾*
1130 A523 200c multi 4.50 1.50
1131 A523 500c multi 11.50 2.75
a. Perf. 13¾x14¼ 11.50 2.75
Issued: Nos. 1130-1131, 9/17/02. No. 1131a, 5/10/05.

Switzerland's Entry Into United Nations — A524

Perf. 13¾x14¼
2002, Sept. 10 Litho.
1132 A524 90c multi .... 2.10 .50

Stamp Day — A525

2002, Nov. 19 *Perf. 13¾x14*
1133 A525 70c multi .... 1.60 .45

World Alpine Skiing Championships, St. Moritz — A526

2002, Nov. 19 *Perf. 14x13¾*
1134 A526 90c multi .... 2.10 .50

Emblem of Switzerland Tourism — A527

Serpentine Die Cut 13¼ Vert.
2002, Nov. 19 Self-Adhesive
1135 A527 (1.30fr) blue & multi .... 3.00 .50
a. Booklet pane of 6 .... 18.00
1136 A527 (1.80fr) red & multi .... 4.25 .75
a. Booklet pane of 6 .... 25.00

Nos. 1135-1136 were valid only on post cards sent to European (#1135) or non-European (#1136) addresses, and could not be used in combination with other stamps. No. 1135a sold for 7.20fr, and No. 1136a for 10fr.

Christmas — A528

2002, Nov. 19 Photo. *Perf. 11½*
Granite Paper
1137 A528 90c multi .... 2.10 .50
See No. 1197b.

Swiss Natl. Association of and for the Blind, Cent. — A529

Litho. & Embossed
2003, Mar. 6 *Perf. 14¾x14½*
1138 A529 70c red & carmine .... 1.60 .45

100th Natl. Horse Market and Show, Saignelégier A530

2003, Mar. 6 Litho. *Perf. 13¼x13½*
1139 A530 90c multi .... 2.10 .50

2003 World Orienteering Championships, Rapperswil and Jona — A531

2003, Mar. 6
1140 A531 90c multi .... 2.10 .50

Intl. Year of Water A532

2003, Mar. 6 *Perf. 13x13¼*
1141 A532 90c multi .... 2.10 .50

Medicinal Plants — A533

Designs: 70c, Hypericum perforatum. 90c, Vinca minor. 110c, Valeriana officinalis. 120c, Arnica montana. 130c, Centaurium minus. 180c, Malva sylvestris. 220c, Matricaria chamomilla.

2003-05 *Perf. 14x13¾*
1142 A533 70c multi .... 1.60 .50
1143 A533 90c multi .... 2.10 .50
1144 A533 110c multi .... 2.50 .65
1145 A533 120c multi .... 2.75 .75
a. Perf. 14x14½ .... 2.75 .40
1146 A533 130c multi .... 3.00 .90
1147 A533 180c multi 4.25 1.10
a. Perf. 14x14½ .... 4.25 .60
1148 A533 220c multi 5.00 1.50
a. Perf. 14x14½ .... 5.00 .70
Nos. 1142-1148 (7) 21.20 5.90

Issued: Nos. 1142-1148, 3/6/03; Nos. 1145a, 1147a, 1148a, 2005.

Europa — A534

2003, May 8 Litho. *Perf. 13¼x13*
1149 A534 90c multi .... 2.10 .50

Comic Strip Art — A535

No. 1150 — Envelope and: a, Woman, birthday cake. b, Man, heart. c, Man, thunder cloud. d, Woman, musical note.
90c, Envelope, woman, duck.

2003, May 8 *Perf. 14¾*
1150 A535 Block of 4 .... 6.50 4.00
a.-d. 70c Any single .... 1.60 .50
Souvenir Sheet
1151 A535 90c multi 2.50 1.25
20th Intl. Comics Festival, Sierre.

Souvenir Sheet

Trilateral Stamp Exhibition, Ticino — A536

2003, May 8   **Perf. 14¾**
1152 A536 Sheet of 2   2.50 2.50
   a.   20c Eagle   .45 .25
   b.   70c Gentian   1.60 .40

Switzerland's Victory in 2003 America's Cup Yacht Races — A537

2003, Mar 7   **Litho.**   **Perf. 13x13¼**
1153 A537 90c multi   2.10 .45

No. 1153 was not sent to standing order subscribers until September.

Minerals Type of 2002

Designs: 300c, Rutilated quartz. 400c, Green fluorite.

2003, Sept. 9   **Perf. 13¾x14¼**
1154 A523 300c multi   7.00 2.00
1155 A523 400c multi   9.25 3.00

Comic Strip "Diddl," by Thomas Goletz — A538

Designs: 70c, Mice reading love letters. 90c, Mouse chasing flying envelopes.

2003, Sept. 9   **Perf. 13¼x13½**
1156 A538 70c multi   1.60 .45
1157 A538 90c multi   2.10 .55

See Nos. 1184-1185.

UNESCO World Heritage Sites — A539

Designs: No. 1158, Jungfrau-Aletsch-Bietschhorn. No. 1159, Three Castles, Bellinzona. No. 1160, Old City, Bern. No. 1161, Convent of St. Gall. No. 1162, Benedictine Convent of St. John, Müstair.

2003, Sept. 9   **Perf. 12¾**
1158 A539 90c multi   2.10 .55
1159 A539 90c multi   2.10 .55
1160 A539 90c multi   2.10 .55
1161 A539 90c multi   2.10 .55
1162 A539 90c multi   2.10 .55
   Nos. 1158-1162 (5)   10.50 2.75

Nos. 1158-1162 each issued in sheets of 6. See NO. 1186.

Stamp Day — A540

     Perf. 13¼x13½
2003, Nov. 19   **Litho.**
1163 A540 70c multi   1.60 .45

Four-leaf Clover — A541

Serpentine Die Cut 12¼ Vert.
2003, Nov. 19   **Self-Adhesive**
1164 A541 130c multi + label   3.00 .65
   a.   Booklet of 10   30.00

Christmas — A542

Ornaments: 70c, Horseman. 90c, Santa Claus.

2003, Nov. 19   **Photo.**   **Perf. 11½**
1165 A542 70c multi   1.60 .45
1166 A542 90c multi   2.10 .55

See Nos. 1197d-1197e.

Swiss Design — A543

Designs: 15c, Rex potato peeler, 1947, designed by Alfred Neweczeral. 50c, Zipper, 1924, designed by M.O. Winterthaler. 85c, Station clock, 1944, designed by Hanls Hilfiker. No. 1169, Le Fauteuil Grand Confort (black armchair), 1928, designed by Le Corbusier. No. 1170, Landi chair (aluminum chair), 1938, designed by Hans Coray.

Serpentine Die Cut 12
2003-04   **Self-Adhesive**   **Litho.**
1167 A543 15c multi   .35 .25
   a.   Booklet pane of 10   3.50
1168 A543 85c multi   2.00 .30
   a.   Booklet pane of 10   19.50
1169 A543 100c multi + etiquette   2.25 .30
   a.   Booklet pane of 10 + 10 etiquettes   25.00
   b.   Nos. 1167-1169 on translucent paper   4.50
1170 A543 100c multi + etiquette   2.25 .30
   a.   Booklet pane of 10 + 10 etiquettes   25.00

Coil Stamp

1171 A543 50c multi   1.15 .25
   Nos. 1167-1171 (5)   8.00 1.40

Issued: 15c, 85c, No. 1169, 12/30; No. 1170, 3/31/04; 50c, 9/7/04. See No. 1206.

FIFA (Fédération Internationale de Football Association), Cent. — A544

2004, Mar. 9   **Perf. 13¼**
1172 A544 100c multi   2.25 .55

UEFA (European Football Union), 50th Anniv. — A545

2004, Mar. 9   **Perf. 13¼x13½**
1173 A545 130c multi   3.00 .65

CERN (European Organization for Nuclear Research), 50th Anniv. — A546

2004, Mar. 9   **Perf. 13½x13¼**
1174 A546 180c multi   4.25 .90

Comic Strip "Titeuf," by Zep — A547

Titeuf: No. 1175, Giving spring flower to Nadia. No. 1176, Sitting in refrigerator. No. 1177, Running through raked leaves. No. 1178, Pointing at snowman.

2004, Mar. 9   **Perf. 14x13½**
1175 A547 85c multi   2.00 .45
1176 A547 85c multi   2.00 .45
1177 A547 85c multi   2.00 .45
1178 A547 85c multi   2.00 .45
   Nos. 1175-1178 (4)   8.00 1.80

Souvenir Sheet

Cycling — A548

No. 1179 — Cyclists and marker for: a, Route 5. b, Route 3.

2004, Mar. 9   **Perf. 14x13½**
1179 A548 Sheet of 2   5.50 5.50
   a.-b.   100c Either single   2.25 .55

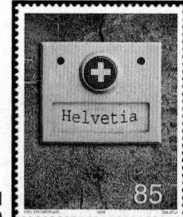

Doorbell Button — A549

2004, May 6   **Perf. 14½x14¼**
1180 A549 85c multi   2.00 .45

Europa A550

2004, May 6   **Perf. 14¼x14½**
1181 A550 100c multi   2.25 .55

2004 Summer Olympics, Athens A551

2004, May 6   **Perf. 13x13¼**
1182 A551 100c multi   2.25 .55
     See No. 12O3.

Zeppelin NT — A552

2004, May 6   **Perf. 14x13½**
1183 A552 180c multi   4.25 .90

Diddl Type of 2003

Designs: 85c, Diddl with teddy bear, Pimboli, and butterflies. 100c, Diddl with flower.

2004, May 6   **Perf. 13¼x13½**
1184 A538 85c multi   2.00 .45
1185 A538 100c multi   2.10 .55

UNESCO World Heritage Type of 2003

Design: Monte San Giorgio.

2004, Sept. 7   **Perf. 13¾x14¼**
1186 A539 100c multi   2.25 .55

Issued in sheets of 6.

Suisse Balance Health Program A553

2004, Sept. 7   **Perf. 13¼x13½**
1187 A553 85c multi   2.00 .45

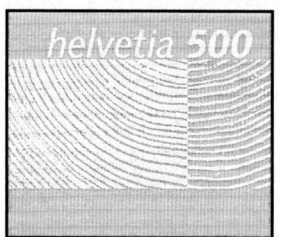

Wood — A554

Silk-screened on Wood
2004, Sept. 7   **Imperf.**
     Self-Adhesive
1188 A554 500c white   11.50 2.75

Cheesemaking A555

Designs: 100c, Cheesemaker inspecting curds and whey. 130c, Cheeses, grapes and nuts.

2004, Sept. 7   **Litho.**   **Perf. 13¼x13½**
1189 A555 100c multi   2.25 .55
1190 A555 130c multi   3.00 .70

Animal Protection A556

2004, Sept. 7   **Perf. 14x13½**
1191 A556   85c Cat   2.00   .45
1192 A556   100c Hedgehog   2.25   .55
1193 A556   130c Pig   3.00   .70
    Nos. 1191-1193 (3)   7.25 1.70
Nos. 1191-1193 each issued in sheets of 6.

Souvenir Sheet

Sitting Helvetia Stamps and Coins, 150th Anniv. — A557

No. 1194: a, Type A17. b, Coin.

Litho. (#1194a), Litho. & Embossed (#1194b)
Perf. 14¼x13¾ on 3 Sides
2004, Sept. 7
1194 A557   Sheet of 2   4.50 4.50
  a.-b.   85c Either single   2.00   .45

Stamp Day — A558

Perf. 13¼x13½
2004, Nov. 23   **Litho.**
1195 A558 85c multi   2.00   .50

Sports A559

2004, Nov. 23   **Litho.**   **Perf. 13x13½**
1196 A559 180c multi   4.25 1.10

No. 1196 is identical to United Nations Offices in Geneva No. 433. The stamp, available for use throughout Switzerland, also served as an official stamp for the International Olympic Committee.

Christmas Ornaments Types of 2000-2003

2004, Nov. 23   **Photo.**   **Perf. 13x13½**
1197   Sheet of 5   12.50 12.50
  a.   A511 85c Snowflake   2.00   .50
  b.   A528 85c Church   2.00   .50
  c.   A498 100c Angel   2.25   .60
  d.   A542 100c Horseman   2.25   .60
  e.   A542 100c Santa Claus   2.25   .60

Photographs by René Burri — A560

No. 1198: a, Children kissing, German inscription. b, Teenagers on bicycle, French inscription. c, Man and woman kissing, Italian

inscription. d, Man and woman in bumper car, Romansch inscription.

Serpentine Die Cut 12
2005, Jan. 3   **Self-Adhesive**   **Litho.**
1198 A560   Block of 4, #a-d + 4 etiquettes   9.25
  a.-d.   100c Any single   2.25   .35
  e.   Booklet pane, 2 each #1198a-1198d + 8 etiquettes   18.50

No. 1198 lacks self-adhesive selvage, and is on a translucent paper that is rouletted on the left and right sides. No. 1198e has a white paper backing, has each stamp and its se-tenant etiquette surrounded by self-adhesive selvage, and is rouletted through the selvage and backing paper.

Swiss Federal Institute of Technology, Zurich, 150th Anniv. A561

2005, Mar. 8   **Perf. 13**
1199 A561 85c multi   2.00   .50

Matterhorn Superimposed Over Inverted Map of Africa — A562

2005, Mar. 8   **Perf. 13x13¼**
1200 A562 85c multi   2.00   .50

Discovery of rocks from Africa making up top of the Matterhorn.

Unspunnen Traditional Costume and Alpine Herdsman's Festival, Bicent. — A563

2005, Mar. 8   **Perf. 13¼x13**
1201 A563 100c multi   2.25   .60

Albert Einstein's Theory of Relativity, Cent. — A564

2005, Mar. 8   **Perf. 13½x13¼**
1202 A564 130c multi   3.00   .75

Cartoon Mouse, by Uli Stein — A565

Mouse with: 85c, Slice of Swiss cheese in typewriter. 100c, Golf club and letter on tee.

2005, Mar. 8   **Perf. 13¼x13½**
1203 A565 85c multi   2.00   .50
1204 A565 100c multi   2.25   .60

Souvenir Sheet

Geneva International Auto Show, Cent. — A566

2005, Mar. 8   **Perf. 13¾x14¼**
1205 A566   Sheet of 2   14.50 14.50
  a.   100c Front of car   2.25   .60
  b.   130c Side of car   3.00   .75

Swiss Design Type of 2003-04

Design: Fixpencil, by Caran d'Ache.

2005, May 10   ***Serpentine Die Cut 12***
Self-Adhesive
1206 A543   220c multi + etiquette   5.00   .75
  a.   Serpentine die cut 12¼x12 + etiquette   5.00   .75
  b.   Booklet pane, 6 #1206, 4 #1206a + 10 etiquettes   50.00

Europa A567

2005, May 10   **Perf. 13x13¼**
1207 A567 100c multi   2.25   .60

Soccer for the Visually Impaired A568

2005, May 10   **Perf. 13¾x14¼**
1208 A568 100c multi   2.25   .60
Printed in sheets of 6.

Opening of Paul Klee Center, Bern — A569

2005, May 10   **Perf. 13¼x14**
1209 A569 100c multi   2.25   .60
Printed in sheets of 6.

Stylized Butterflies A570

Serpentine Die Cut 11¾
2005, May 10   **Self-Adhesive**
1210 A570 100c multi   2.25   .60
  a.   Booklet pane of 10 + 10 labels   25.00

Felix the Bunny, by Annette Langen A571

Felix and: 85c, Lambs, cows. 100c, Swans and Chillon Castle.

2005, May 10   **Perf. 13x13¼**
1211 A571 85c multi   2.00   .50
1212 A571 100c multi   2.25   .60

Subtractive Color Combinations — A572

Additive Color Combinations — A573

Serpentine Die Cut 12½
2005, Sept. 6   **Litho.**
Self-Adhesive
1213 A572 50c multi   1.15   .30
1214 A573 100c multi   2.25   .55

Swiss Timepieces A574

Designs: 100c, Watchmaker, pocket watch and mechanism. 130c, Woman, wristwatches.

2005, Sept. 6   **Perf. 13¼x13½**
1215 A574 100c multi   2.25   .55
1216 A574 130c multi   3.00   .70

Cell Phone Pictures A575

Images: 85c, On Horseback, by Brigit Rohrbach. 100c, Mountain Hike, by Peter Schumacher. 130c, On Top of the World, by Rémy Sager. 180c, Tracks in the Snow, by Debora Ronchi.

2005, Sept. 6   **Perf. 14¼x14**
1217 A575 85c multi   2.00   .45
1218 A575 100c multi   2.25   .55
1219 A575 130c multi   3.00   .70
1220 A575 180c multi   4.25 1.00
    Nos. 1217-1220 (4)   11.50 2.70

Souvenir Sheet

Friends of Nature Switzerland,
Cent. — A576

2005, Sept. 6   **Perf. 13½**
1221   A576   Sheet of 4   11.50   11.50
   a.   85c Skiers   2.00   1.40
   b.   100c Chalet, vert.   2.25   1.60
   c.   110c People fording stream   2.50   1.75
   d.   130c Mountain climber, vert.   3.00   2.10

Stamp
Day — A577

          Perf. 13¼x13½
2005, Nov. 22   **Litho.**
1222   A577   85c multi   2.00   .45

2006 Winter
Olympics,
Turin,
Italy — A578

2005, Nov. 22   **Perf. 13¾**
1223   A578   100c Curling   2.25   .55
Issued in sheets of 6. See No. 12O4.

Swiss
Papal
Guards,
500th
Anniv.
A579

Designs: 85c, Guard and drummers. 100c,
Guards and St. Peter's Basilica.

2005, Nov. 22   **Perf. 14x14¼**
1224   A579   85c multi   2.00   .45
1225   A579   100c multi   2.25   .55
Nos. 1224-1225 each issued in sheets of 6.
See Vatican City Nos. 1315-1316.

Christmas — A580

Designs: 85c, Crozier and miter. 100c, Gingerbread man.

2005, Nov. 22   **Perf. 13½x13¼**
1226   A580   85c multi   2.00   .45
1227   A580   100c multi   2.25   .55

Reintroduction
of Alpine Ibex
in Switzerland,
Cent. — A581

2006, Mar. 7   **Litho.**   **Perf. 13¼x13**
1228   A581   85c multi   2.00   .45

Youth
Soccer — A582

2006, Mar. 7   **Perf. 13¼x13½**
1229   A582   85c multi   2.00   .45

Cuculus
Canorus
A583

Serpentine Die Cut 12
2006, Mar. 7   **Photo.**
       Self-Adhesive
1230   A583   240c multi + eti-
             quette   5.50   .75
   a.   Block of 10 + 10 etiquettes   55.00
No. 1230a is on a backing paper with bar
codes on the reverse.
     See Nos. 1273-1276, 1306-1308, 1341-
1342.

Railroad
Anniversaries
A584

Designs: 85c, Simplon Tunnel, cent. 100c,
Bern-Lötschberg-Simplon Railway, cent.

2006, Mar. 7   **Litho.**   **Perf. 14x13¾**
1231   A584   85c multi   2.00   .45
1232   A584   100c multi   2.25   .55

Art Nouveau Exhibition, La Chaux-de-
Fonds — A585

Designs: 100c, "Fir." 180c, "Petal."

2006, Mar. 7
1233   A585   100c multi   2.25   .55
1234   A585   180c multi   4.25   .90

Post Buses,
Cent. — A586

Various post buses and passengers.

Serpentine Die Cut 10¾x11
2006, Mar. 7   **Self-Adhesive**   **Litho.**
1235   A586   85c blue & multi   2.00   .45
   a.   Block of 4 on backing paper   7.75
1236   A586   100c red & multi   2.25   .55
   a.   Block of 4 on backing paper   9.25
1237   A586   130c grn & multi   3.00   .65
   a.   Block of 4 on backing paper   12.00
   b.   Block of 3, #1235-1237 on
       backing paper   7.25
      Nos. 1235-1237 (3)   7.25   1.65
     Nos. 1235-1237 each were issued in sheets
of 20. Stamps are adjacent on Nos. 1235a-
1237a and on a shiny, but opaque backing
paper.

Kasperli,
Children's
Theater
Puppet — A587

2006, May 9   **Litho.**   **Perf. 14x13¾**
1238   A587   85c multi   2.00   .45

Europa
A588

2006, May 9   **Perf. 13x13¼**
1239   A588   100c multi   2.25   .60

Mountains — A589

     No. 1240: a, Eiger (35x36mm). b, Monch
(30x36mm). c, Jungfrau (39x36mm).

2006, May 9   **Perf. 13¼x13½**
1240   A589   Horiz. strip of 3   6.00   6.00
   a.-c.   85c Any single   2.00   .45

Caricatures of
Cows by
Patrice Killoffer
A590

     Cow: 85c, On back. 100c, In water. 130c,
Seated. 180c, In snow.

2006, May 9   **Perf. 14x14¼**
1241   A590   85c multi   2.00   .45
1242   A590   100c multi   2.25   .60
1243   A590   130c multi   3.00   .75
1244   A590   180c multi   4.25   1.10
      Nos. 1241-1244 (4)   11.50   2.80

First Session of
United Nations
Human Rights
Council
A591

         Perf. 13¾x14¼
2006, June 19   **Litho.**
1245   A591   100c multi   2.25   .60

Dimitri the
Clown — A592

2006, Sept. 7   **Perf. 13¼x13**
1246   A592   100c multi   2.25   .55

Victorinox Swiss
Army
Knives — A593

     Designs: 100c, First model, 1897, khaki
pants. 130c, Modern model, blue jeans.

2006, Sept. 7   **Perf. 14x13¾**
1247   A593   100c multi   2.25   .55
1248   A593   130c multi   3.00   .70

Cocolino the
Cooking Cat,
by Oskar
Weiss — A594

Serpentine Die Cut 10¾x11
2006, Sept. 7   **Self-Adhesive**
1249   A594   85c multi   2.00   .45
   a.   Booklet pane of 10   19.50

Fruit — A595

     Designs: 200c, Gelterkinder cherries. 300c,
Spätlauber apple. 400c, Hauszwetschge
plums.

2006   Photo.   Serpentine Die Cut 12
          Self-Adhesive
1250   A595   200c multi   4.60   1.10
1251   A595   300c multi   6.90   1.60
   a.   Pair, #1250-1251 on backing
       paper   13.80
1252   A595   400c multi   9.20   2.25
      Nos. 1250-1252 (3)   20.70   4.95
     Issued: 200c, 300c, 9/7; 400c, 11/21.Nos.
1250-1252 each were printed in sheets of 50.
See also No. 1314.

Town of Olten,
Boy Wearing Train
Conductor's
Hat — A596

        Perf. 13½x13¼
2006, Nov. 21   **Litho.**
1253   A596   85c multi   2.00   .50
      Stamp Day.

Christmas — A597

Designs: 85c, Star singers. 100c, Advent wreath.

2006, Nov. 21
1254	A597	85c multi	2.00	.50
1255	A597	100c multi	2.25	.60

Women's Soccer — A598

2007, Mar. 6   Litho.   Perf. 13¼x13½
1256	A598	85c multi	2.00	.45

Printed in sheets of 6.

Leonhard Euler (1707-83), Mathematician A599

2007, Mar. 6
1257	A599	130c multi	3.00	.70

Stein am Rhein, 1000th Anniv. — A600

No. 1258: a, Town Hall (28x36mm). b, Houses on Town Hall Square (40x36mm). c, Municipal Fountain (34x36mm).

2007, Mar. 6   Perf. 13¾x13½
1258	A600	Horiz. strip of 3	6.00	6.00
a.-c.		85c Any single	2.00	.45

Legends A601

Designs: 85c, Charlemagne and the Snake. 100c, Fenetta, the Island Maiden. 130c, The Judge of Bellinzona. 180c, Margaretha.

2007, Mar. 6   Perf. 13½x14
1259	A601	85c multi	2.00	.45
1260	A601	100c multi	2.25	.55
1261	A601	130c multi	3.00	.70
1262	A601	180c multi	4.25	1.00
		Nos. 1259-1262 (4)	11.50	2.70

Swiss Club for Bernese Mountain Dogs, Cent. — A602

Serpentine Die Cut 11x10¾
2007, Mar. 6   Self-Adhesive
1263	A602	85c multi	2.00	.45
a.		Block of 4 on backing paper	8.00	

No. 1263 was issued in sheets of 20.

Swiss National Bank, Cent. — A603

Designs: 85c, Banknote security devices. 100c, Artwork from 100-franc banknote.

2007, Mar. 6   Self-Adhesive   Litho.
1264	A603	85c multi	2.00	.45
a.		Block of 4 on backing paper	8.00	
1265	A603	100c multi	2.25	.55
a.		Horiz. pair, #1264-1265	4.25	
b.		Block of 4 on backing paper	9.25	

Nos. 1264-1265 each were printed in sheets of 12.

Roger Federer, Tennis Player — A604

2007, Apr. 10   Perf. 13¾x14¼
1266	A604	100c multi	2.25	.60

Swiss Assoc. of Day Care Centers, Cent. — A605

2007, Apr. 27   Perf. 13½x13¾
1267	A605	85c multi	2.00	.45

Europa — A606

2007, Apr. 27   Perf. 14
1268	A606	100c multi	2.25	.60

Scouting, cent. Printed in sheets of 18 + 12 labels.

Art Brut Movement — A607

Designs: 100c, Saint Adolf-Throne-Rock Face-Flower, by Adolf Wölfli. 180c, Untitled work by Carlo Zinelli.

2007, Apr. 27   Perf. 14¼x14
1269	A607	100c multi	2.25	.60
1270	A607	180c multi	4.25	1.00

Museum of Communications, Cent. — A608

People with: 85c, Lake in background. 100c, Building in background.

Litho. With Three-Dimensional Plastic Affixed
Serpentine Die Cut 10½
2007, Apr. 27   Self-Adhesive
1271	A608	85c multi	2.00	.45
1272	A608	100c multi	2.25	.60

Bird Type of 2006

Designs: 85c, Fringilla coelebs. 100c, Parus major. 110c, Tichodroma muraria. 180c, Aegolius funereus.

Serpentine Die Cut 12
2007, Sept. 6   Photo.
Self-Adhesive
1273	A583	85c multi	2.00	.30
a.		Booklet pane of 10	20.00	
1274	A583	100c multi + etiquette	2.25	.35
a.		Booklet pane of 10 + 10 etiquettes	24.00	
1275	A583	110c multi	2.50	.40
1276	A583	180c multi	4.25	.65
a.		Block of 4, #1273-1276, + 2 etiquettes on backing paper	11.00	
		Nos. 1273-1276 (4)	11.00	1.70

No. 1276 was printed with and without an etiquette.

The Dance, by Nina Corti — A609

2007, Sept. 6   Litho.   Perf. 14¼x14
1277	A609	85c multi	2.00	.50

Illustration for Children's Book "Schnellen-Ursli," by Alois Carigiet — A610

Serpentine Die Cut 10½x11
2007, Sept. 6   Self-Adhesive
1278	A610	85c multi	2.00	.50
a.		Booklet pane of 10	20.00	

Congratulations A611

Designs: 85c, Children and hearts. 100c, Boy and stars. 130c, Woman and starbursts.

2007, Sept. 6
Self-Adhesive   Litho.
1279	A611	85c multi	2.00	.30
1280	A611	100c multi	2.25	.35
1281	A611	130c multi	3.00	.45
a.		Block of 3, #1279-1281, on backing paper	7.25	
		Nos. 1279-1281 (3)	7.25	1.10

Swiss Settings in British Literature A612

Designs: 85c, Mönch, from *Frankenstein*, by Mary Shelley. 100c, Staubbach Falls, from "At Staubbach Falls," by William Wordsworth, vert. 130c, Lake Leman, from "The Prisoner of Chillon," by Lord Byron, vert. 180c, Reichenbach Waterfall, from *The Final Problem*, by Sir Arthur Conan Doyle.

Litho. With Foil Application
Perf. 13¼x13½, 13½x13¼
2007, Sept. 6
1282	A612	85c black & silver	2.00	.50
1283	A612	100c black & silver	2.25	.60
1284	A612	130c black & silver	3.00	.75
1285	A612	180c black & silver	4.25	1.10
		Nos. 1282-1285 (4)	11.50	2.95

Skiers and Swiss Post BeeTagg — A613

Serpentine Die Cut 10¾x10½
2007, Oct. 31   Litho.
Self-Adhesive
1286	A613	100c multi	2.25	.60

The BeeTagg design can be read by camera phones to connect the phones to client websites.

Souvenir Sheet

Einsiedeln Abbey — A614

2007, Nov. 20   Perf. 13¼x14
1287	A614	85c multi	2.00	1.50

Paper Cuttings A615

Paper cuttings: 85c, Heart, by Christian Schwizgebel. 100c, Spring, by Pia Arm. 130c, Family Trip, by Christiane and Jacqueline Saugy. 180c, Minuet, by Verena Kühni.

Serpentine Die Cut 10¾
2007, Nov. 20   Self-Adhesive
1288	A615	85c red & black	2.00	.50
a.		Block of 4 #1288 on backing paper	8.00	
1289	A615	100c green & black	2.25	.60
a.		Block of 4 #1289 on backing paper	9.25	
1290	A615	130c blue & black	3.00	.80
a.		Block of 4 #1290 on backing paper	12.00	
1291	A615	180c org & black	4.25	1.10
a.		Block of 4 #1291 on backing paper	17.00	
b.		Block of 4, #1288-1291 on backing paper	11.50	
		Nos. 1288-1291 (4)	11.50	3.00

Christmas — A616

Designs: 85c, Berne Christmas Fair. 100c, Christmas tree. 130c, Gifts.

2007, Nov. 20   Perf. 13½x13¼
1292	A616	85c multi	2.00	.50
1293	A616	100c multi	2.25	.60
1294	A616	130c multi	3.00	.80
		Nos. 1292-1294 (3)	7.25	1.90

Intl. Year of the Potato — A617

2008, Mar. 4   **Litho.**
1295 A617 85c multi   2.00 .60

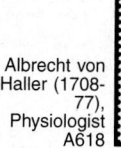

Albrecht von Haller (1708-77), Physiologist A618

2008, Mar. 4   **Perf. 13¼x13½**
1296 A618 85c multi   2.00 .60

The Little Polar Bear, by Hans de Beer — A619

Serpentine Die Cut 10½x11
2008, Mar. 4   **Self-Adhesive**
1297 A619 85c multi   2.00 .60
  a.   Booklet pane of 10   20.00

Euro 2008 Soccer Championships, Austria and Switzerland — A620

Serpentine Die Cut 12x12¼
2008, Mar. 4   **Photo.**
1298 A620 100c green & black   2.25 .65
  Printed in sheets of 10.

Men's Soccer — A621

2008, Mar. 4 Litho. Perf. 13¾x14¼
1299 A621 100c multi   2.25 .65
  Printed in sheets of 6.

Ice Hockey in Switzerland, Cent. — A622

2008, Mar. 4   **Perf. 13x13¼**
1300 A622 100c multi   2.25 .65

Horse Foundation, 50th Anniv. — A623

No. 1301 — Horses and: a, Sun (35x37mm). b, Path and fence (38x37mm). c, Building (31x37mm)

2008, Mar. 4   **Perf. 13½**
1301 A623 Horiz. strip of 3   6.00 6.00
  a.-c.   85c Any single   2.00 .80

Musical Instruments A624

Designs: 85c, Violin. 100c, Swiss accordion. 130c, Electric guitar. 180c, Saxophone.

2008, Mar. 4 Litho. Perf. 13x14
1302 A624 85c multi   2.00 .60
1303 A624 100c multi   2.25 .65
1304 A624 130c multi   3.00 .85
1305 A624 180c multi   4.25 1.10
  Nos. 1302-1305 (4)   11.50 3.20

Birds Type of 2006
Designs: 120c, Picus canus. 130c, Monticola saxatilis. 220c, Podiceps cristatus.

Serpentine Die Cut 12
2008, May 8   **Photo.**
          Self-Adhesive
1306 A583 120c multi   2.75 .50
1307 A583 130c multi   3.00 .50
1308 A583 220c multi + eti-
            quette   5.00 .85
  a.   Block of 3, #1306-1308, on
        backing paper   11.00
  Nos. 1306-1308 (3)   10.75 1.85

No. 1307 was printed with and without etiquette.

UEFA Euro 2008 Soccer Championships, Austria and Switzerland — A625

Serpentine Die Cut 10½x11
2008, May 8   **Litho.**
          Self-Adhesive
1309 A625 85c multi   2.00 .60

No. 1309 was printed in sheets of 10 with a rouletted and slit backing paper. Single stamps also were available on an unslit translucent backing paper.

Swiss Lifesaving Society, 75th Anniv. — A626

2008, May 8   **Perf. 13¼x13½**
1310 A626 100c multi   2.25 .70

2008 Summer Olympics, Beijing — A627

2008, May 8   **Perf. 14x14¼**
1311 A627 100c Mountain biking 2.25 .70
  See No. 1205.

Europa A628

2008, May 8   **Perf. 13x13¼**
1312 A628 100c multi   2.25 .70

24th Universal Postal Congress, Geneva A629

2008, July 23   **Perf. 14x13**
1313 A629 130c multi   3.00 .85

Fruit Type of 2006
Serpentine Die Cut 12
2008, Sept. 4   **Photo.**
          Self-Adhesive
1314 A595 500c Catillac pear 11.50 1.75

No. 1314 was printed in sheets of 50. Single stamps also were available on a translucent paper.

Grains — A630

2008, Sept. 4 Serpentine Die Cut 12
          Self-Adhesive
1315 A630 10c Wheat   .25 .25
1316 A630 15c Barley   .35 .25
1317 A630 20c Rye   .45 .25
1318 A630 50c Oats   1.15 .25
  a.   Block of 4, #1315-1318 on
        backing paper   2.25
  Nos. 1315-1318 (4)   2.20 1.00

Nos. 1315-1318 were each printed in sheets of 50.

Old Rhine Bridge, Bad Sackingen, Germany - Stein, Switzerland — A631

2008, Sept. 4 Litho. Perf. 14
1319 A631 100c multi   2.25 .65

Printed in sheets of 10. See Germany No. 2503.

Drawing by Film Maker Fredi M. Murer A632

2008, Sept. 4   **Perf. 13x13¼**
1320 A632 100c multi   2.25 .65

Swiss Products A633

Designs: 85c, Swiss cheese. 100c, Chocolate. 130c, Clock. 180c, Swiss Army knife tools.

2008, Sept. 4   **Perf. 13¾x13**
1321 A633 85c multi   2.00 .55
1322 A633 100c multi   2.25 .65
1323 A633 130c multi   3.00 .80
1324 A633 180c multi   4.25 1.10
  Nos. 1321-1324 (4)   11.50 3.10

Red Square, by Max Bill (1908-94) — A634

Eggs in a Mirror, Photograph by Hans Finsler (1891-1972) A635

2008, Nov. 21 Litho. Perf. 13½
1325 A634 100c black & red   2.25 .60
1326 A635 130c black & red   3.00 .70

Souvenir Sheet

Stamp Day — A636

2008, Nov. 21   **Perf. 14x13¼**
1327 A636 85c multi   2.00 .45

Christmas — A637

Silver star and: 85c, Christmas ornament. 100c, Gold star. 130c, Bell.

Litho. With Foil Application
2008, Nov. 21   **Perf. 13½x13¼**
1328 A637 85c multi   2.00 .45
1329 A637 100c multi   2.25 .60
1330 A637 130c multi   3.00 .70
  Nos. 1328-1330 (3)   7.25 1.75

European Brown Bear — A638

2009, Mar. 5   **Litho.**
1331 A638 85c multi   2.00 .50
  Pro Natura, Cent.

Hans Ulrich Grubenmann (1709-83), Architect, and Rhine Bridge, Schaffhausen A639

2009, Mar. 5   *Perf. 13¼x13½*
1332 A639 85c multi   2.00 .50

2009 Intl. Ice Hockey Federation World Championships, Bern and Zurich — A640

2009, Mar. 5   *Perf. 13¾x14¼*
Self-Adhesive
1333 A640 100c multi   2.25 .60

Morteratsch Glacier and Lines Showing Glacier's Retreat A641

Litho. & Silk-screened
2009, Mar. 5   *Perf. 14*
1334 A641 100c multi   2.25 .60

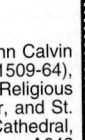 

John Calvin (1509-64), Religious Reformer, and St. Peter's Cathedral, Geneva — A642

2009, Mar. 5   **Litho.**   *Perf. 13½x13¼*
1335 A642 100c multi   2.25 .60

Hans Erni, 100th Birthday — A643

Paintings by Erni: 100c, The Human Mind. 130c, Human Hands.

2009, Mar. 5   *Perf. 14¼x13¾*
1336 A643 100c multi   2.25 .60
1337 A643 130c multi   3.00 .75

 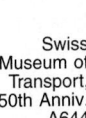

Swiss Museum of Transport, 50th Anniv. A644

Designs: 85c, Steamship Rigi. 100c, Dufaux race car. 130c, Lockheed Orion 9C Special.

2009, Mar. 5   *Perf. 13x13½*
1338 A644 85c multi   2.00 .50
1339 A644 100c multi   2.25 .60
1340 A644 130c multi   3.00 .75
     Nos. 1338-1340 (3)   7.25 1.85

Birds Type of 2006

Designs: 140c, Alectoris graeca. 190c, Milvus milvus.

Serpentine Die Cut 12¼x12
2009, May 8   **Self-Adhesive**
1341 A583 140c multi + etiquette   3.25 .50
1342 A583 190c multi + etiquette   4.50 .70
   a.   Pair, #1341-1342 + 2 etiquettes
       on backing paper   7.75

European Wildcat — A645

2009, May 8   *Perf. 13¾x14¼*
1343 A645 85c multi   2.00 .50

Type Slug and "@" Symbol on Printed Page — A646

2009, May 8   *Perf. 14x13*
1344 A646 100c multi   2.25 .60

Graphics industry in Switzerland, 550th anniv.
See Luxembourg No. 1283.

Location of Helvetia Asteroid — A647

2009, May 8   *Perf. 12¾x13½*
1345 A647 100c multi   2.25 .60

     Europa.

Contemporary Architecture A648

Designs: 100c, Stiva da Morts, Vrin, by Gion A. Caminada. 180c, Pentorama Community Center, Amriswil, by Müller/Sigrist Architects.

2009, May 8   *Perf. 14x13*
1346 A648 100c multi   2.25 .60
1347 A648 180c multi   4.25 1.10

Trees — A649

2009, May 8   *Perf. 13½*
Self-Adhesive
1348 A649 85c Birch   2.00 .50
1349 A649 100c Oak   2.25 .60
1350 A649 130c Willow   3.00 .80
     Nos. 1348-1350 (3)   7.25 1.90

Princess Lillifee, by Monika Finsterbusch A650

Litho. & Silk-screened
2009, Sept. 3   *Serpentine Die Cut 12*
Self-Adhesive
1351 A650 85c multi   2.00 .55
   a.   Booklet pane of 10   20.00

Swiss Stamp Dealers Association, Cent. — A651

2009, Sept. 3 Litho.   *Perf. 13¼x13½*
1352 A651 100c multi   2.25 .65
     Printed in sheets of 12 + 8 labels.

Geneva Conventions, 60th Anniv. — A652

2009, Sept. 3   *Perf. 14x13*
1353 A652 100c multi   2.25 .65

Wedding A653

Anniversary A654

Birth — A655

2009, Sept. 3   *Perf. 13¾x14¼*
Self-Adhesive
1354 A653 100c multi   2.25 .65
1355 A654 100c multi   2.25 .65
1356 A655 100c multi   2.25 .65
     Nos. 1354-1356 (3)   6.75 1.95

Red Flowers With White Crosses A656

Various red flowers with white crosses and German text.

2009, Sept. 3   *Perf. 14x13, 13x14*
1357 A656 85c multi   2.00 .55
1358 A656 100c multi, vert.   2.25 .65
1359 A656 130c multi, vert.   3.00 .85
1360 A656 180c multi   4.25 1.25
     Nos. 1357-1360 (4)   11.50 3.30

Movement of Livestock to New Pastures — A657

No. 1361: a, Sheep and cattle (38x36mm). b, Cattle (32x36mm). c, Cow and horse (34x36mm).

2009, Sept. 3   *Perf. 13¼x13½*
1361 A657   Horiz. strip of 3   6.00 6.00
   a.-c.   85c Any single   2.00 .55

2010 Paralympics, Vancouver A658

2009, Nov. 20   *Perf. 13½*
1362 A658 130c multi   3.00 .85

2010 Winter Olympics, Vancouver — A658a

     Perf. 13¼x13½
2009, Nov. 20   **Litho.**
1362A A658a 100c multi   2.25 2.00

     Souvenir Sheet

Gruyères Castle and Crane — A659

2009, Nov. 20   *Perf. 14x13¼*
1363 A659 85c multi   2.40 2.40

     Stamp Day.

Christmas — A660

Star and: 85c, Cap of Santa Claus. 100c, Christmas tree. 130c, Gift box.

Litho. With Hologram
2009, Nov. 20   *Perf. 13½x13¼*
1364 A660 85c multi   2.00 .60
1365 A660 100c multi   2.25 .65
1366 A660 130c multi   3.00 .85
     Nos. 1364-1366 (3)   7.25 2.10

Basel Carnival Committee, Cent. — A661

No. 1367: a, Four marchers, two carrying parade lantern and sign, Spalentor in background (30x36mm). b, Fifer, drum major, drummer, wagon, Town Hall in background (43x36mm). c, Four musicians, Münster Cathedral in background (30x36mm).

2010, Jan. 12   Litho.   Perf. 13¾x13½
1367 A661   Horiz. strip of 3   7.00 7.00
a.-c.   100c Any single   2.25   .65

University of
Basel, 550th
Anniv. — A662

2010, Mar. 4   Perf. 14x13
1368 A662 85c multi   2.00   .55

Intl. Year of
Biodiversity
A663

2010, Mar. 4   Perf. 14¼x13¾
Self-Adhesive
1369 A663 85c multi   2.00   .55

Swiss Cancer
League,
Cent. — A664

2010, Mar. 4   Perf. 14x13
1370 A664 100c multi   2.25   .65

Powered Flight
in Switzerland,
Cent. — A665

Designs: 85c, Ernest Failloubaz, first holder
of pilot's license, and Grandjean monoplane.
100c, Airbus A340 and Zurich Airport. 130c,
Jorge "Géo" Chavez, first man to fly across the
Alps, and Blériot XI monoplane. 180c, Sport
airplane, glider and hot-air balloons.

2010, Mar. 4   Perf. 13¼x13¾
1371 A665 85c multi   2.00   .55
1372 A665 100c multi   2.25   .65
1373 A665 130c multi   3.00   .85
1374 A665 180c multi   4.25 1.25
    Nos. 1371-1374 (4)   11.50 3.30

2010 Federal
Marksmen's
Festival,
Aarau — A666

2010 Federal
Drumming and
Piping Festival,
Interlaken
A667

Swiss Yodeling
Association,
Cent. — A668

2010 Federal
Costume
Festival,
Schwyz
A669

2010, Mar. 4   Litho.   Perf. 13¾x14¼
1375 A666 100c multi   2.25   .65
**Litho. & Embossed With Foil
Application**
1376 A667 100c multi   2.25   .65
Litho. & Embossed
1377 A668 100c multi   2.25   .65
1378 A669 100c multi   2.25   .65
    Nos. 1375-1378 (4)   9.00 2.60
    No. 1375 has a hole drilled into target in
vignette.

Johann Peter
Hebel (1760-
1826),
Poet — A670

2010, May 6   Litho.   Perf. 13¼x13½
1379 A670 85c multi   2.00   .55

School Boy with
Slate, by Albert
Anker (1831-
1910)
A671

2010, May 6   Perf. 13½x13
1380 A671 85c multi   2.00   .55

Heidi and
Goats — A672

2010, May 6   Perf. 13¼x13
1381 A672 100c multi   2.25   .65
    Europa.

Kunsthaus
Zurich,
Cent.
A673

2010, May 6   Perf. 13¼x13½
Self-Adhesive
1382 A673 100c multi   2.25   .65

Swiss Public
Welfare Society,
Bicent. — A674

2010, May 6   Perf. 13½x13¼
1383 A674 100c multi   2.25   .65

Circus World
Geneva 2010
Circus
Festival — A675

2010, May 6
1384 A675 140c multi   3.25   .85

Railway
Centenaries
A676

Designs: 85c, Niesen Funicular. 100c, Bernina Railway, horiz.

2010, May 6   Perf. 14¼x13¾
1385 A676 85c multi   2.00   .55
                   Perf. 13¾x14¼
1386 A676 100c multi   2.25   .65

Jimmy Flitz,
Character From
Children's Book
by Roland
Zoss — A677

Serpentine Die Cut 12
2010, Sept. 3   Litho.
Self-Adhesive
1387 A677 85c multi   1.75   .60
a.   Booklet pane of 10   17.50

Jeanne Hersch
(1910-2000),
Philosopher
A678

2010, Sept. 3   Perf. 13¼x13½
1388 A678 100c multi   2.00   .65

Words
From "The
Big Dwarf,"
by Franz
Hohler,
Writer
A679

2010, Sept. 3   Perf. 13x13¼
1389 A679 100c green & black   2.00   .65

European Free
Trade
Association,
50th
Anniv. — A680

2010, Sept. 3   Perf. 14x13¾
1390 A680 140c yellow & black   2.75   .90

Gustave
Moynier (1826-
1910) and
Henri Dunant
(1828-1910),
Founders of
Intl. Red
Cross — A681

2010, Sept. 3   Perf. 13¼x13½
1391 A681 190c multi   3.75 1.25

Composers
A682

Designs: 100c, Rolf Liebermann (1910-99).
140c, Heinrich Sutermeister (1910-95).

2010, Sept. 3   Perf. 13x13¼
1392 A682 100c lilac & black   2.00   .65
1393 A682 140c ol brn & blk   2.75   .90

Prehistoric
Animals
A683

Designs: 85c, Theropod. 100c, Ichthyosaur.
140c, Pterosaur.

2010, Sept. 3   Perf. 13¼x13½
1394 A683   85c multi   1.75   .60
1395 A683 100c multi   2.00   .65
1396 A683 140c multi   2.75   .90
    Nos. 1394-1396 (3)   6.50 2.15

A684

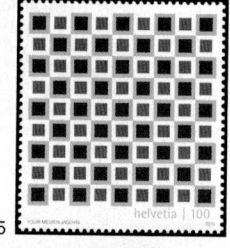

A685

Optical Art by Youri Messen-
Jaschin — A686

2010, Sept. 3   Perf. 14x13¼
Self-Adhesive
1397 A684   85c multi   1.75   .60
1398 A685 100c multi   2.00   .65
1399 A686 140c black & red   2.75   .90
    Nos. 1397-1399 (3)   6.50 2.15

Souvenir Sheet

Zähringer Fountain, Bern — A687

2010, Nov. 4   *Perf. 14x13¼*
1400 A687 85c multi   1.75 .60

Stamp Day.

Handicrafts
A688

Designs: 200c, Bobbin lacemaking. 300c, Wood carving.

2010, Nov. 4   *Serpentine Die Cut 12*
Self-Adhesive
1401 A688 200c multi   4.25 .85
1402 A688 300c multi   6.25 1.25
    a.   Pair, #1401-1402   10.50

Nos. 1401-1402 also were printed in sheets of 10. See Nos. 1418-1419.

Christmas — A689

Designs: 85c, Star, candle, conifer sprigs. 100c, Snowflake. 140c, Star, angel.

Litho. With Hologram
2010, Nov. 4   *Perf. 13½x13¼*
1403 A689 85c multi   1.75 .60
1404 A689 100c multi   2.10 .70
1405 A689 140c multi   3.00 1.00
    Nos. 1403-1405 (3)   6.85 2.30

Pettersson and
Findus,
Children's Book
Characters by
Sven Nordqvist
A690

Serpentine Die Cut 12
2011, Mar. 3   **Self-Adhesive**   **Litho.**
1406 A690 85c multi   1.90 .65
    a.   Booklet pane of 10   19.00

Honeybee and
Flower
A691

2011, Mar. 3   *Perf. 11¾*
1407 A691 85c multi   1.90 .65

Cerebral
Foundation,
50th
Anniv. — A692

2011, Mar. 3   *Perf. 13¼x13½*
1408 A692 85c multi   1.90 .65

14th World
Gymnaestrada,
Lausanne
A693

2011, Mar. 3
1409 A693 85c multi   1.90 .65

Neuchatel,
1000th
Anniv. — A694

2011, Mar. 3
1410 A694 100c multi   2.25 .75

Worldwide
Fund for Nature
(WWF), 50th
Anniv. — A695

2011, Mar. 3
1411 A695 100c multi   2.25 .75

Max Frisch
(1911-91),
Playwright &
Novelist — A696

2011, Mar. 3
1412 A696 100c gray & black   2.25 .75

Model of
Vitamin C
Molecule
A697

Litho. & Embossed
2011, Mar. 3   *Perf. 13x13¼*
1413 A697 100c multi   2.25 .75

Intl. Year of Chemistry.

Flowers — A698

Designs: 85c, Cucurbita pepo. 100c, Pisum sativum. 110c, Allium ursinum. 260c, Cynara scolymus.

Serpentine Die Cut 12
2011, Mar. 3   **Self-Adhesive**   **Litho.**
1414 A698 85c multi   1.90 .65
    a.   Booklet pane of 10   19.00
1415 A698 100c multi + eti-
    quette   2.25 .75
    a.   Booklet pane of 10 + 10 eti-
    quettes   22.50
1416 A698 110c multi   2.40 .80
1417 A698 260c multi   5.75 1.90
    a.   Block of 4, #1414-1417   12.50
    Nos. 1414-1417 (4)   12.30 4.10

Nos. 1414-1415 also were printed in sheets of 50. Nos. 1416-1417 also were printed in sheets of 10. See Nos. 1440-1442, 1481-1482.

Handicrafts Type of 2010

Designs: 400c, Potter shaping pot on wheel. 500c, Blacksmith hammering work on anvil.

Serpentine Die Cut 12
2011, May 5   **Self-Adhesive**   **Litho.**
1418 A688 400c multi   9.25 2.40
1419 A688 500c multi   11.50 3.00
    a.   Pair, #1418-1419   21.00

Nos. 1418-1419 also were printed in sheets of 10.

Art Is
Resistance, by
Thomas
Hirschhorn
A699

2011, May 5   *Perf. 13¾x14¼*
1420 A699 100c multi   2.40 .80

Venice Art Biennale.

Europa
A700

2011, May 5   *Perf. 13½*
1421 A700 100c multi   2.40 .80

Intl. Year of Forests.

Miniature Sheet

Provisional Declaration Naming "Swiss Psalm" as National Anthem, 50th Anniv. — A701

No. 1422: a, Urnerboden (red panels at bottom and right). b, Urnersee bei Flüelen (red panels at left and bottom). c, Urigen (red panels at top and right). d, Schächentaler Windgällen (red panels at left and top).

2011, May 5   *Perf. 13½*
1422 A701   Sheet of 4   2.40 2.40
    a.-d.   25c Any single   .80 .25

On each of the four stamps in the sheet, the first verse of the anthem is printed in fluorescent ink in one of Switzerland's four official languages.

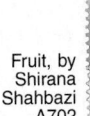 

Fruit, by
Shirana
Shahbazi
A702

2011, Sept. 2   *Perf. 13¼x13½*
1423 A702 100c multi   2.25 .75

See Liechtenstein No. 1522.

Paul
Burkhard
(1911-77),
Composer
A703

2011, Sept. 2   *Perf. 13½*
1424 A703 100c multi   2.25 .75

Works of
Handicapped
Artists — A704

Designs: 85c, Untitled painting by Bajram Mahmuti. 100c, Emmental, painting by Claudia Aebi-Torre, horiz. 140c, Untitled dot picture, by Christian Oppliger, horiz. 190c, Photograph of dancer and wood sculpture, by Flavia Trachsel.

2011, Sept. 2
1425 A704 85c multi   2.00 .65
1426 A704 100c multi   2.25 .75
1427 A704 140c black   3.25 1.10
1428 A704 190c multi   4.50 1.50
    Nos. 1425-1428 (4)   12.00 4.00

Lavaux Vineyard Terraces UNESCO
World Heritage Site — A705

No. 1429: a, Vineyard terraces and steps (26x37mm). b, Village, vineyards, Lake Geneva (41x37mm). c, Open gate and stone wall overlooking Lake Geneva (37x37mm).

2011, Sept. 2   **Litho.**
1429 A705   Horiz. strip of 3   6.75 6.75
    a.-c.   100c Any single   2.25 .75

Muggestutz, King
of the Dwarves,
Book Illustration
by Susanna
Schmid-Germann
A706

2011, Sept. 2   *Serpentine Die Cut 12*
Self-Adhesive
1430 A706 85c multi   2.00 .65
    a.   Booklet pane of 10   20.00

Single examples of No. 1430 on a translucent paper also were made available.

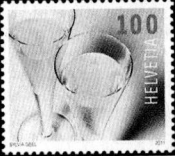

Greetings
Stamps
A707

Designs: No. 1431, Champagne flutes. No. 1432, Heart. No. 1433, Engagement and wedding rings. No. 1434, Baby's pacifier.

2011, Sept. 2   *Perf. 13¼x13½*
Self-Adhesive
1431	A707	100c multi	2.25	.75
1432	A707	100c multi	2.25	.75
1433	A707	100c multi	2.25	.75
1434	A707	100c multi	2.25	.75
		Nos. 1431-1434 (4)	9.00	3.00

Drawing of Swiss Flag, Machine, Clouds, Rainbow and Musical Notes, by Rap Musician Stress
A708

2011, Nov. 17   *Perf. 13½*
1435	A708	100c multi	2.25	.75

Souvenir Sheet

Château de Villa, Sierre — A709

2011, Nov. 17
1436	A709	85c multi	1.90	.65

Stamp Day.

Christmas
A710

Christmas trees and: 85c, Chapel. 100c, Gifts on sleigh, village. 140c, Wreath, chalet.

2011, Nov. 17   *Perf. 13¼x13½*
Self-Adhesive
1437	A710	85c multi	1.90	.65
1438	A710	100c multi	2.25	.75
1439	A710	140c multi	3.25	1.10
		Nos. 1437-1439 (3)	7.40	2.50

Flowers Type of 2011

Designs: 140c, Lycopersicon lucopersicum. 180c, Phaeolus coccineus. 190c, Allium cepa.

2012, Mar. 1   *Serpentine Die Cut 12*
Self-Adhesive
1440	A698	140c multi	3.25	.65
1441	A698	180c multi	4.00	.80
1442	A698	190c multi	4.25	.85
a.		Nos. 1440-1442 on translucent paper	11.50	
		Nos. 1440-1442 (3)	11.50	2.30

Nos. 1440-1442 each were printed in sheets of 10 stamps.

Swiss Brass Band Association, 150th Anniv. — A711

Litho. With Foil Application
2012, Mar. 1   *Perf. 14¼x13¾*
1443	A711	100c multi	2.25	.75

Swiss Civil Code, Cent. A712

2012, Mar. 1   Litho.   *Perf. 13½*
1444	A712	100c multi	2.25	.75

Building of Hermitage in the Steinach Valley by St. Gall (c. 550- c. 645), 1400th Anniv. — A713

2012, Mar. 1   *Perf. 13¼x13½*
1445	A713	100c multi	2.25	.75

Jungfrau Railway, Cent. — A714

2012, Mar. 1
1446	A714	100c multi	2.25	.75

Swiss Tectonic Arena Sardona UNESCO World Heritage Site — A715

No. 1447: a, Buildings in Elm (30x47mm). b, Sun shining through Martinsloch (hole in mountain) (44x47mm). c, Sunshine on Elm Church Tower clock face (30x47mm).

2012, Mar. 1   *Perf. 13½*
1447	A715	Horiz. strip of 3	6.75	6.75
a.-c.		100c Any single	2.25	.75

Beaver — A716

2012, Mar. 1   *Perf. 13½x13¼*
Self-Adhesive
1448	A716	100c multi	2.25	.75

Children's Book Illustration by Janosch (Horst Eckert) — A717

Serpentine Die Cut 12
2012, Mar. 12   **Self-Adhesive**
1449	A717	100c multi	2.25	.75
a.		Serpentine die cut 12¼x12	2.25	.75
b.		Booklet pane of 10 #1449	22.50	

Single examples of No. 1449 were made available on a translucent paper. No.1449a is available only on translucent paper.

Cadastral Surveying in Switzerland, Cent. — A718

2012, May 9   *Perf. 13¾x14¼*
1450	A718	100c multi	2.25	.75

Inauguration of Stanserhorn Cabrio Cable Car — A719

2012, May 9   *Perf. 13¼x13½*
1451	A719	100c multi	2.25	.75

Tidying Up Art, by Ursus Wehrli — A720

2012, May 9   Litho.   *Perf. 13½*
1452	A720	100c multi	2.25	.75

Blood Donation — A721

2012, May 9   *Perf. 13½x13¼*
1453	A721	100c multi	2.25	.75

Europa — A722

2012, May 9   *Perf. 13½*
1454	A722	100c multi	2.25	.75

Tell Theaters A723

Actors at: No. 1455, Tell Theater in Altdorf. No. 1456, Open-air Tell Theater in Interlaken.

2012, May 9   *Perf. 13*
Self-Adhesive
1455	A723	100c multi	2.25	.75
1456	A723	100c multi	2.25	.75

Tell Theaters in Altdorf, 500th anniv.; in Interlaken, cent.

Swimmers in Rhine River Near Basel — A724

Symbols From Arms of Geneva and Colors From International Flags — A725

Intersection in Zurich — A726

2012, Sept. 6   *Perf. 13¼x13½*
Self-Adhesive
1457	A724	100c multi	2.10	.70
1458	A725	100c multi	2.10	.70
1459	A726	100c multi	2.10	.70
		Nos. 1457-1459 (3)	6.30	2.10

Pop Art by Peter Stämpfli A727

Designs: 85c, James Bond (hands on steering wheel). 100c, Bond Street (hand holding bowler hat). 200c, Pudding (molded chocolate pudding and whipped cream).

2012, Sept. 6   *Perf. 14x13½*
Self-Adhesive
1460	A727	85c black	1.90	.65
1461	A727	100c black	2.10	.70
1462	A727	200c multi	4.25	1.40
		Nos. 1460-1462 (3)	8.25	2.75

Woodcuttings of Nature Scenes by Franz Gertsch — A728

Designs: 85c, Butterbur. 100c, Grasses. 140c, Black Water Triptych.

2012, Sept. 6   *Perf. 13½*
Self-Adhesive
1463	A728	85c lt grn & green	1.90	.65
1464	A728	100c lt grn & red	2.10	.70
1465	A728	140c lt grn & gray blue	3.00	1.00
		Nos. 1463-1465 (3)	7.00	2.35

Souvenir Sheet

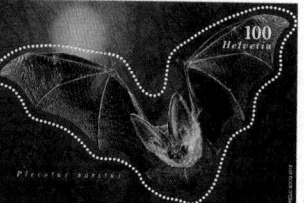

Plecotus Auritus — A729

Litho. & Embossed

2012, Sept. 6   *Perf.*
1466 A729 100c multi   2.10   .70

Yakari, Comic Strip by Derib and Job — A730

Yakari and: No. 1467, Butterfly and flower. No. 1468, Horse and bird.

Serpentine Die Cut 12
2012, Nov. 22   *Litho.*
Self-Adhesive
1467 A730 100c multi   2.25   .75
1468 A730 100c multi   2.25   .75
   a.   Horiz. pair, #1467-1468, on
      translucent backing paper   4.50
   b.   Booklet pane of 10, 5 each
      #1467-1468   22.50

Souvenir Sheet

Altstätten — A731

2012, Nov. 22   *Perf. 13¾*
1469 A731 85c multi   1.90   .65
Stamp Day.

Christmas — A732

Christmas lights and: 85c, Stars, ribbon. 100c, Star, angel, Christmas tree. 140c, Violin, open book, Christmas ornament.

2012, Nov. 22   *Perf. 13½x13¼*
Self-Adhesive
1470 A732 85c multi   1.90   .65
1471 A732 100c multi   2.25   .75
1472 A732 140c multi   3.00 1.00
    Nos. 1470-1472 (3)   7.15 2.40

Swiss Council for Accident Prevention, 75th Anniv. — A733

2013, Mar. 7   *Perf. 13¼x13½*
1473 A733 85c multi   1.90   .65

Swiss Protection and Support Services, 50th Anniv. — A734

2013, Mar. 7
1474 A734 85c multi   1.90   .65

Lötschberg Railway, Cent. — A735

2013, Mar. 7
1475 A735 100c multi   2.10   .70

Gottlieb Duttweiler (1888-1962), Founder of Migros Supermarkets, and Delivery Van — A736

2013, Mar. 7   *Perf. 13½*
1476 A736 100c multi   2.10   .70

Appenzell Cantons in Swiss Confederation, 500th Anniv. — A737

2013, Mar. 7
1477 A737 100c multi   2.10   .70

A738

Children's Book Illustrations by Ernst Kreidolf (1863-1956) — A739

2013, Mar. 7   *Serpentine Die Cut 12*
Self-Adhesive
1478 A738 100c multi   2.10   .70
1479 A739 100c multi   2.10   .70
   a.   Horiz. pair, #1478-1479, on
      translucent paper   4.20
   b.   Booklet pane of 10, 5 each
      #1478-1479   21.00

Miniature Sheet

Swiss Alpine Club, 150th Anniv. — A740

No. 1480: a, Line of skiers and mountain (50x42mm). b, Mountain climber on rock face (28x70mm). c, Hikers on mountain path (78x28mm). d, Mountain hut and Swiss flag (28x42mm).

Perf. 12 on 1, 2, or 3 Sides
2013, Mar. 7
1480 A740   Sheet of 4   11.00 3.75
   a.   85c multi   1.90   .65
   b.   100c multi   2.10   .70
   c.   140c multi   3.00 1.00
   d.   190c multi   4.00 1.40

Flowers Type of 2011

Designs: 130c, Capsicum annuum. 220c, Allium porrum.

2013, May 7   *Serpentine Die Cut 12*
Self-Adhesive
1481 A698 130c multi   2.75   .90
1482 A698 220c multi   4.75 1.60
   a.   Horiz. pair, #1481-1482, on
      translucent paper   7.50
Nos. 1481-1482 each were printed in sheets of 10 stamps.

Faces of Swiss People — A741

2013, May 7   *Perf. 12*
1483 A741 100c multi   2.10   .70

White Stork — A742

2013, May 7   *Perf. 14¼x13¾*
Self-Adhesive
1484 A742 100c multi   2.10   .70

Sculpture of Snake by Valentin Carron — A743

2013, May 7   *Perf. 13¼x13½*
1485 A743 100c multi   2.10   .70
2013 Venice Art Biennale.

Europa A744

Postal vehicles: No. 1486, Tribelhorn delivery van (denomination in blue). No. 1487, Kyburz DXP electric three-wheeler (denomination in brown orange).

2013, May 7   *Perf. 13½*
1486 A744 100c multi   2.10   .70
1487 A744 100c multi   2.10   .70

Swiss Men's Ice Hockey Team's Second-Place Finish in 2013 World Championships A745

2013, May 31   *Litho.*   *Perf. 13¼x13½*
1488 A745 100c multi   2.25   .75

Hillside Buildings, Lausanne A746

Bear, Heraldic Animal of Bern — A747

Buildings and Symbols of Winterthur A748

2013, Sept. 5   *Perf. 13¾x14¼*
Self-Adhesive
1489 A746 100c multi   2.25   .75
1490 A747 100c multi   2.25   .75
1491 A748 100c multi   2.25   .75
    Nos. 1489-1491 (3)   6.75 2.25

Baby Animals A749

Designs: 85c, Chicks. 100c, Calves. 140c, Lambs. 190c, Piglets.

2013, Sept. 5   *Litho.*
Self-Adhesive
1492 A749 85c multi   1.90   .65
1493 A749 100c multi   2.25   .75
1494 A749 140c multi   3.00 1.00
1495 A749 190c multi   4.25 1.40
    Nos. 1492-1495 (4)   11.40 3.80

Smurfs — A750

Designs: No. 1496, Smurfs kissing. No.1497, Papa Smurf.

2013, Sept. 5   *Serpentine Die Cut 12*
Self-Adhesive
1496 A750 100c multi   2.25   .75
1497 A750 100c multi   2.25   .75
   a.   Horiz. pair, #1496-1497 on
      translucent paper   4.50
   b.   Booklet pane of 10, 5 each
      #1496-1497   22.50

Restoration of Waterways — A751

No. 1498 — Waterway and: a, Butterfly (37x37mm). b, Bird (32x37mm). d, Fish (37x37mm).

2013, Sept. 5   *Perf. 13¾x14*
1498 A751   Horiz. strip of 3   6.75 6.75
   a.-c.   100c Any single   2.25   .75

Souvenir Sheet

Obverse of Swiss Gold Vreneli Coin — A752

Litho. & Embossed With Foil Application

2013, Sept. 5   **Perf.**
1499 A752 600c gold & multi   13.00 4.50

Goose With Body of Guitar, by Polo Hofer — A753

2013, Nov. 14   **Litho.**   **Perf. 13½**
1500 A753 100c multi   2.25 .75

Souvenir Sheet

Bell — A754

Litho. & Embossed

2013, Nov. 14   **Perf. 13¼**
1501 A754 85c multi   1.90 .65

Stamp Day.

Souvenir Sheet

Matter Valley Cabins — A755

2013, Nov. 14   **Litho.**   **Perf. 13¼x14**
1502 A755 200c multi   4.50 1.50

Christmas A756

Designs: 85c, Fox, Christmas ornament on tree. 100c, Fawn, lantern. 140c, Owl, Christmas ornament on tree. 190c, Squirrel, lantern.

Perf. 13¾x14¼

2013, Nov. 14   **Litho.**
Self-Adhesive
1503 A756 85c multi   1.90 .65
1504 A756 100c multi   2.25 .75
1505 A756 140c multi   3.25 1.10
1506 A756 190c multi   4.25 1.40
     Nos. 1503-1506 (4)   11.65 3.90

Diplomatic Relations Between Switzerland and Japan, 150th Anniv. — A757

Designs: 100c, Mount Fuji, Japan. 190c, Mountain valley, Switzerland.

2014, Feb. 6   **Litho.**   **Perf. 12¾x13**
1507 A757 100c multi   2.25 .75
1508 A757 190c multi   4.25 1.40
   a.   Horiz. pair, #1507-1508   6.50 6.50

See Japan No. 3646.

Swiss Army Post, 125th Anniv. — A758

2014, Mar. 6   **Litho.**   **Perf. 13¼x13½**
1509 A758 100c multi   2.25 .75

Intl. Year of Crystallography — A759

Litho. With Foil Application

2014, Mar. 6   **Perf. 13x13¼**
1510 A759 85c Epidote   1.90 .65
1511 A759 100c Amethyst   2.25 .75

Swiss Air Force, Cent. — A760

Designs: 100c, F/A-18 Hornets. 140c, F-5 Tigers.

2014, Mar. 6   **Litho.**   **Perf. 13¼x13½**
1512 A760 100c multi   2.25 .75
1513 A760 140c multi   3.25 1.10

Swiss National Park — A761

No. 1514: a, Tree trunk, hiker, text in German (37x37mm). b, Bird, mountain, text in Romansh (32x37mm). c, Mountain, text in Italian (35x37mm).

2014, Mar. 6   **Litho.**   **Perf. 13¾x14**
1514 A761   Horiz. strip of 3   6.75 6.75
  a.-c.   100c Any single   2.25 .75

Mushrooms A762

Designs: 10c, Cantharellus cibarius. 15c, Lactarius lignyotus. 20c, Hydnellum caeruleum. 50c, Strobilomyces strobilaceus.

Serpentine Die Cut 12

2014, Mar. 6   **Litho.**
Self-Adhesive
1515 A762 10c multi   .25 .25
1516 A762 15c multi   .35 .25
1517 A762 20c multi   .45 .25
1518 A762 50c multi   1.10 .35
  a.   Block of 4, #1515-1518, on
      translucent paper   2.25
     Nos. 1515-1518 (4)   2.15 1.10

Nos. 1515-1518 each were printed in sheets of 10.

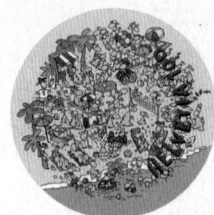

Dinosaurs on Beach A763

Fred the Dinosaur A764

2014, Mar. 6   **Litho.**   **Die Cut**
Self-Adhesive
1519 A763 100c multi   2.25 .75

Serpentine Die Cut 12

1520 A764 100c multi   2.25 .75
  a.   Pair, #1519-1520 on translu-
      cent paper   4.50
  b.   Booklet pane of 9, #1519, 8
      #1520   20.50

Renewable Energy A765

2014, May 8   **Litho.**   **Perf. 13½**
1521 A765 100c multi   2.25 .75

Pilatus Cogwheel Railway, 125th Anniv. — A766

2014, May 8   **Litho.**   **Perf. 13x14**
1522 A766 100c multi   2.25 .75

Special Olympics National Games, Bern — A767

2014, May 8   **Litho.**   **Perf. 13½x13¼**
Self-Adhesive
1523 A767 100c multi   2.25 .75

Diver, Speedboat, Gate and Mount Brè, Lugano — A768

Woman, Lake Lucerne and Chapel Bridge, Lucerne A769

Abbey Cathedral and Tree in Planter, St. Gallen — A770

2014, May 8   **Litho.**   **Perf. 13¼x13½**
Self-Adhesive
1524 A768 100c multi   2.25 .75
1525 A769 100c multi   2.25 .75
1526 A770 100c multi   2.25 .75
     Nos. 1524-1526 (3)   6.75 2.25

Europa — A771

No. 1527: a, Dulcimer and accordion. b, Accordion and alphorn.

2014, May 8   **Litho.**   **Perf. 13½**
1527 A771   Horiz. pair   4.50 4.50
  a.-b.   100c Either single   2.25 .75

Clock Towers and Clocks A772

Designs: 100c, Zytglogge, Bern. 140c, Kazansky Tower, Moscow, Russia.

2014, May 21   **Litho.**   **Perf. 13x13½**
1528 A772 100c multi   2.25 .75
1529 A772 140c multi   3.25 1.10

See Russia No. 7531.

2014 Swiss Skills Competition, Bern — A773

2014, Sept. 4   **Litho.**   **Perf. 13½**
1530 A773 100c multi   2.25 .75

Carriage and Route Map of Lindau Messenger Courier Service — A774

2014, Sept. 4   **Litho.**   **Perf. 13¼x13½**
1531 A774 140c multi   3.00 1.00

Wildlife — A775

Designs: 85c, Mouse weasel. 100c, Alpine marmot. 140c, Nutcracker. 190c, Red deer.

2014, Sept. 4   **Litho.**   **Perf. 13¼x13½**
1532 A775 85c multi   1.90 .40
1533 A775 100c multi   2.25 .45
1534 A775 140c multi   3.00 .60
1535 A775 190c multi   4.25 .85
     Nos. 1532-1535 (4)   11.40 2.30

Garfield, Comic Strip Characters by Jim Davis — A776

Designs: No. 1536, Garfield and Odie making fondue. No. 1537, Garfield eating chocolate, Swiss flag and mountains.

Serpentine Die Cut 12

2014, Sept. 4			Litho.
Self-Adhesive			
1536	A776	100c multi	2.25	.75
1537	A776	100c multi	2.25	.75
a.	Pair, #1536-1537 on translucent paper		4.50
b.	Booklet pane of 10, 5 each #1536-1537		22.50

Souvenir Sheet

Record Label — A777

2014, Sept. 4		Litho.	Rouletted
On Cardboard			
1538	A777	500c multi	11.00 3.75

The stamp from No. 1538 has a circular hole in the center. The sheet margin is coated with a varnish upon which phonograph record grooves have been impressed. The 33⅓rpm recording features a brass band playing the Swiss national anthem.

Tongues — A778

2014, Nov. 13		Litho.	Perf. 12¾x13
1539	A778	100c multi	2.10 .70

Souvenir Sheet

Houses in Emmental Region — A779

2014, Nov. 13		Litho.	Perf. 12
1540	A779	200c multi	4.25 1.40

Christmas A780

Garland and: 85c, Star, gifts, Christmas tree, creche. 100c, Bow, Santa Claus, Christmas stockings hung near fireplace. 140c, Holly, star, candles, dinner table. 190c, Ornament, kitchen, cookies.

		Perf. 13¼x13½	
2014, Nov. 13			Litho.
Self-Adhesive			
1541	A780	85c multi	1.75 .60
1542	A780	100c multi	2.10 .70
1543	A780	140c multi	3.00 1.00
1544	A780	190c multi	4.00 1.40
		Nos. 1541-1544 (4)	10.85 3.70

Expo 2015, Milan A781

Litho. With Foil Application

2015, Mar. 5			Perf. 13x13¼
1545	A781	100c multi	2.10 .70

Stairs, Martinsberg Community Center, Baden, and Murals, Convent of St. John, Müstair — A782

2015, Mar. 5		Litho.	Perf. 13½
1546	A782	100c multi	2.10 .70

Swiss Federal Commission for Monument Preservation, cent.

Swiss Federal Tax Administration, Cent. — A783

2015, Mar. 5		Litho.	Perf. 13½x13¼
1547	A783	100c multi	2.10 .70

Battles A784

Designs: No. 1548, Battle of Morgarten, 1315. No. 1549, Battle of Marignano, 1515.

2015, Mar. 5		Litho.	Perf. 13½
1548	A784	100c multi	2.10 .70
1549	A784	100c multi	2.10 .70

Pets — A785

2015, Mar. 5		Litho.	Perf. 13¾x14¼
Self-Adhesive			
1550	A785	85c Dog	1.75 .60
1551	A785	100c Cat	2.10 .70
1552	A785	140c Rabbit	3.00 1.00
1553	A785	190c Hamster	4.00 1.40
		Nos. 1550-1553 (4)	10.85 3.70

Abbey of St. Maurice, 1500th Anniv. — A786

Designs: No. 1554, Martolet archaeological site. No. 1555, Reliquary of the Children of St. Sigismund. No. 1556, Document and pen. No. 1557, Stained-glass window.

2015, Mar. 5		Litho.	Perf. 13¼x13½
1554	A786	100c multi	2.10 .70
1555	A786	100c multi	2.10 .70
a.	Horiz. pair, #1554-1555		4.25 1.40
1556	A786	100c multi	2.10 .70
1557	A786	100c multi	2.10 .70
a.	Horiz. pair, #1556-1557		4.25 1.40
		Nos. 1554-1557 (4)	8.40 2.80

Rhein Falls — A787

No. 1558: a, Falls, buildings and tour boat (37x37mm). b, Falls, bridge and viewing platform (35x37mm). c, Falls and Laufen Castle (32x37mm).

2015, Mar. 5		Litho.	Perf. 13¾x14
1558	A787	Horiz. strip of 3	6.50 6.50
a.-c.	100c Any single		2.10 .70

Souvenir Sheet

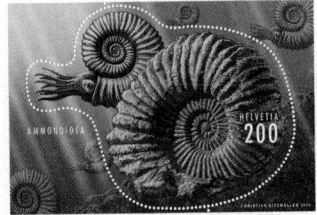

Ammonite and Fossil — A788

Litho. & Embossed

2015, Mar. 5			Perf.
1559	A788	200c multi	4.25 1.40

Swiss Sponsorship for Mountain Communities, 75th Anniv. — A789

2015, May 7		Litho.	Perf. 13½
1560	A789	100c multi	2.10 .70

Skin — A790

2015, May 7		Litho.	Perf. 13¼x13½
Flocked Granite Paper With Ripples			
1561	A790	100c multi	2.10 .70

Exhibition of the works of Pamela Rosenkranz at Venice Biennale. No. 1561 is printed in sheets of 10. The rippling on each stamp in the sheet is different.

Admission of Geneva to Swiss Federation, 200th Anniv. — A791

Admission of Valais to Swiss Federation, 200th Anniv. — A792

Admission of Neuchâtel to Swiss Federation, 200th Anniv. — A793

2015, May 7		Litho.	Perf. 13¼x13½
1562	A791	100c multi	2.10 .70
1563	A792	100c multi	2.10 .70
1564	A793	100c multi	2.10 .70
		Nos. 1562-1564 (3)	6.30 2.10

Nos. 1562-1564 each have cross-shaped hole in upper right corner of stamp.

Europa — A794

Toys: a, Wisa-Gloria rocking duck, 1957. b, Helvetia tricycle, 1949.

2015, May 7		Litho.	Perf. 13½
1565	A794	Horiz. pair	4.25 1.40
a.-b.	100c Either single		2.10 .70

SEMI-POSTAL STAMPS

Nos. B1-B76, B81-B84 were sold at premiums of 2c for 3c stamps, 5c for 5c-20c stamps and 10c for 30c-40c stamps.

Helvetia and Matterhorn — SP2

Perf. 11½, 12

1913, Dec. 1		Typo.	Wmk. 183
Granite Paper			
B1	SP2	5c green	2.75 8.25
		Never hinged	7.75

Boy (Appenzell) SP3

Girl (Lucerne) SP4

1915, Dec. 1			Perf. 11½
B2	SP3	5c green, buff	3.25 8.25
a.	Tête bêche pair		82.50 875.00
		Never hinged	160.00
B3	SP4	10c red, buff	100.00 87.50
		Set, never hinged	225.00

Girl (Fribourg) SP5

Dairy Boy (Bern) SP6

Girl (Vaud) — SP7

1916, Dec. 1

B4	SP5	3c vio, *buff*	5.00	*37.50*
B5	SP6	5c grn, *buff*	11.00	*9.25*
B6	SP7	10c brn red, *buff*	47.50	*77.50*
	Nos. B4-B6 (3)		63.50	*124.25*
	Set, never hinged		175.00	

Girl (Valais)
SP8

Girl (Unter-walden)
SP9

Girl (Ticino) — SP10

1917, Dec. 1

B7	SP8	3c vio, *buff*	3.25	*50.00*
B8	SP9	5c green, *buff*	7.75	*5.50*
B9	SP10	10c red, *buff*	19.00	*22.50*
	Nos. B7-B9 (3)		30.00	*78.00*
	Set, never hinged		87.50	

Uri
SP11

Geneva
SP12

Straw-Surfaced Paper

1918, Dec. 1

B10	SP11	10c red, org & blk	7.75	*25.00*
B11	SP12	15c vio, red, org & blk	9.25	*11.00*
	Set, never hinged		52.50	

Nidwalden
SP13

Vaud
SP14

Obwalden — SP15

Cream-Surfaced Paper

1919, Dec. 1

B12	SP13	7½c gray, red & blk	2.50	*14.00*
B13	SP14	10c lake, grn & blk	2.50	*14.00*
B14	SP15	15c pur, red & blk	5.00	*7.25*
	Nos. B12-B14 (3)		10.00	*35.25*
	Set, never hinged		22.50	

Schwyz
SP16

Zürich
SP17

Ticino — SP18

Cream-Surfaced Paper

1920, Dec. 1

B15	SP16	7½c gray & red	3.75	*11.50*
B16	SP17	10c red & lt bl	5.00	*12.50*
B17	SP18	15c violet, red & bl	2.75	*6.00*
	Nos. B15-B17 (3)		11.50	*30.00*
	Set, never hinged		25.00	

Valais
SP19

Bern
SP20

Switzerland — SP21

Cream-Surfaced Paper

1921, Dec. 1

B18	SP19	10c grn, red & blk	.65	*3.00*
B19	SP20	20c vio, red, org & blk	1.90	*3.50*
B20	SP21	40c blue & red	7.25	*47.50*
	Nos. B18-B20 (3)		9.80	*54.00*
	Set, never hinged		25.00	

Zug
SP22

Fribourg
SP23

Lucerne
SP24

Switzerland
SP25

Cream-Surfaced Paper

1922, Dec. 1

B21	SP22	5c org, pale bl & blk	.50	*5.50*
B22	SP23	10c ol grn & blk	.60	*2.50*
B23	SP24	20c vio, pale bl & blk	1.00	*2.50*
B24	SP25	40c bl & red	8.75	*47.50*
	Nos. B21-B24 (4)		10.85	*58.00*
	Set, never hinged		26.00	

Basel
SP26

Glarus (St. Fridolin)
SP27

Neuchâtel
SP28

Switzerland
SP29

Cream-Surfaced Paper

1923, Dec. 1

B25	SP26	5c org & blk	.40	*3.50*
B26	SP27	10c multi	.40	*1.90*
B27	SP28	20c multi	.45	*1.90*
B28	SP29	40c dk bl & red	7.75	*37.50*
	Nos. B25-B28 (4)		9.00	*44.80*
	Set, never hinged		21.00	

Appenzell
SP30

Solothurn
SP31

Schaffhausen
SP32

Switzerland
SP33

Cream-Surfaced Paper

1924, Dec. 1

B29	SP30	5c dk vio & blk	.25	*1.60*
B30	SP31	10c grn, red & blk	.40	*1.00*
B31	SP32	20c car, yel & blk	.65	*1.00*
B32	SP33	30c bl, red & blk	1.40	*11.00*
	Nos. B29-B32 (4)		2.70	*14.60*
	Set, never hinged		6.50	

St. Gallen (Canton)
SP34

Appenzell-Ausser-Rhoden
SP35

Grisons
SP36

Switzerland
SP37

Cream-Surfaced Paper

1925, Dec. 1

B33	SP34	5c vio, grn & blk	.25	*1.10*
B34	SP35	10c grn & blk	.25	*.85*
B35	SP36	20c multi	.25	*.85*
B36	SP37	30c dk bl, red & blk	1.10	*8.25*
	Nos. B33-B36 (4)		1.85	*11.05*
	Set, never hinged		4.50	

Thurgau
SP38

Basel
SP39

Aargau
SP40

Switzerland
SP41

Cream-Surfaced Paper

1926, Dec. 1

B37	SP38	5c vio, bis & grn	.25	*1.40*
B38	SP39	10c gray grn, red & blk	.25	*1.40*
B39	SP40	20c red, blk & bl	.25	*1.40*
B40	SP41	30c dk bl & red	1.10	*12.50*
	Nos. B37-B40 (4)		1.85	*16.70*
	Set, never hinged		4.50	

Orphan
SP42

Orphan at Pestalozzi School
SP43

SP44

J. H. Pestalozzi
SP45

1927, Dec. 1   Typo.   Wmk. 183
Granite Paper

B41	SP42	5c red vio & yel, *grysh*	.25	*1.60*
B42	SP43	10c grn & fawn, *grnsh*	.25	*.60*

Engr.

B43	SP44	20c red	.25	*.60*

Unwmk.
Photo.

B44	SP45	30c gray bl & blk	1.10	*6.50*
	Nos. B41-B44 (4)		1.85	*9.30*
	Set, never hinged		3.25	

Nos. B43-B44 for the centenary of the death of Johann Heinrich Pestalozzi, the Swiss educational reformer.

Lausanne
SP46

Winterthur
SP47

St. Gallen (City) — SP48

J. H. Dunant
SP49

1928, Dec. 1   Typo.   Wmk. 183
Cream-Surfaced Paper.

B45	SP46	5c dk vio, red & blk	.25	*1.60*
B46	SP47	10c bl grn, org red & blk	.25	*.90*
B47	SP48	20c brn red, blk & yel	.25	*.90*

Unwmk.
Photo.
Thick White Paper

B48	SP49	30c dl bl & red	1.10	*7.00*
	Nos. B45-B48 (4)		1.85	*10.40*
	Set, never hinged		3.50	

No. B48 for the centenary of the birth of Jean Henri Dunant, Swiss author, philanthropist and founder of the Red Cross Society.

Lake Lugano and Mt. Salvatore
SP50

Lake Engstlen and Mt. Titlis
SP51

Mt. Lyskamm
SP52

Nicholas von der Flüe
SP53

1929, Dec. 1 *Perf. 11x11½*

B49 SP50	5c dk vio & red org	.25	*1.40*
B50 SP51	10c ol brn & gray bl	.25	*1.10*
B51 SP52	20c brn garnet & bl	.25	*1.10*
B52 SP53	30c dk blue	1.25	*12.50*
	Nos. B49-B52 (4)	2.00	*16.10*
	Set, never hinged	4.50	

No. B52 for Nicholas von der Flüe, the Swiss patriot. By his advice the Swiss Confederation was continued and Swiss independence was saved.

Fribourg
SP54

Altdorf
SP55

Schaffhausen
SP56

Jeremias Gotthelf
SP57

Wmk. 183

1930, Dec. 1 **Typo.** *Perf. 11½*

Cream-Surfaced Paper

B53 SP54	5c dp grn, dl bl & blk	.25	*1.40*
B54 SP55	10c multicolored	.25	*.90*
B55 SP56	20c multicolored	.30	*.90*

Engr.

White Paper

B56 SP57	30c slate blue	1.25	*6.00*
	Nos. B53-B56 (4)	2.05	*9.20*
	Set, never hinged	4.00	

No. B56 for Jeremias Gotthelf, pen name of Albrecht Bitzius, pastor and author.

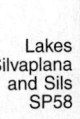

Lakes Silvaplana and Sils
SP58

Wetterhorn
SP59

Lake Geneva
SP60

Alexandre Vinet
SP61

1931, Dec. 1 **Photo.** **Unwmk.**

Granite Paper

B57 SP58	5c dp grn	.45	*1.60*
B58 SP59	10c dk vio	.40	*.85*
B59 SP60	20c brn red	.55	*1.10*

Wmk. 183

Engr.

B60 SP61	30c ultra	4.50	*19.00*
	Nos. B57-B60 (4)	5.90	*22.55*
	Set, never hinged	14.00	

No. B60 for Alexandre Rudolph Vinet, critic and theologian.

Flag Swinger
SP62

Putting the Stone
SP63

Wrestling
SP64

Eugen Huber
SP65

1932, Dec. 1 **Typo.** **Unwmk.**

Granite Paper

B61 SP62	5c dk grn & red	.30	*1.90*
B62 SP63	10c orange	.45	*2.25*
B63 SP64	20c scarlet	.55	*1.90*

Wmk. 183

Engr.

B64 SP65	30c ultra	2.25	*8.75*
	Nos. B61-B64 (4)	3.55	*14.80*
	Set, never hinged	9.50	

No. B64 for Eugen Huber, jurist and author of the Swiss Civil Law Book.

Girl of Vaud — SP66

Girl of Bern — SP67

Girl of Ticino
SP68

Jean Baptiste Girard (Le Père Grégoire)
SP69

1933, Dec. 1 **Photo.** **Unwmk.**

Granite Paper

B65 SP66	5c grn & buff	.30	*1.50*
B66 SP67	10c vio & buff	.30	*1.10*
B67 SP68	20c red & buff	.45	*2.10*

Wmk. 183

Engr.

B68 SP69	30c ultra	2.50	*8.50*
	Nos. B65-B68 (4)	3.55	*13.20*
	Set, never hinged	8.25	

Girl of Appenzell
SP70

Girl of Valais
SP71

Girl of Grisons
SP72

Albrecht von Haller
SP73

1934, Dec. 1 **Photo.** **Unwmk.**

B69 SP70	5c grn & buff	.30	*1.60*
B70 SP71	10c vio & buff	.45	*1.10*
B71 SP72	20c red & buff	.45	*1.60*

Wmk. 183

Engr.

B72 SP73	30c ultra	2.50	*8.75*
	Nos. B69-B72 (4)	3.70	*13.05*
	Set, never hinged	8.25	

Girl of Basel
SP74

Girl of Lucerne
SP75

Girl of Geneva
SP76

Stefano Franscini
SP77

1935, Dec. 1 **Photo.** **Unwmk.**

Granite Paper

B73 SP74	5c grn & buff	.25	*1.75*
B74 SP75	10c vio & buff	.45	*1.10*
B75 SP76	20c red & buff	.45	*2.75*

Wmk. 183

Engr.

B76 SP77	30c ultra	2.50	*8.75*
	Nos. B73-B76 (4)	3.65	*14.35*
	Set, never hinged	8.25	

No. B76 honors Stefano Franscini (1796-1857), political economist and educator.

Alpine Herdsman — SP78

Perf. 11½

1936, Oct. 1 **Photo.** **Unwmk.**

Granite Paper

B77 SP78	10c + 5c vio	.55	*1.00*
B78 SP78	20c + 10c dk red	.85	*4.25*
B79 SP78	30c + 10c ultra	3.75	*20.00*
	Nos. B77-B79 (3)	5.15	*25.25*
	Set, never hinged	11.00	

Souvenir Sheet

B80 SP78	Sheet of 3	35.00	*125.00*
	Never hinged	70.00	
a.	Block of 4 sheets	190.00	*875.00*
	Never hinged	300.00	

Swiss National Defense Fund Drive.

No. B80 contains stamps similar to Nos. B77-B79, but on grilled granite paper with blue and red fibers instead of black and red. Sold for 2fr. Size: 120x130mm.

Johann Georg Nägeli
SP79

Girl of Neuchâtel
SP80

Girl of Schwyz
SP81

Girl of Zurich
SP82

Wmk. 183

1936, Dec. 1 **Engr.** *Perf. 11½*

Granite Paper

B81 SP79	5c grn	.55	*.70*

Unwmk.

Photo.

B82 SP80	10c vio & buff	.55	*.70*
B83 SP81	20c red & buff	.25	*1.90*
B84 SP82	30c ultra & buff	3.50	*30.00*
	Nos. B81-B84 (4)	4.85	*33.30*
	Set, never hinged	11.00	

Gen. Henri Dufour — SP83

Nicholas von der Flüe — SP84

Boy
SP85

Girl
SP86

Perf. 11½

1937, Dec. 1 **Unwmk.** **Engr.**

B85 SP83	5c + 5c bl grn	.25	*.55*
B86 SP84	10c + 5c red vio	.25	*.55*

Photo.

Granite Paper

B87 SP85	20c + 5c red & silver	.30	*.55*
B88 SP86	30c + 10c ultra & sil	1.25	*5.50*
	Nos. B85-B88 (4)	2.05	*7.15*
	Set, never hinged	3.50	

25th anniv. of the Pro Juventute (child welfare) stamps.

Souvenir Sheet

1937, Dec. 20 *Imperf.*

B89	Sheet of 2	6.50	*57.50*
a.	SP85 20c + 5c red & silver	1.60	*17.00*
b.	SP86 30c + 10c ultra & silver	1.60	*17.00*
	Never hinged	7.50	

Simulated perforation in silver. Sheet sold for 1fr.

Tell Chapel, Lake Lucerne
SP87

1938, June 15
Granite Paper   *Perf. 11½*

B90	SP87	10c + 10c brt vio & yel	.45	1.10
		Never hinged	1.10	
a.		Grilled gum	22.50	77.50
		Never hinged	32.50	

National Fête Day.

Salomon Gessner SP88

Girl of St. Gallen SP89

Girl of Uri — SP90

Girl of Aargau — SP91

1938, Dec. 1   Engr.   *Perf. 11½*

B91	SP88	5c + 5c dp bl grn	.25	.50

Photo.
Granite Paper

B92	SP89	10c + 5c pur & buff	.25	.55
B93	SP90	20c + 5c red & buff	.25	.55
B94	SP91	30c + 10c ultra	1.60	6.50
	Nos. B91-B94 (4)		2.35	8.10
	Set, never hinged		4.50	

Castle at Laupen SP92

1939, June 15

B95	SP92	10c + 10c brn, gray & red	.30	1.10
		Never hinged	1.10	

600th anniversary of the Battle of Laupen. The surtax was used to aid needy mothers.

Hans Herzog SP93

Girl of Fribourg SP94

Girl of Nidwalden SP95

Girl of Basel SP96

Perf. 11½
1939, Dec. 1   Unwmk.   Engr.

B96	SP93	5c + 5c dk grn	.25	.45

Photo.
Granite Paper

B97	SP94	10c + 5c rose vio & buff	.25	.45
B98	SP95	20c + 5c org red	.30	1.40
B99	SP96	30c + 10c ultra & buff	1.60	11.50
	Nos. B96-B99 (4)		2.40	13.80
	Set, never hinged		5.00	

Sempach, 1386 — SP97

Giornico, 1478 — SP98

Calven, 1499 SP99

WWI Ranger SP100

1940, Mar. 20   Photo.
Granite Paper

B100	SP97	5c + 5c emer, blk & red	.30	1.25
B101	SP98	10c + 5c brn org, blk & car	.30	.55
B102	SP99	20c + 5c brn red, blk & car	2.25	.95
B103	SP100	30c + 10c brt bl, brn blk & red	1.60	8.25

National Fête Day. The surtax was for the National Fund and the Red Cross.

Redrawn

B104	SP99	20c + 5c brn red, blk & car	9.75	6.50
	Nos. B100-B104 (5)		14.20	17.50
	Set, never hinged		26.00	

The base of statue has been heavily shaded. "Calven 1499" moved nearer to bottom line of base. Top line of base removed.

Souvenir Sheet
Unwmk.
1940, July 16   Photo.   *Imperf.*
Granite Paper

B105		Sheet of 4	250.00	575.00
		Never hinged	425.00	
a.		SP97 5c+5c yel grn, blk & red	11.00	26.00
b.		SP98 10c+5c org yel, blk & red	47.50	210.00
c.		SP99 20c+5c brn red, blk & red (redrawn)	47.50	210.00
d.		SP100 30c+10c chlky bl, blk & red	11.00	26.00

National Fete Day. Sheets measure 125x65mm and sold for 5fr.

Gottfried Keller SP102

Girl of Thurgau SP103

Girl of Solothurn SP104

Girl of Zug SP105

1940, Dec. 1   Engr.   *Perf. 11½*

B106	SP102	5c + 5c dk bl grn	.25	.40

Photo.

B107	SP103	10c + 5c brn & buff	.25	.30
B108	SP104	20c + 5c org red & buff	.25	.40

B109	SP105	30c + 10c dp ultra & buff	1.40	9.50
	Nos. B106-B109 (4)		2.15	10.60
	Set, never hinged		4.00	

Lake Lucerne, Arms of Cantons SP106

Tell Chapel at Chemin Creux SP107

1941, June 15

B110	SP106	10c + 10c multi	.30	.75
B111	SP107	20c + 10c org, red & lt buff	.30	1.25
	Set, never hinged		2.00	

Natl. Fête Day and 650th anniv. of Swiss Independence.

Johann Lavater SP108

Girl of Schaffhausen SP109

Girl of Obwalden SP110

Daniel Jean Richard SP111

1941, Dec. 1   Engr.

B112	SP108	5c + 5c dk grn	.25	.30
B113	SP111	30c + 10c dp ultra	.80	5.00

Photo.

B114	SP109	10c + 5c chnt & buff	.25	.40
B115	SP110	20c + 5c ver & buff	.25	.40
	Nos. B112-B115 (4)		1.55	6.10
	Set, never hinged		3.50	

Souvenir Sheet
Imperf

B116		Sheet of 2	60.00	350.00
a.		SP109 10c +5c chnt & buff	17.00	125.00
b.		SP110 20c +5c ver & buff	17.00	125.00
		Never hinged	100.00	

Issued in sheets measuring 75x70mm and sold for 2fr. The surtax was used for charity.

Ancient Geneva SP113

Soldiers' Monument, Forch SP114

1942, June 15   *Perf. 11½*

B117	SP113	10c + 10c gray blk, red & yel	.25	.50
B118	SP114	20c + 10c cop red, red & buff	.25	.85
	Set, never hinged		1.25	

National Fête Day, 1942. No. B117 for the 2000th anniv. of the City of Geneva.

Souvenir Sheet
Imperf

B119		Sheet of 2	50.00	225.00
a.		SP113 10c +10c gray black, red & yellow	14.00	80.00
b.		SP113 20c +10c copper red, red & buff	14.00	80.00
		Never hinged	82.50	

Issued in sheets measuring 105x63mm in commemoration of National Fete and the 2000th anniv. of the City of Geneva. Sold for 2fr. The surtax was divided between the Swiss Alliance of Samaritans and the National Community Chest.

Niklaus Riggenbach SP116

Girl of Appenzell SP117

Girl of Glarus SP118

Konrad Escher von der Linth SP119

1942, Dec. 1   Engr.   *Perf. 11½*

B120	SP116	5c + 5c deep grn	.25	.50
B121	SP119	30c + 10c royal bl	1.10	4.50

Photo.

B122	SP117	10c + 5c dp brn & buff	.25	.50
B123	SP118	20c + 5c org red	.25	.50
	Nos. B120-B123 (4)		1.85	6.00
	Set, never hinged		3.75	

Intragna SP120

Parliament Buildings, Bern SP121

1943, June 15   Photo.   *Perf. 11½*

B124	SP120	10c + 10c blk brn, buff & dk red	.25	.75
B125	SP121	20c + 10c cop red, buff & dk red	.30	1.50
	Set, never hinged		1.25	

National Fête Day, 1943.

Emanuel von Fellenberg SP122

Silver Thistle SP123

20c+5c, Lady slipper. 30c+10c, Gentian.

1943, Dec. 1   Engr.

B126	SP122	5c + 5c green	.25	.50

Photo.

B127	SP123	10c + 5c sl grn & ocher	.25	.50
B128	SP123	20c + 5c copper red & yel	.25	.50
B129	SP123	30c + 10c royal bl & lt bl	1.10	8.50
	Nos. B126-B129 (4)		1.85	10.00
	Set, never hinged		3.25	

Souvenir Sheets

SP126

1943   **Engr.**   *Imperf.*
B130 SP126   Sheet of 12   37.50   *60.00*
a.   10c black, single stamp   1.10   *3.75*
    Never hinged   77.50

Sold for 5fr. Size: 165x140mm.

SP127

Red Horizontal Lines
B131 SP127   Sheet of 2   42.50   *52.50*
a.   4c black & red   13.00   *20.00*
b.   6c black & red   13.00   *20.00*
    Never hinged   75.00

Sold for 3fr. Size: 70x75mm.

Arms of Geneva — SP128

B132 SP128   Sheet of 2   40.00   *40.00*
a.   5c green & black   11.50   *15.00*
    Never hinged   65.00

Sold for 3fr. Size: 72x72mm. Centenary of
Swiss postage stamps. The surtax aided the
Swiss Red Cross.

Heiden
SP129

St. Jacob
SP130

Mesocco
SP131

Basel
SP132

Perf. 11½
1944, June 15   **Photo.**   **Unwmk.**
B133 SP129   5c + 5c dk bl grn,   .25   *2.25*
    red & buff
B134 SP130   10c + 10c gray blk,   .25   *.50*
    red & buff
B135 SP131   20c + 10c hn, red   .25   *1.00*
    & buff
B136 SP132   30c + 10c brt ultra   2.10   *17.50*
    & red
    Nos. B133-B136 (4)   2.85   *21.25*
    Set, never hinged   6.00

National Fete Day.

Numa Droz
SP133

Edelweiss
SP134

Designs: 20c+5c, Lilium martagon.
30c+10c, Aquilegia alpina.

1944, Dec. 1   **Engr.**
B137 SP133   5c + 5c green   .25   *.35*
      Photo.
B138 SP134   10c + 5c dk sl grn,   .25   *.40*
    yel & gray
B139 SP134   20c + 5c red, yel &   .35   *.40*
    gray
B140 SP134   30c + 10c bl, gray   1.10   *8.50*
    & lt bl
    Nos. B137-B140 (4)   1.95   *9.65*
    Set, never hinged   4.00

Symbol of Faith,
Hope and
Love — SP137

Lifeboat Making a Rescue — SP138

1945, Feb. 20   **Perf. 11½**
B141 SP137   10c + 10c multi   .30   *.50*
B142 SP137   20c + 60c multi   .90   *5.75*
    Set, never hinged   2.50

Imperf
Souvenir Sheet
B143 SP138   3fr + 7fr bl gray   110.00   *225.00*
    Never hinged   200.00

Issued in sheets measuring 70x110mm.
Surtax for the benefit of war victims.

Souvenir Sheet

Dove of Basel — SP139

1945, Apr. 14   **Typo.**
B144 SP139   Sheet of 2   70.00   *95.00*
a.   10c gray, maroon &   16.00   *26.00*
    black
    Never hinged   150.00

Cent. of the Basel Cantonal Stamp. The
sheets measure 71x63mm and sold for 3fr.
The surtax was for the Pro Juventute
Foundation.

Numeral of Value
and Red
Cross — SP140

1945   **Photo.**   *Perf. 12*
B145 SP140   5c + 10c grn & red   .30   *.75*
    Never hinged   .65

Weaver
SP141

Farm of
Jura
SP142

Farm of
Emmental
SP143

Frame House, Eastern
Switzerland — SP144

1945, June 15   **Engr.**   *Perf. 11½*
B146 SP141   5c + 5c bl grn &   .35   *2.00*
    red
      Photo.
B147 SP142   10c + 10c brn,   .35   *.75*
    gray bl &
    red
B148 SP143   20c + 10c hn brn,   .55   *.75*
    buff & red
B149 SP144   30c + 10c saph &   5.50   *35.00*
    red
    Nos. B146-B149 (4)   6.75   *38.50*
    Set, never hinged   14.50

The surtax was for needy mothers.

Ludwig
Forrer — SP145

Susanna
Orelli — SP146

Alpine Dog-
Rose
SP147

Crocus
SP148

1945, Dec. 1   **Engr.**
B150 SP145   5c + 5c dk grn   .25   *.50*
B151 SP146   10c + 10c dk red   .25   *.50*
    brn
      Photo.
B152 SP147   20c + 10c rose brn,   .30   *.50*
    rose & yel org
B153 SP148   30c + 10c dk bl,   1.50   *7.50*
    gray & lil
    Nos. B150-B153 (4)   2.30   *9.00*
    Set, never hinged   4.50

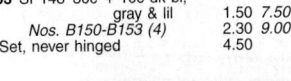

Cheese
Making
SP149

Farm
Buildings
and
Vineyards
SP150

House in
Appenzell
SP151

House in
Engadine
SP152

1946, June 15   **Engr.**
B154 SP149   5c + 5c bl grn &   .35   *2.00*
    red
      Photo.
B155 SP150   10c + 10c brn,   .25   *.75*
    buff & red
B156 SP151   20c + 10c henna,   .35   *.75*
    buff & red
B157 SP152   30c + 10c saph &   3.00   *9.50*
    red
    Nos. B154-B157 (4)   3.95   *13.00*
    Set, never hinged   9.50

Rodolphe
Toepffer
SP153

Narcissus
SP154

20c+10c, Mountain sengreen. 30c+10c,
Blue thistle.

1946, Nov. 30   **Engr.**
B158 SP153   5c + 5c green   .25   *.50*

Photo.

B159 SP154 10c + 10c dk sl grn,
gray & red org .25 .50
B160 SP154 20c + 10c brn car,
gray & yel .30 .75
B161 SP154 30c + 10c dk bl,
gray & pink 1.40 6.00
Nos. B158-B161 (4) 2.20 7.75
Set, never hinged 3.75

Railroad
Laborers
SP157

Railroad
Station,
Rorschach
SP158

Lüen-Castiel Station — SP159

Flüelen
Station
SP160

Perf. 11½

1947, June 14 Engr. Unwmk.
B162 SP157 5c + 5c dk grn
& red .25 2.10

Photo.

B163 SP158 10c + 10c gray
blk, cream &
red .30 .75
B164 SP159 20c + 10c rose lil,
cream & red .30 1.00
B165 SP160 30c + 10c bl, gray
& red 3.50 9.00
Nos. B162-B165 (4) 4.35 12.85
Set, never hinged 10.00

The surtax was for professional education of
invalids and for the fight against cancer.

Jakob
Burckhardt
SP161

Alpine Primrose
SP162

20c+10c, Red lily. 30c+10c, Cyclamen.

1947, Dec. 1 Engr.
B166 SP161 5c + 5c dk grn .25 .45

Photo.

B167 SP162 10c + 10c sl blk,
gray & yel .25 .45
B168 SP162 20c + 10c red brn,
gray & cop red .30 .40
B169 SP162 30c + 10c dk bl,
gray & pink 1.25 5.75
Nos. B166-B169 (4) 2.05 7.05
Set, never hinged 3.50

Sun and
Olympic
Emblem
SP165

Icehockey
Player
SP167

10c+10c, Snowflake and Olympic Emblem.
30c+10c, Ski-runner.

1948, Jan. 15
B170 SP165 5c + 5c dk bl grn &
yel .25 1.50
B171 SP165 10c + 10c choc & bl .30 1.00
B172 SP167 20c + 10c dp mag,
gray & org yel .40 1.50
B173 SP167 30c + 10c dk bl, bl
& gray blk 1.25 5.50
Nos. B170-B173 (4) 2.20 9.50
Set, never hinged 5.50

Issued to publicize the 5th Olympic Winter
Games, St. Moritz, Jan. 30-Feb. 8, 1948.

Frontier
Guard
SP169

House of
Fribourg
SP170

House of
Valais
SP171

House of
Ticino
SP172

1948, June 15 Engr.
B174 SP169 5c + 5c dk grn &
red .25 1.25

Photo.

B175 SP170 10c + 10c sl &
gray .25 .75
B176 SP171 20c + 10c brn red
& pink .30 1.00
B177 SP172 30c + 10c bl &
gray 2.25 7.50
Nos. B174-B177 (4) 3.05 10.50
Set, never hinged 6.00

IMABA 1948 BASEL

Johann R. Wettstein — SP173

1948, Aug. 21 Perf. 11x12½
B178 SP173 Sheet of 2 50.00 65.00
a. 10c rose lilac 14.00 25.00
b. 20c chalky blue 14.00 25.00
Never hinged 77.50

Intl. Phil. Expo., Basel, Aug. 21-29, 1948.
Sheet, size 110x60mm, sold for 3fr, of which
the surtax was used for the exhibition and
charitable purposes.

Gen. Ulrich
Wille
SP174

Foxglove
SP175

20c+10c, Alpine rose. 40c+10c, Lily of
paradise.

1948, Dec. 1 Engr. Perf. 11½
B179 SP174 5c + 5c dk vio brn .25 .45

Photo.

B180 SP175 10c + 10c dk grn,
yel grn & yel .25 .45
B181 SP175 20c + 10c brn, crim
& buff .30 .45
B182 SP175 40c + 10c bl, gray &
org 1.25 5.50
Nos. B179-B182 (4) 2.05 6.85
Set, never hinged 4.50

Postman
SP176

Mountain
Farmhouse
SP177

House of
Lucerne
SP178

House of
Prattigau
SP179

Engraved and Photogravure

1949, June 15 Shield in Carmine
B183 SP176 5c + 5c rose vio .30 1.50

Photo.

B184 SP177 10c + 10c bl grn &
car .30 .75
B185 SP178 20c + 10c dk brn
& cr .30 .75
B186 SP179 40c + 10c bl &
pale bl 2.50 10.00
Nos. B183-B186 (4) 3.40 13.00
Set, never hinged 7.25

The surtax was for professional education of
Swiss youth.

Niklaus Wengi
SP180

Anemone
Sulphureous
SP181

20c+10c, Alpine clematis. 40c+10c, Superb
pink.

1949, Dec. 1 Engr. Perf. 11½
B187 SP180 5c + 5c vio brn .25 .45

Photo.

B188 SP181 10c + 10c grn, gray
& yel .25 .45
B189 SP181 20c + 10c brn, bl &
yel .25 .45
B190 SP181 40c + 10c bl, lav &
yel 1.40 5.50
Nos. B187-B190 (4) 2.15 6.85
Set, never hinged 4.00

Adaptation
of 1850
Design
SP182

Putting the
Stone
SP183

Designs: 20c+10c, Wrestlers. 30c+10c,
Runners. 40c+10c, Target shooting.

1950, June 1 Engr. & Photo.
Shield in Red
B191 SP182 5c + 5c black .25 .75

Photo.

Inscribed: "I. VIII. 1950"
B192 SP183 10c + 10c green .50 .80
B193 SP183 20c + 10c brn ol .50 1.25
B194 SP183 30c + 10c rose lil 3.75 17.00
B195 SP183 40c + 10c dull bl 4.75 11.00
Nos. B191-B195 (5) 9.75 30.80
Set, never hinged 20.00

The surtax was for the Red Cross and the
Society of Swiss History of Art.

Theophil
Sprecher von
Bernegg
SP184

Admiral
Butterfly
SP185

Designs: 20c+10c, Blue Underwing Butterfly. 30c+10c, Bee. 40c+10c, Sulphur Butterfly.

1950, Dec. 1 Engr.
B196 SP184 5c + 5c sepia .25 .30

Photo.

B197 SP185 10c + 10c multi .25 .40
B198 SP185 20c + 10c multi .30 .50
B199 SP185 30c + 10c rose lil,
gray & dk
brn 3.00 13.50
B200 SP185 40c + 10c bl, dk
brn & yel 3.00 9.25
Nos. B196-B200 (5) 6.80 23.95
Set, never hinged 13.50

Arms of Switzerland and
Zurich — SP186

Valaisan
Polka
SP187

20c+10c, Flag-swinging. 30c+10c, Hornus-
sen (natl. game). 40c+10c, Blowing alphorn.

1951, June 1 Engr.
Shield in Red
B201 SP186 5c + 5c gray .25 .50

Photo.

Inscribed: "1. VIII. 1951"
Shield in Red, Figure Shaded in
Gray
B202 SP187 10c + 10c green .40 .50
B203 SP187 20c + 10c ol bis .60 .85
B204 SP187 30c + 10c red vio 4.50 11.50
B205 SP187 40c + 10c brt
blue 4.50 13.50
Nos. B201-B205 (5) 10.25 26.85
Set, never hinged 20.00

The surtax was used primarily for needy
mothers.

Souvenir Sheet

1951, Sept. 29 *Imperf.*
B206 SP187 40c brt bl, sheet 175.00 *190.00*
Never hinged 275.00

No. B206 sold for 3fr, size: 74x56mm. Natl. Phil. Exhib., LUNABA, Sept. 29-Oct. 7, 1951, Lucerne. The net proceeds were used for Swiss schools abroad.

Johanna Spyri SP189

Dragonfly SP190

Butterflies: 20c+10c, Black-Veined. 30c+10c Orange-Tip. 40c+10c, Saturnia pyri.

1951, Dec. 1 **Engr.** ***Perf. 11½***
B207 SP189 5c + 5c red brn .25 *.30*

Photo.

B208 SP190 10c + 10c grn & dk bl .25 *.30*
B209 SP190 20c + 10c rose lil, cr & blk .30 *.50*
B210 SP190 30c + 10c ol grn, gray & org 2.00 *8.50*
B211 SP190 40c + 10c bl, dk brn & car 2.50 *8.50*
Nos. B207-B211 (5) 5.30 *18.10*
Set, never hinged 10.00

Arms of Switzerland, Glarus and Zug — SP191

Doubs River — SP192

Designs: 20c+10c, Lake of St. Gotthard. 30c+10c, Moesa River. 40c+10c, Lake of Marjelen.

1952, May 31 **Engr. & Typo.**
B212 SP191 5c + 5c gray & red .25 *1.00*

Photo.

B213 SP192 10c + 10c bl grn .25 *.50*
B214 SP192 20c + 10c brn car .30 *.50*
B215 SP192 30c + 10c brown 2.50 *6.50*
B216 SP192 40c + 10c blue 3.00 *8.75*
Nos. B212-B216 (5) 6.30 *17.25*
Set, never hinged 12.50

The surtax was used primarily for historical research and popular culture.

See Nos. B222-B226, B233-B236, B243-B246, B253-B256.

Portrait of a Boy, by Albert Anker SP193

Ladybug SP194

20c+10c, Barred-wing butterfly. 30c+10c, Argus butterfly. 40c+10c, Silkworm moth.

Perf. 11½

1952, Dec. 1 **Unwmk.** **Engr.**
B217 SP193 5c + 5c brn car .25 *.35*

Photo.

B218 SP194 10c + 10c bluish grn, blk & org red .25 *.35*
B219 SP194 20c + 10c rose lil, cr & blk .30 *.50*
B220 SP194 30c + 10c brn, blk & gray bl 2.00 *8.25*
B221 SP194 40c + 10c pale vio, brn & buff 1.90 *8.75*
Nos. B217-B221 (5) 4.70 *18.20*
Set, never hinged 10.00

See Nos. B227-B231, B238-B241.

Types Similar to 1952

Designs: 5c+5c, Arms of Switzerland and Bern. 10c+10c, Reuss River. 20c+10c, Sihl Lake. 30c+10c, Bisse River. 40c+10c, Lake of Geneva.

Engraved and Photogravure

1953, June 1
B222 SP191 5c + 5c gray & red .25 *.75*

Photo.

B223 SP192 10c + 10c bl grn .25 *.50*
B224 SP192 20c + 10c brn car .30 *.75*
B225 SP192 30c + 10c brown 2.50 *7.00*
B226 SP192 40c + 10c blue 2.50 *6.50*
Nos. B222-B226 (5) 5.80 *15.50*
Set, never hinged 12.50

The surtax was used for Swiss nationals abroad and for disabled persons.

Booklet Panes

Panes consisting of blocks, strips or pairs removed from large sheets of regular issue and fastened or enclosed within a cover or folder, often by stapling or sewing in the sheet margin, are no longer being listed. Such panes contain no straight edges and can easily be made privately.

Types Similar to 1952, Dated "1953"

5c+5c, Portrait of a girl, by Albert Anker. 10c+10c, Nun moth. 20c+10c, Camberwell beauty butterfly. 30c+10c, Purple longicorn beetle. 40c+10c, Self-portrait, Ferdinand Hodler, facing left.

1953, Dec. 1 **Engr.** ***Perf. 11½***
B227 SP193 5c + 5c rose brn .25 *.35*

Photo.

B228 SP194 10c + 10c multi .25 *.30*
B229 SP194 20c + 10c multi .30 *.50*
a. Sheet of 24 200.00
Never hinged 375.00
b. Bklt. pane, 4 #B229, 2 #B230 32.50
B230 SP194 30c + 10c ol, blk & red 1.90 *8.25*

Engr.

B231 SP193 40c + 10c blue 2.75 *7.00*
Nos. B227-B231 (5) 5.45 *16.40*
Set, never hinged 12.00

No. B229a consists of 16 No. B229 and 8 No. B230, arranged to include four se-tenant pairs and four pairs which are both se-tenant and tête bêche.

Types Similar to 1952, Dated "1954" and

Opening Bars of "Swiss Hymn" — SP195

Views: 10c+10c, Neuchatel lake. 20c+10c, Maggia river. 30c+10c, Cascade, Taubenloch gorge. 40c+10c, Sils lake.

1954, June 1 **Engr.** ***Perf. 11½***
B232 SP195 5c + 5c dk bl grn .25 *.75*

Photo.

B233 SP192 10c + 10c bl grn .25 *.50*
B234 SP192 20c + 10c dp plum .35 *.50*
B235 SP192 30c + 10c dk brn 2.00 *6.75*
B236 SP192 40c + 10c dp bl 2.25 *7.25*
Nos. B232-B236 (5) 5.10 *15.75*
Set, never hinged 12.00

The surtax was used to aid vocational training and home nursing.

No. B232 commemorates the centenary of the death of Alberik Zwyssig, composer of the "Swiss Hymn."

Types Similar to 1952, Dated "1954" and

Jeremias Gotthelf — SP196

Insects: 10c+10c, Garden tiger. 20c+10c, Bumble bee. 30c+10c, Ascalaphus. 40c+10c, Swallow-tail.

1954, Dec. 1 **Engr.**
B237 SP196 5c + 5c dk red brn .25 *.30*

Photo.

B238 SP194 10c + 10c multi .25 *.30*
B239 SP194 20c + 10c multi .35 *.50*
B240 SP194 30c + 10c rose vio, brn & yel 2.00 *6.75*
B241 SP194 40c + 10c multi 2.25 *7.25*
Nos. B237-B241 (5) 5.10 *15.10*
Set, never hinged 11.00

Type Similar to 1952, Dated "1955" and

Federal Institute of Technology, Zurich — SP197

Views: 10c+10c, Saane river. 20c+10c, Lake of Aegeri. 30c+10c, Grappelen Lake. 40c+10c, Lake of Bienne.

1955, June 1 **Engr.** ***Perf. 11½***
B242 SP197 5c + 5c gray .25 *.75*

Photo.

B243 SP192 10c + 10c dp grn .25 *.50*
B244 SP192 20c + 10c rose brn .35 *.50*
B245 SP192 30c + 10c brown 2.00 *6.00*
B246 SP192 40c + 10c dp bl 2.25 *7.50*
Nos. B242-B246 (5) 5.10 *15.25*
Set, never hinged 11.50

The surtax aided mountain dwellers.

No. B242 for the centenary of the Federal Institute of Technology in Zurich.

Charles Pictet de Rochemont SP198

Peacock Butterfly SP199

Insects: 20c+10c, Great Horntail. 30c+10c, Yellow Bear moth. 40c+10c, Apollo butterfly.

1955, Dec. 1 **Engr.** **Unwmk.**
B247 SP198 5c + 5c brn car .25 *.30*

Photo.

Insects in Natural Colors

B248 SP199 10c + 10c yel grn .25 *.30*
B249 SP199 20c + 10c red .30 *.50*
B250 SP199 30c + 10c dk ocher 2.50 *4.75*
B251 SP199 40c + 10c ultra 2.25 *5.75*
Nos. B247-B251 (5) 5.55 *11.60*
Set, never hinged 11.50

Types Similar to 1952, Dated "1956" and

"Woman's Work" — SP200

Designs: 10c+10c, Rhone at St. Maurice. 20c+10c, Katzensee. 30c+10c, Rhine at Trin. 40c+10c, Lake Wallen.

1956, June 1 **Engr.** ***Perf. 11½***
B252 SP200 5c + 5c turq bl .25 *1.00*

Photo.

B253 SP192 10c + 10c green .25 *.50*
B254 SP192 20c + 10c brn car .30 *.75*
B255 SP192 30c + 10c brown 2.00 *4.75*
B256 SP192 40c + 10c ultra 1.75 *5.75*
Nos. B252-B256 (5) 4.55 *12.75*
Set, never hinged 10.00

The surtax was for the National Day Collection, the National Library and Academy of Arts and Letters. No. B252 was issued in honor of Swiss women.

Carlo Maderno SP201

Burnet Moth SP202

Insects: 20c+10c, Purple Emperor. 30c+10c, Blue ground beetle. 40c+10c, Cabbage butterfly.

1956, Dec. 1 **Engr.** ***Perf. 11½***
B257 SP201 5c + 5c brn car .25 *.30*

Photo.

Granite Paper

B258 SP202 10c + 10c grn, dk grn & car rose .25 *.30*
B259 SP202 20c + 10c multi .30 *.30*
B260 SP202 30c + 10c yel & dp bl 1.40 *4.50*
B261 SP202 40c + 10c lt ultra, pale yel & sep 1.40 *5.00*
Nos. B257-B261 (5) 3.60 *10.40*
Set, never hinged 7.50

Red Cross and Swiss Emblems SP203

"Charity" — SP204

Engraved and Photogravure

1957, June 1 **Unwmk.** ***Perf. 11½***
B262 SP203 5c + 5c gray & red .25 *.55*

Photo.

Granite Paper

Cross in Deep Carmine

B263 SP204 10c + 10c brt grn & gray .25 *.30*
B264 SP204 20c + 10c red & bl gray .30 *.30*
B265 SP204 30c + 10c brn & vio gray 1.75 *4.50*
B266 SP204 40c + 10c brt bl & bis 1.90 *5.75*
Nos. B262-B266 (5) 4.45 *11.40*
Set, never hinged 10.00

The surtax went to the Red Cross for the needs of the sick and to combat cancer.

Leonhard Euler — SP205

Clouded Yellow — SP206

Insects: 20c+10c, Magpie moth. 30c+10c, Rose Chafer. 40c+10c, Red Underwing.

1957, Nov. 30 **Engr.** ***Perf. 11½***
B267 SP205 5c + 5c brn car .25 *.30*

Photo.

Granite Paper

B268 SP206 10c + 10c multi .25 *.30*
B269 SP206 20c + 10c lil rose, blk & yel .30 *.50*

B270 SP206 30c + 10c rose brn, ind & brt grn 1.40 4.50
B271 SP206 40c + 10c multi 1.40 3.50
Nos. B267-B271 (5) 3.60 9.10
Set, never hinged 7.50

Catalogue values for unused stamps in this section, from this point to the end of the section, are for Never Hinged items.

Mother and Child — SP207

Fluorite — SP208

Designs: 20c+10c, Ammonite. 30c+10c, Garnet. 40c+10c, Rock Crystal.

Perf. 11½
1958, May 31 Unwmk. Engr.
B272 SP207 5c + 5c brn car .40 .40
Photo.
Granite Paper
B273 SP208 10c + 10c multi .55 .55
B274 SP208 20c + 10c blk, red & ol bis .75 .75
B275 SP208 30c + 10c dl yel & mag 3.25 5.25
B276 SP208 40c + 10c blk, chlky bl & sl bl 3.25 5.00
Nos. B272-B276 (5) 8.20 11.95

The surtax was for needy mothers.
See #B283-B286, B292-B295, B304-B307.

Albrecht von Haller — SP209

Pansy — SP210

Flowers: 20c+10c, China aster. 30c+10c, Morning glory. 40c+10c, Christmas rose.

1958, Dec. 1 Engr. Perf. 11½
B277 SP209 5c + 5c brn car .25 .30
Photo.
Granite Paper
B278 SP210 10c + 10c grn, yel & brn .25 .30
B279 SP210 20c + 10c multi .55 .30
B280 SP210 30c + 10c multi 2.00 3.50
B281 SP210 40c + 10c dk bl, yel & grn 2.00 3.50
Nos. B277-B281 (5) 5.05 7.90
See Nos. B287-B291.

Mineral Type of 1958 and

Globe and Swiss Flags — SP211

Designs: 10c+10c, Agate. 20c+10c, Tourmaline. 30c+10c, Amethyst. 40c+10c, Fossil salamander (andrias).

1959, June 1 Engr. Perf. 11½
B282 SP211 5c + 5c dl grn & red .40 .50
Photo.
Granite Paper
B283 SP208 10c + 10c gray, yel grn & ver .50 .50
B284 SP208 20c + 10c blk, lil rose & bl grn .65 .50
B285 SP208 30c + 10c blk, lt brn & vio 2.25 3.00

B286 SP208 40c + 10c blk, bl & gray 2.50 3.00
Nos. B282-B286 (5) 6.30 7.50

Types of 1958
Designs: 5c+5c, Karl Hilty. 10c+10c, Marigold. 20c+10c, Poppy. 30c+10c, Nasturtium. 50c+10c, Sweet pea.

1959, Dec. 1 Engr. Perf. 11½
B287 SP209 5c +5c brn car .25 .25
Photo.
Granite Paper
B288 SP210 10c + 10c dk grn, grn & yel .30 .25
B289 SP210 20c + 10c mag, red & grn .50 .25
B290 SP210 30c + 10c multi 2.25 3.00
B291 SP210 50c + 10c multi 2.25 3.00
Nos. B287-B291 (5) 5.55 6.75

Mineral Type of 1958 and

Owl, T-Square and Hammer — SP212

Designs: 5c+5c, Smoky quartz. 10c+10c, Feldspar. 20c+10c, Gryphaea, fossil. 30c+10c, Azurite.

1960, June 1 Photo. Perf. 11½
Granite Paper
B292 SP208 5c + 5c blk, bl & ocher .55 .75
B293 SP208 10c + 10c blk, yel grn & pink .60 .50
B294 SP208 20c + 10c blk, lil rose & yel .85 .50
B295 SP208 30c + 10c multi 4.00 3.75
Engr.
B296 SP212 50c + 10c bl & gold 4.75 3.50
Nos. B292-B296 (5) 10.75 9.00

Souvenir Sheet
Imperf
Typo.
B297 Sheet of 4 40.00 20.00
#B297 contains 4 50c+10c stamps of design SP212 in gold & blue. Size: 84x75mm. Sold for 3fr.

Alexandre Calame SP213

Dandelion SP214

Flowers: 20c+10c, Phlox. 30c+10c, Larkspur. 50c+10c, Thorn apple.

1960, Dec. 1 Engr. Unwmk.
B298 SP213 5c + 5c grnsh bl .25 .25
Photo.
Granite Paper
B299 SP214 10c + 10c grn, yel & gray .30 .25
B300 SP214 20c + 10c mag, grn & gray .45 .25
B301 SP214 30c + 10c org brn, grn & bl 3.50 3.50
B302 SP214 50c + 10c ultra & grn 3.50 3.50
Nos. B298-B302 (5) 8.00 7.75
See Nos. B308-B312, B329-B333, B339-B343.

Mineral Type of 1958 and

Book of History with Symbols of Time and Eternity — SP215

Designs: 10c+10c, Fluorite. 20c+10c, Petrified fish. 30c+10c, Lazulite. 50c+10c, Petrified fern.

1961, June 1 Engr. Perf. 11½
B303 SP215 5c + 5c lt blue .35 .50
Photo.
Granite Paper
B304 SP208 10c + 10c gray, grn & pink .50 .35
B305 SP208 20c + 10c gray & car rose .60 .35
B306 SP208 30c + 10c gray, org & grnsh bl 1.60 2.50
B307 SP208 50c + 10c gray, bl & bis 2.25 3.50
Nos. B303-B307 (5) 5.30 7.20

Types of 1960
Designs: 5c+5c, Jonas Furrer. 10c+10c, Sunflower. 20c+10c, Lily of the valley. 30c+10c, Iris. 50c+10c, Silverweed.

1961, Dec. 1 Engr. Perf. 11½
B308 SP213 5c + 5c dk blue .25 .25
Photo.
Granite Paper
B309 SP214 10c + 10c grn, yel & org .25 .25
B310 SP214 20c + 10c dk red, grn & gray .30 .25
B311 SP214 30c + 10c multi 1.75 2.00
B312 SP214 50c + 10c dk bl, yel & grn 2.00 2.50
Nos. B308-B312 (5) 4.55 5.25

Jean Jacques Rousseau SP216

Half-Thaler, Obwalden, 1732 SP217

Coins: 20c+10c, Ducat, Schwyz, ca. 1653. 30c+10c, "Steer Head" Batzen, Uri, 1659. 50c+10c, Nidwalden Batzen.

Perf. 11½
1962, June 1 Unwmk. Engr.
B313 SP216 5c + 5c dk blue .25 .25
Photo.
Granite Paper
B314 SP217 10c + 10c grn & stl bl .25 .25
B315 SP217 20c + 10c car rose & yel .50 .50
B316 SP217 30c + 10c org & sl bl 1.25 1.65
B317 SP217 50c + 10c ultra & vio bl 1.25 1.65
Nos. B313-B317 (5) 3.50 4.30

Apple Blossoms SP218

Mother and Child SP219

Designs: 10c+10c, Boy chasing duck. 30c+10c, Girl and sunflowers. 50c+10c, Forsythia. 1fr+20c, Mother and child, facing right.

1962, Dec. 1 Perf. 11½
Granite Paper
B318 SP218 5c + 5c bl gray, pink, grn & yel .25 .25
B319 SP218 10c + 10c grn, pink & dk grn .25 .25
B320 SP219 20c + 10c org red, brn, grn & pink .60 .50
B321 SP218 30c + 10c org, red & yel 1.10 2.00
B322 SP218 50c + 10c dp bl, yel & brn 1.50 2.50
Nos. B318-B322 (5) 3.70 5.50

Souvenir Sheet
Imperf
B323 SP219 1fr + 20c Sheet of 2 5.25 5.25
50th anniv. of the Pro Juventute (Youth Aid) Foundation. No. B323 sold for 3fr.

Anna Heer, M.D. — SP220

Bandage Roll — SP221

Designs: 20c+10c, Gift parcel. 30c+10c, Plasma bottles. 50c+10c, Red Cross armband.

1963, June 1 Engr. Perf. 11½
B324 SP220 5c + 5c dk blue .25 .25
Photo.
Granite Paper
Cross in Red
B325 SP221 10c + 10c lt & dk grn & gray .25 .25
B326 SP221 20c + 10c rose, gray & blk .50 .25
B327 SP221 30c + 10c multi 1.10 1.50
B328 SP221 50c + 10c bl, gray & blk 1.25 1.50
Nos. B324-B328 (5) 3.35 3.75

Types of 1960
Designs: 5c+5c, Portrait of a Boy by Albert Anker. 10c+10c, Daisy. 20c+10c, Geranium. 30c+10c, Cornflower. 50c+10c, Carnation.

1963, Nov. 30 Engr. Perf. 11½
B329 SP213 5c + 5c blue .25 .30
a. Booklet pane of 4 3.00
Photo.
B330 SP214 10c + 10c grn, gray & yel .30 1.25
a. Booklet pane of 4
B331 SP214 20c + 10c multi 1.40 2.50
a. Booklet pane of 4 5.75
B332 SP214 30c + 10c multi 1.40 1.50
B333 SP214 50c + 10c ultra, lil rose & grn 1.75 1.50
Nos. B329-B333 (5) 5.10 7.05

Nos. B329-B331 were printed on two kinds of paper: I. Fluorescent, with violet fibers. II. Non-fluorescent, the 10c+10c and 20c+10c with mixed red and blue fibers. Nos. B332-B333 exist only on violet-fibered, fluorescent paper. The booklet panes, Nos. B329a, B330a and B331a, exist only on non-fluorescent paper.

Johann Georg Bodmer SP222

Copper Coin, Zurich SP223

Coins: 20c+10c, Doppeldicken, Basel. 30c+10c, Silver taler, Geneva. 50c+10c, Gold half florin, Bern.

Violet Fibers, Fluorescent Paper
1964, June 1 Engr. Perf. 11½
B334 SP222 5c + 5c blue .25 .25
Photo.
B335 SP223 10c + 10c grn, bis & blk .25 .25
B336 SP223 20c + 10c rose car, gray & blk .45 .25
B337 SP223 30c + 10c org, gray & blk .70 .50
Granite Paper, Red and Blue Fibers
B338 SP223 50c + 10c ultra, yel & brn 1.15 .65
Nos. B334-B338 (5) 2.80 1.90

Fluorescent Paper
Paper of Nos. B334-B425, B427 and B429 is fluorescent and has violet fibers.
Nos. B426, B428 and all semipostals from No. B430 onward are fluorescent but lack violet fibers, unless otherwise noted.

Types of 1960

Designs: 5c+5c, Portrait of a Girl by Albert Anker. 10c+10c, Daffodil. 20c+10c, Rose. 30c+10c, Clover. 50c+10c, Water lily.

1964, Dec. 1 Engr. *Perf. 11½*

B339 SP213 5c + 5c grnsh bl .25 .25

Photo.

B340 SP214 10c + 10c dp grn, yel & org .25 .25
B341 SP214 20c + 10c dp car, rose & grn .45 .25
B342 SP214 30c + 10c brn, lil & grn .70 .55
B343 SP214 50c + 10c multi 1.15 .75
Nos. B339-B343 (5) 2.80 2.05

Type of Regular Issue, 1965

Souvenir Sheet

10c, 20r Seated Helvetia. 20c, 40r Seated Helvetia.

1965, Mar. 8 Photo. *Imperf.*

Granite Paper, Nonfluorescent

B344 A153 Sheet of 2 1.50 1.00
a. 10c grn, pale orange & blk .75 .50
b. 20c dark red, yel grn & blk .75 .50

Natl. Postage Stamp Exhib., NABRA, Bern, Aug. 27-Sept. 5, 1965. Sold for 3fr, the net proceeds were used to cover expenses of the exhibition and to promote philately.

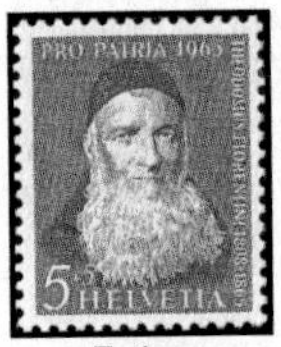
Father Theodosius Florentini SP224

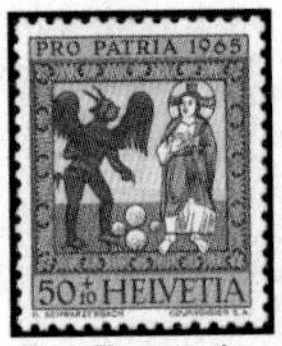
The Temptation of Christ SP225

Ceiling Paintings from Church of St. Martin at Zillis, 12th century: 10c+10c, Symbol of evil (goose with fishtail). 20c+10c, Magi on horseback. 30c+10c, Fishermen on Sea of Galilee.

Perf. 11½

1965, June 1 Unwmk. Engr.

B345 SP224 5c + 5c blue .25 .25

Photo.

B346 SP225 10c + 10c ol grn, ocher & bl .25 .25
B347 SP225 20c + 10c dk brn, red & buff .45 .25
B348 SP225 30c + 10c dk brn, sep & bl .70 .30
B349 SP225 50c + 10c vio bl, bl & brn 1.15 .30
Nos. B345-B349 (5) 2.80 1.35

See Nos. B355-B359, B365-B369.

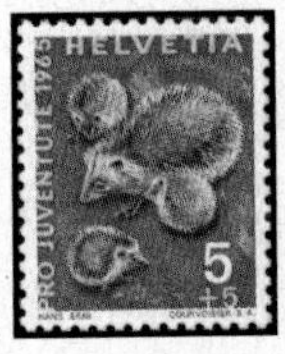
Hedgehogs — SP226

Designs: 10c+10c, Alpine marmots. 20c+10c, Red deer. 30c+10c, European badgers. 50c+10c, Varying hares.

1965, Dec. 1 Photo. *Perf. 11½*

B350 SP226 5c + 5c multi .25 .25
B351 SP226 10c + 10c multi .25 .25
B352 SP226 20c + 10c multi .45 .25
B353 SP226 30c + 10c multi .70 .25
B354 SP226 50c + 10c multi 1.15 .30
Nos. B350-B354 (5) 2.80 1.30

See Nos. B360-B364.

Types of 1965

5c+5c, Heinrich Federer (1866-1928), writer. 10c+10c, Joseph's dream. 20c+10c, Joseph on his way. 30c+10c, Virgin and Child fleeing to Egypt. 50c+10c, Angel leading the way. Nos. B356-B359 from ceiling paintings, Church of St. Martin at Zillis.

1966, June 1 Engr. *Perf. 11½*

B355 SP224 5c + 5c dp blue .25 .25

Photo.

B356 SP225 10c + 10c multi .25 .25
B357 SP225 20c + 10c multi .45 .25
B358 SP225 30c + 10c multi .70 .25
B359 SP225 50c + 10c multi 1.15 .35
Nos. B355-B359 (5) 2.80 1.35

Animal Type of 1965

5c+5c, Ermine. 10c+10c, Red squirrel. 20c+10c, Red fox. 30c+10c, Hares. 50c+10c, Two chamois.

1966, Dec. 1 Photo. *Perf. 11½*

Animals in Natural Colors

B360 SP226 5c + 5c grnsh bl .25 .25
B361 SP226 10c + 10c emer .25 .25
B362 SP226 20c + 10c ver .45 .25
B363 SP226 30c + 10c brt lemon .70 .25
B364 SP226 50c + 10c ultra 1.15 .35
Nos. B360-B364 (5) 2.80 1.35

Types of 1965

Designs: 5c+5c, Dr. Theodor Kocher. 10c+10c, Annunciation to the Shepherds. 20c+10c, Jesus and the Samaritan Woman at the Well. 30c+10c, Adoration of the Magi. 50c+10c St. Joseph. (Ceiling paintings, St. Martin at Zillis).

Perf. 11½

1967, June 1 Unwmk. Engr.

B365 SP224 5c + 5c blue .25 .25

Photo.

B366 SP225 10c + 10c multi .25 .25
B367 SP225 20c + 10c multi .45 .25
B368 SP225 30c + 10c multi .70 .25
B369 SP225 50c + 10c multi 1.15 .35
Nos. B365-B369 (5) 2.80 1.35

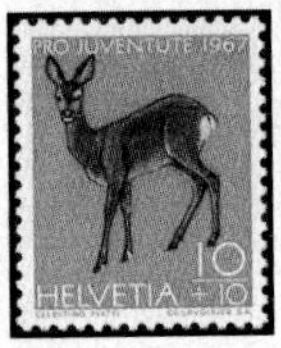
Roe Deer — SP227

Designs: 20c+10c, Pine marten. 30c+10c, Alpine ibex. 50c+20c, Otter.

1967, Dec. 1 Photo. *Perf. 11½*

Animals in Natural Colors

B370 SP227 10c + 10c yel grn .25 .25
B371 SP227 20c + 10c dp car .45 .25
B372 SP227 30c + 10c ol bis .70 .25
B373 SP227 50c + 20c ultra 1.15 .50
Nos. B370-B373 (4) 2.55 1.25

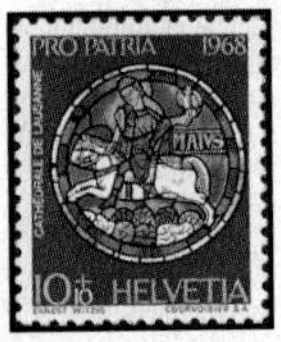
Hunter, Month of May — SP228

Designs from Rose Window, Lausanne Cathedral: 20c+10c, Leo. 30c+10c, Libra. 50c+20c, Pisces.

1968, May 30 Photo. *Perf. 11½*

B374 SP228 10c + 10c multi .25 .25
B375 SP228 20c + 10c multi .45 .25
B376 SP228 30c + 10c multi .70 .30
B377 SP228 50c + 20c multi 1.15 .70
Nos. B374-B377 (4) 2.55 1.50

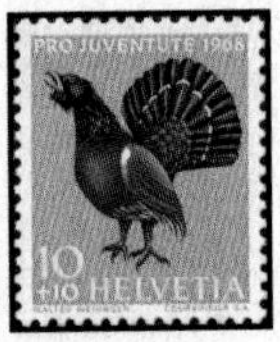
Capercaillie — SP229

Birds: 20c+10c, Bullfinch. 30c+10c, Woodchat shrike. 50c+20c, Firecrest.

1968, Nov. 28 Photo. *Perf. 11½*

Birds in Natural Colors

B378 SP229 10c + 10c dull yel .25 .25
B379 SP229 20c + 10c olive grn .45 .25
B380 SP229 30c + 10c lilac rose .70 .25
B381 SP229 50c + 20c dp violet 1.15 .50
Nos. B378-B381 (4) 2.55 1.25

See Nos. B386-B389.

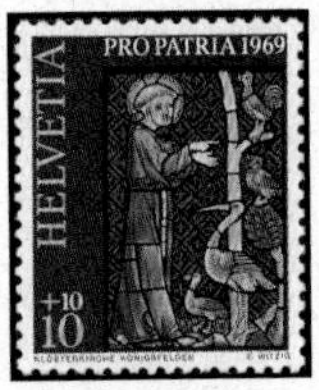
St. Francis — SP230

Designs: 10c+10c, St. Francis Preaching to the Birds, Königsfelden Convent Church. 20c+10c, Israelites Drinking from Spring of Moses, Berne Cathedral. 30c+10c, St. Christopher, Laufelfinger Church (now Basel Museum). 50c+20c, Virgin and Child, Chapel at Grapplang (now National Museum).

1969, May 29 Photo. *Perf. 11½*

B382 SP230 10c + 10c multi .25 .25
B383 SP230 20c + 10c multi .45 .25
B384 SP230 30c + 10c multi .70 .25
B385 SP230 50c + 20c multi 1.15 .45
Nos. B382-B385 (4) 2.55 1.20

Bird Type of 1968

Birds: 10c+10c, European goldfinch. 20c+10c, Golden oriole. 30c+10c, Wall creeper. 50c+20c, Eurasian jay.

1969, Dec. 1 Photo. *Perf. 11½*

Birds in Natural Colors

B386 SP229 10c + 10c gray .25 .25
B387 SP229 20c + 10c green .45 .25
B388 SP229 30c + 10c plum .70 .25
B389 SP229 50c + 20c ultra 1.15 .55
Nos. B386-B389 (4) 2.55 1.30

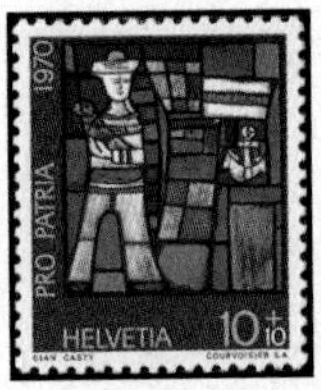
Sailor, by Gian Casty, Gellert Schoolhouse, Basel — SP231

Contemporary Stained Glass Windows: 20c+10c, Abstract composition, by Celestino Piatti. 30c+10c, Bull (Assyrian god Marduk), by Hans Stocker. 50c+20c, Man and Woman, by Max Hunziker and Karl Ganz.

1970, May 29 Photo. *Perf. 11½*

B390 SP231 10c + 10c multi .25 .25
B391 SP231 20c + 10c multi .45 .25
B392 SP231 30c + 10c multi .70 .25
B393 SP231 50c + 20c multi 1.15 .50
Nos. B390-B393 (4) 2.55 1.25

See Nos. B398-B401.

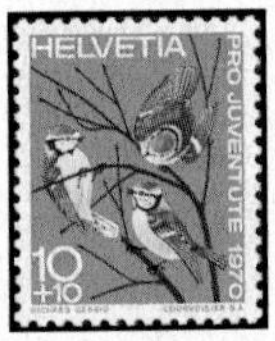
Blue Titmice — SP232

Birds: 20c+10c, Hoopoe. 30c+10c, Greater spotted woodpecker. 50c+20c, Crested grebes.

Birds in Natural Colors

1970, Dec. 1 Photo. *Perf. 11½*

B394 SP232 10c + 10c orange .25 .25
B395 SP232 20c + 10c emerald .45 .25
B396 SP232 30c + 10c brt rose .70 .25
B397 SP232 50c + 20c blue 1.15 .75
Nos. B394-B397 (4) 2.55 1.50

See Nos. B402-B405.

Art Type of 1970

Contemporary Stained Glass Windows: 10c+10c, "Composition," by Jean-François Comment. 20c+10c, Cock, by Jean Prahin. 30c+10c, Fox, by Kurt Volk. 50c+20c, "Composition," by Bernard Schorderet.

1971, May 27 Photo. *Perf. 11½*

B398 SP231 10c + 10c multi .25 .25
B399 SP231 20c + 10c multi .45 .25
B400 SP231 30c + 10c multi .70 .25
B401 SP231 50c + 20c multi 1.15 .45
Nos. B398-B401 (4) 2.55 1.20

Bird Type of 1970

Birds: 10c+10c, European redstarts. 20c+10c, White-spotted bluethroats. 30c+10c, Peregrine falcon. 40c+20c, Mallards.

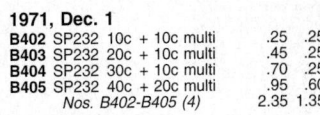

1971, Dec. 1

B402 SP232 10c + 10c multi .25 .25
B403 SP232 20c + 10c multi .45 .25
B404 SP232 30c + 10c multi .70 .25
B405 SP232 40c + 20c multi .95 .60
Nos. B402-B405 (4) 2.35 1.35

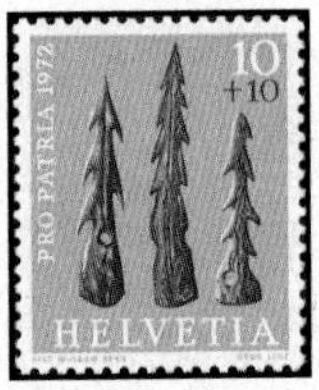
Harpoon Heads, Late Stone Age — SP233

Archaeological Treasures: 20c+10c, Bronze hydria, Hallstadt period. 30c+10c, Gold bust of Emperor Marcus Aurelius, Roman period. 40c+20c, Horseback rider (decorative disk), early Middle Ages.

1972, June 1

B406 SP233 10c + 10c multi .25 .25
B407 SP233 20c + 10c multi .45 .25
B408 SP233 30c + 10c multi .70 .25
B409 SP233 40c + 20c multi .95 .70
Nos. B406-B409 (4) 2.35 1.45

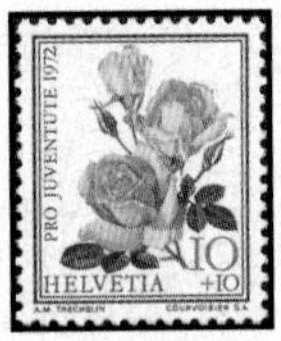
McGredy's Sunset — SP234

Famous Roses: 20c+10c, Miracle. 30c+10c, Papa Meilland. 40c+20c, Madame Dimitriu.

1972, Dec. 1 Photo. *Perf. 11½*

B410 SP234 10c + 10c multi .25 .25
B411 SP234 20c + 10c multi .45 .25
B412 SP234 30c + 10c multi .70 .25
B413 SP234 40c + 20c multi .95 1.10
Nos. B410-B413 (4) 2.35 1.85

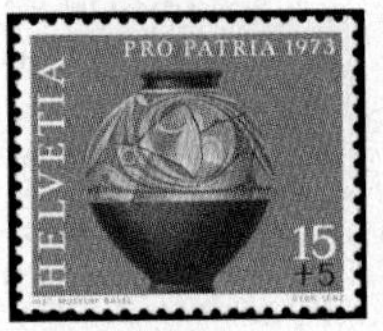
Rauraric (Gallic) Jug — SP235

Archeologic Finds: 30c+10c, Bronze head of a Gaul. 40c+20c, Alemannic dress fasteners (fish), 6th century. 60c+20c, Gold bowl, 6th century B.C.

1973, May 29 Photo. *Perf. 11½*

B414 SP235 15c + 5c multi .35 .25
B415 SP235 30c + 10c multi .70 .25
B416 SP235 40c + 20c multi .95 .60
B417 SP235 60c + 20c multi 1.40 .85
Nos. B414-B417 (4) 3.40 1.95

See Nos. B422-B425.

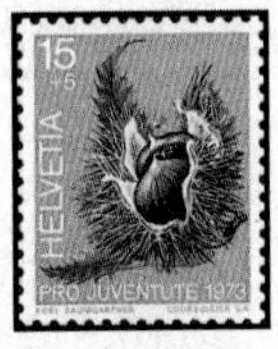
Chestnut — SP236

Fruits of the Forest: 30c+10c, Sweet cherries. 40c+20c, Blackberries. 60c+20c, Blueberries.

1973, Nov. 29 Photo. *Perf. 11½*

B418 SP236 15c + 5c multi .35 .25
B419 SP236 30c + 10c multi .70 .25
B420 SP236 40c + 20c multi .95 .60
B421 SP236 60c + 20c multi 1.40 .70
Nos. B418-B421 (4) 3.40 1.80

Archaeological Type of 1973

Archaeological Finds: 15c+5c, Polychrome glass bowl. 30c+10c, Bull's head. 40c+20c, Gold fibula. 60c+20c, Ceramic bird.

1974, May 30 Photo. *Perf. 11½*

B422 SP235 15c + 5c multi .35 .25
B423 SP235 30c + 10c multi .70 .30
B424 SP235 40c + 20c multi .95 .55
B425 SP235 60c + 20c multi 1.40 .70
Nos. B422-B425 (4) 3.40 1.80

Laurel — SP237

Designs: 30c+20c, Belladonna. 50c+20c, Laburnum. 60c+25c, Mistletoe.

1974, Nov. 29   Photo.   Perf. 11½
B426 SP237 15c + 10c multi   .35   .25
B427 SP237 30c + 20c multi   .70   .25
B428 SP237 50c + 20c multi   1.15   .60
B429 SP237 60c + 25c multi   1.40   .80
     Nos. B426-B429 (4)   3.60   1.90

Gold Fibula, 6th
Century — SP238

Archaeological Treasures: 30c+20c, Bronze head of Bacchus, 2nd century. 50c+20c, Bronze daggers, 1800-1600 B.C. 60c+25c, Colored glass bottle, 1st century.

1975, May 30   Photo.   Perf. 11½
B430 SP238 15c + 10c multi   .35   .25
B431 SP238 30c + 20c multi   .70   .25
B432 SP238 50c + 20c multi   1.15   .70
B433 SP238 60c + 25c multi   1.40   .75
     Nos. B430-B433 (4)   3.60   1.95

Mail Bucket   Hepatica
SP239   SP240

Forest Plants: 30c+20c, Mountain ash berries. 50c+20c, Yellow nettle. 60c+25c, Sycamore maple.

1975, Nov. 27   Photo.   Perf. 11½
B434 SP239 10c + 5c multi   .25   .25
B435 SP240 15c + 10c multi   .35   .30
B436 SP240 30c + 20c multi   .70   .30
B437 SP240 50c + 20c multi   1.15   .65
B438 SP240 60c + 25c multi   1.40   .75
     Nos. B434-B438 (5)   3.85   2.20

See Nos. B443-B446.

Castles
SP241

1976, May 28   Photo.   Perf. 11½
B439 SP241 20c + 10 Kyburg   .45   .25
B440 SP241 40c + 20 Grandson   .95   .30
B441 SP241 40c + 20 Murten   .95   .30
B442 SP241 80c + 20c Bellinzona   2.25   .85
     Nos. B439-B442 (4)   4.60   1.70

See #B447-B450, B455-B458, B463-B466.

Plant Type of 1975

Medicinal Forest Plants: 20c+10c, Barberry. No. B444, Black elder. No. B445, Linden. 80+40c, Pulmonaria.

1976, Nov. 29   Photo.   Perf. 11½
B443 SP240 20c + 10c multi   .45   .25
B444 SP240 40c + 20c lil & multi   .95   .25
B445 SP240 40c + 20c terra cotta & multi   .95   .25
B446 SP240 80c + 40c multi   1.90   .80
     Nos. B443-B446 (4)   4.25   1.55

Castle Type of 1976

1977, May 26   Photo.
B447 SP241 20c + 10c Aigle   .45   .25
B448 SP241 40c + 20c Pratteln   .95   .35
B449 SP241 70c + 30c Sargans   1.60   .90
B450 SP241 80c + 40c Hallwil   1.90   1.00
     Nos. B447-B450 (4)   4.90   2.50

Wild Rose — SP242

Designs: Roses.

1977, Nov. 28   Photo.   Perf. 11½
B451 SP242 20c + 10c multi   .45   .25
B452 SP242 40c + 20c multi   .95   .25
B453 SP242 70c + 30c multi   1.60   .80
B454 SP242 80c + 40c multi   1.90   1.00
     Nos. B451-B454 (4)   4.90   2.30

See Nos. B492-B496.

Castle Type of 1976

1978, May 26   Photo.   Perf. 11½
B455 SP241 20c + 10c Hagenwil   .45   .30
B456 SP241 40c + 20c Burgdorf   .95   .60
B457 SP241 70c + 30c Tarasp   1.60   1.25
B458 SP241 80c + 40c Chillon   1.90   1.50
     Nos. B455-B458 (4)   4.90   3.65

Communal
Arms — SP243

20c+10c, Aarburg. 40c+20c, Gruyeres. 70c+30c, Castasegna. 80c+40c, Wangen an der Aare.

1978, Nov. 28   Photo.   Perf. 11½
B459 SP243 20c + 10c multi   .45   .25
B460 SP243 40c + 20c multi   .95   .25
B461 SP243 70c + 30c multi   1.60   1.00
B462 SP243 80c + 40c multi   1.90   1.25
     Nos. B459-B462 (4)   4.90   2.75

See #B467-B470, B475-B478, B484-B487.

Castle Type of 1976

20c+10c, Oron. 40c+20c, Spiez. 70c+30c, Porrentruy. 80c+40c, Rapperswil.

1979, May 25   Photo.   Perf. 11½
B463 SP241 20c + 10c multi   .45   .30
B464 SP241 40c + 20c multi   .95   .45
B465 SP241 70c + 30c multi   1.60   1.00
B466 SP241 80c + 40c multi   1.90   1.50
     Nos. B463-B466 (4)   4.90   3.25

Arms Type of 1978

20c+10c, Cadro. 40c+20c, Rute. 70c+30c, Schwamendingen. 80c+40c, Perroy.

1979, Nov. 28   Photo.   Perf. 11
B467 SP243 20c + 10c multi   .45   .25
B468 SP243 40c + 20c multi   .95   .25
B469 SP243 70c + 30c multi   1.60   .85
B470 SP243 80c + 40c multi   1.90   1.10
     Nos. B467-B470 (4)   4.90   2.45

Masons' and
Carpenters'
Sign — SP244

40c+20c, Barber. 70c+30c, Hat maker. 80c+40c, Baker.

1980, May 29   Photo.   Perf. 11½
B471 SP244 20c + 10c shown   .45   .30
B472 SP244 40c + 20c multi   .95   .30
B473 SP244 70c + 30c multi   1.60   1.00
B474 SP244 80c + 40c multi   1.90   1.25
     Nos. B471-B474 (4)   4.90   2.85

Arms Type of 1978

20c+10c, Cortaillod. 40c+20c, Sierre. 70c+30c, Scuol. 80c+40c, Wolfenschiessen.

1980, Nov. 26   Photo.   Perf. 11½
B475 SP243 20c + 10c multi   .45   .25
B476 SP243 40c + 20c multi   .95   .25
B477 SP243 70c + 30c multi   1.60   .90
B478 SP243 80c + 40c multi   1.90   .95
     Nos. B475-B478 (4)   4.90   2.35

Icarus in
Flight
SP245

1981, Mar. 9   Photo.
B479 SP245 2fr + 1fr multi   4.75   3.00

Swissair, 50th Anniversary. Surtax was for Pro Aero Foundation Issued in sheet of 8.

Post Office Sign,
Aarburg,
1685 — SP246

Post Office Signs (c. 1849).

1981, May 4   Photo.
B480 SP246 20c + 10c shown   .45   .30
B481 SP246 40c + 20c Fribourg   .95   .50
B482 SP246 70c + 30c Gordola   1.60   1.10
B483 SP246 80c + 40c Splugen   1.90   1.25
     Nos. B480-B483 (4)   4.90   3.15

Arms Type of 1978

1981, Nov. 26   Photo.   Perf. 11½
B484 SP243 20c + 10c Uffikon   .45   .25
B485 SP243 40c + 20c Torre   .95   .30
B486 SP243 70c + 30c Benken   1.60   .60
B487 SP243 80c + 40c Preverenges   1.90   .75
     Nos. B484-B487 (4)   4.90   1.90

Sonne Inn
Sign, Willisau
SP247

40c+20c, A L'Onde, St. Saphorin. 70c+30c, Three Kings, Rheinfelden. 80c+40c, Krone, Winterthur.

1982, May 27   Photo.   Perf. 11½
B488 SP247 20c + 10c shown   .45   .25
B489 SP247 40c + 20c multi   .95   .30
B490 SP247 70c + 30c multi   1.60   .50
B491 SP247 80c + 40c multi   1.90   .70
     Nos. B488-B491 (4)   4.90   1.80

See Nos. B497-B500.

Rose Type of 1977

Designs: 10c+10c, Letter balance. 20c+10c, La Belle Portugaise. 40c+20c, Hugh Dickson. 70c+30c, Mermaid. 80c+40c, Madame Caroline.

1982, Nov. 25   Photo.
B492 SP242 10c + 10c multi   .25   .25
B493 SP242 20c + 10c multi   .45   .25
B494 SP242 40c + 20c multi   .95   .30
B495 SP242 70c + 30c multi   1.60   .80
B496 SP242 80c + 40c multi   1.90   1.10
     Nos. B492-B496 (5)   5.15   2.70

Inn Sign Type of 1982

20c+10c, Lion Inn, Heimiswil, 1669. 40c+20c, Cross Hotel, Sachseln, 1489. 70c+30c, Tankard Inn, 1830. 80c+40c, Au Cavalier Inn, Vaud.

1983, May 26   Photo.
B497 SP247 20c + 10c multi   .45   .30
B498 SP247 40c + 20c multi   .95   .50
B499 SP247 70c + 30c multi   1.60   .80
B500 SP247 80c + 40c multi   1.90   1.00
     Nos. B497-B500 (4)   4.90   2.60

Antique
Toys — SP248

20c+10c, Kitchen stove, 1850. 40c+20c, Rocking horse, 1826. 70c+30c, Doll, 1870. 80c+40c, Steam locomotive, 1900.

1983, Nov. 24
B501 SP248 20c + 10c multi   .45   .25
B502 SP248 40c + 20c multi   .95   .35
B503 SP248 70c + 30c multi   1.60   .55
B504 SP248 80c + 40c multi   1.90   .70
     Nos. B501-B504 (4)   4.90   1.85

Ceramic Tiled
Stoves — SP249

1984, May 24   Photo.   Perf. 11½
B505 SP249 35c + 15c 1566   .80   .40
B506 SP249 50c + 20c 1646   1.15   .50
B507 SP249 70c + 30c 1768   1.60   .70
B508 SP249 80c + 40c 18th cent.   1.90   .90
     Nos. B505-B508 (4)   5.45   2.50

See Nos. B660-B663.

Children's
Stories
SP250

35c+15c, Heidi. 50c+20c, Pinocchio. 70c+30c, Pippi Longstocking. 80c+40c, Max and Moritz.

1984, Nov. 26   Photo.
B509 SP250 35c + 15c multi   .80   .40
B510 SP250 50c + 20c multi   1.15   .50
B511 SP250 70c + 30c multi   1.60   .70
B512 SP260 80c + 40c multi   1.90   .90
     Nos. B509-B512 (4)   5.45   2.50

Musical
Museum
Exhibits
SP251

25c+10c, Music box, 1895. 35c+15c, Rattle box, 18th cent. 50c+20c, Emmenthal necked zither, 1828. 70c+30c, Drum, 1571. 80c+40c, Diatonic accordion, 20th cent.

1985, May 28   Photo.   Perf. 11½
B513 SP251 25c + 10c multi   .60   .25
B514 SP251 35c + 15c multi   .80   .25
B515 SP251 50c + 20c multi   1.15   .25
B516 SP251 70c + 30c multi   1.60   .30
B517 SP251 80c + 40c multi   1.90   .35
     Nos. B513-B517 (5)   6.05   1.40

Surtax for Swiss cultural programs.

Hansel and
Gretel
SP252

Fairy tales by Jakob (1785-1863) and Wilhelm (1786-1859) Grimm — 50c+20c, Snow White. 80c+40c, Little Red Riding Hood. 90c+40c, Cinderella.

1985, Nov. 26   **Photo.**
B518 SP252 35c + 15c shown   .80 .25
B519 SP252 50c + 20c multi   1.15 .25
B520 SP252 80c + 40c multi   1.90 .35
B521 SP252 90c + 40c multi   2.10 .40
Nos. B518-B521 (4)   5.95 1.25

Surtax for Pro Juventute Foundation and youth welfare orgs.

Man, Vitality and Movement SP253

1986, Feb. 11   **Photo.**   *Perf. 12*
B522 SP253 50c + 20c multi   1.15 .25

Surtax for Natl. Sports Federation and cultural programs.

Paintings in Natl. Museums SP254

Swiss art: 35c+15c, Bridge in the Sun, 1907, by Giovanni Giacometti (1868-1933). 50c+20c, The Violet Hat, 1907, by Cuno Amiet (1868-1961). 80c+40c, After the Funeral, 1905, by Max Buri (1868-1915). 90c+40c, Still Life, 1914, by Felix Valloton (1865-1925).

1986, Apr. 22   **Photo.**   *Perf. 11½*
B523 SP254 35c + 15c multi   .80 .25
B524 SP254 50c + 20c multi   1.15 .25
B525 SP254 80c + 40c multi   1.90 .40
B526 SP254 90c + 40c multi   2.10 .45
Nos. B523-B526 (4)   5.95 1.35

Surtax for Natl. Day Collection &monuments preservation, social & cultural organizations.

Children's Toys — SP255

35c+15c, Teddy bear. 50c+20c, Top. 80c+40c, Steamroller. 90c+40c, Doll.

1986, Nov. 25   **Photo.**
B527 SP255 35c + 15c multi   .80 .25
B528 SP255 50c + 20c multi   1.15 .30
B529 SP255 80c + 40c multi   1.90 .50
B530 SP255 90c + 40c multi   2.10 .55
Nos. B527-B530 (4)   5.95 1.60

Surtax was for youth welfare organizations and the Pro Juventute Foundation.

Antique Furniture SP256

Designs: 35c+15c, Saane Valley wall cabinet, 1764, Vieux Pays d'Enhaut Museum, Chateau d'Oex. 50c+20c, Raised chest, 16th cent., Rhaetian Museum, Chur. 80c+40c, Ticino canton cradle, 1782, Valmaggia Museum, Cevio. 90c+40c, Appenzell region wardrobe, 1698, St. Gallen Historical Museum.

1987, May 26   **Photo.**
B531 SP256 35c + 15c multi   .80 .25
B532 SP256 50c + 20c multi   1.15 .35
B533 SP256 80c + 40c multi   1.90 .60
B534 SP256 90c + 40c multi   2.10 .60
Nos. B531-B534 (4)   5.95 1.80

Surtax for Red Cross and patriotic funds.

No. 786 Surcharged in Red

Photo. & Engr.
1987, Sept. 7   *Perf. 13½x13*
B535 A349 50c + 50c multi   1.25 .45

Surtaxed to benefit flood victims.

Christmas SP257   Child Development SP258

50c+20c, Boy, building blocks. 80c+40c, Boy, girl in sandbox. 90c+40c, Father, child.

1987, Nov. 24   **Photo.**   *Perf. 11½*
B536 SP257 25c +10c shown   .60 .25
B537 SP258 35c +15c shown   .80 .25
B538 SP258 50c +20c multi   1.15 .30
B539 SP258 80c +40c multi   1.90 .55
B540 SP258 90c +40c multi   2.10 .60
Nos. B536-B540 (5)   6.55 1.95

Surtax for national youth welfare projects and the Pro Juventute Foundation. See Nos. B555-B558.

Junkers JU-52, 1939, and the Matterhorn SP259

1988, Mar. 8   **Photo.**
B541 SP259 140c +60c multi   3.25 2.50

Pro Aero Foundation, Zurich, 50th Anniv. Issued in sheets of 8.

SP260

Minnesingers — 35c+15c, Count Rudolf of Neuchatel. 50c+20c, Rudolf von Rotenburg. 80c+40c, Master Johannes Hadlaub. 90c+40c, The Hardegger.

1988, May 24   **Photo.**
B542 SP260 35c +15c multi   .80 .25
B543 SP260 50c +20c multi   1.15 .35
B544 SP260 80c +40c multi   1.90 .60
B545 SP260 90c +40c multi   2.10 .65
Nos. B542-B545 (4)   5.95 1.85

700 Years of art and culture.

SP261

1988, Nov. 25   *Perf. 11½*
B546 SP261 35c +15c Reading   .80 .25
B547 SP261 50c +20c Music   1.15 .30
B548 SP261 80c +40c Math   1.90 .55
B549 SP261 90c +40c Art   2.10 .60
Nos. B546-B549 (4)   5.95 1.70

Child development. Surtax for natl. youth welfare projects and the Pro Juventute Foundation.

700 Years of Art and Culture SP262

Illuminations in Zurich Central, Bern Burgher and Lucerne Central libraries: No. B550, King Friedrich II presenting Bern municipal charter, 1218, *Bendicht Tschachtlan Chronicle,* 1470. No. B551, Capt. Adrian von Bubenberg and troops passing through Murten town gate, 1476, *Bern Chronicle,* by Diebold Schilling, 1483. No. B552, Official messenger of Schwyz before the Council of Zurich, c. 1440, *Gerold Edlibach Chronicle,* 1485. No. B553, Schilling presenting manuscript to the mayor and councilmen in the council chamber, Lucerne, c. 1500, *Diebold Schilling's Lucerne Chronicle,* 1513.

1989, May 23
B550 SP262 35c +15c multi   .80 .25
B551 SP262 50c +20c multi   1.15 .30
B552 SP262 80c +40c multi   1.90 .50
B553 SP262 90c +40c multi   2.10 .55
Nos. B550-B553 (4)   5.95 1.60

Surtax to benefit women's and cultural organizations.

Gymnastics SP263

1989, Aug. 25   **Photo.**   *Perf. 11½*
B554 SP263 50c +20c multi   1.15 .30

Surtax to benefit Swiss Natl. Sports Federation, cultural and social work.

Child Development Type of 1987

35c+15c, Community work. 50c+20c, Friendship. 80c+40c, Vocational training. 90c+40c, Higher education and research.

1989, Nov. 24
B555 SP258 35c +15c multi   .80 .25
B556 SP258 50c +20c multi   1.15 .25
B557 SP258 80c +40c multi   1.90 .50
B558 SP258 90c +40c multi   2.10 .55
Nos. B555-B558 (4)   5.95 1.55

Surtax for natl. youth welfare projects and the Pro Juventute Foundation.

700 Years of Art and Culture — SP264

Street criers: No. B559, Fly swatter and starch-sprinkler vendor. No. B560, Clock vendor. No. B561, Knife grinder. No. B562, Pinewood sellers.

1990, May 22   **Photo.**
B559 SP264 35c +15c multi   .80 .25
B560 SP264 50c +20c multi   1.15 .30
B561 SP264 80c +40c multi   1.90 .60
B562 SP264 90c +40c multi   2.10 .60
Nos. B559-B562 (4)   5.95 1.70

Souvenir Sheet

Natl. Philatelic Exhibition, Geneva '90 — SP265

a, Brass badge worn by Geneva Cantonal post drivers before 1849. b, Place du Bourg-

de-Four and entrance to Rue Etienne-Dumont. c, Ile Rousseau and Pont des Bergues. d, No. 2L1 on cover.

1990, Sept. 5
B563 SP265 Sheet of 4   5.50 5.50
a.-d.   50c +25c any single   1.15 .35

Child Development SP266

No. B564, Model making. No. B565, Youth groups. No. B566, Sports. No. B567, Music.

1990, Nov. 20
B564 SP266 35c +15c multi   .80 .25
B565 SP266 50c +20c multi   1.15 .30
B566 SP266 80c +40c multi   1.90 .55
B567 SP266 90c +40c multi   2.10 .60
Nos. B564-B567 (4)   5.95 1.70

700 Years of Art and Culture SP267

Contemporary paintings by: 50c+20c, Wolf Barth. 70c+30c, Helmut Federle. 80c+40c, Matthias Bosshart. 90c+40c, Werner Otto Leuenberger.

1991, May 14   **Photo.**   *Perf. 11½*
B568 SP267 50c +20c multi   1.15 .30
B569 SP267 70c +30c multi   1.60 .45
B570 SP267 80c +40c multi   1.90 .55
B571 SP267 90c +40c multi   2.10 .60
Nos. B568-B571 (4)   6.75 1.90

Woodland Flowers SP268

50c+25c, Allium ursinum. 70c+30c, Geranium sylvaticum. 80c+40c, Campanula trachelium. 90c+40c, Hieracium murorum.

1991, Nov. 26
B572 SP268 50c +25c multi   1.15 .40
B573 SP268 70c +30c multi   1.60 .45
B574 SP268 80c +40c multi   1.90 .55
B575 SP268 90c +40c multi   2.10 .60
Nos. B572-B575 (4)   6.75 2.00

Surtax for youth and family welfare projects and the Pro Juventute Foundation.

Swiss Folk Art — SP269

50c + 20c, Earthenware plate, Heimberg, 18th cent. 70c + 40c, Paper cutout by Johann Jakob Hauswirth (1809-1871). 80c + 40c, Cream spoon, Gruyeres. 90c + 40c, Embroidered silk carnation, Grisons.

1992, May 22   **Photo.**   *Perf. 11½*
B576 SP269 50c +20c multi   1.15 .30
B577 SP269 70c +30c multi   1.60 .45
B578 SP269 80c +40c multi   1.90 .50
B579 SP269 90c +40c multi   2.10 .60
Nos. B576-B579 (4)   6.75 1.85

Surtax for preservation of cultural heritage.

Unfinished Work, by Jean Tinguely SP270

1992, Aug. 25   Photo.   Perf. 12
B580 SP270 50c +20c bl & blk   1.15 .40

Surtax for Natl. Sports Federation and sports-related social and cultural activities.

Wood Puppet of Melchior, 18th Cent. — SP271

Trees — SP272

No. B582, Copper beech. No. B583, Norway maple. No. B584, Common oak. No. B585, Spruce.

1992, Nov. 24   Photo.   Perf. 11½
B581 SP271 50c +25c multi   1.15 .35
B582 SP272 50c +25c multi   1.15 .35
B583 SP272 70c +30c multi   1.60 .50
B584 SP272 80c +40c multi   1.90 .55
B585 SP272 90c +40c multi   2.10 .60
    Nos. B581-B585 (5)   7.90 2.35

Christmas. Surtax for youth and family welfare projects and the Pro Juventute Foundation.

Swiss Folk Art — SP273

Designs: No. B586, Appenzell dairyman's earring. No. B587, Fluhli glassware. 80c + 40c, Painting of cattle drive, by Sylvestre Pidoux. 100c + 40c, Straw hat ornament.

1993, May 5   Photo.   Perf. 11½
B586 SP273 60c +30c multi   1.40 .40
B587 SP273 60c +30c multi   1.40 .40
B588 SP273 80c +40c multi   1.90 .35
B589 SP273 100c +40c multi   2.25 .70
    Nos. B586-B589 (4)   6.95 1.85

Architectural Heritage Type of 1960

Design: 80c+20c, Kapell Bridge and Water Tower, Lucerne.

1993, Sept. 7   Litho.   Perf. 13½x13
B590 A145 80c +20c org & red   1.90 .45

Surtax for reconstruction of Kapell Bridge with any excess for preservation of architectural heritage.

SP274

Woodland plants — No. B591, Christmas wreath. No. B592, Male fern. No. B593, Guelder rose. No. B594, Mnium punctatum.

1993, Nov. 23   Photo.
B591 SP274 60c +30c multi   1.40 .40
B592 SP274 60c +30c multi   1.40 .40
B593 SP274 80c +40c multi   1.90 .55
B594 SP274 100c +50c multi   2.25 .65
    Nos. B591-B594 (4)   6.95 2.00

Christmas. Surtax for youth and family welfare projects and the Pro Juventute Foundation.

SP275

Swiss Folk Art: No. B595, Weight-driven Neuchatel clock. No. B596, Linen-embroidered pomegranate. 80c+40c, Biscuit mold for Krafli. 100c+40c, Paper bird mobile for child's cradle.

1994, May 17   Photo.   Perf. 11½
B595 SP275 60c +30c multi   1.40 .40
B596 SP275 60c +30c multi   1.40 .40
B597 SP275 80c +40c multi   1.90 .55
B598 SP275 100c +40c multi   2.25 .65
    Nos. B595-B598 (4)   6.95 2.00

Christmas SP276

Mushrooms SP277

Designs: No. B600, Wood blewit. 80c+40c, Red boletus. 100c+50c, Shaggy pholiota.

1994, Nov. 28   Litho.   Perf. 11½
B599 SP276 60c +30c multi   1.40 .45
B600 SP277 60c +30c multi   1.40 .45
B601 SP277 80c +40c multi   1.90 .80
B602 SP277 100c +50c multi   2.25 .80
    Nos. B599-B602 (4)   6.95 2.30

Surtax for youth and family welfare projects and the Pro Juventute Foundation.

Swiss Folk Art — SP278

Designs: No. B603, Wooden cream pail. No. B604, Straw hat. 80c+40c, Chest lock, c. 1580. 100c+40c, Langnau pottery sugar bowl.

1995, May 16   Photo.   Perf. 11½
B603 SP278 60c +30c multi   1.40 .50
B604 SP278 60c +30c multi   1.40 .50
B605 SP278 80c +40c multi   1.90 .70
    Complete booklet, 10 #B605   18.50
B606 SP278 100c +40c multi   2.25 .80
    Nos. B603-B606 (4)   6.95 2.50

Surtax for Swiss Pro Patria Foundation and special cultural, social projects.

Souvenir Sheet

Basler Taube '95 Philatelic Exhibition, Basel — SP279

Designs: a, 80c+30c, like Switzerland #3L1. Engraved panorama of Basel, by Matthaus Merian, 17th cent.: b, 60c+30c, Buildings, twin church steeples. c, 100c+50c, Buildings. d, 100c+50c, Buildings, bridge.

1995, May 16   Photo.   Perf. 13x14
B607 SP279 Sheet of 4   8.00 8.00
    a.   80c +30c multi   1.90 .60
    b.   60c +30c black & blue   1.40 .55
    c.-d.   100c +50c any single   2.25 .90

Nos. B607b-B607d are a continuous design.

Christmas SP280

Life In and Around Water — SP281

#B608, Angel from "The Annunciation," by Bartolome. #B609, River trout. 80c+40c, Grey wagtail. 100c+50c, Spotted salamander.

1995, Nov. 28   Photo.   Perf. 11½
B608 SP280 60c +30c multi   1.40 .50
    Complete booklet, 10 #B608   14.00
B609 SP281 60c +30c multi   1.40 .50
B610 SP281 80c +40c multi   1.90 .65
B611 SP281 100c +50c multi   2.25 .80
    Nos. B608-B611 (4)   6.95 2.45

Surtax for Pro Juventute Foundation.

For Sports SP282

1996, Mar. 12   Photo.   Perf. 11½
B612 SP282 70c +30c multi   1.60 .85
    Complete booklet, 10 #B612   16.00

SP283

Restorations, projects: No. B613, Magdalena Chapel, Wolfenschiessen. No. B614, Underground mills, Col-des-Roches. 90c+40c, Pfäfers Baroque spa complex. 110c+50c, Roman road over Great St. Bernhard.

1996, May 14   Photo.   Perf. 11½
B613 SP283 70c +35c multi   1.60 .60
B614 SP283 70c +35c multi   1.60 .60
B615 SP283 90c +40c multi   2.10 .75
    Complete booklet, 10 #B615   21.00
B616 SP283 110c +50c multi   2.50 .90
    Nos. B613-B616 (4)   7.80 2.85

Christmas SP284

Life In and Around Water — SP285

No. B617, Star, constellations. No. B618, Grayling. No. B619, Crayfish. No. B620, Otter.

1996, Nov. 26   Photo.   Perf. 11½
B617 SP284 70c +35c multi   1.60 .55
B618 SP285 70c +35c multi   1.60 .55
    Complete booklet, 10 #B618   16.00
B619 SP285 90c +45c multi   2.10 .70
B620 SP285 110c +55c multi   2.50 .80
    Nos. B617-B620 (4)   7.80 2.60

SP286

Designs: No. B621, St. Valbert Church, Soubey. No. B622, Culture Mill, Lützelflüh. 90c+40c, Ittingen Charterhouse, Thurgau. 110c+50c, Municipal Building, Onsernone Valley.

1997, May 13   Photo.   Perf. 11½
B621 SP286 70c +35c multi   1.60 1.25
B622 SP286 70c +35c multi   1.60 1.25
B623 SP286 90c +40c multi   2.10 1.60
    Complete booklet, 10 #B623   21.00
B624 SP286 110c +50c multi   2.50 2.00
    Nos. B621-B624 (4)   7.80 6.10

Christmas SP287

Life In and Around Water — SP288

Designs: No. B625, Mistletoe twig. No. B626, Three-spined stickleback. 90c+45c, Yellow-bellied toad. 110c+55c, Ruff.

1997, Nov. 20   Photo.   Perf. 11½
B625 SP287 70c +35c multi   1.60 1.25
B626 SP288 70c +35c multi   1.60 1.25
    Complete booklet, 10 #B626   16.00
B627 SP288 90c +45c multi   2.10 1.60
B628 SP288 110c +55c multi   2.50 1.90
    Nos. B625-B628 (4)   7.80 6.00

Surtax for Pro Juventute Foundation.

Pro Patria Stamps, 60th Anniv. SP289

Heritage and landscapes: No. B629, St. Gall Rhine Valley. No. B630, Round Church, Saas Balen. No. B631, Natural forest preserves, Bödmeren. No. B632, St. Gotthard Refuge. 110c +50c, Blacksmiths, Corcelles.

1998, May 12   Photo.   Perf. 11½

B629	SP289	70c + 35c multi	1.60	1.25
B630	SP289	70c + 35c multi	1.60	1.25
B631	SP289	90c + 40c multi	2.10	1.50
	Complete booklet, 10 #B631		21.00	
B632	SP289	90c + 40c multi	2.10	1.50
B633	SP289	110c + 50c multi	2.50	1.90
	Nos. B629-B633 (5)		9.90	7.40

Christmas SP290

Life Near Water — SP291

No. B634, Bell, holly on ribbon. No. B635, Ramshorn snail. 90c+45c, Great crested grebe. 110c+55c, Pike.

1998, Nov. 25   Photo.   Perf. 11½

B634	SP291	70c +35c multi	1.60	1.25
B635	SP291	70c +35c multi	1.60	1.25
B636	SP291	90c +45c multi	2.10	1.60
	Complete booklet, 6 #B634, 4 #B636		18.00	
B637	SP291	110c +55c multi	2.50	1.90
	Nos. B634-B637 (4)		7.80	6.00

Pro Patria — SP292

Heritage and landscapes: No. B638, Chestnut groves, Malcantone. No. B639, La Sarraz Castle. 90c+40c, Lake Lucerne steamship. 110c+50c, St. Paul's Chapel, Rhäzüns.

1999, May 5   Litho.   Perf. 13½

B638	SP292	70c +35c multi	1.60	1.40
B639	SP292	70c +35c multi	1.60	1.40
B640	SP292	90c +40c multi	2.10	1.75
	Complete booklet, 10 #B640		21.00	
B641	SP292	110c +50c multi	2.50	2.10
	Nos. B638-B641 (4)		7.80	6.65

Souvenir Sheet

NABA 2000 Philatelic Exhibition, St. Gallen — SP293

a, 70c+30c, St. Laurenzen Church spire. b, 20c+10c, Top of town house. c, 90c+30c, Oriel window.

1999, Sept. 9   Photo.   Perf. 11¾

Sheet of 3

B642	SP293	#a.-c. + label	4.75	4.75
a.		70c+30c multicolored	1.60	1.25
b.		20c+10c multicolored	.45	.40
c.		90c+30c multicolored	2.10	1.60

Christmas SP294    Nicolo the Clown From Children's Book by Verena Pavoni SP295

Designs: No. B643, Children, snowman. No. B644, Nicolo, circus tent. 90c+45c, Nicolo and his father. 110c+55c, Nicolo and donkey.

Perf. 13½x13¼   Litho.

1999, Nov. 23

B643	SP294	70c +35c multi	1.60	1.40
B644	SP295	70c +35c multi	1.60	1.40
B645	SP295	90c +45c multi	2.10	1.75
	Complete booklet, 6 #B644, 4 #B645		18.00	
B646	SP295	110c +55c multi	2.50	2.10
	Nos. B643-B646 (4)		7.80	6.65

Surtax for Pro Juventute Foundation. See No. B660-B663.

Cities With Pro Patria Foundation Renovation Projects SP296

Perf. 13¼x13½

2000, May 10   Litho. & Engr.

B647	SP296	70c +35c Näfles	1.60	1.25
B648	SP296	70c +35c Tengia	1.60	1.25
B649	SP296	90c +40c Brugg	2.10	1.60
B650	SP296	90c +40c Carouge	2.10	1.60
	Booklet, 10 #B650		21.00	
	Nos. B647-B650 (4)		7.40	5.70

Souvenir Sheet

NABA 2000 Philatelic Exhibition, St. Gallen — SP297

Quadrants of stylized No. 5: a, UL. b, UR. c, LL. d, LR.

2000, May 10   Photo.   Perf. 11¾

B651	SP297	Sheet of 4	5.50	5.50
a.		70c+35c multicolored	1.60	1.25
b.-c.		20c+10c any single	.45	.35
d.		90c+45c multicolored	2.10	1.75

Christmas SP298    Illustrations from Little Albert, by Albert Manser SP299

Designs: No. B652, St. Nicholas and Schmutzli in sleigh. No. B653, Children at fence. No. B654, Little Albert with umbrella. No. B655, Children on sleds.

Perf. 13¼x13½

2000, Nov. 21   Litho.

B652	SP298	70c +35c multi	1.60	1.25
B653	SP299	70c +35c multi	1.60	1.25
B654	SP299	90c +45c multi	2.10	1.50
	Booklet, 6 #B653, 4 #B654		18.00	
B655	SP299	90c +45c multi	2.10	1.50
	Nos. B652-B655 (4)		7.40	5.50

Surtax for Pro Juventute Foundation.

Landmarks SP300

Designs: No. B656, Hauterive Abbey. No. B657, La Chaux-de-Fonds Theater. No. B658, Granary, Rorschach. No. B659, Bishop's Castle, Leuk.

2001, May 9   Litho.   Perf. 13¼x13½

B656	SP300	70c +35c multi	1.60	1.25
B657	SP300	70c +35c multi	1.60	1.25
B658	SP300	90c +40c multi	2.10	1.50
B659	SP300	90c +40c multi	2.10	1.50
	Booklet, 10 #B659		21.00	
	Nos. B656-B659 (4)		7.40	5.50

Surtax for Pro Patria Foundation.

Pro Juventute Types of 1999

Art from children's books: No. B660, What's Santa Claus Doing?, by Karin von Oldershausen. No. B661, Leopold the Leopard, from Leopold and the Sun, by Stephan Brülhart. No. B662, Honeybear, from Leopold and the Sun. No. B663, Tom the Monkey, from Leopold and the Sun.

Perf. 13½x13¼

2001, Nov. 20   Litho.

B660	SP294	70c +35c multi	1.60	1.25
B661	SP295	70c +35c multi	1.60	1.25
B662	SP295	90c +45c multi	2.10	1.60
	Booklet, 6 #B661, 4 #B662		18.00	
B663	SP295	90c +45c multi	2.10	1.60
	Nos. B660-B663 (4)		7.40	5.70

Surtax for Pro Juventute Foundation.

Mills — SP301

Location: No. B664, Bruzella. No. B665, Oberdorf. No. B666, Büren an der Aare. No. B667, Lussery-Villars.

2002, May 15   Litho.   Perf. 13¼x13½

B664	SP301	70c +35c multi	1.60	1.40
B665	SP301	70c +35c multi	1.60	1.40
B666	SP301	90c +40c multi	2.10	1.60
	Booklet, 10 #B666		21.00	
B667	SP301	90c +40c multi	2.10	1.60
	Nos. B664-B667 (4)		7.40	6.00

Surtax for Pro Patria Foundation.

Roses — SP302

Designs: No. B668, Christmas rose (gold background). No. B669, Ingrid Bergman rose (white background). No. B670, Belle Vaudoise rose (orange petals). No. B671, Charmian rose (pink petals). 130c+65c, Frühlingsgold rose.

Perf. 13¾x13¼

2002, Nov. 19   Litho.

B668	SP302	70c +35c multi	1.60	1.40
B669	SP302	70c +35c multi	1.60	1.40
B670	SP302	90c +40c multi	2.10	1.90
	Booklet, 6 #B669, 4 #B670		18.00	

B671	SP302	90c +45c multi	2.10	1.90
B672	SP302	130c +65c multi	3.00	2.60
	Nos. B668-B672 (5)		10.40	9.20

Surtax for Pro Juventute Foundation. No. B668 is impregnated with a pine needle, cinnamon and clove scent, and Nos. B669-B672 with a rose scent.

Bridges SP303

Designs: No. B673, Wynigen Bridge, Burgdorf, 1776. No. B674, Salginatobel Bridge, Schiers, 1929. No. B675, Pont St. Jean, Saint Ursanne, 15th cent. No. B676, Reuss Bridge, Rottenschwil, 1907.

2003, May 8   Litho.   Perf. 13¼x13½

B673	SP303	70c +35c multi	1.60	1.60
B674	SP303	70c +35c multi	1.60	1.60
B675	SP303	90c +40c multi	2.10	2.00
	Booklet, 10 #B675		21.00	
B676	SP303	90c +40c multi	2.10	2.00
	Nos. B673-B676 (4)		7.40	7.20

Rights of the Child — SP304

Children: 70c+35c, Christmas tree, toy tractor, gift. 85c+35c, Playing as storekeeper and shopper. 90c+45c, Skateboarding with dog. 100c+45c, Playing guitar and drums.

Serpentine Die Cut 10½x11

2003, Nov. 19   Litho.

Self-Adhesive

B677	SP304	70c +35c multi	1.75	1.75
a.		Block of 4 on translucent backing paper	7.00	
B678	SP304	85c +35c multi	2.00	1.90
a.		Block of 4 on translucent backing paper	8.00	
B679	SP304	90c +40c multi	2.10	2.10
a.		Block of 4 on translucent backing paper	8.40	
B680	SP304	100c +45c multi	2.25	2.25
a.		Block of 4 on translucent backing paper	9.00	
b.		Nos. B677-B680 on translucent backing paper	8.00	
c.		Booklet, 6 each #B678, B680	22.50	
	Nos. B677-B680 (4)		8.10	8.00

Nos. B677-B680 each were printed in sheets of 20 stamps with a white paper backing.

Small Buildings SP305

Designs: No. B681, Bathing pavilion, Gorgier. No. B682, Granary, Oberramsern. No. B683, Ossuary, Gentilino. No. B684, Dock house, Lucerne.

2004, May 6   Litho.   Perf. 13¾x14¼

B681	SP305	85c +40c multi	2.00	1.90
B682	SP305	85c +40c multi	2.00	1.90
B683	SP305	100c +50c multi	2.40	2.40
B684	SP305	100c +50c multi	2.40	2.40
	Complete booklet, 6 #B681, 4 #B684		22.50	

Complete booklet sold for 14.50fr.

Rights of the Child — SP306

Designs: No. B685, Children playing card game. No. B686, Children, man, giraffe. No. B687, Children, teacher. No. B688, Child, elderly man and woman.

Serpentine Die Cut 10½x11

2004, Nov. 23 **Litho.**

Self-Adhesive

B685 SP306 85c +40c multi 2.25 2.25
a. Block of 4 on translucent paper 9.00
B686 SP306 85c +40c multi 2.25 2.25
a. Block of 4 on translucent paper 9.00
B687 SP306 100c +50c multi 2.75 2.75
a. Block of 4 on translucent paper 11.00
b. Booklet pane, 6 each #B685, B687 30.00
B688 SP306 100c +50c multi 2.75 2.75
a. Block of 4 on translucent paper 11.00
b. Nos. B685-B688 on translucent paper 10.00
Nos. B685-B688 (4) 10.00 10.00

Nos. B685-B688 were each printed in sheets of 20 stamps. No. B687b sold for 17fr.

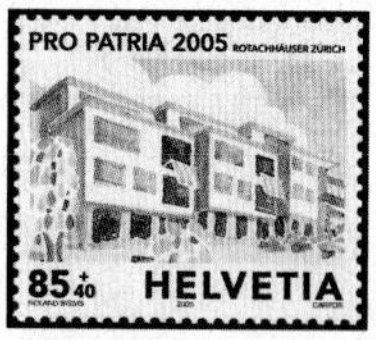

Historic Buildings SP307

Designs: No. B689, Rotach Houses, Zurich. No. B690, Monte Carasso Abbey, Monte Carasso. No. B691, St. Katharinental Abbey, Diessenhofen. No. B692, Palais Wilson, Geneva.

2005, May 10 **Litho.** ***Perf. 13¼x13½***

B689 SP307 85c +40c multi 2.10 2.10
B690 SP307 85c +40c multi 2.10 2.10
B691 SP307 100c +50c multi 2.50 2.50
Complete booklet, 6 #B690, 4 #B691 23.00
B692 SP307 100c +50c multi 2.50 2.50
Nos. B689-B692 (4) 9.20 9.20

Surtax for Pro Patria Foundation.

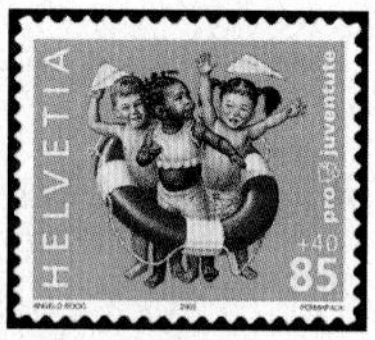

Children's Rights SP308

Children and: No. B693, Life preserver. No. B694, Cherries. No. B695, Computer. No. B696 Candle in window.

Serpentine Die Cut 10½x11

2005, Nov. 22 **Photo.**

Self-Adhesive

B693 SP308 85c +40c multi 2.00 1.90
a. Block of 4 on translucent paper 8.00
B694 SP308 85c +40c multi 2.00 1.90
a. Block of 4 on translucent paper 8.00
B695 SP308 100c +50c multi 2.25 2.25
a. Block of 4 on translucent paper 9.00
b. Booklet pane, 2 each #B693, B695 8.50
Complete booklet, 3 #B695b 26.00
B696 SP308 100c +50c multi 2.25 2.25
a. Block of 4 on translucent paper 9.00
b. Nos. B693-B696 on translucent paper 8.50
Nos. B693-B696 (4) 8.50 8.30

Nos. B693-B696 were each printed in sheets of 20. Complete booklet sold for €17.

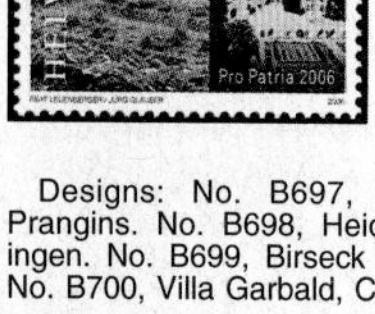

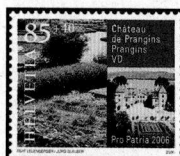

Gardens and Parks — SP309

Designs: No. B697, Prangins Castle, Prangins. No. B698, Heidegg Castle, Gelfingen. No. B699, Birseck Castle, Arlesheim. No. B700, Villa Garbald, Castasegna.

2006, May 9 **Litho.** ***Perf. 14x13¾***

B697 SP309 85c +40c multi 2.10 2.10
B698 SP309 85c +40c multi 2.10 2.10
B699 SP309 100c +50c multi 2.50 2.50
B700 SP309 100c +50c multi 2.50 2.50
Complete booklet, 6 #B698, 4 #B700 24.00
Nos. B697-B700 (4) 9.20 9.20

Complete booklet sold for €14.50.

Souvenir Sheet

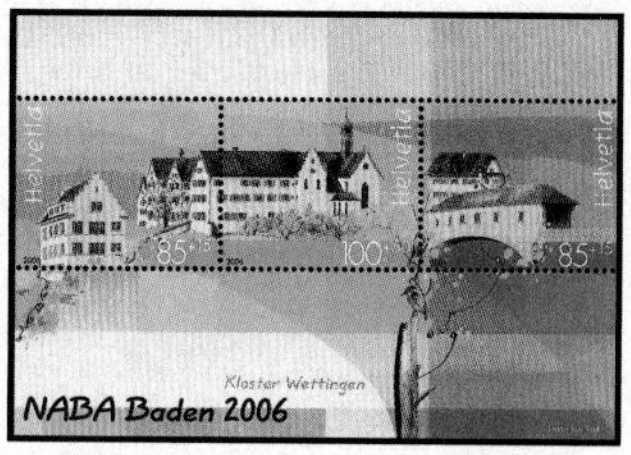

Wettingen Monastery — SP310

No. B701: a, Building, country name at left. b, Building and bridge, country name at right. c, Main building.

2006, May 9 ***Perf. 13¾x14¼***

B701 SP310 Sheet of 3 7.25 7.25
a.-b. 85c+15c Either single 2.00 1.75
c. 100c+50c multi 2.25 2.50

NABA Baden 2006.

Souvenir Sheet

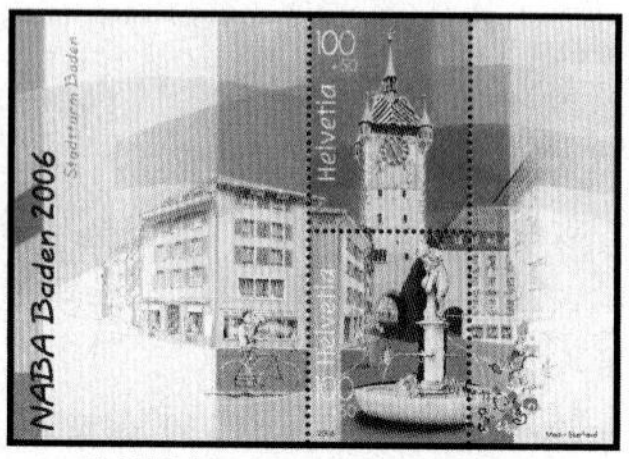

NABA Baden 2006 Philatelic Exhibition — SP311

No. B702: a, Baden City Tower. b, Fountain.

Perf. 14¼x13¾ on 3 Sides

2006, Sept. 7 **Litho.**

B702 SP311 Sheet of 2 5.50 5.50
a.-b. 100c +50c Either single 2.25 2.50

Children's Art Competition SP312

Designs: No. B703, Singer, by Veronica Jesus Garcia Pinto. No. B704, Car in garage, by Stephane Arada. No. B705, Bandaged dog, by Lea Mayer. No. B706, Angel, by Ted Scapa, judge of competition.

Serpentine Die Cut 10¾x11

2006, Nov. 21

Self-Adhesive

B703 SP312 85c +40c multi 2.10 2.10
a. Block of 4, #B703 8.50
B704 SP312 85c +40c multi 2.10 2.10
a. Block of 4, #B704 8.50
B705 SP312 100c +50c multi 2.50 2.50
a. Booklet pane, 6 each #B704-B705 28.00
b. Block of 4, #B705 10.00
B706 SP312 100c +50c multi 2.50 2.50
a. Block of 4, #B703-B706 9.25
b. Block of 4, #B706 10.00
Nos. B703-B706 (4) 9.20 9.20

Surtax for Pro Juventute Foundation. See also Nos. B711-B714, B719-B722.

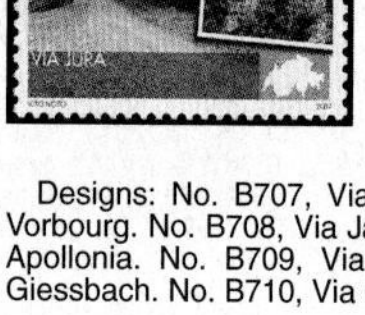

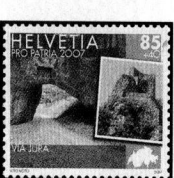

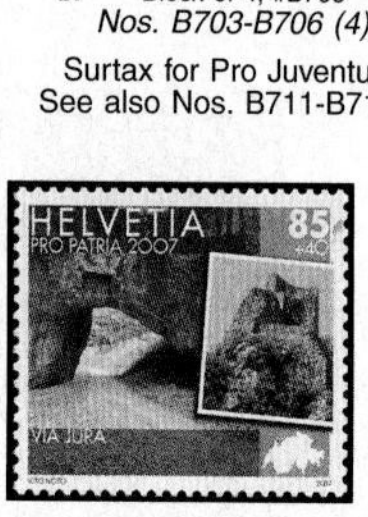

Historic Roads SP313

Designs: No. B707, Via Jura, Chateau de Vorbourg. No. B708, Via Jacobi, Chapel of St. Apollonia. No. B709, Via Cook, Grandhotel Giessbach. No. B710, Via Gottardo, Alte Sust.

2007, Apr. 27 **Litho.** ***Perf. 13½x13¼***

B707 SP313 85c +40c multi 2.10 2.10
B708 SP313 85c +40c multi 2.10 2.10
B709 SP313 100c +50c multi 2.50 2.50
Complete booklet, 6 #B708, 4 #B709 23.00
B710 SP313 100c +50c multi 2.50 2.50
Nos. B707-B710 (4) 9.20 9.20

Surtax for Pro Patria Foundation. See also Nos. B715-B718, B723-B726.

Children's Art Competition Type of 2006

Designs: No. B711, Camping, by Christine Fischer. No. B712, Mountains, by Jonathan Balest. No. B713, Sunshine, by Morena Rufatti. No. B714, Angels, by Ted Scapa, judge of competition.

Serpentine Die Cut 10½x11

2007, Nov. 20 **Litho.**

Self-Adhesive

B711 SP312 85c +40c multi 2.25 2.25
a. Block of 4 #B711 on backing paper 9.00
B712 SP312 85c +40c multi 2.25 2.25
a. Block of 4 #B712 on backing paper 9.00
B713 SP312 100c +50c multi 2.75 2.75
a. Block of 4 #B713 on backing paper 11.00
b. Booklet pane, 6 each #B711, B713 30.00
B714 SP312 100c +50c multi 2.75 2.75
a. Block of 4 #B714 on backing paper 11.00
b. Block of 4, #B711-B714 on backing paper 10.00 10.00
Nos. B711-B714 (4) 10.00 10.00

Surtax for Pro Juventute Foundation.

Historic Roads Type of 2007

Designs: No. B715, Via Romana, East Gate, Avenches, and columns, Nyon. No. B716, Via Sbrinz, Schnitzturm Tower. No. B717, Via Stockalper, Old Hospice, Simplon. No. B718, Via Valtellina, Dürrboden Restaurant, Grisons.

2008, May 8 **Litho.** ***Perf. 13½x13¼***

B715 SP313 85c +40c multi 2.40 2.40
B716 SP313 85c +40c multi 2.40 2.40
B717 SP313 100c +50c multi 3.00 3.00
Complete booklet, 6 #B716, 4 #B717 27.00
B718 SP313 100c +50c multi 3.00 3.00
Nos. B715-B718 (4) 10.80 10.80

Surtax for Pro Patria Foundation.

Children's Art Competition Type of 2006

Designs: No. B719, Friendship Unites (Sun and Moon), by Andrea Andreazzi. No. B720, Friendship Provides Support (boy, girl, child in wheelchair), by Manon Peng. No. B721, Friendship is the Source of Happiness (girls and four-leaf clover), by Delia Candolo. No. B722, Friendship is Uplifting (angels), by Ted Scapa, judge of competition.

Serpentine Die Cut 10¾x11

2008, Nov. 21 **Litho.**

Self-Adhesive

B719 SP312 85c +40c multi 2.10 2.10
B720 SP312 85c +40c multi 2.10 2.10
B721 SP312 100c +50c multi 2.50 2.50
a. Booklet pane, 6 each #B719, B721 28.00
B722 SP312 100c +50c multi 2.50 2.50
a. Block of 4, #B719-B722 on backing paper 9.25
Nos. B719-B722 (4) 9.20 9.20

No. B721a sold for 17fr. Surtax for Pro Juventute Foundation.

Historic Roads Type of 2003

Designs: No. B723, Via Salina and Bern Gate, Murten. No. B724, Via Francigena and Great St. Bernhard Hospice, Bourg-Saint-Pierre. No. B725, Via Rhenana and salt drilling towers, Rheinfelden. No. B726, Via Spluga and Albertini House, Splügen.

2009, May 8 ***Perf. 13½x13¼***

B723 SP313 85c +40c multi 2.25 2.25
B724 SP313 85c +40c multi 2.25 2.25
B725 SP313 100c +50c multi 2.75 2.75
Complete booklet, 6 #B724, 4 #B725 26.00
B726 SP313 100c +50c multi 2.75 2.75
Nos. B723-B726 (4) 10.00 10.00

Complete booklet sold for 14.50fr. Surtax for Pro Patria Foundation.

Souvenir Sheet

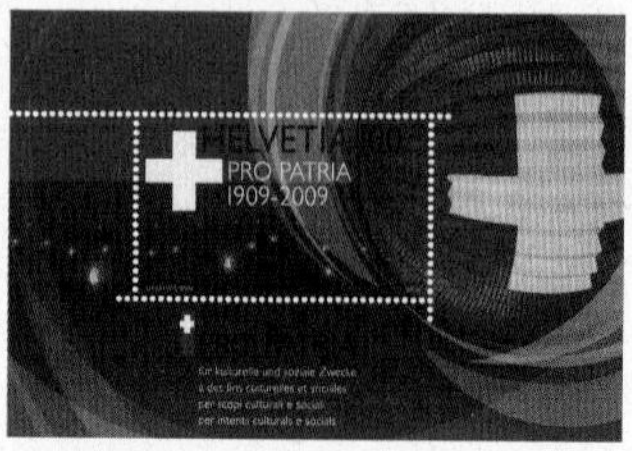

Pro Patria Foundation, Cent. — SP314

2009, May 8 **Litho.** ***Perf. 14x13¼***

B727 SP314 100c +50c multi 2.75 2.75

Surtax for Pro Patria Foundation.

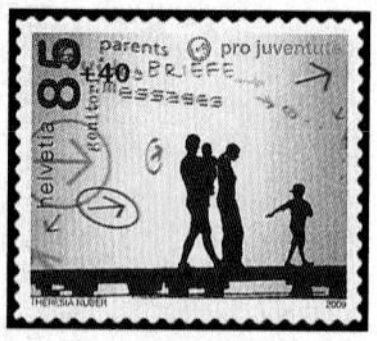

Services of the Pro Juventute Foundation SP315

Designs: No. B728, Letters to Parents (family and arrows). No. B729, Vacation Pass programs (children and tree). No. B730, Advice 147 counseling (boy and girl). No. B731, Semi-postal stamp sales (four children and stylized stamps).

Serpentine Die Cut 12

2009, Nov. 20 **Litho.**

Self-Adhesive

B728 SP315 85c +40c multi 2.50 2.50
a. Block of 4 #B728 on backing paper 10.00
B729 SP315 85c +40c multi 2.50 2.50
a. Block of 4 #B729 on backing paper 10.00
B730 SP315 100c +50c multi 3.00 3.00
a. Booklet pane of 12, 6 each #B728, B730 34.00
b. Block of 4 #B730 on backing paper 12.00
B731 SP315 100c +50c multi 3.00 3.00
a. Block of 4, #B728-B731, on translucent paper 11.00
b. Block of 4 #B731 on backing paper 12.00
Nos. B728-B731 (4) 11.00 11.00

Complete booklet sold for 17fr. Surtax for Pro Juventute Foundation.

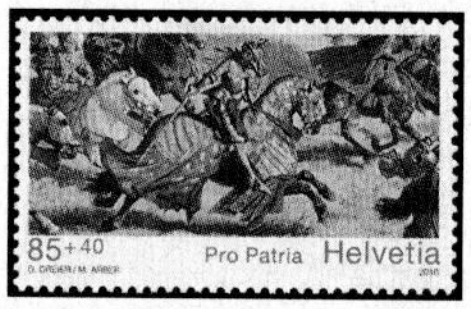

Details From Panorama of Battle of Murten, by Louis Braun — SP316

Desings: No. B732, Retreat of Charles the Bold on caparisoned horse. No. B733, Death of Duke of Somerset near tents. No. B734, Confederate troops with flags and halberds. No. B735, Burgundian Cavalry being attacked by Confederate troops.

2010, May 6 **Litho.** ***Perf. 14***

B732 SP316 85c +40c multi 2.25 2.25
B733 SP316 85c +40c multi 2.25 2.25
B734 SP316 100c +50c multi 2.75 2.75
Complete booklet, 6 #B732, 4 #B734 27.00
B735 SP316 100c +50c multi 2.75 2.75
Nos. B732-B735 (4) 10.00 10.00

Surtax for Pro Patria Foundation. Complete booklet sold for 14.50fr.

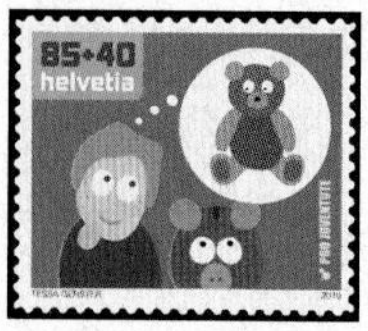

Boy Saving Money SP317

Designs: No. B736, Boy thinking of teddy bear, piggy bank. No. B737, Boy and piggy bank. No. B738, Boy, teddy bear and piggy bank. No. B739, Piggy bank, boy holding gift.

Serpentine Die Cut 12

2010, Nov. 4   Litho.
Self-Adhesive

B736	SP317	85c +40c multi	2.60	2.60
a.	Block of 4 on translucent backing paper		10.50	
B737	SP317	85c +40c multi	2.60	2.60
a.	Block of 4 on translucent backing paper		10.50	
B738	SP317	100c +50c multi	3.25	3.25
a.	Block of 4 on translucent backing paper		13.00	
B739	SP317	100c +50c multi	3.25	3.25
a.	Block of 4, #B736-B739		12.00	
b.	Booklet pane of 12, 6 each #B736, B739		36.00	
c.	Block of 4 on translucent backing paper		13.00	
	Nos. B736-B739 (4)		11.70	11.70

Surtax for Pro Juventute Foundation. No. B739b sold for 17fr.

Lake Steamships SP318

Designs: No. B740, PS Gallia. No. B741, PS Piemonte. No. B742, PS Blümlisalp. No. B743, PS La Suisse.

2011, May 5   Litho.   Perf. 13½
Color of Denomination

B740	SP318	85c+40c green	3.00	3.00
B741	SP318	85c+40c orange	3.00	3.00
B742	SP318	100c+50c yellow	3.50	3.50
	Complete booklet, 6 #B741, 4 #B742		35.00	
B743	SP318	100c+50c brt pink	3.50	3.50
	Nos. B740-B743 (4)		13.00	13.00

Complete booklet sold for 14.50fr. Surtax for Pro Patria Foundation.

Children SP319

Stylized flowers and: No. B744, Young boy, duck, sheep, bear, leaf, crescent moon. No. B745, Two girls, happy face, musical notes, envelope, ice cream cone, heart. No. B746, Two young girls, gift, stars, bell, Christmas tree. No. B747, Boy, sun, fish, ball, paw print.

Color of Denomination

Serpentine Die Cut 12
2011, Nov. 17   Self-Adhesive

B744	SP319	85c +40c blue	2.75	2.75
B745	SP319	85c +40c rose lil	2.75	2.75
B746	SP319	100c +50c dl org	3.50	3.50
B747	SP319	100c +50c green	3.50	3.50
a.	Block of 4, #B744-B747, on translucent paper		12.50	
b.	Booklet pane of 12, 3 each #B744-B747		37.50	
	Nos. B744-B747 (4)		12.50	12.50

Stamps do not touch on No. B747a, but touch on No. B747b. No. B747b sold for 17fr. Surtax for Pro Juventute Foundation.

Girls on Swing SP320

2012, Mar. 1   Serpentine Die Cut 12
Self-Adhesive

B748	SP320	100c +50c multi	3.25	3.25

Pro Juventute Foundation, cent. Surtax for Pro Juventute Foundation.

Architectural Preservation SP321

Designs: No. B749, Eichberg Estate Lion Fountain, Uetendorf. No. B750, Ferme des Troncs storehouse, Mézières. No. B751, Domed stone cellar, Brusio. No. B752, Villa Abendstern summer house, Wädenswil.

2012, May 9   Perf. 14¼x13¾

B749	SP321	85c +40c multi	2.75	2.75
B750	SP321	85c +40c multi	2.75	2.75
B751	SP321	100c +50c multi	3.25	3.25
	Complete booklet, 6 #B749, 4 #B751		32.50	
B752	SP321	100c +50c multi	3.25	3.25
	Nos. B749-B752 (4)		12.00	12.00

Complete booklet sold for 14.50fr. Surtax for Pro Patria Foundation.

2012 National Stamp Exhibiton, Stans — SP322

No. B753: a, Buildings on Stans village square, statue base, mountain peak in background (34x42mm). b, Buildings on village square, clouds in background (34x42mm). c, Statue, exhibition emblem (37x70mm). d, Airplane (68x28mm).

Perf. 13 on 1, 2 or 3 Sides
2012, Sept. 6   Litho.

B753	SP322	Sheet of 4	12.00	12.00
a.-b.	85c+45c Either single		2.75	2.75
c.-d.	100c+55c Either single		3.25	3.25

Pro Juventute Posters — SP323

Designs: 85c+40c, Children Playing, by Margarethe Lipps, 1959. No. B755, Girl with Doll, by Victor Rutz, 1952. No. B756, Child in High Chair, by Celestino Piatti, 1955.

Serpentine Die Cut 12
2012, Nov. 22   Self-Adhesive

B754	SP323	85c +40c multi	2.75	2.75
a.	Block of 4 #B754 on translucent paper		11.00	
B755	SP323	100c +50c multi	3.25	3.25
a.	Block of 4 #B755 on translucent paper		13.00	
B756	SP323	100c +50c multi	3.25	3.25
a.	Nos. B754-B756 on translucent backing paper		9.25	
b.	Booklet pane of 12, 4 each #B754-B756		37.50	
c.	Block of 4 #B756 on translucent paper		13.00	
	Nos. B754-B756 (3)		9.25	9.25

No. B756b sold for 17.50fr. Surtax for Pro Juventute Foundation.

Exhibits in Local Museums SP324

Designs: No. B757, Wax toad, Fram Museum, Einsiedeln. No. B758, Straw hat, Stroh Museum, Wohlen. No. B759, Carved wooden cow, Toggenburger Museum, Lichtensteig. No. B760, Carpenter's plane, Bagnes Museum, Villette.

2013, May 7   Perf. 13¼x13½

B757	SP324	85c +40c multi	2.75	2.75
B758	SP324	85c +40c multi	2.75	2.75
B759	SP324	100c +50c multi	3.25	3.25
B760	SP324	100c +50c multi	3.25	3.25
	Complete booklet, 6 #B758, 4 #B760		31.00	

Surtax for Pro Patria Foundation. Complete booklet sold for 14.50fr.
See Nos. B764-B767, B772-B775.

Children and Swiss Railway Locomotives SP325

Designs: 85c+40c, Girl and Red Arrow RAe 2/4. No. B762, Boy with glasses, Krokodil Ce 6/8. No. B763, Boy, stars, Gotthard Line Ae6/6.

Serpentine Die Cut 12
2013, Nov. 14   Litho.
Self-Adhesive

B761	SP325	85c +40c multi	3.00	3.00
B762	SP325	100c +50c multi	3.50	3.50
B763	SP325	100c +50c multi	3.50	3.50
a.	Sheet of 3, #B761-B763, on translucent paper		10.00	
b.	Booklet pane of 12, 4 each #B761-B763		40.00	
	Nos. B761-B763 (3)		10.00	10.00

Surtax for Pro Juventute Foundation. No. B763b sold for 17.50fr.

Exhibits in Local Museums Type of 2013

Designs: No. B764, Roof tile, Malcantone Museum, Curio. No. B765, Painted larval mask, Ortsmuseum, Binningen. No. B766, Hurdy-gurdy, Musical Instrument Collection, Willisau. No. B767, Apprentice watch by Emile Juillard, Museum Hôtel-Dieu, Porrentruy.

2014, May 8   Perf. 13¾x14¼

B764	SP324	85c +40c multi	3.00	3.00
B765	SP324	85c +40c multi	3.00	3.00
B766	SP324	100c +50c multi	3.50	3.50
B767	SP324	100c +50c multi	3.50	3.50
	Complete booklet, 6 #B765, 4 #B767		33.00	
	Nos. B764-B767 (4)		13.00	13.00

Surtax for Pro Patria Foundation. Complete booklet sold for 14.50fr.

Swiss Family Traditions SP326

Designs: 85c+40c, St. Martin's Day lantern procession. No. B769, Adult reading story to children. No. B770, Family making Christmas cookies.

Serpentine Die Cut 12
2014, Nov. 13   Litho.
Self-Adhesive

B768	SP326	85c +40c multi	2.60	2.60
B769	SP326	100c +50c multi	3.25	3.25
B770	SP326	100c +50c multi	3.25	3.25
a.	Sheet of 3, #B768-B770, on translucent paper		9.25	
b.	Booklet pane of 12, 4 each #B768-B770		37.00	
	Nos. B768-B770 (3)		9.10	9.10

Surtax for Pro Juventute Foundation. No. B770b sold for 17.50fr.

Souvenir Sheet

Horses at Saignelégier Horse Market — SP327

2014, Nov. 13   Litho.   Perf. 14x13½

B771	SP327	100c +50c multi	3.25	3.25

Stamp Day. Surtax for Foundation for the Promotion of Philately.

Exhibits in Local Museums Type of 2013

Designs: No. B772, Tobacco pouch, Appenzell Museum, Appenzell. No. B773, Wine barrel, Wine and Vine Museum, Aigle. No. B774, Carved butter board, 18th cent., Saanen Museum of the Countryside, Saanen. No. B775, Merovingian Period disc brooch from Steckborn-Chilestigli burial ground, Archaeology Museum. Frauenfeld.

2015, May 7   Litho.   Perf. 13¼x13½

B772	SP324	85c +40c multi	2.75	2.75
B773	SP324	85c +40c multi	2.75	2.75
B774	SP324	100c +50c multi	3.25	3.25
B775	SP324	100c +50c multi	3.25	3.25
	Complete booklet, 6 #B773, 4 #B775		32.00	
	Nos. B772-B775 (4)		12.00	12.00

Surtax for Pro Patria Foundation. Complete booklet sold for 14.50fr.

AIR POST STAMPS

Nos. 134 and 139 Overprinted in Carmine

1919-20   Wmk. 183   Perf. 11½
Granite Paper

C1	A25	30c yel brn & pale grn ('20)	110.00	1,250.
C2	A25	50c dp & pale grn	32.50	110.00
	Set, never hinged		350.00	

Counterfeits of overprint and fraudulent cancellations exist.

Airplane AP1

Pilot at Controls of Airplane AP2

Biplane against Sky — AP3

Allegorical Figure of Flight AP4

Perf. 11½, 12 and Compound

1923-25 **Typo.**

C3	AP1 15c brn red & ap grn	2.25	8.25
C4	AP1 20c grn & lt grn ('25)	.90	*6.00*
C5	AP1 25c dk bl & bl	7.75	*22.50*
C6	AP2 35c brn & buff	11.00	*42.50*
C7	AP2 40c vio & gray vio	14.50	*45.00*
C8	AP3 45c red & ind	1.60	*7.25*
C9	AP3 50c blk & red	12.50	17.00

Perf. 11½

C10	AP4 65c gray bl & dp bl ('24)	3.25	*16.00*
C11	AP4 75c org & brn red ('24)	15.00	*55.00*
C12	AP4 1fr vio & dp vio ('24)	42.50	32.50
	Nos. C3-C12 (10)	111.25	*252.00*
	Set, never hinged	275.00	

For surcharges see Nos. C19, C22, C26.

1933-37 **With Grilled Gum**

C4a	AP1	20c grn & lt grn ('37)	.30	.40
C5a	AP1	25c dk bl & bl ('34)	5.00	*50.00*
C8a	AP3	45c red & indigo ('37)	2.50	*52.50*
C9a	AP3	50c gray grn & scar ('35)	1.10	1.60
C10a	AP4	65c gray bl & dp bl ('37)	2.75	*8.50*
C11a	AP4	75c org & brn red ('36)	27.50	*175.00*
C12a	AP4	1fr vio & deep vio	2.10	3.25
		Nos. C4a-C12a (7)	41.25	*291.25*
		Set, never hinged	65.00	

See Grilled Gum note after No. 145.

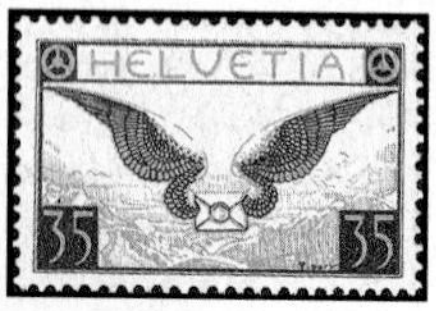

Allegory of Air Mail — AP5

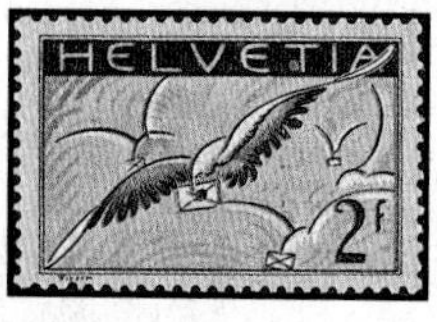

Bird Carrying Letter AP6

1929-30 **Granite Paper**

C13	AP5 35c red brn, bis & claret	15.00	42.50
C14	AP5 40c dl grn, yel grn & bl	57.50	82.50
C15	AP6 2fr blk brn & red brn, *gray* ('30)	85.00	85.00
	Nos. C13-C15 (3)	157.50	210.00
	Set, never hinged	425.00	

1933-35 **With Grilled Gum**

C13a	AP5	35c red brn, bis & cl	5.00	*50.00*
C14a	AP5	40c dk grn, yel grn & bl	37.50	77.50
C15a	AP6	2fr blk brn & red brn ('35)	7.25	12.00
		Nos. C13a-C15a (3)	49.75	*139.50*
		Set, never hinged	140.00	

Front View of Airplane AP7

1932, Feb. 2 **Granite Paper**

C16	AP7 15c dp grn & lt grn	.55	*1.60*
C17	AP7 20c dk red & buff	1.10	*2.50*
C18	AP7 90c dp bl & gray	7.25	*30.00*
	Nos. C16-C18 (3)	8.90	*34.10*
	Set, never hinged	22.50	

Intl. Disarmament Conf., Geneva, Feb. 1932.
For surcharges see Nos. C20-C21, C23-C25.

Nos. C3, C10, C16-C18 Surcharged with New Values and Bars in Black or Red

1935-38

C19	AP1 10c on 15c	4.75	*37.50*
C20	AP7 10c on 15c	.40	.55
a.	Inverted surcharge	*6,500.*	*12,000.*
C21	AP7 10c on 20c ('36)	.45	*2.25*
C22	AP4 10c on 65c ('38)	.25	.40
C23	AP7 30c on 90c ('36)	3.00	*14.00*
C24	AP7 40c on 20c ('37)	3.75	*15.00*
C25	AP7 40c on 90c ('36) (R)	3.25	*14.50*
a.	Vermilion surcharge	92.50	*800.00*
	Never hinged, #C25a	150.00	
	Nos. C19-C25 (7)	15.85	*84.20*
	Set, never hinged	40.00	

Stamp similar to No. C22, but from souvenir sheet, is listed as No. 242a.

Type of Air Post Stamp of 1923 Srchd. in Black

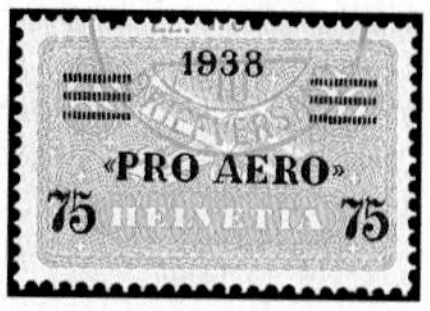

1938, May 22 **Wmk. 183** ***Perf. 11½***

C26 AP3 75c on 50c gray & scar 6.50

"Pro Aero" Meeting, May 21-22.

No. C26 was not sold to the public in the ordinary way, but affixed to air mail letters by postal officials. It was not regularly obtainable unused.

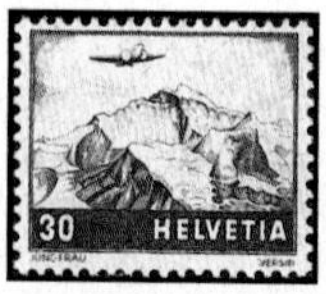

Jungfrau — AP8

Designs: 40c, View of Valais. 50c, Lake Geneva. 60c, Alpstein. 70c, View of Ticino. 1fr, Lake Lucerne. 2fr, The Engadine. 5fr, Churfirsten.

Perf. 11½

1941, May 1 **Unwmk.** **Engr.**

Tinted Granite Paper

C27	AP8 30c ultra	.55	.25
C28	AP8 40c gray blk	.55	.25
C29	AP8 50c slate grn	.55	.30
C30	AP8 60c chestnut	.85	.30
C31	AP8 70c plum	.90	.55
C32	AP8 1fr Prus grn	1.75	.60
C33	AP8 2fr car lake	5.75	3.50
C34	AP8 5fr deep blue	19.00	15.00
	Nos. C27-C34 (8)	29.90	20.75
	Set, never hinged	80.00	

See Nos. C43-C44.

Type of 1941 Overprinted in Red

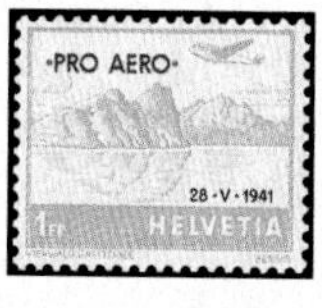

1941, May 12

C35 AP8 1fr blue green 5.50 *19.00*
Never hinged 10.00

Issued to commemorate special flights between Payerne and Buochs, May 28, 1941.

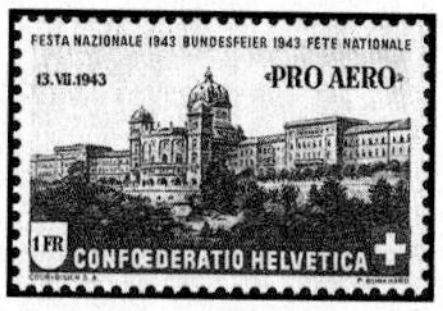

Parliament Buildings, Bern AP16

1943, July 13 **Photo.**

C36 AP16 1fr cop red, buff & blk 1.60 *10.00*
Never hinged 3.75

30th anniv. of the 1st Alpine flight, by Oscar Bider, July 13, 1913.

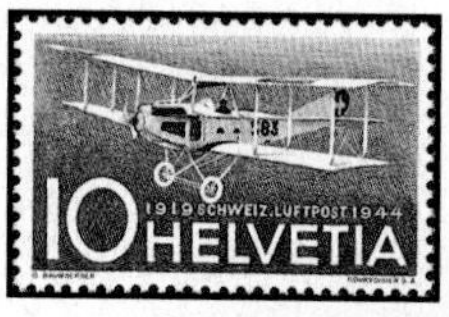

DH-3 Haefeli AP17

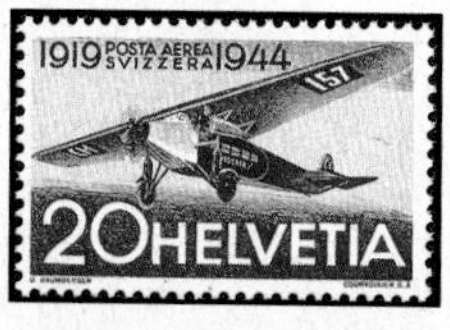

Fokker AP18

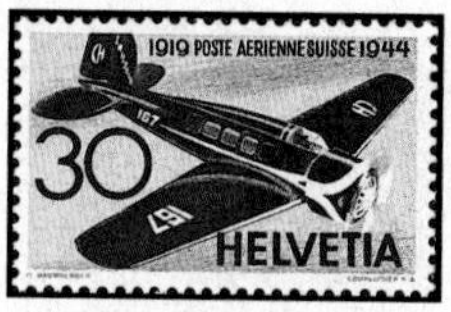

Lockheed-Orion — AP19

1944, Sept. 1

C37	AP17 10c gray brn & pale grn	.25	*.50*
C38	AP18 20c rose car & buff	.30	*.50*
C39	AP19 30c ultra & pale gray	.35	*1.25*
	Nos. C37-C39 (3)	.90	*2.25*
	Set, never hinged	1.50	

25th anniv. of the 1st regular air route in Switzerland.

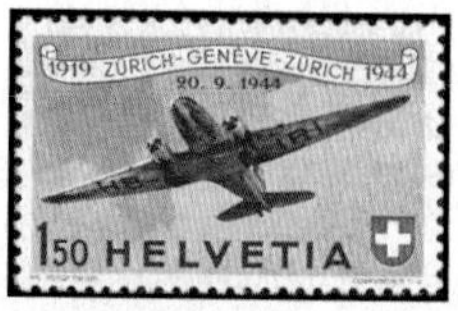

Douglas DC-3 AP20

1944, Sept. 20 **Granite Paper**

C40 AP20 1.50fr multi 5.50 *17.50*
Never hinged 11.00

25th anniv. of the Zurich-Geneva air route.

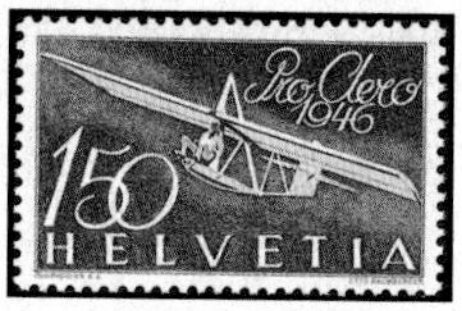

Zoegling Training Glider AP21

1946, May 1 **Granite Paper**

C41 AP21 1.50fr henna brn & gray 11.50 *27.50*
Never hinged 20.00

Valid for use only on two special flights.

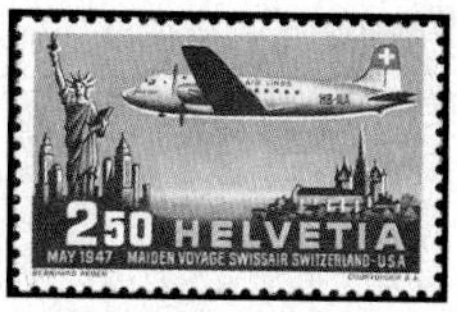

Douglas DC-4 Linking Geneva and New York AP22

1947, Mar. 17 **Granite Paper**

C42 AP22 2.50fr bl gray, dk bl & red 7.00 *20.00*
Never hinged 13.00

Valid only on the Geneva-New York flight of May 2, 1947.

Because of bad weather at NYC the flight ended at Washington.

Types of 1941

1948, Oct. 1 **Engr.**

Tinted Granite Paper

C43	AP8 30c dk slate bl	4.50	*12.50*
C44	AP8 40c deep ultra	21.00	2.75
	Set, never hinged	57.50	

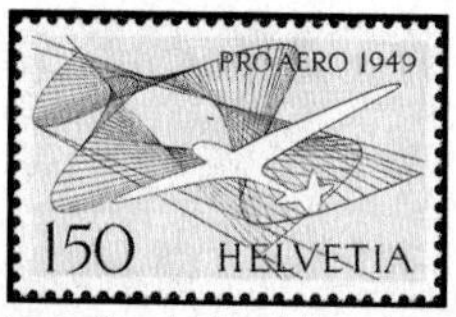

Glider in Symbolized Aerodynamic Buoyancy — AP23

1949, Apr. 11 **Engr. & Typo.**

C45 AP23 1.50fr dk vio & yel 16.00 *37.50*
Never hinged 30.00

Valid only on special flights, Apr. 27-29, 1949. Proceeds were for the advancement of national aviation.

Catalogue values for unused stamps in this section, from this point to the end of the section, are for Never Hinged items.

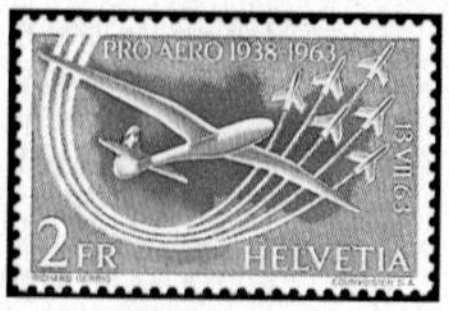

Glider and Jets AP24

1963, June 1 **Photo.** ***Perf. 11½***

Granite Paper

C46 AP24 2fr multicolored 4.00 3.50

50th anniversary of the first Alpine flight by Oscar Bider, July 13, 1913. Valid for postage on July 13, 1963, on flights from Bern to Locarno and Langenbruck to Bern. Proceeds went to the Pro Aero Foundation.

AIR POST SEMI-POSTAL STAMP

Catalogue values for unused stamps in this section are for Never Hinged items.

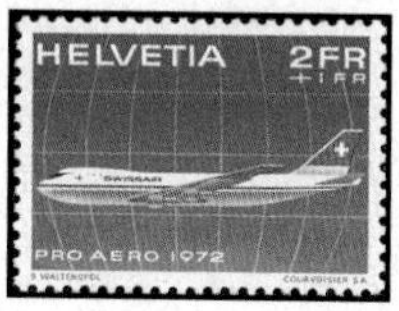

Boeing 747 — SPAP1

1972, Feb. 17 **Photo.** ***Perf. 12½***

Violet Fibers, Fluorescent Paper

CB1 SPAP1 2fr + 1fr dp bl, red & gray 4.50 2.25

50th anniv. of 1st Swiss Intl. flight, Zurich to Nuremberg, and 25th anniv. of 1st Swissair trans-Atlantic flight, Zurich to NYC. Valid on all mail but obligatory on special flights from Geneva to NYC in May, and from Geneva to Nuremberg in June, 1972.

Surtax was for Pro Aero Foundation and the training of young airmen, and for the Swiss Air Rescue Service.

POSTAGE DUE STAMPS

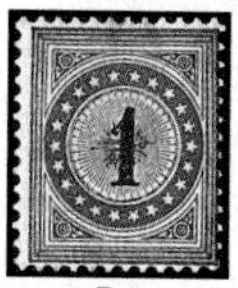

D1

D2

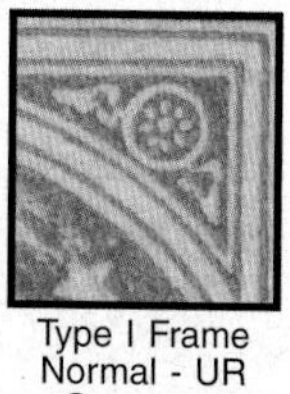

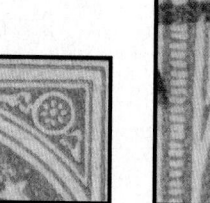

Type I Frame Normal - UR Ornament

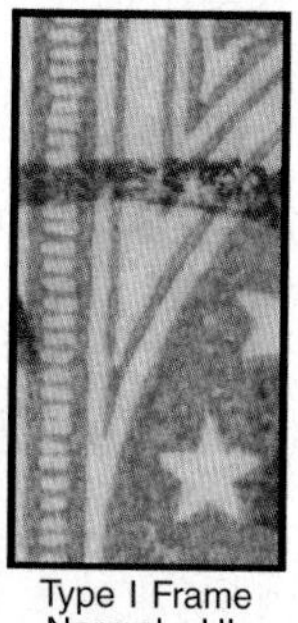

Type I Frame Normal - UL Triangle

Type I Frame Normal: Ornament at UR is undamaged. UL triangle tip and star tip align horizontally. LR triangle tip aligns horizontally with the center of the star.

Wmk. 182

1878-80 **Typo.** ***Perf. 11½***

Type I Frame Normal

J1	D1	1c ultra	2.75	2.50
J2	D2	2c ultra	2.75	2.50
J3	D2	3c ultra	22.50	25.00
J4	D2	5c ultra	25.00	12.50
J5	D2	10c ultra	275.00	10.50
J6	D2	20c ultra	300.00	9.00
J7	D2	50c ultra	575.00	27.50

J8 D2 100c ultra 750.00 25.00
J9 D2 500c ultra 700.00 40.00
Nos. J1-J9 (9) 2,653. 154.50

A 5c in design D1 exists.

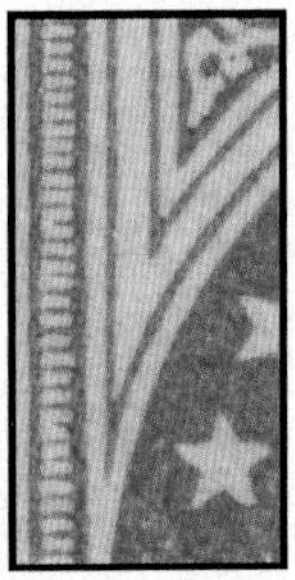

Type I Frame Inverted - UL Triangle

Type I Frame Inverted: Ornament at LL is undamaged. UL triangle tip aligns horizontally with star center. LR triangle tip and star tip align horizontally.

Wmk. 182

1878-80 Typo. *Perf. 11½*

Type I Frame Inverted

J1a 1c ultra 18.00 20.00
J2a 2c ultra 2.75 2.75
J3a 3c ultra 22.50 23.00
J4a 5c ultra 27.00 11.00
J5a 10c ultra 275.00 18.00
J6a 20c ultra 300.00 11.00
J7a 50c ultra 600.00 35.00
J8a 100c ultra 750.00 25.00
J9a 500c ultra 700.00 40.00
Nos. J1a-J9a (9) 2,695. 185.75

Type II Frame Normal - UR Ornament

Type II Frame Normal: Ornament at UR is broken with a white gap in center. UL triangle tip and star tip align horizontally. LR triangle tip aligns horizontally with the center of the star.

Wmk. 182

1878-80 Typo. *Perf. 11½*

Type II Frame Normal

J3b 3c ultra 18.00 17.00
J4b 5c ultra 25.00 22.50
J5b 10c ultra 250.00 10.00
J6b 20c ultra 300.00 8.00
J7b 50c ultra 600.00 30.00
J8b 100c ultra 1,500. 175.00
J9b 500c ultra 700.00 100.00
Nos. J3b-J9b (7) 3,393. 362.50

Type II Frame Inverted - LL Ornament

Type II Frame Inverted: Ornament at LL is broken with a white gap in center. UL triangle tip aligns horizontally with star center. LR triangle tip and star tip align horizontally.

Wmk. 182

1878-80 Typo. *Perf. 11½*

Type II Frame Inverted

J3c 3c ultra 21.00 20.00
J4c 5c ultra 22.50 11.50
J5c 10c ultra 275.00 11.00
J6c 20c ultra 325.00 11.00
J7c 50c ultra 600.00 35.00
J8c 100c ultra 2,250.
J9c 500c ultra 700.00 100.00
Nos. J3c-J9c (7) 1,943. 2,438.

Type II Frame Normal

1882-83 Granite Paper

J10 D2 10c ultra 240.00 57.50
J11 D2 20c ultra 575.00 80.00
J12 D2 50c ultra 3,200. 675.00
J13 D2 100c ultra 1,100. 500.00
J14 D2 500c ultra *21,000.* 325.00

1882-83 Granite Paper

Type II Frame Inverted

J10a 10c ultra 250.00 60.00
J11a 20c ultra 625.00 90.00
J12a 50c ultra 3,250. 800.00
J13a 100c ultra 1,200. 550.00
J14a 500c ultra *22,500.* 350.00

1883-84 Numerals in Red

Type II Frame Inverted

J15 D2 5c blue green 60.00 45.00
J16 D2 10c blue green 110.00 35.00
J17 D2 20c blue green 175.00 30.00
J18 D2 50c blue green 200.00 100.00
J19 D2 100c blue green 575.00 475.00
J20 D2 500c blue green 1,150. 275.00
Nos. J15-J20 (6) 2,270. 960.00

1883-84 Numerals in Red

Type II Frame Normal

J15a 5c blue green 175.00 105.00
J16a 10c blue green 275.00 100.00
J17a 20c blue green 500.00 90.00
J18a 50c blue green 550.00 300.00
J19a 100c blue green 1,500. 1,400.
J20a 500c blue green 2,750. 800.00

1884-97 Numerals in Red

Type II Frame Normal

J21 D2 1c olive green .90 .90
J22 D2 3c olive green 8.00 9.00
J23 D2 5c olive green 2.50 .90
a. 5c yellow green 45.00 15.00
J24 D2 10c olive green 6.75 1.50
a. 10c yellow green 110.00 16.00
J25 D2 20c olive green 13.00 2.25
a. 20c yellow green 190.00 12.00
J26 D2 50c olive green 20.00 5.00
a. 50c yellow green 400.00 125.00
J27 D2 100c olive green 22.50 4.00
a. 100c yellow green 425.00 160.00
J28 D2 500c olive green 175.00 225.00
a. 500c yellow green 800.00 60.00

Numerous shades of Nos. J21-J28 exist.

1908-09 Wmk. 183

Numerals in Red

J29 D2 1c olive green .30 1.10
J30 D2 5c olive green .60 .90
J31 D2 10c olive green 1.50 2.25
J32 D2 20c olive green 3.00 5.00
J33 D2 50c olive green 15.00 1.10
J34 D2 100c olive green 30.00 2.25
Nos. J29-J34 (6) 50.40 12.60

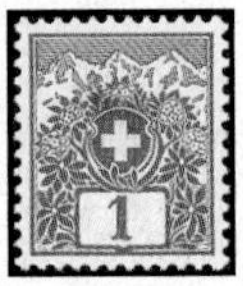

D3

1910 *Perf. 11½, 12*

Numerals in Red

J35 D3 1c blue green .25 .25
J36 D3 3c blue green .25 .25
J37 D3 5c blue green .25 .25
J38 D3 10c blue green 11.00 .25
J39 D3 15c blue green .65 1.10
J40 D3 20c blue green 17.50 .25
J41 D3 25c blue green 1.25 .65
J42 D3 30c blue green 1.25 .55
J43 D3 50c blue green 1.50 1.10
Nos. J35-J43 (9) 33.90 4.65

See Nos. S1-S12.

No. J36 Surcharged

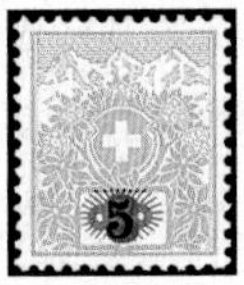

1916

J44 D3 5c on 3c bl grn & red .40 .25

Nos. J35-J36, J43 Surcharged

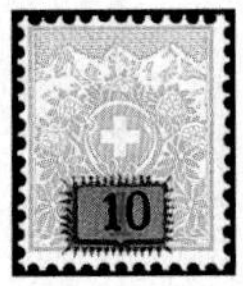

1924

J45 D3 10c on 1c .25 *8.25*
J46 D3 10c on 3c .25 *1.50*
J47 D3 20c on 50c .95 1.50
Nos. J45-J47 (3) 1.45 11.25

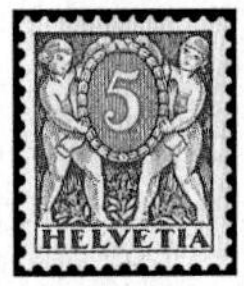

D4

Wmk. 183

1924-26 Typo. *Perf. 11½*

Granite Paper

J48 D4 5c ol grn & red .65 .25
J49 D4 10c ol grn & red 2.75 .25
J50 D4 15c ol grn & red ('26) 2.50 .55
J51 D4 20c ol grn & red 6.00 .25
J52 D4 25c ol grn & red 2.75 .55
J53 D4 30c ol grn & red 2.75 .85
J54 D4 40c ol grn & red ('26) 3.75 .70
J55 D4 50c ol grn & red 3.75 .70
Nos. J48-J55 (8) 24.90 4.10

1924 With Grilled Gum

J48a D4 5c olive green & red .65 .60
J49a D4 10c olive green & red 2.50 1.10
J51a D4 20c olive green & red 4.75 1.50
J52a D4 25c olive green & red 7.25 *65.00*
Nos. J48a-J52a (4) 15.15 *68.20*

See Grilled Gum note after No. 145.

Nos. J50, J53 & J55 Surcharged in Black

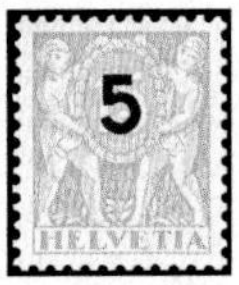

1937

J56 D4 5c on 15c .90 *4.25*
J57 D4 10c on 30c .90 *1.50*
J58 D4 20c on 50c 1.50 *5.00*
J59 D4 40c on 50c 2.50 *12.00*
Nos. J56-J59 (4) 5.80 *22.75*
Set, never hinged 10.50

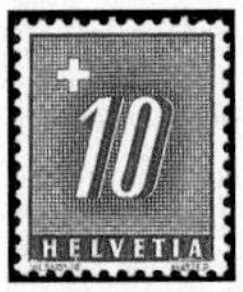

D5

1938 Engr. Unwmk.

J60 D5 5c scarlet .40 .25
J61 D5 10c scarlet .55 .25
J62 D5 15c scarlet 1.25 *2.25*
J63 D5 20c scarlet .95 .25
J64 D5 25c scarlet 1.40 *1.90*
J65 D5 30c scarlet 1.40 1.25
J66 D5 40c scarlet 1.60 .45
J67 D5 50c scarlet 1.90 2.25
Nos. J60-J67 (8) 9.45 *8.85*
Set, never hinged 19.00

1938 With Grilled Gum

J60a D5 5c scarlet .65 *1.60*
J61a D5 10c scarlet .65 *1.25*
J62a D5 15c scarlet 1.40 *2.50*
J63a D5 20c scarlet 1.25 .55
J64a D5 25c scarlet 1.40 *9.50*
J65a D5 30c scarlet 1.40 *2.25*
J66a D5 40c scarlet 2.10 2.10
J67a D5 50c scarlet 2.50 *3.50*
Nos. J60a-J67a (8) 11.35 *23.25*
Set, never hinged 29.00

See Grilled Gum note after No. 145.

OFFICIAL STAMPS

For General Use

With Perforated Cross

In 1935 the government authorized the use of regular postage issues perforated with a nine-hole cross for all government departments. Twenty-seven different stamps were so perforated. These were succeeded in 1938 by the cross overprints.

Values for canceled Official Stamps are for those canceled to order. Postally used stamps sell for considerably more. This note does not apply to Nos. 1O1-1O16, 2O27-2O30, 3O23-3O26.

Counterfeit overprints exist of most official stamps.

Official stamps without unused values were not made available to the public unused.

Regular Issues of 1908-36 Overprinted in Black

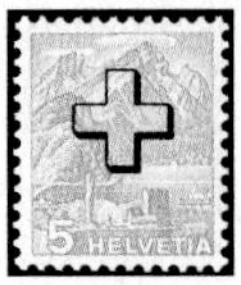

1938 Unwmk. *Perf. 11½*

O1 A53 3c olive .25 .25
O2 A54 5c blue green .25 .25
O3 A55 10c red violet .95 .45
O4 A56 15c orange .25 *1.60*
O5 A68 20c red .45 .25
O6 A58 25c brown .45 *1.40*
O7 A59 30c ultra .60 *1.00*
O8 A60 35c yellow green .60 *1.25*
O9 A61 40c gray .60 *1.00*

Wmk. 183

With Grilled Gum

O10 A25 50c dp grn & pale grn .60 *1.50*
O11 A25 60c brn org & buff 1.25 *2.50*
O12 A25 70c vio & buff 1.25 *4.25*
O13 A25 80c sl & buff 1.25 *3.25*
O14 A36 90c grn & red, *grn* 3.00 *3.25*
O15 A25 1fr dp cl & pale grn 1.50 *3.25*
O16 A36 1.20fr brn rose & red, *rose* 1.50 *4.50*
O17 A36 1.50fr bl & red, *bl* 2.50 *6.00*
O18 A36 2fr gray blk & red, *gray* 3.00 *7.00*
Nos. O1-O18 (18) 20.25 *42.95*
Set, never hinged 65.00

Nos. O14, O16, O17 and O18 are on surface-colored paper.

1938 Unwmk. With Grilled Gum

O1a A53 3c olive 4.50 .45
O2a A54 5c blue green 1.25 .45
O3a A55 10c red violet 1.50 .55
O4a A56 15c orange 2.75 1.25
O5a A68 20c red 1.50 .70
O6a A58 25c brown 75.00 7.75
O7a A59 30c ultra 2.50 1.10
O8a A60 35c yellow green 1.90 1.90
O9a A61 40c gray 2.50 1.00
Nos. O1a-O9a (9) 93.40 15.15
Set, never hinged 190.00

See Grilled Gum note after No. 145.

Postage Stamps of 1936-42 Overprinted in Black

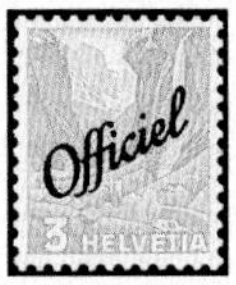

1942-45 Unwmk. *Perf. 11½*

O19 A53 3c olive .30 *2.10*
O20 A54 5c blue green .30 .25
O21 A55 10c dk red brn .55 .55
O21A A55 10c org brn ('45) .25 *.45*
O22 A56 15c orange .60 *1.90*
O23 A68 20c red .60 .45
O24 A58 25c lt brown .60 *2.25*
O25 A59 30c ultra .95 .90
O26 A60 35c yellow grn 1.25 *2.75*
O27 A61 40c gray 1.25 .60
O28 A77 50c dp pur, *grnsh* 3.75 *4.25*
O29 A78 60c red brn, *buff* 4.50 4.25
O30 A79 70c rose vio, *pale lil* 5.00 *8.25*
O31 A80 80c blk, *pale gray* 1.40 *1.60*
O32 A81 90c dk red, *pale rose* 1.60 *2.25*
O33 A82 1fr dk grn, *grnsh* 1.60 1.60
O34 A83 1.20fr red vio, *pale gray* 2.25 *2.75*
O35 A84 1.50fr dk bl, *buff* 2.25 *3.25*
O36 A85 2fr mar, *pale rose* 3.25 *4.00*
Nos. O19-O36 (19) 32.25 *44.40*
Set, never hinged 60.00

Same Overprint on Nos. 329-339

1950 Unwmk. *Perf. 12x11½*

O37 A118 5c orange .40 *.55*
O38 A119 10c yellow grn .65 .55
O39 A120 15c aqua 5.50 *15.00*
O40 A121 20c brown car 2.10 .65
O41 A122 25c red 3.25 *8.25*
O42 A123 30c olive 2.50 *3.25*
O43 A124 35c red brown 3.50 *11.00*
O44 A125 40c deep blue 2.75 *3.25*
O45 A126 50c slate gray 4.50 *5.75*
O46 A127 60c blue green 5.50 *7.75*
O47 A128 70c purple 16.00 *22.50*
Nos. O37-O47 (11) 46.65 *78.50*
Set, never hinged 77.50

FOR THE WAR BOARD OF TRADE

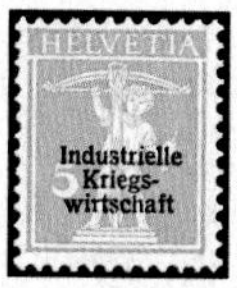

Regular Issues of 1908-18 Overprinted

1918 Wmk. 183 *Perf. 11½, 12*

1O1 A26 3c brown org 110.00 *225.00*
1O2 A26 5c green 10.00 *32.50*
1O3 A26 7½c gray (I) 300.00 *450.00*
a. 7½c slate (II) 550.00 *950.00*
1O4 A28 10c red, *buff* 15.00 *40.00*
1O5 A28 15c vio, *buff* 12.50 *45.00*
1O6 A25 20c red & yel 125.00 *500.00*
1O7 A25 25c dp bl 125.00 *500.00*
1O8 A25 30c yel brn & pale grn 125.00 *450.00*
Nos. 1O1-1O8 (8) 822.50 *2,242.*

Most unused examples of Nos. 1O1-1O8 are reprints made using the original overprint forms.

Counterfeits exist.

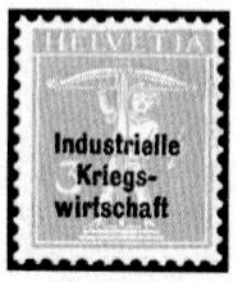

Overprinted

1918

1O9 A26 3c brn org 4.25 *35.00*
1O10 A26 5c green 12.00 *52.50*
1O11 A26 7½c gray 4.50 *22.50*
1O12 A28 10c red, *buff* 45.00 *87.50*
1O13 A28 15c vio, *buff* 82.50
1O14 A25 20c red & yel 8.75 *52.50*
1O15 A25 25c dp blue 8.75 *52.50*
1O16 A25 30c yel brn & pale grn 14.50 *87.50*
Nos. 1O9-1O16 (8) 180.25 390.00

No. 1O13 was never placed in use.

Fraudulent cancellations are found on Nos. 1O1-1O16.

FOR THE LEAGUE OF NATIONS

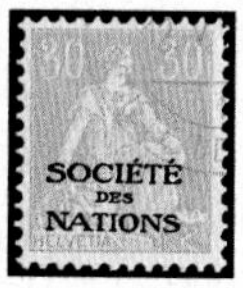

Regular Issues Overprinted

On 1908-30 Issues

1922-31 Wmk. 183 *Perf. 11½, 12*

2O1 A26 2½c ol, *buff* ('28) .45
2O2 A26 3c ultra, *buff* ('30) 8.25
2O3 A26 5c orange, *buff* 5.50
2O4 A26 5c gray vio, *buff* ('26) 2.75
2O5 A26 5c red vio, *buff* ('27) 2.25
2O6 A26 5c dk grn, *buff* ('31) 25.00
2O7 A26 7½c dp grn, *buff* ('28) .55
2O8 A28 10c green, *buff* .55
2O9 A28 10c bl grn, *buff* ('28) 1.10
2O10 A28 10c vio, *buff* ('31) 2.75
2O11 A28 15c brn red, *buff* ('28) 1.10
2O12 A28 20c red vio, *buff* 8.25
2O13 A28 20c car, *buff* ('26) 2.25
2O14 A28 25c ver, *buff* 8.25
2O15 A28 25c car, *buff* 1.10
2O16 A28 25c brn, *buff* ('27) 17.00
2O17 A28 30c dp bl, *buff* ('25) 8.25
2O18 A25 30c yel brn & pale grn 14.00
2O19 A25 35c yel grn & yel 10.00
2O20 A25 40c deep blue 1.40
2O21 A25 40c red vio & grn ('28) 14.00
2O22 A25 50c dp grn & pale grn 11.00
2O23 A25 60c brn org & buff 30.00 1.60
2O24 A25 70c vio & buff ('25) 26.00
2O25 A25 80c slate & buff 2.75
2O26 A25 1fr dp cl & pale grn 6.75
2O27 A29 3fr red 32.50
2O28 A30 5fr ultra 60.00
2O29 A31 10fr dull violet 140.00
2O30 A31 10fr gray grn ('30) 140.00
Nos. 2O1-2O30 (30) 555.35

1930-44 With Grilled Gum

2O2a A26 3c ultra, *buff* ('33) 10.00
2O6a A26 5c dk grn, *buff* ('33) 19.00
2O17a A28 30c dp bl,*buff* 425.00
2O22a A25 50c dp grn & pale grn ('35) .90 2.25
2O23a A25 60c brn org & buff ('44) 25.00 *225.00*
2O24a A25 70c violet & buff ('32) 1.60 2.25
2O25a A25 80c slate & buff ('42) 2.75 2.50
2O26a A25 1fr dp cl & pale grn ('42) 5.25

1935-36 With Grilled Gum

2O31 A36 90c grn & red, *grn* ('36) 5.00
2O32 A36 1.20fr brn rose & red, *rose* ('36) 2.75 *4.50*
b. Inverted overprint *4,250.*
2O33 A36 1.50fr bl & red, *bl* 2.75 *4.50*
2O34 A36 2fr gray blk & red, *gray* ('36) 2.75 *5.25*

1922-25 Ordinary Gum

2O31a A36 90c 14.00
2O32a A36 1.20fr ('25) 14.00
2O33a A36 1.50fr ('25) 13.00
2O34a A36 2fr ('25) 12.00

1928

2O35 A39 5fr blue 87.50

1932 On 1932 Issue

2O36 A41 5c peacock bl 19.00
2O37 A41 10c orange 1.60
2O38 A41 20c cerise 1.60
2O39 A41 30c ultra 55.00
2O40 A41 60c olive brn 15.00

Unwmk.

2O41 A42 1fr ol gray & bl 15.00
Nos. 2O36-2O41 (6) 107.20

On 1934 Issue

1934-35 Wmk. 183

2O42 A46 3c olive .25
2O43 A47 5c emerald .65
2O44 A49 15c orange ('35) 1.50
2O45 A51 25c brown 19.00
2O46 A52 30c ultra 1.60
Nos. 2O42-2O46 (5) 23.00

1937 On 1936 Issue Unwmk.

2O47 A53 3c olive .25 .25
2O48 A54 5c blue green .25 .25
2O49 A55 10c red violet 1.10
2O50 A56 15c orange .45 .55
2O51 A57 20c carmine 1.90
2O52 A58 25c brown .65 1.10
2O53 A59 30c ultra .65 1.00
2O54 A60 35c yellow green .65 1.00
2O55 A61 40c gray .95 1.25
Nos. 2O47-2O55 (9) 8.40

1937 With Grilled Gum

2O47a A53 3c olive .30
2O48a A54 5c blue green .45
2O49a A55 10c red violet 6.25
2O50a A56 15c orange .70
2O51a A57 20c carmine 2.25
2O52a A58 25c brown 1.40
2O53a A59 30c ultra 1.10
2O54a A60 35c yellow green 4.25
2O55a A61 40c gray 4.25
Nos. 2O47a-2O55a (9) 20.95

1937 On 1931 Issue Wmk. 183

2O56 A40 3fr orange brown 190.00

On 1938 Issue

1938 Unwmk. *Perf. 11½*

Granite Paper

2O57 A63 20c red & buff 1.90
2O58 A64 30c blue & lt blue 3.00
2O59 A65 60c brown & buff 5.75
2O60 A66 1fr black & buff 9.25
Nos. 2O57-2O60 (4) 19.90

Regular Issue of 1938 Overprinted in Black or Red

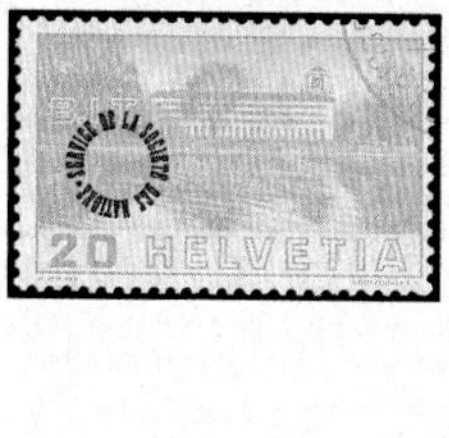

Granite Paper

2O61 A63 20c red & buff 2.25
2O62 A64 30c blue & lt blue 4.00
2O63 A65 60c brown & buff 7.25
2O64 A66 1fr black & buff (R) 12.50
Nos. 2O61-2O64 (4) 26.00

Regular Issue of 1938 Overprinted in Black

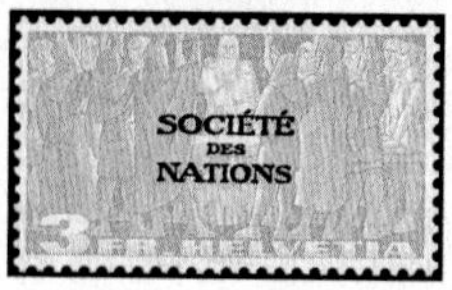

1939

2O65 A69 3fr brn car, *buff* 3.25 *11.00*
2O66 A70 5fr slate bl, *buff* 5.50 *15.00*
2O67 A71 10fr green, *buff* 11.00 *32.50*
Nos. 2O65-2O67 (3) 19.75 *58.50*

Same Overprint in Black on Regular Issues of 1939-42

1942-43

2O68 A55 10c dk red brown .85
2O68A A55 10c orange brn ('43) .40 *.85*
2O69 A68 20c red .50 *1.00*
Nos. 2O68-2O69 (3) *2.70*

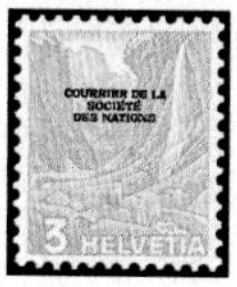

Stamps of 1936-42 Overprinted in Black

1944

2O70 A53 3c olive .25 *.25*
2O71 A54 5c blue green .25 *.25*
2O72 A55 10c orange brown .80 .40
2O73 A56 15c orange .25 *.50*
2O74 A68 20c red .40 *.75*
2O75 A58 25c lt brown .40 *1.00*
2O76 A59 30c ultra .50 *1.00*
2O77 A60 35c yellow green .50 *1.00*
2O78 A61 40c gray .55 *1.25*

Nos. 2O73-2O75 and 2O78 exist with grilled gum. Value each $2,000 unused, $2,250 used.

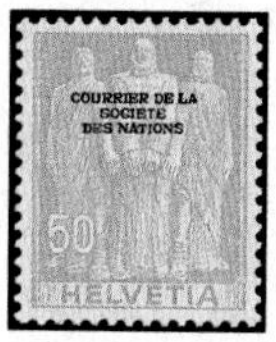

Stamps of 1941 Overprinted in Black

2O79 A77 50c dp pur, *grnsh* 1.00 *1.75*
2O80 A78 60c red brn, *buff* 1.25 *2.50*
2O81 A79 70c rose vio, *pale lil* 1.25 *2.50*
2O82 A80 80c blk, *pale gray* 1.10 *2.00*
2O83 A81 90c dk red, *pale rose* 1.10 *2.00*
2O84 A82 1fr dk grn, *grnsh* 1.10 *2.25*
2O85 A83 1.20fr red vio, *pale gray* 1.75 *3.00*
2O86 A84 1.50fr dk bl, *buff* 2.00 *3.50*
2O87 A85 2fr mar, *pale rose* 2.50 *4.00*

Stamps of 1942 Overprinted in Black

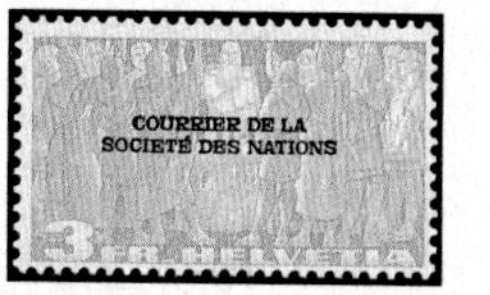

Unwmk. *Perf. 11½*

2O88 A69 3fr brn car, *cr* 4.50 *9.00*
2O89 A70 5fr slate bl, *cr* 7.00 *12.50*
2O90 A71 10fr green, *cr* 12.00 *24.00*
Nos. 2O70-2O90 (21) 40.45 *75.40*
Set, never hinged 65.00

FOR THE INTERNATIONAL LABOR BUREAU

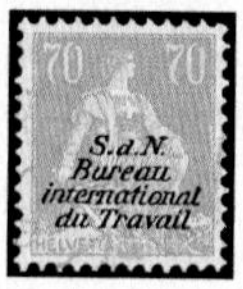

Regular Issues Overprinted

On 1908-30 Issues

1923-30 Wmk. 183 *Perf. 11½, 12*

3O1 A26 2½c ol grn, *buff* ('28) .30
3O2 A26 3c ultra, *buff* ('30) 1.10
3O3 A26 5c org, *buff* .55
3O4 A26 5c red vio, *buff* ('28) .25
3O5 A26 7½c dp grn, *buff* ('28) .45
3O6 A28 10c grn, *buff* .55
3O7 A28 10c bl grn, *buff* ('28) 1.10
3O8 A28 15c brn red, *buff* ('28) 1.10
3O9 A28 20c red vio, *buff* 17.00
3O10 A28 20c car, *buff* ('27) 5.00
3O11 A28 25c car, *buff* 1.25
3O12 A28 25c brn, *buff* ('28) 3.00
3O13 A28 30c dp bl, *buff* ('25) 2.50
3O14 A25 30c yel brn & pale grn 65.00
3O15 A25 35c yel grn & yel 11.00
3O16 A25 40c deep blue 1.25
3O17 A25 40c red vio & grn ('28) 17.00
3O18 A25 50c dp grn & pale grn 5.00
3O19 A25 60c brn org & buff 1.60 *1.90*
3O20 A25 70c vio & buff ('24) 26.00
3O21 A25 80c slate & buff 14.00 2.25
3O22 A25 1fr dp cl & pale grn 2.75
3O23 A29 3fr red 25.00
3O24 A30 5fr ultra 37.50
3O25 A31 10fr dull violet 150.00
3O26 A31 10fr gray grn ('30) 150.00
Nos. 3O1-3O26 (26) 528.80

1937-44 With Grilled Gum

3O18a A25 50c dp grn & pale grn ('42) 1.75 2.25
3O20a A25 70c vio & buff 1.75 2.25
3O21a A25 80c slate & buff ('44) 25.00 *175.00*
3O22a A25 1fr dp cl & pale grn ('42) 3.25

1925-42 With Grilled Gum

3O27 A36 90c grn & red, *grn* ('37) 9.75
a. Ordinary gum 5.00
3O28 A36 1.20fr brn rose & red, *rose* ('42) 14.00 4.00
a. Ordinary gum 4.50
3O29 A36 1.50fr bl & red, *bl* ('37) 2.75 *3.00*
a. Ordinary gum 14.00
3O30 A36 2fr gray blk & red, *gray* ('36) 3.25 *6.25*
a. Ordinary gum 32.50
Nos. 3O27-3O30 (4) 23.00

1928

3O31 A39 5fr blue 82.50

1932 On 1932 Issue

3O32 A41 5c peacock blue 1.10
3O33 A41 10c orange .90
3O34 A41 20c cerise 1.25
3O35 A41 30c ultra 7.75
3O36 A41 60c olive brown 7.75

Unwmk.

3O37 A42 1fr ol gray & bl 10.00
Nos. 3O32-3O37 (6) 28.75

1937 On 1936 Issue

3O38 A53 3c olive .25 .55
3O39 A54 5c blue green .25 .55
3O40 A55 10c red violet 2.75
3O41 A56 15c orange .45 1.10
3O42 A57 20c carmine 2.25
3O43 A58 25c brown .60 *1.40*
3O44 A59 30c ultra .60 *1.10*
3O45 A60 35c yellow green .60 *1.60*
3O46 A61 40c gray .95 *1.90*
Nos. 3O38-3O46 (9) 3.70 *13.20*

1937 With Grilled Gum

3O38a	A53	3c olive	1.10	
3O39a	A54	5c blue green	1.10	
3O40a	A55	10c red violet	1.60	
3O41a	A56	15c orange	1.90	
3O42a	A57	20c carmine	1.60	
3O43a	A58	25c brown	2.25	
3O44a	A59	30c ultra	2.25	
3O45a	A60	35c yellow green	2.75	
3O46a	A61	40c gray	2.25	
		Nos. 3O38a-3O46a (9)	16.80	

1937 On 1931 Issue Wmk. 183

3O47	A40	3fr orange brown	175.00	

On 1934 Issue

3O48	A46	3c olive	5.50	

On 1938 Issue
Granite Paper

1938 Unwmk. *Perf. 11½*

3O49	A63	20c red & buff	1.60	
3O50	A64	30c blue & lt blue	3.25	
3O51	A65	60c brown & buff	6.00	
3O52	A66	1fr black & buff	8.75	
		Nos. 3O49-3O52 (4)	19.60	

Regular Issue of 1938 Overprinted in Black or Red

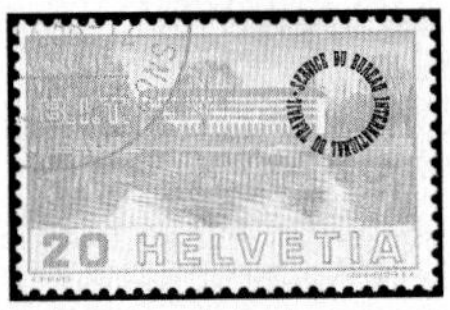

3O53	A63	20c red & buff (Bk)	3.25	
3O54	A64	30c bl & lt bl (Bk)	3.25	
3O55	A65	60c brn & buff (Bk)	6.50	
3O56	A66	1fr blk & buff (R)	7.00	
		Nos. 3O53-3O56 (4)	20.00	

Regular Issue of 1938 Overprinted in Black

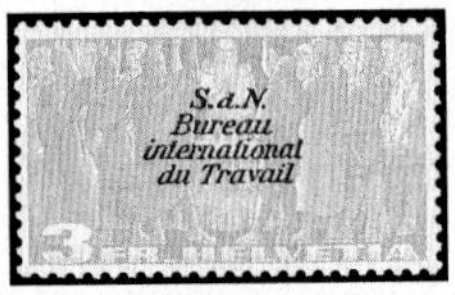

1939

3O57	A69	3fr brn car, *buff*	4.50	*8.25*
3O58	A70	5fr slate bl, *buff*	5.50	*17.00*
3O59	A71	10fr green, *buff*	10.00	*30.00*
		Nos. 3O57-3O59 (3)	20.00	*55.25*

Same Overprint in Black on Regular Issues of 1939-42

1942-43

3O60	A55	10c dark red brown		.80
3O60A	A55	10c orange brn ('43)	.50	*.80*
3O61	A68	20c red	.55	*.80*
		Nos. 3O60-3O61 (3)		*2.40*

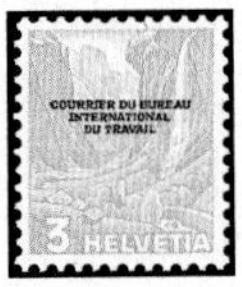

Stamps of 1936-42 Overprinted in Black

1944

3O62	A53	3c olive	.25	.25
3O63	A54	5c blue green	.25	.25
3O64	A55	10c orange brn	.25	.25
3O65	A56	15c orange	.50	.50
3O66	A68	20c red	.35	*.50*
3O67	A58	25c lt brown	.55	*.70*
3O68	A59	30c ultra	.50	*1.10*
3O69	A60	35c yellow grn	.70	*1.25*
3O70	A61	40c gray	.75	*1.40*

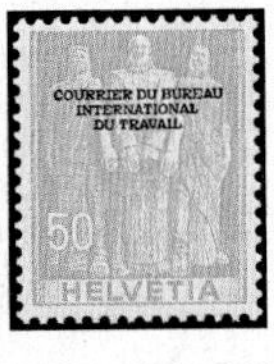

Stamps of 1941 Overprinted

3O71	A77	50c dp pur, *grnsh*	1.50	*8.00*
3O72	A78	60c red brn, *buff*	1.50	*8.00*
3O73	A79	70c rose vio, *pale lil*	1.75	*8.00*
3O74	A80	80c blk, *pale gray*	.45	*1.40*
3O75	A81	90c dk red, *pale rose*	.45	*1.40*
3O76	A82	1fr dk grn, *grnsh*	.45	*1.40*
3O77	A83	1.20fr red vio, *pale gray*	.75	*1.75*
3O78	A84	1.50fr dull bl, *buff*	1.00	*2.25*
3O79	A85	2fr mar, *pale rose*	1.25	*3.00*

Stamps of 1942 Overprinted

3O80	A69	3fr brown car, *cr*	3.25	*6.00*
3O81	A70	5fr slate blue, *cr*	5.00	*10.50*
3O82	A71	10fr green, *cr*	10.00	*20.00*
		Nos. 3O62-3O82 (21)	31.45	*77.90*
		Set, never hinged	60.00	

Nos. 329-339 Overprinted in Black

1950 Unwmk. *Perf. 12x11½*

3O83	A118	5c orange	4.00	*4.75*
3O84	A119	10c yellow green	4.00	*5.25*
3O85	A120	15c aqua	5.00	*7.50*
3O86	A121	20c brn car	5.00	*7.50*
3O87	A122	25c red	6.00	*7.75*
3O88	A123	30c olive	6.00	*7.75*
3O89	A124	35c red brown	6.00	*7.75*
3O90	A125	40c deep blue	6.00	*7.75*
3O91	A126	50c slate gray	7.50	*8.25*
3O92	A127	60c blue green	9.00	*12.50*
3O93	A128	70c purple	10.00	*17.50*
		Nos. 3O83-3O93 (11)	68.50	*94.25*
		Set, never hinged	110.00	

Catalogue values for unused stamps in this section, from this point to the end of the section, are for Never Hinged items.

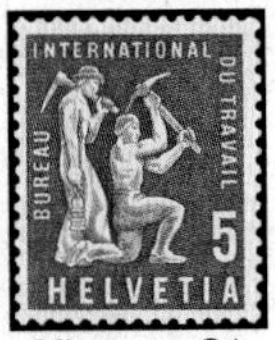

Miners — O1

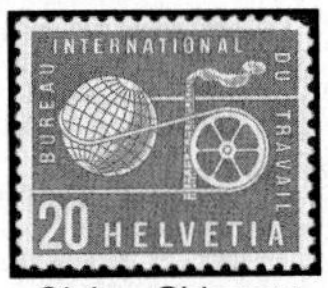

Globe, Chimney and Wheel — O2

1956-60 Unwmk. Engr. *Perf. 11½*

3O94	O1	5c dark gray	.25	.25
3O95	O1	10c green	.25	.25
3O96	O2	20c vermilion	1.25	*2.25*
3O97	O2	20c car rose ('60)	.25	.25
3O98	O2	30c orange ver ('60)	.25	*.40*
3O99	O1	40c blue	1.25	*2.75*
3O100	O1	50c lt ultra ('60)	.25	*.50*
3O101	O2	60c reddish brown	.30	*.50*
3O102	O2	2fr rose violet	1.10	*1.50*
		Nos. 3O94-3O102 (9)	5.15	*8.65*

Type of 1960 Overprinted: "Visite du / Pape Paul VI / Genève / 10 juin 1969"
Violet Fibers, Fluorescent Paper

1969, June 10

3O103	O2	30c orange vermilion	.30	.30

Visit of Pope Paul VI to the Intl. Labor Bureau to celebrate its 50th anniv., Geneva, June 10.

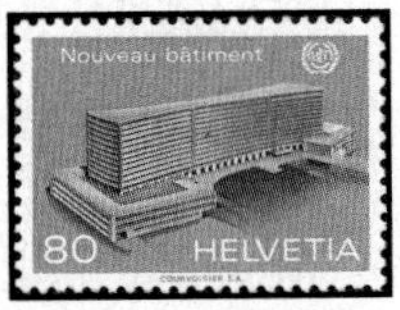

ILO Headquarters, Geneva — O3

Violet Fibers, Fluorescent Paper

1974, May 30 Photo. *Perf. 11½*

3O104	O3	80c blue, yel & gray	1.90	.80

Inauguration of the new International Labor Organization Building.

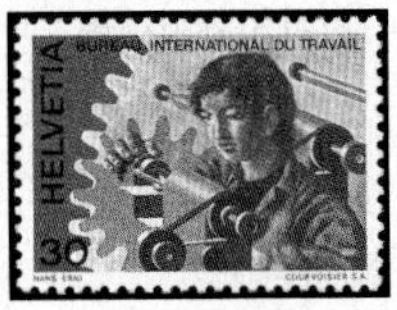

Young Man at Lathe, Cogwheels O4

Designs: 60c, Woman at drilling machine. 90c, Welder and lab assistant using protective devices and clothing. 100c, Surveyor with theodolite and topographical map. 120c, Professional education for youth.

1975-88 Photo. *Perf. 11½*

3O105	O4	30c red brn & dk brn	.70	.30
3O106	O4	60c ultra & blk	1.40	.60
3O107	O4	100c dk green & blk	2.25	1.00
3O108	O4	120c multicolored	2.75	1.25

Perf. 12x11½

3O109	O4	90c multicolored	2.10	1.00
		Nos. 3O105-3O109 (5)	9.20	4.15

Issued: 30c-100c, 2/13; 120c, 8/22/83; 90c, 9/13/88.

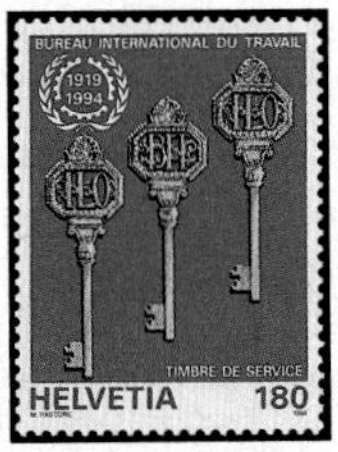

ILO, 75th Anniv. — O5

1994, May 17 Litho. *Perf. 13*

3O110	O5	180c multicolored	2.00	2.00

FOR THE INTERNATIONAL BUREAU OF EDUCATION

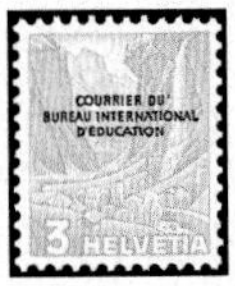

Regular Issues of 1936-42, Overprinted in Black

1944 Unwmk. *Perf. 11½*

4O1	A53	3c olive	.40	*1.00*
4O2	A54	5c blue grn	.55	*1.25*
4O3	A55	10c orange brn	.55	*1.50*
4O4	A56	15c orange	.55	*1.50*
4O5	A68	20c red	.55	*1.50*
4O6	A58	25c lt brown	.65	*1.75*
4O7	A59	30c ultra	.85	*2.25*
4O8	A60	35c yellow grn	.85	*2.25*
4O9	A61	40c gray	1.10	*2.50*

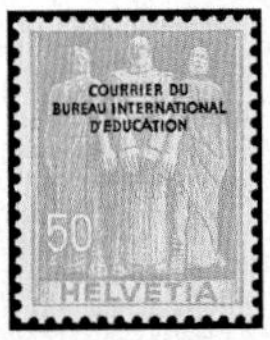

Regular Issue of 1941, Overprinted in Black

4O10	A77	50c dp pur, *grnsh*	5.00	*13.00*
4O11	A78	60c red brn, *buff*	5.00	*13.00*
4O12	A79	70c rose vio, *pale lil*	5.00	*13.00*
4O13	A80	80c blk, *pale gray*	.60	*1.50*
4O14	A81	90c dk red, *pale rose*	.70	*1.75*
4O15	A82	1fr dk grn, *grnsh*	.85	*2.25*
4O16	A83	1.20fr red vio, *pale gray*	1.00	*2.50*
4O17	A84	1.50fr dk bl, *buff*	1.25	*3.00*
4O18	A85	2fr mar, *pale rose*	1.60	*4.00*

Regular Issue of 1942, Overprinted in Black

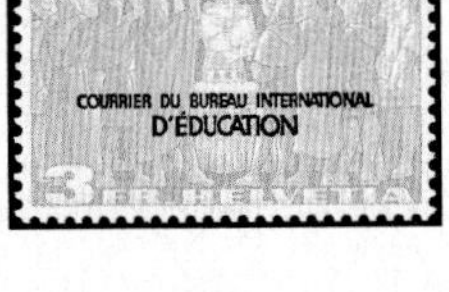

4O19	A69	3fr brn car, *cr*	7.00	*17.00*
4O20	A70	5fr slate bl, *cr*	10.00	*25.00*
4O21	A71	10fr green, *cr*	15.00	*40.00*
		Nos. 4O1-4O21 (21)	59.05	*151.50*
		Set, never hinged	110.00	

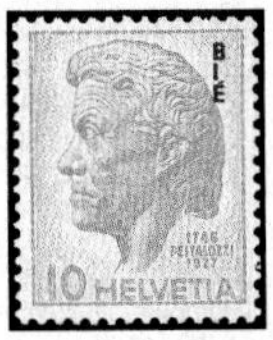

No. 306 Overprinted in Carmine

1946

4O22	A104	10c rose violet	.25	*.50*
		Never hinged	.50	

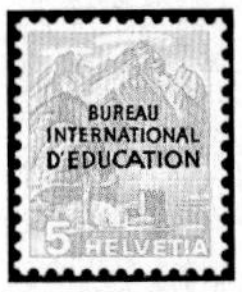

Nos. 316-321 Overprinted in Black

1948 Unwmk. *Perf. 11½*

4O23	A54	5c chocolate	1.75	*3.00*
4O24	A55	10c green	1.75	*3.00*
4O25	A68	20c orange brn	1.75	*3.00*
4O26	A113	25c carmine	1.75	*3.00*
4O27	A59	30c grnsh blue	2.00	*3.00*
4O28	A61	40c ultra	2.00	*3.00*
		Nos. 4O23-4O28 (6)	11.00	18.00
		Set, never hinged	20.00	

Same Overprint on Nos. 329-339

1950 *Perf. 12x11½*

Overprint 18mm wide

4O29	A118	5c orange	.65	*1.75*
4O30	A119	10c yellow grn	.65	*2.10*
4O31	A120	15c aqua	.65	*2.10*
4O32	A121	20c brown car	2.00	*5.75*
4O33	A122	25c red	4.50	*10.50*
4O34	A123	30c olive	4.50	*10.50*
4O35	A124	35c red brn	3.50	*8.75*
4O36	A125	40c deep blue	3.50	*8.75*
4O37	A126	50c slate gray	4.00	*9.75*
4O38	A127	60c blue green	4.75	*11.50*
4O39	A128	70c purple	5.50	*13.50*
		Nos. 4O29-4O39 (11)	34.20	*84.95*
		Set, never hinged	60.00	

Catalogue values for unused stamps in this section, from this point to the end of the section, are for Never Hinged items.

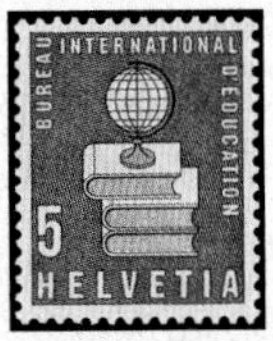

Globe and Books — O1

Designs: 20c, 30c, 60c, 2fr, Pestalozzi Monument at Yverdon.

1958-60 Engr. *Perf. 11½*

4O40	O1	5c dark gray	.25	.25
4O41	O1	10c green	.25	.25
4O42	O1	20c vermilion	2.25	2.25
4O43	O1	20c car rose ('60)	.25	.25
4O44	O1	30c org ver ('60)	.25	*.35*
4O45	O1	40c blue	2.75	2.75
4O46	O1	50c lt ultra ('60)	.30	*.50*
4O47	O1	60c reddish brn	.30	*.50*
4O48	O1	2fr rose violet	1.10	*1.50*
		Nos. 4O40-4O48 (9)	7.70	8.60

FOR THE WORLD HEALTH ORGANIZATION

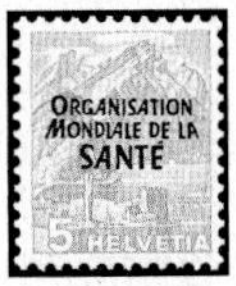

No. 316-319, 321 Overprinted in Black

1948 Unwmk. *Perf. 11½*

5O1	A54	5c chocolate	2.25	*2.50*
5O2	A55	10c green	2.25	*3.50*
5O3	A68	20c orange brn	2.25	*3.50*
5O4	A113	25c carmine	2.25	*4.50*
5O5	A61	40c ultra	2.50	*5.00*
		Nos. 5O1-5O5 (5)	11.50	*19.00*
		Set, never hinged	20.00	

Regular Issues of 1941, 1942 and 1949 Overprinted in Black

1948-50

5O6	A118	5c orange	.50	1.00
5O7	A119	10c yellow grn	.65	1.50
5O8	A120	15c aqua	.90	2.00
5O9	A121	20c brown car	2.25	6.00
5O10	A122	25c red	2.25	6.00
5O11	A123	30c olive	1.50	5.00
5O12	A124	35c red brown	2.10	7.00
5O13	A125	40c deep blue	2.10	3.50
5O14	A126	50c slate gray	2.25	6.00
5O15	A127	60c blue green	2.50	7.00
5O16	A128	70c purple	3.00	7.00
5O17	A80	80c blk, *pale gray* ('48)	2.00	3.75
5O18	A81	90c dk red, *pale rose*	4.25	8.50
5O19	A82	1fr dk grn, *grnsh* ('48)	2.50	4.50
5O20	A83	1.20fr red vio, *pale gray*	5.50	12.00
5O21	A84	1.50fr dk bl, *buff*	11.00	12.00
5O22	A85	2fr mar, *pale rose* ('48)	3.50	6.50
5O23	A69	3fr brn car, *cr*	22.50	37.50
5O24	A70	5fr sl bl, *cr* ('48)	7.50	11.50
5O25	A71	10fr grn, *cr*	45.00	65.00
		Nos. 5O6-5O25 (20)	123.75	213.25
		Set, never hinged	250.00	

> **Catalogue values for unused stamps in this section, from this point to the end of the section, are for Never Hinged items.**

WHO Emblem — O2

1957-60 Unwmk. Engr. Perf. 11½

5O26	O2	5c gray	.25	.25
5O27	O2	10c lt grn	.25	.25
5O28	O2	20c vermilion	2.25	2.25
5O29	O2	20c car rose ('60)	.25	.25
5O30	O2	30c org ver ('60)	.35	.35
5O31	O2	40c blue	2.75	2.75
5O32	O2	50c lt ultra ('60)	.50	.50
5O33	O2	60c red brn	.50	.50
5O34	O2	2fr rose lilac	1.50	1.50
		Nos. 5O26-5O34 (9)	8.60	8.60

No. 5O32 Overprinted

1962, Mar. 19

5O35	O2	50c lt ultra	.75	.75

WHO drive to eradicate malaria.

World Health Organization Emblem — O3

1975-95 Typo. Perf. 11½

5O36	O3	30c multi	.70	.30
5O37	O3	10c lt bl & multi	1.40	.30
5O38	O3	90c lilac & multi	2.10	.90
5O39	O3	100c orange & multi	2.25	1.00

Litho. Perf. 12

5O40	O3	140c lt grn, scar & grn	3.25	1.50

Perf. 13½x13

5O41	O3	180c multicolored	4.25	2.10
		Nos. 5O36-5O41 (6)	13.95	6.10

Issued: 140c, 5/27/86; 180c, 11/28/95; others, 2/13/75.

FOR THE INTERNATIONAL ORGANIZATION FOR REFUGEES

Stamps of 1941 and 1949 Overprinted in Black

1950 Unwmk. Perf. 12x11½, 11½

6O1	A118	5c orange	11.00	14.00
6O2	A119	10c yellow green	11.00	14.00
6O3	A121	20c brn car	11.00	14.00
6O4	A122	25c red	11.00	14.00
6O5	A125	40c deep blue	11.00	14.00
6O6	A80	80c blk, *pale gray*	11.00	14.00
6O7	A82	1fr dk grn, *grnsh*	11.00	14.00
6O8	A85	2fr mar, *pale rose*	11.00	14.00
		Nos. 6O1-6O8 (8)	88.00	112.00
		Set, never hinged	150.00	

FOR THE UNITED NATIONS EUROPEAN OFFICE

See No. 513 for postage issue commemorating the United Nations.

Stamps of 1941-49 Overprinted in Black

1950 Unwmk. Perf. 12x11½, 11½

7O1	A118	5c orange	.25	2.25
7O2	A119	10c yellow grn	.35	2.25
7O3	A120	15c aqua	.55	3.00
7O4	A121	20c brown car	.85	4.25
7O5	A122	25c red	1.10	7.50
7O6	A123	30c olive	1.40	7.50
7O7	A124	35c red brown	1.40	7.50
7O8	A125	40c deep blue	2.10	8.75
7O9	A126	50c slate gray	2.50	10.50
7O10	A127	60c blue green	2.75	12.50
7O11	A128	70c purple	3.50	12.50
7O12	A80	80c blk, *pale gray*	5.50	10.00
7O13	A81	90c dk red, *pale rose*	5.50	10.00
7O14	A82	1fr dk grn, *grnsh*	5.50	10.00
7O15	A83	1.20fr red vio, *pale gray*	6.50	13.00
7O16	A84	1.50fr dk bl, *buff*	6.50	13.00
7O17	A85	2fr mar, *pale rose*	6.50	13.00
7O18	A69	3fr brn car, *cr*	65.00	125.00
7O19	A70	5fr sl bl, *cr*	67.50	125.00
7O20	A71	10fr grn, *cr*	90.00	160.00
		Nos. 7O1-7O20 (20)	275.25	557.50
		Set, never hinged	500.00	

UN Emblem — O1

Statue from UN Building, Geneva — O2

1955-59 Engr. Perf. 11½

7O21	O1	5c dk violet brn	.25	.25
7O22	O1	10c green	.25	.25
7O23	O2	20c vermilion	2.00	4.00
7O24	O2	20c car rose ('59)	.25	.25
7O25	O2	30c org ver ('59)	.25	.30
7O26	O1	40c ultra	2.25	4.50
7O27	O1	50c ultra ('59)	.25	.40
7O28	O1	60c red brown	.25	.50
7O29	O2	2fr lilac	.80	1.50
		Nos. 7O21-7O29 (9)	6.55	12.05
		Set, never hinged	12.50	

See Nos. 7O34-7O37. For overprints see Nos. 7O31-7O32.

United Nations Emblem — O3

1955, Oct. 24 Photo.

7O30	O3	40c dark blue & bister	1.60	3.75
		Never hinged		3.00

10th anniv. of the UN, Oct. 24, 1955.

> **Catalogue values for unused stamps in this section, from this point to the end of the section, are for Never Hinged items.**

Nos. 7O24 Overprinted in Black

Nos. 7O27 Overprinted in Red

1960

7O31	O2	20c carmine rose	.25	.25
7O32	O1	50c ultra (R)	.50	.50

World Refugee Year, 7/1/59-6/30/60.

Palace of Nations, Geneva O4

1960 Granite Paper Perf. 11½

7O33	O4	5fr blue	3.75	4.00

No. 7O34

No. 7O35

Types of 1955 Inscribed

Engraved; Inscription Typographed

1962, Oct. 24 Unwmk. Perf. 11½

7O34	O1	10c green & red	.25	.25
7O35	O2	30c org ver & ultra	.30	.30
7O36	O1	50c ultra & org	.50	.50
7O37	O2	60c red brn & emer	.60	.60
		Nos. 7O34-7O37 (4)	1.65	1.65

Opening of the Philatelic Museum, UN European Office, Geneva.

O5

O6

UNCSAT Emblem

1963, Feb. 4 Engr. Perf. 11½

7O38	O5	50c ultra & car rose	.50	.50
7O39	O6	2fr lilac & emer	2.00	2.00

UN Conf. on the Application of Science and Technology for the Benefit of the Less Developed Areas (UNCSAT), Geneva, Feb. 4-20.

Stamps issued, starting Oct. 4, 1969, by the UN in Swiss currency for use by UN staff members or the public are listed under "United Nations" in Vol. 1 of this catalogue and in Scott's U.S. Specialized Catalogue. These stamps are on sale in various UN post offices, but are valid only in the UN enclave in Geneva. They are not inscribed "Helvetia."

FOR THE WORLD METEOROLOGICAL ORGANIZATION

> **Catalogue values for unused stamps in this section are for Never Hinged items.**

Sun, Cloud, Rain and Snow — O1

Design: 20c, 30c, 60c, 2fr, Direction indicator and anemometer.

1956-60 Unwmk. Engr. Perf. 11½

8O1	O1	5c dark gray	.25	.25
8O2	O1	10c green	.25	.25
8O3	O1	20c vermilion	2.25	2.25
8O4	O1	20c car rose ('60)	.25	.25
8O5	O1	30c org ver ('60)	.35	.35
8O6	O1	40c blue	2.75	2.75
8O7	O1	50c lt ultra ('60)	.50	.50
8O8	O1	60c reddish brn	.60	.60
8O9	O1	2fr rose violet	2.00	2.00
		Nos. 8O1-8O9 (9)	9.20	9.20

WMO Emblem O2

1973, Aug. 30 Engr. Perf. 11½
Violet Fibers, Fluorescent Paper

8O10	O2	30c carmine	.70	.30
8O11	O2	40c blue	.95	.30
8O12	O2	1fr ocher	2.25	1.00
		Nos. 8O10-8O12 (3)	3.90	1.60

Type O2 Inscribed: "OMI / OMM / 1873 / 1973"

1973, Aug. 30 Photo. Perf. 11½
Violet Fibers, Fluorescent Paper

8O13	O2	80c deep violet & gold	1.90	.80

Intl. meteorological cooperation, cent.

FOR THE INTERNATIONAL BUREAU OF THE UNIVERSAL POSTAL UNION

> **Catalogue values for unused stamps in this section are for Never Hinged items.**

See Nos. 98-103, 204-205, 514, 589-590 for postage issues commemorating the UPU.

UPU Monument, Bern — O1

Design: 10c, 20c, 30c, 60c, Pegasus.

1957-60 Unwmk. Engr. Perf. 11½

9O1	O1	5c gray	.25	.25
9O2	O1	10c lt grn	.25	.25
9O3	O1	20c vermilion	2.25	2.25
9O4	O1	20c car rose ('60)	.25	.25

9O5	O1	30c org ver ('60)	.35 .35
9O6	O1	40c blue	2.75 2.75
9O7	O1	50c lt ultra ('60)	.50 .50
9O8	O1	60c red brn	.60 .60
9O9	O1	2fr rose lilac	2.00 2.00
		Nos. 9O1-9O9 (9)	9.20 9.20

First Class
Mail — O2

Parcel
Post — O3

Money
Orders — O4

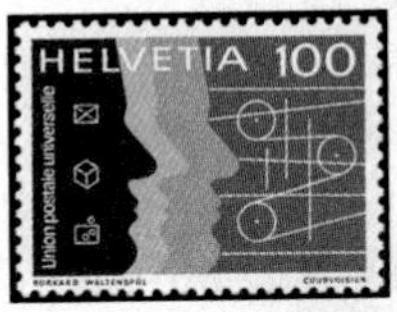

Technical
Cooperation
O5

Intl. Reply
and Notication
Service — O6

Express Mail
Service — O7

Post NET
System
O8

1976-95 Photo. Perf. 11½
Fluorescent Paper

9O10	O2	40c multi	.95 .40
9O11	O3	80c multi	1.90 .80
9O12	O4	90c multi	2.10 .90
9O13	O5	100c multi	2.25 1.00
9O14	O6	120c multi	2.75 1.25
9O15	O7	140c multi	3.25 1.50

Perf. 13½x13

9O16	O8	180c multicolored	4.25 2.10
		Nos. 9O10-9O16 (7)	17.45 7.95

Issued: 120c, 8/22/83; 140c, 3/7/89; 180c,
11/28/95; others, 9/16/76.

UPU, 125th
Anniv.
O9

1999, Mar. 9 Perf. 13
9O17	O9	20c shown	.45 .25
9O18	O9	70c Hand holding rain-bow	1.60 .65

Service Quality
Improvement
O10

2003, Sept. 9 Litho. Perf. 13¾x14¼
9O19	O10	90c multi	2.10 .45

Methods of
Mail Transport
O11

2005, Sept. 6 Litho. Perf. 13½x14¼
9O20	O11	100c multi	2.25 1.60

Postman
O12

2007, Sept. 6 Litho. Perf. 13¼x13½
9O21	O12	180c multi	4.25 3.25

See United Nations No. 944, United Nations
Offices in Geneva No. 475, and United
Nations Offices in Vienna No. 403.

René de Saint-Marceaux (1845-1915),
Sculptor of UPU Monument — O13

Litho. & Engr.
2009, Oct. 9 Perf. 13x13¼
9O22	O13	180c multi	4.25 3.50

See France No. 3724.

Dove — O14

2012, Oct. 9 Litho. Perf. 13¼x13½
9O23	O14	190c multi	4.00 4.00

25th Universal Postal Congress, Doha,
Qatar.

**FOR THE INTERNATIONAL
TELECOMMUNICATION UNION**

Catalogue values for unused
stamps in this section are for
Never Hinged items.

Transmitter — O1

Designs: 20c, 30c, 60c, 2fr, Antenna.

1958-60 Unwmk. Engr. Perf. 11½
1O01	O1	5c dark gray	.25 .25
1O02	O1	10c green	.25 .25
1O03	O1	20c vermilion	2.25 2.25

1O04	O1	20c car rose ('60)	.25 .25
1O05	O1	30c org ver ('60)	.35 .35
1O06	O1	40c blue	2.75 2.75
1O07	O1	50c lt ultra ('60)	.50 .50
1O08	O1	60c redsh brn	.60 .60
1O09	O1	2fr rose vio	2.00 2.00
		Nos. 1O01-1O09 (9)	9.20 9.20

ITU Headquarters,
Geneva — O2

1973, Aug. 30 Photo. Perf. 11½
Violet Fibers, Fluorescent Paper
1O10	O2	80c blue & black	.80 .80

Sound
Waves, ITU
Emblem
O3

Airplane,
Ocean
Liner — O4

Radio Waves,
Face on TV,
Microphone
O5

Photogravure and Engraved
1976, Feb. 12 Perf. 11½
Violet Fibers, Fluorescent Paper
1O11	O3	40c dp org & vio bl	.95 .40
1O12	O4	90c bl, vio bl & yel	2.10 .90
1O13	O5	1fr grn & multi	2.25 1.00
		Nos. 1O11-1O13 (3)	5.30 2.30

ITU activities: world telecommunications,
mobile radio and mass media.

Fiber Optic Communication
Links — O6

1988, Sept. 13 Litho. Perf. 12x11½
1O14	O6	1.40fr multi	3.25 1.40

Radio Waves,
ITU
Emblem — O7

1994, May 17 Litho. Perf. 13½
1O15	O7	1.80fr multicolored	4.25 2.10

Telecommunications — O8

1999, Mar. 9 Photo. Perf. 11½
1O16	O8	10c Teleeducation	.25 .25
1O17	O8	100c Telemedicine	2.25 1.10

Stylized
Face — O9

2003, Sept. 9 Litho. Perf. 13¾x14¼
1O18	O9	90c multi	2.10 .45

**FOR THE WORLD INTELLECTUAL
PROPERTY ORGANIZATION**

Catalogue values for unused
stamps in this section are for
Never Hinged items.

WIPO
Emblem
O1

80c, Headquarters, Geneva. 100c, Industrial symbols. 120c, Educational and artistic
symbols.

1982, May 27 Photo. Perf. 12x11½
1O1	O1	40c shown	.95 .40
1O2	O1	80c multicolored	1.90 .80
1O3	O1	100c multicolored	2.25 1.00
1O4	O1	120c multicolored	2.75 1.25

1985, Sept. 10 Photo. Perf. 12x11½

50c, Mind in action.

1O5	O1	50c multicolored	1.15 .55
		Nos. 1O1-1O5 (5)	9.00 4.00

This is an expanding set. Numbers will
change if necessary.

**FOR THE INTERNATIONAL
OLYMPIC COMMITTEE**

Catalogue values for unused
stamps in this section are for
Never Hinged items.

Olympics Type of Regular Issue

Hand and plant with leaves of Olympic rings
and: 20c, Orange frame. 70c, Green frame.

2000, Sept. 15 Photo. Die Cut
Booklet Stamps
Self-Adhesive
1O1	A496	20c multi	.45 .25
1O2	A496	70c multi	1.60 .80
a.		Booklet pane, #1O1-1O2	2.10
		Booklet, #1O2a	2.10

No. 1O2a is separated from booklet cover
by rouletting. The booklet was sold folded.

**Olympics Type of Regular Issue,
2004**

Design: Runner, "40," Olympic rings, scene
from 1896 Athens Olympics.

2004, May 6 Litho. Perf. 13x13¼
1O3	A551	100c multi	2.25 1.60

2006 Winter Olympics Type of 2005
2005, Nov. 22 Litho. Perf. 13½x13
1O4	A578	130c Ice hockey	3.00 2.00

Issued in sheets of 6.

Summer Olympics Type of 2008
2008, May 8 Litho. Perf. 14x14¼
1O5	A627	180c BMX cycling	4.25 3.50

FRANCHISE STAMPS

These stamps were distributed to many institutions and charitable societies for franking their correspondence.

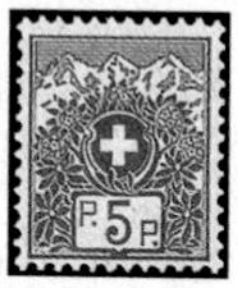

F1

Control Figures Overprinted in Black

214

Perf. 11½, 12

1911-21 Typo. Wmk. 183

Blue Granite Paper

S1	F1	2c ol grn & red	.25	.25
S2	F1	3c ol grn & red	2.50	.55
S3	F1	5c ol grn & red	1.10	.25
S4	F1	10c ol grn & red	1.40	.25
S5	F1	15c ol grn & red	21.00	4.00
S6	F1	20c ol grn & red	5.00	.60
		Nos. S1-S6 (6)	31.25	5.90

Without Control Figures

S1a	F1	2c olive green & red	.55	*19.00*
S2a	F1	3c olive green & red	.55	*25.00*
S3a	F1	5c olive green & red	4.75	*32.50*
S4a	F1	10c olive green & red	8.25	*50.00*
S5a	F1	15c olive green & red	5.25	*125.00*
S6a	F1	20c olive green & red	9.50	*50.00*
		Nos. S1a-S6a (6)	28.85	*301.50*

Control Figures Overprinted in Black

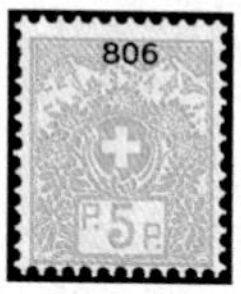

1926

S7	F1	5c ol grn & red	12.50	4.50
S8	F1	10c ol grn & red	7.75	3.25
S9	F1	20c ol grn & red	10.00	3.75
		Nos. S7-S9 (3)	30.25	11.50

Control Figures Overprinted in Black

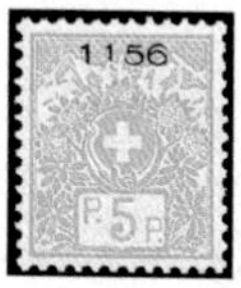

1927 White Granite Paper

S10	F1	5c green & red	5.00	.40
S11	F1	10c green & red	2.50	.25
b.		Grilled gum	325.00	*725.00*
S12	F1	20c green & red	3.50	.30
		Nos. S10-S12 (3)	11.00	.95

Without Control Figures

S10a	F1	5c green & red	32.50	*140.00*
S11a	F1	10c green & red	32.50	*140.00*
c.		Grilled gum	150.00	*650.00*
S12a	F1	20c green & red	32.50	*140.00*

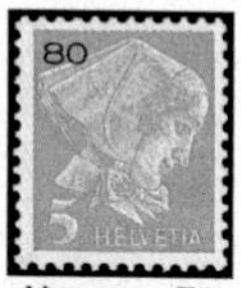

Nurse — F2

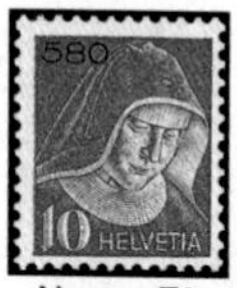

Nun — F3

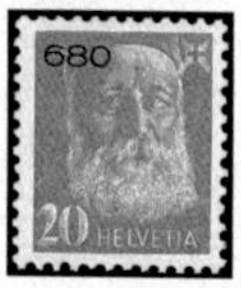

J. H. Dunant — F4

Control Figures Overprinted in Black

1935 *Perf. 11½*

S13	F2	5c turq green	2.25	*5.50*
b.		Grilled gum	3.25	.40
S14	F3	10c lt violet	2.25	*5.50*
b.		Grilled gum	3.25	.25
S15	F4	20c scarlet	2.25	*6.50*
b.		Grilled gum	3.75	.45
		Nos. S13-S15 (3)	6.75	*17.50*
		Nos. S13b-S15b (3)	10.25	1.10

Without Control Figures

S13a	F2	5c turquoise green	1.40	*3.75*
c.		Grilled gum	15.00	1.40
S14a	F3	10c light violet	1.40	*3.75*
c.		Grilled gum	15.00	1.40
S15a	F4	20c scarlet	1.40	*5.00*
c.		Grilled gum	15.00	1.50
		Nos. S13a-S15a (3)	4.20	*12.50*
		Nos. S13c-S15c (3)	45.00	4.30

SYRIA

'sir-ē-ə

LOCATION — Asia Minor, bordering on Turkey, Iraq, Lebanon, Israel and the Mediterranean Sea
GOVT. — Republic
AREA — 71,498 sq. mi.
POP. — 14,972,000 (1997 est.)
CAPITAL — Damascus

Syria was originally part of the Turkish province of Sourya conquered by British and Arab forces in late 1918 and later partitioned. The British assumed control of the Palestine and Transjordan regions; the French were permitted to occupy the sanjaks of Lebanon, Alaouites and Alexandretta; and the remaining territory, including the vilayets of Damascus and Aleppo, was established as an independent Arab kingdom, under which the first Syrian stamps were issued.

French forces from Beirut deposed King Faisal in July 1920, and two years of military occupation followed until Syria was mandated to France in July 1922. Syrian autonomy was substituted for the mandate in 1934, but full independence was not again achieved until 1946. In 1958, Syria and Egypt merged to form the United Arab Republic. Syria left this union in 1961, adopting the name Syrian Arab Republic. UAR issues for Syria are listed following Syria's 1919-20 Issues of the Arabian Government.

10 Milliemes = 1 Piaster
40 Paras = 1 Piaster (Arabian Govt.)
100 Centimes = 1 Piaster (1920)
100 Piasters = 1 Syrian Pound

Catalogue values for unused stamps in this country are for Never Hinged items, beginning with Scott 314 in the regular postage section, Scott B13 in the semipostal section, Scott C124 in the airpost section, Scott CB5 in the airpost semipostal section, Scott J40 in the postage due section, and all of the items in the UAR sections.

Watermarks

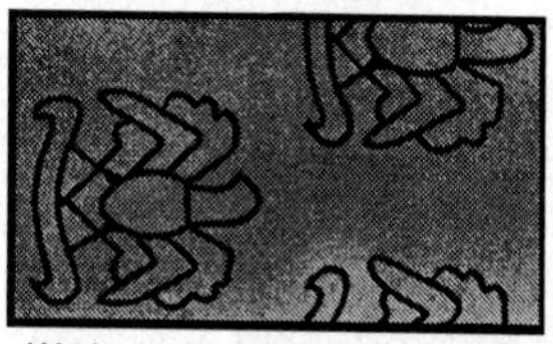

Wmk. 291 — National Emblem Multiple

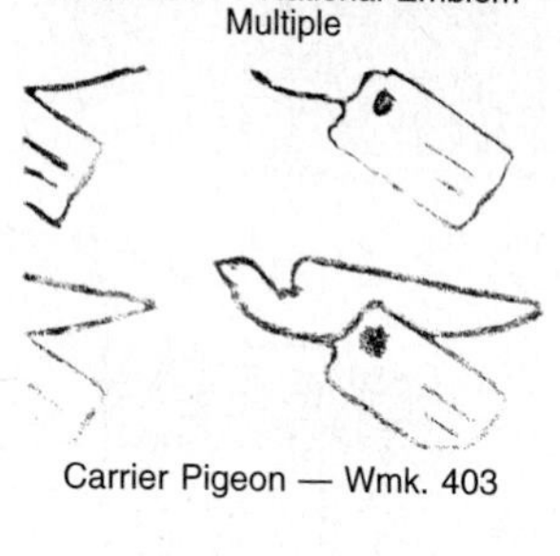

Carrier Pigeon — Wmk. 403

Issued under French Occupation

Stamps of France, 1900-07, Surcharged

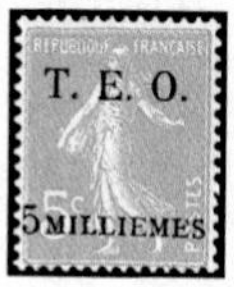

Perf. 14x13½

1919, Nov. 21 Unwmk.

1	A16	1m on 1c gray	250.00	200.00
2	A16	2m on 2c vio brn	600.00	*550.00*
3	A16	3m on 3c red org	300.00	240.00
4	A20	4m on 15c gray grn	60.00	47.50
5	A22	5m on 5c dp grn	35.00	22.50
6	A22	1p on 10c red	50.00	32.50
7	A22	2p on 25c blue	25.00	15.00
8	A18	5p on 40c red & pale bl	32.50	22.50
9	A18	9p on 50c bis brn & lav	65.00	50.00
10	A18	10p on 1fr cl & ol grn	110.00	80.00
		Nos. 1-10 (10)	1,527.	1,260.

The letters "T.E.O." are the initials of "Territoires Ennemis Occupés." There are two types of the numerals in the surcharges on Nos. 2, 3, 8 and 9.

Stamps of French Offices in Turkey, 1902-03, Surcharged

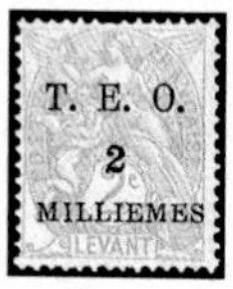

1919

11	A2	1m on 1c gray	1.50	.80
a.		Inverted surcharge	40.00	
12	A2	2m on 2c violet brn	1.50	.80
a.		Inverted surcharge	40.00	
13	A2	3m on 3c red orange	3.25	1.40
14	A3	4m on 15c pale red	1.50	.80
a.		Inverted surcharge	40.00	
15	A2	5m on 5c green	1.50	.80

Overprinted

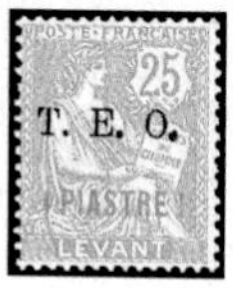

16	A5	1p on 25c blue	1.50	.75
a.		Inverted overprint	40.00	
17	A6	2p on 50c bis brn & lav	2.50	1.25
18	A6	4p on 1fr claret & ol grn	4.00	2.50
19	A6	8p on 2fr gray vio & yel	12.50	8.00
a.		"T.E.O." double	110.00	110.00
20	A6	20p on 5fr dk bl & buff	350.00	210.00
		Nos. 11-20 (10)	379.75	227.10

On Nos. 17-20 "T.E.O." reads vertically up.

Nos. 1-20 were issued in Beirut and mainly used in Lebanon. Nos. 16-20 were also used in Cilicia.

Inverted surcharges exist on several values of this issue.

Stamps of France, 1900-07, Surcharged

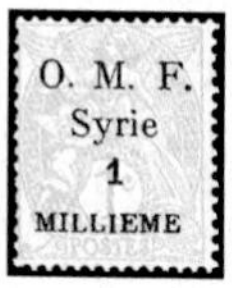

1920

21	A16	1m on 1c gray	5.50	4.50
a.		Inverted surcharge	60.00	
b.		Double surcharge	67.50	
22	A16	2m on 2c vio brn	6.50	4.75
a.		Double surcharge	67.50	
b.		Inverted surcharge	60.00	
23	A22	3m on 5c green	13.00	12.00
a.		Double surcharge	82.50	
b.		Inverted surcharge	100.00	
24	A18	20p on 5fr dk bl & buff	475.00	450.00
		Nos. 21-23 (3)	25.00	21.25

The letters "O.M.F." are the initials of "Occupation Militaire Francaise."

Stamps of France, 1900-07, Surcharged in Black or Red

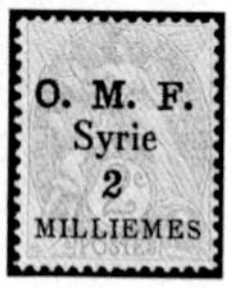

1920

25	A16	1m on 1c gray	1.25	.95
26	A16	2m on 2c vio brn	1.50	1.00
27	A22	3m on 5c green	2.25	2.00
a.		Double surcharge	67.50	
28	A22	5m on 10c red	2.50	2.25
a.		Inverted surcharge	65.00	65.00
b.		Double surcharge	65.00	65.00
29	A18	20p on 5fr dk bl & buff	72.50	70.00
30	A18	20p on 5fr dk bl & buff (R)	300.00	250.00
		Nos. 25-30 (6)	380.00	326.20

Stamps of France, 1900-21, Surcharged in Black or Red

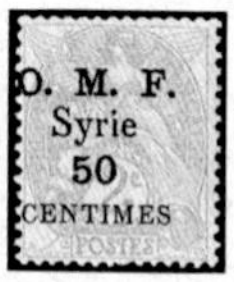

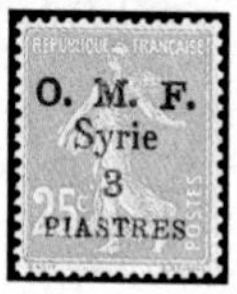

1920-22

31	A16	25c on 1c gray	2.00	1.00
32	A16	50c on 2c vio brn	2.00	1.00
33	A16	75c on 3c red org	2.00	1.00
a.		Inverted surcharge	52.50	52.50
b.		Double surcharge	60.00	60.00
34	A22	1p on 5c grn (R)	2.25	2.00
a.		Double surcharge	60.00	60.00
35	A22	1p on 5c green	1.25	1.00
a.		Inverted surcharge	35.00	35.00
b.		Double surcharge	45.00	45.00
36	A22	1p on 20c red brn ('21)	.75	.25
a.		Inverted surcharge	35.00	35.00
b.		Double surcharge	35.00	35.00
37	A22	1.25p on 25c bl ('22)	1.50	.95
a.		Inverted surcharge	40.00	40.00
b.		Double surcharge	37.50	37.50
38	A22	1.50p on 30c org ('22)	1.60	.80
a.		Inverted surcharge	27.50	40.00
39	A22	2p on 10c red	1.25	1.00
a.		Inverted surcharge	50.00	50.00
40	A22	2p on 25c bl (R)	1.25	1.00
a.		Inverted surcharge	45.00	45.00
b.		Double surcharge	35.00	35.00
41	A18	2p on 40c red & pale bl ('21)	1.60	.75
42	A20	2.50p on 50c dl bl ('22)	1.40	1.10
a.		Final "S" of "Piastres" omitted	24.00	24.00
b.		Inverted surcharge	30.00	30.00
c.		Double surcharge	35.00	35.00
43	A22	3p on 25c bl (R)	1.40	1.10
a.		Inverted surcharge	45.00	45.00
44	A18	3p on 60c vio & ultra ('21)	1.75	1.10
a.		Inverted surcharge	37.50	37.50
45	A20	5p on 15c gray grn	2.50	2.25
a.		Double surcharge	140.00	*150.00*
46	A18	5p on 1fr cl & ol grn ('21)	3.00	1.50
47	A18	10p on 40c red & pale bl	3.75	3.25
48	A18	10p on 2fr org & pale bl ('21)	6.00	3.00
49	A18	25p on 50c bis brn & lav	5.50	4.00
a.		Inverted surcharge	100.00	100.00
50	A18	25p on 5fr dk bl & buff ('21)	110.00	95.00
51	A18	50p on 1fr cl & ol grn	25.00	20.00
a.		"PIASRTES"	*1,650.*	*1,650.*
b.		Double surcharge	1,700.	*1,900.*
52	A18	100p on 5fr dk bl & buff (R)	47.50	45.00
53	A18	100p on 5fr dk bl & buff (Bk)	250.00	225.00
a.		"PIASRTES"	*1,650.*	*1,650.*
		Nos. 31-53 (23)	475.25	413.05

In first printing, space between "Syrie" and numeral is 2mm, second printing, 1mm.

For overprints see Nos. C1-C9.

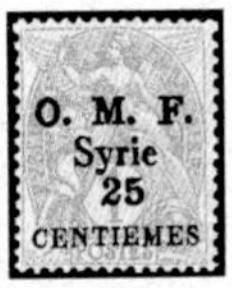

Surcharged in Black or Red

1920-23

54 A16 10c on 2c violet ('23) 1.40 .90
a. Inverted surcharge 35.00 35.00
55 A22 10c on 5c org (R) ('23) 1.00 .65
a. Inverted surcharge 35.00 35.00
56 A16 25c on 1c dk gray 1.10 .90
a. Inverted surcharge 40.00 40.00
b. Double surcharge 52.50 52.50
c. 50c on 1c dk gray (error) 4.50 4.50
57 A22 25c on 5c green ('21) 1.10 .60
a. Inverted surcharge 35.00 35.00
b. Double surcharge 35.00 35.00
58 A22 25c on 5c org ('22) 1.00 .80
a. "CENTIEMES" omitted 37.50 37.50
b. Inverted surcharge 35.00 35.00
c. Double surcharge 37.50 37.50
59 A16 50c on 2c vio brn 1.10 .90
a. Inverted surcharge 35.00 35.00
b. Double surcharge 45.00 45.00
60 A22 50c on 10c red ('21) 1.25 .55
a. Inverted surcharge 35.00 35.00
b. Double surcharge 35.00 35.00
61 A22 50c on 10c grn ('22) 1.50 1.25
a. Inverted surcharge 35.00 35.00
b. Double surcharge 37.50 37.50
c. Double surcharge, one inverted 50.00 50.00
62 A16 75c on 3c red orange 3.00 2.00
a. Inverted surcharge 35.00 35.00
b. Double surcharge 45.00 45.00
63 A20 75c on 15c sl grn ('21) 1.40 .90
a. Double surcharge 35.00 35.00
Nos. 54-63 (10) 13.85 9.45

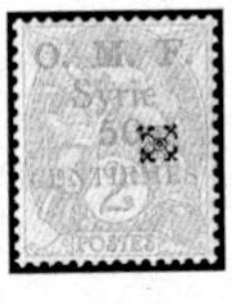

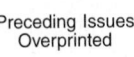

Preceding Issues Overprinted

1920 **Black Overprint**

64 A16 25c on 1c sl gray 12.00 10.00
a. Double overprint 45.00
65 A16 50c on 2c vio brn 13.00 11.00
a. Double overprint 45.00
66 A22 1p on 5c grn 11.00 9.00
a. Double overprint 45.00
67 A22 2p on 25c blue 18.00 14.50
a. Double overprint 82.50
68 A20 5p on 15c gray grn 55.00 47.50
a. Double overprint 140.00 *150.00*
69 A18 10p on 40c red & pale bl 80.00 75.00
a. Double overprint 325.00
70 A18 25p on 50c bis brn & lav 225.00 190.00
a. Double overprint 600.00
71 A18 50p on 1fr cl & ol grn 650.00 625.00
a. Double overprint 2,100.
72 A18 100p on 5fr dk bl & buff 2,000. 1,900.
a. Double overprint 3,900. *4,300.*
Nos. 64-72 (9) 3,064. 2,882.

Red Overprint

73 A16 25c on 1c sl gray 12.50 10.00
74 A16 50c on 2c vio brn 11.00 8.50
75 A22 1p on 5c grn 11.00 8.50
76 A22 2p on 25c bl 9.00 6.50
77 A20 5p on 15c gray grn 55.00 47.50
a. Double overprint 190.00
78 A18 10p on 40c red & pale bl 85.00 75.00
a. Double overprint 170.00
79 A18 25p on 50c bis brn & lav 225.00 180.00
a. Double overprint 450.00 *475.00*
80 A18 50p on 1fr cl & ol grn 475.00 425.00
a. Double surcharge 1,700. *1,900.*
81 A18 100p on 5fr dk bl & buff 1,650. 1,650.
a. Double overprint 3,500. *3,750.*
Nos. 73-81 (9) 2,533. 2,411.

Nos. 64-81 were used only in the vilayet of Aleppo where Egyptian gold currency was still in use.

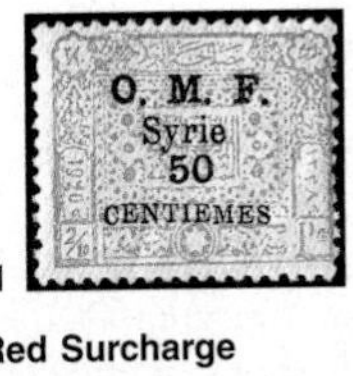

A1

Black or Red Surcharge

1921 ***Perf. 11½***

82 A1 25c on 1/10p lt brn 1.25 .85
a. "25 Centiemes" omitted
83 A1 50c on 2/10p grn 1.25 .85
84 A1 1p on 3/10p yel 1.75 .85
a. "2/10" for "3/10" 12.50 12.50
b. Inverted surcharge 60.00 60.00
85 A1 1p on 5m rose 2.00 1.10
86 A1 2p on 5m rose 2.50 1.25
a. Tête bêche pair 160.00 160.00
b. Inverted surcharge 40.00 40.00
c. Double surcharge 45.00 45.00
87 A1 3p on 1p gray bl 3.00 1.25
a. Inverted surcharge 40.00 40.00
88 A1 5p on 2p bl grn 5.00 3.50
a. Inverted surcharge 45.00 45.00
89 A1 10p on 5p vio brn 11.00 5.75
90 A1 25p on 10p gray (R) 13.00 8.00
a. Inverted surcharge 45.00 45.00
Nos. 82-90 (9) 40.75 23.40

Nos. 82-90 are surcharged on stamps of the Arabian Government Nos. 85, 87-93 and have the designs and sizes of those stamps.

Kilis Issue

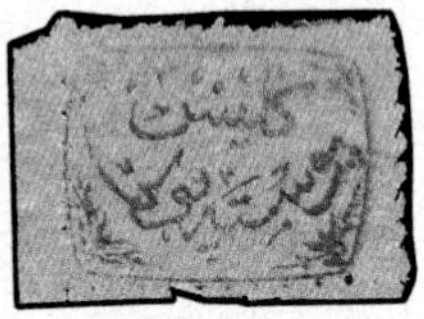

A2

Sewing Machine Perf. 9

1921 **Pelure Paper** **Handstamped**

91 A2 (1p) violet *50.00 45.00*

Issued at Kilis to meet a shortage of the regular issue, caused by the sudden influx of a large number of Armenian refugees from Turkey. The Kilis area was restored to Turkey in Oct. 1923.

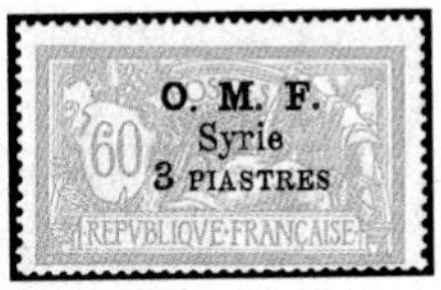

Stamps of France, Surcharged

1921-22 ***Perf. 14x13½***

92 A18 2p on 40c red & pale bl 1.25 .90
a. Inverted surcharge 35.00 35.00
b. Double surcharge 35.00 35.00
c. Triple surcharge 82.50
93 A18 2.50p on 50c bis brn & lav ('22) 1.40 1.00
a. Double surcharge 37.50 37.50
b. 2p on 50c bister brown & lavender (error) 82.50 67.50
94 A18 3p on 60c vio & ultra 1.25 .90
a. Inverted surcharge 35.00 35.00
b. Double surcharge 35.00 35.00
95 A18 5p on 1fr cl & ol grn 7.00 6.00
a. Inverted surcharge 40.00 40.00
96 A18 10p on 2fr org & pale bl 15.00 11.00
97 A18 25p on 5fr dk bl & buff 13.00 10.00
Nos. 92-97 (6) 38.90 29.80

On No. 93 the surcharge reads: "2 PIASTRES 50."

For overprints see Nos. C10-C17.

French Mandate

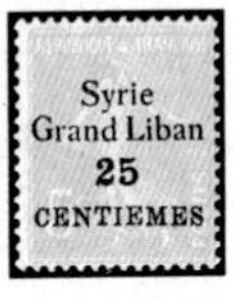

French Stamps of 1900-23 Surcharged

1923

104 A16 10c on 2c vio brn .40 .25
a. Inverted surcharge 27.50 27.50
b. Double surcharge 35.00 35.00
105 A22 25c on 5c orange .75 .75
a. Inverted surcharge 27.50 27.50
106 A22 50c on 10c green .90 .85
a. Inverted surcharge 27.50 27.50
b. Double surcharge 35.00 35.00
c. 25c on 10c green (error) 240.00 240.00
107 A20 75c on 15c sl grn 1.60 1.50
a. Inverted surcharge 35.00 35.00
b. Double surcharge 37.50 37.50
108 A22 1p on 20c red brn .75 .70
a. Inverted surcharge 27.50 27.50
b. Double surcharge 35.00 35.00
109 A22 1.25p on 25c blue 1.40 1.25
a. Inverted surcharge 40.00 40.00
b. Double surcharge 37.50 37.50
110 A22 1.50p on 30c org 1.10 .90
a. Inverted surcharge 27.50 27.50
111 A22 1.50p on 30c red 1.10 .90
112 A20 2.50p on 50c dl bl .70 .60
a. Inverted surcharge 60.00 60.00
b. Double surcharge 35.00 35.00

On Pasteur Stamps of 1923

113 A23 50c on 10c green 2.00 1.75
114 A23 1.50p on 30c red 1.75 1.50
115 A23 2.50p on 50c blue 2.00 1.75

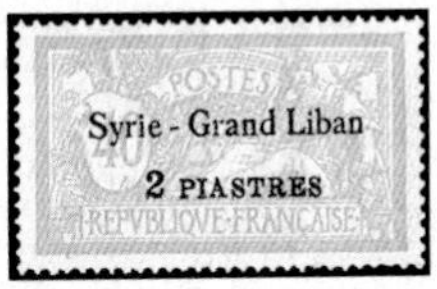

Surcharged

116 A18 2p on 40c red & pale bl .75 .70
a. Inverted surcharge 35.00 35.00
b. Double surcharge 37.50 37.50
c. "Liabn" *450.00 450.00*
117 A18 3p on 60c vio & ultra 1.50 1.25
a. Inverted surcharge 40.00 40.00
b. Double surcharge 75.00 75.00
c. "Liabn" *450.00 450.00*
118 A18 5p on 1fr cl & ol grn 2.00 1.50
a. Inverted surcharge 75.00 75.00
b. "Liabn" *450.00 450.00*
119 A18 10p on 2fr org & pale bl 7.50 7.00
a. "Liabn" *450.00 450.00*
120 A18 25p on 5fr dk bl & buff 22.50 20.00
Nos. 104-120 (17) 48.70 43.15

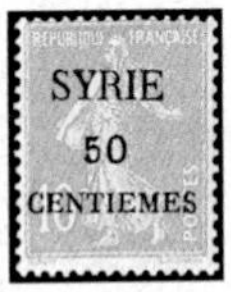

Stamps of France, 1900-21, Surcharged

1924 ***Perf. 14x13½***

121 A16 10c on 2c vio brn .40 .25
a. Inverted surcharge 35.00 35.00
122 A22 25c on 5c orange .70 .60
a. "25" omitted 24.00
123 A22 50c on 10c green .70 .60
a. Inverted surcharge 35.00 35.00
124 A20 75c on 15c sl grn .70 .60
125 A22 1p on 20c red brn .60 .50
a. "1 PIASTRES" 24.00
126 A22 1.25p on 25c blue 1.10 .90
127 A22 1.50p on 30c orange 1.10 .90
128 A22 1.50p on 30c red 1.00 .85
129 A20 2.50p on 50c dl bl 1.00 .85

Same on Pasteur Stamps of France, 1923

1924

130 A23 50c on 10c grn .90 .70
a. Inverted surcharge 47.50 47.50
131 A23 1.50p on 30c red 1.40 1.10
132 A23 2.50p on 50c blue .75 .70
a. Inverted surcharge 35.00 35.00
Nos. 121-132 (12) 10.35 8.55

Olympic Games Issue

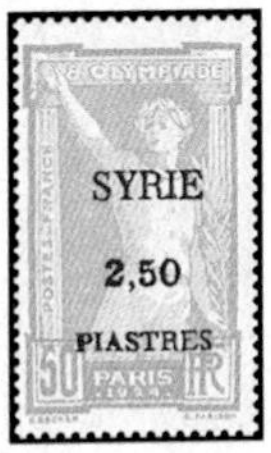

Stamps of France, 1924, Surcharged

1924

133 A24 50c on 10c gray grn & yel grn 30.00 27.50
134 A25 1.25p on 25c rose & dk rose 30.00 27.50
135 A26 1.50p on 30c brn red & blk 30.00 27.50
136 A27 2.50p on 50c ultra & dk bl 30.00 27.50
Nos. 133-136 (4) 120.00 110.00

See Nos. 166-169.

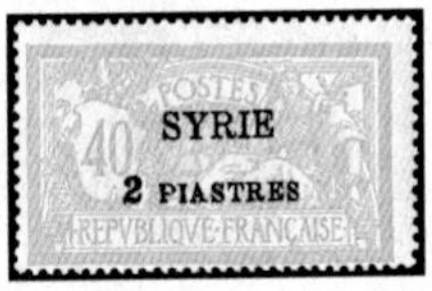

Stamps of France 1900-20 Surcharged

137 A18 2p on 40c red & pale bl .90 .50
138 A18 3p on 60c vio & ultra .70 .65
139 A18 5p on 1fr claret & ol grn 3.50 3.25
140 A18 10p on 2fr org & pale bl 3.50 3.00
141 A18 25p on 5fr dk bl & buff 5.25 4.50
Nos. 137-141 (5) 13.85 11.90

For overprints see Nos. C18-C21.

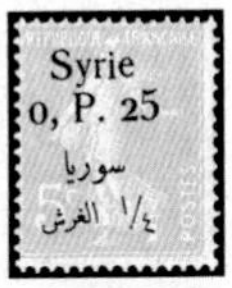

Stamps of France 1900-21, Surcharged

or

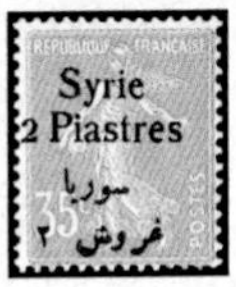

1924-25

143 A16 10c on 2c vio brn .40 .25
a. Double surcharge 35.00 35.00
b. Inverted surcharge 30.00 30.00
144 A22 25c on 5c orange .40 .25
a. Double surcharge 35.00 35.00
145 A22 50c on 10c green .75 .50
a. Double surcharge 35.00 35.00
b. Inverted surcharge 30.00 30.00
146 A20 75c on 15c gray grn .90 .70
a. Double surcharge 35.00 35.00
b. Inverted surcharge 30.00 30.00
147 A22 1p on 20c red brn .60 .40
a. Inverted surcharge 26.00 26.00
148 A22 1.25p on 25c blue .95 .75
a. Inverted surcharge 30.00 30.00
149 A22 1.50p on 30c red .90 .70
a. Double surcharge 35.00 35.00
150 A22 1.50p on 30c orange 26.00 25.00
151 A22 2p on 35c violet ('25) 1.00 .80
152 A18 2p on 40c red & pale bl .75 .50
a. Arabic "Piastre" in singular 1.75 1.75
153 A18 2p on 45c grn & bl ('25) 5.00 4.00
154 A18 3p on 60c vio & ultra 1.10 .75
155 A20 3p on 60c lt vio ('25) 1.25 .75
156 A20 4p on 85c ver .45 .25
157 A18 5p on 1fr cl & ol grn 1.25 .75
158 A18 10p on 2fr org & pale bl 2.00 1.50
159 A18 25p on 5fr dk bl & buff 2.75 1.50
Nos. 143-159 (17) 46.45 39.35

On No. 152a, the surcharge is as illustrated. The correct fourth line ("2 Piastres" -plural), as it appears on Nos. 151, 152 and 153, has four characters, the third resembling "9."

For overprints see Nos. C22-C25.

Same Surcharge on Pasteur Stamps of France

1924-25

160 A23 50c on 10c green 1.25 1.00
161 A23 75c on 15c grn ('25) 1.25 1.00
162 A23 1.50p on 30c red 1.25 1.00
163 A23 2p on 45c red ('25) 1.25 1.00
164 A23 2.50p on 50c blue 1.75 1.25
165 A23 4p on 75c blue 1.75 1.25
Nos. 160-165 (6) 8.50 6.50

Olympic Games Issue

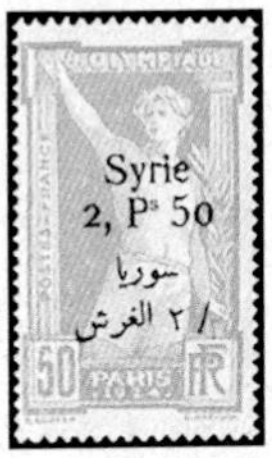

Stamps of France, 1924, Surcharged in French and Arabic

1924 **Same Colors as #133-136**

166 A24 50c on 10c 29.00 29.00
167 A25 1.25p on 25c 29.00 29.00
168 A26 1.50p on 30c 29.00 29.00
169 A27 2.50p on 50c 29.00 29.00
Nos. 166-169 (4) 116.00 116.00

Ronsard Issue

Same Surcharge on France No. 219

1925

170 A28 4p on 75c bl, *bluish* 1.00 .75

Mosque at Hama A3

Mosque at Damascus A5

View of Merkab A4

Designs: 50c, View of Alexandretta. 75c, View of Hama. 1p, Omayyad Mosque, Damascus. 1.25p, Latakia Harbor. 1.50p, View of Damascus. 2p, View of Palmyra. 2.50p, View of Kalat Yamoun. 3p, Bridge of Daphne. 5p, View of Aleppo. 10p, View of Aleppo. 25p, Columns at Palmyra.

Perf. 12½, 13½

1925		Litho.	Unwmk.	
173	A3	10c dark violet	.35	.25
		Photo.		
174	A4	25c olive black	1.00	.55
175	A4	50c yellow green	.50	.25
176	A4	75c brown orange	.60	.25
177	A5	1p magenta	.60	.25
178	A4	1.25p deep green	2.25	1.10
179	A4	1.50p rose red	.75	.25
180	A4	2p dark brown	2.00	.25
181	A4	2.50p peacock blue	1.50	.50
182	A4	3p orange brn	1.50	.25
183	A4	5p violet	1.25	.25
184	A4	10p violet brown	3.50	.30
185	A4	25p ultra	5.75	4.50
		Nos. 173-185 (13)	21.55	8.95

For surcharges see Nos. 186-206, B1-B12, C26-C45, CB1-CB4.

Surcharged in Black or Red

1926-30				
186	A4	1p on 3pi org brn ('30)	2.00	.50
187	A4	2p on 1p25 dp grn (R) ('28)	1.25	.40
a.		Double surcharge	16.00	16.00
188	A4	3.50p on 75c org brn	1.00	.35
a.		Double surcharge	16.00	16.00
189	A4	4p on 25c ol blk	1.50	.35
190	A4	4p on 25c ol blk ('27)	1.40	.45
191	A4	4p on 25c ol blk (R) ('28)	1.25	.35
192	A4	4.50p on 75c brn org	1.40	.35
193	A4	6p on 2p50 pck bl	1.00	.35
194	A4	7.50p on 2p50 pck bl	1.10	.35
195	A4	7.50p on 2p50 pck bl (R) ('28)	3.50	.90
a.		Double surcharge	29.00	
196	A4	12p on 1p25 dp grn	1.50	.40
a.		Surcharge on face and back	50.00	42.50
197	A4	15p on 25p ultra	2.75	.90
198	A4	20p on 1p25 dp grn	2.25	.70
		Nos. 186-198 (13)	21.90	6.35

Size of numerals and arrangement of this surcharge varies on the different denominations.

No. 189 has slanting foot on "4."

No. 190, foot straight.

No. 173 Surcharged in Red

1928				
199	A3	05c on 10c dk vio	1.00	.25

Stamps of 1925 Ovptd. in Red or Blue

1929			*Perf. 13½*	
200	A4	50c yellow grn (R)	3.50	2.75
201	A5	1p magenta (Bl)	3.50	2.75
202	A4	1.50p rose red (Bl)	3.50	2.75
203	A4	3p orange brn (Bl)	3.50	2.75
204	A4	5p violet (R)	3.50	2.75
205	A4	10p violet brn (Bl)	3.50	2.75
206	A4	25p ultra (R)	3.50	2.75
		Nos. 200-206 (7)	24.50	19.25

Industrial Exhibition, Damascus, Sept. 1929.

View of Hama — A6

View of Alexandretta — A9

Citadel at Aleppo A10

Great Mosque of Damascus A11

Ruins of Bosra A13

Mosque at Homs A15

View of Sednaya A16

Citadel at Aleppo A17

Ancient Bridge at Antioch A18

Mosque at Damascus A22

Designs: 20c, Great Mosque, Aleppo. 25c, Minaret, Hama. 2p, View of Antioch. 4p, Square at Damascus. 15p, Mosque at Hama. 25p, Monastery of St. Simeon the Stylite (ruins). 50p, Sun Temple (ruins), Palmyra.

Perf. 12x12½

1930-36		Litho.	Unwmk.	
208	A6	10c red violet	.50	.25
209	A6	10c vio brn ('33)	.50	.35
209A	A6	10c vio brn, redrawn ('35)	.50	.25
210	A6	20c dark blue	.50	.25
211	A6	20c brn org ('33)	.50	.25
212	A6	25c gray green	.50	.25
213	A6	25c dk bl gray ('33)	.80	.45
		Photo.		
		Perf. 13		
214	A9	50c violet	.50	.25
215	A15	75c org red ('32)	.50	.25
216	A10	1p green	.75	.25
217	A10	1p bis brn ('36)	1.75	.40
218	A11	1.50p bister brown	7.50	3.00
219	A11	1.50p dp grn ('33)	1.00	.50
220	A9	2p dark violet	.75	.25
221	A13	3p yellow green	2.00	.70
222	A10	4p yellow orange	.75	.25
223	A15	4.50p rose carmine	1.75	.55
224	A16	6p grnsh black	2.25	.50
225	A17	7.50p dull blue	2.25	.70
226	A18	10p dark brown	2.00	.50
227	A10	15p deep green	3.50	1.00
228	A18	25p violet brown	5.00	1.10
229	A15	50p olive brown	17.50	7.00
230	A22	100p red orange	35.00	15.00
		Nos. 208-230 (24)	88.55	34.25

On No. 209A Arabic inscriptions, upper right, are entirely redrawn with lighter lines. Hyphen added in "Helio-Vaugirard" imprint. Lines in buildings and background more distinct.

On No. 215 the letters of "VAUGIRARD" in the imprint are reversed as in a mirror.

For overprints and surcharges see Nos. 253-268, 346, M1-M2.

Autonomous Republic

Parliament Building A23

abu-al-Ala al-Maarri — A24

President Ali Bek el Abed — A25

Saladin — A26

1934, Aug. 2		Engr.	*Perf. 12½*	
232	A23	10c olive green	2.00	*2.00*
233	A23	20c black	2.00	*2.00*
234	A23	25c red orange	2.50	*2.50*
235	A23	50c ultra	3.00	*3.00*
236	A23	75c plum	3.00	*3.00*
237	A24	1p vermilion	5.50	5.50
238	A24	1.50p green	6.50	6.50
239	A24	2p red brown	6.50	6.50
240	A24	3p Prus blue	6.50	6.50
241	A24	4p brt violet	6.75	6.75
242	A24	4.50p carmine	7.00	7.00
243	A24	5p dark blue	7.00	7.00
244	A24	6p dark brown	8.00	8.00
245	A24	7.50p dark ultra	10.00	10.00
246	A25	10p dark brown	15.00	15.00
247	A25	15p dull blue	25.00	25.00
248	A25	25p rose red	17.50	13.00
249	A26	50p dark brown	35.00	35.00
250	A26	100p lake	60.00	60.00
		Nos. 232-250 (19)	228.75	224.25

Proclamation of the Republic. See Nos. C57-C66. For surcharge see No. M3.

Nos. 232-250 exist imperf. Value: $1,000.

Stamps of 1930-36 Overprinted in Red or Black

1936, Apr. 15				
253	A9	50c violet (R)	2.75	1.50
254	A10	1p bister brn (Bk)	2.75	1.50
255	A9	2p dk violet (R)	2.75	1.50
256	A13	3p yellow grn (Bk)	3.25	1.50
257	A10	4p yellow org (Bk)	3.25	1.50
258	A15	4.50p rose car (Bk)	3.25	1.50
259	A16	6p grnsh blk (R)	4.00	2.00
260	A17	7.50p dull blue (R)	4.75	2.75
261	A18	10p dk brown (Bk)	5.75	3.75
		Nos. 253-261 (9)	32.50	17.50

Industrial Exhibition, Damascus, May 1936. See Nos. C67-C71.

Stamps of 1930 Srchd. in Black

1937-38			*Perf. 13½x13*	
262	A10	2.50p on 4p yel org ('38)	.55	.40
263	A22	10p on 100p red orange	1.00	.90

Stamps of 1930-33 Srchd. in Red or Black

1938			*Perf. 13½*	
264	A15	25c on 75c org red (Bk)	.50	.25
265	A11	50c on 1.50p dp grn (R)	.60	.30
266	A17	2p on 7.50p dl bl (R)	1.00	.60
267	A17	5p on 7.50p dl bl (R)	1.75	.90
268	A15	10p on 50p ol brn (Bk)	2.25	.95
		Nos. 264-268 (5)	6.10	3.00

President Hashem Bek el Atassi — A27

1938-43		Photo.	Unwmk.	
268A	A27	10p dp blue ('42)	1.25	.85
269	A27	12.50p on 10p dp bl (R)	1.50	.90
270	A27	20p dark brown	1.25	.85
		Nos. 268A-270 (3)	4.00	2.60

The 10pi and 20pi exist imperf.

Columns at Palmyra A28

1940		Litho.	*Perf. 11½*	
271	A28	5p pale rose	2.00	.65

Exists imperf.

Museum at Damascus — A29

Hotel at Bloudan A30

Kasr-el-Heir A31

1940   **Typo.**   **Perf. 13x14**

272	A29	10c bright rose	.70	.25
273	A29	20c light blue	.70	.25
274	A29	25c fawn	.75	.25
275	A29	50c ultra	.75	.25

Engr.
Perf. 13

276	A30	1p peacock blue	1.00	.25
277	A30	1.50p chocolate	1.50	.70
278	A30	2.50p dark green	1.00	.30
279	A31	5p violet	1.10	.40
280	A31	7.50p vermilion	2.00	.40
281	A31	50p sepia	3.50	1.30
		Nos. 272-281 (10)	13.00	4.30

For overprints see Nos. 298-299.

President Taj Eddin Hassani A32

1942, Apr. 6   **Litho.**   **Perf. 11½**

282	A32	50c sage green	4.50	2.50
283	A32	1.50p dull gray brn	4.75	2.50
284	A32	6p fawn	5.00	2.50
285	A32	15p light blue	5.50	2.50
		Nos. 282-285,C96-C97 (6)	28.00	18.25

Proclamation of independence by the Allies, Sept. 27, 1941.

President Taj Eddin Hassani — A33

1942   **Photo.**   **Unwmk.**

286	A33	6p rose lake & salmon on rose	4.00	1.25
287	A33	15p dull blue & blue	4.00	1.25
		Nos. 286-287,C98 (3)	12.00	6.50

Nos. 286-287 exist imperf.

President Hassani and Map of Syria — A34

1943   **Litho.**

288	A34	1p light green	4.00	1.50
289	A34	4p buff	4.00	1.50
290	A34	8p pale violet	4.00	1.50
291	A34	10p salmon	4.00	1.50
292	A34	20p dull chalky blue	4.00	1.50
		Nos. 288-292,C99-C102 (9)	32.00	19.50

Proclamation of a United Syria. Exist imperf.

Stamps of 1943 Overprinted with Border in Black

1943

293	A34	1p light green	4.00	1.50
294	A34	4p buff	4.00	1.50
295	A34	8p pale violet	4.00	1.50

296	A34	10p salmon	4.00	1.50
297	A34	20p dl chalky bl	4.25	1.50
		Nos. 293-297,C103-C106 (9)	32.25	19.50

Mourning for President Hassani. Exist imperf.

Nos. 278 and 280 Overprinted in Carmine or Black

1944   **Unwmk.**   **Perf. 13**

298	A30	2.50p dk green (C)	4.50	2.50
299	A31	7.50p vermilion (Bk)	4.75	2.75
		Nos. 298-299,C114-C116 (5)	37.75	33.75

1000th anniv. of the Arab poet and philosopher, abu-al-Ala al-Maarri.

President Shukri el Kouatly — A35

1945, Mar. 15   **Litho.**   **Perf. 11½**

300	A35	4p pale lilac	1.00	.35
301	A35	6p dull blue	1.25	.40
302	A35	10p salmon	1.25	.40
303	A35	15p dark brown	2.00	.50
304	A35	20p slate green	2.00	.50
305	A35	40p orange	3.00	1.00
		Nos. 300-305,C117-C123 (13)	26.60	10.35

Resumption of constitutional government.

Fiscal Stamps Overprinted or Surcharged in Black

A36

A37

A38

A39

1945   **Typo.**   **Perf. 11, 11½x11**

306	A36	12½p on 15p yel grn	4.25	1.25
307	A37	25p buff	8.25	1.75
307A	A38	25p on 25s lt vio brn	5.25	1.40
308	A39	50p on 75p brn org	9.50	2.50
309	A39	75p brown org	12.00	3.25
310	A37	100p yellow grn	19.00	4.00
		Nos. 306-310 (6)	58.25	14.15

Type of 1945 and Nos. 308 and 310 Overprinted in Black

a

b

1945   **Unwmk.**   **Perf. 11**

311	A37(b)	50p magenta	6.00	1.50
312	A39(a)	50p on 75p brn org	4.50	.90
313	A37(b)	100p yellow green	7.75	1.50
		Nos. 311-313 (3)	18.25	3.90

> Catalogue values for unused stamps in this section, from this point to the end of the section, are for Never Hinged items.

Independent Republic

A40

Fiscal Stamp Overprinted in Carmine

1946

314	A40	200p light blue	35.00	10.00

Sun and Ears of Wheat — A41

President Shukri el Kouatly — A42

1946   **Litho.**   **Perf. 13x13½**

315	A41	50c brown orange	.60	.25
316	A41	1p violet	1.00	.25
317	A41	2.50p blue gray	1.25	.30
318	A41	5p lt blue green	1.10	.25

Photo.
Perf. 13½x13, 13x13½

319	A42	7.50p dark brown	.60	.25
320	A42	10p Prussian green	.85	.25
321	A42	12.50p deep violet	2.25	.25
		Nos. 315-321 (7)	7.65	1.80

For overprints see Nos. 328-329, 335-336.

Arab Horse A44

1946-47   **Litho.**

325	A44	50p olive brown	5.75	.90
326	A44	100p dk blue grn ('47)	12.50	2.00
327	A44	200p rose violet ('47)	65.00	5.50
		Nos. 325-327 (3)	83.25	8.40

For overprints and surcharges see Nos. 330, 337, 347, 356-357.

Nos. 320, 321 and 325 Overprinted in Black or Green

1946, Apr. 17

328	A42	10p Prus green	1.25	.45
329	A42	12.50p deep violet	1.75	.65
330	A44	50p olive brown (G)	4.00	1.60
		Nos. 328-330,C135 (4)	9.50	3.70

Evacuation of British and French troops from Syria. For surcharge see No. 347.

President Shukri el Kouatly — A45

1946   **Unwmk.**   **Litho.**   **Perf. 13½x13**

331	A45	15p red	1.00	.25
332	A45	20p violet	1.50	.25
333	A45	25p ultra	2.25	.30
		Nos. 331-333 (3)	4.75	.80

No. 333 Overprinted in Magenta

1946, Aug. 28

334	A45	25p ultra	3.00	1.10
		Nos. 334,C136-C138 (4)	14.50	7.10

8th Arab Medical Cong., Aleppo, 8/28-9/4.

Nos. 328 to 330 With Additional Overprint in Black

e

f

Perf. 13½x13, 13x13½
1947, June 10

335	A42(e)	10p Prus green	1.50	.25
336	A42(e)	12.50p deep violet	1.60	.25
337	A44(f)	50p olive brown	4.50	.75
		Nos. 335-337,C139 (4)	10.10	2.50

Evacuation of British and French troops, 1st anniv.

Hercules and the Lion — A46

Mosaics from Omayyad Mosque, Damascus A47

1947, Nov. 15   **Litho.**   **Perf. 11½**

338	A46	12.50p slate green	3.00	.40
339	A47	25p gray blue	4.25	.85
		Nos. 338-339,C140-C141 (4)	13.75	3.75

1st Arab Archaeological Cong., Damascus, Nov.

See No. C141a.

Courtyard of Azem Palace A48

Telephone Building A49

1947, Nov. 15
340	A48	12.50p deep claret	2.50	.50
341	A49	25p brt blue	3.25	.70
		Nos. 340-341,C142-C143 (4)	11.25	3.95

3rd Congress of Arab Engineers, Damascus, Nov.
See No. C143a.

House of Parliament A50

Pres. Shukri el Kouatly — A51

1948, June 23 Unwmk. Perf. 10½
342	A50	12.50p black & org	1.00	.25
343	A51	25p deep rose	2.00	.45
		Nos. 342-343,C144-C145 (4)	6.15	1.95

Reelection of Pres. Shukri el Kouatly. See No. C145a.

National Emblem — A52

Syrian Flag and Soldier — A53

1948, June 23 Litho.
344	A52	12.50p gray & choc	1.50	.25
345	A53	25p multicolored	2.00	.45
		Nos. 344-345,C146-C147 (4)	6.25	1.75

Inauguration of compulsory military training. See No. C147a.

Nos. 215 and 327 Surcharged with New Value and Bars in Black

1948 Perf. 13, 13x13½
346	A15	50c on 75c org red	.50	.25
347	A44	25p on 200p rose vio	2.75	.30

Col. Husni Zayim — A54

1949, June 20 Litho. Perf. 11½
348	A54	25p blue	2.00	.40

Revolution of Mar. 30, 1949. See No. C153.

A souvenir sheet comprises Nos. 348 and C153, imperf. Value $80.

Ain el Arous A55

Palmyra — A56

1949, June 20
349	A55	12.50p violet	3.75	1.50
350	A56	25p blue	6.50	2.75
		Nos. 349-350,C154-C155 (4)	36.75	22.75

UPU, 75th anniv. See note after No. C155.

Pres. Husni Zayim and Map — A57

Wmk. 291
1949, Aug. 6 Litho. Perf. 11½
351	A57	25p blue & brown	6.50	1.25

Election of President Husni Zayim. See Nos. C156, C156a.

Tel-Chehab Waterfall — A58

Damascus Scene A59

1949
352	A58	5p gray	.75	.25
353	A58	7.50p olive gray	1.00	.25
354	A59	12.50p violet brown	1.25	.25
355	A59	25p blue	2.00	.40
		Nos. 352-355 (4)	5.00	1.15

See No. 376.

Nos. 327 and 326 Surcharged with New Value and Bars in Black

1950 Unwmk. Perf. 13x13½
356	A44	2.50p on 200p rose vio	.40	.25
357	A44	10p on 100p dk bl grn	.50	.25

National Emblem — A60

Road to Damascus A61

Postal Administration Building, Damascus — A62

1950-51 Litho. Perf. 11½
358	A60	50c orange brn	.30	.25
359	A60	2.50p pink	.40	.25
360	A61	10p purple ('51)	.50	.25
361	A61	12.50p sage grn ('51)	.75	.40
362	A62	25p blue ('51)	1.75	.25
363	A62	50p black ('51)	5.25	.60
		Nos. 358-363 (6)	8.95	2.00

Nos. 358 to 363 exist imperforate.

Parliament Building, Damascus A63

1951, Apr. 14
364	A63	12.50p gray blk	.40	.25
365	A63	25p blue	.75	.35
		Nos. 364-365,C162-C163 (4)	2.80	1.85

New constitution adopted Sept. 5, 1950. Nos. 364-365 exist imperforate.

Water Wheel, Hama A64

Palace of Justice, Damascus A65

Perf. 11½
1952, Apr. 22 Litho. Unwmk.
366	A64	50c dark brown	.30	.25
367	A64	2.50p dark blue	.35	.25
368	A64	5p blue green	.40	.25
369	A64	10p red	.45	.25
370	A65	12.50p gray black	.75	.25
371	A65	15p lilac rose	4.00	.25
372	A65	25p deep blue	2.00	.35
373	A65	100p olive brown	7.50	2.00
		Nos. 366-373 (8)	15.75	3.85

Nos. 366-373 exist imperforate.

Type of 1949 and

Crusaders' Fort — A66

Crusaders' Fort — A67

1953 Photo.
374	A67	50c rose red	.40	.25
375	A66	2.50p dark brown	.40	.25
376	A58	7.50p green	.50	.25
377	A67	12.50p deep blue	1.75	.25
		Nos. 374-377 (4)	3.05	1.00

Farm Workers — A68

Family Group A69

Designs: 1pi, 5pi, Farm workers. 10pi, 12½p, Family group. 20pi, 25pi, 50pi, Factory and construction workers.

1954 Perf. 11½
378	A68	1p olive	.25	.25
379	A68	2½p brown red	.30	.25
380	A68	5p deep blue	.40	.25
381	A69	7½p brown red	.50	.25
382	A69	10p black	.60	.25
383	A69	12½p violet	.70	.25
384	A69	20p deep plum	.85	.25
385	A69	25p violet	1.25	.25
386	A69	50p dark green	3.00	.75
		Nos. 378-386 (9)	7.85	2.85

For overprints see Nos. 387-388, UAR 20, 34.

Nos. 382 and 385 Overprinted in Carmine

1954, Oct. 9
387	A69	10p black	1.25	.35
388	A69	25p violet	1.50	.45
		Nos. 387-388,C185-C186 (4)	5.85	3.40

Cotton Festival, Aleppo, October 1954.

Globe — A69a

Arab Postal Union Issue
1955 Photo. Perf. 13½x13
389	A69a	12½p green	.50	.25
390	A69a	25p violet	.95	.35
		Nos. 389-390,C191 (3)	1.85	.85

Founding of the APU, 7/1/54. Exist imperf. For overprints see Nos. 396-399, C203, C207.

Mother and Child — A70

1955, May 13 Litho. Perf. 11½
391	A70	25p red	.80	.25
		Nos. 391,C194-C195 (3)	3.30	1.80

Mother's Day.

United Nations Emblem A71

1955 Photo.
392	A71	7½p crimson	.50	.25
393	A71	12½p Prus green	1.00	.50
		Nos. 392-393,C200-C201 (4)	3.75	1.75

UN, 10th anniv., Oct. 24. For overprints see Nos. 401-402.

Aqueduct at Aleppo
A72

1955 **Litho.** **Unwmk.**
394 A72 7.50p lilac .55 .25
395 A72 12.50p carmine 1.00 .35
Nos. 394-395,C202 (3) 3.55 1.70

New aqueduct bringing water from the Euphrates to Northern Syria. Exist imperf.

Nos. 389-390 Overprinted in Ultramarine or Green

1955 **Photo.** **Perf. 13½x13**
396 A69a 12½p green .40 .25
397 A69a 25p vio (G) 1.25 .40
Nos. 396-397,C203 (3) 2.15 .90

APU Congress held at Cairo, Mar. 15.

Nos. 389-390 Overprinted in Black

1956
398 A69a 12½p green .50 .25
399 A69a 25p violet 1.25 .55
Nos. 398-399,C207 (3) 2.25 1.05

Visit of King Hussein of Jordan to Damascus, Apr. 1956.

Cotton — A73

1956 **Unwmk.** **Litho.** **Perf. 11½**
400 A73 2½p bluish green .50 .25

Issued to publicize a Cotton Festival.

Nos. 392-393 Overprinted in Black

1956 **Photo.** **Perf. 11½**
401 A71 7½p crimson .50 .25
402 A71 12½p Prussian green .75 .35
Nos. 401-402,C221-C222 (4) 4.00 2.45

UN, 11th anniv.

People's Army
A74

1957 **Litho.** **Perf. 11½**
403 A74 5p lilac rose .30 .25
404 A74 20p gray green .50 .25

Formation of the Popular Resistance Movement.

For overprints see Nos. 405-406, 413-414.

Nos. 403-404 Overprinted in Black or Red

1957
405 A74 5p lilac rose .30 .25
406 A74 20p gray green (R) .65 .30

Evacuation of Port Said by British and French troops, Dec. 22, 1956.

Azem Palace, Damascus
A75

1957 **Litho.** **Perf. 11½**
407 A75 12½p lilac .30 .25
408 A75 15p gray .50 .25

For overprint see UAR No. 33.

Map of Near East, Scales and Damascus Skyline — A76

1957 **Wmk. 291** **Perf. 11½**
409 A76 12½p bright green .40 .25
Nos. 409,C240-C241 (3) 1.70 1.05

3rd Congress of the Union of Arab Lawyers, Damascus, Sept. 21-25.

Cotton, Bale and Ship — A77

1957
410 A77 12½p lt bl grn & blk .50 .25
Nos. 410,C242-C243 (3) 2.50 1.15

Cotton Festival, Aleppo, Oct. 3-5.

Children — A78

1957, Oct. 7
411 A78 12½p olive 1.00 .25
Nos. 411,C244-C245 (3) 3.75 1.25

Intl. Children's Day, Oct. 7.
For overprint see UAR Nos. 13A, C10-C11.

Mailing and Receiving Letter
A79

1957 **Unwmk.**
412 A79 5p magenta .50 .25

Intl. Letter Writing Week, Oct. 6-12. See No. C246.

Nos. 403-404 Overprinted in Black or Red

1957 **Perf. 11½**
413 A74 5p lilac rose .40 .25
414 A74 20p gray green (R) .50 .25

Digging of fortifications along the Syrian-Israeli frontier.

Scales, Torch and Map
A80

1957, Nov. 8 **Wmk. 291**
415 A80 20p olive gray .55 .25
Nos. 415,C247-C248 (3) 1.80 1.10

Congress of Afro-Asian Jurists, Damascus.

Glider
A81

1957, Nov. 8 **Litho.** **Perf. 11½**
416 A81 25p red brown 1.10 .30
417 A81 35p green 1.50 .40
418 A81 40p ultra 3.00 .70
Nos. 416-418 (3) 5.60 1.40

Issued to commemorate a glider festival.

Khaled ibn el Walid Mosque, Homs — A82

1957 **Unwmk.** **Perf. 12**
419 A82 2½p dull brown .40 .25

Scroll, Communications Building and Telephone — A83

1958 **Wmk. 291** **Perf. 11½**
420 A83 25p ultra .30 .25
Nos. 420,C249-C250 (3) 1.05 .75

Issues of 1958-61 released by the United Arab Republic are listed following the listings of Syria, Issues of the Arabian Government.

Syrian Arab Republic

Hall of Parliament, Damascus
A83a

1961 **Unwmk.** **Litho.** **Perf. 12**
420A A83a 15p magenta .40 .25
420B A83a 35p olive gray .75 .25

Establishment of Syrian Arab Republic.

Water Wheel, Hama — A84   Roman Arch of Triumph, Latakia — A85

Qalb Lozah Church, Aleppo
A86

7½p, 10p, Khaled ibn el Walid Mosque, Homs.

Perf. 11½x11
1961-62 **Unwmk.** **Litho.**
421 A84 2½p rose red .30 .25
422 A84 5p blue .30 .25
423 A84 7½p blue grn ('62) .30 .25
424 A84 10p orange ('62) .35 .25

Perf. 12x11½
425 A85 12½p gray brn .60 .25
426 A86 17½p olive gray ('62) .50 .25
427 A85 25p dull red brown .70 .25
428 A86 35p dull green ('62) .65 .25
Nos. 421-428 (8) 3.70 2.00

Types of 1961, Regular and Air Post

Designs: 2½p, 5p, 7½p, 10p, Arch, Jupiter Temple. 12½p, 15p, 17½p, 22½p, "The Beauty of Palmyra."

1962 **Perf. 11½x11**
429 A84 2½p gray blue .30 .25
430 A84 5p brown orange .30 .25
431 A84 7½p olive bister .30 .25
432 A84 10p claret .30 .25

Perf. 12x11½
Size: 26x38mm
433 AP68 12½p gray olive .35 .25
434 AP68 15p ultra .50 .25
435 AP68 17½p olive brown .50 .25
436 AP68 22½p grnsh blue .70 .25
Nos. 429-436 (8) 3.25 2.00

Martyrs' Memorial — A87

1962, June 11 **Litho.**
440 A87 12½p tan & sepia .30 .25
441 A87 35p green & bl grn .35 .25

1925 Revolution.

Pres. Nazem el-Kodsi — A88

1962, Dec. 14   **Perf. 12x11½**
442 A88 12½p sepia & lt bl   .30 .25

1st anniv. of the election of Pres. Nazem el-Kodsi. See No. C278.

Queen Zenobia — A89

Central Bank of Syria A90

Designs: 2½p, 5p, "The Beauty of Palmyra." 17½p, Hejaz Railway Station, Damascus. 22½p, Mouassat Hospital, Damascus. 35p, P.T.T. Jalaa Avenue Office, Damascus.

1963   **Unwmk.**   **Perf. 11½x11**
443 A89 2½p dk bl gray   .30 .25
444 A89 5p rose lilac   .30 .25
445 A89 7½p dull blue   .35 .25
446 A89 10p olive gray   .70 .25
447 A89 12½p ultra   1.00 .25
448 A89 15p violet brn   1.50 .25

       Perf. 11½x12
449 A90 17½p dull violet   .60 .25
450 A90 22½p brt violet   .30 .25
451 A90 25p bister brown   .30 .25
452 A90 35p bright pink   .35 .25
   Nos. 443-452 (10)   5.70 2.50

Wheat Emblem and Globe — A91

1963, Mar. 21   **Litho.**   **Perf. 12x11½**
453 A91 12½p ultra & blk   .30 .25

FAO "Freedom from Hunger" Campaign. See No. C291 and souvenir sheet No. C291a.

Cotton Festival Type of Air Post Issue, 1962, Inscribed "1963"

1963, Sept. 26   **Perf. 12x11½**
455 AP75 17½p multi   .30 .25
456 AP75 22½p multi   .35 .25

The 1963 Cotton Festival, Aleppo.

Boy Playing Ball and UN Emblem — A92

1963, Oct. 24   **Perf. 12x11½**
457 A92 12½p emer & sl grn   .30 .25
458 A92 22½p rose red & dk grn   .30 .25

Issued for International Children's Day.

Ugharit Princess — A93

1964   **Litho.**   **Perf. 11½x11**
459 A93 2½p gray   .30 .25
460 A93 5p brown   .30 .25
461 A93 7½p rose claret   .30 .25
462 A93 10p emerald   .30 .25
463 A93 12½p light violet   .30 .25
464 A93 17½p ultra   .30 .25
465 A93 20p rose carmine   .45 .25
466 A93 25p orange   .75 .25
   Nos. 459-466 (8)   3.00 2.00

Map of North Africa and Middle East, Flag of Syria, and Crowd A94

1965, Mar. 8   **Litho.**   **Perf. 11½x12**
467 A94 12½p multicolored   .30 .25
468 A94 17½p multicolored   .30 .25
469 A94 20p multicolored   .30 .25
   Nos. 467-469 (3)   .90 .75

Mar. 8 Revolution, 2nd anniv.

Weather Map and Anemometer — A95

1965, Mar. 23   **Litho.**   **Unwmk.**
470 A95 12½p dl lilac & blk   .30 .25
471 A95 27½p lt blue & blk   .30 .25

Fifth World Meteorological Day.

"Evacuation of Apr. 17, 1946" — A96

1965, Apr. 17   **Litho.**   **Perf. 12x11½**
472 A96 12½p bl & brt yel grn   .30 .25
473 A96 27½p rose red & lt lil   .30 .25

19th anniv. of the evacuation of British and French troops from Syria.

Peasants' Union Emblem — A97

1965, Aug.   **Unwmk.**   **Perf. 11½x11**
474 A97 2½p blue green   .30 .25
475 A97 12½p purple   .30 .25
476 A97 15p maroon   .30 .25
   Nos. 474-476 (3)   .90 .75

Issued to publicize the Peasants' Union.

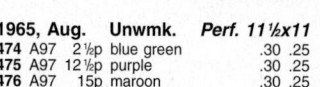

Torch, Map of Arab Countries and Farmer, Soldier, Woman, Intellectual and Worker — A98

1965, Nov. 23   **Perf. 12x11½**
477 A98 12½p multicolored   .30 .25
478 A98 25p multicolored   .30 .25

National Council of the Revolution, a legislative body working for a socialist and democratic society.

Workers, Factory and Emblem — A99

1966, Jan.   **Litho.**   **Perf. 11½x11**
479 A99 12½p blue   .30 .25
480 A99 15p carmine   .30 .25
481 A99 20p dull violet   .30 .25
482 A99 25p olive gray   .30 .25
   Nos. 479-482 (4)   1.20 1.00

Establishment of the General Union of Trade Unions.

Roman Lamp A100

Islamic Vessel, 12th Century A101

1966   **Litho.**   **Perf. 11½x11**
483 A100 2½p slate green   .30 .25
484 A100 5p magenta   .30 .25
485 A101 7½p brown   .30 .25
486 A101 10p brt rose lilac   .30 .25
   Nos. 483-486 (4)   1.20 1.00

"Evacuation of Troops" — A102

1966, Apr. 17   **Litho.**   **Perf. 12x11½**
487 A102 12½p multi   .30 .25
488 A102 27½p multi   .30 .25

20th anniv. of the evacuation of British and French troops from Syria.

Bust of Core, Terra Cotta Vase — A103

Design: 15p, 20p, 25p, 27½p, Bronze vase in form of seated African woman.

1967   **Perf. 11½x11**
489 A103 2½p brt green   .30 .25
490 A103 5p salmon pink   .30 .25
491 A103 10p grnsh blue   .30 .25
492 A103 12½p dull brown   .30 .25
493 A103 15p brt pink   .30 .25
494 A103 20p brt blue   .30 .25

495 A103 25p green   .30 .25
496 A103 27½p violet blue   .30 .25
   Nos. 489-496 (8)   2.40 2.00

Arab Revolution Monument, Damascus A104

1968, Mar. 8   **Litho.**   **Perf. 12x12½**
497 A104 12½p black, yel & brn   .30 .25
498 A104 25p blk, pink & car rose   .30 .25
499 A104 27½p blk, lt grn & grn   .30 .25
   Nos. 497-499 (3)   .90 .75

Mar. 8 Revolution, 5th anniversary.

Map of Syria — A105

1968, Apr. 4   **Litho.**   **Perf. 12x12½**
500 A105 12½p pink & multi   .30 .25
501 A105 60p gray & multi   .40 .25

Arab Baath Socialist Party, 21st anniv.

Hands Holding Wrench, Gun and Torch — A106

1968, Apr. 13
502 A106 12½p tan & multi   .30 .25
503 A106 17½p rose & multi   .30 .25
504 A106 25p yellow & multi   .30 .25
   Nos. 502-504 (3)   .90 .75

Issued to publicize the mobilization effort.

Rising Sun, Power Lines and Railroad Tracks A107

1968, Apr. 17   **Litho.**   **Perf. 12½x12**
505 A107 12½p multicolored   .30 .25
506 A107 27½p violet & multi   .30 .25

22nd anniv. of the evacuation of British and French troops from Syria.

Oil Wells and Oil Pipe Line on Map — A108

1968, May 1
507 A108 12½p lt & dk grn & ultra .30 .25
508 A108 17½p pink, brn & ultra .30 .25

Syrian oil exploitation; completion of the oil pipe line to Tartus.

Map of Palestine and Torch — A109

1968, May   Litho.   Perf. 12x12½
509 A109 12½p ultra, blk & red .75 .35
510 A109 25p ol bis, blk & red 1.00 .35
511 A109 27½p gray, blk & red 1.50 .50
    Nos. 509-511 (3) 3.25 1.20

Issued for Palestine Day.

Citadel of Aleppo, Wheat and Cogwheel A110

1968, July 18   Litho.   Perf. 12x12½
512 A110 12½p multi .30 .25
513 A110 27½p multi .30 .25

Industrial and Agricultural Fair, Aleppo.

Fair Emblem, Globe, Grain, Wheel and Horse — A111

Design: 27½p, Syrian flag, hand with torch, fair emblem, globe, grain and wheel.

Perf. 12x12½, 12½x12
1968, Aug. 25   Litho.
514 A111 12½p dp brn, blk & emer .30 .25
515 A111 27½p multicolored .30 .25
516 A111 60p bl gray, blk & dp org .30 .25
    Nos. 514-516 (3) .90 .75

15th Intl. Damascus Fair, Aug. 25-Sept. 20.

Woman Carrying Cotton, and Castle of Aleppo — A112

1968, Oct. 3   Litho.   Perf. 12x12½
517 A112 12½p multi .30 .25
518 A112 27½p multi .30 .25

13th Cotton Festival, Aleppo.

Al Jahez — A113

1968, Nov. 9   Litho.   Perf. 12x12½
519 A113 12½p black & buff .30 .25
520 A113 27½p black & gray .60 .25

9th Science Week; Al Jahez Abu Uthman Amr ben Bahr (776-868).

Oil Derrick and Pipe Line — A114

1968   Perf. 12x11
521 A114 2½p grnsh bl & dk grn .30 .25
522 A114 5p grn & vio bl .30 .25
523 A114 7½p lt yel grn & bl .30 .25
524 A114 10p brt yel & grn .30 .25
525 A114 12½p yellow & ver .30 .25
526 A114 15p ol bis & dk brn .30 .25
527 A114 27½p dl org & dk red brn .30 .25
    Nos. 521-527 (7) 2.10 1.75

Broken Chains and Sun A115

1969, Mar. 8   Litho.   Perf. 12½x12
Sun in Yellow and Red
528 A115 12½p vio bl & blk .30 .25
529 A115 25p gray & blk .30 .25
530 A115 27½p dull grn & blk .30 .25
    Nos. 528-530 (3) .90 .75

March 8 Revolution, 6th anniversary.

"Sun of Freedom, Young Man and Woman" — A116

1969, Mar. 29   Perf. 12x12½
531 A116 12½p multi .30 .25
532 A116 25p multi .30 .25

Youth Week; 5th Youth Festival, Homs, 4/18-24.

Liberation through Knowledge and Construction A117

1969, Apr. 17   Litho.   Perf. 12x12½
533 A117 12½p yellow & multi .30 .25
534 A117 27½p gray & multi .30 .25

23rd anniv. of the evacuation of British and French troops from Syria.

Mahatma Gandhi — A118

1969, Oct. 7   Litho.   Perf. 12x12½
535 A118 12½p brown & dull yel .30 .25
536 A118 27½p green & yellow .30 .25

Mohandas K. Gandhi (1869-1948), leader in India's fight for independence.

Cotton — A119

1969, Oct. 10
537 A119 12½p multi .30 .25
538 A119 17½p multi .30 .25
539 A119 25p multi .90 .75
    Nos. 537-539 (3) .90 .75

14th Cotton Festival, Aleppo.

Map of Arab Countries A120

Designs: 25p, Arab Academy. 27½p, Damascus University.

1969, Nov. 2   Litho.   Perf. 12½x12
540 A120 12½p ultra & lt grn .30 .25
541 A120 25p dk pur & dp pink .30 .25
542 A120 27½p dp bis & yel grn .30 .25
    Nos. 540-542 (3) .90 .75

10th Science Week, and 6th Arab Scientific Conf. No. 541 also for 50th anniv. of the Arab Academy and No. 542, the 50th anniv. of the Medical School of the Damascus University.

Symbols of Progress A121

1970, Mar. 8   Litho.   Perf. 12½x12
543 A121 12½p brt bl, blk & bis brn .30 .25
544 A121 25p red, blk & dp bl .30 .25
545 A121 27½p lt grn, blk & tan .30 .25
    Nos. 543-545 (3) .90 .75

March 8 Revolution, 7th anniversary.

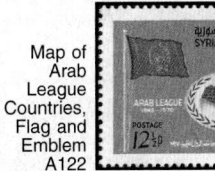

Map of Arab League Countries, Flag and Emblem A122

1970, Mar. 22
546 A122 12½p multi .30 .25
547 A122 25p gray & multi .30 .25
548 A122 27½p multi .35 .25
    Nos. 546-548 (3) .95 .75

25th anniversary of the Arab League.

Sultan Saladin and Battle of Hattin, 1187, between Saracens and Crusaders — A123

1970, Apr. 17   Litho.   Perf. 12½x12
549 A123 15p brn & buff .30 .25
550 A123 35p lilac & buff .35 .25

24th anniv. of the evacuation of British and French troops from Syria.

Development of Agriculture and Industry — A124

1970-71   Litho.   Perf. 11x11½
551 A124 2½p brn & red ('71) .30 .25
552 A124 5p orange & bl .30 .25
553 A124 7½p lil & gray ('71) .30 .25
554 A124 10p lt & dk brn .30 .25
555 A124 12½p blue & org ('71) .30 .25
556 A124 15p grn & red lil .30 .25
557 A124 20p vio & red brn .30 .25
558 A124 22½p red brn & blk ('71) .30 .25
559 A124 25p gray & vio bl .30 .25
560 A124 27½p brt grn & dk brn ('71) .30 .25
561 A124 35p rose red & emer ('71) .35 .25
    Nos. 551-561 (11) 3.35 2.75

Young Man and Woman, Map of Arab Countries A125

1970, May 7   Unwmk.   Perf. 12½x12
569 A125 15p green & ocher .30 .25
570 A125 25p brown & ocher .30 .25

First Youth Week, Latakia, Apr. 23-29. Inscribed "Youth's First Weak" (sic.).

Refugee Family A126

1970, May 15
571 A126 15p multicolored .30 .25
572 A126 25p gray & multi .30 .25
573 A126 35p green & multi .30 .25
    Nos. 571-573 (3) .90 .75

Issued for Arab Refugee Week.

Cotton — A127

1970, Aug. 18   Litho.   Perf. 12½
574 A127 5p shown .30 .25
575 A127 10p Tomatoes .30 .25
576 A127 15p Tobacco .30 .25
577 A127 20p Beets .30 .25
578 A127 35p Wheat .75 .25
    a. Strip of 5, #574-578 2.00 2.00

Industrial and Agricultural Fair, Aleppo.

Boy Scout, Tent, Emblem and Map of Arab Countries A128

1970, Aug. 25   Perf. 12½x12
579 A128 15p gray green   .40 .25
9th Pan-Arab Boy Scout Jamboree, Damascus.

Olive Tree and Emblem A129

1970, Sept. 28   Litho.   Perf. 11½x12
580 A129 15p gray grn, yel & blk   .30 .25
581 A129 25p red brn, yel & blk   .50 .25
Issued to publicize World Olive Year.

Protection of Industry, Agriculture, Arts and Commerce — A130

1971, Mar. 8   Litho.   Perf. 12½x12
582 A130   15p olive, yel & bl   .30 .25
583 A130 22½p red brn, yel & ol   .30 .25
584 A130 27½p bl, yel & red brn   .30 .25
     Nos. 582-584 (3)   .90 .75
March 8 Revolution, 8th anniversary.

Workers Memorial, Hands with Wrench and Olive Branch A131

1971, May 1   Litho.   Perf. 12½x12
585 A131 15p brn vio, yel & bl   .30 .25
586 A131 25p dk bl, bl & yel   .30 .25
Labor Day.

Child and Traffic Lights A132

World Traffic Day: 25p, Road signs, traffic lights, children, vert.

1971, May 4   Perf. 11½x12, 12x11½
587 A132 15p black, red & bl   .30 .25
588 A132 25p gray & multi   .30 .25
589 A132 45p black, red & yel   .30 .25
     Nos. 587-589 (3)   .90 .75

Factories, Cogwheel and Cotton A133

1971, July 15   Litho.   Perf. 12½x12
590 A133 15p lt grn, bl & blk   .30 .25
591 A133 30p red & black   .30 .25
11th Industrial and Agricultural Fair, Aleppo.

Arab Postal Union Emblem — A134

1971, Sep. 1   Perf. 12x12½
592 A134 15p claret & multi   .30 .25
593 A134 20p vio bl & multi   .30 .25
25th anniv. of the Conference of Sofar, Lebanon, establishing the APU.

Flag, Map of Syria, Egypt and Libya — A135

1971, Aug. 13   Perf. 12x11½
594 A135 15p car, dl grn & blk   .30 .25
Confederation of the Arab states of Syria, Libya and Egypt.

Red Pepper and Chemical Factory (Fertilizer Industry) — A136

18th Intl. Damascus Fair: 15p, Electronics industry (TV, telephone, computer). 35p, Glass industry (old map and glass manufacture). 50p, Carpet industry (carpet and looms).

1971, Aug. 25   Perf. 12½
595 A136   5p violet & multi   .30 .25
596 A136 15p dull grn & multi   .30 .25
597 A136 35p multicolored   .30 .25
598 A136 50p yel grn & multi   .50 .25
     Nos. 595-598 (4)   1.40 1.00

Pres. Hafez al Assad and Crowd — A137

1971, Nov.   Litho.   Perf. 12x12½
599 A137 15p vio bl, blk & car   .30 .25
600 A137 20p dk & lt grn, car & blk   .30 .25
1st anniv. of Correctionist Movement of Nov. 16, 1970.

UNESCO Emblem, Radar, Spacecraft, Telephone A138

1971, Dec. 8
601 A138 15p vio bl & multi   .30 .25
602 A138 50p green & multi   .30 .25
25th anniv. of UNESCO.

UNICEF Emblem and Playing Children — A139

1971, Dec. 21
603 A139 15p ultra, dk bl & dp car   .30 .25
604 A139 25p grnsh bl, ocher & dk bl   .30 .25
UNICEF, 25th anniv.

Conference Emblem — A140

1971, Dec.   Perf. 12½x12
605 A140 15p blk, grnsh bl & org   .30 .25
Scholars' Conference.

Book Year Emblem A141

1972, Jan. 2
606 A141 15p tan, lt bl & vio   .30 .25
607 A141 20p brn, lt grn & grn   .30 .25
International Book Year.

Wheel, "8" and Scales of Justice — A142

1972, Mar. 8   Litho.   Perf. 12x12½
608 A142 15p blue grn & vio   .30 .25
609 A142 20p olive bis & car   .30 .25
March 8 Revolution, 9th anniversary.

Baath Party Emblem — A143

1972, Mar. 7
610 A143 15p dk blue & multi   .30 .25
611 A143 20p violet & multi   .30 .25
Arab Baath Socialist Party, 25th anniv.

Eagle, Chimneys, Grain and Oil Rigs — A144

1972, Apr. 17   Perf. 12½x12
612 A144 15p gold, blk & car   .30 .25
Federation of Arab Republics, 1st anniv.

Symbolic Flower, Broken Chain — A145

1972, Apr. 17   Perf. 12x11½
613 A145 15p rose red & gray   .30 .25
614 A145 50p pale bl grn & gray   .30 .25
26th anniv. of the evacuation of British and French troops from Syria.

Hand Holding Wrench and Spade — A146

1972, May 1
615 A146 15p ol grn, bl & blk   .30 .25
616 A146 50p vio bl, brn & blk   .30 .25
Labor Day.

Environment Emblem, Crystals, Microscope A147

1972, June 5
617 A147 15p multicolored   .30 .25
618 A147 50p blue & multi   .35 .25
UN Conference on Human Environment, Stockholm, June 5-16.

Dove over Factory — A148

1972, July 17   Litho.   Perf. 12x11½
619 A148 15p yellow & multi   .30 .25
620 A148 20p yellow & multi   .30 .25
Agricultural and Industrial Fair, Aleppo.

Folk Dance — A149

20p, Women and tambourine player. 50p, Men and drummer.

1972, Aug. 25 Litho. Perf. 12x12½
621 A149 15p shown .30 .25
622 A149 20p multicolored .30 .25
623 A149 50p multicolored .50 .25
   Nos. 621-623 (3) 1.10 .75

19th International Damascus Fair.

Olympic Rings, Discus, Soccer, Swimming — A150

Warriors on Horseback, Olympic Emblems — A151

Design: 60p, Olympic rings, running, gymnastics, fencing.

1972 Litho. Perf. 12½x12
624 A150 15p ol bis, blk & vio .50 .25
625 A150 60p dull bl, blk & org .60 .25

Souvenir Sheet
Imperf
626 A151 75p lt grn, bl & blk 2.00 2.00

20th Olympic Games, Munich, Aug. 26-Sept. 11, 1972.

Emblem of Revolution and Prancing Horse A152

1973, Mar. 8 Litho. Perf. 11½x12
627 A152 15p brt grn, blk & red .30 .25
628 A152 20p dull org, blk & red .30 .25
629 A152 25p blue, blk & red .30 .25
   Nos. 627-629 (3) .90 .75

March 8 Revolution, 10th anniversary.

Heart and WHO Emblem A153

1973, Mar. 21
630 A153 15p gray & multi .30 .25
631 A153 50p lt brown & multi .35 .25

WHO, 25th anniversary.

Cogwheel and Grain Emblem — A154

1973, Apr. 17 Perf. 12x12½
632 A154 15p blue & multi .30 .25
633 A154 20p multicolored .30 .25

27th anniv. of the evacuation of British and French troops from Syria.

Workers and Globe A155

1973, May 1 Perf. 11½x12
634 A155 15p rose & multi .30 .25
635 A155 50p blue & multi .35 .25

Labor Day.

UN, FAO Emblems, People and Symbols — A156

1973, May 7 Perf. 12x11½
636 A156 15p lt grn & red brn .30 .25
637 A156 50p lilac & blue .35 .25

World food program, 10th anniv.

Stock — A157

1973, May 15
638 A157 5p shown .30 .25
639 A157 10p Gardenia .30 .25
640 A157 15p Jasmine .30 .25
641 A157 20p Rose .30 .25
642 A157 25p Narcissus .30 .25
   a. Strip of 5, #638-642 1.50 1.50

Intl. Flower Show, Damascus.

A158

Children and Flame — A158a

Children's Day: 3 children's heads and flame in different arrangements; 25p, 35p, 70p, vertical.

Perf. 11½x12, 12x11½
                  Litho.
1973-74
643 A158 2½p lt olive grn .30 .25
644 A158 5p orange .30 .25
645 A158a 7½p dk brown .30 .25
646 A158a 10p crimson .30 .25
647 A158 15p ultra .30 .25
648 A158a 25p gray .30 .25
649 A158a 35p brt blue .30 .25
650 A158a 55p green .30 .25
651 A158a 70p rose lilac .35 .25
   Nos. 643-651 (9) 2.75 2.25

Issued: 15p, 55p, 70p, 5/73; others, 3/74.

Fair Emblem A159

1973, June 17 Perf. 11½x12
652 A159 15p multicolored .30 .25

13th Agricultural and Industrial Fair, Aleppo.

Euphrates Dam and Power Plant — A160

1973, July 5 Perf. 12½x12
653 A160 15p green & multi .30 .25
654 A160 50p brown & multi .30 .25

Euphrates River diversion and dam project.

Woman from Deir Ezzor — A161

Women's Costumes from: 10p, Hassaké. 20p, As Sahel. 25p, Zakié. 50p, Sarakeb.

1973, July 25 Litho. Perf. 12
655 A161 5p multicolored .30 .25
656 A161 10p multicolored .30 .25
657 A161 20p multicolored .30 .25
658 A161 25p multicolored .30 .25
659 A161 50p multicolored .30 .25
   a. Strip of 5, #655-659 1.50 1.50

20th International Damascus Fair.

Map of Palestine, Barbed Wire, Human Rights Emblem — A162

1973, Aug. 20 Perf. 12x11½
660 A162 15p lt green & multi .90 .50
661 A162 50p lt blue & multi 1.75 .50

25th anniversary of the Universal Declaration of Human Rights.

Citadel of Ja'abar A163

15p, Minaret of Meskeneh, vert. 25p, Statue of Psyche at Anab al Safinah, vert.

Perf. 11½x12, 12x11½
1973, Sept. 5 Litho.
662 A163 10p black, org & blue .30 .25
663 A163 15p black, org & blue .30 .25
664 A163 25p black, org & blue .30 .25
   Nos. 662-664 (3) .90 .75

Salvage of monuments threatened by Euphrates Dam.

WMO Emblem A164

1973, Sept. 12 Perf. 11½x12
665 A164 70p yellow & multi .50 .25

Intl. meteorological cooperation, cent.

Maalula A165

Design: 50p, Ruins of Afamia.

1973, Oct. 22 Litho. Perf. 11½x12
666 A165 15p gray blue & blk .30 .25
667 A165 50p brown & blk .30 .25

Arab Emigrants' Congress, Buenos Aires.

Workers and Soldiers A166

1973, Nov. 16 Litho. Perf. 12½x12
668 A166 15p ultra & yellow .30 .25
669 A166 25p purple & red brn .30 .25

3rd anniv. of Correctionist Movement of Nov. 16, 1970.

Nicolaus Copernicus A167

Design: 25p, Abu-al-Rayhan al-Biruni.

1973, Dec. 15 Perf. 12x11½
670 A167 15p gold & black .30 .25
671 A167 25p gold & black .30 .25

14th Science Week.

Arms of Syria and Emblems A168

1974, Mar. 8 *Perf. 11x12*
672 A168 20p gray & blue .30 .25
673 A168 25p lt green & vio .30 .25
11th anniversary of March 8th Revolution.

UPU Emblem — A169

Air Mail Letter & UPU Emblem — A169a

1974, Mar. 15 *Perf. 12x11½, 11½x12*
674 A169 15p gray & multi .30 .25
675 A169a 20p multicolored .30 .25
676 A169 70p gray & multi .50 .25
Nos. 674-676 (3) 1.10 .75
Centenary of Universal Postal Union.

Arab Postal Institute A170

1974, Apr. 10 *Perf. 11½x12*
677 A170 15p multicolored .30 .25
Inauguration of the Higher Arab Postal Institute, Damascus, Apr. 10.

Sun and Monument A171

1974, Apr. 10
678 A171 15p emerald, blk & org .30 .25
679 A171 20p dp org, blk & org .30 .25
28th anniversary of the evacuation of British and French troops from Syria.

Machine Shop Worker — A172

1974, May 1 *Perf. 12x12½*
680 A172 15p black, yel & bl .30 .25
681 A172 50p black, buff & bl .30 .25
Labor Day.

Abulfeda — A173

Design: 200p, al-Farabi.

1974 *Litho.* *Perf. 11½x11*
682 A173 100p pale green .50 .25
683 A173 200p lt brown 1.00 .45

Damascus Fair Emblem — A174

Design: 25p, Cog wheel and sun.

1974, July 25 *Perf. 11½x11*
684 A174 15p multicolored .30 .25
685 A174 25p blue, blk & yel .30 .25
21st International Damascus Fair.

Figs — A175

Fruits: 15p, Grapes. 20p, Pomegranates. 25p, Cherries. 35p, Rose hips.

1974, Aug. 21 *Perf. 12x12½*
686 A175 5p gray & multi .30 .25
687 A175 15p gray & multi .30 .25
688 A175 20p gray & multi .30 .25
689 A175 25p gray & multi .30 .25
690 A175 35p gray & multi .30 .25
a. Strip of 5, #686-690 2.50 2.50
Agricultural and Industrial Fair, Aleppo.

Burning Fuse and Flowers — A176

20p, Bomb and star-shaped holes in target.

1974, Oct. 6 *Litho.* *Perf. 12x12½*
691 A176 15p multicolored .75 .25
692 A176 20p multicolored 1.00 .25
First anniv. of October Liberation War (Yom Kippur War).

Rook and Knight — A177

Design: 50p, Knight and chess board.

1974, Nov. 23
693 A177 15p blue & black .75 .25
694 A177 50p orange, blk & bl 2.25 .80
Chess Federation, 50th anniversary.

WPY Emblem — A178

1974, Dec. 4 *Litho.* *Perf. 12x12½*
695 A178 50p black, slate & red .30 .25
World Population Year.

Ishtup, Ilum — A179

Ancient Statuettes: 55p, Woman holding pitcher. 70p, Ur-Nina.

1975 *Perf. 12x11½*
696 A179 20p brt green .30 .25
697 A179 55p brown .30 .25
698 A179 70p gray blue .50 .25
Nos. 696-698 (3) 1.10 .75

"A," People and Sun — A180

1975, Mar. 8 *Litho.* *Perf. 12x11½*
699 A180 15p gray & multi .30 .25
12th anniversary, March 8th Revolution.

Postal Savings Bank Emblem, Family — A181

Design: 20p, Family depositing money, and stamped envelope.

1975, Mar. 17
700 A181 15p brt green & multi .30 .25
701 A181 20p orange & black .30 .25
Publicity for Savings Certificates and Postal Savings Bank.

"Sun" and Dove — A182

1975, Apr. 17 *Litho.* *Perf. 12x11½*
702 A182 15p bister, red & blk .30 .25
703 A182 25p bister, grn & blk .30 .25
29th anniversary of the evacuation of British and French troops from Syria.

"Worker and Industry" — A183

1975, May 1 *Litho.* *Perf. 12x11½*
704 A183 15p blue grn & blk .30 .25
705 A183 25p brown, yel & blk .30 .25
Labor Day.

Camomile A184

Flowers: 10p, Chincherinchi. 15p, Carnation. 20p, Poppy. 25p, Honeysuckle.

1975, May 17
706 A184 5p ultra & multi .30 .25
707 A184 10p lilac & multi .30 .25
708 A184 15p blue & multi .35 .25
709 A184 20p gray grn & multi .40 .25
710 A184 25p vio bl & multi .75 .25
a. Strip of 5, #706-710 2.10 2.10
International Flower Show, Damascus.

Kuneitra Destroyed and Rebuilt — A185

1975, June 5 *Perf. 12½*
711 A185 50p black & multi .35 .25
Re-occupation of Kuneitra by Syria.

Apples A186

1975, July 7
712 A186 5p shown .30 .25
713 A186 10p Quince .30 .25
714 A186 15p Apricots .35 .25
715 A186 20p Grapes .40 .25
716 A186 25p Figs .50 .25
a. Strip of 5, #712-716 1.90 1.90
Agricultural and Industrial Fair, Aleppo.

22nd Intl.
Damascus
Fair — A187

1975, July 25   Litho.   Perf. 12x11½
717 A187 15p olive grn & multi   .30 .25
718 A187 35p brown & multi   .30 .25

Pres.
Hafez al
Assad
A188

1975, Nov. 29   Litho.   Perf. 11½x12
719 A188 15p green & multi   .30 .25
720 A188 50p blue & multi   .30 .25

5th anniv. of Correctionist Movement of Nov. 16, 1970.

Farm
Woman — A189

IWY Emblem and: 15p, Mother. 25p, Student. 50p, Laboratory technician.

1975, Nov. 29   Perf. 12x11½
721 A189 10p buff & multi   .30 .25
722 A189 15p rose & black   .30 .25
723 A189 25p dull green & blk   .35 .25
724 A189 50p orange & blk   .50 .25
   Nos. 721-724 (4)   1.45 1.00

International Women's Year.

Horse-shaped
Bronze Lamp
A190

Man's Head
Inkstand
A191

Designs: 10p, 25p, like 20p. 35p, like 30p. 50p, 60p, Nike. 75p, Hera. 100p, Imdugud-Mari (winged animal). 500p, Palmyrene coin of Vasalathus. 1000p, Abraxas coin.

1976   Perf. 11½x12, 12x11½
725 A190 10p brt bluish grn   .30 .25
726 A190 20p lilac rose   .30 .25
727 A190 25p violet blue   .30 .25
728 A191 30p brown   .30 .25
729 A191 35p olive   .30 .25
730 A191 50p brt blue   .30 .25
731 A191 60p violet   .30 .25
732 A191 75p orange   .35 .25
733 A191 100p lilac rose   .50 .25
734 A191 500p grnsh gray   2.00 1.75
735 A191 1000p dk green   4.00 2.25
   Nos. 725-735 (11)   8.95 6.25

See Nos. 798-803.

National
Theater,
Damascus
and Pres.
al Assad
A192

Syria, Arabian Government
#85 — A193

1976, Apr. 12   Perf. 12x12½
738 A193 25p brt green & multi   .30 .25
739 A193 35p blue & multi   .30 .25

Post's Day.

Nurse and
Emblem — A194

1976, Apr. 8   Perf. 12x11½
740 A194 25p blue, blk & red   .30 .25
741 A194 100p violet, blk & red   .50 .30

Arab Red Cross and Red Crescent Societies, 8th Conference, Damascus.

Eagle and
Stars — A195

1976, Apr. 17
742 A195 25p blk, red & brt grn   .30 .25
743 A195 35p blk, red & brt grn   .30 .25

30th anniversary of the evacuation of British and French troops from Syria.

Hand Holding
Wrench — A196

May Day: 60p, Hand holding globe.

1976, May 1
744 A196 25p blue & black   .30 .25
745 A196 60p citron & multi   .40 .25

Cotton and
Factory — A197

1976, Mar. 8   Litho.   Perf. 11½x12
736 A192 25p brt grn, sil & blk   .30 .25
737 A192 35p olive, sil & blk   .30 .25

13th anniversary of March 8 Revolution.

1976, July 1
746 A197 25p vio & multi   .30 .25
747 A197 35p bl & multi   .30 .25

Agricultural and Industrial Fair, Aleppo.

Tulips — A198

1976, July 26
748 A198 5p shown   .30 .25
749 A198 15p Yellow daisies   .30 .25
750 A198 20p Turk's-cap lilies   .30 .25
751 A198 25p Irises   .50 .25
752 A198 35p Freesia   .75 .25
   a.   Strip of 5, #748-752   2.25 2.25

Intl. Flower Show, Damascus.

People,
Globe and
Olive
Branch
A199

60p, Symbolic arrow piercing darkness.

1976, Sept. 2   Perf. 11½x12
753 A199 40p yel & multi   .30 .25
754 A199 60p multi   .35 .25

5th Summit Conference of Non-aligned Countries, Colombo, Sri Lanka, Aug. 9-19.

Soccer, Pan
Arab Games
Emblem
A200

1976, Oct. 6   Litho.   Perf. 12½
755 A200 5p shown   .30 .25
756 A200 10p Swimming   .30 .25
757 A200 25p Running   .30 .25
758 A200 35p Basketball   .30 .25
759 A200 50p Javelin   .30 .25
   a.   Strip of 5, #755-759   1.50 1.50

Souvenir Sheet
Imperf
760 A200 100p Steeplechase   2.00 2.00

5th Pan Arab Sports Tournament.
Size of stamp of No. 760: 55x35mm.

"Development"
A201

1976, Nov. 16   Perf. 12½x12½
761 A201 35p multi   .30 .25

Correctionist Movement pof Nov. 16, 1970.

Syrian Airlines Boeing 747 — A203

1977, Feb.   Litho.   Perf. 12½x12
767 A203 35p multi   .30 .25

Civil Aviation Day.

The Fox and the
Crow — A202

Fairy Tales: 15p, The Hare and the Tortoise, horiz. 20p, Little Red Riding Hood. 25p, The Lamb and the Wolf, horiz. 35p, The Lamb and the Wolf.

1976, Dec. 7   Perf. 12x12½, 12½x12
762 A202 10p multi   .30 .25
763 A202 15p multi   .30 .25
764 A202 20p multi   .30 .25
765 A202 25p multi   .30 .25
766 A202 35p multi   .30 .25
   a.   Strip of 5, #762-766   1.50 1.50

Children's literature.

Muhammad Kurd-
Ali (1876-1953),
Philosopher, Birth
Cent. — A204

1977, Feb.   Perf. 12x12½
768 A204 25p lt grn & multi   .30 .25

Woman Holding
Syrian
Flag — A205

1977, Mar. 8   Litho.   Perf. 12x12½
769 A205 35p multi   .30 .25

14th anniversary of March 8 Revolution.

Warrior on Horseback — A206

1977, Apr. 10   Litho.   Perf. 12½
770 A206 100p multi   .30 .25

31st anniversary of the evacuation of British and French troops from Syria.

APU Emblem — A207

1977, Apr. 12   Litho.   Perf. 12x12½
771 A207 35p silver & multi   .30 .25
Arab Postal Union, 25th anniversary.

Tools and Factories A208

1977, May 1   Perf. 12½x12
772 A208 60p multi   .35 .25
Labor Day.

ICAO Emblem, Plane and Globe A209

1977, May 11
773 A209 100p multi   .50 .25
Intl. Civil Aviation Org., 30th anniv.

Pioneers — A210

1977, Aug. 15   Litho.   Perf. 12x12½
774 A210 35p multi   .30 .25
Al Baath Pioneer Organization.

Citrus Fruit — A211

1977, Aug. 1
775 A211 10p Lemon   .30 .25
776 A211 20p Lime   .30 .25
777 A211 25p Grapefruit   .30 .25
778 A211 35p Oranges   .30 .25
779 A211 60p Tangerines   .40 .25
 a.   Strip of 5, #775-779   1.60 1.60
Agricultural and Industrial Fair, Aleppo.

Flowers A212

1977, Aug. 6   Litho.   Perf. 12½x12
780 A212 10p Mallow   .30 .25
781 A212 20p Coxcomb   .30 .25
782 A212 25p Morning glories   .30 .25
783 A212 35p Almond blossoms   .30 .25
784 A212 60p Lilacs   .30 .25
 a.   Strip of 5, #780-784   1.50 1.50
Intl. Flower Show, Damascus.

Coffeepot and Ornament A213

1977, Sept. 10   Perf. 12x12½
785 A213 25p blk, bl & red   .30 .25
786 A213 60p blk, grn & brn   .35 .25
24th Intl. Damascus Fair.

Blind Man, Globe and Eye — A214

1977, Nov. 17   Litho.   Perf. 12x12½
787 A214 55p multi   .30 .25
788 A214 70p multi   .30 .25
World Blind Week.

Globe and Measures A215

1977, Nov. 5
789 A215 15p grn & multi   .30 .25
World Standards Day, Oct. 14.

Microscope, Book, Harp, UNESCO Emblem — A216

1977, Nov. 5   Perf. 12½x12
790 A216 25p multi   .30 .25
30th anniversary of UNESCO.

Archbishop Capucci, Map of Palestine, Bars — A217

1977, Nov. 17   Perf. 12x12½
791 A217 60p multi   2.00 .50
Palestinian Archbishop Hilarion Capucci, jailed by Israel in 1974.

Fight Cancer Shield, Crab and Surgeon — A218

1977, Nov. 17
792 A218 100p multi   1.00 .50
Fight Cancer Week.

Dome of the Rock, Jerusalem — A219

1977, Dec. 6   Perf. 12
793 A219 5p multi   .50 .25
794 A219 10p multi   .75 .25
Palestinian fighters and their families.

Mural — A220

Designs: 10p, 15p, Murals from Dura-Europos, in National Museum, Damascus.

1978, Jan. 22   Litho.   Perf. 12x11½
795 A220 5p gray grn   .30 .25
796 A220 10p vio bl   .30 .25
797 A220 15p brown, horiz.   .30 .25
   Nos. 795-797 (3)   .90 .75

Types of 1976

Designs: 40p, Man's head inkstand. 55p, Nike. 70p, 80p, Hera. 200p, Arab-Islamic astrolabe. 300p, Palmyrene (Herod) coin.

1978   Litho.   Perf. 12x11½, 11½x12
798 A191 40p pale org   .30 .25
799 A191 55p brt rose   .30 .25
800 A191 70p vermilion   .35 .25
801 A191 80p green   .35 .25
802 A191 200p lt ultra   1.00 .30
803 A190 300p rose lil   1.50 .50
   Nos. 798-803 (6)   3.80 1.80

Pres. Hafez al Assad — A221

1978   Perf. 12x11½
805 A221 50p multi   .40 .25
Anniversary of "Correction Movement."

Blood Circulation, WHO Emblem — A222

1978, Apr. 7   Litho.   Perf. 12x11½
806 A222 100p multi   .50 .25
World Health Day, fight against hypertension.

Factory — A223

1978, Apr. 17
807 A223 35p multi   .30 .25
32nd anniversary of the evacuation of British and French troops from Syria.

Rosette — A224

1978, Apr. 21
808 A224 25p blk & grn   .30 .25
14th Arab Engineering Conference, Damascus, Apr. 21-26.

Map of Arab Countries, Police, Flag and Eye — A225

1978, May
809 A225 35p multi   .30 .25
6th Conf. of Arab Police Commanders.

European Goldfinch
A226

Birds: 20p, Peregrine falcon. 25p, Rock dove. 35p, Eurasian hoopoe. 60p, Old World quail.

1978   **Perf. 11½x12**

810	A226	10p multi	.40 .25
811	A226	20p multi	.40 .25
812	A226	25p multi	.40 .25
813	A226	35p multi	.50 .25
814	A226	60p multi	.60 .25
a.		Strip of 5, #810-814	2.40 2.40

Trout
A227

Designs: Various fish.

1978, July   **Litho.**   **Perf. 11½x12**

815	A227	10p multi	.40 .25
816	A227	20p multi	.40 .25
817	A227	25p multi	.40 .25
818	A227	35p multi	.50 .25
819	A227	60p multi	.55 .25
a.		Strip of 5, #815-819	2.25 2.25

Pres. Assad Type of Air Post, 1978
Miniature Sheet

1978, Sept.   **Litho.**   **Imperf.**

820 AP161 100p gold & multi   1.00 1.00

Reelection of President Assad. Size of stamp: 58x80mm.

Flowering Cactus
A228

Designs: Flowering cacti.

1978   **Litho.**   **Perf. 12½**

821	A228	25p multi	.50 .25
822	A228	30p multi	.50 .25
823	A228	35p multi	.50 .25
824	A228	50p multi	.50 .25
825	A228	60p multi	.50 .25
a.		Strip of 5, #821-825	2.50 2.50

International Flower Show, Damascus.

Fair Emblem — A229

1978   **Litho.**   **Perf. 12x12½**

826	A229	25p sil & multi	.30 .25
827	A229	35p sil & multi	.30 .25

Miniature Sheet
Imperf

828 A229 100p sil & multi   1.00 1.00

25th Intl. Damascus Fair. No. 828 shows different ornament, size of stamp: 40x46mm.

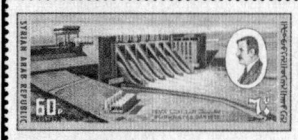

Euphrates Dam and Pres. Assad — A230

1978, Dec.   **Litho.**   **Perf. 12½x12**

829 A230 60p multi   .50 .25

Inauguration of Euphrates Dam.

Pres. Hafez al Assad — A231

1978, Nov. 16   **Litho.**   **Perf. 12x12½**

830 A231 60p multi   .40 .25

Nov. 16 Movement.

Racial Equality Emblem A232

1978, Mar.   **Litho.**   **Perf. 12½**

831 A232 35p multi   .40 .25

International Year to Combat Racism.

Averroes — A233

1979, Mar.

832 A233 100p multi   .75 .25

Averroes (1126-1198), Spanish-Arabian philosopher and physician.

Human Rights Flame and Globe — A234

1978, Dec.   **Perf. 12x12½**

833 A234 60p multi   .50 .25

30th anniversary of Universal Declaration of Human Rights (in 1978).

Symbolic Design — A235

1979, Mar.

834 A235 100p multi   .50 .25

16th anniversary of March 8 Revolution.

Princess, 2nd Century Shield — A236

Designs: 20p, Helmet of Homs. 35p, Ishtar.

1979   **Litho.**   **Perf. 11½**

836	A236	20p green	.30 .25
837	A236	25p rose car	.30 .25
838	A236	35p sepia	.30 .25
		Nos. 836-838 (3)	.90 .75

Flame Emblem — A237

1979   **Litho.**   **Perf. 12x11½**

846 A237 35p multi   .30 .25

Intl. Middle East Dental Congress.

Flame Emblem — A238

1979

847 A238 35p multi   .30 .25

33rd anniversary of evacuation.

Ibn Assaker, 900th Anniv. A239

1979   **Perf. 11½x12**

848 A239 75p multi   .30 .25

Telephone Lineman — A240

1979, May 1   **Litho.**   **Perf. 12x11½**

849	A240	50p multi	.30 .25
850	A240	75p multi	.30 .25

May Day.

Wright Brothers' Plane A241

Designs: 75p, Bleriot's plane crossing English Channel. 100p, Spirit of St. Louis.

1979   **Perf. 11½x12**

851	A241	50p multi	.30 .25
852	A241	75p multi	.30 .25
853	A241	100p multi	.50 .25
		Nos. 851-853 (3)	1.10 .75

75th anniversary of 1st powered flight.

Girl with IYC Emblem — A242

Design: 15p, Boy, globe, IYC emblem.

1979   **Perf. 12x11½**

854	A242	10p multi	.30 .25
855	A242	15p multi	.35 .25

International Year of the Child.

Power Plant — A243

1979   **Perf. 11x11½**

856	A243	5p blue	.30 .25
857	A243	10p lil rose	.30 .25
858	A243	15p gray grn	.30 .25
		Nos. 856-858 (3)	.90 .75

Flags and Pavilion — A244

Design: 75p, Lamppost and flags.

1979   **Photo.**   **Perf. 12x11½**

859	A244	60p multi	.30 .25
860	A244	75p multi	.35 .25

26th International Damascus Fair.

Correction Movement, 9th Anniversary — A245

1979   **Photo.**   **Perf. 11½x12**

861 A245 100p multi   .50 .25

Games
Emblem,
Running
A246

1979, Nov.
862 A246 25p shown .30 .25
863 A246 35p Diving .30 .25
864 A246 50p Soccer .30 .25
Nos. 862-864 (3) .90 .75

8th Mediterranean Games, Split, Yugoslavia, Sept. 15-29.

Butterfly — A247

Designs: Various butterflies.

1979, Dec. Litho. Perf. 12x11½
865 A247 20p multi .50 .25
866 A247 25p multi .50 .25
867 A247 30p multi .50 .25
868 A247 35p multi .50 .25
869 A247 50p multi .50 .25
Nos. 865-869 (5) 2.50 1.25

Damascus
Intl. Flower
Show
A248

Design: Roses.

1980, Jan. 9 Litho. Perf. 12½
870 A248 5p multi .50 .25
871 A248 10p multi .50 .25
872 A248 15p multi .50 .25
873 A248 50p multi .50 .25
874 A248 75p multi .50 .25
875 A248 100p multi .80 .25
Nos. 870-875 (6) 3.30 1.50

March 8
Revolution, 17th
Anniv. — A249

1980, Mar. 25 Litho. Perf. 12x11½
876 A249 40p multi .30 .25

Astrolabe
A250

1980, May 2 Perf. 12½
877 A250 50p violet .30 .25
878 A250 100p sepia .50 .25
879 A250 1000p gray grn 4.00 1.25
Nos. 877-879 (3) 4.80 1.75

2nd International History of Arabic Sciences Symposium, Apr. 5.

Lit Cigarette,
Skull — A251

1980, June 25 Photo. Perf. 12x11½
880 A251 60p Smoker .60 .25
881 A251 100p shown 1.00 .30

World Health Day; anti-smoking campaign.

Evacuation, 34th
Anniversary
A252

1980, June 25 Litho.
882 A252 40p multi .30 .25
883 A252 60p multi .35 .25

Moscow
'80
Emblem
and
Wrestling
A253

1980, July Litho. Perf. 11½x12
884 A253 15p shown .30 .25
885 A253 25p Fencing .30 .25
886 A253 35p Weight lifting .35 .25
887 A253 50p Judo .50 .25
888 A253 75p Boxing 1.00 .25
a. Strip of 5, #884-888 2.50 2.50

Souvenir Sheet
Imperf
888B A253 300p Discus, running 5.00 5.00

22nd Summer Olympic Games, Moscow, July 19-Aug. 3.

Sinbad
the Sailor
A254

25p, Scheherezade and Shahrayar. 35p, Ali Baba and the Forty Thieves. 50p, Hassan the Clever. 100p, Aladdin's Lamp.

1980 Litho. Perf. 11½x12
889 A254 15p shown .30 .25
890 A254 25p multicolored .30 .25
891 A254 35p multicolored .35 .25
892 A254 50p multicolored .50 .25
893 A254 100p multicolored 1.00 .30
a. Strip of 5, #889-893 2.50 2.50

Popular stories.

Savings Certificates — A255

1980
894 A255 25p multicolored .30 .25

Hegira, 1500th Anniv. — A256

1980 Perf. 12½x12
895 A256 35p multicolored .35 .25

Intl. Flower Show,
Damascus
A257

1980 Perf. 12x11½
896 A257 20p Daffodils .50 .25
897 A257 30p Chrysanthemums .50 .25
898 A257 40p Clematis .55 .25
899 A257 60p Yellow roses .60 .25
900 A257 100p Chrysanthemums, diff. .75 .25
a. Strip of 5, #896-900 3.00 3.00

May Day — A258

1980, May
901 A258 35p multicolored .40 .25

Children's
Day — A259

1980
902 A259 25p multicolored .40 .25

November 16th Movement, 10th
Anniv. — A260

1980 Perf. 11½x12
903 A260 100p multicolored 1.00 .25

Steam-powered Passenger
Wagon — A261

1980
904 A261 25p shown .35 .25
905 A261 35p Benz, 1899 .40 .25
906 A261 40p Rolls-Royce, 1903 .60 .25
907 A261 50p Mercedes, 1906 .75 .25
908 A261 60p Austin, 1915 1.00 .30
a. Strip of 5, #904-908 3.25 3.25

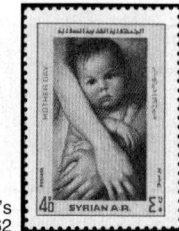

Mother's
Day — A262

1980 Perf. 12x11½
909 A262 40p shown .50 .25
910 A262 100p Mother and child 1.00 .25

27th International Damascus
Fair — A263

1981, Jan. 24 Perf. 11½x12
911 A263 50p multi .45 .25
912 A263 100p multi .80 .25

Army Day — A264

1981, Jan. 24 Perf. 12½x12
913 A264 50p multi .45 .25

A265

1981, Mar. 8 Litho. Perf. 12x11½
914 A265 50p multi .35 .25

18th anniv. of March 8th revolution.

A266

1981, Apr. 17 Litho. Perf. 12x11½
915 A266 50p multi .35 .25
35th anniversary of evacuation.

World Conference on History of Arab
and Islamic Civilization,
Damascus — A267

1981, May 30 Photo. Perf. 12½x12
916 A267 100p multi .60 .25

Intl. Workers'
Solidarity
Day — A268

1981, May 30 Litho. Perf. 12x11½
917 A268 100p multi .60 .25

Housing and
Population
Census — A269

1981, June 1
918 A269 50p multi .35 .25

Umayyad Window A270 · Abdul Malik Gold Coin A270a

10p, figurine. 15p, Rakkla's cavalier, Abbcid
ceramic. 160p, like 5p. 500p, Umar B. Abdul
Aziz gold coin.

1981 Perf. 12x11½, 11½x12
919 A270 5p crim rose .25 .25
920 A270 10p brt grn .25 .25
921 A270 15p dp rose lil .25 .25
922 A270a 75p blue .35 .25
923 A270 160p dk grn .70 .35
924 A270a 500p dk brn 2.50 1.10
Nos. 919-924 (6) 4.30 2.45

Olives A270b · Harbor A270c

1982 Perf. 12x11½
925 A270b 50p ol grn .40 .25
926 A270b 60p bl gray .45 .25
929 A270c 100p lilac .55 .25
930 A270c 180p red 1.10 .55
Nos. 925-930 (4) 2.50 1.30

Saving
Certificates
Plan — A271

1981, June 22
931 A271 50p gldn brn & blk .35 .25

Avicenna (980-
1037),
Philosopher and
Physician
A272

1981, Aug.
932 A272 100p multi .60 .25

Syria-P.L.O.
Solidarity, Intl.
Conference
A273

1981, June 22
933 A273 160p multi 3.50 .90

Grand Mosque, Damascus — A274

1981 Perf. 12½
934 A274 50p Glass lamp, 13th cent. .30 .25
935 A274 180p shown 1.40 .40
936 A274 180p Hunter 1.40 .40
Nos. 934-936 (3) 3.10 1.05

Youth
Festival
A275

1981 Perf. 12½
937 A275 60p multi .40 .25

28th Intl.
Damascus
Fair — A276

1981 Perf. 12x11½
938 A276 50p Ornament .30 .25
939 A276 160p Emblem 1.00 .45

Intl. Palestinian
Solidarity
Day — A277

1981
940 A277 100p multi .75 .25

1300th
Anniv. of
Bulgaria
A278

1981 Perf. 11½x12
941 A278 380p multi 2.25 1.00

Intl.
Children's
Day
A279

1981
942 A279 180p multi 1.10 .45

World
Food Day,
Oct. 16
A280

1981
943 A280 180p multi 1.10 .45

9th Intl. Flower
Show, Damascus
A281

Designs: Flowers.

1981 Perf. 12x11½
944 A281 25p multi .25 .25
945 A281 40p multi .40 .25
946 A281 50p multi .50 .30
947 A281 60p multi .75 .35
948 A281 100p multi 1.10 .50
a. Strip of 5, #944-948 3.00 2.00

Souvenir Sheet

Koran Competition — A282

1981 Litho. Imperf.
949 A282 500p multi 5.00 5.00

11th Anniv. of
Correction
Movement
A283

1981, Nov. Perf. 12x11½
950 A283 60p multi .45 .30

TB
Bacillus
Centenary
A284

1982 Litho. Perf. 11½x12
951 A284 180p multi 1.25 .65

Mothers' Day — A285

1982 Perf. 11½
952 A285 40p green .25 .25
953 A285 75p brown .50 .25

Mar. 8th Revolution, 19th Anniv. — A286

1982, Mar.   **Perf. 12x11½**
954 A286 50p multi   .35 .25

Intl. Year of the Disabled (1981) — A287

1982   **Perf. 12x11½**
955 A287 90p multi   .75 .30

Pres. Hafez al Assad — A288

1982   **Perf. 11½**
956 A288 150p ultra   .90 .50

36th Anniv. of Evacuation A289

1982   **Perf. 12x11½**
957 A289 70p multi   .50 .25

World Traffic Day — A290

1982
958 A290 180p multi   1.25 .65

Intl. Workers' Solidarity Day — A291

1982
959 A291 180p multi   1.25 .65

World Telecommunication Day, May 17 — A292

1982
960 A292 180p multi   1.25 .65

Soldier Holding Rifles — A293

1982   **Photo.**   **Perf. 12x11½**
961 A293 50p multi   .30 .25

Arab Postal Union, 30th Anniv. — A294

1982
962 A294 60p multi   .45 .25

1982 World Cup — A295

Various soccer players. 300p, Ball.

1982, July   **Perf. 12½**
963 A295 40p multi   .25 .25
964 A295 60p multi   .40 .25
965 A295 100p multi   .65 .40
     Nos. 963-965 (3)   1.30 .90
     Size: 75x55mm
     Imperf
966 A295 300p multi   10.00 10.00

10th Intl. Flower Show, Damascus A297

1982   **Perf. 12x11½**
967 A297 50p Honeysuckle   .45 .25
968 A297 60p Geraniums   .60 .30

Scouting Year A298

1982, Nov. 4   **Perf. 11½x12**
969 A298 160p green   1.40 .75

Ladybug A299

1982   **Perf. 12x12½**
970   Strip of 5   .75 .40
  a.   A299 5p Dragonfly   .25 .25
  b.   A299 10p Stag Beetle   .25 .25
  c.   A299 20p shown   .25 .25
  d.   A299 40p Grasshopper   .25 .25
  e.   A299 50p Honeybee   .30 .25

ITU Plenipotentiaries Conference, Nairobi, Sept — A300

1982   **Perf. 11½x12**
971 A300 50p Map   .30 .25
972 A300 180p Dish antenna   1.40 .75

12th Anniv. of Correction Movement A301

1982, Nov.
973 A301 50p dk bl & sil   .35 .25

A302

Factory — A302a

Walled Arch — A302b

Ruins — A302c

1982-83   **Litho.**   **Perf. 11½**
974 A302   30p brown   .25 .25
975 A302a 50p grnish blk   .25 .25
976 A302b 70p green   .35 .25
977 A302c 200p red   1.00 .55
     Nos. 974-977 (4)   1.85 1.30
  Issued: 50p, 11/16/83; others, 11/4/82.

Dove and Satellite — A303

1982   **Litho.**   **Perf. 12x11½**
978 A303 50p multi   .50 .30
  2nd UN Conference on Peaceful Uses of Outer Space, Vienna, Aug. 9-21.

Intl. Palestinian Solidarity Day — A304

1982
979 A304 50p multi   .90 .25

20th Anniv. of March 8th Revolution — A305

1983   **Perf. 12½x12**
980 A305 60p multi   1.00 .50

World Communications Year — A305a

1983
981 A305a 180p multi   1.25 .65

9th Anniv. of Liberation of Al-Kuneitra — A306

1983, June 26   **Litho.**   **Perf. 11½**
982 A306 50p View   1.50 .50
983 A306 100p View, diff.   3.00 .65

Arab Pharmacists' Day, Apr. 2 — A307

1983, Apr. 2   **Perf. 11½x12**
984 A307 100p multi   .75 .30

25th Anniv. of Intl. Maritime Org. — A308

1983, June   *Perf. 12x11½*
985 A308 180p multi   1.40 .75

Namibia Day, Aug. 26 A309

1983, Aug. 26   *Perf. 11½x12*
986 A309 180p multi   1.40 .75

Eibla Sculpture, 3rd Cent. BC A310

1983
987 A310 380p ol & brn   2.50 1.40

World Standards Day — A311

50p, Factory, emblem. 100p, Measuring equipment.

1983, Oct. 14   **Photo.**   *Perf. 11½*
988 A311 50p multicolored   .40 .25
989 A311 100p multicolored   .80 .40

11th Intl. Flower Show, Damascus A312

1983, Oct. 14   **Litho.**   *Perf. 11½*
990 A312 50p multi   .40 .25
991 A312 60p multi, diff.   .50 .25

World Heritage Day — A313

1983, Oct. 14   **Photo.**   *Perf. 11½*
992 A313 60p dk brn   .50 .25

World Food Day A313a

1983, Oct. 16   **Litho.**   *Perf. 11½x12*
992A A313a 180p multi   1.50 .75

Waterwheels of Hama — A314

Perf. 11x11½, 11½x11
1982-84   **Litho.**
993 A314   5p sepia   .25 .25
994 A314   10p violet   .25 .25
995 A314   20p red   .25 .25
997 A314   50p blkish grn   .60 .30
    Nos. 993-997 (4)   1.35 1.05
Issued: 50p, 11/25/82; others, 1/15/84.
On No. 997 "50" is in outlined numbers.

Statue — A316

1983   *Perf. 12*
1003 A316 225p brown   2.00 1.00
Intl. Symposium on History and Archaeology of Deir Ez-zor.

View of Aleppo — A317

1983   *Perf. 12x12½*
1004 A317 245p multi   2.25 1.10
Intl. Symposium on Conservation of Old City of Aleppo, Sept. 26-30.

Mar. 8th Revolution, 21st Anniv. — A318

1984, Mar. 8   *Perf. 12½x12*
1005 A318 60p Alassad Library   .75 .35

Massacre at Sabra and Shatilla A319

1983   **Litho.**   *Perf. 11½x12*
1006 A319 225p Victims, mother & child   2.00 .50

Mothers' Day — A320

1984, Mar. 21   *Perf. 12x11½*
1007 A320 245p Mother & child   2.50 1.25

12th Intl. Flower Show, Damascus A321

Various flowers.

1984, May 25
1008 A321 245p multi   2.50 1.25
1009 A321 285p multi   2.75 1.40

1984 Summer Olympics — A322

1984   **Litho.**   *Perf. 12x11½*
1010   Strip of 5   3.00 2.40
  a.   A322 30p Swimming   .30 .25
  b.   A322 50p Wrestling   .50 .25
  c.   A322 60p Running   .60 .25
  d.   A322 70p Boxing   .65 .35
  e.   A322 90p Soccer   .90 .45

Souvenir Sheet
Imperf
1011 A322 200p Soccer, diff.   3.50 3.50

9th Regional Pioneers' Festival A323

1984   *Perf. 11½x12*
1012 A323 50p Pioneers   .50 .25
1013 A323 60p Pioneers, diff.   .60 .30

Aleppo Agricultural & Industrial Fair — A324

1984, June 12   **Litho.**   *Perf. 12x12½*
1014 A324 150p Peppers, Aleppo Castle   1.25 .50

Supreme Council of Science, 25th Anniv. A325

1985, Feb. 23   *Perf. 12½x12*
1015 A325 65p multi   .40 .25

Aleppo University, 25th Anniv. A326

1985, Feb. 23
1016 A326 45p multi   .25 .25

Syrian Arab Army, 39th Anniv. A327

1985, Feb. 23
1017 A327 65p brn & gldn brn   .40 .25

Pres. Assad, Soldier Saluting, Troops A328

1984, Aug. 1   *Perf. 11½x12*
1018 A328 60p multi   .60 .30
4th General Revolutionary Youth Conference.

ITU Emblem, Satellite Dish, Telephone A329

1984, Oct. 2   *Perf. 12½*
1019 A329 245p multi   1.75 .90
Intl. Telecommunications Day.

APU Emblem and Administration Building, Damascus — A330

1984, Oct. 9
1020 A330 60p multi   .60 .30
Arab Postal Union Day.

Gearwheel,
Arabesque
Pattern — A331

Gold
Necklace — A332

1984, Oct. 27   *Perf. 12x12½, 12x11½*
1021 A331 45p multi .45 .25
1022 A332 100p multi 1.00 .45
    Intl. Fair, Damascus.

Intl. Civil
Aviation
Org., 40th
Anniv.
A333

1984, Oct. 27   *Perf. 11½x12*
1023 A333 45p brt bl & lt bl .25 .25
1024 A333 245p brt ultra, brt bl &
    lt bl 1.25 .60

14th
Anniv. of
11-16-70
Movement
A334

1984, Dec. 3   *Perf. 12½x12*
1025 A334 65p red brn, blk & org .65 .35

Pres. Assad,
Text on Scroll
A335

1984, Nov. 29   *Perf. 12½*
1026 A335 50p grn, brn org & sep .50 .25
    Vow of Dedication taken by Youth of the
Revolution.

Agricultural Exhibition — A336

1984, June 12   *Perf. 12½x12*
1027 A336 65p multi .65 .35

Al-Kuneitra Memorial, Rose — A337

1984
1028 A337 70p multi 1.25 .35

Roman Arch and Colonnades,
Palmyra — A338

1984, Dec. 3
1029 A338 100p multi 1.00 .50
    Intl. Tourism Day.

Woodland Conservation — A339

1984
1030 A339 45p multi .25 .25

March 8
Revolution, 22nd
Anniv. — A340

1985, Apr. 27
1031 A340 60p multi .40 .25

UPU Emblem,
Postal
Headquarters,
Damascus
A341

1985, Apr. 27
1032 A341 285p multi 3.00 1.50
    World Post Day.

APU Building, Damascus — A342

1985, Apr. 27   *Perf. 12½*
1033 A342 245p multi 2.50 1.25
    Arab Parliamentary Union, 10th Anniv.

Natl. Flag,
Map of
Arab
Countries
A343

1985   *Perf. 12½x12*
1034 A343 50p multi .50 .25
    Arab League.

Re-election
of President
Assad
A344

1985, Mar. 12   *Perf. 12½*
1035 A344 200p multi 1.25 .70
1036 A344 300p multi 2.00 1.00
1037 A344 500p multi 3.25 1.75
  a.   Souvenir sheet of 3, #1035-
     1037, imperf. 7.00 5.50
    Nos. 1035-1037 (3) 6.50 3.45

Arab Postal
Union, 12th
Congress,
Damascus
A345

1985, Aug. 12   *Perf. 12x12½*
1038 A345 60p multi .60 .30

Labor
Day — A346

1985, Aug. 12   *Perf. 12½*
1039 A346 60p Order of Labor .60 .30

32nd Intl.
Fair,
Damascus
A347

1986, Feb. 1   *Litho.*   *Perf. 12½*
1040 A347 60p multi .50 .25

2nd Scientific Symposium — A348

1985, Nov. 16   *Perf. 12½*
1041 A348 60p Locomotives .60 .30

UN Child
Survival
Campaign
A349

1985, Nov. 16   *Perf. 12½x12*
1042 A349 60p Malnourished child .50 .25

UN, 40th
Anniv. — A350

1985, Nov. 16   *Perf. 12x12½*
1043 A350 245p multi 2.25 1.10

November 16th Movement, 15th
Anniv. — A351

    Design: Pres. Assad, highway.

1985, Nov. 16   *Perf. 12½*
1044 A351 60p multi .50 .25

Abdul
Rahman
Dakhei in
Andalusia,
1200th
Anniv.
A352

1986, Feb. 1   *Perf. 12½x12*
1045 A352 60p beige & brn .60 .30

Tulips — A353

1986, Feb. 1   *Perf. 12½*
1046 A353 30p multi .30 .25
1047 A353 60p multi, diff. .60 .30
    Intl. Flower Show, Damascus.

Dental Congress, Damascus — A354

1986　　**Perf. 12½x12**
1048 A354 110p yel, grysh grn & bl　　1.10 .55

World Traffic Day — A355

1986　　**Perf. 12x12½**
1049 A355 330p multi　　3.00 1.50

Syrian Investment Certificates, 15th Anniv. — A357

1986　　**Litho.**　　**Perf. 12x11½**
1055 A357 100p multi　　1.00 .50

Liberation of Al-Kuneitra, 12th Anniv. — A358

1986　　**Litho.**　　**Perf. 11½x12**
1056 A358 110p Government Building　　.75 .40

Day of Internal Security Forces — A359

1986　　**Perf. 12x11½**
1057 A359 110p multi　　.75 .40

Labor Day — A360

1986, Aug. 12
1058 A360 330p multi　　1.25 .60

1986 World Cup Soccer Championships, Mexico — A361

500p, Hemispheres, ball.

1986, July 7
1059 A361 330p multi　　3.25 1.75
1060 A361 370p multi　　3.50 1.90
Booklet Stamp
Size: 105x80mm
Imperf
1061 A361 500p multi　　5.00 2.50
　Nos. 1059-1061 (3)　　11.75 6.15

Pres. Hafez al Assad — A362

1986-90　　**Litho.**　　**Perf. 12x11½**
1068 A362　10p rose　　.25 .25
1069 A362　30p dl ultra　　.25 .25
1070 A362　50p claret　　.40 .25
1071 A362　100p brt lt bl　　.65 .30
1072 A362　150p brn vio　　1.40 .65
1073 A362　175p violet　　1.60 .80
1074 A362　200p pale red brn　　1.40 .65
1075 A362　300p brt rose lil　　2.00 1.00
1076 A362　500p orange　　3.25 1.60
1077 A362　550p pink　　5.00 2.50
1078 A362　600p dull grn　　5.25 2.75
1079 A362　1000p brt pink　　6.50 3.25
1080 A362　2000p pale grn　　13.00 6.50
　Nos. 1068-1080 (13)　　40.95 20.75

Issued: 150p, 175p, 550p, 600p, 1988; 50p, 9/30/90.

Intl. Day for Solidarity with the Palestinian People — A363

1986, Aug. 7　　**Litho.**
1081 A363 110p multi　　1.10 .55

Mothers' Day — A364

1986, Aug. 7
1082 A364 100p multi　　1.00 .50

March 8 Revolution, 23rd Anniv. — A365

1986, Aug. 7　　**Perf. 11½x12**
1083 A365 110p multi　　1.10 .55

Arab Post Day A366

1986, Aug. 7
1084 A366 110p multi　　1.10 .55

A367

33rd Intl. Damascus Fair A368

1986, Dec. 9　　**Litho.**　　**Perf. 11½x12**
1085 A367 110p multi　　.90 .45
1086 A368 330p multi　　2.50 .60

14th Intl. Flower Show, Damascus — A369

Various flowers.

1986, Oct. 11　　**Perf. 12½**
1087　Strip of 5　　6.50 5.00
　a. A369 10p multi　　.25 .25
　b. A369 50p multi　　.50 .25
　c. A369 100p multi　　1.00 .50
　d. A369 110p multi　　1.10 .60
　e. A369 330p multi　　3.50 1.75

Syria-Soviet Joint Space Project — A370

1986, Nov. 16　　**Litho.**　　**Perf. 12½**
1088 A370 330p multi　　3.50 1.75

World Children's Day — A371

No. 1090, Youth art exhibition, horiz.

1986　　**Perf. 12x12½, 12½x12**
1089 A371 330p shown　　1.75 .90
1090 A371 330p multi　　1.75 .90

World Post Day A372

1986, Jan. 28　　**Perf. 12½x12**
1091 A372 330p multi　　1.75 .90

Intl. Tourism Day A373

Women wearing folk costumes, landmarks.

1986
1092 A373 330p multi　　1.75 .90
1093 A373 370p multi　　2.00 1.00

Pres. Assad, Tishreen Palace — A374

1986, Nov. 16　　**Litho.**　　**Perf. 12½**
1094 A374 110p multi　　1.25 .60

Nov. 16 Corrective Movement.

March 8th Revolution, 24th Anniv. — A375

1987, Mar. 6
1095 A375 100p multi　　.60 .30

Intl. Peace Year — A376

1987, Mar. 8　　**Perf. 12x11½**
1096 A376 370p multi　　2.25 1.25

Arab Baath Socialist Party, 40th Anniv. A377

1987, Apr. 7　　**Litho.**　　**Perf. 12½**
1097 A377 100p multi　　.60 .30

Arab Post Day, 35th Anniv. A378

1987, May 1   *Perf. 11½x12*
1098 A378 110p multi   .70 .35

Evacuation, Day, 41st Anniv. — A379

1987, Apr. 17   *Perf. 12½x12*
1099 A379 100p multi   .60 .30

Labor Day — A380

1987, May 1   *Perf. 12x11½*
1100 A380 330p multi   2.00 1.00

Hitteen's Battle, 800th Anniv. — A381

1987, June 25   Litho.   *Perf. 12½*
1101 A381 110p multi   1.00 .45

Al-Kuneitra Monument A382

1987, June 25   *Perf. 12x11½*
1102 A382 100p multi   .65 .30

Child Vaccination Campaign — A383

1987, June 25   *Perf. 11½x12*
1103 A383 100p multi   .50 .30
1104 A383 330p multi   2.00 1.10

A384

A385

Syrian-Soviet Joint Space Flight, July 22-30 — A386

Designs: No. 1105, Launch, July 22. No. 1106, Docking at space station, July 24. No. 1107, Landing, July 30, vert. No. 1108a, Lift-off. No. 1108b, Parachute landing. No. 1108c, Docked at space station. No. 1108d, Cosmonauts.

Perf. 12½, 11½x12, 12x11½
1987   Litho.
1105 A384 330p multi   2.00 1.00
1106 A385 330p multi   2.00 1.00
1107 A385 330p multi   2.00 1.00
    Nos. 1105-1107 (3)   6.00 3.00
Souvenir Sheet
Imperf
1108   Sheet of 4   10.00 10.00
a.-d.   A386 300p, any single   2.25 2.25

6th Conference of Arab Ministers of Culture A387

1987, Apr. 21   Litho.   *Perf. 12½*
1109 A387 330p dull blue grn & blk   3.00 1.50

President Assad Conversing with Syrian Cosmonaut — A388

1987, Aug. 12
1110 A388 500p multi   3.50 1.75

10th Mediterranean Games, Latakia — A389

Designs: 100p, Gymnastic rings, weight lifting, vert. 330p, Phoenician sailing ship. 370p, Flags spelling "SYRIA." No. 1115a, Emblem, gymnastics. No. 1115b, Emblem, weight lifting. No. 1115c, Emblem, tennis. No. 1115d, Emblem, soccer.

Perf. 12x11½, 11½x12
1987, Sept. 10
1111 A389 100p brt rose lil & blk   .70 .35
1112 A389 110p shown   .75 .40

Size: 58x28mm
Perf. 12½
1113 A389 330p multi   2.25 1.10
1114 A389 370p multi   2.50 1.25
    Nos. 1111-1114 (4)   6.20 3.10
Souvenir Sheet
Imperf
1115   Sheet of 4   7.75 7.75
a.-d.   A389 300p any single   1.90 1.90

34th Intl. Damascus Fair — A390

1987   *Perf. 12x11½*
1116 A390 330p multi   2.00 1.00

Intl. Flower Show, Damascus A391

1987, Oct. 20   *Perf. 11½x12*
1117 A391 330p Poppies   1.90 1.00
1118 A391 370p Gentian   2.00 1.00

Arbor Day — A392

1987, Oct. 20   *Perf. 12x11½*
1119 A392 330p multi   2.00 1.00

Army Day — A393

1987, Oct. 20   Litho.   *Perf. 12x11½*
1120 A393 100p multi   .60 .30

Intl. Palestine Day — A394

1987, Nov. 16
1121 A394 500p multi   3.50 1.75

Corrective Movement, 17th Anniv. — A395

Design: Assad waving to crowd.

1987, Nov. 16   *Perf. 12½*
1122 A395 150p multi   1.00 .50

World Post Day — A396

1988, Mar. 8   Litho.   *Perf. 12½x12*
1123 A396 500p multi   3.00 1.50

Intl. Tourism Day A397

Women wearing folk costumes and: No. 1124, Palmyra Ruins. No. 1125, Reconstructed Roman amphitheater, Busra.

1988, Feb. 25   Litho.   *Perf. 11½x12*
1124 A397 500p multi   3.00 1.50
1125 A397 500p multi   3.00 1.50
    See Nos. 1147-1148, 1178-1179.

Intl. Children's Day — A398

1988, Feb. 27   *Perf. 12½*
1126 A398 500p multi   3.00 1.50

March 8th Revolution, 25th Anniv. — A399

1988, Mar. 15   Litho.   *Perf. 12x11½*
1127 A399 150p multi   1.00 .50
Size: 110x81mm
Imperf
1128 A399 500p multi, diff.   4.75 4.75

No. 1128 pictures vignette like 150p without denomination, in diff. colors, and Arab Revolt flag, text, outline map; denomination at LR in sheet.

Mothers' Day — A400

1988, Apr. 12 Litho. Perf. 12x12½
1129 A400 500p multi   3.00 1.50

Arab Post Day A401

1988, Apr. 17 Perf. 12½x12
1130 A401 150p multi   1.00 .50

1946 Evacuation A402

1988, Apr. 17 Perf. 12x12½
1131 A402 150p multi   1.00 .50

Labor Day — A403

1988, May 1
1132 A403 550p multi   3.00 1.50

Intl. Flower Show, Damascus A404

1988, May 25 Perf. 12x11½
1133 A404 550p Tiger Lily   3.25 1.60
1134 A404 600p Carnations   3.75 1.90

Arab Engineers' Union — A405

1988, May 25
1135 A405 150p multi   1.00 .50

A406

1988, Aug. 28 Litho. Perf. 12x11½
1136 A406 600p blk, grn & olive   3.50 1.75
Intl. Children's Day.

A407

1988, Aug. 28 Perf. 12½
1137 A407 550p multi   3.00 1.50
Restoration of San'a, Yemen Arab Republic.

Ebla Intl. Symposium on Archaeology of Idlib — A408

175p, Hieroglyphic tablet. 550p, Bas-relief (votive basin). 600p, Gold statue, 3000 B.C.

1988, Aug. 28
1138 A408 175p multicolored   1.00 .50
1139 A408 550p multicolored   3.00 1.50
1140 A408 600p multicolored   3.50 1.75
       Nos. 1138-1140 (3)   7.50 3.75

1988 Summer Olympics, Seoul A409

550p, Cycling. 600p, Soccer. 1200p, Emblem, character trademark.

1988, Sept. 17 Perf. 11½x12
1141 A409 550p multi   3.50 1.60
1142 A409 600p multi   3.75 1.75

Size: 81x61mm
Imperf
1143 A409 1200p multi   12.50 12.50
       Nos. 1141-1143 (3)   19.75 15.85

35th Intl. Fair, Damascus A410

1988, Aug. 28 Perf. 12x11½
1144 A410 600p multi   3.50 1.75

WHO, 40th Anniv. — A411

1988, Aug. 28 Litho. Perf. 12x11½
1145 A411 600p multi   3.25 1.60

Arab Scouting Movement, 50th Anniv. — A412

1988, Sept. 17 Perf. 12½x12
1146 A412 150p multi   1.50 .75

Tourism Type of 1988

Women wearing folk costumes and: 550p, Euphrates Bridge, Deir-ez-Zor. 600p, The Tetrapylon, Latakia.

1988, Oct. 18
1147 A397 550p multi   3.25 1.60
1148 A397 600p multi   3.50 1.75

World Post Day — A413

1988, Dec. 7 Litho. Perf. 12x12½
1149 A413 600p multi   3.50 1.75

Arbor Day — A414

1988, Nov. 16
1150 A414 600p multi   3.50 1.75

Shelter for the Homeless — A415

150p, Arab Housing Day. 175p, Intl. Year of Shelter for the Homeless. 550p, World Housing Day.

1988-89 Perf. 12½x12
1151   A415 150p multicolored   .65 .35
1151A A415 175p multicolored 1.25 .60
1152   A415 550p multicolored 2.50 1.25
1153   A415 600p as No. 1151A 2.75 1.50
       Nos. 1151-1153 (4)   7.15 3.70

The IYSH emblem is pictured on the 175p, 550p and 600p.
Issued: 175p, 2/6/89; others, 10/18/88.

Al-Assad University Hospital — A416

1988, Nov. 16 Litho. Perf. 12½
1154 A416 150p multi   .90 .45
Corrective Movement, 18th anniv.

World Food Day — A417

1988, Oct. 18 Perf. 12x12½
1155 A417 550p multi   2.75 1.40

Birds A418

1989, Mar. 21 Litho. Perf. 11½x12
1156 A418 600p Goldfinch   1.50 .75
1157 A418 600p Turtledove   1.50 .75
1158 A418 600p Bee eater   1.50 .75
       Nos. 1156-1158 (3)   4.50 2.25

Jawaharlal Nehru, 1st Prime Minister of Independent India — A419

1989, Mar. 8 Perf. 12½
1159 A419 550p brn & chest   1.10 .55

Mothers' Day — A420

1989, Mar. 21
1160 A420 550p multi   1.10 .55

Teacher's Day A421

1989, Mar. 8 Litho. Perf. 11½x12
1161 A421 175p multi   .70 .35

5th General Congress of the Union of Women A422

1989, Mar. 8   **Perf. 12½**
1162 A422 150p multi   .30 .25

March 8th Revolution, 26th Anniv. — A423

1989, Mar. 8   **Perf. 11½x12**
1163 A423 150p multi   .30 .25

Arab Board for Medical Specializations, 10th Anniv. — A424

1989, Feb. 6   **Perf. 12½**
1164 A424 175p multi   .60 .30

1946 Evacuation of British and French Troops — A425

1989, Apr. 17   Litho.   Perf. 11½x12
1165 A425 150p multi   .40 .25

Intl. Flower Show, Damascus A426

1989, June 3   **Perf. 12½**
1166   Strip of 5   5.00 4.00
   a.   A426 150p Snapdragon   .30 .25
   b.   A426 150p Canaria   .30 .25
   c.   A426 450p Compositae   .90 .45
   d.   A426 850p Clematis sackmani   1.75 .85
   e.   A426 900p Gesneriaceae   1.75 .90

A427

1989, May 1   **Perf. 12x11½**
1167 A427 850p blue grn & blk   1.75 .90
Labor Day.

A428

1989, June 6   Litho.   Perf. 12x11½
1168 A428 175p multi   .50 .25
13th General Congress of the Arab Teachers' Union.

Arab Post Day — A429

1989, June 6
1169 A429 175p multi   .50 .25

Liberation of Al-Kuneitra, 15th Anniv. — A430

1989, June 26
1170 A430 450p multi   1.25 .60

17th Congress of the Arab Advocates Union A431

1989, June 19   **Perf. 11½x12**
1171 A431 175p multi   .50 .25

World Post Day A432

1989, June 26
1172 A432 550p multi   1.50 .75

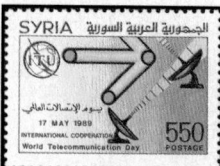

World Telecommunications Day — A433

1989, June 6
1173 A433 550p multi   1.50 .75

Interparliamentary Union, Cent. — A434

1989. July 12   **Perf. 12½**
1174 A434 900p multi   2.50 1.25

Butterflies A435

1989, June 6
1175 A435 550p Small white   1.50 .75
1176 A435 550p Clouded yellow   1.50 .75
1177 A435 550p Painted Lady   1.50 .75
   Nos. 1175-1177 (3)   4.50 2.25

Intl. Tourism Day Type of 1988

Women wearing folk costumes and: 550p, Jaabar Castle, Rakka. 600p, Temple of the Bell, Palmyra.

1989, Oct. 16   Litho.   Perf. 11½x12
1178 A397 550p multicolored   3.75 1.75
1179 A397 600p multicolored   4.00 2.00

36th Intl. Fair, Damascus A436

1989, Oct. 16   **Perf. 12x11½**
1180 A436 450p multicolored   3.00 1.50

Fish A437

1989, Oct. 24   **Perf. 11½x12**
1181 A437 550p Carp   3.75 1.75
1182 A437 600p Trout   4.00 2.00

2nd Anniv. of the Palestinian Uprising — A438

1989, Oct. 24   **Perf. 12x11½**
1183 A438 550p Child's drawing   3.75 1.75

Corrective Movement, 19th Anniv. — A439

1989, Nov. 16   Litho.   Perf. 12½x12
1184 A439 150p multicolored   1.00 .50

World Children's Day — A440

1990, Feb. 13   Litho.   Perf. 12x11½
1185 A440 850p multicolored   1.00 .50

March 8th Revolution, 27th Anniv. — A441

1990
1186 A441 600p multicolored   .70 .35

Revolutionary Youth Union A442

1990   **Perf. 12½**
1187 A442 150p multicolored   .25 .25

World Food Day A443

1990, Feb. 13   Litho.   Perf. 11½x12
1188 A443 850p multicolored   1.00 .50
Dated 1989.

Evacuation of
British and French
Troops,
1946 — A444

1990, Apr. 17   *Perf. 12x11½*
1189 A444 175p multicolored   .25 .25

Mother's
Day — A445

1990, Apr. 17   *Perf. 12½*
1190 A445 550p multicolored   .65 .30

Labor
Day — A446

1990, May 1   Litho.   *Perf. 12x12½*
1191 A446 550p multicolored   .75 .35

World Cup Soccer Championships,
Italy — A447

550p, Denomination at right. 600p, Map,
soccer ball, vert. 1300p, Stadium.

Perf. 11½x12, 12x11½
1990, June 8   **Litho.**
1192 A447   550p shown   .40 .25
1193 A447   550p multi   .40 .25
1194 A447   600p multi   .45 .25
      Nos. 1192-1194 (3)   1.25 .75

Miniature Sheet
Imperf
1195 A447 1300p multi   3.50 1.75

Intl. Flower Show,
Damascus
A448

1990, May 27   *Perf. 12x11½*
1196 A448 600p Lily   1.10 .50
1197 A448 600p Pastelkleurig   1.10 .50
1198 A448 600p Marigold   1.10 .50
1199 A448 600p Viburnum opu-
            lus   1.10 .50
1200 A448 600p Swan river daisy 1.10 .50
      Nos. 1196-1200 (5)   5.50 2.50

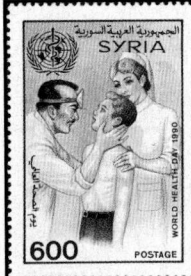

World Health
Day — A449

1990, May 1   Litho.   *Perf. 12½*
1201 A449 600p multicolored   2.50 1.25

Liberation of Al-
Kuneitra, 16th
Anniv. — A450

1990, June 26   *Perf. 12x11½*
1202 A450 550p multicolored   2.50 1.25

Intl. Literacy
Year — A451

1990, June 26
1203 A451 550p multicolored   2.25 1.10

UN Conference on Least Developed
Countries — A452

1990, July 10   *Perf. 11½x12*
1204 A452 600p multicolored   2.40 1.25

37th Damascus
Intl. Fair — A453

1990, Aug. 28   *Perf. 12x11½*
1205 A453 550p multicolored   2.25 1.10

World Meteorology Day — A454

1990, Aug. 28   *Perf. 11½x12*
1206 A454 450p multicolored   1.90 .95

Arbor
Day — A455

1990, Oct. 30   *Perf. 12x11½*
1207 A455 550p multicolored   2.25 1.10

World Food
Day — A456

1990, Oct. 30   *Perf. 12½*
1208 A456 850p multicolored   3.25 1.75

Al Maqdisi,
Cartographer
A457

1990, Nov. 6   *Perf. 12x11½*
1209 A457 550p multicolored   2.25 1.10

A458   A459

Pres.
Hafez al
Assad
A460

1990, Nov. 16   Litho.   *Perf. 11½*
1210 A458   50p claret   .25 .25
1211 A458   70p gray   .25 .25
1212 A458 100p blue   .35 .25
1213 A458 150p brown   .60 .30
          Perf. 12x11½
1214 A459 175p multicolored   .70 .35
1215 A459 300p multicolored   1.25 .55
1216 A459 550p multicolored   2.25 1.10
1217 A459 600p multicolored   2.40 1.25
          Perf. 11½x12
1219 A460 1000p multicolored   4.00 2.00
1220 A460 1500p multicolored   6.00 3.00
1222 A460 2000p multicolored   8.00 4.00
1224 A460 2500p multicolored 10.00 5.00
      Nos. 1210-1224 (12)   36.05 18.30

1992, May 19   Litho.   *Perf. 11½*
Without Date at Right
1225   A458 150p brown   .60 .30
1225A A458 300p violet   1.25 .60
1225B A458 350p gray   1.40 .70
1225C A458 400p red   1.60 .80
      Nos. 1225-1225C (4)   4.85 2.40

Souvenir Sheet

Corrective Movement, 20th
Anniv. — A461

a, Pres. Assad with children. b, Assad
addressing crowd. c, Assad, memorial. d,
Assad, dam.

1990, Nov. 16   *Imperf.*
1227 A461 550p Sheet of 4, #a.-
            d.   9.00 9.00

UN Development Program, 40th
Anniv. — A462

1990, Dec. 11   *Perf. 11½x12*
1228 A462 550p multicolored   2.25 1.10

Arab Civil
Aviation
Day
A463

1990, Dec. 11
1229 A463 175p multicolored   1.00 .50

World Post
Day — A464

1990, Dec. 11   *Perf. 12x11½*
1230 A464 550p multicolored   2.25 1.10

Intl. Children's
Day — A465

1990, Dec. 11
1231 A465 550p multicolored   2.25 1.10

Arab-Spanish Cultural Symposium A466

1990, Dec. 24
1232 A466 550p multicolored 2.25 1.10

World AIDS Day — A467

1990, Dec. 24
1233 A467 550p multicolored 2.25 1.10

March 8th Revolution, 28th Anniv. — A468

1991, Mar. 8   Litho.   Perf. 11½x12
1234 A468 150p multicolored .60 .30

Butterflies A469

No. 1235, Small tortoiseshell. No. 1236, Changeful great mars. No. 1237, Papillion machaon.

1991, Mar. 17   Perf. 12½
1235 A469 550p multicolored 2.25 1.10
1236 A469 550p multicolored 2.25 1.10
1237 A469 550p multicolored 2.25 1.10
    Nos. 1235-1237 (3) 6.75 3.30

Birds — A470

1991, Mar. 17   Perf. 12x11½
1238 A470 600p Golden oriole 2.40 1.25
1239 A470 600p European roller 2.40 1.25
1240 A470 600p House sparrow 2.40 1.25
    Nos. 1238-1240 (3) 7.20 3.75

Mother's Day — A471

1991, Mar. 21
1241 A471 550p multicolored 2.25 1.10

1946 Evacuation of British and French Troops — A472

1991, Apr. 17   Perf. 11½x12
1242 A472 150p multicolored .60 .30

Labor Day A473

1991, May 1
1243 A473 550p multicolored 2.25 1.10

Intl. Flower Show, Damascus — A474

550p, Narcissus. 600p, Monarda didyma.

1991, July 8   Perf. 12x12½
1244 A474 550p multi 2.25 1.10
1245 A474 600p multi 2.40 1.25

Liberation of Kuneitra, 17th Anniv. A475

1991, July 22   Perf. 11½x12
1246 A475 550p multicolored 2.25 1.10

11th Mediterranean Games, Athens — A476

No. 1247, Running. No. 1248, Soccer. No. 1249, Equestrian. No. 1250, Dolphins playing water polo.

1991, July 22
1247 A476 550p multi 2.25 1.10
1248 A476 550p multi 2.25 1.10

1249 A476 600p multi 2.25 1.25
    Size: 80x64mm
    Imperf
1250 A476 1300p multi 5.25 5.25
    Nos. 1247-1250 (4) 12.00 8.70

38th Damascus Intl. Fair — A477

1991, Aug. 28   Perf. 12x12½
1251 A477 550p multicolored 2.25 1.10

Intl. Tourism Day A478

Designs: 450p, Woman at Khan Asaad Pasha El Azem. 550p, Woman at Castle of Arwad Island.

1991, Sept. 27   Perf. 11½x12
1252 A478 450p multicolored 1.90 .95
1253 A478 550p multicolored 2.25 1.10

Housing Day — A479

1991, Oct. 7   Perf. 12x11½
1254 A479 175p multicolored 1.00 .50

Intl. Children's Day — A480

1991, Oct. 16
1255 A480 600p multicolored 2.40 1.25

Physician Abu Bakr Al Razi (Rhazes), Patient A481

1991, Nov. 2   Litho.   Perf. 12½x12
1256 A481 550p multicolored 2.25 1.10
    31st Science Week.

World Post Day A482

1991, Nov. 12
1257 A482 550p multicolored 2.25 1.10

World Food Day A483

1991, Nov. 12
1258 A483 550p multicolored 2.25 1.10

Tomb of Unknown Soldier, Damascus A484

1991, Nov. 16   Perf. 12½
1259 A484 600p multicolored 2.40 1.25
    Size: 65x80mm
    Imperf
1260 A484 1000p multicolored 4.00 2.00

Corrective Movement, 21st Anniv. — A485

1991, Nov. 16   Imperf.
1261 A485 2500p multicolored 10.00 5.00

Protect the Environment — A486

1991, Nov. 20   Perf. 12½x12
1262 A486 175p multicolored .70 .35

World Telecommunications
Fair — A487

1991, Nov. 20   **Perf. 12x12½**
1263 A487 600p multicolored   2.40 1.25

March 8th
Revolution,
29th Anniv.
A488

1992, Mar. 8   **Litho.**   **Perf. 12½**
1264 A488 600p multicolored   2.40 1.25

Re-election of Pres. Assad — A489

1992, Mar. 12   **Litho.**   **Imperf.**
1265 A489 5000p shown   20.00 10.00
Size: 100x85mm
1266 A489 5000p inscription at
         right   20.00 10.00
   Nos. 1265-1266 incorporate designs of Nos.
1036, C496 & C506.

Baath
Party,
45th
Anniv.
A490

1992, Apr. 7   **Perf. 12½x12**
1267 A490 850p multicolored   3.50 1.75

Labor
Day — A491

1992, May 1   **Perf. 12x12½**
1268 A491 900p multicolored   3.50 1.75

Mother's
Day — A492

1992, May 19
1269 A492 900p multicolored   3.50 1.75

Evacuation of British and French
Troops, 46th Anniv. — A493

1992, May 19   **Perf. 12½x12**
1270 A493 900p multicolored   3.50 1.75

Traffic Safety
Day — A494

1992, May 19   **Perf. 12x12½**
1271 A494 850p multicolored   3.50 1.75

Intl. Flower Show,
Damascus
A495

   Designs: 300p, Linum mucronatum, horiz.
800p, Yucca filamentosa. 900p, Zinnia
elegans.

Perf. 11½x12, 12x11½
1992, July 5   **Litho.**
1272 A495 300p multicolored   1.25 .65
1273 A495 800p blue & multi   3.25 1.60
1274 A495 900p multicolored   3.50 1.75
    Nos. 1272-1274 (3)   8.00 4.00

1992 Summer
Olympics,
Barcelona
A496

   No. 1275: a, 150p, Team handball. b, 150p,
Running. c, 450p, Swimming. d, 750p, Wrestling. 5000p, Incorporates designs of Nos.
1275a-1275d.

1992, July 25   **Litho.**   **Perf. 12x11½**
1275 A496   Strip of 4, #a.-d.   6.00 5.00
Imperf
Size: 80x124mm
1276 A496 5000p multicolored 20.00 10.00

Anti-Smoking
Campaign
A497

1992, Aug. 28   **Perf. 12x12½**
1277 A497 750p multicolored   3.00 1.50

39th Intl.
Damascus
Fair — A498

1992, Aug. 28
1278 A498 900p multicolored   3.50 1.75

7th Arab Games, Damascus — A499

   Designs: a, 750p, Soccer. b, 850p, Pommel
horse. c, 900p, Pole vault.

1992, Sept. 4   **Perf. 12½**
1279 A499   Strip of 3, #a.-c.   10.00 5.00

World Post
Day — A500

1992, Oct. 9   **Perf. 12x12½**
1280 A500 600p multicolored   2.40 1.25

World Children's
Day — A501

1992, Nov. 7   **Perf. 12x11½**
1281 A501 850p multicolored   3.50 1.75

Sebtt El Mardini
(826-912)
A502

1992, Nov. 7   **Litho.**   **Perf. 12x11½**
1282 A502 850p multicolored   3.50 1.75

1992 Special
Olympics,
Madrid
A503

1992, Nov. 7   **Perf. 12½**
1283 A503 850p multicolored   3.50 1.75

Corrective Movement, 22nd
Anniv. — A504

1992, Nov. 16   **Perf. 11½x12**
1284 A504 450p multicolored   1.75 .90

Arbor
Day — A505

1992, Dec. 31   **Perf. 12x12½**
1285 A505 600p multicolored   2.40 1.25

2nd Intl. Conference of PACO — A506

   Design: 1150p, Eye surrounded by scenes
of day and night, rainbow.

1993, May 12   **Litho.**   **Perf. 12**
1286 A506 1100p multicolored   1.00 .50

Size: 35½x24mm
Perf. 11½x12
1287 A506 1150p multicolored   1.10   .55
Syrian Ophthamological Society, 25th anniv. (No. 1287).

March 8th Revolution, 30th Anniv. — A507

1993, Mar. 8   **Litho.**   **Perf. 11½x12**
1288 A507 1100p multicolored   .80   .40

Butterflies
A508

Designs: a, 1000p, Common blue. b, 1500p, Silver-washed fritillary. c, 2500p, Precis orithya.

1993, Mar. 13
1289 A508 Strip of 3, #a.-c.   4.75 4.75

Mother's Day — A509

1993, Apr. 17   **Perf. 12x11½**
1290 A509 1100p multicolored   .80   .40

Evacuation of British and French Troops, 47th Anniv. — A510

1993, Apr. 17   **Perf. 11½x12**
1291 A510 1100p multicolored   .80   .40

A511

1993, Apr. 17   **Litho.**   **Perf. 11½x12**
1292 A511 2500p multicolored   1.75   .85

Agricultural Reform, 25th Anniv. — A512

1993, Apr. 20   **Litho.**   **Perf. 11½x12**
1293 A512 1150p multicolored   .90   .45

Labor Day — A513

1993, May 1   **Perf. 12x11½**
1294 A513 1100p multicolored   .80   .40

Intl. Flower Show, Damascus — A514

a, 1000p, Alcea setosa. b, 1100p, Primulaceae. c, 1150p, Gesneriaceae.

1993, June 17   **Litho.**   **Perf. 12x11½**
1295 A514 Strip of 3, #a.-c.   2.25 2.25

Tourism
A515

1993, Sept. 27   **Perf. 11½x12**
1296 A515 1000p Woman, prism tomb   1.00   .50

World Post Day
A516

1993, Oct. 9   **Perf. 12½x12**
1297 A516 1000p multicolored   1.00   .50

World Child Day
A517

1993, Nov. 6   **Perf. 11½x12**
1298 A517 1150p multicolored   1.10   .55

Ibn El Bittar, Chemist — A518

1993, Nov. 6   **Perf. 12x11½**
1299 A518 1150p multicolored   1.10   .55

Corrective Movement, 23rd Anniv. — A519

1993, Nov. 16   **Litho.**   **Imperf.**
1300 A519 2500p multicolored   2.50 2.50

Arabian Horses
A520

1994, Jan.   **Litho.**   **Perf. 12½**
1301 A520 1000p shown   .60   .30
1302 A520 1000p White horse   .60   .30
1303 A520 1500p Tan horse   .90   .45
1304 A520 1500p Black horse   .90   .45
  a.   Strip of 4, #1301-1304   3.00 3.00

Arbor Day
A521

1994, Jan.   **Litho.**   **Perf. 12½x12**
1305 A521 1100p multicolored   1.75   .85

40th Intl. Damascus Fair
A522

1994, Jan.
1306 A522 1100p multicolored   1.75   .85

Basel Al Assad (1962-94) — A523

1994, Mar. 1   **Perf. 12x12½**
1307 A523 2500p multicolored   4.00 2.00

March 8th Revolution, 31st Anniv. — A524

a, Oranges. b, Mandarin oranges. c, Lemons.

1994, Mar. 8   **Perf. 12½x12**
1308 A524 1500p Strip of 3, #a.-c.   7.50 7.50

Evacuation of British and French Troops, 48th Anniv. — A525

1994, Apr. 17
1309 A525 1800p multicolored   2.75 1.40

Mother's Day
A526

1994, May 1   **Litho.**   **Perf. 12½x12**
1310 A526 1800p multicolored   2.75 1.40

Labor Day
A527

1994, May 1
1311 A527 1700p multicolored   2.75 1.40

ILO, 75th
Anniv.
A528

1994, June 1
1312 A528 1700p multicolored 2.75 1.40

1994 World Cup Soccer
Championships, U.S. — A529

Various soccer plays.

1994, June 17 *Perf. 12½*
1313 A529 1700p Pair, #a.-b. 5.75 2.75
Size: 80x80mm
Imperf
1314 A529 4000p multicolored 6.75 6.75

41st Intl. Fair,
Damascus
A530

1994, Aug. 3 Litho. *Perf. 12x12½*
1315 A530 1800p multicolored 1.60 .80

Intl. Flower Show, Damascus — A531

a, Daisies. b, Red flowers. c. Yellow flowers.

1994, Aug. 3 *Perf. 12x11½*
1316 A531 1800p Strip of 3, #a.-
c. 4.50 4.50

Intl. Olympic Committee,
Cent. — A532

1994, Aug. 3 *Perf. 11½x12*
1317 A532 1700p multicolored 1.50 .75

Butterflies — A533

a, Apollo (shown). b, Purple emperor, value
at right. c. Birdwing, value at left.

1994, Aug. 9 Litho. *Perf. 11½x12*
1318 A533 1700p Strip of 3, #a.-
c. 8.25 8.25

4th Natl.
Census
A534

1994, Aug. 15
1319 A534 1000p multicolored 1.50 .75

Science
Week
A535

Design: £10, Al Kindi, philosopher.

1994, Nov. 5 *Perf. 12½*
1320 A535 £10 multicolored 1.50 .75

Corrective Movement, 24th
Anniv. — A536

1994, Nov. 16 *Imperf.*
1321 A536 £25 multicolored 6.50 6.50

ICAO, 50th Anniv. — A537

1994, Dec. 7 Litho. *Perf. 12½*
1322 A537 17p multicolored 1.50 .75

Martyr's
Square
A538

1994, Dec. 7 Litho. *Perf. 11½x12*
1323 A538 £50 purple 7.25 3.75
See Nos. 1472-1474, 1518, 1538.

Intl. Children's
Day — A539

1994, Dec. 19 *Perf. 12x11½*
1324 A539 £10 multicolored 1.50 .75

World Post
Day — A540

1994, Dec. 19
1325 A540 £10 multicolored 1.50 .75

Intl. Tourism
Day — A541

1994, Dec. 19
1326 A541 £17 multicolored 2.50 1.25

March 8 Revolution, 32nd
Anniv. — A542

1995, Mar. 8 Litho. *Perf. 11½x12*
1327 A542 £18 multicolored 2.75 1.40

Arab League,
50th Anniv.
A543

1995, Mar. 22 *Perf. 12½*
1328 A543 £17 multicolored 2.50 1.25

World Water
Day — A544

1995, Apr. 9 Litho. *Perf. 12x12½*
1329 A544 £17 multicolored 1.25 .60

Mother's
Day
A545

1995, Apr. 9 Litho. *Perf. 12½x12*
1330 A545 £17 multicolored 2.00 1.00

Arbor
Day — A546

1995, Apr. 9 Litho. *Perf. 12x12½*
1331 A546 1800p multicolored 1.50 .75

UN, 50th
Anniv. — A547

1995, Aug. 13 Litho. *Perf. 12x11½*
1332 A547 £18 multicolored 2.75 1.40

A548

1995, Aug. 21
1333 A548 £18 multicolored 2.75 1.40
4th World Conference on Women, Beijing.

Desert Festival, Tourism Day A549

1995, June 25   *Perf. 12½x12*
1334   A549   £18 multicolored   1.25   .65

Labor Day — A550

1995, June 25   *Perf. 12x12½*
1335   A550   £10 multicolored   .75   .40

A551

1995, Apr. 30   Litho.   *Perf. 12x11½*
1336   A551   £17 multicolored   1.25   .60

Evacuation of British & French Troops, 49th anniv.

Intl. Year of the Family — A552

1995, Apr. 30   Litho.   *Perf. 12x11½*
1337   A552   £17 multicolored   1.40   .70

Arab Apiculture Union, 1st Anniv. — A553

1995, Apr. 30   Litho.   *Perf. 12x12½*
1338   A553   £17 multicolored   2.00   1.00

FAO, 50th Anniv. A554

1995, June 25   *Perf. 12½x12*
1339   A554   £15 multicolored   1.75   .85

42nd Intl. Fair, Damascus A555

1995, Aug. 28   Litho.   *Perf. 11½x12*
1340   A555   £15 multicolored   1.50   .75

Int'l Flower Show, Damascus A556

No. 1341, Astilbe. No. 1342, Evening primrose. No. 1343, Blue carpet.

1995, July 30   Litho.   *Perf. 12½*
1341   A556   £10 multicolored   .50   .25
1342   A556   £10 multicolored   .50   .25
1343   A556   £10 multicolored   .50   .25
   a.   Strip of 3, #1341-1343   1.50   1.50

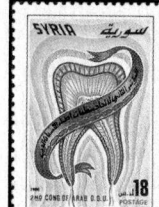

Second Congress of Arab Dentists' Assoc. — A557

1995, Sept. 16   Litho.   *Perf. 12x11½*
1344   A557   £18 multicolored   1.50   .75

Syrian Army, 50th Anniv. A558

1995, Oct. 2   Litho.   *Perf. 11½x12*
1345   A558   £18 multicolored   1.40   .70

World Post Day A559

1995, Oct. 2   Litho.   *Perf. 11½x12*
1346   A559   £15 multicolored   1.60   .85

World Children's Day — A560

1995, Oct. 2   *Perf. 12x11½*
1347   A560   £18 multicolored   2.00   1.00

Ahmed ben Maged, Cartographer, 500th Death Anniv. — A561

1995, Nov. 4   Litho.   *Perf. 11½x12*
1348   A561   £18 multicolored   2.00   1.00

Corrective Movement, 25th Anniv. A562

Design: £50, like No. 1349 with #1044, 720, 1227b, 903.

1995, Nov. 11   Litho.   *Perf. 12½*
1349   A562   £10 multicolored   1.10   .55

Imperf

Size: 100x64mm
1350   A562   £50 multicolored   5.50   2.75

Songbirds — A563

Designs: a, Group on tree branch. b, One in snow, flower. c, One on fence rail.

1995, Dec. 5   Litho.   *Perf. 12½*
1351   A563   £18 Strip of 3, #a.-c.   7.25   7.25

Louis Pasteur (1822-95) A564

1995, Dec. 21   *Perf. 12½x12*
1352   A564   £18 multicolored   2.00   1.00

March 8 Revolution, 33rd Anniv. — A565

Design: Hydro-electric plant.

1996, Mar. 8   Litho.   *Perf. 11½x12*
1353   A565   £25 multicolored   2.00   1.00

Evacuation Day, 50th Anniv. — A566

1996, Apr. 17   *Perf. 12½*
1354   A566   £10 black & multi   .85   .40

1355   A566   £25 bister & multi   2.00   1.00

Size: 57x46mm
Imperf
1356   A566   £25 bis, blk, & multi   5.25   2.75

Liberation of Kuneitra A567

1996, June 26   Litho.   *Perf. 11½x12*
1357   A567   £10 multicolored   .60   .30

1996 Summer Olympic Games, Atlanta A568

1996, July 19   *Perf. 11½x12*
1358   A568   £17 Wrestling   1.10   .55
1359   A568   £17 Swimming   1.10   .55
1360   A568   £17 Running   1.10   .55
   a.   Strip of 3, #1358-1360   3.25   3.25

Size: 55x41mm
Imperf
1361   A568   £25 Soccer   1.60   .80
   Nos. 1358-1361 (4)   4.90   2.45

Intl. Flower Show, Damascus A569

Cactus: No. 1362, Notocactus graessnerii. No. 1363, Mammilaria erythosperma.

1996, July 1   Litho.   *Perf. 12½*
1362   A569   £18 multicolored   1.25   .65
1363   A569   £18 multicolored   1.25   .65

Ba'ath Party, 50th Anniv. A570

1996, July 1   *Perf. 11½x12*
1364   A570   £18 multicolored   1.25   .65

Pres. Hafez al-Assad — A571

1995   Litho.   *Perf. 11½*
1365   A571   100p bright blue   .25   .25
1366   A571   500p bright orange   .55   .25
1367   A571   £10 bright lilac   1.10   .55
1368   A571   £17 rose lake   1.90   .95
1369   A571   £18 slate green   2.00   1.00
   Nos. 1365-1369 (5)   5.80   3.00

Issued: £10, 5/3; 100p, 500p, £17, £18, 12/31.

Arbor Day — A572

1996, Mar. 8 Litho. Perf. 12¼x12½
1370 A572 £17 multicolored .80 .40

Mother's Day — A573

1996, May 1 Perf. 12x11½
1370A A573 £10 multicolored .50 .25

Labor Day — A574

1996, May 1 Perf. 12¼x12½
1371 A574 £15 multicolored .70 .35

Radio, Cent. — A575

1996, Aug. 18 Litho. Perf. 12½
1372 A575 £17 multicolored 1.10 .55

World AIDS Day — A576

1996, Aug. 18 Perf. 12x11½
1373 A576 £17 multicolored 1.10 .55

43rd Intl. Fair, Damascus A577

1996, Aug. 28
1374 A577 £17 multicolored 1.10 .55

NICE, 5th Anniv. A578

1996, Sept. 5 Perf. 11½x12
1375 A578 £18 multicolored 1.10 .60

World Child Day — A579

1996, Oct. 9 Perf. 12x11½
1376 A579 £10 multicolored .65 .30

World Post Day — A580

1996, Oct. 9
1377 A580 £17 multicolored 1.10 .55

UNICEF, 50th Anniv. — A581

1996, Nov. 20
1378 A581 £17 multicolored 1.10 .55

36th Science Week — A582

Design: Musa Iben Shaker's sons.

1996, Nov. 2 Perf. 12½x12
1379 A582 £10 multicolored .65 .35

Corrective Movement, 26th Anniv. A583

1996, Nov. 16 Perf. 12½
1380 A583 £10 multicolored .65 .35
Size: 65x90mm
Imperf
1381 A583 £50 like No. 1380 3.25 1.60

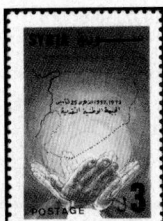

Natl. Advance Party — A584

1997, Mar. 7 Litho. Perf. 12x11½
1382 A584 £3 multicolored .25 .25

March 8 Revolution, 34th Anniv. — A585

1997, Mar. 8
1383 A585 £15 multicolored 1.00 .50

Arbor Day — A586

1997, Apr. 8 Litho. Perf. 12x12½
1384 A586 £10 multicolored .75 .40

Fish — A587

1997, Apr. 8 Perf. 12½x12
1385 £17 Two dorsal fins 1.00 .50
1386 £17 One dorsal fin 1.00 .50
a. A587 Pair, #1385-1386 2.00 2.00

Mother's Day — A588

1997, Apr. 8 Perf. 12x11½
1387 A588 £15 multicolored 1.00 .50

Baath Party Revolution, 50th Anniv. A589

1997, Apr. 3 Perf. 12½
1388 A589 £25 multicolored 1.60 .80
Size: 90x65mm
Imperf
1389 A589 £25 multicolored 1.60 .80

World Tourism Day — A590

1997, Apr. 8 Perf. 12x11½
1390 A590 £17 multicolored 1.10 .60

Evacuation Day, 51st Anniv. — A591

1997, Apr. 17 Perf. 11½x12
1391 A591 £15 multicolored 1.00 .50

Labor Day — A592

1997, May 1 Perf. 12x11½
1392 A592 £15 multicolored 1.00 .50

World Book Day — A592a

1997, June 16 Litho. Perf. 12½
1392A A592a £10 multicolored .50 .25

A592b

1997, June 16 Perf. 12x11½
1392B A592b £18 multicolored .70 .35
No smoking day.

Intl. Flower Show, Damascus — A593

No. 1393, Echino ereus. No. 1394, Iris.

1997, June 21 Litho. Perf. 12x11½
1393 A593 £18 multicolored 1.10 .60
1394 A593 £18 multicolored 1.10 .60
  a. A593 Pair, #1393-1394 2.25 2.25
See Nos. 1412-1413.

4th Congress of Arab Denistry — A594

1997, Sept. 4
1395 A594 £10 multicolored .65 .35

44th Intl. Fair, Damascus A595

1997, Sept. 4
1396 A595 £17 multicolored 1.10 .55

World Post Day A596

1997, Sept. 27
1397 A596 £17 multicolored 1.10 .55

World Children's Day A597

1997, Sept. 27
1398 A597 £17 multicolored 1.10 .55

Intl. Tourism Day A598

1997, Sept. 27
1399 A598 £17 multicolored 1.10 .55

37th Science Week — A599

1997, Nov. 1 Litho. Perf. 12x11½
1400 A599 £17 multicolored 1.10 .55

Corrective Movement, 27th Anniv. A600

1997, Nov. 16 Perf. 12½
1401 A600 £10 multicolored .70 .35
Size: 92x67mm
Imperf
1402 A600 £50 like #1401 3.25 3.25

Islamic Conference, 30th Anniv. — A601

1997, Dec. 9 Litho. Perf. 11½x12
1403 A601 £10 multicolored .70 .35

March 8 Revolution, 35th Anniv. — A602

1998, Mar. 8 Litho. Perf. 12½x12
1404 A602 £17 multicolored 1.10 .55

Mother's Day A603

1998, March 21 Perf. 11½x12
1405 A603 £10 multicolored .70 .35

Evacuation Day, 52nd Anniv. — A604

1998, Apr. 17 Litho. Perf. 12x11½
1406 A604 £10 multicolored .70 .35

Labor Day — A605

1998, May 1
1407 A605 £18 multicolored 1.10 .55

World Tourism Day — A606

Design: Princess of Banias.

1998, July 22 Litho. Perf. 12x11½
1408 A606 £17 multicolored 1.10 .55

Mother Teresa (1910-97) A607

1998, July 22
1409 A607 £18 multicolored 1.10 .55

1998 World Cup Soccer Championships, France — A608

£25, Soccer players, diff.

1998, June 22 Perf. 12x12½
1410 A608 £10 shown .60 .30
Size: 60x55mm
Imperf
1411 A608 £25 multicolored 2.25 1.10

Intl. Flower Show Type of 1997
Flowers: No. 1412, Plum-colored with yellow centers. No. 1413, Red hibiscus.

1998, June 22 Perf. 12x11½
1412 A593 £17 multicolored 1.10 1.10
1413 A593 £17 multicolored 1.10 1.10
  a. Pair, #1412-1413 2.25 2.25

45th Intl. Damascus Fair A609

1998, Sept. 26 Litho. Perf. 11½x12
1414 A609 £18 multicolored 1.10 .55

World Children's Day — A610

1998, Sept. 26 Perf. 12x11½
1415 A610 £18 multicolored 1.10 .55

World Post Day A611

1998, Sept. 26 Litho. Perf. 11½x12
1416 A611 £18 multicolored 1.10 .55

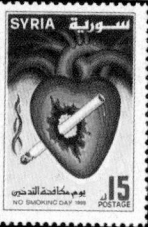

Day to Stop Smoking — A612

1998, Sept. 26 Perf. 12x11½
1417 A612 £15 multicolored .95 .50

Arab Post Day — A613

1998, Sept. 26   *Perf. 12½*
1418 A613 £10 multicolored   .60 .30

Arab-Israeli October War, 25th
Anniv. — A614

1998, Oct. 6   *Imperf.*
1419 A614 £25 multicolored   1.60 .80

Science
Week
A615

1998, Nov. 3   *Perf. 11½x12*
1420 A615 £10 multicolored   .65 .35

Camels
A616

1998, Nov. 25   *Perf. 12½*
1421 A616 £17 multicolored   1.10 .55

Corrective
Movement,
28th Anniv.
A617

1998, Nov. 16   **Litho.**   *Perf. 12½*
1422 A617 £10 multicolored   .65 .30
     Size: 99x65mm
      Imperf
1423 A617 £25 multicolored   .65 .30

Jerusalem — A618

1998, Nov. 25   *Perf. 12½*
1424 A618 £10 multicolored   .65 .30

Re-election
of Pres.
Assad
A619

£50, Portrait with designs from Nos. 1036,
C496, C506, & portrait from No. 1265.

1999, Feb. 11   **Litho.**   *Perf. 12½*
1425 A619 £10 red brn & multi   .50 .25
1426 A619 £17 pale yel & multi   .90 .45
1427 A619 £18 pale grn & multi   .95 .45
     Size: 140x110mm
      Imperf
1428 A619 £50 pale grn & multi   2.50 2.50
    Nos. 1425-1428 (4)   4.85 3.65

Arbor
Day — A620

1999, Apr. 29   **Litho.**   *Perf. 12½*
1429 A620 £17 multicolored   1.10 .55

Evacuation Day,
53rd.
Anniv. — A621

1999, Apr. 29   *Perf. 12x11½*
1430 A621 £18 multicolored   1.10 .55

Mother's
Day — A622

1999, Apr. 29
1431 A622 £17 multicolored   1.10 .55

Intl. Flower Show, Damascus — A623

Designs: a, Jasminum. b, Acanthaceae.

1999, June 20   **Litho.**   *Perf. 12x11½*
1432 A623 £10 Pair, #a.-b.   .85 .45

March 8 Revolution, 36th
Anniv. — A624

No. 1434, Building, monument.

1999, Mar. 8   **Litho.**   *Perf. 12¼x12½*
1433 A624 £25 shown   1.50 .75
     Size: 75x110mm
      Imperf
1434 A624 £25 multicolored   1.50 .75

Declaration of Human Rights, 50th
Anniv. — A625

1999, June 5   *Perf. 11½x12*
1435 A625 £18 multicolored   .95 .45

Labor
Day — A626

1999, June 5   **Litho.**   *Perf. 12x11½*
1436 A626 £10 multicolored   .55 .30

10th
Amity
Festival
A627

1999, Aug. 1   **Litho.**   *Perf. 11½x12*
1437 A627 £10 multicolored   .65 .30

Arab Post
Day — A628

1999, Oct. 12   **Litho.**   *Perf. 12x11½*
1438 A628 £10 multicolored   .65 .30

46th Intl.
Fair,
Damascus
A629

1999, Aug. 28   *Perf. 11½x12*
1439 A629 £15 multicolored   .95 .45

A630

1999, Sept. 21   *Perf. 12x11½*
1440 A630 £17 multicolored   1.10 .55

Arab Dentists Assoc., 7th Congress.

World Children's
Day — A631

1999, Nov. 16
1441 A631 £18 multicolored   1.10 .55

UPU, 125th
Anniv. — A632

1999, Oct. 12
1442 A632 £17 multicolored   1.10 .55

Corrective Movement, 29th
Anniv. — A633

No. 1443, Building, statue. No. 1444, Close-
up of statue. £25, Building statue, fountain.

1999, Nov. 16   *Perf. 12½*
1443 A633 £17 multicolored   1.10 .55
1444 A633 £17 multi, vert.   1.10 .55
      Imperf
     Size: 115x76mm
1445 A633 £25 multicolored   1.60 1.60
    Nos. 1443-1445 (3)   3.80 2.70

Abu Hanifah al-Deilouri,
Botanist — A634

1999, Oct. 12   *Perf. 11½x12*
1446 A634 £17 multicolored   1.10 .55

Christianity, 2000th Anniv. — A635

1999, Nov. 16 *Perf. 12½*
1447 A635 £17 multicolored 1.10 .55

March 8 Revolution, 37th Anniv. A636

2000, Mar. 8 **Litho.** *Perf. 12½*
1448 A636 £18 multicolored 1.10 .55

Mother's Day — A637

2000, Mar. 21
1449 A637 £17 multicolored 1.00 .50

Evacuation Day, 54th Anniv. — A638

2000, Apr. 17 *Imperf.*
1450 A638 £25 multicolored 1.50 1.50

Labor Day — A639

2000, May 1 **Litho.** *Perf. 12x11½*
1451 A639 £10 multicolored .40 .25

Installation of Bashar al-Assad as President A640

2000, July 17 *Perf. 12¼*
1452 Strip of 4 1.90 1.90
a. A640 £3 lt blue & multi .25 .25
b. A640 £10 tan & multi .40 .25
c. A640 £17 bl gray & multi .65 .30
d. A640 £18 gray & multi .65 .35
Imperf
Size: 110x74mm
1453 A640 £50 multi 1.90 1.90

Arab Post Day A641

2000, Aug. 20 **Litho.** *Perf. 11½x12*
1454 A641 £18 multicolored 1.10 .55

47th Damascus Fair — A642

2000, Aug. 20
1455 A642 £15 multicolored .90 .45

2000 Summer Olympics, Sydney — A643

No. 1456: a, £17, Weight lifting. b, £18, Women's shot put.

2000, Oct. 1 **Litho.** *Perf. 12x11½*
1456 A643 Pair, #a-b 1.40 .70
Imperf
Size: 80x77mm
1457 A643 £25 Javelin .95 .50

World Tourism Day — A644

2000, Dec. 6 **Litho.** *Imperf.*
1458 A644 £50 Mosaic 3.00 3.00

World Post Day A645

2000, Aug. 20 *Perf. 11½x12*
1459 A645 £18 multicolored 1.10 .55

Nasir ad-Din at-Tusi (1201-74), Scientist A646

2000, Nov. 1 **Litho.** *Perf. 12½x12¼*
1460 A646 £15 multicolored .60 .30
Science week.

Arbor Day — A647

2000, May 15 *Perf. 12x11½*
1461 A647 £18 multicolored .65 .35

Butterflies — A648

a, £17, Charaxes jasius. b, £18, Apaturairis.

2000, May 15 *Perf. 12½*
1462 A648 Pair, #a-b 1.40 .70

World Children's Day — A649

2000, Aug. 20 **Litho.** *Perf. 12x11½*
1463 A649 £10 multicolored .60 .30

World Meteorological Organization, 50th Anniv. — A650

2000, Dec. 6
1464 A650 £10 multicolored .60 .30

March 8 Revolution, 38th Anniv. — A651

2001 **Litho.** *Perf. 12x11½*
1465 A651 £25 multicolored .95 .50

Mother's Day — A652

2001
1466 A652 £10 multicolored .40 .25

Evacuation Day, 55th Anniv. — A653

2001
1467 A653 £25 multicolored .95 .50

Book and Author's Rights — A654

2001
1468 A654 £10 multi .40 .25

Intl. Flower Show, Damascus — A655

No. 1469: a, Weigela. b, Mertensia.

2001
1469 A655 £10 Horiz. pair, #a-b .75 .40

Syrian Engineering Syndicate, 50th Anniv. A656

2001, Feb. 1 **Litho.** *Perf. 12½*
1470 A656 £17 multi .65 .35

Size: 95x85mm
Imperf
1471 A656 £25 multi .95 .50

Martyr's Square Type of 1994
2001 *Perf. 11½x12*
1472 A538 100p brt blue grn .25 .25
1473 A538 £10 red .35 .25
1474 A538 £50 blue 1.90 .95
Nos. 1472-1474 (3) 2.50 1.45

Labor Day — A657

2001 Litho. *Perf. 12x11½*
1475 A657 £18 multi .75 .40

48th Damascus Fair — A658

2001 Litho. *Perf. 12x11½*
1476 A658 £10 multi .40 .25

Re-occupation of Kuneitra by Syria, 27th Anniv. — A659

2001 *Perf. 11½x12*
1477 A659 £17 multi .65 .35

Anti-Smoking Campaign — A660

2001
1478 A660 £18 multi .70 .35

UN High Commissioner for Refugees, 50th Anniv. — A661

2001
1479 A661 £17 multi .65 .35

Tooth Cross-section A662

2001 *Perf. 12x11½*
1480 A662 £10 multi .40 .25

World Children's Day — A663

2001 *Perf. 12x11½*
1481 A663 £18 multi .70 .35

A664

2001 *Perf. 12x11½*
1482 A664 £10 multi .40 .25

Size: 84x111mm
Imperf
1483 A664 £25 multi 1.00 1.00

A665

Aga Khan Award for Architecture — A666

2001 *Perf. 11½x12*
1484 A665 £10 multi .40 .25
1485 A666 £17 multi .65 .35
1486 A666 £18 multi .70 .35
Nos. 1484-1486 (3) 1.75 .95

Installation of Bashar al-Assad as President, 1st Anniv. — A667

Assad and: a, £10, Silver frame. b, £17, Gold frame.

2001 Litho. *Perf. 12½x12¼*
1487 A667 Horiz. pair, #a-b 1.10 .55

Arab Post Day A668

2001 *Perf. 11½x12*
1488 A668 £18 multi .75 .35

World Post Day A669

2001
1489 A669 £10 multi .40 .25

Arbor Day — A670

2001 *Perf. 12x11½*
1490 A670 £5 multi .25 .25

World Tourism Day — A671

2001 *Perf. 12½*
1491 A671 £17 multi .70 .35

Palestinian Intifada — A672

2001 *Perf. 12x11½*
1492 A672 £17 multi .70 .35

Pres. Hafez al-Assad (1930-2000) — A673

2001 *Perf. 12¼x12½*
1493 A673 £25 multi 1.00 .50

Correctionist Movement, 31st Anniv. — A674

Text color: £5, Black. £15, Red.

2001 *Perf. 11½x12*
1494-1495 A674 Set of 2 .80 .40

Evacuation Day, 56th Anniv. — A675

2002, Apr. 7 Litho. *Perf. 12x11½*
1496 A675 £15 multi .65 .30

Labor Day — A676

2002, May 1 *Perf. 12x12½*
1497 A676 £10 multi .45 .25

Intl. Flower Show, Damascus — A677

No. 1498: a, £15, Yellow flowers. b, £17, White lilies.

2002, May 1 *Perf. 12x11½*
1498 A677 Horiz. pair, #a-b 1.40 .70

March 8 Revolution, 39th Anniv. A678

2002, Mar. 8 Litho. *Perf. 11½x12*
1499 A678 £15 multi .65 .30

Mother's Day — A679

2002, Mar. 21   *Perf. 12x11½*
1500 A679 £25 multi   1.10 .55

Gazelle A680

2002, Mar. 8   *Perf. 12½*
1501 A680 £15 multi   .65 .30

Baath Party, 55th Anniv. A681

2002, Apr. 7   *Perf. 11½x12*
1502 A681 £15 multi   .65 .30

2002 World Cup Soccer Championships, Japan and Korea — A682

No. 1503 — Various players: a, £5. b, £10. £25, Goalie making save, horiz.

2002, May 31   *Perf. 12½*
1503 A682 Horiz. pair, #a-b   .65 .30
Size: 78x65mm
Imperf
1504 A682 £25 multi   1.10 .55

World Tourism Day — A683

2002, Sept. 27   *Perf. 12½*
1505 A683 £10 multi   .40 .25

First Syrian Railroad, Cent. — A684

2002, Nov. 9
1506 A684 £10 multi   .40 .25

Abd al-Rahman al-Kawakibi (1849-1902), Arab Nationalist — A685

2002, Aug. 13   *Perf. 12x11½*
1507 A685 £10 multi   .40 .25

Intifada — A686

Designs: £10, Flag bearer, four rock throwers, tank.
£25, Flag bearer, rock thrower, tank.

2002, Sept. 28   *Perf. 12x11½*
1508 A686 £10 multi   .40 .25
Size: 66x79mm
Imperf
1509 A686 £25 multi   1.10 .55

Birds A687

2002, Sep. 27   *Perf. 11½x12*
1510   Vert. strip of 4   1.40 .70
a.   A687 £3 Sand grouse   .25 .25
b.   A687 £5 Francolin   .25 .25
c.   A687 £10 Duck   .40 .25
d.   A687 £15 Goose   .65 .30

Arab Post Day A688

Frame color: £5, Blue. £10, Red violet.

2002, Aug. 3   *Perf. 11½x12*
1511-1512 A688 Set of 2   .65 .30

49th Intl. Damascus Fair — A689

Emblem and: a, £5, "X's." b, £10, Squares and diamonds.

2002, Aug. 28   *Perf. 12x11½*
1513 A689 Horiz. pair, #a-b   .65 .30

World Post Day — A690

No. 1514: a, Dove, envelope, rainbow. b, Envelope, UPU emblem, horiz.

Perf. 12x11½, 11½x12 (#1514b)
2002, Oct. 9
1514 A690 £10 Horiz. pair, #a-b   .80 .40

Arbor Day — A691

2002, Dec. 26   *Perf. 12x11½*
1515 A691 £10 multi   .40 .25

Intl. Children's Day — A692

2002, Oct. 16   *Perf. 12½*
1516 A692 £10 multi   .40 .25

Corrective Movement, 32nd Anniv. A693

2002, Oct. 16   *Perf. 11½x12*
1517 A693 £10 multi   .40 .25

Martyr's Square Type of 1994
2003, May 5 Litho.   *Perf. 11½x12*
1518 A538 300p brown   .25 .25

March 8 Revolution, 40th Anniv. — A694

2003, Mar. 8   *Perf. 12¼x12½*
1519 A694 £15 multi   .65 .30

Teacher's Day — A695

2003, Mar. 8   *Perf. 12x11½*
1520 A695 £17 multi   .75 .40

Mother's Day — A696

2003, Mar. 21
1521 A696 £32 multi   1.40 .70

Evacuation Day, 57th Anniv. — A697

2003, Apr. 17
1522 A697 £15 multi   .65 .30

Labor Day — A698

2003, May 1
1523 A698 £25 multi   1.10 .55

Intl. Flower Show, Damascus A699

No. 1524: a, Damask roses and violets. b, Anemones. c, Daisies. d, Damask roses and gillyflowers. e, Sunflowers.

2003, June 15   *Perf. 12½x12¼*
1524   Horiz. strip of 5   2.25 1.10
a.-e.   A699 £10 Any single   .45 .25

50th Intl. Damascus Fair — A700

Designs: £32, Flags, emblems. £50, Open orbs, horiz.

2003, Sep. 3   *Perf. 12x12½*
1525 A700 £32 multi   1.40 .70
     Size: 89x66mm
     Imperf
1526 A700 £50 multi   2.25 2.25

World Tourism Day — A701

2003, Sep. 27   *Perf. 12¼x12½*
1527 A701 £32 multi   1.40 .70

Election of Pope John Paul II, 25th Anniv. — A702

2003, Oct. 16   *Perf. 12½x12¼*
1528 A702 £32 multi   1.40 .70

World Post Day A703

2003, Oct. 14 Litho.   *Perf. 11½x12*
1529 A703 £10 multi   .45 .25

Corrective Movement, 33rd Anniv. — A704

2003, Nov. 16   *Perf. 12x11½*
1530 A704 £15 multi   .65 .30

Intl. Children's Day A705

2003, Dec. 8   *Perf. 11½x12*
1531 A705 £15 multi   .65 .30

Birds A706

2003, Dec. 8   *Perf. 12½x12¼*
1532   Horiz. strip of 5   2.75 2.75
  a. A706 £5 Woodcock   .25 .25
  b. A706 £10 Lapwing   .45 .25
  c. A706 £15 European roller   .65 .30
  d. A706 £17 Teal   .70 .35
  e. A706 £18 Bustard   .75 .40

Pres. Bashar al-Assad — A707

     Perf. 11¾x11¼
2003, Dec. 8   **Unwmk.**
1533 A707 £15 brt blue green   .65 .30
1534 A707 £25 blue   1.10 .55
1535 A707 £50 lilac   2.10 1.10
   Nos. 1533-1535 (3)   3.85 1.95

See Nos. 1585-1594. Compare with Nos. 1652-1654.

World Summit on the Information Society, Geneva — A708

2003, Dec. 10   *Perf. 12x11½*
1536 A708 £15 multi   .65 .30

Arbor Day — A709

2003, Dec. 25   **Litho.**
1537 A709 £25 multi   1.10 .55

Martyr's Square Type of 1994
2004   *Perf. 11½x12*
1538 A538 £5 blue   .25 .25

March 8 Revolution, 41st Anniv. — A710

2004, Mar 8   *Perf. 12½x12*
1539 A710 £10 multi   .40 .25

Teacher's Day — A711

2004, Mar. 13   *Perf. 12x11½*
1540 A711 £5 multi   .25 .25

Mother's Day A712

2004, Mar. 21   *Perf. 11½x12*
1541 A712 £15 multi   .65 .30

Evacuation Day, 58th Anniv. — A713

2004, Apr. 17   **Litho.**
1542 A713 £10 multi   .40 .25

Labor Day A714

2004, May 1
1543 A714 £10 multi   .40 .25

A715

A716

A717

A718

FIFA (Fédération Internationale de Football Association), Cent. — A719

2004, May 21   *Perf. 11½x12*
1544 A715 £5 multi   .25 .25
1545 A716 £10 multi   .40 .25
     Perf. 12½x12¼
1546 A717 £15 multi   .60 .30
     Perf. 12¼x12½
1547 A718 £32 multi   1.25 .60
   Nos. 1544-1547 (4)   2.50 1.40
     Imperf
1548 A719 £25 multi   1.00 1.00

Intl. Flower Show, Damascus A720

No. 1549: a, Gladiola lavender. b, Jasmine. c, Iris. d, Orange nesrien. e, Tulip.

2004, June 15   *Perf. 12x11½*
1549   Horiz. strip of 5   1.00 1.00
  a.-e. A720 £5 Any single   .25 .25

Children and War Campaign of Intl. Committee of the Red Cross — A721

2004, June 17   *Perf. 12¼x12½*
1550 A721 £32 red & black   1.25 .60

2004 Summer
Olympics,
Athens — A722

Designs: £5, Track. £10, Boxing, horiz. £25,
Swimming, horiz.

Perf. 12x11½, 11½x12
2004, Aug. 13
1551-1553 A722 Set of 3   1.60   .80

51st Intl.
Damascus
Fair — A723

2004, Sept. 3   **Perf. 12x11½**
1554 A723 £25 multi   1.00   .50

2004
Census
A724

2004, Sept. 14   **Perf. 12½**
1555 A724 £10 multi   .45   .25

World
Tourism
Day
A725

Designs: £5, Locomotive. No. 1557, £10,
Building. No. 1558, £10, Train.

Perf. 11½x12
2004, Sept. 27   **Litho.**   **Unwmk.**
1556-1558 A725 Set of 3   1.00   .50

World Post
Day — A726

2004, Oct. 9   **Litho.**   **Perf. 12x11½**
1559 A726 £17 multi   .70   .35

Intl.
Children's
Day
A727

2004, Oct. 16   **Perf. 11½x12**
1560 A727 £18 multi   .70   .35

Corrective Movement, 34th
Anniv. — A728

2004, Nov. 16   **Perf. 12½x12**
1561 A728 £25 multi   1.00   .50

Arbor
Day — A729

2004, Dec. 30   **Perf. 12x11½**
1562 A729 £10 multi   .40   .25

Northern
Bald
Ibis — A730

Perf. 12½x12¼
2004, Dec. 30   **Litho.**   **Unwmk.**
1563 A730 £10 multi   .40   .25

Farm
Animals
A731

2004, Dec. 30   **Perf. 11½x12**
1564   Vert. strip of 4   2.10 1.10
  a.   A731 £5 Shami goat   .25   .25
  b.   A731 £15 Awassi ewe   .55   .25
  c.   A731 £17 Bull   .65   .30
  d.   A731 £18 Shami cow   .70   .35

March 8 Revolution, 42nd
Anniv. — A732

Perf. 12¼x12½
2005, Mar. 8   **Wmk. 403**
1565 A732 £17 multi   .65   .30

Teacher's
Day
A733

2005, Mar. 13   **Perf. 11½x12**
1566 A733 £25 multi   1.00   .50

Mother's
Day — A734

2005, Mar. 21   **Perf. 12x11½**
1567 A734 £18 multi   .70   .35

Arab League,
60th
Anniv. — A735

2005, Mar. 22
1568 A735 £10 multi   .40   .25

National
Day — A736

2005, Apr. 17
1569 A736 £17 multi   .65   .30

Labor
Day — A737

2005, May 1   **Wmk. 403**
1570 A737 £15 multi   .60   .30

Intl. Flower
Show, Damascus
A738

2005, June 15   **Litho.**
1571   Horiz. strip of 5   2.50 1.25
  a.   A738 £5 Hyacinth   .25   .25
  b.   A738 £10 Sternbergia clusiana   .40   .25
  c.   A738 £15 Primula obconica   .55   .30
  d.   A738 £17 Primula malacoides   .65   .30
  e.   A738 £18 Canaria   .70   .35

Butterflies
A739

No. 1572: a, Papilio ulysses. b, Monarch. c,
Baeotus baeotus. d, Lacewing. e, Tiger
swallowtail.

2005, Aug. 7   **Perf. 12½**
1572   Horiz. strip of 5   2.00 1.00
  a.-e.   A739 £10 Any single   .40   .25

52nd Intl.
Damascus
Fair — A740

2005, Sept. 3   **Perf. 12x11½**
1573 A740 £15 multi   .60   .30

Mevlana
Jalal ad-Din
ar-Rumi
(1207-73),
Islamic
Philosopher
A741

2005, Sept. 25   **Perf. 12½x12¼**
1574 A741 £25 multi   1.00   .50

See Afghanistan Nos. 1449-1451, Iran No.
2911, and Turkey No. 2971.

World
Tourism
Day
A742

2005, Sept. 27   **Perf. 11½x12**
1575 A742 £17 multi   .65   .30

World Post
Day — A743

2005, Oct. 9   **Perf. 12x11½**
1576 A743 £18 multi   .70   .35

Intl. Children's Day — A744

2005, Oct. 16   **Perf. 12¼x12½**
1577 A744 £17 multi   .65   .30

Corrective Movement, 35th
Anniv. — A745

2005, Nov. 16   *Perf. 11½x12*
1578 A745 £25 multi   1.00 .50

World Summit on the Information
Society, Tunis — A746

2005, Nov. 16   *Perf. 12¼x12½*
1579 A746 £17 multi   .65 .30

Poets
A747

No. 1580: a, Nizar Kabbani (1923-98). b,
Sadalah Wannous (1941-97). c, Omar Abu
Reisheh (1910-90).

2005, Dec. 20   *Perf. 12½x12¼*
1580   Horiz. strip of 3   1.75 .85
   a. A747 £10 multi   .40 .25
   b. A747 £17 multi   .65 .30
   c. A747 £18 multi   .70 .35

Arbor
Day — A748

2005, Dec. 25   **Wmk. 403**
1581 A748 £17 multi   .65 .30

March 8
Revolution, 43rd
Anniv. — A749

     Perf. 12x11½
2006, Mar. 8   **Litho.**   **Wmk. 403**
1582 A749 £18 multi   .70 .35

Aleppo,
2006
Capital of
Islamic
Culture
A750

No. 1583: a, £17, Aleppo Castle. b, £18,
Mosque, vert.
£25, Emblem and buildings.

2006, Mar. 16   *Perf. 11½x12, 12x11½*
1583 A750   Pair, #a-b   1.40 .70
     Imperf
    Size: 79x60mm
1584 A750 £25 multi   .95 .50

Pres. Bashir al-Assad Type of 2003
2006   **Wmk. 403**   *Perf. 11¾x11¼*
1585 A707   £1 brt blue   .25 .25
   a.   Dated "2008"   .25 .25
1586 A707   £3 lilac rose   .25 .25
1587 A707   £5 brown   .25 .25
   a.   Dated "2008"   .25 .25
1588 A707   £10 purple   .40 .25
1589 A707   £15 brt blue grn   .60 .30
1590 A707   £17 orange brn   .65 .35
1591 A707   £18 dark blue   .70 .35
1592 A707   £25 blue   .95 .50
1593 A707   £50 lilac   1.90 .95
1594 A707   £100 green   4.00 2.00
    Nos. 1585-1594 (10)   9.95 5.45

Issued: £1, 9/7; £3, 8/24; £5, 8/1; £10, 6/2;
£15, £25, £50, 3/19; £17, 5/11; £18, 6/8; £100,
9/27.

Mother's
Day — A751

     Perf. 12x11½
2006, Mar. 21   **Wmk. 403**
1595 A751 £17 multi   .65 .35

National
Day — A752

No. 1596: a, Sultan Pasha al-Atrach (1889-
1982). b, Yousef al-Azmeh (1884-1920). c,
Sheikh Saleh al-Ali (1885-1950). d, Ibrahim
Hanano (1889-1935). e, Ahmad Moraiwed
(1886-1926).

2006, Apr. 17
1596   Horiz. strip of 5   1.90 .95
   a.-e. A752 £10 Any single   .35 .25

Labor
Day — A753

2006, May 1
1597 A753 £17 multi   .65 .35

Intl. Flower Show, Damascus — A754

No. 1598: a, £5, Hyoscyamus aureus. b,
£10, Cistus salviaefolius.

2006, May 15   *Perf. 11½x12*
1598 A754   Vert. pair, #a-b   .60 .30

2006 World Cup Soccer
Championships, Germany — A755

No. 1599: a, £17, Players, aerial view of
stadium. b, £18, Players under stadium roof.
£50, Players, vert.

2006, June 25   *Perf. 11½x12*
1599 A755   Vert. pair, #a-b   1.40 .70
     Imperf
    Size: 60x80mm
1600 A755 £50 multi   1.90 .95

Diplomatic Relations Between Syria
and People's Republic of China, 50th
Anniv. — A756

2006, Aug. 1   *Perf. 12½x12¼*
1601 A756 £10 multi   .40 .25

Intl. Year of Deserts and
Desertification — A757

2006, Aug. 13   **Wmk. 403**
1602 A757 £10 multi   .40 .25

53rd Intl.
Damascus
Fair — A758

2006, Sept. 3   *Perf. 12x11½*
1603 A758 £10 multi   .40 .25

A759

World Tourism
Day — A760

2006, Sept. 27   *Perf. 11½x12*
1604 A759 £10 multi   .40 .25
             Perf. 12¼x12½
1605 A760 £10 multi   .40 .25

World Post
Day — A761

2006, Oct. 19   *Perf. 12x11½*
1606 A761 £17 multi   .65 .35

Artists — A762

No. 1607: a, Fateh Almudarres (1922-99). b,
Adham Ismail (1922-63). c, Saeed Makhlouf

(1925-2000). d, Burhan Karkutli (1932-2003).
e, Michael Kirsheh (1900-73).

2006, Nov. 12   **Litho.**
1607   Horiz. strip of 5   1.90   .95
a.-e.   A762 £10 Any single   .35   .25

Corrective Movement, 36th
Anniv. — A763

2006, Nov. 16   **Perf. 12½x12¼**
1608   A763 £15 multi   .60   .30

Arbor Day — A764

2006, Dec. 28   **Perf. 12¼x12½**
1609   A764 £15 multi   .60   .30

Fish
A765

No. 1610: a, Light-colored fish, green and
violet seaweed. b, Dark-colored fish, green
and violet seaweed. c, Light-colored fish,
green seaweed.

2006, Dec. 28   **Perf. 11½x12**
1610   A765   £15 Vert. strip of 3,
       #a-c   1.75   .85

March 8 Revolution, 44th
Anniv. — A766

          Perf. 12¼x12½
2007, Mar. 8   **Litho.**   **Wmk. 403**
1611   A766 £17 multi   .65   .35

Mother's
Day — A767

2007, Mar. 21   **Perf. 12½x12¼**
1612   A767 £15 multi   .60   .30

Baath Party,
60th Anniv.
A768

2007, Apr. 7
1613   A768 £25 multi   1.00   .50

National
Day — A769

2007, Apr. 14
1614   A769 £15 multi   .60   .30

Labor
Day — A770

2007, May 1   **Perf. 12½**
1615   A770 £10 multi   .40   .25

Intl. Flower Show, Damascus — A771

No. 1616: a, Freesia. b, Ipomoea purpurea.
c, Plumbago capensis.

2007, June 27   **Perf. 12¼x12½**
1616   A771 £15 Vert. strip of 3,
       #a-c   1.75   .90

Second Term of Pres. Bashar al-
Assad — A772

No. 1617: a, £10, Portrait of Assad. b, £15,
Portrait of Assad, diff.
£25, Assad taking oath, horiz.

         Perf. 12½x12¼
2007, July 17   **Litho.**   **Wmk. 403**
1617   A772   Horiz. pair, #a-b   1.00   .50
       Size: 85x70mm
          Imperf
1618   A772 £25 multi   1.00   .50

54th Intl.
Damascus
Fair — A773

        Perf. 12x11½
2007, Aug. 15   **Litho.**   **Wmk. 403**
1619   A773 £15 multi   .60   .30

Launch of Sputnik 1, 50th
Anniv. — A774

No. 1620 — Sputnik 1, rocket, "50" and
background color of: a, £15, Green. b, £25,
Brown.

2007, Oct. 4
1620   A774   Horiz. pair, #a-b   1.60   .80

World
Tourism
Day
A775

2007, Nov. 4   **Perf. 11½x12**
1621   A775 £10 multi   .40   .25

World Post
Day — A776

2007, Nov. 4   **Perf. 12½**
1622   A776 £25 multi   1.00   .50

Correctionist Movement, 37th
Anniv. — A777

2007, Nov. 16   **Perf. 12½x12¼**
1623   A777 £15 multi   .60   .30

Arbor Day
A778

2007, Dec. 25   **Perf. 11½x12**
1624   A778 £18 multi   .70   .35

Doctors — A779

No. 1625: a, Dr. Hussny Sabah (1900-86).
b, Dr. Wajieh Al-Barudy (1906-96). c, Dr.
Nadim Shoman (1903-84). d, Dr. Tawfik Izzed-
din (1912-75). e, Dr. Abdussalam Al-Ojaily
(1918-2006).

2007, Dec. 25   **Perf. 12x11½**
1625   Horiz. strip of 5   2.00   1.00
a.-e.   A779 £10 Any single   .40   .25

Birds — A780

No. 1626: a, White stork. b, Syrian wood-peckers. c, Shoveler ducks. d, Bee-eater. e, Turtle dove.

2007, Dec. 30   *Perf. 12½x12¼*
1626   Horiz. strip of 5   2.00 1.00
a.-e. A780 £10 Any single   .40 .25

March 8 Revolution, 45th Anniv. A781

2008, Mar. 8   **Litho.**
1627 A781 £15 multi   .60 .30

Mother's Day — A782

2008, Mar. 21   *Perf. 12x11½*
1628 A782 £10 multi   .40 .25

20th Arab Summit, Damascus A783

Emblem, flags and: £10, Map. £25, Horseman.

2008, Mar. 29   *Perf. 12½x12¼*
1629 A783 £10 multi   .40 .25
Imperf
Size: 70x85mm
1630 A783 £25 multi   1.00 .50

Damascus, 2008 Arab Capital of Culture — A784

Designs: £10, Al-Shamieh School. £15, Al-Thaheria Library. £25, Damascus University, vert.

2008, Mar. 30   *Perf. 12¼x12½*
1631-1632 A784   Set of 2   1.00 .50
Imperf
Size: 70x84mm
1633 A784 £25 multi   1.00 1.00

National Day — A785

2008, Apr. 17   *Perf. 12½*
1634 A785 £10 multi   .40 .25

Labor Day — A786

2008, May 1   *Perf. 12x11½*
1635 A786 £20 multi   .80 .40

Aleppo University, 50th Anniv. — A787

2008, May 4   **Wmk. 403**
1636 A787 £15 multi   .60 .30

Intl. Flower Show, Damascus A788

No. 1637: a, Roses. b, Thistles. c, Dahlias. d, Wallflowers. e, Daisies (margreet).

2008, June 25   *Perf. 12½x12¼*
1637   Horiz. strip of 5   2.00 1.00
a.-e. A788 £10 Any single   .40 .25

Arab Postal Day — A789

No. 1638 — Emblem and: a, Camel cara-van. b, Map and pigeon.

2008, Aug. 3   *Perf. 11½*
1638 A789   Horiz. pair   1.40 .70
   a.   £15 multi   .60 .30
   b.   £20 multi   .80 .40

55th Intl. Damascus Fair — A790

2008, Aug. 15   *Perf. 12x11½*
1639 A790 £25 multi   1.00 .50

Hejaz Railway, Cent. — A791

Emblem and: £25, Train on bridge. £50, Train in tunnel, railway map, vert.

2008, Aug. 19   *Perf. 12½x12¼*
1640 A791 £25 multi   1.00 .50
Imperf
Size: 70x85mm
1641 A791 £50 multi   2.00 1.00

2008 Summer Olympics, Beijing — A792

Designs: £5, Weight lifting. £10, Long jump, vert. £25, Swimming.

Perf. 12¼x12½, 12½x12¼
2008, Aug. 19
1642-1643 A792   Set of 2   .60 .30
Imperf
Size: 85x63mm
1644 A792 £25 multi   1.00 .50

Snakes A793

No. 1645: a, Golan snake. b, Eryx jaculus. c, Telescopus fallax syriacus.

2008, Sept. 16   *Perf. 12½*
1645   Horiz. strip of 3   2.40 1.25
a.-c. A793 £20 Any single   .80 .40

World Tourism Day — A794

Designs: £10, Vase. £15, Plate.

2008, Sept. 27   *Perf. 12x11½*
1646 A794 £10 multi   .40 .25

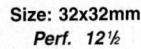

Size: 32x32mm
Perf. 12½
1647 A794 £15 multi   .60 .30

World Post Day — A795

2008, Oct. 19   *Perf. 12x11½*
1648 A795 £18 multi   .80 .40

Corrective Movement, 38th Anniv. — A796

2008, Nov. 16   *Perf. 12¼x12½*
1649 A796 £10 multi   .45 .25

Arbor Day A797

Perf. 11½x12
2008, Dec. 25   **Litho.**   **Wmk. 403**
1650 A797 £17 multi   .75 .35

Louis Braille (1809-52), Educator of the Blind A798

2008, Dec. 27
1651 A798 £17 multi   .75 .35

Pres. Bashir al-Assad Type of 2003 Redrawn
With Sans-Serif Numerals
Perf. 11¾x11¼
2008-09   **Litho.**   **Wmk. 403**
1652 A707   £5 brown   .25 .25
  a.   Dated "2010"   .25 .25
1653 A707   £10 purple   .45 .25
  a.   Dated "2010"   .45 .25
  b.   Dated "2011"   .40 .25
1654 A707   £25 blue   1.10 .55
  a.   grn blue, dated "2011"   1.00 .50
   Nos. 1652-1654 (3)   1.80 1.05

Issued: £25, 2008; £5, £10, 2009. Nos. 1587-1588, 1592 have serifed numerals.

Famous People A799

No. 1655: a, Mustafa Alaakad (1930-2005), film director and producer. b, Nihad Kalaai (1926-93), artist. c, Maha Al-Saleh (1945-2008), artist. d, Abd Allateef Fathy (1916-86), artist. e, Fahd Kaaekati (1924-82), artist.

2009, Feb. 22   *Perf. 12½x12¼*
1655   Horiz. strip of 5   4.50   2.25
a.-e.   A799 £20 Any single   .90   .45

March 8 Revolution, 46th Anniv. — A800

2009, Mar. 8   *Perf. 12x11½*
1656 A800 £10 multi   .45   .25

Mother's Day — A801

2009, Mar. 21   *Perf. 12½*
1657 A801 £18 multi   .80   .40

National Day — A802

2009, Apr. 17   *Perf. 12¼x12½*
1658 A802 £17 multi   .75   .35

Labor Day A803

2009, May 1   *Perf. 11½x12*
1659 A803 £15 multi   .65   .35

Intl. Flower Fair, Damascus A804

No. 1660: a, Wallflowers. b, Maemozas. c, Irises d, Lilies. e Adalias.

2009, June 15   **Wmk. 403**   *Perf. 12*
1660   Horiz. strip of 5   4.50   2.25
a.-e.   A804 £20 Any single   .90   .45

Jerusalem, Capital of Arab Culture A805

2009, Aug. 3   *Perf. 12½x12¼*
1661 A805 £10 multi   .45   .25

56th Intl. Damascus Fair — A806

2009, Aug. 15   *Perf. 12x11½*
1662 A806 £15 multi   .65   .35

World Tourism Day — A807

No. 1663 — Sites in Bosra: a, Bab Al-Hawa. b, Mabrak Al-Naqa Mosque. c, Amphitheater.

2009, Sept. 27   *Perf. 12¼x12½*
1663 A807 £25 Vert. strip of 3, #a-c   3.25   1.60

Birds — A808

No. 1664: a, Thrasher. b, Redstart. c, Blue-headed yellow wagtail. d, Honeyeater. e, Syrian serin.

2009, Oct. 8   **Litho.**   *Perf. 12*
1664   Vert. strip of 5   4.50   2.25
a.-e.   A808 £20 Any single   .90   .45

World Post Day — A809

2009, Oct. 9   *Perf. 12½*
1665 A809 £50 multi   2.25   1.10

Corrective Movement, 39th Anniv. — A810

2009, Nov. 16   *Perf. 12*
1666 A810 £10 multi   .45   .25

Arbor Day — A811

2009, Dec. 31   **Wmk. 403**
1667 A811 £15 multi   .65   .35

March 8 Revolution, 47th Anniv. A812

2010, Mar. 8   **Wmk. 403**   *Perf. 12½*
1668 A812 £25 multi   1.10   .55

Mother's Day — A813

2010, Mar. 21   *Perf. 12*
1669 A813 £10 multi   .45   .25

National Day — A814

2010, Apr. 17   *Perf. 12x11½*
1670 A814 £50 multi   2.25   1.10

Labor Day — A815

2010, May 1   *Perf. 12½x12¼*
1671 A815 £25 multi   1.10   .55

Intl. Year of Biodiversity — A816

2010, May 1   *Perf. 12¼x12½*
1672 A816 £50 multi   2.25   1.10

2010 World Cup Soccer Championships, South Africa — A817

No. 1673 — Emblem and: a, Players with blue shirts celebrating. b, Players chasing ball. £50, Emblem, World Cup, horiz.

2010, May 1   *Perf. 12¼x12½*
1673 A817 £25 Vert. pair, #a-b   2.25   1.10
   Size: 85x67mm
   Imperf
1674 A817 £50 multi   2.25   1.10

50th Aleppo Industrial and Agricultural Production Fair — A818

2010, June 24   **Litho.**   *Perf. 12*
1675 A818 £15 multi   .65   .30

Intl. Flower Fair, Damascus A819

No. 1676: a, Calendula. b, Cyclamen. c, Rose. d, Fuchsia. e, Rosa bracteata.

2010, June 25   *Perf. 12½x12¼*
1676   Horiz. strip of 5   5.50 2.75
a.-e.   A819 £25 Any single   1.10 .55

Historical and Tourism Sites of Brazil and Syria — A820

2010, June 28   *Perf. 12½x12¼*
1677   A820   £50 multi   2.25 1.10

See Brazil No. 3132.

57th Intl. Damascus Fair — A821

2010, July 14   *Perf. 12x11½*
1678   A821   £50 multi   2.25 1.10

Friendship Between Syria and Chile, 200th Anniv. A822

2010, Sept. 23   **Wmk. 403**   *Perf. 12½*
1679   A822   £25 multi   1.10 .55

Mammals A823

No. 1680: a, Squirrel. b, Hedgehog. c, Ichneumon.

2010, Sept. 23   **Litho.**
1680   Horiz. strip of 3   4.50 2.25
a.-b.   A823 £30 Either single   1.25 .65
c.   A823 £40 multi   1.75 .85

World Tourism Day — A824

No. 1681: a, Small plaza with flowers. b, Building, dervishes.

2010, Sept. 27   *Perf. 12*
1681   A824   £25 Horiz. pair, #a-b   2.25 1.10

World Post Day — A825

2010, Oct. 9   **Wmk. 403**
1682   A825   £25 multi   1.10 .55

Corrective Movement, 40th Anniv. A826

2010, Nov. 16
1683   A826   £25 multi   1.10 .55

Miniature Sheet

Lawyers — A827

No. 1684: a, Fatihullah al-Sakal (1893-1970). b, Faris al-Khoubi (1877-1962). c, Saeed al-Gazi (1877-1967). d, Abd-el-Salam al-Tirmanini (1913-2006). e, Mohammad al-Fadel (1919-77). f, Ahmad Fouad al-Koudmani (1905-81)

2010, Dec. 31   *Perf. 12x11½*
1684   A827   £25 Sheet of 6, #a-f   6.50 3.25

March 8 Revolution, 48th Anniv. — A829

Perf. 12x11½
2011, Mar. 8   **Litho.**   **Wmk. 403**
1686   A829   £25 multi   1.10 .55

Mother's Day — A830

2011, Mar. 21
1687   A830   £25 multi   1.10 .55

National Day A831

2011, Apr. 17   *Perf. 11½x12*
1688   A831   £25 multi   1.10 .55

Labor Day A832

2011, May 1   **Wmk. 403**
1689   A832   £50 multi   2.10 1.10

SEMI-POSTAL STAMPS

Nos. 174-185 Srchd. in Red or Black

1926   **Unwmk.**   *Perf. 12½, 13½*
B1   A4   25c + 25c ol blk (R)   2.25 2.00
B2   A4   50c + 25c yel grn   2.25 2.00
B3   A4   75c + 25c brown org   2.25 2.00
B4   A5   1p + 50c magenta   2.25 2.00
B5   A4   1.25p + 50c dp grn (R)   2.25 2.00
B6   A4   1.50p + 50c rose red   2.25 2.00
B7   A4   2p + 75c dk brn (R)   2.25 2.00
B8   A4   2.50p + 75c pck bl (R)   2.25 2.00
B9   A4   3p + 1p org brn (R)   2.25 2.00
B10   A4   5p + 1p violet   2.25 2.00
B11   A4   10p + 2p vio brn   2.25 2.00
B12   A4   25p + 5p ultra (R)   2.25 2.00
   Nos. B1-B12 (12)   27.00 24.00
   Set, never hinged   36.00

On No. B4 the surcharge is set in six lines to fit the shape of the stamp.
The surcharge was a contribution to the relief of refugees from the Djebel Druze War. See Nos. CB1-CB4.

Catalogue values for unused stamps in this section, from this point to the end of the section, are for Never Hinged items.

Syrian Arab Republic

Jordanian Flags on Map of Israel, and Arabs — SP1

1965, June 12   **Litho.**   *Perf. 12x11½*
B13   SP1   12½p + 5p multi   .25 .25
B14   SP1   25p + 5p multi   .25 .25

Issued for Palestine Week.

Father with Children and Red Crescent SP2

1968, May   **Litho.**   *Perf. 12½x12*
B15   SP2   12½p + 2½p multi   .25 .25
B16   SP2   27½p + 7½p multi   .25 .25

The surtax was for refugees.

AIR POST STAMPS

Nos. 35, 45, 47 Handstamped in Violet — a

1920, Dec.   **Unwmk.**   *Perf. 13½*
C1   A22   1p on 5c   160.00 40.00
C2   A20   5p on 15c   290.00 47.50
C3   A18   10p on 40c   425.00 77.50
   Nos. C1-C3 (3)   875.00 165.00

Nos. 36, 46, 48 Overprinted Type "a" in Violet

1921, June 12
C4   A22   1p on 20c   87.50 40.00
C5   A18   5p on 1fr   425.00 150.00
C6   A18   10p on 2fr   425.00 150.00
   Nos. C4-C6 (3)   937.50 340.00

Excellent counterfeits exist of Nos. C1-C6.

Nos. 36, 46, 48 Overprinted — b

1921, Oct. 5
C7   A22   1p on 20c   60.00 18.50
C8   A18   5p on 1fr   150.00 37.50
a.   Inverted overprint   325.00 240.00
C9   A18   10p on 2fr   200.00 47.50
a.   Double overprint   475.00 400.00
   Nos. C7-C9 (3)   410.00 103.50

Nos. 92, 94-96 Ovptd. — c

1922, May 28
C10   A18   2p on 40c   25.00 25.00
a.   Inverted overprint
C11   A18   3p on 60c   25.00 25.00
C12   A18   5p on 1fr   25.00 25.00
C13   A18   10p on 2fr   25.00 25.00
   Nos. C10-C13 (4)   100.00 100.00

Nos. 116-119 Overprinted Type "c"

1923, Nov. 22
C14   A18   2p on 40c   29.00 29.00
b.   Inverted surcharge
C15   A18   3p on 60c   29.00 29.00
C16   A18   5p on 1fr   29.00 29.00
C17   A18   10p on 2fr   29.00 29.00
b.   Double overprint
   Nos. C14-C17 (4)   116.00 116.00

Overprinted "Liabn"

C14a   A18   2p on 40c   400.00 400.00
C15a   A18   3p on 60c   400.00 400.00
C16a   A18   5p on 1fr   400.00 400.00
C17a   A18   10p on 2fr   400.00 400.00

Nos. 137-140 Overprinted Type "c"

1924, Jan. 13

C18 A18 2p on 40c 4.50 4.50
a. Double overprint *27.50*
C19 A18 3p on 60c 4.50 4.50
a. Inverted overprint 47.50
C20 A18 5p on 1fr 4.50 4.50
a. Double overprint *50.00 30.00*
C21 A18 10p on 2fr 4.50 4.50
Nos. C18-C21 (4) 18.00 18.00

Nos. 152, 154, 157-158 Overprinted

1924, July 17

C22 A18 2p on 40c 7.00 7.00
a. Inverted overprint 32.50
C23 A18 3p on 60c 7.00 7.00
a. Inverted overprint 32.50
b. Double overprint 20.00
C24 A18 5p on 1fr 7.00 7.00
C25 A18 10p on 2fr 7.00 7.00
a. Inverted overprint 32.50
Nos. C22-C25 (4) 28.00 28.00

Regular Issue of 1925 Overprinted in Green

1925, Mar. 1

C26 A4 2p dark brown 2.25 2.25
C27 A4 3p orange brown 2.25 2.25
C28 A4 5p violet 2.25 2.25
C29 A4 10p violet brown 2.25 2.25
Nos. C26-C29 (4) 9.00 9.00

Nos.180, 182, 183-184 Ovptd. in Red — f

1926

C30 A4 2p dark brown 2.00 2.00
a. Inverted overprint 40.00 40.00
C31 A4 3p orange brown 2.00 2.00
C32 A4 5p violet 2.50 2.50
a. Inverted overprint 40.00 40.00
b. Double overprint 65.00 65.00
C33 A4 10p violet brown 2.50 2.50
a. Inverted overprint 40.00 40.00
b. Double overprint 65.00 65.00
Nos. C30-C33 (4) 9.00 9.00

Nos. C30-C33 received their first airmail use June 16, 1929, at the opening of the Beirut-Marseille line.

For surcharges see Nos. CB1-CB4.

Regular Issue of 1925 Overprinted Type "f" in Red or Black

1929

C34 A4 50c yellow green (R) 1.25 1.25
a. Inverted overprint 40.00
b. Overprinted on face and back 22.50
c. Double overprint 40.00
d. Double overprint, one inverted 60.00
e. Pair, one without overprint
C35 A5 1p magenta (Bk) 1.75 1.75
a. Reversed overprint
b. Red overprint
C36 A4 25p ultra (R) 5.50 5.50
a. Inverted overprint 82.50
b. Pair, one without overprint
Nos. C34-C36 (3) 8.50 8.50

On No. C35, the overprint is vertical, with plane nose down.

No. 197 Overprinted Type "f" in Red

1929, July 9

C37 A4 15p on 25p ultra 4.25 4.25
a. Inverted overprint

Air Post Stamps of 1926-29 Ovptd. in Various Colors

1929, Sept. 5

C38 A4 50c yellow grn (R) 3.00 3.00
C39 A5 1p magenta (Bl) 3.00 3.00
C40 A4 2p dk brown (V) 3.00 3.00
C41 A4 3p orange brn (Bl) 3.00 3.00
a. Inverted overprint 70.00
C42 A4 5p violet (R) 3.00 3.00
C43 A4 10p violet brn (Bl) 3.00 3.00
C44 A4 25p ultra (R) 3.00 3.00
Nos. C38-C44 (7) 21.00 21.00

Damascus Industrial Exhibition.

AP1

1930, Jan. 30 Red Surcharge

C45 AP1 2p on 1.25p dp grn 3.00 3.00
a. Inverted surcharge
b. Double surcharge 60.00

Plane over Homs AP2

Designs: 1pi, City Wall, Damascus. 2pi, Euphrates River. 3pi, Temple Ruins, Palmyra. 5pi, Deir-el-Zor. 10pi, Damascus. 15pi, Aleppo, Citadel. 25pi, Hama. 50pi, Zebdani. 100pi, Telebisse.

1931-33 Photo. Unwmk.

C46 AP2 50c ocher 1.00 .90
C47 AP2 50c black brn ('33) 1.25 1.00
C48 AP2 1p chestnut brown 1.10 .95
C49 AP2 2p Prus blue 2.75 1.75
C50 AP2 3p blue grn 1.75 1.25
C51 AP2 5p red violet 1.25 1.25
C52 AP2 10p slate grn 1.25 1.25
C53 AP2 15p orange red 2.10 1.50
C54 AP2 25p orange brn 2.75 2.00
C55 AP2 50p black 3.00 2.25
C56 AP2 100p magenta 3.75 2.50
Nos. C46-C56 (11) 21.95 16.60

Nos. C46 to C56 exist imperforate. Value, $425.

For overprints see Nos. C67-C71, C110-C112, C114-C115, MC1-MC4.

Village of Bloudan AP12

1934, Aug. 2 Engr. *Perf. 12½*

C57 AP12 50c yel brown 2.50 2.50
C58 AP12 1p green 3.00 3.00
C59 AP12 2p peacock bl 3.00 3.00
C60 AP12 3p red 3.50 3.50
C61 AP12 5p plum 3.50 3.50
C62 AP12 10p brt violet 30.00 30.00
C63 AP12 15p orange brn 32.50 32.50
C64 AP12 25p dk ultra 37.50 37.50
C65 AP12 50p black 50.00 50.00
C66 AP12 100p red brown 110.00 110.00
Nos. C57-C66 (10) 275.50 275.50

Proclamation of the Republic. Nos. C57-C66 exist imperf. Value, set $1,100. Also exists without figures of value. Value, set $1,500.

Complete set of 29 (Nos. 232-250, C57-66) exist imperf. Value, $2,600.

No. C58 exists without values, imperf. Value, $125.

Air Post Stamps of 1931-33 Overprinted in Red or Black

1936, Apr. 15 *Perf. 13½x13, 13½*

C67 AP2 50c black brown 5.25 4.75
C68 AP2 1p chnt brown (Bk) 5.25 4.75
C69 AP2 2p Prus blue 5.25 4.75
C70 AP2 3p blue green 5.25 4.75
C71 AP2 5p red violet (Bk) 5.25 4.75
Nos. C67-C71 (5) 26.25 23.75

Damascus Fair, May 1936.

Syrian Pavilion at Paris Exposition AP13

1937, July 1 Photo. *Perf. 13½*

C72 AP13 ½p yellow green 2.75 2.75
C73 AP13 1p green 2.75 2.75
C74 AP13 2p lt brown 2.75 2.75
C75 AP13 3p rose red 2.75 2.75
C76 AP13 5p brown orange 2.75 2.75
C77 AP13 10p grnsh black 4.75 4.75
C78 AP13 15p blue 5.25 5.25
C79 AP13 25p dark violet 6.25 6.25
Nos. C72-C79 (8) 30.00 30.00

Paris International Exposition. Exist imperf.

Ancient Citadel at Aleppo AP14

Omayyad Mosque and Minaret of Jesus at Damascus AP15

1937 Engr. *Perf. 13*

C80 AP14 ½p dark violet .65 .65
C81 AP15 1p black .65 .65
C82 AP14 2p deep green .65 .65
C83 AP15 3p deep ultra .65 .65
C84 AP14 5p rose lake 2.00 2.00
C85 AP15 10p red brown 1.10 1.10
C86 AP14 15p lake brown 4.75 4.75
C87 AP15 25p dark blue 6.00 6.00
Nos. C80-C87 (8) 16.45 16.45

No. C80 to C87 exist imperforate. Value, set $175.

For overprint see No. C109.

Maurice Noguès and Route of France-Syria Flight — AP16

1938, July Photo. *Perf. 11½*

C88 AP16 10p dark green 5.00 4.50
a. Souv. sheet of 4, perf. 13½ 50.00 45.00
b. Perf. 13½ 8.00 8.00

10th anniversary of first Marseille-Beirut flight, by Maurice Noguès.

No. C88a exists imperf.; value $800.

Bridge at Deir-el-Zor AP17

1940 Engr. *Perf. 13*

C89 AP17 25c brown black .25 .25
C90 AP17 50c peacock blue .25 .25
C91 AP17 1p deep ultra .30 .30
C92 AP17 2p dk orange brn .45 .45
C93 AP17 5p green .95 .95
C94 AP17 10p rose carmine 1.40 1.00
C95 AP17 50p dark violet 3.00 2.25
Nos. C89-C95 (7) 6.60 5.45

Exist imperf. Value, set $175.

President Taj Eddin Hassani AP18

1942 Litho. *Perf. 11½*

C96 AP18 10p blue gray 4.00 4.00
C97 AP18 50p gray lilac 4.25 4.25

Proclamation of Independence by the Allies, Sept. 27, 1941.

President Taj Eddin Hassani — AP19

1942 Photo.

C98 AP19 10p sl grn & yel grn 4.00 4.00

Exists imperforate. Value, $30.

President Hassani and Map of Syria — AP20

1943 Litho.

C99 AP20 2p dull brown 3.00 3.00
C100 AP20 10p red violet 3.00 3.00
C101 AP20 20p aqua 3.00 3.00
C102 AP20 50p rose pink 3.00 3.00
Nos. C99-C102 (4) 12.00 12.00

Proclamation of United Syria.

Overprinted with Black Border

1943, May 5

C103 AP20 2p dull brown 3.00 3.00
C104 AP20 10p red violet 3.00 3.00
C105 AP20 20p aqua 3.00 3.00
C106 AP20 50p rose pink 3.00 3.00
Nos. C103-C106 (4) 12.00 12.00

Mourning for President Hassani. Exist imperf.

President Shukri el Kouatly — AP21

1944

C107 AP21 200p sepia 9.50 7.50
C108 AP21 500p dull blue 14.00 11.00

For overprints see Nos. C113, C116.

Stamps of 1931-44 Overprinted in Black, Blue or Carmine

1944 *Perf. 13, 13½, 11½*

C109 AP15 10p red brn (Bk) 2.50 2.50
C110 AP2 15p orange red 2.75 2.75
C111 AP2 25p org brown 2.75 2.75

C112	AP2	100p magenta	8.00 6.75
C113	AP21	200p sepia (C)	15.00 12.00
		Nos. C109-C113 (5)	31.00 26.75
		Set, never hinged	50.00

1st congress of Arab lawyers held in Damascus, Sept. 1944.

Nos. C53-C54, C108 Overprinted in Black or Orange

1944

C114	AP2	15p orange red	3.00 3.00
C115	AP2	25p org brown	3.00 3.00
C116	AP21	500p dull blue (O)	22.50 22.50
		Nos. C114-C116 (3)	28.50 28.50
		Set, never hinged	40.00

See note after No. 299.

President Shukri el Kouatly AP22

1945, Mar. 15   Litho.   Perf. 11½

C117	AP22	5p pale green	.50 .25
C118	AP22	10p dull red	.50 .25
C119	AP22	15p orange	.60 .25
C120	AP22	25p lt blue	1.25 .50
C121	AP22	50p lt violet	1.75 .70
C122	AP22	100p deep brown	3.50 1.25
C123	AP22	200p fawn	8.00 4.00
		Nos. C117-C123 (7)	16.10 7.10
		Set, never hinged	25.00

Resumption of constitutional government.

> **Catalogue values for unused stamps in this section, from this point to the end of the section, are for Never Hinged items.**

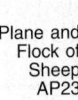

Plane and Flock of Sheep AP23

Kattineh Dam AP24

Kanawat, Djebel Druze AP25

Sultan Ibrahim Mosque AP26

1946-47   Perf. 13x13½

C124	AP23	3p rose brown	.50 .25
C125	AP23	5p lt bl grn ('47)	.50 .25
C126	AP23	6p dp org ('47)	.50 .25
C127	AP24	10p sl gray ('47)	.35 .25
C128	AP24	15p scarlet ('47)	.35 .25
C129	AP24	25p blue	.45 .25
C130	AP25	50p violet	.75 .25
C131	AP25	100p blue green	1.75 .40
C132	AP25	200p brown ('47)	4.00 1.25
C133	AP26	300p red brn ('47)	16.00 2.50
C134	AP26	500p ol gray ('47)	17.50 3.50
		Nos. C124-C134 (11)	42.65 9.40

For overprints and surcharges see Nos. C135-C139, C148-C152, C157, C172.

No. C129 Overprinted in Red

1946, Apr. 17

C135	AP24	25p blue	2.50 1.00

Evacuation of British and French troops from Syria.

Nos. C129-C131 Overprinted in Magenta

1946, Aug. 28

C136	AP24	25p blue	2.50 1.25
C137	AP25	50p violet	3.00 1.75
C138	AP25	100p blue green	6.00 3.00
		Nos. C136-C138 (3)	11.50 6.00

See note after No. 334.

No. C135 with Additional Overprint in Black

1947, June 10   Perf. 13x13½

C139	AP24	25p blue	2.50 1.25

1st anniv. of the evacuation of British and French troops from Syria.

Window at Kasr El-Heir El-Gharbi AP27

Ram-headed Sphinxes Carved in Ivory, from King Hazael's Bed — AP28

1947, Nov. 15   Litho.   Perf. 11½

C140	AP27	12.50p dark violet	1.50 .50
C141	AP28	50p brown	5.00 2.00
	a.	Souv. sheet of 4, #338-339, C140-C141	65.00 65.00

1st Arab Archaeological Cong., Damascus, Nov.

No. C141a sold for 125 piasters.

Kasr El-Heir El-Charqui AP29

Congress Emblem — AP30

1947, Nov. 15

C142	AP29	12.50p olive black	1.00 .50
C143	AP30	50p dull violet	4.50 2.25
	a.	Souv. sheet of 4, #340, 341, C142, C143	65.00 65.00

3rd Cong. of Arab Engineers, Damascus, Nov.

No. C143a sold for 125 piasters.

Kouatly Types of Regular Issue

1948, June 22   Litho.   Perf. 10½

C144	A50	12.50p dp bl & vio brn	.65 .25
C145	A51	50p violet brn & grn	2.50 1.00
	a.	Souv. sheet #342, 343, C144, C145, imperf	150.00 150.00

Reelection of Pres. Shukri el Kouatly.

Military Training Types of Regular Issue

1948, June 22

C146	A52	12.50p blue & dk bl	.75 .25
C147	A53	50p green, car & blk	2.00 .80
	a.	Souv. sheet of 4, #344, 345, C146, C147, imperf.	140.00 140.00

Inauguration of compulsory military training.

Nos. C124, C126 and C132 to C134 Surcharged with New Value and Bars in Black or Carmine

1948, Oct. 18   Perf. 13x13½

C148	AP23	2.50p on 3p	.30 .25
C149	AP23	2.50p on 6p	.35 .25
C150	AP25	25p on 200p (C)	.80 .25
C151	AP26	50p on 300p	10.00 .75
C152	AP26	50p on 500p	10.00 .75
		Nos. C148-C152 (5)	21.45 2.25

Husni Zayim Type of Regular Issue

1949, June 20   Litho.   Perf. 11½

C153	A54	50p brown	3.75 2.50

Revolution of March 30, 1949.

Pigeons and Globe AP36

Husni Zayim and View of Damascus AP37

1949, June 20   Unwmk.

C154	AP36	12.50p claret	7.50 6.00
C155	AP37	50p gray black	19.00 12.50

UPU, 75th anniv. A souvenir sheet of 4 contains #349, 350, C154, C155. Value $125.

Election Type of Regular Issue

Wmk. 291

1949, Aug. 6   Litho.   Perf. 11½

C156	A57	50p car rose & dk grnsh bl	3.75 2.50
	a.	Souv. sheet of 2, #351, C156, imperf.	175.00 175.00

Election of Pres. Husni Zayim.

No. C131 Surcharged with New Value and Bars in Black

1950   Unwmk.   Perf. 13x13½

C157	AP25	2.50p on 100p bl grn	.40 .25

Port of Latakia AP38

1950, Dec. 25   Perf. 11½

C158	AP38	2.50p dull lilac	.50 .25
C159	AP38	10p grnsh blue	1.10 .25
C160	AP38	15p orange brown	2.50 .40
C161	AP38	25p bright blue	5.50 .35
		Nos. C158-C161 (4)	9.60 1.25

Exist imperf. Value, $35. See No. C173. For overprint see No. C169.

Symbolical of Constitution AP39

1951, Apr. 14   Unwmk.

C162	AP39	12.50p crimson rose	.40 .25
C163	AP39	50p brown violet	1.25 1.00

New constitution adopted Sept. 5, 1950. Exist imperf.

Ruins, Palmyra AP40

Citadel at Aleppo AP41

1952, Apr. 22   Litho.   Perf. 11½

C164	AP40	2.50p vermilion	.30 .25
C165	AP40	5p green	.35 .25
C166	AP40	15p violet	.50 .25
C167	AP41	25p deep blue	.75 .35
C168	AP41	100p lilac rose	5.50 1.00
		Nos. C164-C168 (5)	7.40 2.10

Nos. C164-C168 exist imperforate. For overprints see Nos. C170-C171, C186.

Stamps of 1946-52 Overprinted in Black

1953, Feb. 16   Perf. 13x13½, 11½

C169	AP38	10p grnsh blue	2.00 1.00
C170	AP40	15p violet	2.25 1.10
C171	AP41	25p deep blue	3.25 1.60
C172	AP25	50p violet	8.00 2.25
		Nos. C169-C172 (4)	15.50 5.95

UN Social Welfare Seminar, Damascus, Dec. 8-20, 1952.

Type of 1950 and

Post Office, Aleppo AP42

1953, Oct.   Photo.   Perf. 11½

C173	AP38	10p violet blue	.50 .25
C174	AP42	50p red brown	1.60 .30

For overprint see No. C185.

Building at Hama and
PTT Emblem — AP43

University
of Syria,
Damascus
AP44

1954

C175	AP43	5p violet	.25	.25
C176	AP43	10p brown	.30	.25
C177	AP43	15p dull green	.35	.25
C178	AP44	30p dark brown	.45	.25
C179	AP44	35p blue	.80	.25
C180	AP44	40p orange	1.75	.40
C181	AP44	50p deep plum	1.25	.60
C182	AP44	70p purple	3.25	.70
		Nos. C175-C182 (8)	8.40	2.95

For overprints see UAR Nos. C27-C28.

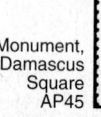

Monument,
Damascus
Square
AP45

Mosque and Syrian
Flag — AP46

1954, Sept. 2

C183	AP45	40p carmine rose	1.00	.45
C184	AP46	50p green	1.25	.55

Damascus Fair, Sept. 1954.
Nos. C183-C184 exist imperforate.

**Nos. C174 and C168 Overprinted in
Blue or Black**

1954, Oct. 9

C185	AP42	50p red brown (Bl)	1.10	1.00
C186	AP41	100p lilac rose	2.00	1.60

Cotton Festival, Aleppo, October 1954.

Virgin of Sednaya
Convent — AP47

1955, Mar. 27   Photo.   Perf. 11½

C187	AP47	25p deep purple	.60	.40
C188	AP47	75p deep blue green	1.75	1.25

50th anniv. of the founding of Rotary Intl.
Exist imperforate.

Omayyad
Mosque — AP48

1955, Mar. 26

C189	AP48	35p cerise	.95	.60
C190	AP48	65p deep green	1.75	1.10

1955 Regional Cong. of Rotary Intl.,
Damascus.

**Arab Postal Union Type of Regular
Issue**

1955, Jan. 1   Perf. 13½x13

C191	A69a	5p yellow brown	.40	.25

Founding of the APU, July 1, 1954.
For overprints see Nos. C203, C207.

Young
Couple and
View of
Damascus
AP49

60p, Tank and planes leading advancing
troops.

1955, Apr. 16   Litho.   Perf. 11½

C192	AP49	40p dark rose lake	.60	.30
C193	AP49	60p ultra	2.25	.35

9th anniv. of the evacuation of British and
French troops from Syria.

Mother's Day Type of Regular Issue

1955, May 13   Unwmk.

C194	A70	35p violet	1.00	.60
C195	A70	40p black	1.50	.95

Issued to publicize Mother's Day.

Emigrants under
Syrian Flag — AP51

15p, Airplane over globe and fountain.

1955, July 26   Perf. 11½

C196	AP51	5p magenta	.55	.25
C197	AP51	15p light blue	.75	.40

Emigrants' Congress. Exist imperf.

Mother and
Child — AP52

1955, Oct. 3   Photo.

C198	AP52	25p deep blue	.75	.50
C199	AP52	50p plum	1.25	.90

International Children's Day.

Globe,
Scales and
Dove
AP53

1955, Oct. 30

C200	AP53	15p ultra	.75	.40
C201	AP53	35p brown black	1.50	.60

10th anniv. of the UN, Oct. 24, 1955.
For overprints see Nos. C221-C222.

Aqueduct Type of Regular Issue

1955, Nov. 21   Litho.   Unwmk.

C202	A72	30p dark blue	2.00	1.10

No. C191
Overprinted in
Ultramarine

1955, Dec. 29   Photo.   Perf. 13½x13

C203	A69a	5p yellow brown	.50	.25

APU Congress, Cairo, Mar. 15, 1955.

Liberation
Monument — AP54

Designs: 65p, Winged figure with shield
and sword. 75p, President Shukri el Kouatly.

1956, Apr. 17   Litho.   Perf. 11½

C204	AP54	35p black brown	.60	.40
C205	AP54	65p rose red	1.00	.60
C206	AP54	75p dk slate green	1.90	1.00
		Nos. C204-C206 (3)	3.50	2.00

10th anniv. of the evacuation of British and
French troops from Syria.

No. C191
Overprinted in Black

1956, Apr. 11   Photo.   Perf. 13½x13

C207	A69a	5p yellow brown	.50	.25

Visit of King Hussein of Jordan to Damascus, Apr. 1956.

President Shukri el
Kouatly — AP55

1956, July 7   Litho.   Perf. 11½

C208	AP55	100p black	1.25	1.00
C209	AP55	200p violet	2.50	1.25
C210	AP55	300p dull rose	4.00	2.75
C211	AP55	500p dk bl grn	7.50	5.00
		Nos. C208-C211 (4)	15.25	10.00

**Nos. CB5-CB8 Overprinted with 3
Bars Obliterating Surtax**

1956

C212	SPAP1	25p gray black	.60	.25
C213	SPAP2	35p ultra	.75	.25
C214	SPAP2	40p rose lilac	1.50	.60
C215	SPAP1	70p Prus green	1.75	.90
		Nos. C212-C215 (4)	4.60	2.00

Gate of Kasr el Heir,
Palmyra — AP56

Designs: 20p, Hand loom and modern mill.
30p, Ox-drawn plow and tractor. 35p, Cogwheels and galley. 50p, Textiles and vase.

1956, Sept. 1   Unwmk.

C216	AP56	15p gray	.50	.50
C217	AP56	20p brt ultra	.75	.75
C218	AP56	30p blue green	1.00	1.00
C219	AP56	35p blue	1.25	1.25
C220	AP56	50p rose lilac	1.50	1.50
		Nos. C216-C220 (5)	5.00	5.00

3rd International Fair, Damascus.

Nos. C200-
C201
Ovptd. in
Red or
Green

1956, Oct. 30   Photo.   Perf. 11½

C221	AP53	15p ultra (R)	1.00	.60
C222	AP53	35p brown blk (G)	1.75	1.25

United Nations, 11th anniversary.

Clay Tablet
with First
Alphabet
AP57

Helmet of Syrian
Legionary and
Ornament — AP58

50p, Lintel from Temple of the Sun, Palmyra.

1956, Oct. 8   Typo.

C223	AP57	20p gray	1.00	.40
C224	AP58	30p magenta	1.25	.50
C225	AP57	50p gray brown	1.90	1.00
		Nos. C223-C225 (3)	4.15	1.90

Intl. Museum Week (UNESCO), Oct. 8-14.

Trees and
Mosque
AP59

1956, Dec. 27   Litho.   Perf. 11½

C226	AP59	10p olive bister	.40	.25
C227	AP59	40p slate green	.90	.45

Day of the Tree, Dec. 27, 1956.
See UAR No. 36. For overprint see UAR No.
49.

Mother and
Child — AP60

Design: 60p, Mother holding infant.

1957, Mar. 21   **Unwmk.**
C228 AP60 40p ultra   .75 .60
C229 AP60 60p vermilion   1.25 .85

Mother's Day, 1957.

Sword and
Shields — AP61

Designs: 15p, 35p, Map and "Syria" holding
torch. 25p, Pres. Kouatly.

1957, Apr. 20   **Wmk. 291**
C230 AP61 10p redsh brn   .30 .25
C231 AP61 15p bl grn   .40 .25
C232 AP61 25p violet   .50 .35
C233 AP61 35p cerise   .75 .50
C234 AP61 40p gray   1.10 .60
    Nos. C230-C234 (5)   3.05 1.95

British-French troop evacuation, 11th anniv.

Ship
Loading — AP62

Sugar
Production
AP63

30p, 40p, Harvesting grain and cotton.

1957, Sept. 1   **Unwmk.**   *Perf. 11½*
C235 AP62 25p magenta   .50 .30
C236 AP62 30p light red brown   .60 .35
C237 AP63 35p light blue   .75 .40
C238 AP62 40p blue green   1.00 .50
C239 AP62 70p olive bister   1.25 .90
    Nos. C235-C239 (5)   4.10 2.45

4th International Fair, Damascus.

Arab Lawyers Type of Regular Issue
1957, Sept. 21   **Litho.**   **Wmk. 291**
C240 A76 17½p red   .40 .30
C241 A76 40p black   .90 .50

Cotton Festival Type of Regular Issue
1957, Oct. 17
C242 A77 17½p org & blk   .75 .40
C243 A77 40p lt bl & blk   1.25 .50

Children's Day Type of Regular Issue
1957, Oct. 3
C244 A78 17½p ultra   1.25 .50
C245 A78 20p red brn   1.50 .50

International Children's Day, Oct. 7.
For overprints see UAR Nos. C10-C11.

Family
Writing
and
Reading
Letters
AP64

1957, Oct. 18   **Litho.**   **Unwmk.**
C246 AP64 5p brt grn   .40 .25

Intl. Letter Writing Week Oct. 6-12.
For overprint see No. C26.

Afro-Asian Jurists Type of Regular Issue
1957, Nov.   **Wmk. 291**   *Perf. 11½*
C247 A80 30p lt bl grn   .50 .35
C248 A80 50p lt vio   .75 .50

Type of Regular Issue and

Radio, Telegraph and
Telephone — AP65

1958, Feb. 12   *Perf. 11½*
C249 A83 10p brt grn   .35 .25
C250 AP65 15p brown   .40 .25

Syrian Arab Republic
Souvenir Sheet

Syrian Flag — AP67

1961   **Unwmk.**   **Litho.**   *Imperf.*
C253 AP67 50p multi   2.75 2.75

Establishment of Syrian Arab Republic.

"The Beauty of
Palmyra" — AP68

Archway,
Palmyra — AP69

Design: 200p, 300p, 500p, 1000p, Niche,
King Zahir Bibar's tomb.

1961-63   **Litho.**   *Perf. 12x11½*
C255 AP68 45p citron   .40 .25
C256 AP68 50p red org   .50 .25
C257 AP69 85p sepia   1.00 .30
C258 AP69 100p lilac   1.25 .35
C259 AP69 200p sl grn ('62)   2.25 .65
C260 AP69 300p dk bl ('62)   2.75 .75
C261 AP69 500p lilac ('63)   4.00 1.50
C262 AP69 1000p dk gray
      ('63)   8.25 2.75
    Nos. C255-C262 (8)   20.40 6.80

See Nos. 433-436.

Arab League
Building, Cairo,
and
Emblem — AP70

1962, Apr. 1   *Perf. 12x11½*
C264 AP70 17½p Prus grn & yel
      grn   .30 .25
C265 AP70 22½p dk & lt bl   .30 .25
C266 AP70 50p dk brn & dl org   .75 .30
    Nos. C264-C266 (3)   1.35 .80

Arab League Week, Mar. 22-28.

Malaria
Eradication
Emblem — AP71

1962, Apr. 7
C267 AP71 12½p ol, lt bl & pur   .40 .25
C268 AP71 50p brn, yel & grn   .75 .40

WHO drive to eradicate malaria.

Rearing
Horse — AP72

Gen. Yusef al-
Azmeh
AP73

1962, Apr. 17
C269 AP72 45p vio & org   .55 .25
C270 AP73 55p vio bl & lt bl   .75 .25

Evacuation Day, 1962.

Martyrs' Square
Memorial, Globe
and Handshake
AP74

Design: 40p, 45p, Eastern Gate at Fair.

1962, Aug. 25   **Litho.**   *Perf. 12x11½*
C271 AP74 17½p rose cl & brn   .30 .25
C272 AP74 22½p ver & magenta   .30 .25
C273 AP74 40p vio brn & lt brn   .30 .25
C274 AP74 45p grnsh bl & lt
      grn   .50 .25
    Nos. C271-C274 (4)   1.40 1.00

9th International Damascus Fair.

Cotton and
Cogwheel
AP75

1962, Sept. 20   *Perf. 12x11½*
C275 AP75 12½p multi   .35 .25
C276 AP75 50p multi   .50 .25

Cotton Festival, Aleppo. See Nos. 455-456.

President Type of Regular Issue
1962, Dec. 14   **Unwmk.**
C278 A88 50p bl gray & tan   .75 .25

1st anniv. of the election of Pres. Nazem el-
Kodsi.

Queen Zenobia
of
Palmyra — AP76

1962, Dec. 28   *Perf. 12x11½*
C279 AP76 45p violet   1.00 .25
C280 AP76 50p rose red   1.00 .25
C281 AP76 85p blue green   1.00 .30
C282 AP76 100p rose claret   1.25 .55
    Nos. C279-C282 (4)   4.25 1.35

Saad Allah El
Jabri — AP77

1962, Dec. 30   **Litho.**
C283 AP77 50p dull blue   .50 .25

Saad Allah El Jabri (1894-1947), a leader in
Syria's struggle for independence.

Woman from
Mohardé — AP78

Regional Costumes: 40p, Marje Sultan. 45p,
Kalamoun. 55p, Jabal-Al-Arab. 60p, Afrine.
65p, Hauran.

1963   *Perf. 12*
Costumes in Original Colors
C285 AP78 40p pale lil & blk   .55 .25
C286 AP78 45p pink & blk   .60 .25
C287 AP78 50p lt grn & blk   .60 .25
C288 AP78 55p lt bl & blk   .75 .30
C289 AP78 60p tan & blk   .80 .30
C290 AP78 65p pale grn & blk   1.00 .40
    Nos. C285-C290 (6)   4.30 1.75

Hunger Type of Regular Issue

50p, Wheat emblem & bird feeding nestlings.

Perf. 12x11½

1963, Mar. 21   **Unwmk.**
C291 A91 50p ver & blk   .45 .25
   a. Souv. sheet of 2, #453, C291,
     imperf.   1.50 1.50

FAO "Freedom from Hunger" campaign.

Eagle in Flight — AP79

1963, Apr. 18   **Litho.**
C292 AP79 12½p brt grn   .30 .25
C293 AP79 50p lilac rose   .35 .25

Revolution of Mar. 8, 1963.

Faris el Khouri — AP80

Arms and Wreath — AP81

1963, Apr. 27   **Perf. 12x11½**
C294 AP80 17½p gray   .30 .25
C295 AP81 22½p bl grn & blk   .30 .25

Evacuation Day, 1963.

abu-al-Ala al-Maarri — AP82

1963, Aug. 19   **Perf. 12x11½**
C296 AP82 50p violet blue   .40 .25

abu-al-Ala al-Maarri (973-1057), poet and philosopher.

Copper Pitcher, Arch and Fair — AP83

1963, Aug. 25
C297 AP83 37½p ultra, yel & brn   .45 .25
C298 AP83 50p brt bl, yel & brn   .50 .25

10th International Damascus Fair.

Centenary Emblem — AP84

50p, Centenary emblem and globe.

1963, Sept. 19   **Litho.**
C299 AP84 15p chlky bl, red & blk   .40 .25
C300 AP84 50p yel grn, blk & red   .50 .25

Centenary of the International Red Cross.

Abou Feras al Hamadani AP85

1963, Nov. 13   **Perf. 12x11½**
C301 AP85 50p yel ol & dk brn   .50 .25

Abou Feras (932-968), poet.

Heads of Three Races and Flame — AP86

1964, Jan. 6   **Unwmk.**
C302 AP86 17½p multi   .30 .25
C303 AP86 22½p grn, blk & red   .30 .25
C304 AP86 50p vio, blk & red   .40 .25
   a. Souv. sheet of 3   1.10 1.10
     Nos. C302-C304 (3)   1.00 .75

Universal Declaration of Human Rights, 15th anniv. No. C304a contains 3 imperf. stamps similar to Nos. C302-C304 with simulated perforations.

Flag, Torch and Map of Arab Countries AP87

1964, Mar. 8   **Unwmk.**   **Perf. 11½**
C305 AP87 15p multi   .30 .25
C306 AP87 17½p multi   .30 .25
C307 AP87 22½p multi   .30 .25
     Nos. C305-C307 (3)   .90 .75

Revolution of Mar. 8, 1963, 1st anniv.

Kaaba, Mecca, and Mosque, Damascus AP88

1964, Mar. 14   **Litho.**   **Perf. 11½x12**
C308 AP88 12½p bl & blk   .30 .25
C309 AP88 22½p rose lil & blk   .30 .25
C310 AP88 50p lt grn & blk   .35 .25
     Nos. C308-C310 (3)   .95 .75

First Arab Conference of Moslem Wakf Ministers, Damascus.

Young Couple and View of Damascus AP89

1964, Apr. 17   **Unwmk.**
C311 AP89 20p blue   .30 .25
C312 AP89 25p rose car   .30 .25
C313 AP89 60p emerald   .35 .25
     Nos. C311-C313 (3)   .95 .75

Evacuation Day, Apr. 17, 1964.

Abul Kasim (Albucasis) AP90

1964, Apr. 21   **Perf. 12x11½**
C314 AP90 60p brown   .40 .25

4th Arab Congress of Dental and Oral Surgery, Damascus.

Mosaic, Chahba, Thalassa AP91

     Perf. 11½x12
1964, June-July   **Litho.**
C315 AP91 27½p car rose   .30 .25
C316 AP91 45p gray   .30 .25
C317 AP91 50p brt grn   .40 .25
C318 AP91 55p slate grn   .40 .25
C319 AP91 60p ultra   .50 .25
     Nos. C315-C319 (5)   1.90 1.25

Hanging Lamp, Fair Emblem — AP92

Globe and Fair Emblem — AP93

1964, Aug. 28   **Perf. 12x11½**
C320 AP92 20p multi   .30 .25
C321 AP93 25p multi   .30 .25

11th International Damascus Fair.

Industrial and Agricultural Symbols — AP94

1964, Sept. 22   **Litho.**   **Unwmk.**
C322 AP94 25p multi   .30 .25

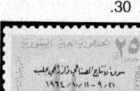

No. C322 Overprinted in Red and Arabic

C323 AP94 25p multi   .30 .25

Cotton Festival, Aleppo. Overprint on No. C323 translates: "Market for Industrial and Agricultural Products."

Arms of Syria and Aero Club Emblem AP95

1964, Oct. 8   **Litho.**   **Perf. 11½x12**
C324 AP95 12½p emer & blk   .30 .25
C325 AP95 17½p crim & blk   .30 .25
C326 AP95 20p brt bl & blk   .40 .25
     Nos. C324-C326 (3)   1.00 .75

10th anniversary of Syrian Aero Club.

Arab Postal Union Emblem — AP96

1964, Nov. 12   **Litho.**   **Perf. 12x11½**
C327 AP96 12½p org & blk   .30 .25
C328 AP96 20p emer & blk   .30 .25
C329 AP96 25p dp lil rose & blk   .30 .25
     Nos. C327-C329 (3)   .90 .75

10th anniv. of the permanent office of the APU.

Grain and Hands Holding Book — AP97

1964, Nov. 30   **Unwmk.**
C330 AP97 12½p emer & blk   .30 .25
C331 AP97 17½p mar & blk   .30 .25
C332 AP97 20p dp bl & blk   .30 .25
     Nos. C330-C332 (3)   .90 .75

Burning of the library of Algiers, 6/7/62.

Tennis Player — AP98

17½p, Wrestlers and drummer. 20p, Weight lifter. 100p, Wrestlers and drummer.

1965, Feb. 7   *Perf. 12x11½*
C333 AP98 12½p multi .30 .25
C334 AP98 17½p multi .30 .25
C335 AP98 20p multi, horiz. .30 .25
   Nos. C333-C335 (3) .90 .75
Souvenir Sheet
C336 AP98 100p multi 1.25 1.25
18th Olympic Games, Tokyo, 10/10-25/64.
No. C336 contains one 45x33mm stamp.

Ramses Battling the Hittites AP99

Design: 50p, Two statues of Ramses II.

1965, Mar. 21   **Litho.**   *Perf. 11x12*
C337 AP99 22½p emer, ultra & blk .30 .25
C338 AP99 50p ultra, emer & blk .40 .25
UNESCO world campaign to save historic monuments in Nubia.

Al-Sharif Al-Radi — AP100

1965, Apr. 3   **Litho.**   *Perf. 12x11½*
C339 AP100 50p gray brn .50 .25
5th Poetry Festival held in Latakia; Al-Sharif Al-Radi (970-1015), poet.

Hippocrates and Avicenna — AP101

1965, Apr. 19   *Perf. 11½*
C340 AP101 60p dl bl grn & blk .55 .30
"Medical Days of the Near and Middle East," a convention held at Damascus Apr. 19-25.

Dagger in Map of Palestine AP102

1965, May 15
C341 AP102 12½p multi .90 .25
C342 AP102 60p multi 1.00 .25
Deir Yassin massacre, Apr. 9, 1948.

ITU Emblem, Old and New Communication Equipment — AP103

    Perf. 11½x12
1965, May 24   **Litho.**   **Unwmk.**
C343 AP103 12½p multi .30 .25
C344 AP103 27½p multi .30 .25
C345 AP103 60p multi .50 .25
   Nos. C343-C345 (3) 1.10 .75
ITU, centenary.

Syrian Welcoming AP104

1965, Aug.   **Unwmk.**   *Perf. 12x11½*
C346 AP104 25p pur & multi .30 .25
C347 AP104 100p blk & multi .75 .25
Issued to welcome Arab immigrants.

Bridge and Gate — AP105

27½p, Fair emblem. 60p, Jug & ornaments.

1965, Aug. 28   **Litho.**
C348 AP105 12½p blk, brt ultra & brn .30 .25
C349 AP105 27½p multi .30 .25
C350 AP105 60p multi .40 .25
   Nos. C348-C350 (3) 1.00 .75
12th International Damascus Fair.

Fair Emblem and Cotton Pickers — AP106

1965, Sept. 30   *Perf. 12x11½*
C351 AP106 25p olive & multi .30 .25
10th Cotton Festival, Aleppo.

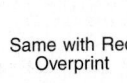

Same with Red Overprint

1965, Sept. 30
C352 AP106 25p olive & multi .30 .25
Industrial and Agricultural Fair, Aleppo.

View of Damascus and ICY Emblem AP107

1965, Oct. 24   *Perf. 11½x12*
C353 AP107 25p multi .30 .25
International Cooperation Year.

Radio Transmitter, Globe, Syrian Flag and View of Damascus AP108

1966, Feb. 16   **Litho.**   *Perf. 12x11½*
C354 AP108 25p multi .30 .25
C355 AP108 60p multi .35 .25
3rd Conference of Arab Information Ministers, Damascus, Feb. 14-18.

Hand (shaped like a dove) Holding Flower — AP109

Design: 17½p, Stylized people, horiz.

1966, Mar. 8   *Perf. 12x11½, 11½x12*
C356 AP109 12½p multi .30 .25
C357 AP109 17½p multi .30 .25
C358 AP109 50p multi .75 .25
   Nos. C356-C358 (3) 1.35 .75
March 8 Revolution, 3rd anniversary.

Statues of Ramses II from Abu Simbel — AP110

1966, Mar. 15   *Perf. 12x11½*
C359 AP110 25p dark blue .30 .25
C360 AP110 60p dark slate green .40 .25
Arab "Save the Nubian Monument Week."

UN Headquarters Building and Emblem — AP111

Design: 100p, UN Flag.

1966, Apr. 11   **Litho.**   *Perf. 11½x12*
C361 AP111 25p blk & gray .30 .25
C362 AP111 50p blk & pale grn .35 .25
Souvenir Sheet
Imperf
C363 AP111 100p yel, brt bl & blk 1.25 1.25
20th anniv. (in 1965) of the UN. No. C363 contains one stamp 42x36mm.

Marching Workers AP112

1966, May 1   **Litho.**   *Perf. 11½x12*
C364 AP112 60p multi .40 .25
Issued for May Day.

Inauguration of WHO Headquarters, Geneva — AP113

1966, May 3
C365 AP113 60p blk, bl & yel .40 .25

Map of Arab Countries and Traffic Signals — AP114

1966, May 4   *Perf. 12x11½*
C366 AP114 25p gray & multi .30 .25
Issued to publicize Traffic Day.

Astarte & Tyche, 1st cent. Basrelief, Palmyra AP115

1966, July 26   **Litho.**   *Perf. 12x11½*
C367 AP115 50p pale brn .35 .25
C368 AP115 60p slate .50 .25

Symbolic Flag, Wheat, Globe and Fair Emblem AP116

1966, Aug. 25   **Litho.**   *Perf. 12x11½*
C369 AP116 12½p multi .30 .25
C370 AP116 60p multi .35 .25
13th Intl. Damascus Fair, Aug. 25-Sept. 20.

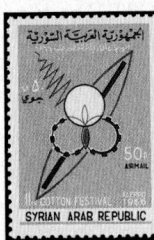

Shuttle and Symbols of Agriculture, Industry and Cotton — AP117

1966, Sept. 9   **Litho.**   *Perf. 12x11½*
C371 AP117 50p sil, blk & plum .35 .25
11th Cotton Festival, Aleppo.

Symbolic Water Cycle — AP118

1966, Oct. 24   Litho.   Perf. 12x11½
C372 AP118 12½p emer, blk & org   .30 .25
C373 AP118 60p ultra, blk & org   .35 .25
Hydrological Decade (UNESCO), 1965-74.

Abd-el Kader — AP119

1966, Nov. 7
C374 AP119 12½p brt grn & blk   .30 .25
C375 AP119 50p brt grn & red
      brn   .35 .25
Transfer from Damascus to Algiers of the ashes of Abd-el Kader (1807?-1883), Emir of Mascara.

Clasped Hands over Map of South Arabia — AP120

1967, Feb. 8   Litho.   Perf. 12x11½
C376 AP120 20p pink & multi   .30 .25
C377 AP120 25p multi   .30 .25
3rd Congress of Solidarity with the Workers and People of Aden, Damascus, Jan. 15-18.

Pipelines and Pigeons AP121

1967, Mar. 8   Litho.   Perf. 12x11½
C378 AP121 17½p multi   .30 .25
C379 AP121 25p multi   .30 .25
C380 AP121 27½p multi   .30 .25
   Nos. C378-C380 (3)   .90 .75
4th anniversary of March 8 Revolution.

Soldier, Woman and Man Holding Flag — AP122

Workers' Monument, Damascus AP123

1967, Apr. 17   Litho.   Perf. 12x11½
C381 AP122 17½p green   .30 .25
C382 AP122 25p dp claret   .30 .25
C383 AP122 27½p vio blue   .30 .25
   Nos. C381-C383 (3)   .90 .75
21st anniv. of the evacuation of British and French troops from Syria.

1967, May 1
C384 AP123 12½p bl grn   .30 .25
C385 AP123 50p brt pink   .35 .25
Issued for Labor Day, May 1.

Fair Emblem and Gate, Minaret, Omayyad Mosque — AP124

1967, Aug. 25   Litho.   Perf. 12x12½
C386 AP124 12½p multi   .30 .25
C387 AP124 60p multi   .35 .25
14th Intl. Damascus Fair, Aug. 25-Sept. 20.

Statue of Ur-Nina and ITY Emblem AP125

1967, Sept. 2   Perf. 12½x12
C388 AP125 12½p lt bl, brt rose
      lil & blk   .30 .25
C389 AP125 25p lt bl, ver & blk   .30 .25
C390 AP125 27½p lt bl, dk bl &
      blk   .30 .25
   Nos. C388-C390 (3)   .90 .75
Souvenir Sheet
Imperf
C391 AP125 60p lt bl & vio bl   1.00 1.00
Intl. Tourist Year.

Cotton Boll and Cogwheel Segment AP126

1967, Sept. 28   Litho.   Perf. 12x12½
C392 AP126 12½p ocher, brn & blk   .30 .25
C393 AP126 60p ap grn, brn &
      blk   .40 .25
12th Cotton Festival, Aleppo.

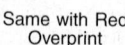

Same with Red Overprint

1967, Sept. 28
C394 AP126 12½p multi   .30 .25
C395 AP126 60p multi   .35 .25
Industrial and Agricultural Production Fair, Aleppo.

Head of Young Man, Amrith, 4th-5th Century B.C. — AP127

100p, 500p, Bronze bust of a Princess, 2nd cent.

1967, Oct. 7
C396 AP127 45p orange   .30 .25
C397 AP127 50p brt pink   .40 .25
C398 AP127 60p grnsh bl   .50 .25
C399 AP127 100p green   .60 .30
C400 AP127 500p brn red   2.25 1.50
   Nos. C396-C400 (5)   4.05 2.55

Ibn el-Naphis AP128

1967, Dec. 28   Litho.   Perf. 12x12½
C401 AP128 12½p grn & org   .30 .25
C402 AP128 27½p dk bl & lil rose   .30 .25
700th death anniv. of Ibn el-Naphis (1210-1288), Arab physician.

Human Rights Flame and People AP129

Design: 100p, Heads of various races and Human Rights flame.

1968, Feb. 21   Litho.   Perf. 12½x12
C403 AP129 12½p lt grnsh bl, bl
      & blk   .30 .25
C404 AP129 60p pink, blk & dl
      red   .40 .25
Souvenir Sheet
Imperf
C405 AP129 100p multi   1.00 1.00
20th anniv. of the Declaration of Human Rights; Intl. Human Rights Year.

Old Man and Woman Reading AP130

Design: 17½p, 45p, Torch and book.

1968, Mar. 3   Perf. 12x12½
C406 AP130 12½p rose car, blk
      & org   .30 .25
C407 AP130 17½p multi   .30 .25
C408 AP130 25p grn, blk & org   .30 .25
C409 AP130 45p bl & multi   .30 .25
   Nos. C406-C409 (4)   1.20 1.00
Issued to publicize the literacy campaign.

Euphrates Dam Project — AP131

1968, Apr. 11   Litho.   Perf. 12½x12
C410 AP131 12½p multi   .30 .25
C411 AP131 17½p multi   .30 .25
C412 AP131 25p multi   .30 .25
   Nos. C410-C412 (3)   .90 .75
Proposed dam across Euphrates River.

WHO Emblem and Avenzoar (1091-1162) — AP132

WHO Emblem and: 25p, Rhazes (Razi, 850-923). 60p, Geber (Jabir 721-776).

1968, June 10   Litho.   Perf. 12½x12
C413 AP132 12½p brn, grn & sal   .30 .25
C414 AP132 25p brn, gray & sal   .30 .25
C415 AP132 60p brn, gray bl &
      sal   .40 .25
   Nos. C413-C415 (3)   1.00 .75
WHO, 20th anniv.

Monastery of St. Simeon the Stylite AP133

Designs: 17½p, El Tekkieh Mosque, Damascus, vert. 22½p, Columns, Palmyra, vert. 45p, Chapel of St. Paul, Bab Kisan. 50p, Theater of Bosra.

Perf. 12½x12, 12x12½
1968, Oct. 10   Litho.
C416 AP133 15p pale grn &
      rose brn   .30 .25
C417 AP133 17½p redsh brn &
      dk red brn   .30 .25
C418 AP133 22½p grn gray & dk
      red brn   .30 .25
C419 AP133 45p yel & dk red
      brn   .30 .25
C420 AP133 50p lt bl & dk red
      brn   .30 .25
   Nos. C416-C420 (5)   1.50 1.25

Hammer Throw — AP134

Designs: 25p, Discus. 27½p, Running. 60p, Basketball. 50p, Polo, horiz.

1968, Dec. 19   Litho.   Perf. 12x12½
C421 AP134 12½p brt pink, blk &
      grn   .30 .25
C422 AP134 25p red, grn & blk   .30 .25

C423 AP134 27½p blk, gray & grn .30 .25
C424 AP134 60p multi .30 .25
Nos. C421-C424 (4) 1.20 1.00

Souvenir Sheet
Imperf

C425 AP134 50p multi 1.00 1.00

19th Olympic Games, Mexico City, Oct. 12-27. No. C425 contains one 52x80mm horiz. stamp.

Construction of Damascus Intl. Airport — AP135

1969, Jan. 20 Litho. Perf. 12½x12
C426 AP135 12½p yel, brt bl & grn .30 .25
C427 AP135 17½p org, pur & lt grn .30 .25
C428 AP135 60p car, blk & yel .40 .25
Nos. C426-C428 (3) 1.00 .75

Baal Shamin Temple, Palmyra AP136

Designs: 45p, Interior of Omayyad Mosque, Damascus, vert. 50p, Amphitheater, Palmyra. 60p, Khaled ibn-al-Walid Mosque, Homs, vert. 100p, Ruins of St. Simeon, Djebel Samaan.

1969, Jan. 20 Photo. Perf. 12x11½
C429 AP136 25p multi .30 .25
C430 AP136 45p bl & multi .30 .25
C431 AP136 50p multi .30 .25
C432 AP136 60p multi .30 .25
C433 AP136 100p vio & multi .60 .25
Nos. C429-C433 (5) 1.80 1.25

Workers, ILO Emblem, Cogwheel AP137

Design: 60p, ILO emblem.

1969, May 1 Litho. Perf. 12½x12
C434 AP137 12½p multi .30 .25
C435 AP137 27½p multi .30 .25

Miniature Sheet
Imperf

C436 AP137 60p multi .60 .60

ILO, 50th anniv. No. C436 contains one stamp 53½x47mm.

Ballet Dancers AP138

Designs: 12½p, Russian dancers. 45p, Lebanese singer and dancers. 55p, Egyptian dancer and musicians. 60p, Bulgarian dancers.

1969, Aug. 25 Litho. Perf. 12½x12
C437 AP138 12½p multi .30 .25
C438 AP138 27½p bl & multi .30 .25
C439 AP138 45p multi .30 .25

C440 AP138 55p multi .30 .25
C441 AP138 60p multi .40 .25
a. Strip of 5, #C437-C441 1.75 1.75

16th Intl. Fair, Damascus, Aug. 25-Sept. 20.

Children Playing — AP139

1969, Oct. 6 Litho. Perf. 12x12½
C442 AP139 12½p aqua, dk bl & emer .30 .25
C443 AP139 25p brn red, dk bl & lt vio .30 .25
C444 AP139 27½p ultra, dk bl & gray .30 .25
Nos. C442-C444 (3) .90 .75

Issued for Children's Day.

Fortuna — AP140

Designs: 25p, Seated woman from Palmyra. 60p, Motherhood. All sculptures from Greco-Roman period.

1969, Oct. 10
C445 AP140 17½p blk, yel grn & grn .30 .25
C446 AP140 25p dk brn, red brn & lt grn .30 .25
C447 AP140 60p blk, lt gray & bl gray .40 .25
Nos. C445-C447 (3) 1.00 .75

9th Intl. Congress for Classical Archaeology, Oct. 11-20.

Damascus Agricultural Museum — AP141

1969, Dec. 24 Litho. Perf. 12½x12
C448 AP141 12p Cock .30 .25
C449 AP141 17½p Cow .30 .25
C450 AP141 20p Corn .30 .25
C451 AP141 50p Olives .30 .25
a. Strip of 4, #C448-C451 + label 1.25 1.25

Weather Balloon Tracking and UN Emblem AP142

1970, Mar. 23 Litho. Perf. 12½x12
C452 AP142 25p blk, sl grn & yel .30 .25
C453 AP142 60p blk, dk bl & yel .35 .25

10th World Meteorological Day.

Lenin (1870-1924) AP143

1970, Apr. 15 Litho. Perf. 12x12½
C454 AP143 15p red & dk brn .30 .25
C455 AP143 60p red & grn .35 .25

Workers' Syndicate Emblem AP144

1970, May 1 Litho. Perf. 12½x12
C456 AP144 15p dk brn & brt grn .30 .25
C457 AP144 60p dk brn & org .35 .25

Issued for Labor Day.

Radar and Open Book AP145

1970, May 17
C458 AP145 15p brt pink & blk .30 .25
C459 AP145 60p bl & blk .35 .25

International Telecommunications Day.

Opening of UPU Headquarters, Bern — AP146

1970, May 30
C460 AP146 15p multi .30 .25
C461 AP146 60p multi .35 .25

"Zahier Piebers and Maarouf" — AP147

Folk Tales: 10p, Two warriors on horseback. 15p, Two warriors on white horses. 20p, Lady and warrior on horseback. 60p, Warriors, woman and lion.

1970, Aug. 12 Litho. Perf. 12½
C462 AP147 5p lt bl & multi .30 .25
C463 AP147 10p lt bl & multi .30 .25
C464 AP147 15p lt bl & multi .30 .25
C465 AP147 20p lt bl & multi .30 .25
C466 AP147 60p lt bl & multi .50 .25
a. Strip of 5, #C462-C466 1.75 1.75

Al Aqsa Mosque on Fire AP148

1970, Aug. 21 Perf. 12½x12
C467 AP148 15p multi .30 .25
C468 AP148 60p multi .35 .25

1st anniv. of the burning of Al Aqsa Mosque, Jerusalem.

Wood Carving — AP149

Handicrafts: 20p, Jewelry. 25p, Glass making. 30p, Copper engraving. 60p, Shellwork.

1970, Aug. 25 Perf. 12½
C469 AP149 15p vio & multi .30 .25
C470 AP149 20p ol & multi .30 .25
C471 AP149 25p multi .30 .25
C472 AP149 30p multi .30 .25
C473 AP149 60p multi .50 .25
a. Strip of 5, #C469-C473 1.75 1.75

17th Intl. Fair, Damascus.

Education Year Emblem AP150

1970, Nov. 2 Litho. Perf. 12
C474 AP150 15p dl grn & dk brn .30 .25
C475 AP150 60p vio bl & dk brn .35 .25

International Education Year.

UN Emblem, Symbols of Progress, Justice and Peace AP151

1970, Nov. 3
C476 AP151 15p lt ultra, red & blk .30 .25
C477 AP151 60p bl, yel & blk .35 .25

United Nations, 25th anniversary.

Khaled ibn-al-Walid AP152

1970-71 Perf. 12x11½, 12½x12½
C478 AP152 45p brt pink .30 .25
C479 AP152 50p green .35 .25
C480 AP152 60p vio brn .50 .25
C481 AP152 100p dk bl .60 .25
C482 AP152 200p grnsh gray ('71) 1.10 .50
C483 AP152 300p lil ('71) 1.50 .95
C484 AP152 500p gray ('71) 3.00 1.60
Nos. C478-C484 (7) 7.35 4.05

Woman with Garland AP153

1971, Apr. 17　Litho.　Perf. 12
C485 AP153 15p dl red, blk & grn　.30　.25
C486 AP153 60p grn, blk & dk grn　.35　.25
25th anniv. of the evacuation of British and French troops from Syria.

People Dancing Around Globe AP154

1971, Apr. 28　Litho.　Perf. 12½x12
C487 AP154 15p vio & multi　.30　.25
C488 AP154 60p grn & multi　.30　.25
Intl. Year against Racial Discrimination.

Pres. Hafez al Assad and Council Chamber — AP155

1971, Sept. 30　Litho.　Perf. 12½x12
C489 AP155 15p grn & multi　.30　.25
C490 AP155 65p bl & multi　.60　.25
People's Council and presidential election.

Gamal Abdel Nasser (1918-1970), President of Egypt — AP156

1971, Oct. 17　　Perf. 12x12½
C491 AP156 15p lt ol grn & brn　.30　.25
C492 AP156 20p gray & brn　.30　.25

Globe and Arrows AP157

1972, May 17　Litho.　Perf. 11½
C493 AP157 15p bl, vio bl & pink　.30　.25
C494 AP157 50p org, yel & sep　.30　.25
4th World Telecommunications Day.

Pres. Hafez al Assad — AP158

1972, July　Litho.　Perf. 12x11½
C495 AP158 100p dk grn　.60　.25
C496 AP158 500p dk brn　3.00　1.10

Airline Emblem, Eastern Hemisphere AP159

1972, Sept. 16　Litho.　Perf. 12x11½
C497 AP159 15p blk, lt bl & Prus bl　.30　.25
C498 AP159 50p blk, gray & Prus bl　.30　.25
Syrianair, Syrian airline, 25th anniversary.

Pottery — AP160

Handicraft Industries: 25p, Rugs. 30p, Metal (weapons). 35p, Straw (baskets, mats). 100p, Wood carving.

1976, July　Litho.　Perf. 12x12½
C499 AP160 10p multi　.30　.25
C500 AP160 25p multi　.30　.25
C501 AP160 30p multi　.30　.25
C502 AP160 35p multi　.30　.25
C503 AP160 100p multi　.50　.30
　a.　Strip of 5, #C499-C503　1.75　1.75
23rd Intl. Damascus Fair.

Pres. Hafez al Assad AP161

1978, Sept.　Litho.　Perf. 12½x12
C504 AP161 25p sil & multi　.50　.25
C505 AP161 35p grn & multi　.50　.25
C506 AP161 60p gold & multi　.50　.25
　Nos. C504-C506 (3)　1.50　.75
Reelection of Pres. Assad. See No. 820.

AIR POST SEMI-POSTAL STAMPS

Nos. C30-C33 Surcharged Like Nos. B1-B12 in Black and Red

1926, Apr. 1　Unwmk.　Perf. 13½
CB1 A4 2p + 1p dk brown　3.00　2.75
CB2 A4 3p + 2p org brn　2.75　2.75
CB3 A4 5p + 3p violet　2.75　2.75
CB4 A4 10p + 5p vio brn　2.75　2.75
　Nos. CB1-CB4 (4)　11.25　11.00

The new value is in red and rest of the surcharge in black on Nos. CB1-CB3. The entire surcharge is black on No. CB4.
See note following Nos. B1-B12.

> Catalogue values for unused stamps in this section, from this point to the end of the section, are for Never Hinged items.

Fair Entrance SPAP1

Industry, Handicraft and Farming SPAP2

Design: 70p+10p, Fairgrounds.

Perf. 11½, Imperf.
1955　Litho.　Unwmk.
CB5 SPAP1 25p + 5p gray black　.40　.40
CB6 SPAP2 35p + 5p ultra　.40　.40
CB7 SPAP2 40p + 10p rose lilac　.60　.60
CB8 SPAP1 70p + 10p Prus grn　1.10　1.10
　Nos. CB5-CB8 (4)　2.50　2.50
Intl. Fair, Damascus, Sept. 1955.
For overprint see Nos. C212-C215.

United Nations Refugee Emblem SPAP3

1966, Dec. 12　Litho.　Perf. 11½x12
CB9 SPAP3 12½p + 2½p ultra & blk　.25　.25
CB10 SPAP3 50p + 5p grn & blk　.50　.25
UN Day, 21st anniv.; Refugee Week, Oct. 24-31.

POSTAGE DUE STAMPS

Under French Occupation

French Offices in the Turkish Empire, 1902-03, Surcharged

O. M. F. Syrie Ch. taxe 1 PIASTRE

1920　Unwmk.　Perf. 14x13½
J1 A3 1p on 10c rose red　160.00　160.00
J2 A3 2p on 20c brn vio　160.00　160.00
J3 A3 3p on 30c lil　160.00　160.00
J4 A4 4p on 40c red & pale bl　160.00　160.00
　Nos. J1-J4 (4)　640.00　640.00

Postage Due Stamps of France, 1893-1920, Surcharged in Black or Red

O. M. F. Syrie 2 PIASTRES

1920
J5 D2 1p on 10c brown　3.25　3.25
J6 D2 2p on 20c ol grn (R)　3.25　3.25
　a.　"PIASTRE"　900.00　900.00
J7 D2 3p on 30c red　3.25　3.25
　a.　"PIASTRE"
J8 D2 4p on 50c brn vio　4.75　4.75
　a.　3p in setting of 4p　525.00　525.00
　Nos. J5-J8 (4)　14.50　14.50

1921-22
J9 D2 50c on 10c brown　1.40　1.40
　a.　"75" instead of "50"　90.00
　b.　"CENTI MES" instead of "CEN-TIEMES"　7.50
J10 D2 1p on 20c ol grn　1.40　1.40
J11 D2 2p on 30c red　3.25　3.25
J12 D2 3p on 50c brn vio　3.50　3.50
J13 D2 5p on 1fr red brn, straw　5.00　5.00
　Nos. J9-J13 (5)　14.55　14.55

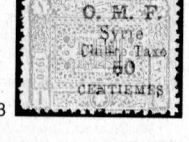
O. M. F. Syrie Chiffre Taxe 50 CENTIEMES
D3

1921　Red Surcharge　Perf. 11½
J14 D3 50c on 1p black　3.75　3.75
J15 D3 1p on 1p black　3.75　3.75

O. M. F. Syrie 4 PIASTRES
D4

1922
J16 D4 2p on 5m rose　10.00　6.50
　a.　"AX" of "TAXE" inverted　175.00　175.00
J17 D4 3p on 1p gray bl　15.00　12.00

French Mandate

Postage Due Stamps of France, 1893-1920, Surcharged

Syrie Grand Liban 2 PIASTRES

1923
J18 D2 50c on 10c brown　1.50　1.50
J19 D2 1p on 20c ol grn　2.25　2.25
J20 D2 2p on 30c red　1.90　1.90
J21 D2 3p on 50c vio brn　1.90　1.90
J22 D2 5p on 1fr red brn, straw　3.75　3.75
　Nos. J18-J22 (5)　11.30　11.30

Postage Due Stamps of France, 1893-1920, Surcharged

SYRIE 1 PIASTRE

1924
J23 D2 50c on 10c brown　1.00　1.00
J24 D2 1p on 20c ol grn　1.00　1.00
J25 D2 2p on 30c red　1.10　1.10
J26 D2 3p on 50c vio brn　1.50　1.50
J27 D2 5p on 1fr red brn, straw　1.50　1.50
　Nos. J23-J27 (5)　6.10　6.10

Postage Due Stamps of France, 1893-1920, Surcharged

Syrie 2 Piastres

1924
J28 D2 50c on 10c brown　.75　.75
J29 D2 1p on 20c ol grn　.75　.75
J30 D2 2p on 30c red　1.00　1.00
J31 D2 3p on 50c vio brn　1.40　1.40
J32 D2 5p on 1fr red brn, straw　1.75　1.75
　Nos. J28-J32 (5)　5.65　5.65

Water Wheel at Hama D5

Bridge at Antioch — D6

Designs: 2p, The Tartous. 3p, View of Banias. 5p, Chevaliers' Castle.

1925 Photo. Perf. 13½

J33	D5	50c brown, yel	.25	.25
J34	D6	1p violet, rose	.25	.25
J35	D5	2p black, blue	.55	.55
J36	D5	3p black, red org	1.25	1.25
J37	D5	5p black, bl grn	1.50	1.50
		Nos. J33-J37 (5)	3.80	3.80

D7

Lion — D8

1931

J38	D7	8p black, gray blue	3.50	3.50
J39	D8	15p black, dull rose	6.00	6.00

Catalogue values for unused stamps in this section, from this point to the end of the section, are for Never Hinged items.

Syrian Arab Republic

D9

1965 Unwmk. Litho. Perf. 11½x11

J40	D9	2½p violet blue	.25	.25
J41	D9	5p black brown	.25	.25
J42	D9	10p green	.25	.25
J43	D9	17½p carmine rose	.25	.25
J44	D9	25p blue	.25	.25
		Nos. J40-J44 (5)	1.25	1.25

MILITARY STAMPS

Free French Administration

Syria No. 222 Surcharged in Black

1942 Unwmk. Perf. 13

M1	A10	50c on 4p yel org	9.00 8.00

Lebanon Nos. 155 and 142A Surcharged in Carmine

M2	A13	1fr on 5p grnsh bl	9.00 8.00
M3	A25	2.50fr on 12½p dp ultra	9.00 8.00

Camel Corps, Palmyra — M1

Perf. 11½x11¾

1942 Unwmk. Litho.
Bistre Background

M4	M1	1fr deep rose	.75	.55
M5	M1	1.50fr bright violet	.75	.55
M6	M1	2fr orange	.75	.55
M7	M1	2.50fr brown gray	1.00	.85
M8	M1	3fr Prussian blue	1.25	1.10
M9	M1	4fr deep green	2.00	1.60
M10	M1	5fr deep claret	2.25	1.75
		Nos. M4-M10 (7)	8.75	6.95

Nos. M4 to M10 exist imperforate. Value: unused $125; never hinged $200.
For surcharges see Nos. MB1-MB2, MC10.

MILITARY SEMI-POSTAL STAMPS

Free French Administration

Military Stamps of 1942 Srchd. in Black

1943 Unwmk. Perf. 11½

MB1	M1	1fr + 9fr deep rose	15.00 17.50
MB2	M1	5fr + 20fr deep claret	15.00 17.50

MILITARY AIR POST STAMPS

Free French Administration

Syria Nos. C55-C56 Srchd. in Black, Carmine or Orange

1942 Unwmk. Perf. 13

MC1	AP2	4fr on 50p blk (C)	8.25	8.25
MC2	AP2	6.50fr on 50p blk (C)	8.25	8.25
MC3	AP2	8fr on 50p blk (O)	8.25	8.25
MC4	AP2	10fr on 100p mag	8.25	8.25
		Nos. MC1-MC4 (4)	33.00	33.00

Winged Shields and Cross of Lorraine MAP1

1942 Litho. Perf. 11½

MC5	MAP1	6.50fr pale pink & rose car	4.00 4.00
MC6	MAP1	10fr lt bl & dl vio	4.50 4.50

Nos. MC5 and MC6 exist imperforate.
See Nos. MC7-MC8. For surcharges see Nos. MC9, MCB1-MCB2.

Souvenir Sheets

1942 Without Gum Perf. 11

MC7		Sheet of 2	37.50 40.00
a.	MAP1	6.50fr pale pink & rose carmine	15.00 15.00
b.	MAP1	10fr lt bl & dl violet	15.00 15.00

Imperf

MC8		Sheet of 2	37.50 40.00
a.	MAP1	6.50fr pale pink & rose carmine	15.00 15.00
b.	MAP1	10fr lt bl & dl violet	15.00 15.00

No. MC5 Surcharged in Rose Carmine With New Value and Bars

1942 Perf. 11½

MC9	MAP1	4fr on 6.50fr	4.00 4.00

Military Stamp of 1942 Srchd. in Black

1943

MC10	M1	4fr on 3fr Prus blue	2.50 2.50

MILITARY AIR POST SEMI-POSTAL STAMPS

Free French Administration
Military Air Post Stamps of 1942 Surcharged in Black

1943 Unwmk. Perf. 11½

MCB1	MAP1	6.50fr + 48.50fr	35.00 37.50
MCB2	MAP1	10fr + 100fr	35.00 37.50

POSTAL TAX STAMPS

Revenue Stamps Overprinted in Red or Black

R1

a

1945 Unwmk. Perf. 10½x11½

RA1	R1(a)	5p dark blue (R)	110.00 22.50

On Stamps Overprinted — b

RA2	R1(a)	5p dk bl (Bk+Bk)	100.00 27.50
RA3	R1(a)	5p dk bl (Bk+R)	115.00 27.50
RA4	R1(a)	5p dk bl (R+R)	110.00 27.50
RA5	R1(b)	5p dk bl (R+R)	105.00 24.00

On Stamps Overprinted

RA6	R1(a)	5p dk bl (Bk+Bk)	100.00 30.00
RA7	R1(a)	5p dk bl (Bk+R)	100.00 30.00
RA8	R1(a)	5p dk bl (R+R)	100.00 30.00
RA9	R1(b)	5p dk bl (R+R)	120.00 30.00
		Nos. RA1-RA9 (9)	960.00 249.00

The tax was for national defense.

Revenue Stamp Surcharged in Black

R2

1945 Unwmk. Perf. 11

RA10	R2	5p on 25c on 40c rose red	100.00 32.50

The surcharge reads "Tax (postal) for Syrian Army."

Revenue Stamp Surcharged in Black

1945

RA11	R2	5p on 25c on 40c rose red	110.00 32.50

No. RA11 Overprinted in Black

RA12	R2	5p on 25c on 40c	90.00

The tax on Nos. RA11-RA12 was for the army.
This overprint exists on No. RA10.

Revenue stamps without overprints occasionally were used as postage on covers through at least 1948.

ISSUES OF THE ARABIAN GOVERNMENT

The following issues replaced the British Military Occupation (E.E.F.) stamps (Palestine Nos. 2-14) which were used in central and eastern Syria from Nov. 1918 until Jan. 1920.

Turkish Stamps of 1913-18 Handstamped in Various Colors

Also Handstamp Surcharged with New Values as

1 millieme

1 Egyptian piaster

The Seal reads: "Hakuma al Arabie" (The Arabian Government)

Perf. 11½, 12, 12½, 13½

1919-20				**Unwmk.**	
1	A24	1m on 2pa red lil (254)		.85	.85
2	A25	1m on 4pa dk brn (255)		.85	.85
3	A26	2m on 5pa vio brn (256)		1.40	1.40
4	A15	2m on 5pa on 10pa gray grn (291)		.95	.95
5	A18	2m on 5pa ocher (304)		22.50	22.50
6	A41	2m on 5pa grn (345)		275.00	250.00
7	A18	2m on 5pa ocher (378)		47.50	47.50
8	A28	4m on 10pa grn (258)		6.50	6.50

9	A28	4m on 10pa grn (271)	.85	.85
10	A22	4m on 10pa bl grn (329)	1.75	1.75
11	A41	4m on 10pa car (346)	37.50	37.50
12	A23	4m on 10pa grn (415)	7.25	7.25
13	A44	4m on 10pa grn (424)	1.25	1.25
14	A11	4m on 10pa on 20pa vio brn (B38)	1.25	1.25
15	A41	4m on 10pa car (B42)	.85	.85
16	SP1	4m on 10pa red vio (B46)	1.40	1.40
17	SP1	4m on 10pa on 20pa car rose (B47)	1.40	1.40
19	A21	5pa ocher (317)		
21	A21	20pa car rose (153)	92.50	110.00
22	A29	20pa red (259)	1.40	1.40
23	A29	20pa red (272)	275.00	275.00
24	A17	20pa car (299)	2.75	2.75
25	A21	20pa car rose (318)	2.75	2.75
26	A22	20pa car rose (330)	11.00	11.00
27	A21	20pa car rose (342)	5.00	5.00
28	A41	20pa ultra (347)	2.75	2.75
29	A16	20pa mag (363)	11.00	11.00
30	A17	20pa car (371)	2.75	2.75
31	A18	20pa car (379)	7.75	7.75
32	A45	20pa dp rose (425)	3.75	3.75
33	A21	20pa car rose (B8)	2.75	2.75
34	A22	20pa car rose (B33)	2.75	2.75
35	A22	20pa car rose (B36)	13.00	13.00
36	A41	20pa ultra (B43)	.55	.55
37	A16	20pa mag (P140)	2.75	2.75
38	A17	20pa car (P144)	250.00	250.00
39	A30	1pi bl (260)	2.75	2.75
40	A31	1pi on 1½pi car & blk (261)	375.00	375.00
41	A30	1pi bl (273)	92.50	92.50
42	A30	1pi on 1pi bl (273)	125.00	125.00
43	A17	1pi blue (300)	4.75	4.75
44	A18	1pi blue (307)	57.50	57.50
45	A22	1pi ultra (331)	5.75	5.75
46	A21	1pi ultra (343)	10.00	10.00
47	A41	1pi vio & blk (348)	1.75	1.75
48	A18	1pi brt bl (389)	5.75	5.75
49	A46	1pi dl vio (426)	1.75	1.75
50	A47	1pi on 50pa ultra (428)	1.10	1.10
51	A21	1pi ultra (B9)	6.00	6.00
52	A22	1pi ultra (B15)	10.00	10.00
53	A18	1pi brt bl (B21)	6.00	6.00
54	A18	1pi blue (B23)	15.00	15.00
55	A22	1pi ultra (B34)	12.50	12.50
56	A41	1pi vio & blk (B44)	2.75	2.75
57	A33	2pi grn & blk (263)	72.50	72.50
58	A13	2pi brn org (289)	2.00	2.00
59	A18	2pi slate (308)	27.50	27.50
60	A18	2pi slate (314)	27.50	27.50
61	A21	2pi bl blk (320)	5.25	5.25
62	A17	2pi org (373)	4.25	4.25
63	A18	2pi brn (310)	12.00	12.00
64	A22	2pi dl vio (333)	23.50	23.50
65	A41	5pi yel brn & blk (349)	4.75	4.75
66	A41	5pi yel brn & blk (418)	4.75	4.75
67	A53	5pi on 2pa Prus bl (547)	7.75	7.75
68	A21	5pi dk vio (B10)	275.00	275.00
69	A17	5pi lil rose (B20)	47.50	47.50
70	A41	5pi yel brn & blk (B45)	4.75	4.75
72	A50	10pi dk grn (431)	130.00	130.00
73	A50	10pi dk vio (432)	110.00	110.00
74	A50	10pi dk brn (433)	375.00	
75	A18	10pi org brn (B2)	350.00	350.00
76	A37	10pi ol grn (267)	350.00	350.00
77	A40	25pi on 200pi grn & blk (287)	500.00	500.00
78	A17	25pi brn (303)	375.00	375.00
79	A51	25pi car, straw (434)	92.50	92.50
81	A52	50pi ind (438)	200.00	200.00

The variety "surcharge omitted" exists on Nos. 1-5, 12-13, 16, 32, 49-50, 67.

A few examples of No. 377 (50pi) and No. 269 (100pi) were overprinted but not regularly issued.

Overprinted

The Inscription reads "Hakum Soria Arabie" (Syrian-Arabian Government)
On Stamp of 1913

83	A26	2m on 5pa vio brn (256)	5.00	5.00

On Stamp of 1916-18

| 84 | A45 | 20pa dp rose (425) | .55 | .55 |

A1

		Litho.		**Perf. 11½**
85	A1	5m rose	.55	.55
a.		Tête bêche pair	22.50	10.00
b.		Imperf.		

Independence Issue
Arabic Overprint in Green
"Souvenir of Syrian Independence March 8, 1920"

86	A1	5m rose	250.00	150.00
a.		Tête bêche pair		
b.		Inverted overprint	375.00	375.00

A2

Litho.
Size: 22x18mm

87	A2	1/10pi lt brn	.25	.25

Size: 28x22mm

88	A2	2/10pi yel grn	.30	.25
a.		2/10pi yellow (error)	10.00	10.00
89	A2	3/10pi yellow	.40	.30
90	A2	1pi gray blue	.35	.25
91	A2	2pi blue grn	2.00	1.00

Size: 31x25mm

92	A2	5pi vio brn	2.75	1.50
93	A2	10pi gray	2.75	2.00
		Nos. 86-93 (8)	258.80	155.55

Nos. 86-93 exist imperf.
For overprint see No. J5.

PF1   PF2

Revenue Stamps Surcharged as on Postage Stamps, for Postal Use

1920		**Unwmk.**		**Perf. 11½**
94	PF1	5m on 5pa red	.50	.35
95	PF2	1m on 5pa red	.50	.25
96	PF2	2m on 5pa red	.40	.25
97	PF2	1pi on 5pa red	1.00	.65

Surcharged in Syrian Piasters

98	PF2	2pi on 5pa red	.35	.25
99	PF2	3pi on 5pa red	.35	.25
		Nos. 94-99 (6)	3.10	2.00

ISSUES OF THE ARABIAN GOVERNMENT POSTAGE DUE STAMPS

Postage Due Stamps of Turkey, 1914, Handstamped and Surcharged

No. J1   No. J4

1920		**Unwmk.**		**Perf. 12**
J1	D1	2m on 5pa claret	6.75	6.75
J2	D2	20pa red	6.75	6.75
J3	D3	1pi dark blue	6.75	6.75
J4	D4	2pi slate	6.75	6.75
		Nos. J1-J4 (4)	27.00	27.00

Type of Regular Issue

		Litho.		**Perf. 11½**
J5	A2	1pi black	1.25	1.25

UNITED ARAB REPUBLIC

Catalogue values for unused stamps in this section are for Never Hinged items.

See Egypt for stamps of types A1, A4, A7, A8, A14, A17, A19, A20, A24 with denomination in "M" (milliemes).

Issues for Syria

Linked Maps of Egypt and Syria — A1

		Perf. 11½		
1958, Feb. 1		**Unwmk.**		**Litho.**
1	A1	12½p yellow & green	.25	.25

Establishment of UAR. See No. C1.
See also Egypt No. 436.

Freedom Monument A2

1958, May				
2	A2	5p yel & vio	.40	.25
3	A2	15p yel grn & brn red	.65	.35
		Nos. 2-3,C2-C3 (4)	3.00	1.35

British-French troop evacuation, 12th anniv.

Bronze Rattle — A3

Antique Art: 15p, Goddess. 20p, Lamgi Mari. 30p, Mithras fighting bull. 40p, Aspasia. 60p, Minerva. 75p, Flask. 100p, Enameled Vase. 150p, Mosaic from Omayyad Mosque, Damascus.

1958, Sept. 14		**Litho.**		**Perf. 12**
4	A3	10p lt ol grn	.25	.25
5	A3	15p brown org	.25	.25
6	A3	20p rose lilac	.25	.25
7	A3	30p lt brown	.25	.25
8	A3	40p gray	.30	.25
9	A3	60p green	.50	.25
10	A3	75p blue	.80	.30
11	A3	100p brown car	1.20	.40
12	A3	150p dull purple	2.25	.60
		Nos. 4-12 (9)	6.05	2.80

Archaeological collections and museums.

Hand Holding Torch, Broken Chain and Flag — A4

1958, Oct. 14				**Perf. 11½**
13	A4	12.50p car rose	.25	.25

Establishment of Republic of Iraq.
See Egypt No. 454.

Syria No. 411 Overprinted

1958, Oct. 6		**Wmk. 291**		**Perf. 11½**
13A	A78	12½p olive	55.00	55.00
		Nos. 13A,C10-C11 (3)	145.00	145.00

Intl. Children's Day, 1958.

View of Damascus — A5

1958, Dec. 10				**Unwmk.**
14	A5	12½p green	.25	.25

4th Near East Regional Conference, Damascus, Dec. 10-20. See No. C14.

Secondary School, Damascus — A6

1959, Feb. 26		**Litho.**		**Perf. 12**
15	A6	12½p dull green	.25	.25

See No. 26.

Flags of UAR and Yemen A7

Perf. 13x13½

1959, Mar. 8   Photo.   Wmk. 318
16   A7   12½p grn, red & blk   .25   .25

1st anniversary of United Arab States.
See Egypt No. 465.

Arms of UAR — A8

Perf. 12x11½

1959, Feb. 22   Litho.   Wmk. 291
17   A8   12½p grn, blk & red   .25   .25

United Arab Republic, 1st anniv.
See Egypt No. 462.

Mother and
Children — A9

1959, Mar. 21   Perf. 11½
18   A9   15p carmine rose   .25   .25
19   A9   25p dk slate grn   .30   .25

Arab Mother's Day, Mar. 21.
For overprints see Nos. 41-42.

**Syria No. 378 Surcharged "U.A.R."
in Arabic and English, and New
Value in Red**

1959, Apr. 6   Photo.   Unwmk.
20   A68   2½p on 1p olive   .25   .25

Type of 1959 and

A10

Boys' School, Damascus — A11

Designs: 5p, 7½p, 10p, Various
arabesques. 12½p, St. Simeon's Monastery.
17½p, Hittin school. 35p, Normal School for
Girls, Damascus.

1959-61   Unwmk.   Litho.   Perf. 11½
21   A10   2½p violet   .25   .25
22   A10   5p olive bister   .25   .25
23   A10   7½p ultra   .25   .25
24   A10   10p bl grn   .25   .25
25   A11   12½p lt bl ('61)   .25   .25
26   A6   17½p brt lilac ('60)   .25   .25
27   A11   25p brt grnsh bl   .30   .25
28   A11   35p brown ('60)   .40   .25
            Nos. 21-28 (8)   2.20 2.00

Male Profile and
Fair Emblem — A12

Fair Emblem and Globe — A13

1959, Aug. 30   Unwmk.   Perf. 11½
30   A12   35p gray, grn & vio   .40   .25

Souvenir Sheet
Imperf
31   A13   30p dl yel & grn   1.50 1.50

6th International Damascus Fair.

Shield and
Cogwheel — A14

Perf. 13½x13

1959, Oct. 20   Wmk. 328
32   A14   50p sepia   .60   .35

Issued for Army Day, 1959.
See Egypt No. 491.

Syria Nos.
408 and
386 with
Red
Overprint
Similar to

1959   Unwmk.   Litho.   Perf. 11½
33   A75   15p gray   .25   .25

Photo.
34   A69   50p dk grn   .60   .40

The overprints differ in size and lettering:
No. 33 is 28x8½mm; No. 34 is 21x6mm. A
period follows "R" on Nos. 33-34. The Arabic
overprint means "United Arab Republic."
See Nos. C26-C28.

Cogwheel, Wheat
and Cotton — A15

1959, Oct. 30   Litho.
35   A15   35p gray, bl & ocher   .40   .25

Industrial and Agricultural Production Fair,
Aleppo. For overprint see No. 46.

**Type of Syria Air Post, 1956,
Inscribed "U.A.R."**

1959, Dec. 31   Unwmk.   Perf. 13½
36   AP59   12½p gray ol & bister   .25   .25

Day of the Tree. For overprint see No. 49.

A. R.
Kawakbi — A16

1960, Jan. 11   Perf. 12x11½
37   A16   15p dark green   .25   .25

Kawakbi, Arabic writer, 50th death anniv.

Arms and
Flag — A17

Perf. 13½x13

1960, Feb. 22   Photo.   Wmk. 328
38   A17   12½p red & dk sl grn   .25   .25

United Arab Republic, 2nd anniversary.
See Egypt No. 499.

Diesel Train and Old Town — A18

Perf. 11½x11

1960, Mar. 15   Litho.   Unwmk.
39   A18   12½p brn & brt bl   .35   .25

Construction of the Latakia-Aleppo railroad.

Arab
League
Center,
Cairo,
and Arms
of UAR
A19

Perf. 13x13½

1960, Mar. 22   Photo.   Wmk. 328
40   A19   12½p dl grn & blk   .25   .25

Opening of the Arab League Center and the
Arab Postal Museum in Cairo.
See Egypt No. 502.

Nos. 18-19
Overprinted in
Black or Magenta

Wmk. 291
1960, Apr. 3   Litho.   Perf. 11½
41   A9   15p car rose   .25   .25
42   A9   25p dk slate grn (M)   .35   .25

Issued for Arab Mother's Day.

Refugees
Pointing
to Map of
Palestine
A20

Perf. 13x13½

1960, Apr. 7   Photo.   Wmk. 328
43   A20   12½p car rose   .40   .25
44   A20   50p green   .70   .30

World Refugee Year, 7/1/59-6/30/60.
See Egypt Nos. 503-504.

Evacuation Day, 1960 — A21

Perf. 11½

1960, May 12   Unwmk.   Litho.
45   A21   12½p vio, rose & pale grn   .25 .25

No. 35 Overprinted
in Red

1960
46   A15   35p gray, bl & ocher   .30   .25

1960 Industrial and Agricultural Production
Fair, Aleppo.

Souvenir Sheet

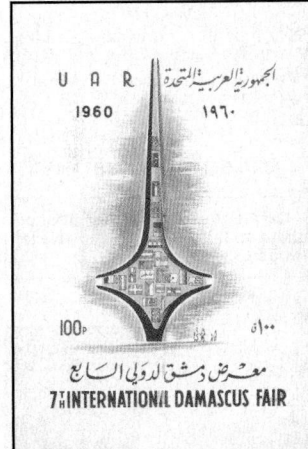

Flags in Symbolic Design — A22

1960   Unwmk.   Imperf.
47   A22   100p gray, brn & lt bl   1.50 1.50

7th Intl. Damascus Fair.

Child — A23

1960   Litho.   Perf. 11½
48   A23   35p dk grn & fawn   .40   .25

Issued for Children's Day.

No. 36 Overprinted in Carmine

1960   **Unwmk.**   *Perf. 11½*
49   AP59   12½p gray ol & bis   .25   .25
Issued to publicize the Day of the Tree.

Coat of Arms and
Victory
Wreath — A24

Perf. 13½x13
1961, Feb. 22   **Photo.**   **Wmk. 328**
50   A24   12½p lt vio   .25   .25
United Arab Republic, 3rd anniversary.
See Egypt No. 517.

Cogwheel, Retort
and Ear of
Wheat — A25

Perf. 11½
1961, June 8   **Unwmk.**   **Litho.**
51   A25   12½p multi   .25   .25
Industrial and Agricultural Fair, Aleppo.

UAR SEMI-POSTAL STAMP

> Catalogue values for unused
> stamp in this section is for a Never
> Hinged item.

Postal
Emblem — SP1

Perf. 13½x13
1959, Jan. 2   **Photo.**   **Wmk. 318**
B1   SP1   20p + 10p bl grn, red &
          blk   .40   .40
Issued for Post Day. The surtax went to the
social fund for postal employees.
   See Egypt No. B18 for similar stamp with
denomination in "M" (milliemes).

UAR AIR POST STAMPS

> Catalogue values for unused
> stamps in this section are for
> Never Hinged items.

Map Type of Regular Issue
Perf. 11½
1958, Apr. 3   **Unwmk.**   **Litho.**
C1   A1   17½p ultra & brn   .35   .25

Broken
Chain,
Dove and
Olive
Branch
AP1

1958, May 17
C2   AP1   35p rose & blk   .70   .35
C3   AP1   45p bl & brn   1.25   .40
British-French troop evacuation, 12th anniv.

Scout
Putting
up
Tent
AP2

1958, Aug. 31   *Perf. 12*
C4   AP2   35p dk brn   3.00   1.50
C5   AP2   40p ultra   4.00   2.00
3rd Pan-Arab Boy Scout Jamboree.

View of Damascus Fair — AP3

UAR Flag and Fair Emblem — AP4

Designs: 30p, Minaret, vase and emblem,
vert. 45p, Mosque, chimneys and wheel, vert.

1958, Sept. 1   **Litho.**   *Perf. 11½*
C6   AP3   25p vermilion   .70   .60
C7   AP3   30p brt bl grn   1.00   .60
C8   AP3   45p violet   .80   .55
    Nos. C6-C8 (3)   2.50   1.75
Souvenir Sheet
Imperf
C9   AP4   100p brt grn, car &
          blk   50.00   50.00
Fifth Damascus International Fair.

Syria Nos. C244-
C245 Overprinted

1958, Oct. 6   **Wmk. 291**   *Perf. 11½*
C10   A78   17½p ultra   45.00   45.00
C11   A78   20p red brn   45.00   45.00
International Children's Day.

Cotton and
Cotton
Material — AP5

1958, Oct. 10   **Unwmk.**   *Perf. 12*
C12   AP5   25p brn & yel   .40   .40
C13   AP5   35p brn & brick red   .70   .50
Cotton Festival, Aleppo, Oct. 9-11.

Type of Regular Issue, 1958
1958, Dec. 10
C14   A5   17½p brt vio   .25   .25

Children and
Glider — AP6

1958, Dec. 1   **Litho.**   *Perf. 12*
C15   AP6   7½p gray green   .50   .30
C16   AP6   12½p olive   2.00   1.25
1958 glider festival.

UN
Emblem — AP7

1958, Dec. 10
C17   AP7   25p dl pur   .25   .25
C18   AP7   35p light blue   .35   .25
C19   AP7   40p brn red   .45   .30
    Nos. C17-C19 (3)   1.05   .80
10th anniv. of the signing of the Universal
Declaration of Human Rights.

Globe, Radio and Telegraph — AP8

1959, Mar. 1   *Perf. 12*
C20   AP8   40p grn & blk   .50   .35
Arab Union of Telecommunications.
   See Egypt No. 464 for similar stamp with
denomination in "M" (milliemes).

Same Overprinted in Red

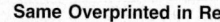

1959, Mar. 1
C21   AP8   40p grn & blk   .40   .25
2nd Conference of the Arab Union of Telecommunications, Damascus.

Laurel and Map
of Syria — AP9

Design: 35p, Torch and broken chain.

1959, Apr. 17   *Perf. 12x11½*
C22   AP9   15p ocher & green   .25   .25
C23   AP9   35p gray & carmine   .40   .25
British-French troop evacuation, 13th anniv.

"Emigration" — AP10

1959, Aug. 4   **Unwmk.**   *Perf. 11½x12*
C24   AP10   80p brt grn, blk & red   .70   .40
Convention of the Assoc. of Arab Emigrants
in the US.

Refinery
AP11

1959, Aug. 12   **Litho.**
C25   AP11   50p bl, blk & car   .90   .40
Opening of first oil refinery in Syria.

Syria Nos. C246 and C181-C182
Overprinted like Nos. 33-34

1959   *Perf. 11½*
C26   AP64   5p bright green   .25   .25
C27   AP44   50p deep plum   .40   .25
C28   AP44   70p purple   .70   .30
    Nos. C26-C28 (3)   1.35   .80
   The overprints differ in size and lettering:
No. C26 is 25½x9½mm; Nos. C27-C28 are
27x8mm. A period follows "R" on Nos. C27-
C28.

Cotton Boll and
Thread — AP12

1959, Oct. 1   Litho.   Perf. 11½
C29 AP12 45p gray blue   .40 .25
C30 AP12 50p claret   .40 .30
Cotton Festival, Aleppo.
For overprints see Nos. C33-C34.

Boy and Building Blocks — AP13

1959, Oct. 5
C31 AP13 25p dl lil, red & dk bl   .25 .25
Issued for Children's Day.

Crane and Compass AP14

1960   Unwmk.   Perf. 11½
C32 AP14 50p lt brn, crim & blk   .40 .30
7th Damascus International Fair.

Nos. C29-C30 Overprinted in Claret or Gray Blue

1960   Litho.   Perf. 11½
C33 AP12 45p gray blue (C)   .40 .25
C34 AP12 50p claret (GB)   .45 .30
1960 Cotton Festival, Aleppo.

17th Olympic Games, Rome — AP15

1960, Dec. 27   Unwmk.   Perf. 12
C35 AP15 15p Basketball   .25 .25
C36 AP15 20p Swimmer   .35 .25
C37 AP15 25p Fencing   .35 .25
C38 AP15 40p Horsemanship   .60 .30
   Nos. C35-C38 (4)   1.55 1.05

Globe, Laurel and "UN" — AP16

1960, Dec. 31
C39 AP16 35p multi   .35 .25
C40 AP16 50p bl, red & yel   .40 .25
United Nations, 15th anniversary.

Ibrahim Hanano — AP17

1961   Litho.   Perf. 12x11½
C41 AP17 50p buff & slate grn   .80 .25
Hanano, leader of liberation movement.

Soldier with Flag — AP18

1961, Apr. 17   Wmk. 291   Perf. 11½
C42 AP18 40p gray green   1.00 .25
Issued for Evacuation Day, 1961.

Arab and Map of Palestine — AP19

1961, May 15   Perf. 12
C43 AP19 50p ultra & blk   2.00 .25
Issued for Palestine Day.

Abu-Tammam AP20

1961, July 20   Unwmk.   Perf. 11½
C44 AP20 50p brown   .50 .25
Abu-Tammam (807-845?), Arabian poet.

Discus Thrower and Lyre AP21

1961, Aug. 23   Litho.   Perf. 11½
C45 AP21 15p crimson & blk   .25 .25
C46 AP21 35p bl grn & vio   .50 .25
5th University Youth Festival.
A souvenir sheet contains one each of Nos. C45-C46 imperf.

Fair Emblem — AP22

UAR Pavilion — AP23

1961, Aug. 25
C47 AP22 17½p vio & grn   .25 .25
C48 AP23 50p brt lil & blk   .35 .25
   a. Black omitted
8th International Damascus Fair.

St. Simeon's Monastery AP24

1961, Oct.   Litho.   Perf. 12
C49 AP24 200p violet blue   1.50 .90
No. C49 was issued by the Syrian Arab Republic after dissolution of the UAR.

UAR AIR POST SEMI-POSTAL STAMP

Catalogue value for the unused stamp in this section is for a Never Hinged item.

Eye, Hand and UN Emblem SPAP1

Perf. 12x11½
1961, Apr. 29   Litho.   Wmk. 291
CB1 SPAP1 40p + 10p sl grn & blk   .30 .30
UN welfare program for the blind.

TAHITI

tə-ˈhēt-ē

LOCATION — An island in the South Pacific Ocean, one of the Society group
GOVT. — A part of the French Oceania Colony
AREA — 600 sq. mi.
POP. — 19,029
CAPITAL — Papeete

The stamps of Tahiti were replaced by those of French Oceania (see French Polynesia in Vol. 2).

100 Centimes = 1 Franc

Counterfeits exist of surcharges and overprints on Nos. 1-31.

Stamps of French Colonies Surcharged in Black

a   b

c   d

1882   Unwmk.   Imperf.
1   A8(a) 25c on 35c dk vio, org   425. 350.
1A   A8(b) 25c on 35c dk vio, org   4,500. 4,500.
1B   A8(a) 25c on 40c ver, straw   6,250. 6,750.

Nos. 1-1B exist with surcharges inverted. Values for Nos. 1 and 1A are approximately the same as for normal stamps; No. 1B with surcharge inverted is worth about half the value of a normal stamp.
Surcharge exists reading either up or down on Nos. 1 and 1A, and double, one inverted on No. 1B. See Scott Classic Specialized Catalogue of Stamps and Covers for detailed listings of these and later Tahiti issues.

1884   Perf. 14x13½
2   A9(c) 5c on 20c red, yel grn   300. 240.
3   A9(d) 10c on 20c red, yel grn   350. 300.

Imperf
4   A8(b) 25c on 1fr brnz grn, straw   750. 650.

Inverted and vertical surcharges on Nos. 2-4 are same value as normally placed surcharges.

Handstamped in Black

1893   Perf. 14x13½
5   A9 1c blk, lil bl   950.00 875.00
6   A9 2c brown, buff   3,200. 2,500.
7   A9 4c claret, lav   1,500. 1,250.
8   A9 5c green, grnsh   55.00   47.50
9   A9 10c black, lav   60.00   52.50
10   A9 15c blue   60.00   47.50
11   A9 20c red, green   72.50   65.00
12   A9 25c yel, straw   8,750. 7,250.
13   A9 25c blk, rose   55.00   47.50
14   A9 35c violet, org   2,600. 2,200.
15   A9 75c carmine, rose   87.50   87.50
16   A9 1fr brnz grn, straw 92.50   92.50

Nearly all values of this set are known with overprint sloping up, sloping down and horizontal. Some occur double. Values the same as for the listed stamps.
For Nos. 6//16 with inverted overprint, see the Scott Classic Specialized Catalogue of Stamps and Covers.
Nos. 6, 12 and 14 are valued in the grade of Fine.

Overprinted in Black

1893

17	A9	1c blk, *lil bl*	925.00	800.00
18	A9	2c brn, *buff*	3,750.	2,750.
19	A9	4c claret, *lav*	1,850.	1,500.
20	A9	5c grn, *grnsh*	1,100.	950.00
21	A9	10c black, *lav*	350.00	350.00
22	A9	15c blue	55.00	50.00
23	A9	20c red, *grn*	60.00	55.00
24	A9	25c yel, *straw*	50,000.	42,500.
25	A9	25c black, *rose*	55.00	50.00
26	A9	35c violet, *org*	2,600.	2,200.
27	A9	75c carmine, *rose*	60.00	55.00
	b.	Double overprint	400.00	
28	A9	1fr brnz grn, *straw*	75.00	60.00

Inverted Overprint

17a	A9	1c blk, *lil bl*	1,350.	1,200.
18a	A9	2c brn, *buff*	4,000.	3,900.
19a	A9	4c claret, *lav*	2,000.	1,900.
20a	A9	5c grn, *grnsh*	1,600.	1,500.
21a	A9	10c black, *lav*	950.	900.
22a	A9	15c blue	250.	225.
23a	A9	20c red, *grn*	250.	225.
25a	A9	25c black, *rose*	250.	225.
26a	A9	35c violet, *org*	3,000.	2,800.
27a	A9	75c carmine, *rose*	300.	250.
28a	A9	1fr brnz grn, *straw*	300.	275.

Stamps of French Polynesia Surcharged in Black or Carmine

g   h

1903

29	A1 (g)	10c on 15c bl (Bk)	11.00	11.00
	a.	Double surcharge	67.50	67.50
	b.	Inverted surcharge	72.50	72.50
30	A1 (h)	10c on 25c blk, *rose* (C)	11.00	11.00
	a.	Double surcharge	67.50	67.50
	b.	Inverted surcharge	80.00	80.00

31	A1 (h)	10c on 40c red, *straw* (Bk)	13.00	13.00
	a.	Double surcharge	80.00	80.00
	b.	Inverted surcharge	80.00	80.00
		Nos. 29-31 (3)	35.00	35.00

In the surcharges on Nos. 29-31 there are two varieties of the "1" in "10," i. e. with long and short serif.

SEMI-POSTAL STAMPS

Stamps of French Polynesia Overprinted in Red

1915   Unwmk.   Perf. 14x13½

B1	A1	15c blue	300.00	300.00
	a.	Inverted overprint	1,100.	1,000.
B2	A1	15c gray	35.00	35.00
	a.	Inverted overprint	425.00	425.00

Counterfeits exist.

POSTAGE DUE STAMPS

Counterfeits exist of overprints on Nos. J1-J26.

Inverted overprints exist on most, and double overprints on many, Tahiti postage due stamps. See the *Scott Classic Specialized Catalogue of Stamps and Covers* for detailed listings.

Postage Due Stamps of French Colonies Handstamped in Black like Nos. 5-16

1893   Unwmk.   *Imperf.*

J1	D1	1c black	400.	400.
J2	D1	2c black	400.	400.
J3	D1	3c black	450.	450.
J4	D1	4c black	450.	450.
J5	D1	5c black	450.	450.
J6	D1	10c black	450.	450.
J7	D1	15c black	450.	450.
J8	D1	20c black	350.	350.
J9	D1	30c black	450.	450.
J10	D1	40c black	450.	450.
J11	D1	60c black	525.	525.
J12	D1	1fr brown	1,100.	1,100.
J13	D1	2fr brown	1,100.	1,100.
		Nos. J1-J13 (13)	7,025.	7,025.

Overprinted in Black like Nos. 17-28

1893

J14	D1	1c black	2,400.	2,400.
J15	D1	2c black	550.	550.
J16	D1	3c black	550.	550.
J17	D1	4c black	550.	550.
J18	D1	5c black	550.	550.
J19	D1	10c black	550.	550.
J20	D1	15c black	550.	550.
J21	D1	20c black	550.	550.
J22	D1	30c black	550.	550.
J23	D1	40c black	550.	550.
J24	D1	60c black	550.	550.
J25	D1	1fr brown	550.	550.
J26	D1	2fr brown	550.	550.
		Nos. J14-J26 (13)	9,000.	9,000.

TAJIKISTAN

tä-jik-i-'stan

(Tadzhikistan)

LOCATION — Asia, bounded by Uzbekistan, Kyrgyzstan, People's Republic of China and Afghanistan
GOVT. — Republic
AREA — 55,240 sq. mi.
POP. — 6,102,854 (1999 est.)
CAPITAL — Dushanbe

With the breakup of the Soviet Union on Dec. 26, 1991, Tajikistan became independent.

100 Kopecks = 1 Ruble
100 Tanga = 1 Ruble
100 Dirams = 1 Somoni (2000)

Catalogue values for all unused stamps in this country are for Never Hinged items.

Gold Statue of Man on Horse — A1

1992, May 20   Litho.   Perf. 12x12½
1   A1   50k multicolored   .35   .35
For surcharge see No. 12.

Sheik Muslihiddin Mosque A2

1992, May 25   Photo.   Perf. 11½
2   A2   50k multicolored   .30   .30
For surcharges, see Nos. 13-14.

Musical Instruments of Tajikistan — A3

Photo. & Engr.
1992, Aug. 15   Perf. 12x11½
3   A3   35k multicolored   .30   .30
For surcharges see Nos. 5-7.

Ram — A4

1992, Aug. 21   Photo.   Perf. 12x12½
4   A4   30k multicolored   .40   .40

No. 3 Surcharged in Black or Blue

Photo. & Engr.
1992, Nov. 12   Perf. 12x11½
5   A3   15r on 35k   .85   .85
6   A3   15r on 35k (Bl)   2.25   2.25
7   A3   50r on 35k   .85   .85
   Nos. 5-7 (3)   3.95   3.95

Russia No. 5838 Surcharged

1992, Jan. 4   Litho.   Perf. 12x12½
8   A2765   3r on 1k   .35   .35
9   A2765   100r on 1k   2.10   2.10

Russia No. 5984 Surcharged in Violet Blue or Green

No. 1 Surcharged in Black

1992, May 7   Litho.   Perf. 12x12½
10   A2765   10r on 2k (VB)   .95   .95
11   A2765   15r on 2k (Gr)   .95   .95
12   A1   60r on 50k   1.90   1.90
   Nos. 10-12 (3)   3.80   3.80
Location and size of lettering on Nos. 10-11 varies.

No. 2 Surcharged

Methods and Perfs as Before
1992, Sept. 18
13   A2   5r on 50k multi   .45   .45
14   A2   25r on 50k multi   1.10   1.10

Wild Animals A5

Designs: 3r, Ursus arctos. 10r, Cervas elaphus. 15r, Capra falconeri. 25r, Hystrix leucura. 100r, Uncia uncia.

1993, June 8   Litho.   Perf. 13½
15   A5   3r multicolored   .25   .25
16   A5   10r multicolored   .35   .25
17   A5   15r multicolored   .35   .25
18   A5   25r multicolored   .60   .25
19   A5   100r multicolored   2.25   .40
   Nos. 15-19 (5)   3.80   1.40
For surcharge, see No. 372.

Fortress, 19th Cent. — A6

Academy — A6a

1r, Statue of Rudaki, poet, vert. 5r, Mountains, river. 10r, Statue with oriental inscription, vert. 15r, Mausoleum of Aini, poet, vert. 20r, Map, flag. 35r, Post office. 50r, Aini Opera House. #29, Theater. #30, Flag, map, diff. #31, Observatory. #32, Academy.

1993-94
20   A6   1r multicolored   .25   .25
22   A6   5r multicolored   .25   .25
23   A6   10r multicolored   .25   .25
24   A6   15r multicolored   .25   .25
25   A6   20r green & multi   .25   .25
26   A6   25r multicolored   .40   .40
27   A6   35r multicolored   .25   .25
28   A6   50r multicolored   .60   .60
29   A6   100r multicolored   .55   .55
30   A6   100r blue & multi   1.10   1.10
31   A6   160r multicolored   .65   .65
32   A6a   160r shown   .65   .65
   Nos. 20-32 (12)   5.45   5.45

Issued: 1r, 5r, 15r, 20r, 25r, 50r, No. 30, 6/8/93, others, 9/8/94.
This is an expanding set. Numbers will change if necessary.
For surcharges, see Nos. 169-171, 231-232, 301, 373.

Souvenir Sheet

1992 Summer Olympics, Barcelona — A7

1993, June 8
33   A7   50r multicolored   8.75   8.75
For surcharge see No. 52A.

Epic Poem "Book of Kings", by Ferdowsi, 1000th Anniv. A8

Designs: 5r, Combat with swords. 20r, Two men on horseback fighting with spears. 30r, Men in combat stopped by guide on giant bird, vert. 50r, Ferdowsi (c. 935-c. 1020), vert.

1993, June 8   Litho.   Perf. 13½
34   A8   5r multicolored   .50   .50
35   A8   20r multicolored   1.40   1.40
36   A8   30r multicolored   1.75   1.75
  a.   Sheet, 2 each # 34-36, + 4 labels   14.00   —
   Nos. 34-36 (3)   3.65   3.65
Souvenir Sheet
37   A8   50r multicolored   3.25   3.25
No. 37 contains one 30x45mm stamp.

Traditional Art Pattern — A8a

1993, July 1   Litho.   Perf. 12x11½
37A   A8a   1.50r multicolored   .70   .70
Dated 1992.
For surcharges see Nos. 62-65.

Ali Hamadani (1314-85), Persian Mystic — A9

1994, Feb. 22   Litho.   Perf. 13½
38   A9   1000r multicolored   3.00   3.00
39   A9   1000r multicolored   3.00   3.00
Name in latin letters on No. 38 and in cyrillic letters on No. 39.

Natl. Arms — A10

1994, Feb. 22
40   A10   10r black brown & multi   .25   .25
41   A10   15r purple & multi   .25   .25
43   A10   35r olive & multi   .25   .25
44   A10   50r red & multi   .25   .25
46   A10   100r green & multi   .30   .30
47   A10   160r blue & multi   .50   .50
   Size: 23x36mm
50   A10   500r blue & multi   .75   .75
52   A10   1000r brown & multi   1.25   1.25
   Nos. 40-52 (8)   3.80   3.80
This is an expanding set. Numbers will change if necessary.

No. 33 Overprinted

1994, Apr. 13   Litho.   Perf. 13½
52A   A7   50r multicolored   7.50   7.50

Prehistoric Animals A11

Designs: No. 53, Diatryma. No. 54, Triceratops. No. 55, Anatosaurus. No. 56, Tyrannosaurus. No. 57, Parasaurolophus. No. 58, Incorrectly inscribed "Tyrannosaurus," with

horns, resembling an Ankalysaurus. No. 59, Spinosaurus. No. 60, Stegosaurus.

1994, Sept. 8 Litho. Perf. 13½
53-60 A11 500r Set of 8   7.25 2.50

Issued both in separate sheetlets of nine and together in a se-tenant sheetlet of nine, containing Nos. 53-60 and one label. Values: set of nine sheetlets, $60; se-tenant sheetlet, $40.

No. 37A Surcharged in Green

1995, Mar. 10 Litho. Perf. 12x11½
62 A8a 100r on 1.50r multi   .25 .25
63 A8a 600r on 1.50r multi   .50 .50
64 A8a 1000r on 1.50r multi   .90 .90
65 A8a 5000r on 1.50r multi   4.25 4.25
  a. Strip, #64-65, 2 ea #62-63   9.00 9.00
  Nos. 62-65 (4)   5.90 5.90

Issued in sheets of 36 stamps. Each vertical and horizontal strip has stamps in different order.

For surcharges see Nos. 111-114.

Membership Admissions — A13

Designs: No. 66, Member of UN. No. 67, Member of UPU, vert. No. 68, Member of OSCE (Organization of Security & Cooperation in Europe), vert.

1995, May 4 Litho. Perf. 13½
66 A13 1000r multicolored   1.25 1.00
67 A13 1000r multicolored   1.25 1.00
68 A13 1000r multicolored   1.25 1.00
  Nos. 66-68 (3)   3.75 3.00

Lizards A14

#69, Alsophylax loricatus. #70, Varanus griseus. #71, Phrynocephalus mystaceus. #72, Phrynocephalus helioscopus. #73, Phrynocephalus sogdianus. #74, Teratoscincus scineus.

5000r, Eumeces schneideri.

1995, May 4 Litho. Perf. 13½
69 A14 500r multicolored   .60 .60
70 A14 500r multicolored   .60 .60
71 A14 500r multicolored   .60 .60
72 A14 500r multicolored   .60 .60
73 A14 500r multicolored   .60 .60
74 A14 500r multicolored   .60 .60
  Nos. 69-74 (6)   3.60 3.60

Souvenir Sheet
75 A14 5000r multicolored   6.25 3.75

For overprints see Nos. 77-78.

Souvenir Sheet

End of World War II, 50th Anniv. — A15

1995, May 8 Litho. Perf. 13½
76 A15 5000r multicolored   6.50 6.50
  a. As #76, color diff.   5.50 5.50

On No. 76 emblem in margin is bister, black & red. No. 76a emblem is yellow, black & red with missing letter "E" from second line of text.

No. 70 Ovptd.

No. 71 Ovptd.

1995, Dec. 1 Litho. Perf. 13½
77 A14 500r on #70   4.25 4.25
78 A14 500r on #71   4.25 4.25

Singapore '95 (#77), Beijing '95 (#78).

New Natl. Arms — A16

1995, Dec. 20
79 A16 1r olive & multi   .30 .30
80 A16 2r brown & multi   .30 .30
81 A16 5r green & multi   .30 .30
82 A16 12r red & multi   .50 .50
83 A16 40r green blue & multi   1.00 1.00
  Nos. 79-83 (5)   2.40 2.40

Birds A17

Designs: No. 84, Syrrhaptes tibetana. No. 85, Perdix daurica turcomana. No. 86, Tetraogallus tibetanus. No. 87, Otis undulata macqueeni. No. 88, Larus brunnicephalus. No. 89, Anser indicus.

600r, Phasianus colchicus.

1996, Feb. 1
84 A17 200r multicolored   1.40 1.40
85 A17 200r multicolored   1.40 1.40
86 A17 200r multicolored   1.40 1.40
87 A17 200r multicolored   1.40 1.40
88 A17 200r multicolored   1.40 1.40
89 A17 200r multicolored   1.40 1.40
  Nos. 84-89 (6)   8.40 8.40

Souvenir Sheet
90 A17 600r multicolored   6.75 6.75

Two each of Nos. 84-89 were issued in sheet of 12 + label.

UN, 50th Anniv. A18

Designs: 100r, UN headquarters, New York. 500r, Headquarters at night.

1996
90A A18 100r multicolored   1.00 1.00
Souvenir Sheet
90B A14 500r multicolored   4.00 4.00
  Issued: 100r, 4/10; 500r, 2/1.

Souvenir Sheet

Save the Aral Sea — A19

Designs: a, Felis caracal. b, Salmo trutta aralensis. c, Hyaena hyaena. d, Pseudoscaphirhynchus kaufmanni. e, Aspiolucius esocinus.

1996, May 3 Litho. Perf. 14
91 A19 100r Sheet of 5, #a.-e.   6.00 6.00

See Kazakhstan No. 145, Kyrgyzstan No. 107, Turkmenistan No. 52, Uzbekistan No. 113.

A20

A20a

Designs: Nos. 92-95, 98, Otocolobus manul (different views). No. 96, Felis chaus oxiana. No. 97, Felix lynx isabellina.

1996, June 28 Litho. Perf. 13½
92 A20 100r brown & multi   2.00 2.00
93 A20 100r yellow & multi   2.00 2.00
94 A20 150r blue & multi   2.00 2.00
95 A20 150r lilac & multi   2.00 2.00
96 A20 200r multicolored   2.00 2.00
97 A20 200r multicolored   2.00 2.00
  Nos. 92-97 (6)   12.00 12.00

Souvenir Sheet
98 A20a 500r multicolored   8.00 8.00

World Wildlife Fund (#92-95).

1996 Summer Olympic Games, Atlanta A21

1996, July 12 Litho. Perf. 13½
99 A21 200r Judo   1.90 1.90
100 A21 200r Diving   1.90 1.90
101 A21 200r Hammer throw   1.90 1.90
102 A21 200r Soccer   1.90 1.90
103 A21 200r Pierre de
          Coubertin   1.90 1.90
  Nos. 99-103 (5)   9.50 9.50

Kamol Khujandi, Poet — A22

1996, Sept. 7 Litho. Perf. 13½
104 A22 500r Cyrillic name
          14mm long   5.00 5.00
  a. Cyrillic name 13mm long   11.00 11.00
105 A22 500r English inscriptions   5.00 5.00

Central Asian Postal Union, 5th Anniv. A23

1996, Dec. 25 Perf. 12¾
106 A23 100r multicolored   5.50 5.50

Mountains A24

1997, July 16 Perf. 13x12¾
107 A24 100r Communism Peak   1.50 1.50
108 A24 100r Peak Korzhenevskoj   1.50 1.50
109 A24 100r Lenin Peak   1.50 1.50
  a. Strip of 3, #107-109   6.50 6.50
Souvenir Sheet
110 A24 500r Mountain climber   6.50 6.50

Nos. 62-65 Srchd.

1997, Oct. 27 Litho. Perf. 12x11½
111 A8a (A) on 100r #62   1.00 1.00
112 A8a (A) on 600r #63   1.00 1.00
113 A8a (A) on 1000r #64   1.00 1.00
114 A8a (A) on 5000r #65   1.00 1.00
  a. Strip, #113-114, 2 ea #111-112   6.00 6.00
  Nos. 111-114 (4)   4.00 4.00

A25

Traditional Costumes: #115, Woman with red shawl draped over head, carrying pitcher. #116, Woman in long formal dress, cape, tiara. #117, Man wearing long striped coat. #118, Man wearing long blue coat.

1998, Feb. 20 Litho. Perf. 12½x13
115 A25 100r multicolored   1.00 1.00
116 A25 100r multicolored   1.00 1.00
117 A25 150r multicolored   1.50 1.50
  a. Pair, #115, 117   2.50 2.50
118 A25 150r multicolored   1.50 1.50
  a. Pair, #116, 118   2.50 2.50
  Nos. 115-118 (4)   5.00 5.00

Handicrafts — A26

1998, Feb. 20 Litho. Perf. 12¾
119 A26 30r Urn   .50 .50
119A A26 100r Cradles   1.50 1.50

Size: 64x64mm

Imperf

120	A26	300r Ceramic tile	4.00	4.00
	Nos. 119-120 (3)		6.00	6.00

A27

Flowers: 12r, Tulipa greigii. 30r, Crocus korolkowii. 70r, Iris darwasica. 150r, Petilium eduardii. 300r, Juno nicolai.

1998, Apr. 3   Litho.   Perf. 12½x13

121	A27	12r multicolored	.40	.40
122	A27	30r multicolored	.60	.60
123	A27	70r multicolored	1.25	1.25
124	A27	150r multicolored	2.75	2.75
a.	Sheet of 4, #121-124		5.50	5.50
	Nos. 121-124 (4)		5.00	5.00

Souvenir Sheet

125	A27	300r multicolored	5.00	5.00

Stamps in No. 124a have margins continuing the background design of the sheet.

Butterflies
A28

12r, Catocala timur. 30r, Celerio chamyla apocyni. 70r, Colias sieversi. 150r, Papilio alexanor.
300r, Anthocharis tomyris.

1998, Apr. 3   Perf. 13x12½

126	A28	12r multicolored	.75	.75
127	A28	30r multicolored	.90	.90
128	A28	70r multicolored	1.25	1.25
129	A28	150r multicolored	2.50	2.50
a.	Sheet of 4, #126-129		7.00	7.00
	Nos. 126-129 (4)		5.40	5.40

Souvenir Sheet

130	A28	300r multicolored	6.50	6.50

Stamps of No. 129a have margins continuing the background design of the sheet.

Gems
A29

1998, Aug. 21   Litho.   Perf. 13x12¾

131	A29	1r Sapphire	.25	.25
132	A29	1r Ruby	.25	.25
133	A29	12r Lapis lazuli	.35	.35
134	A29	12r Tourmaline	.35	.35
135	A29	150r Spinel	1.90	1.90
136	A29	150r Amethyst	1.90	1.90
a.	Sheet of 6, #131-136, + 2 labels		5.00	5.00
	Nos. 131-136 (6)		5.00	5.00

Souvenir Sheet

137	A29	350r Agate	5.25	5.25

Bobojon Ghafurov,
Academician
(1908-98) — A30

1998, Aug. 21   Perf. 12¾x13

138	A30	12r blue & multi	.30	.30
139	A30	150r red & multi	2.10	2.10

Each printed in sheets of 10.

Aleksander Pushkin (1799-1837),
Russian Poet — A31

100r, Self-portrait drawing. 270r, Painting by Kiprensky.

1999, June   Litho.   Perf. 13¼x13½

140		100r multicolored	.75	.75
141		270r multicolored	2.25	2.25
a.	A31 Pair, #140-141		3.00	3.00

For surcharges see Nos. 332-335.

"ILLEGAL" STAMPS

Tajikistan postal officials have declared as "illegal" the following items.

Sheets of nine stamps of various denominations depicting:

Elvis Presley, Barry White, Michael Douglas, Robert DeNiro, Grace Kelly, the television show "Ally McBeal," Harry Potter, Batman, Superman (two different sheets), Warner Brothers cartoon characters, U.S. Political Cartoons concerning the 2000 Presidential election, Mushrooms, Mushrooms in Art, Major League Baseball players, Sydney 2002 Olympic Games (two different sheets), Various golfers, U.S. Open Golf Championship, Golfer Eduardo Romero, Tiger Woods (two different sheets), Pope John Paul II, and Masonic emblems.

Sheet of 3 stamps of various denominations depicting Marilyn Monroe.

A32

A32a

A32b

1999, June 5   Litho.   Perf. 13½

142	A32	(40r) multi	.30	.30
143	A32a	(100r) multi	.80	.80
144	A32b	(270r) multi	1.90	1.90
	Nos. 142-144 (3)		3.00	3.00

For surcharge see No. 358.

Samanid
Dynasty — A33

1999, Aug.   Litho.   Perf. 12¾x13

145	A33	30r Lion figurine	.25	.25
146	A33	50r Round emblem	.45	.45
147	A33	100r Handled figurine	.90	.90
148	A33	270r Three figurines	2.50	2.50
	Nos. 145-148 (4)		4.10	4.10

Souvenir Sheet

149	A33	500r King	5.50	5.50
a.	Sheet, #149, 2 ea #145-148		10.00	10.00

Samanid Dynasty, 1100th
Anniv. — A34

No. 150: a, 100r, King. b, 500r, Pres. Emomali Rakhmonov.

1999, Oct.   Litho.   Perf. 13½x13

150	A34	Sheet of 2, #a.-b.	11.00	11.00

Mushrooms
A35

Designs: Nos. 151, 153a, 100r, Pleurotus eryngii. Nos. 152, 153b, 270r, Lepista nuda. 500r, Morchella steppicola.

1999, Nov.   Perf. 13¼x13

151	A35	100r multi	1.25	1.25
152	A35	270r multi	4.00	4.00

Miniature Sheet

153	A35	Sheet, 2 ea #153a-153b	3.75	3.75

Souvenir Sheet

154	A35	500r multi	3.00	3.00

Nos. 151-152 have white borders, and Nos. 153a-153b have borders which continue the sheet's central design.
For surcharge see No. 229.

Fish — A36

Designs: 40r, Ophiocephalus argus. 100r, Barbus brachycephalus. 230r, Schizopygopsis stoliczkai. 270r, Pseudoscaphirhynchus fedtschenkoi.
500r, Pseudoscaphirhynchus kaufmanni.

2000   Litho.   Perf. 13¼x13

155-158	A36	Set of 4	4.25	4.25
158a		Souvenir sheet, #155-158	5.00	5.00

Souvenir Sheet

159	A36	500r multi	5.00	5.00

On Nos. 158-159, Pseudoscaphirhynchus is misspelled "Pseudoscaphihynchus."
For surcharge see No. 218.

UPU, 125th
Anniv. (in
1999) — A37

2000

160	A37	270r multi	1.25	1.25

100 Dinars = 1 Somoni (2000)

Birds of
Prey
A38

Designs: 10d, Pandion haliaetus. 27d, Aquila chrysaetus, vert. 50d, Gyps himalayensis. 70d, Circaetus ferox, vert. 1s, Falco peregrinus, vert.

2001, Jan. 23   Litho.   Perf. 14

161-164	A38	Set of 4	6.75	6.75

Souvenir Sheet

165	A38	1s multi	4.25	4.25

No. 165 contains one 42x56mm stamp. Dated 2000.

Chess — A39

Designs: 15d, Mikhail Botvinnik. 41d, Bobby Fischer.
No. 168: a, 10d, Wilhelm Steinitz. b, 25d, Chess board, five people. c, 50d, José Raul Capablanca. d, 70d, Emanuel Lasker. e, 90d, Chess board, four people. f, 1s, Alexander Alekhine.

2001, May 29   Perf. 14¼x14

166-167	A39	Set of 2	3.00	3.00

Souvenir Sheet

168	A39	Sheet of 6, #a-f	10.00	10.00

No. 26 Surcharged in Green, Red or Black

a

b

c

2001, June 4   Perf. 13½

169	A6(a)	(6d) multi (G)	.65	.65
170	A6(b)	(15d) multi (R)	1.25	1.25
171	A6(c)	(41d) multi (Bk)	3.75	3.75
	Nos. 169-171 (3)		5.65	5.65

Souvenir Sheet

Satellite Communications — A40

2001, July 25   Perf. 13¼x13

172	A40	1.50s multi	3.75	3.75

For overprint, see No. 408.

Souvenir Sheets

Nurec Hydroelectric Station — A41

Pres. Emomali Rakhmonov — A42

Independence, 10th Anniv. — A43

No. 175: a, 41d, Map, flag and arms (29x29mm). b, 54d, Emblem (29x29mm). c, 95d, Ratification of constitution (49x29mm).

2001, Sept. 7   **Perf. 13¼x13¾**
173   A41   2.50s multi   30.00   30.00
           Perf. 12¾x13¼
174   A42   3s multi   35.00   35.00
           Perf. 14x13¾
175   A43   Sheet of 3, #a-c 25.00   25.00
      Independence, 10th anniv.

Tajikistan postal officials have declared as "illegal" the following items:
     Sheets of nine stamps of various denominations depicting Bruce Lee, Michael Jordan, Osama bin Laden, Captain America, Fantastic Four, Queen Mother's 100th Birthday, Formula 1 Racing, Motor Sports and the Netherlands Royal Wedding.
     Sheets of six stamps of various denominations depicting Pope John Paul II and Motorcycle racers.
     Sheet of three stamps of various denominations depicting Pope John Paul II.

Transportation — A44

Designs: 1s, Tu-154M Airplane.
No. 177: a, 41d, Vehicles on road. b, 90d, Locomotive.

2001, Dec. 12   **Litho.**   **Perf. 14x13¼**
176   A44   1s multi   2.75   2.75
           Souvenir Sheet
177   A44   Sheet of 3, #176,
             177a, 177b   6.50   6.50

Commonwealth of Independent States, 10th Anniv. — A45

2001, Dec. 17   **Perf. 14¼x14**
178   A45   50d multi   2.00   2.00

Souvenir Sheet

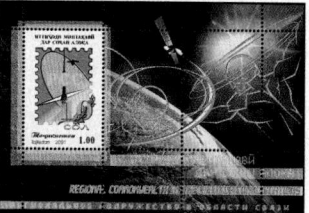

Regional Communications Accord — A46

2001, Dec. 17
179   A46   1s multi + 2 labels   3.50   3.50
      For overprint, see No. 407.

Avesta, 2700th Anniv. — A47

Zoroastrian: 2d, Goddess Anahita. 3d, Priest.
No. 182: a, 70d, Goddess Haoma. b, 90d, God Farroh. c, 1s, God Surush. d, 2s, Goddess Din.

2002, Jan. 1   **Litho.**   **Perf. 10**
180-181 A47   Set of 2   2.00   2.00
          Souvenir Sheet
182   A47   Sheet of 4, #a-d   13.50   13.50
     No. 182 contains four 27x44mm stamps. Dated 2001.

Miniature Sheet

UN High Commissioner for Refugees, 50th Anniv. (in 2001) — A48

No. 183: a, Mothers holding children, refugees. b, Military helicopter, sun, refugees. c, Cloud, rainbow, moon, soldier, child.

2002, Jan. 1
183   A48   50d Sheet of 3, #a-c   5.25   5.25
      Dated 2001.

Flora and Fauna of Central Asia — A49

No. 184: a, Bird facing right. b, Bird facing left. c, Mushrooms and snail. d, Rodent. e, Butterfly. f, Butterfly and tulip. g, Cat. h, Cat and tulip.

2002, Apr. 12   **Litho.**   **Perf. 13¾x13½**
184   Miniature sheet of 8   9.00   9.00
  a.   A49   6d multi   .50   .50
  b.   A49   15d multi   .50   .50
  c.   A49   41d multi   .50   .50
  d.   A49   50d multi   .60   .60
  e.   A49   95d multi   1.10   1.10
  f.-h. A49   1.50s any single   1.75   1.75
     No. 184 exists imperf. Value, $20.

Worldwide Fund for Nature (WWF) — A50

Reed cats: a, 1s, Two cats. b, 1.50s, One cat walking. c, 2s, One cat resting. d, 2s, Three kittens.

2002, Apr. 12   **Perf. 14x14¼**
185   A50   Block of 4, #a-d   7.00   7.00
  e.   Sheet, 2 #185   16.00   16.00

Dushanbe Zoo, 40th Anniv. — A51

Designs: 2d, Pan troglodytes. 3d, Cervus nippon hortulorum. 10d, Panthera tigris altaice. 41d, Diceros bicornis michaeli. 50d, Giraffa camelopardis reticulata. 1s, Panthera leo.

2002, Aug. 29   **Litho.**   **Perf. 14¼x14**
186-191 A51   Set of 6   5.75   5.75

Souvenir Sheet

Navruz — A52

No. 192: a, 1s, Wheat bundle. b, 50d, Dancers in red costumes. c, 1s, Dancer in purple costume.

2002, Aug. 29
192   A52   Sheet of 3, #a-c   5.00   5.00

A53   A54

Istravashan, 2500th Anniv.
A55   A56

2002, Sept. 6
193   A53   50d brown & multi   1.00   1.00
194   A54   50d green & multi   1.00   1.00
195   A55   50d brown & multi   1.00   1.00
196   A56   50d green & multi   1.00   1.00
     Nos. 193-196 (4)   4.00   4.00

No. 168 Overprinted "2002" on Stamps and With Text in Margin
Souvenir Sheet

Designs as before.

2002, Sept. 20   **Litho.**   **Perf. 14¼x14**
197   A39   Sheet of 6, #a-f   11.00   11.00
     No. 197 exists imperf. Value $300.
     No. 197 also exists with violet overprint. Value: perf, $30; imperf $350.

Tajikistan postal officials have declared as "illegal" the following items.

Sheets of nine stamps of various denominations depicting: 20th Century Dreams (6 different sheets), Elephants and Rotary Intl. emblem, Owls, mushrooms and Rotary International emblem, Pandas, Chess, The Beatles, Locomotives, Princess Diana, the movie The Blair Witch Project, Defenders of Peace and Freedom, 2002 Brazilian World Cup Soccer Team, Harry Potter, Cartoon characters from South Park (Christmas), Warner Brothers Cartoon Characters (Christmas).

Sheets of six stamps of various denominations depicting Pokemon characters (eight sheets), Pope John Paul II, Dinosaurs.

Sheet of three stamps of various denominations depicting Elvis Presley.

Souvenir sheets of one stamp with 25.00 denomination depicting Harry Potter (2 different sheets), Penguins,

Souvenir sheet of one stamp of one with 20.00 denomination depicting Pope John Paul and New York fireman.

New Year 2002 (Year Of the Horse) — A57

No. 198: a, 2d, Thoroughbred racing. b, 3d, Harness racing. c, 95d, Troika. d, 95d, Polo.

No. 199: a, 50d, Dressage. b, 50d, Fox hunting. c, 1s, Steeplechase. d, 1s, Show jumping.

1.50s, Horses in circus act, vert.

2002, Oct. 15 Litho. Perf. 14x14¼
Blocks of 4, #a-d
198-199 A57 Set of 2   8.00 8.00
Souvenir Sheet
Perf. 14¼x14
200 A57 1.50s multi + 2 labels   4.25 4.25

Oriental Bazaar — A58

No. 201: a, Man in donkey cart. b, Man on donkey. c, Melon vendor. d, Man cooking shashliks.

2002, Dec. 25 Litho. Perf. 14¼x14
201 A58 65d Block of 4, #a-d   5.50 5.50

Traditional Sports A59

Designs: 1d, Archery. 20d, Horse racing. 53d, Polo. 65d, Stone throwing. 1s, Buzkashi. 1.24s, Wrestling.

2002, Dec. 25 Perf. 14x14¼
202-207 A59 Set of 6   6.00 6.00

Lunar Calendar — A60

Designs: 53d, Sun and zodiac animals. 65d, Zodiac animals and ram. 1s, Ram in circle. 1.50s, Ram.

2003, Mar. 11 Perf. 14¼x14
208-210 A60 Set of 3   5.50 5.50
Souvenir Sheet
211 A60 1.50s multi + 2 labels   4.50 4.50

Monument to Ismail Somoni — A61

2003, Mar. 11 Perf. 13¼x14
212 A61 1d emerald   .80 .80
213 A61 2d red violet   .80 .80
214 A61 3d blue green   .80 .80
215 A61 4d purple   .80 .80
216 A61 12d brown   .80 .80
217 A61 20d blue   .80 .80
    Nos. 212-217 (6)   4.80 4.80

No. 158a Surcharged in Purple
Souvenir Sheet

No. 218: a, 8d on 40r, Ophiocephalus argus. b, 20d on 100r, Barbus brachycephalus. c, 53d on 230r, Schizopygopsis stoliczkai. d, 66d on 270r, Pseudoscaphirhynchus fedtschenkoi.

2003, May 12 Litho. Perf. 13¼x13
218 A36 Sheet of 4, #a-d   8.00 8.00

2004 Summer Olympics, Athens and 2008 Summer Olympics, Beijing — A62

No. 219: a, 53d, Archery. b, 1s, Track and field. c, 1.23s, Soccer. d, 2s, Gymnastics.

2003, May 20 Perf. 14x13½
219 A62 Sheet of 4, #a-d, +
          2 labels   10.00 10.00
No. 219 exists imperf. with additional designs in margin. Value $32.50.
For overprint, see No. 389.

Philatelic Exhibitions and Fauna — A63

No. 220: a, 8d, 16th Asian Intl. Stamp Exhibition, China. b, 20d, Panthera tigris. c, 53d, Inachis io. d, 66d, Bangkok 2003 World Philatelic Exhibition. e, 1s, Rupicapra rupicapra. f, 1.50s, Ailuropoda melanoleuca. g, 1.50s, Leontopithecus rosalia. h, 2s, Elephas maximus.

2003, May 20
220 A63 Sheet of 8, #a-h   14.00 14.00
No. 220 exists imperf. Value $35.
For overprint see No. 341.

Intl. Forum on Fresh Water — A64

Designs: No. 221, 1.50s, Peak of Moskvin. No. 222, 1.50s, Iskanderkul.

2003, June 7 Perf. 13½
221-222 A64 Set of 2   6.00 6.00
Nos. 221-222 were printed setenant, both vertically and horizontally, in one sheet.

Famous Men — A65

Designs: No. 223, 1.23s, Nosir Khusrav (1004-88), poet. No. 224, 1.23s, Sadridin Aini (1878-1954), writer.

2003, Sept. 1
223-224 A65 Set of 2   4.75 4.75

Intl. Association of Academies of Science, 10th Anniv. — A66

No. 225: a, Head, satellite dish, airplane, chemicals. b, Association emblem, cosmonaut, robotic hand, computer.

2003, Sept. 1
225 A66 1.23s Horiz. pair, #a-b 5.50 5.50

Intl. Year of Fresh Water — A67

Children's art: a, Fish above lake. b, Sun, river, tree and hills. c, River, hills and trees. d, Waterfalls.

2003, Oct. 20 Perf. 14x14¼
226 A67 66d Block of 4, #a-d   5.00 5.00

Racing Airplanes — A68

No. 227: a, Aero L-29A Delfin Akrobat. b, Yak-55. c, Cessna 172. d, SIAI-Marchetti SF-260. e, Europa XS. f, MBB BO 209 Monsun. g, Mudry Cap 10. h, Soko 2.

2003, Oct. 28 Perf. 14x13½
227 A68 1s Sheet of 8, #a-h   14.00 14.00
No. 227 exists imperf. Value $40.

Fauna of Central Asia — A69

No. 228: a, 8d, Mimas tiliae. 20d, Mustela erminea. 53d, Testudo horsfieldii. 64d, Mantis religiosa. 1.23s, Lanius collurio. 1.27s, Canis aureus. 1.76s, Capra falconeri. 2.29s, Alcedo atthis.

2003, Oct. 28
228 A69 Sheet of 8, #a-h   15.00 15.00
No. 228 exists imperf. Value $40.

No. 153 Surcharged in Red

2004, Jan. 4 Litho. Perf. 13¼x13
229 A35 Miniature sheet, 2
          each #a-b   7.00 7.00
  a. 20d on 100r #153a   1.75 1.75
  b. 66d on 270r #153b   3.25 3.25
No. 229 exists surcharged in green. Value, $21.

National Dances — A70

No. 230 — Various dancers and frame color of: a, Brown. b, Purple. c, Green. d, Bright pink.

2004, Jan. 19   Litho.   Perf. 14¼x14
230 A70 53d Block of 4, #a-d   4.75 4.75

Adjacent blocks in sheet are tete-beche. No. 230 exists with visible tagging that reads "Belarus."

No. 28
Surcharged in
Black and Red

2004, Apr. 26   Litho.   Perf. 13½
231 A6 A on 50r multi   .90   .90

Sold for 8d on day of issue.

No. 31
Surcharged in
Black

2004, Apr. 26
232 A6 b on 160r multi   .90   .90

Sold for 20d on day of issue.

Miniature Sheet

New Year 2004 (Year of the
Monkey) — A71

No. 233: a, 1s, Monkey covering eyes. b, 1.20s, Monkey covering ears. c, 1.50s, Monkey covering mouth.

2004, Aug. 13   Perf. 13¾x13½
233 A71 Sheet of 3, #a-c   6.50 6.50

Dushanbe
Buildings — A72

Designs: 1d, National Circus. 2d, Ferdowsi National Library. 3d, National Bank. 8d, Finance Ministry. 20d, Communications Ministry. 50d, City Government Building.

2004, Aug. 13   Perf. 13¾x13¼
234 A72 1d multi   .60   .60
235 A72 2d multi   .60   .60
236 A72 3d multi   .60   .60
237 A72 8d multi   .60   .60
238 A72 20d multi   .60   .60
239 A72 50d multi   1.25   1.25
      Nos. 234-239 (6)   4.25   4.25

FIFA (Fédération Internationale de
Football Association), Cent. — A73

Designs: 50d, Goalie, World Cup. 70d, FIFA General Secretariat Building, Zurich. 1s, Player with red shirt, vert. 2s, Player with yellow shirt, vert.

Perf. 13½x13¾, 13¾x13½
2004, Aug. 30
240-243 A73 Set of 4   8.00 8.00

Nos. 240-243 exist imperf. Value, set $35.

Miniature Sheet

2004 Summer Olympics,
Athens — A74

No. 244: a, 30d, Wrestling. b, 45d, Track. c, 55d, Basketball. d, 60d, Shooting. e, 75d, Equestrian. f, 80d, Women's archery. g, 1.50s, Soccer. h, 2.50s, Rhythmic gymnastics.

2004, Sept. 6   Perf. 14x13½
244 A74 Sheet of 8, #a-h   13.00 13.00

No. 244 exists imperf. Value $35.

Miniature Sheet

Dushanbe Circus — A75

No. 245: a, 20d, Circus building. b, 50d, Tightrope walkers. c, 1s, Elephant and trainer. d, 1.10s, Genie, lamp and cat. e, 1.50s, Man riding donkey, dog. f, 1.70s, Bareback rider.

2004, Dec. 21   Perf. 14x13½
245 A75 Sheet of 6, #a-f   10.00 10.00

No. 245 exists imperf. Value $25.

Miniature Sheet

Vehicles — A76

No. 246: a, Fire engine. b, Ambulance and helicopter. c, Police cars. d, Postal van and train. e, Wrecker and damaged car. f, School bus.

2004, Dec. 21
246 A76 1s Sheet of 6, #a-f   10.00 10.00

No. 246 exists imperf. Value $25.

Miniature Sheet

Dushanbe as Capital City, 80th
Anniv. — A77

No. 247: a, 20d, New apartment buildings on Rudaki Ave. b, 46d, Aini State Opera and Ballet Theater. c, 53d, National Bank. d, 62d, City Government Building. e, 1.27s, Parliament Building. f, 1.76s, Presidential Palace.

2004, Nov. 16   Litho.   Perf. 11½
247 A77 Sheet of 6, #a-f   14.00 14.00

Musical Instruments — A78

No. 248: a, Gejak and bow. b, Adirna.

2004, Nov. 29   Perf. 11½x11¾
248 A78 2.50s Horiz. pair, #a-b 11.00 11.00

See Kazakhstan No. 470.

Fruit — A79

Designs: Nos. 249, 255, Apples. Nos. 250, 256, Apricots. Nos. 251, 257, Plums. Nos. 252, 258, Pears. Nos. 253, 259, Quince. Nos. 254, 260, Pomegranates.

2005, Mar. 19   Perf. 14x14¼
Panel Color
White Background
249 A79 6d lilac   .25   .25
250 A79 7d blue   .25   .25
251 A79 8d brn orange   .25   .25
252 A79 10d rose   .30   .25
253 A79 11d green   .30   .25
254 A79 12d yel orange   .30   .25
Pale Yellow Background
255 A79 20d purple   .50   .45
256 A79 50d violet   1.00   .90
257 A79 55d red   1.10   1.00
258 A79 75d red violet   1.50   1.25
259 A79 2s dk olive   4.00   3.50
260 A79 3s brown red   6.00   5.50
      Nos. 249-260 (12)   15.75 14.10

Lake Sarez — A80

No. 261: a, Katta Nardjonoi Bay (denomination in white). b, Iriht Bay (denomination in black).

2005, Apr. 4   Perf. 13½
261 A80 2s Horiz. pair, #a-b   7.00 7.00

Souvenir Sheet

End of World War II, 60th
Anniv. — A81

No. 262: a, 18d. b, 75d.

2005, Apr. 15   Perf. 14¼x14
262 A81   Sheet of 2, #a-b, +
           central label   4.25 4.25

Souvenir Sheet

Hunting — A82

No. 263: a, 1s, Hunter facing left. b, 1.70s, Hunter facing right. c, 2.30s, Like 1s.

2005, July 27   Perf. 13¾x13½
263 A82 Sheet of 3, #a-c   10.00 10.00

Compare with Type A89.

Airbus A-380 — A83

No. 264 — Inset of airplane and: a, 1.50s, Left wing. b, 1.50s, Nose. c, 1.80s, Tail. d, 1.80s, Right wing.

2005, July 27   Perf. 13½x14
264 A83 Block of 4, #a-d   12.50 12.50

No. 264 exists imperf. Value $25.

Miniature Sheet

Mammals — A84

No. 265: a, 20d, Hyena on cliff. b, 20d, Turkestan lynx on tree branch. c, 75d, Badger. d, 75d, Fox. e, 80d, Snow leopard. f, 1s, Bear. g, 1.50s, Leopard. h, 1.80s, Tiger.

2005, Aug. 10   Perf. 13½x14
265 A84 Sheet of 8, #a-h   12.50 12.50

No. 265 exists imperf. Value $25.
For overprint, see No. 370.

Worldwide Fund for Nature (WWF) — A85

No. 266 — Various views of bharals: a, 1s. b, 1.45s. c, 1.70s. d, 2.25s.

2005, Aug. 26   **Perf. 13½x14**
266 A85   Block of 4, #a-d   5.00 5.00

No. 266 exists imperf. Value $17.50.

Avicenna (980-1037), Scientist — A86

2005, Oct. 3   **Perf. 13¼x13¾**
267 A86   6d Prus bl & blk   .25 .25
268 A86   8d brn & black   .25 .25
269 A86   10d purple & lilac   .25 .25
270 A86   12d blue   .45 .45
271 A86   50d blue green   1.40 1.40
272 A86   1s orange   3.00 3.00
    Nos. 267-272 (6)   5.60 5.60

World Post Day — A87

2005, Oct. 3   **Perf. 13¼x13¾**
273 A87   5d blue & black   .30 .30
274 A87   7d brown   .30 .30
275 A87   11d green & lt grn   .30 .30
276 A87   20d purple   .50 .50
277 A87   55d gray blue   1.50 1.50
278 A87   75d orange   3.25 3.25
    Nos. 273-278 (6)   6.15 6.15

Mountains — A88

No. 279: a, 1s, Pendjikent. b, 1.50s, Muminabod. c, 2s, Pamir. d, 2.50s, Isfara.

2005, Dec. 6   **Perf. 13½**
279 A88   Block of 4, #a-d   12.50 12.50

Souvenir Sheet

Hunting — A89

No. 280: a, Hunter holding falcon. b, Hunter killing leopard.

2005, Dec. 31   **Perf. 13¾x13½**
280 A89 2.50s Sheet of 2, #a-
    b, + central la-
    bel   10.00 10.00

Compare with type A82.
No. 280 exists imperf. Value $30.

Fairy Tales — A90

No. 281: a, 55d, The Peasant and the Bear. b, 75d, Three Brothers. c, 2s, Iradj-bogatyr. d, 3s, The Gold Fox.

2006, Mar. 20   **Perf. 14¼x14**
281 A90   Block of 4, #a-d   10.50 10.50
Stamps in vertical columns are tete-beche.

Traditional Costumes — A91

No. 282: a, 75d, Man from Samarkand wearing red headdress. b, 75d, Man from Sugd wearing blue headdress. c, 1s, Woman from Bukhara with arms together. d, 1s, Woman from Kalayhum with arms apart.

2006, June 20   **Litho.**   **Perf. 14¼x14**
282 A91   Block or horiz. strip of
    4, #a-d   6.00 6.00
Printed in sheets of eight containing two of each stamp.

Miniature Sheet

Fauna of Asia — A92

No. 283: a, 8d, Aquila chrysaetos. b, 20d, Panthera tigris longipilis. c, 55d, Hystrix hirsutirostris. d, 70d, Alluropoda melanoleuca. e, 75d, Meles meles. f, 1.60s, Ursus arctos. g, 1.92s, Mustela erminea. h, 2s, Bubo coromandus.

2006, June 29   **Perf. 13¾x13½**
283 A92   Sheet of 8, #a-h   13.00 13.00
No. 283 exists imperf. Value $27.50.

2006 World Cup Soccer Championships, Germany — A93

No. 284: a, 1.50s, Five players. b, 1.50s, Three players and goalie. c, 1.50s, Four players. d, 2s, Three players and goalie, diff.

2006, June 29   **Perf. 13½x13¾**
284 A93   Block of 4, #a-d   10.00 10.00
   e.   Miniature sheet, 2 each
      #284a-284d   20.00 20.00

Souvenir Sheet

Kulob, 2700th Anniv. — A94

No. 285: a, Anniversary emblem, flag of Tajikistan. b, Mausoleum of Mir Said Ali Hamadoni.

2006, Aug. 30
285 A94 2s Sheet of 2, #a-b   8.00 8.00

Miniature Sheet

Independence, 15th Anniv. — A95

No. 286: a, 1.50s, Presidential Palace. b, 2.50s, Arms of Tajikistan. c, 3s, Flag of Tajikistan, Pres. Emomali Rakhmonov.

2006, Aug. 30   **Perf. 14x14¼**
286 A95   Sheet of 3, #a-c, +
    3 labels   13.00 13.00

Souvenir Sheet

Commonwealth of Independent States, 15th Anniv. — A96

No. 287: a, Emblem of Commonwealth of Independent States, flags of member nations. b, Emblem of Regional Communications Commonwealth.

2006, Sept. 12   **Perf. 14¼x14**
287 A96 1.50s Sheet of 2, #a-b,
    + central label   6.50 6.50

Cotton — A97

2006, Dec. 15   **Perf. 13½x13¾**
Background Color
288 A97   5d olive green   .35 .35
289 A97   6d rose   .35 .35
290 A97   7d lilac   .35 .35
291 A97   8d light blue   .35 .35
292 A97   20d green   .55 .55
293 A97   75d blue   1.50 1.50
    Nos. 288-293 (6)   3.45 3.45

Headdresses — A98

No. 294 — Various headdresses with gray geometrical design at: a, LR. b, LL. c, UR. d, UL.

2006, Dec. 28   **Perf. 14x14¼**
294 A98 1.50s Block of 4, #a-d   9.50 9.50
No. 294 exists imperf. Value $25.

Dogs — A99

Designs: 20d, West Siberian laika. 55d, Perdiguero de burgos. 75d, Afghan hound. 1s, Sredneasiatckaia ovtcharka. 2s, Saluki. 3s, Tosa.

2006, Dec. 28   **Perf. 13¾x13½**
295-300 A99   Set of 6   12.00 12.00
Nos. 295-300 exist imperf. Value, set $25.

No. 32 Surcharged

Methods and Perfs As Before
2007, Mar. 31
301 A6a 75d on 160r #32   2.25 2.25

Souvenir Sheet

Snakes — A100

No. 302: a, Echis carinatus. b, Naja oxiana.

2007, Apr. 30   **Litho.**   **Perf. 14**
302 A100 2s Sheet of 2, #a-b   10.00 10.00

A101

A102

Mevlana (c. 1207-73),
Poet — A103

2007, Aug. 30   **Perf. 13¼x13¾**
303	A101	5d red	.30	.30
304	A101	10d bright blue	.30	.30
305	A101	20d green	.30	.30
306	A101	(25d) dark blue	.45	.45
307	A102	(1.35s) brown violet	2.25	2.25
308	A103	(2.15s) red violet	3.75	3.75
		Nos. 303-308 (6)	7.35	7.35

Jewelry — A104

No. 309: a, 50d, Earring. b, 2s, Necklace. c,
2.50s, Necklace, diff. d, 3s, Earring, diff.

2007, Dec. 18   **Perf. 14¼x14**
309	A104	Block of 4, #a-d	11.00	11.00

Miniature Sheet

Transportation — A105

No. 310: a, 50d, Camels. b, 60d, Steam
locomotive. c, 70d, Airplane and helicopter. d,
80d, Pickup truck. e, 90d, Donkey cart. f,
1.50s, Train. g, 1.70s, Bus. h, 2s, Dump truck.

2007, Dec. 27   **Perf. 14x13½**
310	A105	Sheet of 8, #a-h	11.00	11.00

Birds — A106

Designs: Nos. 311, 317a, 1s, Aquila
chrysaetos. Nos. 312, 317b, 1.10s, Pha-
sianinae. Nos. 313, 317c, 1.20s, Aix galericu-
lata. Nos. 314, 317d, 1.30s, Otididae. Nos.
315, 317e, 1.40s, Falco cherrug. Nos. 316,
317f, 1.60s Haliaeetus albicilla.

2007, Dec. 27   **Perf. 14x13½**
Stamps With White Frames
311-316	A106	Set of 6	12.50	12.50

Stamps With Colored Frames
317	A106	Sheet of 6, #a-f	12.50	12.50

2008
Summer
Olympics,
Beijing
A107

Designs: 1.50s, Soccer. No. 319, 2s, Hammer throw. No. 320, 2s, Judo. No. 321, 2s,
Boxing.

2008, Feb. 28 Litho.   **Perf. 12½x13**
318-321	A107	Set of 4	7.50	7.50
321a		Miniature sheet, 2 each		
		#318-321	15.00	15.00

Cooking
Pot — A108

Pitcher — A109

Pot With
Lid — A110

Pitcher — A111

2008, Mar. 28   **Perf. 14x14¼**
322	A108	20d brown	.35	.35
323	A108	25d dark blue	.45	.45
324	A109	50d purple	.90	.90
325	A109	1s indigo	1.75	1.75
326	A110	1.35s dark green	2.40	2.40
327	A111	2s brown	3.75	3.75
328	A110	2.15s dark blue	4.00	4.00
329	A111	3s dark red	5.50	5.50
		Nos. 322-329 (8)	19.10	19.10

Souvenir Sheet

Intl. Conference on Water Related
Disaster Reduction, Dushanbe — A112

No. 330: a, Avalanche. b, Tornado.

2008, June 19   **Perf. 14¼x14**
330	A112	2.50s Sheet of 2, #a-b,		
		+ label	9.50	9.50

Souvenir Sheet

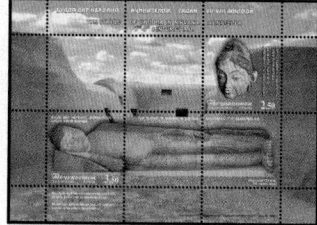

Buddha Statues, Ajinateppa — A113

No. 331: a, 2.50s, Head of Buddha. b,
3.50s, Buddha reclining.

2008, June 19   **Perf. 14x14¼**
331	A113	Sheet of 2, #a-b, +		
		4 labels	10.00	10.00

Nos. 140-141 Surcharged in Black or Red

Methods and Perfs. As Before
2008, July 4   **Black Surcharge**
332		1s on 100r #140	3.25	3.25
333		1s on 100r #141	3.25	3.25
a.		A31 Pair, #332-333	6.50	6.50

Red Surcharge
334		1s on 100r #140	3.25	3.25
335		1s on 100r #141	3.25	3.25
a.		A31 Pair, #334-335	6.50	6.50
		Nos. 332-335 (4)	13.00	13.00

Souvenir Sheet

Rudaki (c. 859-940), Poet — A114

No. 336 — Rudaki facing: a, Right. b, Left.

2008, July 9 Litho.   **Perf. 14¼x14**
336	A114	2.50s Sheet of 2, #a-b,		
		+ label	8.25	8.25

Plants and Insects — A115

No. 337: a, 1.50s, Ribwort and grasshopper.
b, 1.50s, Coltfoot and ladybug. c, 2s, Dandelion and beetle. d, 2s, Calendula and bee.

2008, Sept. 29   **Perf. 14x14¼**
337	A115	Block of 4, #a-d	11.00	11.00

Souvenir Sheet

Snakes — A116

No. 338 — Snake facing: a, Right. b, Left.

2008, Sept. 29   **Perf. 13½x14**
338	A116	2.50s Sheet of 2, #a-b	9.50	9.50

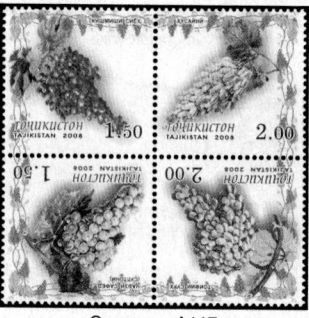

Grapes — A117

No. 339 — Color of grapes: a, 1.50s, Purple
(Djaus). b, 1.50s, Pink (Black sultana). c, 2s,
White (Ladies' fingers). d, 2s, Red (Red Taffi).

2008, Dec. 1   **Perf. 14x14¼**
339	A117	Block of 4, #a-d	10.50	10.50

Musical Instruments — A118

No. 340: a, Gijak of Badahshon. b,
Khoirasan local dotaar.

2008, Dec. 1 Litho.   **Perf. 14x14¼**
340	A118	Horiz. pair +		
		central label	11.00	11.00
a.-b.		3s Either single	5.50	5.50

See Iran No. 2976.

No. 220 Overprinted

Designs as before.

Methods and Perfs As Before
2009, Feb. 1
341	A63	Sheet of 8, #a-h		
		(#220)	14.50	14.50

Souvenir Sheet

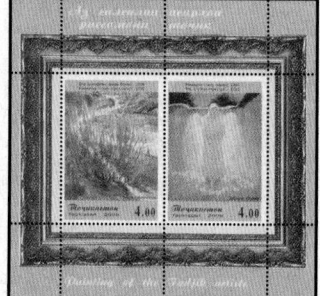

Paintings — A119

No. 342: a, Flowering Indian Lilac — Luchob, by Zuhur Habibuloev. b, My Mother — My wings, by Sabzali Sharif.

2009, Mar. 31 Litho. Perf. 13½
342 A119 4s Sheet of 2, #a-b 11.50 11.50

Imam Azam's Celebration Year — A120

2009, July 28
343 A120 4s multi 5.00 5.00

Worldwide Fund for Nature (WWF) A121

Cervus elaphus bactrianus: 1.50s, Head of doe, bucks fighting. 2s, Buck. 2.50s, Buck, two does. 3s, Two does and fawn.

2009, July 28 Perf. 13½x13¾
344-347 A121 Set of 4 5.50 5.50
347a Sheet of 16, 4 each #344-347 22.00 22.00

Nos. 344-347, 347a exist imperf.

Animals — A122

Designs: No. 348, 1s, Equus przewalskii. No. 349, 1s, Panthera tigris tigris. No. 350, 1.50s, Camelus bactrianus. No. 351, 1.50s, Caracal caracal. No. 352, 2s, Ailuropoda melanoleuca. No. 353, 2s, Macaca fuscata. No. 354, 2.30s, Elephas maximus. No. 355, 2.30s, Ovis vignei.

2009, July 28 Perf. 13¾x13½
348-355 A122 Set of 8 11.00 11.00
355a Sheet of 8, #348-355 11.00 11.00

Nos. 348-355 were each printed in sheets of 9 + label.

Souvenir Sheet

Animal Circus Performers — A123

No. 356: a, Cat on ball. b, Dog balancing ball on nose.

2009, Sept. 14 Perf. 14x14¼
356 A123 3.50s Sheet of 2, #a-b 10.50 10.50

Souvenir Sheet

Tajikistan Glaciers — A124

No. 357 — Glaciers on mountain peaks: a, Abu ali ibn Sino. b, Ismoili Somoni.

2009, Sept. 14 Perf. 13½
357 A124 4s Sheet of 2, #a-b 11.00 11.00

No. 144 Surcharged

Method and Perf. As Before
2009, Dec. 1
358 A32b 15d on (270r) #144 .40 .40

Melons — A125

No. 359: a, 1.50s, Green melon (whole melon and quarter melon), and large green leaves. b, 1.50s, Yellow and brown melon (whole melon and ⅛ melon slice) and gray leaves. c, 2s, Yellow and brown melon (whole melon and half melon) and gray leaves. d, 2s, Yellow and brown melon (whole melon and quarter melon) and large green leaves.

2009, Dec. 3 Litho. Perf. 14x14¼
359 A125 Block of 4, #a-d 10.50 10.50

Stamps of same denomination are se-tenant within the block. No. 359 exists imperf. Value, $20.

Victory in World War II, 65th Anniv. — A126

No. 360: a, 1.35s, Soldiers and airplanes. b, 2.15s, Soviet Union soldiers holding Nazi flags near Kremlin in Moscow.

2010, Mar. 15 Litho. Perf. 14¼x14
360 A126 Pair, #a-b 3.75 3.75

Printed in sheets containing 3 #360a, 2 #360b + label.

Peonies — A127

No. 361 — Peony with butterfly at: a, 2s, Right. b, 3.20s, Left.

2010, Mar. 30 Perf. 12½
361 A127 Pair, #a-b 5.25 5.25
c. Souvenir sheet, #361b 3.25 3.25

Printed in sheets containing 3 each #361a-361b.

Rogun Hydroelectric Project — A128

Designs: 10d, Vakhsh River Dam. 15d, Transmission towers and lines. 20d, Turbines. 10s, Tunnel-boring machine.

2010, May 20 Perf. 13¼x14
362-365 A128 Set of 4 9.25 9.25

Khaje Abdullah Ansari (1006-88), Mystic A129

2010, July 25 Perf. 13½
366 A129 5s multi 5.75 5.75

See Afghanistan No. and Iran No. 3016.

Miniature Sheet

Mammals — A130

No. 367: a, 2.50s, Canis lupus. b, 3s, Lynx lynx. c, 3.50s, Elephas maximus. d, 4.50s, Panthera tigris.

2010, Aug. 2 Perf. 14¼x14
367 A130 Sheet of 4, #a-d + 2 labels 11.50 11.50

Bangkok 2010 Intl. Stamp Exhibition, Portugal 2010 World Philatelic Exhibition.

Souvenir Sheet

Ancient Coins — A131

No. 368: a, 4s, Silver Sasani coin. b, 5s, Gold Shahanshoh Vasudeva coin.

2010, Nov. 19 Perf. 13½x14
368 A131 Sheet of 2, #a-b 11.00 11.00

Souvenir Sheet

Traditional Men's Dances — A132

No. 369: a, Man dancing, old man, boy, birds. b, Three men dancing.

2010, Nov. 19 Perf. 14¼x14
369 A132 4s Sheet of 2, #a-b 10.50 10.50

No. 265 Overprinted

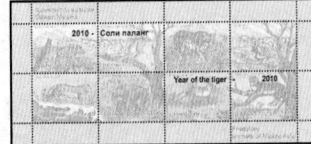

Methods and Perfs As Before
2010, Apr. 30
370 A84 Sheet of 8, #265c, 265e, 265f, 265h, 370a-370d 15.50 15.50
a. 20d "2010 -" on #265a .45 .45
b. 20d Cyrillic text overprinted on #265b .45 .45
c. 75d "Year of the tiger" overprinted on #265d 1.75 1.75
d. 1.50s "- 2010" overprinted on #265g 3.50 3.50

Souvenir Sheet

New Year 2011 (Year of the Rabbit) — A133

No. 371: a, Rabbit and carrots. b, Rabbit and cat.

2011, Apr. 1 Litho. Perf. 14¼x14
371 A133 2s Sheet of 2, #a-b 5.75 5.75

Nos. 18 and 27 Surcharged

Methods and Perfs As Before
2011, Apr. 27
372 A5 10d on 25r #18 .75 .75
373 A6 15d on 35r #27 1.10 1.10

Locomotives — A134

No. 374: a, 1-5-0, 1947. b, 1-4-0, 1912. c, 1-3-1, 1925. d, 2-3-1, 1925.

2011, June 3　Litho.　Perf. 14x14¼
374　A134　1.50s　Block of 4, #a-d　6.25　6.25

Apricot Blossoms — A135

No. 375 — Various blossoms: a, 3.50s. b, 4s.

2011, Aug. 10　　　　　　Perf. 13
375　A135　Horiz. pair, #a-b　5.50　5.50

Miniature Sheet

Independence, 20th Anniv. — A136

No. 376: a, 2.50s, Norak Hydropower Plant (40x28mm). b, 2.50s, Sangtuda Hydropower Plant (40x28mm). c, 2.50s, Rogun Hydropower Plant (40x28mm). d, 3s, President Emomali Rakhmonov (40x84mm).

2011, Aug. 26　　　　　Perf. 14x14¼
376　A136　Sheet of 4, #a-d　12.00　12.00

Souvenir Sheet

Commonweath of Independent States, 20th Anniv. — A137

2011, Aug. 26　　　　Perf. 14¼x14
377　A137　3.50s multi　9.50　9.50

Souvenir Sheet

Regional Communications Commonwealth, 20th Anniv. — A138

2011, Sept. 8
378　A138　2.50s multi　9.25　9.25

Sogdian Terra Cotta Heads — A139

Various terra cotta heads from 5th-8th cent.: 10d, Man with crown. 15d, Head of Rurel. 20d, Female figure in high relief. 25d, King.

2011, Dec. 23　Litho.　Perf. 14x14¼
379-382　A139　Set of 4　1.40　1.40

Lunar Calendar Animals — A140

Designs: 2s, Dragon. 2.50s, Fish.

2012, Mar. 16
383-384　A140　Set of 2　5.25　5.25

A141

Native Costumes — A142

2012, June 19　　　　Perf. 14¼x14
385　A141　1.35s multi　1.90　1.90
386　A142　2.15s multi　3.00　3.00

Miniature Sheet

2012 Summer Olympics, London — A143

No. 387: a, Judo. b, Taekwondo. c, Hammer throw. d, Boxing.

2012, June 19
387　A143　2s Sheet of 4, #a-d　7.75　7.75

Souvenir Sheet

Paintings — A144

No. 388: a, The Pomegranate, by Batyr Allabergenov, 2009. b, Wake Up!, by Rahim Safarov, 2004.

2012, June 19　　　　　　Perf. 13
388　A144　4s Sheet of 2, #a-b　7.25　7.25

No. 219 Overprinted in Blue and Bluish Black

Methods and Perfs As Before
2012, July 26
389　A62　Sheet of 4, #219b,
　　　　　219d, 389a, 389b,
　　　　　+ 2 labels　13.00　13.00
　a.　53d With Cyrillic text over-
　　　printed　1.50　1.50
　b.　1.23s With Cyrillic text over-
　　　printed　3.50　3.50
2012 Summer Olympics, London.

A145

Flowers and Butterflies — A146

No. 390 — Stamps inscribed with flower names: a, 1.60s, Rose and grasshopper. b, 2.50s, Golden daisy and yellow, black and red butterfly. c, 3s, Golden daisy and orange, black and white butterfly. d, 3s, Rose and ladybug.
No. 391 — Stamps inscribed "Butterflies of Central Asia": a, 1.60s, Orange, black and

---

white butterfly on flower. b, 2.50s, Red, black and white butterfly on flower. c, 3s, Blue butterfly on orange flower. d, 3s, Yellow, black and red butterfly on pink flower.

2012, Oct. 25　　　　　Perf. 14x14¼
390　A145　Block of 4, #a-d　9.25　9.25
391　A146　Block of 4, #a-d　9.25　9.25

Singers — A147

No. 392: a, Gurminj Zavqibekov (1929-2003). b, Khikmat Rizo.

2012, Dec. 30　Litho.　Perf. 14x13½
392　A147　3s Pair, #a-b　5.00　5.00

Souvenir Sheet

New Year 2013 (Year of the Snake) — A148

No. 393: a, Snake with crown, denomination at UL. b, Snake wrapped around tree. c, Snake with crown, denomination at UR.

2013, Apr. 11　Litho.　Perf. 14x13½
393　A148　2.50s Sheet of 3, #a-c　6.50　6.50

Cats — A149

Designs: No. 394, 2s, Maine Coon cat (maykun). No. 395, 2s, La Perm cat. No. 396, 2s, British shorthair cat.

2013, Apr. 11　Litho.　Perf. 14x13½
394-396　A149　Set of 3　6.00　6.00
Nos. 394-396 each were printed in sheets of 9 + label.

Worldwide Fund for Nature (WWF) — A150

Mustela altaica: No. 397, 4.50s, Head. No. 398, 4.50s, Standing on rock. No. 399, 5s, Carrying prey. No. 400, 5s, Two animals.

2013, Apr. 22　Litho.　Perf. 14x14¼
397-400　A150　Set of 4　8.25　8.25
400a　　　Sheet of 16, 4 each
　　　　　#397-400　33.00　33.00
Nos. 397-400 each were printed in sheets of 10.

Tajikistan Academy of Science, 20th Anniv. — A151

No. 401 — Emblems and: a, 1.60s, Flasks, books, molecular model, microscope, biological hazard emblem. b, 2.50s, Oil refinery, computer, telephone, satellite, satellite dish.

2013, July 16   Litho.   *Perf. 13*
401   A151   Horiz. pair, #a-b   4.50 4.50

Trains — A152

No. 402: a, EU 733. b, TE 33 A emerging from tunnel, towers in background. c, TE 33 A emerging from tunnel, hill in background. d, TE 33 A on bridge over river.

2013, July 16   Litho.   *Perf. 14x14¼*
402   A152   1.60s Block of 4, #a-d   6.75 6.75

Mobile Communications — A153

Emblems of telecommunications companies, satellite dish, and: 10d, Globe, denomination in blue. 15d, Like 10d, denomination in orange. 1.60s, Presidential palace.

2013, July 16   Litho.   *Perf. 14x14¼*
403-405   A153   Set of 3   3.75 3.75

Transportation — A154

No. 406 — Emblem of Regional Communications Commonwealth and: a, Aiplane flying right, train. b, Airplane flying left, train. c, Yellow car with red, white and green stripes. d, Airplane and red Tajik Post car.

2013, July 16   Litho.   *Perf. 14x14¼*
406   A154   2.50s Block of 4, #a-d   11.50 11.50

Nos. 172 and 179 Overprinted in Red

Methods and Perfs As Before
2013, July 26
407   A46   1s on #179   7.50 7.50
408   A40   1.50s on #172   11.50 11.50

Space flight of Valentina Tereshkova, first woman in space, 50th anniv.

Animals
A155

Designs: No. 409, 1.60s, Tiger. No. 410, 1.60s, Bear. No. 411, 1.60s, Fox.

2013, Nov. 19   Litho.   *Perf. 14x14¼*
409-411   A155   Set of 3   7.00 7.00
411a   Souvenir sheet of 6, 2
                 each #409-411   14.00 14.00

Nos. 409-411 each were printed in sheets of 7 + label.

Birds — A156

No. 412: a, Partridges. b, Eagle and mountain. c, Eagle and rabbit. d, Owl (otus scops).

2013, Nov. 19   Litho.   *Perf. 14x14¼*
412   A156   2s Block of 4, #a-d   8.75 8.75

Fish — A157

No. 413: a, Goldfish. b, Silurus. c, Salmo trutta. d, Sazan.

2013, Nov. 19   Litho.   *Perf. 14x14¼*
413   A157   2s Block of 4, #a-d   8.75 8.75

Miniature Sheet

Architecture — A158

No. 414: a, Mausoleum of Mir Said Ali Hamadoni. b, Fortress of Hulbuk. c, New Mosque, Dushanbe. d, Fortress of Hisor.

2013, Nov. 19   Litho.   *Perf. 14x14¼*
414   A158   3s Sheet of 4, #a-d   11.50 11.50

Horses — A159

No. 415: a, 1.60s, White horse running right. b, 1.60s, White horse running left. c, 2.50s,

Brown horse running left. d, 2.50s, Brwon horse running right.

2014, Feb. 7   Litho.   *Perf. 14x14¼*
415   A159   Block of 4, #a-d   7.50 7.50

2014 Winter Olympics, Sochi, Russia — A160

No. 416 — Emblem of Regional Communications Commonwealth and: a, 1.60s, Figure skating. b, 1.60s, Ice hockey. c, 2.50s, Skiing. d, 3s, Speed skating.
No. 417, 3s — Emblem of Regional Communication Commonwealth and design: a, Like #416a. b, Like #416b.

2014, Mar. 7   Litho.   *Perf. 14x14¼*
416   A160   Block of 4, #a-d   9.50 9.50

Souvenir Sheet
Perf. 13½x14
417   A160   3s Sheet of 2, #a-b   12.50 12.50

No. 416 was printed in sheets of 10 containing 3 each Nos. 416a-416b and 2 each Nos. 416c-416d.

No. 225 Overprinted

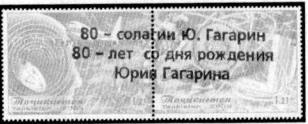

Method and Perf. As Before
2014, Mar. 8
418   A66   1.23s on #225   8.75 8.75

Yuri Gagarin (1934-68), first man in space.

Dushanbe
A161   A162

Designs: 10d, Rudaki Garden. 30d, S. Ayni Opera and Ballet Theater. 50d, Civil registry office. 1s, Palace of Nations. 2.50s, Arms of Dushanbe.

2014, June 11   Litho.   *Perf. 14x13½*
419   A161   10d multi   .25 .25
420   A161   30d multi   .35 .35
421   A161   50d multi   .60 .60
422   A161   1s multi   1.25 1.25

Perf. 13½x14
423   A162   2.50s multi   3.00 3.00
       Nos. 419-423 (5)   5.45 5.45

Khujand Intl. Airport — A163

No. 424: a, 2.50s, Airplanes on ground and in flight. b, 3s, Airplane over terminal.

2014, June 11   Litho.   *Perf. 14x14¼*
424   A163   Horiz. pair, #a-b   5.50 5.50

Mammals
A164

Designs: 1.60s, Arkhar ram. 2s, Wolf. 2.50s, Wild boar.

2014, June 11   Litho.   *Perf. 14x14¼*
425-427   A164   Set of 3   7.50 7.50
427a   Souvenir sheet of 6, 2
                 each #425-427   15.00 15.00

No. 284 Overprinted in Red

Method and Perf. As Before
2014, June 13
428   A93   on #284   11.50 11.50
a.-c.   1.50s Any single   2.60 2.60
d.   2s multi   3.50 3.50

2014 World Cup Soccer Championships, Brazil.

TANGANYIKA

,tan-gə-'nyē-kə

LOCATION — Southeastern Africa bordering on the Indian Ocean
GOVT. — Republic within British Commonwealth
AREA — 362,688 sq. mi.
POP. — 9,404,000 (est. 1961)
CAPITAL — Dar es Salaam

Before World War I, this area formed part of German East Africa. It was mandated to Britain after World War I and (in 1946) became a trust territory under the United Nations. In 1935, stamps of the mandate were replaced by those used jointly by Kenya, Uganda and Tanganyika (see Kenya, Uganda and Tanzania). On Dec. 9, 1961, Tanganyika became independent. On Dec. 9, 1962, it became a republic. April 26, 1964, it joined Zanzibar to form the United Republic of Tanganyika and Zanzibar (later renamed Tanzania). See Tanzania.

100 Cents = 1 Rupee
100 Cents = 1 Shilling (1922)
20 Shillings = 1 Pound

> **Catalogue values for unused stamps in this country are for Never Hinged items, beginning with Scott 45 in the regular postage section and Scott O1 in the officials section.**

Stamps of East Africa & Uganda Protectorates Overprinted

G.E.A.

1921		**Wmk. 4**		**Perf. 14**
1	A1	12c gray	9.00	110.00
2	A1	15c ultra	7.00	11.00
3	A1	50c dull violet & blk	14.00	100.00

Overprinted

G.E.A.

4	A2	2r black & red, *blue*	42.50	140.00
5	A2	3r gray green & violet	100.00	275.00
7	A2	5r dull violet & ultra	150.00	400.00
		Nos. 1-7 (6)	322.50	1,036.

Overprinted in Red or Black

G.E.A.

1922				
8	A1	1c black (R)	1.25	21.00
9	A1	10c orange (Bk)	2.50	16.00

A3

Giraffe — A4

		Perf. 14½x14		
1922-25		**Engr.**		**Wmk. 4**
10	A3	5c dk violet & blk	2.75	.25
11	A3	5c grn & blk ('25)	9.00	1.75
12	A3	10c green & blk	3.25	.95
13	A3	10c yel & blk ('25)	9.00	1.75
14	A3	15c carmine & blk	3.75	.25
15	A3	20c orange & blk	4.25	.25
16	A3	25c black	7.50	7.50
17	A3	25c blue & blk ('25)	4.50	20.00
18	A3	30c blue & blk	5.75	5.75
19	A3	30c dull vio & blk ('25)	6.50	16.00
20	A3	40c brown & black	3.25	5.25
21	A3	50c gray black	5.50	1.75
22	A3	75c bister & black	4.50	21.00
		Perf. 14		
23	A4	1sh green & black	4.75	12.50
a.		Wmk. sideways	8.50	22.00
24	A4	2sh brn vio & blk	5.25	32.50
a.		Wmk. sideways	8.50	22.50
25	A4	3sh blk, wmk. sideways	40.00	37.50
26	A4	5sh red & black	30.00	85.00
a.		Wmk. sideways	60.00	100.00
27	A4	10sh dp blue & blk	85.00	160.00
a.		Wmk. sideways	170.00	375.00
28	A4	£1 orange & black	300.00	475.00
a.		Wmk. sideways	350.00	500.00
		Nos. 10-28 (19)	534.50	884.95

On No. 28 the words of value are in a curve between the circle and "POSTAGE & REVENUE."

King George V
A5   A6

1927-31				**Typo.**
29	A5	5c green & black	2.00	.25
30	A5	10c yellow & black	2.25	.25
31	A5	15c red & black	2.00	.25
32	A5	20c orange & black	3.00	.25
33	A5	25c ultra & black	4.25	2.25
34	A5	30c dull violet & blk	3.25	3.00
35	A5	30c ultra & blk ('31)	29.00	.35
36	A5	40c brown & black	2.25	7.50
37	A5	50c gray & black	2.90	1.10
38	A5	75c olive grn & blk	2.25	22.50
39	A6	1sh green & black	4.75	3.25
40	A6	2sh violet brn & blk	30.00	6.00
41	A6	3sh black	45.00	85.00
42	A6	5sh scarlet & blk	30.00	24.00
43	A6	10sh ultra & black	85.00	120.00
44	A6	£1 brown org & blk	225.00	400.00
		Nos. 29-44 (16)	472.90	675.95

> **Catalogue values for unused stamps in this section, from this point to the end of the section, are for Never Hinged items.**

Independent State

A7   A8

Designs: 5c, Teacher instructing villagers, horiz. 10c, Nurse and infant. 15c, Coffee picker. 20c, Harvesting corn. 30c, Flag, horiz. 50c, Serengeti lions. 1sh, Nurse showing infant to mother, hospital horiz. 1sh30c, Torch and Mt. Kilimanjaro. 2sh, Dar es Salaam harbor, horiz. 5sh, Tractor & field workers, horiz. 10sh, Diamond mine & rose diamond, horiz. 20sh, Torch and Mt. Kilimanjaro, diff.

		Perf. 14x14½, 14½x14		
1961, Dec. 9		**Photo.**		**Unwmk.**
45	A7	5c sepia & yel grn	.30	.30
46	A7	10c Prus grn	.30	.30
47	A7	15c sepia & blue	.30	.30
b.		Blue omitted	1,400.	
48	A7	20c orange brown	.30	.30
49	A7	30c dp grn, blk & yel	.30	.30
50	A7	50c sepia & yellow	.30	.30
		Perf. 14½		
51	A8	1sh cit brn & gray bl	.30	.30
52	A8	1sh30c multicolored	4.00	.30
53	A8	2sh multicolored	1.10	.30
54	A8	5sh Prus grn & dp org	1.10	.30
55	A8	10sh blk, bl & rose	17.50	5.25
a.		Rose (diamond) omitted	200.00	150.00
56	A8	20sh multicolored	4.50	10.00
		Nos. 45-56 (12)	30.30	18.25

Tanganyika's independence, Dec. 9, 1961. For overprints see Nos. O21-O28.

Pres. Julius Nyerere with Pickax — A9

Designs: 50c, Flag hoisting on Mt. Kilimanjaro. 1sh30c, Presidential emblem. 2sh50c, Independence monument, Mnazi Moja.

1962, Dec. 9			**Perf. 14½x14**	
57	A9	30c bright green	.25	.25
58	A9	50c multicolored	.25	.25
59	A9	1sh30c multicolored	.25	.25
60	A9	2sh50c dk blue, blk & red	.75	.50
		Nos. 57-60 (4)	1.50	1.25

Issued to commemorate the establishment of the Republic of Tanganyika, Dec. 9, 1962.

OFFICIAL STAMPS

> **Catalogue values for unused stamps in this section are for Never Hinged items.**

Issued for use by the Tanganyika Government

Stamps of Kenya, Uganda & Tanganyika, 1954-59, Overprinted

OFFICIAL

		Perf. 12½x13, 13x12½		
1959		**Engr.**		**Wmk. 4**
O1	A18a	5c choc & blk	.25	1.25
O2	A19	10c carmine	.25	1.25
O3	A20	15c lt bl & blk (on #106)	.35	1.25
O4	A19	20c org & blk	.25	.25
a.		Double overprint		1,300.
O5	A18a	30c ultra & black	.25	.95
O6	A19	50c dp red lilac	.75	.25
O7	A19	1sh dp mag & blk	.25	.85
O8	A20	1sh30c pur & red org	5.50	2.25
O9	A20	2sh dp grn & gray	1.40	1.10
O10	A20	5sh black & org	4.00	3.50
O11	A20	10sh ultra & blk	2.25	4.00
O12	A21	£1 black & ver	7.50	17.50
		Nos. O1-O12 (12)	23.00	34.40

Stamps of Kenya, Uganda & Tanganyika, 1960, Overprinted

OFFICIAL

		Perf. 14½x14		
1960, Oct. 1		**Photo.**		**Wmk. 314**
O13	A23	5c dull blue	.25	2.00
O14	A23	10c lt olive green	.25	2.00
O15	A23	15c dull purple	.25	2.00
O16	A23	20c brt lilac rose	.25	.55
O17	A23	30c brt vermilion	.25	.25
O18	A23	50c dull violet	.35	1.10

Nos. 129 & 133 of Kenya, Uganda & Tanganyika Overprinted

		Engr.		**Perf. 14**
O19	A24	1sh violet & lilac red	.45	.30
O20	A24	5sh rose red & lilac	16.00	1.50
		Nos. O13-O20 (8)	18.05	9.70

Nos. 45-51 and 54 Overprinted "OFFICIAL" in Sans-serif Type of Various Sizes

		Perf. 14x14½, 14½x14		
1961, Dec. 9				**Unwmk.**
O21	A7	5c sepia & yellow grn	.25	.25
O22	A7	10c Prussian green	.25	.25
O23	A7	15c sepia & blue	.25	.25
O24	A7	20c orange brown	.25	.25
O25	A7	30c dp grn blk & yel	.25	.25
O26	A7	50c sepia & yellow	.25	.25
O27	A8	1sh citron brn & gray bl	.25	.25
O28	A8	5sh Prus grn & dp org	1.00	1.00
		Nos. O21-O28 (8)	2.75	2.75

TANNU TUVA

ˈtä-nə ˈtü-və

(Tuva People's Republic)

LOCATION — Between Siberia and northwestern Mongolia at the sources of the Yenisei, in the basin formed by the Tannu-Ola and Sayan Mountains.

GOVT. — A former republic closely identified with Soviet Russia in Asia

AREA — 64,000 sq. mi. (approx.)

POP. — 95,000 (1941 est.)

CAPITAL — Kyzyl

This region, traditionally called Uriankhai, was ruled by the Mongols until the mid-18th century, when it became part of the Chinese Empire. Russia and China struggled for control of the country 1914-21, until it became independent as the Tannu Tuva People's Republic in 1921. In 1944 it was incorporated into the U.S.S.R. as an autonomous region of the Russian Soviet Federated Socialist Republic.

Russian, later Soviet, stamps were used in Tuva prior to 1926 and after 1944.

100 Mongo=1 Tugrik
100 Kopecks = 1 Ruble
100 Kopecks = 1 Tugrik (1934)
100 Kopecks = 1 Aksha (1936)

Watermarks

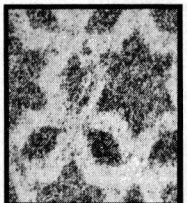

Wmk. 204 — Stars and Diamonds

Wmk. 170 — Greek Border and Rosettes

Most used examples of Nos. 1-38, 45-52a, 54-92 and C1-C18 on the market are cancelled to order, and the used values below are for such stamps.

Tuvan stamps, except for Nos. 117-123 and most of the overprints, were printed by the State Security Printers in Moscow.

Wheel of Truth — A1

1926 Litho. Wmk. 204 Perf. 13½

Size: 20x26mm

1	A1	1k red	1.50	1.50
2	A1	2k light blue	1.50	1.50
3	A1	5k orange	1.50	1.50
4	A1	8k yel green	2.00	1.75
5	A1	10k violet	2.00	1.75
6	A1	30k dark brown	2.00	1.75
7	A1	50k gray black	2.25	1.75

Size: 22½x30mm
Perf. 10½

8	A1	1r blue green	6.00	3.00
9	A1	3r red brown	8.00	5.75
10	A1	5r dark ultra	13.50	8.00
		Nos. 1-10 (10)	40.25	28.25
		Set, never hinged	77.50	

Nos. 1-10 have crackled white gum. Reprints can be distinguished by their smooth gum.

Nos. 1-10 in different colors are proofs.

Nos. 7-10 Surcharged in Red or Black

Surcharged in Kyzyl.

1927 Perf. 13½

11	A1	8k on 50k	25.00	12.50
a.		Inverted surcharge	65.00	
b.		Double surcharge	100.00	

Perf. 10½

12	A1	14k on 1r	25.00	12.50
a.		Inverted surcharge	75.00	
b.		Double surcharge	85.00	
13	A1	18k on 3r (Bk)	25.00	12.50
a.		Inverted surcharge	90.00	
b.		Double surcharge	75.00	
14	A1	28k on 5r (Bk)	25.00	12.50
a.		Inverted surcharge	90.00	
b.		Double surcharge	75.00	
		Nos. 11-14 (4)	100.00	50.00
		Set, never hinged	200.00	

Nos. 11-14 were surcharged with a shiny ink. Reprints are overprinted with a dull ink and are often smudged.

Tuvan Woman — A3

Map of Tannu Tuva A8

Sheep Herding — A11

Fording a Stream — A13

Tuvan Riding Reindeer — A16

Designs: 2k, Stag. 3k, Mountain goat. 4k, Tuvan and tent. 5k, Tuvan man. 10k, Archery competition. 14k, Camel caravan. 28k, Landscape. 50k, Weaving. 70k, Tuvan on horseback.

Printed in Moscow.

1927 Litho. Perf. 12½

15	A3	1k blk, lt brn & red	1.00	.60
16	A3	2k pur, dp brn & grn	1.20	.55
17	A3	3k blk, bl grn & yel	2.00	.60
18	A3	4k vio bl & choc	.90	.60
19	A3	5k org, blk & dk bl	.90	.65

Perf. 12½x12

20	A8	8k ol brn, pale bl & red brn	1.00	.65
21	A8	10k blk, grn & brn	5.50	1.00
22	A8	14k vio bl & red org	10.00	3.50

Perf. 10½

23	A11	18k dk bl & red brn	10.00	5.00
24	A11	28k emer & blk brn	7.25	2.75
25	A13	40k rose & bl grn	5.00	2.50
26	A13	50k blk, grn & red brn	3.50	2.00
27	A13	70k dl red & bis	7.00	4.00
28	A16	1r yel brn & vio	16.00	6.75
		Nos. 15-28 (14)	71.25	31.15
		Set, never hinged	142.50	

Nos. 15-28 were issued with a crackled white gum. Reprints of the 1k-5k values exist and can be distinguished by their smooth gum.

Nos. 15-28 in different colors are proofs.

Nos. 25-27, 20-22 Surcharged in Various Colors

Surcharged in Moscow.

1932

29	A13	1k on 40k (Bk)	9.00	10.00
30	A13	2k on 50k (Br)	10.00	10.00
31	A13	3k on 70k (Bl)	10.00	10.00
a.		Inverted surcharge	300.00	
32	A8	5k on 8k (Bk)	10.00	10.00
33	A8	10k (Bk)	10.00	10.00
34	A8	15k on 14k (Bk)	15.00	15.00
		Nos. 29-34 (6)	64.00	65.00
		Set, never hinged	128.00	

Issued in connection with the Romanization of the alphabet.

No. 31 with black surcharge was prepared but not issued.

Nos. 20, 22-24 Surcharged in Black

No. 37

No. 38

Surcharged by numbering machine in Kyzyl.

1932-33 Wmk. 204

35	A8	10k on 8k	180.00	100.00
36	A8	15k on 14k	300.00	200.00
37	A11	35k on 18k (#23)	150.00	100.00
b.		Pair, one without surcharge	—	
c.		Inverted surcharge	500.00	
38	A11	35k on 28k	150.00	100.00
a.		Pair, one without surcharge	—	
		Nos. 35-38 (4)	780.00	500.00
		Set, never hinged	1,550.	

Revenue Stamps Surcharged — A19

Surcharged in Kyzyl

Three types: type 1, figures of value 6.7mm high; type 2, figures of value 6.7mm high, letter "p" lengthened at bottom; type 3, figures of value 5.1mm high.

1933 Perf. 12x12½

39	A19	15k on 6k org yel, type 1	300.00	150.00
40	A19	15k on 6k org yel, type 2	300.00	150.00
b.		Inverted surcharge	—	
41	A19	15k on 6k org yel, type 3	500.00	300.00
42	A19	35k on 15k red brn, type 1	—	4,000.
43	A19	35k on 15k red brn, type 2	—	4,000.
44	A19	35k on 15k red brn, type 3	1,500.	800.00

Mounted Hunter — A20

Tuvan Inside of Yurt — A21

Tuvan Milking Yak — A22

Die I   Die II

Designs: 2k, Hunter stalking game. 4k, Tractor. 10k, Camel caravan. 15k, Herdsman lassoing reindeer. 20k, Hunter shooting fox with arrow.

Two dies on 10k: Die I, Crown at center top is light and matches the shade of the sky below; Die II, Crown at center top is bold, consistent with rest of design and darker than the sky.

Printed by State Security Printers, Moscow.

Wmk. 170

1934, Apr. Photo. Perf. 12

45	A20	1k red orange	1.50	1.00
46	A20	2k olive green	1.50	1.00
47	A21	3k rose red	1.50	1.00
48	A21	4k slate purple	3.50	1.75
49	A22	5k ultramarine	3.50	1.75
50	A22	10k brown, die II	3.50	1.75
51	A22	15k dark lilac	3.50	1.75
52	A22	20k gray black	4.75	2.75
		Nos. 45-52 (8)	23.25	12.75
		Set, never hinged	50.00	
		Set, imperf	50.00	
		Set, imperf., never hinged	100.00	

Nos. 45-52 are inscribed "REGISTERED," but were used as regular postage stamps.

Nos. 46, 48 and 50 exist perf 11, and No. 50 also exists perf 11x10. No. 48 exists perf 11½, reportedly as a color trial proof.

No. 51 Surcharged in Black

Surcharged by numbering machine in Kyzyl.

1935

53	A22	20k on 15k	175.00	325.00
a.		Inverted surcharge		400.00

Map of Tuva — A23

Rocky Outcropping — A24

Designs: 3k, 5k, 10k, Different scenes of Yenisei River. 25k, Bei-kem rapids. 50k, Mounted hunters.
Printed by State Security Printers, Moscow.

Wmk. 170

1935, Mar.		**Photo.**		**Perf. 14**
54	A23	1k yellow orange	2.25	1.75
55	A23	3k deep green	2.25	1.75
56	A23	5k carmine red	3.00	2.00
57	A23	10k violet	3.25	2.00
b.		Pair, imperf between		
58	A24	15k olive green	3.50	2.50
59	A24	25k violet blue	4.00	2.50
60	A24	50k dark brown	5.75	2.75
		Nos. 54-60 (7)	24.00	15.25
		Set, never hinged	45.00	

Nos. 54-60 in different colors, perf and imperf, are proofs.

Badger
A25

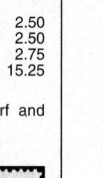

Squirrel — A26

Fox — A27

Elk — A28

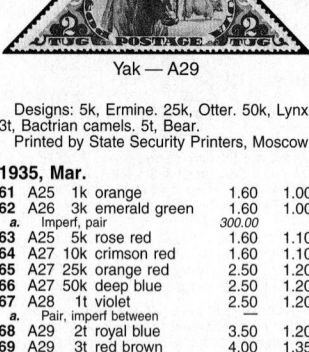

Yak — A29

Designs: 5k, Ermine. 25k, Otter. 50k, Lynx. 3t, Bactrian camels. 5t, Bear.
Printed by State Security Printers, Moscow.

1935, Mar.

61	A25	1k orange	1.60	1.00
62	A26	3k emerald green	1.60	1.00
a.		Imperf, pair	300.00	
63	A25	5k rose red	1.60	1.10
64	A27	10k crimson red	1.60	1.10
65	A27	25k orange red	2.50	1.20
66	A27	50k deep blue	2.50	1.20
67	A28	1t violet	2.50	1.20
a.		Pair, imperf between		
68	A29	2t royal blue	3.50	1.20
69	A29	3t red brown	4.00	1.35
70	A28	5t indigo	5.00	1.75
a.		Imperf, pair	300.00	
b.		Pair, imperf between	—	
		Nos. 61-70 (10)	26.40	12.10
		Set, never hinged	50.00	

Nos. 61-70 in different colors are proofs.

Tuvan Arms — A30

Wrestlers — A31

Herdsman on Bull — A32

Athletic Competitions — A33

Soldiers
A34

Designs: 2k, Pres. Chürmit-Dazhy. 3k, Tuvan with Bactrian camel. 5k, 8k, Archer. 10k, 15k, Spearfishing. 12k, 20k, Bear-hunting. 30k, Camel and train. 40k, 50k, Horse race. 80k, Partisans. 3t, Partisans confiscating cattle. 5t, 1921 battle scene.
Printed by State Security Printers, Moscow.

1936, July			**Perf. 11, 14**	
71	A30	1k bronze green	2.00	.70
72	A30	2k dark brown	2.50	1.50
73	A30	3k indigo blue	3.25	.75
74a	A31	4k orange red	3.50	.75
75	A31	5k brown purple	5.00	.70
76	A31	6k myrtle green	4.75	.70
77	A31	8k plum	4.75	.70
78a	A31	10k rose red	5.25	.75
79	A31	12k black brown	7.50	1.25
80	A31	15k bronze green	11.00	1.50
81	A31	20k deep blue	11.00	1.20
82	A32	25k orange red	6.00	1.20
83	A32	30k plum	30.00	1.25
84	A32	35k rose red	6.00	1.50
85a	A32	40k deep brown	7.00	1.50
86a	A32	50k indigo blue	13.00	1.50
87a	A33	70k plum	9.50	2.50
88a	A33	80k green	9.50	2.50
89b	A34	1a orange red	9.50	3.00
90	A34	2a rose red	11.00	3.00
91	A33	3a indigo blue	17.50	2.00
92	A33	5a black brown	15.00	2.50
		Nos. 71-92 (22)	194.50	32.95
		Set, never hinged	333.00	

15th anniversary of independence.
Values for Nos. 71-92 are for the most common varieties. For detailed listings, see the *Scott Classic Specialized Catalogue*.
Imperfs are remainders, later sold by the Soviet Postal Museum.

Values for Nos. 93-98 and 104-116 are for genuine examples. Expertization is essential for these issues.

Issues of 1934-36 Handstamped with Large Numerals and Old Values Obliterated with Bars or Blocks

1938, Aug.

93	A34	5k on 2a (#90a)	400.00
94	AP5	5k on 2a (#C17)	375.00
95	AP1	10k on 1t (#C8)	350.00
96	A24	20k on 50k (#60)	350.00
97	AP5	30k on 2a (#C17)	350.00
98	AP5	30k on 3a (#C18)	325.00

Types of 1935-36 with Modified Designs and New Colors

1938, Dec.		**Unwmk.**	**Perf. 12½**
99	A25	5k deep green	60.00	—
100	A31	10k indigo (dates removed)	60.00	—
101	AP3	15k red brown ("AIR MAIL," dates removed)	60.00	—
102	A31	20k orange red (dates removed)	85.00	—
103	A33	30k maroon (dates removed)	60.00	—
		Nos. 99-103 (5)	325.00	
		Set, never hinged	500.00	

Some experts believe that these stamps were issued in March 1941.

Stamps of 1934-35 Handstamp Surcharged with New Values in Black or Violet at Kyzyl

1939

104	AP1	10k on 1t (#C8)	225.00
105	AP1	10k on 1t (#B8) (V)	225.00
106	A24	20k on 50k (#60) (V)	200.00

Old values obliterated on Nos. 104-106.

Stamps of 1934-36 Handstamp Surcharged with New Values at Kyzyl

1940, Oct.-1941

107	AP1	10k on 1t (#C8)	—	125.00
a.		Double surcharge	—	—
108	A24	20k on 50k (#60)	—	150.00
109	A27	20k on 50k (#66)	—	350.00
110	A32	20k on 50k (#86a)	—	350.00
111	AP4	20k on 50k (#C14)	—	100.00
112	A33	20k on 70k (#87a)	—	500.00
113	AP4	20k on 75k (#C15)	—	110.00
114	A33	20k on 80k (#88)	—	500.00

The old values are not obliterated on Nos. 107 or 108.

Nos. 91, 92 Handstamp Surcharged with New Values at Kyzyl

1942

115	A33	25k on 3a (#91)	1,200.	—
116	A33	25k on 5a (#92)	—	—

Government House — A35

Exhibition Hall — A36

Tuvan Woman — A37

1942		**Typo.**	**Unwmk.**	**Imperf.**
117	A35	25k steel blue	950.00	100.00
118	A36	25k steel blue	950.00	100.00
119	A37	25k steel blue	950.00	150.00
		Nos. 117-119 (3)	2,850.	350.00

21st anniversary of independence.
Nos. 117-119 were hand-printed together in small sheetlets of five (117+119+118+117+119), so various se-tenant combinations are possible.
Two additional values, a 25k depicting a Tuvan man and a 50k depicting a soldier on a horse, were prepared, but not issued. A collective proof sheetlet of five, containing Nos. 117-119 and these two values, in the same color as the issued stamps, is also known.

Coat of Arms — A38

Government Building — A39

1943		**Perf. 11 (1 or 2 Sides)**	
		Buff Paper	
120	A38	25k slate blue	100.00	—
		Vertical strip of 5	900.00	
121	A38	25k black	100.00	—
122	A38	25k blue green	90.00	—
123	A39	50k blue green	90.00	—
		Nos. 120-123 (4)	380.00	

		White Paper		
120a	A38	25k slate blue	90.00	—
b.		Strip of 3, imperf between		250.00

121a	A38	25k black	125.00	—
		Vertical strip of five	600.00	
122a	A38	25k blue green	95.00	—
123a	A39	50k blue green	95.00	—
		Nos. 120a-123a (4)	405.00	

22nd anniversary of independence.

Nos. 120 and 121 were each printed in vertical strips of five, perforated 11 between stamps and imperf on outside edges, so that these stamps may be perforated on top edge only, bottom edge only, or on both top and bottom edges. To make maximum use of limited wartime paper supplies, they were sometimes printed in strips of four. These smaller strips are rare.

Nos. 122 and 123 were printed together in blocks of four, containing a vertical pair of the 25k and a vertical pair of the 50k, perforated internally both vertically and horizontally and imperf on the outer edges. Setenant pairs, Value $225 (#122+123), $275 (#122a+123a).

Nos. 121 and 123a were issued with gum, No. 123a both with and without gum, and the balance of the set without gum.

Used examples and covers exist but are extremely rare.

AIR POST STAMPS

Airplane and Yaks — AP1

Airplane and Capercaillie — AP2

Designs, airplane over: 5k, 15k, Camels. 25k, Argali (wild sheep). 75k, Ox and cart. 2t, Roe deer.

Printed by State Security Printers, Moscow.

Wmk. 170

		1934, Apr. 4	**Photo.**	**Perf. 14**	
C1	AP1	1k orange red		1.40	1.00
C2	AP1	5k emer green		1.40	1.00
C3	AP2	10k purple brown		4.50	3.00
C4	AP1	15k rose red		2.75	1.00
C5	AP2	25k slate purple		2.75	1.00
C6	AP1	50k dp bl green		2.75	1.00
C7	AP2	75k lake		2.75	1.00
C8	AP1	1t royal blue		3.50	2.00
C9	AP2	2t ultra, 61x31mm		20.00	25.00
a.		54.5x29mm		40.00	—
		Nos. C1-C9 (9)		41.80	36.00
		Set, never hinged		55.00	

Nos. C1-C9 imperf or perf 11½ and stamps printed in different colors are proofs.

Tuvan Leading Laden Yak — AP3

Horseman and Zeppelin AP4

Seaplane Above Dragon — AP5

Designs: 10k, Tuvan plowing. 50k, Villagers with biplane overhead.

Printed by State Security Printers, Moscow.

		1936	**Unwmk.**	
C10	AP3	5k indigo & beige	3.00	1.50
C11	AP3	10k pur & cinn	4.50	1.50
C12	AP3	15k blk brn & pale gray	4.50	1.75
C13	AP4	25k plum & cream	6.00	2.50
c.		Horiz. pair, perf 11, imperf between	—	—
C14	AP4	50k rose red & cream	6.50	2.50
C15	AP4	75k emer grn & pale yel	10.00	4.00
C16	AP5	1a bl grn & pale bl grn	12.00	5.00
C17	AP5	2a rose red & cream	9.50	3.75
C18	AP5	3a dk brn & beige	9.50	3.75
		Nos. C10-C18 (9)	65.50	26.25
		Set, never hinged	120.00	

15th anniversary of independence.

Nos. C10-C18 exist imperf.

TANZANIA

ˌtan-zə-ˈnē-ə

(Tanganyika and Zanzibar)

LOCATION — Southeastern Africa bordering on the Indian Ocean, and a group of islands about 20 miles off the coast

GOVT. — United republic in British Commonwealth

AREA — 364,886 sq. mi.

POP. — 31,270,820 (1999 est.)

CAPITAL — Dodoma

Tanganyika joined Zanzibar on April 26, 1964, to form the United Republic of Tanganyika and Zanzibar. In October 1965 the name was changed to United Republic of Tanzania.

Zanzibar stamps include two (Nos. 331, 334) inscribed "Tanzania."

100 Cents = 1 Shilling

> **Catalogue values for all unused stamps in this country are for Never Hinged items.**

Watermark

Wmk. 387 — Squares and Rectangles

Map — A1

Design: 30c, 1sh30c, Emblem (hands holding torch and spear).

		Perf. 14x14½		
		1964, July 7	**Photo.**	**Unwmk.**
1	A1	20c blue & emerald	.25	.25
2	A1	30c brn, dk & lt bl	.25	.25
3	A1	1.30sh ultra, blk & org	.30	.30
4	A1	2.50sh ultra & purple	.65	.65
		Nos. 1-4 (4)	1.45	1.45

Union of Tanganyika and Zanzibar. Not sold in Zanzibar, nor valid there.

Flag A2

Native Handicraft A3

Designs: 5c, Hale hydroelectric plant. 15c, Army squad. 20c, Road building. 40c, Giraffes. 50c, Zebras. 65c, Mt. Kilimanjaro. 1sh, Dar es Salaam harbor. 1.30sh, Zinjanthropus skull and Olduvai Gorge excavation. 2.50sh, Sailfish, dhow and map of Mafia Island. 5sh, Sisal industry. 10sh, State House, Dar es Salaam. 20sh, Tanzania coat of arms.

		Perf. 14x14½, 14½x14		
		1965, Dec. 9	**Photo.**	**Unwmk.**
		Size: 21x17½mm, 17½x21mm		
5	A2	5c orange & ultra	.40	.60
6	A2	10c ultra, grn, yel & blk	.40	.60
7	A3	15c grn, bl, brn & buff	.40	.60
8	A2	20c blue & brown	.40	.60
9	A3	30c black & red brn	.40	.60
10	A3	40c blue, yel grn & brn	.40	.60
11	A2	50c yellow grn & blue	.40	.60
12	A2	65c ultra, grn & red brn	.50	.75

		Perf. 14½		
		Size: 41½x25, 25x41½mm		
13	A2	1sh bl, grn, yel & brn	.60	.60
14	A2	1.30sh multicolored	.90	.60
15	A2	2.50sh blue & red brn	1.35	.95
16	A2	5sh bl, brt grn & red brn	2.75	1.40
17	A2	10sh blue & yellow	5.50	4.00
18	A3	20sh gray & multi	10.50	9.00
		Nos. 5-18 (14)	24.90	21.50

For overprints see Nos. O1-O8.

Turkeyfish — A4

Fish: 5c, Cardinalfish. 10c, Mudskipper. 15c, Toby puffer. 20c, Two sea horses. 30c, Batfish. 40c, Sweetlips. 50c, Birdfish. 65c, Butterflyfish. 70c, Grouper. 1.30sh, Surgeonfish. 1.50sh, Caesio xanthonotus. 2.50sh, Emperor snapper. 5sh, Moorish idol. 10sh, Striped trigerfish. 20sh, Squirrelfish.

		1967-71	**Photo.**	**Perf. 14x14½**	
		Size: 21x17½mm			
		Fish in Natural Colors			
19	A4	5c black & citron		.25	.25
20	A4	10c brown & olive		.25	.25
21	A4	15c brown & blue		.25	.25
22	A4	20c brn & dk bl grn		.25	.25
23	A4	30c black & yel grn		.25	.25
24	A4	40c brown & emerald		.25	.25
25	A4	50c blk & dull bl grn		.25	.25
26	A4	65c blk & gray grn		.70	.70
27	A4	70c blk & olive ('69)		.55	.55

		Perf. 14½		
		Size: 41x25mm		
28	A4	1sh brown & multi	.45	.25
29	A4	1.30sh black & olive	.70	.25
30	A4	1.50sh black & ol ('69)	.80	.25
31	A4	2.50sh brn yel & grn	1.40	.25
32	A4	5sh black & bl grn	2.25	.25
33	A4	10sh brn & gray grn	4.75	.60
34	A4	20sh blk & gray olive	11.50	1.40
		Nos. 19-34 (16)	24.85	6.25

Issued: #27, 30, 9/15/69; others, 12/9/67. Values of Nos. 28-34 are for canceled-to-order stamps with printed cancellations. Postally used examples sell for higher prices. For overprints see Nos. O9-O16.

Papilio Hornimani A5

Euphaedra Neophron A6

Butterflies: 10c, Colotis ione. 15c, Amauris makuyuensis. 20c, Libythea laius. 30c, Danaus chrysippus. 40c, Sallya rosa. 50c, Axiocerses styx. 60c, Eurema hecabe. 70c, Acraea insignis. 1.50sh, Precis octavia. 2.50sh, Charaxes eupale. 5sh, Charaxes pollux. 10sh, Salamis parhassus. 20sh, Papilio ophidicephalus.

		1973, Dec. 3	**Photo.**	**Perf. 14½x14**	
35	A5	5c yellow grn & multi		.35	.35
a.		Booklet pane of 4		1.40	
36	A5	10c lt brown & multi		.35	.35
a.		Booklet pane of 4		1.40	
37	A5	15c ultra & multi		.35	.35
38	A5	20c fawn & multi		.35	.35
a.		Booklet pane of 4		1.40	
39	A5	30c yellow & multi		.35	.35
a.		Booklet pane of 4		1.50	
40	A5	40c multicolored		.35	.35
a.		Booklet pane of 4		1.60	
41	A5	50c citron & multi		.35	.35
a.		Booklet pane of 4		1.50	
42	A5	60c multicolored		.35	.35
43	A5	70c brt green & multi		.35	.35
a.		Booklet pane of 4		1.75	

		Perf. 14½		
44	A6	1sh green & multi	.60	.60
45	A6	1.50sh orange & multi	1.00	1.00
46	A6	2.50sh multicolored	1.75	1.75
47	A6	5sh multicolored	4.00	4.00
48	A6	10sh lt green & multi	7.50	7.50
49	A6	20sh blue & multi	16.50	15.00
		Nos. 35-49 (15)	34.50	33.00

For surcharges and overprints see Nos. 50-53, 135-136, O17-O26.

Nos. 42, 45-46, 49 Surcharged with New Value and 2 Bars

		Perf. 14½x14, 14½		
		1975, Nov. 17	**Photo.**	
50	A5	80c on 60c multi	4.00	3.75
51	A6	2sh on 1.50sh multi	8.00	7.50
52	A6	3sh on 2.50sh multi	24.00	29.00
53	A6	40sh on 20sh multi	12.00	14.00
		Nos. 50-53 (4)	48.00	54.25

A6a

Designs: 50c, Microwave tower. 1sh, Cordless switchboard and operators, horiz. 2sh, Telephones of 1880, 1930 and 1976. 3sh, Message switching center, horiz.

1976, Apr. 15 Litho. *Perf. 14½*

54	A6a 50c blue & multi	.25	.25
55	A6a 1sh red & multi	.25	.25
56	A6a 2sh yellow & multi	.25	.30
57	A6a 3sh multicolored	.35	.40
a.	Souvenir sheet of 4	2.25	2.25
	Nos. 54-57 (4)	1.10	1.20

Telecommunications development in East Africa. No. 57a contains 4 stamps similar to Nos. 54-57 with simulated perforations.

Exist imperf. from Format International liquidation stock.

A6b

Designs: 50c, Akii Bua, Ugandan hurdler. 1sh, Filbert Bayi, Tanzanian runner. 2sh, Steve Muchoki, Kenyan boxer. 3sh, Olympic torch, flags of Kenya, Tanzania and Uganda.

1976, July 5 Litho. *Perf. 14½*

58	A6b 50c blue & multi	.25	.25
59	A6b 1sh red & multi	.25	.25
60	A6b 2sh yellow & multi	.25	.25
61	A6b 3sh blue & multi	.30	.35
a.	Souv. sheet of 4, #58-61, perf. 13	4.25	4.25
	Nos. 58-61 (4)	1.05	1.10

21st Olympic Games, Montreal, Canada, July 17-Aug. 1.

Exist imperf. from Format International liquidation stock.

A6c

Rail Transport in East Africa: 50c, Tanzania-Zambia Railway. 1sh, Nile Bridge, Uganda. 2sh, Nakuru Station, Kenya. 3sh, Class A locomotive, 1896.

1976, Oct. 4 Litho. *Perf. 14½*

62	A6c 50c lilac & multi	.25	.25
63	A6c 1sh emerald & multi	.30	.25
64	A6c 2sh brt rose & multi	.60	.35
65	A6c 3sh yellow & multi	.90	.60
a.	Souv. sheet of 4, #62-65, perf. 13	7.00	7.00
	Nos. 62-65 (4)	2.05	1.45

A6d

1977, Jan. 10 Litho. *Perf. 14½*

66	A6d 50c Nile perch	.25	.25
67	A6d 1sh Tilapia	.50	.45
68	A6d 3sh Sailfish	1.25	1.00
69	A6d 5sh Black marlin	2.25	2.25
a.	Souvenir sheet of 4, #66-69	4.25	3.50
	Nos. 66-69 (4)	4.25	3.95

A6e

50c, Masai tribesmen bleeding cow. 1sh, Dancers from Uganda. 2sh, Makonde sculpture. 3sh, Tribesmen skinning hippopotamus.

1977, Jan. 15 *Perf. 13½x14*

70	A6e 50c multicolored	.25	.25
71	A6e 1sh multicolored	.25	.25
72	A6e 2sh multicolored	.40	.30
73	A6e 3sh multicolored	.65	.45
a.	Souvenir sheet of 4, #70-73	2.25	2.25
	Nos. 70-73 (4)	1.55	1.25

2nd World Black and African Festival, Lagos, Nigeria, Jan. 15-Feb. 12.

A6f

50c, Automobile passing through village. 1sh, Winner at finish line. 2sh, Car going through washout. 5sh, Car, elephants and Mt. Kenya.

1977, Apr. 5 Litho. *Perf. 14*

74	A6f 50c multicolored	.25	.25
75	A6f 1sh multicolored	.25	.25
76	A6f 2sh multicolored	.55	.30
77	A6f 5sh multicolored	1.40	.85
a.	Souvenir sheet of 4, #74-77	3.25	3.25
	Nos. 74-77 (4)	2.45	1.65

25th Safari rally, Apr. 7-11.

A6g

Designs: 50c, Rev. Canon Apolo Kivebulaya. 1sh, Uganda Cathedral. 2sh, Early grass-topped Cathedral. 5sh, Early tent congregation, Kigezi.

1977, June 20 Litho. *Perf. 14*

78	A6g 50c multicolored	.25	.25
79	A6g 1sh multicolored	.25	.25
80	A6g 2sh multicolored	.25	.25
81	A6g 5sh multicolored	.65	.55
a.	Souvenir sheet of 4, #78-81	2.50	2.50
	Nos. 78-81 (4)	1.40	1.30

Church of Uganda, centenary.

A6h

Endangered species: 50c, Pancake tortoise. 1sh, Nile crocodile. 2sh, Hunter's hartebeest. 3sh, Red Colobus monkey. 5sh, Dugong.

1977, Sept. 26 Litho. *Perf. 14x13½*

82	A6h 50c multicolored	1.00	.35
83	A6h 1sh multicolored	2.40	.60
84	A6h 2sh multicolored	4.75	2.25
85	A6h 3sh multicolored	8.00	3.25
86	A6h 5sh multicolored	10.50	6.00
a.	Souvenir sheet of 4, #83-86	12.00	12.00
	Nos. 82-86 (5)	26.65	12.45

Prince Philip and Julius Nyerere, 1961 — A7

5sh, Queen Elizabeth II, Prince Philip, Prime Minister Nyerere in London, 1975. 10sh, Royal crown, flags of Tanzania and Commonwealth nations. 20sh, Coronation.

1977, Nov. 23 Litho. *Perf. 14x13½*

87	A7 50c multicolored	.25	.25
88	A7 5sh multicolored	.25	.25
89	A7 10sh multicolored	.25	.25
90	A7 20sh multicolored	.40	.40
a.	Souvenir sheet of 4, #87-90	1.25	1.25
	Nos. 87-90 (4)	1.15	1.15

25th anniv. of reign of Elizabeth II.

For overprints see Nos. 99-102, 179-180.

Women Fetching Water from Stream and Tap — A8

1sh, Flag raising. 3sh, Health care, laboratory and hospital. 5sh, Pres. Julius Nyerere.

1978, Feb. 5 Litho. *Perf. 13½x14*

91	A8 50c multicolored	.25	.25
92	A8 1sh multicolored	.25	.25
93	A8 3sh multicolored	.25	.25
94	A8 5sh multicolored	.35	.35
a.	Souvenir sheet of 4, #91-94	1.25	1.25
	Nos. 91-94 (4)	1.10	1.10

First anniversary of the New Revolutionary Party (Chama cha Mapinduzi).

A8a

50c, Soccer scene and Joe Kadenge. 1sh, Mohammed Chuma receiving trophy, and his portrait. 2sh, Shot on goal and Omari S. Kidevu. 3sh, Backfield defense and Polly Ouma.

1978, Apr. 17 Litho. *Perf. 14x13½*

95	A8a 50c green & multi	.25	.25
96	A8a 1sh lt brown & multi	.25	.25
97	A8a 2sh lilac & multi	.25	.25
98	A8a 3sh dk blue & multi	.35	.35
a.	Souvenir sheet of 4, #95-98	2.50	2.50
	Nos. 95-98 (4)	1.10	1.10

World Soccer Cup Championships, Argentina '78, June 1-25.

Nos. 87-90a Overprinted in Large Serifed Letters: "25th ANNIVERSARY / CORONATION / 2nd JUNE 1953"

1978, June 2

99	A7 50c multicolored	.25	.25
100	A7 5sh multicolored	.25	.25
101	A7 10sh multicolored	.25	.25
102	A7 20sh multicolored	.30	.30
a.	Souvenir sheet of 4, #99-102	1.00	1.00
	Nos. 99-102 (4)	1.05	1.05

25th anniv. of coronation of Elizabeth II.

Nos. 99-102a also exist overprinted with smaller, sans serif letters, perf. 12. Same values or less. The perf. 12 set does not exist without overprint.

"Do not Drink when Driving" — A9

Designs: 1sh, "Courtesy to the young, old and handicapped." 3sh, "Observe highway code." 5sh, "Do not drive faulty vehicle."

1978, July 1 Litho. *Perf. 13½x13*

103	A9 50c multicolored	.25	.25
104	A9 1sh multicolored	.25	.25
105	A9 3sh multicolored	.40	.40
106	A9 5sh multicolored	1.60	1.60
a.	Souv. sheet, #103-106, perf. 14	2.75	2.75
	Nos. 103-106 (4)	2.50	2.50

Road Safety Campaign.

Lake Manyara Hotel — A10

Designs: 1sh, Lobo Wildlife Lodge. 3sh, Ngorongoro Crater Lodge. 5sh, Ngorongoro Wildlife Lodge. 10sh, Mafia Island Lodge. 20sh, Mikumi Wildlife Lodge.

1978, Sept. 11 Litho. *Perf. 13½*

107	A10 50c multicolored	.25	.25
108	A10 1sh multicolored	.25	.25
109	A10 3sh multicolored	.25	.25
110	A10 5sh multicolored	.40	.40
111	A10 10sh multicolored	.80	.80
112	A10 20sh multicolored	1.75	1.75
a.	Souvenir sheet of 6, #107-112	7.75	7.75
	Nos. 107-112 (6)	3.70	3.70

Game Lodges of Tanzania.

Chained African — A11

1sh, Division of races (black and white heads). 2.50sh, Racial harmony (black and white handshake and heads). 5sh, End of suppression and rise of freedom (hands breaking loose from chains).

1978, Oct. 24 Litho. *Perf. 14½x14*

113	A11 50c multicolored	.25	.25
114	A11 1sh multicolored	.25	.25
115	A11 2.50sh multicolored	.40	.40
116	A11 5sh multicolored	.80	.80
a.	Souvenir sheet of 4, #113-116	2.25	2.25
	Nos. 113-116 (4)	1.70	1.70

Anti-Apartheid Year.

Fokker Friendship at Dar Es Salaam Airport — A12

Designs: 1sh, Single-engine Dragon, 1930, Zanzibar. 2sh, British Airways Concorde. 5sh, Wright Brothers' Flyer 1, 1903.

1978, Dec. 28 Litho. *Perf. 13½*

117	A12 50c multicolored	.30	.30
118	A12 1sh multicolored	.45	.45
119	A12 2sh multicolored	.85	.85
120	A12 5sh multicolored	2.10	2.10
a.	Souvenir sheet of 4, #117-120	4.25	4.25
	Nos. 117-120 (4)	3.70	3.70

75th anniversary of 1st powered flight.

Emblem A13

Design: 5sh, Headquarters buildings.

1979, Feb. 3 Litho. *Perf. 14½x14*

121	A13 50c multicolored	.25	.25
122	A13 5sh multicolored	.65	.65
a.	Souvenir sheet of 2, #121-122	1.60	1.60

Tanzania Post and Telecommunications Corporation, 1st anniversary.

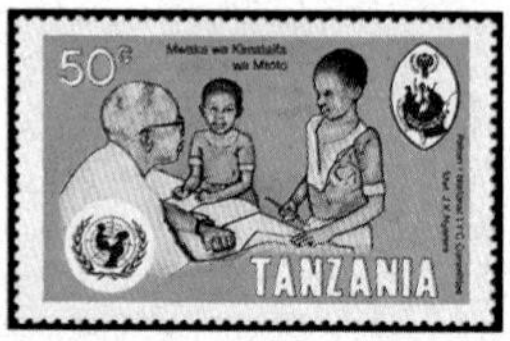

Pres. Nyerere and Children — A14

Designs (UNICEF and Tanzanian IYC Emblems and): 1sh, Kindergarten. 2sh, Vaccination of infant. 5sh, Emblems.

1979, June 25 Litho. *Perf. 14½*

123 A14 50c multicolored .25 .25
124 A14 1sh multicolored .25 .25
125 A14 2sh multicolored .25 .25
126 A14 5sh multicolored .50 .50
a. Souvenir sheet of 4, #123-126 2.25 2.25
Nos. 123-126 (4) 1.25 1.25

International Year of the Child.

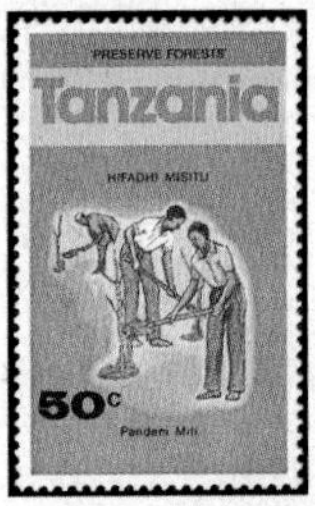

Tree Planting — A15

Forest Preservation and Expansion: 1sh, Seedling. 2sh, Rainfall. 5sh, Forest fire.

1979, Sept. 29 Litho. *Perf. 14½*

127 A15 50c multicolored .25 .25
128 A15 1sh multicolored .35 .35
129 A15 2sh multicolored .60 .60
130 A15 5sh multicolored 1.60 1.60
Nos. 127-130 (4) 2.80 2.80

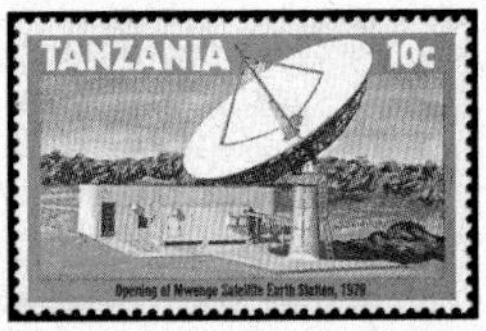

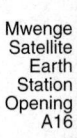

Mwenge Satellite Earth Station Opening A16

1979, Dec. 3 Litho. *Perf. 13½*

131 A16 10c multicolored .25 .25
132 A16 40c multicolored .25 .25
133 A16 50c multicolored .25 .25
134 A16 1sh multicolored .25 .25
Nos. 131-134 (4) 1.00 1.00

Nos. 36, 43 Surcharged

1979 Litho. *Perf. 14½x14*

135 A5 40c (10 + 30) multi 4.00 4.00
136 A5 50c on 70c multi 6.00 6.00

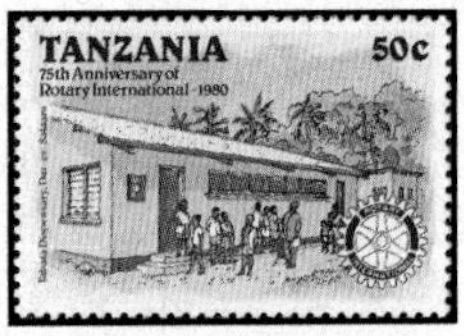

Tabata Dispensary, Dar-es-Salaam, Rotary Emblem — A17

1sh, Ngomvu water project. 5sh, Flying doctor service. 20sh, Torch, anniversary emblem.

1980, Mar. 1 Litho. *Perf. 13x13½*

137 A17 50c shown .25 .25
138 A17 1sh multicolored .25 .25
139 A17 5sh multicolored .45 .45
140 A17 20sh multicolored 2.00 2.00
a. Souvenir sheet of 4, #137-140 2.75 2.75
Nos. 137-140 (4) 2.95 2.95

Rotary International, 75th anniversary.
For overprints see Nos. 149-152.

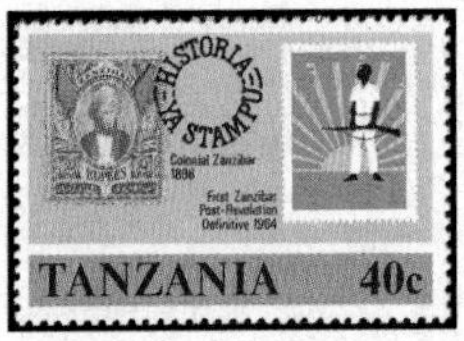

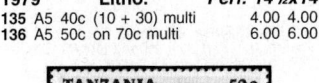

Zanzibar Nos. 49 and 309, "Stamp History" Cancel A18

Cancel and: 50c, Tanganyika #58, postal worker, vert. 10sh, Tanganyika #16, 52. 20sh, Penny Black, Rowland Hill, vert.

1980, Apr. *Perf. 14*

141 A18 40c multicolored .25 .25
142 A18 50c multicolored .25 .25
143 A18 10sh multicolored .50 .50
144 A18 20sh multicolored 1.00 1.00
a. Souvenir sheet of 4, #141-144 2.75 2.75
Nos. 141-144 (4) 2.00 2.00

Sir Rowland Hill (1795-1879), originator of penny postage; Tanzanian stamp history.

Overprinted: "LONDON 1980" / PHILATELIC EXHIBITION

1980, May 6 Litho. *Perf. 14*

145 A18 40c multicolored .25 .25
146 A18 50c multicolored .25 .25
147 A18 10sh multicolored .50 .50
148 A18 20sh multicolored 1.00 1.00
a. Souvenir sheet of 4, #145-148 2.75 2.75
Nos. 145-148 (4) 2.00 2.00

London 80 Intl. Stamp Exhib., May 6-14.

Nos. 137-140a with Additional Inscription on 1 or 2 Lines: "District 920-55th Annual / Conference, Arusha, Tanzania"

1980, June 23 Litho. *Perf. 13x13½*

149 A17 50c multicolored .25 .25
150 A17 1sh multicolored .25 .25
151 A17 5sh multicolored .65 .65
152 A17 20sh multicolored 2.75 2.75
a. Souvenir sheet of 4, #149-152 4.00 4.00
Nos. 149-152 (4) 3.90 3.90

District 920 Rotary Club, 55th Annual Conference, Arusha.

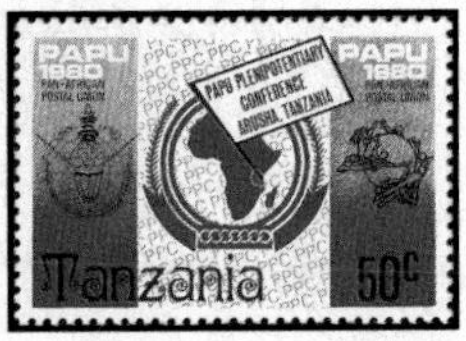

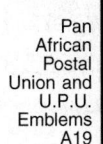

Pan African Postal Union and U.P.U. Emblems A19

1980, July 1 *Perf. 13x13½*

153 A19 50c purple & blk .25 .25
154 A19 1sh ultra & blk .25 .25
155 A19 5sh red orange & blk .50 .50
156 A19 10sh green & blk 1.00 1.00
Nos. 153-156 (4) 2.00 2.00

Pan African Postal Union Plenipotentiary Conference, Arusha, Jan. 8-18.

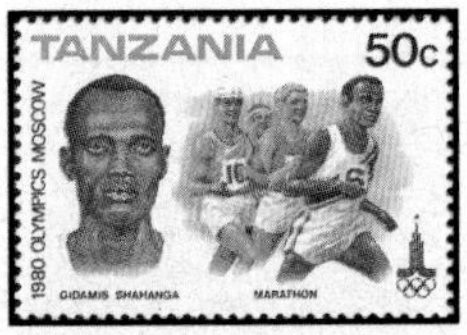

Gidamis Shahanga, Marathon — A20

Tanzanian Olympic Team: 1sh, Nzael Kyomo and sprinters. 10sh, Zakayo Malekwa and javelin. 20sh, William Lyimo and boxers.

1980, Aug. 18 Litho. *Perf. 13x13½*

157 A20 50c multicolored .25 .25
158 A20 1sh multicolored .25 .25
159 A20 10sh multicolored .75 .75
160 A20 20sh multicolored 1.75 1.75
a. Souvenir sheet of 4, #157-160 3.50 3.50
Nos. 157-160 (4) 3.00 3.00

22nd Summer Olympic Games, Moscow, July 19-Aug. 3.
Issued also in sheets of 20 (5 of each value).

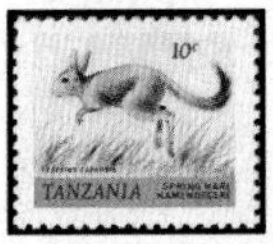

Spring Hare — A21

1980, Oct. 1 Litho. *Perf. 14*

161 A21 10c shown .25 .25
162 A21 20c Genet .25 .25
163 A21 40c Mongoose .25 .25
164 A21 50c Ratel .25 .25
165 A21 75c Rock hyrax .25 .25
166 A21 80c Leopard .25 .25

Perf. 14½

Size: 40x24mm

167 A21 1sh Impalas .25 .25
168 A21 1.50sh Giraffes .25 .25
169 A21 2sh Zebras .25 .25
170 A21 3sh Buffalo .25 .25
171 A21 5sh Lions .30 .40
172 A21 10sh Rhinoceros .65 .80
173 A21 20sh Elephants 1.30 1.60
174 A21 40sh Cheetahs 2.60 3.25
Nos. 161-174 (14) 7.35 8.55

For overprints see Nos. O27-O36.

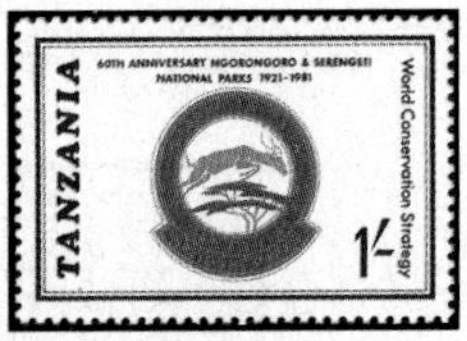

National Parks Emblem A22

50c, Ngorongoro Park. 5sh, Friends of Serengeti. 20sh, Friends of Ngorongoro.

1981, Jan. 26 Litho. *Perf. 13x13½*

175 A22 50c multicolored .25 .25
176 A22 1sh shown .25 .25
177 A22 5sh multicolored .50 .50
178 A22 20sh multicolored 2.00 2.00
Nos. 175-178 (4) 3.00 3.00

Ngorongoro & Serengeti Parks, 60th anniv.
For overprints see Nos. 299-302.

Nos. 89-90 Overprinted

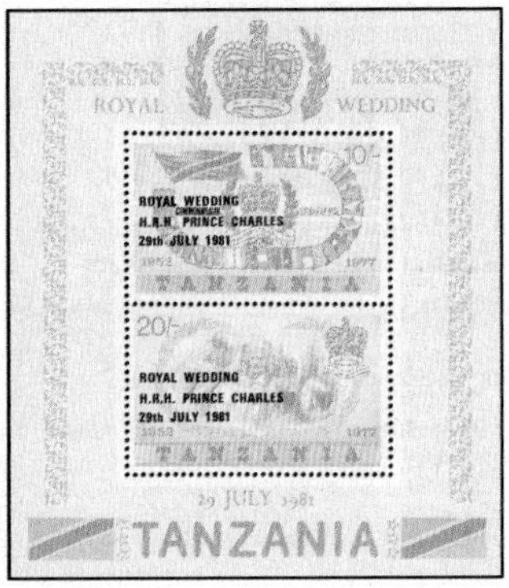

1981, July 29 Litho. *Perf. 14x13½*

179 A7 10sh multicolored .35 .35
180 A7 20sh multicolored .65 .65
a. Souvenir sheet of 2, #179-180 5.50 5.50

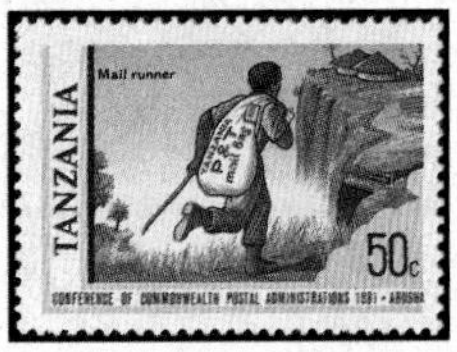

Mail Runner A23

1sh, Letter sorting. 5sh, Post horn, carrier pigeon. 10sh, Commonwealth members' flags.

1981, Oct. 23 Litho. *Perf. 12½x12*

181 A23 50c shown .25 .25
182 A23 1sh multicolored .25 .25
183 A23 5sh multicolored .55 .55
184 A23 10sh multicolored 1.20 1.20
a. Souvenir sheet of 4, #181-184 2.75 2.75
Nos. 181-184 (4) 2.25 2.25

Commonwealth Postal Administrations Conference, Arusha, June 29-July 10.

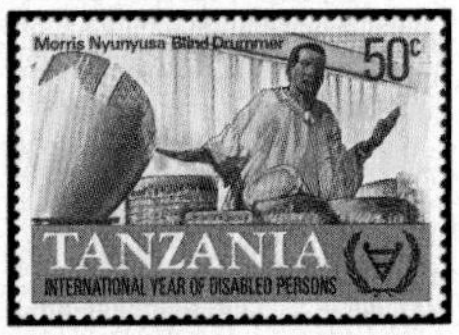

Intl. Year of the Disabled A24

1981, Nov. 30 Litho. *Perf. 14*

185 A24 50c Morris Nyunyusa, blind drummer .30 .30
186 A24 1sh Sewing .40 .40
187 A24 5sh Prostheses 1.40 1.40
188 A24 10sh Children 2.75 2.75
Nos. 185-188 (4) 4.85 4.85

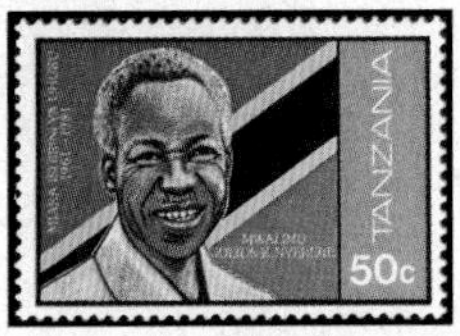

20th Anniv. of Independence — A25

1982, Jan. 13 Litho. *Perf. 13x13½*

189 A25 50c Pres. Nyerere, flag .25 .25
190 A25 1sh Zanzibar Electricity Plant .25 .25
191 A25 3sh Sisal plant, weaver .50 .50
192 A25 10sh Pupils 1.75 1.75
a. Souvenir sheet of 4, #189-192 3.00 3.00
Nos. 189-192 (4) 2.75 2.75

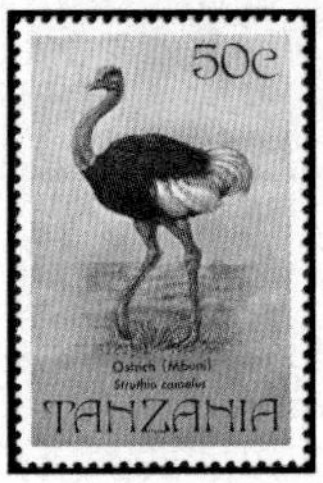

Ostrich — A26

1982, Jan. 25 Litho. *Perf. 13½*

193 A26 50c shown .65 .65
194 A26 1sh Secretary bird 1.00 1.00
195 A26 5sh Kori bustard 4.25 4.25
196 A26 10sh Saddle-bill stork 8.00 8.00
Nos. 193-196 (4) 13.90 13.90

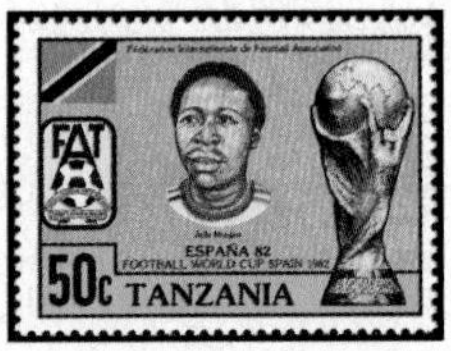

1982 World Cup A27

1982, June 2 Litho. *Perf. 14*

197 A27 50c Jella Mtagwa .35 .35
198 A27 1sh Stadium .35 .35
199 A27 10sh Diego Armando Maradona 3.00 3.00
200 A27 20sh Globe 6.50 6.50
a. Souvenir sheet of 4, #197-200 10.50 10.50
Nos. 197-200 (4) 10.20 10.20

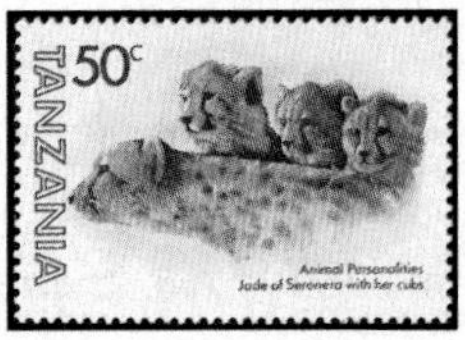

Jade of Seronera and her Cubs A28

Animals Appearing in Movies or TV Shows: 1sh, Wild dog and puppies, Havoc. 5sh, Fifi and sons, Gombe. 10sh, Bahati and twins Rashidi and Ramadhani, Lake Manyara.

1982, July 15 Litho. *Perf. 14*

201 A28 50c multicolored .25 .25
202 A28 1sh multicolored .30 .30
203 A28 5sh multicolored 1.25 1.25
204 A28 10sh multicolored 2.75 2.75
a. Souv. sheet, #201-204, perf. 14½ 5.50 5.50
Nos. 201-204 (4) 4.55 4.55

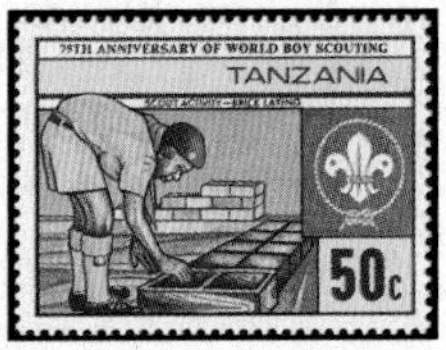

Scouting Year A29

1982, Aug. 25

205 A29 50c Brick laying .25 .25
206 A29 1sh Camping .25 .25
207 A29 10sh Tracing marks 1.75 1.75
208 A29 20sh Baden-Powell 3.75 3.75
a. Souvenir sheet of 4, #205-208 6.50 6.50
Nos. 205-208 (4) 6.00 6.00

For overprint see No. 303.

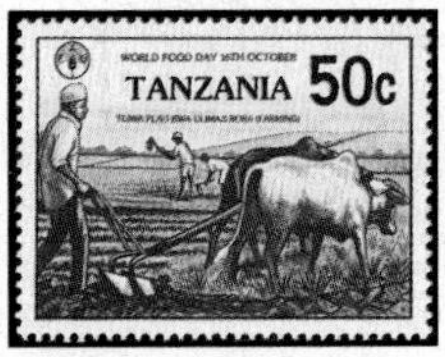

World Food Day — A30

1982, Oct. 16 Litho. *Perf. 14*

209 A30 50c Plowing .25 .25
210 A30 1sh Dairy cows .25 .25
211 A30 5sh Corn harvest .90 .90

212 A30 10sh Grain storage 1.75 1.75
a. Souvenir sheet of 4, #209-212 3.25 3.25
Nos. 209-212 (4) 3.15 3.15

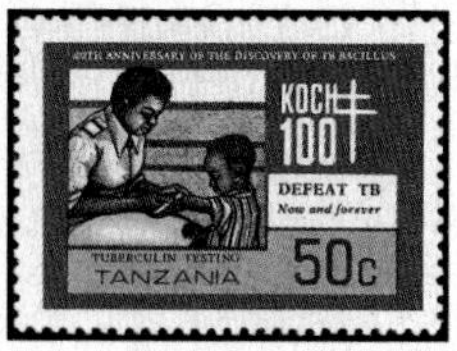

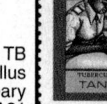

TB Bacillus Centenary A31

1982, Dec. 5 *Perf. 12½x12*
213 A31 50c Child immunization .25 .25
214 A31 1sh Koch .25 .25
215 A31 5sh TB emblem .90 .90
216 A31 10sh WHO emblem 1.75 1.75
Nos. 213-216 (4) 3.15 3.15

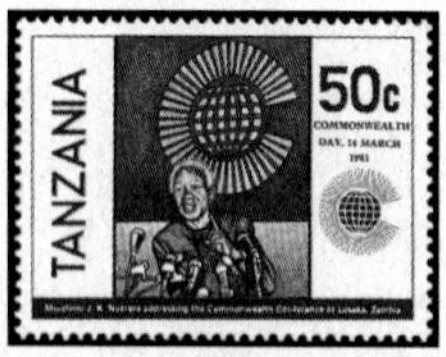

A31a

1983, Mar. 14 **Litho.** *Perf. 14*
217 A31a 50c Pres. Nyerere .25 .25
218 A31a 1sh Running, boxing .25 .25
219 A31a 5sh Flags .75 .75
220 A31a 10sh Pres. Nyerere, Royal Family 1.50 1.50
a. Souvenir sheet of 4, #217-220 3.00 3.00
Nos. 217-220 (4) 2.75 2.75

Commonwealth Day. For overprint see #407.

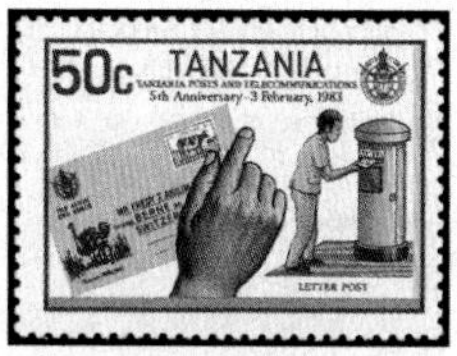

5th Anniv. of Posts and Telecommunications Dept. — A32

1983, Feb. 3 **Litho.** *Perf. 12½x12*
221 A32 50c Letter post .25 .25
222 A32 1sh Training Institute .25 .25
223 A32 5sh Satellite communications .80 .80
224 A32 10sh Emblems 1.60 1.60
a. Souvenir sheet of 4, #221-224 3.00 3.00
Nos. 221-224 (4) 2.90 2.90

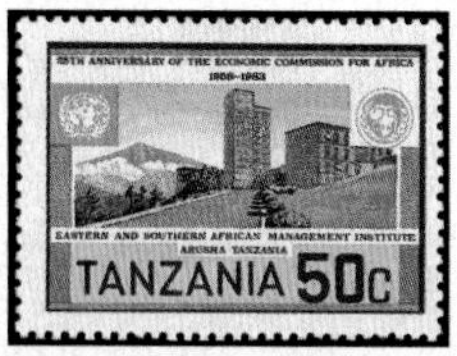

25th Anniv. of Economic Commission for Africa — A33

50c, Eastern & Southern African Management Institute, Arusha. 1sh, Emblems. 5sh, Mineral collections. 10sh, Emblems, diff.

1983, Sept. 12 **Litho.** *Perf. 12½x12*
225 A33 50c multicolored .45 .45
226 A33 1sh multicolored .60 .60
227 A33 5sh multicolored 2.40 2.40
228 A33 10sh multicolored 4.75 4.75
a. Souvenir sheet of 4, #225-228 8.25 8.25
Nos. 225-228 (4) 8.20 8.20

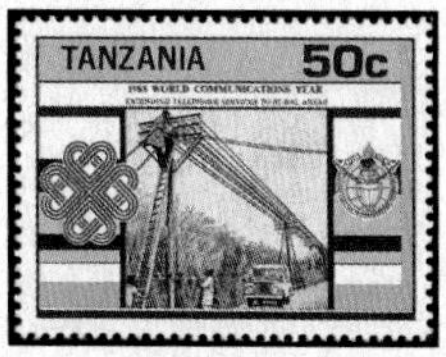

World Communications Year — A34

1983, Oct. 17 **Litho.** *Perf. 14*
229 A34 50c Rural telephone service .25 .25
230 A34 1sh Emblems .25 .25
231 A34 5sh Post Office 1.00 1.00
232 A34 10sh Microwave tower 2.00 2.00
a. Souvenir sheet of 4, #229-232 3.50 3.50
Nos. 229-232 (4) 3.50 3.50

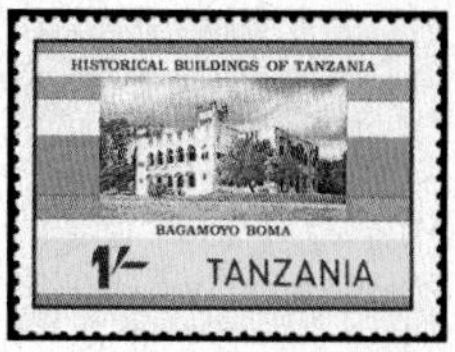

Historical Buildings A35

1983, Dec. 12 **Litho.** *Perf. 12½x12*
233 A35 1sh Bagamoyo Boma .25 .25
234 A35 1.50sh Beit-El-Ajaib .30 .30
235 A35 5sh Anglican Church .70 .70
236 A35 10sh State House, old and new 1.25 1.25
a. Souvenir sheet of 4, #233-236 3.00 3.00
Nos. 233-236 (4) 2.50 2.50

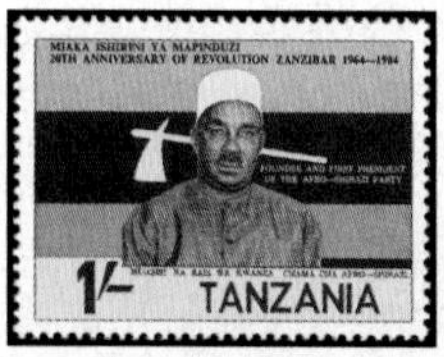

20th Anniv. of Revolution A36

1sh, Muasisi Kwanza. 1.50sh, Clove farming. 5sh, Industrial development. 10sh, Housing developments. 15sh, Map, ship.

1984, June 18 **Litho.** *Perf. 14*
237 A36 1sh multicolored .25 .25
238 A36 1.50sh multicolored .30 .30
239 A36 5sh multicolored .90 .90
240 A36 10sh multicolored 1.75 1.75
Nos. 237-240 (4) 3.20 3.20

Souvenir Sheet

241 A36 15sh multicolored 3.25 3.25

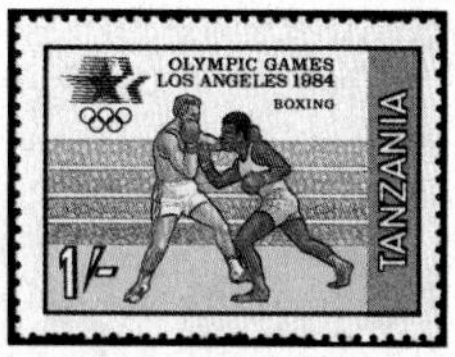

1984 Summer Olympics A37

1984, Aug. 6 *Perf. 12½x12*
242 A37 1sh Boxing .25 .25
243 A37 1.50sh Running .25 .25
244 A37 5sh Basketball .70 .70
245 A37 20sh Soccer 2.00 2.00
a. Souvenir sheet of 4, #242-245 3.50 3.50
Nos. 242-245 (4) 3.20 3.20

For overprints see Nos. 275-278.

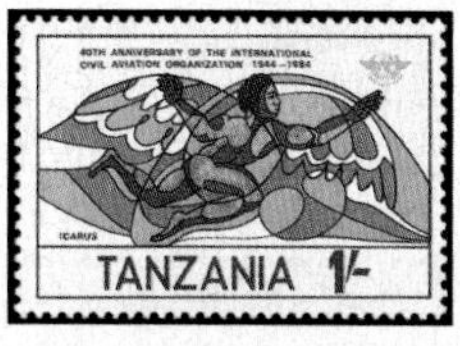

Intl. Civil Aviation Org. 40th Anniv. A38

1sh, Icarus. 1.50sh, Air Tanzania jets, traffic controller. 5sh, Aircraft maintenance. 10sh, ICAO emblem.

1984, Nov. 15 **Litho.** *Perf. 13*
246 A38 1sh multicolored .25 .25
247 A38 1.50sh multicolored .25 .25
248 A38 5sh multicolored .90 .90
249 A38 10sh multicolored 1.40 1.40
a. Souvenir sheet of 4, #246-249 3.25 3.25
Nos. 246-249 (4) 2.80 2.80

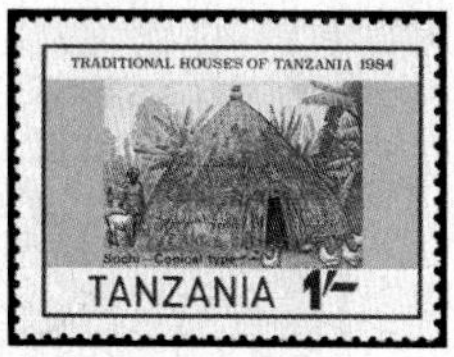

Traditional Houses A39

1984, Dec. 20 *Perf. 12½x12*
250 A39 1sh Sochi .25 .25
251 A39 1.50sh Isyenga .25 .25
252 A39 5sh Tembe .60 .60
253 A39 10sh Banda 1.10 1.10
a. Souvenir sheet of 4, #250-253 2.50 2.50
Nos. 250-253 (4) 2.20 2.20

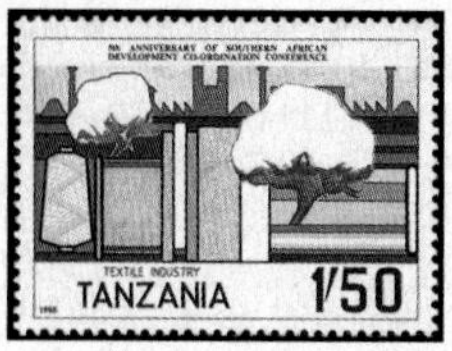

Textile Industry A40

5th anniversary of the Southern Africa Development Coordination Conference — 4sh, Mining. 5sh, Transportation and communications. 20sh, Flags of member nations.

1985, Apr. 1 *Perf. 14*
254 A40 1.50sh shown .50 .50
255 A40 4sh multicolored 1.25 1.25
256 A40 5sh multicolored 1.40 1.40
257 A40 20sh multicolored 6.00 6.00
a. Souvenir sheet of 4, #254-257 10.00 10.00
Nos. 254-257 (4) 9.15 9.15

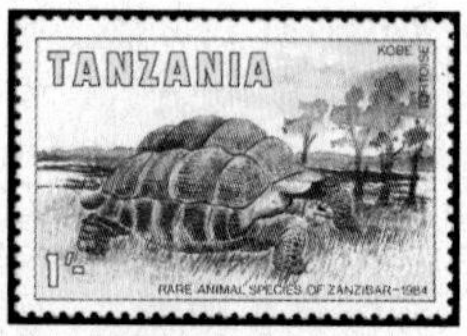

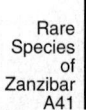

Rare Species of Zanzibar A41

Perf. 13½x13, 13x13½

1985, May 8 **Litho.**
258 A41 1sh Tortoise .50 .50
259 A41 4sh Leopard 1.50 1.50
260 A41 10sh Civet cat 3.00 3.00
261 A41 17.50sh Red colobus, vert. 4.75 4.75
Nos. 258-261 (4) 9.75 9.75

Souvenir Sheet

262 Sheet of 2 3.75 3.75
a. A41 15sh Black rhinoceros 1.50 1.50
b. A41 20sh Giant ground pangolin 2.25 2.25

For overprints see Nos. 408-409, 411.

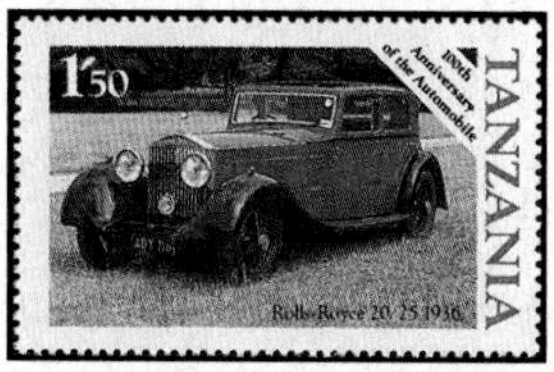

Automobile Centenary — A42

Classic autos manufactured by Rolls-Royce.

1985, May 14 *Perf. 14½x14*
263 A42 1.50sh 1936 20/25 .25 .25
264 A42 5sh 1933 Phantom II .25 .25
265 A42 10sh 1926 Phantom I .25 .25
266 A42 30sh 1907 Silver Ghost .70 .70
a. Souvenir sheet of 4, #263-266 1.75 1.75
Nos. 263-266 (4) 1.45 1.45

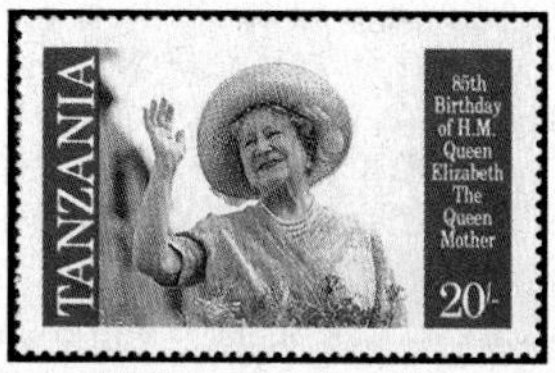

Queen Mother, 85th Birthday — A43

1985, Sept. 30
267 A43 20sh Waving .25 .25
268 A43 20sh Facing left .25 .25
269 A43 100sh Wearing green hat .25 .25
a. Souvenir sheet, #267, 269 .75 .75
270 A43 100sh Facing right .25 .25
a. Souvenir sheet, #268, 270 .75 .75
Nos. 267-270 (4) 1.00 1.00

For overprints see Nos. 295-298.

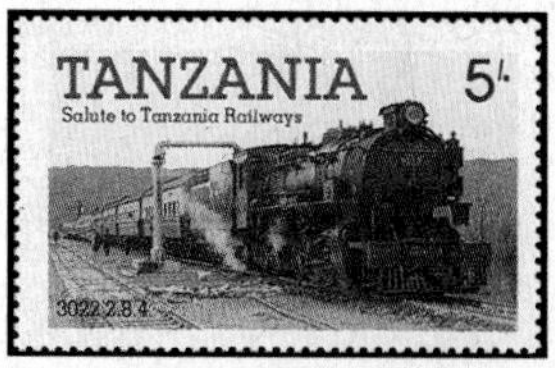

Tanzania Railways Locomotives — A44

1985, Oct. 7 **Litho.** *Perf. 14½x14*
271 A44 5sh No. 3022 .25 .25
272 A44 10sh No. 3107 .25 .25
273 A44 20sh No. 6004 .35 .35
274 A44 30sh No. 3129 .55 .55
a. Souvenir sheet of 4, #271-274 1.25 1.25
Nos. 271-274 (4) 1.40 1.40

Nos. 242-245 Ovptd. with Winners and "GOLD MEDAL" in 2 or 3 Lines

1985, Oct. 22 *Perf. 12½x12*
275 A37 1sh Henry Tillman, USA .30 .30
276 A37 1.50sh USA .30 .30
277 A37 5sh USA .70 .70
278 A37 20sh France 2.10 2.10
a. Souvenir sheet of 4, #275-278 8.75 8.75
Nos. 275-278 (4) 3.40 3.40

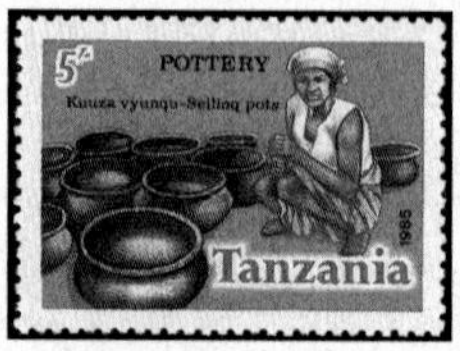

Pottery A45

1.50sh, Water and cooking pots. 2sh, Frying pot and caldron. 5sh, Woman selling pots. 40sh, Beer pot.
30sh, Water pot.

1985, Nov. 4
279 A45 1.50sh multicolored .25 .25
280 A45 2sh multicolored .25 .25
281 A45 5sh multicolored .40 .40
282 A45 40sh multicolored 3.25 3.25
Nos. 279-282 (4) 4.15 4.15

Souvenir Sheet

283 A45 30sh multicolored 4.25 4.25

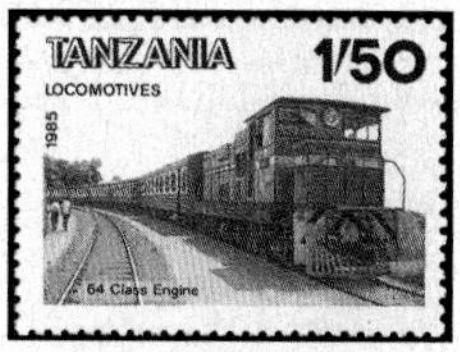

Locomotives — A46

1.50sh, Class 64. 2sh, Class 36. 5sh, Shunting DFH1013. 10sh, Diesel Electric DE1001. 30sh, Zanzibar, 1906.

1985, Nov. 25
284 A46 1.50sh multi .25 .25
285 A46 2sh multi .25 .25
286 A46 5sh multi .60 .60
287 A46 10sh multi 1.25 1.25
288 A46 30sh multi 3.50 3.50
Nos. 284-288 (5) 5.85 5.85

Souvenir Sheet

289 Sheet of 2 10.00 10.00
a. A46 15sh Class 30 steam 4.50 4.50
b. A46 20sh Class 11 steam 5.50 5.50

For overprints see Nos. 381A-381E.

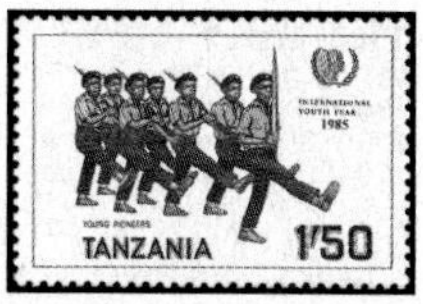

Intl. Youth Year — A47

1986, Jan. 20 *Perf. 14*
290 A47 1.50sh Young Pioneers .25 .25
291 A47 4sh Health care .50 .50
292 A47 10sh Uhuru torch race 1.00 1.00
293 A47 20sh World map 1.75 1.75
Nos. 290-293 (4) 3.50 3.50

Souvenir Sheet

294 A47 30sh Agriculture 3.50 3.50

Nos. 267-270 Ovptd. "CARIBBEAN/ ROYAL VISIT/ 1985" in Silver or Gold

1986, Feb. 10 *Perf. 14½x14*
295 A43 20sh on #267 *9.00 9.00*
296 A43 20sh on #268 *9.00 9.00*
297 A43 100sh on #269 *9.00 9.00*
a. Souvenir sheet, #295, 297 *20.00* —
298 A43 100sh on #270 *9.00 9.00*
a. Souvenir sheet, #296, 298 *20.00* —
Nos. 295-298 (4) 36.00 36.00

See footnote following No. 303.

Nos. 175-178, 208a Ovptd. "75th ANNIVERSARY GIRL GUIDES/ 1910-1985" in Silver or Black

1986, Feb. Litho. *Perf. 13x13½, 14*

299	A22	50c multicolored (S)	15.00 15.00
300	A22	1sh multicolored	15.00 15.00
301	A22	5sh multicolored	15.00 15.00
302	A22	20sh multicolored	15.00 15.00

Souvenir Sheet

303		Sheet of 4	45.00 45.00
a.		A29 50c multicolored	— —
b.		A29 1sh multicolored	— —
c.		A29 10sh multicolored	— —
d.		A29 20sh multicolored	— —

The status of this set, the Caribbean Royal Visit set and at least 12 stamps overprinted congratulating the Duke and Duchess of York on their marriage are in question.

Rotary Intl., World Chess Championships — A48

1986, Mar. 17 *Perf. 14*

304	A48	20sh shown	.25 .25
305	A48	100sh Chess board	1.25 1.25
a.		Souvenir sheet of 2, #304-305	1.75 1.75

Audubon Birth Bicent. — A49

Illustrations of American bird species by Audubon.

1986, May 22

306	A49	5sh Mallard	.30 .30
307	A49	10sh American eider	.30 .30
308	A49	20sh Scarlet ibis	.55 .55
309	A49	30sh Roseate spoonbill	.85 .85
a.		Souvenir sheet of 4, #306-309	3.00 3.00
		Nos. 306-309 (4)	2.00 2.00

Gemstones A50

1986, May 22

310	A50	1.50sh Pearls	.65 .65
311	A50	2sh Sapphires	.80 .80
312	A50	5sh Tanzanite	2.25 2.25
313	A50	40sh Diamonds	12.50 12.50
		Nos. 310-313 (4)	16.20 16.20

Souvenir Sheet

314	A50	30sh Rubies	17.00 17.00

Indigenous Flowers — A51

1.50sh, Hibiscus calyphyllus. 5sh, Aloe graminicola. 10sh, Nersium oleander. 30sh, Nymphaea caerulea.

1986, June 2

315	A51	1.50sh multicolored	.25 .25
316	A51	5sh multicolored	.25 .25
317	A51	10sh multicolored	.25 .25
318	A51	30sh multicolored	.50 .50
a.		Souvenir Sheet of 4, #315-318	1.25 1.25
		Nos. 315-318 (4)	1.25 1.25

Endangered Wildlife — A52

1986, June 30 Litho. *Perf. 14x14½*

319	A52	5sh Oryx	.25 .25
320	A52	10sh Giraffe	.25 .25
321	A52	20sh Rhinoceros	.30 .30
322	A52	30sh Cheetah	.40 .40
a.		Miniature sheet of 4, #319-322	1.40 1.40
		Nos. 319-322 (4)	1.20 1.20

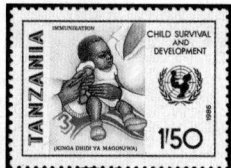

UN Child Survival Campaign A53

1.50sh, Immunization. 2sh, Growth monitoring. 5sh, Oral rehydration therapy. 40sh, Breast feeding. 30sh, Healthy child.

1986, July 29 *Perf. 12½x12*

323	A53	1.50sh multicolored	.35 .35
324	A53	2sh multicolored	.35 .35
325	A53	5sh multicolored	.35 .35
326	A53	40sh multicolored	3.00 3.00
		Nos. 323-326 (4)	4.05 4.05

Souvenir Sheet

327	A53	30sh multicolored	2.00 2.00

For overprints see Nos. 406, 410, 412.

Marine Life A54

1986, Aug. 20

328	A54	1.50sh Butterflyfish	.80 .80
329	A54	4sh Parrotfish	1.75 1.75
330	A54	10sh Sea turtle	3.00 3.00
331	A54	20sh Octopus	4.50 4.50
		Nos. 328-331 (4)	10.05 10.05

Souvenir Sheet

332	A54	30sh Coral	3.75 3.75

Queen Elizabeth II, 60th Birthday — A55

Photographs: 5sh, Royal family, Buckingham Palace balcony. 10sh, With princes in open carriage. 40sh, Elizabeth II. 60sh, Greeting crowd.

1987, Mar. 24 Litho. *Perf. 14*

333	A55	5sh multicolored	.20
334	A55	10sh multicolored	.20
335	A55	40sh multicolored	.60
336	A55	60sh multicolored	1.00
a.		Souvenir sheet of 4, #333-336	2.00
		Nos. 333-336 (4)	2.00

1986 World Cup Soccer Championships, Mexico — A57

Designs: 1.50sh, Map, team captains, officials. 2sh, Foul. 10sh, Goal. 20sh, Goalie save. 30sh, Argentine natl. team.

1986, Oct. 30 Litho. *Perf. 14*

341	A57	1.50sh multicolored	.30 .30
342	A57	2sh multicolored	.30 .30
343	A57	10sh multicolored	.65 .65
344	A57	20sh multicolored	1.25 1.25
		Nos. 341-344 (4)	2.50 2.50

Souvenir Sheet

345	A57	30sh multicolored	1.50 1.50

Hair Styles — A58

1987, Mar. 16 *Perf. 14½*

346	A58	1.50sh Nungu Nungu	.40 .40
347	A58	2sh Upanga wa Jogoo	.60 .60
348	A58	10sh Morani	1.25 1.25
349	A58	20sh Twende Kilioni	1.75 1.75
		Nos. 346-349 (4)	4.00 4.00

Souvenir Sheet

350	A58	30sh Kusuka Nywele	4.00 4.00

Intl. Peace Year A59

Designs: 1.50sh, Julius K. Nyerere, Beyond War Award winner. 2sh, Peace among nations. 10sh, Peaceful use of outer space. 20sh, Emblem, UN building. 30sh, Emblem, handshake.

1986, Dec. 22 Litho. *Perf. 14½*

351	A59	1.50sh multicolored	.55 .55
352	A59	2sh multicolored	.85 .85
353	A59	10sh multicolored	2.10 2.10
354	A59	20sh multicolored	3.00 3.00
		Nos. 351-354 (4)	6.50 6.50

Souvenir Sheet

355	A59	30sh multicolored	2.75 2.75

Natl. Bank of Commerce, 20th Anniv. — A60

1.50sh, Mobile bank. 2sh, Headquarters. 5sh, Pres. Mwinyi laying foundation stone. 20sh, Cotton harvest.

1987, Feb. 6 Litho. *Perf. 14*

356	A60	1.50sh multicolored	.50 .50
357	A60	2sh multicolored	.85 .85
358	A60	5sh multicolored	1.40 1.40
359	A60	20sh multicolored	3.50 3.50
		Nos. 356-359 (4)	6.25 6.25

New Revolutionary Party (CCM), 10th Anniv. — A61

2sh, Soldiers in formation . 3sh, Woman picking coffee beans. 10sh, Speaker at podium. 30sh, Nyerere, Mwinyi.

1987, Apr. 10 *Perf. 14½x14*

360	A61	2sh multicolored	.25 .25
361	A61	3sh multicolored	.25 .25
362	A61	10sh multicolored	.40 .40
363	A61	30sh multicolored	1.10 1.10
		Nos. 360-363 (4)	2.00 2.00

Arush Declaration, 20th anniv.

Insects A62

1987, Apr. 22 *Perf. 12½x12*

364	A62	1.50sh Bees	.70 .70
365	A62	2sh Greater grain borer	.95 .95
366	A62	10sh Tse-tse fly	2.10 2.10
367	A62	20sh Wasp	3.50 3.50
		Nos. 364-367 (4)	7.25 7.25

Souvenir Sheet

368	A62	30sh Mosquito	6.00 6.00

Reptiles A63

1987, July 2

369	A63	2sh Crocodiles	.70 .70
370	A63	3sh Black-striped grass snake	.70 .70
371	A63	10sh Adder	1.40 1.40
372	A63	20sh Green mamba	2.75 2.75
		Nos. 369-372 (4)	5.55 5.55

Souvenir Sheet

373	A63	30sh Tortoise	2.00 2.00

Posts and Telecommunications, Railways Emblems — A64

8sh, Air Tanzania, Port Authority. 20sh, Modes of communication and transportation.

1987, July 27 *Perf. 14*

374	A64	5sh shown	.60 .60
375	A64	8sh multicolored	1.40 1.40

Souvenir Sheet

376	A64	20sh multicolored	5.00 5.00

Traditional Crafts A65

1987, Dec. 15 Litho. *Perf. 12½x12*

377	A65	2sh Baskets	.30	.30
378	A65	3sh Gourds	.30	.30
379	A65	10sh Stools	.50	.50
380	A65	20sh Makonde carvings	.90	.90
		Nos. 377-380 (4)	2.00	2.00

Souvenir Sheet

381	A65	40sh Makonde carver at work	2.00	2.00

Nos. 284-288 Ovptd.

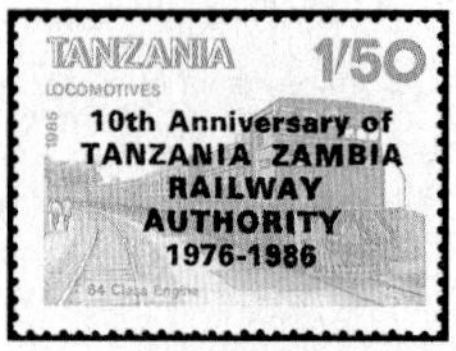

1987, Dec. 30 Litho. *Perf. 12½x12*

381A	A46	1.50sh multicolored	.70	.70
381B	A46	2sh multicolored	.70	.70
381C	A46	5sh multicolored	.85	.85
381D	A46	10sh multicolored	1.75	1.75
381E	A46	30sh multicolored	5.25	5.25
		Nos. 381A-381E (5)	9.25	9.25

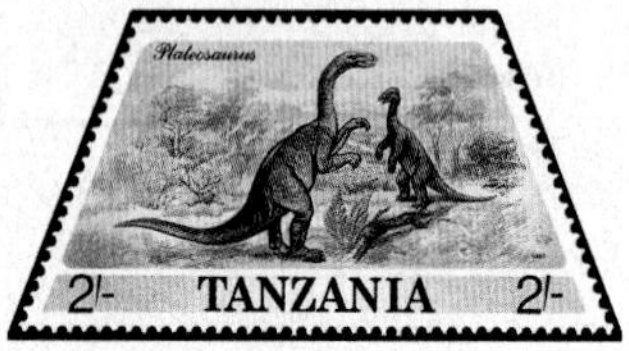

Plateosaurus — A66

1988, Apr. 22 *Perf. 12½*

382	A66	2sh shown	.65	.65
383	A66	3sh Pteranodon	.65	.65
384	A66	5sh Brontosaurus	.65	.65
385	A66	7sh Lions	.70	.70
386	A66	8sh Tiger	.70	.70
387	A66	12sh Orangutans	.80	.80
388	A66	20sh Elephants	1.10	1.10
389	A66	100sh Stegosaurus	2.75	2.75
		Nos. 382-389 (8)	8.00	8.00

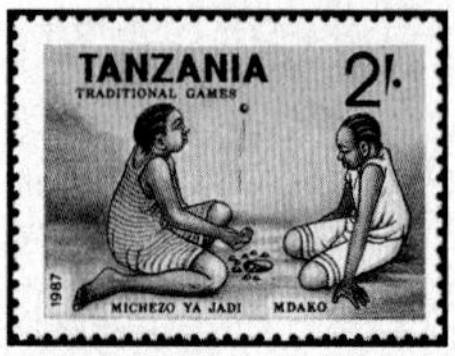

Traditional Games A67

1988, Feb. 15 Litho. *Perf. 12½x12*

390	A67	2sh Mdako (marbles)	.50	.50
391	A67	3sh Mieleka (wrestling)	.50	.50
392	A67	8sh Bull fight	.50	.50
393	A67	20sh Bao (African chess)	.80	.80
		Nos. 390-393 (4)	2.30	2.30

Souvenir Sheet

394	A67	30sh Kulenga shabaha (archery)	2.00	2.00

Dated 1987.

Miniature Sheets

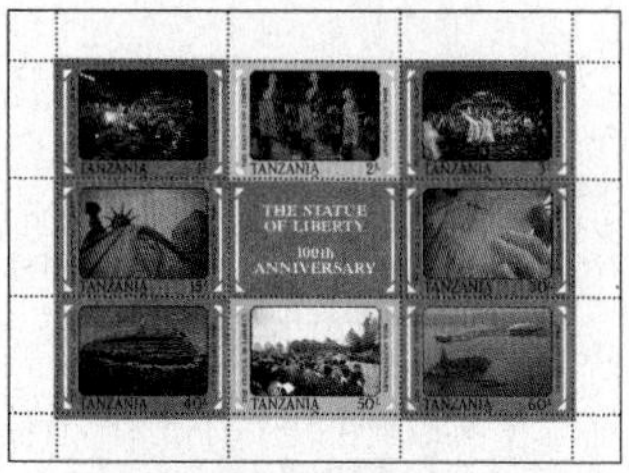

Statue of Liberty, Cent. (in 1986) — A68

No. 395: 1sh, Re-opening gala (evening), 1986. 2sh, Musicians performing. 3sh, Cheerleaders. 15sh, Statue holding tablet. 30sh, Tablet inscription. 40sh, Liberty Island. 50sh, Re-opening gala (afternoon), 1986. 60sh, Blimps over Liberty Island.

No. 396: 4sh, Statue, blimp. 5sh, Torch. 6sh, Torch and crown observatories lit at night, scaffolding. 7sh, Worker gilding torch. 8sh, Statue shrouded in scaffolding. 10sh, Two workers, torch. 12sh, Head, scaffolding. 18sh, Celebrant at re-opening (evening). 20sh, Goodyear blimp, skirt of Statue. 25sh, Boys' choir, statue. 35sh, Torch held aloft, full moon. 45sh, Worker cleaning tablet.

1988, June 15 Litho. *Perf. 14*

395		Sheet of 8 + label	9.00	9.00
a.	A68	1sh multicolored	.25	.25
b.	A68	2sh multicolored	.25	.25
c.	A68	3sh multicolored	.25	.25
d.	A68	15sh multicolored	.60	.60
e.	A68	30sh multicolored	1.25	1.25
f.	A68	40sh multicolored	1.60	1.60
g.	A68	50sh multicolored	2.00	2.00
h.	A68	60sh multicolored	2.40	2.40
396		Sheet of 12	9.00	9.00
a.	A68	4sh multicolored	.25	.25
b.	A68	5sh multicolored	.25	.25
c.	A68	6sh multicolored	.25	.25
d.	A68	7sh multicolored	.25	.25
e.	A68	8sh multicolored	.35	.35
f.	A68	10sh multicolored	.40	.40
g.	A68	12sh multicolored	.45	.45
h.	A68	18sh multicolored	.75	.75
i.	A68	20sh multicolored	.80	.80
j.	A68	25sh multicolored	1.00	1.00
k.	A68	35sh multicolored	1.40	1.40
l.	A68	45sh multicolored	1.75	1.75

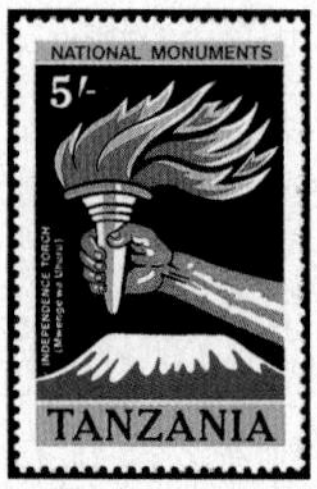

Natl. Monuments — A69

5sh, Independence Torch. 12sh, Arusha Declaration. 30sh, Askari. 60sh, Independence. 100sh, Soldier (Askari detail).

1988, June 15 Litho.

397	A69	5sh multicolored	.25	.25
398	A69	12sh multicolored	.25	.25
399	A69	30sh multicolored	.30	.30
400	A69	60sh multicolored	.50	.50
		Nos. 397-400 (4)	1.30	1.30

Souvenir Sheet

401	A69	100sh multicolored	2.50	2.50

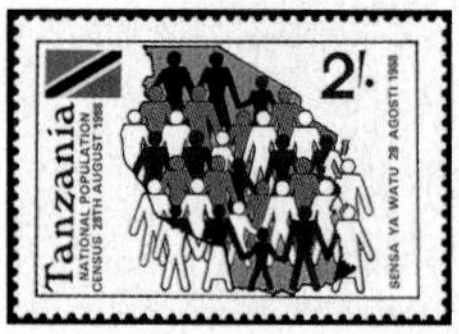

3rd Natl. Census, Aug. 28 — A70

3sh, Enumeration. 10sh, Health care. 20sh, Population figures.
40sh, Segments of economy and society.

1988, Aug. 8

402	A70	2sh shown	.25	.25
403	A70	3sh multicolored	.25	.25
404	A70	10sh multicolored	.30	.30
405	A70	20sh multicolored	.45	.45
		Nos. 402-405 (4)	1.25	1.25

Souvenir Sheet

405A	A70	40sh multicolored	1.25	1.25

Stamps of 1983-86 Overprinted

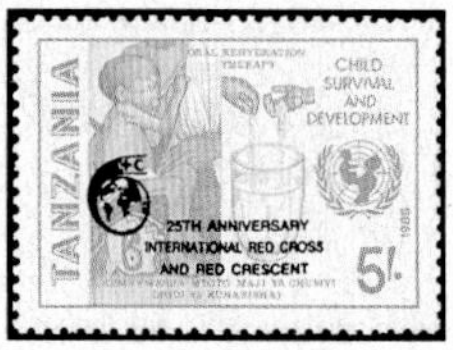

Nos. 406 & 410, 412 Overprinted

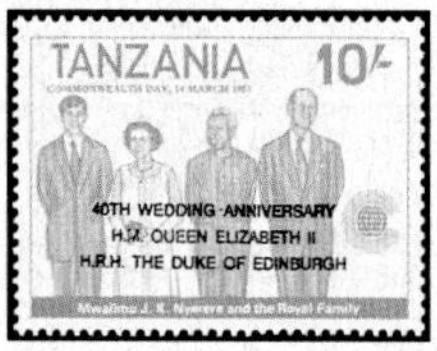

No. 408 Ovptd.

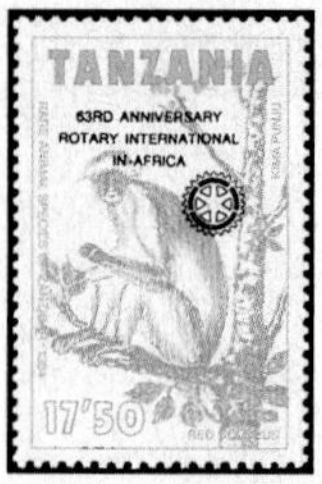

Nos. 407 & 409, 411 Overprinted

1988, Aug. 15 *Perfs. as Before*

406	A53	5sh on #325	1.10	1.10
407	A31a	10sh on #220	15.00	15.00
a.		Souv. sheet of 4, #218-220, 407	10.00	10.00
408	A31a	10sh on #260	5.50	5.50
409	A41	17.50sh on #261	10.00	10.00
410	A53	40sh on #326	13.00	13.00
		Nos. 406-410 (5)	44.60	44.60

Souvenir Sheets

411		Sheet of 2	6.75	6.75
a.	A41	15sh on #262a	1.75	1.75
b.	A41	20sh on #262b	3.75	3.75
412	A53	30sh on #327	6.75	6.75

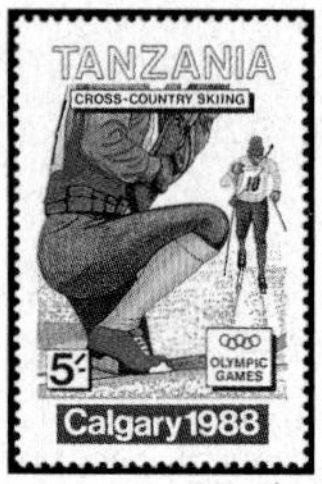

1988 Olympics, Seoul and Calgary — A71

1988, Aug. 29 *Perf. 14*

414	A71	5sh Biathlon	.50	.50
415	A71	10sh Soccer	.25	.25
416	A71	20sh Cycling	.80	.80
417	A71	25sh Pairs figuring skating	.90	.90
418	A71	50sh Fencing	.85	.85
419	A71	50sh Downhill skiing	1.60	1.60
420	A71	70sh Volleyball	1.00	1.00
421	A71	75sh Bobsled	1.90	1.90
		Nos. 414-421 (8)	7.80	7.80

Souvenir Sheets

422	A71	100sh Flags, hockey sticks	4.00	4.00
423	A71	100sh Gymnastics	4.00	4.00

For overprint see No. 534A-534J.

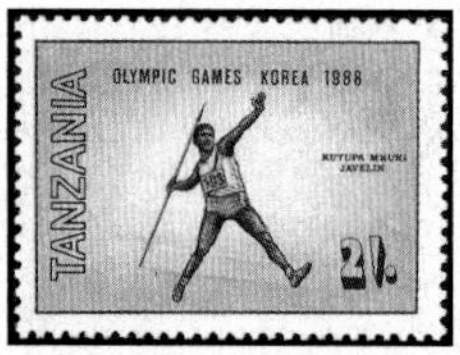

1988 Summer Olympics, Seoul A71a

1988, Sept. 5 Litho. *Perf. 12½x12*

423A	A71a	2sh Javelin	.90	.90
423B	A71a	3sh Hurdles	.95	.95
423C	A71a	7sh Long distance running	1.50	1.50
423D	A71a	12sh Relay race	2.00	2.00
		Nos. 423A-423D (4)	5.35	5.35

A souvenir sheet exists.

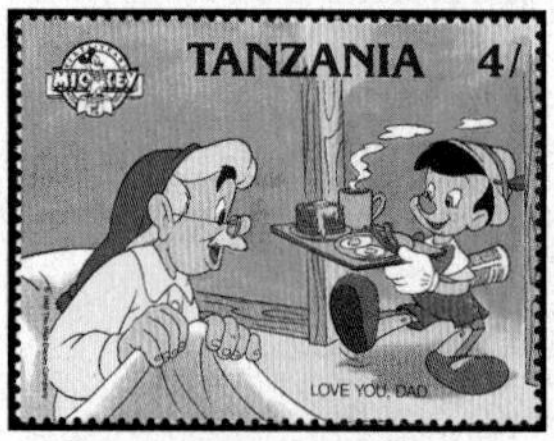

Disney Characters, Special Occasions — A72

1988, Sept. 9 *Perf. 14*

424	A72	4sh Love You, Dad	.30	.30
425	A72	5sh Happy Birthday	.30	.30
426	A72	10sh Trick or Treat	.45	.45
427	A72	12sh Be Kind to Animals	.45	.45
428	A72	15sh Love	.55	.55
429	A72	20sh Let's Celebrate	.80	.80
430	A72	30sh Keep In Touch	1.75	1.75
431	A72	50sh Love You, Mom	3.50	3.50
		Nos. 424-431 (8)	8.10	8.10

Souvenir Sheets

432	A72	150sh Let's Work Together	4.50	4.50
433	A72	150sh Have a Super Sunday	4.50	4.50

Mickey Mouse, 60th anniv.

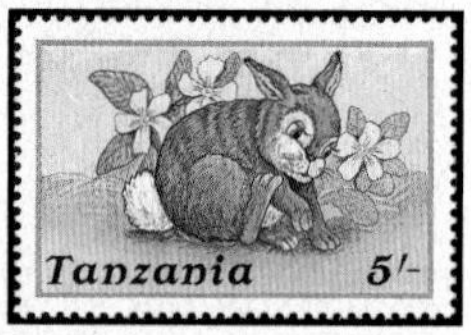

Domestic Animals A73

1988, Sept. 9

434	A73	4sh Goat, vert.	.60	.60
435	A73	5sh Rabbit	.60	.60
436	A73	8sh Cows	.85	.85
437	A73	10sh Cat	1.10	1.10
438	A73	12sh Horse, vert.	1.50	1.50
439	A73	20sh Dog, vert.	2.25	2.25
		Nos. 434-439 (6)	6.90	6.90

Souvenir Sheet

440	A73	100sh Chicken	4.50	4.50

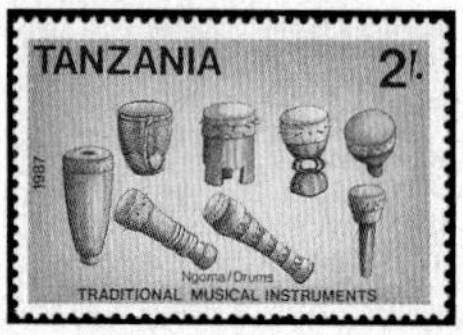

Traditional Musical Instruments — A74

1988, Sept. 30 Litho. *Perf. 14*

441	A74	2sh Drums	.70	.70
442	A74	3sh Xylophones	.70	.70
443	A74	10sh Thumb pianos	1.50	1.50
444	A74	20sh Fiddles	2.10	2.10
		Nos. 441-444 (4)	5.00	5.00

Souvenir Sheet

445	A74	40sh Violins with calabash resonators	2.00	2.00

Dated 1987.

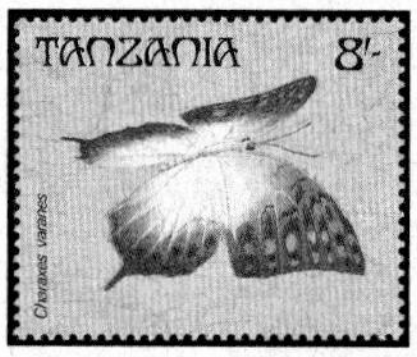

Butterflies A75

8sh, Charaxes varanes. 30sh, Neptis melicerta. 40sh, Mylothris chloris. 50sh, Charaxes bohemani. 60sh, Myrina ficedula. 75sh, Papilio phorcas. 90sh, Cyrestis camillus. 100sh, Salamis temora.
200sh, Asterope rosa. 250sh, Kallima rumia.

1988, Oct. 17 *Perf. 14½*

446	A75	8sh multicolored	.75	.75
447	A75	30sh multicolored	1.40	1.40
448	A75	40sh multicolored	1.40	1.40
449	A75	50sh multicolored	1.75	1.75
450	A75	60sh multicolored	2.10	2.10
451	A75	75sh multicolored	2.75	2.75
452	A75	90sh multicolored	3.25	3.25
453	A75	100sh multicolored	3.25	3.25
		Nos. 446-453 (8)	16.65	16.65

Souvenir Sheets

454	A75	200sh multicolored	7.50	7.50
455	A75	250sh multicolored	8.50	8.50

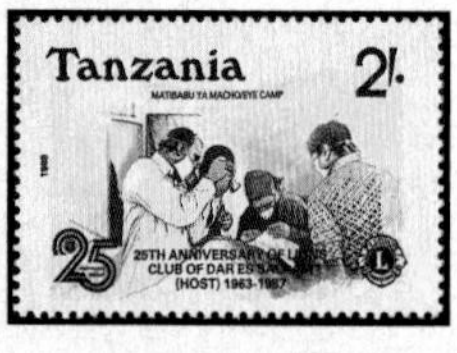

Intl. Lions Club at Dar es Salaam, 25th Anniv. A76

1988, Nov, 30 Litho. *Perf. 14½*

456	A76	2sh Eye operation	.40	.40
457	A76	3sh Shallow water well	.40	.40
458	A76	7sh Map, rhinoceros	1.25	1.25
459	A76	12sh Donating school desks	.50	.50
		Nos. 456-459 (4)	2.55	2.55

Souvenir Sheet

460	A76	40sh Emblem	2.00	2.00

Community services: Matibabu Ya Macho Eye Camp (2sh); sanitary water supply in Dar

es Salaam (3sh); wildlife conservation (7sh); aid to local schools (12sh).

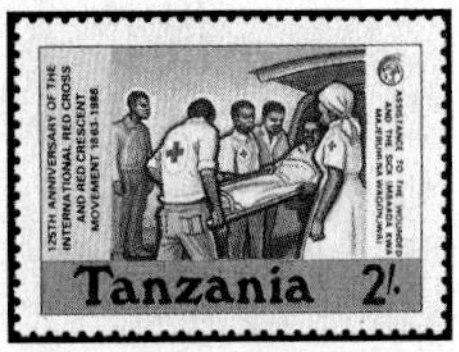

Intl. Red Cross and Red Crescent Organizations, 125th Annivs. — A77

Design: 2sh, Assisting the wounded and sick. 3sh, Postnatal care clinic. 7sh, Red Cross flag. 12sh, Jean-Henry Dunant, founder. 40sh, Dunant, Thomas Maunier, Louis Appia, Gustave Moynier and Gen. Guillaume Henri Dufour, members of intl. committee that sponsored the conference in 1863 where the Red Cross was founded.

1988, Dec. 30 Litho. *Perf. 12½x12*

461	A77	2sh multicolored	.50	.50
462	A77	3sh multicolored	.50	.50
463	A77	7sh multicolored	.55	.55
464	A77	12sh multicolored	.80	.80
		Nos. 461-464 (4)	2.35	2.35

Souvenir Sheet

465	A77	40sh multicolored	2.00	2.00

Miniature Sheet

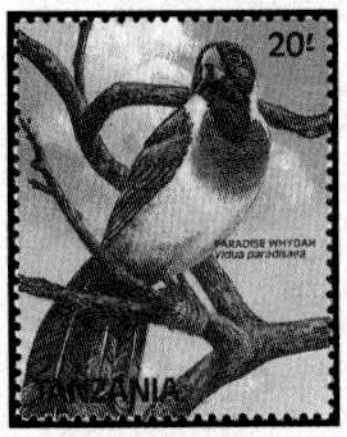

Paradise Whydah — A78

Birds: a, Paradise whydah. b, Black-collared barbet. c, Bataleur eagle. d, Openbill storks, lilac-breasted roller. e, Scarlet-tufted malachite sunbird. f, Dark chanting goshawk. g, White-fronted bee-eater, little bee-eater, carmine bee-eater. h, Marabou stork, Narina's trocon. i, African gray parrot. j, Hoopoe. k, Yellow-collared lovebird. l, Yellow-billed hornbill. m, Hammerkop. n, Flamingos, violet-crested turaco. o, Malachite kingfisher. p, Greater flamingo. q, Yellow-billed stork. r, Shoebill stork. s, Saddle-billed stork, blacksmith plover. t, Crowned crane.

1989, Jan. 10 *Perf. 14*

466		Sheet of 20	30.00	30.00
a.-t.	A78	20sh any single	.75	.75

Souvenir Sheets

467	A78	350sh Helmeted guineafowl	8.00	8.00
467A	A78	350sh Ostrich	8.00	8.00

No. 466 has a continuous design.

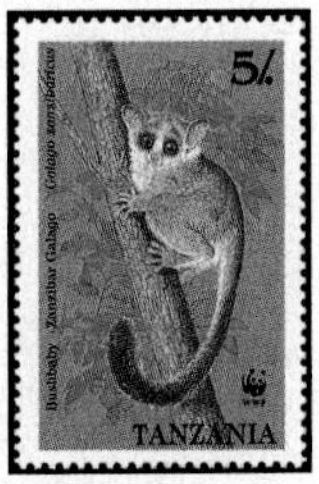

Endangered Species — A79

World Wildlife Fund: Various bushbabies, *Galago zanzibaricus*. 350sh, African palm civet.

1989, Jan. 24 *Perf. 14*

468	A79	5sh shown	.85	.85
469	A79	10sh multi, horiz.	1.00	1.00
470	A79	20sh multi, diff.	1.40	1.40
471	A79	45sh multi, diff., horiz.	2.75	2.75
		Nos. 468-471 (4)	6.00	6.00

Souvenir Sheet

472	A79	350sh multi, horiz.	10.00	10.00

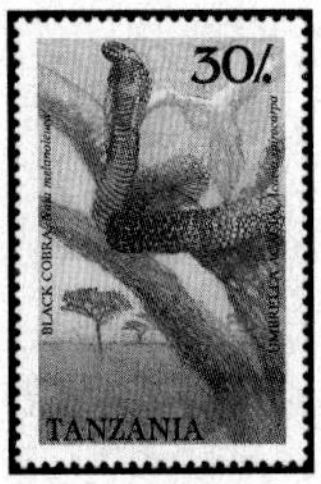

Endangered Species — A80

30sh, Black cobra, umbrella acacia. 70sh, Red-tailed tropic bird, tree fern. 100sh, African tree frog, cocoa tree. 150sh, African black-necked heron, Egyptian papyrus. 350sh, Pink-backed pelicans, baobab tree.

1989, Jan. 24

473	A80	30sh shown	1.00	1.00
474	A80	70sh multicolored	4.50	4.50
475	A80	100sh multicolored	5.25	5.25
476	A80	150sh multicolored	8.00	8.00
		Nos. 473-476 (4)	18.75	18.75

Souvenir Sheet

477	A80	350sh multicolored	9.25	9.25

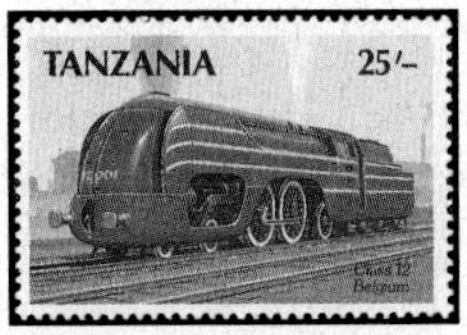

Steam Locomotives — A81

10sh, Class P36, USSR. 25sh, Class 12, Belgium. 60sh, Class C62, Japan. 75sh, Class T1, Pennsylvania R.R. 80sh, Class WP, India. 90sh, Class 59, East African Railways. 150sh, People Class 4-6-2, China. 200sh, Southern Pacific Daylight Express, US.

No. 486, Stephenson's Planet, Britain. No. 487, Coronation Scot, Britain.

1989, Jan. 31

478	A81	10sh multicolored	.85	.85
479	A81	25sh multicolored	.90	.90
480	A81	60sh multicolored	1.35	1.35
481	A81	75sh multicolored	1.60	1.60
482	A81	80sh multicolored	1.75	1.75
483	A81	90sh multicolored	2.00	2.00
484	A81	150sh multicolored	3.25	3.25
485	A81	200sh multicolored	3.25	3.25
		Nos. 478-485 (8)	14.95	14.95

Souvenir Sheets

486	A81	350sh multicolored	6.75	6.75
487	A81	350sh multicolored	6.75	6.75

Nos. 486-487 vert.

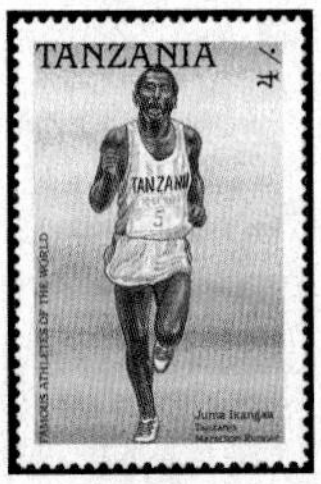

World-Class Athletes — A82

Designs: 4sh, Juma Ikangaa, Tanzania, marathon. 8.50sh, Steffi Graf, West Germany, tennis. 12sh, Yannick Noah, France, tennis. 40sh, Pele, Brazil, soccer. 100sh, Erhard Keller, West Germany, speed skater. 125sh, Sadanoyama, Japan, Sumo wrestler. 200sh, Taino, Japan, Sumo wrestler. 250sh, I. Aoki, Japan, golfer. No. 496, Joe Louis, US, world heavyweight boxing champion, 1937-1949. No. 497, T. Nakajima, Japan, golfer.

1989, Feb. 7

488	A82	4sh multicolored	.40	.40
489	A82	8.50sh multicolored	.40	.40
490	A82	12sh multicolored	.40	.40
491	A82	40sh multicolored	1.25	1.25
492	A82	100sh multicolored	3.00	3.00
493	A82	125sh multicolored	3.50	3.50
494	A82	200sh multicolored	5.25	5.25
495	A82	250sh multicolored	6.75	6.75
		Nos. 488-495 (8)	20.95	20.95

Souvenir Sheets

496	A82	350sh multicolored	8.50	8.50
497	A82	350sh multicolored	8.50	8.50

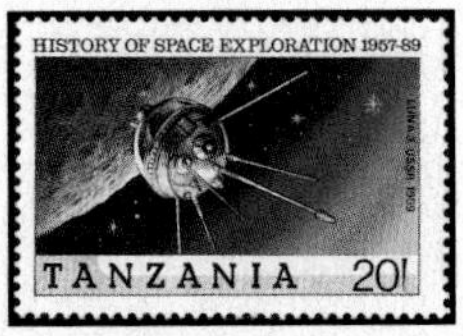

History of Space Exploration and 20th Anniv. of the 1st Moon Landing — A83

20sh, Luna 3. 30sh, Rendezvous of Gemini 6 & 7. 40sh, 1st US space walk. 60sh, First man on Moon. 70sh, Experiments on Moon. 100sh, Apollo 15 lunar rover. 150sh, Apollo-Soyuz. 200sh, Spacelab.

No. 506, Futuristic space station. No. 507, Eagle lunar module.

1989, July 20

498	A83	20sh multicolored	.50	.50
499	A83	30sh multicolored	.60	.60
500	A83	40sh multicolored	.65	.65
501	A83	60sh multicolored	.90	.90
502	A83	70sh multicolored	1.00	1.00
503	A83	100sh multicolored	1.35	1.35
504	A83	150sh multicolored	1.75	1.75
505	A83	200sh multicolored	2.25	2.25
		Nos. 498-505 (8)	9.00	9.00

Souvenir Sheets

506	A83	250sh multicolored	3.75	3.75
507	A83	250sh multicolored	3.75	3.75

History of space exploration (Nos. 498-500, 503-506); others 20th anniv. of 1st Moon Landing.

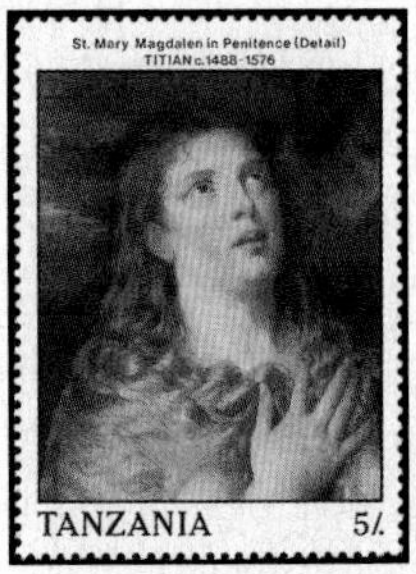

St. Mary Magdalene in Penitence A84

Details from paintings by Titian: 10sh, Averoldi Polyptych. 15sh, St. Margaret. 50sh, Venus and Adonis. 75sh, Venus and the Lutenist. 100sh, Tarquin and Lucretia. 125sh, St. Jerome. 150sh, Madonna and Child with Saints. No. 516, St. Catherine of Alexandria at Prayer. No. 517, Adoration of the Holy Trinity. No. 517A, The Supper at Emmaus.

1989, Nov. 15 Litho. *Perf. 13½x14*

508	A84	5sh multicolored	.35	.35
509	A84	10sh multicolored	.35	.35
510	A84	15sh multicolored	.35	.35
511	A84	50sh multicolored	.80	.80
512	A84	75sh multicolored	1.30	1.30
513	A84	100sh multicolored	1.50	1.50
514	A84	125sh multicolored	1.90	1.90
515	A84	150sh multicolored	2.25	2.25
		Nos. 508-515 (8)	8.80	8.80

Souvenir Sheets

516	A84	300sh multicolored	4.00	4.00
517	A84	300sh multicolored	4.00	4.00
517A	A84	300sh multicolored	4.00	4.00

500th birth anniv. of Titian.
#517A was not available until Jan. 8, 1991.

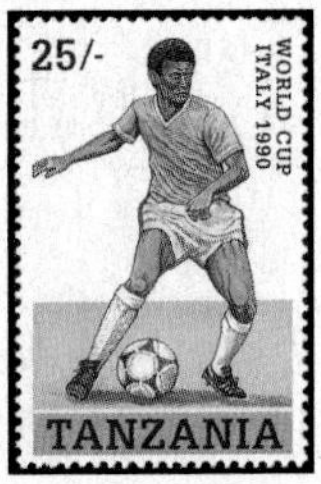

World Cup Soccer Championships, Italy — A85

1989, Nov. 15 *Perf. 14*

Uniform colors

518	A85	25sh grn, red & yel	1.00	1.00
519	A85	60sh grn, yel & blue	2.10	2.10
520	A85	75sh orange & blue	2.75	2.75
521	A85	200sh blue & white	7.00	7.00
		Nos. 518-521 (4)	12.85	12.85

Souvenir Sheets

522	A85	350sh org & bl, diff.	5.75	5.75
523	A85	350sh grn, yel & bl, diff.	5.75	5.75

Souvenir Sheet

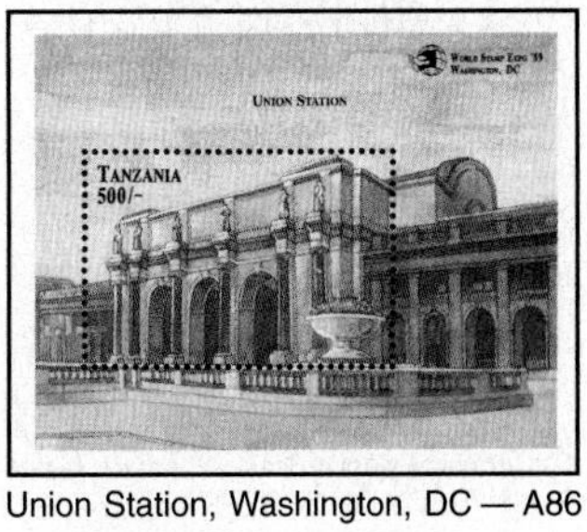

Union Station, Washington, DC — A86

1989, Nov. 17

524	A86	500sh multicolored	9.50	9.50

World Stamp Expo '89.

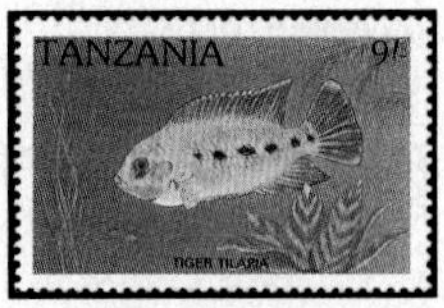

Fish A87

9sh, Tiger tilapia. 13sh, Picasso fish. 20sh, Powder-blue surgeonfish. 40sh, Butterflyfish. 70sh, Guenther's notho. 100sh, Ansorge's noelebias. 150sh, Lyretail panchax. 200sh, Regal angelfish.

No. 533, Batfish. No. 534, Jewel cichlid.

1989, Dec. 14

525	A87	9sh multicolored	.40	.40
526	A87	13sh multicolored	.40	.40
527	A87	20sh multicolored	.55	.55
528	A87	40sh multicolored	1.00	1.00
529	A87	70sh multicolored	1.75	1.75
530	A87	100sh multicolored	2.60	2.60
531	A87	150sh multicolored	4.00	4.00
532	A87	200sh multicolored	5.50	5.50
		Nos. 525-532 (8)	16.20	16.20

Souvenir Sheets

533	A87	350sh multicolored	7.50	7.50
534	A87	350sh multicolored	7.50	7.50

Nos. 533-534 each contain one 38x51mm stamp.

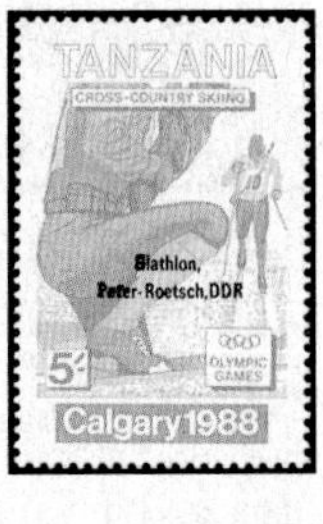

Nos. 414-423 Ovptd. and Similarly

No. 534B, "Gold - USSR / Silver - Brazil / Bronze - W. Germany". No. 534C, "Men's Match Sprint / Lutz Hesslich, DDR". No. 534D, "Pairs, Gordeeva & Grinkov, USSR". No. 534E, "Epee, Schmitt, W. Germany". No. 534F, "Zurbriggen, Switzerland". No. 534G, "Men's Team, USA". No. 534H, "Gold-USSR / Silver-DDR / Bronze-DDR".

No. 534I, "Ice Hockey: / Gold-USSR". No. 534J, "Women's Team, / Gold-USSR".

Perfs. as Before

1989, Dec. 19 Litho.

534A	A71	5sh shown	.55	.55
534B	A71	10sh multicolored	.75	.75
534C	A71	20sh multicolored	3.00	3.00
534D	A71	25sh multicolored	1.50	1.50
534E	A71	50sh multicolored	2.40	2.40
534F	A71	50sh multicolored	2.40	2.40
534G	A71	70sh multicolored	3.75	3.75
534H	A71	75sh multicolored	3.00	3.00
		Nos. 534A-534H (8)	17.35	17.35

Souvenir Sheets

534I	A71	100sh multicolored	11.00	11.00
534J	A71	100sh multicolored	4.00	4.00

Silver and Bronze medalists overprinted on margins of souvenir sheets.

Inter-Parliamentary Union, Cent. — A88

Designs: 9sh, Secret ballot. 13sh, Parliament, Dar Es Salaam. 40sh, Sir William Randal Cremer, Frederic Passy. 80sh, Parliament in session. 100sh, IPU emblem.

1989, Dec. 22   **Perf. 12½x12**
535	A88	9sh multicolored	.25	.25
536	A88	13sh multicolored	.25	.25
537	A88	80sh multicolored	.70	.70
538	A88	100sh lt bl, dp bl & blk	.80	.80
		Nos. 535-538 (4)	2.00	2.00

Souvenir Sheet
| 539 | A88 | 40sh multicolored | 1.40 | 1.40 |

Pan-African Postal Union, 10th Anniv. A89

9sh, PAPU emblem. 13sh, Post offices boxes. 70sh, Mail early, prompt delivery. 100sh, Modes of mail delivery.

40sh, Tanzania Post, PAPU, UPU emblems.

1990, Jan. 17   **Perf. 13½**
540	A89	9sh multicolored	.35	.35
541	A89	13sh multicolored	.35	.35
542	A89	70sh multicolored	1.40	1.40
543	A89	100sh multicolored	2.40	2.40
		Nos. 540-543 (4)	4.50	4.50

Souvenir Sheet
| 544 | A89 | 40sh multicolored | 1.60 | 1.60 |

Extinct Animals A90

25sh, Tecopa pupfish. 40sh, Thylacine. 50sh, Quagga. 60sh, Passenger pigeon. 75sh, Rodriguez saddleback tortoise. 100sh, Toolache wallaby. 150sh, Texas red wolf. 200sh, Utah lake sculpin.

No. 553, Hawaiian O-O, vert. No. 554, South island whekau.

1990, Feb. 4   **Perf. 14**
545	A90	25sh multicolored	.75	.75
546	A90	40sh multicolored	1.10	1.10
547	A90	50sh multicolored	1.50	1.50
548	A90	60sh multicolored	1.75	1.75
549	A90	75sh multicolored	2.25	2.25
550	A90	100sh multicolored	2.75	2.75
551	A90	150sh multicolored	4.25	4.25
552	A90	200sh multicolored	5.50	5.50
		Nos. 545-552 (8)	19.85	19.85

Souvenir Sheets
| 553 | A90 | 350sh multicolored | 8.00 | 8.00 |
| 554 | A90 | 350sh multicolored | 8.00 | 8.00 |

Nina, Admiral's Flag A91

60sh, Pinta, flag. 75sh, Santa Maria, flag. 200sh, Map of Columbus' first voyage. 350sh, Ships, bird's head.

1990, Feb. 20
555	A91	50sh shown	2.10	2.10
556	A91	60sh multicolored	2.50	2.50
557	A91	75sh multicolored	3.00	3.00
558	A91	200sh multicolored	8.25	8.25
		Nos. 555-558 (4)	15.85	15.85

Souvenir Sheet
| 559 | A91 | 350sh multicolored | 9.50 | 9.50 |

Discovery of America, 500th anniv. (in 1992).

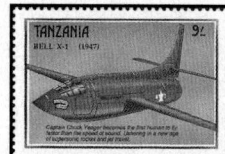

Modern Discoveries — A92

Designs: 9sh, Bell X-1 breaking the sound barrier. 13sh, Bathyscaph Trieste reaches the deepest ocean bottom. 150sh, Transistor and computer chips. 250sh, Discovery of DNA structure. 350sh, Voyager 2 visits Neptune.

1990, Feb. 20
560	A92	9sh multicolored	.65	.65
561	A92	13sh multicolored	.65	.65
562	A92	150sh multicolored	1.50	1.50
563	A92	250sh multicolored	2.50	2.50
		Nos. 560-563 (4)	5.30	5.30

Souvenir Sheet
| 564 | A92 | 350sh multicolored | 5.75 | 5.75 |

Girl Guides, 60th Anniv. A93

1990, Feb. 22   **Perf. 12½x12**
565	A93	9sh Hiking	.25	.25
566	A93	13sh Planting trees	.25	.25
567	A93	50sh Teaching writing	.70	.70
568	A93	100sh Teaching health care	1.40	1.40
		Nos. 565-568 (4)	2.60	2.60

Souvenir Sheet
Perf. 12x12½
| 569 | A93 | 40sh Nursing school, vert. | 1.60 | 1.60 |

Disney Characters, Automobiles — A94

20sh, Herbie, The Love Bug. 30sh, The Absent-Minded Professor's car. 45sh, Chitty-Chitty Bang-Bang. 60sh, Mr. Toad's wild ride. 75sh, Scrooge's limousine. 100sh, Shaggy dog's car. 150sh, Donald Duck's car. 200sh, Firetruck in "Dumbo".

No. 578, Cruella de Vil. No. 579, Mickeymobile.

1990, Mar. 20   **Perf. 14x13½**
570	A94	20sh multicolored	.45	.45
571	A94	30sh multicolored	.50	.50
572	A94	45sh multicolored	.65	.65
573	A94	60sh multicolored	.90	.90
574	A94	75sh multicolored	1.10	1.10
575	A94	100sh multicolored	1.50	1.50
576	A94	150sh multicolored	2.40	2.40
577	A94	200sh multicolored	2.50	2.50
		Nos. 570-577 (8)	10.00	10.00

Souvenir Sheets
| 578 | A94 | 350sh multicolored | 6.00 | 6.00 |
| 579 | A94 | 350sh multicolored | 6.00 | 6.00 |

Black Entertainers A95

1990, Mar. 30   **Litho.**   **Perf. 14**
580	A95	9sh Miriam Makeba	.25	.25
581	A95	13sh Manu Dibango	.25	.25
582	A95	25sh Fela	.25	.25

583	A95	70sh Smokey Robinson	1.00	1.00
584	A95	100sh Gladys Knight	1.25	1.25
585	A95	150sh Eddie Murphy	2.25	2.25
586	A95	200sh Sammy Davis, Jr.	3.00	3.00
587	A95	250sh Stevie Wonder	3.00	3.00
		Nos. 580-587 (8)	11.25	11.25

Souvenir Sheets
Perf. 14½
| 588 | A95 | 350sh Bill Cosby | 3.75 | 3.75 |
| 589 | A95 | 350sh Michael Jackson | 3.75 | 3.75 |

Union of Tanganyika and Zanzibar, 25th Anniv. (in 1989) — A95a

Designs: 9sh, Fishing. 13sh, Grapes. 50sh, Cloves. 100sh, Presidents Nyerere and Karume exchanging Union instruments, vert. 40sh, Natl. arms, vert.

Perf. 12½x12, 12x12½
1990, Apr. 25   **Litho.**
589A	A95a	9sh multicolored	.55	.55
589B	A95a	13sh multicolored	.55	.55
589C	A95a	50sh multicolored	1.75	1.75
589D	A95a	100sh multicolored	3.50	3.50
		Nos. 589A-589D (4)	6.35	6.35

Souvenir Sheet
| 589E | A95a | 40sh multicolored | 2.75 | 2.75 |

Southern Africa Development Coordinating Conf. (SADCC), 10th Anniv. — A96

8sh, Railway transport. 11.50sh, Paper industry. 25sh, Tractor production. 100sh, Flags, map.

50sh, Map.

1990, Aug. 8   **Perf. 13½**
590	A96	8sh multicolored	.50	.50
591	A96	11.50sh multicolored	.50	.50
592	A96	25sh multicolored	.90	.90
593	A96	100sh multicolored	2.75	2.75
		Nos. 590-593 (4)	4.65	4.65

Souvenir Sheet
Perf. 12½
| 594 | A96 | 50sh multicolored | 2.50 | 2.50 |

A97

Pope John Paul II's Visit to Tanzania: 15sh, Wearing red vestments. 20sh, Wearing miter. 100sh, Papal arms. No. 599: a, Pope with arms outstretched. b, St. Joseph's Cathedral, Dar Es Salaam. c, Christ the King Cathedral, Moshi. d, Saint Theresa's Cathedral, Tabora. e, Cathedral of the Epiphany, Bugando Mwanza. f, St. Mathias Mulumba Kalemba Cathedral, Songea.

1990, Sept. 1   **Litho.**   **Perf. 14**
595	A97	10sh shown	.30	.30
596	A97	15sh multicolored	.45	.45
597	A97	20sh multicolored	.50	.50
598	A97	100sh multicolored	1.25	1.25
		Nos. 595-598 (4)	2.50	2.50

Souvenir Sheet
| 599 | | Sheet of 6 | 7.00 | 7.00 |
| a.-f. | A97 | 50sh any single | .60 | .60 |

A98

Players from participating countries.

1990, Sept. 28
600	A98	10sh West Germany	1.00	1.00
601	A98	60sh Italy	1.75	1.75
602	A98	100sh Scotland	3.00	3.00
603	A98	300sh Yugoslavia	5.25	5.25
		Nos. 600-603 (4)	11.00	11.00

Souvenir Sheets
| 604 | A98 | 400sh Costa Rica | 6.00 | 6.00 |
| 605 | A98 | 400sh Belgium | 6.00 | 6.00 |

World Cup Soccer Championships, Italy.

Birds — A99

5sh, Masked weaver. 9sh, Emerald cuckoo. 13sh, Little bee-eater. 15sh, Red bishop. 20sh, Bateleur. 25sh, Scarlet-chested sunbird. 30sh, Pigeons. 40sh, Lesser flamingo. 70sh, Helmeted guineafowl. 100sh, White pelican. 170sh, Saddle-billed stork. 200sh, Crowned crane. 300sh, Pied crow. 400sh, White-headed vulture. 500sh, Ostrich.

1990-91   **Litho.**   **Perf. 14**
606	A99	5sh multi	.45	.45
607	A99	9sh multi	.45	.45
608	A99	13sh multi	.80	.80
609	A99	15sh multi	.80	.80
610	A99	20sh multi	1.00	1.00
611	A99	25sh multi	1.00	1.00
a.		Bklt. pane, 2 ea #606-611	9.00	9.00
611B	A99	30sh multi	1.00	1.00

Size: 42x28mm
612	A99	40sh multi	1.00	1.00
613	A99	70sh multi	1.10	1.10
614	A99	100sh multi	1.25	1.25
615	A99	170sh multi	1.75	1.75
616	A99	200sh multi	2.00	2.00
616A	A99	300sh multi	2.25	2.25
616B	A99	400sh multi	2.50	2.50
617	A99	500sh multi	2.50	2.50
		Nos. 606-617 (15)	19.85	19.85

Souvenir Sheet
Stamp size: 42x28mm
617A		Sheet of 2	6.25	6.25
b.	A99	40sh Superb starling	1.10	1.10
c.	A99	60sh Lilac-breasted roller	1.60	1.60

Issued: 30sh, 300sh, 400sh, 1991; others, 10/1/90.

For surcharges, see Nos. 1723A, 1723B, 2157-2159C, 2267.

Boats A100

1990, Oct. 10   **Litho.**   **Perf. 12½x12**
618	A100	9sh Canoe	.45	.45
619	A100	13sh Outrigger canoe	.45	.45
620	A100	25sh Dhow	.75	.75
621	A100	100sh Freighter	3.00	3.00
		Nos. 618-621 (4)	4.65	4.65

Souvenir Sheet
| 622 | A100 | 40sh Boat | 3.50 | 3.50 |

Commonwealth Games, New Zealand — A101

1990, Oct. 22 *Perf. 14*

623	A101	9sh Sprinting	.45	.45
624	A101	13sh Netball, vert.	.75	.75
625	A101	25sh Pole vault	1.05	1.05
626	A101	100sh Long jump, vert.	3.50	3.50
		Nos. 623-626 (4)	5.75	5.75

Souvenir Sheet

627	A101	40sh Boxing	2.50	2.50

Orchids — A102

10sh, Phalaenopsis. 25sh, Lycaste. 30sh, Vuylstekeara, Cambria "Plush". 50sh, Vuylstekeara, Monica "Burnham". 90sh, Odontocidium. 100sh, Oncidioda. 250sh, Sophrolaeliocattleya. 300sh, Laeliocattleya.

No. 636, Cymbidium, Baldoyle "Melbury". No. 637, Cymbidium, Tapestry "Long Beach".

1990, Nov. 12

628	A102	10sh multicolored	.40	.40
629	A102	25sh multicolored	.40	.40
630	A102	30sh multicolored	.45	.45
631	A102	50sh multicolored	.70	.70
632	A102	90sh multicolored	1.25	1.25
633	A102	100sh multicolored	1.60	1.60
634	A102	250sh multicolored	4.00	4.00
635	A102	300sh multicolored	4.50	4.50
		Nos. 628-635 (8)	13.30	13.30

Souvenir Sheets

636	A102	400sh multicolored	6.25	6.25
637	A102	400sh multicolored	6.25	6.25

Expo '90, the Intl. Garden and Greenery Exposition, Osaka, Japan.

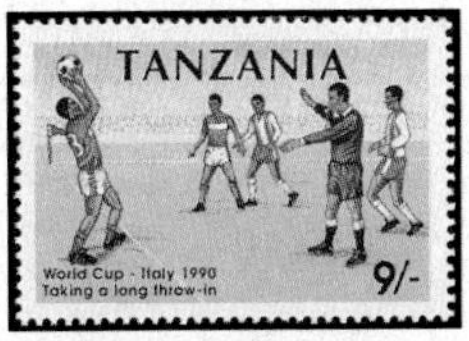

1990 World Cup Soccer Championships, Italy — A102a

1990, Nov. 17 **Litho.** *Perf. 14*

637A	A102a	9sh Long throw-in	.75	.75
637B	A102a	13sh Penalty kick	.75	.75
637C	A102a	25sh Dribbling	1.25	1.25
637D	A102a	100sh Corner kick	4.25	4.25
		Nos. 637A-637D (4)	7.00	7.00

Souvenir Sheet

637E	A102a	50sh Trophy, map	4.50	4.50

Racing A103

5sh, Olympic Soling Class Yacht racing. 20sh, Olympic downhill ski racing. 30sh, Tour de France bicycle race. 40sh, Le Mans 24 hour endurance auto race. 75sh, Olympic 2-man bobsled. 100sh, Belgian Grand Prix motorcycle race. 250sh, Indianapolis 500 auto race. 300sh, Power boat gold cup racing. #646, Colorado 500 enduro motorcycle race. #647, Schneider Trophy air races.

1990, Nov. 19

638	A103	5sh multicolored	.45	.45
639	A103	20sh multicolored	.85	.85
640	A103	30sh multicolored	1.40	1.40
641	A103	40sh multicolored	1.40	1.40
642	A103	75sh multicolored	1.60	1.60
643	A103	100sh multicolored	2.40	2.40
644	A103	250sh multicolored	3.00	3.00
645	A103	300sh multicolored	3.25	3.25
		Nos. 638-645 (8)	14.35	14.35

Souvenir Sheets

646	A103	400sh multicolored	7.00	7.00
647	A103	400sh multicolored	7.00	7.00

1992 Summer Olympics, Barcelona — A104

5sh, Archery. 10sh, Women's gymnastics. 25sh, Boxing. 50sh, Two-man kayak race. 100sh, Men's volleyball. 150sh, Mens' gymnastics. 200sh, 4x100 meter relay. 300sh, Judo.

No. 656, Men's 400 meter hurdles. No. 657, Men's cycling.

1990, Nov. 30

648	A104	5sh multicolored	.30	.30
649	A104	10sh multicolored	.30	.30
650	A104	25sh multicolored	.30	.30
651	A104	50sh multicolored	.55	.55
652	A104	100sh multicolored	1.10	1.10
653	A104	150sh multicolored	1.75	1.75
654	A104	200sh multicolored	2.25	2.25
655	A104	300sh multicolored	3.50	3.50
		Nos. 648-655 (8)	10.05	10.05

Souvenir Sheets

656	A104	400sh multicolored	5.50	5.50
657	A104	400sh multicolored	5.50	5.50

Cog Railroads A105

Cog locomotives: 8sh, Petersberg Cog Railway, West Germany. 25sh, Engine *Waumbek* on Mt. Washington Cog Railway, US. 50sh, Doubleheaded cog engines on Dubrovnik-Sarajevo line, Yugoslavia. 100sh, Cog Railway, Budapest, Hungary 1874. 150sh, Vordenberg-Eisenerz line, Austria. 200sh, Rimutaka Incline, New Zealand, 1955. 250sh, John Stevens' cog engine, Hoboken, NJ, 1825. 300sh, Pilatusbahn Cog Railway, Switzerland, 1889. No. 666, Schneebergbahn of the OBB, Austria. No. 667, Sylvester Marsh, Mt. Washington Cog Railway, 1869.

1990, Dec. 8

658	A105	8sh multicolored	.30	.30
659	A105	25sh multicolored	.30	.30
660	A105	50sh multicolored	.60	.60
661	A105	100sh multicolored	1.10	1.10
662	A105	150sh multicolored	1.75	1.75
663	A105	200sh multicolored	2.25	2.25
664	A105	250sh multicolored	3.25	3.25
665	A105	300sh multicolored	3.75	3.75
		Nos. 658-665 (8)	13.30	13.30

Souvenir Sheets

666	A105	400sh multicolored	6.50	6.50
667	A105	400sh multicolored	6.50	6.50

First Postage Stamps, 150th Anniv. A106

Designs: No. 668, German Post Office at Dar Es Salaam, German East Africa No. 16. No. 669, Mailboat S.S. Reichstag, 1890, Germany No. 40 cancelled in Zanzibar. No. 670, Dhows used as mailboats, Zanzibar No. 1. No. 671, Mailplane Singapore I on Lake Victoria, 1928, Tanganyika No. 22. No. 672, Mailplane, Livingston's House, Zanzibar No. 316. No. 673, Passenger-mail train at Moshi Station, Tanganyika No. 52. No. 674, Royal mail coach, 1840. 150sh, Stephenson's *Rocket*, mail car, 1838. 200sh, Handley Page HP-42 mailplane. No. 677, Hand delivery of mail, Thurn & Taxis No. 44 on cover. No. 678, Sir Rowland Hill.

1990, Dec. 12

668	A106	50sh multicolored	1.10	1.10
669	A106	50sh multicolored	1.10	1.10
a.		Pair, #668-669	1.10	1.10
670	A106	75sh multicolored	1.40	1.40
671	A106	75sh multicolored	1.40	1.40
a.		Pair, #670-671	1.50	1.50
672	A106	100sh multicolored	2.10	2.10
673	A106	100sh multicolored	2.10	2.10
a.		Pair, #672-673	2.25	2.25
674	A106	100sh multicolored	2.10	2.10
675	A106	150sh multicolored	3.00	3.00
676	A106	200sh multicolored	3.00	3.00
		Nos. 668-676 (9)	17.30	17.30

Souvenir Sheets

677	A106	350sh multicolored	6.75	6.75
678	A106	350sh multicolored	6.75	6.75

500th anniv. of Thurn and Taxis Post (No. 677).

For overprints see Nos. 928-934.

Intl. Literacy Year — A107

Nos. 679a-681i depict various Walt Disney characters and a letter of the alphabet.

No. 682, Mickey's train hauls Russian alphabet. No. 683, Children learning Hebrew.

1990, Dec. 27 *Perf. 13½x14*

Miniature Sheets

679		Sheet of 9	7.50	7.50
a.	A107	1sh "ABC"	.25	.25
b.	A107	2sh "A"	.25	.25
c.	A107	3sh "B"	.25	.25
d.	A107	15sh "C"	.25	.25
e.	A107	55sh "D"	.45	.45
f.	A107	80sh "E"	.65	.65
g.	A107	120sh "F"	.95	.95
h.	A107	145sh "G"	1.10	1.10
i.	A107	200sh "H"	1.60	1.60
680		Sheet of 9	7.25	7.25
a.	A107	10sh "I"	.25	.25
b.	A107	20sh "J"	.25	.25
c.	A107	30sh "K"	.25	.25
d.	A107	40sh "L"	.30	.30
e.	A107	50sh "M"	.40	.40
f.	A107	60sh "N"	.50	.50
g.	A107	100sh "O"	.80	.80
h.	A107	125sh "P"	1.00	1.00
i.	A107	150sh "Q"	1.25	1.25
681		Sheet of 9	7.50	7.50
a.	A107	5sh "R"	.25	.25
b.	A107	18sh "S"	.25	.25
c.	A107	25sh "T"	.25	.25
d.	A107	35sh "U"	.30	.30
e.	A107	45sh "V"	.35	.35
f.	A107	75sh "W"	.60	.60
g.	A107	90sh "X"	.70	.70
h.	A107	160sh "Y"	1.25	1.25
i.	A107	175sh "Z"	1.40	1.40

Souvenir Sheets

682	A107	600sh multicolored	8.50	8.50
683	A107	600sh multicolored	8.50	8.50

Intl. Literacy Year A108

9sh, Learning to read. 13sh, Learning to write. 25sh, Blackboard, books. 100sh, Reading newspapers.

50sh, Adult education.

1991, Mar. 15 **Litho.** *Perf. 14*

684	A108	9sh multicolored	.30	.30
685	A108	13sh multicolored	.40	.40
686	A108	25sh multicolored	.55	.55
687	A108	100sh multicolored	.275	2.75
		Nos. 684-687 (4)	1.53	4.00

Souvenir Sheet

688	A108	50sh multicolored	2.50	2.50

For surcharge see No. 1431A.

Mickey Mouse — A109

Character roles: 5sh, Western cowboy. 10sh, Boxer. 15sh, Astronaut. 20sh, Romantic lead with Minnie. 100sh, Swashbuckling hero. 200sh, Detective with Donald Duck and Pistol Pete. 350sh, King with Donald as court jester. 450sh, Sailor with Donald and Goofy. No. 697, Minnie, Mickey as archaeologists in Egypt, Donald as a mummy. No. 698, Mickey as Canadian Mountie.

1991, Feb. 11 **Litho.** *Perf. 14x13½*

689	A109	5sh multicolored	.45	.45
690	A109	10sh multicolored	.50	.50
691	A109	15sh multicolored	.50	.50
692	A109	20sh multicolored	.50	.50
693	A109	100sh multicolored	2.00	2.00
694	A109	200sh multicolored	4.00	4.00
695	A109	350sh multicolored	4.50	4.50
696	A109	450sh multicolored	4.50	4.50
		Nos. 689-696 (8)	16.95	16.95

Souvenir Sheets

697	A109	600sh multicolored	8.50	8.50
698	A109	600sh multicolored	8.50	8.50

Craters and Caves — A109a

Designs: 3sh, Ngorongoro Crater. 5sh, Kondoa Caves, prehistoric rock paintings. 9sh, Mount Kilimanjaro's inner crater. 12sh, Olduvai Gorge.

Amboni Caves: No. 698f, Open area of cave. g, People viewing cave, large stalactite. h, Woman seated beside welcome sign. i, Man climbing up to view cave.

1991, Mar. 28 **Litho.** *Perf. 14½*

698A	A109a	3sh multi	3.25	3.25
698B	A109a	5sh multi	3.25	3.25
698C	A109a	9sh multi	4.25	4.25
698D	A109a	12sh multi	6.25	6.25
		Nos. 698A-698D (4)	17.00	17.00

Souvenir Sheet

698E	A109a	10sh Sheet of 4, #f.-i.	8.00	8.00

Nos. 698A-698E were not available to the philatelic community until Mar. 1994.

Miniature Sheet

Peter Paul Rubens, 350th Death Anniv. — A110

Cycle of Decius Mus: No. 699a, Proclamation of the Vision. b, Divining of the Entrails. c, Dispatch of the Lictors. d, Dedication to Death. e, Victory and Death of Decius Mus. f, Funeral Rites. No. 700, Trophy of War, vert.

1991, Apr. 10 **Litho.** *Perf. 14x13½*

699	A110	85sh Sheet of 6, #a.-f.	14.00	14.00

Souvenir Sheet

Perf. 13½x14

700	A110	500sh multicolored	12.00	12.00

Tanzania Investment Bank, 20th Anniv. — A111

Designs: 10sh, Dairy farming. 13sh, Industrial development. 25sh, Engineering. 100sh, Tea harvesting.

1991, June 7 *Perf. 14*

701	A111	10sh multicolored	.40	.40
702	A111	13sh multicolored	.40	.40
703	A111	25sh multicolored	.40	.40
704	A111	100sh multicolored	2.25	2.25
a.		Souvenir sheet of 4, #701-704	3.25	3.25
		Nos. 701-704 (4)	3.45	3.45

Phila Nippon '91 A112

Japanese locomotives: 10sh, First Japanese steam. 25sh, Series 4500 steam. 35sh, C 62 steam. 50sh, Mikado steam. 75sh, Series 6250 steam. 100sh, C 11 steam. 200sh, E 10 steam. 300sh, Series 8550 steam. No. 713, EF 58 electric. No. 714, DD 51 diesel. No. 715, Series 400 electric. No. 716, EH 10 electric.

1991, Aug. 15 **Litho.** *Perf. 14*

705	A112	10sh multicolored	1.00	1.00
706	A112	25sh multicolored	1.50	1.50
707	A112	35sh multicolored	1.75	1.75
708	A112	50sh multicolored	2.00	2.00
709	A112	75sh multicolored	2.50	2.50
710	A112	100sh multicolored	3.00	3.00
711	A112	200sh multicolored	3.50	3.50
712	A112	300sh multicolored	4.75	4.75
		Nos. 705-712 (8)	20.00	20.00

Souvenir Sheets

713	A112	400sh multicolored	4.75	4.75
714	A112	400sh multicolored	4.75	4.75
715	A112	400sh multicolored	4.75	4.75
716	A112	400sh multicolored	4.75	4.75

Fauna in Natl. Game Parks A113

Species and park: 10sh, Common zebra, golden-winged sunbird, Ngorongoro Crater Conservation Area. 25sh, Greater kudu, African elephant, Ruaha. 30sh, Sable antelope, red and yellow barbet, Mikumi. 50sh, Wildebeest, leopard, Serengeti. 90sh, Giraffe, white-starred bush robin, Ngurdoto Crater. 100sh, Eland, Abbot's duiker, Kilimanjaro. 250sh, Lion, impala, Lake Manyara. 300sh, Black rhinoceros, ostrich, Tarangire. No. 725, Paradise whydah, oryx, Mkomazi Game Reserve. No. 726, Blue-breasted kingfisher, defassa waterbuck, Selous Game Reserve.

1991, Aug. 22 **Litho.** *Perf. 14*

717	A113	10sh multicolored	.30	.30
718	A113	25sh multicolored	.65	.65
719	A113	30sh multicolored	.80	.80
720	A113	50sh multicolored	1.25	1.25
721	A113	90sh multicolored	2.10	2.10
722	A113	100sh multicolored	2.50	2.50
723	A113	250sh multicolored	6.00	6.00
724	A113	300sh multicolored	7.50	7.50
		Nos. 717-724 (8)	21.10	21.10

Souvenir Sheets

725	A113	400sh multicolored	9.75	9.75
726	A113	400sh multicolored	9.75	9.75

Butterflies — A114

Designs: 10sh, Vine leaf vagrant. 15sh, Blue spot commodore. 35sh, Orange admiral. 75sh, Wanderer. 100sh, Jackson's leaf. 150sh, Painted empress. 200sh, Double-banded orange. 300sh, Crawshay's sapphire blue. No. 735, Noble swallowtail. No. 736, Club-tailed charaxes. No. 737, Satyr charaxes. No. 738, Green patch swallowtail.

1991, Aug. 28 **Litho.** *Perf. 14*

727	A114	10sh multicolored	.45	.45
728	A114	15sh multicolored	.45	.45
729	A114	35sh multicolored	.95	.95
730	A114	75sh multicolored	1.90	1.90
731	A114	100sh multicolored	2.50	2.50
732	A114	150sh multicolored	4.00	4.00
733	A114	200sh multicolored	5.00	5.00
734	A114	300sh multicolored	7.50	7.50
		Nos. 727-734 (8)	22.75	22.75

Souvenir Sheets

735	A114	400sh multicolored	5.50	5.50
736	A114	400sh multicolored	5.50	5.50
737	A114	400sh multicolored	5.50	5.50
738	A114	400sh multicolored	5.50	5.50

While Nos. 727-736 have the same issue date as Nos. 737-738, the dollar value of Nos. 737-738 was lower when they were released.

Intelsat, 25th Anniv. A115

Designs: 10sh, Microwave link. 25sh, Earth. 100sh, Mwenge standard "B" Earth station. 500sh, Mwenge standard "A" Earth station. 50sh, World map.

1991, Sept. 5 **Litho.** *Perf. 14*

739	A115	10sh multicolored	.40	.40
740	A115	25sh multicolored	.55	.55
741	A115	100sh multicolored	2.00	2.00
742	A115	500sh multicolored	8.00	8.00
		Nos. 739-742 (4)	10.95	10.95

Souvenir Sheet

743	A115	50sh multicolored	4.00	4.00

UN Development Program, 40th Anniv. — A116

Designs: 10sh, Irrigated rice farming. 15sh, Vocational training. 100sh, Terrace farming. 500sh, Architectural renovations, vert. 40sh, Helping people to help themselves, vert.

1991, Sept. 16 *Perf. 13½*

744	A116	10sh multicolored	.30	.30
745	A116	15sh multicolored	.30	.30
746	A116	100sh multicolored	1.50	1.50
747	A116	500sh multicolored	7.00	7.00
		Nos. 744-747 (4)	9.10	9.10

Souvenir Sheet

Perf. 13x12½

748	A116	40sh black & blue	2.00	2.00

All Africa Games, Cairo — A117

Perf. 12x12½, 12½x12

1991, Sept. 20

749	A117	10sh Netball	.50	.50
750	A117	15sh Soccer, horiz.	.50	.50
751	A117	100sh Tennis	2.50	2.50
752	A117	200sh Running	3.25	3.25
753	A117	500sh Baseball, horiz.	7.25	7.25
		Nos. 749-753 (5)	14.00	14.00

Souvenir Sheet

754	A117	500sh Basketball	10.50	10.50

Telecom '91 — A118

1991, Oct. 1 *Perf. 13½x14, 14x13½*

755	A118	10sh shown	.30	.30
756	A118	15sh Telecom '91, horiz.	.30	.30
757	A118	35sh arrows	.40	.40
758	A118	100sh like #757, horiz.	1.10	1.10
		Nos. 755-758 (4)	2.10	2.10

World Telecommunications Day (Nos. 757-758).

Dinosaurs A119

1991, Oct. 28 *Perf. 12x12½*

759	A119	10sh Stegosaurus	.30	.30
760	A119	15sh Triceratops	.30	.30
761	A119	25sh Edmontosaurus	.45	.45
762	A119	30sh Plateosaurus	.60	.60
763	A119	35sh Diplodocus	.70	.70
764	A119	100sh Iguanodon	1.90	1.90
765	A119	200sh Silviasaurus	3.75	3.75
		Nos. 759-765 (7)	8.00	8.00

Souvenir Sheet

766	A119	150sh Rhamphorhynchus	4.75	4.75

Animals and Fish A120

No. 767 — Horses: a, Shire. b, Thoroughbred. c, Kladruber. d, Appaloosa. e, Hanoverian. f, Arab. g, Breton. h, Exmoor. i, Connemara. j, Lipizzaner. k, Shetland. l, Percheron. m, Pinto. n, Orlov. o, Palomino. p, Welsh cob.

No. 768 — Cats: a, Japanese bobtail. b, Cornish rex. c, Malayan. d, Tonkinese. e, Abyssinian. f, Russian blue. g, Cymric. h, Somali. i, Siamese. j, Himalayan. k, Singapura. l, Manx. m, Oriental shorthair. n, Maine coon. o, Persian. p, Birman.

No. 769, vert. — African elephants: a, One walking left. b, Two with tusks entangled. c, One facing forward. d, One under tree. e, Adult and calf in water, zebra. f, Adult and calf walking into water. g, Two adults and calf in water. h, Adult and calf standing in water. i, One walking right. j, Two, one raising trunk in air. k, One raising trunk in air. l, One facing forward, trunk down, zebra. m, Adult, calf at edge of water, antelope. n, Adult and calf, two more in background. o, One walking toward water. p, Adult with trunk on calf.

No. 770 — Aquarium fish: a, Jewel tetra. b, Five-banded barb. c, Simpson platy. d, Guppy, e, Zebra danio. f, Neon tetra. g, Siamese fighting fish. h, Tiger barb. i, Red lyretail. j, Goldfish. k, Pearl gourami. l, Angelfish. m, Clown loach. n, Red swordtail. o, Brown discus. p, Rosy barb.

No. 771 — Birds: a, Budgerigar. b, Rainbow bunting. c, Golden-fronted leafbird. d, Black-headed caique. e, Java sparrow. f, Diamond sparrow. g, Peach-faced lovebird. h, Golden conure. i, Military macaw. j, Celestial parrotlet. k, Sulphur-crested cockatoo. l, Spectacled Amazon parrot. m, Paradise tanager. n, Gouldian finch. o, Masked lovebird. p, Hill mynah.

1991, Oct. 28 **Litho.** *Perf. 14*

767	A120	50sh Sheet of 16, #a.-p.	19.00	19.00
768	A120	50sh Sheet of 16, #a.-p.	19.00	19.00
769	A120	75sh Sheet of 16, #a.-p.	19.00	19.00
770	A120	75sh Sheet of 16, #a.-p.	19.00	19.00
771	A120	75sh Sheet of 16, #a.-p.	19.00	19.00
		Nos. 767-771 (5)	95.00	95.00

For overprints see Nos. 1529-1530.

Paintings by Vincent Van Gogh A121

Designs: 10sh, Peasant Woman Sewing. 15sh, Head of a Peasant Woman with Greenish Lace Cap. 35sh, Flowering Orchard. 75sh, Portrait of a Girl. 100sh, Portrait of a Woman with a Red Ribbon. 150sh, Vase with Flowers. 200sh, Houses in Antwerp. 400sh, Seated Peasant Woman with White Cap. No. 780, The Parsonage Garden at Nuenen in the Snow, horiz. No. 781, Bulb Fields, horiz.

1991, Nov. 20 **Litho.** *Perf. 13½x14*

772	A121	10sh multicolored	.30	.30
773	A121	15sh multicolored	.30	.30
774	A121	35sh multicolored	.80	.80
775	A121	75sh multicolored	1.60	1.60
776	A121	100sh multicolored	2.00	2.00
777	A121	150sh multicolored	3.00	3.00
778	A121	200sh multicolored	4.00	4.00
779	A121	400sh multicolored	8.00	8.00
		Nos. 772-779 (8)	20.00	20.00

Size: 127x102mm

Imperf

780	A121	400sh multicolored	8.50	8.50
781	A121	400sh multicolored	8.50	8.50

Walt Disney Christmas Cards — A122

Design and date of card: 10sh, "Joy", 1968. 25sh, Mickey, Pluto and Goofy at fireplace, 1981. 35sh, Robin Hood and merry men celebrating, 1973. 75sh, Tree of greetings, Mickey, 1967. 100sh, Goofy, Mickey and Donald trying to catch Santa coming down chimney, 1969, vert. 150sh, Mickey on top of Christmas ornament, 1976, vert. 200sh, Clarabelle Cow with bells, 1935, vert. 300sh, Orphan mice reading book of tricks, 1935, vert. No. 790, Mickey wearing Santa hat and surrounded by Disney characters, 1968, vert. No. 791, Mickey with present for Donald, 1935, vert.

Perf. 13½x14, 14x13½

1991, Dec. **Litho.**

782	A122	10sh multicolored	.30	.30
783	A122	25sh multicolored	.55	.55
784	A122	35sh multicolored	.70	.70
785	A122	75sh multicolored	1.40	1.40
786	A122	100sh multicolored	2.00	2.00
787	A122	150sh multicolored	2.50	2.50
788	A122	200sh multicolored	3.00	3.00
789	A122	300sh multicolored	4.00	4.00
		Nos. 782-789 (8)	14.45	14.45

Souvenir Sheets

790	A122	500sh multicolored	8.50	8.50
791	A122	500sh multicolored	8.50	8.50

Elephants A123

Designs: 10sh, 15sh, 25sh, 100sh, Various pictures of elephas maximus. 30sh, 35sh, 200sh, Various pictures of loxodonta africana. 400sh, Mammut mammuthus.

Perf. 12x12½,12½x12

1991, Nov. 28 **Litho.**

792	A123	10sh multi, vert.	.60	.60
793	A123	15sh multi, vert.	.60	.60
794	A123	25sh multi, vert.	.90	.90
795	A123	30sh multi, vert.	1.25	1.25
796	A123	35sh multicolored	1.50	1.50
797	A123	100sh multicolored	4.00	4.00
798	A123	200sh multicolored	7.50	7.50
		Nos. 792-798 (7)	16.35	16.35

Souvenir Sheet

799 A123 400sh multicolored 7.25 7.25

Locomotives — A124

10sh, USSR 1930. 15sh, Japan 1964. 25sh, Russia 1834, vert. 35sh, France 1979. 60sh, France 1972. 100sh, United Kingdom 1972. 300sh, Russia 1837, vert.

No. 807, 100sh, France, 1952, vert.

1991, Dec. 10 *Perf. 12½x12, 12x12½*

800	A124	10sh multicolored	.25	.25
801	A124	15sh multicolored	.25	.25
802	A124	25sh multicolored	.40	.40
803	A124	35sh multicolored	.65	.65
804	A124	60sh multicolored	1.10	1.10
805	A124	100sh multicolored	1.60	1.60
806	A124	300sh multicolored	5.25	5.25
		Nos. 800-806 (7)	9.50	9.50

Souvenir Sheet

807 A124 100sh multicolored 2.50 2.50

Entertainers — A125

Nos. 808a-808i, 812, Various portraits of Elvis Presley.

Nos. 809a-809i, 813, Various portraits of Marilyn Monroe.

Nos. 810a-810i, 814, Various portraits of Bruce Lee.

Black entertainers: No. 811: a, Scott Joplin. b, Sammy Davis, Jr. c, Joan Armatrading. d, Louis Armstrong. e, Miriam Makeba. f, Lionel Ritchie. g, Whitney Houston, h, Bob Marley. i, Tina Turner. No. 815, Kouyate family.

1992, Feb. 15 *Perf. 14*

808	A125	75sh Sheet of 9, #a.-i.	9.75	9.75
809	A125	75sh Sheet of 9, #a.-i.	9.75	9.75
810	A125	75sh Sheet of 9, #a.-i.	9.75	9.75
811	A125	75sh Sheet of 9, #a.-i.	9.75	9.75
		Nos. 808-811 (4)	39.00	39.00

Souvenir Sheets

812	A125	500sh multicolored	8.75	8.75
813	A125	500sh multicolored	8.75	8.75
814	A125	500sh multicolored	8.75	8.75
815	A125	500sh multicolored	8.75	8.75
		Nos. 812-815 (4)	35.00	35.00

Nos. 812-815 each contain one 29x43mm stamp.

See #949 for #808 inscribed "15th Anniversary."

Fish of Tanzania A126

Designs: 10sh, Malacanthus latovittatus. 15sh, Lamprologus tretocephalus. 25sh, Lamprologus calvus. 35sh, Hemichromis bimaculatusl. 60sh, Aphyosemion bivittatum. No. 821, Synanceia verrucosa. 300sh, Aphyosemion ahli. No. 823, Regalecus glesne.

1992, Mar. 8 *Perf. 12½x12*

816	A126	10sh multicolored	.55	.55
817	A126	15sh multicolored	.70	.70
818	A126	25sh multicolored	.90	.90
819	A126	35sh multicolored	1.10	1.10
820	A126	60sh multicolored	1.50	1.50
821	A126	100sh multicolored	2.00	2.00
822	A126	300sh multicolored	5.25	5.25
		Nos. 816-822 (7)	12.00	12.00

Souvenir Sheet

823 A126 100sh multicolored 3.00 3.00

World War II in the Pacific A127

Designs: No. 824a, British-designed radar at Pearl Harbor. b, Churchill declares war on Japan. c, Repulse destroyed. d, Prince of Wales sunk. e, Singapore falls to Japanese. f, Hermes is sunk off Ceylon. g, Airfields in Malaya attacked. h, Hong Kong falls to Japanese. i, Japanese Daihatsu landing craft. j, Japanese cruiser Haguro in Java Sea.

1992, Apr. 27 *Perf. 14½x15*

824 A127 75sh Sheet of 10, #a.-j. 22.50 22.50

Visits of Pope John Paul II — A128

No. 825, 100sh: a, Dominican Republic, 1979. b, Mexico, 1979. c, Poland, 1979. d, Ireland, 1979. e, UN, New York, 1979. f, US, 1979. g, Turkey, 1979. h, Zaire, 1980. i, Congo, 1980. j, Kenya, 1980. k, Ghana, 1980. l, Upper Volta, 1980.

No. 826, 100sh: a, Ivory Coast, 1980. b, France, 1980. c, Brazil, 1980. d, West Germany, 1980. e, Pakistan, 1981. f, Philippines, 1981. g, Guam, 1981. h, Japan, 1981. h, Alaska, 1981. i, Nigeria, 1982. j, Benin, 1982. l. Gabon, 1982.

No. 827, 100sh: a, Equatorial Guinea, 1982. b, Portugal, 1982. c, Great Britain, 1982. d, Argentina, 1982. e, UN, Geneva, 1982. f, San Marino, 1982. g, Spain, 1982. h, Costa Rica, 1983. i, Panama, 1983. j, El Salvador, 1983. k, Nicaragua, 1983. l, Guatemala, 1983.

No. 828, 100sh: a, Honduras, 1983. b, Belize, 1983. c, Haiti, 1983. d, Poland, 1983. e, France, 1983. f, Austria, 1983. g, Alaska, 1984. h, South Korea, 1984. i, Papua New Guinea, 1984. j, Solomon Islands, 1984. k, Thailand, 1984. l, Switzerland, 1984.

No. 829, 100sh: a, Canada, 1984. b, Dominican Republic, 1984. c, Puerto Rico, 1984. d, Venezuela, 1985. e, Ecuador, 1985. f, Peru, 1985. g, Trinidad & Tobago, 1985. h, Netherlands, 1985. i, Luxembourg, 1985. j, Belgium, 1985. k, Togo, 1985. l, Ivory Coast, 1985.

No. 830, 100sh: a, Cameroun, 1985. b, Central African Republic, 1985. c, Zaire, 1985. d, Kenya, 1985. e, Morocco, 1985. f, Liechtenstein, 1985. g, India, 1986. h, Colombia, 1986. i, St. Lucia, 1986. j, France, 1986. k, Bangladesh, 1986. l, Singapore, 1986.

No. 831, 100sh: a, Fiji, 1986. b, New Zealand, 1986. c, Australia, 1986. d, Seychelles, 1986. e, Uruguay, 1987. f, Chile, 1987. g, Argentina, 1987. h, West Germany, 1987. i, Poland, 1987. j, US, 1987. k, Canada, 1987. l, Uruguay, 1988.

No. 832, 100sh: a, Bolivia, 1988. b, Peru, 1988. c, Paraguay, 1988. d, Austria, 1988. e, Zimbabwe, 1988. f, Botswana, 1988. g, Lesotho, 1988. h, Swaziland, 1988. i, Mozambique, 1988. j, France, 1988. k, Madagascar, 1989. l, Reunion, 1989.

No. 833, 100sh: a, Zambia, 1989. b, Malawi, 1989. c, Norway, 1989. d, Iceland, 1989. e, Finland, 1989. f, Denmark, 1989. g, Sweden, 1989. h, Spain, 1989. i, South Korea, 1989. j, Indonesia, 1989. k, Mauritius, 1989. l, Cape Verde, 1990.

No. 834, 100sh: a, Mali, 1990. b, Guinea-Bissau, 1990. c, Burkina Faso, 1990. d, Chad, 1990. e, Czechoslovakia, 1990. f, Mexico, 1990. g, Curacao, 1990. h, Malta, 1990. i, Tanzania, 1990. j, Burundi, 1990. k, Rwanda, 1990. l, Ivory Coast, 1990.

1992, Apr. 13 *Perf. 14*

Sheets of 12 + 4 Labels

825-834 A128 Set of 10 200.00 200.00

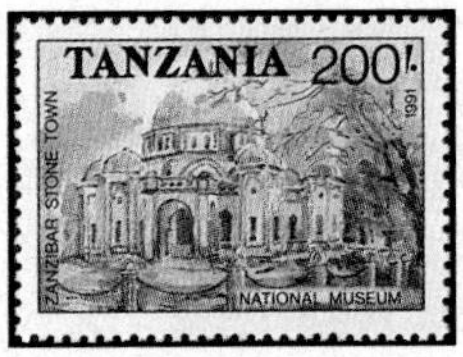

Zanzibar Stone Town A129

10sh, Balcony. 20sh, Bahlnara mosque. 30sh, High Court bldg. 200sh, Natl. museum. No. 839a, 150sh, Old fort. b, 300sh, Maruhubi ruins.

1992, Apr. 15 *Perf. 12x12½, 12½x12*

835	A129	10sh multicolored	.60	.60
836	A129	20sh multicolored	1.40	1.40
837	A129	30sh multicolored	2.00	2.00
838	A129	200sh multicolored	8.00	8.00
		Nos. 835-838 (4)	12.00	12.00

Souvenir Sheet

839 A129 Sheet of 2, #a.-b. 10.00 10.00

Nos. 835-837 are vert.

Wolfgang Amadeus Mozart, Death Bicent. A130

Designs: 10sh, Marcella Sembrich as Zerlina in Don Giovanni. 50sh, Symphony Number 41, Jupiter. 300sh, Luciano Pavarotti as Idamente in Idomeneo. 500sh, Wolfgang Amadeus Mozart, vert.

1992, Aug. 1 *Perf. 14*

840	A130	10sh violet & blk	1.50	1.50
841	A130	50sh multicolored	3.50	3.50
842	A130	300sh violet & blk	8.00	8.00
		Nos. 840-842 (3)	13.00	13.00

Souvenir Sheet

843 A130 500sh olive brn & blk 11.50 11.50

While No. 843 has the same issue date as Nos. 840-842, the dollar value was lower when it were released.

No. 843 contains one 38x50mm stamp.

1992, Aug. 1

Designs: 10sh, Insignia, giraffe and elephant. 15sh, Scouts in canoe. 400sh, John Glenn's Gemini space capsule orbiting Earth. 500sh, Boy scout, vert.

844	A130	10sh multicolored	.45	.45
845	A130	15sh multicolored	.45	.45
846	A130	400sh multicolored	10.50	10.50
		Nos. 844-846 (3)	11.40	11.40

Souvenir Sheet

847 A130 500sh multicolored 8.50 8.50

Lord Robert Baden-Powell, Founder of Boy Scouts, 50th Death Anniv. (in 1991).

While No. 847 has the same issue date as Nos. 844-846, the dollar value was lower when it were released.

No. 847 contains one 38x50mm stamp.

1992, Aug. 1

Charles de Gaulle (1890-1970): 25sh, French Resistance Monument and medal. 30sh, First Free French tank at Omaha beach, Normandy. 150sh, Concorde at de Gaulle Airport. 500sh, France #439 with Cross of Lorraine overprint and Free French stamp, vert.

848	A130	25sh multicolored	.90	.90
849	A130	30sh multicolored	1.00	1.00
850	A130	150sh multicolored	10.00	10.00
		Nos. 848-850 (3)	11.90	11.90

Souvenir Sheet

851 A130 500sh multicolored 13.00 13.00

While No. 851 has the same issue date as Nos. 848-850, the dollar value was lower when it was released.

No. 851 contains one 38x50mm stamp.

Common Chimpanzee A131

Various chimpanzees in natural habitat.

No. 860, Swinging from tree. No. 861, Eating termites.

1992

852	A131	10sh multicolored	.35	.35
853	A131	15sh multicolored	.35	.35
854	A131	35sh multicolored	.85	.85
855	A131	75sh multicolored	1.90	1.90
856	A131	100sh multicolored	2.25	2.25
857	A131	150sh multicolored	3.50	3.50
858	A131	200sh multicolored	4.50	4.50
859	A131	300sh multicolored	7.00	7.00
		Nos. 852-859 (8)	20.70	20.70

Souvenir Sheets

860	A131	400sh multicolored	6.50	6.50
861	A131	400sh multicolored	6.50	6.50

Spanish Art — A132

Drawings by Goya: 25sh, A Picador mounted on the shoulders of a Chulo, spears a Bull. 100sh, The Dream of Reason brings forth Monsters, vert. 150sh, Another Madness (of Martincho) in the Plaza de Zaragoza. 200sh, Recklessness of Martincho in the Plaza de Zaragoza.

No. 866, Seascape, by Mariano Salvador Maella.

1992 *Perf. 13*

862	A132	25sh blk & red brn	.50	.50
863	A132	100sh black & brn	1.75	1.75
864	A132	150sh blk & red brn	2.75	2.75
865	A132	200sh blk & red brn	3.00	3.00

Size: 120x95mm

Imperf

866	A132	400sh multicolored	5.00	5.00
		Nos. 862-866 (5)	13.00	13.00

Granada '92.

1992 *Perf. 13*

Drawings by Diego da Silva Velazquez: 35sh, Philip IV at Fraga. 50sh, The Head of the Stag. 75sh, The Cardinal Infante Don Fernando as a Hunter. 300sh, Pablo de Valladolid. No. 871, Two Men at Table.

867	A132	35sh multicolored	.75	.75
868	A132	50sh multicolored	.90	.90
869	A132	75sh multicolored	1.40	1.40
870	A132	300sh multicolored	3.75	3.75

Size: 120x95mm

Imperf

871	A132	400sh multicolored	5.00	5.00
		Nos. 867-871 (5)	11.80	11.80

Granada '92.

A133

Chimpanzees of Gombe — A134

Designs: No. 872, Melisa and Mike. No. 873, Leakey and David Greybeard. No. 874, Fifi eating termites. No. 875 Galahad.

No. 876a, 10sh, Leakey. b, 15sh, Fifi. c, 20sh, Faben. d, 30sh, David Greybeard. e, 35sh, Mike. f, 50sh, Galahad. g, 100sh, Melisa. h, 200sh, Flo.

No. 877, Fifi, Flo, and Faben.

1992, May 29 Litho. *Perf. 14*

872 A133 10sh multicolored 1.00 1.00
873 A133 15sh multicolored 1.25 1.25
874 A133 30sh multicolored 1.75 1.75
875 A133 35sh multicolored 2.00 2.00
Nos. 872-875 (4) 6.00 6.00

Miniature Sheet

876 A134 Sheet of 8, #a.-h. 12.00 12.00

Souvenir Sheet

877 A133 100sh multicolored 4.50 4.50

Natl. Bank of Commerce, 25th Anniv. — A135

Designs: 10sh, Sorghum plants. 15sh, Samora Avenue branch, computer operator, vert. 30sh, Head office. 35sh, Bankers Training Center. 40sh, Batik tie dyeing.

1992, June 22

878 A135 10sh multicolored .70 .70
879 A135 15sh multicolored .80 .80
880 A135 35sh multicolored 1.25 1.25
881 A135 40sh multicolored 1.25 1.25
Nos. 878-881 (4) 4.00 4.00

Souvenir Sheet

882 A135 30sh multicolored 2.50 2.50

Traditional Dress — A136

Designs: 3sh, Gogo, central area. 5sh, Swahili, coastal area. 9sh, Hehe, southern highlands and Makonde, southern area. 12sh, Maasai, northern area. 40sh, Mwarusha.

1992, Apr. 30 Litho. *Perf. 14½*

883 A136 3sh multicolored .70 .70
884 A136 5sh multicolored .80 .80
885 A136 9sh multicolored .90 .90
886 A136 12sh multicolored 1.20 1.20
Nos. 883-886 (4) 3.60 3.60

Souvenir Sheet

887 A136 40sh multicolored 4.50 4.50

Dated 1989.

1992 Summer Olympics, Barcelona A137

1992, July 23 *Perf. 12x12½*

888 A137 40sh Basketball .80 .80
889 A137 100sh Billiards 1.25 1.25
890 A137 200sh Table tennis 2.00 2.00
891 A137 400sh Darts 4.25 4.25
Nos. 888-891 (4) 8.30 8.30

Souvenir Sheet

892 A137 500sh Weight lifting 6.00 6.00

Fish A138

No. 893: a, Tilapia mariae. b, Capoeta hulstaerti. c, Tropheus moorii. d, Synodontis angelicus. e, Julidochromis dickfeldi. f, Tilapia nilotica. g, Nothobranchius rachovii. h, Pseudotropheus crabro. i, Lamprologus leleupi. j, Pseudotropheus zebra. k, Julidochromis marlieri. l, Chalinochromis brichardi.

Designs: No. 894, Haplochromis "electric blue." No. 895, Lamprologus brevis. No. 896, Nothobranchius palmqvisti.

1992, Oct. Litho. *Perf. 13½*

893 A138 100sh Sheet of 12, #a.-l. 19.00 19.00

Souvenir Sheets

894 A138 500sh multicolored 6.50 6.50
895 A138 500sh multicolored 6.50 6.50
896 A138 500sh multicolored 6.50 6.50

Discovery of America, 500th Anniv. A139

1992, Oct. Litho. *Perf. 14*

897 A139 70sh Sailing ship 1.75 1.75
898 A139 300sh Columbus 6.00 6.00

Souvenir Sheet

899 A139 500sh Columbus, diff. 5.00 5.00

Miniature Sheet

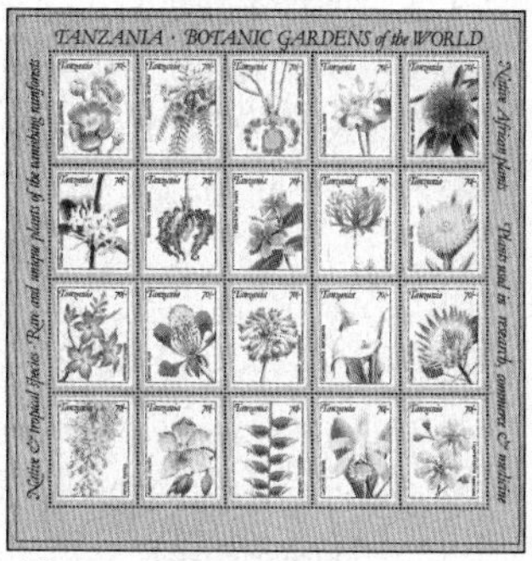

Flowers in Rio de Janeiro Botanical Garden — A140

No. 900: a, Couroupita guianensis. b, Jacaranda acutifolia. c, Psychopsis papilio. d, Nelumbo nucifera. e, Brownea grandiceps. f, Coffea arabica. g, Monodora myristica. h, Calaranthus rosea. i, Hibiscus schizopetalus. j, Carpobrotus edulis. k, Adenium obesum. l, Delonix regia. m, Agapanthus praecox. n, Zantedeschia aethiopica. o, Protea cynaroides. p, Cassia fistula. q, Aganisia cyanea. r, Heliconia rostrata. s, Cattelya luteola. t, Lagerstroemia speciosa.

500sh, Avenue of Royal Palms, Rio.

1992, Nov. 5 Litho. *Perf. 14½*

900 A140 70sh Sheet of 20, #a.-t. 24.00 24.00

Souvenir Sheet

901 A140 500sh multicolored 7.50 7.50

Dinosaurs — A141

No. 902: a, Iguanodon. b, Saltasaurus. c, Cetiosaurus. d, Camarasaurus. e, Spinosaurus. f, Stegosaurus. g, Allosaurus. h, Ceratosaurus. i, Lesothosaurus. j, Anchisaurus. k, Ornithomimus. l, Baronyx. m, Pachycephalosaurus. n, Heterodontosaurus. o, Dryosaurus. p, Coelophysis.

1992, Nov. 5 Litho. *Perf. 14*

902 A141 100sh Sheet of 16, #a.-p. 22.00 22.00

1992 Olympics, Albertville and Barcelona A142

Designs: 20sh, 4000-meter pursuit cycling, vert. 40sh, Double sculls. 50sh, Water polo. 70sh, Women's single luge. 100sh, Marathon. 150sh, Uneven parallel bars. 200sh, Ice hockey, vert, 400sh, Rings, vert.

No. 911, Tennis, vert. No. 912, Soccer, vert.

1992, Nov. 16 Litho. *Perf. 14*

903 A142 20sh multicolored .35 .35
904 A142 40sh multicolored .55 .55
905 A142 50sh multicolored .60 .60
906 A142 70sh multicolored .85 .85
907 A142 100sh multicolored 1.25 1.25
908 A142 150sh multicolored 1.75 1.75
909 A142 200sh multicolored 2.40 2.40
910 A142 400sh multicolored 4.75 4.75
Nos. 903-910 (8) 12.50 12.50

Souvenir Sheets

911 A142 500sh multicolored 6.00 6.00
912 A142 500sh multicolored 6.00 6.00

Mickey's Portrait Gallery A142a

Donald Duck in scenes from Disney movies: No. 915, Sea Scouts, 1939. 35sh, Fire Chief, 1940. 50sh, Truant Officer Donald, 1941. 500sh, With Daisy in Mr. Duck Steps Out, 1940.

No. 925, Daisy in Don Donald, 1937.

Disney characters in scenes from Disney movies: No. 913, Hawaiian Holiday, 1937. No. 914, Society Dog Show, 1939. 75sh, Clock Cleaners, 1937. No. 919, Magician Mickey, 1937. No. 920, Goofy and Wilbur, 1939. 200sh, The Nifty Nineties, 1941. 300sh, Society Dog Show, 1939. 400sh, Pluto's Quin-Puplets, 1937. No. 926, Brave Little Tailor, 1938, horiz. No. 927, Forever Goofy.

1992, Nov. 30 Litho. *Perf. 13½x14*

913 A142a 25sh multicolored .50 .50
914 A142a 25sh multicolored .50 .50
915 A142a 25sh multicolored .50 .50
916 A142a 35sh multicolored .65 .65
917 A142a 50sh multicolored .90 .90
918 A142a 75sh multicolored 1.10 1.10
919 A142a 100sh multicolored 1.25 1.25
920 A142a 100sh multicolored 1.25 1.25
921 A142a 200sh multicolored 2.00 2.00
922 A142a 300sh multicolored 2.75 2.75
923 A142a 400sh multicolored 3.00 3.00
924 A142a 500sh multicolored 3.00 3.00
Nos. 913-924 (12) 17.40 17.40

Souvenir Sheets

925 A142a 600sh multicolored 5.00 5.00

Perf. 14x13½

926 A142a 600sh multicolored 5.00 5.00

Perf. 13½x14

927 A142a 600sh multicolored 5.00 5.00

Nos. 668-673 & 678 Ovptd. in Black or Red

1992 Litho. *Perf. 14*

928 A106 50sh on #668 .35 .35
929 A106 50sh on #669 .35 .35
a. Pair, #928-929 .70 .70
930 A106 75sh on #670 .55 .55
931 A106 75sh on #671 .55 .55
a. Pair, #930-931 1.10 1.10
932 A106 100sh on #672 .75 .75
933 A106 100sh on #673 .75 .75
a. Pair, #932-933 1.50 1.50
Nos. 928-933 (6) 3.30 3.30

Souvenir Sheet

934 A106 350sh on #678 (R) 2.50 2.50

Overprint appears on one line in sheet margin of No. 934.

Traditional Hunting A143

Designs: 20sh, Slingshots used on birds. 40sh, Various weapons. 70sh, Bow and arrow used on gazelles. 100sh, Long knife, wooden club used on gazelles. 150sh, Spear and shield used on lion.

1992 Litho. *Perf. 13½*

935 A143 20sh multicolored 1.40 1.40
936 A143 70sh multicolored 1.75 1.75
937 A143 100sh multicolored 2.75 2.75
938 A143 150sh multicolored 4.00 4.00
Nos. 935-938 (4) 9.90 9.90

Souvenir Sheet

Perf. 12½

939 A143 40sh multicolored 3.25 3.25

Shells — A144

Designs: 10sh, Lambis truncata Humphrey. 15sh, Cypraecassis rufa. 25sh, Vexillum rugosum. 30sh, Conus litteratus. 35sh, Corculum cardissa. 50sh, Murex ramosus. 250sh, Melo melo. 300sh, Tridacha gigas.

1992, June 30 *Perf. 12x12½*

940 A144 10sh multicolored .45 .45
941 A144 15sh multicolored .55 .55
942 A144 25sh multicolored .75 .75
943 A144 30sh multicolored .75 .75
944 A144 35sh multicolored .75 .75
945 A144 50sh multicolored 1.10 1.10
946 A144 250sh multicolored 4.50 4.50
Nos. 940-946 (7) 8.85 8.85

Souvenir Sheet

947 A144 300sh multicolored 6.00 6.00

No. 808 Inscribed Vertically "15th Anniversary"

1992 Litho. *Perf. 14*

949 A125 75sh Sheet of 9, #a.-i. 12.00 12.00

Marine Life
A145

1992 **Litho.** **Perf. 14**
950 A145 20sh Seal 1.25 1.25
951 A145 30sh Whale 3.00 3.00
952 A145 70sh Shark 1.75 1.75
953 A145 100sh Walrus 3.00 3.00
Nos. 950-953 (4) 9.00 9.00

Souvenir Sheet
954 A145 500sh Sea turtle 10.00 10.00

A146

Anniversaries and Events — A147

Designs: 30sh, Count Ferdinand von Zeppelin. 70sh, Apollo-Soyuz. No. 957, Child being offered apple. No. 958, African elephant. No. 959, Lions Intl. emblem, man being given glasses. No. 960, Zebra. 300sh, Graf Zeppelin. No. 962, Space shuttle in Earth orbit. No. 963, Wolfgang Amadeus Mozart.
No. 964, Voyager 2. No. 965, Unidentified zeppelin. No. 966, African elephant, diff. No. 967, Scene from "The Magic Flute."

1992 **Litho.** **Perf. 14**
955 A146 30sh multicolored 3.25 3.25
956 A146 70sh multicolored 4.50 4.50
957 A146 150sh multicolored 2.00 2.00
958 A146 150sh multicolored 3.25 3.25
959 A146 200sh multicolored 2.40 2.40
960 A146 200sh multicolored 3.25 3.25
961 A146 300sh multicolored 3.25 3.25
962 A146 400sh multicolored 4.50 4.50
963 A147 400sh multicolored 3.25 3.25
Nos. 955-963 (9) 29.65 29.65

Souvenir Sheets
964 A146 500sh multicolored 4.50 4.50
965 A146 500sh multicolored 4.50 4.50
966 A146 500sh multicolored 4.50 4.50
967 A147 800sh multicolored 6.50 6.50

Count Zeppelin, 75th death anniv. (#955, 961, 965). Intl. Space Year (#956, 962, 964). Intl. Conference on Nutrition (#957). Earth Summit, Rio de Janeiro (#958, 960, 966). Lions Intl., 75th anniv. (#959). Wolfgang Amadeus Mozart, bicent. of death (in 1991) (#963, 967).
Issued: Nos. 955-956, 961-962, 964-965, Nov.; Nos. 957-960, 966, Dec.

Cats — A147a

20sh, Abyssinian. 30sh, Havana. 50sh, Persian black. 70sh, Persian blue. 100sh, European silver tabby. 150sh, Persian silver tabby. 200sh, Maine.
300sh, European.

1992, Dec. 3 **Litho.** **Perf. 12x12½**
967A A147a 20sh multi .75 .75
967B A147a 30sh multi .75 .75
967C A147a 50sh multi .90 .90
967D A147a 70sh multi 1.10 1.10
967E A147a 100sh multi 1.30 1.30

967F A147a 150sh multi 1.60 1.60
967G A147a 200sh multi 2.00 2.00
Nos. 967A-967G (7) 8.40 8.40

Souvenir Sheet
967H A147a 300sh multi 5.00 5.00

Model Trains
A148

Lionel models: 10sh, B & O Tunnel locomotive #5, 2⅞-inch gauge, 1904. 20sh, Liberty Bell #385E, standard gauge, 1930. 30sh, Armored motor car #203, standard gauge, 1917. 50sh, Open trolley #202, standard gauge, 1910-14. 70sh, Macy special #450, standrad gauge. 100sh, Milwaukee Road bipolar electric #381E, standard gauge, 1929. 200sh, New York Central "S" type, standard gauge, 1912. 300sh, 4-4-0 American #7 (thick rim), standard gauge, 1914.
No. 976, Wind-up hand car with Mickey and Minnie Mouse, O-27 gauge, 1936. No. 977, Clear plastic F-3 display model, O gauge, 1947.

1992, Dec. 10 **Litho.** **Perf. 14**
968 A148 10sh multicolored .65 .65
969 A148 20sh multicolored .75 .75
970 A148 30sh multicolored .80 .80
971 A148 50sh multicolored 1.25 1.25
972 A148 70sh multicolored 1.50 1.50
973 A148 100sh multicolored 1.60 1.60
974 A148 200sh multicolored 2.25 2.25
975 A148 300sh multicolored 3.00 3.00
Nos. 968-975 (8) 11.80 11.80

Souvenir Sheets
976 A148 500sh multicolored 5.00 5.00
977 A148 500sh multicolored 5.00 5.00

Genoa '92.

Birds — A149

5sh, Superb starling. 10sh, Canary. 15sh, Four-colored bush shrike. 25sh, Grey-headed kingfisher. 30sh, Common kingfisher. 35sh, Yellow-billed oxpecker. 150sh, Black throated honeyquide.
300sh, European cuckoo, horiz.

1992, Dec. 10 **Litho.** **Perf. 12x12½**
978 A149 5sh multicolored .90 .90
979 A149 10sh multicolored 1.10 1.10
980 A149 15sh multicolored 1.10 1.10
981 A149 25sh multicolored 1.25 1.25
982 A149 30sh multicolored 1.25 1.25
983 A149 35sh multicolored 1.25 1.25
984 A149 150sh multicolored 3.00 3.00
Nos. 978-984 (7) 9.85 9.85

Souvenir Sheet
Perf. 12½x12
985 A149 300sh multicolored 6.00 6.00

Makonde Art — A149a

Various carved faces.

1992, Dec. 24 **Litho.** **Perf. 12x12½**
985A A149a 20sh multicolored .30 .30
985B A149a 30sh multicolored .30 .30
985C A149a 50sh multicolored .50 .50
985D A149a 70sh multicolored .70 .70
985E A149a 100sh multicolored 1.00 1.00

985F A149a 150sh multicolored 1.50 1.50
985G A149a 200sh multicolored 2.00 2.00
Nos. 985A-985G (7) 6.30 6.30

Souvenir Sheet
985H A149a 350sh multicolored 5.00 5.00

Bicycles
A149b

20sh, Russia, 1813. 30sh, Germany, 1840. 50sh, Germany, 1818. 70sh, Germany, 1850. 100sh. Italy, 1988. 150sh, Sweden, 1982. 300sh, Italy, 1989.
350sh, Great Britain, 1887.

1992, Dec. 30 **Litho.** **Perf. 12½x12**
985I A149b 20sh multicolored .45 .45
985J A149b 30sh multicolored .45 .45
985K A149b 50sh multicolored .65 .65
985L A149b 70sh multicolored .65 .65
985M A149b 100sh multicolored .70 .70
985N A149b 150sh multicolored 1.50 1.50
985O A149b 300sh multicolored 1.75 1.75
Nos. 985I-985O (7) 6.15 6.15

Souvenir Sheet
985P A149b 350sh multicolored 5.00 5.00

Discovery of America, 500th Anniv. — A150

Designs: 10sh, Symbols of luck. 15sh, "Is this course right?," compass, chart. 25sh, "Earth!," first sight of land. 30sh, First meetings, horiz. 35sh, Nina, horiz. 75sh, Santa Maria, horiz. 200sh, Ship running aground, vert. 200sh, Columbus.

Perf. 12x12½, 12½x12
1992, Sept. 30 **Litho.**
986 A150 10sh multicolored .35 .35
987 A150 15sh multicolored .40 .40
988 A150 25sh multicolored .55 .55
989 A150 30sh multicolored .60 .60
990 A150 35sh multicolored .70 .70
991 A150 75sh multicolored 1.25 1.25
992 A150 250sh multicolored 2.25 2.25
Nos. 986-992 (7) 6.10 6.10

Souvenir Sheet
993 A150 200sh multicolored 6.00 6.00

— PAINTINGS FROM THE LOUVRE —

— BICENTENNIAL 1793 – 1993 —

Louvre Museum, Bicent. — A151

No. 994 — Paintings by Jean-Baptiste-Simeon Chardin (1699-1779): a, Young Artist. b, The Buffet. c, The Provider. d, A Mother Working. e, Grace. f, The Copper Fountain. g, House of Cards. h, Child with Teetotum. 500sh, The Ray, horiz.

1993, Mar. 8 **Litho.** **Perf. 12**
994 A151 100sh Sheet of 8, #a.-h. + label 12.00 12.00

Souvenir Sheet
Perf. 14½
995 A151 500sh multicolored 6.00 6.00
No. 995 contains one 88x55mm stamp.

Coronation of Queen Elizabeth II, 40th Anniv.
A152

No. 996: a, 100sh, Official coronation photograph. b, 150sh, Exeter salt. c, 200sh, Photograph of ceremony, 1953. d, 300sh, Queen, Prince Andrew.
500sh, Princess Elizabeth Opening the New Broadgate Coventry, by Dame Laura Knight, 1948.

1993, June 2 **Litho.** **Perf. 13½x14**
996 A152 Sheet, 2 ea #a.-d. 14.00 14.00

Souvenir Sheet
Perf. 14
997 A152 500sh multicolored 6.00 6.00
No. 997 contains one 28x43mm stamp.

Famous Women — A153

Designs: a, 20sh, Valentina Tereshkova. b, 40sh, Marie Curie. c, 50sh, Indira Gandhi. d, 70sh, Wilma Rudolph. e, 100sh, Margaret Mead. f, 150sh, Golda Meir. g, 200sh, Dr. Elizabeth Blackwell. h, 400sh, Margaret Thatcher.
No. 999, Mother Teresa.

1993, July 15 **Perf. 14**
998 A153 Sheet of 8, #a.-h. 15.00 15.00

Souvenir Sheet
999 A153 500sh multicolored 7.00 7.00

Wildlife — A154

No. 1000 — Wildlife at watering hole: No. 1000: a, Elephant. b, Gazelles. c, Hartebeest. d, Duiker. e, Genet. f, Civet. g, Pelicans. h, Waterbuck. i, Blacksmith plovers. j, Pied kingfisher. k, Black-winged stilts. l, Bush pig.
No. 1000M: n, Brown-hooded kingfisher. o, Sable antelope (n). p, Impala (q). q, Buffalo. r, Leopard. s, Aardvark (t). t, Hippopotamus. u, Spotted hyena. v, Crowned crane (w). w, Crocodile. x, Flamingo. y, Baboon.
No. 1001 — Wildlife on the plains: No. 1001: a, Potto. b, Flamingos. c, Grey-headed kingfisher. d, Red colobus monkey. e, Dik-dik. f, Aardwolf. g, Black-backed jackal. h, Tree pangolin. i, Serval. j, Yellow-billed hornbill. k, Pygmy mongoose. l, Bat-eared fox.
No. 1001M: n, Bushbaby. o, Egyptian vulture. p, Ostrich. q, Greater kudu. r, Diana monkey. s, Giraffe (w). t, Cheetah (s). u, Wildebeeest (t). v, Chimpanzee. w, Warthog. x, Zebra. y, Rhinoceros.
No. 1002, Lions, horiz. No. 1003, African elephants, horiz.

1993, June 30
1000	A154	100sh Sheet of 12, #a.-l.	12.00	12.00
1000M	A154	100sh Sheet of 12, #n.-y.	12.00	12.00
1001	A154	100sh Sheet of 12, #a.-l.	12.00	12.00
1001M	A154	100sh Sheet of 12, #n.-y.	12.00	12.00
		Nos. 1000-1001M (4)	48.00	48.00

Souvenir Sheets
1002	A154	500sh multi	6.50	6.50
1003	A154	500sh multi	6.50	6.50

For overprints see Nos. 1531, 1534.

Pancake Tortoise A155

1993, June 30
1004	A155	20sh On rock	.60	.50
1005	A155	30sh Drinking	.90	.75
1006	A155	50sh Crawling from under rocks	1.05	.90
1007	A155	70sh Hatchling	1.35	1.20
		Nos. 1004-1007 (4)	3.90	3.35

World Wildlife Federation.

Mushrooms A156

Designs: 20sh, Macrolepiota rhacodes. 40sh, Mycena pura. 50sh, Chlorophyllum molybdites. 70sh, Agaricus campestris. 100sh, Volvariella volvacea. 150sh, Leucoagaricus naucinus. 200sh, Oudemansiella radicata. 300sh, Clitocybe nebularis.

No. 1016, Omphalotus olearius. No. 1017, Lepista nuda.

1993, June 18   Litho.   Perf. 14
1008	A156	20sh multicolored	.35	.35
1009	A156	40sh multicolored	.55	.55
1010	A156	50sh multicolored	.60	.60
1011	A156	70sh multicolored	.85	.85
1012	A156	100sh multicolored	1.40	1.40
1013	A156	150sh multicolored	1.75	1.75
1014	A156	200sh multicolored	2.40	2.40
1015	A156	300sh multicolored	4.00	4.00
		Nos. 1008-1015 (8)	11.90	11.90

Souvenir Sheets
1016	A156	500sh multicolored	5.00	5.00
1017	A156	500sh multicolored	5.00	5.00

Sports — A157

1992, May 28   Litho.   Perf. 12x12½
1018	A157	20sh Boxing	.35	.35
1019	A157	50sh Field hockey	.80	.80
1020	A157	70sh Horse racing	.65	.65
1021	A157	100sh Marathon	.75	.75
1022	A157	150sh Soccer	.95	.95
1023	A157	200sh Diving	1.25	1.25
1024	A157	400sh Basketball	2.40	2.40
		Nos. 1018-1024 (7)	7.15	7.15

Souvenir Sheet
Perf. 12½x12
1025	A157	300sh High jump, horiz.	4.00	4.00

Animals A158

No. 1026: a, Female Grant's zebra, running. b, Male Grant's zebra, standing. c, Female Grant's gazelle. d, Male Grant's gazelle. e, Thompson's gazelle. f, White-bearded gnu, calf.

No. 1027: a, Female cheetah, cubs. b, Young cheetah. c, Lioness carrying her cub. d, Two hunting dogs. e, Three hunting dogs. f, Hunting dogs before an attack.

No. 1028, African rhinoceros. No. 1029, African elephant.

1993, June 30   Litho.   Perf. 14
1026	A158	100sh Sheet of 6, #a.-f.	9.00	9.00
1027	A158	100sh Sheet of 6, #a.-f.	9.00	9.00

Souvenir Sheets
1028	A158	500sh multicolored	10.00	10.00
1029	A158	500sh multicolored	10.00	10.00

For overprints see Nos. 1532-1533, 1535.

A159

1994 Winter Olympics, Lillehammer, Norway: 300sh, Matti Nykanen, ski jumping, 1988. 400sh, Stefan Krause, Jan Behrendt, double luge, 1992. 500sh, Downhill skiing, 1972.

1993, June 10   Litho.   Perf. 14
1030	A159	300sh multicolored	2.25	2.25
1031	A159	400sh multicolored	2.75	2.75

Souvenir Sheet
1032	A159	500sh multicolored	3.50	3.50

A160

100sh, Telescope. 300sh, Radio telescope. 500sh, Copernicus.

1993, June 10
1033	A160	100sh multicolored	.70	.70
1034	A160	300sh multicolored	2.25	2.25

Souvenir Sheet
1035	A160	500sh multicolored	3.50	3.50

Copernicus, 450th anniv. of death.

Picasso (1881-1973) A160a

Various details of painting, Guernica, 1937.

1993, June 10   Litho.   Perf. 14
1035A	A160a	30sh multi	.25	.25
1035B	A160a	200sh multi	1.40	1.40
1035C	A160a	300sh multi	2.00	2.00
		Nos. 1035A-1035C (3)	3.65	3.65

Souvenir Sheet
1035D	A160a	500sh multi	3.50	3.50

Flowers — A161

Designs: 20sh, Leopard orchid. 30sh, African violet. 40sh, Stapelia semota lutea. 50sh, Busy Lizzie. 60sh, Senecio petraeus. 70sh, Kalanchoe velutina. 100sh, Dwarf ginger lily. 150sh, Nymphaea colorata. 200sh, Thunbergia battiscombei. 250sh, Crossandra nilotica. 300sh, African tulip tree. 350sh, Ruttya fruticosa.

No. 1048, False African violet. No. 1049, Glory lily.

1993, Nov. 8   Litho.   Perf. 13½
1036	A161	20sh multicolored	.50	.50
1037	A161	30sh multicolored	.55	.55
1038	A161	40sh multicolored	.55	.55
1039	A161	50sh multicolored	.55	.55
1040	A161	60sh multicolored	.80	.80
1041	A161	70sh multicolored	.90	.90
1042	A161	100sh multicolored	1.00	1.00
1043	A161	150sh multicolored	1.60	1.60
1044	A161	200sh multicolored	1.90	1.90
1045	A161	250sh multicolored	1.90	1.90
1046	A161	300sh multicolored	2.25	2.25
1047	A161	350sh multicolored	2.25	2.25
		Nos. 1036-1047 (12)	14.75	14.75

Souvenir Sheets
Perf. 13
1048	A161	500sh multicolored	4.25	4.25
1049	A161	500sh multicolored	4.25	4.25

Polska '93 — A162

Paintings: 200sh, Stone Masons, by Aleksander Kobzdej, 1952. 300sh, Child Wearing Plumed Helmut, by Z. Waliszewski, 1932.

500sh, In the Marketplace, by Stanislaw Ososticwicz, 1939.

1993   Litho.   Perf. 14
1050	A162	200sh multicolored	1.75	1.75
1051	A162	300sh multicolored	2.50	2.50

Souvenir Sheet
1052	A162	500sh multicolored	3.75	3.75

Butterflies A163

No. 1053: a, Gold-banded forester. b, Twin dotted border. c, Aphnaeus flavescens. d, Orange-and-lemon. e, Club-tailed charaxes. f, Broad blue-banded swallowtail. g, African map. h, Buxton's hairstreak. i, Bush charaxes. j, Lilac nymph. k, Large striped swordtail. l, Charaxes acuminatus. m, African leaf. n, African wood white. o, Trimen's false acraea. p, Red line sapphire. q, Mother-of-pearl. r, Flame-bordered charaxes. s, Large blue charaxes. t, Emperor swallowtail.

No. 1054: a, Angled grass yellow. b, Figtree blue. c, Iolaus ismenias. d, Green-veined charaxes. e, Commodore. f, African monarch. g, Bush scarlet. h, Eyed pansy. i, Zebra white. j, Azure hairstreak. k, Yellow pansy. l, Regal purple tip.

No. 1054M: n, Iolaus aphnaeoides. o, Green charaxes. p, Beautiful monarch. q, Short-tailed admiral. r, Dusky dotted border. s, Charaxes anticlea. t, Blue salamis. u, Nepheronia argia. v, Acraea pseudolycia. w, Blue-banded diadem. x, Golden tip. y, Acraea bonasia.

No. 1055, Blood-red cymothoe. No. 1056, Precis octavia. No. 1056A, Noble swallowtail. No. 1056B, Violet-spotted charaxes.

1993, Nov. 8   Litho.   Perf. 13
1053	A163	100sh Sheet of 20, #a.-t.	30.00	30.00
1054	A163	100sh Sheet of 12, #a.-l.	20.00	20.00
1054M	A163	100sh Sheet of 12, #n.-y.	20.00	20.00

Souvenir Sheets
1055	A163	500sh multi	7.00	7.00
1056	A163	500sh multi	7.00	7.00
1056A	A163	500sh multi	7.00	7.00
1056B	A163	500sh multi	7.00	7.00

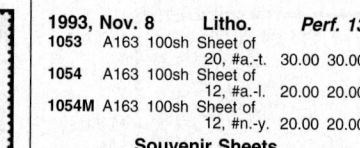

A164

Players, country: 20sh, Gullit, Holland. 30sh, Sheehy, Ireland. 50sh, Giannini, Italy. 70sh, Cesar, Brazil. 250sh, Barnes, England; Grun, Belgium. 300sh, Chendo, Spain. 350sh, Rijkaard, Holland. 400sh, Matthaeus, Germany.

No. 1065, 500sh, Berti, Italy; Caligiuri, US. No. 1066, 500sh, Walker, England; Gilhaus, Holland.

1993, Dec.   Perf. 14
1057-1064	A164	Set of 8	9.50	9.50

Souvenir Sheets
1065-1066	A164	Set of 2	9.50	9.50

1994 World Cup Soccer Championships, US.

A165

Hummel Figurines: 20sh, Boy with accordian. 40sh, Girl with guitar, boy with banjo. 50sh, Boy with tuba. 70sh, Boy with harmonica, bird. 100sh, Bird in tree, boy seated on fence. 150sh, Boy playing horn. 200sh, Boy with horn, bird. 300sh, Girl playing banjo. 350sh, Boy with cello on back. 400sh, Girls with banjo and sheet music.

No. 1077, 500sh, Four carolers. No. 1078, 500sh, Two figures in tower blowing horns at angel below.

1994, Feb. 10
1067-1076	A165	Set of 10	12.50	12.50

Souvenir Sheets
1077-1078	A165	Set of 2	11.00	11.00

Black Athletes — A166

No. 1079: a, 20sh, Arthur Ashe. b, 40sh, Michael Jordan. c, 50sh, Daley Thompson. d, 70sh, Jackie Robinson. e, 100sh, Kareem Abdul-Jabbar. f, 150sh, Florence Joyner. g, 200sh, Jesse Owens. h, 400sh, Jack Johnson. 500sh, Muhammad Ali, horiz.

1993, July 15
1079	A166	Sheet of 8, #a.-h.	9.00	9.00

Souvenir Sheet
1080	A166	500sh multicolored	5.50	5.50

First US Gas Balloon Flight, Bicent. A167

Designs: 200sh, Balloons filling with hot air. 400sh, Jean-Pierre Blanchard (1753-1809), balloon. 500sh, Hot air balloons in flight, vert.

1994, Apr. 25   **Litho.**   *Perf. 14*
1081 A167 200sh multicolored   2.25   2.25
1082 A167 400sh multicolored   4.25   4.25

Souvenir Sheet
1083 A167 500sh multicolored   6.50   6.50

Royal Air Force, 75th Anniv. A168

Designs: 200sh, Sopwith Camel. 400sh, BAE Harrier. 500sh, Supermarine Spitfire.

1993, Dec.
1084 A168 200sh multicolored   2.50   2.50
1085 A168 400sh multicolored   4.50   4.50

Souvenir Sheet
1086 A168 500sh multicolored   7.00   7.00

Automotive Anniversaries — A171

Designs: No. 1099, 200sh, 1893 Benz, 1993 500 SEL. No. 1100, 200sh, Henry Ford, 1922 Model T. No. 1101, 400sh, Karl Benz, emblem. No. 1102, 400sh, 1893 Ford, Mustang Cobra.
No. 1103, 500sh, Emblem, 1937 540 K. No. 1104, 500sh, Henry Ford, first Ford factory.

1994, Apr. 25   **Litho.**   *Perf. 14*
1099-1102 A171 Set of 4   11.00   11.00

Souvenir Sheets
1103-1104 A171 Set of 2   10.00   10.00

First Benz 4-wheel motor car, cent. (#1099, 1101, 1103). First Ford motor, cent. (#1100, 1102, 1104).

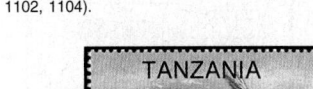

Birds A172

No. 1105, vert.: a, 20sh, African hawk eagle. b, 30sh, Shoe-bill stork. c, 50sh, Harrier eagle. d, 70sh, Casqued hornbill. e, 100sh, Crowned crane. f, 150sh, Greater flamingo.
No. 1106: a, 200sh, Pelican. b, 250sh, Jacana, black crake. c, 300sh, Ostrich. d, 350sh, Helmeted guinea fowl. e, 400sh, Malachite kingfisher. f, 500sh, Saddle-billed stork.

1994, May 11
1105 A172 Sheet of 6, #a.-f.   10.50   10.50
1106 A172 Sheet of 6, #a.-f.   12.50   12.50

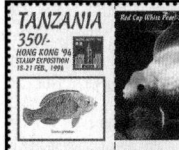

Hong Kong '94 A173

Red-cap white pearl-scale goldfish and: No. 1107, Scarus ghobban. No. 1108, Regal angelfish.

1994, Feb. 18
1107 A173 350sh multicolored   2.25   2.25
1108 A173 350sh multicolored   2.25   2.25
   a.   Pair, #1107-1108   4.50   4.50

Nos. 1107-1108 issued in sheets of 5 pairs. No. 1108a is a continuous design.

Mickey Mouse, 65th Anniv. — A176

Disney characters on tour: 10sh, Boarding plane. 20sh, Dancing, Tonga. 30sh, Lawn bowling, Australia. 40sh, Building igloo, Arctic region. 50sh, Royal Palace Guard, London. 60sh, Esna bazaar, Egypt. 70sh, Zsambox cowboys, Hungary, vert. 100sh, Grand Canal, Venice, vert. 150sh, Dancing, Bali, Indonesia, vert. 200sh, Monks studying text, Bangkok, Thailand, vert. 300sh, Water skiing, Taj Mahal, India, vert. 400sh, Himalayas, Nepal.
No. 1125, Kilimanjaro Uhuru Peak, Kibo, Tanzania, vert. No. 1126, Kigoma railway station, Dar es Salaam, Tanzania, vert. No. 1127, Memorial to Dr. Livingstone, shores of Lake Tanganyika, Tanzania.

1994, Apr. 6   *Perf. 14x13½, 13½x14*
1113 A176 10sh multicolored   .30   .30
1114 A176 20sh multicolored   .30   .30
1115 A176 30sh multicolored   .30   .30
1116 A176 40sh multicolored   .45   .45
1117 A177 50sh multicolored   .50   .50
1118 A176 60sh multicolored   .55   .55
1119 A176 70sh multicolored   .75   .75
1120 A176 100sh multicolored   1.05   1.05
1121 A176 150sh multicolored   1.50   1.50
1122 A176 200sh multicolored   2.10   2.10
1123 A176 300sh multicolored   3.00   3.00
1124 A176 400sh multicolored   4.00   4.00
   Nos. 1113-1124 (12)   14.80   14.80

Souvenir Sheets
1125 A176 500sh multicolored   4.75   4.75
1126 A176 500sh multicolored   4.75   4.75
1127 A176 500sh multicolored   4.75   4.75

Reptiles A177

Designs: 20sh, Geochelone elephantopus, vert. 50sh, Iguana iguana, vert. 70sh, Varanus salvator. 100sh, Naja oxiana, vert. 150sh, Chamaeleo jacksonii. 200sh, Eunectes murinus. 250sh, Alligator mississippensis. 500sh, Vipera berus, vert.

Perf. 12x12½, 12½x12
1993, June 28   **Litho.**
1128-1134 A177 Set of 7   6.75   6.75

Souvenir Sheet
1135 A177 500sh multicolored   5.25   5.25

Nos. 1128-1135 were were not available until July 1994.

Sharks A178

Designs: 20sh, Isurus oxyrinchus. 30sh, Etmopterus hillianus. 50sh, Galeocerdo cuvier. 70sh, Squatina africana. 100sh, Pristiophorus cirratus. 150sh, Triaenodon obesus. 200sh, Sphyrna lewini.
350sh, Hexanchus griseus, vert.

1993, July 27   *Perf. 12½x12*
1136-1142 A178 Set of 7   5.25   5.25

Souvenir Sheet
Perf. 12x12½
1143 A178 350sh multicolored   3.25   3.25

Nos. 1136-1143 were not available until July 1994.

Dogs — A179

Designs: 20sh, Gordon setter. 30sh, Zwergschnauzer. 50sh, Labrador retriever. 70sh, Wire fox terrier. 100sh, English springer spaniel. 150sh, Newfoundlander. 200sh, Moscow toy terrier.
350sh, Doberman pinscher.

1993, Sept. 27   *Perf. 12x12½*
1144-1150 A179 Set of 7   5.75   5.75

Souvenir Sheet
1151 A179 350sh multicolored   2.75   2.75

Nos. 1144-1151 were not available until July 1994.

Horses A180

Designs: 20sh, Norman-Arab. 40sh, Nonius. 50sh, Boulonnais. 70sh, Arab. 100sh, Anglo-Arab. 150sh, Tarpan. 200sh, Thoroughbred.
No. 1159, Anglo-Norman.

1993, Nov. 30   *Perf. 12½x12*
1152-1158 A180 Set of 7   6.00   6.00

Souvenir Sheet
Perf. 12x12½
1159 A180 400sh multicolored   3.00   3.00

Nos. 1152-1159 were not available until July 1994.

Military Aircraft A181

Designs: 20sh, ALFA jet. 30sh, Northrup F-5E. 50sh, Mirage 3NG. 70sh, MB-339C. 100sh, MIG-31. 150sh, C-101 AVIOJET. 200sh, F-16B.
500sh, EAP fighter, vert.

1994, Apr. 25   **Litho.**   *Perf. 12½x12*
1160-1166 A181 Set of 7   6.00   6.00

Souvenir Sheet
Perf. 12x12½
1167 A181 500sh multicolored   3.50   3.50

A182

Customs Co-operation Council Meeting, Arusha — A183

Designs: 20sh, Trans-border trade. 50sh, Customs-international trade by ship. 100sh, Customs-air transportation. 150sh, Postal service-customs co-operation, Customs and UPU emblems.
500sh, Emblem.

1994, Aug. 23   **Litho.**   *Perf. 13½*
1168-1171 A182 Set of 4   5.00   5.00

Souvenir Sheet
Perf. 12½
1172 A183 500sh multicolored   6.00   6.00

1994 World Cup Soccer Championships, US — A184

No. 1173: a, Giuseppe Signori. b, Ruud Gullit. c, Roberto Mancini. d, Marco Van Basten. e, Dennis Bergkamp. f, Oscar Ruggeri. g, Frank Rijkaard. h, Peter Schmeichel.
1000sh, World Cup trophy.

1994, Sept. 26   *Perf. 14*
1173 A184 300sh Sheet of 8, #a.-h.   10.00   10.00

Souvenir Sheet
1174 A184 1000sh multi   5.50   5.50

1994 World Cup Soccer Championships, US — A184a

Letter in soccer ball: 40sh, B. 50sh, C. 70sh, D. 100sh, E. 170sh, A. 200sh, none. 250sh, F. 500sh, Two players and goalie.

1994, Sept. 30   **Litho.**   *Perf. 12½x12*
1174A-1174G A184a Set of 7   10.00   10.00
   i.   Souv. sheet of 6, #1174A-1174E, 1174G + 3 labels   8.00   8.00

Souvenir Sheet
1174H A184a 500sh multi   5.50   5.50

Dogs — A185

No. 1175, 120sh: a, Alsatian (German Shepherd). b, Japanese chin. c, Shetland sheepdog. d, Italian spinone. e, Great dane. f, English setter. g, Pembroke (welsh corgi). h, St. Bernard. i, Irish wolfhound.
No. 1176, 120sh: a, Afghan hound. b, Basenji (Congo dog). c, Siberian husky. d, Irish setter. e, Norwegian elkhound. f, Bracco Italiano (Italian hound). g, Australian cattle dog. h, German short haired pointer. i, Rhodesian ridgeback.
No. 1177, 120sh: a, Alaskan malamute. b, Scottish cairn terrier. c, American foxhound. d, British bulldog. e, Boston terrier. f, Borzoi (Russian wolfhound). g, Shar pei (Chinese fighting dog). h, Saluki (Persian greyhound). i, Bernese mountain dog.
No. 1178, 120sh: a, Doberman pinscher. b, Chihuahua. c, Bloodhound. d, Keeshond (Dutch barge dog). e, Tibetan spaniel. f, Japanese akita. g, Tervueren (Belgian shepherd dog). h, Chow chow (Chinese Spitz). i, Pharaoh hound.
No. 1179, 1000sh, Like #1175e. No. 1180, 1000sh, Like #1176b.

1994, Sept. 30 Sheets of 9, #a-i
1175-1178 A185 22.00 22.00
Souvenir Sheets
1179-1180 A185 Set of 2 13.50 13.50

Miniature Sheets of 8

Orchids — A186

No. 1181, 200sh: a, Rangaeris amaniensis. b, Eulophia macowanii. c, Cyrtorchis arcuata. d, Centrostigma occultans. e, Cirrhopetalum umbellatum. f, Ansellia gigantea. g, Angraecum ramosum. h, Disa englerana.
No. 1182, 200sh: a, Nervilia stolziana. b, Satyrium orbiculare. c, Schzochilus sulphureus. d, Disa stolzii. e, Platycoryne mediocris. f, Satyrium breve. g, Eulophia nuttii. h, Disa ornithantha.
No. 1183, 1000sh, Eulophia thomsonii, horiz. No. 1184, 1000sh, Phaius P. tankervilliae, horiz.

1994, Oct. 7 Sheets of 8, #a-h
1181-1182 A186 Set of 2 35.00 35.00
Souvenir Sheets
1183-1184 A186 Set of 2 20.00 20.00

Natl. Parks A187

Designs: 20sh, Ngorongoro Crater. 50sh, Ngurdoto Crater. 70sh, Kilimanjaro Natl. Park. 100sh, Gombe Natl. Park. 150sh, Selous Natl. Park. 200sh, Mikumi Natl. Park. 250sh, Serengeti Natl. Park.
500sh, Lake Manyara Natl. Park, vert.

1993, Oct. 29 Litho. Perf. 12
1185-1191 A187 Set of 7 4.50 4.50
Souvenir Sheet
1192 A187 500sh multicolored 2.75 2.75
Nos. 1185-1192 are dated 1993 but were not available until Oct. 1994.

Historical African Costumes A188

Designs: 20sh, Berts style. 40sh, Galla style. 50sh, Guinean warrior. 70sh, Goloff style. 100sh, Peul style. 150sh, Abyssinian warrior. 200sh, Pahuin style.
350sh, Zulu style.

1993, Dec. 30
1193-1199 A188 Set of 7 3.25 3.25
Souvenir Sheet
1200 A189 350sh multicolored 2.00 2.00
Nos. 1193-1200 are dated 1993 but were not available until Oct. 1994.

1994 Winter Olympics, Lillehammer A189

Designs: 40sh, Downhill skiing. 50sh, Ice hockey. 70sh, Speed skating. 100sh, Bobsled. 120sh, Figure skating. 170sh, Free style skiing. 250sh, Biathlon.
500sh, Slalom skiing.

1994, Feb. 12
1201-1207 A189 Set of 7 4.50 4.50
Souvenir Sheet
1208 A189 500sh multicolored 2.50 2.50

Sailing Ships — A190

Designs: 40sh, Jahazi. 50sh, Caravel. 70sh, Carrack. 100sh, Galeas. 170sh, Line of battle ship. 200sh, Frigate. 250sh, Brig.
No. 1210, Bark.

1994, Apr. 20
1209-1215 A190 Set of 7 4.00 4.00
Souvenir Sheet
1216 A190 500sh multicolored 2.50 2.50

Prehistoric Animals — A191

Designs: 40sh, Diatruma. 50sh, Tyranosaurus. 100sh, Uintaterius. 120sh, Stiracosaurus. 170sh, Diplodocus. 250sh, Archaeopteryx. 300sh, Sordes.
500sh, Dimetrodon, vert.

1994, June 30
1217-1223 A191 Set of 7 8.00 8.00
Souvenir Sheet
1224 A191 500sh multicolored 3.50 3.50

Intl. Year of the Family — A192

Designs: 40sh, Family. 120sh, Father playing ball with children. 170sh, People at clinic, horiz. 250sh, Woman harvesting in field.
300sh, Emblem.

Perf. 12x12½, 12½x12
1994, Aug. 30 Litho.
1225-1228 A192 Set of 4 4.00 4.00
Souvenir Sheet
1229 A192 300sh multicolored 4.00 4.00

Zanzibar Revolution, 30th Anniv. — A193

Designs: 40sh, Pres. Salmin Amour. 70sh, Abeid Amani Karume, first president. 120sh, Processing cloves, horiz. 250sh, Zanzibar door.
500sh, Hands clasped over map.

1994, Aug. 1
1230-1233 A193 Set of 4 4.00 4.00
Souvenir Sheet
1234 A193 500sh multicolored 3.50 3.50

Arachnids A194

Designs: 40sh, Trombidium. 50sh, Eurypelma. 100sh, Salticus. 120sh, Micrommata rosea, vert. 170sh, Araneus, vert. 250sh, Micrathena, vert. 300sh, Araneus diadematus, vert.
500sh, Hadogenes, vert.

Perf. 12½x12, 12x12½
1994, Aug. 31
1235-1241 A194 Set of 7 5.50 5.50
Souvenir Sheet
1242 A194 500sh multicolored 2.50 2.50

Butterflies and Flowers A195

No. 1243, 120sh: a, Lunaria biennis, papilio glaucus. b, Phlox paniculata, danaus plexippus. c, Rudbeckia gloriosa, papilio troilus. d, Tithonia rotundifolia, hypolimnas antevorta. e, Osteospermum, cirrochroa imperatrix. f, Ursinia anethoides, vanessa atalanta. g, Wahlenbergia gloriosa, limenitis archippus. h, Mentzelia lindleyi, hypolimnas pandarus. i, Paeonia suffruticosa, anthocharis belia.
No. 1244, 120sh: a, Coreopsis laneolata, limenitis sydyi. b, Lantana camara, agraulis vanillae. c, Asclepias tuberosa, danaus chrysippus. d, Verbena canadensis, eurytides marcellus. e, Lonicera japonica, artopoetes pryeri. f, Pentas bussei, heliconius charitonius. g, Echinacea purpurea, limenitis weidemeyerii. h, Myosotis alpestris, phoebis sennae. i, Aster amellus, timelaea albescens.
No. 1245, 1000sh, Buddleia davidii, papilio polyxenes. No. 1246, 1000sh, Helianthus annuus, vanessa cardui.

1994, Nov. 19 Perf. 14
Sheets of 9, #a-i
1243-1244 A195 Set of 2 18.00 18.00
Souvenir Sheets
1245-1246 A195 Set of 2 13.50 13.50

First Manned Moon Landing, 25th Anniv. A196

No. 1247, 150sh: a, Map of landing site. b, Location of Sea of Tranquility shown on Moon. c, Craters. d, Launch. e, Second stage separation. f, Separation of lunar modules. g, Command module, "Columbia," landing module, "Eagle." h, "Eagle" descending. i, Inside module.
No. 1248, 150sh: a, Michael Collins, Neil Armstrong, Edwin "Buzz" Aldrin. b, "Eagle" on lunar surface. c, Stepping foot on moon. d,

---

Erecting solar wind devices. e, Gathering soil samples. f, Reflection in helmet. g, Astronaut, US flag. h, Carrying equipment. i, "Eagle" ascending from lunar surface.
No. 1249, 150sh: a, "Columbia" above lunar surface, Earth on horizon. b, "Eagle" above lunar surface. c, Release of S-4B rocket. d, Heading toward Earth. e, Re-entering atmosphere. f, Splashdown. g, Pickup at sea. h, Helicopter lifting men on board. i, Astronauts in quarantine.

1994, Nov. 30 Sheets of 9, #a-i
1247-1249 A196 Set of 3 30.00 30.00

Dinosaurs — A198

No. 1250: a, Brontosaurus (e). b, Albertosaurus. c, Parasaurolophus. d, Pteranodon. e, Stegosaurus. f, Tyrannosaurus. g, Triceratops. h, Ornitholestes. i, Camarasaurus. j, Ankylosaurus. k, Trachodon. l, Allosaurus. m, Corythosaurus. n, Struthiomimus. o, Camptosaurus. p, Heterodontosaurus.
No. 1251: a, Deinonychus. b, Styracosaurus. c, Anatosaurus. d, Plateosaurus. e, Iguanodon. f, Oviraptor. g, Dimorphodon. h, Ornithomimus. i, Lambeosaurus. j, Megalosaurus. k, Cetiosaurus. l, Hypsilophodon. m, Rhamphorhynchus. n, Scelidosaurus. o, Antrodemus. p, Dimetrodon.
1000sh, Brachiosaurus, vert.

1994, Dec. 26
1250 A197 120sh Sheet of 16, #a-p. 15.00 15.00
1251 A198 120sh Sheet of 16, #a-p. 15.00 15.00
Souvenir Sheet
1252 A197 1000sh multi 8.25 8.25
No. 1250 is a continuous design.

Mickey Mouse, Safari Club — A199

Designs: No. 1253, 70sh, Donald, Mickey, lion cubs. No. 1254, 70sh, Goofy leaning on Donald. No. 1255, 100sh, Donald wearing tree disguise. No. 1256, 100sh, Donald under elephant. No. 1257, 120sh, Donald, hippopotamus. No. 1258, 120sh, Mickey writing in diary. No. 1259, 150sh, Goofy carrying gear, Donald, Mickey. No. 1260, 150sh, Mickey, elephant, Donald, Goofy in rain. No. 1261, 200sh, Donald, Goofy, Mickey reading book, lion. No. 1262, 200sh, Goofy, zebras. No. 1263, 250sh, Mickey, giraffe. No. 1264, 250sh, Donald filming picture.
No. 1265, 1000sh, Goofy hanging from tree, vert. No. 1266, 1000sh, Goofy holding camera, Donald, vert. No. 1267, 1000sh, Mickey holding camera, vert.

1994, Dec. 26 Perf. 14x13½
1253-1264 A199 Set of 12 13.00 13.00
Souvenir Sheets
Perf. 13½x14
1265-1267 A199 Set of 3 16.00 16.00

Tanzania A200

Olympic Gold Medalists — A201

Designs: 350sh, Kristin Otto, Germany, 50m free-style swimming, 1988. 500sh, Carl Lewis, US, track & field, 1984, 1988.
1000sh, Oksana Baiul, Ukraine, women's figure skating, 1994.

1994, Dec. 12   Litho.   Perf. 14
1268 A200 350sh multicolored   1.75 1.75
1269 A200 500sh multicolored   2.50 2.50
          Souvenir Sheet
1270 A201 1000sh multicolored   5.00 5.00
    Intl. Olympic Committee, cent. (#1270).

D-Day, 50th Anniv. A202

350sh, Combined forces attack Atlantic wall. 600sh, Waterproofed tanks support Marines at Omaha Beach.
No. 1273, 200sh: a, Gen. Eisenhower, US forces, Omaha Beach. b, P-51 Mustang, D-Day armada. c, US Coast Guard cutter, landing craft. d, US troops approaching Omaha Beach. e, US troops landing on Omaha Beach. f, US forces on Omaha Beach.
No. 1274, 200sh: a, Gen. Montgomery, White Ensign flies over Normandy beach. b, British forces with Churchill Avre tank, Gold Beach. c, USS Thompson refueled en route to Omaha Beach. d, HMS Warspite fires on German positions, Sword Beach. e, Royal Marine commandoes landing, Juno Beach. f, Sherman Crab flail tank landing on Normandy beach.
No. 1275, 200sh: a, Supermarine Spitfire over Normandy beaches. b, Bren gun carriers, Gold Beach. c, Le Regiment de la Chaudiere, Juno Beach. d, Canadian forces land on Juno Beach. e, Sherman tank on Normandy beach. f, German artillery fires on D-Day Armada.
No. 1276, 1000sh, US forces prepare to embark from England to Normandy beaches. No. 1277, 1000sh, US forces on Utah Beach. No. 1278, 1000sh, Beach obstacles.

1994, Dec. 12   Litho.   Perf. 14
1271 A202 350sh multicolored   1.75 1.75
1272 A202 600sh multicolored   3.25 3.25
          Sheets of 6, #a-f
1273-1275 A202 Set of 3   20.00 20.00
          Souvenir Sheets
1276-1278 A202 Set of 3   16.00 16.00

Raptors A203

Designs: 40sh, Terathopius ecaudatus, vert. 50sh, Spizaetus ornatus, vert. 100sh, Pandion haliaetus, vert. 120sh, Vultur gryphus, vert. 170sh, Haliaetus vocifer. 250sh, Sarcoramphus papa, vert. 400sh, Falco peregrinus.
500sh, Pseudogyps africanus, vert.

Perf. 12x12½, 12½x12
1994, Sept. 30
1279-1285 A203 Set of 7   9.00 9.00
          Souvenir Sheet
1286 A203 500sh multicolored   3.50 3.50

Endangered Species — A204

Designs: 40sh, Phascolasctos cinereus. 70sh, Ailurus fulgens. 100sh, Aguila. 120sh, Loxodonta africana. 250sh, Monachus tropicalis. 400sh, Eschrichtius gibbosus. 500sh, Cetacea.
500sh, Panthera tigris, vert.

1994, July 29   Perf. 12½x12
1287-1293 A204 Set of 7   8.50 8.50
          Souvenir Sheet
          Perf. 12x12½
1294 A204 500sh multicolored   3.75 3.75
    No. 1288 shows a Giant Panda, and is incorrectly inscribed with the scientific name of the Lesser Panda.

Crabs — A205

Designs: 40sh, Astacus leptodactytus, horiz. 100sh, Eriocheir sinensis. 120sh, Caneer opillo. 170sh, Cardisoma quanhumi, horiz. 250sh, Birgus latro. 300sh, Menippe mercenaria, horiz. 400sh, Dromia vulgaris.
No. 1302, Callinectes sapidus, horiz.

Perf. 12½x12, 12x12½
1994, Nov. 30   Litho.
1295-1301 A205 Set of 7   6.75 6.75
          Souvenir Sheet
1302 A205 500sh multicolored   2.00 2.00

Flowers — A206

Designs: 40sh, Dicentra spectabilis. 100sh, Thunbergia alata. 120sh, Cyrtanthus minimiflorus. 170sh, Nepenthes hybrida. 250sh, Allamanda cathartica. 300sh, Encyclia pentotis. 400sh, Protea lacticolor. 500sh, Tradescantia.

1995, Oct. 31   Perf. 12x12½
1303-1309 A206 Set of 7   6.50 6.50
          Souvenir Sheet
1310 A206 500sh multicolored   2.50 2.50
          Dated 1994.

Woodstock Music Festival, 25th Anniv. — A207

No. 1311, Jimi Hendrix. No. 1312, Carlos Santana. No. 1313, John Lee Hooker.

1995   Imperf.
          Size: 124x84mm
1311 A207 2000sh multi   10.00 10.00
          Souvenir Sheet
          Self-Adhesive
1312 A207 2000sh multi   10.00 10.00
          Size: 115x122mm
          Imperf
          Self-Adhesive
1313 A207 2000sh multi   11.00 11.00
    Issued: No. 1311, 2/27; No. 1312, 5/15; No. 1313, 8/22.

Space Probes and Satellites A208

Designs: 40sh, Hubble telescope. 100sh, Mariner. 120sh, Voyager 2. 170sh, Work Package 03. 250sh, Orbiting solar observatory (OSO). 300sh, Magellan. 400sh, Galileo. 500sh, FOBOS.

1994, Dec. 30   Litho.   Perf. 12½x12
1319-1325 A208 Set of 7   6.75 6.75
          Souvenir Sheet
1326 A208 500sh multicolored   3.50 3.50

Sierra Club, Cent. A209

No. 1327, 150sh, vert: a, Black rhinoceros. b, Aye-aye. c, Aye-aye, holding claw at mouth. d, Giraffes, Masai Mara Reserve. e, Red lechwe, group. f, Red lechwe running. g, White-handed gibbon, white coat. h, White-handed gibbon, dark coat. i, White-handed gibbon, ready to climb tree.
No. 1328, 150sh: a, Aye-aye. b, Black rhinoceros facing each other. c, Black rhinoceros. d, Red lechwe. e, Lions fighting, Masai Mara Reserve. f, Hyena, Masai Mara Reserve. g, Nile crocodile in water. h, Nile crocodile, mouth open. i, Nile crocodile in grass.

1995, July 6   Litho.   Perf. 14
          Sheets of 9, #a-i
1327-1328 A209 Set of 2   18.00 18.00

Fruit A210

Designs: 70sh, Coconuts. 100sh, Pineapple. 150sh, Pawpaw. 200sh, Tomato. 500sh, Coconuts.

1995, June 30
1329-1332 A210 Set of 4   6.00 6.00
          Souvenir Sheet
1333 A210 500sh multicolored   5.25 5.25
          Miniature Sheets of 9

The Beatles — A211

No. 1334, 100sh: a, George Harrison. b, d, e, f, h, Various group portraits. c, Ringo Starr. g, Paul McCartney. i, John Lennon.
No. 1335, 100sh, vert.: a-i, Various portraits of John Lennon.
No. 1336, 500sh, John Lennon, vert. No. 1337, 500sh, Paul McCartney.

1995   Sheets of 9, #a-i   Perf. 12½
1334-1335 A211 Set of 2   13.00 13.00
          Souvenir Sheets
1336-1337 A211 Set of 2   13.00 13.00
    No. 1336 contains one 51x76mm stamp.
    No. 1337 contains one 57x51mm stamp.

Trains A212

No. 1338, 200sh: a, 0-6-0 Italy. b, 0-4-4-OT Mallet, Germany. c, 4-8-0 Tender Engine, Ghana. d, Mallet Tanks, Germany. e, 0-6-2T on the Zillertalbahn, Switzerland. f, Rack Lines, Austria. g, Sweden Jodemans Railway, Norway. h, 4-6-0 Portugal. i, 60CM gauge, Mine Railway, Spain.
No. 1339, 200sh: a, 640 Class 2-6-0s, Italy. b, Norway electric. c, Gordon Highlander 4-40s. d, High Line 9600 class 2-8-0 Japan. e, 4-6-0 Henschel, Portugal. f, Federal German State Railway 220 hydraulic. g, Caledonian 4-2-2, Scotland. h, M2 Locomotive, Denmark. i, Denver & Rio Grande, Western US.
No. 1340, 1000sh, Karl Golsdorf 2-6-0 tank engine, "Germany." No. 1341, 1000sh, High speed ET 403, Germany. No. 1342, 1000sh, AKO 1920, US. No. 1343 1000sh, Porter 2-4-0S, Hawaii.

1995, July 5   Litho.   Perf. 14
          Sheets of 9, #a-i
1338-1339 A212 Set of 2   25.00 25.00
          Souvenir Sheets
1340-1343 A212 Set of 4   27.50 27.50
          Singapore '95.

FAO, 50th Anniv.— A213

No. 1344: a, Boy eating. b, Baby, mother eating. c, Two young people eating.
    1000sh, Woman picking fruit, horiz.

1995, Aug. 14
1344 A213 250sh Strip of 3,
              #a.-c.   4.50 4.50
          Souvenir Sheet
1345 A213 1000sh multicolored   5.25 5.25
    No. 1344 is a continuous design.

Rotary International, 90th Anniv. — A214

Designs: 600sh, Paul Harris, Rotary emblem. 1000sh, Natl. flag, Rotary emblem.

1995, Aug. 14
1346 A214 600sh multicolored 3.25 3.25

Souvenir Sheet
1347 A214 1000sh multicolored 5.25 5.25

Queen Mother, 95th Birthday — A215

No. 1348: a, Drawing. b, With Queen Elizabeth II. c, Formal portrait. d, In black outfit. 1000sh, Blue dress with pearls.

1995, Aug. 14   Perf. 13½x14
1348 A215 250sh Block or strip of 4, #a.-d. 5.00 5.00

Souvenir Sheet
1349 A215 1000sh multicolored 5.25 5.25

No. 1348 was issued in sheets of 8 stamps. Sheets of Nos. 1348-1349 exist with black borders overprinted in sheet margins and text "In Memoriam 1900-2002."

End of World War II, 50th Anniv. A216

No. 1350 — Flags of countries shaped as "VJ:" a, Singapore. b, Fiji. c, Malaysia. d, Marshall Islands. e, Philippines. f, Solomon Islands.

No. 1351: a, Pearl Harbor. b, North Africa. c, Battle of Atlantic. d, War in Soviet Union. e, "D" Day, June 6, 1944. f, Holocaust. g, War in Pacific. h, Hiroshima, Enola Gay, mushroom cloud.

No. 1352, 1000sh, Battle of Britain. No. 1353, 1000sh, British soldier, donkey with backpack.

1995, Aug. 14   Litho.   Perf. 14
1350 A216 250sh Sheet of 6, #a.-f. + label 8.50 8.50
1351 A216 250sh Sheet of 8, #a.-h. + label 8.50 8.50

Souvenir Sheets
1352-1353 A216 Set of 2 17.50 17.50

Reptiles A217

No. 1354: a, African rock python. b, Bell's hinged tortoise. c, Gaboon viper. d, Royal python. e, Savannah monitor. f, Nile monitor. g, Three-horned chameleon. h, Nile crocodile. i, Rough-scaled bush viper. j, Puff adder. k, Rhinocerous viper. l, Leopard tortoise.

No. 1355, 1000sh, Bush viper. No. 1356, 1000sh, Spitting cobra.

1995, Sept. 5
1354 A217 200sh Sheet of 12, #a.-l. 13.00 13.00

Souvenir Sheets
1355-1356 A217 Set of 2 12.00 12.00

UN, 50th Anniv. — A218

No. 1357 — Various races of people, within group: a, Woman holding baby on shoulders. b, Man holding child in arms. c, One child standing.

1000sh, UN soldier using binoculars.

1995, Aug. 14   Litho.   Perf. 14
1357 A218 250sh Strip of 3, #a.-c. 5.25 5.25

Souvenir Sheet
1358 A218 1000sh multicolored 5.25 5.25

No. 1357 is a continuous design.

Summer Olympics Gold Medal Winners — A219

No. 1359 — 200sh, a, Tommie Smith, US, 1968. b, Jack Lovelock, New Zealand, 1936. c, Al Oerter, US, 1956-68. d, Daley Thompson, Great Britain, 1980. e, Greg Louganis, US, 1984-88. f, Sammy Lee, US, 1948. g, Dan Gable, US, 1972. h, Helen Meany, US, 1928. i, Sugar Ray Leonard, US, 1976.

No. 1360, 200sh: a, Robert Mathias, US, 1948-52 . b, Larissa Latynina, USSR, 1956. c, Martin Sheridan, US, 1904-08. d, Vera Caslavska, Czechoslovakia, 1968. e, Edwin Moses, US, 1984. f, Jesse Owens, US, 1936. g, Mary Lou Retton, US, 1984. h, Bobby Morrow, US, 1956. i, Joan Benoit, US, 1984.

No. 1361, 1000sh, Florence Griffith Joyner, Jackie Joyner-Kersee, US, 1988. No. 1362, 1000sh, Vasily Alexeyev USSR, 1972-76.

1995, Sept. 18   Sheets of 9, #a-i
1359-1360 A219 Set of 2 16.00 16.00

Souvenir Sheets
1361-1362 A219 Set of 2 10.00 10.00

Wild Animals A220

No. 1363: a, Snake, vulture. b, Vulture. c, Giraffe (d, g, h, k, l). d, African bateleur. e, Elephants (f). f, Kob, rhino (b, e, i, j, n). g, Rhinos. h, Baboon. i, Kob (m, n). j, Saddle billed stork, warthog (n). k, Cheetahs (g, j, n). l, African lion (h, k, o, p). m, Vulture. n, Dikdiks. o, Lion cubs. p, Lions (o).

No. 1364: a, Elands. b, Zebras. c, Lions. d, Baboons.

No. 1365, 1000sh, Rhinoceros. No. 1366, 1000sh, Leopard.

1995, Sept. 15
1363 A220 100sh Sheet of 16, #a.-p. 8.50 8.50
1364 A220 250sh Sheet of 4, #a.-d. 5.50 5.50

Souvenir Sheets
1365-1366 A220 Set of 2 10.00 10.00

UN, 50th Anniv. A221

Designs: 70sh, Corn farming, vert. 100sh, Cultivating land. 150sh, Women spinning cotton in factory. 200sh, Boy drawing at desk, vert.

500sh, UN emblem, "50."

Wmk. 387
1995, Oct. 24   Litho.   Perf. 14
1367-1370 A221 Set of 4 4.75 4.75

Souvenir Sheet
1371 A221 500sh multicolored 5.25 5.25

East African Treaty, 2nd Anniv. A222

Designs: 100sh, Heads of State. 150sh, Map, flags, vert. 180sh, Map, cotton, vert. 200sh, Fishing on Lake Victoria.

500sh, Heads of State.

1995, Oct. 24
1373-1376 A222 Set of 4 5.50 5.50

Souvenir Sheet
1377 A222 500sh multicolored 5.50 5.50

Hoofed Animals — A224

Designs: 70sh, Hippopotamus amphibius, horiz. 100sh, Litocranius walleri. 150sh, Sincerus caffer, horiz. 180sh, Antilocapridae, horiz. 200sh, Alcelphus buselaphus. 260sh, Taurotragus oryx. 380sh, Strepsiceros.

500sh, Giraffa camelopardalis.

Perf. 12½x12, 12x12½
1995, May 31   Litho.
1380-1386 A224 Set of 7 7.25 7.25

Souvenir Sheet
1387 A224 500sh multicolored 6.75 6.75

Cactus Flowers — A225

Designs: 70sh, Weingartia fidaiana. 100sh, Rebutia spegazziniana. 150sh, Caralluma lugarii. 180sh, Cerochlamys pachyphylla. 200sh, Schlumbergera orssighiana. 260sh, Epiphyllum darrahii. 380sh, Ceropegia nilotica.

500sh, Neoporteria nigrihorrida.

1995, Aug. 31   Perf. 12x12½
1388-1394 A225 Set of 7 7.25 7.25

Souvenir Sheet
1395 A225 500sh multicolored 6.75 6.75

Bats A226

Designs: 70sh, Cheiromeles torquatus, vert. 100sh, Hypsignatus monstrosus, vert. 150sh, Rhinolophus, ferrum-equinum, vert. 180sh, Plecotus auritus. 200sh, Syconycteris australis, vert. 260sh, Plecotus auritus, vert. 380sh, Otomops martiensseni.

500sh, Pteropus.

1995, July 31   Perf. 12x12½, 12½x12
1396-1402 A226 Set of 7 7.25 7.25

Souvenir Sheet
1403 A226 500sh multicolored 6.50 6.50

Marine Life of Coral Reefs A227

Designs: 70sh, Medusa. 100sh, Surgeonfish. 150sh, Angelfish. 180sh, Octopus. 200sh, Zebra fish. 260sh, Shark. 380sh, Ray. 500sh, Turtle.

1995, June 15   Perf. 12½x12
1404-1410 A227 Set of 7 7.25 7.25

Souvenir Sheet
1411 A227 500sh multicolored 6.75 6.75

Jerry Garcia (d. 1995), Musician A228

Scenes of Grateful Dead performing on stage and: No. 1413A, Bears. No. 1413B, Skeletons.

1995   Litho.   Perf. 12½
1412 A228 200sh multi 10.00 10.00

Souvenir Sheet
1413 A228 1000sh multi 9.50 9.50

Size: 140x92mm
Imperf
Self-Adhesive
1413A A228 2000sh multi 8.25 8.25
1413B A228 2000sh multi 8.25 8.25

No. 1412 was issued in sheets of 9. No. 1413 contains one 51x57mm stamp.

Issued: #1412-1413, 11/15/95; #1413A-1413B, 12/21/95.

Rock and Roll Stars A229

No. 1414: a, Chuck Berry. b, Bob Dylan. c, Aretha Franklin. d, The Supremes. e, Buddy Holly. f, Bruce Springsteen. g, Elton John. h, The Rolling Stones. i, Michael Jackson.

1000sh, The Beach Boys (Al Jardin, Mike Love, Brian Wilson, Carl Wilson, Dennis Wilson), horiz.

1995, Dec. 1   Perf. 13½x14
1414 A229 250sh Sheet of 9, #a.-i. 15.00 15.00

Souvenir Sheet
Perf. 14x13½
1415 A229 1000sh multi 8.50 8.50

Motion
Pictures,
Cent.
A230

No. 1416: a, Noah's Ark, Dolores Costello.
b, Ben-Hur, 1926, Ramon Novarro. c, Ben-
Hur, 1926, Francis X. Bushman. d, Ben-Hur,
1959, Charlton Heston. e, Ben-Hur, 1959,
Haya Harareet. f, Ben-Hur, 1959, Sam Jaffe.
g, The Ten Commandments, 1923, Theodore
Roberts. h, Samson and Delilah, Victor
Mature. i, Samson and Delilah, Hedy Lamarr.
No. 1417, The Ten Commandments, Theo-
dore Roberts.

1995, Dec. 1   **Perf. 13½x14**
1416 A230 250sh Sheet of 9,
    #a.-i.   19.00 19.00
Souvenir Sheet
1417 A230 1000sh multi   8.50 8.50

World Tourism Organization, 20th
Anniv. — A231

Designs: 100sh, Olduvai Gorge, "Cradle of
Mankind." 300sh, First State House,
Bagamoyo. 400sh, Mount Kilimanjaro.
500sh, Rhinoceroses, Ngorongoro Crater.

1995, Dec. 18   **Litho.**   **Perf. 14**
1418-1420 A231 Set of 3   6.50 6.50
Souvenir Sheet
1421 A231 500sh multicolored   6.25 6.25

Predatory
Animals
A232

Designs: 70sh, Acinonyx jubatus. 100sh,
Felus serval. 150sh, Huaena buana. 200sh,
Otocyon megalotis. 250sh, Lucaon pictus.
280sh, Pantera pardus. 300sh, Pantera leo.
500sh, Alligator.

1995, Sept. 30   **Litho.**   **Perf. 12½x12**
1422-1428 A232 Set of 7   10.50 10.50
Souvenir Sheet
1429 A232 500sh multicolored   5.50 5.50

Horses — A233

No. 1430: a, True black Freisian. b,
Appaloosa. c, Arab. d, Paint. e, Chestnut saddlebred. f, Standard thoroughbred. g, Belgian.
h, Liver chestnut quarter. i, Hackney.
1000sh, Clydesdale.

1995   **Perf. 14**
1430 A233 250sh Sheet of 9,
    #a.-i.   19.00 19.00
Souvenir Sheet
1431 A233 1000sh multi   10.50 10.50

No. 685 Surcharged

1995, May 30   **Litho.**   **Perf. 14**
1431A A108 70sh on 13sh #685

Paintings from
the
Metropolitan
Museum of
Art — A234

No. 1432, 200sh: a, La Orana Maria, by
Gauguin. b, Young Herdsman with Cows, by
Cuyp. c, Moses and the Burning Bush by,
Domenichino. d, Path in the Ile Saint-Martin,
Vétheuil, by Monet. e, Dances, Pink and
Green, by Degas. f, Terrace at Sainte-
Adresse, by Monet. g, The Rehearsal
Onstage, by Degas. h, Study for "A Sunday on
La Grande Jatte," by Seurat.
No. 1433, 200sh: a, Madame Marsollier and
Daughter, by Nattier. b, Christ and the Woman
of Samaria, by Rembrandt. c, Rubens and His
Wife and Son, by Rubens. d, Portrait of a
Young Woman, by Vermeer. e, Portrait of a
Man, by Van Dyck. f, Young Woman with a
Water Jug, by Vermeer. g, Self Portrait, by
Rembrandt. h, Young Man and Woman in an
Inn, by Hals.
No. 1434, 1000sh, On the Beach at
Trouville, by Boudin. No. 1435, 1000sh, A
Dance in the Country, by G.D. Tiepolo.

1996, Mar. 7   **Perf. 13½x14**
Sheets of 8, #a-h, + Label
1432-1433 A234   Set of 2   32.50 32.50
Souvenir Sheets
Perf. 14
1434-1435 A234   Set of 2   20.00 20.00
Nos. 1434-1435 each contain one
81x53mm stamp.

Miniature Sheet

Cats and Dogs — A235

No. 1436 — Cats: a, Siberian. b, Classic
silver tabby Persian. c, Brown Burmese. d,
Norwegian forest. e, Tabby. f, Blue & white
maine coon. g, Brown California spangled cat.
h, Black & white bicolor Persian. i, Shaded
silver American shorthair.
No. 1437 — Dogs: a, Red labrador. b, St.
Bernard. c, Cocker spaniel. d, Black labrador.
e, Bernese mountain dog. f, Beagle. g, Miniature pincher. h, Basset hound. i, German
shepherd.
No. 1438, Silver tabby British shorthair. No.
1439, Alaskan malamute.

1996, Mar. 4   **Litho.**   **Perf. 14**
1436 A235 250sh Sheet of 9,
    #a.-i.   15.00 15.00
1437 A235 250sh Sheet of 9,
    #a.-i.   15.00 15.00
Souvenir Sheets
1438 A235 1000sh multi   8.50 8.50
1439 A235 1000sh multi   8.50 8.50

Souvenir Sheets

Janis Joplin (1943-70), Rock Musician
— A235a

Design: No. 1439B, Joplin seated atop a
psychedelically-painted Porsche, horiz.

1996, Apr. 10   **Litho.**   **Imperf.**
Self-Adhesive
1439A A235a 2000sh shown   22.50 22.50
1439B A235a 2000sh multi   22.50 22.50

Elvis Presley (1935-77) — A235b

Various photographs with EPE (Elvis Presley Enterprises) official product emblem.

1996, Mar. 13   **Litho.**   **Perf. 12½**
1439C A235b 200sh Sheet of
    9, #d.-l.   13.00 13.00

New
Year
1996
(Year of
the Rat)
A236

No. 1440: a, Arvicola oryzivora. b, Meriones
hudsonicus. c, Mus missouriensis. d, Mus
aureolus.
500sh, Fiber zibethicus.

1996, Apr. 12
1440 A236 200sh Block of 4, #a.-
    d.   4.25 4.25
   e.   Souvenir sheet of 1 #1440   4.25 4.25
Souvenir Sheet
1442 A236 500sh multicolored   4.25 4.25
No. 1440 was issued in sheets of 16 stamps.

Deng
Xiaoping,
Chinese
Communist
Leader
A237

Various portraits.

1996, May 6   **Litho.**   **Perf. 13**
1443 A237 250sh Sheet of 6,
    #a.-f.   13.00 13.00
Souvenir Sheet
1444 A237 500sh multicolored   5.50 5.50
CHINA '96, 9th Asian Intl. Philatelic Exhibition (#1443).

Butterflies
A238

Designs: 70sh, Dirphia multicolor. 100sh,
Inachis io, vert. 150sh, Automerisio. 200sh,
Saturnia pyri. 250sh, Arctia villica. 260sh, Arctia caja. 300sh, Celerio euforbiae, vert.
500sh, Zygaena laeta.

Perf. 12½x12, 12x12½
1996, Jan.   **Litho.**
1445-1451 A238 Set of 7   12.00 12.00
Souvenir Sheet
1452 A238 500sh multicolored   6.00 6.00

Frogs
A239

Designs: 100sh, Bufo bufo laur. 140sh, Pyx-
icephalus adspersus. 180sh, Megalixalus
laevis. 200sh, Xenopus laevis. 210sh,
Hemisus marmoratus. 260sh, Rana beccarii.
300sh, Hyperolius cinctiventrus.
500sh, Rana goliaph.

1996, Jan. 31   **Perf. 12½x12**
1453-1459 A239 Set of 7   8.50 8.50
Souvenir Sheet
1460 A239 500sh multicolored   7.00 7.00

Souvenir Sheet

China 1996 Intl. Philatelic
Exhibition — A239a

1996, June 5   Litho.   Perf. 12½
1460A A239a 300sh multi   5.50 5.50

Souvenir Sheet

Shanghai Intl. Tea Culture
Festival — A239b

1996   Litho.   Perf. 12½
1460B A239b 300sh multi   5.00 5.00

Queen Elizabeth II, 70th
Birthday — A240

No. 1461: a, Portrait. b, As young woman in
evening dress. c, Wearing tiara, jewels.
1000sh, Portrait as young woman.

1996, July 3   Litho.   Perf. 13½x14
1461 A240 300sh Strip of 3,
         #a.-c.   7.00 7.00
Souvenir Sheet
1462 A240 1000sh multicolored 8.00 8.00
No. 1461 was issued in sheets of 9 stamps.

Crocodiles, Alligators — A241

Designs: 100sh, Melanosuchus niger.
150sh, Caiman latirostris. 200sh, Alligator mis-
sisspiensis. 250sh, Gavialis gangeticus.
260sh, Crocodylus niloticus. 300sh, Crocodylus cataphractus. 380sh, Crocodylus
rhombifer.
500sh, Crocodile.

1996   Perf. 12½x12
1463-1469 A241 Set of 7   9.50 9.50
Souvenir Sheet
1470 A241 500sh multicolored   7.50 7.50

Snakes
A242

Designs: 100sh, Naja pallida. 140sh, Agkistrodon contortrix. 180sh, Bungarus fasciatus.
200sh, Micrurus frontalis, vert. 260sh, Bitis
gabonica, vert. 300sh, Elaphe moellendorffi,
vert. 400sh, Vipera ursini, vert.
700sh, Corallus caninus, vert.

1996   Perf. 12½x12, 12x12½
1471-1477 A242 Set of 7   9.50 9.50
Souvenir Sheet
1478 A242 700sh multicolored   7.50 7.50

Famous People,
Events — A243

No. 1479, 250sh: a, Gandhi. b, Mao Tse-
tung. c, Jonas Salk. d, John F. Kennedy. e,
Neil Armstrong. f, Mikhail Gorbachev. g, Nel-
son Mandela. h, Gen. Colin Powell.
No. 1480, 250sh: a, Orville, Wilbur Wright.
b, Battle of Verdun, 1916. c, Charles
Lindbergh. d, Al Jolson. e, Alexander Fleming.
f, Amelia Earhart. g, Franklin Roosevelt,
Joseph Stalin, Winston Churchill, Yalta Confer-
ence, 1945. h, Atomic bomb blast, 1945,
Enrico Fermi.
No. 1481, 1000sh, Deng Xiaoping.

1996, July 15   Litho.   Perf. 14
Sheets of 8, #a-h
1479-1480 A243 Set of 2   17.00 17.00
Souvenir Sheet
1481 A243 multicolored   8.50 8.50

A244

Fruits of East Africa: 140sh, Pineapple.
180sh, Orange, lime. 200sh, Pear, apple.
300sh, Bananas.

1996, Sept. 4   Litho.   Perf. 13
1482-1485 A244 Set of 4   7.50 7.50
1485a   Souv. sheet of 1 #1485 4.25 4.25

Birds — A245

No. 1486, 300sh: a, Vidua_macroura. b,
Tockus erythrorynchus. c, Trachyphonus
erythrocephalus. d, Bubo capensis. e, Gyps
ruppellii. f, Sarkidiornis melanotus. g, Dendrocygna bicolor. h, Struthio camelus.
No. 1487, 300sh: a, Gypohierax angolensis.
b, Aquila chrysaetos. c, Spilornis rufipectus. d,
Eutriorchis astur. e, Haliaeetus albicilla. f,
Ichthyophaga ichthyaetus. g, Spilornis holospi-
lus. h, Dryotriorchis spectabilis.
No. 1488, 1000sh: African paradise flycatcher. No. 1489, 1000sh: Haliaeetus
leucocephala, horiz.

1996, Sept. 16   Perf. 14
Sheets of 8, #a-h
1486-1487 A245 Set of 2   30.00 30.00
Souvenir Sheets
1488 A245 multicolored   9.00 9.00
1489 A245 multicolored   9.00 9.00

Reef Fish
A246

Designs: 100sh, Yellowtail wrasse. 150sh,
Jewel grouper. 250sh, Barred thick-lipped
wrasse. 500sh, Bullethead parrotfish.
No. 1494: a, Golden cardinal fish. b, Yel-
lowhead butterfly fish. c, Common banner fish
(diver). d, Zanzibar butterfly fish. e, Lemon
damsel. f, Blue and gold fusilier. g, Red
firegoby. h, Threadfin fairy basslet. i, Rein rock
basslet.
No. 1495, 1000sh, African pygmy angelfish.
No. 1496, 1000sh, Blue green chromis.

1996, Sept. 23
1490-1493 A246 Set of 4   8.50 8.50
1494 A246 200sh Sheet of 9,
         #a.-i.   13.00 13.00
Souvenir Sheets
1495-1496 A246 Set of 2   8.50 8.50

Ferrari
Cars
A247

No. 1497: a, 1964 250LM. b, 1992 456 GT.
c, 1995 F50. d, 1995 F512 M "Testarossa." e,
1984 BB 512. f, 1955 410 S coupe.
1000sh, 1964 250 GTO.

1996, Sept. 27   Litho.   Perf. 14
1497 A247 250sh Sheet of 6,
         #a.-f.   12.50 12.50
Souvenir Sheet
1498 A247 1000sh multi   8.50 8.50
No. 1498 contains one 85x28mm stamp.

Radio, Cent.
A248

Designs: 70sh, Franklin D. Roosevelt, 1st
fireside chat, 1933. 100sh, Harry S. Truman

announces US use of atomic bomb, 1945.
150sh, Orson Welles, "Alien Invasion" broadcast, 1938. 200sh, Fiorello La Guardia reads
newspaper comics via radio.
1000sh, Robin Williams as Adrian
Cronauer, "Good Morning Viet Nam."

1996, July 15   Litho.   Perf. 13½x14
1499-1502 A248 Set of 4   4.25 4.25
Souvenir Sheet
1503 A248 1000sh multicolored 8.50 8.50

Mercedes-Benz Automobiles — A249

No. 1504: a, 1952 300SL Coupè 1. b, 1932
680S. c, 1934 500K. d, 1934 Type 150. e,
1934 Type 150 Sport Roadster "Heck." f, 1937
W125.
1000sh, 1936 540K Roadster Class A.

1996, Sept. 27   Perf. 14
1504 A249 250sh Sheet of 6,
         #a.-f.   12.00 12.00
Souvenir Sheet
1505 A249 1000sh multi   8.50 8.50

UNICEF, 50th
Anniv. — A250

Designs: 200sh, Child holding bowl. 250sh,
Mother breastfeeding infant. 500sh, Tetsuko
Kuroyanaga holding child.
1000sh, Girl.

1996, Oct. 4
1506-1508 A250 Set of 3   7.50 7.50
Souvenir Sheet
1509 A250 1000sh multicolored 7.75 7.75

UNESCO, 50th Anniv. — A251

Designs: 200sh, Ngorongoro Conservation
Area, Tanzania. 250sh, Los Katios Natl. Park,
Colombia. 600sh, Kilwa Kisiwani Makutani
Complex, Tanzania.
1000sh, Kilimanjaro Natl. Park, Tanzania.

1996, Oct. 4
1510-1512 A251 Set of 3   11.00 11.00
Souvenir Sheet
1513 A251 1000sh multi   11.00 11.00

Flowers — A252

No. 1514, 300sh: a, Lily of the valley. b,
Spanish iris. c, Spiderwort. d, Morning glory.
e, Gazania. f, Pansy. g, Begonia. h, Madonna
lily.
No. 1515, 300sh: a, Snowdrop. b, Treesia.
c, Cosmos. d, Daffodil. e, Blue himalayan

poppy. f, Blue daisy. g, Zinnia flore-pleno. h, Oriental poppy.
No. 1516, 1000sh, Fuchsia. No. 1517, 1000sh, Hanson's lily.

1996, Oct. 25
Sheets of 8, #1-h + Label
1514-1515 A252 Set of 2   35.00   35.00

Souvenir Sheets
1516-1517 A252 Set of 2   20.00   20.00

Domestic
Cats
A253

Designs: 100sh, Lilac point Siamese. 150sh, Somali. 200sh, British blue shorthair.
No. 1521: a, American shorthair silver tabby. b, Scottish fold. c, Persian blue. d, Ocicat.
1000sh, Ragdoll.

1996, Dec. 10   **Litho.**   **Perf. 14**
1518-1520 A253 Set of 3   3.50   3.50
1521 A253 300sh Sheet of 4,
     #a.-d.   8.00   8.00

Souvenir Sheet
1522 A253 1000sh multicolored   8.50   8.50

Dogs
A254

Designs: 70sh, Shar-pei. 250sh, Beagle. 600sh, Keeshond.
No. 1527: a, St. Bernard. b, Shetland sheepdog. c, Samoyed. d, Australian cattle dog.
1000sh, Collie.

1996, Dec. 10   **Litho.**   **Perf. 14**
1524-1526 A254 Set of 3   6.50   6.50
1527 A254 300sh Sheet of 4,
     #a.-d.   9.50   9.50

Souvenir Sheet
1528 A254 1000sh multicolored   8.50   8.50

Nos. 767-768, 1001-1002, 1026-1028
Ovptd.

a

b

c

1996, Dec. 16
1529 A120(a-b) 50sh Sheet
     of 16,
     #a.-p.
     (#767)   9.75   9.75
1530 A120(c) 50sh Sheet
     of 16,
     #a.-p.
     (#768)   9.75   9.75
1531 A154(a-b) 100sh Sheet
     of 12,
     #a.-l.
     (#1001) 14.50 14.50

1532 A158(c) 100sh Sheet
     of 6,
     #a.-f.
     (#1026)   7.25   7.25
1533 A158(c) 100sh Sheet
     of 6,
     #a.-f.
     (#1027)   7.25   7.25

Souvenir Sheets
1534 A154(c) 500sh on
     #1002   6.00   6.00
1535 A158(a) 500sh on
     #1028   6.00   6.00

Size and location of overprint varies.
Overprints types a-b appear on alternating stamps of Nos. 1529, 1531.
Nos. 1529-1533 have additional overprints in sheet margin.

Mushrooms
A255

No. 1536, 300sh: a, Amanita phalloides. b, Amanita muscaria. c, Morchella vulgaris. d, Tricholoma aurantium. e, Amanita caesarea. f, Psalliota haemorrhoidaria. g, Russula virescens. h, Boletus crocipodius.
No. 1537, 300sh: a, Coprinus comatus. b, Amanitopsis vaginata. c, Clitocybe geotropa. d, Cortinarius violaceus. e, Russula sardonia. f, Cortinarius collinitus. g, Boletus aereus. h, Lepiota procera.
No. 1538, 1000sh, Ganoderma lucidum. No. 1539, 1000sh, Collybia distorta.

1996, Dec. 17   **Sheets of 8, #a-h**
1536-1537 A255 Set of 2   32.50   32.50

Souvenir Sheets
1538-1539 A255 Set of 2   18.00   18.00

Souvenir Sheet

Watercolor Painting — A256

1996, May 6   **Litho.**   **Perf. 13**
1540 A256 500sh multicolored   4.75   4.75

China '96. No. 1540 was not available until March 1997.

Sun Yat-Sen
(1866-1925)
A257

Various portraits.

1997   **Perf. 14**
1541 A257 300sh Sheet of 6,
     #a.-f.   13.00   13.00

Souvenir Sheet
1542 A257 1000sh multi   8.50   8.50

Hong Kong '97.

Horses
A258

No. 1543: a, Blue Arabian horse. b, English thoroughbred. c, Tennessee walking horse. d, Anglo-Arab horse.
No. 1544: a, Trakehner. b, American saddlebred. c, Morgan. d, Frederiksborg. e, Mirror of #d. f, Mirror of #c. g, Mirror of #b. h, Mirror of #a.
No. 1545, 1000sh, Wielkopolski. No. 1546, 1000sh, Thiawari, vert.

1997, Mar. 20   **Litho.**   **Perf. 14**
1543 A258 250sh Strip of 4,
     #a.-d.   8.50   8.50
1544 A258 250sh Sheet of 8,
     #a.-h.   15.00   15.00

Souvenir Sheets
1545-1546 A258 Set of 2   15.00   15.00

No. 1543 was issued in sheets of 8 stamps with second strip in reverse order.

COMESA
A259

Designs140sh, Tourism. 180sh, Fishing. 200sh, Dar es Salaam Port. 300sh, TAZARA Railway.

1997   **Perf. 13**
1547-1550 A259 Set of 4   7.00   7.00

Souvenir Sheet
1551 A259 500sh Cotton   4.75   4.75

UN
Volunteers,
25th Anniv.
A260

Designs: 140sh, Health of mother and child. 200sh, Food distribution. 260sh, Clean water distribution. 300sh, Public education. 500sh, Refugee camp.

1997
1552-1555 A260 Set of 4   7.50   7.50

Souvenir Sheet
1556 A260 500sh multicolored   5.50   5.50

Birds
A261

Designs: 150sh, Mockingbird. 200sh, House finch. 410sh, Bridled titmouse. 500sh, Cactus wren.
No. 1561: a, Sooty tern. b, Nunbird. c, Mottled wood owl. d, Turquoise-browed mot mot. e, Emerald toucanet. f, Dusky-headed conure.
No. 1562: a, Maguari stork. b, Spoonbills. c, Flamingo. d, Hammerkop. e, Limpkin. f, Pink-backed pelican.
No. 1563, 1000sh, Masked booby. No. 1564, 1000sh, Brown pelican.

1997, May 5   **Litho.**   **Perf. 14**
1557-1560 A261 Set of 4   8.50   8.50
1561 A261 140sh Sheet of 6,
     #a.-f.   6.00   6.00
1562 A261 370sh Sheet of 6,
     #a.-f.   13.00   13.00

Souvenir Sheets
1563-1564 A261 Set of 2   16.00   16.00

Flowers
A262   A263

Designs: 100sh, Plumeria rubra acutifolia. 140sh, 150sh, Liliaceae. 180sh, Alamanda. 200sh, Liliaceae, diff. 210sh, Zinnia. 260sh, Malvaviscus penduliflorus. 300sh, Carna. 380sh, Nerium oleander carneum. 400sh, Hibiscus rosa sinensis. 500sh, Catharanthus roseus. 600sh, Cartharanthus roseus. 700sh, Bougainvillea formosa. 750sh, Acalypha.
No. 1577: a, like #1571. b, like #1569. c, like #1572. d, like #1575.

1997-2004(?)   **Perf. 14½x15**
1565 A262 100sh multi   .40   .40
1566 A262 140sh multi   .60   .60
1566A A262 150sh multi
1567 A262 180sh multi   .75   .75
1568 A262 200sh multi   .80   .80
1569 A262 210sh multi   .85   .85
1570 A262 260sh multi   1.00   1.00
1571 A262 300sh multi   1.25   1.25
1572 A262 380sh multi   1.50   1.50
1573 A262 400sh multi   1.60   1.60
1573A A262 500sh multi   1.00   1.00
1574 A262 600sh multi   2.50   2.50
1575 A262 700sh multi   3.00   3.00
1576 A262 750sh multi   3.50   3.50
Nos. 1565-1566,1567-1576 (13) 18.75 18.75

Souvenir Sheet
Perf. 14½x14
1577 A263 125sh Sheet of 4,
     #a.-d.   2.50   2.50

Issued: #1566A, 1997; #1573A, 2004(?); others, 5/19.
For overprint see No. O49. For surcharges see Nos. 2268, 2335, 2337.

Modern Olympic Games, Cent., 1996
Summer Olympic Games,
Atlanta, — A264

1996   **Litho.**   **Perf. 11½**
1578 A264 100sh Tennis   .90   .90
1579 A264 150sh Baseball   1.40   1.40
1580 A264 200sh Soccer   1.60   1.60
1581 A264 300sh Boxing   2.75   2.75
Nos. 1578-1581 (4)   6.65   6.65

Chernobyl
Disaster,
10th Anniv.
A265

Designs: No. 1582, Chabad's Children of Chernobyl. No. 1583, UNESCO.

1997, Apr. 25   **Litho.**   **Perf. 13½x14**
1582 A265 700sh multicolored   5.50   5.50
1583 A265 700sh multicolored   5.50   5.50

Flowers — A266

No. 1583A: b, Prunus dulcis. c, Spassky Clock tower. d, Crataegus monogyna. e, Amica montana. f, Campanula patula. g, Papaver orientalis.

No. 1584: a, Malus niedzwetzkayana. b, Golden domes of the Cathedral of the Annunciation, Moscow. c, Polygonatum multiflorum. d, Leucanthemum vulgare, e, Hypencum perforatum. f, Pulsatilla vulgaris.

No. 1585, 1000sh, Laburnum anagyroides, St. Basil's Cathedral, vert. No. 1585A, 1000sh, Rosa canina, Church of Christ Resurrection, Moscow.

1997			**Perf. 14x14½**	
1583A	A266	200sh Sheet of 6,		
		#b.-g.	9.50	9.50
1584	A266	300sh Sheet of 6,		
		#a.-f.	14.50	14.50
Souvenir Sheets				
1585-1585A	A266	Set of 2	20.00	20.00

No. 1585 contains one 30x38mm stamp.

World AIDS Day A267

Designs: 140sh, Condom protects against AIDS, vert. 310sh, Caution, you may contract AIDS. 370sh, Control of AIDS is our responsibility. 410sh, Care and support AIDS orphans. 500sh, Like #1586.

1997		**Litho.**	**Perf. 13**	
1586-1589	A267	Set of 4	9.50	9.50
Souvenir Sheet				
1590	A267	500sh multicolored	5.00	5.00

Paintings by Hiroshige (1797-1858) A268

No. 1591: a, Aoi Slope, Outside Toranomon Gate. b, Bikuni Bridge in Snow. c, Mount Atago, Shiba. d, Akasaka Kiribatake. e, Zojoji Pagoda & Akabane. f, Hibiya & Soto-Sakurada from Yamashita-cho.

No. 1592, 1000sh, Shiba Shinmei Shrine. No. 1593, 1000sh, Kanasugibashi Shibaura.

1997, July 21		**Litho.**	**Perf. 13½x14**	
1591	A268	250sh Sheet of 6,		
		#a.-f.	10.50	10.50
Souvenir Sheets				
1592-1593	A268	Set of 2	7.00	7.00

Queen Elizabeth II and Prince Philip, 50th Anniv. A269

No. 1594: a, Engagement picture of Queen. b, Royal arms. c, Queen, Prince in casual attire. d, Prince, Queen. e, Balmoral Castle. f, Prince Philip.

1500sh, Formal portrait.

1997, July 21		**Litho.**	**Perf. 14**	
1594	A269	370sh Sheet of 6,		
		#a.-f.	10.50	10.50
Souvenir Sheet				
1595	A269	1500sh multi	10.50	10.50

Return of Hong Kong to China — A270

No. 1596 — Split design comparing modern and early photographs of: a, Clock Tower, Tsim Sha Tsu, former terminal of Kowloon-Canton Railways. b, Legislative Council Building, previously Supreme Court.

No. 1597: a, Signing of Sino-British Joint Declaration on Question of Hong Kong, 1984. b, Deng Xiaoping, Chinese leaders, c, C.F. Tung, first Chinese chief executive of Hong Kong, 1996.

1997, July 21			**Perf. 14½**	
1596	A270	1000sh Sheet of 2,		
		#a.-b.	11.00	11.00
1597	A270	1000sh Sheet of 3,		
		#a.-c.	16.00	16.00

No. 1597 contains 3 59x28mm stamps.

Grimm's Fairy Tales A271

Mother Goose — A272

No. 1598 — Rumpelstiltskin: a, Woman at spinning wheel, Prince. b, Woman, Rumpelstiltskin at spinning wheel. c, Prince, woman playing mandolin.

No. 1599, Girl whistling. No. 1600, Rumpelstiltskin.

1997			**Perf. 13½x14**	
1598	A271	400sh Sheet of 3,		
		#a.-c.	7.25	7.25
Souvenir Sheets				
		Perf. 14		
1599	A272	1000sh multicolored	7.25	7.25
		Perf. 13½x14		
1600	A271	1500sh multicolored	7.25	7.25

1998 Winter Olympic Games, Nagano — A273

Designs: 100sh, Torvill & Dean, ice dancing. 200sh, Katarina Witt, figure skating. 500sh, First Olympic winter games, 1924, curling introduced. 600sh, Pirmin Zurbriggen, downhill skiing.

No. 1605: a, Dan Jansen, 1000m speed skating. b, Alberto Tomba, slalom & giant slalom skiing. c, Herma Plank-Szabo, figure skating. d, Donna Weinbrecht, mogul skiing.

No. 1606, 1000sh, Yukio Kasaya, ski jump. No. 1607, 1000sh, Barbara Ann Scott, figure skating.

1997, Oct. 6		**Litho.**	**Perf. 14**	
1601-1604	A273	Set of 4	9.00	9.00
1605	A273	250sh Block or strip of 4,		
		#a.-d.	6.50	6.50
Souvenir Sheets				
1606-1607	A273	Set of 2	12.50	12.50

Sinking of MV Bukoba A274

Designs: 140sh, Ship sinking. 350sh, Removing bodies. 370sh, Identification of the dead. 410sh, Mass funeral.

500sh, MV Bukoba.

1997, May 21		**Litho.**	**Perf. 14**	
1608-1611	A274	Set of 4	8.50	8.50
Souvenir Sheet				
		Perf. 14½		
1612	A274	500sh multicolored	4.25	4.25

Tourist Attractions of East Africa — A275

Designs: 140sh, Mount Kilimanjaro. 310sh, Masai. 370sh, Zanzibar old stonetown. 410sh, Buffalo, plains of Ruaha.

500sh, Mount Kilimanjaro Kibo Peak.

1997, Oct. 9			**Perf. 13½**	
1613-1616	A275	Set of 4	8.50	8.50
Souvenir Sheet				
1617	A275	500sh multicolored	4.25	4.25

1998 World Cup Soccer Championships, France — A276

Teams: 100sh, Italy, 1938. 150sh, Brazil, 1970. 200sh, Uruguay, 1930. 250sh, W. Germany, 1954. 500sh, Argentina, 1978. 600sh, England, 1966.

No. 1624, 250sh, vert. — Players: a, Muller, W. Germany. b, Kocsis, Hungary. c, Pele, Brazil. d, Schillaci, Italy. e, Fontaine, France. f, Nejedly, Czechoslovakia. g, Rahn, W. Germany. h, Lineker, England.

No. 1625, 250sh — Stadiums: a, The Rose Bowl, US, 1994. b, Torino Stadium, Italy, 1934. c, Olympia Stadium, Germany, 1974. d, Azteca Satdium, Mexico, 1970, 1986. e, Wembley, England, 1966. f, Maracana, Brazil,

1950. g, Centenary Stadium, Uruguay, 1930. h, Bernabeu Stadium, Spain, 1982.

No. 1626, 1000sh, Pele, Brazil. No. 1627, 1000sh, Eusebio, Portugal.

1997, Oct. 20		**Perf. 14x13½, 13½x14**		
1618-1623	A276	Set of 6	6.50	6.50
Sheets of 8, #a-h, + Label				
1624-1625	A276	Set of 2	14.50	14.50
Souvenir Sheet				
1626-1627	A276	Set of 2	8.50	8.50

Endangered Species — A277

Fauna A278

No. 1628, 250sh — Animals of Asia: a, Tiger. b, Japanese macaque. c, Slender loris. d, Musk deer. e, Przewalski's horse. f, Red panda.

No. 1629, 250sh — Animals of Latin America: a, Night monkey. b, Woolly opossum. c, Jaguar. d, Red uakaris. e, Ringtailed coati. f, Cotton-top tamarin.

No. 1630, 250sh — Animals of North America: a, Bobcat. b, Moose. c, American bison. d, Mountain goat. e, Walrus. f, Common racoon.

No. 1630G — Animals of Africa: h, Cheetah. i, Zebra. j, Gorilla. k, Brown lesser mouse lemur. l, Rhinoceros. m. Chimpanzee.

No. 1631, 250sh — Northern wilderness animals: a, Great horned owl. b, Bald eagle. c, Coyotes. d, Grizzly bear. e, Caribou (d). f, Walrus. g, Hooded seal. h, Humpback whale (g). i, Harp seal.

No. 1632, 250sh — African safari animals a, Barbary macaque. b, Turaco. c, Giraffe (f). d, Mountain gorilla, African elephant (a, b, e, g, h). e, Zebra. f, Grant's gazelle, g, Monarch butterfly, meerkat. h, African lion. i, Rhinoceros (f).

No. 1633, 1500sh, Maned wolf. No. 1634, 1500sh, Giant panda. No. 1635, 1500sh, Gray wolf. No. 1636, 1500sh, African elephant, diff.

1997, Oct. 30			**Perf. 14**	
Sheets of 6, #a-f				
1628-1630	A277	Set of 3	55.00	55.00
1630G	A277	250sh Sheet of 6, #h.-m.	18.00	18.00
Sheets of 9, #a-i				
1631-1632	A278	250sh Set of 2	50.00	50.00
Souvenir Sheets				
1633-1636	A277	1500sh Set of 4	60.00	60.00

A279

No. 1637 — Modern architecture: a, Sydney Opera House, Australia. b, Brasilia Cathedral, Brazil. c, Metropolitan Cathedral of Christ the King, Liverpool, England. d, Einstein Tower, Potsdam, Berlin, Germany. e, Solomon Guggenheim Museum, New York City, US. f, Palace of the Natl. Congress, Brasilia.

No. 1638 — Ancient wonders of the world, vert.: a, Temple of Artemis at Ephesus. b, Great Pyramid of Cheops. c, Mausoleum at Halicarnassus. d, Statue of Zeus at Olympia. e, Hanging Gardens of Babylon. f, Colossus of Rhodes.

No. 1639, 1000sh, Notre Dame Du Haut Chapel, Ronchamp, France. No. 1640, 1000sh, Lighthouse of Alexandria.

1997, Nov. 5   **Perf. 14**
1637 A279 140sh Sheet of 6,
                   #a.-f.   6.80 6.80
1638 A279 370sh Sheet of 6,
                   #a.-f.   17.00 17.00
Souvenir Sheets
1639-1640 A279 Set of 2   17.50 17.50

Nos. 1639-1640 contain one 42x57mm or 57x42mm stamp, respectively.

A280

Coastal Birds: 140sh, Red hornbill. 350sh, Sacred ibis, horiz. 370sh, Sea gulls, horiz. 410sh, Ring-necked dove, horiz.
500sh, Hornbill, ibis, gulls, doves, horiz.

1997, Nov. 28   **Wmk. 233**
1641-1644 A280 Set of 4   9.00 9.00
Souvenir Sheet
1645 A280 500sh multicolored   3.75 3.75

Aircraft
A281

Fighter Planes: 100sh, P-51D. 200sh, Lockheed P-38J Lightning. 350sh, B-29 Superfortress. 400sh, Lockheed P-80 Shooting Star P-80 A1. 500sh, Curtiss P-36A.

No. 1651, 150sh — Spitfires: a, MK IX providing altitude cover for bomber formations. b, MK Vc dog fighting. c, PRMK XIX, Photographic Reconnaissance Development Unit, RAF. d, MK Vb over North Africa. e, FR XIVE firing rockets. f, MK VIII (ZPZ), Japanese bomber. g, Supermarine Seafire being catapulted from HMS Indomitable. h, MK IX during D-Day landings. i, MK XII attacking V1 Flying Bomb.

No. 1652, 150sh — Spitfires: a, MK IXc, escorting crippled Lancaster Bomber. b, MK 1a dog fighting. c, PR MK XI, 14th Photo Sqdn., US 8th Air Force. d, MK Vb, North Africa. e, MK VIII with lightning bolt on nose. f, MK Vc with RAF, Yugoslav, American markings. g, Supermarine Seafire landing on British carrier. h, MK IXc D-Day. i, MK XII destroying V-1 Flying Bomb.

No. 1653: a, MKII in desert. b, Hurribomber dog fighting. c, MK 24, photo reconnaissance. d, Canadian MK 1 foreign squadron. e, Mark IXC convoy protection. f, Spitfire with clipped wings flanked by MK 22. g, Hurricanes MKII in desert. h, Hurribomber.

No. 1654, 1000sh, Boeing P-26. No. 1655, 1000sh, SR-71A. No. 1656, 1000sh, MK Vb. No. 1657, 1000sh,MK V Float plane. No. 1658, 1000sh, MK 1.

1997, Dec. 23   **Litho.**   **Perf. 14**
1646-1650 A281 Set of 5   11.00 11.00

Sheets of 9, #a-i
1651-1652 A281 Set of 2   15.00 15.00
1653 A281 250sh Sheet of 8,
                  #a.-h.   25.00 25.00
Souvenir Sheets
1654-1658 A281 Set of 5   40.00 40.00

No. 1656 contains one 85x28mm stamp. Nos. 1657-1658 each contain one 57x42mm stamp.

Jackie Chan, Movie Star A282

Various portraits.

1997, Dec. 30
1659 A282 370sh Sheet of 6,
                  #a.-f.   15.00 15.00

PAPU (Pan African Postal Union), 18th Anniv. A283

Designs: 150sh, Natl. flag of Tanzania, flag of PAPU. 250sh, PAPU emblem. 400sh, Delivery by EMS motorcycles. 500sh, Giraffes.

1998, Jan. 18   **Perf. 13½**
1660-1663 A283 Set of 4   9.50 9.50

A284

1998   **Litho.**   **Perf. 14**
1664 A284 410sh Mt. Kilimanjaro   3.00 3.00

A285

Diana, Princess of Wales (1961-97): 150sh, In red jacket. 250sh, In lilac dress.
1000sh, In teal suit with Prince Harry (in sheet margin).

1998, Jan. 23
1665 A285 150sh multicolored   1.10 1.10
1666 A285 250sh multicolored   1.90 1.90
Souvenir Sheet
1667 A285 1000sh multicolored   7.00 7.00

Nos. 1665-1666 were each issued in sheets of 9.

Marine Life and Sea Birds A286

No. 1668: a, Black-browed albatross. b, Unidentified bird. c, Xantusi murrelet. d, Empress angelfish. e, Bottle nosed dolphins. f, Queen angelfish. g, Red sponge. h, Unidentified red and tan fish. i, Reef shark. j, Sea star. k, Unidentified white and black fish. l, Stingray.

No. 1669, 250sh: a, Black-saddled pufferfish. b, Harlequin tuskfish. c, Emperor angelfish. d, Foxface. e, Yellow tang. f, Catalina goby. g, Fifteen-spined stickleback. h, Banded pipefish. i, Weather loach.

No. 1670, 250sh, vert.: a, Octopus. b, Pantherfish. c, Hawksbill turtle. d, Skate. e, Jellyfish. f, White tip shark. g, Blue starfish. h, Brain coral. i, Anemone.

No. 1671, 1000sh, Clown fish. No. 1672, 1000sh, Shark. No. 1673, 1000sh, Yellow seahorse, vert.

1998, Jan. 30
1668 A286 200sh Sheet of 12,
                  #a.-l.   18.00 18.00
Sheets of 9, #a-i
1669-1670 A286 Set of 2   40.00 40.00
Souvenir Sheets
1671-1673 A286 Set of 3   25.00 25.00

For overprints see #1697-1702.

Traditional Weapons — A287

Designs: 150sh, Slingshot. 250sh, Cutlass and club. 400sh, Gun. 500sh, Bow, arrows.

1998, Mar. 16   **Litho.**   **Perf. 14**
1674-1677 A287 Set of 4   9.00 9.00

New Year 1998 (Year of the Tiger) — A288

No. 1678 — Stylized tiger: a, Walking right. b, Walking left. c, Lying down. d, Seated. 1500sh, Tiger standing.

1998, Mar. 30   **Litho.**   **Perf. 13½**
1678 A288 370sh Sheet of 4,
                  #a.-d.   10.00 10.00
Souvenir Sheet
1679 A288 1500sh multi   10.00 10.00

John Denver (1943-97), Rock Musician — A288a

No. 1679A: c, Wearing green sweater. d, Wearing brown sweater (shoulders in middle of stamp). e, Wearing brown sweater (shoulder near corner of stamp). f, Wearing green sweater, hand at face.
1500sh, Wearing blue shirt.

1998, Apr. 30   **Litho.**   **Perf. 14**
1679A A288a 370sh Sheet of
                   4, #c-f   5.00 5.00
Souvenir Sheet
1679B A288a 1500sh multi   5.00 5.00

Most examples of Nos. 1679A-1679B were not available in the philatelic marketplace until Dec. 2002.

Antique Automobiles — A289

No. 1680, 370sh: a, 1901 Mercedes 35hp. b, 1903 Ford Model A. c, 1908 Legnano Type A. d, 1908-09 Rolls Royce 40-50hp Silver Ghost. e, 1910 Renault Petit Duc. f, 1913 Fischer Torpedo.

No. 1681, 370sh: a, 1923-24 Peugeot 18cv. b, 1926 Daimler 25-85hp. c, 1932 Bugatti Type 50T. d, 1933 Pierce-Arrow V12 "Silver Arrow." e, 1934 Tatra V8. f, 1937 Grosser Mercedes Benz.

No. 1682, 1000sh, 1900 Benz. No. 1683, 1000sh, 1893 Duryea.

1998, Aug. 4   **Litho.**   **Perf. 14**
Sheets of 6, #a-f
1680-1681 A289 Set of 2   35.00 35.00
Souvenir Sheets
1682-1683 A289 Set of 2   17.50 17.50

Nos. 1682-1683 each contain one 64x48mm stamp.

Flowers and Insects — A290

No. 1684, vert: a, Euanthe sanderiana, teirataenia surinama. b, "Clown Mixed." c, Pansies, caterpiller of papilio polyxenes. d, "Prelude." e, Dendrobium primulinum, wasp beetle. f, Carrion beetle, clematis "Lasurstern." g, Sunflowers, "Autumn Beauty" & "Italian White," elder borer, painted daisy. h, Grape hyacinth.

No. 1685, 250sh: a, Platinum sun. b, Vespid wasp, oriental poppy. c, Anemone. d, Ipomoea alba, king's bee hawkmoth. e, Aussie delight, potter wasp. f, Colorado potato beetle, Japanese iris. g, Bomarea caldasii, azure damselfly. h, Hybrid macranthe, queen bumblebee. i, Love with lace iris, click beetle.

No. 1686, 250sh: a, Golden ray lily, South African longhorn beetle. b, Oncidium macianthum. c, Agelia petali, dendrobium. c, Cobaea scandens. d, Goldsmith beetle, paphiopedilum gilda. e, Iceland poppies, potter wasp. f, Pink beauty. g, Annual chrysanthemums. h, Little mal, m. femurrubrum.

No. 1687, 1500sh, Carolina Queen. No. 1688, 1500sh, Robert E. Lee daffodils. No. 1689, 1500sh, Orange scarlet hybrid "Tempo." No. 1690, 1500sh, Pansies.

1998, Aug. 18   **Litho.**   **Perf. 14**
1684 A290 250sh Sheet of 8,
                  #a.-h.   25.00 25.00
Sheets of 9, #a-i
1685-1686 A290 Set of 2   27.50 27.50
Souvenir Sheets
1687-1690 A290 Set of 4   42.50 42.50

A291

Endangered Species — A292

No. 1691: a, Hyacinth macaw. b, Gibbon. c, Bosman's potto. d, Scarlet crowned barbets. e, Giant anteater. f, Cacomistle. g, Tiger. h, Mara. i, Mandrill. j, Crocodile. k, Wood turtle. l, Baribusa.

No. 1692: a, Giant sable antelope. b, Cheetah. c, Giraffe. d, Black bear. e, African elephant. f, Giant panda.

No. 1693: a, Tiger. b, Bald eagle (a, c). c, Mountain gorilla. d, Sea lion. e, Green sea turtle. f, Hippopotamus.

No. 1694, Emerald tanager.

No. 1695, 1500sh, Florida manatee. No. 1696, 1500sh, Orangutan.

1998, Aug. 31   Litho.   Perf. 14
1691 A291 200sh Sheet of 12,
　　　#a.-l.　　　　　　　17.00 17.00
1692 A292 370sh Sheet of 6,
　　　#a.-f.　　　　　　　15.00 15.00
1693 A292 370sh Sheet of 6,
　　　#a.-f.　　　　　　　15.00 15.00
Souvenir Sheets
1694 A291 1500sh multi　　　13.00 13.00
1695-1696 A292 Set of 2　　26.00 26.00

Nos. 1692, 1695 each contain 51x38mm stamps. No. 1696 contains 43x28mm stamps.

Nos. 1668-1673 Ovptd.
1998, Sept. 2   Litho.   Perf. 14
1697 A286 200sh Sheet of 12,
　　　#a.-l.
　　　(#1668)　　　　　22.50 22.50
1698 A286 250sh Sheet of 9
　　　#a.-i.
　　　(#1669)　　　　　13.00 13.00
1699 A286 250sh Sheet of 9
　　　#a.-i.
　　　(#1670)　　　　　13.00 13.00
Souvenir Sheets
1700 A286 1000sh multi
　　　(#1671)　　　　　10.00 10.00
1701 A286 1000sh multi
　　　(#1672)　　　　　10.00 10.00
1702 A286 1000sh multi
　　　(#1673)　　　　　10.00 10.00

The stamps of Nos. 1697-1699, 1701-1702 were ovptd. with Intl. Year of the Ocean emblem and the sheet margins contain one or two emblems with words "INTERNATIONAL YEAR OF THE OCEAN." No. 1700 has overprint only on sheet margin.

Aircraft
A293

No. 1703, 300sh: a, Antoinette IV, 1908. b, Deperdussin Racer, 1912. c, Demoiselle, 1909. d, Bleriot XI, 1909. e, Avro FAV Roe, 1912. f, Breguet IV, 1910.

No. 1704, 300sh: a, Deperdussin. b, Ultralight, 1979-86. c, Amphibian, 1929-30. d, Pitts Special, 1930. e, AK-221, 1960. f, Avro Tutor, 1931.

No. 1705, 300sh: a, KI-44 Tojo. b, Hawker Fury. c, Mustang. d, Zero. e, Travel Air Mystery Ship. f, F8F Bearcat.

No. 1706, 1000sh, USAAF Curtiss P-40M. No. 1707, 1000sh, Biplane. No. 1708, 1000sh, Balloon.

1998, Aug. 4   Litho.   Perf. 14
Sheets of 6, #a-f
1703-1705 A293　Set of 3　40.00 40.00
Souvenir Sheets
1706-1708 A293　Set of 3　27.50 27.50

No. 1704a incorrectly inscribed 1900.

Eagles
A294

No. 1709: a, Pallas's fish. b, Bateleur. c, Martial. d, Golden. e, Wedge-tailed. f, Java hawk.

1500sh, Wedge-tailed, diff.

1998, Aug. 31
1709 A294 370sh Sheet of 6,
　　　#a.-f.　　　　　　　15.00 15.00
Souvenir Sheet
1710 A294 1500sh multi　　11.00 11.00

Fauna and Flora
A295

Designs: 250sh, Takahe. 410sh, Lear's macaw. 500sh, Ring-tailed lemur. 600sh, Arabian oryx.

No. 1715, 370sh, ; a, Japanese crested ibis. b, Kuai O'o. c, Bourke's hairstreak. d, Quokka. e, Tahitian lorikeet. f, Black-faced tamarin.

No. 1716, 370sh: a, Loggerhead turtle. b, Snow leopard. c, Gurney's pitta. d, Lowland gorilla. e, Echo parakeet. f, Orangutan.

No. 1717, 1500sh, Giant panda. No. 1718, 1500sh, Bengal tiger.

1998, Aug. 31   Perf. 14x14½
1711-1714 A295　Set of 4　14.00 14.00
Sheets of 6, #a-f
1715-1716 A295　Set of 2　24.00 24.00
Souvenir Sheets
1717-1718 A295　Set of 2　16.00 16.00

Children's Rights
A296

Designs: 150sh, Equal rights for boys and girls. 250sh, Right to education. 400sh, Right not to be beaten, vert. No. 1722, 500sh, Right to be loved, vert.

No. 1723, Right to education.

1998   Perf. 13
1719-1722 A296　Set of 4　8.00 8.00
Souvenir Sheet
1723 A296　500sh multicolored　3.25 3.25

Nos. 608, 610
Surcharged

1998   Method and Perf. as Before
1723A A99 150sh on 13sh #608
1723B A99 150sh on 20sh #610　　—　—

Issued: No. 723A, 1/26; No. 1723B, 3/16.

World Stamp Day — A297

Designs: 150sh, UPU Emblem. 250sh, Letter facing and date stamping. 400sh, Trusted messenger. 500sh, Letter posting.

No. 1728, Trusted messenger, letter posting, UPU emblem.

1998, Oct. 9   Wmk. 387   Perf. 14
1724-1727 A297　Set of 4　8.00 8.00
Souvenir Sheet
1728 A297　500sh multicolored　3.25 3.25

A298

Marine Life, Sea Birds
A299

Designs: 150sh, Equal sea star. 250sh, Mountain crab. 400sh, Wolffish. 500sh, Purple sea urchin.

No. 1733: a, Barred antshrike. b, Yellow-nosed albatross, common tern. c, Common tern, killer whale. d, Crimson-rumped toucanet. e, French angelfish. f, Grey shark (e). g, Manta ray (f, h). h, Yellow-backed damselfish. i, Green parrot wrasse. j, Silver badgerfish, pyjama wrasse. k, Skate, red-knobbed starfish (h). l, Striped snapper.

No. 1734: a, Common dolphin. b, Blue marlin. c, Arctic tern. d, Blackedge moray. e, Loggerhead turtle. f, Blacktip shark. g, Two-spotted octopus. h, Manta ray. i, Sailfin tang.

No. 1735, 1000sh, Aequipecten opercularis. No. 1736, 1000sh, Chrysaora quinquecirrha. 1500sh, Skate.

1998, Oct. 12
1729-1732 A298　Set of 4　9.00 9.00
1733 A299 200sh Sheet of 12,
　　　#a.-l.　　　　　　18.00 18.00
1734 A298 300sh Sheet of 9,
　　　#a.-i.　　　　　　22.00 22.00
Souvenir Sheets
1735-1736 A298　Set of 2　12.00 12.00
1737 A299 1500sh multi　　9.00 9.00

Intl. Year of the Ocean (#1733-1737).

Mushrooms and Insects — A300

Designs: 140sh, Cardinal beetle, tricholoma batschii. 150sh, Tricholoma catigatum, painted lady. 200sh, Lyophylum decastes, speckled wood butterfly. 250sh, Tricholoma flavovfrens, speckled bush cricket. 370sh, Boletus chrysenteron, shieldbug. 410sh, Boletus zelleri, darter dragonfly. 500sh, Gyroporus castaneus, tortoise beetle. 600sh, Hissing cockroach, boletus satanas.

No. 1746, 250sh: a, Hygrocybe miniata, shieldbug. b, Peacock butterfly, cystolepiata adulterina. c, Collybia dryophila, bush cricket. d, Omphalotus olearius, halloween pennant butterfly. e, Macrolepiota rhacodes, helicon butterfly. f, Macrole piota puellaris, hornet. g, Carpenter bee. h, Mycena epipteryia, South African longhorn beetle. i, Amanita muscaria, skipper butterfly.

No. 1747 250sh, vert.: a, Leaf hopper cicadia, pleurotus ostreatus. b, Amanita muscaria, froghopper beetle. c, Wasp, amanita umbrinolutea. d, Butterfly, oninia tomentosa. e, Monarch butterfly, ganoderma lucidum. f, Broad-bodied libellua, macrolepiota procera. g, Butterfly anthocharis, suillus granulatus. h, Egyptian grasshopper, cortinarius praestans. i, Flying bush cricket, marasmius ramealis.

No. 1748, 1500sh, Coprinus silvaticus, thornbug. No. 1749, 1500sh, Black swallowtail, chroogomphus rutilus.

1998, Nov. 27
1738-1745 A300　Set of 8　17.00 17.00
Sheets of 9, #a-i
1746-1747 A300　Set of 2　35.00 35.00
Souvenir Sheets
1748-1749 A300　Set of 2　22.50 22.50

Rudolph the Red-Nosed Reindeer
A301

No. 1752, 200sh: a, Milo. b, Rudolph (face). c, Leonard. d, Stormella. e, Ridley. f, Boone.

No. 1753, 200sh: a, Santa. b, Rudolph. c, Doggle. d, Edgar. e, Baby Rudolph. f, Toys.

No. 1754, 1000sh, Leonard, horiz. No. 1755, 1000sh, Rudolph. No. 1756, 1000sh, Baby Rudolph with ball on nose, diff. No. 1757, 1000sh, Santa with Rudolph.

Perf. 13½x14, 14x13½
1998, Dec. 15   Litho.
1752-1753 A301　Set of 2　12.00 12.00
Souvenir Sheets
1754-1757 A301　Set of 4　22.50 22.50

Ferrari Automobiles — A301a

No. 1757A: c, GTO. d, F40. e, 512S. 100sh, Breadvan.

1998, Dec. 16   Litho.   Perf. 14
1757A A301a 500sh Sheet of
　　　3, #c-e　　　　　12.00 12.00
Souvenir Sheet
Perf. 13¾x14¼
1757B A301a 1000sh multi　8.00 8.00

No. 1757A contains three 39x25mm stamps.

Diana, Princess of Wales (1961-97)
A302

1998, Dec. 16   Perf. 14
1758 A302 600sh multicolored　3.50 3.50

No. 1758 was issued in sheets of 6.

Picasso — A303

Paintings: No. 1759, 400sh, Jacquelin with Crossedhand, 1954. No. 1760, 400sh, Straw Hat with Blue Foilage, 1936. 500sh, Reading the Letter, 1921.

1500sh, Woman Writing, 1934.

1998, Dec. 16   Perf. 14½
1759-1761 A303　Set of 3　7.50 7.50
Souvenir Sheet
1762 A303　1500sh multicolored　8.50 8.50

Mohandas Gandhi — A304

1998, Dec. 16   Perf. 14
1763 A304　370sh Portrait　3.25 3.25

Souvenir Sheet

1764 A304 1500sh Jawaharlal
Nehru 11.00 11.00

No. 1763 was issued in sheets of 4.

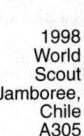 

1998 World Scout Jamboree, Chile A305

No. 1765: a, US Pres. William Howard Taft greets scouts during early years, 1908. b, Early Cub Scout pack enjoys musical camp break, 1930's. c, Dan Beard demonstrates tomahawk throw at Silver Bay, 1912.
1500sh, Ernest Thompson Seton (1860-1946), first Chief Scout.

1998, Dec. 16   Litho.   Perf. 14
1765 A305 600sh Sheet of 3,
#a.-c. 10.50 10.50

Souvenir Sheet
1766 A305 1500sh multi 9.50 9.50

Royal Air Force, 80th Anniv. A306

No. 1767: a, Panavia Tornado F3. b, Sepe-cat Jaguar GR1A. c, Jaguar GR1A. d, Jaguar GR1A, diff.
No. 1768, 1000sh, Harrier, Eurofighter. No. 1769, 1000sh, Biplane, hawk.

1998, Dec. 16   Perf. 14
1767 A306 500sh Sheet of 4,
#a.-d. 13.00 13.00

Souvenir Sheets
1768-1769 A306 Set of 2 14.00 14.00

New Year 1999 (Year of the Rabbit) A307

No. 1770 — Color of rabbit : a, Red brown. b, Spotted. c, Yellow. d, Brown.
1500sh, White.

1999, Jan. 18   Perf. 14
1770 A307 250sh Sheet of 4,
#a.-d. 7.00 7.00

Souvenir Sheet
1771 A307 1500sh multicolored 9.50 9.50

Tourism in Zanzibar A308

Designs: 100sh, Dhow Harbor, vert. 150sh, Girl on giant tortoise, vert. 250sh, Children with giant tortoise. 300sh, Street in Stone Town, vert. 400sh, Old fort. 500sh, Red colobus monkeys.
600sh, Girl on tortoise, street in Stone Town.

1998, Nov. 10   Litho.   Perf. 14
1772-1777 A308 Set of 6 11.50 11.50

Souvenir Sheet
1778 A308 600sh multicolored 5.00 5.00

Tanzanian Posts Corp., 5th Anniv. A309

Designs: 150sh, Rural post office. 250sh, Overnight mail service. 350sh, Money fax service. 400sh, Post shop business.
500sh, Exterior view of high rise building, vert.

1999, Jan. 1
1779-1782 A309 Set of 4 7.00 7.00

Souvenir Sheet
1783 A309 500sh multicolored 3.50 3.50

Butterflies A310

200sh, Calycopis cecrops. 250sh, Heliconis melpomena, vert. 370sh, Citheras menander, vert. 410sh, Heliconis antiochus, vert.
No. 1788, 200sh: a, Acraea cerasa. b, Acraea semivitrea. c, Euchrysops scintilla. d, Papilio phorcas. e, Euphaedra eusemoides. f, Acraea masamba. g, Phyciodes emerantia. h, Hypothiris tricolor. i, Orimba jansoni.
No. 1789, 200sh: a, Papilio zagreus. b, Chlosyne narva. c, Phyciodes alsina. d, Pyronia bathseba. e, Eurema daira. f, Eurytides xanticles. g, Clossiana titania. h, Euphydryas cynthia. i, Polygonia c-album.
No. 1790, 1500sh, Ornithoptera priamus, vert. No. 1791, 1500sh, Phyciodes, vert.

1999, Feb. 18
1784-1787 A310 Set of 4 7.50 7.50

Sheets of 9, #a-i
1788-1789 A310 Set of 2 15.00 15.00

Souvenir Sheets
1790-1791 A310 Set of 2 19.00 19.00

Birds A311

No. 1792, 370sh: a, Yellow billed stork. b, Black egret. c, Crowned lapwing. d, Snowy plover. e, Crowned crane. f, Saddlebilled stork.
No. 1793, 370sh: a, Great blue heron. b, Chinese egret. c, Horned puffins. d, White faced ibis. e, Greater flamingo. f, Blue footed boobie.
No. 1794, 370sh: a, Blacksmith plover. b, Brolga crane. c, Green-backed heron. d, Straw-necked ibis. e, Little bittern. f, Marabou stork.
No. 1795, 370sh, vert.: a, Sandhill crane. b, Great egret. c, Spoonbill. d, Yellow-crowned night heron. e, Glossy ibis. f, Willet.
No. 1796, 1500sh, Purple heron. No. 1797, 1500sh, Kittliz's sandplover, vert. No. 1798, 1500sh, Black-crowned night heron. No. 1799, 1500sh, Black-headed heron.

1999, Feb. 18   Sheets of 6, #a-f
1792-1795 A311 Set of 4 40.00 40.00

Souvenir sheets
1796-1799 A311 Set of 4 35.00 35.00

A312   A313

Cats A314

Designs: No. 1800, 200sh, Bengal, horiz. No. 1801, 250sh, Seal lynx point birman. No. 1802, 370sh, Calico British shorthair, horiz. No. 1803, 420sh, Blue & white cornish rex.

Nos. 1804, 100sh, Burmese. No. 1805, 140sh, Burmilla. No. 1806, 150sh, Turkish van. No. 1807, 200sh, Snowshoe. No. 1808, 250sh, Bombay. No. 1809, 370sh, Seychellois longhair.
No. 1810: a, Silver classic tabby. b, Auburn Turkish van. c, Seal bicolor ragdoll. d, European shorthair. e, Black & white British shorthair. f, Gold California spangled. g, Chocolate tipped Burmilla. h, Red classic tabby manx.
No. 1811, 370sh: a, Pekeface Persian. b, American curl shorthair. c, Korat. d, Himalayan Persian. e, Exotic shorthair. f, Scottish fold.
No. 1812, 370sh: a, European shorthair. b, Chartreux. c, British shorthair. d, Maine coon. e, Japanese bobtail. f, Birman.
No. 1813 — Kittens chasing butterflies: a, Black & white kitten, butterfly UL. b, Black & white kitten, butterfly UR. c, Black & yellow kitten, butterfly UR. d, Yellow kitten, butterfly UL.
No. 1814, 1500sh, Black & white Persian, horiz. No. 1815, 1500sh, Cream tabby European shorthair.
No. 1816, 1500sh, American shorthair. No. 1817, 1500sh, American wirehair. No. 1818, Kitten, butterfly, vert.

1999, Feb. 23
1800-1803 A312 Set of 4 9.00 9.00
1804-1809 A313 Set of 6 9.00 9.00
1810 A312 250sh Sheet of 8,
#a.-h. 11.00 11.00

Sheets of 6, #a-f
1811-1812 A313 Set of 2 24.00 24.00
1813 A314 500sh Sheet of 4,
#a.-d. 11.00 11.00

Souvenir Sheets
1814-1815 A312 Set of 2 20.00 20.00
1816-1817 A313 Set of 2 20.00 20.00
1818 A314 1500sh multi 10.00 10.00

19th Century Ships A315

No. 1819, 370sh: a, Prince Consort (1). b, USS Kearsage (2). c, HMS Victoria (3). d, USS Brooklyn (4). e, Mount Stewart (5). f, Hougomont (6).
No. 1820, 370sh: a, Charles W. Morgan (1). b, RMS Britannia (2). c, Great Britain (3). d, Flying Cloud (4). e, HMS Warrior (5). f, Lightning (6).
No. 1821, 1500sh, Cutty Sark. No. 1822, 1500sh, Great Eastern.

1999, Feb. 9   Litho.   Perf. 14
Sheets of 6, #a-f
1819-1820 A315 Set of 2 29.00 29.00

Souvenir Sheets
1821-1822 A315 Set of 2 19.00 19.00

Nos. 1821-1822 each contain one 57x43mm stamp.

Military Helicopters — A316

No. 1823: a, Germany DF 4. b, Germany. c, France. d, US, with rocket pods. e, US, with suspended lift sling. f, France, red on tail boom & stabilizers.

1999
1823 A316 370sh Sheet of 6,
#a.-f. 15.00 15.00

Unidentified Flying Objects (UFOs) — A317

No. 1824, 370sh: a, US, 1968. b, Trinidad, 1958. c, Belgium, 1990. d, Finland, 1970. e, New Zealand, 1951. f, Australia, 1954.

No. 1825, 370sh: a, McMinnville, 1950. b, Albuquerque, 1963. c, Gulf Breeze, 1988. d, Madre de Dios, 1952. e, Merlin, 1964. f, Mexico City, 1991.
No. 1826, 1500sh, The Arnold Sighting, 1947. No. 1827, 1500sh, The Mantell case, 1948.

1999   Sheets of 6, #a-f
1824-1825 A317 Set of 2 17.00 17.00

Souvenir Sheets
1826-1827 A317 Set of 2 20.00 20.00

Dogs — A318

No. 1828: a, Boston terrier. b, Tyrolean hound. c, Rottweiler. d, Golden retriever. e, English bulldog. f, Spanish greyhound. g, Long-haired dachshund. h, Scottish terrier. i, Pekingese.
1500sh, English cocker spaniel.

1999
1828 A318 200sh Sheet of 9,
#a.-i. 10.00 10.00

Souvenir Sheet
1829 A318 1500sh multi 9.50 9.50

Dinosaurs — A319

Designs: 200sh, Stegosaurus (inscribed Edmontonia). 250sh, Archaeopteryx. 370sh, Stegosaurus. 410sh, Lagosuchus.
No. 1834, 370sh: a, Dromiceiomimus. b, Saurolophus. c, Camarosaurus. d, Protoceratops. e, Psittacosaurus. f, Stegoceras.
No. 1835, 370sh: a, Gallimimus. b, Peteinosaurus. c, Lambeosaurus. d, Coelophysis. e, Parasaurolophus. f, Tyrannosaurus rex.
No. 1836, 1500sh, Quetzalcoatlus. No. 1837, 1500sh, Rhomaleosaurus.

1999, Apr. 30   Litho.   Perf. 14
1830-1833 A319 Set of 4 7.50 7.50

Sheets of 6, #a-f
1834-1835 A319 Set of 2 29.00 29.00

Souvenir Sheets
1836-1837 A319 Set of 2 19.00 19.00

Tourism A320

No. 1838: a, Hoofed animals. b, Mount Kilimanjaro, crater. c, Animal life. d, Sacred ibis. e, Ngorongoro crater. f, Giraffe. g, Lions. h, Dik diks. i, Vulture. j, Lion cubs. k, Elephants. l, African lion. m, Stone Town, Zanzibar. n, National Museum. o, Carved door, Zanzibar. p, Map showing Zanzibar, Pemba, Indian Ocean. q, Herding animals. r, Fishing. s, Lion cub. t, Buildings, boats along shore. u, Masai. v, Birds wading in water. w, Buffalo stampede. x, Like #1838b, closer view.

1999   Perf. 14½x14
Booklet Stamps
1838   Souvenir Booklet   11.00
a.-x.   A320 150sh any single   .45   .45
y.   Booklet pane, #1838a-1838f   2.75
z.   Booklet pane, #1838g-1838l   2.75
aa. Bklt. pane, #1838m-1838r   2.75
ab. Bklt. pane, #1838s-1838x   2.75

Space Exploration — A321

Designs: 70sh, Edward White. 100sh, Gemini 7. 150sh, Mir, Russian space station, vert. 200sh, Laika, Russian space dog. 250sh, Apollo Command & Service Modules. 370sh, Apollo Lunar Module.
1500sh, Saturn V Moon Rocket, vert.

1999   *Perf. 14*
1839-1844 A321 Set of 6   8.50   8.50
Souvenir Sheet
1845 A321 1500sh multi   10.00   10.00

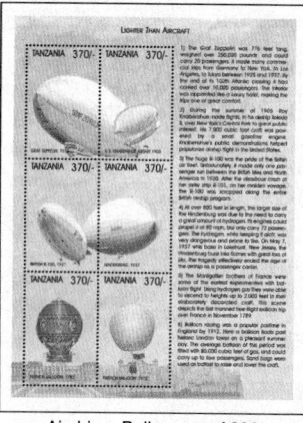

Airships, Balloons — A322

No. 1846: a, Graf Zeppelin, 1935 (b). b, Knabenshue Airship, 1905. c, British R-100, 1931. d, Hindenburg, 1937 (c). e, French Balloon, 1783. f, French Balloon, 1912.
1500sh, Sport ballooning.

1999
1846 A322 370sh Sheet of 6,   #a.-f.   13.00   13.00
Souvenir Sheet
1847 A322 1500sh multi   8.50   8.50

Marine Life
A323

Designs: 200sh, Powder blue surgeon. 250sh, Frilled anemone. 310sh, Red-finned batfish. 410sh, Red beard sponge.
No. 1852, 250sh: a, Right whale. b, Fin whale. c, Humpback whale. d, Tucuxi. e, Gray's beaked whale. f, Sperm whale. g, Bottlenose dolphin. h, Hector's dolphin. i, Hourglass dolphin.
No. 1853, 250sh: a, Horn shark. b, Nurse shark. c, Bonnethead. d, Tiger shark. e, Bull shark. f, Leopard shark. g, Blue shark. h, Zebra shark. i, Oceanic whitetip.
No. 1854, 1500sh, Pacific Electric ray, vert. No. 1855, 1500sh, Loggerhead turtle, vert.

1999, Feb. 9   **Litho.**   *Perf. 14*
1848-1851 A323 Set of 4   5.50   5.50
Sheets of 9, #a.-i.
1852-1853 A323 Set of 2   29.00   29.00
Souvenir Sheets
1854-1855 A323 Set of 2   17.00   17.00

Airplanes
A324

Designs: 20sh, Oiseau Bleu, 1929. 100sh, Beechcraft Model 17, 1934. No. 1858, 140sh, US Army Air Corps Beechcraft YC-43. No.

1859, 140sh, Deperdussin, 1913. 150sh, Beechcraft E17B, 1937. 200sh, Beechcraft B17L, 1936. 250sh, Beechcraft Model-G175, 1946. 370sh, Beechcraft Staggerwing Model-C17L.
No. 1864: a, Bird of Passage, Voisin Brothers, 1909. b, BS1, Geoffrey de Havilland, 1913. c, Taube-IGO Etrich, 1910. d, Curtiss Rheims Flyer, Glenn Curtiss, 1909. e, Wright Flyer III, Wright Brothers, 1905. f, Russky Vitvas, Igor Sikorsky, 1913.
No. 1865: a, Sikorsky S-38. b, EFA Eurofighter. c, F-16. d, Hawker Hurricane. e, Artiplast. f, Islander.
No. 1866, 1500sh, Piper Cherokee. No. 1867, 1500sh, MiG.

1999, Feb. 14
1856-1863 A324 Set of 8   8.50   8.50
Sheets of 6
1864 A324 370sh Sheet of 6,   #a.-f.   10.50   10.50
1865 A324 370sh Sheet of 6,   #a.-f.   10.50   10.50
Souvenir Sheets
1866-1867 A324 Set of 2   19.00   19.00
Nos. 1866-1867 contain one 56x42mm stamp.
Stamp inscriptions are incorrect on Nos. 1865b, 1865c, and perhaps others.

African Wildlife A325

Designs: 100sh, Black rhinoceros. 140sh, Zebra, vert. 150sh, Hippopotomus. 200sh, Nile crocodile. 250sh, African elephant, vert. 370sh, Cape buffalo.
No. 1874, 1500sh, Royal python. No. 1875, 1500sh, Giraffe.

1999, Feb. 18
1868-1873 A325 Set of 6   8.00   8.00
Souvenir Sheets
1874-1875 A325 Set of 2   18.00   18.00

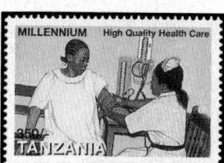

Millennium — A326

Designs: 350sh, High quality health care. 400sh, Good upbringing. 700sh, An abundance of food. 750sh, Clean water for all.
1500sh, Ostrich, "Enhancement of tourism promotion," vert.

1999, Mar. 29
1876-1879 A326 Set of 4   13.00   13.00
Souvenir Sheet
1880 A326 1500sh multi   9.50   9.50

Sharks
A327

Designs: 200sh, Sand tiger. 250sh, Mako. 370sh, Great white. 410sh, Bull.
No. 1885: a, Basking. b, Whale. c, Tiger. d, Thresher. e, Caribbean reef. f, Nurse.
No. 1886, 1500sh, Scalloped hammerhead. No. 1887, 1500sh, Blue.

1999   **Litho.**   *Perf. 14*
1881-1884 A327 Set of 4   7.00   7.00
1885 A327 370sh Sheet of 6,   #a.-f.   14.00   14.00
Souvenir Sheets
1886-1887 A327 Set of 2   18.50   18.50

Rotary Club of Dar Es Salaam, 50th Anniv. A328

Designs: 150sh, Emblem. 250sh, Polio plus immunization, vert. 350sh, Paul P. Harris, founder of Rotary, Intl., vert. 400sh, Water supply.
500sh, Emblem, vert.

1999, June 30
1888-1891 A328 Set of 4   6.50   6.50
Souvenir Sheet
1892 A328 500sh multicolored   3.25   3.25

Endangered or Extinct Species — A330

No. 1898: a, Atitlan grebe. b, Cabot's tragopan. c, Spider monkey. d, Dibatag. e, Right whale. f, Imperial parrot. g, Cheetah. h, Brown-eared pheasant. i, Leatherback turtle. j, Imperial woodpecker. k, Andean condor. l, Barbary deer. m, Gray gentle lemur. n, Cuban parrot. o, Numbat. p, Short-tailed albatross. q, Green turtle. r, White rhinoceros. s, Diademed sifaka. t, Galapagos penguin.
No. 1899 — Tigers, horiz.: a, Caspian. b, Bengal. c, Javan. d, Indochinese. e, In white phase. f, Sumatran. g, Chinese. h, Bali. i, Siberian.
No. 1900, 1500sh, Rabbit-eared bandicoot. No. 1901, 1500sh, Grenada dove.

1999, Feb. 18
1898 A330 100sh Sheet of 20,   #a.-t.   10.00   10.00
1899 A330 250sh Sheet of 9,   #a.-i.   11.00   11.00
Souvenir Sheets
1900-1901 A330 Set of 2   15.00   15.00

Queen Mother (b. 1900) — A331

No. 1902: a, In Kenya, 1959. b, In 1980. c, With Prince Charles, 1950. d, Iin 1990. 1500sh, In Kenya, 1959, diff.

1999, Aug. 4   **Litho.**   *Perf. 14*
1902 A331 600sh Sheet of 4,   #a.-d. +   label   10.00   10.00
Souvenir Sheet
Perf. 13¾
1903 A331 1500sh black   7.00   7.00
No. 1903 contains one 38x51mm stamp.

UPU, 125th Anniv. A332

Designs: 150sh, Mail conveyance. 300sh, Letter writing competition. 350sh, UPU committee meeting. 400sh, EMS Post net track and trace.
500sh, UPU emblem.

Wmk. 387
1999, Aug. 10   **Litho.**   *Perf. 14*
1904-1907 A332 Set of 4   5.50   5.50
Souvenir Sheet
1908 A332 500sh multicolored   2.50   2.50
Souvenir Sheets

Philex France 99 — A333

Trains: No. 1909, 1500sh, 4-8-2 compound express locomotive. No. 1910, 1500sh, TGV.

1999, Aug. 20   **Litho.**   *Perf. 13¾*
1909-1910 A333 Set of 2   14.00   14.00
Inscriptions are misspelled on Nos. 1909-1910.

Birds of Japan A334

No. 1911, 250sh: a, Steller's sea eagle. b, Japanese blue flycatcher. c, Great gray shrike. d, Kingfisher. e, Hen harrier. f, Siberian meadow bunting. g, Mandarin duck. h, Red-necked grebe. i, Fairy pitta.
No. 1912, 250sh: a, Laysan albatross. b, Collared Scops owl. c, Ryukyu robin. d, Japanese green woodpecker. f, Lidth's jay. g, White-naped crane. h, Copper pheasant. i, Okinawa rail.
No. 1913, 1500sh, Gyrfalcon. No. 1914, 1500sh, Japanese yellow bunting.

1999, Aug. 20   **Sheets of 9, #a.-i.**
1911-1912 A334 Set of 2   22.50   22.50
Souvenir Sheets
1913-1914 A334 Set of 2   15.00   15.00
Inscription on No. 1912b, and perhaps others, is misspelled.
APS StampShow '99 (#1911-1912).

Hokusai Paintings — A335

No. 1915: a, A Ferry Boat at Onmayagashi. b, A Drum Bridge at Kameido. c, Sea Life (fish). d, Sea Life (Octopus). e, Measuring a Pine Tree at Mishima Pass. f, Mount Fuji Seen From the Banks of Minobu River.

1500sh, Mount Fuji and Edo Castle Seen From Nihonbashi, vert.

1999, Aug. 20
1915 A335 400sh Sheet of 6,
#a.-f.   13.00 13.00
Souvenir Sheet
1916 A335 1500sh multi   7.50 7.50

Masks — A336

Various masks: 150sh, 250sh, 300sh, 350sh.

1999, Aug. 20   *Perf. 14*
1917-1920 A336 Set of 4   5.00 5.00
Souvenir Sheet
1921 A336 1500sh multicolored   7.00 7.00

Military Scenes — A337

150sh, British defeat Spanish Armada, 1588, horiz. No. 1923, 250sh, Battle of Waterloo. No. 1924, 250sh, Rorke's Drift, 24th Regiment, South Wales Borderers. No. 1925, 250sh, Special Air Services, Desert Storm. No. 1926, 300sh, Soldier on horseback. No. 1927, 300sh, World War I, horiz. No. 1928, 300sh, Bland's Dragoons, Battle of Dettingen. No. 1929, 350sh, Battle of Trafalgar, horiz. No. 1930, 350sh, Light Brigade. No. 1931, 350sh, Squadron 617, the "Dam Busters." No. 1932, 400sh, World War I tank, horiz. No. 1933, 400sh, Battle of Inkerman. No. 1934, 400sh, Battle of Salamanca, horiz. No. 1935, 500sh, Gen. James Wolfe, Battle of Quebec. No. 1936, 500sh, Parachute Regiment, Battle of Arnhem. No. 1937, 500sh, Battle of the Bulge. No. 1938, 1500sh, Battle of the Nile. No. 1939, 1500sh, Battle of Albuhera.

1999, Sept. 30
1922-1937 A337 Set of 16   28.00 28.00
Souvenir Sheets
1938-1939 A337 Set of 2   14.00 14.00

Ships A338

No. 1940, 400sh: a, Bayan. b, Flying Cloud. c, Mayflower. d, Santa Maria. e, Morning Star. f, Ben Venue.
No. 1941, 400sh: a, Georg Stag. b, E. Starr Jones. c, Indiana. d, Brazilian coasting vessel. e, Nova Queen. f, Rainbow.
No. 1942, 1500sh, Dutch East Indiaman. No. 1943, 1500sh, Junk.

1999, Sept. 30   **Sheets of 6, #a.-f.**
1940-1941 A338 Set of 2   22.50 22.50
Souvenir Sheets
1942-1943 A338 Set of 2   15.00 15.00

Trains A339

No. 1944, 400sh: a, Adler 2-2-2, 1835. b, Beuth 2-2-2, 1843. c, Class 500 4-6-0, 1900. d, Northumbrian 0-2-2, 1830. e, Class 4-6-2, 1901. f, Claud Hamilton class 4-4-0.
No. 1945, 400sh: a, Firefly class 2-2-2, 1840. b, Single, 1854. c, 4-4-0, 1891. d, Medoc class 2-4-0, 1857. e, 4-4-0, 1893. f, Numar, 1846.
No. 1946, 1500sh, Planet class 2-2-0, 1830. No. 1947, 1500sh, Vauxhall 2-2-0, 1834. No. 1948, 1500sh, Class PB 4-6-0, 1906. No. 1949, 1500sh, 4-4-0, 1855.

1999, Sept. 30   **Sheets of 6, #a.-f.**
1944-1945 A339 Set of 2   22.50 22.50
Souvenir Sheets
1946-1949 A339 Set of 4   15.00 15.00

Airplanes A340

Designs: 200sh, Amref. No. 1951, 250sh, Westwind 2. 300sh, Morning Star. 400sh, Piper Warrior III.
No. 1954: a, Glasair Super II. b, Glastar. c, Cessna 120. d, Europa XS. e, Beechcraft Bonanza. f, Comache GTO. g, Lancir IV. h, Comanche 400.
No. 1955, 1500sh, Glastar, diff. No. 1956, 1500sh, Piper Archer III.

1999, Sept. 30   **Litho.**   *Perf. 14*
1950-1953 A340 Set of 4   6.25 6.25
1954 A340 250sh Sheet of 8,
#a.-h.   9.00 9.00
Souvenir Sheets
1955-1956 A340 Set of 2   15.00 15.00

Automobiles — A341

No. 1957, 400sh: a, Audi TT Coupe. b, Mitsubishi SST Spyder. c, Honda Dream. d, Renault 20. e, Renault Spider. f, Hyundai Euro I.
No. 1958, 400sh: a, Pininfarina Ethos. b, Jaguar XK120. c, Pininfarina Ethos II. d, Rinspeed E-GO Rocket. e, Volkswagen W12 Roadster. f, Chrysler Pronto Cruiser.
No. 1959, 1500sh, Ferrari Mythos. No. 1960, 1500sh, Hyundai Euro I, diff.

1999, Sept. 30   **Sheets of 6, #a.-f.**
1957-1958 A341 Set of 2   22.50 22.50
Souvenir Sheets
1959-1960 A341 Set of 2   14.00 14.00

Flowers A342

Designs; 150sh, Lilium longiflorum. 250sh, Strelitzia reginae. 400sh, Zantedeschia anim lily. 500sh, Iris. 600sh, Like 400sh.

1999, Oct. 6   **Litho.**   *Perf. 14*
1961-1964 A342 Set of 4   6.25 6.25
Souvenir Sheet
1965 A342 600sh multicolored   3.00 3.00

Butterflies — A343

No. 1966: a, Basilarchia archippus. b, Eueides isabella. c, Colobura dirce. d, Papilio cresphontes. e, Agrias claudia. f, Callicore maimuna.
No. 1967, 1500sh, Anteos clorinade, horiz. No. 1968, 1500sh, Tithorea harmonia, horiz.

1999, Nov. 15
1966 A343 400sh Sheet of 6,
#a.-f.   12.00 12.00
Souvenir Sheets
1967-1968 A343 Set of 2   16.00 16.00

Sea Birds A344

Designs: 150sh, Rockhopper penguin, vert. No. 1970, 250sh, Jackass penguin, vert. 300sh, Adelie penguin, vert. 350sh, White tern. 400sh, Great frigatebird. 500sh, Brown pelican.
No. 1975, 250sh: a, Manx shearwater. b, Ring-billed gull. c, Herring gull. d, Red-tailed tropic bird. e, Laysan albatross. f, Black-headed gull. g, Blue-footed booby. h, Parakeet auklet. i, Red-legged cormorant.
No. 1976, 250sh: a, Razorbill. b, Southern giant petrel. c, Atlantic puffin. d, Great cormorant. e, Northern gannet. f, Masked booby. g, Tufted puffin. h, Galapagos penguin. i, Macaroni penguin.
No. 1977, 1500sh, King penguin, vert. No. 1978, 1500sh, Emperor penguin, vert.

1999, Nov. 15
1969-1974 A344 Set of 6   10.00 10.00
Sheets of 9, #a.-i.
1975-1976 A344 Set of 2   22.50 22.50
Souvenir Sheets
1977-1978 A344 Set of 2   14.00 14.00

Dogs A345

No. 1979: a, Boxer. b, Mixed breed. c, Afghan hound. d, Chihuahua. e, Basset hound. f, Cavalier King Charles. 1500sh, Cocker spaniel.

1999, Nov. 15
1979 A345 400sh Sheet of 6,
#a.-f.   10.00 10.00
Souvenir Sheet
1980 A345 1500sh multi   8.00 8.00

Paintings by Xu Beihong (1895-1953) A346

No. 1981: a, Chang K'uei. b, Fisherman. c, Orchid. d, Cock and Sunflower. e, Eagle. f, Sprite of the Mountain. g, Horse. h, Geese. i, Pigeon and Bamboo. j, Cat and Bamboo.
No. 1982: a, Spring Rain of Li River, horiz. b, The Himalayas, horiz.

1999   *Perf. 12½*
1981 A346 150sh Sheet of 10,
#a.-j.   7.50 7.50
Perf. 13
1982 A346 600sh Sheet of 2,
#a.-b.   6.00 6.00

China 1999 World Philatelic Exhibition.

Return of Macao to People's Republic of China — A347

No. 1983 — Nam Van: a, In 1850s. b, In 1930s. c, At present. d, View of lakes project.

1999   **Litho.**   *Perf. 13¾*
1983 A347 300sh Sheet of 4,
#a.-d.   6.50 6.50

China 1999 World Philatelic Exhibition.

Animals of the Central American Rain Forest — A348

No. 1984: a, Red howler monkey. b, Scarlet macaw. c, Rainbow boa, tree sloth. d, Iguana. e, Fruit bat. f, Rainbow boa. g, Crocodile. h, Manatee. i, Jaguar.
1500sh, Jaguar, diff.

1999, Nov. 15   **Litho.**   *Perf. 14*
1984 A348 350sh Sheet of 9,
#a.-i.   9.50 9.50
Souvenir Sheet
1985 A348 1500sh multi   4.50 4.50

Dinosaurs — A349

No. 1986: a, Tyrannosaurus. b, Coelurus. c, Stegosaurus. d, Corythosaurus. e, Thadeosaurus. f, Brachiosaurus.
1500sh, Ceratosaurus.

1999, Nov. 15
1986 A349 400sh Sheet of 6,
#a.-f.   6.50 6.50
Souvenir Sheet
1987 A349 1500sh multi   4.25 4.25

Nos. 1986-1987 dated 1998. Inscription on No. 1986f is misspelled.

Cats A350

No. 1988: a, Si-Rex. b, Spotted Mist. c, Angora. d, Persian. e, Sphynx. f, Alaskan Snow.
1500sh, Ragdoll.

1999, Nov. 15
1988 A350 400sh Sheet of 6,
#a.-f.   7.00 7.00
Souvenir Sheet
1989 A350 1500sh multi   4.75 4.75

150/- TANZANIA
Mushrooms
A351

150sh, Tricholoma portentosum. 250sh, Tricholomopsis rutilans. 300sh, Russula foetens. 350sh, Russula aeruginea. #1994, 400sh, Cortinarius varius. 500sh, Hygrocybe coccineocrenata.

No. 1996, 400sh: a, Agaricus abruptibulbus. b, Anellaria semiovata. c, Cystoderma carcharias. d, Amanita rubescens. e, Amanita fulva. f, Tricholoma sulphureum.

No. 1997, 400sh: a, Xerocomus rubellus. b, Geastrum rufescens. c, Lactarius salmonicolor. d, Gomphus clavatus. e, Russula rhodopoda. f, Russula paludosa.

No. 1998, 1500sh, Owl. No. 1999, 1500sh, Chipmunk and Stropharia hornemanii, horiz.

1999, Nov. 15
1990-1995 A351 Set of 6   5.50 5.50
Sheets of 6, #a.-f.
1996-1997 A351 Set of 2   13.00 13.00
Souvenir Sheets
1998-1999 A351 Set of 2   7.75 7.75

TANZANIA 300/-
Flora and Fauna
A352

Designs: No. 2000, 150sh, Lion, vert. No. 2001, 150sh, Mountain gorilla, vert. No. 2002, 250sh, Pygmy hippopotamus, vert. No. 2003, 250sh, Japanese macaque, vert. No. 2004, 300sh, Cheetah. No. 2005, 300sh, Desert hare, vert. No. 2006, 350sh, Horned puffin. No. 2007, 350sh, Salvin's Amazon parrot. No. 2008, 400sh, Blueberries. No. 2009, 400sh, Bird's foot violet. No. 2010, 500sh, Orange groundsel. No. 2011, 500sh, Iguana.

No. 2012, 400sh: a, Polar bear. b, Woodland caribou. c, Snowy owl. d, Arctic fox. e, Willow ptarmigan. f, Arctic hare.

No. 2013, 400sh: a, White-tailed deer. b, Monarch butterfly. c, Yellow trumpet pitcher plants. d, Great blue heron. e, Yellow mud turtle. f, American alligator.

No. 2014, 400sh: a, Three-toed sloth. b, Emerald toucan. c, Praying mantis. d, Mouse opossum. e, Green palm viper. f, Phyllomedusa tarsier.

No. 2015, 400sh: a, Ficus stupenda. b, Slow loris. c, Sambar deer. d, Thick-billed green pigeon. e, Bush cricket. f, Monitor lizard.

No. 2016, 1500sh, Three-toed jacamar. No. 2017, 1500sh, Chuckwallas. No. 2018, 1500sh, Swallowtail butterfly. No. 2019, 1500sh, Otter, vert.

1999, Nov. 15
2000-2011 A352 Set of 12   11.00 11.00
Sheets of 6, #a.-f.
2012-2015 A352 Set of 4   14.00 14.00
Souvenir Sheets
2016-2019 A352 Set of 4   15.00 15.00

TANZANIA 150/-
Flowers — A353

Designs: 150sh, Foxglove. 250sh, Chrysanthemum. 400sh, Amaryllis. 500sh, Hidden lilies.

No. 2024, 350sh, horiz.: a, Gerbara daisies. b, Begonias. c, Clematis. d, Violas. e, Southern magnolia. f, Dwarf balloon flowers. g, Camellias. h, Day lilies. i, Roses.

No. 2025, 350sh, horiz.: a, Daffodils. b, Columbines. c, Nasturtiums. d, Gazanias. e, Rose. f, Crocuses. g, Trumpet vine. h, Dahlia. i, Oriental poppies.

No. 2026, 1500sh, Siberian iris. No. 2027, 1500sh, Water lily, horiz.

1999, Nov. 15   Litho.   Perf. 14
2020-2023 A353 Set of 4   3.25 3.25
Sheets of 9, #a.-i.
2024-2025 A353 Set of 2   16.00 16.00
Souvenir Sheets
2026-2027 A353 Set of 2   7.50 7.50

TANZANIA 1500/-
Military Vehicles — A354

No. 2028, 400sh: a, French Hotchkiss H35 tank. b, German Panzer IV tank. c, US M4 tank. d, German Tiger tank. e, US Half track. f, British Cromwell tank.

No. 2029, 400sh: a, British MK IV tank. b, Japanese Type 95 tank. c, German Hunting Panther tank. d, French AMX30 tank. e, Israeli Merkava tank. f, US M1 tank.

No. 2030, 1500sh, AH-64A Apache helicopter. No. 2031, 1500sh, Austin armored car, vert.

1999, Sept. 30   Litho.   Perf. 14
Sheets of 6, #a.-f.
2028-2029 A354 Set of 2   12.00 12.00
Souvenir Sheets
2030-2031 A354 Set of 2   8.00 8.00

150/-
African Flowers — A355

Designs: 150sh, Canarina abyssinica. 250sh, Diaphananthe kamerunensis. 350sh, Protea barbigera. 500sh, Angraecum scottianum.

No. 2036, 400sh: a, Bolusanthus speciosus. b, Cassia abbreviata. c, Erythrina lysistemon. d, Leucodendron discolor. e, Romulea fischeri. f, Lupinus princei.

No. 2037, 400sh: a, Ansellia africana. b, Kigelia africana. c, Aerangis brachycarpa. d, Brachcorythis kalbreyeri. e, Begonia meyeriijohannis. f, Saintpaulia ionantha.

No. 2038, 1500sh, Nymphaea caerulea. No. 2039, 1500sh, Aloe petricola.

1999, Nov. 15
2032-2035 A355 Set of 4   3.25 3.25
Sheets of 6, #a.-f.
2036-2037 A355 Set of 2   12.00 12.00
Souvenir Sheets
2038-2039 A355 Set of 2   7.50 7.50

TANZANIA 1500/-
African Wildlife — A356

No. 2040, horiz.: a, Mountain gorilla. b, Zebras. c, East African elephant. d, Crowned cranes. e, Cheetah. f, Tiger. g, Pygmy chimpanzee. h, Hippopotamus.

No. 2041, 1500sh, Giraffes. No. 2042, 1500sh, Rhinoceros.

1999, Nov. 15
2040 A356 300sh Sheet of 8,
          #a.-h.   11.00 11.00
Souvenir Sheets
2041-2042 A356 Set of 2   10.00 10.00

TANZANIA 350/-
Marine Life
A357

Designs: 350sh, Beluga whale. 400sh, Ghost crab. 500sh, Emperor penguin, vert.

No. 2046: a, Herring gulls. b, Dusky dolphin. c, Sandwich tern. d, Humpback whale. e, Right whale. f, Dusky dolphin, sergeant major. g, White-tipped shark. h, Manta ray, trunkfish. i, Purple moon angel. j, Scalloped hammerhead shark. k, Manatee. l, Striped fingerfish.

No. 2047, 1500sh, Humpback whales. No. 2048, 1500sh, Tiger shark.

1999, Nov. 15
2043-2045 A357 Set of 3   5.00 5.00
2046 A357 250sh Sheet of 12,
          #a.-l.   11.00 11.00
Souvenir Sheets
2047-2048 A357 Set of 2   10.00 10.00

Tanzania 300/-
Ballet
A358

Designs: 300sh, Romeo and Juliet. 350sh, The Dying Swan. 400sh, Giselle, vert. 500sh, Spartacus, vert.

No. 2053, 1500sh, The Firebird, vert. No. 2054, 1500sh, Swan Lake, vert.

1999, Aug. 20   Litho.   Perf. 14
2049-2052 A358 Set of 4   5.00 5.00
Souvenir Sheets
2053-2054 A358 Set of 2   9.00 9.00

TANZANIA 1500/-
17th and 18th Century Indian
Art — A359

No. 2055, 500sh: a, Krishna and the Gopis (large tree). b, Krishna Painting the Feet of Radha. c, Krishna Yearning for the Moon (woman with fan). d, Games of Krishna and Radha (boat).

No. 2056, 500sh: a, Balwant Singh Having His Beard Cut. b, Festival of Hou (women at right). c, Ragini Bialvali (woman with fan, woman on seat). d, Krishna Holding a Ball of Butter.

No. 2057, 1500sh, Portrait of Emperor Jahanoir (man with necklace), vert. No. 2058, 1500sh, Krishna and the Gopis, diff., vert.

Illustration reduced.

1999, Aug. 20   Perf. 13¾
Sheets of 4, #a-d
2055-2056 A359 Set of 2   10.00 10.00
Souvenir Sheets
2057-2058 A359 Set of 2   8.00 8.00

VALENTINO GARAVANI
BORN 1932

Valentino became the official couturier to Jacqueline Kennedy, Elizabeth Taylor, and the first lady of Italy, Vittoria Leone. Flamboyant satin ruffles, elaborate embroidery and black became his trademark.

VALENTINO

Fashion Designers — A360

No. 2059: a, Christian Dior. b, Model wearing Dior fashions. c, Bottle of Chanel No. 5, model wearing Chanel Fashions. d, Gabrielle "Coco" Chanel. e, Gianni Versace. f, Model wearing Versace fashions. g, Model wearing Yves Saint Laurent fashions. h, Yves Saint Laurent.

1500sh, Valentino Garavani.

1999, Aug. 20   Perf. 14
2059 A360 300sh Sheet of 8,
          #a-h   6.00 6.00
Souvenir Sheet
2060 A360 1500sh multi   4.00 4.00
Nos. 2059b-2059c, 2059f-2059g are 53x39mm.

Locomotives — A361

No. 2061: a, Class EF 81 Bo-Bo, Japan. b, Class 120 Bo-Bo, West Germany. c, Shao Shan I Co-Co, China. d, TGV, France. e, F40 PH Bo-Bo, US. f, LRC Bo-Bo, Canada.
1500sh, Class 401 Intercity Express, Germany.

1999, Sept. 30
2061 A361 400sh Sheet of 6, #a-f 6.00 6.00
Souvenir Sheet
2062 A361 1500sh multi 3.75 3.75

Marine Life A362

Designs: 150sh, Great barracuda. 250sh, Common squid. No. 2065, 300sh, Atlantic salmon. 350sh, Ocean sunfish. 400sh, Lobster. 500sh, Yellowfin tuna.
No. 2069, 300sh: a, Flying fish. b, Sailfish. c, Common dolphin. d, Sperm whale. e, Spinner dolphin. f, Manta ray. g, Green turtle. h, Hammerhead shark. i, Marlin.
No. 2070, 300sh: a, Walrus. b, Killer whale. c, Arctic tern. d, White shark. e, Narwhal. f, Blue whale. g, Giant clam. h, Octopus. i, Conger eel.
No. 2071, 1500sh, Whale shark. No. 2072, 1500sh, Beluga, vert.

1999, Nov. 15
2063-2068 A362 Set of 6 6.00 6.00
Sheets of 9, #a-i
2069-2070 A362 Set of 2 14.00 14.00
Souvenir Sheets
2071-2072 A362 Set of 2 7.50 7.50

Pres. Julius K. Nyerere (1922-99) A363

Nyerere: 200sh, As young man and old man. 500sh, With Edward Moringe Sokoine. 600sh, The Compassionate leader, vert. 800sh, During the early days of independence, vert.
1000sh, Mausoleum.

2000, Apr. 13 Perf. 13
2073-2076 A363 Set of 4 5.00 5.00
Souvenir Sheet Perf. 13x13½
2077 A363 1000sh multi 2.50 2.50
No. 2077 contains one 35x28mm stamp.

Tourism A364

Designs: 400sh, Lion, Seronera Wildlife Lodge. No. 2079, 800sh, Hippopotami and hyenas, Selous Game Reserve. No. 2080, 800sh, Fish, Mafia Island. No. 2081, 800sh, Giraffes, Lobo Wildlife Lodge. No. 2082, 800sh, Rhinoceros, Ngorongoro Crater Wildlife Lodge. No. 2083, 800sh, Elephant, Mikumi Natl. Park. No. 2084, 800sh, Elephant, Lake Manyara Natl. Park. No. 2085, 800sh, Elephants, rhinoceros, Kibo Peak, Mt. Kilimanjaro.
1000sh, Lion, giraffes, elephant, rhinoceros, Lake Manyara Natl. Park, vert.

Perf. 13x13½, 13½x13
2000, June 10 Litho.
2078-2085 A364 Set of 8 20.00 20.00
Souvenir Sheet
2086 A364 1000sh multi 4.25 4.25
See Nos. 2102-2125.

Activities of World Vision A365

Designs: 200sh, Children with water pots on heads. 600sh, Family preparing food. 800sh, Nurse, family. 1000sh, Education of children.

2000, July 20 Litho. Perf. 13x13¼
2087-2090 A365 Set of 4 6.00 6.00
Souvenir Sheet
2091 A365 500sh Two children 1.25 1.25

2000 Summer Olympics, Sydney A366

Designs: 150sh, Soccer. 350sh, Basketball, vert. 400sh, Women's 1500-meter race, vert. 800sh, Boxing.
500sh, Medal ceremony, vert.

2000, Sept. 15 Perf. 13¾
2092-2095 A366 Set of 4 4.50 4.50
Souvenir Sheet
2096 A366 500sh multi 1.25 1.25

Universities of East Africa A367

Designs: 150sh, Medical students, Muhimbili University College of Health Sciences. 200sh, Zanzibar University. 600sh, Makerere University, Uganda, vert. 800sh, Egerton University, Kenya.
500sh, Emblem of Inter-university Council for East Africa.

2000 Perf. 13x13¼, 13¼x13
2097-2100 A367 Set of 4 4.25 4.25
Perf. 14½
Size: 84x83mm
2101 A367 500sh multi 1.25 1.25

Tourism Type of 2000
No. 2102, 400sh, No. 2110, 500sh, No. 2118, 600sh, Like #2079. No. 2103, 400sh, No. 2111, 500sh, No. 2119, 600sh, Like #2080. No. 2104, 400sh, No. 2112, 500sh, No. 2120, 600sh, Like #2081. No. 2105, 400sh, No. 2113, 500sh, No. 2121, 600sh, Like #2082. No. 2106, 400sh, No. 2114, 500sh, No. 2122, 600sh, Like #2083. No. 2107, 400sh, No. 2115, 500sh, No. 2123, 600sh, Like #2084. No. 2108, 400sh, No. 2116, 500sh, No. 2124, 600sh, Like #2085. No. 2109, 500sh, No. 2117, 600sh, No. 2125, 800sh, Like #2078.

2000, June 1 Litho. Perf. 13x13½
2102-2125 A364 Set of 24 50.00 50.00

Flowers A368

150sh, Bacciflava. 250sh, Hybridus pendulus. #2128, 300sh, Rhaphiolepis umbellata. 350sh, Magnoliaeflora. 400sh, Magnolia, vert. 500sh, Margot Koster, vert.
No. 2132, 300sh: a, Viola pedata. b, Magnolia. c, Felicia amelloides. d, Lythrum. e, Hemerocallis. f, Tithonia rotundifolia. g, Lilium. h, Iris. i, Stokesia laevis.

No. 2133, 300sh, vert.: a, Prunus subhirtella. b, Sanguinaria canadensis. c, Rosa palustris. d, Gordonia lasianthius. e, Aquilegia caerulea. f, Fremontodendron. g, Hypericum calycinum. h, Anemone vitifolia. i, Clematis.
No. 2134, 1500sh, Iris cristata, vert. No. 2134A, 1500sh, Aster prikartil.

2000 Perf. 14
2126-2131 A368 Set of 6 5.00 5.00
Sheets of 9, #a-i
2132-2133 A368 Set of 2 13.00 13.00
Souvenir Sheet
2134-2134A A368 Set of 2 7.50 7.50

Social Security Fund A369

Designs: 200sh, Retirement. 350sh, Employment injury. 600sh, Invalidity. 800sh, Health insurance.

2000 Wmk. 387 Perf. 13¾
2135-2138 A369 Set of 4 5.00 5.00
Souvenir Sheet
2139 A369 500sh Maternity 1.25 1.25

Environmental Care — A370

Designs: 200sh, Tree planting campaign. 400sh, Water sources protection. 600sh, Cleaning sewage. 800sh, Protecting forests.

2000 Wmk. 387 Perf. 13x13¼
2140-2143 A370 Set of 4 5.00 5.00
Souvenir Sheet
2144 A370 1000sh Mountain 2.50 2.50

Zanzibar Millennium A371

Designs: 150sh, Fishing industry. 200sh, Trade and tourism. 400sh, Child and emblem, vert. 800sh, Right to higher learning, vert.
500sh, Peace and tranquility, vert.

2000 Wmk. 387 Perf. 13¾
2145-2148 A371 Set of 4 4.50 4.50
Souvenir Sheet
2149 A371 500sh multi 1.25 1.25

Orchids A372

Designs: 200sh, Vanilla planifolia. 250sh, Pleurothallus tuerckheimii. No. 2152, 370sh, Trichopilia fragrans.
No. 2153, 370sh: a, Cyrtopodium andersonii. b, Cochleanthes discolor. c, Catasetum barbatum. d, Caularthron bicornutum. e, Broughtonia sanguinea. f, Brassavola nodosa.
No. 2154, 370sh: a, Oeceoclades maculata. b, Isochilus linearis. c, Eulophia alta. d, Ionopsis utricularioides. e, Epidendrum ciliare. f, Dimerandra emarginata.
No. 2155, 1500sh, Brassavola cucullata. No. 2156, 1500sh, Epidendrum nocturnum.

2000 Litho. Perf. 14
2150-2152 A372 Set of 3 3.50 3.50
Sheets of 6, #a-f
2153-2154 A372 Set of 2 14.00 14.00
Souvenir Sheets
2155-2156 A372 Set of 2 8.00 8.00

Nos. 607, 610, 612, 615, 617
Surcharged

Methods and perfs as before
1998-2001
2157 A99 100sh on 40sh multi
2158 A99 150sh on 9sh multi
2159 A99 200sh on 170sh multi
2159A A99 230sh on 20sh multi — —
2159B A99 230sh on 170sh multi
2159C A99 800sh on 500sh multi 2.00 2.00

Issued: No. 2158, 1/26/98; No. 2157, 8/6/98; No. 2159, 6/4/00; No. 2159C, 4/6/00; No. 2159B, 11/20/00; No. 2159A, 11/20/01.

Rare Birds A373

Designs: 150sh, Taita falcon. 300sh, Banded green. 400sh, Spotted ground thrush. 500sh, Fischer's turaco. 600sh, Blue swallow.

2000 Litho. Perf. 14
2160 A373 150sh multi .75 .75
2161 A373 300sh multi 1.25 1.25
2162 A373 400sh multi 1.75 1.75
2163 A373 500sh multi 2.00 2.00
Souvenir Sheet
2164 A373 600sh multi 3.00 3.00

Architecture — A374

Designs: 150sh, Ruins of Great Mosque, Kilwa Kisiwani. 200sh, German Boma, Mikindani. 250sh, German Boma, Bagamoyo. 300sh, Butiama Museum, Mara. 350sh, Chief Government Chemist Office. 400sh, Old Post Office, Dar es Salaam. 500sh, Dr. David Livingstone Lodge, Kwihara Tabora. 600sh, Original and present State Houses, vert. 700sh, Ngoni-Nyamwezi traditional houses. 800sh, The People's Palace Beit Elajaib, Zanzibar. 900sh, Tongoni Ruins, Tanga. 1000sh, Karimjee Hall, Dar es Salaam.
1500sh, Old Boma, Mikindani.

2000 (?)   Litho.   *Perf. 13*
2165 A374 150sh multi
2166 A374 200sh multi
2166A A374 250sh multi
2167 A374 300sh multi
2167A A374 350sh multi
2168 A374 400sh multi
2168A A374 500sh multi
2169 A374 600sh multi
2169A A374 700sh multi
2170 A374 800sh multi
2170A A374 900sh multi
2171 A374 1000sh multi
Souvenir Sheet
2172 A374 1500sh multi

For surcharge see No. 2336.

Flora and Fauna — A375

Designs: 100sh, Common babbler. 140sh, Eastern blue darner. 150sh, Cavalier mushroom. 200sh, Orange-barred sulphur. 250sh, Harlequin bug. No. 2179, 370sh, Brassolae liocattleya.
No. 2180, 370sh: a, Common yellowthroat. b, Great orange tip. c, Tiger lily. d, Shaggy mane. e, Sri Lanka grasshopper. f, Woodhouse's toad.
No. 2181, 370sh: a, Golden-crowned warbler. b, Fuchsia. c, Alfalfa butterfly. d, Lycaste aquila. e, Snail. f, Ground beetle.
No. 2182, 1500sh, Rufous-collared sparrow, horiz. No. 2183, 1500sh, Monarch butterfly, horiz.

2000   Litho.   *Perf. 14*
2174-2179 A375 Set of 6   3.00 3.00
Sheets of 6, #a-f
2180-2181 A375 Set of 2   11.00 11.00
Souvenir Sheets
2182-2183 A375 Set of 2   8.00 8.00

Activities of World Vision — A375a

Design: 200sh, Children have a right to education, horiz. 600sh, Children have a right to happiness, horiz. 800sh, Children have a right not to be exploited. 1000sh, Children have a right to be heard.

2001, Apr. 30   Litho.   *Perf. 13*
2183A A375a 200sh multi   — —
2183B A375a 600sh multi   — —
2183C A375a 800sh multi   — —
2183D A375a 1000sh multi   — —
Souvenir Sheet
2183E A375a 500sh multi   — —

Endangered Animals A376

Designs: 200sh, Leopard. 400sh, Rhinoceros. No. 2186, 600sh, Crocodile. 800sh, Hunting wild dogs.

No. 2188, 600sh, Cheetah.
2001, June 15   Litho.   *Perf. 13*
2184-2187 A376 Set of 4   5.00 5.00
Souvenir Sheet
2188 A376 600sh multi   1.75 1.75

UN High Commissioner for Refugees, 50th Anniv. — A377

Designs: 200sh, Refugee child being vaccinated. 400sh, Refugees crossing Lake Tanganyika. 600sh, Refugee woman, vert. 800sh, Fleeing refugees, vert.

2001, July 31
2189-2192 A377 Set of 4   5.00 5.00
2191a   Souvenir sheet of 1   1.75 1.75

Landscapes A378

Designs: 200sh, Rufiji River, Selous Game Reserve. 400sh, Mangapwani Beach, Zanzibar. 600sh, Mountains, Mikumi Natl. Park. 800sh, Balancing Stones, Shore of Lake Victoria, Mwanza, vert.
700sh, Ruaha Natl. Park, vert.

2001, Nov. 30   Litho.   *Perf. 13*
2193-2196 A378 Set of 4   5.00 5.00
Souvenir Sheet
2197 A378 700sh multi   1.75 1.75

Year of Dialogue Among Civilizations A379

Designs: 200sh, Talking with children. 400sh, Formal dress. 600sh, Exchanging ideas. 800sh, Letter writing.
700sh, Communication linkages, vert.

2001, Oct. 9   Litho.
2198-2201 A379 Set of 4   4.50 4.50
Souvenir Sheet
2202 A379 700sh multi   1.50 1.50

Conservation of Zanzibar Rare Species — A380

Designs: 250sh, Dolphins. 300sh, Coral reefs. 450sh, Coral reefs, diff. 800sh, Zanzibar red colobus, vert.
700sh, Zanzibar red colobus, diff.

2002, Aug. 30   Litho.   *Perf. 13*
2203-2206 A380 Set of 4   4.50 4.50
Souvenir Sheet
2207 A380 700sh multi   1.75 1.75

Historic Sites of East Africa A381

Designs: 250sh, Fort Kilwa. 300sh, Maruhubi Palace ruins, Zanzibar. 400sh, Old Provincial Office, Nairobi, 1913. 800sh, Mparu Tombs, Hoima, Uganda.
700sh, Map of East Africa, ship.

2001, Oct. 19
2208-2211 A381 Set of 4   3.75 3.75
Souvenir Sheet
2212 A381 700sh multi   1.50 1.50

Independence, 40th Anniv. — A382

Designs: 180sh, Tea estates. 230sh, Regional integration with Uganda and Kenya, vert. 350sh, University graduates, vert. 450sh, 1000sh, Lion, elephant, buffalo, cheetah, rhinoceros, Mt. Kilimanjaro. 650sh, Referral hospitals. 950sh, Mining industry.

2001, Dec. 30   Litho.   *Perf. 14*
2213-2218 A382 Set of 6   6.00 6.00
Souvenir Sheet
2219 A382 1000sh multi   2.10 2.10

Ceremonial Costumes — A383

Designs: 250sh, Makonde mask dance. 350sh, Zanzibar Mwaka koga festival. 400sh, Lizombe dancer. 450sh, Zaramo bride's celebration.
500sh, Like 400sh.

Wmk. 387
2002, Mar. 30   Litho.   *Perf. 13¾*
2220-2223 A383 Set of 4   4.00 4.00
Souvenir Sheet
2224 A383 500sh multi   1.50 1.50

Mountains A384

Designs: 250sh, Mt. Kilimanjaro. 350sh, Usambara Mountains. 400sh, Uluguru Mountains. 450sh, Mwanihana Peak, Udzungwa Mountains.
500sh, Like 250sh.

2002, June 30   Wmk. 387
2225-2228 A384 Set of 4   4.00 4.00
Souvenir Sheet
2229 A384 500sh multi   1.50 1.50

National Census A385

Census emblem and: 200sh, School children, vert. 250sh, Group of people. 350sh, Family. 600sh, Boy, census figures.
800sh, Group of people, vert.

Perf. 13x13¼ Sync., 13¼x13 Sync.
2002, Aug. 13   Unwmk.
2230-2233 A385 Set of 4   4.00 4.00
Souvenir Sheet
Perf. 13x13¼
2234 A385 800sh multi   1.75 1.75

Arts of Zanzibar A386

Designs: 200sh, Mat making. 250sh, Hand-sewn hats. 350sh, Chair making. 600sh, Hina painting.
800sh, Zanzibar door.

2002, Sept. 13   Unwmk.   *Perf. 13¼*
2235-2238 A386 Set of 4   3.75 3.75
Souvenir Sheet
Perf. 13
2239 A386 800sh multi   1.75 1.75

Souvenir Sheet

Wildlife — A387

No. 2240: a, Leopard. b, Elephant. c, Rhinoceros. d, Lion. e, Buffalo.

Perf. 13x14
2002, Apr. 30   Wmk. 387
2240 A387 250sh Sheet of 5, #a-e   3.75 3.75
Compare No. 2240 with No. 2251.

Archaeology A388

Designs: 250sh, Ancient city of Kisimkazi, Zanzibar, vert. 400sh, Ruins of Kaole town, Bagamoyo. 450sh, Kondoa Irangi rock paintings, vert. 600sh, Great Mosque, Kilwa Kisiwani.
1000sh, Like 450sh.

Perf. 13¼
2002, Sept. 30   Unwmk.   Litho.
2241-2244 A388 Set of 4   3.50 3.50
Souvenir Sheet
Perf. 13
2245 A388 1000sh multi   2.25 2.25

Wildlife A389

Designs: 400sh, Rhinoceroses. 500sh, Elephant. 600sh, Lion. 800sh, Leopard, vert. 1000sh, Buffalo.
1500sh, Rhinoceros, elephant, lion, leopard, buffalo, vert.

Perf. 13¼x12¾, 12¾x13¼
2003, Apr. 22   Litho.   Wmk. 387
2246-2250 A389 Set of 5   8.00 8.00
Size: 85x115mm
Imperf
2251 A389 1500sh multi   4.00 4.00
Compare No. 2251 with No. 2240.

Cash Crops — A390

Designs: 250sh, Cotton. 300sh, Cashews. 600sh, Sisal. 800sh, Cloves. 1000sh, Tea, horiz.

Perf. 13x13¼ Syncopated
2003, June 10   Unwmk.
2252-2255 A390 Set of 4   3.75 3.75
Souvenir Sheet
Perf. 13¼x13 Syncopated
2256 A390 1000sh multi   2.25 2.25

Activities of World Vision A391

Designs: 300sh, Better nutrition with vitamin A. 600sh, Education opportunity for all children. 800sh, Clean and safe water for all, vert. 1000sh, Malaria prevention with treated mosquito nets.
500sh, Children have a right to be heard.

2003, July 3   **Perf. 13**
2257-2260 A391 Set of 4   5.25 5.25
Souvenir Sheet
2261 A391 500sh multi   1.25 1.25

Traditional Dances A392

Dances: 300sh, Nyamwezi. 500sh, Luo. 600sh, Pemba. 800sh, Baganda. 1000sh, Masai.

Perf. 13¼x13 Syncopated
2003, July 25
2262-2265 A392 Set of 4   4.25 4.25
Souvenir Sheet
2266 A392 1000sh multi   2.00 2.00

Nos. 612 and 1567 Surcharged

Northern Circuit Tourist Attractions A393

Methods and Perfs As Before
2002
2267 A99 250sh on 40sh #612   .75 .75
2268 A262 250sh on 180sh #1567   .90 .90

Issued: No. 2267, 7/23/02; No. 2268, 8/30/02.

Designs: 300sh, Lion, lioness, Mt. Kilimanjaro. 350sh, Kibo Peak, Mt. Kilimanjaro. 400sh, Zebras, Serengeti Natl. Park. 500sh, Elephants, Kilimanjaro Natl. Park. 600sh, Leopards, Serengeti Natl. Park. 800sh, Rhinoceros, Ngorongoro Crater.
1000sh, Buffalo, Arusha Natl. Park.

2003, Apr. 30 Litho. **Perf. 13¼x13**
2269-2274 A393 Set of 6   5.75 5.75
Souvenir Sheet
2275 A393 1000sh multi   2.00 2.00

Landscapes A394

Designs: 300sh, Rufiji Delta. 400sh, Zanzibar shore. 500sh, Lake Manyara, Rift Valley. 800sh, Kalambo Falls, vert.
1000sh, Coastal mangroves.

2003, July 22 Litho. **Perf. 13¼x13**
2276-2279 A394 Set of 4   4.00 4.00
Souvenir Sheet
2280 A394 1000sh multi   1.90 1.90

Zanzibar Tourist Attractions A395

Designs: 300sh, Old Fort. 500sh, Door, Beit al Ajaib, vert. 600sh, Coconut palm tree, Michamvi Beach, vert. 800sh, Dhow, Beit al Ajaib.

Perf. 13¼x13, 13x13¼
2003, Sept. 30   Litho.
2281-2284 A395 Set of 4   4.25 4.25
2284a Souvenir sheet, #2281, 2283, 2284   3.25 3.25

Marine Mammals A396

Designs: 300sh, Common dolphin. 350sh, Sperm whale. 400sh, Southern right whale. 600sh, Dugong.
500sh, Bottlenose dolphin.

2003, Oct. 11 Litho. **Perf. 13¼x13**
2285-2288 A396 Set of 4   4.25 4.25
Souvenir Sheet
2289 A396 500sh multi   1.75 1.75

Religious Festivals — A396a

Designs: 300sh, Muslims on pilgrimage to Mecca. 500sh, Choir at Christmas. 600sh, Prophet Mohammed's Birthday. 800sh, Church at Christmas.
1000sh, Crucifixion of Jesus.

Wmk. 387
2003, Nov. 4 Litho. **Perf. 14**
2289A-2289D A396a Set of 4   4.25 4.25
Souvenir Sheet
2289E A396a 1000sh multi   1.90 1.90

Tanzania Posts Corporation, 10th Anniv. — A397

Designs: 350sh, Counter automation. 400sh, Overnight mail delivery services. 600sh, Workers' participation. 800sh, Expedited mail services.
1000sh, Post Cargo.

Unwmk.
2004, Jan. 19 Litho. **Perf. 13**
2290-2293 A397 Set of 4   4.00 4.00
2293a Souvenir sheet, #2290-2293   4.00 4.00
Souvenir Sheet
2294 A397 1000sh multi   1.90 1.90

Western Union Money Transfer A398

Designs: 300sh, Exchange of American and Tanzanian currency. 400sh, Busalanga Primary School. 500sh, Woman, child, Tanzanian currency, vert. 600sh, World map.
800sh, Like 300sh, without Western Union emblem.

Perf. 13¼x13, 13x13¼
2004, Feb. 3   Litho.
2295-2298 A398 Set of 4   3.25 3.25
Souvenir Sheet
2299 A398 800sh multi   1.50 1.50

Girl Guides in Tanzania, 75th Anniv. A399

Designs: 300sh, Guides demonstrating solar cookers. 400sh, Camp training. 600sh, Bravery training. 800sh, Guides assisting at a mother and child clinic session.
1000sh, Like 800sh.

2004, May 15 **Perf. 13¼x13**
2300-2303 A399 Set of 4   3.75 3.75
Souvenir Sheet
2304 A399 1000sh multi   1.90 1.90

Tanganyika Christian Refugee Service, 40th Anniv. A400

Designs: 350sh, Truck carrying refugees and bicycles. 600sh, Public water source. 800sh, Students in classroom. 1000sh, Afforestation campaign.
1200sh, Four vignettes combined.

Unwmk.
2004, May 24 Litho. **Perf. 14**
2305-2308 A400 Set of 4   5.00 5.00
Souvenir Sheet
Perf. 14¼
2309 A400 1200sh multi   2.25 2.25

No. 2309 contains one 44x34mm stamp.

Zanzibar Watercraft Races A401

Designs: 350sh, Crowd cheering race winners. 400sh, Punt race. 600sh, Dhow race. 800sh, Sailboat race.
1000sh, Dhow, vert.

2004, June 25   **Perf. 13**
2310-2313 A401 Set of 4   4.00 4.00
2313a Souvenir sheet, #2310-2313   4.00 4.00
Souvenir Sheet
2314 A401 1000sh multi   1.90 1.90

Flora, Fauna and Mushrooms — A402

No. 2315, 550sh, horiz. — Animals: a, Red colobus monkey. b, Leopard. c, Giraffe. d, Eland. e, Zebra. f, African elephant.
No. 2316, 550sh, horiz. — Birds: a, European roller. b, Little swift. c, African gray parrot. d, Bateleur. e, European bee-eater. f, Hoopoe.
No. 2317, 550sh, horiz. — Butterflies: a, Gold-banded forester. b, Two-tailed pasha. c, Plain tiger. d, Common dotted border. e, African migrant. f, Forest queen.
No. 2318, 550sh, horiz. — Orchids: a, Cynorkis kassnerana. b, Habenaria rhodocheila. c, Vanilla planifola. d, Ansellia africana. e, Disa uniflora. f, Calathe rosea.
No. 2319, 550sh, horiz. — Mushrooms: a, Fly mushroom. b, Rosy-gill fairy helmet. c, Purple coincap. d, Velvet shank. e, Thickfooted morel. f, King bolete.
No. 2320, 2000sh, Olive baboon. No. 2321, 2000sh, Gray crowned crane. No. 2322, 2000sh, Blue diadem butterfly. No. 2323, 2000sh, Disa uniflora, diff. No. 2324, 2000sh, Sharp-scaled parasol mushroom.

2004, July 19   **Perf. 14**
Sheets of 6, #a-f
2315-2319 A402 Set of 5   30.00 30.00
Souvenir Sheets
2320-2324 A402 Set of 5   18.50 18.50

Mining A403

Designs: 350sh, Diamond mining at Williamson Diamond Mwadui. 500sh, Semiprocessed jewels. No. 2327, 600sh, Drillers in deep mine. 800sh, Gold miners.
No. 2329, Unprocessed gemstones.

2004, July 30   **Perf. 13¼x12¾**
2325-2328 A403 Set of 4   4.25 4.25
2328a Souvenir sheet, #2325-2328   4.25 4.25
Souvenir Sheet
2329 A403 600sh multi   1.40 1.40

Southern African Development Community, 24th Anniv. A404

Designs: 350sh, Removal of water hyacinths from beach. 500sh, Irrigation ditch in corn field. 600sh, irrigation ditch at rice paddy. 800sh, Workers installing pipe in borehole, vert.
1000sh, Farm workers hoeing corn field irrigation ditches.

2004, Aug. 17   **Perf. 14x13, 13x14**
2330-2333 A404 Set of 4   4.25 4.25
2333a Souvenir sheet, #2330-2333, perf. 13½x13, 13x13½   4.25 4.25
Souvenir Sheet
2334 A404 1000sh multi   1.90 1.90

Nos. 1565, 1569 and 2166 Surcharged

#2335

#2336

Methods and Perfs As Before

2004, Nov. 13
2335	A262	350sh on 100sh #1565	—	—
2336	A374	350sh on 200sh #2166	—	—
2337	A262	350sh on 210sh #1569	—	—

Children's Rights A405

Inscriptions: No. 2338, 350sh, Involve children in school development. No. 2339, 350sh, Let's equip children with life skills. 400sh, Children need education before employment. 500sh, 1000sh, Disabled children need to be educated.

2004, Nov. 4   Litho.   Perf. 13¼x12¾
2338-2341	A405	Set of 4	3.00	3.00

Souvenir Sheet
2342	A405	1000sh multi	1.90	1.90

Law and Peace in the Great Lakes Zone — A405a

Designs: 350sh, Julius K. Nyerere acting as facilitator in Burundi peace negotiations. 500sh, Burundi refugees at border. No. 2342C, 600sh, Nelson Mandela and Tanzania Pres. Banjamin W. Mkapa at Arusha peace talks. 800sh, Pres. Mkapa with Uganda Pres. Yoweri Musaveni and Burundi Pres. Domitien Ndayizeye at Dar es Salaam peace talks.
No. 2342E, 600sh, Arusha Intl. Conference Center.

2004, Oct. 15   Litho.   Perf. 14x13
2342A-2342D	A405a	Set of 4	4.25	4.25
2342Df		Souvenir sheet, #2342A-2342D	4.25	4.25

Souvenir Sheet
2342E	A405a	600sh multi	1.10	1.10

Rotary International, Cent. — A406

Designs: 350sh, Rotary officials honor Tanzania Pres. Julius Nyerere. 500sh, Emblem of Dar es Salaam North Tanzania Club, vert. No. 2345 600sh, Eradication of polio. 800sh, Map and flags of District 9200 countries, Eritrea, Ethiopia, Uganda, Kenya and Tanzania, vert.
No. 2347: a, Environmental project. b, Self-reliance to the handicapped. c, Basic health care project, vert. d, Jaipur foot project. e, Malaria project. f, Eradication of river blindness project.
1000sh, Centenary emblem, vert.

2005, Feb. 23   Litho.   Perf. 13
2343-2346	A406	Set of 4	4.25	4.25
2347	A406	600sh Sheet of 6, #a-f	6.50	6.50

Souvenir Sheet
2348	A406	1000sh multi	1.90	1.90

Safari Circuit Animals — A407

Designs: 350sh, Lionesses. 500sh, Cheetahs, horiz. No. 2351, 600sh, Red colobus monkey. 800sh, Zebras, horiz.
No. 2353, horiz.: a, Elephants. b, Rhinoceroses. c, Giraffes. d, Crocodile. e, Chimpanzees. f, Buffaloes.
No. 2354, horiz.: a, Leopard. b, Wild hunting dogs.

Perf. 12¾x13¼, 13¼x12¾

2005, Apr. 30
2349-2352	A407	Set of 4	4.25	4.25
2353	A407	600sh Sheet of 6, #a-f	6.50	6.50
2354	A407	1000sh Sheet of 2, #a-b	3.75	3.75

Zanzibar Heritage and Culture A408

Designs: 350sh, Bull fighting. 400sh, Narrow street in Stone Town, vert. No. 2357, 600sh, Women's traditional dress, vert. 800sh, Clove harvesting, vert.
No. 2359, 600sh: a, House of Wonders. b, Local Taarabu musicians. c, Man holding fish. d, Coconut palm. e, Women's indoor traditional dress. f, Old museum building.
500sh, Pemba-Zanzibar ferry boat.

Perf. 13½x13, 13x13½

2005, June 30   Litho.
2355-2358	A408	Set of 4	4.00	4.00
2359	A408	600sh Sheet of 6, #a-f	6.50	6.50

Souvenir Sheet
2360	A408	500sh multi	1.25	1.25

2004 Summer Olympics, Athens — A409

Designs: No. 2361, 350sh, Greco-Roman wrestlers. No. 2362, 350sh, Baron Godefroy de Blonay, vert. 500sh, Commemorative medal for 1928 Amsterdam Summer Olympics, vert. 1000sh, Greek javelin thrower sculpture, vert.

2005, May 2   Litho.   Perf. 13¼
2361-2364	A409	Set of 4	4.00	4.00

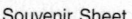

Reign of Pope John Paul, 25th Anniv. (in 2003) — A410

No. 2365: a, Pope as boy, with mother, 1921. b, Visit to Poland, 1979. c, Meeting with Pres. George W. Bush, 2001. d, In Armenia, 2001.

2005, May 2   Perf. 13½
2365	A410	1000sh Sheet of 4, #a-d	8.00	8.00

Locomotives, Bicent. — A411

No. 2366: a, West Side Lumber 3-truck shay, Georgetown Loop Railroad. b, LK&P 0-4-0 Saddletanker. c, Double-headed C&T steam locomotive. d, Baldwin 4-6-0, Huckleberry Railroad.
2500sh, Heber Valley Railroad 2-8-0.

2005, May 2
2366	A411	1000sh Sheet of 4, #a-d	7.25	7.25

Souvenir Sheet
2367	A411	2500sh multi	4.50	4.50

FIFA (Fédération Internationale de Football Association) Cent. (in 2004) — A412

No. 2368: a, Franco Baresi. b, Daniel Passarella. c, Miroslav Klose. d, Michel Platini. 2500sh, Gianfranco Zola.

2005, May 2   Litho.   Perf. 13½
2368	A412	1000sh Sheet of 4, #a-d	7.25	7.25

Souvenir Sheet
2369	A412	2500sh multi	4.50	4.50

D-Day, 60th Anniv. (in 2004) — A413

No. 2370, vert.: a, Map of invasion. b, Gen. Dwight D. Eisenhower. c, American troops landing at Omaha Beach. d, British Mosquitos. e, Fleet Admiral Ernest J. King. f, Gen. George C. Marshall.
2500sh, Battle for Fox Green Beach.

2006, May 2
2370	A413	600sh Sheet of 6, #a-f	6.50	6.50

Souvenir Sheet
2371	A413	2500sh multi	4.50	4.50

Jules Verne (1828-1905), Writer — A414

No. 2372, 800sh: a, Voyages Extraordinaires. b, Twenty Thousand Leagues Under the Sea. c, A Floating City (book cover). d, Adventures of Three Englishmen and Three Russians in South Africa.
No. 2373, 800sh: a, Mathias Sandorf. b, The Steam House, The Demon of Cawnpore. c, Hector Servadec on the Career of a Comet. d, An Antarctic Mystery.
No. 2374, 800sh: a, Around the World in Eighty Days. b, Dr. Ox's Experiment. c, The Purchase of the North Pole. d, Adrift in the Pacific.
No. 2375, 800sh: a, The Archipelago on Fire. b, The Vanished Diamond. c, Mistress Branican. d, The Castle of the Carpathians.
No. 2376, 800sh: a, The Invasion of the Sea. b, The Floating Island. c, A Floating City (men near ship railing). d, Dick Sands, Boy Captain.
No. 2377, 2000sh, Around the World in Eighty Days, diff. No. 2378, 2000sh, Five Weeks in a Balloon. No. 2379, 2000sh, The Mysterious Island. No. 2380, 2000sh, The Adventures of a Chinaman. No. 2381, 2000sh, The Invasion of the Sea, diff.

2005, May 16   Perf. 13½
Sheets of 4, #a-d
2372-2376	A414	Set of 5	29.00	29.00

Souvenir Sheets
2377-2381	A414	Set of 5	18.00	18.00

Fish of Lake Victoria A415

Designs: No. 2382, 350sh, Labeo victorianus. 400sh, Lates niloticus. 600sh, Pundamilia nyererei. 800sh, Brycinus sadleri.
No. 2386, 350sh: a, Haplochromis sharpsnout. b, Haplochromis chilotes. c, Mormyrus kannume. d, Clarias gariepinus. e, Synodontis afrofischeri. f, Protopterus aethiopicus.
500sh, Oreochromis niloticus.

2005, Aug. 30   *Perf. 13¼x13¾*
2382-2385 A415   Set of 4   3.75 3.75
2386 A415 350sh Sheet of 6, #a-
     f   3.75 3.75

Souvenir Sheet

2387 A415 500sh multi   1.25 1.25

Pope John Paul II (1920-2005), and Pres. Bill Clinton — A416

2005, Sept. 22   *Perf. 12¾*
2388 A416 1500sh multi   2.75 2.75

Printed in sheets of 4, with each stamp having a slightly different background.

Rotary International, Cent. — A417

No. 2389: a, Child receiving polio vaccine. b, Dr. Jonas E. Salk, polio researcher. c, Hands, test tube.
2500sh, Salk and Rotary International centenary emblem.

2005, Sept. 22
2389 A417 1200sh Sheet of 3,
     #a-c   6.50 6.50

Souvenir Sheet

2390 A417 2500sh multi   4.50 4.50

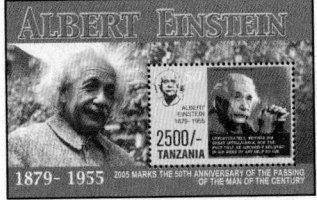

Albert Einstein (1879-1955), Physicist — A418

No. 2391 — Sketch of Einstein and: a, 1979 Swiss 5-franc coin. b, Time Magazine cover. c, Israel #117.
2500sh, Portrait of Einstein.

2005, Sept. 22
2391 A418 1300sh Sheet of 3,
     #a-c   7.00 7.00

Souvenir Sheet

2392 A418 2500sh multi   4.50 4.50

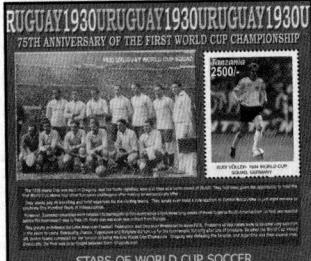

First World Cup Soccer Championships, 75th Anniv. — A419

No. 2393: a, Christian Ziege. b, Marko Rehmer. c, Jens Nowotny.
2500sh, Rudi Völler.

2005, Sept. 22   *Perf. 13¼*
2393 A419 1200sh Sheet of 3,
     #a-c   6.50 6.50

Souvenir Sheet

2394 A419 2500sh multi   4.50 4.50

Butterflies A420

Designs: 350sh, Papilio ufipa. No. 2396, 500sh, Mylothris sagala mahale. No. 2397, 600sh, Amauris tartarea tukuyuensis. 800sh, Charaxes lucyae gabriellae.
No. 2399, 600sh: a, Like 350sh. b, Euphaedra neophron kiellandi. c, Like 800sh. d, Abisara zanzibarica. e, Acrae utengulensis.
No. 2400, 500sh, Charaxes usambarae maridula.

2005, Oct. 27   *Perf. 13¾x13½*
2395-2398 A420   Set of 4   4.00 4.00
2399 A420 600sh Sheet of 6,
     #2397,
     2399a-2399e   6.50 6.50

Souvenir Sheet

2400 A420 500sh multi   .90 .90

Anniversaries and Events A421

Designs: 350sh, Person with amputated leg. No. 2402, 500sh, Line of people at polling station. No. 2403, 600sh, Pope John Paul II, kneeling at airport. 800sh, Laurean Cardinal Rugambwa, Pope John Paul II and Pres. Alis Hassan Mwinyi.
No. 2405, 600sh: a, Pres. Julius Nyerere and Abeid Aman Karume signing Union Treaty. b, Woman holding child, casting ballot. c, Pope John Paul II, Pres. Mwinyi and Julius and Maria Nyerere. d, Pope John Paul II and Cardinal Rugambwa and car roof. e, Majimaji Museum, Songea. f, President B. W. Mkapa at fire.
No. 2406, 500sh, Majimaji Monument, vert.

2005, Dec. 9   *Perf. 13¼x12¾*
2401-2404 A421   Set of 4   4.00 4.00
2405 A421 600sh Sheet of 6, #a-
     f   6.25 6.25

Souvenir Sheet
Perf. 12¾x13¼

2406 A421 600sh multi   1.25 1.25

World Diabetes Day (350sh); 2005 general elections (#2402, 2405b); Visit of Pope John Paul II, 15th anniv. (800sh, #2405c, 2405d).

Birds A422

Designs: 350sh, Rufous-winged sunbird. No. 2408, 500sh, Pemba white-eye. No. 2409, 600sh, Kilombero weaver. 800sh, Usambara eagle owl.
No. 2411, 600sh: a, Pemba scops owl. b, Spike-heeled lark. c, Pemba green pigeon. d, Uluguru bush shrike. e, Yellow-collared love birds. f, Usambara nightjar.
No. 2412, 500sh, Moreau's sunbird, vert.

2006, Mar. 25   *Perf. 13*
2407-2410 A422   Set of 4   4.00 4.00
2411 A422 600sh Sheet of 6, #a-
     f   6.50 6.50

Souvenir Sheet

2412 A422 500sh multi   1.10 1.10

No. 2412 contains one 39x49mm stamp.

2006 World Cup Soccer Championships, Germany — A423

Designs: 350sh, New National Stadium, Dar es Salaam. 500sh, Map of Africa and flags of participating countries, vert. No. 2415, 600sh, Pres. Jakaya Kikwete holding World Cup trophy. 800sh, Mascot for 2006 World Cup, vert. No. 2417, 600sh, World Cup Trophy and 2006 World Cup emblem.

Perf. 13¼x12¾, 12¾x13¼
2006, Mar. 25
2413-2416 A423   Set of 4   3.75 3.75
2416a   Miniature sheet, #2413-
     2416   3.75 3.75

Souvenir Sheet

2417 A423 600sh multi   1.50 1.50

Miniature Sheet

Wolfgang Amadeus Mozart (1756-91), Composer — A424

No. 2418: a, Portrait of Mozart (blue panel). b, Mozart's birthplace, Salzburg. c, Poster for Don Giovanni. d, Portrait of Mozart (purple panel).

2006, June 13   *Perf. 12¾*
2418 A424 1200sh Sheet of 4,
     #a-d   8.00 8.00

Release of Elvis Presley Movie, *Jailhouse Rock*, 50th Anniv. — A425

No. 2419 — Presley with: a, Both arms at side. b, Arm raised above head. c, Arms outstretched and jacket pulled up behind head. d, Hand in front of chest.

2006, June 13   *Perf. 13½*
2419 A425 1200sh Sheet of 4,
     #a-d   9.00 9.00

Queen Elizabeth II, 80th Birthday — A426

No. 2420 — Queen: a, Wearing blue robe. b, On reviewing stand. c, On horse. d, Wearing feathered hat.
2500sh, Wearing tiara.

2006, June 13   *Perf. 14¼*
2420 A426 1200sh Sheet of 4,
     #a-d   9.50 9.50

Souvenir Sheet

2421 A426 2500sh multi   5.25 5.25

Rembrandt (1606-69), Painter — A427

No. 2422 — Painting details: a, Jan Pellicorne and His Son Caspar (Jan Pellicorne). b, Jan Pellicorne and His Son Caspar (Caspar). c, Susanna Van Collen, Wife of Jan Pellicorne, and Her Daughter, Eva Susanna (Susanna). d, Susanna Van Collen, Wife of Jan Pellicorne, and Her Daughter, Eva Susanna (Eva Susanna).
3000sh, A Turk.

2006, June 13   *Perf. 13¼*
2422 A427 1000sh Sheet of 4,
     #a-d   6.75 6.75

Imperf
Size: 70x100mm

2423 A427 3000sh multi   5.00 5.00

Beauty of Zanzibar A428

Designs: 350sh, Man and woman in traditional Zanzibar dress. No. 2425, 500sh, Zanzibar Museum. No. 2426, 600sh, Maruhubi Palace ruins. 800sh, Man climbing coconut tree.
No. 2428, 600sh: a, Green turtle at Mnemba Island. b, Red colobus monkey. c, Giant tortoise at Changuu Island. d, Dhow, Zanzibar sunset. e, Dhow sailing near Matemwe. f, Coconut crab, Chumbe Island.
No. 2429, 500sh, vert.: a, Clove foliage and enlargement of flower buds. b, Light Signal Tower.

2006, June 30   *Perf. 13½x13*
2424-2427 A428   Set of 4   4.00 4.00
2428 A428 600sh Sheet of 6, #a-
     f   6.00 6.00

Souvenir Sheet
Perf. 13x13½

2429 A428 500sh Sheet of 2, #a-
     b   1.75 1.75

Mountains — A429

Designs: 350sh, Mt. Kenya. 400sh, Udzungwa Mountain Range. 600sh, Sanje Falls, vert. 800sh, Ruwenzori Range.
No. 2434, 1000sh: a, Kiko Summit and Mawenzi, Mt. Kilimanjaro. b, Giraffe and Mt. Kilimanjaro.
No. 2435, 1000sh: a, Cattle, herder and Ol Doinyo Lengai. b, Ol Doinyo Lengai summit and crater, vert.

Perf. 13½x13¾, 13¾x13½

2006, Aug. 24

2430-2433	A429	Set of 4	3.50	3.50

Sheets of 2, #a-b

2434-2435	A429	Set of 2	6.50	6.50

Miniature Sheet

Tazara Railway, 30th Anniv. — A430

No. 2436: a, 350sh, Map of Tanzania and Zambia, waterfall, mountain, people waving, and men signing agreement. b, 350sh, Men and train, elephant and antelope. c, 600sh, Dar es Salaam Station, sign and wreaths with Chinese inscriptions. d, 600sh, New Kapiri Mposhi Station, people near train. e, 800sh, Train, bridge and tunnel, zebra and giraffe. f, 800sh, Train on bridge, lion and lioness.

2006, Oct. 25   **Perf. 12**

2436	A430	Sheet of 6, #a-f	6.00	6.00

Worldwide Fund for Nature (WWF) — A431

No. 2437 — Damaliscus lunatus jimela: a, Males butting heads. b, Close-up view of head. c, Adult and juvenile. d, Adult on mound.

2006, Nov. 24   **Perf. 13¼**

2437	A431	Horiz. or vert. strip	7.00	7.00
a.-d.		600sh Any single	1.25	1.25
e.		Miniature sheet, 2 each #2437a-2437d	8.00	8.00

Zanzibar Flora and Fauna — A432

No. 2438, 1000sh: a, Coconut crab. b, Frangipane. c, Sykes monkey. d, Green sea turtle.

No. 2439, 1000sh: a, African civet. b, Four-toed elephant shrew. c, Lesser bushbaby. d, Pemba sunbird.

No. 2440, 3000sh, Protoreaster lincki. No. 2441, 3000sh, Tauraco fischeri.

2006, Nov. 24   **Perf. 13¼**

Sheets of 4, #a-d

2438-2439	A432	Set of 2	13.50	13.50

Souvenir Sheets

2440-2441	A432	Set of 2	10.00	10.00

Space Achievements — A433

No. 2442 — Intl. Space Station: a, Two rows of solar panels at top, part of Space Station at bottom. b, Connection point for arms holding solar panels. c, Main junction of Space Station. d, Space Station, denomination at UR. e, Space Shuttle with cargo door open. f, Space Station, "International Space Station" just above country name.

No. 2443 — Mars Reconnaissance Orbiter: a, Mars, launch of rocket. b, Orbiter, country name in white at UR. c, Orbiter, country name in red and black at LL. d, Orbiter, country name in white at UL.

No. 2444, 2500sh, Calipso and Cloudsat satellites. No. 2445, 2500sh, Muses-C probe.

2006, June 13   **Litho.**   **Perf. 14**

2442	A433	800sh Sheet of 6, #a-f	7.75	7.75
2443	A433	1150sh Sheet of 4, #a-d	7.50	7.50

Souvenir Sheets

2444-2445	A433	Set of 2	8.00	8.00

Phila Africa 06 Stamp Exhibition, Dar es Salaam A434

2006, Aug. 24   **Perf. 13¾**

2446	A434	(700sh) multi	1.10	1.10

Souvenir Sheet

2447	A434	600sh multi	.90	.90

No. 2447 contains one 47x32mm stamp.

Independence, 45th Anniv. — A435

Designs: 350sh, Pres. Julius K. Nyerere with torch. No. 2449, 400sh, University of Dar es Salaam, horiz. No. 2450, 600sh, Vice-president Abeid A. Karume, country name in green. 800sh, Nyerere.

No. 2452, 600sh: a, Prime Minister Rashidi Mfaume Kawawa. b, Nyerere, diff. c, Karume, country name in blue. d, Pres. Ali Hassan Mwinyi. e, Pres. Benjamin W. Mkapa. f, Pres. Jakaya Mrisho Kikwete.

No. 2453, National Uhuru Monument.

2006, Dec. 9   **Perf. 13½**

2448-2451	A435	Set of 4	3.50	3.50
2452	A435	600sh Sheet of 6, #a-f	5.75	5.75

Souvenir Sheet

2453	A435	400sh multi	.65	.65

Safari Hunt Animals A436

Designs: 400sh, Wild dog. 600sh, Warthog. No. 2456, 700sh, Zebras. 800sh, Female monkeys and young.

No. 2458, 700sh: a, Elephant. b, Leopard in grass. c, Buffaloes. d, Lion and lioness. e, Leopard in foliage (66x46mm). 1000sh, Lionesses.

2007, Feb. 23   **Perf. 13¾**

2454-2457	A436	Set of 4	4.00	4.00
2458	A436	700sh Sheet of 5, #a-e	5.75	5.75

Souvenir Sheet

2459	A436	1000sh multi	1.60	1.60

No. 2459 contains one 47x32mm stamp.

Historical Zanzibar — A437

Designs: 400sh, Ruins. 600sh, Coral reef and fish west of Pemba, horiz. No. 2462, 700sh, Bet El Ajaib, cloves. 800sh, Coral reef and fish, diff.

No. 2464, 700sh, horiz.: a, Beach. b, Kizimbani Persian Bath. c, Maruhubi Ruins. d, Livingstone House. e, Old Dispensary. f, Cave.

No. 2465, 700sh, Colobus monkey, horiz.

2007, Apr. 26

2460-2463	A437	Set of 4	4.00	4.00
2464	A437	700sh Sheet of 6, #a-f	6.75	6.75

Souvenir Sheet

2465	A437	700sh multi	1.10	1.10

Activities of World Vision A438

Designs: No. 2466, 400sh, Food security. 600sh, Income generation and nutrition. No. 2468, 700sh, Advocating for children and rights. 800sh, Children's immunization. 1000sh, Education for development.

No. 2471, 700sh: a, Children's immunization. b, Education for development.

No. 2472, 400sh, Income generation and nutrition.

2007, May 31   **Litho.**   **Perf. 13¾x13½**

2466-2470	A438	Set of 5	5.50	5.50
2471	A438	700sh Sheet of 3, #2468, 2471a, 2471b	3.50	3.50

Souvenir Sheet

2472	A438	400sh multi	.65	.65

Environmental Care — A439

Designs: No. 2473, 400sh, Prof. Mark Mwandosya planting tree at Kiroka Secondary School, Morogoro. No. 2474, 500sh, Shinyanga. 700sh, Kihansi Waterfall, Nectophrynoides aspersginis. 800sh, Natural regeneration of the land.

No. 2477, 400sh: a, Illegal mining. b, Tree planting, Morogoro. c, Planted trees in degraded areas. d, Traditional soil and moisture conservation method. e, Tree seedlings for rehabilitating degraded areas. f, Agriculture on steep mountains.

No. 2478, 500sh, Nguru Mountains catchment area.

2007, June 5   **Litho.**   **Perf. 14**

2473-2476	A439	Set of 4	4.00	4.00
2477	A439	400sh Sheet of 6, #a-f	4.00	4.00

Souvenir Sheet

2478	A439	500sh multi	.80	.80

Campaign Against AIDS — A440

Inscriptions: No. 2479, 400sh, Let us talk with our children about AIDS. 700sh, Be faithful in your marriage. 800sh, Fight against AIDS is our duty. 1000sh, Examine your health to be free.

No. 2483, 400sh: a, Let us get education about AIDS. b, Prevent yourself from new infection. c, Let us sing to stop AIDS. d, Let us not segregate the people with AIDS.

No. 2484, 400sh, Stop AIDS, keep the promise.

2007, July 14   **Litho.**   **Perf. 13¾x13½**

2479-2482	A440	Set of 4	4.50	4.50
2483	A440	400sh Sheet of 4, #a-d	2.50	2.50

Souvenir Sheet

2484	A440	400sh multi	.65	.65

Reign of Aga Khan, 50th Anniv. A441

Designs: 400sh, Zanzibar Madrasa Resource Center. No. 2486, 600sh, Aga Khan Hospital, Dar es Salaam, gold frame. 700sh, Lake Manyara Serena Safari Lodge. 800sh, Zanzibar Serena Inn.

No. 2489, 600sh: a, Exterior of Stone Town Cultural Center, Zanzibar. b, View from balcony of Stone Town Cultural Center. c, Medical personnel treating patient at Aga Khan Hospital. d, Aga Khan Hospital, white frame.

1000sh, Women at Zanzibar Madrasa Resource Center, vert.

2007, Aug. 18   **Litho.**   **Perf. 14½**

2485-2488	A441	Set of 4	4.00	4.00
2489	A441	600sh Sheet of 4, #a-d	3.75	3.75

Souvenir Sheet

2490	A441	1000sh multi	1.60	1.60

Campaign Against Corruption A442

Emblem of Prevention of Corruption Bureau: No. 2491, 400sh, Group of people in map of Tanzania. 500sh, Police officer escorting arrested man. 700sh, Man with briefcase as marionette, vert. 800sh, Man initiating bribe.

No. 2495: a, 400sh, Emblem with bright yellow background. b, 600sh, Man, police officer, bus.

No. 2496, 400sh, Emblem with olive green background.

2007, Oct. 9   **Litho.**   **Perf. 13¼**

2491-2494	A442	Set of 4	4.25	4.25
2495	A442	Sheet of 5, #2492-2494, 2495a, 2495b	5.25	5.25

Souvenir Sheet

2496	A442	400sh multi	.70	.70

Ceremonial Costumes — A443

Designs: No. 2497, 400sh, Iringa Hehe tribesman in traditional outfit. 600sh, Haya girls in bark cloth outfit. No. 2499, 700sh, Msewe dancers in Pemba, horiz. 800sh, Wabena tribesmen in traditional ceremony, horiz.

No. 2501, 700sh: a, Maasai girls. b, Maasai dancing. c, Singida Nyaturu girl. d, Sambaa tribesman in traditional outfit. e, Wabena woman grinding corn. f, Wairaq man and wife in leather outfit.

No. 2502, 400sh, Wanyaturu girls, horiz.

2007, Oct. 9   **Perf. 14**

2497-2500	A443	Set of 4	4.50	4.50
2501	A443	700sh Sheet of 6, #a-f	7.50	7.50

Souvenir Sheet

2502	A443	400sh multi	.70	.70

Pope Benedict
XVI — A444

2007, Oct. 24   Litho.   Perf. 13½
2503 A444 600sh multi   1.10 1.10
Printed in sheets of 8.

Wedding of Queen Elizabeth II and
Prince Philip, 60th Anniv. — A445

No. 2504: a, Queen and flowers. b, Couple.

2007, Oct. 24
2504 A445 750sh Pair, #a-b   2.60 2.60
Printed in sheets containing three of each
stamp.

Princess Diana (1961-97) — A446

No. 2505 — Diana wearing: a, Purple and
red hat, close-up. b, Blue and beige hat, close-
up. c, Black and white hat. d, Blue and beige
hat. e, Purple and red hat. f, Black and white
hat, close-up.
3500sh, Blue and white hat.

2007, Oct. 24
2505 A446 750sh Sheet of 6,
      #a-f   7.75 7.75
Souvenir Sheet
2506 A446 3500sh multi   6.00 6.00

First Helicopter Flight, Cent. — A447

No. 2507: a, Hiller UH-12 Raven. b, Kamov
Ka-25 Hormone. c, Cierva autogyro. d,
Eurocopter Tiger.
3000sh, Bristol Sycamore.

2007, Oct. 24
2507 A447 1200sh Sheet of 4,
      #a-d   8.25 8.25
Souvenir Sheet
2508 A447 3000sh multi   5.25 5.25

Paintings by Qi Baishi (1864-
1957) — A448

No. 2509: a, Wisteria and Bees. b, Pine and
Cicada. c, Narcissus, Rock and Quail. d,
Pumpkins.
3000sh, Begonias and Butterfly.

2007, Oct. 24   Perf. 12½
2509 A448 1000sh Sheet of 4,
      #a-d   7.00 7.00
Souvenir Sheet
Perf. 13½
2510 A448 3000sh multi   5.25 5.25
No. 2509 contains four 32x80mm stamps.

Animals
A449

Designs: 400sh, Wildebeests and zebras
grazing. No. 2512, 600sh, Lion and lioness,
vert. 700sh, Lioness descending tree, vert.
800sh, Giraffes, vert.
No. 2515, 600sh: a, Leopard on tree, vert. b,
Young chimpanzee, vert. c, Lioness resting on
tree, vert. d, Adult male chimpanzee, vert. e,
Cheetah with a kill. f, Baboons.
No. 2616, 600sh: a, Leopard and cubs. b,
Impala.

Perf. 13¾x13½, 13½x13¼
2008, Jan. 30   Litho.
2511-2514 A449 Set of 4   4.25 4.25
2515 A449 600sh Sheet of 6, #a-
      f   6.25 6.25
Souvenir Sheet
2516 A449 600sh Sheet of 2, #a-
      b   2.10 2.10

Miniature Sheet

2008 Summer Olympics,
Beijing — A450

No. 2517: a, Basketball. b, Marathon. c,
Swimming. d, Javelin.

2008, Apr. 8   Litho.   Perf. 12¾
2517 A450 700sh Sheet of 4, #a-
      d   4.50 4.50

Spices of
Zanzibar
A451

Designs: 400sh, Nutmeg. No. 2519, 600sh,
Man picking cloves. 700sh, Drying cloves,
vert. 1000sh, Cardamom (iliki) seeds.
No. 2522, 600sh: a, Cardamom plants. b,
Vanilla beans. c, Ginger. d, Cinnamon
(mdalasini). e, Black pepper. f, Paprika
peppers.
No. 2523, 600sh, Turmeric (binzari).

Perf. 13¼
2008, Apr. 26   Litho.   Perf. 13¼
2518-2521 A451 Set of 4   4.50 4.50

2522 A451 600sh Sheet of 6, #a-
      f   6.00 6.00
Souvenir Sheet
2523 A451 600sh multi   1.00 1.00

Marine
Life — A452

Designs: 400sh, Sea turtle. No. 2525,
600sh, Dugongs. 700sh, Octopus. 1000sh,
Whale shark.
No. 2528, 600sh: a, Lizard fish. b, Eel. c,
Sea turtle, diff. d, Lionfish. e, Anemone fish. f,
Coelacanths.
No. 2529, 600sh, Seahorses, vert.

2008, Aug. 15   Perf. 13¾x13½
2524-2527 A452 Set of 4   4.75 4.75
Perf. 13¾
2528 A452 600sh Sheet of 6, #a-
      f   6.25 6.25
Souvenir Sheet
2529 A452 600sh multi   1.10 1.10
No. 2528 contains six 42x32mm stamps.
No. 2529 contains one 35x50mm stamp.

Visit to
United
States of
Pope
Benedict
XVI — A453

2008, Sept. 3   Litho.   Perf. 13¼
2530 A453 1000sh multi   1.75 1.75
Printed in sheets of 4.

Miniature Sheet

Elvis Presley (1935-77) — A454

No. 2531 — Movies: a, Jailhouse Rock. b,
Wild in the Country. c, Flaming Star. d,
Roustabout.

2008, Sept. 3
2531 A454 1200sh Sheet of 4,
      #a-d   8.50 8.50

Botanical
Gardens —
A454a

Designs: 400sh, Flowers, Kitulo Natl. Park.
No. 2531F, 600sh, Chameleon and butterfly,
Amani Forest. 700sh, Monkey and waterfall,
Udzungwa Mountains Forest. 1000sh, Trees,
Saadani Natl. Park.
No. 2531I, 600sh: k, Flowers, Kitulo Natl.
Park. l, Gazrden House, Vuga-Lushoto. m,
Flowers, Udzingwa Mountains. n, Bird at Lake
Rushwa, Kagera. o, Rufiji River, Selous Game
Reserve. p, Rhinoceros, Ngorongoro Crater.
No. 2531J, 600sh, Bird, Kitulo Natl. Park.

Perf. 13¾x13½
2008, Nov. 15   Litho.
2531E-2531H A454a Set of 4   4.25 4.25
2531I A454a 600sh Sheet of 6,
      #k-p   5.75 5.75

Souvenir Sheet
Perf. 13¾
2531J A454a 600sh multi   .95   .95
No. 2531J contains one 50x35mm stamp.

Tanzania
Posts
Corporation,
15th
Anniv. — A455

Designs: 400sh, Window clerk. 600sh,
Headquarters, vert.

Perf. 13¾x13½, 13½x13¾
2009, Jan. 20
2532-2533 A455 Set of 2   1.50 1.50

Miniature Sheet

Inauguration of US Pres. Barack
Obama — A456

No. 2534 — Pres. Obama and: a, White
background. b, Flag. c, Window. d, Wife,
Michelle.

2009, Jan. 20   Litho.   Perf. 11½x12
2534 A456 1500sh Sheet of 4,
      #a-d   8.75 8.75

Souvenir Sheet

Signing of Millennium Challenge
Compact Aid Package, 1st
Anniv. — A457

No. 2535: a, US Pres. George W. Bush. b,
Tanzania Pres. Jakaya Kikwete.

2009, Jan. 27   Perf. 13½
2535 A457 1500sh Sheet of 2,
      #a-b   4.75 4.75

Space Exploration, 50th Anniv. (In
2007) — A458

No. 2536: a, 1200sh, Sputnik III. b, 1500sh,
Sputnik III and clouds.
No. 2537: a, 1200sh, Cassini orbiter and technician.
b, Cassini orbiter and Huygens probe in
manufacturing facility. c, Titan IV-B/ Centaur
launch vehicle. d, Cassini-Huygens in space.
e, Saturn, Titan, Huygens probe. f, Huygens
probe on Titan.
No. 2538, 1200sh: a, Sputnik II. b, Laika on
Monument to the Conquerors of Space, Mos-
cow. c, Statue of Laika. d, Laika the dog.
No. 2539, 1200sh: a, Vostok I. b, Yuri
Gagarin. c, Vostok 8K72K. d, Statue of
Gagarin.
No. 2540, 1200sh: a, Explorer I and techni-
cians. b, Dr. James Van Allen, Explorer I. c,
Explorer I atop Juno I. d, Explorer I in space.
No. 2541, 1200sh — Spitzer Space tele-
scope: a, In space. b, In manufacturing facility,

name in black at left. c, In manufacturing facility, name in white at right. d, In space, above Earth.

No. 2542, 3500sh, Sputnik III, horiz. No. 2543, 3500sh, Hubble Space Telescope, horiz.

2009, Mar. 13   Litho.   Perf. 14
2536	A458	Pair, #a-b	4.25 4.25
2537	A458	750sh Sheet of 6, #a-f	6.75 6.75

Sheets of 4, #a-d
2538-2541	A458	Set of 4	29.00 29.00

Souvenir Sheets
2542-2543	A458	Set of 2	10.50 10.50

No. 2536 was printed in sheets containing 2 pairs.

Peonies
A459

2009, Apr. 10   Perf. 13¼
2544	A459	570sh multi	.85 .85

Printed in sheets of 8.

Butterflies and Moths — A459a

Designs: 400sh, Mkuranga moth. No. 2544B, 600sh, Udzungwa butterfly, vert. 700sh, Acraea petraea. 800sh, Acraea petraea, diff.

No. 2544E, 600sh: f, Cymothoe alcimeda. g, Junonia octavia sesamus. h, Junonia oenone oenone. i, Hypolimnas misippus.

No. 2544J, 600sh, Vanessa cardui. No. 2544K, 600sh, Axiocerses tjoane, vert.

Perf. 13¼x13½, 13½x13¼
2009, June 30
Granite Paper
2544A-2544D	A459a	Set of 4	3.75 3.75
2544E	A459a	600sh Sheet of 4, #f-i	3.75 3.75

Souvenir Sheets
2544J-2544K	A459a	Set of 2	1.90 1.90

Zanzibar Attractions — A459b

Designs: No. 2544L, 400sh, Red colobus monkey. No. 2544M, 600sh, House of Wonders, horiz. No. 2544N, 700sh, Carved door. No. 2544O, 1000sh, Coffee seller.

No. 2544P, 600sh: r, Man dragging outrigger canoe. s, Zanzibar seafront, horiz. t, Giant tortoise, horiz. u, Face of red colobus monkey. v, Chake Chake's Courthouse, horiz. w, Zumari, horiz.

No. 2544Q, 600sh, Zanzibar seafront and dhow, horiz.

2009, July 30   Perf. 14
2544L-2544O	A459b	Set of 4	4.25 4.25
2544P	A459b	600sh Sheet of 6, #r-w	5.50 5.50

Souvenir Sheet
2544Q	A459b	600sh multi	.95 .95

Miniature Sheets

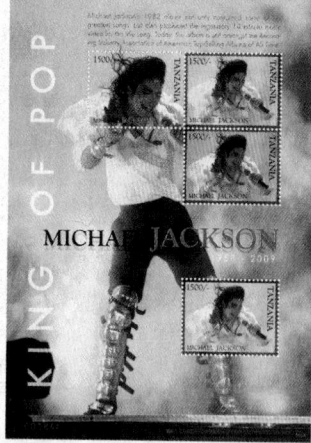

A460

Michael Jackson (1958-2009), Singer — A461

No. 2545: a, Dull blue background, no frame. b, Yellow background, with gray frame. c, Orange background, with gray frame. d, Blue background, with gray frame.

No. 2546 — Various photographs with: a, Black background, purple denomination. b, Blue background, purple denomination. c, Blue background, white denomination. d, Black background, white denomination.

2009, Sept. 3   Perf. 11½x12
2545	A460	1500sh Sheet of 4, #a-d	9.25 9.25

Perf. 12x11½
2546	A461	1500sh Sheet of 4, #a-d	9.25 9.25

Chinese Aviation, Cent. — A462

No. 2547 — Helicopters: a, Z-5. b, Z-6. c, Z-8. d, Z-11.
2700sh, Z-9 helicopter.

2009, Nov. 12   Perf. 14
2547	A462	950sh Sheet of 4, #a-d	5.75 5.75

Souvenir Sheet
Perf. 14¼
2548	A462	2700sh multi	4.25 4.25

Aeropex 2009, Beijing. No. 2547 contains four 42x28mm stamps.

Youths at Play — A462a 2548A

Designs: 400sh, Girls playing Mdako game. No. 2548B, 600sh, Girls playing tennis. 700sh, Youths dancing. 1000sh, Boy on swing.

No. 2548E, 600sh: g, Boys playing Bao game. h, Boys playing basketball. i, Girls playing handball. j, Boys playing baseball. k, Boys running. l, Girls skipping rope.
No. 2548F, 600sh, Boys playing soccer.

2009, Dec. 30   Perf. 14
2548A-2548D	A462a	Set of 4	4.00 4.00
2548E	A462a	600sh Sheet of 6, #g-l	5.50 5.50

Souvenir Sheet
2548F	A462a	600sh multi	.90 .90

Miniature Sheet

Chinese Zodiac Animals — A463

No. 2549: a, Tiger. b, Ox. c, Rat. d, Horse. e, Rabbit. f, Dragon. g, Snake. h, Pig. i, Dog. j, Cock. k, Monkey. l, Goat.

2010, Jan. 4   Litho.   Perf. 12¼
2549	A463	300sh Sheet of 12, #a-l	5.50 5.50

Souvenir Sheet

New Year 2010 (Year of the Tiger) — A464

No. 2550 — Tiger facing: a, Right. b, Left.

2010, Jan. 4   Perf. 12
2550	A464	2700sh Sheet of 2, #a-b	8.25 8.25

Miniature Sheets

Election of Pres. John F. Kennedy, 50th Anniv. — A465

No. 2551, 1400sh — Pres. Kennedy (brown red panels) with: a, Pres. Dwight D. Eisenhower. b, Wife, Jacqueline, and children. c, Wife and crowd. d, Crowd.

No. 2552, 1400sh — Pres. Kennedy (violet blue panels): a, Shaking woman's hand. b, Leaving Air Force One with wife. c, With wife. d, Looking into space capsule.

2010, June 4   Perf. 11½
Sheets of 4, #a-d
2551-2552	A465	Set of 2	15.50 15.50

Antverpia 2010 National and European Championship of Philately, Antwerp, Belgium (#2551).

Souvenir Sheet

Boy Scouts of America, Cent. — A466

No. 2553: a, Emblem of Charles L. Sommers National High Adventure Base, Scouts in canoe. b, Emblem of Northern Tier-Bissett National High Adventure Base, Scout skiing. c, Wmblem of Northern Tier-Rogert's Atikokan National High Adventure Base, Scout fishing.

2010, July 15   Perf. 13¼
2553	A466	1900sh Sheet of 3, #a-c	7.50 7.50

Miniature Sheets

A467

Princess Diana (1961-97) — A468

No. 2554 — Diana wearing: a, Pink hat with brim with red edge. b, White gown and tiara, looking left. c, Hat with flower. d, Tiara, pink dress and necklace.

No. 2555 — Diana wearing: a, Black and white hat and dress. b, Pink hat. c, White gown and tiara, looking right. d, Tiara, red dress, touching face.

2010, Oct. 14   Perf. 13¼x13
2554	A467	1400sh Sheet of 4, #a-d	7.50 7.50
2555	A468	1400sh Sheet of 4, #a-d	7.50 7.50

Miniature Sheets

Characters From Star Trek Television Shows — A469

No. 2556, 1400sh — Characters from Star Trek Voyager: a, Capt. Kathryn Janeway. b, Tuvok. c, B'Elanna Torres. d, Chakotay.

No. 2557, 1400sh, vert. — Characters from Star Trek Deep Space Nine: a, Kira Nerys. b, Capt. Benjamin Sisko. c, Quark. d, Jadzia Dax.

2010, Oct. 14   Perf. 11½x12, 12x11½
Sheets of 4, #a-d
2556-2557 A469 Set of 2   15.00 15.00

A470

National Aeronautics and Space Administration, 50th Anniv. — A471

No. 2558: a, Earth, nose of Space Shuttle. b, Mars, fuselage of Space Shuttle. c, Jupiter. d, Neptune, astronaut.
No. 2559: a, Launch of Apollo 11, July 16, 1969. b, Launch of Space Shuttle Atlantis, May 14, 2010.

2010, Oct. 14
2558 A470 1400sh Sheet of 4, #a-d   7.50 7.50
Souvenir Sheet
Perf. 13¼x13
2559 A471 1400sh Sheet of 2, #a-b   3.75 3.75

Reign of Pope Benedict XVI, 5th Anniv. A472

Pope Benedict XVI: No. 2560, 1400sh, Holding censer. No. 2561, 1400sh, And St. Peter's Basilica.

2010, Dec. 23   Perf. 12
2560-2561 A472 Set of 2   3.75 3.75
Nos. 2560-2561 each were printed in sheets of 4.

Miniature Sheets

A473

Hu Jintao, President of People's Republic of China — A474

No. 2562 — Pres. Hu and: a, Chinese characters at left, English name in white, pale yellow area above first "0" in denomination. b, Chinese characters at right, English name in white, country name and denomination over pink area. c, Chinese characters at right, English name in black, denomination over pale yellow area. d, As "c," denomination over pink area. e, As "a," without pale yellow area above first "0" in denomination. f, As "b," hyphen at right over pale yellow area.
No. 2563 — Pres. Hu: a, Waving. b, Wearing red tie, with black door and knocker in background. c, Wearing blue tie, red and black background. d, Wearing red striped tie, gray background.

2010, Dec. 23
2562 A473 900sh Sheet of 6, #a-f   7.25 7.25
2563 A474 1100sh Sheet of 4, #a-d   6.00 6.00
Beijing 2010 Intl. Philatelic Exhibition.

Miniature Sheets

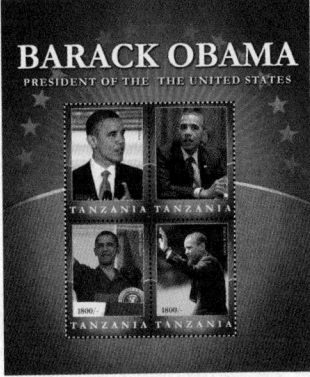
Pres. Barack Obama — A475

No. 2564, 1800sh — Pres. Obama (red and blue frames): a, With finger pointed up. b, Sitting, with arms on desk. c, Behind lectern, with arm raised. d, Waving.
No. 2565, 1800sh — Pres. Obama (purple panels at bottom): a, Writing. b, Standing, with shirt sleeves rolled up. c, Standing, wearing suit and red tie. d, Saluting.

2010, Dec. 23   Litho.
Sheets of 4, #a-d
2564-2565 A475 Set of 2   19.50 19.50

Start of Chimpanzee Research at Gombe by Jane Goodall, 50th Anniv. — A476

No. 2566, 2500sh: a, Black-and-white photograph of Goodall with chimpanzee. b, Goodall writing. c, Chimpanzees embracing.
No. 2567, 2500sh: a, Goodall shoveling dirt. b, Local people embracing. c, Goodall holding chimpanzee.
No. 2568, 4000sh, Goodall following chimpanzee in forest. No. 2569, 4000sh, Goodall holding camera, looking at chimpanzee. No. 2570, 4000sh, Goodall extending hand to three chimpanzees. No. 2571, 4000sh, Goodall in forest. No. 2572, 4000sh, Chimpanzee looking at ant-covered stick. No. 2573, 4000sh, Goodall holding binoculars, vert. No. 2574, 4000sh, Two chimpanzees, vert.

2010, Dec. 23   Perf. 12
Sheets of 3, #a-c
2566-2567 A476 Set of 2   20.50 20.50
Souvenir Sheets
2568-2574 A476 Set of 7   38.00 38.00

Souvenir Sheet

New Year 2011 (Year of the Rabbit) — A477

No. 2575: a, Rabbit standing on hind legs, word "Rabbit" hyphenated. b, Rabbit on all four legs, word "Rabbit" not hyphenated.

2010, Dec. 23
2575 A477 2250sh Sheet of 2, #a-b   6.25 6.25

Pan African Postal Union, 30th Anniv. A478

Emblem and: 400sh, Electronic money transfer. 500sh, Integrating physical mail into the digital world. 700sh, Track and trace of postal items.
600sh, Post office internet café service.

2010, Jan. 18   Perf. 14½
2576-2578 A478 Set of 3   2.40 2.40
Souvenir Sheet
2579 A478 600sh multi   .90 .90

Wild Animals — A479

Designs: 400sh, Chimpanzees. 500sh, Lion and lioness, horiz. No. 2582, 600sh, Grant's red colobus monkeys, horiz. 700sh, Elephants. 800sh, Gnus, horiz. 1000sh, Waterbuck. 1800sh, Elephant looking for foliage. 2000sh, Zebras, horiz. 2500sh, Hunting dogs, horiz. 3000sh, Buffalo, horiz. 5000sh, Zebras and gazelles grazing, horiz.
No. 2591, 600sh, horiz.: a, Kirk's red colobus monkey. b, Lioness guarding her cubs. c, Udzungwa monkey. d, Female kongoni and juvenile. e, Female hippopotamus with juvenile. f, Leopard with cub.
No. 2592, 600sh, Male giraffe, horiz.

2010, Oct. 28   Perf. 14
2580-2590 A479 Set of 11   25.00 25.00
2591 A479 600sh Sheet of 6, #a-f   5.00 5.00
Souvenir Sheet
2592 A479 600sh multi   .80 .80

School of St. Jude, Arusha A480

Designs: No. 2593, 400sh, Teacher and three students. No. 2594, 400sh, Four students. 600sh, Students in cafeteria, three students with food bowls. 700sh, One student. 800sh, Students on bus.

2010, Oct. 28   Perf. 13x13¼
2593-2597 A480 Set of 5   4.00 4.00
2597a   Souvenir sheet of 4, #2594-2597   3.50 3.50

Wonders of Zanzibar A481

Designs: 400sh, Giant tortoise, Prison Island. 600sh, Red colobus monkey, Jozani Forest, vert. 700sh, Pemba flying fox. 800sh, Slave chambers, Manga Pwani.
No. 2602, 600sh: a, Ruins of Friday Mosque, Tumbatu Island. b, Beit el Mtoni. c, Anglican Cathedral. d, Beit el Jaib. e, Maruhubi Palace ruins. f, Old Fort.
No. 2603, 600sh, Chumbe Island Lighthouse, vert.

Perf. 14, 13¾x13½ (#2602)
2011, Feb. 22
2598-2601 A481 Set of 4   3.25 3.25
2602 A481 600sh Sheet of 6, #a-f   4.75 4.75
Souvenir Sheet
2603 A481 600sh multi   .80 .80
No. 2602 contains six 35x25mm stamps. No. 2603 contains one 40x60mm stamp.

Whales — A482

No. 2604: a, Orca (Killer whale). b, Sperm whale. c, Beluga whale. d, Humpback whale. e, Gray whale. f, Right whale. 3800sh, Blue whale.

2011, Mar. 31   Perf. 13 Syncopated
2604 A482 1250sh Sheet of 6,
#a-f, + la-
bel   10.00 10.00
Souvenir Sheet
Perf. 12
2605 A482 3800sh multi   5.00 5.00

Grasshoppers and Crickets — A483

Designs: No. 2606, 500sh, Truxalis species.
No. 2607, 700sh, Common milkweed locust.
No. 2608, 800sh, Common stick grasshopper.
No. 2609, 900sh, Red locust.
No. 2610, 700sh: a, Migratory locust. b,
Foam locust. c, Green milkweed locust. d, Edi-
ble grasshopper. e, Male cricket. f, Green
bush cricket.
600sh, Elegant grasshopper.

2011, Apr. 15   Perf. 14
2606-2609 A483   Set of 4   4.00 4.00
2610 A483 700sh Sheet of 6, #a-
f   5.75 5.75
Souvenir Sheet
2611 A483 600sh multi   .80   .80

Beatification of Pope John Paul
II — A484

No. 2612 — Pope John Paul II: a, With children, country name at bottom. b, Greeting
crowd, country name at bottom. c, As "b,"
country name at top. d, As "a," country name
at top.
4000sh, Pope John Paul II, vert.

2011, May 16   Perf. 13 Syncopated
2612 A484 1800sh Sheet of 4,
#a-d   9.25 9.25
Souvenir Sheet
Perf. 12½
2613 A484 4000sh multi   5.25 5.25
No. 2613 contains one 38x51mm stamp.

Tourist
Attractions
A485

Designs: 500sh, Kibo Peak, Mt. Kilimanjaro.
700sh, Pemba Floating Island. 800sh, Giraffes
in Serengeti National Park. 900sh, Lions in
Serengeti National Park.

Serpentine Die Cut 14
2011, May 16   Litho.
Booklet Stamps
Self-Adhesive
2614 A485 500sh multi   .65   .65
  a.   Booklet pane of 8   5.25
2615 A485 700sh multi   .90   .90
  a.   Booklet pane of 8   7.25
2616 A485 800sh multi   1.00 1.00
  a.   Booklet pane of 8   8.00
2617 A485 900sh multi   1.25 1.25
  a.   Booklet pane of 8   10.00
     Nos. 2614-2617 (4)   3.80 3.80

Traditional
Grain
Storage
A486

Designs: No. 2618, 500sh, People and grain
storage baskets. No. 2619, 700sh, Pole hanging grain storage. No. 2620, 800sh, Tree hanging grain storage. No. 2621, 900sh, Outdoor
granary.
No. 2622: a, Covered granary on platform.
b, Outdoor granaries, thatched roof. c, Corn
(maize) granary. d, Granary container. e, Outdoor granary next to building. f, Indoor
granary.
600sh, Outdoor grain storage (building on
stilts).

2011, Aug. 25   Litho.   Perf. 14
2618-2621 A486   Set of 4   3.75 3.75
2622 A486 700sh Sheet of 6, 3a-
f   5.25 5.25
Souvenir Sheet
2623 A486 600sh multi   .75   .75

Flowers — A487

No. 2624: a, African foxglove. b, Bird of paradise. c, Water hyacinth. d, Torch lily.
3800sh, Fan aloe.

2011, Sept. 7   Perf. 12
2624 A487 1500sh Sheet of 5,
#2624a-
2624c, 2
#2624d   9.25 9.25
Souvenir Sheet
Perf. 13¼
2625 A487 3800sh multi   4.75 4.75
No. 2625 contains one 44x44mm stamp.

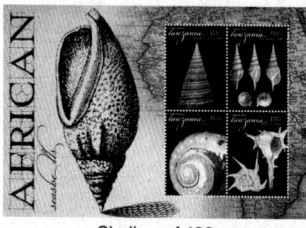

Shells — A488

No. 2626: a, Telescopium telescopium. b,
Tibia insulaechorab. c, Turbo sarmaticus. d,
Bolinus cornutus.
3800sh, Oxymeris maculata, horiz.

2011, Sept. 7   Perf. 13¼x13
2626 A488 1700sh Sheet of 4,
#a-d   8.50 8.50
Souvenir Sheet
Perf. 13¼
2627 A488 3800sh multi   4.75 4.75
No. 2627 contains one 50x30mm stamp.

Sept. 11, 2001 Terrorist Attacks, 10th
Anniv. — A489

No. 2628: a, American flag on Pentagon. b,
Tribute in Light. c, World Trade Center.
4000sh, World Trade Center, diff.

2011, Sept. 11   Perf. 13 Syncopated
2628 A489 2000sh Sheet of 3,
#a-c   7.50 7.50
Souvenir Sheet
2629 A489 4000sh multi   5.00 5.00

Activities of
World
Vision
A490

Inscriptions: 500sh, A child drawing safe
and clean water. 800sh, Food security is one
of our focus. 900sh, Children enjoy good
health. 1000sh, Advocating for child's rights.

2011, Sept. 30   Perf. 14x13¼
2630-2633 A490   Set of 4   3.75 3.75

Animals of Serengeti National
Park — A491

No. 2634: a, Lion eating antelope. b, One
hunting dog, horiz. c, Two hunting dogs, horiz.
d, Two cheetahs.
1000sh, Zebras and gnus, horiz.

Perf. 13¼x13, 13x13¼x14x13
(#2634b, 2634c)
2011, Nov. 15
2634 A491 800sh Sheet of 4,
#a-d   4.00 4.00
Souvenir Sheet
Perf. 13½x13
2635 A491 1000sh multi   1.25 1.25
No. 2635 contains one 45x35mm stamp.

Birds — A492

No. 2636, 1700sh: a, Senegal parrot. b, African gray parrot. c, Lilac-breasted roller. d,
Southern masked weaver.
No. 2637, 1700sh: a, Pied crow. b, Ground
woodpecker. c, Greater honeyguide. d, Bird
with stripe above eye (misidentified as ground
woodpecker).
No. 2638, 3800sh, Black-collared barbet.
No. 2639, 3800sh, White-headed mousebird.

2011, Nov. 20   Perf. 13 Syncopated
Sheets of 4, #a-d
2636-2637 A492   Set of 2   16.50 16.50
Souvenir Sheets
2638-2639 A492   Set of 2   9.25 9.25

Butterflies and Moths — A493

No. 2640, 1700sh: a, Fig eater butterfly. b,
Green-veined emperor. c, Scarce forest
emperor. d, Western blue charaxes.
No. 2641, 1700sh: a, Madagascar sunset
moth. b, Angola white lady. c, Congo kuba
cloth. d, Eggfly.
No. 2642, 3800sh, Mother of pearl. No.
2643, 3800sh, Monarch.

2011, Nov. 20   Perf. 12
Sheets of 4, #a-d
2640-2641 A493   Set of 2   16.50 16.50
Souvenir Sheets
Perf. 12½
2642-2643 A493   Set of 2   9.25 9.25
Nos. 2642-2643 each contain one
51x38mm stamp.

Independence, 50th Anniv. — A494

No. 2644 — Tanzania flag and: a, Crowd
celebrating complete independence. b, Stu-
dents in Adult Education program. c, Presi-
dents Julius K. Nyerere of Tanzania, Kenneth
Kaunda of Zambia, Samora Machel of
Mozambique. d, Pres. Nyerere and Edward
Moringe Sokoine, 1982. e, Presidents Nyerere
and Machel.
Tanzanian flag and: No. 2645, Pres. Nyer-
ere and South African Pres. Nelson Mandela.
No. 2646, Tanzania Pres. Jakaya Kikwete
meeting with U. S. Pres. Barack Obama.
No. 2647, vert. — Tanzanian flag and: a,
Pres. Nyerere, sepia-toned photograph. b,
Pres. Al Haj Hassan Mwinyi. c, Pres. Mzee
Benjamin William Mkapa. d, Pres. Kikwete. e,
Vice-President Mzee Abeid Aman Karume. f,
Prime Minister Mzee Rashid Mfaume
Kawama. g, Prime Minister Edward Moringe
Sokoine. h, Pres. Nyerere, color photograph.
No. 2648 — Tanzanian flag and: a, State
House. b, Parliament of Tanzania, Dodoma. c,
University of Dodoma. d, University of Dar es
Salaam.
No. 2649 — Tanzanian flag and: a, 800sh,
Pres. Nyerere and Cuban Pres. Fidel Castro.
b, 800sh, Pres. Nyerere and Ghana Pres.
Kwame Nkrumah. c, 900sh, Pres. Kikwete and
Pres. Hu Jintao of People's Republic of China.
No. 2650, 900sh — Tanzanian flag and: a,
Like #2645. b, Presidents Kikwete, Mwinyi and
Mkapa.

2011, Dec. 9   Perf. 13x13¼
2644   Horiz. strip of 5   3.25 3.25
  a.-e.   A494 500sh Any single .65   .65
2645 A494 800sh multi   1.00 1.00
2646 A494 900sh multi   1.25 1.25
  a.   Perf. 14x13¼x13x13¼
        (#2649)   1.25 1.25
  b.   Perf. 13x13¼x14x13¼
        (#2650)   1.25 1.25
     Nos. 2644-2646 (3)   2.90 2.90
Perf. 13¼x13
2647 A494 700sh Sheet of 8,
#a-h   7.25 7.25

Souvenir Sheets
Perf. 13x13¼

2648	A494	700sh Sheet of 4, #a-d	3.50	3.50
2649	A494	Sheet of 4, #2646a, 2649a- 2649c	4.50	4.50
d.		As "c," perf. 13x13¼x14x13¼ (#2650)	1.25	1.25

Perf. 13x13¼x14x13¼

2650	A494	900sh Sheet of 4, #2646d, 2649d, 2650a, 2650b	5.00	5.00
		Nos. 2647-2650 (4)	20.25	20.25

Material
Culture
A495

Designs: No. 2651, 500sh, Beer pot with three mouths, cow-shaped water container. No. 2652, 700sh, Fiddle with calabash resonator. No. 2653, 800sh, Maasai beaded necklaces. No. 2654, 900sh, Container with lid, corn storage basket. No. 2655, 1000sh, Bamboo milk mugs, decorated calabash.

No. 2656, 800sh: a, Bao game. b, Grain storage. c, Cooking and storage pots. d, Drum on platform, wedding drums. e, Winnowing trays, drinking mug, storage basket. f, Fruit storage, dish cover.

2012, Mar. 15   **Perf. 14x13½**

2651-2655	A495	Set of 5	5.00	5.00
2655a		Souvenir sheet of 1 #2655	1.25	1.25

Miniature Sheet

2656	A495	800sh Sheet of 6, #a-f	6.25	6.25

Miniature Sheet

2012 Summer Olympics, London — A496

No. 2657: a, Basketball. b, Boxing. c, 3000-meter steeplechase. d, 5000-meter race.

2012, June 27   **Perf. 14**

2657	A496	1300sh Sheet of 4, #a-d	6.50	6.50

Miniature Sheet

Muhammad Ali, Boxer — A497

No. 2658 — Ali: a, Showing fist. b, Dodging opponent's punch. c, In profile. d, Training with punching bag.

2012, Sept. 10   **Perf. 12½**

2658	A497	2000sh Sheet of 4, #a-d	10.50	10.50

Miniature Sheet

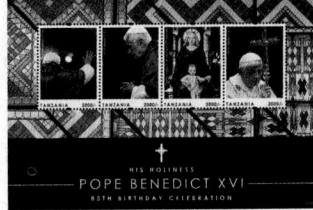

Pope Benedict XVI, 85th Birthday — A498

No. 2659: a, Pope Benedict XVI waving. b, Pope Benedict XVI praying. c, Madonna and Child stained-glass window, Vatican City Museum. d, Pope Benedict XVI with cross.

2012, Nov. 28   **Perf. 13 Syncopated**

2659	A498	2000sh Sheet of 4, #a-d	10.00	10.00

Zanzibar
Attractions
A499

Designs: 500sh, New House of Representatives Building. 700sh, Four doors. No. 2662, 800sh, Ngalawa sailing off Jambian Coast, vert. 900sh, Huts.

No. 2664, 800sh: a, Zanzibar Pres. Ali Mohammed Shein harvesting cloves. b, Shein and First Vice-president Maalim Seif Sharif Hamad and others touring Zanzibar. c, Shein greeting students. d, Shein harvesting rice in paddy. e, Shein, Hamad and Second Vice-president Seif Ali Iddi. f, Shein and First Lady Mwanamwema Shein assisting in the separation of clove buds.

1000sh, Darajani Market.

Perf. 14x13¼, 13¼x14

2012, Apr. 26   **Litho.**

2660-2663	A499	Set of 4	3.75	3.75
2664	A499	800sh Sheet of 6, #a-f	6.25	6.25

Souvenir Sheet

2665	A499	1000sh multi	1.25	1.25

A500

Birds — A501

No. 2666, 1000sh: a, Superb starling. b, Buffalo weaver. c, Quelea quelea. d, Bubalornis albirostris.

No. 2667, 1000sh: a, Malachite kingfisher. b, Gray-headed kingfisher. c, Woodland kingfisher. d, Pied kingfisher.

No. 2668, 1000sh: a, Verreaux's eagle owl. b, Augur buzzard. c, Red-tailed buzzard. d, Bateleur eagle. e, Adult Verreaux's eagle. f, Chanting goshawk. g, Immature Verreaux's eagle. h, Terathopius ecaudatus.

No. 2669, 800sh, Secretary bird. No. 2670, 800sh, Superb starling, horiz.

2012, July 10   **Litho.**   **Perf. 14**

Sheets of 4, #a-d

2666-2667	A500	Set of 2	10.50	10.50
2668	A500	1000sh Sheet of 8, #a-h	10.50	10.50

Souvenir Sheets

2669-2670	A501	Set of 2	2.00	2.00

Miniature Sheets

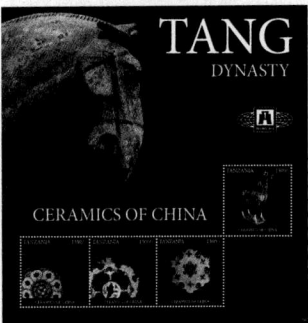

Tang Dynasty Ceramics — A502

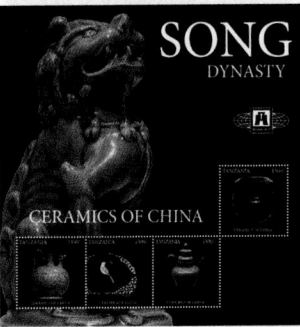

Song Dynasty Ceramics — A503

Ming Dynasty Ceramics — A504

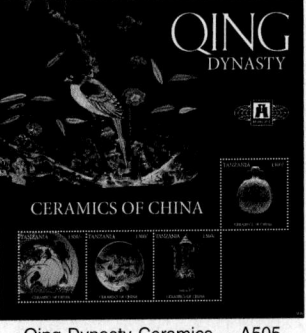

Qing Dynasty Ceramics — A505

No. 2671: a, Plate with lotus flowers. b, Plate with bird. c, Hexagonal plate with upturned edges. d, Horse.

No. 2672: a, Pitcher with green glaze. b, Plate with bird, diff. c, Pitcher with gray glaze. d, Bowl.

No. 2673: a, Plate depicting building and people. b, Lidded bowl. c, Buddha. d, Plate with birds and flowers.

No. 2674: a, Plate with birds and flowers, diff. b, Plate with building and man on rock. c, Pitcher, diff. d, Round container.

2012, Oct. 10   **Litho.**   **Perf. 13¾**

2671	A502	1300sh Sheet of 4, #a-d	6.50	6.50
2672	A503	1300sh Sheet of 4, #a-d	6.50	6.50
2673	A504	1300sh Sheet of 4, #a-d	6.50	6.50
2674	A505	1300sh Sheet of 4, #a-d	6.50	6.50
		Nos. 2671-2674 (4)	26.00	26.00

2013 Beijing Intl. Stamp Exhibtion.

Dragon — A506

Snake — A507

Snake
A508

2012, Oct. 10   **Litho.**   **Perf. 13¼x13**

2675	A506	350sh multi	.45	.45
2676	A507	350sh multi	.45	.45

Perf. 12

2677	A508	2000sh multi	2.50	2.50
		Nos. 2675-2677 (3)	3.40	3.40

New Year 2013 (Year of the Snake). No. 2677 was printed in sheets of 4.

Chinese
Character
With Fish,
Flowers and
Butterfly
A509

Chinese
Character
With Reindeer
A510

Chinese
Character
With Cranes
A511

Chinese
Character
With Birds
and Flowers
A512

500/-
TANZANIA

Snake
A513

500/-
TANZANIA

2012, Oct. 10   Litho.   Perf. 13¼
2678   Sheet of 20, #2678a-
2678d, 16 #2678e   13.00 13.00
  a. A509 500sh multi   .65
  b. A510 500sh multi   .65
  c. A511 500sh multi   .65
  d. A512 500sh multi   .65
  e. A513 500sh multi   .65
  New Year 2013 (Year of the Snake).

Miniature Sheet

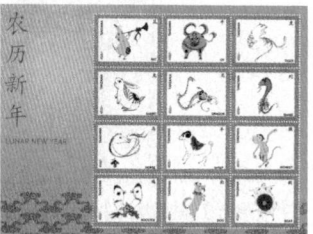

Chinese Zodiac Animals — A514

No. 2679: a, Rat. b, Ox. c, Tiger. d, Rabbit.
e, Dragon. f, Snake. g, Horse. h, Sheep. i,
Monkey. j, Rooster. k, Dog. l, Boar.

2012, Oct. 10   Litho.   Perf. 14
2679 A514 450sh Sheet of 12,
    #a-l   6.75 6.75

Pres. Abraham Lincoln (1809-
65) — A515

No. 2680: a, Lincoln without beard. b, Presidential campaign poster of 1860 depicting Lincoln and Hannibal Hamlin. c, "In Defense of
the Union and the Constitution" poster. d, Lincoln with beard.
  5500sh, Lincoln with beard, diff.

2012, Nov. 28   Litho.   Perf. 12
2680 A515 1700sh Sheet of 4,
    #a-d   8.50 8.50

Souvenir Sheet
Perf.
2681 A515 5500sh multi   7.00 7.00
  No. 2681 contains one 43x33mm elliptical
stamp.

Election of Pope Francis — A517

No. 2682: a, Pope Francis wearing miter,
carrying crucifix. b, Pope Francis holding rail in
Popemobile. c, Pope Francis with flag and St.
Peter's Basilica in background. d, Crowd in St.
Peter's Square.

2013, July 7   Litho.   Perf. 14
2682 A516   2000sh Sheet of
    4, #a-d   10.00 10.00

**Litho., Margin Embossed With Foil
Application**
Souvenir Sheet
Imperf
2683 A517 13,000sh multi   16.50 16.50

Miniature Sheet

A518

Paintings of Flowers — A519

No. 2684: a, Roses, building, dragonfly, bird
and nest. b, Begonias and butterfly at UL. c,
Red flowers with long green leaves, mountain
in background. d, White lilies. e, Passion flowers. f, Small pink flowers, mountains in background. g, Water lily, mosque in background.
h, Hydrangea and butterfly at UR.
No. 2685: a, Hyacinths. b, Carnations. c,
Four primrose plants, mountains in background. d, Tulips. e, Strelitzia. f, Two primrose
plants. g, Lotuses. h, Pitcher plants and bird.

2013, July 7   Litho.   Perf. 12¾
2684 A518 1200sh Sheet of 8,
    #a-h   12.00 12.00
2685 A519 1200sh Sheet of 8,
    #a-h   12.00 12.00

Insects — A520

No. 2686: a, African bush grasshopper. b,
Devil's flower mantis. c, African moon moth. d,
Common pond damsel.
  5500sh, Giant African fruit beetle.

Perf. 13 Syncopated
2013, July 7   Litho.
2686 A520 2000sh Sheet of 4,
    #a-d   10.00 10.00

Souvenir Sheet
2687 A520 5500sh multi   7.00 7.00

African Animals — A521

No. 2688: a, Zebra. b, Rhinoceros. c, Hippopotami. d, African elephants.
  5500sh, Giraffes.

2013, July 7   Litho.   Perf. 12
2688 A521 2000sh Sheet of 4,
    #a-d   10.00 10.00

Souvenir Sheet
2689 A521 5500sh multi   7.00 7.00
  No. 2689 contains one 30x50mm stamp.

Miniature Sheets

A522

Cats — A523

No. 2690: a, Gray tabby cat with gray green
eyes looking up. b, Sleeping cat. c, Cat with
brown eyes. d, Gray cat with gray green eyes
looking down.
No. 2691: a, Cat in grass. b, Gray tabby
sleeping. c, Brown tabby sleeping, black background. d, Two cats.

2013, Aug. 26   Litho.   Perf. 13¾
2690 A522 2000sh Sheet of 4,
    #a-d   10.00 10.00
2691 A523 2000sh Sheet of 4,
    #a-d   10.00 10.00

Paintings by Dong Qichang (1555-
1636) — A524

No. 2692: a, Valley with trees from *Eight
Views of Autumn Moods* (leaf one). b, Trees
and mountains from *Eight Views of Autumn
Moods* (leaf four). c, Trees and body of water
from *Eight Views of Autumn Moods* (leaf five).
d, *Landscapes in the Manner of Old Masters.*
  5500sh, *Wanluan Thatched Hall* (incorrectly
inscribed *Eight Views of Autumn Moods.*),
vert.

2013, Aug. 26   Litho.   Perf. 13¾
2692 A524 2000sh Sheet of 4,
    #a-d   10.00 10.00

Souvenir Sheet
Perf. 12½
2693 A524 5500sh multi   7.00 7.00
  China International Collection Expo 2013,
Beijing. No. 2693 contains one 38x51mm
stamp.

Fruit — A525

No. 2694: a, Watermelon. b, Calabashes. c,
Passion fruit. d, Horned melons. e, Figs. f,
Safous.
  5500sh, Fig, safou, horned melon, passion
fruit, calabash, watermelon, horiz.

2013, Aug. 26   Litho.   Perf. 13¾
2694 A525 1500sh Sheet of 6,
    #a-f   11.50 11.50

Souvenir Sheet
Perf. 12
2695 A525 5500sh multi   7.00 7.00
  No. 2695 contains one 80x30mm stamp.

Birth of Prince George of
Cambridge — A526

No. 2696: a, Queen Elizabeth II holding
Prince Charles. b, Princess Diana holding
Prince William. c, Duchess of Cambridge holding Prince George. d, Duke and Duchess of
Cambridge, Prince George.
  8000sh, Prince George in arms of Duchess
of Cambridge.

2013, Sept. 17   Litho.   Perf. 12½
2696 A526 2000sh Sheet of 4,
    #a-d   10.00 10.00

Souvenir Sheet
Perf.
2697 A526 8000sh multi   10.00 10.00
  No. 2697 contains one 38mm diameter
stamp.

A527

Neslon Mandela (1918-2013),
President of South Africa — A528

No. 2698 — Mandela: a, Wearing black and
gray shirt. b, Wearing suit and tie, with arm
raised. c, Wearing blue shirt with circular
designs. d, In crowd, wearing blue shirt with
circular designs. e, Wearing sports jersey, with
arm raised. f, Holding dove.
No. 2699 — Mandela: a, Wearing blue shirt
with circular designs, with arm raised. b,
Wearing black and white shirt, with arm raised.
c, Wearing green and black shirt. d, Wearing
suit, vest and tie, fist clenched. e, Wearing suit
and tie. f, Wearing jacket with Olympic rings.
No. 2700, 5500sh, Sepia-toned photograph
of Mandela as young man, vert. No. 2701,
5500sh, Color photograph of Mandela wearing
blue and white shirt, vert.

2013, Dec. 15		**Litho.**		**Perf. 13¾**
2698	A527	1550sh	Sheet of 6,	
			#a-f	12.00 12.00
2699	A528	1550sh	Sheet of 6,	
			#a-f	12.00 12.00

Souvenir Sheets
Perf. 12½

2700-2701	A528	Set of 2	14.00 14.00

Nos. 2700-2701 each contain one
38x51mm stamp.

Miniature Sheet

Mao Zedong (1893-1976), Chinese
Communist Leader — A531

Various photographs dated: a, 1949. b,
1952. c, 1954. d, 1959. e, 1961. f, 1965.

2013, Sept. 10		**Litho.**		**Perf. 14**
2712	A531	350sh	Sheet of 6, #a-f	2.60 2.60

Reptiles — A534

No. 2725: a, Two-horned chameleon. b,
Strange-nosed chameleon. c, Jackson's chameleon. d, Lined day gecko.
5500sh, Satanic leaf-tailed gecko.

2013, Dec. 31		**Litho.**		**Perf. 12**
2725	A534	2000sh	Sheet of 4, #a-d	10.00 10.00

Souvenir Sheet
Perf. 12¾

2726	A534	5500sh multi	7.00 7.00

No. 2726 contains one 51x38mm stamp.

Sunbirds — A535

No. 2727: a, Fraser's sunbird. b, Anchieta's
sunbird. c, Collared sunbird. d, Olive sunbird.
5500sh, Nile Valley sunbird, horiz.

2013, Dec. 31		**Litho.**		**Perf. 14**
2727	A535	2000sh	Sheet of 4, #a-d	10.00 10.00

Souvenir Sheet
Perf. 12¾

2728	A535	5500sh multi	7.00 7.00

No. 2728 contains one 51x38mm stamp.

Dogs — A536

No. 2729, 2000sh: a, Scotch collie. b, Standard schnauzer. c, Sloughi. d, Saluki.
No. 2730, 2000sh: a, Taigan. b, Pyrenean
mastiff. c, Thai ridgeback. d, Wirehaired pointing griffon.
No. 2731, 5500sh, Thai ridgeback, horiz.
No. 2732, 5500sh, Siberian husky, horiz.

Perf. 14, 12 (#2730)

2013, Dec. 31			**Litho.**

Sheets of 4, #a-d

2729-2730	A536	Set of 2	20.00 20.00

Souvenir Sheets
Perf. 12¾

2731-2732	A536	Set of 2	14.00 14.00

Nos. 2731-2732 each contain one
51x38mm stamp.

Orchids — A538

No. 2739, 2000sh: a, Anacamptis fein-
bruniae. b, Ophrys holosericea. c, Orchis
boryi. d, Anacamptis caspia.
No. 2740, 2000sh: a, Bulbophyllum guttu-
latum. b, Orchis punctulata. c, Phaius wallichii.
d, Vanilla phalaenopsis.
No. 2741, 6000sh, Dactylorhiza dinglensis.
No. 2742, 6000sh, Orchis purpurea.

2014, Mar. 10		**Litho.**		**Perf. 12x12½**

Sheets of 4, #a-d

2739-2740	A538	Set of 2	20.00 20.00

Souvenir Sheets

2741-2742	A538	Set of 2	15.00 15.00

SEMI-POSTAL STAMPS

Natl.
Solidarity
Walk — SP1

1988, July 1		**Litho.**		**Perf. 14½**
B1	SP1	2sh +1sh	Flag, crowd	.70 .70
B2	SP1	3sh +1sh	Map, Pres. Mwinyi	.70 .70

Souvenir Sheet

B3	SP1	50sh +1sh Flag, Pres. Mwinyi	1.75 1.75

Surtax for Chama Cha Mapinduzi party
activities.

Natl.
Solidarity
Walk — SP2

1989, July 1		**Litho.**		**Perf. 14½**
B4	SP2	5sh +1sh	Party flag	.45 .45
B5	SP2	10sh +1sh	Pres. Mwinyi, walk	.45 .45

Souvenir Sheet

B6	SP2	50sh +1sh Pres. Mwinyi	1.40 1.40

Natl.
Solidarity
Walk
SP3

Designs: 4sh + 1sh, Pres. Mwinyi marching
with crowd. 9sh + 1sh, Crowd around party
flag. 13sh + 1sh, Pres. Mwinyi. 30sh + 1sh,
Pres. Mwinyi planting tree. No. B11, Pres.
Mwinyi sorting cloves. No. B12, Handshake
across map, vert.

1991-92		**Litho.**		**Perf. 13½**
B7	SP3	4sh +1sh multi ('92)		.75 .75
B8	SP3	9sh +1sh multicolored		1.00 1.00
B9	SP3	13sh +1sh multicolored		1.00 1.00
B10	SP3	30sh +1sh multi ('92)		1.75 1.75
		Nos. B7-B10 (4)		4.50 4.50

Souvenir Sheets
Perf. 12½

B11	SP3	50sh +1sh multicolored	3.00 3.00
B12	SP3	50sh +1sh multicolored	2.40 2.40

Issued: Nos. B8-B9, 7/6/90. Nos. B7, B10,
7/5/91.

POSTAGE DUE STAMPS

D1

Perf. 13¾x14

1978, July 31		**Litho.**		**Unwmk.**
J1	D1	5c red		.75 1.00
J2	D1	10c green		.75 1.00
J3	D1	20c dark blue		.75 1.00
J4	D1	30c reddish brown		.75 1.00
J5	D1	40c bright rose lilac		.75 1.00
J6	D1	1sh orange		1.25 2.25
		Nos. J1-J6 (6)		5.00 7.25

1967, Jan. 3				**Perf. 14x13½**
J1a	D1	5c red		.35 3.00
J2a	D1	10c green		.35 3.00
J3a	D1	20c dark blue		.55 5.25
J4a	D1	30c reddish brown		.90 7.50
J5a	D1	40c bright rose lilac		1.25 10.50
J6a	D1	1sh orange		3.25 22.50
		Nos. J1a-J6a (6)		6.65 51.75

1969-71				**Perf. 14x15**
J1b	D1	5c red		.70 3.00
J2b	D1	10c green		.70 3.00
J3b	D1	20c dark blue		1.50 5.25
J4b	D1	30c reddish brown		2.10 7.50
J5b	D1	40c bright rose lilac		2.75 10.50
J6b	D1	1sh orange ('71)		7.25 22.50
		Nos. J1b-J6b (6)		15.00 51.75

1973, Dec. 12				**Perf. 15**
J1c	D1	5c red		.40 3.25
J2c	D1	10c green		.40 3.25
J3c	D1	20c dark blue		.60 6.25
J4c	D1	30c reddish brown		.90 9.50
J5c	D1	40c bright rose lilac		1.25 13.00
J6c	D1	1sh orange		3.00 32.50
		Nos. J1c-J6c (6)		6.55 67.75

1984?				**Perf. 14¾x14**
J1d	D1	5c red brown		— —
J2d	D1	10c green		— —
J4d	D1	30c reddish brown		— —

Additional stamps of this type with this perforation have been reported. The editors
would like to examine any examples.

D2

1990		**Litho.**		**Perf. 15x14**
J7	D2	50c dark green		.35 .35
J8	D2	80c bright blue		.35 .35
J9	D2	1sh orange brown		.35 .35
J10	D2	2sh light olive green		.35 .35
J11	D2	3sh purple		.35 .35
J12	D2	5sh gray		.35 .35
J13	D2	10sh brown		.35 .35
J14	D2	20sh bister		.35 .35
		Nos. J7-J14 (8)		2.80 2.80

OFFICIAL STAMPS

**Nos. 5-9, 11, 13 and 16 Overprinted:
"OFFICIAL"**
Perf. 14x14½, 14½x14

1965, Dec. 9		**Photo.**	**Unwmk.**

Size: 21x17½mm, 17½x21mm

O1	A2	5c orange & ultra	.25 .25
O2	A2	10c multicolored	.25 .25
O3	A3	15c grn bl, brn & buff	.25 .25
O4	A2	20c blue & brown	.25 .25
O5	A3	30c black & red brn	.25 .25
O6	A2	50c yellow grn & blk	.25 .25

Perf. 14½
Size: 41½x25mm

O7	A2	1sh multicolored	.30 .25
O8	A2	5sh bl, brt grn & red brn	1.50 1.00
		Nos. O1-O8 (8)	3.30 2.75

Overprint size: 17mm on 5c, 10c, 20c, 50c.
14mm on 15c, 30c. 29x3½mm on 1sh, 5sh.
The overprint was also applied in 1967 in
Dar es Salaam to 50c, 1sh and 5sh. Size:
29x3mm.

Nos. 19-23, 25, 27
and 30 Overprinted

Fish in Natural Colors
Size: 21x17½mm
Overprint Litho., 17mm Wide

1967, Dec. 9		**Photo.**	**Perf. 14x14½**
O9	A4	5c black & citron	.50 1.25
O10	A4	10c brown & olive	.50 .60
O11	A4	15c brown & blue	.50 .40
O12	A4	20c brown & dk blue grn	.50 .40
O13	A4	30c black & yel grn	.50 .40
O14	A4	50c black & dull bl grn	.50 1.00

Perf. 14½
Size: 41x25mm
Overprint 29mm Wide

O15	A4	1sh brown & multi	1.00 2.00
O16	A4	5sh black & blue grn	4.00 8.00
		Nos. O9-O16 (8)	8.00 14.05

Overprint Typo., 17½mm Wide

1970-73			
O9a	A4	5c black & citron	.55 .55
O10a	A4	10c brown & olive	.55 .55
O12a	A4	20c brn & dk bl grn	.55 .55

O13a A4 30c blk & yel grn .80 .55
O13B A4 40c multicolored ('73)
Nos. O9a-O13a (4) 2.45 2.20

The overprint was also applied in 1973 to 15c, 50c, 1sh (28mm wide), and 5sh.

Nos. 35-36, 38, 40-41, 43-47 Overprinted

a    b

1973, Dec. 10 Photo. Perf. 14½x14
O17 A5(a) 5c multicolored 1.10 4.00
O18 A5(a) 10c multicolored 1.40 .70
O19 A5(a) 20c multicolored 1.50 .70
O20 A5(a) 40c multicolored 2.25 .70
O21 A5(a) 50c multicolored 2.25 .70
O22 A5(a) 70c multicolored 2.25 .70

Perf. 14½
O23 A6(b) 1sh multicolored 3.25 .80
O24 A6(b) 1.50sh multicolored 3.75 4.00
O25 A6(b) 2.50sh multicolored 5.50 6.00
O26 A6(b) 5sh multicolored 7.50 10.00
Nos. O17-O26 (10) 30.75 28.30

A larger overprint (17½mm wide instead of 14½mm) was applied locally to 10c, 20c, 40c, and 50c.
Provisional use of some values for regular postage is known.

Nos. 161-171 Overprinted

1980, Oct. 1 Perf. 14
O27 A21 10c multicolored .70 .70
O28 A21 20c multicolored .70 .70
O29 A21 50c multicolored .70 .70
O30 A21 50c multicolored .70 .70
O31 A21 75c multicolored .70 .70
O32 A21 80c multicolored .70 .70

Perf. 14½
O33 A21 1sh multicolored .70 .70
O33A A21 1.50sh multicolored
O34 A21 2sh multicolored 1.40 1.40
O35 A21 3sh multicolored 1.90 1.90
O36 A21 5sh multicolored 3.25 3.25
Nos. O27-O33,O34-O36 (10) 11.45 11.45

Overprint measures 13mm on Nos. O33-O36; reads up or down.

Nos. 606-614 Inscribed "OFFICIAL"
1990-91 Litho. Perf. 14
O37 A99 5sh multi .60 .60
O38 A99 9sh multi .60 .60
O39 A99 13sh multi .60 .60
O40 A99 15sh multi .60 .60
O41 A99 20sh multi .90 .90
O42 A99 25sh multi 1.00 1.00
O42A A99 30sh multi ('91) 1.40 1.40
O43 A99 40sh multi 1.75 1.75
O44 A99 70sh multi 3.00 3.00
O45 A99 100sh multi 4.50 4.50
Nos. O37-O45 (10) 14.95 14.95

Inscription on Nos. O37-O42A is 15½mm long. Insription on Nos. O43-O45 is 19mm long.

Nos. 1565, 1566, 1568, 1570, 1571, and 1572 Overprinted

1997 (?) Litho. Perf. 14½x15
O47 A262 100sh multi — —
O48 A262 140sh multi — —
O49 A262 200sh multi — —
O50 A262 260sh multi — —
O51 A262 300sh multi — —
O52 A262 380sh multi — —

The editors suspect there are additional stamps in this set, and would like to examine any examples.

TETE

'tāt-ə

LOCATION — In southeastern Africa between Nyasaland and Southern Rhodesia
GOVT. — A district of the Portuguese East Africa Colony
AREA — 46,600 sq. mi. (approx.)
POP. — 367,000 (approx.)
CAPITAL — Tete

This district was formerly a part of Zambezia. Stamps of Mozambique replaced those of Tete. See Mozambique.

100 Centavos = 1 Escudo

Vasco da Gama Issue of Various Portuguese Colonies Surcharged

1913 Unwmk. Perf. 12½, 16
On Stamps of Macao
1 CD20 ¼c on ½a bl grn 5.00 5.00
2 CD21 ½c on 1a red 2.00 2.10
3 CD22 1c on 2a red vio 2.00 2.10
4 CD23 2½c on 4a yel grn 2.00 2.10
5 CD24 5c on 8a dk blue 2.00 2.10
6 CD25 7½c on 12a vio brn 2.40 3.00
7 CD26 10c on 16a bis brn 2.00 2.10
8 CD27 15c on 24a bister 2.00 2.10
Nos. 1-8 (8) 19.40 20.60

On Stamps of Portuguese Africa
9 CD20 ¼c on 2½r bl grn 2.00 2.10
10 CD21 ½c on 5r red 2.00 2.10
11 CD22 1c on 10r red vio 2.00 2.10
12 CD23 2½c on 25r yel grn 2.00 2.10
13 CD24 5c on 50r dk blue 2.00 2.10
14 CD25 7½c on 75r vio brn 2.40 3.00
15 CD26 10c on 100r bis brn 2.00 2.10
16 CD27 15c on 150r bister 2.00 2.10
Nos. 9-16 (8) 16.40 17.70

On Stamps of Timor
17 CD20 ¼c on ½a bl grn 2.00 2.10
18 CD21 ½c on 1a red 2.00 2.10
19 CD22 1c on 2a red vio 2.00 2.10
a. Inverted overprint 30.00 30.00
20 CD23 2½c on 4a yel grn 2.00 2.10
21 CD24 5c on 8a dk blue 2.00 2.10
22 CD25 7½c on 12a vio brn 2.40 3.00
23 CD26 10c on 16a bis brn 2.00 2.10
24 CD27 15c on 24a bister 2.00 2.10
Nos. 17-24 (8) 16.40 17.70
Nos. 1-24 (24) 52.20 56.00

Common Design Types pictured following the introduction.

Ceres — A1

1914 Typo. Perf. 15x14
Name and Value in Black
25 A1 ¼c olive brn 1.40 2.25
26 A1 ½c black 1.40 2.25
27 A1 1c blue grn 1.40 2.25
28 A1 1½c lilac brn 1.40 2.25
29 A1 2c carmine 1.40 2.25
30 A1 2½c light vio 1.40 2.25
31 A1 5c deep blue 1.40 2.25
32 A1 7½c yel brn 3.00 3.25
33 A1 8c slate 3.00 3.25
34 A1 10c org brn 3.00 4.00
35 A1 15c plum 5.00 4.50
36 A1 20c yel green 5.00 4.50
37 A1 30c brn, *green* 5.00 4.50
38 A1 40c brn, *pink* 8.00 7.00
39 A1 50c org, *salmon* 10.00 9.00
40 A1 1e grn, *blue* 12.00 10.00
Nos. 25-40 (16) 63.80 65.75

THAILAND

'tī-,land

(Siam)

LOCATION — Western part of the Malay peninsula in southeastern Asia
GOVT. — Republic
AREA — 198,250 sq. mi.
POP. — 60,609,046 (1999 est.)
CAPITAL — Bangkok

32 Solot = 16 Atts = 8 Sio =
4 Sik = 2 Fuang = 1 Salung
4 Salungs = 1 Tical
100 Satangs (1909) = 1 Tical
= 1 Baht (1912)

Catalogue values for unused stamps in this country are for Never Hinged items, beginning with Scott 264 in the regular post-age section, Scott B34 in the semi-postal section, Scott C20 in the airpost section, and Scott O1 in the official section.

Watermarks

Wmk. 176 — Chakra

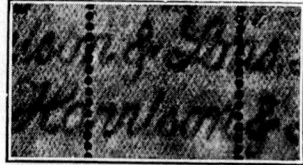

Wmk. 233 — Harrison & Sons, London in Script Letters

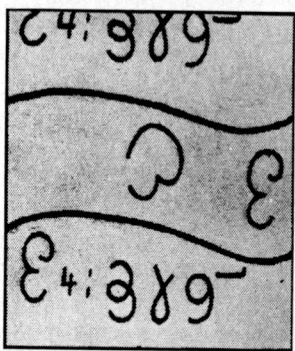

Wmk. 299 — Thai Characters and Wavy Lines

Wmk. 329 — Zigzag Lines

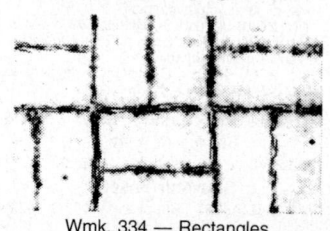

Wmk. 334 — Rectangles

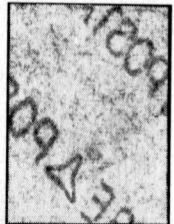

Wmk. 340 — Alternating Interlaced Wavy Lines

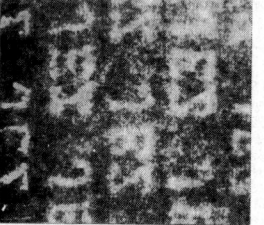

Wmk. 356 — POSTAGE

Wmk. 368 — JEZ Multiple

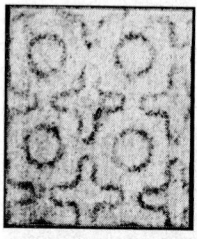

Wmk. 371 — Wavy Lines

Wmk. 374 — Circles and Crosses

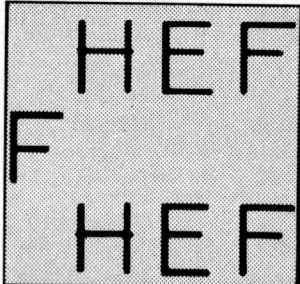

Wmk. 375 — Letters

Wmk. 377 — Interlocking Circles

Wmk. 385 — CARTOR

Wmk. 387 — Squares and Rectangles

King Chulalongkorn
A1   A2

A4

Perf. 14½, 15

			Unwmk.	Engr.
1883, Aug. 4				
1	A1	1sol blue	14.00	14.00
b.	Imperf., pair			4,500.
2	A1	1att carmine	16.00	16.00
3	A1	1sio vermilion	24.00	24.00
4	A2	1sik yellow	15.00	19.00
5	A4	1sa orange	62.50	62.50
a.	1sa ocher		70.00	70.00
	Nos. 1-5 (5)		131.50	135.50

There are three types of No. 1, differing mainly in the background of the small oval at the top.

A 1 fuang red, of similar design to the foregoing, was prepared but not placed in use. Value, $1,500.

For surcharges see Nos. 6-8, 19.

No. 1 Handstamp Surcharged in Red

a   b

c

1 Tical   **1 Tical**
d   *e*

1885, July 1

6	A1	(a)	1t on 1sol blue	475.	475.
7	A1	(b)	1t on 1sol blue	375.	375.
c.	"1" inverted			1,100.	1,100.
8	A1	(c)	1t on 1sol blue	500.	500.

Surcharges of Nos. 6-8 have been counterfeited.

Types "d" and "e" are typeset *official reprints.*

As is usual with handstamps, double impressions, etc., exist.

King
Chulalongkorn — A7

1887-91 Typo. Wmk. 176 Perf. 14

11	A7	1a green ('91)	6.50	2.00
12	A7	2a green & car	6.50	2.00
13	A7	3a grn & blue	12.00	4.00
14	A7	4a grn & org brn	12.00	4.75
15	A7	8a green & yel	12.00	7.00
16	A7	12a lilac & car	17.50	3.50
17	A7	24a lilac & blue	24.00	4.00
18	A7	64a lil & org brn	87.50	29.00
	Nos. 11-18 (8)		178.00	56.25

The design of No. 11 has been redrawn and differs in many minor details from Nos. 12-18.
Issue dates: Nos. 12-18, Apr. 1; No. 11, Feb.

For surcharges see Nos. 20-69, 109, 111, 126.

No. 3 Handstamp Surcharged

1889, Aug. Unwmk. Perf. 15

19	A1	1a on 1sio	19.00	19.00

Three different handstamps were used. Doubles, etc. exist.

Nos. 12 and 13 Handstamp Surcharged

1889-90 Wmk. 176 Perf. 14

20	A7	1a on 2a	4.00	3.00
a.	"1" omitted		275.00	275.00
c.	1st Siamese character invtd.			
d.	First Siamese character omitted		300.00	300.00
21	A7	1a on 3a ('90)	9.00	9.00
a.	Inverted "1"		150.00	150.00

For surcharge see No. 29.

22	A7	1a on 2a grn & car	475.00	475.00

24	A7	1a on 2a grn & car	225.00	225.00

25	A7	1a on 2a grn & car	1,000.	1,000.

26	A7	1a on 3a grn & bl	

Some authorities consider No. 26 a forgery. Doubles, etc., exist in this issue.
Issue dates: Nov. 1889. Sept. 1890.

No. 13 Handstamp Surcharged

1891

27	A7	2a on 3a grn & bl	65.00	65.00

28	A7	2a on 3a grn & bl	55.00	55.00
a.	Double surcharge		250.00	250.00
b.	"2" omitted		250.00	

No. 21 with Additional 2 Att Surcharge

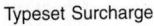

29	A7	2a on 1a on 3a grn & bl	1,500.	1,500.

On No. 29 the 2a surcharge consists of Siamese numeral like No. 27 and English numeral like No. 28.

Most examples of No. 29 show attempts to remove the "1" of the first surcharge.

Typeset Surcharge

30	A7	2a on 3a grn & bl	45.00	45.00

There are 7 types of this surcharge in the setting.
Issued: #27-28, Jan.; #29, Feb.; #30, Mar.

No. 17 Handstamp Surcharged

f   g

1892, Oct.

33	A7	(f) 4a on 24a lil & bl	50.00	50.00
34	A7	(g) 4a on 24a lil & bl	35.00	35.00

Surcharges exist double on Nos. 33-34 and inverted on No. 33.

Nos. 33-34 Handstamp Surcharged in English

1892, Nov.

35	A7	4a on 24a lil & bl	9.00	9.00
c.	Inverted "s"		45.00	45.00

36	A7	4a on 24a lil & bl	14.00	10.00
a.	Inverted "s"		40.00	40.00

37	A7	4a on 24a lil & bl	12.50	12.50

38	A7	4a on 24a lil & bl	15.00	15.00

Numerous inverts., doubles, etc., exist. Nos. 35 and 37 are surcharged examples of No. 33. Nos. 36 and 38 are surcharged examples of No. 34. The "4 atts" surcharge is small on Nos. 35 and 36, and large on Nos. 37 and 38.

Nos. 18 and 17 Typeset Srchd. in English (Shown) and Siamese

1894

39	A7	1a on 64a lil & org brn	3.50	3.50
a.	Inverted "s"		45.00	45.00
b.	Inverted surcharge		900.00	900.00
d.	Italic "s"		60.00	60.00
e.	Italic "1"		60.00	60.00

40	A7	1a on 64a lil & org brn	2.00	2.00
a.	Inverted capital "S" added to the surcharge		200.00	200.00

h   j

k   l

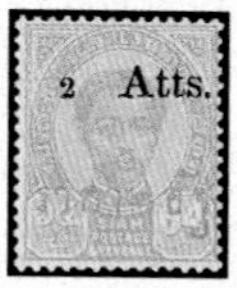

m

2 Atts.
i

41	A7 (h) 2a on 64a	26.00	26.00
a.	Inverted "s"	*42.50*	*42.50*
b.	Double surcharge	*100.00*	*100.00*
42	A7 (i) 2a on 64a	*3,000.*	*3,000.*
43	A7 (j) 2a on 64a	62.50	62.50
44	A7 (k) 2a on 64a	37.50	37.50
45	A7 (l) 2a on 64a	57.50	57.50
46	A7 (m) 2a on 64a	3.00	3.00
a.	"Att.s"	*45.00*	*45.00*

Nos. 41-46 were in one plate of 120 subjects. The quantities were: h, 38; i, 1; j, 8; k, 18; l, 11 and m, 44.

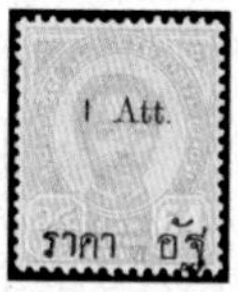

1894, Oct. 12

47	A7 1a on 64a	3.00	3.00
a.	Surcharged on face and back	*150.00*	
b.	As "a," surcharge on back inverted	*200.00*	
c.	Double surcharge	*475.00*	
d.	Inverted surcharge	*500.00*	
e.	Siamese surcharge omitted	*400.00*	

See No. 67.

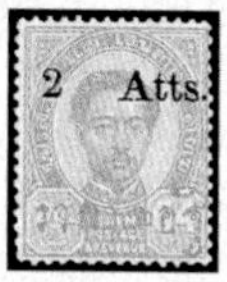

48	A7 2a on 64a	3.00	3.00
a.	"Att"	*35.00*	*35.00*
b.	Inverted surcharge	*300.00*	*300.00*
c.	Surch. on face and back	*400.00*	*400.00*
d.	Surcharge on back inverted	*400.00*	*400.00*
e.	Double surcharge	*300.00*	*300.00*
f.	Double surch., one inverted	*1,100.*	*1,100.*
g.	Inverted "s"	*42.50*	*42.50*

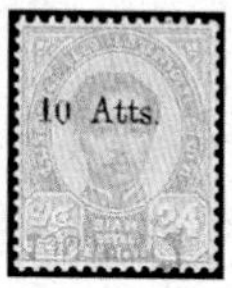

1895, July 23

49	A7 10a on 24a lil & bl	7.00	2.00
a.	Inverted "s"	*45.00*	*45.00*
b.	Surch. on face and back	*175.00*	*175.00*
c.	Surcharge on back inverted	*175.00*	*175.00*

No. 16 Surcharged in English (Shown) and Siamese

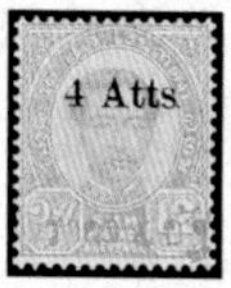

1896

50	A7 4a on 12a lil & car	15.00	8.00
a.	Inverted "s"	*50.00*	*50.00*
b.	Surcharged on face and back	*175.00*	*175.00*
c.	Double surcharge on back	*175.00*	*175.00*

Two types of surcharge.

Nos. 16-18 Surcharged in English (Shown) and Siamese Antique Surcharges

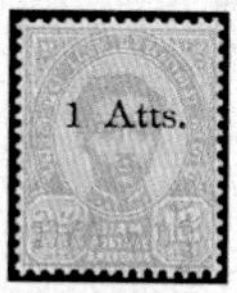

a

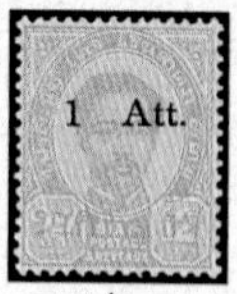

b

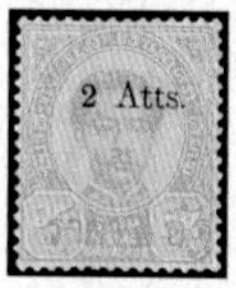

c

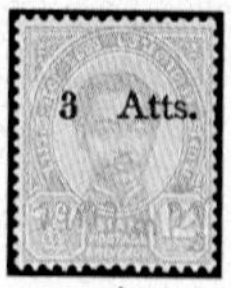

d

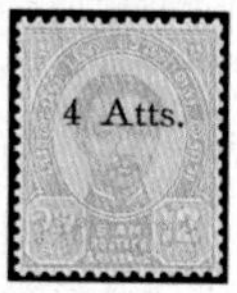

e

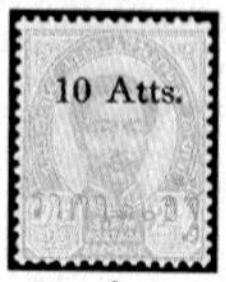

f

Atts.

Antique Letters

Atts.

Roman Letters

1898-99

51	A7 (a) 1a on 12a	360.00	360.00
52	A7 (b) 1a on 12a	18.00	7.00
53	A7 (c) 2a on 64a ('99)	30.00	9.00
54	A7 (d) 3a on 12a	12.00	4.00
a.	Double surcharge	*350.00*	*350.00*
55	A7 (e) 4a on 12a	12.00	5.00
a.	Double surcharge	*350.00*	*350.00*
56	A7 (e) 4a on 24a ('99)	40.00	14.00
57	A7 (f) 10a on 24a ('99)	825.00	825.00
	Nos. 51-57 (7)	1,297.	1,224.

Roman Surcharges

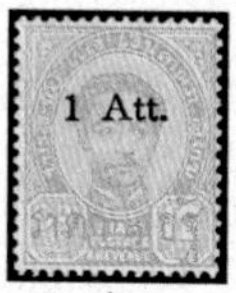

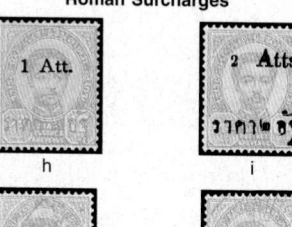

h

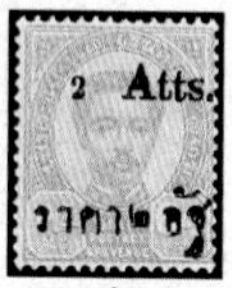

i

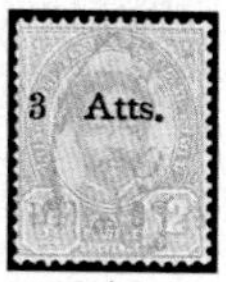

j

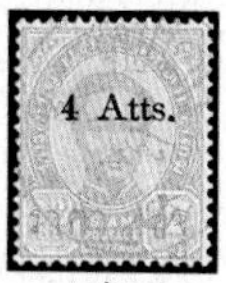

k

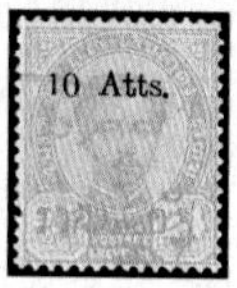

l

1 Atts.
g

58	A7 (g) 1a on 12a	450.00	450.00
59	A7 (h) 1a on 12a	45.00	20.00
60	A7 (i) 2a on 64a ('99)	35.00	10.00
61	A7 (j) 3a on 12a	85.00	19.00
62	A7 (k) 4a on 12a	40.00	14.00
a.	Double surcharge	*175.00*	*175.00*
b.	No period after "Atts."	*35.00*	*35.00*
63	A7 (k) 4a on 24a ('99)	60.00	29.00
64	A7 (l) 10a on 24a ('99)	750.00	750.00
	Nos. 58-64 (7)	1,465.	1,292.

In making the settings to surcharge Nos. 51 to 64 two fonts were mixed.

Antique and Roman letters are frequently found on the same stamp. Such stamps sell for more.

Issue dates: Nos. 54-55, 61-62, Feb. 22. Nos. 51-52, 58-59, June 4. Nos. 56-57, 63-64, Oct. 3.

Nos. 16 and 18 Surcharged in English (Shown) and Siamese Surcharged

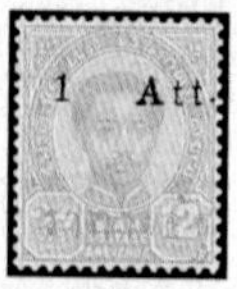

m

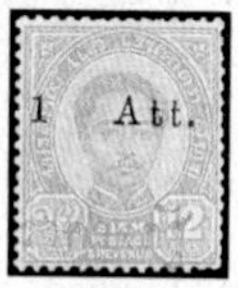

n

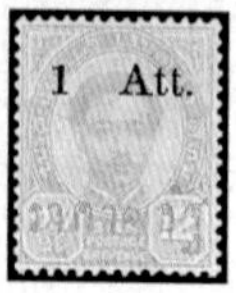

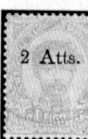

o

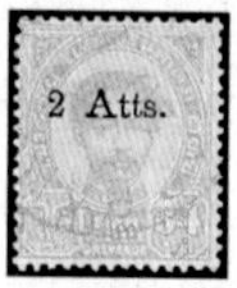

p

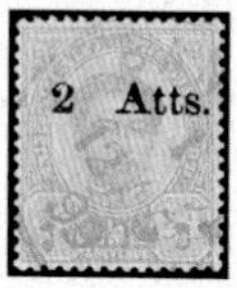

r

1894-99

65	A7 (m) 1a on 12a	20.00	6.00
66	A7 (n) 1a on 12a	20.00	6.00
a.	Inverted "1"	*150.00*	*150.00*
b.	Inverted 1st "t"	*150.00*	*150.00*
67	A7 (o) 1a on 64a	5.00	5.00
68	A7 (p) 2a on 64a	24.00	8.00
a.	"1 Atts."	*500.00*	*500.00*
69	A7 (r) 2a on 64a	24.00	8.00
	Nos. 65-69 (5)	93.00	33.00

Issued: No. 67, 10/12/94; others, 2/14/99.
See No. 47.

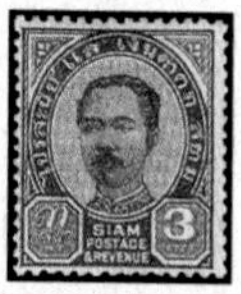

A13

1899, Oct. Typo. Unwmk.

70	A13 1a dull green	200.	85.
71	A13 2a dl grn & rose	350.	85.
72	A13 3a car & blue	600.	125.
73	A13 4a black & grn	2,200.	325.
74	A13 10a car & grn	2,500.	500.
	Nos. 70-74 (5)	5,850.	1,120.

The King rejected Nos. 70-74 in 1897, but some were released by mistake to three post offices in Oct. 1899. Used values are for stamps canceled to order at Korat in Dec. 1899. Values for postally used stamps are listed in the Scott Classic Specialized catalog.

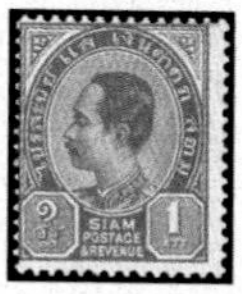

A14

1899-1904

75	A14 1a gray green	2.00	1.00
76	A14 2a yellow green	2.25	1.25
77	A14 2a scarlet & bl	4.00	2.00
78	A14 3a red & blue	7.00	2.00
79	A14 3a green	20.00	12.00
80	A14 4a dark rose	4.00	1.50
81	A14 4a vio brn & rose	8.00	2.00
82	A14 6a dk rose	35.00	14.00
83	A14 8a dk grn & org	9.00	2.00
84	A14 10a ultra	9.00	3.00
85	A14 12a brn vio & rose	40.00	2.00
86	A14 14a ultra	23.00	18.00
87	A14 24a brn vio & bl	375.00	29.00
88	A14 28a vio brn & bl	25.00	25.00
89	A14 64a brn vio & org brn	70.00	11.00
	Nos. 75-89 (15)	633.25	125.75

Two types of 1a differ in size and shape of Thai "1" are in drawing of spandrel ornaments.

Issue dates: 6a, 14a, 28a, Nos. 77, 79, 81, Jan. 1, 1904; others, Sept. 1899.

For surcharges see Nos. 90-91, 112, 125, 127.

Nos. 78 and 85 With Typewritten Srch. of 6 or 7 Siamese Characters (1 line) in Violet

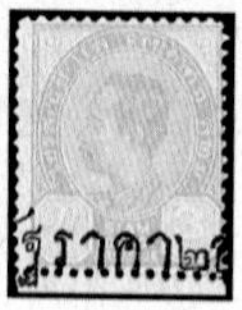

1902

78a	A14 2a on 3a	*5,000.*	*5,250.*
85a	A14 10a on 12a	*5,000.*	*5,250.*

Nos. 78a and 85a were authorized provisionals, surcharged and issued by the Battambang postmaster.

Nos. 86 and 88 Surcharged in Black

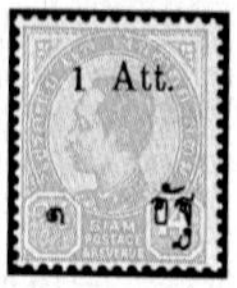

1905, Feb.

90	A14 1a on 14a	10.00	10.00
a.	No period after "Att"	*45.00*	*45.00*
b.	Double surcharge	*125.00*	*125.00*
91	A14 2a on 28a	12.00	12.00
a.	Double surcharge	*125.00*	*125.00*
b.	No period after "Att"	*45.00*	*45.00*

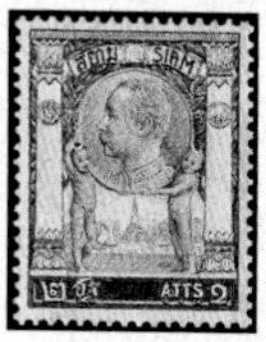

King Chulangkorn — A15

1905-08 Engr.

92	A15 1a orange & green	2.50	1.00
93	A15 2a violet & slate	3.00	1.00
94	A15 2a green ('08)	11.00	4.00
95	A15 3a green	4.00	2.00
96	A15 3a vio & sl ('08)	12.00	6.25
97	A15 4a gray & red	6.00	1.50
98	A15 4a car & rose ('08)	9.50	2.00
99	A15 5a carmine & rose	8.00	3.00
100	A15 8a blk & ol bis	8.75	1.50
101	A15 9a blue ('08)	23.50	9.00
102	A15 12a blue	18.00	4.00
103	A15 18a red brn ('08)	60.00	22.50
104	A15 24a red brown	34.00	8.00
105	A15 1t dp bl & brn org	45.00	10.00
	Nos. 92-105 (14)	245.25	75.75

Issue dates: Dec. 1905, Apr. 1, 1908.

For surcharges and overprints see Nos. 110, 113-117, 128-138, 161-162, B15, B21.

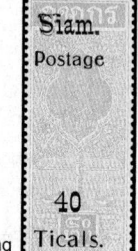

King Chulalongkorn — A16

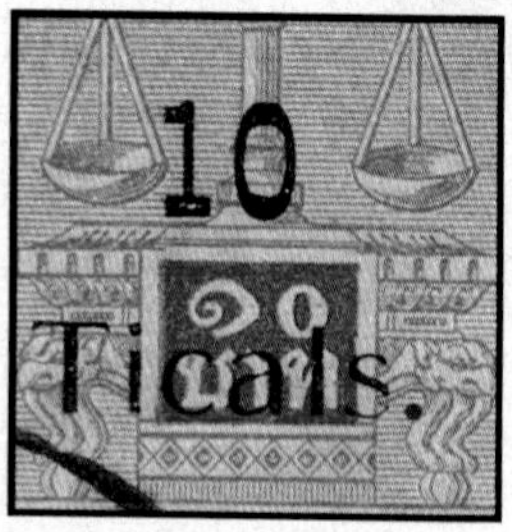

No. 106

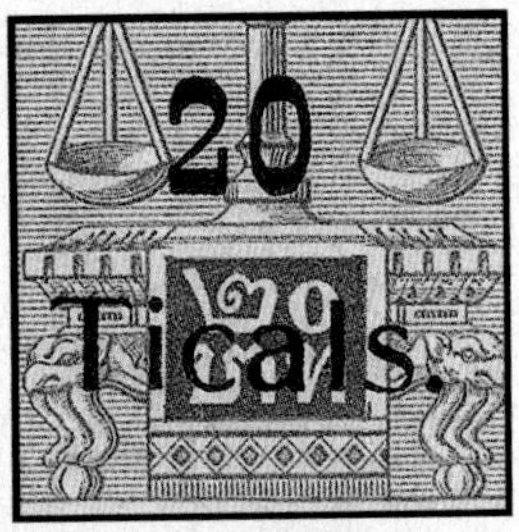

No. 107

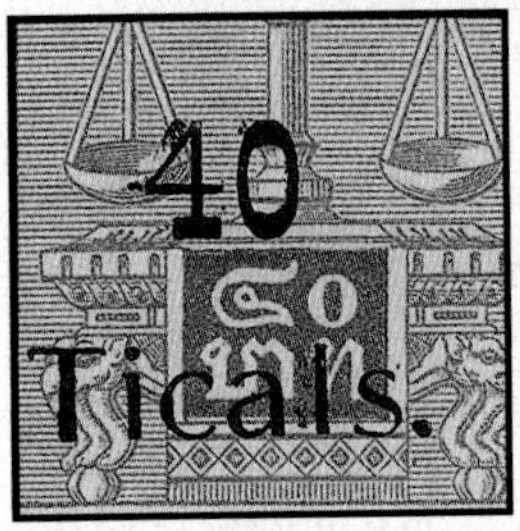

No. 108

1907, Apr. 24 **Black Surcharge**

106	A16	10t gray green	600.00	100.00
107	A16	20t gray green	4,750.	350.00
108	A16	40t gray green	3,400.	475.00
		Nos. 106-108 (3)	*8,750.*	*925.00*

Counterfeits of Nos. 106-108 exist. In the genuine, the surcharged figures correspond to the Siamese value inscriptions on the basic revenue stamps.

No. 17 Surcharged

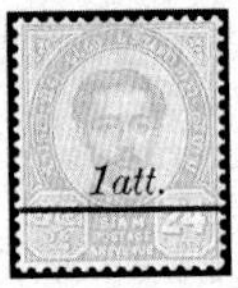

1907, Dec. 16

109	A7	1a on 24a lil & bl	4.50	1.50
a.		Double surcharge	400.00	

No. 99 Surcharged

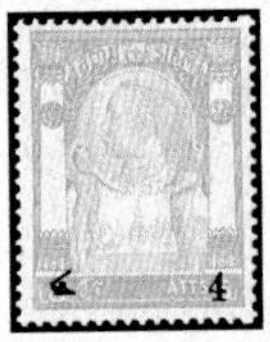

1908, Sept.

110	A15	4a on 5a car & rose	11.00	4.00

The No. 110 surcharge is found in two spacings of the numerals: normally 15mm apart, and a narrow, scarcer spacing of 13½mm.

Nos. 17 and 84 Surcharged in Black

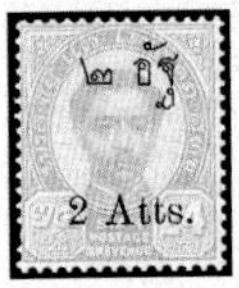

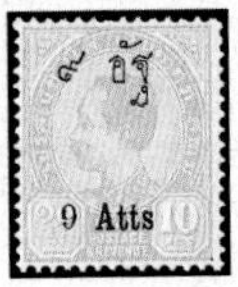

111	A7	2a on 24a lil & bl	4.50	1.20
a.		Inverted surcharge	*325.00*	*325.00*
112	A14	9a on 10a ultra	13.50	5.00
a.		Inverted surcharge	*325.00*	*325.00*

Jubilee Issue

Nos. 92, 95, 110, 100 and 103 Overprinted in Black or Red

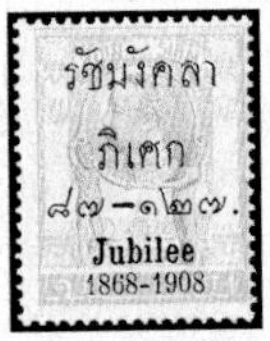

1908, Nov. 11

113	A15	1a	3.25	1.60
a.		Siamese date "137" instead of "127"	*950.00*	*950.00*
b.		Pair, one without ovpt.		
114	A15	3a	5.50	3.25
115	A15	4a on 5a	5.50	3.25
a.		Horiz. pair, imperf. btwn.	*500.00*	
116	A15	8a (R)	21.00	21.00
117	A15	18a	32.50	24.00
		Nos. 113-117 (5)	*67.75*	*53.10*

40th year of the reign of King Chulalongkorn. Nos. 113 to 117 exist with a small "i" in "Jubilee."

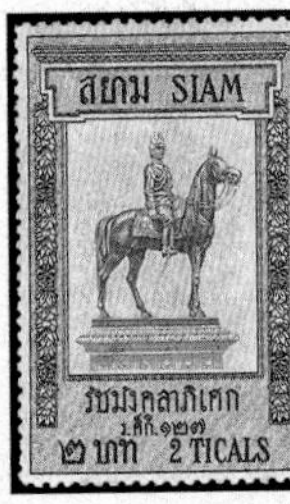

Statue of King Chulalongkorn A19

1908, Nov. 11 **Engr.** ***Perf. 13½***

118	A19	1t green & vio	52.50	8.00
119	A19	2t red vio & org	72.50	20.00
120	A19	3t pale ol & bl	105.00	16.00
121	A19	5t dl vio & dk grn	160.00	27.50
122	A19	10t bister & car	*1,250.*	87.50
123	A19	20t gray & red brn	525.00	87.50
124	A19	40t sl bl & blk brn	525.00	300.00
		Nos. 118-124 (7)	*2,690.*	*546.50*

The inscription at the foot of the stamps reads: "Coronation Commemoration-Forty-first year of the reign-1908."

Stamps of 1887-1904 Surcharged

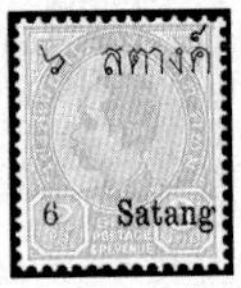

1909 ***Perf. 14***

125	A14	6s on 6a dk rose	2.50	2.00
126	A7	14s on 12a lil & car	110.00	100.00
127	A14	14s on 14a ultra	20.00	18.00
		Nos. 125-127 (3)	*132.50*	*120.00*

Nos. 92-102 Surcharged with Bar and

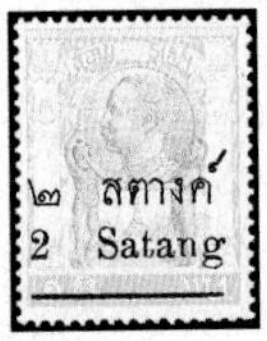

1909, Aug. 15

128	A15	2s on 1a #92	2.50	1.20
129	A15	2s on 2a #93	60.00	60.00
130	A15	2s on 2a #94	2.75	1.20
a.		"2" omitted	*85.00*	
131	A15	3s on 3a #95	12.00	7.50
132	A15	3s on 3a #96	4.50	1.00
133	A15	6s on 4a #97	64.00	64.00
134	A15	6s on 4a #98	8.00	2.00
135	A15	6s on 5a #99	12.00	8.75
136	A15	12s on 8a #100	7.00	1.40
137	A15	14s on 9a #101	11.00	3.00
138	A15	14s on 12a #102	22.50	21.00
		Nos. 128-138 (11)	206.25	171.05

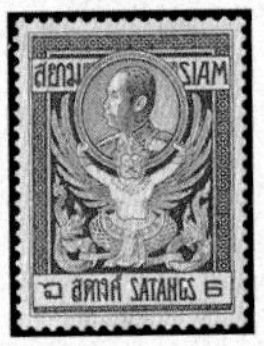

King Chulalongkorn — A20

1910 **Engr.** ***Perf. 14x14½***

139	A20	2s org & green	2.50	1.50
140	A20	3s green	2.50	1.50
141	A20	6s carmine	6.50	2.50
142	A20	12s blk & ol brn	12.00	2.50
143	A20	14s blue	20.00	2.50
144	A20	28s red brown	47.50	10.00
		Nos. 139-144 (6)	91.00	20.50

Issue dates: 12s, June 5. Others, May 5.
For surcharges see Nos. 163, 223-224.

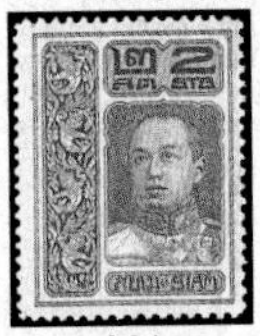

A21

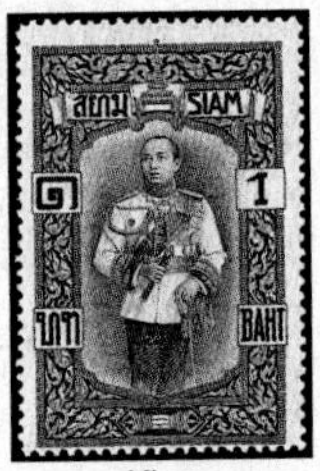

King Vajiravudh — A22

Printed at the Imperial Printing Works, Vienna

1912 ***Perf. 14½***

145	A21	2s brn org	3.25	1.20
a.		Vert. pair, imperf. btwn.	*500.00*	*500.00*
b.		Horiz. pair, imperf. btwn.	*500.00*	*500.00*
146	A21	3s yellow green	3.25	1.20
a.		Horiz. pair, imperf. btwn.	*500.00*	*500.00*
b.		Vert. pair, imperf. btwn.	*500.00*	*500.00*
147	A21	6s car rose	4.00	1.50
148	A21	12s gray blk & brn	5.50	2.00
149	A21	14s ultramarine	7.00	2.50
150	A21	28s chocolate	20.00	12.00
151	A22	1b blue & blk	30.00	2.00
a.		Vert. pair, imperf. btwn.	*1,250.*	*1,250.*
b.		Horiz. pair, imperf. btwn.	*1,250.*	*1,250.*
152	A22	2b car rose & ol brn	35.00	4.00
153	A22	3b yel grn & bl blk	40.00	6.50
154	A22	5b vio & blk	50.00	12.00
155	A22	10b ol grn & vio brn	300.00	95.00
156	A22	20b sl bl & red brn	475.00	95.00
		Nos. 145-156 (12)	973.00	234.90

See Nos. 164-175.

For surcharges and overprints see Nos. 157-160, 176-186, 206, B1-B14, B16-B20, B22, B31-B33.

Nos. 147-150 Surcharged in Red or Blue

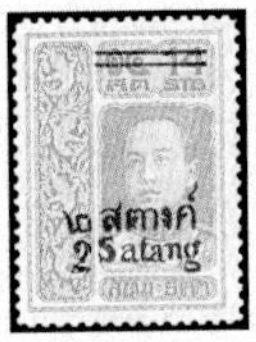

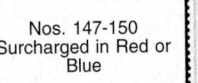

1914-15

157	A21	2s on 14s (R) ('15)	2.75	.70
a.		Vert. pair, imperf. btwn.	*900.00*	*900.00*
b.		Double surcharge	*62.50*	*40.00*
158	A21	5s on 6s (Bl)	5.00	.50
a.		Horiz. pair, imperf. btwn.	*900.00*	*900.00*
b.		Double surcharge	*67.50*	*67.50*
159	A21	10s on 12s (R)	5.00	.50
a.		Double surcharge	*67.50*	*67.50*
160	A21	15s on 28s (Bl)	8.50	2.50
		Nos. 157-160 (4)	21.25	4.20

The several settings of the surcharges on Nos. 157-160 show variations in the figures and letters.

Nos. 92-93 Surcharged

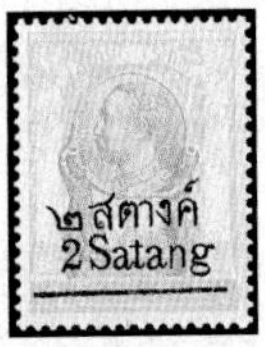

1915, Apr. 3

161	A15	2s on 1a org & grn	7.00	5.00
a.		Pair, one without surcharge	*350.00*	*350.00*
162	A15	2s on 2a vio & slate	7.00	4.50

No. 143 Surcharged in Red

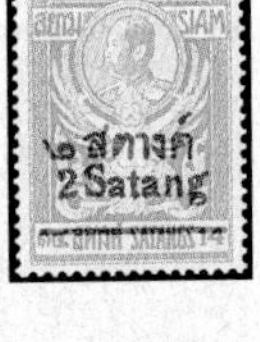

1916, Oct.

163	A20	2s on 14s blue	4.50	2.00

Types of 1912 Re-engraved

Printed by Waterlow & Sons, London

1917, Jan. 1 ***Perf. 14***

164	A21	2s orange brown	2.50	1.20
165	A21	3s emerald	2.50	2.50
166	A21	5s rose red	4.00	1.20
167	A21	10s black & olive	3.50	1.20
168	A21	15s blue	4.00	1.40
170	A22	1b bl & gray blk	25.00	4.50
171	A22	2b car rose & brn	70.00	35.00
172	A22	3b yellow grn & blk	525.00	275.00
173	A22	5b dp violet & blk	275.00	190.00
174	A22	10b ol gray & vio brn	425.00	32.50
a.		Perf. 12½	500.00	47.50
175	A22	20b sea grn & brn	600.00	70.00
a.		Perf. 12½	625.00	85.00
		Nos. 164-175 (11)	1,936.	614.50

The re-engraved design of the satang stamps varies in numerous minute details from the 1912 issue. Four lines of the background appear between the vertical strokes of the "M" of "SIAM" in the 1912 issue and only three lines in the 1917 stamps.

The 1912 stamps with value in bahts are 37½mm high; those of 1917 are 39mm. In the latter the king's features, especially the eyes and mouth, are more distinct and the uniform and decorations are more sharply defined.

The 1912 stamps have seven pearls between the earpieces of the crown. On the 1917 stamps there are nine pearls in the same place. Nos. 174 and 175 exist imperforate.

Nos. 164-173 Overprinted in Red

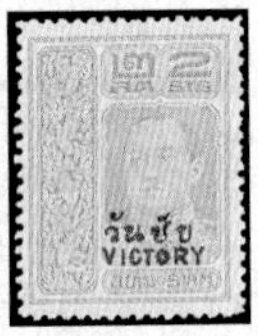

1918, Dec. 2

176	A21	2s orange brown	3.25	3.25
a.		Double overprint	110.00	110.00
177	A21	3s emerald	3.25	3.25
178	A21	5s rose red	4.50	4.50
a.		Double overprint	150.00	150.00
179	A21	10s black & olive	6.75	6.75
180	A21	15s blue	6.75	6.75
181	A22	1b bl & gray blk	27.50	24.00
182	A22	2b car rose & brn	65.00	47.50
183	A22	3b yel grn & blk	190.00	120.00
184	A22	5b dp vio & blk	400.00	325.00
		Nos. 176-184 (9)	707.00	541.00

Counterfeits of this overprint exist.

Nos. 147-148 Surcharged in Green or Red

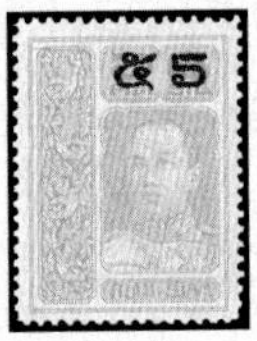

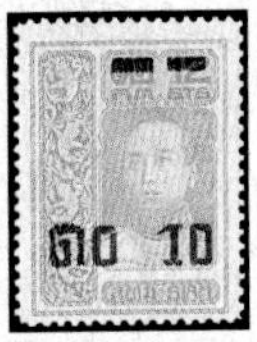

1919-20

185	A21	5s on 6s (G)	2.75	1.90
186	A21	10s on 12s (R) ('20)	6.00	1.50

Issue dates: 5s, Nov. 11. 10s, Jan. 1.

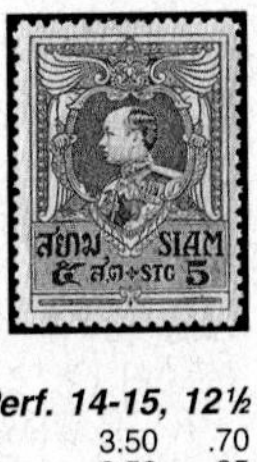

King Vajiravudh — A23

1920-26 **Engr.** ***Perf. 14-15, 12½***

187	A23	2s brn, *yel* ('21)	3.50	.70
188	A23	3s grn, *grn* ('21)	3.50	.95
189	A23	3s chocolate ('24)	3.25	.70
190	A23	5s rose, *pale rose*	4.50	.70
191	A23	5s green ('22)	34.00	6.00
192	A23	5s dk vio, *lil* ('26)	7.50	.95
193	A23	10s black & org ('21)	7.00	.70
194	A23	15s bl, *bluish* ('21)	8.50	.70
195	A23	15s carmine ('22)	44.00	6.00
196	A23	25s chocolate ('21)	24.00	2.75
197	A23	25s dk blue ('22)	32.50	1.40
198	A23	50s ocher & blk ('21)	32.50	2.00
		Nos. 187-198 (11)	201.50	22.85

For overprints see Nos. 205, B23-B30.

Throne Room — A24

1926, Mar. 5 ***Perf. 12½***

199	A24	1t gray vio & grn	16.00	3.50
200	A24	2t car & org red	35.00	6.00
201	A24	3t ol grn & bl	67.50	25.00
202	A24	5t dl vio & ol grn	95.00	45.00
203	A24	10t red & ol bis	325.00	32.50
204	A24	20t gray bl & brn	375.00	110.00
		Nos. 199-204 (6)	913.50	222.00

This issue was intended to commemorate the fifteenth year of the reign of King Vajiravudh. Because of the King's death the stamps were issued as ordinary postage stamps.

Nos. 195 and 150 with Surcharge similar to 1914-15 Issue in Black or Red

1928, Jan.

205	A23	5s on 15s car	7.00	3.50
206	A21	10s on 28s choc (R)	12.00	2.00

King Prajadhipok
A25 A26

1928 **Engr.** ***Perf. 12½***

207	A25	2s dp red brn	.65	.65
208	A25	3s deep green	.65	.65
209	A25	5s dark violet	.65	.30
210	A25	10s deep rose	.75	.30
211	A25	15s dark blue	.90	.40
212	A25	25s black & org	4.00	1.00
213	A25	50s brn org & blk	2.00	1.25
214	A25	80s blue & black	4.00	2.50
216	A26	1b dk blue & blk	6.00	2.50
217	A26	2b car rose & blk brn	12.00	5.00
218	A26	3b yellow grn & blk	12.00	6.00
219	A26	5b dp vio & gray blk	20.00	6.75
220	A26	10b ol grn & red vio	40.00	10.00
221	A26	20b Prus grn & brn	80.00	18.50
222	A26	40b dk grn & ol brn	160.00	80.00
		Nos. 207-222 (15)	343.60	135.80
		Set, never hinged	500.00	

On the single colored stamps, type A25, the lines in the background are uniform; those of the bicolored values are shaded and do not extend to the frame.

Issue dates: 5s, 10s, 2b-40b, Apr. 15; 2s, 3s, 15s, 25s, 50s, May 1; 1b, June 1; 80s, Nov. 15.

For overprints & surcharge see Nos. 300-301, B34.

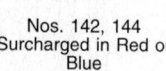

Nos. 142, 144 Surcharged in Red or Blue

1930 ***Perf. 14***

223	A20	10s on 12s blk & ol brn	8.75	2.75
224	A20	25s on 28s red brn (Bl)	30.00	2.25
		Set, never hinged	50.00	

King Prajadhipok and Chao P'ya Chakri
A27 A28

Statue of Chao P'ya Chakri — A29

1932, Apr. 1 **Engr.** ***Perf. 12½***

225	A27	2s dark brown	2.00	.40
226	A27	3s deep green	3.25	.85
227	A27	5s dull violet	2.00	.40
228	A28	10s red brn & blk	2.00	.25
229	A28	15s dull blue & blk	9.50	1.50
230	A28	25s violet & black	12.50	2.00
231	A28	50s claret & black	55.00	6.00
232	A29	1b blue black	77.50	15.00
		Nos. 225-232 (8)	163.75	26.40
		Set, never hinged	225.00	

150th anniv. of the Chakri dynasty, the founding of Bangkok in 1782, and the opening of the memorial bridge across the Chao Phraya River.

Assembly Hall, Bangkok A30

1939, June 24 **Litho.** ***Perf. 11, 12***

233	A30	2s dull red brown	4.50	2.00
234	A30	3s green	9.50	4.00
235	A30	5s dark violet	6.50	.80
236	A30	10s carmine	14.00	.80
237	A30	15s dark blue	35.00	2.00
		Nos. 233-237 (5)	69.50	9.60
		Set, never hinged	90.00	

7th anniv. of the Siamese Constitution.

Chakri Palace, Bangkok — A31

1940 **Typo.** ***Perf. 12½***

238	A31	2s dull brown	4.50	1.00
239	A31	3s dp yellow grn	8.00	2.50
	a.	Cliché of 5s in plate of 3s	900.00	*725.00*
240	A31	5s dark violet	5.50	.50
241	A31	10s carmine	20.00	.50
242	A31	15s dark blue	40.00	1.00
		Nos. 238-242 (5)	78.00	5.50
		Set, never hinged	125.00	

Issued: 2s, 3s, 5/13; 5s, 5/24; 15s, 5/28; 10s, 5/30.

King Ananda Mahidol — A32

Plowing Rice Field — A33

Royal Pavilion at Bang-pa-in — A34

1941, Apr. 17 **Engr.**

243	A32	2s brown	2.00	.45
244	A32	3s deep green	2.75	.85
245	A32	5s violet	1.60	.45
246	A32	10s dark red	1.60	.45
247	A33	15s dp bl & gray blk	2.75	.95
248	A33	25s slate & org	3.50	1.10
249	A33	50s red org & gray	3.25	1.20
250	A34	1b brt ultra & gray	15.00	3.50
251	A34	2b dk car rose & gray	14.00	2.00
252	A34	3b dp grn & gray	35.00	4.25
253	A34	5b blk & rose red	60.00	20.00
	a.	Horiz. pair, imperf. btwn.		
254	A34	10b ol blk & yel	95.00	50.00
		Nos. 243-254 (12)	236.45	85.20
		Set, never hinged	375.00	

King Ananda Mahidol — A35

1943, May 1 **Unwmk.** ***Perf. 11***

255	A35	1b dark blue	21.00	2.75
	a.	Horiz. pair, imperf. btwn.	100.00	100.00
	b.	Vert. pair, imperf. btwn.	100.00	100.00

See No. 274.

Indo-China War Monument — A36

1943 **Engr.** ***Perf. 11, 12½***

256	A36	3s dark green	20.00	17.50

Litho.

Perf. 12½x11

257	A36	3s dull green	4.00	2.50

Issue dates: #256, June 1. #257, Nov. 2.

Bangkhaen Monument — A37

Two types of 10s:
I — Size 19½x24mm.
II — Size 20¾x25¼mm.

1943, Nov. 25 ***Perf. 12½, 12½x11***

258	A37	2s brown orange	2.50	3.25
259	A37	10s car rose (I)	4.00	.80
	a.	Type II	8.00	5.00

10th anniv. of the quelling of a counter-revolution led by a member of the royal family on Oct. 11, 1933.

Stamps of similar design, but with values in "cents," are listed under Malaya, Occupation Stamps. See Nos. 2N1-2N6.

King Bhumibol Adulyadej — A38

1947, Dec. 5 ***Pin-perf. 12½x11***

260	A38	5s orange	2.75	3.00
261	A38	10s olive ('48)	2.75	3.00
	a.	10s light brown	80.00	80.00
262	A38	20s blue	7.00	2.40
263	A38	50s blue green	14.00	4.75
		Nos. 260-263 (4)	26.50	13.15

Coming of age of King Bhumibol Adulyadej. Issued with and without gum.

Catalogue values for unused stamps in this section, from this point to the end of the section, are for Never Hinged items.

King Bhumibol Adulyadej — A39

1947-49 **Unwmk.** **Engr.** ***Perf. 12½***

Size: 20x25mm

264	A39	5s violet	2.00	.30
265	A39	10s red	4.50	.50
266	A39	20s chocolate	2.00	.30
267	A39	50s olive	4.50	.30

Size: 22x27mm

268	A39	1b vio & dp bl	16.00	.45
269	A39	2b ultra & green	55.00	1.60
270	A39	3b brn red & blk	70.00	3.00
271	A39	5b bl grn & brn red	87.50	6.00
272	A39	10b dk brn & pur	325.00	3.00
273	A39	20b blk & rose brn	400.00	9.00
		Nos. 264-273 (10)	966.50	24.45

Issued: 5s, 20s, 11/15/47; 10s, 50s, 1/3/49; 1b-20b, 11/1/48.

For surcharges see Nos. 302-303.

Type of 1943

Perf. 11½, 12½x11½

1948, Jan. **Litho.**

274	A35	1b chalky blue	50.00	8.00
	a.	Horiz. pair, imperf. btwn.	150.00	150.00
	b.	Vert. pair, imperf. btwn.	150.00	150.00

King Bhumibol Adulyadej and Palace — A40

Perf. 12½

1950, May 5 **Unwmk.** **Engr.**

275	A40	5s red violet	2.00	.40
276	A40	10s red	2.50	.40
277	A40	15s purple	13.00	5.00
278	A40	20s chocolate	2.50	.40
279	A40	80s green	25.00	5.00
280	A40	1b deep blue	6.00	.40
281	A40	2b orange yellow	27.50	2.00
282	A40	3b gray	100.00	12.00
		Nos. 275-282 (8)	178.50	25.60

Coronation of Bhumibol Adulyadej as Rama IX, May 5, 1950.

King Bhumibol Adulyadej and Palace — A41

1951-60 ***Perf. 12½, 13x12½***

283	A41	5s rose lilac	2.50	.25
284	A41	10s deep green	2.00	.25
285	A41	15s red brown	2.50	.40
285A	A41	20s chocolate	3.00	.40
286	A41	25s carmine	1.20	.25
287	A41	50s gray olive	3.00	.40
288	A41	1b deep blue	6.50	.40
289	A41	1.15b deep blue	2.00	.50
290	A41	1.25b orange brn	10.00	.50
291	A41	2b dull blue grn	15.00	.50
292	A41	3b gray	20.00	.80
293	A41	5b aqua & red	65.00	2.00
294	A41	10b black brn & vio	325.00	6.00
295	A41	20b gray & olive	325.00	21.00
		Nos. 283-295 (14)	782.70	33.65

Issued: 25s, 2/15; 5s, 10s, 1b, 6/4; 2b, 3b, 12/1; 15s, 2/15/52; 1.15b, 9/1/53; 1.25b, 10/1/54; 5b, 10b, 20b, 2/1/55; 50s, 10/15/56; 20s, 1960.

United Nations Day — A42

1951, Oct. 24
296 A42 25s ultramarine 5.00 4.75

Overprinted in
Carmine

1952, Oct.
297 A42 25s ultramarine 3.50 2.75

Overprinted in
Carmine

1953, Oct.
298 A42 25s ultramarine 2.75 2.00

Overprinted in
Carmine

1954, Oct. 24
299 A42 25s ultramarine 6.00 4.00
Nos. 296-299 (4) 17.25 13.50

For more overprints see Nos. 315, 320.

Nos. 209 and 210
Overprinted in Black

1955, Jan. 4 Perf. 12½
300 A25 5s dark violet 9.50 20.00
301 A25 10s deep rose 9.50 20.00

**No. 266 Surcharged with New Value
in Black or Carmine**
302 A39 5s on 20s choc 3.50 .75
303 A39 10s on 20s choc (C) 5.00 .75
Nos. 300-303 (4) 27.50 41.50

King Naresuan
(1555-1605), on War
Elephant — A43

Perf. 13½
1955, Feb. 15 Unwmk. Engr.
304 A43 25s brt carmine 2.75 .45
305 A43 80s rose violet 25.00 5.00
306 A43 1.25b dark olive grn 70.00 3.00
307 A43 2b deep blue 15.00 2.00
308 A43 3b henna brown 60.00 3.00
Nos. 304-308 (5) 172.75 13.45

Tao Suranari — A44

1955, Apr. 15 Perf. 12x13½
309 A44 10s purple 2.50 .40
310 A44 25s emerald 1.90 .40
311 A44 1b brown 40.00 3.00
Nos. 309-311 (3) 44.40 3.80

Lady Mo, called Tao Suranari (Brave
Woman) for her role in stopping an 1826
rebellion.

King Taksin Statue at
Thonburi — A45

1955, May 1 Perf. 12½x12
312 A45 5s violet blue 1.90 .30
313 A45 25s Prus green 11.00 .30
314 A45 1.25b red 45.00 3.00
Nos. 312-314 (3) 57.90 3.60

King Somdech P'ya Chao Taksin (1734-
1782).

No. 296 Overprinted
in Red

1955, Oct. 24 Perf. 12½
315 A42 25s ultramarine 5.00 4.00

United Nations Day, Oct. 24, 1955.

Don Jedi
Monument — A46

1956, Feb. 1 Perf. 13½x13
316 A46 10s emerald 4.75 3.00
317 A46 50s reddish brown 27.50 2.00
318 A46 75s violet 8.00 1.00
319 A46 1.50b brown orange 25.00 1.50
Nos. 316-319 (4) 65.25 8.00

No. 296 Overprinted
in Red Violet

1956, Oct. 24
320 A42 25s ultramarine 6.00 4.50

United Nations Day, Oct. 24, 1956.

Dharmachakra and
Deer — A47

20s, 25s, 50s, Hand of peace and
Dharmachakra. 1b, 1.25b, 2b, Pagoda of
Nakon Phatom.

Wmk. 329
1957, May 13 Photo. Perf. 13½
321 A47 5s dark brown 1.50 .65
322 A47 10s rose lake 1.50 .65
323 A47 15s brt green 3.25 1.75
324 A47 20s orange 3.25 2.00
325 A47 25s reddish brown 1.10 .65
326 A47 50s magenta 2.50 .70
327 A47 1b olive brown 2.90 .85
328 A47 1.25b slate blue 35.00 6.00
329 A47 2b deep claret 8.00 1.25
Nos. 321-329 (9) 59.00 14.50

2500th anniversary of birth of Buddha.

UN Day — A48

1957, Oct. 24 Perf. 13½
330 A48 25s olive 1.60 .80
331 A48 25s bright ocher ('58) 1.60 .80
332 A48 25s indigo ('59) 2.40 .80
Nos. 330-332 (3) 5.60 2.40
Issued: Oct. 24.

Thai Archway — A49

Designs (inscribed "SEAP Games 1959"):
25s, Royal tiered umbrellas. 1.25b, Thai
archer, ancient costume. 2b, Wat Arun pagoda
and prow of royal barge.

1959, Oct. 15 Photo. Perf. 13½
333 A49 10s orange 1.10 .25
334 A49 25s dk carmine
rose 1.40 .25
335 A49 1.25b bright green 5.50 1.50
336 A49 2b light blue 4.75 .85
Nos. 333-336 (4) 12.75 2.85

Issued to publicize the South-East Asia
Peninsula Games, Bangkok, Dec. 12-17.

Wat Arun, WRY
Emblem — A50

1960, Apr. 7
337 A50 50s chocolate 1.60 .40
338 A50 2b yellow green 2.40 1.20

WRY, July 1, 1959-June 30, 1960.

Wat Arun,
Bangkok — A51

1960, Aug. Wmk. 329 Perf. 13½
339 A51 50s carmine rose .75 .25
340 A51 2b ultramarine 4.75 1.00

Anti-leprosy campaign.

Elephants in Teak
Forest — A52

1960, Aug. 29 Photo. Perf. 13½
341 A52 25s emerald 1.60 .40

5th World Forestry Cong., Seattle, WA, Aug.
29-Sept. 10.

Globe and
SEATO
Emblem — A53

1960, Sept. 8
342 A53 50s chocolate 1.60 .40

SEATO Day, Sept. 8.

Siamese
Child — A54

1960, Oct. 3 Wmk. 329
343 A54 50s magenta 1.75 .25
344 A54 1b orange 5.00 .75

Children's Day, 1960.

Hand with Pen and
Globe — A55

1960, Oct. 3
345 A55 50s carmine rose 1.50 .50
346 A55 2b blue 5.50 1.60

Intl. Letter Writing Week, Oct. 3-9.

UN Emblem and
Globe — A56

1960, Oct. 24 Perf. 13½
347 A56 50s purple 1.75 .40

15th anniversary of the United Nations.
See Nos. 369, 390.

King Bhumibol
Adulyadej — A57

Perf. 13½x13
1961-68 Engr. Wmk. 334
348 A57 5s rose cl ('62) .80 .40
349 A57 10s green ('62) .80 .40
350 A57 15s red brn ('62) .80 .40
351 A57 20s brown ('62) .80 .40
352 A57 25s carmine ('63) .80 .40
353 A57 50s olive ('62) .80 .40
354 A57 80s orange ('62) 5.00 2.00
355 A57 1b vio bl & brn 5.00 .80
355A A57 1.25b red & citron
('65) 8.50 2.00
356 A57 1.50b dk vio & yel
green 2.50 .80
357 A57 2b red & violet 2.50 2.00
358 A57 3b brn & bl 13.00 .65
358A A57 4b olive bis &
blk ('68) 15.00 3.00
359 A57 5b blue & green 32.50 2.00
360 A57 10b red org & blk 90.00 3.00
361 A57 20b emer & ultra 100.00 6.00
362 A57 25b green & blue 45.00 2.00
362A A57 40b yellow & blk
('65) 110.00 9.00
Nos. 348-362A (18) 433.80 38.65

For overprint see No. 588.

Children in Garden — A58

Wmk. 329

1961, Oct. 2　Photo.　Perf. 13½
363 A58 20s indigo　　1.75 .70
364 A58 2b purple　　4.50 1.50
Issued for Children's Day.

Pen and Envelope with Map — A59

1b, 2b, Pen and letters circling globe.

1961, Oct. 9
365 A59 25s gray green　　.70 .25
366 A59 50s rose lilac　　.35 .25
367 A59 1b bright rose　　2.00 .40
368 A59 2b ultramarine　　2.50 .70
　Nos. 365-368 (4)　　5.55 1.60
Intl. Letter Writing Week, Oct. 2-8.

UN Type of 1960

1961, Oct. 24　Wmk. 329　Perf. 13½
369 A56 50s maroon　　1.60 .70
Issued for United Nations Day, Oct. 24.

Scout Emblem — A60　Scouts Saluting and Tents — A61

Design: 2b, King Vajiravudh and Scouts.

1961, Nov. 1　　　Photo.
370 A60 50s carmine rose　　.70 .30
371 A61 1b bright green　　1.75 .50
372 A61 2b bright blue　　2.75 1.20
　Nos. 370-372 (3)　　5.20 2.00
Thai Boy Scouts, 50th anniversary.

Malaria Eradication Emblem and Siamese Designs
A62　　A63

1962, Apr. 7　Wmk. 329　Perf. 13
373 A62 5s orange brown　　.30 .25
374 A62 10s sepia　　.30 .25
375 A62 20s blue　　1.10 .25
376 A62 50s carmine rose　　.30 .25
377 A63 1b green　　1.50 .25
378 A63 1.50b dk car rose　　3.50 .65
379 A63 2d dark blue　　2.00 .35
380 A63 3b violet　　5.50 2.50
　Nos. 373-380 (8)　　14.50 4.75
WHO drive to eradicate malaria.

View of Bangkok and Seattle Fair Emblem A64

1962, Apr. 21　Wmk. 329　Perf. 13
381 A64 50s red lilac　　1.50 .30
382 A64 2b deep blue　　7.00 .75
"Century 21" Intl. Expo., Seattle, WA, Apr. 21-Oct. 12.

Mother and Child — A65

Wmk. 329

1962, Oct. 1　Photo.　Perf. 13
383 A65 25s lt blue green　　1.25 .30
384 A65 50s bister brown　　1.50 .25
385 A65 2b bright pink　　6.75 .75
　Nos. 383-385 (3)　　9.50 1.30
Issued for Children's Day.

Globe, Letters, Carrier Pigeons — A66

Design: 1b, 2b, Quill pen and scroll.

1962, Oct. 8
386 A66 25s violet　　.70 .30
387 A66 50s red　　.50 .25
388 A66 1b lemon　　3.50 .60
389 A66 2b lt bluish green　　7.00 .70
　Nos. 386-389 (4)　　11.70 1.85
Intl. Letter Writing Week, Oct. 7-13.

UN Type of 1960

1962, Oct. 24　　　Perf. 13½
390 A56 50s carmine rose　　1.00 .80
United Nations Day, Oct. 24.

Exhibition Emblem — A67

1962, Nov. 1　　　Unwmk.
391 A67 50s olive bister　　1.90 .25
Students' Exhibition, Bangkok.

Woman Harvesting Rice — A68

Wmk. 334

1963, Mar. 21　Engr.　Perf. 14
392 A68 20s green　　2.00 .65
393 A68 50s ocher　　1.50 .25
FAO "Freedom from Hunger" campaign.

Temple Lion — A69

1963, Apr. 1　Wmk. 329　Perf. 13½
394 A69 50s green & bister　　2.00 .25
1st anniv. of the formation of the Asian-Oceanic Postal Union, AOPU.

New and Old Post and Telegraph Buildings — A70

Wmk. 334

1963, Aug. 4　Engr.　Perf. 14
395 A70 50s org, bluish blk & grn　　2.40 .80
396 A70 3b grn, dk red & brn　　6.50 1.50
80th anniv. of the Post and Telegraph Dept.

King Bhumibol Adulyadej — A71

Perf. 13x13½

			Photo.	
1963-71　Wmk. 329
397 A71 5s dk car rose　　.80 .40
398 A71 10s dark green　　.80 .40
399 A71 15s red brown　　.80 .40
400 A71 20s black brown　　.80 .40
401 A71 25s carmine　　.80 .40
402 A71 50s olive gray　　1.60 .40
402A A71 75s brt vio ('71)　　1.50 .25
403 A71 80s dull orange　　6.50 1.60
404 A71 1b dk bl & dk brn　　4.00 .40
404A A71 1.25b org brn & ol ('65)　　16.00 4.50
405 A71 1.50b vio bl & grn　　4.50 .80
406 A71 2b dk red & vio　　4.50 .40
407 A71 3b brn & dk bl　　4.50 .80
407A A71 4b dp bis & blk ('68)　　7.00 2.40
408 A71 5b blue & green　　3.25 .80
409 A71 10b orange & blk　　27.50 1.50
410 A71 20b brt grn & ind　　180.00 8.00
411 A71 25b dk grn & bl　　12.00 1.50
411A A71 40b yel & blk ('65)　　225.00 9.50
　Nos. 397-411A (19)　　501.85 34.85
Nos. 397-403 were issued in 1963; Nos. 404, 405-407, 408-411 in 1964.
For overprint see No. 589.

Child with Dolls — A72

1963, Oct. 7　Litho.　Perf. 13½
412 A72 50s rose red　　2.00 .25
413 A72 2b dull blue　　8.50 .75
Issued for Children's Day.

Garuda Carrying Letter — A73

Design: 2b, 3b, Thai women writing letters.

1963, Oct. 7　　　Wmk. 329
414 A73 50s lt blue & claret　　2.75 .45
415 A73 1b lt grn & vio brn　　4.75 .80
416 A73 2b yel brn & turq bl　　34.00 3.50
417 A73 3b org brn & yel grn　　18.00 3.50
　Nos. 414-417 (4)　　59.50 7.75
Intl. Letter Writing Week, Oct. 6-12.

UN Emblem — A74

1963, Oct. 24　Wmk. 329　Perf. 13½
418 A74 50s bright blue　　1.50 .40
United Nations Day, Oct. 24.

King Bhumibol Adulyadej — A75

1963, Dec. 5　Photo.　Perf. 13½
419 A75 1.50b blue, org & ind　　5.00 1.50
420 A75 5b brt lil rose, org & blk　　24.00 4.50
King Bhumibol's 36th birthday.

UNICEF Emblem — A76

1964, Jan. 13　　　Litho.
421 A76 50s blue　　1.00 .40
422 A76 2b olive green　　4.50 .80
17th anniv. of UNICEF.

Hand (flags), Pigeon and Globe — A77

Designs: 1b, Girls and world map. 2b, Pen, pencil and unfolded world map. 3b, Globe and hand holding quill.

1964, Oct. 5　Wmk. 329　Perf. 13½
423 A77 50s lilac & lt grn　　2.40 .40
424 A77 1b red brown & grn　　6.00 1.50
425 A77 2b yellow & vio bl　　14.50 1.50
426 A77 3b blue & dk brown　　9.50 3.25
　Nos. 423-426 (4)　　32.40 6.65
Intl. Letter Writing Week, Oct. 5-11.

UN Emblem and Globe — A78

1964, Oct. 24　Photo.　Perf. 13½
427 A78 50s gray　　1.50 .40
United Nations Day, Oct. 24.

King and Queen — A79

1965, Apr. 28   Wmk. 329   Perf. 13½
428 A79 2b brown & multi   16.00   .80
429 A79 5b violet & multi   25.00 4.00
15th wedding anniversary of King Bhumibol Adulyadej and Queen Sirikit.

ITU Emblem, Old and New Communications Equipment — A80

1965, May 17   Photo.
430 A80 1b bright green   7.00 1.50
Cent. of the ITU.

World Map, Letters and Goddess — A81

2b, 3b, World map, letters and handshake.

1965, Oct. 3   Wmk. 329   Perf. 13½
431 A81 50s dp plum, gray & sal   1.75   .60
432 A81 1b dk vio bl, lt vio & yel   5.00   .80
433 A81 2b dk gray, bis & dp org 14.00 1.20
434 A81 3b multicolored   17.50 4.00
    Nos. 431-434 (4)   38.25 6.60
Intl. Letter Writing Week, Oct. 3-9.

A82
Gates of Royal Chapel of Emerald Buddha.

Engr. & Litho.
Perf. 13½x14
1965, Oct. 24   Wmk. 356
435 A82 50s slate grn, bl & ocher 2.00 .40
International Cooperation Year, 1965.

A83
Map of Thailand and UPU monument, Bern.

Wmk. 329
1965, Nov. 1   Litho.   Perf. 13½
436 A83 20s dk blue & lilac   1.00   .40
437 A83 50s gray & blue   2.25   .40
438 A83 1b orange brn & vio bl   7.00   .45
439 A83 3b green & bister   14.00 2.50
    Nos. 436-439 (4)   24.25 3.75
80th anniv. of Thailand's admission to the UPU.

Lotus Blossom and Child — A84

Design: 1b, Boy with book walking up steps.
1966, Jan. 8   Wmk. 334   Perf. 13½
440 A84 50s henna brn & blk   1.50   .40
441 A84 1b green & black   4.00 1.60
Issued for Children's Day, 1966.

Bicycling — A85

1966, Aug. 4   Photo.   Wmk. 329
442 A85 20s shown   1.00   .45
443 A85 25s Tennis   1.40   .45
444 A85 50s Running   1.00   .25
445 A85 1b Weight lifting   4.50 1.50
446 A85 1.25b Boxing   6.50 4.00
447 A85 2b Swimming   9.50 1.20
448 A85 3b Netball   19.00 4.00
449 A85 5b Soccer   52.50 14.00
    Nos. 442-449 (8)   95.40 25.85
5th Asian Games, Bangkok.

Trade Fair Emblem and Temple of Dawn — A86

1966, Sept. 1   Litho.   Perf. 13½
450 A86 50s lilac   1.75   .80
451 A86 1b brown red   4.50 1.60
1st Intl. Asian Trade Fair, Bangkok.

Letter Writer A87

Design: 50s, 1b, Letters, maps and pen.
1966, Oct. 3   Photo.   Wmk. 329
452 A87 50s scarlet   1.60   .40
453 A87 1b orange brown   3.25   .80
454 A87 2b brt violet   12.00   .80
455 A87 3b brt blue grn   7.00 2.40
    Nos. 452-455 (4)   23.85 4.40
Intl. Letter Writing Week, Oct. 6-12.

UN Emblem — A88

Wmk. 334
1966, Oct. 24   Litho.   Perf. 13½
456 A88 50s ultramarine   1.60   .40
United Nations Day, Oct. 24.

Rice Field A89

1966, Nov. 1   Engr.   Wmk. 329
457 A89 50s dp bl & grnsh bl   4.00   .80
458 A89 3b plum & pink   16.00 4.50
Intl. Rice Year under sponsorship of the FAO.

Pra Buddha Bata Monastery, UNESCO Emblem — A90

1966, Nov. 4   Photo.   Wmk. 329
459 A90 50s black & yel grn   1.25   .25
20th anniv. of UNESCO.

Thai Boxing A91

Designs: 1b, Takraw (three men playing ball). 2b, Kite fighting. 3b, Cudgel play.

1966, Dec. 9   Wmk. 329   Perf. 13½
460 A91 50s black, brn & red   2.00   .80
461 A91 1b black, brn & red   6.50 2.00
462 A91 2b black, brn & red   29.00 4.50
463 A91 3b black, brn & red   27.50 14.00
    Nos. 460-463 (4)   65.00 21.30
5th Asian Games.

Snakehead — A92

Pigmy Mackerel — A93

Fish: 3b, Barb. 5b, Siamese fighting fish.

1967, Jan. 1   Photo.
464 A92 1b brt blue & multi   7.00 1.50
465 A93 2b multicolored   27.50 3.00
466 A93 3b yel grn & multi   15.00 7.00
467 A92 5b pale grn & multi   20.00 8.00
    Nos. 464-467 (4)   69.50 19.50

Dharmachakra, Globe and Temples — A94

Wmk. 329
1967, Jan. 15   Litho.   Perf. 13½
468 A94 2b black & yellow   6.50 1.20
Establishment of the headquarters of the World Fellowship of Buddhists in Thailand.

Great Hornbill — A95

Birds: 25s, Hill myna. 50s, White-rumped shama. 1b, Diard's fireback pheasant. 1.50b, Spotted dove. 2b, Sarus crane. 3b, White-breasted kingfisher. 5b, Asiatic open-bill (stork).

1967, Feb. 1   Photo.
469 A95 20s tan & multi   1.40   .80
470 A95 25s lt gray & multi   2.00 1.60
471 A95 50s yel grn & multi   3.50   .80
472 A95 1b olive & multi   5.00 1.50
473 A95 1.50b dull yel & multi   5.00 2.40
474 A95 2b pale sal & multi   29.00 3.25
475 A95 3b gray & multi   18.50 7.75
476 A95 5b multicolored   29.00 8.00
    Nos. 469-476 (8)   93.40 26.10

Ascocentrum Curvifolium — A96

Orchids: 20s, Vandopsis parishii. 80s, Rhynchostylis retusa. 1b, Rhynchostylus gigantea. 1.50b, Dendrobium falconerii. 2b, Paphiopedilum callosum. 3b, Dendrobium formosum. 5b, Dendrobium primulinum.

1967, Apr. 1   Wmk. 329   Perf. 13½
477 A96 20s black & multi   1.40   .80
478 A96 50s brt blue & multi   2.00   .40
479 A96 80s black & multi   3.50 1.60
480 A96 1b blue & multi   5.25 1.25
481 A96 1.50b black & multi   5.25 1.25
482 A96 2b ver & multi   24.00 3.25
483 A96 3b brown & multi   18.50 7.75
484 A96 5b multicolored   29.00 6.25
    Nos. 477-484 (8)   88.90 22.55

Thai Architecture — A97

1967, Apr. 6   Engr.
485 A97 50s Mansion   2.00   .80
486 A97 1.50b Pagodas   5.50 3.25
487 A97 2b Bell tower   24.00 3.00
488 A97 3b Temple   16.00 5.50
    Nos. 485-488 (4)   47.50 12.55

Grand Palace and Royal Barge on Chao Phraya River — A98

1967, Sept. 15   Wmk. 329   Perf. 13½
489 A98 2b ultra & sepia   9.50 2.00
International Tourist Year, 1967.

Globe, Dove, People and Letters A99

2b, 3b, Clasped hands, globe and doves.

1967, Oct. 8   Photo.
490 A99 50s dk blue & multi   .85   .40
491 A99 1b multicolored   3.25   .80
492 A99 2b brt yel grn & blk   7.00   .80
493 A99 3b brown & blk   12.50 3.00
    Nos. 490-493 (4)   23.60 5.00
Intl. Letter Writing Week, Oct. 6-12.

UN Emblem — A100

1967, Oct. 24   Wmk. 329   Perf. 13½
494 A100 50s multicolored   1.40   .25
Issued for United Nations Day, Oct. 24.

Flag and Map of Thailand — A101

1967, Dec. 5   Photo.   Perf. 13½
495 A101 50s greenish blue, red
                 & vio bl   1.60   .80
496 A101 2b ol gray, red & vio
                 bl   7.00 1.60
50th anniversary of the flag.

Elephant Carrying Teakwood — A102

1968, Mar. 1   Engr.   Wmk. 329
497 A102 2b rose claret & gray ol 7.00   .75
See Nos. 537, 566.

Syncom Satellite over Thai Tracking Station — A103

1968, Apr. 1   Photo.   Perf. 13
498 A103 50s multicolored   .70   .25
499 A103 3b multicolored   3.50 1.25

Earth Goddess — A104

1968, May 1   Wmk. 329   Perf. 13
500 A104 50s blk, gold, red & bl
                 grn   2.40   .40
Hydrological Decade (UNESCO), 1965-74.

Snake-skinned Gourami — A105

Fish: 20s, Red-tailed black "shark." 25s, Tor tambroides. 50s, Pangasius sanitwongsei. 80s, Bagrid catfish. 1.25b, Vaimosa rambaiae. 1.50b, Catlocarpio siamensis.   4b, Featherback.

1968, June 1   Photo.   Perf. 13
501 A105 10s multicolored   1.00   .40
502 A105 20s multicolored   1.75   .40
503 A105 25s multicolored   1.75   .40
504 A105 50s multicolored   4.50   .40
505 A105 80s multicolored   6.00 3.25
506 A105 1.25b multicolored   6.50 4.75
507 A105 1.50b multicolored 24.00 4.00
508 A105 4b multicolored   50.00 17.50
    Nos. 501-508 (8)   95.50 31.10

Arcturus Butterfly — A106

Various butterflies.

1968, July 1   Wmk. 329   Perf. 13
509 A106 50s lt blue & multi   5.00   .30
510 A106 1b multicolored   8.00   1.50
511 A106 3b multicolored   22.50   7.00
512 A106 4b buff & multi   32.50 12.00
    Nos. 509-512 (4)   68.00 20.80

Queen Sirikit — A107

Designs: Various portraits of Queen Sirikit.

Photogravure and Engraved
Perf. 13½x14
1968, Aug. 12   Wmk. 334
513 A107 50s gold & multi   .80   .45
514 A107 2b gold & multi   4.50   1.60
515 A107 3b gold & multi   10.00   3.00
516 A107 5b gold & multi   16.00   5.50
    Nos. 513-516 (4)   31.30 10.55
Queen Sirikit's 36th birthday, or third 12-year "cycle."

WHO Emblem and Medical Apparatus — A108

1968, Sept. 1   Photo.   Perf. 12½
517 A108 50s olive, blk & gray 1.60   .25
20th anniv. of the WHO.

Globe, Pen and Envelope — A109

1b, 3b, Pen nib, envelope and globe.

1968, Oct. 6   Wmk. 329   Perf. 13½
518 A109 50s brown & multi   .30   .30
519 A109 1b pale brown &
                 multi   1.40   .55
520 A109 2b multicolored   2.75   .70
521 A109 3b violet & multi   9.50   2.00
    Nos. 518-521 (4)   13.95   3.55
Intl. Letter Writing Week, Oct. 7-13.

UN Emblem and Flags — A110

1968, Oct. 24
522 A110 50s multicolored   1.20   .25
Issued for United Nations Day.

Human Rights Flame and Bas-relief — A111

1968, Dec. 10   Photo.   Perf. 13½
523 A111 50s sl grn, red & vio 1.60   .25
International Human Rights Year.

King Rama II — A112

1968, Dec. 30   Engr.   Wmk. 329
524 A112 50s sepia & bister   1.60   .40
Rama II (1768-1824), who reigned 1809-24.

National Assembly Building — A113

Photogravure and Engraved
1969, Feb. 10   Wmk. 329   Perf. 13½
525 A113 50s multicolored   1.00   .25
526 A113 2b multicolored   5.25 1.20
First constitutional election day.

ILO Emblem and Cogwheels — A114

1969, May 1   Photo.   Perf. 13½
527 A114 50s rose vio & dk bl .85   .25
50th anniv. of the ILO.

Ramwong Dance — A115

Designs: 1b, Candle dance. 2b, Krathop Mai dance. 3b, Nohra dance.

1969, July 15   Wmk. 329   Perf. 13
528 A115 50s multicolored   .65   .30
529 A115 1b multicolored   1.60   .65
530 A115 2b multicolored   2.75   .65
531 A115 3b multicolored   3.25   1.50
    Nos. 528-531 (4)   8.25   3.10

Posting and Receiving Letters — A116

Design: 2b, 3b, Writing and posting letters.

1969, Oct. 5   Photo.   Wmk. 334
532 A116 50s multicolored   .65   .40
533 A116 1b multicolored   1.25   .45
534 A116 2b multicolored   2.40   .65
535 A116 3b multicolored   3.25   1.40
    Nos. 532-535 (4)   7.55   2.90
International Letter Writing Week.

Hand Holding Globe — A117

1969, Oct. 24   Wmk. 329   Perf. 13
536 A117 50s multicolored   1.40   .40
Issued for United Nations Day.

Teakwood Type of 1968
1969, Nov. 18   Engr.   Perf. 13½
537 A102 2b Tin mine   5.00   .65
Issued to publicize tin export, and the 2nd Technical Conf. of the Intl. Tin Council, Bangkok.

Loy Krathong Festival — A118

Designs: 1b, Marriage ceremony. 2b, Khwan ceremony. 5b, Songkran festival.

1969, Nov. 23   Wmk. 329
538 A118 50s gray & multi   1.00   .25
539 A118 1b multicolored   1.75   .65
540 A118 2b multicolored   2.75   .55
541 A118 5b multicolored   5.50 1.75
    Nos. 538-541 (4)   11.00 3.20

Biplane, Mailmen and Map of First Thai Airmail Flight, 1919 — A119

1969, Dec. 10   Engr.   Perf. 13½
542 A119 1b multicolored   1.75   .45
50th anniversary of Thai airmail service.

Shadow Play — A120

Photogravure and Engraved
1969, Dec. 18   Wmk. 329
543 A120 50s Phra Rama   .65   .30
544 A120 2b Ramasura   3.50   .40
545 A120 3b Mekhala   3.25   1.20
546 A120 5b Ongkhot   6.00   1.40
    Nos. 543-546 (4)   13.40   3.30

Symbols of Agriculture, Industry and Shipping — A121

1970, Jan. 1   **Photo.**
547 A121 50s multicolored   .60 .25
    Productivity Year 1970.

World Map, Thai Temples and Emblem — A122

1970, Jan. 31   **Litho.**
548 A122 50s brt blue & blk   1.25 .30
    19th triennial meeting of the Intl. Council of Women, Bangkok.

Earth Station Radar and Satellite — A123

Perf. 14½x15
1970, Apr. 1   **Litho.**   **Wmk. 356**
549 A123 50s multicolored   .65 .25
    Communication by satellite.

Household and Population Statistics — A124

Perf. 13x13½
1970, Apr. 1   **Photo.**   **Wmk. 329**
550 A124 1b multicolored   .95 .40
    Issued to publicize the 1970 census.

Inauguration of New UPU Headquarters, Bern — A125

Lithographed and Engraved
1970, June 15   **Wmk. 334**   **Perf. 13½**
551 A125 50s lt bl, lt grn & grn   .95 .30

Khun Ram Kamhang Teaching (Mural) — A126

1970, July 1   **Litho.**
552 A126 50s black & multi   1.40 .30
    Issued for International Education Year.

Swimming Stadium — A127

1.50b, Velodrome. 3b, Subhajalasaya Stadium. 5b, Kittikachorn Indoor Stadium.

Lithographed and Engraved
1970, Sept. 1   **Wmk. 329**   **Perf. 13½**
553 A127   50s yellow, red & pur   .85 .30
554 A127   1.50b ultra, grn & dk red   2.00 .65
555 A127   3b gold, black & dk red   2.50 1.10
556 A127   5b brt grn, ultra & dk red   4.00 1.20
    Nos. 553-556 (4)   9.35 3.25
    6th Asian Games, Bangkok.

Children Writing Letters — A128

Designs: 1b, Woman writing letter. 2b, Two women reading letters. 3b, Man reading letter.

1970, Oct. 4   **Photo.**   **Perf. 13½**
557 A128 50s black & multi   .65 .25
558 A128 1b black & multi   1.50 .45
559 A128 2b black & multi   3.50 .65
560 A128 3b black & multi   3.50 1.60
    Nos. 557-560 (4)   9.15 2.95
    Intl. Letter Writing Week, Oct. 6-12.

Royal Palace, Bangkok, and UN Emblem — A129

1970, Oct. 24   **Photo.**   **Perf. 13½**
561 A129 50s multicolored   1.40 .40
    25th anniversary of the United Nations.

Heroes of Bangrachan — A130

1b, Monument to Thao Thepkrasattri & Thao Sri Sunthon. 2b, Queen Suriyothai riding elephant. 3b, Phraya Phichaidaphak and battle scene.

1970, Oct. 25   **Engr.**   **Perf. 13½**
562 A130 50s pink & violet   .65 .45
563 A130 1b violet & maroon   1.40 .65
564 A130 2b rose & brown   3.50 .65
565 A130 3b blue & green   5.00 1.60
    Nos. 562-565 (4)   10.55 3.35
    Heroes from Thai history.

Teakwood Type of 1968
1970, Nov. 1   **Engr.**
566 A102 2b Rubber plantation   3.25 .70
    Issued to publicize rubber export.

King Bhumibol Lighting Flame — A131

1970, Dec. 9   **Photo.**   **Wmk. 329**
567 A131 1b multicolored   2.00 .65
    Opening of 6th Asian Games, Bangkok.

Woman Playing So Sam Sai — A132

Women Playing Classical Thai Musical Instruments: 2b, Khlui Phiang-O. 3b, Krachappi. 5b, Thon Rammana.

1970, Dec. 20
568 A132 50s multicolored   .65 .40
569 A132 2b multicolored   2.00 .65
570 A132 3b multicolored   2.75 .95
571 A132 5b multicolored   5.25 1.25
    Nos. 568-571 (4)   10.65 3.25

Chocolate Point Siamese Cats — A133

Siamese Cats: 1b, Blue point. 2b, Seal point. 3b, Pure white cat and kittens.

Perf. 13½x14
1971, Mar. 15   **Litho.**   **Wmk. 356**
572 A133 50s multicolored   .65 .45
573 A133 1b multicolored   4.50 1.00
574 A133 2b multicolored   6.00 1.10
575 A133 3b multicolored   8.50 2.75
    Nos. 572-575 (4)   19.65 5.30

Muang Nakhon Temple — A134

Temples: 1b, Phanom. 3b, Pathom Chedi. 4b, Doi Suthep.

Lithographed and Engraved
1971, Mar. 30   **Wmk. 329**   **Perf. 13½**
576 A134 50s rose, black & brn   .70 .30
577 A134 1b emerald, bis & pur   1.40 .40
578 A134 3b org, brn & dk brn   3.00 .65
579 A134 4b ultra, ocher & brn   5.25 2.75
    Nos. 576-579 (4)   10.35 4.10

Corn and Tractor in Field A135

1971, Apr. 20   **Engr.**   **Wmk. 329**
580 A135 2b multicolored   2.00 .65
    Export promotion.

Buddha's Birthplace, Lumbini, Nepal — A136

Buddha's: 1b, Place of Enlightenment, Bihar. 2b, Place of first sermon, Benares. 3b, Place of death, Kusinara.

1971, May 9   **Engr.**   **Perf. 13½**
581 A136 50s violet blue & blk   1.00 .30
582 A136 1b green & black   1.25 .55
583 A136 2b dull yellow & blk   3.25 .90
584 A136 3b red & black   2.75 1.50
    Nos. 581-584 (4)   8.25 3.05
    20th anniv. of World Fellowship of Buddhists.

King Bhumibol and Subjects — A137

Perf. 13½
1971, June 9   **Unwmk.**   **Litho.**
585 A137 50s silver & multi   1.40 .30
    King Bhumibol's Silver Jubilee.

Floating Market — A138

1971, June 20   **Photo.**   **Wmk. 329**
586 A138 4b gold & multi   2.75 .65
    Visit Asia Year.

Boy Scouts Saluting — A139

1971, July 1   **Litho.**
587 A139 50s orange & multi   1.25 .40
    60th anniversary of Thai Boy Scouts.

**Blocks of four of Nos. 354 and 403
Overprinted in Dark Blue**

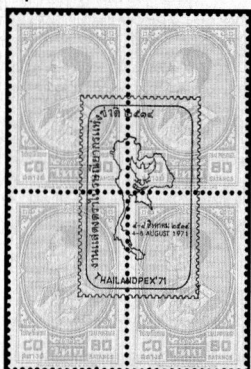

a

b

Perf. 13½x13
1971, Aug.   Wmk. 334   Engr.
588 A57 (a) Block of 4   8.00 8.00
a.   80s orange, single stamp   2.00 2.00

Perf. 13x13½
Photo.   Wmk. 329
589 A71 (b) Block of 4   8.00 8.00
a.   80s dull orange, single stamp 2.00 2.00
THAILANDPEX '71, Philatelic Exhib., Aug. 4-8.

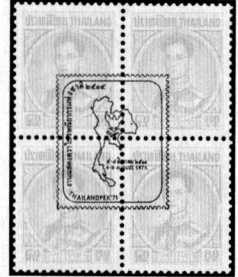

Woman Writing Letter — A140

Designs: 1b, Women reading mail. 2b, Woman sitting on porch. 3b, Man handing letter to woman.

Wmk. 334
1971, Oct. 3   Litho.   Perf. 13½
590 A140 50s gray & multi   .70 .25
591 A140 1b red brown & multi   1.00 .25
592 A140 2b ultra & multi   1.75 .50
593 A140 3b lt gray & multi   2.75 1.25
       Nos. 590-593 (4)   6.20 2.25
Intl. Letter Writing Week, Oct. 6-12.

Wat Benchamabopit (Marble Temple), Bangkok — A141

Perf. 13½x14
1971, Oct. 24   Litho.   Unwmk.
594 A141 50s multicolored   1.50 .45
United Nations Day, Oct. 24.

Duck Raising — A142

Rural occupations: 1b, Raising tobacco. 2b, Fishermen. 3b, Rice winnowing.

Wmk. 329
1971, Nov. 15   Photo.   Perf. 12½
595 A142 50s lt blue & multi   .65 .25
596 A142 1b multicolored   1.00 .40
597 A142 2b blue & multi   1.60 .40
598 A142 3b buff & multi   3.25 1.60
       Nos. 595-598 (4)   6.50 2.65

UNICEF Emblem, Mother and Child — A143

1971, Dec. 11   Wmk. 334   Perf. 13½
599 A143 50s blue & multi   .65 .25
25th anniv. of UNICEF.

Thai Costumes, 17th Century — A144

Thai Costumes: 1b, 13th-14th cent. 1.50b, 14th-17th cent. 2b, 18th-19th cent.

Perf. 13½x14
1972, Jan. 12   Litho.   Unwmk.
600 A144 50s multicolored   .80 .40
601 A144 1b multicolored   1.25 .70
602 A144 1.50b multicolored   3.25 .80
603 A144 2b blue & multi   6.00 1.60
       Nos. 600-603 (4)   11.30 3.50

Globe A145

Perf. 13x13½
1972, Apr. 1   Photo.   Wmk. 334
604 A145 75s violet blue   1.10 .25
Asian-Oceanic Postal Union, 10th anniv.

King Bhumibol Adulyadej — A146

Perf. 13½x13
1972-77   Litho.   Wmk. 329
Size: 21x26mm
605 A146 10s yellow green   .45 .25
606 A146 20s blue   .70 .25
607 A146 25s rose red   .70 .25
608 A146 75s lilac   1.50 .25

Engr.
609 A146 1.25b yel grn & pink   3.00 .40
610 A146 2.75b red brn & blue grn 2.50 .65
611 A146 3b brn & dk blue ('74) 5.50 .65

612 A146 4b blue & org red ('73) 3.25 .65
613 A146 5b dk vio & red brown   3.50 .70
614 A146 6b green & vio   7.50 .70
615 A146 10b ver & black   6.00 .65
616 A146 20b org & yel grn   6.00 1.10
617 A146 40b dp bis & lilac ('74) 32.50 10.00
618 A146 50b pur & brt grn ('77) 45.00 3.50
619 A146 100b dp org & dk bl ('77) 65.00 5.50
       Nos. 605-619 (15)   183.10 25.50
See Nos. 835-838, 907-908.
For surcharges, see Nos. 2248, 2281-2282.

Iko Women — A147

Hill Tribes: 2b, Musoe musician. 4b, Yao weaver. 5b, Maeo farm woman.

Wmk. 334
1972, May 11   Photo.   Perf. 13½
620 A147 50s multicolored   .30 .25
621 A147 2b dark gray & multi   1.60 .40
622 A147 4b multicolored   8.00 3.50
623 A147 5b multicolored   11.00 1.00
       Nos. 620-623 (4)   20.90 5.15

Ruby A148

Precious Stones: 2b, Yellow sapphire. 4b, Zircon. 6b, Star sapphire.

1972, June 7   Litho.
624 A148 75s gray & multi   1.75 .25
625 A148 2b multicolored   8.75 1.00
626 A148 4b multicolored   12.00 4.50
627 A148 6b crimson & multi   15.00 5.00
       Nos. 624-627 (4)   37.50 10.75

Prince Vajiralongkorn A149

Perf. 13½x13
1972, July 28   Photo.   Wmk. 329
628 A149 75s tan & multi   2.00 .40
20th birthday of Prince Vajiralongkorn, heir apparent.

Thai Costume A150

Designs: Costumes of Thai women.

Perf. 14x13½
1972, Aug. 12   Litho.   Wmk. 356
629 A150 75s tan & multi   1.00 .25
630 A150 2b multicolored   2.00 .70
631 A150 4b yellow & multi   5.50 3.25

632 A150 5b gray & multi   6.00 2.50
a.   Souvenir sheet of 4, #629-632 47.50 40.00
       Nos. 629-632 (4)   14.50 6.70

Rambutan — A151

Fruits: 1b, Mangosteen. 3b, Durian. 5b, Mango.

1972, Sept. 7   Wmk. 334   Perf. 13½
633 A151 75s multicolored   1.00 .25
634 A151 1b multicolored   2.40 .55
635 A151 3b pink & multi   6.00 1.40
636 A151 5b lt ultra & multi   12.00 2.50
       Nos. 633-636 (4)   21.40 4.70

Lod Cave, Phangnga — A152

1.25b, Kang Krachan Reservoir. 2.75b, Erawan Waterfalls, Kanchanaburi. 3b, Nok-Kaw Cliff, Loei.

1972, Nov. 15   Litho.   Wmk. 334
637 A152 75s multicolored   .80 .25
638 A152 1.25b multicolored   1.60 1.00
639 A152 2.75b multicolored   5.50 .65
640 A152 3b multicolored   4.50 1.75
       Nos. 637-640 (4)   12.40 3.65
Intl. Letter Writing Week, Oct. 9-15.

Princess Mother Visiting Old People — A153

1972, Oct. 21   Photo.   Wmk. 329
641 A153 75s dk green & ocher   5.00 1.00
Princess Mother Sisangwan, 72nd birthday.

UN Emblem and Globe — A154

Wmk. 334
1972, Nov. 15   Litho.   Perf. 14
642 A154 75s blue & multi   .80 .65
25th anniversary of the Economic Commission for Asia and the Far East (ECAFE).

Educational Center and Book Year Emblem — A155

1972, Dec. 8   Perf. 13½
643 A155 75s multicolored   .65 .25
International Book Year 1972.

Crown Prince
Vajiralongkorn
A156

1972, Dec. 28   Photo.   Wmk. 329
644 A156 2b brt blue & multi   1.90 .40
Investiture of Prince Vajiralongkorn
Salayacheevin as Crown Prince.

Flag, Soldiers and Civilians — A157

1973, Feb. 3   Wmk. 334   Perf. 13½
645 A157 75s multicolored   1.20 .25
25th anniversary of Veterans Day.

Savings Bank,
Emblem and
Coin — A158

1973, Apr. 1   Wmk. 329
646 A158 75s emerald & multi   .85 .25
60th anniv. of Government Savings Bank.

WHO Emblem and Deity — A159

1973, Apr. 1   Wmk. 329
647 A159 75s brt green & multi   .80 .25
25th World Health Organization Day.

Water
Lily
A160

Designs: Various water lilies (Thai lotus).

Perf. 11x13
1973, May 15   Litho.   Wmk. 356
648 A160 75s violet & multi   1.00 .25
649 A160 1.50b brown & multi   2.00 .35
650 A160 2b dull grn & multi   3.50 .75
651 A160 4b black & multi   9.00 3.50
    Nos. 648-651 (4)   15.50 4.85

King Bhumibol
Adulyadej — A161

Perf. 14x13½
1973-81   Photo.   Wmk. 334
652 A161 5s purple   1.75 .55
653 A161 20s blue   1.75 .55
a.   Perf. 14½, wmk. 233   .30 .25
654 A161 25s rose carmine   2.25 .45

Wmk. 233   Perf. 14½
655 A161 25s brown red ('81)   .30 .25
656 A161 50s dk olive grn ('79)   1.50 .25
657 A161 75s violet   1.25 .25
a.   Perf. 14x13½, wmk. 334   2.25 .45

Wmk. 334
Engr.   Perf. 13
658 A161 5b vio & brn   12.50 1.50
659 A161 6b grn & vio   7.50 1.60
660 A161 10b red & black   14.00 2.00
661 A161 20b org & yel grn
    ('75)   175.00 8.00
    Nos. 652-661 (10)   217.80 15.40
For surcharges see Nos. 1168A, 1548, 2249.

Silversmiths — A162

1973, June 15   Litho.   Perf. 13½
662 A162 75s shown   .65 .25
663 A162 2.75b Lacquerware   2.25 .55
664 A162 4b Pottery   5.50 3.00
665 A162 5b Paper umbrel-
    las   5.75 1.00
    Nos. 662-665 (4)   14.15 4.80
Thai handicrafts.

Fresco from Temple of the Emerald
Buddha — A163

Designs: Frescoes illustrating Ramayana in
Temple of the Emerald Buddha.

1973, July 17   Photo.   Wmk. 329
666 A163 25s multicolored   1.00 .40
667 A163 75s multicolored   1.00 .40
668 A163 1.50b multicolored   3.25 1.25
669 A163 2b multicolored   5.50 1.60
670 A163 2.75b multicolored   2.75 .65
671 A163 3b multicolored   10.00 2.00
672 A163 5b multicolored   13.50 6.75
673 A163 6b multicolored   6.00 2.50
    Nos. 666-673 (8)   43.00 15.55

Development of Postal
Service — A164

2b, Telecommunications development.

1973, Aug. 4   Perf. 13½
674 A164 75s multicolored   .70 .40
675 A164 2b multicolored   2.00 .95
90th anniv. of Post and Telegraph Dept.

No. 1 and Other Stamps — A165

Various Stamps and: 1.25b, No. 147. 1.50b,
No. 209. 2b, No. 244.

1973, Aug. 4   Photo. & Engr.
676 A165 75s dp rose & dk
    bl   .65 .25
677 A165 1.25b blue & dp rose   1.75 .50
678 A165 1.50b olive & vio blk   5.50 1.60
679 A165 2b org & sl grn   4.00 .65
a.   Souvenir sheet of 4   21.00 17.50
    Nos. 676-679 (4)   11.90 3.00
2nd Natl. Phil. Exhib., THAIPEX '73, Aug. 4-
8. No. 679a contains 4 stamps with simulated
perforations similar to Nos. 676-679.

INTERPOL Emblem — A166

1973, Sept. 3   Photo.
680 A166 75s gray & multi   1.00 .25
Intl. Criminal Police Organization, 50th anniv.

"Lilil Pralaw" — A167

Designs: Scenes from Thai literature.

Perf. 11x13
1973, Oct. 7   Litho.   Wmk. 368
681 A167 75s green & multi   .40 .25
682 A167 1.50b blue & multi   1.60 .60
683 A167 2b multicolored   3.50 1.40
684 A167 5b blue & multi   9.50 2.00
a.   Souvenir sheet of 4, #681-
    684, perf. 13x14   40.00 27.50
    Nos. 681-684 (4)   15.00 4.25
Intl. Letter Writing Week, Oct. 7-13.

Wat Suan Dok,
Chiangmai; UN
Emblem — A168

1973, Oct. 24   Perf. 13x11
685 A168 75s blue & multi   1.20 .35
United Nations Day.

Schomburgk's Deer — A169

25s, Kouprey. 75s, Gorals. 1.25b, Water
buffalos. 1.50b, Javan rhinoceros. 2b, Eld's
deer. 2.75b, Asiatic 2-horned rhinoceros. 4b,
Serows.

Wmk. 329
1973, Nov. 14   Photo.   Perf. 13½
686 A169 20s shown   .80 .30
687 A169 25s multicolored   .80 .30
688 A169 75s multicolored   1.40 .30
689 A169 1.25b multicolored   1.90 .95
690 A169 1.50b multicolored   8.00 3.25
691 A169 2b multicolored   10.00 3.25
692 A169 2.75b multicolored   8.00 1.00
693 A169 4b multicolored   12.00 8.00
    Nos. 686-693 (8)   42.90 17.35
Protected animals.

Human Rights Flame — A170

Wmk. 371
1973, Dec. 10   Litho.   Perf. 12½
694 A170 75s multicolored   1.40 .45
25th anniversary of the Universal Declaration of Human Rights.

Children and
Flowers — A171

1974, Jan. 12   Litho.   Perf. 13
695 A171 75s multicolored   1.50 .30
Children's Day.

Siriraj Hospital and Statue of Prince
Nakarin — A172

Perf. 13x13½
1974, Mar. 17   Photo.   Wmk. 368
696 A172 75s multicolored   1.25 .40
84th anniversary of Siriraj Hospital, oldest
medical school in Thailand.

Phala Piang
Lai — A173

Classical Thai Dances: 2.75b, Phra Lux
Phlaeng Rit. 4b, Chin Sao Sai. 5b, Charot
Phra Sumen.

Wmk. 334
1974, June 25   Litho.   Perf. 14
697 A173 75s pink & multi   1.20 .40
698 A173 2.75b gray bl & multi   3.00 .65
699 A173 4b gray & multi   6.75 4.00
700 A173 5b yellow & multi   6.75 3.25
    Nos. 697-700 (4)   17.70 8.30

Large Teak Tree in Uttaradit
Province — A174

1974, July 5   Wmk. 329   Perf. 12½
701 A174 75s multicolored   1.00 .40
15th Arbor Day.

People and WPY Emblem — A175

Perf. 10½x13
1974, Aug. 19   Litho.   Wmk. 368
702 A175 75s multicolored   .95   .30
World Population Year, 1974.

Ban Chiang Painted Vase — A176

75s, Royal chariot. 2.75b, Avalokitesavara Bodhisattva. 3b, King Mongkut, Rama IV.

1974, Sept. 19   Wmk. 262   Perf. 12½
703 A176   75s blue & multi   .85   .40
704 A176   2b black, brn & bis   2.25   .85
705 A176   2.75b black, brn & tan 3.00   .70
706 A176   3b black & multi   4.00 2.25
   Nos. 703-706 (4)   10.10 4.20
Centenary of National Museum. Inscribed "BATH" in error.

Purging Cassia — A177

1974, Oct. 6   Wmk. 368   Perf. 11x13
707 A177   75s shown   .75   .25
708 A177   2.75b Butea   2.75   .65
709 A177   3b Jasmine   5.50 1.00
710 A177   4b Lagerstroemia   4.75 2.00
a.   Souvenir sheet of 4, #707-
     710, perf. 13½x14   45.00 45.00
   Nos. 707-710 (4)   13.75 3.90
Intl. Letter Writing Week, Oct. 6-12.

"UPU" and UPU Emblem — A178

1974, Oct. 9   Wmk. 371   Perf. 12½
711 A178 75s dk green & multi   1.10   .45
Centenary of Universal Postal Union.

Wat Suthat Thepvararam — A179

Wmk. 329
1974, Oct. 24   Photo.   Perf. 13
712 A179 75s multicolored   1.50   .45
United Nations Day.

Elephant Roundup — A180

Wmk. 371
1974, Nov. 16   Engr.   Perf. 12½
713 A180 4b multicolored   4.75 2.00
Tourist publicity.

Vanda Coerulea — A181

Orchids: 2.75b, Dendrobium aggregatum. 3b, Dendrobium scabrilingue. 4b, Aerides falcata.

Perf. 11x13
1974, Dec. 5   Photo.   Wmk. 368
714 A181   75s red & multi   .95   .30
715 A181   2.75b multicolored   2.25   .70
716 A181   3b olive & multi   4.50 2.00
717 A181   4b green & multi   4.50 2.25
a.   Souvenir sheet of 4, #714-
     717, perf. 13½x14   45.00 45.00
   Nos. 714-717 (4)   12.20 5.25
See Nos. 745-748.

Boy — A182

Perf. 14x13½
1975, Jan. 11   Litho.   Wmk. 374
718 A182 75s vermilion & multi 2.40   .55
Children's Day.

Democracy Monument — A183

Designs: 2b, Mother with children and animals, bas-relief from Democracy Monument. 2.75b, Workers, bas-relief from Democracy Monument. 5b, Top of Democracy Monument and quotation from speech of King Rama VII.

Perf. 14x14½
1975, Jan. 26   Wmk. 233
719 A183   75s dull grn & multi   .95   .30
720 A183   2b multicolored   2.50   .65
721 A183   2.75b blue & multi   4.50   .70
722 A183   5b multicolored   4.75   .90
   Nos. 719-722 (4)   12.70 3.55
Movement of Oct. 14, 1973, to re-establish democratic institutions.

Marbled Tiger Cat — A184

1975, Mar. 5   Wmk. 334   Perf. 13½
723 A184   20s shown   1.00   .65
724 A184   75s Gaurs   2.40   .65
725 A184   2.75b Asiatic elephant 8.00 1.25

726 A184   3b Clouded leop-
            ard   7.00 3.25
   Nos. 723-726 (4)   18.40 5.80
Protected animals.

White-eyed River Martin — A185

Birds: 2b, Paradise flycatchers. 2.75b, Long-tailed broadbills. 5b, Sultan tit.

Wmk. 371
1975, Apr. 2   Litho.   Perf. 12½
727 A185   75s ocher & multi   1.60   .95
728 A185   2b lt blue & multi   3.75 1.60
729 A185   2.75b lt violet & multi 4.00 1.60
730 A185   5b rose & multi   8.00 2.75
   Nos. 727-730 (4)   17.35 6.90

King Bhumibol Adulyadej and Queen Sirikit — A186

3b, King, Queen, different background design.

Perf. 10½x13
1975, Apr. 28   Photo.   Wmk. 368
731 A186 75s violet bl & multi 2.40   .65
732 A186 3b multicolored   4.50 1.50
25th wedding anniversary of King Bhumibol Adulyadej and Queen Sirikit.

Round-house Kick — A187

Thai Boxing: 2.75b, Reverse elbow. 3b, Flying knee. 5b, Ritual homage.

Wmk. 371
1975, May 20   Litho.   Perf. 12½
733 A187   75s green & multi   1.60   .45
734 A187   2.75b blue & multi   4.00 1.20
735 A187   3b orange & multi   4.75 2.40
736 A187   5b orange & multi   14.00 4.00
   Nos. 733-736 (4)   24.35 8.05

Tosakanth Mask — A188

Masks: 2b, Kumbhakarn. 3b, Rama. 4b, Hanuman.

1975, June 10   Litho.   Wmk. 371
737 A188   75s dark gray & multi 1.75   .30
738 A188   2b dull vio & multi 4.75   .65
739 A188   3b purple & multi   5.50 1.75
740 A188   4b multicolored   13.00 6.00
   Nos. 737-740 (4)   25.00 8.70
Thai art and literature.

THAIPEX 75 Emblem — A189

THAIPEX 75 Emblem and: 2.75b, Stamp designer. 4b, Stamp printing plant. 5b, Stamp collector.

1975, Aug. 4   Wmk. 371   Perf. 12½
741 A189   75s yellow & multi   .65   .30
742 A189   2.75b orange & multi 1.75   .65
743 A189   4b lt blue & multi   2.75 1.75
744 A189   5b carmine & multi   3.25   .65
   Nos. 741-744 (4)   8.40 3.35
THAIPEX 75, Third National Philatelic Exhibition, Aug. 4-10.

Orchid Type of 1974

Orchids: 75s, Dendrobium cruentum. 2b, Dendrobium parishii. 2.75b, Vanda teres. 5b, Vanda denisoniana.

Perf. 11x13
1975, Aug. 12   Photo.   Wmk. 368
745 A181   75s olive & multi   .85   .55
746 A181   2b multicolored   2.25 1.40
747 A181   2.75b scarlet & multi 4.00 1.40
748 A181   5b ultra & multi   6.75 2.25
a.   Souv. sheet, #745-748, perf
     13½   52.50 52.50
   Nos. 745-748 (4)   13.85 5.60

Mytilus Smaragdinus — A190

Sea Shells: 1b, Turbo marmoratus. 2.75b, Oliva mustelina. 5b, Cypraea moneta.

Perf. 14x14½
1975, Sept. 5   Litho.   Wmk. 375
749 A190   75s yellow & multi   2.00   .85
750 A190   1b ver & multi   1.75   .25
751 A190   2.75b blue & multi   5.50   .40
752 A190   5b green & multi   11.00 3.75
   Nos. 749-752 (4)   20.25 5.25

Yachting and Games Emblem — A191

Designs: 1.25b, Badminton. 1.50b, Volleyball. 2b, Target shooting.

Perf. 11x13
1975, Sept. 20   Litho.   Wmk. 368
753 A191   75s ultra & black   1.00   .30
754 A191   1.25b brt rose & blk 1.40   .95
755 A191   1.50b red & black   2.50 1.75
756 A191   2b apple grn &
            blk   3.50 1.90
a.   Souv. sheet, #753-756, perf
     13½   40.00 40.00
   Nos. 753-756 (4)   8.40 4.90
8th SEAP Games, Bangkok, Sept. 1975.

Pataya Beach A192

Views: 2b, Samila Beach. 3b, Prachuap Bay. 5b, Laem Singha Bay.

1975, Oct. 5 **Wmk. 371** *Perf. 12½*

757	A192	75s orange & multi	1.10	.65
758	A192	2b orange & multi	2.40	1.50
759	A192	3b orange & multi	6.00	.85
760	A192	5b orange & multi	7.00	2.00
		Nos. 757-760 (4)	16.50	5.00

Intl. Letter Writing Week, Oct. 6-12.

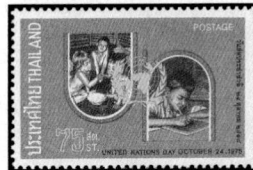

"u n," UN Emblem, Food and Education for Children — A193

1975, Oct. 24 **Litho.** **Wmk. 371**

761	A193	75s ultra & multi	1.40	.45

United Nations Day.

Morse Telegraph — A194

Design: 2.75b, Teleprinter and radar.

Perf. 14x14½

1975, Nov. 4 **Litho.** **Wmk. 334**

762	A194	75s multicolored	1.50	.70
763	A194	2.75b blue & multi	2.25	.80

Centenary of telegraph system.

Sukhrip Khrong Mueang Barge — A195

Thai ceremonial barges: 1b, Royal escort barge Anekchat Phuchong. 2b, Royal barge Anantanakarat. 2.75b, Krabi Ran Ron Rap barge. 3b, Asura Wayuphak barge. 4b, Asura paksi barge. 5b, Royal barge Sri Suphanahong, 6b, Phali Rang Thawip barge.

Wmk. 371

1975, Nov. 18 **Litho.** *Perf. 12½*

764	A195	75s multicolored	2.40	.45
765	A195	1b multicolored	4.00	1.90
766	A195	2b lilac & multi	6.00	2.00
767	A195	2.75b multicolored	6.75	2.25
768	A195	3b yellow & multi	8.00	2.75
769	A195	4b multicolored	8.00	6.00
770	A195	5b gray & multi	15.00	6.50
771	A195	6b blue & multi	12.00	6.00
		Nos. 764-771 (8)	62.15	27.85

Thai Flag, Arms of Chakri Royal Family — A196

King Bhumibol Adulyadej — A197

Perf. 15x14

1975, Dec. 5 **Litho.** **Wmk. 375**

772	A196	75s multicolored	2.75	.85
773	A197	5b multicolored	5.00	1.50

King Bhumibol's 48th birthday.

Shot Put and SEAP Emblem — A198

2b, Table tennis. 3b, Bicycling. 4b, Relay race.

1975, Dec. 9 **Wmk. 368** *Perf. 11x13*

774	A198	1b orange & black	.80	.25
775	A198	2b brt green & blk	2.75	1.60
776	A198	3b ocher & blk	3.25	1.75
777	A198	4b violet & blk	3.50	2.40
a.		Souvenir sheet of 4, #774-777, perf. 13½	37.50	37.50
		Nos. 774-777 (4)	10.30	6.00

8th SEAP Games, Bangkok, Dec. 9-20.

IWY Emblem and Globe — A199

Perf. 14x14½

1975, Dec. 20 **Wmk. 375**

778	A199	75s blk, org & vio bl	1.10	.30

International Women's Year.

Children Writing on Slate — A200

Perf. 13x14

1976, Jan. 10 **Litho.** **Wmk. 368**

779	A200	75s lt green & multi	1.60	.70

Children's Day.

Macrobrachium Rosenbergii — A201

Designs: 2b, Penaeus merguiensis. 2.75b, Panulirus ornatus. 5b, Penaeus monodon.

1976, Feb. 18 *Perf. 11x13*

780	A201	75s multicolored	2.50	.30
781	A201	2b multicolored	4.00	2.00
782	A201	2.75b multicolored	4.00	.65
783	A201	5b multicolored	9.50	4.50
		Nos. 780-783 (4)	20.00	7.45

Shrimp and lobster exports.

Golden-backed Three-toed Woodpecker A202

Birds: 1.50b, Greater green-billed malcoha. 3b, Pomatorhinus hypoleucos. 4b, Green magpie.

Wmk. 371

1976, Apr. 2 **Litho.** *Perf. 12½*

784	A202	1b multicolored	.80	.45
785	A202	1.50b multicolored	.80	.65
786	A202	3b yellow & multi	4.00	1.20
787	A202	4b rose & multi	3.00	.95
		Nos. 784-787 (4)	8.60	3.25

Ban Chiang Vase — A203

Designs: Ban Chiang painted pottery, various vessels, Bronze Age.

Perf. 14½x14

1976, May 5 **Litho.** **Wmk. 375**

788	A203	1b olive & multi	1.25	.25
789	A203	2b dp blue & multi	5.25	.65
790	A203	3b green & multi	3.75	.55
791	A203	4b org red & multi	6.00	3.50
		Nos. 788-791 (4)	16.25	4.95

Mailman, 1883 — A204

Designs: 3b, Mailman, 1935. 4b, Mailman, 1950. 5b, Mailman, 1974.

Wmk. 377

1976, Aug. 4 **Litho.** *Perf. 12½*

792	A204	1b multicolored	.95	.30
793	A204	3b multicolored	2.75	1.60
794	A204	4b multicolored	4.25	2.40
795	A204	5b multicolored	6.00	1.60
		Nos. 792-795 (4)	13.95	5.90

Development of mailmen's uniforms.

Kinnari — A205

Thai Mythology: 2b, Suphan-mat-cha. 4b, Garuda. 5b, Naga.

1976, Oct. 3 **Wmk. 368** *Perf. 11x13*

796	A205	1b green & multi	6.00	1.75
797	A205	2b ultra & multi	1.60	.30
798	A205	4b gray & multi	2.40	.40
799	A205	5b slate & multi	3.50	.80
		Nos. 796-799 (4)	13.50	3.25

International Letter Writing Week.

UN Emblem, Drug Addicts, Alcohol, Cigarettes, Drugs — A206

Wmk. 329

1976, Oct. 24 **Photo.** *Perf. 13½*

800	A206	1b ultra & multi	1.20	.40

United Nations Day.

Old and New Telephones — A207

Perf. 14x14½

1976, Nov. 10 **Litho.** **Wmk. 375**

801	A207	1b multicolored	1.20	.40

Centenary of first telephone call by Alexander Graham Bell, Mar. 10, 1876.

Sivalaya-Mahaprasad Hall — A208

Royal Houses: 2b, Cakri-Mahaprasad. 4b, Mahisra-Prasad. 5b, Dusit-Mahaprasad.

Perf. 14x15

1976, Dec. 5 **Wmk. 375** **Litho.**

802	A208	1b multicolored	.95	.25
803	A208	2b multicolored	6.75	.75
804	A208	4b multicolored	4.00	2.40
805	A208	5b multicolored	5.00	1.60
		Nos. 802-805 (4)	16.70	5.00

Banteng — A209

Protected animals: 2b, Tapir and young. 4b, Sambar deer and fawn. 5b, Hog deer family.

Wmk. 334

1976, Dec. 26 **Litho.** *Perf. 11*

806	A209	1b multicolored	5.50	2.40
807	A209	2b multicolored	6.50	2.75

Wmk. 368

808	A209	4b multicolored	3.00	.95
809	A209	5b multicolored	3.25	1.00
		Nos. 806-809 (4)	18.25	7.10

Child Casting Shadow of Man — A210

Wmk. 329

1977, Jan. 8 **Photo.** *Perf. 13½*

810	A210	1b multicolored	1.40	.30

National Children's Day.

Alsthom's Electric Engine — A211

Locomotives: 2b, Davenport's electric engine. 4b, Pacific's steam engine. 5b, George Egestoff's steam engine.

Perf. 11x13

			Wmk. 368	
811	A211	1b multicolored	1.50	.95
812	A211	2b multicolored	6.00	2.50
813	A211	4b multicolored	13.50	8.00
814	A211	5b multicolored	20.00	6.00
		Nos. 811-814 (4)	41.00	17.45

80th anniv. of State Railroad of Thailand.

Chulalongkorn University Auditorium — A212

1977, Mar. 26 **Photo.**

815	A212	1b multicolored	1.50	.40

Chulalongkorn University, 60th anniversary.

Flags of AOPU Members — A213

Wmk. 371
1977, Apr. 1 **Litho.** *Perf. 12½*

816	A213	1b multicolored	1.50	.40

Asian-Oceanic Postal Union (AOPU), 15th anniv.

Invalid in Wheelchair and Soldiers — A214

Wmk. 329
1977, Apr. 2 **Photo.** *Perf. 13½*

817	A214	5b multicolored	1.75	.45

Sai-Jai-Thai Day, to publicize Sai-Jai-Thai Foundation which helps wounded soldiers.

Phra Aphai Mani and Phisua Samut A215

Puppets: 3b, Rusi and Sutsakhon. 4b, Nang Vali and Usren. 5b, Phra Aphai Mani and Nang Laweng's portrait.

Perf. 11x13

			Wmk. 368	
818	A215	2b multicolored	.80	.25
819	A215	3b multicolored	2.00	.40
820	A215	4b multicolored	1.60	.40
821	A215	5b multicolored	2.40	.65
		Nos. 818-821 (4)	6.80	1.70

Thai plays and literature.

Drum Dance — A216

Designs: 3b, Dance of dip nets. 4b, Harvest dance. 5b, Kan dance.

1977, July 14 **Photo.** *Perf. 13x11*

822	A216	2b rose & multi	.30	.25
823	A216	3b lt green & multi	1.60	.45
824	A216	4b yellow & multi	1.40	.40
825	A216	5b lt violet & multi	1.60	.45
		Nos. 822-825 (4)	4.90	1.55

Thailand No. 609, Various Stamps and Thaipex Emblem — A217

Wmk. 377
1977, Aug. 4 **Litho.** *Perf. 12½*

826	A217	75s multicolored	1.40	.40

THAIPEX 77, 4th National Philatelic Exhibition, Aug. 4-12.

Scenes from Thai Literature — A218

Perf. 11x13

1977, Oct. 5 **Photo.** **Wmk. 368**

827	A218	75s multicolored	2.40	.30
828	A218	2b multi, diff.	2.40	.80
829	A218	5b multi, diff.	3.00	.30
830	A218	6b multi, diff.	4.00	.95
		Nos. 827-830 (4)	11.80	2.55

Intl. Letter Writing Week, Oct. 6-12.

Old and New Buildings, UN Emblem — A219

1977, Oct. 5 **Litho.** *Perf. 11x13*

831	A219	75s multicolored	1.90	.30

United Nations Day.

King Bhumibol as Scout Leader, Camp and Emblem — A220

1977, Nov. 21 **Photo.** **Wmk. 368**

832	A220	75s multicolored	2.50	.30

9th National Jamboree, Nov. 21-27.

Diseased Hand and Elbow — A221

1977, Dec. 20 *Perf. 11x13*

833	A221	75s multicolored	1.25	.30

World Rheumatism Year.

Map of South East Asia and ASEAN Emblem — A222

Wmk. 377
1977, Dec. 1 **Litho.** *Perf. 12½*

834	A222	5b multicolored	2.25	.45

ASEAN, 10th anniv.

King Type of 1972-74 Redrawn
1976 *Perf. 12½x13*

Size: 21x27mm

835	A146	20s blue	6.00	.65
836	A146	75s lilac	6.00	.65

Engr.

837	A146	10b vermilion & blk	55.00	3.50
838	A146	40b bister & lilac	12.00	2.25
		Nos. 835-838 (4)	79.00	7.05

Numerals are taller and thinner and leaves in background have been redrawn.

Children Carrying Flag of Thailand — A223

Wmk. 329
1978, Jan. 9 **Photo.** *Perf. 13½*

839	A223	75s multicolored	1.75	.45

Children's Day.

Dendrobium Heterocarpum — A224

Orchids: 1b, Dendrobium pulchellum. 1.50b, Doritis pulcherrima. 2b, Dendrobium hercoglossum. 2.75b, Aerides odorata. 3b, Trichoglottis fasciata. 5b, Dendrobium wardianum. 6b, Dendrobium senile.

Perf. 11x14

1978, Jan. 18 **Wmk. 368**

840	A224	75s multicolored	1.60	.55
841	A224	1b multicolored	2.50	1.00
842	A224	1.50b multicolored	3.25	2.00
843	A224	2b multicolored	.65	.25
844	A224	2.75b multicolored	5.50	.25
845	A224	3b multicolored	.65	.25
846	A224	5b multicolored	1.00	.25
847	A224	6b multicolored	1.40	1.25
		Nos. 840-847 (8)	16.55	5.80

9th World Orchid Conference.

Census Chart, Symbols of Agriculture — A225

Wmk. 377
1978, Mar. 1 **Litho.** *Perf. 12½*

848	A225	75s multicolored	.65	.25

Agricultural census, Apr. 1978.

Anabas Testudineus — A226

Fish: 2b, Datnioides microlepis. 3b, Kryptopterus apogon. 4b, Probarbus Jullieni.

Perf. 11x13

1978, Apr. 13 **Photo.** **Wmk. 368**

849	A226	1b multicolored	2.40	1.60
850	A226	2b multicolored	1.50	.40
851	A226	3b multicolored	1.50	.40
852	A226	4b multicolored	2.25	.50
		Nos. 849-852 (4)	7.65	2.90

Birth of Prince Siddhartha — A227

Murals: 3b, Prince Siddhartha cuts his hair. 5b, Buddha descending from Tavatimsa Heaven. 6b, Buddha entering Nirvana.

Wmk. 329
1978, June 15 **Photo.** *Perf. 13½*

853	A227	2b multicolored	2.40	.70
854	A227	3b multicolored	4.75	1.10
855	A227	5b multicolored	9.50	3.75
856	A227	6b multicolored	5.50	2.40
		Nos. 853-856 (4)	22.15	7.95

Story of Gautama Buddha, murals in Puthi Savan Hall, National Museum, Bangkok.

Bhumibol Dam — A228

Dams and Reservoirs: 2b, Sirikit dam. 2.75b, Vajiralongkorn dam. 6b, Ubol Ratana dam.

Perf. 14x14½

1978, July 28 **Litho.** **Wmk. 233**

857	A228	75s multicolored	1.10	.25
858	A228	2b multicolored	1.40	.25
859	A228	2.75b multicolored	2.75	.25
860	A228	6b multicolored	4.25	2.00
		Nos. 857-860 (4)	9.50	2.75

Idea Lynceus — A229

Butterflies: 3b, Sephisa chandra. 5b, Charaxes durnfordi. 6b, Cethosia penthesilea methypsia.

Perf. 11x13
1978, Aug. 25   Litho.   Wmk. 368
861 A229 2b lilac, blk & red   2.00   .70
862 A229 3b multicolored   3.25   .70
863 A229 5b multicolored   3.75 1.75
864 A229 6b multicolored   5.00 2.75
Nos. 861-864 (4)   14.00 5.90

Chedi Chai Mongkhon Temple — A230

Temples: 2b, That Hariphunchai. 2.75b, Borom That Chaiya. 5b, That Choeng Chum.

1978, Oct. 8   Perf. 13x11
865 A230 75s multicolored   1.40   .30
866 A230 2b multicolored   2.00   .30
867 A230 2.75b multicolored   3.25   .30
868 A230 5b multicolored   3.25 1.40
Nos. 865-868 (4)   9.90 2.30

Intl. Letter Writing Week, Oct. 6-12.

Mother and Children, UN Emblem — A231

Perf. 14½x14
1978, Oct. 24   Litho.   Wmk. 375
869 A231 75s multicolored   .95   .25

United Nations Day.

Boxing, Soccer, Pole Vault — A232

Designs: 2b, Javelin, weight lifting, running. 3b, Ball games and sailing. 5b, Basketball, hockey stick and boxing gloves.

Perf. 14x14½
1978, Oct.   Wmk. 233   Litho.
870 A232 75s multicolored   .80   .25
871 A232 2b multicolored   1.10   .55
872 A232 3b multicolored   2.10   .80
873 A232 5b multicolored   4.50 2.40
Nos. 870-873 (4)   8.50 4.00

8th Asian Games, Bangkok.

Five Races and World Map A233

1978, Nov.
874 A233 75s multicolored   .95   .25

Anti-Apartheid Year.

Children Painting Thai Flag — A234

Children and Children's SOS Village, Tambol Bangpu — A235

1979, Jan. 17   Perf. 14x14½
875 A234 75s multicolored   .65   .25
876 A235 75s multicolored   1.40   .45

International Year of the Child.

Matuta Lunaris — A236

Crabs: 2.75b, Matuta planipes fabricius. 3b, Portunus pelagicus. 5b, Scylla serrata.

Wmk. 377
1979, Mar. 22   Litho.   Perf. 12½
877 A236 2b multicolored   1.60   .65
878 A236 2.75b multicolored   4.75   .80
879 A236 3b multicolored   3.25   .65
880 A236 5b multicolored   5.00 2.75
Nos. 877-880 (4)   14.60 4.85

A237

1979, June 25
881 A237 1b Sweetsop   1.75   .30
882 A237 2b Pineapple   1.75   .95
883 A237 5b Bananas   4.00 1.00
884 A237 6b Longans (litchi)   2.75 2.00
Nos. 881-884 (4)   10.25 4.25

See Nos. 1145-1148.

A238

Young man and woman planting tree.

Perf. 13x11
1979, July 10   Litho.   Wmk. 368
885 A238 75s multicolored   .80   .25

20th Arbor Day.

Pencil, Pen, Thaipex '79 Emblem — A239

Thaipex '79 Emblem and: 2b, Envelopes. 2.75b, Stamp album. 5b, Magnifying glass and tongs.

1979, Aug. 4   Perf. 11x13
886 A239 75s multicolored   .65   .25
887 A239 2b multicolored   1.10   .25
888 A239 2.75b multicolored   1.25   .25
889 A239 5b multicolored   3.50 1.40
Nos. 886-889 (4)   6.50 2.15

Thaipex '79, 5th National Philatelic Exhibition, Bangkok, Aug. 4-12.

Floral Arrangement A240

Designs: Decorative arrangements.

Perf. 14½x14
1979, Oct. 7   Wmk. 233
890 A240 75s multicolored   .65   .25
891 A240 2b multicolored   1.10   .25
892 A240 2.75b multicolored   1.75   .25
893 A240 5b multicolored   2.90 1.25
Nos. 890-893 (4)   6.40 2.00

Intl. Letter Writing Week, Oct. 8-14.

UN Day — A241

1979, Oct. 24   Litho.   Perf. 14½x14
894 A241 75s multicolored   .85   .25

Frigate Makut Rajakumarn — A242

Thai Naval Ships: 3b, Frigate Tapi. 5b, Fast strike craft, Prabparapak. 6b, Patrol boat T-91.

Wmk. 329
1979, Nov. 20   Photo.   Perf. 13½
895 A242 2b multicolored   2.10   .40
896 A242 3b multicolored   2.10   .85
897 A242 5b multicolored   5.00 2.00
898 A242 6b multicolored   7.50 2.75
Nos. 895-898 (4)   16.70 6.00

Thai Royal Orders (Medallions and Ribbons) — A243

Designs: #900a, Rajamitrabhorn Order. #902a, House of Chakri. #904a, The nine gems. #906a, Chula Chom Klao. Pairs have continuous design.

Perf. 13x11
1979, Dec. 5   Litho.   Wmk. 368
899 1b multicolored   1.40   .40
900 1b multicolored   1.40   .40
  a. A243 Pair, #899-900   3.00 3.00
901 2b multicolored   1.50   .30
902 2b multicolored   1.50   .30
  a. A243 Pair, #901-902   3.25 3.25
903 5b multicolored   3.00   .70
904 5b multicolored   3.00   .70
  a. A243 Pair, #903-904   6.50 6.50
905 6b multicolored   3.75 1.40
906 6b multicolored   3.75 1.40
  a. A243 Pair, #905-906   8.00 8.00
Nos. 899-906 (8)   19.30 5.60

See Nos. 1278-1285.

King Type of 1972-77
Perf. 13½x13
1979, Dec. 23   Litho.   Wmk. 329
Size: 21x26mm
907 A146 50s olive green   .60   .25
Engr.
908 A146 2b org red & lilac   1.25   .25

Rice Planting — A245

Children's Day: No. 910, Family in rice field.

Perf. 13x11
1980, Jan. 12   Litho.   Wmk. 368
909 A245 75s multicolored   .85   .25
910 A245 75s multicolored   .85   .25

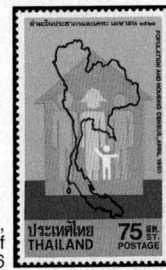

Family, House, Map of Thailand — A246

Perf. 15x14
1980, Feb. 1   Litho.   Wmk. 233
911 A246 75s multicolored   .70   .30

Natl. Population & Housing Census, Apr.

Gold-fronted Leafbird — A247

2b, Yellow-cheeked tit. 3b, Chestnut-tailed siva. 5b, Scarlet minivet.

Perf. 13x11

			Wmk. 368	
1980, Feb. 26				
912	A247	75s shown	.70	.25
913	A247	2b multicolored	1.00	.30
914	A247	3b multicolored	2.50	.40
915	A247	5b multicolored	4.50	1.25
		Nos. 912-915 (4)	8.70	2.20

Intl. Commission for Bird Preservation, 9th Conf. of Asian Section, Chieng-mai, 2/26-29.

Smokers and Lungs, WHO Emblem — A248

1980, Apr. 7   Wmk. 329   Perf. 13½
916 A248 75s multicolored   .70 .25

World Health Day; fight against cigarette smoking.

Garuda and Rotary Emblem — A249

1980, May 6   Wmk. 368   Perf. 13x11
917 A249 5b multicolored   1.90 .45

Rotary International, 75th anniversary.

Sai Yok Falls, Kanchanaburi — A250

2b, Punyaban Falls, Ranong. 5b, Heo Suwat Falls, Nakhon Ratchasima. 6b, Siriphum Falls, Chiang Mai.

Perf. 14x15

1980, July 1			**Litho.**	**Wmk. 233**	
918	A250	1b shown		.65	.25
919	A250	2b multicolored		.80	.25
920	A250	5b multicolored		2.40	1.00
921	A250	6b multicolored		2.10	1.40
		Nos. 918-921 (4)		5.95	2.90

Queen Sirikit — A251

Family with Cattle, Ceres Medal (Reverse) — A252

No. 924, Ceres medal (obverse), potters.

Perf. 13½, 11x13 (5b)
Wmk. 329, 368 (5b)

1980, Aug. 12			**Litho.**	
922	A251	75s multicolored	.65	.25
923	A252	1.75b multicolored	1.75	.80
924	A252	5b multicolored	1.75	.80
		Nos. 922-924 (3)	4.15	1.85

Queen Sirikit's 48th birthday.

Khao Phanomrung Temple, Buri Ram — A253

Intl. Letter Writing Week, Oct. 6-12 (Temples): 2b, Prang Ku, Chailyaphum. 2.75b, Phimai, Nakhon Ratchasima. 5b, Sikhoraphum, Surin.

Perf. 11x13

1980, Oct. 5			**Wmk. 368**	
925	A253	75s multicolored	.80	.30
926	A253	2b multicolored	.80	.30
927	A253	2.75b multicolored	1.20	.45
928	A253	5b multicolored	2.00	1.00
		Nos. 925-928 (4)	4.80	2.05

Princess Mother — A254

Perf. 15x14

1980, Oct. 21		**Litho.**	**Wmk. 233**	
929	A254	75s multicolored	2.75	.55
	Complete booklet, 10 #929		65.00	

Princess Mother, 80th birthday.

Golden Mount, Bangkok — A255

1980, Oct. 24
930 A255 75s multicolored   .65 .30
  Complete booklet, 10 #930   16.00

United Nations Day.

King Bhumibol Adulyadej — A256

Type I

Type II Redrawn

Two types of Nos. 936-938: Type I, asymmetrical shape to mouth and small eye pupils. Type II, symmetrical mouth and large eye pupils.

Perf. 11x13

1980-86(?)			**Litho.**	**Wmk. 368**	
932	A256	25s salmon		2.00	.25
933	A256	50s olive green		4.50	.25
	b.	Wmk. 233, perf. 14x15		7.50	.40
	c.	Wmk. 387, perf. 11x13		1.50	.25
934	A256	75s lilac		.70	.25
935	A256	1.25b yellow green		.70	.25
	a.	Wmk. 387, perf. 11x13		2.25	.25
	b.	Wmk. 233, perf. 14x15		6.00	.25

Perf. 13½x13

			Engr.	**Wmk. 329**	
936	A256	3b brn & dk bl (II)		.70	.25
	a.	Type I		20.00	1.20
937	A256	5b pur & brn (II)		1.40	.30
	a.	Type I		20.00	1.20
938	A256	6b dk grn & pur (II)		1.40	.25
	a.	Type I		20.00	1.20
939	A256	8.50b grn & brn org		2.00	.50
940	A256	9.50b olive & dk grn		2.50	.55
		Nos. 932-940 (9)		15.90	2.85

Issued: 25s, 75s, 12/5/80; Nos. 933, 935, 9/7/81; #933b, 12/5/81; Nos. 933b, 935b, 6/8/83; Nos. 936a, 937a, 938a, 8.50b, 9.50b, 12/5/83. Nos. 933c, 935a, 1984. Nos. 936-938, 1985-86.
See Nos. 1080-1093. For surcharges see Nos. 1226-1226A, 2250.

King Rama VII Monument Inauguration A257

Perf. 15x14
1980, Dec. 10   Wmk. 233
946 A257 75s multicolored   .75 .30

Bencharongware Bowl — A258

Perf. 11x13

1980, Dec. 15			**Wmk. 368**	
947	A258	2b shown	1.20	.40
948	A258	2.75b Covered bowls	1.20	.40
949	A258	3b Covered jar	1.75	.60
950	A258	5b Stem plates	1.75	1.00
		Nos. 947-950 (4)	5.90	2.40

King Vajiravudh Birth Centenary A259

1981, Jan. 1   Wmk. 233   Perf. 15x14
951 A259 75s multicolored   1.40 .25
  Complete booklet, 10 #951   32.50

Children's Day — A260

Perf. 13x11
1981, Jan. 16   Wmk. 368
952 A260 75s multicolored   1.10 .25
  Complete booklet, 10 #952   16.00

Hegira, 1500th Anniv. — A261

Wmk. 377
1981, Jan. 18   Litho.   Perf. 12½
953 A261 5b multicolored   3.25 .75

Dolls in Native Costumes — A262

Wmk. 368

1981, Feb. 6			**Perf. 13½**	
954	A262	75s Palm-leaf fish mobile	.45	.25
	Complete booklet, 10 #954		12.50	
955	A262	75s Teak elephants	.45	.25
	Complete booklet, 10 #955		12.50	
956	A262	2.75b shown	1.25	.60
957	A262	2.75b Baskets	1.25	.60
		Nos. 954-957 (4)	3.40	1.70

CONEX '81 International Crafts Exhibition.

Scout Leader and Boy on Crutches — A263

1981, Feb. 28   Perf. 13x11
958 A263 75s shown   .45 .25
  Complete booklet, 10 #958   10.00
959 A263 5b Diamond cutter in wheelchair   1.60 .60

International Year of the Disabled.

Dindaeng-Tarua Expressway Opening — A264

1981, Oct. 29   *Perf. 13½*
960 A264 1b Klongtoey .65 .25
961 A264 5b Vipavadee Rangsit Highway 2.25 .65

Ongkhot, Khon Mask — A265

Designs: Various Khon masks.

1981, July 1   **Litho.**   *Perf. 13x11*
962 A265 75s shown .45 .25
963 A265 2b Maiyarab 1.00 .25
964 A265 3b Sukrip 1.60 .50
965 A265 5b Indrajit 2.00 1.25
    Nos. 962-965 (4) 5.05 2.25

Exhibition Emblem, No. 83 — A266

     Wmk. 370
1981, Aug. 4   **Litho.**   *Perf. 12*
966 A266 75s shown .45 .25
967 A266 75s No. 144 .45 .25
968 A266 2.75b No. 198 1.25 .60
969 A266 2.75b No. 226 1.25 .60
    Nos. 966-969 (4) 3.40 1.70

A267

     Perf. 15x14
1981, Aug. 26   **Wmk. 233**
970 A267 1.25b multicolored .85 .25
   Complete booklet, 10 #970 16.00

Luang Praditphairo, court Musician, birth centenary. THAIPEX '81 Intl. Stamp Exhibition.

A268

Designs: Dwarfed trees.

1981, Oct. 4   **Wmk. 329**
971 A268 75s Mai hok-hian .65 .25
972 A268 2b Mai kam-ma-lo 1.00 .40
973 A268 2.75b Mai khen 1.40 .30
974 A268 5b Mai khabuan 2.75 1.25
    Nos. 971-974 (4) 5.80 2.20

25th Intl. Letter Writing Week, Oct. 6-12.

World Food Day A269

     Wmk. 370
1981, Oct. 16   **Litho.**   *Perf. 12*
975 A269 75s multicolored .65 .25

United Nations Day — A270

1981, Oct. 24   **Wmk. 368**   *Perf. 13½*
976 A270 1.25b Samran Mukha-mat Pavilion .85 .25

King Cobra A271

1981, Dec. 1   **Wmk. 329**   *Perf. 13½*
977 A271 75s shown .65 .25
978 A271 2b Banded krait 1.40 .65
979 A271 2.75b Thai cobra 1.60 .25
980 A271 5b Malayan pit viper 2.00 1.00
    Nos. 977-980 (4) 5.65 2.15

Children's Day — A272

1982, Jan. 9   **Wmk. 370**   *Perf. 12*
981 A272 1.25b multicolored .75 .25
   Complete booklet, strip of 4 #981 10.00

Scouting Year — A273

1982, Feb. 22
982 A273 1.25b multicolored .70 .25
   Complete booklet, strip of 4 #982 10.00

Bicentenary of Bangkok (Thai Capital) A274

Chakri Dynasty kings. (Rama I-Rama IX) — 1b, Buddha Yod-Fa (1736-1809). 2b, Buddha Lert La Naphalai (1767-1824). 3b, Nang Klao (1787-1851). 4b, Mongkut (1804-1868). 5b, Chulalongkorn (1853-1910). 6b, Vajiravudh (1880-1925). 7b, Prachathipok (1893-1941). 8b, Ananda Mahidol (1925-1946). 9b, Bhumibol Adulyadej (b. 1927).

1982, Apr. 4   **Litho.**   *Perf. 12*
983 A274 1b multicolored 1.20 .45
984 A274 1.25b shown 1.20 .45
   Complete booklet, strip of 4 #984 6.50
985 A274 2b multicolored 1.40 .45
986 A274 3b multicolored 2.25 .65
987 A274 4b multicolored 1.60 .80
988 A274 5b multicolored 2.75 .85
989 A274 6b multicolored 2.75 .85
990 A274 7b multicolored 5.25 4.00
991 A274 8b multicolored 2.75 1.50
992 A274 9b multicolored 3.25 1.75
  a. Souv. sheet of 10, 205x142mm 52.50 52.50
  b. Souv. sheet of 10, 195x180mm 52.50 52.50
    Nos. 983-992 (10) 24.40 11.75

Nos. 992a-992b each contain Nos. 983-992. No. 992a sold for 60b, No. 992b for 70b. Values for #992a-992b include folder.

TB Bacillus Centenary — A275

     Wmk. 368
1982, Apr. 7   **Litho.**   *Perf. 13½*
993 A275 1.25b multicolored .95 .25
   Complete booklet, strip of 4 #993 6.50

Local Flowers — A276

1.25b, Quisqualis indica. 1.50b, Murraya aniculata. 6.50b, Mesua ferrea. 7b, Desmos chinensis.

     Perf. 14x14½
1982, June 30   **Wmk. 233**
994 A276 1.25b multicolored .35 .25
   Complete booklet, strip of 4 #994 4.00
995 A276 1.50b multicolored .55 .30
996 A276 6.50b multicolored 2.00 1.00
997 A276 7b multicolored 1.60 .50
    Nos. 994-997 (4) 4.50 2.05

Buddhist Temples in Bangkok — A277

4.25b, Wat Pho. 6.50b, Mahathat Yuwarat Rangsarit. 7b, Phra Sri Rattana Satsadaram.

1982, Aug. 4   **Wmk. 368**   *Perf. 13½*
998 A277 1.25b shown .45 .25
   Complete booklet, strip of 4 #998 4.00

---

999 A277 4.25b multicolored 1.10 .40
1000 A277 6.50b multicolored 1.60 .95
1001 A277 7b multicolored 2.25 .65
  a. Souv. sheet of 4, #998-1001, perf. 12½ 90.00 90.00
    Nos. 998-1001 (4) 5.40 2.25

BANGKOK '83 Intl. Stamp Exhibition, Aug. 4-13, 1983. No. 1001a sold for 30b. See Nos. 1025-1026.

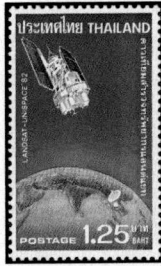

A278

Design: LANDSAT Satellite.

1982, Aug. 9   **Wmk. 370**   *Perf. 12*
1002 A278 1.25b multicolored .95 .30
   Complete booklet, strip of 4 #1002 6.50

2nd UN Conference on Peaceful Uses of Outer Space, Vienna, Aug. 9-21.

A279

Prince Purachatra of Kambaengbejra (1882-1936).

1982, Sept. 14   **Wmk. 233**   *Perf. 14*
1003 A279 1.25b multicolored 1.25 .30
   Complete booklet, strip of 4 #1003 8.00

26th Intl. Letter Writing Week, Oct. 6-12 — A280

Sangalok Pottery — 1.25b, Covered glazed jar. 3b, Painted jar. 4.25b, Glazed plate. 7b, Painted plate.

1982, Oct. 3   **Wmk. 329**   *Perf. 13½*
1004 A280 1.25b multicolored .50 .25
   Complete booklet, strip of 4 #1004 6.50
1005 A280 3b multicolored 1.75 .50
1006 A280 4.25b multicolored 1.00 .65
1007 A280 7b multicolored 2.25 1.00
    Nos. 1004-1007 (4) 5.50 2.40

UN Day — A281

Design: Loha Prasat Tower.

1982, Oct. 24
1008 A281 1.25b multicolored .85 .25
   Complete booklet, strip of 4 #1008 8.00

Musical Instruments — A282

50s, Chap, ching. 1b, Pi nai, pi nok. 1.25b, Klong that, taphon. 1.50b, Khong mong, krap. 6b, Khong wong yai. 7b, Khong wong lek. 8b, Ranat ek. 9b, Ranat thum.

1982, Nov. 30   Wmk. 370   Perf. 12

1009	A282	50s multicolored	.25	.25
1010	A282	1b multicolored	.70	.25
1011	A282	1.25b multicolored	.40	.25
		Complete booklet, strip of 4 #1011	6.50	
1012	A282	1.50b multicolored	.40	.30
1013	A282	6b multicolored	5.00	1.75
1014	A282	7b multicolored	2.00	.65
1015	A282	8b multicolored	1.75	.90
1016	A282	9b multicolored	1.75	.90
		Nos. 1009-1016 (8)	12.25	5.25

Pileated Gibbon — A283

3b, Pig-tailed macaque. 5b, Slow loris. 7b, Silvered leaf monkey.

1982, Dec. 26

1017	A283	1.25b shown	.65	.25
		Complete booklet, strip of 4 #1017	4.00	
1018	A283	3b multicolored	2.00	.45
1019	A283	5b multicolored	1.50	.55
1020	A283	7b multicolored	1.60	.80
		Nos. 1017-1020 (4)	5.75	2.05

ASEAN Members' Flags — A284

1982, Dec. 26   Wmk. 233

1021	A284	6.50b multicolored	1.75	.65

15th Anniv. of Assoc. of Southeast Asian Nations.

Children's Day — A285

Perf. 14½x14

1983, Jan. 8   Litho.   Wmk. 233

1022	A285	1.25b multicolored	.70	.25
		Complete booklet, strip of 4 #1022	8.50	

First Anniv. of Postal Code A286

1983, Feb. 25   Wmk. 329   Perf. 13½

1023	A286	1.25b Codes	.60	.25
		Complete booklet, strip of 4 #1023	7.50	
1024	A286	1.25b Code on envelope	.60	.25
		Complete booklet, strip of 4 #1024	7.50	

BANGKOK '83 Type of 1982

Design: Old General Post Office.

1983, Feb. 25   Wmk. 368   Photo.

1025	A277	7b multicolored	1.75	.30
1026	A277	10b multicolored	2.75	.65
a.		Souv. sheet of 2, #1025-1026, perf. 12½	32.50	32.50

25th Anniv. of Intl. Maritime Org. — A287

Perf. 14x14½

1983, Mar. 17   Litho.   Wmk. 233

1029	A287	1.25b Chinese junks	.70	.25
		Complete booklet, strip of 4 #1029	6.50	

Civil Servants' Day — A288

1983, Apr. 1   Wmk. 370   Perf. 12

1030	A288	1.25b multicolored	.65	.25
		Complete booklet, strip of 4 #1030	6.50	

Prince Sithiporn Kridakara (1883-1971) — A289

Perf. 14½x14

1983, Apr. 11   Wmk. 233

1031	A289	1.25b multicolored	.70	.25
		Complete booklet, strip of 4 #1031	6.50	

Domestic Satellite Communications System Inauguration — A290

Design: Map, dish antenna, satellite.

Wmk. 368

1983, Aug. 4   Litho.   Perf. 13½

1032	A290	2b multicolored	.95	.25

BANGKOK '83 Intl. Stamp Show, Aug. 4-13 — A291

1.25b, Mail collection. 7.50b, Posting letters. 8.50b, Mail transport. 9.50b, Mail delivery.

1983, Aug. 4   Wmk. 370   Perf. 12

1033	A291	1.25b multicolored	.25	.25
		Complete booklet, strip of 4 #1033	2.40	
1034	A291	7.50b multicolored	1.00	.60
1035	A291	8.50b multicolored	1.25	.75
1036	A291	9.50b multicolored	1.75	.75
a.		Souv. sheet of 4, #1033-1036	32.50	32.50
		Nos. 1033-1036 (4)	4.25	2.35

No. 1036a exist imperf, sold for 50b. Value, $200.

A292

Prince Bhanurangsi memorial statue.

Perf. 15x14

1983, Aug. 4   Litho.   Wmk. 233

1037	A292	1.25b multicolored	.80	.25
		Complete booklet, strip of 4 #1037	8.00	

A293

Wmk. 370

1983, Sept. 27   Litho.   Perf. 12

1038	A293	1.25b multicolored	.25	.25
		Complete booklet, strip of 4 #1038	3.50	
1039	A293	7b multicolored	1.50	.75

Malaysia/ Thailand/ Singapore submarine cable inauguration.

Intl. Letter Writing Week — A294

1983, Oct. 6   Wmk. 329   Perf. 13½

1040	A294	2b Acropora asper	.70	.25
1041	A294	3b Platygyra lamellina	1.60	.25
1042	A294	4b Fungia	1.00	.70
1043	A294	7b Pectinia lactuca	2.00	1.10
		Nos. 1040-1043 (4)	5.30	2.30

Prince Mahidol of Songkhla — A295

Wmk. 370

1983, Oct. 10   Litho.   Perf. 12

1044	A295	9.50b multicolored	2.00	.75

Siriraj Hospital Faculty of Medicine and Rockefeller Foundation, 60th Anniv. of cooperation.

World Communications Year — A296

3b, Telecommunications equipment, diff.

Perf. 14x14½

1983, Oct. 24   Litho.   Wmk. 233

1045	A296	2b multicolored	.70	.25
1046	A296	3b multicolored	.85	.30

United Nations Day — A297

1983, Oct. 24

1047	A297	1.25b multicolored	.65	.25
		Complete booklet, strip of 4 #1047	4.50	

Thai Alphabet, 700th Anniv. — A298

Designs: 3b, Painted pottery, Sukothai period. 7b, Thai characters, reign of King Ramkamhaeng. 8b, Buddha, Sukothai period. 9b, Mahathat Temple, Sukothai province.

1983, Nov. 17   Wmk. 370   Perf. 12

1048	A298	3b multicolored	1.00	.25
1049	A298	7b multicolored	1.90	.45
1050	A298	8b multi, vert.	1.60	.50
1051	A298	9b multi, vert.	1.75	.65
		Nos. 1048-1051 (4)	6.25	1.85

National Development Program — A299

#1052, King and Queen initiating Royal Projects. #1053, Technical aid. #1054, Terrace farming, Irrigation dam. #1055, Gathering grain. #1056, Receiving the peoples' gratitude.

1984, May 5

1052	A299	1.25b multicolored	.65	.25
1053	A299	1.25b multicolored	.65	.25
1054	A299	1.25b multicolored	.65	.25

1055	A299	1.25b multicolored	.65	.25
1056	A299	1.25b multicolored	.65	.25
a.		Strip of 5, #1052-1056	3.25	3.25

Children's Day — A300

1984, Jan. 14   Wmk. 329   Perf. 13½

1057	A300	1.25b multicolored	.80	.25
		Complete booklet, strip of 4 #1057	8.00	

17th Natl. Games, Jan. 22-28 — A301

1984, Jan. 22

1058	A301	1.25b Running	.65	.25
		Complete booklet, strip of 4 #1058	6.50	
1059	A301	3b Soccer	.65	.25

5th Rheumatology Congress, Jan. 22-27 — A302

Design: Rheumatic joints.

Perf. 14x15
1984, Jan. 22   Wmk. 233

1060	A302	1.25b multicolored	.75	.25
		Complete booklet, strip of 4 #1060	6.50	

Armed Forces Day — A303

Design: King Naresuan, tanks, jet, ship.

1984, Jan. 25   Perf. 15x14

1061	A303	1.25b multicolored	.85	.25
		Complete booklet, strip of 4 #1061	8.00	

50th Anniv. of Royal Institute — A304

1984, Mar. 31

1062	A304	1.25b multicolored	.70	.25
		Complete booklet, strip of 4 #1062	6.50	

Thammasat University, 50th Anniv. — A305

1984, June 27   Perf. 14x15

1063	A305	1.25b Dome Building	.70	.25
		Complete booklet, strip of 4 #1063	6.50	

Asia-Pacific Broadcasting Union, 20th Anniv. — A306

1984, July 1   Wmk. 387   Perf. 12

1064	A306	4b Map, emblem	1.25	.40

Seated Buddha, Chiang Saen Style — A307

Seated Buddhas in various styles.

Perf. 14½x14
1984, July 12   Wmk. 233

1065	A307	1.25b shown	.35	.25
1066	A307	7b Sukhothai	1.60	.70
1067	A307	8.50b U-Thong	1.75	1.00
1068	A307	9.50b Ayutthaya	2.40	1.00
		Nos. 1065-1068 (4)	6.10	2.95

Intl. Letter Writing Week — A308

Medicinal Succulents: 1.50b, Alocasia indica. 2b, Aloe barbadensis. 4b, Gynura pseudochina DC. 10b, Rhoeo spathacea.

Wmk. 385
1984, Oct. 7   Litho.   Perf. 13½

1069	A308	1.50b multicolored	.40	.25
1070	A308	2b multicolored	.65	.25
1071	A308	4b multicolored	1.10	.45
1072	A308	10b multicolored	3.00	1.75
		Nos. 1069-1072 (4)	5.15	2.70

Princess Mother (b. 1900) — A309

Perf. 15x14
1984, Oct. 21   Wmk. 233

1073	A309	1.50b Portrait	.70	.25

UN Day — A310

Design: Woman threshing rice.

1984, Oct. 24   Wmk. 233

1074	A310	1.50b multicolored	.65	.25

Local Butterflies — A311

2b, Bhutanitis lidderdalei. 3b, Stichophthalma louisa. 5b, Parthenos sylvia. 7b, Stichophthalma godfreyi.

Wmk. 329
1984, Nov. 27   Photo.   Perf. 13½

1075	A311	2b multicolored	.65	.30
1076	A311	3b multicolored	.80	.35
1077	A311	5b multicolored	1.40	.90
1078	A311	7b multicolored	2.40	.90
		Nos. 1075-1078 (4)	5.25	2.40

King Type of 1980
Perf. 13½x13, 14x15 (1.50b, 2b)
Wmk. 329, 233 (1.50b, 2b)

1984-87   Litho.

1080	A256	1b Prus blue	.70	.30
1081	A256	1.50b brt yel org ('85)	4.50	1.75
1082	A256	2b dk car ('85)	2.25	.25
a.		Wmk. 387, perf. 11x13½ ('86?)	4.75	.30
b.		Wmk. 387, perf. 14½x14 ('87)	2.40	.30

Engr.

1083	A256	2b hn brn & gray vio	13.00	.40
1084	A256	4b turq bl & hn brn	1.20	.25
1085	A256	6.50b dk yel grn & ol brn	1.50	.70
1086	A256	7b dl red brn & sep	1.90	.40
1087	A256	7.50b dk org & saph ('85)	1.50	.65
1088	A256	8b brn vio & ol grn ('85)	1.75	.55
1089	A256	9b int bl & dk ol bis ('85)	2.25	.70
1090	A256	10b hn brn & sl grn	2.25	.70
1091	A256	20b dk org & grn	5.25	.65
1092	A256	50b dp vit & grn	10.00	1.75
1093	A256	100b dp org & dk bl	18.00	3.25
		Nos. 1080-1093 (14)	66.05	12.30

For surcharges see Nos. 1212, 2251.

Issued: 1b, 1/25/84; No. 1083, 4b, 6.50b, 7b, 10b, 50b, 100b, 12/5/84; 7.50b, 8b, 9b, 1/25/85; 1.50b, 4/6/85; No. 1082, 8/4/85; No. 1082a, 3/3/86; No. 1082b, 6/19/87.

Children's Day — A313

Children's drawings — No. 1101, Pedestrians, overpass. No. 1102, Climbing overpass, vert.

Wmk. 385
1985, Jan. 12   Litho.   Perf. 13½

1101	A313	1.50b multicolored	.40	.25
1102	A313	1.50b multicolored	.40	.25

Bangkok Mail Center Opening — A314

1985, Feb. 25

1103	A314	1.50b multicolored	.70	.25

Phuket Province Heroes Bicent. — A315

Perf. 15x14
1985, Mar. 13   Wmk. 233

1104	A315	2b multicolored	.70	.25

Tao-Thep-Krasattri, Tao-Sri-Sundhorn Monument.

Government Savings Bank, 72nd Anniv. — A316

Design: King Rama VI, headquarters.

1985, Apr. 1   Perf. 14x15

1105	A316	1.50b multicolored	.65	.25

Intl. Telecommunications Satellite Org., 20th Anniv. — A317

1985, Apr. 6   Wmk. 387   Perf. 12

1106	A317	2b multicolored	.70	.25

Thai Airways Intl., 25th Anniv. — A318

Wmk. 385
1985, May 1   Litho.   Perf. 13

1107	A318	2b DC-6	.40	.25
1108	A318	7.50b DC-10	1.60	.80
1109	A318	8.50b Airbus A-300	2.00	.90
1110	A318	9.50b Boeing 747	2.40	1.00
		Nos. 1107-1110 (4)	6.40	2.95

Natl. Flag and UPU Emblem — A319

10b, Flag and ITU emblem.

1985, July 1   **Wmk. 387**   *Perf. 12*
1111 A319   2b shown   .55   .25

Perf. 13½
Wmk. 385
1112 A319   10b multicolored   1.60   .90
Thai membership to UPU and Intl. Telecommunications Union, cent.

Natl. Communications Day, Aug. 5 — A320

1985, Aug. 4   **Wmk. 329**   *Perf. 13½*
1113 A320   2b multicolored   .70   .25

THAIPEX '85, Aug. 4-13 — A321

2b, Aisvarya Pavilion, vert. 3b, Varopas Piman Pavilion. 7b, Vehas Camrun Pavilion. 10b, Vitoon Tassana Tower, vert.

1985, Aug. 4   **Wmk. 385**
1114 A321   2b multicolored   .50   .25
1115 A321   3b multicolored   .80   .25
1116 A321   7b multicolored   1.75   .65
1117 A321   10b multicolored   2.60   .95
   a.   Souv. sheet of 4, #1114-1117   65.00   65.00
     Nos. 1114-1117 (4)   5.65   2.10
No. 1117a exists imperf, sold for 40b. Value, $700.

Natl. Science Day, Aug. 18 — A322

Design: King Rama IV, solar eclipse.

1985, Aug. 18   **Wmk. 387**   *Perf. 12*
1118 A322   2b multicolored   1.20   .25

1885 Seal, Modern Map and Crest — A323

Perf. 14½x15
1985, Sept. 3   **Wmk. 233**
1119 A323   2b multicolored   .70   .25
Royal Thai Survey Department, Cent.

13th SEA Games, Bangkok, Dec. 8-17 — A324

Designs: a, Boxing. b, Shot put. c, Badminton. d, Javelin. e, Weight lifting.

1985, Oct. 1   **Wmk. 387**   *Perf. 12*
1120   Strip of 5   8.50   2.50
  a.-e.   A324 2b, any single   .85   .25
  f.   Souv. sheet of 5, #a.-e. + label   35.00   35.00
No. 1120f sold for 20b.

Climbing Plants — A325

2b, Allemanda cathartica. 3b, Jasminum auriculatum. 7b, Passiflora laurifolia. 10b, Antigonon leptopus.

1985, Oct. 6   **Wmk. 385**   *Perf. 13½*
1121 A325   2b multicolored   .65   .25
1122 A325   3b multicolored   .90   .25
1123 A325   7b multicolored   1.60   .70
1124 A325   10b multicolored   2.00   .85
     Nos. 1121-1124 (4)   5.15   2.05
International Letter Writing Week.

UN Child Survival Campaign A326

1985, Oct. 24
1125 A326   2b multicolored   .70   .25
UN Day.

Prince Kromamun Bidyalabh Bridhyakorn (1885-1974), Govt. Minister — A327

1985, Nov. 7
1126   A327   2b multi   7.00   .25
1126A A327   2b multi, diff.   1.00   .25
  b.   Pair, #1126-1126A   37.50   37.50
No. 1126A has flower design framing portrait reversed.

Rangsit (1885-1951), Prince of Jainad — A328

Perf. 15x14½
1985, Nov. 12   **Wmk. 233**
1127 A328   1.50b multicolored   .85   .25

Asian-Pacific Postal Union, 5th Congress, Nov. 25-Dec. 4 — A329

1985, Nov. 25   **Wmk. 385**   *Perf. 13½*
1128 A329   2b multicolored   .40   .25
1129 A329   10b multicolored   2.00   .85

Intl. Youth Year A330

Perf. 14x15
1985, Nov. 26   **Wmk. 233**
1130 A330   2b multicolored   1.00   .30

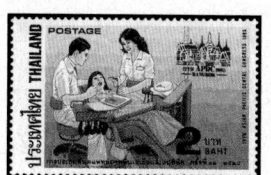

12th Asian-Pacific Dental Congress, Bangkok, Dec. 5-10 — A331

1985, Dec. 5
1131 A331   2b multicolored   .85   .25

13th SEA Games — A332

1985, Dec. 8   **Wmk. 387**   *Perf. 12*
1132 A332   1b Volleyball   .25   .25
1133 A332   2b Sepak-takraw   .50   .25
1134 A332   3b Women's gymnastics   .80   .30
1135 A332   4b Bowling   1.00   .50
  a.   Souv. sheet, #1132-1135 + label   32.50   32.50
     Nos. 1132-1135 (4)   2.55   1.30
No. 1135a sold for 20b.

French Envoys — A333

1985, Dec. 12   **Wmk. 385**   *Perf. 13½*
1136 A333   2b shown   .55   .25
1137 A333   8.50b Thai envoys   1.60   .70
Diplomatic relations with France, 300th anniv.

Domestic Express Mail Service Inauguration — A334

1986, Jan. 1
1138 A334   2b multicolored   .85   .25
     Complete booklet, strip of 5 #1138   8.00
Intl. Express Mail Service, EMS, 3rd anniv.

Wildlife Conservation — A335

Marine turtles — 1.50b, Chelonia mydas. 3b, Eretmochelys imbricata. 5b, Dermochelys coriacea. 10b, Lepidochelys olivacea.

1986, Jan. 8   **Wmk. 329**
1139 A335   1.50b multicolored   .70   .30
1140 A335   3b multicolored   1.50   .30
1141 A335   5b multicolored   3.00   .70
1142 A335   10b multicolored   2.40   1.00
     Nos. 1139-1142 (4)   7.60   2.30

Natl. Children's Day — A336

Design: Children picking lotus, by Areeya Makarabhundhu, age 12.

1986, Jan. 11   **Wmk. 385**
1143 A336   2b multicolored   .75   .25
     Complete booklet, strip of 5 #1143   8.00

Statue of Sunthon Phu, Poet — A337

1986, June 26
1144	A337 2b multicolored	.75	.25
	Complete booklet, strip of 5 #1144	8.00	

Fruit Type of 1979

1986, June 26 — Wmk. 385
1145	A237 2b Watermelon	1.50	.25
	Complete booklet, strip of 5 #1145	12.50	
1146	A237 2b Malay apple	1.50	.25
	Complete booklet, strip of 5 #1146	12.50	
1147	A237 6b Pomelo	1.50	.65
1148	A237 6b Papaya	1.50	.65
	Nos. 1145-1148 (4)	6.00	1.80

Nos. 1145-1148 horiz.

Natl. Year of the Trees A338

1986, July 21
1149	A338 2b multicolored	.70	.25
	Complete booklet, strip of 5 #1149	5.25	

Communications Day — A339

1986, Aug. 4
1150	A339 2b multicolored	.70	.25
	Complete booklet, strip of 5 #1150	5.25	

Bamboo Baskets — A340

1986, Oct. 5
1151	A340 2b Chalom	.50	.25
	Complete booklet, strip of 5 #1151	5.25	
1152	A340 2b Krabung	.50	.25
	Complete booklet, strip of 5 #1152	5.25	
1153	A340 6b Kratib	1.00	.45
1154	A340 6b Kaleb	1.00	.45
	Nos. 1151-1154 (4)	3.00	1.40

Intl. Letter Writing Week.

Intl. Peace Year A341

1986, Oct. 24
1155	A341 2b multicolored	.70	.25
	Complete booklet, strip of 5 #1155	6.50	

Productivity Year — A342

1986, Oct. 24 — Wmk. 329
1156	A342 2b multicolored	.65	.25
	Complete booklet, strip of 5 #1156	5.25	

6th ASEAN Orchid Congress — A343

2b, Vanda varavuth, vert. 3b, Ascocenda emma, vert. 4b, Dendrobium sri-siam. 5b, Dendrobium ekapol panda.

1986, Nov. 7 — Wmk. 385
1157	A343 2b multicolored	.70	.25
	Complete booklet, strip of 5 #1157	5.25	
1158	A343 3b multicolored	.80	.50
1159	A343 4b multicolored	1.40	1.10
1160	A343 5b multicolored	1.40	.95
a.	Souv. sheet of 4, #1157-1160	110.00	110.00
	Nos. 1157-1160 (4)	4.30	2.80

No. 1160a sold for 25b.

Fungi A344

No. 1161, Volvariella volvacea. No. 1162, Pleurotus ostreatus. No. 1163, Auricularia polytricha. No. 1164, Pleurotus cystidiosus.

Perf. 13x13½

1986, Nov. 26 — Wmk. 329 — Photo.
1161	A344 2b multicolored	.90	.25
	Complete booklet, strip of 5 #1161	6.50	
1162	A344 2b multicolored	.90	.25
	Complete booklet, strip of 5 #1162	6.50	
1163	A344 6b multicolored	2.50	.65
1164	A344 6b multicolored	2.50	.65
	Nos. 1161-1164 (4)	6.80	1.80

Fisheries Dept., 60th Anniv. — A345

No. 1165, Morulius chrysophekadion. No. 1166, Notopterus blanci. No. 1167, Scleropages formosus. No. 1168, Pangasianodon gigas.

Wmk. 385

1986, Dec. 16 — Litho. — **Perf. 13½**
1165	A345 2b multicolored	.60	.25
	Complete booklet, strip of 5 #1165	5.25	
1166	A345 2b multicolored	.60	.25
	Complete booklet, strip of 5 #1166	5.25	
1167	A345 7b multicolored	1.40	.65
1168	A345 7b multicolored	1.40	.65
	Nos. 1165-1168 (4)	4.00	1.80

No. 653 Surcharged in Dark Olive Green

Perf. 14x13½

1986, Dec. — Photo. — Wmk. 233
1168A	A161 1b on 20s blue	.70	.25

Children's Day — A346

Child's drawing.

Perf. 14½x15

1987, Jan. 10 — Litho. — Wmk. 387
1169	2b School, playground	.70	.25
1170	2b Pool	.70	.25
a.	A346 Pair, #1169-1170	1.90	1.60

No. 1170a has continuous design.

F-16 & F-5 Fighter Planes, Pilot — A347

1987, Mar. 27 — Wmk. 385 — **Perf. 13½**
1171	A347 2b multicolored	1.10	.25
	Complete booklet, strip of 5 #1171	10.50	

Royal Thai Air Force, 72nd anniv.

King Rama III (Nang Klao, 1787-1851) — A348

Perf. 15x14½

1987, Mar. 31 — Wmk. 387
1172	A348 2b multicolored	1.00	.40
	Complete booklet, strip of 5 #1172	10.50	

Ministry of Communications, 75th Anniv. — A349

1987, Apr. 1
1173	A349 2b multicolored	.70	.25
	Complete booklet, strip of 5 #1173	5.25	

Forestry Year — A350

1987, July 11 — Wmk. 385 — **Perf. 13½**
1174	A350 2b multicolored	.70	.25
	Complete booklet, strip of 5 #1174	5.25	

THAIPEX '87 — A351

Gold artifacts — No. 1175, Peacock, vert. No. 1176, Hand mirrors, vert. No. 1177, Water urn, finger bowls. No. 1178, Dragon vase.

1987, Aug. 4 — Wmk. 385
1175	A351 2b multicolored	.40	.25
	Complete booklet, strip of 5 #1175	3.75	
1176	A351 2b multicolored	.40	.25
	Complete booklet, strip of 5 #1176	3.75	
1177	A351 6b multicolored	1.10	.55
1178	A351 6b multicolored	1.10	.55
a.	Souv. sheet of 4, #1175-1178	55.00	55.00
	Nos. 1175-1178 (4)	3.00	1.60

No. 1178a exists imperf. Value, $450.

ASEAN, 20th Anniv. — A352

1987, Aug. 20
1179	A352 2b multicolored	.40	.25
	Complete booklet, strip of 5 #1179	2.75	
1180	A352 3b multicolored	.60	.30
1181	A352 4b multicolored	.70	.40
1182	A352 5b multicolored	.95	.45
	Nos. 1179-1182 (4)	2.65	1.40

Natl. Communications Day — A353

1987, Aug. 4
1183	A353 2b multicolored	.80	.25
	Complete booklet, strip of 5 #1183	6.50	

Chulachamklao Royal Military Academy, Cent. — A354

Design: School crest, King Rama V, and King Rama IX conferring sword on graduating officer.

1987, Aug. 5
1184	A354 2b multicolored	1.75	.30
	Complete booklet, strip of 5 #1184	21.00	

Intl. Literacy Day — A355

1987, Sept. 8
1185	A355 2b multicolored	.70	.25
	Complete booklet, strip of 5 #1185	6.50	

Tourism Year — A356

2b, Flower-offering ceremony, Saraburi province. 3b, Duan Sib Festival, Nakhon Si Thammarat province. 5b, Bang Fai Festival, Yasothon province. 7b, Loi Krathong Festival, Sukhothai province.

1987, Sept. 18
1186	A356	2b multicolored	.30	.25
		Complete booklet, strip of 5		
		#1186	4.00	
1187	A356	3b multicolored	.60	.30
1188	A356	5b multicolored	.90	.40
1189	A356	7b multicolored	1.25	.60
		Nos. 1186-1189 (4)	3.05	1.55

Auditor General's Office, 72nd Anniv. — A357

1987, Sept. 18
1190	A357	2b multicolored	.70	.25
		Complete booklet, strip of 5		
		#1190	6.50	

Diplomatic Relations Between Thailand and Japan, Cent. — A358

1987, Sept. 26   **Wmk. 329**
1191	A358	2b multicolored	.85	.30
		Complete booklet, strip of 5		
		#1191	8.00	

Intl. Letter Writing Week — A359

Floral garlands.

1987, Oct. 4   **Wmk. 385**
1192	A359	2b Floral tassel	.35	.25
		Complete booklet, strip of 5		
		#1192	2.75	
1193	A359	3b Tasselled garland	.65	.30
1194	A359	5b Wrist garland	.75	.40
1195	A359	7b Double-ended garland	1.25	.65
		Nos. 1192-1195 (4)	3.00	1.60

Thai Pavilion — A360

1987, Oct. 9   **Wmk. 387**   *Perf. 15*
1196	A360	2b multicolored	.95	.25
		Complete booklet, strip of 5		
		#1196	6.50	

Social Education and Cultural Center inauguration.

A361

A362

King Bhumibol Adulyadej, 60th Birthday — A363

Royal ciphers and: #1197, Adulyadej as a child. #1198, King and Queen, wedding portrait, 1950. #1199, King taking the Oath of Accession, 1950. #1200, King dressed as a monk, collecting alms. #1201, Greeting 100 year-old woman. #1202, In military uniform holding pen and with hill tribes. #1203, Royal couple visiting wounded servicemen. #1204, Visiting farm. #1205, Royal family. #1206, King, Queen Sirikit. #1207, Princess Mother Somdej Phra Sri Nakarindra Boromrajjonnani, emblem of Medical Volunteer Assoc. #1208, Crown Prince Maha Vajiralongkorn, crown prince's royal standard. #1209, Princess Maha Chakri Sirindhorn, emblem of Sai Jai Thai Foundation. #1210, Princess Chulabhorn, Albert Einstein gold medal awarded by UNESCO.

Wmk. 329
1987, Dec. 5   **Photo.**   *Perf. 13½*
1197	A361	2b shown	.70	.30
1198	A361	2b multicolored	.70	.30
1199	A361	2b multicolored	.70	.30
1200	A361	2b multicolored	.70	.30
1201	A361	2b multicolored	.70	.30
1202	A361	2b multicolored	.70	.30
1203	A361	2b multicolored	.70	.30
1204	A361	2b multicolored	.70	.30
	a.	Souv. sheet, #1197-1204	37.50	37.50

Litho.
Wmk. 385
1205	A362	2b multicolored	1.20	.40
1206	A362	2b multicolored	1.20	.40
1207	A362	2b multicolored	1.20	.40
1208	A362	2b multicolored	1.20	.40
1209	A362	2b multicolored	1.20	.40
1210	A362	2b multicolored	1.20	.40

Litho. & Embossed
1211	A363	100b vio blue & gold	65.00	65.00
		Nos. 1197-1211 (15)	77.80	69.80

Size of Nos. 1206-1210: 45x27mm. No. 1211 printed in sheets of 10. Value, $750. No. 1204a sold for 40b.

No. 1081 Surcharged

1987   **Litho.**   **Wmk. 233**   *Perf. 14x15*
1212	A256	2b on 1.50b brt yel org	.85	.25

Children's Day — A364

Perf. 14x14½
1988, Jan. 9   **Litho.**   **Wmk. 387**
1213	A364	2b multicolored	.70	.25
		Complete booklet, strip of 5		
		#1213	5.25	

Thai Agricultural Cooperatives, 72nd Anniv. — A365

Design: Prince Bridhyalongkorn, founder.

1988, Feb. 26   **Wmk. 387**
1214	A365	2b multicolored	.70	.25
		Complete booklet, strip of 5		
		#1214	5.25	

Royal Siam Soc., 84th Anniv. A366

1988, Mar. 10   *Perf. 14½x14*
1215	A366	2b multicolored	.65	.25
		Complete booklet, strip of 5		
		#1215	5.25	

Cultural Heritage Preservation — A367

Ruins in Sukhothai Historic Park — 2b, Wat Phra Phai Luang. 3b, Wat Traphang Thonglang. 4b, Wat Maha That. 6b, Thewalai Maha Kaset.

1988, Apr. 2   *Perf. 14½x14*
1216	A367	2b multicolored	.30	.25
		Complete booklet, strip of 5		
		#1216	4.50	
1217	A367	3b multicolored	.60	.30
1218	A367	4b multicolored	.90	.60
1219	A367	6b multicolored	1.25	.70
		Nos. 1216-1219 (4)	3.05	1.85

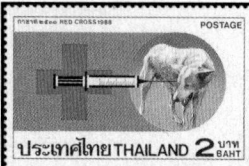

Red Cross Fair A368

Design: Prevention of rabies.

1988, Apr.   **Wmk. 387**   *Perf. 14*
1220	A368	2b multicolored	.70	.25
		Complete booklet, strip of 5		
		#1220	5.25	

King Rama V, Founder — A369

Perf. 14x14½
1988, Apr. 26   **Wmk. 387**
1221	A369	5b multicolored	2.75	.70

Siriraj Hospital, cent.

Pheasants — A370

Wmk. 329
1988, June 15   **Photo.**   *Perf. 13½*
1222	A370	2b Crested fireback	.30	.25
		Complete booklet, strip of 5		
		#1222	2.75	
1223	A370	3b Kalij	.60	.25
1224	A370	6b Silver pheasant	1.25	.60
1225	A370	7b Hume's pheasant	1.50	.75
		Nos. 1222-1225 (4)	3.65	1.85

Nos. 935a, 935 Surcharged

a   b

Perf. 11x13
1988-92   **Litho.**   **Wmk. 387**
1226	A256(a)	1b on 1.25b	.80	.25
1226A	A256(b)	1b on 1.25b	.85	.25
	b.	Wmk. 368	1.75	.30

Issued: #1226, 1988; #1226A, Dec. 5, 1992.

Intl. Council of Women, Cent. — A371

1988, June 26   **Wmk. 385**   *Perf. 13½*
1227	A371	2b multicolored	.70	.25
		Complete booklet, strip of 5		
		#1227	5.25	

King Bhumibol Adulyadej
A372   A372a

Perf. 13½x13
1988-95   **Litho.**   **Wmk. 387**
1228	A372	25s brown	.40	.25

Perf. 14x14½
1229	A372	50s olive	.55	.25
	a.	Wmk. 329, perf. 13½x13	.65	.25
1230	A372	1b brt blue	.55	.25
		Complete booklet, 5 #1230	6.00	
	a.	Photo, wmk. 233	.80	.25

b. Photo., wmk. 340, perf.
13½x13¾ .55 .25
1233 A372 2b scarlet .70 .25
Complete booklet, 5 #1233 7.50
a. Wmk. 329 .55 .25
b. Photo., wmk. 340, perf.
13½x13¾ .70 .25
Complete booklet, 5 #1233b 6.00

Photo.
Wmk. 233
Perf. 14½

1236 A372 1b bright blue .80 .25
Nos. 1228-1236 (5) 3.00 1.25

No. 1236 has blue background without halo effect around head. See #1230.
Issued: 25s, 8/12/92; 1b-2b, 7/2/88; 50s, 7/28/93; #1230a, 1236, 1990; #1233a, 1992; #1230b, 1233b, 12/5/94; #1229a, 1995.

Perf. 13½x13

			Wmk. 329
1988-90		Engr.	
1241	A372a	3b brn & bluish gray	.80 .25
1242	A372a	4b brt bl & red brn	.95 .30
1243	A372a	5b violet & brn	1.10 .30
1244	A372a	6b green & vio	1.10 .35
1245	A372a	7b red brn & dk brn	.80 .25
1246	A372a	8b red brn & gray ol	1.10 .40
1247	A372a	9b dk blue & brn	1.75 .40
1248	A372a	10b hen brn & blk	1.60 .25
1249	A372a	20b brn org & sage grn	2.40 1.75
1250	A372a	25b ol grn & dk bl	4.50 .90
1251	A372a	50b violet & grn	8.00 1.00
1252	A372a	100b brn org & bluish blk	13.00 2.25
		Nos. 1241-1252 (12)	37.10 8.40

Issued:3b, 10b, 50b, 100b, 12/5; 5b, 6b, 8b, 9b, 7/1/89; 4b, 7b, 20b, 12/5/89; 25b, 1/9/90.

A373

A374

King Bhumibol's Reign (since 1950) — A375

Designs: No. 1253, King Bhumibol.
Regalia: No. 1254, Great Crown of Victory. No. 1255, Sword of Victory and matching scabbard. No. 1256, Scepter. No. 1257, Fan and feather fly swatter. No. 1258, Royal slippers.
Canopied thrones in the Grand Palace: No. 1259, Queen's round ottoman on 1-tier dais in front of decorative screen. No. 1260, King's throne on 1-tier dais in front of decorative screen. No. 1261, 3-Tier throne with 3 gilded trees. No. 1262, 3-Canopy throne on high gold dais. No. 1263, 3-Tier throne with 4 gilded trees, altar in background. No. 1264, 3-Canopy throne on 5-stair dais, in front of arch flanked by columns.

Wmk. 385

1988, July 2		Litho.	**Perf. 13½**
1253	A373	2b shown	2.50 .40

Photo.
Wmk. 329

1254	A374	2b multi, vert.	.65 .30
1255	A374	2b multicolored	.65 .30
1256	A374	2b multicolored	.65 .30
1257	A374	2b multicolored	.65 .30
1258	A374	2b multicolored	.65 .30

Litho.
Perf. 14x14½
Wmk. 387

1259	A375	2b multicolored	.80 .30
1260	A375	2b multicolored	.80 .30
1261	A375	2b multicolored	.80 .30
1262	A375	2b multicolored	.80 .30
1263	A375	2b multicolored	.80 .30
1264	A375	2b multicolored	.80 .30
a.		Souv. sheet of 6, #1259-1264	60.00 60.00
		Nos. 1253-1264 (12)	10.55 3.70

No. 1264a sold for 25b.

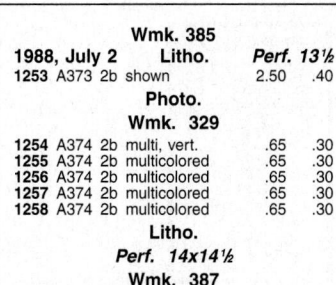

Arbor Year A376

Perf. 14½x14

1988, July 29		Litho.	Wmk. 387
1265	A376	2b multicolored	.65 .25
		Complete booklet, strip of 5 #1265	5.25

Natl. Communications Day — A377

Wmk. Alternating Interlaced Wavy Lines (340)

1988, Aug. 4			Perf. 13½
1266	A377	2b multicolored	.85 .25
		Complete booklet, strip of 5 #1266	6.50

Intl. Letter Writing Week — A378

Designs: Coconut leaf sculptures.

Perf. 14½x14

1988, Oct. 9			Wmk. 387
1267	A378	2b Grasshopper	.40 .25
		Complete booklet, strip of 5 #1267	2.75
1268	A378	2b Fish	.40 .25
		Complete booklet, strip of 5 #1268	2.75
1269	A378	6b Bird	1.10 .50
1270	A378	6b Takro (box)	1.10 .50
		Nos. 1267-1270 (4)	3.00 1.50

Housing Development — A379

Wmk. 233

1988, Oct. 24		Litho.	Perf. 14
1271	A379	2b multicolored	.65 .25
		Complete booklet, strip of 5 #1271	5.25

Traffic Safety — A380

1988, Nov. 11		Wmk. 329	Perf. 13½
1272	A380	2b multicolored	.65 .25
		Complete booklet, strip of 5 #1272	6.50

King's Bodyguard, 120th Anniv. — A381

1988, Nov. 11			Wmk. 385
1273	A381	2b Chulalongkorn	4.00 .70
		Complete booklet, strip of 5 #1273	50.00

New Year — A382

Flowers — No. 1274, Crotalaria sessiliflora. No. 1275, Uvaria grandiflora. No. 1276, Reinwardtia trigyna. No. 1277, Impatiens griffithii.

1988, Dec. 1			Wmk. 387
1274	A382	1b multicolored	.65 .30
1275	A382	1b multicolored	.65 .30
1276	A382	1b multicolored	.65 .30
1277	A382	1b multicolored	.65 .30
		Nos. 1274-1277 (4)	2.60 1.20

Thai Royal Orders Type of 1979

Floral background: Nos. 1278-1279, Knight Grand Commander, Order of Rama, 1918. Nos. 1280-1281, Knight Grand Cordon, Order of the White Elephant, 1861. Nos. 1282-1283, Knight Grand Cordon, Order of the Crown of Thailand, 1869. Nos. 1284-1285, Ratana Varabhorn Order of Merit, 1911. Pairs have continuous designs.

1988, Dec. 5			Wmk. 385
1278	A243	2b multicolored	.30 .25
1279	A244	2b multicolored	.30 .25
a.		Pair, #1278-1279	.80 .40
1280	A243	3b multicolored	.65 .25
1281	A244	3b multicolored	.65 .25
a.		Pair, #1280-1281	1.75 .90
1282	A243	5b multicolored	1.00 .40
1283	A244	5b multicolored	1.00 .40
a.		Pair, #1282-1283	2.75 1.40
1284	A243	7b multicolored	1.20 .55
1285	A244	7b multicolored	1.20 .55
a.		Pair, #1284-1285	4.00 2.00
		Nos. 1278-1285 (8)	6.30 2.90

A383

Buddha Monthon Celebrations, Tambol Salaya — A384

2b, Birthplace. 3b, Enlightenment place. 4b, Location of 1st sermon. 5b, Place Buddha achieved nirvana. 6b, Statue.

Perf. 14x15, 15x14

1988, Dec. 5			Wmk. 233
1286	A383	2b multicolored	.35 .25
		Complete booklet, strip of 5 #1286	2.75
1287	A383	3b multicolored	.45 .25
1288	A383	4b multicolored	.65 .45
1289	A383	5b multicolored	.85 .40
1290	A384	6b multicolored	1.00 .50
		Nos. 1286-1290 (5)	3.30 1.85

Souvenir Sheet
Perf. 14½x14

1291	A384	6b like No. 1290	27.50 27.50

No. 1291 sold for 15b.

Children's Day — A385

"Touch" paintings by blind youth: No. 1292, *Floating Market*, by Thongbai Siyam. No. 1293, *Flying Bird*, by Kwanchai Kerd-Daeng. No. 1294, *Little Mermaid*, by Chalermpol Jiengmai. No. 1295, *Golden Fish*, by Natetip Korsantirak.

Wmk. 387

1989, Jan. 14		Litho.	Perf. 13½
1292	A385	2b multicolored	.45 .25
		Complete booklet, strip of 5 #1292	4.00
1293	A385	2b multicolored	.45 .25
		Complete booklet, strip of 5 #1293	4.00
1294	A385	2b multicolored	.45 .25
		Complete booklet, strip of 5 #1294	4.00
1295	A385	2b multicolored	.45 .25
		Complete booklet, strip of 5 #1295	4.00
		Nos. 1292-1295 (4)	1.80 1.00

Communications Authority of Thailand, 12th Anniv. — A386

1989, Feb. 25			Perf. 14½x14
1296	A386	2b multicolored	.70 .25
		Complete booklet, strip of 5 #1296	5.25

Chulalongkorn University, 72nd Anniv. — A387

Design: 2b, Statue of Chulalongkorn and King Vajiravudh in front of university auditorium.

1989, Mar. 26			
1297	A387	2b multicolored	.80 .25
		Complete booklet, strip of 5 #1297	8.00

A388

Perf. 15x14

1989, Mar. 31   Litho.   Wmk. 233
1298 A388 2b shown   .70 .30
   Complete booklet, strip of 5
   #1298   5.25

Wmk. 387
Perf. 13½

1299 A388 10b Emblem   1.50 .60

Thai Red Cross Society, 96th anniv. (2b);
Intl. Red Cross and Red Crescent organizations, 125th annivs. (10b).

A389

Phra Nakhon Khiri Historical Park: 2b, Wat
Phra Kaeo. 3b, Chatchawan Wiangchai
Observatory. 5b, Phra That Chom Phet Stupa.
6b, Wetchayan Wichian Prasat Throne Hall.

Perf. 14x14½

1989, Apr. 2   Wmk. 387
1300 A389 2b multicolored   .55 .25
   Complete booklet, strip of 5
   #1300   4.00
1301 A389 3b multicolored   .90 .45
1302 A389 5b multicolored   1.40 .95
1303 A389 6b multicolored   1.60 1.10
   Nos. 1300-1303 (4)   4.45 2.75

Natl. Lottery Office, 50th
Anniv. — A390

1989, Apr. 5   Perf. 13½
1304 A390 2b multicolored   .65 .25
   Complete booklet, strip of 5
   #1304   5.25

Seashells — A391

2b, Conus thailandis. 3b, Spondylus
princeps. 6b, Cyprea guttata. 10b, Nautilus
pompilius.

1989, June 28 Wmk. 329 Perf. 13½
1305 A391 2b multicolored   .30 .25
   Complete booklet, strip of 5
   #1305   2.75
1306 A391 3b multicolored   .70 .30
1307 A391 6b multicolored   1.00 .75
1308 A391 10b multicolored   3.00 1.60
   Nos. 1305-1308 (4)   5.00 2.90

Arts
and
Crafts
Year
A392

No. 1309, Ceramic figurines. No. 1310,
Gold niello ginger jar, chicken. No. 1311, Textiles. No. 1312, Gemstone flower ornament.

Wmk. 387
1989, June 28   Litho.   Perf. 13½
1309 A392 2b multicolored   .40 .25
   Complete booklet, strip of 5
   #1309   2.75
1310 A392 2b multicolored   .40 .25
   Complete booklet, strip of 5
   #1310   2.75
1311 A392 6b multicolored   1.10 .50
1312 A392 6b multicolored   1.10 .50
   Nos. 1309-1312 (4)   3.00 1.50

Asia-Pacific Telecommunications
Organization, 10th Anniv. — A393

APT emblem, map of submarine cable network and satellites of member nations.

1989, July 1   Wmk. 329   Perf. 13½
1313 A393 9b multicolored   1.25 .75

Phya Anuman
Rajadhon (1888-
1969),
Ethnologist
A394

1989, July 1   Wmk. 387   Perf. 13½
1314 A394 2b multicolored   .65 .25
   Complete booklet, strip of 5
   #1314   5.25

9th Natl. Phil.
Exhib., Aug. 4-
13 — A395

Various mailboxes.

1989, Aug. 4 Wmk. 233 Perf. 15x14
1315 A395 2b multicolored   .40 .25
   Complete booklet, strip of 5
   #1315   2.75
1316 A395 3b multi, diff.   .45 .25
1317 A395 4b multi, diff.   .65 .35
1318 A395 5b multi, diff.   .80 .40
1319 A395 6b multi, diff.   .95 .50
  a. Souv. sheet, #1315-1319,
    perf 14   35.00 35.00
   Nos. 1315-1319 (5)   3.25 1.75

No. 1319a sold for 30b. No. 1319a exists
imperf. Value, $125.

A396

Wmk. 387
1989, June 26   Perf. 13½
1320 A396 2b multicolored   .55 .25
   Complete booklet, strip of 5
   #1320   5.25

Intl. Anti-drug Day.

A397

1989, Aug. 4 Wmk. 233 Perf. 14x15
1321 A397 2b multicolored   .70 .25
   Complete booklet, strip of 5
   #1321   5.25

Post and Telecommunications School, cent.

A398

1989, Aug. 4   Wmk. 387   Perf. 13½
1322 A398 2b multicolored   .55 .25
   Complete booklet, strip of 5
   #1322   5.25

Natl. Communications Day.

Dragonflies — A399

Wmk. 329
1989, Oct. 8   Photo.   Perf. 13½
1323 A399 2b shown   .65 .25
   Complete booklet, strip of 5
   #1323   .95
1324 A399 5b multi, diff.   .75 .50
1325 A399 6b multi, diff.   1.25 .60
1326 A399 10b Damselfly   1.60 1.00
  a. Souv. sheet of 4, #1323-
    1326   30.00 30.00
   Nos. 1323-1326 (4)   4.25 2.35

Intl. Letter Writing Week. #1326a sold for
40b.

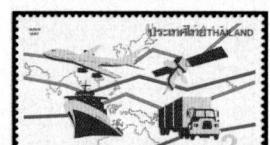

Transport and Communications
Decade for Asia and the
Pacific — A400

Perf. 14½x14
1989, Oct. 24   Litho.   Wmk. 387
1327 A400 2b multicolored   .55 .25
   Complete booklet, strip of 5
   #1327   5.25

Mental Health
Care,
Cent. — A401

1989, Nov. 1 Wmk. 233 Perf. 15x14
1328 A401 2b multicolored   .55 .25
   Complete booklet, strip of 5
   #1328   5.25

New Year
1990 — A402

Flowering plants.

Perf. 14x14½
1989, Nov. 15   Wmk. 387
1329 A402 1b Hypericum uralum   .30 .30
1330 A402 1b Uraria rufescens   .30 .30
1331 A402 1b Manglietia garrettii   .30 .30
1332 A402 1b Aeschynanthus
    macranthus   .30 .30
  a. Souv. sheet of 4, #1329-1332 6.50 6.50
   Nos. 1329-1332 (4)   1.20 1.20

No. 1332a sold for 14b.

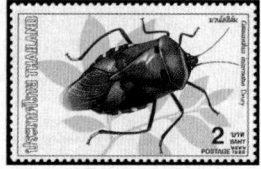

Insects — A403

2b, Catacanthus incarnatus. 3b, Aristobia
approximator. 6b, Chrysochroa chinensis.
10b, Enoplotrupes sharpi.

Wmk. 329
1989, Nov. 15   Photo.   Perf. 13½
1333 A403 2b multicolored   .40 .25
   Complete booklet, strip of 5
   #1333   2.75
1334 A403 3b multicolored   .60 .30
1335 A403 6b multicolored   .90 .50
1336 A403 10b multicolored   1.60 1.25
   Nos. 1333-1336 (4)   3.50 2.30

Population and Housing Census of
1990 — A404

Wmk. 387
1990, Jan. 1   Litho.   Perf. 13½
1337 A404 2b multicolored   .80 .25
   Complete booklet, strip of 5
   #1337   5.75

Children's Day — A405

Perf. 15x14

1990, Jan. 13   **Wmk. 233**
1338 A405 2b Jumping rope, horiz.   .60 .25
  Complete booklet, strip of 5
  #1338   4.00
1339 A405 2b Sports   .60 .25
  Complete booklet, strip of 5
  #1339   4.00

Emblems — A406

1990, Mar. 29   **Wmk. 387**   **Perf. 13½**
1340 A406 2b multicolored   .70 .25
  Complete booklet, strip of 5
  #1340   5.75

WHO Fight AIDS Worldwide campaign and the Natl. Red Cross Soc.

Thai Heritage Conservation Day — A407

Prize-winning inlaid mother-of-pearl containers: No. 1341, Tiap (footed bowl with lid), vert. No. 1342, Phan waenfa (two-tiered vessel), vert. No. 1343, Lung (lidded bowl). No. 1344, Chiat klom (spade-shaped lidded container signifying noble rank).

1990, Apr. 2   **Photo.**   **Wmk. 329**
1341 A407 2b multicolored   .25 .25
1342 A407 2b multicolored   .25 .25
1343 A407 8b multicolored   1.10 .90
1344 A407 8b multicolored   1.10 .90
  Nos. 1341-1344 (4)   2.70 2.30

A408

Minerals.

Perf. 14x14½

1990, June 29   **Litho.**   **Wmk. 387**
1345 A408 2b Tin   .45 .25
1346 A408 3b Zinc   .70 .40
1347 A408 5b Lead   .85 .60
1348 A408 6b Fluorite   1.00 .80
  a.   Souv. sheet of 4, #1345-1348   6.25 6.25
  Nos. 1345-1348 (4)   3.00 2.05

No. 1348a sold for 30b. Exists imperf, value same as perf.

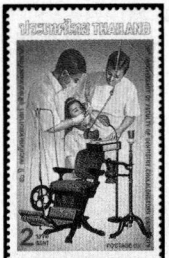

A409

1990, May 16
1349 A409 2b multicolored   .50 .25

Faculty of Dentistry, Chulalongkorn Univ., 50th anniv.

Communications Day — A410

1990, Aug. 4   **Perf. 14½x14**
1350 A410 2b multicolored   .65 .25
  Complete booklet, strip of 5
  #1350   5.75

Asian-Pacific Postal Training Center, 20th Anniv. — A411

1990, Sept. 10
1351 A411 2b multicolored   .45 .25
  Complete booklet, strip of 5
  #1351   5.00
1352 A411 8b multicolored   1.40 .70

Rotary Intl. in Thailand, 60th Anniv. — A412

1990, Sept. 16   **Perf. 13½**
1353 A412 2b Health care   .45 .25
  Complete booklet, strip of 5
  #1353   3.00
1354 A412 3b Immunizations   .60 .30
1355 A412 6b Literacy project   .60 .55
1356 A412 8b Thai museum project   1.20 1.00
  Nos. 1353-1356 (4)   2.85 2.10

Intl. Letter Writing Week, 1990 — A413

1990, Oct. 7   **Perf. 14**
1357 A413 2b multicolored   .45 .25
1358 A413 3b multi, diff.   .70 .40
1359 A413 5b multi, diff.   .85 .60
1360 A413 6b multi, diff.   1.00 .80
  a.   Souv. sheet of 4, #1357-1360   6.25 6.25
  Nos. 1357-1360 (4)   3.00 2.05

No. 1360a sold for 30b. Exists imperf, value same as perf.

Dept. of Comptroller-General, Cent. — A414

1990, Oct. 7   **Perf. 14½x14**
1361 A414 2b multicolored   1.00 .25
  Complete booklet, strip of 5
  #1361   5.75

A415

1990, Oct. 21   **Perf. 14x14½**
1362 A415 2b multicolored   4.00 .60
  Complete booklet, strip of 5
  #1362   32.50

Princess Mother, 90th birthday.

A416

Flowers: No. 1363, Cyrtandromoea grandiflora. No. 1364, Rhododendron arboreum. No. 1365, Merremia vitifolia. No. 1366, Afgekia mahidolae.

1990, Nov. 15   **Wmk. 233**   **Perf. 14½**
1363 A416 1b multicolored   .45 .25
1364 A416 1b multicolored   .45 .25
1365 A416 1b multicolored   .45 .25
1366 A416 1b multicolored   .45 .25
  a.   Sheet of 4, #1363-1366   4.50 4.50
  Nos. 1363-1366 (4)   1.80 1.00

New Year 1991. No. 1366a sold for 10b. Exists imperf, value same as perf. See Nos. 1417-1420.

Wiman Mek Royal Hall — A417

Royal Throne Rooms in the Dusit Palace: 3b, Ratcharit Rungrot Royal House. 4b, Aphisek Dusit Royal Hall. 5b, Amphon Sathan Palace. 6b, Udon Phak Royal Hall. 8b, Anantasamakhom Throne Hall.

Wmk. 329
1990, Dec. 5   **Photo.**   **Perf. 13½**
1367 A417 2b multicolored   .45 .25
  Complete booklet, strip of 5
  #1367   3.25
1368 A417 3b multicolored   .65 .25
1369 A417 4b multicolored   .65 .40
1370 A417 5b multicolored   .75 .50
1371 A417 6b multicolored   1.00 .60
1372 A417 8b multicolored   1.60 .90
  Nos. 1367-1372 (6)   5.10 2.90

Somdet Phra Maha Samanachao Kromphra Paramanuchitchinorot (1790-1853), Supreme Patriarch — A418

1990, Dec. 11   **Wmk. 387**   **Perf. 13½**
1373 A418 2b multicolored   .60 .25
  Complete booklet, strip of 5
  #1373   6.25

Petroleum Authority, 12th Anniv. — A419

Perf. 14½x14
1990, Dec. 29   **Litho.**   **Wmk. 387**
1374 A419 2b multicolored   .55 .25
  Complete booklet, strip of 5
  #1374   5.25

Locomotives — A420

Designs: 2b, No. 6, Krauss & Co., Germany, 1908. 3b, No. 32, Kyosan Kogyo, Japan, 1949. 5b, No. 715, C56, Japan, 1946. 6b, No. 953, Mikado, Japan, 1949-1951.

Perf. 14½x14
1990, Dec. 29   **Litho.**   **Wmk. 387**
1375 A420 2b multicolored   .70 .25
1376 A420 3b multicolored   1.10 .35
1377 A420 5b multicolored   1.40 1.40
1378 A420 6b multicolored   1.75 1.40
  a.   Souv. sheet of 4, #1375-1378   7.50 7.50
  Nos. 1375-1378 (4)   4.95 3.40

No. 1378a sold for 25b. Exists imperf, value same as perf.

Children's Day — A421

Children's games: 2b, Tops. 5b, Race. 6b, Blind-man's buff.

1991, Jan. 12
1379 A421 2b multicolored   .45 .25
  Complete booklet, strip of 5
  #1379   3.50
1380 A421 3b shown   .60 .30
1381 A421 5b multicolored   .80 .40
1382 A421 6b multicolored   1.10 .50
  Nos. 1379-1382 (4)   2.95 1.45

A422

1991, Feb. 17   **Perf. 14x14½**
1383 A422 2b multicolored   .55   .25
Complete booklet, strip of 5
#1383   5.50

Land titling project.

A423

Perf. 14x14½
1991, Mar. 30   **Litho.**   **Wmk. 387**
1384 A423 2b Princess Maha   2.50   .25
Complete booklet, strip of 5
#1384   20.00
a.   Souvenir sheet of 1   5.00   5.00

Red Cross. No. 1384a sold for 8b. Exists imperf, value same as perf.

Cultural Heritage A424

Floral decorations: 2b, Indra's heavenly abode. 3b, Celestial couch. 4b, Crystal ladder. 5b, Crocodile.

Wmk. 329
1991, Apr. 2   **Photo.**   **Perf. 13½**
1385 A424 2b multicolored   .40   .25
1386 A424 3b multicolored   .50   .30
1387 A424 4b multicolored   .75   .50
1388 A424 5b multicolored   .85   .60
a.   Souv. sheet of 4, #1385-1388   8.00   8.00
   Nos. 1385-1388 (4)   2.50   1.65

No. 1388a sold for 30b. Exists imperf, value same as perf.

Songkran Day — A425

Perf. 14x14½
1991, Apr. 13   **Wmk. 387**   **Litho.**
1389 A425 2b Demon on sheep   2.50   1.00
Complete booklet, strip of 5
#1389   22.50
a.   Souvenir sheet of 1   17.00   17.00

No. 1389a sold for 8b. Exists imperf, value same as perf.
See #1467, 1530, 1566, 1606, 1662, 1724, 1801, 1869, 1940, 1970, 2017.

Prince Narisranuvattivongs (1863-1947) — A426

1991, Apr. 28   **Perf. 14½x14**
1390 A426 2b brown & yellow   .50   .25
Complete booklet, strip of 5
#1390   5.00

Mosaics — A427

Various lotus flowers.

1991, May 28   **Perf. 13½**
1391 A427 2b multi, vert.   .35   .25
Complete booklet, strip of 5
#1391   4.00
1392 A427 3b multi, vert.   .55   .25
1393 A427 5b multi   .80   .45
1394 A427 6b multi   1.00   .55
   Nos. 1391-1394 (4)   2.70   1.50

Natl. Communications Day — A428

Wmk. 387
1991, Aug. 4   **Litho.**   **Perf. 13½**
1395 A428 2b multicolored   .70   .25
Complete booklet, strip of 5
#1395   7.25

Thaipex '91, Natl. Philatelic Exhibition A429

Various fabric designs.

1991, Aug. 4   **Perf. 14x14½**
1396 A429 2b multicolored   .25   .25
1397 A429 4b multicolored   .40   .35
1398 A429 6b multicolored   .70   .40
1399 A429 8b multicolored   .90   .60
a.   Souv. sheet of 4, #1396-1399   6.00   6.00
   Nos. 1396-1399 (4)   2.25   1.60

No. 1399a sold for 30b. Exists imperf, value $32.50. No. 1399a overprinted with Philanippon emblem in lower left corner of margin sold for 200b. Value, $190.

Intl. Productivity Congress — A430

Perf. 14½x14
1991, Sept. 3   **Litho.**   **Wmk. 387**
1400 A430 2b multicolored   .55   .25
Complete booklet, strip of 5
#1400   5.00

26th Intl. Council of Women Triennial — A431

Wmk. 387
1991, Sept. 23   **Litho.**   **Perf. 13½**
1401 A431 2b multicolored   .55   .25
Complete booklet, strip of 5
#1401   5.00

Bantam Chickens — A432

Wmk. 329
1991, Oct. 6   **Photo.**   **Perf. 13½**
1402 A432 2b Black bantams   .45   .25
1403 A432 3b Black-tailed buff bantams   .80   .25
1404 A432 6b Fancy bantams   1.25   .30
1405 A432 8b White bantams   1.75   .80
a.   Souv. sheet of 4, #1402-1405   7.50   7.50
   Nos. 1402-1405 (4)   4.25   1.60

No. 1405a sold for 35b. Exists imperf, value same as perf.
Intl. Letter Writing Week.

World Bank/Intl. Monetary Fund Annual Meetings — A433

Temples, meeting emblem and: 2b, Silver coin of King Rama IV. 4b, Pod Duang money. 8b, Chieng and Hoi money. 10b, Funan, Dvaravati and Srivijaya money.

Perf. 14½x14
1991, Oct. 15   **Litho.**   **Wmk. 387**
1406 A433 2b multicolored   .25   .25
Complete booklet, strip of 5
#1406   3.25
1407 A433 4b multicolored   .45   .30
1408 A433 8b multicolored   .90   .60
1409 A433 10b multicolored   1.10   .75
a.   Souv. sheet of 4, #1406-1409   6.25   6.25
   Nos. 1406-1409 (4)   2.70   1.90

No. 1409a sold for 35b. Exists imperf, value same as perf.

1993 World Philatelic Exhibition, Bangkok — A434

1991, Oct. 23   **Perf. 14x14½**
1410 A434 2b No. 118   .25   .25
1411 A434 3b No. 119   .30   .25
1412 A434 4b No. 120   .40   .30
1413 A434 5b No. 121   .55   .40
1414 A434 6b No. 122   .65   .45
1415 A434 7b No. 123   .75   .50
1416 A434 8b No. 124   .85   .60
a.   Souvenir sheet of 1   5.00   5.00
   Nos. 1410-1416 (7)   3.75   2.75

No. 1416a sold for 15b. Exists imperf, value same as perf.

Flower Type of 1990

1991, Nov. 5   **Perf. 13½**
1417 A416 1b Dillenia obovata   .25   .25
1418 A416 1b Melastoma sanguineum   .25   .25
1419 A416 1b Commelina diffusa   .25   .25
1420 A416 1b Plumbago indica   .25   .25
a.   Souv. sheet of 4, #1417-1420   5.00   5.00
   Nos. 1417-1420 (4)   1.00   1.00

No. 1420a sold for 10b. Exists imperf, value same as perf.

Asian Elephants — A435

Wmk. 329
1991, Nov. 5   **Photo.**   **Perf. 13½**
1421 A435 2b shown   .45   .25
1422 A435 4b Pulling logs   .90   .30
1423 A435 6b Lying down   1.00   .45
1424 A435 8b In river   2.00   .90
a.   Souvenir sheet of 1, litho.   7.50   7.50
   Nos. 1421-1424 (4)   4.35   1.90

No. 1424a sold for 22b and stamp does not have border. No. 1424a exists imperf, value same as perf.

Wild Animals — A436

Perf. 14½x14
1991, Dec. 26   **Wmk. 387**   **Litho.**
1425 A436 2b Viverra zibetha   .55   .25
Complete booklet, strip of 5
#1425   3.00
1426 A436 3b Prionodon linsang   .70   .25
1427 A436 6b Felis temmincki   1.00   .50
1428 A436 8b Ratufa bicolor   1.50   .65
a.   Sheet of 4, #1425-1428   6.25   8.50
   Nos. 1425-1428 (4)   3.75   1.65

No. 1428a sold for 30b. Exists imperf, value same as perf.

Prince Mahidol of Songkla (1891-1929), Medical Pioneer — A437

1992, Jan. 1   **Perf. 14x14½**
1429 A437 2b multicolored   1.00   .25
Complete booklet, strip of 5
#1429   7.25

Department of Mineral Resources, Cent. — A438

No. 1430, Locating fossils. No. 1431, Mining excavation. No. 1432, Drilling for natural gas and petroleum. No. 1433, Digging artesian wells.

Perf. 14½x14
1992, Jan. 1   **Litho.**   **Wmk. 387**
1430 A438 2b multicolored   .90   .25
Complete booklet, strip of 5
#1430   4.50
1431 A438 2b multicolored   .90   .25
Complete booklet, strip of 5
#1431   4.50
1432 A438 2b multicolored   .90   .25
Complete booklet, strip of 5
#1432   4.50
1433 A438 2b multicolored   .90   .25
Complete booklet, strip of 5
#1433   4.50
   Nos. 1430-1433 (4)   3.60   1.00

Children's Day — A439

Children's drawings on "World Under the Sea": 2b, Divers, fish. 3b, Fish, sea grass. 5b, Mermaid.

1992, Jan. 11   Wmk. 329   Perf. 13½
1434	A439	2b multicolored	.45	.25
		Complete booklet, strip of 5		
		#1434	3.00	
1435	A439	3b multicolored	.45	.30
1436	A439	5b multicolored, vert.	.90	.50
		Nos. 1434-1436 (3)	1.80	1.05

Duel on Elephants, 400th Anniv. — A440

Perf. 14½x14
1992, Jan. 18   Litho.   Wmk. 387
1437	A440	2b multicolored	.80	.25
		Complete booklet, strip of 5		
		#1437	7.25	

Orchids (Paphiopedilum) — A441

1992, Jan. 20
1438	A441	2b Bellatulum	.25	.25
1439	A441	2b Exul	.25	.25
1440	A441	3b Concolor	.35	.30
1441	A441	3b Godefroyae	.35	.30
1442	A441	6b Niveum	.70	.55
1443	A441	6b Villosum	.70	.55
1444	A441	10b Parishii	1.25	.90
a.		Souv. sheet of 4, #1438, 1440, 1442, 1444	5.00	5.00
1445	A441	10b Sukhakulii	1.25	.90
a.		Souv. sheet of 4, #1439, 1441, 1443, 1445	5.00	5.00
		Nos. 1438-1445 (8)	5.10	4.00

Fourth Asia Pacific Orchid Conference. Nos. 1444a-1445a each sold for 30b. Each exists imperf, value same as perf.

21st Intl. Society of Sugar Cane Technologists Conf. — A442

1992, Mar. 5   Perf. 14x14½
1446	A442	2b multicolored	1.60	.25
		Complete booklet, strip of 5		
		#1446	6.00	

Intl. Red Cross A443

Perf. 14½x14
1992, Mar.   Litho.   Wmk. 387
1447	A443	2b multicolored	.50	.25
		Complete booklet, strip of 5		
		#1447	4.00	

Ministry of Justice, Cent. — A444

Designs: 3b, Prince Rabi Badhanasakdi of Ratchaburi, founder of Thailand's School of Law. 5b, King Rama V, reformer of court system.

1992, Mar. 25   Perf. 13½
1448	A444	3b multicolored	.80	.30
1449	A444	5b multicolored	1.25	.40

Ministry of Agriculture and Cooperatives, Cent. — A445

1992, Apr. 1   Perf. 14½x14
1450	A445	2b gray & multi	.45	.25
		Complete booklet, strip of 5		
		#1450	3.25	
1451	A445	3b lil & multi	.60	.30
1452	A445	4b pink & multi	.80	.35
1453	A445	5b gray bl & multi	1.00	.40
		Nos. 1450-1453 (4)	2.85	1.30

A446

Ministry of Interior, Cent.: No. 1454, Prince Damrong Rajanubharb, first Minister of the Interior. No. 1455, People voting. No. 1456, Police and fire protection. No. 1457, Water and electricity provided to remote areas.

1992, Apr. 1   Perf. 14x14½
1454	A446	2b multicolored	.35	.25
		Complete booklet, strip of 5		
		#1454	4.00	
1455	A446	2b multicolored	.35	.25
		Complete booklet, strip of 5		
		#1455	4.00	
1456	A446	2b multicolored	.35	.25
		Complete booklet, strip of 5		
		#1456	4.00	
1457	A446	2b multicolored	.35	.25
		Complete booklet, strip of 5		
		#1457	4.00	
		Nos. 1454-1457 (4)	1.40	1.00

A447

1992, Apr. 1
1458	A447	2b Ships, truck	.25	.25
		Complete booklet, strip of 5		
		#1458	3.25	

Ministry of Education, Cent. — A448

1459	A447	3b Truck, bus, train	.40	.30
1460	A447	5b Airplanes	.60	.40
1461	A447	6b Truck, satellites	.75	.50
		Nos. 1458-1461 (4)	2.00	1.45

Ministry of Transport and Communications, 80th anniv.

Perf. 14x14½
1992, Apr. 1   Litho.   Wmk. 387
1462	A448	2b multicolored	.45	.25
		Complete booklet, strip of 5		
		#1462	4.00	

Carts A449

1992, Apr. 2   Perf. 14½x14
1463	A449	2b West	.25	.25
		Complete booklet, strip of 5		
		#1463	3.25	
1464	A449	3b North	.35	.25
1465	A449	5b Northeast	.55	.40
1466	A449	10b East	1.10	.90
a.		Souv. sheet of 4, #1463-1466	4.50	
		Nos. 1463-1466 (4)	2.25	1.80

Heritage Conservation Day. No. 1466a sold for 30b. Exists imperf without sheet price in margin, value same as perf.

Songkran Day Type of 1991
1992, Apr. 13   Perf. 14x14½
1467	A425	2b Demon on monkey, zodiac	1.40	.25
		Complete booklet, strip of 5		
		#1467	7.00	
a.		Souvenir sheet of 1	4.00	4.00

No. 1467a sold for 8b. Exists imperf with sale price in different colors, value same as perf.

Department of Livestock Development, 50th Anniv. — A451

Perf. 14½x14
1992, May 5   Litho.   Wmk. 387
1468	A451	2b multicolored	.65	.25
		Complete booklet, strip of 5		
		#1468	4.00	

Wisakhabucha Day — A452

Scenes from Buddha's life: 2b, Birth. 3b, Enlightenment. 5b, Death.

Meteorological Department, 50th Anniv. — A453

Wmk. 387
1992, May 16   Litho.   Perf. 14½
1469	A452	2b multicolored	.35	.25
1470	A452	3b multicolored	.70	.30
1471	A452	5b multicolored	1.00	.65
		Nos. 1469-1471 (3)	2.05	1.20

1992, June 23   Perf. 14x14½
1472	A453	2b multicolored	.65	.25
		Complete booklet, strip of 5		
		#1472	4.00	

1993 World Philatelic Exhibition, Bangkok — A454

Perf. 14x14½
1992, July 1   Litho.   Wmk. 387
1473	A454	2b No. 18	.25	.25
		Complete booklet, strip of 5		
		#1473	3.25	
1474	A454	3b No. 156	.35	.25
1475	A454	5b No. 222	.55	.40
1476	A454	7b No. 255	.85	.50
1477	A454	8b No. 273	1.00	.65
a.		Souv. sheet of 5, #1473-1477 + label	6.00	6.00
		Nos. 1473-1477 (5)	3.00	2.05

No. 1477a sold for 35b. Exists imperf. with sheet price in blue, value same as #1477a.

Visit ASEAN Year — A455

Designs: 2b, Bua Tong field, Mae Hong Son Province. 3b, Klong Larn Waterfall, Kamphaeng Phet Province. 4b, Coral, Chumphon Province. 5b, Khao Ta-Poo, Phangnga Province.

1992, July 1
1478	A455	2b multicolored	.30	.25
		Complete booklet, strip of 5		
		#1478	3.25	
1479	A455	3b multicolored	.40	.25
1480	A455	4b multicolored	.50	.35
1481	A455	5b multicolored	.60	.40
		Nos. 1478-1481 (4)	1.80	1.25

Prince Chudadhuj Dharadilok of Bejraburna (1892-1923) A456

Wmk. 368

1992, July 5   Litho.   *Perf. 13½*
1482 A456 2b multicolored   .60   .25
  Complete booklet, strip of 5
    #1482   5.00

Natl. Communications Day — A457

Perf. 14½x14
1992, Aug. 4   Litho.   Wmk. 387
1483 A457 2b multicolored   .55   .25
  Complete booklet, strip of 5
    #1483   4.00

ASEAN, 25th
Anniv. — A458

Flags and: 2b, Cultures and sports. 3b, Tourist attractions. 5b, Transportation, communications. 7b, Agriculture.

1992, Aug. 8   Wmk. 368   *Perf. 13½*
1484 A458 2b multicolored   .25   .25
  Complete booklet, strip of 5
    #1484   3.25
1485 A458 3b multicolored   .35   .25
1486 A458 5b multicolored   .55   .40
1487 A458 7b multicolored   .85   .55
    Nos. 1484-1487 (4)   2.00 1.45

Queen Sirikit, 60th Birthday — A459

#1488, Wedding, with King, Queen being anointed. #1489, Coronation, King and Queen on throne. #1490, Being crowned, Queen with crown, being anointed. #1491, Formal portrait, Queen seated. #1492, Visiting wounded. #1493, Visiting public.

Wmk. 329

1992, Aug. 12   Photo.   *Perf. 13½*
1488 A459 2b multicolored   .70   .25
  Complete booklet, strip of 5
    #1488   6.00
1489 A459 2b multicolored   .70   .25
  Complete booklet, strip of 5
    #1489   6.00
1490 A459 2b multicolored   .70   .25
  Complete booklet, strip of 5
    #1490   6.00
1491 A459 2b multicolored   .70   .25
  Complete booklet, strip of 5
    #1491   6.00
1492 A459 2b multicolored   .70   .25
  Complete booklet, strip of 5
    #1492   6.00
1493 A459 2b multicolored   .70   .25
  Complete booklet, strip of 5
    #1493   6.00
  a.   Souv. sheet of 6, #1488-1493   5.00 5.00
    Nos. 1488-1493 (6)   4.20 1.50

No. 1493a sold for 30b. Exists imperf with sale price in different colors, value same as perf.

Royal Regalia
of Queen
Sirikit — A460

No. 1494, Tray. No. 1495, Kettle. No. 1496, Bowl. No. 1497, Box. No. 1498, Covered dish.

1992, Aug. 12   Background Colors
1494 A460 2b dark blue   .45   .25
1495 A460 2b violet   .45   .25
1496 A460 2b yellow green   .45   .25
1497 A460 2b Prussian blue   .45   .25
1498 A460 2b dark green   .45   .25
    Nos. 1494-1498 (5)   2.25 1.25

Opening of Sirikit Medical
Center — A461

Perf. 14½x14
1992, Aug. 12   Litho.   Wmk. 387
1499 A461 2b multicolored   .45   .25
  Complete booklet, strip of 5
    #1499   4.00

Queen Sirikit, 60th Birthday — A462

Litho. & Embossed
1992, Aug. 12   *Perf. 13½*
1500 A462 100b blue & gold   17.50 17.50

No. 1500 was printed in sheets of 10. Value, $190.

A463

Wmk. 387
1992, Aug. 25   Litho.   *Perf. 13½*
1501 A463 2b multicolored   .60   .25
  Complete booklet, strip of 5
    #1501   5.00

Prince Wan Waithayakon Krommun Naradhip Bongsprabandh (1891-1976).

A464

1992, Sept. 15   *Perf. 14x14½*
1502 A464 2b multicolored   .60   .25
  Complete booklet, strip of 5
    #1502   5.00

Professor Silpa Bhirasri, Sculptor, cent. of birth.

Coral
A465

2b, Catalaphyllia jardinei. 3b, Porites lutea. 6b, Tubastraea coccinea. 8b, Favia pallida.

Perf. 14½x14
1992, Oct. 4   Litho.   Wmk. 387
1503 A465 2b multicolored   .55   .25
  Complete booklet, strip of 5
    #1503   3.25
1504 A465 3b multicolored   .80   .25
1505 A465 6b multicolored   1.10   .50
1506 A465 8b multicolored   1.60   .70
  a.   Souv. sheet of 4, #1503-1506   5.25
    Nos. 1503-1506 (4)   4.05 1.70

Intl. Letter Writing Week. No. 1506a sold for for 30b.

New Year
1993 — A466

Flowers: No. 1507, Rhododendron simsii. No. 1508, Cynoglossum lanceolatum. No. 1509, Tithonia diversifolia. No. 1510, Agapetes parishii.

Perf. 14x13½
1992, Nov. 15   Wmk. 368   Litho.
1507 A466 1b multicolored   .35   .25
1508 A466 1b multicolored   .35   .25
1509 A466 1b multicolored   .35   .25
1510 A466 1b multicolored   .35   .25
  a.   Souv. sheet of 4, #1507-1510   3.00 2.00
    Nos. 1507-1510 (4)   1.40 1.00

Nos. 1510a sold for 10b. Exists imperf with sheet price in green, value same as perf.

1st Asian
Congress of
Allergies and
Immunology
A467

1992, Nov. 22   *Perf. 13½*
1511 A467 2b black, red & yellow   .45   .25
  Complete booklet, strip of 5
    #1511   5.00

Natl. Assembly, 60th Anniv. — A468

Wmk. 387
1992, Dec. 10   Litho.   *Perf. 13½*
1512 A468 2b multicolored   .60   .25
  Complete booklet, strip of 5
    #1512   6.00

Bank of Thailand, 50th Anniv. — A469

1992, Dec. 10   *Perf. 14½x14*
1513 A469 2b multicolored   .60   .25
  Complete booklet, strip of 5
    #1513   5.50

Children's Day — A470

Children's drawings: No. 1514, River scene. No. 1515, Wild animals, forest. No. 1516, Trains, planes, monorail.

1993, Jan. 9   Wmk. 368   *Perf. 13½*
1514 A470 2b multicolored   .35   .25
  Complete booklet, strip of 5
    #1514   4.00
1515 A470 2b multicolored   .35   .25
  Complete booklet, strip of 5
    #1515   4.00
1516 A470 2b multicolored   .35   .25
  Complete booklet, strip of 5
    #1516   4.00
    Nos. 1514-1516 (3)   1.05   .75

Pottery — A471

Designs: 3b, Jug with bird's neck spout, two bottles. 6b, Pear-shaped vase, two jars. 7b, Three bowls. 8b, Three jars.

1993, Jan. 9   Photo.   Wmk. 329
1517 A471 3b multicolored   .35   .25
1518 A471 6b multicolored   .70   .50
1519 A471 7b multicolored   .80   .55
1520 A471 8b multicolored   .95   .70
  a.   Souv. sheet of 4, #1517-1520   5.50 4.00
    Nos. 1517-1520 (4)   2.80 2.00

1993 World Philatelic Exhibition, Bangkok. No. 1520a sold for 35b.

Thai Teachers'
Training Institute,
Cent. — A472

Perf. 13½x14
1993, Jan. 16   Litho.   Wmk. 368
1521 A472 2b multicolored   .45   .25
  Complete booklet, strip of 5
    #1521   6.00

Kasetsart University, 50th
Anniv. — A473

1993, Feb. 2   Wmk. 329   *Perf. 13½*
1522 A473 2b multicolored   .60   .25
  Complete booklet, strip of 5
    #1522   6.00

Maghapuja Day — A474

Wmk. 387
1993, Mar. 7   Litho.   Perf. 14½
1523 A474 2b multicolored   .70   .25

Queen Sri Bajarindra — A475

1993, Mar. 27   Perf. 14x14½
1524 A475 2b multicolored   .80   .25
       Complete booklet, strip of 5
       #1524   7.25

Thai Red Cross, cent.

Office of Attorney General, Cent. — A476

1993, Apr. 1   Wmk. 368   Perf. 12½
1525 A476 2b multicolored   .60   .25
       Complete booklet, strip of 5
       #1525   6.00

Heritage Conservation Day — A477

Historical landmarks, Si Satchanalai Park: 3b, Wat Chedi Chet Thaeo. 4b, Wat Chang Lom. 6b, Wat Phra Si Rattanamahathat (Chaliang). 7b, Wat Suan Kaeo Utthayan Noi.

Wmk. 368
1993, Apr. 2   Litho.   Perf. 13½
1526 A477 3b multicolored   .35   .25
1527 A477 4b multicolored   .45   .30
1528 A477 6b multicolored   .70   .50
1529 A477 7b multicolored   .80   .55
   a.   Souv. sheet of 4, #1526-1529   4.50   3.50
       Nos. 1526-1529 (4)   2.30   1.60

No. 1529a sold for 25b.
See Nos. 1561-1564, 1650-1653, 1797-1800.

Songkran Day Type of 1991

Design: Demon on rooster's back, zodiac.

Perf. 14x14½
1993   Litho.   Wmk. 387
1530 A425 2b multicolored   .40   .25
       Complete booklet, strip of 5
       #1530   2.50
   a.   Souvenir sheet of 1   2.50   1.00
   b.   As "a," ovptd. in gold   15.00 15.00

No. 1530b overprinted on sheet margin in both Thai and Chinese for Chinpex '93.
Nos. 1530a-1530b sold for 8b and exist imperf. with sale price in different colors. Values same as for perf.
Issued: Nos. 1530, 1530a, 4/13.

Mushrooms — A478

Wmk. 368
1993, July 1   Litho.   Perf. 13½
1531 A478 2b Marasmius   .25   .25
       Complete booklet, strip of 5
       #1531   3.50
1532 A478 4b Coprinus   .50   .30
1533 A478 6b Mycena   .70   .45
1534 A478 8b Cyathus   1.00   .60
   a.   Souv. sheet of 4, #1531-1534   4.25   4.25
       Nos. 1531-1534 (4)   2.45   1.60

No. 1534a sold for 30b.

Natl. Communications Day — A479

1993, Aug. 4   Wmk. 387   Perf. 13½
1535 A479 2b multicolored   .45   .25
       Complete booklet, strip of 5
       #1535   5.00

Post and Telegraph Department, 110th Anniv. — A480

Wmk. 387
1993, Aug. 4   Litho.   Perf. 13½
1536 A480 2b multicolored   1.00   .25
       Complete booklet, strip of 5
       #1536   10.50

Queen Suriyothai's Monument — A481

1993, Aug. 12
1537 A481 2b multicolored   .60   .25
       Complete booklet, strip of 5
       #1537   6.00

Fruit — A482

Wmk. 368
1993, Oct. 1   Photo.   Perf. 13½
1538 A482 2b Citrus reticulata   .25   .25
       Complete booklet, strip of 5
       #1538   2.50
1539 A482 3b Musa sp.   .40   .25
1540 A482 6b Phyllanthus dis-
            tichus   .75   .45
1541 A482 8b Bouea burmanica   1.00   .60
       Nos. 1538-1541 (4)   2.40   1.55

Thai Ridgeback Dogs — A483

Various dogs.

1993, Oct. 1
1542 A483 2b multicolored   .55   .25
       Complete booklet, strip of 5
       #1542   2.75
1543 A483 3b multicolored   .55   .25
1544 A483 5b multicolored   .80   .40
1545 A483 10b multicolored   2.10   .75
   a.   Souv. sheet of 4, #1542-1545   4.50   4.00
       Nos. 1542-1545 (4)   4.00   1.65

Intl. Letter Writing Week. No. 1545a sold for 30b.

5th Conference & Exhibition of ASEAN Council on Petroleum (ASCOPE) — A484

Wmk. 387
1993, Nov. 2   Litho.   Perf. 13½
1546 A484 2b multicolored   .60   .25
       Complete booklet, strip of 5
       #1546   6.00

King Rama VII (1893-1941) A485

1993, Nov. 8   Perf. 14x14½
1547 A485 2b multicolored   1.00   .25
       Complete booklet, strip of 5
       #1547   9.00

No. 655 Surcharged

1993   Photo.   Wmk. 233   Perf. 14½
1548 A161 1b on 25s brown red   .70   .25

Bencharong and Lai Nam Thong Wares — A486

Designs: 3b, Bencharong cosmetic jar, divinity design. 5b, Bencharong cosmetic jar, gold knob. 6b, Lai Nam Thong cosmetic jar, floral design. 7b, Lai Nam Thong cosmetic jar, floral design, diff.

Wmk. 368
1993, Oct. 1   Photo.   Perf. 13½
1549 A486 3b multicolored   .35   .25
1550 A486 5b multicolored   .55   .40
1551 A486 6b multicolored   .65   .45
1552 A486 7b multicolored   .80   .55
   a.   Souv. sheet of 4, #1549-1552   4.00   4.00
       Nos. 1549-1552 (4)   2.35   1.65

Bangkok '93. No. 1552a sold for 30b.
No. 1552a exists imperf. Value, $22.50.

New Year 1994 — A487

Perf. 14½x14
1993, Nov. 15   Litho.   Wmk. 387
1553 A487 1b Ipomoea cairica   .25   .25
1554 A487 1b Decaschistia
            parviflora   .25   .25
1555 A487 1b Hibiscus tiliaceus   .25   .25
1556 A487 1b Passiflora foetida   .25   .25
   a.   Souv. sheet of 4, #1553-1556   2.00   1.75
       Nos. 1553-1556 (4)   1.00   1.00

No. 1556a sold for 10b.

THAICOM, Natl. Satellite Project — A488

1993, Dec. 1   Perf. 14x14½
1557 A488 2b multicolored   .50   .25
       Complete booklet, strip of 5
       #1557   5.00

Children's Day — A489

1994, Jan. 8   Perf. 14½x14
1558 A489 2b Play land   .45   .25
       Complete booklet, strip of 5
       #1558   4.00

Administrative Building, Chulalongkorn Hospital, 80th Anniv. — A490

Perf. 14½x14
1994, Mar. 30   Litho.   Wmk. 387
1559 A490 2b multicolored   .45   .25
       Complete booklet, strip of 5
       #1559   4.00

Thai Red Cross.

Royal Institute, 60th Anniv. — A491

1994, Mar. 31   Perf. 14x14½
1560 A491 2b multicolored   .40   .25
       Complete booklet, strip of 5
       #1560   4.00

Heritage Conservation Day Type of 1993

Historical landmarks, Phra Nakhon Si Ayutthaya Park: 2b, Wat Ratchaburana. 3b, Wat Maha That. 6b, Wat Maheyong. 9b, Wat Phra Si Samphet.

1994, Apr. 2   **Perf. 14½x14**
1561 A477 2b multicolored .30 .25
    Complete booklet, strip of 5 #1561   2.50
1562 A477 3b multicolored .40 .25
1563 A477 6b multicolored .80 .50
1564 A477 9b multicolored 1.25 .95
  a. Souv. sheet of 4, #1561-1564 3.25 3.25
  Nos. 1561-1564 (4) 2.75 1.95

No. 1564a sold for 25b.

Opening of Friendship Bridge, Thailand-Laos — A492

1994, Apr. 8
1565 A492 9b multicolored 1.75 .75

Songkran Day Type of 1991

Design: Demon on dog's back, zodiac.

1994, Apr. 13   **Litho.**
1566 A425 2b multicolored .35 .25
    Complete booklet, strip of 5 #1566   3.25
  a. Souvenir sheet of 1 2.00 1.75
  b. As "a," inscribed in margin 4.50 4.50

No. 1566a sold for 8b and exists imperf with frame around stamp and sale price in different color. Value same as perf.

Sheet margin of No. 1566b has no value inscription and is overprinted in violet with Thai and Chinese inscriptions for Beijing Stamp Exhibition. Issued: May 1994. No. 1566b also exists imperf. Value same as perf.

Intl. Olympic Committee, Cent. — A493

Wmk. 387
1994, June 23   **Litho.**   **Perf. 14**
1567 A493 2b Soccer .25 .25
    Complete booklet, strip of 5 #1567   1.75
1568 A493 3b Running .35 .25
1569 A493 5b Swimming .60 .45
1570 A493 6b Weight lifting .80 .55
1571 A493 9b Boxing 1.10 .80
  Nos. 1567-1571 (5) 3.10 2.30

Thammasat University, 60th Anniv. — A494

Wmk. 387
1994, June 27   **Litho.**   **Perf. 14**
1572 A494 2b multicolored 1.60 .45
    Complete booklet, strip of 5 #1572   8.00

Asalhapuja Day — A495

1994, July 22   **Wmk. 329**   **Perf. 13½**
1573 A495 2b multicolored .45 .25

Natl. Communications Day — A496

1994, Aug. 4   **Wmk. 368**
1574 A496 2b multicolored .45 .25
    Complete booklet, strip of 5 #1574   4.00

Crabs A497

3b, Phricotelphusa limula. 5b, Thaipotamon chulabhorn. 6b, Phricotelphusa sirindhorn. 10b, Thaiphusa sirikit.

Wmk. 340 (340)
1994, Aug. 12   **Photo.**   **Perf. 13½x13**
1575 A497 3b multicolored .55 .25
1576 A497 5b multicolored .80 .45
1577 A497 6b multicolored .80 .55
1578 A497 10b multicolored 1.60 .90
  a. Souv. sheet of 4, #1575-1578 4.50 4.50
  b. As "a," inscribed in margin 7.25 5.50
  Nos. 1575-1578 (4) 3.75 2.15

No. 1578b has PHILAKOREA '94 Exhibition emblem added to sheet margin.

Intl. Letter Writing Week — A498

Winning paintings in design contest: 2b, Gold niello bowls, octagonal footed tray. 6b, Pumpkin shaped bowls. 8b, Silver niello betelnut set. 9b, Covered square bowl with gold finial, small lotus-shaped footed tray.

Wmk. 368
1994, Oct. 9   **Photo.**   **Perf. 13½**
1579 A498 2b multicolored .25 .25
    Complete booklet, 5 #1579   2.50
1580 A498 6b multicolored .80 .55
1581 A498 8b multicolored 1.00 .70
1582 A498 9b multicolored 1.10 .80
  a. Souv. sheet of 4, #1579-1582 4.00 4.00
  Nos. 1579-1582 (4) 3.15 2.30

No. 1582a sold for 30b.

ILO, 75th Anniv. A499

Perf. 15x14
1994, Oct. 29   **Litho.**   **Wmk. 387**
1583 A499 2b multicolored .30 .25
    Complete booklet, 5 #1583   4.00

New Year 1995 — A500

Herbs: No. 1584, Utricularia delphinioides. No. 1585, Utricularia minutissima. No. 1586, Eriocaulon odoratum. No. 1587, Utricularia bifida.

1994, Nov. 15   **Perf. 14x14½**
1584 A500 1b multicolored .25 .25
1585 A500 1b multicolored .25 .25
1586 A500 1b multicolored .25 .25
1587 A500 1b multicolored .25 .25
  a. Souv. sheet of 4, #1584-1587 2.00 1.75
  Nos. 1584-1587 (4) 1.00 1.00

No. 1587a sold for 10b.

Suan Dusit Teachers College, 60th Anniv. — A501

Perf. 14½x14
1994, Dec. 4   **Litho.**   **Wmk. 387**
1588 A501 2b multicolored .60 .25
    Complete booklet, 5 #1588   5.50

Council of State, 120th Anniv. — A502

1994, Dec. 5   **Wmk. 368**   **Perf. 13½**
1589 A502 2b multicolored 1.40 .25
    Complete booklet, 5 #1589   12.50

ICAO, 50th Anniv. A503

Perf. 14½x14
1994, Dec. 7   **Wmk. 387**
1590 A503 2b multicolored .35 .25
    Complete booklet, 5 #1590   5.50

Pharmacy in Thailand, 80th Anniv. — A504

Grinding stones: 2b, Dvaravati, 7th-11th cent. 6b, Lopburi Period, 11th-13th cent. 9b, Bangkok Period, 18th-20th cent.

1994, Dec. 13
1591 A504 2b multicolored .30 .25
    Complete booklet, 5 #1591   3.00
1592 A504 6b multicolored .80 .50
1593 A504 9b multicolored 1.10 .80
  Nos. 1591-1593 (3) 2.20 1.55

Bar Assoc., 80th Anniv. — A505

Design: 2b, First Bar Assoc. headquarters, King Vajiravudh, King Bhumibol.

1995, Jan. 1   **Wmk. 368**   **Perf. 13½**
1594 A505 2b multicolored .60 .25
    Complete booklet, 5 #1594   6.25

A506

Children's drawings: No. 1595, Kites Decorate the Summer Sky. No. 1596, Trees and Streams, horiz. No. 1597, Youths and Religion, horiz.

1995, Jan. 14   **Wmk. 387**   **Perf. 14**
1595 A506 2b multicolored .55 .25
    Complete booklet, 5 #1595   3.00
1596 A506 2b multicolored .55 .25
    Complete booklet, 5 #1596   3.00
1597 A506 2b multicolored .55 .25
    Complete booklet, 5 #1597   3.00
  Nos. 1595-1597 (3) 1.65 .75

Children's Day.

A507

1995, Mar. 4
1598 A507 2b multicolored .35 .25
    Complete booklet, 5 #1598   5.00

First Thai newspaper, Bangkok Recorder, 150th anniv.

Royal Thai Air Force, 80th Anniv. A508

1995, Mar. 27   **Wmk. 368**   **Perf. 13½**
1599 A508 2b multicolored .25 .25
    Complete booklet, 5 #1599   4.00

Red Cross Floating Clinic, Wetchapha — A509

1995, Mar. 30
1600 A509 2b multicolored .25 .25
    Complete booklet, 5 #1600   4.00

Phimai Historical Park — A510

Paintings: 3b, Naga Bridge. 5b, Brahmin Hall. 6b, Gateway of the Inner Wall. 9b, Main Pagoda.

Perf. 14½x14

1995, Apr. 2 **Wmk. 387**
1601	A510 3b multicolored	.35	.25
1602	A510 5b multicolored	.60	.35
1603	A510 6b multicolored	.80	.50
1604	A510 9b multicolored	1.10	.80
a.	Souv. sheet of 4, #1601-1604	4.00	4.00
	Nos. 1601-1604 (4)	2.85	1.90

Heritage Conservation Day.
No. 1604a sold for 30b.

Ministry of Defense, 108th Anniv. — A511

Design: 2b, Admin. building, King Rama V.

1995, Apr. 8 **Wmk. 387** **Perf. 14**
1605	A511 2b multicolored	.70	.25
	Complete booklet, 5 #1605	7.50	

Songkran Day Type of 1991

Design: Demon on boar's back, zodiac.

1995, Apr. 13 **Perf. 11x13**
1606	A425 2b multicolored	.30	.25
a.	Souvenir sheet of 1	1.75	1.00
	Complete booklet, 5 #1606	3.25	

No. 1606a sold for 8b and exists imperf with sale price in different color. Value same as perf. No. 1606a and the similar imperf sheet exist with a red marginal inscription in Thai and Chinese (without sale price). Value, each $5.50.

Ministry of Foreign Affairs, 120th Anniv. — A512

2b, Saranrom Palace, King Rama V.

1995, Apr. 14 **Perf. 14**
1607	A512 2b multicolored	.80	.25
	Complete booklet, 5 #1607	7.50	

Visakhapuja Day — A513

Sculptures of Buddha: 2b, Emerald Buddha, temple of Wat Phra Si Rattana Satsadaram, Bangkok. 6b, Phra Phuttha Chinnarat, Wat Phra Si Rattana Maha That, Phitsanulok Province. 8b, Phra Phuttha Sihing, Wat Phra Sing, Chiang Mai Province. 9b, Phra Sukhothai Traimit, Wat Traimit Witthayaram, Bangkok.

Wmk. 340

1995, May 13 **Photo.** **Perf. 13½**
1608	A513 2b multicolored	.25	.25
1609	A513 6b multicolored	.80	.50
1610	A513 8b multicolored	1.00	.70

1611	A513 9b multicolored	1.10	.80
a.	Souv. sheet of 4, #1608-1611	4.50	4.50
	Nos. 1608-1611 (4)	3.15	2.25

No. 1611a sold for 35b.

ASEAN Environment Year — A514

1995, June 5 **Litho.** **Wmk. 368**
1612	A514 2b multicolored	.25	.25
	Complete booklet, 5 #1612	4.00	

Information Technology Year — A515

1995, June 9 **Wmk. 340**
1613	A515 2b multicolored	.25	.25
	Complete booklet, 5 #1613	4.00	

Thailand-People's Republic of China Diplomatic Relations, 20th Anniv. — A516

#1614, Elephants walking right into water.
#1615, Elephants walking left into water.

Wmk. 340

1995, July 1 **Photo.** **Perf. 13½**
1614	A516 2b multicolored	.50	.25
1615	A516 2b multicolored	.50	.25
a.	Pair, Nos. 1614-1615	1.75	1.75
b.	Souv. sheet, #1614-1615	3.50	
c.	As "b," diff. inscriptions in sheet margin	18.00	

No. 1615c contains Jakarta '95 exhibition emblem and does not have sheet value in margin.
#1615b sold for 8b. #1615c sold for 28b.
No. 1615b exists with serial number in sheet margin, The same number is on China (PRC) No. 2462a. These two souvenir sheets were sold as a set. Value, set $26.50.
See People's Republic of China Nos. 2579-2580.

Natl. Communications Day — A517

1995, Aug. 4 **Litho.** **Perf. 14½x14**
1616	A517 2b multicolored	.30	.25
	Complete booklet, 5 #1616	4.50	

A518

Domestic cats: 3b, Khoa Manee. 6b, Korat or Si-Sawat. 7b, Seal point Siamese. 9b, Burmese.

1995, Aug. 4 **Photo.** **Perf. 13½**
1617	A518 3b multicolored	.55	.25
1618	A518 6b multicolored	.80	.50
1619	A518 7b multicolored	1.00	.60
1620	A518 9b multicolored	1.60	.80
a.	Souv. sheet, Nos. 1617-1620	5.50	5.50
b.	As "a," diff. inscriptions in margin	35.00	35.00
	Nos. 1617-1620 (4)	3.95	2.15

Thaipex '95.
No. 1620b contains Singapore '95 exhibition emblem added to sheet margin and does not have value inscription.
No. 1620a sold for 35b. No. 1620b sold for 46b.
No. 1620a exists imperf. Value $21.00.

Revenue Department, 80th Anniv. — A519

1995, Sept. 2 **Litho.** **Perf. 14x14½**
1621	A519 2b multicolored	.25	.25
	Complete booklet, 5 #1621	4.50	

Natl. Auditing & Office of Auditor General, 120th Anniv. — A520

1995, Sept. 18 **Perf. 14½x14**
1622	A520 2b multicolored	.25	.25
	Complete booklet, 5 #1622	4.00	

Intl. Letter Writing Week — A521

Wicker: No. 1623, Vase with handles, legs. No. 1624, Oval-shaped container. No. 1625, Lamp shade. No. 1626, Vase.

Wmk. 340

1995, Oct. 8 **Photo.** **Perf. 13½**
1623	A521 2b multicolored	.25	.25
	Complete booklet, 5 #1623	2.75	
1624	A521 2b multicolored	.25	.25
	Complete booklet, 5 #1624	2.75	
1625	A521 9b multicolored	1.10	.80
1626	A521 9b multicolored	1.10	.80
a.	Souv. sheet, #1623-1626	4.50	4.50
	Nos. 1623-1626 (4)	2.70	2.10

FAO, 50th Anniv. A522

1995, Oct. 16 **Litho.** **Perf. 14½x14**
1627	A522 2b multicolored	.25	.25
	Complete booklet, 5 #1627	3.50	

Total Solar Eclipse in Thailand — A523

1995, Oct. 24 **Perf. 13½**
1628	A523 2b multicolored	.45	.25
	Complete booklet, 5 #1628	2.50	

UN, 50th Anniv. A524

Perf. 13½x14

1995, Oct. 24 **Wmk. 387**
1629	A524 2b multicolored	.25	.25
	Complete booklet, 5 #1629	2.50	

World Agricultural and Industrial Exhibition, Nkhon Ratchasima Province — A525

2b, Worldtech '95 Thailand Symbol Tower, vert. 5b, Farming equipment, food products, vert. 6b, Computers, equipment. 9b, Factory, beach.

Perf. 14x14½, 14½x14

1995, Nov. 4 **Wmk. 340**
1630	A525 2b multicolored	.25	.25
	Complete booklet, 5 #1630	2.50	
1631	A525 5b multicolored	.60	.40
1632	A525 6b multicolored	.80	.50
1633	A525 9b multicolored	1.10	.80
	Nos. 1630-1633 (4)	2.75	1.95

New Year 1996 — A526

#1634, Adenium obesum. #1635, Bauhinia acuminata. #1636, Cananga odorata. #1637, Thunbergia erecta.

1995, Dec. 9 **Perf. 13½**
1634	A526 2b multicolored	.25	.25
1635	A526 2b multicolored	.25	.25
a.	Souvenir sheet, #1634-1635	4.50	
1636	A526 2b multicolored	.25	.25
1637	A526 2b multicolored	.25	.25
a.	Souvenir sheet #1634-1637	2.75	2.25
b.	As "a," inscribed in margin	13.50	10.00
c.	Souvenir sheet, #1636-1637	8.00	7.00
	Nos. 1634-1637 (4)	1.00	1.00

No. 1637a sold for 15b.
Nos. 1635a, 1637c have "CHINA '96" emblem inscribed in sheet margin and sold for 22b each. No. 1637b is inscribed in sheet margin with "Indonesia '96" emblem and has the gold 15b value removed. No. 1637b sold for 14b.
Issued: #1635a, 1637b-1637c, 5/18/96.

Veterinary Science in Thailand, 60th Anniv. — A527

1995, Dec. 9   **Perf. 14½x14**
1638 A527 2b multicolored   .50 .25
    Complete booklet, 5 #1638   4.00

A528

Perf. 14x14½
1996, Jan. 12   **Litho.**   **Wmk. 340**
1639 A528 2b multicolored   .50 .25
    Complete booklet, 5 #1639   5.00

Siriraj School of Nursing and Midwifery, cent.

A529

Paintings of Buddha instructing people with: No. 1640, Bright light, deer. No. 1641, Children, animal, person reclined, horiz. No. 1642, Followers, large tree, river.

1996, Jan. 13   **Wmk. 387**   **Perf. 13½**
1640 A529 2b multicolored   .50 .25
    Complete booklet, 5 #1640   2.75
1641 A529 2b multicolored   .50 .25
    Complete booklet, 5 #1641   2.75
1642 A529 2b multicolored   .50 .25
    Complete booklet, 5 #1642   2.75
    Nos. 1640-1642 (3)   1.50 .75

Natl. Children's Day.

Natl. Aviation Day — A530

Perf. 14½x14
1996, Jan. 13   **Wmk. 340**
1643 A530 2b multicolored   .30 .25
    Complete booklet, 5 #1643   4.00

Asia-Europe Economic Meeting — A531

Perf. 14x14½
1996, Mar. 1   **Litho.**   **Wmk. 340**
1644 A531 2b multicolored   .25 .25
    Complete booklet, 5 #1644   4.00

Maghapuja Day — A532

Scenes from the Ten Jataka stories: 2b, Man on knee, another holding chariot. 6b, Two people flying over sea. 8b, Archer approaching man with arrow in side. 9b, Charioteer pointing.

Wmk. 340
1996, Mar. 3   **Photo.**   **Perf. 13½**
1645 A532 2b multicolored   .25 .25
1646 A532 6b multicolored   .80 .50
1647 A532 8b multicolored   1.00 .70
1648 A532 9b multicolored   1.10 .80
  a. Souvenir Sheet, #1645-1648   6.25 5.50
    Nos. 1645-1648 (4)   3.15 2.25

No. 1648a sold for 36b.

Cremation of Princess Mother Somdej Phra Sri Nakharindra Barommarajjonnani — A533

Litho. & Embossed
Perf. 14½x14
1996, Mar. 10   **Wmk. 340**
1649 A533 2b gold & multi   .80 .25
    Complete booklet, 5 #1649   6.25

Heritage Conservation Day Type of 1993

Historical landmarks, Kamphaeng Phet Park: 2b, Wat Phra Kaeo. 3b, Wat Phra Non. 6b, Wat Chang Rop. 9b, Wat Phra Si Iriyabot.

Wmk. 387
1996, Apr. 2   **Litho.**   **Perf. 13½**
1650 A477 2b multicolored   .25 .25
    Complete booklet, 5 #1650   2.75
1651 A477 3b multicolored   .45 .25
1652 A477 6b multicolored   .80 .50
1653 A477 9b multicolored   1.10 .80
  a. Souvenir sheet, #1650-1653   3.75 3.75
    Nos. 1650-1653 (4)   2.60 1.80

No. 1653a sold for 28b.

Chiang Mai, 700th Anniv. — A534

Anniv. logo of Chiang Mai and: 2b, Buddhist Pagoda of Wat Chiang Man. 6b, Sculpted angel on wall, Wat Chet Yot's Pagoda. 8b, Insignia of Wat Phan Tao's Vihara. 9b, Sattaphanta.

Wmk. 340
1996, Apr. 12   **Photo.**   **Perf. 13½**
1654 A534 2b multicolored   .25 .25
    Complete booklet, 5 #1654   2.75
1655 A534 6b multicolored   .80 .50
1656 A534 8b multicolored   1.00 .70
1657 A534 9b multicolored   1.10 .80
  a. Souvenir sheet, #1654-1657   3.25 3.25
    Nos. 1654-1657 (4)   3.15 2.25

No. 1657a sold for 37b.

Second Intl. Asian Hornbill Workshop A535

#1658, White-crowned. #1659, Rufous-necked. #1660, Plain-pouched. #1661, Rhinoceros.

1996, Apr. 12
1658 A535 3b multicolored   .35 .25
1659 A535 3b multicolored   .35 .25
1660 A535 9b multicolored   1.10 .80
1661 A535 9b multicolored   1.10 .80
  a. Souvenir sheet, #1658-1661   5.50 5.50
  b. As "a," inscribed in margin   10.00 8.00
    Nos. 1658-1661 (4)   2.90 2.10

No. 1661a sold for 35b. No. 1661b was issued 6/8/96, contains CAPEX '96 exhibition emblem in sheet margin, no value inscription, and sold for 47b.

Songkran Day Type of 1991

Design: Demon on rat's back, zodiac.

Perf. 13½x14
1996, Apr. 13   **Litho.**   **Wmk. 387**
1662 A425 2b multicolored   .25 .25
    Complete booklet, 5 #1662   3.50
  a. Souvenir sheet of 1   2.75 2.75
  b. Souv. sheet, #1389, 1467,
     1530, 1566, 1606, 1662   4.00 4.00
  c, As "a," inscribed in margin   6.00 6.00
  d. As "b," inscribed in margin   17.50 15.00

No. 1662c contains CHINA '96 exhibition emblem and "CHINA '96-9th Asian International Philatelic Exhibition" in Chinese and English and no value inscription in sheet margin. No. 1662d contains CHINA '96 and Hong Kong '96 exhibition emblems in margin and no value inscription.

#1662a sold for 8b. #1662b sold for 20b. #1662c, issued 5/15/96, sold for 14b. #1662d, issued 5/10/96, sold for 25b. #1662a-1662d exist imperf.

King Bhumibol Adulyadej, 50th Anniv. of Assession to the Throne A537

Designs: No. 1663, Royal Ablutions Ceremony. No. 1664, Pouring of the Libation. No. 1665, Grand Audience. No. 1666, Royal Progress by Land. No. 1667, Audience from Balcony.

1996, June 9   **Photo.**   **Perf. 11½**
Granite Paper
1663 A536 3b multicolored   .45 .25
  a. Souvenir sheet   1.50
1664 A536 3b multicolored   .45 .25
  a. Souvenir sheet   1.50
1665 A536 3b multicolored   .45 .25
  a. Souvenir sheet   1.50
1666 A536 3b multicolored   .45 .25
  a. Souvenir sheet   1.50
1667 A536 3b multicolored   .45 .25
  a. Souvenir sheet   1.50

Litho. & Typo.
Wmk. 387
Perf. 13½
1668 A537 100b gold & multi   13.50 9.00
    Nos. 1663-1668 (6)   15.75 10.25

Nos. 1663a 1664a, 1665a, 1666a, 1667a have a continuous design and each sold for 8b.

No. 1668 was issued in panes of 10. Value, $150.

Development Programs of King Bhumibol Adulyadej — A538

#1669, Using Vetiver grass to prevent soil erosion. #1670, Chai pattana aerator to improve water quality. #1671, Rain making project to counter droughts. #1672, Dam, natural water resource development. #1673, Reforestation.

Wmk. 340
1996, June 9   **Litho.**   **Perf. 13½**
1669 A538 3b multicolored   .35 .25
1670 A538 3b multicolored   .35 .25
1671 A538 3b multicolored   .35 .25
1672 A538 3b multicolored   .35 .25
1673 A538 3b multicolored   .35 .25
  a. Souv. sheet, #1669-1673+label   4.00 3.50
    Nos. 1669-1673 (5)   1.75 1.25

No. 1671 has a holographic image. Soaking in water may affect the hologram. No. 1673a sold for 25b.

Royal Utensils — A539

#1674, Gold-enameled cuspidor, golden spittoon. #1675, Royal betel, areca-nut set, vert. #1676, Royal water urn, vert.

Wmk. 329
1996, June 9   **Photo.**   **Perf. 13½**
1674 A539 3b green & multi   .35 .25
1675 A539 3b blue & multi   .35 .25
1676 A539 3b purple & multi   .35 .25
  a. Souvenir sheet, #1674-1676   3.00 2.25
    Nos. 1674-1676 (3)   1.05 .75

No. 1676a sold for 17b.

Modern Olympic Games, Cent. — A540

2b, Pierre de Coubertin, grave site. 3b, 1st lighting of Olympic torch, Olympia, Greece. 5b, Olympic Stadium, Athens, Olympic flag. 9b, Discus thrower, medal from 1896 games.

Perf. 14x14½
1996, June 23   **Litho.**   **Wmk. 340**
1677 A540 2b multicolored   .25 .25
    Complete booklet, 5 #1677   2.50
1678 A540 3b multicolored   .35 .25
1679 A540 5b multicolored   .60 .45
1680 A540 9b multicolored   1.10 .80
    Nos. 1677-1680 (4)   2.30 1.75

A536

Nat. Communications Day — A541

1996, Aug. 4   **Wmk. 340**
1681 A541 2b King using radio   .55   .25
    Complete booklet, 5 #1681   4.00

Royal Forest Department, Cent. — A542

Perf. 14½x14
1996, Sept. 18   **Litho.**   **Wmk. 340**
Type of Forest
1682 A542 3b Tropical rain   .30   .25
1683 A542 6b Hill evergreen   .80   .50
1684 A542 7b Swamp   .90   .60
1685 A542 9b Mangrove   1.10   .80
   a.   Souvenir sheet, #1682-1685   5.00   5.00
    Nos. 1682-1685 (4)   3.10   2.15

No. 1685a sold for 35b.

Intl. Letter Writing Week — A543

Classical Thai novels, characters: No. 1686, "Ramayana," King Rama following deer. No. 1687, "Inao," Inao kidnapping Budsaba, taking her to cave. No. 1688, "Ngao Pa," Lumhap touring forest. No. 1689, "Mathanapatha," Nang Mathana being cursed.

Wmk. 340
1996, Oct. 6   **Photo.**   **Perf. 13½**
1686 A543 3b multicolored   .35   .25
1687 A543 3b multicolored   .35   .25
1688 A543 9b multicolored   1.10   .80
1689 A543 9b multicolored   1.10   .80
   a.   Souvenir sheet, #1686-1689   5.00   5.00
    Nos. 1686-1689 (4)   2.90   2.10

No. 1689a sold for 36b. For surcharges, see Nos. 2530-2531.

Rotary Intl. 1996 Asia Regional Conference A544

Perf. 14x14½
1996, Oct. 25   **Litho.**   **Wmk. 340**
1690 A544 2b multicolored   .25   .25
    Complete booklet, 5 #1609   2.50

UNESCO, 50th Anniv. — A545

1996, Nov. 4   **Perf. 14½x14**
1691 A545 2b multicolored   .25   .25
    Complete booklet, 5 #1691   2.50

Royal Barge — A546

1996, Nov. 7   **Unwmk.**   **Perf. 11½**
Granite Paper
1692 A546 9b multicolored   1.75   1.25
   a.   Souvenir sheet of 1   3.25   2.75

No. 1692a sold for 16b.

New Year 1997 — A547

Designs: No. 1693, Limnocharis flava. No. 1694, Crinum thaianum, vert. No. 1695, Monochoria hastata, vert. No. 1696, Nymphoides indicum.

Perf. 14x14½, 14½x14
1996, Nov. 15   **Litho.**   **Wmk. 387**
1693 A547 2b multicolored   .25   .25
1694 A547 2b multicolored   .25   .25
1695 A547 2b multicolored   .25   .25
1696 A547 2b multicolored   .25   .25
   a.   Souvenir sheet, #1693-1696   2.75   2.75
   b.   As "a," inscribed in margin   7.50   7.50
    Nos. 1693-1696 (4)   1.00   1.00

No. 1696a sold for 15b. No. 1696b inscribed in sheet margin with Hong Kong '97 emblem and vertical Chinese inscription. No. 1696b issued 2/12/97.

Ducks A548

#1697, Sarkidiornis melanotos. #1698, Dendrocygna javanica, vert. #1699, Cairina scutulata, vert. #1700, Nettapus coromandelianus.

Wmk. 340
1996, Dec. 1   **Photo.**   **Perf. 13½**
1697 A548 3b multicolored   .35   .25
1698 A548 3b multicolored   .35   .25
1699 A548 7b multicolored   .90   .60
1700 A548 7b multicolored   .90   .60
   a.   Souvenir sheet, #1697-1700   5.50   5.50
    Nos. 1697-1700 (4)   2.50   1.70

No. 1700a sold for 33b.

UNICEF, 50th Anniv. — A549

Perf. 14½x14
1996, Dec. 11   **Litho.**   **Wmk. 340**
1701 A549 2b multicolored   .25   .25
    Complete booklet, 5 #1701   2.50

King Bhumibol Adulyadej — A550

Perf. 14x14½
1996, Dec. 5   **Litho.**   **Wmk. 340**
1702 A550 2b carmine   .35   .25
    Complete booklet, 5 #1702   4.50
   a.   Unwmkd., granite paper   .50   .25
    No. 1702a issued 9/1/98.
See Nos. 1725-1729, 1743-1745, 1756-1757, 1794-1795, 1819-1820, 1876-1879, 2067, 2212-2213, 2435, 2465A.

Thailand's 1st Olympic Gold Medal, 1996 — A552

Litho. & Embossed
Perf. 14½x14
1996, Dec. 16   **Wmk. 340**
1704 A552 6b multicolored   .80   .50

Mahavajiravudh School, Songkhla, Cent. — A553

Perf. 14x14½
1997, Jan. 1   **Wmk. 387**
1705 A553 2b multicolored   .25   .25
    Complete booklet, 5 #1705   2.50

Children's Day — A554

Children' paintings: No. 1706, Children processing fish. No. 1707, Monument, children in praise.

1997, Jan. 11   **Wmk. 340**
1706 A554 2b multicolored   .25   .25
    Complete booklet, 5 #1706   1.75
1707 A554 2b multicolored   .25   .25
    Complete booklet, 5 #1707   1.75

Communications Authority of Thailand, 20th Anniv. — A555

Perf. 14½x14
1997, Feb. 25   **Litho.**   **Wmk. 340**
1708 A555 2b multicolored   .25   .25
    Complete booklet, 5 #1708   2.50

Statue of Prince Bhanurangsi A556

1997, Feb. 25   **Perf. 14x14½**
1709 A556 2b multicolored   .25   .25
    Complete booklet, 5 #1709   2.50

Laksi Mail Center A557

#1710, Outside view of building. #1711, Computerized mail sorting machine.

1997, Feb. 25   **Perf. 14½x14**
1710 A557 2b multicolored   .45   .25
1711 A557 2b multicolored   .45   .25
   a.   Pair, #1710-1711   1.00   .50

State Railway, Cent. — A558

3b, 0-6-0 Type. 4b, Garratt. 6b, Sulzer diesel. 7b, Hitachi diesel leaving tunnel.

Wmk. 387
1997, Mar. 26   **Litho.**   **Perf. 13**
1712 A558 3b multicolored   .35   .25
   a.   Souvenir sheet of 1   2.75   2.75
1713 A558 4b multicolored   .50   .35
1714 A558 6b multicolored   .80   .50
1715 A558 7b multicolored   1.00   .60
   a.   Souv. sheet of 4, #1712-1715   4.00   4.00
    Nos. 1712-1715 (4)   2.65   1.70

No. 1712a sold for 20b, No. 1715a sold for 30b.

Chulalongkorn University, 80th Anniv. — A559

Designs: No. 1716, Palace of Prince Maha Vajirunhis. No. 1717, Faculty of Arts building.

Perf. 14½x14
1997, Mar. 26   **Wmk. 340**
1716 A559 2b yellow & multi   .45   .25
    Complete booklet, 5 #1716   2.00
1717 A559 2b rose & multi   .45   .25
    Complete booklet, 5 #1717   2.00

Thai Red Cross A560

1997, Mar. 28
1718 A560 3b Rajakarun building   .35   .25

Govt. Savings Bank, 84th Anniv. — A561

1997, Apr. 1
1719 A561 2b multicolored .25 .25
   Complete booklet, 5 #1719 2.00

Heritage Conservation Day — A562

Phanomrung historical Park: No. 1720, Outer stairway. No. 1721, Pavilion. No. 1722, Passage, stairway to sanctuary. No. 1723, Naga balustrade, Central Gate of Eastern Gallery.

1997, Apr. 2
1720 A562 3b multicolored .35 .25
1721 A562 3b multicolored .35 .25
1722 A562 7b multicolored .90 .60
1723 A562 7b multicolored .90 .60
   a. Souvenir sheet, #1720-1723 4.00 4.00
   Nos. 1720-1723 (4) 2.50 1.70

No. 1723a sold for 30b.

Songkran Day Type of 1991

Design: Demon on ox's back, zodiac.

1997-2002 Wmk. 340 Perf. 14x14½
1724 A425 2b multicolored .30 .25
   Complete booklet, 5 #1724 1.60
   a. Souvenir sheet of 1 2.25 1.60
   b. Unwmkd., granite paper .25 .25

Issued: Nos. 1724, 1724a, 4/13/97; No. 1724b, 4/13/02. No. 1724b issued only in No. 2017b.
No. 1724a sold for 8b and exists imperf. Values same.

King Bhumibol Adulyadej Type of 1996

Litho, Litho & Engraved (#1728-1729)
Perf. 14x14½

1997, May 5 Wmk. 340
1725 A550 4b blue & red brown 1.25 .25
   a. Perf. 13¼, unwmkd. 1.00 .25
   b. Unwmkd., granite paper 1.00 .25
1726 A550 5b pur & org brn 1.25 .30
   a. Perf. 13½, unwmk., granite paper 1.75 .30
   b. Unwmkd., granite paper 1.25 .25
1727 A550 7b pink & green 1.40 1.40

Wmk. 329
Perf. 13½x13
1728 A550 10b org & dk brn 2.25 .90
1729 A550 20b violet & maroon 3.75 1.75
   Nos. 1725-1729 (5) 9.90 4.60

Issued: No. 1726a, 12/28/98; No. 1725a, 10/8/99. 1725b, 1726b, 12/1/00.

Waterfowl — A563

Designs: No. 1730, Pheasant-tailed jacana. No. 1731, Bronze-winged jacana. No. 1732, Painted stork. No. 1733, Black-winged stilt.

Perf. 11½x12
1997, May 15 Photo. Unwmk.
Granite Paper
1730 A563 3b multicolored .55 .55
1731 A563 3b multicolored .55 .55
1732 A563 7b multicolored 1.25 1.25

1733 A563 7b multicolored 1.25 1.25
   a. Souvenir sheet, #1730-1733 6.00 6.00
   b. As "a," with added inscription 10.00 10.00
   Nos. 1730-1733 (4) 3.60 3.60

No. 1733a sold for 30b. No. 1733b has PACIFIC 97 emblem in sheet margin, while sales price has been removed from sheet margin. No. 1728b sold for 42b.

King Bhumibol Adulyadej, National Telecommunications — A564

2b, King using hand-held radio, "Suthee" aerial. 3b, King using hand-held radio for communication in local areas. 6b, King using computer. 9b, King, classroom using satellite information.

Perf. 14½x14
1997, June 9 Wmk. 340
1734 A564 2b multicolored .35 .35
   Complete booklet, 5 #1734 2.00
1735 A564 3b multicolored .55 .55
1736 A564 6b multicolored 1.10 1.10
1737 A564 9b multicolored 1.75 1.75
   a. Souvenir sheet, #1734-1737 6.00 6.00
   Nos. 1734-1737 (4) 3.75 3.75

No. 1737a sold for 30b. For surcharges, see Nos. 2407-2408, 2532, 2586.

Motion Pictures in Thailand, Cent. — A565

Designs: No. 1738, King Rama VII filming movie, film showing King Chulalongkorn's state visit to Europe. No. 1739, Early motion picture equipment, advertisement, Prince Sanbassatra, founder of Thai motion picures. No. 1740, Poster from "Double Luck," band playing in front of movie theater. No. 1741, Open air theater, poster from "Going Astray."

1997, June 10
1738 A565 3b multicolored .55 .55
1739 A565 3b multicolored .55 .55
1740 A565 7b multicolored 1.25 1.25
1741 A565 7b multicolored 1.25 1.25
   Nos. 1738-1741 (4) 3.60 3.60

Faculty of Medicine, Chulalongkorn University, 50th Anniv. — A566

King Rama VIII, building, operating room.

1997, June 11
1742 A566 2b multicolored .45 .25
   Complete booklet, 5 #1742 2.25

King Bhumibol Adulyadej Type of 1996
Perf. 14x14½
1997, July 19 Litho. Wmk. 340
1743 A550 4b grn & gray vio .40 .30
1744 A550 9b dk bl & brn org .60 .45

Litho. & Engr.
Wmk. 329
Perf. 13½x13
1745 A550 100b lem & dk bl grn 6.25 4.75
   Nos. 1743-1745 (3) 7.25 5.50

Thai-Russian Diplomatic Relations, Cent. — A567

Design: Peterhof Palace, King Chulalongkorn (King Rama V).

1997, July 3 Litho. Perf. 14½x14
1746 A567 2b multicolored .35 .25
   Complete booklet, 5 #1746 3.25

Asalhapuja Day — A568

3b, Mahosathajataka (scene with man on elephant). 4b, Bhuridattajataka (scene with two men, large snake). 6b, Candakumarajataka (scene with pot of fire, three men on knees, man in sky, Buddha). 7b, Naradajataka (scene with people praising human figure with four arms hovering above roof).

Perf. 11½ Syncopated
1997, July 19 Photo. Unwmk.
Granite Paper
1747 A568 3b multicolored .55 .55
   a. Souvenir sheet of 1 1.75 .90
   b. As "a," inscribed in margin 3.25 3.25
1748 A568 4b multicolored .70 .70
   a. Souvenir sheet of 1 1.75 .90
   b. As "a," inscribed in margin 3.25 3.25
1749 A568 6b multicolored 1.10 1.10
   a. Souvenir sheet of 1 1.75 .90
   b. As "a," inscribed in margin 3.25 3.25
1750 A568 7b multicolored 1.25 1.25
   a. Souvenir sheet of 1 2.75 1.75
   b. Souvenir sheet, #1747-1750 6.00 4.50
   c. As "a," inscribed in margin 27.50 27.50
   Nos. 1747-1750 (4) 3.60 3.60

#1747a sold for 6b; #1748a for 8b; #1749a for 10b; #1750a for 12b; #1750b for 30b.
Sheet margins of lack value inscriptions, but contain Shanghai '97 exhibition emblem (#1747b, 1748b), Chinese insription; Bangkok '97 exhibition emblem (#1749b, 1750c).
No. 1750b exists imperf. It was issued for sale only at overseas stamp exhibitions.
For surcharges see Nos. 2380, 2382.

1997 Thailand Philatelic Exhibition — A569

Houses from: 2b, Northern region. 5b, Central region. 6b, Northeastern region. 9b, Southern region.

Wmk. 329
1997, Aug. 2 Litho. Perf. 13½
1751 A569 2b multicolored .25 .25
   Complete booklet, 5 #1751 1.60
1752 A569 5b multicolored .70 .70
1753 A569 6b multicolored .80 .80
1754 A569 9b multicolored 1.25 1.25
   a. Souvenir sheet, #1751-1754 17.50 17.50
   Nos. 1751-1754 (4) 3.00 3.00

No. 1754a sold for 32b.
No. 1754a exists imperf, sold with an exhibition book. Value, $15.

Natl. Communications Day — A570

Perf. 14x14½
1997, Aug. 4 Wmk. 340
1755 A570 2b multicolored .25 .25
   Complete booklet, 5 #1755 2.00

Greeting Stamps — A570a

Lotus flowers: No. 1755A, Nymphaea capensis. No. 1755B, Nymphaea stellata.

Perf. 14x14½
1997, Aug. 4 Litho. Wmk. 387
Booklet Stamps
1755A A570a (2b) multi 1.50 1.50
1755B A570a (2b) multi 1.50 1.50
   c. Bklt. pane, 5 ea #1755A-1755B + 4 labels 30.00
   Complete bklt., #1755Bc 35.00

Nos. 1755A-1755B were sold only at 7-11 stores, not at post offices or philatelic agencies.

King Bhumibol Adulyadej Type of 1996
Litho. & Engr.
Perf. 13½x13
1997, Aug. 8 Wmk. 329
1756 A550 25b bl grn & ol blk 8.00 3.25
1757 A550 200b lil rose & vio blk 17.50 9.00

ASEAN, 30th Anniv. — A571

Designs: No. 1758, Thi Lo Su Falls, Tak. No. 1759, Luang Chiang Dao Mountain, Chiang Mai. No. 1760, Phromthep Cape, Phuket. No. 1761, Thalu Island, Chumphon.

Perf. 14½x14
1997, Aug. 8 Wmk. 340
1758 A571 2b multicolored .25 .25
   Complete booklet, 5 #1758 1.25
1759 A571 2b multicolored .25 .25
   Complete booklet, 5 #1759 1.25
1760 A571 9b multicolored 1.25 1.25
1761 A571 9b multicolored 1.25 1.25
   Nos. 1758-1761 (4) 3.00 3.00

Dinosaurs — A572

Designs: 2b, Phuwiangosaurus sirindhornae. 3b, Siamotyrannus isanensis. 6b, Siamosaurus suteethorni. 9b, Psittacosaurus sattayaraki.

Perf. 13½x13 Syncopated
1997, Aug. 28 Photo. Unwmk.
1762 A572 2b multicolored .25 .25
   Complete booklet, 5 #1762 1.25
1763 A572 3b multicolored .35 .25
1764 A572 6b multicolored .50 .35

1765	A572	9b multicolored	1.00	.60
a.		Souvenir sheet, #1762-1765	3.25	2.00
		Nos. 1762-1765 (4)	2.10	1.45

No. 1765a sold for 30b.
For surcharge see No. 2355.

King Chulalongkorn's Visit to Switzerland, Cent. — A573

Perf. 14x14½
1997, Sept. 12   Litho.   Wmk. 340

1766	A573	2b multicolored	.45	.25
		Complete booklet, 5 #1766	6.75	

Intl. Letter Writing Week — A574

Winning drawings: No. 1767, Tricycle, combining rickshaw and tricycle. No. 1768, Tricycle with side seat. No. 1769, Motor tricycle. No. 1770. Motor tricycle with light on roof.

Perf. 11½x12
1997, Oct. 5   Photo.   Unwmk.
Granite Paper

1767	A574	3b multicolored	.25	.25
1768	A574	3b multicolored	.25	.25
1769	A574	9b multicolored	.90	.50
1770	A574	9b multicolored	.90	.50
a.		Souvenir sheet, #1767-1770	2.75	2.00
		Nos. 1767-1770 (4)	2.30	1.50

No. 1770a sold for 30b.

Shells of Thailand and Singapore A575

Designs: No. 1771, Drupa morum. No. 1772, Nerita chamaelon. No. 1773, Littoraria melanostoma. No. 1774, Cryptospira elgans.

1997, Oct. 9   Litho.   Perf. 11½
Granite Paper

1771	A575	2b multicolored	.25	.25
		Complete booklet, 5 #1771	1.75	
1772	A575	2b multicolored	.25	.25
		Complete booklet, 5 #1772	1.75	
1773	A575	9b multicolored	.90	.45
1774	A575	9b multicolored	.90	.45
a.		Souvenir sheet, #1771-1774	2.75	2.75
		Nos. 1771-1774 (4)	2.30	1.40

No. 1774a sold for 30b. See Singapore Nos. 825-828A.

Chalerm Prakiat Energy Conserving Building — A576

Perf. 14½x14
1997, Nov. 10   Litho.   Wmk. 340

1775	A576	2b multicolored	.25	.25
		Complete booklet, 5 #1775	2.00	

Christening of Suphannahong Royal Barge, 86th Anniv. — A577

Perf. 11½
1997, Nov. 13   Photo.   Unwmk.
Granite Paper

1776	A577	9b multicolored	.80	.50
a.		Souvenir sheet of 1	2.25	1.75
b.		As "a," ovptd. in margin	4.00	2.75
c.		As "a," ovptd. in margin	7.25	7.25

#1776a, 1776b, 1776c sold for 20b.
The sheet margin of #1776b is ovptd in gold with Thai and Chinese inscriptions for Bangkok/China 98. Issued 10/16/98.
No. 1776c overprinted in margin with World Stamp Expo 2000 emblem in gold. Issued 7/7/00.
For surcharge, see No. 2512.

New Year 1998 — A578

Flowers: No. 1777, Cassia alata. No. 1778, Strophanthus caudatus. No. 1779, Clinacanthus nutans. No. 1780, Acanthus ilicifolius.

1997, Nov. 15   Litho.   Perf. 13½x13
Granite Paper

1777	A578	2b multicolored	.25	.25
1778	A578	2b multicolored	.25	.25
1779	A578	2b multicolored	.25	.25
1780	A578	2b multicolored	.25	.25
a.		Souvenir sheet, #1777-1780	1.75	.90
b.		As "a," with added inscription	3.50	2.75
		Nos. 1777-1780 (4)	1.00	1.00

No. 1780a sold for 15b. No. 1780b contains Indepex '97 exhibition emblem, but no value inscription in sheet margin.

King Bhumibol Adulyadej's 70th Birthday — A579

#1781, Playing saxophone. #1782, Painting picture. #1783, Building sailboat. #1784, Wearing gold medal, sailboats. 6b, Taking photograph. 7b, Writing book. 9b, Working at computer.

1997, Dec. 5   Photo.   Perf. 11½
Granite Paper

1781	A579	2b multicolored	.25	.25
1782	A579	2b multicolored	.25	.25
1783	A579	2b multicolored	.25	.25
1784	A579	2b multicolored	.25	.25
1785	A579	6b multicolored	.50	.35
1786	A579	7b multicolored	.70	.45
1787	A579	9b multicolored	.90	.50
		Nos. 1781-1787 (7)	3.10	2.30

For surcharge see No. 2381.

A580

Winners in Yuvabadhana Foundation, "Sports Develop Mind and Body" drawing competition: No. 1788, Children in wheelchair race. No. 1789, Flying kites. No. 1790, Gymnastics. No. 1791, Windsurfing.

Perf. 14x14½
1998, Jan. 10   Litho.   Wmk. 340

1788	A580	2b multicolored	.25	.25
		Complete booklet, 5 #1788	3.25	
1789	A580	2b multicolored	.25	.25
		Complete booklet, 5 #1789	3.25	
1790	A580	2b multicolored	.25	.25
		Complete booklet, 5 #1790	3.25	
1791	A580	2b multicolored	.25	.25
a.		Complete booklet, 5 #1791	3.25	
		Nos. 1788-1791 (4)	1.00	1.00

Natl. Childrens' Day.

A581

1998, Jan. 17   Unwmk.
Granite Paper

1792	A581	2b multicolored	.25	.25
		Complete booklet, 5 #1792	3.50	

20th Asia Pacific Dental Congress.

A582

1998, Feb. 3   Wmk. 340

1793	A582	2b multicolored	.25	.25
		Complete booklet, 5 #1793	3.25	

Veteran's Day, 50th anniv.

King Bhumibol Adulyadej Type of 1996
1998, Feb. 25   Photo.   Perf. 11½x12
Granite Paper

1794	A550	50s dk ol & lt ol	.35	.25

Litho. & Engr.
Perf. 13½x13
Wmk. 329

1795	A550	50s dp vio & dk grn	7.25	2.25

A583

Perf. 14x14½
1998, Mar. 27   Litho.   Wmk. 340

1796	A583	2b Queen Sirikit	.35	.25
		Complete booklet, 5 #1796	5.00	

1998 Thai Red Cross Fair.

Heritage Conservation Day Type of 1993

Paintings of Phanomrung Historical Park: 3b, Main Tower. 4b, Minor Tower. 6b, Scripture Repository. 7b, Lintel depicting Vishnu sleeping in ocean, doorway of Main Tower.

Perf. 14½x14
1998, Apr. 2   Litho.   Wmk. 340

1797	A477	3b multicolored	.25	.25
1798	A477	4b multicolored	.25	.25
1799	A477	6b multicolored	.45	.45
1800	A477	7b multicolored	.50	.50
a.		Souvenir sheet, #1797-1800	2.75	2.75

No. 1800a sold for 27b.

Songkran Day Type of 1991

Design: Demon on tiger's back, zodiac.

1998-2002   Perf. 14x14½

1801	A425	2b multicolored	.25	.25
		Complete booklet, 5 #1801	3.25	
a.		Souvenir sheet of 1	1.75	1.00
b.		As "a," inscribed in margin	3.50	2.25
c.		Unwmkd., granite paper	.25	.25

Issued: Nos. 1801-1801b, 4/13/98. No. 1801c, 4/13/02. No. 1801c issued only in No. 2017b.
No. 1801a sold for 8b and exists imperf. Values same.
Sheet margin of No. 1801b contains flags of Thailand and China (PRC), Thai and Chinese inscriptions, no value inscription, and exists imperf.
No. 1801b sold for 8b and was issued 10/16/98.

Wild Cats A584

Paintings: 2b, Felis viverrina. 4b, Panthera tigris. 6b, Panthera pardus. 8b, Felis chaus.

1998, Apr. 13   Perf. 14½x14

1802	A584	2b multicolored	.35	.25
		Complete booklet, 5 #1802	4.00	
1803	A584	4b multicolored	.50	.25
1804	A584	6b multicolored	.50	.45
1805	A584	8b multicolored	.70	.50
a.		Souvenir sheet, #1802-1805	3.50	2.75
		Nos. 1802-1805 (4)	2.05	1.45

No. 1805a sold for 30b.

AEROTHAI (Aeronautical Radio of Thailand, Ltd.), 50th Anniv. — A585

1998, Apr. 15

1806	A585	2b multicolored	.25	.25
		Complete booklet, 5 #1806	3.25	

Visakhapuja Day — A586

Paintings of the "Ten Jataka Stories:" 3b, Riding horse above buildings, Vidhurajataka. 4b, In chariot, Vessantarajataka. 6b, Two figures seated before larger figure, Vessantarajataka. 7b, Figures in front of building, Vessantarajataka.

1998, May 10   Perf. 13½

1807	A586	3b multicolored	.35	.25
1808	A586	4b multicolored	.50	.25
1809	A586	6b multicolored	.70	.45
1810	A586	7b multicolored	.90	.50
a.		Souvenir sheet, #1807-1810	2.75	2.00
		Nos. 1807-1810 (4)	2.45	1.45

No. 1810a sold for 30b.

Adm. Abhakara Kiartiwongse (1880-1923), Father of Royal Thai Navy — A587

1998, May 19   **Perf. 14½x14**
1811	A587	2b multicolored	.35 .25
		Complete booklet, 5 #1811	5.00

Educational Development — A588

1998, June 15   **Litho.**   **Wmk. 340**
1812	A588	2b multicolored	.25 .25
		Complete booklet, 5 #1812	4.00

King Chulalongkorn's 1st State Visit to Europe, Cent. — A589

Unwmk.
1998, July 1   **Litho.**   **Perf. 13**
Granite Paper
1813	A589	6b multicolored	.70 .45

Litho. & Embossed
1814	A589	20b multicolored	1.75 1.25

Intl. Year of the Ocean A590

2b, Orchaella brevirostris. 3b, Tursiops truncatus. 6b, Physeter catodon. 9b, Dugong dugon.

1998, July 19   **Litho.**   **Perf. 14½x14**
Granite Paper
1815	A590	2b multicolored	.35 .25
		Complete booklet, 5 #1815	2.75
1816	A590	3b multicolored	.35 .25
1817	A590	6b multicolored	.55 .45
1818	A590	9b multicolored	.90 .50
a.		Souvenir sheet, #1815-1818	4.50 4.50
		Nos. 1815-1818 (4)	2.15 1.45

No. 1818a sold for 30b.
For surcharges see Nos. 2356-2357.

King Bhumibol Adulyadej Type of 1996

1998 Photo. Unwmk. Perf. 11½x12
Granite Paper
1819	A550	2b carmine	.50 .25
1820	A550	9b violet & brn org	1.25 .45

For surcharges, see Nos. 2335, 2585.

Irrigation Engineering in Thailand, 60th Anniv. — A591

Perf. 14½x14
1998, Aug. 1   **Litho.**   **Unwmk.**
Granite Paper
1821	A591	2b multicolored	.25 .25
		Complete booklet, 5 #1821	3.25

Natl. Communications Day — A592

1998, Aug. 4   **Granite Paper**
1822	A592	2b multicolored	.25 .25
		Complete booklet, 5 #1822	3.25

School of Political Science, Chulalongkorn University, 50th Anniv. — A593

1998, Aug. 19   **Granite Paper**
1823	A593	2b multicolored	.25 .25
		Complete booklet, 5 #1823	3.25

Sukhothai Thammathirat Open University, Award for Excellence — A594

1998, Sept. 5   **Litho.**   **Perf. 14½x14**
Granite Paper
1824	A594	2b multicolored	.25 .25
		Complete booklet, 5 #1824	3.25

Amazing Thailand, 1998-99, Thai Arts and Culture A595

1998, Sept. 15   **Perf. 13½**
Granite Paper
1825	A595	3b With bow & arrow	.25 .25
1826	A595	3b Combat	.25 .25
1827	A595	7b Seizing opponent	.70 .50
1828	A595	7b Sky hovering	.70 .50
		Nos. 1825-1828 (4)	1.90 1.50

Chinese Stone Statues — A596

Warriors holding: No. 1829, Staff with loop. No. 1830, Spear with slightly curved blade. No. 1831, Mace. No. 1832, Spear with jagged blade.

1998, Sept. 15   **Perf. 14x14½**
Granite Paper
1829	A596	2b multicolored	.25 .25
		Complete booklet, 5 #1829	2.50
1830	A596	2b multicolored	.25 .25
		Complete booklet, 5 #1830	3.25
1831	A596	10b multicolored	.90 .60
1832	A596	10b multicolored	.90 .60
a.		Souvenir sheet, #1829-1832, perf 13¼	3.25 2.25
b.		As "a," with added marginal inscription	20.00 16.00
		Nos. 1829-1832 (4)	2.30 1.70

China 1999 World Philatelic Exhibition (#1832b). #1832a-1832b sold for 35b.
#1832 is perf 13¼ and was issued 8/21/99.

Intl. Letter Writing Week — A597

Himavanta mythical animals created by ancient Thai artists: #1836, Kraisara Rajasiha, 3 king lions, white body, golden collars. #1837, Gajasiha, 2 tusked lions. #1838, Kesara Singha, 2 hoofed lions. #1839, Singha, 3 gray lions.

Perf. 11½
1998, Oct. 3   **Photo.**   **Unwmk.**
Granite Paper
1836	A597	2b multicolored	.25 .25
		Complete booklet, 5 #1836	3.25
1837	A597	2b multicolored	.25 .25
		Complete booklet, 5 #1837	3.25
1838	A597	12b multicolored	.70 .70
1839	A597	12b multicolored	.70 .70
a.		Souvenir sheet, #1836-1839	3.50 2.75
		Nos. 1836-1839 (4)	1.90 1.90

No. 1839a sold for 40b.

Thai Presidency of the Intl. Assoc. of Lions Clubs — A598

1998, Oct. 8   **Litho.**   **Perf. 14½x14**
Granite Paper
1840	A598	2b multicolored	.25 .25
		Complete booklet, 5 #1840	4.00

New Year 1999 — A599

Flowers: No. 1841, Barleria lupulina. No. 1842, Gloriosa superba. No. 1843, Asclepias curassavica. No. 1844, Sesamum indicum.

Perf. 14½x14
1998, Nov. 15   **Photo.**   **Unwmk.**
Granite Paper
1841	A599	2b multicolored	.25 .25
1842	A599	2b multicolored	.25 .25
1843	A599	2b multicolored	.25 .25
1844	A599	2b multicolored	.25 .25
a.		Souvenir sheet, #1841-1844	2.00 1.75
		Nos. 1841-1844 (4)	1.00 1.00

No. 1844a sold for 15b.

Knight Grand Cross, Most Admirable Order of the Direkgunabhorn — A600

Perf. 14x14½
1998, Dec. 5   **Litho.**   **Unwmk.**
Granite Paper
1845		15b shown	1.25 .70
1846		15b Decoration	1.25 .70
a.		A600 Pair, #1845-1846	3.25 1.60

Children's Day — A601

Paintings from competition, "Sports develop body and mind:" No. 1847, Sepak Takraw (game of kicking ball over net). No. 1848, Swimming. No. 1849, Volleyball. No. 1850, Equestrian sports.

Perf. 14½x14
1999, Jan. 9   **Litho.**   **Unwmk.**
Granite Paper
1847	A601	2b multicolored	.35 .25
		Complete booklet, 5 #1847	3.25
1848	A601	2b multicolored	.35 .25
		Complete booklet, 5 #1848	3.25
1849	A601	2b multicolored	.35 .25
		Complete booklet, 5 #1849	3.25
1850	A601	2b multicolored	.35 .25
		Complete booklet, 5 #1850	3.25
		Nos. 1847-1850 (4)	1.40 1.00

Asian and Pacific Decade of Disabled Persons — A602

1999, Jan. 10   **Granite Paper**
1851	A602	2b multicolored	.45 .25
a.		Complete booklet, 5 #1851	3.25

Thai Rice Production — A603

#1852, Planting rice. #1853, Harvesting rice by hand. #1854, Harvesting rice with machinery. #1855, Rice in field, bowl of rice.

1999, Feb. 25   **Litho.**   **Perf. 14½x14**
Granite Paper
1852	A603	6b multicolored	.45 .45
1853	A603	6b multicolored	.45 .45
1854	A603	12b multicolored	.90 .90
1855	A603	12b multicolored	.90 .90
a.		Souvenir sheet, #1852-1855	3.25 3.25
		Nos. 1852-1855 (4)	2.70 2.70

No. 1855a sold for 45b.

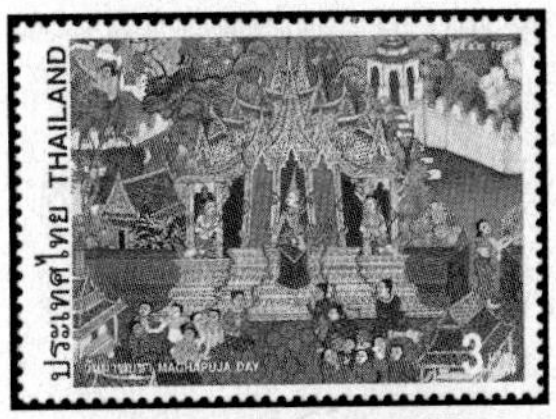

Maghapuja Day (Buddhist Holiday) — A604

Designs: 3b, Birth of Mahajanaka. 6b, Mani Mekkhala carrying Mahajanaka to Mithila City. 9b, Two mango trees. 15b, Mahajanaka founding an educational institution.

1999, Mar. 1 Litho. *Perf. 13½*
Granite Paper

1856 A604 3b multicolored .30 .25
1857 A604 6b multicolored .60 .45
1858 A604 9b multicolored .80 .60
1859 A604 15b multicolored 1.25 1.00
a. Souvenir sheet, #1856-1859 4.50 3.50
Nos. 1856-1859 (4) 2.95 2.30

No. 1859a sold for 45b.

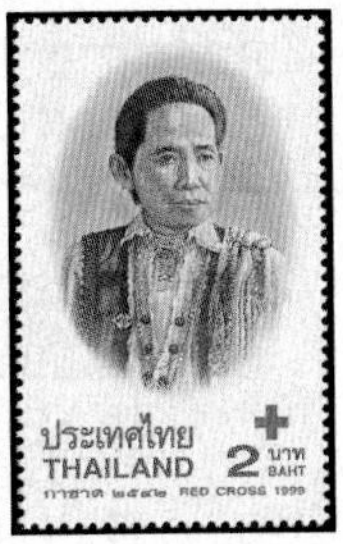

Somdetch Phra Sri Savarindira Baromma Raja Devi Phra Phan Vassa Ayika Chao, Queen Grandmother A605

Perf. 14x14½
1999, Mar. 30 Litho. Wmk. 340

1860 A605 2b multicolored .35 .25
Complete booklet, 5 #1860 5.00

1999 Red Cross Fair.

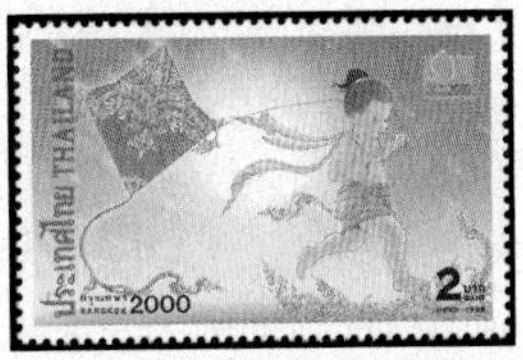

Bangkok 2000 World Youth Stamp Expo, 13th Asian Intl. Stamp Expo — A606

Thai children's games: No. 1861, Kite flying. No. 1862, Wheel rolling. No. 1863, Catching last one in line (children going under arms). No. 1864, Snatching baby from mother snake.

Perf. 14½x14
1999, Mar. 30 Unwmk.
Granite Paper

1861 A606 2b multicolored .35 .25
1862 A606 2b multicolored .35 .25
1863 A606 15b multicolored 1.10 1.00
1864 A606 15b multicolored 1.10 1.00
a. Souvenir sheet, #1861-1864, perf. 13½ 4.50
Nos. 1861-1864 (4) 2.90 2.50

No. 1864a sold for 45b.

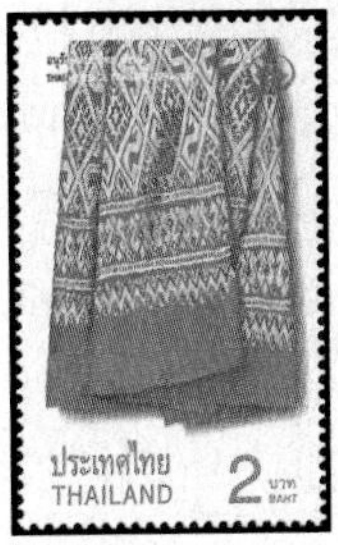

Heritage Conservation Day — A607

Various Thai silk designs for "Mudmee" textiles.

1999, Apr. 2 *Perf. 14x14½*
Granite Paper

1865 A607 2b bl grn & multi .25 .25
Complete booklet, 5 #1865 3.25
1866 A607 4b red & multi .45 .25
1867 A607 12b vermilion & multi 1.00 .90
1868 A607 15b black & multi 1.40 1.10
a. Souvenir sheet, #1865-1868 4.50 3.50
Nos. 1865-1868 (4) 3.10 2.50

No. 1868a sold for 45b.

Songkran Day Type of 1991

Design: Woman on rabbit's back, zodiac.

1999, Apr. 13 Granite Paper

1869 A425 2b multicolored .25 .25
Complete booklet, 5 #1869 3.25
a. Souvenir sheet of 1 1.40 1.40
b. As "a," with added marginal inscription 5.00 5.00

China 1999 World Philatelic Exhibition (#1869b). #1869a-1869b sold for 8b and exist imperf. Values same.
Issued: #1869b, 8/21.

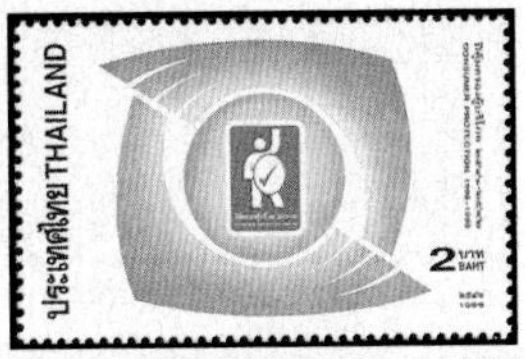

Consumer Protection Years, 1998-99 — A608

1999, Apr. 30 *Perf. 14½x14*
Granite Paper

1870 A608 2b multicolored .35 .25
Complete booklet, 5 #1870 3.50

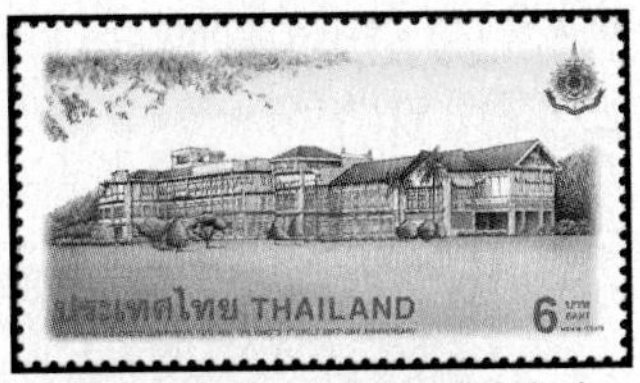

King Bhumibol Adulyadej's 72nd Birthday — A609

Royal palaces: No. 1871, Chitralada Villa, Dusit Palace, Bangkok, tree branch at UL. No. 1872, Phu Phing Ratchaniwet Palace, circular drive, white fence. No. 1873, Phu Phan Ratchaniwet Palace, adjoining buildings, light posts. No. 1874, Thaksin Ratchaniwet Palace, four trees reaching to second story windows.

1999, May 5 Photo. *Perf. 11½*
Granite Paper

1871 A609 6b multicolored .65 .45
1872 A609 6b multicolored .65 .45
1873 A609 6b multicolored .65 .45
1874 A609 6b multicolored .65 .45
a. Souvenir sheet, #1871-1874 4.50 3.50
Nos. 1871-1874 (4) 2.60 1.80

No. 1874a sold for 40b.

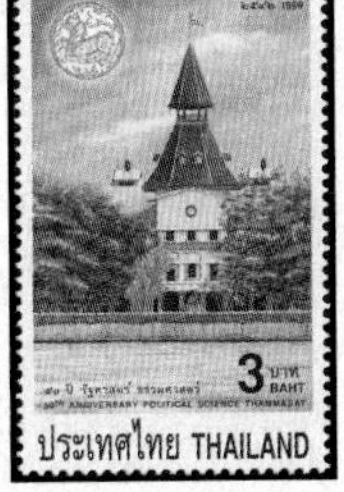

Political Science Dept., Thammasat University, 50th Anniv. — A610

1999, June 14 Litho. *Perf. 14x14½*

1875 A610 3b multicolored .25 .25

King Bhumibol Adulyadej Type of 1996

Litho. & Engr.
1999 Wmk. 329 *Perf. 13*

1876 A550 12b bl grn & bl 1.25 .80
1877 A550 15b yel brn & grn 2.00 .45
1878 A550 30b pink & brown 2.90 2.00

Size: 25x30mm
Perf. 12¾x13¼

1879 A550 500b org & claret 35.00 19.00
Nos. 1876-1879 (4) 41.15 22.25

Issued: 12b, 15b, 30b, 7/1; 500b, 9/10.

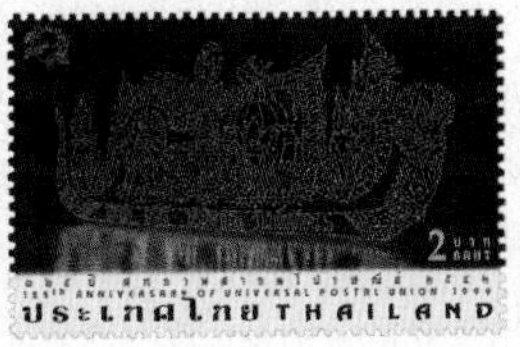

UPU, 125th Anniv. A611

Designs: 2b, Floating Vessel of Light Festival. 15b, Buddhist Candle Festival, Ubon Ratchathani.

1999, July 1 Litho. *Perf. 14½x14*
Granite Paper

1880 A611 2b multicolored .35 .25
Complete booklet, 5 #1880 2.90
1881 A611 15b multicolored 1.10 1.00

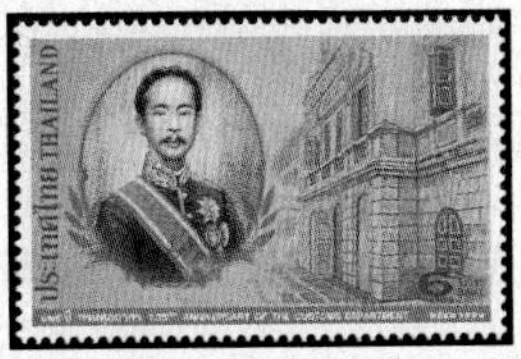

Customs Dept., 125th Anniv. — A612

1999, July 3

1882 A612 6b multicolored .60 .45

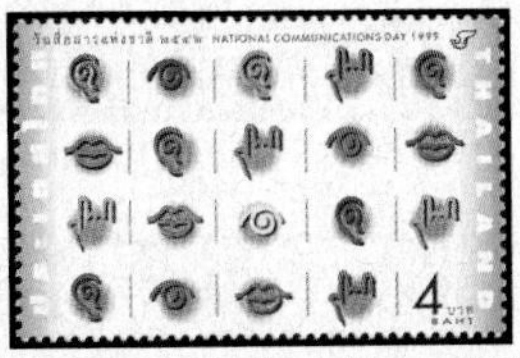

Natl. Communications Day — A613

1999, Aug. 4 Litho. *Perf. 14½x14*
Granite Paper

1883 A613 4b multicolored .25 .25

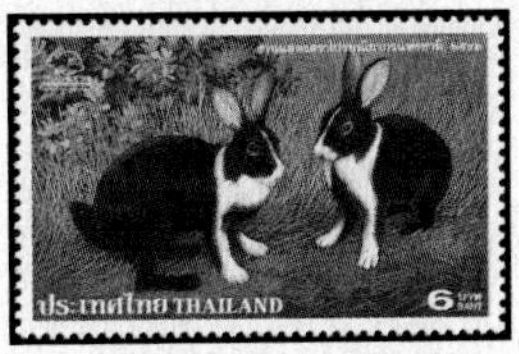

Thaipex '99 — A614

1999, Aug. 4 Granite Paper
Color of Rabbits

1884 A614 6b black & white .60 .45
1885 A614 6b gldn brn, brn .60 .45
1886 A614 12b white 1.00 .80
1887 A614 12b gray 1.00 .80
a. Souvenir sheet, #1884-1887, perf. 13½ 4.00 4.00
Nos. 1884-1887 (4) 3.20 2.50

No. 1887a sold for 50b and exists imperf. Value, $15.

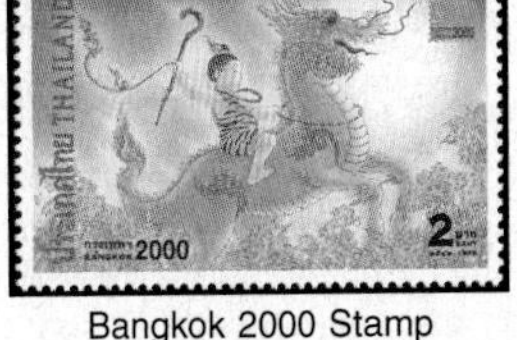

Bangkok 2000 Stamp Exhibition — A615

Scenes from Thai folk tales and literature: No. 1888, Boy on dragon-like horse. No. 1889, Rishi transforming tiger cub and calf into humans. No. 1890, Boy exiting conch shell. No. 1891, Children playing with kitchenware.

1999, Aug. 4 *Perf. 14½x14*
Granite Paper

1888 A615 2b multicolored .35 .25
1889 A615 2b multicolored .35 .25
1890 A615 15b multicolored 1.10 1.00
1891 A615 15b multicolored 1.10 1.00
a. Souvenir sheet, #1888-1891, perf. 13½ 4.50 3.50
Nos. 1888-1891 (4) 2.90 2.50

No. 1891a sold for 45b.

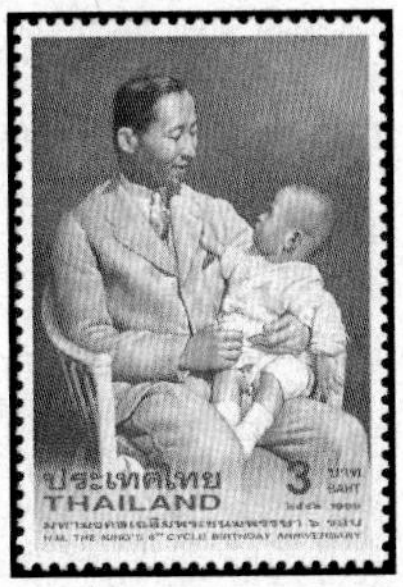

King Bhumibol Adulyadej's 72nd Birthday A616

King: No. 1892, On father's knee. No. 1893, With mother, sister and brother. No. 1894, With brother, in suits. No. 1895, With brother, in military uniforms. No. 1896, With wife on wedding day. No. 1897, At coronation ceremony. No. 1898, As Buddhist monk. No. 1899, With Queen, Prince and Princesses. No. 1900, Wearing royal robe.

1999, Sept. 10 Photo. *Perf. 11¾*
Granite Paper

1892 A616 3b multicolored .35 .25
1893 A616 3b multicolored .35 .25
1894 A616 3b multicolored .35 .25
1895 A616 6b multicolored .60 .35
1896 A616 6b multicolored .60 .35
1897 A616 6b multicolored .60 .35
1898 A616 12b multicolored 1.25 .80
1899 A616 12b multicolored 1.25 .80
1900 A616 12b multicolored 1.25 .80
a. Souvenir sheet, #1892-1900 10.50 9.00
Nos. 1892-1900 (9) 6.60 4.20

No. 1900a sold for 90b.

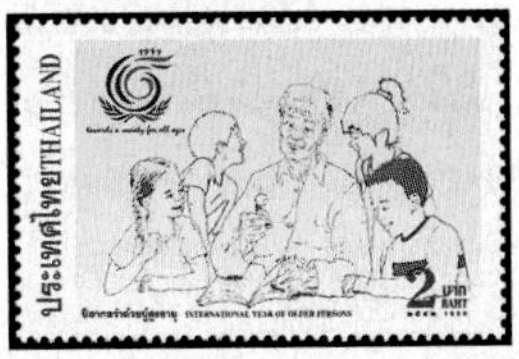

Intl. Year of Older Persons — A617

1999, Oct. 1 Litho. *Perf. 14½x14*
Granite Paper

1901 A617 2b multi .35 .25
Complete booklet, 5 #1901 3.50

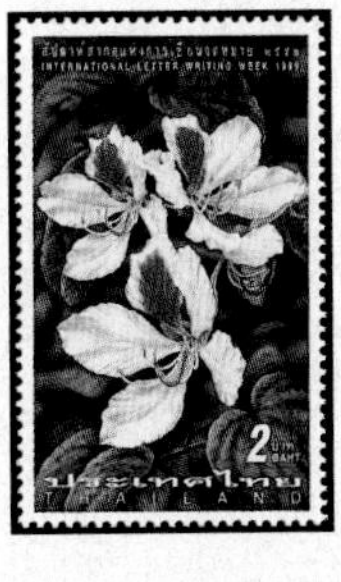

Bauhinia Variegata — A618

Intl. Letter Writing Week: No. 1903, Bombax ceiba. No. 1904, Radermachera ignea (orange flowers). No. 1905, Bretschneidera sinensis (pink flowers).

1999, Oct. 2 *Perf. 14x14½*
Granite Paper

1902 A618 2b shown .35 .25
Complete booklet, 5 #1902 2.40
1903 A618 2b multi .35 .25
Complete booklet, 5 #1903 3.25
1904 A618 12b multi 1.10 .80
1905 A618 12b multi 1.10 .80
a. Souvenir sheet, #1902-1905, perf. 13¼ 3.50 2.75
Nos. 1902-1905 (4) 2.90 2.10

No. 1905a sold for 35b.

King Bhumibol Adulyadej's 72nd
Birthday — A619

King: #1906, And vehicle. #1907, And Buddhist monks. #1908, And Queen. #1909, And soldiers. #1910, And crowd. #1911, And disabled boy. #1912, Wearing green army uniform. #1913, In white suit with camera. #1914, With crowd waving flags.

1999, Oct. 21   Photo.   Perf. 14½
Granite Paper

1906	A619	3b multi	.25	.25
1907	A619	3b multi	.25	.25
1908	A619	3b multi	.25	.25
1909	A619	6b multi	.50	.35
1910	A619	6b multi	.50	.35
1911	A619	6b multi	.50	.35
1912	A619	12b multi	1.10	.80
1913	A619	12b multi	1.10	.80
1914	A619	12b multi	1.10	.80
a.		Souvenir sheet, #1906-1914	7.25	6.25
		Nos. 1906-1914 (9)	5.55	4.20

No. 1914a sold for 90b. Numbers have been reserved for additional stamps in this set.

Design
A39 — A620

**Litho. & Embossed with Foil
Application**
1999, Dec. 5   Wmk. 387   Perf. 13¼

1915	A620	100b blue & bronze	7.00	7.00
1916	A620	100b blue & silver	7.00	7.00
1917	A620	100b blue & gold	7.00	7.00
a.		Souvenir sheet, #1915-1917	25.00	20.00
		Nos. 1915-1917 (3)	21.00	21.00

King Bhumibol Adulyadej's 72nd birthday. No. 1917a sold for 350b.

New Year
2000 — A621

Medicinal plants: No. 1918, Thunbergia laurifolia. No. 1919, Gmelina arborea. No. 1920, Prunus cerasoides. No. 1921, Fagraea fragrans.

Perf. 14½x14¼
1999, Nov. 15   Litho.
Granite Paper

1918	A621	2b multi	.25	.25
1919	A621	2b multi	.25	.25
1920	A621	2b multi	.25	.25
a.		Souv. sheet, 5 ea #1918-1920 + 10 labels	30.00	
1921	A621	2b multi	.35	.25
a.		Souvenir sheet #1918-1921	2.25	1.75
		Nos. 1918-1921 (4)	1.10	1.00

No. 1921a sold for 15b.
No. 1920a was issued 3/25/00 and sold for 60b. For an additional fee the blank labels could be personalized with photos taken at a booth not operated by the Thailand postal authorities at the Bangkok 2000 Stamp Exhibition.

Investiture of
Crown Prince
Vajiralongkorn,
27th
Anniv. — A622

1999, Dec. 28   Perf. 14x14½
Granite Paper

1922	A622 3b multi		.60 .25

Lake of Lilies, Thale Noi — A623

Kulap Khao Flowers, Doi Chang
Dao — A624

Krachieo Flowers, Pa Hin
Ngam — A625

Bua Tong Flowers, Doi Mae
Ukor — A626

Perf. 14½x14¼
2000   Litho.   Unwmk.
Granite Paper

1923	A623	Sheet of 12, #a-l	8.00	5.50
a.-l.		3b Any single	.55	.35
1924	A624	Sheet of 12, #a-l	8.00	5.50
a.-l.		3b Any single	.55	.35
1925	A625	Sheet of 12, #a-l	8.00	5.50
a.-l.		3b Any single	.55	.35
1926	A626	Sheet of 12, #a-l	8.00	5.50
a.-l.		3b Any single	.55	.35
		Nos. 1923-1926 (4)	32.00	22.00

Issued: #1923, 1/1; #1924, 2/25; #1925, 7/16. #1926, 11/15.

Bees — A627

#1927, Apis andreniformis. #1928, Apis florea. #1929, Apis cerana. #1930, Apis dorsata.

2000, Mar. 19   Photo.   Perf. 11¾
Granite Paper

1927-1930		A627 3b Set of 4	1.75	1.40
		Souvenir Sheets of 1		
1927a-1930a		Set of 4	4.50	3.00

Nos. 1927a-1930a do not have white margin on stamps and sold for 8b each.

Bangkok 2000 Stamp
Exhibition — A628

Ceremonies: #1931, 2b, 1st month blessing (family & baby). #1932, 2b, Tonsure. #1933, 15b, Teacher respect (teacher, 3 children). #1934, 15b, Novice ordination.

2000, Mar. 25   Litho.   Perf. 14½x14
Granite Paper

1931-1934	A628	Set of 4	4.00	3.25
1934a		Souvenir sheet, #1931-1934, perf. 13½x14	5.50	4.50

No. 1934a sold for 45b. No 1934a exists imperf. Value, $20.

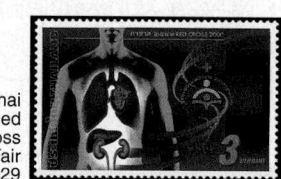

Thai
Red
Cross
Fair
A629

2000, Mar. 30   Perf. 14½x14
Granite Paper

1935	A629 3b multi	.35	.35

Thai Heritage Conservation — A630

Chok cloths from: 3b, Hat Seio. 6b, Mae Chaem. 8b, Ban Rai. 12b, Khu Bua.

2000, Apr. 2   Wmk. 387   Perf. 13¼

1936-1939	A630	Set of 4	4.75	3.75
1939a		Souvenir sheet, #1936-1939	5.50	4.50

No. 1939a sold for 40b.

Songkran Day Type of 1991
Perf. 14x14½
2000, Apr. 13   Litho.   Unwmk.
Granite Paper

1940	A425	2b Angel on serpent	.35	.25
		Booklet, 5 #1940	3.75	
a.		Souvenir sheet of 1	1.60	.75

No. 1940a sold for 8b and exists imperf.

50th Wedding Anniv. of King and
Queen — A631

No. 1941 — King Bhumibol Adulyadej and Queen Sirikit: a, Sitting on grass. b, Standing. c, Sitting on thrones. d, With family. e, Standing, wearing regalia.

2000, Apr. 28   Photo.   Perf. 11¾
Granite Paper

1941		Vert. strip of 5	6.50	5.00
a.-e.	A631	10b Any single	1.25	1.00

Asalhapuja
Day — A632

2000, July 16   Litho.   Perf. 14x14½
Granite Paper

1942	A632 3b multi	.65	.35

Crown Prince Maha Vajiralongkorn,
48th Birthday — A633

2000, July 28   Perf. 14½x14
Granite Paper

1943	A633	2b multi	.45	.25
		Booklet, 5 #1943	5.00	
a.		Souvenir sheet of 1, perf. 13¼	1.60	.80

No. 1943a sold for 8b.

Natl. Communications Day — A634

2000, Aug. 4   Granite Paper

1944	A634 3b multi	.35	.25

A635

Intl. Letter Writing Week — A636

Various tea sets.

Perf. 14½x14
2000, Oct. 7   Litho.   Unwmk.
Granite Paper

1945	A635	6b shown	.65	.55
1946	A635	6b multi, diff.	.65	.55
1947	A636	12b shown	1.25	1.10
1948	A636	12b multi, diff.	1.25	1.10
a.		Souvenir sheet, #1945-1948, perf. 13¼	5.00	4.50
		Nos. 1945-1948 (4)	3.80	3.30

No. 1948a sold for 45b.

Princess Srinagarindra, Birth
Cent. — A637

2000, Oct. 21   Granite Paper
1949 A637 2b multi   .45   .25
    Booklet, 5 #1949   3.75
  a. Souvenir sheet of 1, perf. 13¼ 1.60   .80
        No. 1949a sold for 8b.

Royal Barge Anantanakkharat — A638

Perf. 13¼x14
2000, Nov. 15   Photo.   Wmk. 340
1950 A638 9b multi   1.00   .75
  a. Souvenir sheet of 1   2.25   1.60
        No. 1950a sold for 15b.

New Year
2001 — A639

Flowers: No. 1951, 2b, Clerodendrum philippinum. No. 1952, 2b, Capparis micracantha.
No. 1953, 2b, Belamcanda chinensis. No.
1954, 2b, Memecylon caeruleum.

Perf. 14½x14¼
2000, Nov. 15   Litho.   Unwmk.
Granite Paper
1951-1954 A639   Set of 4   1.25   .85
1954a   Souvenir sheet, #1951-1954   2.25   1.60
        No. 1954a sold for 15b.

Parrots — A640

Designs: 2b, Psittacula alexandri. 5b, Psittacula eupatria. 8b, Psittinus cyanurus. 10b,
Psittacula roseata.

2001, Jan. 13   Perf. 14x14½
Granite Paper
1955-1958 A640   Set of 4   3.50   2.25
    Booklet, 5 #1955   3.75
  a. Souvenir sheet,
        #1955-1958, perf.
        13¼   4.50   3.25
  b. As "a," without price
        and with show em-
        blem in margin   20.00 15.00
No. 1955a sold for 35b. No. 1955b, Hong
Kong 2001 Stamp Exhibition, sold for 50b.

King
Chulalongkorn
and Land
Deed — A641

2001, Feb. 17   Granite Paper
1959 A641 5b multi   .55   .45
        Dept. of Lands, cent.

Marine Life — A642

Designs: a, Ray. b, Turtle. c, Jellyfish. fish.
d, Lionfish. e, Black, yellow fish, coral. f, Eel. g,
School of striped fish, angelfish, coral, vert. h,
Pufferfish, blue fish, vert. i, Shark, fish.
Stamp sizes: Nos. 1960a-1960f, 29x24mm.
Nos. 1960g-1960h, 29x48mm. No. 1960i,
58x42mm.

Perf. 13¾x14¼
2001, Mar. 15   Photo.
Granite Paper
1960 A642   Sheet of 9   6.50   5.50
a.-f.   3b Any single   .55   .35
g.-i.   6b Any single   .75   .55
        For surcharge, see No. 2511.

Gems
A643

Designs: 3b, Diamond. 4b, Green sapphire.
6b, Pearl. 12b, Blue sapphire.

2001   Litho.   Perf. 14½x14
Granite Paper
1961-1964 A643   Set of 4   2.25   2.25
  a. Souvenir sheet, #1961-1964,
        perf. 13½x14   4.50   3.25
  b. As "a," ovptd. in margin in
        gold   13.00 11.00
Issued, Nos. 1961-1964a, 3/30; No. 1964b,
6/9.
No. 1964a sold for 35b.
No. 1964b has Belgica 2001 emblem
overprint.

Red
Cross
A644

Perf. 14½x14
2001, Apr. 1   Litho.   Unwmk.
Granite Paper
1965 A644 4b multi   .60   .25

Ancient Brocades
From Nakhon Si
Thammarat
National
Museum — A645

Colors of brocade: 2b, Orange red, lilac, and
gold. 3b, Green and gold. No. 1968, 10b,
Orange and gold. No. 1969, 10b, Bright pink
and gold.

2001, Apr. 2   Perf. 14x14½
Granite Paper
1966-1969 A645   Set of 4   3.00   2.25
    Booklet, 5 #1966   3.00
  a. Souvenir sheet, #1966-1969, perf.
        13¼   4.50   3.25
    Heritage Conservation Day.
No. 1969a sold for 35b.

Songkran Day Type of 1991

2b, Man on snake, zodiac.

Perf. 13½x13¾
2001-2002   Wmk. 387
1970 A425 2b multicolored   .60   .25
    Booklet, 5 #1970   3.75
  a. Souvenir sheet of 1   1.60   1.10
  b. Unwmkd., granite paper, perf.
        14x14½   3.00   3.00
Issued: Nos. 1970-1970a, 4/13/01. No.
1970b, 4/13/02. No. 1970b issued only in No.
2017b.
No. 1970a sold for 8b and exists imperf.

Visakhapuja
Day — A646

2001, May 7   Unwmk.   Perf. 14x14½
Granite Paper
1971 A646 3b multi   .55   .35

Demon
Statues — A647

Designs: 2b,   Maiyarap.   5b,
Wirunchambang.   10b,   Thotsakan.   12b,
Sahatsadecha.

Perf. 14x14½
2001, June 13   Litho.   Unwmk.
Granite Paper
1972-1975 A647   Set of 4   3.50   2.60
    Booklet, 5 #1972   4.00
1975a   Souvenir sheet, #1972-
        1975, perf. 13½   4.50   3.25
        No. 1975a sold for 33b.

Prince Purachartra
Jayakara and
Rotary Intl.
Emblem — A648

2001, July 1   Granite Paper
1976 A648 3b multi   .50   .25
        Rotary Intl. in Thailand, 66th anniv.

Mushrooms — A649

Designs: 2b, Schizophyllum commune. 3b,
Lentinus giganteus. 5b, Pleurotus citrinopileatus. 10b, Pleurotus flabellatus.

2001, July 4   Photo.   Perf. 13¾x14
Granite Paper
1977-1980 A649   Set of 4   2.75   2.00
    Booklet, 5 #1977   3.75
1980a   Souvenir sheet, #1977-
        1980, perf. 13½   4.50   3.25
        No. 1980 sold for 26b.

Insects
A650

Designs: 2b, Cheirotonus parryi. 5b, Mouhotia batesi. 6b, Cladognathus giraffa. 12b,
Mormolyce phyllodes.

2001, July 4   Wmk. 329   Perf. 13½
1981-1984 A650   Set of 4   2.90   2.25
    Booklet, 5 #1981   3.75
  a. Souvenir sheet, #1981-1984   5.50   4.50
  b. As "a," with Phila Nippon '01
        emblem in margin   13.00 12.00
        No. 1984a sold for 34b.
No. 1984b sold for 34b, and was issued 8/1.

Natl. Communications Day — A651

Perf. 14½x14
2001, Aug. 4   Litho.   Unwmk.
Granite Paper
1985 A651 4b multi   .50   .45

Thaipex '01 — A652

Various domesticated fowl: 3b, 4b, 6b, 12b.

2001, Aug. 4   Photo.   Perf. 13¼
Granite Paper
1986-1989 A652   Set of 4   3.00   2.25
1989a   Souvenir sheet, #1986-
        1989   4.50   3.25
No. 1989a sold for 33b. No. 1989a also
exists imperf. Value, $17.50.

Queen Suriyothai, Heroine of Thailand — A653

2001, Aug. 12 Litho. *Perf. 14x14¾*
Granite Paper
1990 A653 3b multi   .55   .45
  a.   Souvenir sheet of 1, perf. 13¼   2.75 1.25
     No. 1990a sold for 10b.

Queen Sirikit's Visit to the People's Republic of China — A654

2001, Aug. 12   *Perf. 14¾x14*
Granite Paper
1991 A654 5b multi   .75   .45

Butterflies — A655

Designs: 2b, Pachliopta aristolochiae goniopeltis. 4b, Rhinopalpa polynice. 10b, Poritia erycinoides. 12b, Spindasis lohita.

Perf. 13½ Syncopated
2001, Sept. 10   Photo.
1992-1995 A655 Set of 4   4.00 2.75
     Booklet, 5 #1992   3.00
1995a   Souvenir sheet, #1992-
        1995   5.50 4.50
1995b   As "a," with Hafnia '01
        emblem in margin   16.00 16.00
     No. 1995a sold for 40b.
No. 1995b issued 11/16. No. 1995b sold for 43b.

Intl. Letter Writing Week — A656

Medicinal herbs: 2b, Piper nigrum. 3b, Solanum trilobatum. 5b, Boesenbergia rotunda. 10b, Ocimum tenuiflorum.

Perf. 14x14½
2001, Oct. 6   Litho.   Unwmk.
Granite Paper
1996-1999 A656 Set of 4   2.75 1.90
     Booklet, 5 #1996   3.75
1999a   Souvenir sheet, #1996-
        1999, perf. 13½x13¼   3.75 3.25
     No. 1999a sold for 25b.

Police Cadet Academy, Cent. — A657

2001, Oct. 13 Litho. *Perf. 14½x14*
Granite Paper
2000 A657 5b multi   .75   .55

Royal Barge Anekkachat Puchong — A658

2001, Nov. 15   Photo.   *Perf. 14¼*
Granite Paper
2001 A658 9b multi   1.00   .90
  a.   Souvenir sheet of 1   3.25 2.25
     No. 2001a sold for 17b.

New Year 2002 — A659

Flowers: No. 2002, 2b, Pedicularis siamensis. No. 2003, 2b, Schoutenia glomerata. No. 2004, 2b, Gentiana crassa. No. 2005, 2b, Colquhounia coccinea.

2001, Nov. 15 Litho. *Perf. 14x14½*
Granite Paper
2002-2005 A659 Set of 4   1.10 1.00
2005a   Souvenir sheet, #2002-
        2005   2.25 1.75
     No. 2005a sold for 11b.

Laying of Foundation Stone for Suvarnabhumi Airport Passenger Terminal — A660

2002, Jan. 19 Litho. *Perf. 14½x14*
Granite Paper
2006 A660 3b multi   .50   .35

Rose — A661

2002, Feb. 1   *Perf. 13¾*
Granite Paper
2007 A661 4b multi   3.75 1.50

12th World Congress of Gastroenterology A662

2002, Feb. 24   *Perf. 14x14½*
Granite Paper
2008 A662 3b multi   .50   .30

Communications Authority of Thailand, 25th Anniv. — A663

No. 2009: a, Satellite dish, CAT Telecom Co. emblem. b, Envelope, mailbox, Thailand Post emblem.

2002, Feb. 25   *Perf. 14½x14*
Granite Paper
2009 A663 3b Horiz. pair, #a-b 1.10 .75
  c.   Souvenir sheet, #2009, perf.
       13¼x13½   1.60 1.10
     No. 2009c sold for 10b.

Maghapuja Day — A664

2002, Feb. 26   *Perf. 14½x14*
Granite Paper
2010 A664 3b multi   1.60 1.10

2002 Red Cross Fair A665

2002, Mar. 30   Granite Paper
2011 A665 4b multi   .50   .40

Ministry of Transport and Communications, 90th Anniv. — A666

2002, Apr. 1 Litho. *Perf. 14½x14*
Granite Paper
2012 A666 3b multi   .50   .30

Heritage Conservation Day — A667

String puppets: No. 2013, 3b, Man. No. 2014, 3b, Woman. 4d, Demon. 15b, Monkey.

2002, Apr. 2   *Perf. 14x14½*
Granite Paper
2013-2016 A667 Set of 4   2.50 2.50
2016a   Souvenir sheet, #2013-
        2016, perf. 13¼   4.50 3.50
     No. 2016a sold for 30b.

Songkran Day Type of 1991
Design: Angel on horse, zodiac.

2002, Apr. 13   *Perf. 14x14½*
Granite Paper
2017 A425 2b multicolored   .60   .25
  a.   Souvenir sheet of 1   2.00 2.00
  b.   Souvenir sheet, #1724b,
       1801c, 1869, 1940,
       1970b, 2017   3.00 3.00
  c.   As "b," with Beijing 2002
       emblem in margin and
       selling price removed   17.50 17.50
Nos. 2017a and 2017b sold for 8b and 14b respectively. Both exist imperf.
Issued: No. 2017c, 9/29. No. 2017c sold for 30b.

Fighting Fish A668

Designs: No. 2018, 3b, Betta imbellis. No. 2019, 3b, Betta splendens. 4b, Betta splendens, diff. 15b, Betta splendens, diff.

2002, May 15 Litho. *Perf. 14½x14*
Granite Paper
2018-2021 A668 Set of 4   3.00 2.50
2021a   Souvenir sheet, #2018-
        2021, perf. 13½   4.50 4.00
2021b   As "a," with Amphilex
        2002 emblem and sell-
        ing price removed   15.00 15.00
     Issued: No. 2021b, 8/30. No. 2021a sold for 30b; No. 2021b sold for 31b.

Temples — A669

Designs: No. 2022, 3b, Wat Phra Si Rattanasatsadaram. No. 2023, 3b, Wat Phra Chetuphon Wimon Mangkhalaram. 4b, Wat Arun Ratchawararam. 12b, Wat Benchamabophit Dusit Wanaram.

2002, June 17   *Perf. 14½x14*
Granite Paper
2022-2025 A669 Set of 4   3.00 2.25
2025a   Souvenir sheet, #2022-
        2025, perf. 13½   3.25 2.75
2025b   As "a," with Philakorea
        2002 emblem and sell-
        ing price removed   15.00 15.00
     Issued: No. 2025b, 8/2. Nos. 2025a and 2025b each sold for 27b.

Crown Prince Maha Vajiralongkorn, 50th Birthday — A670

2002, July 28   *Perf. 14x14½*
Granite Paper
2026 A670 3b multi   .55   .30

Natl. Communications Day — A671

2002, Aug. 4   Granite Paper
2027 A671 4b multi   .50   .40

Thailand — Australia Diplomatic Relations, 50th Anniv. — A672

Designs: No. 2028, 3b, Nelumbo nucifera (pink flower). No. 2029, 3b, Nymphaea immutabilis (purple flower).

2002, Aug. 6 **Perf. 14½x14**
Granite Paper
2028-2029 A672 Set of 2 1.10 .75
2029a Souvenir sheet, #2028-
2029, perf. 13½ 1.60 1.50

See Australia Nos. 2072-2073. No. 2029a sold for 9b.

Queen Sirikit, 70th Birthday — A673

Designs: No. 2030, 3b, Queen and roses. No. 2031, 3b, Queen Sirikit rose. 4b, Queen Sirikit orchid. 15b, Queen Sirikit dona shrub.

2002, Aug. 12 **Perf. 14½x14**
Granite Paper
2030-2033 A673 Set of 4 2.25 2.25
2033a Souvenir sheet, #2030-
2033, perf. 13½ 3.75 3.50

No. 2033a sold for 31b.

National Archives, 50th Anniv. — A674

2002, Aug. 18 **Perf. 14½x14**
2034 A674 3b multi .50 .30

Thai Bank Notes, Cent. A675

2002, Sept. 7 **Engr.** **Perf. 13½**
Granite Paper
2035 A675 5b org & brown .75 .50
a. Souvenir sheet of 1 3.75 3.25

No. 2035a sold for 11b.

Vimanmek Mansion Art Objects — A676

Designs: No. 2036, 3b, Round, lidded betel nut box. No. 2037, 3b, Bowl. 4b, Bowl, diff. 12b, Rectangular betel nut box.

2002, Sept. 7 **Litho.** **Perf. 14½x14**
Granite Paper
2036-2039 A676 Set of 4 2.75 2.00
2039a Souvenir sheet, #2036-
2039, perf. 13½ 3.25 3.25

No. 2039a sold for 26b.

Royal Palaces A677

Designs: No. 2040, 4b, Thailand. No. 2041, 4b, Sweden.

Perf. 12½x13½ Syncopated
2002, Oct. 5 **Litho. & Engr.**
2040-2041 A677 Set of 2 1.10 .75

See Sweden No. 2445.

Intl. Letter Writing Day A678

Designs: No. 2042, 3b, Animal-shaped coconut grater. No. 2043, 3b, Strainer. 4b, Coconut shell ladle. 15b, Earthenware stove and pot.

2002, Oct. 5 **Litho.** **Perf. 14½x14**
Granite Paper
2042-2045 A678 Set of 4 2.25 2.00
2045a Souvenir sheet, #2042-
2045, perf. 13½ 4.50 3.25

No. 2045a sold for 31b.

Bangkok 2003 World Philatelic Exhibition — A679

Foods from: No. 2046, 3b, Central Thailand (red tablecloth). No. 2047, 3b, Southern Thailand (brown and yellow tablecloth). 4b, Northeastern Thailand. 15b, Northern Thailand.

2002, Oct. 5 **Perf. 14½x14**
2046-2049 A679 Set of 4 2.90 2.25
2049a Souvenir sheet, #2046-2049,
perf. 13½ 4.50 3.50

No. 2049a sold for 30b.

New Year 2003 — A680

Flowers: No. 2050, 3b, Guaiacum officinale. No. 2051, 3b, Nyctanthes arbor-tristis. No. 2052, 3b, Barleria cristata. No. 2053, 3b, Thevetia peruviana.

Perf. 14½x14¼
2002, Nov. 15 **Litho.**
Granite Paper
2050-2053 A680 Set of 4 1.50 1.10
2053a Souvenir sheet, #2050-
2053 2.75 2.25

No. 2053a sold for 16b.

20th World Scout Jamboree — A681

Designs: 3b, Scouts. 12b, Jamboree site.

2002, Dec. 28 **Perf. 14½x14**
Granite Paper
2054-2055 A681 Set of 2 1.90 1.25

New Year 2003 (Year of the Goat) — A682

2003, Jan. 1 **Perf. 13**
Granite Paper
2056 A682 3b multi .50 .25
See Nos. 2108, 2161, 2341a.

National Children's Day — A683

Pangpond and his: a, Dog, Big (blue background). b, Friend, Hanuman (orange background). c, Girlfriend, Namo (green background). d, Teacher (red background).

2003, Jan. 11 **Perf. 14½x14**
Granite Paper
2057 A683 3b Block of 4, #a-d 1.25 1.00

Rose — A684

2003, Feb. 1 **Perf. 13**
Granite Paper
2058 A684 4b multi .75 .30

No. 2058 is impregnated with rose scent. Compare with Type A716.

Blue Green, by Fua Haribhitak A685

Portrait of Chira Chongkon, by Chamras Kietkong A686

Moonlight, by Prasong Padmanuja A687

Lotus Flowers, by Thawee Nandakwang — A688

2003, Feb. 24 **Perf. 13¼**
Granite Paper
2059 A685 3b multi .35 .25
2060 A686 3b multi .35 .25
2061 A687 3b multi .35 .25
2062 A688 15b multi 1.40 1.25
Nos. 2059-2062 (4) 2.45 2.00

Bangkok 2003 World Philatelic Exhibition — A689

Tourist attractions: No. 2063, 3b, Doi Inthanon Temple, Chiang Mai. No. 2064, 3b, River Kwai Bridge, Kanchanaburi. No. 2065, 3b, Phu Kradung (cliff), Loei. 15b, Maya Bay, Krabi.

2003, Mar. 3 **Perf. 14½x14**
Granite Paper
2063-2066 A689 Set of 4 2.60 2.10
2066a Souvenir sheet, #2063-
2066, perf. 13¼ 4.50 3.25

No. 2066a sold for 29b.

King Bhumibol Adulyadej Type of 1996
Perf. 14x14½
2003, Mar. 14 **Litho.** **Unwmk.**
Granite Paper
2067 A550 1b blue .45 .25

2003 Red Cross Fair — A690

2003, Mar. 28 **Perf. 14x14½**
Granite Paper
2068 A690 3b multi .50 .30

Kick Boxing — A691

Designs: No. 2069, 3b, Boxers punching. No. 2070, 3b, Boxer in black trunks with knee raised. No. 2071, 3b, Boxer in red trunks kicking. 15b, Boxer in red trunks kicking, diff.

2003, Apr. 2 **Litho.** **Perf. 13¼**
Granite Paper
2069-2072 A691 Set of 4 3.00 2.10
2072a Souvenir sheet, #2069-
2072 4.50 3.50
2072b As "a," with China 2003
Philatelic Exhibition
emblem in margin 13.00 11.00

No. 2072a sold for 29b.
Issued: No. 2072b, 11/20. No. 2072b sold for 29b.

Princess Maha
Chakri Sirindhorn,
48th
Birthday — A692

2003, Apr. 2   **Perf. 14x14½**
Granite Paper
2073 A692 3b multi   .50   .25

Princess Galyani
Vadhana, 80th
Birthday — A693

2003, May 6   **Granite Paper**
2074 A693 3b multi   1.00   .50

Kings
Chulalongkorn
and Vajiravudh
A694

2003, May 6   **Granite Paper**
2075 A694 3b multi   .55   .30
Inspector General Dept., cent.

King Prajadhipok Day — A695

2003, May 30   **Perf. 14½x14**
Granite Paper
2076 A695 3b multi   .55   .30

Bantam
Chickens — A696

Designs: No. 2077, 3b, White ears jungle
fowl. No. 2078, 3b, Sugarcane husk colored.
No. 2079, 3b, Black-tailed white. 15b, Dark
gray.

2003   **Litho.**   **Perf. 13**
Granite Paper
2077-2080 A696   Set of 4   3.00   2.10
2080a   Souvenir sheet, #2077-
    2080   4.50   3.25
2080b   As "a," with Lanka
    Philex 2003 emblem in
    margin   20.00   16.00
   Issued: Nos. 2077-2080, 2080a, 6/10; No.
2080b, 7/31. Nos. 2080a and 2080b each sold
for 29b.

Asalhapuja
Day — A697

2003, July 13   **Perf. 14x14½**
Granite Paper
2081 A697 3b multi   1.40   .40

National Communications Day — A698

2003, Aug. 4   **Perf. 14½x14**
Granite Paper
2082 A698 3b multi   .50   .25

Communications Organization
Emblems — A699

   No. 2083: a, Thailand Post Company Limited. b, Communications Authority of Thailand
(23x27mm). c, CAT Telecom Public Company
Limited.

       Perf. 14¼x14½
2003, Aug. 14   **Litho.**   **Wmk. 340**
2083 A699 3b Horiz. strip of 3,
     #a-c   1.25   .90

King
Chulalongkorn
(1853-1910)
A700

Litho. & Embossed
2003, Sept. 20   **Unwmk.**   **Perf. 13¼**
2084 A700 100b gold & multi   8.25   6.50
  a.   Souvenir sheet of 4   35.00   35.00
   No. 2084a issued 9/30.
   No. 2084a exists imperf. with Bangkok 2003
emblem at lower left. Value, $50.

Government Housing Bank, 50th
Anniv. — A701

2003, Sept. 24   **Litho.**   **Perf. 14½x14**
Granite Paper
2085 A701 3b multi   .50   .25

Bangkok 2003 World Philatelic
Exhibition — A702

   Handicrafts: No. 2086, 3b, Basketry. No.
2087, 3b, Pottery. No. 2088, 3b, Leatherwork.
15b, Wood carving.

2003, Oct. 4   **Granite Paper**
2086-2089 A702   Set of 4   2.60   2.10
2089a   Souvenir sheet, #2086-
    2089, perf. 13¼   3.75   3.25
   A varnish with a rough surface was applied
to portions of the designs.
   No. 2089a sold for 29b. No 2089a exists
imperf. Value, $16.

Trees of Thailand and Canada — A703

   No. 2090: a, Cassia fistula (Thailand). b,
Maple leaves (Canada).

2003, Oct. 4   **Perf. 14x14½**
Granite Paper
2090 A703 3b Horiz. pair, #a-b   1.25   1.10
  c.   Souvenir sheet, #2090, perf.
    13¼   2.50   2.50
   No. 2090c sold for 9b.

Lychees — A704

Rose
Apples — A705

   Fruit: No. 2093, Coconuts. 15b, Jackfruit.

2003, Oct. 4   **Granite Paper**
2091 A704   3b shown   .45   .25
2092 A705   3b shown   .45   .25
2093 A704   3b multi   .45   .25
2094 A704   15b multi   1.60   1.25
  a.   Souvenir sheet, #2091-2094,
    perf. 13¼   4.50   3.25
    Nos. 2091-2094 (4)   2.95   2.00
   International Letter Writing Week. No.
2094a sold for 29b.

Oct. 14, 1973 Student Uprisings, 30th
Anniv. — A706

2003, Oct. 14   **Perf. 14½x14**
Granite Paper
2095 A706 3b multi   .50   .25

Asia-Pacific Economic Cooperation
Meeting — A707

2003, Oct. 20   **Granite Paper**
2096 A707 3b multi   .50   .25

New Year
2004 — A708

   Flowers: No. 2097, 3b, Bougainvillea
spectabilis. No. 2098, 3b, Eucrosia bicolor.
No. 2099, 3b, Canna x generalis. No. 2100,
3b, Zinnia violacea.

2003, Nov. 15   **Perf. 14½x14¼**
Granite Paper
2097-2100 A708   Set of 4   1.25   1.10
2100a   Souvenir sheet, #2097-
    2100   2.25   1.75
2100b   As "a," with 2004 Hong
    Kong Stamp Expo em-
    blem in margin   7.00   6.50
   No. 2100a sold for 16b.
   Issued: No. 2100a, 1/30/04. No. 2100b sold
for 16b.

Thailand Flag
A709

Thai Pavilion
A710

Elephants
A711

Cassia Fistula
A712

2003, Dec. 1   **Perf. 14¼x14½**
Granite Paper
2101 A709 3b multi   .45   .25
2102 A710 3b multi   .45   .25
2103 A711 3b multi   .45   .25
2104 A712 3b multi   .45   .25
    Nos. 2101-2104 (4)   1.80   1.00
   Compare with types A865a-A865d.

Elephants — A713

   No. 2105: a, Asian elephant. b, African
elephants.

2003, Dec. 9 — Perf. 14½x14
Granite Paper
2105 A713 3b Horiz. pair, #a-b 1.00 .75
c.   Souvenir sheet, #2105a, perf.
     13¼ 2.75 2.25

No. 2105c sold for 9b.
Thailand-South Africa diplomatic relations,
10th anniv. See South Africa No. 1330.

King Bhumibol Adulyadej Type of 1996
2003, Dec. 3 — Perf. 14x14½
Granite Paper
2106 A550 50s olive brown .75 .25
2107 A550 1b blue .75 .25

Issued: 50s, 12/3, 1b, 1/22/04

Zodiac Animal Type of 2003
2004, Jan. 1 — Litho. — Perf. 13
Granite Paper
2108 A682 3b Monkey .50 .25

See No. 2341b.

Children's Day — A714

2004, Jan. 10 — Perf. 14½x14
Granite Paper
2109 A714 3b multi .50 .25

Paintings of
Hem Vejakorn
A715

Designs: No. 2110, 3b, A Scene in Thai History (dancers). No. 2111, 3b, Maha Bharatayudh (charioteer). No. 2112, 3b, Khun Chang — Khun Phaen (women with horse). No. 2113, 3b, Phra Lor (woman and rooster).

2004, Jan. 17 — Perf. 13¼
Granite Paper
2110-2113 A715 Set of 4 1.40 1.10
2113a   Souvenir sheet, #2110-2113 3.25 2.25

No. 2113a sold for 16b.

Rose — A716

2004, Feb. 1 — Perf. 13
Granite Paper
2114 A716 4b multi .65 .30

Compare with type A684. No. 2114 is impregnated with rose scent.

Turtles — A717

Designs: No. 2115, 3b, Cuora amboinensis. No. 2116, 3b, Platysternon megacephalum.

No. 2117, 3b, Indotestudo elongata. No. 2118, 3b, Heosemys spinosa.

2004, Mar. 1 — Perf. 14½x14
Granite Paper
2115-2118 A717 Set of 4 1.75 1.25
2118a   Souvenir sheet, #2115-2118, perf. 13¼ 3.25 3.00
2118b   Similar to "a," with 2004 Singapore World Stamp Championship emblem in margin 8.75 7.50

Issued: No. 2118b, 8/28.
Nos. 2118a and 2118b sold for 16b.

Siam Society, Cent. — A718

2004, Mar. 10 — Perf. 14½x14
2119 A718 3b multi .50 .25

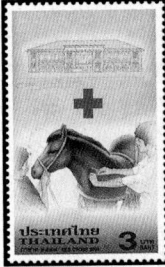

2004 Red Cross
Fair — A719

2004, Mar. 29 — Perf. 14x14½
Granite Paper
2120 A719 3b multi .50 .25

Heritage
Conservation
Day — A720

Fringe colors of hand woven clothes: No. 2121, 3b, Rose red. No. 2122, 3b, Blue. No. 2123, 3b, Green. No. 2124, 3b, Orange red. Denomination is at LL on Nos. 2122, 2124.

2004, Apr. 2 — Litho. — Perf. 14x14½
Granite Paper
2121-2124 A720 Set of 4 1.60 1.25
2124a   Souvenir sheet, #2121-2124, perf. 13¼ 3.25 2.75
2124b   As "a," with España 2004 emblem in margin, perf. 13¼ 10.00 9.00

Issued: No. 2124b, 5/22. No. 2124a sold for 16b; No. 2124b for 18b.

Architecture in Thailand and
Italy — A721

No. 2125: a, Golden Mountain Temple, Bangkok. b, Colosseum, Rome.

2004, Apr. 21 — Perf. 14½x14
Granite Paper
2125 A721 3b Horiz. pair, #a-b 2.75 2.50
2125c   Souvenir sheet, #2125, perf. 13¼ 24.00 20.00

No. 2125c sold for 10b.
See Italy No. 2602.

Sculpture
A722

Designs: No. 2126, 3b, One-sided Drum, by Chit Rienpracha (yellow green background). No. 2127, 3b, Dance Drama, by Sitthidet Saenghiran (rose red background). No. 2128, 3b, Heavenly Flute, by Khien Yimsiri (Prussian blue background). No. 2129, 3b, The Calf, by Paitun Muangsomboom, horiz.

2004, May 3 — Perf. 13¼
2126-2129 A722 Set of 4 1.40 .95

Unseen Tourist Attractions — A723

No. 2130: a, Non Ngai Buddha, Suphan Buri. b, Khao Laem Dam, Kanchanaburi. c, Mural, Temple for the Emerald Buddha, Bangkok. d, Ko Li-Pe, Satun. e, Buddha, Wat Phra Thong, Phuket. f, Khao Luang National Park, Nakhon Si Thammarat. g, Miracle Beach, Ko Damikhwan, Krabi. h, Hornbill, Hala-Bala Forest, Narathiwat. i, Long Ru Waterfall, Ubon Ratchathani. j, Prasat Hin Phanom Rung, Buri Ram. k, Red maple leaves, Phu Kradueng National Park, Loei. l, Phukhao Ya, Ranong. m, Ko Kradat, Trat. n, Op Luang National Park, Chiang Mai. o, Dusky leaf monkey, Phetchaburi. p, Lalu, Sra Kaeo. q, Pu Kai, Mu Ko Similan, Phang-Nga. r, Tha Le Noi Waterfowl Park. Phatthalung. s, Phu Pha Thoep, Mukdahan National Park. t, Phi Maen Cave, Mae Hong Son.

2004, May 31 — Perf. 13
Granite Paper
2130 A723 3b Sheet of 20, #a-t 10.00 8.00

See Nos. 2137, 2147, 2158.

Buddha
Sculptures
A724

No. 2131: a, Phra Nangpaya. b, Phra Kampaeng Soumkhor. c, Phra Somdej Wat Rakangkhositaram. d, Phar Rod. e, Phra Phongsuphan.

Litho. & Embossed
2004, June 1 — Perf. 13¼
Granite Paper
2131   Horiz. strip of 5 12.00 9.50
a.-e.   A724 9b Any single 2.40 1.75
f.   Souvenir sheet, #2131a-2131e 20.00 20.00

No. 2131f sold for 53b.

Visakhapuja
Day — A725

2004, June 2 — Litho. — Perf. 14x14½
Granite Paper
2132 A725 3b multi .50 .25

Bridges — A726

Designs: No. 2133, 5b, Phra Buddha Yodfa Bridge. No. 2134, 5b, Rama VI Bridge. No. 2135, 5b, Rama VIII Bridge. No. 2136, 5b, Rama IX Bridge.

2004, July 1 — Litho. — Perf. 14¼x14½
Granite Paper
2133-2136 A726 Set of 4 2.25 1.25

On Nos. 2135 and 2136 portions of the design were produced by a thermographic process which produces a shiny, raised effect.

Unseen Tourist Attractions Type of 2004

No. 2137: a, Wat Pho Prathap Chang, Phichit. b, Phra Prathan Chaturathit, Wat Phumin, Nan. c, Thalenai, Angthong Archipelago, Surat Thani. d, Wat Na Phra Men, Phra Nakhon Si Ayutthaya. e, Sanam Chan Palace, Nakhon Pathom. f, Piyamitr Tunnel, Yala. g, Ban Khamchanot, Udon Thani. h, Rail line along Pasak Cholasit Dam, Lop Buri. i, Khlong Lan Waterfall, Khlong Lan National Park, Kamphaeng Phet. j, Mo-I-Daeng Cliff, Khao Phra Wihan National Park, Si Sa Ket. k, Changkra Wild Orchid Park, Khon Kaen. l, Canoeists at Ti Lo Re, Tak. m, Khao Ta Mong Lai, Prachuap Khiri Khan. n, Suriya Patithin solar calendar, Prasat Phu Phek, Sakon Nakhon. o, Traditional boat racing, Chumphon. p, Mokochu Range Mae Wong National Park, Nakhon Sawan. q, Ordination by elephant in the sixth month, Surin. r, Rock climbing, Tan Rattana Waterfall, Khao Yai National Park, Prachin Buri. s, Monks collecting alms on horseback, Chiang Rai. t, Cycling in Thung Salaeng Luang, Phitsanulok.

2004, July 28 — Perf. 13
Granite Paper
2137 A723 3b Sheet of 20, #a-t 10.00 8.00

Jasmine
Flower — A727

Litho. & Embossed
2004, Aug. 2 — Perf. 13
Granite Paper
2138 A727 5b multi .55 .30

No. 2138 is impregnated with a jasmine scent.

Princess Maha Chakri Sirindhorn Information Technology Program — A728

2004, Aug. 4   Litho.   Perf. 14x14½
Granite Paper
2139 A728 3b multi   .50   .25

National Communications Day — A729

2004, Aug. 4   Perf. 14½x14
Granite Paper
2140 A729 3b multi   .50   .25

Opening of First Subway Line — A730

2004, Aug. 12   Litho.   Perf. 14½x14
Granite Paper
2141 A730 3b multi   .50   .25

Queen Sirikit, 72nd Birthday A731

Litho. & Embossed
2004, Aug. 12   Perf. 13¼
2142 A731 100b multi   7.00   4.50

Boats A732

Designs: No. 2143, 3b, Thai junk. No. 2144, 3b, Sampan boat. No. 2145, 3b, Krachaeng boat. 15b, Packet boat.

2004-05   Litho.   Perf. 14½x14
Granite Paper
2143-2146 A732   Set of 4   2.00   1.40
2146a   Souvenir sheet, #2143-
             2146, perf. 13¼   3.25   3.00
    b. As "a," with Pacific Explorer
         2005 emblem in margin   9.00   8.00
  No. 2146a sold for 29b. No. 2146b sold for 30b.
  Issued: Nos. 2143-2146a, 9/1/04; No. 2146b, 4/21/05.

Unseen Tourist Attractions Type of 2004

No. 2147: a, Phra Nang Din, Phayad. b, Phra That Kong Khao Noi, Yasothon. c, Phra Atchana, Wat Sri Chum, Sukothai. d, Wat Bang Kung, Samut Songkhram. e, Ku Kut, Wat Phrathat Chamthewi, Lamphun. f, Dolphin watching, Chachoengsao. g, Tak Bat Dok Mai tradition, Saraburi. h, Hat Chao Lao, Chanthaburi. i, Phu Kum Khao dinosaur fossils, Kalasin. j, Reversed stupa, Wat Phra That Lampang Luang, Lampang. k, Khu Khut Waterfowl Park, Songkhla. l, Plant Market Khlong 15, Nakhon Nayok. m, Huppatad, Uthai Thani. n, Thai Muang Beach, Nakhon Phanom. o, Wild gaur, Khao Yai National Park, Nakhon Ratchasima. p, Canoeing, Le Khao Kop Cave, Trang. q, Sea of flowers, Pru Soi Dao, Uttaradit. r, Kolae boat, Ban Paseyawo, Pattani. s, Sea of Mist, Thap Boek, Phu Hin Rongkla National Park, Phetchabun. t, Bats, Khao Chung Phran, Ratchaburi.

2004, Sept. 28   Perf. 13
Granite Paper
2147 A723 3b Sheet of 20, #a-t   10.00   8.00

Intl. Letter Writing Week — A733

Kites: No. 2148, 3b, Snake. No. 2149, 3b, Star-shaped. No. 2150, 3b, Diamond-shaped with tail. 15b, Buffalo.

2004, Oct. 9   Litho.   Perf. 14x14½
Granite Paper
2148-2151 A733   Set of 4   2.00   1.40
2151a   Souvenir sheet, #2148-
             2151, perf. 13¼   3.25   3.00
2151b   Similar to "a," with Beijing
             2004 emblem in margin 9.00   8.00
  Issued: No. 2151b, 10/28. No. 2151a sold for 29b; No. 2151b for 30b.

King Mongkut (1804-68) A734

2004, Oct. 18   Perf. 14x14½
Granite Paper
2152 A734 4b multi   .50   .25

E-customs System — A735

2004, Nov. 15   Perf. 14½x14
Granite Paper
2153 A735 3b multi   .50   .25

New Year 2005 — A736

Flowers: No. 2154, 3b, Wrightia sirikitiae. No. 2155, 3b, Eria amica. No. 2156, 3b, Burmannia coelestris. No. 2157, 3b, Utricularia bifida.

2004, Nov. 15   Perf. 14¼x14½
Granite Paper
2154-2157 A736   Set of 4   3.00   2.00
2157a   Souvenir sheet, #2154-
             2157, perf. 14¼x14½   5.00   5.00
  No. 2157a sold for 16b.

Unseen Tourist Attractions Type of 2004

No. 2158: a, Phra That Cho Hae, Phrae. b, Wat Karuna, Chai Nat. c, Wat Nang Sao, Samut Sakhon. d, Phra Mutao Pagoda, Nonthaburi. e, Phu Kao Phu Phan Kham National Park, Nong Bua Lam Phu. f, Airvata (three-headed elephant), Erawan Museum, Samut Prakan. g, Wat Chedi Hoi, Pathum Thani. h, White krajiaw field, Chaiyaphum. i, Chet Si Waterfall, Nong Khai. j, Summer Palace, Ko Si Chang, Choi Buri. k, Traditional Drum-making village (Ban Bang Phae), Ang Thong. l, Ko Thalu, Rayong. m, Kosamphi Forest Park, Maha Sarakham. n, Cannonball tree, Wat Phra Non Chaksi, Sing Buri. o, Tung Kula Rong Hai, Roi Et. p, Phu Sra Dok Bua, Amnat Charoen.

2004, Nov. 26   Perf. 13
Granite Paper
2158 A723 3b Sheet of 16, #a-p,
            + 4 labels   9.00   8.00

Bangkok Fashion City Initiative — A737

No. 2159: a, 3b, Man and woman. b, 3b, Woman in pink dress. c, 3b, Woman with green shirt. d, 15b, Woman with brown eyeshade.

2004, Dec. 5   Perf. 14x14½
Granite Paper
2159 A737   Horiz. strip of 4, #a-
             d   2.25   2.25
    e. Souvenir sheet, #2159a-2159d,
         perf. 13½   3.25   2.75
  No. 2159e sold for 30b.

Queen Rambhai Bharni (1904-84) A738

2004, Dec. 20   Perf. 14x14½
Granite Paper
2160 A738 3b multi   .50   .25

Zodiac Animal Type of 2003
2005, Jan. 1   Perf. 13
Granite Paper
2161 A682 3b Cock   .50   .30
  See No. 2341c.

Children's Day — A739

2005, Jan. 8   Perf. 14½x14
Granite Paper
2162 A739 3b multi   .50   .25

Thailand - Argentina Diplomatic Relations, 50th Anniv. — A740

No. 2163: a, Tango dancers, Argentina. b, Tom-tom dancers, Thailand.

2005, Feb. 2   Perf. 13¼
Granite Paper
2163 A740 3b Horiz. pair, #a-b   1.10   1.00
  See Argentina Nos. 2312-2313.

Rose — A741

2005, Feb. 10   Perf. 12½
Flocked Paper
2164 A741 10b multi   1.10   .80
  No. 2164 is impregnated with rose scent.

Maghapuja Day — A742

2005, Feb. 23   Perf. 14x14½
Granite Paper
2165 A742 3b multi   .50   .25

Rotary International, Cent. — A743

2005, Feb. 23   Perf. 14½x14
Granite Paper
2166 A743 3b multi   .50   .25

Red Cross A744

2005, Mar. 30   Litho.
Granite Paper
2167 A744 3b multi   .50   .25

Princess
Maha Chakri
Sirindhorn,
50th Birthday
— A774a

2005, Apr. 2   Litho.   Perf. 13¼
Granite Paper
2167A A774a 3b multi   .50 .25

A745

Hanging
Art — A746

2005, Apr. 2   Litho.   Perf. 13¼
Granite Paper
2168 A745 3b shown   .35 .25
2169 A746 3b shown   .35 .25
2170 A746 3b multi, diff.   .35 .25
2171 A745 15b multi, diff.   1.40 .55
  a.   Souvenir sheet, #2168-2171   3.25 2.75
  Nos. 2168-2171 (4)   2.45 1.30

Heritage Conservation Day. No. 2171 sold
for 30b.

Authors Born in 1905 — A747

Designs: No. 2172, 3b, Dokmaisod (olive
green background). No. 2173, 3b, Sri Burapha
(Prussian blue background). No. 2174, 3b,
Maimuangderm (dark blue background). No.
2175, 3b, Arkatdumkeung Rabibhadana (rose
pink background).

2005, May 5   Perf. 14½x14
Granite Paper
2172-2175 A747 Set of 4   2.25 2.10
2175a   Souvenir sheet, #2172-
        2175, perf. 13¼   5.00 4.50

No. 2175a sold for 17b.

Insects — A748

No. 2176: a, Coccinella transversalis. b,
Chrysochroa buqueti rugicollis (47x28mm). c,

Sagra femorata. d, Chrysochroa maruyamai
(47x28mm).

Litho. & Embossed
2005, May 31   Perf. 14¼x14½
Granite Paper
2176   Horiz. strip or block of
       4   2.25 1.60
  a.-d. A748 5b Any single   .55 .40
  e.   Sheet, 2 each #2176a-2176d 3.00 3.00

Embossed portions of stamps are covered
with a glossy varnish.
No. 2176e issued May 2006, Washington
2006 World Philatelic Exhibition. No. 2176e
sold for 54b.

Heart Balloons
and Mail
Truck — A749

Balloons —
A749a

2005   Litho.   Perf. 13
Granite Paper
2177   A749   3b multi   .75 .50
2177A A749a 3b multi   .75 .50

Issued: No. 2177, June; No. 2177A, 7/15.
Nos. 2177 and 2177A were issued in sheets of
12 + 12 personalizable labels the same size as
the stamp.

Buddha
Amulets —
A750

No. 2178: a, Phra Ruang Lang Rang Puen.
b, Phra Hu Yan. c, Phra Chinnarat Bai Sema.
d, Phra Mahesuan. e, Phra Tha Kradan.

Litho. & Embossed
2005, June 19   Perf. 13¼
Granite Paper
2178   Horiz. strip of 5   4.50 4.50
  a.-e. A750 9b Any single   .90 .90
  f.   Souvenir sheet, #2178a-
       2178e   12.00 12.00
  g.   As "f," with Taipei 2005 em-
       blem in margin   12.00 12.00

No. 2178f sold for 55b.
No. 2178g issued 8/19/05. No. 2178g sold
for 85b.

Thailand - People's Republic of China
Diplomatic Relations, 30th
Anniv. — A751

Panda: a, Showing tongue. b, Feeding on
bamboo.

2005, July 1   Litho.   Perf.
Granite Paper
2179   A751   Horiz. pair   1.10 .90
  a.-b. 3b Either single   .45 .30
  c.   Souvenir sheet, #2179a-2179b 3.25 2.75

No. 2179 has perf. 13¼ line of perforations
between the two stamps, and the surrounding

selvage is rouletted 11¾. No. 2179c, which
sold for 15b, lacks the perforations between
the stamps and has no rouletting.

Thaipex
2005 — A752

Dancers in play "Chuck Nark": No. 2180, 3b,
Pra Rama and Princess Srida. No. 2181, 3b,
Hanuman (white mask). No. 2182, 3b, Thot-
sakan (green mask). 15b, Pra Rama and
Thotsakan.

Litho. with Foil Application
2005, Aug. 3   Perf. 13¼
Granite Paper
2180-2183 A752 Set of 4   2.60 2.00
2183a   Souvenir sheet, #2180-
        2183   4.50 3.25

No. 2183a sold for 30b. No. 2183a exists
imperf. Value $25.

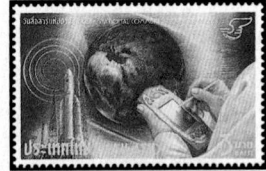

Natl. Communications Day — A753

2005, Aug. 4   Litho.   Perf. 14½x14
Granite Paper
2184   A753   3b multi   .50 .25

Building Gables — A754

No. 2185: a, Prasat Phanom Rung. b, Phra
Prang at Wat Phra Phai Luang. c, Uposatha
Hall at Wat Khao Bandai It. d, Scripture
Library at Wat Phra Sing Woramahawihan.

Perf. 13¼x13½
2005, Aug. 4   Photo.   Wmk. 340
2185   Horiz. strip of 4 + cen-
       tral label   2.75 2.25
  a.-d. A754 5b Any single   .55 .40

Orchids — A755

Designs: No. 2189, 3b, Rhynchostylis
gigantea Alba (white flowers). No. 2190, 3b,
Rhynchostylis gigantea (pink and red flowers).
No. 2191, 3b, Dendrobium gratiosissimum.
15b, Dendrobium thyrsiflorum.

Perf. 14½
2005, Sept. 1   Litho.   Unwmk.
Granite Paper
2189-2192 A755 Set of 4   2.50 2.50
2192a   Souvenir sheet, #2189-
        2192, perf. 13¼   3.50 3.50

No. 2192a sold for 30b.

Intl. Day of
Peace — A756

2005, Sept. 21   Perf. 13
Granite Paper
2193   A756   3b multi   .50 .25

Intl. Letter Writing Week — A757

Water buffalo: No. 2194, 3b, Head. No.
2195, 3b, Standing in field. No. 2196, 3b, In
mud. 15b, Attached to plow.

Perf. 14½x14
2005, Oct. 8   Litho.   Unwmk.
Granite Paper
2194-2197 A757 Set of 4   2.50 2.50
2197a   Souvenir sheet, #2194-
        2197, perf. 13¼   4.50 3.25

National Library, Cent. — A758

2005, Oct. 12   Perf. 14½x14
Granite Paper
2198   A758   3b multi   .50 .25

Abolition of Slavery, Cent. — A759

2005, Oct. 23   Litho.
Granite Paper
2199   A759   3b multi   .50 .30

New Year
2006 — A760

Flowers: No. 2200, 3b, Beaumontia
murtonii. No. 2201, 3b, Hibiscus mutabilis. No.
2202, 3b, Hibiscus rosa-sinensis. No. 2203,
3b, Cochlospermum religiosum.

2005, Nov. 15   Perf. 14x14½
Granite Paper
2200-2203 A760 Set of 4   1.25 1.25
2203a   Souvenir sheet, #2200-
        2203   2.25 2.00

No. 2203a sold for 17b.

Princess
Bejaratana, 80th
Birthday — A761

2005, Nov. 24   Perf. 14x14½
Granite Paper
2204 A761 3b multi   .50   .30

Siamese
Roosters — A762

Designs: No. 2205, 3b, Golden Rooster, by Pichai Nirand (olive green panel). No. 2206, 3b, Rooster at Dawn, by Prayat Pongdam (black panel). No. 2207, 3b, Legendary Rooster, by Chakrabhand Posayakrit (dancing woman, brown panel). No. 2208, 3b, Divine Rooster, by Chalermchai Kositpipat (blue panel), horiz.

Perf. 14x14½, 14½x14
2005, Nov. 24
2205-2208 A762 Set of 4   1.25 1.25

King Bhumibol Adulyadej's "New
Theory" Agriculture — A763

No. 2209: a, King, easel, farmers, animals. b, King and farmers.

2005, Dec. 5   Perf. 14¼x14½
Granite Paper
2209   Horiz. pair, #a-b, +
             central label   .85   .85
  a.-b.   A763 3b Either single   .35   .30

Buddhist
Monks
A764

No. 2210: a, Somdet Phra Phutthachan (1788-1872). b, Phra Ratchamuni Samiram Khunupamachan (1582-1682). c, Phra Achan Man Bhuridatto (1870-1949). d, Khruba Si wichai (1877-1938).

Litho. & Engr.
2005, Dec. 5   Perf. 13½
Granite Paper
2210   Horiz. strip of 4   2.25 2.25
  a.-d.   A764 5b Any single   .55   .50
  e.   Souvenir sheet, #2210a-2210d 3.50 3.50

No. 2210e sold for 30b.

Dec. 26, 2004 Tsunami, 1st
Anniv. — A765

No. 2211: a, Wave. b, Undivided Kindness of Thai People, by Chanipa Temprom.

2005, Dec. 26   Litho.   Perf. 14½x14
Granite Paper
2211 A765 3b Horiz. pair, #a-b   2.50 1.75

**King Bhumibol Adulyadej Type of
1996**
2006   Litho.   Perf. 14x14½
Granite Paper
2212 A550 10b orange & brown   2.00 1.00
2213 A550 15b yel brn & green   3.00 1.50

New Year 2006
(Year of the
Dog) — A766

2006, Jan. 1   Litho.   Perf. 13
Granite Paper
2214 A766 3b multi   .50   .30

Prince Chaturantarasmi Krom Phra
Chakrabardibongse (1856-1900),
Finance Minister — A767

2006, Jan. 13   Perf. 14x14½
Granite Paper
2215 A767 3b multi   .50   .30

Natl. Children's Day — A768

Winning designs in children's stamp design competition with panel colors of: No. 2216, 3b, Orange brown. No. 2217, 3b, Blue. No. 2218, 3b, Red violet. No. 2219, 3b, Green.

2006, Jan. 14   Perf. 14½x14
Granite Paper
2216-2219 A768 Set of 4   1.25 1.25

Rose — A769

Litho. & Embossed
2006, Feb. 7   Perf. 13
Granite Paper
2220 A769 5b multi   .75   .50

Diplomatic Relations Between
Thailand and Iran, 50th Anniv. — A770

2006, Feb. 11   Litho.   Perf. 14½x14
Granite Paper
2221 A770 3b multi   .50   .30

Queen Sirikit Center for Breast
Cancer — A771

2006, Mar. 29   Perf. 14½x14
Granite Paper
2222 A771 3b multi   .50   .25

Heritage
Conservation
Day — A772

Sites in Phu Phrabat Historical Park: No. 2223, 3b, Buddha's Footprint (monument). No. 2224, 3b, Upright rocks and trees, horiz. No. 2225, 3b, Thao Barot horse stable (rock overhang), horiz. 15b, Nang Usa rock pillar.

2006, Apr. 2   Perf. 14x14½, 14½x14
Granite Paper
2223-2226 A772 Set of 4   2.50 2.50
  2226a   Souvenir sheet, #2223-
             2226, perf. 13¼   4.50 3.25

No. 2226a sold for 36b.

Thon Buri Palace — A773

No. 2227: a, Throne Hall. b, King Taksin's Shrine. c, Two Chinese-style residences. d, King Pinklao's residence.

2006, Apr. 2   Perf. 14½x14
Granite Paper
2227 A773 3b Block of 4, #a-d   1.40 1.40
  e.   Souvenir sheet, #2227, perf.
             13¼   2.75 2.25

No. 2227e sold for 17b.

A774

King
Bhumibol
Adulyadej,
60th
Anniv. of
Accession
A775

King Bhumibol Adulyadej: No. 2228, 3b, Wearing tie, red brown background (shown). No. 2229, 3b, Wearing tie, blue background. No. 2230, 3b, Wearing tie, olive brown background. No. 2231, 3b, Without tie, blue violet background. No. 2232, 3b, Without tie, green background. No. 2233, 3b, Without tie, brown background.

2006   Photo.   Perf. 13¼
Granite Paper
2228-2233 A774 Set of 6   8.00 7.00
  2233a   Miniature sheet, #2228-
             2233   16.00 16.00
**Litho. & Embossed With Foil
Application**
2234 A775 100b gold & multi   9.00 9.00

Issued: Nos. 2228-2233, 2233a, 5/5; No. 2234, 6/9. No. 2233a sold for 30b.

Visakhapuja
Day — A776

2006, May 12   Litho.   Perf. 14x14½
Granite Paper
2235 A776 3b multi   .50   .30

Buddhadasa
Bhikkhu (1906-
93), Buddhist
Philosopher
A777

No. 2236: a, Buddhadasa seated between trees. b, Profile of Buddhadasa. c, Gathering of monks. d, Stone fence.

2006, May 27   Perf. 13
Granite Paper
2236   Horiz. strip of 4   1.60 1.60
  a.-d.   A777 3b Any single   .30   .30
  e.   Miniature sheet, #2236a-2236d 2.00 2.00

No. 2236e sold for 17b.

Anemonefish — A778

Designs: No. 2237, 3b, Amphiprion clarkii. No. 2238, 3b, Amphiprion perideraion. No. 2239, 3b, Amphiprion ocellaris. No. 2240, 3b, Amphiprion polymnus.

2006, June 24   Perf. 14½x14
Granite Paper

2237-2240	A778	Set of 4	1.40	1.40
2240a		Miniature sheet, #2237-2240, perf. 13½	2.75	2.25
2240b		As "a", with Belgica '06 emblem in margin	11.00	11.00

Issued: Nos. 2237-2240, 2240a, 6/24; No. 2240b, Dec. No. 2240a sold for 20b; No. 2240b, for 30b.

Natl. Communications Day — A779

2006, Aug. 4   Litho.
Granite Paper

2241	A779	3b multi	.50	.30

Mitrephora Sirikitiae — A780

Litho. & Embossed
2006, Aug. 12   Perf. 13
Granite Paper

2242	A780	5b multi	.55	.40

Royal Dog Tongdaeng A781

Dog: No. 2243, 3b, Sitting. No. 2244, 3b, Standing. No. 2245, 3b, Laying down. No. 2246, 3b, With puppies.

2006   Litho.   Perf. 13½
Granite Paper

2243-2246	A781	Set of 4	1.40	1.10
2246a		Miniature sheet, #2243-2246	2.25	2.25
2246b		As "a", with MonacoPhil 2006 emblem in margin	10.00	10.00

Issued: Nos. 2243-2246, 2246a, 9/1; No. 2246b, Dec. No. 2246a sold for 17b; No. 2246b, for 26b.

Suvarnabhumi Airport — A782

2006, Sept. 28   Perf. 14½x14
Granite Paper

2247	A782	3b multi	.50	.30

Nos. 606, 653a, 934 and 1081 Surcharged

Methods, Perfs and Watermarks As Before
2006, Sept. 15

2248	A146	2b on 20s #606	16.00	16.00
2249	A161	2b on 20s #653a	1.10	.35
a.		2b on 20s #653	75.00	75.00
2250	A256	2b on 75s #934	2.75	2.75
2251	A256	2b on 1.50b #1081	2.75	2.75
		Nos. 2248-2251 (4)	22.60	21.85

Location and size of surcharges differs.

Fireworks — A783

2006, Apr. 20   Litho.   Perf. 13
Granite Paper

2252	A783	3b multi + label	2.75	2.75

Printed in sheets of 10 stamps + 10 labels that could be personalized. Sheets sold for 100b. Value, $32.50.

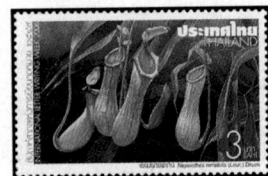

Intl. Letter Writing Week — A784

Carnivorous plants: No. 2253, 3b, Nepenthes mirabilis. No. 2254, 3b, Rafflesia kerrii. No. 2255, 3b, Sapria poilanei. 15b, Drosera burmannii.

2006   Litho. Unwmk.   Perf. 14½x14
Granite Paper

2253-2256	A784	Set of 4	2.50	1.60
2256a		Miniature sheet, #2253-2256, perf. 13½	3.25	2.75
2256b		As "a," with Beijing 2006 emblem in margin	10.00	10.00

Issued: Nos. 2253-2256, 2256a, 10/9; No. 2256b, Dec. No. 2256a sold for 29b; No. 2256b, for 44b.

New Year 2007 — A785

Flowers: No. 2257, 3b, Hypoxis aurea. No. 2258, 3b, Murdannia gigantea. No. 2259, 3b, Impatiens phuluangensis. No. 2260, 3b, Caulokaempferia alba.

2006, Nov. 15   Perf. 14½x14
Granite Paper

2257-2260	A785	Set of 4	1.25	.90
2260a		Miniature sheet, #2257-2260	2.50	2.25

No. 2260a sold for 16b.

Royal Thai Naval Academy, Cent. — A786

2006, Nov. 20   **Granite Paper**

2261	A786	3b multi	.50	.30

King Bhumibol Adulyadej, 60th Anniv. of Accession A787

King Bhumibol Adulyadej: No. 2262, 5b, Standing in forest. No. 2263, 5b, Seated on walkway, taking notes. No. 2264, 5b, Standing on wooden plank over water. No. 2265, 5b, Pointing to ground. No. 2266, 5b, Riding cow. No. 2267, 5b, Walking up hill.

2006, Dec. 5   Photo.   Perf. 13½
Granite Paper

2262-2267	A787	Set of 6	3.75	2.50
2267a		Miniature sheet, #2262-2267	5.50	5.50

No. 2267a sold for 44b. No. 2267a exists imperf. Value, $275.

Opening of Second Thai-Lao Friendship Bridge — A788

No. 2268 — Bridge and flag of: a, Thailand (denomination at LL). b, Laos (denomination at LR).

2006, Dec. 20   Litho.   Perf. 14½x14
Granite Paper

2268	A788	3b Horiz. pair, #a-b	1.10	1.10

New Year 2007 (Year of the Pig) — A789

2007, Jan. 1   Perf. 13
Granite Paper

2269	A789	3b multi	.50	.30

See No. 2341d.

Natl. Children's Day — A790

No. 2270 — Children's drawings: a, Rainbow, birds and butterflies. b, Cat with green face and butterflies. c, Spotted animals. d, Birds, cloud, sun and girl riding horse.

2007, Jan. 13   Perf. 14½x14
Granite Paper

2270	A790	3b Block of 4, #a-d	2.25	1.25

Siam Commercial Bank Public Company, Cent. — A791

2007, Jan. 30   Perf. 14x14½
Granite Paper

2271	A791	3b multi	.50	.30

Bangkok 2007 Intl. Stamp Exhibition — A792

Various carved wooden dolls depicting Thai children with background colors of: No. 2272, 5b, Blue. No. 2273, 5b, Olive green. No. 2274, 5b, Brown olive. No. 2275, 5b, Rose.

Litho. With Foil Application
2007, Feb. 1   Perf. 13
Granite Paper

2272-2275	A792	Set of 4	2.25	1.75
2275a		Miniature sheet, #2272-2275	3.75	3.25

No. 2275a sold for 33b.

Yellow Rose — A793

2007, Feb. 7   Litho.   Perf. 13
Granite Paper

2276	A793	5b multi	.55	.40

No. 2276 is impregnated with a rose scent.

A794

A795

A796

Carved Fruits and Vegetables — A797

2007, Mar. 1   Litho.   Perf. 14½x14
Granite Paper
2277	A794	5b multi	.55	.40
2278	A795	5b multi	.55	.40
2279	A796	5b multi	.55	.40
2280	A797	5b multi	.55	.40
a.		Souvenir sheet, #2277-2280, perf. 13¼	3.50	3.25
		Nos. 2277-2280 (4)	2.20	1.60

No. 2280a sold for 26b.

No. 617 Surcharged
in Bronze and Black

**Methods, Perfs and Watermarks As
Before**
2007, Mar. 29
2281	A146	50b on 40b #617	6.50	6.50
2282	A146	100b on 40b #617	10.00	10.00

Postman on
Scooter — A798

Unwmk.
2007, Mar. 29   Litho.   Perf. 13
Granite Paper
2283	A798	3b multi	.35	.30

No. 2283 was printed in sheets of 10 and in
sheets of 10 + 10 labels that could be
personalized.

Thailand Red Cross Tuberculosis
Laboratory — A799

2007, Mar. 29   Litho.   Perf. 14½x14
2285	A799	3b multi	.35	.30

A800

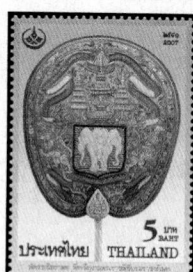

A801

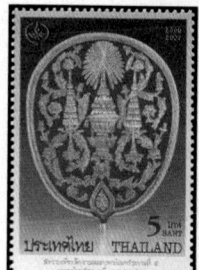

A802

Buddhist
Ecclesiastical
Ceremonial
Fans of King
Chulalongkorn
Era — A803

Litho. With Foil Application
2007, Apr. 2   Perf. 13¼
Granite Paper
2286	A800	5b multi	.55	.40
2287	A801	5b multi	.55	.40
2288	A802	5b multi	.55	.40
2289	A803	5b multi	.55	.40
a.		Souvenir sheet, #2286-2289	3.75	3.25
		Nos. 2286-2289 (4)	2.20	1.60

No. 2289a sold for 27b.

Flowers — A804

No. 2290: a, Lotus flower at UR, sunflowers
in center and LR. b, Sunflower at UR, two lotus
flowers. c, Rose, sunflower and lotus flowers.
d, Three roses.

2007, Apr. 23   Litho.   Perf. 13
Granite Paper
2290		Vert. strip of 4	1.60	1.60
a.-d.	A804	3b Any single	.35	.30

King Bhumibol Adulyadej, 80th
Birthday — A805

**Litho. & Embossed With Foil
Application**
2007, May 5   Perf. 13¼
Granite Paper
2291	A805	9b multi	1.40	1.40

Princess Galyani
Vadhana, 84th
Birthday — A806

2007, May 6   Litho.   Perf. 14x14½
2292	A806	3b multi	.65	.50

Visakhapuja Day — A807

2007, May 31   Perf. 14¼x14½
Granite Paper
2293	A807	3b multi	.45	.40

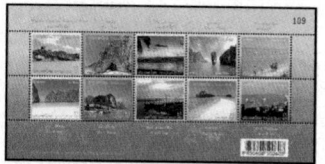

Seaside Tourist Areas — A808

No. 2294: a, Mu Ko Similan National Park.
b, Ko Khai. c, Ko Chang. d, Khao Tapu. e, Hat
Cha-am. f, Ao Maya. g, Ko Panyi. h, Hat Chao
Mai. i, Thale Waek. j, Hat Pattaya.

2007, June 1   Perf. 14½x14
Granite Paper
2294	A808	Sheet of 10	11.00	11.00
a.-j.		15b Any single	1.10	1.10

The original printing of No. 2294 has the bar
code in the bottom margin. A later printing with
a smaller margin has the bar code at the right
side.

Waterfalls — A809

Waterfall at: No. 2295, 3b, Doi Inthanon
National Park. No. 2296, 3b, Thung Salaeng
Luang National Park. No. 2297, 3b, Khuean
Srinagarindra National Park. No. 2298, 3b,
Phu Hin Rong Kla National Park.

2007, June 1   Perf. 14½x14
Granite Paper
2295-2298	A809	Set of 4	1.40	1.40
2298a		Souvenir sheet, #2295-2298, perf. 13½	2.90	2.25

No. 2298a sold for 16b.

Phi Takhon Masks — A810

No. 2299 — Masks with rice steamer hat in:
a, White, black background. b, Black, white

background. c, Red, black background. d,
White, white background.
10b, Two people wearing masks.

2007, June 23   Perf. 13¼
Granite Paper
2299	A810	3b Horiz. strip of 4,		
		#a-d	1.60	1.60

Souvenir Sheet
Perf. 14x14½
2300	A810	10b multi	2.00	2.00

No. 2300 contains one 60x48mm stamp.

A811

A812

A813

Rock Formations in Pa Hin Ngam
National Park — A814

2007, July 2   Litho.   Perf. 13¼x12¾
2301	A811	5b multi	.55	.40
2302	A812	5b multi	.55	.40
2303	A813	5b multi	.55	.40
2304	A814	5b multi	.55	.40
a.		Souvenir sheet, #2301-2304	4.75	3.75
		Nos. 2301-2304 (4)	2.20	1.60

No. 2304a sold for 39b. Portions of the
designs of Nos. 2301-2304 and 2304a were
printed with a thermographic process producing a shiny, raised effect. A gritty substance
was added to these areas to produce a rough
texture.

Temples — A815

Designs: No. 2305, 5b, Wat Rajaorasaram.
No. 2306, 5b, Wat Rajapradit
Sathitmahasimaram. No. 2307, 5b, Wat
Rajabopit Sathitmahasimaram. No. 2308, 5b,
Wat Suthatthepwararam.

2007, July 2   Litho.   Perf. 14½x14
Granite Paper
2305-2308	A815	Set of 4	2.25	1.75
2308a		Souvenir sheet, #2305-2308, perf. 13¼	3.50	3.25

No. 2308a sold for 27b.

Bird
Figurines
A816

Bird figurines covered with beetle wing: No. 2309, 5b, Duck with wings spread. No. 2310, 5b, Bird on rock. No. 2311, 5b, Bird with long tail feathers. No. 2312, 5b, Rooster.

Litho. With Foil Application
2007, Aug. 3   *Perf. 14x14½*
Granite Paper
2309-2312 A816   Set of 4   2.60 1.75
2312a   Souvenir sheet, #2309-
            2312   3.75 3.25

No. 2312a sold for 33b. Bangkok 2007 Intl. Stamp Exhibition.

Natl. Communications Day — A817

2007, Aug. 4   Litho.   *Perf. 14½x14*
Granite Paper
2313 A817 3b multi   .30   .30

24th Summer
Universiade,
Bangkok — A818

2007, Aug. 8   *Perf. 13¼*
Granite Paper
2314 A818 3b multi   .30   .30

Miniature Sheet

Association of South East Asian
Nations (ASEAN), 40th Anniv. — A819

No. 2315: a, Secretariat Building, Bandar Seri Begawan, Brunei. b, National Museum of Cambodia. c, Fatahillah Museum, Jakarta, Indonesia. d, Typical house, Laos. e, Malayan Railway Headquarters Building, Kuala Lumpur, Malaysia. f, Yangon Post Office, Myanmar (Burma). g, Malacañang Palace,

Philippines. h, National Museum of Singapore. i, Vimanmek Mansion, Bangkok. j, Presidential Palace, Hanoi, Viet Nam.

2007, Aug. 8   *Perf. 13¼*
Granite Paper
2315 A819 3b Sheet of 10, #a-j 5.50 4.50

See Brunei No. 607, Burma No. 370, Cambodia No. 2339, Indonesia Nos. 2120-2121, Laos Nos. 1717-1718, Malaysia No. 1170, Philippines Nos. 3103-3105, Singapore No. 1265, and Viet Nam Nos. 3302-3311.

Miniature Sheet

Diplomatic Relations Between
Thailand and Japan, 120th
Anniv. — A820

No. 2316: a, Buddhist statue. b, Pagoda. c, Elephant. d, Dragon. e, Pink and white orchids. f, White flowers. g, Thai dancer. h, Japanese dancer.

2007, Sept. 26   Litho.   *Perf. 13¼*
Granite Paper
2316 A820   3b Sheet of 8, #a-h 4.50 3.25

See Japan No. 2998.

Intl. Letter Writing Week — A821

Utensils: No. 2317, 3b, Betel nut scissors. No. 2318, 3b, Betel nut masher. No. 2319, 3b, Cylinder-and-piston igniter. No. 2320, 3b, Earthenware oil lamp or incense dish.

2007, Oct. 8   Litho.   *Perf. 14½x14*
Granite Paper
2317-2320 A821   Set of 4   1.75 1.10
2320a   Miniature sheet, #2317-2320,
            perf. 13¼   3.00 2.75

No. 2320a sold for 18b.

Miniature Sheets

Provincial Seals — A822

No. 2321, 3b — Seals of: a, Bangkok. b, Krabi. c, Kanchanaburi. d, Kalasin. e, Kamphaeng Phet. f, Khon Kaen. g, Chanthaburi. h, Chachoengsao. i, Chon Buri. j, Chai Nat.
No. 2322, 3b — Seals of: a, Chaiyaphum. b, Chumphon. c, Chiang Rai. d, Chiang Mai. e, Trang. f, Trat. g, Tak. h, Nakhon Nayok. i, Nakhon Pathom. j, Nakhon Phanom.

**Litho. & Embossed With Foil
Application**
2007, Oct. 11   *Perf. 13½*
Granite Paper
Sheets of 10, #a-j
2321-2322 A822   Set of 2   5.50 5.50

Miniature Sheet

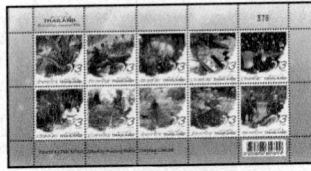

People at Work — A823

No. 2323: a, People in palm tree. b, Cook feeding people on wooden walkway. c, People near elephant carving. d, Buddhist monk in canoe. e, People under lanterns. f, Artisan with hammer. g, Woman with flowers. h, Man weaving fishing basket. i, People in boats filled with fruits and vegetables. j, People logging with elephants.

2007, Oct. 26   Litho.   *Perf. 13*
Granite Paper
2323 A823 3b Sheet of 10, #a-j 5.50 5.50

Ministry of
Defense, 120th
Anniv. — A824

2007, Nov. 11   *Perf. 14x14½*
Granite Paper
2324 A824 3b multi   .35   .30

New Year
2008 — A825

Designs: No. 2325, 3b, Pink Plumeria rubra, denomination in red. No. 2326, 3b, Plumeria obtusa. No. 2327, 3b, White and yellow Plumeria rubra, denomination in pink. No. 2328, 3b, Red Plumeria rubra, denomination in red.

2007, Nov. 15   *Perf. 14x14½*
Granite Paper
2325-2328 A825   Set of 4   1.25 1.25
2328a   Souvenir sheet, #2325-
            2328   2.90 2.90

No. 2328a sold for 18b.

Patrol
Boat — A826

        Perf. 14½x14¼
2007, Nov. 20   Litho.
Granite Paper
2329 A826 3b multi   .55   .30

White Elephant of King Bhumibol
Adulyadej — A827

Designs: No. 2330, 5b, King touching elephant's trunk. No. 2331, 5b, Elephant on lawn. No. 2332, 5b, Elephant on lawn with handlers, vert. No. 2333, 5b, King touching elephant's head, vert.

        Perf. 14¾x14, 14x14¾
2007, Dec. 5   Litho.
Granite Paper
2330-2333 A827   Set of 4   1.75 1.75
2333a   Souvenir sheet, #2333,
            perf. 13½   2.75 2.25

No. 2333a sold for 10b.

Miniature Sheet

King Bhumibol Adulyadej, 80th
Birthday — A828

No. 2334 — King: a, 5b, As small boy. b, 5b, As boy, sitting in wagon. c, 5b, As student, reading book. d, 5b, Wearing suit, sepia photograph. e, 5b, Wearing cap. f, 5b, Wearing red uniform. g, 5b, Wearing suit and red tie. h, 5b, Wearing gold robe. i, 80b, Wearing Buddhist robe.

**Litho., Litho. & Embossed With
Hologram Affixed (80b)**
2007, Dec. 5   *Perf. 13¼x13½*
2334 A828   Sheet of 9, #a-i 16.00 12.00

No. 1820
Surcharged in Gold

Methods and Perfs As Before
2007, Dec. 18   **Granite Paper**
2335 A550 15b on 9b #1820   2.00   .75

Busabok
Mala
A829

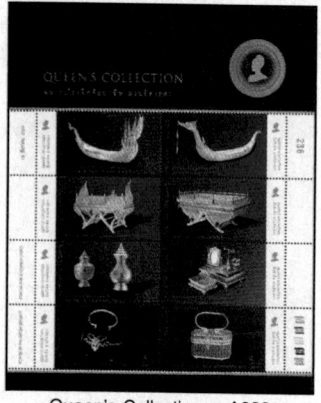

Queen's Collection — A830

No. 2337: a, Miniature model of royal barge Anantanakharai. b, Miniature model of royal barge Suphannahongse. c, Sappagab Phragajatarn. d, Sappagab Khram. e, Water jars. f, Miniature vanity set. g, Yan Lipao basketry. h, Evening bag.

Litho. & Embossed With Foil Application
2007, Dec. 18   Perf. 13¼x13½
2336 A829 20b multi   3.00 3.00
　a.　Souvenir sheet of 1   6.00 6.00
Granite Paper
Perf. 13
2337 A830 5b Sheet of 8, #a-h   4.50 3.75
　　　No. 2336a sold for 40b.

Nos. B78-B79 Surcharged in Black

Methods, Perfs and Watermarks As Before
2007, Jan. 16
2338 　　Horiz. strip of 4 (#B78)   —   —
　a.-d. SP13 5b on 2b+1b #B78a-B78d,
　　　　　Any single   —   —
2339 　　Horiz. strip of 4 (#B79)   —   —
　a.-d. SP13 5b on 2b+1b #B79a-B79d,
　　　　　Any single   —   —

New Year Types of 2003-2007 and

New Year 2008 (Year of the Rat) — A831

Unwmk.
2008, Jan. 1   Litho.   Perf. 13
Granite Paper
2340 A831 3b multi   .35   .30
2341 　　Sheet of 6, #2214,
　　　　　2340, 2341a-2341d   3.50 3.25
　a.　A682 3b As #2056, with gold
　　　　rings with colored centers .30   .30
　b.　A682 3b As #2108, with gold
　　　　rings with colored centers —   —
　c.　A682 3b As #2161, with gold
　　　　rings with colored centers .30   .30
　d.　A789 3b As #2269, with gold
　　　　rings and dots   .30   .30
　e.　As #2341, with Taipei 2008
　　　　emblem in margin   10.00 10.00
　　　No. 2341 sold for 30b. On Nos. 2056, 2108 and 2161, gold rings have white centers. No. 2269 has gold dots only.

A832

A833

A834

A835

Children's Art — A836

No. 2342: a, Stilt walkers, by Kemtis Kumsrijan. b, Flying kites, by Natapol Saelim. c, Puppet show, by Sirada Chokeyangkul. d, Thien Phansa, by Salinthip Narongpun. e, People thanking rice plants, by Amornthep Jitnak.

2008, Jan. 12   Litho.   Perf. 14½x14
Granite Paper
2342 　　Horiz. strip of 5   2.00 2.00
　a.　A832 3b multi   .35   .30
　b.　A833 3b multi   .35   .30
　c.　A834 3b multi   .35   .30
　d.　A835 3b multi   .35   .30
　e.　A836 3b multi   .35   .30
　　　　　Children's Day.

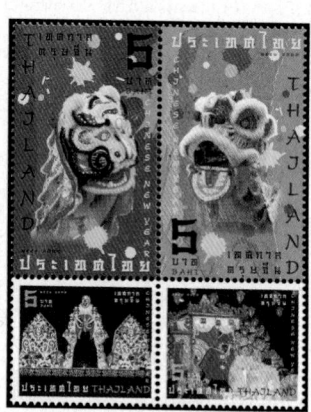

Chinese New Year — A837

No. 2343: a, Mask, black denomination at UR (29x48mm). b, Mask, black denomination at LL (29x48mm). c, Masks, green denomination at UL (29x24mm). d, People celebrating, green denomination at LL (29x24mm).

2008, Feb. 1   Litho.   Perf. 14½x14¼
Granite Paper
2343 A837 5b Block of 4, #a-d   2.25 2.25
　e.　Souvenir sheet, #2343a-2343b 2.50 2.50
　　　No. 2343e sold for 20b. For surcharges, see No. 2358.

Pink Rose — A838

2008, Feb. 7   Litho.   Perf. 13
Granite Paper
2344 A838 5b multi   .45   .40
　　　No. 2344 is impregnated with a rose scent.

Postman in Boat — A839

2008, Mar. 3   Perf. 14¼
Granite Paper
2345 A839 3b multi   .25   .25

Stylized People Holding Heart — A840

2008, Mar. 17   Granite Paper
2346 A840 3b multi   .35   .30
　　　Printed in sheets of 10 and in sheets of 10 + 10 labels that could be personalized.

Nos. B78-B79 Surcharged in Gold and Black

Methods, Perfs and Watermarks As Before
2008, Mar. 26
2347 　　Horiz. strip of 4 (#B78) 4.00 3.00
　a.-d. SP13 15b on 2b+1b #B78a-
　　　　　B78d, Any single   1.00   .75
2348 　　Horiz. strip of 4 (#B79) 4.00 3.00
　a.-d. SP13 15b on 2b+1b #B79a-
　　　　　B79d, Any single   1.00   .75

Miniature Sheet

Chatukham Rammathep — A841

No. 2349: a, Statue, maroon panels, "Chatukham" above denomination. b, Gold amulet, light gray background. c, Statue, maroon panels, "Rammathep" above denomination. d, Statue, yellow panels, "Chatukham" above denomination. e, Gold amulet with inner ring, dark gray background. f, Statue, yellow panels, "Rammathep" above denomination. g, Silver and brown amulet, bister background. h, Silver amulet, blue background. i, Silver and red amulet, orange brown background. j, Silver and red amulet, olive green background. k, Black amulet, pale blue green background. l, Red brown amulet, pink background.

Litho. & Embossed
Perf. 13½x13¼
2008, Mar. 29   Unwmk.
2349 A841 9b Sheet of 12, #a-
　　　　l   10.00 10.00
　　　No. 2349 was printed in sheets of 12 with and without a row of perforations through the center of the sheet. For surcharges, see No. 2588.

A842

A843

A844

Angels and Demons — A845

2008, Apr. 2   Litho.   Perf. 14x14½
Granite Paper
2350 A842 3b multi   .35   .30
2351 A843 3b multi   .35   .30
2352 A844 3b multi   .35   .30
2353 A845 3b multi   .35   .30
　a.　Miniature sheet, #2350-2353,
　　　　perf. 13¼   3.00 3.00
　　　Nos. 2350-2353 (4)   1.40 1.20
　　　No. 2353a sold for 20b.

Miniature Sheet

Provincial Seals — A846

No. 2354 — Seals of: a, Nakhon Ratchasima. b, Nakhon Si Thammarat. c, Nakhon Sawan. d, Nonthaburi. e, Narathiwat. f, Nan. g, Buri Ram. h, Pathum Thani. i, Prachuap Khiri Khan. j, Prachin Buri.

Litho. & Embossed With Foil Application
2008, Apr. 2 **Perf. 13**
Granite Paper
2354 A846 3b Sheet of 10, #a-j 5.50 5.50

Nos. 1764, 1817-1818 Surcharged in Gold and Black

c

Methods and Perfs As Before
2008
2355 A572(c) 15b on 6b #1764 .95 .95

Granite Paper
2356 A590(c) 15b on 6b #1817 .95 .95
2357 A590(c) 15b on 9b #1818 .95 .95
Nos. 2355-2357 (3) 2.85 2.85

Nos. 2343a, 2343c, 2343d, and Items Similar to Nos. 2343b and 2343e Surcharged in Gold and Black — d

Methods and Perfs As Before
2008, Apr. 25 **Granite Paper**
2358 Block of 4 (#2343) 4.50 4.50
a. A837(d) 15b on 5b #2343a 1.10 1.10
b. A837(d) 15b on 5b stamp similar to #2343a 1.10 1.10
c.-d. A837(c) 15b on 5b Either single, #2343c-2343d 1.10 1.10
e. A837(d) 15b on 5b sheet similar to #2343e 4.50 3.75

No. 2358b is a surcharge on an unissued stamp similar to No. 2343b that was printed with the incorrectly-spelled inscription "Chinese Neww Year." The extra "w" is obliterated by a gold circle in the surcharge on No. 2358b found in in the block of four or in the souvenir sheet, No. 2358e.

Diplomatic Relations Between Thailand and Turkey, 50th Anniv. — A847

No. 2359: a, Flag of Thailand, Wat Rajannada, Bangkok. b, Flag of Turkey, Blue Mosque, Istanbul.

2008, May 12 **Litho.** **Perf. 13¼**
Granite Paper
2359 A847 3b Horiz. pair, #a-b .55 .55
See Turkey Nos. 3108-3109.

Sunflowers A848

2008, May 16 **Perf. 13**
Granite Paper
2360 A848 3b multi .25 .25

Visakhapuja Day — A849

2008, May 19 **Perf. 14¼x14½**
Granite Paper
2361 A849 3b multi .35 .30

A850

A851

A852

World Environment Day — A853

2008, June 5 **Perf. 13½**
Granite Paper
2362 A850 3b multi .25 .25
2363 A851 3b multi .25 .25
2364 A852 3b multi .25 .25
2365 A853 3b multi .25 .25
Nos. 2362-2365 (4) 1.00 1.00

Miniature Sheet

Orchids — A854

No. 2366: a, Brassocattleya Ploenpit Star. b, Aerides falcata. c, Arachnis Hookeriana x Vanda Doctor Anek. d, Phalaenopsis Little

---

Mary. e, Dendrobium sutiknoi. f, Paphiopedilum callosum. g, Grammatophyllum speciosum. h, Vascostylis Prapawan. i, Vanda Robert's Delight.

2008, June 13 **Litho.** **Perf. 14x14½**
Granite Paper
2366 A854 3b Sheet of 9, #a-i 3.25 3.25

A855

A856

A857

A858

A859

A860

A861

A862

A863

Bangkok Attractions A864

2008, July 11 **Perf. 13¼x13½**
Granite Paper
2367 Sheet of 10 4.50 4.50
a. A855 3b multi .35 .25
b. A856 3b multi .35 .25
c. A857 3b multi .35 .25
d. A858 3b multi .35 .25
e. A859 3b multi .35 .25
f. A860 3b multi .35 .25
g. A861 3b multi .35 .25
h. A862 3b multi .35 .25
i. A863 3b multi .35 .25
j. A864 3b multi .35 .25

Miniature Sheet

Mountain Region Attractions — A865

No. 2368: a, Phu Chi Fa. b, Phu Pha Thoep. c, Heo Narok Waterfall. d, Phang-Ung. e, Sun Crack. f, Phu Khao Hin Pakarang. g, Phae Mueang Phi Earth Pillar. h, Phu Kradueng. i, Phu Soi Dao. j, Khun Mae Ya.

2008, July 11 **Litho.**
Granite Paper
2368 A865 15b Sheet of 10, #a-j 11.00 11.00

Thailand Flag — A865a

Thai Pavilion A865b

Elephants — A865c

Cassia Fistula — A865d

2008, July 25 **Litho.** **Perf. 14¼x14½**
2368K A865a 3b multi .45 .25
2368L A865b 3b multi .45 .25
2368M A865c 3b multi .45 .25
2368N A865d 3b multi .45 .25
Nos. 2368K-2368N (4) 1.80 1.00

Nos. 2368K-2368N were printed by a different printer than Nos. 2101-2104.

No. 2368K has a taller, rounder "3" than No. 2101.

No. 2368L has a black line under the building railing at bottom. On No. 2102, the railing touches the white frame of the stamp.

On No. 2368M, the country name, having small dots of color in the lettering, appears pale gray, and the entire vignette has a fuzzy appearance. On No. 2103, the country name is all white and the vignette is sharper.

On No. 2368N, the area without flowers has a blue appearance, and the flowers have a greener appearance. On No. 2104, the area without flowers has a purple appearance, and the flowers appear browner. The screens used on these stamps differ, with No. 2368N having coarser dots than No. 2104. Under magnification the bottom edge of the vignette has more of a saw-tooth appearance on No. 2368N than on No. 2104.

Postman, Tree and Dove — A866

2008, Aug. 1   *Perf. 14¼*
Granite Paper

2369	A866	3b multi	.35	.30
a.		Perf. 13	4.50	4.50

A867

Thailand Postal Service, 125th
Anniv. — A868

Designs: No. 2370, 3b, Unissued 1-fuang
stamp of 1883 and various modern Thailand
stamps. No. 2371, 3b, Old and modern post
offices. No. 2372, 3b, Old and modern post
office counters. No. 2373, 3b, Old and modern
postal delivery men. No. 2374, 3b, Old and
modern postal trucks.
No. 2375: a, 5b, Thailand #2 in black and
Post Office. b, 5b, Thailand #3. c, 5b, Thailand
#4. d, 10b, Thailand #5a. e, 25b, Hologram of
Thailand #1 with added Thai words.

**Litho., Litho. With Hologram Affixed
(#2375e)**

2008, Aug. 4   *Perf. 14½x14*
Granite Paper

2370-2374	A867	Set of 5	1.60	1.10
		Perf. 13¼x13½		
2375	A868	Sheet of 5 #a-e	4.50	4.50

Communications
Day — A869

2008, Aug. 4 Litho.   Perf. 14x14½
Granite Paper

2376	A869	3b multi	.35	.30

End of telegraph message service in
Thailand.

Painting of
Flowers by
Princess Maha
Chakri Sirindhorn
A870

2008, Aug. 4   *Perf. 13½x13¼*
Granite Paper

2377	A870	5b multi	.45	.40

Peacocks
A871

Designs: No. 2378, 10b, Peacock on
branch. No. 2379, 10b, Peacock with tail feathers raised.

**Litho. & Embossed With Hologram
Affixed**

2008, Aug. 9   *Perf. 13¼*
Granite Paper

2378-2379	A871	Set of 2	2.00	1.60
2379a		Souvenir sheet, #2378-		
		2379	3.75	3.25

No. 2379a sold for 30b.

**Nos. 1749-1750, 1785 Surcharged in
Black**

Methods and Perfs As Before

2008, Oct. 1   **Granite Paper**

2380	A568	10b on 6b #1749	3.25	3.25
2381	A579	10b on 6b #1785	3.25	3.25
2382	A568	50b on 7b #1750	7.50	7.50
		Nos. 2380-2382 (3)	14.00	14.00

Diplomatic Relations Between
Thailand and Republic of Korea, 50th
Anniv. — A872

No. 2383: a, Chakri Maha Prasat Throne
Hall, Thailand (denomination at L). b,
Juhamnu Mansion, Changdeok Palace, Korea
(denomination at R).

2008, Oct. 1   Litho.   Perf. 14½x14
Granite Paper

2383	A872	3b Horiz. pair, #a-b	.55	.55

See South Korea No. 2295.

Intl. Letter Writing
Week — A873

Shadow puppets: No. 2384, 3b, Rishi. No.
2385, 3b, Shiva. No. 2386, 3b, Shadow play
preluder. No. 2387, 3b, Theng the Jester.

2008, Oct. 4   *Perf. 14x14½*
Granite Paper

2384-2387	A873	Set of 4	.90	.90
2387a		Souvenir sheet, #2384-		
		2387, perf. 13½	2.40	2.40

No. 2387a sold for 18b.

Miniature Sheet

Provincial Seals — A874

No. 2388 — Seal of: a, Pattani. b, Phra
Nakhon Si Ayutthaya. c, Phang-Nga. d,
Phatthalung. e, Phayao. f, Phichit. g, Phit-
sanulok. h, Phetchaburi. i, Phetchabun. j,
Phrae.

**Litho. & Embossed With Foil
Application**

2008, Oct. 10   *Perf. 13¾*
Granite Paper

2388	A874	3b Sheet of 10, #a-j	4.50	4.50

Thailand No.
119 — A875

2008, Oct. 23 Litho.   Perf. 13½x13¼
Granite Paper

2389	A875	5b multi	.45	.40

Equestrian statue of King Chulalongkorn,
cent.

New Year
2009 — A876

Water lilies: No. 2390, 3b, Nymphaea
"Suwanna." No. 2391, 3b, Nymphaea "Tan-
khwan." No. 2392, 3b, Nymphaea "Tanpong."
No. 2393, 3b, Nymphaea "Mangala-Ubol."

2008, Nov. 15 Litho.   Perf. 14x14½
Granite Paper

2390-2393	A876	Set of 4	.70	.55
2393a		Souvenir sheet of 4,		
		#2390-2393	.95	.75

No. 2393a sold for 17b. A sheet similar to
No. 2393a, with the China 2009 World Stamp
Exhibition emblem in the sheet margin, sold
for 30b.

Miniature Sheet

Cremation of Princess Galyani
Vadhana (1933-2008) — A877

No. 2394 — Princess: a, As child. b, Wearing sash. c, Wearing cap. d, Wearing red
dress.

2008, Nov. 11   *Perf. 14x14¾*
Granite Paper

2394	A877	5b Sheet of 4, #a-d	3.00	1.75

No. 2394 exists imperf. Value, $160.

Miniature Sheet

King
Bhumibol
Adulyadej,
81st Birthday
A878

2008, Dec. 3   *Perf. 13¼*
Granite Paper

2395	A878	3b multi	.25	.25

Somdet Chao
Phraya Borom
Maha
Sisuriyawong
(1808-83),
Regent of King
Chulalongkorn
A879

2008, Dec. 23   *Perf. 14x14¾*
Granite Paper

2396	A879	3b multi	.35	.30

New Year 2009
(Year of the
Ox) — A880

2009, Jan. 2   Litho.   Perf. 14¼
Granite Paper

2397	A880	3b multi	.35	.30
a.		Perf. 13 (#2796a)	.30	.25

Issued: No. 2397a, 1/1/14.

Miniature Sheet

Children's Day — A881

No. 2398 — Characters from "Phra Abhai
Manee," poem by Phra Sunthorn Voharn: a,
Sri Suvan with pole. b, Phra Abhai Manee with
flute. c, Mermaid and fish. d, Giant woman in
water. e, Sud Sakhon falling. f, Old man with
tiger skin clothes. g, Naked man with stick. h,
King's daughter.

2009   *Perf. 14¾x14*
Granite Paper

2398	A881	3b Sheet of 8, #a-h	6.50	6.50
i.		Souvenir sheet, #2398a-2398d,		
		perf. 13¼	9.00	9.00

Issued: No. 2398, 1/10, No. 2398i, May.
Honk Kong 2009 Intl. Philatelic Exhibition (No.
2398i).

A882

A883

A884

Prince Bhanurangsi (1860-1928), Founder of Thai Postal Service — A885

2009, Jan. 11   *Perf. 14x14¾*
Granite Paper

2399	A882	3b multi	.35 .30
2400	A883	3b multi	.35 .30
2401	A884	3b multi	.35 .30
2402	A885	3b multi	.35 .30
a.		Souvenir sheet of 4, #2399-2402, perf. 13½	2.25 2.25
		Nos. 2399-2402 (4)	1.40 1.20

No. 2402a sold for 20b. No. 2402a exists imperf. Value, $27.50.

White Rose — A886

Litho. & Embossed
2009, Feb. 6   *Perf. 13*
Granite Paper

2403 A886 5b multi   .45 .40

School of Postal Services — A887

2009, Feb. 22   **Litho.**   *Perf. 14¾x14*
Granite Paper

2404 A887 3b multi   .35 .30

Red Cross A888

2009, Mar. 30   **Granite Paper**
2405 A888 3b multi   .35 .30

Prince Krom Luang Wongsa Dhiraj Snid (1808-71), Physician — A889

2009, Mar. 30   *Perf. 14x14¾*
Granite Paper
2406 A889 3b multi   .35 .30

Nos. 1736-1737 Surcharged in Gold

Methods, Perfs and Watermarks As Before

2009, Apr. 1

2407	A564	30b on 6b #1736	*22.50 11.00*
2408	A564	46b on 9b #1737	*37.50 16.00*

Prasat Ta Muean, Surin Province — A890

Prasat Ta Muean Thom, Surin Province — A891

Prasat Ta Muean Tot, Surin Province — A892

Prasat Sadok Kok Thom, Sa Kaeo Province — A893

Perf. 14¾x14
2009, Apr. 2   **Litho.**   **Unwmk.**
Granite Paper

2409	A890	3b multi	.35 .30
2410	A891	3b multi	.35 .30
2411	A892	3b multi	.35 .30
2412	A893	3b multi	.35 .30
a.		Souvenir sheet of 4, #2409-2412, perf. 13½	2.00 2.00
		Nos. 2409-2412 (4)	1.40 1.20

Royal Headgear A894

Designs: No. 2413, 5b, Gold brocade hat. No. 2414, 5b, Felt hat. No. 2415, 5b, Battle helmet. No. 2416, 5b, Grand diamond hat.

2009, Apr. 6   *Perf. 13*
Granite Paper

2413-2416	A894	Set of 4	1.75 1.75
2416a		Souvenir sheet of 4, #2413-2416	2.40 2.40

No. 2416a sold for 25b.

Visakhapuja Day — A895

2009, May 8   *Perf. 14¼x14½*
Granite Paper
2417 A895 3b multi   .35 .30

Statues of Hindu Gods — A896

Designs: No. 2418, 5b, Ganesa. No. 2419, 5b, Brahma. No. 2420, 5b, Narayana. No. 2421, 5b, Siva.

Litho. & Embossed
2009, June 2   *Perf. 13¼*
Granite Paper

2418-2421	A896	Set of 4	1.75 1.75
2421a		Souvenir sheet of 4, #2418-2421	2.40 2.40

No. 2421a sold for 25b. No. 2421a exists imperf. Value, $125.

Orchids — A897

Designs: No. 2422, 3b, Cattleya Queen Sirikhit. No. 2423, 3b, Paphiopedilum Princess Sangwan. No. 2424, 3b, Sirindhornia

---

pulchella. No. 2425, 3b, Phalaenopsis Princess Chulabhorn. No. 2426, 3b, Dendrobium "Pink Nagarindra." No. 2427, 3b, Ascocenda Sukontharat. No. 2428, 3b, Dendrobium "Soamsawali."

2009, June 5   **Litho.**   *Perf. 14½x14*
Granite Paper

2422-2428	A897	Set of 7	1.25 .95
2428a		Sheet of 7, #2422-2428, perf. 13¼	1.75 1.40

No. 2428a sold for 30b.

Diplomatic Relations Between Thailand and the Philippines, 60th Anniv. — A898

No. 2429 — Stick dancers with denomination in: a, Pale yellow. b, Light blue.

2009, June 14   **Granite Paper**
2429 A898 3b Horiz. pair, #a-b   .35 .30

Thammasat University, 75th Anniv. — A899

2009, June 27   *Perf. 14x14½*
2430 A899 3b multi   .35 .30

A900

A901

A902

Candle
Procession
Festival — A903

2009, July 6   **Perf. 14x14½**
2431 A900 3b multi   .55 .50
2432 A901 3b multi   .55 .50
2433 A902 3b multi   .55 .50
2434 A903 3b multi   .55 .50
   a.   Souvenir sheet of 4, #2431-
     2434, perf. 13¼   3.00 3.00
   Nos. 2431-2434 (4)   2.20 2.00
     No. 2434a sold for 20b.

**King Bhumibol Adulyadej Type of
1996**

Die Cut Perf. 13¼x13¾
2009, Aug. 4   **Litho.**
Self-Adhesive
2435 A550 3b bister brn & bl   .35 .30

Natl. Communications Day — A904

2009, Aug. 4   **Perf. 14½x14**
Granite Paper
2436 A904 3b multi   .35 .30

Hun Lakorn Lek Puppetry — A905

Puppets and puppeteers with: No. 2437,
25b, Orange panel at right. No. 2438, 25b,
Orange panel at left.
No. 2439, 25b, No orange panel.

**Litho. With Three-Dimensional
Plastic Affixed**
2009, Aug. 4   **Perf. 17**
Self-Adhesive
2437-2438 A905 Set of 2   5.50 5.50
Souvenir Sheet
Perf. 12¼x12
2439 A905 25b multi   5.50 5.50

Miniature Sheet

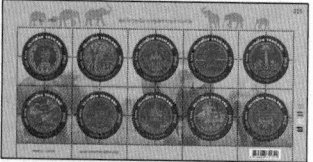

Provincial Seals — A906

No. 2440 — Seals of: a, Phuket. b, Maha
Sarakham. c, Mukdahan. d, Mae Hong Son. e,
Yasothon. f, Yala. g, Roi Et. h, Ranong. i,
Rayong. j, Ratchaburi.

**Litho. & Embossed With Foil
Application**
2009, Sept. 7   **Perf. 13**
Granite Paper
2440 A906 3b Sheet of 10, #a-j   3.25 3.25

Guan Yin
Bodhisat
A907

2009, Sept. 9 Litho.   **Perf. 14½x14¼**
Granite Paper
2441 A907 9b multi   1.00 1.00
   a.   Souvenir sheet of 1   1.60 1.60
     No. 2441a sold for 15b. No. 2441a exists
imperf. without gum. Value, $160.

Natl. Telecommunications
Commission — A908

2009, Oct. 1   **Perf. 14x14½**
Granite Paper
2442 A908 3b multi   .35 .30

Royal
Carriages
A909

Designs: No. 2443, 3b, Four-wheeled dog
cart. No. 2444, 3b, Postillion landau. No. 2445,
3b, C-spring phaeton. No. 2446, 3b, Glass
state coach.

2009, Oct. 7   **Perf. 13¼x13½**
Granite Paper
2443-2446 A909 Set of 4   1.25 1.25
2446a   Souvenir sheet of 4,
     #2443-2446   2.25 2.25
     No. 2446a sold for 20b.

A910

A911

A912

Intl. Letter Writing
Week — A913

2009, Oct. 9   **Perf. 14x14½**
Granite Paper
2447 A910 3b multi   .35 .30
2448 A911 3b multi   .35 .30
2449 A912 3b multi   .35 .30
2450 A913 3b multi   .35 .30
   a.   Souvenir sheet of 4, #2447-
     2450, perf. 13½   2.25 2.25
   Nos. 2447-2450 (4)   1.40 1.20
     No. 2450a sold for 20b.

New Year
2010 — A914

Flowers: No. 2451, 3b, Drosera peltata. No.
2452, 3b, Sonerila griffithii. No. 2453, 3b, Cya-
notis arachnoidea. No. 2454, 3b,
Caulokaempferia saxicola.

2009, Nov. 15   **Perf. 14½x14**
Granite Paper
2451-2454 A914 Set of 4   1.25 1.25
2454a   Souvenir sheet of 4,
     #2451-2454   1.60 1.60
     No. 2454a sold for 15b.

Princess
Bejaratana
Ratsuda, 84th
Birthday — A915

2009, Nov. 24   **Perf. 13¼**
Granite Paper
2455 A915 3b multi   .45 .40

Royal Thai Army Medical Department,
110th Anniv. — A916

Designs: No. 2456, 3b, Building, medic
treating soldier. No. 2457, 3b, Soldier with
rifle, knapsack and medical bag, soldiers carrying litter to medical helicopter. No. 2458, 3b,
Medic treating soldier, doctors in surgery. No.
2459, 3b, Hospital, soldier saluting.

2009, Nov. 25   **Perf. 14½x14**
Granite Paper
2456-2459 A916 Set of 4   1.25 1.25
2459a   Souvenir sheet of 4,
     #2456-2459   16.00 —

King Bhumibol Adulyadej, 82nd
Birthday — A917

2009, Dec. 5   **Perf. 14½x14**
Granite Paper
2460 A917 9b multi   1.00 1.00

Thailand Earth Observation
Satellite — A918

2009, Dec. 5   **Litho.**
Granite Paper
2461 A918 3b multi   .35 .30
A gritty substance has been applied to portions of the design.

Education for the Blind — A919

2009, Dec. 12   **Litho. & Embossed**
Granite Paper
2462 A919 3b multi   .35 .30

New Year 2010
(Year of the
Tiger) — A920

2010, Jan. 1   **Litho.**   **Perf. 13**
Granite Paper
2463 A920 3b multi   .25 .25

2010 Population and Housing
Census — A921

2010, Jan. 5   Litho.   Perf. 13½
Granite Paper

2465 A921 3b multi   .25   .25

**King Bhumibol Adulyadej Type of
1996**

2010, Jan. 8   Perf. 14x14½
Granite Paper

2465A A550 3b bister brn & bl   .25   .25

Young
Phra
Sang
A922

Chao Ngo and Nang
Rotchana — A923

Phra
Sang
A924

Phra Sang Playing Polo — A925

2010, Jan. 9   Perf. 14½x14
Granite Paper

2466 A922 3b multi   .25   .25
2467 A923 3b multi   .25   .25
2468 A924 3b multi   .25   .25
2469 A925 3b multi   .25   .25
      Nos. 2466-2469 (4)   1.00   1.00

Characters from Sang Thong. National Children's Day.

Euah
Suntornsanan
(1910-81),
Composer and
Musician — A926

2010, Jan. 21   Perf. 14x14½
Granite Paper

2470 A926 3b multi   .25   .25

Child Praying
A927

Flowers
A929

Birthday Cake
A928

Heart
A930

Moon and
Stars
A931

Balloons
A932

2010, Jan. 28   Litho.   Perf. 14x14½
Granite Paper (#2471-2476)

2471 A927 3b multi   .25   .25
2472 A928 3b multi   .25   .25
2473 A929 3b multi   .25   .25
2474 A930 3b multi   .25   .25
2475 A931 3b multi   .25   .25
2476 A932 3b multi   .25   .25
      Nos. 2471-2476 (6) 1.50   1.50

Litho. With Holographic Film
Self-Adhesive
Die Cut Perf. 13½x13¾

2477 A927 3b multi   .25   .25
2478 A928 3b multi   .25   .25
2479 A929 3b multi   .25   .25
2480 A930 3b multi   .25   .25
2481 A931 3b multi   .25   .25
2482 A932 3b multi   .25   .25
a.   Sheet of 6, #2477-2482 1.50
      Nos. 2477-2482 (6) 1.50   1.50

No. 2482a sold for 25b.

Red
Rose — A933

Litho. & Embossed
2010, Feb. 5   Perf. 13
Granite Paper

2483 A933 5b multi   .30   .25

A rose-scented scratch-and-sniff panel was applied over a rose leaf. A souvenir sheet containing one No. 2483 sold for 14b.

A934

A935

Chinese
Deities — A936

2010, Feb. 8   Litho.   Perf. 14x14½
Granite Paper

2484 A934 5b multi   .30   .25
2485 A935 5b multi   .30   .25
2486 A936 5b multi   .30   .25
a.   Souvenir sheet of 3, #2484-
      2486, perf. 13½x13¼   1.50   1.10
      Nos. 2484-2486 (3)   .90   .75

No. 2486a sold for 24b.

A937

A938

A939

Fantasy World Painting
Competition — A940

2010, Feb. 25   Litho.   Perf. 13½
Granite Paper

2487 A937 5b multi   .30   .25
2488 A938 5b multi   .30   .25
2489 A939 5b multi   .30   .25
2490 A940 5b multi   .30   .25
a.   Souvenir sheet of 4, #2487-
      2490   1.75   1.40
      Nos. 2487-2490 (4)   1.20   1.00

Bangkok 2010 Intl. Stamp Exhibition. No. 2490a sold for 28b.

Red
Cross — A941

2010, Mar. 30   Perf. 13½
Granite Paper

2491 A941 3b multi   .25   .25

Postman
Carrying
Parcel — A942

2010, Mar. 30   Perf. 13
Granite Paper

2492 A942 3b multi   .25   .25

Heritage Conservation Day — A943

Designs: No. 2493, 3b, Jalimangalasana Residence, Sanam Chandra Palace. No. 2494, 3b, Phiman Chakri Hall, Phyathai Palace. No. 2495, 3b, Phra Ram Ratchaniwet Palace. No. 2496, 3b, Main Building, Srapathum Palace.

2010, Apr. 2   Perf. 14½x14
Granite Paper

2493-2496 A943 Set of 4   .75   .55
2496a   Souvenir sheet of 4,
           #2493-2496, perf. 13½ 1.25   .95

No. 2496a sold for 19b.

King Chao
Phraya
Chakkri
(Rama I)
(1736-1809)
A944

2010, Apr. 6   Perf. 13¼
Granite Paper

2497 A944 3b multi   .25   .25

Wedding of King Bhumibol Adulyadej
and Queen Sirikit, 60th Anniv. — A945

King and Queen: No. 2498, 15b, As young couple. No. 2499, 15b, As older couple.

Litho. & Embossed With Foil Application

2010, Apr. 28			**Perf. 13¼**
2498-2499	A945	Set of 2	1.90 1.40
2499a		Souvenir sheet of 2, #2498-2499	3.75 3.00

Values for Nos. 2498-2499 are for stamps with surrounding selvage. No. 2499a sold for 60b.

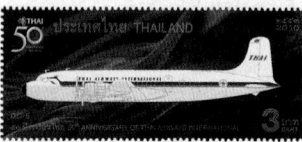

Thai Airways International, 50th Anniv. — A946

Airplanes: No. 2500, 3b, DC-6. No. 2501, 3b, DC-10. No. 2502, 3b, Boeing 747-400. No. 2503, 3b, Airbus A340-600.

Litho. & Embossed

2010, May 1			**Perf. 14¼x14½**
		Granite Paper	
2500-2503	A946	Set of 4	.75 .55
2503a		Souvenir sheet of 4, #2500-2503	1.40 1.10

No. 2503a sold for 22b.

Coronation of King Bhumibol Adulyadej, 60th Anniv. A947

2010, May 5		**Litho.**	**Perf. 13¼**
		Granite Paper	
2504	A947	9b multi	.55 .40

Visakhapuja Day — A948

2010, May 28			**Perf. 14¼x14½**
		Granite Paper	
2505	A948	3b multi	.25 .25
a.		Souvenir sheet of 4, #2293, 2361, 2417, 2505	1.25 .95

No. 2505a sold for 20b.

Tourism Authority of Thailand, 50th Anniv. — A949

Designs: No. 2506, 3b, Wat Arun, Bangkok. No. 2507, 3b, Royal barge. No. 2508, 3b, Canoeists near shore. No. 2509, 3b, Tourists on elephants fording river.

2010, June 1			**Litho.**
		Granite Paper	
2506-2509	A949	Set of 4	.75 .55

Election Commission, 12th Anniv. — A950

2010, June 9			**Perf. 13½**
		Granite Paper	
2510	A950	3b multi	.25 .25

No. 1960 Surcharged in Silver
Miniature Sheet

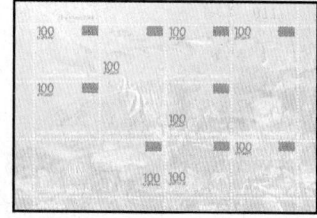

Designs as before.

Method and Perf. As Before

2010, June 16			**Granite Paper**
2511	A642	Sheet of 9	55.00 42.50
a.-f.		100b on 3b Any single	6.00 4.50
g.-i.		100b on 6b Any single	6.00 4.50

No. 1776 Surcharged in Gold

Method and Perf. As Before

2010, June 16			**Granite Paper**
2512	A577	200b on 9b #1776	12.50 9.50

Bangkok General Post Office Building, 70th Anniv. — A951

Designs: No. 2513, 3b, Sculptures of Type A15 stamp, Garuda. No. 2514, 3b, Sculptures of Type A29 stamp, man at table. 5b, General Post Office Building, horiz. (57x23mm).

		Perf. 14x14½, 14½x14	
2010, June 24			**Litho.**
		Granite Paper	
2513-2515	A951	Set of 3	.70 .55

King Nang Khlao Chao Youhua (Rama III) (1787-1851) A952

2010, July 21			**Perf. 13¼**
		Granite Paper	
2516	A952	3b multi	.25 .25

Miniature Sheet

Provincial Seals — A953

No. 2517 — Seals of: a, Lop Buri. b, Lampang. c, Lamphun. d, Loei. e, Si Sa Ket. f, Sakon Nakhon. g, Songkhla. h, Satun. i, Samut Prakan. j, Samut Songkhram.

Litho. With Foil Application

2010, July 23			**Perf. 13**
		Granite Paper	
2517	A953	3b Sheet of 10, #a-j	1.90 1.40

National Communications Day — A954

2010, Aug. 4		**Litho.**	**Perf. 14½x14**
		Granite Paper	
2518	A954	3b multi	.25 .25

Peacock A955

Inscriptions: No. 2519, 15b, Thai Silk. No. 2520, 15b, Thai Silk Blend. No. 2521, 25b, Classic Thai Silk. No. 2522, 25b, Royal Thai Silk.

Litho. With Foil Application on Affixed Silk Oval

2010, Aug. 4			**Perf. 13¼**
2519-2522	A955	Set of 4	5.00 3.75

Bangkok 2010 Intl. Stamp Exhibition. A souvenir sheet containing one No. 2522 sold for 60b.

Orchids — A956

Rhynchostylis gigantea varieties: No. 2523, 3b, Speckle. No. 2524, 3b, Kultana strain. No. 2525, 3b, Alba. No. 2526, 3b, Rubrum.

2010, Aug. 5		**Litho.**	**Perf. 14x14½**
		Granite Paper	
2523-2526	A956	Set of 4	.75 .55
2526a		Souvenir sheet of 4, #2523-2526, perf. 13½	1.25 .95

No. 2526a sold for 20b. A sheet similar to No. 2526a with the emblem of the 4th Siam Paragon Bangkok Royal Orchid Paradise sold for 80b.

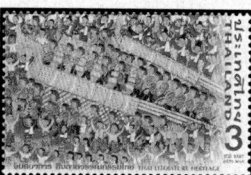

Thai Literature Heritage — A957

2010, Aug. 7			**Perf. 14½x14**
		Granite Paper	
2527	A957	3b multi	.25 .25

Flag of Thailand — A958   Cassia Flowers — A959

2010, Aug. 12			**Perf. 14¼x14½**
		Granite Paper	
2528	A958	3b multi	.25 .25
2529	A959	3b multi	.25 .25

Nos. 1687 and 1689 Surcharged

Methods, Perfs. and Watermarks As Before

2010, Aug. 27			
2530	A543	10b on 9b #1688	.65 .50
2531	A543	10b on 9b #1689	.65 .50

No. 1736 Surcharged in Gold

Method, Perf. and Watermark As Before

2010, Sept. 1			
2532	A564	10b on 6b #1736	.65 .50

Miniature Sheet

Queen Savang Vadhana (1862-1955) — A960

No. 2533: a, Queen Savang Vadhana. b, Prince Mahidol and his wife, Princess Srinagarindra. c, King Bhumibol Adulyadej and women (denomination in yellow), horiz. d, King Bhumibol Adulyadej and Queen Sirikit (denomination in dark blue), horiz.

Perf. 13¼ (#2533a),
13¼x13¼x14½x13¼ (#2533b),
14½x14

2010, Sept. 10   Litho.   Unwmk.
Granite Paper
2533 A960 3b Sheet of 4, #a-d   .80   .60

Royal Thai Mint, 150th Anniv. — A961

No. 2534: a, Coin, old Mint building, denomination at LR. b, Coin, new Mint building, denomination at LL.

Litho. & Embossed
2010, Sept. 17   Perf. 13¼
Granite Paper
2534	A961	Horiz. pair	.70 .55
a.-b.		5b Either single	.35 .25
c.		Souvenir sheet of 2, #2534a-2534b	1.40 1.10

No. 2534c sold for 20b.

National Youth Day — A962

2010, Sept. 20   Litho.   Perf. 14½x14
Granite Paper
2535 A962 3b multi   .25   .25

Tin Toys — A963

Designs: No. 2536, 3b, Wind-up rabbit and chicken. No. 2537, 3b, Chinese rattle drums. No. 2538, 3b, Pop gun. No. 2539, 3b, Boats. No. 2540, 3b, Boy on tricycle. No. 2541, 3b, Tops.

2010, Oct. 5   Perf. 13
Granite Paper
2536-2541 A963 Set of 6   1.25   .95
A souvenir sheet containing Nos. 2536-2538 and a souvenir sheet containing Nos. 2539-2541 exist. Each sold for 20b.

Curves — A964

2010, Oct. 5   Perf. 13¼
Granite Paper
2542	A964	3b green	.25 .25
2543	A964	3b lemon	.25 .25
2544	A964	3b blue	.25 .25
		Nos. 2542-2544 (3)	.75 .75

Department of Comptroller General,
120th Anniv. — A965

2010, Oct. 7   Perf. 14½x14
Granite Paper
2545 A965 3b multi   .25   .25

Goddess Guan
Yin — A966

2010, Oct. 10   Perf. 14½x14¼
Granite Paper
2546 A966 9b multi   .60   .45
a.   Souvenir sheet of 1   1.10   .85
No. 2546a sold for 15b.

King Bhumibol
Adulyadej — A967

2010   Litho.   Perf. 13½x13¼
Granite Paper
2547	A967	1b blue	.25 .25
2548	A967	2b lake	.25 .25
2549	A967	3b green	.25 .25
2550	A967	5b fawn	.35 .30
2551	A967	6b violet	.40 .30
2552	A967	7b lilac rose	.50 .35
2553	A967	9b yel bister	.60 .45
2554	A967	10b brown & blk	.70 .55
2555	A967	12b bl grn & gray bl	.80 .60
2556	A967	15b bis & dk grn	1.00 .75
a.		Souvenir sheet of 10, #2547-2556	5.25 4.25

Litho. & Engr.
2557	A967	50b pur & bl grn	3.50 2.60
2558	A967	100b apple grn & grn	6.75 5.25
2559	A967	200b rose & brn	13.50 10.00

Size:24x29mm
2560	A967	500b org brn & brn	34.00 26.00
a.		Souvenir sheet of 4, #2557-2560	60.00 45.00
		Nos. 2547-2560 (14)	62.85 47.90

Issued: Nos. 2547-2556, 2556a, 10/10; Nos. 2557-2560, 2560a, 11/11.

King
Chulalongkorn
(Rama V)
(1853-1910)
A968

2010, Oct. 15   Litho.   Perf. 13¼
Granite Paper
2561 A968 9b multi   .60   .45

Vajiravudh College, Cent. — A969

2010, Nov. 11   Perf. 13½
Granite Paper
2562 A969 3b multi   .25   .25

A970

A971

A972

Fireworks
A973

2010, Nov. 15   Perf. 13½
Granite Paper
2563	A970	3b multi	.25 .25
2564	A971	3b multi	.25 .25
2565	A972	3b multi	.25 .25
2566	A973	3b multi	.25 .25
a.		Souvenir sheet of 4, #2563-2566	1.40 1.10
		Nos. 2563-2566 (4)	1.00 1.00

No. 2566a sold for 20b.

King
Bhumibol
Adulyadej,
83rd Birthday
A974

Litho. With Rice Grain Affixed
2010, Dec. 5   Perf. 13¼
Granite Paper
2567 A974 9b multi   .60   .45

New Year 2011
(Year of the
Rabbit) — A975

2011, Jan. 1   Litho.   Perf. 13
Granite Paper
2568 A975 3b multi   .25   .25

Khun Chang — A976

Khun Phaen — A977

Kumanthong — A978

Pimpiralai — A979

2011, Jan. 8   Perf. 13¼
Granite Paper
2569	A976	3b multi	.25 .25
2570	A977	3b multi	.25 .25
2571	A978	3b multi	.25 .25
2572	A979	3b multi	.25 .25
		Nos. 2569-2572 (4)	1.00 1.00

Khun Chang Khun Phaen, epic poem.

Fruits and
Vegetables
A980

Designs: No. 2573, 3b, Bottle gourd. No. 2574, 3b, Lime. No. 2575, 3b, Tomato. No. 2576, 3b, Pumpkin.

2011, Jan. 15   Perf. 13½
Granite Paper
2573-2576 A980 Set of 4   .80   .60

Li Tie
Guai — A981

Han Zhong
Li — A982

Lu Dong
Bin — A983

Zhang Guo
Lao — A984

Lan Cai
He — A985

He Xian
Gu — A986

Han Xiang
Zi — A987

Cao Guo
Jiu — A988

2011, Feb. 1   Litho. & Embossed
Granite Paper

2577	A981	3b multi	.25 .25
2578	A982	3b multi	.25 .25
2579	A983	3b multi	.25 .25
2580	A984	3b multi	.25 .25
2581	A985	3b multi	.25 .25
2582	A986	3b multi	.25 .25
2583	A987	3b multi	.25 .25
2584	A988	3b multi	.25 .25
a.		Souvenir sheet of 8, #2577-2584	2.60 2.00

Nos. 2577-2584 (8)   2.00 2.00

Eight Chinese Immortals.

No. 1820
Surcharged in Gold

No. 1737 Surcharged in Gold

No. 2349
Surcharged

Methods, Perfs and Papers As Before

2011

2585	A550	12b on 9b #1820	.80 .60
2586	A564	50b on 9b #1737	3.25 2.50
2588	A841	Sheet of 12	39.00 39.00
a.-l.		50b on 9b Any single, #2349a-2349l	3.25 2.50

Issued: Nos. 2585, 2586, 2588, 2/2.

Charoen Krung
Road, 150th
Anniv. — A989

2011, Feb. 5   Litho.   Perf. 14½x14¼
Granite Paper

2589 A989 3b multi   .25 .25

Love — A990

No. 2590 — Heart of: a, Roses. b, Concentric lines.

2011, Feb. 7   Perf. 13
Granite Paper

2590 A990 5b Horiz. pair, #a-b   .65 .50

Suankularb Long Building, Bangkok,
Cent. — A991

2011, Mar. 8   Perf. 14½x14
Granite Paper

2591 A991 3b multi   .25 .25

Fine Arts
Department,
Cent. — A992

2011, Mar. 27   Perf. 14x14½
Granite Paper

2592 A992 3b multi   .25 .25

Princess Maha
Chakri Sirindhorn
Wearing Red
Cross
Uniform — A993

2011, Mar. 30   Perf. 13¼
Granite Paper

2593 A993 3b multi   .25 .25

A994

A995

A996

Muang Tam Religious Sanctuary,
Prakhon Chai — A997

2011, Apr. 2   Perf. 14½x14
Granite Paper

2594	A994	3b multi	.25 .25
2595	A995	3b multi	.25 .25
2596	A996	3b multi	.25 .25
2597	A997	3b multi	.25 .25
a.		Souvenir sheet of 4, #2594-2597	1.40 1.10

Nos. 2594-2597 (4)   1.00 1.00

Thai Heritage Conservation Day. No. 2597a
sold for 20b.

Momrajawongse
Kukrit Pramoj
(1911-95), Prime
Minister — A998

Kukrit Pramoj: No. 2598, 3b, Wearing uniform with sash, yellow orange panel at right.
No. 2599, 3b, Wearing traditional costume, olive green panel at right. No. 2600, 3b, With dogs, brown panel at right, horiz. No. 2601, 3b, With Mao Zedong, gray panel at right, horiz.

2011, Apr. 20   Perf. 13¼
Granite Paper

2598-2601 A998 Set of 4   .80 .60

Diplomatic Relations Between
Thailand and Laos, 60th
Anniv. — A999

No. 2602: a, Woman, denomination at LR.
b, Woman, denomination at LL. c, Cassia fistula flowers, denomination at LR. d, Plumeria flowers, denomination at LL.

2011, Apr. 22   Perf. 14x14½
Granite Paper

2602 A999 3b Block of 4, #a-d   .80 .60

See Laos Nos. 1836-1839.

Postman With
Fork, Spoon and
Foods — A1000

2011, May 10   Litho.   Perf. 13
Granite Paper

2603 A1000 3b multi   .25 .25

Self-Adhesive
Serpentine Die Cut 12

2604 A1000 3b multi   .25 .25

Pridi Banomyong (1900-83), Prime
Minister — A1001

No. 2605 — Banomyong: a, In suit and tie.
b, Wearing uniform and sash.

2011, May 11   Perf. 13¼
Granite Paper

2605 A1001 3b Horiz. pair, #a-b   .40 .30

Panyananda Bhikkhu (1911-2007),
Buddhist Monk — A1002

Bhikkhu and: No. 2606, 3b, Thai text. No.
2607, 3b, Buddhist temple. No. 2608, 3b,
Sculpture. No. 2609, 3b, Shell-shaped award.

2011, May 11   Perf. 13¼
Granite Paper

2606-2609 A1002   Set of 4   .80   .60

Visakhapuja
Day — A1003

2011, May 17   Perf. 14½x14¼
Granite Paper

2610 A1003 3b multi   .25   .25

A souvenir sheet containing one example of
No. 2610 sold for 10b.

Orchid Varieties
A1004

Designs: No. 2611, 3b, Dendrobium
"Cherluk Red." No. 2612, 3b, Dendrobium "Lai
Sirin." No. 2613, 3b, Dendrobium "Suree
Peach." No. 2614, 3b, Dendrobium "Cheetah."

2011, June 2   Perf. 14x14½
Granite Paper

2611-2614 A1004   Set of 4   .80   .60
2614a   Souvenir sheet of 4,
          #2611-2614, perf. 13½   1.40 1.10

No. 2614a sold for 20b. A sheet similar to
No. 2614a, but with the emblem of the 5th
Siam Paragon Bangkok Royal Orchid Paradise
and the date of the show, sold for 100b.

Department of Science Service, 120th
Anniv. — A1005

2011, June 23   Perf. 14½x14
Granite Paper

2615 A1005 3b multi   .25   .25

No. 2615 was printed in sheets of 20 with
stamps from the right column having purple
engine turning lines in the background.

Scouting in Thailand, Cent. — A1006

2011, July 1   Perf. 13¼
Granite Paper

2616 A1006 3b multi   .25   .25

A1007

Diplomatic Relations Between
Thailand and Portugal, 500th
Anniv. — A1008

No. 2617: a, Portuguese caravel, rowboats,
Thai buildings and temples. b, Elephant and
riders at dockside.
No. 2618: a, Portuguese caravel, Thai buildings. b, Thai boats and buildings.

2011, July 20   Perf. 13½
Granite Paper

2617 A1007 3b Horiz. pair, #a-b   .40   .30
2618 A1008 3b Horiz. pair, #a-b   .40   .30

See Portugal Nos. 3334-3335.

Miniature Sheet

Provincial Seals — A1009

No. 2619 — Seals of: a, Samut Sakhon. b,
Sa Kaeo. c, Saraburi. d, Sing Buri. e,
Sukhothai. f, Suphan Buri. g, Surat Thani. h,
Surin. i, Nong Khai. j, Nong Bua Lam Phu.

**Litho. & Embossed With Foil
Application**
2011, July 20   Perf. 13½
Granite Paper

2619 A1009 3b Sheet of 10, #a-j   2.00 1.50

Sheets of ten identical stamps were available, but these appear to have been sold locally and not through the philatelic bureau.

Thai Alphabet
A1010

No. 2620 — Various characters of Thai
alphabet that are the first consonants of the
word for: a, Chicken. b, Eggs. c, Bottles. d,
Water buffalo. e, Person wearing red shirt. f,
Bell. g, Snake. h, Plates. i, Cymbals on string.
j, Elephant. k, Chain on stump. l, Trees. m,
Woman weaing pink blouse. n, Headdress. o,
Javelin. p, Pedestal. q, Mandodari (girl wearing headdress). r, Old man. s, Child wearing
Buddhist monk's robe. t, Child in overalls. u,
Turtle. v, Bags. w, Soldier. x, Flag.
No. 2621 — Various characters of Thai
alphabet that are the first consonants of the
word for: a, Mouse. b, Leaves. c, Fish. d, Bee
on flowers. e, Lids of pots. f, Bowl. g, Teeth. h,
Sailboat. i, Horse. j, Yaksha (Buddhist giant).
k, Boat. l, Monkey. m, Ring. n, Pavilion. o,

Hermit in cave. p, Tiger. q, Chest. r, Kite. s,
Basin with flower. t, Owl.

2011, July 29   Litho.   Perf. 14¼
Granite Paper

2620   Sheet of 24   6.00 6.00
  a.-x. A1010 1b Any single   .25   .25
2621   Sheet of 20 + 4 labels 5.00 5.00
  a.-t. A1010 1b Any single   .25   .25

Communications
Day — A1011

2011, Aug. 4   Perf. 14x14½
Granite Paper

2622 A1011 3b multi   .25   .25

A1012

A1013

A1014

Likay Performers
A1015

Litho. With Glitter Affixed
2011, Aug. 4   Perf. 14x14½
Granite Paper

2623 A1012 5b multi   .35   .30
2624 A1013 5b multi   .35   .30
2625 A1014 5b multi   .35   .30
2626 A1015 5b multi   .35   .30
  a.   Souvenir sheet of 4, #2623-
          2626, perf. 13½   2.00 1.50
  Nos. 2623-2626 (4)   1.40 1.20

Thaipex 2011 Intl. Philatelic Exhibition,
Bangkok. No. 2626a sold for 30b.

Philatelists Association of
Thailand — A1016

2011, Aug. 9   Litho.   Perf. 13¼
Granite Paper

2627 A1016 3b multi   .25   .25

Miniature Sheet

Queen Savang Vadhana (1862-
1955) — A1017

No. 2628 — Queen Savang Vadhana: a, As
child, with King Chulalongkorn (pink back-
ground). b, With Crown Prince Maha
Vajirunhis (olive green background). c, With
Prince Mahitala Dhibesra Adulyadej Vikrom
and Princess Valaya Alongkorn (blue violet
background), horiz. d, With King Ananda
Mahidol, King Bhumibol Adulyadej, Princess
Galyani Vadhana, and Prince Rangsit
Prayurasakdi (blue green background), horiz.

2011, Sept. 10   Perf. 13¼
Granite Paper

2628 A1017 3b Sheet of 4, #a-d   .80   .60

Worldwide Fund for Nature
(WWF) — A1018

Cats: No. 2629, 3b, Marbled cat. No. 2630,
3b, Asiatic golden cat. No. 2631, 3b, Leopard
cat. No. 2632, 3b, Flat-headed cat.

2011, Sept. 26   Perf. 13
Granite Paper

2629-2632 A1018   Set of 4   .80   .60
2632a   Souvenir sheet of 4, #2629-
          2632, + label   1.40 1.10

No. 2632a sold for 20b.

International
Letter Writing
Week — A1019

Designs: No. 2633, 3b, Girl and boy writing
letters. No. 2634, 3b, Girl bringing letter to mail
box. No. 2635, 3b, Postman delivering letter to
girl. No. 2636, 3b, Boy and girl reading letters.

2011, Oct. 4 — Granite Paper

2633-2636	A1019	Set of 4	.80	.60
2636a		Souvenir sheet of 4, #2633-2636	1.40	1.10

No. 2636a sold for 20b.

King Bhumibol Adulyadej in Carpentry Shop — A1020

2011, Oct. 21 — Perf. 13¼
Granite Paper

2637	A1020	3b multi	.25	.25

Cabinet declaration of King Bhumibol Adulyadej as "Father of the Thai Workmanship Standard."

Princess Mother Srinigarindra (1900-95) A1021

2011, Oct. 21 — Litho.
Granite Paper

2638	A1021	3b multi	.25	.25

Children's Projects of Princess Maha Chakri Sirindhorn, 30th Anniv. A1022

2011, Oct. 21 — Perf. 13¼
Granite Paper

2639	A1022	3b multi	.25	.25

Lotus Flower — A1023

2011, Nov. 7 — Perf. 13
Granite Paper

2640	A1023	3b multi	.25	.25

Festivals — A1024

Designs: No. 2641, 3b, Loy Krathong and Candle Festival, Sukhothai. No. 2642, 3b, Festival of Illuminated Boat Procession, Nakhon Phanom. No. 2643, 3b, Yi-Peng Festival, Chiang Mai. No. 2644, 3b, Loi Krathong Sai Festival, Tak.

2011, Nov. 10 — Perf. 13¼
Granite Paper

2641-2644	A1024	Set of 4	.80	.60
2644a		Souvenir sheet of 4, #2641-2644	1.50	1.10

No. 2644a sold for 22b.

Medallions of Monks — A1025

Designs: No. 2645, 9b, Luang Pho Klan, Wat Phrayathkaram. No. 2646, 9b, Luang Pu lam, Wat Nang Ratchaworawihan. No. 2647, 9b, Luang Pu Suk, Wat Pak Khlong Makham Thao. No. 2648, 9b, Luang Pho Khong, Wat Bang Kaphom. No. 2649, 9b, Luang Pho Chui, Wat Khongkharam.

Litho. & Embossed
2011, Nov. 11 — Perf. 13¼
Granite Paper

2645-2649	A1025	Set of 5	3.00	2.25
2649a		Souvenir sheet of 5, #2645-2649	4.00	3.00

No. 2649a sold for 60b.

A1026

A1027

A1028

Fireworks A1029

Stamps With White Frames
Litho. With Glitter Affixed
2011, Nov. 15 — Granite Paper

2650	A1026	3b multi	.25	.25
2651	A1027	3b multi	.25	.25
2652	A1028	3b multi	.25	.25
2653	A1029	3b multi	.25	.25
		Nos. 2650-2653 (4)	1.00	1.00

Souvenir Sheet
Stamps Without White Frames

2654		Sheet of 4	1.50	1.10
a.	A1026	3b multi	.35	.25
b.	A1027	3b multi	.35	.25
c.	A1028	3b multi	.35	.25
d.	A1029	3b multi	.35	.25

No. 2654 sold for 22b.

A1030

A1031

A1032

A1033

A1034

A1035

A1036

Coins Depicting King Bhumibol Adulyadej — A1037

Awards of King Bhumibol Adulyadej — A1038

No. 2663: a, Agricola Medal inscribed: "Golden Jubilee of His Majesty's Reign". b, World Health Organization Award (plate on stand). c, Human Development Lifetime Achievement Award (silver bowl on stand). d, International Rice Award (medallion dated 1996). e, Award inscribed "Glory to the Greatest Inventor." f, WIPO Global Leader Award. g, Brussels Eureka medal.

Litho. & Embossed With Foil Application
2011, Dec. 5 — Perf. 12¼
Granite Paper

2655	A1030	5b multi	.35	.25
2656	A1031	5b multi, inscribed "7 Cycle"	.35	.25
a.		Inscribed "7th Cycle"	.65	.50
2657	A1032	5b multi	.35	.25
2658	A1033	5b multi	.35	.25
2659	A1034	5b multi	.35	.25
2660	A1035	5b multi	.35	.25
2661	A1036	5b multi	.35	.25
a.		Sheet of 7, #2655, 2656a, 2657-2661	4.75	3.50
2662	A1037	100b multi	6.50	5.00
		Nos. 2655-2662 (8)	8.95	6.75

Miniature Sheet

2663	A1038	5b Sheet of 7, #a-g	2.40	1.75

King Bhumibol Adulyadej, 84th birthday. No. 2661a sold for 70b.

Diplomatic Relations Between Thailand and Pakistan, 60th Anniv. A1039

2011, Dec. 13 Litho. *Perf. 13¼*
Granite Paper
2664 A1039 3b multi .25 .25

New Year 2012 (Year of the Dragon) A1040

2012, Jan. 1 *Perf. 13*
Granite Paper
2665 A1040 3b multi .25 .25

Prince Mahidol Adulyadej (1892-1929), Father of King Bhumibol Adulyadej A1041

2012, Jan. 1 *Perf. 13¼*
Granite Paper
2666 A1041 3b multi .25 .25

A1042

A1043

A1044

Children's Day — A1045

2012, Jan. 14 *Perf. 14½x14*
Granite Paper
2667 A1042 3b multi .25 .25
2668 A1043 3b multi .25 .25
2669 A1044 3b multi .25 .25
2670 A1045 3b multi .25 .25
Nos. 2667-2670 (4) 1.00 1.00

King Bhumibol Adulyadej and Map — A1046

2012, Jan. 16 *Perf. 13¼*
Granite Paper
2671 A1046 3b multi .25 .25

Caishenye, God of Wealth — A1047

Various depictions with background color of: No. 2672, 3b, Red. No. 2673, 3b, Olive green.

2012, Jan. 23 Litho.
Granite Paper
2672-2673 A1047 Set of 2 .40 .30
A souvenir sheet containing Nos. 2672-2673 sold for 15b.

Chiang Rai, 750th Anniv. — A1048

2012, Jan. 26 *Perf. 14x14½*
Granite Paper
2674 A1048 3b multi .25 .25

Love — A1049

No. 2675, 5b: a, Heart as padlock. b, Heart on key.
No. 2676, 5b: a, Teddy bear with padlock heart. b, Teddy bear with key.

2012, Feb. 7 *Perf. 13*
Granite Paper
Horiz. Pairs, #a-b
2675-2676 A1049 Set of 2 1.40 1.10

Excise Department, 80th Anniv. — A1050

2012, Feb. 17 *Perf. 13¼*
Granite Paper
2677 A1050 3b multi .25 .25

Red Cross — A1051

2012, Mar. 30 *Perf. 14x14½*
Granite Paper
2678 A1051 3b multi .25 .25

Asian-Pacific Postal Union, 50th Anniv. — A1052

2012, Apr. 1 *Perf. 14½x14*
Granite Paper
2679 A1052 3b multi .25 .25

King Vajiravudh (1881-1925) and Bank Building — A1053

King Prajadhipok (1893-1941) and Bank Building — A1054

King Ananda Mahidol (1925-46) and Bank Building — A1055

King Bhumibol Adulyadej and Bank Building — A1056

2012, Apr. 1 *Perf. 14x14½*
Granite Paper
2680 A1053 3b multi .25 .25
2681 A1054 3b multi .25 .25
2682 A1055 3b multi .25 .25
2683 A1056 3b multi .25 .25
Nos. 2680-2683 (4) 1.00 1.00
Government Savings Bank, 99th anniv.

Ministry of Transport, Cent. — A1057

Designs: No. 2684, 3b, Aerial view of highway. No. 2685, 3b, Bridge and train. No. 2686, 3b, Ship. No. 2687, 3b, Airplane and airport.

2012, Apr. 1 Litho.
Granite Paper
2684-2687 A1057 Set of 4 .80 .60

Cultural Preservation — A1058

No. 2688, 3b: a, Monument No. 1, Muang Sing Historical Park. b, Radiating Bodhisattva Avalokitesavara, Muang Sing Historical Park.
No. 2689, 3b: a, Prang Si Thep, Si Thep Historical Park. b, Stone Dharmachakra, Si Thep Historical Park.

2012, Apr. 2 *Perf. 13¼*
Granite Paper
Horiz. Pairs, #a-b
2688-2689 A1058 Set of 2 .80 .60
2689c Souvenir sheet of 4, #2688a-2688b, 2689a-2689b 1.40 1.10
No. 2689c sold for 20b.

Miniature Sheets

Royal Thai Air Force, Cent. — A1059

No. 2690, 3b: a, Nieuport IIN. b, Breguet III. c, Biplane (Thai inscriptions). d, Ki-30. e, F8F-1. f, F-84G. g, F-86F. h, F-5A.
No. 2691, 3b: a, F-5B. b, F-5E. c, F-16 ADF. d, Gripen C. e, Avro. f, Boeing 737-800. g, Bell 412EP helicopter. h, S-92A helicopter.

2012 **Sheets of 8, #a-h** **Litho.**
Granite Paper
2690-2691 A1059 Set of 2 3.00 2.25
Issued: No. 2690, 4/9; No. 2691, 7/2.

Buddha
Statues
A1060

Designs: No. 2692, 5b, Phra Phutthasothon, Wat Sothonwararam Worawihan (olive brown inscriptions). No. 2693, 5b, Luang Pho To, Wat Bang Phli Yai Nai (dark blue inscriptions). No. 2694, 5b, Luang Pho Wat Rai Khing, Wat Rai Khing (red brown inscriptions). No. 2695, 5b, Luang Pho Wat Ban Laem, Wat Phetchasamut Worawihan (green inscriptions). No. 2696, 5b, Luang Pho Wat Khao Ta-Khrao, Wat Khao Ta-Khrao (purple inscriptions).

2012, May 5 **Perf. 13¼**
Granite Paper
2692-2696 A1060 Set of 5 1.60 1.25
2696a Souvenir sheet of 5, #2692-2696 2.60 2.00
No. 2696a sold for 40b.

2012 Rotary International Convention, Bangkok A1061

2012, May 6 **Perf. 14x14½**
Granite Paper
2697 A1061 3b multi .25 .25

Vesak Day — A1062

2012, June 2 **Perf. 13¼**
Granite Paper
2698 A1062 3b multi .25 .25

Miniature Sheet

Provincial Seals — A1063

No. 2699 — Seals of: a, Ang Thong. b, Udon Thani. c, Uttaradit. d, Uthai Thani. e, Ubon Ratchathani. f, Amnat Charoen. g, Chang Thai. h, Ratchaphruek. i, Sala Thai. j, Bueng Kan.

Litho. & Embossed With Foil Application
2012, June 28 **Granite Paper**
2699 A1063 3b Sheet of 10, #a-j 1.90 1.40
Sheets of ten identical stamps were available, but these appear to have been sold locally and not through the philatelic bureau.

Office of the Prime Minister, 80th Anniv. — A1064

2012, June 28 **Litho.** **Perf. 14½x14**
Granite Paper
2700 A1064 3b multi .25 .25

Miniature Sheet

Coastlines — A1065

No. 2701: a, Phromthep Cape, Phuket, denomination at LR. b, Phromthep Cape, denomination at UR. c, Muko Ang Thong National Park, Surat Thani, denomination at LR. d, Muko Ang Thong National Park, denomination at UR. e, Rai Le Bay, Krabi, denomination at LR. f, Rai Le Bay, denomination at UR. g, Hong Island, Krabi, denomination at LR. h, Hong Island, denomination at UR. i, Panyi Island, Phang-nga, denomination at LR. j, Panyi Island, denomination at UR.

2012, July 5 **Perf. 14¼x14½**
Granite Paper
2701 A1065 15b Sheet of 10, #a-j 9.50 7.25

Ranong, 150th Anniv. — A1066

2012, July 21 **Perf. 14½x14**
Granite Paper
2702 A1066 3b multi .25 .25

Prince Maha Vajiralongkorn, 60th Birthday — A1067

Litho. With Foil Application
2012, July 28 **Perf. 13¼**
Granite Paper
2703 A1067 9b multi .60 .45

National Communications Day — A1068

2012, Aug. 4 **Litho.** **Perf. 14½x14**
Granite Paper
2704 A1068 3b multi .25 .25

Miniature Sheet

Queen Sirikit, 80th Birthday — A1069

No. 2705 — Queen Sirikit: a, 5b, As child, with ribbon in hair. b, 5b, As young girl, wearing white dress and necklace. c, 5b, As young woman, with necklace. d, 5b, As young woman, with hair decoration. e, 5b, With bare shoulder showing, color photograph. f, 5b, With bird decoration on shoulder. g, 5b, Wearing red dress. h, 5b, Wearing blue earring. i, 40b, Profile.

Litho., Litho. & Embossed With Foil Application (#2705i)
2012, Aug. 12 **Perf. 13**
Granite Paper
2705 A1069 Sheet of 9, #a-i 5.25 4.00
j. Souvenir sheet of 4, #2705a-2705d 2.10 1.60
k. Souvenir sheet of 4, #2705e-2705h 2.10 1.60
Nos. 2705j and 2705k each sold for 33b.

Miniature Sheet

Queen Savang Vadhana (1862-1955) — A1070

No. 2706 — Queen Savang Vadhana: a, As child (brown background). b, As young woman (green background). c, As woman (gray background). d, As older woman (blue background).

2012, Sept. 10 **Litho.** **Perf. 13¼**
Granite Paper
2706 A1070 3b Sheet of 4, #a-d .80 .60

Thailand 2013 World Stamp Exhibition — A1071

No. 2707: a, Lanna-style lantern. b, Paper umbrellas. c, Bung Fai rocket. d, Reed mouth organ, circular panpipes. e, Courtier dolls. f, Pottery. g, Kolek boat. h, Wooden bird cage.

2012, Oct. 3 **Granite Paper**
2707 A1071 Block of 8 2.80 2.00
a.-h. 5b Any single .35 .25
i. Souvenir sheet of 2, #2702a-2702b 1.00 .75
j. Souvenir sheet of 2, #2702c-2702d 1.00 .75
k. Souvenir sheet of 2, #2702e-2702f 1.00 .75
l. Souvenir sheet of 2, #2702g-2702h 1.00 .75
Nos. 2707i-2707l each sold for 15b.

Somdet Phra Nyanasamvara, Supreme Buddhist Patriarch of Thailand, 99th Birthday — A1072

2012, Oct. 3 **Perf. 13¼**
Granite Paper
2708 A1072 5b multi .35 .25
A souvenir sheet containing one of No. 2708 sold for 15b.

International Letter Writing Week — A1073

Designs: No. 2709, 3b, Girl bowing to grandparents, girl writing letter (denomination in red at LL). No. 2710, 3b, Girl and mother on parke bench, girl writing letter (denomination in dark blue at LR). No. 2711, 3b, Girl and boy, girl writing letter (denomination in red at LR). No. 2712, 3b, Classmates, girl writing letter (denomination in blue at LL).

2012, Oct. 8 **Litho.**
Granite Paper
2709-2712 A1073 Set of 4 .80 .60
2712a Souvenir sheet of 4, #2709-2712 1.40 1.10
No. 2712a sold for 20b.

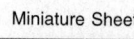

Prince Nares Varariddhi (1855-1925) — A1074

2012, Oct. 14   *Perf. 13¼*
Granite Paper
2713 A1074 3b multi   .25   .25

Souvenir Sheet

Visit of King Chulalongkorn to Austria, 115th Anniv. — A1075

No. 2714: a, 5b, King Chulalongkorn. b, 15b, Emperor Franz Josef of Austria.

2012, Nov. 10   **Litho.**
Granite Paper
2714 A1075   Sheet of 2, #a-b   1.40 1.10
     See Austria No. 2409.

Fireworks
A1076

Various fireworks with background color of: No. 2715, 3b, Violet blue. No. 2716, 3b, Green. No. 2717, 3b, Red. No. 2718, 3b, Light blue.

Litho. With Glitter Affixed
2012, Nov. 15   **Granite Paper**
2715-2718 A1076   Set of 4   .80   .60
2718a   Souvenir sheet of 4,   1.60 1.25
      #2715-2718
     No. 2718a sold for 24r.

Princess
Chulabhorn
A1077

Litho. With Foil Application
2012, Dec. 1   **Granite Paper**
2719 A1077 5b multi   .35   .25

Prince Damrong Rajanubhab (1862-1943) and Military Parade — A1078

Prince Damrong Rajanubhab and Luk Khun Hall — A1079

Prince Damrong Rajanubhab and Books Written by Him — A1080

Prince Damrong Rajanubhab and Woradis Palace — A1081

2012, Dec. 1   **Litho.**
Granite Paper
2720 A1078 3b multi   .25   .25
2721 A1079 3b multi   .25   .25
2722 A1080 3b multi   .25   .25
2723 A1081 3b multi   .25   .25
a.   Souvenir sheet of 4, #2720-   1.40 1.10
      2723
    Nos. 2720-2723 (4)   1.00 1.00

King
Bhumibol
Adulyadej,
85th Birthday
A1082

Litho. with Foil Application
2012, Dec. 5   **Granite Paper**
2724 A1082 9b multi   .60   .45

Princess Bajrakitiyabha, Chairperson of the United Nations Commission on Crime Prevention and Criminal Justice — A1083

2012, Dec. 7   *Perf. 13¼*
Granite Paper
2725 A1083 5b multi   .35   .25

New Year 2013
(Year of the
Snake) — A1084

2013, Jan. 1   **Litho.**   *Perf. 13*
Granite Paper
2726 A1084 3b multi   .25   .25

Children's Day — A1085

2013, Jan. 12   *Perf. 13*
Granite Paper
2727 A1085 5b multi   .35   .25

Tai Sui
God — A1086

Tai Sui God with background color of: No. 2728, 5b, Red. No. 2729, 5b, Blue. No. 2730, 5b, Green.

Litho. With Foil Application
2013, Feb. 7   **Granite Paper**
2728-2730 A1086   Set of 3   1.00   .75
2730a   Souvenir sheet of 3,   2.00 1.50
      #2728-2730
     No. 2730a sold for 30b.

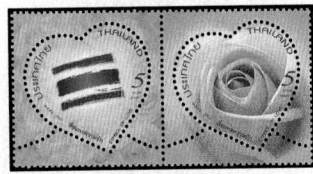

Love — A1087

No. 2731: a, Flag of Thailand. b, Pink rose.

2013, Feb. 7   **Litho.**
2731 A1087 5b Horiz. pair, #a-b   .70   .55

Miniature Sheet

Thailand 2013 World Stamp Exhibition, Bangkok — A1088

No. 2732: a, Gilded black lacquer cabinet (lai rot nam technique). b, Plaster dragon. c, Khon mask. d, Vessel with mother-of-pearl inlay. e, Figurine of elephant (metal beating). f, Molded sculpture of mythical being. g, Carved wood Buddha. h, Figurine with mirrored-glass inlay.

2013, Mar. 22   **Litho.**   *Perf. 13*
Granite Paper
2732 A1088 5b Sheet of 8, #a-h   2.75 2.10
i.   Souvenir sheet of 2, #2732a-   1.25   .95
      2732b
j.   Souvenir sheet of 2, #2732c-   1.25   .95
      2732d
k.   Souvenir sheet of 2, #2732e-   1.25   .95
      2732f
l.   Souvenir sheet of 2, #2732g-   1.25   .95
      2732h
    Nos. 2732i-2732l each sold for 18b.

King
Chulalongkorn
and Queen
Srisavarindira
A1089

2013, Mar. 29   **Litho.**   *Perf. 13¼*
Granite Paper
2733 A1089 3b multi   .25   .25
    Thai Red Cross, 120th anniv.

First Government Savings Bank, 1913 — A1090

Government Savings Bank, 1934 — A1091

Government Savings Bank, 1950 — A1092

Government Savings Bank, 1966 — A1093

2013, Apr. 1   *Perf. 14¾x14*
Granite Paper
2734 A1090 3b multi   .25   .25
2735 A1091 3b multi   .25   .25
2736 A1092 3b multi   .25   .25
2737 A1093 3b multi   .25   .25
    Nos. 2734-2737 (4)   1.00 1.00
    Government Savings Bank, cent.

Heritage Conservation Day — A1094

No. 2738 — Theatrical masks: a, Phra Shiva. b, Phra Vishnu. c, Phra Brahma. d, Phra Parakontap. e, Phra Panjasikorn. f, Phra kanes. g, Phra Vishnukam. h, Phra Indra.

2013, Apr. 2   **Perf. 13¼**

Granite Paper

2738   A1094   3b   Block of 8, #a-h   1.75   1.40

A souvenir sheet containing Nos. 2738a-2738c sold for 20b.

Bangkok, 2013 World Book Capital — A1095

2013, Apr. 23   **Perf. 14x13¼**

2739   A1095   5b multi   .35   .25

A souvenir sheet containing No. 2739 sold for 20b.

Vesak Day — A1096

2013, May 24   Litho.   Perf. 14¼x14½

Granite Paper

2740   A1096   3b multi   .25   .25

Thai Engineering, Cent. — A1097

Designs: No. 2741, 5b, Electrical engineering (workers and generators, gear at left). No. 2742, 5b, Civil engineering (workers and bridge, gear at left). No. 2743, 5b, Mechanical engineering (workers and machine, gear at right).

Litho. & Embossed

2013, June 1   **Perf. 13½x13¾**

2741-2743   A1097   Set of 3   1.00   .75

Royal Irrigation Department, 111th Anniv. — A1098

2013, June 13   Litho.   Perf. 13¼

Granite Paper

2744   A1098   3b multi   .25   .25

Owls — A1099

Designs: No. 2745, 5b, Bubo sumatranus. No. 2746, 5b, Tyto alba. No. 2747, 5b, Otus lettia. No. 2748, 5b, Glaucidium brodiei.

2013, July 29   Litho.   Perf. 14x14½

Granite Paper

2745-2748   A1099   Set of 4   1.25   .95
2748a   Souvenir sheet of 4,
       #2745-2748, perf. 13¼   2.25   1.75

No. 2748a sold for 35b.

Phra Si Sakkaya Thotsaphonlayan Phrathan Phutthamonthon Suthat Statue, by Silpa Bhirasri — A1100

Fishing Village, by Damrong Wong-Uparas — A1101

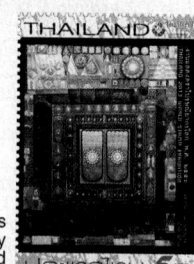

Lord Buddha's Footprint, by Pichai Nirand A1102

Leela, by Sawat Tantisuk — A1103

Phra Mahathat Chalermaj Sattha, by Wanida Phuensuntom A1104

Full Moon, by Manit Poo-aree — A1105

White Ubosot of Wat Rong Khun, by Chalermchai Kositpipat A1106

Bull, by Thawan Duchanee — A1107

2013, Aug. 2   Litho.   Perf. 13¼

Granite Paper

2749   Sheet of 8 + 4 labels   2.80   2.00
  a.   A1100 5b multi   .35   .25
  b.   A1101 5b multi   .35   .25
  c.   A1102 5b multi   .35   .25
  d.   A1103 5b multi   .35   .25
  e.   A1104 5b multi   .35   .25
  f.   A1105 5b multi   .35   .25
  g.   A1106 5b multi   .35   .25
  h.   A1107 5b multi   .35   .25
  i.   Souvenir sheet of 2, #2749a-2749b   1.40   1.40
  j.   Souvenir sheet of 2, #2749c-2749d   1.40   1.40
  k.   Souvenir sheet of 2, #2749e-2749f   1.40   1.40
  l.   Souvenir sheet of 2, #2749g-2749h   1.40   1.40

Thailand 2013 World Stamp Exhibition, Bangkok. Nos. 2749i-2749l each sold for 20b.

National Communications Day — A1108

Die Cut Perf. 11x10

2013, Aug. 4   **Litho.**

Self-Adhesive

2750   A1108   9b multi   .60   .45

A lottery code number appears under the scratch-off panel on the stamp. Values for unused stamps are for stamps with unscratched panel.

Thailand No. 1 Under Magnifying Glass A1109

2013, Aug. 4   Litho.   Perf. 13¼

Granite Paper

2751   A1109   5b multi   .35   .25

Thai postal services, 130th anniv.

Bangkok General Post Office Building — A1110

Designs: No. 2753, Plaster renditions of Thailand Nos. 1 and 75. No. 2754, Garuda emblem from Post Office door.

2013, Aug. 4   Litho.   Perf. 14½x14

Granite Paper

2752   A1110   5b shown   .35   .25

Litho. & Embossed

2753   A1110   5b multi   .35   .25

Litho. & Embossed With Foil Application

2754   A1110   5b multi   .35   .25
     Nos. 2752-2754 (3)   1.05   .75

A souvenir sheet with one perf. 13¼ example of No. 2754 sold for 16b.

A1111

A1112

A1113

A1114

A1115

Queen
Sirikit — A1116

2013, Aug. 12 Litho. *Perf. 14x14½*
Granite Paper

2755	Miniature sheet of 6	1.50	1.10
a.	A1111 3b multi	.25	.25
b.	A1112 3b multi	.25	.25
c.	A1113 3b multi	.25	.25
d.	A1114 3b multi	.25	.25
e.	A1115 3b multi	.25	.25
f.	A1116 3b multi	.25	.25

Designation of Queen Sirikit as "Pre-eminent Protector of Arts and Crafts."

Paknam
Incident, 120th
Anniv.
A1117

2013, Aug. 13 Litho. *Perf. 13x13¼*
Granite Paper

2756	A1117 5b multi	.35	.25

A souvenir sheet of one sold for 16b.

Thailand Post as Public Company,
10th Anniv. — A1118

2013, Aug. 14 Litho. *Perf. 14¼*
Granite Paper

2757	A1118 10b multi	.65	.50

A1119

A1120

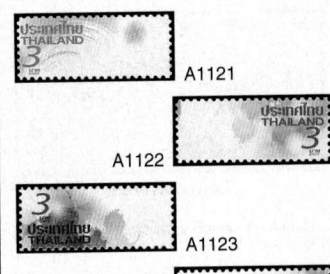

A1121

A1122

A1123

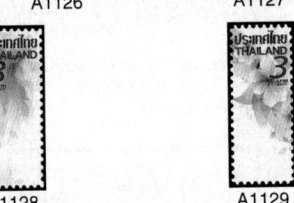

A1124

A1125

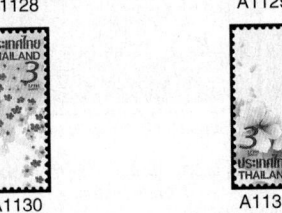

A1126

A1127

A1128

A1129

A1130

A1131

A1132

A1133

A1134

2013, Sept. 4 Litho. *Perf. 13¼x14¼*
Granite Paper

2758	A1119 3b multi	.25	.25
2759	A1120 3b multi	.25	.25
2760	A1121 3b multi	.25	.25
2761	A1122 3b multi	.25	.25
2762	A1123 3b multi	.25	.25
2763	A1124 3b multi	.25	.25
2764	A1125 3b multi	.25	.25
2765	A1126 3b multi	.25	.25

Perf. 14¼x13¼

2766	A1127 3b multi	.25	.25
2767	A1128 3b multi	.25	.25
2768	A1129 3b multi	.25	.25
2769	A1130 3b multi	.25	.25
2770	A1131 3b multi	.25	.25
2771	A1132 3b multi	.25	.25
2772	A1133 3b multi	.25	.25
2773	A1134 3b multi	.25	.25
	Nos. 2758-2773 (16)	4.00	4.00

Flag of Thailand — A1135

Perf. 14¼x13¼
2014, Sept. 12 Litho.
Granite Paper

2775	A1135 15b multi	.95	.70

Government
Housing Bank,
60th
Anniv. — A1136

2013, Sept. 24 Litho. *Perf. 14x14½*
Granite Paper

2776	A1136 3b multi	.25	.25

Somdet Phra Nyanasamvara (1913-
2013), Supreme Patriarch of
Thailand — A1137

Somdet Phra Nyanasamvara: No. 2777, 5b, As young monk. No. 2778, 5b, As older monk. No. 2779, 5b, Holding bowl for food offerings. No. 2780, 5b, Seated, giving donations to students.

2013, Oct. 3 Litho. *Perf. 13¼*
Granite Paper

2777-2780	A1137 Set of 4	1.40	1.10
2780a	Souvenir sheet of 4, #2777-2780	1.90	1.90

No. 2780a sold for 30b.

A1138

A1139

A1140

Intl. Letter Writing Week — A1141

2013, Oct. 7 Litho. *Perf. 13¼*
Granite Paper

2781	A1138 3b multi	.25	.25
2782	A1139 3b multi	.25	.25
2783	A1140 3b multi	.25	.25
2784	A1141 3b multi	.25	.25
	Nos. 2781-2784 (4)	1.00	1.00

Silpakorn
University,
70th Anniv.
A1142

Depictions of Ganesh with denomination in:
No. 2785, 3b, Silver. No. 2786, 3b, Black.

2013, Oct. 12 Litho. *Perf. 13¼*
Granite Paper

2785-2786	A1142 Set of 2	.40	.30

Use of Family
Names in
Thailand,
Cent. — A1143

2013, Oct. 14 Litho. *Perf. 13*
Granite Paper

2787	A1143 3b multi	.25	.25

Democracy Day — A1144

2013, Oct. 14 Litho. *Perf. 13¼*
Granite Paper

2788	A1144 5b multi	.35	.25

Prince Narisaranuvattiwongse (1863-
1947) and Wat Rajathiwas
Rajaworavihara — A1146

2013, Nov. 11 Litho. *Perf. 14½x14*
Granite Paper

2790	A1146 3b multi	.25	.25

Miniature Sheet

Flags and National Flowers of ASEAN
Countries — A1147

Designs: a, Dillenia suffruticosa, flag of Brunei. b, Mitrella mesnyi, flag of Cambodia. c,
Phalaenopsis amabilis, flag of Indonesia. d,
Plumeria alba, flag of Laos. e, Hibiscus rosa-
sinensis, flag of Malaysia. f, Pterocarpus
macrocarpus, flag of Myanmar. g, Jasminum
sambac, flag of Philippines. h, Vanda "Miss
Joaquim" orchid, flag of Singapore. i, Cassia
fistula, flag of Thailand. j, Nelumbo nucifera,
flag of Viet Nam.

Perf. 14¼x14½
2013, Nov. 15   Litho.
Granite Paper
2791 A1147 3b Sheet of 10, #a-j 1.90 1.90

King Bhumibol Adulyadej and
Humanitarian Soil Scientist
Medal — A1148

Litho. With Foil Application
2013, Dec. 5   **Perf. 13¼x13**
Granite Paper
2792 A1148 9b multi   .60 .45
86th birthday of King Bhumibol Adulyadej.

Siam Cement Factory, Cent. — A1150

2013, Dec. 8 Litho.   **Perf. 14½x14**
Granite Paper
2794 A1150 3b multi   .25 .25

Map of Thailand and Digital Television
Mascot — A1151

2013, Dec. 11 Litho.   **Perf. 13¼**
Granite Paper
2795 A1151 3b multi   .25 .25

New Year 2014
(Year of the
Horse) — A1152

2014, Jan. 1 Litho.   **Perf. 13**
Granite Paper
2796 A1152 3b multi   .25 .25
  a. Souvenir sheet of 6, #2397a,
      2463, 2568, 2665, 2726,
      2796   1.90 1.90
No. 2796a sold for 30b. A sheet containing
twelve 3b stamps similar to the 2003-14 New

Year stamps but with reflective gold animals
sold for 99b.

Chiang Mai University, 50th
Anniv. — A1153

2014, Jan. 1 Litho.   **Perf. 14½x14**
Granite Paper
2797 A1153 3b multi   .25 .25

National Children's Day — A1154

Children in national costume, greetings, and
flags from: a, Thailand and Viet Nam. b, Philippines and Singapore. c, Malaysia and
Myanmar. d, Indonesia and Laos. e, Brunei
and Cambodia

2014, Jan. 11 Litho.   **Perf. 14½x14**
Granite Paper
2798   Vert. strip of 5   .95 .70
a.-e. A1154 3b Any single   .25 .25
No. 2798 was printed in sheets containing
two vertical strips.

Thammasat University, 80th
Anniv. — A1155

2014, Jan. 15 Litho.   **Perf. 14½x14**
Granite Paper
2799 A1155 3b multi   .25 .25

Laughing Buddha — A1156

Litho. With Foil Application
2015, Jan. 24   **Perf. 13¼**
Granite Paper
2800 A1156 5b multi   .30 .25
      Chinese New Year.

Khon Kaen University, 50th
Anniv. — A1157

2014, Jan. 25 Litho.   **Perf. 13¼**
2801 A1157 3b multi   .25 .25

Love — A1158

Cut-out in center of stamp: a, Hand signing
"I love you." b, Heart.

2014, Feb. 7 Litho.   **Perf. 13¾**
Granite Paper
2802 A1158 5b Horiz. pair, #a-b .65 .50
No. 2802 is impregnated with a rose scent.

Zoological Park
Organization, 60th
Anniv. — A1159

2014, Feb. 15 Litho.   **Perf. 14x14½**
Granite Paper
2803 A1159 3b multi   .25 .25

Postal School, 125th Anniv. — A1160

2014, Feb. 22 Litho.   **Perf. 14½x14**
Granite Paper
2804 A1160 3b multi   .25 .25

Thai Heritage Conservation
Day — A1162

Masks: a, Tosakanth. b, Kumbhakarn. c,
Pipek. d, Thut. e, Khorn. f, Trisian. g,
Samanakkha. h, Indrajit.

2014, Apr. 2 Litho.   **Perf. 13¼**
Granite Paper
2806 A1162 3b Block of 8, #a-h 1.50 1.10
A souvenir sheet of 1 containing No. 2806a
sold for 13b.

First Thailand-Laos Friendship Bridge,
20th Anniv. — A1163

Bridge and: a, Sai Buddha Image Proces-
sion Festival, Nong Khai, Thailand. b, Pho
Chai Temple, Nong Khai, and On Thu Temple,
Vientiane, Laos.

2014, Apr. 5 Litho.   **Perf. 14½x14**
Granite Paper
2807 A1163 3b Horiz. pair, #a-b .40 .30
See Laos No. 1881.

Thailand Tobacco Monopoly, 75th
Anniv. — A1164

2014, Apr. 19 Litho.   **Perf. 13¼**
Granite Paper
2808 A1164 3b multi   .25 .25

Vesak Day — A1165

2014, May 13 Litho.   **Perf. 13**
Granite Paper
2809 A1165 3b multi   .25 .25

Kings
Chulalongkorn
and Vajiravudh,
King
Chulalongkorn
Memorial
Hospital — A1166

2014, May 30 Litho.   **Perf. 14x14½**
Granite Paper
2810 A1166 3b multi   .25 .25
King Chulalongkorn Memorial Hospital, cent.

Don Mueang International Airport,
Bangkok, Cent. — A1168

Centenary emblem and: No. 2812, 3b,
Breguet 14 B mail plane. No. 2813, 3b, Terminal, 1973. No. 2814, 3b, Terminal and movable
boarding platform, 2014. No. 2815, 3b, Prince
Chakrabongse Bhuvanath (1883-1920), commander of Royal Aeronautical Service, vert.

Perf. 14½x14, 14x14½
2014, July 1 Granite Paper Litho.
2812-2815 A1168 Set of 4   .75 .55

Amphibians — A1169

Designs: No. 2816, 5b, Ingerophrynus
macrotis. No. 2817, 5b, Rhacophorus kio. No.
2818, 5b, Megophrys nasuta. No. 2819, 5b,
Hylarana erythraea.

2014, July 10 Litho.   **Perf. 14½x14**
Granite Paper
2816-2819 A1169 Set of 4   1.25 .95
2819a   Souvenir sheet of 4,
           #2816-2819, perf. 13¼   2.25 2.25
No. 2819a sold for 35b.

Communications Day — A1170

2014, Aug. 4   Litho.   Perf. 14½x14
Granite Paper
2820 A1170 3b multi   .25   .25

Thailand Waterworks, Cent. — A1171

2014, Aug. 15   Litho.   Perf. 13¼
Granite Paper
2821 A1171 3b multi   .25   .25

Synod of
Ayutthaya,
350th
Anniv.
A1172

2014, Aug. 15   Litho.   Perf. 13¼
Granite Paper
2822 A1172 5b multi   .35   .25

See Vatican City No. 1573.

SEMI-POSTAL STAMPS

Nos. 164-175
Overprinted in Red

1918, Jan. 11   Unwmk.   Perf. 14
B1 A21 2s orange
              brown   2.40   2.40
B2 A21 3s emerald   2.40   2.40
B3 A21 5s rose red   4.75   4.75
B4 A21 10s black & olive 8.00   6.00
B5 A21 15s blue   8.75   6.00
B6 A22 1b blue & gray
              blk   45.00   32.50
B7 A22 2b car rose &
              brn   65.00   27.50
B8 A22 3b yel grn & blk 100.00   55.00
B9 A22 5b dp vio & blk   250.00   80.00
  a.   Double overprint   775.00 400.00
B10 A22 10b ol grn & vio
              brn   625.00 240.00
B11 A22 20b sea grn &
              brn   2,250. 1,400.
    Nos. B1-B11 (11)   3,361. 1,856.

Excellent counterfeit overprints are known.
These stamps were sold at an advance over
face value, the excess being given to the Siamese Red Cross Society.

Stamps of 1905-19
Handstamp
Overprinted

1920, Feb.
On Nos. 164, 146, 168
B12 A21 2s (+ 3s) org
              brn   42.50   42.50
B13 A21 3s (+ 2s) green   45.00   45.00
B14 A21 15s (+ 5s) blue 140.00 120.00

On No. 105
B15 A15 1t (+ 25s)   375.00 350.00
On Nos. 185-186
B16 A21 5s on 6s (+ 5s)   62.50   62.50
  a.   Overprint inverted
B17 A21 10s on 12s (+
              5s)   70.00   70.00
    Nos. B12-B17 (6)   735.00 690.00
    Set, never hinged   1,125.

Sold at an advance over face value, the
excess being for the benefit of the Wild Tiger
Corps. Counterfeits exist.

Stamps of 1905-20
Handstamp
Overprinted

On Nos. 164, 146, 168
B18 A21 2s (+ 3s) org brn 40.00   40.00
B19 A21 3s (+ 2s) green   40.00   40.00
  a.   Pair, one without ovpt.
B20 A21 15s (+ 5s) blue   65.00   65.00
On No. 105
B21 A15 1t (+ 25s)   290.00 290.00
On No. 186
B22 A21 10s on 12s (+ 5s) 65.00   65.00
On No. 190
B23 A23 5s (+ 5s)   100.00 100.00
    Nos. B18-B23 (6)   600.00 600.00
    Set, never hinged   925.00

Sold at an advance over face value, the
excess being for the benefit of the Wild Tiger
Corps. Counterfeits exist.

Nos. 187-188, 190,
193-194, 196, 198
Overprinted in Blue or
Red

1920, Dec. 21
B24 A23 2s brown, yel   15.00   15.00
B25 A23 3s grn, grn (R)   15.00   15.00
B26 A23 5s rose, pale rose 15.00   15.00
B27 A23 10s blk & org (R) 15.00   15.00
B28 A23 15s bl, bluish (R) 30.00   30.00
B29 A23 25s chocolate   100.00 100.00
B30 A23 50s ocher & blk (R) 225.00 225.00
    Nos. B24-B30 (7)   415.00 415.00
    Set, never hinged   625.00

Nos. B12-B30 were sold at an advance over
face value, the excess being for the benefit of
the Wild Tiger Corps. Counterfeits exist.

Nos. 170-172
Surcharged in Red

1939, Apr. 6   Unwmk.   Perf. 14
B31 A22 5s + 5s on 1b   22.50   22.50
B32 A22 10s + 5s on 2b   27.50   27.50
B33 A22 15s + 5s on 3b   27.50   27.50
    Nos. B31-B33 (3)   77.50   77.50
    Set, never hinged   130.00

Founding of the Intl. Red Cross Soc., 75th
anniv.
Bottom line of overprint is different on Nos.
B32-B33.

**Catalogue values for unused
stamps in this section, from this
point to the end of the section, are
for Never Hinged items.**

No. 214 Surcharged
in Carmine

1952   Unwmk.   Perf. 12½
B34 A25 80s + 20s blue & blk 22.50   15.00
New constitution.

Red Cross and
Dancer — SP1

Lithographed, Cross Typographed
1953, Apr. 6   Wmk. 299   Perf. 11
Cross in Red, Dancer Dark Blue
B35 SP1 25s + 25s yellow grn 12.50   5.00
B36 SP1 50s + 50s brt rose   25.00   8.00
B37 SP1 1b + 1b lt blue   32.50   9.00
    Nos. B35-B37 (3)   70.00 22.00

60th anniv. of the founding of the Siamese
Red Cross Society.

Nos. B35-B37
Overprinted in
Black

1955, Apr. 3
Cross in Red, Dancer Dark Blue
B38 SP1 25s + 25s yel grn   24.00   16.00
B39 SP1 50s + 50s brt rose   160.00 110.00
B40 SP1 1b + 1b lt blue   210.00 160.00
    Nos. B38-B40 (3)   394.00 286.00

Counterfeits exist.

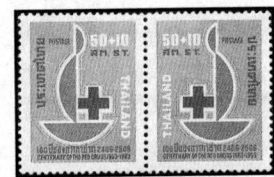

Red Cross Cent. Emblem — SP2

1963   Wmk. 334   Litho.   Perf. 13½
B41 50s + 10s cross at right .80   .40
B42 50s + 10s cross at left   .80   .40
  a.   SP2 Pair, #B41-B42   2.40 1.60

Cent. of the Intl. Red Cross.

Nos. B41-B42
Surcharged

1973, Feb. 15
B43 SP2 75s + 25s on 50s + 10s 1.40 1.20
B44 SP3 75s + 25s on 50s + 10s 1.40 1.20
  a.   Pair, #B43-B44   3.00 2.40

Red Cross Fair, Feb. 15-19.

Nos. B41-B42
Surcharged

1974, Feb. 2
B45 SP2 75s + 25s on 50s + 10s 1.40 1.40
B46 SP3 75s + 25s on 50s + 10s 1.40 1.40
  a.   Pair, #B45-B46   2.90 2.90

Red Cross Fair, Feb. 1974. Position of
surcharge reversed on No. B46.

Nos. B41-B42
Surcharged

1975, Feb 11 52
B47 SP2 75s + 25s on 50s + 10s 1.40 1.40
B48 SP3 75s + 25s on 50s + 10s 1.40 1.40
  a.   Pair, #B47-B48   2.90 2.90

Red Cross Fair, Feb. 1975. Position of
surcharge reversed on No. B48.

Nos. B41-B42
Surcharged

1976, Feb. 26
B49 SP2 75s + 25s on 50s + 10s 1.40 1.40
B50 SP3 75s + 25s on 50s + 10s 1.40 1.40
  a.   Pair, #B49-B50   2.90 2.90

Red Cross Fair, Feb. 16-Mar. 1. Position of
surcharge reversed on #B50.

Nos. B41-B42
Surcharged

1977, Apr. 6   Wmk. 334   Perf. 13½
B51 SP2 75s + 25s on 50s + 10s 1.40   .65
B52 SP3 75s + 25s on 50s + 10s 1.40   .65
  a.   Pair, #B51-B52   2.90 2.90

Red Cross Fair 1977.

Red Cross Blood
Collection — SP4

Wmk. 329
1978, Apr. 6   Photo.   Perf. 13
B53 SP4 2.75b + 25s multi   2.25 2.00

"Give blood, save life."
For surcharge see No. B58.

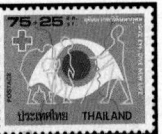

Eye and Blind
People — SP5

Perf. 14x13½
1979, Apr. 6   Litho.   Wmk. 368
B54 SP5 75s + 25s multi   .85   .50

"Give an eye, save new life." Red Cross Fair.
Surtax was for Thai Red Cross.
For surcharge see No. B59.

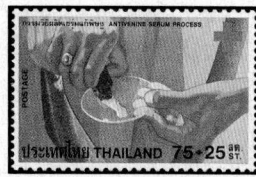

Extracting Snake Venom, Red
Cross — SP6

1980, Apr.   **Perf. 11x13**
B55 SP6 75s + 25s multi   1.10   .95
  Complete booklet, 10 #B55   24.00

Red Cross Fair. Surtax was for Thai Red
Cross.
For surcharge see No. B60.

Nurse Helping Victim — SP7

1981, Apr. 6   Wmk. 377   Perf. 12½
B56 SP7 75 + 25s red & gray grn 1.50 1.40

Red Cross Fair (canceled). Surtax was for
Thai Red Cross.
For surcharge see No. B65.

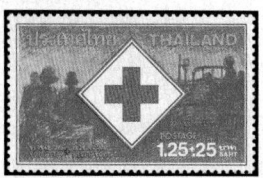

Red
Cross
Fair
SP8

Perf. 13x13½
1983, Apr. 6   Litho.   Wmk. 329
B57 SP8 1.25b + 25s multi   1.20 1.00

Surtax was for Thai Red Cross.

No. B53 Surcharged

1984, Apr. 6   Photo.   Perf. 13
B58 SP4 3.25b + 25s on 2.75b +
  25s   2.25 4.50

Red Cross Fair. Surtax was for Thai Red
Cross. Overprint translates: Red Cross
Donation.

No. B54
Surcharged

Wmk. 368
1985, Mar. 30   Litho.   Perf. 13
B59 SP5 2b + 25c on 75s + 25s 1.90 1.90

Surtax for the Thai Red Cross.

No. B55 Overprinted and Surcharged

1986, Apr. 6   Wmk. 368   Perf. 11x13
B60 SP6 2b + 25s on 75s + 25s 2.25 2.25

Natl. Children's Day. Surtax for Natl. Red
Cross Society. Overprint translates "Red
Cross Donation."

Natl. Scouting Movement, 75th Anniv.,
15th Asia-Pacific Conference,
Thailand — SP9

#B61, Scouts, saluting, community service.
#B62, Scout activities. #B63, King & queen at
ceremony. #B64, 15th Asia-Pacific conf.

1986, Nov. 7   Wmk. 385   Perf. 13½
B61 SP9 2b + 50s multi   .50 .35
B62 SP9 2b + 50s multi   .50 .35
B63 SP9 2b + 50s multi   .50 .35
B64 SP9 2b + 50s multi   .50 .35
  Nos. B61-B64 (4)   2.00 1.40

Surtax for the Natl. Scouting Fund.

No. B56 Surcharged

1987, Apr.   Wmk. 377   Perf. 12½
B65 SP7 2b + 50s on 75s + 25s 2.00 1.60

Sports — SP10

Designs: No. B66, Hurdles, medal winners.
No. B67, Race, nurse treating injured cyclist.
No. B68, Boxers training. No. B69, Soccer.

1989, Dec. 16   Wmk. 387   Perf. 13½
B66 SP10 2b +1b multi   .40 .30
B67 SP10 2b +1b multi   .40 .30
B68 SP10 2b +1b multi   .40 .30
B69 SP10 2b +1b multi   .40 .30
  Nos. B66-B69 (4)   1.60 1.20

Surtax for sports welfare organizations.

Sports — SP11

1990, Dec. 16
B70 SP11 2b +1b Judo   .60 .35
B71 SP11 2b +1b Archery   .60 .35
B72 SP11 2b +1b High jump   .60 .35
B73 SP11 2b +1b Windsurfing   .60 .35
  Nos. B70-B73 (4)   2.40 1.40

Surtax for sports welfare organization.

Sports — SP12

Wmk. 387
1991, Dec. 16   Litho.   Perf. 13½
B74 SP12 2b +1b Jogging   .35 .35
B75 SP12 2b +1b Cycling   .35 .35
B76 SP12 2b +1b Soccer, jump-
  ing rope   .35 .35
B77 SP12 2b +1b Swimming   .35 .35
  Nos. B74-B77 (4)   1.40 1.40

Surtax for sports welfare organizations.

18th South East Asian Games, Chiang
Mai — SP13

No. B78: a, Water polo. b, Tennis. c, Hur-
dles. d, Gymnastics.
No. B79: a, Fencing. b, Pool. c, Diving. d,
Pole vault.

1994, Dec. 16   Wmk. 340
B78 SP13 2b +1b Strip of 4,
  #a.-d.   2.25 1.75
  e. Souvenir sheet, #B78   2.00 2.00

Wmk. 387
B79 SP13 2b +1b Strip of 4,
  #a.-d.   2.25 1.75
  e. Souvenir sheet, #B79   2.00 2.00
  Nos. B78e, B79e sold for 15b.
Issued: #B78, 12/16/94; #B79, 12/9/95.
For surcharges see Nos. 2338-2339, 2347-
2348.

13th Asian Games, Bangkok — SP14

1998, Mar. 27   Perf. 14½x14
B80 SP14 2b +1b Shooting   .25 .25
B81 SP14 3b +1b Rhythmic
  gymnastics   .35 .25
B82 SP14 4b +1b Swimming   .45 .35
B83 SP14 7b +1b Wind-surfing   .70 .55
  Nos. B80-B83 (4)   1.75 1.40

13th Asian Games, Bangkok — SP15

Perf. 14½x14
1998, Dec. 6   Litho.   Unwmk.
Granite Paper
B84 SP15 2b +1b Field hockey   .35 .25
B85 SP15 3b +1b Wrestling   .45 .25
B86 SP15 4b +1b Rowing   .55 .35
B87 SP15 7b +1b Equestrian   .90 .55
  Nos. B84-B87 (4)   2.25 1.40

AIR POST STAMPS

Garuda — AP1

1925   Unwmk.   Engr.   Perf. 14, 14½
C1 AP1 2s brown, yel   8.00   .50
C2 AP1 3s dark brown   8.00   .50
C3 AP1 5s green   20.00   .55
C4 AP1 10s black & org   32.50   1.00
C5 AP1 15s carmine   8.00   1.50
C6 AP1 25s dark blue   16.00   1.50

C7 AP1 50s brown org &
  blk   60.00   9.00
C8 AP1 1b blue & brown   40.00 11.00
  Nos. C1-C8 (8)   192.50 25.55
  Set, never hinged   290.00

Issue dates: 2s, 50s, Apr. 21; others, Jan. 3.

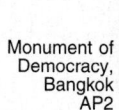 

Nos. C1-C8 received this overprint
("Government Museum 2468") in 1925,
but were never issued. The death of
King Vajiravudh caused cancellation of
the fair at which this set was to have
been released.
They were used during 1928 only in
the interdepartmental service for
accounting purposes of the money-
order sections of various Bangkok post
offices, and were never sold to the public. Values for set: unused, $1,200;
used, $45.

1930-37   Perf. 12½
C9 AP1 2s brown, yel   9.50   1.00
C10 AP1 5s green   2.40   .40
C11 AP1 10s black & org   8.00   .40
C12 AP1 15s carmine   32.50   8.00
C13 AP1 25s dark blue ('37) 4.00   1.20
  a. Vert. pair, imperf. btwn. 450.00
C14 AP1 50s brn org & blk
  ('37)   4.00   2.40
  Nos. C9-C14 (6)   60.40 13.40
  Set, never hinged   90.00

Monument of
Democracy,
Bangkok
AP2

1942-43   Engr.   Perf. 11
C15 AP2 2s dk org brn
  ('43)   3.25   2.40
C16 AP2 3s dk grn ('43)   32.50 24.00
  a. Vert. pair, imperf. btwn. 100.00 100.00
C17 AP2 5s deep claret   3.25   1.20
  a. Horiz. pair, imperf. btwn. 75.00 75.00
  b. Vert. pair, imperf. btwn. 75.00 75.00
C18 AP2 10s carmine ('43) 15.00   1.20
  a. Vert. pair, imperf. btwn. 100.00 100.00
C19 AP2 15s dark blue   5.25   2.00
  a. Vert. pair, imperf. btwn. 100.00 100.00
  Nos. C15-C19 (5)   59.25 30.80
  Set, never hinged   90.00

> **Catalogue values for unused
> stamps in this section, from this
> point to the end of the section, are
> for Never Hinged items.**

Garuda and
Bangkok
Skyline — AP3

1952-53   Perf. 13x12½
C20 AP3 1.50b red violet ('53) 5.50 1.20
C21 AP3 2b dark blue   16.00   2.50
C22 AP3 3b gray ('53)   20.00   1.40
  Nos. C20-C22 (3)   41.50   5.10

Issue dates: June 15, 1952. Sept. 15, 1953.

OFFICIAL STAMPS

> **Catalogue values for unused
> stamps in this section are for
> Never Hinged items.**

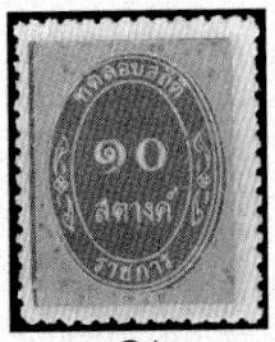
O1

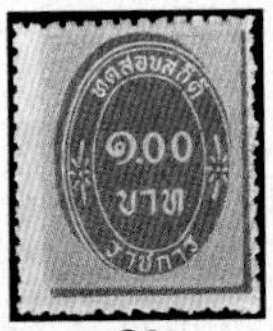
O2

Perf. 10½ Rough

1963, Oct. 1 Typo. Unwmk.

Without Gum

O1 O1 10s pink & dp car .25 .25
O2 O1 20s brt grn & car rose .25 .25
O3 O1 25s blue & dp car .30 *.35*
O4 O1 50s deep carmine 1.10 *2.00*
O5 O2 1b silver & car rose 1.25 *3.00*
O6 O2 2b bronze & car rose 2.25 2.25
Nos. O1-O6 (6) 5.40 8.10

Issued as an official test from Oct. 1, 1963, to Jan. 31, 1964, to determine the amount of mail sent out by various government departments.

Nos. O5, O9, O10 exist with oval frame of type O1.

1964 Without Gum

O7 O1 20s green .50 .50
O8 O1 25s blue .50 .50
O9 O2 1b silver 1.00 1.00
O10 O2 2b bister 2.50 2.50
Nos. O7-O10 (4) 4.50 4.50

Others values exist printed in one color.

THRACE

'thrās

LOCATION — In southeastern Europe between the Black and Aegean Seas
GOVT. — Former Turkish Province
AREA — 89,361 sq. mi. (approx.)

Thrace underwent many political changes during the Balkan Wars and World War I. It was finally divided among Turkey, Greece and Bulgaria.

100 Lepta = 1 Drachma
40 Paras = 1 Piaster
100 Stotinki = 1 Leva (1919)

A large number of minor overprint errors exist on most issues of Thrace. See the *Scott Classic Specialized Catalogue of Stamps and Covers 1840-1940* for much more specialized listings.

Giumulzina District Issue

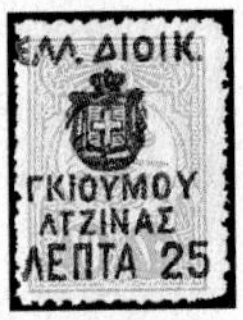

Turkish Stamps of 1909 Surcharged in Blue or Red

1913 Unwmk. *Perf. 12, 13½*

1 A21 10 l on 20pa rose (Bl) 45.00 45.00
a. Inverted overprint 170.00
b. Double overprint 170.00
2 A21 25 l on 10pa bl grn 67.50 70.00
a. Inverted overprint 175.00
b. Double overprint 175.00
3 A21 25 l on 20pa rose (Bl) 67.50 70.00
a. Inverted overprint 170.00
b. Double overprint 170.00
c. Béhié ovpt. (#162) 200.00
4 A21 25 l on 1pi ultra 110.00 115.00
a. Inverted overprint 220.00
b. Double overprint 220.00
Nos. 1-4 (4) 290.00 300.00

Counterfeits exist of Nos. 1-4.

Eight other values exist, bearing surcharges differing in color or denomination from Nos. 1-4. These stamps were not issued. Values, each: unused $175; never hinged $350.

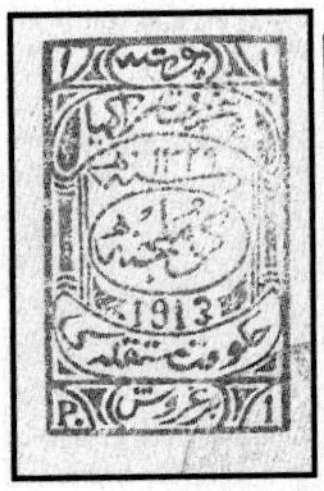
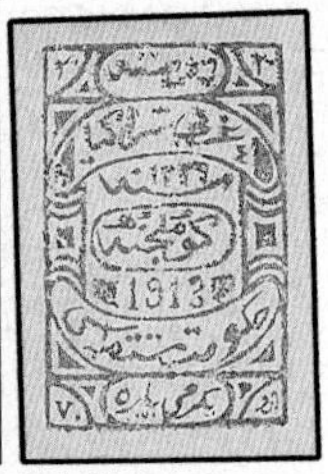

Turkish Inscriptions
A1 A2

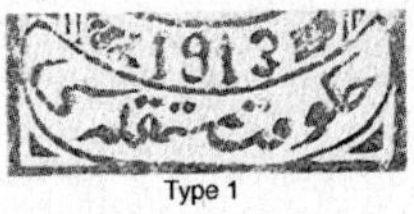
Type 1

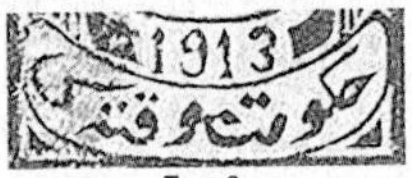
Type 2

1913 Litho. *Imperf.*

Laid Paper

Control Mark in Rose

Without Gum

5 A1 1pi blue, type 1 17.00 17.00
a. Double print 250.00
b. Type 2 80.00 75.00
6 A1 2pi violet 17.00 17.00
a. Double print 500.00 190.00
b. Type 2 190.00

Wove Paper

7 A2 10pa vermilion 35.00 30.00
8 A2 20pa blue 35.00 30.00
9 A2 1pi violet 37.50 30.00
Nos. 5-9 (5) 141.50 124.00

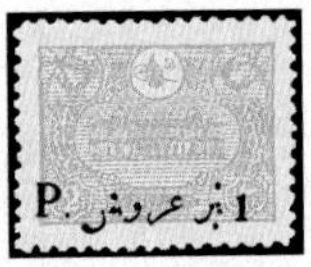

Turkish Stamps of 1913 Surcharged in Red or Black

1913 *Perf. 12*

10 A22 1pi on 2pa ol grn (R) 25.00 25.00
10A A22 1pi on 2pa ol grn 25.00 25.00
11 A22 1pi on 5pa ocher 25.00 25.00
11A A22 1pi on 5pa ocher (R) 25.00 25.00
12 A22 1pi on 20pa rose 32.50 32.50
13 A22 1pi on 5pi dk vio (R) 65.00 65.00
13A A22 1pi on 5pi dk vio 65.00 65.00
14 A22 1pi on 10pi dl red 110.00 *120.00*
15 A22 1pi on 25pi dk grn 475.00 *500.00*
Nos. 10-15 (9) 847.50 882.50

On Nos. 13-15 the surcharge is vertical, reading up. No. 15 exists with double surcharge, one black, one red.

Nos. 10-15 exist with forged surcharges.

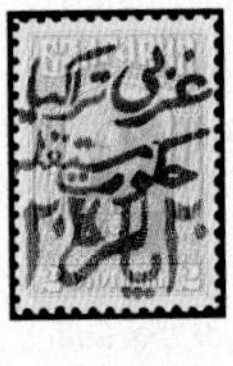

Bulgarian Stamps of 1911 Handstamped Surcharged in Red or Blue

1913

16 A20 10pa on 1s myr grn (R) 20.00 20.00
a. Top ovpt. inverted 100.00
b. Top ovpt. double 100.00
c. Top ovpt. omitted 150.00
d. Bottom ovpt. omitted 150.00
e. Bottom ovpt. inverted 100.00
17 A21 20pa on 2s car & blk 20.00 20.00
a. Inverted overprint 60.00
18 A23 1pi on 5s grn & blk (R) 20.00 20.00
a. Inverted overprint 125.00 125.00
19 A22 2pi on 3s lake & blk 28.00 28.00
a. Inverted overprint 80.00 80.00
20 A24 2½pi on 10s dp red & blk 40.00 40.00
b. 2½pi on 2s 260.00
21 A25 5pi on 15s brn bis 70.00 70.00
a. Inverted overprint 250.00
Nos. 16-21 (6) 198.00 198.00

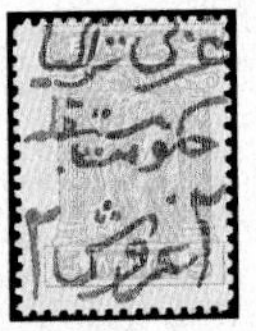

Same Surcharges on Greek Stamps

On Issue of 1911

1913 *Serrate Roulette 13½*

22 A24 10pa on 1 l grn (R) 22.50 22.50
23 A24 10pa on 1 l grn 23.00 23.00
24 A26 10pa on 5 l grn 110.00 110.00
25 A25 10pa on 25 l ultra (R) 32.50 32.50
26 A25 20pa on 2 l car rose 22.50 22.50
27 A24 1pi on 3 l ver 22.50 22.50
a. Value omitted 65.00 65.00
b. Red overprint 22.50 22.50
27C A24 1pi on 10 l car rose 550.00
28 A26 2pi on 5 l grn (R) 60.00 60.00
29 A24 2½pi on 10 l car rose 60.00 60.00
30 A25 5pi on 40 l dp bl (R) 110.00 110.00
Nos. 22-30 (9) 463.00 463.00

On Occupation Stamps of 1912

31 O1 10pa on 1 l brn 20.00 15.00
a. Value omitted 100.00
b. Value srch. inverted 50.00
32 O1 20pa on 1 l brn 20.00 15.00
33 O1 1pi on 1 l brn 20.00 15.00
Nos. 31-33 (3) 60.00 45.00

These surcharges were made with handstamps, two of which were required for each surcharge. The upper handstamp, reads "Administration of Autonomous Western Thrace" in old Turkish. The lower handstamp expresses the new value. On horizontal designs, the text appears on the right, and the value appears on the left. On inverted overprints on horizontal stamps, this is reversed. One or both parts may be found inverted or omitted.

Nos. 16-33 exist with forged surcharges.

OCCUPATION STAMPS

Issued under Allied Occupation

Bulgarian Stamps of 1915-19 Handstamped in Violet Blue

Perf. 11½, 11½x12, 14

1919 Unwmk.

N1b A43 1s black 2.50 2.00
N2 A43 2s olive green 2.50 2.00
N3 A44 5s green .85 .85
N4 A44 10s rose .85 .85
N5 A44 15s violet .85 .85
N6 A26 25s indigo & black .85 .85
Nos. N1b-N6 (6) 8.40 7.40

The overprint on Nos. N1-N6 exists applied both ascending and descending, as well as inverted in both positions. On the 1s value, the usual position of the overprint is upright, reading from lower left to upper right; on the rest of the set, the overprint is usually inverted, reading from lower right to upper left. See the *Scott Classic Specialized Catalogue of Stamps and Covers* for detailed listings.

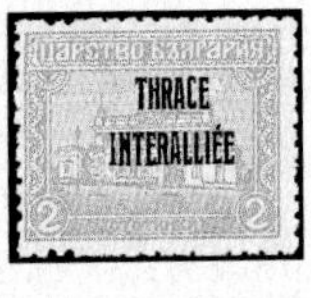

Bulgarian Stamps of 1911-19 Overprinted in Red or Black

1919

N7 A43 1s black (R) .25 .25
N8 A43 2s olive green .25 .25
c. Inverted ovpt. 40.00
N9 A44 5s green .25 .25
c. Inverted ovpt.
d. Pair, one without ovpt.
e. Double ovpt. 40.00
N10 A44 10s rose .25 .25
d. Pair, one without ovpt.
e. Double ovpt. 30.00
N11 A44 15s violet .25 .25
N12 A26 25s indigo & black .25 .25
N13 A29 1 l chocolate 5.00 5.00
N14 A37a 2 l brown orange 9.00 9.00
N15 A38 3 l claret 12.00 12.00
Nos. N7-N15 (9) 27.50 27.50

Overprint is vertical, reading up, on Nos. N9-N13.

The following varieties are found in the setting of "INTERALLIEE": Inverted "V" for "A," second "L" inverted, "F" instead of final "E."

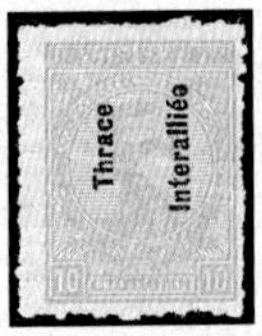

Bulgarian Stamps of 1919 Overprinted

1920

N16 A44 5s green .25 .25
d. Imperf, pair 70.00
N17 A44 10s rose .25 .25
N18 A44 15s violet .25 .25
N19 A44 50s yel brn, ovpt. reading up 1.50 1.50
d. Ovpt. reading down 25.00 *30.00*
h. As "d," imperf, pair 140.00
Nos. N16-N19 (4) 2.25 2.25

Various typographical errors in the overprint are found on all values.

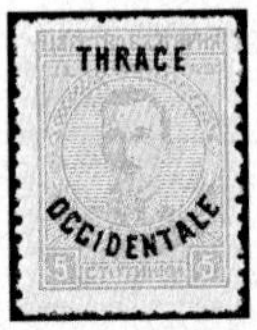

Bulgarian Stamps of 1919 Overprinted

1920 *Perf. 12x11½*

N20 A44 5s green .25 .25
a. Inverted overprint 32.50 *50.00*
b. Pair, one without ovpt. 42.50 *65.00*
c. Imperf, pair 45.00 *65.00*
d. As "c," inverted overprint 55.00 *75.00*
N21 A44 10s rose .25 .25
a. Inverted overprint 28.00 *37.50*
b. Double ovpt., one on gum side 45.00 *65.00*
c. Imperf, pair 45.00 *65.00*
d. As "c," inverted overprint 55.00 *75.00*
N22 A44 15s violet .25 .25
a. Inverted overprint 28.00 *37.50*
b. Imperf, pair 45.00 *65.00*
c. As "c," inverted overprint 55.00 *75.00*
N23 A44 25s deep blue .25 .25
a. Inverted overprint 28.00 *37.50*
b. Imperf, pair 45.00 *65.00*
c. As "c," inverted overprint 55.00 *75.00*
d. Double ovpt., one on gummed side 45.00
N24 A44 50s ocher .25 .25
a. Inverted overprint 32.50 *50.00*
b. Imperf, pair 45.00 65.00
c. As "b," inverted ovpt. 55.00 80.00

Imperf

N25 A44 30s chocolate 1.50 1.50
a. Inverted overprint 32.50 *55.00*
b. Perforated 20.00
Nos. N20-N25 (6) 2.75 2.75

No. N25 is not known without overprint.

ISSUED UNDER GREEK OCCUPATION

Counterfeits exist of Nos. N26-N84.

For Use in Western Thrace

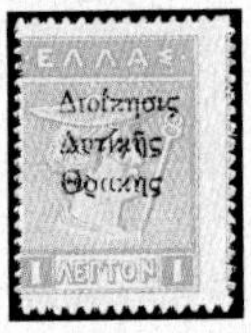

Greek Stamps of 1911-19 Overprinted "Administration Western Thrace" in Greek

Serrate Roulette 13½

1920 Litho. Unwmk.

N26 A24 1 l green .25 *.25*
a. Inverted overprint 20.00
b. Double overprint 20.00
c. Double overprint, one inverted 75.00
N27 A25 2 l rose .25 *.25*
N28 A24 3 l vermilion .25 *.25*
a. Inverted overprint 30.00
N29 A26 5 l green .25 *.25*
a. Inverted overprint 25.00
b. Double overprint 25.00
N30 A24 10 l rose .40 *.85*
N31 A25 15 l dull blue .40 *.75*
a. Inverted overprint 20.00
b. Double overprint 20.00
c. Dbl. ovpt., one inverted 30.00

N32	A25	25 l blue	.40	*.85*
N34	A25	40 l indigo	2.00	*4.00*
N35	A26	50 l violet brn	2.00	*6.00*
N36	A27	1d ultra	9.00	*15.00*
N37	A27	2d vermilion	30.00	*35.00*
a.		Double overprint	75.00	
		Nos. N26-N37 (11)	45.20	*63.45*

The 20 l value with this overprint was not issued. Values: unused $25; never hinged $65.

Engr.

N38	A25	2 l car rose	1.00	1.00
N39	A24	3 l vermilion	1.00	1.00
N39A	A25	20 l slate	27.50	
N39B	A25	25 l blue	32.50	
N39C	A25	30 l rose	40.00	
N40	A27	1d ultra	27.50	25.00
N41	A27	2d vermilion	40.00	35.00
N42	A27	3d car rose	60.00	*80.00*
N43	A27	5d ultra	25.00	*30.00*
N44	A27	10d deep blue	25.00	*30.00*
		Nos. N38-N44 (10)	279.50	

Nos. N38-N44 were not issued. Values for used examples of Nos. N38-N39 and N40-N44 are for cancelled-to-order stamps.

Nos. N42-N44 are overprinted on the reissues of Greece Nos. 210-212. See footnote below Greece No. 213.

Overprinted

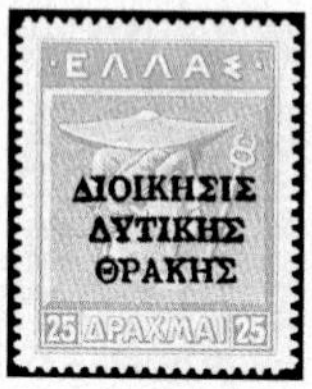

N45	A28	25d deep blue	60.00	35.00

This overprint reads: "Administration Western Thrace."

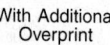

With Additional Overprint

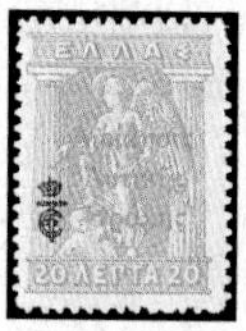

Litho.

N46	A24	1 l green	5.00	3.00
N47	A25	2 l rose	.25	*.50*
a.		Inverted overprint	65.00	
N47B	A26	5 l green	25.00	
N48	A24	10 l rose	.60	*.80*
a.		Inverted overprint	17.50	
N49	A25	20 l slate	.60	*.80*
a.		Inverted overprint	17.50	
N49B	A25	25 l blue	45.00	
N50	A26	30 l rose (#240)	.65	*1.00*

Engr.

N50A	A26	30 l rose (#244)	75.00	
N51	A27	2d vermilion	35.00	30.00
N52	A27	3d car rose	45.00	30.00
N53	A27	5d ultra	40.00	32.50
N54	A27	10d deep blue	35.00	22.50
		Nos. N46-N54 (12)	307.10	*121.10*

Nos. N46, N47B, N49B, N50A, N51, N53 and N54 were not issued. Used values for Nos. N46, N51, N53 and N54 are for canceled-to-order stamps.

For Use in Eastern and Western Thrace

Greek Stamps of 1911-19 Overprinted "Administration Thrace" in Greek

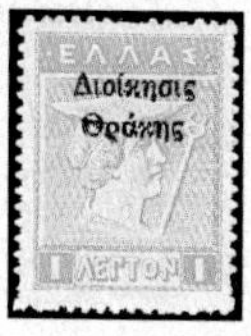

1920 **Litho.**

N55	A24	1 l green	.25	*1.00*
a.		Inverted overprint	15.00	
b.		Double overprint	15.00	
N56	A25	2 l rose	.25	*.50*
a.		Inverted overprint	12.50	
b.		Double overprint	15.00	
c.		Triple overprint	25.00	
N57	A24	3 l vermilion	.25	*.50*
a.		Inverted overprint	12.50	
b.		Double overprint	15.00	
c.		Double overprint, one inverted	17.50	
N58	A26	5 l green	.25	*.50*
a.		Inverted overprint	20.00	
b.		Double overprint	35.00	
N59	A24	10 l rose	.50	*.75*
a.		Double overprint	85.00	
N59B	A25	15 l dull blue	60.00	
a.		Inverted overprint	60.00	
N60	A25	20 l slate	.65	*1.30*
a.		Inverted overprint	17.50	
b.		Double overprint	15.00	
N61	A25	25 l blue	1.75	*2.50*
N62	A25	40 l indigo	2.50	*7.00*
N63	A26	50 l violet brn	3.00	*6.50*
N64	A27	1d ultra	15.00	*30.00*
N65	A27	2d vermilion	32.50	*45.00*

Engr.

N65A	A25	2 l rose	2.50	*4.00*
N66	A24	3 l vermilion	2.50	*4.00*
N67	A25	20 l gray lilac	7.50	*22.50*
N68	A28	25d deep blue	70.00	*100.00*
		Nos. N55-N68 (16)	199.40	*226.05*

Nos. N59B and N65A-N68 were not issued. Used values for Nos. N65A-N68 are for canceled-to-order stamps.

With Additional Overprint

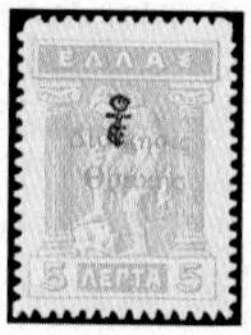

Litho.

N68A	A24	1 l green	12.50	*6.00*
N69	A25	2 l car rose	.25	*.50*
a.		Inverted overprint	35.00	
b.		Double overprint	30.00	
N70	A26	5 l green	7.50	*8.00*
N71	A25	20 l slate	.25	*.50*
a.		Double overprint	350.00	325.00
N72	A26	30 l rose	.25	*.50*

Engr.

N73	A27	3d car rose	15.00	*25.00*
a.		Inverted overprint		—
N74	A27	5d ultra	25.00	*45.00*
N75	A27	10d deep blue	40.00	*60.00*
		Nos. N68A-N75 (8)	100.75	*145.50*

Nos. N68A, N70 and N74-N75 were not issued. Used values are for canceled-to-order stamps.

Turkish Stamps of 1916-20 Srchd. in Blue, Black or Red

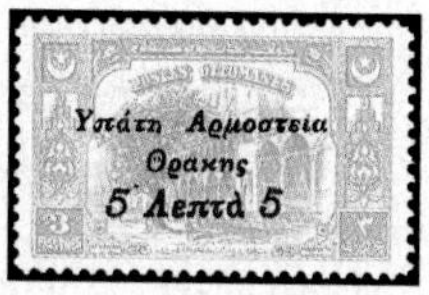

1920 ***Perf. 11½, 12½***

N76	A43	1 l on 5pa org (Bl)	.40	*.50*
a.		Inverted overprint	35.00	35.00
b.		Double overprint	30.00	30.00
c.		Double overprint, one inverted	50.00	50.00
d.		Double overprint, one on gummed side	35.00	
N77	A32	5 l on 3pi blue	.40	*.50*
a.		Inverted overprint	100.00	100.00
b.		Double overprint	70.00	70.00
N78	A30	20 l on 1pi bl grn	.55	*.75*
a.		Inverted overprint	27.50	27.50
b.		Double overprint	27.50	27.50
c.		Double overprint, one inverted	40.00	40.00
d.		Double overprint, one on gummed side	37.50	
N79	A53	25 l on 5pi on 2pa Prus bl (R)	.80	*.90*
a.		Inverted overprint	50.00	50.00
b.		Double overprint	50.00	50.00
N80	A49	50 l on 5pi bl & blk (R)	6.00	*7.00*
N81	A45	1d on 20pa dp rose (Bl)	1.75	1.50
a.		Double overprint	40.00	40.00
N82	A22	2d on 10pa ol grn (R)	2.50	*2.50*
a.		Double overprint	60.00	60.00
N83	A57	3d on 1pi dp bl (R)	11.00	11.00
a.		Inverted overprint	60.00	60.00
b.		Double overprint	65.00	65.00
N84	A23	5d on 20pa rose	10.00	10.00
a.		Inverted overprint	75.00	70.00
b.		Double overprint, one inverted	75.00	70.00
		Nos. N76-N84 (9)	33.40	34.65

On Nos. N83 and N84, the normal overprint is reading down. On the inverted overprints, it is reading up.

Nos. N77, N78 and N84 are on the 1920 issue with designs modified. Nos. N81, N82 and N83 are on stamps with the 1919 overprints.

POSTAGE DUE STAMPS

Issued under Allied Occupation

1919 Bulgarian Postage Due Stamps Overprinted, Reading Vertically Up

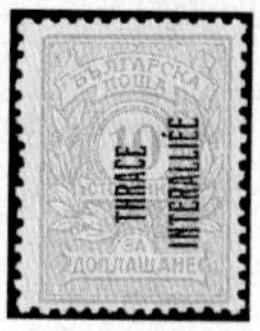

1919 **Unwmk.** ***Perf. 12x11½***

NJ1	D6	5s emerald	.45	.50
NJ2	D6	10s purple	.90	1.00
NJ3	D6	50s blue	2.75	3.00
		Nos. NJ1-NJ3 (3)	4.10	4.50

Type of Bulgarian Postage Due Stamps of 1919-22 Overprinted

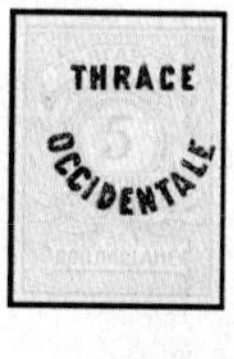

1920 ***Imperf.***

NJ4	D6	5s emerald	.25	.50
a.		Inverted overprint	40.00	
NJ5	D6	10s deep violet	2.00	2.00
a.		Inverted overprint	40.00	
NJ6	D6	20s salmon	1.00	1.00
NJ7	D6	50s blue	1.50	1.50

Perf. 12x11½

NJ8	D6	10s deep violet	1.25	1.25
		Nos. NJ4-NJ8 (5)	6.00	6.25

No. NJ6 issued without gum.

TIBET

tə-ˈbet

LOCATION — A high tableland in Central Asia

GOVT. — A semi-independent state, nominally under control of China (under Communist China since 1950-51). In 1965 Tibet became a nominally autonomous region of the People's Republic of China.

AREA — 463,200 sq. mi.

POP. — 1,500,000 (approx.)

CAPITAL — Lhasa

Tibet's postage stamps were valid only within its borders.

6 ⅔ Trangka = 1 Sang

"Stamps" produced by the "Tibetan Government in Exile" have no postal value. These include four-value sets for Himalayan animals and the UPU that were put on sale in the early 1970s.

Excellent counterfeits of Nos. 1-18 exist. Numerous shades of all values.

All stamps issued without gum.

Small bits of foreign matter (inclusions) are to be expected in Native Paper. These do not reduce the value of the stamp unless they have caused serious damage to the design or paper.

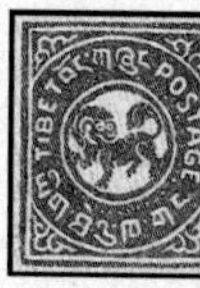

A1

1912-50 **Unwmk.** **Typo.** ***Imperf.***

Native Paper

1	A1	⅙t green	40.00	*45.00*
2	A1	⅓t blue	40.00	*55.00*
a.		⅓t ultramarine	50.00	*60.00*
3	A1	½t violet	40.00	*55.00*
4	A1	⅔t carmine	50.00	*60.00*
a.		"POTSAGE"	150.00	*175.00*
5	A1	1t vermilion	55.00	*75.00*
6	A1	1s sage green ('50)	100.00	*110.00*
		Nos. 1-6 (6)	325.00	*400.00*

The "POTSAGE" error is found on all shades of the ⅔t (positions 6 and 7).

Pin-perf. examples of Nos. 1 and 3 exist.

Issued in sheets of 12.

Beware of private reproductions of #1-5 that were printed in the US around 1986. Sheets of 12 bear "J. Crow Co." imprint. The set of 5 sheets was sold for $5.

Printed Using Shiny Enamel Paint

1920

1a	A1	⅙t green	60.00	40.00
2b	A1	⅓t blue	500.00	500.00
3d	A1	½t purple	100.00	*110.00*
4h	A1	⅔t carmine	100.00	*110.00*
i.		"POTSAGE"	*225.00*	*250.00*
5c	A1	1t carmine	350.00	400.00

In some 1920-30 printings, European enamel paint was used instead of ink. It has a glossy surface.

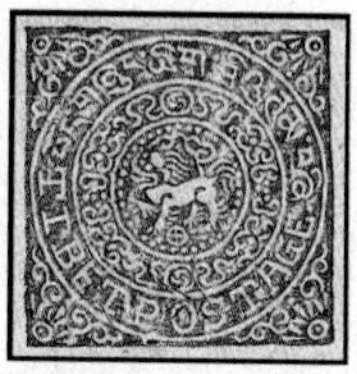

Lion — A2

1914

7	A2	4t milky blue	750.	*850.*
a.		4t dark blue	1,100.	1,100.
8	A2	8t carmine rose	165.	175.
a.		8t carmine	1,100.	*1,100.*

Issued in sheets of 6.

Printed Using Shiny Enamel Paint

1920

7b	A2	4t blue	1,350.	*1,500.*
8b	A2	8t carmine	1,350.	*1,500.*

See note following No. 5c.

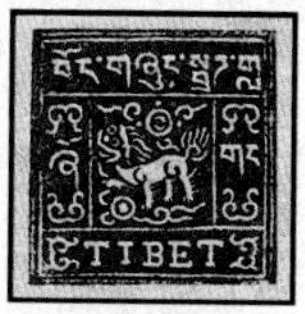

A3

Thin White Native Paper

1933 ***Pin-perf.***

9	A3	½t orange	95.00	*100.00*
10	A3	⅔t dark blue	95.00	*120.00*
11	A3	1t rose carmine	95.00	*120.00*
12	A3	2t scarlet	95.00	*120.00*
13	A3	4t emerald	95.00	*120.00*
		Nos. 9-13 (5)	475.00	*580.00*

Issued in sheets of 12.

Exist imperf.

Heavy Toned Native Paper

1934 ***Imperf.***

14	A3	½t yellow	16.00	*18.00*
15	A3	⅔t blue	14.00	*15.00*
16	A3	1t orange ver	14.00	*15.00*
a.		1t carmine	16.00	*18.00*
17	A3	2t red	14.00	*15.00*
a.		2t orange vermilion	14.00	*15.00*
18	A3	4t green	14.00	*15.00*
a.		25x25mm instead of 24x24mm	55.00	*65.00*
		Nos. 14-18 (5)	72.00	*78.00*

Nos. 14-18 are also known with a private pin-perf.

The ½t and 1t exist printed on both sides.

Issued in sheets of 12.

OFFICIAL STAMPS

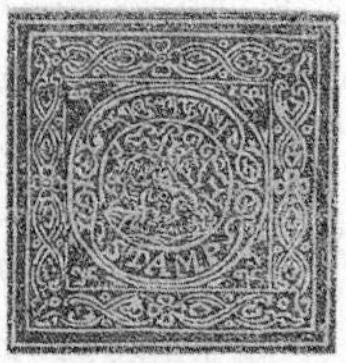

O1

O2

Sizes: No. O1, 32½x32½mm. No. O2, 38x28½mm. No. O3, 34x33mm. No. O4, 44x44mm. No. O5, 66x66mm.

Various Designs and Sizes Inscribed "STAMP"

1945 Unwmk. Typo. *Imperf.*
Native Paper

O1	O1	⅓t bronze green		
O2	O2	⅓t slate black		
O3	O1	⅔t reddish brown		
O4	O1	1⅓t olive green		
O5	O1	1s dark gray blue		

The status of Nos. O1-O5 is in question. Other values exist.

TIMOR

'tē-,mor

LOCATION — The eastern part of Timor island, Malay archipelago
GOVT. — Former Portuguese Overseas Territory
AREA — 7,330 sq. mi.
POP. — 660,000 (est. 1974)
CAPITAL — Dili

The Portuguese territory of Timor was annexed by Indonesia May 3, 1976. Timor-Leste achieved independent statehood status on May 20, 2002.

1000 Reis = 1 Milreis
78 Avos = 1 Rupee (1895)
100 Avos = 1 Pataca
100 Centavos = 1 Escudo (1960)
100Cents = 1 Dollar (2000)

Catalogue values for unused stamps in this country are for Never Hinged items, beginning with Scott 256 in the regular postage section, Scott J31 in the postage due section, and Scott RA11 in the postal tax section.

Watermark

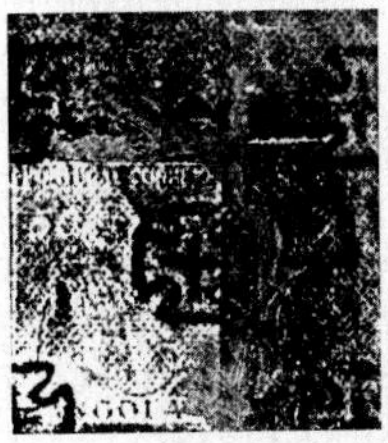

Wmk. 232 — Maltese Cross

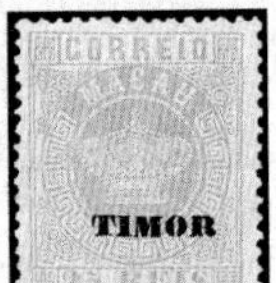

Stamps of Macao Overprinted in Black or Carmine

1885 Unwmk. *Perf. 12½, 13½*

1	A1	5r black (C)	6.00	1.60
a.		Double overprint	50.00	50.00
b.		Triple overprint	115.00	
2	A1	10r green	8.00	3.50
a.		Overprint on Mozambique stamp	22.50	14.00
b.		Overprinted on Portuguese India stamp	210.00	150.00
3	A1	20r rose, perf. 13½	9.00	4.50
a.		Double overprint	27.50	
b.		Perf. 12½	9.50	5.00
4	A1	25r violet	4.00	1.10
a.		Perf. 13½	30.00	17.50
5	A1	40r yellow	6.00	3.00
a.		Double overprint	17.50	
b.		Inverted overprint	21.00	21.00
c.		Perf. 13½	14.00	11.00
6	A1	50r blue	8.00	2.00
a.		Perf. 13½	15.00	12.00
7	A1	80r slate	12.50	4.00
8	A1	100r lilac	8.00	1.75
a.		Double overprint	25.00	
b.		Perf. 13½	9.00	3.50
9	A1	200r org, perf. 13½	11.00	4.00
a.		Perf. 12½	12.50	4.75
10	A1	300r brown	10.00	3.50
		Nos. 1-10 (10)	82.50	28.95

The 20r bister, 25r rose and 50r green were prepared for use but not issued.

The reprints are printed on a smooth white chalky paper, ungummed, with rough perforation 13½, and on thin white paper with shiny white gum and clean-cut perforation 13½.

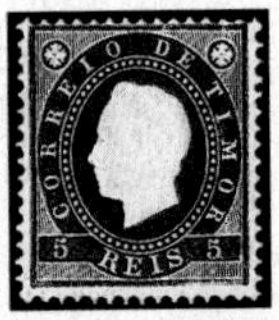

King Luiz — A2

1887 Embossed *Perf. 12½*

11	A2	5r black	2.50	1.90
12	A2	10r green	4.00	3.00
13	A2	20r bright rose	4.25	3.00
14	A2	25r violet	8.00	3.50
15	A2	40r chocolate	14.00	5.25
16	A2	50r blue	15.00	6.00
17	A2	80r gray	16.50	8.00
18	A2	100r yellow brown	25.00	10.50
19	A2	200r gray lilac	32.50	17.50
20	A2	300r orange	35.00	18.50
		Nos. 11-20 (10)	156.75	77.15

Reprints of Nos. 11, 16, 18 and 19 have clean-cut perforation 13½.

For surcharges see Nos. 34-43, 83-91.

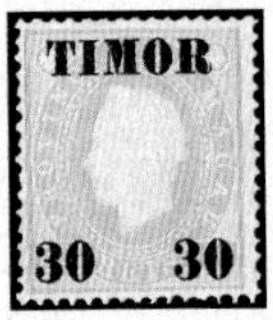

Macao No. 44 Surcharged in Black

1892 Without Gum *Perf. 12½, 13*

21	A7	30r on 300r orange	12.00	6.75

For surcharge see No. 44.

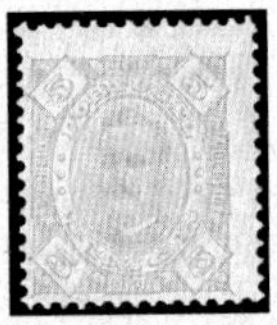

King Carlos — A3

1894 Typo. *Perf. 11½*

22	A3	5r yellow	1.25	.65
23	A3	10r red violet	1.75	.65
24	A3	15r chocolate	3.00	.95
25	A3	20r lavender	3.75	1.10
26	A3	25r green	4.50	.80
27	A3	50r light blue	5.75	3.50
a.		Perf. 13½	*160.00*	*125.00*
28	A3	75r rose	7.25	2.75
29	A3	80r light green	7.75	4.25
30	A3	100r brown, *buff*	5.75	2.75
31	A3	150r car, *rose*	13.00	8.00
32	A3	200r dk bl, *lt bl*	13.50	10.50
33	A3	300r dk bl, *salmon*	15.00	12.00
		Nos. 22-33 (12)	82.25	47.90

For surcharges and overprints see Nos. 92-102, 120-122, 124-128, 131-133, 183-193, 199.

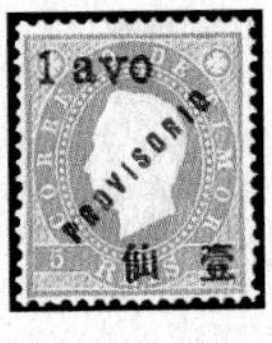

Stamps of 1887 Surcharged in Red, Green or Black

1895 Without Gum *Perf. 12½*

34	A2	1a on 5r black (R)	1.50	.85
35	A2	2a on 10r green	1.50	.85
a.		Double surcharge	25.00	
36	A2	3a on 20r brt rose (G)	4.00	1.75
37	A2	4a on 25r violet	4.00	1.10
38	A2	6a on 40r choc	6.00	3.00
39	A2	8a on 50r blue (R)	5.00	2.25
40	A2	13a on 80r gray	15.50	10.00
41	A2	16a on 100r yellow brn	20.00	7.75
42	A2	31a on 200r gray lilac	32.50	20.00
43	A2	47a on 300r org (G)	35.00	22.50
		Nos. 34-43 (10)	125.00	70.05

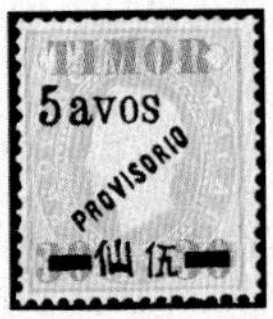

No. 21 Surcharged

1895 Without Gum *Perf. 12½, 13*

44	A7	5a on 30r on 300r org	20.00	5.75

Common Design Types pictured following the introduction.

Vasco da Gama Issue
Common Design Types

1898 Engr. *Perf. 14 to 15*

45	CD20	½a blue green	1.50	.85
46	CD21	1a red	1.50	.85
47	CD22	2a red violet	1.50	.85
48	CD23	4a yellow green	1.50	.85
49	CD24	8a dark blue	3.00	1.25
50	CD25	12a violet brown	3.50	1.40
51	CD26	16a bister brown	4.00	1.90
52	CD27	24a bister	5.00	2.50
		Nos. 45-52 (8)	21.50	10.45

400th anniversary of Vasco da Gama's discovery of the route to India.

For overprints and surcharge see Nos. 148-155.

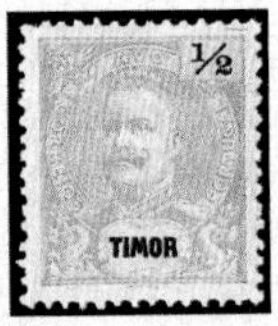

King Carlos — A5

1898-1903 Typo. *Perf. 11½*
Name & Value in Black Except #79

53	A5	½a gray	.35	.25
a.		Perf. 12½	2.50	1.75
54	A5	1a orange	.35	.30
a.		Perf. 12½	2.50	1.75
55	A5	2a light green	.35	.30
56	A5	2½a brown	1.25	1.10
57	A5	3a gray violet	1.25	1.10
58	A5	3a gray green ('03)	1.50	1.00
59	A5	4a sea green	1.60	1.00
60	A5	5a rose ('03)	1.50	1.00
61	A5	6a pale yel brn ('03)	1.50	1.00
62	A5	8a blue	2.00	1.10
63	A5	9a red brown ('03)	1.50	1.25
64	A5	10a slate blue ('00)	2.00	1.10
65	A5	10a gray brown ('03)	1.50	1.00
66	A5	12a rose	4.25	3.00
67	A5	12a dull blue ('03)	20.00	10.00
68	A5	13a violet	4.50	3.75
69	A5	13a red lilac ('03)	3.50	1.75
70	A5	15a gray lilac ('03)	5.50	3.75
71	A5	16a dark bl, *bl*	4.50	3.75
72	A5	20a brn, *yelsh* ('00)	6.00	3.75
73	A5	22a brn org, *pink* ('03)	6.00	3.50
74	A5	24a brown, *buff*	5.50	3.75
75	A5	31a red lil, *pinkish*	5.50	3.75
76	A5	31a brn, *straw* ('03)	10.00	3.50
77	A5	47a dk blue, *rose*	12.00	4.25
78	A5	47a red vio, *pink* ('03)	10.00	3.50
79	A5	78a blk & red, *bl* ('00)	12.50	6.75
80	A5	78a dl bl, *straw* ('03)	20.00	10.00
		Nos. 53-80 (28)	146.40	80.25

Most of Nos. 53-80 were issued without gum.

For surcharges & overprints see #81-82, 104-119, 129-130, 134-147, 195-196.

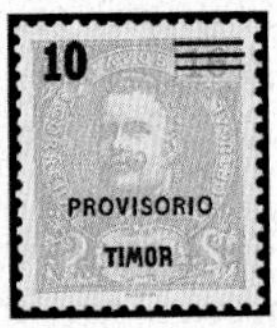

King Carlos — A6

1899 Black Surcharge

81	A6	10a on 16a dk bl, *bl*	3.75	2.50
82	A6	20a on 31a red lil, *pnksh*	3.75	2.50

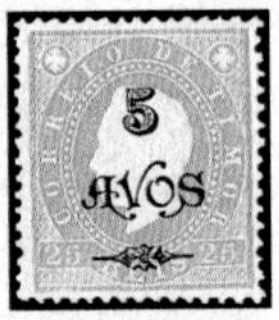

Surcharged in Black

1902 On Issue of 1887

83	A2	5a on 25r violet	2.50	1.75
84	A2	5a on 200r gray lil	4.00	2.50
85	A2	6a on 10r blue grn	100.00	50.00
86	A2	6a on 300r orange	3.75	3.50
87	A2	9a on 40r choc	4.50	3.50
88	A2	9a on 100r yel brn	4.50	3.50
89	A2	15a on 20r rose	4.50	3.50
90	A2	15a on 50r blue	100.00	50.00
91	A2	22a on 80r gray	8.75	6.50
		Nos. 83-91 (9)	232.50	124.75

Reprints of Nos. 83-88, 90-91, 104A have clean-cut perf. 13½.

On Issue of 1894

92	A3	5a on 5r yellow	2.00	1.10
a.		Inverted surcharge	40.00	30.00
93	A3	5a on 25r green	3.00	1.10
94	A3	5a on 50r lt blue	3.00	1.40
95	A3	6a on 20r lavender	3.00	1.40
96	A3	9a on 15r choc	3.00	1.40
97	A3	9a on 75r rose	3.00	1.40
98	A3	15a on 10r red vio	4.00	2.25
99	A3	15a on 100r brn, *buff*	4.00	2.25
100	A3	15a on 300r bl, *sal*	4.00	2.25
101	A3	22a on 80r lt green	6.00	4.00
102	A3	22a on 200r bl, *blue*	8.00	4.00

On Newspaper Stamp of 1893

103	N2	6a on 2½r brn	1.00	.85
a.		Inverted surcharge	27.50	27.50
		Nos. 92-103 (12)	44.00	23.40

Nos. 93-97, 99-102 issued without gum.

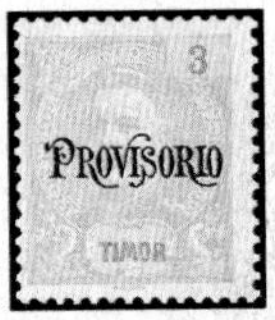

Stamps of 1898 Overprinted in Black

104	A5	3a gray violet	4.00	1.90
104A	A5	12a rose	6.00	3.75

Reprint noted after No. 91.

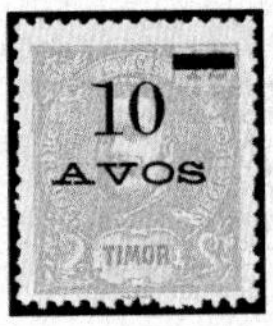

No. 67 Surcharged in Black

1905

105	A5	10a on 12a dull blue	8.25	4.25

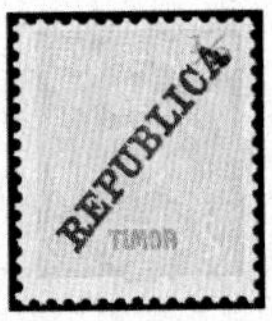

Stamps of 1898-1903 Overprinted in Carmine or Green

1911

106	A5	½a gray	.30	.30
a.		Inverted overprint	*20.00*	*20.00*
107	A5	1a orange	.30	.30
a.		Perf. 12½	*16.00*	*16.00*
108	A5	2a light green	.40	.35
109	A5	3a gray green	.50	.35
110	A5	5a rose (G)	.50	.35
111	A5	6a yel brown	.50	.35
112	A5	9a red brown	.75	.45
113	A5	10a gray brown	.75	.45
114	A5	13a red lilac	.80	.50
115	A5	15a gray lilac	1.60	1.25
116	A5	22a brn org, *pink*	1.60	1.25
117	A5	31a brown, *straw*	1.60	1.25
118	A5	47a red vio, *pink*	3.00	2.50
119	A5	78a dl bl, *straw*	4.75	3.50
		Nos. 106-119 (14)	17.35	13.15

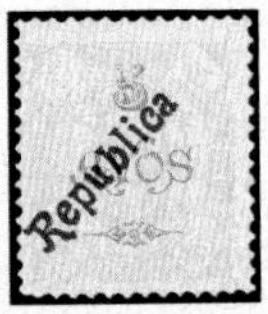

Preceding Issues Overprinted in Red

1913 **Without Gum**

On Provisional Issue of 1902

120	A3	5a on 5r yellow	7.00	4.00
121	A3	5a on 25r green	7.00	4.00
122	A3	5a on 50r lt bl	8.00	7.00
123	N2	6a on 2½r brn	8.00	7.00
124	A3	6a on 20r lavender	7.00	4.00
125	A3	9a on 15r choc	7.00	4.00
126	A3	15a on 100r brn, *buff*	8.00	5.50
127	A3	22a on 80r lt grn	9.00	8.00
128	A3	22a on 200r bl, *bl*	8.00	7.50

On Issue of 1903

129	A5	3a gray green	8.00	*7.50*

On Issue of 1905

130	A5	10a on 12a dull bl	8.00	4.00
		Nos. 120-130 (11)	85.00	*62.50*

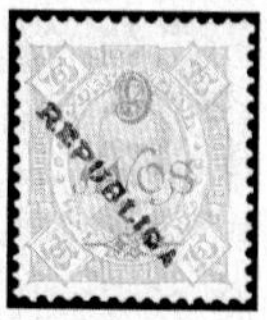

Overprinted in Green or Red

On Provisional Issue of 1902

1913

131	A3	9a on 75r rose (G)	7.00	6.00
132	A3	15a on 10r red vio (G)	6.00	5.00
a.		Inverted overprint	*35.00*	*35.00*
133	A3	15a on 300r bl, *sal* (R)	9.00	8.00
a.		"REUBPLICA"	19.00	19.00
b.		"REPBLICAU"	19.00	19.00

On Issue of 1903

134	A5	5a rose (G)	5.00	4.00
		Nos. 131-134 (4)	27.00	23.00

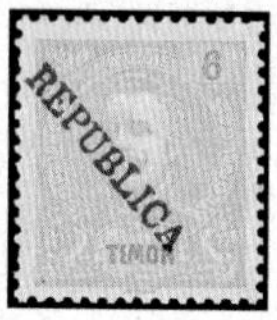

Stamps of 1898-1903 Overprinted in Red

1913

135	A5	6a yellow brown	5.00	1.75
136	A5	9a red brown	5.00	1.75
137	A5	10a gray brown	5.00	1.75
138	A5	13a violet	7.00	2.50
a.		Inverted overprint	40.00	40.00
139	A5	13a red lilac	6.00	2.50
140	A5	15a gray lilac	6.00	3.25
141	A5	22a brn org, *pnksh*	7.00	3.50
142	A5	31a red lil, *pnksh*	8.00	3.50
143	A5	31a brown, *straw*	10.00	5.50
144	A5	47a blue, *pink*	11.00	5.50
145	A5	47a red vio, *pink*	12.00	8.00
146	A5	78a dl bl, *straw*	15.00	6.50

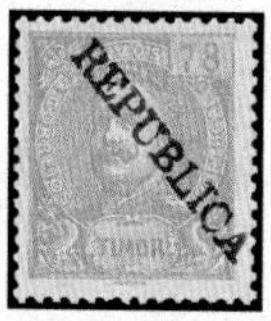

No. 79 Overprinted in Red

147	A5	78a blk & red, *bl*	15.00	8.00
		Nos. 135-147 (13)	112.00	54.00

Vasco da Gama Issue of 1898 Overprinted or Surcharged in Black

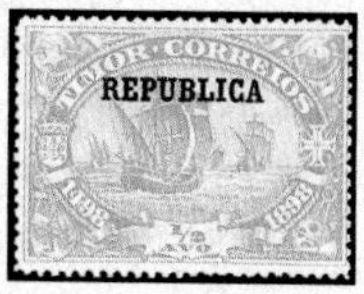

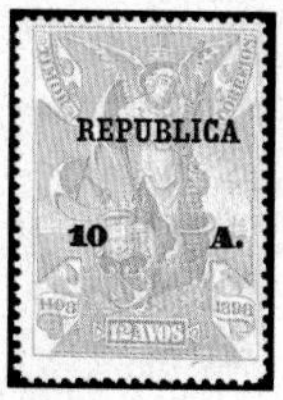

1913

148	CD20	½a blue green	.65	.60
149	CD21	1a red	.65	.60
150	CD22	2a red violet	.65	.60
151	CD23	4a yellow green	.65	.60
152	CD24	8a dark blue	1.40	1.10
153	CD25	10a on 12a vio brn	2.50	2.00
154	CD26	16a bister brown	2.00	1.75
155	CD27	24a bister	2.75	2.25
		Nos. 148-155 (8)	11.25	9.50

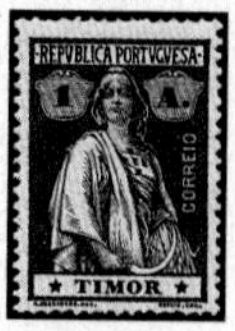

Ceres — A7

Name and Value in Black

Chalky Paper

1914 **Typo.** ***Perf. 15x14***

156	A7	½a olive brown	.25	.25
157	A7	1a black	.25	.25
158	A7	2a blue green	.25	.25
159	A7	3a lilac brown	1.00	.75
160	A7	4a carmine	1.00	.75
161	A7	6a light violet	1.00	.75
162	A7	10a deep blue	1.25	.75
163	A7	12a yellow brown	1.50	1.25
164	A7	16a slate	2.25	4.25
165	A7	20a org brown	16.50	6.75
166	A7	40a plum	10.00	5.00
167	A7	58a brown, *grn*	11.00	7.25
168	A7	76a brown, *rose*	13.00	7.25
169	A7	1p org, *salmon*	24.50	12.50
170	A7	3p green, *blue*	40.00	27.50
		Nos. 156-170 (15)	123.75	75.50

For surcharges see Nos. 200-201, MR1.

1920

Ordinary Paper

171	A7	1a black	.60	.45

1922-26 ***Perf. 12x11½***

173	A7	½a olive brown	.45	.40
174	A7	1a black	.45	.40
175	A7	1½a yel grn ('23)	.60	*1.10*
176	A7	2a blue green	.45	.40
177	A7	4a carmine	2.75	2.00
178	A7	7a lt green ('23)	1.75	*1.75*
179	A7	7½a ultra ('23)	3.25	*3.50*
180	A7	9a blue ('23)	4.00	*6.75*
181	A7	11a gray ('23)	4.00	*6.75*
182	A7	12a yellow brown	2.25	1.90
182A	A7	15a lilac ('23)	9.00	*8.00*
182B	A7	18a dp blue ('23)	11.00	7.00
182C	A7	19a gray grn ('23)	11.00	6.00
182D	A7	36a turq blue ('23)	10.00	4.75
182E	A7	54a choc ('23)	11.00	8.00
182F	A7	72a brt rose ('23)	17.50	17.50

Glazed Paper

182G	A7	5p car rose ('23)	92.00	60.00
		Nos. 173-182G (17)	181.45	136.20

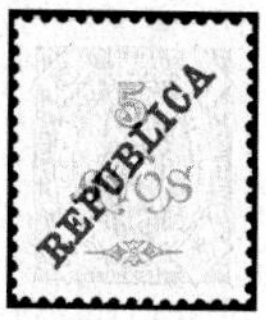

Preceding Issues Overprinted in Carmine

1915 ***Perf. 11½***

On Provisional Issue of 1902

183	A3	5a on 5r yellow	1.00	.55
184	A3	5a on 25r green	1.00	.55
185	A3	5a on 50r lt blue	1.00	.55
186	A3	6a on 20r lavender	1.00	.55
187	A3	9a on 15r chocolate	1.00	.55
188	A3	9a on 75r rose	1.50	.55
189	A3	15a on 10r red vio	1.50	1.50
190	A3	15a on 100r brn, *buff*	2.00	1.50
191	A3	15a on 300r bl, *sal*	2.00	3.00
192	A3	22a on 80r lt grn	3.25	2.75
193	A3	22a on 200r bl, *bl*	5.00	5.00

On No. 103

194	N2	6a on 2½r, perf. 13½	1.00	.55
a.		Perf. 12½	2.00	1.25
b.		Perf. 11½	4.00	1.75

On No. 104

195	A5	3a gray violet	1.00	.60

On No. 105

196	A5	10a on 12a dull bl	1.10	.60
		Nos. 183-196 (14)	23.35	18.80

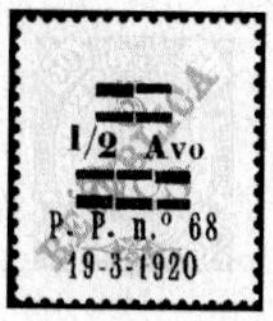

Type of 1915 with Additional Surcharge in Black

Perf. 11½

199	A3	½a on 5a on 50r lt bl	20.00	8.50
a.		Perf. 13½	35.00	12.50

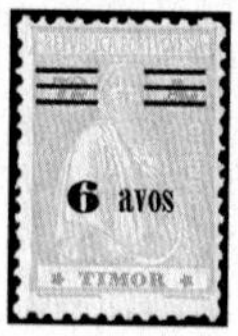

Nos. 178 and 169 Surcharged

1932 ***Perf. 12x11½***

200	A7	6a on 72a brt rose	1.50	1.25
201	A7	12a on 15a lilac	1.50	1.25

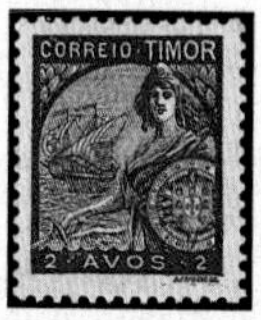

"Portugal" and Vasco da Gama's Flagship "San Gabriel" — A8

Perf. 11½x12

1935 **Typo.** **Wmk. 232**

202	A8	½a bister	.25	.25
203	A8	1a olive brown	.25	.25
204	A8	2a blue green	.25	.25
205	A8	3a red violet	.60	.60
206	A8	4a black	.60	.30
207	A8	5a gray	.70	.65
208	A8	6a brown	.85	.60
209	A8	7a bright rose	1.00	1.00
210	A8	8a bright blue	1.10	1.10
211	A8	10a red orange	1.60	1.20
212	A8	12a dark blue	2.75	2.10
213	A8	14a olive green	3.25	2.10
214	A8	15a maroon	3.00	2.75
215	A8	20a orange	3.50	2.75
216	A8	30a apple green	5.00	3.00
217	A8	40a violet	9.00	5.00
218	A8	50a olive bister	10.00	5.00
219	A8	1p light blue	24.50	14.00
220	A8	2p brn orange	50.00	25.00
221	A8	3p emerald	67.50	40.00
222	A8	5p dark violet	100.00	52.50
		Nos. 202-222 (21)	285.70	160.40

Common Design Types

1938 **Unwmk.** **Engr.** ***Perf. 13½x13***

Name and Value in Black

223	CD34	1a gray green	.25	.25
224	CD34	2a orange brown	.25	.30
225	CD34	3a dk violet brn	.25	.30
226	CD34	4a brt green	.25	.65
227	CD35	5a dk carmine	.25	*2.50*
228	CD35	6a slate	.45	.25
229	CD35	8a rose violet	.65	1.10
230	CD37	10a brt red violet	.65	1.75
231	CD37	12a red	1.10	2.50
232	CD37	15a orange	1.75	2.50
233	CD36	20a blue	1.75	.80
234	CD36	40a gray black	3.75	1.25
235	CD36	50a brown	3.75	1.25
236	CD38	1p brown carmine	7.50	5.00
237	CD38	2p olive green	17.50	4.00
238	CD38	3p blue violet	22.50	9.50
239	CD38	5p red brown	45.00	14.00
		Nos. 223-239 (17)	107.60	47.90

For overprints see Nos. 245A-245K.

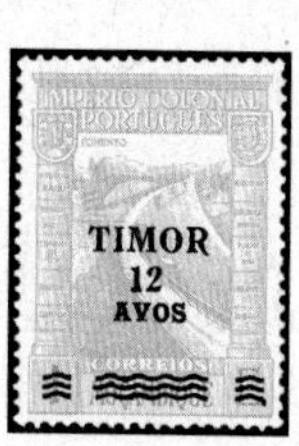

Mozambique Nos. 273, 276, 278, 280, 282 and 283 Surcharged in Black

1946 ***Perf. 13½x13***

240	CD34	1a on 15c dk vio brn	9.00	5.50
241	CD35	4a on 35c brt grn	9.00	5.50
242	CD35	8a on 50c brt red vio	9.00	5.50
243	CD36	10a on 70c brn vio	9.00	5.50
244	CD36	12a on 1e red	9.00	5.50
245	CD37	20a on 1.75e blue	9.00	5.50
		Nos. 240-245 (6)	54.00	33.00

Nos. 223-227 and 229-234 Overprinted "Libertacao"

1947

245A	CD34	1a gray green	22.00	15.00
245B	CD34	2a org brown	37.50	17.50
245C	CD34	3a dk vio brn	15.00	8.50
245D	CD34	4a brt green	15.00	10.00
245E	CD35	5a dark car	7.50	3.50
245F	CD35	8a rose violet	3.00	2.00
245G	CD37	10a brt red vio	10.00	5.00
245H	CD37	12a red	12.50	6.00
245I	CD37	15a orange	6.00	3.50
245J	CD36	20a blue	77.50	60.00
m.		Inverted overprint	*125.00*	*100.00*
245K	CD36	40a gray black	25.00	14.00
		Nos. 245A-245K (11)	231.00	145.00

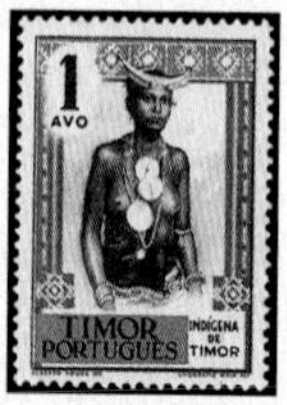

Timor Woman — A9

Designs: 3a, Gong ringer. 4a, Girl with basket. 8a, Aleixo de Ainaro. 10a, 1p, 3p, Heads of various chieftains. 20a, Warrior and horse.

1948 **Litho.** ***Perf. 14***

246	A9	1a aqua & dk brn	.50	.50
247	A9	3a gray & dk brn	1.10	.60
248	A9	4a pink & dk grn	1.40	.60
249	A9	8a red & blue blk	1.10	.50
250	A9	10a blue grn & org	1.10	.60
251	A9	20a ultra, aqua & bl	1.40	.50
252	A9	1p org, bl & ultra	19.00	4.00
253	A9	3p vio & dk brn	21.50	6.50
a.		Sheet of 8, #246-253	90.00	90.00
		Nos. 246-253 (8)	47.10	13.80

No. 253a sold for 5p.

Lady of Fatima Issue

Common Design Type

1948, Oct.

254	CD40	8a slate gray	3.00	3.00

UPU Issue

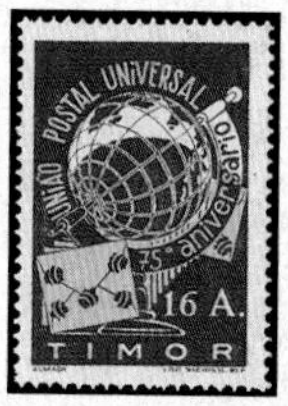

UPU Symbols — A10

1949 **Unwmk.** ***Perf. 14.***

255	A10	16a brown & buff	9.50	*10.50*

UPU, 75th anniversary.

Catalogue values for unused stamps in this section, from this point to the end of the section, are for Never Hinged items.

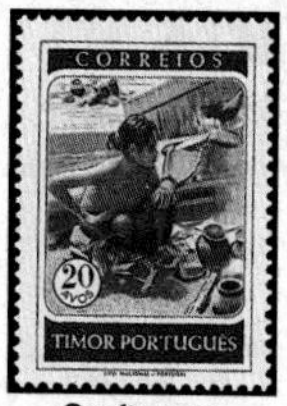

Craftsman A11

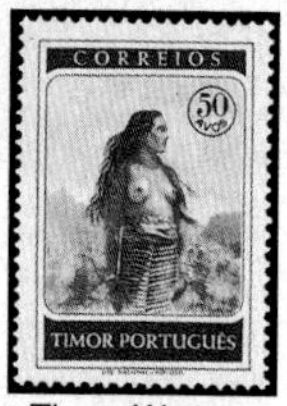

Timor Woman A12

1950 ***Perf. 14½***

256	A11	20a dull vio blue	1.10	.70
257	A12	50a dull brown	6.00	1.90

Holy Year Issue

Common Design Types

1950, May ***Perf. 13x13½***

258	CD41	40a green	1.50	1.25
259	CD42	70a black brown	2.25	2.00

Blackberry
Lily — A13

Designs: Various flowers.

1950   Unwmk.   Litho.   Perf. 14½
260	A13	1a multicolored	.35	.30
261	A13	3a multicolored	1.40	1.00
262	A13	10a multicolored	1.75	1.00
263	A13	16a multicolored	3.50	1.25
264	A13	20a multicolored	1.40	1.00
265	A13	30a multicolored	1.75	1.10
266	A13	70a multicolored	2.25	1.25
267	A13	1p multicolored	4.00	3.50
268	A13	2p multicolored	7.50	6.00
269	A13	5p multicolored	12.75	8.00
		Nos. 260-269 (10)	36.65	24.40

Holy Year Extension Issue
Common Design Type

1951   Perf. 14
270	CD43	86a bl & pale bl + label	2.00 1.75

Stamp without label attached sells for much less.

Medical Congress Issue
Common Design Type

Design: Weighing baby.

1952   Litho.   Perf. 13½
271	CD44	10a ol blk & brn	1.00 1.00

St. Francis Xavier Issue

Statue of St. Francis
Xavier — A14

Designs: 16a, Miraculous Arm of St. Francis. 1p, Tomb of St. Francis.

1952, Oct. 25   Perf. 14
272	A14	1a black	.25	.25
273	A14	16a blk brn & brn	1.00	.80
274	A14	1p dk car & gray	5.00	2.00
		Nos. 272-274 (3)	6.25	3.05

400th death anniv. of St. Francis Xavier.

Madonna and
Child — A15

1953   Perf. 13x13½
275	A15	3a dk brn & dull gray	.25	.25
276	A15	16a dk brown & cream	1.00	.60
277	A15	50a dk bl & dull gray	3.00	1.40
		Nos. 275-277 (3)	4.25	2.25

Exhibition of Sacred Missionary Art, Lisbon, 1951.

Stamp Centenary Issue

Stamp of Portugal
and Arms of
Colonies — A16

1953   Photo.   Perf. 13
278	A16	10a multicolored	1.10 1.00

Sao Paulo Issue
Common Design Type

1954   Litho.   Perf. 13½
279	CD46	16a dk brn red, bl & blk	.85 .70

Map of
Timor — A17

1956   Unwmk.   Perf. 14x12½
Inscription and design in brown, red, green, ultramarine & yellow
280	A17	1a pale salmon	.25	.25
281	A17	3a pale gray blue	.25	.25
282	A17	8a buff	.30	.25
283	A17	24a pale green	.40	.25
284	A17	32a lemon	.50	.25
285	A17	40a pale gray	.75	.30
286	A17	1p yellow	1.75	1.10
287	A17	3p pale blue	4.25	1.50
		Nos. 280-287 (8)	8.45	4.15

For surcharges see Nos. 291-300.

Brussels Fair Issue

Exhibition Emblems
and View — A18

1958   Perf. 14½
288	A18	40a multicolored	.50 .40

Tropical Medicine Congress Issue
Common Design Type

Design: Calophyllum inophyllum.

1958   Perf. 13½
289	CD47	32a multicolored	3.00 2.75

Symbolical
Globe — A19

1960   Unwmk.   Litho.   Perf. 13½
290	A19	4.50e multicolored	.50 .35

500th death anniv. of Prince Henry the Navigator.

Nos. 280-287 Surcharged with New value and Bars
Inscription and design in brown, red, green, ultramarine & yellow

1960   Unwmk.   Perf. 14x12½
291	A17	5c on 1a pale salmon	.25	.25
292	A17	10c on 3a pale gray bl	.25	.25
293	A17	20c on 8a buff	.25	.25
294	A17	30c on 24a pale grn	.30	.25
295	A17	50c on 32a lemon	.40	.25
296	A17	1e on 40a pale gray	.50	.25
297	A17	2e on 40a pale gray	.60	.25
298	A17	5e on 1p yellow	.75	1.00
299	A17	10e on 3p pale blue	1.75	2.50
300	A17	15e on 3p pale blue	2.50	2.00
		Nos. 291-300 (10)	7.55	7.25

Carved Elephant
Jar — A20

Native Art: 10c, House on stilts. 20c, Madonna and Child. 30c, Silver rosary. 50c, Two men in boat, horiz. 1e, Silver box in shape of temple. 2.50e, Archer. 4.50e, Elephant. 5e, Man climbing tree. 10e, Woman carrying pot on head. 20e, Cockfight. 50e, House on stilts and animals.

Multicolored Designs

1961   Litho.   Perf. 11½x12
301	A20	5c pale violet	.25	.30
302	A20	10c pale green	.25	.30
a.		Value & legend inverted	72.50	72.50
303	A20	20c pale blue	.25	.30
304	A20	30c rose	.25	.25
305	A20	50c pale grnsh bl	.25	.25
306	A20	1e bister	.70	.25
307	A20	2.50e pale ol bis	.50	.25
308	A20	4.50e lt salmon	.50	.25
309	A20	5e lt gray	.60	.25
310	A20	10e gray	1.40	.30
311	A20	20e yellow	2.75	1.00
312	A20	50e lt bluish gray	9.25	2.50
		Nos. 301-312 (12)	16.95	6.20

Sports Issue
Common Design Type

Sports: 50c, Duck hunting. 1e, Horseback riding. 1.50e, Swimming. 2e, Gymnastics. 2.50e, Soccer. 15e, Big game hunting.

1962, Mar. 22   Unwmk.   Perf. 13½
Multicolored Designs
313	CD48	50c gray & bis	.25	.25
314	CD48	1e olive bister	.60	.30
315	CD48	1.50e gray & bl grn	.70	.40
316	CD48	2e buff	.85	.35
317	CD48	2.50e gray	1.00	.50
318	CD48	15e salmon	3.00	1.90
		Nos. 313-318 (6)	6.40	3.70

Anti-Malaria Issue
Common Design Type

Design: Anopheles sundaicus.

1962   Litho.   Perf. 13½
319	CD49	2.50e multicolored	.75 .60

National Overseas Bank Issue
Common Design Type

Design: 2.50e, Manuel Pinheiro Chagas.

1964, May 16   Unwmk.   Perf. 13½
320	CD51	2.50e grn, gray, yel, lt bl & blk	.75 .60

ITU Issue
Common Design Type

1965, May 17   Litho.   Perf. 14½
321	CD52	1.50e multicolored	1.50 .90

National Revolution Issue
Common Design Type

Design: 4.50e, Dr. Vieira Machado Academy and Dili Health Center.

1966, May 28   Litho.   Perf. 11½
322	CD53	4.50e multicolored	1.50 .90

Navy Club Issue
Common Design Type

10c, Capt. Gago Coutinho and gunboat Patria. 4.50e, Capt. Sacadura Cabral and seaplane Lusitania.

1967, Jan. 31   Litho.   Perf. 13
323	CD54	10c multicolored	2.00	1.00
324	CD54	4.50e multicolored	2.00	1.00

Sepoy Officer,
1792 — A21

Designs: 1e, Officer, 1815. 1.50e, Infantry soldier, 1879. 2e, Infantry soldier, 1890. 2.50e, Infantry officer, 1903. 3e, Sapper, 1918. 4.50e, Special forces soldier, 1964. 10e, Paratrooper, 1964.

1967, Feb. 12   Photo.   Perf. 13½
325	A21	35c multicolored	.25	.30
326	A21	1e multicolored	1.50	1.00
327	A21	1.50e multicolored	.60	.30
328	A21	2e multicolored	.60	.25
329	A21	2.50e multicolored	.60	.25
330	A21	3e multicolored	1.00	.35
331	A21	4.50e multicolored	1.50	.45
332	A21	10e multicolored	3.00	.65
		Nos. 325-332 (8)	9.05	3.55

Our Lady of
Fatima — A22

1967, May 13   Litho.   Perf. 12½x13
333	A22	3e multicolored	.60 .30

Apparition of the Virgin Mary to three shepherd children at Fatima, Portugal, 50th anniv.

Cabral Issue

Map of Brazil, by Lopo Homem-Reinéis, 1519 — A23

1968, Apr. 22   Litho.   Perf. 14
334	A23	4.50e multicolored	.80 .50

See note after Macao No. 416.

Admiral Coutinho Issue
Common Design Type

Design: 4.50e, Adm. Coutinho and frigate Adm. Gago Coutinho.

1969, Feb. 17   Litho.   Perf. 14
335	CD55	4.50e multicolored	1.10 .85

View of Dili,
1834 — A24

1969, July 25   Litho.   Perf. 14
336	A24	1e multicolored	.30 .25

Bicentenary of Dili as capital of Timor.

Vasco da Gama Issue

da Gama Medal in
St. Jerome's
Convent — A25

1969, Aug. 29   Litho.   Perf. 14
337	A25	5e multicolored	.40 .30

Vasco da Gama (1469-1524), navigator.

Administration Reform Issue
Common Design Type

1969, Sept. 25   Litho.   Perf. 14
338	CD56	5e multicolored	.40 .25

King Manuel I Issue

Emblem of King
Manuel, St.
Jerome's
Convent — A26

1969, Dec. 1   Litho.   Perf. 14
339	A26	4e multicolored	.40 .25

King Manuel I, 500th birth anniv.

Capt. Ross Smith, Arms of Great
Britain, Portugal and Australia, and
Map of Timor
A27

1969, Dec. 9
340 A27 2e multicolored .50 .40
50th anniv. of the first England to Australia
flight of Capt. Ross Smith and Lt. Keith Smith.

Marshal Carmona Issue
Common Design Type

Antonio Oscar Carmona in civilian clothes.

1970, Nov. 15 Litho. Perf. 14
341 CD57 1.50e multicolored .25 .25

Lusiads Issue

Sailing Ship and
Monks Preaching
to
Islanders — A28

1972, May 25 Litho. Perf. 13
342 A28 1e brown & multi .25 .35
4th centenary of publication of The Lusiads
by Luiz Camoens.

Olympic Games Issue
Common Design Type

Design: 4.50e, Soccer, Olympic emblem.

1972, June 20 Perf. 14x13½
343 CD59 4.50e multicolored .50 .50

Lisbon-Rio de Janeiro Flight Issue
Common Design Type

Design: 1e, Sacadura Cabral and Gago
Coutinho in cockpit of "Lusitania."

1972, Sept. 20 Litho. Perf. 13½
344 CD60 1e multicolored .25 .40

WMO Centenary Issue
Common Design Type

1973, Dec. 15 Litho. Perf. 13
345 CD61 20e multicolored 1.75 2.00

**United Nations Transitional
Authority in East Timor**

A30

2000, Apr. 29 Litho. Perf. 12x11¾
350 A30 Dom. red & multi 35.00 50.00
351 A30 Int. blue & multi 50.00 75.00
No. 350 sold for 10c and No. 351 sold for
50c on day of issue.

**INDEPENDENT STATE OF TIMOR-
LESTE**

Independence — A31

Designs: 25c, Crocodile. 50c, Palm fronds.
$1, Coffee beans and picker. $2, Flag.

2002, May 20 Litho. Perf. 14½x14
352-355 A31 Set of 4 20.00 35.00

A32

Flag and: 10c, Pres. Xanana Gusmao. 50c,
Map of country.

2002 Litho. Perf. 13x13¼
356-357 A32 Set of 2 12.50 15.00

A33

Independence From Portugal, 30th
Anniv. — A34

Designs: 15c, Timorese flag, old man. 25c,
Timorese flag, child. 50c, Timorese coin,
rooster. 75c, Timorese flag, Pres. Nicolau
Lobato.

2005, Nov. 28 Litho. Perf. 12x12½
358 A33 15c multi .75 .75
359 A33 25c multi 1.00 1.00
360 A33 50c multi 2.00 2.00
361 A34 75c multi 3.00 3.00
Nos. 358-361 (4) 6.75 6.75

AIR POST STAMPS

Common Design Type
**1938 Unwmk. Engr. Perf. 13½x13
Name and Value in Black**
C1 CD39 1a scarlet .85 .45
C2 CD39 2a purple .90 .55
C3 CD39 3a orange .90 .60
C4 CD39 5a ultra 1.00 .65
C5 CD39 10a lilac brown 2.00 1.50
C6 CD39 20a dark green 3.50 1.75
C7 CD39 50a red brown 6.00 4.00
C8 CD39 70a rose carmine 9.00 7.50
C9 CD39 1p magenta 17.50 8.25
Nos. C1-C9 (9) 41.65 25.25

No. C7 exists with overprint "Exposicao
Internacional de Nova York, 1939-1940" and
Trylon and Perisphere. Counterfeits exist.
For overprints see Nos. C15-C23.

Mozambique Nos.
C3, C4, C6, C7 and
C9 Surcharged in
Black

1946 Unwmk. Perf. 13½x13
C10 CD39 8a on 50c orange 9.00 5.00
C11 CD39 12a on 1e ultra 9.00 5.00
C12 CD39 40a on 3e dk green 9.00 5.00
C13 CD39 50a on 5e red brn 9.00 5.00
C14 CD39 1p on 10e mag 9.00 5.00
Nos. C10-C14 (5) 45.00 25.00

**Nos. C1-C9 Overprinted
"Libertacao"**

1947
C15 CD39 1a scarlet 25.00 19.00
C16 CD39 2a purple 25.00 19.00
C17 CD39 3a orange 26.50 20.00
C18 CD39 5a ultra 25.00 19.00
C19 CD39 10a lilac brown 8.00 4.75
C20 CD39 20a dark green 8.75 5.50
C21 CD39 50a red brown 8.00 4.50
C22 CD39 70a rose carmine 35.00 14.00
C23 CD39 1p magenta 15.00 7.50
Nos. C15-C23 (9) 176.25 113.25

POSTAGE DUE STAMPS

D1

**1904 Unwmk. Typo. Perf. 12
Without Gum
Name and Value in Black**
J1 D1 1a yellow green .75 .50
J2 D1 2a slate .75 .50
J3 D1 5a yellow brown 2.50 1.50
J4 D1 6a red orange 2.75 2.25
J5 D1 10a gray brown 3.00 2.00
J6 D1 15a red brown 4.75 3.25
J7 D1 24a dull blue 7.50 6.00
J8 D1 40a carmine 9.00 6.75
J9 D1 50a orange 14.00 8.00
J10 D1 1p dull violet 22.50 15.00
Nos. J1-J10 (10) 67.50 45.75

Overprinted in
Carmine or Green

1911 Without Gum
J11 D1 1a yellow green .25 .25
J12 D1 2a slate .30 .25
a. Inverted overprint
J13 D1 5a yellow brown .60 .40
J14 D1 6a deep orange .80 .50
J15 D1 10a gray brown 1.50 .70
J16 D1 15a brown 1.75 1.10
J17 D1 24a dull blue 2.50 2.00
J18 D1 40a carmine (G) 3.25 2.50
J19 D1 50a orange 3.75 2.50
J20 D1 1p dull violet 7.50 7.00
Nos. J11-J20 (10) 22.20 17.20

Nos. J1-J10
Overprinted in Red
or Green

1913 Without Gum
J21 D1 1a yellow green 9.00 9.00
J22 D1 2a slate 9.00 9.00
J23 D1 5a yellow brown 7.00 6.00
J24 D1 6a deep orange 7.00 6.00
a. Inverted surcharge 30.00
J25 D1 10a gray brown 7.00 6.00
J26 D1 15a red brown 7.00 6.00
J27 D1 24a dull blue 8.00 7.00
J28 D1 40a carmine (G) 8.00 7.00
J29 D1 50a orange 10.00 12.00
J30 D1 1p gray violet 10.00 12.00
Nos. J21-J30 (10) 82.00 80.00

**Catalogue values for unused
stamps in this section, from this
point to the end of the section, are
for Never Hinged items.**

Common Design Type
**1952 Photo. & Typo. Perf. 14
Numeral in Red, Frame Multicolored**
J31 CD45 1a chocolate .40 .40
J32 CD45 3a brown .40 .40
J33 CD45 5a dark green .40 .40
J34 CD45 10a green .40 .40

J35 CD45 30a purple .65 .65
J36 CD45 1p brown carmine 1.25 1.25
Nos. J31-J36 (6) 3.50 3.50

WAR TAX STAMP

Regular Issue of 1914
Surcharged in Red

**1919 Unwmk. Perf. 15x14
Without Gum**
MR1 A7 2a on ½a ol brn 30.00 22.50
a. Inverted surcharge 100.00 100.00
See note after Macao No. MR2.

NEWSPAPER STAMPS

King Luiz — N1

**Stamps of Macao Surcharged in
Black**

**1892 Unwmk. Perf. 12½
Without Gum**
P1 N1 2½r on 20r brt rose 2.00 .75
a. "TIMOR" inverted
P2 N1 2½r on 40r chocolate 2.00 .75
a. "TIMOR" inverted
b. Perf. 13½ 4.50 3.00
c. As "a," perf. 13½
P3 N1 2½r on 80r gray 2.00 .75
a. "TIMOR" inverted
b. Perf. 13½ 18.00 11.50
Nos. P1-P3 (3) 6.00 2.25

N2

N3

1893-95 Typo. Perf. 11½, 13½
P4 N2 2½r brown .40 .35
a. Perf. 12½ 2.00 1.50
P5 N3 ½a on 2½r brn ('95) .45 .30
For surcharges see Nos. 103, 123, 194.

POSTAL TAX STAMPS

Pombal Issue
Common Design Types

1925 Unwmk. Perf. 12½
RA1 CD28 2a lake & black .30 .30
RA2 CD29 2a lake & black .30 .30
RA3 CD30 2a lake & black .30 .30
Nos. RA1-RA3 (3) .90 .90

**Type of War Tax Stamp of
Portuguese India Overprinted in
Red**

1934-35 Perf. 12
RA4 WT1 2a green & blk 6.50 8.00
RA5 WT1 5a green & blk 8.00 8.00

Surcharged in Black

RA6 WT1 7a on ½a rose & blk ('35) 10.00 9.00
Nos. RA4-RA6 (3) 24.50 25.00

The tax was for local education.

Type of War Tax Stamp of Portuguese India Overprinted in Black

Assistência
D. L. nº 72
10 avos

1936 **Perf. 12x11½**
RA7 WT1 10a rose & black 7.00 9.00

1937 **Perf. 11½**
RA8 WT1 10a green & blk 5.50 8.25

REPÚBLICA PORTUGUESA
10 avos
TIMOR
Assistência
PT1

1948 Unwmk. Typo. Perf. 11½
Without Gum
RA9 PT1 10a dark blue 3.00 2.00
RA10 PT1 20a green 3.50 3.00

The 20a bears a different emblem.

> **Catalogue values for unused stamps in this section, from this point to the end of the section, are for Never Hinged items.**

REPÚBLICA PORTUGUESA
$70
TIMOR
ASSISTÊNCIA
PT2

1960 Without Gum Perf. 11½
RA11 PT2 70c dark blue 1.50 1.25
RA12 PT2 1.30e green 2.25 2.25

See Nos. RA13-RA16. For surcharges see Nos. RA20-RA25.

Type of 1960 Redrawn

1967 Typo. Perf. 10½
Without Gum
RA13 PT2 70c deep blue 12.00 12.00
RA14 PT2 1.30e emerald 16.00 12.50

The denominations of Nos. RA13-RA14 are 2mm high. They are 2½mm high on Nos. RA11-RA12. Other differences exist. The printed area of No. RA13 measures 18x31mm; "Republica" 16mm.

Type of 1960

1967 Serif Type Face
RA14A PT2 70c deep blue 12.00 10.00

Type of 1960, 2nd Redrawing

1967-68 Typo. Perf. 10½
Without Gum
RA15 PT2 70c violet blue .60 .60
RA16 PT2 1.30e bluish grn ('68) 1.25 1.25

The printed area measures 13x30mm on Nos. RA15-RA16; "Republica" measures 10½mm.

REPÚBLICA
ASSISTÊNCIA
TIMOR
$50
PORTUGUESA
Woman and Star — PT3

1969-70 Litho. Perf. 13½
RA17 PT3 30c vio bl & lt bl ('70) .25 .25
RA18 PT3 50c dl org & maroon .25 .25
RA19 PT3 1e yellow & brown .25 .25
Nos. RA17-RA19 (3) .75 .75

The 2.50e and 10e in design PT3 were revenue stamps. Value $1.50 each.

REPÚBLICA
D. L. nº 776
$30
TIMOR
ASSISTENCIA

Nos. RA15-RA16 Surcharged in Red or Carmine

1970 Typo. Perf. 10½
Without Gum
RA20 PT2 30c on 70c 7.00 6.00
RA21 PT2 30c on 1.30e 6.00 6.00
RA22 PT2 50c on 70c 275.00 200.00
RA23 PT2 50c on 1.30e 7.25 7.25
RA24 PT2 1e on 70c (C) 325.00 225.00
RA25 PT2 1e on 1.30e 10.00 10.00
Nos. RA20-RA25 (6) 630.25 454.25

POSTAL TAX DUE STAMPS

Pombal Issue
Common Design Types

1925 Unwmk. Perf. 12½
RAJ1 CD28 4a lake & black .40 1.00
RAJ2 CD29 4a lake & black .40 1.00
RAJ3 CD30 4a lake & black .40 1.00
Nos. RAJ1-RAJ3 (3) 1.20 3.00

TOBAGO

tə-ˈbā-ˌgō

LOCATION — An island in the West Indies lying off the Venezuelan coast north of Trinidad
GOVT. — British Colony
AREA — 116 sq. mi.
POP. — 25,358
CAPITAL — Scarborough (Port Louis)

In 1889 Tobago, then an independent colony, was united with Trinidad under the name of Colony of Trinidad and Tobago. It became a ward of that colony January 1, 1899.

12 Pence = 1 Shilling
20 Shillings = 1 Pound

ONE SHILLING
Queen Victoria — A1

Wmk. Crown and C C (1)
1879 Typo. Perf. 14
1 A1 1p rose 140.00 100.00
2 A1 3p blue 140.00 85.00
3 A1 6p orange 65.00 80.00
4 A1 1sh green 425.00 80.00
a. Half used as 6p on cover —
5 A1 5sh slate 900.00 800.00
6 A1 £1 violet 4,500.

Stamps of the above set with revenue cancellations sell for a small fraction of the price of postally used examples.
Stamps of Type A1, watermarked Crown and C A, are revenue stamps.

1880 Manuscript Surcharge
7 A1 1p on half of 6p org 5,500. 875.

HALFPENNY
Queen Victoria — A2

1880
8 A2 ½p brown violet 65.00 100.00
9 A2 1p red brown 140.00 70.00
a. Half used as ½p on cover 2,250.
10 A2 4p yellow green 325.00 37.50
a. Half used as 2p on cover 2,250.
11 A2 6p bister brown 400.00 125.00
12 A2 1sh bister 100.00 130.00
a. Imperf.
Nos. 8-12 (5) 1,030. 462.50

2½ PENCE

No. 11 Surcharged in Black

1883
13 A2 2½p on 6p bister brn 100.00 100.00
a. Double surcharge 4,000. 2,250.

1882-96 Wmk. Crown and C A (2)
14 A2 ½p brown vio ('82) 2.50 20.00
15 A2 ½p dull green ('86) 4.25 1.50
16 A2 1p red brown ('82) 12.00 3.25
a. Diagonal half used as ½p on cover —
17 A2 1p rose ('89) 6.50 1.75
18 A2 2½p ultra ('83) 15.00 1.25
a. 2½p dull blue ('83) 65.00 3.75
b. 2½p bright blue 14.00 1.25
19 A2 4p yel grn ('82) 225.00 100.00
20 A2 4p gray ('85) 7.50 4.00
a. Imperf., pair 2,250.
21 A2 6p bis brn ('84) 625.00 550.00
a. Imperf.
22 A2 6p brn org ('86) 2.75 7.50
23 A2 1sh olive bis ('94) 4.00 27.50
24 A2 1sh brn org ('96) 26.00 130.00

Stamps of 1882-96 Surcharged in Black

½ PENNY
2½ PENNY

2½ PENCE
FOUR PENCE

Nos. 25-29  No. 30

1886-92
25 A2 ½p on 2½p ultra 10.00 25.00
a. Inverted surcharge
b. Pair, one without surcharge 15,000.
c. Space between "½" and "PENNY" 3mm 35.00 75.00
d. Double surcharge 2,500. 2,000.
26 A2 ½p on 4p gray 29.00 85.00
a. Space between "½" and "PENNY" 3mm 75.00
b. Double surcharge 3,500.
27 A2 ½p on 6p bis brn 3.75 25.00
a. Inverted surcharge 3,250.
b. Space between "½" and "PENNY" 3mm 30.00 125.00
c. Double surcharge 3,750.
28 A2 ½p on 6p brn org 150.00 200.00
a. Space between "½" and "PENNY" 3mm 375.00 450.00
b. Double surcharge 2,750.
29 A2 1p on 2½ ultra 110.00 22.50
a. Space between "1" and "PENNY" 4mm 300.00 90.00
b. Half used as ½p on cover 1,650.
30 A2 2½p on 4p gray 22.50 10.00
a. Double surcharge 3,500. 3,500.
Nos. 25-30 (6) 325.25 367.50

½d
POSTAGE

Revenue Stamp Type A1 Surcharged in Black

1896
31 A1 ½p on 4p lilac & rose 100.00 55.00
a. Space between "½" and "d" 150.00 82.50
1 ½ to 2 ½mm

Tobago stamps were replaced by those of Trinidad or Trinidad and Tobago.

TOGO

'tō-ˌgō

LOCATION — Western Africa, bordering on the Gulf of Guinea
GOVT. — Republic
AREA — 20,400 sq. mi.
POP. — 4,320,000 (1997 est.)
CAPITAL — Lome

The German Protectorate of Togo was occupied by Great Britain and France in World War I, and later mandated to them. The British area became part of Ghana. The French area was granted internal autonomy in 1956 and achieved independence in 1958.

100 Pfennig = 1 Mark
12 Pence = 1 Shilling
100 Centimes = 1 Franc

Catalogue values for unused stamps in this country are for Never Hinged items, beginning with Scott 309 in the regular postage section, Scott B11 in the semi-postal section, Scott C14 in the airpost section, Scott J32 in the postage due section, and Scott O1 in the official section.

Watermark

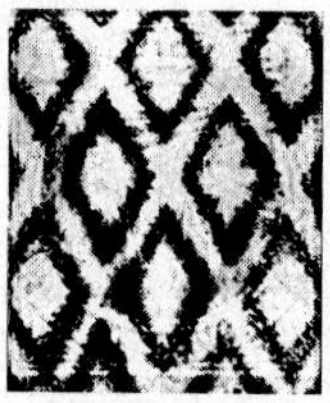

Wmk. 125 — Lozenges

German Protectorate

AREA — 34,934 sq. mi.
POP. — 1,000,368 (1913)

Stamps of Germany Overprinted in Black

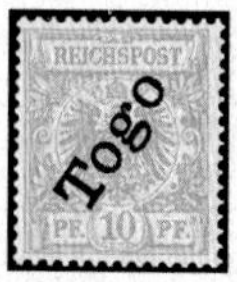

1897 Unwmk. Perf. 13½x14½

1	A9	3pf dark brown	5.25	6.00
a.		3pf yellow brown	9.25	25.00
b.		3pf reddish brown	47.50	140.00
c.		3pf pale gray brown	1,600.	1,200.
2	A9	5pf green	4.75	2.75
3	A10	10pf carmine	5.50	3.00
4	A10	20pf ultra	5.50	12.50
5	A10	25pf orange	35.00	55.00
6	A10	50pf red brown	35.00	55.00
		Nos. 1-6 (6)	91.00	134.25

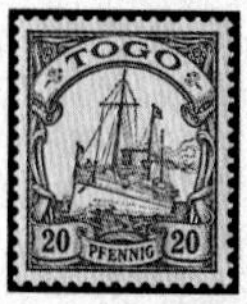

A3

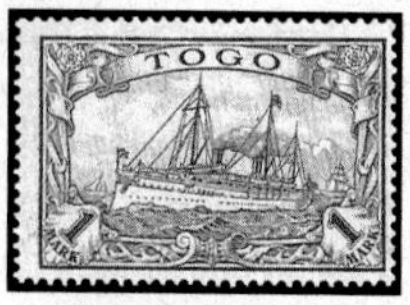

Kaiser's Yacht, the "Hohenzollern" — A4

1900 Typo. Perf. 14

7	A3	3pf brown	1.00	1.25
8	A3	5pf green	11.00	2.00
9	A3	10pf carmine	20.00	1.60
10	A3	20pf ultra	1.00	1.50
11	A3	25pf org & blk, *yel*	1.00	9.50
12	A3	30pf org & blk, *sal*	1.25	9.50
13	A3	40pf lake & blk	1.00	9.50
14	A3	50pf pur & blk, *sal*	1.25	7.25
15	A3	80pf lake & blk, *rose*	2.40	16.00

Engr.
Perf. 14½x14

16	A4	1m carmine	3.25	52.50
17	A4	2m blue	5.25	80.00
18	A4	3m black vio	6.75	14.00
19	A4	5m slate & car	120.00	475.00
		Nos. 7-19 (13)	175.15	679.60

Counterfeit cancellations are found on Nos. 10-19 and 22.

1909-19 Wmk. 125 Typo. Perf. 14

20	A3	3pf brown ('19)	.80	
21	A3	5pf green	1.25	2.00
22	A3	10pf carmine ('14)	1.60	110.00

Engr.
Perf. 14½x14

23	A4	5m slate & carmine ('19)	22.50	
		Nos. 20-23 (4)	26.15	

Nos. 20 and 23 were never placed in use.

British Protectorate

Nos. 7, 10-19, 21-22 Overprinted or Surcharged

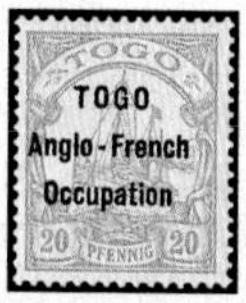

First (Wide) Setting
3mm between Lines
2mm between "Anglo" & "French"
Wmk. 125 (5pf, 10pf); Unwmkd.

1914, Oct. 1 Perf. 14, 14½

33	A3	½p on 3pf brn	160.00	140.00
a.		Thin "y" in "penny"	400.00	350.00
34	A3	1p on 5pf grn	160.00	140.00
a.		Thin "y" in "penny"	400.00	350.00
35	A3	3pf brown	130.00	100.00
36	A3	5pf green	130.00	100.00
37	A3	10pf carmine	130.00	100.00
a.		Inverted overprint	10,000.	3,000.
b.		Unwmk.		5,500.
38	A3	20pf ultra	42.50	50.00
39	A3	25pf org & blk, *yel*	40.00	47.50
40	A3	30pf org & blk, *sal*	47.50	60.00
41	A3	40pf lake & blk	225.00	250.00
42	A3	50pf pur & blk, *sal*	12,000.	10,000.
43	A3	80pf lake & blk, *rose*	275.00	275.00
44	A4	1m carmine	5,000.	2,750.
45	A4	2m blue	12,000.	14,000.
a.		Inverted overprint	15,000.	
b.		"Occupation" double	22,000.	15,000.

On Nos. 33-34, the surcharge line ("Half penny" or "One penny") was printed separately and its position varies in relation to the 3-line overprint. On Nos. 46-47, the surcharge and overprint lines were printed simultaneously.

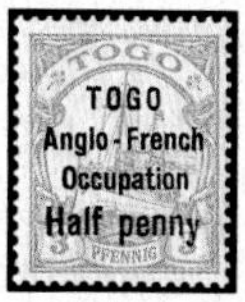

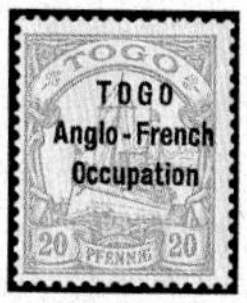

Second (Narrow) Setting
2mm between Lines
2mm between "Anglo" & "French"

1914, Oct.

46	A3	½p on 3pf brown	47.50	26.00
a.		Thin "y" in "penny"	75.00	60.00
b.		"TOG"	425.00	300.00
47	A3	1p on 5pf green	8.00	4.25
a.		Thin "y" in "penny"	12.00	15.00
b.		"TOG"	130.00	110.00
48	A3	3pf brown	6,500.	1,100
a.		"Occupation" omitted		
49	A3	5pf green	1,500.	750.00
50	A3	10pf carmine		3,000.
51	A3	20pf ultra	30.00	12.00
a.		"TOG"	3,500.	2,500.
b.		Vert. pair, #51 & #38	9,000.	
52	A3	25pf org & blk, *yel*	40.00	32.50
a.		"TOG"	12,000.	
53	A3	30pf org & blk, *sal*	20.00	29.00
54	A3	40pf lake & blk	6,000.	1,600.
55	A3	50pf pur & blk, *sal*		9,000.
56	A3	80pf lake & blk, *rose*	3,250.	2,250.
57	A4	1m carmine	8,000.	4,250.
58	A4	2m blue		13,000.
59	A4	3m black violet		65,000.
60	A4	5m slate & car		65,000.

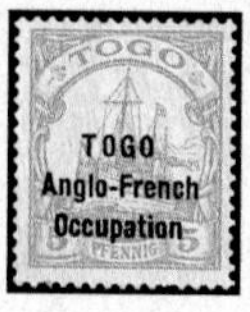

Third Setting
1¼mm btwn. "Anglo" & "French"
2mm between Lines
"Anglo-French" 15mm Wide

1915, Jan. 7

61	A3	3pf brown	9,000.	2,500.
62	A3	5pf green	225.	130.
63	A3	10pf carmine	200.	130.
64	A3	20pf ultra	1,400.	400.
64A	A3	40pf lake & blk		9,000.
65	A3	50pf pur & blk, *sal*	16,000.	11,000.

Stamps of Gold Coast Overprinted Locally

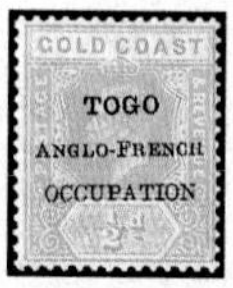

1915, May Wmk. 3 Perf. 14

66	A7	½p green	.35	3.75
a.		Double overprint		
67	A8	1p scarlet	.35	.60
a.		Double ovpt.	350.00	475.00
b.		Inverted ovpt.	175.00	250.00
c.		As "b," "Togo" omitted	8,000.	
68	A7	2p gray	.35	1.50
69	A7	2½p ultra	4.00	7.00

Chalky Paper

70	A7	3p violet, *yel*	3.50	6.00
71	A7	6p dl vio & red vio	2.75	2.00
72	A7	1sh black, *grn*	2.50	11.00
a.		Double overprint	1,500.	
73	A7	2sh vio & bl, *bl*	15.00	22.50
74	A7	2sh6p blk & red, *bl*	5.50	30.00
75	A7	10sh grn & red, *grn*	50.00	60.00
76	A7	20sh vio & blk, *red*	150.00	160.00

Surfaced-Colored Paper

77	A7	3p violet, *yel*	4.00	24.00
78	A7	5sh grn & red, *yel*	9.50	15.00
		Nos. 66-78 (13)	247.80	343.35

Nos. 66-78 exist with small "F" in "French" and thin "G" in "Togo." Several values are known without the hyphen between "Anglo-French" and all but No. 77 without the first "O" in "Occupation."

Stamps of Gold Coast Overprinted in London

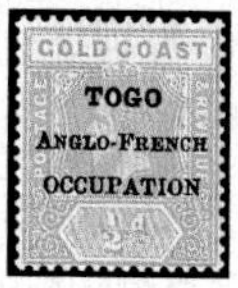

1916, Apr. Ordinary Paper

80	A7	½p green	.35	2.75
81	A8	1p scarlet	.35	.85
a.		Inverted ovpt.		
82	A7	2p gray	.60	3.00
83	A7	2½p ultra	.70	1.50

Chalky Paper

84	A7	3p violet, *yel*	6.00	1.25
85	A7	6p dl vio & red vio	2.50	2.00
86	A7	1sh black, *grn*	8.00	13.00
a.		1sh black, *emerald*	400.00	850.00
b.		1sh black, *bl grn, ol back*	12.00	18.00
87	A7	2sh vio & ultra, *bl*	4.50	8.50
88	A7	2sh6p blk & red, *bl*	4.50	7.00
89	A7	5sh grn & red, *yel*	37.50	27.50
90	A7	10sh grn & red, *bl grn, ol back* ('20)	21.00	75.00
a.		10sh green & red, *grn*	27.50	65.00
91	A7	20sh vio & blk, *red*	160.00	190.00
		Nos. 80-91 (12)	246.00	332.35

The overprint on Nos. 80-91 is in heavier letters than on Nos. 66-78 and the 2nd and 3rd lines are each ½mm longer. The letter "O" on Nos. 80-91 is narrower and more oval.

Issued under French Occupation

Stamps of German Togo Surcharged

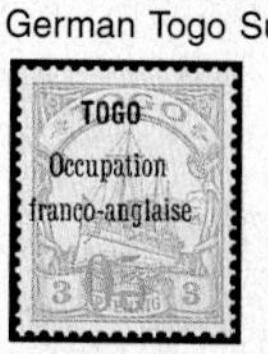

c

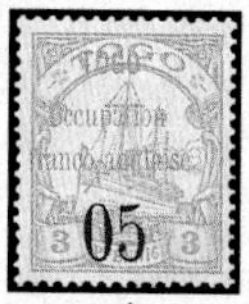

d

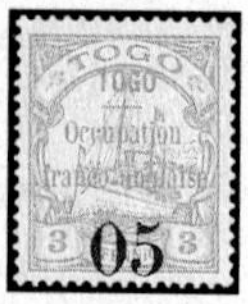

e

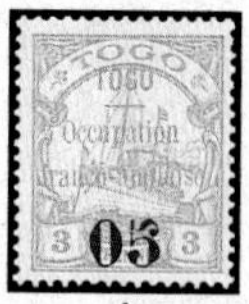

f

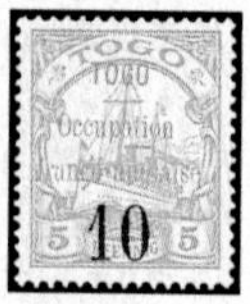

g

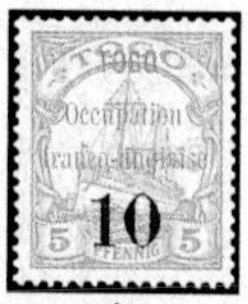

h

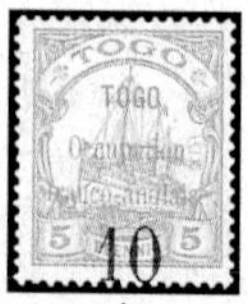

i

Wmk. Lozenges (5pf and 10pf) (125), Unwmk. (other values)

1914 Perf. 14, 14½

151	A3(c+d)	5c on 3pf brn	70.00	70.00
152	A3(c+e)	5c on 3pf brn	67.50	67.50
153	A3(c+f)	5c on 3pf brn	77.50	77.50
154	A3(c+g)	10c on 5pf grn	25.00	25.00
a.		Double surcharge	1,200.	1,200.
155	A3(c+h)	10c on 5pf grn	25.00	25.00
156	A3(c+i)	10c on 5pf grn	50.00	50.00
158	A3(c)	20pf ultra	55.00	55.00
a.		3½mm between "TOGO" and "Occupation"	875.00	875.00
159	A3(c)	25pf org & blk, *yel*	80.00	80.00
160	A3(c)	30pf org & blk, *sal*	100.00	100.00
161	A3(c)	40pf lake & black	600.00	625.00
162	A3(c)	80pf lake & blk, *rose*	600.00	625.00
		Nos. 151-162 (11)	1,750.	1,800.

Surcharged or Overprinted in Sans-Serif Type

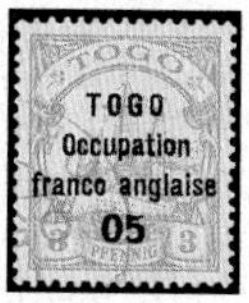

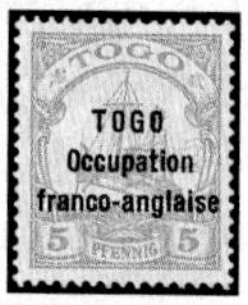

1915

164	A3	5c on 3pf brown	21,000.	4,500.
165	A3	5pf green	1,050.	450.
166	A3	10pf carmine	1,150.	450.
a.		Inverted overprint	27,000.	16,500.
167	A3	20pf ultra	1,400.	1,050.
168	A3	25pf org & blk, *yel*	15,000.	7,000.
169	A3	30pf org & blk, *sal*	15,000.	7,000.
170	A3	40pf lake & blk	15,000.	7,000.
171	A3	50pf pur & blk, *sal*	21,000.	12,500.
171A	A3	80pf red & blk, *rose*		—
172	A4	1m carmine		—
173	A4	2m blue	—	—
174	A4	3m black vio	—	—
175	A4	5m slate & car	—	—

Stamps of Dahomey, 1913-17, Overprinted

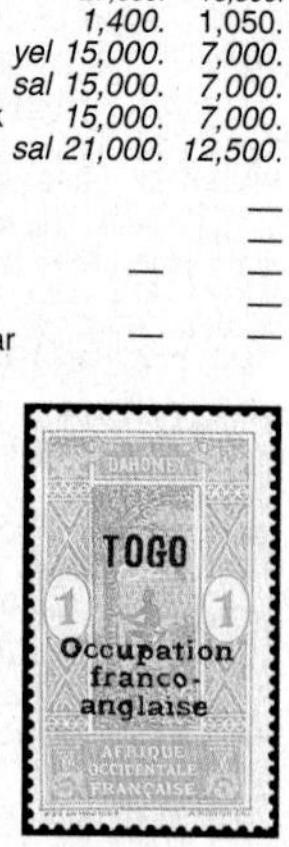

1916-17 Unwmk. Perf. 13½x14

176	A5	1c violet & blk	.35	.50
177	A5	2c choc & rose	.35	.50
178	A5	4c black & brn	.35	.80
a.		Double overprint	500.00	500.00
179	A5	5c yel grn & bl grn	.70	.70
180	A5	10c org red & rose	.70	.70

181 A5 15c brn org & dk vio ('17) 1.75 1.75
182 A5 20c gray & choc .70 1.10
183 A5 25c ultra & dp bl 1.10 1.10
184 A5 30c choc & vio 1.10 1.40
185 A5 35c brown & blk 1.75 2.10
186 A5 40c blk & red org 1.40 1.75
187 A5 45c gray & ultra 1.75 2.10
188 A5 50c choc & brn 1.75 2.10
189 A5 75c blue & vio 7.00 8.00
190 A5 1fr bl grn & blk 8.50 10.50
191 A5 2fr buff & choc 12.00 14.00
192 A5 5fr vio & do bl 14.00 16.00
Nos. 176-192 (17) 55.25 65.10

All values of the 1916-17 issue exist on chalky paper and all but the 15c, 25c and 35c on ordinary paper. See the *Scott Classic Specialized Catalogue of Stamps & Covers* for detailed listings.

French Mandate

AREA — 21,893 sq. mi.
POP. — 780,497 (1938)

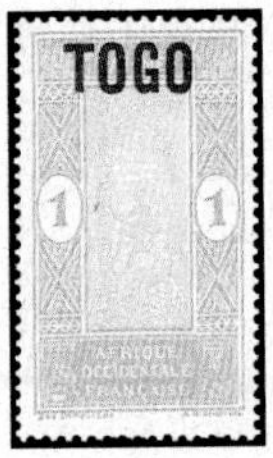

Type of Dahomey, 1913-39, Overprinted

1921

193 A5 1c gray & yel grn .35 .35
a. Overprint omitted 125.00 125.00
194 A5 2c blue & org .35 .35
195 A5 4c ol grn & org .35 .35
196 A5 5c dull red & blk .35 .35
a. Overprint omitted 410.00 425.00
197 A5 10c bl grn & yel grn .35 .70
198 A5 15c brown & car .70 .70
199 A5 20c bl grn & org 1.10 1.10
200 A5 25c slate & org 1.10 1.10
201 A5 30c dp rose & ver 1.40 1.75
202 A5 35c red brn & yel grn 1.10 1.40
203 A5 40c bl grn & ol 2.10 1.75
204 A5 45c red brn & ol 2.10 2.10
205 A5 50c deep blue 2.10 1.40
206 A5 75c dl red & ultra 2.10 2.10
207 A5 1fr gray & ultra 2.10 2.10
208 A5 2fr ol grn & rose 7.00 7.00
209 A5 5fr orange & blk 10.50 10.50
Nos. 193-209 (17) 35.15 35.10

Stamps and Type of 1921 Surcharged

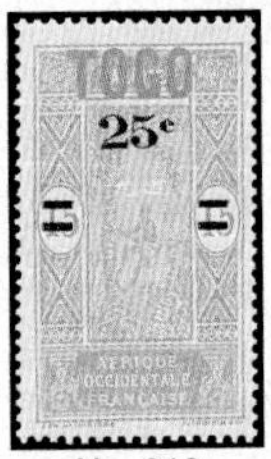

No. 210

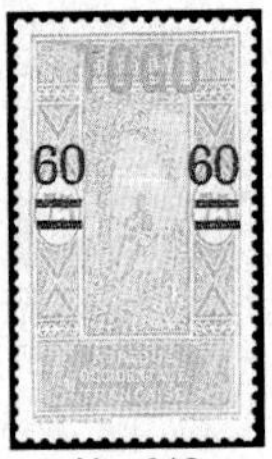

No. 213

1922-25

210 A5 25c on 15c ol brn & rose red .35 .55
211 A5 25c on 2fr ol grn & rose .70 .80
212 A5 25c on 5fr org & blk .70 .80
a. "TOGO" omitted 275.00 275.00
213 A5 60c on 75c vio, *pnksh* 1.10 1.40
a. "60" omitted 200.00 210.00
214 A5 65c on 45c red brn & ol 1.40 1.75
a. "TOGO" omitted 190.00 200.00
215 A5 85c on 75c dull red & ultra 2.10 2.75
Nos. 210-215 (6) 6.35 8.05

Issue years: #213, 1922; #211-212, 1924; others, 1925.

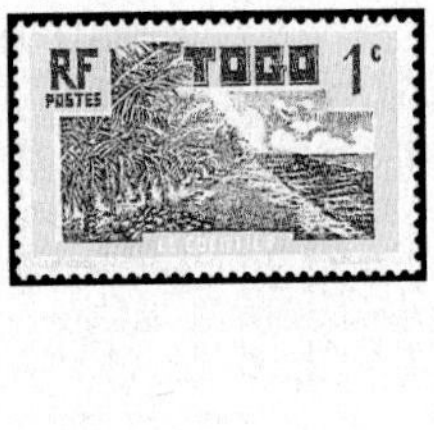

Coconut Grove A6

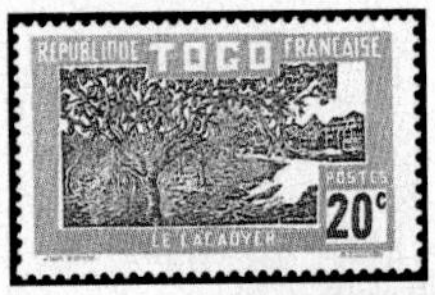

Cacao Trees — A7

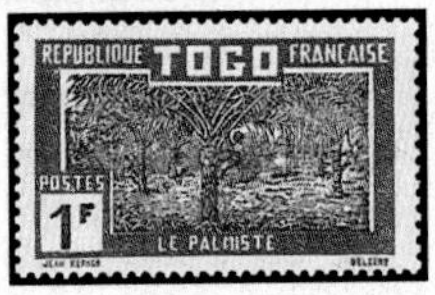

Oil Palms A8

1924-38 **Typo.**

216 A6 1c yellow & blk .25 .35
217 A6 2c dp rose & blk .25 .35
218 A6 4c dk blue & blk .25 .35
219 A6 5c dp org & blk .25 .35
220 A6 10c red vio & blk .25 .35
221 A6 15c green & blk .25 .35
222 A7 20c gray & blk .30 .50
223 A7 25c grn & blk, *yel* .70 .70
224 A7 30c gray grn & blk .35 .35
225 A7 30c dl grn & lt grn ('27) .70 .70
226 A7 35c lt brown & blk .70 .70
227 A7 35c dp bl grn & grn ('38) .70 .70
228 A7 40c red org & blk .35 .35
229 A7 45c carmine & blk .35 .35
230 A7 50c ocher & blk, *bluish* .35 .70
231 A7 55c vio bl & car rose ('38) 1.10 1.10
232 A7 60c vio brn & blk, *pnksh* .35 .35
233 A7 60c dp red ('26) .35 .70
234 A7 65c gray lil & brn .70 .70
235 A7 75c blue & black .70 .70
236 A7 80c ind & dl vio ('38) 1.75 1.75
237 A7 85c brn org & brn 1.10 1.10
238 A7 90c brn red & cer ('27) 1.10 1.10
239 A8 1fr red brn & blk, *bluish* 1.10 1.10
240 A8 1fr blue ('26) .70 .70
241 A8 1fr gray lil & grn ('28) 2.75 2.75
242 A8 1fr dk red & red org ('38) 1.10 1.10
243 A8 1.10fr vio & dk brn ('28) 4.25 5.50
244 A8 1.25fr mag & rose ('33) 1.40 1.75
245 A8 1.50fr bl & lt bl ('27) .70 1.10
246 A8 1.75fr bis & pink ('33) 8.50 5.25
247 A8 1.75fr vio bl & ultra ('38) 1.40 1.40
248 A8 2fr bl blk & blk, *bluish* 1.10 1.40
249 A8 3fr bl grn & red org ('27) 1.40 1.75
250 A8 5fr red org & blk, *bluish* 2.10 3.50
251 A8 10fr ol brn & rose ('26) 2.50 2.75
252 A8 20fr brn red & blk, *yel* ('26) 3.50 3.50
Nos. 216-252 (37) 45.65 48.20

For surcharges see Nos. 253, 301-302, B8-B9.

No. 240 Surcharged with New Value and Bars in Red

1926

253 A8 1.25fr on 1fr lt bl .70 .70

Common Design Types pictured following the introduction.

Colonial Exposition Issue

Common Design Types

Engr., "TOGO" Typo. in Black

1931, Apr. 13 ***Perf. 12½***

254 CD70 40c deep green 5.50 5.50
255 CD71 50c violet 5.50 5.50
256 CD72 90c red orange 5.50 5.50
257 CD73 1.50fr dull blue 5.50 5.50
Nos. 254-257 (4) 22.00 22.00
Set, never hinged 42.00

Paris International Exposition Issue

Common Design Types

1937 ***Perf. 13***

258 CD74 20c deep violet 1.60 1.60
259 CD75 30c dark green 1.60 1.60
260 CD76 40c car rose 1.60 1.60
261 CD77 50c dark brown 1.60 1.60
262 CD78 90c red 1.75 1.75
263 CD79 1.50fr ultra 1.75 1.75
Nos. 258-263 (6) 9.90 9.90
Set, never hinged 17.50

Colonial Arts Exhibition Issue

Souvenir Sheet

Common Design Type

1937 ***Imperf.***

264 CD77 3fr Prus bl & blk 10.50 10.50
Never hinged 14.00

Caillié Issue

Common Design Type

1939, Apr. 5 ***Perf. 12½x12***

265 CD81 90c org brn & org .35 1.10
266 CD81 2fr brt violet .35 1.10
267 CD81 2.25fr ultra & dk bl .35 1.10
Nos. 265-267 (3) 1.05 3.30
Set, never hinged 2.10

New York World's Fair Issue

Common Design Type

1939, May 10

268 CD82 1.25fr carmine lake .70 1.40
Never hinged 1.10
269 CD82 2.25fr ultra .70 1.40
Never hinged 1.10

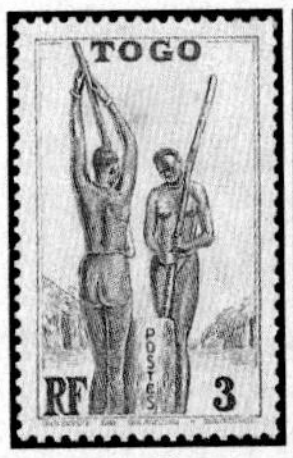

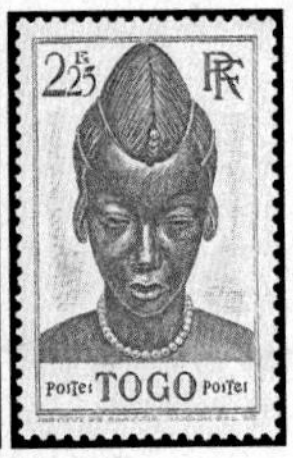

Togolese Women
A9 A12

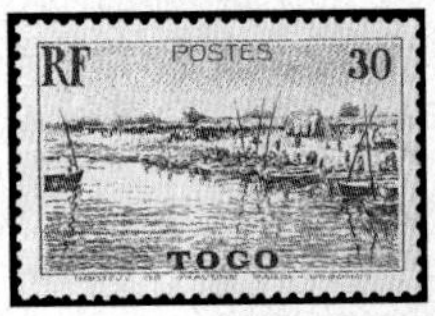

Mono River Bank A10

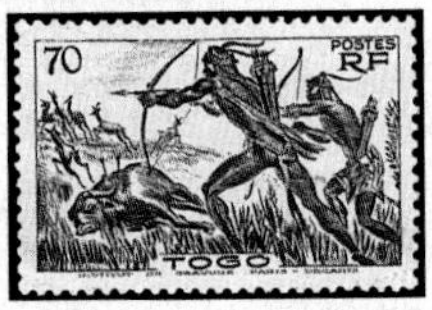

Hunters A11

1941 **Engr.** ***Perf. 12½***

270 A9 2c brown vio .25 .30
271 A9 3c yellow grn .35 .35
272 A9 4c brown blk .25 .30
273 A9 5c lilac rose .25 .30
274 A9 10c light blue .25 .30
275 A9 15c chestnut .25 .25
276 A10 20c plum .25 .25
277 A10 25c violet blue .25 .25
278 A10 30c brown blk .25 .25
279 A10 40c dk carmine .35 .35
280 A10 45c dk green .35 .35
281 A10 50c chestnut .35 .35
282 A10 60c red violet .35 .70
283 A11 70c black .70 1.10
284 A11 90c lt violet 1.40 1.40
285 A11 1fr yellow grn .35 .70
286 A11 1.25fr cerise 1.10 1.40
287 A11 1.40fr orange brn .70 .70
288 A11 1.60fr orange .70 1.10
289 A11 2fr lt ultra .70 .70
290 A12 2.25fr ultra 1.40 2.10
291 A12 2.50fr lilac rose 1.10 1.10
292 A12 3fr brown vio 1.10 1.10
293 A12 5fr vermilion 1.10 1.10
294 A12 10fr rose violet 1.75 1.75
295 A12 20fr brown blk 2.50 2.50
Nos. 270-295 (26) 18.35 21.05
Set, never hinged 26.00

For surcharges see Nos. 303-308, B7, B10.

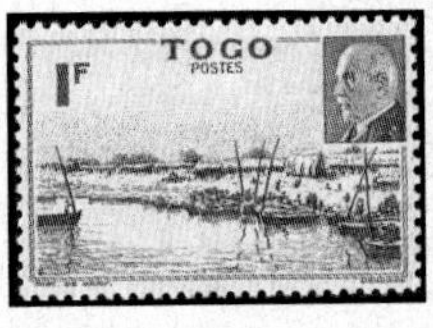

Mono River Bank and Marshal Pétain A12a

1941 **Engr.** ***Perf. 12½x12***

296 A12a 1fr green .35
297 A12a 2.50fr blue .35
Set, never hinged 1.40

Nos. 296-297 were issued by the Vichy government in France, but were not placed on sale in Togo.

For surcharges, see Nos. B10D-B10E.

Types of 1941 Without "RF"

1942-44 ***Perf. 12½***

298 A9 10c blue green .35
299 A9 15c yel brn & black .70
300 A10 20c lil brn & blk .70
300A A11 1fr yellow grn 1.10
300B A11 1.50fr lilac & green .70
300C A12 3fr brown violet 1.10
300D A12 5fr red brown 1.10
300E A12 10fr rose violet 1.40
300F A12 20fr black 1.40
Nos. 298-300F (9) 8.55
Set, never hinged 12.00

Nos. 298-300F were issued by the Vichy government in France, but were not placed on sale in Togo.

Nos. 231, 238, 284 Surcharged in Various Colors

a

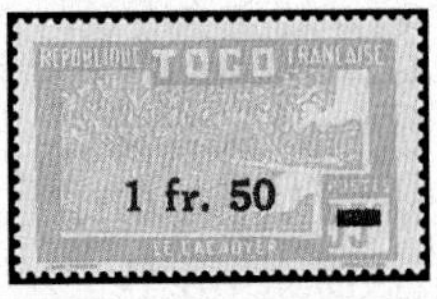

b

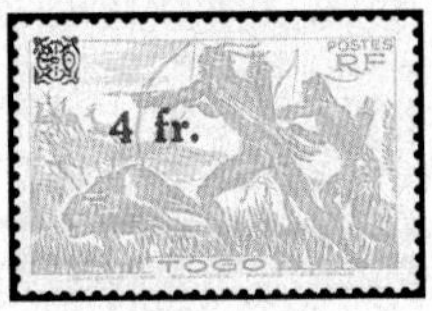

Perf. 14x13½, 12½

1943-44 **Unwmk.**

301 A7(a) 1.50fr on 55c (Bk) 1.10 1.10
302 A7(a) 1.50fr on 90c (Bk) 1.10 1.10
303 A11(b) 3.50fr on 90c (Bk) .70 .70
304 A11(b) 4fr on 90c (R) 1.40 1.40
305 A11(b) 5fr on 90c (Bl) 2.10 2.10
306 A11(b) 5.50fr on 90c (Br) 2.10 2.10
307 A11(b) 10fr on 90c (G) ('44) 2.10 2.10
308 A11(b) 20fr on 90c (R) 3.50 3.50
Nos. 301-308 (8) 14.10 14.10
Set, never hinged 17.50

Catalogue values for unused stamps in this section, from this point to the end of the section, are for Never Hinged items.

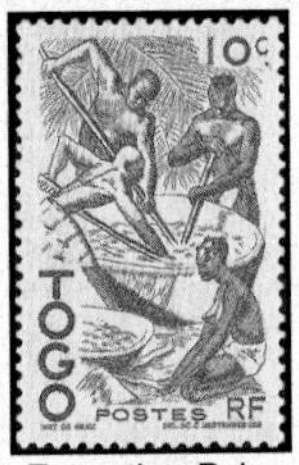

Extracting Palm Oil — A13

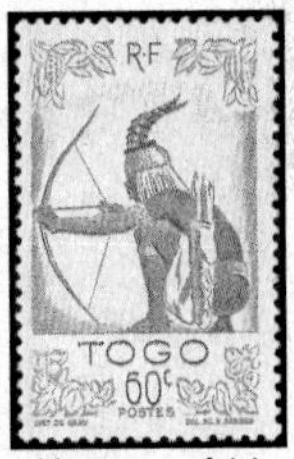

Hunter — A14

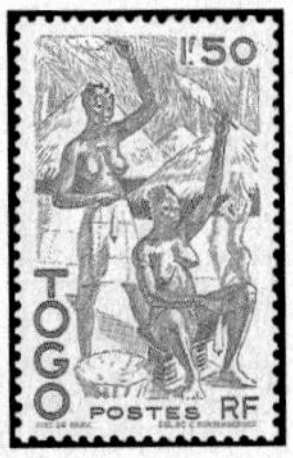

Cotton Spinners — A15

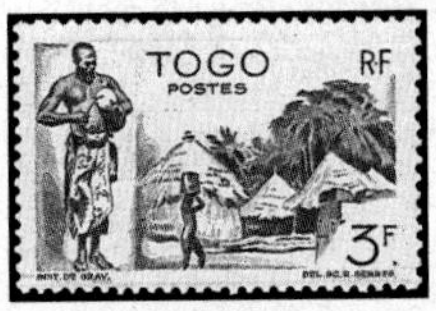

Village of Atakpamé A16

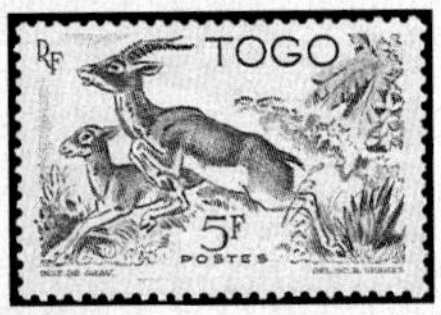

Red-fronted Gazelles — A17

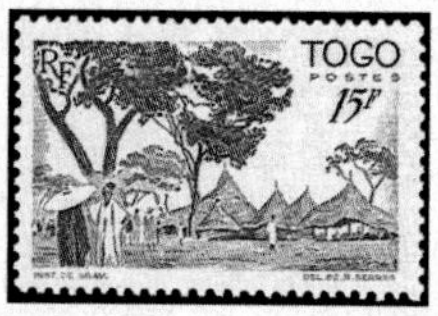

Houses of
the Cabrais
A18

1947, Oct. 6 Engr. *Perf. 12½*

309 A13 10c dark red .70 .35
310 A13 30c brt ultra .70 .35
311 A13 50c bluish green .70 .35
312 A14 60c lilac rose .70 .35
313 A14 1fr chocolate .70 .35
314 A14 1.20fr yellow grn 1.10 .70
315 A15 1.50fr brown org 1.10 .70
316 A15 2fr olive 1.10 .70
317 A15 2.50fr gray blk 1.75 1.40
318 A16 3fr slate 1.10 .70
319 A16 3.60fr rose car 1.10 1.10
320 A16 4fr Prus green 1.10 .35
321 A17 5fr black brn 2.10 .70
322 A17 6fr ultra 2.10 1.40
323 A17 10fr orange red 2.75 .70
324 A18 15fr dp yel grn 2.75 .70
325 A18 20fr grnsh black 2.10 .70
326 A18 25fr lilac rose 2.75 1.10
Nos. 309-326 (18) 26.40 12.70

Military Medal Issue

Common Design Type

Engr. & Typo.

1952, Dec. 1 *Perf. 13*

327 CD101 15fr multicolored 5.50 4.75

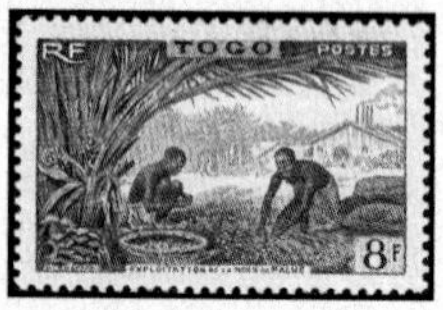

Gathering
Palm Nuts
A19

1954, Nov. 29 Engr.

328 A19 8fr vio & vio brn 1.40 .70
329 A19 15fr indigo & dk brn 1.75 .70

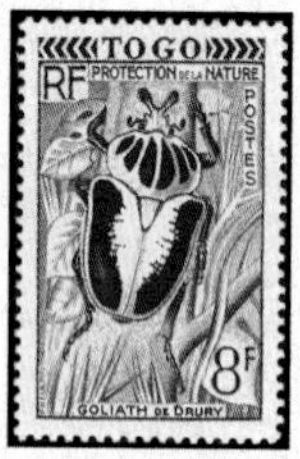

Goliath
Beetle — A20

1955, May 2

330 A20 8fr black & green 3.25 1.40

Intl. Exhibition for Wildlife Protection, Paris, May 1955.

FIDES Issue

Common Design Type

Design: 15fr, Teacher and children planting tree.

1956 Unwmk. *Perf. 13x12½*

331 CD103 15fr dk vio brn & org brn 4.25 2.10

Republic

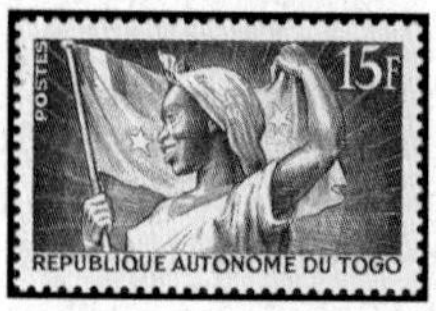

Woman
Holding
Flag — A21

1957, June 8 Engr. *Perf. 13*

332 A21 15fr dk bl grn, sepia & red .70 .25

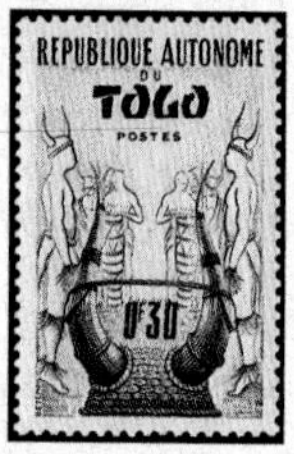

Konkomba
Helmet — A22

Teak Forest
A23

Design: 4fr, 5fr, 6fr, 8fr, 10fr, Buffon's kob.

1957, Oct. Unwmk.

333 A22 30c violet & claret .25 .25
334 A22 50c indigo & blue .25 .25
335 A22 1fr pur & lil rose .25 .25
336 A22 2fr dk brn & olive .25 .25
337 A22 3fr black & green .25 .25
338 A22 4fr blue & gray .60 .25
339 A22 5fr bluish gray & mag .60 .25
340 A22 6fr crim rose & bl gray .75 .25
341 A22 8fr bluish gray & vio .75 .25
342 A22 10fr grn & red brn .75 .25
343 A23 15fr multicolored .50 .25
344 A23 20fr violet, mar & org .60 .25
345 A23 25fr indigo & bis brn .75 .25
346 A23 40fr dk brn, ol & dk grn 1.10 .35
Nos. 333-346 (14) 7.65 3.60

See Nos. 350-363.

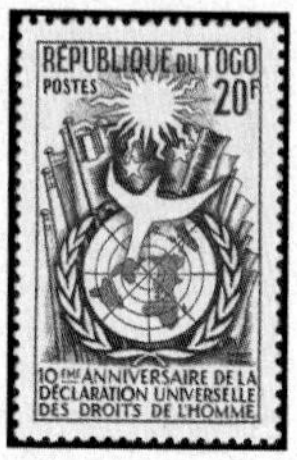

Flags, Dove and UN
Emblem — A24

1958, Dec. 10 Engr. *Perf. 13*

347 A24 20fr dk grn & rose red .65 .25

Universal Declaration of Human Rights, 10th anniversary.

Flower Issue

Common Design Type

Designs: 5fr, Flower of Bombax tree (kapok). 20fr, Tectona grandis (teakwood) flower, horiz.

Perf. 12x12½, 12½x12

1959, Jan. 15 Photo. Unwmk.

348 CD104 5fr dp bl, rose & grn .55 .25
349 CD104 20fr black, yel & grn .55 .25

Types of 1957
Inscribed:"Republique du Togo"

1959, Jan. 15 Engr. *Perf. 13*

Designs as Before

350 A22 30c ultra & gray .45 .25
351 A22 50c org & brt grn .45 .25
352 A22 1fr red lil & lt ol grn .45 .25
353 A22 2fr olive & bl grn .45 .25
354 A22 3fr vio & rose car .45 .25
355 A22 4fr lil rose & pale pur .45 .25
356 A22 5fr green & brown .45 .25
357 A22 6fr ultra & gray bl .45 .25
358 A22 8fr sl grn & bis .45 .25
359 A22 10fr vio & lt brn .45 .25
360 A23 15fr dk brn, bis & cl .45 .25
361 A23 20fr blk, bl grn & brn .45 .25
362 A23 25fr sep, red brn, ol & vio .60 .25
363 A23 40fr dk grn, org brn & bl .60 .25
Nos. 350-363 (14) 6.60 3.50

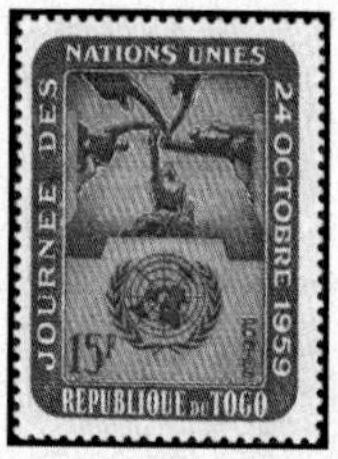

"Five Continents,"
Ceiling Painting,
Palais des
Nations,
Geneva — A25

1959, Oct. 24 Engr. *Perf. 12½*

Centers in Dark Ultramarine

364 A25 15fr brown .35 .25
365 A25 20fr purple .35 .25
366 A25 25fr dark orange .35 .25
367 A25 40fr dark green .55 .25
368 A25 60fr carmine rose .60 .30
Nos. 364-368 (5) 2.20 1.30

Issued for United Nations Day, Oct. 24.

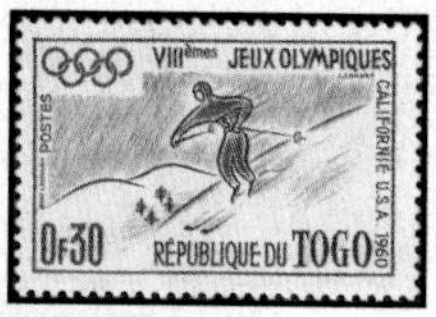

Skier
A26

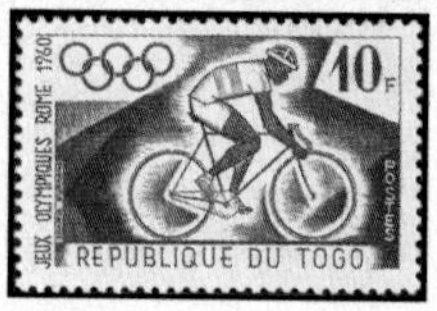

Bicyclist
A27

Sports: 50c, Ice Hockey. 1fr, Tobogganing. 15fr, Discus thrower, vert. 20fr, Boxing, vert. 25fr, Runner.

1960 Unwmk. *Perf. 13*

369 A26 30c sl grn, car & bl grn .45 .25
370 A26 50c red & black .45 .25
371 A26 1fr red, blk & emer .45 .25
372 A27 10fr brown, ultra & sl .45 .25
373 A27 15fr dk red brn & grn .45 .25
374 A27 20fr dk grn, gldn brn & brn .55 .25
375 A27 25fr orange, mag & brn .65 .25
Nos. 369-375 (7) 3.45 1.75

8th Winter Olympic Games, Squaw Valley, Calif. (Nos. 369-371); 17th Olympic Games, Rome (Nos. 372-375).

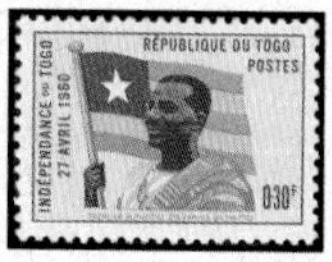

Prime Minister
Sylvanus Olympio
and Togo
Flag — A28

1960, Apr. 27 Litho.

Center in Green, Red, Yellow & Brown

376 A28 30c black & buff .25 .25
377 A28 50c brown & buff .25 .25
378 A28 1fr lilac & buff .25 .25
379 A28 10fr blue & buff .25 .25
380 A28 20fr red & buff .25 .25
381 A28 25fr green & buff .25 .25
Nos. 376-381 (6) 1.50 1.50

Proclamation of Togo's full independence, Apr. 27, 1960.

See Nos. C31-C33.

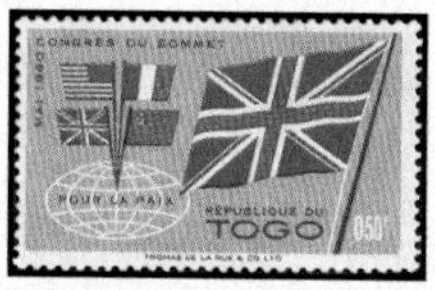

Flags of
"Big Four,"
and British
Flag — A29

1960, May 21 *Perf. 14x14½*

382 A29 50c shown .35 .25
383 A29 1fr USSR .35 .25
384 A29 20fr France .35 .25
385 A29 25fr US .35 .25
Nos. 382-385 (4) 1.40 1.00

Summit Conference of France, Great Britain, United States and USSR, Paris, May 16.

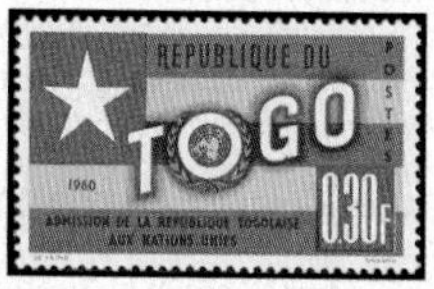

Flag of
Togo and
UN
Emblem
A30

1961, Jan. 6 *Perf. 14½x15*

Flag in red, olive green & yellow

386 A30 30c red .30 .25
387 A30 50c brown .30 .25
388 A30 1fr ultramarine .30 .25
389 A30 10fr maroon .30 .25
390 A30 25fr black .30 .25
391 A30 30fr violet .30 .25
Nos. 386-391 (6) 1.80 1.50

Togo's admission to United Nations.

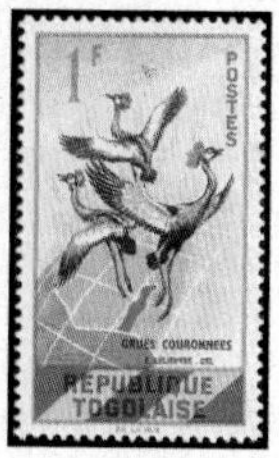

Crowned Cranes
over Map — A31

1961, Apr. 1 *Perf. 14½x15*

392 A31 1fr multicolored .40 .25
393 A31 10fr multicolored .40 .25
394 A31 25fr multicolored .50 .25
395 A31 30fr multicolored .70 .25
Nos. 392-395 (4) 2.00 1.00

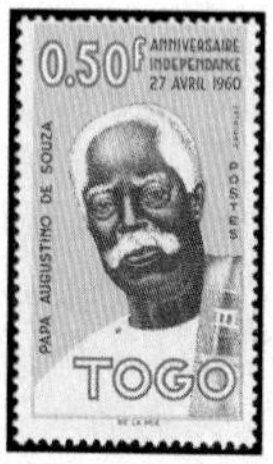

Augustino de
Souza — A32

1961, Apr. 27 Litho. *Perf. 15*

396 A32 50c yellow, red & blk .35 .25
397 A32 1fr emerald, brn & blk .35 .25
398 A32 10fr grnsh bl, vio & blk .35 .25
399 A32 25fr salmon, grn & blk .35 .25
400 A32 30fr rose lil, bl & blk .35 .25
Nos. 396-400 (5) 1.75 1.25

1st anniv. of independence; "Papa" Augustino de Souza, leader of the independence movement.

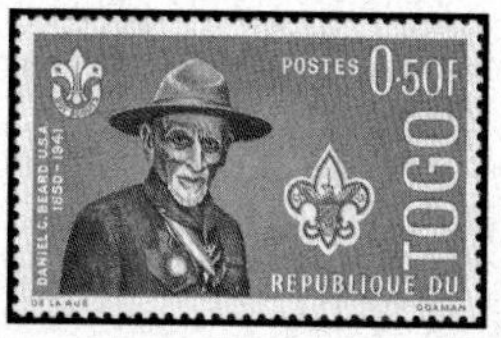

Daniel
C.
Beard
A33

Designs: 1fr, Lord Baden-Powell. 10fr, Togolese Scout and emblems. 25fr, Togolese Scout and flag, vert. 30fr, Symbolic tents and fire, vert. 100fr, Three hands of different races giving Scout sign.

1961, Oct. 7 Photo. *Perf. 13*

401 A33 50c brt rose & grn .45 .25
402 A33 1fr dp violet & car .45 .25
403 A33 10fr dk gray & brn .45 .25
404 A33 25fr multicolored .45 .25
405 A33 30fr grn, red & org brn .55 .25
406 A33 100fr rose car & bl 1.25 .25
Nos. 401-406 (6) 3.60 1.50

Togolese Boy Scouts; 20th anniv. of the deaths of Daniel C. Beard and Lord Baden-Powell.

Four imperf. souvenir sheets each contain the six stamps, Nos. 401-406. Two sheets have a solid background of bright yellow, two a background of pale grayish brown. One yellow and one brown sheet have simulated perforations around the stamps. Size: 120x145mm. "REPUBLIQUE DU TOGO" is inscribed in white on bottom sheet margin. Value, each $4.

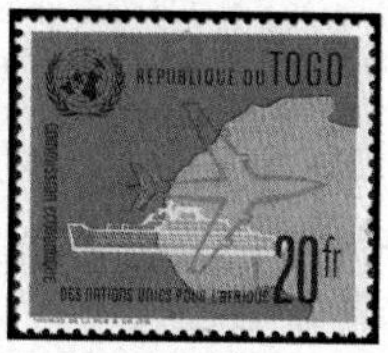

Plane, Ship
and Part of
Map of
Africa — A34

Part of Map of Africa and: 25fr, Electric train and power mast. 30fr, Tractor and oil derricks. 85fr, Microscope and atomic symbol.

1961, Oct. 24 Litho.

Black Inscriptions; Map in Ocher

407 A34 20fr vio bl, org & yel .50 .25
408 A34 25fr gray, org & yel .50 .25
409 A34 30fr dk red, yel & org .60 .25
410 A34 85fr blue, yel & org 1.10 .25
a. Souvenir sheet of 4 4.00 2.75
Nos. 407-410 (4) 2.70 1.00

UN Economic Commission for Africa. No. 410a contains one each of Nos. 407-410, imperf., printed without separating margin

between the individual stamps to show a complete map of Africa.

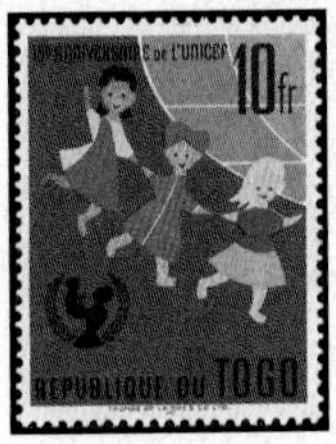

Children Dancing around Globe — A35

UNICEF Emblem, children and globe.

1961, Dec. 9 Unwmk. *Perf. 13½*
Black Inscription; Multicolored Design

411	A35	1fr ultra	.40	.25
412	A35	10fr red brown	.40	.25
413	A35	20fr lilac	.40	.25
414	A35	25fr gray	.40	.25
415	A35	30fr bright blue	.45	.25
416	A35	85fr deep lilac	.85	.25
a.		Souvenir sheet of 6	5.00	3.50
		Nos. 411-416 (6)	2.90	1.50

UNICEF, 15th anniv.
Nos. 411-416a assembled in two rows show the globe and children of various races dancing around it.

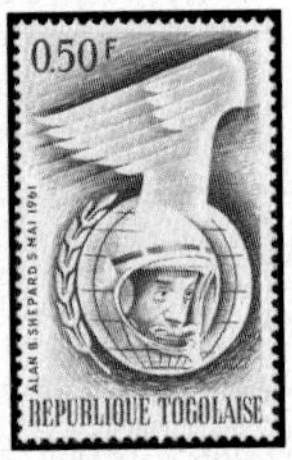

Cmdr. Alan B. Shepard — A36

Designs: 1fr, 30fr, Yuri A. Gagarin. 25fr, Shepherd.

1962, Feb. 24 *Perf. 15x14*

417	A36	50c green	.25	.25
418	A36	1fr carmine rose	.25	.25
419	A36	25fr blue	.30	.25
420	A36	30fr purple	.45	.25
		Nos. 417-420 (4)	1.25	1.00

Astronauts of 1961.
Issued in sheets of 50 and in miniature sheets of 12 stamps plus four central labels showing photographs of Alan B. Shepard (US), Virgil I. Grissom (US), Yuri A. Gagarin (USSR), Gherman S. Titov (USSR).

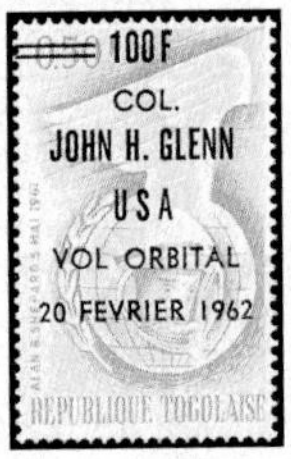

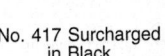

No. 417 Surcharged in Black

1962, Apr. 7

421	A36	100fr on 50c green	2.00	.50
a.		Carmine surcharge	2.00	.50

Orbital flight of Lt. Col. John H. Glenn, Jr., US, Feb. 20, 1962.

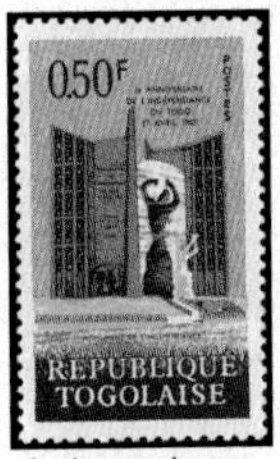

Independence Monument, Lomé — A37

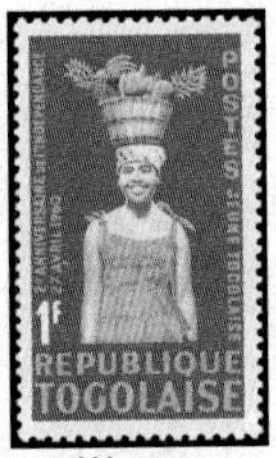

Woman Carrying Fruit Basket — A38

1962, Apr. 27 Litho. *Perf. 13½x14*

422	A37	50c multicolored	.25	.25
423	A38	1fr green & pink	.25	.25
424	A37	5fr multicolored	.25	.25
425	A38	20fr purple & yel	.35	.25
426	A37	25fr multicolored	.40	.25
427	A38	30fr red & yellow	.40	.25
a.		Souv. sheet of 3, #424-425, 427, imperf.	2.40	1.75
		Nos. 422-427 (6)	1.90	1.50

2nd anniversary of Togo's independence.

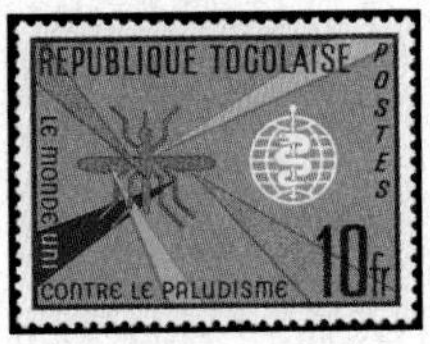

Malaria Eradication Emblem A39

1962, June 2 *Perf. 13½x13*
Multicolored Design

428	A39	10fr yellow green	.35	.25
429	A39	25fr pale lilac	.50	.25
430	A39	30fr ocher	.55	.25
431	A39	85fr light blue	1.10	.25
		Nos. 428-431 (4)	2.50	1.00

WHO drive to eradicate malaria.

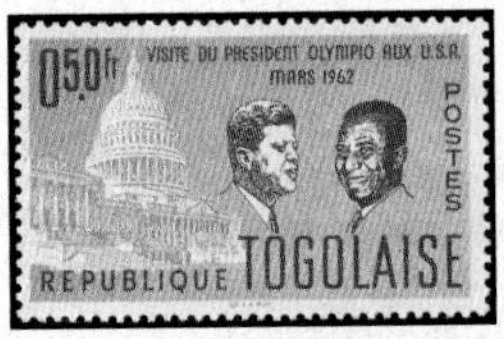

Capitol, Pres. John F. Kennedy and Pres. Sylvanus Olympio — A40

1962, July 4 Unwmk. *Perf. 13*
Inscription and Portraits in Slate Green

432	A40	50c yellow	.25	.25
433	A40	1fr blue	.25	.25
434	A40	2fr vermilion	.25	.25
435	A40	5fr lilac	.25	.25
436	A40	25fr pale violet	.45	.25
437	A40	100fr brt green	1.75	.80
a.		Souvenir sheet, imperf.	5.50	5.75
		Nos. 432-437 (6)	3.20	2.05

Visit of Pres. Sylvanus Olympio of Togo to the US, Mar. 1962.

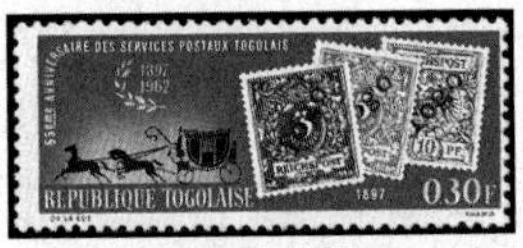

Mail Coach and Stamps of 1897 — A41

50c, Mail ship, stamps of 1900. 1fr, Mail train, stamps of 1915. 10fr, Motorcycle truck, stamp of 1924. 25fr, Mail truck, stamp of 1941. 30fr, DC-3, stamp of 1947.

1963, Jan. 12 Photo. *Perf. 13*

438	A41	30c multicolored	.25	.25
439	A41	50c multicolored	.25	.25
440	A41	1fr multicolored	.35	.25
441	A41	10fr vio, dp org & blk	.40	.25
442	A41	25fr dk red brn, blk & yel grn	.75	.25
443	A41	30fr ol brn & lil rose	.75	.25
		Nos. 438-443,C34 (7)	4.35	1.95

65th anniv. of Togolese mail service.
For souvenir sheet see No. C34a.

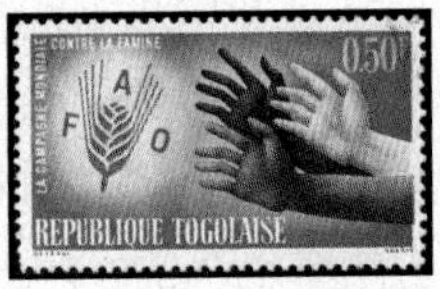

Hands Reaching for FAO Emblem A42

1963, Mar. 21 *Perf. 14*

444	A42	50c bl, org & dk brn	.25	.25
445	A42	1fr ol grn, org & dk brn	.25	.25
446	A42	25fr brn, dk brn & org	.75	.25
447	A42	30fr vio, dk brn & org	1.10	.25
		Nos. 444-447 (4)	2.35	1.00

FAO "Freedom from Hunger" campaign.

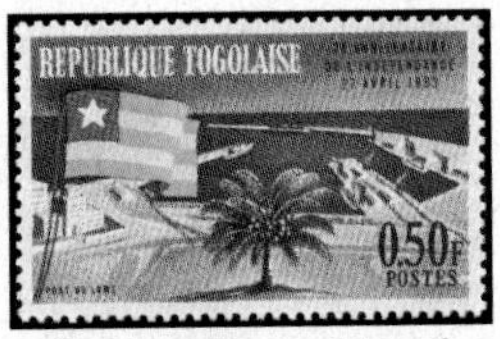

Togolese Flag and Lomé Harbor — A43

1963, Apr. 27 Litho. *Perf. 13x12½*
Flag in Red, Green and Yellow

448	A43	50c red brn & blk	.25	.25
449	A43	1fr dk car rose & blk	.25	.25
450	A43	25fr dull bl & blk	.35	.25
451	A43	50fr bister & blk	.40	.25
		Nos. 448-451 (4)	1.25	1.00

3rd anniversary of independence.

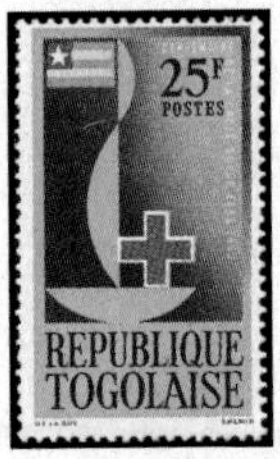

Centenary Emblem — A44

1963, June 1 Photo. *Perf. 14*
Flag in Red, Olive Green, Yellow

452	A44	25fr blue, blk & red	1.00	.25
453	A44	30fr dull grn, blk & red	1.20	.25

International Red Cross centenary.

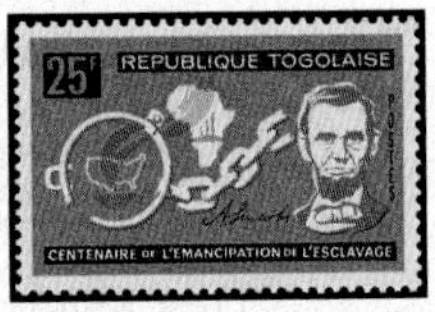

Lincoln, Broken Fetters, Maps of Africa and US. — A45

1963, Oct. Unwmk. *Perf. 13x14*

454	A45	50c multicolored	.25	.25
455	A45	1fr multicolored	.25	.25
456	A45	25fr multicolored	.35	.25
		Nos. 454-456,C35 (4)	2.35	1.20

Centenary of the emancipation of the American slaves. See souvenir sheet No. C35a.
For overprints see Nos. 473-475, C41.

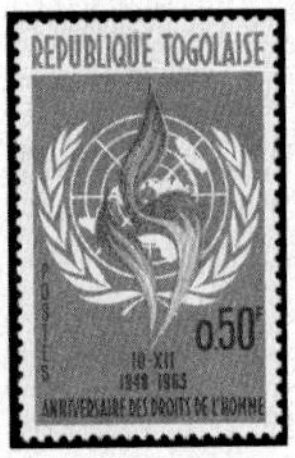

UN Emblem and "15" — A46

1963, Dec. 10 Photo. *Perf. 14x13*

457	A46	50c ultra, dk bl & rose red	.25	.25
458	A46	1fr yel grn, dk bl & rose red	.25	.25
459	A46	25fr lil, dk bl & rose red	.50	.25
460	A46	85fr gold, dk bl & rose red	1.10	.30
		Nos. 457-460 (4)	2.10	1.05

15th anniv. of the Universal Declaration of Human Rights.

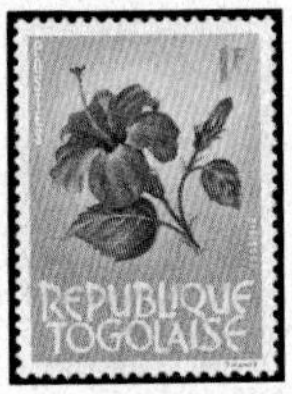

Hibiscus — A47

Designs: 50c, Orchid. 2fr, Butterfly. 5fr, Hinged tortoise. 8fr, Ball python. 10fr, Bunea alcinoe (moth). 20fr, Octopus. 25fr, John Dory (fish). 30fr, French angelfish. 40fr, Hippopotamus. 60fr, Bohor reedbuck. 85fr, Anubius baboon.

1964 Size: 22½x31mm *Perf. 14*

461	A47	50c multicolored	.25	.25
462	A47	1fr yellow, car & grn	.25	.25
463	A47	2fr lilac, yel & blk	.35	.25
464	A47	5fr gray & multi	.25	.25
465	A47	8fr cit, red brn & blk	.45	.25
466	A47	10fr multicolored	1.20	.25
467	A47	20fr dl bl, yel & brn	1.40	.25
468	A47	25fr dl bl, grn & yel	1.40	.25
469	A47	30fr multicolored	1.55	.25
470	A47	40fr grn, red brn & blk	2.10	.25
471	A47	60fr grnsh bl & red brn	4.50	.25
472	A47	85fr lt grn, brn & org	5.50	.25
		Nos. 461-472 (12)	19.20	3.00

See Nos. 511-515, C36-C40, J56-J63.

Nos. 454-456 Overprinted Diagonally: "En Mémoire de / JOHN F. KENNEDY / 1917-1963"

1964, Mar. 7 *Perf. 13x14*

473	A45	50c multicolored	.25	.25
474	A45	1fr multicolored	.25	.25
475	A45	25fr multicolored	.50	.25
		Nos. 473-475 (3)	1.00	.75

Issued in memory of John F. Kennedy.
See No. C41 and note on souvenir sheets following it.

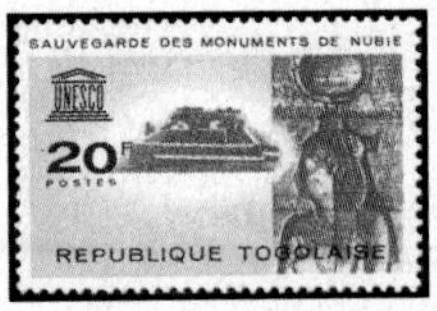

Isis of Kalabsha A48

Designs: 25fr, Head of Ramses II. 30fr, Colonnade of Birth House at Philae.

1964, Mar. 8 Litho. *Perf. 14*

476	A48	20fr blk, pale grn & red	.35	.25
477	A48	25fr black & lil rose	.45	.25
478	A48	30fr black & citron	.70	.25
a.		Souvenir sheet of 3	2.75	2.50
		Nos. 476-478 (3)	1.50	.75

UNESCO world campaign to save historic monuments in Nubia. No. 478a contains three imperf. stamps similar to Nos. 476-478 with simulated perforations.

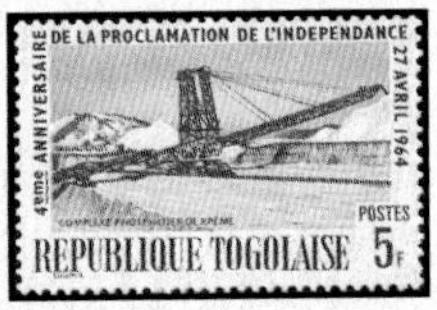

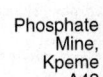

Phosphate Mine, Kpeme A49

25fr, Phosphate plant, Kpeme. 60fr, Phosphate train. 85fr, Loading ship with phosphate.

1964, Apr. 27 Unwmk. *Perf. 14*

479	A49	5fr brown & bis brn	.30	.25
480	A49	25fr dk pur & brn car	.30	.25
481	A49	60fr dk green & olive	.70	.25
482	A49	85fr vio blk & Prus bl	1.00	.25
		Nos. 479-482 (4)	2.30	1.00

Fourth anniversary of independence.

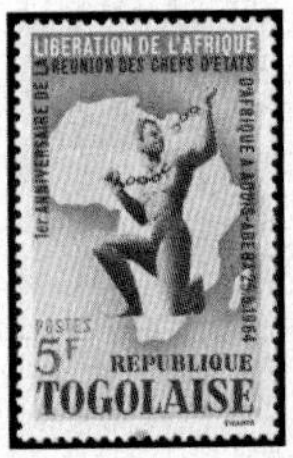

African Breaking Slavery Chain, and Map — A50

1964, May 25 Photo. *Perf. 14x13*

483	A50	5fr dp orange & brn	.25	.25
484	A50	25fr olive grn & brn	.40	.25
485	A50	85fr rose car & brn	1.00	.25
		Nos. 483-485,C42 (4)	3.15	1.05

1st anniv. of the meeting of African heads of state at Addis Ababa.

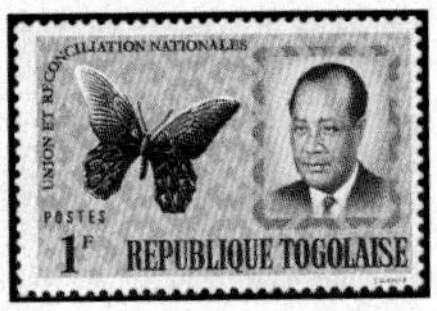

Pres. Nicolas Grunitzky and Butterfly A51

1964, Aug. 18   Litho.   Perf. 14
486	A51	1fr shown	.55	.25
487	A51	5fr Dove	.55	.25
488	A51	25fr Flower	.55	.25
489	A51	45fr as 1fr	.90	.25
490	A51	85fr Flower	1.75	.25
		Nos. 486-490 (5)	4.30	1.25

National Union and Reconciliation.

Soccer — A52

1964, Oct.   Photo.   Perf. 14
491	A52	1fr shown	.25	.25
492	A52	5fr Runner	.30	.25
493	A52	25fr Discus	.50	.25
494	A52	45fr as 1fr	.65	.25
		Nos. 491-494,C43 (5)	2.95	1.30

18th Olympic Games, Tokyo, Oct. 10-25.
For souvenir sheet see No. C43a.

Cooperation Issue
Common Design Type

1964, Nov. 7   Engr.   Perf. 13
495	CD119	25fr mag, dk brn & ol bis	.70	.25

Dirigible and Balloons — A53

25fr, 45fr, Otto Lilienthal's glider, 1894;
Wright Brothers' plane, 1903; Boeing 707.

1964, Dec. 5   Photo.   Perf. 14x13
496	A53	5fr org lil & grn	.25	.25
497	A53	10fr brt grn, dl bl & dk red	.30	.25
498	A53	25fr bl, vio bl & org	.50	.25
499	A53	45fr brt pink, vio bl & grn	1.10	.25
a.		Souv. sheet of 4	8.75	7.25
		Nos. 496-499,C44 (5)	3.65	1.50

Inauguration of the national airline, Air Togo.
#499a contains 4 imperf. stamps similar to
#497-499 and #C44 with simulated perfs.

Orbiting Geophysical Observatory and
Mariner — A54

Space Satellites: 15fr, 25fr, Tiros, Telstar
and Orbiting Solar Observatory. 20fr, 50fr,
Nimbus, Syncom and Relay.

1964, Dec. 12   Litho.   Perf. 14
500	A54	10fr dp rose, bl & yel	.40	.25
501	A54	15fr multi	.40	.25
502	A54	20fr yel, grn & vio	.40	.25
503	A54	25fr multi	.40	.25
504	A54	45fr brt grn, dk bl & yel	.55	.25
505	A54	50fr yel, grn & org	.75	.25
a.		Souv. sheet, #502-505, imperf.	3.00	2.50
		Nos. 500-505 (6)	2.90	1.50

Intl. Quiet Sun Year.

Togo Olympic
Stamps Printed in
Israel — A55

Arms of Israel and Togo — A56

Pres. Nicolas Grunitzky of Togo and: 20fr,
Church of the Mount of Beatitudes. 45fr, Ruins
of Synagogue at Capernaum.

Perf. 13½x14½, 14x13½

1964, Dec. 26   Photo.
506	A55	5fr rose violet	.40	.25
507	A56	20fr grnsh bl, grn & dl pur	.40	.25
508	A56	25fr red & bluish grn	.40	.25
509	A56	45fr dl yel, ol & dl pur	.85	.25
510	A56	85fr mag & bluish grn	.65	.25
a.		Souv. sheet of 4, imperf.	4.50	3.50
		Nos. 506-510 (5)	2.70	1.25

Israel-Togo friendship.

Type of Regular Issue, 1964

1965, June   Unwmk.   Perf. 14

Designs: 3fr, Morpho aega butterfly. 4fr,
Scorpion. 6fr, Bird-of-paradise flower. 15fr,
Flap-necked chameleon. 45fr, Ring-tailed
palm civet.

Size: 23x31mm
511	A47	3fr bister & multi	1.20	.25
512	A47	4fr org & bluish blk	.30	.25
513	A47	6fr multi	.45	.25
514	A47	15fr brt pink, yel & brn	1.75	.25
515	A47	45fr dl grn, org & brn	3.50	.25
		Nos. 511-515 (5)	7.20	1.25

Syncom Satellite, Radar Station and
ITU Emblem — A57

1965, June   Perf. 13x14
516	A57	10fr Prus blue	.45	.25
517	A57	20fr olive bister	.45	.25
518	A57	25fr bright blue	.45	.25
519	A57	45fr crimson	.65	.25
520	A57	50fr green	.75	.25
		Nos. 516-520 (5)	2.75	1.25

ITU, centenary.

Abraham
Lincoln — A58

1965, June 26   Photo.   Perf. 13x14
521	A58	1fr magenta	.25	.25
522	A58	5fr dull green	.25	.25
523	A58	20fr brown	.40	.25
524	A58	25fr slate	.40	.25
		Nos. 521-524,C45 (5)	3.30	1.35

Death cent. of Abraham Lincoln. For souvenir sheet see No. C45a.

Discus Thrower,
Flags of Togo and
Congo — A59

Flags and: 10fr, Javelin thrower. 15fr, Handball player. 25fr, Runner.

1965, July   Unwmk.   Perf. 14x13
Flags in Red, Yellow and Green
525	A59	5fr deep magenta	.25	.25
526	A59	10fr dark blue	.25	.25
527	A59	15fr brown	.35	.25
528	A59	25fr dark purple	.90	.25
		Nos. 525-528,C46 (5)	3.50	1.35

1st African Games, Brazzaville, July 18-25.

Winston Churchill
and "V" — A60

Stalin, Roosevelt and Churchill at
Yalta — A61

Perf. 13½x14, 14x13½

1965, Aug. 7   Photo.
529	A60	5fr dull green	.25	.25
530	A61	10fr brt vio & gray	.25	.25
531	A60	20fr brown	.50	.25
532	A61	45fr Prus bl & gray	.85	.25
		Nos. 529-532,C47 (5)	3.35	1.40

Sir Winston Spencer Churchill (1874-1965),
British statesman and World War II leader.

Unisphere and New York
Skyline — A62

10fr, Togolese dancers & drummer, Unisphere. 50fr, Michelangelo's Pieta &
Unisphere.

1965, Aug. 28   Photo.   Perf. 14
533	A62	5fr grnsh bl & vio blk	.35	.25
534	A62	10fr yel grn & dk brn	.35	.25
535	A62	25fr brn org & dk grn	.35	.25
536	A62	50fr vio & sl grn	.50	.25
537	A62	85fr rose red & brn	1.10	.30
a.		Souvenir sheet of 2	2.75	1.75
		Nos. 533-537 (5)	2.65	1.30

New York World's Fair, 1964-65. No. 537a
contains two imperf. stamps similar to Nos.
536-537 with simulated perforations.

"Constructive Cooperation" and Olive
Branch — A63

Designs: 25fr, 40fr, Hands of various races
holding globe and olive branch. 85fr, Handclasp, olive branch and globe.

1965, Sept. 25   Unwmk.   Perf. 14
538	A63	5fr violet, lt bl & org	.35	.25
539	A63	15fr brn, org & gray	.35	.25
540	A63	20fr blue & orange	.35	.25
541	A63	40fr dp car, gray & org	.55	.25
542	A63	85fr green & org	1.00	.30
		Nos. 538-542 (5)	2.60	1.30

International Cooperation Year.

Major White and Gemini 4 — A64

25fr, Lt. Col. Alexei Leonov and Voskhod 2.

1965, Nov. 25   Photo.   Perf. 13½x14
543	A64	25fr dp bl & brt car rose	.60	.25
544	A64	50fr green & brown	1.00	.25

"Walks in Space" of Lt. Col. Alexei Leonov
(USSR), and Major Edward H. White (US).
Printed in sheets of 12 with ornamental
borders.
For overprints and surcharges see Nos.
563-566.

Adlai E. Stevenson and UN
Headquarters — A65

5fr, "ONU" and doves. 10fr, UN emblem and
headquarters. 20fr, "ONU" and orchids.

1965, Dec. 15   Perf. 14x13½
545	A65	5fr dk brn, yel & lt bl	.40	.25
546	A65	10fr org, dk bl & grn	.40	.25
547	A65	20fr brn, yel grn & org brn	.40	.25
548	A65	25fr brt yel, dk bl & blu- ish grn	.40	.25
		Nos. 545-548,C48 (5)	3.35	1.40

UN, 20th anniv.; Adlai E. Stevenson (1900-
1965), US ambassador to the UN.

Pope Paul VI, Plane and UN
Emblem — A66

15fr, 30fr, Pope addressing UN General
Assembly & UN emblem, vert. 20fr, Pope,
NYC skyline with UN Headquarters.

1966, Mar. 5   Litho.   Perf. 12
549 A66 5fr blue & multi   .25   .25
550 A66 15fr lt violet & multi   .25   .25
551 A66 20fr bister & multi   .35   .25
552 A66 30fr lt ultra & multi   .50   .25
   Nos. 549-552,C49-C50 (6)   3.90   1.50

Visit of Pope Paul VI to the UN, New York City, Oct. 4, 1965.

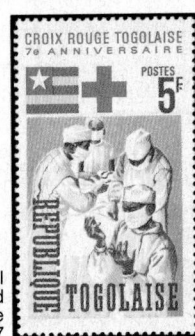

Surgical Operation and Togolese Flag — A67

Togolese Flag and: 10fr, 30fr, Blood transfusion. 45fr, Profiles of African man and woman.

1966, May 7   Litho.   Perf. 12
553 A67 5fr multicolored   .40   .25
554 A67 10fr multicolored   .40   .25
555 A67 15fr multicolored   .40   .25
556 A67 30fr multicolored   .40   .25
557 A67 45fr multicolored   .60   .25
   Nos. 553-557,C51 (6)   4.45   1.60

Togolese Red Cross, 7th anniversary.

Talisman Roses and WHO Headquarters, Geneva — A68

Various flowers & WHO Headquarters.

1966, May   Litho.   Perf. 12
558 A68 5fr lt yel grn & multi   .25   .25
559 A68 10fr pale pink & multi   .35   .25
560 A68 15fr dull yel & multi   .45   .25
561 A68 20fr pale gray & multi   .55   .25
562 A68 30fr tan & multi   .70   .25
   Nos. 558-562,C52-C53 (7)   4.70   1.75

Inauguration of WHO Headquarters, Geneva.

Nos. 543-544 Overprinted or Surcharged in Red

No. 563, Envolée Surveyor 1. No. 564, Envolée Gemini 9. No. 565, Envolée Luna 9. No. 566, Envolée Venus 3.

1966, July 11   Photo.   Perf. 13½x14
563 A64 50fr multi   .70   .25
564 A64 50fr multi   .70   .25
   a. Pair, #563-564   1.50   .60
565 A64 100fr on 25fr multi   1.60   .25
566 A64 100fr on 25fr multi   1.60   .25
   a. Pair, #565-566   3.50   .90
   Nos. 563-566 (4)   4.60   1.00

US and USSR achievements in Space.

Wood Carver — A69

Arts and Crafts: 10fr, Basket maker. 15fr, Woman weaver. 30fr, Woman potter.

1966, Sept.   Photo.   Perf. 13x14
567 A69 5fr blue, yel & dk brn   .25   .25
568 A69 10fr emer, org & dk brn   .25   .25
569 A69 15fr ver, yel & dk brn   .30   .25
570 A69 30fr lilac, dk brn & yel   .40   .25
   Nos. 567-570,C55-C56 (6)   4.00   1.50

Togolese Dancer — A70

Designs: 5fr, Togolese man. 20fr, Woman dancer from North Togo holding branches. 25fr, Male dancer. 30fr, Male dancer from North Togo with horned helmet. 45fr, Drummer.

1966, Nov.   Photo.   Perf. 13x14
571 A70 5fr emerald & multi   .25   .25
572 A70 10fr dl yel & multi   .25   .25
573 A70 20fr lt ultra & multi   .40   .25
574 A70 25fr dp orange & multi   .50   .25
575 A70 30fr red violet & multi   .55   .25
576 A70 45fr blue & multi   .95   .25
   Nos. 571-576,C57-C58 (8)   5.10   2.00

Soccer Players and Jules Rimet Cup — A71

Various Soccer Scenes.

1966, Dec. 14   Photo.   Perf. 14x13
577 A71 5fr blue, brn & red   .25   .25
578 A71 10fr brick red & multi   .30   .25
579 A71 20fr ol, brn & dk grn   .40   .25
580 A71 25fr vio, brn & org   .25   .25
581 A71 30fr ocher & multi   .50   .25
582 A71 45fr emerald, brn & mag   .85   .25
   Nos. 577-582,C59-C60 (8)   4.95   2.00

England's victory in the World Soccer Cup Championship, Wembley, July 30. For souvenir sheet see No. C60a.

African Mouthbreeder and Sailboat — A72

Designs: 10fr, Yellow jack and trawler. 15fr, Banded distichodus and seiner. 25fr, Jewelfish and galley. 30fr, like 5fr.

1967, Jan. 14   Photo.   Perf. 14
Fish in Natural Colors
583 A72 5fr lt ultra & blk   .25   .25
584 A72 10fr brn org & brn   .40   .25
585 A72 15fr brt rose & dk bl   .45   .25
586 A72 25fr olive & blk   .70   .25
587 A72 30fr grnsh bl & blk   .85   .25
   Nos. 583-587,C61-C62 (7)   5.90   1.85

African Boy and Greyhound — A73

UNICEF Emblem and: 10fr, Boy and Irish setter. 20fr, Girl and doberman.

1967, Feb. 11   Photo.   Perf. 14x13½
588 A73 5fr orange, plum & blk   .25   .25
589 A73 10fr yel grn, red brn & dk grn .35 .25
590 A73 15fr brt rose, brn & blk   .50   .25
591 A73 20fr bl, vio bl & blk   .60   .25
592 A73 30fr ol, sl grn & blk   1.10   .25
   Nos. 588-592,C63-C64 (7)   5.95   1.85

UNICEF, 20th anniv. (in 1966).

French A-1 Satellite — A74

5fr, Diamant rocket, vert. 15fr, Fr-1 satellite, vert. 20fr, 40fr, D-1 satellite. 25fr, A-1 satellite.

Perf. 14x13½, 13½x14
1967, Mar. 18   Photo.
593 A74 5fr multi   .25   .25
594 A74 10fr multi   .25   .25
595 A74 15fr multi   .35   .25
596 A74 20fr multi   .40   .25
597 A74 25fr multi   .55   .25
598 A74 40fr multi   .75   .25
   Nos. 593-598,C65-C66 (8)   5.30   2.05

French achievements in space.

Johann Sebastian Bach and Organ — A75

UNESCO Emblem and: 10fr, Ludwig van Beethoven, violin and oboe. 15f, Duke Ellington, saxophone, trumpet, drums. 20fr, Claude A. Debussy, piano and harp. 30fr, like 15fr.

1967, Apr. 15   Photo.   Perf. 14x13½
599 A75 5fr org & multi   .25   .25
600 A75 10fr multi   .50   .25
601 A75 15fr multi   .70   .25
602 A75 20fr lt bl & multi   1.10   .25
603 A75 30fr lil & multi   1.50   .25
   Nos. 599-603,C67-C68 (7)   6.05   1.75

20th anniv. (in 1966) of UNESCO.

EXPO Emblem, British Pavilion and Day Lilies — A76

10fr, French pavilion, roses. 30fr, African village, bird-of-paradise flower.

1967, May 30   Photo.   Perf. 14
604 A76 5fr brt pink & multi   .25   .25
605 A76 10fr dull org & multi   .25   .25
606 A76 30fr blue & multi   .55   .25
   Nos. 604-606,C69-C72 (7)   5.65   2.05

EXPO '67 Intl. Exhibition, Montreal, Apr. 28-Oct. 27.
For overprints see Nos. 628-630, C86-C89.

Lions Emblem — A77

20fr, 45fr, Lions emblem and flowers.

1967, July 29   Photo.   Perf. 13x14
607 A77 10fr yellow & multi   .45   .25
608 A77 20fr multicolored   .45   .25
609 A77 30fr green & multi   .55   .25
610 A77 45fr blue & multi   .80   .25
   Nos. 607-610 (4)   2.25   1.00

50th anniversary of Lions International.

Montagu's Harriers — A78

5fr, Bohor reedbucks. 15fr, Zebras. 20fr, 30fr, Marsh harriers. 25fr, Leopard.

1967, Aug. 19   Photo.   Perf. 14x13½
611 A78 5fr lilac & org brn   .55   .25
612 A78 10fr dk red, yel & dl bl   .55   .25
613 A78 15fr grn, blk & lil   .55   .25
614 A78 20fr dk brn, yel & dl bl   .55   .25
615 A78 25fr brn, ol & yel   .55   .25
616 A78 30fr vio, yel & dl bl   .65   .25
   Nos. 611-616,C79-C80 (8)   6.10   2.00

Stamp Auction and Togo Nos. 16 and C42 — A79

10fr, 45fr, Exhibition, #67 (British) & 520. 15fr, 30fr, Stamp store, #230. 20fr, Stamp packet vending machine, #545.

Stamps on Stamps in Original Colors

1967, Oct. 14   Photo.   Perf. 14x13
617 A79 5fr purple   .30   .25
618 A79 10fr dk brown   .30   .25
619 A79 15fr deep blue   .30   .25
620 A79 20fr slate green   .35   .25

621 A79 30fr red brown .50 .25
622 A79 45fr Prus blue .80 .25
Nos. 617-622,C82-C83 (8) 5.80 2.15

70th anniv. of the 1st Togolese stamps. For souvenir sheet see No. C82a.
See Nos. 853-855, C205.

Monetary Union Issue
Common Design Type

1967, Nov. 4 **Engr.** **Perf. 13**
623 CD125 30fr dk bl, vio bl & brt grn .60 .25

Broad Jump, Summer Olympics Emblem and View of Mexico City — A80

15fr, Ski jump, Winter Olympics emblem, ski lift. 30fr, Runners, Summer Olympics emblem, view of Mexico City. 45fr, Bobsledding, Winter Olympics emblem, ski lift.

1967, Dec. 2 **Photo.** **Perf. 13x14**
624 A80 5fr orange & multi .50 .25
625 A80 15fr multicolored .50 .25
626 A80 30fr multicolored .50 .25
627 A80 45fr multicolored .65 .25
Nos. 624-627,C84-C85 (6) 5.15 1.95

1968 Olympic Games. For souvenir sheet see No. C85a.

Nos. 604-606 Overprinted:
"JOURNÉE NATIONALE / DU TOGO / 29 SEPTEMBRE 1967"

1967, Dec. **Perf. 14**
628 A76 5fr multicolored .30 .25
629 A76 10fr multicolored .30 .25
630 A76 30fr blue & multi .40 .25
Nos. 628-630,C86-C89 (7) 5.40 1.85

National Day, Sept. 29, 1967.

The Gleaners, by François Millet and Phosphate Works, Benin — A81

Industrialization of Togo: 20fr, 45fr, 90fr, The Weaver at the Loom, by Vincent van Gogh, and textile plant, Dadia.

1968, Jan. **Photo.** **Perf. 14**
631 A81 10fr olive & multi .45 .25
632 A81 20fr multicolored .45 .25
633 A81 30fr brown & multi .55 .25
634 A81 45fr multicolored .65 .25
635 A81 60fr dk blue & multi .95 .25
636 A81 90fr multicolored 1.60 .25
Nos. 631-636 (6) 4.65 1.50

Togolese Women Brewing Beer — A82

The Beer Drinkers, by Edouard Manet — A83

Design: 45fr, Modern beer bottling plant.

1968, Mar. 26 **Litho.** **Perf. 14**
637 A82 20fr emerald & multi .55 .25
638 A83 30fr dk car & multi .70 .25
639 A82 45fr orange & multi .85 .25
Nos. 637-639 (3) 2.10 .75

Publicity for local beer industry.

Symbolic Water Cycle, Flower and Cogwheels A84

1968, Apr. 6
640 A84 30fr multicolored .65 .25

Hydrological Decade (UNESCO), 1965-74.
See No. C90.

Viking Ship and Portuguese Brigantine — A85

10fr, Fulton's steamship and modern steamship. 20fr, Harbor activities and map of Africa.

1968, Apr. 26 **Photo.** **Perf. 14x13½**
641 A85 5fr brt green & multi .25 .25
642 A85 10fr dp orange & multi .25 .25
643 A85 20fr green & multi .40 .25
644 A85 30fr yel grn & multi .85 .25
Nos. 641-644,C91-C92 (6) 4.85 1.50

Inauguration of Lomé Harbor.

Adenauer and 1968 Europa Emblem — A86

1968, May 25 **Photo.** **Perf. 14**
645 A86 90fr olive grn & brn org 1.90 .25

Konrad Adenauer (1876-1967), chancellor of West Germany (1949-63).

Adam and Eve Expelled from Paradise, by Michelangelo — A87

Paintings: 20fr, The Anatomy Lesson of Dr. Tulp, by Rembrandt. 30fr, The Anatomy Lesson, by Rembrandt (detail). 45fr, Jesus Healing the Sick, by Raphael.

1968, June 22 **Photo.** **Perf. 14**
646 A87 15fr crimson & multi .35 .25
647 A87 20fr multicolored .40 .25
648 A87 30fr green & multi .70 .25
649 A87 45fr multicolored 1.00 .25
Nos. 646-649,C93-C94 (6) 4.70 1.50

WHO, 20th anniv.

Olympic Monument, San Salvador Island, Bahamas — A88

1968, July 27 **Perf. 14x13½**
650 A88 15fr Wrestling .25 .25
651 A88 20fr Boxing .40 .25
652 A88 30fr Judo .60 .25
653 A88 45fr Running .75 .25
Nos. 650-653,C95-C96 (6) 4.10 1.50

19th Olympic Games, Mexico City, 10/12-27.

Chick Holding Lottery Ticket — A89

45fr, Lottery ticket, horseshoe & 4-leaf clover.

1968, Oct. 5 **Litho.** **Perf. 14**
654 A89 30fr dk green & multi .65 .25
655 A89 45fr multicolored .75 .25

2nd anniversary of National Lottery.

Scout Before Tent — A90

10fr, 45fr, Scout leader training cub scouts, horiz. 20fr, First aid practice, horiz. 30fr, Scout game.

1968, Nov. 23
656 A90 5fr dp org & multi .25 .25
657 A90 10fr emerald & multi .25 .25
658 A90 20fr multicolored .40 .25
659 A90 30fr multicolored .50 .25
660 A90 45fr blue & multi .70 .25
Nos. 656-660,C97-C98 (7) 4.50 1.85

Issued to honor the Togolese Boy Scouts.

Adoration of the Shepherds, by Giorgione — A91

Paintings: 20f, Adoration of the Magi, by Pieter Brueghel. 30fr, Adoration of the Magi, by Botticelli. 45fr, Adoration of the Magi, by Durer.

1968, Dec. 28 **Litho.** **Perf. 14**
661 A91 15fr green & multi .35 .25
662 A91 20fr multicolored .40 .25
663 A91 30fr multicolored .55 .25
664 A91 45fr multicolored .90 .25
Nos. 661-664,C100-C101 (6) 4.80 1.60

Christmas.

Martin Luther King, Jr. — A92

Portraits and Human Rights Flame: 20fr, Professor René Cassin (author of Declaration of Human Rights). 45fr, Pope John XXIII.

1969, Feb. 1 **Photo.** **Perf. 13½x14**
665 A92 15fr brn org & sl grn .25 .25
666 A92 20fr grnsh bl & vio .40 .25
667 A92 30fr ver & slate bl .60 .25
668 A92 45fr olive & car rose 1.25 .25
Nos. 665-668,C102-C103 (6) 4.90 1.65

International Human Rights Year.
For overprints see Nos. 683-686, C110-C111.

Omnisport Stadium and Soccer — A93

Stadium and: 15fr, Handball. 20fr, Volleyball. 30fr, Basketball. 45fr, Tennis.

1969, Apr. 26 **Photo.** **Perf. 14x13½**
669 A93 10fr emer, dp car & dk brn .25 .25
670 A93 15fr org, ultra & dk brn .35 .25
671 A93 20fr yel, ol & dk brn .40 .25
672 A93 30fr dl grn, bl & dk brn .55 .25
673 A93 45fr org, lil & dk brn .70 .25
Nos. 669-673,C105-C106 (7) 4.60 1.80

Opening of Omnisport Stadium, Lomé.

Astronaut and Eagle on Moon, Earth and Stars in Sky — A94

Designs: 1f, 30f, Lunar Module Eagle Landing on Moon. 45fr, Astronaut and Eagle on moon, earth and stars in sky.

1969, July 21 **Litho.** **Perf. 14**
674 A94 1fr green & multi .25 .25
675 A94 20fr brown & multi .25 .25
676 A94 30fr scarlet & multi .40 .25
677 A94 45fr ultra & multi .70 .25
Nos. 674-677,C107-C108 (6) 4.00 1.75

Man's 1st landing on the moon, 7/20/69. US astronauts Neil A. Armstrong & Col. Edwin E. Aldrin, Jr., with Lieut. Col. Michael Collins piloting Apollo 11.
For overprints see #710-712, C120-C121.

Christ at Emmaus, by Velazquez A95

Paintings: 5fr, The Last Supper, by Tintoretto. 20fr, Pentecost, by El Greco. 30fr, The Annunciation, by Botticelli. 45fr, Like 10fr.

1969, Aug. 16   Litho.   Perf. 14
678 A95 5fr red, gold & multi   .25   .25
679 A95 10fr multicolored   .35   .25
680 A95 20fr grn, gold & multi   .55   .25
681 A95 30fr multicolored   .75   .25
682 A95 45fr pur, gold & multi   1.25   .25
    Nos. 678-682,C109 (6)   5.25   1.75

Nos. 665-668
Overprinted

1969, Sept. 1   Photo.   Perf. 13½x14
683 A92 15fr brn org & sl grn   .30   .25
684 A92 20fr grnsh bl & vio   .50   .25
685 A92 30fr ver & slate bl   .55   .25
686 A92 45fr olive & car rose   1.00   .25
    Nos. 683-686,C110-C111 (6)   4.50   1.55

Gen. Dwight D. Eisenhower (1890-1969), 34th President of the US.

African
Development
Bank and
Emblem — A96

Designs: 45fr, Bank emblem and hand holding railroad bridge and engine.

1969, Sept. 10   Photo.   Perf. 13x14
687 A96 30fr ultra, blk gold & multi .65   .25
688 A96 45fr grn, dk bl, gold &
          dk red   2.00   .35

5th anniv. of the African Development Bank. See No. C112.

Louis Pasteur and Help for 1968 Flood Victims — A97

Designs: 15fr, Henri Dunant and Red Cross workers meeting Biafra refugees at airport. 30fr, Alexander Fleming and help for flood victims. 45fr, Wilhelm C. Roentgen and Red Cross workers with children in front of Headquarters.

1969, Sept. 27   Litho.   Perf. 14
689 A97 15fr red & multi   .35   .25
690 A97 20fr emerald & multi   .40   .25
691 A97 30fr purple & multi   .75   .25
692 A97 45fr brt blue & multi   .90   .25
    Nos. 689-692,C113-C114 (6)   4.50   1.70

League of Red Cross Societies, 50th anniv.

Glidji
Agricultural
Center
A98

Designs (Emblem of Young Pioneer and Agricultural Organization and): 1fr, Corn harvest. 3fr, Founding meeting of Agricultural Pioneer Youths, Mar. 7, 1967. 4fr, Class at Glidji Agricultural School. 5fr, Boys forming

human pyramid. 7fr, Farm students threshing. 8fr, Instruction in gardening. 10fr, 50fr, Cooperative village. 15fr, Gardening School. 20fr, Cattle breeding. 25fr, Chicken farm. 30fr, Independence parade. 40fr, Boys riding high wire. 45fr, Tractor and trailer. 60fr, Instruction in tractor driving.

1969-70   Litho.   Perf. 14
693 A98 1fr multi ('70)   .25   .25
694 A98 2fr multi   .25   .25
695 A98 3fr multi ('70)   .25   .25
696 A98 4fr multi ('70)   .25   .25
697 A98 5fr ultra & multi   .25   .25
698 A98 7fr multi ('70)   .25   .25
699 A98 8fr red & multi   .25   .25
700 A98 10fr bl & multi ('70)   .25   .25
701 A98 15fr red & multi ('70)   .30   .25
702 A98 20fr lilac & multi   .35   .25
703 A98 25fr multi ('70)   .50   .25
704 A98 30fr brt bl & multi   .50   .25
705 A98 40fr brt yel & multi   .70   .25
706 A98 45fr rose lil & multi   .75   .25
707 A98 50fr blue & multi   .85   .25
708 A98 60fr orange & multi   .85   .25
    Nos. 693-708,C115-C119 (21)   25.40   6.55

Books and
Map of
Africa
A99

1969, Nov. 27   Litho.   Perf. 14
709 A99 30fr lt blue & multi   .60   .25

12th anniv. of the Intl. Assoc. for the Development of Libraries in Africa.

Christmas Issue
Nos. 674-675, 677 Overprinted
"JOYEUX NOEL"

1969, Dec.   Litho.   Perf. 14
710 A94 1fr green & multi   .60   .25
711 A94 20fr brown & multi   1.90   .35
712 A94 45fr ultra & multi   2.60   .65
    Nos. 710-712,C120-C121 (5)   13.85   2.35

George
Washington — A100

Portraits: 20fr, Albert Luthuli. 30fr, Mahatma Gandhi. 45fr, Simon Bolivar.

1969, Dec. 27   Photo.   Perf. 14x13½
713 A100 15fr dk brn, emer &
           buff   .35   .25
714 A100 20fr dk brn, org & buff   .35   .25
715 A100 30fr dk brn, grnsh bl &
           ocher   .60   .25
716 A100 45fr dk brn, sl grn & dl
           yel   1.00   .25
    Nos. 713-716,C122-C123 (6)   4.70   1.60

Issued to honor leaders for world peace.
For overprint & surcharges see #764-766, C143.

Plower, by
M.K. Klodt
and ILO
Emblem
A101

Paintings and ILO Emblem: 10fr, Gardening, by Camille Pissarro. 20fr, Fruit Harvest, by Diego Rivera. 30fr, Spring Sowing, by Vincent van Gogh. 45fr, Workers, by Rivera.

1970, Jan. 24   Litho.   Perf. 12½x13
717 A101 5fr gold & multi   .25   .25
718 A101 10fr gold & multi   .35   .25
719 A101 20fr gold & multi   .60   .25

720 A101 30fr gold & multi   1.40   .25
721 A101 45fr gold & multi   1.40   .25
    Nos. 717-721,C124-C125 (7)   8.50   1.75

ILO, 50th anniversary.

Togolese Hair Styles — A102

Various hair styles. 20fr, 30fr, vertical.

1970, Feb. 21   Perf. 13x12½, 12½x13
722 A102 5fr multicolored   .25   .25
723 A102 10fr ver & multi   .35   .25
724 A102 20fr purple & multi   .50   .25
725 A102 30fr yellow grn & multi 1.25   .25
    Nos. 722-725,C126-C127 (6)   5.00   1.65

Togo No. C127 and Independence Monument, Lomé — A103

30fr, Pres. Etienne G. Eyadéma, Presidential Palace and Independence Monument. 50fr, Map of Togo, dove and Independence Monument, vert.

Perf. 13x12½, 12½x13
1970, Apr. 27   Litho.
726 A103 20fr multicolored   .50   .25
727 A103 30fr multicolored   .70   .25
728 A103 50fr multicolored   1.20   .25
    Nos. 726-728,C128 (4)   3.25   1.00

10th anniv. of independence.

Inauguration of UPU Headquarters, Bern — A104

1970, May 30   Photo.   Perf. 14x13½
729 A104 30fr orange & pur   1.20   .25

See No. C129.

Soccer, Jules Rimet Cup and Flags of Italy and Uruguay — A105

Designs (Various Scenes from Soccer, Rimet Cup and Flags of): 10fr, Great Britain and Brazil. 15fr, USSR and Mexico. 20fr, Germany and Morocco. 30fr, Romania and Czechoslovakia.

1970, June 27   Litho.   Perf. 13x14
730 A105 5fr olive & multi   .25   .25
731 A105 10fr pink & multi   .30   .25
732 A105 15fr yellow & multi   .50   .25
733 A105 20fr multicolored   .60   .25
734 A105 30fr emerald   1.20   .25
    Nos. 730-734,C130-C132 (8)   6.40   2.10

Soccer Championships for the Jules Rimet Cup, Mexico City, May 30-June 21, 1970.

Lenin and
UNESCO
Emblem
A106

1970, July 25   Litho.   Perf. 12½
735 A106 30fr fawn & multi   1.75   .25

Lenin (1870-1924), Russian communist leader. See No. C133.
For surcharge see No. C179.

EXPO '70 Emblem and View of US Pavilion — A107

Designs: 2fr, Paper carp flying over Sanyo pavilion. 30fr, Russian pavilion. 50fr, Tower of the Sun pavilion. 60fr, French and Japanese pavilions.

1970, Aug. 8   Litho.   Perf. 13
Size: 56½x35mm
736 A107 2fr gray & multi   .25   .25
Size: 50x33mm
737 A107 20fr blue & multi   .30   .25
738 A107 30fr blue & multi   .50   .25
739 A107 50fr blue & multi   1.00   .25
740 A107 60fr blue & multi   1.25   .25
  a.   Strip of 4, #737-740   3.50   1.90
    Nos. 736-740 (5)   3.30   1.25

EXPO '70 Intl. Exhibition, Osaka, Japan, Mar. 15-Sept. 13. No. 740a has continuous view of EXPO. See No. C134.

Neil A.
Armstrong,
Michael
Collins and
Edwin E.
Aldrin,
Jr. — A108

Designs: 2fr, US flag, moon rocks and Apollo 11 emblem. 20fr, Astronaut checking Surveyor 3 on moon, and Apollo 12 emblem. 30fr, Charles Conrad, Jr., Richard F. Gordon, Jr., Alan L. Bean and Apollo 12 emblem. 50fr, US flag, moon rocks and Apollo 12 emblem.

1970, Sept. 26
741 A108 1fr multi   .25   .25
742 A108 2fr multi   .25   .25
743 A108 20fr multi   .40   .25
744 A108 30fr multi   .75   .25
745 A108 50fr multi   1.20   .25
    Nos. 741-745,C135 (6)   5.75   2.00

Moon landings of Apollo 11 and 12.
For overprints see Nos. 746-750, C136.

**Nos. 741-745 Inscribed:
"FELICITATIONS / BON RETOUR
APOLLO XIII"**

1970, Sept. 26
746 A108 1fr multi   .25   .25
747 A108 2fr multi   .25   .25
748 A108 20fr multi   .40   .25
749 A108 30fr multi   .75   .25
750 A108 50fr multi   1.20   .25
    Nos. 746-750,C136 (6)   5.60   1.85

Safe return of the crew of Apollo 13.

Forge of Vulcan, by Velazquez, and
ILO Emblem — A109

Paintings and Emblems of UN Agencies:
15fr, Still Life, by Delacroix, and FAO emblem.
20fr, Portrait of Nicholas Kratzer, by Holbein,
and UNESCO emblem. 30fr, UN Headquarters, New York, and UN emblem. 50fr, Portrait
of a Little Girl, by Renoir, and UNICEF
emblem.

1970, Oct. 24   Litho.   Perf. 13x12½
751 A109 1fr car, gold & dk brn   .65   .25
752 A109 15fr ultra, gold & blk   .65   .25
753 A109 20fr grnsh bl, gold &
                dk grn   .65   .25
754 A109 30fr lil & multi   .80   .25
755 A109 50fr org brn, gold & se-
                pia   1.25   .25
      Nos. 751-755,C137-C138 (7)   6.85   1.80

United Nations, 25th anniversary.

Euchloron Megaera — A110

Butterflies and Moths: 2fr, Cymothoe
chrysippus. 30fr, Danaus chrysippus. 50fr,
Morpho.

1970, Nov. 21   Litho.   Perf. 13x14
756 A110 1fr yellow & multi   2.00   .25
757 A110 2fr lt vio & multi   2.00   .25
758 A110 30fr multicolored   2.00   .25
759 A110 50fr orange & multi   3.75   .25
      Nos. 756-759,C139-C140 (6)   20.25 1.50

For surcharge see No. 859.

Nativity, by Botticelli — A111

Paintings: 20fr, Adoration of the Shepherds,
by Veronese. 30fr, Adoration of the Shepherds, by El Greco. 50fr, Adoration of the
Kings, by Fra Angelico.

1970, Dec. 26   Litho.   Perf. 12½x13
760 A111 15fr gold & multi   .65   .25
761 A111 20fr gold & multi   .65   .25
762 A111 30fr gold & multi   .65   .25
763 A111 50fr gold & multi   1.10   .25
      Nos. 760-763,C141-C142 (6)   6.80   1.55

Christmas.

**Nos. 715, C123, 714 Surcharged and
Overprinted: "EN MEMOIRE /
Charles De Gaulle / 1890-1970"**
1971, Jan. 9   Photo.   Perf. 14x13½
764 A100 30fr multicolored   2.00   .25
765 A100 30fr on 90fr multi   2.00   .25
766 A100 150fr on 20fr multi   8.50   .35
      Nos. 764-766,C143 (4)   24.00 1.45

"Aerienne" obliterated with heavy bar on No.
765.

De Gaulle
and
Churchill
A112

De Gaulle and: 30fr, Dwight D. Eisenhower.
40fr, John F. Kennedy. 50fr, Konrad
Adenauer.

1971, Feb. 20   Photo.   Perf. 13x14
767 A112 20fr blk & brt blue   .90   .25
768 A112 30fr blk & crimson   .90   .25
769 A112 40fr blk & dp green   1.40   .25
770 A112 50fr blk & brown   1.60   .25
      Nos. 767-770,C144-C145 (6)   10.00 1.50

Nos. 764-770 issued in memory of Charles
de Gaulle (1890-1970), President of France.

Resurrection, by Raphael — A113

Easter: 30fr, Resurrection, by Master of
Trebon. 40fr, like 1fr.

1971, Apr. 10   Litho.   Perf. 10½x11½
771 A113 1fr gold & multi   .50   .25
772 A113 30fr gold & multi   .50   .25
773 A113 40fr gold & multi   .50   .25
      Nos. 771-773,C146-C148 (6)   5.20   1.55

Cmdr. Alan B. Shepard, Jr. — A114

Designs: 10fr, Edgar D. Mitchell and astronaut on moon. 30fr, Stuart A. Roosa, module
on moon. 40fr, Take-off from moon, and
spaceship.

1971, May   Litho.   Perf. 12½
774 A114 1fr blue & multi   .40   .25
775 A114 10fr green & multi   .40   .25
776 A114 30fr dull red & multi   .40   .25
777 A114 40fr dk green & multi   .45   .25
      Nos. 774-777,C149-C151 (7)   5.90   2.55

Apollo 14 moon landing, Jan. 31-Feb. 9.
For overprints see Nos. 788, C162-C164.

Cacao Tree and Pods — A115

Designs: 40fr, Sorting and separating
beans and pods. 50fr, Drying cacao beans.

1971, June 6   Litho.   Perf. 14
778 A115 30fr multicolored   .40   .25
779 A115 40fr ultra & multi   .60   .25
780 A115 50fr multicolored   .75   .25
      Nos. 778-780,C152-C154 (6)   4.85   1.85

International Cacao Day, June 6.

Napoleon, Death Sesquicentennial —
A115a

Die Cut Perf. 12
1971, June 11   Embossed
780A A115a 1000fr gold   37.50 37.50
   b.   Sheet of 1, imperf.   27.50 27.50

No. 780Ab contains one 48x69mm stamp.

Control Tower and
Plane — A116

1971, June 26   Litho.   Perf. 14
781 A116 30fr multicolored   1.00   .25

10th anniv. of the Agency for the Security of
Aerial Navigation in Africa and Madagascar
(ASECNA). See No. C155.

Great Market, Lomé — A117

Tourist publicity: 30fr, Bird-of-paradise
flower and sculpture of a man. 40fr, Aledjo
Gorge and anubius baboon.

1971, July 17
782 A117 20fr multicolored   .35   .25
783 A117 30fr multicolored   .55   .25
784 A117 40fr multicolored   .85   .25
      Nos. 782-784,C156-C158 (6)   4.05   1.65

For surcharge and overprint see Nos. 804,
C172.

Great Fetish of Gbatchoume — A118

Religions of Togo: 30fr, Chief Priest in front
of Atta Sakuma Temple. 40fr, Annual ceremony of the sacred stone.

1971, July 31   Litho.   Perf. 14½
785 A118 20fr multicolored   .30   .25
786 A118 30fr multicolored   .40   .25
787 A118 40fr multicolored   .70   .25
      Nos. 785-787,C159-C161 (6)   3.65   1.50

**No. 777 Overprinted in Silver "EN
MEMOIRE / DOBROVOLSKY —
VOLKOV — PATSAYEV / SOYUZ 11"**
1971, Aug.   Perf. 12½
788 A114 40fr multicolored   1.10   .25
      Nos. 788,C162-C164 (4)   5.40   1.65

Russian astronauts Lt. Col. Georgi T.
Dobrovolsky, Vladislav N. Volkov and Victor I.
Patsayev, who died during the Soyuz 11 space
mission, June 6-30, 1971.

Sapporo '72 Emblem and Speed
Skating — A119

Sapporo '72 Emblem and: 10fr, Slalom skiing. 20fr, Figure skating, pairs. 30fr, Bobsledding. 50fr, Ice hockey.

1971, Oct. 30   Perf. 14
789 A119 1fr multicolored   .25   .25
790 A119 10fr multicolored   .25   .25
791 A119 20fr multicolored   .35   .25
792 A119 30fr multicolored   .50   .25
793 A119 50fr multicolored   1.00   .25
      Nos. 789-793,C165 (6)   4.45   1.75

11th Winter Olympic Games, Sapporo,
Japan, Feb. 3-13, 1972.

Toy Crocodile and UNICEF
Emblem — A120

Toys and UNICEF Emblem: 30fr, Fawn and
butterfly. 40fr, Monkey. 50fr, Elephants.

1971, Nov. 27
794 A120 20fr multicolored   .35   .25
795 A120 30fr violet & multi   .35   .25
796 A120 40fr green & multi   .45   .25
797 A120 50fr bister & multi   .65   .25
      Nos. 794-797,C167-C168 (6)   3.20   1.50

UNICEF, 25th anniv.
For overprints see Nos. 918, C263-C264.

Virgin and
Child, by
Botticelli
A121

Virgin and Child by: 30fr, Master of the Life
of Mary. 40fr, Dürer. 50fr, Veronese.

1971, Dec. 24   Perf. 14x13
798 A121 10fr purple & multi   .25   .25
799 A121 30fr green & multi   .40   .25
800 A121 40fr brown & multi   .85   .25
801 A121 50fr dk blue & multi   .95   .25
      Nos. 798-801,C169-C170 (6)   5.20   1.80

Christmas.

St. Mark's Basilica — A122

Design: 40fr, Rialto Bridge.

1972, Feb. 26   Litho.   Perf. 14
802 A122 30fr multicolored   .90 .25
803 A122 40fr multicolored   1.40 .25
  Nos. 802-803,C171 (3)   4.05 1.05
UNESCO campaign to save Venice.

No. 784 Surcharged with New Value, Two Bars and "VISITE DU PRESIDENT / NIXON EN CHINE / FEVRIER 1972"

1972, Mar.   Litho.   Perf. 14
804 A117 300fr on 40fr multi   3.25 1.60
Visit of Pres. Richard M. Nixon to the People's Republic of China, Feb. 20-27.
See No. C172.

Easter
A123

Paintings: 25s, Crucifixion, by Master MS. 30fr, Pieta, by Botticelli. 40fr, Like 25fr.

1972, Mar. 31
805 A123 25fr gold & multi   .60 .25
806 A123 30fr gold & multi   .95 .25
807 A123 40fr gold & multi   1.20 .25
  Nos. 805-807,C173-C174 (5)   5.95 1.25

Heart, Smith, WHO
Emblem — A124

Heart, WHO Emblem and: 40fr, Typist. 60fr, Athlete with javelin.

1972, Apr. 4
808 A124 30fr multicolored   .50 .25
809 A124 40fr multicolored   .55 .25
810 A124 60fr multicolored   .90 .25
  Nos. 808-810,C175 (4)   3.20 1.20
"Your heart is your health," World Health Day.

Org. of African and Malagasy Union
Conf. — A124a

Die Cut Perf. 12x12½
1972, Apr. 24   Litho. & Embossed Self-adhesive
810A A124a 1000fr gold, red &
                    grn   9.00 9.00
On No. 810A embossing may cut through stamp and embossed backing paper may not adhere well to the unused stamps.
For overprint see No. 893A.

Video
Telephone — A125

1972, June 24   Litho.   Perf. 14
811 A125 40fr violet & multi   1.00 .25
4th World Telecommunications Day. See No. C176.
For overprints see Nos. 880, C229.

Grating
Cassava — A126

25fr, Cassava collection by truck, horiz.

1972, June 30
812 A126 25fr yellow & multi   .45 .25
813 A126 40fr multicolored   .60 .25
  Nos. 812-813,C177-C178 (4)   3.40 1.00
Cassava production.
For overprint & surcharge see #866-867.

Basketball
A127

1972, Aug. 26   Litho.   Perf. 14
814 A127 30fr shown   .40 .25
815 A127 40fr Running   .65 .25
816 A127 50fr Discus   .85 .25
  Nos. 814-816,C180-C181 (5)   4.30 1.90
20th Olympic Games, Munich, 8/26-9/11.
For overprints see Nos. C234-C235.

Pin-tailed
Whydah — A128

Birds: 30fr, Broad-tailed widowbird. 40fr, Yellow-shouldered widowbird. 60fr, Yellow-tailed widowbird.

1972, Sept. 9
817 A128 25fr citron & multi   .55 .25
818 A128 30fr lt blue & multi   .75 .25
819 A128 40fr multicolored   1.10 .25
820 A128 60fr lt green & multi   2.10 .25
  Nos. 817-820,C182 (5)   7.25 1.45

Paul P. Harris,
Rotary
Emblem — A129

50fr, Flags of Togo and Rotary Club.

1972, Oct. 7   Litho.   Perf. 14
821 A129 40fr green & multi   .40 .25
822 A129 50fr multicolored   .45 .25
  a. Souvenir sheet of 2   2.10 1.25
  Nos. 821-822,C183-C185 (5)   3.65 1.60
Rotary International, Lomé. No. 822a contains 2 stamps with simulated perforations similar to Nos. 821-822.
For overprints see Nos. 862, 898, C212-C213, C244-C235.

Mona Lisa,
by
Leonardo
da Vinci
A130

40fr, Virgin and Child, by Giovanni Bellini.

1972, Oct. 21
823 A130 25fr gold & multi   1.50 .25
824 A130 40fr gold & multi   1.60 .25
  Nos. 823-824,C186-C188 (5)   8.50 1.50

West African Monetary Union Issue
Common Design Type
Design: 40fr, African couple, city, village and commemorative coin.

1972, Nov. 2   Engr.   Perf. 13
825 CD136 40fr red brn, rose red
                    & gray   .60 .25

Presidents Pompidou and Eyadema,
Party Headquarters — A131

1972, Nov. 23   Litho.   Perf. 14
826 A131 40fr purple & multi   1.60 .25
Visit of Pres. Georges Pompidou of France to Togo, Nov. 1972. See No. C189.

Christmas
A132

Paintings: 25fr, Anunciation, Painter Unknown. 30fr, Nativity, Master of Vyshchibrod. 40fr, Like 25fr.

1972, Dec. 23
827 A132 25fr gold & multi   .40 .25
828 A132 30fr gold & multi   .65 .25
829 A132 40fr gold & multi   1.00 .25
  Nos. 827-829,C191-C193 (6)   5.65 1.80

Raoul Follereau and Lepers — A133

1973, Jan. 23   Photo.   Perf. 14x13½
830 A133 40fr violet & green   1.75 .25
World Leprosy Day and 20th anniv. of the Raoul Follereau Foundation. See No. C194.

WHO
Emblem — A134

1973, Apr. 7   Photo.   Perf. 14x13
831 A134 30fr blue & multi   .50 .25
832 A134 40fr dp yellow & multi   .65 .25
WHO, 25th anniv.

Christ on the
Cross — A135

1973, Apr. 21   Litho.   Perf. 14
833 A135 25fr shown   .50 .25
834 A135 30fr Pietá   .50 .25
835 A135 40fr Ascension   .60 .25
  Nos. 833-835,C195 (4)   3.00 1.15
Easter.

Eugene Cernan, Ronald Evans,
Harrison Schmitt, Apollo 17
Badge — A136

Design: 40fr, Lunar rover on moon.

1973, June 2   Litho.   Perf. 14
836 A136 25fr multicolored   .50 .25
837 A136 40fr multicolored   .60 .25
  Nos. 836-837,C196-C197 (4)   5.95 1.60
Apollo 17 moon mission, Dec. 7-19, 1972.

Scouts Pitching Tent — A137

20fr, Campfire, horiz. 30fr, Rope climbing.

1973, June 30
838	A137	10fr multicolored	.25	.25
839	A137	20fr multicolored	.40	.25
840	A137	30fr violet & multi	.65	.25
841	A137	40fr ocher & multi	.90	.25
	Nos. 838-841,C198-C199 (6)		5.95	2.15

24th Boy Scout World Conference (1st in Africa), Nairobi, Kenya, July 16-21.
For overprints see Nos. C265-C266.

Nicolaus Copernicus, 500th Anniv. Birth — A138

Designs: 10fr, Heliocentric system. 20fr, Nicolaus Copernicus. 30fr, Seated figure of Astronomy and spacecrafts around earth and moon. 40fr, Astrolabe.

1973, July 18
842	A138	10fr multicolored	.25	.25
843	A138	20fr multicolored	.40	.25
844	A138	30fr multicolored	.85	.25
845	A138	40fr lilac & multi	1.10	.25
	Nos. 842-845,C200-C201 (6)		6.10	1.80

Red Cross Ambulance Crew A139

1973, Aug. 4
846	A139	40fr multicolored	1.40	.25

Togolese Red Cross. See No. C202.
For overprints see Nos. 942, C294.

Teacher and Students — A140

40fr, Hut and man reading under tree, vert.

1973, Aug. 18   Litho.   Perf. 14
847	A140	30fr multicolored	.50	.25
848	A140	40fr multicolored	.65	.25
	Nos. 847-848,C203 (3)		2.65	.85

Literacy campaign.

African Postal Union Issue
Common Design Type

1973, Sept. 12   Engr.   Perf. 13
849	CD137	100fr yel, red & claret	1.00	.35

INTERPOL Emblem and Headquarters A141

1973, Sept. 29   Photo.   Perf. 13½x14
850	A141	30fr yel, brn & gray grn	.55	.25
851	A141	40fr yel grn, bl & mag	.65	.25

50th anniv. of Intl. Criminal Police Org.

Weather Vane and WMO Emblem — A142

1973, Oct. 4   Perf. 14x13
852	A142	40fr yel, dp brn & grn	1.00	.25

Intl. meteorological cooperation, cent. See No. C204.

Type of 1967

Designs: 25fr, Old and new locomotives, No. 795. 30fr, Mail coach and bus, No. 613. 90fr, Mail boat and ship, Nos. C61 and 469.

1973, Oct. 20   Photo.   Perf. 14x13
853	A79	25fr multicolored	.60	.25
854	A79	30fr purple & green	.80	.25
855	A79	90fr dk blue & multi	2.10	.35
	Nos. 853-855,C205 (4)		6.00	1.20

Togolese postal service, 75th anniv.

John F. Kennedy and Adolf Schaerf — A143

Designs: 30fr, Kennedy and Harold MacMillan. 40fr, Kennedy and Konrad Adenauer.

1973, Nov. 22   Litho.   Perf. 14
856	A143	20fr blk, gray & vio	.55	.25
857	A143	30fr blk, rose & brn	.55	.25
858	A143	40fr blk, lt grn & grn	.65	.25
	Nos. 856-858,C206-C208 (6)		9.10	2.55

John F. Kennedy (1917-1963).

No. 758 Surcharged with New Value, 2 Bars and Overprinted in Ultramarine: "SECHERESSE SOLIDARITE AFRICAINE"

1973, Dec.   Photo.   Perf. 13x14
859	A110	100fr on 30fr multi	1.40	.50

African solidarity in drought emergency.

Virgin and Child, Italy, 15th Century — A144

30fr, Adoration of the Kings, Italy, 15th cent.

1973, Dec. 22   Litho.   Perf. 14
860	A144	25fr gold & multi	.60	.25
861	A144	30fr gold & multi	.70	.25
	Nos. 860-861,C210-C211 (4)		3.90	1.30

Christmas.

No. 821 Overprinted: "PREMIERE CONVENTION / 210eme DISTRICT / FEVRIER 1974 / LOME"

1974, Feb. 21   Litho.   Perf. 14
862	A129	40fr green & multi	.40	.25
	Nos. 862,C212-C213 (3)		2.05	.85

First convention of Rotary Intl., District 210, Lomé, Feb. 22-24.

Soccer and Games' Cup A145

Various soccer scenes and games' cup.

1974, Mar. 2   Litho.   Perf. 14
863	A145	20fr lt blue & multi	.35	.25
864	A145	30fr yellow & multi	.50	.25
865	A145	40fr lilac & multi	.55	.25
	Nos. 863-865,C214-C216 (6)		5.30	2.65

World Soccer Championships, Munich, Germany, June 13-July 7.

Nos. 812-813 Overprinted and Surcharged: "10e ANNIVERSAIRE DU P.A.M."

1974, Mar. 25   Litho.   Perf. 14
866	A126	40fr multicolored	.65	.25
867	A126	100fr on 25fr multi	1.40	.50

10th anniv. of World Food Program. Overprint on No. 866 is in one line; 2 lines on No. 867 and 2 bars through old denomination.

Girl Before Mirror, by Picasso — A146

Paintings by Picasso: 30fr, The Turkish Shawl. 40fr, Mandolin and Guitar.

1974, Apr. 6
868	A146	20fr vio blue & multi	.40	.25
869	A146	30fr maroon & multi	.65	.25
870	A146	40fr multicolored	.85	.25
	Nos. 868-870,C217-C219 (6)		9.50	2.45

Pablo Picasso (1881-1973), Spanish painter.

Kpeme Village and Wharf A147

Design: 40fr, Tropicana tourist village.

1974, Apr. 20
871	A147	30fr multicolored	.45	.25
872	A147	40fr multicolored	.45	.25
	Nos. 871-872,C220-C221 (4)		3.25	1.10

Mailman, UPU Emblem — A148

Design: 40fr, Mailman, different uniform.

1974, May 10   Litho.   Perf. 14
873	A148	30fr salmon & multi	.45	.25
874	A148	40fr multicolored	.50	.25
	Nos. 873-874,C222-C223 (4)		2.90	1.10

UPU, centenary.

Map and Flags of Members — A148a

1974, May 29   Litho.   Perf. 13x12½
875	A148a	40fr blue & multi	.60	.25

15th anniversary of the Council of Accord.

Fisherman with Net A149

40fr, Fisherman casting net from canoe.

1974, June 22   Litho.   Perf. 14
876	A149	30fr multicolored	.55	.25
877	A149	40fr multicolored	.65	.25
	Nos. 876-877,C224-C226 (5)		5.70	1.65

Lagoon fishing.

Pioneer Communicating with Earth — A150

30fr, Radar station and satellite, vert.

1974, July 6   Perf. 14
878	A150	30fr multicolored	.35	.25
879	A150	40fr multicolored	.40	.25
	Nos. 878-879,C227-C228 (4)		3.65	1.50

US Jupiter space probe.

No. 811 Overprinted with INTERNABA Emblem in Silver Similar to No. C229

1974, July
880	A125	40fr multicolored	3.00	.50

INTERNABA 1974 Intl. Philatelic Exhibition, Basel, June 7-16. See No. C229.
No. 880 exists overprint in black. Value, unused $10.

Tympanotomus Radula — A151

Designs: Seashells.

1974, July 13   Litho.   Perf. 14
881	A151	10fr shown	.85	.25
882	A151	20fr Tonna galea	.85	.25
883	A151	30fr Conus mercator	1.00	.25
884	A151	40fr Cardium costatum	1.40	.25
	Nos. 881-884,C230-C231 (6)		8.10	1.70

Groom with Horses A152

Design: 40fr, Trotting horses.

1974, Aug. 3   Litho.   *Perf. 14*
885 A152 30fr multicolored .90 .25
886 A152 40fr multicolored 1.10 .25
Nos. 885-886,C232-C233 (4) 6.50 1.20
Horse racing.

Leopard
A153

1974, Sept. 7   Litho.   *Perf. 14*
887 A153 20fr shown .70 .25
888 A153 30fr Giraffes .70 .25
889 A153 40fr Elephants .95 .25
Nos. 887-889,C236-C237 (5) 6.70 1.50
Wild animals of West Africa.

1974, Oct. 14
890 A153 30fr Herding cattle .40 .25
891 A153 40fr Milking cow .55 .25
Nos. 890-891,C238-C239 (4) 3.30 1.10
Domestic animals.

Churchill
and Frigate
F390
A154

Design: 40fr, Churchill and fighter planes.

1974, Nov. 1   Photo.   *Perf. 13x13½*
892 A154 30fr multicolored .55 .25
893 A154 40fr multicolored .70 .25
Nos. 892-893,C240-C241 (4) 5.25 1.55
Winston Churchill (1874-1965).

No. 810A Ovptd. "Inauguration de l'hotel de la Paix 9-1-75"
Litho. & Embossed
1975, Jan. 9   *Perf. 12½*
Self-adhesive
893A A124a 1000fr gold, red & grn 10.00 10.00

On No. 893A embossing may cut through stamp and embossed backing paper may not adhere well to the unused stamps.

Chlamydocarya Macrocarpa — A155

Flowers of Togo: 25fr, Strelitzia reginae, vert. 30fr, Storphanthus sarmentosus, vert. 60fr, Clerodendrum scandens.

1975, Feb. 15   Litho.   *Perf. 14*
894 A155 25fr multicolored .35 .25
895 A155 30fr multicolored .50 .25
896 A155 40fr multicolored .80 .25
897 A155 60fr multicolored 1.10 .25
Nos. 894-897,C242-C243 (6) 7.25 1.80

No. 821 Overprinted: "70e ANNIVERSAIRE / 23 FEVRIER 1975"
1975, Feb. 23   Litho.   *Perf. 14*
898 A129 40fr green & multi .55 .25
Nos. 898,C244-C245 (3) 2.45 .85
Rotary Intl., 70th anniv.

Radio
Station,
Kamina
A156

30fr, Benedictine Monastery, Zogbegan. 40fr, Causeway, Atchinedji. 60fr, Ayome Waterfalls.

1975, Mar. 1   Photo.   *Perf. 13x14*
899 A156 25fr multicolored .35 .25
900 A156 30fr multicolored .35 .25
901 A156 40fr multicolored .45 .25
902 A156 60fr multicolored .65 .25
Nos. 899-902 (4) 1.80 1.00

Jesus Mocked, by
El Greco — A157

Paintings: 30fr, Crucifixion, by Master Janoslet. 40fr, Descent from the Cross, by Bellini. 90fr, Pietà, painter unknown.

1975, Apr. 19   Litho.   *Perf. 14*
903 A157 25fr black & multi .35 .25
904 A157 30fr black & multi .45 .25
905 A157 40fr black & multi .55 .25
906 A157 90fr black & multi 1.10 .30
Nos. 903-906,C246-C247 (6) 5.45 1.85
Easter.

Stilt
Walking,
Togolese
Flag
A158

Design: 30fr, Flag and dancers.

1975, Apr. 26   Litho.   *Perf. 14*
907 A158 25fr multicolored .40 .25
908 A158 30fr multicolored .40 .25
Nos. 907-908,C248-C249 (4) 2.00 1.00
15th anniv. of independence.

Rabbit
Hunter with
Club
A159

40fr, Beaver hunter with bow and arrow.

1975, May 24   Photo.   *Perf. 13x13½*
909 A159 30fr multicolored .75 .25
910 A159 40fr multicolored .95 .25
Nos. 909-910,C250-C251 (4) 5.55 1.10

Pounding
Palm Nuts
A160

Design: 40fr, Man extracting palm oil, vert.

1975, June 28   Litho.   *Perf. 14*
911 A160 30fr multicolored .95 .25
912 A160 40fr multicolored .95 .25
Nos. 911-912,C252-C253 (4) 5.65 1.50
Palm oil production.

Apollo-Soyuz Link-up — A161

1975, July 15
913 A161 30fr multicolored .40 .25
Nos. 913,C254-C258 (6) 5.80 1.85

Apollo Soyuz space test project (Russo-American cooperation), launching July 15; link-up July 17.

Women's Heads, IWY
Emblem — A162

1975, July 26   Litho.   *Perf. 12½*
914 A162 30fr blue & multi .50 .25
915 A162 40fr multicolored .60 .25
International Women's Year.

Dr. Schweitzer and Children — A163

1975, Aug. 23   Litho.   *Perf. 14x13½*
916 A163 40fr multicolored .75 .25
Nos. 916,C259-C261 (4) 4.50 1.30
Dr. Albert Schweitzer (1875-1965), medical missionary and musician.

Merchant Writing
Letter, by Vittore
Carpaccio
A164

1975, Oct. 9   Litho.   *Perf. 14*
917 A164 40fr multicolored .60 .25
Intl. Letter Writing Week. See No. C262.

No. 797 Overprinted: "30ème Anniversaire / des Nations-Unies"
1975, Oct. 24   Litho.   *Perf. 14*
918 A120 50fr multi .50 .25
Nos. 918,C263-C264 (3) 1.85 .75
UN, 30th anniv.

Virgin and Child,
by Mantegna
A165

Paintings of the Virgin and Child: 30fr, El Greco. 40fr, Barend van Orley.

1975, Dec. 20   Litho.   *Perf. 14*
919 A165 20fr red & multi .35 .25
920 A165 30fr bl & multi .40 .25
921 A165 40fr red & multi .50 .25
Nos. 919-921,C267-C269 (6) 4.70 1.75
Christmas.

Crashed
Plane and
Pres.
Eyadema
A166

1976, Jan. 24   Photo.   *Perf. 13*
922 A166 50fr multi 11.00 .45
923 A166 60fr multi 26.00 .50
Airplane crash at Sara-kawa, Jan. 24, 1974, in which Pres. Eyadema escaped injury.

1976
Summer
Olympics,
Montreal —
A166a

Litho. & Embossed
1976, Feb. 24   *Perf. 11*
923A A166a 1000fr Diving 15.00 —
923B A166a 1000fr Track 15.00 —
923C A166a 1000fr Pole vault 15.00 —
923D A166a 1000fr Equestrian 15.00 —
923E A166a 1000fr Cycling 15.00 —
Nos. 923A-923E (5) 75.00
Exist imperf.

Frigates on the Hudson — A167

American Bicentennial: 50fr, George Washington, by Gilbert Stuart, and Bicentennial emblem, vert.

1976, Mar. 3   Litho.   *Perf. 14*
924 A167 35fr multicolored .45 .25
925 A167 50fr multicolored .65 .25
Nos. 924-925,C270-C273 (6) 5.50 1.80
For overprints see Nos. C280-C283.

ACP and
CEE
Emblems
A168

50fr, Map of Africa, Europe and Asia.

1976, Apr. 24   Photo.   *Perf. 13x14*
926 A168 10fr orange & multi .30 .25
927 A168 50fr pink & multi .50 .30
Nos. 926-927,C274-C275 (4) 2.00 1.05
First anniv. of signing of treaty between Togo and European Common Market, Lomé, Feb. 28, 1975.

Cable-laying Ship — A169

30fr, Telephone, tape recorder, speaker.

1976, Mar. 10   Photo.   *Perf. 13x14*
928 A169 25fr ultra & multi .25 .25
929 A169 30fr pink & multi .35 .25
Nos. 928-929,C276-C277 (4) 1.70 1.15
Centenary of first telephone call by Alexander Graham Bell, Mar. 10, 1876.

908 TOGO

Blind Man and
Insect — A170

1976, Apr. 8   **Perf. 14x13**
930 A170 50fr brt grn & multi   .75 .25
World Health Day: "Foresight prevents blindness." See No. C278.

Air Post Type, 1976, and

Marine Exhibition
Hall — A171

10fr, Pylon, flags of Ghana, Togo and
Dahomey.

1976   **Litho.**   **Perf. 14**
931 A171 5fr multicolored   .25 .25
932 AP19 10fr multicolored   .50 .25
933 A171 50fr multicolored   .70 .45
    Nos. 931-933,C279 (4)   2.45 1.20
Marine Exhibition, 10th anniv. (5fr, 50fr).
Ghana-Togo-Dahomey electric power grid, 1st
anniversary (10fr).
Issue dates: 50fr, May 8; 5fr, 10fr, August.

Running — A172

Montreal Olympic Emblem and: 30fr, Kayak.
50fr, High jump.

1976, June 15   **Photo.**   **Perf. 14x13**
934 A172 25fr multicolored   .30 .25
935 A172 30fr multicolored   .30 .25
936 A172 50fr multicolored   .45 .25
    Nos. 934-936,C284-C286 (6)   4.10 2.05
21st Olympic Games, Montreal, Canada,
July 17-Aug. 1.
For overprints see Nos. 947, C298-C299.

Titan 3 and Viking Emblem — A173

50fr, Viking trajectory, Earth to Mars.

1976, July 15   **Litho.**   **Perf. 14**
937 A173 30fr blue & multi   .35 .25
938 A173 50fr rose & multi   .50 .25
    Nos. 937-938,C287-C290 (6)   4.70 2.00
US Viking Mars missions.

Young Routy at
Celeyran, by
Toulouse-Lautrec
A174

Paintings by Toulouse-Lautrec: 20fr, Model
in Studio. 35fr, Louis Pascal, portrait.

1976, Aug. 7   **Litho.**   **Perf. 14**
939 A174 10fr black & multi   .25 .25
940 A174 20fr black & multi   .50 .25
941 A174 35fr black & multi   .65 .25
    Nos. 939-941,C291-C293 (6)   5.80 1.80
Henri Toulouse-Lautrec (1864-1901),
French painter, 75th death anniversary.

**No. 846 Overprinted: "Journée /
Internationale / de l'Enfance"**

1976, Nov. 27   **Litho.**   **Perf. 14**
942 A139 40fr multi   .40 .25
Intl. Children's Day. See No. C294.

Adoration of the Shepherds, by
Pontormo — A175

Paintings: 30fr, Nativity, by Carlo Crivelli.
50fr, Virgin and Child, by Jacopo da Pontormo.

1976, Dec. 18
943 A175 25fr multi   .35 .25
944 A175 30fr multi   .50 .25
945 A175 50fr multi   .85 .25
    Nos. 943-945,C295-C297 (6)   5.10 2.35
Christmas.

Mohammed Ali
Jinnah, Flags of
Togo and
Pakistan — A176

1976, Dec. 24   **Litho.**   **Perf. 13**
946 A176 50fr multi   .60 .25
Jinnah (1876-1948), first Governor General
of Pakistan.

**No. 936 Overprinted: "CHAMPIONS
OLYMPIQUES / SAUT EN HAUTEUR
/ POLOGNE"**

1976, Dec.   **Photo.**   **Perf. 14x13**
947 A172 50fr multi   .55 .25
    Nos. 947,C298-C299 (3)   2.95 1.15
Olympic winners.

Queen
Elizabeth II,
Silver
Jubilee —
A176a

Designs: No. 947A, Portrait. No. 947B,
Wearing coronation regalia.

Litho. & Embossed
1977, Jan. 10   **Perf. 11**
947A A176a 1000fr silver & multi   7.00
Souvenir Sheet
947B A176a 1000fr silver & multi   8.50
Exist imperf.

Kpeme
Phosphate
Mine, Sara-
kawa Crash
A177

1977, Jan. 13   **Photo.**   **Perf. 13x14**
948 A177 50fr multi   .55 .25
    Nos. 948,C300-C301 (3)   1.95 .85
Presidency of Etienne Eyadema, 10th anniv.

Musical
Instruments
A178

1977, Feb. 7   **Litho.**   **Perf. 14**
949 A178 5fr Gongophone   .25 .25
950 A178 10fr Tamtam, vert.   .25 .25
951 A178 25fr Dondon   .60 .25
    Nos. 949-951,C302-C304 (6)   4.40 1.55

Victor Hugo
and his
Home
A179

1977, Feb. 26   **Perf. 13x14**
952 A179 50fr multi   .65 .25
Victor Hugo (1802-1885), French writer,
175th birth anniversary. See No. C305.
For overprints see Nos. 959, C316.

Beethoven
and
Birthplace,
Bonn
A180

50fr, Bronze bust, 1812, & Heiligenstadt
home.

1977, Mar. 7   **Perf. 14**
953 A180 30fr multi   .50 .25
954 A180 50fr multi   .75 .25
    Nos. 953-954,C306-C307 (4)   4.60 1.45

Benz, 1894, Germany — A181

Early Automobiles: 50fr, De Dion Bouton,
1903, France.

1977, Apr. 11   **Litho.**   **Perf. 14**
955 A181 35fr multi   .65 .25
956 A181 50fr multi   .90 .25
    Nos. 955-956,C308-C311 (6)   6.05 2.10

Lindbergh, Ground Crew and Spirit of
St. Louis — A182

50fr, Lindbergh and Spirit of St. Louis.

1977, May 9
957 A182 25fr multi   .35 .25
958 A182 50fr multi   .70 .25
    Nos. 957-958,C312-C315 (6)   4.15 1.55
Charles A. Lindbergh's solo transatlantic
flight from New York to Paris, 50th anniv.

**No. 952 Overprinted: "10ème
ANNIVERSAIRE DU / CONSEIL
INTERNATIONAL / DE LA LANGUE
FRANCAISE"**

1977, May 17   **Litho.**   **Perf. 14**
959 A179 50fr multi   .70 .25
Intl. French Language Council, 10th anniv.
See No. C316.

African Slender-snouted
Crocodile — A183

Endangered wildlife: 15fr, Nile crocodile.

1977, June 13
960 A183 5fr multi   .35 .25
961 A183 15fr multi   .35 .25
    Nos. 960-961,C317-C320 (6)   5.90 1.60

Agriculture
School,
Tove
A184

1977, July 11   **Litho.**   **Perf. 14**
962 A184 50fr multi   .50 .25
    Nos. 962,C321-C323 (4)   3.60 1.20
Agricultural development.

Landscape with Cart, by Peter Paul
Rubens (1577-1640) — A185

Rubens Painting: 35fr, Exchange of the
Princesses at Hendaye, 1623.

1977, Aug. 8
963 A185 15fr multi   .45 .25
964 A185 35fr multi   .60 .25
    Nos. 963-964,C324-C325 (4)   3.35 1.00

Orbiter 101 on Ground — A186

Designs: 30fr, Launching of Orbiter, vert.
50fr, Ejection of propellant tanks at take-off.

1977, Oct. 4   Litho.   Perf. 14
965 A186 20fr multi   .30 .25
966 A186 30fr multi   .40 .25
967 A186 50fr multi   .50 .25
Nos. 965-967,C326-C328 (6)   4.50 1.60

Space shuttle trials in the US.

Lafayette Arriving in Montpelier, Vt. — A187

Design: 25fr, Lafayette, age 19, vert.

1977, Nov. 7   Perf. 14x13, 13x14
968 A187 25fr multi   .35 .25
969 A187 50fr multi   .60 .25
Nos. 968-969,C329-C330 (4)   2.70 1.00

Arrival of the Marquis de Lafayette in North America, 200th anniv.

Lenin, Cruiser Aurora, Red Flag A188

1977, Nov. 7   Litho.   Perf. 12
970 A188 50fr multi   1.20 .25

Russian October Revolution, 60th anniv.

Virgin and Child, by Lorenzo Lotto — A189

Virgin and Child by: 30fr, Carlo Crivelli. 50fr, Cosimo Tura.

1977, Dec. 19   Perf. 14
971 A189 20fr multi   .25 .25
972 A189 30fr multi   .35 .25
973 A189 50fr multi   .50 .25
Nos. 971-973,C331-C333 (6)   4.20 1.65

Christmas.

Edward Jenner — A190

Design: 20fr, Vaccination clinic, horiz.

Perf. 14x13, 13x14
1978, Jan. 9   Litho.
974 A190 5fr multi   .25 .25
975 A190 20fr multi   .25 .25
Nos. 974-975,C334-C335 (4)   1.25 1.00

Worldwide eradication of smallpox.

Orville and Wilbur Wright — A191

Design: 50fr, Wilbur Wright flying at Kill Devil Hill, 1902.

1978, Feb. 6   Litho.   Perf. 14
976 A191 35fr multi   .40 .25
977 A191 50fr multi   .55 .25
Nos. 976-977,C336-C339 (6)   6.55 1.95

75th anniversary of first motorized flight.

Anniversaries and Events — A192

Designs: No. 978, High jump. No. 979, Westminster Abbey. No. 980, Soccer players, World Cup. No. 981, Apollo 8. No. 982, Duke of Wellington, by Goya. No. 983, Hurdles. No. 984, Coronation coach. No. 985, Soccer players. No. 986, Apollo launch. No. 987, Dona Isabel Cobos de Porcel, by Goya.

1978, Mar. 13   Litho.   Perf. 11
978 A192 1000fr gold & multi   9.00
979 A192 1000fr gold & multi   9.00
980 A192 1000fr gold & multi   9.00
981 A192 1000fr gold & multi   9.00
982 A192 1000fr gold & multi   9.00

Souvenir Sheets
983 A192 1000fr gold & multi   12.00
984 A192 1000fr gold & multi   12.00
985 A192 1000fr gold & multi   12.00
986 A192 1000fr gold & multi   12.00
987 A192 1000fr gold & multi   12.00

Nos. 978, 983, 1980 Summer Olympics, Moscow. Nos. 979, 984, Coronation of Queen Elizabeth II, 25th anniv. Nos. 980, 985, 1978 World Cup Soccer Championships, Argentina. Nos. 981, 986, 1st manned lunar orbit, 10th anniv. Nos. 982, 987, Death sesquicent. of Francisco Goya.
For overprints see Nos. 1056A-1056B, 1094A-1094B.
Exist imperf.

John, the Evangelist and Eagle — A197

Evangelists: 10fr, Luke and ox. 25fr, Mark and lion. 30fr, Matthew and angel.

1978, Mar. 20   Litho.   Perf. 13½x14
988 A197 5fr multi   .25 .25
989 A197 10fr multi   .25 .25
990 A197 25fr multi   .25 .25
991 A197 30fr multi   .35 .25
  a.   Souvenir sheet of 4   1.25 .60
Nos. 988-991 (4)   1.10 1.00

No. 991a contains one each of Nos. 988-991 with simulated perforations.

Anchor, Fishing Harbor, Lomé A199

1978, Apr. 26   Photo.   Perf. 13
997 A199 25fr multi   .25 .25
Nos. 997,C340-C342 (4)   3.05 1.15

Venera I, USSR — A200

Designs: 30fr, Pioneer, US, horiz. 50fr, Venera, fuel base and antenna.

1978, May 8   Litho.   Perf. 14
998 A200 20fr multi   .25 .25
999 A200 30fr multi   .30 .25
1000 A200 50fr multi   .40 .25
Nos. 998-1000,C343-C345 (6)   3.90 1.60

US Pioneer and USSR Venera space missions.

Soccer — A201

50fr, Soccer players and Argentina '78 emblem.

1978, June 5   Perf. 14
1001 A201 30fr multi   .30 .25
1002 A201 50fr multi   .45 .25
Nos. 1001-1002,C346-C349 (6)   5.40 1.95

11th World Cup Soccer Championship, Argentina, June 1-25.

Celerifère, 1818 A202

History of the Bicycle: 50fr, First bicycle sidecar, c. 1870, vert.

Perf. 13x14, 14x13
1978, July 10   Photo.
1003 A202 25fr multi   .35 .25
1004 A202 50fr multi   .75 .25
Nos. 1003-1004,C350-C353 (6)   4.25 1.70

Thomas A. Edison, Sound Waves — A203

Design: 50fr, Victor's His Master's Voice phonograph, 1905, and dancing couple.

1978, July 8   Photo.   Perf. 14x13
1005 A203 30fr multicolored   .30 .25
1006 A203 50fr multicolored   .40 .25
Nos. 1005-1006,C354-C357 (6)   5.35 1.85

Centenary of the phonograph, invented by Thomas Alva Edison.

Dunant's Birthplace, Geneva — A204

Designs: 10fr, Henri Dunant and red cross. 25fr, Help on battlefield, 1864, and red cross.

1978, Sept. 4   Photo.   Perf. 14x13
1007 A204 5fr Prus bl & red   .25 .25
1008 A204 10fr red brn & red   .25 .25
1009 A204 25fr grn & red   .25 .25
Nos. 1007-1009,C358 (4)   1.20 1.00

Dunant (1828-1910), founder of Red Cross.

Threshing, by Raoul Dufy — A205

50fr, Horsemen on Seashore, by Paul Gauguin.

1978, Nov. 6   Litho.   Perf. 14
1010 A205 25fr multi   .30 .25
1011 A205 50fr multi   .50 .25
Nos. 1010-1011,C359-C362 (6)   4.70 2.15

Eiffel Tower, Paris — A206

1978, Nov. 27   Photo.   Perf. 14x13
1012 A206 50fr multi   .60 .25
Nos. 1012,C365-C367 (4)   3.45 1.70

Centenary of the Congress of Paris.

Virgin and Child, by Antonello da Messina — A207

Paintings (Virgin and Child): 30fr, by Carlo Crivelli. 50fr, by Francesco del Cossa.

1978, Dec. 18   Litho.   Perf. 14
1013 A207 20fr multi   .30 .25
1014 A207 30fr multi   .40 .25
1015 A207 50fr multi   .50 .25
Nos. 1013-1015,C368-C370 (6)   4.65 2.20

Christmas.

Capt. Cook's Ship off New Zealand — A208

Design: 50fr, Endeavour in drydock, N.E. Coast of Australia, horiz.

1979, Feb. 12　　Litho.　　Perf. 14
1016　A208　25fr multi　　　　.25　.25
1017　A208　50fr multi　　　　.45　.25
　　Nos. 1016-1017,C371-C374 (6)　4.25　2.55
200th death anniv. of Capt. James Cook.

Entry into Jerusalem A209

Easter: 40fr, The Last Supper, horiz. 50fr, Descent from the Cross, horiz.

1979, Apr. 9
1018　A209　30fr multi　　　　.30　.25
1019　A209　40fr multi　　　　.35　.25
1020　A209　50fr multi　　　　.40　.25
　　Nos. 1018-1020,C375-C377 (6)　3.70　2.10

Einstein Observatory, Potsdam — A210

Design: 50fr, Einstein and James Ramsay MacDonald, Berlin, 1931.

1979, July 2　　Photo.　　Perf. 14x13
1021　A210　35fr multi　　　　.30　.25
1022　A210　50fr multi　　　　.45　.25
　　Nos. 1021-1022,C380-C383 (6)　4.65　2.45
Albert Einstein (1879-1955), theoretical physicist.

Children and Children's Village Emblem — A211

IYC: 10fr, Mother and children. 15fr, Map of Africa, Children's Village emblem, horiz. 20fr, Woman and children walking to Children's Village, horiz. 25fr, Children sitting under African fan palm. 30fr, Map of Togo with location of Children's Villages.

1979, July 30　　Photo.　　Perf. 14x13
1023　A211　5fr multi　　　　.25　.25
1024　A211　10fr multi　　　　.25　.25
1025　A211　15fr multi　　　　.25　.25
1026　A211　20fr multi　　　　.25　.25
1027　A211　25fr multi　　　　.25　.25
1028　A211　30fr multi　　　　.25　.25
　a.　Souv. sheet of 2, #1027-1028　.75　.45
　　Nos. 1023-1028 (6)　　　1.50　1.50

Man Planting Tree — A212

1979, Aug. 13　　　　Perf. 14x13
1029　A212　50fr lilac & green　.60　.25
Second Arbor Day. See No. C384.

Sir Rowland Hill (1795-1879), Originator of Penny Postage — A213

30fr, French mail-sorting office, 18th cent., horiz. 50fr, Mailbox, Paris, 1850.

1979, Aug. 27
1030　A213　20fr multi　　　　.25　.25
1031　A213　30fr multi　　　　.30　.25
1032　A213　50fr multi　　　　.40　.25
　　Nos. 1030-1032,C385-C387 (6)　3.80　2.05

Norris Locomotive, 1843 — A214

35fr, Stephenson's "Rocket," 1829, vert.

1979, Oct. 1　　Litho.　　Perf. 14
1033　A214　35fr multi　　　　.50　.25
1034　A214　50fr multi　　　　.55　.25
　　Nos. 1033-1034,C388-C391 (6)　4.90　2.60

Olympic Flame, Lake Placid 80 Emblem, Slalom — A215

1980 Olympic Emblems, Olympic Flame and: 30fr, Yachting 50fr, Discus.

1979, Oct. 18　　Litho.　　Perf. 13½
1035　A215　20fr multi　　　　.25　.25
1036　A215　30fr multi　　　　.25　.25
1037　A215　50fr multi　　　　.55　.25
　　Nos. 1035-1037,C392-C394 (6)　3.90　2.05
13th Winter Olympic Games, Lake Placid, NY, 2/12-24/80 (90fr); 22nd Summer Olympic Games, Moscow, 7/19-8/3/80.

Catholic Priests A216

Design: 30fr, Native praying, vert.

1979, Oct. 29　　　　Perf. 13x14
1038　A216　30fr multi　　　　.25　.25
1039　A216　50fr multi　　　　.40　.25
　　Nos. 1038-1039,C396-C397 (4)　1.70　1.05
Religions in Togo.

Astronaut Walking on Moon — A217

Design: 50fr, Space capsule orbiting moon.

1979, Nov. 5
1040　A217　35fr multi　　　　.30　.25
1041　A217　50fr multi　　　　.40　.25
　　Nos. 1040-1041,C398-C401 (6)　5.25　2.65
Apollo 11 moon landing, 10th anniversary.

Telecom 79 — A218

1979, Nov. 26　　Photo.　　Perf. 13x14
1042　A218　50fr multi　　　　.35　.25
3rd World Telecommunications Exhibition, Geneva, Sept. 20-26. See No. C402.

Holy Family — A219

Christmas: 30fr, Virgin and Child. 50fr, Adoration of the Kings.

1979, Dec. 17　　Litho.　　Perf. 14
1043　A219　20fr multi　　　　.25　.25
1044　A219　30fr multi　　　　.30　.25
1045　A219　50fr multi　　　　.50　.25
　　Nos. 1043-1045,C403-C405 (6)　4.15　2.20

Rotary Emblem — A220

Rotary Emblem and: 30fr, Anniversary emblem. 40fr, Paul P. Harris, Rotary founder.

1980, Jan. 14
1046　A220　20fr multi　　　　.25　.25
1047　A220　30fr multi　　　　.35　.25
1048　A220　40fr multi　　　　.40　.25
　　Nos. 1046-1048,C406-C408 (6)　4.25　2.45
Rotary International, 75th anniversary.

Biathlon, Lake Placid '80 Emblem — A221

1980, Jan. 31　　Litho.　　Perf. 13½
1049　A221　50fr multi　　　　.40　.25
　　Nos. 1049,C409-C411 (4)　　3.00　1.50
13th Winter Olympic Games, Lake Placid, NY, Feb. 12-24. See No. C412.

1980 Winter Olympics, Lake Placid — A221a

Gold medalist: No. 1049F, Hanni Wenzel, Liechtenstein, women's slalom. No. 1049G, Eric Heiden, US, men's speed skating. No. 1049H, Jouko Tormanen, Finland, 90-meter ski jumping. No. 1049I, Erich Schaerer, Josef Benz, Switzerland, 2-man bobsled. No. 1049J, US, ice hockey.

1980　　　　Litho.　　Perf. 11
1049A　A221a　1000fr multi　20.00　4.50
1049B　A221a　1000fr multi　20.00　4.50
1049C　A221a　1000fr multi　20.00　4.50
1049D　A221a　1000fr multi　20.00　4.50
1049E　A221a　1000fr multi　20.00　4.50
　　Nos. 1049A-1049E (5)　100.00　22.50

Souvenir Sheets
1049F　A221a　1000fr gold & multi　—
1049G　A221a　1000fr gold & multi　—
1049H　A221a　1000fr gold & multi　—
1049I　A221a　1000fr gold & multi　—
1049J　A221a　1000fr gold & multi　—

Exist imperf.

Swimming, Moscow '80 Emblem — A222

1980, Feb. 29　　Litho.　　Perf. 13½
1050　A222　20fr shown　　　　.25　.25
1051　A222　30fr Gymnastics　　.30　.25
1052　A222　50fr Running　　　.50　.25
　　Nos. 1050-1052,C413-C415 (6)　5.20　3.25
22nd Summer Olympic Games, Moscow, July 19-Aug. 3.

Christ and the Angels, by Andrea Mantegna
A223

Easter 1980 (Paintings by): 40fr, Carlo Crivelli. 50fr, Jacopo Pontormo.

1980, Mar. 31   **Perf. 14**
1053	A223	30fr multi	.30	.25
1054	A223	40fr multi	.55	.25
1055	A223	50fr multi	.55	.25
		Nos. 1053-1055,C416-C418 (6)	4.05	2.00

Jet over Map of Africa
A224

1980, Mar. 24   **Litho.**   **Perf. 12½**
| 1056 | A224 | 50fr multi | .60 | .25 |

ASECNA (Air Safety Board), 20th anniv. See No. C419.

Nos. 979, 984 Ovptd. "Londres / 1980"

Litho. & Embossed
1980, May 6   **Perf. 11**
| 1056A | A192 | 1000fr gold & multi | 6.50 | — |

Souvenir Sheet
| 1056B | A192 | 1000fr gold & multi | 7.25 | — |

12th World Telecommunications Day — A225

1980, May 17   **Photo.**   **Perf. 14x13½**
| 1057 | A225 | 50fr multi | .50 | .25 |

See No. C420.

Red Cross over Globe Showing Lomé, Togo — A226

1980, June 16   **Photo.**   **Perf. 14x13**
| 1058 | A226 | 50fr multi | .60 | .25 |

Togolese Red Cross. See No. C421.

Jules Verne (1828-1905), French Science Fiction Writer — A227

50fr, Shark (20,000 Leagues Under the Sea).

1980, July 14   **Litho.**   **Perf. 14**
1059	A227	30fr multi	.30	.25
1060	A227	50fr multi	.55	.25
		Nos. 1059-1060,C422-C425 (6)	4.05	2.00

Baroness James de Rothschild, by Ingres — A228

Paintings by Jean Auguste Dominique Ingres (1780-1867): 30fr, Napoleon I on Imperial Throne. 40fr, Don Pedro of Toledo and Henri IV.

1980, Aug. 29   **Litho.**   **Perf. 14**
1061	A228	25fr multi	.25	.25
1062	A228	30fr multi	.35	.25
1063	A228	40fr multi	.40	.25
		Nos. 1061-1063,C426-C428 (6)	4.25	2.05

Minnie Holding Mirror for Leopard
A229

Disney Characters and Animals from Fazao Reserve: 2fr, Goofy (Dingo) cleaning teeth of hippopotamus. 3fr, Donald holding snout of crocodile. 4fr, Donald dangling over cliff from horn of rhinoceros. 5fr, Goofy riding water buffalo. 10fr, Monkey taking picture of Mickey. 100fr, Mickey as doctor examining giraffe with sore throat. 200fr, Pluto in party hat. No. 1071, Elephant giving shower to Goofy. No. 1072, Lion carrying Goofy by seat of his pants. No. 1072A, Pluto.

1980, Sept. 15   **Perf. 11**
1064	A229	1fr multi	.25	.25
1065	A229	2fr multi	.25	.25
1066	A229	3fr multi	.25	.25
1067	A229	4fr multi	.25	.25
1068	A229	5fr multi	.25	.25
1069	A229	10fr multi	.25	.25
1070	A229	100fr multi	.75	.35
1070A	A229	200fr multi	1.50	.75
1071	A229	300fr multi	2.25	1.10
		Nos. 1064-1071 (9)	6.00	3.70

Souvenir Sheets
| 1072 | A229 | 300fr multi | 8.00 | 3.00 |
| 1072A | A229 | 300fr multi | 4.00 | 1.50 |

50fr anniv. of the Disney character Pluto.

Market Activities, Women Preparing Meat
A230

1fr, Grinding savo. 3fr, Truck going to market. 4fr, Unloading produce. 5fr, Sugar cane vendor. 6fr, Barber curling child's hair, vert. 7fr, Vegetable vendor. 8fr, Sampling mangos, vert. 9fr, Grain vendor. 10fr, Spiced fish vendor. 15fr, Clay pot vendor. 20fr, Straw baskets. 25fr, Selling lemons and onions, vert. 30fr, Straw baskets, diff. 40fr, Shore market. 45fr, Vegetable stall. 50fr, Women carrying produce, vert. 60fr, Rice wine.

1980-81   **Perf. 14**
1073	A230	1fr multicolored	.25	.25
1074	A230	2fr shown	.25	.25
1075	A230	3fr multicolored	.25	.25
1076	A230	4fr multicolored	.25	.25
1077	A230	5fr multicolored	.25	.25
1078	A230	6fr multicolored	.25	.25
1079	A230	7fr multicolored	.25	.25
1080	A230	8fr multicolored	.25	.25
1081	A230	9fr multicolored	.25	.25
1082	A230	10fr multicolored	.25	.25
1083	A230	15fr multicolored	.25	.25
1084	A230	20fr multicolored	.25	.25
1085	A230	25fr multicolored	.25	.25
1086	A230	30fr multicolored	.25	.25
1087	A230	40fr multicolored	.30	.25
1087A	A230	45fr multicolored	.30	.25
1088	A230	50fr multicolored	.40	.25
1088A	A230	60fr multicolored	.40	.25
		Nos. 1073-1088A (18)	4.90	4.50

Issued: 45fr, 60fr, 3/8/81; others, 3/17/80. Nos. 1087A, 1088A dated 1980. See Nos. C440-C445, J68-J71. For overprints see Nos. C486-C487.

Commemorative Wreath — A231

Famous Men of the Decade: 40fr, Mao Tsetung, vert.

1980, Feb. 11   **Perf. 14x13**
1089	A231	25fr multi	.40	.25
1090	A231	40fr emer grn & dk grn	.60	.25
		Nos. 1089-1090,C429-C431 (5)	5.10	1.80

World Tourism Conference, Manila, Sept. 27 — A232

1980, Sept. 15   **Litho.**   **Perf. 14**
| 1091 | A232 | 50fr Hotel tourism emblem, vert. | .35 | .25 |
| 1092 | A232 | 150fr shown | 1.10 | .75 |

Map of Australia and Human Rights Flame
A233

1980, Oct. 13   **Photo.**   **Perf. 13x14**
1093	A233	30fr shown	.30	.25
1094	A233	50fr Europe and Asia map	.50	.25
		Nos. 1093-1094,C432-C433 (4)	2.20	1.25

Declaration of Human Rights, 30th anniv.

Nos. 980, 985 Ovptd. in Gold & Black

Litho. & Embossed
1980, Nov. 24   **Perf. 11**
| 1094A | A192 | 1000fr gold & multi | 8.50 | — |

Souvenir Sheet
| 1094B | A192 | 1000fr gold & multi | 7.00 | — |

No. 1094B ovptd. with additional text and black bars in sheet margin.

Melk Monastery, Austria, 18th Century
A234

30fr, Tarragon Cathedral, Spain, 12th cent. 50fr, St. John the Baptist, Florence, 1964.

Perf. 14½x13½
1980, Dec. 22   **Litho.**
1095	A234	20fr shown	.25	.25
1096	A234	30fr multicolored	.35	.25
1097	A234	50fr multicolored	.55	.25
		Nos. 1095-1097,C435-C437 (6)	4.35	2.25

Christmas.

African Postal Union, 5th Anniversary
A235

1980, Dec. 24   **Photo.**   **Perf. 13½**
| 1098 | A235 | 100fr multi | .75 | .35 |

February 2nd Hotel Opening
A236

1981, Feb. 2   **Litho.**   **Perf. 12½x13**
| 1099 | A236 | 50fr multi | .60 | .25 |

See No. C437B.

A236a

1981, Dec. 21   **Litho.**   **Perf. 12½**
| 1100 | A236a | 70fr lt grn & multi | .70 | .35 |

West African Rice Development Assoc. See No. C461.

A237

Easter (Rembrandt Paintings): 30fr, Rembrandt's Father. 40fr, Self-portrait. 50fr, Artist's father as an old man. 60fr, Rider on Horseback.

1981, Apr. 13   *Perf. 14½x13½*
1101	A237	30fr multi	.35	.25
1102	A237	40fr multi	.40	.25
1103	A237	50fr multi	.50	.25
1104	A237	60fr multi	.60	.30
	Nos. 1101-1104,C438-C439 (6)		4.50	2.15

Wedding of Prince Charles and Lady Diana Spencer — A237a — 1105

1981, July 29   **Litho.**   *Perf. 11*
1105	A237a	1000fr gold & multi	4.00	2.50

Souvenir Sheet
Litho. & Embossed
1106	A237a	1000fr Charles & Diana, diff.	5.00	3.00

No. 1105 printed with embossed se-tenant label.
For overprints see Nos. 1143A-1143B.

Red-headed Rock Fowl — A238

40fr, Splendid sunbird. 60fr, Violet-backed starling. 90fr, Red-collared widowbird.

1981, Aug. 10   *Perf. 13½x14½*
1107	A238	30fr shown	.45	.25
1108	A238	40fr multicolored	.55	.25
1109	A238	60fr multicolored	.90	.25
1110	A238	90fr multicolored	1.40	.30
	Nos. 1107-1110,C446-C447 (6)		5.60	1.65

1982 World Soccer Championships, Spain — A238a

Flags (Nos. 1110A-1110E) or Players (Nos. 1110F-1110J) and stadiums: Nos. 1110A, 1110F, Athletico de Madrid. Nos. 1110B, 1110G, Real Madrid C.F. Nos. 1110C, 1110H, R.C.D. Espanol. Nos. 1110D, 1110I, Real Zaragoza. Nos. 1110E, 1110J, Valencia.

Set of 5
Litho. & Embossed
1981, Aug. 17   *Perf. 11*
1110A-1110E	A238a	1000fr	40.00 10.00

Souvenir Sheets
1110F-1110J	A238a	1000fr	35.00 10.00

African Postal Union Ministers, 6th Council Meeting, July 28-20 A239

1981, Aug. 31   **Litho.**   *Perf. 12½*
1111	A239	70fr Dish antenna	.50	.25
1112	A239	90fr Computer operator, vert.	.70	.35
1113	A239	105fr Map	.80	.40
	Nos. 1111-1113 (3)		2.00	1.00

Intl. Year of the Disabled A240

1981, Aug. 31   *Perf. 14*
1114	A240	70fr Blind man	.85	.45
	Nos. 1114,C448-C449 (3)		3.25	1.70

See No. C449A.

Woman with Hat, by Picasso, 1961 — A241

Picasso Birth Centenary: Sculptures.

1981, Sept. 14   *Perf. 14½x13½*
1116	A241	25fr shown	.30	.25
1117	A241	50fr She-goat	.50	.25
1118	A241	60fr Violin, 1915	.55	.25
	Nos. 1116-1118,C450-C452 (6)		5.75	2.55

Aix-la-Chapelle Cathedral, Germany — A242

World Heritage Year: 40fr, Geyser, Yellowstone Natl. Park. 50fr, Nahanni Natl. Park, Canada. 60fr, Stone churches, Ethiopia.

1981, Sept. 28   *Perf. 13½x14½*
1119	A242	30fr multi	.25	.25
1120	A242	40fr multi	.30	.25
1121	A242	50fr multi	.40	.25
1122	A242	60fr multi	.50	.35
	Nos. 1119-1122,C453-C454 (6)		4.00	2.35

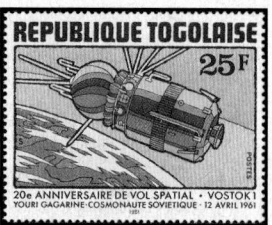

Yuri Gagarin's Vostok I, 20th. — A243

Space Anniversaries: 50fr, 20th Anniv. of Alan Shepard's Flight. 60fr, Lunar Orbiter I, 15th.

1981, Nov.   *Perf. 14*
1123	A243	25fr multi	.25	.25
1124	A243	50fr multi	.45	.25
1125	A243	60fr multi	.55	.25
	Nos. 1123-1125,C455-C456 (5)		2.60	1.25

Christmas A244

Rubens Paintings: 20fr, Adoration of the Kings. 30fr, Adoration of the Shepherds. 50fr, St. Catherine.

Perf. 14½x13½
1981, Dec. 10   **Litho.**
1126	A244	20fr multi	.25	.25
1127	A244	30fr multi	.25	.25
1128	A244	50fr multi	.40	.25
	Nos. 1126-1128,C457-C459 (6)		5.20	2.75

15th Anniv. of Natl. Liberation — A245

1982, Jan. 13   **Litho.**   *Perf. 12½*
1129	A245	70fr Dove, flag	.70	.35
1130	A245	90fr Citizens, Pres. Eyadema, vert.	.90	.45
	Nos. 1129-1130,C462-C463 (4)		3.20	1.55

Scouting Year A246

1982, Feb. 25   **Litho.**   *Perf. 14*
1131	A246	70fr Pitching tent	.55	.25
	Nos. 1131,C464-C467 (5)		4.50	1.80

Easter — A247

Designs: The Ten Commandments.

1982, Mar. 15   *Perf. 14x14½*
1132	A247	10fr multi	.25	.25
1133	A247	25fr multi	.25	.25
1134	A247	30fr multi	.25	.25
1135	A247	45fr multi	.30	.25
1136	A247	50fr multi	.35	.25
1137	A247	70fr multi	.45	.25
1138	A247	90fr multi	.60	.30
	Nos. 1132-1138,C469-C470 (9)		3.95	2.55

Papilio Dardanus A248

1982, July 15   **Litho.**   *Perf. 14½x14*
1139	A248	15fr shown	.35	.25
1140	A248	20fr Belenois calypso	.55	.25
1141	A248	25fr Palla decius	.55	.25
	Nos. 1139-1141,C474-C475 (5)		4.80	1.60

1982 World Cup — A249

Designs: Various soccer players.

1982, July 26   *Perf. 14x14½*
1142	A249	25fr multi	.25	.25
1143	A249	45fr multi	.35	.25
	Nos. 1142-1143,C477-C479 (5)		4.90	2.50

For overprints see Nos. 1150-1155.

Nos. 1105-1106 Overprinted on one or two lines

1982, Oct. 28   **Litho.**   *Perf. 11*
1143A	A237a	1000fr gold & multi	8.00	4.00

Souvenir Sheet
Litho. & Embossed
1143B	A237a	1000fr gold & multi	9.25	3.50

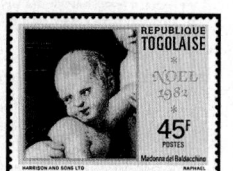

Christmas A250

Madonna of Baldacchino, by Raphael. #1144-1148 show details; #1149 entire painting.

1982, Dec. 24   **Litho.**   *Perf. 14½x14*
1144	A250	45fr multi	.45	.25
1145	A250	70fr multi	.65	.25
1146	A250	105fr multi	.85	.25
1147	A250	130fr multi	1.20	.30
1148	A250	150fr multi	1.40	.35
	Nos. 1144-1148 (5)		4.55	1.40

Souvenir Sheet
Perf. 14x14½
1149	A250	500fr multi, vert.	3.75	1.75

Nos. 1142-1143, C477-C480 Overprinted: VAINQUER / COUPE DU MONDE / FOOTBALL 82 / "ITALIE"

1983, Jan. 31   **Litho.**   *Perf. 14x14½*
1150	A249	25fr multi	.25	.25
1151	A249	45fr multi	.35	.25
1152	A249	105fr multi	.75	.35
1153	A249	200fr multi	1.40	.55
1154	A249	300fr multi	2.10	.85
	Nos. 1150-1154 (5)		4.85	2.25

Souvenir Sheet
1155	A249	500fr multi	4.25	2.50

Italy's victory in 1982 World Cup. Nos. 1152-1155 airmail.

20th Anniv. of West African Monetary Union (1982) — A251

1983, May   Litho.   Perf. 12½x12
1156	A251	70fr Map	.60	.25
1157	A251	90fr Emblem	.80	.30

Visit of Pres. Mitterand of France, Jan. 13-15 — A252

35fr, Sokode Regional Hospital. 45fr, Citizens joining hands. 70fr, Soldiers, vert. 90fr, Pres. Mitterand. 105fr, Pres. Eyadema, Mitterand, vert. 130fr, Greeting crowd.

1983, Jan. 13   Litho.   Perf. 13
1158	A252	35fr multicolored	.25	.25
a.		Souvenir sheet, imperf.	1.00	.55
1159	A252	45fr multicolored	.40	.25
a.		Souvenir sheet, imperf.	1.00	.55
1160	A252	70fr multicolored	.60	.25
a.		Souvenir sheet, imperf.	1.00	.55
1161	A252	90fr multicolored	.70	.30
a.		Souvenir sheet, imperf.	1.00	.55
1162	A252	105fr multicolored	.90	.35
a.		Souvenir sheet, imperf.	1.00	.55
1163	A252	130fr multicolored	1.25	.45
a.		Souvenir sheet, imperf.	1.00	.55
		Nos. 1158-1163 (6)	4.10	1.85

Nos. 1161-1163 airmail.

Easter — A253

Paintings: 35fr, Mourners at the Death of Christ, by Bellini. 70fr, Crucifixion, by Raphael. 90fr, Descent from the Cross, by Carracci. 500fr Christ, by Reni.

1983   Litho.   Perf. 13½x14½
1164	A253	35fr multi	.35	.25
1165	A253	70fr multi, vert.	.55	.25
1166	A253	90fr multi	.85	.25
		Nos. 1164-1166 (3)	1.75	.75

Souvenir Sheet
Perf. 14½x13½
1167	A253	500fr multi	3.75	1.75

90fr, 500fr airmail.

Folkdances — A254

1983, Dec. 1   Perf. 14½x14
1168	A254	70fr Kondona	.55	.25
1169	A254	90fr Kondona, diff.	.65	.25
1170	A254	105fr Toubole	.85	.30
1171	A254	130fr Adjogbo	1.00	.25
		Nos. 1168-1171 (4)	3.05	1.05

90fr, 105fr, 130fr airmail.

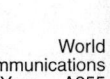

World Communications Year — A255

1983, June 20   Litho.   Perf. 14x14½
1172	A255	70fr Drummer	.60	.25
1173	A255	90fr Modern communication	.70	.25

90fr airmail.

Christmas — A256

70fr, Catholic Church, Kante. 90fr, Altar, Dapaong Cathedral. 105fr, Protestant Church, Dapaong. 500fr, Ecumenical Church, Pya.

1983, Dec.   Perf. 13½x14½
1174	A256	70fr multicolored	.55	.25
1175	A256	90fr multicolored	.65	.25
1176	A256	105fr multicolored	.80	.25
		Nos. 1174-1176 (3)	2.00	.75

Souvenir Sheet
1177	A256	500fr multicolored	4.50	1.75

90fr, 105fr, 500fr airmail.

Sarakawa Presidential Assassination Attempt, 10th Anniv. — A257

70fr, Wrecked plane. 90fr, Plane, diff. 120fr, Memorial Hall. 270fr, Pres. Eyadema statue, vert.

1984, Jan. 24   Litho.   Perf. 13
1178	A257	70fr multicolored	.60	.25
1179	A257	90fr multicolored	.70	.25
1180	A257	120fr multicolored	1.00	.25
1181	A257	270fr multicolored	2.25	.45
		Nos. 1178-1181 (4)	4.55	1.20

120fr, 270fr airmail.

20th Anniv. of World Food Program (1983) A258

1984, May 2   Litho.   Perf. 13
1182	A258	35fr Orchard	.25	.25
1183	A258	70fr Fruit tree	.50	.25
1184	A258	90fr Rice paddy	.65	.25
		Nos. 1182-1184 (3)	1.40	.75

Souvenir Sheet
1185	A258	300fr Village, horiz.	3.00	1.90

25th Anniv. of Council of Unity — A259

1984, May 29   Perf. 12
1186	A259	70fr multi	.55	.25
1187	A259	90fr multi	.70	.25

Easter 1984 — A260

Various stained-glass windows.

1984   Litho.   Perf. 14x14½
1188	A260	70fr multi	.55	.25
1189	A260	90fr multi	.65	.25
1190	A260	120fr multi	.85	.25
1191	A260	270fr multi	1.90	.50
1192	A260	300fr multi	2.10	.55
		Nos. 1188-1192 (5)	6.05	1.80

Souvenir Sheet
1193	A260	500fr multi	4.50	3.50

Nos. 1189-1193 airmail.

Centenary of German-Togolese Friendship — A261

#1194, Degbenou Catholic Mission, 1893. #1195, Kara Bridge, 1911. #1196, Treaty Site, Baguida, 1884. #1197, Degbenou Students, 1893. #1198, Sansane Administrative Post, 1908. #1199, Adjido Official School. #1200, Sokode Cotton Market, 1910. #1201, William Fountain, Atakpame, 1906. #1202, Lome Main Street, 1895, No. 19. #1203, Police, 1905. #1204, Lome Railroad Construction. #1205, Governor's Palace, Lome, 1905. #1206, No. 9, Commerce Street, Lome. #1207, Nos. 10, 17. #1208, Lome Wharf, 1903. #1209, G. Nachtigal. #1210, Wilhelm II. #1211, O.F. de Bismark. #1212, J. de Puttkamer. #1213, A. Koehler. #1214, W. Horn. #1215, J.G. de Zech. #1216, E. Bruckner. #1217, A.F. de Mecklenburg. #1218, H.G. de Doering. #1219, Land Development, 1908. #1220, Postal Courier, No. 8. #1221, Treaty Signers, 1885. 150fr, German & Togolese Children, Flags. #1223, Aneho Line Locomotive, 1905. #1224, Mallet Locomotive, 1907. #1225, German Ship "Mowe," 1884. #1226, "La Sophie," 1884. 300fr, Pres. Eyadema, Helmut Kohl.

1984, July 5   Litho.   Perf. 13
1194	A261	35fr multi	.50	.25
1195	A261	35fr multi	.50	.25
1196	A261	35fr multi, vert.	.50	.25
1197	A261	35fr multi	.50	.25
1198	A261	35fr multi	.50	.25
1199	A261	35fr multi	.50	.25
1200	A261	35fr multi	.50	.25
1201	A261	45fr multi, vert.	.50	.25
1202	A261	45fr multi	.50	.25
1203	A261	45fr multi	.50	.25
1204	A261	45fr multi	.50	.25
1205	A261	45fr multi	.50	.25
1206	A261	45fr multi	.50	.25
1207	A261	70fr multi	.60	.25
1208	A261	70fr multi	.60	.25
1209	A261	90fr multi, vert.	.75	.25
1210	A261	90fr multi, vert.	.75	.25
1211	A261	90fr multi, vert.	.75	.25
1212	A261	90fr multi, vert.	.75	.25
1213	A261	90fr multi, vert.	.75	.25
1214	A261	90fr multi, vert.	.75	.25
1215	A261	90fr multi, vert.	.75	.25
1216	A261	90fr multi, vert.	.75	.25
1217	A261	90fr multi, vert.	.75	.25
1218	A261	90fr multi, vert.	.75	.25
1219	A261	90fr multi	.75	.25
1220	A261	120fr multi, vert.	1.00	.25
1221	A261	120fr multi	1.00	.25
1222	A261	150fr multi, vert.	1.25	.25
1223	A261	270fr multi	2.25	.45
1224	A261	270fr multi	2.25	.45
1225	A261	270fr multi	2.25	.45
1226	A261	270fr multi	2.25	.45
1227	A261	300fr multi	2.40	.50
		Nos. 1194-1227 (34)	30.60	9.55

Souvenir sheets of one exist for each design. Stamp size: 65x80mm. Value, set of 34, $35.

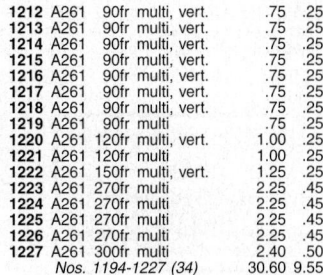

Donald Duck, 50th Anniv. A262

1fr, Donald, Chip. 2fr, Donald, Chip and Dale. 3fr, Louie, Chip and Dale. 5fr, Donald, Chip. 10fr, Daisy Duck, Donald. 15fr, Goofy, Donald. 105fr, Huey, Dewey and Louie. 500fr, Nephews, Donald. No. 1238, 1000fr, Nephews, Donald.
No. 1239, Surprised Donald. No. 1240, Perplexed Donald.

1984, Sept. 21   Litho.   Perf. 11
1230	A262	1fr multi	.55	.25
1231	A262	2fr multi	.55	.25
1232	A262	3fr multi	.55	.25
1233	A262	5fr multi	.55	.25
1234	A262	10fr multi	.55	.25
1235	A262	15fr multi	.55	.25
1236	A262	105fr multi	.80	.25
1237	A262	500fr multi	3.75	.70
1238	A262	1000fr multi	8.25	1.40
		Nos. 1230-1238 (9)	16.10	3.85

Souvenir Sheets
Perf. 14
1239	A262	1000fr multi	7.50	7.50
1240	A262	1000fr multi	7.50	7.50

Nos. 1236-1240 airmail.
For overprints see Nos. C551-C554.

Endangered Mammals — A263

45fr, Manatee swimming. 70fr, Manatee eating. 90fr, Manatees floating. 105fr, Young manatee, mother.
No. 1245, Olive Colobus monkey, vert. No. 1246, Galago (Bushbaby)

1984, Oct. 1   Litho.   Perf. 15x14½
1241	A263	45fr multi	1.60	.50
1242	A263	70fr multi	2.25	.50
1243	A263	90fr multi	2.25	1.00
1244	A263	105fr multi	2.75	1.00
		Nos. 1241-1244 (4)	8.85	3.00

Souvenir Sheets
Perf. 14x15, 15x14
1245	A263	1000fr multi	10.00	6.00
1246	A263	1000fr multi	10.00	6.00

Nos. 1243-1246 airmail. See #1444-1447.

Birth Centenary of Eleanor Roosevelt A264

90fr, Mrs. Roosevelt, Statue of Liberty.

1984, Oct. 10　　Litho.　　Perf. 13½
1247	A264	70fr shown	.55	.25
1248	A264	90fr multicolored	.70	.25

No. 1248 airmail.

Classic Automobiles — A265

1984, Nov. 15　　Litho.　　Perf. 15
1249	A265	1fr 1947 Bristol	.25	.25
1250	A265	2fr 1925 Frazer Nash	.25	.25
1251	A265	3fr 1950 Healey	.25	.25
1252	A265	4fr 1925 Kissell	.25	.25
1253	A265	50fr 1927 La Salle	.80	.25
1254	A265	90fr 1921 Minerva	.65	.25
1255	A265	500fr 1950 Morgan	4.00	.70
1256	A265	1000fr 1921 Napier	8.00	1.40
		Nos. 1249-1256 (8)	14.45	3.60

Souvenir Sheets
1257	A265	1000fr 1941 Nash	8.00	2.00
1258	A265	1000fr 1903 Peugeot	8.00	2.00

Nos. 1254-1258 airmail.
For overprints see Nos. 1328-1331, C542-C544, C564-C565.

Christmas
A266

70fr, Connestable Madonna. 290fr, Cowper Madonna. 300fr, Alba Madonna. 500fr, Madonna of the Curtain. 1000fr, Madonna with Child.

Perf. 14½x13½

1984, Nov. 23　　　　　　Litho.
1259	A266	70fr multi	.50	.25
1260	A266	290fr multi	2.00	.50
1261	A266	300fr multi	2.10	.55
1262	A266	500fr multi	3.50	.85
		Nos. 1259-1262 (4)	8.10	2.15

Souvenir Sheet
1263	A266	1000fr multi	7.00	6.75

Nos. 1260-1263 airmail.

African Locomotives — A267

1fr, Decapod, Madeira. 2fr, 2-6-0, Egypt. 3fr, 4-8-2+2-8-4, Algeria. 4fr, Congo-Ocean diesel. 50fr, 0-4-0+0-4-0, Libya. 90fr, #49, Malawi. 105fr, 1907 Mallet, Togo. 500fr, 4-8-2, Rhodesia. 1000fr, Beyer-Garratt, East Africa.
No. 1273, 2-8-2, Ghana. No. 1274, Locomotive, Senegal.

1984, Nov. 30　　Litho.　　Perf. 15
1264	A267	1fr multi	.25	.25
1265	A267	2fr multi	.25	.25
1266	A267	3fr multi	.25	.25
1267	A267	4fr multi	.25	.25
1268	A267	50fr multi	.25	.25
1269	A267	90fr multi	.75	.25
1270	A267	105fr multi	.90	.25
1271	A267	500fr multi	3.75	.80
1272	A267	1000fr multi	6.50	1.60
		Nos. 1264-1272 (9)	13.15	4.15

Souvenir Sheets
1273	A267	1000fr multi	9.00	6.00
1274	A267	1000fr multi	9.00	6.00

Nos. 1269-1274 airmail.
For overprints see Nos. 1343-1346, 1356-1360, C541, C566.

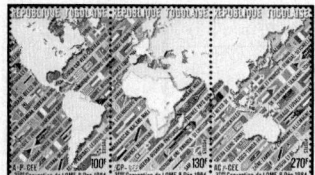

Economic Convention, Lome — A268

100fr, Map of the Americas. 130fr, Map of Eurasia, Africa. 270fr, Map of Asia, Australia. 500fr, President Eyadema.

1984, Dec. 8　　Litho.　　Perf. 12½
1275	A268	100fr multicolored	.70	.25
1276	A268	130fr multicolored	1.00	.25
1277	A268	270fr multicolored	1.90	.50
a.		A268 Strip of 3, #1275-1277	3.75	3.75

Souvenir Sheet
1278	A268	500fr multicolored	3.75	3.25

No. 1277a has continuous design.

Intl. Civil Aviation Org., 40th Anniv. A269

Map of Togo, ICAO emblem and: 70fr, Lockheed Constellation, 1944. 105fr, Boeing 707, 1954. 200fr, Doublas DC-8-61, 1966. 500fr, Bac/Sud Concorde, 1966. 1000fr, Icarus, by Hans Erni.

1984, Oct. 15　　Litho.　　Perf. 15x14
1279	A269	70fr multi	.65	.25
1280	A269	105fr multi	.85	.25
1281	A269	200fr multi	1.40	.25
1282	A269	500fr multi	3.75	.75
		Nos. 1279-1282 (4)	6.65	1.50

Souvenir Sheet
1283	A269	1000fr multi	6.50	6.00

Nos. 1280-1283 airmail.

Mosaic of the 12 Apostles, Baptistry of the Aryans, Ravenna, Italy, — A270

Designs: 1fr, St. Paul. 2fr, St. Thomas. 3fr, St. Matthew. 4fr, St. James the Younger. 5fr, St. Simon. 70fr, St. Thaddeaus Judas. 90fr, St. Bartholomew. 105fr, St. Philip. 200fr, St. John. 270fr, St. James the Greater. 400fr, St. Andrew. 500fr, St. Peter. No. 1296, The Last Supper, by Andrea del Castagno, c. 1421-1457, horiz. No, 1297, Coronation of the Virgin, by Raphael, 1483-1520, horiz.

1984, Dec. 14　　　　　　　Perf. 15
1284	A270	1fr multi	.25	.25
1285	A270	2fr multi	.25	.25
1286	A270	3fr multi	.25	.25
1287	A270	4fr multi	.25	.25
1288	A270	5fr multi	.25	.25
1289	A270	70fr multi	1.20	.25
1290	A270	90fr multi	.80	.25
1291	A270	105fr multi	.95	.25
1292	A270	200fr multi	1.75	.25
1293	A270	270fr multi	2.25	.35
1294	A270	400fr multi	3.50	.45
1295	A270	500fr multi	4.75	.55
		Nos. 1284-1295 (12)	16.45	3.60

Souvenir Sheets
1296-1297	A270	1000fr each	10.00	4.50

Nos. 1290-1297 airmail.
For overprints see Nos. C545-C547.

1f République Togolaise

Race Horses A271

1fr, Allez France. 2fr, Arkle, vert. 3fr, Tingle Creek, vert. 4fr, Interco. 50fr, Dawn Run. 90fr, Seattle Slew, vert. 500fr, Nijinsky. No. 1305, 1000fr, Politician.
No. 1306, Shergar. No. 1307, Red Rum.

1985, Jan. 10
1298	A271	1fr multi	.25	.25
1299	A271	2fr multi	.25	.25
1300	A271	3fr multi	.25	.25
1301	A271	4fr multi	.25	.25
1302	A271	50fr multi	.75	.25
1303	A271	90fr multi	.75	.25
1304	A271	500fr multi	3.75	.60
1305	A271	1000fr multi	6.00	1.25
		Nos. 1298-1305 (8)	12.25	3.35

Souvenir Sheets
1306	A271	1000fr multi	7.00	5.50
1307	A271	1000fr multi	7.00	5.50

Nos. 1303-1307 airmail.
For overprints see Nos. 1353-1355A.

Easter — A272

Paintings by Raphael (1483-1520) — 70fr, Christ and His Flock. 90fr, Christ and the Fishermen. 135fr, The Blessed Christ, vert. 150fr, The Entombment, vert. 250fr, The Resurrection, vert. 1000fr, The Transfiguration.

Perf. 13½x14½, 14½x13½

1985, Mar. 7
1308	A272	70fr multi	.65	.25
1309	A272	90fr multi	.70	.25
1310	A272	135fr multi	1.20	.25
1311	A272	150fr multi	1.25	.25
1312	A272	250fr multi	2.10	.35
		Nos. 1308-1312 (5)	5.90	1.35

Souvenir Sheet
1313	A272	1000fr multi	8.50	6.50

Nos. 1309-1313 airmail.

Technical & Cultural Cooperation Agency, 15th Anniv. — A273

1985, Mar. 20　　　　　　　Perf. 12½
1314	A273	70fr multi	.60	.25
1315	A273	90fr multi	.60	.25

Philexafrica '85, Lome — A274

No. 1316, Woman carrying fruit basket. No. 1317, Man plowing field.

1985, May 9　　　　　　　　Perf. 13
1316	A274	200fr multi	1.75	.25
1317	A274	200fr multi	1.75	.25
a.		Pair, #1316-1317 + label	4.00	4.00

Scarification Ritual — A275

25fr, Kabye (Pya). 70fr, Mollah (Kotokoli). 90fr, Maba (Dapaong). 105fr, Kabye (Pagouda). 270fr, Peda.

1985, May 14　　　　　　Perf. 14x15
1318	A275	25fr multi	.60	.25
1319	A275	70fr multi	.60	.25
1320	A275	90fr multi	.60	.25
1321	A275	105fr multi	.75	.25
1322	A275	270fr multi	1.75	.30
		Nos. 1318-1322 (5)	4.30	1.30

Nos. 1320-1322 airmail.

Seashells A276

70fr, Clavatula muricata. 90fr, Marginella desjardini. 120fr, Clavatula nifat. 135fr, Cypraea stercoraria. 270fr, Conus genuanus. 1000fr, Dancers wearing traditional shell decorations.

1985, June 1　　　　　　Perf. 15x14
1323	A276	70fr multi	.85	.25
1324	A276	90fr multi	.90	.25
1325	A276	120fr multi	1.10	.25
1326	A276	135fr multi	1.40	.25
1327	A276	270fr multi	2.75	.35
		Nos. 1323-1327 (5)	7.00	1.35

Souvenir Sheet
1327A	A276	1000fr multi	8.50	6.00

Nos. 1324-1327A airmail.

Nos. 1253, 1256-1258 Overprinted "Exposition Mondiale 1985 / Tsukuba, Japon"

1985, June　　　　　　　　Perf. 15
1328	A265	50fr #1253	1.50	.25
1329	A265	11fr #1256	11.50	3.50

Souvenir Sheets
1330	A265	1000fr #1257	9.75	3.75
1331	A265	1000fr #1258	9.75	3.75

EXPO '85.

Audubon Birth Bicent. — A277

Illustrations by artist-naturalist J.J. Audubon (1785-1851) — 90fr, Larus bonapartii. 120fr, Pelecanus occidentalis. 135fr, Cassidix mexicanus. 270fr, Aquila chrysaetos. 500fr, Picus erythrocephalus. 1000fr, Dendroica petechia.

1985, Aug. 13　　　　　　　Perf. 13
1332	A277	90fr multi	.95	.25
1333	A277	120fr multi	1.25	.25
1334	A277	135fr multi	1.25	.25
1335	A277	270fr multi	2.50	.35
1336	A277	500fr multi	4.50	.60
		Nos. 1332-1336 (5)	10.45	1.70

Souvenir Sheet
1337	A277	1000fr multi	9.50	7.50

Nos. 1332, 1334 and 1336-1337 airmail.

Dove, UN Emblem — A278

Kara Port Construction — A279

Designs: 115fr, Hands, UN emblem. 250fr, Millet crop, Atalote Research Facility. 500fr, UN, Togo flags, statesmen.

1985, Oct. 24   **Litho.**   **Perf. 13**
1338	A278	90fr multi	.70	.25
1339	A278	115fr multi	.95	.25
1340	A279	150fr multi	1.25	.25
1341	A279	250fr multi	1.60	.35
1342	A279	500fr multi	3.50	.65
		Nos. 1338-1342 (5)	8.00	1.75

UN, 40th anniv. Nos. 1340-1342 are airmail.

Nos. 1267, 1270, 1272, 1273 Ovptd. with Rotary Emblem and "80e ANNIVERSAIRE DU / ROTARY INTERNATIONAL"

1985   **Litho.**   **Perf. 15**
1343	A267	4fr multi	.60	.40
1344	A267	105fr multi	1.10	1.00
1345	A267	1000fr multi	11.00	5.00
		Nos. 1343-1345 (3)	12.70	6.40

Souvenir Sheet
| 1346 | A267 | 1000fr multi | 12.50 | 6.50 |

Nos. 1344-1346 are airmail.

Christmas A280

Religious paintings and statuary: 90fr, The Garden of Roses Madonna. 115fr, Madonna and Child, Byzantine, 11th cent. 150fr, Rest During the Flight to Egypt, by Gerard David (1450-1523). 160fr, African Madonna, 16th cent. 250fr, African Madonna, c. 1900. 500fr, Mystic Madonna, by Sandro Botticelli (1444-1510).

Perf. 14½x13½
1985, Dec. 10   **Litho.**
1347	A280	90fr multi	.70	.25
1348	A280	115fr multi	.90	.25
1349	A280	150fr multi	1.10	.25
1350	A280	160fr multi	1.10	.25
1351	A280	250fr multi	2.00	.40
		Nos. 1347-1351 (5)	5.80	1.40

Souvenir Sheet
| 1352 | A280 | 500fr multi | 4.50 | 3.50 |

Nos. 1348-1352 air airmail. No. 1352 contains one stamp 36x51mm.

Nos. 1302, 1305-1307 Ovptd. "75e Anniversaire / du Scoutisme Feminin"

1986, Jan.   **Perf. 15**
| 1353 | A271 | 50fr multi | 1.60 | .30 |
| 1354 | A271 | 1000fr multi | 15.00 | 3.50 |

Souvenir Sheet
| 1355 | A271 | 1000fr multi | 9.50 | 7.50 |
| 1355A | A271 | 1000fr multi | 9.50 | 7.50 |

Nos. 1354-1355A airmail.

Nos. 1268-1269, 1271, 1273-1274 Ovptd. "150e ANNIVERSAIRE / DE CHEMIN FER 'LUDWIG"

1985, Dec. 27   **Litho.**   **Perf. 15**
1356	A267	70fr multi	1.25	.35
1357	A267	90fr multi	1.25	.60
1358	A267	500fr multi	8.00	3.50
		Nos. 1356-1358 (3)	10.50	4.45

Souvenir Sheets
| 1359 | A267 | 1000fr No. 1273 | 9.00 | 6.50 |
| 1360 | A267 | 1000fr No. 1274 | 9.00 | 6.50 |

Halley's Comet A281

Designs: 70fr, Suisei space probe, comets. 90fr, Vega-1 probe. 150fr, Space telescope. 200fr, Giotto probe, comet over Togo. 1000fr, Edmond Halley, Sir Isaac Newton.

1986, Mar. 27   **Perf. 13**
1361	A281	70fr multi	.70	.25
1362	A281	90fr multi	.70	.30
1363	A281	150fr multi	1.20	.45
1364	A281	200fr multi	1.75	.60
		Nos. 1361-1364 (4)	4.35	1.60

Souvenir Sheet
| 1365 | A281 | 1000fr multi | 7.00 | 6.50 |

Nos. 1362-1365 are airmail.
For overprints see Nos. 1405-1409.

Flowering and Fruit-bearing Plants A282

70fr, Anacardium occidentale. 90fr, Ananas comosus. 120fr, Persea americana. 135fr, Carica papaya. 290fr, Mangifera indica, vert.

1986, June   **Perf. 14**
1366	A282	70fr multi	.55	.25
1367	A282	90fr multi	.80	.30
1368	A282	120fr multi	.90	.40
1369	A282	135fr multi	1.10	.45
1370	A282	290fr multi	2.25	.90
		Nos. 1366-1370 (5)	5.60	2.30

Nos. 1368-1370 airmail.

1986 World Cup Soccer Championships, Mexico — A283

Various soccer plays.

1986, May 5   **Litho.**   **Perf. 15x14**
1371	A283	70fr multi	.55	.25
1372	A283	90fr multi	.55	.30
1373	A283	130fr multi	.85	.40
1374	A283	300fr multi	2.00	.90
		Nos. 1371-1374 (4)	3.95	1.85

Souvenir Sheet
| 1375 | A283 | 1000fr multi | 7.00 | 5.50 |

Nos. 1372-1375 are airmail.
For overprints see Nos. 1394-1397.

Mushrooms — A284

70fr, Ramaria moelleriana. 90fr, Hygrocybe firma. 150fr, Kalchbrennera corallocephala. 200fr, Cookeina tricholoma.

1986, June 9   **Perf. 13x12½**
1376	A284	70fr multi	1.10	.25
1377	A284	90fr multi	1.40	.30
1378	A284	150fr multi	2.25	.45
1379	A284	200fr multi	3.00	.60
		Nos. 1376-1379 (4)	7.75	1.60

Intl. Youth Year — A285

1986, June   **Perf. 13½x14½**
| 1380 | A285 | 25fr shown | .80 | .25 |
| 1381 | A285 | 90fr Youths, doves | 2.10 | .30 |

Dated 1985.

Wrestling — A286

15fr, Single-leg takedown move. 20fr, Completing takedown. 70fr, Pinning combination. 90fr, Riding.

1986, July 16   **Perf. 14x15, 15x14**
1382	A286	15fr multicolored	.40	.25
1383	A286	20fr multicolored	.40	.25
1384	A286	70fr multicolored	.65	.25
1385	A286	90fr multicolored	.95	.35
		Nos. 1382-1385 (4)	2.40	1.10

Nos. 1384-1385 horiz. No. 1385 is airmail.

Wedding of Prince Andrew and Sarah Ferguson — A287

No. 1386, Sarah Ferguson. No. 1387, Prince Andrew.
No. 1388, Couple.

1986, July 23   **Perf. 14**
| 1386 | A287 | 10fr multi | .50 | .25 |
| 1387 | A287 | 1000fr multi | 6.50 | 2.75 |

Souvenir Sheet
| 1388 | A287 | 1000fr multi | 7.50 | 6.00 |

Nos. 1387-1388 are airmail.

Easter A288

Paintings (details): 25fr, 1000fr, The Resurrection, by Andrea Mantegna (1431-1506), vert. 70fr, The Calvary, by Paolo Veronese (1528-1588), vert. 90fr, The Last Supper, by Jacopo Tintoretto (1518-1594). 200fr, Christ at the Tomb, by Alonso Berruguette (1486-1561).

Perf. 14x15, 15x14
1986, Mar. 24   **Litho.**
1389	A288	25fr multi	.25	.25
1390	A288	70fr multi	.50	.25
1391	A288	90fr multi	.75	.30
1392	A288	200fr multi	1.60	.60
		Nos. 1389-1392 (4)	3.10	1.40

Souvenir Sheet
| 1393 | A288 | 1000fr multi | 7.50 | 5.00 |

Nos. 1391-1393 are airmail.

Nos. 1371-1374 Overprinted

No. 1394

No. 1395

No. 1396

No. 1397

1986, Aug. 4   **Litho.**   **Perf. 15x14**
1394	A283	70fr multi	.60	.25
1395	A283	90fr multi	.75	.30
1396	A283	130fr multi	1.00	.40
1397	A283	300fr multi	2.40	.90
		Nos. 1394-1397 (4)	4.75	1.85

Nos. 1395-1397 are airmail.

Hotels — A289

1986, Aug. 18   **Perf. 12½**
1398	A289	70fr Fazao	.55	.25
1399	A289	90fr Sarakawa	.60	.35
1400	A289	120fr Le Lac	1.00	.40
		Nos. 1398-1400 (3)	2.15	1.00

Nos. 1399-1400 are airmail.

Keran Natl. Park A290

1986, Sept. 15   **Litho.**   *Perf. 14½*
1401	A290	70fr Wild ducks	.95	.25
1402	A290	90fr Antelope	1.10	.25
1403	A290	100fr Elephant	1.25	.30
1404	A290	130fr Waterbuck	1.75	.35
		Nos. 1401-1404 (4)	5.05	1.15

Nos. 1402-1404 are airmail.

**Nos. 1361-1365 Ovptd. with Halley's
Comet Emblem in Silver**

1986, Oct. 9   *Perf. 13*
1405	A281	70fr multi	1.60	.25
1406	A281	90fr multi	1.90	.30
1407	A281	150fr multi	3.25	.50
1408	A281	200fr multi	4.25	.65
		Nos. 1405-1408 (4)	11.00	1.70

Souvenir Sheet

1409	A281	1000fr multi	21.00	7.25

Nos. 1406-1409 are airmail.

Frescoes from Togoville Church — A291

Togoville Church — A292

45fr, Annunciation. 120fr, Nativity. 130fr, Adoration of the Magi. 200fr, Flight into Egypt.

1986, Dec. 22   **Litho.**   *Perf. 14½x15*
1410	A291	45fr multicolored	.40	.25
1411	A291	120fr multicolored	.90	.30
1412	A291	130fr multicolored	1.10	.35
1413	A291	200fr multicolored	1.50	.55
		Nos. 1410-1413 (4)	3.90	1.45

Souvenir Sheet

1414	A292	1000fr multicolored	7.00	5.50

Christmas. Nos. 1411-1414 are airmail.

Phosphate Mining — A293

Natl. Liberation, 20th Anniv. — A294

50fr, Sugar refinery, Anie. 70fr, Nangbeto Dam. 90fr, Hotel, post office in Lome. 100fr, Post office, Kara. 120fr, Peace monument. 130fr, Youth vaccination campaign.

1987, Jan. 13   **Litho.**   *Perf. 12½*
1415	A293	35fr shown	.30	.25
1416	A293	50fr multicolored	.40	.25
1417	A293	70fr multicolored	.50	.25
1418	A293	90fr multicolored	.70	.40
1419	A293	100fr multicolored	.80	.40
1420	A293	120fr multicolored	.90	.45
1421	A293	130fr multicolored	1.00	.60
		Nos. 1415-1421 (7)	4.60	2.60

Souvenir Sheet
Perf. 13

1422	A294	500fr shown	3.50	3.25

Nos. 1419-1422 are airmail.

Easter — A295

Paintings in Nadoba Church, Keran: 90fr, The Last Supper. 130fr, Christ on the Cross. 300fr, The Resurrection. 500fr, Evangelization in Tamberma, fresco, horiz.

1987, Apr. 13   **Litho.**   *Perf. 14½x15*
1423	A295	90fr multi	.65	.35
1424	A295	130fr multi	.95	.45
1425	A295	300fr multi	2.10	1.00
		Nos. 1423-1425 (3)	3.70	1.80

Souvenir Sheet
Perf. 15x14½

1426	A295	500fr multi	4.00	3.75

Nos. 1424-1426 are airmail.

World Rugby Cup A296

70fr, Dive. 130fr, Running with the ball. 300fr, Scrimmage.
1000fr, Stands, goal, vert.

1987, May 11   *Perf. 15x14½*
1427	A296	70fr multicolored	.75	.25
1428	A296	130fr multicolored	1.50	.45
1429	A296	300fr multicolored	3.00	1.10
		Nos. 1427-1429 (3)	5.25	1.80

Souvenir Sheet
Perf. 14½x15

1430	A296	1000fr multicolored	9.50	9.50

Nos. 1427-1429 are horiz. Nos. 1428-1430 are airmail.

Indigenous Flowers A297

70fr, Adenium obesum. 90fr, Amorphophallus abyssinicus, vert. 100fr, Ipomoea mauritana. 120fr, Salacia togoica, vert.

1987, June 22   **Litho.**   *Perf. 13*
1431	A297	70fr multi	.70	.25
1432	A297	90fr multi	.85	.25
1433	A297	100fr multi	.95	.30
1434	A297	120fr multi	1.25	.35
		Nos. 1431-1434 (4)	3.75	1.15

Nos. 1432-1434 are airmail.

Fish A298

70fr, Chaetodon hoefleri. 90fr, Tetraodon lineatus. 120fr, Chaetodipterus goreensis. 130fr, Labeo parvus.

1987, Sept. 8   **Litho.**   *Perf. 13*
1435	A298	70fr multi	.75	.30
1436	A298	90fr multi	.85	.35
1437	A298	120fr multi	1.10	.50
1438	A298	120fr multi	1.25	.55
		Nos. 1435-1438 (4)	3.95	1.70

1988 Summer Olympics, Seoul — A299

Buddha and athletes

1987, Sept. 14   *Perf. 12½*
1439	A299	70fr Long jump	.60	.30
1440	A299	90fr Relay	.75	.35
1441	A299	200fr Cycling	1.75	.80
1442	A299	250fr Javelin	2.25	.85
		Nos. 1439-1442 (4)	5.35	2.30

Souvenir Sheet

1443	A299	1000fr Tennis	7.50	5.50

Nos. 1440-1443 are airmail.

World Wildlife Fund Type of 1984

1987, Dec. 15   **Litho.**   *Perf. 14*
Size: 32x24mm
1444	A263	60fr like 45fr	1.10	.30
1445	A263	75fr like 70fr	1.25	.30
1446	A263	80fr like 90fr	1.75	.30
1447	A263	100fr like 105fr	2.75	.50
		Nos. 1444-1447 (4)	6.85	1.40

No. 1447 is airmail.

Christmas A300

Paintings: 40fr, Springtime in Paradise, horiz. 45fr, Creation of Man, Sistine Chapel, by Michelangelo, horiz. 105fr, Presentation in the Temple. 270fr, Original Sin. 500fr, Nativity, horiz.

Perf. 15x14, 14x15
1987, Dec. 15			**Litho.**	
1448	A300	40fr multi	.40	.25
1449	A300	45fr multi	.45	.25
1450	A300	105fr multi	1.10	.45
1451	A300	270fr multi	2.75	1.00
		Nos. 1448-1451 (4)	4.70	1.95

Souvenir Sheet

1452	A300	500fr multi	4.50	4.00

Nos. 1450-1452 are airmail.

Eradication of Tuberculosis A301

80fr, Inoculation, horiz. 90fr, Family under umbrella. 115fr, Hospital, horiz.

1987, Dec. 28   *Perf. 12½x13, 13x12½*
1453	A301	80fr multicolored	.55	.30
1454	A301	90fr multicolored	.65	.30
1455	A301	115fr multicolored	.80	.40
		Nos. 1453-1455 (3)	2.00	1.00

Health for all by the year 2000. Nos. 1454-1455 are airmail.

Intl. Fund for Agricultural Development (IFAD), 10th Anniv. — A302

1988, Feb. 25   **Litho.**   *Perf. 13½*
1456	A302	90fr multi	.75	.30

Easter 1988 — A303

Stained-glass windows: 70fr, Jesus and the Disciples at Emmaus. 90fr, Mary at the Foot of the Cross. 120fr, The Crucifixion. 200fr, St. Thomas Touching the Resurrected Christ. 500fr, The Agony of Jesus on the Mount of Olives.

1988, June 6   **Litho.**   *Perf. 14x15*
1457	A303	70fr multi	.55	.25
1458	A303	90fr multi	.85	.35
1459	A303	120fr multi	.85	.50
1460	A303	200fr multi	1.60	.85
		Nos. 1457-1460 (4)	3.85	1.95

Souvenir Sheet

1461	A303	500fr multi	3.50	2.75

Nos. 1459-1461 are airmail.

Paintings by Picasso (1881-1973) — A304

Designs: 45fr, The Dance. 160fr, Portrait of a Young Girl. No. 1464, Gueridon. No. 1465, Mandolin and Guitar.

1988, Apr. 25   **Litho.**   *Perf. 12½x13*
1462	A304	45fr multi	.50	.25
1463	A304	160fr multi	1.60	.75
1464	A304	300fr multi	3.00	1.50
		Nos. 1462-1464 (3)	5.10	2.50

Souvenir Sheet

1465	A304	300fr multi	2.75	2.00

Nos. 1464-1465 are airmail.

1988 Summer Olympics, Seoul — A305

1988, Aug. 30   *Perf. 14x15*
1466	A305	70fr Basketball	.55	.30
1467	A305	90fr Tennis	.70	.35
1468	A305	120fr Archery	.90	.50
1469	A305	300fr Discus	1.75	.80
		Nos. 1466-1469 (4)	3.90	1.95

Souvenir Sheet

1470	A305	500fr Marathon	3.50	2.75

Nos. 1468-1470 are airmail.

Various women dancing.

1992, Aug. 24
1600	A344	90fr multicolored	.70	.30
1601	A344	125fr multicolored	.90	.45
1602	A344	190fr multicolored	1.40	.65
		Nos. 1600-1602 (3)	3.00	1.40

Dated 1991.

A345

1994 World Cup Soccer
Championships, US — A346

Various soccer players in action: 5fr, 10fr,
25fr, 60fr, 90fr, 100fr, 200fr, 1000fr.
1500fr, Player in white & green uniform.
3000fr, Two players in air, horiz.

1994, Nov. 15   **Litho.**   **Perf. 14**
| 1603-1610 | A345 | Set of 8 | 6.75 | 3.50 |

Souvenir Sheets
| 1611 | A346 | 1500fr multicolored | 7.50 | 3.50 |
| 1612 | A346 | 3000fr multicolored | 12.50 | 6.25 |

UPU, 120th
Anniv. — A347

1994, July 29   **Perf. 13½**
| 1613 | A347 | 180fr multicolored | .70 | .35 |

A miniature sheet may exist.

Stamp
Day — A348

1994, Oct. 9
| 1614 | A348 | 90fr pale bl & multi | .60 | .25 |
| 1615 | A348 | 125fr pale yel & multi | .75 | .40 |

Intl. Olympic Committee,
Cent. — A348a

Designs, each 300fr: b, Pierre de Coubertin,
Olympic Hymn. c, Original members of IOC. d,
Olympic flame.
900fr, Pierre de Coubertin holding
document.

1994, Oct.   **Litho.**   **Perf. 13½**
| 1615A | A348a | Strip of 3, #b.-d. | 4.25 | 4.25 |

Souvenir Sheet
| 1615E | A348a | 900fr multicolored | 4.25 | 2.10 |

Nos. 1615A, 1615E exist imperf. No. 1615c
is 60x51mm. No. 1615E is airmail and contains one 36x51mm stamp.

Birds
A349

Designs: #1616, 5fr, Secretary bird, vert.
#1617, 10fr, Paradise flycather, vert. #1618,
25fr, African spoonbill. #1619, 60fr, Cordon
bleu waxbill. #1620, 90fr, Orange-breasted
sunbird, vert. #1621, 100fr, Yellow-billed hornbill, vert. #1621A, 180fr, Barn owl. #1622,
200fr, African hoopoe. #1622A, 300fr, Fire-
crowned bishop, vert. #1623, 1000fr, Red-
throated bee eater, vert.

1995   **Litho.**   **Perf. 14**
| 1616-1623 | A349 | Set of 10 | 7.75 | 3.75 |

Souvenir Sheet
| 1624 | A349 | 1500fr Vulture | 7.50 | 3.50 |

Issued: 180fr, 300fr, 8/7; others, 1/23.

A350

Motion Picture, Alien: a, Alien creature. b,
Humans in combat with creature. c, Sigourney
Weaver.

1994   **Litho.**   **Perf. 13½**
| 1625 | A350 | 600fr Strip of 3, #a.-c. | 7.50 | 3.75 |

No. 1625b is 60x48mm. No. 1625 is a continuous design and exists in souvenir sheets of
1.

First Manned Moon
Landing, 25th
Anniv. — A351

No. 1626, each 600fr: a, Edwin "Buzz"
Aldrin. b, Eagle, olive branch, Neil Armstrong.
c, Michael Collins.
No. 1627, each 600fr: a, Apollo emblem,
footprint. b, Crew of Apollo 11. c, Moon rock,
NASA emblem.

1994   **Strips of 3, #a.-c.**
| 1626-1627 | A351 | Set of 2 | 15.00 | 7.50 |

Nos. 1626b, 1627b are each 60x47mm.
Nos. 1626-1627 are continuous designs and
exist in souvenir sheets of 1.

Dinosaurs — A352

| | 125fr, | Polacanthus. | 180fr, |
Pachycephalosaurus. 425fr, Coelophysis.
480fr, Brachiosaurus. 500fr, Dilophosaurus.
1500fr, Scutellosaurus.
No. 1634, Velociraptor, vert.

1994
| 1628-1633 | A352 | Set of 6 | 13.00 | 6.50 |

Souvenir Sheet
| 1634 | A352 | 1500fr multicolored | 6.25 | 3.00 |

No. 1634 is airmail.

Flowers — A353

Designs: 15fr, Belvache de Madagascar.
90fr, Oeuillets. 125fr, Agave, horiz.

1995, May 12
| 1635-1637 | A353 | Set of 3 | 1.10 | .55 |

Easter — A354

Details or entire paintings: 90fr, The Resurrection, by A. Mantegna. 180fr, Calvary, by
Veronese. 190fr, The Last Supper, by Tintoretto, horiz.

1995, May 12
| 1638-1640 | A354 | Set of 3 | 2.10 | 1.10 |

Fish
A355

10fr, Pike. 90fr, Capitaine. 180fr, Carp.

1995, May 12
| 1641-1643 | A355 | Set of 3 | 2.10 | 1.10 |

Miniature Sheets of 6 and 8

VJ Day, 50th Anniv. — A356

Japanese leaders: No. 1644a, Adm. Isoroko
Yamamoto. b, Gen. Hideki Tojo. c, Vice Adm.
Shigeru Fukudome. d, Adm. Shigetaro
Shimada. e, Contre-Adm. Chuichi Nagumo. f,
Gen. Shizu Ichi Tanaka.
VE Day: No. 1645a, 200fr, German fighter
planes making final attacks. b, 200fr, Allies win
Battle of the Atlantic. c, 200fr, Ludendorf
Bridge at Remagen is taken intact. d, 200fr,
Russian rockets fired at Berlin. e, 45fr, Hostili-
ties suspended in Italy. f, 90fr, Russians cap-
ture devastated Warsaw. g, 125fr, Russian
tanks enter Berlin. h, 500fr, UN flag.
No. 1646, Japanese signing peace agree-
ment. No. 1647, German U-236 surrenders.

1995, July 20   **Litho.**   **Perf. 14**
| 1644 | A356 | 200fr #a.-f. | 4.75 | 2.50 |
| 1645 | A356 | #a.-h. | 6.25 | 3.25 |

Souvenir Sheets
| 1646 | A356 | 1500fr multicolored | 6.00 | 3.00 |
| 1647 | A356 | 1500fr multicolored | 10.00 | 5.00 |

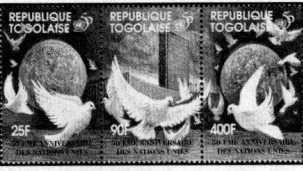

UN, 50th Anniv. — A357

No. 1648: a, 25fr, Doves, earth from space.
b, 90fr, Doves, UN headquarters. c, 400fr,
Doves, earth from space.
1000fr, Earth, dove.

1995, June 26
| 1648 | A357 | Strip of 3, #a.-c. | 2.40 | 1.25 |

Souvenir Sheet
| 1649 | A357 | 1000fr multicolored | 6.25 | 3.00 |

1995 Boy Scout
Jamboree,
Holland — A358

Designs: 90fr, Nat. flag. 190fr, Scout oath.
300fr, Lord Baden-Powell.
1500fr, Scout salute.

1995, July 20
| 1650-1652 | A358 | Set of 3 | 2.75 | 1.40 |

Souvenir Sheet
| 1653 | A358 | 1500fr multicolored | 6.00 | 3.00 |

Queen Mother, 95th Birthday — A359

No. 1654: a, Formal portrait. b, Cutting
cake. c, As younger woman wearing jewels,
waving. d, Drawing.
No. 1654E, Holding umbrella. No. 1654F,
Formal portrait as young woman.
No. 1655, Royal attire, pearls.
No. 1655A, Early picture of King George VI,
Queen Mother.

1995, July 20   **Perf. 13½x14**
1654	A359	250fr Strip of 4,		
		#a.-d.	5.00	2.50
1654E	A359	250fr multicolored	1.25	.65
1654F	A359	250fr multicolored	1.25	.65
g.		Block or strip of 4, #1654a,		
		1654d, 1654E, 1654F	5.00	2.50
		Nos. 1654-1654F (3)	7.50	3.80

Souvenir Sheets
| 1655 | A359 | 1000fr multicolored | 4.00 | 2.00 |
| 1655A | A359 | 1000fr multicolored | 4.00 | 2.00 |

Nos. 1654, 1654Fg were issued in sheets of
8 stamps.
Issued: #1654, 1655, 7/20; # 1654E, 1654F,
1655A, 11/22.

FAO, 50th Anniv. — A360

No. 1656: a, 45fr, Cattle. b, 125fr, Water buffalo. c, 200fr, Boy, man with water buffaloes.
1000fr, Woman milking cow.

1995, Mar. 3   **Litho.**   *Perf. 14*
1656 A360   Strip of 3, #a.-c.   2.25 1.10
    Souvenir Sheet
1657 A360   1000fr multicolored   4.50 2.10
   No. 1656 is a continuous design.

Nobel Prize Winners — A361

No. 1658, each 200fr: a, Elihu Root, peace, 1912. b, Alfred Fried, peace, 1911. c, Henri Moissan, chemistry, 1906. d, Charles Barkla, physics, 1917. e, Rudolf Eucken, literature, 1908. f, Carl von Ossietzky, peace, 1935. g, Sir Edward Appleton, physics. 1947. h, Camillo Golgi, physiology, 1906. i, Wilhelm Roentgen, physics, 1901.
No. 1659, each 200fr: a, Manfred Eigen, chemistry, 1967. b, Donald J. Cram, chemistry, 1987. c, Paul J. Flory, chemistry, 1974. d, Johann Deisenhofer, chemistry, 1988. e, P.W. Bridgman, physics, 1946. f, Otto Stern, physics, 1943. g, Arne Tiselius, chemistry, 1948. h, J. Georg Bednorz, physics, 1987. i, Albert Claude, medicine, 1974.
Each 1500fr: No. 1660, Albert Einstein, physics, 1921. No. 1661, Woodrow Wilson, peace, 1919.

1995, Aug. 21
   Miniature Sheets of 9, a-i
1658-1659 A361   Set of 2   25.00 12.00
    Souvenir Sheets
1660-1661 A361   Set of 2   12.50 6.50

Rotary Intl., 90th Anniv. — A362

No. 1663, Natl. flag, Rotary emblem.

1995, July 20
1662 A362   1000fr shown   4.25 2.00
    Souvenir Sheet
1663 A362   1000fr multi   4.25 2.00

    Miniature Sheets

Fauna A363

Primates, each 200fr, vert: No. 1664a, Black-faced monkey in tree. b, Brown monkey in tree. c, Black monkey. d, Baboon.
Wild animals, each 200fr: No. 1665a, Hyena. b, Hyrax. c, Mongoose. d, Elephant. e, Mandrill. f, Okapi. g, Hippopotamus. h, Flamingo. i, Wild boar.
1500fr, Potto.

1995, Oct. 2   **Litho.**   *Perf. 14*
1664 A363   Sheet of 4, #a.-d.   3.25 1.60
1665 A363   Sheet of 9, #a.-i.   7.25 3.50
    Souvenir Sheet
1666 A363   1500fr multicolored   6.00 3.00

FAO, 50th Anniv. A364

1995, Mar. 3   **Litho.**   *Perf. 14*
1667 A364   125fr shown   .50 .25
    Souvenir Sheet
1668 A364   300fr like No. 1667   1.50 .75

Sir Rowland Hill (1795-1879) A365

1995, June 3   *Perf. 13½*
1669 A365   125fr multicolored   .75 .40

UN, 50th Anniv. — A366

1995, June 26
1670 A366   180fr multicolored   .90 .50

    Miniature Sheets of 8

Mushrooms A367

No. 1671: a, Cortinarius violaceus. b, Hygrocybe flavescens. c, Mycena haematopus. d, Coprinus micaceus. e, Helvella lacunosa. f, Flammulina velutipes. g, Aleuria aurantia. h, Geastrum triplex.
No. 1672: a, Russula laurocerasi. b, Phyllotopsis nidulans. c, Xeromphalina campanella. d, Psathyrella hydrophila. e, Entoloma murraii. f, Hygrophorus speciosus. g, Mycena leaiana. h, Cystoderma amianthinum.
No. 1673, each 200fr: a, Amanita muscaria. b, Amanita virosa. c, Galerina autumnalis. d, Omphalotus illudens. e, Naematoloma fasciculare. f, Paxillus involutus. g, Russula emetica. h, Scleroderma citrinum.
No. 1674, each 200fr: a, Armillaria ponderosa. b, Agaricus augustus. c, Gomphidius subroseus. d, Morchella esculenta. e, Stropharia rugoso. f, Boletus edulis. g, Clitocybe nuda. h, Lactarius deliciosus.
Each 1500fr: No. 1675, Trametes versicolor. No. 1676, Collybia iocephala.

1995, Nov. 1   *Perf. 14*
1671 A367   180fr #a.-h.   9.00 4.50
1672 A367   195fr #a.-h.   10.00 4.75
1673-1674 A367   Set of 2, #a.-   h.   21.00 10.50
    Souvenir Sheets
1675-1676 A367   Set of 2   20.00 10.00

    Miniature Sheets

History of Transportation — A368

Steam locomotives: No. 1677, each 200fr: a, SNCF Class 231 D Le Havre-Paris Express. b, Princess Royal Class Pacific, England. c, Class 52 2-10-0, German Railroad. d, Class "15A" 4-6-4+4-6-4 Beyer-Garratt, Rhodesia. e, Japanese 2-8-0. f, Class 940, 2-8-2 engine, Italy.
Various vehicles: No. 1678, each 200fr: a, Semi truck. b, Roman chariot. c, Motorcycle. d, Hummer 4-wheel drive. e, Bicycle. f, London autobus. g, Lunar rover. h, 1954 Jaguar XK 140. i, Ski-doo.
No. 1679, First land vehicle to break sound barrier.

1995, Dec. 1   **Litho.**   *Perf. 14*
1677 A368   Sheet of 6, #a.-f.   5.50 2.75
1678 A368   Sheet of 9, #a.-i.   8.00 3.75
    Souvenir Sheet
1679 A368   1500fr multicolored   6.50 3.50
   No. 1679 contains one 85x28mm stamp.

World Post Day A369

Designs: 220fr, Selling stamps. 315fr, Sorting stamps. 335fr, Post office workers handling large sacks of mail.

1995   **Litho.**   *Perf. 13½*
1680-1682 A369   Set of 3   4.50 2.25

Christmas A370

Paintings: 90fr, Nativity scene, vert. 325fr, Adoration of the Magi, vert. 340fr, 500fr, Adoration of the shepherds.

1995, Sept. 13   **Litho.**   *Perf. 13½*
1683-1685 A370   Set of 3   4.00 2.00
    Souvenir Sheet
    Perf. 12½
1686 A370   500fr multi, vert.   3.75 1.90

    Sheets of 6

Wildlife of Africa — A371

No. 1687: a, Gorilla. b, Uroota suraka. c, Pan troglodytes. d, Panthera pardus. e, Crocodylus niloticus. f, Leptailurus serval.
No. 1688a, Papilio tyndareaus. b, Bongo taurotragus. c, Epiphora aldiba. d, Cephalophus zebra. e, Cercopithecus cephus. f, Arctocebus calabarensis.

1996, May 10   **Litho.**   *Perf. 14*
1687 A371   150fr #a.-f.   3.75 1.90
1688 A371   180fr #a.-f.   4.75 2.50
China '96, 9th Asian Intl. Philatelic Exhibition.

A372

Designs: 50fr, Olympic Stadium, Mexico, 1968, horiz. 90fr, Yevgeny Petrov, skeet shooter, Mexico, 1968, horiz. 220fr, Lia Manoliu, women's discus, Mexico, 1968, horiz. 325fr, Dumb-bell lifting, discontinued sport.
Medal winners from past games: No. 1693, each 200fr: a, China, Women's Volleyball, 1984. b, Wayne Wells, wrestling, 1972. c, Bob Beaman, long jump, 1968. d, Victor Kurentsov, weight lifting, 1968. e, Shirley Strong, 100m hurdles, 1984. f, Nadia Comaneci, balance beam, 1976. g, Giovanni Parisi, boxing, 1988. h, Emil Zatopek, 10,000m, 1948. i, USSR, Brazil, Germany, soccer, 1988.
1000fr, Helen Mayer, fencing, 1936.

1996, July 8   **Litho.**   *Perf. 14*
1689-1692 A372   Set of 4   2.75 1.40
1693 A372   Sheet of 9, #a.-i.   7.25 3.50
    Souvenir Sheet
1694 A372   1000fr multicolored   4.00 2.00

1996 Summer Olympics, Atlanta — A373

100fr, Women's gymnastics. 150fr, Women's tennis. 200fr, Javelin. 300fr, Men's field hockey. 400fr, Weight lifting. 500fr, Men's soccer.
1000fr, Synchronized swimming.

1996, Mar. 25   *Perf. 12½*
1695-1700 A373   Set of 6   7.50 3.75
    Souvenir Sheet
1701 A373   1000fr multicolored   5.50 2.75

Butterflies A374

Designs: 40fr, Euphaedra eleus, vert. 90fr, Papilio dardanus, vert. 220fr, Iolaus timon. 315fr, Charaxes cynthia.

1996, June 17   **Litho.**   *Perf. 13*
1702-1705 A374   Set of 4   2.75 1.50

Beetles — A375

Designs: 100fr, Purpuricenus kaehleri. 150fr, Carabus auronitens. 200fr, Semanotus rassicus. 300fr, Rosalia alpina. 400fr, Mylabris variabilis. 500fr, Odontolabis cuvera.
1000fr, Psalidognathus atys.

1996, May 5
1706-1711 A375   Set of 6   7.75 3.75
    Souvenir Sheet
    Perf. 12½
1712 A375   1000fr multicolored   5.50 2.75
   No. 1712 contains one 40x32mm stamp.

1998 World Cup Soccer Championships, France — A376

French flag, various action scenes: 100fr, 150fr, 200fr, 300fr, 400fr, 500fr.

1996, Apr. 10   **Perf. 12½**
1713-1718 A376 Set of 6   7.75 3.75
Souvenir Sheet
1719 A376 1000fr multicolored   5.50 2.75

World Wildlife Fund — A377

Designs: a, 325fr, Cephalophus drosalis. b, 220fr, Cephalophus maxwelli. c, 180fr, Cephalophus rufilatus. d, 370fr, Cephalophus syvicultor.
1500fr, Cephalophus dorsalis, diff.

1996, July 30   **Perf. 14**
1720 A377 Block of 4, #a.-d.   7.00 3.00
Souvenir Sheet
1721 A377 1500fr multicolored   8.25 4.00
No. 1720 was issued in sheets of 16 stamps.

Endangered Species — A378

Designs, vert: 220fr, Zebra. 315fr, Cheetah. 325fr, Antelope. 335fr, Madoqua Kirki.
No. 1726, each 200fr: a, African elephants. b, Toucan (c, d, e, f.) c, Mamba (f). d, Lionesses. e, Impala. f, Nyala. g, Hippoppotamus. h, Crocodile. i, Kingfisher.
Each 1500 fr: No. 1727, Buphagus erythrorhynchus, vert. No. 1728, Leopard, vert.

1996, July 30
1722-1725 A378 Set of 4   8.50 4.00
1726 A378 Sheet of 9, #a.-i.   9.50 4.75
Souvenir Sheets
1727-1728 A378 Set of 2   17.00 9.25

Endangered Species A379

75fr, Elephant. 90fr, Crocodile. 315fr, Deer.

1996, July 30   **Litho.**   **Perf. 13**
1729-1731 A379 Set of 3   5.50 3.00

Traditional Musical Instruments A380

90fr, Gongs. 220fr, Cymbals (balafon). 325fr, String instrument. 500fr, Drums.

1996, July 15
1732-1735 A380 Set of 4   5.00 2.50

Traditional Dances A381

Designs: 10fr, Kamou dance, Kabyes. 90fr, Kondona dance, Kabyes. 220fr, Bassar. 315fr, Kloto. 335fr, Voudoussis.

1996, June 30
1736-1740 A381 Set of 5   8.00 4.00

New Year 1997 (Year of the Ox) — A382

Paintings, by Ren Bonian (1840-95): No. 1741: a, Herdboy on Buffalo. b, Return from the Pasture. c, Grazing by the Pond.
500fr, Reading Beside an Ox.

1997, Jan. 2   **Litho.**   **Perf. 14**
1741 A382 180fr Strip of 3, #a.-c.   2.50 2.50
   d.   Souvenir sheet of 6, 2x #a-c   5.00 5.00
Souvenir Sheet
Perf. 13½x14
1742 A382 500fr multicolored   2.75 2.75
No. 1741 was issued in sheets of 6 stamps. No. 1742 contains one 34x46mm stamp.

Fruits A383

100fr, Mango. 150fr, Bananas. 200fr, Peaches. 300fr, Papaya. 400fr, Lemon. 500fr, Coconuts.
1000fr, Various fruits.

1996, June 2   **Litho.**   **Perf. 12½**
1743-1748 A383 Set of 6   7.25 7.25
Souvenir Sheet
Perf. 13
1749 A383 1000fr multicolored   5.25 5.25
No. 1749 contains one 40x32mm stamp.

Souvenir Sheet

Chinese Stone Carving — A384

1996, May 10   **Litho.**   **Perf. 12**
1750 A384 370fr multicolored   1.50 1.50
China '96. No. 1750 was not available until March 1997.

Jaffar Ballogou, Boxer — A384a

1996   **Litho.**   **Perf. 13**
1750A A384a 90fr red & multi   —
1750B A384a 220fr blk & multi   —
1750C A384a 315fr red & multi   —

World Telecommunications Day.

UNESCO, 50th Anniv. A385

World Heritage Sites: No. 1751, each 235fr: a, Axum archaeological site, Ethiopia. b, Victoria Falls, Zambia. c, Archaeological site, Zimbabwe. d, Nature reserve, Niger. e, Arguin Natl. Park, Mauritania. f, Goree Island, Senegal. g, Timgad Ruins, Algeria. h, Ait Ben-Haddou, Morocco.
No. 1752, each 235fr: a, Kyoto, Japan. b, Waterfalls, Colombia. c, Necropolis, Egypt. d, Old Rama Church, Finland. e, Palladian villa, Vicenza, Italy. f, Rock paintings, China. g, Church, Ouro Preto, Brazil. h, Rhodes, Greece.
No. 1753, each 235fr: a, Exterior of Cistercian Abbey, Fontenay, France. b, Dubrovnik, Croatia. c, Interior of Cistercian Abbey, Fontenay. d, e, Quedlinberg, Germany. f, Ironbridge Gorge, England. g, Grand Canyon, US. h, Village, Ironbridge Gorge, England.
Each 1000fr: No. 1754, Kyoto, Japan, horiz. No. 1755, Mt. Huangshan, China, horiz. No. 1756, Village, Ironbridge, England, horiz.

1997, Mar. 24   **Litho.**   **Perf. 14**
Sheets of 8, a-h, + Label
1751-1753 A385 Set of 3   25.00 25.00
Souvenir Sheets
1754-1756 A385 Set of 3   12.50 12.50

Cats A386

150fr, American shorthair. 200fr, Siamese, vert. 300fr, Java. 400fr, "Ocicat," vert. 500fr, Scottish fold. No. 1762, 1000fr, Persian, vert. No. 1763, Colorpoint shorthair, vert.

1997   **Litho.**   **Perf. 12½**
1757-1762 A386 Set of 6   12.00 12.00
Souvenir Sheet
1763 A386 1000fr multicolored   4.50 4.50
No. 1763 contains one 32x40mm stamp.

Military Uniforms — A387

Designs: 150fr, Officer of cuirassiers. 200fr, Norman regiment officer. 300fr, Volunteer battalion foot soldier. 400fr, Berlin Campaign Militiaman. 500fr, Foot soldier. No. 1769, 1000fr, Musketeer.

No. 1770, Belling Regiment Hussar.

1997   **Perf. 13x12½**
1764-1769 A387 Set of 6   12.00 12.00
Souvenir Sheet
1770 A387 1000fr multicolored   4.50 4.50
No. 1770 contains one 40x32mm stamp.

Return of Hong Kong to China — A388

Deng Xiaoping (1904-97) — A388a

Views of city: 220fr, Chinese flag as inscription, skyscraper. 315fr, Chinese flag as inscription, night scene. 325fr, Circular stair railing, skyscraper at night. 340fr, Chinese flag, view of city through inscription. 370fr, Deng Xiaoping (1904-97), fireworks over city.
#1775A: a, shown. b, Looking left.

1997, June 2   **Perf. 14**
1771-1775 A388 Set of 5   7.50 7.50
Sheet of 2
Perf. 13½
1775A A388a 500fr #a.-b.   4.50 4.50
Nos. 1771-1773 are 28x44mm and were each issued in sheets of 4. Nos. 1774-1775 were each issued in sheets of 3.

Queen Elizabeth II and Prince Philip, 50th Wedding Anniv. A389

No. 1776: a, Queen. b, Royal arms. c, Queen in yellow hat, Prince in military uniform. d, Queen in white hat, Prince. e, Windsor Castle. f, Prince.
1000fr, Portrait of Queen, Prince.

1997, June 25
1776 A389 315fr Sheet of 6, #a.-f.   7.50 7.50
Souvenir Sheet
1777 A389 1000fr multicolored   4.50 4.50

Locomotives — A390

150fr, Light locomotive, Adams Bridges. 200fr, Norris Type, England 1866. 300fr, Jones and Ports locomotive with long boiler, 1848. 400fr, Cargo and passenger locomotive, Ansaldo, 1850. 500fr, Birkenhead, Italy, 1863. #1783, 1000fr, Quarter locomotive, New York, 1890.
#1783A, Six-wheeled locomotive, Robert Stephenson, 1830, vert.

1996, Dec. 5   **Litho.**   **Perf. 12½x12**
1778-1783 A390 Set of 6   12.00 12.00
Souvenir Sheet
Perf. 12½
1783A A390 1000fr multi   4.50 4.50

Birds — A391

150fr, Poephila guttata. 200fr, Lonchura malacca. 300fr, Acanthis cannabina. 400fr, Fringilla coelebs. 500fr, Emblema guttata. #1789, 1000fr, Passerina amoena. #1789A, Chloebia gouldiae.

1996, Nov. 27   **Perf. 13**
1784-1789 A391 Set of 6   11.00 11.00

Souvenir Sheet
1789A A391 1000fr multi   4.50 4.50

Nos. 1784-1789 are dated 1996.
No. 1789A contains one 32x40mm stamp.

Turtles — A392

Designs: 150fr, Asterochelys yniphora. 200fr, Staurotypus triporcatus. 300fr, Puxidea mouhoti. 400fr, Geomyda spengleri. 500fr, Cuora galbinifrons. #1795, 1000fr, Malaclemys terrapin. #1795A, Asterochelys radiata.

1996, Nov. 30
1790-1795 A392 Set of 6   11.00 11.00

Souvenir Sheet
1795A A392 1000fr multi   4.50 4.50

Nos. 1790-1795 are dated 1996.
No. 1795A contains one 40x32mm stamp.

Natl. Liberation, 30th Anniv. — A393

1997   **Litho.**   **Perf. 13½**
1796 A393 90fr yellow & multi   .30 .30
1797 A393 220fr green & multi   .75 .75

Diana, Princess of Wales (1961-97) A394

Nos. 1798a-1798i: Various portraits of Princess Diana in designer gowns, each 180fr.

Views up close, each 180fr: No. 1799, like #1798a. No. 1799A, Like #1798b. No. 1800, like #1798c. No. 1801, like #1798d. No. 1802, like #1798e. No. 1802A, Like #1798f. No. 1802B, Like #1798g. No. 1803, like #1798h. No. 1804, like #1798i.

1997
1798 A394 Sheet of 9, #a.-i.   7.50 7.50

Souvenir Sheets
1799-1804 A394 Set of 9   50.00 50.00

Diana, Princess of Wales (1961-97) — A395

Nos. 1805-1807, Various pictures of Diana during her lifetime as Princess of Wales.
Each 1000fr: Pictures of Diana with (in margin): No. 1808, French Pres. Giscard d'Estaing. No. 1809, Mother Teresa. No. 1810, US First Lady Hillary Clinton.

1998, Jan. 2   **Sheets of 6**   **Perf. 14**
1805 A395 240fr #a.-f.   5.00 5.00
1806 A395 315fr #a.-f.   6.50 6.50
1807 A395 340fr #a.-f.   7.25 7.25

Souvenir Sheets
1808-1810 A395 Set of 3   10.50 10.50

Souvenir Sheet

Marilyn Monroe (1926-62) — A396

1997   **Litho.**   **Perf. 13½**
1811 A396 2000fr multicolored   8.50 8.50

New Year 1998 (Year of the Tiger) — A397

Various paintings of tigers, by Liu Jiyou (1918-83): No. 1812: a, 180fr. b, 200fr. No. 1813: a, 90fr. b, 100fr. c, 180fr. d, 200fr.

1998, Jan. 5   **Litho.**   **Perf. 14**
1812 A397 Sheet of 2, #a.-b.   1.25 1.25
1813 A397 Sheet of 4, #a.-d.   2.00 2.00

No. 1812 contains two 26x65mm stamps.

Hiroshige (1797-1858), Painter — A398

Paintings: No. 1814: a, Sixty-Nine Stations of the Kisokaido Road: Mochizuki. b, Eight Views of Lake Biwa Evening Snow at Mt. Hira. c, Kinkizan Temple on Enoshima Island, Sagami Provence. d, Cherry Blossoms. e, Evening Snow at Asakusa. f, Miyanokoshi.
No. 1815: a, Two Terrapins (Fan print). b, Swimming Carp. c, Takanawa by Moonlight. d, Night Rain at Karasaki. e, Chiryu: The Summer Horse Fair. f, Shower over the Nihonbashi.
No. 1816, vert: a, Takata Riding Grounds. b, Sugatami & Omokage Bridges & Jariba at Takata. c, Dam on the Otonashi River at Oji. d, Basho's Hermitage and Camellia Hill. e, Fudo Falls, Oji. f, Takinogawa Oji.

Each 1000fr: No. 1817, Bird in a Tree. No. 1818, Title Page for Hiroshige's One Hundred Views of Edo, by Baisotei. No. 1819, Memorial Portrait of Hiroshige, by Utagawa. No. 1820, Street Stalls and Tradesmen in Jouricho. No. 1821, Cherry Blossom, Morning Glory, Cranes and Rabbits. No. 1822, Three Wild Geese Flying Across the Moon. No. 1823, Suwa Bluff, Nippori. Nos. 1817-1823 are vert.

Perf. 14x13½, 13½x14
1998, Mar. 2   **Sheets of 6**   **Litho.**
1814 A398 220fr #a.-f.   5.50 5.50
1815 A398 315fr #a.-f.   7.50 7.50
1816 A398 370fr #a.-f.   8.50 8.50

Souvenir Sheets
Perf. 13½x14
1817-1823 A398 Set of 7   30.00 30.00

Nos. 1817-1823 each contain one 26x72mm stamp.

Fauna, Flora, Minerals — A399

Dolphins and whales: No. 1824: a, Souffleur nesarnack. b, Lagenorhynque. c, Sotalie du cameroun. d, Petit rorqual. e, Rorqual commun. f, Faux orque.
Insects and spiders: No. 1825: a, Lasius niger. b, Sceliphron spirifex. c, Peucetia. d, Mygale. e, Theraphoside. f, Dynaste hercule.
Precious stones, minerals: No. 1826: a, Ruby. b, Diamond in kimberlite. c, Cut diamond. d, Rock salt. e, Tiger's eye. f, Uraninite.
Moths and butterflies: No. 1827: a, Pirate. b, Euchromie des liserons. c, Asterope. d, Psalis de kiriakoff. e, Sphinx de fabricius. f, Pensee bleue.
Mushrooms: No. 1828: a, Lepiote. b, Hypholome. c, Lactaire. d, Russule fetide. e, Russule doree. f, Strophaire.
Each 2000fr: No. 1829, Tricholome a odeur de savon. No. 1830, Potto.

1998(?)   **Litho.**   **Perf. 13½**
Sheets of 6
1824 A399 180fr #a.-f.   4.00 4.00
1825 A399 250fr #a.-f.   5.75 5.75
1826 A399 300fr #a.-f.   6.75 6.75
1827 A399 400fr #a.-f.   9.00 9.00
1828 A399 450fr #a.-f.   10.25 10.25

Souvenir Sheets
1829-1830 A399 Set of 2   15.50 15.50

Intl. Scouting, 90th Anniv. (#1825, 1827-1830). Nos. 1829-1830 each contain one 41x60mm stamp.

Jerry Garcia (1942-95) — A400

Various portraits.

1998   **Litho.**   **Perf. 13½**
1831 A400 250fr Sheet of 9, #a.-i.   7.75 7.75

Souvenir Sheet
1832 A400 2000fr multicolored   7.00 7.00

No. 1832 contains one 42x51mm stamp.

Dinosaurs — A401

Various unidentified dinosaurs.

1998
1833 A401 290fr Sheet of 9, #a.-i.   10.00 10.00

Souvenir Sheet
1834 A401 2000fr multicolored   7.50 7.50

No. 1834 contains one 42x51mm stamp.

1998 Winter Olympic Games, Nagano — A402

No. 1835: a, Hockey. b, Speed skating. c, Pairs figure skating. d, Luge. e, Curling. f, Bobsledding.
No. 1836: a, Downhill skiing. b, Freestyle ski jumping (blue skis). c, Ski jumping. d, Downhill skiier in tuck. e, Snow boarding. f, Freestyle skiing (red skis).

1998   **Sheets of 6**
1835 A402 250fr #a.-f.   5.75 5.75
1836 A402 300fr #a.-f.   6.75 6.75

Nos. 1835-1836 each have 3 labels.

1998 World Cup Soccer Championships, France — A403

Player, country, vert: No. 1837, Kluivert, Netherlands. No. 1838, Asprilla, Colombia. No. 1839, Bergkamp, Netherlands. No. 1840, Gascoigne, England. No. 1841, Ravanelli, Italy. No. 1842, Sheringham, England.
No. 1843: a, Paul Gascoigne, England, diff. b, Ryan Giggs, Wales. c, Roy Keane, Ireland. d, Stuart Pearce, England. e, Tony Adams, England. f, Teddy Sheringham, England, diff. g, Paul Ince, England. h, Steve McManaman, England.
No. 1844: a, Rossi, Italy. b, Lineker, England. c, Lato, Poland. d, Futre, Poland. e, Klinsmann, Germany. f, Hurst, England. g, Kempes, Argentina. h, McCoist, Scotland.
World Cup Champions, year, vert. — #1845: a, Argentina, 1978. b, Italy, 1982. c, England, 1966. d, Uruguay, 1930. e, Germany, 1954. f, Argentina, 1986. g, Brazil, 1994.
Each 1500fr: No. 1846, Ronaldo, Brazil, vert. No. 1847, Gary Lineker, England, vert. No. 1848, Shearer, England, vert.

Perf. 13½x14, 14x13½
1998, July 10   **Litho.**
1837-1842 A403 370fr Set of 6 10.00 10.00

Sheets of 8 + Label

1843	A403	220fr #a.-h.	6.50	7.75
1844	A403	315fr #a.-h.	11.00	11.00

Sheet of 7 + 2 Labels

1845	A403	325fr #a.-g.	10.00	10.00

Souvenir Sheets

1846-1848	A403	Set of 3	18.00	18.00

Bella Bellow (d. 1973), Singer — A403a

1998-2002		Litho.	Perf. 13½
1848A	A403a	5fr yel orange	
1848B	A403a	10fr ol grn	
1848C	A403a	25fr emerald	
1848D	A403a	40fr violet	
1848E	A403a	50fr grnsh blk	
	s.	gray green, dated "2002"	—
1848F	A403a	75fr yel orange	
1848G	A403a	100fr orange	
1848H	A403a	125fr blue	
1848I	A403a	200fr brt purple	
1848J	A403a	240fr red violet	
1848K	A403a	280fr green	
1848L	A403a	300fr Prus blue	
1848M	A403a	320fr red org	
1848N	A403a	340fr car lake	
1848O	A403a	390fr car rose	
1848P	A403a	450fr brt blue ('02)	
1848R	A403a	500fr gray ol ('02)	
1848T	A403a	1000fr gray	—

No. 1848E is dated "1998." At least three additional values were issued in this set. The editors would like to examine any examples. See Nos. 1990A-1990J.

Star Wars Movies — A404

Return of the Jedi — #1849: a, Princess Leia. b, Darth Vader. c, Han Solo. d, R2-D2, C-3PO. e, Emperor Palpatine. f, Chewbacca. g, Leia on speeder. h, Luke Skywalker. i, Storm trooper on speeder.

Empire Strikes Back — #1850: a, Lando Calrissian. b, Yoda. c, Chewbacca. d, C-3PO, R2-D2. e, Luke Skywalker. f, Darth Vader. g, Battle on snow planet. h, Leia. i, Rider on snow planet.

2000fr, Han Solo, Luke Skywalker, Princess Leia, R2-D2.

1997		Litho.	Perf. 13½
		Sheets of 9	
1849	A404	190fr #a.-i.	6.50	6.50
1850	A404	350fr #a.-i.	11.50	11.50
		Souvenir Sheet	
1851	A404	2000fr multicolored	8.00	8.00

No. 1851 contains one 42x60mm.

Jacqueline Kennedy Onassis (1929-94) — A405

No. 1852: Various portraits.
No. 1853: Various portraits of John F. Kennedy (1917-63).

1997			Sheets of 9	
1852	A405	250fr #a.-i.	10.00	10.00
1853	A405	400fr #a.-i.	12.00	12.00

Diana, Princess of Wales (1961-97) — A406

No. 1854: Various portraits.
2000fr, Diana in black (Mother Teresa in sheet margin).

1997		Sheet of 8 + Label	
1854	A406	500fr #a.-h.	16.00	16.00
		Souvenir Sheet	
1854I	A406	2000fr multicolored	10.00	10.00

Marilyn Monroe (1926-62) — A407

Various portraits, each 300fr.

1997		Litho.	Perf. 13½
1855	A407	Sheet of 9, #a.-i.	11.00	11.00

Minerals A408

Designs: 100fr, Calcite. 150fr, Turquoise, vert. 200fr, Pyrite, vert. 300fr, Tourmaline, vert. 400fr, Pyrargirite, vert. 500fr, Malachite. 1000fr, Beryl, vert.

1999		Litho.	Perf. 12¾
1856-1861	A408	Set of 6	6.00	6.00
		Souvenir Sheet	
		Perf. 13	
1861A	A408	1000fr multicolored	4.00	4.00

No. 1861A contains one 32x40mm stamp.

Butterflies — A408a

Designs: 100fr, Quercusia quercus. 150fr, Pseudacraea boisduvali. 200fr, Argynnis paphia. 300fr, Erebia pandrose. 400fr, Euphydryas maturna. 500fr, Pyronia tithonus. 1000fr, Charaxes pollux.

1999, June 7		Litho.	Perf. 12¾
1861B-1861G	A408a	Set of 6	5.75	5.75
		Souvenir Sheet	
		Perf. 13	
1861H	A408a	1000fr multi	3.75	3.75

No. 1861H contains one 40x32mm stamp.

Flowers — A409

Designs: No. 1862, Caralluma burchardii. No. 1863, Dimorphotheca barberiae. No. 1864, Hoya carnosa. No. 1865, Amaryllis belladonna. No. 1866, Watsonia beatricis. No. 1867, Anthurium schezerianum. No. 1868, Thumbergia alata. No. 1869, Arctotis breviscapa. No. 1870, Glauciun flavum. No. 1871, Impatiens petersiana. No. 1872, Chrysanthemum segetum. No. 1873, Zantedeschia aethiopica, horiz.

1999			Perf. 12¼	
1862	A409	100fr brown	.30	.30
1863	A409	100fr violet	.30	.30
1864	A409	100fr pale red	.30	.30
1865	A409	150fr dark grn bl	.55	.55
1866	A409	150fr red brown	.55	.55
1867	A409	150fr violet blue	.55	.55
1868	A409	200fr orange	.75	.75
1869	A409	200fr bright grn bl	.75	.75
1870	A409	300fr olive	1.10	1.10
1871	A409	300fr blue	1.10	1.10
1872	A409	500fr brown	1.75	1.75
1873	A409	1000fr bright pink	3.75	3.75
		Nos. 1862-1873 (12)	11.75	11.75

1998 World Cup Soccer Championship, France — A410

Predominant colors of player's shirts. No. 1874: a, Yellow. b, White. c, Blue. d, Red.
No. 1875: a, White. b, Blue. c, Red. d, Green.
No. 1876: a, White, with black shorts. b, Yellow, with blue shorts. c, Yellow, with yellow shorts. d, White, with white shorts.
No. 1877: a, Red. b, Green. c, White. d, Red & white striped.
No. 1878: a, Blue. b, Yellow. c, Red. d, White.
No. 1879: a, Orange. b, White. c, Red. d, Multicolored diamonds.
No. 1880: a, White, with black shorts. b, White, with blue and red chest stripes. c, White, with green trim. d, White, with red and blue arm stripes.
No. 1881: a, Blue & white stripes. b, Red & white checks. c, Yellow & green. d, Blue. 2000fr, Player, map of France.

1998		Litho.	Perf. 13¼
		Sheets of 4	
1874	A410	180fr #a.-d.	3.25	3.25
1875	A410	200fr #a.-d.	3.50	3.50
1876	A410	250fr #a.-d.	4.25	4.25
1877	A410	290fr #a.-d.	5.00	5.00
1878	A410	300fr #a.-d.	5.25	5.25
1879	A410	350fr #a.-d.	6.25	6.25
1880	A410	400fr #a.-d.	6.75	6.75
1881	A410	425fr #a.-d.	7.25	7.25
		Nos. 1874-1881 (8)	41.50	41.50
		Souvenir Sheet	
1882	A410	2000fr multicolored	7.50	7.50

Birds 1882A

Designs: 100fr, Luscinia svecica. 150fr, Oriolus oriolus. 200fr, Carduelis carduelis. 300fr, Parus caeruleus. 400fr, Fringilla coelebs. 500fr, Parus montanus. 1000fr, Regulus ignicapillus.

1999		Litho.	Perf. 12¾
1882A-1882F	A410a	Set of 6	6.00	6.00
		Souvenir Sheet	
		Perf. 13x13¼	
1882G	A410a	1000fr multi	4.00	4.00

No. 1882G contains one 40x32mm stamp.

Antique Automobiles — A410b

Designs: 100fr, 1913 Peugeot Bebe. 150fr, 1950 Rolls-Royce. 200fr, 1921 Stutz Bearcat. 300fr, 1923 Ford Model T. 400fr, 1907 Packard. 500fr, 1950 Citroen II Legere sedan. 1000fr, 1929 Ford Model A Tudor sedan.

1999 **Perf. 12¾**
1882H-1882M A410b Set of 6 6.00 6.00
Souvenir Sheet
Perf. 13
1882N A410b 1000fr multi 4.00 4.00
No. 1882N contains one 40x32mm stamp.

Mushrooms —
A410c

Designs: 100fr, Ganoderma lucidum. 150fr, Cantharellus lutescens. 200fr, Lactarius deliciosus. 300fr, Amanita caesarea. 400fr, Cortinarius violaceus. 500fr, Amanita rubescens. 1000fr, Clitopilus prunulus.

1999, Feb. 23 **Litho.** **Perf. 12¾**
1882O-1882T A410c Set of 6 — —
Souvenir Sheet
Perf. 13¼
1882U A410c 1000fr multi — —

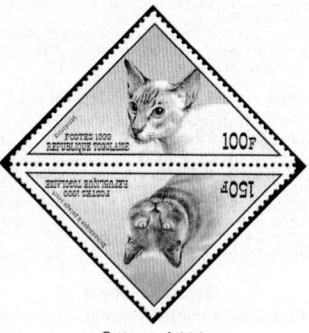

Cats — A411

No. 1883: a, 100fr, Colorpoint. b, 150fr, British shorthair.
No. 1884: a, 200fr, Ocicat. b, 300fr, Ragdoll.
No. 1885: a, 400fr, Balinese. b, 500fr, California Spangled.
1000fr, Somali.

1999 **Litho.** **Perf. 12½**
1883 A411 Pair, #a.-b. .85 .85
1884 A411 Pair, #a.-b. 1.90 1.90
1885 A411 Pair, #a.-b. 3.50 3.50
Nos. 1883-1885 (3) 6.25 6.25
Souvenir Sheet
1886 A411 1000fr multicolored 4.00 4.00

Millennium
A412

No. 1886A, Invention of Paper by Chinese (with millennium emblem).
No. 1887 — Chinese Science & Technology: a, Lacquerware. b, Counting rods. c, Sericulture. d, Acupuncture. e, "Tuned chime bell." f, Piston bellows. g, Compass. h, Manufacture of steel. i, Crossbow. j, Spinning wheel. k, Water conservancy. l, Pulse taking. m, Multi-tube seed drill. n, Rotary winnowing fan. o, Like #1886A (no millennium emblem). p, Silk loom (60x40mm). q, Wheelbarrow.
No. 1888 — Highlights of the 11th Century: a, Chinese invent gunpowder. b, Islamic bronze griffin. c, Battle of Clontarf. d, William becomes Duke of Normandy. e, Norman knight. f, Spinning wheels in use in China. g, Yaroslav becomes Grand Prince of Kiev. h, Polyphonic singing introduced. i, Macbeth becomes King of Scotland. j, Edward the Confessor becomes King of England. k, Astrolabe. l, Harp introduced in Europe. m, Trier Cathedral. n, Mandingo Empire founded in Africa. o, Toltecs invade Yucatan. p, Vikings reach North

Americam (60x40mm). q, Movable type used in China.
No. 1889 — Western Paintings of the 20th century by: a, Henri Matisse. b, Pablo Picasso. c, Marc Chagall. d, Wassily Kandinsky. e, Fernand Léger. f, Piet Mondrian. g, George Bellows. h, Georgia O'Keeffe. i, Salvador Dali. j, Francis Bacon. k, Edward Hopper. l, Andy Warhol. m, Helen Frankenthaler. n, Richard Anuszkiewicz. o, Audrey Flack. p, Jackson Pollack. q, Lee Krasner (60x40mm). q, Jean-Michel Basquiat.

1999 **Litho.** **Perf. 13¼x13**
1886A A412 120fr multi .70 .70
Sheets of 17
Perf. 12½
1887 A412 120fr #a.-q. + label
9.00 9.00
1888 A412 130fr #a.-q. + label
9.00 9.00
1889 A412 140fr #a.-q. + label
11.00 11.00
Inscriptions on Nos. 1887b, 1887e, 1888i, and perhaps others, are incorrect or misspelled.
Issued: 130fr, 7/20.

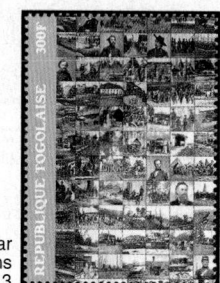

US Civil War
Photographs
A413

Various Civil War photographs making up a photomosaic of Abraham Lincoln, each 300fr.

1999, July 20 **Litho.** **Perf. 13½**
1890 A413 Sheet of 8, #a.-h. 10.00 10.00
See Nos. 1939-1940.

Free Trade
Zone, 10th
Anniv. — A414

Symbol and: 125fr, Map. 240fr, Clouds. 340fr, Wall.

1999 **Litho.** **Perf. 12¾**
1891 A414 125fr multi .45 .45
1892 A414 240fr multi .85 .85
1893 A414 340fr multi 1.25 1.25
Nos. 1891-1893 (3) 2.55 2.55

Rural Development Council, 40th
Anniv. — A414a

1999 **Litho.** **Perf. 13x13¼**
1893A A414a 100fr grn & multi —
1893B A414a 125fr blue & multi —
1893C A414a 240fr red & multi —
1893D A414a 380fr vio & multi —
1893E A414a 390fr blk & multi —
Other stamps for this subject may exist. The editors would like to examine any examples. Numbers may change.

Goldfish
A415

Various depictions of Carassius auratus auratus: 100fr, 150fr, 200fr, 300fr, 400fr, 500fr.

1999
1894-1899 A415 Set of 6 6.00 6.00
Souvenir Sheet
Perf. 13
1899A A415 1000fr multi 4.00 4.00
No. 1899A contains one 40x31mm stamp.

SOS Children's
Villages, 50th
Anniv. — A416

1999 **Litho.** **Perf. 13¼x13**
1900 A416 125fr multi ('01) .70 .70
1901 A416 240fr multi
1902 A416 340fr multi
Additional stamps may have been issued in this set. The editors would like to examine any examples.

Sailing
Vessels —
A417

Designs: 100fr, Phoenician boat. 150fr Roman cargo boat. 200fr, New Guinea fishing boat. 300fr, Caravel, vert. 400fr, 16th cent. English ship, vert. 500fr, 17th cent. English ship, vert.
1000fr, Steamship with sails.

1999 **Litho.** **Perf. 12½**
1905-1910 A417 Set of 6 6.00 6.00
Souvenir Sheet
Perf. 12¼x12
1911 A417 1000fr multi 4.00 4.00
No. 1911 contains one 42x30mm stamp.

Dogs — A417a

Designs: 100fr, St. Bernard. 150fr, Teckel. 200fr, German shepherd. 300fr, Italian hound. 400fr, Yorkshire terrier. 500fr, Schnauzer. 1000fr, Afghan hound.

1999 **Litho.** **Perf. 12¾**
1911A-1911F A417a Set of 6 6.00 6.00
Souvenir Sheet
Perf. 12½
1911G A417a 1000fr multi 4.00 4.00
No. 1911G contains one 40x31mm stamp.

Trains
A417b

Designs: 100fr, Baldwin 0-4-0. 150fr, Baldwin 2-6-2. 200fr, Baldwin gasoline locomotive. 300fr, H.K. Porter 0-4-0. 400fr, H.K. Porter 2-6-2. 500fr, Vulcan 0-4-0.
1000fr, Jordanian locomotive.

1999 **Litho.** **Perf. 12¾**
1911H-1911M A417b Set of 6 6.00 6.00
Souvenir Sheet
1911N A417b 1000fr multi 4.00 4.00
No. 1911N contains one 40x31mm stamp.

Orchids
A417c

Designs: 100fr, Gramangis ellisii. 150fr, Habenaria columbae. 200fr, Epidendrum atroporpureum. 300fr, Odontoglossum majale. 400fr, Oncidium splendidum. 500fr, Zygopetalum mackai.
1000fr, Paphiopedilum pairieanum.

1999, Nov. 8 **Litho.** **Perf. 12x12¼**
1911O-1911T A417c Set of 6 7.25 7.25
Souvenir Sheet
Perf. 12½
1911U A417c 1000fr multi 4.00 4.00
No. 1911U contains one 31x39mm stamp.

New Year 2000
(Year of the
Dragon) — A418

Various views of dragon: 100fr, 150fr, 200fr, 300fr, 400fr, 500fr.
1000fr, Head of dragon, horiz.

2000 **Perf. 12¾x12**
1912-1917 A418 Set of 6 6.25 6.25
Souvenir Sheet
Perf. 13¼
1918 A418 1000fr multi 3.50 3.50
No. 1918 contains one 40x32mm stamp.

Wild
Cats
A419

Designs: 100fr, Panthera tigris. 150fr, Acinonyx jubatus. 200fr, Felis concolor. 300fr, Panthera leo, female. 400fr, Felis pardalis. 500fr, Panthera leo, male.
1000fr, Panthera tigris, diff.

2000 **Perf. 13**
1919-1924 A419 Set of 6 6.25 6.25
Souvenir Sheet
1925 A419 1000fr multi 3.50 3.50
No. 1925 contains one 40x32mm stamp.

Flowers — A420

No. 1926, 290fr: a, Cyrtanthus contractus. b, Sandersonia aurantiaca. c, Anomateca grandiflora. d, Helichrysum ecklonis. e, Striga elegans. f, Nymphaea odorata.

No. 1927, 290fr: a, Leomotis leonii. b, Strelitzia reginae. c, Freesia refracta. d, Garzania nivea. e, Dimophotheca sinuata. f, Pelargonium domesticum.

No. 1928, 290fr: a, Gloriosa rothchiliana. b, Clematis vitalba. c, Rochea falcato. d, Plumbago capensis. e, Thunbergia alata. f, Lampranthus coccineus.

No. 1929, 1500fr, Epiphyllum hybrid. No. 1930, 1500fr, Agapanthus africanus.
Illustration reduced.

2000, July 28   Litho.   Perf. 14
Sheets of 6, #a-f
1926-1928 A420 Set of 3   24.00 24.00
Souvenir Sheets
1929-1930 A420 Set of 2   13.50 13.50

Wildlife
A421

Designs: 200fr, Thompson's gazelle. 300fr, Felis margarita. 400fr, Blesbok. 500fr, Kob.

No. 1935, 290fr, vert.: a, Hoopoe. b, Harpactira spider. c, Marabou. d, Bee-eater. e, Oryx. f, Okapi. g, Wart hog. h, Baboon.

No. 1936, 290fr, vert.: a, Hornbill. b, Pygmy kingfisher. c, Vulture. d, Bateaur eagle. e, Kudu. f, Hyena. g, Gorilla. h, Lizard.

No. 1937, 1500fr, Eland, vert. No. 1938, 1500fr, Mongoose, vert.

2000, July 28
1931-1934 A421 Set of 4   6.75 6.75
Sheets of 8, #a-h
1935-1936 A421 Set of 2   22.50 22.50
Souvenir Sheets
1937-1938 A421 Set of 2   13.50 13.50

Mushrooms
A421a

Designs: 100fr, Hebeloma crustuliniforme. 150fr, Polyporellus squamosus, horiz. 200fr, Morchella deliciosa. 300fr, Disciotis venosa, horiz. 400fr, Cantharellus tubiforms. 500fr, Otidea onotica, horiz.
1000fr, Ixocomus granulatus, horiz.

2000, July 30   Litho.   Perf. 12¾
1938A-1938F A421a Set of 6   6.25 6.25
Souvenir Sheet
Perf. 13
1938G A421a 1000fr multi   3.50 3.50
No. 1938G contains one 39x31mm stamp.

Civil War Photographs Type of 1999

No. 1939, 290fr: Various photographs with a science theme making up a photomosaic of Albert Einstein.

No. 1940, 290fr: Various photographs with an Oriental theme making up a photomosaic of Mao Zedong.

2000, Sept. 5   Perf. 13¾
Sheets of 8, #a-h
1939-1940 A413 Set of 2   24.00 24.00

Queen Mother, 100th Birthday — A422

No. 1941: a, With Princesses Elizabeth and Margaret, 1931. b, With daughter, 1940. c, Black and white photo. d, In 1990.
1500fr, With Princess Margaret, 1939.

2000, Sept. 5   Perf. 14
1941 A422 650fr Sheet of 4,
#a-d, + label   12.50 12.50
Souvenir Sheet
Perf. 13¾
1942 A422 1500fr multi   7.25 7.25
No. 1942 contains one 38x51mm stamp.

Popes — A423

No. 1943, 400fr: a, Anastasius I, 399-401. b, Boniface I, 418-22. c, Gaius, 283-96. d, Hilarius, 461-68. e, Hyginus, 136-40. f, Innocent I, 402-17.

No. 1944, 400fr: a, Martin I, 649-55. b, Nicholas I, 858-67. c, Paschal I, 817-24. d, Paul I, 757-67. e, Pelagius, 556-61. f, Pelagius II, 579-90.

No. 1945, 400fr: a, Sergius, 687-701. b, Sergius II, 844-47. c, Severinus, 640. d, Sisinnius, 708. e, Stephen II, 752-57. f, Stephen IV, 816-17.

No. 1946, 1500fr, Pontian, 230-35. No. 1947, 1500fr, Pelagius II, diff. No. 1948, 1500fr, Stephen V, 885-91.
Illustration reduced.

2000, Sept. 5   Perf. 12x12¼
Sheets of 6, #a-f
1943-1945 A423 Set of 3   32.50 32.50
Souvenir Sheets
1946-1948 A423 Set of 3   20.00 20.00

British Monarchs — A424

No. 1949, 400fr: a, Charles II, 1660-85. b, Anne, 1702-14. c, George I, 1714-27. d, George IV, 1820-30. e, James II, 1685-88. f, George II, 1727-60.

No. 1950, 400fr: a, Elizabeth II, 1952-present. b, Edward VIII, 1936. c, George VI, 1936-52. d, George V, 1910-36. e, Edward VII, 1901-10. f, William IV, 1830-37.

No. 1951, 1500fr, William III and Mary, 1689-1702. No. 1952, 1500fr, Victoria, 1837-1901.

2000, Sept. 5   Sheets of 6, #a-f
1949-1950 A424 Set of 2   22.50 22.50
Souvenir Sheets
1951-1952 A424 Set of 2   13.50 13.50

Millennium Type of 1999

Highlights of 1950-59: a, US sends troops to defend South Korea. b, Rock and roll hits the air waves. c, Death of Eva Peron. d, Structure of DNA revealed by Watson and Crick. e, Sir Edmund Hillary and Tenzing Norgay reach peak of Mt. Everest. f, John F. Kennedy marries Jacqueline Bouvier. g, Coronation of Queen Elizabeth II. h, Millionth Volkswagen produced. i, German soccer team wins World Cup. j, Roger Bannister runs 1st 4-minute mile. k, Dr. Jonas Salk develops polio vaccine. l, 1st McDonald's franchise. m, New phone lines cross Atlantic. n, Soviet Union launches Sputnik. o, Jack Kerouac writes "On the Road." p, China begins "Great Leap Forward." q, Communist revolution in Cuba. r, Computer chip patented.

2000   Perf. 12¾x12½
1953 A412 200fr Sheet of 18,
#a-r, + label   17.50 17.50

36th Organization of African Unity
Summit, Lomé — A425

OAU emblem, map of Africa, doves and panel color of: 10fr, Bright yellow. 25fr, Green. 100fr, Dull yellow. 125fr, Blue violet. 250fr, Red violet. 375fr, Red. 400fr, Brown. 425fr, Orange.

No. 1954: a, Peace dove statue. b, Hotel du 2 Février. c, Congress building, Lomé. d, Alédjo Fault. e, Temberma hut. f, Cacao plantation.

No. 1955: a, Pres. Gnassingbé Eyadema, map of Europe and Africa, handshakes. b, Algerian Pres. Abdelazir Bouteflika, Pres. Eyadema, and map of Africa. c, Pres. Eyadema and OAU emblem. d, Map of Africa, doves, OAU emblem.
Illustration reduced.

2000   Litho.   Perf. 14x13¾
1953S-1953Z A425 Set of 8   7.25 7.25
Sheets of 6 and 4
1954 A425 350fr #a-f   7.50 7.50
1955 A425 550fr #a-d   7.75 7.75

Trains — A426

No. 1956, 425fr: a, Richard Trevethick's engine. b, Stephenson's Adler. c, Crampton Continent. d, Atlantic Coastlines 4-4-2. e, Great Northern Railway Ivatt Atlantic. f, Great Western Railway City of Truro 4-4-0.

No. 1957, 425fr: a, Paris-Lyon-Mediterranean Railway, compound 4-8-2. b, Canadian Pacific Railway Royal Hudson 4-6-4. c, London-Midland Railway Duchess. d, New York Central Twentieth Century Limited. e, New Zealand Government Railway J class 4-8-4. f, British Railways Evening Star 5-10-0.

No. 1958, 1800fr, Eurostar. No. 1959, 1800fr, TGV Atlantique.

2000, Sept. 8   Litho.   Perf. 14
Sheets of 6, #a-f
1956-1957 A426 Set of 2   22.50 22.50
Souvenir Sheets
1958-1959 A426 Set of 2   16.00 16.00

Ships — A427

No. 1960, 425fr: a, Norse knaar. b, Hanseatic cog. c, Iberian caravel. d, Henri Grace à Dieu. e, Ark Royal. f, Dutch Hooker.

No. 1961, 425fr: a, HMS Victory. b, HMS Warrior. c, Cutty Sark. d, USS Olympia. e, Empress of Canada. f, James Clark Ross.

No. 1962, 1800fr, Discovery. No. 1963, 1800fr, Sea Cat ferry.

2000, Sept. 8   Litho.   Perf. 14
Sheets of 6, #a-f
1960-1961 A427 Set of 2   22.50 22.50
Souvenir Sheets
1962-1963 A427 Set of 2   16.00 16.00

Dogs and
Cats — A428

Designs: 275fr, Bloodhound. 300fr, Sphinx cat. 325fr, Basset hound. 350fr, Cocker spaniel. No. 1968, 375fr, American curl cat. 400fr, Scottish fold cat.

No. 1970, 375fr, horiz. — Dogs: a, Bearded collie. b, Chow chow. c, Boxer. d, Irish setter. e, Bracco Italiano. f, Pointer.

No. 1971, 375fr, horiz. — Cats: a, Devon Rex. b, Cornish Rex. c, Siamese. d, Balinese. e, Birman. f, Korat.

No. 1972, 1500fr, Yorkshire terrier. No. 1973, 1500fr, Chinchilla cat.

Perf. 13½x13¼, 13¼x13½
2001, Dec. 17   Litho.
1964-1969 A428 Set of 6   10.00 10.00
Sheets of 6, #a-f
1970-1971 A428 Set of 2   22.50 22.50
Souvenir Sheets
1972-1973 A428 Set of 2   15.00 15.00

Marine Life — A429

No. 1974, 200fr (31x31mm): a, Priacanthus arenatus. b, Diplodus annularis. c, Lithognathus mormyrus. d, Selene vomer. e, Penaeus duorarum. f, Arbacia lixula. g, Serranus scriba. h, Trachurus trachurus. i, Lepas anatifera. j, Octopus vulgaris. k, Scorpaena scrofa. l, Dardanus arrosor.

No. 1975, 250fr (31x31mm): a, Porcupine fish. b, Blue shark. c, Sting ray. d, Physalia physalis. e, Turtles. f, Coryphaena hippurus. g, Caranx hippos. h, Sawfish. i, Todaropsis eblanae. j, Pompano. k, Diplodus cervinus. l, Barracuda.

No. 1976, 1500fr, Octopus vulgaris, diff. No. 1977, 1500fr, Blue shark, diff.

2001, Dec. 17   **Perf. 12½**
Sheets of 12, #a-l
1974-1975 A429   Set of 2   26.00 26.00
Souvenir Sheets
Perf. 13¼x13½
1976-1977 A429   Set of 2   15.00 15.00

African Wildlife A430

Designs: 150fr, Okapia johnstoni, vert. 200fr, Sagittarius serpentarius. 250fr, Lemur catta, vert. 300fr, Gorilla gorilla. 350fr, Genetta genetta, vert. 400fr, Fennecus zerda.

No. 1984, 380fr: a, Papio hamadryas. b, Felis serval. c, Suricata suricatta. d, Orycteropus afer. e, Connochataetes taurinus. f, Tragelaphus strepsiceros.

No. 1985, 380fr: a, Panthera pardus. b, Loxodonta africana. c, Cercopithecus hamlyni. d, Ephippiorhynchuus senegalensis. e, Hippopotamus amphibius. f, Hippotragus niger.

No. 1986, 415fr: a, Equus burchelli boehmi. b, Ceratotherium simum. c, Achionyx jubatus. d, Gazella dama. e, Crocuta crocuta. f, Lyacon pictus.

No. 1987, 1500fr, Crocodylus niloticus. No. 1988, 1500fr, Panthera leo, vert. No. 1989, 1500fr, Giraffa camelopardalis.

Perf. 13½x13¼, 13¼x13½
2001, Dec. 17
1978-1983 A430   Set of 6   8.00 8.00
Sheets of 6, #a-f
1984-1986 A430   Set of 3   35.00 35.00
Souvenir Sheets
1987-1989 A430   Set of 3   22.50 22.50

United We Stand A431

2002, Mar. 18   **Litho.**   **Perf. 14**
1990 A431 400fr multi   2.00 2.00

Bella Bellow Type of 1998-2002

2002-04   **Litho.**   **Perf. 13½**
1990A A403a   20fr yel green   — —
1990B A403a   30fr brown   — —
1990C A403a   110fr blue green   — —
1990D A403a   150fr aquamarine   — —
1990E A403a   250fr red   — —
1990F A403a   400fr yellow
          green   —
1990G A403a   550fr pale orange   —
1990H A403a   650fr black   —
1990I A403a   1000fr rose   —
1990J A403a   3000fr light blue   —

The editors suspect that additional stamps were issued in this set and would like to examine any examples.
Numbers may change.

2004 Summer Olympics, Athens — A432

Designs: 150fr, Chariot rider and horses. 300fr, Pin from 1960 Rome Olympics, vert. 450fr, Emblem of 1960 Squaw Valley Winter Olympics, vert. 500fr, Diver, vert.

2004, Aug. 25   **Litho.**   **Perf. 13¼**
1991-1994 A432   Set of 4   6.50 6.50

Pres. Gnassingbé Eyadema (1935-2005) A433

2004   **Perf. 13½x13¼**
Panel Color
1995 A433   25fr dark blue   .25 .25
1996 A433   50fr yel green   .25 .25
1997 A433   150fr olive green   .60 .60
1998 A433   400fr dull brown   1.60 1.60
1999 A433   550fr green   2.25 2.25
2000 A433   650fr brt blue   2.75 2.75
2001 A433   1000fr lilac   4.25 4.25
2002 A433   2000fr salmon pink   8.25 8.25
2003 A433   3000fr blue green   12.50 12.50
   Nos. 1995-2003 (9)   32.70 32.70

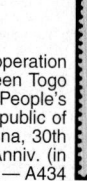

Cooperation Between Togo and People's Republic of China, 30th Anniv. (in 2002) — A434

2004, Mar. 1   **Perf. 12**
Frame Color
2004 A434 300fr gray   —

Two additional stamps exist in this set. The editors would like to examine any examples.

Pope John Paul II (1920-2005) A435

2006, Jan. 24   **Perf. 13½**
2007 A435 550fr multi   2.50 2.50
   Printed in sheets of 4.

Jules Verne (1828-1905), Writer — A436

No. 2008: a, Home of Verne from 1882-1900. b, Monument to Verne, Amiens, France. c, Sculpture of Verne, Amiens. d, Mysterious Island.

2006, Jan. 24   **Litho.**   **Perf. 13½**
2008 A436 550fr Sheet of 4,
     #a-d   10.00 10.00

Rotary International, Cent. (in 2005) — A437

No. 2009 — Children and denomination in: a, Yellow in upper right. b, Red. c, Yellow in upper left.
1000fr, Child.

2006, Jan. 24
2009 A437 700fr Sheet of 3,
     #a-c   10.00 10.00
Souvenir Sheet
2010 A437 1000fr multi   4.50 4.50

Friedrich von Schiller (1759-1805), Writer — A438

No. 2011, vert. — Schiller: a, Monument. b, Bust. c, Portrait.
1000fr, Birthplace of Schiller.

2006, Jan. 24
2011 A438 700fr Sheet of 3,
     #a-c   10.00 10.00
Souvenir Sheet
2012 A438 1000fr multi   4.50 4.50

World Cup Soccer Championships, 75th Anniv. (in 2005) — A439

No. 2013: a, David Beckham. b, Ronaldo Nazario. c, Fernando Hierro.
1000fr, Eusebio.

2006, Jan. 24
2013 A439 700fr Sheet of 3,
     #a-c   10.00 10.00
Souvenir Sheet
2014 A439 1000fr multi   4.50 4.50

V-E Day, 50th Anniv. (in 2005) — A440

No. 2015, vert.: a, Monument to victory. b, New York Times front page with war reports. c, Soldiers at Battle of the Bulge, 1944. d, Airplanes. e, Sculpture of Holocaust victim.
1000fr, DUKW.

2006, Jan. 24   **Litho.**   **Perf. 13¼**
2015 A440 400fr Sheet of 5, #a-
     e   7.50 7.50
Souvenir Sheet
2016 A440 1000fr multi   3.75 3.75

V-J Day, 50th Anniv. (in 2005) — A441

No. 2017: a, USS Charles Carroll. b, BB-35. c, LCT-515. d, LST-388. e, Destroyer Thompson DD-627. f, USS Thomas Jefferson.
1000fr, Battle of Iwo Jima.

2006, Jan. 24
2017 A441 350fr Sheet of 6, #a-
     f   7.75 7.75
Souvenir Sheet
2018 A441 1000fr multi   3.75 3.75

Railroads, Bicent. — A442

No. 2019: a, DX5287. b, W192. c, Central Pacific Jupiter. d, LWDHAM.
No. 2020, 1000fr, Rovos Ralf Class 25NC.
No. 2021, 1000fr, Class 242 streamlined tank locomotive.

2006, Jan. 24
2019 A442 550fr Sheet of 4, #a-d   8.25 8.25

Souvenir Sheets
2020-2021 A442 Set of 2   7.50 7.50

Léopold Sédar Senghor Year — A443

2006, July 28

2022	A443	150fr multi	.60	.60
2023	A443	550fr multi	2.25	2.25
2024	A443	650fr multi	2.60	2.60
2025	A443	1000fr multi	4.00	4.00
2026	A443	2000fr multi, horiz.	8.00	8.00
2027	A443	3000fr multi, horiz.	12.00	12.00
2028	A443	5000fr multi, horiz.	20.00	20.00
2029	A443	10,000fr multi, horiz.	40.00	40.00
	Nos. 2022-2029 (8)		89.45	89.45

Souvenir Sheet

Wolfgang Amadeus Mozart (1756-91), Composer — A444

2006, Dec. 21   **Perf. 14**
2030 A444 1500fr multi   6.00 6.00

Space Achievements — A445

Designs: 150fr, Luna 9. 300fr, Hayabusa probe. 450fr, Venus Express. 500fr, Space Shuttle Discovery, vert.
No. 2035: a, Intl. Space Station. b, Deep Impact probe. c, Muse Asteroid. d, Artist's view of L1 spacecraft. e, Odyssey. f, Calipso.
No. 2036: a, Viking 1 in oribit around Mars. b, Viking 1. c, Phobos. d, Viking Lander 1.
No. 2037, 1500fr, Mars Reconnaissance Orbiter. No. 2038, 1500fr, Apollo 11, vert.

2006, Dec. 21   **Perf. 13¼**
2031-2034 A445 Set of 4   5.75 5.75
2035 A445 400fr Sheet of 6, #a-f   9.50 9.50
2036 A445 550fr Sheet of 4, #a-d   8.75 8.75

Souvenir Sheets
2037-2038 A445 Set of 2   12.00 12.00

Worldwide Fund for Nature (WWF) — A446

No. 2039 — Cyclanorbis senegalensis: a, On sand, facing left. b, With foliage, facing left. c, Head. d, With foliage, facing right.

2006, Dec. 28
2039 A446 350fr Block or strip of 4, #a-d   5.75 5.75
  e. Minature sheet, 2 each #a-d   11.50 11.50

Oiseaux Aquatique

Birds — A447

No. 2040: a, Platnea alba. b, Ceryle rudis. c, Ardea alba. d, Ephipphorhynchus senegalensis.
1500fr, Ephipphorhynchus senegalensis, diff.

2006, Dec. 28   **Perf. 14**
2040 A447 450fr Sheet of 4, #a-d   7.25 7.25

Souvenir Sheet
2041 A447 1500fr multi   6.00 6.00

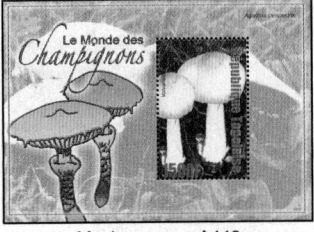

Mushrooms — A448

No. 2042: a, Coprinus micaceus. b, Cookeina sulcipes. c, Hygrocybe firma. d, Chlorophyllum molybdites.
1500fr, Volvariella esculenta.

2006, Dec. 28
2042 A448 450fr Sheet of 4, #a-d   7.25 7.25

Souvenir Sheet
2043 A448 1500fr multi   6.00 6.00

Papillons du TOGO

Butterflies — A449

No. 2044, horiz.: a, Papilio nobilis. b, Colotis celimene. c, Salamis anacardii. d, Eronia cleodora.
1500fr, Colotis regina.

2006, Dec. 28   **Perf. 14**
2044 A449 450fr Sheet of 4, #a-d   7.25 7.25

Souvenir Sheet
2045 A449 1500fr multi   6.00 6.00

LA BELLE ORCHIDÉE

Orchids — A450

No. 2046, vert.: a, Triphora trianthophora. b, Amerorchis rotundifolia. c, Cypripedium x andrewsii. d, Pogonia ophioglossoides.
1500fr, Platanthera x keenanii.

2006, Dec. 28   **Perf. 14**
2046 A450 450fr Sheet of 4, #a-d   7.25 7.25

Souvenir Sheet
2047 A450 1500fr multi   6.00 6.00

Rembrandt (1606-69), Painter A451

Designs: 50fr, Three Oriental Figures (Jacob and Laban). 100fr, The Pancake Woman. 150fr, The Goldsmith. 250fr, The Golf Player. 325fr, The Persian. 350fr, Jacob and Rachel Listening to an Account of Joseph's Dreams.
1250fr, The Conspiracy of Julius Civilis, horiz.

2006   **Perf. 14¼**
2048-2053 A451 Set of 6   5.00 5.00
          Imperf
          Size: 106x76mm
2054 A451 1250fr multi   5.00 5.00

Souvenir Sheets

A452

Elvis Presley (1935-77) — A453

No. 2055 — Country name in: a, Pale blue. b, Pale yellow. c, Pink. d, Pale green.
No. 2056 — Country name in: a, Pale blue. b, Pale yellow. c, Pink. d, Pale green.

2006, Dec. 21 Litho. Perf. 14
2055 A452 550fr Sheet of 4, #a-d 8.75 8.75
2056 A453 550fr Sheet of 4, #a-d 8.75 8.75

New Year 2007 (Year of the Pig) A454

2008, Jan. 21 Litho. Perf. 13½
2057 A454 275fr multi   1.25 1.25
Printed in sheets of 4.

Pope Benedict XVI — A455

2008, Jan. 21 Perf. 12½x12¾
2058 A455 300fr multi   1.40 1.40
Printed in sheets of 8.

Miniature Sheet

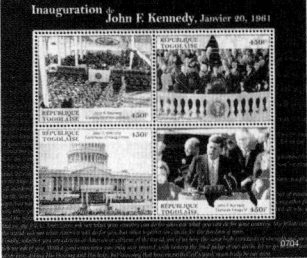

Inauguration of Pres. John F. Kennedy, 47th Anniv. — A456

No. 2059: a, Band passing reviewing stand. b, Kennedy taking oath of office. c, Capitol. d, Kennedy giving inaugural address.

2008, Jan. 21   **Perf. 13¼**
2059 A456 450fr Sheet of 4, #a-d   8.00 8.00

Wedding of Queen Elizabeth II and Prince Philip, 60th Anniv. — A457

No. 2060: a, Couple, white frame. b, Queen, pink frame. c, Couple, light blue frame. d, Queen, light blue frame. e, Couple, pink frame. f, Queen, white frame.
1250fr, Couple, diff., green frame.

2008, Jan. 21   **Perf. 12¾**
2060 A457 400fr Sheet of 6,
       #a-f   11.00 11.00

Souvenir Sheet
2061 A457 1250fr multi   5.75 5.75

Princess Diana (1961-97) — A458

No. 2062, vert.: a, Wearing double-stranded pearl necklace, large photo. b, Wearing white hat, cropped photo. c, Wearing black and white houndstooth dress, large photo. d, Wearing double-stranded pearl necklace, cropped photo. e, Wearing white hat, large photo. f, Wearing black and white houndstooth dress, cropped photo.
1500fr, Wearing black jacket.

2008, Jan. 21
2062 A458 400fr Sheet of 6,
       #a-f   11.00 11.00

Souvenir Sheet
2063 A458 1500fr multi   6.75 6.75

Campaign to Prevent AIDS — A459

Red AIDS ribbon and: 200fr, Colored squares. 350fr, Hand, horiz. 650fr, Man and woman carrying Togo flags, horiz.

2008, Feb. 8   **Perf. 11½**
2064-2066 A459 Set of 3   5.75 5.75
     Dated 2007.

Miniature Sheet

2008 Summer Olympics, Beijing — A460

No. 2067: a, Swimming. b, Running. c, Soccer. d, Sailing.

2008, Aug. 18   **Litho.**   **Perf. 12**
2067 A460 240fr Sheet of 4, #a-d   4.50 4.50

Peony A461

2009, Apr. 10   **Litho.**   **Perf. 13¼**
2068 A461 200fr multi   .80 .80
     Printed in sheets of 8.

Miniature Sheet

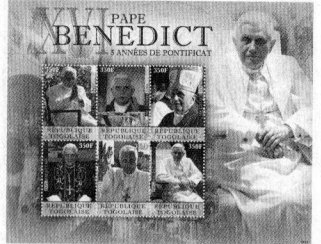

Pope Benedict XVI — A462

No. 2069 — Pope Benedict XVI: a, Seated, with hands in prayer. b, With covered chalices. c, Wearing miter. d, Wearing red vestments and red and gold stole. e, Wearing white vestments, hand raised. f, Seated with hands crossed.

2010, Feb. 11   **Perf. 11½**
2069 A462 350fr Sheet of 6, #a-f   8.75 8.75

Miniature Sheet

U.S. Pres. Barack Obama — A463

No. 2070 — Pres. Obama: a, With people in background. b, With blue sky in background. c, On telehone. d, Wearing suit, with hand raised.

2010, Feb. 11   **Perf. 12x11½**
2070 A463 450fr Sheet of 4,
     #a-d   7.50 7.50

A464

A465

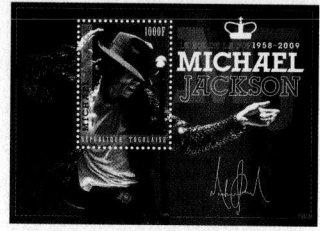

Michael Jackson (1958-2009), Singer — A466

No. 2071 — Jackson with microphone: a, Near mouth, gray area at top. b, Near eyes, black area behind head. c, Near eyes, tan area behind head. d, Near mouth, black area behind head.
No. 2072 — Jackson wearing: a, White costume with pearls. b, Black costume with sequins. c, Sunglasses, with hands together. d, Sunglasses, hands not visible.

2010, Feb. 11   **Perf. 11½x12**
2071 A464 450fr Sheet of 4, #a-d   7.50 7.50

             Perf. 11½
2072 A465 450fr Sheet of 4, #a-d   7.50 7.50

Souvenir Sheet
2073 A466 1000fr black & gray   4.25 4.25

A467

A468

A469

Phataginus Tricuspis A470

2010, Mar. 6   **Perf. 13x13¼**
2074   Horiz. strip of 4   9.00 9.00
   a. A467 550fr multi   2.25 2.25
   b. A468 550fr multi   2.25 2.25
   c. A469 550fr multi   2.25 2.25
   d. A470 550fr multi   2.25 2.25
   e. Sheet of 8, 2 each #2074a-
      2074d, + 2 labels   18.00 18.00

SEMI-POSTAL STAMPS

Curie Issue
Common Design Type
1938   **Unwmk.**   **Engr.**   **Perf. 13**
B1 CD80 1.75fr + 50c brt ultra 20.00 20.00
    Never hinged   32.50

French Revolution Issue
Common Design Type
Photo., Name and Value Typo. in Black
1939
B2 CD83 45c + 25c green   8.50 8.50
B3 CD83 70c + 30c brown   8.50 8.50
B4 CD83 90c + 35c red
     org   8.50 8.50
B5 CD83 1.25fr + 1fr rose
     pink   8.50 8.50
B6 CD83 2.25fr + 2fr blue   8.50 8.50
    Nos. B2-B6 (5)   42.50 42.50
    Set, never hinged   70.00

French Revolution, 150th anniv. Surtax for defense of the colonies.

Nos. 281, 236, 245, 289 Srchd. in Red or Black

1941   **Perf. 14 x 13½, 12½**
B7 A10 50c + 1fr   3.50 3.50
B8 A7 80c + 2fr   7.00 7.00
B9 A8 1.50fr + 2fr   7.00 7.00
B10 A11 2fr + 3fr (R)   7.00 7.00
    Nos. B7-B10 (4)   24.50 24.50
    Set, never hinged   50.00

Catalogue values for unused stamps in this section, from this point to the end of the section, are for Never Hinged items.

Common Design Type and

Togolese Militiaman SP1

Military Infirmary SP2

1941   **Photo.**   **Perf. 13½**
B10A SP1 1fr + 1fr red   1.10
B10B CD86 1.50fr + 3fr maroon   1.10
B10C SP2 2.50fr + 1fr blue   1.10
    Nos. B10A-B10C (3)   3.30

Nos. B10A-B10C were issued by the Vichy government in France, but were not placed on sale in Togo.

Nos. 296-297 Surcharged in Black or Red

1944 Engr. Perf. 12x12½
B10D 50c + 1.50fr on 2.50fr deep blue (R) .70
B10E + 2.50fr on 1fr green .70

Colonial Development Fund.
Nos. B10D-B10E were issued by the Vichy government in France, but were not placed on sale in Togo.

Tropical Medicine Issue
Common Design Type

1950 Engr. Perf. 13
B11 CD100 10fr + 2fr indigo & dk bl 5.00 3.50

The surtax was for charitable work.

Republic

Patient on
Stretcher — SP3

Designs: 30fr+5fr, Feeding infant. 50fr+10fr, Blood transfusion.

1959 Engr. Perf. 13
B12 SP3 20fr + 5fr multicolored .75 .75
  a. Souvenir sheet of 4 5.00 5.00
B13 SP3 30fr + 5fr bl, car & brn .75 .75
  a. Souvenir sheet of 4 5.00 5.00
B14 SP3 50fr + 10fr emer, brn & car .75 .75
  a. Souvenir sheet of 4 5.00 5.00
  Nos. B12-B14 (3) 2.25 2.25

Issued for the Red Cross.
Nos. B12a, B13a, B14a exist imperf.; same values.

Uprooted Oak
Emblem — SP4

No. B16 similar to No. B15, with emblem on top.

1960 Unwmk. Perf. 13
B15 SP4 25fr + 5fr dk bl, brn & yel grn .45 .45
B16 SP4 45fr + 5fr dk bl, brn & ol .80 .80

World Refugee Year, July 1, 1959-June 30, 1960. The surtax was for aid to refugees.

AIR POST STAMPS

Common Design Type

1940 Unwmk. Engr. Perf. 12½x12
C1 CD85 1.90fr ultra .35 .35
C2 CD85 2.90fr dark red .35 .35
C3 CD85 4.50fr dk gray grn .35 .35
C4 CD85 4.90fr yellow bister .70 .70
C5 CD85 6.90fr deep orange 1.40 1.40
  Nos. C1-C5 (5) 3.15 3.15
Set, never hinged 5.00

Common Design Type
Inscribed "Togo" across top

1942
C6 CD88 50c car & bl .25
C7 CD88 1fr brn & blk .35
C8 CD88 2fr grn & red brn .50
C9 CD88 3fr dk bl & scar .65
C10 CD88 5fr vio & brn red .70

Frame Engraved, Center Typographed
C11 CD89 10fr ultra, ind & org 1.10
C12 CD89 20fr rose car, mag & gray blk 1.10

C13 CD89 50fr yel grn, dl grn & lt vio 2.10 —
  Nos. C6-C13 (8) 6.75
Set, never hinged 10.50

There is doubt whether Nos. C6-C12 were officially placed in use.

Elephants — AP1

Plane — AP2

Plane — AP3

Post Runner and Plane — AP4

1947, Oct. 6 Engr. Perf. 12½
C14 AP1 40fr blue 8.50 3.50
C15 AP2 50fr lt ultra, & red vio 4.25 1.40
C16 AP3 100fr emer & dk brn 8.50 2.10
C17 AP4 200fr lilac rose 13.00 3.50
  Nos. C14-C17 (4) 34.25 10.50

UPU Issue
Common Design Type

1949, July 4 Perf. 13
C18 CD99 25fr multi 8.50 7.00

Liberation Issue
Common Design Type

1954, June 6
C19 CD102 15fr indigo & pur 7.00 5.50

Freight
Highway — AP5

1954, Nov. 29
C20 AP5 500fr indigo & dk grn 52.50 42.50

Republic

Independence Allegory — AP6

Unwmk.
1957, Oct. 29 Engr. Perf. 13
C21 AP6 25fr bl, olive bister & ver .60 .30
1st anniv. of Togo's autonomy.

Flag and Torch — AP7

Great White Egret — AP8

1957, Oct. 29
C22 AP7 50fr multi .65 .35
C23 AP7 100fr multi 1.10 .60
C24 AP7 200fr multi 2.25 1.00
C25 AP8 500fr ind, lt bl & grn 18.00 6.75
  Nos. C22-C25 (4) 22.00 8.70

Types of 1957 Inscribed "Republique du Togo" and

Flag, Plane and
Map — AP9

1959, Jan. 15 Engr. Perf. 13
C26 AP9 25fr ultra, emer & vio brn .40 .25
C27 AP7 50fr dk bl, dl grn & red .60 .35
C28 AP7 100fr multi 1.40 .60
C29 AP7 200fr dk grn, red & ultra 3.50 1.25
C30 AP8 500fr blk brn, rose lil & grn 14.00 3.50
  Nos. C26-C30 (5) 19.90 5.95

Hotel Le
Benin
AP10

Eagle and Map of
Togo — AP11

Perf. 14½x15, 15x14½
1960, Apr. 27 Litho. Unwmk.
C31 AP10 100fr crim, emer & yel 1.75 .25
C32 AP10 200fr multi 4.00 .40
C33 AP11 500fr grn & gldn brn 8.50 1.00
  Nos. C31-C33 (3) 14.25 1.65

Proclamation of Togo's full independence, Apr. 27, 1960.

Mail Service Type
100fr, Boeing 707 and stamps of 1960.

1963, Jan. 12 Photo. Perf. 13
C34 A41 100fr multi 1.60 .45
  a. Souvenir sheet of 4 4.50 3.50

No. C34a contains 4 stamps similar to Nos. 441-443 and C34, with simulated perforations.

Emancipation Type
1963, Oct. Unwmk. Perf. 13x14
C35 A45 100fr multi 1.50 .45
  a. Souv. sheet of 4, #454-456, C35, imperf. 2.50 2.00

For overprint see No. C41.

Type of 1964 Regular Issue
50fr, Pirenestes ostrinus. 100fr, Spermestes bicolor. 200fr, Agapornis pullaria. 250fr, Psittacus erithacus. 500fr, Trachyphonus margaritaceus.

1964-65 Photo. Perf. 14
Size: 22½x31mm
Birds in Natural Colors
C36 A47 50fr yel grn 3.00 .30
C37 A47 100fr ocher 6.00 .35
C38 A47 200fr dl bl grn 11.50 .90
C39 A47 250fr dl rose ('65) 15.50 1.10
C40 A47 500fr violet 30.00 1.60
  Nos. C36-C40 (5) 66.00 4.25

No. C35
Ovptd.
Diagonally

1964, Feb. Perf. 13x14
C41 A45 100fr multi 1.75 .30

Issued in memory of John F. Kennedy.
Same overprint was applied to stamps of No. C35a, with black border and commemorative inscription added. Two sheets exist: with and without gray silhouetted head of Kennedy covering all four stamps. Value: without silhouette, $15; with silhouette, $25.

Liberation Type
1964, May 25 Perf. 14x13
C42 A50 100fr dl bl grn & dk brn 1.50 .30

Olympic Games Type
1964, Oct. Photo. Perf. 14
C43 A52 100fr Tennis 1.25 .30
  a. Souv. sheet of 3, #493-494, C43, imperf. 2.50 2.00

Flag of Togo and Jet — AP12

1964, Dec. 5 Unwmk. Perf. 14x13
C44 AP12 100fr multi 1.50 .50

Inauguration of the national airline "Air Togo." For souvenir sheet see No. 499a.

Lincoln Type
1965, June Photo. Perf. 13½x14
C45 A58 100fr ol gray 2.00 .35
  a. Souv. sheet, #545, C45, imperf 3.00 2.25

Sports Type

100fr, Soccer player, flags of Togo and Congo.

1965, July Unwmk. *Perf. 14x13*
C46 A59 100fr multi 1.75 .35

Churchill Type

1965, Aug. 7 Photo. *Perf. 13½x14*
C47 A60 85fr car rose 1.50 .40
a. Souv. sheet, #532, C47, imperf 2.50 2.00

UN Type

100fr, Apple, grapes, wheat and "ONU."

1965, Dec. 15 *Perf. 14x13½*
C48 A65 100fr dk bl & bis 1.75 .40
a. Souvenir sheet of 2 2.40 1.75

No. C48a contains two imperf. stamps similar to Nos. 548 and C48 with simulated perforations.

Pope Type

Designs: 45fr, Pope speaking at UN rostrum, world map and UN emblem. 90fr, Pope, plane and UN emblem.

1966, Mar. 5 Litho. *Perf. 12*
C49 A66 45fr emer & multi .80 .25
C50 A66 90fr gray & multi 1.75 .25
a. Souvenir sheet of 2, #C49-C50 3.00 2.00

Red Cross Type

Jean Henri Dunant and Togolese Flag.

1966, May 7 Litho. *Perf. 12*
C51 A67 100fr multi 2.25 .35

WHO Type

Flowers: 50fr, Daisies and WHO Headquarters. 90fr, Talisman roses and WHO Headquarters.

1966, May Litho. *Perf. 12*
C52 A68 50fr lt bl & multi .90 .25
C53 A68 90fr gray & multi 1.50 .25
a. Souvenir sheet of 2, #C52-C53 3.00 2.00

Air Afrique Issue
Common Design Type

1966, Aug. 31 Photo. *Perf. 13*
C54 CD123 30fr brt grn, blk & lem .80 .25

Arts and Crafts Type

60fr, Basket maker. 90fr, Wood carver.

1966, Sept. *Perf. 13x14*
C55 A69 60fr ultra, org & blk 1.40 .25
C56 A69 90fr brt rose, yel & blk 1.40 .25

Dancer Type

50fr, Woman from North Togo holding branches. 60fr, Man from North Togo with horned helmet.

1966, Nov. Photo. *Perf. 13x14*
C57 A70 50fr multi .95 .25
C58 A70 60fr olive & multi 1.25 .25

Soccer Type

Designs: Different Soccer Scenes.

1966, Dec. 14 Photo. *Perf. 14x13*
C59 A71 50fr org, brn & pur .85 .25
C60 A71 60fr ultra, brn & org 1.40 .25
a. Souv. sheet of 3, #582, C59-C60, imperf. 3.25 2.40

Fish Type

Designs: 45fr, Yellow jack and trawler. 90fr, Banded distichodus and seiner.

1967, Jan. 14 Photo. *Perf. 14*
Fish in Natural Colors
C61 A72 45fr org & brn 1.25 .25
C62 A72 90fr emer & dk bl 2.00 .35

UNICEF Type

UNICEF Emblem and: 45fr, Girl and miniature poodle. 90fr, African boy and greyhound.

1967, Feb. 11 Photo. *Perf. 14x13½*
C63 A73 45fr yel, red brn & blk 1.25 .25
C64 A73 90fr ultra, dk grn & blk 1.90 .35
a. Souvenir sheet of 2 4.00 2.25

No. C64a contains 2 imperf., lithographed stamps with simulated perforations similar to Nos. C63-C64.

Satellite Type

50fr, Diamant rocket. 90fr, Fr-1 satellite.

1967, Mar. 18 Photo. *Perf. 13½x14*
C65 A74 50fr multi, vert. 1.00 .25
C66 A74 90fr multi, vert. 1.75 .30
a. Souvenir sheet of 2 3.00 1.75

No. C66a contains 2 imperf. stamps similar to Nos. C65-C66 with simulated perforations.

Musician Type

UNESCO Emblem and: 45fr, Johann Sebastian Bach and organ. 90fr, Ludwig van Beethoven, violin and oboe.

1967, Apr. 15 Photo. *Perf. 14x13½*
C67 A75 45fr multi .75 .25
C68 A75 90fr pink & multi 1.25 .25
a. Souvenir sheet of 2 3.50 1.40

No. C68a contains 2 imperf. stamps similar to Nos. C67-C68 with simulated perforations.

EXPO '67 Type

EXPO '67 Emblem and: 45fr, French pavilion, roses. 60fr, British pavilion, day lilies. 90fr, African village, bird-of-paradise flower. 105fr, US pavilion, daisies.

1967, May 30 Photo. *Perf. 14*
C69 A76 45fr multi .75 .25
C70 A76 60fr multi .85 .25
C71 A76 90fr yel & multi 1.25 .30
a. Souv. sheet, #C69-C71, imperf 3.50 2.50
C72 A76 105fr multi 1.75 .50
Nos. C69-C72 (4) 5.10 1.05

For overprints see Nos. C86-C89.

Mural by José Vela Zanetti — AP13

The designs are from a mural in the lobby of the UN Conf. Building, NYC. The mural depicting mankind's struggle for a lasting peace is shown across 3 stamps twice in the set: on the 5fr, 15fr, 30fr and 45fr, 60fr, 90fr.

1967, July 15 Litho. *Perf. 14*
C73 AP13 5fr multi .40 .25
C74 AP13 15fr org & multi .40 .25
C75 AP13 30fr multi .45 .25
C76 AP13 45fr multi .70 .25
C77 AP13 60fr car & multi 1.10 .25
C78 AP13 90fr ind & multi 1.75 .30
a. Souvenir sheet of 3, #C76-C78 3.50 2.50
Nos. C73-C78 (6) 4.80 1.55

Issued to publicize general disarmament.

Animal Type

1967, Aug. 19 Photo. *Perf. 14x13½*
C79 A78 45fr Lion 1.10 .25
C80 A78 60fr Elephant 1.60 .25

African Postal Union Issue, 1967
Common Design Type

1967, Sept. 9 Engr. *Perf. 13*
C81 CD124 100fr bl, brt grn & ol brn 1.90 .30

Stamp Anniversary Type

Designs: 90fr, Stamp auction and Togo Nos. 16 and C42. 105fr, Father and son with stamp album and No. 474.

1967, Oct. 14 Photo. *Perf. 14x13*
Stamps on Stamps in Original Colors
C82 A79 90fr olive 1.25 .25
a. Souvenir sheet of 3 3.00 2.50
C83 A79 105fr dk car rose 2.00 .40

No. C82a contains 3 imperf. stamps similar to Nos. 621-622 and C82 with simulated perforations.

Pre-Olympics Type

View of Mexico City, Summer Olympics emblem and: 60fr, Runners. 90fr, Broad jump.

1967, Dec. 2 *Perf. 13x14*
C84 A80 60fr pink & multi 1.50 .45
C85 A80 90fr multi 1.50 .50
a. Souv. sheet of 3, #627, C84-C85, imperf. 5.00 3.00

Nos. C69-C72 Overprinted

1967, Dec. Photo. *Perf. 14*
C86 A76 45fr multi .60 .25
C87 A76 60fr multi .90 .25
C88 A76 90fr yel & multi 1.40 .25
C89 A76 105fr multi 1.50 .35
Nos. C86-C89 (4) 4.40 1.00

Issued for National Day, Sept. 29, 1967.

Hydrological Decade Type

1968, Apr. 6 Litho. *Perf. 14*
C90 A84 60fr multi 1.75 .25

Ship Type

Designs: 45fr, Fulton's and modern steamships. 90fr, US atomic ship Savannah and atom symbol.

1968, Apr. 26 Photo. *Perf. 14x14½*
C91 A85 45fr yel & multi 1.10 .25
C92 A85 90fr bl & multi 2.00 .25
a. Souvenir sheet of 2 3.75 1.75

No. C92a contains 2 imperf. stamps similar to Nos. C91-C92 with simulated perforations.

WHO Type

Paintings: 60fr, The Anatomy Lesson, by Rembrandt (detail). 90fr, Jesus Healing the Sick, by Raphael.

1968, June 22 Photo. *Perf. 14*
C93 A87 60fr multi 1.00 .25
C94 A87 90fr pur & multi 1.25 .25
a. Souvenir sheet of 2 3.50 2.50

No. C94a contains 2 imperf. stamps similar to Nos. C93-C94 with simulated perforations.

Olympic Games Type

1968, July 27 *Perf. 14x13½*
C95 A88 60fr Wrestling .85 .25
C96 A88 90fr Running 1.25 .25
a. Souvenir sheet of 2 2.50 2.10

No. C96a contains 2 imperf. stamps similar to Nos. C95-C96 with simulated perforations.

Boy Scout Type

60fr, First aid practice, horiz. 90fr, Scout game.

1968, Nov. 23 Litho. *Perf. 14*
C97 A90 60fr ol & multi 1.00 .25
C98 A90 90fr org & multi 1.40 .35
a. Souvenir sheet of 2 3.00 1.75

No. C98a contains 2 imperf. stamps with simulated perforations similar to Nos. C97-C98.

PHILEXAFRIQUE Issue

The Letter, by Jean Auguste Franquelin AP14

1968, Nov. 9 Photo. *Perf. 12½x12*
C99 AP14 100fr multi 2.75 1.75

PHILEXAFRIQUE Philatelic Exhibition in Abidjan, Feb. 14-23. Printed with alternating light ultramarine label.

Christmas Type

Paintings: 60fr, Adoration of the Magi, by Pieter Brueghel. 90fr, Adoration of the Magi, by Dürer.

1968, Dec. 28 Litho. *Perf. 14*
C100 A91 60fr red & multi 1.10 .25
C101 A91 90fr multi 1.50 .35
a. Souvenir sheet 3.75 1.75

No. C101a contains 2 imperf. stamps similar to Nos. C100-C101 with simulated perforations.

Human Rights Type

Human Rights Flame and: 60fr, Robert F. Kennedy. 90fr, Martin Luther King, Jr.

1969, Feb. 1 Photo. *Perf. 13½x14*
C102 A92 60fr brt rose lil & vio bl 1.00 .25
C103 A92 90fr emer & brn 1.40 .40
a. Souvenir sheet 2.50 1.75

No. C103a contains 2 imperf. stamps similar to Nos. C102-C103 with simulated perforations.

For overprints see Nos. C110-C111.

2nd PHILEXAFRIQUE Issue
Common Design Type

Design: 50fr, Togo #16 and Aledjo Fault.

1969, Feb. 14 Engr. *Perf. 13*
C104 CD128 50fr red brn, grn & car rose 2.25 .45

Sports Type

Stadium and: 60fr, Boxing. 90fr, Bicycling.

1969, Apr. 26 Photo. *Perf. 14x13½*
C105 A93 60fr bl, red & dk brn .95 .25
C106 A93 90fr ultra, brt pink & dk brn 1.40 .30
a. Souvenir sheet 2.50 1.75

No. C106a contains 2 imperf. stamps similar to Nos. C105-C106 with simulated perforations.

Lunar Type

Designs: 60fr, Astronaut exploring moon surface. 100fr, Astronaut gathering rocks.

1969, July 21 Litho. *Perf. 14*
C107 A94 60fr dk bl & multi .90 .25
C108 A94 100fr multi 1.50 .50
a. Souvenir sheet 14.00 5.00

No. C108a contains 4 imperf. stamps with simulated perforations similar to Nos. 676-677 and C107-C108, magenta margin. No. C108a also exists with colors of 30fr and 100fr stamps changed, and margin in orange. Value, unused $6, used $2.

For overprints see Nos. C120-C121.

Painting Type

Painting: 90fr, Pentecost, by El Greco.

1969, Aug. 16 Litho. *Perf. 14*
C109 A95 90fr multi 2.10 .50
a. Souvenir sheet 2.75 1.50

No. C109a contains two imperf. stamps with simulated perforations similar to Nos. 682 and C109.

Nos. C102-C103 Overprinted Like Nos. 683-686

1969, Sept. 1 Photo. *Perf. 13½x14*
C110 A92 60fr brt rose lil & vio bl .90 .25
C111 A92 90fr emer & brn 1.25 .30
a. Souv. sheet of 2 3.00 2.00

#C111a is #C103a with Eisenhower overprint.

Bank Type

Design: 100fr, Bank emblem and hand holding cattle and farmer.

1969, Sept. 10 Photo. *Perf. 13x14*
C112 A96 100fr multi 1.10 .40

Red Cross Type

60fr, Wilhelm C. Roentgen & Red Cross workers with children in front of Togo Headquarters. 90fr, Henri Dunant & Red Cross workers meeting Biafra refugees at airport.

1969, Sept. 27 Litho. *Perf. 14*
C113 A97 60fr brn & multi .85 .30
C114 A97 90fr ol & multi 1.25 .40
a. Souv. sheet of 2 2.75 2.10

No. C114a contains 2 imperf. stamps with simulated perforations similar to Nos. C113-C114.

Agricultural Center Type

Emblem of Young Pioneer and Agricultural Organization and: 90fr, Manioc harvest. 100fr, Instruction in gardening. 200fr, Corn harvest. 250fr, Marching drum corps. 500fr, Parade of Young Pioneers.

1969-70 Litho. *Perf. 14*

C115 A98 90fr multi 1.20 .25
C116 A98 100fr org & multi 1.40 .30
C117 A98 200fr multi ('70) 2.75 .40
C118 A98 250fr ol & multi 4.25 .70
C119 A98 500fr multi ('70) 9.00 .90
Nos. C115-C119 (5) 20.00 2.50

Christmas Issue

Nos. C107-C108, C108a Overprinted: "JOYEUX NOEL"

1969, Dec. Litho. *Perf. 14*

C120 A94 60fr multi 3.50 .45
C121 A94 100fr multi 5.25 .65
a. Souvenir sheet of 4 60.00 60.00

Peace Leaders Type

60fr, Friedrich Ebert. 90fr, Mahatma Gandhi.

1969, Dec. 27 Litho. *Perf. 14x13½*

C122 A100 60fr dk brn, dk red & yel 1.00 .25
C123 A100 90fr dk brn, vio bl & ocher 1.40 .35

For surcharges see Nos. 765, C143.

ILO Type

Paintings and ILO Emblem: 60fr, Spring Sowing, by Vincent van Gogh. 90fr, Workers, by Diego de Rivera.

1970, Jan. 24 Litho. *Perf. 12½x13*

C124 A101 60fr gold & multi 1.75 .25
C125 A101 90fr gold & multi 2.75 .25
a. Souvenir sheet of 2 3.50 1.40

No. C125a contains two stamps similar to Nos. C124-C125, with simulated perforations.

Hair Styles Type

Various hair styles. 45fr, vert. 90fr, horiz.

1970, Feb. 21 *Perf. 12½x13, 13x12½*

C126 A102 45fr car & multi .90 .25
C127 A102 90fr multi 1.75 .40

Independence Type

Design: 60fr, Togo No. C33 and Independence Monument, Lomé.

1970, Apr. 27 Litho. *Perf. 13x12½*

C128 A103 60fr yel & multi .85 .25

UPU Type

1970, May 30 Photo. *Perf. 14x13½*

C129 A104 50fr grnsh bl & dk car .90 .25

Soccer Type

Various Scenes from Soccer, Rimet Cup and Flags of: 50fr, Sweden and Israel. 60fr, Bulgaria and Peru. 90fr, Belgium and Salvador.

1970, June 27 Litho. *Perf. 13x14*

C130 A105 50fr multi .75 .25
C131 A105 60fr lil & multi .90 .25
C132 A105 90fr multi 1.90 .35
a. Souvenir sheet of 4 4.00 4.00
Nos. C130-C132 (3) 3.75 .75

No. C132a contains 4 stamps similar to Nos. 734, C130-C132, but imperf. with simulated perforations.

Lenin Type

Design: 50fr, Lenin Meeting Peasant Delegation, by V. A. Serov, and UNESCO emblem.

1970, July 25 Litho. *Perf. 12½*

C133 A106 50fr multi 1.95 .25

For overprint see No. C179.

EXPO '70 Type

Souvenir Sheet

150fr, Mitsubishi pavilion, EXPO '70 emblem.

1970, Aug. 8 Litho. *Perf. 13*

C134 A107 150fr yel & multi 5.00 3.50
a. Inscribed "AERINNE"

No. C134 contains one stamp 86x33mm.

Astronaut Type

Design: 200fr, James A. Lovell, Fred W. Haise, Jr. and Tom Mattingly (replaced by John L. Swigert, Jr.) and Apollo 13 emblem.

1970, Sept. 26

C135 A108 200fr multi 2.90 .75
a. Souv. sheet of 3 3.75 2.50

Space flight of Apollo 13. No. C135a contains 3 stamps similar to Nos. 741, 744 and C135, with simulated perforations.
For overprint see No. C136.

Nos. C135, C135a Inscribed: "FELICITATIONS / BON RETOUR APOLLO XIII"

1970, Sept. 26

C136 A108 200fr multi 2.75 .60
a. Souvenir sheet of 3 3.75 2.50

Safe return of the crew of Apollo 13.

UN Type

Paintings and Emblems of UN Agencies: 60fr, The Mailman Roulin, by van Gogh, and UPU emblem. 90fr, The Birth of the Virgin, by Vittore Carpaccio, and WHO emblem.

1970, Oct. 24 Litho. *Perf. 13x12½*

C137 A109 60fr grn, gold & blk 1.10 .25
C138 A109 90fr red org, gold & brn 1.75 .30
a. Souvenir sheet of 4 3.50 2.50

No. C138a contains one each of Nos. 754-755 and C137-C138 with simulated perforations.

Moth Type

Moths: 60fr, Euchloron megaera. 90fr, Pseudacraea boisduvali.

1970, Nov. 21 Photo. *Perf. 13x14*

C139 A110 60fr multi 5.25 .25
C140 A110 90fr multi 5.25 .25

Christmas Type

Paintings: 60fr, Adoration of the Magi, by Botticelli. 90fr, Adoration of the Kings, by Tiepolo.

1970, Dec. 26 Litho. *Perf. 12½x13*

C141 A111 60fr gold & multi 1.50 .25
C142 A111 90fr gold & multi 2.25 .30
a. Souv. sheet of 2, #C141-C142 3.50 1.75

No. C122 Surcharged and Overprinted: "EN MEMOIRE / Charles De Gaulle / 1890-1970"

1971, Jan. 9 Photo. *Perf. 14x13½*

C143 A100 200fr on 60fr 11.50 .60

De Gaulle Type

Designs: 60fr, De Gaulle and Pope Paul VI. 90fr, De Gaulle and satellite.

1971, Feb. 20 Photo. *Perf. 13x14*

C144 A112 60fr blk & dp vio 2.20 .25
C145 A112 90fr blk & bl grn 3.00 .25
a. Souvenir sheet of 4 8.50 3.00

Nos. C143-C145 issued in memory of Charles De Gaulle (1890-1970), President of France. No. C145a contains 4 imperf. stamps similar to Nos. 769-770, C144-C145.

Easter Type

Paintings: 50fr, Resurrection, by Matthias Grunewald. 60fr, Resurrection, by Master of Trebon. 90fr, Resurrection, by El Greco.

1971, Apr. 10 Litho. *Perf. 10½x11½*

C146 A113 50fr gold & multi .85 .25
C147 A113 60fr gold & multi 1.25 .25
C148 A113 90fr gold & multi 1.60 .30
a. Souvenir sheet of 4, #773, C146-C148 4.50 2.50
Nos. C146-C148 (3) 3.70 .70

Apollo 14 Type

Designs: 50fr, 200fr, Apollo 14 badge. 100fr, Take-off from moon, and spaceship.

1971, May Litho. *Perf. 12½*

C149 A114 50fr grn & multi .65 .25
C150 A114 100fr multi 1.10 .45
C151 A114 200fr org & multi 2.50 .85
a. Souv. sheet of 4 5.75 5.50
Nos. C149-C151 (3) 4.25 1.50

No. C151a contains 4 stamps similar to Nos. 777 and C149-C151 with simulated perforations.
For surcharge and overprints see Nos. C162-C164.

Cacao Type

60fr, Ministry of Agriculture. 90fr, Cacao tree and & pods. 100fr, Sorting & separating beans from pods.

1971, June 6 Litho. *Perf. 14*

C152 A115 60fr multi .75 .25
C153 A115 90fr multi 1.10 .40
C154 A115 100fr multi 1.25 .45
Nos. C152-C154 (3) 4.10 1.05

ASECNA Type

1971, June 26

C155 A116 100fr multi 1.60 .35

Tourist Type

Designs: 50fr, Château Viale and antelope. 60fr, Lake Togo and crocodile. 100fr, Old lime furnace, Tokpli, and hippopotamus.

1971, July 17

C156 A117 50fr multi .55 .25
C157 A117 60fr multi .75 .25
C158 A117 100fr multi 1.00 .40
Nos. C156-C158 (3) 3.60 .80

For overprint see No. C172.

Religions Type

Designs: 50fr, Mohammedans praying in front of Lomé Mosque. 60fr, Protestant service. 90fr, Catholic bishop and priests.

1971, July 31 Litho. *Perf. 14½*

C159 A118 50fr multi .55 .25
C160 A118 60fr multi .75 .25
C161 A118 90fr multi .95 .25
a. Souvenir sheet of 4, #787, C159-C161 4.25 2.50
Nos. C159-C161 (3) 2.35 .65

Nos. C149-C151 Overprinted and Surcharged in Black or Silver: "EN MEMOIRE / DOBROVOLSKY — VOLKOV — PATSAYEV / SOYUZ 11"

1971, Aug. *Perf. 12½*

C162 A114 90fr on 50fr multi 1.00 .35
C163 A114 100fr multi (S) 1.20 .40
C164 A114 200fr multi 2.10 .65
a. Souvenir sheet of 4, #788, C162-C164 7.00 7.00
Nos. C162-C164 (3) 5.65 1.40

See note after No. 788.

Olympic Type

200fr, Sapporo '72 emblem and Ski jump.

1971, Oct. 30 Litho. *Perf. 14*

C165 A119 200fr multi 2.10 .50
a. Souvenir sheet of 4 4.25 3.50

No. C165 contains 4 stamps with simulated perforations similar to Nos. 791-793 and C165 printed on glazed paper.

African Postal Union Issue

Common Design Type

Design: 100fr, Adjogbo dancers and UAMPT Building, Brazzaville, Congo.

1971, Nov. 13 Photo. *Perf. 13x13½*

C166 CD135 100fr bl & multi 1.25 .40

Intl. Organization for the Protection of Children (U.I.P.E.) — AP14a

Die Cut Perf. 10½

1971, Nov. 13 Embossed

C166A AP14a 1500fr gold 20.00

UNICEF Type

Toys: 60fr, Turtle. 90fr, Parrot.

1971, Nov. 27 Litho. *Perf. 14*

C167 A120 60fr lt bl & multi .55 .25
C168 A120 90fr multi .85 .25
a. Souvenir sheet of 4 2.75 2.50

No. C168a contains 4 stamps with simulated perforations similar to Nos. 796-797 and C167-C168.
For overprints see Nos. C263-C264.

Christmas Type

Virgin and Child by: 60fr, Giorgione. 100fr, Raphael.

1971, Dec. 24 *Perf. 14x13*

C169 A121 60fr olive & multi 1.00 .30
C170 A121 100fr multi 1.75 .50
a. Souvenir sheet of 4 5.25 2.25

No. C170a contains 4 stamps with simulated perforations similar to Nos. 800-801, C169-C170.

Venice Type

Design: 100fr, Ca' d'Oro, Venice.

1972, Feb. 26 Litho. *Perf. 14*

C171 A122 100fr multi 1.75 .55
a. Souvenir sheet of 3 5.75 2.50

No. C171a contains 3 stamps similar to Nos. 802-803, C171 with simulated perforations.

No. C156 Overprinted "VISITE DU PRESIDENT / NIXON EN CHINE / FEVRIER 1972"

1972, Mar. Litho. *Perf. 14*

C172 A117 50fr multi .90 .25

Visit of Pres. Richard M. Nixon to the People's Republic of China, Feb. 20-27.

Easter Type

Paintings: 50fr, Resurrection, by Thomas de Coloswa. 100fr, Ascension by Andrea Mantegna.

1972, Mar. 31

C173 A123 50fr gold & multi 1.10 .25
C174 A123 100fr gold & multi 2.10 .25
a. Souvenir sheet of 4 3.00 1.50

No. C174a contains 4 stamps similar to Nos. 806-807, C173-C174 with simulated perforations.

Heart Type

100fr, Heart, WHO emblem and smith.

1972, Apr. 4

C175 A124 100fr multi 1.25 .45
a. Souvenir sheet of 2 3.25 1.40

No. C175a contains 2 stamps similar to Nos. 810 and C175 with simulated perforations.

Telecommunications Type

Design: 100fr, Intelsat 4 over Africa.

1972, June 24 *Perf. 14*

C176 A125 100fr multi 1.60 .30

For overprint see No. C229.

Cassava Type

60fr, Truck and cassava processing factory, horiz. 80fr, Children, mother holding tapioca cake.

1972, June 30

C177 A126 60fr multi 1.10 .25
C178 A126 80fr multi 1.25 .25

No. C133 Surcharged in Deep Carmine: "VISITE DU PRESIDENT / NIXON EN RUSSIE / MAI 1972"

1972, July 15 Litho. *Perf. 12½*

C179 A106 300fr on 50fr multi 4.75 1.40

President Nixon's visit to the USSR, May 1972. Old denomination obliterated with 6x5mm rectangle.

Olympic Type

1972, Aug. 26 Litho. *Perf. 14*

C180 A127 90fr Gymnastics .65 .40
a. Souv. sheet of 2 3.25 1.60
C181 A127 200fr Basketball 1.75 .75

No. C180a contains 2 stamps with simulated perforations similar to Nos. 816 and C180.
For overprints see Nos. C234-C235.

Bird Type

Bird: 90fr, Rose-ringed parakeet.

1972, Sept. 9

C182 A128 90fr multi 2.75 .45
a. Souvenir sheet of 4 13.00 2.60

No. C182a contains 4 stamps similar to Nos. 818-820, C182 with simulated perforations.

Rotary Type

Rotary Emblem and: 60fr, Map of Togo, olive branch. 90fr, Flags of Togo and Rotary Club. 100fr, Paul P. Harris.

1972, Oct. 7   Litho.   *Perf. 14*
C183 A129 60fr brn & multi   .65   .25
C184 A129 90fr multi   .90   .40
C185 A129 100fr multi   1.25   .45
    Nos. C183-C185 (3)   3.25 1.35

For overprints see Nos. C212-C213, C244-C245.

Type of 1972 Painting

Designs: 60fr, Mystical Marriage of St. Catherine, by Assistant to the P. M. Master. 80fr, Self-portrait, by Leonardo da Vinci. 100fr, Sts. Mary and Agnes by Botticelli.

1972, Oct. 21
C186 A130 60fr gold & multi   1.40   .25
C187 A130 80fr gold & multi   1.75   .30
C188 A130 100fr gold & multi   2.25   .45
   a.   Souvenir sheet of 4   4.50 2.00
    Nos. C186-C188 (3)   8.15   .95

No. C188a contains 4 stamps with simulated perforations similar to Nos. 824, C186-188.

Presidential Visit Type

Design: 100fr, Pres. Pompidou and Col. Etienne Eyadema, front view of party headquarters.

1972, Nov. 23   Litho.   *Perf. 14*
C189 A131 100fr multi   2.40   .40

Johann Wolfgang von Goethe (1749-1832), German Poet and Dramatist AP15

1972, Dec. 2   Photo.   *Perf. 13x14*
C190 AP15 100fr grn & multi   1.40   .40

Christmas Type

Paintings: 60fr, Nativity, by Master Vyshchibrod. 80fr, Adoration of the Kings, anonymous. 100fr, Flight into Egypt, by Giotto.

1972, Dec. 23   Litho.   *Perf. 14*
C191 A132 60fr gold & multi   1.00   .25
C192 A132 80fr gold & multi   1.20   .35
C193 A132 100fr gold & multi   1.40   .45
   a.   Souvenir sheet of 4   5.00 1.75
    Nos. C191-C193 (3)   4.95 1.05

No. C193a contains 4 stamps with simulated perforations similar to Nos. 829, C191-C193.

Leprosy Day Type

Design: 100fr, Dr. Armauer G. Hansen, apparatus, microscope and Petri dish.

1973, Jan. 23   Photo.   *Perf. 14x13½*
C194 A133 100fr rose car & bl   2.75   .40

World Leprosy Day and centenary of the discovery of the Hansen bacillus, the cause of leprosy.

Miniature Sheets

1972 Summer Olympics, Munich — AP15a

Medalists, each 1500fr: #C194A, Mark Spitz, US, swimming. #C194B, L. Linsenhoff, West Germany, equestrian. #C194C, D. Morelon, France, cycling.

Litho. & Embossed

1973, Jan.   *Perf. 13½*
C194A-C194C AP15a Set of 3   375.00
    Exist imperf.

Miniature Sheet

Apollo 17 Moon Landing — AP15b

1973, Jan.
C194D AP15b 1500fr gold & multi   55.00
    Exists imperf.

Easter Type

1973, Apr. 21   Litho.   *Perf. 14*
C195 A135 90fr Christ in Glory   1.40   .40
   a.   Souvenir sheet of 2   2.75 1.75

No. C195a contains one each of Nos. 835 and C195 with simulated perforations.

Apollo 17 Type

Designs: 100fr, Astronauts on moon and orange rock. 200fr, Rocket lift-off at Cape Kennedy and John F. Kennedy.

1973, June 2   Litho.   *Perf. 14*
C196 A136 100fr multi   1.60   .45
C197 A136 200fr multi   3.25   .65
   a.   Souvenir sheet of 2   4.25 3.00

No. C197a contains 2 stamps similar to Nos. C196-C197 with simulated perforations.

Boy Scout Type

100fr, Canoeing, horiz. 200fr, Campfire, horiz.

1973, June 30   Litho.   *Perf. 14*
C198 A137 100fr bl & multi   1.25   .45
C199 A137 200fr bl & multi   2.50   .70
   a.   Souvenir sheet of 2   3.50 2.10

No. C199a contains 2 stamps similar to Nos. C198-C199 with simulated perforations. For overprints see Nos. C265-C266.

Copernicus Type

Designs: 90fr, Heliocentric system. 100fr, Nicolaus Copernicus.

1973, July 18
C200 A138 90fr multi   1.60   .35
C201 A138 100fr bis & multi   1.90   .45
   a.   Souv. sheet of 2, #C200-C201   3.00 1.60

Red Cross Type

Design: 100fr, Dove carrying Red Cross letter, sun, map of Togo.

1973, Aug. 4
C202 A139 100fr multi   3.00   .35
    For overprint see No. C294.

Literacy Type

Design: 90fr, Woman teacher in classroom.

1973, Aug. 18   Litho.   *Perf. 14*
C203 A140 90fr multi   1.50   .35

WMO Type

1973, Oct. 4   Photo.   *Perf. 14x13*
C204 A142 200fr dl bl, pur & brn   2.00   .60

Type 1967

Early & contemporary planes, #758, C36.

1973, Oct. 20   Photo.   *Perf. 14x13*
C205 A79 100fr multi   2.50   .35
   a.   Souvenir sheet of 2   3.00 1.75

75th anniversary of Togolese postal service. No. C205a contains 2 stamps similar to Nos. 855 and C205 with simulated perforations.

Kennedy Type

Designs: 90fr, Kennedy and Charles De Gaulle. 100fr, Kennedy and Nikita Krushchev. 200fr, Kennedy and model of Apollo spacecraft.

1973, Nov. 22   Litho.   *Perf. 14*
C206 A143 90fr blk & pink   1.60   .45
C207 A143 100fr blk, lt bl & bl   1.75   .60
C208 A143 200fr blk, buff & brn   4.00   .75
   a.   Souvenir sheet of 2   4.00 2.00
    Nos. C206-C208 (3)   7.35 1.80

No. C208a contains 2 stamps similar to Nos. C207-208 with simulated perforations.

Human Rights Flame and People — AP16

1973, Dec. 8   Photo.   *Perf. 13x14*
C209 AP16 250fr lt bl & multi   2.75   .80

25th anniversary of the Universal Declaration of Human Rights.

Christmas Type

Paintings: 90fr, Virgin and Child. 100fr, Adoration of the Kings. Both after 15th century Italian paintings.

1973, Dec. 22   Litho.   *Perf. 14*
C210 A144 90fr gold & multi   1.10   .35
C211 A144 100fr gold & multi   1.50   .45
   a.   Souvenir sheet of 2   2.75 1.50

No. C211a contains 2 stamps with simulated perforations similar to Nos. C210-C211.

Nos. C183 and C185 Overprinted: "PREMIERE CONVENTION / 210eme DISTRICT / FEVRIER 1974 / LOME"

1974, Feb. 21   Litho.   *Perf. 14*
C212 A129 60fr brn & multi   .65   .25
C213 A129 100fr multi   1.00   .35

First convention of Rotary International, District 210, Lomé, Feb. 22-24.

Soccer Type

Various soccer scenes and games' cup.

1974, Mar. 2   Litho.   *Perf. 14*
C214 A145 90fr multi   .90   .45
C215 A145 100fr multi   1.00   .50
C216 A145 200fr multi   2.00   .95
   a.   Souvenir sheet of 2   3.75 2.10
    Nos. C214-C216 (3)   5.00 1.90

No. C216a contains 2 stamps with simulated perforations similar to Nos. C215-C216.

Picasso Type

Paintings: 90fr, The Muse. 100fr, Les Demoiselles d'Avignon. 200fr, Sitting Nude.

1974, Apr. 6   Litho.   *Perf. 14*
C217 A146 90fr brn & multi   1.60   .40
C218 A146 100fr pur & multi   2.00   .45
C219 A146 200fr multi   4.00   .85
   a.   Souvenir sheet of 3   7.00 4.00
    Nos. C217-C219 (3)   7.60 1.70

No. C219a contains 3 stamps similar to Nos. C217-C219 with simulated perforations.

Coastal Views Type

Designs: 90fr, Fishermen on Lake Togo. 100fr, Mouth of Anecho River.

1974, Apr. 20
C220 A147 90fr multi   1.10   .25
C221 A147 100fr multi   1.25   .35
   a.   Souvenir sheet of 2   2.50 1.25

No. C221a contains 2 stamps similar to Nos. C220-C221 with simulated perforations.

UPU Type

Designs: Old mailmen's uniforms.

1974, May 10   Litho.   *Perf. 14*
C222 A148 50fr multi   .70   .25
C223 A148 100fr multi   1.25   .35
   a.   Souvenir sheet of 2   40.00 17.00

No. C223a contains 2 stamps similar to Nos. C222-C223, rouletted.

Fishing Type

Designs: 90fr, Fishermen bringing in net with catch. 100fr, Fishing with rod and line. 200fr, Fishing with basket, vert.

1974, June 22   Litho.   *Perf. 14*
C224 A149 90fr multi   1.00   .25
C225 A149 100fr multi   1.10   .25
C226 A149 200fr multi   2.40   .65
   a.   Souvenir sheet of 3   5.25 2.50
    Nos. C224-C226 (3)   4.50 1.15

No. C226a contains 3 stamps with simulated perforations similar to Nos. C224-C226.

Jupiter Probe Type

Designs: 100fr, Rocket take-off, vert. 200fr, Satellite in space.

1974, July 6   *Perf. 14*
C227 A150 100fr multi   .90   .35
C228 A150 200fr multi   2.00   .65
   a.   Souvenir sheet of 2   5.50 4.00

No. C228a contains 2 stamps similar to Nos. C227-C228 with simulated perforations; imperf. or rouletted.

No. C176 Overprinted in Black

1974, July   *Perf. 14*
C229 A125 100fr multi   3.50 1.20

INTERNABA 1974 Intl. Philatelic Exhibition, Basel, June 7-16.
No. C229 exists overprinted in silver. Value, unused $11.

Seashell Type

1974, July 13   *Perf. 14*
C230 A151 90fr Alcithoe ponsonbyi   1.75   .30
C231 A151 100fr Casmaria iredalei   2.25   .40
   a.   Souvenir sheet of 2   4.50 1.40

No. C231a contains 2 stamps similar to Nos. C230-C231 with simulated perforations.

Horse Racing Type

90fr, Steeplechase. 100fr, Galloping horses.

1974, Aug. 3   Litho.   *Perf. 14*
C232 A152 90fr multi   2.10   .30
C233 A152 100fr multi   2.40   .40
   a.   Souvenir sheet of 2   6.50 2.25

No. C233a contains one each of Nos. C232-C233 with simulated perforations.

Nos. C180, C180a and C181 Overprinted: "COUPE DU MONDE / DE FOOTBALL / VAINQUEURS / REPUBLIQUE FEDERALE / d'ALLEMAGNE"

1974, Aug. 19
C234 A127 90fr multi   .75   .25
   a.   Souvenir sheet of 2   18.00   —
C235 A127 200fr multi   1.50   .65

World Cup Soccer Championship, Munich, 1974, victory of German Federal Republic. For description of No. C234a see note after No. C181.

Animal Type

1974, Sept. 7   *Perf. 14*
C236 A153 90fr Lions   2.10   .35
C237 A153 100fr Rhinoceroses   2.25   .40
   a.   Souvenir sheet of 3   3.75 1.90

Wild animals of West Africa. No. C237a contains 3 stamps similar to Nos. 889, C236-C237 with simulated perforations.

1974, Oct. 14

C238 A153 90fr Herd at waterhole 1.10 .25
C239 A153 100fr Village and cows 1.25 .35
a. Souvenir sheet of 2 2.50 1.25

Domestic animals. No. C239a contains 2 stamps with simulated perforations similar to Nos. C238-C239.

Churchill Type

Designs: 100fr, Churchill and frigate. 200fr, Churchill and fighter planes.

1974, Nov. 1 Photo. *Perf. 13x13½*

C240 A154 100fr multi 1.25 .35
C241 A154 200fr org & multi 2.75 .70
a. Souvenir sheet of 2 4.50 2.10

No. C241a contains 2 stamps similar to Nos. C240-C241; perf. or imperf.

Flower Type

Flowers of Togo: 100fr, Clerodendrum thosonae. 200fr, Gloriosa superba.

1975, Feb. 15 Litho. *Perf. 14*

C242 A155 100fr multi 1.75 .30
C243 A155 200fr multi 2.75 .50
a. Souvenir sheet of 2 7.00 1.90

No. C243a contains one each of Nos. C242-C243, perf. 13x14 or imperf.

Nos. C184-C185 Overprinted: "70e ANNIVERSAIRE / 23 FÉVRIER 1975"

1975, Feb. 23 Litho. *Perf. 14*

C244 A129 90fr multi .90 .25
C245 A129 100fr multi 1.00 .35

Rotary International, 70th anniversary.

Easter Type

Paintings: 100fr, Christ Rising from the Tomb, by Master MS. 200fr, Holy Trinity (detail), by Dürer.

1975, Apr. 19 Litho. *Perf. 14*

C246 A157 100fr multi 1.00 .25
C247 A157 200fr multi 2.00 .55
a. Souvenir sheet of 2 3.50 2.00

No. C247a contains 2 stamps similar to Nos. C246-C247 with simulated perforations.

Independence Type

50fr, National Day parade, flag and map of Togo. 60fr, Warriors' dance and flag of Togo.

1975, Apr. 26 Litho. *Perf. 14*

C248 A158 50fr multi, vert. .50 .25
C249 A158 60fr multi .70 .25
a. Souvenir sheet of 2 1.50 .75

No. C249a contains 2 stamps similar to Nos. C248-C249 with simulated perforations.

Hunt Type

Designs: 90fr, Running deer. 100fr, Wild boar hunter with shotgun.

1975, May 24 Photo. *Perf. 13x13½*

C250 A159 90fr multi 1.75 .30
C251 A159 100fr multi 2.10 .30

Palm Oil Type

Designs: 85fr, Selling palm oil in market, vert. 100fr, Oil processing plant, Alokoegbe.

1975, June 28 Litho. *Perf. 14*

C252 A160 85fr multi 1.75 .50
C253 A160 100fr multi 2.00 .50

Apollo-Soyuz Type and

Soyuz Spacecraft AP17

Designs: 60fr, Donald K. Slayton, Vance D. Brand and Thomas P. Stafford. 90fr, Aleksei A. Leonov and Valery N. Kubasov. 100fr, Apollo-Soyuz link-up, American and Russian flags. 200fr, Apollo-Soyuz emblem and globe.

1975, July 15

C254 AP17 50fr yel & multi .50 .25
C255 A161 60fr lil & multi .70 .25
C256 A161 90fr bl & multi .85 .25
C257 A161 100fr grn & multi 1.25 .40
C258 A161 200fr yel & multi 2.10 .45
a. Souv. sheet of 4, #C255-C258 6.00 3.50
Nos. C254-C258 (5) 5.40 1.50

See note after No. 913.

Schweitzer Type

Dr. Schweitzer: 80fr, playing organ, vert. 90fr, with pelican, vert. 100fr, and Lambarene Hospital.

1975, Aug. 23 Litho. *Perf. 14x13½*

C259 A163 80fr multi 1.10 .30
C260 A163 90fr multi 1.25 .35
C261 A163 100fr multi 1.40 .40
Nos. C259-C261 (3) 3.75 1.05

Letter Writing Type

80fr, Erasmus Writing Letter, by Hans Holbein.

1975, Oct. 9 Litho. *Perf. 14*

C262 A164 80fr multi 1.00 .25

Nos. C167-C168a Overprinted: "30ème Anniversaire / des Nations-Unies"

1975, Oct. 24 Litho. *Perf. 14*

C263 A120 60fr multi .60 .25
C264 A120 90fr multi .75 .25
a. Souvenir sheet of 4 3.00 1.90

UN, 30th anniv. #C264a contains Nos. 796 (with overprint), 918, C263-C264.

Nos. C198-C199 Overprinted: "14ème JAMBORÉE / MONDIAL / DES ÉCLAIREURS"

1975, Nov. 7

C265 A137 100fr multi .90 .25
C266 A137 200fr multi 1.75 .50
a. Souvenir sheet of 2 3.25 2.00

14th World Boy Scout Jamboree, Lillehammer, Norway, July 29-Aug. 7. No. C266a contains one each of Nos. C265-C266 with simulated perforations.

Christmas Type

Paintings of the Virgin and Child: 90fr, Nativity, by Federico Barocci. 100fr, Bellini. 200fr, Correggio.

1975, Dec. 20 Litho. *Perf. 14*

C267 A165 90fr bl & multi .80 .25
C268 A165 100fr red & multi .90 .25
C269 A165 200fr bl & multi 1.75 .50
a. Souv. sheet of 2, #C268-C269 3.50 2.00
Nos. C267-C269 (3) 3.45 1.00

Bicentennial Type

Paintings (and Bicentennial Emblem): 60fr, Surrender of Gen. Burgoyne, by John Trumbull. 70fr, Surrender at Trenton, by Trumbull, vert. 100fr, Signing of Declaration of Independence, by Trumbull. 200fr, Washington Crossing the Delaware, by Emanuel Leutze.

1976, Mar. 3 Litho. *Perf. 14*

C270 A167 60fr multi .65 .25
C271 A167 70fr multi .75 .25
C272 A167 100fr multi 1.00 .25
C273 A167 200fr multi 2.00 .55
a. Souv. sheet of 2, #C272-C273 4.00 2.00
Nos. C270-C273 (4) 4.40 1.20

No. C273a also exists imperf. Value $22.50.
For overprints see Nos. C280-C283.

Common Market Type

Designs: 60fr, ACP and CEE emblems. 70fr, Map of Africa, Europe and Asia.

1976, Apr. 24 Photo. *Perf. 13x14*

C274 A168 60fr lt bl & multi .55 .25
C275 A168 70fr yel & multi .65 .25

Telephone Type

Designs: 70fr, Thomas A. Edison, old and new communications equipment. 105fr, Alexander Graham Bell, old and new telephones.

1976, Mar. 10 Photo. *Perf. 13x14*

C276 A169 70fr multi .50 .25
C277 A169 105fr multi .60 .40
a. Souv. sheet of 2, #C276-C277 2.25 1.40

No. C277a exists imperf. Value $10.00.

Eye Examination AP18

1976, Apr. 8 *Perf. 14x13*

C278 AP18 60fr dk red & multi .60 .25

World Health Day: "Foresight prevents blindness."

Pylon, Flags of Ghana, Togo, Dahomey — AP19

1976, May 8 Litho. *Perf. 14*

C279 AP19 60fr multi 1.00 .25

Ghana-Togo-Dahomey electric power grid, 1st anniv. See No. 932.

Nos. C270-C273, C273a, Overprinted: "INTERPHIL / MAI 29-JUIN 6, 1976"

1976, May 29

C280 A167 60fr multi .50 .25
C281 A167 70fr multi .55 .25
C282 A167 100fr multi .80 .25
C283 A167 200fr multi 1.60 .55
a. Souvenir sheet of 2 3.00 3.00
Nos. C280-C283 (4) 3.45 1.30

Interphil 76 Intl. Philatelic Exhibition, Philadelphia, Pa., May 29-June 6. Overprint on No. C281 in 3 lines; overprint on No. C283a applied to each stamp.

Olympic Games Type

Montreal Olympic Emblem and: 70fr, Yachting. 105fr, Motorcycling. 200fr, Fencing.

1976, June 15 Photo. *Perf. 14x13*

C284 A172 70fr multi .60 .25
C285 A172 105fr multi .85 .40
C286 A172 200fr multi 1.60 .65
a. Souvenir sheet of 2, #C285-C286, perf. 14 3.00 2.25
Nos. C284-C286 (3) 3.05 1.30

For overprints see Nos. C298-C299.

Viking Type

60fr, Viking landing on Mars. 70fr, Nodus Gordii (view on Mars). 105fr, Lander over Mare Tyrrhenum. 200fr, Landing on Mars.

1976, July 15 Litho. *Perf. 14*

C287 A173 60fr bis & multi .55 .25
C288 A173 70fr multi .65 .25
C289 A173 105fr bl & multi .90 .40
C290 A173 200fr multi 1.75 .60
a. Souv. sheet of 2, #C289-C290, perf. 14x13½ 3.50 2.25
Nos. C287-C290 (4) 3.85 1.40

Toulouse-Lautrec Type, 1976

Paintings: 60fr, Carmen, portrait. 70fr, Maurice at the Somme. 200fr, "Messalina."

1976, Aug. 7 Litho. *Perf. 14*

C291 A174 60fr blk & multi 1.00 .25
C292 A174 70fr blk & multi 1.00 .25
C293 A174 200fr blk & multi 2.40 .55
a. Souv. sheet of 2, #C292-C293, perf. 13½x14 5.00 2.25
Nos. C291-C293 (3) 4.65 1.00

No. C202 Overprinted: "Journeé / Internationale / de l'Enfance"

1976, Nov. 27 Litho. *Perf. 14*

C294 A139 100fr multi .55 .35

International Children's Day.

Christmas Type

Paintings: 70fr, Holy Family, by Lorenzo Lotto. 105fr, Virgin and Child with Saints, by Jacopo da Pontormo. 200fr, Virgin and Child with Saints, by Lotto.

1976, Dec. 18

C295 A175 70fr multi .55 .25
C296 A175 105fr multi 1.10 .45
C297 A175 200fr multi 1.75 .90
a. Souv. sheet of 2, #C296-C297 1.75 2.00
Nos. C295-C297 (3) 4.30 1.55

No. C284 Overprinted

No. C286 Overprinted

1976, Dec. Photo. *Perf. 14x13*

C298 A172 70fr multi .65 .25
C299 A172 200fr multi 1.75 .65
a. Souvenir sheet of 2 3.50 2.50

Olympic winners. No. C299a (on No. C286a) contains Nos. C285 and C299.

Eyadema Anniversary Type

60fr, National Assembly Building. 100fr, Pres. Eyadema greeting people at Aug. 30th meeting.

1977, Jan. 13 Photo. *Perf. 13x14*

C300 A177 60fr multi .55 .25
C301 A177 100fr multi .85 .35
a. Souv. sheet of 2, #C300-C301 1.75 1.10

Musical Instrument Type

Musical Instruments: 60fr, Atopani. 80fr, African violin, vert. 105fr, African flutes, vert.

1977, Feb. 7 Litho. *Perf. 14*

C302 A178 60fr multi .80 .25
C303 A178 80fr multi 1.00 .25
C304 A178 105fr multi 1.50 .30
a. Souv. sheet of 2, #C303-C304 2.75 1.50
Nos. C302-C304 (3) 3.30 .70

Victor Hugo Type

Victor Hugo in exile on Guernsey Island.

1977, Feb. 26 *Perf. 13x14*

C305 A179 60fr multi .70 .25
a. Souvenir sheet of 2, #952, C305 1.25 .75

For overprint see No. C316.

Beethoven Type

Designs: 100fr, Beethoven's piano and 1818 portrait. 200fr, Beethoven on his deathbed and Holy Trinity Church, Vienna.

1977, Mar. 7 *Perf. 14*

C306 A180 100fr multi 1.25 .35
C307 A180 200fr multi 2.10 .60
a. Souv. sheet of 2, #C306-C307 3.25 1.50

Automobile Type

Early Automobiles: 60fr, Cannstatt-Daimler, 1899, Germany. 70fr, Sunbeam, 1904, England. 100fr, Renault, 1908, France. 200fr, Rolls Royce, 1909, England.

1977, Apr. 11 Litho. *Perf. 14*

C308 A181 60fr multi .80 .25
C309 A181 70fr multi .85 .25
C310 A181 100fr multi 1.10 .35
C311 A181 200fr multi 1.75 .75
a. Souv. sheet of 2, #C310-C311 5.00 1.75
Nos. C308-C311 (4) 5.35 1.50

Lindbergh Type

Designs: 60fr, Lindbergh and son Jon, birds in flight. 85fr, Lindbergh home in Kent, England. 90fr, Spirit of St. Louis over Atlantic Ocean. 100fr, Concorde over NYC.

1977, May 9

C312 A182 60fr multi .50 .25

C313 A182 85fr multi .75 .25
C314 A182 90fr multi .75 .25
C315 A182 100fr multi 1.10 .30
a. Souv. sheet of 2, #C314-C315 2.40 1.20
Nos. C312-C315 (4) 3.70 .90

No. C305 Overprinted: "10ème ANNIVERSAIRE DU / CONSEIL INTERNATIONAL / DE LA LANGUE FRANCAISE"

1977, May 17 Litho. *Perf. 14*
C316 A179 60fr multi .70 .25

10th anniv. of the French Language Council.

Wildlife Type

60fr, Colobus monkeys. 90fr, Chimpanzee, vert. 100fr, Leopard. 200fr, West African manatee.

1977, June 13
C317 A183 60fr multi .70 .25
C318 A183 90fr multi 1.00 .25
C319 A183 100fr multi 1.10 .25
C320 A183 200fr multi 2.40 .35
a. Souv. sheet of 2, #C319-C320 4.00 1.75
Nos. C317-C320 (4) 5.20 .95

Agriculture Type

Designs: 60fr, Corn silo. 100fr, Hoeing and planting by hand. 200fr, Tractor on field.

1977, July 11 Litho. *Perf. 14*
C321 A184 60fr multi .50 .25
C322 A184 100fr multi .85 .25
C323 A184 200fr multi 1.75 .45
a. Souv. sheet of 2, #C322-C323, perf. 13x14 3.40 1.60
Nos. C321-C323 (3) 3.10 .85

Rubens Type

Paintings: 60fr, Heads of Black Men, 1620. 100fr, Anne of Austria, 1624.

1977, Aug. 8
C324 A185 60fr multi .90 .25
C325 A185 100fr multi 1.40 .25
a. Souv. sheet of 2, #C324-C325, perf. 14x13 2.10 1.25

Orbiter Type

90fr, Retrieval of unmanned satellite in space. 100fr, Satellite's return to space after repairs. 200fr, Manned landing of Orbiter.

1977, Oct. 4 Litho. *Perf. 14*
C326 A186 90fr multi, vert. .75 .25
C327 A186 100fr multi .80 .25
C328 A186 200fr multi 1.75 .35
a. Souv. sheet of 2, #C327-C328 3.00 1.50
Nos. C326-C328 (3) 3.30 .75

Lafayette Type

60fr, Lafayette landing in New York, 1824. 105fr, Lafayette and Washington at Valley Forge.

1977, Nov. 7 *Perf. 13x14*
C329 A187 60fr multi .65 .25
C330 A187 105fr multi 1.10 .25
a. Souv. sheet of 2, #C329-C330 1.75 1.00

Christmas Type

Virgin & Child by: 90fr, 200fr, Carlo Crivelli, diff. 1 00fr, Bellini.

1977, Dec. 19 *Perf. 14*
C331 A189 90fr multi .70 .25
C332 A189 100fr multi .90 .25
C333 A189 200fr multi 1.50 .40
a. Souv. sheet of 2, #C332-C333 3.25 1.75
Nos. C331-C333 (3) 3.65 .80

Jenner Type

Designs: 50fr, Edward Jenner. 60fr, Smallpox vaccination clinic, horiz.

1978, Jan. 9 *Perf. 14x13, 13x14*
C334 A190 50fr multi .35 .25
C335 A190 60fr multi .40 .25
a. Souvenir sheet of 2 1.40 .65

No. C335a contains 2 stamps with simulated perforations similar to Nos. C334-C335.

Wright Brothers Type

Designs: 60fr, Orville Wright's 7½-minute flight. 70fr, Orville Wright injured in first aircraft accident, 1908. 200fr, Wrights' bicycle shop, Dearborn, Mich. 300fr, First flight, 1903.

1978, Feb. 6 Litho. *Perf. 14*
C336 A191 60fr multi 1.00 .25
C337 A191 70fr multi 1.10 .25
C338 A191 200fr multi 1.40 .35
C339 A191 300fr multi 2.10 .60
a. Souvenir sheet of 2 9.25 5.25
Nos. C336-C339 (4) 6.25 1.35

No. C339a contains one each of Nos. C338-C339 with simulated perforations.

Port of Lomé Type, 1978

Anchor and: 60fr, Industrial harbor. 100fr, Merchant marine harbor. 200fr, Bird's-eye view of entire harbor.

1978, Apr. 26 Photo. *Perf. 13*
C340 A199 60fr multi .45 .25
C341 A199 100fr multi .75 .25
C342 A199 200fr multi 1.60 .40
a. Souv. sheet of 2, #C341-C342 3.00 1.50
Nos. C340-C342 (3) 2.80 .80

Space Type

Designs: 90fr, Module camera, horiz. 100fr, Module antenna. 200fr, Pioneer, US, in orbit.

1978, May 8 Litho. *Perf. 14*
C343 A200 90fr multi .70 .25
C344 A200 100fr multi .75 .25
C345 A200 200fr multi 1.50 .35
a. Souv. sheet of 2, #C344-C345, perf. 13½x14 2.50 1.50
Nos. C343-C345 (3) 2.95 .75

Soccer Type

Various soccer scenes & Argentina '78 emblem.

1978, June 5 *Perf. 14*
C346 A201 60fr multi .50 .25
C347 A201 80fr multi .65 .25
C348 A201 200fr multi 1.40 .40
C349 A201 300fr multi 2.10 .55
a. Souvenir sheet of 2, #C348-C349, perf. 13½x14 3.25 1.90
Nos. C346-C349 (4) 5.30 1.35

Bicycle Type

History of Bicycle: 60fr, Bantam, 1896, vert. 85fr, Fold-up bicycle for military use, 1897. 90fr, Draisienne, 1816, vert. 100fr, Penny-farthing, 1884, vert.

Perf. 14x13, 13x14
1978, July 10 Photo.
C350 A202 60fr multi .50 .25
C351 A202 85fr multi .70 .25
C352 A202 90fr multi .85 .35
C353 A202 100fr multi 1.10 .35
a. Souv. sheet of 2, #C352-C353 2.75 1.10
Nos. C350-C353 (4) 4.15 1.10

Phonograph Type

60fr, Edison's original phonograph, horiz. 80fr, Emile Berliner's phonograph, 1888. 200fr, Berliner's improved phonograph, 1894, horiz. 300fr, His Master's Voice phonograph, 1900, horiz.

Perf. 13x14, 14x13
1978, July 8 Photo.
C354 A203 60fr multi .45 .25
C355 A203 80fr multi .60 .25
C356 A203 200fr multi 1.40 .35
C357 A203 300fr multi 2.20 .50
a. Souv. sheet of 2, #C356-C357 3.50 2.00
Nos. C354-C357 (4) 4.65 1.25

Red Cross Type

Design: 60fr, Red Cross and other pavilions at Paris Exhibition, 1867.

1978, Sept. 4 Photo. *Perf. 14x13*
C358 A204 60fr pur & red .45 .25
a. Souv. sheet, #1009, C358 1.10 .55

Paintings Type

60fr, Langlois Bridge, by Vincent van Gogh. 70fr, Witches' Sabbath, by Francisco Goya. 90fr, Jesus among the Doctors, by Albrecht Dürer. 200fr, View of Arco, by Dürer.

1978, Nov. 6 Litho. *Perf. 14*
C359 A205 60fr multi .60 .25
C360 A205 70fr multi .65 .30
C361 A205 90fr multi .90 .40
C362 A205 200fr multi 1.75 .70
a. Souv. sheet of 2, #C361-C362 3.25 1.40
Nos. C359-C362 (4) 3.90 1.60

Birth and death anniversaries of famous painters.

Philexafrique II — Essen Issue
Common Design Types

#C363, Warthog and Togo No. C36. #C364, Firecrest and Thurn and Taxis No. 1.

1978, Nov. 1 Litho. *Perf. 13x12½*
C363 CD138 100fr multi 1.40 .50
C364 CD139 100fr multi 1.40 1.00
a. Pair, #C363-C364 + label 3.00 1.50

Congress of Paris Type

60fr, Mail ship "Slieve Roe" 1877, post horn. 105fr, Congress of Paris medal. 200fr, Locomotive, 1870. All horizontal.

1978, Nov. 27 Photo. *Perf. 14x13*
C365 A206 60fr multi .55 .25
C366 A206 105fr multi .90 .45
C367 A206 200fr multi 1.40 .75
a. Souv. sheet of 2, #C366-C367 2.50 1.20
Nos. C365-C367 (3) 3.40 1.40

Christmas Type

Paintings (Virgin and Child): 90fr, 200fr, by Carlo Crivelli, diff. 100fr, by Cosimo Tura.

1978, Dec. 18
C368 A207 90fr multi .75 .35
C369 A207 100fr multi .95 .40
C370 A207 200fr multi 1.75 .70
a. Souv. sheet of 2, #C369-C370 3.25 1.40
Nos. C368-C370 (3) 3.45 1.45

Capt. Cook Type

Designs: 60fr, "Freelove," Whitby Harbor, horiz. 70fr, Trip to Antarctica, 1773, horiz. 90fr, Capt. Cook. 200fr, Sails of Endeavour.

1979, Feb. 12 Litho. *Perf. 14*
C371 A208 60fr multi .50 .25
C372 A208 70fr multi .55 .25
C373 A208 90fr multi .75 .30
C374 A208 200fr multi 1.75 1.25
a. Souv. sheet of 2, #C373-C374 3.00 1.75
Nos. C371-C374 (4) 3.55 2.00

Easter Type

60fr, Resurrection. 100fr, Ascension. 200fr, Jesus appearing to Mary Magdalene.

1979, Apr. 9
C375 A209 60fr multi .45 .25
C376 A209 100fr multi .70 .40
C377 A209 200fr multi 1.50 .70
a. Souv. sheet of 2, #C376-C377 2.75 1.40
Nos. C375-C377 (3) 2.65 1.30

UPU Emblem, Drummer — AP20

Design: 100fr, UPU emblem, hands passing letter, satellites.

1979, June 8 Engr. *Perf. 13*
C378 AP20 60fr multi 1.40 .50
C379 AP20 100fr multi 1.20 1.00

Philexafrique II, Libreville, Gabon, June 8-17.

Einstein Type

Designs: 60fr, Sights and actuality diagram. 85fr, Einstein playing violin, vert. 100fr, Atom symbol and formula of relativity, vert. 200fr, Einstein portrait, vert.

Perf. 14x13, 13x14
1979, July 2 Photo.
C380 A210 60fr multi .50 .25
C381 A210 85fr multi .80 .40
C382 A210 100fr multi .85 .45
C383 A210 200fr multi 1.75 .85
a. Souv. sheet of 2, #C382-C383 3.00 1.50
Nos. C380-C383 (4) 4.05 1.90

Tree Type

Design: 60fr, Man watering tree.

1979, Aug. 13 *Perf. 14x13*
C384 A212 60fr blk & brn .40 .25

Rowland Hill Type

Designs: 90fr, Bellman, England, 1820. 100fr, "Centercycles" used for parcel delivery, 1883, horiz. 200fr, French P.O. railroad car, 1848, horiz.

1979, Aug. 27 Photo.
C385 A213 90fr multi .65 .30
C386 A213 100fr multi .70 .35
C387 A213 200fr multi 1.50 .65
a. Souv. sheet of 2, #C386-C387 2.50 1.25
Nos. C385-C387 (3) 2.85 1.30

Train Type

Historic Locomotives: 60fr, "Le General," 1862. 85fr, Stephenson's, 1843. 100fr, "De Witt Clinton," 1831. 200fr, Joy's "Jenny Lind," 1847.

1979, Oct. 1 Litho. *Perf. 14*
C388 A214 60fr multi .55 .25
C389 A214 85fr multi .70 .45
C390 A214 100fr multi .85 .50
C391 A214 200fr multi 1.75 .90
a. Souv. sheet of 2, #C390-C391 6.00 3.00
Nos. C388-C391 (4) 4.50 2.05

Olympic Type

1980 Olympic Emblems and: 90fr, Ski jump. No. C393, Doubles canoeing, Olympic flame. No. C394, Rings. No. C395a, Bobsledding, horiz. No. C395b, Gymnast, horiz.

1979, Oct. 18 Litho. *Perf. 13½*
C392 A215 90fr multi .70 .30
C393 A215 100fr multi .75 .35
C394 A215 200fr multi 1.40 .65
Nos. C392-C394 (3) 2.95 1.30

Souvenir Sheet

C395 Sheet of 2 2.50 1.25
a. A215 100fr multi .65 .35
b. A215 200fr multi 1.40 .65

Religion Type

Designs: 60fr, Moslems praying. 70fr, Protestant ministers.

1979, Oct. 29 *Perf. 13x14*
C396 A216 60fr multi .50 .25
C397 A216 70fr multi .55 .30
a. Souv. sheet, #C396-C397 1.40 .50

Apollo 11 Type

60fr, Astronaut leaving Apollo 11. 70fr, US flag. 200fr, Sun shield. 300fr, Lunar take-off.

1979, Nov. 5
C398 A217 60fr multi .45 .25
C399 A217 70fr multi .50 .25
C400 A217 200fr multi 1.50 .65
C401 A217 300fr multi 2.10 1.00
a. Souv. sheet of 2, #C400-C401 4.00 1.75
Nos. C398-C401 (4) 4.55 2.10

Telecom Type

Design: 60fr, Telecom 79, dish antenna.

1979, Nov. 26 Photo. *Perf. 14x13*
C402 A218 60fr multi .55 .25

Miniature Sheets

President Eyadema, 10th Anniv. of the People's Republic — AP21

Litho. & Embossed
1979, Nov. 30 *Perf. 13½*
C402A AP21 1000fr In uniform 6.00 —

Imperf
C402B AP21 1000fr In suit, vert. 6.00 —

Exist imperf.

Christmas Type

90fr, Adoration of the Kings. 100fr, Presentation of Infant Jesus. 200fr, Flight into Egypt.

1979, Dec. 17 Litho. *Perf. 14*
C403 A219 90fr multi .55 .35
C404 A219 100fr multi .80 .40
C405 A219 200fr multi 1.75 .70
a. Souv. sheet of 2, #C404-C405 3.50 1.50
Nos. C403-C405 (3) 3.35 1.45

Rotary Type

3-H Emblem and: 90fr, Man reaching for sun. 100fr, Fish, grain. 200fr, Family, globe.

1980, Jan. 14
C406 A220 90fr multi .80 .40
C407 A220 100fr multi .85 .45
C408 A220 200fr multi 1.60 .85
a. Souv. sheet of 2, C407-C408 3.25 1.60
Nos. C406-C408 (3) 3.25 1.70

Rotary Intl., 75th anniv.; 3-H program (health, hunger, humanity).

Winter Olympic Type, 1980

1980, Jan. 31 Litho. *Perf. 13½*

C409 A221 60fr Downhill skiing .45 .25
C410 A221 100fr Speed skating .75 .35
C411 A221 200fr Cross-country skiing 1.40 .65
Nos. C409-C411 (3) 2.60 1.20

Souvenir Sheet

C412 Sheet of 2 2.50 1.25
a. A221 100fr Ski jump, horiz. .65 .35
b. A221 200fr Hockey, horiz. 1.25 .65

Olympic Type

1980, Feb. 29 Litho. *Perf. 13½*

C413 A222 100fr Fencing .65 .45
C414 A222 200fr Pole vault 1.40 .80
C415 A222 300fr Hurdles 2.10 1.25
a. Souv. sheet of 2, #C414-C415 3.75 1.75
Nos. C413-C415 (3) 5.00 2.50

Easter Type

Easter 1980 (Paintings by): 60fr, Lorenzo Lotto. 100fr, El Greco. 200fr, Carlo Crivelli.

1980, Mar. 31 *Perf. 14*

C416 A223 60fr multi .50 .25
C417 A223 100fr multi .75 .35
C418 A223 200fr multi 1.40 .65
a. Souv. sheet of 2, #C417-C418 2.50 1.25
Nos. C416-C418 (3) 2.70 1.20

ASECNA Type

1980, Mar. 24 Litho. *Perf. 12½*

C419 A224 60fr multi .60 .25

Telecommunications Type

1980, May 17 Photo. *Perf. 13½x14*

C420 A225 60fr "17 MAI", vert. .60 .25

Red Cross Type

1980, June 16 Photo. *Perf. 14x13*

C421 A226 60fr Nurses, patient .60 .25

Jules Verne Type

Designs: 60fr, Rocket (From Earth to Moon). 80fr, Around the World in 80 Days. 100fr, Rocket and moon (From Earth to Moon). 200fr, Octopus (20,000 Leagues Under the Sea).

1980, July 14 Litho. *Perf. 14*

C422 A227 60fr multi .45 .25
C423 A227 80fr multi .55 .25
C424 A227 100fr multi .80 .35
C425 A227 200fr multi 1.40 .65
a. Souv. sheet of 2, #C424-C425, perf. 13½x14 2.50 1.25
Nos. C422-C425 (4) 3.45 1.45

Ingres Type

Ingres Paintings: 90fr, Jupiter and Thetis. 100fr, Countess d'Haussonville. 200fr, "Tu Marcellus Eris."

1980, Aug. 29 Litho. *Perf. 14*

C426 A228 90fr multi .80 .30
C427 A228 100fr multi .85 .35
C428 A228 200fr multi 1.60 .65
a. Souv. sheet of 2, #C427-C428 3.00 1.25
Nos. C426-C428 (3) 3.25 1.30

Famous Men Type

90fr, Salvador Allende, vert. 100fr, Pope Paul VI, vert. 200fr, Jomo Kenyatta, vert.

1980, Feb. 11 Litho. *Perf. 14x13*

C429 A231 90fr ultra & lt bl grn 1.00 .30
C430 A231 100fr pur & pink 1.10 .35
C431 A231 200fr brn & yel bis 2.00 .65
a. Souv. sheet of 2, #C430-C431 2.50 1.25
Nos. C429-C431 (3) 4.10 1.30

Human Rights Type

1980, Oct. 13 *Perf. 13x14*

C432 A233 60fr Map of Americas .40 .25
C433 A233 150fr Map of Africa 1.00 .50
a. Souv. sheet of 2, #C432-C433 1.75 1.25

American Order of Rosicrucians Emblem — AP22

1980, Nov. 17 Litho. *Perf. 13*

C434 AP22 60fr multi .60 .25

General Conclave of the American Order of Rosicrucians, meeting of French-speaking countries, Lome, Aug.

Christmas Type

Designs: 100fr, Cologne Cathedral, Germany, 13th cent. 150fr, Notre Dame, Paris, 12th cent. 200fr, Canterbury Cathedral, England, 11th cent.

1980, Dec. 22 *Perf. 14½x13½*

C435 A234 100fr multi .70 .35
C436 A234 150fr multi 1.10 .50
C437 A234 200fr multi 1.40 .65
a. Souv. sheet of 2, #C436-C437 3.00 1.40
Nos. C435-C437 (3) 3.20 1.50

Hotel Type of 1981

1981, Feb. 2 Litho. *Perf. 12½x13*

C437B A236 60fr multi .60 .25

Easter Type of 1981

Rembrandt Paintings: 100fr, Artist's Mother. 200fr, Man in a Ruff.

1981, Apr. 13 Litho. *Perf. 14½x13½*

C438 A237 100fr multi .90 .40
C439 A237 200fr multi 1.75 .70
a. Souv. sheet of 2, #C438-C439 3.50 1.50

Market Type

1981, Mar. 8 Litho. *Perf. 14*

C440 A230 90fr Fabric dealer .60 .30
C441 A230 100fr Bananas .65 .35
C442 A230 200fr Clay pottery 1.40 .65
C443 A230 250fr Setting up 1.60 .80
C444 A230 500fr Selling 3.50 1.60
C445 A230 1000fr Measuring grain 6.50 3.50
Nos. C440-C445 (6) 14.25 7.20

For overprints see Nos. C486-C487.

Bird Type

50fr, Violet-backed sunbird. 100fr, Red bishop.

Perf. 13½x14½

1981, Aug. 10 Litho.

C446 A238 50fr multi .80 .25
C447 A238 100fr multi 1.50 .35
a. Souv. sheet, #1110, C447 5.50 2.50

IYD Type

90fr, Carpenter. 200fr, Basketball players. 300fr, Weaver.

1981, Aug. 31 *Perf. 14*

C448 A240 90fr multi .80 .40
C449 A240 200fr multi 1.60 .85

Souvenir Sheet

C449A A240 300fr multi 2.75 1.60

Picasso Type

90fr, Violin and Bottle on Table, 1916. 100fr, Baboon and Young. 200fr, Mandolin and Clarinet, 1914.

1981, Sept. 14 *Perf. 14½x13½*

C450 A241 90fr multi .90 .40
C451 A241 100fr multi 1.10 .50
C452 A241 200fr multi 2.40 .90
a. Souv. sheet of 2, #C451-C452 3.50 1.40
Nos. C450-C452 (3) 4.70 1.80

World Heritage Year Type

100fr, Cracow Museum, Poland. 200fr, Goree Isld., Senegal.

1981, Sept. 28 *Perf. 13½x14½*

C453 A242 100fr multi .80 .40
C454 A242 200fr multi 1.75 .85
a. Souv. sheet of 2, #C453-C454 2.75 1.25

Space Type

1981, Nov. *Perf. 14*

C455 A243 90fr multi .65 .25
C456 A243 100fr multi .70 .25

Souvenir Sheet

Perf. 13x14

C456A A243 300fr multi, vert. 2.25 1.25

10th anniv. of Soyuz 10 (90fr) and Apollo 14 (100fr).

Christmas Type

Rubens Paintings: 100fr, Adoration of the Kings. 200fr, Virgin and Child. 300fr, Virgin giving Chasuble to St. Idefonse.

Perf. 14½x13½

1981, Dec. 10 Litho.

C457 A244 100fr multi .70 .35
C458 A244 200fr multi 1.50 .65
C459 A244 300fr multi 2.10 1.00
a. Souv. sheet of 2, #C458-C459 4.00 1.90
Nos. C457-C459 (3) 4.30 2.00

West African Rice Development Assoc. Type

1981, Dec. 21 Litho. *Perf. 12½*

C461 A236a 105fr yel & multi .70 .35

Liberation Type

Designs: 105fr, Citizens holding hands, Pres. Eyadema, vert. 130fr, Hotel.

1982, Jan. 13 Litho. *Perf. 12½*

C462 A245 105fr multi .70 .35
C463 A245 130fr multi .90 .40

Scouting Year Type

1982, Feb. 25 Litho. *Perf. 14*

C464 A246 90fr Semaphore .75 .30
C465 A246 120fr Tower 1.00 .40
C466 A246 130fr Scouts, canoe 1.10 .40
C467 A246 135fr Scouts, tent 1.10 .45
Nos. C464-C467 (4) 3.95 1.55

Souvenir Sheet

Perf. 13x14

C468 A246 500fr Baden-Powell 4.25 1.60

Easter Type

1982, Apr. *Perf. 14x14½*

C469 A247 105fr multi .70 .35
C470 A247 120fr multi .80 .40

Souvenir Sheet

C471 A247 500fr multi 4.00 1.60

PHILEXFRANCE '82 Intl. Stamp Exhibition, Paris, June 11-21 — AP23

1982 Litho. *Perf. 13*

C472 AP23 90fr shown .70 .30
C473 AP23 105fr ROMOLYMPHIL '82, vert. .90 .35

Issue dates: 90fr, June 11; 105fr, May 19.

Butterfly Type

90fr, Euxanthe eurionome. 105fr, Mylothris rhodope.
500fr, Papilio zalmoxis.

1982, July 15 *Perf. 14½x14*

C474 A248 90fr multi 1.60 .40
C475 A248 105fr multi 1.75 .45

Souvenir Sheet

C476 A248 500fr multi 4.25 1.60

World Cup Type

1982, July 26 *Perf. 14x14½*

C477 A249 105fr multi .80 .35
C478 A249 200fr multi 1.40 .65
C479 A249 300fr multi 2.10 1.00
Nos. C477-C479 (3) 4.30 2.00

Souvenir Sheet

C480 A249 500fr multi 3.75 1.65

For overprints see Nos. 1152-1155.

Pre-Olympics, 1984 Los Angeles — AP24

1983, Oct. 3 Photo. *Perf. 12½*

C481 AP24 70fr Boxing .55 .25
C482 AP24 90fr Hurdles .70 .25
C483 AP24 105fr Pole vault .80 .25
C484 AP24 130fr Runner .90 .25
Nos. C481-C484 (4) 2.95 1.00

Souvenir Sheet

C485 AP24 500fr Runner, diff. 4.00 1.50

Nos. C443-C444 Overprinted: "19E CONGRES UPU HAMBOURG 1984"

1984, June Litho. *Perf. 14*

C486 A230 250fr multi 1.75 1.00
C487 A230 500fr multi 3.75 2.00

1984 Summer Olympics — AP25

1984, July 27 *Perf. 13*

C488 AP25 70fr Pole vault .45 .25
C489 AP25 90fr Bicycling .45 .25
C490 AP25 120fr Soccer .75 .25
C491 AP25 250fr Boxing 1.50 .40
C492 AP25 400fr Running 2.25 .65
Nos. C488-C492 (5) 5.40 1.80

Souvenir Sheet

C493 AP25 1000fr like 120fr, without flag 7.50 6.50

Nos. C488-C490, C493 vert.

Olympic Champions AP26

No. C494, Jim Thorpe, US. No. C495, Jesse Owens, US. No. C496, Muhammad Ali, US. No. C497, Bob Beamon, US.
No. C498, Bill Steinkraus, US. No. C499, New Zealand rowing team. No. C500, Pakistani hockey team. No. C501, Yukio Endo, Japan.

1984, Nov. 15 Litho. *Perf. 15*

C494 AP26 500fr multi 7.25 3.25
C495 AP26 500fr multi 7.25 3.25
C496 AP26 500fr multi 40.00 3.25
C497 AP26 500fr multi 7.25 3.25
Nos. C494-C497 (4) 61.75 13.00

Souvenir Sheets

C498 AP26 500fr multi 7.25 3.25
C499 AP26 500fr multi 7.25 3.25
C500 AP26 500fr multi 7.25 3.25
C501 AP26 500fr multi 7.25 3.25

West German Olympians

No. C502, Dietmar Mogenburg. No. C503, Fredy Schmidtke. No. C504, Matthias Behr. No. C505, Sabine Everts.
No. C506, Karl-Heinz Radschinsky. No. C507, Pasquale Passarelli. No. C508, Michale Gross. No. C509, Jurgen Hingsen.

1984, Nov. 15

C502 AP26 500fr multi 7.25 3.25
C503 AP26 500fr multi 7.25 3.25
C504 AP26 500fr multi 7.25 3.25
C505 AP26 500fr multi 7.25 3.25
Nos. C502-C505 (4) 29.00 13.00

Souvenir Sheets

C506 AP26 500fr multi 7.25 3.25
C507 AP26 500fr multi 7.25 3.25
C508 AP26 500fr multi 7.25 3.25
C509 AP26 500fr multi 7.25 3.25

For overprints see Nos. C521-C536, C563.

Peace and Human Rights — AP28

230fr, Map of Togo, globe, doves. 270fr, Palm tree, emblem. 500fr, Opencast mining

operation. 1000fr, Human Rights Monument, UN, NYC.

1985, Jan. 14 Litho. Perf. 13½x14

C510	AP28	230fr multi	1.50	.25
C511	AP28	270fr multi	1.90	.30
C512	AP28	350fr multi	3.50	.50
C513	AP28	1000fr multi	7.00	1.00
	Nos. C510-C513 (4)		13.90	2.05

Tribal Dances AP29

120fr, Adifo, Adangbe. 135fr, Fouet (whip), Kente. 290fr, Idjombi, Pagouda. 500fr, Moba, Dapaong.

1985, July Perf. 15x14

C514	AP29	120fr multicolored	.85	.25
C515	AP29	135fr multicolored	.85	.25
C516	AP29	290fr multicolored	2.00	.30
C517	AP29	500fr multicolored	3.50	.50
	Nos. C514-C517 (4)		7.20	1.30

Visit of Pope John Paul II — AP30

90fr, The Pope outside Lome Cathedral. 130fr, Blessing crowd in St. Peter's Square. 500fr, Greeting Pres. Eyadema.

1985, Aug. 9 Perf. 13

C518	AP30	90fr multi	.75	.25
C519	AP30	130fr multi, vert.	1.25	.25
C520	AP30	500fr multi	3.50	.50
	Nos. C518-C520 (3)		5.50	1.00

Nos. C495, C497, C499, C502, C505-508 Overprinted with Winners Names, Country and Type of Olympic Medal

No. C521, Kirk Baptiste, US. No. C522, Carl Lewis, US. No. C523, Patrik Sjoberg, Sweden. No. C524, Glynis Nunn, Australia.

No. C525, Rowing eights, Canada. No. C526, Rolf Milser, W. Germany. No. C527, Takashi Irie, Japan. No. C528, Frederic Delcourt, France.

1985, Aug. Perf. 15

C521	AP26	500fr multicolored	6.50	1.50
C522	AP26	500fr multicolored	6.50	1.50
C523	AP26	500fr multicolored	6.50	1.50
C524	AP26	500fr multicolored	6.50	1.50
	Nos. C521-C524 (4)		26.00	6.00

Souvenir Sheets

C525	AP26	500fr multicolored	3.50	3.00
C526	AP26	500fr multicolored	3.50	3.00
C527	AP26	500fr multicolored	3.50	3.00
C528	AP26	500fr multicolored	3.50	3.00

Nos. C494, C496, C503-C504, C498, C500, C501, C509 Ovptd. with Winners Names, Country and Type of Olympic Medal

No. C529, Italy. No. C530, Kevin Barry. No. C531, Rolf Golz. No. C532, Philippe Boisse. No. C533, Karen Stives. No. C534, R.F.A. (West Germany). No. C535, Koji Gushiken. No. C536, Daley Thompson.

1985, Sept. 19 Litho. Perf. 15

C529	AP26	500fr multicolored	6.50	1.50
C530	AP26	500fr multicolored	6.50	1.50
C531	AP26	500fr multicolored	6.50	1.50
C532	AP26	500fr multicolored	6.50	1.50
	Nos. C529-C532 (4)		26.00	6.00

Souvenir Sheets

C533	AP26	500fr multicolored	3.50	3.00
C534	AP26	500fr multicolored	3.50	3.00
C535	AP26	500fr multicolored	3.50	3.00
C536	AP26	500fr multicolored	3.50	3.00

Traditional Instruments — AP31

Youth and Development — AP32

Designs: No. C537, Xylophone, Kante horn, tambour. No. C538, Bongo drums, castanets, bassar horn. No. C539, Communications. No. C540, Agriculture and industry.

1985 Litho. Perf. 13

C537	AP31	100fr multi	.90	.60
C538	AP31	100fr multi	.90	.60
a.		Pair, #C537-C538	3.00	3.00
C539	AP32	200fr multi	1.75	1.25
C540	AP32	200fr multi	1.75	1.25
a.		Pair, #C539-C540	7.50	7.50
	Nos. C537-C540 (4)		5.30	3.70

PHILEXAFRICA '85, Lome, Togo, 11/16-24. Issued: 100fr, Nov. 4; 200fr, Nov. 16.

No. 1274 Ovptd. with Organization Emblem and "80e Anniversaire du Rotary International."

1985, Nov. 15 Litho. Perf. 15

Souvenir Sheet

C541	A267	1000fr multi	20.00 6.50

Nos. 1254-1255, 1258 Ovptd. "10e ANNIVERSAIRE DE APOLLO-SOYUZ" in 1 or 2 lines

1985, Dec. 27 Litho. Perf. 15

C542	A265	90fr multi	1.25	.40
C543	A265	500fr multi	6.75	2.00

Souvenir Sheet

C544	A265	1000fr multi	8.50 2.90

Nos. 1294-1295, 1297 Ovptd. "75e ANNIVERSAIRE DE LA MORT DE HENRI DUNANT FONDATEUR DE LA CROIX ROUGE" in 2 or 4 lines

1985, Dec. 27

C545	A270	400fr multi	4.75	1.50
C546	A270	625fr multi	6.25	2.00

Souvenir Sheet

C547	A270	1000fr multi	7.50 6.00

Statue of Liberty, Cent. — AP33

70fr, Eiffel Tower. 90fr, Statue of Liberty. 500fr, Empire State Building.

1986, Apr. 10 Perf. 13

C548	AP33	70fr multicolored	.55	.25
C549	AP33	90fr multicolored	.65	.25
C550	AP33	500fr multicolored	3.75	1.40
	Nos. C548-C550 (3)		4.95	1.90

Nos. 1237-1240 Ovptd. with AMERIPEX '86 Emblem

1986, May 22 Perf. 11

C551	A262	500fr multi	6.50	1.40
C552	A262	1000fr multi	12.50	2.75

Souvenir Sheets

Perf. 14

C553	A262	1000fr No. 1239	8.50 3.50
C554	A262	1000fr No. 1240	8.50 3.50

Air Africa, 25th Anniv. AP34

1986, Dec. 29 Litho. Perf. 12½x13

C555	AP34	90fr multi	.75 .25

Konrad Adenauer (1876-1967) West German Chancellor — AP35

120fr, At podium. No. C557, 500fr, With Pres. Kennedy, 1962. No. C558, 500fr, Portrait, vert.

1987, July 15 Litho. Perf. 12½x13

C556	AP35	120fr multi	.90 .60
C557	AP35	500fr multi	3.50 3.00

Souvenir Sheet

Perf. 13x12½

C558	AP35	500fr multi	3.50 3.00

Berlin, 750th Anniv. AP36

Designs: 90fr, Wilhelm I (1781-1864) coin, Victory statue. 150fr, Frederick III (1831-1888) coin, Brandenburg Gate. 300fr, Wilhelm II (1882-1951) coin, Reichstag building. 750fr, Otto Leopold von Bismarck (1815-1898), first chancellor of the German empire, and Charlottenburg Palace.

1987, Aug. 31 Litho. Perf. 13½

C559	AP36	90fr multi	.60	.30
C560	AP36	150fr multi	1.00	.50
C561	AP36	300fr multi	2.00	1.00
	Nos. C559-C561 (3)		3.60	1.80

Souvenir Sheet

C562	AP36	750fr multi	5.50 4.25

Nos. C506, 1258, 1273 and 1274 Overprinted in Black for Philatelic Exhibitions

a

b

c

d

1988, Apr. 25 Litho. Perf. 15

Souvenir Sheets

C563	AP26 (a)	500fr #C506	9.50	3.00
C564	A265 (b)	1000fr #1258	10.00	5.50
C565	A265 (c)	1000fr #1273	10.00	5.50
C566	A267 (d)	1000fr #1274	10.00	5.50
	Nos. C563-C566 (4)		39.50	19.50

Additional overprints appear on souvenir sheets away from stamps.

AIR POST SEMI-POSTAL STAMPS

Nursery — SPAP1

Perf. 13½x12½

1942, June 22 Unwmk. Photo.

CB1	SPAP1	1.50fr + 3.50fr green	.55	5.50
CB2	SPAP1	2fr + 6fr brown	.55	5.50
	Set, never hinged		1.40	

Native children's welfare fund.

Nos. CB1-CB2 were issued by the Vichy government in France, but were not placed on sale in Togo.

Colonial Education Fund
Common Design Type

1942, June 22 Engr.

CB3	CD86a	1.20fr + 1.80fr blue & red	.35	5.50
	Set, never hinged		.70	

No. CB3 was issued by the Vichy government in France, but was not placed on sale in Togo.

POSTAGE DUE STAMPS

Postage Due Stamps of Dahomey, 1914 Overprinted

1921 Unwmk. Perf. 14x13½

J1	D2	5c green	.65	.85
J2	D2	10c rose	.65	.90
J3	D2	15c gray	1.25	1.75
J4	D2	20c brown	2.50	2.50
J5	D2	30c blue	2.50	2.75
J6	D2	50c black	2.10	2.50
J7	D2	60c orange	2.10	2.50
J8	D2	1fr violet	3.75	4.50
	Nos. J1-J8 (8)		15.50	18.25

Cotton Field — D3

1925 Typo. Unwmk.

J9	D3	2c blue & blk	.25	.35
J10	D3	4c dl red & blk	.25	.35
J11	D3	5c ol grn & blk	.25	.35
J12	D3	10c cerise & blk	.35	.45
J13	D3	15c orange & blk	.70	.85
J14	D3	20c red vio & blk	.35	.55
J15	D3	25c gray & blk	1.10	1.10
J16	D3	30c ocher & blk	.35	.55
J17	D3	50c brown & blk	1.10	1.10
J18	D3	60c green & blk	1.10	1.10
J19	D3	1fr dk vio & blk	1.10	1.10
	Nos. J9-J19 (11)		6.90	7.85

Type of
1925 Issue
Surcharged

1927

J20	D3	2fr on 1fr rose red & vio	7.00 7.00
J21	D3	3fr on 1fr org brn, blk & ultra	7.00 7.00

Mask — D4

1941   **Engr.**   **Perf. 13**

J22	D4	5c brown black	.25 .30
J23	D4	10c yellow green	.25 .30
J24	D4	15c carmine	.25 .30
J25	D4	20c ultra	.30 .30
J26	D4	30c chestnut	.55 .65
J27	D4	50c olive green	1.40 1.75
J28	D4	60c violet	.70 .85
J29	D4	1fr light blue	.90 1.00
J30	D4	2fr orange vermilion	.85 .90
J31	D4	3fr rose violet	.85 1.10
		Nos. J22-J31 (10)	6.30 7.50
		Set, never hinged	8.00

For type D4 without "RF," see Nos. J31A-J31F.

Type of 1941 Without "RF"

1942-44

J31A	D4	5c brown black	.25
J31B	D4	10c green & violet	.30
J31C	D4	15c car rose & brn	.35
J31D	D4	30c brown & black	.55
J31E	D4	2fr brn org & brn vio	.70
J31F	D4	3fr violet & green	.70
		Nos. J31A-J31F (6)	2.85
		Set, never hinged	3.50

Nos. J31A-J31F were issued by the Vichy government in France, but were not placed on sale in Togo.

Catalogue values for unused stamps in this section, from this point to the end of the section, are for Never Hinged items.

Carved Figures — D5

1947

J32	D5	10c brt ultra	.30 .30
J33	D5	30c red	.30 .30
J34	D5	50c dp yellow grn	.30 .30
J35	D5	1fr chocolate	.50 .50
J36	D5	2fr carmine	.50 .50
J37	D5	3fr gray blk	.50 .50
J38	D5	4fr ultra	.80 .80
J39	D5	5fr sepia	1.10 .90
J40	D5	10fr dp orange	1.10 1.00
J41	D5	20fr dk blue vio	1.50 1.40
		Nos. J32-J41 (10)	6.90 6.50

Republic

Konkomba
Helmet — D6

1957   **Engr.**   **Perf. 14x13**

J42	D6	1fr brt violet	.25 .25
J43	D6	2fr brt orange	.25 .25
J44	D6	3fr dk gray	.25 .25
J45	D6	4fr brt red	.25 .25
J46	D6	5fr ultra	.25 .25
J47	D6	10fr dp green	.35 .35
J48	D6	20fr dp claret	.50 .50
		Nos. J42-J48 (7)	2.10 2.10

Konkomba
Helmet — D7

1959   **Perf. 14x13**

J49	D7	1fr orange brn	.25 .35
J50	D7	2fr lt blue grn	.25 .35
J51	D7	3fr orange	.25 .35
J52	D7	4fr blue	.25 .45
J53	D7	5fr lilac rose	.25 .45
J54	D7	10fr violet blue	.45 .65
J55	D7	20fr black	.80 .85
		Nos. J49-J55 (7)	2.50 3.45

Type of Regular Issue

Shells: 1fr, Conus papilionaceus. 2fr, Marginella faba. 3fr, Cypraea stercoraria. 4fr, Strombus latus. 5fr, Costate cockle (sea shell). 10fr, Cancellaria cancellata. 15fr, Cymbium pepo. 20fr, Tympanotomus radula.

1964-65   **Unwmk.**   **Photo.**   **Perf. 14**
Size: 20x25½mm

J56	A47	1fr gray grn & red brn ('65)	.25 .25
J57	A47	2fr tan & ol grn ('65)	.25 .25
J58	A47	3fr gray, brn & yel ('65)	.25 .25
J59	A47	4fr tan & multi ('65)	.30 .25
J60	A47	5fr sep, org & grn	.70 .30
J61	A47	10fr sl bl, brn & bis	.95 .40
J62	A47	15fr grn & brn	2.75 1.00
J63	A47	20fr sl, dk brn & yel	3.25 1.25
		Nos. J56-J63 (8)	8.70 3.95

Tomatoes — D8

1969-70   **Litho.**   **Perf. 14**

J64	D8	5fr yellow & multi	.25 .25
J65	D8	10fr blue & multi	.45 .25
J66	D8	15fr multi ('70)	.70 .30
J67	D8	20fr multi ('70)	1.00 .40
		Nos. J64-J67 (4)	2.40 1.20

Market Type

1981, Mar. 8   **Litho.**   **Perf. 14**
Size: 23x32mm, 32x23mm

J68	A230	5fr Millet, vert.	.25 .25
J69	A230	10fr Packaged goods	.25 .25
J70	A230	25fr Chickens	.25 .25
J71	A230	50fr Ivory vendor	.50 .25
		Nos. J68-J71 (4)	1.25 1.00

OFFICIAL STAMPS

Catalogue values for unused stamps in this section are for never hinged items.

O1

1991?   **Litho.**   **Perf. 13½**

O1	O1	15fr multicolored	— —
O2	O1	100fr multicolored	— —
O3	O1	125fr multicolored	— —
O4	O1	500fr multicolored	— —

1991?

O5	O1	10fr multicolored	— —
O6	O1	90fr yellow & multi	— —

1991?

O7	O1	180fr ap grn & multi	— —

1991

O8	O1	50fr yellow & multi	— —
O9	O1	300fr ap grn & multi	— —

The editors would like information on dates of issue and stamps of other denominations. The catalogue numbers will change.

TOKELAU

ˈtō-kə-ˌlau

(Union Islands)

LOCATION — Pacific Ocean 300 miles north of Apia, Western Samoa
GOVT. — A dependency of New Zealand
AREA — 4 sq. mi.
POP. — 1,487 (1996)

The Tokelau islands consist of three atolls: Atafu, Nukunono and Fakaofo, which span 100 miles of ocean.

12 Pence = 1 Shilling
100 Cents = 1 Dollar (1967)

Catalogue values for all unused stamps in this country are for Never Hinged items.

Map and Scene on Atafu — A1

Nukunono Dwelling and Map — A2

Fakaofo Shore Line and Map — A3

Perf. 13½x13

1948, June 22   **Wmk. 253**   **Engr.**

1	A1	½p red brown & rose lilac	.25 .45
2	A2	1p dp green & orange brn	.25 .35
3	A3	2p deep ultra & green	.30 .35
		Nos. 1-3 (3)	.80 1.15

For surcharges see Nos. 5, 9-11.

Coronation Issue

Queen Elizabeth II — A3a

1953, May 25   **Photo.**   **Perf. 14x14½**

4	A3a	3p brown	3.75 2.75

No. 1 Srchd. in Black

Perf. 13½x13

1956, Mar. 27   **Engr.**   **Wmk. 253**

5	A1	1sh on ½p	4.00 4.00

Postal-Fiscal Type of New Zealand, 1950, Surcharged

Wmk. 253

1966, Nov.   **Typo.**   **Perf. 14**

6	A109	6p light blue	1.75 1.50
7	A109	8p light green	2.25 1.75
8	A109	2sh pink	2.75 2.00
		Nos. 6-8 (3)	6.75 5.25

Nos. 1-3 Surcharged with New Value and Dots Obliterating Old Denomination

1967, July 10   **Engr.**   **Perf. 13½x13**

9	A2	1c on 1p	.45 1.25
10	A3	2c on 2p	.90 1.75
11	A1	10c on ½p	3.25 3.50
		Nos. 9-11 (3)	4.60 6.50

The 1c and 2c surcharges include two dots, the 10c surcharge has only one.

Postal Fiscal Type of New Zealand, 1950, Surcharged

1967, July 10   **Typo.**   **Perf. 14**

12	A109	3c light lilac	.35 .35
13	A109	5c light blue	.70 .70
14	A109	7c light green	1.10 1.10
15	A109	20c pink	2.50 2.50
		Nos. 12-15 (4)	4.65 4.65

1877, British Protectorate — A4

History of Tokelau: 10c, 1916, part of Gilbert and Ellice Islands Colony. 15c, 1925, administration transferred to New Zealand. 20c, 1948, New Zealand Territory.

Perf. 13x12½

1969, Aug. 8   **Litho.**   **Wmk. 253**

16	A4	5c ultra, yellow & blk	1.10 .45
17	A4	10c rose red, yel & blk	1.25 .85
18	A4	15c dull grn, yel & blk	1.40 1.40
19	A4	20c brown, yel & blk	1.75 1.75
		Nos. 16-19 (4)	5.50 4.45

Nativity, by Federico Fiori — A4a

1969, Oct. 1   **Photo.**   **Perf. 13½x14**

20	A4a	2c multicolored	.40 .40

Christmas.

Adoration, by Correggio — A4b

Perf. 12½

1970, Oct. 1   **Unwmk.**   **Litho.**

21	A4b	2c multicolored	.40 .40

Christmas.

"Dolphin," 1765, Map of Atafu — A5

Designs: 10c, "Pandora," 1791, and map of Nukunono. 25c, "General Jackson," 1835, and map of Fakaofo, horiz.

1970, Dec. 9   Unwmk.   Perf. 13½
22	A5	5c yellow & multi	1.10	.80
23	A5	10c multicolored	2.50	1.50
24	A5	25c pink & multi	5.50	4.50
		Nos. 22-24 (3)	9.10	6.80

Discovery of Tokelau Islands.

Fan — A6

Native Handicrafts: 2c, Round vessel. 3c, Hexagonal box. 5c, Shoulder bag. 10c, Handbag. 15c, Jewelry box with beads. 20c, Outrigger canoe model. 25c, Fish hooks.

1971, Oct. 20   Litho.   Perf. 14
25	A6	1c olive & multi	.25	.25
26	A6	2c red & multi	.30	.30
27	A6	3c dk violet & multi	.45	.45
28	A6	5c dull blue & multi	.50	.50
29	A6	10c dp orange & multi	.60	.60
30	A6	15c emerald & multi	.85	.85
31	A6	20c multicolored	1.10	1.10
32	A6	25c violet blue & multi	1.25	1.25
		Nos. 25-32 (8)	5.30	5.30

Windmill Pump, Map of Atafu — A7

South Pacific Commission Emblem and: 10c, Community well, map of Fakaofo. 15c, Eradication of rhinoceros beetle, map of Nukunono. 20c, members.

1972, Sept. 6   Litho.   Perf. 14x13½
33	A7	5c lt blue grn & multi	.90	.30
34	A7	10c grnsh blue & multi	1.10	.55
35	A7	15c lilac & multi	1.30	.70
36	A7	20c violet bl & multi	1.75	1.10
		Nos. 33-36 (4)	5.05	2.65

South Pacific Commission, 25th anniversary. On 15c, "PACIFIC" reads "PACFIC."

Horny Coral — A8

1973, Sept. 12   Litho.   Perf. 13x13½
37	A8	3c shown	1.40	1.10
38	A8	5c Soft coral	1.40	1.25
39	A8	15c Mushroom coral	2.25	2.10
40	A8	25c Staghorn coral	2.75	2.50
		Nos. 37-40 (4)	7.80	6.95

Cowrie (Cypraea Mauritiana) A9

Cowrie shells: 5c, Cypraea tigris. 15c, Cypraea talpa. 25c, Cypraea argus.

1974, Nov. 13   Litho.   Perf. 14
41	A9	3c apple grn & multi	1.50	1.10
42	A9	5c dk blue & multi	1.75	1.10
43	A9	15c blue & multi	2.50	2.25
44	A9	25c green & multi	2.75	2.50
		Nos. 41-44 (4)	8.50	6.95

Moorish Idol — A10

Fish: 10c, Long-nosed butterflyfish. 15c, Lined butterflyfish. 25c, Red firefish.

1975, Nov. 19   Litho.   Perf. 14
45	A10	5c blue & multi	.70	.30
46	A10	10c brown & multi	1.25	.65
47	A10	15c lilac & multi	1.90	1.10
48	A10	25c multicolored	3.25	2.10
		Nos. 45-48 (4)	7.10	4.15

Canoe Making A11

Designs: 2c, Reef fishing. 3c, Woman preparing pandanus leaves for weaving. 5c, Communal kitchen (umu). 9c, Wood carving. 20c, Husking coconuts. 50c, Wash day. $1, Meal time. 9c, 20c, 50c, $1, vertical.

1976, Oct. 27   Litho.   Perf. 14
49	A11	1c pink & multi	.55	1.10
50	A11	2c multicolored	.40	1.40
51	A11	3c lt blue & multi	.35	.70
52	A11	5c yellow & multi	.40	.70
53	A11	9c bister & multi	.25	.85
54	A11	20c multicolored	.25	.70
55	A11	50c tan & multi	.35	.85
56	A11	$1 multicolored	.70	2.10
		Nos. 49-56 (8)	3.25	8.40

1981, July 17   Perf. 15
49a	A11	1c	.50	.65
51a	A11	3c	.50	.65
52a	A11	5c	.50	.65
53a	A11	9c	.90	1.00
54a	A11	20c	.90	1.00
55a	A11	50c	1.75	2.00
56a	A11	$1	5.00	5.00
		Nos. 49a-56a (7)	10.05	10.95

White Tern — A12

Birds of Tokelau: 10c, Turnstone. 15c, White-capped noddy. 30c, Brown noddy.

1977, Nov. 16   Litho.   Perf. 14½x15
57	A12	8c multicolored	.50	.35
58	A12	10c multicolored	.65	.40
59	A12	15c multicolored	.80	.65
60	A12	30c multicolored	1.75	1.40
		Nos. 57-60 (4)	3.70	2.80

Westminster Abbey — A13

10c, King Edward's Chair. 15c, Scepter, Crown, Orb, Bible and Staff of State. 30c, Elizabeth II.

1978, June 28   Litho.   Perf. 14
61	A13	8c multicolored	.25	.25
62	A13	10c multicolored	.35	.35
63	A13	15c multicolored	.55	.55
64	A13	30c multicolored	1.00	1.00
		Nos. 61-64 (4)	2.15	2.15

25th anniv. of coronation of Elizabeth II.

Canoe Racing A14

Designs: Various canoe races.

1978, Nov. 8   Litho.   Perf. 13½x14
65	A14	8c multicolored	.40	.40
66	A14	12c multicolored	.55	.55
67	A14	15c multicolored	.65	.65
68	A14	30c multicolored	1.10	1.10
		Nos. 65-68 (4)	2.70	2.70

1979, Nov. 7   Photo.   Perf. 14
69	A14	10c Rugby	.35	.35
70	A14	15c Cricket	.70	.70
71	A14	20c Rugby, diff.	.70	.70
72	A14	30c Cricket, diff.	.85	.85
		Nos. 69-72 (4)	2.60	2.60

1980, Nov. 5   Litho.   Perf. 13½
73	A14	10c Surfing	.25	.25
74	A14	20c Surfing, diff.	.30	.25
75	A14	30c Swimming	.45	.40
76	A14	50c Swimming, diff.	.60	.55
		Nos. 73-76 (4)	1.60	1.45

1981, Nov. 4   Photo.   Perf. 14
77	A14	10c Pole vaulting, vert.	.35	.35
78	A14	20c Volleyball, vert.	.40	.35
79	A14	30c Running, vert.	.50	.40
80	A14	50c Volleyball, vert., diff.	.60	.60
		Nos. 77-80 (4)	1.85	1.70

Wood Carving — A15

1982, May 5   Litho.   Perf. 13½x13
81	A15	10s shown	.35	.35
82	A15	22s Bow-drilling sea shells	.35	.35
83	A15	34s Bowl finishing	.50	.50
84	A15	60s Basket weaving	1.00	1.00
		Nos. 81-84 (4)	2.20	2.20

Octopus Lure Fishing — A16

Designs: Fishing Methods.

1982, Nov. 3   Litho.   Perf. 14
85	A16	5s shown	.25	.25
86	A16	18s Multiple-hook	.25	.25
87	A16	23s Ruvettus	.25	.25
88	A16	34s Netting flying fish	.40	.40
89	A16	63s Noose	.70	.70
90	A16	75s Bonito	.85	.85
		Nos. 85-90 (6)	2.70	2.70

Outrigger Canoe A17

1983, May 4   Litho.   Perf. 13½x14
91	A17	5s shown	.25	.25
92	A17	18s Whale boat	.25	.25
93	A17	23s Aluminium whale boat	.25	.25
94	A17	34s Alia fishing boat	.30	.30
95	A17	63s Cargo ship	.65	.65
96	A17	75s Seaplane	.90	.90
		Nos. 91-96 (6)	2.60	2.60

Traditional Games A18

1983, Nov. 2   Litho.   Perf. 14
97	A18	5s Javelin throwing	.25	.25
98	A18	18s Tifaga string game	.25	.25
99	A18	23s Fire making	.25	.25
100	A18	34s Shell throwing	.25	.25
101	A18	50s Handball	.50	.50
102	A18	75s Mass wrestling	.75	.75
		Nos. 97-102 (6)	2.25	2.25

Planting, Harvesting Copra — A19

Copra Industry: b, Husking, splitting. c, Drying, cutting. d, Bagging, weighing. e, Shipping. Continuous design.

1984, May 2   Litho.   Perf. 13½x13
103		Strip of 5	3.00	3.00
a.-e.		A19 48s any single	.45	.45

Local Fish — A20

1984, Dec. 5   Litho.   Perf. 14½x14
104	A20	1c Manini	.25	.25
105	A20	2c Hahave	.25	.25
106	A20	5c Uloulo	.25	.25
107	A20	9c Ume Ihu	.25	.25
108	A20	23c Lifilafi	.30	.30
109	A20	34c Fagamea	.45	.45
110	A20	50c Kakahi	.55	.55
111	A20	75c Palu Po	1.00	1.00
112	A20	$1 Mokoha	1.25	1.25
113	A20	$2 Hakula	2.25	2.25
		Nos. 104-113 (10)	6.80	6.80

No. 110 exists overprinted "STAMPEX 86 / 4-10 AUGUST / 1986." These overprinted stamps were not available at post offices in Tokelau. Used examples were sent to the islands for cancellation.

Trees, Fruits and Herbs — A21

1985, June 26   Litho.   Perf. 13½
114	A21	5c Mati	.25	.25
115	A21	18c Nonu	.25	.25
116	A21	32c Ulu	.40	.40
117	A21	48c Fala	.55	.55
118	A21	60c Kanava	.75	.75
119	A21	75c Niu	.90	.90
		Nos. 114-119 (6)	3.10	3.10

Public Buildings and Churches
A22

Designs: 5c, Administration Center, Atafu. 18c, Administration Center, Nukunonu. 32c, Administration Center, Fakaofo. 48c, Congregational Church, Atafu. 60c, Catholic Church, Nukunonu. 75c, Congregational Church, Fakaofo.

1985, Dec. 4

120	A22	5c multicolored	.25	.25
121	A22	18c multicolored	.25	.25
122	A22	32c multicolored	.40	.40
123	A22	48c multicolored	.55	.55
124	A22	60c multicolored	.75	.75
125	A22	75c multicolored	.90	.90
		Nos. 120-125 (6)	3.10	3.10

Hospitals and Schools
A23

Designs: 5c, Atafu Hospital. 18c, St. Joseph's Hospital, Nukunonu. 32c, Fenuafala Hospital, Fakaofo. 48c, Matauala School, Atafu. 60c, Matiti School, Nukunonu. 75c, Fenuafala School, Fakaofo.

1986, May 7 *Perf. 13½*

126	A23	5c multicolored	.25	.25
127	A23	18c multicolored	.25	.25
128	A23	32c multicolored	.40	.40
129	A23	48c multicolored	.55	.55
130	A23	60c multicolored	.75	.75
131	A23	75c multicolored	.90	.90
		Nos. 126-131 (6)	3.10	3.10

Fauna
A24

1986, Dec. 3 **Litho.** *Perf. 14*

132	A24	5c Coconut crab	.25	.25
133	A24	18c Pigs	.25	.25
134	A24	32c Chickens	.40	.40
135	A24	48c Turtles	.65	.65
136	A24	60c Goats	.80	.80
137	A24	75c Ducks	.95	.95
		Nos. 132-137 (6)	3.30	3.30

Flora
A25

1987, May 6

138	A25	5c Gahu	.50	.50
139	A25	18c Puka	.75	.75
140	A25	32c Higano	.95	.95
141	A25	48c Tialetiale	1.30	1.30
142	A25	60c Gagie	1.50	1.50
143	A25	75c Puapua	1.60	1.60
		Nos. 138-143 (6)	6.60	6.60

Olympic Sports
A26

1987, Dec. 2 **Litho.** *Perf. 14x14½*

144	A26	5c Javelin	.35	.35
145	A26	18c Shot put	.60	.60
146	A26	32c Long jump	.75	.75
147	A26	48c Hurdles	.85	.85
148	A26	60c Running	1.05	1.05
149	A26	75c Wrestling	1.45	1.45
		Nos. 144-149 (6)	5.05	5.05

Australia Bicentennial, SYDPEX '88 — A27

Re-enactment of the arrival of the First Fleet in Sydney Harbor, Jan. 26, 1988 (in a continuous design): a, Ships in harbor, building (LL). b, Ships in harbor, tall ship (LR). c, Ships in harbor, Sydney Opera House. d, Bridge. e, North Sydney.

1988, July 30 **Litho.** *Perf. 13½x13*

150		Strip of 5	11.00	11.00
a.-e.		A27 50c any single	1.90	1.90

Political Development
A28

Designs: 5c, Transfer of administration from the New Zealand Department of Maori and Island Affairs to the Ministry of Foreign Affairs, 1975. 18c, The General Fono empowered as the decision-making body of Tokelau, 1977. 32c, 1st Visit of New Zealand's prime minister, 1985. 48c, 1st Visit of UN representatives, 1976. 60c, 1st Tokelau delegation to go to the UN, 1987. 75c, 1st Tokelau appointed to the office of Official Secretary, 1987.

1988, Aug. 10 *Perf. 14½*

151	A28	5c multicolored	.25	.25
152	A28	18c multicolored	.35	.35
153	A28	32c multicolored	.75	.75
154	A28	48c multicolored	1.10	1.10
155	A28	60c multicolored	1.30	1.30
156	A28	75c multicolored	1.75	1.75
		Nos. 151-156 (6)	5.50	5.50

Island Christmas
A29

Designs: 5c, Three Wise Men *(Na Makoi)*. 20c, Holy family *(He Tala)*. 40c, Escape into Egypt *(Fakagagalo ki Aikupito)*. 60c, Christmas presents *(Meaalofa Kilihimahi)*. 70c, Christ child *(Pepe ko Iesu)*. $1, Christmas parade *(Holo Tamilo)*.

1988, Dec. 7 **Litho.** *Perf. 13½*

157	A29	5c multicolored	.25	.25
158	A29	20c multicolored	.25	.25
159	A29	40c multicolored	.65	.65
160	A29	60c multicolored	1.00	1.00
161	A29	70c multicolored	1.10	1.10
162	A29	$1 multicolored	1.60	1.60
		Nos. 157-162 (6)	4.85	4.85

Food Gathering — A30

Fishing and gathering coconuts. Printed se-tenant in continuous designs.

No. 163: a, Launching outrigger canoe. b, Outrigger canoe and sailboat starboard side. c, Outrigger canoe and sailboat stern.

No. 164: a, Outrigger and sailboat port side. b, Islander carrying baskets of coconuts. c, Gathering coconuts from palm trees.

1989, June 28 **Litho.** *Perf. 14x14½*

163	A30	Strip of 3	4.25	4.25
a.-c.		50c any single	1.30	1.30
164	A30	Strip of 3	4.25	4.25
a.-c.		50c any single	1.30	1.30

Women's Work and Leisure — A31

1990, May 2 **Litho.** *Perf. 14½*

165	A31	5c Weavers	.65	.65
166	A31	20c Washing clothes	1.00	1.00
167	A31	40c Resting among palm trees	1.60	1.60
168	A31	60c Weaving mat	2.00	2.00
169	A31	80c Weaving, diff.	2.75	2.75
170	A31	$1 Basket weaver	3.00	3.00
		Nos. 165-170 (6)	11.00	11.00

Souvenir Sheet

Penny Black, 150th Anniv. — A32

1990, May 3 **Litho.** *Perf. 11½*

171	A32	$3 multicolored	17.50	17.50

Men's Handicrafts — A33

1990, Aug. 1 **Photo.** *Perf. 13*

172	A33	50c shown	1.30	1.10
173	A33	50c Carving pots	1.30	1.10
174	A33	50c Tying rope on pot	1.30	1.10
a.		Strip of 3, #172-174	5.00	5.00
175	A33	50c Finishing pots	1.30	1.10
176	A33	50c Shaping a canoe	1.30	1.10
177	A33	50c Three men working	1.30	1.10
a.		Strip of 3, #175-177	5.00	5.00

1992 Summer Olympics, Barcelona — A34

1992, July 8 **Litho.** *Perf. 13½*

178	A34	40c Swimming	.75	.75
179	A34	60c Long jump	1.10	1.10
180	A34	$1 Volleyball	2.50	2.50
181	A34	$1.80 Running	3.25	3.25
		Nos. 178-181 (4)	7.60	7.60

Discovery of America, 500th Anniv.
A35

1992, Dec. 18

182	A35	40c Santa Maria	1.00	1.00
183	A35	60c Columbus	1.20	1.20
184	A35	$1.20 Columbus' fleet	2.75	2.75
185	A35	$1.80 Landfall	4.00	4.00
		Nos. 182-185 (4)	8.95	8.95

Coronation of Queen Elizabeth II, 40th Anniv.
A36

25c, Queen, early portrait. 40c, Prince Philip. $1, Queen, recent portrait. $2, Queen & Prince Philip.

1993, July 8 **Litho.** *Perf. 13½*

186	A36	25c multicolored	.65	.65
187	A36	40c multicolored	1.10	1.10
188	A36	$1 multicolored	1.90	1.90
189	A36	$2 multicolored	3.25	3.25
		Nos. 186-189 (4)	6.90	6.90

Birds
A37

25c, Numenius tahitiensis. 40c, Phaethon rubricauda. $1, Egretta sacra. $2, Pluvialis fulva.

1993-94 **Litho.** *Perf. 13½*

190	A37	25c multicolored	.90	.90
191	A37	40c multicolored	1.35	1.35
192	A37	$1 multicolored	2.25	2.25
193	A37	$2 multicolored	3.00	3.00
a.		Souvenir sheet of 4, #190-193, perf. 14x14½	8.00	8.00
		Nos. 190-193 (4)	7.50	7.50

No. 193a contains Hong Kong '94 emblem, inscription in Chinese and English in sheet margin and sold for $20 HK at the show.

Issued: #190-193, 12/15/93; #193a, 2/1/94.

PHILAKOREA '94 — A38

1994, Aug. 16 **Litho.** *Perf. 12*

194	A38	$2 White heron	3.50	3.50
a.		Souvenir sheet of 1	5.25	5.25

No. 194a has a continuous design.

Handicrafts
A39

1995 **Litho.** *Perf. 13½*

195	A39	5c Outrigger canoe	.25	.25
196	A39	25c Plaited fan	.30	.30
197	A39	40c Plaited baskets	.45	.45
198	A39	50c Fishing box	.60	.60
199	A39	80c Water bottle	.85	.85
200	A39	$1 Fishing hook	1.25	1.25
201	A39	$2 Coconut gourds	2.25	2.25
202	A39	$5 Shell necklace	6.00	6.00
		Nos. 195-202 (8)	11.95	11.95

Souvenir Sheet

New Year 1995 (Year of the Boar) — A40

1995, Feb. 3 **Litho.** *Perf. 14*

203	A40	$5 multicolored	8.50	8.50
a.		Ovptd. in sheet margin	16.00	16.00
b.		Ovptd. in sheet margin	11.00	11.00

No. 203a ovptd. in red in sheet margin "POST'X 95 / 3-6 February / 1995 / AUCKLAND" surrounded by simulated perforations.

No. 203b ovptd. in red in sheet margin with Singapore '95 exhibition emblem.

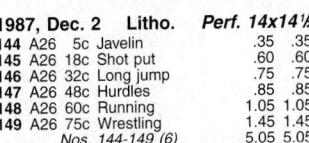

Pacific Imperial Pigeon A41

1995, Apr. 27   Litho.   Perf. 13½
204	A41	25c shown	.75	.75
205	A41	40c Full view	1.20	1.20
206	A41	$1 In tree, red berries	1.90	1.90
207	A41	$2 Nesting	3.50	3.50
		Nos. 204-207 (4)	7.35	7.35

World Wildlife Fund.

Reef Fish — A42

Designs: 25c, Long nosed butterfly fish. 40c, Emperor angelfish. $1, Moorish idol. $2, Lined butterfly fish.
$3, Red fire fish.

1995, Sept. 1   Litho.   Perf. 12
208	A42	25c multicolored	.45	.45
209	A42	40c multicolored	.65	.65
210	A42	$1 multicolored	1.60	1.60
211	A42	$2 multicolored	3.50	3.50
		Nos. 208-211 (4)	6.20	6.20

Souvenir Sheet
212	A42	$3 multicolored	4.75	4.75

No. 212 contains one 40x35mm stamp and is inscribed in sheet margin for Singapore '95.

Butterflies — A43

Designs: 25c, Danaus plexippus. 40c, Precis villida samoensis. $1, Hypolimnas bolina. $2, Euploea leweni.

1995, Oct. 16   Litho.   Perf. 12
213	A43	25c multicolored	.60	.60
214	A43	40c multicolored	1.00	1.00
215	A43	$1 multicolored	2.40	2.40
216	A43	$2 multicolored	3.50	3.50
		Nos. 213-216 (4)	7.50	7.50

Sea Turtles A44

1995, Nov. 27   Litho.   Perf. 12
217	A44	25c Hawksbill	.70	.70
218	A44	40c Leatherback	1.00	1.00
219	A44	$1 Green	2.40	2.40
220	A44	$2 Loggerhead	3.50	3.50
		Nos. 217-220 (4)	7.60	7.60

Souvenir Sheet
221	A44	$3 like #220	5.25	5.25

No. 221 contains one 50x40mm stamp and is a continuous design.

Souvenir Sheet

New Year 1996 (Year of the Rat) — A45

1996, Feb. 19   Litho.   Perf. 12
222	A45	$3 Pacific rat	4.75	4.75
a.		Ovptd. in sheet margin	4.75	4.75
b.		Ovptd. in sheet margin	4.75	4.75

Overprinted in sheet margin with red exhibition emblem: No. 222a, CHINA '96; No. 222b, TAIPEI '96.

Common Design Types pictured following the introduction.

Queen Elizabeth II, 70th Birthday
Common Design Type

Various portraits of Queen, scenes of Tokelau: 40c, Nukunonu. $1, Atafu, silhouette of island, boat. $1.25, Atafu, building on island, boat. $2, Atafu, huts.
$3, Queen wearing tiara, formal dress.

1996, Apr. 22   Litho.   Perf. 13½
223	CD354	40c multicolored	.50	.50
224	CD354	$1 multicolored	1.60	1.60
225	CD354	$1.25 multicolored	1.90	1.90
226	CD354	$2 multicolored	2.60	2.60
		Nos. 223-226 (4)	6.60	6.60

Souvenir Sheet
227	CD354	$3 multicolored	4.75	4.75

Dolphins — A46

1996, July 15   Litho.   Perf. 14
228	A46	40c Fraser's	1.20	1.20
229	A46	$1 Common	2.60	2.60
230	A46	$1.25 Striped	2.60	2.60
231	A46	$2 Spotted	3.75	3.75
		Nos. 228-231 (4)	10.15	10.15

Shells A47

Designs: 40c, Cypraea talpa. $1, Cypraea mauritiana. $1.25, Cypraea argus. $2, Cypraea tigris.
$3, Cypraea mauritana, diff.

1996, Oct. 16   Litho.   Perf. 12
232	A47	40c multicolored	.70	.70
233	A47	$1 multicolored	1.60	1.60
234	A47	$1.25 multicolored	2.10	2.10
235	A47	$2 multicolored	3.00	3.00
		Nos. 232-235 (4)	7.40	7.40

Souvenir Sheet
236	A47	$3 multicolored	4.75	4.75

No. 236 contains one 50x40mm stamp with a continuous design.

Souvenir Sheet

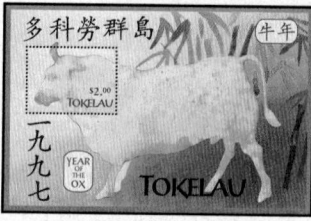

New Year 1997 (Year of the Ox) — A48

1997, Feb. 12   Litho.   Perf. 15x14
237	A48	$2 multicolored	4.00	4.00
a.		Overprinted in gold	5.00	5.00
b.		Overprinted in red	8.00	8.00

No. 237a ovptd. in sheet margin HONG KONG '97 / STAMP EXHIBITION" in English and Chinese.
No. 237b overprinted in sheet margin with Pacific 97 emblem. Issued 5/29.

Humpback Whale A49

Designs: 40c, With school of fish. $1, Calf, adult, young adult. $1.25, With mouth open, school of fish. $2, Adult, calf.
$3, Mouth, head of whale.

1997, May 29   Litho.   Perf. 12
238	A49	40c multicolored	.60	.60
239	A49	$1 multicolored	1.40	1.40
240	A49	$1.25 multicolored	2.00	2.00
241	A49	$2 multicolored	2.75	2.75
		Nos. 238-241 (4)	6.75	6.75

Souvenir Sheet
242	A49	$3 multicolored	4.75	4.75
a.		Ovptd. in sheet margin	5.00	5.00

No. 242a ovptd. in sheet margin, "AUPEX '97 / 13-16 NOVEMBER / NZ NATIONAL / STAMP EXHIBITION." Issued: 11/13.

South Pacific Commission, 50th Anniv. — A50

1997, Sept. 17   Litho.   Perf. 14
243	A50	40c Church, waterfront	.60	.60
244	A50	$1 Beach, child	1.50	1.50
245	A50	$1.25 Island	1.90	1.90
246	A50	$2 Atoll	3.00	3.00
		Nos. 243-246 (4)	7.00	7.00

Year of the Coral Reef — A51

Designs: No. 247, Gorgonian coral, emperor angelfish. No. 248, Soft coral. No. 249, Mushroom coral. No. 250, Staghorn coral. No. 251, Staghorn coral, Moorish idol.

1997, Oct. 20   Litho.   Perf. 13½
247	A51	$1 multicolored	1.20	1.20
248	A51	$1 multicolored	1.20	1.20
249	A51	$1 multicolored	1.20	1.20
250	A51	$1 multicolored	1.20	1.20
251	A51	$1 multicolored	1.20	1.20
a.		Strip of 5, #247-251	6.00	6.00

Souvenir Sheet

New Year 1998 (Year of the Tiger) — A52

1998, Jan. 28   Litho.   Perf. 14x14½
252	A52	$2 multicolored	2.75	2.75
a.		Ovptd. in sheet margin	4.00	4.00

No. 252a overprinted in sheet margin with emblem of Singpex '98 Stamp Exhibition, Singapore.

Diana, Princess of Wales (1961-97)
Common Design Type

Designs: No. 252B, Holding yellow flowers. No. 253: a, Wearing high-collared ruffled blouse. b, Wearing red beret. c, Wearing pink and yellow jacket.

1998, May 15   Litho.   Perf. 14½x14
252B	CD355	$1 multi	2.50	2.50

Souvenir Sheet
253	CD355	$1 Sheet of 4, #252B, 253a-253c	4.25	4.25

No. 253 sold for $4 + 50c, with surtax from international sales being donated to the Princess Diana Memorial Fund and surtax from national sales being donated to designated local charity.

Souvenir Sheet

First Stamps of Tokelau, 50th Anniv. — A53

Designs: a, #3. b. #1. c, #2.

1998, June 22   Litho.   Perf. 14½
254	A53	$1 Sheet of 3, #a.-c.	3.50	3.50

Beetles A54

Designs: 40c, Oryctes rhinoceros. $1, Tribolium castaneum. $1.25, Coccinella repanda. $2, Amarygmus hyorophiloides.
$3, Coccinella repanda, diff.

1998, Aug. 24   Litho.   Perf. 14
255	A54	40c multicolored	.55	.55
256	A54	$1 multicolored	1.50	1.50
257	A54	$1.25 multicolored	1.90	1.90
258	A54	$2 multicolored	2.75	2.75
		Nos. 255-258 (4)	6.70	6.70

Souvenir Sheet
259	A54	$3 multicolored	4.00	4.00

Tropical Flowers A55

40c, Ipomoea pes-caprae. $1, Ipomoea littoralis. $1.25, Scaevola taccada. $2, Thespesia populnea.

1998, Nov. 19   **Litho.**   **Perf. 14**
260	A55	40c multicolored	.60	.60
261	A55	$1 multicolored	1.50	1.50
262	A55	$1.25 multicolored	2.00	2.00
263	A55	$2 multicolored	3.00	3.00
		Nos. 260-263 (4)	7.10	7.10

Souvenir Sheet

New Year 1999 (Year of the
Rabbit) — A56

1999, Feb. 16   **Litho.**   **Perf. 14**
264	A56	$3 multicolored	4.50	4.50
a.		Ovptd. in sheet margin	4.50	4.50

No. 264a overprinted in sheet margin with emblem of IBRA '99 Intl. Stamp Exhibtion, Nuremburg. Issued: 4/27.

Souvenir Sheet

Australia '99, World Stamp
Exhibition — A57

1999, Mar. 19
265	A57	$3 HMS Pandora	5.50	5.50

First Manned
Moon Landing,
30th Anniv. — A58

Designs: 25c, Lift-off. 50c, Separation of stages. 75c, Aldrin deploying instruments on moon. $1, Planting flag. $1.25, Returning to Earth. $2, Splashdown.
$3, Apollo 11, Moon, Earth.

Perf. 13½x13¼
1999, Aug. 31   **Litho.**
266	A58	25c multicolored	.30	.30
267	A58	50c multicolored	.60	.60
268	A58	75c multicolored	.85	.85
269	A58	$1 multicolored	1.30	1.30
270	A58	$1.25 multicolored	1.75	1.75
271	A58	$2 multicolored	2.50	2.50
		Nos. 266-271 (6)	7.30	7.30

Souvenir Sheet
272	A58	$3 multicolored	4.00	4.50
a.		Ovptd. in silver "World Stamp Expo 2000 7-16 July Anaheim - U.S.A." on sheet margin	10.00	10.00

Crabs
A59

1999   **Litho.**   *Perf. 14¼x14½*
273	A59	40c Coconut	.55	.55
274	A59	$1 Ghost	1.40	1.40
275	A59	$1.25 Land hermit	1.90	1.90
276	A59	$2 Purple hermit	2.75	2.75
		Nos. 273-276 (4)	6.60	6.60

Souvenir Sheet
277	A59	$3 Ghost, diff.	4.00	4.00

Black-naped
Tern — A60

Designs: 40c, Chick and egg. $1, On nest. $1.25, Pair near water. $2, Pair in flight.

Perf. 13½x14
1999, Dec. 31   **Litho.**   **Unwmk.**
278-281	A60	Set of 4	6.25	6.25

Souvenir Sheet

New Year 2000 (Year of the
Dragon) — A61

2000   **Litho.**   **Perf. 14x14¼**
282	A61	$3 multi	5.50	5.50
a.		Overprinted in sheet margin	5.50	5.50

No. 282a overprinted in sheet margin with emblem "Bangkok 2000," "World Youth Stamp Exhibition" and Thai text.

Souvenir Sheet

The Stamp Show 2000,
London — A62

Unwmk.
2000, May 22   **Litho.**   **Perf. 14**
283	A62	$6 multi	7.75	7.75

Queen Mother,
100th
Birthday — A63

Various photos. Denominations 40c, $1.20, $1.80, $3.

Perf. 14½x14¼
2000, Aug. 4   **Wmk. 373**
284-287	A63	Set of 4	8.50	8.50

Lizards
A64

Designs: 40c, Gehyra oceanica. $1, Lepidodactylus lugubris. $1.25, Gehyra mutilata. $2, Emoia cyanura.

2001, Feb. 1   **Litho.**   **Perf. 14**
288-291	A64	Set of 4	8.50	8.50

Souvenir Sheet

New Year 2001 (Year of the
Snake) — A65

2001, Feb. 1
292	A65	$3 multi	6.00	6.00
a.		With gold ovpt. in margin	7.00	7.00

Overprint in margin on No. 292a is for Hong Kong 2001 Stamp Exhibition.

Hippocampus
Histrix — A66

Various views of seahorses. Denominations: 40c, $1, $1.25, $2.

2001, Aug. 23   **Litho.**   **Perf. 14**
293-296	A66	Set of 4	7.00	7.00

Souvenir Sheet
297	A66	$3 multi	4.75	4.75

Island
Scenery
A67

Designs: 40c, Sky over Atafu. $1, Waters of Fakaofo. $2, Sunrise over Nukunonu village. $2.50, Ocean, Nukunonu.

Unwmk.
2001, Dec. 17   **Litho.**   **Perf. 14**
298-301	A67	Set of 4	9.00	9.00
a.		Souvenir sheet, #298-301	9.00	9.00

Issued: No. 301a issued 5/27/06 for Washington 2006 World Philatelic Exhibition.

Reign Of Queen Elizabeth II, 50th Anniv. Issue
Common Design Type

Designs: Nos. 302, 306a, 40c, Princess Elizabeth, Prince Philip on honeymoon, 1947. Nos. 303, 306b, $1, Wearing purple hat. Nos. 304, 306c, $1.25, Holding Prince Charles, 1948. Nos. 305, 306d, $2, In 1996. No. 306e, $3, 1955 portrait by Annigoni (38x50mm).

Perf. 14¼x14½, 13¾ (#306e)
2002, Feb. 6   **Litho.**   **Wmk. 373**
With Gold Frames
302	CD360	40c multicolored	.60	.60
303	CD360	$1 multicolored	1.50	1.50
304	CD360	$1.25 multicolored	1.90	1.90
305	CD360	$2 multicolored	3.00	3.00
		Nos. 302-305 (4)	7.00	7.00

Souvenir Sheet
Without Gold Frames
306	CD360	Sheet of 5, #a-e	10.00	10.00

Souvenir Sheet

New Year 2002 (Year of the
Horse) — A68

2002, Feb. 12   **Litho.**   **Perf. 14**
307	A68	$4 multi	6.00	6.00
a.		As #307, with gold ovpt. in margin	6.50	6.50

No. 307a was issued 2/22 and has overprint reading "STAMPEX 2002 / HONG KONG / 22-24 FEBRUARY 2002."

Worldwide Fund for Nature
(WWF) — A69

Various views of Pelagic thresher shark: 40c, $1, $2, $2.50.

2002, July 2   **Litho.**   **Perf. 14¼**
308-311	A69	Set of 4	9.00	9.00

Queen Mother Elizabeth (1900-2002)
Common Design Type

Designs: 40c, Wearing broad-brimmed hat (black and white photograph). $2, Wearing blue hat.
No. 314: a, $2.50, Wearing hat (black and white photograph). b, $4, Wearing purple hat.

Wmk. 373
2002, Aug. 5   **Litho.**   **Perf. 14¼**
With Purple Frames
312	CD361	40c multicolored	.75	.75
313	CD361	$2 multicolored	4.00	4.00

Souvenir Sheet
Without Purple Frames
Perf. 14½x14¼
314	CD361	Sheet of 2, #a-b	9.50	9.00

New
Zealand
Navy Ships
That Have
Stopped at
Tokelau
A70

Designs: 40c, HMNZS Kaniere. $1, HMNZS Endeavour. $2, HMNZS Wellington. $2.50, HMNZS Monowai.

2002, Dec.   **Litho.**   **Unwmk.**   **Perf. 14**
315-318	A70	Set of 4	9.25	9.25

Souvenir Sheet

New Year 2003 (Year of the
Ram) — A71

2003, Feb. 3
319	A71	$4 multi	6.50	6.50
a.		With Bangkok 2003 overprint in gold in margin	6.50	6.50

Issued: No. 319a, 10/13.

Coronation of Queen Elizabeth II, 50th Anniv.
Common Design Type

Designs: Nos. 320, 322a, \$2.50, Queen with maids of honor. Nos. 321, 322b, \$4, Queen with Prince Philip.

Perf. 14¼x14½

2003, June 2   Litho.   Wmk. 373
Vignettes Framed, Red Background
320 CD363 \$2.50 multicolored   3.75 3.75
321 CD363 \$4 multicolored   6.25 6.25

Souvenir Sheet
Vignettes Without Frame, Purple Panel
322 CD363   Sheet of 2, #a-b   10.00 10.00

Prince William, 21st Birthday
Common Design Type

No. 323: a, Color photograph at right. b, Color photograph at left.

Wmk. 373

2003, June 21   Litho.   Perf. 14¼
323   Horiz. pair   7.25 7.25
a.   CD364 \$1.50 multi   2.25 2.25
b.   CD364 \$3 multi   5.00 5.00

Souvenir Sheet

Welpex 2003 Stamp Show, Wellington, New Zealand — A72

Unwmk.

2003, Nov. 7   Litho.   Perf. 14
324 A72 \$4 multi   6.00 6.00

Souvenir Sheet

New Year 2004 (Year of the Monkey) — A73

2004   Litho. with Foil Application
325 A73 \$4 multi   6.50 6.50
a.   With 2004 Hong Kong Stamp Expo emblem in gold in margin   6.50 6.50

Issued: No. 325, 1/22; No. 325a, 1/28.

Island Scenes A74

Designs: 40c, Atafu dawn. \$1, Return of the fishermen, Nukunonu. \$2, A Fakaofo calm evening glow. \$2.50, Solitude in Atafu.

2004, June 30   Litho.   Perf. 14¼x14
326-329 A74   Set of 4   8.00 8.00

No. 324 Overprinted in Silver

2004, Aug. 8   Litho.   Perf. 14
330 A72 \$4 multi   7.00 7.00

Fregata Ariel A75

Designs: 40c, Bird on nest. \$1, Birds in flight. \$2, Birds on nest and in flight. \$2.50, Bird on nest, diff.

2004, Dec. 20   Litho.   Perf. 14
331-334 A75   Set of 4   10.00 10.00

Souvenir Sheet

New Year 2005 (Year of the Rooster) — A76

2005, Feb. 9
335 A76 \$4 multi   7.50 7.50
a.   Ovptd. in gold in margin with Pacific Explorer 2005 emblem   7.50 7.50

No. 335a issued 4/21/05.

Pope John Paul II (1920-2005) A77

2005, Aug. 18   Litho.   Perf. 14
336 A77 \$1 multi   1.90 1.90

Visit of HMNZS Te Kaha A78

Various views of ship: 40c, \$1, \$2, \$2.50.

2005, Dec. 15   Litho.   Perf. 14
337-340 A78   Set of 4   10.50 10.50

Souvenir Sheet

New Year 2006 (Year of the Dog) — A79

2006, Jan. 29
341 A79 \$4 multi   8.25 8.25

Queen Elizabeth II, 80th Birthday A80

Queen: 40c, With head on hands. \$1, In wedding gown. No. 344, \$2, Wearing tiara. No. 345, \$2.50, Wearing blue hat. No. 346: a, \$2, Like \$1. b, \$2.50, Like #344. No. 347: a, #346a overprinted "KIWIPEX." b, #346b overprinted "2006"

2006   Litho.   Perf. 14
With White Frames
342-345 A80   Set of 4   9.50 9.50
Souvenir Sheets
Without White Frames
346 A80   Sheet of 2, #a-b   7.00 7.00
Overprinted in Metallic Blue
347 A80   Sheet of 2, #a-b   8.50 8.50

Issued: Nos. 342-346, 4/21; No. 347, 11/2. No. 347 is also overprinted in sheet margin "National Stamp Exhibition, Christchurch, New Zealand."

Souvenir Sheet

New Year 2007 (Year of the Pig) — A81

2007, Feb. 18   Litho.   Perf. 14
348 A81 \$4 multi   9.00 9.00

Worldwide Fund for Nature (WWF) A82

Pacific golden plover: 40c, Flock of birds. \$1, Head. \$2, Bird standing on one leg. \$2.50, Birds and driftwood.

2007, Oct. 19   Litho.   Perf. 14
349-352 A82   Set of 4   10.00 10.00
352a   Miniature sheet of 16, 4 each #349-352   40.00 40.00

Marine Life — A83

Designs: 10c, Bicolor angelfish. 20c, Staghorn coral. 40c, Black-tipped reef sharks. 50c, Sea star. \$1, Porcupine fish. \$1.50, Thorny seahorses. \$2, Spotted eagle rays. \$2.50, Small giant clams. \$5, Green turtles. \$10, Slate pencil urchin.

2007, Dec. 19   Perf. 14½x14¼
353 A83   10c multi   .25 .25
354 A83   20c multi   .30 .30
355 A83   40c multi   .65 .65
356 A83   50c multi   .80 .80
357 A83   \$1 multi   1.60 1.60
358 A83   \$1.50 multi   2.40 2.40
359 A83   \$2 multi   3.25 3.25
360 A83   \$2.50 multi   4.00 4.00
361 A83   \$5 multi   7.75 7.75
362 A83   \$10 multi   15.50 15.50
a.   Miniature sheet, #353-362   42.50 42.50
Nos. 353-362 (10)   36.50 36.50

Souvenir Sheet

New Year 2008 (Year of the Rat) — A84

2008, Feb. 7   Perf. 14
363 A84 \$4 multi   8.00 8.00

Sir Edmund Hillary (1919-2008), Mountaineer A85

Hillary: 50c, As young man. \$1, Wearing plaid shirt. \$2, Wearing hat and glasses. \$2.50, Wearing blue jacket. \$5, On mountain, horiz.

2008, Nov. 5   Litho.   Perf. 14¼
364-367 A85   Set of 4   10.00 10.00
Souvenir Sheet
Perf. 13¾x13¼
368 A85 \$5 multi   8.50 8.50

Local Scenes A86

Designs: 50c, Buildings near seashore. \$1, Boats on beach. \$2, Trees. \$2.50, Boat anchored near buildings. \$5, Islets.

2008, Nov. 7   Perf. 14¼
369-372 A86   Set of 4   10.00 10.00
Souvenir Sheet
Perf. 13¾x13¼
373 A86 \$5 multi   7.50 7.50

Tarapex National Exhibition, New Plymouth, New Zealand (#373).

Souvenir Sheet

New Year 2009 (Year of the Ox) — A87

2009, Jan. 26   Litho.   Perf. 14
374 A87 \$4 multi   7.25 7.25

Coins of the Pacific Area — A88

Obverse and reverse of: 50c, Chile 1875 one-peso. $1, Great Britain 1911 one-sovereign. $2, New Zealand 1950 half-crown. $2.50, Tokelau 1997 ten-dollar.

2009, Dec. 22   Litho.   Perf. 14x14¼
375-378 A88   Set of 4   9.00 9.00
378a   Souvenir sheet of 4, #375-   9.00 9.00
          378

For overprint, see No. 380.

Souvenir Sheet

New Year 2010 (Year of the Tiger) — A89

2010, Feb. 12   Perf. 13¼x13½
379 A89 $4 multi   6.50 6.50

No. 378a Overprinted in Gold

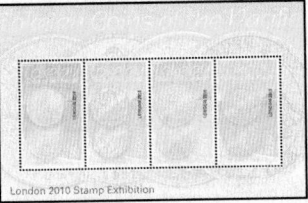

Designs as before.

Method and Perf. As Before
2010, May 8
380 A88   Sheet of 4, #a-d   8.25 8.25
            London 2010 Festival of Stamps.

2009 Tokelauan Bible Translation A90

Open Bible and: 50c, Atafu Church. $1, Fakaofo Church. $2, Nukunonu Church. $2.50, Closed Tokelauan Bibles.

Perf. 13½x13¼
2010, Sept. 21   Litho.
381-384 A90   Set of 4   9.00 9.00

Souvenir Sheet

New Year 2011 (Year of the Rabbit) — A91

Perf. 13¼x13¾
2011, Feb. 3   Unwmk.
385 A91 $5 multi   7.75 7.75

Worldwide Fund for Nature (WWF) A92

Yellow-bellied sea snake: 50c, On rocks. $1, On beach. $2, In sea. $2.50, Three in sea.

2011, Mar. 25   Unwmk.   Perf. 13½
386-389 A92   Set of 4   9.50 9.50
389a   Miniature sheet of 16, 4   38.00 38.00
          each #386-389

Souvenir Sheet

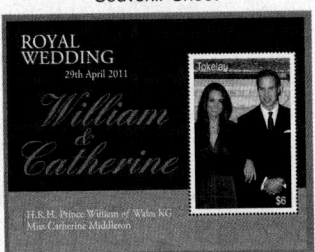

Wedding of Prince William and Catherine Middleton — A93

Perf. 14¾x14¼
2011, Apr. 29   Wmk. 406
390 A93 $6 multi   9.50 9.50

Christmas — A94

Designs: 40c, Christmas tree. 45c, Ornament. $1.40, Stocking. $2, Angel.

2011, Nov. 16   Unwmk.   Perf. 13½
391-394 A94   Set of 4   6.75 6.75

Island Scenes A95

Designs: 10c, Man in coconut palm. 20c, Clouds over island. 25c, Small inhabited island. 40c, Snorkelers. 45c, Sailboat. 50c, House and boats. $1, Beach and trees. $1.40, Fisherman. $2, Beach and trees, diff.

2012, Apr. 11   Perf. 13½x13¼
395 A95   10c multi   .25   .25
396 A95   20c multi   .35   .35
397 A95   25c multi   .40   .40
398 A95   40c multi   .65   .65
399 A95   45c multi   .75   .75
400 A95   50c multi   .80   .80
401 A95 $1 multi   1.60 1.60
402 A95 $1.40 multi   2.25 2.25
403 A95 $2 multi   3.25 3.25
       Nos. 395-403 (9)   10.30 10.30

Reign of Queen Elizabeth II, 60th Anniv. A96

Photograph of Queen Elizabeth II from: $2, 1963. $3, 2012.

2012, May 23
404-405 A96   Set of 2   7.75 7.75
405a   Souvenir sheet of 2, #404-   7.75 7.75
          405

Fish A97

Designs: 40c, Yellowfin tuna. 45c, Ruby snapper. $1.40, Wahoo. $2, Common dolphinfish.

2012, Oct. 3
406-409 A97   Set of 4   7.00 7.00
409a   Souvenir sheet of 4, #406-   7.00 7.00
          409

Christmas — A98

Designs: 45c, Santa Claus, sleigh, reindeer over Atafu. $2, Reindeer over Nukunonu. $3, Reindeer over Fakaofo.

2012, Nov. 21   Perf. 13¼x13½
410-412 A98   Set of 3   9.25 9.25
412a   Horiz. strip of 3, #410-412   9.25 9.25
412b   Souvenir sheet of 3, #410-
          412   9.25 9.25

Coronation of Queen Elizabeth II, 60th Anniv. A99

Designs: $2, Queen Elizabeth II and Prince Philip waving from Buckingham Palace balcony. $3, Queen Elizabeth II and family.

2013, May 8   Perf. 13½x13¼
413-414 A99   Set of 2   8.00 8.00
414a   Souvenir sheet of 2, #413-
          414   8.00 8.00

Butterflies A100

Designs: 45c, Female Blue moon butterfly. $1, Male Blue moon butterfly. $1.40, Common crow butterfly. $3, Meadow argus butterfly.

2013, Aug. 7   Perf. 13½
415-418 A100   Set of 4   9.50 9.50
418a   Souvenir sheet of 4, #415-
          418   9.50 9.50

Christmas — A101

Designs: 45c, Journey to Bethlehem. $1.40, Nativity. $2, Shepherds. $3, Magi.

Perf. 13¼x13½
2013, Nov. 20   Litho.
419-422 A101   Set of 4   11.50 11.50
422a   Souvenir sheet of 4, #419-
          422   11.50 11.50

Woven Items A102

Designs: 45c, Taulima (bracelets). $1.40, Pupu (water containers). $2, Tapili (fan). $3, Ato (basket).

2014, Apr. 23   Litho.   Perf. 13½x13¼
423-426 A102   Set of 4   12.00 12.00
426a   Souvenir sheet of 4,
          #423-426   12.00 12.00

Vakas — A103

Designs: 45c, Vakas in water. $1.40, Men building vaka. $2, Men rowing vaka. $3, Men bringing vaka ashore.

Perf. 13¼x13½
2014, June 14   Litho.
427-430 A103   Set of 4   12.00 12.00
430a   Souvenir sheet of 4,
          #427-430   12.00 12.00

Tokelau Language Week A104

Stylized people and speech balloons with English and Tokelauan words for: 45c, "Hello." $1.40, "How are you?" $2, "What is your name?" $3, "Farewell then."

2014, Oct. 15   Litho.   Perf. 13½x13¼
431-434 A104   Set of 4   11.00 11.00
434a   Souvenir sheet of 4,
          #431-434   11.00 11.00

Christmas A105

Designs: 45c, Shepherds. $2, Holy Family. $3, Magi.

Perf. 13¼x13½
2014, Dec. 10   Litho.
435-437 A105   Set of 3   8.50 8.50
437a   Souvenir sheet of 3, #435-
          437   8.50 8.50

TONGA

'täŋgə

LOCATION — A group of islands in the south Pacific Ocean, south of Samoa
GOVT. — Kingdom in British Commonwealth
AREA — 289 sq. mi.
POP. — 109,082 (1999 est.)
CAPITAL — Nuku'alofa

This group, also known as the Friendly Islands, became a British Protectorate in 1900 under the Anglo-German Agreement of 1899. On June 4, 1970, the United Kingdom ceased to have any responsibility for the external relations of Tonga.

12 Pence = 1 Shilling
20 Shillings = 1 Pound
100 Seniti = 1 Pa'anga (1967)

Catalogue values for unused stamps in this country are for Never Hinged items, beginning with Scott 87 in the regular postage section, Scott B1 in the semipostal section, Scott C1 in the air post section Scott CE1 in the air post special delivery section, Scott CO1 in the air post official section, and Scott O11 in the officials section.

Watermarks

Wmk. 62 — NZ and Small Star Wide Apart

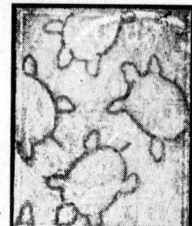

Wmk. 79 — Turtles

King George I — A1

Perf. 12x11½

			Typo.	Wmk. 62	
1886-92					
1	A1	1p car rose ('87)		11.50	4.00
a.		Perf. 12½		450.00	7.00
b.		Perf. 12½x10			
2	A1	2p violet ('87)		42.50	3.50
a.		Perf. 12½		57.50	14.00
3	A1	6p ultra ('88)		57.50	2.75
a.		Perf. 12½		67.50	4.00
4	A1	6p org yel ('92)		18.00	30.00
5	A1	1sh blue grn ('88)		62.50	7.25
a.		Perf. 12½		110.00	4.50
b.		Half used as 6p on cover			
		Nos. 1-5 (5)		192.00	47.50

For surcharges and overprints see #6-9, 24.

Nos. 1 and 2 Surcharged or Overprinted in Black

a   b

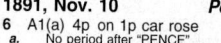

1891, Nov. 10   Perf. 12x11½

6	A1(a)	4p on 1p car rose (Bl)	3.50	12.50
a.		No period after "PENCE"	57.50	125.00
7	A1(a)	8p on 2p violet	40.00	100.00

Type I

Two types of overprint:
I — Solid stars, rays pointed and short.
II — Open-center stars, rays blunt and long.

1891, Nov. 23   Perf. 12½

8	A1(b)	1p car rose (I)	50.00	65.00
a.		Overprinted with 3 stars (I)	400.00	
b.		Overprinted with 4 stars (I)	550.00	
c.		Overprinted with 5 stars (I)	800.00	
d.		Type II	50.00	65.00
e.		Perf. 12x11½ (I or II)	350.00	
9	A1(b)	2p violet (I)	80.00	42.50
a.		Type II	80.00	42.50
b.		Perf. 12x11½ (I or II)	425.00	

Coat of Arms   George I
A4   A5

1892, Nov. 10   Typo.   Perf. 12x11½

10	A4	1p rose	14.00	25.00
a.		Diagonal half used as ½p on cover	975.00	
11	A5	2p olive gray	27.50	18.00
12	A4	4p red brown	55.00	80.00
13	A5	8p violet	62.50	200.00
14	A5	1sh brown	90.00	125.00
		Nos. 10-14 (5)	249.00	448.00

For surcharges and overprints see Nos. 15-23, 25-28, 36-37, O1-O10.

Types A4 and A5 Surcharged in Carmine or Black

c   d

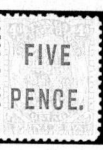 

e   f

1893

15	A4(c)	½p on 1p ultra (C)	26.00	30.00
a.		Surcharge omitted		
16	A4(c)	½p on 1p ultra	50.00	55.00
17	A5(d)	2½p on 2p blue grn (C)	21.00	13.50
18	A5(d)	2½p on 2p blue grn	19.00	19.00
a.		Double surcharge	3,000.	2,000.
19	A4(e)	5p on 4p org yel (C)	4.50	7.50
20	A5(f)	7½p on 8p rose (C)	27.50	85.00
		Nos. 15-20 (6)	148.00	210.00

Stamps of 1886-92 Surcharged in Blue or Black

g   h

1894

21	A4	½p on 4p red brn (Bl)	2.25	8.00
a.		"SURCHARGE"	10.00	22.50
b.		Pair, one without surcharge		
c.		"HALF PENNY" omitted		
22	A5	½p on 1sh brn (Bk)	2.75	12.50
a.		Double surcharge	310.00	
b.		"SURCHARGE"	11.50	45.00
c.		As "b," double surcharge	1,000.	
23	A5	2½p on 8p vio (Bk)	8.00	9.25
a.		No period after "SURCHARGE"	37.50	62.50
24	A1	2½p on 1sh blue grn (Bk), perf. 12½	65.00	27.50
a.		No period after "SURCHARGE"	200.00	
b.		Perf. 12x11½	17.50	47.50
		Nos. 21-24 (4)	78.00	57.25

Type A5 with Same Surcharges in Carmine

1895   Unwmk.

25	A5(g)	1p on 2p lt blue	30.00	30.00
26	A5(h)	1½p on 2p lt bl, perf. 12x11	55.00	45.00
a.		Perf. 12	70.00	45.00
27	A5(h)	2½p on 2p lt blue	45.00	50.00
b.		Without period	250.00	250.00
28	A5(h)	7½p on 2p lt bl, perf. 12x11	70.00	50.00
a.		Perf. 12	475.00	
		Nos. 25-28 (4)	220.00	175.00

King George II — A13

1895, Aug. 16   Perf. 12

29	A13	1p gray green	27.50	30.00
a.		Diagonal half used as ½p on cover		850.00
b.		Horiz. pair, imperf. btwn.		7,500.
30	A13	2½p dull rose	24.00	15.00
31	A13	5p brt blue, perf. 12x11	26.00	57.50
a.		Perf. 12	32.50	57.50
b.		Perf. 11	400.00	
32	A13	7½p yellow	37.50	55.00
		Nos. 29-32 (4)	115.00	157.50

Type A13 Redrawn and Surcharged "g" or "h" in Black

33	A13(g)	½p on 2½p red	47.50	37.50
a.		"SURCHARCE"	85.00	70.00
b.		Period after "Postage"	95.00	75.00
34	A13(g)	1p on 2½p red	95.00	95.00
a.		Period after "Postage"	170.00	110.00
35	A13(h)	7½p on 2½p red	62.50	75.00
a.		Period after "Postage"	110.00	120.00
		Nos. 33-35 (3)	205.00	162.50

Nos. 26 and 28 with Additional Surcharge in Violet and Black

1896, May   Perf. 12x11

36	A5	½p on 1½p on 2p	500.00	
a.		Tongan surch. reading up	475.00	475.00
b.		Perf. 12	475.00	475.00
c.		As "a," perf. 12	500.00	500.00
d.		"Haalf"	3,500.	
37	A5	½p on 7½p on 2p	97.50	125.00
a.		"Half penny" inverted	3,250.	
b.		"Half penny" double		
c.		Tongan surch. reading up	97.50	125.00
d.		Tongan surcharge as "c" and double		
e.		"Hafl Penny"	2,200.	2,500.
f.		"Hafl" only	5,500.	
g.		"Hwif"		
h.		Periods instead of hyphens after words		1,100.
j.		Perf. 12	925.00	

Coat of Arms — A17    Ovava Tree — A18

George II — A19

Prehistoric Trilithon, Tongatabu — A20

Breadfruit   Coral
A21   Formations
           A22

View of Haabai — A23

Red-breasted Musk Parrot — A24

View of Vavau — A25

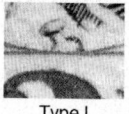 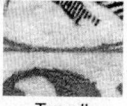

Type I   Type II

Two types of 2p:
I — Top of sword hilt shows above "2."
II — No hilt shows.

Wmk. 79 Sideways

			Engr.	Perf. 14	
1897-1934					
38	A17	½p dark blue		.70	3.00
39	A17	½p green ('34)		1.10	1.40
40	A18	1p dp red & blk		.90	.90
41	A19	2p bis & sep (I)		20.00	7.00
a.		bister & gray, type II		35.00	3.75
42	A19	2½p lt blue & blk		8.00	1.60
a.		"½" without fraction bar		110.00	75.00
43	A20	3p ol grn & blk		4.00	9.75
44	A21	4p dull vio & grn		4.25	4.50
45	A19	5p orange & blk		35.00	16.00
46	A22	6p red		9.00	7.00
47	A19	7½p green & blk		20.00	26.00
a.		Center inverted		6,500.	
48	A19	10p carmine & blk		50.00	55.00
49	A19	1sh red brn & blk		16.00	9.00
a.		"SILENI-E-TAHA" missing second hyphen		350.00	
50	A23	2sh dk ultra & blk		30.00	32.50
51	A24	2sh6p dk violet		65.00	50.00
52	A25	5sh dull red & blk		26.00	32.50
		Nos. 38-52 (15)		289.95	256.15

See Nos. 73-74, 77-78, 80-81. For surcharges see Nos. 63-69.

Stamp of 1897
Overprinted in
Black

1899, June 1
53	A18	1p red & black	40.00	72.50
a.		"1889" instead of "1899"	250.00	400.00
b.		Comma omitted after June		
c.		Double overprint		

Marriage of George II to Lavinia, June 1, 1899. The letters "T L" are the initials of Taufa'ahau, the King's family name, and Lavinia.

No. 53 exists with serifed "T" and "L". Some specialists consider it to be an essay or proof.

Queen
Salote — A26

Dies of 2p:
Die I — Ball of "2" smaller.
Die II — Ball of "2" larger. "U" has spur at left.

1920-35		**Engr.**	**Wmk. 79**	
54	A26	1½p gray blk ('35)	.55	3.50
55	A26	2p violet & sepia	12.00	15.00
56	A26	2p dl vio & blk (I) ('24)	15.00	2.75
a.		Die II	6.00	9.50
57	A26	2½p blue & black	9.00	45.00
58	A26	2½p ultra ('34)	5.00	1.10
59	A26	5p red org & blk	3.75	5.50
60	A26	7½p green & blk	2.00	2.00
61	A26	10p carmine & blk	2.90	5.50
62	A26	1sh red brown & blk	1.40	2.90
		Nos. 54-62 (9)	51.60	83.25

See Nos. 75-76, 79.

Stamps of 1897
Srchd. in Dark
Blue or Red

1923
63	A19	2p on 5p org & blk	1.10	1.00
64	A19	2p on 7½p grn & blk	27.50	32.50
65	A19	2p on 10p car & blk	18.00	57.50
66	A19	2p on 1sh red brn & blk	75.00	25.00
a.		"SILENI-E-TAHA" missing second hyphen	600.00	
67	A23	2p on 2sh ultra & blk (R)	12.00	7.00
68	A24	2p on 2sh6p dk vio (R)	35.00	7.50
69	A25	2p on 5sh dull red & blk (R)	3.50	2.50
		Nos. 63-69 (7)	172.10	133.00

Queen
Salote — A27

Inscribed "1918-1938"

1938, Oct. 12			**Perf. 14**	
70	A27	1p carmine & blk	.65	4.00
71	A27	2p violet & blk	8.00	3.00
72	A27	2½p ultra & blk	8.00	3.75
		Nos. 70-72 (3)	16.65	10.75
		Set, never hinged	32.00	

Accession of Queen Salote Tupou, 20th anniv.
See Nos. 82-86.

Types of 1897-1920
Die III of 2p:
Foot of "2" longer than in Die II, extending beyond curve of loop.

1942		**Engr.**	**Wmk. 4**	
73	A17	½p green	.30	2.75
74	A18	1p scarlet & blk	1.75	2.75
75	A26	2p dull vio & blk	4.50	3.00
a.		Die III	5.50	10.00
76	A26	2½p ultra (II)	1.10	2.00
77	A20	3p green & black	.40	4.25
78	A22	6p orange red	2.00	2.25
79	A26	1sh red brown & gray blk	3.00	3.50
80	A24	2sh6p dk violet	25.00	30.00
81	A25	5sh dull red & brn blk	12.00	60.00
		Nos. 73-81 (9)	50.05	110.50
		Set, never hinged	70.00	

Type of 1938, Inscribed "1918-1943"
1944, Jan. 25				
82	A27	1p rose car & blk	.25	1.10
83	A27	2p purple & blk	.25	1.10
84	A27	3p dk yel grn & blk	.25	1.10
85	A27	6p red orange & blk	.40	2.00
86	A27	1sh dk red brn & blk	.25	2.00
		Nos. 82-86 (5)	1.40	7.30
		Set, never hinged	2.00	

25th anniv. of the accession of Queen Salote.

> **Catalogue values for unused stamps in this section, from this point to the end of the section, are for Never Hinged items.**

UPU Issue
Common Design Types
Engr.; Name Typo. on 3p, 6p
Perf. 13½, 11x11½
1949, Oct. 10			**Wmk. 4**	
87	CD306	2½p ultra	.40	.90
88	CD307	3p deep olive	1.75	3.25
89	CD308	6p deep carmine	.55	.55
90	CD309	1sh red brown	.55	.55
		Nos. 87-90 (4)	3.25	5.25

Common Design Types pictured following the introduction.

A28

A29

Queen
Salote — A30

1950, Nov. 1		**Photo.**	**Perf. 12½**	
91	A28	1p cerise	1.20	3.00
92	A29	5p green	1.20	2.75
93	A30	1sh violet	1.20	3.00
		Nos. 91-93 (3)	3.60	8.75

50th anniv. of the birth of Queen Salote.

Map and Island
Scene — A31

Badges
and Royal
Palace
A32

2½p, Queen Salote & coastal scene. 3p, Queen Salote & ship "Bellona." 5p, Flag of Tonga, island view. 1sh, Arms of Tonga & Great Britain.

Perf. 13x13½ (1p), 13½x13, 12½ (3p)
1951, July 2		**Engr.**	**Wmk. 4**	
94	A31	½p deep green	.30	3.25
95	A32	1p carmine & black	.30	3.25
96	A32	2½p choc & dp grn	.60	3.25
97	A31	3p ultra & org yel	2.75	3.25
98	A32	5p dp green & car	3.75	1.50
99	A32	1sh purple & orange	3.75	1.50
		Nos. 94-99 (6)	11.45	16.00

50th anniv. of the treaty of friendship between Tonga and Great Britain.

Royal
Palace,
Nukualofa
A33

Map of Tonga
Islands — A34

Designs: 1½p, Fisherman. 2p, Canoe and schooners. 3p, Swallows' Cave, Vavau. 3½p, Map of Tongatabu. 4p, Vavau harbor. 5p, Post Office, Nukualofa. 6p, Fuaamotu airport. 8p, Wharf, Nukualofa. 2sh, Beach at Lifuka, Haapai. 5sh, Mutiny on the Bounty. 10sh, Queen Salote. £1, Arms of Tonga.

Perf. 11½x11, 11x11½
1953, July 1			**Wmk. 79**	
100	A33	1p chocolate & blk	.30	.25
101	A33	1½p emerald & ultra	.30	.25
102	A33	2p black & aqua	.30	.25
103	A34	3p dk grn & ultra	.30	.25
104	A33	3½p carmine & yel	.30	.25
105	A33	4p rose car & yel	.30	.25
106	A33	5p choc & ultra	.30	.25
107	A33	6p black & dp ultra	.40	.25
108	A33	8p purple & emer	.45	.25
109	A34	1sh black & ultra	.75	.40
110	A33	2sh choc & ol grn	5.00	.90
111	A33	5sh purple & yel	15.00	5.00
112	A34	10sh black & yellow	9.00	6.00
113	A34	£1 ultra, car & yel	11.00	10.50
		Nos. 100-113 (14)	43.70	25.05

For surcharges and overprints see Nos. 119-126, 158-174, 182-202, 210-215, 218-221, 237, 269-273, C34-C39, C47-C54, C87-C91, CO4-CO6, CO11-CO20, CO27-CO43.

Whaling
Ship and
Longboat
A35

1p, Stamp of 1886. 4p, Post Office, Customs & Treasury Building & Queen Salote. 5p, Diesel-driven ship Aoniu. 1sh, Plane over Tongatabu.

1961, Dec. 1		**Photo.**	**Perf. 14½x13½**	
114	A35	1p brn org & car rose	.30	.25
115	A35	2p ultra	.90	.30
116	A35	4p bright green	.30	.30
117	A35	5p purple	.90	.30
118	A35	1sh red brown	1.00	.60
		Nos. 114-118 (5)	3.40	1.75

75th anniversary of postal service.
For surcharges & overprints see #146-151, 216-221, C16-C21, C55-C57, CO1-CO3, CO9-CO10.

Stamps of
1953 &
1961 Ovptd.
in Red

Perf. 11½x11, 11x11½, 14½x13
Engr.; Photo. (4p)
1962, Feb. 7			**Wmk. 79**	
119	A33	1p choc & blk	.25	.60
120	A35	4p brt green	.25	.65
121	A33	5p choc & ultra	.25	.65
122	A33	6p black & dp ultra	.25	1.10
123	A33	8p purple & emer	.50	1.60
124	A34	1sh black & ultra	.35	.80
125	A34	2sh on 3p dk grn & ultra	.60	3.75
126	A33	5sh purple & yellow	6.25	3.75
		Nos. 119-126 (8)	8.70	12.90

Cent. of emancipation. See Nos. CO1-CO6.
Nos. 119-126 were overprinted locally. Nos. 124-125 exist with inverted overprint. No. 125 exists surcharged "2/" instead of "2/-".

Freedom from Hunger Issue
Common Design Type with Portrait of Queen Salote
Perf. 14x14½
1963, June 4		**Wmk. 79**	**Photo.**	
127	CD314	11p ultra	.70	.35

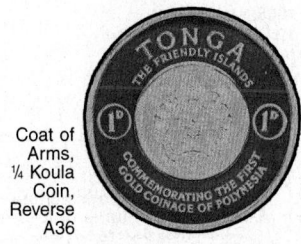

Coat of
Arms,
¼ Koula
Coin,
Reverse
A36

Designs: 2p, 9p, 2sh, Queen Salote (head), ¼-koula coin, obverse.

Litho.; Embossed on Gilt Foil
1963, July 15		**Unwmk.**	**Die Cut**	
		Diameter: 40mm		
128	A36	1p dp carmine	.50	.40
129	A36	2p violet blue	.50	.40
130	A36	6p dp green	.50	.40
131	A36	9p magenta	.50	.40
132	A36	1sh6p violet	.70	.70
133	A36	2sh emerald	.75	.75
		Nos. 128-133,C1-C6,CO7 (13)	16.10	15.70

1st gold coinage of Polynesia. Backed with paper inscribed in salmon-colored alternating rows: "TONGA" and "THE FRIENDLY ISLANDS" in multiple.
For surcharges see #140-145, C11-C15, CO8.

Red Cross Centenary Issue
Common Design Type with Portrait of Queen Salote
Wmk. 79
1963, Sept. 2		**Litho.**	**Perf. 13**	
134	CD315	2p black & red	.25	.25
135	CD315	11p ultra & red	.75	1.00

Queen Salote on ¼-Koula Coin
A37

Litho.; Embossed on Gilt Foil
1964, Oct. 19   Unwmk.   Die Cut
136 A37 3p pink   .50 .40
137 A37 9p light blue   .50 .40
138 A37 2sh yellow green   .50 .50
139 A37 5sh pale lilac   1.50 1.50
   Nos. 136-139,C7-C10 (8)   6.45 6.25

Pan-Pacific and Southeast Asia Women's Association Conf., Nukualofa, Aug. 1964. See note on paper backing after No. 133.
For surcharges & overprints see #152-157, 263-268.

Nos. 128-133 Surcharged in Red, White or Black

1965, Mar. 18
140 A36 1sh3p on 1sh6p (R)   1.00   .50
141 A36 1sh9p on 9p (W)   1.00   .50
142 A36 2sh6p on 6p (R)   1.50   .75
143 A36 5sh on 1p   29.00 29.00
144 A36 5sh on 2p   5.00 5.00
145 A36 5sh on 2sh   2.50 2.00
   Nos. 140-145,C11-C15,CO8 (12) 110.75 106.00

Nos. 114-115 Overprinted and Surcharged in Purple or Red

Perf. 14½x13½
1966, June 18   Photo.   Wmk. 79
146 A35 1p (P)   .25   .25
147 A35 3p on 1p (P)   .25   .25
148 A35 6p on 2p (R)   .25   .25
149 A35 1sh2p on 2p (R)   .30   .25
150 A35 2sh on 2p (R)   .40   .25
151 A35 3sh on 2p (R)   .40   .30
   Nos. 146-151,C16-C21,CO9-CO10 (14)   6.60 4.45

Centenary of Tupou College and of secondary education.

Nos. 136-137 Ovptd. and Srchd. in Silver on Black or Ultramarine

Litho.; Embossed on Gilt Foil
1966, Dec. 16   Unwmk.   Die Cut
152 A37 3p pink (U)   .50   .40
153 A37 5p on 9p lt blue   .50   .40
154 A37 9p lt bl   .50   .40
155 A37 1sh7p on 3p pink (U) 1.25   .65
156 A37 3sh6p on 9p lt blue 1.50 1.00
157 A37 6sh6p on 3p pink (U) 2.00 1.25
   Nos. 152-157,C22-C26 (11) 12.25 9.90

Nos. 100-110, 147 and 151 Srchd. in Black or Red

No. 158-165 Surcharged

Nos. 166-167 Surcharged

No. 168 Surcharged

No. 169 Surcharged

Nos. 170-171, 173 Surcharged

Nos. 172, 174 Surcharged

Perf. 11½x11, 11x11½, 14½x13½
1967, Mar. 25   Wmk. 79
158 A33 1s on 1p   .25   .25
159 A33 2s on 4p   .25   .25
160 A33 3s on 5p   .25   .25
161 A33 4s on 5p   .25   .25
162 A33 5s on 3½p   .25   .25
163 A33 6s on 8p   .25   .25
164 A33 7s on 1½p   .25   .25
165 A33 8s on 6p   .25   .25
166 A34 9s on 3p   .25   .25
167 A34 10s on 1sh   .30   .30
168 A35 11s on 3p on 1p   .40   .40
169 A33 21s on 3sh on 2p   .60   .60
170 A33 23s on 1p   .65   .65
171 A33 30s on 2sh (R) (1-line surcharge) 1.40 1.40
172 A33 30s on 2sh (R) (3-line surcharge) 1.50 1.50
173 A33 50s on 6p (R)   1.75 1.75
174 A33 60s on 2p (R)   2.25 2.25
   Nos. 158-174 (17)   11.10 11.10

The size, typeface and arrangement of surcharge vary on the different denominations.

King Taufa'ahau IV — A38

Designs: 1s, 4s, 28s, 1pa, Coat of Arms, reverse of new palladium coins.
Diameter: 1s, 44mm; 2s, 50s, 52mm; 4s, 59mm; 15s, 68mm; 28s, 40mm; 1pa, 74mm

Litho.; Embossed on Palladium Foil
1967, July 4   Unwmk.   Die Cut
175 A38 1s orange & brt bl   .50   .40
176 A38 2s brt bl & dp mag   .50   .40
177 A38 4s emerald & mag   .50   .40
178 A38 15s blue grn & vio   .50   .40
179 A38 28s blk & brt red lil .60   .60
180 A38 50s red & vio bl   1.10 1.10
181 A38 1pa ultra & brt rose 2.75 2.75
   Nos. 175-181,C27-C33 (14) 14.80 14.10

Coronation of King Taufa'ahau IV, July 4, 1967. Backed with paper inscribed in yellow alternating rows: "Tonga The Friendly Islands" and "Historically The First Palladium Coinage."
For surcharges and overprints see Nos. 203-209, C40-C46, CO21-CO24,

Types of Regular Issue, 1953, Surcharged

Wmk. 79
1967, Dec. 15   Engr.   Die Cut
182 A33 1s on 1p yellow & blk   .25   .25
183 A33 2s on 2p car & ultra   .25   .25
184 A34 3s on 3p brn org & yel .25   .25
185 A33 4s on 4p purple & yel   .25   .25
186 A33 5s on 5p green & yel   .25   .25
187 A34 10s on 10p rose red & yel .25   .25
188 A33 20s on 2sh car & ultra   .35   .35
189 A33 50s on 5sh sepia & yel 3.00 3.00
190 A34 1pa on 10sh org red   1.00   .75
   Nos. 182-190,C34-C36,CO12-CO14 (15)   9.95 9.60

Arrival of US Peace Corps.

Nos. 100-111 Srchd. in Red, Black or Ultra

Perf. 11½x11, 11x11½
1968, Apr. 6   Engr.   Wmk. 79
191 A33 1s on 1p (R)   .25   .25
192 A33 2s on 4p   .25   .25
193 A34 3s on 3p (U)   .25   .25
194 A33 4s on 5p (R)   .25   .25
195 A33 5s on 2p (R)   .25   .25
196 A33 6s on 6p (R)   .25   .25
197 A33 7s on 1½p (R)   .25   .25
198 A33 8s on 8p (R)   .25   .25
199 A33 9s on 3½p   .30   .30
200 A34 10s on 1sh (R)   .30   .30
201 A33 20s on 5sh (R)   2.00 2.00
202 A33 2pa on 2sh (R)   3.00 3.00
   Nos. 191-202,C37-C39,CO15-CO18 (19)   15.75 15.50

Surcharge on 3s and 10s is vertical.

Nos. 175-181 Overprinted: "H.M'S BIRTHDAY / 4 July 1968" in Gold on Red Panel on 1s, 4s, 28s and 1pa. "HIS MAJESTY'S 50th BIRTHDAY" in Silver on Blue Panel on 2s, 15s and 50s

Litho.; Embossed on Palladium Foil
1968, July 4   Unwmk.   Die Cut
203 A38 1s orange & brt bl   .25   .25
204 A38 2s brt bl & dp mag   .25   .25
205 A38 4s emerald & mag   .25   .25
206 A38 15s blue grn & vio   .55   .55
207 A38 28s blk & brt red lil 1.10 1.10

208 A38 50s red & vio bl   1.90 1.90
209 A38 1pa ultra & brt rose 4.00 4.00
   Nos. 203-209,C40-C46,CO21-CO24 (18)   33.20 29.15

Types of 1953 Surcharged in Red, Black or Green: "Friendly Islands / Field & Track Trials / South Pacific Games / Port Moresby 1969"

Designs as before.

Wmk. 79
1968, Dec. 19   Engr.   Die Cut
210 A33 5s on 5p grn & yel (R) .25   .25
211 A34 10s on 1sh cer & buff   .25   .25
212 A33 15s on 2sh rose car & bl .25   .25
213 A33 25s on 2p rose car & bl .55   .55
214 A34 50s on 1p yel & blk   .75   .75
215 A34 75s on 10sh org (G)   1.10 1.10
   Nos. 210-215,C47-C54,CO19-CO20 (16)   9.30 7.30

Issued to publicize the field and track trials for the third South Pacific Games, Port Moresby, 1969. The overprint is in 5 lines on the vertical stamps, in 7 lines on vertical stamps. On the vertical stamps "Trial" is printed on the line ahead of "Field & Track." On #215 the denomination is spelled out.

Nos. 149-150 and Types of 1953 Surcharged

Nos. 216-217 Surcharged

Nos. 218, 221 Surcharged

No. 219 Surcharged

No. 220 Surcharged

Perf. 14½x13½
1968   Photo.   Wmk. 79
216 A35 1s on 1sh2p on 2p   1.60 1.60
217 A35 1s on 2sh on 2p   1.60 1.60
**   Engr.   Die Cut**
218 A33 1s on 6p yel & blk   .90   .90
219 A33 2s on 3½p dk blue   1.00 1.00
220 A33 1s on 2½p lt green   1.00 1.00
221 A33 4s on 8p blk & pale grn 1.10 1.10
   Nos. 216-221,C55-C57 (9)   12.00 10.20

Banana — A39

Unwmk.
1969, Apr. 21   Typo.   Die Cut
**   Self-adhesive**
222 A39 1s yellow, black & red   1.00   .85
223 A39 2s yel, black & emer   1.10 1.00
224 A39 3s yellow, black & lil 1.25 1.10
225 A39 4s yellow, black & ultra 1.40 1.10
226 A39 5s yel, blk & ol grn   1.75 1.75
   Nos. 222-226 (5)   6.50 5.80

Packed in boxes of 200. See Nos. 248-252, 297-301, O11-O15, design A75.

Peelable Backing Inscribed

Starting in 1969, self-adhesive stamps are attached to peelable paper backing printed with "TONGA where time begins" in multiple rows and various colors, unless otherwise stated.

Shot-putter — A40

1969, Aug. 13   Litho.   Die Cut
Self-adhesive

227	A40	1s bister, red & blk	.25	.25
228	A40	3s bis, red & emer	.25	.25
229	A40	6s bister, red & bl	.25	.25
230	A40	10s bister, red & pur	.25	.25
231	A40	30s bister, red & bl	.40	.40

Nos. 227-231,C58-C62,CO25-CO26 (12)   8.95   8.95

3rd Pacific Games, Port Moresby, Papua and New Guinea, Aug. 13-23.

Oil Derrick and Map of Tonga Islands — A41

1969, Dec. 23   Litho.   Die Cut
Self-adhesive

232	A41	3s brown & multi	.50	.50
233	A41	7s brt blue & multi	.60	.60
234	A41	20s multicolored	1.00	1.00
235	A41	25s orange & multi	1.10	1.10
236	A41	35s henna brn & multi	1.50	1.50

Type of Regular Issue, 1953, Surcharged in Red: "1969 / OIL / SEARCH / T$1.10" and Oil Derrick Obliterating Old Denomination

Wmk. 79   Die Cut

237	A34	1.10pa on £1 grn & multi	4.50	4.50

Nos. 232-237,C63-C67,CO27 (12)   18.40   18.40

First scientific search for oil in Tonga.

British and Tongan Royal Families — A42

Litho.; Gold Embossed
1970, Mar. 7   Self-adhesive   Die Cut

238	A42	3s multicolored	.25	.25
239	A42	5s multicolored	.25	.25
240	A42	10s multicolored	.55	.40
241	A42	25s multicolored	1.25	.90
242	A42	50s multicolored	2.75	2.00

Nos. 238-242,C68-C72,CO28-CO30 (13)   27.55   18.85

Visit of Elizabeth II, Prince Philip and Princess Anne, Mar. 1970.

Open Book, George Tupou I and II, Salote Tupou III, Taufa'ahau Tupou IV and Tonga Flag — A43

Litho.; Gold Embossed
1970, June 4   Die Cut
Self-adhesive

243	A43	3s multicolored	.50	.50
244	A43	7s multicolored	.65	.65
245	A43	15s multicolored	1.00	1.00
246	A43	25s multicolored	1.25	1.25
247	A43	2.00 multicolored	2.00	2.00

Nos. 243-247,C73-C77,CO31-CO33 (13)   32.10   24.60

Tonga's independence and entry into the British Commonwealth of Nations.

For surcharges see Nos. CO49-CO51, CO71.

Banana Type of 1969 redrawn and

Coconut — A44

1970, June 9   Typo.
Self-adhesive

248	A39	1s yellow, blk & mag	.40	.40
249	A39	2s yellow, blk & bl	.50	.50
250	A39	3s yellow, blk & brn	.50	.50
251	A39	4s yellow, blk & grn	.50	.50
252	A39	5s yellow, blk & org	.55	.55

Typo.; Embossed on Gilt Foil
Coconut Brown

253	A44	6s blue, grn & mag	.65	.65
254	A44	7s purple & green	.70	.70
255	A44	8s gold, grn & vio bl	.75	.75
256	A44	9s carmine & green	.85	.85
257	A44	10s gold, grn & org	.85	.85

Nos. 248-257,O11-O20 (20)   16.00   16.00

Nos. 248-252 have no white shading in upper part of the banana, Nos. 222-226 have white shading. Nos. 253-256 have self-adhesive control numbers in lower left corner of paper backing. Paper backing is green on Nos. 253-257.

See Nos. 302-306, O26-O30.

Red Cross and Arms of Tonga A45

1970, Oct. 17   Litho.   Die Cut
Self-adhesive

258	A45	3s red, black & grn	.25	.25
259	A45	7s red, blk & vio bl	.25	.25
260	A45	15s red, blk & red lil	.55	.55
261	A45	25s red, black & brt grn	.90	.90
262	A45	75s red, black & brn	4.50	4.50

Nos. 258-262,C78-C82,CO34-CO36 (13)   29.35   29.35

Centenary of the British Red Cross.

Nos. 153, 152 Surcharged

Litho.; Embossed on Gilt Foil
1971, Jan. 31   Die Cut

263	A37	2s on 9p lt blue	.25	.25
264	A37	3s on 9p lt blue	.25	.25
265	A37	5s on 3p pink	.35	.25
266	A37	15s on 9p lt blue	1.10	.65
267	A37	25s on 3p pink	1.50	1.00
268	A37	50s on 3p pink	3.50	2.10

Nos. 263-268,C83-C86,CO37-CO40 (14)   35.10   24.55

In memory of Queen Salote (1900-65). The "In Memoriam" inscription is in silver on black panel on the 2s, 3s and 15s; in silver on ultramarine panel on the 5s, 25s and 50s. The dates and denominations are all on black panels in silver and metallic red, green, bronze, magenta or gold respectively.

Type of Regular Issue, 1953, Surcharged in Red and Black

1971   Engr.   Wmk. 79   Imperf

269	A33	3s on 8p blk & pale grn	.25	.25
270	A33	7s on 4p pur & yel	.25	.25
271	A33	25s on 1p yel & blk	.55	.40
272	A33	75s on 2sh car & ultra	3.25	2.10

Nos. 269-272,C87-C89,CO41-CO43 (10)   14.05   9.40

Philatokyo 71, Philatelic Exposition, Tokyo, Apr. 19-29.

Type of Regular Issue, 1971, Surcharged

1971

273	A34	15s on 1sh car & buff	.50	.50

Nos. 273,C90-C91 (3)   4.00   4.00

Centenary of Japanese postal service.

Self-adhesive & Die Cut

Starting with Nos. 274-278, all issues are self-adhesive and die cut, unless otherwise stated.

Pole Vault — A46

1971, July   Litho.   Unwmk.   Die Cut

274	A46	3s green, blk & brn	.25	.25
275	A46	7s red, blk & brn	.25	.25
276	A46	15s green, blk & brn	.35	.35
277	A46	25s rose lil, blk & brn	.50	.50
278	A46	50s dk bl, blk & brn	1.00	1.00

Nos. 274-278,C92-C96,CO44-CO46 (13)   14.80   14.80

4th South Pacific Games, Papeete, French Polynesia, Sept. 8-19.
For surcharges see Nos. 332, C140.

Gold Medal of Merit — A47

24s, Silver Medal of Merit. 38s, Bronze Medal of Merit, obverse (King Taufa'ahau IV).

Litho; Embossed
1971, Oct. 30   Imperf.

279	A47	3s gold & multi	.25	.25
280	A47	24s silver & multi	.45	.45
281	A47	38s bronze & multi	.85	.85

Nos. 279-281,C99-C101,CO49-CO51 (9)   10.65   10.65

First investiture of Tongan Medal of Merit.
For surcharges see Nos. 333-336.

Juggler, UNICEF Emblem A48

1971, Dec.   Litho.   Die Cut

282	A48	2s violet & multi	.25	.25
283	A48	4s multicolored	.25	.25
284	A48	8s blue & multi	.25	.25
285	A48	16s emerald & multi	.35	.35
286	A48	30s lil rose & multi	.70	.70

Nos. 282-286,C102-C106,CO52-CO54 (13)   15.40   15.40

25th anniv. of UNICEF.

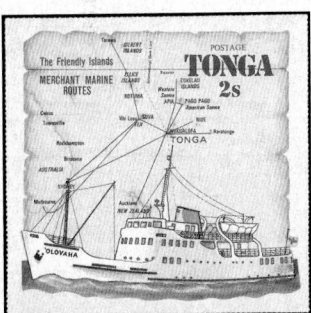

Merchant Marine Routes from Tonga and "Olovaha" — A49

1972, Apr. 14

287	A49	2s blue & multi	.35	.35
288	A49	10s magenta & multi	.85	.35
289	A49	17s brown & multi	1.25	.35
290	A49	21s dk green & multi	1.40	.50
291	A49	60s multicolored	6.50	4.00

Nos. 287-291,C107-C111,CO55-CO57 (13)   41.95   28.75

Togan Merchant Marine publicity
For surcharges see Nos. C124, CO66-CO69.

King Taufa'ahau IV Coronation Coin,
¼ Hau — A50

Litho.; Embossed on Metallic Foil

1972, July 15

292	A50	5s silver & multi	.25	.25
293	A50	7s silver & multi	.25	.25
294	A50	10s silver & multi	.25	.25
295	A50	17s silver & multi	.40	.40
296	A50	60s silver & multi	1.40	1.40

    Nos. 292-296,C112-
C116,CO58-CO60 (13)   15.45 15.45

Coronation of King Taufa'ahau IV, 5th anniv.

Coconut Type of 1970 and

Banana
A51

Watermelon — A52

1972, Sept. 30   **Typo.**

297	A51	1s brt yel, red & blk	.35	.25
298	A51	2s brt yel, bl & blk	.40	.25
299	A51	3s brt yel, emer & blk	.45	.25
300	A51	4s brt yel & blk	.45	.25
301	A51	5s brt yel & brn blk	.45	.25
302	A44	6s brn, org & grn	.50	.25
303	A44	7s brn, ultra & grn	.55	.30
304	A44	8s brn, mag & grn	.55	.30
305	A44	9s brn, red & grn	.55	.30
306	A44	10s bl & grn	.65	.35
307	A52	15s green, org brn & ultra	1.40	.50
308	A52	20s grn, bl & red	1.50	.70
309	A52	25s grn, red & brn	1.75	.80
310	A52	40s grn, bl & org	3.00	1.75
311	A52	50s grn, dk bl & yel	3.00	2.00

    Nos. 297-311,O21-O35 (30)   28.85 17.35

Paper backing is brown on Nos. 302-311.
Nos. 302-306 have self-adhesive control number in lower left corner of paper backing.

Flag Raising, Minerva Reef — A53

1972, Dec. 9   **Litho.**

312	A53	5s black & multi	.25	.25
313	A53	7s green & multi	.25	.25
314	A53	10s purple & multi	.25	.25
315	A53	15s orange & multi	.40	.40
316	A53	40s ultra & multi	1.50	1.50

    Nos. 312-316,C119-
C123,CO63-CO65 (13)   13.75 13.75

Tonga's proclamation of sovereignty over the Minerva Reefs, June 1972.

Tongan Coins and Bank
Building — A54

1973, Mar. 30   **Litho.**

317	A54	5s silver & multi	.25	.25
318	A54	7s silver & multi	.25	.25
319	A54	10s silver & multi	.25	.25
320	A54	20s silver & multi	.45	.25
321	A54	30s silver & multi	.60	.35

    Nos. 317-321,C125-
C129,CO66-CO68 (13)   17.95 17.10

Establishment of Bank of Tonga.

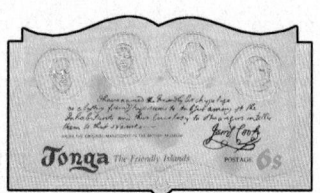

Handshake, Outrigger Canoe — A55

1973, June 29

322	A55	5s silver & multi	.30	.25
323	A55	7s silver & multi	.45	.25
324	A55	15s silver & multi	1.40	.55
325	A55	21s silver & multi	1.90	.70
326	A55	50s silver & multi	6.75	3.25

    Nos. 322-326,C130-
C134,CO69-CO71 (13)   135.00 70.10

Tongan Boy Scout Movement, 25th anniv.

Capt. Cook's Report and Tongan
Rulers — A56

Litho.; Embossed on Gilt Foil

1973, Oct. 2

327	A56	6s multicolored	.50	.45
328	A56	8s multicolored	.50	.45
329	A56	11s multicolored	.70	.55
330	A56	35s multicolored	4.75	1.90
331	A56	40s multicolored	4.75	2.25

    Nos. 327-331,C135-
C139,CO72-CO74 (13)   60.00 31.45

Bicentenary of Capt. Cook's arrival. Design is from the manuscript in British Museum.

**Nos. 278, 281, C100-C101 and 280
Srchd. & Ovptd. in Silver or Gold on
Red (12s, 14s) or Black Panels (5s,
20s, 50s): "Commonwealth Games
Christchurch 1974"**

1973, Dec. 19   **Litho.**

332	A46	5s on 50s (G)	.25	.25

Litho.; Embossed

333	A47	12s on 38s (S)	.50	.50
334	A47	14s on 75s (S)	.50	.50
335	A47	20s on 1pa (G)	.85	.85
336	A47	50s on 24s (S)	1.60	1.60

    Nos. 332-336,C140-
C144,CO75-CO77 (13)   17.10 16.45

10th British Commonwealth Games, Christchurch, N.Z., Jan. 24-Feb. 2, 1974.

Letter Addressed to Tonga, Names
of UPU Members — A57

1974, June 20   **Typo.**

337	A57	5s tan & multi	.25	.25
338	A57	10s tan & multi	.25	.25
339	A57	15s tan & multi	.45	.45
340	A57	20s tan & multi	.50	.50
341	A57	50s tan & multi	1.60	1.60

    Nos. 337-341,C154-
C158,CO87-CO89 (13)   14.55 14.55

Centenary of Universal Postal Union.

Girl Guide Badges — A58

1974, Sept. 11   **Litho.**

342	A58	5s multicolored	.45	.30
343	A58	10s multicolored	.85	.50
344	A58	20s multicolored	2.00	1.25
345	A58	40s multicolored	4.00	2.40
346	A58	60s multicolored	5.50	3.25

    Nos. 342-346,C159-
C163,CO90-CO92 (13)   49.00 29.20

Girl Guides of Tonga.
For surcharges see Nos. C189, C192.

Sailing
Ship
and
Anchors
A59

1974, Dec. 11

347	A59	5s blue & multi	.40	.35
348	A59	10s blue & multi	.90	.45
349	A59	25s blue & multi	2.00	.80
350	A59	50s blue & multi	4.00	2.75
351	A59	75s blue & multi	6.00	4.50

    Nos. 347-351,C164-
C168,CO93-CO95 (13)   47.00 27.00

Establishment of Royal Marine Institute.

Dateline Hotel, Nukualofa — A60

1975, Mar. 11

352	A60	5s blue & multi	.25	.25
353	A60	10s green & multi	.25	.25
354	A60	15s scarlet & multi	.35	.35
355	A60	30s purple & multi	.75	.75
356	A60	1pa orange & multi	2.75	2.75

    Nos. 352-356,C169-
C173,CO96-CO98 (13)   15.15 15.15

First meeting of South Pacific area Prime Ministers. See note after No. 226.

Boxing and Games' Emblem — A61

1975, June 11   **Litho.**

357	A61	5s black & multi	.25	.25
358	A61	10s green & multi	.35	.35
359	A61	20s brown & multi	.55	.55
360	A61	25s orange & multi	.65	.65
361	A61	65s violet & multi	1.40	1.40

    Nos. 357-361,C174-
C178,CO99-CO101 (13)   13.35 13.35

5th South Pacific Games, Guam, Aug. 1-10. See note after No. 226.
For surcharges see Nos. 412, 482.

King
Taufa'ahau IV
Coin — A62

Designs (FAO Coins): 5s, Chicken. 20s, like 1pa, (small coin, 27mm). 50s, School of fish. 2pa, Animals and plants on reverse, King on obverse (large coin, 42mm).

1975, Sept. 3

362	A62	5s red, sil & blk	.25	.25
363	A62	20s ultra, grn, sil & blk	.55	.55
364	A62	50s blue, sil & blk	1.10	1.10
365	A62	1pa silver & black	2.25	2.25
366	A62	2pa silver & black	3.75	3.75

    Nos. 362-366,C179-C183 (10)   13.25 13.25

Coinage issued for the benefit of the FAO. Size of paper backing of 2pa: 82x50mm; others 45x45mm. See note after No. 226.
For surcharge see Nos. 413.

Coat of Arms, 5pa Coin,
Reverse — A63

George Tupou I Coin, Reverse and
Obverse — A64

Coins: 20s, King Taufa'ahau IV. 50s, King George Tupou II, 50pa obverse and reverse. 75s, 20pa reverse.

Litho.; Embossed on Gilt Foil
1975, Nov. 4
Pink Background
367 A63 5s black, sil & vio bl .30 .30
368 A64 10s gold, blk & red .40 .40
369 A63 20s black, sil & grn .75 .75
370 A64 50s gold, blk & vio 1.75 1.75
371 A63 75s black, sil & red lil 2.75 2.75
Nos. 367-371,C184-
C188,CO102-CO104 (13) 18.10 18.10

Centenary of Constitution of Tonga. Size of paper backing of Nos. 367 and 369: 65x60mm; of No. 371, 87x78mm. See note after No. 226.
For surcharges see Nos. C232, C296.

Montreal Olympic Games Emblem — A65

1976, Feb. 24 Litho.
372 A65 5s red, ultra & blk .40 .35
373 A65 10s red, green & blk .60 .35
374 A65 25s red, lt brown & blk 1.40 .80
375 A65 35s red, lilac & blk 1.75 1.10
376 A65 70s red, bister & blk 3.50 2.75
Nos. 372-376,C189-
C193,CO105-CO107 (13) 31.00 20.05

21st Olympic Games, Montreal, Canada, July 17-Aug. 1. See note after No. 226.
For surcharges see Nos. 414, 478.

William Hooper, William Floyd, John Penn, Francis Lightfoot Lee — A66

Signers of Declaration of Independence, Flags of US and Tonga: 10s, Benjamin Franklin, Thomas Nelson, Jr., Benjamin Harrison, William Ellery. 15s, Oliver Wolcott, Lyman Hall, William Whipple, Carter Braxton. 25s, George Taylor, Thomas Stone, Arthur Middleton, Richard Stockton. 75s, Stephen Hopkins, Elbridge Gerry, James Wilson, Francis Hopkinson.

1976, May 26 Litho.
377 A66 9s buff & multi .45 .25
378 A66 15s buff & multi .45 .25
379 A66 15s buff & multi .65 .50
380 A66 25s buff & multi 1.00 1.00
381 A66 75s buff & multi 5.75 4.50
Nos. 377-381,C194-
C198,CO108-CO110 (13) 34.50 21.45

American Bicentennial. Printed on peelable buff paper backing, inscribed in carmine with facsimile of Declaration of Independence.
For surcharges see #481, C233, C236-C237, C297.

Nathaniel Turner and John Thomas — A67

1976, Aug. 25
382 A67 5s yellow & multi .25 .25
383 A67 10s multicolored .40 .25
384 A67 20s multicolored .90 .50
385 A67 25s multicolored 1.00 .55
386 A67 85s multicolored 2.75 2.75
Nos. 382-386,C199-
C203,CO111-CO113 (13) 18.75 16.65

Sesquicentennial of the arrival of Methodist missionaries and establishment of Christianity in Tonga. Printed on peelable paper backing inscribed in manuscript with segments of John Thomas's Tonga diary.
For surcharges see Nos. 415-416, 479-480.

Wilhelm I and George Tupou I — A68

1976, Nov. 1
387 A68 9s yellow & multi .35 .35
388 A68 15s yellow & multi .55 .50
389 A68 22s yellow & multi .85 .85
390 A68 50s yellow & multi 1.50 1.50
391 A68 73s yellow & multi 2.00 2.00
Nos. 387-391,C204-
C208,CO114-CO116 (13) 17.50 17.45

Tonga-Germany Friendship Treaty, centenary. Printed on peelable paper backing showing reproduction of original treaty.

Queen Salote in Coronation Procession, 1953 — A69

1977, Feb. 7 Litho.
392 A69 11s blue & multi .40 .40
393 A69 20s green & multi .50 .50
394 A69 30s vio blue & multi .30 .30
395 A69 50s lt green & multi .45 .45
396 A69 75s violet & multi .80 .80
Nos. 392-396,C209-
C213,CO117-CO119 (13) 45.80 23.55

25th anniv. of the reign of Elizabeth II. Printed on peelable paper backing showing replica of handwritten Proclamation of Accession.
For surcharge see No. 417.

Various Coins — A70

1977, July 4
397 A70 10s multicolored .25 .25
398 A70 15s multicolored .30 .30
399 A70 25s multicolored .40 .40
400 A70 50s multicolored .85 .85
401 A70 75s multicolored 1.50 1.50
Nos. 397-401,C214-
C218,CO120-CO122 (13) 13.50 13.50

10th anniversary of coronation of King Taufa'ahau IV. Printed on peelable paper backing showing multicolored replicas of Tongan stamps.

Capt. Cook's Resolution — A71

1977, Sept. 27 Litho.
402 A71 10s multicolored 1.00 .75
403 A71 17s multicolored 2.25 1.25
404 A71 25s multicolored 2.50 2.50
405 A71 30s multicolored 3.50 3.00
406 A71 40s multicolored 3.50 3.00
Nos. 402-406,C219-
C223,CO123-CO125 (13) 81.95 61.90

Bicentenary of Capt. Cook's farewell voyage.

Humpback Whale — A72

1977, Dec. 16
407 A72 15s ultra & black 4.25 .85
408 A72 22s green & black 4.50 1.50
409 A72 31s orange & black 5.25 2.00
410 A72 38s lilac & black 5.50 5.25
411 A72 64s red & black 9.25 5.50
Nos. 407-411,C224-
C228,CO126-CO128 (13) 87.25 38.15

Whale protection.

Stamps of 1975-77 Surcharged in Black, Green, Brown or Black on Silver

1978, Feb. 17
412 A61 15s on 20s (#359;B) 2.00 1.75
413 A62 15s on 5s (#362;B) 2.00 1.75
414 A65 15s on 10s (#373;G) 2.00 1.75
415 A67 15s on 5s (#382;Br) 2.00 1.75
416 A67 15s on 10s (#383;B) 2.00 1.75
417 A69 15s on 11s (#392;B on S) 2.00 3.00

418 OA11 15s on 38s (#CO99;B) 2.00 1.75
Nos. 412-418,C229-C238 (17) 79.75 70.50

The surcharge on No. 413 is only the "1," and on No. 418 includes "postage."

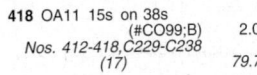

Flags of Canada and Tonga A73

1978, May 5 Litho.
419 A73 10s red & multi .25 .25
420 A73 15s red & multi .35 .35
421 A73 20s red & multi .45 .45
422 A73 25s red & multi .60 .60
423 A73 45s red & multi 2.00 2.00
Nos. 419-423,C239-
C243,CO129-CO131 (13) 14.05 14.05

11th Commonwealth Games, Edmonton, Canada, Aug. 3-12. See note after No. 226.

King Taufa'ahau IV — A74

1978, July 4
424 A74 2s multicolored .25 .25
425 A74 5s multicolored .25 .25
426 A74 10s multicolored .25 .25
427 A74 25s multicolored .65 .65
428 A74 75s multicolored 2.00 2.00
Nos. 424-428,C244-
C248,CO132-CO134 (13) 13.10 13.10

60th birthday of King Taufa'ahau IV. See note after No. 226.

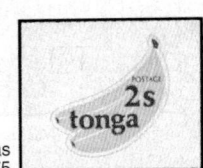

Two Bananas A75

Coconut — A76

Designs: 1s to 5s, Bananas. 6s to 10s, Coconuts. 15s to 1pa, Pineapples.

1978, Sept. 29 Typo.
429 A75 1s yellow & black .30 .30
430 A75 2s yellow & dk blue .30 .30
431 A75 3s multicolored .40 .40
432 A75 4s multicolored .40 .40
433 A75 5s multicolored .40 .40
434 A76 6s multicolored .60 .60
435 A76 7s multicolored .60 .60
436 A76 8s multicolored .60 .60
437 A76 9s multicolored .60 .60
438 A76 10s brown & green .60 .60
439 A76 15s green & lt brown 1.75 1.75
440 A76 20s multicolored 2.00 2.00
441 A76 30s multicolored 2.25 2.25
442 A76 50s multicolored 2.75 2.75
443 A76 1pa multicolored 3.25 3.25
Nos. 429-443,O36-O50 (30) 31.95 31.95

Nos. 429-443 issued in coils; self-adhesive control numbers on paper backing, except on 1s and 5s. See note after No. 226.

See No. 529.

Whale — A77

1978, Dec. 15   Litho. & Typo.
444 A77 15s shown   4.00 2.00
445 A77 18s Bat   4.00 2.00
446 A77 25s Turtle   4.00 2.00
447 A77 28s Parrot   6.50 3.00
448 A77 60s like 15s   10.50 6.00
    Nos. 444-448,C249-
    C253,CO150-CO152 (13)   85.75 45.50

Wildlife conservation. See note after No. 226.

Introduction of Metric System — A78

Shipping Routes, South Pacific
Map — A79

Peace
Corps — A80

22s, New church buildings. 50s, Air routes
to Auckland, Suva, Apia & Pago Pago.

1979, Feb. 16   Litho.
449 A78 5s multicolored   .25 .25
450 A79 11s multicolored   .60 .60
451 A80 18s multicolored   .60 .60
452 A79 22s multicolored   .60 .60
453 A79 50s multicolored   2.25 2.25
    Nos. 449-453,C254-
    C258,CO153-CO155 (13)   19.30 16.30

Decade of Progress. Paper backing shows
map of Tonga.

Tongan First Day Covers — A81

1979, June 1   Litho.
454 A81 5s multicolored   .30 .25
455 A81 10s multicolored   .40 .30
456 A81 25s multicolored   .70 .60
457 A81 50s multicolored   1.25 1.25
458 A81 1pa multicolored   1.75 1.75
    Nos. 454-458,C259-
    C263,CO156-CO158 (13)   14.15 12.65

10th anniversary of introduction of self-
adhesive stamps and for Bernard Mechanick,
inventor of self-adhesive, free-form stamps;
death centenary of Sir Rowland Hill.
Printed on peelable paper backing showing
advertisement.
For surcharges and overprints see Nos.
469-473.

Eua Island through Camera
Lens — A82

1979, Nov. 23   Litho.
459 A82 10s multicolored   .40 .40
460 A82 18s multicolored   .45 .45
461 A82 31s multicolored   .80 .80
462 A82 50s multicolored   1.25 1.25
463 A82 60s multicolored   1.40 1.40
    Nos. 459-463,C275-
    C279,CO170-CO172 (13)   13.35 13.35

Printed on peelable paper backing showing
film and camera.

King George Tupou I, Admiral du
Bouzet, Map of Tonga — A83

1980, Jan. 9   Litho.
464 A83 7s multicolored   .30 .30
465 A83 10s multicolored   .40 .40
466 A83 14s multicolored   .50 .50
467 A83 50s multicolored   1.50 1.50
468 A83 75s multicolored   2.00 2.00
    Nos. 464-468,C280-
    C284,CO173-CO175 (13)   14.85 14.85

Tongan-French Friendship Treaty, 125th
anniversary. Printed on peelable paper; multicolored backing shows map of Tonga.

**Nos. 454-458 Surcharged and
Overprinted in Black on Silver:
"1980 OLYMPIC GAMES," Moscow
'80 and Bear Emblems**

1980, Apr. 30   Litho.
469 A81 13s on 5s multi   .50 .50
470 A81 20s on 10s multi   .75 .75
471 A81 25s multicolored   .90 .90
472 A81 33s on 50s multi   1.10 1.10
473 A81 1pa multicolored   3.50 3.50
    Nos. 469-473,C285-
    C289,CO176-CO178 (13)   18.15 18.15

Boy Scout Cooking over
Campfire — A84

1980, Sept. 30   Litho.
474 A84 9s multicolored   .25 .25
475 A84 13s multicolored   .40 .40
476 A84 15s multicolored   .45 .45
477 A84 30s multicolored   .90 .90
    Nos. 474-477,C290-
    C293,CO179-CO180 (10)   17.00 17.00

Boy Scout Jamboree; Rotary Intl., 75th
anniv. Peelable backing shows map of Tonga.

**Nos. 361, 375, 380, 384-385
Surcharged**

1980, Dec. 3   Litho.
478 A65 9s on 35s multi   .50 .50
479 A67 13s on 20s multi   .75 .75
480 A67 13s on 25s multi   .75 .75
481 A66 19s on 25s multi   1.10 1.10
482 A61 1pa on 65s multi   6.25 6.25
    Nos. 478-482,C294-
    C299,CO181 (12)   27.85 27.85

Intl. Year of the Disabled — A85

1981, Sept. 9   Litho.
483 A85 2pa multicolored   3.25 3.25
484 A85 3pa multicolored   5.00 5.00
    Nos. 483-484,C300-C302 (5)   10.45 10.45

Prince
Charles and
Lady
Diana — A86

Designs: 13s, Charles, King Taufa'ahau.
47s, 1.50pa, Couple, diff.

1981, Oct. 21   Litho.
485 A86 13s multicolored   .25 .25
486 A86 47s multicolored   .50 .50
487 A86 1.50pa multicolored   1.75 1.75
488 A86 3pa multicolored   3.50 3.50
    Nos. 485-488 (4)   6.00 6.00

Royal Wedding and Gt. Britain-Tonga
Friendship Treaty centenary. Issued in sheets
of 20 (2x10) and 5 labels in vert. center row.
For surcharge see No. B1.

Bicentenary
of Discovery
of Vavau by
Francisco
Maurelle
A87

18th century Spanish engravings and maps.

1981, Nov. 25   Litho.
489 A87 9s multicolored   .60 .50
490 A87 13s multicolored   .90 .60
491 A87 47s multicolored   2.75 1.40
492 A87 1pa multicolored   6.75 6.75
     a. Souvenir sheet, imperf.   13.00 13.00
    Nos. 489-492 (4)   11.00 9.25

No. 492a contains one No. 492 (32x25mm).

Bible Class, 1830 Print — A88

1981, Nov. 25
493 A88 9s Open book   .30 .30
494 A88 13s Book, diff.   .50 .40
495 A88 32s Type   1.10 1.10
496 A88 47s shown   1.60 1.60
    Nos. 493-496 (4)   3.50 3.40

Christmas 1981 and sesquicentennial of
books printed in Tonga.

175th Anniv. of Capture of The Port-
au-Prince — A89

1981, Dec. 16   Litho.
497 A89 29s Battle   1.00 .75
498 A89 32s Battle, diff.   1.25 .90
499 A89 47s Map   1.60 1.50
500 A89 47s Sinking ship   1.60 1.50
     a. Pair, #499-500   3.25
501 A89 1pa Ship   3.50 3.50
    Nos. 497-501 (5)   8.95 8.15

Nos. CO179-CO180 Surcharged

1982, Jan. 4   Litho.
502 OA19 5pa on 25s multi   17.50 17.50
503 OA19 5pa on 2pa multi   17.50 17.50

Scouting
Year — A90

29s, Brownsea Isld. Camp, 1907. 32s,
Baden-Powell, horse. 47s, Imperial Jamboree,
1924. 1.50pa, "Scouting for Boys". 2.50pa,
Mafeking stamp.

1982, Feb. 22   Litho.
504 A90 29s multicolored   1.00 .60
505 A90 32s multicolored   1.00 .65
506 A90 47s multicolored   1.50 1.00
507 A90 1.50pa multicolored   4.50 3.00
508 A90 2.50pa multicolored   8.00 5.00
    Nos. 504-508 (5)   16.00 10.25

1982 World Cup — A91

Designs: Various soccer players, map showing match sites.

1982, July 7   Litho.
509	A91	32s multicolored	.85	.60
510	A91	47s multicolored	1.25	.85
511	A91	75s multicolored	1.90	1.40
512	A91	1.50pa multicolored	3.50	2.50
		Nos. 509-512 (4)	7.50	5.35

Inter-island Transport A92

9s, 13s, Ferry Olovaha. 47s, 1pa SPIA Twin Otter (Niuatoputapu Airport opening).

1982, Aug. 11
513	A92	9s multicolored	.50	.25
514	A92	13s multicolored	.60	.30
515	A92	47s multicolored	2.00	1.00
516	A92	1pa multicolored	4.00	2.75
		Nos. 513-516 (4)	7.10	4.30

Tin Can Mail Centenary A93

13s, 32s, 47s, Collecting mail. 2pa, Map. Nos. 517-519 form continuous design.

1982, Sept. 29   Litho.
517	A93	13s multicolored	.25	.25
518	A93	32s multicolored	.55	.55
519	A93	47s multicolored	.90	.90
a.		Souv. sheet of 3 (13s, 32s, 47s)	2.00	2.00
520	A93	2pa multicolored	3.50	3.50
a.		Souvenir sheet of 1	3.50	3.50
		Nos. 517-520 (4)	5.20	5.20

No. 520 comes with different labels. For surcharges see Nos. 526-528.

Tonga College Centenary — A94

1982, Oct. 25   Size: 42x30mm (5s)
521	A94	5s Students	.35	.35
522	A94	29s King George Tupou I		
			2.25	2.25
523	A94	29s Monument	2.25	2.25
a.		Pair, #522-523	5.00	
		Nos. 521-523 (3)	4.85	4.85

Nos. 521-523 inscribed in English or Tongan.

12th Commonwealth Games, Brisbane, Australia, Sept. 30-Oct. 9 — A95

1982, Oct. 25
524	A95	32s Decathlon, vert.	1.60	.75
525	A95	1.50pa Opening ceremony	8.25	8.25

Nos. 517-519 Overprinted in Red or Silver in 1 or 2 Lines: "Christmas / Greetings / 1982"

1982, Nov. 17
526	A93	13s multicolored	.30	.30
527	A93	32s multicolored	.70	.70
528	A93	47s multicolored	1.00	1.00
		Nos. 526-528 (3)	2.00	2.00

Pineapple Type of 1978 and

Fruit — A96

1982, Nov. 17
529	A76	13s multicolored	5.50	5.50
530	A96	2pa multicolored	12.00	12.00
531	A96	3pa multicolored	15.00	15.00
		Nos. 529-531 (3)	32.50	32.50

Capt. Cook's Resolution, 1777 and Canberra, 1983 — A96a

32s, like 29s. 47s, 1.50pa, Montgolfier Bros. balloon, 1783, Concorde. 2.50pa, Concorde, Canberra. 29s se-tenant with label showing Resolution.

1983, Feb. 22   Litho.
532	A96a	29s multicolored	2.25	1.50
533	A96a	32s multicolored	3.00	1.50
534	A96a	47s multicolored	4.25	2.50
535	A96a	1.50pa multicolored	11.00	11.00
		Nos. 532-535 (4)	20.50	16.50

Souvenir Sheet

536	A96a	2.50pa multicolored	6.50	6.50

Pacific Forum of Sea and Air Transport (29s, 32s, 2.50pa); manned flight bicentenary (47s, 1.50pa).
For overprints see Nos. O68-O70.

A96b

29s, Map. 32s, Dancers. 47s, Fishermen. 1.50pa, King Taufa'ahau IV, flag.

1983, Mar. 14
537	A96b	29s multi	1.40	1.40
538	A96b	32s multi	1.60	1.60
539	A96b	47s multi	2.25	2.25
540	A96b	1.50pa multi	7.00	7.00
		Nos. 537-540 (4)	12.25	12.25

Commonwealth Day.

Niuafo'ou Airport Opening A97

1983, May 11   Litho.
541	A97	32s De Havilland Otter	.90	.50
542	A97	47s like 32s	1.25	.50
543	A97	1pa Boeing 707	2.10	1.40
544	A97	1.50pa like 1pa	3.75	2.10
		Nos. 541-544 (4)	8.00	4.50

World Communications Year — A98

1983, June 22   Litho.
545	A98	29s Intelsat IV	.50	.50
546	A98	32s Intelsat IV-A	.60	.60
547	A98	75s Intelsat V	1.40	1.40

Size: 45x32mm
548	A98	2pa Apollo 15 Moon post cover	3.50	3.50
		Nos. 545-548 (4)	6.00	6.00

10th Anniv. of Bank of Tonga A99

Various banknotes.

1983, Aug. 3   Litho.
549	A99	1pa multicolored	2.25	2.25
550	A99	2pa multicolored	4.25	4.25

Printing Press, 1830 — A100

1983, Sept. 22   Litho.
551	A100	13s shown	.30	.30
552	A100	32s Woon's arrival, 1831	.75	.75
553	A100	1pa Print	1.75	1.75
554	A100	2pa Tonga Chronicle	3.75	3.75
		Nos. 551-554 (4)	6.55	6.55

Sesquicentennial of printing in Tonga (by missionary William Woon).

Christmas 1983 A101

Designs: Various sailboats off Vava'u.

1983, Nov. 17   Litho.
555	A101	29s multicolored	.50	.40
556	A101	32s multicolored	.60	.50
557	A101	1.50pa multicolored	2.40	2.40
558	A101	2.50pa multicolored	4.25	4.25
		Nos. 555-558 (4)	7.75	7.55

Abel Tasman, Discoverer of Tonga, and his Zeehan — A102

Navigators and Explorers of the Pacific and their Ships — 47s, Samuel Wallis, Dolphin. 90s, William Bligh, Bounty. 1.50pa, James Cook, Resolution.

1984, Mar. 12   Litho.
559	A102	32s shown	2.00	2.00
560	A102	47s multi	2.75	2.75
561	A102	90s multi	5.00	5.00
562	A102	1.50pa multi	9.00	9.00
		Nos. 559-562 (4)	18.75	18.75

See Nos. 593-596.

Swainsonia Casta — A103

Shells, fish — 2s, Porites (coral). 3s, Holocentrus ruber. 5s, Cypraea mappa viridis. 6s, Dardanus megistos (crab). 9s, Stegostoma fasciatum. 10s, Conus bullatus. 13s, Pterois volitans. 15s, Conus textile. 20s, Dascyllus aruanus. 29s, Conus aulicus. 32s, Acanthurus leucosternon. 47s, Lambis truncata. 1pa, Millepora dichotoma (coral). 2pa, Birgus latro (crab). 3pa, Chicoreus palma-rosae. 5pa, Thunnus albacares.

1984-85   Litho.
563	A103	1s shown	.50	1.90
564	A103	2s multi	1.25	1.90
565	A103	3s multi	1.60	2.25
566	A103	5s multi	.60	1.90
567	A103	6s multi	1.60	2.25
568	A103	9s multi	1.60	.90
a.		Perf. 14½ ('85)	1.60	.90
569	A103	10s multi	1.25	.95
570	A103	13s multi	1.90	.95
571	A103	15s multi	1.25	2.25
572	A103	20s multi	2.75	2.75
573	A103	29s multi	2.25	1.25
574	A103	32s multi	4.00	1.25
575	A103	47s multi	4.00	2.00

Size: 39x25mm
576	A103	1pa multi	12.00	12.00
577	A103	2pa multi	17.50	19.00
578	A103	3pa multi	11.00	19.00
579	A103	5pa multi	13.50	22.50
		Nos. 563-579 (17)	78.55	95.00

See Nos. 682-692, 701-709, 756-759. For surcharges and overprints see Nos. 618-625, 808-810, O52-O67, O71-O77.

Tonga Chronicle, 20th Anniv. — A104

1984, June 26
580	A104	3s multicolored	.25	.25
a.		Sheet of 12	.75	
581	A104	32s multicolored	.50	.50
a.		Sheet of 12	7.00	

Nos. 580-581 issued in sheets of 12; sheet backgrounds show pages of Chronicle, giving each stamp different background.

1984 Summer Olympics A105

1984, July 23
582	A105	29s Running	.40	.40
583	A105	47s Javelin	.65	.65
584	A105	1.50pa Shot put	2.00	2.00
585	A105	3pa Torch	4.25	4.25
		Nos. 582-585 (4)	7.30	7.30

Intl. Dateline Centenary — A106

47s, George Airy, Greenwich Meridian pioneer. 2pa, Sandford Fleming, time zone pioneer.

1984, Aug. 20
586	A106	47s multicolored	2.00	1.50
587	A106	2pa multicolored	9.00	6.00

Ausipex '84 — A107

1984, Sept. 17
588	A107	32s Australia #18	1.25	.85
589	A107	1.50pa Tonga #51	5.50	3.75

Souvenir Sheet
589A		Sheet of 2, #588-589	5.50	5.50

Nos. 588-589 each printed se-tenant with label showing exhibition emblem.

No. 589A contains two imperf. stamps similar to Nos. 588-589, but with denomination replacing logo. No. 589A without denominations was not valid for postage.

Christmas 1984 — A108

Christmas Carols in local settings.

1984, Nov. 12 Litho.
590	A108	32s Silent Night	.90	.50
591	A108	47s Away in a Manger	1.60	.80
592	A108	1pa I Saw Three Ships	3.25	3.25
		Nos. 590-592 (3)	5.75	4.55

Explorers Type of 1984

Designs: 32s, Willem Schouten (c. 1580-1625), The Eendracht, 1616. 47s, Jakob Le Maire (1585-1616), The Hoorn, 1615. 90s, Lt. Fletcher Christian, The Bounty, 1789. 1.50pa, Francisco Maurelle, La Princessa, 1781.

1985, Feb. 27 Litho. Die Cut
593	A102	32s multicolored	2.50	1.50
a.		Perf. 14	50.00	
594	A102	47s multicolored	3.75	1.75
595	A102	90s multicolored	6.75	5.00
596	A102	1.50pa multicolored	12.00	7.75
		Nos. 593-596 (4)	25.00	16.00

Nos. 593-596 each printed se-tenant with self-adhesive label picturing anchor.

Geological Survey of Tonga Trench for Oil — A110

Designs: 29s, Tonga Trench and islands. 32s, Marine exploration, seismic surveying. 47s, Search for oil off Tongatapu, vert. No. 600, Exploration of sea bed, vert. No. 601, Angler fish.

1985, Apr. 10
597	A110	29s multicolored	1.50	1.10
598	A110	32s multicolored	1.60	1.10
599	A110	47s multicolored	2.50	1.60
600	A110	1.50pa multicolored	8.25	8.25
		Nos. 597-600 (4)	13.85	12.05

Souvenir Sheet
601	A110	1.50pa multicolored	13.00	7.75
a.		Perf. 14	13.00	7.75

Nos. 597-600 printed in sheets of 40, 2 panes of 20 separated by labels inscribed "Proof 1," etc.

Adventures of Will Mariner — A111

29s, Readying Port au Prince for sail, Gravesend, 1805. 32s, Captured & set afire, 1806. 47s, Mariner taken prisoner by Chief Finow, Tonga. 1.50pa, Passage to China aboard brig Favourite. 2.50pa, Returning to England aboard East Indiaman Cuffnells, 1810.

1985, June 18 Die Cut
602	A111	29s multicolored	.60	.50
a.		Perf. 14	.60	.50
603	A111	32s multicolored	.65	.55
a.		Perf. 14	.65	.55
604	A111	47s multicolored	1.00	.80
a.		Perf. 14	1.00	.80
605	A111	1.50pa multicolored	3.75	3.75
a.		Perf. 14	3.75	3.75
606	A111	2.50pa multicolored	6.00	6.00
a.		Perf. 14	6.00	6.00
		Nos. 602-606 (5)	12.00	11.60
		Nos. 602a-606a (5)	12.00	11.60

Mutiny on the Bounty, Film 50th Anniv. A112

Designs: a, Byron Russell (Quintal), Stanley Fields (Muspratt) and Charles Laughton (Capt. Bligh). b, Laughton, Donald Crisp (Burkitt), Eddie Quillon (Ellison) and David Thursby (Maxwell). c, Clark Gable (Fletcher Christian). d, Russell, Alec Craig (McCoy), Laughton and Fields. e, Laughton and Franchot Tone (Roger Byam).

1985, July 16 Perf. 14
607		Strip of 5	62.50	62.50
a.-e.		A112 47s, any single	10.00	5.00

Sheets consist of four strips of 5 and a central strip of labels showing film credits.

Queen Mother, 85th Birthday A113

Designs: 32s, Age 10. 47s, At Hadfield Girl Guides rally, 1931. 1.50pa, In Guide uniform. 2.50pa, Portrait by Norman Parkinson, 1985.

1985, Aug. 20 Imperf.
608	A113	32s multicolored	1.25	.90
a.		Perf. 14	2.00	1.50
609	A113	47s multicolored	2.00	1.50
a.		Perf. 14	3.25	2.40

610	A113	1.50pa multicolored	6.00	6.00
a.		Perf. 14	9.25	9.25
611	A113	2.50pa multicolored	9.75	9.75
a.		Perf. 14	15.00	15.00
		Nos. 608-611 (4)	19.00	18.15
		Nos. 608a-611a (4)	29.50	28.15

Girl Guides movement, 75th anniv.

Christmas — A114

32s, No room at the inn. 42s, Shepherds follow star. 1.50pa, The three kings. 2.50pa, Holy family.

1985, Nov. 12
612	A114	32s multicolored	.50	.35
613	A114	42s multicolored	.75	.50
614	A114	1.50pa multicolored	2.75	2.75
615	A114	2.50pa multicolored	4.25	4.25
		Nos. 612-615 (4)	8.25	7.85

Self-adhesive Discontinued
In 1986, die cut self-adhesive stamps attached to peelable paper backing were no longer issued, unless otherwise stated.

Halley's Comet A115

Designs: Nos. 616a, 617a, Comet. Nos. 616b, 617b, Edmond Halley. Nos. 616c, 617c, Solar system. Nos. 616d, 617d, Telescope. Nos. 616e, 617e, Giotto space probe.

1986, Mar. 26 Perf. 14
616		Strip of 5	19.00	19.00
a.-e.		A115 42s, any single	3.00	3.00
617		Strip of 5	19.00	19.00
a.-e.		A115 57s, any single	3.00	3.00

Nos. 564, 570, 565, 568, 567, 572, 577 and 579 Surcharged

1986, Apr. 16 Die Cut
Self-adhesive
618	A103	4s on 2s, #564	1.10	2.25
619	A103	4s on 13s, #570	1.10	2.25
620	A103	42s on 3s, #565	2.90	1.75
621	A103	42s on 9s, #568	2.90	1.75
622	A103	57s on 6s, #567	3.50	2.50
623	A103	57s on 20s, #572	3.50	2.50
624	A103	2.50pa on 2pa, #577	11.00	11.00
625	A103	2.50pa on 5pa, #579	11.00	11.00
		Nos. 618-625 (8)	37.00	35.00

Royal Links with the United Kingdom A116

1986, May 22 Perf. 14
626	A116	57s Taufa'ahau IV	1.50	1.50
627	A116	57s Elizabeth II	1.50	1.50
a.		Pair, #626-627	3.50	3.50

Size: 40x40mm
628	A116	2.50pa King and queen	6.00	6.00
		Nos. 626-628 (3)	9.00	9.00

Queen Elizabeth II, 60th birthday. No. 628 printed in sheets of 5 + one label.

AMERIPEX '86, Chicago, May 22-June 1 — A117

Peace Corps activities: No. 629, Health care. No. 630, Education.

1986, May 22
629	A117	57s multicolored	1.10	1.10
630	A117	1.50pa multicolored	3.00	3.00
a.		Souv. sheet, #629, 630, imperf	4.75	4.75
b.		Pair, #629-630	5.75	5.75

Peace Corps in Tonga, 20th anniv.

Intl. Sporting Events — A118

Designs: 42s, 1986 Field Hockey World Cup, London. 57s, Women's basketball, 13th Commonwealth Games, Scotland. 1pa, Boxing, Commonwealth Games. 2.50pa, 1986 World Cup Soccer Championships, Mexico.

1986, July 23 Litho. Perf. 14
631	A118	42s multicolored	1.25	1.25
632	A118	57s multicolored	2.00	2.00
633	A118	1pa multicolored	3.25	3.25
634	A118	2.50pa multicolored	8.00	8.00
		Nos. 631-634 (4)	14.50	14.50

Postage Stamp Cent. A119

Stamps on stamps: No. 635, #1. No. 636, #47a. No. 637, #91. No. 638, #628. No. 639a, #40, UL portion of #C29. No. 639b, UR portion of #C29, left side #245. No. 639c, Center of #245, Type AP10. No. 639d, Left side #245, #C148. No. 639e, LL portion of #C29, #429, #440. No. 639f, LR portion of #C29, #C135. No. 639g, #507. No. 639h, #514. Nos. 639a-639h, vert.

1986, Aug. 27
635	A119	32s multi	2.50	1.75
636	A119	42s multi	2.75	2.00
637	A119	57s multi	3.50	2.00
638	A119	2.50pa multi	5.75	5.75
		Nos. 635-638 (4)	14.50	11.50

Souvenir Sheet
639		Sheet of 8	15.00	15.00
a.-h.		A119 50s, any single	1.50	1.50

Christmas — A120

Designs: 32s, Girls wearing shell jewelry. 42s, Boy, totem poles, vert. 57s, Folk dancers, vert. 2pa, outrigger canoe.

1986, Nov. 12 Litho. Perf. 14
640	A120	32s multicolored	2.50	.75
641	A120	42s multicolored	2.75	1.00
642	A120	57s multicolored	3.00	1.50
643	A120	2pa multicolored	6.25	6.25
		Nos. 640-643 (4)	14.50	9.50

Nos. 641-642 Ovptd. with Jamboree Emblem and "BOY SCOUT / JAMBOREE / 5th-10th DEC '86" in Silver

1986, Dec. 2	**Litho.**	**Perf. 14**	
644	A120	42s multicolored	3.50 3.50
645	A120	57s multicolored	3.75 3.75

Dumont d'Urville's Second Voyage A121

Designs: 32s, D'Urville and ship Astrolabe. 42s, Four Tongan girls, detail from D'Urville's engraving, Voyage au Pole et dans l'Oceanie. 1pa, Map of voyage. 2.50pa, Wreck of the Astrolabe.

1987, Feb. 24			
646	A121	32s multicolored	4.25 2.00
647	A121	42s multicolored	4.25 2.00
648	A121	1pa multicolored	10.00 6.00
649	A121	2.50pa multicolored	16.00 16.00
		Nos. 646-649 (4)	34.50 26.00

Dumont d'Urville (1790-1842), explorer and admiral.

Wildlife Conservation — A122

Fauna: a, Noah's Ark. b, Eagles. c, Giraffes, birds. d, Seagulls. e, Elephants. f, Elephant. g, Lions, zebras, antelopes. h, Chimpanzees. i, Antelope, frogs. j, Tigers, lizard. k, Tiger, snake. l, Butterfly.

1987, May 6		**Perf. 13½**	
650	A122	Sheet of 12	67.50 67.50
a.-l.		42s any single	4.25 4.25

1st Inter-island Canoe Race, Tonga to Samoa — A123

1987, July 1		**Perf. 14**	
651	A123	32s Two paddlers	.55 .45
652	A123	42s Five paddlers	.85 .70
653	A123	57s Three paddlers	1.10 .90
654	A123	1.50pa Two, diff.	3.00 3.00
a.		Souvenir sheet of 4, #651-654	10.00 10.00
		Nos. 651-654 (4)	5.50 5.05

Coronation of King Taufa'ahau IV, 20th Anniv. — A124

Booklet Stamps

1987-88	**Self-Adhesive**		**Imperf.**
655	A124	1s green & yel grn	.35 .85
655A	A124	2s blk & pale yel org	4.00 4.00
656	A124	5s black & brt pink	.35 .85
a.		Bklt. pane of 12 (6 5s plus 1 5s, 2 10s, 3 15s with gutter between)	5.00
657	A124	10s black & bluish lil	.45 .95
658	A124	15s brn blk & org ver	.60 .95
a.		Bklt. pane of 12 (1s, 2 2s, 3 10s, plus 2 5s, 10s, 3 15s with gutter between) ('88)	14.00

659	A124	32s Prus bl & aqua	.70 1.00
a.		Bklt. pane, 4 32s, 2 15s + 4 10s, 2 1s with gutter between)	7.00
b.		Bklt. pane, 6 32s + 2 2s, 4 1s with gutter btwn. ('88)	14.00
		Nos. 655-659 (6)	6.45 8.60

Issued: 2s, 7/4/88; others, 7/1/87.

Parliament, 125th Anniv. — A125

1987, Sept. 2		**Litho.**	**Perf. 14½**
660	A125	32s multicolored	.50 .50
661	A125	42s multicolored	.75 .75
662	A125	75s multicolored	1.50 1.50
663	A125	2pa multicolored	3.00 3.00
		Nos. 660-663 (4)	5.75 5.75

Christmas 1987 — A126

Cartoons featuring Octopus as Santa Claus and mouse as his helper.

1987, Nov. 18		**Litho.**	**Perf. 14**
664	A126	42s Sack of gifts	1.50 .80
665	A126	57s Delivering them by canoe	1.75 1.75
666	A126	1pa By automobile	3.25 3.25
667	A126	3pa Sipping tropical drinks	8.00 8.00
		Nos. 664-667 (4)	14.50 13.80

King Taufa'ahau Tupou IV, 70th Birthday — A127

Portrait and: 32s, M.V. Olovaha inter-island ship, athlete pole vaulting and offshore oil derrick. 42s, Banknote and coins, Ha'Amonga Trilithon and traditional craftsman. 57s, Rowing, Red Cross nurse and communications satellite. 2.50pa, Tonga Scouts emblem, No. 506 and Friendly Islands Airways passenger plane.

1988, July 4		**Litho.**	**Perf. 11½**
668	A127	32s multicolored	2.25 1.00
669	A127	42s multicolored	1.60 1.10
670	A127	57s multicolored	1.75 1.10
671	A127	2.50pa multicolored	8.00 8.00
		Nos. 668-671 (4)	13.60 11.20

See Nos. 744-747 for stamps inscribed for the silver jubilee.

Souvenir Sheet

Australia Bicentennial — A128

Designs: a, Cook and his journal. b, List of stores shipped aboard the Lady Juliana, the ship, Arthur Philip, 1st gov. of New South Wales, 1788, and left half of the list of sentences of all the prisoners tried at Glo'ster Assizes. c, Right half of list of sentences, Australia Type A59 redrawn and aerial view of an early settlement. d, Robert O'Hara Burke (1820-61) and W.J. Wills (1834-61), the 1st explorers to cross Australia from south to north. e, Emu pictured on a Player's cigarette card, U.R. Stuart's (gold) prospecting license and opals. f, Australian Commonwealth Military Forces emblem, WW I recruit on cigarette card, and war poster. g, Souv. card commemorating 1st overland mail delivery by transcontinental railway, and Australia Type A4 on cover. h, Hand-canceled cover commemorating the 1st England-Australia transcontinental airmail flight, Nov. 12-Dec.10, 1919, aviator Capt. Ross Smith (1892-1922) and Great Britain #588. i, Don Bradman and Harold Larwood, cricket champions of the 1930s, on cigarette cards, and era newspaper frontispiece. j, Frontispiece of Hulton's natl. weekly Picture Post Victory Special issue, and WW II campaign medals. k, Australia #676 and a sheep station. l, Sydney Harbor Bridge, Opera House and theater tickets to The Bartered Bride.

1988, July 11		**Litho.**	**Perf. 13½**
672	A128	Sheet of 12	45.00 45.00
a.-l.		42s any single	3.00 3.00

1988 Summer Olympics, Seoul — A129

1988, Aug. 11			**Perf. 14**
673	A129	57s Running	.90 .90
674	A129	75s Yachting	1.10 1.10
675	A129	2pa Cycling	5.50 5.50
676	A129	3pa Women's tennis	6.50 6.50
		Nos. 673-676 (4)	14.00 14.00

Music of Tonga A130

1988, Sept. 9		**Litho.**	**Perf. 14**
677	A130	32s shown	.45 .35
678	A130	42s Choir	.65 .50
679	A130	57s Tonga Police Band	.80 .70
680	A130	2.50pa The Jets	3.50 3.50
		Nos. 677-680 (4)	5.40 5.05

Souvenir Sheet

681		Sheet of 2	3.50 3.50
a.		A130 57s like 2.50pa	1.10 1.10
b.		A130 57s Olympic eternal flame	1.10 1.10

SPORT AID '88.

Marine Type of 1984

Two types of background shading on No. 690:

Type I: Shading at top and sides extends to vert. & horiz. edges of design.
Type II: Shading is oval shaped.

1988		**Litho.**	**Perf. 14½**
		Size: 27x34mm	
682	A103	1s like No. 563	.30 .30
683	A103	2s like No. 564	.40 .40
684	A103	5s like No. 566	.55 .55
685	A103	6s like No. 567	1.10 .65
686	A103	10s like No. 569	.65 .65
687	A103	15s like No. 571	.65 .65
688	A103	20s like No. 572	.95 .95
689	A103	32s like No. 574	1.10 1.10
690	A103	42s Fregata ariel, type I	4.00 .95
a.		Type II	35.00
691	A103	57s Sula leucogaster	4.75 1.25
		Size: 41x27mm	
		Perf. 14	
692	A103	3pa Like No. 578	3.00 9.00
		Nos. 682-692 (11)	17.45 16.90

Issued: 1s, 5s, 10s, 20s, 32s, Oct. 4; 2s, 6s, 15s, 42s, 57s, 3pa, Oct. 18.
Nos. 683-684, 686, 689 exist inscribed "1990."
See #701-709. For surcharge see #808.

Tonga-US Treaty, Cent. A131

1988, Oct. 20			**Perf. 14**
693	A131	42s Resolution	1.00 .75
694	A131	57s Santa Maria	1.50 1.10
695	A131	2pa Capt. Cook, Columbus	5.50 5.50
a.		Souvenir sheet of 3, #693-695	7.25 7.25
		Nos. 693-695 (3)	8.00 7.35

Christmas — A132

Designs (a, Intl. Red Cross, b, Natl. Red Cross): 15s, Girl, teddy bear. 32s, Nurse reading to child. 42s, Checking pulse. 57s, Tucking child into bed. 1.50pa, Boy in wheelchair.

1988, Nov. 17		**Litho.**	**Perf. 14½**
696	A132	15s Pair, #a.-b.	.50 .50
697	A132	32s Pair, #a.-b.	1.00 1.00
698	A132	42s Pair, #a.-b.	1.10 1.10
699	A132	57s Pair, #a.-b.	1.90 1.90
700	A132	1.50pa Pair, #a.-b.	4.75 4.75
		Nos. 696-700 (5)	9.25 9.25

Intl. Red Cross 125th anniv. and 25th anniv. of the natl. Red Cross.

Marine Type of 1984

7s, Diomedea exulans. 35s, Hippocampus. 1pa, Chelonia mydas. 1.50pa, Megaptera novaeangliae.

1989, Mar. 2			**Litho.**
		Size: 27x34mm	
701	A103	4s like No. 570	1.90 1.90
702	A103	7s multicolored	4.50 3.00
703	A103	35s multicolored	4.00 3.25
704	A103	50s like No. 573	4.50 2.40
		Size: 41x27mm	
		Perf. 14	
705	A103	1pa multicolored	7.25 5.50
706	A103	1.50pa multicolored	14.50 9.00
707	A103	2pa like No. 577	10.50 10.50
709	A103	5pa like No. 579	17.00 20.00
		Nos. 701-709 (8)	64.15 55.55

Mutiny on the Bounty, Bicent. — A133

32s, Map of Tofua & Kao Isls., breadfruit. 42s, Bounty, chronometer. 57s, William Bligh & castaways in longboat. 2pa, Mutineers on the Bounty, vert. 3pa, Castaways.

Perf. 13½x14, 14x13½

1989, Apr. 28			Photo.
710	A133	32s multicolored	4.50	2.50
711	A133	42s multicolored	7.50	3.25
712	A133	57s multicolored	10.00	4.75
		Nos. 710-712 (3)	22.00	10.50

Souvenir Sheet

713		Sheet of 2	17.00	17.00
a.	A133	2pa multicolored	5.00	5.00
b.	A133	3pa multicolored	7.50	7.50

Butterflies
A134

42s, Hypolimnas bolina. 57s, Jamides bochus. 1.20pa, Melanitis leda solandra. 2.50pa, Danaus plexippus.

1989, May 15		Litho.	Perf. 14½
714	A134	42s multi	1.25	.85
715	A134	57s multi	1.60	1.10
716	A134	1.20pa multi	3.75	2.75
717	A134	2.50pa multi	7.25	7.25
		Nos. 714-717 (4)	13.85	11.95

Opening of the Natl. Sports Stadium
and the South Pacific Mini Games,
Aug. 22
A135

Rugby (No. 718): a, Rugby Public School, 1870. b, Dave Gallaher and the Springboks vs. East Midlands, 1906. c, King George V inspecting Cambridge team of 1922 and Wavell Wakefield, captain of England. d, Ernie Crawford, captain of Ireland, Danie Craven demonstrating the dive pass and cigarette cards from the 1930's. e, Sioni Mafi, captain of Tonga, and match scene.
Tennis (No. 719): a, Royal tennis, 1659. b, Walter Clopton Wingfield and game of lawn tennis, 1873. c, Oxford and Cambridge teams of 1884. d, Bunny Ryan in 1910 and cigarette cards. e, Tennis players, 1980's.
Cricket (No. 720): a, Match in 1743 and bronze memorial to Fuller Pilch. b, W.G. Grace, 19th cent. c, The Boys Own Paper, 1909. d, Australian team of 1909 and cigarette cards. e, The Ashes trophy and modern match scene.

1989, Aug. 22		Litho.	Perf. 14
718		Strip of 5	6.25	6.25
a.-e.	A135	32s any single	1.00	1.00
719		Strip of 5	9.50	9.50
a.-e.	A135	42s any single	1.50	1.50
720		Strip of 5	14.50	14.50
a.-e.	A135	57s any single	2.50	2.50
		Nos. 718-720 (3)	30.25	30.25

Printed in sheets of 10 containing descriptions and emblem.

Natl. Aviation
History — A136

Designs: 42s, Short S30. 57s, Vought F4U Corsair. 90s, Boeing 737. 3pa, Montgolfier brothers' hot-air balloon, the Wright Flyer, Concorde jet and space shuttle.

1989, Oct. 23		Litho.	Perf. 14½x14
721	A136	32s multicolored	3.25	1.60
722	A136	57s multicolored	3.75	2.00
723	A136	90s multicolored	6.50	6.00

Size: 97x126½mm

724	A136	3pa multicolored	16.00	16.00
		Nos. 721-724 (4)	29.50	25.60

1st Flight to Tonga, 1939 (42s); military base on the island, 1943 (57s); civil aviation, Fua'amotu Airport (90s); aviation through the ages (3pa).

Flying Home for
Christmas
A137

32s, Aircraft landing. 42s, Islanders waving, aircraft. 57s, Tongan in outrigger canoe, aircraft. 3pa, Islanders waving, aircraft, diff.

1989, Nov. 9			Perf. 14x13½
725	A137	32s multi	2.40	1.10
726	A137	42s multi	2.75	1.10
727	A137	57s multi	3.00	1.50
728	A137	3pa multi	8.00	8.00
		Nos. 725-728 (4)	16.15	11.70

World
Stamp
Expo '89
A138

20th UPU Congress, Washington,
DC — A139

Postal history and communications (No. 730): a, Sir Rowland Hill, penny blacks on Mulready envelope. b, Clipper ship, early train. c, Pony Express advertisement, stagecoach, post rider. d, Hot-air balloon and flight cover. e, Samuel Morse, miniature, telegraph key. f, Early Royal Mail truck, mailbox. g, Biplane and early aviators. h, Zeppelin flight cover, HMS Queen Mary. i, Helicopter, truck. j, Computer operator, facsimile machine. k, Apollo 11 mission emblem, flight cover, planetary bodies. l, American space shuttle, UPU monument.

1989, Nov. 17		Litho.	Perf. 14
729	A138	57s Pair, #730k-730 l	3.50	3.50

Souvenir Sheet

Perf. 13½

730	A139	Sheet of 12	42.50	42.50
a.-l.	A139	57s any single	2.50	2.50

A140

1990, Feb. 14		Litho.	Perf. 14
731	A140	42s Boxing	1.25	.75
732	A140	57s Archery	2.25	1.50
733	A140	1pa Bowls	3.00	3.00
734	A140	2pa Swimming	5.00	5.00
		Nos. 731-734 (4)	11.50	10.25

1990 Commonwealth Games.

A141

Protect the Environment: 32s, Wave power, ocean pollution. 57s, Wind power, acid rain. $1.20, Solar power, ozone layer. $2.50, Green earth, rain forests.

1990, Apr. 11		Litho.	Perf. 14
735	A141	32s multicolored	2.50	.90
736	A141	57s multicolored	3.50	1.50
737	A141	1.20pa multicolored	7.00	7.00
		Nos. 735-737 (3)	13.00	9.40

Souvenir Sheet

738	A141	2.50pa multicolored	13.00	13.00

First
Postage
Stamps,
150th
Anniv.
A142

1990		Litho.	Perf. 14
739	A142	42s G. B. #1	2.10	1.50
740	A142	42s G. B. #2	2.10	1.50
a.		Pair, #739-740	3.75	3.75
741	A142	57s Tonga #1	2.50	1.50
742	A142	1.50pa Tonga #CO180	6.00	6.00
743	A142	2.50pa Tonga #736	9.00	9.00
		Nos. 739-743 (5)	21.70	19.50

**King's Birthday Type of 1988
Inscribed "Silver Jubilee of His
Majesty King Taufa'ahau Tupou IV
1965-1990"**

1990, July 4			Perf. 11½
744	A127	32s like No. 668	1.50	1.00
745	A127	42s like No. 669	1.50	1.00
746	A127	57s like No. 670	2.25	1.25
747	A127	2.50pa like No. 671	7.75	7.75
		Nos. 744-747 (4)	13.00	11.00

Native
Catamaran — A143

1990, June 6			Perf. 14½
748	A143	32s buff & green	1.60	.75
749	A143	42s buff & bl, diff.	1.60	.85
750	A143	1.20pa buff & brn, diff.	4.25	4.25
751	A143	3pa buff & vio, diff.	8.50	8.50
		Nos. 748-751 (4)	15.95	14.35

Banded
Iguana
A144

1990, Sept. 12		Litho.	Perf. 14
752	A144	32s multicolored	2.00	1.25
753	A144	42s multi, diff.	2.50	1.75
754	A144	57s multi, diff.	3.25	2.25
755	A144	1.20pa multi, diff.	8.25	4.75
		Nos. 752-755 (4)	16.00	10.00

Marine Type of 1984

1990, July 6			Perf. 14
		Size: 20x22mm		
756	A103	2s like No. 564	1.25	.85
a.		Booklet pane of 10	12.50	12.50
757	A103	5s like No. 566	1.25	.85
a.		Booklet pane of 10	12.50	12.50
758	A103	10s like No. 569	1.25	.85
a.		Booklet pane of 10	12.50	12.50

759	A103	32s like No. 574	2.25	2.25
a.		Booklet pane of 10	22.50	22.50
		Nos. 756-759 (4)	6.00	4.80

Nos. 756-758 exist inscribed "1992."
For surcharges see Nos. 809-810.
Issue date: #756a-759a, Sept. 4.

UN Development Program, 40th
Anniv. — A145

1990, Oct. 25		Litho.	Perf. 14
760	A145	57s Tourism	2.00	2.00
761	A145	57s Agriculture, fisheries	2.00	2.00
a.		Pair, #760-761	4.50	4.50
762	A145	3pa Education	10.00	10.00
763	A145	3pa Healthcare	10.00	10.00
a.		Pair, #762-763	22.50	22.50
		Nos. 760-763 (4)	24.00	24.00

Rotary
Intl. — A146

1990, Nov. 28			
764	A146	32s shown	1.00	.55
765	A146	42s Two boys	1.50	.80
766	A146	2pa Three children	5.00	5.00
767	A146	3pa Two girls	6.50	6.50
		Nos. 764-767 (4)	14.00	12.85

Accident Prevention — A147

No. 768: a, d, Care at work; hard hats save lives. b, c, Keep matches and medicines out of children's reach. e, as "d," corrected inscription
No. 769: a, d, Don't drink and drive. b, c, Crash helmets save lives; mind cyclists and children.
No. 770: a, d, Listen to forecasts; learn to swim. b, c, Swim from safe beaches; beware of broken glass.
"a" and "b" have English inscriptions, denominations at top; "c" and "d" have Tongan inscriptions, denominations at bottom.

Strips of 4 + Label

1991, Apr. 10		Litho.	Perf. 14½
768	A147	32s #a.-d.	5.25	5.25
f.		Strip of 4, #a.-c., e.	35.00	
769	A147	42s #a.-d.	7.50	7.50
770	A147	57s #a.-d.	9.25	9.25
		Nos. 768-770 (3)	22.00	22.00

Center label is a progressive proof.
No. 768d was incorrectly inscribed, "Ngauo tokanga." No. 768e was issued 8/11/91 with correct inscription, "Ngaue tokanga."
For surcharges see No. 811, 1124.

A148

1991, July 2		Litho.	Perf. 14½
771	A148	42s Fish	.80	.70
772	A148	57s Island, boat	.95	.85
773	A148	2pa Fruit, island	3.50	3.50
774	A148	3pa Turtle, beach	6.25	6.25
		Nos. 771-774 (4)	11.50	11.30

Heilala week.

A149

Racing yachts: a, Red spinnaker. b, Yellow spinnaker. c, Green striped spinnaker. d, Yacht at sunset. e, Yacht, moon.

Miniature Sheet of 5 + Label

1991, July 2
775 A149 1pa #775a-775e   13.00 13.00
Around the world yacht race.

Church of Jesus Christ of Latter Day Saints in Tonga, Cent. — A150

1991, Aug. 19
776 A150 42s Tonga Temple   1.75 1.75
777 A150 57s Temple at night 2.75 2.75

Rowing Festival A151

42s, Women's coxed eight. 57s, Men's longboat. 1pa, Outrigger. No. 781, Bow of large canoe. No. 782, Stern of large canoe.

1991, Oct. 29   Litho.   *Perf. 14*
778 A151 42s multicolored   1.00 1.00
779 A151 57s multicolored   1.50 1.50
780 A151 1pa multicolored   2.75 2.75
781 A151 2pa multicolored   5.25 5.25
782 A151 2pa multicolored   5.25 5.25
  a.   Pair, #781-782   11.00 11.00
      Nos. 778-782 (5)   15.75 15.75

For surcharges see Nos. 898-899C.

Telecommunications — A152

No. 783: a, Recording television program. b, Communications Satellite. c, Watching television program.
No. 784: a, Man on telephone, woman at computer. b, Communications satellite, diff. c, Man in city on telephone.
No. 785: a, Seaman on sinking ship broadcasting SOS. b, Man on telephone, satellite relay station. c, Rescue missions.
No. 786: a, Weather satelite. b, Men at computers. c, Television weather report, storm.

1991, Oct. 15   Litho.   *Perf. 14½*
783 A152 15s Strip of 3, #a.-c.   1.50 1.50
784 A152 32s Strip of 3, #a.-c.   3.00 3.00
785 A152 45s Strip of 3, #a.-c.   4.25 4.25
786 A152 57s Strip of 3, #a.-c.   6.00 6.00
      Nos. 783-786 (4)   14.75 14.75

For surcharges, see 1095-1098.

Christmas — A153

Designs: 32s, Turtles pulling Santa's sleigh. 42s, Santa on roof. 57s, Family with presents. 3.50pa, Waving goodbye to Santa.

1991, Nov. 11   *Perf. 14*
787 A153 32s multicolored   1.00 .70
788 A153 42s multicolored   1.25 .90
789 A153 57s multicolored   1.75 1.75
790 A153 3.50pa multicolored 10.00 10.00
      Nos. 787-790 (4)   14.00 13.35

For surcharges, see 1120-1122.

Armed Forces — A154

1991, Dec. 15
791 42s Royal Tonga Marine   1.00 1.00
792 42s Patrol boat Pangai   1.00 1.00
  a. A154 Pair, #791-792   2.50 2.50
793 57s Patrol boat Neiafu   1.50 1.50
794 57s Tonga Royal Guards   1.50 1.50
  a. A154 Pair, #793-794   3.50 3.50
795 2pa King Tupou IV, military parade 5.25 5.25
796 2pa Patrol boat Savea   5.25 5.25
  a. A154 Pair, #795-796   11.00 11.00
      Nos. 791-796 (6)   15.50 15.50

Miniature Sheet

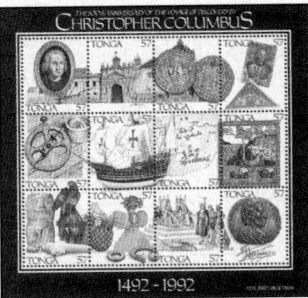

Discovery of America, 500th Anniv. — A155

Designs: a, Columbus. b, Monastery of Santa Maria de la Chevas. c, Obverse and reverse of coin of Ferdinand and Isabella. d, Spain #C48, #426. e, Compass, astrolabe. f, Santa Maria. g, Map, Columbus' signature. h, Columbus arriving in New World. i, Lucayan artifacts, parrot. j, Pineapple, artifacts. k, Columbus announcing his discovery. l, Medal of Columbus, signature.

1992, Apr. 28   Litho.   *Perf. 13½*
797 A155 57s Sheet of 12, #a.-l.   42.50 42.50

Marine Type of 1984 and

A155a

1s, Swainsonia casta. 3s, Holocentrus ruber. 5s, Cypraea mappa viridis. 10s, Conus bullatus. 20s, Dascyllus aruanus. 45s, Lambis truncata. 60s, Conus aulicus. 80s, Pterois volitans.

Perf. 13x13½, 14 (15s, 20s, 10pa)
1992-93   Litho.
798 A155a 1s multicolored   .25 .25
799 A155a 3s multicolored   .25 .25
800 A155a 5s multicolored   .25 .25

801 A155a 10s multicolored   .25 .25
802 A103 15s like #567   .30 .30
803 A155a 20s multicolored   .35 .35
804 A155a 45s multicolored   .75 .75
805 A155a 60s multicolored 1.00 1.00
806 A155a 80s multicolored 1.40 1.40
        Size: 27x41mm
807 A103 10pa like #568   20.00 20.00
        Nos. 798-807 (10)   24.80 24.80

Issued: 1s, 3s, 5s, 10s, 20s, 45s, 60s, 80s, May 12, 1993. 15s, 10pa, May 5, 1992.
See Nos. 874-884. Area covered by background colors on Nos. 874, 876-879 has been reduced in size. See Nos. 920-924.
For inscribed stamps see Nos. O78-O87.

Surcharges

On #688

On #756 in Blue

On #759

On #769 in Red and Black

1992-93   Litho.   *Perf. 14½, 14*
808 A103 1s on 20s #688   .25 .25
809 A103 10s on 2s #756 65.00 65.00
810 A103 45s on 32s #759 4.00 4.00
811 A147 60s on 42s Strip of 4, #a.-d. + label 16.00 16.00

Issued: 1s, 5/19; 45s, 60s, 8/11; 10s, 1993.

Miniature Sheet

World War II in Pacific, 50th Anniv. A156

Designs: a, Newspaper headline, Japanese attack on Pearl Harbor. b, Map of Bataan, Corregidor, and Manila, pilot's wings, airplanes. c, Newspaper headline, troops landing in Gilbert Islands, Marine Corps emblem, dogtags. d, Uniform patch, B-29 "Enola Gay," troops landing on Iwo Jima. e, Map of Battle of Midway, Admiral Nimitz. f, Southwest Pacific campaign map, Gen. MacArthur. g, Map of Saipan and Tinian, Lt. Gen. Holland Smith. h, Map outling bombing of Japan, Maj. Gen. Curtis Lemay. i, Mitsubishi A6M Zero. j, Douglas SBD Dauntless. k, Grumman F4F Wildcat. l, Supermarine Seafire.

1992, May 26   Litho.   *Perf. 14*
814 A156 42s Sheet of 12, #a.-l.   30.00 30.00

1992 Summer Olympics, Barcelona — A157

1992, June 16
815 A157 42s Boxing   1.25 .85
816 A157 57s Diving   1.75 1.10
817 A157 1.50pa Tennis 4.50 4.50
818 A157 3pa Cycling   9.50 9.50
      Nos. 815-818 (4)   17.00 15.95

For surcharges, see 1123, 1125.

King Taufa'ahau IV, 25th Anniv. of Coronation A158

Designs: 45s, 2pa, King, Queen Halaevalu. No. 820a, King, crown. b, Extract from investiture ceremony. c, King, #C33.

1992, July 4   *Perf. 13½x13*
819 A158 45s multicolored   1.25 .90
        Size: 51x38mm
        Perf. 12½x12
820 A158 80s Strip of 3, #a.-c.   6.50 6.50
821 A158 2pa multicolored   5.25 5.25
      Nos. 819-821 (3)   13.00 12.65

Sacred Bats of Kolovai — A159

Designs: No. 822a, Bats in flight. b, Close-up of flying bat. c, Flying bats, tree. d, Bats hanging in tree. e, Bat hanging from tree limb.
Origin of sacred bats: No. 823a, 45s, Kula leaving for Upolu to be tattooed as Tongan chief. b, 45s, Kula looking through path of fires. c, 2pa, Kula walking down path, Hina. d, 2pa, Hina waving, Kula leaving with pet fruit bats.
Nos. 823a-823d are horiz.

1992, Oct. 20   Litho.   *Perf. 14*
822 A159 60s Strip of 5, #a.-e.   13.00 13.00
        Souvenir Sheet
        Perf. 14½
823 A159 Sheet of 4, #a.-d.   14.00 14.00

Christmas A160

1992, Nov. 10   *Perf. 14*
824 A160 60s Pearls   1.50 1.10
825 A160 80s Reef fish   2.00 1.40
826 A160 2pa Pacific orchids 4.75 4.75
827 A160 3pa Eua parrots   7.25 7.25
      Nos. 824-827 (4)   15.50 14.50

For surcharges see Nos. 894-897.

Anniversaries and Events — A161

Designs: 60s, Tonga flag, Rotary emblem. 80sh, John F. Kennedy, Peace Corps emblem. 1.50pa, FAO, WHO emblems. 3.50pa, Globe, Rotary Foundation emblem.

1992, Dec. 15   *Perf. 14½*
828 A161 60s multicolored   1.40 1.00
829 A161 80s multicolored   1.90 1.40
830 A161 1.50pa multicolored 3.50 3.50
831 A161 3.50pa multicolored 8.50 8.50
      Nos. 828-831 (4)   15.30 14.40

Rotary Intl. in Tonga, 25th anniv. (#828). Peace Corps in Tonga, 25th anniv. (#829). Intl. Conference of FAO and WHO (#830). Rotary Foundation of Rotary Intl., 75th anniv. (#831).
For overprint see No. 869.

Family Planning — A163

Outdoor silhouette scenes: No. 832, Mother, girl, butterflies. No. 833, Child on tricycle pulling kite. No. 834, Girl, kittens. No. 835, Adult, child playing chess.

1993, Jan. 26			**Perf. 14x13½**	
832	A163	15s Pair, #a.-b.	2.50	2.50
833	A163	45s Pair, #a.-b.	3.50	3.50
834	A163	60s Pair, #a.-b.	5.00	5.00
835	A163	2pa Pair, #a.-b.	15.00	15.00
	Nos. 832-835 (4)		26.00	26.00

Nos. 832a-835a have Tongan inscriptions. Nos. 832b-835b have English inscriptions and are mirror images of Nos. 832a-835a.

Health and Fitness — A164

Designs: 60s, Fresh fruit, fish, anti-smoking symbol. 80s, Anti-smoking symbol, weight training. 1.50pa, Anti-smoking symbol, water sports. 2.50pa, Fresh fruit, fish, cyclist, jogger.

1993, Mar. 16		**Litho.**	**Perf. 14**	
836	A164	60s multicolored	2.00	2.00
837	A164	80s multicolored	2.75	2.75
838	A164	1.50pa multicolored	5.25	5.25
839	A164	2.50pa multicolored	8.50	8.50
	Nos. 836-839 (4)		18.50	18.50

Tonga Fire Service, 25th Anniv. A165

No. 840, Fireman's badge. No. 841, Police van, badge. No. 842, Police band. No. 843, Putting out fire. No. 844, Fire truck at station. No. 845, Policeman, police dog.

1993, May 18		**Litho.**	**Perf. 14**	
840	A165	45s multi	2.00	2.00
841	A165	45s multi	2.00	2.00
a.		Pair, #840-841	4.50	3.50
842	A165	60s multi	2.50	2.50
843	A165	60s multi	2.50	2.50
a.		Pair, #842-843	5.50	4.50
844	A165	2pa multi	9.00	9.00
845	A165	2pa multi	9.00	9.00
a.		Pair, #844-845	20.00	15.00
	Nos. 840-845 (6)		27.00	27.00

Tonga Police Training College, 25th anniv. (#841-842, 845).
For surcharges see Nos. 943-948.

A166

Abel Tasman's Voyage to Eua, 350th Anniv.: 30s, Map of islands. 60s, Sailing ships, Heemskirk and Zeehaen. 80s, Sailing ships, natives in canoes. 3.50pa, Landing on Eua.

1993, June 21				
846	A166	30s multicolored	.80	.50
847	A166	1.75s multicolored	1.75	1.10
848	A166	80s multicolored	2.25	2.25
849	A166	3.50pa multicolored	10.00	10.00
	Nos. 846-849 (4)		14.80	13.85

A167

King Taufa'ahau IV, 75th Birthday: 45s, 2pa, Musical instruments.

No. 851a, Sporting events. b, Ancient landmarks. c, Royal Palace.

1993, July 1		**Litho.**	**Perf. 13x13½**	
850	A167	45s multicolored	.65	.65
		Perf. 12x12½		
		Size: 37x48mm		
851	A167	80s Strip of 3, #a.-c.	5.00	5.00
852	A167	2pa multicolored	3.00	3.00
	Nos. 850-852 (3)		8.65	8.65

A168

Children's Stamp Designs: Nos. 853a, 854a, Beach scene. Nos. 853b, 854b, "Maui-The Fisher of the Islands." Nos. 853c, 854c, Raft on ocean. Nos. 853d, 854d, Woman with hands in mixing bowl. Nos. 853e, 854e, "Maui and his Hook." Nos. 853f, 854f, "Communication in the South Pacific."

1993, Dec. 1		**Litho.**	**Perf. 14**	
853	A168	10s Strip of 6, #a.-f.	3.00	3.00
854	A168	80s Strip of 6, #a.-f.	14.00	14.00

A168a

Christmas traditions: 60s, Festive dinner. 80s, Shooting cannon. 1.50pa, Musicians. 3pa, Going to church.

1993, Nov. 10		**Litho.**	**Perf. 14**	
855	A168a	60s multicolored	1.50	1.25
856	A168a	80s multicolored	2.00	1.50
857	A168a	1.50pa multicolored	3.75	3.75
858	A168a	3pa multicolored	7.75	7.75
	Nos. 855-858 (4)		15.00	14.25

Miniature Sheet

Kindness to Animals — A169

Designs: a, 80s, Boy holding puppy. b, 80s, Girl holding kitten. c, 60s, Boy holding rooster (b). d, 60s, Girl with butterfly. e, 60s, Three dogs. f, 60s, Boy, puppy.

1994, Jan. 14			**Perf. 14½**	
859	A169	Sheet of 6, #a.-f.	17.50	17.50

For overprint see No. 868.

Game Fishing — A170

60s, Tiger shark. 80s, Dolphin fish. 1.50pa, Yellow fin tuna. 2.50pa, Pacific blue marlin.

1994, Feb. 28		**Litho.**	**Perf. 12**	
860	A170	60s multicolored	1.50	1.00
861	A170	80s multicolored	2.00	1.40
862	A170	1.50pa multicolored	4.00	4.00
863	A170	2.50pa multicolored	6.50	6.50
	Nos. 860-863 (4)		14.00	12.90

1994 World Cup Soccer Championships, US — A171

Designs: No. 864a, Player's legs. No. 864b, World Cup trophy. No. 865a, American player in red, white, & blue. No. 865b, German player in black shorts, white shirt.

1994, June 1			**Perf. 14x14½**	
864	A171	80s Pair, #a.-b.	4.00	4.00
865	A171	2pa Pair, #a.-b.	10.00	10.00

Pan Pacific & South East Asia Women's Assoc. Conference — A172

Career women: No. 866a, Lawyer. No. 866b, Policewoman. No. 867a, Doctor. No. 867b, Nurse.

1994, Aug. 18		**Litho.**	**Perf. 14**	
866	A172	45s Pair, #a.-b.	3.50	3.50
867	A172	2.50pa Pair, #a.-b.	10.50	10.50

No. 859 Overprinted

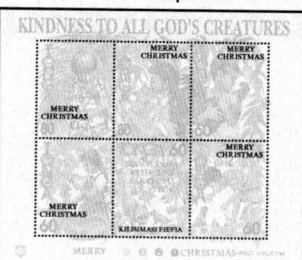

1994, Nov. 10		**Litho.**	**Perf. 14½**	
868	A169	Sheet of 6, #a.-f.	8.50	8.50

No. 831 Ovptd. in Dark Blue

1994, Nov. 17		**Litho.**	**Perf. 14½**	
869	A161	60s on 3.50pa multi	4.00	4.00

Types of 1969-85 and

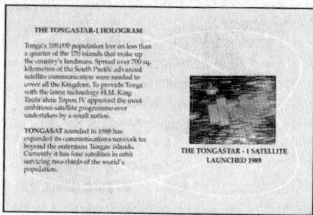

Tongastar 1 Satellite — A173

Design: a, 10s, Type A39 banana, size 22x11mm. b, 25s, Type AP12. c, Booklet pane, 12 #870a, 3 #870b. d, 45s, like #608. e, 45s, like #609. f, 45s, like #610. g, 45s, like #611. h, Booklet pane of 3 each #870d-870e, 2 #870f, 1 #870g. i, 60s, Type A72. j, 60s, Type OA19. k, 80s, Type OA17. l, Booklet pane, #870i-870k. m, 2pa, Tongastar 1. n, Booklet pane of 1 #870m.

Unwmk.

1994, Dec. 14		**Litho.**	**Die Cut**	
			Self-adhesive	
870	A173	Souvenir booklet		27.50

First full-scale production of self-adhesive stamps by Tonga, 25th anniv. (#870). Satellite communications network for Tongan Islands (#870m).

No. 870b is airmail. Nos. 870j-870k are air post official stamps.

No. 870m contains a holographic image. Soaking in water may affect the hologram.

Marine Type of 1992-93 Redrawn

1994-95			**Perf. 14**	
874	A155a	10s like #801	.25	.25
876	A155a	20s like #803	.35	.35
877	A155a	45s like #804	.80	.80
878	A155a	60s like #805	1.10	1.10
879	A155a	80s like #806	1.40	1.40
		Size: 41x27mm, 41x27mm		
880	A155a	1pa like #705, horiz.	2.25	2.25
881	A155a	2pa like #577, horiz.	4.25	4.25
882	A155a	3pa like #578, horiz.	6.25	6.25
883	A155a	5pa like #706	10.00	10.00
884	A155a	10pa like #568	21.00	21.00
	Nos. 874-884 (10)		47.65	47.65

Area covered by background colors on Nos. 874, 876-879 has been reduced in size.

Issued: 1pa, 2pa, 3pa, 6/21/94; 5pa, 9/21/94; 10pa, 1/18/95; 10s, 20s, 45s, 60s, 80s, 9/25/95.

For overprints, see Nos. O78-O87.

FAO, 50th Anniv. A174

1995, May 16		**Litho.**	**Perf. 14**	
886	A174	5pa multicolored	17.00	17.00

Tonga's Entry into British Commonwealth, 25th Anniv. — A175

Children with bicycles from parts of Commonwealth.

1995, June 6				
887	A175	45s Polynesia	1.10	.90
888	A175	60s Asia	1.50	1.25
889	A175	80s Africa	1.75	1.75
890	A175	2pa India	4.50	4.50
891	A175	2.50pa Europe	6.00	6.00
	Nos. 887-891 (5)		14.85	14.40

1995 Rugby World Cup, South Africa — A176

Designs: No. 892a, Player running right with ball, two others. b, Two players. No. 893a, Three players. b, Player ready to catch ball.

1995, June 20		Perf. 14½	
892	A176	80s Pair, #a.-b.	6.00 6.00
893	A176	2pa Pair, #a.-b.	13.50 13.50

Nos. 892-893 were each issued in sheets of 4 stamps.
For surcharges see Nos. 954A, 956A.

Nos. 824-827 Surcharged

i

j

1995, June 30		Litho.	Perf. 14	
894		60s Pair	4.50	4.50
a.	A160(i)	on #824	2.00	2.00
b.	A160(j)	on #824	2.00	2.00
895		60s Pair	4.50	4.50
a.	A160(i)	on 80s #825	2.00	2.00
b.	A160(j)	on 80s #825	2.00	2.00
896		60s Pair	4.50	4.50
a.	A160(i)	on 2pa #826	2.00	2.00
b.	A160(j)	on 2pa #826	2.00	2.00
897		60s Pair	4.50	4.50
a.	A160(i)	on 3pa #827	2.00	2.00
b.	A160(j)	on 3pa #827	2.00	2.00
		Nos. 894-897 (4)	18.00	18.00

Nos. 779-782 Surcharged

1995, June 30		Litho.	Perf. 14	
898	A151	60s on 57s #779	1.60	1.60
899	A151	80s on 2pa #781	2.00	2.00
899A	A151	80s on 2pa #782	2.00	2.00
b.		Pair, #899-899A	4.00	4.00
899C	A151	1pa on #780	2.50	2.50
		Nos. 898-899C (4)	8.10	8.10

Victory in the Pacific, 50th Anniv. — A177

Nos. 900, 901: a, Soldier climbing from rope ladder. b, Ship, soldiers. c, Ship, landing craft with troops, soldiers up close. d, Ship, landing craft with troops. e, Map.

1995, Aug. 1		Litho.	Perf. 14x14½	
900	A177	60s Strip of 5, #a.-e.	10.00	10.00
901	A177	80s Strip of 5, #a.-e.	12.00	12.00

Nos. 900-901 are continuous designs and were issued together in sheet containing ten stamps.

Singapore '95 — A178

Designs: No. 902a, 45s, #887. b, 60s, #888. 2pa, Boy cycling in Singapore.

1995, Sept. 1		Litho.	Perf. 12	
902	A178	Pair, #a.-b.	3.75	3.75

Souvenir Sheet

903	A178	2pa multicolored	5.25	5.25

Souvenir Sheet

Beijing Intl. Coin & Stamp Show '95 — A179

Design: 1.40pa, Mount Song, Henan Province, China.

1995, Sept. 14			Perf. 14½	
904	A179	1.40pa multicolored	5.00	5.00

End of World War II, UN, 50th Anniv. — A180

No. 905a, Holocaust survivors. b, UN emblem, "50." c, Children of Holocaust survivors in celebration.
No. 906a, Mushroom cloud from atom bomb explosion. b, Like #905b. c, Space shuttle.

1995, Oct. 20		Litho.	Perf. 13	
905	A180	60s Strip of 3, #a.-c.	4.00	4.00
906	A180	80s Strip of 3, #a.-c.	7.50	7.50

Nos. 905b, 906b are 23x31mm.

Christmas and New Year — A181

Orchids: 20s, Calanthe triplicata. Nos. 908, Spathoglottis plicata, inscribed "MERRY CHRISTMAS." No. 909, like #908, inscribed "A HAPPY 1996." No. 910, Dendrobium platygastrium, inscribed "MERRY CHRISTMAS". No. 911, like #910, inscribed "A HAPPY 1996." 80s, Dendrobium toki. 2.50pa, Phaius tankervilliae.

1995, Nov. 15		Litho.	Perf. 14x14½	
907	A181	20s multicolored	.75	.75
908	A181	45s multicolored	1.00	1.00
909	A181	45s multicolored	1.00	1.00
910	A181	60s multicolored	1.25	1.25
911	A181	60s multicolored	1.25	1.25
912	A181	80s multicolored	1.75	1.75
913	A181	2pa multicolored	5.00	5.00
914	A181	2.50pa multicolored	6.00	6.00
		Nos. 907-914 (8)	18.00	18.00

Humpback Whale — A182

1996, Jan. 7			Perf. 14	
915	A182	45s In water	2.10	2.10
916	A182	60s With calf	3.25	3.25
917	A182	1.50pa Sounding	6.50	6.50
918	A182	2.50pa Breaching	9.25	9.75
		Nos. 915-918 (4)	21.10	21.60

World Wildlife Fund.

Miniature Sheet

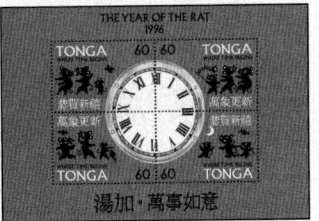

New Year 1996 (Year of the Rat) — A183

Denomination: a, UR. b, UL. c, LR. d, LL.

1996, Feb. 23				
919	A183	60s Sheet of 4,		
		#a.-d.	7.50	7.50

No. 919 is a continuous design.
See Nos. 930-932, 932E, 942, 986.

Marine Type of 1992-93 Redrawn

1996, May 31		Litho.	Perf. 14	
		Size: 40x26mm		
920	A155a	1pa like #880	2.25	2.25
921	A155a	2pa like #881	4.75	4.75
922	A155a	3pa like #882	7.50	7.50
923	A155a	5pa like #883	12.00	12.00
924	A155a	10pa like #884	25.00	25.00
		Nos. 920-924 (5)	51.50	51.50

Size of "TONGA" on Nos. 920-923 is smaller than on Nos. 880-883. Name of species appears at top instead of bottom on Nos. 920-924. Background colors vary. Inscribed "1996."

1996 Summer Olympic Games, Atlanta — A184

Statues of classical Greek figures, modern athletes: 45s, Zeus, runner. 80s, The Discus Thrower. 2pa, The Javelin Thrower. 3pa, The Horseman, dressage competitor.

1996, July 2		Litho.	Perf. 14	
925	A184	45s multicolored	1.25	.80
926	A184	80s multicolored	2.00	1.90
927	A184	2pa multicolored	5.75	5.75
928	A184	3pa multicolored	9.00	9.00
		Nos. 925-928 (4)	18.00	17.45

For surcharges & overprint see Nos. 949-952.

13th Congress of Intl. Union of Preshistoric and Protohistoric Sciences — A185

a, Prehistoric man using fire, knife, bow & arrow, animals. b, Ancient Egyptians, Greeks, Romans.

1996, Sept. 5		Litho.	Perf. 12	
929	A185	1pa Pair, #a.-b.	7.50	7.50

No. 929 was issued in sheets of 6 stamps.

New Year 1996 (Year of the Rat) Type

Denomination: a, UR. b, UL. c, LR. d, LL.

1996, June 27		Litho.	Perf. 14	
		Sheets of 4		
930	A183	10s #a.-d.	1.40	1.40
931	A183	20s #a.-d.	2.75	2.75
932	A183	45s #a.-d.	6.75	6.75
932E	A183	60s #a.-d.	10.00	10.00

The denominations are larger on No. 932E than those on No. 919.

Christmas A186

Paintings: 20s, Virgin and Child, by Sassoferrato. 60s, Adoration of the Shepherds, by Murillo. 80s, Virgin and Child, by Delaroche. 1pa, Adoration of the Shepherds, by Champaigne.

1996, Oct. 29		Litho.	Perf. 14	
933	A186	20s multicolored	.75	.50
934	A186	60s multicolored	2.50	1.50
935	A186	80s multicolored	2.75	2.50
936	A186	1pa multicolored	8.50	8.50
		Nos. 933-936 (4)	14.50	13.00

UNICEF, 50th Anniv. — A187

Children in sports activities: a, Running, playing rugby. b, Tennis. c, Cycling.

1996, Oct. 29				
937	A187	80s Strip of 3, #a.-c.	9.00	9.00

No. 937 is a continuous design.

Queen Halaevalu Mata'aho, 70th Birthday — A188

Designs: 60s, Queen, natl. flag. No. 939a, Queen, coin with portrait. No. 939b, Coin with natl. arms, Queen.

1996, Nov. 27		Litho.	Perf. 12	
938	A188	60s multicolored	3.50	3.50
939	A188	2pa Pair, #a.-b.	10.50	10.50

Towards the Year 2000 — A189

Year "2000" rising out of Pacific, Tonga landmarks: Nos. 940a, 941a, The Ha'amonga stone monument, globe, Kao Island. Nos. 940b, 941b, Mount Talau overlooking Port of Reguge, Royal Palance, Tongatapu, communication satellite.

1996, Dec. 9				
940	A189	80s Pair, #a.-b.	4.00	4.00
941	A189	2pa Pair, #a.-b.	9.50	9.50

New Year Type of 1996 Redrawn with Ox

Denomination located: a, 60s, UR. b, 60s, UL. c, 80s, LR. d, 2pa, LL.

1997, Jan. 24   Litho.   Perf. 14
942 A183 Sheet of 4, #a.-d.   11.00 11.00
New Year 1997 (Year of the Ox).

Nos. 840-845 Surcharged

1997, Mar. 3   Litho.   Perf. 14
943 A165 10s on 45s #840   3.50 3.25
944 A165 10s on 45s #841   3.50 3.25
a.   Pair, #943-944   6.00 6.00
945 A165 10s on 60s #842   3.50 3.25
946 A165 10s on 60s #843   3.50 3.25
a.   Pair, #945-946   6.00 6.00
947 A165 20s on 2pa #844   4.00 3.75
948 A165 20s on 2pa #845   4.00 3.75
a.   Pair, #947-948   7.00 7.00
    Nos. 943-948 (6)   22.00 20.50

Nos. 925-928 Surcharged & Overprinted.

1997, Mar. 24   Litho.   Perf. 14
949 A184 10s on 45s #925   .90 .90
950 A184 10s on 80s #926   .90 .90
951 A184 10s on 2pa #927   .90 .90
952 A184 3pa #928   9.25 9.25
    Nos. 949-952 (4)   11.95 11.95
Size and location of surcharge varies.

Nos. 892-893 Surcharged

a   b

1997, Mar. 24   Perf. 14½
Sheets of 4
954A A176 10s on 80s   2.00 2.00
956A A176 1pa on 2pa   15.00 15.00

#954A contains #892a (a), #892b (b), #892a (b). #956A contains #893a (a), #893b (a), #893b (b), #893a (b).

Christianity in Tonga, Birth of King George Tupou I, Bicent. — A190

#957, 961a, 962a, Arrival of missionary ship, Duff, Captain James Wilson. #958, King George Tupou I, village. #959, 961b, 962b, People in water, rowboats coming ashore from Duff. #960, 961c, 962c, Natives, missionaries, Duff.

1997, Apr. 28   Perf. 14
957 A190 10s multicolored   .25 .25
958 A190 10s multicolored   .25 .25
959 A190 10s multicolored   .25 .25

960 A190 10s multicolored   .25 .25
a.   Sheet of 6, #957, 959-960, 3 #958   4.00 4.00
961 A190 60s Strip of 3, #a.-c.   5.00 5.00
962 A190 80s Strip of 3, #a.-c.   7.00 7.00
Nos. 961-962 were each issued in sheets of 9 stamps. See Nos. 972-975.

Souvenir Sheet

Pacific Swallow, Golden Gate Bridge — A191

1997, May 30
963 A191 2pa multicolored   7.50 7.50
Pacific '97.

Tonga High School, 50th Anniv. A192

Designs: 20s, Students in uniforms outside of school. 60s, Dressed for sports. 80s, Brass band. 3.50pa, Running competition.

1997, June 4
964 A192 20s multicolored   .75 .40
965 A192 60s multicolored   1.75 1.10
966 A192 80s multicolored   2.25 1.50
967 A192 3.50pa multicolored   9.25 9.25
    Nos. 964-967 (4)   14.00 12.25

A193

Nos. 968, 970: a, Queen, King with bowed heads, royal escorts. b, Coronation ceremony. c, Queen, King. 45s, 2pa, King's crown.

1997, June 30   Litho.   Perf. 13x13½
968 A193 10s Strip of 3, #a.-c.
969 A193 45s multicolored   1.25 1.25
    1.75 1.75
Size: 34x47mm
Perf. 12
970 A193 60s Strip of 3, #a.-c.   7.00 7.00
971 A193 2pa multicolored   8.50 8.50
King Taufa'ahau IV, Queen Halaevalu Mata'aho, 50th wedding anniv., coronation, 30th anniv.

Christianity in Tonga Type of 1997

1997, Aug. 27   Perf. 14
Size: 27x18mm
972 A190 10s like #957   .25 .25
973 A190 10s like #958   .25 .25
974 A190 10s like #959   .25 .25
975 A190 10s like #960   .25 .25
a.   Sheet of 12, 6 #973, 2 each #972, #974-975   6.00 6.00

A194

Mushrooms: Nos. 976a, 977a, Lenzites elegans. Nos. 976b, 977b, Marasmiellus semiustus. No. 976c, 978a, Aseroe rubra. Nos. 976d, 978b, Podoscypha involuta. Nos. 976e, 979a, Microporus xanthopus. Nos. 976f, 979b, Lentinus tuberregium.

1997, Oct. 1   Litho.   Perf. 14
976 A194 10s Strip of 6, #a.-f.   2.25 2.25
Size: 26x40mm
977 A194 20s Pair, #a.-b.   2.00 2.00
978 A194 60s Pair, #a.-b.   6.00 6.00
979 A194 2pa Pair, #a.-b.   19.00 19.00
c.   Sheet of 6, #977-979   32.50 32.50
No. 976 is a continuous design.

Diana, Princess of Wales (1961-97)
Common Design Type

Various portraits: a, 10s. b, 80s, c, 1pa. d, 2.50pa.

Perf. 13½x14
1998, May 29   Litho.   Unwmk.
980 CD355 Sheet of 4, #a.-d   5.75 5.75
No. 980 sold for 4.40pa + 50s with surtax from international sales going to the Princess Diana Memorial Fund and surtax from local sales going to designated local charity.
For surcharge, see No. 1192.

Flying Home for Christmas A195

Designs: 60s, Airplane on ground, people waving. 80s, People waving, house, plane overhead. 1.50pa, Man in outrigger canoe waving to airplane. 3.50pa, Man, woman, people in boat on lake waving, airplane overhead.

1997, Oct. 20   Litho.   Perf. 14x13½
981 A195 60s bister & red   .90 .90
982 A195 80s bister & red   1.20 1.20
983 A195 1.50pa bister & red   2.20 2.20
984 A195 3.50pa bister & red   5.20 5.20
    Nos. 981-984 (4)   9.50 9.50

King Taufa'ahau Tupou IV, 80th Birthday — A196

1998, July 4   Litho.   Perf. 14
985 A196 2.70pa multicolored   7.00 7.00
a.   Souv. sheet, #985, Niuafo'ou #207   10.00 10.00

New Year 1998 (Year of the Tiger)
Tiger: a, 55s, Leaping down. b, 80s, Lying down. c, 1pa, Leaping upward. d, 1pa, Stalking.

1998, July 23
986 A183 Sheet of 4, #a.-d.   6.00 6.00
No. 986 is a continuous design. Singpex '98.
For surcharges, see No. 1098.

Birds A197

5s, Fairy tern, vert. 10s, Tongan whistler, vert. 15s, Common barn owl, vert. 20s, Purple swamp hen, vert. 30s, Red-footed booby, vert. 40s, Banded rail. 50s, Swamp harrier. 55s, Blue-crowned lorikeet, vert. 60s, Great frigate bird, vert. 70s, Friendly ground dove. 80s, Red-tailed tropic bird, vert. 1pa, Red shining parrot, vert. 2pa, Pacific pigeon, vert. 3pa, Pacific golden plover. 5pa, Tongan megapode.

Perf. 14x14½, 14½x14
1998, Aug. 26   Litho.
992 A197 5s multicolored   .25 .25
993 A197 10s multicolored   .25 .25
994 A197 15s multicolored   .25 .25
995 A197 20s multicolored   .30 .30
996 A197 30s multicolored   .50 .50
997 A197 40s multicolored   .65 .65
998 A197 50s multicolored   .75 .75
999 A197 55s multicolored   .90 .90
1000 A197 60s multicolored   .95 .95
1001 A197 70s multicolored   1.10 1.10
1002 A197 80s multicolored   1.25 1.25
1003 A197 1pa multicolored   1.60 1.60
1004 A197 2pa multicolored   3.00 3.00
1005 A197 3pa multicolored   4.75 4.75
1006 A197 5pa multicolored   8.00 8.00
    Nos. 992-1006 (15)   24.50 24.50
For surcharges, see Nos. 1077A, 1077B, 1099-1114, 1126, 1147.

Fish A198

Designs: a, 10s, Chaetodon pelewensis. b, 55s, Chaetodon lunula. c, 1pa, Chaetodon ephippium.

1998, Sept. 23   Litho.   Perf. 14
1008 A198 Strip of 3, #a.-c.   4.75 4.75
Intl. Year of the Ocean. No. 1008 was issued in sheets of 9 stamps.

Christmas A199

Designs: 10s, Angel, "Kilisimasi Fiefia." 80s, Angel, "Merry Christmas." 1pa, Children, candle, "Ta'u Fo'ou Monu'ia." 1.60pa, Children, candle, "Happy New Year."

1998, Nov. 12   Litho.   Perf. 14x14½
1009 A199 10s multicolored   .60 .40
1010 A199 80s multicolored   2.50 1.25
1011 A199 1pa multicolored   2.75 2.25
1012 A199 1.60pa multicolored   3.50 3.50
    Nos. 1009-1012 (4)   9.35 7.40

New Year 1999 (Year of the Rabbit) — A200

a, 10s, Three rabbits. b, 55s, Rabbit eating. c, 80s, Rabbit looking upward. d, 1pa, Rabbit hopping.

1999, Feb. 16   *Perf. 14*
1013 A200 Sheet of 4, #a.-d.   4.50   4.50

Explorers — A201

Explorer, ship: 55s, Tasman, Heemskerck, 1643. 80s, La Perouse, Astrolabe, 1788. 1pa, William Bligh, Bounty, 1789. 2.50pa, James Cook, Resolution, 1777.

1999, Mar. 19   Litho.   *Perf. 14*
1014 A201	55s multicolored	1.10	.65
1015 A201	80s multicolored	1.60	1.10
1016 A201	1pa multicolored	2.25	2.00
1017 A201	2.50pa multicolored	5.00	5.00
a.	Souvenir sheet of 1	5.25	5.25
	Nos. 1014-1017 (4)	9.95	8.75

Australia '99 World Stamp Expo (#1017a).

Scenic Views, Vava'u A202

Designs: 10s, Neiafu. 55s, Boats on water, Port of Refuge. 80s, Aerial view, Port of Refuge. 1pa, Sunset, Neiafu. 2.50pa, Mounu Island.

1999, May 19   *Perf. 14½*
1018 A202	10s multicolored	.50	.40
1019 A202	55s multicolored	1.00	.60
1020 A202	80s multicolored	1.60	.80
1021 A202	1pa multicolored	1.75	1.40
1022 A202	2.50pa multicolored	3.50	3.50
	Nos. 1018-1022 (5)	8.35	6.70

For surcharge see No. 1148.

Flowers A203

Designs: 10s, Fagraea berteroana. 80s, Garcinia pseudoguttfera. 1pa, Phlaeria disperma, vert. 2.50pa, Gardenia taitensis, vert.

Perf. 13¼x13, 13x13¼
1999, Sept. 29   Litho.
1023 A203	10s multicolored	.30	.30
1024 A203	80s multicolored	1.40	1.40
1025 A203	1pa multicolored	1.75	1.75
1026 A203	2.50pa multicolored	4.25	4.25
	Nos. 1023-1026 (4)	7.70	7.70

Millennium — A204

Designs: a, 55s, Ha'amonga monument, people, clocks at 11:15 to 11:25. b, 80s, Monument, people, clocks at 11:30 to 11:40. c, 1pa, People, clocks at 11:45 to 11:55. d,

---

2.50pa, King Taufa'ahau IV, clocks at 12:00, 12:05.

1999, Dec. 1
1027 A204   Strip of 4, #a.-d.   7.00   7.00

Millennium — A205

Clock, dove and: 10s, Flowers. 1pa, Ha'amonga Monument. 2.50pa, Native boat. 2.70pa, Crown.

Litho. & Embossed
2000, Jan. 1   *Perf. and Die Cut*
1028 A205	10s multi	.25	.25
1029 A205	1pa multi	1.50	1.50
1030 A205	2.50pa multi	3.50	3.50
1031 A205	2.70pa multi	4.00	4.00
a.	Souv. sheet, #1030-1031	8.00	8.00
	Nos. 1028-1031 (4)	9.25	9.25

Values are for stamps with attached selvage.

Souvenir Sheet

New Year 2000 (Year of the Dragon) — A206

Various dragons; a, 10s. b, 55s, c, 80s. d, 1pa.

Litho. with Foil Application
2000, Feb. 4   *Perf. 14½*
1032 A206   Sheet of 4, #a.-d.   5.00   5.00

Souvenir Sheet

The Stamp Show 2000, London — A207

Litho. with Foil Application
2000, May 22   *Perf. 13x13¼*
1033 A207	Sheet of 2	5.50	5.50
a.	1pa Queen Mother	1.50	1.50
b.	2.50pa Queen Salote Tupou III	3.50	3.50

Geostationary Orbital Slot Program — A208

Designs: 10s, Proton RU500 lauch vehicle, vert. 1pa, LM3 launch vehicle. 2.50pa, Apstar 1. 2.70pa, Gorizont.

Litho. with Foil Application
2000, July 5   *Perf. 14½x15, 15x14½*
1034-1037 A208	Set of 4	9.00	9.00
1037a	Souvenir sheet, #1036-1037	8.25	8.25

World Stamp Expo 2000, Anaheim.

2000 Summer Olympics, Sydney — A209

No. 1038: a, Runner, koalas, sailboats. b, Boxers, kangaroos, Ayers Rock. c, Torchbearers, Ayers Rock, Sydney Opera House (60x45mm). d, Discus thrower, Sydney Harbour Bridge, flower. e, Weight lifter, kookaburra, fish.

2000, Sept. 15   Litho.   *Perf. 14*
1038 A209	Horiz. strip of 5	5.50	5.50
a-e.	80s Any single	1.00	1.00

Commonwealth Membership, 30th Anniv. — A210

Designs: 10s, Education. 55s, Arts. 80s, Health. 2.70pa, Agriculture.

2000, Oct. 25
1039-1042 A210   Set of 4   5.50   5.50
For surcharge see No. 1149.

Souvenir Sheet

New Year 2001 (Year of the Snake) — A211

No. 1043 — Various snakes: a, 10s. b, 55s, c, 80s, d, 1pa.

Litho. with Foil Application
2001, Feb. 1   *Perf. 14¼*
1043 A211   Sheet of 4, #a-d   4.50   4.50
Hong Kong 2001 Stamp Exhibition.

Dance — A212

Designs: 10s, Ma'ulu'ulu. 55s, Me'etupaki. 80s, Tau'olunga. 2.70pa, Faha'iula.

2001, Apr. 4   Litho.   *Perf. 13¼*
1044-1047 A212   Set of 4   5.50   5.50
For surcharge see No. 1151.

Year of the Mangrove A213

Designs: 10s, Fiddler crab. 55s, Black duck, gray mullet, vert. 80s, Red mangrove, emperor fish, vert. 1pa, Reef heron, mangrove. 2.70pa, Mangrove crab.

2001, May 5   Litho.   *Perf. 13¾*
1048-1052 A213	Set of 5	6.75	6.75
1052a	Souvenir sheet, #1048-1052, perf. 13½	7.25	7.25

For surcharge see No. 1150.

Sport Fishing — A214

2001, July 31   *Perf. 14¾x14*
1053 A214	Horiz. strip of 4 with central label	8.25	8.25
a.	45s Sailfish	.50	.50
b.	80s Blue marlin	1.00	1.00
c.	2.40pa Wahoo	3.00	3.00
d.	2.60pa Dorado	3.25	3.25

Fruit — A215

2001, Sept. 19   *Serpentine Die Cut Self-Adhesive*
1054	Horiz. strip of 5	6.25	6.25
a.	A215 10s Banana	.25	.25
b.	A215 45s Coconut	.50	.50
c.	A215 60s Pineapple	.75	.75
d.	A215 80s Watermelon	.85	.85
e.	A215 2.40pa Passion fruit	2.40	2.40

Shells A216

Designs: 10s, Haliotis ovina. 80s, Turbo petholatus. 1pa, Trochus niloticus. 2.70pa, Turbo marmoratus.

Perf. 12¾
2001, Dec. 13   Litho.   Unwmk.
1055-1058 A216   Set of 4   7.00   7.00
Values are for stamps with surrounding selvage.

Reign Of Queen Elizabeth II, 50th Anniv. Issue
Common Design Type
Souvenir Sheet

No. 1059: a, 15s, Princess Elizabeth as child. b, 90s, Wearing yellow hat. c, 1.20pa, With Princess Anne and Prince Charles. d, 1.40pa, Wearing crown. e, 2.25pa, 1955 portrait by Annigoni (38x50mm).

Perf. 14¼x14½, 13¾ (2.25pa)
2002, Feb. 6   Litho.   Wmk. 373
1059 CD360 Sheet of 5, #a-e   8.00   8.00

Souvenir Sheet

New Year 2002 (Year of the Horse) — A217

Various horses: a, 65s. b, 80s. c, 1pa. d, 2.50pa.

Litho. With Foil Application
2002, Feb. 12   Unwmk.   *Perf. 14*
1060 A217   Sheet of 4, #a-d   7.50   7.50

Intl. Year of Ecotourism — A218

Designs: 5s, Whale, surfer. 15s, Woman, shoreline. 70s, Beach, fish. 1.40pa, Arch, man. 2.25pa, Boats, man.

2002, Apr. 9   Litho.   *Perf. 13¼x13¾*
1061-1065 A218   Set of 5   6.75   6.75

Pearls
A219

Pearls and: 90s, Workers preparing oysters for pearl cultivation. 1pa, Diver checking strung oysters. 1.20pa, Woman, pearl on necklace. 2.50pa, Islands.

2002, June 12   Litho.   *Perf. 13½*
1066-1069 A219   Set of 4   8.00   8.00
1069a   Souvenir sheet, #1068-1069   6.00   6.00
Values are for stamps with surrounding selvage.

Participation of Tongan Team in Rugby Sevens Tournament — A220

Designs: 15s, Player leaping for ball. 30s, Players ready for scrum. 90s, Player attempting tackle. 4pa, Players on ground.

2002, July 27
1070-1073 A220   Set of 4   9.00   9.00
Values are for stamps with surrounding selvage.

Weaving — A221

Designs: 30s, Woman and young girl. 90s, Woman with work hanging on line, boy with baskets. 1.40pa, Women weaving baskets. 2.50pa, Woman weaving basket lid.

2002, Sept. 17   *Perf. 12¼*
1074-1077 A221   Set of 4   7.00   7.00

No. 999 Surcharged

Type 1 — Slash Over First "5"

No. 1003 Surcharged

Methods and Perfs As Before
2002, Sept.
1077A A197   5s on 55s #999,
            Type 1   65.00   —
1077B A197   15(s) on $1 #1003   75.00   —
     See Nos. 1099-1114 for additional surcharges on No. 999.

'Eua National Park, 10th Anniv. — A222

Various depictions of red shining parrots 45s, 1pa, 1.50pa, 2.50pa.

2002, Nov. 27   Litho.   *Perf. 12¼*
1078-1081 A222   Set of 4   7.50   7.50

New Year 2003 (Year of the Ram) — A223

No. 1082: a, 65s, One ram. 80s, Three sheep. 1pa, Three sheep, diff. 2.50pa, Two sheep.

2003, Apr. 14   Litho.   *Perf. 13¼*
1082 A223   Sheet of 4, #a-d   7.00   7.00

Coronation of Queen Elizabeth II, 50th Anniv. — A224

Designs: 90s, Queen Elizabeth II in coach. 1.20pa, Queen Salote of Tonga. 1.40pa, Queen Salote in coach. 2.50pa, Queen Elizabeth II.

Litho. With Foil Application
2003, June 2
1083-1086 A224   Set of 4   10.00   10.00

Boats of Abel Tasman — A225

Various boats: 15s, 75s, 90s, 2.50pa.

2003, Aug. 7   Litho.   *Perf. 13¼*
1087-1090 A225   Set of 4   9.00   9.00
1090a   Souvenir sheet, #1087-1090   9.00   9.00

Beaches — A226

Flower and: 15s, Euakafa Beach. 90s, Pangaimotu Beach. 1.40pa, Fafa Beach. 2.25pa, Nuku Beach.

2003, Sept. 11
1091-1094 A226   Set of 4   8.50   8.50

Nos. 784, 785a, 785b, 785c, 786 Surcharged

Methods and Perfs As Before
2003, Sept.
1095   A152   10s on 32s Horiz.
          strip of 3,
          #784a-784c   150.00   —
1096   A152   10s on 42s
          #785a   —
1097   A152   10s on 42s
          #785b   —
1097A A152   10s on 42s #785c   —
1098   A152   10s on 57s Horiz.
          strip of 3,
          #786a-786c   150.00   —

No. 999 Surcharged

Type 2 — Small numerals and cent sign

Type 3 — Small numerals and "s"

Type 4 — Thin numerals and "s"

Type 5 — Large numerals and "s"

Type 6 — Medium-sized numerals and "s"

Type 7 — Very large, bold numerals and "c"

Methods and Perfs As Before
2003-04
1099 A197   05s on 55s, Type 3   150.00   —
  a.   Obliterators 2x1 ½mm   —
1100 A197   05s on 55s, Type 4   350.00   —
1101 A197   5s on 55s, Type 5   20.00   —
1102 A197   5c on 55s, Type 7   10.00   —
1103 A197   10s on 55s, Type 4   50.00   —
1104 A197   10s on 55s, Type 5   45.00   —
1105 A197   10c on 55s, Type 7   25.00   —
1106 A197   15c on 55s, Type 2   75.00   —
1107 A197   15s on 55s, Type 4   350.00   —
1108 A197   15s on 55s, Type 5   20.00   —
1109 A197   15s on 55s, Type 6   25.00   —
1110 A197   20c on 55s, Type 2   65.00   —
1111 A197   20s on 55s, Type 4   25.00   —
1112 A197   20s on 55s, Type 5   50.00   —
1113 A197   45c on 55s, Type 2   50.00   —
1114 A197   45s on 55s, Type 6   75.00   —

     Earliest known uses: Nos. 1099, 1106, 1110, 10/03; Nos. 1100, 1103, 1107, 1111, 12/03; Nos. 1101, 1108, 2/04; Nos. 1113, 4/04; Nos. 1104, 1112, 1114, 6/04; Nos. 1105, 1109, 8/04; No. 1102, 9/04;

Churches
A227

Designs: 15s, Catholic Church, Neiafu, Vava'u. 90s, Wesleyan Church, Uiha, Ha'apai.

1.40pa, Cathedral of the Immaculate Conception of Mary. 2.25pa, Free Wesleyan Church, Nuku'alofa.

2003, Nov. 10
1115-1118 A227 Set of 4 8.50 8.50
Christmas.

Year of the Monkey 2004

New Year 2004 (Year of the Monkey) — A228

No. 1119: a, 60s, Spider monkey. b, 80s, Ring-tailed lemur. c, 1pa, Cotton-top tamarin. d, 2.50pa, White-cheeked gibbon.

2004, Feb. 12   Litho.   Perf. 13¼
1119 A228   Sheet of 4, #a-d   6.00 6.00

Nos. 770, 787, 788, 815, 816, 1001, Niuafo'ou Nos. 140, 141 and 145 Surcharged

Type 1 — Small denomination and obliterator

Type 2 — Large denomination and obliterator

Methods and Perfs As Before
2004
1120 A153 10s on 32s #787   50.00 —
1121 A153 10s on 42s #788,
            Type 1   —   —
1122 A153 10s on 42s #788,
            Type 2   150.00   —
1123 A157 10s on 42s #815 350.00   —
1124 A147 10s on 57s Horiz.
            strip of 4, +
            central label,
            #770a-770d   350.00   —
1125 A157 10s on 57s #816   90.00   —
1126 A197 60s on 70s #1001 30.00   —

On Stamps of Niuafo'ou
1127 A25   10s on 42s #140 350.00   —
1128 A26   10s on 42s #145 110.00   —
1129 A25   10s on 57s #141 350.00   —

Size and location of obliterators and new denominations varies. Earliest known use: No. 1126, 3/04; Nos. 1120, 1121, 4/04; Nos. 1122, 1123, 1124, 1125, 1127, 1128, 1129, 6/04. The surcharged Niuafo'ou stamps were not necessarily sent only to Niuafo'ou for sale there.

Fruit
Plants — A229

Designs: 45s, Mango. 60s, Pineapple. 80s, Coconut. 1.80pa, Banana.

2004, Sept. 21   Litho.   Perf. 14¼x14
1130-1133 A229   Set of 4   4.50 4.50

Christmas
A230

Designs: 65s, Madonna and Child. 80s, Journey to Bethlehem. 1.20pa, Annunciation to the Shepherds. 2.50pa, Magi.

2004, Dec.   Perf. 14
1134-1137 A230   Set of 4   8.25 8.25

Royalty — A231

Designs: 65s, King George Tupou I. 90s, King George Tupou II. 1.40pa, Queen Salote Tupou III. 3.05pa, King Taufa'ahau Tupou IV.

2004, July 7   Litho.   Perf. 14
1138-1141 A231   Set of 4   6.75 6.75
1141a   Souvenir sheet of 4, #1138-
           1141   6.75 6.75

Souvenir Sheet

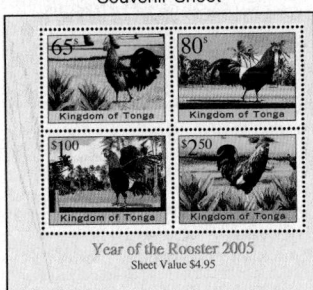

Year of the Rooster 2005
Sheet Value $4.95

New Year 2005 (Year of the Rooster) — A232

No. 1142 — Various roosters with panel color of: a, 65s, Yellow orange. b, 80s, Light green. c, 1pa, Tan. d, 2.50pa, Gray blue.

2005, Feb. 12
1142 A232   Sheet of 4, #a-d   8.50 8.50

Souvenir Sheet

Whales — A233

No. 1143 — Various whales with denominations in: a, 65s, Purple. b, 80s, Yellow. c, 1pa, Green. d, 2.50pa, Pink.

2005, May 4   Perf. 13¼
1143 A233   Sheet of 4, #a-d   8.25 8.25

Coronation of
King Siaosi Tupou
V — A234

King Siaosi Tupou V wearing: 30s, Uniform and sash. 1pa, Tuxedo and sash. 5pa, Robe and crown.

Litho. With Foil Application
2008, Aug. 1   Perf. 14
1144-1145 A234   Set of 2   1.50 1.50
Souvenir Sheet
1146 A234 5pa multi   5.50 5.50
No. 1146 contains one 30x60mm stamp.

Tonga Nos. 999, 1019, 1040, 1045, 1049, and Niuafo'ou Nos. 203, 211, 225 and 235 Surcharged

Type 1 — Serifed
Surcharge

Type 2 — Unserifed Surcharge

Methods and Perfs As Before
2008-10   On Stamps of Tonga
1147 A197 30s on 55s
            #999, type
            1
1148 A202 30s on 55s
            #1019, type
            1   60.00
   a. Surcharge double   120.00
1149 A210 30s on 55s
            #1040, type
            2   40.00 900.00
1150 A213 30s on 55s
            #1049, type
            2   40.00
1151 A212 70s on 55s
            #1045, type
            1   50.00

On Stamps of Niuafo'ou
1152 A41   30s on 55s
            #203, type
            2
1153 A44   30s on 55s
            #211, type
            2
1154 A52   30s on 55s
            #225, type
            2
1155 A41   70s on 55s
            #203, type
            2   90.00
1156 A56   70s on 55s
            #235, type
            2

Size, location and obliterators of surcharges vary. Surcharged Niuafo'ou stamps were used in Tonga.
Issued: No. 1147, Nov. 2009; No. 1148, Nov. 2008; Nos. 1149, 1153, July 2008; No. 1150, Feb. 2010; No. 1151, June 2010; Nos. 1152, 1154, 2008; Nos. 1155, 1156, May 2010.
No. 1149 used is valued on cover.

Christmas — A235

No. 1157: a, 3pa, Lighthouse ornament on Christmas tree. b, 5pa, Christmas lights and Free Church of Tonga Cathedral.

2011, Dec. 24   Litho.   Perf. 14
1157 A235   Horiz. pair, #a-b   9.25 9.25

Birds
A236

Designs: 60s, Prosopeia tabuensis. 2.25pa, Anas superciliosa. 2.40pa, Halcyon chloris. 2.50pa, Egretta novaehollandiae. 2.70pa, Aplonis tabuensis. 3pa, Megapodius pritchardii. 3.40pa, Megapodius pritchardii, diff. 4pa, Lalage maculosa. 5pa, Tyto alba. 6.60pa, Halcyon chloris, diff. 7.30pa, Prosopeia tabuensis, diff. 10pa, Swamp harrier.

2012, Feb. 6   Perf. 14
Stamps With White Frames
1158 A236 60s multi   .75   .75
1159 A236 2.25pa multi 2.75 2.75
1160 A236 2.40pa multi 3.00 3.00
1161 A236 2.50pa multi 3.00 3.00
1162 A236 2.70pa multi 3.25 3.25
1163 A236 3pa multi   3.75 3.75
1164 A236 3.40pa multi 4.00 4.00
1165 A236 4pa multi   4.75 4.75
1166 A236 5pa multi   6.00 6.00
1167 A236 6.60pa multi 8.00 8.00
1168 A236 7.30pa multi 8.75 8.75
1169 A236 10pa multi   12.00 12.00
   Nos. 1158-1169 (12)   60.00 60.00

Stamps Without White Frames
1170   Sheet of 12 60.00 60.00
   a. A236 60s multi   .75   .75
   b. A236 2.25pa multi 2.75 2.75
   c. A236 2.40pa multi 3.00 3.00
   d. A236 2.50pa multi 3.00 3.00
   e. A236 2.70pa multi 3.25 3.25
   f. A236 3pa multi   3.75 3.75
   g. A236 3.40pa multi 4.00 4.00
   h. A236 4pa multi   4.75 4.75
   i. A236 5pa multi   6.00 6.00
   j. A236 6.60pa multi 8.00 8.00
   k. A236 7.30pa multi 8.75 8.75
   l. A236 10pa multi   12.00 12.00

Reign of Queen
Elizabeth II, 60th
Anniv. — A237

2012, Mar. 6   Perf. 14¾x14
1171 A237 3.40pa multi   4.00 4.00
Souvenir Sheet
1172 A237 10pa multi   12.00 12.00

Worldwide Fund for Nature
(WWF) — A238

Various depictions of Thorny seahorse: 45s, 2pa, 2.40pa, 3.40pa.

2012, Mar. 12   Perf. 14¼x14
1173-1176 A238   Set of 4   9.75 9.75
1176a   Sheet of 16, 4 each
           #1173-1176   39.00 39.00

Miniature Sheet

Reconstruction and Development Porjects — A239

No. 1177: a, 45s, Nuku'alofa construction. b, 85s, Vuna Wharf. c, 2.70pa, Vaiola Hospital. d, 5pa, New construction. e, 8pa, New Vuna Wharf. f, 10pa, Nuku'alofa sidewalks.

2012, May 30   **Perf. 12½**
1177   A239   Sheet of 6, #a-f
                                    30.00 30.00

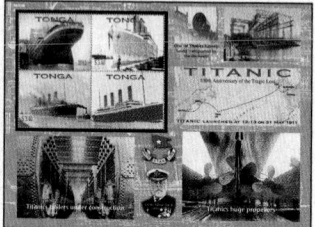

Sinking of the Titanic, Cent. — A240

No. 1178: a, Titanic under construction with ship under gantries. b, Titanic at dock, ropes at right. c, Titanic and tuboat. d, Titanic at sea. No. 1179a, Like #1178a.

2012, June 6   **Perf. 12½**
1178   A240   3.40pa   Sheet of 4,
                             #a-d   16.00 16.00
       Souvenir Sheet
1179   A240   Sheet of 2,
                             #1178c, 1179a   4.50 4.50
   a.   45s multi   .50   .50

ANZAC Day — A241

Designs: 45s, Council of the South Pacific Scout Association emblem. 1pa, Flag of Tonga. 2.40pa, Tonga Girl Guides Emblem. 3.40pa, Rotary International emblem.
No. 1184: a, 3.40pa, Scouts and leaders. b, 5pa, Scouts and leaders, diff.

2012, June 25   **Perf. 13½**
1180-1183 A241   Set of 4   8.25 8.25
       Souvenir Sheet
1184   A241   Sheet of 2, #a-b   9.50 9.50

2012 Summer Olympics, London — A242

Designs: 45s, Boxing. 1.40pa, Track. 3.40pa, Swimming.

2012, June 25   **Perf. 13¾**
1185-1187 A242   Set of 3   6.00 6.00
1187a   Souvenir sheet of 3,
                             #1185-1187   6.00 6.00
1187b   Souvenir sheet of 6, 2
                             each #1185-1187 12.00 12.00

Personalizable Stamp A243

2012, Aug. 8   **Perf. 13¼**
1188   A243   3pa multi   3.50 3.50

Tongan Monarchs — A244

2012, Aug. 20   **Imperf.**
1189   A244   20pa multi   23.00 23.00

Miniature Sheets

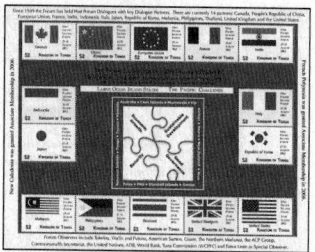

43rd Pacific Islands Forum — A245

No. 1190 — Flags of: a, Canada. b, People's Republic of China. c, European Union. d, France. e, India. f, Indonesia. g, Italy. h, Japan. i, Republic of Korea. j, Malaysia. k, Philippines. l, Thailand. m, United Kingdom. n, United States.
No. 1191 — Flags of: a, Australia. b, Cook Islands. c, Fiji. d, Kiribati. e, Micronesia. f, Nauru. g, New Zealand. h, Niue. i, Palau. j, Papua New Guinea. k, Marshall Islands. l, Samoa. m, Solomon Islands. n, Tonga. o, Tuvalu. p, Vanuatu.

2012, Aug. 31   **Perf. 14**
1190   A245   2pa Sheet of 14,
                             #a-n   32.50 32.50
1191   A245   2pa Sheet of 16,
                             #a-p   37.50 37.50

No. 980 Surcharged in Gold and Black

No. 1192: a, 5pa on 10s. b, 5pa on 80s. c, 5pa on 1pa. d, 5pa on 2.50pa.

2012, Sept. 4   **Litho.**
1192   CD355   Sheet of 4, #a-
                             d   23.00 23.00

Overprint is printed across the four stamps of the sheet. It reads "In Loving Memory of Diana, Princess of Wales / 31 August 1997 / Her Legacy will live on forever. / William and Kate, Duke and Duchess of Cambridge / 1st Anniversary of their Royal Wedding 2011".

Miniature Sheet

Christmas — A246

No. 1193 — Mystical Nativity, by Sandro Botticelli: a, Angel in red robe at left, angels with white and brown robes at center. b, White angel's robe at UL, angels in brown and red robes at center. c, Parts of five angels, with angel with red robe at right. d, Angels and manger roof. e, Virgin Mary, heads of cow and donkey. f, Angel with green robe to left of manger post. g, Infant Jesus. h, Angels to right of manger post. i, Angel in green robe embracing man. j, Angel in white robe embracing man. k, Angel in red robe embracing man.

2012, Nov. 21   **Perf. 14¾x14¼**
1193   A246   1pa Sheet of 11,
                             #a-k, + 2 la-
                             bels   13.00 13.00

Wedding of Crown Prince Tupouto'a 'Ulukulala and Sinaitakala Fakafanua — A247

Designs: No. 1194, Photograph of bride, groom and families.
No. 1195: a, King Tupou VI and Queen Nanasipau'u (36x36mm). b, Like No. 1194, without top panel. c, Procession of dignitaries (36x36mm). d, Bride and groom in robes (36x36mm). e, Limousine (36x36mm).

2012, Dec. 14   **Perf. 13¼**
1194   A247   3pa multi   3.50 3.50
1195   A247   3pa Sheet of 5, #a-
                             e   17.50 17.50

Miniature Sheet

New Year 2012 (Year of the Snake) — A248

No. 1196: a, Olive green snake with yellow green underside. b, Red brown snake with green underside. c, Yellow green snake with orange red underside. d, Purple snake with yellow green underside.

2013, Feb. 20   **Perf. 14¾x14¼**
1196   A248   2.45pa Sheet of 4,
                             #a-d   11.50 11.50

A249

A250

A251

A252

A253

A254

A255

Turtles A256

2013, Feb. 21   **Perf. 14**
Stamps With White Backgrounds
1197   Horiz. strip of 4   19.00 19.00
   a.   A249 4pa multi   4.75 4.75
   b.   A250 4pa multi   4.75 4.75
   c.   A251 4pa multi   4.75 4.75
   d.   A252 4pa multi   4.75 4.75
1198   Horiz. strip of 4   23.00 23.00
   a.   A253 5pa multi   5.75 5.75
   b.   A254 5pa multi   5.75 5.75
   c.   A255 5pa multi   5.75 5.75
   d.   A256 5pa multi   5.75 5.75

Miniature Sheets
Stamps With Colored Backgrounds
1199   Sheet of 4   19.00 19.00
   a.   A249 4pa multi   4.75 4.75
   b.   A250 4pa multi   4.75 4.75
   c.   A251 4pa multi   4.75 4.75
   d.   A252 4pa multi   4.75 4.75
1200   Sheet of 4   23.00 23.00
   a.   A253 5pa multi   5.75 5.75
   b.   A254 5pa multi   5.75 5.75
   c.   A255 5pa multi   5.75 5.75
   d.   A256 5pa multi   5.75 5.75

Souvenir Sheet

Australia 2013 World Stamp Expo, Melbourne — A257

No. 1201: a, Koala. b, Royal Exhibition Building, Melbourne. c, Red kangaroo.

2013, May 10   **Perf. 13¼**
1201 A257   3pa Sheet of 3,
         #a-c   10.00 10.00

Miniature Sheet

Blow Holes and Fish — A258

No. 1202 — Fish: a, 3pa, Chaetodon flavirostris, Pseudanthias pleurotaenia. b, 3pa, Pygoplites diacathus, Amblyglyphidodon melanopterus. c, 4pa, Acanthurus guttatus, Myripristis hexagona. d, 4pa, Pseudanthias pleurotaenia, Zanclus comutus. e, 5pa, Zanclus comutus, Pygoplites diacanthus. f, 5pa, Amblyglyphidodon melanopterus, Myripristis hexagona.

2013, June 4   **Perf. 13¾**
1202 A258   Sheet of 6, #a-f   27.00 27.00

Birds and Flora A259

Designs: 10s, Halcyon chloris, Adenanthera pavonina. 20s, Aplonis tabuensis, Myristica hypagyraea. 30s, Vini australis, Artocarpus altilis. 40s, Fregata minor, Hibiscus tiliaceus. 50s, Sula sula, Terminalia catappa. 80s, Phaeton rubricauda, Cocos nucifera. 90s, Anous minutus, Elattostachys falcata. 1.10pa, Lalage maculosa, Tarenina sambucina. 1.20pa, Porzana tabuensis, Mimosa pigra. 2pa, Foulehaio caruncultatus, Solanum mauritianum. 12.50pa, Prosopeia tabuensis, Adenanthera pavonina. 20pa, Ptilinopus perousii, Psidium guajava.

2013, June 6   **Perf. 14**
Stamps With White Frames
1203	A259	10s multi	.25	.25
1204	A259	20s multi	.25	.25
1205	A259	30s multi	.35	.35
1206	A259	40s multi	.45	.45
1207	A259	50s multi	.55	.55
1208	A259	80s multi	.90	.90
1209	A259	90s multi	1.00	1.00
1210	A259	1.10pa multi	1.25	1.25
1211	A259	1.20pa multi	1.40	1.40
1212	A259	2pa multi	2.25	2.25
1213	A259	12.50pa multi	14.00	14.00
1214	A259	20pa multi	22.50	22.50
	Nos. 1203-1214 (12)		45.15	45.15

Miniature Sheet
Stamps Without White Frames
1215		Sheet of 12	46.00	46.00
a.	A259	10s multi	.25	.25
b.	A259	20s multi	.25	.25
c.	A259	30s multi	.35	.35
d.	A259	40s multi	.45	.45
e.	A259	50s multi	.55	.55
f.	A259	80s multi	.90	.90
g.	A259	90s multi	1.00	1.00
h.	A259	1.10pa multi	1.25	1.25
i.	A259	1.20pa multi	1.40	1.40
j.	A259	2pa multi	2.25	2.25
k.	A259	12.50pa multi	14.00	14.00
l.	A259	20pa multi	22.50	22.50

Fire Dancers, Hana's Cave, Oholei Beach Resort A260

Designs: 15s, Girl clapping. 1.75pa, Dancers. 4.70pa, Dancers with three torches. No. 1219, vert.: a, 5.25pa, Dancer with torch burining on both ends. b, 7.85pa, Dancer holding torch well above head. c, 8.65pa, Dancer holding torch close to mouth.

2013, Aug. 14   **Perf. 13¾**
1216-1218 A260   Set of 3   7.25 7.25
Souvenir Sheet
Perf. 13¾x13½
1219 A260   Sheet of 3, #a-c   23.50 23.50

Birth of Prince George of Cambridge A261

Designs: 1.75pa, Baby's feet on adult's hands. 2.40pa, Adult's hands touching baby's feet. 2.60pa, Baby's hand holding adult's finger. 3.40pa, Baby's hand holding adult's finger, diff.
11.30pa, Baby's hand in adult's hand.

2013, Aug. 30   **Perf. 13¾**
1220-1223 A261   Set of 4   11.00 11.00
Souvenir Sheet
1224 A261   11.30pa multi   12.50 12.50

Miniature Sheet

Giant Pandas — A262

No. 1225 — Panda: a, Sitting under tree. b, In snow. c, Chewing on long stick. d, Face. e, Eating bamboo leaves.

2013, Sept. 26   **Perf. 12**
1225 A262   2.50pa Sheet of 5,
         #a-e   14.00 14.00

Souvenir Sheet

China International Collection Expo 2013, Beijing — A263

No. 1226: a, Painting by Paul Gauguin. b, Beijing Exhibition Center.

2013, Sept. 26   **Perf. 12**
1226 A263   2pa multi   4.50 4.50

Watercraft and Tin Can Island Mail Cans — A264

Design: 2.25pa, Ship and mail can at sea. 5.40pa, Canoe, mail can on shore.

2013, Sept. 27   **Perf. 14¼**
1227 A264   2.25pa multi   2.50 2.50
Souvenir Sheet
1228 A264   5.40pa multi   6.00 6.00

Dragon A265

2013, Oct. 15   **Perf. 12**
1229 A265   8pa multi   8.75 8.75
No. 1229 was printed in sheets of 2.

Souvenir Sheets

A266

Diplomatic Relations Between Tonga and People's Republic of China, 15th Anniv. — A267

No. 1230: a, Vaipua Bridge, Tonga. b, MA60 airplane.
No. 1231: a, Great Wall of China. b, Haamonga Trilithon, Tonga.

2013, Nov. 2   **Litho.**   **Perf. 13½x13¾**
1230 A266   3pa Sheet of 2, #a-b   6.75 6.75
Perf. 13x13¼
1231 A267   3pa Sheet of 2, #a-b   6.75 6.75

King Tupou VI — A268

2013, Nov. 12   **Litho.**   **Perf. 14¼**
Panel Color
1232	A268	45s blue gray	.50	.50
1233	A268	50s dull org	.55	.55
1234	A268	75s yel bister	.80	.80
1235	A268	1.05pa dull yel grn	1.10	1.10
1236	A268	2.40pa brown	2.60	2.60
1237	A268	2.60pa dull yel org	2.75	2.75
1238	A268	3.40pa dull brn	3.75	3.75
	Nos. 1232-1238 (7)		12.05	12.05

Christmas A269

Paintings by: 1.75pa, Simon Vouet. 2.35pa, Giotto di Bondone. 2.60pa, Jan van Eyck.

2013, Nov. 13   **Litho.**   **Perf. 13½**
1239-1241 A269   Set of 3   7.25 7.25

Miniature Sheets

Cruise Ships and Wharves — A270

No. 1242: a, 1.75pa, Ocean Princess at New Vuna Wharf. b, 1.75pa, MS Amadea. c, 1.75pa, Seabourne Quest. d, 2.40pa, MS Columbus. e, 2.40pa, MS Europa. f, 2.40pa, New Vuna Wharf.
No. 1243: a, 2.60pa, Pacific Jewel. b, 2.60pa, MS Dawn Princess. c, 2.60pa, MS Artania. d, 3.40pa, Sea Princess. e, 3.40pa, MS Regatta. f, 3.40pa, New Vuna Wharf, diff.

2013, Dec. 11   **Litho.**   **Perf. 14**
1242	A270	Seeht of 6, #a-f	13.50	13.50
1243	A270	Sheet of 6, #a-f	19.50	19.50

Souvenir Sheet

Christening of Prince George of Cambridge — A271

2014, Jan. 3   **Litho.**   **Perf. 13¼**
1244 A271   10pa multi   11.00 11.00

Miniature Sheet

New Year 2014 (Year of the Horse) — A272

No. 1245: a, Horse's head. b, Horse facing left, leaping. c, Horse facing right, walking. d, Horse facing right, leaping.

2014, Jan. 6   **Litho.**   **Perf. 13¾**
1245 A272   2.45pa Sheet of 4,
         #a-d   10.50 10.50

Chinese
Space
Program
A273

Spacecraft and: 1.75pa, Astronaut Liu Yang.
2.40pa, Map of People's Republic of China.
2.60pa, Astronaut Jing Haipeng. 3.40pa, Jing
Haipeng, diff.

2014, Feb. 3   Litho.   Perf. 14¾x14¼
1246-1249 A273   Set of 4   11.00 11.00

Miniature Sheet

EASTER 2014

Easter — A274

No. 1250 — Various paintings of the resurrected Christ by Tiziano Vecellio (Titian): a,
2.35pa. b, 3pa. c, 4.60pa. d, 6.95pa.

2014, Apr. 7   Litho.   Perf. 13¼
1250 A274   Sheet of 4, #a-d   18.50 18.50

Bactrian Camels, by Wu Zuoren
(1908-97) — A275

2014, Apr. 9   Litho.   Perf. 14¾x14¼
1251 A275   5pa multi   5.50 5.50

No. 1251 was printed in sheets of 4.

Souvenir Sheet

Young Nelson Mandela

*Never, never and never again shall it be that
this beautiful land will again experience the
oppression of one by another.*
— Nelson Mandela

July 18, 1918 - December 5, 2013

Nelson Mandela (1918-2013),
President of South Africa — A276

No. 1252 — Mandela: a, Carrying book and
papers. b, Wearing necklace.

2014, May 13   Litho.   Perf. 14¾x14¼
1252 A276   5pa Sheet of 2, #a-
              b   11.00 11.00

Pacific Small Island
Developing
States — A277

No. 1253: a, Rising sea levels. b, Tropical
Cyclone Ian. c, Emblem of Pacific Small Island
Developing States. d, Map of Tonga and Fiji. e,
Island Voices Global Choices emblem. f, Sail-
boat. g, Cruise ship. h, USS Cleveland. i, Fish-
ing boat. j, Landing Craft Utility 1665. k, Tubas-
traea micranthus. l, Pseudanthias
squamipinnis. m, Amphiprion ocellaris. n,
Rhincodon typus. o, Laticauda colubrina. p,
Flag of Tonga.
   No. 1254: a, Like #1253a. b, Like #1253p. c,
Like #1253b. d, Like #1253c. e, Like #1253d. f,
Like #1253e.
   No. 1255: a, Like #1253f. b, Like #1253p. c,
Like #1253g. d, Like #1253h. e, Like #1253i. f,
Like #1253j.
   No. 1256: a, Like #1253k. b, Like #1253p. c,
Like #1253l. d, Like #1253m. e, Like #1253n. f,
Like #1253o.

2014, May 20   Litho.   Perf. 13¼
1253   Block of 18, #1253a-
             1253o, 3 #1253p   9.00 9.00
a.-p. A277 45s Any single   .50   .50
          Miniature Sheets
1254   Sheet of 6   11.50 11.50
a.-f. A277 1.75pa Any single 1.90 1.90
1255   Sheet of 6   15.00 15.00
a.-f. A277 2.35pa Any single 2.50 2.50
1256   Sheet of 6   15.00 15.00
a.-f. A277 2.60pa Any single 2.75 2.75
         Nos. 1254-1256 (3) 41.50 41.50

No. 1253 was printed in sheets containing 3
blocks of 18. The frame on each stamp in the

sheet, depicting a map of the Pacific Ocean,
differs.

Birds — A278

No. 1257: a, 11.30pa, Barn owl. b, 16.90pa,
Blue-crowned lorikeet. c, 28pa, Buff-banded
rail.

2014, Sept. 15   Litho.   Perf. 13¼
1257 A278   Horiz. strip of 3,
            #a-c, + 3 labels   57.50 57.50

Miniature Sheet

Tongan Participation in the
Commonwealth Games, 40th
Anniv. — A279

No. 1258: a, 1.75pa, Boxing. b, 2.35pa, Pole
vault. c, 2.40pa, Rugby sevens. d, 2.60pa,
Judo. e, 3.40pa, Weight lifting.

2014, Sept. 17   Litho.   Perf. 14
1258 A279   Sheet of 5, #a-e,
            + label   13.00 13.00

Miniature Sheet

Christmas — A280

Bells and: a, Musical score with five staffs,
denomination in white. b, Musical score with
five staffs, denomination in black. c, Musical
score with three staffs, denomination in black.
d, Curving staff with G clef and notes, denomination in white.

2014, Dec. 15   Litho.   Perf. 13¾
1259 A280 2.25pa Sheet of 4,
            #a-d   9.25 9.25

A281

New Year 2015 (Year of the
Sheep) — A282

No. 1261 — Sheep with background colors
of: a, 11.30pa, Yellow green and green. b,
16.90pa, Yellow brown and brown.

2015, Jan. 5   Litho.   Perf. 13¼
1260 A281 8pa multi   7.75 7.75
            Souvenir Sheet
            Self-Adhesive
            Die Cut Perf. 13½
1261 A282   Sheet of 2, #a-b 27.00 27.00

No. 1261 has rouletting in sheet margin
allowing the entire sheet to be folded into a
hangable lantern.

SEMI-POSTAL STAMP

**Catalogue values for unused
stamps in this section are for
Never Hinged items.**

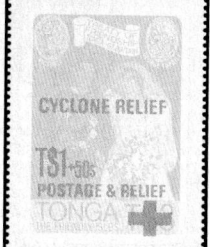

No. 488
Surcharged
in Silver

1982, Apr. 14   Litho.
B1   A86 3pa + 50s multi   7.00 7.00

AIR POST STAMPS

**Catalogue values for unused
stamps in this section are for
Never Hinged items.**

Type of Regular Gold Coin Issue

Designs: 10p, 1sh1p, Queen Salote standing, ½-koula coin, obverse. 11p, Coat of arms,
½-koula coin, reverse. 2sh1p, 2sh9p, Queen
Salote standing, 1-koula coin, obverse. 2sh4p,
Coat of arms, 1-koula coin, reverse.

Litho.; Embossed on Gilt Foil
1963, July 15   Unwmk.   *Die Cut*
         Diameter: 54mm
C1 A36 10p dp carmine   .50   .50
C2 A36 11p green   .70   .70
C3 A36 1sh1p violet blue   .70   .70
         Diameter: 80mm
C4 A36 2sh1p magenta   1.25 1.25
C5 A36 2sh4p emerald   1.25 1.25
C6 A36 2sh9p violet   2.00 2.00
         Nos. C1-C6 (6)   6.40 6.40

See note after No. 133.

Map of Tongatabu and ¼-Koula
Coin — AP1

Litho.; Embossed on Gilt Foil
1964, Oct. 19
C7	AP1	10p deep green	.30 .30
C8	AP1	1sh2p black	.45 .45
C9	AP1	3sh6p carmine	.95 .95
C10	AP1	6sh6p purple	1.75 1.75
		Nos. C7-C10 (4)	3.45 3.45

Pan-Pacific and Southeast Asia Women's
Association Conf., Nukualofa, Aug. 1964. See
note after No. 133.
For overprints and surcharges see Nos.
C22-C26, C83-C86.

Nos. C1-C2, C4-C6 Srchd. like
Regular Issue, 1965, in Black, White
or Red

1965, Mar. 18
C11	A36	2sh3p on 10p (B)	2.00 1.00
C12	A36	2sh9p on 11p (W)	3.50 2.00
C13	A36	4sh6p on 2sh1p	22.50 22.50
C14	A36	4sh6p on 2sh4p	22.50 22.50
C15	A36	4sh6p on 2sh9p	13.50 13.50
		Nos. C11-C15 (5)	54.25 54.25

Nos. 114-115, 117-118 Ovptd. or
Srchd.

Perf. 14½x13½
1966, June 18   Wmk. 79
C16	A35	5p purple	.25 .25
C17	A35	10p on 1p brn org & car rose	.25 .25
C18	A35	1sh red brown	.40 .25
C19	A35	2sh9p on 2p ultra	.50 .25
C20	A35	3sh6p on 5p purple	.50 .25
C21	A35	4sh6p on 1sh red brn	.25 .25
		Nos. C16-C21 (6)	2.25 1.20

Centenary of Tupou College and secondary
education. The overprint or surcharge is
spaced differently on other values.
For Surcharges see Nos. C55-C57.

Nos. C7-C8 Ovptd. and Srchd. in
Silver or Gold on Black, or in Black
on Gold

Litho.; Embossed on Gilt Foil
1966, Dec. 16   Unwmk.   Die Cut
C22	AP1	10p (S on B)	.50 .40
C23	AP1	1sh2p (B on G)	.50 .40
C24	AP1	4sh on 10p (S on B)	1.00 1.00

C25	AP1	5sh6p on 1sh2p (B on G)	1.50 1.50
C26	AP1	10sh6p on 1sh2p (G on B)	2.50 2.50
		Nos. C22-C26 (5)	5.40 5.40

In memory of Queen Salote (1900-65). See
Nos. C83-C86.

King Taufa'ahau Type of Regular
Issue, 1967

Designs: 7s, 11s, 23s, 2pa, Taufa'ahau IV,
obverse of new palladium coins. 9s, 21s, 29s,
Coat of Arms, reverse.

Litho.; Embossed on Palladium Foil
1967, July 4

Diameter: 7s, 44mm; 9s, 29s, 52mm; 11s,
59mm; 21s, 68mm; 23s, 40mm; 2pa, 74mm.

C27	A38	7s red & black	.50 .40
C28	A38	9s maroon & emer	.50 .40
C29	A38	11s brt blue & org	.50 .40
C30	A38	21s black & emer	.55 .55
C31	A38	23s magenta & emer	.60 .60
C32	A38	29s vio blue & emer	.70 .70
C33	A38	2pa magenta & orange	5.00 5.00
		Nos. C27-C33 (7)	7.60 7.60

See note after No. 181.

Regular
Issues of
1953 Srchd.
in Red or
Black

Wmk. 79
1967, Dec. 15   Engr.   Die Cut
C34	A33	11s on 3½p ultra (R)	.30 .30
C35	A33	21s on 1½p emerald	.40 .35
C36	A33	23s on 3½p ultra (R)	.40 .35
		Nos. C34-C36 (3)	1.00 1.00

Arrival of the United States Peace Corps.

No. 112 Surcharged
in Red

1968, Apr. 6   Engr.   Perf. 11x11½
C37	A34	11s on 10sh blk & yel	.50 .50
C38	A34	21s on 10sh blk & yel	.65 .65
C39	A34	23s on 10sh blk & yel	.65 .65
		Nos. C37-C39 (3)	1.65 1.65

Nos. C27-C33 Overprinted "HIS
MAJESTY'S 50th BIRTHDAY" in
Silver on Blue Panel on 7s, 11s, 23s
and 2pa. "H.M.'s BIRTHDAY / 4.
JULY. 1968" in Gold on Red Panel
on 9s, 21s and 29s

Litho.; Embossed on Palladium Foil
1968, July 4   Unwmk.   Die Cut
C40	A38	7s red & black	.25 .25
C41	A38	9s maroon & emer	.25 .25
C42	A38	11s brt blue & org	.25 .25
C43	A38	21s black & emerald	.75 .35
C44	A38	23s mag & emerald	.75 .35
C45	A38	29s vio blue & emer	1.00 .40
C46	A38	2pa magenta & org	6.75 6.00
		Nos. C40-C46 (7)	9.90 7.70

50th birthday of King Taufa'ahau IV.

Types of 1953 Surcharged "Friendly
Islands / Field & Track Trials / South
Pacific Games / Port Moresby 1969 /
AIRMAIL"

Designs as before.

1968, Dec. 19   Engr.   Wmk. 79
C47	A33	6s on 6p yel& blk	.25 .25
C48	A33	7s on 4p purple & yel	.25 .25
C49	A33	8s on 8p blk & lt grn	.25 .25
C50	A33	9s on 1½p emerald	.25 .25
C51	A34	11s on 3p brn org & yel	.25 .25
C52	A33	21s on 3½p dk blue	.30 .30
C53	A33	38s on 5sh sepia & yel	2.10 .85
C54	A34	1pa on 10sh orange yel	1.00 .60
		Nos. C47-C54 (8)	4.40 2.40

Issued to publicize the field and track trials
for the third South Pacific Games, Port
Moresby, 1969. The overprint is in 5 lines on
the horizontal stamps, in 7 lines on the vertical
stamps. On the vertical stamps "Trial" is

---

printed on the line ahead of "Field & Track." On
No. C54 the denomination is spelled out.

Nos. C19-
C21 Srchd.

Perf. 14½x13½
1968   Photo.   Wmk. 79
C55	A35	1s on 2sh9p on 2p ultra	1.60 1.00
C56	A35	1s on 3sh6p on 5p pur	1.60 1.00
C57	A35	1s on 4sh6p on 1sh red brown	1.60 1.00
		Nos. C55-C57 (3)	4.80 3.00

Pacific Games Type of Regular
Issue

Design: Boxer.

1969, Aug. 13   Litho.   Die Cut
Self-adhesive
C58	A40	9s orange, blk & pur	.35 .35
C59	A40	11s orange, blk & dk bl	.35 .35
C60	A40	20s org, blk & yel grn	.55 .55
C61	A40	29s orange, blk & scar	1.40 1.40
C62	A40	1pa orange, blk & grn	1.90 1.90
		Nos. C58-C62 (5)	4.10 4.10

See note after No. 231.

Oil Derrick on
Map of
Tongatabu and
King Taufa'ahau
IV — AP2

Litho.; Gold Embossed
1969, Dec. 23   Self-adhesive
C63	AP2	9s multicolored	.55 .55
C64	AP2	10s multicolored	.55 .55
C65	AP2	24s multicolored	1.00 1.00
C66	AP2	29s multicolored	1.10 1.10
C67	AP2	38s multicolored	1.50 1.50
		Nos. C63-C67 (5)	3.90 3.90

1st scientific search for oil in Tonga.

King Taufa'ahau IV and Queen
Elizabeth II — AP3

Litho.; Gold Embossed
1970, Mar. 7   Self-adhesive
C68	AP3	7s multicolored	.40 .30
C69	AP3	10s multicolored	.50 .35
C70	AP3	24s multicolored	1.25 .65
C71	AP3	29s multicolored	1.50 .75
C72	AP3	38s multicolored	2.10 1.00
		Nos. C68-C72 (5)	5.75 3.05

See note after No. 242.

King Taufa'ahau Tupou IV
Medal — AP4

Litho.; Gold Embossed
1970, June 4   Self-adhesive
C73	AP4	9s grnsh bl, ver & gold	.35 .35
C74	AP4	10s lilac, bl & gold	.35 .35
C75	AP4	24s yel, grn & gold	.80 .80
C76	AP4	29s ultra, org & gold	1.10 1.10
C77	AP4	38s ocher, emer & gold	1.60 1.60
		Nos. C73-C77 (5)	4.05 4.05

See note after No. 247.

Red Cross Type of Regular Issue
Without Coat of Arms
1970, Oct. 17   Litho.   Die Cut
Self-adhesive
C78	A45	9s red & silver	.25 .25
C79	A45	10s red & magenta	.25 .25
C80	A45	18s red & brt green	.75 .75
C81	A45	38s red & brt blue	2.75 2.75
C82	A45	1pa red & green	6.00 6.00
		Nos. C78-C82 (5)	10.00 10.00

Centenary of the British Red Cross.

Nos. C22-C24 Surcharged

Lithographed; Embossed on Gilt
Foil
1971, Jan. 31   Die Cut
C83	AP1	9s on #C22 (S on B)	.70 .25
C84	AP1	24s on #C24 (G on B)	1.50 1.00
C85	AP1	29s on #C23 (R on B)	2.10 1.25
C86	AP1	38s on #C23 (G on B)	3.25 1.60
		Nos. C83-C86 (4)	7.55 4.05

In memory of Queen Salote (1900-1965).

Regular
Issues of
1953, Srchd.
in Red and
Black

1971   Engr.   Wmk. 79   Imperf
C87	A33	9s on 1½p green	.25 .25
C88	A33	10s on 4p purple & yel	.25 .25
C89	A33	38s on 1p yellow & blk	1.10 .60
		Nos. C87-C89 (3)	1.60 1.00

See note after No. 272.

Types of Regular Issue Srchd. in
Purple or Black "AIRMAIL," New
Denomination and "HONOURING
JAPANESE POSTAL CENTENARY
1871-1971"

1971
C90	A34	18s on 1sh car & buff (P)	.50 .50
C91	A33	1pa on 2sh car & ultra	3.00 3.00

Surcharge on #C90 in 6 lines, on #C91 in 4.

Self-adhesive & Die Cut
Starting with Nos. C92-C96, all airmail issues are self-adhesive and die
cut, unless otherwise stated.

High Jump — AP5

1971, July   Litho.   Unwmk.

C92	AP5	9s brown, mag & blk	.25	.25
C93	AP5	10s brown, blue & blk	.25	.25
C94	AP5	24s brn, dk grn & blk	.45	.45
C95	AP5	29s brown, vio & blk	.75	.75
C96	AP5	38s brown, red & blk	1.00	1.00
		Nos. C92-C96 (5)	2.60	2.60

4th South Pacific Games, Papeete, French Polynesia, Sept. 8-19.
For surcharges see Nos. C141-C142.

Prehistoric
Trilithon,
King's Watch
and Portrait
AP6

Litho. and Embossed
1971, July 20

C97	AP6	14s dk brown & multi	.75	.75
C98	AP6	21s ocher & multi	1.10	1.10

2nd anniversary of man's first landing on the moon and the placement of a Bulova Accutron there. See Nos. C117-118, CO47-CO48, CO61-CO62. Advertisement on peelable paper backing.

Medal Type of Regular Issue

Designs: 10s, Gold Medal of Merit, obverse (King Taufa'ahau IV). 75s, Silver Medal of Merit, obverse (King Taufa'ahau IV). 1pa, Bronze Medal of Merit, reverse.

1971, Oct. 30   Litho. & Embossed

C99	A47	10s gold & multi	.25	.25
C100	A47	75s silver & multi	1.60	1.60
C101	A47	1pa bronze & multi	1.75	1.75
		Nos. C99-C101 (3)	3.60	3.60

Girl with Blocks
and UNICEF
Emblem — AP7

1971, Dec.   Litho.

C102	AP7	10s multicolored	.30	.30
C103	AP7	15s multicolored	.40	.40
C104	AP7	65s multicolored	.65	.65
C105	AP7	50s multicolored	1.50	1.50
C106	AP7	1pa multicolored	2.75	2.75
		Nos. C102-C106 (5)	5.40	5.40

25th anniversary of UNICEF.

Ship Type of Regular Issue

Design: Map of Merchant Marine routes from Tonga and cargo ship "Niuvakai."

1972, Apr. 14

C107	A49	9s ver & multi	.85	.35
C108	A49	12s multicolored	1.10	.35
C109	A49	14s dk pur & multi	1.25	.35
C110	A49	75s olive & multi	6.75	5.00
C111	A49	90s black & multi	7.00	6.50
		Nos. C107-C111 (5)	16.95	12.55

For surcharge and overprint see No. C124.

Coin Type of Regular Issue

Design: Coins on top; panel at bottom inscribed "5th anniversary world's first palladium coinage."

Litho.; Embossed on Metallic Foil
1972, July 15

C112	A50	9s silver & multi	.30	.30
C113	A50	12s silver & multi	.35	.35
C114	A50	14s silver & multi	.50	.50
C115	A50	21s silver & multi	.75	.75
C116	A50	75s silver & multi	2.25	2.25
		Nos. C112-C116 (5)	4.15	4.15

Watch Type of 1971
Litho. and Embossed
1972, July 20

C117	AP6	17s multicolored	.85	.85
C118	AP6	38s multicolored	1.75	1.75

Advertisement on peelable paper backing.

Proclamation of Sovereignty — AP8

1972, Dec. 9   Litho.

C119	AP8	9s ultra & multi	.25	.25
C120	AP8	12s red brown & multi	.25	.25
C121	AP8	14s magenta & multi	.40	.40
C122	AP8	38s brn org & multi	1.10	1.10
C123	AP8	1pa olive & multi	3.00	3.00
		Nos. C119-C123 (5)	4.55	4.55

Tonga's proclamation of sovereignty over the Minerva Reefs, June 1972.

No. C107 Surcharged

1972, Nov.   Litho.

C124	A49	7s on 9s multicolored	3.00	3.00

Inauguration of internal airmail service Nukualofa-Vavau, Nov. 1972.

Tongan Bank Notes and Bank
Building — AP9

1973, Mar. 30   Litho.

C125	AP9	9s multicolored	.25	.25
C126	AP9	12s ultra & multi	.25	.25
C127	AP9	17s dp car & multi	.40	.25

C128	AP9	50s lt blue & multi	1.50	1.25
C129	AP9	90s multicolored	2.75	2.75
		Nos. C125-C129 (5)	5.15	4.60

Establishment of Bank of Tonga.

Boy Scout Emblem — AP10

1973, June 29   Litho.

C130	AP10	9s silver & multi	.70	.35
C131	AP10	12s silver & multi	.85	.45
C132	AP10	14s silver & multi	1.25	.70
C133	AP10	17s silver & multi	1.40	.85
C134	AP10	1pa silver & multi	15.00	9.25
		Nos. C130-C134 (5)	19.20	11.60

See note after No. 326.
For surcharges see Nos. C143-C144.

"Resolution" — AP11

1973, Oct. 2   Litho.

C135	AP11	9s multicolored	.80	.40
C136	AP11	14s multicolored	1.50	.60
C137	AP11	29s multicolored	4.50	2.75
C138	AP11	38s multicolored	5.50	3.00
C139	AP11	75s multicolored	10.50	4.25
		Nos. C135-C139 (5)	22.80	11.00

Bicentenary of Capt. Cook's arrival.

Nos. 277, C96, C94, C130 and C132 Surcharged in Silver, Violet or Black: "Commonwealth Games Christchurch 1974"

1973, Dec. 19

C140	A46	7s on 25s multi (S)	.25	.25
C141	AP5	9s on 38s multi (V)	.30	.25
C142	AP5	24s multicolored (B)	1.00	.65
C143	AP10	29s on 9s multi (V)	1.25	1.10
C144	AP10	40s on 14s multi (B)	1.60	1.50
		Nos. C140-C144 (5)	4.10	2.35

10th British Commonwealth Games, Christchurch, New Zealand, Jan. 24-Feb. 2, 1974. No. C140 is overprinted "AIRMAIL" in black; the silver surcharge and overprint are on black panels.

Parrot of
Eua — AP12

1974, Mar. 20   Litho.

C145	AP12	7s multicolored	.50	.25
C146	AP12	9s multicolored	.60	.30
C147	AP12	12s multicolored	.60	.30
C148	AP12	14s multicolored	.90	.45

C149	AP12	17s multicolored	1.00	.50
C150	AP12	29s multicolored	1.75	.90
C151	AP12	38s multicolored	2.50	1.25
C152	AP12	50s multicolored	3.00	1.50
C153	AP12	75s multicolored	4.50	2.25
		Nos. C145-C153 (9)	15.35	7.70

Printed in rolls of 500. Self-adhesive rose red control number in upper left corner.

Carrier Pigeon Scattering Letters over
Tonga — AP13

1974, June 20   Typo.

C154	AP13	14s lt blue & multi	.45	.45
C155	AP13	21s lt blue & multi	.55	.55
C156	AP13	60s lt blue & multi	1.75	1.75
C157	AP13	75s lt blue & multi	1.90	1.90
C158	AP13	1pa lt blue & multi	2.50	2.50
		Nos. C154-C158 (5)	7.15	7.15

Centenary of Universal Postal Union.

Girl Guide Leaders — AP14

1974, Sept. 11   Litho.

C159	AP14	14s blue & multi	.80	.50
C160	AP14	16s blue & multi	1.40	.80
C161	AP14	29s blue & multi	2.75	1.60
C162	AP14	31s blue & multi	3.50	2.10
C163	AP14	75s blue & multi	7.50	4.50
		Nos. C159-C163 (5)	15.95	9.50

Girl Guides of Tonga.
For surcharges and overprints see Nos. C190-C191, C193.

Freighter "James Cook" and List of
Tongan Merchantmen — AP15

1974, Dec. 11

C164	AP15	9s blue & multi	.80	.30
C165	AP15	14s blue & multi	1.40	.55
C166	AP15	17s blue & multi	1.50	.60
C167	AP15	60s blue & multi	5.50	3.75
C168	AP15	90s blue & multi	8.75	4.75
		Nos. C164-C168 (5)	17.95	9.95

Establishment of Royal Marine Institute.

Beach
AP16

Designs: 12s, 14s, like 9s. 17s, 38s, Surf.

1975, Mar. 11				**Litho.**
C169	AP16	9s gold & multi	.25	.25
C170	AP16	12s gold & multi	.25	.25
C171	AP16	14s gold & multi	.30	.30
C172	AP16	17s gold & multi	.30	.30
C173	AP16	38s gold & multi	.95	.95
	Nos. C169-C173 (5)		*2.00*	*2.00*

First meeting of South Pacific area Prime Ministers. See note after No. 226.
For surcharges see Nos. C229, C298.

Women's Discus and Games'
Emblem — AP17

1975, June 11				
C174	AP17	9s multicolored	.35	.35
C175	AP17	12s multicolored	.45	.45
C176	AP17	14s multicolored	.45	.45
C177	AP17	17s black & multi	.60	.60
C178	AP17	90s olive & multi	2.40	2.40
	Nos. C174-C178 (5)		*4.25*	*4.25*

5th South Pacific Games, Guam, Aug. 1-10.
See note after No. 226.
For surcharges see Nos. C230-C231.

FAO Type of 1975

Designs (FAO Coins): 12s, Coins showing cattle, corn and pig. 14s, Cornucopias; coins showing king, family planning emblem and melons. 25s, Bananas and treasure chest. 50s, King Taufa'ahau. 1pa, Palms.

1975, Sept. 3				
C179	A62	12s multicolored	.45	.45
C180	A62	14s blue & multi	.45	.45
C181	A62	25s silver, blk & org	.70	.70
C182	A62	50s car, sil & blk	1.25	1.25
C183	A62	1pa silver & black	2.50	2.50
	Nos. C179-C183 (5)		*5.35*	*5.35*

Size of paper backing of 14s: 82x50mm;
others 45x45mm. See note after No. 226.

Coin Type of 1975

Coins: 9s, King Taufa'ahau IV, obverse. 12s, Queen Salote III, 75pa reverse and obverse. 14s, 10pa reverse. 38s, King Taufa'ahau IV, 10pa reverse and observe. 1pa, Heads of four constitutional monarchs.

1975, Nov. 4		**Lt. Blue Background**		
C184	A63	9s black, sil & red	.40	.40
C185	A63	12s gold, blk & grn	.50	.50
C186	A63	14s black, sil & ol	.50	.50
C187	A63	38s gold, blk & org	1.25	1.25
C188	A63	1pa black, sil & blue	3.00	3.00
	Nos. C184-C188 (5)		*4.85*	*4.00*

Size of paper backing of 1pa: 87x78mm,
others 65x60mm. See note after No. 226.

**Nos. 344-345, C160, C163 Srchd.
and Ovptd. in Carmine on Silver,
Green or Gold**

a

b

1976, Feb. 24				**Litho.**
C189	A58 (a)	12s on 20s (S)	.80	.50
C190	AP14 (b)	14s on 16s (Gr)	.80	.50
C191	AP14 (b)	16s (G)	1.00	.50
C192	A58 (a)	38s on 40s (G)	2.50	.70
C193	AP14 (b)	75s (S)	4.50	2.75
	Nos. C189-C193 (5)		*9.60*	*4.95*

21st Olympic Games, Montreal, Canada,
July 17-Aug. 1. See note after No. 226.

Bicentennial Type of 1976

Signers of Declaration of Independence, Flags of US and Tonga: 12s, Abraham Clark, George Ross, Thomas Lynch, Jr., Charles Carroll, Roger Sherman (no flags). 14s, Robert Treat Paine, Thomas Jefferson, Thomas McKean, John Adams. 17s, Button Gwinnett, Lewis Morris, Caesar Rodney, Richard Henry Lee. 38s, John Hart, Samuel Huntington, Philip Livingston, John Morton. 1pa, John Hancock, Joseph Hewes, Josiah Bartlett, John Witherspoon.

1976, May 26				
C194	A66	12s buff & multi	.65	.25
C195	A66	14s buff & multi	.75	.25
C196	A66	17s buff & multi	.80	.45
C197	A66	38s buff & multi	3.50	1.00
C198	A66	1pa buff & multi	6.75	4.25
	Nos. C194-C198 (5)		*12.45*	*6.10*

See note after No. 381.

Missionary Ship "Triton" — AP18

1976, Aug. 25				**Litho.**
C199	AP18	9s pink & multi	.35	.30
C200	AP18	12s multicolored	.55	.40
C201	AP18	14s multicolored	.60	.45
C202	AP18	17s buff & multi	.80	.55
C203	AP18	38s multicolored	1.40	.90
	Nos. C199-C203 (5)		*3.70*	*2.60*

See note after No. 386.
For surcharges see Nos. C234, C294, C299.

Treaty Signing Ceremony,
Nukualofa — AP19

1976, Nov. 1				
C204	AP19	11s multicolored	.45	.45
C205	AP19	17s multicolored	.60	.60
C206	AP19	18s multicolored	.65	.65
C207	AP19	31s multicolored	1.25	1.25
C208	AP19	39s multicolored	1.40	1.40
	Nos. C204-C208 (5)		*4.20*	*3.80*

See note after No. 391.
For surcharges see Nos. C235, C295.

Elizabeth II and Taufa'ahau IV — AP20

1977, Feb. 7				
C209	AP20	15s gray & multi	1.60	.55
C210	AP20	17s gray & multi	2.25	.80
C211	AP20	22s gray & multi	22.50	10.00
C212	AP20	31s gray & multi	3.00	1.75
C213	AP20	39s gray & multi	6.00	3.00
	Nos. C209-C213 (5)		*35.35*	*16.10*

See note after No. 396.

Coronation Coin — AP21

1977, July 4				**Litho.**
C214	AP21	11s multicolored	.40	.40
C215	AP21	17s multicolored	.50	.50
C216	AP21	18s multicolored	.50	.50
C217	AP21	39s multicolored	.80	.80
C218	AP21	1pa multicolored	2.75	2.75
	Nos. C214-C218 (5)		*4.95*	*4.95*

See note after No. 401.
See Nos. CO120-CO122.

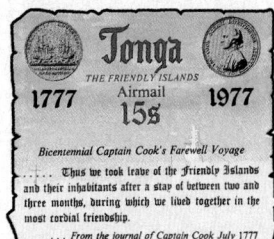

Capt. Cook Medal and Journal
Quotation — AP22

1977, Sept. 27				
C219	AP22	15s multicolored	.90	.75
C220	AP22	22s multicolored	1.40	1.25
C221	AP22	31s multicolored	3.50	3.00
C222	AP22	50s multicolored	10.00	5.00
C223	AP22	1pa multicolored	21.00	9.00
	Nos. C219-C223 (5)		*36.80*	*19.00*

Bicentenary of Capt. Cook's farewell voyage.
See Nos. CO123-CO125.

Sei and Fin Whales — AP23

1977, Dec. 16				
C224	AP23	11s blk, vio & bl	4.25	.80
C225	AP23	17s blk, red & bl	4.75	.90
C226	AP23	18s blk, grn & bl	4.75	1.10
C227	AP23	39s blk, brn & bl	5.75	2.25
C228	AP23	50s blk, mag & bl	7.25	3.50
	Nos. C224-C228 (5)		*26.75*	*8.55*

Whale protection.
See Nos. CO126-CO128.

Stamps of 1975-77 Surcharged in
Various Colors

1978				
C229	AP16	17s on 38s (#C173;Gr)	2.25	1.50
C230	AP17	17s on 9s (#C174;B)	2.25	1.50
C231	AP17	17s on 12s (#C175;DBl)	2.25	1.50
C232	A63	17s on 38s (#C187;B)	2.25	1.50
C233	A66	17s on 12s (#C194; R on G)	2.25	1.50
C234	AP18	17s on 9s (#C199; B)	2.25	1.50
C235	AP19	17s on 18s (#C206; G on Brn)	2.25	1.50
C236	A66	1pa on 75s (#381; Gr on S)	11.75	9.50
C237	A66	1pa on 38s (#C197; DBl on G)	11.75	9.50
C238	OA15	1pa on 1.10pa (#CO119; S on DBl)	26.50	27.50

Edmonton Games Type of 1978

Canadian Maple leaf and Tongan coat of arms.

1978, May 5				**Litho.**
C239	A73	17s red & multi	.45	.45
C240	A73	35s red & multi	.90	.90
C241	A73	38s red & multi	.95	.95
C242	A73	40s red & multi	2.00	2.00
C243	A73	65s red & multi	1.50	1.50
	Nos. C239-C243 (5)		*5.80*	*5.80*

See note after No. 423.

King Type of 1978

Design: Head of King Taufa'ahau IV within 6-pointed star.

1978, July 4				
C244	A74	11s multicolored	.25	.25
C245	A74	15s multicolored	.35	.35
C246	A74	17s multicolored	.45	.45
C247	A74	39s multicolored	1.00	1.00
C248	A74	1pa multicolored	2.50	2.50
	Nos. C244-C248 (5)		*4.55*	*4.55*

See note after No. 226.

Wildlife Type of 1978

1978, Dec. 15			**Litho. & Typo.**	
C249	A77	17s Whale	4.00	2.00
C250	A77	22s Bat	4.00	2.00
C251	A77	31s Turtle	4.00	2.00
C252	A77	39s Parrot	8.50	3.50
C253	A77	45s like 17s	8.75	4.00
	Nos. C249-C253 (5)		*29.25*	*13.50*

Wildlife conservation. See note after No. 226.

Types of 1979

Designs: 15s, like No. 453. 17s, like No. 450. 31s, Rotary emblem. 39s, Ministry and tourism buildings, Bank of Tonga, GPO. 1pa, Dish antenna and map of Tonga.

1979, Feb. 16   **Litho.**

C254	A79	15s multicolored	1.25	.50
C255	A79	17s multicolored	1.25	.50
C256	A78	31s vio blue & gold	1.25	.75
C257	A79	39s multicolored	1.25	.75
C258	A79	1pa multicolored	3.50	3.50
		Nos. C254-C258 (5)	5.50	3.35

Decade of Progress. Paper backing shows map of Tonga.

Type of 1979

Tongan self-adhesive, free-form stamps.

1979, June 1

C259	A81	15s multicolored	.45	.35
C260	A81	17s multicolored	.55	.45
C261	A81	18s multicolored	.65	.60
C262	A81	31s multicolored	.85	.85
C263	A81	39s multicolored	1.00	1.00
		Nos. C259-C263 (5)	3.15	3.15

See note after No. 458.

Jet — AP24

1979, Aug. 17

C264	AP24	5s multicolored	.60	.60
C265	AP24	11s multicolored	.65	.65
C266	AP24	14s multicolored	.65	.65
C267	AP24	15s multicolored	.70	.70
C268	AP24	17s multicolored	.70	.70
C269	AP24	18s multicolored	.75	.75
C270	AP24	22s multicolored	.90	.90
C271	AP24	31s multicolored	1.25	1.25
C272	AP24	39s multicolored	1.50	1.50
C273	AP24	75s multicolored	2.50	1.75
C274	AP24	1pa multicolored	3.50	2.50
		Nos. C264-C274 (11)	13.70	11.95

Nos. C264-C274 issued in coils; self-adhesive control number in lower left corner of paper backing except on 14s, 18s, 22s, 75s. See note after No. 226.
See Nos. C303-C305.

View Type of 1979

Design: Kao Island. See note after No. 463.

1979, Nov. 23

C275	A82	5s multicolored	.30	.30
C276	A82	15s multicolored	.50	.50
C277	A82	17s multicolored	.50	.50
C278	A82	39s multicolored	1.25	1.25
C279	A82	75s multicolored	1.75	1.75
		Nos. C275-C279 (5)	3.85	3.85

Friendship Treaty Type of 1980

George Tupou I, Napoleon III, Adventure. See notes over #464 & after #468.

1980, Jan. 9   **Litho.**

C280	A83	15s multicolored	.50	.50
C281	A83	17s multicolored	.60	.60
C282	A83	22s multicolored	.65	.65
C283	A83	31s multicolored	.90	.90
C284	A83	39s multicolored	1.00	1.00
		Nos. C280-C284 (5)	3.45	3.45

Nos. C259-C263 Surcharged and Overprinted in Black on Silver "1980 OLYMPIC GAMES," Moscow '80 and Bear Emblems

1980, Apr. 30   **Litho.**

C285	A81	9s on 15s multi	.30	.30
C286	A81	16s on 17s multi	.65	.65
C287	A81	29s on 18s multi	1.00	1.00
C288	A81	32s on 31s multi	1.10	1.10
C289	A81	47s on 39s multi	1.75	1.75
		Nos. C285-C289 (5)	4.80	4.80

22nd Summer Olympic Games, Moscow, July 19-Aug. 3.

Scouting Activities in Rotary Emblem — AP25

1980, Sept. 30   **Litho.**

C290	AP25	29s multicolored	1.00	1.00
C291	AP25	32s multicolored	1.00	1.00
C292	AP25	47s multicolored	1.50	1.50
C293	AP25	1pa multicolored	3.00	3.00
		Nos. C290-C293 (4)	6.50	6.50

Boy Scout Jamboree; Rotary International, 75th anniversary. Peelable backing shows map of Tonga.

Nos. C170, C185, C195, C200-C201, C208 Surcharged

1980, Dec. 3   **Litho.**

C294	AP18	29s on 14s multi	1.75	1.75
C295	AP19	29s on 39s multi	1.75	1.75
C296	A63	32s on 12s multi	2.00	2.00
C297	A66	32s on 14s multi	2.00	2.00
C298	AP16	47s on 39s multi	2.75	2.75
C299	AP18	47s on 12s multi	2.75	2.75
		Nos. C294-C299 (6)	13.00	13.00

IYD Type of 1981

1981, Sept. 9   **Litho.**

Size: 25x32mm

C300	A85	29s multicolored	.50	.50
C301	A85	32s multicolored	.60	.60
C302	A85	47s multicolored	1.10	1.10
		Nos. C300-C302 (3)	2.20	2.20

Jet Type of 1979

1982, Nov. 17   **Litho.**

C303	AP24	29s pink & black	12.00	5.00
C304	AP24	32s pale yel & blk	12.00	5.00
C305	AP24	47s lt brown & blk	12.00	5.00
		Nos. C303-C305 (3)	36.00	15.00

AIR POST SPECIAL DELIVERY STAMP

Catalogue values for unused stamps in this section are for Never Hinged items.

Owl — APSD1

1990, Feb. 21   **Litho.**   **Perf. 11½**

CE1	APSD1	10pa multi	17.00 17.00

APSD2

APSD3

APSD4

Short-eared Owl — APSD5

2012, Aug. 30   **Perf. 14¼**
Stamps With White Frame All Around

CE2	APSD2	25pa multi	28.00	28.00
CE3	APSD3	25pa multi	28.00	28.00
CE4	APSD4	25pa multi	28.00	28.00
CE5	APSD5	25pa multi	28.00	28.00
		Nos. CE2-CE5 (4)	112.00	112.00

Stamps With White Frame on Two Sides

CE6		Sheet of 4	112.00	112.00
a.		APSD2 25pa multi	28.00	28.00
b.		APSD3 25pa multi	28.00	28.00
c.		APSD4 25pa multi	28.00	28.00
d.		APSD5 25pa multi	28.00	28.00

A sheet of 16 containing four of each of types APSD2-APSD5 without white frames on the stamps was produced in a limited printing.

AIR POST OFFICIAL STAMPS

Catalogue values for unused stamps in this section are for Never Hinged items.

Nos. 115, 117-118, 111-113 Overprinted "OFFICIAL AIR MAIL / 1862 / TAU'ATAINA / EMANCIPATION / 1962" in Red

Engr.; Photo. (A35)

1962, Feb. 7   **Wmk. 79**

CO1	A35	2p ultra	16.00	7.50
CO2	A35	5p purple	16.00	8.00
CO3	A35	1sh red brown	9.00	4.00
CO4	A33	5sh pur & yel	90.00	55.00
CO5	A34	10sh black & yel	42.50	22.50
CO6	A34	£1 ultra, car & yel	75.00	37.50
		Nos. CO1-CO6 (6)	248.50	134.50

Centenary of emancipation.
Nos. CO1-CO6 were overprinted locally. Overprint varieties of nos. CO1-CO6 exist with "OFFICIAI" instead of "OFFICIAL" and "MAII" instead of "MAIL".

Type of Regular Gold Coin Issue

Design: 15sh, Queen Salote standing, 1-koula coin, obverse.

Litho.; Embossed on Gilt Foil
1963, July 15   **Unwmk.**   **Die Cut**
Diameter: 80mm

CO7	A36	15sh black	6.25 6.25

Note after No. 133 also applies to No. CO7.

No. CO7 Surcharged like Regular Issue of 1965 in Black

1965, Mar. 18

CO8	A36	30sh on 15sh black	6.75 6.75

No. 116 Surcharged in Italic Letters Similarly to Nos. C16-C21

Perf. 14½x13½

1966, June 18   **Wmk. 79**

CO9	A35	10sh on 4p brt green	1.00	.60
CO10	A35	20sh on 4p brt green	1.10	.75

Centenary of Tupou College and secondary education.

No. 111 Srchd. in Red

1967, Mar. 25   **Engr.**   **Perf. 11½x11**

CO11	A33	1p on 5sh pur & yel	3.00 3.00

Type of Regular Issue Surcharged

1967, Dec. 15   **Wmk. 79**   **Die Cut**

CO12	A34	30s on £1 multi	.60	.60
CO13	A34	70s on £1 multi	.90	.90
CO14	A34	1.50pa on £1 multi	1.50	1.50
		Nos. CO12-CO14 (3)	2.60	2.60

Arrival of US Peace Corps.

No. 113 Surcharged with New Value and "OFFICIAL/AIRMAIL"

1968, Apr. 6   **Engr.**   **Perf. 11x11½**

CO15	A34	40s on £1 multi	.85	.85
CO16	A34	60s on £1 multi	1.25	1.00
CO17	A34	1pa on £1 multi	1.75	1.75
CO18	A34	2pa on £1 multi	2.50	2.50
		Nos. CO15-CO18 (4)	5.50	5.50

Type of 1953 Surcharged: "Friendly Islands / Trials / Field & Track / South Pacific / Games / Port Moresby / 1969 / OFFICIAL AIRMAIL"

Wmk. 79

1968, Dec. 19   **Engr.**   **Die Cut**

CO19	A34	20s on £1 grn & multi	.40	.40
CO20	A34	1pa on £1 grn & multi	1.10	1.10

No. 176 Overprinted and Surcharged in Gold on Colored Panels (Green, Emerald, Violet or Lilac) like Nos. 203-209

Litho.; Embossed on Palladium Foil
1968   **Unwmk.**

CO21	A38	40s on 2s (G)	1.90	.90
CO22	A38	60s on 2s (E)	2.50	1.60
CO23	A38	1pa on 2s (V)	3.75	3.75
CO24	A38	2pa on 2s (L)	6.75	6.75
		Nos. CO21-CO24 (4)	14.90	13.00

50th birthday of King Taufa'ahau IV.

Pacific Games Type of Regular Issue

Design: Boxer.

1969, Aug. 13   Litho.   Die Cut
Self-adhesive
CO25	A40	70s gray, red & grn	1.40	1.40
CO26	A40	80s gray, red & org	1.60	1.60

See note after No. 231.

Type of Regular Issue, 1953, Surcharged "OFFICIAL AIRMAIL / 1969 OIL / SEARCH / 90s" and Oil Derrick Obliterating Old Denomination

1969, Dec. 23   Die Cut Wmk. 79
CO27	A34	90s on £1 grn & multi	4.50	4.50

First scientific search for oil in Tonga.

Type of Regular Issue, 1953, Surcharged "Royal Visit / MARCH / 1970 / OFFICIAL / AIRMAIL" in Black, Violet Blue or Emerald

1970, Mar. 7   Engr.   Wmk. 79
CO28	A34	75s on 1sh	4.25	3.00
CO29	A34	1pa on 1sh (VBl)	5.50	4.00
CO30	A34	1.25pa on 1sh (E)	7.00	5.00
	Nos. CO28-CO30 (3)		16.75	12.00

See note after No. 242.

Regular Issue Srchd. in Black, Red or Emerald

1970, June 4   Wmk. 79   Die Cut
CO31	A33	50s on 5sh (B)	6.50	4.00
CO32	A33	90s on 5sh (R)	7.50	5.00
CO33	A33	1.50pa on 5sh (E)	8.50	6.00
	Nos. CO31-CO33 (3)		8.00	8.00

See note after No. 247.

Regular Issue of 1953, Srchd. in Red and Purple or Black

1970, Oct. 17   Engr.   Die Cut
CO34	A33	30s on 1½p (B & R)	1.90	1.90
CO35	A33	80s on 5sh (P & R)	5.00	5.00
CO36	A33	90s on 5sh (P & R)	6.00	6.00
	Nos. CO34-CO36 (3)		12.90	12.90

Centenary of the British Red Cross.

Type of Regular Issue, 1953, Surcharged in Black, Purple, Blue or Green

1971, Jan. 31   Engr.   Die Cut
CO37	A34	20s on 10sh (Bk)	1.25	.85
CO38	A34	30s on 10sh (P)	2.10	1.25
CO39	A34	50s on 10sh (Bl)	3.50	2.10
CO40	A34	2pa on 10sh (G)	13.75	11.75
	Nos. CO37-CO40 (4)		20.60	15.95

In memory of Queen Salote (1900-1965).

Type of Regular Issue, 1953, Surcharged in Red and Blue, Black or Purple

1971   Engr.   Wmk. 79   Imperf
Colors: Green & Yellow
CO41	A33	30s on 5p (R & Bl)	1.40	.80
CO42	A33	80s on 5p (R & Bk)	3.25	2.10
CO43	A33	90s on 5p (R & P)	3.50	2.40
	Nos. CO41-CO43 (3)		8.15	5.30

See note after No. 272.

Self-adhesive & Die Cut
Starting with Nos. CO44-CO46, all airmail official issues are self-adhesive and die cut, unless otherwise stated.

Soccer Ball — OA1

1971, July   Litho.   Unwmk.
CO44	OA1	50s multi	1.75	1.75
CO45	OA1	90s multi	2.75	2.75
CO46	OA1	1.50s multi	5.25	5.25
	Nos. CO44-CO46 (3)		4.85	4.85

4th South Pacific Games, Papeete, French Polynesia, Sept. 8-19.
For overprints see Nos. CO75-CO77.

Watch Type of Air Post Issues
Litho. and Embossed

1971, July 20
CO47	AP6	14s brown & multi	1.25	1.25
CO48	AP6	21s brn red & multi	1.75	1.75

Advertisement on peelable paper backing.

Nos. 243-244, 246 Surcharged

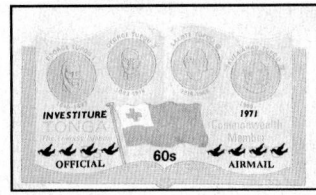

Litho.; Gold Embossed
1971, Oct. 30
CO49	A43	60s on 3s multi	1.50	1.50
CO50	A43	80s on 25s multi	1.75	1.75
CO51	A43	1.10pa on 7s multi	2.25	2.25
	Nos. CO49-CO51 (3)		4.50	4.50

First investiture of Tongan Medal of Honor.

"UNICEF" — OA2

1971, Dec.   Litho.
CO52	OA2	70s black & multi	2.25	2.25
CO53	OA2	80s multicolored	2.75	2.75
CO54	OA2	90s multicolored	3.00	3.00
	Nos. CO52-CO54 (3)		7.00	7.00

25th anniversary of UNICEF.
For overprint see No. CO70.

Ship Type of Regular Issue

Design: Map of Merchant Marine routes from Tonga and tanker "Aoniu."

1972, Apr. 14
CO55	A49	20s multi	1.90	.90
CO56	A49	50s multi	4.00	2.75
CO57	A49	1.20pa multi	8.75	7.00
	Nos. CO55-CO57 (3)		14.65	10.65

Coin Type of Regular Issue

Design: Coins in center, inscription panel above, date below coins.

Litho.; Embossed on Metallic Foil
1972, July 15
CO58	A50	50s silver & multi	1.75	1.75
CO59	A50	70s silver & multi	2.50	2.50
CO60	A50	1.50pa silver & multi	4.50	4.50
	Nos. CO58-CO60 (3)		8.75	8.75

Watch Type of Air Post Issue

1972, July 20   Litho.; Embossed
CO61	AP6	17s multicolored	1.25	1.25
CO62	AP6	38s ocher & multi	2.50	2.50

Advertisement on peelable paper backing.

Flags and Map of Tonga Islands — OA3

1972, Dec. 9   Litho.
CO63	OA3	25s black & multi	.60	.60
CO64	OA3	75s multicolored	1.75	1.75
CO65	OA3	1.50pa multicolored	3.75	3.75
	Nos. CO63-CO65 (3)		5.65	2.15

Tonga's proclamation of sovereignty over the Minerva Reefs, June 1972.

No. 290 Surcharged in Black, Ultramarine or Green

1973, Mar. 30   Litho.
CO66	A49	40s on 21s (B)	2.00	2.00
CO67	A49	85s on 21s (U)	4.00	4.00
CO68	A49	1.25pa on 21s (G)	5.00	5.00
	Nos. CO66-CO68 (3)		11.00	11.00

Establishment of Bank of Tonga.

Nos. CO55 Ovptd. & Srchd. in Silver

No. CO53 Ovptd. in Silver

No. 247 Srchd. & Ovptd. in Silver on Dark Blue Panels

1973, June 29
CO69	A49	30s on 20s	15.00	4.00
CO70	OA2	80s multi	37.50	14.50
CO71	A43	1.40pa on 90s	52.50	35.00
	Nos. CO69-CO71 (3)		105.00	53.50

25th anniv. of Tongan Boy Scout movement.

Tanker James Cook and Cook Medal — OA4

1973, Oct. 2   Litho.
CO72	OA4	25s multi	4.00	1.60
CO73	OA4	80s multi	10.00	5.00
CO74	OA4	1.30pa multi	12.00	8.25
	Nos. CO72-CO74 (3)		26.00	14.85

Bicentenary of Capt. Cook's arrival.

Nos. CO44-CO46 Overprinted in Dark Blue, Black or Green with Games' Emblems and "1974 / Commonwealth / Games / Christchurch"

1973, Dec. 19
CO75	OA1	50s multi (DBl)	1.75	1.75
CO76	OA1	90s multi (B)	3.00	3.00
CO77	OA1	1.50pa multi (G)	4.25	4.25
	Nos. CO75-CO77 (3)		7.25	6.50

10th British Commonwealth Games, Christchurch, N.Z., Jan. 24-Feb. 2, 1974.

Peace Dove OA5

1974, Mar. 20   Litho.
CO78	OA5	7s multicolored	.50	.25
CO79	OA5	9s multicolored	.65	.35
CO80	OA5	12s multicolored	.65	.35
CO81	OA5	14s multicolored	.90	.50
CO82	OA5	17s multicolored	1.00	.65
CO83	OA5	29s multicolored	1.75	1.10
CO84	OA5	38s multicolored	2.50	1.40
CO85	OA5	50s multicolored	3.00	3.00
CO86	OA5	75s multicolored	4.25	4.25
	Nos. CO78-CO86 (9)		15.20	11.85

Printed in rolls of 500. Self-adhesive lilac control number in upper left corner.

"UPU Centenary" — OA6

1974, June 20   Typo.
CO87	OA6	25s red, green & blk	1.00	1.00
CO88	OA6	35s yel, red lil & blk	1.10	1.10
CO89	OA6	70s dp org, bl & blk	2.25	2.25
	Nos. CO87-CO89 (3)		4.35	4.35

Centenary of Universal Postal Union.

Lady Baden-Powell — OA7

1974, Sept. 11 **Litho.**
CO90 OA7 45s emer & multi 4.50 2.75
CO91 OA7 55s emer & multi 6.50 3.75
CO92 OA7 1pa emer & multi 9.25 5.50
Nos. CO90-CO92 (3) 20.25 12.00

Girl Guides of Tonga.
For overprints see Nos. CO105-CO107.

Handshake and Institute's
Emblem — OA8

Institute's Emblem and
Banknotes — OA9

1974, Dec. 11
CO93 OA8 30s multicolored 3.25 1.60
CO94 OA8 35s multicolored 3.75 2.10
CO95 OA9 80s red & multi 8.75 4.50
Nos. CO93-CO95 (3) 15.75 8.20

Establishment of Royal Marine Institute.

Arch and Palms — OA10

Designs: 75s, 1.25pa, Dawn over lagoon.

1975, Mar. 11 **Litho.**
CO96 OA10 50s multi 1.75 1.75
CO97 OA10 75s multi 3.00 3.00
CO98 OA10 1.25pa multi 4.00 4.00
Nos. CO96-CO98 (3) 8.75 8.75

First meeting of South Pacific area Prime
Ministers. See note after No. 226.

Track and Games' Emblem — OA11

1975, June 11
CO99 OA11 38s multi 1.00 1.00
CO100 OA11 75s multi 1.90 1.90
CO101 OA11 1.20pa multi 3.00 3.00
Nos. CO99-CO101 (3) 5.90 5.90

5th South Pacific Games, Guam, Aug. 1-10.
See note after No. 226.
For surcharge see No. 418.

Four Constitutional Monarchs — OA12

Litho.; Embossed on Gilt Foil
1975, Nov. 4
CO102 OA12 17s multicolored 1.00 1.00
CO103 OA12 60s multicolored 2.50 2.50
CO104 OA12 90s multicolored 3.00 3.00
Nos. CO102-CO104 (3) 5.40 5.00

**No. CO90-CO92 Ovptd. in Carmine
on Blue, Silver or Gold**

1976, Feb. 24 **Litho.**
CO105 OA7 45s multi (B) 3.50 1.40
CO106 OA7 55s multi (S) 3.50 1.60
CO107 OA7 1pa multi (G) 6.75 6.75
Nos. CO105-CO107 (3) 13.75 9.75

21st Olympic Games, Montreal, Canada,
July 17-Aug. 1. See note after No. 226.

Bicentennial Type of 1976

Signers of Declaration of Independence:
20s, William Paca, Francis Lewis, George
Read, Edward Rutledge, Thomas Heyward,
Jr. 50s, George Walton, Matthew Thornton, Rob-
ert Morris, William Williams, James Smith.
1.15pa, Benjamin Rush, Samuel Adams,
Samuel Chase, George Wythe, George
Clymer.

1976, May 26
CO108 A66 20s buff & multi 1.25 1.00
CO109 A66 50s buff & multi 4.00 2.50
CO110 A66 1.15pa buff & multi 8.50 5.25
Nos. CO108-CO110 (3) 13.75 8.75

See note after No. 381.

Inside View of Lifuka Chapel — OA13

1976, Aug. 25 **Litho.**
CO111 OA13 65s multi 2.75 2.75
CO112 OA13 85s multi 3.00 3.00
CO113 OA13 1.15pa multi 4.00 4.00
Nos. CO111-CO113 (3) 9.75 9.75

See note after No. 386.
For surcharge see No. CO181.

OA14

1976, Nov. 1
CO114 OA14 30s silver &
multi .90 .90
CO115 OA14 60s silver &
multi 2.25 2.25
CO116 OA14 1.25pa silver &
multi 4.75 4.75
Nos. CO114-CO116 (3) 7.35 7.35

See note after No. 391.

Flags of Great Britain and
Tonga — OA15

1977, Feb. 7 **Litho.**
CO117 OA15 35s multi 5.00 3.25
CO118 OA15 45s multi 1.00 .50
CO119 OA15 1.10pa multi 2.00 1.25
Nos. CO117-CO119 (3) 8.00 5.00

See note after No. 396.
For surcharge see No. C238.

Coin Type of Air Post Stamps 1977

Design: Coronation coin, inscriptions in
round upper panel.

1977, July 4
CO120 AP21 20s multicolored .75 .75
CO121 AP21 40s multicolored 1.50 1.50
CO122 AP21 80s multicolored 3.00 3.00
Nos. CO120-CO122 (3) 5.25 5.25

See note after No. 401.

**Capt. Cook Type of Air Post Stamps
1977**

Design: Inscription and flying dove.

1977, Sept. 27
CO123 AP22 20s gold & multi 1.40 1.40
CO124 AP22 55s on 20s multi 10.00 10.00
CO125 AP22 85s on 20s multi 21.00 21.00
Nos. CO123-CO125 (3) 32.40 32.40

Printed on peelable paper backing showing
dark brown replica of entry in Capt. Cook's
diary.

**Whale Type of Air Post Stamps
1977**

Design: Blue whale.

1977, Dec. 16
CO126 AP23 45s multicolored 7.75 3.50
CO127 AP23 65s multicolored 11.00 5.00
CO128 AP23 85s multicolored 13.00 6.00
Nos. CO126-CO128 (3) 31.75 14.50

Whale protection.

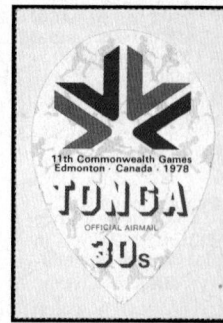

Games'
Emblem
and
Athletes
OA16

1978, May 5 **Litho.**
CO129 OA16 30s red & multi .70 .70
CO130 OA16 60s red & multi 1.40 1.40
CO131 OA16 1pa red & multi 2.50 2.50
Nos. CO129-CO131 (3) 4.60 4.60

See note after No. 423.

King Type of 1978

Head of King Taufa'ahau IV on medal.

1978, July 4
CO132 A74 26s multicolored .65 .65
CO133 A74 85s multicolored 2.00 2.00
CO134 A74 90s multicolored 2.50 2.50
Nos. CO132-CO134 (3) 5.15 5.15

See note after No. 226.

Wildlife Type of 1978

1978, Dec. 15 **Litho. & Typo.**
CO150 A77 40s Whale 8.25 4.00
CO151 A77 50s Bat 8.25 4.00
CO152 A77 1.10pa Turtle 11.00 9.00
Nos. CO150-CO152 (3) 27.50 17.00

Wildlife conservation. See note after No. 226.

Types of 1979

Designs: 38s, Red Cross and star. 74s, like
No. 451. 80s, like No. 450.

1979, Feb. 16 **Litho.**
CO153 A78 38s multicolored 1.50 1.00
CO154 A80 74s multicolored 2.00 2.00
CO155 A79 80s multicolored 3.00 3.00
Nos. CO153-CO155 (3) 5.60 3.70

Decade of Progress. Paper backing shows
map of Tonga.

Hands Peeling off No. CO118 — OA17

1979, June 1

CO156 OA17 45s multicolored 1.50 1.25
CO157 OA17 65s multicolored 2.00 1.75
CO158 OA17 80s multicolored 2.75 2.25
Nos. CO156-CO158 (3) 5.25 5.25

See note after No. 458.
For surcharges see Nos. CO176-CO178.

Parrot — OA18

1979, Aug. 1

CO159 OA18 5s multicolored .60 .60
CO160 OA18 11s multicolored .65 .65
CO161 OA18 14s multicolored .65 .65
CO162 OA18 15s multicolored .70 .70
CO163 OA18 17s multicolored .70 .70
CO164 OA18 18s multicolored .70 .70
CO165 OA18 22s multicolored .80 .80
CO166 OA18 31s multicolored 1.10 1.10
CO167 OA18 39s multicolored 1.50 1.50
CO168 OA18 75s multicolored 2.25 2.25
CO169 OA18 1pa multicolored 2.75 2.75
Nos. CO159-CO169 (11) 12.40 12.40

Nos. CO159-CO169 issued in coils. See note after No. 226.

The 5s exists with denomination in magenta and the leaves behind the bird missing. This seems to be a special printing that was not available for postal purposes.

View Type of 1979

Design: Niuatoputapu and Tafahi Islands. See note after No. 463.

1979, Nov. 23 **Litho.**

CO170 A82 35s multicolored 1.00 1.00
CO171 A82 45s multicolored 1.25 1.25
CO172 A82 1pa multicolored 2.50 2.50
Nos. CO170-CO172 (3) 4.20 4.20

Friendship Treaty Type of 1980

Design: Church. See note after No. 468.

1980, Jan. 9 **Litho.**

CO173 A83 40s multicolored 1.25 1.25
CO174 A83 55s multicolored 1.75 1.75
CO175 A83 1.25pa multicolored 3.50 3.50
Nos. CO173-CO175 (3) 5.75 5.75

Nos. CO156-CO158 Srchd. & Ovptd. in Black on Silver "1980 OLYMPIC GAMES," Moscow '80 and Bear Emblems

1980, Apr. 30 **Litho.**

CO176 OA17 26s on 45s 1.00 1.00
CO177 OA17 40s on 65s 1.60 1.60
CO178 OA17 1.10pa on 80s 4.00 4.00
Nos. CO176-CO178 (3) 6.60 6.60

22nd Summer Olympic Games, Moscow, July 19-Aug. 3.

Tents and Rotary Emblem — OA19

1980, Sept. 30 **Litho.**

CO179 OA19 25s multicolored 1.75 1.75
CO180 OA19 2pa multicolored 6.75 6.75

Boy Scout Jamboree; Rotary Intl., 75th anniv. Peelable backing shows map of Tonga.

For surcharges see Nos. 502-503.

No. CO111 Surcharged

1980, Dec. 3 **Litho.**

CO181 OA13 2pa on 65s multi 5.50 5.50

OFFICIAL STAMPS

Types of Postage Issue of 1892 Overprinted in Carmine

Perf. 12x11½

1893, Feb. 13 **Wmk. 62**

O1 A4 1p ultra 11.50 *55.00*
a. Half used as ½p on cover
O2 A5 2p ultra 30.00 *62.50*
O3 A4 4p ultra 55.00 *110.00*
O4 A5 8p ultra 100.00 *200.00*
O5 A5 1sh ultra 110.00 *210.00*
Nos. O1-O5 (5) 306.50 *637.50*

Values are for stamps of good color. Faded and discolored stamps sell for much less.

The overprinted initials stand for "Gaue Faka Buleaga" (On Government Service).

Nos. O1-O5 with Additional Surcharge Handstamped in Black

1893

O6 A4 ½p on 1p ultra 20.00 *57.50*
O7 A5 2½p on 2p ultra 27.50 *50.00*
O8 A4 5p on 4p ultra 27.50 *50.00*
O9 A5 7½p on 8p ultra 27.50 *92.50*
O10 A5 10p on 1sh ultra 32.50 *95.00*
Nos. O6-O10 (5) 135.00 *345.00*

Catalogue values for unused stamps in this section, from this point to the end of the section, are for Never Hinged items.

Redrawn Banana and Coconut Types of Regular Issue, 1970, Inscribed "Official Post"

1970, June 9 **Typo.** ***Die Cut***

Self-adhesive

O11 A39 1s yel, blk & dp car .55 .55
O12 A39 2s yel, blk & blue .70 .70
O13 A39 3s yel, blk & brn .70 .70
O14 A39 4s yel, blk & emer .70 .70
O15 A39 5s yel, blk & org .80 .80

Litho.; Embossed on Gilt Foil

O16 A44 6s brown & multi .95 .95
O17 A44 7s brown & multi 1.00 1.00
O18 A44 8s brown & multi 1.10 1.10
O19 A44 9s brown & multi 1.50 1.50
O20 A44 10s brown & multi 1.75 1.75
Nos. O11-O20 (10) 9.75 9.75

Nos. O13, O17-O18 and O20 have self-adhesive control numbers in lower left corner of paper backing.

Types of Regular Issue 1970-72

1972, Sept. 30 **Typo.** ***Die Cut***

Self-adhesive

O21 A51 1s yel, red & brn .25 .25
O22 A51 2s yel, grn & brn .30 .25
O23 A51 3s yel, emer & brn .35 .25
O24 A51 4s yel, blk & brn .35 .25
O25 A51 5s yellow & brn .35 .25
O26 A44 6s brown & green .45 .25
O27 A44 7s brown & green .50 .30
O28 A44 8s brown & green .50 .30
O29 A44 9s brown & green .50 .30
O30 A44 10s brown & green .60 .35
O31 A52 15s green & ultra 1.00 .50
O32 A52 20s green & ver 1.25 .70
O33 A52 25s green & dk brn 1.40 .90
O34 A52 40s green & org 2.50 1.75
O35 A52 50s green & vio bl 3.00 2.25
Nos. O21-O35 (15) 13.30 8.70

Paper backing is brown on Nos. O26-O35. Nos. O30-O35 have self-adhesive control number in lower left corner, Nos. O21-O29 lower right corner.

Types of Regular Issue 1978

Designs: 1s-5s, Bananas (similar to type A75). 6s-10s, Coconuts. 15s-1pa, Pineapples.

1978, Sept. 29 **Typo.** ***Die Cut***

Self-Adhesive

O36 A75 1s yellow & lilac .30 .30
O37 A75 2s yellow & brown .30 .30
O38 A75 3s multicolored .40 .40
O39 A75 4s multicolored .40 .40
O40 A75 5s multicolored .40 .40
O41 A76 6s multicolored .60 .60
O42 A76 7s multicolored .60 .60
O43 A76 8s multicolored .60 .60
O44 A76 9s multicolored .60 .60
O45 A76 10s multicolored .60 .60
O46 A76 15s multicolored 1.50 1.50
O47 A76 20s multicolored 1.60 1.60
O48 A76 30s multicolored 1.75 1.75
O49 A76 50s multicolored 2.25 2.25
O50 A76 1pa multicolored 3.25 3.25
Nos. O36-O50 (15) 15.15 15.15

Nos. O36-O50 issued in coils; self-adhesive control numbers on paper backing except on 1s. See note after No. 226.

Type of 1984 Overprinted "OFFICIAL"

1984-85 **Litho.** ***Die Cut***

Self-Adhesive

O52 A103 1s multicolored .50 .50
O53 A103 2s multicolored .50 .50
O54 A103 3s multicolored .50 .50
O55 A103 5s multicolored .50 .50
O56 A103 6s multicolored .50 .50
O57 A103 9s multicolored .75 .75
a. Perf. 14½ ('85) .75 .75
O58 A103 10s multicolored .75 .75
O59 A103 13s multicolored 1.25 1.25
O60 A103 15s multicolored 1.25 1.25
O61 A103 20s multicolored 1.50 1.50
O62 A103 29s multicolored 1.75 1.75
O63 A103 32s multicolored 1.75 1.75
O64 A103 47s multicolored 2.00 2.00
O65 A103 1pa multicolored 4.00 4.00
O66 A103 2pa multicolored 7.00 7.00
O67 A103 5pa multicolored ('85) 12.00 12.00
Nos. O52-O67 (16) 36.50 36.50

Nos. 532-534 Ovptd. "OFFICIAL"

1983, Feb. 22 **Litho.** ***Die Cut***

Self-Adhesive

O68 A96a 29s multicolored 4.75 4.75
O69 A96a 32s multicolored 4.75 4.75
O70 A96a 47s multicolored 10.00 10.00
Nos. O68-O70 (3) 19.50 19.50

O68-O70 handstamped.

Nos. 618-624 Overprinted

1986, Apr. 16 **Litho.** ***Die Cut***

Self-adhesive

O71 A103 4s on 2s, #618 1.00 1.00
O72 A103 4s on 13s, #619 1.00 1.00
O73 A103 42s on 3s, #620 3.25 3.25
O74 A103 42s on 9s, #621 3.25 3.25
O75 A103 57s on 6s, #622 3.50 3.50
O76 A103 57s on 20s, #623 3.50 3.50
O77 A103 2.50pa on 2pa, #624 12.00 12.00
Nos. O71-O77 (7) 27.50 27.50

Marine Type Inscribed "POSTAGE & REVENUE" and "OFFICIAL"

1995-96 **Litho.** ***Perf. 14***

O78 A155a 10s multicolored .60 .60
O79 A155a 20s multicolored .90 .40
O80 A155a 45s multicolored 1.10 .70
O81 A155a 60s multicolored 1.40 .95
O82 A155a 80s multicolored 1.75 1.25
O83 A155a 1pa multicolored 2.25 1.75
O84 A155a 2pa multicolored 4.00 4.00
O85 A155a 3pa multicolored 5.00 5.00
O86 A155a 5pa multicolored 9.75 9.75
O87 A155a 10pa multicolored 14.00 14.00
Nos. O78-O87 (10) 40.75 38.40

Issued: 10s-80s, 9/25/95; 1pa-10pa, 5/31/96.

NIUAFO'OU

Tin Can Island

Catalogue values for all unused stamps in this country are for Never Hinged items.

Nos. 1-63 are die cut self-adhesive stamps on peelable inscribed backing paper.

Niuafo'ou Airport Type of Tonga

1983, May 11 **Litho.** ***Die Cut***

1 A97 29s multicolored 1.75 1.75
2 A97 1pa multicolored 4.75 4.75

Map of Niuafo'ou — A1

1983, May 11

3 A1 1s buff, blk & red .45 .45
4 A1 2s buff, blk & brt green .45 .45
5 A1 3s buff, blk & brt blue .45 .45
6 A1 3s buff, blk & brn org .45 .45
7 A1 5s buff, blk & deep rose lil .45 .45
8 A1 6s buff, blk & grnsh blue .45 .45
9 A1 9s buff, blk & lt ol grn .45 .45
10 A1 10s buff, blk & brt bl .45 .45
11 A1 13s buff, blk & brt grn .50 .50
12 A1 15s buff, blk & brn org .60 .60
13 A1 20s buff, blk & grnsh blue .75 .75
14 A1 29s buff, blk & deep rose lil 1.25 1.25
15 A1 32s buff, blk & lt ol grn 1.40 1.40
16 A1 47s buff, blk & red 1.90 1.90
Nos. 3-16 (14) 10.00 10.00

See Nos. 19-22.

Tonga No. 520 Surcharged or Ovptd. in Purple or Gold "NIUAFO'OU / Kingdom of Tonga"

1983, May 11

17 A93 1pa on 2pa multi (P) 3.25 3.25
18 A93 2pa multicolored (G) 6.75 6.75

Nos. 17-18 each exist se-tenant with label.

Map Type of 1983

Value Typo. in Violet Blue

1983, May 30

19 A1 3s buff & black .30 .30
20 A1 5s buff & black .30 .30
21 A1 32s buff & black 1.50 1.50
22 A1 2pa buff & black 8.00 8.00
Nos. 19-22 (4) 10.10 10.10

The denomination on Nos. 19-22 added like a surcharge and is larger than on Nos. 5-7, 15, covering part of the design.

Nos. 19-22 each exist se-tenant with label.

Eruption of Niuafo'ou, Sept. 9, 1946 — A2

29s, Lava flow. 32s, Moving to high ground. 1.50pa, Evacuation to Eua.

1983, Sept. 29

23 A2 5s shown .50 .35
24 A2 29s multicolored 1.90 1.25
25 A2 32s multicolored 2.10 1.25
26 A2 1.50pa multicolored 6.50 6.50
Nos. 23-26 (4) 11.00 9.35

Birds — A3

1s, Purple swamphen. 2s, White-collared kingfisher. 3s, Red-headed parrotfinch. 5s, Banded rail. 6s, Niuafo'ou megapode. 9s, Giant forest honeyeater. 10s, Purple swamphen, drinking. 13s, Banded rail, diff. 15s, Niuafo'ou megapode, diff. 29s, Red-headed parrotfinch, diff. 32s, White-collared kingfisher, diff.

1983, Nov. 15

27	A3	1s multicolored	1.00	1.00
28	A3	2s multicolored	1.00	1.00
29	A3	3s multicolored	1.00	1.00
30	A3	5s multicolored	1.25	1.25
31	A3	6s multicolored	1.60	1.60
32	A3	9s multicolored	2.50	2.50
33	A3	10s multicolored	2.50	2.50
34	A3	12s multicolored	2.75	2.75
35	A3	15s multicolored	2.75	2.75

Size: 25x39mm

36	A3	20s like #34	3.25	3.25
37	A3	29s multicolored	3.50	3.50
38	A3	32s multicolored	3.50	3.50
39	A3	47s like #35	4.25	4.25

Size: 32x42mm

40	A3	1pa like #33	8.00	9.75
41	A3	2pa like #35	11.00	14.00
		Nos. 27-41 (15)	49.85	54.60

Nos. 34-36, 39 and 41 horiz.
For surcharges see Nos. 66-73.

Wildlife
A4

29s, Green turtle. 32s, Flying fox, vert. 47s, Humpback whale. 1.50pa, Niuafo'ou megapode, vert.

1984, Mar. 7

42	A4	29s multicolored	.90	.90
43	A4	32s multicolored	.90	.90
44	A4	47s multicolored	3.25	2.10
45	A4	1.50pa multicolored	6.00	8.25
		Nos. 42-45 (4)	11.05	12.15

Map
A5

47s, Intl. Date Line, Cent.

1984, Aug. 20

46	A5	47s multicolored	1.10	1.10
47	A5	2pa shown	3.75	3.75

AUSIPEX
'84 — A6

1984, Sept. 17

48	A6	32s Australia No. 15	.90	.90
49	A6	1.50pa No. 10	4.50	4.50

Souvenir Sheet

50	Sheet of 2	5.00	5.00

No. 50 contains two imperf. stamps similar to Nos. 48-49, but with denomination replacing logo. No. 50 without denominations was not valid for postage.

A7

Jacob Le Maire, 400th Birth Anniv.: 13s, Dutch band entertaining natives. 32s, Natives preparing kava. 47s, Native outrigger canoes. 1.50pa, Le Maire's ship at anchor.

1985, Feb. 20

51	A7	13s multicolored	.50	.50
52	A7	32s multicolored	1.10	1.10
53	A7	47s multicolored	1.50	1.50
54	A7	1.50pa multicolor	4.50	5.50
		Nos. 51-54 (4)	7.60	8.60

Souvenir Sheet

55	A7	1.50pa multicolored	4.00	4.00

Mail Ships
A8

1985, May 22 Die Cut

56	A8	9s Ysabel, 1902	.60	.60
a.		Perf. 14	.90	.90
57	A8	13s Tofua I, 1908	1.25	1.25
a.		Perf. 14	1.90	1.90
58	A8	47s Mariposa, 1934	1.90	1.90
a.		Perf. 14	2.75	2.75
59	A8	1.50pa Matua, 1936	4.25	6.00
a.		Perf. 14	6.50	9.00
		Nos. 56-59 (4)	8.00	9.75
		Nos. 56a-59a (4)	12.05	14.55

Rocket Mail — A9

Designs: 32s, Preparing to fire rocket. 42s, Rocket airborne. 57s, Captain watching rocket's progress. 1.50pa, Islanders reading mail.

1985, Nov. 5

60	A9	32s multicolored	1.50	.90
61	A9	42s multicolored	2.00	1.10
62	A9	57s multicolored	2.75	1.50
63	A9	1.50pa multicolored	5.75	6.50
		Nos. 60-63 (4)	12.00	10.10

Self-adhesive stamps discontinued.

Halley's Comet — A10

Nos. 64, 65: a, Drawing of Comet in 684. b, Comet shown in Bayeux Tapestry, 1066. c, Edmond Halley. d, Comet, 1910. e, Infrared photography, 1986.

1986, Mar. 26 Perf. 14

64	A10	42s Strip of #a.-e.	36.00	32.50
65	A10	57s Strip of #a.-e.	36.00	32.50

Nos. 32-39 Surcharged in Blue

1986, Apr. 16 Die Cut

Self-Adhesive

66	A3	4s on 9s #32	1.50	2.75
67	A3	4s on 10s #33	1.50	2.75
68	A3	42s on 13s #34	3.75	2.75
69	A3	42s on 15s #35	3.75	2.75
70	A3	57s on 29s #37	4.75	3.25
71	A3	57s on 32s #38	4.75	3.25
72	A3	2.50pa on 20s #36	13.00	14.00
73	A3	2.50pa on 47s #39	13.00	14.00
		Nos. 66-73 (8)	46.00	45.50

Placement of surcharge varies.

AMERIPEX '86 Type of Tonga

1986, May 22 Perf. 14

74	A117	57s Surveying	3.00	3.00
75	A117	1.50pa Agriculture	5.50	5.50
a.		Souv. sheet of 2, #74-75, imperf.	10.00	10.00

Peace Corps in Tonga, 25th anniv.

First Tongan Postage Stamps, Cent.
A11

42s, Swimmers with mail. 57s, Loading tin can mail into canoe. 1pa, Rocket mail. 2.50pa, Outrigger canoe.
No. 80, Outrigger canoe, diff.

1986, Aug. 27

76	A11	42s multicolored	1.60	1.60
77	A11	57s multicolored	2.10	2.10
78	A11	1pa multicolored	3.75	3.75
79	A11	2.50pa multicolored	6.50	6.50
		Nos. 76-79 (4)	13.95	13.95

Souvenir Sheet

80	A11	2.50pa multicolored	14.00	14.00

Red Cross — A12

15s, Balanced diet. 42s, Post-natal care. 1pa, Insects spread disease. 2.50pa, Fight against drugs, alcohol, smoking.

1987, Mar. 11 Perf. 14x14½

81	A12	15s multicolored	1.25	1.25
82	A12	42s multicolored	3.25	3.25
83	A12	1pa multicolored	4.75	4.75
84	A12	2.50pa multicolored	7.50	7.50
		Nos. 81-84 (4)	16.75	16.75

Sharks A13

1987, Apr. 29 Perf. 14

85	A13	29s Hammerhead	3.00	2.75
86	A13	32s Tiger	3.00	2.75
87	A13	47s Gray nurse	3.50	3.00
88	A13	1pa Great white	6.00	8.25
		Nos. 85-88 (4)	15.50	16.75

Souvenir Sheet

89	A13	2pa Shark attack	18.00	18.00

Aviators and Aircraft A14

Designs: 42s, Capt. E. C. Musick and Sikorsky S-42. 57s, Capt. J.W. Burgess and Shorts S-30. 1.50pa, Sir Charles Kingsford Smith and Fokker F.VIIb-3m. 2pa, Amelia Earhart and Lockheed Electra 10A.

1987, Sept. 2

90	A14	42s multicolored	2.50	1.75
91	A14	57s multicolored	3.00	2.00
92	A14	1.50pa multicolored	4.50	4.50
93	A14	2pa multicolored	5.25	5.25
		Nos. 90-93 (4)	15.25	13.50

First Niuafo'ou Postage Stamps, 5th Anniv.
A15

Designs: 42s, 57s, Niuafo'ou megapode, No. 15. 1pa, 2pa, Concorde, No. 1.

1988, May 18

94	A15	42s multicolored	1.50	1.00
95	A15	57s multicolored	1.50	1.10
96	A15	1pa multicolored	5.00	3.75
97	A15	2pa multicolored	6.00	4.75
		Nos. 94-97 (4)	14.00	10.60

#96-97, Niuafo'ou Airport Inauguration, 5th anniv.

Settlement of Australia, Bicent. Type of Tonga
Miniature Sheet

Designs: a, Arrival of First Fleet, Sydney Cove, Jan. 1788. b, Aborigines. c, Early settlement. d, Soldier on guard. e, Herd of sheep. f, Horseman. g, Locomotive, kangaroos. h, Train, kangaroos. i, Flying doctor service. j, Cricket players. k, Stadium, batsman guarding wicket. l, Sydney Harbor Bridge, Opera House.

1988, July 11 Perf. 13½

98	A128	42s Sheet of 12,	50.00	50.00
		#98a-98 l		

Polynesian Islands — A16

Birds and landmarks: 42s, Audubon's shearwater, blowholes at Houma, Tonga. 57s, Kiwi, Akaroa Harbor, New Zealand. 90s, Red-tailed tropicbird, Rainmaker Mountain, Samoa. 2.50pa, Laysan albatross, Kapoho Volcano, Hawaii.

1988, Aug. 18 Perf. 14

99	A16	42s multicolored	1.50	1.00
100	A16	57s multicolored	2.50	1.60
101	A16	90s multicolored	2.75	2.75
102	A16	2.50pa multicolored	5.25	5.25
		Nos. 99-102 (4)	12.00	10.60

Miniature Sheet

Mutiny on the Bounty, Bicent. — A17

Designs: a, Sextant. b, William Bligh. c, Royal Navy lieutenant. d, Midshipman. e, Contemporary newspaper, Tahitian girl. f, Breadfruit. g, Mutiny on the Bounty excerpt, pistol grip. h, Pistol barrel, illustration of Bounty castaways. i, Tahitian girl, newsprint. j, Bligh's and Fletcher Christian's signatures. k, Christian, Pitcairn Island. l, Tombstone of John Adams.

1989, Apr. 28 Perf. 13½

103	A17	42s Sheet of 12, #a.-l.	30.00	30.00

Marine Conservation — A18

1989, June 2 Perf. 14

104	A18	32s Hatchet fish	1.40	1.40
105	A18	42s Snipe eel	1.60	1.60
106	A18	57s Viper fish	2.00	2.00
107	A18	1.50pa Angler fish	5.00	5.00
		Nos. 104-107 (4)	10.00	10.00

Evolution of the Earth — A19

Designs: 1s, Formation of the crust. 2s, Cross-section of crust. 5s, Volcanism. 10s, Surface cools. 13s, Gem stones. 15s, Oceans form. 20s, Mountains develop. 32s, River valley. 42s, Silurian Era plant life. 45s, Early marine life. 50s, Trilobites, Cambrian Era marine life. 57s, Carboniferous Era forest, coal seams. 60s, Dinosaurs feeding. 80s, Dinosaurs fighting. 1pa, Carboniferous Era insect, amphibians. 1.50pa, Stegosaurus, Jurassic Era. 2pa, Birds and mammals, Jurassic Era. 5pa, Hominid family, Pleistocene Era. 10pa, Mammoth, saber tooth tiger.

			1989-93		Perf. 14½
108	A19	1s multicolored	.70	.70
109	A19	2s multicolored	.70	.70
110	A19	5s multicolored	.90	.90
111	A19	10s multicolored	.90	.90
111A	A19	13s multicolored	1.10	1.10
112	A19	15s multicolored	.90	.90
113	A19	20s multicolored	.90	.90
114	A19	32s multicolored	1.10	1.10
115	A19	42s multicolored	1.50	1.50
115A	A19	45s multicolored	1.50	1.50
116	A19	50s multicolored	1.60	1.60
117	A19	57s multicolored	1.60	1.60
117A	A19	60s multicolored	1.75	1.75
117B	A19	80s multicolored	2.10	2.10

Size: 26x40mm
Perf. 14

118	A19	1pa multicolored	3.00	3.00
119	A19	1.50pa multicolored	4.75	4.75
120	A19	2pa multicolored	4.75	4.75
121	A19	5pa multicolored	9.25	9.25

Perf. 14

121A	A19	10pa multicolored	16.00	16.00
		Nos. 108-121A (19)	55.00	55.00

Issued: 1s-10s, 15s-42s, 50s-57s, 6/6/89; 13s, 45s, 60s, 80s, 5/3/93; 10pa, 9/14/93; others, 8/1/89.

A20

1989, Nov. 17   **Perf. 14**

122	A20	57s multicolored	1.90	1.90

Miniature Sheet

Nos. 108-121 with UPU emblem: Nos. 123a-123e, #108-112, Nos. 123f-123j, #113-117, Nos. 123k-123n, #118-121.

123		Sheet of 15, #a.-n., 122	27.50	27.50
a.-e.		A19 32s any single, perf. 14½	1.00	1.00
f.-j.		A19 42s any single, perf. 14½	1.50	1.50
k.-n.		A19 57s any single, perf. 14	2.00	2.00

Miniature Sheet

Lake Vai Lahi, Niuafo'ou — A21

a, d, Left part of lake. b, e, Small islands in center of lake. c, f, Small islet in right side of lake.

1990, Apr. 4   **Perf. 14**

124	A21	Sheet of 6	11.00	11.00
a.-c.		42s any single	1.00	1.00
d.-f.		1pa any single	2.25	2.25

Nos. 124a-124c and 124d-124f printed in continuous designs.

Penny Black, 150th Anniv. A22

Tin Can Mail and: 42s, Penny Black. 57s, US #2. 75s, Western Australia #1. 2.50pa, Cape of Good Hope #178.

1990, May 1

125	A22	42s multicolored	1.75	1.40
126	A22	57s multicolored	1.90	1.60
127	A22	75s multicolored	2.10	2.10
128	A22	2.50pa multicolored	7.25	7.00
		Nos. 125-128 (4)	13.00	12.10

Polynesian Whaling — A23

Designs: 15s, Whale surfacing. 42s, Whale diving beneath outrigger canoe. 57s, Tail flukes. 1pa, 2pa, Old man, two whales.

1990   **Perf. 11½**

129	A23	15s multicolored	2.50	2.50
130	A23	42s multicolored	3.50	3.50
131	A23	57s multicolored	3.75	3.75
132	A23	2pa multicolored	9.75	9.75
		Nos. 129-132 (4)	19.50	19.50

Souvenir Sheet
Perf. 14x14½

133	A23	1pa multicolored	20.00	20.00

Issue dates: #133, Sept. 4, others, June 6.
The entire souvenir sheet, No. 133, shows a modified No. 132. The 37½x30½mm stamp shows the two whales.
For surcharges see Nos. 139, 174-178.

UN Development Program, 40th Anniv. — A24

Designs: No. 134a, Agriculture and fisheries. No. 134b, Education. No. 135a, Health care. No. 135b, Communications.

1990, Oct. 25   **Perf. 14**

134	A24	57s Pair, #a.-b.	3.00	3.00
135	A24	2.50pa Pair, #a.-b.	12.00	12.00

Charting of Niuafo'ou, Bicent. — A24a

Designs: No. 136a, 32s, The Bounty. b, 42s, Chart showing location of Niuafo'ou and Tonga. c, 57s, The Pandora.
No. 137a, 2pa, Capt. Edwards of the Pandora. b, 3pa, Capt. Bligh of the Bounty.

1991, July 25   **Litho.**   **Perf. 14½**

136	A24a	Strip of 3, #a.-c.	6.00	6.00

Souvenir Sheet

137	A24a	Sheet of 2, #a.-b.	18.00	18.00

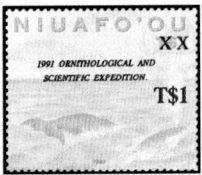

No. 133 Surcharged in Dark Blue Violet

1991, July 31   **Litho.**   **Perf. 14x14½**

139	A23	1pa on 1pa #133	13.00	13.00

"1991 Ornithological and Scientic Expedition" overprint appears on souvenir sheet at top center.

Ceresium Unicolor — A25

42s, Larva stage. 57s, Mature beetle. 1.50pa, Larva stage, diff. 2.50pa, Mature beetle on tree limb.

1991, Sept. 11   **Perf. 14½x14**

140	A25	42s multicolored	1.25	1.25
141	A25	57s multicolored	1.50	1.50
142	A25	1.50pa multicolored	3.75	3.75
143	A25	2.50pa multicolored	6.50	6.50
		Nos. 140-143 (4)	13.00	13.00

For surcharges, see Tonga Nos. 1127, 1129.

Christmas A26

Legend of the origin of the coconut tree: 15s, No. 146a, Heina bathing in lake being watched by eel. 42s, No. 146b, Heina weeping over plant growing from eel's grave. No. 146c, 1.50pa, Heina's boy climbing coconut tree. No. 146d, 3pa, "Eel's face" on coconut.

1991, Nov. 12   **Litho.**   **Perf. 14½**

144	A26	15s multicolored	.75	.75
145	A26	42s multicolored	2.00	2.00
146	A26	Sheet of 4, #a.-d.	17.50	17.50
		Nos. 144-146 (3)	20.25	20.25

For surcharge, see Tonga No. 1128.

Nos. 144-145 inscribed "Christmas Greetings 1991." No. 146 contains Nos. 144-145, 146a-146d inscribed "A Love Story."

Miniature Sheet

Discovery of America, 500th Anniv. — A27

Designs: a, Columbus. b, Queen Isabella, King Ferdinand. c, Columbus being blessed by Abbot of Palos. d, Men in boat, 15th century compass. e, Wooden traverse, wind rose, Nina. f, Bow of Santa Maria. g, Stern of Santa Maria. h, Pinta. i, Two men raising cross. j, Explorers, natives. k, Columbus kneeling before King and Queen. l, Columbus' second coat of arms.

1992, Apr. 28   **Litho.**   **Perf. 13½**

147	A27	57s Sheet of 12, #a.-l.	35.00	35.00

Miniature Sheet

World War II in Pacific, 50th Anniv. — A28

Newspaper headline and: a, Battleship ablaze at Pearl Harbor. b, Destroyed aircraft. c, Japanese A6M Zero fighter. d, Declaration of war, Pres. Franklin D. Roosevelt. e, Japanese T95 tank, Gen. MacArthur, Japanese naval ensign. f, Douglas SBD Dauntless dive bomber, Admiral Nimitz. g, Bren gun, Gen. Sir Thomas Blamey. h, Australian mortar crew, Kokoda Trail. i, US battleship, Maj. Gen. Julian C. Smith. j, Aircraft carrier USS Enterprise. k, American soldier, flag, Maj. Gen. Curtis Lemay. l, B-29 bomber, surrender ceremony on USS Missouri in Tokyo bay.

1992, May 12   **Litho.**   **Perf. 14**

148	A28	42s Sheet of 12, #a.- l.	27.50	27.50

King Taufa'ahau IV, 25th Anniv. of Coronation A29

45s, 2pa, King, Queen Halaevalu during coronation. No. 150a, King, Tongan national anthem. b, Extract from investiture ceremony. c, Tongan national anthem, singers.

1992, July 4   **Perf. 13½x13**

149	A29	45s multicolored	1.10	1.10

Size: 51x38mm
Perf. 12½x12

150	A29	80s Strip of 3, #a.-c.	6.00	6.00
151	A29	2pa multicolored	5.00	5.00
		Nos. 149-151 (3)	12.10	12.10

Megapodius Pritchardii — A30

1992, Sept. 15   **Litho.**   **Perf. 14**

152	A30	45s Female & male	2.25	2.25
153	A30	60s Female with egg	2.75	2.75
154	A30	80s Chick	4.00	4.00
155	A30	1.50pa Head of male	7.00	7.00
		Nos. 152-155 (4)	16.00	16.00

World Wildlife Fund.

First Niuafo'ou Postage Stamps, 10th Anniv. A31

1993, May 3   **Litho.**   **Perf. 14x14½**

156	A31	60s Nos. 4, 117A	1.90	1.90
157	A31	80s Nos. 7, 117B	2.40	2.40

Aviation in Niuafo'ou, 10th Anniv. — A32

Airplanes of: 1pa, South Pacific Island Airways. 2.50pa, Friendly Islands Airways.

1993, May 3

158	A32	1pa multicolored	3.50	3.50
159	A32	2.50pa multicolored	7.50	7.50

King's 75th Birthday Type of Tonga

King and: 45s, 2pa, Patrol boat Pangai. No. 161a, Sporting events. b, Aircraft and communications. c, Musical instruments.

1993, July 1   *Perf. 13x13½*
160 A167 45s multicolored   1.00   1.00

Perf. 12x12½
Size: 37x48mm
161 A167 80s Strip of 3, #a.-
    c.   5.50   5.50
162 A167 2pa multicolored   4.25   4.25
Nos. 160-162 (3)   10.75   10.75

Wildlife — A33

Designs: a, Two parrots. b, Bird with fish. c, Butterfly, beetle. d, Birds, dragonfly, butterfly. e, Bird in flight, two on ground.

1993, Aug. 10   Litho.   *Perf. 14*
163 A33 60s Strip of 5, #a.-e.   8.00   8.00

No. 163 is a continuous design.

Winners of Children's Painting
Competition — A34

Designs: Nos. 164a, 165a, Ofato Beetle Grubs of Niuafo'ou, by Peni Finau. Nos. 164b, 165b, Crater Lake Megapode, Volcano, by Paea Puletau.

1993, Dec. 10   Litho.   *Perf. 14*
164 A34 10s Pair, #a.-b.   1.00   1.00
165 A34 1pa Pair, #a.-b.   7.50   7.50

Beetles
A35

1994, Mar. 15   Litho.   *Perf. 14*
168 A35   60s Scarabaeidea   1.75   1.75
169 A35   80s Coccinellidea   2.10   2.10
170 A35 1.50pa Cerambycidea   3.75   3.75
171 A35 2.50pa Pentatomidae   6.75   6.75
Nos. 168-171 (4)   14.35   14.35

A36

Sailing Ships: a, Stern of HMS Bounty. b, Bow of HMS Bounty. c, HMS Pandora. d, Whaling ship. e, Trading schooner.

1994, June 21   Litho.   *Perf. 14*
172 A36 80s Strip of 5, #a.-e.   17.50   17.50

No. 172 is a continuous design.

A37

1946 Volcanic Eruption: a, Blue-crowned lorikeet, lava flow. b, Black Pacific ducks, lava flow. c, Megapodes, palm trees (b). d, White-tailed tropic birds, people evacuating island (c). e, People wading out to sailboats, Pacific reef heron.

1994, Sept. 21   Litho.   *Perf. 14½*
173 A37 80s Strip of 5, #a.-e.   9.50   9.50

No. 173 is a continuous design.

Nos. 129-133 Surcharged in Blue

1995, June 30   Litho.   *Perf. 11½*
174 A23   60s on 42s #130   3.00   3.00
175 A23   80s on 15s #129   3.75   3.75
176 A23   80s on 57s #131   4.00   4.00
177 A23   2pa on 32s #132   9.25   9.25
Nos. 174-177 (4)   20.00   20.00

Souvenir Sheet
178 A23 1.50pa on 1pa #133   11.00   11.00

Size and location of surcharge varies. Surcharge on No. 178 includes "COME WHALE WATCHING / IN THE SOUTH PACIFIC."

Victory in the Pacific Type of Tonga

Nos. 179, 180: a, Soldier holding rifle. b, Soldier aiming rifle, tank. c, Front of tank. d, Troops coming off boat, firing weapons. e, Troops on beach.

1995, Aug. 1   Litho.   *Perf. 14x14½*
179 A177 60s Strip of 5, #a.-e.   13.00   13.00
180 A177 80s Strip of 5, #a.-e.   17.00   17.00

Nos. 179-180 are continuous designs and were issued together in sheets containing 10 stamps.

Singapore '95 Type of Tonga

Designs, vert: No. 181a, 45s, like #117A. b, 60s, like #117B.
2pa, Plesiosaurus.

1995, Sept. 1   Litho.   *Perf. 12*
181 A178 Pair, #a.-b.   4.25   4.25

Souvenir Sheet
182 A178 2pa multicolored   5.75   5.75

Beijing Intl. Coin & Stamp Show '95 Type of Tonga
Souvenir Sheet

Design: 1.40pa, The Great Wall of China.

1995, Sept. 14   *Perf. 14½*
183 A179 1.40pa multicolored   5.50   5.50

End of World War II, UN, 50th Anniv. Type of Tonga

No. 184: a, London blitz. b, UN emblem, "50." c, Concorde.
No. 185: a, Building of Siam-Burma Railway by Allied prisoners of war. b, Like #184b. c, Japanese bullet train.

1995, Oct. 20   Litho.   *Perf. 14*
184   A180 60s Strip of 3, #a.-
    c.   5.50   5.50
185   A180 80s Strip of 3, #a.-
    c.   7.50   7.50

Nos. 184b, 185b are 23x31mm.

Mailmen of Niuafo'ou
A38

Portrait, illustration of postal history: 45s, Charles Stuart Ramsey, companions, floating with poles. 60s, Ramsey with can of mail encountering shark. 1pa, Walter George Quensell, mail being lowered from ship to canoes. 3pa, Quensell, original "tin can" mail cancels.

1996, Aug. 21   Litho.   *Perf. 14*
186 A38 45s multicolored   1.25   1.25
187 A38 60s multicolored   1.75   1.75
188 A38 1pa multicolored   3.00   3.00
189 A38 3pa multicolored   9.00   9.00
Nos. 186-189 (4)   15.00   15.00

Congress of Preshistoric and Protohistoric Sciences Type of Tonga

a, Prehistoric man making drawings, fire, living in huts, animals. b, Ancient Egyptians, Romans.

1996, Sept. 5   *Perf. 12*
190 A185 1pa Pair, #a.-b.   7.00   7.00

Evacuation of Niuafo'ou, 50th
Anniv. — A39

a, Island, two canoes. b, Volcano, four canoes. c, Edge of island, canoe. d, Canoe. e, People boarding MV Matua.

1996, Dec. 2   *Perf. 14*
191 A39 45s Strip of 5, #a.-e.   6.00   6.00
192 A39 60s Strip of 5, #a.-e.   9.00   9.00

Nos. 191-192 are continuous designs and were issued together in sheet containing 10 stamps.

UNICEF, 50th Anniv. Type of Tonga

Children's toys on checkerboard: a, Dolls, truck, balls on pegs. b, Tricycle, car, balls on pegs, teddy bear, train. c, Car, helicopter, roller skates, books, blocks.

1996, Oct. 29   Litho.   *Perf. 14*
193 A187 80s Strip of 3, #a.-c.   6.50   6.50

No. 193 is a continuous design.

Ocean Environment — A40

Various zooplankton and phytoplankton.

1997, May 19   Litho.   *Perf. 14*
194 A40   60s red & multi   1.50   1.50
195 A40   80s brown & multi   2.00   2.00
196 A40 1.50pa blue & multi   4.00   4.00
197 A40 2.50pa green & multi   7.00   7.00
Nos. 194-197 (4)   14.50   14.50

Pacific '97 Type of Tonga
Souvenir Sheet

Design: Oakland Bay Bridge, back-naped tern.

1997, May 30
198 A191 2pa multicolored   7.00   7.00

1997 Wedding Anniv., Coronation Anniv. Type of Tonga

No. 199: a, King Taufa'ahau, Queen Halaevalu Mata'aho on wedding day. b, King in coronation regalia.
5pa, King in coronation procession, horiz.

1997, June 30   Litho.   *Perf. 12*
Size: 34x47mm
199 A193 80s vert. pair, #a.-
    b.   5.00   5.00

Souvenir Sheet
200 A193 5pa multicolored   13.00   13.00

No. 199 was issued in sheets of 6 stamps.

Diana, Princess of Wales (1961-97)
Common Design Type

Various portraits: a, 10s. b, 80s, c, 1pa. d, 2.50pa.

Perf. 13½x14
1998, May 29   Litho.   *Unwmk.*
201 CD355 Sheet of 4, #a.-d.   7.75   7.75

No. 201 sold for 4.40pa + 50s with surtax from international sales going to the Princess Diana Memorial Fund and surtax from local sales going to designated local charity.
For surcharge, see No. 291.

Blue Crowned
Lorikeet — A41

World Wildlife Fund: 10s, Young birds in nest. 55s, Adult on branch of flower. 80s, Adult on branch of bush. 3pa, Two adults on tree branch.

1998, May 15   Litho.   *Perf. 14½x15*
202 A41 10s multicolored   1.25   1.25
203 A41 55s multicolored   2.75   2.75
204 A41 80s multicolored   3.25   3.25
205 A41 3pa multicolored   10.00   10.00
   a.   Sheet, 2 each #202-205   37.50   37.50
    Nos. 202-205 (4)   17.25   17.25

For surcharges see Tonga Nos. 1152, 1155.

King Taufa'ahau Tupou IV Type of Tonga

1998, July 4   Litho.   *Perf. 14*
207 A196 2.70pa multicolored   5.00   5.00

See Tonga #985a for souvenir sheet containing one #207.

Fish — A43

a, 10s, Amphiprion melanopus. b, 55s, Amphipiron perideraion. c, 80s, Amphipiron chrysopterus.

1998, Sept. 23   Litho.   *Perf. 14*
208 A43 Strip of 3, #a.-c.   2.50   2.50

Intl. Year of the Ocean. No. 208 was issued in sheets of 9 stamps.

Year of the Tiger Type of Tonga

Designs: a, 55s, Head of tiger with mouth open. b, 80s, Two tigers standing. c, 1pa, Two tigers lying down. 1pa, Head of tiger.

1998, July 23   Litho.   *Perf. 14*
209 A183 Sheet of 4, #a.-d.   6.00   6.00

No. 209 is a continuous design. Singpex '98.

Christmas
A44

Designs: 20s, Angel playing mandolin. 55s, Angel playing violin. 1pa, Children singing, bells. 1.60pa, Children singing, candles.

1998, Nov. 12   *Perf. 14x14½*
210	A44	20s multicolored	.40	.40
211	A44	55s multicolored	1.10	1.10
212	A44	1pa multicolored	2.00	2.00
213	A44	1.60pa multicolored	3.00	3.00
		Nos. 210-213 (4)	6.50	6.50

For surcharge see Tonga No. 1153.

New Year 1999 (Year of the Rabbit) A45

Stylized rabbits: a, 10s. b, 55s. c, 80s. d, 1pa.

1999, Feb. 16   *Perf. 14*
214	A45	Sheet of 4, #a.-d.	4.25	4.25

Jakob le Maire (1585-1616), Explorer — A46

1999, Mar. 19   Litho.   *Perf. 14*
215	A46	80s shown	1.40	1.40
216	A46	2.70pa Tongiaki canoe	4.50	4.50
a.		Souvenir sheet, #215-216	6.00	6.00

Australia '99 World Stamp Expo (#216a).

Flowers A47

55s, Cananga odorata. 80s, Gardenia tannaensis, vert. 1pa, Coleus amboinicus. 2.50pa, Hernandia moerenhoutiana.

Perf. 13x13¼, 13¼x13
1999, Sept. 29   Litho.
217	A47	55s multicolored	.75	.75
218	A47	80s multicolored	1.25	1.25
219	A47	1pa multicolored	1.50	1.50
220	A47	2.50pa multicolored	4.00	4.00
		Nos. 217-220 (4)	7.50	7.50

Souvenir Sheet

Millennium — A48

a, 1pa, Dove. b, 2.50pa, Native boat.

2000, Jan. 1   Litho.   *Perf. 14½x15*
221	A48	Sheet of 2, #a.-b.	5.00	5.00

Souvenir Sheet

New Year 2000 (Year of the Dragon) — A49

Various dragons; a, 10s. b, 55s, c, 80s. d, 1pa.

Litho. with Foil Application
2000, Feb. 4   *Perf. 14½*
222	A49	Sheet of 4, #a.-d.	4.50	4.50

Souvenir Sheet

The Stamp Show 2000, London — A50

Litho. with Foil Application
2000, May 22   *Perf. 13x13¼*
223	A50	Sheet of 2	6.25	6.25
a.		$1.50 Queen Mother	2.00	2.00
b.		$2.50 Queen Salote Tupou III	3.25	3.25

Souvenir Sheet

World Stamp Expo 2001, Anaheim — A51

No. 224: a, 10s, Man and woman. b, 2.50pa, Satellite dish. c, 2.70pa, Intelsat.

2000, July 7   Litho.   *Perf. 13x13¼*
224	A51	Sheet of 3, #a-c	8.25	8.25

Butterflies — A52

Designs: 55s, Jamides bochus. 80s, Blue moon. 1pa, Eurema hecabe aprica. 2.70pa, Monarch.

2000, Oct. 25   *Perf. 14*
225-228	A52	Set of 4	8.00	8.00

For surcharge see Tonga No. 1154.

Souvenir Sheet

New Year 2001 (Year of the Snake) — A53

No. 229 — Various snakes: a, 10s. b, 55s, c, 80s, d, 1pa.

Litho. with Foil Application
2001, Feb. 1   *Perf. 14¼*
229	A53	Sheet of 4, #a-d	4.25	4.25

Hong Kong 2001 Stamp Exhibition.

Fish — A54

Designs: 80s, Prognichthys sealei. 1pa, Xiphias gladius. 2.50pa, Katsuwonus pelamis.

2001, June 5   Litho.   *Perf. 13¾*
230-232	A54	Set of 3	7.25	7.25
232a		Souvenir sheet, #230-232	7.25	7.25

Souvenir Sheet

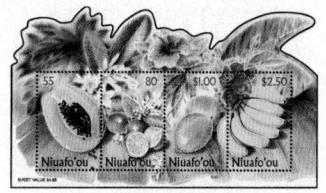

Fruit — A55

No. 233: a, 55s, Papaya. b, 80s, Limes. c, 1pa, Mangos. d, 2.50pa, Bananas.

Perf. 14¼x14
2001, Sept. 19   Litho.   Unwmk.
233	A55	Sheet of 4, #a-d	8.50	8.50

Barn Owl A56

Designs: Nos. 234, 238a, 10s, Owl in flight. Nos. 235, 238b, 55s, Adult feeding young. Nos. 236, 238c, 2.50pa, Four owls. Nos. 237, 238d, 2.70pa, Owl's head.

2001, Nov. 21   *Perf. 12¾x13¼*
Without Vertical Bister Line Separating Panels
234-237	A56	Set of 4	10.00	10.00

Souvenir Sheet
With Vertical Bister Line Separating Panels
238	A56	Sheet of 4, #a-d	10.00	10.00

For surcharge see Tonga No. 1156.

Reign Of Queen Elizabeth II, 50th Anniv. Issue
Common Design Type
Souvenir Sheet

No. 239: a, 15s, Princess Elizabeth with Queen Mother. b, 90s, Wearing purple hat. c, 1.20pa, As young woman. d, 1.40pa, Wearing red hat. e, 2.25pa, 1955 portrait by Annigoni (38x50mm).

Perf. 14¼x14½, 13¾ (2.25pa)
2002, Feb. 6   Litho.   Wmk. 373
239	CD360	Sheet of 5, #a-e	7.00	7.00

Souvenir Sheet

New Year 2002 (Year of the Horse) — A517

Various horses; a, 65s. b, 80s. c, 1pa. d, 2.50pa.

Litho. With Foil Application
2002, Feb. 12   Unwmk.   *Perf. 14*
240	A57	Sheet of 4, #a-d	8.50	8.50

Megapodius Pritchardii A58

Designs: 15s, Bird, eggs. 70s, Two birds. 90s, Bird, vert. 2.50pa, Two birds, vert.

Perf. 14x13½, 13½x14
2002, Apr. 9   Litho.
241-244	A58	Set of 4	7.00	7.00
244a		Souvenir sheet, #243-244	6.00	6.00

Nos. 243-244 lack white frame around stamp.

Cephalopods A59

Designs: 80s, Octopus vulgaris. 1pa, Sepioteuthis lessoniana. 2.50pa, Nautilus belauensis.

2002, July 25   Litho.   *Perf. 13¾*
245-247	A59	Set of 3	7.00	7.00
247a		Souvenir sheet, #245-247	7.00	7.00

Souvenir Sheet

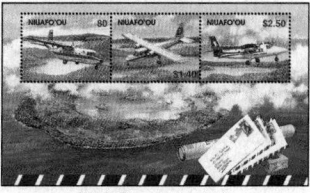

Mail Planes — A60

No. 248: a, 80c, Casa C-212 Aviocar. b, 1.40pa, Britten-Norman Islander. c, 2.50pa, DHC 6-300 Twin Otter.

2002, Nov. 27   Litho.   *Perf. 12¾*
248	A60	Sheet of 3, #a-c	8.00	8.00

New Year 2003 (Year of the Ram) Type of Tonga

No. 249: a, 65s, One ram. 80s, Three sheep. 1pa, Three sheep, diff. 2.50pa, Two sheep.

2003, Apr. 14   Litho.   *Perf. 13¼*
249	A223	Sheet of 4, #a-d	6.00	6.00

Coronation of Queen Elizabeth II, 50th Anniv. Type of Tonga

Designs: 90s, Queen Elizabeth II. 1.20pa, Queen Elizabeth II seated. 1.40pa, Queen Salote of Tonga in coach. 2.50pa, Queen Salote.

2003, June 2   Litho.
250-253	A224	Set of 4	10.00	10.00

New Year (Year of the Monkey) Type of Tonga

No. 254: a, 60s, Spider monkey. b, 80s, Ring-tailed lemur. c, 1pa, Cotton-top tamarin. d, 2.50pa, White-cheeked gibbon.

2004, Feb. 12　Litho.　Perf. 13¼
254　A228　Sheet of 4, #a-d　6.00　6.00

Trees Type of Tonga

Designs: 45s, Pawpaw (papaya). 60s, Banana. 80s, Coconut. 1.80pa, Lime.

2004　Litho.　Perf. 14¼x14
255-258　A229　Set of 4　4.50　4.50

Christmas Type of Tonga

Designs: 15s, Madonna and Child. 90s, Journey to Bethlehem. 1.20pa, Annunciation to the Shepherds. 2.60pa, Magi.

2004, Dec.　Perf. 14
259-262　A230　Set of 4　5.75　5.75

Royalty Type of Tonga

Designs: 30s, King George Tupou I. 65s, King George Tupou II. 80s, Queen Salote Tupou III. 3.05pa, King Taufa'ahau Tupou IV.

2004, July 7　Litho.　Perf. 14
263-266　A231　Set of 4　5.75　5.75
266a　Souvenir sheet, #263-266　5.75　5.75

New Year 2005 (Year of the Rooster) Type of Tonga
Souvenir Sheet

No. 267 — Various roosters with panel color of: a, 65s, Gray. b, 80s, Grayish tan. c, 1pa, Gray. d, 2.50pa, Yellow green.

2005, Feb. 12
267　A232　Sheet of 4, #a-d　5.25　5.25

Christmas — A61

No. 268: a, 3.40pa, Palm frond and Christmas lights. b, 5pa, Grass and snowflakes.

2011, Dec. 24
268　A61　Horiz. pair, #a-b　9.75　9.75

Miniature Sheets

Megaptera Novaeangliae — A62

No. 269 — Various depictions of humpback whale: a, 1pa. b, 1.40pa. c, 1.60pa.
No. 270 — Various depictions of humpback whale: a, 2pa. b, 2.25pa. c, 2.40pa.

2012, Jan. 16
269　A62　Sheet of 3, #a-c, + label　4.75　4.75
270　A62　Sheet of 3, #a-c, + label　8.00　8.00

Worldwide Fund for Nature (WWF) — A63

Various depictions of Zebra shark: 45s, 2pa, 2.40pa, 3.40pa.

2012, Mar. 12　Perf. 14¼x14
271-274　A63　Set of 4　9.75　9.75
274a　Sheet of 16, 4 each #271-274　39.00　39.00

Butterflies — A64

Designs: 45s, Australian meadow-argus. 1.95pa, Crow butterfly. 2pa, Monarch butterfly. 2.40pa, Monarch butterfly, diff. 2.50pa, Blue moon butterfly. 3pa, Australian meadow-argus, diff. 3.40pa, Crow butterfly, diff. 4pa, Blue moon butterfly, diff. 5pa, Monarch butterfly, diff. 6pa, Blue moon butterfly, diff. 7.30pa, Crow butterfly, diff. 8pa, Australian meadow-argus, diff.

2012, Apr. 20　Perf. 12¾x12½
Stamps With White Backgrounds
275	A64	45s multi	.55	.55
276	A64	1.95pa multi	2.25	2.25
277	A64	2pa multi	2.40	2.40
278	A64	2.40pa multi	2.75	2.75
279	A64	2.50pa multi	3.00	3.00
280	A64	3pa multi	3.50	3.50
281	A64	3.40pa multi	4.00	4.00
282	A64	4pa multi	4.75	4.75
283	A64	5pa multi	6.00	6.00
284	A64	6pa multi	7.00	7.00
285	A64	7.30pa multi	8.50	8.50
286	A64	8pa multi	9.50	9.50
		Nos. 275-286 (12)	54.20	54.20

Stamps With Light Blue Background
287		Sheet of 12	55.00	55.00
a.	A64	45s multi	.55	.55
b.	A64	1.95pa multi	2.25	2.25
c.	A64	2pa multi	2.40	2.40
d.	A64	2.40pa multi	2.75	2.75
e.	A64	2.50pa multi	3.00	3.00
f.	A64	3pa multi	3.50	3.50
g.	A64	3.40pa multi	4.00	4.00
h.	A64	4pa multi	4.75	4.75
i.	A64	5pa multi	6.00	6.00
j.	A64	6pa multi	7.00	7.00
k.	A64	7.30pa multi	8.50	8.50
l.	A64	8pa multi	9.50	9.50

Titanic Type of Tonga

No. 288: a, Titanic facing left at dock. b, Photograph of Titanic facing right. c, Titanic facing left at sea. d, Color painting of Titanic at sea.
No. 289a, Like #288d.

2012, June 6　Perf. 12½
288　A240　3.40pa Sheet of 4, #a-d　16.00　16.00
Souvenir Sheet
289　A240　Sheet of 2, #288a, 289a　4.50　4.50
a.　　45s multi　.50　.50

Personalizable Stamp — A65

2012, Aug. 8　Perf. 14x14¾
290　A65　3pa multi　3.50　3.50

No. 201 Surcharged in Gold and Black

No. 1192: a, 4pa on 10s. b, 4pa on 80s. c, 4pa on 1pa. d, 4pa on 2.50pa.

2012, Sept. 4　Litho.
291　CD355　Sheet of 4, #a-d　18.50　18.50

Overprint is printed across the four stamps of the sheet. It reads "In Loving Memory of Diana, Princess of Wales / 31 August 1997 / Her Legacy will live on forever. / William and Kate, Duke and Duchess of Cambridge / 1st Anniversary of their Royal Wedding 2011".

Miniature Sheet

Christmas — A66

No. 292 — Nativity, by Giotto di Bondone: a, Angels, manger roof at LR, denomination at UL. b, Angels, manger roof at LL, denomination at LL. c, Angels in sky, no roof visible. d, Angels, manger post at left. e, Angels, manger post at right. f, Angel and tree. g, Madonna and Child, cow and donkey. h, Two shepherds. i, Joseph. j, Attendant holding infant Jesus. k, Attendant and sheep. l, Sheep and legs of shepherds.

2012, Nov. 21　Perf. 14¾x14¼
292　A66　1pa Sheet of 12, #a-l, + 2 labels　14.00　14.00

New Year 2013 (Year of Snake) Type of Tonga

No. 293: a, Red snake with yellow green spots. b, Dark green snake with blue spots. c, Purple snake with green spots. d, Yellow green snake with green spots.

2013, Feb. 20
293　A248　2.45pa Sheet of 4, #a-d　11.50　11.50

Tin Can Island Mail Cans — A67

Designs: 2.25pa, Can on beach, ship at sea. 5.40pa, Can on beach, ship at sea, diff.

2013, Aug. 21　Litho.　Perf. 14x14¾
294-295　A67　Set of 2　8.25　8.25

Birth of Prince George of Cambridge A68

Designs: 2.15pa, Baby's feet in adult's hand. 3.20pa, Baby's hand and foot. 4.10pa, Baby's hand in adult's hand. 4.70pa, Baby's hand.
16.90pa, Baby's feet in adult's hand, diff.

2013, Aug. 30　Litho.　Perf. 13¾
296-299　A68　Set of 4　15.50　15.50
Souvenir Sheet
300　A68　16.90pa multi　18.50　18.50

Butterflies and Flowers A69

Designs: 20s, Blue moon butterfly, Jasmine. 30s, Monarch butterfly, Hibiscus. 40s, Meadow argus butterfly, Elder. 50s, Crow butterfly, Heilala. 60s, Blue moon butterfly, Blue wild indigo. 80s, Monarch butterfly, Purple coneflowers. 90s, Meadow argus butterfly, Yellow bell. 1.10pa, Crow butterfly, Frangipani. 1.20pa, Blue moon butterfly, Tahitian gardenia. 10pa, Blue moon butterfly, Frangipani. 12.50pa, Monarch butterfly, diff. 20pa, Meadow argus butterfly, Tahitian vanilla orchid.

2013, Sept. 6　Litho.　Perf. 14
Stamps With White Frames
301	A69	20s multi	.25	.25
302	A69	30s multi	.35	.35
303	A69	40s multi	.45	.45
304	A69	50s multi	.55	.55
305	A69	60s multi	.65	.65
306	A69	80s multi	.90	.90
307	A69	90s multi	1.00	1.00
308	A69	1.10pa multi	1.25	1.25
309	A69	1.20pa multi	1.40	1.40
310	A69	10pa multi	11.00	11.00
311	A69	12.50pa multi	13.50	13.50
312	A69	20pa multi	22.00	22.00
		Nos. 301-312 (12)	53.30	53.30

Miniature Sheet
Stamps With Blue Frames
313		Sheet of 12	54.00	54.00
a.	A69	20s multi	.25	.25
b.	A69	30s multi	.35	.35
c.	A69	40s multi	.45	.45
d.	A69	50s multi	.55	.55
e.	A69	60s multi	.65	.65
f.	A69	80s multi	.90	.90
g.	A69	90s multi	1.00	1.00
h.	A69	1.10pa multi	1.25	1.25
i.	A69	1.20pa multi	1.40	1.40
j.	A69	10pa multi	11.00	11.00
k.	A69	12.50pa multi	13.50	13.50
l.	A69	20pa multi	22.00	22.00

China International Collection Expo Type of Tonga of 2013
Souvenir Sheet

No. 314: a, 2.35pa, Painting by Paul Gauguin. b, 2.60pa, Beijing Exhibition Center.

2013, Sept. 26　Litho.　Perf. 12
314　A263　Sheet of 2, #a-b　5.50　5.50

Christmas Type of Tonga of 2013

Paintings of angels by: 1.75pa, Pietro Perugino. 2.35pa, Melozzo da Forli. 2.60pa, Sandro Botticelli.

2013, Nov. 13　Litho.　Perf. 13½
315-317　A269　Set of 3　7.25　7.25

Miniature Sheet

New Year 2014 (Year of the Horse) — A70

No. 318: a, Brown horse, black denomination at UL. b, White horse, white denomination at UR. c, Two horses. d, White horse, white denomination at UL.

2014, Jan. 6　Litho.　Perf. 13¾
318　A70　$1.50 Sheet of 4, #a-d　6.50　6.50

Miniature Sheet

Easter — A71

No. 319 — Various paintings depicting the resurrected Christ by Pietro Perugino: a, 1.75pa. b, 2.25pa. c, 2.75pa. d, 4.55pa.

2014, Apr. 7   Litho.   Perf. 13¼
319 A71   Sheet of 4, #a-d   12.50 12.50

Souvenir Sheet

Nelson Mandela (1918-2013), President of South Africa — A72

No. 320 — Mandela's: a, 2.25pa, Head. b, 5.40pa, Head and hands.

2014, May 13   Litho.   Perf. 14¾x14¼
320 A72   Sheet of 2, #a-b   8.25 8.25

Butterflies — A73

No. 321: a, 11.30pa, Small greasy butterfly. b, 16.90pa, Spotted crow butterfly. c, 28pa, Monarch butterfly.

2014, May 22   Litho.   Perf. 13¼
321 A73 Horiz. strip of 3, #a-
           c, + 3 labels   60.00 60.00

Miniature Sheet

Christmas — A74

Bells and: a, Curved staff and notes in foreground, slanted musical score in background. b, Faint musical score with three staffs in background. c, G clef and musical notes, faint musical score with six staffs. d, Curving staff with G clef and notes, faint musical score with four staffs in background.

2014, Dec. 15   Litho.   Perf. 13¾
322 A74 2.25pa Sheet of 4, #a-d 9.25 9.25

Souvenir Sheet

New Year 2015 (Year of the Sheep) — A75

Sheep with background color of: a, 3.40pa, Blue. b, 4.60pa, Purple.

2015, Jan. 5   Litho.   Perf. 13¼
323 A75   Sheet of 2, #a-b   7.75 7.75

AIR POST SPECIAL DELIVERY STAMPS

APSD1

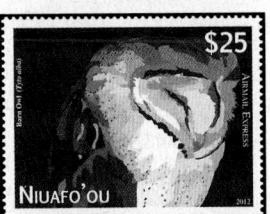

APSD2

APSD3

Barn Owl — APSD4

2012, Aug. 30   Litho.   Perf. 14¼
Stamps With White Frame All Around
CE1 APSD1 25pa multi   28.00 28.00
CE2 APSD2 25pa multi   28.00 28.00
CE3 APSD3 25pa multi   28.00 28.00
CE4 APSD4 25pa multi   28.00 28.00
     Nos. CE1-CE4 (4)   112.00 112.00

Stamps With White Frame on Two Sides

CE5   Sheet of 4   112.00 112.00
  a. APSD1 25pa multi   28.00 28.00
  b. APSD2 25pa multi   28.00 28.00
  c. APSD3 25pa multi   28.00 28.00
  d. APSD4 25pa multi   28.00 28.00

A sheet of 16 containing four of each of types APSD1-APSD4 without white frames on the stamps was produced in a limited printing.

TRANSCAUCASIAN FEDERATED REPUBLIC

ˌtranˌt s-ko-ˈkā-zhən ˈfe-də-rāted ri-ˈpə-blik

LOCATION — In southeastern Europe, south of the Caucasus Mountains between the Black and Caspian Seas
GOVT. — Former republic
AREA — 71,255 sq. mi.
POP. — 5,851,000 (approx.)
CAPITAL — Tiflis

The Transcaucasian Federation was made up of the former autonomies of Armenia, Georgia and Azerbaijan. Its stamps were replaced by those of Russia.

100 Kopecks = 1 Ruble

Russian Stamps of 1909-17 Overprinted in Black or Red

1923   Unwmk.   Perf. 14½x15
1   A15 10k dark blue   4.00   5.00
2   A14 10k on 7k lt bl   4.00   5.00
3   A11 25k grn & gray vio   4.00   5.00
4   A11 35k red brn & grn (R) 4.00   5.00
  a.   Double overprint   75.00 75.00
5   A8   50k brn red & grn   4.00   5.00
6   A9   1r pale brn, brn &
          org   12.00 12.00
7   A12 3½r mar & lt grn   35.00
          Imperf
8   A9   1r pale brn, brn &
          red org   6.50   6.00
     Nos. 1-8 (8)   73.50
     Nos. 1-6,8 (7)   43.00

No. 7 was prepared but not issued.

Overprinted on Stamps of Armenia Previously Handstamped

a   c

          Perf. 14½x15
9   A11(c) 25k grn & gray
            vio   250.00 250.00
10 A8(c) 50k vio & grn 250.00 150.00
          Perf. 13½
11 A9(a) 1r pale brn, brn
            & org   100.00 50.00
12 A9(c) 1r pale brn, brn
            & org   150.00 50.00
          Imperf
13 A9(c) 1r pale brn, brn
            & red org   35.00 35.00
     Nos. 9-13 (5)   785.00 535.00

Counterfeit overprints exist.

Oil Fields — A1

Soviet Symbols — A2

1923   Perf. 11½
14 A1   40,000r red violet   3.00   3.50
15 A1   75,000r dark grn   3.00   3.50
16 A1 100,000r blk vio   3.00   3.50
17 A1 150,000r red   3.00   3.50
18 A2 200,000r dull grn   3.00   3.50
19 A2 300,000r blue   3.00   3.50
20 A2 350,000r dark brn   3.00   3.50
21 A2 500,000r rose   3.00   3.50
     Nos. 14-21 (8)   24.00 28.00

Nos. 14-15 Srchd. in Brown

1923
22 A1 700,000r on 40,000r   3.00   5.00
  a. Imperf., pair   40.00
23 A1 700,000r on 75,000r   3.00   5.00
  a. Imperf., pair   40.00

Types of Preceding Issue with Values in Gold Kopecks
1923, Oct. 24
25 A2   1k orange   2.50   2.50
26 A2   2k blue green   2.50   2.50
27 A2   3k rose   3.50   2.50
28 A2   4k gray brown   2.25   2.50
29 A1   5k dark violet   2.25   2.50
30 A1   9k deep blue   2.25   2.50
31 A1 18k slate   2.25   2.50
     Nos. 25-31 (7)   17.50 17.50

Nos. 14-21, 25-31 exist imperf. but are not known to have been issued in that condition. Value, $14 each.

TRANSVAAL

tran̦țs-'väl

(South African Republic)

LOCATION — Southern Africa
GOVT. — A former British Colony
AREA — 110,450 sq. mi.
POP. — 1,261,736 (1904)
CAPITAL — Pretoria

Transvaal was known as the South African Republic until 1877 when it was occupied by the British. The republic was restored in 1884 and continued until 1900 when it was annexed to Great Britain and named "The Transvaal."

12 Pence = 1 Shilling
20 Shillings = 1 Pound

Most unused stamps between Nos. 1-96, 119-122 and 136-137 were issued with gum, but do not expect gum on scarcer stamps as few examples retain their original gum. In many cases removal of the remaining gum may enhance the preservation of the stamps. Otherwise, values for unused stamps are for examples with original gum as defined in the catalogue introduction.

Very fine imperforate stamps will have adequate to large margins. However, rouletted stamps are valued as partly rouletted, with straight edges, and rouletted just into the design, as the rouletting methods were quite inaccurate.

First Republic

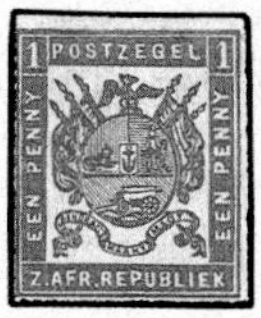

Coat of Arms — A1

A1 has spread wings on eagle.

Mecklenburg Printings
By Adolph Otto, Gustrow
Fine Impressions
Thin Paper

1869 Unwmk. *Imperf.*
1 A1 1p brown lake 500.00
a. 1p red 675.00 675.00
2 A1 6p ultra 230.00 230.00
3 A1 1sh dark green 800.00 800.00
a. Tete beche pair —

Rouletted 15½, 16
4 A1 1p red 125.00
5 A1 6p ultra 115.00 *115.00*
6 A1 1sh blue green 150.00 *150.00*
a. 1sh yellow green 200.00 *185.00*
b. 1sh deep green 260.00 *275.00*

Nos. 1-6 were printed from 2 sets of plates, differing in the spacing between the stamps.

The only known example of No. 3a is in a museum.

See Nos. 9-24, 26-33, 35-36, 38-39, 41-42, 43-49, 119, 122. For overprints see Nos. 53-61, 63-66, 68-72, 75-78, 81-83, 86-87, 90-91, 94.

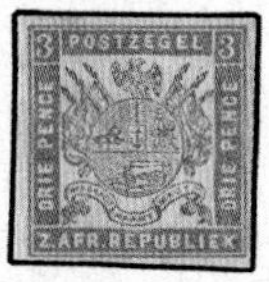

Coat of Arms — A2

1871-74
7 A2 3p lilac 92.50 *100.00*
a. 3p violet 110.00 115.00
8 A2 6p brt ultra ('74) 70.00 27.50
a. Half used as 3p on cover *1,650.*

Many forgeries exist in colors duller or lighter than the genuine stamps.

In forgeries of type A1, all values, the "D" of "EENDRAGT" is not noticeably larger than the other letters and does not touch the top of the ribbon. In type A1 genuine stamps, the "D" is large and touches the ribbon top. The eagle's eye is a dot and its face white on the genuine stamps; the eye is a loop or blob attached to the beak, and the beak is strongly hooked, on the forgeries. Many forgeries of the 1sh have the top line of the ribbon broken above "EENDRAGT."

Forgeries of type A2 usually can be detected only by color.

A sharply struck cancellation of a numeral in three rings is found on many of these forgeries. The similar genuine cancellation is always roughly or heavily struck.

See Nos. 25, 34, 437, 40, 42B, 120-121. For overprints see Nos. 50-52, 62, 67, 73-74, 79-80, 84-85, 88-89, 92-93, 95-96.

Local Printings

(A) By M. J. Viljoen, Pretoria
Poor Impressions,
Overinked and Spotted

1870 Thin Soft Paper *Imperf.*
9 A1 1p pink 92.50
a. 1p rose red 115.00
b. 1p carmine 80.00 *92.50*
10 A1 6p dull ultra 375.00 80.00
a. Tete beche pair —

The only known examples of No. 10a are in museums.

Rouletted 15½, 16
11 A1 1p carmine 800.00 300.00
a. Rouletted 6½ 1,100.
12 A1 6p dull ultra 230.00 135.00

Hard Paper, Thick to Medium
Imperf
13 A1 1p carmine 100.00 *100.00*
14 A1 6p ultra —
15 A1 1sh gray green 150.00 140.00
a. 1sh dark green —
b. Tete beche pair *23,000.*
c. Half used as 6p on cover *2,100.*

The existence of No. 14 is questionable.

Rouletted 15½, 16
16 A1 1p light carmine 125.00 *100.00*
a. 1p carmine 62.50 *70.00*
17 A1 6p ultra 125.00 125.00
a. Tete beche pair *30,000.* *21,000.*
18 A1 1sh dark green 185.00 92.50
a. 1sh gray green 750.00 750.00

Examples of Nos. 16-18 are sometimes so heavily inked as to be little more than blots of color.

(B) By J. P. Borrius, Potchefstroom
Clearer Impressions Though Often
Overinked

1870 Thick Porous Paper *Imperf.*
19 A1 1p black 160.00 135.00
20 A1 6p indigo —

Rouletted 15½, 16
21 A1 1p black 25.00 32.50
22 A1 6p gray blue 160.00 70.00
a. 6p indigo 115.00 92.50
b. 6p bright ultra —

Thin Transparent Paper
23 A1 1p black 225.00 *750.00*
24 A1 1p brt carmine 200.00 62.50
a. 1p deep carmine 80.00 47.50
25 A2 3p gray lilac 125.00 75.00
26 A1 6p ultra 80.00 35.00
27 A1 1sh yellow green 100.00 50.00
a. 1sh deep green 100.00 50.00
b. Half used as 6p on cover — *2,100.*

Thick Soft Paper
28 A1 1p dull rose 450.00 85.00
a. 1p brown rose 575.00 140.00
b. Printed on both sides —
29 A1 6p dull blue 100.00 50.00
a. 6p bright blue 230.00 75.00
b. 6p ultramarine 200.00 75.00
c. Rouletted 6½ —
30 A1 1sh yellow green 975.00 750.00

The paper of Nos. 28 to 30 varies considerably in thickness.

(C) By P. Davis & Son, Natal
Thin to Medium Paper

1874 *Perf. 12½*
31 A1 1p red 150.00 50.00
a. 1p brownish red 150.00 50.00
32 A1 6p deep blue 200.00 70.00
a. 6p blue 185.00 62.50
b. Horiz. pair, imperf. between —

(D) By the Stamp Commission, Pretoria
Pelure Paper

1875-76 *Imperf.*
33 A1 1p pale red 70.00 65.00
a. 1p orange red 65.00 32.50
b. 1p brown red 80.00 40.00
c. Pin perf. 775.00 475.00
34 A2 3p gray lilac 80.00 55.00
a. 3p dull violet 90.00 55.00
b. Pin perf. — 500.00
35 A1 6p blue 77.50 55.00
a. 6p pale blue 77.50 62.50
b. 6p dark blue 82.50 57.50
c. Tete beche pair, thin opaque paper *20,000.*
d. Tete beche pair, pelure, transparent paper —
e. Pin perf. — 400.00

The only known examples of No. 35c are in museums.

Rouletted 15½, 16
36 A1 1p orange red 450.00 155.00
a. Rouletted 6½ 1,250. 250.00
37 A2 3p dull violet 500.00 165.00
a. Rouletted 6½ *1,100.* 320.00
38 A1 6p blue 215.00 130.00
a. Rouletted 6½ 1,275. 140.00

The paper of this group varies slightly in thickness and is sometimes divided into pelure and semipelure. We believe there was only one lot of the paper and that the separation is not warranted.

Thick Hard Paper
Imperf
39 A1 1p org red ('76) 32.50 25.00
40 A2 3p lilac 425.00 140.00
41 A1 6p deep blue 70.00 25.00
a. 6p blue 115.00 27.50
b. Tete beche pair *20,000.*

Rouletted 15½, 16
42 A1 1p org red ('76) 475.00 175.00
a. Rouletted 6½ ('75) 700.00 175.00
42B A2 3p lilac 400.00
43 A1 6p deep blue *700.00* 325.00
a. 6p blue *875.00* 125.00
b. Rouletted 6½ ('75) *750.00* 300.00

Soft Porous Paper
Imperf
44 A1 1p orange red 150.00 62.50
45 A1 6p deep blue 225.00 650.00
a. 6p dull blue 400.00 110.00
46 A1 1sh yellow green 460.00 140.00
a. Half used as 6p on cover 1,850.

Rouletted 15½, 16
47 A1 1p orange red — 425.00
a. Rouletted 6½ — *525.00*
48 A1 6p deep blue — *185.00*
a. Rouletted 6½ — *1,275.*
49 A1 1sh yellow grn 800.00 400.00
a. Rouletted 6½ — 1,400.
b. Rouletted 15½-16x16½ 800.00 400.00

First British Occupation

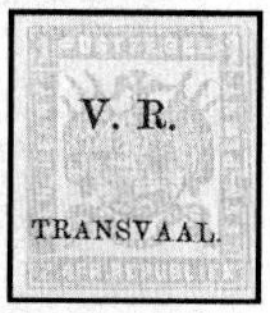

Stamps and Types of 1875 Overprinted

Red Overprint
Pelure Paper

1877 Unwmk. *Imperf.*
50 A2 3p lilac 1,500. 210.00
a. Overprinted on back 3,750. *3,750.*
b. Double ovpt., red and black *7,000.*

Rouletted 15½, 16
51 A2 3p lilac — *1,850.*
a. Rouletted 6½ — *2,600.*

Thin Hard Paper
Imperf
52 A2 3p lilac 1,500. 350.00

Soft Porous Paper
53 A1 6p blue 1,850. *210.00*
a. 6p deep blue — *300.00*
b. Inverted overprint *6,000.*
c. Double overprint 5,250. 1,150.
54 A1 1sh yellow grn 750.00 210.00
a. Inverted overprint *5,250.*
b. Half used as 6p on cover *2,100.*

Rouletted 15½, 16
55 A1 6p blue *2,000.*
a. Rouletted 6½ *2,750.*
56 A1 1sh yellow grn 2,000. 875.00
a. Rouletted 6½ 4,750. *2,750.*
b. As "a.", overprint inverted *7,500.*

Black Overprint
Pelure Paper
Imperf
57 A1 1p red 360.00 145.00

Rouletted 15½, 16
58 A1 1p red — *1,350.*

Thick Hard Paper
Imperf
59 A1 1p red 35.00 27.50
a. Inverted overprint 650.00 575.00

Rouletted 15½, 16
60 A1 1p red 185.00 57.50
a. Rouletted 6½ 750.00 350.00
b. Inverted overprint
c. Double overprint *1,275.*

Soft Porous Paper
Imperf
61 A1 1p red 35.00 40.00
a. Double overprint 1,400.
62 A2 3p lilac 110.00 52.50
a. 3p deep lilac 200.00 97.50
b. Inverted overprint —
63 A1 6p dull blue 200.00 100.00
a. 6p bright blue 185.00 35.00
b. 6p dark blue 185.00 *250.00*
d. Inverted overprint 1,650. —
e. Double overprint *4,000.* 2,400.
64 A1 6p blue, *rose* 115.00 55.00
a. Tete beche pair —
b. Inverted overprint 140.00 55.00
c. Overprint omitted 4,000. 2,900.
d. Half used as 3p on cover
65 A1 1sh yellow grn 150.00 65.00
a. Tete beche pair 23,500. *24,000.*
b. Inverted overprint 1,400. 500.00
c. Half used as 6p on cover *1,750.*

The only known examples of No. 64a are in museums.

Rouletted 15½, 16
66 A1 1p red 100.00 85.00
a. Rouletted 6½ 750.00 175.00
67 A2 3p lilac 240.00 75.00
a. Rouletted 6½ *875.00*
68 A1 6p dull blue 240.00 75.00
a. Inverted overprint — *875.00*
b. Rouletted 6½ — *1,400.*
c. As "a," rouletted 6½ *4,750.*
69 A1 6p blue, *rose* 300.00 80.00
a. Inverted overprint 650.00 80.00
b. Rouletted 6½
c. Tete beche pair
d. Overprint omitted
e. As "a," rouletted 6½ 750.00
f. As "d," rouletted 6½
70 A1 1sh yellow grn 325.00 125.00
a. Inverted overprint 1,400. 575.00
b. Rouletted 6½ 550.00 150.00
c. As "a," rouletted 6½ 1,750. 700.00

In this issue the space between "V. R." and "TRANSVAAL" is normally 8½mm but in position 11 it is 12mm. In this and the following issues there are numerous minor varieties of the overprint, missing periods, etc.

The only known examples of No. 69c are in museums.

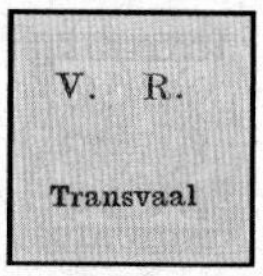

Types A1 and A2 Overprinted

1877-79 *Imperf.*
71 A1 1p red, *blue* 70.00 35.00
a. "Transvral" *6,500.* *2,900.*
b. Inverted overprint *925.00* 475.00
c. Double overprint *4,750.*
d. Overprint omitted —
72 A1 1p red, *org* ('78) 37.50 24.00
a. Printed on both sides —
b. Pin perf. —
73 A2 3p lilac, *buff* 75.00 50.00
a. Inverted overprint 875.00
b. Pin perf. —
74 A2 3p lilac, *grn* ('79) 175.00 70.00
a. Inverted overprint 2,350.
b. Double overprint —
c. Pin perf. —
75 A1 6p blue, *grn* 115.00 45.00
a. Tete beche pair *20,000.*
b. Inverted overprint *1,275.*
c. Half used as 3p on cover —
d. Pin perf. —
76 A1 6p blue, *bl* ('78) 80.00 32.50
a. Tete beche pair —
b. Overprint omitted *2,750.*
c. Inverted overprint *1,275.*
d. Half used as 3p on cover *925.00*
e. Double overprint 3,750.
f. Pin perf. —
Nos. 71-76 (6) 552.50 256.50

The only known examples of No. 76a are in museums.

Rouletted 15½, 16
77 A1 1p red, *blue* 125.00 45.00
a. "Transvral" 3,500.
b. Inverted overprint —
c. Double overprint —
78 A1 1p red, *org* ('78) 47.50 32.50
a. Horiz. pair, imperf. vert.
b. Rouletted 6½ 300.00 115.00
79 A2 3p lilac, *buff* 125.00 32.50
a. Inverted overprint 3,500.
b. Vert. pair, imperf. horiz. 875.00
c. Rouletted 6½ 115.00
80 A2 3p lilac, *grn* ('79) 800.00 175.00
a. Inverted overprint
b. Rouletted 6½ 750.00 325.00
81 A1 6p blue, *green* 110.00 32.50
a. Inverted overprint *750.00*
b. Overprint omitted *4,750.*
c. Tete beche pair —
d. Half used at 3p on cover 800.00
e. Rouletted 6½ — *1,275.*
82 A1 6p blue, *bl* ('78) 325.00 65.00
a. Inverted overprint — 1,050.
b. Overprint omitted — 4,000.
c. Tete beche pair —
d. Horiz. pair, imperf. vert. —
e. Half used as 3p on cover *900.00*
f. Double overprint —
g. Rouletted 6½ 350.00
h. As "a," rouletted 6½ —
Nos. 77-82 (6) 1,532. 382.50

The only known examples of No. 81c are in museums. The existence of No. 82c is questioned.

Types A1 and A2 Overprinted

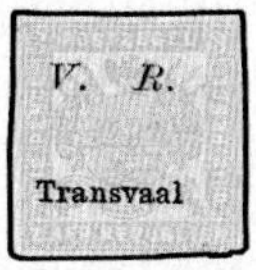

Imperf

83 A1 1p red, *org* ('78) 80.00 52.50
84 A2 3p lilac, *buff* ('78) 92.50 40.00
a. Pin perf. 875.00 875.00
85 A2 3p lilac, *grn* ('79) 160.00 40.00
a. Inverted overprint 2,300.
b. Overprint omitted —
c. Printed on both sides 1,150.
86 A1 6p blue, *bl* ('78) 160.00 50.00
a. Tete beche pair 18,000.
b. Inverted overprint 800.00
Nos. 83-86 (4) 492.50 182.50

Rouletted 15½, 16

87 A1 1p red, *org* ('78) 200.00 140.00
a. Rouletted 6½ 350.00
88 A2 3p lilac, *buff* ('78) 210.00 125.00
a. Vert. pair, imperf. horiz. —
b. Rouletted 6½ 400.00
89 A2 3p lilac, *grn* ('79) 800.00 175.00
a. Inverted overprint —
b. Overprint omitted —
c. Rouletted 6½ ('97) 350.00
90 A1 6p blue, *bl* ('78) 500.00 125.00
a. Tete beche pair —
b. Inverted overprint — 1,275.
d. Rouletted 6½ 400.00
e. As "b," rouletted 6½

Types A1 and A2 Overprinted

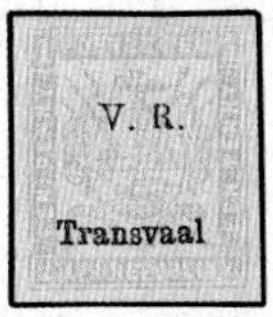

1879 ***Imperf.***

91 A1 1p red, *orange* 55.00 50.00
a. 1p red, *yellow* 57.50 55.00
b. Small capital "T" 350.00 200.00
92 A2 3p lilac, *green* 52.50 40.00
a. Small capital "T" 300.00 115.00
93 A2 3p lilac, *blue* 57.50 35.00
a. Small capital "T" 325.00 110.00
Nos. 91-93 (3) 165.00 125.00

Rouletted 15½, 16

94 A1 1p red, *yellow* 400.00 240.00
a. 1p red, *orange* 875.00 450.00
b. Small capital "T" 1,100. 750.00
c. Rouletted 6½ 750.00 750.00
d. Pin perf. 875.00
95 A2 3p lilac, *green* 875.00 300.00
a. Small capital "T" 1,000.
b. Rouletted 6½ 1,150. 750.00
96 A2 3p lilac, *blue* 210.00
a. Small capital "T" 800.00
b. Rouletted 6½ 950.00
c. Pin perf. 1,000.

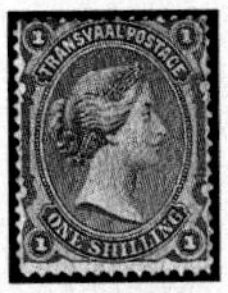

Queen Victoria — A3

1878-80 **Engr.** ***Perf. 14, 14½***

97 A3 ½p vermilion ('80) 30.00 100.00
98 A3 1p red brown 19.00 5.25
99 A3 3p claret 30.00 9.25
100 A3 4p olive green 32.50 9.25
101 A3 6p slate 19.00 6.50
a. Half used as 3p on cover —
102 A3 1sh green 140.00 55.00
103 A3 2sh blue 225.00 95.00
Nos. 97-103 (7) 495.50 280.25

For surcharges see Nos. 104-118, 138-139.

No. 101 Surcharged in Red or Black

(a) Surcharged

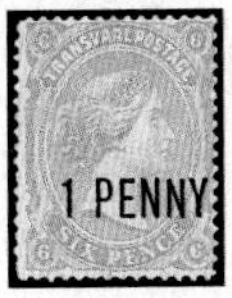

Surcharge distinction: "PENNY" in gothic capitals.

1879

104 A3 1p on 6p slate (R) 200.00 95.00
105 A3 1p on 6p slate (Bk) 55.00 27.50

(b) Surcharged

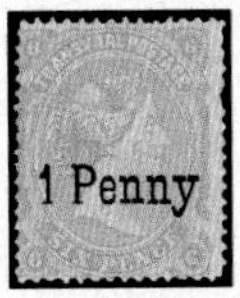

Surcharge distinction: "1" has heavy serif at base; "P," thin serif at base.

106 A3 1p on 6p slate (R) 750.00 400.00
107 A3 1p on 6p slate (Bk) 275.00 95.00

(c) Surcharged

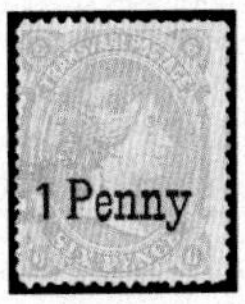

Surcharge distinction: No serif at base of "1."

108 A3 1p on 6p slate (R) 750.00 400.00
109 A3 1p on 6p slate (Bk) 275.00 95.00

(d) Surcharged

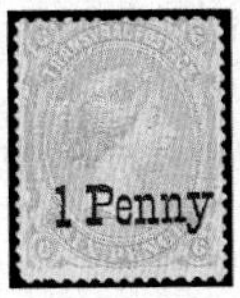

Surcharge distinction: Heavy serifs at base of "1" and "p."

110 A3 1p on 6p slate (R) 375.00 210.00
111 A3 1p on 6p slate (Bk) 110.00 55.00
a. Pair, one without surcharge —

(e) Surcharged

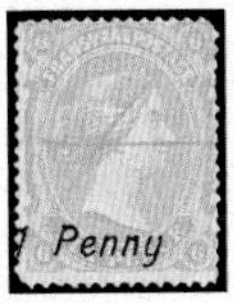

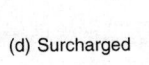

Surcharge distinction: Italics.

112 A3 1p on 6p slate (R) 700.00 375.00
113 A3 1p on 6p slate (Bk) 240.00 87.50

(f) Surcharged

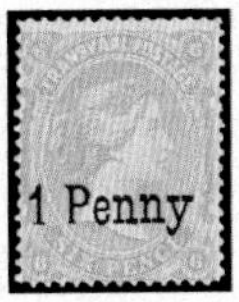

Surcharge distinction: "1" has long, sloping serif at top, thin serif at base.

114 A3 1p on 6p slate (R) 325.00 185.00
115 A3 1p on 6p slate (Bk) 110.00 50.00

(g) Surcharged **1 Penny**

Surcharge distinction: Tail of "y" missing.

116 A3 1p on 6p slate (R) 7,000. 1,850.
117 A3 1p on 6p slate (Bk) 700.00 185.00

Second Republic

No. 100 Surcharged

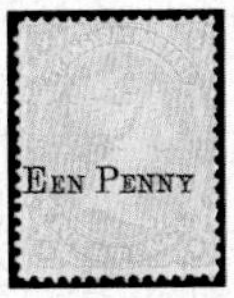

1882 **Unwmk.** ***Perf. 14, 14½***

118 A3 1p on 4p olive grn 20.00 7.00
a. Inverted surcharge 375.00 250.00

1883 ***Perf. 12***

119 A1 1p black 8.00 3.00
a. Imperf. —
b. Vert. pair, imperf. horiz. 650.00 400.00
c. Horiz. pair, imperf. vert. 325.00
120 A2 3p red 17.50 3.50
a. Horiz. pair, imperf. vert. — 1,000.
b. Half used as 1p on cover 750.00
121 A2 3p black, *rose* 32.50 7.50
a. Half used as 1p on cover 750.00
122 A1 1sh green 80.00 7.00
a. Tete beche pair 1,150. 185.00
b. Half used as 6p on cover 550.00
Nos. 119-122 (4) 138.00 21.00

The so-called reprints of this issue are forgeries. They were made from the counterfeit plates described in the note following No. 8, plus a new false plate for the 3p. The false 3p plate has many small flaws and defects.

Forgeries of No. 120 are in dull orange red, clearly printed on whitish paper, and those of No. 121 in brownish or grayish black on bright rose. Genuine examples of No. 120 lack the orange tint and the paper is yellowish; genuine examples of No. 121 are in black without gray or brown shade, on dull lilac rose paper.

A 6p in slate on white, apparently of this issue, is a late print from the counterfeit plate.

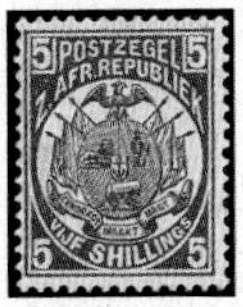

A4

Perf. 13½, 11½x12, 12½, 12½x12

1885-93 **Typo.**

123 A4 ½p gray 1.75 .25
a. Imperf. at top and bottom (used strip of 4) —
124 A4 1p rose 1.20 .25
125 A4 2p brown 3.00 4.00
126 A4 2p olive bis ('87) 2.40 .25
127 A4 2½p purple ('93) 3.50 .65
128 A4 3p violet 3.75 2.50
129 A4 4p bronze green 5.25 1.50
130 A4 6p blue 4.50 3.75
a. Imperf. —
131 A4 1sh green 3.75 1.50
132 A4 2sh6p yellow 14.00 3.75
133 A4 5sh steel blue 10.00 6.50
134 A4 10sh pale brown 40.00 13.00
135 A4 £5 dk grn ('92) 4,000. 225.00
Nos. 123-134 (12) 93.10 37.90

Reprints of Nos. 123-137, 140-163, 166-174 closely resemble the originals. Paper is whiter; perf. 12½, large holes.

Excellent counterfeits of No. 135 exist.

For overprint and surcharges see Nos. 140-147, 163, 213.

Nos. 120, 122 Surcharged

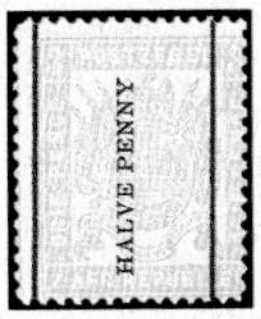

1885 ***Perf. 12***

136 A2 ½p on 3p red 8.75 13.00
a. Surcharge reading down 8.75 13.00
137 A1 ½p on 1sh green 32.50 65.00
a. Surcharge reading down 32.50 65.00
b. Tete beche pair 1,000. 450.00

Almost all examples of No. 137b have telegraph cancellations. Postally used examples are rare.

Nos. 101, 128 Surcharged in Red or Black

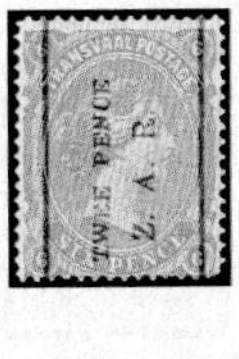

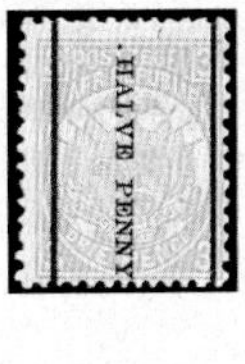

Perf. 14

138 A3 ½p on 6p slate 85.00 115.00
139 A3 2p on 6p slate 11.00 17.50
a. Horiz. pair, imperf. vert. —

Perf. 11½x12, 12½x12

140 A4 ½p on 3p vio (Bk) 7.50 7.50
a. "PRNNY" 55.00 75.00
b. 2nd "N" of "PENNY" invtd. 105.00 115.00

No. 128 Surcharged

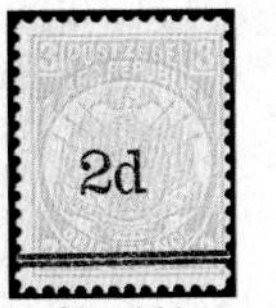

No. 141

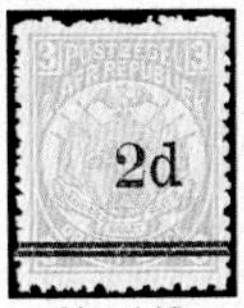

No. 142

1887

141 A4 2p on 3p violet 2.40 5.00
a. Double surcharge 210.00 210.00
142 A4 2p on 3p violet 11.50 10.50
a. Double surcharge — 400.00

Nos. 126, 130, 131 Surcharged

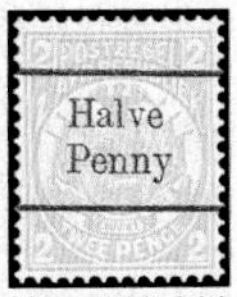

Nos. 143-144

Nos. 145-146

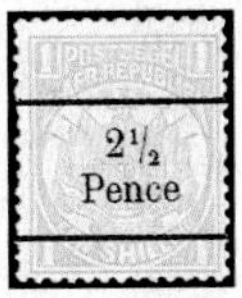

No. 147

1893 **Red Surcharge**

143 A4 ½p on 2p olive bis .90 3.00
a. Inverted surcharge 3.00 3.50
b. Bars 14mm apart 1.75 3.75
c. As "b," inverted 5.75 11.50

Black Surcharge

144 A4 ½p on 2p olive bis 1.00 3.00
a. Inverted surcharge 5.25 5.75
b. Bars 14mm apart 1.75 3.75
c. As "b," inverted 23.00 18.50
145 A4 1p on 6p blue 2.00 2.00
a. Inverted surcharge 2.60 3.00
b. Double surcharge 65.00 52.50
c. Pair, one without surcharge 260.00
d. Bars 14mm apart 3.00 3.00
e. As "d," inverted 6.50 5.25
f. As "d," double 95.00
146 A4 2½p on 1sh green 2.60 6.25
a. Inverted surcharge 8.00 8.50
b. Fraction line misplaced "2/12" 50.00 87.50
c. As "b," inverted 400.00 350.00
d. Bars 14mm apart 3.75 8.75
e. As "d," inverted 11.00 21.00
147 A4 2½p on 1sh green 8.00 7.00
a. Inverted surcharge 10.00 10.00
b. Bars 14mm apart 13.00 13.00
c. As "b," inverted 24.00 24.00
d. Double surcharge 92.50 105.00
Nos. 143-147 (5) 14.50 21.25

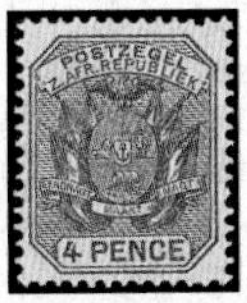

A13

Wagon with Two Shafts

1894 **Typo.** ***Perf. 12½***

148 A13 ½p gray 1.50 .90
149 A13 1p rose 2.40 .25
150 A13 2p olive bister 2.40 .25
151 A13 6p blue 3.25 .60
152 A13 1sh yellow grn 17.50 22.00
Nos. 148-152 (5) 27.05 24.00

Counterfeits of Nos.148-152 are plentiful.
See note following No. 135 for reprints.

1895-96 **Wagon with Pole**

153 A13 ½p gray 1.50 .25
154 A13 1p rose 1.50 .25
155 A13 2p olive bister 1.75 .35
156 A13 3p violet 3.00 1.00
157 A13 4p slate 3.50 1.00
158 A13 6p blue 3.50 1.00
159 A13 1sh green 4.00 1.75
160 A13 5sh slate blue ('96) 20.00 35.00
161 A13 10sh red brown ('96) 20.00 8.00
Nos. 153-161 (9) 58.75 48.60

Most of the unused examples of Nos. 153-161 now on the market are reprints.

See Nos. 166-174. For surcharge see No. 162.

See note following No. 135 for reprints.

Nos. 159, 127 Surcharged in Red or Green

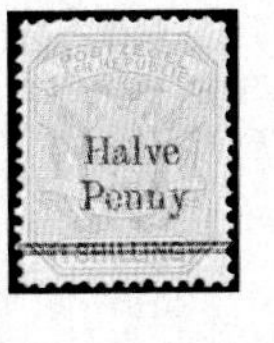

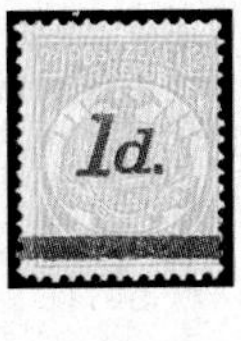

1895

162 A13 ½p on 1sh green (R) 1.75 .25
a. Inverted surcharge 5.25 5.25
b. "Pennij" instead of "Penny" 70.00 80.00
c. Double surcharge 75.00 105.00

163 A4 1p on 2½p pur (G) .60 .30
a. Inverted surcharge 20.00 20.00
b. Surcharge sideways — —
c. Surcharge on back 4,000.
d. Space between "1" and "d" 1.50 *1.75*

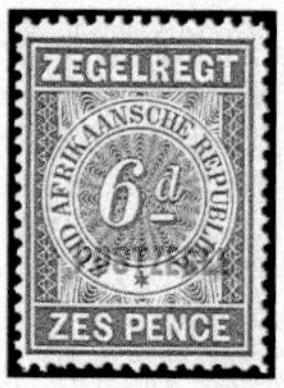

A16

1895 ***Perf. 11½***
164 A16 6p rose (G) 2.40 2.60
a. Vertical pair, imperf. between —

Counterfeits of No. 164 are on the 6p dark red revenue stamp of 1898, and have a shiny green ink for the overprint. The false overprint is also found on other revenue denominations, though only the 6p rose was converted to postal use.

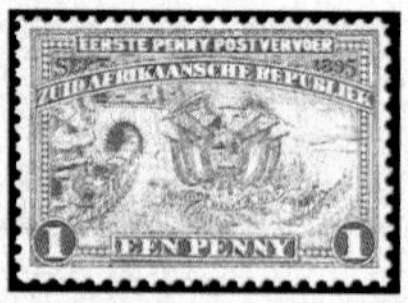

Coat of Arms, Wheat Field and Railroad Train — A17

1895, Sept. 6 **Litho.**
165 A17 1p red 2.40 *2.60*
a. Imperf. —
b. Vertical pair, imperf. between 150.00 *160.00*

Penny Postage in Transvaal. Horiz. pair, imperf. between also exists.
For overprint see No. 245.

Arms Type of 1894 With Pole

1896 **Typo.** ***Perf. 12½***
166 A13 ½p green 1.20 .25
167 A13 1p rose & grn 1.20 .25
168 A13 2p brown & grn 1.20 .25
169 A13 2½p ultra & grn 2.40 .25
170 A13 3p red vio & grn 3.00 3.00
171 A13 4p olive & grn 3.00 *3.50*
172 A13 6p violet & grn 2.00 2.00
173 A13 1sh bister & grn 2.60 .80
174 A13 2sh6p lilac & grn 3.00 *3.50*
Nos. 166-174 (9) 19.60 13.80

See note following No. 135 for reprints.
For overprints and surcharges see Nos. 202-212, 214-235, 237-244, 246-251, Cape of Good Hope Nos. N5-N8.

Pietersburg Issue

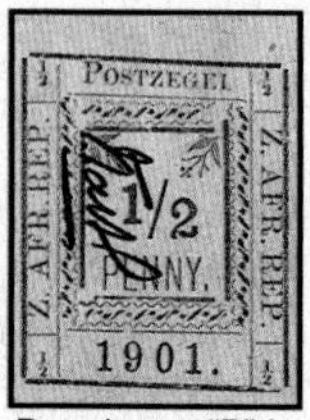

Date large; "P" in Postzegel large — A18

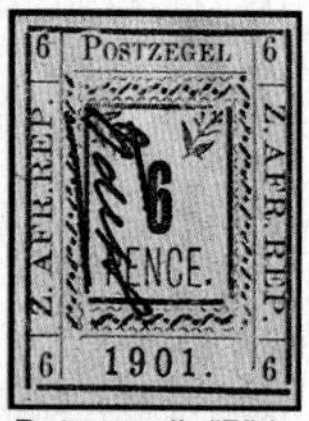

Date small; "P" in Postzegel large — A19

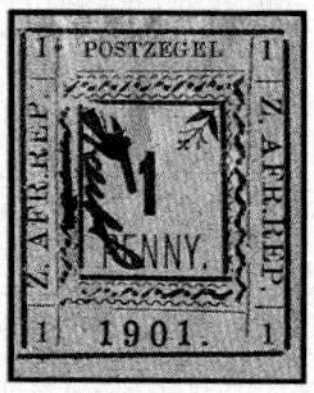

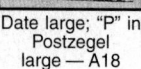

Date small; "P" in Postzegel small — A20

1901 **Typeset** ***Imperf.***
Initials in Red
175 A18 ½p black, *green* 37.50
a. Initials omitted 125.00
b. Initials in black 45.00
176 A19 ½p black, *green* 50.00
a. Initials omitted 125.00
b. Initials in black 52.50
177 A20 ½p black, *green* 50.00
a. Initials omitted 125.00
b. Initials in black 52.50

Initials in Black
178 A18 1p black, *rose* 5.00
179 A19 1p black, *rose* 6.50
180 A20 1p black, *rose* 8.00
181 A18 2p black, *orange* 7.50
182 A19 2p black, *orange* 20.00
183 A20 2p black, *orange* 25.00
184 A18 4p black, *dull blue* 12.50
185 A19 4p black, *dull blue* 15.00
186 A20 4p black, *dull blue* 40.00
187 A18 6p black, *green* 16.50
188 A19 6p black, *green* 20.00
189 A20 6p black, *green* 55.00
190 A18 1sh black, *yellow* 12.50
191 A19 1sh black, *yellow* 20.00
192 A20 1sh black, *yellow* 30.00

Perf. 11½
Initials in Red
193 A18 ½p black, *green* 6.50
194 A19 ½p black, *green* 20.00
195 A20 ½p black, *green* 15.00

Initials in Black
196 A18 1p black, *rose* 3.00
a. Horiz. pair, imperf. vert. 65.00
197 A19 1p black, *rose* 3.50
a. Horiz. pair, imperf. vert. 100.00
198 A20 1p black, *rose* 6.50
a. Horiz. pair, imperf. vert. 100.00
199 A18 2p black, *orange* 7.50
200 A19 2p black, *orange* 9.50
201 A20 2p black, *orange* 17.00

Nos. 193-201 inclusive are always imperforate on one side.
The setting consisted of 12 stamps of type A18, 6 of type A19, and 6 of type A20. Numerous type-setting varieties exist. The perforated stamps are from the first printing and were put into use first. Used stamps are not valued because all seem to show evidence of having been canceled to order.

Second British Occupation Issued under Military Authority

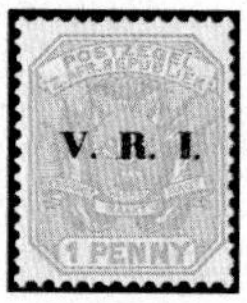

Nos. 166-174, 160-161, 135 Overprinted

1900 **Unwmk.** ***Perf. 12½***
202 A13 ½p green .35 .60
a. "V.I.R." 700.00
203 A13 1p rose & grn .35 .50
204 A13 2p brown & grn 4.00 3.00
a. "V.I.R." 700.00 *750.00*
205 A13 2½p ultra & grn 1.25 *3.00*
206 A13 3p red vio & grn 1.25 *2.60*
207 A13 4p olive & grn 3.75 3.25
a. "V.I.R." 700.00
208 A13 6p violet & grn 3.75 2.00
209 A13 1sh bister & grn 3.75 *4.50*
210 A13 2sh6p hel & grn 4.75 *14.00*
211 A13 5sh slate blue 9.50 20.00
212 A13 10sh red brown 11.50 22.00
213 A4 £5 dark green 2,500. 925.00
Nos. 202-212 (11) 44.20 75.45

Nos. 202-213 have been extensively counterfeited. The overprint on the forgeries is clear and clean, with small periods and letters showing completely. In the genuine, letters are worn and lack many or all serifs; the periods are large and oval.
The genuine overprint exists inverted; double; with period missing after "V," after "R," after "I," etc.

Issued in Lydenburg

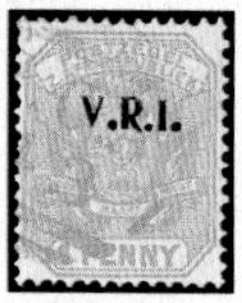

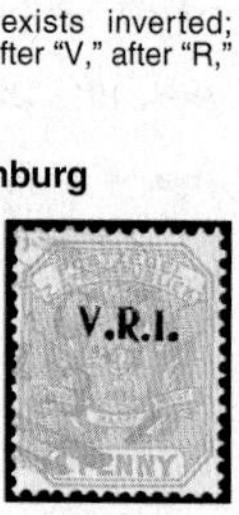

Nos. 166-169, 171-173 Overprinted in Black

1900
214 A13 ½p green 160.00 160.00
215 A13 1p rose & grn 150.00 140.00
216 A13 2p brown & grn 1,400. 1,000.
217 A13 2½p ultra & grn 2,600. 1,050.
218 A13 4p olive & grn 3,750. 1,050.
219 A13 6p violet & grn 3,250. 1,000.
220 A13 1sh bister & grn 5,500. 3,250.

Beware of counterfeits.

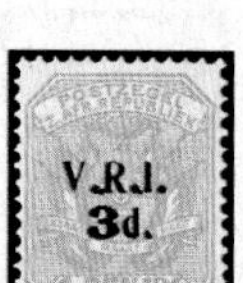

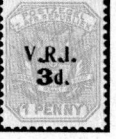

No. 167 Surcharged

221 A13 3p on 1p rose & grn 130.00 110.00

Issued in Rustenburg

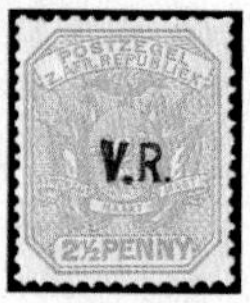

Nos. 166-170, 172-174 Handstamped in Violet

1900 ***Perf. 12½***
223 A13 ½p green 175.00 130.00
224 A13 1p rose & grn 130.00 100.00
225 A13 2p brown & grn 375.00 190.00
226 A13 2½p ultra & grn 210.00 130.00
227 A13 3p red vio & grn 300.00 175.00
229 A13 6p violet & grn 1,400. 500.00
230 A13 1sh bister & grn 2,000. 1,100.
231 A13 2sh6p hel & grn *8,000.*

Issued in Schweizer Reneke
Nos. 166-168 and 172 Handstamped "BESIEGED" in Black

1900 **Typo.** ***Perf. 12½***
232 A13 ½p green 290.00
233 A13 1p rose & green 300.00
234 A13 2p brown & green 450.00
235 A13 6p violet & green 1,150.
Nos. 232-235 (4) 2,190.

Same Overprint on Cape of Good Hope No. 59 and Type of 1893
Perf. 14
236 A15 ½p green 600.00
236A A15 1p carmine 600.00

In 1902 five revenue stamps overprinted "V.R.I." are said to have been used postally in Volksrust. There seems to be some doubt that this issue was properly authorized for postal use.

Issued in Wolmaransstad

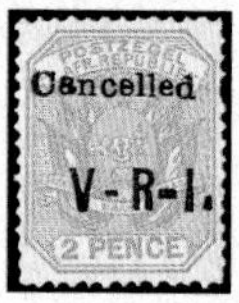

Nos. 166-173 Handstamped in Blue or Red

1900
237 A13 ½p green 290.00 *450.00*
238 A13 1p rose & grn 200.00 *325.00*
239 A13 2p brown & grn 2,100. 2,100.
240 A13 2½p ultra & grn (R) 2,100.
241 A13 3p red vio & grn 3,500. *3,750.*
242 A13 4p olive & grn 4,750. *5,250.*
243 A13 6p violet & grn 5,250. *5,750.*
244 A13 1sh bister & grn *11,000.*

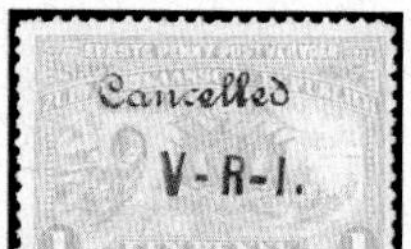

No. 165 Overprinted in Blue

245 A17 1p red 200.00 *350.00*

Regular Issues
No. 166-168, 170-171, 174 Surcharged or Overprinted

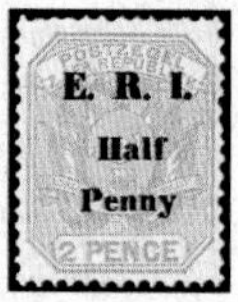

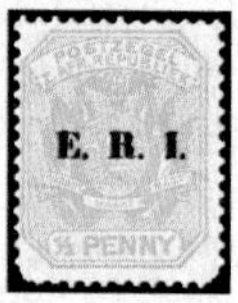

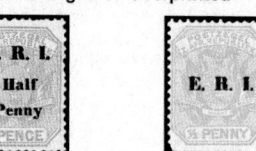

1901-02
246 A13 ½p on 2p brn & grn .80 1.20
247 A13 ½p green .60 *1.75*
248 A13 1p rose & grn .60 .25
a. Overprint "E" omitted 87.50
249 A13 3p red vio & grn 2.60 *4.25*
250 A13 4p olive & grn 2.75 *6.25*
251 A13 2sh6p hel & grn 10.50 *30.00*
Nos. 246-251 (6) 17.85 43.70

Excellent counterfeits of Nos. 246-251 are plentiful. See note after No. 213 for the recognition marks of the counterfeits.

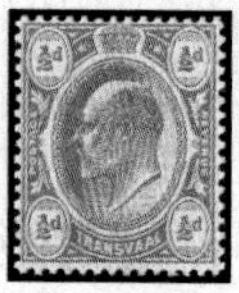

Edward VII — A27

Nos. 260, 262 to 267 and 275 to 280 have "POSTAGE" at each side; the other stamps of type A27 have "REVENUE" at the right.

Wmk. Crown and C A (2)

1902-03 **Typo.** ***Perf. 14***
252 A27 ½p gray grn & blk 2.00 .25
253 A27 1p rose & blk 1.50 .25
254 A27 2p violet & blk 5.00 1.20
255 A27 2½p ultra & blk 11.50 1.50
256 A27 3p ol grn & blk 10.50 1.00
257 A27 4p choc & blk 10.50 2.00
258 A27 6p brn org & blk 5.00 1.20
259 A27 1sh ol grn & blk 16.50 *20.00*
260 A27 1sh red brn & blk 15.00 5.00
261 A27 2sh brown & blk 60.00 *70.00*
262 A27 2sh yel & blk 17.50 *18.50*
263 A27 2sh6p black & vio 18.50 17.50
264 A27 5sh vio & blk, *yel* 35.00 *45.00*
265 A27 10sh vio & blk, *red* 75.00 47.50
266 A27 £1 violet & grn 325.00 190.00
267 A27 £5 violet & org 1,650. 750.00
Nos. 252-266 (15) 608.50 420.90

Issue dates: 3p, 4p, Nos. 260, 262, £1, £5, 1903. Others, Apr. 1, 1902.

1904-09 **Wmk. 3**
268 A27 ½p gray grn & blk 10.50 3.50
269 A27 1p rose & blk 8.00 1.20
270 A27 2p violet & blk 15.00 2.40
271 A27 2½p ultra & blk 22.00 10.00
272 A27 3p ol grn & blk 4.00 .60
273 A27 4p choc & blk 5.50 .80
274 A27 6p brn org & blk 13.00 2.40
275 A27 1sh red brn & blk 10.50 .60
276 A27 2sh yellow & blk 27.50 10.50
277 A27 2sh6p blk & red vio 55.00 10.00
278 A27 5sh vio & blk, *yel* 29.00 1.75
279 A27 10sh vio & blk, *red* 80.00 3.50
280 A27 £1 violet & grn 350.00 40.00
Nos. 268-280 (13) 630.00 87.25

The 2p and 3p are on chalky paper, the 2½p, 4p, 6p and £1 on both chalky and ordinary, and the other values on ordinary paper only.
Issue years: ½p, 1p, 5sh, 1904. 2½p, 6p, 1sh, 1905. 2p, 3p, 4p, 2sh, 1906. 10sh, 1907. £1, 1908. 2sh6p, 1909.

1905-10
281 A27 ½p green 2.75 .25
a. Booklet pane of 6 —
282 A27 1p carmine 1.50 .25
a. Wmk. 16 (anchor) ('07) — *375.00*
b. Booklet pane of 6 — —
283 A27 2p dull vio ('10) 4.00 .75
284 A27 2½p ultra ('10) 20.00 10.00
Nos. 281-284 (4) 28.25 11.25

Wmk. 16 is illustrated in the Cape of Good Hope.
Some of the above stamps are found with the overprint "C. S. A. R." for use by the Central South African Railway, the control mark being applied after the stamps had left the post office.

POSTAGE DUE STAMPS

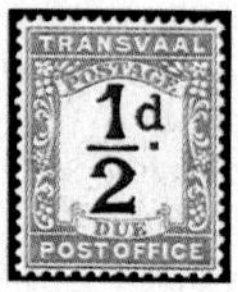

D1

Wmk. Multiple Crown and C A (3)

1907 **Typo.** ***Perf. 14***
J1 D1 ½p green & blk 4.00 1.50
J2 D1 1p carmine & blk 4.75 1.00
J3 D1 2p brown org 5.75 1.50
J4 D1 3p blue & blk 8.75 5.00
J5 D1 5p violet & blk 2.75 *14.00*
J6 D1 6p red brown & blk 5.00 *14.00*
J7 D1 1sh black & car 14.00 10.00
Nos. J1-J7 (7) 45.00 47.00

Most canceled stamps of #J1-J7 were used outside the Transvaal under the Union of South Africa administration in 1910-16.

The stamps of Transvaal were replaced by those of South Africa.

TRINIDAD

ˈtri-nə-ˌdad

LOCATION — West Indies, off the Venezuelan coast
GOVT. — British Colony which became part of the Colony of Trinidad and Tobago in 1889
AREA — 1,864 sq. mi.
POP. — 387,000
CAPITAL — Port of Spain

12 Pence = 1 Shilling
20 Shillings = 1 Pound

In 1847 David Bryce, owner of the "Lady McLeod," issued a blue, lithographed, imperf. stamp to prepay his 5-cent rate for carrying letters on his sail-equipped steamer between Port of Spain and San Fernando, another Trinidad port. The stamp pictures the "Lady McLeod" above the monogram "LMcL," expressing no denomination. Value, unused, $50,000, used (pen canceled), $12,500. Used stamps canceled by having a corner skinned off are worth less.

Values for unused stamps are for examples with original gum as defined in the catalogue introduction. However, Nos. 9-12 are seldom found with gum, and these are valued without gum.

Values for Nos. 18-26 are for stamps with pin perforations on two or three sides. Stamps with pin perforations on all four sides are not often seen and command large premiums.

Very fine examples of Nos. 27-47 will have perforations touching the design on one or more sides due to the narrow spacing of the stamps on the plates and imperfect perforating methods. These stamps with perfs clear of the design on all four sides are scarce and command substantially higher prices.

"Britannia" — A1

1851-56   Unwmk.   Engr.   Imperf.
Blued Paper

1	A1	(1p) brick red ('56)	200.00	85.00
a.		(1p) brown red ('53)	360.00	77.50
2	A1	(1p) purple brown	21.00	90.00
3	A1	(1p) blue	22.00	72.50
a.		(1p) deep blue, deeply blued paper	175.00	95.00

4	A1	(1p) gray brn ('53)	57.50	90.00
a.		(1p) gray ('52)	90.00	77.50
		Nos. 1-4 (4)	300.50	337.50

1854-57   White Paper

6	A1	(1p) brown red ('57)	3,250.	77.50
7	A1	(1p) gray	55.00	95.00
8	A1	(1p) black violet	32.50	100.00

See Nos. 14, 18, 22, 27, 33, 39, 43, 45, 48, 58. For surcharges see Nos. 62-64.

"Britannia" — A2

1852   Litho.
Fine Impressions
Yellowish Paper

9	A2	(1p) blue	11,500.	1,950.
a.		(1p) deep blue	11,500.	1,950.
b.		White paper		1,950.

1853   Bluish Paper

10	A2	(1p) blue	10,000.	2,400.

Same, Lines of Background More or Less Worn

1855-60   Thin Paper

11	A2	(1p) slate blue	5,500.	800.00
12	A2	(1p) blue	5,000.	500.00
a.		(1p) greenish blue		800.00
13	A2	(1p) rose	17.50	750.00
a.		(1p) dull red	17.50	725.00

A3

1859   Engr.   Imperf.
White Paper

14	A1	(1p) dull rose	—	—
15	A3	4p gray lilac	125.00	400.00
a.		4p dull lilac		
16	A3	6p green	15,000.	525.00
17	A3	1sh slate blue	125.00	425.00

Pin-perf. 12½

18	A1	(1p) dull rose red	2,000.	70.00
a.		(1p) lake	2,250.	70.00
19	A3	4p brown lilac		1,250.
a.		4p dull purple	7,500.	1,250.
20	A3	6p deep green	3,500.	250.00
a.		6p yellow green	3,500.	250.00
21	A3	1sh black violet	9,000.	1,750.

Pin-perf. 14

22	A1	(1p) rose red	275.00	35.00
a.		(1p) carmine	325.00	37.50
23	A3	4p brown lilac	250.00	150.00
a.		4p violet	600.00	160.00
b.		4p dull violet	1,650.	125.00
24	A3	6p deep green	800.00	100.00
25	A3	6p yellow green	200.00	160.00
a.		Vert. pair, imperf. between	8,000.	
26	A3	1sh black violet	9,000.	1,150.

1860   Clean-cut Perf. 14 to 15½

27	A1	(1p) dull rose	190.00	67.50
a.		(1p) carmine	100.00	40.00
b.		Horiz. pair, imperf. vert.	3,000.	
29	A3	4p violet brown	200.00	95.00
a.		4p dull violet		375.00
30	A3	6p deep green	300.00	175.00
31	A3	6p yellow green	550.00	110.00
32	A3	1sh black violet		

1861   Rough Perf. 14 to 16½

33	A1	(1p) dull rose	170.00	32.50
34	A3	4p gray lilac	750.00	100.00
35	A3	4p brown lilac	325.00	85.00
a.		4p dull violet	750.00	115.00

36	A3	6p green	475.00	85.00
37	A3	1sh indigo	1,000.	350.00
a.		1sh purplish blue	1,675.	550.00

Thick Paper

1863   Perf. 11½ to 12

39	A1	(1p) carmine	160.00	25.00
a.		Perf. 11½-12x11	2,000.	600.00
40	A3	4p dull violet	225.00	72.50
41	A3	6p dp blue green	1,350.	100.00
a.		Perf. 11½-12x11		8,000.
42	A3	1sh indigo	2,750.	110.00

Perf. 12½

43	A1	(1p) lake	60.00	25.00

Perf. 13

45	A1	(1p) lake	50.00	25.00
46	A3	6p emerald	500.00	60.00
47	A3	1sh brt violet	4,500.	300.00

1864-72   Wmk. 1   Perf. 12½

48	A1	(1p) red	65.00	3.50
a.		(1p) lake	65.00	7.25
b.		(1p) rose	65.00	3.00
c.		(1p) carmine	70.00	3.75
d.		Imperf., pair	800.00	800.00
49	A3	4p brt violet	150.00	18.00
a.		4p pale violet	250.00	21.00
b.		Imperf.	600.00	
50	A3	4p lilac	200.00	21.00
a.		4p gray lilac		
51	A3	4p gray ('72)	160.00	7.50
52	A3	6p blue green	175.00	9.00
a.		6p emerald	110.00	17.50
53	A3	6p yellow grn	100.00	6.00
a.		6p dp grn	500.00	9.00
b.		Imperf., pair	800.00	
54	A3	1sh purple	200.00	10.00
a.		1sh lilac	150.00	10.00
b.		1sh violet	150.00	10.00
c.		1sh red lilac	160.00	11.00
d.		Imperf.	750.00	
55	A3	1sh orange yel ('72)	175.00	2.00
		Nos. 48-55 (8)	1,225.	77.00

See Nos. 59-61A, 65. For surcharge see No. 67.

Queen Victoria — A4

1869-94   Typo.   Perf. 12½

56	A4	5sh dull lake	200.00	90.00
a.		Imperf., pair	1,250.	

Perf. 14

57	A4	5sh claret ('94)	67.50	100.00

For overprint see No. O7.

1876   Engr.   Perf. 14

58	A1	(1p) carmine	45.00	2.75
a.		(1p) red	60.00	2.75
b.		(1p) lake	45.00	2.75
c.		Half used as ½p on cover		750.00
59	A3	4p gray	140.00	1.75
60	A3	6p yellow green	120.00	4.00
a.		6p deep green	150.00	3.00
61	A3	1sh orange yellow	150.00	4.50
		Nos. 58-61 (4)	455.00	13.00

Perf. 14x12½

61A	A3	6p yellow green		6,750.

Value for No. 61A is for stamp with perfs barely touching the design.

Type A1 Surcharged in Black

1879   Wmk. 1   Perf. 14

62	A1	½p lilac	18.00	11.00

Same Surcharge

1882   Wmk. Crown and C A (2)

63	A1	½p lilac	250.00	90.00
64	A1	1p carmine	65.00	20.00
a.		Half used as ½p on cover		675.00

Type of 1859

1882   Wmk. 2

65	A3	4p gray	215.00	13.00

No. 60 Surcharged by pen and ink in Black or Red

1882   Wmk. 1

67	A3	1p on 6p green (R)	14.00	8.00
a.		Half used as ½p on cover		400.00
b.		Black surcharge		1,900.

Counterfeits of No. 67b are plentiful. Various handwriting exists on both 60 and 60a.

A7

1883-84   Typo.   Wmk. 2

68	A7	½p green	9.50	1.50
69	A7	1p rose	20.00	.60
a.		Half used as ½p on cover		950.00
70	A7	2½p ultra	25.00	.70
a.		2½p blue	22.50	.75
71	A7	4p slate	4.00	.70
72	A7	6p olive brn ('84)	7.00	6.50
73	A7	1sh orange brn ('84)	12.00	5.50
		Nos. 68-73 (6)	77.50	15.50

For overprints see Nos. O1-O6.

A8    A9

ONE   ONE
Type I   Type II

ONE PENNY:
Type I — Round "O" in "ONE."
Type II — Oval "O" in "ONE."

1896-1904 *Perf. 14*

74	A8	½p lilac & green	4.00	.35
75	A8	½p gray grn ('02)	1.00	2.40
76	A8	1p lil & car, type I	4.25	.25
77	A8	1p lil & car, type II ('00)	400.00	4.75
78	A8	1p blk, *red*, type II ('01)	3.50	.25
a.		Value omitted	36,000.	
79	A8	2½p lilac & ultra	7.25	.25
80	A8	2½p vio & bl, *bl* ('02)	22.50	.75
81	A8	4p lilac & orange	7.75	22.50
82	A8	4p grn & ultra, *buff* ('02)	2.25	21.00
83	A8	5p lilac & violet	9.50	16.00
84	A8	6p lilac & black	9.00	6.50
85	A8	1sh grn & org brn	8.25	7.75
86	A8	1sh blk & bl, *yel* ('04)	22.50	6.50

Wmk. C A over Crown (46)

87	A9	5sh green & org	55.00	90.00
88	A9	5sh lil & red vio ('02)	60.00	77.50
89	A9	10sh grn & ultra	250.00	425.00
		Revenue cancel		30.00
90	A9	£1 grn & car	180.00	275.00
		Nos. 74-90 (17)	1,046.	956.75

No. 82 also exists on chalky paper. Values: unused $3.50, used $14. Nos. 88 and 90 exist on both ordinary and chalky paper.

Circular "Registrar General" cancels are revenue usage and of minimal value.

See Nos. 92-104.

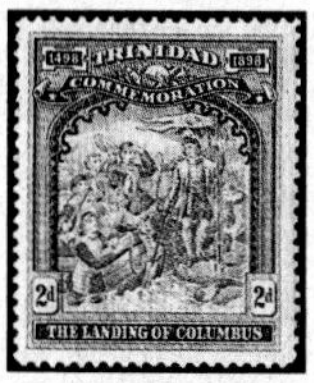

Landing of Columbus — A10

1898 **Engr.** **Wmk. 1**

91	A10	2p gray vio & yel brn	2.50	1.25
		Overprinted "SPECIMEN"	60.00	

400th anniv. of the discovery of the island of Trinidad by Columbus, July 31, 1498.

1904-09 **Wmk. 3** **Chalky Paper**

92	A8	½p gray green	9.00	2.25
a.		Ordinary paper	7.00	1.25
93	A8	1p blk, *red*, type II	11.00	.25
a.		Ordinary paper	11.00	.25
94	A8	2½p vio & bl, *bl*	27.50	1.10
95	A8	4p blk & car, *yel* ('06)	5.00	12.00
96	A8	6p lilac & blk ('05)	21.00	18.00
97	A8	6p vio & dp vio ('06)	8.50	15.00
98	A8	1sh blk & bl, *yel*	24.00	9.50
99	A8	1sh vio & bl, *yel*	14.00	24.00
100	A8	1sh blk, *grn* ('06)	2.25	1.50
101	A9	5sh lil & red vio ('07)	70.00	110.00
102	A9	£1 grn & car ('07)	225.00	300.00
		Nos. 92-102 (11)	417.25	493.60

For overprints see Nos. O8-O9.

1906-07

103	A8	1p carmine ('07)	9.50	.25
104	A8	2½p ultramarine	7.00	.25

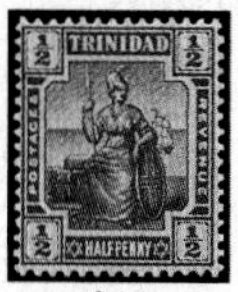

A11

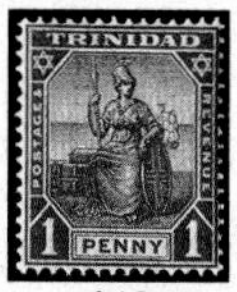

A12

1909 **Ordinary Paper**

105	A11	½p gray green	9.00	.25
106	A12	1p carmine	9.00	.25
107	A11	2½p ultramarine	24.00	3.75
		Nos. 105-107 (3)	42.00	4.25

For overprint see No. O10.

POSTAGE DUE STAMPS

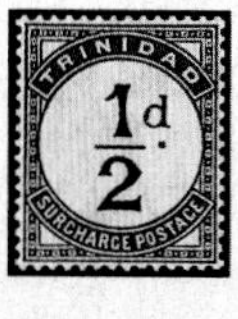

D1

Wmk. Crown and C A (2)

1885, Jan. 1 **Typo.** *Perf. 14*

J1	D1	½p black	22.50	55.00
J2	D1	1p black	11.00	.25
J3	D1	2p black	42.50	.25
J4	D1	3p black	60.00	.50
J5	D1	4p black	50.00	6.00
J6	D1	5p black	27.50	.70
J7	D1	6p black	47.50	10.00
J8	D1	8p black	65.00	4.00
J9	D1	1sh black	80.00	9.00
		Nos. J1-J9 (9)	406.00	85.70

1906-07 **Wmk. 3**

J10	D1	1p black	8.00	.25
J11	D1	2p black	37.50	.25
J12	D1	3p black	15.00	3.25
J13	D1	4p black	15.00	19.00
J14	D1	5p black	17.50	19.00
J15	D1	6p black	7.25	14.00
J16	D1	8p black	16.00	18.00
J17	D1	1sh black	22.50	42.50
		Nos. J10-J17 (8)	138.75	116.25

See Trinidad and Tobago Nos. J1-J16.

OFFICIAL STAMPS

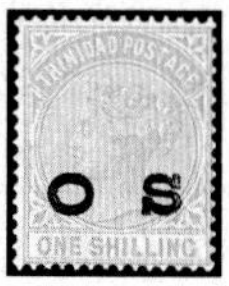

Postage Stamps of 1869-84 Overprinted in Black

1893-94 **Wmk. 2** *Perf. 14*

O1	A7	½p green	42.50	65.00
O2	A7	1p rose	45.00	72.50
O3	A7	2½p ultra	55.00	110.00
O4	A7	4p slate	57.50	115.00
O5	A7	6p olive brown	57.50	115.00
O6	A7	1sh orange brown	77.50	160.00

Wmk. Crown and C C (1)

Perf. 12½

O7	A4	5sh dull lake	190.00	750.00
		Nos. O1-O7 (7)	525.00	1,387.

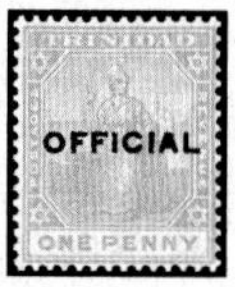

Nos. 92 and 103 Overprinted

1909-10 **Wmk. 3** *Perf. 14*

O8	A8	½p gray green	2.75	9.00
O9	A8	1p carmine	2.50	10.00
a.		Double overprint		375.00
b.		Inverted overprint	900.00	275.00
c.		Vertical overprint	140.00	160.00

Same Overprint on No. 105

1910

O10	A11	½p gray green	9.50	13.50

Stamps of Trinidad have been superseded by those inscribed "Trinidad and Tobago."

TRINIDAD & TOBAGO

'tri-nə-ˌdad and tə-'bā-ˌgō

LOCATION — West Indies off the coast of Venezuela
GOVT. — Republic
AREA — 1,980 sq. mi.
POP. — 1,102,096 (1999 est.)
CAPITAL — Port-of-Spain

The two British colonies of Trinidad and Tobago were united from 1889 until 1899, when Tobago became a ward of the united colony. From 1899 until 1913 postage stamps of Trinidad were used. The two islands became a state in August 1962, and the independent Republic of Trinidad and Tobago on August 1, 1976.

12 Pence = 1 Shilling
20 Shillings = 1 Pound
100 Cents = 1 Dollar (1935)

Catalogue values for unused stamps in this country are for Never Hinged items, beginning with Scott 62 in the regular postage section and Scott J9 in the postage due section.

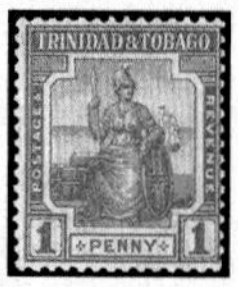

"Britannia" — A1

1913 **Typo.** **Wmk. 3** *Perf. 14*

Ordinary Paper

1	A1	½p green	3.50	.25
2	A1	1p scarlet	1.75	.25
a.		1p carmine	2.75	.25
4	A1	2½p ultra	8.00	.50

Chalky Paper

5	A1	4p scar & blk, *yel*	.80	7.00
6	A1	6p red vio & dull vio	11.00	8.00
7	A1	1sh black, *emerald*	1.75	3.50
a.		1sh black, *green*	2.00	5.00
b.		1sh black, *bl grn*, ol back	13.00	10.00
		Nos. 1-2,4-7 (6)	26.80	19.50

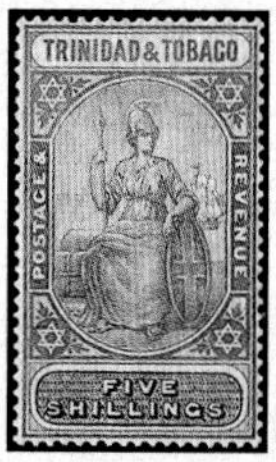

"Britannia" — A2

1914 **Surface-colored Paper**

8	A1	4p scar & blk, *yel*	2.00	11.00
9	A1	1sh black, *green*	1.60	15.00

Chalky Paper

10	A2	5sh dull vio & red vio	75.00	110.00
11	A2	£1 green & car	250.00	300.00
		Nos. 8-11 (4)	328.60	436.00

1921-22 **Ordinary Paper** **Wmk. 4**

12	A1	½p green	3.50	2.75
13	A1	1p scarlet	.75	.40
14	A1	1p brown ('22)	.75	1.90
15	A1	2p gray ('22)	1.25	1.50
16	A1	2½p ultra	1.00	22.50
17	A1	3p ultra ('22)	6.50	4.00

Chalky Paper

18	A1	6p red vio & dull vio	4.25	19.00
19	A2	5sh dull vio & red vio	70.00	170.00
20	A2	£1 green & car	180.00	375.00
		Nos. 12-20 (9)	268.00	597.05

For overprints see #B2-B3, MR1-MR13, O1-O5.

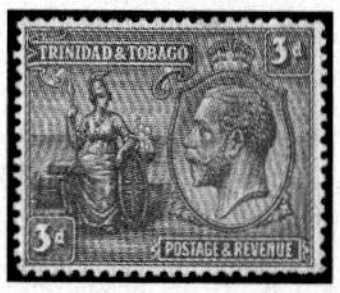

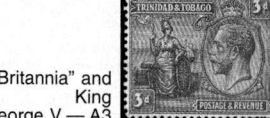

"Britannia" and King George V — A3

1922-28 **Ordinary Paper**

21	A3	½p green	.55	.25
22	A3	1p brown	.55	.25
23	A3	1½p rose red	2.75	.25
24	A3	2p gray	.55	1.40
25	A3	3p ultra	.55	1.40

Chalky Paper

26	A3	4p red & blk, *yel* ('28)	3.75	3.75
27	A3	6p red vio & dl vio	2.50	29.00
28	A3	6p red & grn, *emer* ('24)	1.40	.70
29	A3	1sh blk, *emer* ('25)	6.25	2.00
30	A3	5sh vio & dull vio	26.00	42.50
31	A3	£1 rose & green	150.00	275.00

Wmk. Multiple Crown and C A (3)

Chalky Paper

32	A3	4p red & blk, *yel*	3.75	17.00
33	A3	1sh blk, *emerald*	4.00	11.00
		Nos. 21-33 (13)	202.60	384.50

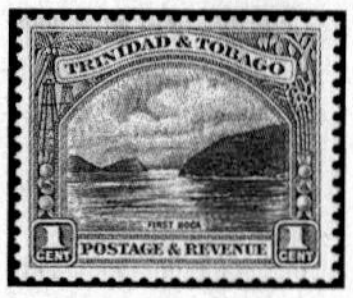

First Boca — A4

Designs: 2c, Agricultural College. 3c, Mt. Irvine Bay, Tobago. 6c, Discovery of Lake Asphalt. 8c, Queen's Park, Savannah. 12c, Town Hall, San Fernando. 24c, Government House. 48c, Memorial Park. 72c, Blue Basin.

1935-37 **Engr.** **Wmk. 4** *Perf. 12*

34	A4	1c emer & bl, perf. 12½ ('36)	.40	.25
a.		Perf. 12	.50	1.10
35	A4	2c lt brn & ultra, perf. 12	2.00	1.25
a.		Perf. 12½ ('36)	1.75	.25
36	A4	3c red & blk, perf. 12½ ('36)	3.25	.40
a.		Perf. 12	2.75	.40
37	A4	6c bl & brn, perf. 12	5.00	3.00
a.		Perf. 12½ ('37)	13.00	7.50
38	A4	8c red org & yel grn	4.50	4.25
39	A4	12c dk violet & blk	4.00	2.25
a.		Perf. 12½ ('37)	14.00	9.50
40	A4	24c ol grn & blk	8.00	2.75
a.		Perf. 12½ ('37)	22.50	16.00
41	A4	48c slate green	11.00	19.00
42	A4	72c mag & sl grn	40.00	40.00
		Nos. 34-42 (9)	78.15	73.15

Common Design Types pictured following the introduction.

Silver Jubilee Issue

Common Design Type

1935, May 6 *Perf. 11x12*

43	CD301	2c black & ultra	.40	1.00
44	CD301	3c car & blue	.40	2.25
45	CD301	6c ultra & brn	2.00	2.50
46	CD301	24c brn vio & ind	9.50	22.00
		Nos. 43-46 (4)	12.30	27.75
		Set, never hinged	22.00	

Coronation Issue

Common Design Type

1937, May 12 *Perf. 13½x14*

47	CD302	1c deep green	.25	.25
48	CD302	2c yellow brown	.25	.25
49	CD302	8c deep orange	.50	.50
		Nos. 47-49 (3)	1.00	1.00
		Set, never hinged	1.50	

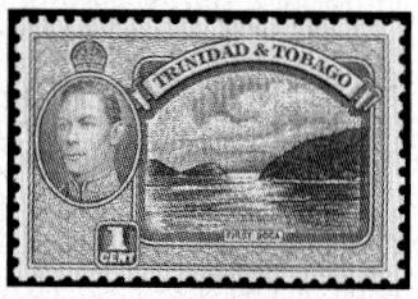

First Boca — A13

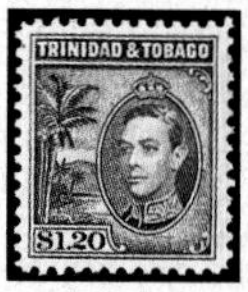

George VI — A14

Various Frames and: 2c, Agricultural College. 3c, Mt. Irvine Bay, Tobago. 4c, Memorial Park. 5c, General Post Office and Treasury. 6c, Discovery of Lake Asphalt. 8c, Queen's Park, Savannah. 12c, Town Hall, San Fernando. 24c, Government House. 60c, Blue Basin.

Perf. 11½x11

1938-41 **Wmk. 4** **Engr.**

50	A13	1c emer & blue	.50	.25
51	A13	2c lt brn & ultra	.60	.25
52	A13	3c dk car & blk	7.50	1.00
52A	A13	3c vio brn & bl grn ('41)	.25	.25
53	A13	4c brown	19.00	2.50
53A	A13	4c red ('41)	.30	.25
54	A13	5c mag ('41)	.30	.25
55	A13	6c brt bl & sep	1.25	.75
56	A13	8c red org & yel grn	1.50	1.00
57	A13	12c dk vio & blk	2.00	.25

58	A13	24c dk ol grn & blk	2.75	.25
59	A13	60c mag & sl grn	7.00	1.75

Perf. 12

60	A14	$1.20 dk grn ('40)	8.50	1.50
61	A14	$4.80 rose pink ('40)	24.00	*50.00*
		Nos. 50-61 (14)	75.45	60.25
		Set, never hinged	125.00	

Watermark sideways on Nos. 50-59.

Catalogue values for unused stamps in this section, from this point to the end of the section, are for Never Hinged items.

Peace Issue
Common Design Type
Perf. 13½x14

1946, Oct. 1		Engr.	Wmk. 4
62	CD303	3c brown	.25 .25
63	CD303	6c deep blue	.25 .25

Silver Wedding Issue
Common Design Types

1948, Nov. 22	Photo.	Perf. 14x14½
64	CD304	3c red brown	.25 .25

Perf. 11½x11
Engr.

65	CD305	$4.80 rose car	32.50 38.00

UPU Issue
Common Design Types
Engr.; Name Typo. on 6c, 12c
Perf. 13½, 11x11½

1949, Oct. 10			Wmk. 4
66	CD306	5c red violet	.35 .35
67	CD307	6c indigo	1.90 1.90
68	CD308	12c rose violet	.45 .45
69	CD309	24c olive	.45 .45
		Nos. 66-69 (4)	3.15 3.15

University Issue
Common Design Types
Inscribed: "Trinidad"

1951, Feb. 16	Engr.	Perf. 14x14½
70	CD310	3c choc & grn	.25 .25
71	CD311	12c purple & blk	.50 .50

Types of 1938 with Portrait of Queen Elizabeth II

1953, Apr. 20			Perf. 11½x11
72	A13	1c yel grn & dp blue	.25 .25
73	A13	2c org brn & sl blue	.25 .25
74	A13	3c vio brn & blue grn	.25 .25
75	A13	4c red	.25 .25
76	A13	5c magenta	.25 .25
77	A13	6c blue & brown	.55 .35
78	A13	8c red org & dp grn	2.50 .35
79	A13	12c dk violet & blk	.35 .25
80	A13	24c dk ol grn & blk	2.50 .35
81	A13	60c rose car & grnsh blk	25.00 1.25

Perf. 11½

82	A14	$1.20 dark green	1.40 .65
a.		Perf. 12	2.50 1.00
83	A14	$4.80 rose pink	9.00 *19.00*
a.		Perf. 12	12.00 *17.00*
		Nos. 72-83 (12)	42.55 23.45

For surcharge see No. 85.

Coronation Issue
Common Design Type

1953, June 3	Perf. 13½x13
84	CD312	3c dark green & blk	.25 .25

No. 73 Surcharged "ONE CENT"
Perf. 11½x11

1956, Dec. 20			Wmk. 4
85	A13	1c on 2c org brn & sl blue	1.60 *1.75*

West Indies Federation
Common Design Type
Perf. 11½x11

1958, Apr. 22	Engr.	Wmk. 314
86	CD313	5c green	.25 .25
87	CD313	6c blue	.25 *.40*
88	CD313	12c carmine rose	.25 .25
		Nos. 86-88 (3)	.75 .90

Cipriani Memorial, Port-of-Spain
A27

Queen's Hall, Port-of-Spain
A28

Designs: 5c, Whitehall. 6c, Treasury Building. 8c, Governor General's House. 10c, General Hospital, San Fernando. 12c, Oil refinery. 15c, Crest of colony. 25c, Scarlet ibis. 35c, Lake Asphalt (Pitch). 50c, Jinnah Memorial Mosque. 60c, Anthurium lilies. $1.20, Copper-rumped hummingbird and hibiscus. $4.80, Map.

Perf. 13½x14, 14x13½

1960, Sept. 24	Photo.	Wmk. 314

Size: 22½x25mm, 25x22½mm

89	A27	1c dark gray & buff	.25 .25
a.		Wmkd. sideways ('66)	.50 .50
90	A28	2c ultra	.25 .25
91	A28	5c dark blue	.25 .25
92	A28	6c lt red brown	.25 .25
93	A28	8c yellow green	.25 *.35*
94	A28	10c light purple	.25 .25
95	A28	12c bright red	.25 .25
96	A28	15c orange	2.75 .90
97	A28	25c dk blue & crim	.90 .25
98	A28	35c green & black	4.00 .25
99	A28	50c blue, yel & olive	.40 *1.00*
100	A27	60c multicolored	.55 .25
a.		Perf. 14 ('65)	185.00 40.00

Size: 48x25mm

101	A28	$1.20 multicolored	17.50 4.00
102	A28	$4.80 lt bl & lt yel grn	27.50 17.50
		Nos. 89-102 (14)	55.35 26.00

See #116. For overprints see #123-124, 126.

Scouts and Map of Trinidad and Tobago — A29

1961, Apr. 4		Perf. 13½x14
103	A29	8c multicolored	.25 .25
104	A29	25c multicolored	.30 .30

2nd Caribbean Scout Jamboree, Valsayn Park, Trinidad, Apr. 4-14.

Independent State

Underwater Scene from Painting by Carlisle Chang — A30

Designs: 8c, Elizabeth II and new Terminal Building, Piarco Airport. 25c, Elizabeth II and Hilton Hotel. 35c, Map and greater bird of paradise. 60c, Map and scarlet ibis.

1962, Aug. 31	Photo.	Perf. 14½
105	A30	5c blue green	.25 .25
106	A30	8c slate	.45 .60
107	A30	25c purple	.30 .25
108	A30	35c emer, yel, brn & blk	2.75 .25
109	A30	60c ultra, black & ver	3.50 *3.50*
		Nos. 105-109 (5)	7.25 4.85

Issued to mark Trinidad and Tobago's independence, Aug. 31, 1962.

Freedom from Hunger Issue

Protein Food — A31

1963, June 1		Perf. 14x13½
110	A31	5c henna brown	.25 .25
111	A31	8c citron	.25 .25
112	A31	25c violet blue	.50 .50
		Nos. 110-112 (3)	1.00 1.00

See note in Common Design section.

Girl Guide Emblem
A32

Perf. 14½x14

1964, Sept. 15		Wmk. 314
113	A32	6c red, dk blue & yel	.25 .25
114	A32	25c brt blue, dk bl & yel	.25 .25
115	A32	35c lt green, dk bl & yel	.30 .30
		Nos. 113-115 (3)	.80 .80

50th anniv. of the Trinidad and Tobago Girl Guide Association.

Arms of Independent State — A33

1964, Sept. 15	Perf. 14x13½
116	A33	15c orange	.40 .40

For overprint see No. 125.

ICY Emblem A34

Unwmk.

1965, Nov. 15	Litho.	Perf. 12
	Granite Paper	
117	A34	35c dull yel, red brn & grn	.70 .70

International Cooperation Year, 1965.

Eleanor Roosevelt — A35

Perf. 13½x14

1965, Dec. 10		Wmk. 314
118	A35	25c vio blue, red & blk	.40 .40

Issued to honor Eleanor Roosevelt and to publicize the Eleanor Roosevelt Memorial Foundation.

"Redhouse," Parliament Building — A36

8c, Map of Trinidad & Tobago, royal yacht "Britannia," arms of State. 25c, Flag, map. 35c, Flag, Trinity Hills, General Post Office, sugar cane, coconut palms, derricks.

1966, Feb. 8	Photo.	Wmk. 314
119	A36	5c ultra, red, blk & grn	.80 .25
120	A36	8c ultra, sil, blk & yel brn	2.25 .30
121	A36	25c red, blk & emerald	2.25 1.25
122	A36	35c ultra, red, blk & grn	2.25 1.50
		Nos. 119-122 (4)	7.55 3.30

Visit of Elizabeth II and Prince Philip.

Nos. 93, 94, 116 and 100 Overprinted "FIFTH YEAR OF / INDEPENDENCE / 31st AUGUST 1967"
Perf. 14x13½, 13½x14

1967, Aug. 31	Photo.	Wmk. 314
123	A28	8c yellow green	.25 .25
124	A28	10c lt purple	.25 .25
125	A32	15c orange	.25 .25
126	A27	60c multicolored	.30 .30
		Nos. 123-126 (4)	1.05 1.05

On 60c, the overprint is arranged in 5 lines.

Carnival Symbols — A37

Designs: 10c, Calypso King, vert. 15c, Steel band. 25c, Chinese masks. 35c, Carnival King, vert. 60c, Carnival Queen, vert.

Unwmk.

1968, Feb. 16	Litho.	Perf. 12
127	A37	5c pink & multi	.25 .25
128	A37	10c vio blue & multi	.25 .25
129	A37	15c multicolored	.25 .25
130	A37	25c multicolored	.25 .25
131	A37	35c dk purple & multi	.25 .25
132	A37	60c brown ol & multi	.45 .45
		Nos. 127-132 (6)	1.70 1.70

Issued to publicize the Trinidad Carnival.

WHO Emblem and Eye Examination — A38

Wmk. 314

1968, May 7	Photo.	Perf. 14
133	A38	5c rose red, gold & blk	.25 .25
134	A38	25c orange, gold & blk	.30 .30
135	A38	35c brt blue, gold & blk	.35 .35
		Nos. 133-135 (3)	.90 .90

Dancing Children and Human Rights Flame — A39

1968, Aug. 5		Perf. 14
136	A39	5c carmine, yel & blk	.25 .25
137	A39	10c brt blue, yel, & blk	.25 .25
138	A39	25c yel grn, yel & blk	.25 .25
		Nos. 136-138 (3)	.75 .75

International Human Rights Year.

Bicycling and Map — A40

Designs (Olympic Rings, Map of Trinidad and Tobago and): 15c, Weight lifting. 25c, Relay race. 35c, Running. $1.20, Map of Mexico and flags of Mexico and Trinidad and Tobago.

Photo.; Gold Impressed (except $1.20)

1968, Oct. 12		Perf. 14
139	A40	5c vio, gold & multi	.25 .25
140	A40	15c red, gold & multi	.25 .25
141	A40	25c org, gold & multi	.25 .25

142	A40	35c brt grn, gold & multi	.35	.25
143	A40	$1.20 blue, gold & multi	1.10	.75
		Nos. 139-143 (5)	2.20	1.75

19th Olympic Games, Mexico City, 10/12-27.

Cacao
A41

Designs: 3c, Sugar refinery. 5c, Redtailed chachalaca. 6c, Oil refinery. 8c, Fertilizer plant. 10c, Green hermit (hummingbird) vert. 12c, Citrus fruit, vert. 15c, Coat of arms, vert. 20c, 25c, Flag and map of islands, vert. 30c, Wild poinsettia, vert. 40c, Scarlet ibis. 50c, Maracas Bay. $1, Blooming tabebuia (tree) vert. $2.50, Fishermen hauling in net. $5, Red House, Port-of-Spain.

Photo.; Silver or Gold Impressed

1969, Apr. 1		Wmk. 314	Perf. 14	
144	A41	1c silver & multi	.25	.25
145	A41	3c gold & multi	.25	.25
a.		Wmk. upright ('74)	.90	.60
146	A41	5c gold & multi	1.00	.25
a.		Wmk. upright ('73)	8.00	4.50
147	A41	6c silver & multi	.25	.25
a.		Wmk. upright ('74)	.75	
148	A41	8c gold & multi	1.00	.25
149	A41	10c gold & multi	1.00	.25
b.		Wmk. 373 ('76)	1.50	.25
150	A41	12c silver & multi	.25	.25
151	A41	15c gold & multi	.25	.25
152	A41	20c gold & multi	.25	.25
153	A41	25c gold & multi	.30	.25
154	A41	30c silver & multi	.35	.25
155	A41	40c gold & multi	.55	.35
156	A41	50c silver & multi	.70	.50
157	A41	$1 gold & multi	1.75	.90
158	A41	$2.50 gold & multi	3.75	4.50
159	A41	$5 gold & multi	7.50	6.00
		Nos. 144-159 (16)	19.40	15.00

For overprint see No. 187.

Capt. A. A.
Cipriani,
ILO
Emblem
and Gate
A42

ILO, 50th Anniv.: 15c, Industrial Court's & ILO emblems, & Woodford Square gate.

Unwmk.

1969, May 1		Photo.	Perf. 12	
160	A42	6c dp car, gold & blk	.25	.25
161	A42	15c brt blue, gold & blk	.25	.25

Union Jack
and Flags
of CARIFTA
Members
A43

Designs: 6c, Cornucopia, vert. 30c, Map of Caribbean, vert. 40c, Jet plane and "Strength through Unity" emblem.

1969, Aug. 1		Perf. 14x13½, 13½x14		
162	A43	6c lilac, gold & multi	.25	.25
163	A43	10c multicolored	.25	.25
164	A43	30c red, emer, blk & gold	.25	.25
165	A43	40c blue, blk, grn & gold	.35	.35
		Nos. 162-165 (4)	1.10	1.10

Caribbean Free Trade Area (CARIFTA).

Moon Landing and Earth — A44

40c, Lunar landing module & astronauts on moon. $1, Astronauts Aldrin at control panel, Armstrong collecting rocks.

1969, Sept. 1		Litho.	Perf. 14	
166	A44	6c multi	.25	.25
167	A44	40c multi, vert.	.30	.30
168	A44	$1 multi	.65	.65
		Nos. 166-168 (3)	1.20	1.20

See note after US No. C76.

Maces of Senate and House of
Representatives — A45

10c, Chamber of Parliament. 15c, View of Kennedy Complex, University of the West Indies at St. Augustine. 40c, Cannon & view of Scarborough from Fort King George.

		Perf. 14x13½		
1969, Oct. 23		**Photo.**	**Wmk. 314**	
169	A45	10c multicolored	.25	.25
170	A45	15c multicolored	.25	.25
171	A45	30c lt blue & multi	.25	.25
172	A45	40c multicolored	.25	.25
		Nos. 169-172 (4)	1.00	1.00

15th Conf. of the Commonwealth Parliamentary Assoc., Port-of-Spain, Oct. 4-19.

Congress Emblem
and
Landscape — A46

6c, Congress emblem (steel drum and bird). 30c, Palms, landscape and emblem, horiz.

		Perf. 14x13½, 13½x14		
1969, Nov. 2		**Litho.**	**Unwmk.**	
173	A46	6c red, black & gold	.25	.25
174	A46	30c lt blue, plum & gold	.25	.25
175	A46	40c ultra, black & gold	.25	.25
		Nos. 173-175 (3)	.75	.75

24th Cong. of the Intl. Junior Chamber of Commerce.

Carnival King as
"Man in the
Moon" — A47

Designs: 6c, Carnival Queen as "City Beneath the Sea." 15c, Bambara god (antelope) from the Band of the Year. 30c, Pheasant Queen (Chanticleer) of Malaya. 40c, Steel Band of the Year with 1969 Calypso and Road March Kings, horiz.

1970, Feb. 2		Wmk. 314	Perf. 14	
176	A47	5c dk brown & multi	.25	.25
177	A47	6c dk blue & multi	.25	.25
178	A47	15c violet bl & multi	.25	.25
179	A47	30c dk green & multi	.25	.25
180	A47	40c green & multi	.25	.25
		Nos. 176-180 (5)	1.25	1.25

Issued to publicize the Trinidad Carnival.

Mahatma
Gandhi and
Indian
Flag — A48

Design: 10c, Gandhi monument, vert.

"Culture,
Science,
Arts and
Technology"
A49

UN, 25th Anniv.: 10c, Children of various races, map of Trinidad and Tobago and "UNICEF." 20c, Noah's ark, rainbow, dove and UN emblem.

		Unwmk.		
1970, Mar. 2		**Photo.**	**Perf. 12**	
181	A48	10c ultra & multi	.60	.50
182	A48	30c crimson & multi	1.40	1.10

Mohandas K. Gandhi (1869-1948), leader in India's fight for independence.

1970, June 26		Photo.	Perf. 13½	
183	A49	5c multicolored	.25	.25
184	A49	10c multicolored	.50	.50
185	A49	20c multicolored	.75	.75
		Nos. 183-185 (3)	1.50	1.50

UPU Headquarters, Bern — A50

1970, June 26		Unwmk.	Perf. 12	
186	A50	30c ultra & multi	.50	.50

Opening of new UPU Headquarters in Bern.

**No. 146 Overprinted "NATIONAL /
COMMERCIAL / BANK /
ESTABLISHED / 1.7.70"**

Photo.; Gold Embossed

1970, July 1		Wmk. 314	Perf. 14	
187	A41	5c gold & multi	.30	.25

San Fernando Town Hall — A51

Designs: 3c, East Indian Immigrants, 1820, after painting by Cazabon, vert. 40c, Ships in San Fernando Harbor, 1860, after painting by Michel J. Cazabon.

		Perf. 14x13½, 13½x14		
1970, Nov.		**Litho.**	**Wmk. 314**	
188	A51	3c bister & multi	.25	.25
189	A51	5c lemon & multi	.25	.25
190	A51	40c lemon & multi	.65	.65
		Nos. 188-190 (3)	1.15	1.15

Municipality of San Fernando, 125th anniv.

Madonna
and Child,
by
Titian — A52

Paintings: 3c, Adoration of the Shepherds, School of Saville. 30c, Adoration of the Shepherds, by Louis Le Nain. 40c, Virgin and Child with St. John and Angel, by Morando. $1, Adoration of the Magi, by Paolo Veronese.

		Perf. 13½		
1970, Dec. 8		**Unwmk.**	**Litho.**	
191	A52	3c dull org & multi	.25	.25
a.		Booklet pane of 2	.20	

192	A52	5c brt pink & multi	.25	.25
a.		Booklet pane of 2	.25	.25
193	A52	30c lt utra & multi	.25	.25
a.		Booklet pane of 2	.60	
194	A52	40c yellow grn & multi	.25	.25
a.		Booklet pane of 2	.75	
b.		Souvenir sheet of 4, #191-194	2.50	2.50
195	A52	$1 pale lilac & multi	.50	.50
		Nos. 191-195 (5)	1.50	1.50

Brocket Deer — A53

		Perf. 14x13½		
1971, Aug. 9		**Litho.**	**Wmk. 314**	
196	A53	3c shown	.35	.25
197	A53	5c Collared peccary	.40	.25
198	A53	6c Paca	.50	.40
199	A53	30c Agouti	1.60	3.00
200	A53	40c Ocelot	1.60	2.25
		Nos. 196-200 (5)	4.45	6.15

Capt. A. A.
Cipriani — A54

Design: 30c, Chaconia medal (for distinction in social field).

1971, Aug. 31			Perf. 14	
201	A54	5c multicolored	.25	.25
202	A54	30c multicolored	.30	.30

9th anniversary of independence. Capt. Arthur Andrew Cipriani (died 1945) was mayor of Port of Spain and member of First Executive Council.

Virgin and Child with
St. John, by
Bartolommeo — A55

Christmas: 5c, Local creche. 10c, Virgin and Child with Sts. Jerome and Dominic, by Filippino Lippi. 15c, Virgin and Child with St. Anne, by Gerolamo dai Libri.

1971, Oct. 25		Litho.	Perf. 14x14½	
203	A55	3c yellow & multi	.25	.25
204	A55	5c dull blue & multi	.25	.25
205	A55	10c red & multi	.25	.25
206	A55	15c orange & multi	.35	.35
		Nos. 203-206 (4)	1.10	1.10

Satellite
Earth
Station,
Matura
A56

Dish Antenna A57

Design: 40c, Satellite over earth (Africa).

1971, Nov. 18   **Perf. 14**

207	A56	10c ultra & multi	.25	.25
208	A57	30c green & multi	.25	.25
209	A57	40c black & multi	.35	.35
a.		Souvenir sheet of 3	2.25	2.25
		Nos. 207-209 (3)	.85	.85

Opening of Satellite Earth Station at Matura. No. 209a contains 3 imperf. stamps with simulated perforations similar to Nos. 207-209.

Morpho Hybrid A58

Butterflies: 5c, Purple mort bleu. 6c, Jaune d'abricot. 10c, Purple king shoemaker. 20c, Southern white pape. 30c, Little jaune.

1972, Feb. 18   **Photo.**   **Wmk. 314**

210	A58	3c olive & multi	1.00	.80
211	A58	5c ocher & multi	1.50	.25
212	A58	6c yellow & multi	1.75	.80
213	A58	10c yel grn & multi	2.00	.30
214	A58	20c lilac & multi	3.00	2.40
215	A58	30c dull grn & multi	4.50	3.00
		Nos. 210-215 (6)	13.75	7.55

S.S. Lady McLeod and Stamp A59

10c, Map of Trinidad and Tobago. 30c, Commemorative inscription.

1972, Apr. 12   **Litho.**   **Perf. 14½x14**

216	A59	5c blue & multi	.25	.25
217	A59	10c blue & multi	.25	.25
218	A59	30c blue & multi	.65	.65
a.		Souvenir sheet of 3, #216-218	1.75	1.75
		Nos. 216-218 (3)	1.15	1.15

125th anniv. of the Lady McLeod stamp.

Trinity Cross — A60

Medals: 10c, Chaconia medal. 20c, Hummingbird medal. 30c, Medal of Merit.

1972, Aug. 28   **Photo.**   **Perf. 13½x13**

219	A60	5c blue & multi	.25	.25
220	A60	10c multicolored	.25	.25
221	A60	20c yellow grn & multi	.25	.30
222	A60	30c brt rose & multi	.25	.40
a.		Souvenir sheet of 4, #219-222	1.25	1.25
		Nos. 219-222 (4)	1.00	1.20

10th anniversary of independence. See Nos. 235-238.

Olympic Rings, Relay Race Medal, 1964 A61

Olympic Rings and: 20c, Bronze medal, 200-meters, 1964. 30c, Bronze medals, weight lifting, 1952. 40c, Silver medal, 400-meters, 1964. 50c, Silver medal, weight lifting, 1948.

1972, Sept. 7   **Litho.**   **Perf. 14**

223	A61	10c yellow & multi	.25	.25
224	A61	20c multicolored	.30	.30
225	A61	30c lilac & multi	.35	.35
226	A61	40c lt blue & multi	.45	.45
227	A61	50c orange & multi	.55	.55
a.		Souv. sheet of #223-227 + label	2.25	2.25
		Nos. 223-227 (5)	1.90	1.90

20th Olympic Games, Munich, 8/26-9/11.

Holy Family, by Titian A62

Christmas: 3c, Adoration of the Kings, by Dosso Dossi. 30c, Like 5c.

1972, Nov. 9   **Photo.**   **Wmk. 314**

228	A62	3c blue & multi	.25	.25
229	A62	5c rose lilac & multi	.25	.25
230	A62	30c lt green & multi	.50	.50
a.		Souvenir sheet of 3, #228-230	2.00	2.00
		Nos. 228-230 (3)	1.00	1.00

ECLA Headquarters, Santiago, Chile — A63

Designs: 20c, INTERPOL emblem. 30c, WMO emblem. 40c, University of West Indies Administration Building.

1973, Aug. 15   **Litho.**   **Wmk. 314**

231	A63	10c orange & multi	.25	.25
232	A63	20c multicolored	.25	.25
233	A63	30c ultra & multi	.35	.35
234	A63	40c lilac & multi	.40	.40
a.		Souvenir sheet of 4, #231-234	1.40	1.40
		Nos. 231-234 (4)	1.25	1.25

Economic Commission for Latin America, 25th anniv. (10c); Intl. Criminal Police Organization, 50th anniv. (20c); Intl. Meteorological cooperation, cent. (30c); Admission of 1st students to the University of West Indies, 25th anniv. (40c).

Medal Type of 1972 Redrawn

Medals: 10c, Trinity Cross. 20c, Medal of Merit. 30c, Chaconia medal. 40c, Hummingbird medal.

1973, Aug. 30   **Photo.**   **Perf. 14½x14**

235	A60	10c dark green & multi	.25	.25
236	A60	20c dark brown & multi	.25	.25
237	A60	30c dark blue & multi	.25	.25
238	A60	40c deep violet & multi	.35	.35
a.		Souv. sheet of 4, #235-238, perf. 14	1.25	1.25
		Nos. 235-238 (4)	1.10	1.10

11th anniv. of independence. "Trinidad and Tobago" in one line on #235-238.

General Post Office, Port of Spain A64

40c, Conference Hall & flags, Chagaramas.

1973, Oct. 8   **Photo.**   **Perf. 14**

239	A64	30c multicolored	.25	.25
240	A64	40c multicolored	.30	.30
a.		Souvenir sheet of 2, #239-240	1.10	1.10

2nd Commonwealth Conf. of Postal Administrations, Trinidad, Oct. 8-20. On #240a the perforations extend through margin and divide map.

Virgin and Child, by Murillo — A65

1973, Oct. 22   **Perf. 14½x14**

241	A65	5c pink & multi	.25	.25
242	A65	$1 lt blue & multi	.65	.65
a.		Souv. sheet, #241-242, perf. 14	1.10	1.10

Christmas 1973.

Post Office and UPU Emblem — A66

UPU, Cent.: 50c, Map of Islands, UPU emblem, means of transportation.

1974, Nov. 18   **Photo.**   **Perf. 13½x14**

243	A66	40c brt purple & multi	.50	.50
244	A66	50c blue gray & multi	.70	.70
a.		Souvenir sheet of 2, #243-244	17.50	17.50

Humming Bird I, Transatlantic Crossing, 1960 — A67

Design: 50c, Globe, Humming Bird II, Harold and Kwailan La Borde.

1974, Dec. 2   **Perf. 14½**

245	A67	40c multicolored	.60	.60
246	A67	50c multicolored	.75	.75
a.		Souvenir sheet of 2, #245-246	3.50	3.50

First anniversary of the voyage around the world by Harold and Kwailan La Borde aboard Humming Bird II, 1969-1973.

"Equality" and IWY Emblem A68

1975, June 23   **Litho.**   **Wmk. 314**

247	A68	15c multicolored	.25	.25
248	A68	30c multicolored	.40	.40

International Women's Year 1975.

Dr. Pawan and Laboratory Equipment — A69

25c, Vampire bat, microscope, syringe, bat's head.

Perf. 14x14½

1975, Sept. 23   **Photo.**   **Wmk. 373**

249	A69	25c yellow & multi	.45	.45
250	A69	30c lt blue & multi	.55	.55

Isolation of rabies virus by Dr. Joseph Lennox Pawan (1887-1957).

Boeing 707, BWIA Emblem, Air Routes A70

Designs: 30c, Boeing 707 on ground. 40c, Boeing 707 in the air.

Wmk. 373

1975, Nov. 27   **Litho.**   **Perf. 14½**

251	A70	20c dark blue & multi	.50	.50
252	A70	30c deep ultra & multi	.65	.65
253	A70	40c dull green & multi	.85	.85
a.		Souvenir sheet of 3, #251-253	2.50	2.50
		Nos. 251-253 (3)	2.00	2.00

British West Indian Airways, 35th anniv.

Land of the Hummingbird Costume — A71

Carnival 1976: $1, Carib Prince riding pink ibis. Designs show prize-winning costumes from 1974 carnival.

1976, Jan. 12   **Photo.**   **Perf. 14½**

254	A71	30c multicolored	.35	.35
255	A71	$1 multicolored	.95	.95
a.		Souvenir sheet of 2, #254-255	1.50	1.50

Angostura Building, Port of Spain A72

Designs (Exposition Medals, obverse and reverse): 35c, New Orleans, 1885-86. 45c, Sydney, 1879. 50c, Brussels, 1897.

1976, July 14   **Litho.**   **Perf. 13**

256	A72	5c bister & multi	.25	.25
257	A72	35c yellow grn & multi	.25	.25
258	A72	45c blue & multi	.25	.25
259	A72	50c violet & multi	.25	.25
a.		Souv. sheet of 4, #256-259, perf. 14	1.10	1.10
		Nos. 256-259 (4)	1.00	1.00

Sesquicentennial of the manufacture of Angostura Bitters.

Map of West Indies, Bats, Wicket and Ball A72a

Prudential Cup — A72b

1976, Oct. 4   **Unwmk.**   **Perf. 14**

260	A72a	35c lt blue & multi	.40	.40
261	A72b	45c lilac rose & blk	.65	.65
a.		Souvenir sheet of 2, #260-261	2.50	2.50

World Cricket Cup, won by West Indies Team, 1975.

Columbus Sailing through the Bocas, by A. Camps-Campins — A73

Paintings: 10c, View, by Jean Michael Cazabon. 20c, Landscape, by Cazabon. 35c, Los Gallos Point, by Cazabon. 45c, Corbeaux Town, by Cazabon.

1976, Nov. 1   Litho.   Wmk. 373
262	A73	5c ocher & multi	.55	.55
263	A73	10c lilac & multi	.55	.55
264	A73	20c green & multi	.55	.55
265	A73	35c red orange & multi	.55	.55
266	A73	45c blue & multi	.65	.65
a.		Souvenir sheet of 5, #262-266	2.50	2.50
		Nos. 262-266 (5)	2.85	2.85

For overprints see Nos. 325, 327.

Hasely Crawford and Gold Medal A74

1977, Jan. 4   Litho.   Perf. 12½
267	A74	25c multicolored	.40	.40
a.		Souvenir sheet of 1	.70	.70

Hasely Crawford, winner of 100-meter dash at Montreal Olympic Games.

Sikorsky S-38 (Lindbergh's Plane) — A75

Designs: 35c, Charles Lindbergh delivering first airmail to Port of Spain, 1927. 45c, Boeing 707, British West Indies Airways. 50c, Boeing 747, British Airways.

1977, Apr.   Wmk. 373   Perf. 13
268	A75	20c lt blue & multi	.30	.30
269	A75	35c lt blue & multi	.55	.55
270	A75	45c lt blue & multi	.65	.65
271	A75	50c lt blue & multi	1.25	1.00
a.		Souv. sheet, #268-271, perf. 14	5.00	5.00
		Nos. 268-271 (4)	2.75	2.50

Airmail to Trinidad & Tobago, 50th anniv.

Trinidad and Tobago Flag — A76

35c, Coat of arms. 45c, Government House.

1977, July 26   Litho.   Perf. 13½x13
272	A76	20c yellow & multi	.40	.40
273	A76	35c red & multi	.70	.70
274	A76	45c lt blue & multi	.90	.90
a.		Souv. sheet, #272-274, perf. 14	2.00	2.00
		Nos. 272-274 (3)	2.00	2.00

Inauguration of the Republic, Aug. 1, 1976.

White Poinsettia — A77

Christmas: 45c, 50c, Red poinsettia.

1977, Oct. 11   Litho.   Perf. 14½
275	A77	10c multicolored	.25	.25
276	A77	35c multicolored	.35	.35
277	A77	45c multicolored	.50	.50
278	A77	50c multicolored	.55	.55
a.		Souvenir sheet of 4, #275-278	1.75	1.75
		Nos. 275-278 (4)	1.65	1.65

Robinson Crusoe Hotel, Tobago A78

15c, Turtle Beach Hotel, Tobago. 25c, Mount Irvine Hotel, Tobago. 70c, Mount Irvine beach, Tobago. $5, Holiday Inn, Trinidad.

Wmk. 373
1978, Jan. 17   Litho.   Perf. 14
279	A78	6c multicolored	.25	.25
280	A78	15c multicolored	.25	.25
281	A78	25c multicolored	.25	.25
282	A78	70c multicolored	.40	.40
283	A78	$5 multicolored	3.00	3.00
a.		Souvenir sheet of 5, #279-283	4.00	4.00
		Nos. 279-283 (5)	4.15	4.15

For overprint see No. 326.

Paphinia Cristata A79

Orchids: 30c, Caularthron bicornutum. 40c, Miltassia. 50c, Oncidium ampiliatum. $2.50, Oncidium papilio.

1978, June 7   Wmk. 373   Perf. 14
284	A79	12c multicolored	.70	.70
285	A79	30c multicolored	.80	.80
286	A79	40c multicolored	1.00	1.00
287	A79	50c multicolored	1.25	1.25
288	A79	$2.50 multicolored	6.25	6.25
a.		Souvenir sheet of 5, #284-288	8.50	8.50
		Nos. 284-288 (5)	10.00	10.00

Miss Universe and Trophy — A80

Designs: 35c, Portrait with crown. 45c, Miss Universe in evening dress.

1978, Aug. 2   Litho.   Perf. 14½
289	A80	10c multicolored	.45	.45
290	A80	35c multicolored	.70	.70
291	A80	45c multicolored	.85	.85
a.		Souvenir sheet of 3, #289-291	1.75	1.75
		Nos. 289-291 (3)	2.00	2.00

Janelle (Penny) Commissiong, Miss Universe, 1977.

Tayra A81

1978, Nov. 7   Perf. 13½x14
292	A81	15c shown	.25	.25
293	A81	25c Ocelot	.30	.30
294	A81	40c Porcupine	.50	.50
295	A81	70c Yellow anteater	1.00	1.00
a.		Souvenir sheet of 4, #292-295	2.25	2.25
		Nos. 292-295 (4)	2.05	2.05

"Burst of Beauty" — A82

Costumes: 10c, Rain worshipper. 35c, Zodiac. 45c, Praying mantis. 50c, Eye of the hurricane. $1, Steel orchestra.

1979, Feb. 1   Litho.   Perf. 13½
296	A82	5c multicolored	.25	.25
297	A82	10c multicolored	.25	.25
298	A82	35c multicolored	.25	.25
299	A82	45c multicolored	.25	.25
300	A82	50c multicolored	.30	.30
301	A82	$1 multicolored	.40	.40
		Nos. 296-301 (6)	1.70	1.70

Day Care Center — A83

IYC Emblem and: 10c, School lunch program. 35c, Dental care. 45c, Nursery school. 50c, Free school bus. $1, Medical care.

Unwmk.
1979, June 5   Litho.   Perf. 13
302	A83	5c multicolored	.25	.25
303	A83	10c multicolored	.25	.25
304	A83	35c multicolored	.25	.25
305	A83	45c multicolored	.25	.25
306	A83	50c multicolored	.30	.30
307	A83	$1 multicolored	.50	.50
a.		Souvenir sheet of 6, #302-307	1.75	1.75
		Nos. 302-307 (6)	1.80	1.80

International Year of the Child.

Geothermal Exploration A84

Designs: 35c, Hydrogeology. 45c, Petroleum exploration. 70c, Preservation of the environment.

1979, July 3   Wmk. 373
308	A84	10c multicolored	.25	.25
309	A84	35c multicolored	.35	.35
310	A84	45c multicolored	.40	.40
311	A84	70c multicolored	.60	.60
a.		Souvenir sheet of 4, #308-311	2.25	2.25
		Nos. 308-311 (4)	1.60	1.60

4th Latin American Geological Cong., July 7-15.

Map of Tobago and Tobago No. 1 — A85

15c, Tobago #2, 7. 35c, Tobago #28, 11. 45c, Tobago #25, 4. 70c, Great Britain #28 used in Scarborough and Tobago #5. $1, General Post Office, Scarborough and Tobago #6.

Perf. 13½x14
1979, Aug. 1   Litho.   Wmk. 373
312	A85	10c multicolored	.25	.25
313	A85	15c multicolored	.25	.25
314	A85	35c multicolored	.25	.25
315	A85	45c multicolored	.30	.30
316	A85	70c multicolored	.35	.35
317	A85	$1 multicolored	.50	.50
a.		Souvenir sheet of 6, #312-317	2.25	2.25
		Nos. 312-317 (6)	1.90	1.90

Centenary of Tobago's postage stamps.

Rowland Hill, Trinidad and Tobago No. 109 — A86

Hill and: 45c, Trinidad and Tobago #273. $1, Trinidad #62, Tobago #10.

1979, Oct. 4   Perf. 13
318	A86	25c multicolored	.25	.25
319	A86	45c multicolored	.35	.35
320	A86	$1 multicolored	.70	.70
a.		Souvenir sheet of 3, #318-320	2.00	2.00
		Nos. 318-320 (3)	1.30	1.30

Sir Rowland Hill (1795-1879), originator of penny postage.

Poui Tree A87

Designs: 10c, Court House. 50c, Royal Train locomotive. $1.50, Bacchante freighter.

Wmk. 373
1980, Jan. 21   Litho.   Perf. 14½
321	A87	5c multicolored	.25	.25
322	A87	10c multicolored	.25	.25
323	A87	50c multicolored	.40	.40
324	A87	$1.50 multicolored	1.10	1.10
a.		Souvenir sheet of 4, #321-324	2.50	2.50
		Nos. 321-324 (4)	2.00	2.00

Princes Town centenary.

Nos. 262, 279, 263 Overprinted in 3 or 5 Lines "1844-1980 POPULATION CENSUS 12th MAY 1980"

1980, Apr. 8   Litho.   Perf. 14
325	A73	5c multicolored	.25	.25
326	A78	6c multicolored	.25	.25
327	A73	10c multicolored	.25	.25
		Nos. 325-327 (3)	.75	.75

Scarlet Ibis Hen and Nest — A88

Scarlet Ibis: b, Nest and eggs. c, Chick in nest. d, Male. e, Male and female.

Wmk. 373

1980, May 6   Litho.   Perf. 14½

328   Strip of 5, multi   5.00 5.00
a.-e. A88 single stamp   .70 .70

Bronze and Silver Medals, 1948, 1952 — A89

15c, Hasely Crawford, 1976 gold medal. 70c, 1964 silver, bronze medals. $2.50, Moscow '80 emblem, vert.

Wmk. 373

1980, July 22   Litho.   Perf. 14

329 A89 10c shown   .25 .25
330 A89 15c multicolored   .25 .25
331 A89 70c multicolored   .40 .40
     Nos. 329-331 (3)   .90 .90

Souvenir Sheet

332 A89 $2.50 multicolored   2.40 2.40

22nd Summer Olympic Games, Moscow, July 19-Aug. 3.

Charcoal Production — A90

Wmk. 373

1980, Sept. 8   Litho.   Perf. 14

333 A90 10c shown   .25 .25
334 A90 55c Logging   .25 .25
335 A90 70c Teak plantation   .35 .35
336 A90 $2.50 Watershed management   1.00 1.00
a.   Souvenir sheet of 4, #333-336   2.50 2.50
     Nos. 333-336 (4)   1.85 1.85

11th Commonwealth Forestry Conference.

Elizabeth Bourne, Judiciary and Isabella Tesbier, Government — A91

Decade for Women: No. 338, Beryl McBurnie, dance and culture; Audrey Jeffers, social work. No. 339, Dr. Stella Abidh, public health; Louise Horne, nutrition.

1980, Sept. 29

337 A91 $1 multicolored   .50 .50
338 A91 $1 multicolored   .50 .50
339 A91 $1 multicolored   .50 .50
     Nos. 337-339 (3)   1.50 1.50

Stadium and Netball League Emblem — A92

1980, Oct. 21

340 A92 70c multicolored   .40 .40

1979 World Netball Tournament, Port-of-Spain.

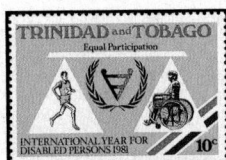

Athlete, Man in Wheelchair, IYD Emblem — A93

Wmk. 373

1981, Apr. 6   Litho.   Perf. 14½

341 A93 10c shown   .25 .25
342 A93 70c Amputee with crutch   .30 .30
343 A93 $1.50 Blind people   .50 .50
344 A93 $2 IYD emblem   .90 .90
     Nos. 341-344 (4)   1.95 1.95

International Year of the Disabled.

Marine Preservation — A94

1981, July 7   Litho.   Perf. 13x13½

345 A94 10c Land   .25 .25
346 A94 55c shown   .30 .30
347 A94 $3 Sky   2.00 2.00
a.   Souvenir sheet of 3, #345-347   4.75 4.75
     Nos. 345-347 (3)   2.55 2.55

World Food Day — A95

1981, Oct. 16   Litho.   Perf. 14½x14

348 A95 10c Produce   .25 .25
349 A95 15c Rice threshing, mill   .25 .25
350 A95 45c Bigeye   .30 .30
351 A95 55c Cow, pig, goats   .40 .40
352 A95 $1.50 Poultry   1.00 1.00
353 A95 $2 Smallmouth grunt   1.40 1.40
a.   Souvenir sheet of 6, #348-353   4.25 4.25
     Nos. 348-353 (6)   3.60 3.60

President Awards — A96

1981, Nov. 30   Perf. 14

354 A96 10c First aid   .25 .25
355 A96 70c Motor mechanics   .50 .50
356 A96 $1 Hiking   .65 .65
357 A96 $2 President giving award   1.20 1.20
     Nos. 354-357 (4)   2.60 2.60

Commonwealth Pharmaceutical Conference — A97

1982, Feb. 12   Litho.   Perf. 14½x14

358 A97 10c Pharmacist   .50 .50
359 A97 $1 Pluchea symphitfolia   2.25 2.25
360 A97 $2 Nopalea cochenilifera   4.50 4.50
     Nos. 358-360 (3)   7.25 7.25

Scouting Year — A98

1982, June 28   Litho.   Perf. 14

361 A98 15c Production   .60 .60
362 A98 55c Tolerance   1.75 1.75
363 A98 $5 Discipline   7.50 7.50
     Nos. 361-363 (3)   9.85 9.85

25th Anniv. of Tourist Board — A99

Perf. 13½x14

1982, Oct. 18   Litho.   Wmk. 373

364 A99 55c Charlotteville   .40 .40
365 A99 $1 Boating   .60 .60
366 A99 $3 Fort George   2.00 2.00
     Nos. 364-366 (3)   3.00 3.00

Pa Pa Bois — A100

Designs: Various folklore characters.

1982, Nov. 8

367 A100 10c multicolored   .25 .25
368 A100 15c multicolored   .25 .25
369 A100 65c multicolored   .40 .40
370 A100 $5 multicolored   3.25 3.25
a.   Souvenir sheet of 4, #367-370   7.00 7.00
     Nos. 367-370 (4)   4.15 4.15

Canefarmers' Centenary — A101

1982, Dec. 13   Litho.   Perf. 14

371 A101 30c Harvest   .30 .30
372 A101 70c Loading bullock cart   .60 .60
373 A101 $1.50 Field   1.25 1.25
a.   Souvenir sheet of 3, #371-373, perf. 14½   2.75 2.75
     Nos. 371-373 (3)   2.15 2.15

20th Anniv. of Independence — A102

10c, Natl. Stadium. 35c, Caroni Arena Water Treatment Plant. 50c, Mount Hope Maternity Hospital. $2, Natl. Insurance Board Mall, Tobago.

1982, Dec. 28   Perf. 13½x14

374 A102 10c multicolored   .45 .45
375 A102 35c multicolored   .90 .90
376 A102 50c multicolored   1.75 1.75
377 A102 $2 multicolored   2.25 2.25
     Nos. 374-377 (4)   5.35 5.35

Commonwealth Day — A103

1983, Mar. 14   Perf. 14

378 A103 10c Flags   .25 .25
379 A103 55c Satellite view   .35 .35
380 A103 $1 Oil industry, vert.   .50 .50
381 A103 $2 Maps, vert.   1.00 1.00
     Nos. 378-381 (4)   2.10 2.10

10th Anniv. of CARICOM — A104

1983, July 11   Litho.   Perf. 14

382 A104 35c Jet, map   2.00 2.00

World Communications Year — A105

15c, Operator. 55c, Scarborough PO, Tobago. $1, Textel Building. $3, Morne Bleu Receiving Station.

1983, Aug. 5   Perf. 14½

383 A105 15c multicolored   .25 .25
384 A105 55c multicolored   .55 .55
385 A105 $1 multicolored   .90 .90
386 A105 $3 multicolored   2.50 2.50
     Nos. 383-386 (4)   4.20 4.20

Commonwealth Finance Ministers Conference — A106

Wmk. 373

1983, Sept. 19   Litho.   Perf. 14

387 A106 $2 multicolored   .90 .90

World Food Day — A107

1983, Oct. 17   Perf. 14x13½

388 A107 10c Kingfish   .45 .45
389 A107 55c Flying fish   .90 .90
390 A107 70c Queen conch   1.25 1.25
391 A107 $4 Red shrimp   7.00 7.00
     Nos. 388-391 (4)   9.60 9.60

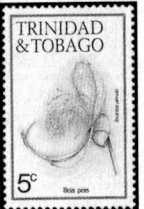

Flowers — A108

5c, Bois pois. 10c, Maraval Lily. 15c, Star grass. 20c, Bois caco. 25c, Strangling fig. 30c, Cassia moschata. 50c, Chalice flower. 65c, Black stick. 80c, Columnea scandens. 95c,

Cats Claws. $1, Bois l'agli. $1.50, Eustoma exeltatum. $2, Chaconia, horiz. $2.50, Chysothemis pulchella, horiz. $5, Centratherum punctatum, horiz. $10, Savanna flower, horiz.

1983, Dec. 14 Wmk. 373 *Perf. 14*
No Year Imprint Below Design

392 A108 5c multicolored .25 .25
b. Imprint "1989" .25 .25
393 A108 10c multicolored .25 .25
b. Imprint "1985" .25 .25
c. Imprint "1986" .25 .25
d. Imprint "1987" .25 .25
e. Imprint "1989" .25 .25
394 A108 15c multicolored .25 .25
395 A108 20c multicolored .25 .25
396 A108 25c multicolored .25 .25
397 A108 30c multicolored .25 .25
398 A108 50c multicolored .60 .65
399 A108 65c multicolored .70 *.85*
400 A108 80c multicolored .90 *1.00*
401 A108 95c multicolored .95 *1.25*
402 A108 $1 multicolored 1.00 *1.25*
403 A108 $1.50 multicolored 1.50 *2.00*

Size: 38½x26mm

404 A108 $2 multicolored 2.00 *2.25*
405 A108 $2.50 multicolored 2.50 *3.00*
406 A108 $5 multicolored 5.00 *6.00*
407 A108 $10 multicolored 10.00 *12.00*
Nos. 392-407 (16) 26.65 31.75

1984, Oct.
"1984" Imprint Below Design

392a A108 5c multicolored 3.75 *4.00*
393a A108 10c multicolored 2.75 *3.00*
394a A108 15c multicolored 2.75 *3.00*
396a A108 25c multicolored 4.50 *5.00*
Nos. 392a-396a (4) 13.75 *15.00*

1985-89 Wmk. 384
"1985" Imprint Below Design

392f A108 5c multicolored 1.25 1.25
401f A108 95c multicolored .80 .80
402f A108 $1 multicolored .85 .85
406f A108 $5 multicolored 3.25 3.25
407f A108 $10 multicolored 6.50 6.50
Nos. 392f-407f (5) 12.65 12.65

"1986" Imprint Below Design

393g A108 10c multicolored .25 .25

"1987" Imprint Below Design

393h A108 10c multicolored .25 .25
397h A108 30c multicolored .25 .25
399h A108 65c multicolored .60 .60
400h A108 80c multicolored .75 .75
401h A108 95c multicolored .85 .85
402h A108 $1 multicolored 1.00 .60
403h A108 $1.50 multicolored 1.50 1.50
404h A108 $2 multicolored 1.90 1.90
406h A108 $5 multicolored 5.00 5.00
407h A108 $10 multicolored 10.00 10.00
Nos. 393h-407h (10) 22.10 21.70

"1988" Imprint Below Design

393i A108 10c multicolored .85 .85
395i A108 20c multicolored .35 .25
396i A108 25c multicolored .85 .85
397i A108 30c multicolored .35 .25
399i A108 65c multicolored .60 .40
400i A108 80c multicolored .75 .75
401i A108 95c multicolored .95 .95
402i A108 $1 multicolored — —
406i A108 $5 multicolored 5.00 5.00
407i A108 $10 multicolored 10.00 10.00
Nos. 393i-407i (9) 19.70 19.30

"1989" Imprint Below Design

393j A108 10c multicolored .25 .25
395j A108 20c multicolored .35 .25
396j A108 25c multicolored .85 .85
397j A108 30c multicolored .35 .25
399j A108 65c multicolored .60 .40
402j A108 $1 multicolored 1.00 .60
403j A108 $1.50 multicolored 1.50 1.50
404j A108 $2 multicolored 1.90 1.90
405j A108 $2.50 multicolored 2.50 2.50
406j A108 $5 multicolored 5.00 5.00
407j A108 $10 multicolored 10.00 10.00
Nos. 393j-407j (11) 24.30 23.50

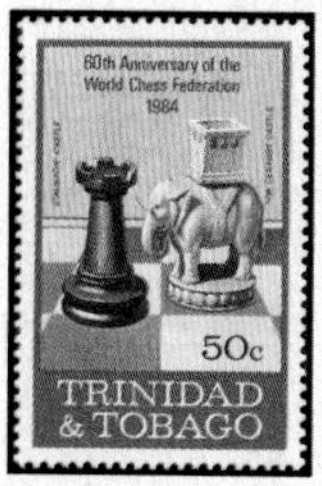

Castles on Chess Board — A109

World Chess Federationn, 60th Anniv.: Various chess pieces.

Wmk. 373
1984, Sept. 12 Litho. *Perf. 14*

408 A109 50c multicolored 1.60 1.60
409 A109 70c multicolored 2.25 2.25
410 A109 $1.50 multicolored 5.00 5.00
411 A109 $2 multicolored 7.00 7.00
Nos. 408-411 (4) 15.85 15.85

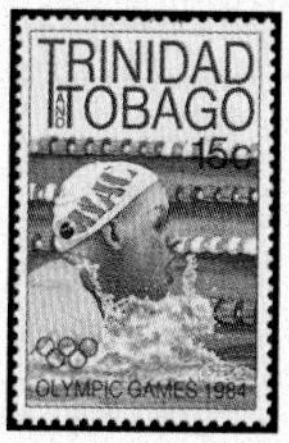

1984 Summer Olympics — A110

1984, Sept. 21 *Perf. 14x14½*

412 A110 15c Swimming .30 .30
413 A110 55c Running .75 .75
414 A110 $1.50 Yachting 1.75 1.75
415 A110 $4 Bicycling 4.50 4.50
a. Souvenir sheet of 4, #412-415 8.00 8.00
Nos. 412-415 (4) 7.30 7.30

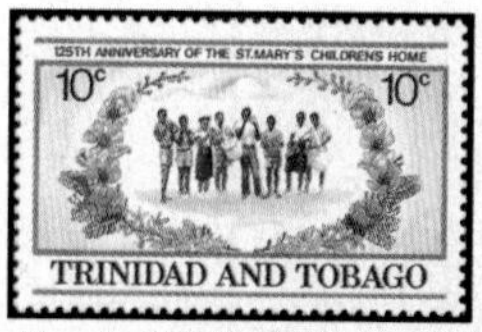

St. Mary's Children's Home, 125th Anniv. — A111

1984, Nov. 13 Litho. *Perf. 13½*

416 A111 10c Children's band .25 .25
417 A111 70c St. Mary's Home .90 .90
418 A111 $3 Group scene 3.50 3.50
Nos. 416-418 (3) 4.65 4.65

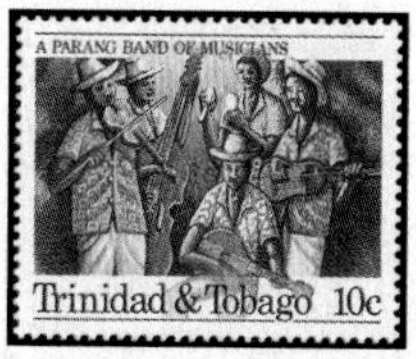

Christmas 1984 A112

10c, Parang Band. 30c, Musical notes, Poinsettia. $1, Bandola, Cuatro, Bandolin. $3, Fiddle, Guitar, Double Bass.

1984, Nov. Litho. *Perf. 14*

419 A112 10c multicolored .35 .35
420 A112 30c multicolored .40 .40
421 A112 $1 multicolored 1.50 1.50
422 A112 $3 multicolored 4.50 4.50
Nos. 419-422 (4) 6.75 6.75

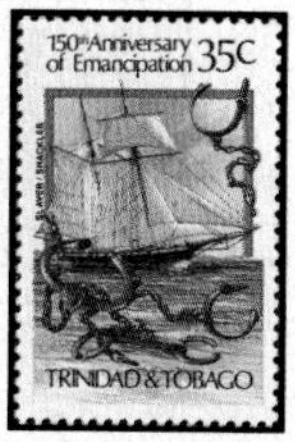

Emancipation, 150th Anniv. — A113

35c, Slave ship. 55c, Map, Slave Triangle. $1, Book by Eric Williams. $2, Toussaint L'Ouverture.

1984, Oct. 22 Litho. *Perf. 13½x13*

423 A113 35c multicolored .85 .85
424 A113 55c multicolored 1.40 1.40
425 A113 $1 multicolored 2.50 2.50
426 A113 $2 multicolored 5.25 5.25
a. Souvenir sheet of 4, #423-426 11.00 11.00
Nos. 423-426 (4) 10.00 10.00

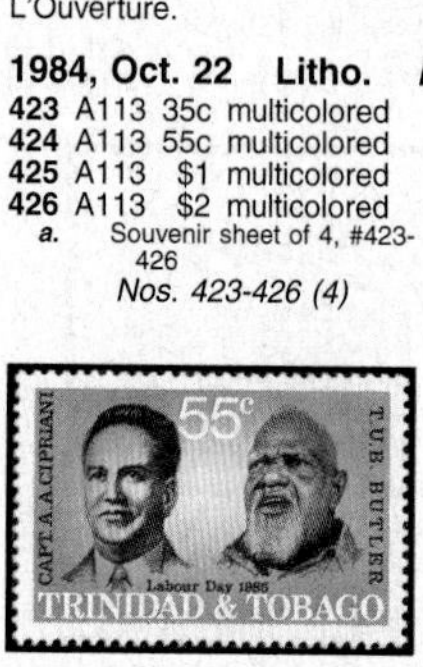

Labor Day — A114

Labor leaders: No. 427, A.A. Cipriani and T.U.B. Butler. No. 428, A. Cola Rienzi and C.T.W.E. Worrell. No. 429, C.P. Alexander and Q. O'Connor.

Wmk. 373
1985, June 17 Litho. *Perf. 14*

427 A114 55c dull rose & blk 2.00 2.00
428 A114 55c brt green & blk 2.00 2.00
429 A114 55c lt orange & blk 2.00 2.00
Nos. 427-429 (3) 6.00 6.00

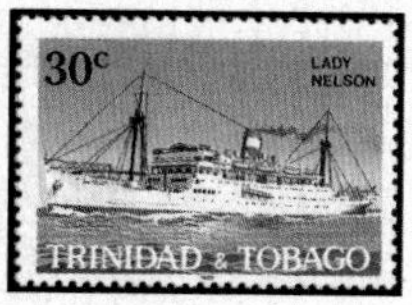

Ships A115

Wmk. 373
1985, Aug 20 Litho. *Perf. 14½*

430 A115 30c Lady Nelson .50 .50
431 A115 95c Lady Drake 1.50 1.50
432 A115 $1.50 Federal Palm 2.25 2.25
433 A115 $2 Federal Maple 2.75 2.75
Nos. 430-433 (4) 7.00 7.00

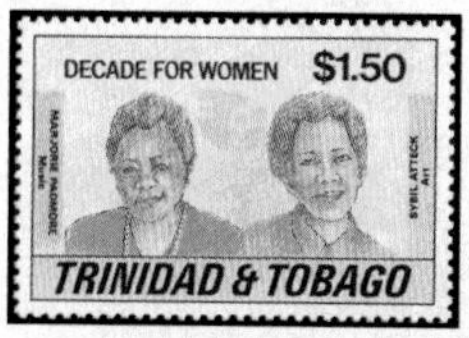

UN Decade for Women A116

Women in the arts, public service and education: No. 434, Sybil Atteck, Marjorie Padmore. No. 435, May Cherrie, Evelyn Tracey. No. 436, Jessica Smith-Phillips, Irene Omilta McShine.

1985, Oct. 30 Wmk. 384 *Perf. 14*

434 A116 $1.50 multicolored 2.40 2.40
435 A116 $1.50 multicolored 2.40 2.40
436 A116 $1.50 multicolored 2.40 2.40
Nos. 434-436 (3) 7.20 7.20

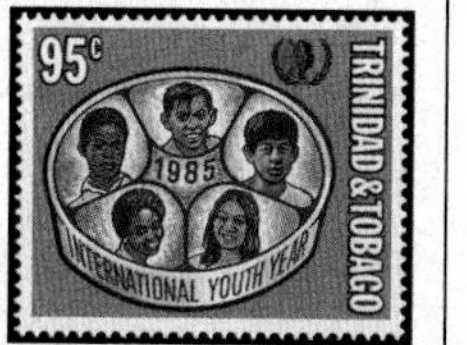

Intl. Youth Year — A117

Anniversaries and events: 10c, Natl. Cadet Force, 75th anniv. 65c, Girl Guides, 75th anniv.

1985, Nov. 27 *Perf. 14x14½*

437 A117 10c Cadet emblem .90 .90
438 A117 65c Badges, anniv. emblem 2.25 2.25
439 A117 95c shown 3.00 3.00
Nos. 437-439 (3) 6.15 6.15

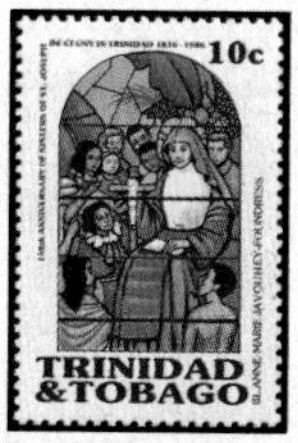

A118

Sisters of St. Joseph de Cluny in Trinidad, 150th Anniv.: 10c, Sister Anne-Marie Javouhey, founder. 65c, Sister St. Joseph's Convent, Port-of-Spain. 95c, Statue of Sr. Anne-Marie.

Perf. 14x14½
1986, Mar. 19 Litho. Wmk. 384

440 A118 10c multicolored .25 .25
441 A118 65c multicolored .55 .55
442 A118 95c multicolored .95 .95
Nos. 440-442 (3) 1.75 1.75

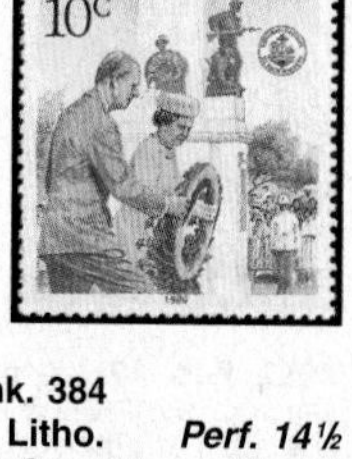

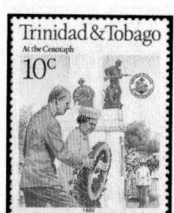

A119

Wmk. 384
1986, Apr. 21 Litho. *Perf. 14½*

443 A119 10c At the Cenotaph .35 .35
444 A119 15c Aboard HMY Britannia .35 .35
445 A119 30c With Pres. Clarke .35 .35
446 A119 $5 Receiving bouquet 4.50 4.50
Nos. 443-446 (4) 5.55 5.55

Queen Elizabeth II, 60th birthday.

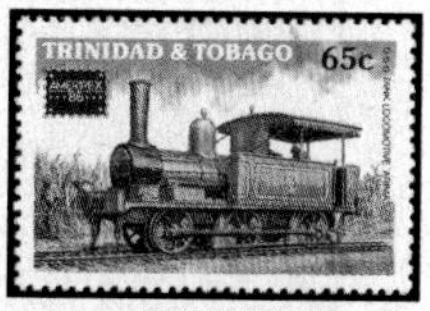

Locomotives, AMERIPEX '86 — A120

Perf. 14½x14
1986, May 26 Wmk. 373

447 A120 65c Arma tank locomotive .35 .35
448 A120 95c Canadian-built No. 22 .60 .65
449 A120 $1.10 Tender engine .70 .75
450 A120 $1.50 Saddle tank .95 .95
a. Souvenir sheet of 4, #447-450 3.50 3.50
Nos. 447-450 (4) 2.60 2.70

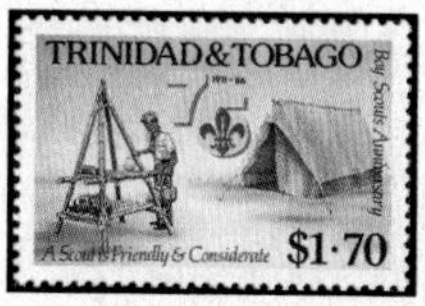

Boy Scouts, 75th Anniv. A121

1986, July 21 Wmk. 384 *Perf. 14*

451 A121 $1.70 Campsite 1.60 1.60
452 A121 $2 Uniforms, 1911, 1986 2.25 2.25

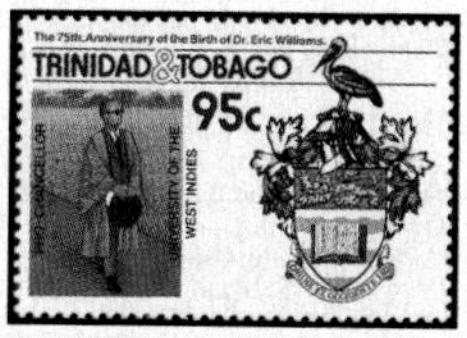

Dr. Eric Williams (1911-1981), First Prime Minister — A122

10c, Graduating college, 1935. 30c, Wearing red tie. 95c, Pro-Chancellor of UWI. $5, Williams, prime minister's residence.

Wmk. 373
1986, Sept. 25 Litho. *Perf. 14*

453 A122 10c multicolored .75 .75
454 A122 30c multicolored 1.00 1.00
a. Black tie 1.25 1.25
455 A122 95c multicolored 1.75 1.75
456 A122 $5 multicolored 5.75 5.75
a. Souvenir sheet of 4, #453-456 10.00 10.00
Nos. 453-456 (4) 9.25 9.25

Nos. 453-454 vert.

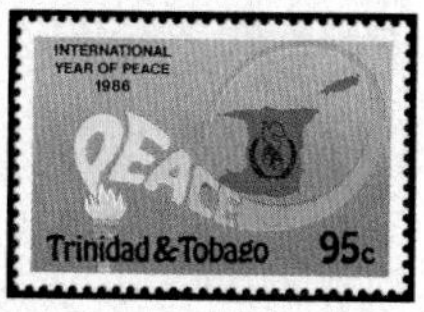

Intl. Peace Year A123

1986, Oct. 30 Wmk. 384

457 A123 95c shown .50 .50
458 A123 $3 Dove 2.00 2.00

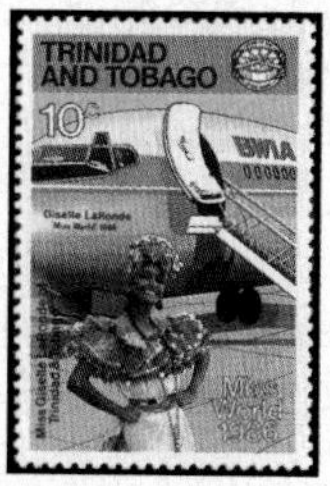

Giselle LaRonde, Miss World 1986 — A124

Wmk. 384
1987, July 27 Litho. *Perf. 14*

459 A124 10c Wearing folk costume .90 .90
460 A124 30c Bathing suit 2.00 2.00
461 A124 95c Crown 3.75 3.75
462 A124 $1.65 Crown and sash 5.75 5.75
Nos. 459-462 (4) 12.40 12.40

Republic Bank, 150th Anniv. A125

Designs: 10c, Colonial Bank, Port of Spain. 65c, Cocoa plantation. 95c, Oil fields. $1.10, Tramcar, Belmont Tramway Co.

Wmk. 373
1987, Dec. 21		**Litho.**	**Perf. 14**	
463	A125	10c buff, red brn & blk	.65	.65
464	A125	65c buff, red brn & blk	.90	.90
465	A125	95c buff, red brn & blk	2.60	2.60
466	A125	$1.10 buff, red brn & blk	3.00	3.00
		Nos. 463-466 (4)	7.15	7.15

Defense Force, 25th Anniv. — A126

Various army, coast guard and navy uniforms.

Wmk. 384
1988, Feb. 29		**Litho.**	**Perf. 14**	
467	A126	10c Army	1.60	1.60
468	A126	30c Army (women)	3.00	3.00
469	A126	$1.10 Navy, army, coast guard	4.25	4.25
470	A126	$1.50 Navy	5.25	5.25
		Nos. 467-470 (4)	14.10	14.10

Cricket A127

Bat, wicket posts, ball, 18th cent. belt buckle and batters: 30c, George John. 65c, Learie Constantine. 95c, Sonny Ramadhin. $1.50, Gerry Gomez. $2.50, Jeffrey Stollmeyer.

Wmk. 373
1988, June 6		**Litho.**	**Perf. 14**	
471	A127	30c multicolored	1.75	1.75
472	A127	65c multicolored	3.25	3.25
473	A127	95c multicolored	3.50	3.50
474	A127	$1.50 multicolored	4.25	4.25
475	A127	$2.50 multicolored	5.50	5.50
		Nos. 471-475 (5)	18.25	18.25

Oilfield Workers' Trade Union, 50th Anniv. — A128

50, Star, oil well and: 10c, Uriah Buzz Butler, labor leader. 30c, Adrian C. Rienzi, pres. from 1937-42. 65c, John Rojas, pres. from 1943-62. $5, George Weekes, pres. from 1962-87.

Wmk. 384
1988, July 11		**Litho.**	**Perf. 14½**	
476	A128	10c multicolored	.25	.25
477	A128	30c multicolored	.30	.30
478	A128	65c multicolored	.60	.60
479	A128	$5 multicolored	3.00	3.00
		Nos. 476-479 (4)	4.15	4.15

Borough of Arima, Cent. A129

20c, Mary Werges, Santa Rosa Church. 30c, Gov. W. Robinson, royal charter. $1.10, Mayor C.P. Lopez greeting Gov. Robinson at train station. $1.50, Mayor J.F. Wallen, centennial emblem.

Wmk. 384
1988, Aug. 22		**Litho.**	**Perf. 14½**	
480	A129	20c multicolored	.35	.35
481	A129	30c multicolored	.35	.35
482	A129	$1.10 multicolored	2.00	2.00
483	A129	$1.50 multicolored	2.00	2.00
		Nos. 480-483 (4)	4.70	4.70

Lloyds of London, 300th Anniv.
Common Design Type

Designs: 30c, Queen Mother at the "Topping Out" ceremony of new Lloyds's building, 1984. $1.10, BWIA Tristar 500, horiz. $1.55, ISCOTT iron and steel mill, horiz. $2, *Atlantic Empress* on fire off Tobago.

1988, Nov. 21		**Litho.**	**Perf. 14**	
484	CD341	30c multicolored	.85	.85
485	CD341	$1.10 multicolored	3.00	1.75
486	CD341	$1.55 multicolored	2.75	2.40
487	CD341	$2 multicolored	5.25	3.50
		Nos. 484-487 (4)	11.85	8.50

Unification of the Islands, Cent. — A130

Torch and: 40c, Natl. arms, 1889, and 1p Type A1. $1, Badge from Tobago flag and Tobago No. 31. $1.50, Badge from Trinidad flag and Trinidad No. 71. $2.25, Natl. arms, 1989, and No. 274.

Wmk. 384
1989, Mar. 20		**Litho.**	**Perf. 14½**	
488	A130	40c multicolored	1.40	1.40
489	A130	$1 multicolored	3.25	3.25
490	A130	$1.50 multicolored	3.50	3.50
491	A130	$2.25 multicolored	4.00	4.00
		Nos. 488-491 (4)	12.15	12.15

Rare Species A131

Designs: a, Pipile pipile. b, Phyllodytes auratus. c, Cebus albifrons trinitatis. d, Tamandua tetradactyla. e, Lutra longicaudis. Printed in a continuous design.

Perf. 14x14½
1989, July 31		**Wmk. 373**	
492	Strip of 5	22.50	22.50
a.-e.	A131 $1 any single	2.40	2.40

A132

10c, Men using walking sticks. 40c, City Hall. $1, Guides and leader. $2.25, Volunteers, anniv. emblem.

1989, Oct. 2			**Perf. 14½**	
493	A132	10c multi	1.50	1.50
494	A132	40c multi	.90	.90
495	A132	$1 multi	3.50	3.50
496	A132	$2.25 multi	4.25	4.25
		Nos. 493-496 (4)	10.15	10.15

Blind Welfare, 75th anniv. (10c), Port-of-Spain City Hall, 75th anniv. (40c), Girl Guides, 75th anniv. ($1), and Red Cross, 50th anniv. ($2.25).

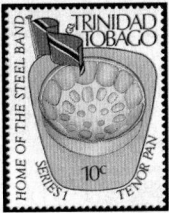

A133

Drum instruments played in a steel band.

		Perf. 14½x14		
1989, Nov. 30			**Wmk. 384**	
497	A133	10c Tenor	.45	.45
498	A133	40c Guitar	.45	.45
499	A133	$1 Cello	.80	.80
500	A133	$2.25 Bass	2.00	2.00
		Nos. 497-500 (4)	3.70	3.70

Mushrooms A134

10c, Xeromphalina tenuipes. 40c, Dictyophora indusiata. $1, Leucocoprinus birnbaumii. $2.25, Crinipellis perniciosa.

1990, May 3			**Perf. 14x13½**	
501	A134	10c multicolored	.40	.40
502	A134	40c multicolored	.80	.80
503	A134	$1 multicolored	2.00	2.00
504	A134	$2.25 multicolored	4.00	4.00
		Nos. 501-504 (4)	7.20	7.20

Stamp World London '90.

Scarlet Ibis A135

1990, Sept. 7			**Perf. 14**	
505	A135	40c Immature bird	2.25	2.25
506	A135	80c Mating display	2.50	2.50
507	A135	$1 Adult male	3.00	3.00
508	A135	$2.25 Adult, egg & young	5.25	5.25
		Nos. 505-508 (4)	13.00	13.00

World Wildlife Fund.

Yellow Oriole — A136

No. 510, Green rumped parrotlet. No. 511, Fork-tailed flycatcher. No. 512, Copper rumped hummingbird. No. 513, Bananaquit. No. 514, Semp. No. 515, Channel-billed toucan. No. 516, Bay headed tanager. No. 517, Green honeycreeper. No. 518, Cattle egret. No. 519, Golden olive woodpecker. No. 520, Peregrine falcon.

1990, Dec. 17		**Litho.**	**Wmk. 384**	
509	A136	20c shown	.40	.40
510	A136	25c multicolored	1.25	.30
511	A136	40c multicolored	.50	.25
512	A136	50c multicolored	.35	.25
513	A136	$1 multicolored	1.00	.40
514	A136	$2 multicolored	2.75	2.75
515	A136	$2.25 multicolored	1.75	1.75
516	A136	$2.50 multicolored	1.25	1.25
517	A136	$5 multicolored	2.75	2.75
518	A136	$10 multicolored	3.25	3.25
519	A136	$20 multicolored	6.00	6.00
520	A136	$50 multicolored	20.00	20.00
		Nos. 509-520 (12)	41.25	39.35

For overprints & surcharges see Nos. 565-568, 597A, 609, 889, 897, 898.

1994-98			**Wmk. 373**	
510a	A136	25c	.90	.90
512a	A136	50c	.60	.60
513a	A136	$1	.90	.90
514a	A136	$2	2.00	2.00
516a	A136	$2.50	2.40	2.40
517a	A136	$5	4.75	4.75
b.		Souvenir sheet of 1, wmk. 373, dated "1997"	5.25	5.25
518a	A136	$10	9.75	9.75
519a	A136	$20	20.00	20.00

Issued: #510a, 8/94; #512a, 4/95; #513a, 514a, 3/3/97; #516a, 518a, 519a, 10/14/98; #517a, 6/1996.

#510a, 512a, 513a, 514a, 516a, 517a, 518a, 519a are dated 1990. No. 517b issued 2/3/97 for Hong Kong '97.

Two additional items were issued in this set. The editors would like to examine any examples of them.

University of the West Indies A137

Chancellors and Campus Buildings: 40c, HRH Princess Alice, Administration Building. 80c, Sir Hugh Wooding, Main Library. $1, Sir Allen Lewis, Faculty of Engineering. $2.25, Sir Shridath Ramphal, Faculty of Medical Studies.

		Perf. 13½x14		
1990, Oct. 15		**Litho.**	**Wmk. 373**	
521	A137	40c multicolored	.75	.75
522	A137	80c multicolored	1.25	1.25
523	A137	$1 multicolored	1.75	1.75
524	A137	$2.25 multicolored	4.25	4.25
		Nos. 521-524 (4)	8.00	8.00

British West Indies Airways, 50th Anniv. A138

Airplanes: 40c, Lockheed Lodestar. 80c, Vickers Viking 1A. $1, Vickers Viscount 702. $2.25, Boeing 707. $5, Lockheed TriStar 500.

1990, Nov. 27			**Perf. 14**	
525	A138	40c multicolored	1.75	1.75
526	A138	80c multicolored	2.50	2.50
527	A138	$1 multicolored	2.75	2.75
528	A138	$2.25 multicolored	5.25	5.25
		Nos. 525-528 (4)	12.25	12.25

Souvenir Sheet
529	A138	$5 multicolored	8.25	8.25

Ferns A139

40c, Lygodium volubile. 80c, Blechnum occidentale. $1, Gleichenia bifida. $2.25, Polypodium lycopodiodes.

1991, July 1			**Perf. 13½**	
530	A139	40c multicolored	.60	.60
531	A139	80c multicolored	1.10	1.10
532	A139	$1 multicolored	1.50	1.50
533	A139	$2.25 multicolored	3.25	3.25
		Nos. 530-533 (4)	6.45	6.45

Trinidad & Tobago in World War II — A140

Designs: 40c, Firing practice by Trinidad & Tobago regiment. 80c, Fairey Barracuda surprises U-boat. $1, Avro Lancaster returns from bombing raid. $2.25, River class frigate on convoy duty. No. 538a, Supermarine Spitfire. b, Vickers Wellington.

Perf. 13½x14

1991, Dec. 7		**Litho.**	**Wmk. 384**
534	A140	40c multicolored	1.25 1.25
535	A140	80c multicolored	2.75 2.75
536	A140	$1 multicolored	3.50 3.50
537	A140	$2.25 multicolored	7.50 7.50
	Nos. 534-537 (4)		15.00 15.00

Souvenir Sheet of 2

538	A140	$2.50 #a.-b.	22.50 22.50

H. E. Rapsey — A141

Inca Clathrata Quesneli — A142

Holy Name Convent — A143

1992, Mar. 30	**Wmk. 373**		**Perf. 14**
539	A141	40c multicolored	.75 .75
540	A142	80c multicolored	1.50 1.50
541	A143	$1 multicolored	2.00 2.00
	Nos. 539-541 (3)		4.25 4.25

#539, Building and Loan Assoc., cent. #540, Trinidad & Tobago Field Naturalists' Club. #541, Holy Name Convent, cent.

Religions of Trinidad and Tobago — A145

No. 544, Baptist, baptism by immersion. No. 545, Muslim, minaret. No. 546, Hindu, Brahman..the source of all. No. 547, Christianity, cross. No. 548, Baha'i, slogan.

1992, Apr. 21		**Litho.**	**Perf. 14**
544	A145	40c multicolored	1.50 1.50
545	A145	40c multicolored	1.50 1.50
546	A145	40c multicolored	1.50 1.50
547	A145	40c multicolored	1.50 1.50
548	A145	40c multicolored	1.50 1.50
	Nos. 544-548 (5)		7.50 7.50

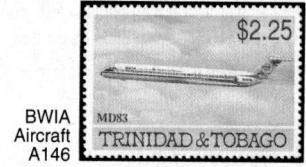

BWIA Aircraft A146

Wmk. 373

1992, Aug. 6	**Litho.**		**Perf. 14**
549	A146	$2.25 MD83	4.00 4.00
550	A146	$2.25 L1011	4.00 4.00

Natl. Museum and Art Gallery, Cent. A147

Wmk. 384

1992, Dec. 7	**Litho.**		**Perf. 14½**
551	A147	$1 multicolored	.75 .75

Christmas — A148

1992, Dec. 21			
552	A148	40c multicolored	.50 .50

Trinidad Guardian, 75th Anniv. — A149

1992, Dec. 23			
553	A149	40c multicolored	.50 .50

Philatelic Society of Trinidad & Tobago, 50th Anniv. A150

1992, Dec. 30			
554	A150	$2.25 multicolored	1.75 1.75

CARICOM (Caribbean Economic Community), 20th Anniv. — A151

Map of CARICOM nations, portraits of West Indian men: 50c, $1.50, $2.75, $3, Derek Walcott, Sir Shridath Ramphal, William Demas.
$6, Order of the Caribbean Community.

Perf. 13x13½

1994, Jan. 31	**Litho.**		**Wmk. 373**
555	A151	50c pink & multi	.25 .25
556	A151	$1.50 green & multi	.85 .85
557	A151	$2.75 gray & multi	1.60 1.60
558	A151	$3 violet & multi	1.75 1.75
	Nos. 555-558 (4)		4.45 4.45

Souvenir Sheet

Perf. 13½x13

559	A151	$6 multicolored	4.25 4.25

No. 559 contains one 34x56mm stamp.

Drum Instruments Played in a Steel Band — A152

1994, Feb. 11			**Perf. 14x15**
560	A152	50c Quadrophonic pan	.40 .40
561	A152	$1 Tenor base pan	.85 .85
562	A152	$2.25 Six pan	1.75 1.75
563	A152	$2.50 Rocket pan	2.00 2.00
	Nos. 560-563 (4)		5.00 5.00

Aldwyn Roberts Kitchener, Calypso Singer — A153

1994, Feb. 11			**Perf. 14**
564	A153	50c multicolored	3.00 3.00

Nos. 510-511, 514, 518 Ovptd. with Hong Kong '94 Exhibition Emblem

Wmk. 384

1994, Feb. 18	**Litho.**		**Perf. 14**
565	A136	25c multicolored	.35 .35
566	A136	40c multicolored	.35 .35
567	A136	$2 multicolored	1.25 1.25
568	A136	$10 multicolored	7.25 7.25
	Nos. 565-568 (4)		9.20 9.20

Hotels & Lodges A154

#569, Trinidad Hilton. #570, Sandy Point Village, Tobago. #571, Asa Wright Nature Center and Lodge. #572, ML's Bed and Breakfast.

Wmk. 373

1994, Aug. 10	**Litho.**		**Perf. 14**
569	A154	$3 multicolored	1.50 1.50
570	A154	$3 multicolored	1.50 1.50
571	A154	$3 multicolored	1.50 1.50
572	A154	$3 multicolored	1.50 1.50
	Nos. 569-572 (4)		6.00 6.00

Snakes A155

50c, Boa constrictor. $1.25, Horse whip or vine snake. $2.50, Bushmaster. $3, Large coral snake.

Wmk. 373

1994, Sept. 19	**Litho.**		**Perf. 14**
573	A155	50c multicolored	.35 .35
574	A155	$1.25 multicolored	1.00 1.00
575	A155	$2.50 multicolored	2.00 2.00
576	A155	$3 multicolored	2.25 2.25
	Nos. 573-576 (4)		5.60 5.60

Trinidad Art Society, 50th Anniv. — A156

Artworks: No. 577, Copper sculpture, by Ken Morris. No. 578, Fisherman, by Sybil Atteck. No. 579, Snowballman, by Mahmoud P. Alladin.

1995, Mar. 6			**Wmk. 384**
577	A156	50c multicolored	1.00 1.00
578	A156	50c multicolored	1.00 1.00
579	A156	50c multicolored	1.00 1.00
	Nos. 577-579 (3)		3.00 3.00

Conservation — A157

Designs: $1.25, Leatherback turtle. $2.50, POS Lighthouse, vert. $3, "Knowsley" Ministry of Foreign Affairs.

1995, Aug. 7			
580	A157	$1.25 multicolored	.85 .85
581	A157	$2.50 multicolored	1.75 1.75
582	A157	$3 multicolored	2.10 2.10
	Nos. 580-582 (3)		4.70 4.70

Brian Lara, Cricket Hero — A158

Designs: $1.25, Batting. $2.50, In batting stance. $3, Batting, diff.
No. 587: a, $3.75, With arms raised at crowd. b, $5.01, Down on one knee with bat.

Perf. 13x13½

1996, May 15	**Litho.**		**Wmk. 373**
583	A158	50c multicolored	.35 .35
584	A158	$1.25 multicolored	.90 .90
585	A158	$2.50 multicolored	1.60 1.60
586	A158	$3 multicolored	2.00 2.00
	Nos. 583-586 (4)		4.85 4.85

Souvenir Sheet

587	A158	Sheet of 2, #a.-b.	8.75 8.75

Trinidad & Tobago Remembers World War II — A159

50c, Red Cross Economy Label. $1.25, Battleship USS Missouri. $2.50, US servicemen playing baseball, Queen's Park, Savannah, 1942. $3, Fulmar 1, Royal Naval Air Station.
No. 592: a, Grumman Goose seaplane. b, US Navy Airship.

Wmk. 373

1996, June 7	**Litho.**		**Perf. 14**
588	A159	50c multicolored	.50 .50
589	A159	$1.25 multicolored	1.25 1.25
590	A159	$2.50 multicolored	2.50 2.50
591	A159	$3 multicolored	3.00 3.00
	Nos. 588-591 (4)		7.25 7.25

Souvenir Sheet of 2

592	A159	$3 #a.-b.	11.00 11.00

A160

Wendy Fitzwilliam, 1998 Miss Universe: $1.25, Lying on beach. $2.50, In traditional costume. $3, Wearing evening gown.
$5, After coronation.

1999, May 3 **Litho.** ***Perf. 14***

593 A160 50c multicolored .75 .75
594 A160 $1.25 multicolored 1.50 1.50
595 A160 $2.50 multicolored 2.75 2.75
596 A160 $3 multicolored 3.00 3.00
Nos. 593-596 (4) 8.00 8.00

Souvenir Sheet

597 A160 $5 multicolored 8.75 8.75

No. 511 Surcharged

1999 **Method and Perf. as Before**

597A A136 75c on 40c multi —

A161

Angostura Bitters, 175th Anniv.: 75c, Angostura Bitters bottle. $3, Distillery. $4.50, Bitters bottle, cocktails.

Self-Adhesive

Serpentine Die Cut

2000, Jan. 27 **Litho.**

598 A161 75c multi .60 .60
599 A161 $3 multi 2.40 2.40
600 A161 $4.50 multi 3.50 3.50
a. Souvenir sheet, #598-600 6.25 6.25
Nos. 598-600 (3) 6.50 6.50

Tourism A162

Shoreline scenes: 75c, Maracas Bay. $1, Pirates Bay. $3.75, Pigeon Point. $5, Toco, North Coast.

2000, July 25 **Litho.** ***Perf. 14¼x14½***

601 A162 75c multi .50 .50
602 A162 $1 multi .75 .75
603 A162 $3.75 multi 3.50 3.50
604 A162 $5 multi 4.00 4.00
Nos. 601-604 (4) 8.75 8.75

For surcharge, see No. 890.

Christmas A163

Design: 75c, Caroni landscape. $3.75, Pastelles, sorrel and ginger beer. $4.50, Musicians under palm trees. $5.25, Angels with steel drums.

Perf. 14¼x14½

2000, Nov. 14 **Litho.**

605 A163 75c multi .40 .40
606 A163 $3.75 multi 2.75 2.75
607 A163 $4.50 multi 3.00 3.00
608 A163 $5.25 multi 3.75 3.75
Nos. 605-608 (4) 9.90 9.90

No. 515 Surcharged

Method and Perf. as Before

2001?

609 A136 75c on $2.25 multi —

National Mail Center A164

Designs: $3, Building entrance. $10, Side of building.

Perf. 14¼x14½

2000, Nov. 20 **Litho.**

610-611 A164 Set of 2 7.50 7.50

Endangered Fauna A165

Designs: 25c, Paca, 50c, Prehensile-tailed porcupine. 75c, Iguana. $1, Leatherback turtle. $2, Golden tegu. $2, Red howler monkey. $4, Weeping capuchin monkey, vert. $5, River otter. $10, Ocelot. $20, Trinidad piping guan, vert.

Perf. 14¼x14½, 14½x14¼

2001, Feb. 6 **Litho.**

612 A165 25c multi .35 .35
613 A165 50c multi .55 .55
614 A165 75c multi .75 .75
615 A165 $1 multi .85 .85
616 A165 $2 multi 1.50 1.50
617 A165 $3 multi 1.75 1.75
618 A165 $4 multi 2.25 2.25
619 A165 $5 multi 2.75 2.75
620 A165 $10 multi 5.75 5.75
621 A165 $20 multi 12.00 12.00
Nos. 612-621 (10) 28.50 28.50

Salvation Army in Trinidad & Tobago, Cent. — A166

Designs: 75c, Emblem. $2, William Booth Memorial Hall.

2001, Aug. 9 ***Perf. 14½x14¼***

622-623 A166 Set of 2 2.00 2.00
623a Souvenir sheet, #622-623, perf. 13¾x14¼ 2.00 2.00

Natl. Library, 150th Anniv. A167

Designs: 75c, Port of Spain Public Library, Carnegie Free Library. $3.25, New National Library building.

2001, Aug. 9 ***Perf. 14¼x14½***

624-625 A167 Set of 2 3.00 3.00
625a Souvenir sheet, #624-625 3.00 3.00

Under 17 World Soccer Championships — A168

Designs: $2, Emblem of Soca Warriors. $3.25, National flag. $4.50, Lion holding flag. $5.25, Stadiums.

2001, Sept. 6 ***Perf. 14½x14***

626-629 A168 Set of 4 9.50 9.50
629a Souvenir sheet, #626-629 9.50 9.50

Flowers — A169

Designs: $1, Pachystachys coccinea. $2.50, Heliconia psittacorum. $3.25, Brownea latifolia, horiz. $3.75, Oncidium papilio.

2001 ***Perf. 14½x14¼, 14¼x14½***

630-633 A169 Set of 4 9.00 9.00

Christmas — A170

People and: $1, Boats, church. $3.75, Flowers. $4.50, House, flowers. $5.25, Church, post office.

2001 ***Perf. 14½x14¼***

634-637 A170 Set of 4 9.00 9.00
637a Souvenir sheet, #634-637 9.50 9.50

Butterflies A171

Designs: $1, Cracker. $3.75, Tiger. $4.50, Four continent. $5.25, "89."

2002, June 19 **Litho.** ***Perf. 13¼x13***

638-641 A171 Set of 4 11.00 11.00

Hummingbirds A172

Designs: $1, Rufous-breasted hermit. $2.50, Black-throated mango. $3.25, Tufted coquette. $3.75, White-chested emerald.

2002 ? ***Perf. 13x13¼***

642-645 A172 Set of 4 9.75 9.75

Historic Forts A173

Designs: $1, Fort Picton. $3.75, Fort George. $4.50, Fort King George. $5.25, Fort James.

2002 ? ***Perf. 13¼x13***

646-649 A173 Set of 4 9.50 9.50
649a Souvenir sheet, #646-649 10.00 10.00

Reign of Queen Elizabeth II, 50th Anniv. A174

Queen: $3.75, At Governor General's House. $4.50, With Mayor E. Taylor of Port of Spain. $5.25, At Red House, addressing Parliament, #119, and former personal flag of the Queen.
$10, In limousine, waving to crowd.

2002 **Litho.** ***Perf. 13¾***

650-652 A174 Set of 3 10.00 10.00

Souvenir Sheet

653 A174 $10 multi 11.00 11.00

Independence, 40th Anniv. — A175

2002

654 A175 $1 multi 1.50 1.50

Christmas A176

Designs: $1, Child opening gift of steel drum, vert. $2.50, People, musicians, house. $3.75, Houses. $5.25, Santa Claus on horse-drawn cart, vert.

Perf. 14½x14¼, 14¼x14½

2002, Nov. 20 **Litho.**

655-658 A176 Set of 4 9.50 9.50

Pan-American Health Organization, Cent. — A177

Designs: $1, Emblem. $2.50, National headquarters, Port of Spain. $3.25, Steel drum with symbols. $4.50, Joseph L. Pawan (1887-1957), discoverer of vampire bat rabies.

2002, Dec. 2   **Perf. 14½x14¼**
659-662 A177   Set of 4   9.00 9.00

Cricket Players — A178

Designs: $1, Ian Raphael Bishop. $2.50, Deryck Lance Murray. $4.50, Augustine Lawrence Logie. $5.25, Ann Browne John.

2003, Feb. 7   **Perf. 13**
663-666 A178   Set of 4   10.00 10.00

Carnival A179

Various costumed participants: $1, $2.50, $3.75, vert., $4.50, vert., $5.25, vert.

Perf. 14¼x14½, 14½x14¼
2003, Feb. 25   **Litho.**
667-671 A179   Set of 5   10.00 10.00
671a   Souvenir sheet of 1   5.00 5.00

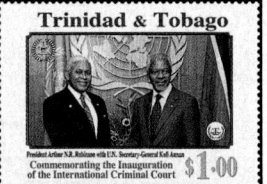

Inauguration of Intl. Criminal Court — A180

Designs: $1, Trinidad & Tobago Pres. Arthur N. R. Robinson and UN Secretary General Kofi Annan. $2.50, Robinson, Prof. Benjamin Ferencz, Prof. Cherif Bassiouni, Philippe Kirsch, UN Undersecretary for Legal Affairs Hans Corell. $3.75, Robinson and Corell. $4.50, Robinson, Emma Bonino, and Italian Pres. Carlo Ciampi.
$6, Robinson, vert.

Perf. 14¾x14½, 14½x14¾
2003, Feb. 25
672-675 A180   Set of 4   9.50 9.50
Souvenir Sheet
676 A180 $6 multi   5.50 5.50

Rainforest Flora & Fauna — A181

No. 677: a, Mountain immortelle. b, Blue-crowned motmot. c, Red howler monkey. d, Butterfly orchid. e, Channel-billed toucan. f, Ocelot. g, Bromeliads. h, Lineated woodpecker. i, Tamandua. j, Emperor butterfly.

Serpentine Die Cut 12½
2003, Feb. 24   **Litho.**
Self-Adhesive
677   Booklet pane of 10   11.00
   a.-j.   A181 $1 Any single   .75 .75

Lighthouses A182

Designs: $1, Port-of-Spain. $3.75, Chacachacare. $4.50, Port-of-Spain, diff. $5.25, Chacachacare, diff.
No. 681B, Like No. 679, spelled "Chacacharie." No. 681C, Like No. 681, spelled "Chacacharie."

2002-03   **Perf. 14½x14¼**
678-681 A182   Set of 4   13.50 13.50
681a   Souvenir sheet, #678-681   13.50 13.50
681B A182 $3.75 multi   — —
681C A182 $5.25 multi   — —

Nos. 678, 680, 681B and 681C were issued on 11/6/02 and all were withdrawn from sale later that day when the incorrect spelling of the lighthouse was discovered. Nos. 678 and 680 were put back on sale, along with new stamps with the corrected spelling of the lighthouse, Nos. 679 and 681, and the souvenir sheet with the stamps with the corrected spelling, No. 681a, on 5/26/03. The editors would like to examine any examples of the souvenir sheet with stamps with the incorrect spelling.

Scenes of Village Life — A183

Designs: $1, Dancing the cocoa. $2.50, Dirt oven. $3.75, River washing. $4.50, Box cart racing. $5.25, Pitching marbles.

2003, Oct. 28
682-686 A183   Set of 5   10.00 10.00

Marine Life — A184

Designs: $1, Boulder brain coral. $2.50, Hawksbill turtle. $3.75, Green moray eel. $4.50, Creole wrasse. $5.25, Black-spotted sea goddess.
$10, Queen angelfish.

2003, Oct. 28   **Perf. 14¼x14½**
687-691 A184   Set of 5   11.00 11.00
Souvenir Sheet
692 A184 $10 multi   11.00 11.00

Christmas — A185

Paintings by Jean Michel Cazabon (1813-88): $1, View of Port-of-Spain from Laventille Hill. $2.50, View of Diego Martin from Fort George. $3.75, Corbeaux Town, Trinidad. $4.50, Rain Clouds over Cedros. $5.25, Los Galos, Icacos Bay.
No. 698: a, $5, River at St. Ann's. b, $6.50, House in Trinidad.

2003, Nov. 17   **Perf. 13¾**
693-697 A185   Set of 5   10.00 10.00
Souvenir Sheet
698 A185   Sheet of 2, #a-b   10.00 10.00

World AIDS Day — A186

Designs: $1, Unite against AIDS. $2.50, Stigma isolates. $3.75, Care stops AIDS, vert. $4.50, Family protects, vert.
$10, People and AIDS ribbon.

2003, Nov. 21
699-702 A186   Set of 4   8.75 8.75
Souvenir Sheet
703 A186 $10 multi   8.50 8.50

2004 Carnival — A187

Calypso musicians: $1, Aldric Farrel, "The Lord Pretender." $2.50, Roy Lewis, "The Mystic Prowler." $3.75, Lord Kitchener, The Mighty Sparrow and The Roaring Lion. $4.50, McArthur Linda Sandy-Rose, "Calypso Rose." $5.25, Nap Hepburne, Lord Brynner and The Mighty Sparrow.
$10, McArthur Linda Sandy-Rose, diff.

2004, Feb. 18
704-708 A187   Set of 5   8.75 8.75
Souvenir Sheet
709 A187 $10 multi   8.25 8.25

2004 Summer Olympics, Athens — A188

Designs: $1, Track and field. $2.50, Boxing. $3.75, Taekwondo. $4.50, Swimming.

2004, July 19   **Litho.**   **Perf. 13**
710-713 A188   Set of 4   8.00 8.00

Intl. Year Commemorating the Struggle Against Slavery and Its Abolition — A189

Designs: $1, Slave ship. $2.50, Rada community, Belmont. $3.75, Daaga, Prince of Popo. $4.50, Slaves singing freedom songs, horiz. $5.25, Providence Estate Aqueduct, Tobago, horiz.
$15, Sandy's escape, horiz.

2004, Sept. 23   **Litho.**   **Perf. 13**
714-718 A189   Set of 5   9.00 9.00
Souvenir Sheet
719 A189 $15 multi   7.75 7.75

Christmas A190

Paintings by Arthur Aldwin "Boscoe" Holder: $1, Lady with Ginger Lilies. $2.50, View from Maracas Lookout. $3.75, Lady in Peacock Chair. $4.50, Caribbean Beauty in White, horiz. $5.25, Teteron Bay, Chaguaramas, horiz.
$10, Creole Ladies in Straw Hats, horiz.

2004, Nov. 22
720-724 A190   Set of 5   9.00 9.00
Souvenir Sheet
725 A190 $10 multi   6.00 6.00

Fruits — A191

Designs: $1, Mango. $2.50, Lime. $3.75, Pineapple. $4.50, Coconut, horiz. $5.25, Orange, horiz.
$10, Guava, horiz.

2004, June 7
726-730 A191   Set of 5   9.00 9.00
Souvenir Sheet
731 A191 $10 multi   7.50 7.50

Carnival — A192

Designs: $1, Dame Lorraine. $2.50, Jab Jab. $3.25, Burrokeet, horiz. $3.75, Midnight Robber. $4.50, Fancy Indian.
$15, Fancy Sailor.

2005, Jan. 18   **Litho.**   **Perf. 13**
732-736 A192   Set of 5   8.50 8.50
Souvenir Sheet
737 A192 $15 multi   8.75 8.75

Brian Lara, Cricket Player — A193

Various photos of Lara in action: $1, $2.50, $3.75, $4.50, $5.25.
$15, Lara walking under raised cricket bats.

2005, Apr. 12   **Litho.**   **Perf. 13**
738-742 A193   Set of 5   12.00 12.00
Souvenir Sheet
743 A193 $15 multi   12.00 12.00

Tobago Heritage Festival — A194

Designs: $1, Belé. $2.50, Dancing the jig. $3.75, Goat race, horiz. $4.50, Harvest Festival, horiz. $5.25, Drumming Festival, horiz. $15, Traditional Tobago wedding.

Perf. 13½x13¼, 13¼x13½

2005, Aug. 15
744-748 A194 Set of 5   8.00 8.00
Souvenir Sheet
Perf. 13¼
749 A194 $15 multi   8.00 8.00

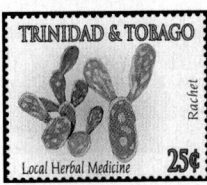

Medicinal Herbs
A195

Designs: 25c, Rachet. 50c, Chandelier. 75c, Worm grass. $1, Black sage. $3, Wonder of the world. $3.25, Vervine. $4, Aloe vera. $5, Senna. $10, Bois bande. $20, Herbal garden.

2005, May 18   **Perf. 13¼x13**
750 A195 25c multi   .25 .25
751 A195 50c multi   .30 .30
752 A195 75c multi   .50 .50
753 A195 $1 multi   .60 .60
754 A195 $3 multi   1.25 1.25
755 A195 $3.25 multi   1.50 1.50
756 A195 $4 multi   1.75 1.75
757 A195 $5 multi   2.00 2.00
758 A195 $10 multi   3.50 3.50
759 A195 $20 multi   7.00 7.00
   Nos. 750-759 (10)   18.65 18.65

Fish and Marine Life — A196

No. 760: a, Foureye butterfly fish. b, Caribbean reef squid. c, Hawksbill turtle. d, Southern sting ray. e, Queen angelfish. f, Giant anemone. g, Peppermint shrimp. h, Rough file clam. i, White-speckled hermit crab. j, Christmas tree worm.

Serpentine Die Cut 12½

2005, May 1   **Self-Adhesive**   **Litho.**
760   Booklet of 10   9.00
  a.-j. A196 $1 Any single   .60 .60

Sir Solomon Hochoy (1905-83), First Governor-General — A197

Hochoy and: $1, Prime Minister Dr. Eric E. Williams. $2.50, Haile Selassie. $3.75, His wife, Thelma. $4.50, Queen Elizabeth II. $5.25, Honor Guard. $15, Hochoy in uniform.

2005, Aug. 22   **Perf. 13½x13**
761-765 A197 Set of 5   9.00 9.00
Souvenir Sheet
Perf. 13½x13¼
766 A197 $15 multi   9.00 9.00
   For surcharge, see No. 891.

Introduction of Women Police, 50th Anniv. — A198

2005, Sept. 30   **Perf. 12¾**
767 A198 $15 black   10.00 10.00

Souvenir Sheet

Children Against Cancer — A199

2005, Nov. 7   **Perf. 13½x13¼**
768 A199 $15 multi   10.00 10.00
   No. 768 sold for $20.

Anansi and the Cricket Match — A200

Anansi: $1, And friends reading cricket brochure. $2.50, And friends hiding in bathroom. $3.75, And friends under umbrella. $4.50, Holding bag, talking to woman. $5.25, Laughing at friends paying woman. $15, Anansi rubbing stomach.

2005, Dec. 12   **Perf. 13½x13**
769-773 A200 Set of 5   9.00 9.00
Souvenir Sheet
774 A200 $15 multi   8.75 8.75

Pope John Paul II (1920-2005) A201

Scenes from Pope's 1985 visit to Trinidad & Tobago: $1, Leaving airplane. $2.50, Kissing ground. $3.75, Shaking hands with priest. $4.50, With bishop, waving. $5.25, Celebrating mass. $15, Waving to crowd from police vehicle.

2006, Apr. 10   **Litho.**   **Perf. 13½x13¼**
775-779 A201 Set of 5   8.50 8.50
Souvenir Sheet
780 A201 $15 multi   7.50 7.50

2006 World Cup Soccer Championships, Germany — A202

Various images of Trinidad & Tobago soccer players in action: $1, $2.50, $3.75, $4.50.

Perf. 13¼x13½
2006, June 28   **Litho.**
781-784 A202 Set of 4   11.00 11.00
Initial reports said this set was available only with the purchase of a first day cover for $50, but the stamps have been made available individually at face value.

CARICOM Single Market and Economy A203

Designs: $1, Cables, palm tree. $2.50, Lighthouse, check. $3.75, Cell phone, diver. $4.50, Sprinter's hands, beach, horiz. $5.25, Hands on computer keyboard, globe, horiz. $15, Map of Caribbean, horiz.

Perf. 13½x13¼, 13¼x13½
2006, July 3
785-789 A203 Set of 5   9.00 9.00
Souvenir Sheet
790 A203 $15 multi   8.50 8.50

Souvenir Sheet

Orchid Society, 50th Anniv. — A204

2006, Sept. 5   **Perf. 13½x13¼**
791 A204 $15 multi   9.00 9.00

Arrival of Chinese to Trinidad and Tobago, Bicent. A205

Art: $1, Guayaguayare Beach, by Ou Hing Wan. $2.50, Hosay, by Carlisle Chang. $3.75, Saddle Road, by Amy Leong Pang, vert. $4.50, Mother & Child, sculpture by Patrick Chu Foon, vert. $5.25, Still Life, by Sybil Atteck, vert. $15, Inherent Nobility of Man, by Chang, vert.

Perf. 14¼x14½, 14½x14¼
2006, Oct. 11
792-796 A205 Set of 5   9.75 9.75
Souvenir Sheet
Perf. 13x13¼
797 A205 $15 multi   7.50 7.50

Children's Games — A206

Designs: $1, Rim driving. $2.50, Top spinning. $3.75, Playing 3A. $4.50, Farmer in the Den. $15, Tire swing.

2006, Nov. 29   **Perf. 13¼**
798-801 A206 Set of 4   7.00 7.00
Souvenir Sheet
802 A206 $15 multi   7.00 7.00

2007 Cricket World Cup, West Indies — A207

2007 Cricket World Cup emblem, Cricket World Cup and: $1, Batsman. $2, Bowler. $2.50, Bowler, diff. $3.75, Batsman, diff. $4.50, Wicketkeeper. $15, Cricket World Cup.

2007, Mar. 15   **Litho.**   **Perf. 13**
803-807 A207 Set of 5   6.00 6.00
Souvenir Sheet
Perf. 13½
808 A207 $15 multi   6.00 6.00
   No. 808 contains one 27x45mm stamp.

Reopening of Red House, Cent. — A208

Designs: $1, Red House, c. 1907. $2.50, Parliament Chamber. $3.75, Cenotaph and Eternal Flame. $5.25, Rotunda and fountain. $15, Dome.

2007, Sept. 14   **Perf. 13½x13¼**
809-812 A208 Set of 4   4.00 4.00
Souvenir Sheet
813 A208 $15 multi   4.75 4.75

St. Mary's Children's Home, 150th Anniv. — A209

Designs: $1, Main entrance, c. 1930. $2.50, Fountain. $3.75, St. Mary's Anglican Church. $4.50, St. Mary's Children's Home Cub Scout pack.

2007, Sept. 21
814-817 A209 Set of 4   3.75 3.75

Historic Buildings A210

Designs: $1, Roomor. $2, Killarney. $2.50, Queen's Royal College. $3.25, Hayes Court. $3.75, Knowsley. $4.50, Mille Fleurs. $10, Boissiere House. $20, Archbishop's House. $50, White Hall.

2007, Dec. 14		Litho.	Perf. 13	
818	A210	$1 multi	.35	.35
819	A210	$2 multi	.65	.65
820	A210	$2.50 multi	.80	.80
821	A210	$3.25 multi	1.10	1.10
822	A210	$3.75 multi	1.25	1.25
823	A210	$4.50 multi	1.50	1.50
824	A210	$10 multi	3.25	3.25
825	A210	$20 multi	6.50	6.50
826	A210	$50 multi	16.00	16.00
Nos. 818-826 (9)			31.40	31.40

Souvenir Sheet

Ozone Layer Protection — A211

2008, Jan. 24   Litho.   Perf. 13x13¼
827   A211 $15 multi   6.00   6.00

Miniature Sheet

2008 Summer Olympics, Beijing — A212

No. 828: a, Running. b, Table tennis. c, Cycling. d, Swimming.

2008, June 16   Perf. 12
828   A212 $3.50 Sheet of 4, #a-d   5.25   5.25

Scouting, Cent. (in 2007) A213

Designs: $1, Cub scouts. $2.50, Scouts. $3.75, Venturers. $4.50, Leaders. $15, Lord Robert Baden-Powell, vert.

2008, July 29   Litho.   Perf. 13¼x13½
829-832   A213   Set of 4   4.00   4.00
Souvenir Sheet
Perf. 13½x13¼
833   A213 $15 multi   5.00   5.00

University of the West Indies, 60th Anniv. — A214

Designs: $1, Sir Arthur Lewis, first West Indian principal. $2.50, Princess Alice, Countess of Athlone, first Chancellor. $3.75, Sir Philip Sherlock, first principal of St. Augustine Campus. $4.50, Administration Building, St. Augustine Campus, horiz. $5.25, Samaan tree, St. Augustine Campus, horiz.
$15, Administration Building, St. Augustine Campus, at night.

Perf. 13½x13¼, 13¼x13½
2008, Oct. 3
834-838   A214   Set of 5   5.50   5.50
Souvenir Sheet
839   A214 $15 multi   5.00   5.00

For surcharge, see No. 892.

Worldwide Fund for Nature (WWF) — A215

No. 840 — Brazilian porcupine: a, Adult on branch (shown). b, Head. c, Adult and juvenile. d, Juvenile on branch.

2008, Nov. 3   Perf. 13½x13¼
840   Strip or block of 4   5.00   5.00
   a.-d.   A215 $3.75 Any single   1.25   1.25
   e.   Miniature sheet, 2 each
      #840a-840d   10.00   10.00

Commonwealth Heads of Government Meeting, Port of Spain — A216

Designs: $1, International Finance Center, Waterfront Complex, Port of Spain. $2.50, Steel drums. $3.75, Pigeon Point, Tobago. $4.50, Queen Elizabeth II and Commonwealth Secretaries-General chief Emeka Anyaoku, Kamalesh Sharma, Sir Shridath Ramphal, and Sir Donald McKinnon. $5.25, Scarlet ibis.
$15, Emblem of Commonwealth Heads of Government Meeting.

2009, Nov. 16   Perf. 13¼
841-845   A216   Set of 5   5.50   5.50
Souvenir Sheet
Perf. 14x13¾
846   A216 $15 multi   4.75   4.75

No. 846 contains one 33x45mm stamp. For surcharge, see No. 893.

Souvenir Sheet

Trinidad & Tobago Postal Corporation, 10th Anniv. — A217

No. 847: a, Head office. b, Retail counter.

Litho. & Embossed
2009, Dec. 18   Perf. 13¾x13¼
847   A217 $10 Sheet of 2, #a-b   6.50   6.50

Miniature Sheets

Intl. Year of Biodiversity — A218

No. 848: a, $1, Collared peccary. b, $1, No Man's Land, Bon Accord, Tobago. c, $2.50, Butterfly orchid. d, $2.50, Hot peppers. e, $3.75, Paria Bay, Trinidad. f, $3.75, Ornate hawk eagle. g, $4.50, Trinidad piping-guan. h, $4.50, Royal poinciana tree. i, $5.25, Trinidad select hybrid cocoa pods. j, $5.25, Water buffalos, Aripo Livestock Station.
No. 849: a, $1, Agouti. b, $1, Fishermen at Grafton Beach, Tobago. c, $2.50, Caroni Swamp and Bird Sanctuary, Trinidad. d, $2.50, Red bracket deer. e, $3.75, Turkey vulture. f, $3.75, White-chested emerald hummingbird. g, $4.50, Leatherback turtle. h, $4.50, Nariva Swamp, Trinidad. i, $5.25, Soldado Rock, Gulf of Paria. j, $5.25, Orchid.

2010, May 26   Litho.   Perf. 13¼x12½
Sheets of 10, #a-j
848-849   A218   Set of 2   21.50   21.50

London 2010 Festival of Stamps.

Syrians and Lebanese in Trinidad & Tobago, Cent. — A219

Designs: $1, Rahme Sabga, peddler. $2.50, Kashish, peddler. $3.75, Grand Bazaar Shopping Center. $4.50, Nicholas Tower.
$15, Woman wearing traditional Arab head covering.

2010, July 20   Perf. 13¼x13
850-853   A219   Set of 4   3.75   3.75
Souvenir Sheet
854   A219 $15 multi   4.75   4.75

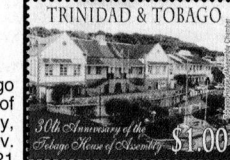

Trinidad & Tobago Cadet Force, Cent. — A220

Various photographs of cadets: $1, $2.50, $3.75, $4.50, $5.25.
$15, Rifles, Sir George Ruthven Le Hunte, Cadet Force founder, and Pres. George Maxwell Richards.

2010, Dec. 1   Perf. 13x13¼
855-859   A220   Set of 5   5.50   5.50
Souvenir Sheet
860   A220 $15 multi   4.75   4.75

Tobago House of Assembly, 30th Anniv. A221

Designs: $1, Tobago House of Assembly. $2.50, Englishman's Bay. $3.75, St. Patrick's Anglican Church. $4.50, Fort King George. $5.25, Buccoo Goat Race.
$15, Pigeon Point Heritage Park.

2010, Dec. 4   Perf. 13x13¼
861-865   A221   Set of 5   5.50   5.50
Souvenir Sheet
Perf. 13¼
866   A221 $15 multi   4.75   4.75

Festivities A222

Designs: $1, Spiritual Baptist Liberation Day. $2.50, Eid ul-Fitr. $3.75, Christmas. $4.50, Diwali.
$15, Parang.

2010, Dec. 10   Perf. 13¼x13
867-870   A222   Set of 4   3.75   3.75
Souvenir Sheet
Perf. 13¼
871   A222 $15 multi   4.75   4.75

Carnival — A223

Designs: $1, Participant in Sky People costume designed by Peter Minshall. $2.50, Children portraying Pierrot Grenade. $3.75, Junior Carnival Queen on Broadway. $4.50, Children's Carnival on Frederick Street. $5.25, Participant in Black Indian Chief costume designed by Larrie Approo.
$15, Participant in Pan Woman costume designed by Wendy Kallicharan.

2011, Mar. 1   Perf. 12
872-876   A223   Set of 5   5.50   5.50
Souvenir Sheet
877   A223 $15 multi   4.75   4.75

Dr. Eric Williams (1911-81), Prime Minister — A224

Designs: $1, Williams with Sir V. S. Naipaul, Michael Anthony, and Andre Deutsch. $1.50, Williams playing cricket with C. L. R. James and Sir Learie Constantine. $2.50, Williams and Kwame Nkrumah. $3.75, Painting of Williams by Georgia M. Cordner. $4.50, Williams with John Lennon and Ringo Starr. $5.25, Williams and Jawaharlal Nehru.
$15, Williams with Sir Winston Churchill.

2011, Apr. 5   Litho.   Perf. 13¼x13
878-883 A224 Set of 6   6.00 6.00
Souvenir Sheet
884 A224 $15 multi   4.75 4.75

Independence, 50th Anniv. — A225

Designs: No. 885, $1, Flag of Trinidad & Tobago. No. 886, $1, Arms of colonial and independent Trinidad & Tobago. No. 887, $1, Sir Solomon Hochoy, first Governor-General and Dr. Eric E. Williams, first Prime Minister. No. 888, $1, 50th anniversary emblem, vert.

2012, Aug. 8   Perf. 13¼
885-888 A225 Set of 4   1.40 1.40

No. 515 Surcharged

Method, Perf. and Watermark As Before
2012 ?
889 A136 $1 on $2.25 #515   —   —
  a.   Inverted surcharge

Nos. 604, 765, 838 and 845 Surcharged in Blue

Methods and Perfs As Before
2013, July 4
890 A162 $1 on $5 #604   .35 .35
891 A197 $1 on $5.25 #765   .35 .35
892 A214 $1 on $5.25 #838   .35 .35
893 A216 $1 on $5.25 #845   .35 .35
        Nos. 890-893 (4)   1.40 1.40

The new denomination on Nos. 890-893 obliterates the old denomination.

A226

World Food Day A227

Designs: $1, Sorrel drink. $2.50, Sorrel plant. $3.75, Capsular fruit of Hibiscus sabdariffa. $4.50, Biodiversity of sorrel in Trinidad & Tobago. $5.25, Flower of Hibiscus sabdariffa. $50, Mature Hibiscus sabdariffa calyces.

2013, Dec. 4   Litho.   Perf. 13¾
894 A226 $1 multi   .35 .35
Self-Adhesive
Serpentine Die Cut
895 A227 $50 multi   16.00 16.00
Miniature Sheet
Serpentine Die Cut 12¼
896   Sheet of 5   5.50
  a.   A226 $1 multi   .30 .30
  b.   A226 $2.50 multi   .80 .80
  c.   A226 $3.75 multi   1.25 1.25
  d.   A226 $4.50 multi   1.40 1.40
  e.   A226 $5.25 multi   1.75 1.75

Sorrel seeds were placed under a circle of plastic affixed to Nos. 895 and 896a-896e.

No. 516 Surcharged Like No. 889
Method, Perf. and Watermark As Before
2013?
897 A136 $1 on $2.50 #516   .55 .55

No. 516 Surcharged

Method, Perf. and Watermark As Before
2013, Nov. 8
898 A136 $1 on $2.50 #516   .35 .35

SEMI-POSTAL STAMPS

Emblem of Red Cross SP1

Perf. 11, 12
1914, Sept. 18   Typo.   Unwmk.
B1 SP1 (½p) red (on cover)   250.00

This stamp was allowed to pay ½p postage on one day, Sept. 18, 1914, on circulars distributed by the Red Cross. Value on cover is for proper Red Cross usage. Value unused, $15.

No. 2 Overprinted in Red (Cross) and Black (Date)

a   b

1915, Oct. 21   Wmk. 3   Perf. 14
B2 A1 (a) 1p scarlet   2.25 2.25

1916, Oct. 19
B3 A1 (b) 1p scarlet   .80 3.25
  a.   Date omitted

POSTAGE DUE STAMPS

D1

1923-45   Typo.   Wmk. 4   Perf. 14
J1 D1 1p black   3.75 3.75
J2 D1 2p black   7.00 1.90
J3 D1 3p black ('25)   7.00 5.00
J4 D1 4p black ('29)   7.00 27.50
J5 D1 5p black ('45)   42.50 110.00
J6 D1 6p black ('45)   75.00 42.50
J7 D1 8p black ('45)   52.50 200.00
J8 D1 1sh black ('45)   90.00 140.00
      Nos. J1-J8 (8)   284.75 530.65

> Catalogue values for unused stamps in this section, from this point to the end of the section, are for Never Hinged items.

Denominations in Cents
1947, Sept. 1
J9   D1 2c black   2.50 3.25
J10 D1 4c black   1.50 4.50
J11 D1 6c black   1.90 9.00
J12 D1 8c black   1.90 27.50
J13 D1 10c black   1.90 4.00
J14 D1 12c black   1.90 22.50
J15 D1 16c black   3.50 52.50
J16 D1 24c black   12.50 11.00
      Nos. J9-J16 (8)   27.60 134.25

Nos. J9-J16 also exist on chalky paper.

Wmk. 4a (error)
J9a   D1 2c   60.00
J11a D1 6c   125.00
J14a D1 12c   150.00

D2

1970   Unwmk. Litho. Perf. 14x13½
Size: 18x23mm
J17 D2 2c green   .25 2.75
J18 D2 4c carmine rose   .25 4.25
J19 D2 6c brown   .55 5.50
J20 D2 8c lt violet   .70 6.25
J21 D2 10c brick red   .70 6.25
J22 D2 12c dull orange   1.00 6.25
J23 D2 16c brt yellow grn   1.00 4.25
J24 D2 24c gray   1.00 4.50
J25 D2 50c blue   1.00 5.00
J26 D2 60c olive green   1.00 5.00
      Nos. J17-J26 (10)   7.45 50.00

Perf. 13½x14
1976-77   Litho.   Unwmk.
Size: 17x21mm
J27 D2 2c green   .25 1.75
J28 D2 4c carmine rose   .25 1.75
J29 D2 6c brown   .25 2.40
J30 D2 8c lt violet   .30 2.40
J31 D2 10c brick red   .30 2.40
J32 D2 12c dull orange   .45 3.25
      Nos. J27-J32 (6)   1.80 13.95

Issued: 4c, 12c, 4/1/76; 2c, 6c, 8c, 10, 1977.
The letters in the top label on Nos. J27-J32 are larger with D's and O's more squarish than the oval letters on Nos. J17-J26. "Postage Due" is 13mm long and is composed of finer letters than on Nos. J17-J26, which have a 14mm inscription.

WAR TAX STAMPS

Nos. 1-2 Overprinted

1917   Wmk. 3   Perf. 14
MR1 A1 1p scarlet   4.00 4.25
  a.   Invtd. overprint   225.00 300.00

Overprinted

MR2 A1 ½p green   1.50 .40
  a.   Overprinted on face and back   425.00
  b.   Pair, one without overprint   275.00
MR3 A1 1p scarlet   1.25 2.25
  a.   Pair, one without overprint   425.00 800.00
  b.   Double overprint   125.00

Overprinted

MR4 A1 ½p green   .30 6.50
MR5 A1 1p scarlet   .30 1.00

Overprinted

MR6 A1 ½p green   .30 3.25
MR7 A1 1p scarlet   3.50 1.25

Overprinted

MR8 A1 ½p green   .30 3.25
MR9 A1 1p scarlet   35.00 27.50

Overprinted

MR10 A1 1p scarlet   .80 1.40
  a.   Inverted overprint   100.00 100.00

Overprinted

MR11 A1 1p scarlet 1.75 .30
  a. Double overprint 200.00 200.00
  b. Inverted overprint 125.00 125.00

Overprinted

1918
MR12 A1 ½p green .30 2.00
MR13 A1 1p scarlet .90 1.75
  a. Double overprint 125.00
  b. Horiz. pair, one without
    overprint 1,000.

The War Tax Stamps show considerable variations in the colors, thickness of the paper, distinctness of the watermark, and the gum. Counterfeits exist of the errors of Nos. MR1-MR13.

OFFICIAL STAMPS

Regular Issue of 1913
Overprinted

1913 Wmk. 3 Perf. 14
O1 A1 ½p green 1.50 14.00

Same Overprinted

1914
O2 A1 ½p green 3.25 20.00

Same Overprinted

1916
O3 A1 ½p green 4.00 7.50
  a. Double overprint 50.00

Same Overprint without Period
1917
O4 A1 ½p green 4.75 22.50

Same Overprinted

1917, Aug. 22
O5 A1 ½p green 5.00 25.00

The official stamps are found in several shades of green and on paper of varying thickness.

TRIPOLITANIA

tri-,pä-lə-'tā-nyə

LOCATION — In northern Africa, bordering on Mediterranean Sea
GOVT. — A former Italian Colony
AREA — 350,000 sq. mi. (approx.)

POP. — 570,716 (1921)
CAPITAL — Tripoli

Formerly a Turkish province, Tripolitania became part of Italian Libya. See Libya.

100 Centesimi = 1 Lira

Used values in italics are for postally used stamps. CTO's or stamps with fake cancels sell for about the same as unused, hinged stamps.

Watermark

Wmk. 140 —
Crowns

Propaganda of the Faith Issue
Italian Stamps Overprinted

1923, Oct. 24 Wmk. 140 Perf. 14
1 A68 20c ol grn & brn
    org 11.00 47.50
2 A68 30c claret & brn
    org 11.00 47.50
  a. Double overprint 2,250.
  b. Vert. pair, imperf. btwn and
    at bottom 1,100. 1,650.
3 A68 50c vio & brn org 7.50 55.00
4 A68 1 l blue & brn org 7.50 85.00
  Nos. 1-4 (4) 37.00 235.00
  Set, never hinged 92.50

Fascisti Issue

Italian Stamps
Overprinted in Red
or Black

1923, Oct. 29 Unwmk.
5 A69 10c dk green (R) 15.00 18.50
6 A69 30c dk violet (R) 15.00 18.50
7 A69 50c brown car 15.00 18.50
  Wmk. 140
8 A70 1 l blue 15.00 47.50
9 A70 2 l brown 15.00 60.00
  a. Double overprint 1,650.
10 A71 5 l blk & bl (R) 15.00 90.00
  Nos. 5-10 (6) 90.00 253.00
  Set, never hinged 225.00

Manzoni Issue
Stamps of Italy, 1923, Overprinted in Red

1924, Apr. 1 Wmk. 140 Perf. 14
11 A72 10c brown red &
    blk 12.00 75.00
12 A72 15c blue grn & blk 12.00 75.00
13 A72 30c black & slate 12.00 75.00
  a. Imperf.

14 A72 50c org brn & blk 12.00 75.00
15 A72 1 l blue & blk 75.00 450.00
16 A72 5 l violet & blk 500.00 3,000.
  Nos. 11-16 (6) 623.00 3,750.
  Set, never hinged 1,530.

On Nos. 15 and 16 the overprint is placed vertically at the left side.

Victor Emmanuel Issue

Italy Nos. 175-177
Overprinted

1925-26 Unwmk. Perf. 11
17 A78 60c brown car 2.25 13.50
18 A78 1 l dark blue 3.00 13.50
  a. Perf. 13½ 10.50 42.50
  Perf. 13½
19 A78 1.25 l dk bl ('26) 3.75 37.50
  a. Perf. 11 2,000. 2,600.
  Nos. 17-19 (3) 9.00 64.50
  Set, #17-19, 18a, 19a,
  never hinged 4,000.

Saint Francis of Assisi Issue
Italy Nos. 178-180 Overprinted

1926, Apr. 12 Wmk. 140 Perf. 14
20 A79 20c gray green 2.25 13.50
  a. Vert. pair, one without ovpt. 5,250.
21 A80 40c dark violet 2.25 13.50
22 A81 60c red brown 2.25 26.00

Italy No. 182 and Type of A83
Overprinted in Red

  Unwmk.
23 A82 1.25 l dark blue 2.25 35.00
24 A83 5 l + 2.50 l ol grn 7.50 67.50
  a. Horiz. pair, imperf. btwn. 2,250.
  Nos. 20-24 (5) 16.50 155.50
  Set, never hinged 25.00

Volta Issue

Type of Italy
Overprinted

1927, Oct. 10 Wmk. 140 Perf. 14
25 A84 20c purple 4.50 37.50
26 A84 50c deep orange 7.50 26.00
  a. Double overprint 190.00
27 A84 1.25 l brt blue 13.50 60.00
  Nos. 25-27 (3) 25.50 123.50
  Set, never hinged 62.50

Monte Cassino Issue
Types of Italy Overprinted in Red or Blue

1929, Oct. 14
28 A96 20c dk green (R) 6.00 21.00
29 A96 25c red org (Bl) 6.00 21.00
30 A98 50c + 10c crim (Bl) 6.00 22.50

31 A98 75c + 15c ol brn
    (R) 6.00 22.50
32 A96 1.25 l + 25c dk vio
    (R) 13.50 42.50
33 A98 5 l + 1 l saph (R) 13.50 45.00

Overprinted in Red

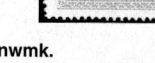

  Unwmk.
34 A100 10 l + 2 l gray brn 13.50 67.50
  Nos. 28-34 (7) 64.50 242.00
  Set, never hinged 160.00

Royal Wedding Issue

Type of
Italy
Overprinted

1930, Mar. 17 Wmk. 140
35 A101 20c yellow green 3.00 9.00
36 A101 50c + 10c dp org 2.25 9.00
37 A101 1.25 l + 25c rose red 2.25 18.00
  Nos. 35-37 (3) 7.50 36.00
  Set, never hinged 19.00

Ferrucci Issue

Types of
Italy
Overprinted
in Red or
Blue

1930, July 26
38 A102 20c violet (R) 6.00 6.00
39 A103 25c dk green (R) 6.00 6.00
40 A103 50c black (R) 6.00 11.00
41 A103 1.25 l dp bl (R) 6.00 21.00
42 A104 5 l + 2 l dp car
    (Bl) 13.50 45.00
  Nos. 38-42, C1-C3 (8) 73.50 196.00
  Set, never hinged 180.00

Virgil Issue

Types of
Italy
Overprinted
in Red or
Blue

1930, Dec. 4 Photo.
43 A106 15c violet black 1.10 11.50
44 A106 20c orange brown 1.10 4.50
45 A106 25c dark green 1.10 4.50
46 A106 30c lt brown 1.10 4.50
47 A106 50c dull violet 1.10 4.50
48 A106 75c rose red 1.10 9.00
49 A106 1.25 l gray blue 1.10 11.50
  Unwmk.
  Engr.
50 A106 5 l + 1.50 l dk vio 4.50 45.00
51 A106 10 l + 2.50 l ol brn 4.50 67.50
  Nos. 43-51, C4-C7 (13) 37.70 306.50
  Set, never hinged 90.00

Saint Anthony of Padua Issue

Types of
Italy
Overprinted
in Blue or
Red

1931, May 7 Photo. Wmk. 140
52 A116 20c brown (Bl) 1.50 21.00
53 A116 25c green (R) 1.50 7.50
54 A118 30c gray brn (Bl) 1.50 7.50
55 A118 50c dull vio (Bl) 1.50 7.50
56 A120 1.25 l slate bl (R) 1.50 37.50

Overprinted in Red or Black

Unwmk.   Engr.

57	A121	75c black (R)	1.50	21.00
58	A122	5 l + 2.50 l dk brn (Bk)	10.50	75.00
		Nos. 52-58 (7)	19.50	177.00
		Set, never hinged	47.50	

Native Village Scene A14

1934, Oct. 16   Wmk. 140

73	A14	5c ol grn & brn	5.25	21.00
74	A14	10c brown & black	5.25	21.00
75	A14	20c scar & indigo	5.25	19.00
76	A14	50c pur & brn	5.25	19.00
77	A14	60c org brn & ind	5.25	26.00
78	A14	1.25 l dk bl & grn	5.25	45.00
		Nos. 73-78,C43-C48 (12)	63.00	302.00
		Set, never hinged	155.00	

2nd Colonial Arts Exhibition, Naples.

SEMI-POSTAL STAMPS

Many issues of Italy and Italian Colonies include one or more semipostal denominations. To avoid splitting sets, these issues are generally listed as regular postage, airmail, etc., unless all values carry a surtax.

Holy Year Issue
Italian Stamps of 1924 Overprinted in Black or Red

1925   Wmk. 140   Perf. 12

B1	SP4	20c+ 10c dk grn & brn	3.75	22.50
B2	SP4	30c+ 15c dk brn & brn	3.75	24.00
B3	SP4	50c+ 25c vio & brn	3.75	22.50
B4	SP4	60c+ 30c dp rose & brn	3.75	30.00
B5	SP8	1 l + 50c dp bl & vio (R)	3.75	37.50
B6	SP8	5 l + 2.50 l org brn & vio (R)	3.75	57.50
		Nos. B1-B6 (6)	22.50	194.00
		Set, never hinged	55.00	

Colonial Institute Issue

Peace Substituting Spade for Sword — SP1

1926, June 1   Typo.   Perf. 14

B7	SP1	5c + 5c brown	1.10	9.50
B8	SP1	10c + 5c ol brn	1.10	9.50
B9	SP1	20c + 5c bl grn	1.10	9.50
B10	SP1	40c + 5c brn red	1.10	9.50
B11	SP1	60c + 5c orange	1.10	9.50
B12	SP1	1 l + 5c blue	1.10	20.00
		Nos. B7-B12 (6)	6.60	67.50
		Set, never hinged	16.50	

The surtax was for the Italian Colonial Institute.

> Fiera Campionaria Tripoli
> See Libya for stamps with this inscription.

Types of Italian Semi-Postal Stamps of 1926 Overprinted like Nos. 17-19

1927, Apr. 21   Unwmk.   Perf. 11

B19	SP10	40c + 20c dk brn & blk	3.75	40.00
B20	SP10	60c + 30c brn red & ol brn	3.75	40.00
B21	SP10	1.25 l + 60c dp bl & blk	3.75	60.00
B22	SP10	5 l + 2.50 l dk grn & blk	6.00	92.50
		Nos. B19-B22 (4)	17.25	232.50
		Set, never hinged	42.50	

The surtax was for the charitable work of the Voluntary Militia for Italian National Defense.

Allegory of Fascism and Victory — SP2

1928, Oct. 15   Wmk. 140

B29	SP2	20c + 5c bl grn	3.25	13.50
B30	SP2	30c + 5c red	3.25	13.50
B31	SP2	50c + 10c pur	3.25	22.50
B32	SP2	1.25 l + 20c dk bl	4.00	30.00
		Nos. B29-B32 (4)	13.75	79.50
		Set, never hinged	32.50	

46th anniv. of the Società Africana d'Italia. The surtax aided that society.

Types of Italian Semi-Postal Stamps of 1928 Ovptd.

1929, Mar. 4   Unwmk.   Perf. 11

B33	SP10	30c + 10c red & blk	4.50	26.00
B34	SP10	50c + 20c vio & blk	4.50	28.00
B35	SP10	1.25 l + 50c brn & bl	6.75	50.00
B36	SP10	5 l + 2 l ol grn & blk	6.75	97.50
		Nos. B33-B36 (4)	22.50	201.50
		Set, never hinged	55.00	

The surtax on these stamps was for the charitable work of the Voluntary Militia for Italian National Defense.

Types of Italian Semi-Postal Stamps of 1926, Overprinted in Black or Red Like Nos. B33-B36

1930, Oct. 20

B50	SP10	30c + 10c dp grn & bl grn (Bk)	35.00	52.50
B51	SP10	50c + 10c dk grn & vio (R)	35.00	97.50
B52	SP10	1.25 l + 30c blk brn & red brn (R)	35.00	97.50
B53	SP10	5 l + 1.50 l ind & grn (R)	110.00	260.00
		Nos. B50-B53 (4)	215.00	507.50
		Set, never hinged	525.00	

Ancient Arch — SP3

1930, Nov. 27   Photo.   Wmk. 140

B54	SP3	50c + 20c ol brn	3.75	24.00
B55	SP3	1.25 l + 20c dp bl	3.75	24.00
B56	SP3	1.75 l + 20c green	3.75	32.50
B57	SP3	2.55 l + 50c purple	9.00	45.00
B58	SP3	5 l + 1 l deep car	9.00	92.50
		Nos. B54-B58 (5)	29.25	218.00
		Set, never hinged	72.50	

25th anniv. of the Italian Colonial Agricultural Institute. The surtax was for the benefit of that institution.

AIR POST STAMPS

Ferrucci Issue
Type of Italian Air Post Stamps Overprinted in Blue or Red like #38-42

1930, July 26   Wmk. 140   Perf. 14

C1	AP7	50c brown vio (Bl)	6.00	13.50
C2	AP7	1 l dk blue (R)	6.00	18.50
C3	AP7	5 l + 2 l dp car (Bl)	24.00	75.00
		Nos. C1-C3 (3)	36.00	107.00
		Set, never hinged	90.00	

Virgil Issue
Types of Italian Air Post Stamps Overprinted in Red or Blue like #43-51

1930, Dec. 4   Photo.

C4	AP8	50c deep green	2.25	12.00
C5	AP8	1 l rose red	2.25	12.00

Unwmk.   Engr.

C6	AP8	7.70 l + 1.30 l dk brn	8.25	60.00
C7	AP8	9 l + 2 l gray	8.25	60.00
		Nos. C4-C7 (4)	21.00	144.00
		Set, never hinged	50.00	

Airplane over Columns of the Basilica, Leptis — AP1

Arab Horseman Pointing at Airplane AP2

1931-32   Photo.   Wmk. 140

C8	AP1	50c rose car	.75	.25
C9	AP1	60c red org	2.25	10.50
C10	AP1	75c dp bl ('32)	2.25	9.00
C11	AP1	80c dull violet	12.00	16.50
C12	AP2	1 l deep blue	1.50	.25
C13	AP2	1.20 l dk brown	30.00	22.50
C14	AP2	1.50 l org red	13.50	22.50
C15	AP2	5 l green	35.00	35.00
		Nos. C8-C15 (8)	97.25	116.50
		Set, never hinged	210.00	

For surcharges and overprint see Nos. C29-C32.

Agricultural Institute, 25th Anniv. AP3

1931, Dec. 7

C16	AP3	50c dp blue	3.00	24.00
C17	AP3	80c violet	3.00	24.00
C18	AP3	1 l gray black	3.00	35.00

C19	AP3	2 l deep green	9.00	45.00
C20	AP3	5 l + 2 l rose red	13.50	92.50
		Nos. C16-C20 (5)	31.50	220.50
		Set, never hinged	80.00	

Graf Zeppelin Issue

Mercury, by Giovanni da Bologna, and Zeppelin AP4

Designs: 3 l, 12 l, Mercury. 10 l, 20 l, Guido Reni's "Aurora." 5 l, 15 l, Arch of Marcus Aurelius.

1933, May 5

C21	AP4	3 l dark brown	12.00	120.00
C22	AP4	5 l purple	12.00	120.00
C23	AP4	10 l deep green	12.00	225.00
C24	AP4	12 l deep blue	12.00	240.00
C25	AP4	15 l carmine	12.00	260.00
C26	AP4	20 l gray black	12.00	350.00
		Nos. C21-C26 (6)	72.00	1,315.
		Set, never hinged	180.00	

For overprints and surcharges see Nos. C38-C42.

North Atlantic Flight Issue

Airplane, Lion of St. Mark AP7

1933, June 1

C27	AP7	19.75 l blk & ol brn	20.00	650.00
C28	AP7	44.75 l dk bl & lt grn	20.00	650.00
		Set, never hinged	95.00	

Type of 1931 Ovptd. or Srchd.

1934, Jan. 20

C29	AP2	2 l on 5 l org brn	4.50	90.00
C30	AP2	3 l on 5 l grn	4.50	90.00
C31	AP2	5 l ocher	4.50	105.00
C32	AP2	10 l on 5 l rose	6.00	105.00
		Nos. C29-C32 (4)	19.50	390.00
		Set, never hinged	52.50	

For use on mail to be carried on a special flight from Rome to Buenos Aires.

Types of Libya Airmail Issue Overprinted in Black or Red

1934, May 1   Wmk. 140

C38	AP4	50c rose red	13.50	160.00
C39	AP4	75c lemon	13.50	160.00
C40	AP4	5 l + 1 l brn	13.50	160.00
C41	AP4	10 l + 2 l dk bl	240.00	850.00
C42	AP5	25 l + 3 l pur	240.00	850.00
		Nos. C38-C42,CE1-CE2 (7)	547.50	2,500.
		Set, never hinged	1,300.	

"Circuit of the Oases."

Plane Shadow on Desert AP11

Designs: 25c, 50c, 75c, Plane shadow on desert. 80c, 1 l, 2 l, Camel corps.

1934, Oct. 16 **Photo.**

C43	AP11	25c sl bl & org red	5.25	21.00
C44	AP11	50c dk grn & ind	5.25	19.00
C45	AP11	75c dk brn & org red	5.25	19.00
C46	AP11	80c org brn & ol grn	5.25	21.00
C47	AP11	1 l scar & ol grn	5.25	26.00
C48	AP11	2 l dk bl & brn	5.25	45.00
		Nos. C43-C48 (6)	31.50	151.00
		Set, never hinged	77.50	

Second Colonial Arts Exhibition, Naples.

AIR POST SEMI-POSTAL STAMPS

King Victor Emmanuel III SPAP1

1934, Nov. 5 **Wmk. 140** ***Perf. 14***

CB1	SPAP1	25c + 10c gray grn	9.00	26.00
CB2	SPAP1	50c + 10c brn	9.00	26.00
CB3	SPAP1	75c + 15c rose red	9.00	26.00
CB4	SPAP1	80c + 15c blk brn	9.00	26.00
CB5	SPAP1	1 l + 20c red brn	9.00	26.00
CB6	SPAP1	2 l + 20c brt bl	9.00	26.00
CB7	SPAP1	3 l + 25c pur	26.00	120.00
CB8	SPAP1	5 l + 25c org	26.00	120.00
CB9	SPAP1	10 l + 30c rose vio	26.00	120.00
CB10	SPAP1	25 l + 2 l dp grn	26.00	120.00
		Nos. CB1-CB10 (10)	158.00	636.00
		Set, never hinged	390.00	

65th birthday of King Victor Emmanuel III; non-stop flight from Rome to Mogadiscio.
For overprint see No. CBO1.

AIR POST SEMI-POSTAL OFFICIAL STAMP

Type of Air Post Semi-Postal Stamps Ovptd. Crown and "SERVIZIO DI STATO" in Black

1934 **Wmk. 140** ***Perf. 14***

CBO1	SPAP1	25 l + 2 l cop red	2,450.	6,000.
		Never hinged	4,850.	

AIR POST SPECIAL DELIVERY STAMPS

Type of Libya Overprinted in Black Like Nos. C38-C42

1934, May 1 **Wmk. 140** ***Perf. 14***

CE1	APSD1	2.25 l red orange	13.50	160.00
CE2	APSD1	4.50 l + 1 l dp rose	13.50	160.00
		Set, never hinged	65.00	

AUTHORIZED DELIVERY STAMP

Authorized Delivery Stamp of Italy 1930, Overprinted like Nos. 38-42

1931, Mar. **Wmk. 140** ***Perf. 14***

EY1	AD2	10c reddish brown	18.00	45.00
		Never hinged	45.00	

TRISTAN DA CUNHA

ˌtris-tən-də-ˈkü-nə

LOCATION — Group of islands in the south Atlantic Ocean midway between the Cape of Good Hope and South America
GOVT. — A dependency of St. Helena
AREA — 40 sq. mi.
POP. — 313 (1988)

12 Pence = 1 Shilling
100 Cents = 1 Rand (1961)
12 Pence = 1 Shilling (1963)
20 Shillings = 1 Pound
100 Pence = 1 Pound (1971)

Catalogue values for all unused stamps in this country are for Never Hinged items.

Stamps of St. Helena, 1938-49, Overprinted in Black

1952, Jan. 1 **Wmk. 4** ***Perf. 12½***

1	A24	½p purple	.25	2.75
2	A24	1p blue grn & blk	1.00	1.90
3	A24	1½p car rose & blk	1.00	1.90
4	A24	2p carmine & blk	1.00	1.90
5	A24	3p gray	1.25	1.90
6	A24	4p ultra	7.00	3.00
7	A24	6p gray blue	7.00	3.00
8	A24	8p olive	7.00	7.50
9	A24	1sh sepia	6.00	2.50
10	A24	2sh6p deep claret	25.00	17.50
11	A24	5sh brown	37.50	22.50
12	A24	10sh violet	60.00	37.50
		Nos. 1-12 (12)	154.00	103.85
		Set, hinged	85.00	

Common Design Types pictured following the introduction.

Coronation Issue
Common Design Type

1953, June 2 **Engr.** ***Perf. 13½x13***

13	CD312	3p dk green & black	1.00	1.75

Tristan Crayfish — A1

Carting Flax — A2

Designs: 1½p, Rockhopper penguin. 2p, Factory. 2½p, Mollymauk. 3p, Island boat. 4p, View of Tristan. 5p, Potato patches. 6p, Inaccessible Island. 9p, Nightingale Island. 1sh, St. Mary's Church. 2sh 6p, Elephant seal. 5sh, Flightless rail. 10sh, Island spinning wheel.

1954-58 ***Perf. 12½***

14	A1	½p choc & red	.25	.25
a.		Bklt. pane of 4 ('58)	2.50	
15	A2	1p green & choc	.25	.60
a.		Bklt. pane of 4 ('58)	4.00	
16	A1	1½p dp plum & blk	2.00	1.40
a.		Bklt. pane of 4 ('58)	7.00	
17	A2	2p org & vio blue	.35	.25
18	A2	2½p carmine & blk	1.75	.70
19	A1	3p ol grn & ultra	.80	1.40
a.		Bklt. pane of 4 ('58)	10.50	
20	A2	4p dp bl & aqua	.80	.75
a.		Bklt. pane of 4 ('58)	13.00	
21	A2	5p gray & bl grn	.80	.75
22	A2	6p vio & dk ol grn	.80	.75
23	A2	9p henna brn & rose lil	.80	.55
24	A2	1sh choc & ol grn	.80	.55
25	A2	2sh6p blue & choc	19.00	10.00
26	A2	5sh red org & blk	50.00	15.00
27	A2	10sh red vio & org	24.00	16.00
		Nos. 14-27 (14)	102.40	48.95
		Set, hinged	70.00	

Starfish — A3

Fish: 1p, Concha. 1½p, Klipfish. 2p, Heron fish (saury). 2½p, Snipefish ("swordfish"). 3d, Tristan crawfish. 4p, Soldier fish. 5p, Five finger fish. 6p, Mackeral scad. 9p, Stumpnose. 1sh, Bluefish. 2sh6p, Snoek (snake mackerel). 5sh, Shark. 10sh, Atlantic right whale.

Perf. 12½x13

1960, Feb. 1 **Engr.** **Wmk. 314**

28	A3	½p org & blk	.25	.25
a.		Booklet pane of 4	1.50	
29	A3	1p rose lil & blk	.25	.25
a.		Booklet pane of 4	2.50	
30	A3	1½p grnsh bl & blk	.30	.25
a.		Booklet pane of 4	2.60	
31	A3	2p green & black	.40	.35
32	A3	2½p brown & black	.45	.35
33	A3	3p rose red & blk	1.20	1.40
a.		Booklet pane of 4	7.25	
34	A3	4p gray ol & blk	1.10	.65
a.		Booklet pane of 4	6.50	
35	A3	5p org yel & blk	1.40	.70
36	A3	6p blue & black	1.40	.80
37	A3	9p rose car & blk	1.60	.70
38	A3	1sh brn org & blk	2.40	.60
39	A3	2sh6p vio blue & blk	11.00	12.50
40	A3	5sh emerald & blk	13.00	16.00
41	A3	10sh violet & blk	45.00	50.00
		Nos. 28-41 (14)	79.75	84.80

1961, Apr. 15 ***Perf. 12½x13***

42	A3	½c like No. 28	.25	.25
43	A3	1c like No. 29	.25	.25
44	A3	1½c like No. 30	.40	.40
45	A3	2c like No. 32	.75	.75
46	A3	2½c like No. 33	1.10	1.10
47	A3	3c like No. 34	1.10	1.10
48	A3	4c like No. 35	1.40	1.40
49	A3	5c like No. 36	1.40	1.40
50	A3	7½c like No. 37	1.40	1.40
51	A3	10c like No. 38	1.60	1.60
52	A3	25c like No. 39	9.00	9.00
53	A3	50c like No. 40	17.50	17.50
54	A3	1r like No. 41	40.00	40.00
		Nos. 42-54 (13)	76.15	76.15

Nos. 46, 49-51 surcharged for "Tristan Relief" are listed as St. Helena Nos. B1-B4.

Types of St. Helena, 1961 Overprinted

Perf. 11½x12, 12x11½

1963, Apr. 12 **Photo.** **Wmk. 4**

55	A29	1p rose, ultra, yel & grn	.25	1.00
56	A29	1½p bis, sep, yel & grn	.25	.40
57	A29	2p gray & red	.25	1.00
58	A30	3p dk bl, rose & grnsh bl	.30	1.00
a.		Double overprint		
59	A29	4½p slate, brn & grn	.55	.70
60	A29	6p cit, brn & dp car	.80	.40
61	A29	7p vio, blk & red brn	.55	.40
62	A29	10p bl & dp claret	.55	.40
63	A29	1sh red brn, grn & yel	.55	.40
64	A29	1sh6p gray bl & blk	5.00	1.10
65	A29	2sh6p grnsh bl, yel & red	1.75	.75
66	A29	5sh grn, brn & yel	6.50	1.75
67	A29	10sh gray bl, blk & sal	6.50	1.75
		Nos. 55-67 (13)	23.80	11.05

Freedom from Hunger Issue
Common Design Type

Perf. 14x14½

1963, Oct. 2 **Photo.** **Wmk. 314**

68	CD314	1sh6p rose carmine	.90	.40

Red Cross Centenary Issue
Common Design Type

1964, Jan. 2 **Litho.** ***Perf. 13***

69	CD315	3p black & red	.55	.40
70	CD315	1sh6p ultra & red	.95	.60

Flagship of Tristáo da Cunha, 1506 — A4

Queen Elizabeth II — A5

½p, Map of South Atlantic Ocean. 1½p, Dutch ship Heemstede, first landing, 1643. 2p, New England whaler. 3p, Confederate ship Shenandoah. 4½p, H.M.S. Galatea, 1867. 6p, H.M.S. Cilicia, 1942. 7p, H.M. Royal Yacht Britannia, 1957. 10p, H.M.S. Leopard, Evacuation, 1961. 1sh, Dutch ship Tjisadane, 1961. 1sh6p, M.V. Tristania. 2sh6p, M.V. Boissevain, returning islanders, 1963. 5sh, M.S. Bornholm, returning islanders, 1963.

Perf. 11x11½

1965, Feb. 17 **Engr.** **Wmk. 314**

71	A4	½p black & dk blue	.25	.25
a.		Booklet pane of 4	.25	
72	A4	1p black & emerald	.85	.25
a.		Booklet pane of 4	4.25	
73	A4	1½p black & ultra	.85	.25
a.		Booklet pane of 4	4.25	
74	A4	2p black & lilac	.85	.25
75	A4	3p blk & grnsh bl	.85	.25
a.		Booklet pane of 4	4.25	
76	A4	4½p black & brown	.85	.25
77	A4	6p black & green	.70	.30
a.		Booklet pane of 4	4.25	
78	A4	7p black & ver	.85	.40
79	A4	10p black & dk brn	.85	.40
80	A4	1sh black & lil rose	.85	.50
81	A4	1sh6p black & olive	4.00	2.75
82	A4	2sh6p black & brn org	2.50	3.00
83	A4	5sh black & violet	5.00	4.00

Perf. 11½x11

84	A5	10sh lil rose & dk bl	1.75	1.50
		Nos. 71-84 (14)	21.00	14.35

See Nos. 113-115. For surcharges see Nos. 108, 141-152. For overprints see Nos. 132.

ITU Issue
Common Design Type

1965, May 11 **Litho.** ***Perf. 11x11½***

85	CD317	3p vermilion & gray	.50	.25
86	CD317	6p purple & orange	.65	.40

Intl. Cooperation Year Issue
Common Design Type

1965, Oct. 25 **Wmk. 314** ***Perf. 14½***

87	CD318	1p blue grn & claret	.25	.30
88	CD318	6p lt violet & green	1.10	.45

Churchill Memorial Issue
Common Design Type

Wmk. 314

1966, Jan. 24 **Photo.** ***Perf. 14***

Design in Black, Gold and Carmine Rose

89	CD319	1p bright blue	.25	.25
90	CD319	3p green	.35	.25
91	CD319	6p brown	1.35	.70
92	CD319	1sh6p violet	4.00	1.50
		Nos. 89-92 (4)	5.95	2.70

World Cup Soccer Issue
Common Design Type

1966 **Litho.** ***Perf. 14***

93	CD320	3p multicolored	.25	.25
94	CD321	2sh6p multicolored	1.00	.55

Nos. 93-94 were issued Oct. 1 in Tristan da Cunha, but on July 1 in St. Helena.

Light Dragoon of 19th Century and Sailing Ship — A6

Wmk. 314

1966, Aug. 15   Litho.   Perf. 14½
95	A6	3p pale green & multi	.25	.25
96	A6	6p tan & multi	.25	.25
97	A6	1sh6p gray & multi	.40	.30
98	A6	2sh6p multicolored	.55	.45
		Nos. 95-98 (4)	1.45	1.25

150th anniv. of the establishment of a garrison on Tristan da Cunha.

WHO Headquarters Issue
Common Design Type

1966, Oct. 1   Litho.   Perf. 14
99	CD322	6p multicolored	.30	.25
100	CD322	5sh multicolored	1.60	1.00

UNESCO Anniversary Issue
Common Design Type

1966, Dec. 1   Litho.   Perf. 14
101	CD323	10p "Education"	.30	.25
102	CD323	1sh6p "Science"	.60	.40
103	CD323	2sh6p "Culture"	1.10	.75
		Nos. 101-103 (3)	2.00	1.40

Calshot Harbor A7

Perf. 14x14½

1967, Jan. 2   Litho.   Unwmk.
104	A7	6p dull green & multi	.25	.25
105	A7	10p brown & multi	.25	.25
106	A7	1sh6p dull blue & multi	.25	.25
107	A7	2sh6p orange brn & multi	.25	.30
		Nos. 104-107 (4)	1.00	1.05

Opening of the artificial Calshot Harbor.

No. 76 Surcharged with New Value and Three Bars
Perf. 11x11½

1967, May 10   Engr.   Wmk. 314
108	A4	4p on 4½p blk & brn	.45	.30

Tristan da Cunha, Prince Alfred, Queen Elizabeth II and Prince Philip — A8

1967, July 10   Litho.   Perf. 14x14½
109	A8	3p blue grn, dk grn & blk	.25	.25
110	A8	6p dk carmine & blk	.25	.25
111	A8	1sh6p brt grn, gray grn & blk	.25	.25
112	A8	2sh6p dull ultra, sep & blk	.25	.30
		Nos. 109-112 (4)	1.00	1.05

Cent. of the visit of Prince Alfred, First Duke of Edinburgh, to Tristan da Cunha.

Types of 1965

Designs: 4p, H.M.S. Challenger, 1870. 10sh, South African research vessel, R.S.A. £1, Queen Elizabeth II.

Perf. 11x11½

1967, Sept. 1   Engr.   Wmk. 314
113	A4	4p black & orange	4.50	3.75
114	A4	10sh black & dull grn	14.00	14.00

Perf. 11½x11
115	A5	£1 brn org & dk blue	14.00	17.50
		Nos. 113-115 (3)	32.50	35.25

Wandering Albatross Nest — A9

Birds: 1sh, Big-billed buntings. 1sh6p, Tristan thrushes. 2sh6p, Great shearwaters.

Perf. 14x14½

1968, May 15   Photo.   Wmk. 314
116	A9	4p multicolored	.25	.25
117	A9	1sh multicolored	.50	.30
118	A9	1sh6p multicolored	.85	.50
119	A9	2sh6p multicolored	1.20	.85
		Nos. 116-119 (4)	2.80	1.90

Union Jack and St. Helena Flag — A10

Design: 9p, 2sh6p, Map showing locations of St. Helena and Tristan da Cunha.

1968, Nov. 1   Litho.   Wmk. 314
120	A10	6p violet & multi	.25	.25
121	A10	9p brn, bl grn & vio bl	.25	.25
122	A10	1sh6p green & multi	.25	.25
123	A10	2sh6p dp car, bl grn & vio bl	.25	.35
		Nos. 120-123 (4)	1.00	1.10

30th anniv. of Tristan da Cunha as a Dependency of St. Helena.

Frigate A11

Designs: 1sh, Cape Horner. 1sh6p, Barque. 2sh6p, Tea Clipper.

Perf. 11x11½

1969, June 1   Engr.   Wmk. 314
124	A11	4p brt blue	.25	.25
125	A11	1sh rose carmine	.40	.40
126	A11	1sh6p green	.55	.50
127	A11	2sh6p sepia	.95	.90
		Nos. 124-127 (4)	2.15	2.05

Islanders Going to First Religious Service, 1851 — A12

Designs: 4p, Tristan da Cunha, birds and ship. 1sh6p, Landing at the beach. 2sh6p, St. Mary's Church, 1969, and procession.

Perf. 14½x14

1969, Nov. 1   Litho.   Wmk. 314
128	A12	4p multicolored	.25	.40
129	A12	9p multicolored	.25	.40
130	A12	1sh6p multicolored	.30	.55
131	A12	2sh6p multicolored	.40	.55
		Nos. 128-131 (4)	1.20	1.90

Issued to honor the work of the United Society for the Propagation of the Faith.

No. 77 Overprinted in Deep Orange: "NATIONAL / SAVINGS"
Perf. 11x11½

1970, May 15   Engr.   Wmk. 314
132	A4	6p black & green	.45	.25

Issued to promote national savings. No. 132 also used as savings stamp.
In 1971, No. 132 was locally surcharged "2½p" and 3 short bars by means of a rubber handstamp. Value $7.

Globe and Red Cross A13

1sh9p, 2sh6p, British & Red Cross flags, vert.

Perf. 13½x13, 13x13½

1970, June 1   Litho.
133	A13	4p emer, red & grnsh bl	.25	.25
134	A13	9p bister, red & grnsh bl	.35	.25
135	A13	1sh9p gray, vio bl & red	.55	.35
136	A13	2sh6p rose cl, vio bl & red	.75	.60
		Nos. 133-136 (4)	1.90	1.45

Centenary of the British Red Cross Society.

Rock Lobster and Lobster Men Placing Trap — A14

10p, 2sh6p, Workers in processing plant and side view of rock lobster (jasus tristani).

Perf. 12½x13

1970, Nov. 1   Litho.   Wmk. 314
137	A14	4p lilac rose & multi	.25	.30
138	A14	10p dull yel & multi	.25	.35
139	A14	1sh6p brown org & multi	.60	.60
140	A14	2sh6p olive & multi	.90	.75
		Nos. 137-140 (4)	2.00	2.00

Tristan da Cunha rock lobster (crawfish) industry.

Nos. 72-74, 77-83, 113-114 Surcharged with New Value and Three Bars
Perf. 11x11½

1971, Feb. 15   Engr.   Wmk. 314
141	A4	½p on 1p	.25	.25
142	A4	1p on 2p	.25	.25
143	A4	1½p on 4p	.30	.25
144	A4	2½p on 6p	.30	.25
145	A4	3p on 7p	.30	.25
146	A4	4p on 10p	.30	.25
147	A4	5p on 1sh	.30	.25
148	A4	7½p on 1sh6p	1.90	2.10
149	A4	12½p on 2sh6p	2.50	3.00
150	A4	15p on 1½p	2.50	3.50
151	A4	25p on 5sh	2.50	6.25
152	A4	50p on 10sh	3.75	12.50
		Nos. 141-152 (12)	15.15	29.10

"Quest" — A15

4p, Presentation of Scout Troop flag in front of Tristan school. 7½p, Great Britain #167a with Tristan da Cunha cancellation. 12½p, Sir Ernest Henry Shackleton, boat & expedition cancellations.

Perf. 13½x14

1971, June 1   Litho.   Wmk. 314
153	A15	1½p lt blue & multi	.95	.25
154	A15	4p buff, yel grn & blk	.95	.45
155	A15	7½p pale grn, rose lil & blk	.95	1.00
156	A15	12½p lt blue & multi	1.60	2.00
		Nos. 153-156 (4)	4.45	3.70

50th anniversary of the Shackleton-Rowett South Atlantic expedition.

"Victory" at Trafalgar and Thomas Swain Catching Nelson — A16

Ships and Island Families: 2½p, "Emily of Stonington" and inscribed P. W. Green, 1836. 4p, "Italia" and inscribed Gaetano Lavarello, 1892, and Andrea Repetto. 7½p, "Falmouth" and Corp. William Glass, 1816. 12½p, American Whaler and inscribed 1836 Joshua Rogers, 1849, Capt. Andrew Hangan.

1971, Nov. 1
157	A16	1½p bister & multi	.25	.25
158	A16	2½p multicolored	.25	.25
159	A16	4p gray & multi	.40	.55
160	A16	7½p multicolored	.65	.85
161	A16	12½p blue & multi	1.00	1.40
		Nos. 157-161 (5)	2.55	3.30

Cow Pudding — A17

Native Flora: 1p, Peak berry and crater lake. 1½p, Sand flower, horiz. 2½p, New Zealand flax, horiz. 3p, Island tree. 4p, Bog fern and snow-capped mountain. 5p, Dog catcher and albatrosses. 7½p, Celery and terns. 12½p, Pepper tree and waterfall. 25p, Foul berry, horiz. 50p, Tussock and penguins. £1, Tussac and islands, horiz.

Perf. 13½x13, 13x13½

1972, Feb. 26   Wmk. 314
162	A17	½p gray & multi	.25	.25
163	A17	1p salmon & multi	.25	.25
164	A17	1½p green & multi	.25	.25
165	A17	2½p multicolored	.25	.25
166	A17	3p multicolored	.25	.25
167	A17	4p lemon & multi	.30	.30
168	A17	5p yel grn & multi	.45	.30
169	A17	7½p dull yel & multi	1.90	1.75
170	A17	12½p multicolored	1.25	1.00
171	A17	25p gray & multi	2.50	2.40

Litho. and Engr.
172	A17	50p multicolored	6.00	4.50
173	A17	£1 lt blue & multi	11.00	4.50
		Nos. 162-173 (12)	24.65	16.00

Coxswain — A18

2½p, Launching longboat. 4p, Men rowing longboat. 12½p, Longboat under sail.

1972, June 1   Litho.   Perf. 14
174	A18	2½p multi, horiz.	.25	.25
175	A18	4p multi, horiz.	.25	.25
176	A18	7½p multi	.50	.40
177	A18	12½p multi	.85	.50
		Nos. 174-177 (4)	1.85	1.40

Silver Wedding Issue, 1972
Common Design Type

Design: Queen Elizabeth II, Prince Philip, thrush and wandering albatrosses.

Perf. 14x14½

1972, Nov. 20   Photo.   Wmk. 314
178	CD324	2½p multicolored	.25	.25
179	CD324	7½p ultra & multi	.45	.45

Altar, St. Mary's Church — A19

1973, July 8   Litho.   Perf. 13½
180 A19 25p dk blue & multi   1.10 1.10
St. Mary's Church, Tristan da Cunha, 50th anniv.

"Challenger" off Tristan, Steil's Sounding Instrument — A20

Designs: 4p, Challenger's laboratory. 7½p, Challenger off Nightingale Island. 12½p, Map of Challenger's voyage. Each stamp shows an instrument for deep sea soundings.

Perf. 13½x14
1973, Oct. 15   Wmk. 314
181 A20 4p multicolored   .25 .25
182 A20 5p multicolored   .25 .25
183 A20 7½p multicolored   .40 .40
184 A20 12½p multicolored   .80 .80
a. Souv. sheet, #181-184, perf. 13½   2.25 2.25
Nos. 181-184 (4)   1.70 1.70
Centenary of "Challenger's" visit to Tristan da Cunha during oceanographic exploration world trip, 1872-76.

View of English Port from Shipboard — A21

5p, Inspectors at volcano rim. 7½p, Islanders disembarking from "Bornholm." 12½p, Islanders on board ship approaching Tristan da Cunha.

1973, Nov. 10   Perf. 14½
185 A21 4p yellow, blk & gold   .25 .25
186 A21 5p multicolored   .25 .25
187 A21 7½p multicolored   .40 .30
188 A21 12½p multicolored   .50 .40
Nos. 185-188 (4)   1.40 1.20
10th anniversary of return of islanders to Tristan da Cunha.

Princess Anne's Wedding Issue
Common Design Type
1973, Nov. 14   Wmk. 314   Perf. 14
189 CD325 7½p multicolored   .25 .25
190 CD325 12½p bl grn & multi   .25 .25

Rockhopper Penguin — A22

Designs: Rockhopper penguins.

1974, May 1   Litho.
191 A22 2½p shown   2.60 1.25
192 A22 5p Colony   3.00 1.65
193 A22 7½p Penguins fishing   3.25 2.00
194 A22 25p Penguin and fledgling   6.50 5.00
Nos. 191-194 (4)   15.35 9.90

Souvenir Sheet

Map of Tristan da Cunha, Penguin and Sea Gull — A23

1974, Oct. 1   Wmk. 314   Perf. 13½
195 A23 35p multicolored   5.25 5.25

Blenheim Palace A24

25p, Churchill and Queen Elizabeth II.

Wmk. 373
1974, Nov. 30   Litho.   Perf. 14
196 A24 7½p black & yellow   .25 .25
197 A24 25p black & brown   .40 .40
a. Souvenir sheet of 2, #196-197   .90 .90
Sir Winston Churchill (1874-1965).

Plocamium Fuscorubrum — A25

Aquatic Plants: 5p, Ulva lactuca. 10p, Epymenia flabellata. 20p, Macrocystis pyrifera.

Perf. 13x14
1975, Apr. 16   Wmk. 314
198 A25 4p lilac & multi   .25 .25
199 A25 5p ultra & multi   .25 .25
200 A25 10p yellow & multi   .30 .30
201 A25 20p lt green & multi   .65 .65
Nos. 198-201 (4)   1.45 1.45

Killer Whales — A26

Wmk. 314
1975, Nov. 1   Litho.   Perf. 13½
202 A26 2p shown   .30 .25
203 A26 3p Rough-toothed dolphins   .55 .25
204 A26 5p Atlantic right whale   1.50 .85
205 A26 20p Finback whales   3.75 1.90
Nos. 202-205 (4)   6.10 3.25

Tristan da Cunha No. 1 A27

Designs: 9p, Tristan da Cunha #13, vert. 25p, Freighter Tristania II.

Perf. 13½x14, 14x13½
1976, May 6   Litho.   Wmk. 373
206 A27 5p lilac, vio & blk   .25 .25
207 A27 9p bluish gray, grn & blk   .25 .25

208 A27 25p multicolored   .60 .60
a. Souvenir sheet of 3   3.25 3.25
Nos. 206-208 (3)   1.10 1.10
Festival of Stamps 1976. #208a contains one each of Ascension #214, St. Helena #297 and Tristan da Cunha #208.

The Patches A28

Views, by Roland Svensson: 3p, Tristan house, vert. 10p, Tristan Settlement and Cliffs. 20p, Huts at Nightingale, vert.

1976, Oct. 4   Litho.   Perf. 14
209 A28 3p multicolored   .25 .25
210 A28 5p multicolored   .25 .25
211 A28 10p multicolored   .30 .30
212 A28 20p multicolored   .45 .45
a. Souvenir sheet of 4, #209-211   1.60 1.60
Nos. 209-212 (4)   1.25 1.25
An artist's view of Tristan da Cunha. See Nos. 234-237, 268-271.

Royal Yacht Britannia — A29

15p, Royal standard. 25p, Royal family.

1977, Feb. 7   Wmk. 373   Perf. 13
213 A29 10p multicolored   .25 .25
214 A29 15p multicolored   .25 .25
215 A29 25p multicolored   .25 .25
Nos. 213-215 (3)   .75 .75
25th anniv. of the reign of Elizabeth II. For surcharges see Nos. 220-221.

H.M.S. Eskimo, Sept. 1970 A30

Royal Naval Ships and Arms: 10p, Naiad, Nov. 1968. 15p, Jaguar, Mar. 1964. 20p, London, Dec. 1964. Dates of visits to island.

1977, Oct. 1   Litho.   Perf. 14½
216 A30 5p multicolored   .25 .25
217 A30 10p multicolored   .25 .25
218 A30 15p multicolored   .25 .25
219 A30 20p multicolored   .30 .30
a. Souvenir sheet of 4, #216-219   1.75 1.75
Nos. 216-219 (4)   1.05 1.05

Nos. 214-215 Surcharged with New Value and Bar
1977, Oct. 13   Wmk. 373   Perf. 13
220 A29 4p on 15p multi   2.50 6.50
221 A29 7½p on 25p multi   2.50 6.50

Giant Fulmars — A31

1p, Pterodroma macroptera, horiz. 2p, Fregetta marina, horiz. 3p, Macronectes giganteus. 4p, Pterodroma mollis. 5p, Diomedea exulans. 10p, Pterodroma brevirostris. 15p, Sterna vittata. 20p, Puffinus gravis. 25p, Pachyptila vittata. 50p, Catharacta skua. £1, Pelecanoides urinatrix. £2, Diomedea chlororynchos.

Perf. 13½x14, 14x13½
1977, Dec. 1   Litho.
222 A31 1p multicolored   .25 .45
223 A31 2p multicolored   .25 .75
224 A31 3p multicolored   .25 .75
225 A31 4p multicolored   .25 .85
226 A31 5p multicolored   .25 .85
227 A31 10p multicolored   .30 .85
228 A31 15p multicolored   .50 1.25
229 A31 20p multicolored   .65 1.25
230 A31 25p multicolored   .80 1.25
231 A31 50p multicolored   1.75 1.25
232 A31 £1 multicolored   2.50 2.25
233 A31 £2 multicolored   5.25 3.00
Nos. 222-233 (12)   13.00 14.75
Nos. 224-233 are vertical. For overprints see Nos. 318-319.

Painting Type of 1976
Views by Roland Svensson: 5p, St. Mary's Church. 10p, Longboats. 15p, A Tristan home. 20p, Harbor, 1970.

Wmk. 373
1978, Mar. 1   Litho.   Perf. 14½
234 A28 5p multicolored   .25 .25
235 A28 10p multicolored   .25 .25
236 A28 15p multicolored   .30 .30
237 A28 20p multicolored   .45 .45
a. Souvenir sheet of 4, #234-237   1.75 1.75
Nos. 234-237 (4)   1.25 1.25
An artist's view of Tristan da Cunha.

Elizabeth II Coronation Anniversary
Common Design Types
Souvenir Sheet
1978, Apr. 21   Unwmk.   Perf. 15
238 Sheet of 6   1.50 1.50
a. CD326 25p King's Bull   .30 .30
b. CD327 25p Elizabeth II   .30 .30
c. CD328 25p Tristan crawfish   .30 .30
No. 238 contains 2 se-tenant strips of Nos. 238a-238c, separated by horizontal gutter with commemorative and descriptive inscriptions and showing central part of coronation procession with coach.

Sodalite — A32

Local Minerals: 5p, Aragonite. 10p, Sulphur. 20p, Lava containing pyroxene crystal.

Perf. 13½x14
1978, June 9   Litho.   Wmk. 373
239 A32 3p multicolored   .40 .45
240 A32 5p multicolored   .45 .45
241 A32 10p multicolored   .70 .70
242 A32 20p multicolored   1.10 1.10
Nos. 239-242 (4)   2.65 2.65

Fish A33

1978, Sept. 29   Litho.   Perf. 14
243 A33 5p Klipfish   .30 .30
244 A33 10p Fivefinger   .30 .30
245 A33 15p Concha   .35 .35
246 A33 20p Soldier   .40 .40
Nos. 243-246 (4)   1.35 1.35

Orangeleaf and Navy Flag — A34

Royal Fleet Auxiliary Vessels: 10p, Tarbatness. 20p, Tidereach. 25p, Reliant.

1978, Nov. 24   Litho.   Perf. 12½
247 A34 5p multicolored   .25 .25
248 A34 10p multicolored   .25 .25
249 A34 20p multicolored   .25 .25

250	A34 25p multicolored	.30	.30
a.	Souvenir sheet of 4, #247-250	1.40	2.75
	Nos. 247-250 (4)	1.05	1.05

Fur Seals — A35

Wildlife conservation: 5p, Elephant seal. 15p, Tristan thrush. 20p, Tristan buntings.

Wmk. 373

1979, Jan. 3		**Litho.**	**Perf. 14**
251	A35 5p multicolored	.25	.25
252	A35 10p multicolored	.25	.25
253	A35 15p multicolored	.30	.30
254	A35 20p multicolored	.35	.35
	Nos. 251-254 (4)	1.15	1.15

Tristan Longboat — A36

Ships: 10p, Queen Mary. 15p, Queen Elizabeth. 20p, QE II. 25p, QE II, longboat, view of Tristan.

1979, Feb. 8			**Perf. 14½**
255	A36 5p multicolored	.25	.25
256	A36 10p multicolored	.25	.25
257	A36 15p multicolored	.25	.25
258	A36 20p multicolored	.35	.35
	Nos. 255-258 (4)	1.10	1.10

Souvenir Sheet

259	A36 50p multicolored	1.00	1.50

Visit of cruise ship QE II, Feb. 8. No. 259 contains one 132x28mm stamp.

Tristan da Cunha No. 12 A37

Tristan da Cunha Stamps: 10p, No. 26. 25p, No. 58, vert. 50p, 1p-local "potatoe" stamp.

Perf. 14½x14, 14x14½

1979, Aug. 27		**Litho.**	**Wmk. 373**
260	A37 5p multicolored	.25	.25
261	A37 10p multicolored	.25	.25
262	A37 25p multicolored	.40	.40
	Nos. 260-262 (3)	.90	.90

Souvenir Sheet

263	A37 50p multicolored	.75	.75

Sir Rowland Hill (1795-1879), originator of penny postage.

The Padre's House, IYC Emblem A38

IYC Emblem, Children's Drawings: 10p, "Houses in the Village." 15p, "St. Mary's Church." 20p, "Rockhopper Penguins."

1979, Nov. 26		**Litho.**	**Perf. 14**
264	A38 5p multicolored	.25	.25
265	A38 10p multicolored	.25	.25
266	A38 15p multicolored	.25	.25
267	A38 20p multicolored	.25	.25
	Nos. 264-267 (4)	1.00	1.00

International Year of the Child.

Painting Type of 1976

Views (Sketches by Roland Svensson): 5p, Stoltenhoff Island. 10p, Nightingale from the East. 15p, The Administrator's abode, vert. 20p, "Ridge where the goat jumped off," vert.

1980, Feb.		**Litho.**	**Perf. 14**
268	A28 5p multicolored	.25	.25
269	A28 10p multicolored	.25	.25
270	A28 15p multicolored	.25	.25
271	A28 20p multicolored	.25	.25
a.	Souvenir sheet of 4, #268-271	1.00	1.00
	Nos. 268-271 (4)	1.00	1.00

Mail Pickup Boat — A40

1980, May 6		**Litho.**	**Perf. 14**
272	A40 5p shown	.25	.25
273	A40 10p Unloading mail	.25	.25
274	A40 15p Truck transport	.25	.25
275	A40 20p Delivery bell	.25	.25
276	A40 25p Distribution	.25	.25
	Nos. 272-276 (5)	1.25	1.25

London 80 Intl. Stamp Exhib., May 6-14.

Queen Mother Elizabeth Birthday
Common Design Type

1980, Aug. 11		**Litho.**	**Perf. 14**
277	CD330 14p multicolored	.45	.45

Golden Hinde — A41

1980, Sept. 6			**Perf. 14½**
278	A41 5p shown	.25	.25
279	A41 10p Drake's route	.25	.25
280	A41 20p Sir Francis Drake	.25	.25
281	A41 25p Queen Elizabeth I	.25	.25
	Nos. 278-281 (4)	1.00	1.00

Sir Francis Drake's circumnavigation, 400th anniversary.

Humpty Dumpty A42

Wmk. 373

1980, Oct. 31		**Litho.**	**Perf. 13½**
282	Sheet of 9	1.90	1.90
a.	A42 15p shown	.25	.25
b.	A42 15p Mary had a Little Lamb	.25	.25
c.	A42 15p Little Jack Horner	.25	.25
d.	A42 15p Hey Diddle Diddle	.25	.25
e.	A42 15p London Bridge	.25	.25
f.	A42 15p Old King Cole	.25	.25
g.	A42 15p Sing a Song of Sixpence	.25	.25
h.	A42 15p Tom Tom the Piper's Son	.25	.25
i.	A42 25p Owl and the Pussy Cat	.25	.25

Christmas 1980.

Islands on Mid-Atlantic Ridge, Society Emblem — A43

Royal Geographical Soc., 150th Anniv. (Maps and Expeditions): 10p, Tristan da Cunha, Francis Beaufort, 1806. 15p, Tristan Island, Norwegian expedition, 1937-1938. 20p, Gough Island, scientific survey, 1955-1956.

1980, Dec. 15			
283	A43 5p multicolored	.25	.25
284	A43 10p multicolored	.25	.25
285	A43 15p multicolored	.25	.25
286	A43 20p multicolored	.25	.25
	Nos. 283-286 (4)	1.00	1.00

Rev. Edwin Dodgson A44

Wmk. 373

1981, Mar. 23		**Litho.**	**Perf. 14**
287	A44 10p portrait, vert.	.25	.25
288	A44 20p shown	.30	.30
289	A44 30p Dodgson preaching, vert.	.40	.40
a.	Souvenir sheet of 3, #287-289	.90	.90
	Nos. 287-289 (3)	.95	.95

Centenary of arrival of Rev. Edwin H. Dodgson, who saved population from starvation.

Map of Tristan da Cunha showing L'heure du Berger Route, 1767 (Dalrymple's Map, 1781) — A45

Early Maps and Charts By: 5p, 21p, Capt. Denham, 1853 (diff.). 35p, Ivan Keulen, 1700.

1981, May 22			
290	A45 5p multicolored	.25	.25
291	A45 14p multicolored	.30	.30
292	A45 21p multicolored	.45	.45
	Nos. 290-292 (3)	1.00	1.00

Souvenir Sheet

293	A45 35p multicolored	.65	.85

Royal Wedding Issue
Common Design Type

Wmk. 373

1981, July 22		**Litho.**	**Perf. 14**
294	CD331 5p Bouquet	.25	.25
295	CD331 20p Charles	.25	.25
296	CD331 50p Couple	.40	.40
	Nos. 294-296 (3)	.90	.90

Hiking — A46

1981, Sept. 14			
297	A46 5p shown	.25	.25
298	A46 10p Camping	.25	.25
299	A46 20p Map reading	.25	.25
300	A46 25p Prince Philip	.25	.25
	Nos. 297-300 (4)	1.00	1.00

Duke of Edinburgh's Awards, 25th anniv.

Inaccessible Island Rail — A47

1981, Nov. 1		**Litho.**	**Perf. 13½x14**
301	Strip of 4	1.20	1.20
a.	A47 10p Nest	.30	.30
b.	A47 10p Eggs	.30	.30
c.	A47 10p Chicks	.30	.30
d.	A47 10p Adult rail	.30	.30

Six-gilled Shark A48

1982, Feb. 8		**Litho.**	**Perf. 13½x14**
302	A48 5p shown	.25	.25
303	A48 14p Porbeagle shark	.40	.30
304	A48 21p Blue shark	.65	.55
305	A48 35p Hammerhead shark	.90	.85
	Nos. 302-305 (4)	2.20	1.95

Marcella — A49

1982, Apr. 5		**Litho.**	**Perf. 14**
306	A49 5p shown	.35	.35
307	A49 15p Eliza Adams	.35	.35
308	A49 30p Corinthian	.50	.50
309	A49 50p Samuel & Thomas	.80	.80
	Nos. 306-309 (4)	2.00	2.00

See Nos. 324-327.

Princess Diana Issue
Common Design Type

Perf. 14½x14

1982, July 1		**Litho.**	**Wmk. 373**
310	CD333 5p Arms	.25	.25
311	CD333 15p Diana	.55	.25
312	CD333 30p Wedding	1.10	.35
313	CD333 50p Portrait	1.75	.60
	Nos. 310-313 (4)	3.65	1.45

Scouting Year — A50

5p, Baden-Powell, vert. 20p, Brownsea Isld. camp, 1907, vert. No. 316, 50p, Saluting. No. 317, 50p, Tree illustration, vert.

Perf. 13½x13, 13x13½

1982, Aug. 23			**Litho.**
314	A50 5p multicolored	.25	.25
315	A50 20p multicolored	.30	.30
316	A50 50p multicolored	.75	.75
	Nos. 314-316 (3)	1.30	1.30

Souvenir Sheet
Perf. 14

317	A50 50p multicolored	1.40	1.25

Nos. 226, 230 Overprinted: "1st PARTICIPATION / COMMONWEALTH / GAMES 1982"
Perf. 13½x14

1982, Sept. 28		**Litho.**	**Wmk. 373**
318	A31 5p multicolored	.25	.25
319	A31 25p multicolored	.40	.40

12th Commonwealth Games, Brisbane, Australia, Sept. 30-Oct. 9.

Formation of Volcanic Island A51

1982, Nov. 1 — Perf. 14x14½

320 A51 5p shown		.30	.30
321 A51 15p Surface cinder cones		.40	.40
322 A51 25p Eruption		.50	.50
323 A51 35p 1961 eruption		.60	.60
Nos. 320-323 (4)		1.80	1.80

Ship Type of 1982

1983, Feb. 1 — Litho. — Perf. 14

324 A49 5p Islander, vert.		.25	.25
325 A49 20p Roscoe		.40	.40
326 A49 35p Columbia		.75	.60
327 A49 50p Emeline, vert.		1.00	.90
Nos. 324-327 (4)		2.40	2.15

Tractor Pulling Trailer A52

1983, May 2 — Litho. — Perf. 14

328 A52 5p shown		.25	.25
329 A52 15p Pack mules		.25	.25
330 A52 30p Oxen pulling cart		.40	.40
331 A52 50p Jeep		.60	.60
Nos. 328-331 (4)		1.50	1.50

Map of South Atlantic A53

Island History — 3p, Tristao d'Acunha's flagship. 4p, Landing, 1643. 5p, 17th cent. views. 10p, Landing party, 1815. 15p, Settlement. 18p, Governor Glass's house. 20p, Rev. W.F. Taylor, Peter Green. 25p, Three-master John and Elizabeth. 50p, Dependency declaration of St. Helena, 1938. £1, Commissioning ceremony. £2, Evacuation, 1961.

Wmk. 373

1983, Aug. 1 — Litho. — Perf. 14

332 A53 1p multicolored		.25	.25
333 A53 3p multicolored		.25	.25
334 A53 4p multicolored		.25	.25
335 A53 5p multicolored		.25	.25
336 A53 10p multicolored		.25	.25
337 A53 15p multicolored		.35	.45
338 A53 18p multicolored		.40	.50
339 A53 20p multicolored		.45	.60
340 A53 25p multicolored		.70	.90
341 A53 50p multicolored		1.25	1.75
342 A53 £1 multicolored		2.50	3.50
343 A53 £2 multicolored		5.25	7.25
Nos. 332-343 (12)		12.15	16.20

Raphael, 500th Birth Anniv. — A54

1983, Oct. 27 — Litho. — Perf. 14½

344 A54 10p multicolored		.25	.25
345 A54 25p multicolored		.50	.50
346 A54 40p multicolored		.90	.90
Nos. 344-346 (3)		1.65	1.65

Souvenir Sheet

347 A54 50p multi, horiz.		1.50	1.25

Details from Christ's Charge to St. Peter.

St. Helena Colony Sesquicentenary — A55

1984, Jan. 3 — Litho. — Perf. 14

348 A55 10p No. 7		.25	.25
349 A55 15p No. 9		.25	.25
350 A55 25p No. 10		.40	.40
351 A55 60p No. 12		1.10	1.00
Nos. 348-351 (4)		2.00	1.90

Local Fungi A56

10p, Agrocybe praecox, vert. 20p, Laccaria tetraspora, vert. 30p, Agrocybe cylindracea. 50p, Sarcoscypha coccinea.

1984, Mar. 26

352 A56 10p multicolored		.50	.75
353 A56 20p multicolored		.85	.85
354 A56 30p multicolored		1.35	1.35
355 A56 50p multicolored		2.10	2.10
Nos. 352-355 (4)		4.80	5.05

Constellations A57

1984, July 30 — Perf. 14½

356 A57 10p Orion		.25	.25
357 A57 20p Scorpius		.55	.45
358 A57 25p Canis Major		.60	.55
359 A57 50p Crux		1.20	1.10
Nos. 356-359 (4)		2.60	2.35

Sheep Shearing — A58

1984, Oct. 1

360 A58 9p shown		.25	.25
361 A58 17p Carding wool		.35	.30
362 A58 29p Spinning		.60	.50
363 A58 45p Knitting		.95	.85
a. Souvenir sheet of 4, #360-363		2.25	2.25
Nos. 360-363 (4)		2.15	1.90

Stamps from No. 363a do not have white border around the design.

Christmas 1984 A59

1984, Dec. 3 — Perf. 14

364 A59 10p Three angels, Christmas dinner		.25	.25
365 A59 20p Two angels, cart		.40	.35
366 A59 30p Candles, sailboat		.65	.55
367 A59 50p Trees, Nativity		1.00	.85
Nos. 364-367 (4)		2.30	2.00

Shipwrecks — A60

10p, HMS Julia, 1817, vert. 25p, Bell from Mabel Clark, 1878, vert. 35p, Barque Glenhuntley, 1898.

60p, Map of shipwreck sites.

1985, Feb. 4 — Perf. 14x13½, 13½x14

368 A60 10p multicolored		.70	.45
369 A60 25p multicolored		1.10	1.10
370 A60 50p multicolored		1.60	1.50
Nos. 368-370 (3)		3.40	3.05

Souvenir Sheet

371 A60 60p multicolored		2.25	2.00

No. 371 contains one 48x32mm stamp. See Nos. 393-396, 412-415.

Queen Mother 85th Birthday
Common Design Type

10p, With Prince Charles, 1954. 20p, With Margaret at Ascot. 30p, Queen Mother. 50p, Holding Prince Henry. 80p, With Anne.

Perf. 14½x14

1985, June 7 — Litho. — Wmk. 384

372 CD336 10p multicolored		.25	.25
373 CD336 20p multicolored		.45	.45
374 CD336 30p multicolored		.70	.70
375 CD336 50p multicolored		.85	.85
Nos. 372-375 (4)		2.25	2.25

Souvenir Sheet

376 CD336 80p multicolored		2.75	2.75

Flags A61

10p, Jonathan Lambert & flag of 1811, Isles of Refreshment. 15p, Cannon & flag of 21st Light Dragoons, 1816-17, Fort Malcolm. 25p, HMS Falmouth, 1816, & flag of HMS Atlantic Isle, HMS JOB 9, 1942-46. 60p, View of Tristan & Union Jack, 1816 to date.

1985, Sept. 30 — Wmk. 373 — Perf. 14

377 A61 10p multicolored		.45	.45
378 A61 15p multicolored		.60	.60
379 A61 25p multicolored		1.05	1.05
380 A61 60p multicolored		2.75	2.40
Nos. 377-380 (4)		4.85	4.50

Nos. 378-380 vert.

Loss of The Lifeboat, Cent. — A62

1985, Nov. 28

381 A62 10p Lifeboat, barque West Riding		.25	.25
382 A62 30p Map		.75	.75
383 A62 50p Death toll		1.25	1.25
Nos. 381-383 (3)		2.25	2.25

Halley's Comet A63

10p, Bayeux Tapestry, c. 1092. 20p, Trajectory around Earth. 30p, Comet over Inaccessible Is. 50p, Ship Paramour.

1986, Mar. 3 — Wmk. 384

384 A63 10p multicolored		.50	.50
385 A63 20p multicolored		.80	.80
386 A63 30p multicolored		1.10	1.10
387 A63 50p multicolored		1.75	1.75
Nos. 384-387 (4)		4.15	4.15

Queen Elizabeth II 60th Birthday
Common Design Type

Designs: 10p, With Prince Charles, 1950. 15p, Birthday Parade, wearing uniform of Scots Guards, 1976. 25p, At Westminster Abbey, London, 1972, wearing mantle and robes of the Most Noble Order of Bath. 45p,

Silver Jubilee Tour, Canada, 1977. 65p, Visiting Crown Agents' offices, 1983.

1986, Apr. 21 — Perf. 14½

388 CD337 10p scarlet, blk & sil		.25	.25
389 CD337 15p ultra & multi		.30	.30
390 CD337 25p green & multi		.50	.50
391 CD337 45p violet & multi		.80	.80
392 CD337 65p rose vio & multi		1.15	1.15
Nos. 388-392 (5)		3.00	3.00

For overprints see Nos. 429-433.

Shipwrecks Type of 1985

9p, SV Allanshaw, 1893. 20p, Church font from Edward Vittery, 1881. 40p, Figurehead, 1940.
65p, Barque Italia, 1892.

1986, June 2 — Perf. 13½

393 A60 9p multicolored		.45	.45
394 A60 20p multicolored		.90	.90
395 A60 40p multicolored		1.75	1.75
Nos. 393-395 (3)		3.10	3.10

Souvenir Sheet
Perf. 13½x13

396 A60 65p multicolored		3.25	3.25

Nos. 394-395 vert.

Royal Wedding Issue, 1986
Common Design Type

Designs: 10p, Informal portrait. 40p, Andrew operating helicopter.

1986, July 23 — Perf. 14

397 CD338 10p multicolored		.25	.25
398 CD338 40p multicolored		1.15	1.15

A64

5p, Wandering albatross. 10p, Daisy. 20p, Vanessa butterfly. 25p, Wilkins's bunting. 50p, Ring-eye.

1986, Sept. 30

399 A64 5p multicolored		.25	.25
400 A64 10p multicolored		.50	.50
401 A64 20p multicolored		1.00	1.00
402 A64 25p multicolored		1.25	1.25
403 A64 50p multicolored		2.40	2.40
Nos. 399-403 (5)		5.40	5.40

Flora & fauna of Inaccessible Island.

A65

Indigenous Flightless Species and Habitats: 10p, Flightless moth, Edinburgh Settlement. 25p, Strap-winged fly, Crater Lake. 35p, Flightless rail, Inaccessible Island. 50p, Gough Island moorhen, Gough Island.

1987, Jan. 23 — Perf. 14½

404 A65 10p multicolored		.45	.45
405 A65 20p multicolored		1.10	1.10
406 A65 35p multicolored		1.50	1.50
407 A65 50p multicolored		2.25	2.25
Nos. 404-407 (4)		5.30	5.30

Rockhopper Penguins A66

1987, June 22

408	A66	10p Swimming	.60	.60
409	A66	20p Nesting	1.30	1.30
410	A66	30p Adult and young	1.90	1.90
411	A66	50p Adult's head	3.50	3.50
		Nos. 408-411 (4)	7.30	7.30

Shipwrecks Type of 1985

Designs: 11p, Castaways attacking sea elephant, vert. 17p, Henry A. Paull, 1879, Sandy Point. 45p, Gustav Stoltenhoff, Stoltenhoff Is., vert. 70p, Map of wrecks off Inaccessible Is.

1987, Apr. 2 — Perf. 14

412	A60	11p olive gray & blk	.55	.55
413	A60	17p dark violet & blk	.90	.90
414	A60	45p myrtle green & blk	2.60	2.60
		Nos. 412-414 (3)	4.05	4.05

Souvenir Sheet

415	A60	70p light blue, royal blue & apple grn	4.50 4.50

Norwegian Scientific Expedition, 50th Anniv. — A67

10p, Microscope and textbooks symbolic of expedition results. 20p, Scientists tagging a mollymawk. 30p, Expedition headquarters on the island. 50p, S.S. Thorshammer.

Wmk. 384

1987, Dec. 7 — Litho. — Perf. 14

416	A67	10p multicolored	.95	.90
417	A67	20p multicolored	1.90	1.50

Wmk. 373

418	A67	30p multicolored	2.75	2.10
419	A67	50p multicolored	4.00	3.50
		Nos. 416-419 (4)	9.60	8.00

Fauna of Nightingale Island — A68

1988, Mar. 21 — Wmk. 384 — Perf. 14

420	A68	5p Tristan bunting	.30	.30
421	A68	10p Tristan thrush	.55	.55
422	A68	20p Yellow-nosed albatross	.90	.90
423	A68	25p Great shearwater	1.10	1.10
424	A68	50p Elephant seal	2.50	2.50
		Nos. 420-424 (5)	5.35	5.35

Handicrafts A69

1988, May 30 — Perf. 14½

425	A69	10p Painted penguin eggs	.35	.35
426	A69	15p Moccasins	.50	.50
427	A69	35p Woolen clothing	1.25	1.25
428	A69	50p Model canvas boats	1.75	1.75
		Nos. 425-428 (4)	3.85	3.85

Nos. 388-392 Ovptd. "40TH WEDDING ANNIVERSARY" in Silver

1988, Mar. 9

429	CD337	10p scar, blk & sil	.25	.25
430	CD337	15p ultra & multi	.35	.35
431	CD337	25p green & multi	.50	.50
432	CD337	50p violet & multi	.90	.90
433	CD337	65p rose vio & multi	1.40	1.40
		Nos. 429-433 (5)	3.40	3.40

19th Cent. Whaling A70

1988, Oct. 6 — Perf. 14x14½

434	A70	10p "Trying out" blubber	.70	.70
435	A70	20p Harpoon guns	1.25	1.25
436	A70	30p Scrimshaw	2.10	2.10
437	A70	50p Ships	3.25	3.25
		Nos. 434-437 (4)	7.30	7.30

Souvenir Sheet

438	A70	£1 Right whale	5.00	5.00

Lloyds of London, 300th Anniv.
Common Design Type

10p, Lloyds's new building, 1988. 25p, Cargo ship *Tristania II*, horiz. 35p, Supply ship *St. Helena*, horiz. 50p, Square-rigger *Kobenhavn*, lost at sea.

1988, Nov. 7 — Perf. 14

439	CD341	10p multicolored	.60	.60
440	CD341	25p multicolored	1.75	1.75
441	CD341	35p multicolored	2.25	2.25
442	CD341	50p multicolored	3.00	3.00
		Nos. 439-442 (4)	7.60	7.60

Paintings of the Island, 1824, by Augustus Earle (1793-1838) — A71

Designs: 1p, Government House. 3p, Squall off Tristan. 4p, Rafting Blubber. 5p, Tristan. 10p, Man Killing an Albatross. 15p, View on the Summit. 20p, Nightingale Island. 25p, Tristan, diff. 35p, "Solitude," Watching the Horizon. 50p, North Eastern. £1, Tristan, diff. £2, Governor Glass and His Companions.

1988, Dec. 10

443	A71	1p multicolored	.25	.25
444	A71	3p multicolored	.25	.25
445	A71	4p multicolored	.25	.25
446	A71	5p multicolored	.25	.25
447	A71	10p multicolored	.35	.35
448	A71	15p multicolored	.45	.60
449	A71	20p multicolored	.60	1.10
450	A71	25p multicolored	.80	1.25
451	A71	35p multicolored	1.10	2.00
452	A71	50p multicolored	1.40	2.75
453	A71	£1 multicolored	3.00	5.50
454	A71	£2 multicolored	6.00	10.50
		Nos. 443-454 (12)	14.70	25.05

Gough Is. Fauna — A72

1989, Feb. 6 — Litho. — Wmk. 384

455	A72	5p Giant petrel	.45	.45
456	A72	10p Gough moorhen	.80	.80
457	A72	20p Gough bunting	1.50	1.50
458	A72	25p Sooty albatross	1.75	1.75
459	A72	50p Amsterdam fur seal	3.50	3.50
		Nos. 455-459 (5)	8.00	8.00

Ferns — A73

10p, Eriosorus cheilanthoides. 25p, Asplenium alvarezense. 35p, Elaphoglossum hybridum. 50p, Ophioglossum opacum.

1989, May 22 — Wmk. 373 — Perf. 14

460	A73	10p multicolored	.55	.55
461	A73	25p multicolored	1.40	1.40
462	A73	35p multicolored	2.10	2.10
463	A73	50p multicolored	2.60	2.60
		Nos. 460-463 (4)	6.65	6.65

A74

1989, Nov. 20 — Wmk. 384

464	A74	10p Cattle egret	1.30	1.10
465	A74	25p Spotted sandpiper	2.75	2.50
466	A74	35p Purple gallinule	4.00	3.50
467	A74	50p Barn swallow	5.25	4.75
		Nos. 464-467 (4)	13.30	11.85

Artifacts on Exhibit in the Nautical Museum A75

10p, Surgeon's mortar. 20p, Parts of a harpoon. 35p, Compass with binnacle hood. 60p, Rope-twisting device.

1989, Sept. 25

468	A75	10p multicolored	.55	.55
469	A75	20p multicolored	1.10	1.10
470	A75	30p multicolored	1.75	1.75
471	A75	60p multicolored	3.50	3.50
		Nos. 468-471 (4)	6.90	6.90

Moths A76

10p, Peridroma saucia. 15p, Ascalapha odorata. 35p, Agrius cingulata. 60p, Eumorpha labruscae.

1990, Feb. 1 — Perf. 14

472	A76	10p multicolored	.70	.70
473	A76	15p multicolored	1.10	1.10
474	A76	35p multicolored	2.75	2.75
475	A76	60p multicolored	5.00	5.00
		Nos. 472-475 (4)	9.55	9.55

Starfish (Echinoderms) A77

1990, June 12 — Perf. 14x13½

476	A77	10p shown	.80	.80
477	A77	20p multi, diff.	1.10	1.50
478	A77	30p multi, diff.	2.60	2.25
479	A77	60p multi, diff.	4.50	4.50
		Nos. 476-479 (4)	9.00	9.05

Queen Mother, 90th Birthday
Common Design Types

25p, Queen Mother at the Coliseum. £1, Broadcasting to women of the empire, 1939.

1990, Aug. 4 — Wmk. 384 — Perf. 14x15

480	CD343	25p multicolored	1.10	1.10

Perf. 14½

481	CD344	£1 multicolored	4.50	4.50

Dunnottar Castle, 1942 — A78

Designs: 15p, RMS St. Helena, 1977-1990. 35p, Launching new RMS St. Helena, 1989. 60p, Duke of York launching new RMS St. Helena. £1, New RMS St. Helena.

1990, Sept. 13 — Wmk. 373 — Perf. 14½

482	A78	10p multicolored	.95	.95
483	A78	15p multicolored	1.50	1.50
484	A78	35p multicolored	4.00	3.25
485	A78	60p multicolored	6.25	5.50
		Nos. 482-485 (4)	12.70	11.20

Souvenir Sheet

486	A78	£1 multicolored	8.75	8.75

See Ascension Nos. 493-497, St. Helena Nos. 535-539.

Royal Navy Warships A79

Perf. 14½x14

1990, Nov. 30 — Litho. — Wmk. 373

487	A79	10p Pyramus, 1829	1.25	1.25
488	A79	25p Penguin, 1815	3.00	3.00
489	A79	35p Thalia, 1886	4.25	4.25
490	A79	50p Sidon, 1858	6.00	6.00
		Nos. 487-490 (4)	14.50	14.50

See Nos. 547-550.

1991, Feb. 4

491	A79	10p Milford, 1938	2.10	1.60
492	A79	25p Dublin, 1923	3.25	2.75
493	A79	35p Yarmouth, 1919	4.50	4.00
494	A79	50p Carlisle, 1938	5.00	6.00
		Nos. 491-494 (4)	14.85	14.35

Souvenir Sheet

Royal Viking Sun — A80

Wmk. 384

1991, Apr. 1 — Litho. — Perf. 14

495	A80	£1 multicolored	10.00	10.00

Prince Philip, 70th Birthday A81

Designs: 10p, HMS Galatea, Prince Alfred. 25p, Royal Visit, 1957. 30p, HMY Britannia, Prince Philip. 50p, Settlement of Edinburgh, Prince Philip.

1991, June 10 — Wmk. 373

496	A81	10p multicolored	1.50	1.25
497	A81	25p multicolored	3.25	3.00
498	A81	30p multicolored	4.00	3.50
499	A81	50p multicolored	6.25	6.00
		Nos. 496-499 (4)	15.00	13.75

Birds
A82

1991, Oct. 1
500	A82	8p Gough moorhens	2.50	1.60
501	A82	10p Gough bunting	2.50	1.90
502	A82	12p Gough moorhen in nest	2.75	1.90
503	A82	15p Gough bunting with chicks	3.00	2.25
		Nos. 500-503 (4)	10.75	7.65

World Wildlife Fund.

Discovery of America, 500th
Anniv. — A83

10p, STV Eye of the Wind. 15p, STV Soren Larsen. 35p, STV Pinta, Nina, Santa Maria. 60p, Columbus, Santa Maria.

1992, Jan. 23
504	A83	10p multicolored	.95	.75
505	A83	15p multicolored	1.25	1.10
506	A83	35p multicolored	3.00	2.75
507	A83	60p multicolored	5.50	4.75
		Nos. 504-507 (4)	10.70	9.35

World Columbian Stamp Expo '92, Chicago and Genoa '92 Intl. Philatelic Exhibitions.

Queen Elizabeth II's Accession to the Throne, 40th Anniv.
Common Design Type

1992, Feb. 6
508	CD349	10p multicolored	.55	.55
509	CD349	20p multicolored	1.15	1.10
510	CD349	25p multicolored	1.40	1.25
511	CD349	35p multicolored	1.90	1.90
512	CD349	65p multicolored	3.75	3.50
		Nos. 508-512 (5)	8.75	8.30

Fish — A84

Designs: 10p, Caesioperca coatsii. 15p, Mendosoma lineatum. 35p, Physiculus karrerae. 60p, Decapterus longimanus.

1992, June 1
513	A84	10p multicolored	.80	.55
514	A84	15p multicolored	1.50	1.10
515	A84	35p multicolored	2.75	2.40
516	A84	60p multicolored	5.00	4.25
		Nos. 513-516 (4)	10.05	8.30

Wreck of the Italia, Cent. — A85

Designs: 10p, Italia leaving Greenock. 45p, In mid-Atlantic. 65p, Driving ashore on Stony Beach. £1, Italia in peaceful waters.

1992, Sept. 18   Perf. 13½x14
517	A85	10p multicolored	.85	.80
518	A85	45p multicolored	3.50	3.50
519	A85	65p multicolored	5.25	5.25
		Nos. 517-519 (3)	9.60	9.55

Souvenir Sheet
520	A85	£1 multicolored	9.75	9.75

Genoa '92 Intl. Philatelic Exhibition (#520).

Insects — A86

15p, Stenoscelis hylastoides. 45p, Trogloscaptomyza brevilamellata. 60p, Senilites tristanicola.

Perf. 14x13½
1993, Feb. 2   Litho.   Wmk. 384
521	A86	15p multicolored	1.25	1.25
522	A86	45p multicolored	3.50	3.50
523	A86	60p multicolored	4.00	4.00
		Nos. 521-523 (3)	8.75	8.75

Coronation of Queen Elizabeth II, 40th Anniv. — A87

Designs: 10p, Ampulla, spoon. 15p, Orb. 35p, Imperial State Crown. 60p, St. Edward's Crown.

1993, June 14   Perf. 14½
524	A87	10p green & black	.70	.70
525	A87	15p red vio & black	1.10	1.10
526	A87	35p purple & black	2.40	2.40
527	A87	60p blue & black	4.25	4.25
		Nos. 524-527 (4)	8.45	8.45

Resettlement to Tristan, 30th
Anniv. — A88

Ships: No. 528, Tristania, Frances Repetto. No. 529, Boissevain. 50p, Bornholm.

1993, Nov. 10   Perf. 13½x14
528	A88	35p multicolored	2.75	2.50
529	A88	35p multicolored	2.75	2.50
a.		Pair, #528-529	6.50	6.00
530	A88	50p multicolored	4.50	4.25
		Nos. 528-530 (3)	10.00	9.25

Christmas — A89

Entire paintings or details: 5p, Madonna with Child, School of Botticelli. 15p, The Holy Family, by Daniel Gran. 35p, The Holy Virgin and Child, by Rubens. 65p, The Mystical Marriage of St. Catherine with the Holy Child, by Jan Van Balen.

1993, Nov. 30   Wmk. 373   Perf. 13
531	A89	5p multicolored	.60	.60
532	A89	15p multicolored	1.75	1.25
533	A89	35p multicolored	3.75	2.75
534	A89	65p multicolored	6.00	5.25
		Nos. 531-534 (4)	12.10	9.85

Ships
A90

Designs: 1p, Duchess of Atholl, 1929. 3p, Empress of Australia, 1935. 5p, Anatolia, 1937. 8p, Viceroy of India, 1939. 10p, Rangitata, 1943. 15p, Caronia, 1950. 20p, Rotterdam, 1960. 25p, Leonardo da Vinci, 1972. 35p, Vistafjord, 1974. £1, World Discoverer, 1984. £2, Astor, 1984. £5, RMS St. Helena, 1992.

1994, Feb. 3   Wmk. 384   Perf. 14
535	A90	1p multicolored	.30	.35
536	A90	3p multicolored	.30	.35
537	A90	5p multicolored	.30	.35
538	A90	8p multicolored	.30	.35
539	A90	10p multicolored	.40	.50
540	A90	15p multicolored	.60	.70
541	A90	20p multicolored	.80	.90
542	A90	25p multicolored	1.00	1.10
543	A90	35p multicolored	1.50	1.75
544	A90	£1 multicolored	3.75	4.50
545	A90	£2 multicolored	7.75	9.00
546	A90	£5 multicolored	20.00	17.00
		Nos. 535-546 (12)	37.00	36.85

Royal Navy Warships Type of 1990

10p, HMS Nigeria, 1948. 25p, HMS Phoebe, 1949. 35p, HMS Liverpool, 1949. 50p, HMS Magpie, 1955.

1994, May 2   Wmk. 373
547	A79	10p multicolored	1.00	1.00
548	A79	25p multicolored	2.50	2.50
549	A79	35p multicolored	3.25	3.25
550	A79	50p multicolored	5.25	5.25
		Nos. 547-550 (4)	12.00	12.00

Sharks
A91

1994, Aug.   Wmk. 384
551	A91	10p Blue shark	.95	.95
552	A91	45p Seven-gill shark	3.75	3.75
553	A91	65p Mako shark	5.25	5.25
		Nos. 551-553 (3)	9.95	9.95

Farm Animals — A92

1994, Nov.   Wmk. 373
554	A92	10p Donkeys	.75	.75
555	A92	20p Cattle	1.75	1.75
556	A92	35p Ducks, geese	3.25	3.25
557	A92	60p Girl feeding lamb	5.75	5.75
		Nos. 554-557 (4)	11.50	11.50

See Nos. 601-604.

Local
Transport
A93

Designs: 15p, Pick-up truck. 20p, Leyland Daf Sherpa van. 45p, Yamaha motorcycle, scooter. 60p, Administrator's Landrover.

Wmk. 384
1995, Feb. 27   Litho.   Perf. 14
558	A93	15p multicolored	1.15	1.15
559	A93	20p multicolored	1.35	1.35
560	A93	45p multicolored	3.25	3.25
561	A93	60p multicolored	4.50	4.50
		Nos. 558-561 (4)	10.25	10.25

End of World War II, 50th Anniv.
Common Design Types

Designs: 15p, Lewis gun instruction, 1943. 20p, Tristan defense volunteers, 1943-46. 45p,

Radio, weather stations. 60p, HNS Birmingham, 1942. £1, Reverse of War Medal, 1939-45.

Perf. 13x13½
1995, June 19   Litho.   Wmk. 373
562	CD351	15p multicolored	1.50	1.50
563	CD351	20p multicolored	2.10	2.10
564	CD351	45p multicolored	4.00	4.00
565	CD351	60p multicolored	5.75	5.75
		Nos. 562-565 (4)	13.35	13.35

Souvenir Sheet
Perf. 14
566	CD352	£1 multicolored	6.75	6.75

Souvenir Sheet

Queen Mother, 95th Birthday — A94

1995, Aug. 4   Litho.   Perf. 14½x14
567	A94	£1.50 multicolored	9.00	9.00

UN, 50th Anniv.
Common Design Type

20p, Bedford 4-ton truck. 30p, Saxon armored personnel carrier. 45p, Mi26 heavy lift helicopter. 50p, RFA Sir Tristram transporting UN vehicles.

1995, Oct. 24   Perf. 13½x13
568	CD353	20p multicolored	1.75	1.75
569	CD353	30p multicolored	3.00	3.00
570	CD353	45p multicolored	4.00	4.00
571	CD353	50p multicolored	4.75	4.75
		Nos. 568-571 (4)	13.50	13.50

Seals
A95

Sub Antarctic fur seal: 10p, On rock. 35p, Coming out of water with young.
Southern elephant seal: 45p, On beach with young. 50p, In water.

1995, Nov. 3   Perf. 13½
572	A95	10p multicolored	.70	.70
573	A95	35p multicolored	2.75	2.75
574	A95	45p multicolored	4.00	4.00
575	A95	50p multicolored	4.25	4.25
		Nos. 572-575 (4)	11.70	11.70

Queen Elizabeth II, 70th Birthday
Common Design Type

Various portraits of Queen, island scenes: 15p, Tristan from sea. 20p, Traditional cottage. 45p, The Residency. 60p, With Prince Philip.

1996, Apr. 22   Litho.   Perf. 13½
576	CD354	15p multicolored	.90	.90
577	CD354	20p multicolored	1.20	1.20
578	CD354	45p multicolored	2.75	2.75
579	CD354	60p multicolored	3.50	3.50
		Nos. 576-579 (4)	8.35	8.35

New Harbor — A96

15p, View of Old Harbor. 20p, Earthmoving, New Harbor construction. 45p, Crane, new construction. 60p, View of New Harbor. Nos. 581-582 are 45x28mm.

1996, July 5   Wmk. 373   Perf. 13

580	A96	15p multicolored	1.75	1.75
581	A96	20p multicolored	2.75	2.75
582	A96	45p multicolored	3.50	3.50
583	A96	60p multicolored	4.50	4.50
		Nos. 580-583 (4)	12.50	12.50

Nos. 581-582 are 45x28mm.

A97

Gough Island Birds: 15p, Gough moorhen. 20p, Wandering albatross. 45p, Sooty albatross. 60p, Gough bunting.

1996, Oct. 1   Perf. 14

584	A97	15p multicolored	.90	.90
585	A97	20p multicolored	1.35	1.35
586	A97	45p multicolored	3.25	3.25
587	A97	60p multicolored	4.50	4.50
a.		Souvenir sheet of 1	5.00	5.00
		Nos. 584-587 (4)	10.00	10.00

No. 587a for return of Hong Kong to China, July 1, 1997. Issued 6/20/97.

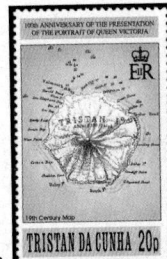

A98

Presentation of Portrait of Queen Victoria, Cent.: 20p, 19th cent. map of Trista da Cunha. 30p, HMS Magpie. 45p, Peter Green, former governor. 50p, Detail of portrait of Queen Victoria, by Heinrich Von Angell.

1996, Dec. 18   Perf. 13½

588	A98	20p multicolored	1.40	1.40
589	A98	30p multicolored	2.25	2.25
590	A98	45p multicolored	3.25	3.25
591	A98	50p multicolored	3.50	3.50
		Nos. 588-591 (4)	10.40	10.40

Atlantic Marine Fauna of the Cretaceous — A99

Designs: a, Archelon. b, Trinacromerum. c, Platecarpus. d, Clidastes.

1997, Feb. 10   Wmk. 384   Perf. 14

592	A99	35p Sheet of 4, #a.-d.	10.50	10.50

See No. 619.

Visual Communications — A100

Designs: No. 593, Smoke signals. No. 594, HMS Eurydice. No. 595, HMS Challenger. No. 596, Flag hoists. No. 597, Semaphore. No. 598, HMS Carlisle. No. 599, Light signals. No. 600, HMS Cilicia.

1997   Litho.   Wmk. 384   Perf. 14½

593		10p multicolored	.65	.65
594		10p multicolored	.65	.65
a.	A100	Pair, #593-594	1.50	1.50
595		15p multicolored	.90	.90
596		15p multicolored	.90	.90
a.	A100	Pair, #595-596	2.40	2.40
597		20p multicolored	1.10	1.10
598		20p multicolored	1.10	1.10
a.	A100	Pair, #597-598	3.00	3.00
599		35p multicolored	1.90	1.90
600		35p multicolored	1.90	1.90
a.	A100	Pair, #599-600	5.00	5.00
		Nos. 593-600 (8)	9.10	9.10

Farm Animals Type of 1994

1997, Aug. 26   Litho.   Perf. 14

601	A92	20p Chickens	1.30	1.30
602	A92	30p Cattle	2.25	2.25
603	A92	45p Sheep	3.25	3.25
604	A92	50p Dogs	3.25	3.25
		Nos. 601-604 (4)	10.05	10.05

Queen Elizabeth II and Prince Philip, 50th Wedding Anniv. — A101

Designs: No. 605, Queen up close. No. 606, Prince riding polo pony. No. 607, Queen with horse. No. 608, Prince up close. No. 609, Prince in military attire, Queen in green coat. No. 610, Princess Anne riding horse. £1.50, Queen, Prince riding in open carriage, horiz.

1997, Nov. 20   Wmk. 373   Perf. 14

605		15p multicolored	.90	.90
606		15p multicolored	.90	.90
a.	A101	Pair, #605-606	2.40	2.40
607		20p multicolored	1.30	1.30
608		20p multicolored	1.30	1.30
a.	A101	Pair, #607-608	4.25	4.25
609		45p multicolored	2.75	2.75
610		45p multicolored	2.75	2.75
a.	A101	Pair, #609-610	8.75	8.75
		Nos. 605-610 (6)	9.90	9.90
		Souvenir Sheet		
611	A101	£1.50 multicolored	12.50	12.50

First Lobster Survey, 50th Anniv. — A102

Ships: 15p, Hilary, Melodie. 20p, Tristania II, Hekla. 30p, Pequena, Frances Repetto. 45p, Tristania, Gillian Gaggins. 50p, MFV. Kelso, MV. Edinburgh. £1.20, Fr. C.P. Lawrence, lobster.

1998, Feb. 6   Perf. 14½

612	A102	15p multicolored	.75	.75
613	A102	20p multicolored	1.10	1.10
614	A102	30p multicolored	1.60	1.60
615	A102	45p multicolored	2.75	2.75
616	A102	50p multicolored	2.75	2.75
		Nos. 612-616 (5)	8.95	8.95
		Souvenir Sheet		
617	A102	£1.20 multicolored	10.50	10.50

Diana, Princess of Wales (1961-97)
Common Design Type

a, In beige dress. b, In white top with black collar. c, In striped top. d, In lilac & white print dress.

1998, May 15   Perf. 14½x14

618	CD355	35p Strip of 4, #a.-d.	5.00	5.00

No. 618 sold for £1.40 + 20p with surtax from international sales going to the Princess Diana Memorial Fund and surtax from local sales going to a designated local charity.

Atlantic Marine Fauna Type of 1997

Fauna of the Miocene Epoch: a, Carcharodon. b, Orycterocetus. c, Eurhinodelphis. d, Hexanchus (six gilled shark), myliobatis.

1998, July 8   Perf. 14

619	A99	45p Sheet of 4, #a.-d.	16.00	16.00

Visiting Cruise Ships A103

1998, Sept. 15   Perf. 14

620	A103	15p Livonia	1.35	1.35
621	A103	20p Professor Molchanov	1.90	1.90
622	A103	45p Explorer	4.25	4.25
623	A103	60p Hanseatic	5.50	5.50
		Nos. 620-623 (4)	13.00	13.00

Sailing Ships A104

15p, H.G. Johnson, 1892. 35p, Theodore, 1893. 45p, Hesperides, 1893. 50p, Bessfield, 1894.

1998, Nov. 23   Wmk. 373   Perf. 14½

624	A104	15p multicolored	1.40	1.40
625	A104	35p multicolored	3.00	3.00
626	A104	45p multicolored	4.25	4.25
627	A104	50p multicolored	4.50	4.50
		Nos. 624-627 (4)	13.15	13.15

1999, Mar. 19

20p, Derwent, 1895. 30p, Strathgryffe, 1898. 50p, Celestial Empire, 1898. 60p, Lamorna, 1902.

628	A104	20p multicolored	2.00	2.00
629	A104	30p multicolored	2.75	2.75
630	A104	45p multicolored	4.25	4.25
631	A104	60p multicolored	4.50	4.50
		Nos. 628-631 (4)	13.50	13.50
		Nos. 624-631 (8)	28.00	28.00

Wandering Albatross — A105

World Wildlife Fund: 5p, Two adults. 8p, Adult, juvenile in nest. 12p, Adult spreading wings. 15p, Two in flight.

1999, Apr. 27   Wmk. 373   Perf. 14

632	A105	5p multicolored	.60	.60
633	A105	8p multicolored	.65	.65
634	A105	12p multicolored	.70	.70
635	A105	15p multicolored	.80	.80
a.		Strip of 4, #632-635	3.00	3.00
		Nos. 632-635 (4)	2.75	2.75

Issued in sheets of 16.

Wedding of Prince Edward and Sophie Rhys-Jones
Common Design Type

Perf. 13¾x14

1999, June 18   Litho.   Wmk. 384

636	CD356	45c Separate portraits	2.25	2.25
637	CD356	£1.20 Couple	5.25	5.25

Queen Mother's Century
Common Design Type

Queen Mother: 20p, With Princess Elizabeth on her 18th birthday. 30p, With King George VI at Balmoral. 50p, With Royal Family. 60p, As colonel-in-chief of Black Watch. £1.50, Age 5 photo, airplanes from Battle of Britain, 1940.

1999, Aug. 18   Wmk. 384   Perf. 13½

638	CD358	20p multi	1.00	1.00
639	CD358	30p multi	1.75	1.75
640	CD358	50p multi	2.75	2.75
641	CD358	60p multi	3.50	3.50
		Nos. 638-641 (4)	9.00	9.00
		Souvenir Sheet		
642	CD358	£1.50 black	9.00	9.00

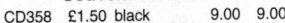

Millennium — A106

Various birds.

2000, Jan. 1   Wmk. 373   Perf. 14
Color of Queen's Head

643	A106	20p bister	1.25	1.25
644	A106	30p green	2.10	2.10
645	A106	50p blue	4.00	4.00
646	A106	60p brown	4.75	4.75
		Nos. 643-646 (4)	12.10	12.10

Royalty — A107

British monarchs on 8p-£5: 1p, King Manuel I of Portugal. 3p, Frederick Henry, Prince of Orange. 5p, Empress Maria Theresa of Austria. 8p, King George III. 10p, King George IV. 15p, King Willian IV. 20p, Queen Victoria. 25p, Edward VII. 35p, George V. £1, Edward VIII. £2, George VI. £5, Elizabeth II.

2000, Feb. 1   Wmk. 384   Perf. 14

647	A107	1p multi	.25	.25
648	A107	3p multi	.25	.25
649	A107	5p multi	.25	.25
650	A107	8p multi	.30	.30
651	A107	10p multi	.40	.40
652	A107	15p multi	.55	.80
653	A107	20p multi	.70	1.00
654	A107	25p multi	.90	1.10
655	A107	35p multi	1.40	1.90
656	A107	£1 multi	3.50	5.25
657	A107	£2 multi	7.50	10.00
658	A107	£5 multi	18.00	24.50
		Nos. 647-658 (12)	34.00	46.00

The Stamp Show 2000, London A108

Designs: 15p, Longboat under oars. 45p, Longboat under sail. 50p, Cutty Sark, 1876. 60p, Cutty Sark, 2000. £1.50, Cutty Sark visiting Tristan da Cunha, 1876.

Wmk. 373

2000, May 22   Litho.   Perf. 14

659	A108	15p multi	1.50	1.50
660	A108	45p multi	3.50	3.50
661	A108	50p multi	4.00	4.00
662	A108	60p multi	4.75	4.75
		Nos. 659-662 (4)	13.75	13.75
		Souvenir Sheet		
663	A108	£1.50 multi	13.00	13.00

Prince William, 18th Birthday
Common Design Type

William: Nos. 664, 668a, As toddler, with Princes Charles and Harry, vert. Nos. 665, 668b, Holding paper, vert. Nos. 666, 668c, Wearing scarf. Nos. 667, 668d, Wearing suit and wearing sweater. No. 668e, As child, with Shetland pony.

Perf. 13¾x14¼, 14¼x13¾
2000, June 21   Litho.   Wmk. 373
Stamps With White Border

664	CD359	45p multi	2.25 2.25
665	CD359	45p multi	2.25 2.25
666	CD359	45p multi	2.25 2.25
667	CD359	45p multi	2.25 2.25
		Nos. 664-667 (4)	9.00 9.00

Souvenir Sheet
Stamps Without White Border
Perf. 14¼

668	CD359	45p Sheet of 5, #a-e	12.50 12.50

Ships and Helicopters — A109

No. 669, 10p: a, SA Agulhas. b, SA 330J Puma, 1999.
No. 670, 15p: a, HMS London. b, Westland Wessex HAS 1, 1964.
No. 671, 20p: a, HMS Endurance. b, Westland Lynx HAS 3, 1996.
No. 672, 50p: a, USS Spiegel Grove. b, Sikorsky UH-19F, 1963.

Wmk. 373
2000, Sept. 4   Litho.   Perf. 14
Pairs, #a-b

669-672	A109	Set of 4	14.50 14.50

First Election of Winston Churchill to Parliament, Cent. — A110

Designs: 20p, During siege of Sidney Street, 1911. 30p, With Franklin D. Roosevelt, 1941. 50p, VE Day broadcast, 1945. 60p, Greeting Queen Elizabeth, 1955.

Perf. 13¾x14
2000, Oct. 2   Wmk. 373

673-676	A110	Set of 4	10.00 10.00

Souvenir Sheet

New Year 2001 (Year of the Snake) — A111

No. 677: a, 30p, Inaccessible Island rail. b, 45p, Black-faced spoonbill.

Wmk. 373
2001, Feb. 1   Litho.   Perf. 14½

677	A111	Sheet of 2, #a-b	10.00 10.00

Hong Kong 2001 Stamp Exhibition.

Age of Victoria A112

Designs: 15p, Letter, 1846. 20p, Prince Alfred, Duke of Edinburgh, vert. 30p, HMS

Galatea. 35p, Queen Victoria, vert. 50p, Charles Dickens, vert. 60p, Resupplying ships. £1.50, Jubilee celebrations.

Wmk. 373
2001, May 24   Litho.   Perf. 14

678-683	A112	Set of 6	10.50 10.50

Souvenir Sheet

684	A112	£1.50 multi	8.00 8.00

Longboats — A113

No. 685: a, Boat with dark and light blue striped sails, island in distance. b, Boat with red and blue striped and white sails, boat with blue, red and yellow striped and blue and white striped sails. c, Prow and sail of boat, two boats in distance. d, Boat with blue red and yellow striped and blue and white striped sails. e, Boat with dark and light blue sails near shore. f, Boat with red and blue striped and white sails. g, Boat with gray, red and white striped sails. h, Boat with sails down.

2001, July 12

685	A113	30p Sheet of 8, #a-h	12.00 12.00

Nos. 669-672 Overprinted in Blue Violet

Wmk. 373
2001, Sept. 17   Litho.   Perf. 14

686	A109	10p Pair, #a-b	2.00 2.00
687	A109	15p Pair, #a-b	2.75 2.75
688	A109	20p Pair, #a-b	3.50 3.50
689	A109	50p Pair, #a-b	9.00 9.00
		Nos. 686-689 (4)	17.25 17.25

Souvenir Sheet

Birdlife International World Bird Festival — A114

Spectacled petrel: a, Head. b, Diving (island in background). c, In flight with legs extended. d, Diving (sea in background). e, Chick.

Wmk. 373
2001, Oct. 1   Litho.   Perf. 14½

690	A114	35p Sheet of 5, #a-e	14.00 14.00

Royal Navy Ships A115

Designs: No. 691, 20p, HMS Penguin, 1815. No. 692, 20p, HMS Julia, 1817. No. 693, 35p, HMS Beagle, 1901. No. 694, 35p, HMS Puma, 1962. No. 695, 60p, HMS Monmouth, 1997. No. 696, 60p, HMS Somerset, 1999.

Wmk. 373
2001, Oct. 31   Litho.   Perf. 14

691-696	A115	Set of 6	14.00 14.00

Churches A116

Designs: No. 697, 35p, Exterior, St. Joseph's Catholic Church. No. 698, 35p, Exterior, St. Mary's Anglican Church. No. 699, 60p, Stained glass window, St. Joseph's. No. 700, 60p, Altar, St. Mary's.

Perf. 13¼x13½, 13½x13¼
2001, Nov. 27

697-700	A116	Set of 4	13.00 13.00

Christmas, Arrival of first USPG missionary, 150th anniv.

Tristan da Cunha Postage Stamps, 50th Anniv. A117

Designs: Nos. 701, 45p, 705a, 45p, #5, 6, 9, 10 canceled. Nos. 702, 20p, 705, 45p, #7, 8, 11, 12 canceled. Nos. 703, 50p, 705c, 45p, #1-4 canceled. Nos. 704, 60p, 705d, 45p, Men at post office, 1952.

2002, Jan. 1   Perf. 13½
Without "Tristan da Cunha" in Script

701-704	A117	Set of 4	12.00 12.00

Souvenir Sheet
With "Tristan da Cunha" in Script at Top or Bottom of Stamps

705	A117	45p Sheet of 4, #a-d	11.50 11.50

Reign Of Queen Elizabeth II, 50th Anniv. Issue
Common Design Type

Designs: Nos. 706, 710a, 15p, Princess Elizabeth, 1947. Nos. 707, 710b, 30p, Wearing tiara, 1991. Nos. 708, 710c, 45p, Wearing red coat. Nos. 709, 710d, 50p, Wearing purple hat, 1997. No. 710e, 60p, 1955 portrait by Annigoni (38x50mm).

Perf. 14¼x14½, 13¾ (#710e)
2002, Feb. 6   Litho.   Wmk. 373
With Gold Frames

706	CD360	15p multicolored	.95 .95
707	CD360	30p multicolored	1.80 1.80
708	CD360	45p multicolored	2.50 2.50
709	CD360	50p multicolored	2.75 2.75
		Nos. 706-709 (4)	8.00 8.00

Souvenir Sheet
Without Gold Frames

710	CD360	Sheet of 5, #a-e	10.50 10.50

Fishing Industry A118

Designs: 20p, Pelagic armorhead. 35p, Yellowtail. 50p, Splendid alfonsino. 60p, Ship San Liberatore.

Wmk. 373
2002, May   Litho.   Perf. 14

711-713	A118	Set of 3	6.75 6.75
714		Souvenir sheet, #711-713, 714a	8.50 8.50
a.		A118 60p multi	1.75 1.75

Queen Mother Elizabeth (1900-2002)
Common Design Type

Designs: 20p, Wearing hat (black and white photograph). £1.50, Wearing blue green hat. No. 717: a, 75p, Holding baby (black and white photograph). b, 75p, Wearing dark blue hat.

Wmk. 373
2002, Aug. 5   Litho.   Perf. 14¼
With Purple Frames

715	CD361	20p multicolored	1.00 1.00
716	CD361	£1.50 multicolored	6.25 6.25

Souvenir Sheet
Without Purple Frames
Perf. 14½x14¼

717	CD361	Sheet of 2, #a-b	9.00 9.00

Marine Mammals — A119

No. 718: a, Gray's beaked whale. b, Dusky dolphin. c, False killer whale. d, Long-finned pilot whale. e, Sperm whale. f, Shepherd's beaked whale.
£2, Humpback whale.

Wmk. 373
2002, Sept. 24   Litho.   Perf. 13¼

718	A119	30p Sheet of 6, #a-f	13.50 13.50

Souvenir Sheet

719	A119	£2 multi	16.00 16.00

HMS Herald Survey, 150th Anniv. — A120

Designs: 20p, Captain Denham and officers. 35p, HMS Herald in Bay of Biscay. 50p, Surveying, Oct. 30, 1852. 60p, HMS Herald and Torch at sunset, 1852.

2002, Nov. 11   Perf. 14x14¾

720-723	A120	Set of 4	8.75 8.75

Guinness Book of World Records — A121

No. 724: a, Great Barrier Reef (longest reef). b, Greenland (biggest island). c, Sahara Desert (biggest desert). d, Amazon and Nile Rivers (longest rivers). e, Mt. Everest (biggest mountain). f, Tristan da Cunha (most remote inhabited island).
£2, Like No. 724f.

Wmk. 373
2003, Jan. 10   Litho.   Perf. 13¾

724	A121	30p Sheet of 6, #a-f	9.50 9.50

Souvenir Sheet

725	A121	£2 multi	11.00 11.00

Atlantic Yellow-
nosed
Albatross
A122

Designs: Nos. 726, 730a, 15p, Heads of two birds. Nos. 727, 730b, 30p, Bird on nest, vert. Nos. 728, 730c, 45p, Bird in flight, vert. Nos. 729, 730d, Two birds in flight. No. 730e, £1, Two birds in flight, diff.

Perf. 14¼x13¾, 13¾x14¼
2003, May 7   Litho.
Stamps With White Frames
726-729 A122   Set of 4   7.50 7.50
Souvenir Sheet
Stamps Without Frames
Perf. 14¼x14½
730 A122   Sheet of 5, #a-e   11.00 11.00
Birdlife International.

Head of Queen Elizabeth II
Common Design Type
Wmk. 373
2003, June 2   Litho.   Perf. 13¾
731 CD362 £2.80 multi   10.00 10.00

Coronation of Queen Elizabeth II, 50th Anniv.
Common Design Type

Designs: Nos. 732, 20p, 734a, Queen and extended family. Nos. 733, £1.50, 734b, Bishops paying homage to Queen at coronation.

Perf. 14¼x14½
2003, June 2   Litho.   Wmk. 373
Vignettes Framed, Red Background
732 CD363   20p multicolored   1.00 1.00
733 CD363   £1.50 multicolored 7.00 7.00
Souvenir Sheet
Vignettes Without Frame, Purple Panel
734 CD363 75p Sheet of 2, #a-b 8.75 8.75

Prince William, 21st Birthday
Common Design Type

No. 735: a, William in polo uniform at right. b, In sweater at left.

Wmk. 373
2003, June 21   Litho.   Perf. 14¼
735   Horiz. pair   6.00 6.00
a.-b. CD364 50p Either single 2.60 2.60

William Glass (1787-1853), Governor — A123

No. 736: a, Arrival of Glass on HMS Falmouth, 1816. b, As corporal, stationed on Tristan da Cunha. c, Glass and family onshore, 1817. d, Glass family with dog. e, Gov. Glass conducting daughter's marriage ceremony, 1833. f, Glass as old man.

Perf. 14¼x14½
2003, Nov. 24   Litho.   Wmk. 373
736 A123 30p Sheet of 6, #a-f, + 6 labels   9.00 9.00

Royal Navy Ships — A124

No. 737, 20p: a, RFA Tideflow. b, RFA Tidespring.
No. 738, 35p: a, RFA Gold Rover. b, RFA Diligence.
No. 739, 60p: a, RFA Wave Chief. b, HMY Britannia.

Wmk. 373
2003, Dec. 8   Litho.   Perf. 14
Horiz. pairs, #a-b
737-739 A124   Set of 3   12.00 12.00

History of Writing Implements — A125

Designs: 15p, Cave paintings and pigment blocks. 20p, Clay tablet. 35p, Egyptian writing palette. 45p, Goose quill pen. 50p, Fountain pen. 60p, Ballpoint pen. £1.50, Word processing.

2004, Jan. 8   Perf. 13¾
740-745 A125 Set of 6   9.25 9.25
Souvenir Sheet
Litho. with Margin Embossed
746 A125 £1.50 multi   8.00 8.00

Worldwide Fund for Nature (WWF) — A126

Subantarctic fur seal: No. 747, 35p, Underwater. No. 748, 35p, Pair on rocks. No. 749, 35p, Seal on rock. No. 750, 35p, Head.

Wmk. 373
2004, July 12   Litho.   Perf. 14
747-750 A126 Set of 4   6.00 6.00
750a   Sheet, 4 each #747-750 26.00 26.00

New Flag — A127

2004, July 27   Unwmk.   Die Cut
Self-Adhesive
Booklet Stamp
751 A127 30p multi   1.35 1.35
a.   Booklet pane of 6   8.25
      Complete booklet, 2 #751a 16.50

Merchant Ships A128

Designs: No. 752, 20p, RMS Dunnottar Castle. No. 753, 20p, RMS Caronia. No. 754, 35p, SA Agulhas. No. 755, 35p, MV Edinburgh. No. 756, 60p, MV Explorer. No. 757, 60p, MV Hanseatic.

Wmk. 373
2004, Nov. 9   Litho.   Perf. 13¼
752-757 A128 Set of 6   11.00 11.00

Battle of Trafalgar, Bicent. — A129

Designs: 15p, Admiral Horatio Nelson's quadrant. 20p, HMS Royal Sovereign breaks the line, horiz. 25p, Thomas Swain aids the wounded Nelson, horiz. 35p, HMS Victory breaks the line, horiz. 50p, Nelson. 60p, HMS Victory, horiz.
No. 764: a, Capt. Thomas Masterman Hardy. b, HMS Victory.

Perf. 13¼
2005, Jan. 20   Litho.   Unwmk.
758-763 A129 Set of 6   11.50 11.50
Souvenir Sheet
764 A129 75p Sheet of 2, #a-b 9.50 9.50

No. 763 has particles of wood from the HMS Victory embedded in the areas covered by a thermographic process that produces a shiny, raised effect.

Island Flora, Fauna and Scenes A130

No. 765 — Tristan da Cunha: a, Rockhopper penguins. b, Southern elephant seals. c, Tristan rock lobster. d, Crowberry. e, Tristan da Cunha island settlement and volcano.
No. 766 — Gough Island: a, Gough moorhen. b, Subantarctic fur seal. c, Bluefish. d, Gough tree fern. e, South African Weather Station.
No. 767 — Inaccessible Island: a, Inaccessible rail. b, Dusky dolphins. c, Sebastes capensis. d, Pepper tree. e, Inaccessible Island Waterfall.
No. 768 — Nightingale Island: a, Tristan thrush. b, Southern right whale. c, Fivefinger fish. d, Tussock grass. e, Nightingale Island.
No. 769 — Middle Island: a, Broad-billed prion. b, False killer whale. c, Wreckfih. d, Fern. e, Middle Island.
No. 770 — Stoltenhoff Island: a, Brown skua. b, Shepherd's beaked whales. c, Snoeks. d, Sea bind weed. e, Stoltenhoff Island.

2005   Wmk. 373   Perf. 13¾
765   Horiz. strip of 5   11.00 11.00
a.-e. A130 50p Any single   2.25 2.25
766   Horiz. strip of 5   11.00 11.00
a.-e. A130 50p Any single   2.25 2.25
767   Horiz. strip of 5   11.00 11.00
a.-e. A130 50p Any single   2.25 2.25
768   Horiz. strip of 5   11.00 11.00
a.-e. A130 50p Any single   2.25 2.25
769   Horiz. strip of 5   11.00 11.00
a.-e. A130 50p Any single   2.25 2.25
770   Horiz. strip of 5   11.00 11.00
a.-e. A130 50p Any single   2.25 2.25

Issued: No. 765, 2/21; No. 766, 3/28; No. 767, 4/18; No. 768, 2/7/06; No. 769, 3/30/06; No. 770, 9/27/06.
See No. 796.

Birds A131

Designs: 1p, Kerguelen petrel. 3p, Sooty albatross. 5p, Antarctic tern. 8p, Tristan bunting. 10p, Cape petrel. 15p, Tristan moorhen. 20p, Giant fulmar. 25p, Brown skua. 35p, Great-winged petrel. £1, Broad-billed prion. £2, Soft-plumaged petrel. £5, Rockhopper penguin.

Perf. 14¼x14¾
2005, June 1   Litho.   Wmk. 373
771 A131 1p multi   .25 .25
772 A131 3p multi   .25 .25
773 A131 5p multi   .25 .25
774 A131 8p multi   .30 .30
775 A131 10p multi   .35 .35
776 A131 15p multi   .55 .55
777 A131 20p multi   .75 .75
778 A131 25p multi   .90 .90
779 A131 35p multi   1.25 1.25
780 A131 £1 multi   4.00 4.00
781 A131 £2 multi   7.25 8.75
782 A131 £5 multi   18.00 21.00
   Nos. 771-782 (12) 34.10 38.60

Pope John Paul II (1920-2005) A132

Wmk. 373
2005, Aug. 18   Litho.   Perf. 14
783 A132 50p multi   3.00 3.00

Battle of Trafalgar, Bicent. — A133

Designs: 20p, HMS Victory. 70p, Ships in battle, horiz. £1, Admiral Horatio Nelson.

Perf. 13¼
2005, Oct. 18   Litho.   Unwmk.
784-786 A133 Set of 3   12.00 12.00

Discovery of Tristan da Cunha, 500th Anniv. — A134

No. 787: a, 30p, Discovery by Tristao d'Acunha, 1506. b, 30p, First survey, 1767. c, 30p, Jonathan Lambert of Salem, 1810. d, 50p, William Glass, 1816. e, 50p, Duke of Gloucester (ship), 1824. f, 80p, Wreck of the Emily, 1836.
No. 788: a, 30p, Thomas Swain (1774-1862). b, 30p, HMS Challenger, 1873. c, 30p, Rev. Edwin Dodgson arrives, 1881. d, 50p, Wreck of the Italia, 1892. e, 50p, HMS Milford, 1938. f, 80p, Norwegian Expedition, 1937-38.
No. 789: a, 30p, World War II TDV training. b, 30p, HMS Atlantic Isle, 1944. c, 30p, Hands holding potatoes, 1946 potato stamp. d, 50p, Tristan da Cunha #5. e, 50p, Volcano eruption and evacuation, 1961. f, 80p, Gough Island Scientific Expedition, 1955.
No. 790: a, 30p, Royal Society Expedition, 1962. b, 30p, Resettlement, 1963. c, 30p, Denstone Expedition to Inaccessible Island, 1982. d, 50p, RMS St. Helena, 1992. e, 50p, New coat of arms, 2002. f, 80p, Hurricane disaster, 2001.

Perf. 14¼x14½
2006   Litho.   Wmk. 373
787 A134 Sheet of 6, #a-f 15.00 15.00
788 A134 Sheet of 6, #a-f 15.00 15.00
Perf. 14¼x14¾
789 A134 Sheet of 6, #a-f 16.00 16.00
790 A134 Sheet of 6, #a-f 16.00 16.00
   Issued: Nos. 787-788, 2/2; Nos. 789-790, 6/1.

Queen Elizabeth II, 80th Birthday A135

Queen: No. 791, 60p, As child. No. 792, 60p, Wearing feathered hat. No. 793, 60p, Wearing red hat. No. 794, 60p, Wearing sunglasses.

No. 795: a, 50p, Like No. 792. b, 50p, Like No. 793.

2006, Apr. 21   **Perf. 14**
791-794 A135   Set of 4   12.00 12.00
Souvenir Sheet
795 A135 50p Sheet of 2, #a-b   5.25 5.25

Island Flora, Fauna and Scenes Type of 2005-06
Miniature Sheet

No. 796: a, Map of Tristan da Cunha, flag. b, Map of Inaccessible Island, wandering albatross. c, Map of Nightingale Island, humpback whale. d, Map of Middle Island, traditional longboats. e, Map of Stoltenhoff Island, mackerel. f, Map of Gough Island, sub-antarctic fur seal.

Wmk. 373
2007, Jan. 22   **Litho.**   **Perf. 13¾**
796   Sheet of 6   15.00 15.00
a.-f. A130 50p Any single   2.40 2.40

Local Vehicles A136

Designs: 15p, Wave Dancer fishery patrol boat. 20p, Ambulance. 30p, Inshore rescue craft. 45p, Police Land Rover. 50p, Fire engine. 85p, Administrator's Land Rover.

Perf. 12½x13
2007, Apr. 17   **Litho.**   **Unwmk.**
797-802 A136   Set of 6   13.00 13.00

Wedding of Queen Elizabeth II and Prince Philip, 60th Anniv. — A137

Designs: No. 803, 50p, Shown. No. 804, 50p, Queen waving. No. 805, 50p, Queen and Prince (black and white photograph). No. 806, 50p, Queen and Prince (color photograph). £2, Queen in wedding gown.

2007, June 1   **Wmk. 373**   **Perf. 13¾**
803-806 A137   Set of 4   9.50 9.50
Souvenir Sheet
Perf. 14
807 A137 £2 multi   9.50 9.50
No. 807 contains one 42x57mm stamp.

Miniature Sheet

BirdLife International — A138

No. 808 — Great shearwater: a, In flight, facing right. b, In flight, facing left, showing land and sky. c, On ground, showing land and sky. d, In flight facing left, showing land and water. e, On ground, showing land only. f, Chick.

2007, July 1   **Unwmk.**   **Perf. 13¾**
808 A138 50p Sheet of 6, #a-f   16.00 16.00

Scouting, Cent. A139

Designs: 15p, Scout J. W. S. Marr and his book, *Into the Frozen South*, hands tying knot. 20p, The Quest frozen in, Marr, hands tightening rope. £1.25, Flag raising ceremony, hand with compass. £1.40, Children of Tristan da Cunha, trumpeter.

No. 813, vert.: a, Marr and Questie, the ship's cat. b, Lord Robert Baden-Powell.

2007, July 9   **Wmk. 373**
809-812 A139   Set of 4   15.00 15.00
Souvenir Sheet
813 A139 £1.50 Sheet of 2, #a-b   15.00 15.00

A140

A141

A142

A143

A144

Princess Diana (1961-97) A145

Perf. 13x12½
2007, Nov. 30   **Litho.**   **Unwmk.**
814 A140 50p multi   2.40 2.40
815 A141 50p multi   2.40 2.40
816 A142 50p multi   2.40 2.40
817 A143 50p multi   2.40 2.40
818 A144 50p multi   2.40 2.40
819 A145 50p multi   2.40 2.40
   Nos. 814-819 (6)   14.40 14.40

Military Uniforms — A146

Designs: No. 820, 15p, Officer, 21st Light Dragoon. No. 821, 15p, Corporal, Royal Artillery. No. 822, 20p, Privates, Royal Artillery. No. 823, 20p, Lieutenant, Royal Artillery. No. 824, £1, Soldiers from Cape Regiment. No. 825, £1, Soldiers from South Africa Army Engineering Corps.

Unwmk.
2007, Dec. 10   **Litho.**   **Perf. 14**
820-825 A146   Set of 6   15.00 15.00

Marine Invertebrates A147

Designs: 15p, Tristan rock lobster. 20p, Trumpet anemone. 35p, Starfish. No. 829, 60p, Tristan urchin. No. 830, 60p, Sponge. 85p, Strawberry anemone.

2007, Dec. 10   **Unwmk.**   **Perf. 13¼**
826-831 A147   Set of 6   12.50 12.50

A148

Royal Air Force, 90th Anniv. — A149

Designs: No. 832, 30p, Royal Aircraft Factory S. E. 5a. No. 833, 30p, Hawker Hart. No. 834, 30p, Hawker Typhoon. No. 835, 30p, Avro Vulcan. No. 836, 30p, SEPECAT Jaguar. £1.50, Sir Hugh Trenchard reviewing troops.

Wmk. 373
2008, Apr. 1   **Litho.**   **Perf. 14**
832-836 A148   Set of 5   8.00 8.00
Souvenir Sheet
837 A149 £1.50 black   8.00 8.00
Nos. 832-836 each were printed in sheets of 8 + central label.

Tristan Fisheries, 60th Anniv. — A150

Designs: 15p, Fishing boats in harbor. 20p, Fishing boats. 30p, Offloading and loading fish. 70p, Sorting tails. 80p, Wrapping and packaging of rock lobster tails. £1.25, Shipping for export.

Perf. 13¼x13
2008, July 1   **Litho.**   **Unwmk.**
838-843 A150   Set of 6   15.00 15.00

Allan B. Crawford (1912-2007), Writer — A151

Designs: 15p, Crawford. 20p, Local Tristan da Cunha stamp. 50p, First map of Tristan da Cunha. 60p, Members of 1937-38 Norwegian Scientific Expedition, Crawford's book, *I Went to Tristan*, horiz. 85p, Men at opening of Marion Island Meteorological Office, Crawford's book, *Tristan da Cunha and the Roaring Forties*, horiz. £1.20, Crawford and his book, *Penguins, Potatoes and Postage Stamps*, horiz.

Perf. 13x13¼, 13¼x13
2008, Aug. 1   **Litho.**   **Unwmk.**
844-849 A151   Set of 6   15.00 15.00

End of World War I, 90th Anniv. A152

Paintings: No. 850, 50p, End of Richthofen, by Charles H. Hubbell. No. 851, 50p, Lion Leads in Jutland, by W. L. Wyllie. No. 852, 50p, Oppy Wod, by John Nash. No. 853, 50p, A Battery Shelled, by Percy Wyndham Lewis. No. 854, 50p, Somme Tank, by Louis Dauphin. No. 855, 50p, The Angels of Mons, by R. Crowhurst, vert.

£1, Wreath of Remembrance, vert.

Wmk. 406
2008, Sept. 16   **Litho.**   **Perf. 14**
850-855 A152   Set of 6   12.50 12.50
Souvenir Sheet
856 A152 £1 multi   4.50 4.50

Ships A153

Tristao da Cunha (1460-1540), Explorer — A154

Designs: No. 857, 50p, Mary Rose. No. 858, 50p, Endurance. No. 859, 50p, Cutty Sark. No. 860, 50p, Suomen Joutsen. No. 861, 50p, RFA Lyme Bay. No. 862, 50p, MS Explorer.

Wmk. 406
2009, Mar. 9   **Litho.**   **Perf. 14**
857-862 A153   Set of 6   11.50 11.50
Souvenir Sheet
863 A154 £1 multi   4.00 4.00

Naval Aviation, Cent.
A155

Designs: 25p, Felixstowe F.2A. 35p, Short S.27. No. 866, 50p, Blackburn Dart. No. 867, 50p, Sikorsky Hoverfly helicopter.
£1.50, Lieutenant Commander C. R. Samson in Short S.27 taking off from HMS Hibernia, 1912.

Wmk. 406
2009, Apr. 17   Litho.   Perf. 14
864-867 A155 Set of 4   9.25 9.25
Souvenir Sheet
868 A155 £1.50 multi   6.50 6.50
Nos. 864-867 each were printed in sheets of 8 + central label.

Space Exploration
A156

Designs: 25p, Goddard Rocket, 1936. 35p, X-24B Spaceplane, 1972. 60p, Launch of Apollo 11, 1969. 90p, Space Shuttle Discovery ferried by Boeing 747, 2005. £1, X-43C experimental hypersonic aircraft.
£1.50, Astronauts on Moon, painting by Capt. Alan Bean, vert.

Wmk. 406
2009, July 20   Litho.   Perf. 13¼
869-873 A156 Set of 5   12.50 12.50
Souvenir Sheet
Perf. 13x13½
874 A156 £1.50 multi   6.50 6.50
First man on the Moon, 40th anniv. No. 874 contains one 40x60mm stamp.

Potato Production — A157

No. 875, 25p: a, Preparing seed potatoes. b, Planting.
No. 876, 35p: a, Digging out. b, Harvesting.
No. 877, £1.10: a, Potato blossoms. b, Potato fields.

Unwmk.
2009, Aug. 3   Litho.   Perf. 13
Horiz. Pairs, #a-b
875-877 A157 Set of 3   13.50 13.50

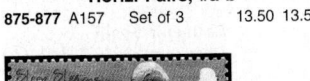

Island Traditions
A158

Designs: 25p, Sheep shearing. 35p, Ratting Day. 70p, Longboats to Nightingale. £1.60, Old Year's Night Okalolies.

2009, Sept. 28
878-881 A158 Set of 4   10.50 10.50
See Nos. 927-930.

Mail Delivery on Tristan da Cunha
A159

Designs: 25p, Mail arriving by ship. 35p, Transporting mail to post office. £1, Hitting the gong. £1.60, Giving out the mail.

Unwmk.
2009, Nov. 23   Litho.   Perf. 13
882-885 A159 Set of 4   12.50 12.50

British History
A160

Designs: No. 886, 35p, Battle of Hastings. No. 887, 35p, Peasants' Revolt. No. 888, 35p, King Henry VIII. No. 889, 35p, English Reformation. No. 890, 35p, Elizabethan era. No. 891, 35p, English Civil War. No. 892, 35p, Scientific innovation. No. 893, 35p, Bonnie Prince Charlie.

Wmk. 406
2010, Jan. 15   Litho.   Perf. 13¼
886-893 A160 Set of 8   11.00 11.00
See Nos. 902-909, 944-951.

A161

A162

A163

A164

A165

Battle of Britain, 70th Anniv.
A166

Design: £1.50, Sir Douglas Bader, vert.

Wmk. 406
2010, Mar. 18   Litho.   Perf. 13
894 A161 25p black & gray   1.05 1.05
895 A162 25p black & gray   1.05 1.05
896 A163 50p black & gray   2.10 2.10
897 A164 50p black & gray   2.10 2.10
898 A165 70p black & gray   2.75 2.75
899 A166 70p black & gray   2.75 2.75
Nos. 894-899 (6)   11.80 11.80
Souvenir Sheet
900 A166 £1.50 black & gray   5.75 5.75

Souvenir Sheet

Great Britain No. 159 — A167

2010, May 8   Perf. 14x14¼
901 A167 £1.50 multi   5.50 5.50
London 2010 Festival of Stamps.

British History Type of 2010
Designs: No. 902, 35p, Thomas Becket. No. 903, 35p, Battle of Agincourt. No. 904, 35p, Battle of Trafalgar. No. 905, 35p, Engineering & transportation. No. 906, 35p, Wireless age. No. 907, 35p, Votes for women. No. 908, 35p, The Great Depression. No. 909, 35p, Second World War.

Wmk. 406
2010, July 16   Litho.   Perf. 13¼
902-909 A160 Set of 8   11.00 11.00

Surnames of Island Families
A168

Surnames of island families, flags and birds: No. 910, 50p, Hagan and Rogers, US flag, bald eagle. No. 911, 50p, Repetto and Lavaretto, Italian flag, hoopoe. No. 912, 50p, Glass, Scottish flag, golden eagle. No. 913, 50p, Green, Netherlands flag, oystercatcher. No. 914, 50p, Swain, English flag, avocet.

Perf. 12½x13
2010, Sept. 6   Unwmk.
910-914 A168 Set of 5   10.50 10.50

Conservation — A169

Designs: 1p, New Conservation R1 boat. 3p, Eradication of New Zealand flax on Nightingale Island. 5p, Banding Tristan albatross. 8p, Hag's Tooth, Gough Island UNESCO World Heritage Site. 10p, Inaccessible rail. 15p, Inaccessible Island UNESCO World Heritage Site. 25p, Counting seals. 35p, Eradication of Sagina plant on Gough Island. 70p, Eradication of Loganberry plants at Sandy Point. £1, Banding Yellow-nosed albatross. £2, Gough bunting. £5, Counting penguins.

2010, Nov. 1   Litho.   Perf. 13
915 A169 1p multi   .30 .30
916 A169 3p multi   .30 .30
917 A169 5p multi   .30 .30
918 A169 8p multi   .30 .30
919 A169 10p multi   .40 .40
920 A169 15p multi   .55 .55
921 A169 25p multi   .90 .90
922 A169 35p multi   1.30 1.30
923 A169 70p multi   2.60 2.60
924 A169 £1 multi   3.75 3.75
925 A169 £2 multi   7.50 7.50
926 A169 £5 multi   19.00 19.00
Nos. 915-926 (12)   37.20 37.20

Island Traditions Type of 2009
Designs: 25p, Thatching a roof. 35p, Bullock cart. 70p, Music. £1.60, Pillow dance.

2010, Nov. 24
927-930 A158 Set of 4   11.00 11.00

Service of Queen Elizabeth II and Prince Philip — A170

Designs: 25p, Queen Elizabeth II. 35p, Queen and Prince Philip. No. 933, 50p, Queen and Prince Philip, diff. No. 934, 50p, Queen (wearing hat) and Prince Philip. No. 935, 70p, Queen and Prince Philip, diff. No. 936, 70p, Prince Philip.
£1.50, Queen and Prince Philip, diff.

2011, Mar. 14   Perf. 13¼
931-936 A170 Set of 6   11.00 11.00
936a   Souvenir sheet of 6, #931-936, + 3 labels   11.00 11.00
Souvenir Sheet
937 A170 £1.50 multi   5.50 5.50

Cruise Ships — A171

Designs: 25p, MV Professor Multanovskiy. 35p, MV Aleksey Maryshev. 70p, MV Professor Molchanov. £1.10, MV Plancius. £1.50, MV Plancius.

Perf. 14x14¾
2011, Apr. 12   Unwmk.
938-941 A171 Set of 4   8.50 8.50
Souvenir Sheet
942 A171 £1.50 multi   5.50 5.50

Souvenir Sheet

Wedding of Prince William and Catherine Middleton — A172

Perf. 14¾x14¼
2011, Apr. 29   Wmk. 406
943 A172 £3 multi   11.00 11.00

British History Type of 2010
Designs: No. 944, 35p, Magna Carta. No. 945, 35p, Wars of the Roses. No. 946, 35p, The Gunpowder Plot. No. 947, 35p, Great Fire of London. No. 948, 35p, Battle of Waterloo. No. 949, 35p, Age of Empire. No. 950, 35p, Industry and Commerce. No. 951, 35p, First World War.

2011, May 24   Wmk. 406   Perf. 13¼
944-951 A160 Set of 8   9.25 9.25

Photographs of Wedding of Prince William and Catherine Middleton — A173

Couple: No. 952, 70p, Standing, holding hands. No. 953, 70p, Kissing. No. 954, 70p, In coach, waving, horiz. No. 955. 70p, In car, waving, horiz.

2011, Sept. 1　　Unwmk.　　Perf. 12½
952-955　A173　Set of 4　　9.00　9.00

Eruption of Queen Mary's Peak, 50th Anniv. A174

Queen Mary's Peak and: No. 956, 25p, Tholoid. No. 957, 35p, October 1961 eruption. No. 958, 95p, Islanders leave aboard the MV Tjisadane. No. 959, £1.10, Islanders arrive in Cape Town.
No. 960, MV Tjisadane.

2011, Oct. 10　　Unwmk.　　Perf. 14
956-959　A174　Set of 4　　8.50　8.50
Souvenir Sheet
960　A174　£2 multi　　6.25　6.25

See Nos. 961-965, 999-1003, 1006-1010.

Volcano Eruption Type of 2011

Queen Mary's Peak and: No. 961, 25p, Returning with the report. No. 962, 35p, Resettlement survey team. No. 963, 95p, HMS Protector Whirlwind helicopter. No. 964, £1.10, Royal Society members.
No. 965, £2, Landing party.

2012, Jan. 30　　Unwmk.　　Perf. 14
961-964　A174　Set of 4　　8.50　8.50
Souvenir Sheet
965　A174　£2 multi　　6.50　6.50

Reign of Queen Elizabeth II, 60th Anniv. — A175

Queen Elizabeth II: 25p, Color photograph. 35p, Color photograph, diff. No. 968, 50p, Black-and-white photograph. No. 969, 50p, Color photograph, diff. No. 970, 70p, Color photograph, diff. No. 971, 70p, Black-and-white photograph.
£1.50, Queen Elizabeth II wearing crown.

2012, Feb. 6　　Unwmk.　　Perf. 13¼
966-971　A175　Set of 6　　9.50　9.50
971a　　Sheet of 6, #966-971, + 3 labels　　9.50　9.50
Souvenir Sheet
972　A175　£1.50 multi　　4.75　4.75

Miniature Sheet

Sinking of the Titanic, Cent. — A176

No. 973: a, Titanic being built in Harland & Wolff Shipyard. b, First class dining room. c, Titanic's propellers. d, Sinking of the ship. e, Captain. E. J. Smith and crew. f, Survivors in lifeboat. g, Titanic setting sail. h, Newspaper reports. i, Passengers strolling on board. j, Discovery of the wreck.

2012, Feb. 27　　Unwmk.　　Perf. 13¼
973　A176　50p Sheet of 10, #a-j, + 5 labels　　16.00　16.00

Ships A177

Designs: No. 974, 35p, Agulhas I at sea. No. 975, 35p, Agulhas II at sea. 70p, Agulhas I near land. £1.10, Agulhas II near land.

2012, Sept. 17　　　　Perf. 14
974-977　A177　Set of 4　　8.00　8.00

Miniature Sheet

Royal Navy Ships and Their Crests — A178

No. 978: a, 35p, HMS Portland, 2005. b, 35p, HMS Edinburgh, 2006. c, 70p, HMS Clyde, 2011. d, 70p, HMS Montrose, 2012.

2012, Oct. 15　　　　Perf. 13¼x13½
978　A178　Sheet of 4, #a-d　　6.75　6.75

Members of Shackleton-Rowett Antarctic Expedition — A179

Designs: No. 979, 70p, Frank Wild, Inaccessible Island. No.980, 70p, Hubert Wilkins, Gough Island. No. 981, 70p, James Marr, Tristan da Cunha. No. 982, 70p, Frank Worsley, Nightingale Island.

2012, Nov. 28　　　　Perf. 14
979-982　A179　Set of 4　　9.00　9.00

Worldwide Fund for Nature (WWF) — A180

Tristan albatross: Nos. 983, 987a, 35p, Bird on nest. Nos. 984, 987b, 45p, Two birds. Nos. 985, 987c, 70p, Two birds, diff. Nos. 986, 987d, £1.10, Bird in flight.
£3, Bird landing.

2013, Jan. 28　　Litho.　　Perf. 13¼x13½
Stamps With White Frames
983-986　A180　Set of 4　　8.25　8.25
Stamps Without White Frames
987　A180　Horiz. strip of 4, #a-d 8.25　8.25
Souvenir Sheet
988　A180　£3 multi　　9.50　9.50
No. 988 contains one 48x30mm stamp.

Tristan Song Project A181

Designs: 35p, Recorder and lyrics of "When Fish Get the Flu." 45p, Violin and lyrics of "Rockhopper Penguins." 70p, Guitar and lyrics of "The Volcano's Black." £1.10, Accordion and lyrics to "The Molly."

2013, Feb. 14　　　　Perf. 13¼x13½
989-992　A181　Set of 4　　8.25　8.25

Items Produced for Coronations — A182

Coronation of Queen Elizabeth II, 60th Anniv. — A183

Items produced for coronation of: 35p, Queen Victoria. 45p, King Edward VII. 70p, King George V. £1.10, King George VI. £1.50, Queen Elizabeth II.

2013, Apr. 15　　　　Perf. 14
993-997　A182　Set of 5　　13.00　13.00
Souvenir Sheet
Perf. 14¾x14
998　A183　£2 multi　　6.25　6.25
Nos. 993-997 each were printed in sheets of 8 + label.

Volcano Eruption Type of 2011

Queen Mary's Peak and: 25p, Returning islanders sitting near their possessions. 35p, Returning islanders walking toward possessions. 95p, Islanders on shore waiting for ships transporting their possessions. £1.10, Islanders returning to their homes in a tractor-pulled wagon.
£2, Islanders pulling longboat over rocks on shore.

2013, Nov. 11　　Litho.　　Perf. 14
999-1002　A174　Set of 4　　8.50　8.50
Souvenir Sheet
1003　A174　£2 multi　　6.50　6.50

Christmas A184

No. 1004: a, St. Mary's Anglican Church, Tristan da Cunha. b, Canterbury Cathedral, Canterbury, England.
No. 1005: a, St. Joseph's Catholic Church, Tristan da Cunha. b, St. Peter's Basilica, Vatican City.

Perf. 13¼x13½
2013, Nov. 18　　　　Litho.
1004　　Horiz. pair + central label　　5.00　5.00
a.　A184 35p multi　　1.25　1.25
b.　A184 £1.10 multi　　3.75　3.75
1005　　Horiz. pair + central label　　5.00　5.00
a.　A184 35p multi　　1.25　1.25
b.　A184 £1.10 multi　　3.75　3.75

Volcano Eruption Type of 2011

Queen Mary's Peak and: 25p, HMS Puma. 35p, HMS Jaguar. 95p, MV Tristania. £1.10, MV Stirling Castle.
£2, MV Bornholm.

2013, Dec. 9　　Litho.　　Perf. 14
1006-1009　A174　Set of 4　　8.75　8.75
Souvenir Sheet
1010　A174　£2 multi　　6.50　6.50

Polar Explorers and Their Ships A185

Designs: 35p, James Weddell (1787-1834) and Jane. 45p, George Nares (1831-1915) and HMS Challenger. 70p, Carsten Borchgrevink (1864-1934) and SS Antarctic. £1.50, Dr. Alexander Macklin (1889-1967) and Quest.

2014, Apr. 7　　Litho.　　Perf. 13¼x13½
1011-1014　A185　Set of 4　　10.00　10.00

Royal Christenings A186

Photographs of British royalty with christened infants: 35p, Queen Elizabeth II, 1926. 45p, Prince Charles, 1948. £1.10, Prince William, 1982. £1.50, Prince George, 2013.

2014, May 21　　Litho.　　Perf. 13¼
1015-1018　A186　Set of 4　　11.50　11.50

Finches A187

Designs: 35p, Gough finch, Gough Island. 45p, Dunn's finch, Inaccessible Island. 50p, Nightingale finch, Nightingale Island Group. £1.50, Wilkin's finch, Nightingale Island.
£2, Inaccessible finch, Inaccessible Island.

2014, June 18　　　　Perf. 14
1019-1022　A187　Set of 4　　9.75　9.75
Souvenir Sheet
1023　A187　£2 multi　　7.00　7.00

Paintings by Augustus Earle (1793-1838) A188

Designs: No. 1024, 50p, Scudding Before a Heavy Westerly Gale Off the Cape, Latitude 44 Degrees (brown panel). No. 1025, 50p, On Board the Duke of Gloucester, Margate Hoy, Between Rio de Janeiro and Tristan de Acunha (olive green panel). No. 1026, 70p, Tristan da Cunha (blue panel). No. 1027, 70p, Solitude, Watching the Horizon at Sunset, in the Hopes of Seeing a Vessel, Tristan de Acunha in the South Atlantic (brown panel).

2014, July 10　　Litho.　　Perf. 13¾
1024-1027　A188　Set of 4　　8.25　8.25

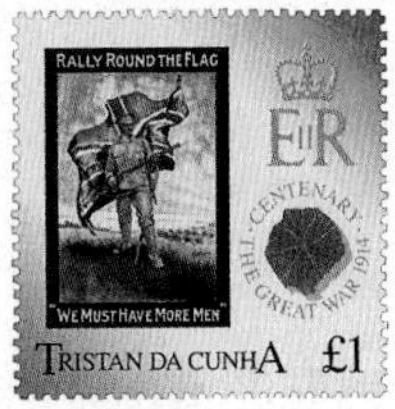

World War I, Cent. — A189

Poppies and war posters inscribed: No. 1028, £1, "Rally Round the Flag / We Must Have More Men." No. 1029, £1, "Join the Royal Marines." No. 1030, £1, "The Empire Needs Men." No. 1031, £1, "National Service / Women's Land Army."

2014, Aug. 4 **Litho.** ***Perf. 13¼***

1028-1031	A189	Set of 4	13.50 13.50

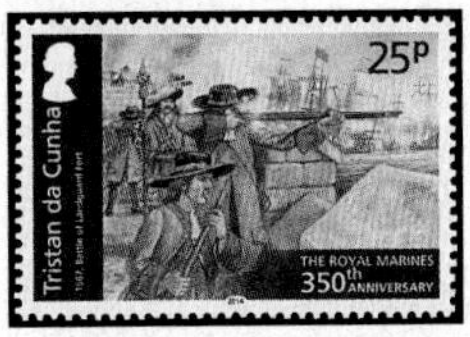

Royal Marines, 350th Anniv. A190

Designs: 25p, Battle of Landguard Fort, 1667. 35p, Capture of Gibraltar, 1704. 40p, Zeebrugge Raid, 1918. 60p, Normandy Invasion, 1944. 80p, Falklands Conflict, 1982. £1.10, Marines in Afghanistan, 2013.

2014, Oct. 28 **Litho.** ***Perf. 14***

1032-1037	A190	Set of 6	11.50 11.50

Miniature Sheet

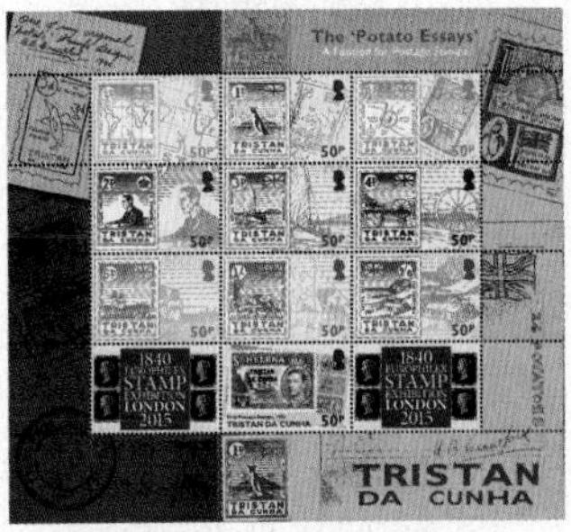

Potato Essays of 1937 and First Tristan da Cunha Postage Stamps — A191

No. 1038: a, Essay for ½p stamp. b, Essay for 1p stamp. c, Essay for 1½p stamp. d, Essay for 2p stamp. e, Essay for 3p stamp. f, Essay for 4p stamp. g, Essay for 6p stamp. h, Essay for 1sh stamp. i, Essay for 2sh6p stamp. j, Tristan da Cunha #1-3.

2015, Apr. 8 **Litho.** ***Perf. 13¼x13½***

1038	A191	50p	Sheet of 10, #a-j, + 2 labels	15.50 15.50

POSTAGE DUE STAMPS

Type of Barbados 1934-47

Perf. 14

1957, Feb. 1 **Wmk. 4** **Typo.**

Chalky Paper

J1	D1	1p	rose red	3.50	*7.00*
J2	D1	2p	orange yellow	4.25	*9.25*
J3	D1	3p	green	4.50	*11.50*
J4	D1	4p	ultramarine	5.25	*13.50*
J5	D1	5p	deep claret	6.50	*16.00*
			Nos. J1-J5 (5)	24.00	*57.25*

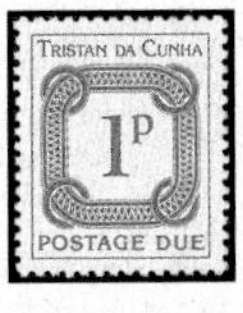

Numeral — D2

Perf. 13½x14

1976, Sept. 3 **Litho.** **Wmk. 373**

J6	D2	1p	lilac rose	.25	*.70*
J7	D2	2p	grayish green	.25	*1.00*
J8	D2	4p	violet	.25	*1.00*
J9	D2	5p	light blue	.25	*1.00*
J10	D2	10p	brown	.65	*1.50*
			Nos. J6-J10 (5)	1.65	*5.20*

1976, May 31 **Wmk. 314**

J6a	D2	1p	lilac rose	.35	*.70*
J7a	D2	2p	grayish green	.35	*1.00*
J8a	D2	4p	violet	.35	*1.00*
J9a	D2	5p	light blue	.35	*1.00*
J10a	D2	10p	brown	.75	*1.50*
			Nos. J6a-J10a (5)	2.15	*5.20*

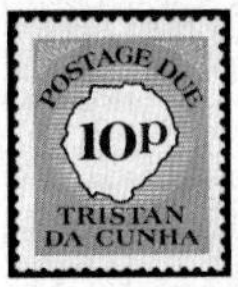

Outline Map of Tristan da Cunha — D3

Perf. 15x14

1986, Nov. 20 **Litho.** **Wmk. 384**

J11	D3	1p	pale yel brn & brn	.25	*.45*
J12	D3	2p	orange & brown	.25	*.45*
J13	D3	5p	crimson rose & brn	.25	*.45*
J14	D3	7p	lt lilac & black	.25	*.45*
J15	D3	10p	pale ultra & blk	.30	*.55*
J16	D3	25p	lt green & blk	.75	*1.60*
			Nos. J11-J16 (6)	2.05	*3.95*

TRUCIAL STATES

'trü-shəl 'stāts

LOCATION — Qatar Peninsula, Persian Gulf
GOVT. — Sheikdoms under British Protection
AREA — 32,300 sq. mi.
POP. — 86,000
CAPITAL — Dubai

The Trucial States are: Abu Dhabi, Ajman, Dubai, Fujeira, Ras al Khaima, Sharjah and Kalba, and Umm al Qiwain.

Stamps inscribed "Trucial States" were issued and used only in Dubai. Beginning Aug. 1972 all Trucial States used the stamps of United Arab Emirates.

100 Naye Paise = 1 Rupee

Catalogue values for all unused stamps in this country are for Never Hinged items.

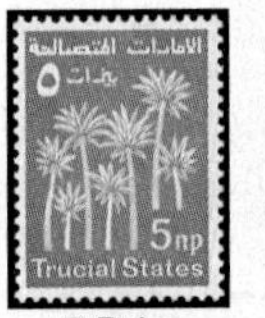

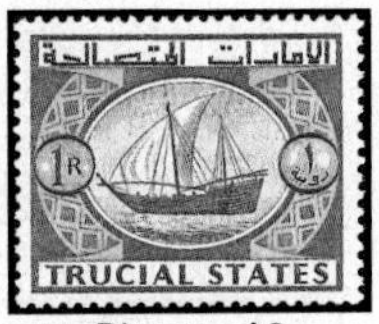

7 Palm Trees — A1

Dhow — A2

Perf. 14½x14

1961, Jan. 7 **Photo.** **Unwmk.**

1	A1	5np	emerald	1.75	.40
2	A1	15np	red brown	.75	.40
3	A1	20np	ultra	1.60	.40
4	A1	30np	orange	.75	.35
5	A1	40np	purple	.75	.40
6	A1	50np	brown olive	.75	.40
7	A1	75np	gray	1.00	.40
			Engr.	***Perf. 13x12½***	
8	A2	1r	emerald	9.00	4.00
9	A2	2r	black	9.00	*24.00*
10	A2	5r	rose red	11.00	*26.50*
11	A2	10r	violet blue	17.50	*27.50*
			Nos. 1-11 (11)	53.85	*84.75*

Stamps inscribed "Trucial States" were withdrawn in June, 1963, when the individual states began issuing their own stamps.

TUNISIA

tü-'nē-zh,ē,ə

LOCATION — Northern Africa, bordering on the Mediterranean Sea
GOVT. — Republic
AREA — 63,362 sq. mi.
POP. — 9,513,603 (1999 est.)
CAPITAL — Tunis

The former French protectorate became a sovereign state in 1956 and a republic in 1957.

100 Centimes = 1 Franc
1000 Millimes = 1 Dinar (1959)

Catalogue values for unused stamps in this country are for Never Hinged items, beginning with Scott 163 in the regular postage section, Scott B78 in the semi-postal section, Scott C13 in the airpost section, Scott CB1 in the airpost semi-postal section, and Scott J33 in the postage due section.

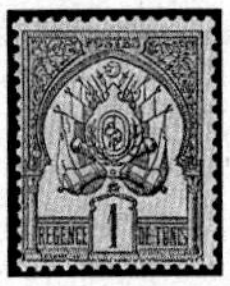

Coat of Arms — A1

Perf. 14x13½

1888-97 **Typo.** **Unwmk.**

1	A1	1c	black, *blue*	5.50	3.50
2	A1	2c	pur brn, *buff*	7.00	3.50
3	A1	5c	green, *grnsh*	35.00	17.50
4	A1	15c	blue, *grysh*	55.00	27.50
5	A1	25c	black, *rose*	110.00	70.00
6	A1	40c	red, *straw*	110.00	77.50
7	A1	75c	car, *rose*	110.00	85.00
8	A1	5fr	gray vio, *grysh*	510.00	275.00
			Nos. 1-8 (8)	942.50	559.50

All values exist imperforate.

Reprints were made in 1893 and some values have been reprinted twice since then. The shades usually differ from those of the originals. Stamps from the 1897 printing are on thicker paper, with white gum instead of grayish, and have a background of horizontal ruled lines.

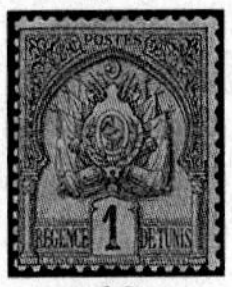

A2

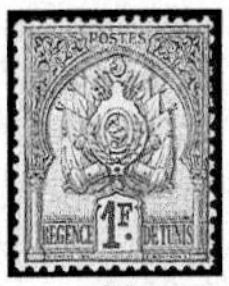

A3

1888-1902

9	A2	1c	blk, *lil bl*	1.75	1.10
10	A2	2c	pur brn, *buff*	1.75	1.10
11	A2	5c	grn, *grnsh*	7.00	1.10
12	A2	5c	yellow grn ('99)	7.00	1.10
13	A2	10c	blk, *lav* ('93)	14.00	2.10
14	A2	10c	red ('01)	7.00	1.10
15	A2	15c	blue, *grysh*	50.00	1.10
16	A2	15c	gray ('01)	11.00	2.10
17	A2	20c	red, *grn* ('99)	21.00	2.10
18	A2	25c	blk, *rose*	25.00	2.10
19	A2	25c	blue ('01)	21.00	2.75
20	A2	35c	brown ('02)	55.00	3.50
21	A2	40c	red, *straw*	21.00	2.10
22	A2	75c	car, *rose*	170.00	80.00
23	A2	75c	dp vio, *org* ('93)	35.00	11.00
24	A3	1fr	olive, *olive*	35.00	9.00
25	A3	2fr	dull violet ('02)	175.00	130.00
26	A3	5fr	red lil, *lav*	200.00	77.50
			Bar cancellation		1.00
			Quadrille Paper		
27	A2	15c	bl, *grysh* ('93)	50.00	1.40
			Nos. 9-27 (19)	907.50	332.25

For surcharges see Nos. 28, 58-61.

No. 27 Surcharged in Red

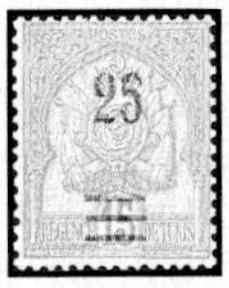

1902

28	A2	25c	on 15c blue	3.50	3.50

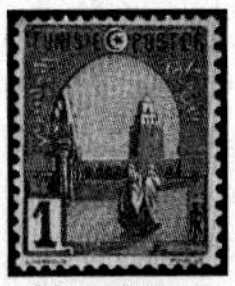

Mosque at Kairouan A4

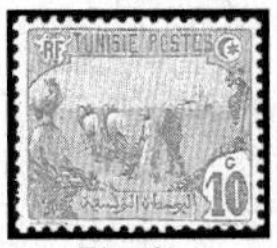

Plowing A5

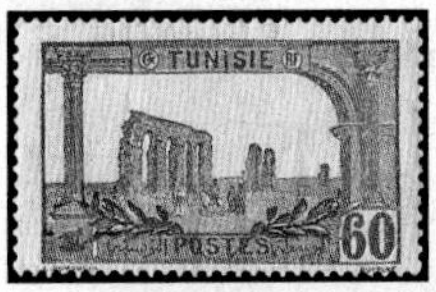

Ruins of Hadrian's Aqueduct A6

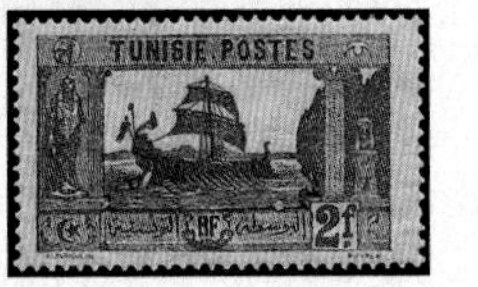

Carthaginian Galley — A7

1906-26 **Typo.**

29	A4	1c	blk, *yel*	.25	.25
30	A4	2c	red brn, *straw*	.25	.25
31	A4	3c	lt red ('19)	.25	.25
32	A4	5c	grn, *grnsh*	.35	.25
33	A4	5c	orange ('21)	.35	.25
34	A5	10c	red	.35	.30
35	A5	10c	green ('21)	.35	.35
36	A5	15c	vio, *pnksh*	1.40	.30
a.			Imperf., pair	175.00	
37	A5	15c	brn, *org* ('23)	.35	.35
38	A5	20c	brn, *pnksh*	.35	.30
39	A5	25c	deep blue	2.10	.70
a.			Imperf., pair		
40	A5	25c	violet ('21)	.35	.35
41	A6	30c	red brn & vio ('19)	1.10	.70
42	A5	30c	pale red ('21)	1.10	.70
43	A6	35c	ol grn & brn	10.50	2.10
44	A6	40c	blk brn & red brn	5.50	.70
45	A5	40c	blk, *pnksh* ('23)	1.20	.80
46	A5	40c	gray grn ('26)	.25	.25
47	A5	50c	blue ('21)	1.10	.70
48	A6	60c	ol grn & vio ('21)	1.10	1.10
49	A6	60c	ver & rose ('25)	.70	.35
50	A6	75c	red brn & red	1.10	.70
51	A6	75c	ver & dl red ('26)	.50	.50
52	A7	1fr	red & dk brn	1.10	.70
53	A7	1fr	ind & ultra ('25)	.35	.35
54	A7	2fr	brn & ol grn	6.50	2.00
55	A7	2fr	grn & red, *pink* ('25)	1.10	.35
56	A7	5fr	violet & blue	12.50	5.50
57	A7	5fr	gray vio & grn ('25)	1.10	.70
			Nos. 29-57 (29)	53.50	22.10

For surcharges and overprints see Nos. 62-64, 70-73115-116, B1-B23, B25-B27, B29-B30, B32-B36, C1-C6.

Stamps and Type of 1888-1902 Surcharged

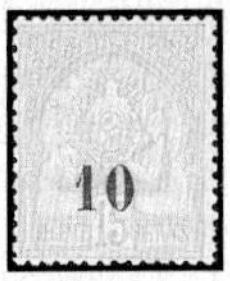

1908, Sept.

58	A2	10c	on 15c gray, *lt gray* (R)	2.10	2.10
59	A3	35c	on 1fr ol, *ol* (R)	5.50	5.50
60	A3	40c	on 2fr dl vio (Bl)	10.50	10.50
61	A3	75c	on 5fr red lil, *lav* (Bl)	7.00	7.00
			Nos. 58-61 (4)	25.10	25.10

No. 36 Surcharged

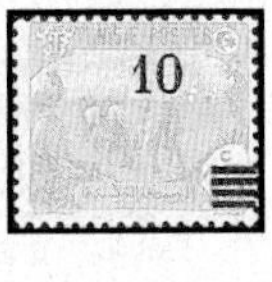

1911

62	A5	10c	on 15c vio, *pinkish*	1.75	.70
a.			Inverted surcharge		2,100.

No. 34 Surcharged

1917, Mar. 16

63	A5	15c on 10c red	1.10	.35
a.		"15c" omitted	40.00	
b.		Double surcharge	87.50	

No. 36 Surcharged

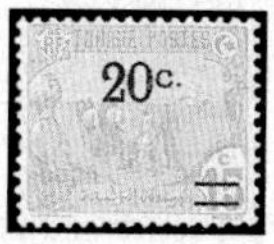

1921

64	A5	20c on 15c vio, *pinkish*	1.10	.35
a.		grayish paper (#36b)	1.40	.45

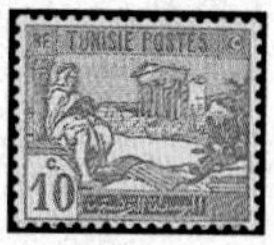

Arab and Ruins of Dougga — A9

1922-26 Typo. *Perf. 13½x14*

65	A9	10c green	.25	.25
66	A9	10c rose ('26)	.30	.30
67	A9	30c rose	1.10	1.10
68	A9	30c lilac ('26)	.45	.45
69	A9	50c blue	.70	.70
		Nos. 65-69 (5)	2.80	2.80

For surcharges see Nos. 117, B24, B28, B31.

Stamps and Type of 1906 Surcharged in Red or Black

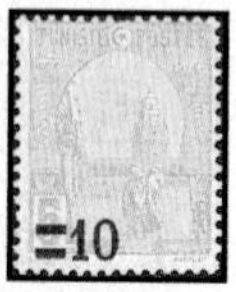

a

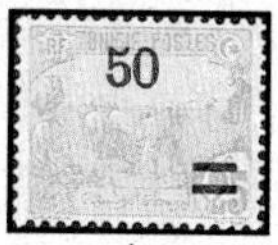

b

1923-25

70	A4(a)	10c on 5c grn, *grnsh* (R)	.35	.35
a.		Double surcharge	80.00	
b.		Inverted surcharge	115.00	
c.		Double surcharge, one inverted	115.00	
71	A5(b)	20c on 15c vio (Bk)	1.10	.35
a.		Double surcharge	115.00	
72	A5(b)	30c on 20c yel brn (Bk) ('25)	.35	.35
73	A5(b)	50c on 25c blue (R)	1.10	.35
a.		Double surcharge	110.00	
b.		Inverted surcharge	110.00	
		Nos. 70-73 (4)	2.90	1.40

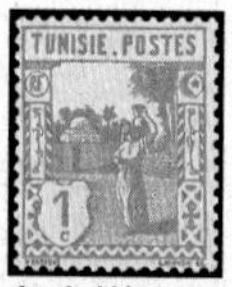

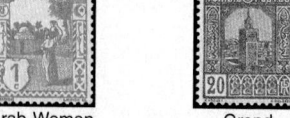

Arab Woman Carrying Water — A10

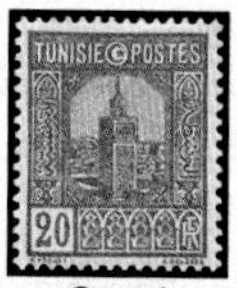

Grand Mosque at Tunis — A11

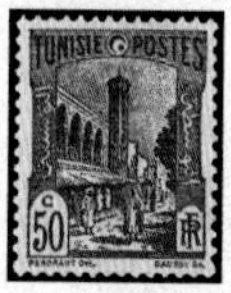

Mosque, Tunis — A12

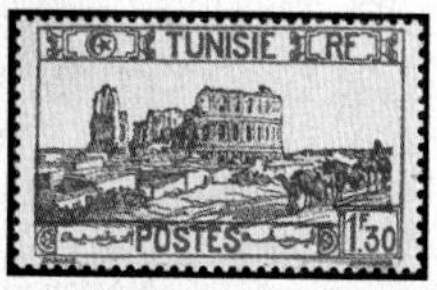

Roman Amphitheater, El Djem (Thysdrus) — A13

1926-46 Typo. *Perf. 14x13½*

74	A10	1c lt red	.25	.25
75	A10	2c olive grn	.25	.25
76	A10	3c slate blue	.25	.25
77	A10	5c yellow grn	.25	.25
78	A10	10c rose	.25	.25
78A	A12	10c brown ('46)	.25	.25
79	A11	15c gray lilac	.25	.25
80	A11	20c deep red	.30	.25
81	A11	25c gray green	.45	.30
82	A11	25c lt violet ('28)	.70	.30
83	A11	30c lt violet	.45	.35
84	A11	30c bl grn ('28)	.35	.30
84A	A12	30c dk ol grn ('46)	.25	.25
85	A11	40c deep brown	.25	.25
85A	A12	40c lil rose ('46)	.30	.30
86	A11	45c emer ('40)	1.10	1.10
87	A12	50c black	.25	.25
88	A12	50c ultra ('34)	.70	.35
88B	A12	50c emer ('40)	.25	.25
88C	A12	50c lt blue ('46)	.30	.30
89	A12	60c red org ('40)	.25	.25
89A	A12	60c ultra ('45)	.25	.25
90	A12	65c ultra ('38)	.70	.35
91	A12	70c dk red ('40)	.25	.25
92	A12	75c vermilion	.35	.70
93	A12	75c lil rose ('28)	1.10	.35
94	A12	80c blue green	1.10	.70
94A	A12	80c blk brn ('40)	.30	.30
94B	A12	80c emer ('45)	.45	.30
95	A12	90c org red ('28)	.35	.35
96	A12	90c ultra ('39)	10.00	10.00
97	A12	1fr brown violet	.70	.70
97A	A12	1fr rose ('40)	.25	.25
98	A13	1.05fr dl bl & mag	.70	.70
98A	A12	1.20fr blk brn ('45)	.35	.30
99	A13	1.25fr gray bl & dk bl	.70	.70
100	A13	1.25fr car rose ('40)	1.10	1.10
100A	A13	1.30fr bl & vio bl ('42)	.35	.30
101	A13	1.40fr brt red vio ('40)	1.20	1.20
102	A13	1.50fr bl & dp bl ('28)	1.40	.50
102A	A13	1.50fr rose red & red org ('42)	.35	.50
102B	A12	1.50fr rose lil ('46)	.25	.25
103	A13	2fr rose & ol brn	1.40	.35
104	A13	2fr red org ('39)	.35	.35
104A	A12	2fr Prus grn ('45)	.35	.25
105	A13	2.25fr ultra ('39)	.70	.90
105A	A13	2.40fr red ('46)	.65	.50
106	A13	2.50fr green ('40)	.80	.80
107	A13	3fr dl bl & org	1.75	.70
108	A13	3fr violet ('39)	.35	.35
108A	A13	3fr blk brn ('46)	.35	.25
108B	A13	4fr ultra ('45)	1.10	.55
109	A13	5fr red & grn, *grnsh*	2.75	1.40
110	A13	5fr dp red brn ('40)	1.25	1.25
110A	A13	5fr dk grn ('46)	.45	.45
110B	A13	6fr dp ultra ('45)	.70	.45
111	A13	10fr brn red & blk, *bluish*	11.00	3.50
112	A13	10fr rose pink ('40)	.80	.80
112A	A13	10fr ver ('46)	.70	.45
112B	A13	10fr ultra ('46)	.65	.35
112C	A13	15fr rose lil ('45)	.35	.25
113	A13	20fr lil & red, *pnksh* ('28)	2.50	1.10
113A	A13	20fr dk grn ('45)	.70	.45
113B	A13	25fr violet ('45)	.70	.65
113C	A13	50fr carmine ('45)	1.75	.85
113D	A13	100fr car rose ('45)	2.10	1.10
		Nos. 74-113D (66)	64.05	44.65

See Nos. 152A-162, 185-189, 199-206.

For surcharges and overprints see Nos. 114, 118-121, 143-152, B74-B77, B87-B88, B91-B95, B98, C7-C12.

No. 99 Surcharged with New Value and Bars in Red

1927, Mar. 24

114	A13	1.50fr on 1.25fr	.80	.30

Stamps of 1921-26 Surcharged

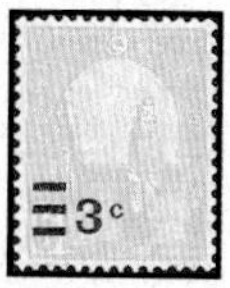

1928, May 1

115	A4	3c on 5c orange	.35	.25
116	A5	10c on 15c brn, *org*	.70	.30
c.		Double surcharge	125.00	
117	A9	25c on 30c lilac	.70	.70
118	A12	40c on 80c bl grn	.70	.45
119	A12	50c on 75c ver	1.10	.50
		Nos. 115-119 (5)	3.55	2.20

No. 83 Surcharged

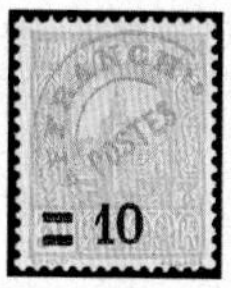

1929

120	A11	10c on 30c lt violet	1.75	1.10

No. 120 exists precanceled only. The value in first column is for a stamp which has not been through the post and has original gum. The value in the second column is for a postally used, gumless stamp. See No. 199a.

No. 85 Surcharged with New Value and Bars

1930

121	A11	50c on 40c dp brn	5.50	.70

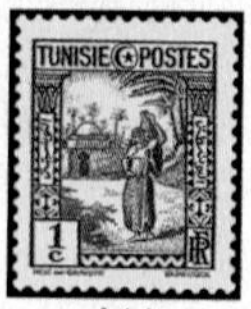

A14

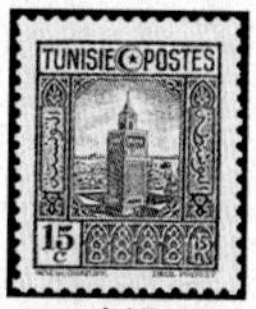

A15

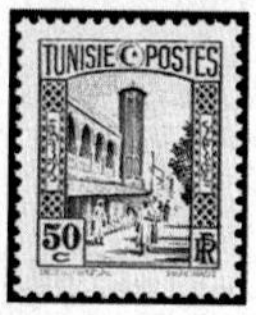

A16

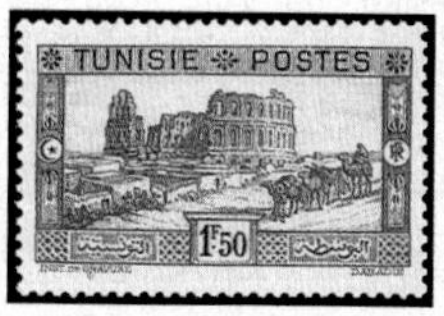

A17

Perf. 11, 12½, 12½x13

1931-34 Engr.

122	A14	1c deep blue	.25	.25
123	A14	2c yellow brn	.25	.25
124	A14	3c black	.35	.35
125	A14	5c yellow grn	.25	.25
126	A14	10c red	.25	.25
127	A15	15c dull violet	.70	.70
128	A15	20c dull brown	.25	.25
129	A15	25c rose red	.35	.35
130	A15	30c deep green	.35	.70
131	A15	40c red orange	.35	.35
132	A16	50c ultra	.35	.35
133	A16	75c yellow	2.10	2.10
134	A16	90c red	.70	.70
135	A16	1fr olive black	.35	.70
136	A16	1fr dk brn ('34)	.50	.45
137	A17	1.50fr brt ultra	1.00	.70
138	A17	2fr deep brown	.70	1.00
139	A17	3fr blue green	10.50	10.50
140	A17	5fr car rose	28.00	21.00
a.		Perf. 12½	37.50	35.00
141	A17	10fr black	50.00	35.00
142	A17	20fr dark brown	62.50	45.00
		Nos. 122-142 (21)	160.05	121.20

For surcharges see Nos. B54-B73.

Nos. 88, 102 Surcharged in Red or Black

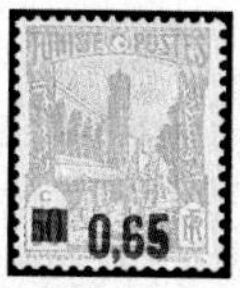

1937 *Perf. 14x13½*

143	A12	65c on 50c (R)	.70	.35
b.		Double surcharge	105.00	87.50
144	A13	1.75fr on 1.50fr (R)	5.50	1.40
a.		Double surcharge	95.00	95.00
b.		In pair with unsurcharged stamp	250.00	

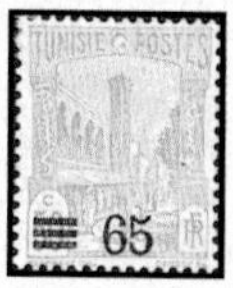

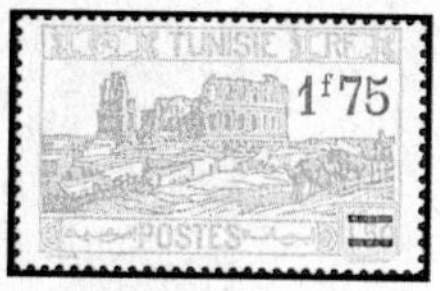

1938

145	A12	65c on 50c (Bk)	.70	.35
a.		Double surcharge, one inverted	175.00	175.00
146	A13	1.75fr on 1.50fr (R)	10.50	7.00

Stamps of 1938-39 Surcharged in Red or Carmine

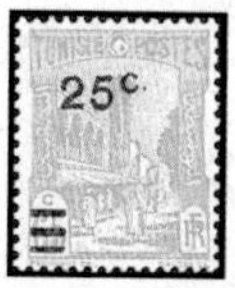

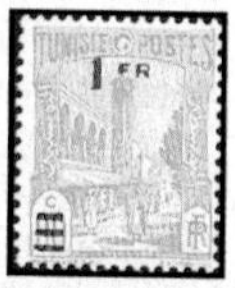

1940

147	A12	25c on 65c ultra (C)	.25	.25
148	A12	1fr on 90c ultra (R)	.50	.50
a.		Double surcharge	120.00	

Stamps of 1938-40 Surcharged in Red or Black

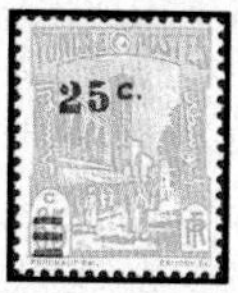

1941

149	A12	25c on 65c ultra (R)	.35	.35
150	A13	1fr on 1.25fr car rose	.70	.35
151	A13	1fr on 1.40fr brt red vio	.70	.70
152	A13	1fr on 2.25fr ultra (R)	.70	.70
		Nos. 149-152 (4)	2.45	2.10

Types of 1926 Without RF

1941-45 Typo. *Perf. 14x13½*

152A	A11	30c carmine ('45)	.25	.25
152B	A12	1.20fr int blue ('45)	.25	.25
153	A12	1.50fr brn red ('42)	.35	.45
154	A13	2.40fr car & brt pink ('42)	.45	.45
155	A13	2.50fr dk bl & lt bl	.35	.45
156	A13	3fr lt violet ('42)	.30	.30
157	A13	4fr blk & bl vio ('42)	.35	.45
158	A13	4.50fr ol grn & brn ('42)	.70	.70
159	A13	5fr brown blk ('42)	.70	.55
160	A13	10fr lil & dull vio	.35	.50
161	A13	15fr henna brn ('42)	5.50	4.50
162	A13	20fr lt vio & car	2.75	1.50
		Nos. 152A-162 (12)	12.30	10.35

Catalogue values for unused stamps in this section, from this point to the end of the section, are for Never Hinged items.

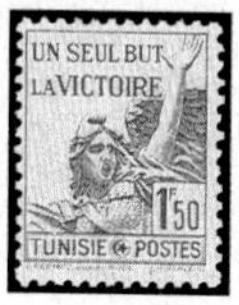

One Aim Alone - Victory — A18

1943 Litho. *Perf. 12*

163	A18	1.50fr rose	.35	.25

Mosque and Olive
Tree — A19

1944-45   Unwmk.   Perf. 11½

Size: 15½x19mm

165	A19	30c yellow ('45)	.35 .25
166	A19	40c org brn ('45)	.35 .25
168	A19	60c red org ('45)	.70 .45
169	A19	70c rose pink ('45)	.35 .25
170	A19	80c Prus grn ('45)	.35 .30
171	A19	90c violet ('45)	.35 .30
172	A19	1fr red ('45)	.35 .30
173	A19	1.50fr dp bl ('45)	.35 .30

Size: 21¼x26½mm

175	A19	2.40fr red	.70 .45
176	A19	2.50fr red brn	.70 .45
177	A19	3fr lt vio	1.10 .65
178	A19	4fr brt bl vio	.70 .45
179	A19	4.50fr apple grn	.70 .45
180	A19	5fr gray	1.10 .65
181	A19	6fr choc ('45)	.70 .45
182	A19	10fr brn lake ('45)	1.10 .70
183	A19	15fr copper brn	1.10 .70
184	A19	20fr lilac	1.10 .80
		Nos. 165-184 (18)	12.15 8.15

For surcharge see No. B79.

Types of 1926

1946-47   Typo.   Perf. 14x13½

185	A12	2fr emerald ('47)	.70 .45
186	A12	3fr rose pink	.35 .25
187	A12	4fr violet ('47)	.85 .45
188	A13	4fr violet ('47)	1.10 .50
189	A12	6fr carmine ('47)	.35 .25
		Nos. 185-189 (5)	3.35 1.90

Neptune,
Bardo
Museum
A20

1947-49   Engr.   Perf. 13

190	A20	5fr dk grn & bluish blk	1.10 .90
191	A20	10fr blk brn & bluish blk	.55 .30
192	A20	18fr dk bl gray & Prus bl ('48)	1.75 1.40
193	A20	25fr dk bl & bl grn ('49)	2.10 1.10
		Nos. 190-193 (4)	5.50 3.30

For surcharge see No. B108.

Detail from
Great
Mosque at
Kairouan
A21

1948-49

194	A21	3fr dk bl grn & bl grn	1.10 .55
195	A21	4fr dk red vio & red vio	.70 .45
196	A21	6fr red brn & red	.35 .25
197	A21	10fr purple ('49)	.65 .35
198	A21	12fr henna brn	1.10 .65
198A	A21	12fr dk brn & org brn ('49)	.90 .55
198B	A21	15fr dk red ('49)	.80 .55
		Nos. 194-198B (7)	5.60 3.35

See No. 225. For surcharge see No. B103.

Types of 1926

1947-49   Typo.   Perf. 14x13½

199	A12	2.50fr brown orange	.70 .45
a.		2.50fr brown	1.50 .80
200	A12	4fr brown org ('49)	1.20 .45
201	A12	4.50fr lt ultra	1.10 .45
202	A12	5fr blue ('48)	.70 .35
203	A12	5fr lt bl grn ('49)	1.20 .25
204	A13	6fr rose red	.35 .25
205	A12	15fr rose red	1.20 .65
206	A13	25fr red orange	2.10 .90
		Nos. 199-206 (8)	8.55 3.95

No. 199a is known only precanceled. See
note after No. 120.

Dam on the
Oued
Mellegue
A22

1949, Sept. 1   Engr.   Perf. 13

207	A22	15fr grnsh black	3.50 .70

UPU Symbols and
Tunisian Post
Rider — A23

1949, Oct. 28   Bluish Paper

208	A23	5fr dark green	1.75 1.40
209	A23	15fr red brown	1.75 1.40
		Nos. 208-209,C13 (3)	6.00 4.55

UPU, 75th anniversary.
Nos. 208-209 exist imperf.

Berber Hermes at
Carthage — A24

1950-51

210	A24	15fr red brown	1.10 .70
211	A24	25fr indigo ('51)	1.10 .70
212	A24	50fr dark green ('51)	2.50 .70
		Nos. 210-212 (3)	4.70 2.10

Horse, Carthage
Museum — A25

1950, Dec. 26   Typo.   Perf. 13½x14

Size: 21½x17½mm

213	A25	10c aquamarine	.30 .25
214	A25	50c brown	.30 .25
215	A25	1fr rose lilac	.30 .25
216	A25	2fr gray	.35 .30
217	A25	4fr vermilion	.55 .45
218	A25	5fr blue green	.35 .25
219	A25	8fr deep blue	.55 .35
220	A25	12fr red	1.40 .65
221	A25	15fr carmine rose ('50)	.55 .45
		Nos. 213-221 (9)	4.65 3.20

See Nos. 222-224, 226-228.

1951-53   Engr.   Perf. 13x14

Size: 22x18mm

222	A25	15fr carmine rose	1.20 .65
223	A25	15fr ultra ('53)	1.40 .55
224	A25	30fr deep ultra	2.50 .70
		Nos. 222-224 (3)	5.10 1.90

Type of 1948-49

1951, Aug. 1   Perf. 13

225	A21	30fr dark blue	1.40 1.10

Horse Type of 1950

1952   Typo.   Perf. 13½x14

226	A25	3fr brown orange	.70 .45
227	A25	12fr carmine rose	1.40 .45
228	A25	15fr ultra	.70 .25
		Nos. 226-228 (3)	2.80 1.15

Charles
Nicolle — A26

1952, Aug. 4   Engr.   Perf. 13

229	A26	15fr black brown	2.10 .90
230	A26	30fr deep blue	2.10 .90

Founding of the Society of Medical Sciences
of Tunisia, 50th anniv.

Flags, Pennants
and Minaret — A27

1953, Oct. 18

231	A27	8fr black brn & choc	1.40 1.10
232	A27	12fr dk green & emer	1.40 1.10
233	A27	15fr indigo & ultra	1.40 1.10
234	A27	18fr dk pur & pur	1.40 1.10
235	A27	30fr dk car & car	2.10 1.40
		Nos. 231-235 (5)	7.70 5.80

First International Fair of Tunis.

Courtyard at
Sousse — A28

Sidi Bou
Maklouf
Mosque
A29

Designs: 1fr, Courtyard at Sousse. 2fr, 4fr,
Citadel, Takrouna. 5fr, 8fr, View of Tatahouine.
10fr, 12fr, Oasis of Matmata. 15fr, Street Corner, Sidi Bou Said. 20fr, 25fr, Genoese fort,
Tabarka. 30fr, 40fr, Bab-El-Khadra gate. 50fr,
75fr, Four-story building, Medenine.

Perf. 13½x13 (A28), 13

1954, May 29

236	A28	50c emerald	.30 .25
237	A28	1fr carmine rose	.30 .25
238	A28	2fr violet brown	.35 .30
239	A28	4fr turq blue	.55 .30
240	A28	5fr violet	.55 .25
241	A28	8fr black brown	.55 .30
242	A28	10fr dk blue grn	.55 .25
243	A28	12fr rose brown	.55 .30
244	A28	15fr dp ultra	2.25 .35
245	A29	18fr chocolate	2.00 .65
246	A29	20fr dp ultra	1.25 .30
247	A29	25fr indigo	1.25 .30
248	A29	30fr dp claret	1.40 .30
249	A29	40fr dk Prus grn	1.50 .65
250	A29	50fr dk violet	2.50 .30
251	A29	75fr carmine rose	5.50 2.10

Typo.

Perf. 14x13½

252	A28	15fr ultra	.80 .25
		Nos. 236-252 (17)	22.15 7.40

Imperforates exist. Value $50. See Nos.
271-287. For surcharge see No. B125.

Mohammed al-
Amin, Bey of
Tunis — A30

1954, Oct.   Perf. 13

253	A30	8fr bl & dk bl	1.10 .85
254	A30	12fr lil gray & indigo	1.10 .85
255	A30	15fr dp car & brn lake	1.20 .85
256	A30	18fr red brn & blk brn	1.20 .90
257	A30	30fr bl grn & dk bl grn	1.75 1.40
		Nos. 253-257 (5)	6.35 4.90

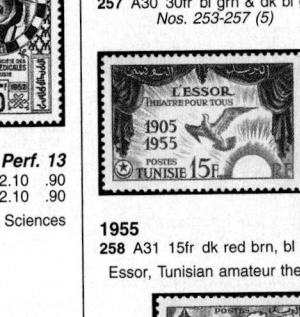

Theater
Drapes,
Dove and
Sun — A31

1955

258	A31	15fr dk red brn, bl & org	1.10 .85

Essor, Tunisian amateur theatrical society.

Rotary Emblem, Map and Symbols of
Punic, Roman, Arab and French
Civilizations
A32

1955, May 14   Unwmk.

259	A32	12fr vio brn & blk brn	1.10 .85
260	A32	15fr vio gray & dk brn	1.10 .85
261	A32	18fr rose vio & dk pur	1.20 .90
262	A32	25fr blue & dp ultra	1.20 .90
263	A32	30fr dk Prus grn & ind	1.75 1.40
		Nos. 259-263 (5)	6.35 4.90

Rotary International, 50th anniv.

Bey of Tunis — A33

1955   Engr.   Perf. 13½x13

264	A33	15fr dark blue	.70 .25

Embroiderers — A34

15fr, 18fr, Potters. 20fr, 30fr, Florists.

1955, July 25   Perf. 13

265	A34	5fr rose brown	1.10 .85
266	A34	12fr ultra	1.10 .85
267	A34	15fr Prussian green	1.10 .90
268	A34	18fr red	1.10 .90
269	A34	20fr dark violet	1.40 1.10
270	A34	30fr violet brown	1.40 1.10
		Nos. 265-270 (6)	7.20 5.70

For surcharge see No. B126.

Independent Kingdom
Types of 1954 Redrawn with "RF"
Omitted

1956, Mar. 1   Perf. 13½x13, 13 (A29)

271	A28	50c emerald	.25 .25
272	A28	1fr carmine rose	.25 .25
273	A28	2fr violet brown	.25 .25
274	A28	4fr turquoise blue	.30 .25
275	A28	5fr violet	.30 .25
276	A28	8fr black brown	.30 .25
277	A28	10fr dk blue grn	.30 .25
278	A28	12fr rose brown	.30 .25
279	A28	15fr deep ultra	1.10 .25
280	A29	18fr chocolate	.35 .25
281	A29	20fr deep ultra	.30 .25
282	A29	25fr indigo	.30 .25
283	A29	30fr deep claret	1.10 .25
284	A29	40fr dk Prus grn	1.10 .25
285	A29	50fr dark violet	1.00 .25
286	A29	75fr carmine rose	1.75 1.10

Perf. 14x13
Typo.

287 A28 15fr ultra   .70   .25
    Nos. 271-287 (17)   9.95 5.10

Mohammed al-Amin
Bey of Tunis — A35

Designs: 12fr, 18fr, 30fr, Woman and Dove.
5fr, 20fr, Bey of Tunis.

1956   Unwmk.   Engr.   Perf. 13
288 A35 5fr deep blue   .25   .25
289 A35 12fr brown violet   .30   .35
290 A35 15fr red   .30   .35
291 A35 18fr dk blue gray   .45   .40
292 A35 20fr dark green   .45   .40
293 A35 30fr copper brown   .85   .50
    Nos. 288-293 (6)   2.60 2.25

Issued to commemorate Tunisian autonomy.

Farhat
Hached — A36

1956, May 1
294 A36 15fr rose brown   .30   .30
295 A36 30fr indigo   .35   .35

Farhat Hached (1914-1952), nationalist
leader.

Grapes — A37

Fruit
Market
A38

Designs: 15fr, Hand holding olive branch.
18fr, Wheat harvest. 20fr, Man carrying food
basket ("Gifts for the wedding").

1956-57   Unwmk.   Engr.   Perf. 13
296 A37 12fr lil, vio & vio brn   .55   .25
297 A37 15fr ind, dk ol grn & red
           brn   .65   .25
298 A37 18fr brt violet blue   .90   .40
299 A37 20fr brown orange   .90   .40
300 A38 25fr chocolate   1.25 .80
301 A38 30fr deep ultra   1.40 .65
    Nos. 296-301 (6)   5.65 2.75

Habib
Bourguiba — A39

Farmers and
Workers
A40

Perf. 14 (A39), 11½x11 (A40)
1957, Mar. 20
302 A39 5fr dark blue   .25   .25
303 A40 12fr magenta   .25   .25
304 A39 20fr ultra   .30   .30
305 A40 25fr green   .35   .25
306 A39 30fr chocolate   .45   .35
307 A40 50fr crimson rose   .80   .55
    Nos. 302-307 (6)   2.40 1.95

First anniversary of independence.

Dove and
Handclasp
A41

Labor Bourse,
Tunis — A42

1957, July 5   Engr.   Perf. 13
308 A41 18fr dk red violet   .30   .30
309 A42 20fr crimson   .35   .35
310 A41 25fr green   .35   .35
311 A42 30fr dark blue   .45   .45
    Nos. 308-311 (4)   1.45 1.45

5th World Congress of the Intl. Federation of
Trade Unions, Tunis, July 5-13.

Republic

Officer and
Soldier — A43

1957, Aug. 8   Typo.   Perf. 11
312 A43 20fr rose pink   14.00 20.00
313 A43 25fr light violet   14.00 19.00
314 A43 30fr brown orange   14.00 19.00
    Nos. 312-314 (3)   42.00 58.00

Proclamation of the Republic.

Bourguiba
in Exile, Ile
de la Galité
A44

1958, Jan. 18   Engr.   Perf. 13
315 A44 20fr blue & dk brn   .55   .40
316 A44 25fr lt blue & vio   .55   .40

6th anniv. of Bourguiba's deportation.

Map of
Tunisia — A45

25fr, Woman & child. 30fr, Hand holding
flag.

1958, Mar. 20   Perf. 13
317 A45 20fr dk brown & emer   .40   .25
318 A45 25fr blue & sepia   .40   .25
319 A45 30fr red brown & red   .55   .25
    Nos. 317-319 (3)   1.35 .75

2nd anniv. of independence. See No. 321.

Andreas Vesalius and Abderrahman
ibn Khaldoun — A46

1958, Apr. 17   Unwmk.
320 A46 30fr bister & slate grn   .65   .25

World's Fair, Brussels, Apr. 17-Oct. 19.

Redrawn Type of 1958
1958, June 1   Engr.   Perf. 13
321 A45 20fr brt bl & ocher   .65   .25

Date has been changed to "1 Juin 1955-
1958."
3rd anniv. of the return of Pres. Habib
Bourguiba.

Gardener — A47

1958, May 1
322 A47 20fr multicolored   .65   .30

Labor Day, May 1.

A48

1958, July 25   Unwmk.   Perf. 13
Blue Paper
323 A48 5fr dk vio brn & ol   .45   .25
324 A48 10fr dk grn & yel grn   .45   .25
325 A48 15fr org red & brn lake   .45   .25
326 A48 20fr vio, ol grn & yel   .45   .25
327 A48 25fr red lilac   .45   .25
    Nos. 323-327 (5)   2.25 1.25

First anniversary of the Republic.

Pres. Habib
Bourguiba — A49

1958, Aug. 3   Unwmk.   Perf. 13
328 A49 20fr vio & brn lake   .65   .25

Pres. Bourguiba's 55th birthday.

Fishermen Casting
Net — A50

1958, Oct. 18   Engr.   Perf. 13
329 A50 25fr dk brn, grn & red   .65   .30

6th International Fair, Tunis.

UNESCO
Building,
Paris
A51

1958, Nov. 3
330 A51 25fr grnsh black   .65   .30

Opening of UNESCO Headquarters, Nov. 3.

Woman Opening
Veil — A52

1959, Jan. 1   Engr.   Perf. 13
331 A52 20m greenish blue   .65   .25

Emancipation of Tunisian women.

Hand Planting
Symbolic
Tree — A53

Habib
Bourguiba
at Borj le
Boeuf
A54

10m, Shield with flag and people holding
torch. 20m, Habib Bourguiba at Borj le Boeuf,
Sahara.

1959, Mar. 2   Unwmk.   Perf. 13
332 A53 5m vio brn, car & sal   .25   .25
333 A53 10m multicolored   .30   .25
334 A53 20m blue   .40   .25
335 A54 30m grnsh bl, ind & org
           brn   .70   .40
    Nos. 332-335 (4)   1.65 1.15

25th anniv. of the founding of the Neo-
Destour Party at Kasr Helal, Mar. 2, 1934.

"Independence" — A55

1959, Mar. 20
336 A55 50m olive, blk & red   .85   .40

3rd anniversary of independence.

Map of Africa and Drawings — A56

1959, Apr. 15   Litho.   Perf. 13
337 A56 40m lt bl & red brn   .85 .40
Africa Freedom Day, Apr. 15.

Camel Camp and Mosque, Kairouan A57

Horseback Rider — A58

Olive Picker — A59

Open Window A58a

Designs: ½m, Woodcock in Ain-Draham forest. 2m, Camel rider. 3m, Saddler's shop. 4m, Old houses of Medenine, gazelle and youth. 6m, Weavers. 8m, Woman of Gafsa. 10m, Unveiled woman holding fruit. 12m, Ivory craftsman. 15m, Skanes Beach, Monastir, and mermaid. 16m, Minaret of Ez-Zitouna University, Tunis. 20m, Oasis of Gabès. 25m, Oil, flowers and fish of Sfax. 30m, Modern and Roman aqueducts. 40m, Festival at Kairouan (drummer and camel). 45m, Octagonal minaret, Bizerte (boatman). 50m, Three women of Djerba island. 60m, Date palms, Djerid. 70m, Tapestry weaver. 75m, Pottery of Nabeul. 90m, Le Kef (man on horse). 100m, Road to Sidi-bou-Said. 200m, Old port of Sfax. ½d, Roman temple, Sbeitla. 1d, Farmer plowing with oxen, Beja.

1959-61   Unwmk.   Engr.   Perf. 13
338 A58 ½m emer, brn &
             bl grn ('60)   .25   .25
339 A58   1m lt bl & ocher   .25   .25
340 A58   2m multicolored   .25   .25
341 A58   3m slate green   .25   .25
342 A57   4m red brn ('60)   .25   .25
343 A58   5m gray green   .25   .25
344 A58   6m rose violet   .25   .25
345 A58   8m vio brn ('60)   .75   .30
346 A58 10m ol, dk grn &
             car   .25   .25
347 A58 12m vio bl & ol
             bis ('61)   .60   .25
348 A57 15m brt blue ('60)   .30   .25
349 A57 16m grnsh blk
             ('60)   .35   .25
350 A58a 20m grnsh blue   1.10   .30
351 A58a 20m grnsh blk, ol
             & mar ('60)   2.00   .25
352 A57 25m multi ('60)   .30   .25
353 A58a 30m brn, grnsh bl
             & ol   .45   .25
354 A59 40m dp grn ('60)   1.80   .25
355 A58a 45m brt grn ('60)   .75   .30
356 A58a 50m Prus grn, dk
             bl & rose
             ('60)   1.10   .25
357 A58a 60m grn & red
             brn ('60)   1.10   .40
358 A59 70m multi ('60)   1.60   .55
359 A59 75m ol gray ('60)   1.50   .60
360 A58a 90m brt grn, ultra
             & choc ('60)   1.50   .60
361 A59 95m multicolored   2.00   1.10
362 A58a 100m dk bl, ol &
             brn   2.10   1.00
363 A58a 200m brt bl, bis &
             car   5.25   2.40
363A A59 ½d lt brn ('60)   12.00 6.75

363B A58a 1d sl grn & bis
             ('60)   22.50 13.50
    Nos. 338-363B (28)   61.05 31.80

UN Emblem and Clasped Hands — A60

1959, Oct. 24
364 A60 80m org brn, brn & ultra   .75 .60
UN Day, Oct. 24.

Dancer and Coin — A61

1959, Nov. 4
365 A61 50m grnsh bl & blk   .75 .60
Central Bank of Tunisia, first anniversary.

Uprooted Oak Emblem — A62

Doves and WRY Emblem A63

1960, Apr. 7   Engr.   Perf. 13
366 A62 20m blue black   .60 .35
367 A63 40m red lil & dk grn .75 .50
World Refugee Year, 7/1/59-6/30/60.

Girl, Boy and Scout Badge — A64

Designs: 25m, Hand giving Scout sign. 30m, Bugler and tent. 40m, Peacock and Scout emblem. 60m, Scout and campfire.

1960, Aug. 9
368 A64 10m lt blue green   .30   .30
369 A64 25m green, red & brn   .45   .35
370 A64 30m vio bl, grn & mar   .50   .35
371 A64 40m black, car & bl   .75   .45
372 A64 60m dk brn, vio blk &
             lake   1.10 .60
    Nos. 368-372 (5)   3.10 2.05
4th Arab Boy Scout Jamboree, Tunis, Aug.

Cyclist — A65

Designs: 10m, Olympic rings forming flower. 15m, Girl tennis player and minaret. 25m, Runner and minaret. 50m, Handball player and minaret.

1960, Aug. 25
373 A65 5m dk brown & olive   .30   .30
374 A65 10m sl, red vio & emer   .30   .30
375 A65 15m rose red & rose car .30   .30
376 A65 25m grnsh bl & gray bl   .45   .45
377 A65 50m brt green & ultra   .80   .85
    Nos. 373-377 (5)   2.15 2.20
17th Olympic Games, Rome, 8/25-9/11.

Symbolic Forest Design — A66

Designs: 15m, Man working in forest. 25m, Tree superimposed on leaf. 50m, Symbolic tree and bird.

1960, Aug. 29
378 A66 8m multicolored   .30   .25
379 A66 15m dark green   .45   .25
380 A66 25m dk pur, crim & brt
             grn   .60   .30
381 A66 50m Prus grn, yel grn &
             rose lake   1.10 .55
    Nos. 378-381 (4)   2.45 1.35
5th World Forestry Congress, Seattle, Wash., Aug. 29-Sept. 10.

National Fair Emblems — A67

1960, June 1
382 A67 100m black & green   .60 .50
5th Natl. Fair, Sousse, May 27-June 12.

Pres. Bourguiba Signing Constitution A68

Pres. Bourguiba A69

1960, June 1
383 A68 20m choc, red & emer   .30 .25
384 A69 20m grayish blk   .25 .25
385 A69 30m blue, dl red & blk   .35 .25
386 A69 40m grn, dl red & blk   .55 .25
    Nos. 383-386 (4)   1.40 1.00
Promulgation of the Constitution (No. 383).

UN Emblem and Arms — A70

1960, Oct. 24   Engr.   Perf. 13
387 A70 40m mag, ultra & gray grn .60 .50
15th anniversary of the United Nations.

Dove and "Liberated Tunisia" — A71

Design: 75m, Globe and arms.

1961, Mar. 20   Perf. 13
388 A71 20m maroon, bis & bl   .25 .25
389 A71 30m blue, vio & brn   .35 .25
390 A71 40m yel grn & ultra   .65 .45
391 A71 75m bis, red lil & Prus
             bl   .80 .55
    Nos. 388-391 (4)   2.05 1.50
5th anniversary of independence.

Map of Africa, Woman and Animals — A72

Map of Africa: 60m, Negro woman and Arab. 100m, Arabic inscription and Guinea masque. 200m, Hands of Negro and Arab.

1961, Apr. 15   Engr.   Unwmk.
392 A72 40m bis brn, red brn &
             dk grn   .30 .25
393 A72 60m sl grn, blk & org
             brn   .35 .30
394 A72 100m sl grn, emer & vio .75 .45
395 A72 200m dk brn & org brn   1.40 1.10
    Nos. 392-395 (4)   2.80 2.10
Africa Freedom Day, Apr. 15.

Mother and Child with Flags — A73

Designs: 50m, Tunisians. 95m, Girl with wings and half-moon.

1961, June 1   Unwmk.   Perf. 13
396 A73 25m pale vio, red & brn   .30 .25
397 A73 50m bl grn, sep & brn   .45 .25
398 A73 95m pale vio, rose lil &
             ocher   .70 .35
    Nos. 396-398 (3)   1.45 .85
National Feast Day, June 1.

Dag Hammarskjold — A74

1961, Oct. 24   Photo.   Perf. 14
399 A74 40m ultramarine   .60 .30

UN Day; Dag Hammarskjold (1905-1961), Secretary General of the UN, 1953-61.

Arms of Tunisia — A75

1962, Jan. 18   Perf. 11½
Arms in Original Colors
400 A75 1m black & yellow   .25 .25
401 A75 2m black & pink   .25 .25
402 A75 3m black & lt blue   .25 .25
403 A75 6m black & gray   .30 .25
    Nos. 400-403 (4)   1.05 1.00

Tunisia's campaign for independence, 10th anniv.

Mosquito in Spider Web and WHO Emblem — A76

Designs: 30m, Symbolic horseback rider spearing mosquito. 40m, Hands crushing mosquito, horiz.

1962, Apr. 7   Engr.   Perf. 13
404 A76 20m chocolate   .50 .30
405 A76 30m red brn & slate grn .50 .30
406 A76 40m dk brn, mar & grn .90 .35
    Nos. 404-406 (3)   1.90 .95

WHO drive to eradicate malaria.

Boy and Map of Africa — A77   African Holding "Africa" — A78

1962, Apr. 15   Photo.   Perf. 14
407 A77 50m brown & orange   .50 .35
408 A78 100m blue, blk & org   .75 .50

Africa Freedom Day, Apr. 15.

Farm Worker — A79   Industrial Worker — A80

1962, May 1   Unwmk.
409 A79 40m multicolored   .50 .25
410 A80 60m dark red brown   .60 .35

Labor Day.

"Liberated Tunisia" — A81

1962, June 1   Typo.   Perf. 13½x14
411 A81 20m salmon & blk   .65 .35

National Feast Day, June 1.

Woman of Gabès — A82

Women in costume of various localities: 10m, 30m, Mahdia. 15m, Kairouan. 20m, 40m, Hammamet. 25m, Djerba. 55m, Ksar Hellal. 60m, Tunis.

1962-63   Photo.   Perf. 11½
412 A82 5m multi   .65 .25
413 A82 10m multi   .75 .35
414 A82 15m multi ('63)   1.20 .50
415 A82 20m multi   1.20 .65
416 A82 25m multi ('63)   1.20 .65
417 A82 30m multi   1.40 .75
418 A82 40m multi   1.40 .75
419 A82 50m multi   1.40 .85
420 A82 55m multi ('63)   2.10 1.10
421 A82 60m multi ('63)   2.90 1.40
    Nos. 412-421 (10)   14.20 7.25

6 stamps issued July 25, 1962 (July 25) for the 6th anniv. of Tunisia's independence. 4 issued June 1, 1963 for Natl. Feast Day. See Nos. 470-471.

UN Emblem, Flag and Dove — A83

30m, Leaves, globe, horiz. 40m, Dove, globe.

1962, Oct. 24   Unwmk.
422 A83 20m gray, blk & scar   .30 .25
423 A83 30m multicolored   .45 .25
424 A83 40m claret brn, blk & bl .70 .25
    Nos. 422-424 (3)   1.45 .85

Issued for United Nations Day, Oct. 24.

Aboul-Qasim Chabbi — A84

1962, Nov. 20   Engr.   Perf. 13
425 A84 15m purple   .65 .25

Aboul-Qasim Chabbi (1904-34), Arab poet.

Pres. Habib Bourguiba — A85

1962, Dec. 7   Photo.   Perf. 12½x13½
426 A85 20m bright blue   .25 .25
427 A85 30m rose claret   .25 .25
428 A85 40m green   .25 .25
    Nos. 426-428 (3)   .75 .75

Hached Telephone Exchange — A86

Designs: 10m, Carthage Exchange. 15m, Sfax telecommunications center. 50m, Telephone operators. 100m, Symbol of automatization. 200m, Belvedere Central Exchange.

1962, Dec. 7   Litho.
429 A86 5m multicolored   .30 .25
430 A86 10m multicolored   .35 .25
431 A86 15m multicolored   .50 .35
432 A86 50m multicolored   .80 .50
433 A86 100m multicolored   1.90 1.00
434 A86 200m multicolored   2.75 1.60
    Nos. 429-434 (6)   6.60 3.95

1st Afro-Asian Philatelic Exhibition; automation of the telephone system.

Dove over Globe — A87   "Hunger" — A88

1963, Mar. 21   Engr.   Perf. 13
435 A87 20m brt bl & brn   .35 .25
436 A88 40m bis brn & dk brn   .65 .25

FAO "Freedom from Hunger" campaign.

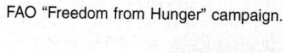

Runner and Walker — A89

1963, Feb. 17   Litho.   Perf. 13
437 A89 30m brn, blk & grn   .45 .50

Army Sports Day; 13th C.I.S.M. cross country championships.

Centenary Emblem — A90

1963, May 8   Engr.   Perf. 13
438 A90 20m brn, gray & red   1.10 .30

Centenary of International Red Cross.

"Human Rights" — A91

1963, Dec. 10   Unwmk.   Perf. 13
439 A91 30m grn & dk brn   .60 .30

15th anniv. of the Universal Declaration of Human Rights.

Hand Raising Gateway of Great Temple of Philae — A92

1964, Mar. 8   Engr.
440 A92 50m red brn, bis & bluish blk .55 .30

UNESCO world campaign to save historic monuments in Nubia.

Sunshine, Rain and Barometer — A93

1964, Mar. 8   Unwmk.   Perf. 13
441 A93 40m brn, red lil & slate .55 .25

4th World Meteorological Day, Mar. 23.

Mohammed Ali — A94

1964, May 15   Engr.
442 A94 50m sepia   .60 .35

Mohammed Ali (1894-1928), labor leader.

Map of Africa and Symbolic Flower — A95

1964, May 25   Photo.   Perf. 13x14
443 A95 60m multicolored   .60 .30

Addis Ababa charter on African Unity, 1st anniv.

Pres. Habib
Bourguiba — A96

1964, June 1   Engr.   Perf. 12½x13½
444 A96 20m vio bl   .30   .25
445 A96 30m black   .30   .25

"Ship and
Torch" — A97

1964, Oct. 19   Photo.   Perf. 11½x11
446 A97 50m blk & grn   .60   .30

Neo-Destour Congress, Bizerte. "Bizerte" in
Arabic forms the ship and "Neo-Destour Congress 1964" the torch of the design.

Communication Equipment and ITU
Emblem — A98

1965, May 17   Engr.   Perf. 13
447 A98 55m gray & blue   .60   .30

ITU, centenary.

Carthaginian
Coin — A99

Perf. 12½x14
1965, July 9   Photo.   Unwmk.
448 A99 5m grn & blk brn   .25   .25
449 A99 10m bis & blk brn   .30   .25
450 A99 75m bl & blk brn   .75   .25
     Nos. 448-450 (3)   1.30 .75

Festival of Popular Arts, Carthage.

Girl with
Book — A100

1965, Oct. 1   Engr.   Perf. 13
451 A100 25m brt bl, blk & red   .30   .25
452 A100 40m blk, bl & red   .35   .25
453 A100 50m red, bl & blk   .45   .35
  a.   Souvenir sheet of 3, #451-453   5.00 5.00
     Nos. 451-453 (3)   1.10 .85

Girl Students' Center; education for women.
No. 453a sold for 200m. Issued perf. and
imperf.; same value.

Links and ICY
Emblem — A101

1965, Oct. 24
454 A101 40m blk, brt bl & rose lil   .60   .25

International Cooperation Year.

Man Pouring
Water — A102

Symbolic Designs: 10m, Woman and pool.
30m, Woman pouring water. 100m, Mountain
and branches.

Inscribed "Eaux Minerales"

1966, Jan. 18   Photo.   Perf. 13x14
455 A102 10m gray, ocher & dk
              red   .30   .25
456 A102 20m multicolored   .45   .35
457 A102 30m yel, bl & red   .45   .35
458 A102 100m ol, bl & yel   1.20 .70
     Nos. 455-458 (4)   2.40 1.65

Mineral waters of Tunisia.

President
Bourguiba
and Hands
A103

"Promotion of
Culture" — A104

25m, "Independence" (arms raised), flag
and doves. 40m, "Development."

1966, June 1   Engr.   Perf. 13
459 A103 5m dl pur & vio   .25   .25
460 A103 10m gray grn & sl grn   .25   .25

Perf. 11½
Photo.
461 A104 25m multi   .25   .25
462 A104 40m multi, horiz.   .55   .25
463 A104 60m multi   .85   .35
     Nos. 459-463 (5)   2.15 1.35

10th anniversary of independence.

Map of Africa
through View
Finder, Plane and
UN
Emblem — A105

1966, Sept. 12   Engr.   Perf. 13
464 A105 15m lilac & multi   .30   .25
465 A105 35m blue & multi   .35   .25
466 A105 40m multicolored   .50   .35
  a.   Souvenir sheet, #464-466   10.00 10.00
     Nos. 464-466 (3)   1.15 .85

2nd UN Regional Cartographic Conference
for Africa, held in Tunisia, Sept. 12-24.
No. 466a sold for 150m. Issued perf. and
imperf.; same value.

UNESCO
Emblem
and Nine
Muses
A106

1966, Nov. 4   Perf. 13
467 A106 100m blk & brn   1.10 .35

UNESCO, 20th anniv.

Runners and
Mediterranean
Map — A107

1967, Mar. 20   Engr.   Perf. 13
468 A107 20m dk red, brn ol & bl   .30   .25
469 A107 30m brt bl & blk   .60   .35

Mediterranean Games, Sept. 8-17.

**Types of 1962-63 and 1965-66 with
EXPO '67 Emblem, Inscription and**

Symbols of Various
Activities — A108

Designs: 50m, Woman of Djerba. 75m,
Woman of Gabes. 155m, Pink flamingoes.

Photo.; Engr. (A108)
1967, Apr. 28   Perf. 11½, 13 (A108)
470 A82 50m multicolored   .45   .25
471 A82 75m multicolored   .70   .30
472 A108 100m dk grn, sl bl &
              blk   1.10 .30
473 A108 110m dk brn, ultra &
              red   1.40 .55
474 AP6 155m multicolored   2.10 .75
     Nos. 470-474 (5)   5.75 2.15

EXPO '67, Intl. Exhibition, Montreal, Apr.
28-Oct. 27.

Tunisian Pavilion, Pres. Bourguiba and
Map of Tunisia — A109

Designs: 105m, 200m, Tunisian Pavilion
and bust of Pres. Bourguiba.

1967, June 13   Engr.   Perf. 13
475 A109 65m red lil & dp org   .45   .35
476 A109 105m multicolored   .50   .35
477 A109 120m brt bl   .65   .40
478 A109 200m red, lil & blk   1.10 .50
     Nos. 475-478 (4)   2.70 1.60

Tunisia Day at EXPO '67.

"Tunisia"
Holding 4-
leaf Clovers
A110

Woman Freeing
Doves — A111

1967, July 25   Litho.   Perf. 13½
479 A110 25m multicolored   .30   .25
480 A111 40m multicolored   .45   .25

10th anniversary of the Republic.

Tennis Courts, Players and Games'
Emblem — A112

10m, Games' emblem & sports emblems,
vert. 15m, Swimming pool & swimmers. 35m,
Sports Palace & athletes. 75m, Stadium &
athletes.

1967, Sept. 8   Engr.   Perf. 13
481 A112 5m sl grn & hn brn   .25   .25
482 A112 10m brn red & multi   .25   .25
483 A112 15m black   .30   .25
484 A112 35m dk brn & Prus bl   .45   .25
485 A112 75m dk car rose, vio &
              bl grn   .80   .45
     Nos. 481-485 (5)   2.05 1.45

Mediterranean Games, Tunis, Sept. 8-17.

Bird, Punic
Period — A113

History of Tunisia: 20m, Sea horse, medallion from Kerkouane. 25m, Hannibal, bronze
bust, Volubilis. 30m, Stele, Carthage. 40m,
Hamilcar, coin. 60m, Mask, funereal pendant.

1967, Dec. 1   Litho.   Perf. 13½
486 A113 15m gray grn, pink &
              blk   .30   .25
487 A113 20m dp bl, red & blk   .30   .25
488 A113 25m dk grn & org brn   .45   .25
489 A113 30m grnsh gray, pink &
              blk   .45   .25
490 A113 40m red brn, yel & blk   .55   .25
491 A113 60m multicolored   .65   .35
     Nos. 486-491 (6)   2.70 1.60

"Mankind" and
Human Rights
Flame — A114

1968, Jan. 18   Engr.   Perf. 13
492 A114 25m brick red   .55   .35
493 A114 60m deep blue   .55   .25

International Human Rights Year.

Computer Fantasy A115

1968, Mar. 20   Engr.   Perf. 13
494 A115 25m mag, bl vio & ol   .40 .35
495 A115 40m ol grn, red brn &   .40 .35
      brn
496 A115 60m ultra, slate & brn   .50 .40
    Nos. 494-496 (3)   1.30 1.10

Introduction of electronic equipment for postal service.

Physician and Patient — A116

1968, Apr. 7   Engr.   Perf. 13
497 A116 25m dp grn & brt grn   .45 .35
498 A116 60m magenta & carmine   .65 .35

WHO, 20th anniversary.

Arabian Jasmine — A117

Flowers: 5m, Flax. 6m, Canna indica. 10m, Pomegranate. 15m, Rhaponticum acaule. 20m, Geranium. 25m, Madonna lily. 40m, Peach blossoms. 50m, Caper. 60m, Ariana rose. 100m, Jasmine.

Granite Paper
1968-69   Photo.   Perf. 11½
499 A117 5m multicolored   .25 .25
500 A117 6m multicolored   .25 .25
501 A117 10m multicolored   .30 .25
502 A117 12m multicolored   .30 .25
503 A117 15m multicolored   .35 .25
504 A117 20m multicolored   .45 .25
505 A117 25m multicolored   .45 .30
506 A117 40m multicolored   .65 .30
507 A117 50m multicolored   .80 .35
508 A117 60m multicolored   1.20 .60
509 A117 100m multicolored   1.75 .80
    Nos. 499-509 (11)   6.75 3.85

Issued: 12, 50, 60, 100m, 4/9/68; others, 3/20/69.

Flower with Red Crescent and Globe — A118

25m, Dove with Red Crescent and globe.

1968, May 8   Engr.   Perf. 13
510 A118 15m Prus bl, grn & red   .40 .35
511 A118 25m brt rose lil & red   .50 .35

Red Crescent Society.

Flutist — A119

1968, June 1   Litho.   Perf. 13
512 A119 20m vio & multi   .50 .25
513 A119 50m multicolored   .55 .35

Stamp Day.

Jackal A120

Animals: 8m, Porcupine. 10m, Dromedary. 15m, Dorcas gazelle. 20m, Desert fox (fennec). 25m, Desert hedgehog. 40m, Arabian horse. 60m, Boar.

1968-69   Photo.   Perf. 11½
514 A120 5m dk brn, lt bl & bis   .30 .25
515 A120 8m dk vio brn & yel   .45 .25
      grn
516 A120 10m dk brn, lt bl &   .65 .25
      ocher
517 A120 15m dk brn, ocher &   .70 .25
      yel grn
518 A120 20m dl yel & dk brn   1.10 .45
519 A120 25m blk, tan & brt grn   1.40 .60
520 A120 40m blk, lil & pale grn   1.75 .90
521 A120 60m dk brn, buff & yel   2.75 1.20
      grn
    Nos. 514-521 (8)   9.10 4.15

Issued: 5, 8, 20, 60m, 9/15/68; others, 1/18/69.

Worker and ILO Emblem — A121

60m, Young man & woman holding banner.

1969, May 1   Engr.   Perf. 13
522 A121 25m Prus bl, blk & bis   .45 .35
523 A121 60m rose car, bl & yel   .65 .40

ILO, 50th anniversary.

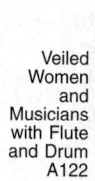 

Veiled Women and Musicians with Flute and Drum A122

1969, June 20   Litho.   Perf. 14x13½
524 A122 100m dp yel grn & multi 1.25 .35

Stamp Day.

Tunisian Coat of Arms — A123

1969, July 25   Photo.   Perf. 11½
525 A123 15m yel & multi   .30 .25
526 A123 25m pink & multi   .45 .25
527 A123 40m gray & multi   .60 .25
528 A123 60m lt bl & multi   .75 .25
    Nos. 525-528 (4)   2.10 1.00

Symbols of Industry — A124

1969, Sept. 10   Perf. 13x12
529 A124 60m blk, red & yel   .60 .30

African Development Bank, 5th anniv.

Lute — A125

Musical Instruments: 50m, Zither, horiz. 70m, Rebab (2-strings). 90m, Drums and flute, horiz.

1970, Mar. 20   Photo.   Perf. 11½
Granite Paper
530 A125 25m multicolored   .45 .35
531 A125 50m multicolored   .60 .35
532 A125 70m multicolored   .80 .35
533 A125 90m multicolored   1.20 .35
    Nos. 530-533 (4)   3.05 1.40

Nurse and Maghrib Flags — A126

1970, May 4   Photo.   Perf. 11½
534 A126 25m lilac & multi   .60 .25

6th Medical Seminar of Maghrib Countries (Morocco, Algeria, Tunisia and Libya), Tunis, May 4-10.

Common Design Types pictured following the introduction.

UPU Headquarters Issue
Common Design Type
1970, May 20   Engr.   Perf. 13
535 CD133 25m dl red & dk ol bis   .60 .25

Mail Service Symbol A127

35m, Mailmen of yesterday and today, vert.

1970, Oct. 15   Litho.   Perf. 12½x13
Size: 37x31½mm
536 A127 25m pink & multi   .30 .25
Size: 22x37½mm
Perf. 13x12½
537 A127 35m blk & multi   .45 .25

Stamp Day.

Dove, Laurel and UN Emblem A128

1970, Oct. 24   Photo.   Perf. 13x12½
538 A128 40m multicolored   .65 .25

United Nations, 25th anniversary.

Jasmine Vendor and Veiled Woman — A129

Scenes from Tunisian Life: 25m, "The 3rd Day of the Wedding." 35m, Perfume vendor. 40m, Fish vendor. 85m, Waiter in coffeehouse.

1970, Nov. 9   Photo.   Perf. 14
539 A129 20m dk grn & multi   .25 .25
540 A129 25m multicolored   .30 .25
541 A129 35m multicolored   .45 .35
542 A129 40m dp car & multi   .50 .35
543 A129 85m brt bl & multi   .85 .35
  a. Souvenir sheet of 5, #539-543 7.00 7.00
    Nos. 539-543 (5)   2.35 1.55

No. 543a sold for 500m. Issued perf. and imperf.; same value.

Lenin, after N.N. Joukov — A130

1970, Dec. 28   Engr.   Perf. 13
544 A130 60m dk car rose   2.10 .30

Lenin (1870-1924), Russian communist leader.

Radar, Flags and Carrier Pigeon — A131

1971, May 17   Litho.   Perf. 13x12½
545 A131 25m lt bl & multi   .60 .35

Coordinating Committee for Post and Telecommunications Administrations of Maghrib Countries.

UN Headquarters, Symbolic Flower — A132

1971, May 10   Photo.   Perf. 12½x13
546 A132 80m brt rose lil, blk & yel   .50 .30

Intl. year against racial discrimination.

"Telecommunications" — A133

1971, May 17   *Perf. 13x12½*
547 A133 70m sil, blk & lt grn   .50 .25

3rd World Telecommunications Day.

Earth,
Moon,
Satellites
A134

Design: 90m, Abstract composition.

1971, June 21   Photo.   Perf. 13x12½
548 A134 15m brt bl & blk   .40 .25
549 A134 90m scar & blk   .75 .30

Conquest of space.

"Pottery
Merchant"
A135

Life in Tunisia (stylized drawings): 30m, Esparto weaver selling hats and mats. 40m, Poultry man. 50m, Dyer.

1971, July 24   Photo.   Perf. 14x13½
550 A135 25m gold & multi   .50 .25
551 A135 30m gold & multi   .60 .25
552 A135 40m gold & multi   .70 .25
553 A135 50m gold & multi   .80 .25
    a.   Sheet of 4, #550-553, perf. 13½   7.50 7.50
         Nos. 550-553 (4)   2.60 1.00

No. 553a sold for 500m. Issued perf. and imperf.; same value.

Pres.
Bourguiba
Sick in
1938
A136

Designs: 25m, Bourguiba and "8," vert. 50m, Bourguiba carried in triumph, vert. 80m, Bourguiba and irrigation dam.

1971, Oct. 11   Perf. 13½x13, 13x13½
554 A136 25m multicolored   .30 .25
555 A136 30m multicolored   .35 .25
556 A136 50m multicolored   .35 .30
557 A136 80m blk, ultra & grn   .50 .30
         Nos. 554-557 (4)   1.50 1.10

8th Congress of the Neo-Destour Party.

Shah Mohammed
Riza Pahlavi and
Stone Head 6th
Century
B.C. — A137

50m, King Bahram-Gur hunting, 4th cent. 100m, Coronation, from Persian miniature, 1614.

1971, Oct. 17   *Perf. 11½*
Granite Paper
558 A137 25m multicolored   .30 .30
559 A137 50m multicolored   .35 .25
560 A137 100m multicolored   .70 .30
    a.   Souvenir sheet of 3, #558-560   4.25 4.25
         Nos. 558-560 (3)   1.35 .85

2500th anniv. of the founding of the Persian empire by Cyrus the Great. No. 560a sold for 500m. Issued perf. and imperf.; same value.

Pimento
and
Warrior
A138

2m, Mint & farmer. 5m, Pear & 2 men under pear tree. 25m, Oleander & girl. 60m, Pear & sheep. 100m, Grapefruit & fruit vendor.

1971, Nov. 15   Litho.   Perf. 13
561 A138 1m lt bl & multi   .25 .25
562 A138 2m gray & multi   .30 .30
563 A138 5m citron & multi   .35 .35
564 A138 25m lilac & multi   .60 .35
565 A138 60m multicolored   1.20 .35
566 A138 100m buff & multi   1.75 .45
    a.   Souvenir sheet of 6, #561-566   7.50 7.50
         Nos. 561-566 (6)   4.45 1.95

Fruit, flowers and folklore. No. 566a sold for 500m. Exists imperf.; same value.

Dancer and
Musician — A139

1971, Nov. 22   Photo.   Perf. 11½
567 A139 50m blue & multi   .60 .25

Stamp Day.

Map of Africa,
Communication
Symbols — A139a

Perf. 13½x12½
1971, Nov. 30   **Litho.**
568 A139a 95m multicolored   .60 .45

Pan-African telecommunications system.

UNICEF Emblem,
Mother and
Child — A140

1971, Dec. 6   Photo.   Perf. 11½
569 A140 110m multicolored   .60 .45

UNICEF, 25th anniv.

Symbolic Olive Tree
and Oil Vat — A141

1972, Jan. 9   Litho.   Perf. 13½
570 A141 60m multicolored   .60 .25

International Olive Year.

Gondolier in Flood
Waters — A142

Designs: 30m, Young man and Doge's Palace. 50m, Gondola's prow and flood. 80m, Rialto Bridge and hand holding gondolier's hat, horiz.

1972, Feb. 7   Photo.   Perf. 11½
571 A142 25m lt bl & multi   .30 .25
572 A142 30m blk & multi   .50 .25
573 A142 50m yel grn, gray & blk   .50 .40
574 A142 80m bl & multi   .95 .40
         Nos. 571-574 (4)   2.25 1.30

UNESCO campaign to save Venice.

Man Reading and
Book Year
Emblem — A143

1972, Mar. 27   Photo.   Perf. 11½
Granite Paper
575 A143 90m brn & multi   .60 .45

International Book Year.

"Your Heart is Your
Health" — A144

World Health Day: 60m, Smiling man pointing to heart.

1972, Apr. 7   *Perf. 13x13½*
576 A144 25m grn & multi   .50 .25
577 A144 60m red & multi   .70 .35

"Only One Earth" Environment
Emblem — A145

1972, June 5   Engr.   Perf. 13
578 A145 60m lemon & slate green   .75 .25

UN Conference on Human Environment, Stockholm, June 5-16.

Hurdler,
Olympic
Emblems
A146

1972, Aug. 26   Photo.   Perf. 11½
579 A146 5m Volleyball   .25 .25
580 A146 15m shown   .30 .25
581 A146 20m Athletes   .30 .25
582 A146 25m Soccer   .30 .25
583 A146 60m Swimming, wo-
         men's   .50 .25
584 A146 80m Running   .65 .30
    a.   Souv. sheet of 6   4.50 4.50
         Nos. 579-584 (6)   2.30 1.55

20th Olympic Games, Munich, Aug. 26-Sept. 11. No. 584a contains 6 imperf. stamps similar to Nos. 579-584. Sold for 500m.

Chessboard and
Pieces — A147

1972, Sept. 25   Photo.   Perf. 11½
585 A147 60m grn & multi   3.00 1.00

20th Men's Chess Olympiad, Skopje, Yugoslavia, Sept.-Oct.

Fisherman
A148

1972, Oct. 23   Litho.   Perf. 13½
586 A148 5m shown   .25 .25
587 A148 10m Basket maker   .25 .25
588 A148 25m Musician   .35 .25
589 A148 50m Married Berber
         woman   .75 .25
590 A148 60m Flower merchant   1.00 .25
591 A148 80m Festival   1.20 .45
    a.   Souvenir sheet of 6, #586-591   4.50 4.50
         Nos. 586-591 (6)   3.80 1.70

Life in Tunisia. No. 591a sold for 500m; exists imperf.

Post
Office,
Tunis
A149

Litho. & Engr.
1972, Dec. 8   *Perf. 13*
592 A149 25m ver, org & blk   .50 .25

Stamp Day.

Dome of
the Rock,
Jerusalem
A150

1973, Jan. 22   Photo.   Perf. 13½
593 A150 25m multicolored   .60 .35

Globe, Pen and Quill — A151

Design: 60m, Lyre and minaret.

1973, Mar. 19   Photo.   Perf. 14x13½
594 A151 25m gold, brt mag & brn   .30 .25
595 A151 60m bl & multi   .45 .25

9th Congress of Arab Writers.

Family — A152

Family Planning: 25m, profiles and dove.

1973, Apr. 2   Perf. 11½
596 A152 20m grn & multi   .30 .25
597 A152 25m lil & multi   .50 .35

"10" and Bird Feeding Young A153

Design: 60m, "10" made of grain and bread, and hand holding spoon.

1973, Apr. 26   Photo.   Perf. 11½
598 A153 25m multicolored   .60 .25
599 A153 60m multicolored   .60 .25

World Food Program, 10th anniversary.

Roman Head and Ship A154

Drawings of Tools and: 25m, Mosaic with ostriches and camel. 30m, Mosaic with 4 heads and 4 emblems. 40m, Punic stele to the sun, vert. 60m, Outstretched hand & arm of Christian preacher; symbols of 4 Evangelists. 75m, 17th cent. potsherd with Arabic inscription, vert.

1973, May 6
600 A154   5m multicolored   .50   .25
601 A154 25m multicolored   .75   .40
602 A154 30m multicolored   .75   .40
603 A154 40m multicolored   1.10   .40
604 A154 60m multicolored   1.40   .40
605 A154 75m multicolored   1.50   .50
 a.   Souvenir sheet of 6   12.00 12.00
      Nos. 600-605 (6)   6.00 2.35

UNESCO campaign to save Carthage. No. 605a contains 6 imperf. stamps similar to Nos. 600-605. Sold for 500m.

Overlapping Circles — A155

Design: 75m, Printed circuit board.

1973, May 17   Photo.   Perf. 14x13½
606 A155 60m yel & multi   .75 .25
607 A155 75m vio & multi   .90 .25

5th Intl. Telecommunications Day.

Map of Africa as Festival Emblem — A156

40m, African heads, festival emblem in eye.

1973, July 15   Photo.   Perf. 13½x13
608 A156 25m multicolored   .40 .35
609 A156 40m multicolored   .50 .35

Pan-African Youth Festival, Tunis.

Scout Emblem and Pennants — A157

1973, July 23   Litho.   Perf. 13½x13
610 A157 25m multicolored   .60 .35

International Boy Scout Organization.

Crescent-shaped Racing Cars — A158

1973, July 30   Perf. 13x13½
611 A158 60m multicolored   .65 .40

2nd Pan-Arab auto race.

Highway Cloverleaf A159

Traffic Lights and Signs — A160

Perf. 12½x13, 13x12½
1973, Sept. 28   Litho.
612 A159 25m lt bl & multi   .65 .40
613 A160 30m multicolored   .75 .35

Highway safety campaign.

Stylized Camel — A161

Stamp Day: 10m, Stylized bird and philatelic symbols, horiz.

1973, Oct. 8   Photo.   Perf. 13½
614 A161 10m multicolored   .50 .25
615 A161 65m multicolored   .60 .40

Copernicus — A162

Lithographed and Engraved
1973, Oct. 16   Perf. 13x12½
616 A162 60m blk & multi   2.50 .30

African Unity — A163

1973, Nov. 4   Photo.   Perf. 14x13½
617 A163 25m blk & multi   .65 .25

10th anniv. of the OAU.

Handshake and Emblems A164

1973, Nov. 15   Litho.   Perf. 14½x14
618 A164 65m yel & multi   .65 .40

25th anniv. of Intl. Criminal Police Org.

Globe, Hand Holding Carnation — A165

1973, Dec. 10   Photo.   Perf. 11½
619 A165 60m blk & multi   .75 .35

25th anniv. of Universal Declaration of Human Rights.

National Meteorological Institute and World Meteorological Organization Emblem — A166

Design: 60m, Globe and emblem.

1973, Dec. 24   Litho.   Perf. 14x14½
620 A166 25m multicolored   .55 .25
621 A166 60m multicolored   .75 .30

Intl. meteorological cooperation, cent.

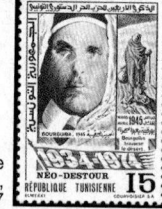

Bourguiba in the Desert, 1945 — A167

Portraits of Pres. Habib Bourguiba: 25m, Exile transfer from Galite Island to Ile de la Groix, France, 1954. 60m, Addressing crowd, 1974. 75m, In Victory Parade, 1955. 100m, In 1934.

1974, Mar. 2   Photo.   Perf. 11½
622 A167 15m plum & multi   .45 .25
623 A167 25m multicolored   .45 .25
624 A167 60m multicolored   .45 .25
625 A167 75m multicolored   .60 .25
626 A167 100m multicolored   .75 .40
 a.   Souvenir sheet of 5, #622-626 3.00 3.00
      Nos. 622-626 (5)   2.70 1.40

40th anniv. of the Neo-Destour Party. No. 626a sold for 500m. Issued perf. and imperf.; same value.

Scientist with Microscope A168

1974, Mar. 21   Perf. 14
627 A168 60m multicolored   1.10 .50

6th African Congress of Micropaleontology, Mar. 21-Apr. 3.

Woman with Telephones and Globe — A169

60m, Telephone dial, telephones, wires.

1974, July 1   Photo.   Perf. 11½
628 A169 15m multicolored   .50 .40
629 A169 60m multicolored   .80 .50

Introduction of international automatic telephone dialing system.

WPY Emblem and Symbolic Design A170

1974, Aug. 19   Photo.   Perf. 11½
630 A170 110m multicolored   .75 .40

World Population Year.

Pres. Bourguiba
and Sun Flower
Emblem — A171

60m, Bourguiba and cactus flower, horiz.
200m, Bourguiba and verbena, horiz.

1974, Sept. 12   Photo.   Perf. 11½
631 A171 25m blk, ultra & grnsh
             bl   .35   .25
632 A171 60m red, car & yel   .40   .25
633 A171 200m blk, brt lil & grn   1.50   .60
 a.   Souv. sheet, #631-633, imperf. 3.75 3.75
       Nos. 631-633 (3)   2.25 1.10

Congress of the Socialist Destour Party.

Jets
Flying
over
Old
World
Map
A172

1974, Sept. 23   Litho.   Perf. 12½
634 A172 60m brn & multi   .65   .40

25th anniversary of Tunisian aviation.

Symbolic Carrier
Pigeons — A173

Handshake,
Letter, UPU
Emblem — A174

1974, Oct. 9   Photo.   Perf. 13
635 A173 25m multicolored   .40   .25
636 A174 60m multicolored   .75   .35

Centenary of Universal Postal Union.

Le Bardo, National
Assembly — A175

Pres. Bourguiba
Ballot — A176

1974, Nov. 3   Photo.   Perf. 11½
637 A175 25m grn, bl & blk   .40   .30
638 A176 100m org & blk   1.00   .40

Legislative (25m) and presidential elections
(100m), Nov. 1974.

Mailman with Letters
and Bird — A177

1974, Dec. 5   Litho.   Perf. 14½x14
639 A177 75m lt vio & multi   .65   .25

Stamp Day.

Water
Carrier — A178

1975, Feb. 17   Photo.   Perf. 13½
640 A178   5m shown   .30   .25
641 A178   15m Perfume vendor   .30   .25
642 A178   25m Laundresses   .30   .25
643 A178   60m Potter   .65   .25
644 A178 110m Fruit vendor   1.40   .65
 a.   Souvenir sheet of 5, #640-644 7.00 7.00
       Nos. 640-644 (5)   2.95 1.65

Life in Tunisia. No. 644a sold for 500m.
Issued perf. and imperf.; same value.

Steel Tower,
Skyscraper — A179

Geometric
Designs
and Arrow
A180

Perf. 14x13½, 13½x14
1975, Mar. 17   Photo.
645 A179 25m yel, org & blk   .30   .25
646 A180 65m ultra & multi   .80   .35

Union of Arab Engineers, 13th Conference,
Tunis, Mar. 17-21.

Brass Coffeepot and Plate — A181

15m, Horse and rider. 25m, Still life. 30m,
Bird cage. 40m, Woman with earrings. 60m,
Design patterns.

1975, Apr. 14   Perf. 13x14, 14x13
647 A181 10m blk & multi   .25   .25
648 A181 15m blk & multi   .25   .25
649 A181 25m blk & multi   .45   .25
650 A181 30m blk & multi, vert. .50 .25
651 A181 40m blk & multi, vert. .50 .25
652 A181 60m blk & multi   .95   .30
       Nos. 647-652 (6)   2.90 1.55

Artisans and their works.

Communications and Weather
Symbols — A182

1975, May 17   Photo.   Perf. 11½
653 A182 50m lt bl & multi   .50   .25

World Telecommunications Day (communications serving meteorology).

Youth and
Hope — A183

65m, Bourguiba arriving at La Goulette,
Tunis.

1975, June 1   Photo.   Perf. 11½
654 A183 25m multi   .25   .25
655 A183 65m multi, horiz.   .50   .25

Victory (independence), 20th anniversary.

Tunisian Woman,
IWY
Emblem — A184

1975, June 19   Litho.   Perf. 14x13½
656 A184 110m multicolored   .75   .35

International Women's Year.

Children
Crossing
Street
A185

1975, July 5   Photo.   Perf. 13½x14
657 A185 25m multicolored   .60   .25

Highway safety campaign, July 1-Sept. 30.

Djerbian
Minaret,
Hotel
and
Marina,
Jerba
A186

Old & new Tunisia: 15m, 17th cent. minaret
& modern hotel, Tunis. 20m, Fortress, earring
& hotel, Monastir. 65m, View of Sousse, hotel
& pendant. 500m, Town wall, mosque &
palms, Tozeur. 1d, Mosques & Arab ornaments, Kairouan.

1975, July 12   Litho.   Perf. 14x14½
658 A186   10m multicolored   .25   .25
659 A186   15m multicolored   .25   .25
660 A186   20m multicolored   .25   .25
661 A186   65m multicolored   .75   .25
662 A186 500m multicolored   4.75 1.75
663 A186   1d multicolored   7.50 2.50
       Nos. 658-663 (6)   13.75 5.40

Victors — A187

Symbolic
Ship
A188

1975, Aug. 23   Photo.   Perf. 13½
664 A187 25m olive & multi   .25   .25
665 A188 50m blue & multi   .50   .25

7th Mediterranean Games, Algiers, 8/23-9/6.

Flowers in Vase,
Birds Holding
Letters — A189

1975, Sept. 29   Litho.   Perf. 13½x13
666 A189 100m blue & multi   .65   .25

Stamp Day.

Sadiki College, Young
Bourguiba — A190

Engr. & Litho.
1975, Nov. 17   Perf. 13
667 A190 25m sepia, orange &
             olive   .50   .25

Sadiki College, centenary.

Duck — A191

Vergil — A192

Mosaics: 10m, Fish. 25m, Lioness, horiz.
60m, Head of Medusa, horiz. 75m, Circus
spectators.

1976, Feb. 16   Photo.   Perf. 13
668 A191   5m multicolored   .30   .25
669 A191 10m multicolored   .45   .25
670 A192 25m multicolored   .75   .25
671 A192 60m multicolored   1.00   .50
672 A192 75m multicolored   1.10   .50

673 A192 100m multicolored   1.40   .50
a.   Souvenir sheet of 6, #668-673   6.50   6.50
      Nos. 668-673 (6)   5.00   2.50

Tunisian mosaics, 2nd-5th centuries.
No. 673a sold for 500m. Issued perf. and
imperf.; same value.

Telephone
A193

1976, Mar. 10   Litho.   Perf. 14x13½
674 A193 150m blue & multi   .70   .35

Centenary of first telephone call by Alexander Graham Bell, Mar. 10, 1876.

Pres.
Bourguiba
and
"20" — A194

Pres. Bourguiba and: 100m, "20" and symbolic Tunisian flag. 150m, "Tunisia" rising from darkness, and 20 flowers.

1976, Mar. 20   Photo.   Perf. 11½
675 A194 40m multicolored   .25   .25
676 A194 100m multicolored   .55   .25
677 A194 150m multicolored   .80   .35
      Nos. 675-677 (3)   1.60   .85

Souvenir Sheets
Perf. 11½, Imperf.
678   Sheet of 3   3.50   3.50
a.   A194 50m like 40m   .50   .50
b.   A194 200m like 100m   1.00   1.00
c.   A194 250m like 150m   1.50   1.50

20th anniversary of independence.

Blind Man with
Cane — A195

1976, Apr. 7   Engr.   Perf. 13
679 A195 100m black & red   .60   .25

World Health Day: "Foresight prevents blindness."

Procession and
Buildings — A196

1976, May 31   Photo.   Perf. 12x11½
680 A196 40m multicolored   .60   .25

Habitat, UN Conf. on Human Settlements, Vancouver, Canada, May 31-June 11.

Face and Hands
Decorated with
Henna — A197

Old and new Tunisia: 50m, Sponge fishing at Jerba. 65m, Textile industry. 110m, Pottery of Guellala.

1976, June 15   Photo.   Perf. 13x13½
681 A197 40m multicolored   .25   .25
682 A197 50m multicolored   .55   .25
683 A197 65m multicolored   .55   .25
684 A197 110m multicolored   .75   .50
      Nos. 681-684 (4)   2.10   1.25

The
Spirit of
'76, by
Archibald
M.
Willard
A198

1976, July 4   Perf. 13x14
685 A198 200m multicolored   1.75   .85

Souvenir Sheets
Perf. 13x14, Imperf.
686 A198 500m multicolored   5.00   5.00

American Bicentennial.

Running
A199

Montreal Olympic Games Emblem and: 75m, Bicycling. 120m, Peace dove.

1976, July 17   Photo.   Perf. 11½
687 A199 50m gray, red & blk   .25   .25
688 A199 75m red, yel & blk   .45   .25
689 A199 120m orange & multi   .70   .35
      Nos. 687-689 (3)   1.40   .85

21st Olympic Games, Montreal, Canada, July 17-Aug. 1.

Child
Reading — A200

1976, Aug. 23   Litho.   Perf. 13
690 A200 100m brown & multi   .60   .25

Books for children.

Heads and
Bird — A201

1976, Sept. 30   Litho.   Perf. 13
691 A201 150m orange & multi   .75   .25

Non-aligned Countries, 15th anniv. of 1st Conference.

Mouradite
Mausoleum, 17th
Century — A202

Cultural Heritage: 100m, Minaret, Kairouan Great Mosque and psalmodist. 150m, Monastir Ribat monastery and Alboracq (sphinx). 200m, Barber's Mosque, Kairouan and man's bust.

1976, Oct. 25   Photo.   Perf. 14
692 A202 85m multicolored   .40   .25
693 A202 100m multicolored   .50   .25
694 A202 150m multicolored   .75   .25
695 A202 200m multicolored   1.10   .40
      Nos. 692-695 (4)   2.75   1.15

Globe
and
Emblem
A203

1976, Dec. 24   Photo.   Perf. 13x14
696 A203 150m multicolored   .95   .35

25th anniv. of UN Postal Administration.

Electronic Tree
and ITU
Emblem — A204

1977, May 17   Photo.   Perf. 14x13½
697 A204 150m multicolored   1.25   .50

9th World Telecommunications Day.

"Communication," Sassenage Castle,
Grenoble — A205

1977, May 19   Litho.   Perf. 13½x13
698 A205 100m multicolored   1.50   .40

10th anniv. of Intl. French Language Council.

Soccer
A206

1977, June 27   Photo.   Perf. 13½
699 A206 150m multicolored   1.25   .50

Junior World Soccer Tournament, Tunisia, June 27-July 10.

Gold Coin, 10th
Century — A207

Cultural Heritage: 15m, Stele, Gorjani Cemetery, Tunis, 13th century. 20m, Floral design, 17th century illumination. 30m, Bird and flowers, glass painting, 1922. 40m, Antelope, from

11th century clay pot. 50m, Gate, Sidi Bou Said, 20th century.

1977, July 9   Photo.   Perf. 13
700 A207 10m multicolored   .25   .25
701 A207 15m multicolored   .25   .25
702 A207 20m multicolored   .25   .25
703 A207 30m multicolored   .40   .25
704 A207 40m multicolored   .50   .25
705 A207 50m multicolored   .50   .25
a.   Miniature sheet of 6, #700-705   3.75   3.75
      Nos. 700-705 (6)   2.15   1.50

"The Young
Republic" and
Bourguiba
A208

Habib Bourguiba and: 100m, "The Confident Republic" and 20 doves. 150m, "The Determined Republic" and 20 roses.

1977, July 25   Photo.   Perf. 13x13½
706 A208 40m multicolored   .40   .25
707 A208 100m multicolored   .50   .25
708 A208 150m multicolored   .85   .35
a.   Souvenir sheet of 3, #706-708   2.75   2.75
      Nos. 706-708 (3)   1.75   .85

20th anniv. of the Republic. No. 708a sold for 500m. Exists imperf., same value.

Symbolic Cancellation, APU
Emblem — A209

1977, Aug. 16   Litho.   Perf. 13x12½
709 A209 40m multicolored   .50   .25

Arab Postal Union, 25th anniversary.

Diseased Knee,
Gears and
Globe — A210

1977, Sept. 26   Photo.   Perf. 14x13½
710 A210 120m multicolored   .95   .35

World Rheumatism Year.

Farmer, Road, Water and
Electricity — A211

1977, Dec. 15   Photo.   Perf. 13½
711 A211 40m multicolored   .60   .25

Rural development.

Factory Workers — A212

Designs: 20m, Bus driver and trains, horiz. 40m, Farmer driving tractor, horiz.

1978, Mar. 6   *Perf. 13x14, 14x13*
712 A212   20m rose red & multi   .25   .25
713 A212   40m black & green   .35   .25
714 A212   100m multicolored   .75   .35
      Nos. 712-714 (3)   1.35   .85

5th development plan, creation of new jobs.

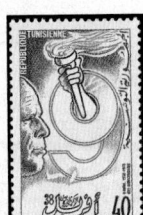

Pres. Bourguiba, Torch and "9" — A213

1978, Apr. 9   **Engr.**   *Perf. 13*
715 A213   40m shown   .30   .25
716 A213   60m Bourguiba and "9"   .30   .25

40th anniv. of 1st fight for independence, 4/9/38.

A214

1978, May 2   **Photo.**   *Perf. 13x13½*
717 A214   150m Policeman   1.10   .35

6th Regional African Interpol Conference, Tunis, May 2-5.

A215

Designs: 40m, Tunisian Goalkeeper. 150m., Soccer player, maps of South America and Africa, flags.

1978, June 1   **Photo.**   *Perf. 13x14*
718 A215   40m multicolored   .35   .25
719 A215   150m multicolored   1.00   .40

11th World Cup Soccer Championship, Argentina, June 1-25.

Destruction of Apartheid, Map of South Africa — A216

Fight Against Apartheid: 100m, White and black doves flying in unison.

1978, Aug. 30   **Litho.**   *Perf. 13½x14*
720 A216   50m multicolored   .25   .25
721 A216   100m multicolored   .60   .35

"Pollution is a Plague" — A217

Designs: 50m, "The Sea, mankind's patrimony." 120m, "Greening of the desert."

1978, Sept. 11   **Photo.**   *Perf. 14x13*
722 A217   10m multicolored   .25   .25
723 A217   50m multicolored   .60   .25
724 A217   120m multicolored   1.25   .35
      Nos. 722-724 (3)   2.10   .85

Protection of the environment.

"Eradication of Smallpox" — A218

1978, Oct. 16   **Litho.**   *Perf. 12½*
725 A218   150m multicolored   .95   .40

Global eradication of smallpox.

Jerba Wedding A219

5m, Horseman from Zlass. 75m, Women potters from the Mogods. 100m, Dove over Marabout Sidi Mahrez cupolas, Tunis. 500m, Plowing in Jenduba. 1d, Spring Festival in Tozeur (man on swing).

1978, Nov. 1   **Photo.**   *Perf. 13*
726 A219   5m multi, vert.   .25   .25
727 A219   60m multi   .35   .25
728 A219   75m multi   .50   .25
729 A219   100m multi   .50   .25
730 A219   500m multi   3.75   1.25
731 A219   1d multi   6.00   2.50
      Nos. 726-731 (6)   11.35   4.75

Traditional Arab calligraphy.

Lenin and Red Banner over Kremlin — A220

1978, Nov. 7   *Perf. 13½*
732 A220   150m multicolored   1.60   .50

Russian October Revolution, 60th anniv.

Farhat Hached, Union Emblem — A221

1978, Dec. 5   **Photo.**   *Perf. 14*
733 A221   50m multicolored   .60   .25

Farhat Hached (1914-1952), founder of General Union of Tunisian Workers.

Family — A222

1978, Dec. 15   **Photo.**   *Perf. 13½*
734 A222   50m multicolored   .60   .25

Tunisian Family Planning Assoc., 10th anniv.

Sun with Man's Face — A223

1978, Dec. 25   *Perf. 14*
735 A223   100m multicolored   .75   .25

Sun as a source of light and energy.

Plane, Weather Map and Instruments — A224

1978, Dec. 29
736 A224   50m multicolored   .60   .25

Tunisian civil aviation and meteorology, 20th anniv.

Habib Bourguiba and Constitution — A225

1979, May 31   **Photo.**   *Perf. 14x13½*
737 A225   50m multicolored   .60   .25

20th anniversary of Constitution.

El Kantaoui Port A226

1979, June 3   *Perf. 13½x14*
738 A226   150m multicolored   1.25   .35

Development of El Kantaoui as a resort area.

Landscapes — A227

1979, July 14   *Perf. 12½x13½*
739 A227   50m Korbous   .25   .25
740 A227   100m Mides   .50   .25

Bow Net Weaving — A228

1979, Aug. 15   **Photo.**   *Perf. 11½*
741 A228   10m shown   .30   .25
742 A228   50m Beekeeping   .70   .25

Pres. Bourguiba, "10" and Hands — A229

1979, Sept. 5
743 A229   50m multicolored   .50   .25

Socialist Destour Party, 10th Congress.

Modes of Communication, ITU Emblem — A230

1979, Sept. 20   **Litho.**   *Perf. 11½*
744 A230   150m multicolored   1.00   .50

3rd World Telecommunications Exhibition, Geneva, Sept. 20-26.

Arab Achievements — A231

1979, Oct. 1   *Perf. 14½*
745 A231   50m multicolored   .50   .25

Children Crossing Street, IYC Emblem — A232

1979, Oct. 16   *Perf. 14x13½*
746 A232 50m shown   .30 .25
747 A232 100m Child and birds   .75 .25
International Year of the Child.

Dove, Olive Tree, Map of Tunisia — A233

1979, Nov. 1   *Litho.*   *Perf. 12*
748 A233 150m multicolored   1.10 .40
2nd International Olive Oil Year.

Woman Wearing Crown — A234

1979, Nov. 3   *Perf. 14½*
749 A234 50m multicolored   .50 .25
Central Bank of Tunisia, 20th anniversary.

Children and Jujube Tree — A235

1979, Dec. 25   *Litho.*   *Perf. 15x14½*
750 A235 20m shown   .30 .25
751 A235 30m Peacocks   .60 .25
752 A235 70m Goats   1.10 .35
753 A235 85m Girl, date palm   1.10 .40
   Nos. 750-753 (4)   3.10 1.25

Postal Code Introduction — A236

1980, Mar. 20   *Photo.*   *Perf. 14*
754 A236 50m multicolored   .55 .25

Fight Against Cigarette Smoking A237

1980, Apr. 7
755 A237 150m multicolored   .85 .25

Pres. Bourguiba in Flower, Open Book — A238

1980, June 1   *Photo.*   *Perf. 11½*
756 A238 50m shown   .25 .25
757 A238 100m Dove, Bourguiba, mosque   1.00 .40
Victory (independence), 25th anniversary.

Butterfly and Gymnast A239

1980, June 3   *Photo.*   *Perf. 12x11½*
Granite Paper
758 A239 100m multicolored   .60 .25
Turin Gymnastic Games, June 1-7.

Artisans
A240   A241

1980, July 21   *Photo.*   *Perf. 13½*
759 A240 30m multicolored   .35 .25
760 A241 75m multicolored   .75 .25

ibn-Khaldun (1332-1406), Historian — A242

1980, July 28   *Perf. 14*
761 A242 50m multicolored   .60 .25

Avicenna (Arab Physician), Birth Millenium — A243

1980, Aug. 18   *Engr.*   *Perf. 12½x13*
762 A243 100m redsh brn & sepia   .75 .30

Arab Achievements — A244

1980, Aug. 25   *Photo.*   *Perf. 13½x14*
763 A244 50m multicolored   .85 .25

Port Sidi bou Said A245

1980, Sept. 4   *Perf. 14*
764 A245 100m multicolored   .50 .30

World Tourism Conference, Manila, Sept. 27 — A246

1980, Sept. 27   *Photo.*   *Perf. 14*
765 A246 150m multicolored   .75 .25

Wedding in Jerba, by Yahia (1903-1969) — A247

1980, Oct. 1   *Perf. 12*
766 A247 50m multicolored   .75 .40

Tozeur-Nefta International Airport Opening — A248

1980, Oct. 13   *Photo.*   *Perf. 13x13½*
767 A248 85m multicolored   .60 .25

Eye and Text A249

1980, Oct. 26   *Litho.*   *Perf. 13½x14*
768 A249 100m multicolored   1.00 .50
7th Afro-Asian Ophthalmologic Congress.

Hegira, 1500th Anniv. A250

1980, Nov. 9
769 A250 50m Spiderweb   .25 .25
770 A250 80m City skyline   .50 .25

Film Strip and Woman's Head — A251

1980, Nov. 15   *Photo.*   *Perf. 14x13½*
771 A251 100m multicolored   .75 .35
Carthage Film Festival.

Orchid A252

1980, Nov. 17   *Perf. 13½x14*
772 A252 20m shown   .55 .30
773 A252 25m Wild cyclamen   .70 .30
   Size: 39x27mm
   Perf. 14
774 A252 50m Mouflon   1.40 .30
775 A252 100m Golden eagle   3.00 .40
   Nos. 772-775 (4)   5.65 1.30

Campaign to Save Kairouan Mosque A253

1980, Dec. 29   *Photo.*   *Perf. 12*
Granite Paper
776 A253 85m multicolored   .55 .25

Heinrich von Stephan (1831-1897), Founder of UPU — A254

1981, Jan. 7
777 A254 150m multicolored   .90 .40

Blood Donors' Assoc., 20th Anniv. — A255

1981, Mar. 5   *Litho.*   *Perf. 14x13½*
778 A255 75m multicolored   .90 .50

Pres. Bourguiba and Flag — A256

1981, Mar. 20 Photo. *Perf. 12x11½*
Granite Paper

779	A256	50m shown	.25	.25
780	A256	60m Stork, "25"	.50	.25
781	A256	85m Doves	.75	.40
782	A256	120m Victory on winged horse	.75	.40
a.		Souvenir sheet of 4, #779-782	4.00	4.00
		Nos. 779-782 (4)	2.25	1.30

25th anniversary of independence. No. 782 sold for 500m. Exists imperf., same value.

Pres. Bourguiba and Flower A257

1981, Apr. 10 Photo. *Perf. 12x11½*

783	A257	50m shown	.25	.25
784	A257	75m Bourguiba, flower, diff.	.50	.25

Destourien Socialist Party Congress.

Mosque Entrance, Mahdia A258

1981, Apr. 20 *Perf. 13½*

785	A258	50m shown	.35	.25
786	A258	85m Tozeur Great Mosque, vert.	.50	.35
787	A258	100m Needle Rocks, Tabarka	.60	.25
		Nos. 785-787 (3)	1.45	.85

A259

1981, May 17 Litho. *Perf. 14x15*

788	A259	150m multicolored	.95	.35

13th World Telecommunications Day.

Youth Festival — A260

1981, June 2 Photo. *Perf. 11½*
Granite Paper

789	A260	100m multicolored	.65	.25

A261

1981, June 15 Photo. *Perf. 14*

790	A261	150m multicolored	.95	.35

Kemal Ataturk (1881-1938), 1st president of Turkey.

A262

1981, July 15 Photo. *Perf. 11½x12*

791	A262	150m Skifa, Mahdia	.80	.40

Mohammed Tahar Ben Achour (1879-1973), Scholar — A263

1981, Aug. 6 *Perf. 13*

792	A263	200m multicolored	1.50	.50

25th Anniv. of Personal Status Code (Women's Liberation) — A264

1981, Aug. 13

793	A264	50m Woman	.25	.25
794	A264	100m shown	.75	.35

Intl. Year of the Disabled — A265

1981, Sept. 21 Photo. *Perf. 13½*

795	A265	250m multicolored	1.50	.65

Pilgrimage to Mecca — A266

1981, Oct. 7 Photo. *Perf. 13½*

796	A266	50m multicolored	.60	.25

World Food Day — A267

1981, Oct. 16 Litho. *Perf. 12*
Granite Paper

797	A267	200m multicolored	1.50	.65

Traditional Jewelry A268

150m, Mneguech silver earrings. 180m Mahfdha (silver medallion worn by married women). 200m, Essalta gold headdress.

1981, Dec. 7 Photo. *Perf. 14*

798	A268	150m multi, vert.	.75	.35
799	A268	180m multi	.90	.40
800	A268	200m multi, vert.	1.10	.50
		Nos. 798-800 (3)	2.75	1.25

Bizerta Bridge A269

1981, Dec. 14 Litho. *Perf. 12x11½*
Granite Paper

801	A269	230m multicolored	1.25	.50

A270

Chemist compounding honey mixture, manuscript miniature, 1224.

1982, Apr. 3 Photo. *Perf. 13*

802	A270	80m multicolored	.95	.35

Arab Chemists' Union, 16th anniv.

A271

1982, May 12 Photo. *Perf. 13½*

803	A271	150m multicolored	1.25	.60

Oceanic Enterprise Symposium, Tunis, 5/12-14.

A272

1982, June 26 *Perf. 12½*
Granite Paper

804	A272	80m multicolored	.60	.25

The Productive Family Employment campaign.

A273

25th Anniv. of Republic: Pres. Bourguiba and Various Women.

1982, July 25 Litho. *Perf. 14x13½*

805	A273	80m multicolored	.40	.25
806	A273	100m multicolored	.60	.35
807	A273	200m multicolored	1.00	.40
		Nos. 805-807 (3)	2.00	1.00

Scouting Year — A274

Perf. 14½x14, 14x14½

1982, Aug. 23

808	A274	80m multicolored	.50	.25
809	A274	200m multicolored	1.10	.25

75th anniv. of scouting and 50th anniv. of scouting in Tunisia (80m, horiz.).

Tunisian Fossils — A274a

Designs: 80m, Pseudophillipsia azzouzi, vert. 200m, Mediterraneotrigonia cherahilensis, vert. 280m, Numidiopleura enigmatica. 300m, Micreschara tunisiensis, vert. 500m, Mantelliceras pervinquieri, vert. 1000m, Elephas africanavus.

1982, Sept. 20 Photo. *Perf. 11½x12*

809A	A274a	80m multi	.90	.40
809B	A274a	200m multi	1.80	.50
809C	A274a	280m multi	2.10	.65
809D	A274a	300m multi	2.75	.90
809E	A274a	500m multi	5.25	1.40
809F	A274a	1000m multi	11.00	2.75
		Nos. 809A-809F (6)	23.80	6.60

A275

1982, Sept. 29 *Perf. 14x13½*

810	A275	80m shown	.60	.25

Size: 23x40mm

811	A275	200m Woman, buildings	1.00	.50

30th Anniv. of Arab Postal Union.

A276

1982, Oct. 1   Photo.   *Perf. 12*
Granite Paper
812 A276 200m multicolored   1.00 .25
ITU Plenipotentiaries Conf., Nairobi

World Food Day — A277

1982, Oct. 16   Litho.   *Perf. 13*
813 A277 200m multicolored   1.00 .35

Tahar Haddad (1899-1935), Social Reformer — A278

1982, Oct. 25   Engr.
814 A278 200m dark brown   1.00 .25

TB Bacillus Centenary A279

1982, Nov. 16   Litho.   *Perf. 13½*
815 A279 100m multicolored   1.25 .25

Folk Songs and Stories — A280

20m, Dancing in the Rain. 30m, Woman Sweeping. 70m, Fisherman and the Child. 80m, Rooster and the Oranges, horiz. 100m, Woman and the Mirror, horiz. 120m, The Two Girls, horiz.

1982, Nov. 22   Photo.   *Perf. 14*
816 A280 20m multi   .30 .25
817 A280 30m multi   .30 .25
818 A280 70m multi   .30 .25
819 A280 80m multi   .40 .25
820 A280 100m multi   .60 .25
821 A280 120m multi   .85 .30
    Nos. 816-821 (6)   2.75 1.55

Intl. Palestinian Solidarity Day — A281

1982, Nov. 30   Litho.   *Perf. 13x12*
822 A281 80m multicolored   .60 .25

Farhat Hached (1914-1952) — A282

1982, Dec. 6   Engr.   *Perf. 13*
823 A282 80m brown red   .60 .25

Bourguiba Dam Opening — A283

1982, Dec. 20   Litho.   *Perf. 13½*
824 A283 80m multicolored   .75 .25

Environmental Training College Opening — A284

1982, Dec. 29   Photo.   *Perf. 11½*
Granite Paper
825 A284 80m multicolored   .60 .25

World Communications Year — A285

1983, May 17   Litho.   *Perf. 13½x14*
826 A285 200m multicolored   .80 .35

20th Anniv. of Org. of African Unity — A286

1983, May 25   Photo.   *Perf. 12*
Granite Paper
827 A286 230m ultra & grnsh bl   .90 .50

30th Anniv. of Customs Cooperation Council — A287

1983, May 30   Litho.   *Perf. 13½*
828 A287 100m multicolored   .60 .25

Aly Ben Ayed (1930-1972), Actor — A288

1983, Aug. 15   Engr.   *Perf. 13*
829 A288 80m dk car, dl red & gray   .60 .35

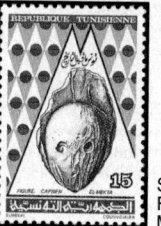

Stone-carved Face, El-Mekta — A289

Pre-historic artifacts: 20m, Neolithic necklace, Kel el-Agab. 30m, Mill and grindstone, Redeyef. 40m, Orynx head rock carving, Gafsa. 80m, Dolmen Mactar. 100m, Acheulian Bi-face flint, El-Mekta.

1983, Aug. 20   Photo.   *Perf. 11½x12*
830 A289 15m multicolored   .25 .25
831 A289 20m multicolored   .45 .25
832 A289 30m multicolored   .45 .25
833 A289 40m multicolored   .45 .25
834 A289 80m multicolored   .60 .40
835 A289 100m multicolored   .75 .40
    Nos. 830-835 (6)   2.95 1.80

Sports for All A290

1983, Sept. 27   Litho.   *Perf. 12½*
836 A290 40m multicolored   .45 .25

World Fishing Day A291

1983, Oct. 17   *Perf. 14½*
837 A291 200m multicolored   1.25 .25

Evacuation of French Troops, 20th Anniv. — A292

1983, Oct. 17   Litho.   *Perf. 14x13½*
838 A292 80m multicolored   .50 .25

Tapestry Weaver, by Hedi Khayachi (1882-1948) — A293

1983, Nov. 22   Photo.   *Perf. 11½*
Granite Paper
839 A293 80m multicolored   .90 .40

Natl. Allegiance — A294

1983, Nov. 30   Litho.   *Perf. 14½*
840 A294 100m Children, flag   .50 .25

Jet, Woman's Head, Emblem — A295

1983, Dec. 21   *Perf. 13½*
841 A295 150m multicolored   .80 .25

Pres. Bourguiba A296

Destourien Socialist Party, 50th Anniv.: Portraits of Bourguiba. 200m, 230m horiz.

Perf. 12½x12, 12x12½
1984, Mar. 2   Photo.
Granite Paper
842 A296 40m multicolored   .25 .25
843 A296 70m multicolored   .25 .25
844 A296 80m multicolored   .40 .25
  a.   Pair, #843-844   .75 .75
845 A296 150m multicolored   .65 .40
  a.   Pair, #842, 845   1.00 1.00
846 A296 200m multicolored   .85 .40
847 A296 230m multicolored   .90 .60
  a.   Pair, #846-847   2.00 2.00
    Nos. 842-847 (6)   3.30 2.15

Nos. 844a, 845a and 847a were printed checkerwise in sheets of ten.

4th Molecular Biology Symposium A297

1984, Apr. 3   *Perf. 13½x13*
848 A297 100m Map, diagram   .80 .35

Ibn El Jazzar, Physician — A298

1984, May 15   Photo.   Perf. 14x13
849 A298 80m multicolored   .70   .40

Economic Development Program, 20th Anniv. — A299

1984, June 15   Perf. 11½
Granite Paper
850 A299 230m Merchant, worker   1.25   .40

Coquette, The Sorceress and the Fairy Carabosse A300

80m, Counting with fingers. 100m, Boy riding horse, vert.

Perf. 13½x14, 14x13½
1984, Aug. 27   Photo.
851 A300 20m shown   .30   .25
852 A300 80m multicolored   .50   .25
853 A300 100m muticolored   .65   .25
     Nos. 851-853 (3)   1.45   .75

Legends and folk tales.

Family and Education Org., 20th Anniv. — A301

1984, Sept. 4   Perf. 13x14
854 A301 80m Family looking into future   .50   .25

Natl. Heritage Protection A302

1984, Sept. 13   Perf. 14
855 A302 100m Medina Mosque Minaret, hand   .60   .35

Aboul-Qasim Chabbi, Poet (1909-1934) — A303

1984, Oct. 9   Engr.   Perf. 12½x13
856 A303 100m multicolored   —   .25

40th Anniv., ICAO A304

1984, Oct. 25   Photo.   Perf. 13
857 A304 200m Aircraft tail, bird   1.00   .60

Sahara Festival A305

1984, Dec. 3   Litho.   Perf. 14½
858 A305 20m Musicians   .80   .25

20th Anniv., Intelsat A306

Perf. 13½x14½
1984, Dec. 25   Photo.
859 A306 100m Tunisian Earth Station   .70   .25

Mediterranean Landscape, by Jilani Abdelwaheb (Abdul) — A307

1984, Dec. 31   Photo.   Perf. 14½
860 A307 100m multicolored   .80   .40

EXPO '85, Tsukuba, Japan A308

1985, Mar. 20   Photo.   Perf. 12
861 A308 200m multicolored   1.00   .50

Civil Protection Week — A309

1985, May 13   Litho.   Perf. 14
862 A309 100m Hands, water and fire   .75   .40

Pres. Habib Bourguiba, Crowded Pier — A310

Pres. Bourguiba: 75m, On horseback, vert. 200m, Wearing hat, vert. 230m, Waving to crowd.

1985, June 1   Perf. 12½
863 A310 75m multicolored   .50   .50
864 A310 100m multicolored   .80   .80
865 A310 200m multicolored   1.10   1.10
866 A310 230m multicolored   1.40   1.40
     Nos. 863-866 (4)   3.80   3.80

Natl. independence, 30th anniv.

Head of a Statue, Carthage and Pres. Bourguiba A311

1985, June 4   Perf. 14
867 A311 250m multicolored   1.00   .65

EXPO '85.

Intl. Amateur Film Festival, Kelibia — A312

1985, July 20   Perf. 14½x13
868 A312 250m multicolored   1.40   .65

Natl. Folk Tales — A313

25m, Sun, Sun Shine Again, horiz. 50m, I Met a Man With Seven Wives. 100m, Uncle Shisbene.

1985, July 29   Perf. 14
869 A313 25m multi   .25   .25
870 A313 50m multi   .25   .25
871 A313 100m multi   .40   .25
     Nos. 869-871 (3)   .90   .75

Intl. Youth Year — A314

1985, Sept. 30   Perf. 14½x13½
872 A314 250m multicolored   1.10   .60

The Perfumers' Courtyard, 1912, by Hedi Larnaout — A315

1985, Oct. 4   Perf. 14
873 A315 100m multicolored   .65   .25

Regional Bridal Costumes — A316

1985, Oct. 22   Perf. 12
874 A316 20m Matmata   .30   .25
875 A316 50m Moknine   .30   .25
876 A316 100m Tunis   .75   .25
     Nos. 874-876 (3)   1.35   .75

UN, 40th Anniv. — A317

1985, Oct. 24   Perf. 14x13½
877 A317 250m multicolored   1.00   .60

Self-Sufficiency in Food Production — A318

Perf. 13½x14½
1985, Nov. 26   Photo.
878 A318 100m Makhtar stele of feast   .60   .25

League of Arab States, 40th Anniv. A319

1985, Nov. 29   Litho.   Perf. 13½x14
879 A319 100m multicolored   .50   .25

Aziza Othmana (d. 1669) — A320

1985, Dec. 16   Engr.   Perf. 12½x13
880 A320 100m dk grn, hn brn & brn   .75   .25

Land Law, Cent. — A321

1985, Dec. 25   Litho.   Perf. 13½
881   A321   100m multicolored   .65   .25

Natl. Independence, 30th Anniv. — A322

Perf. 13x13½, 13½x13
1986, Mar. 20   Photo.
882   A322   100m Dove, vert.   .45   .25
883   A322   120m Rocket   .50   .25
884   A322   280m Horse and rider   1.40   .65
885   A322   300m Balloons, vert.   1.60   .75
   a.   Souvenir sheet of 4, #882-885   4.00   4.00
         Nos. 882-885 (4)   3.95   1.90

No. 885a exists imperf. Same value.

A323   A324

1986, Apr. 30   Litho.   Perf. 14x13½
886   A323   300m multicolored   1.50   .40
887   A324   380m multicolored   2.00   .50

Prof. Hulusi Behcet (1889-1948), discovered virus causing Behcet's Disease affecting eyes and joints. 3rd Mediterranean Rheumatology Day (#886). Intl. Geographical Ophtalmological Soc. Cong. (#887).

12th Destourian Socialist Party Congress A325

1986, June 19   Photo.   Perf. 12
888   A325   120m shown   .50   .25
889   A325   300m Torchbearer   1.50   .75

A326

Regional bridal costumes.

1986, Aug. 25   Litho.   Perf. 14
890   A326   40m Homi-Souk   .25   .25
891   A326   280m Mahdia   1.00   .60
892   A326   300m Nabeul   1.40   .65
         Nos. 890-892 (3)   2.65   1.50

A327

1986, Sept. 20   Engr.   Perf. 13
893   A327   160m dark red   .80   .25

Hassen Husni Abdul-Wahab (1883-1968), historian, archaeologist

Founding of Carthage, 2800th Anniv. — A328

1986, Oct. 18   Engr.   Perf. 13
894   A328   2d dark violet   9.00   3.00

Protohistoric Artifacts — A329

Design: 10m, Flint arrowhead, El Borma, c. 3000 B.C. 20m, Rock cut-out dwelling, Sejnane, c. 1000 B.C. 50m, Lintel bas-relief from a cult site in Tunis, c. 1000 B.C., horiz. 120m, Base of a Neolithic vase, Kesra. 160m, Phoenician trireme, petroglyph, c. 800 B.C., horiz. 250m, Ceramic pot, c. 700 B.C., found at Sejnane, vert.

1986, Oct. 30   Litho.   Perf. 13½
895   A329   10m multicolored   .35   .25
896   A329   20m multicolored   .35   .25
897   A329   50m multicolored   .60   .25
898   A329   120m multicolored   .95   .25
899   A329   160m multicolored   1.25   .40
900   A329   250m multicolored   2.40   .60
         Nos. 895-900 (6)   5.90   2.00

Bedouins, by Ammar Farhat — A330

1986, Nov. 20   Photo.   Perf. 13½
901   A330   250m multicolored   1.60   .40

Intl. Peace Year A331

1986, Nov. 24   Perf. 13½x13
902   A331   300m multicolored   1.25   .40

FAO, 40th Anniv. — A332

1986, Nov. 27   Perf. 13x13½
903   A332   280m multicolored   1.25   .60

Computer Education Inauguration A333

1986, Dec. 8   Perf. 13½
904   A333   2d multicolored   9.50   2.75

Breast-feeding for Child Survival — A334

1986, Dec. 22   Photo.   Perf. 14
905   A334   120m multicolored   .50   .25

Wildlife, Natl. Parks — A335

Designs: 60m, Mountain gazelle, Chambi Natl. Park. 120m, Addax, Bou. Hedma. 350m, Seal, Zembretta. 380m, Greylag goose, Ichkeul.

Granite Paper
1986, Dec. 29   Perf. 12
906   A335   60m multicolored   .25   .25
907   A335   120m multicolored   .55   .35
908   A335   350m multicolored   1.60   1.00
909   A335   380m multicolored   1.90   1.10
         Nos. 906-909 (4)   4.30   2.70

City of Monastir, Cent. — A336

1987, Jan. 24   Litho.   Perf. 12x11½
Granite Paper
910   A336   120m Pres. Bourguiba, city arms   .60   .25

Invention of the Telegraph by Samuel F.B. Morse, 150th Anniv. — A337

1987, June 15   Litho.   Perf. 13½x14
911   A337   500m multicolored   2.25   1.00

30th Anniv. of the Republic A338

Pres. Bourguiba and women of various sects.

1987, July 25   Photo.   Perf. 13½
912   A338   150m multi   .45   .25
913   A338   250m multi   .80   .35
914   A338   350m multi, diff.   1.10   .55
915   A338   500m multi, diff.   1.60   .75
   a.   Souvenir sheet of 4, #912-915   5.00   5.00
         Nos. 912-915 (4)   3.95   1.90

No. 915a sold for 1.50d. Exists imperf.

UN Universal Vaccination by 1990 Campaign — A339

1987, Sept. 14   Perf. 12
Granite Paper
916   A339   250m multicolored   1.00   .50

The Street, by Azouz ben Raiz (1902-1962) A340

1987, Sept. 22   Granite Paper
917   A340   250m multicolored   1.25   .50

Arab Day for Shelter of the Homeless A341

1987, Oct. 5   Photo.   Perf. 12x11½
Granite Paper
918   A341   150m multicolored   .65   .25

Advisory Council for Postal Research, 30th Anniv. A342

1987, Oct. 9   Perf. 14
919   A342   150m Express mail   .65   .25
920   A342   350m Use postal code   1.50   .60

The Arabs, by Ibn-Mandhour (1233-1312), Lexicographer A343

1987, Oct. 26   Engr.   Perf. 13
921   A343   250m plum   1.10   .50

Pasteur
Institute,
Tunis
A344

1987, Nov. 21   *Perf. 13x12½*
922 A344 250m blk, grn & rose
    lake   2.50 .50
Pasteur Institute, Paris, cent.

Intl. Year of the
Vine
(Wine) — A345

1987, Nov. 27   **Photo.**   *Perf. 14*
923 A345 250m multicolored   1.50 .50

6th Volleyball
Championships of
African
Nations — A346

1987, Dec. 2   **Litho.**   *Perf. 14x13½*
924 A346 350m multicolored   1.60 .70

African Basketball
Championships
A347

1987, Dec. 15
925 A347 350m multicolored   1.60 .70

Folk
Costumes — A348

1987, Dec. 25   **Photo.**
926 A348 20m Midoun   .25 .25
927 A348 30m Tozeur   .25 .25
928 A348 150m Sfax   .75 .40
    Nos. 926-928 (3)   1.25 .90

Flowering
Plants — A349

1987, Dec. 29   *Perf. 14½*
929 A349 30m Narcissus tazetta   .25 .25
930 A349 150m Gladiolus com-
    munis   .60 .30
931 A349 400m Iris xiphium   1.50 .80
932 A349 500m Tulipa sylvestris   1.90 1.00
    Nos. 929-932 (4)   4.25 2.35

Declaration
of Nov. 7,
1987
A350

Cameo portrait of Pres. Zine el Abidine Ben
Ali and: 150m, Scales of Justice. 200m, Girl
with flowers (party badges) in her hair, vert.
350m, Mermaid, doves, natl. coat of arms.
370m, "CMA," emblem of the Maghreb states
(Tunisia, Mauritania, Morocco, Algeria and
Libya), vert.

1988, Mar. 21   **Photo.**   *Perf. 12*
Granite Paper
933 A350 150m multicolored   .60 .25
934 A350 200m multicolored   .70 .30
935 A350 350m multicolored   1.25 .55
936 A350 370m multicolored   1.25 .60
    Nos. 933-936 (4)   3.80 1.70

Youth and
Change
A351

1988, Mar. 22   **Litho.**   *Perf. 14x14½*
937 A351 75m shown   .25 .25
938 A351 150m Happy family   .55 .25

Martyr's
Day, 50th
Anniv.
A352

Perf. 13x13½, 13½x13
1988, Apr. 9   **Photo.**
939 A352 150m shown   .65 .25
940 A352 500m Monument, vert.   1.75 .75

Opening Conference of the
Constitutional Democratic
Assembly — A353

1988, July 30   *Perf. 12x11½*
Granite Paper
941 A353 150m Flag, Pres. Ben Ali .60 .25

1988
Summer
Olympics,
Seoul
A354

1988, Sept. 20   **Photo.**   *Perf. 13½*
942 A354 150m shown   .60 .25
943 A354 430m Running, boxing,
    weight lifting,
    wrestling   1.60 1.00

A355

1988, Sept. 21
944 A355 200m multicolored   .75 .35
Restoration of the City of San'a, Yemen.

A356

1988, Nov. 7   **Photo.**   *Perf. 14*
945 A356 150m multicolored   .50 .30
Appointment of Pres. Zine El Abidine Ben
Ali, 1st anniv.

Amilcar Beach, 1942, by A.
Debbeche — A357

1988, Nov. 21   **Photo.**   *Perf. 13½x13*
946 A357 100m multicolored   .75 .25

Tunis Air,
40th Anniv.
A358

1988, Nov. 28   **Photo.**   *Perf. 12x11½*
Granite Paper
947 A358 500m multicolored   1.60 .80

UN Declaration of
Human Rights,
40th
Anniv. — A359

1988, Dec. 10   *Perf. 12*
Granite Paper
948 A359 370m black   1.25 .60

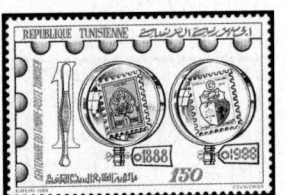

Tunisian Postage Stamp Cent. — A360

1988, Dec. 16   *Perf. 12½*
Granite Paper
949 A360 150m multicolored   .75 .40

A361

Decorative doorways.

1988, Dec. 26   *Perf. 14x13½*
950 A361 50m multi   .30 .25
951 A361 70m multi, diff.   .30 .25
952 A361 100m multi, diff.   .30 .25
953 A361 150m multi, diff.   .50 .25
954 A361 370m multi, diff.   1.00 .40
955 A361 400m multi, diff.   1.25 .40
    Nos. 950-955 (6)   3.65 1.80

A362

1989, Mar. 7   **Engr.**   *Perf. 13½x13*
956 A362 1000m dark blue   3.25 1.60
Ali Douagi (1909-49).

Natl. Day for the
Handicapped
A363

1989, May 30   **Photo.**   *Perf. 13½*
957 A363 150m multicolored   .65 .25

Education
A364

1989, July 10   *Perf. 14*
958 A364 180m multicolored   .65 .25

Family Planning
Assoc., 20th
Anniv. — A365

1989, Aug. 14   **Litho.**   *Perf. 14*
959 A365 150m multicolored   .65 .25

Family
Care
A366

1989, Aug. 14   **Litho.**   *Perf. 14*
960 A366 150m multicolored   .65 .25

Fauna
A367

1989, Aug. 28   Photo.   Perf. 13½x14
961 A367 250m Tortoise   1.10   .50
962 A367 350m Oryx   1.50   .65

Intl. Fair,
Tunis — A368

1989, Oct. 16   Photo.   Perf. 14
963 A368 150m shown   .50   .25
964 A368 370m Pavilion, horiz. 1.25   .60

Mohamed Beyram
V (1840-1889)
A369

1989, Oct. 28   Engr.   Perf. 13
965 A369 150m blk & dp rose lil   .65   .25

Theater,
Carthage — A370

1989, Nov. 3   Photo.   Perf. 14
966 A370 300m multicolored   1.00   .40

Monument — A371

1989, Nov. 7   Perf. 11½x12
Granite Paper
967 A371 150m multicolored   .65   .25
Appointment of Pres. Zine El Abidine Ben
Ali, 2nd Anniv.

Nehru — A372

1989, Nov. 29   Engr.   Perf. 13
968 A372 300m dark brown   1.25   .35
Jawaharlal Nehru, 1st prime minister of
independent India.

Flags — A373

1990, Jan. 15   Photo.   Perf. 12x11½
Granite Paper
969 A373 200m multicolored   .75   .35
Maghreb Union summit, Tunis.

Museum
of Bardo,
Cent.
A374

1990, Feb. 20   Litho.   Perf. 13½
970 A374 300m multicolored   1.00   .50

Pottery
A375

1990, Mar. 22   Perf. 14
971 A375 75m multicolored   .35   .25
972 A375 100m multi, diff.   .50   .35

Sheep Museum — A376

1990, Apr. 13   Litho.   Perf. 13½
973 A376 400m Sheep   1.25   .75
974 A376 450m Ram's head   1.75   .85
  a.   Souvenir sheet of 2, #973-974   4.50   4.50
No. 974a sold for 1000m, exists imperf. Nos.
973-974 inscribed 1989.

Tunisian Olympic Movement — A377

1990, May 27
975 A377 150m multicolored   .65   .25

Child's
Drawing
A378

1990, June 5   Perf. 14
976 A378 150m multicolored   .65   .25

A379

Traditional costumes.

1990, July 13   Photo.   Perf. 14x14½
977 A379 150m Sbiba   .75   .35
978 A379 500m Bou Omrane   2.00   .85

A380

Relic from Punic city of Dougga.

1990, Aug. 1   Litho.   Perf. 14
979 A380 300m multicolored   1.00   .50

Intl.
Literacy
Year
A381

1990, Sept. 8   Photo.   Perf. 12x11½
Granite Paper
980 A381 120m multicolored   .65   .25

A382

1990, Oct. 15   Perf. 11½x12
Granite Paper
981 A382 150m multicolored   .75   .25
Importance of water.

A383

1990, Nov. 7   Granite Paper
982 A383 150m shown   .50   .25
983 A383 150m Clock tower   .50   .25
Appointment of Pres. Zine El Abidine Ben
Ali, 3rd anniv.

A384

1990, Nov. 16   Engr.   Perf. 13½x13
984 A384 150m green   .65   .25
Kheireddine Et-Tounsi (1822-1889), politician.

A385

Fauna and flora — 150m, Cervus elaphus
barbarus. 200m, Cynara cardenculus. 300m,
Bubalus bubalis. 600m, Ophris lutea.

1990, Dec. 17   Photo.   Perf. 13½
985 A385 150m multicolored   .50   .25
986 A385 200m multicolored   .80   .35
987 A385 300m multicolored   1.25   .40
988 A385 600m multicolored   2.60   .85
  Nos. 985-988 (4)   5.15 1.85

Maghreb Arab
Union, 2nd
Anniv. — A386

1991, Jan. 21   Photo.   Perf. 13½
989 A386 180m multicolored   .75   .25

Harbor of
Tabarka — A387

1991, Mar. 17
990 A387 450m multicolored   1.50   .50

Fish — A388

1991, Sept. 10   Photo.   Perf. 14x13
991 A388 180m Pagre   .70   .25
992 A388 350m Rouget de roche   1.40   .40
993 A388 450m Maquereau   1.40   .60
994 A388 550m Pageot commun   2.40   .90
  Nos. 991-994 (4)   5.90 2.15

Child Welfare — A389

1991, Sept. 29   *Perf. 14*
995 A389 450m multicolored   2.10 .85

A390

1991, Oct. 9   *Perf. 13½x14*
996 A390 400m multicolored   1.75 .50

A391

Jewelry.

     Perf. 14x13, 13x14
1991, Oct. 22   **Litho.**
997 A391 120m Ring, bracelets,
           horiz.   .45 .25
998 A391 180m Necklace   .55 .25
999 A391 220m Earrings   .70 .35
1000 A391 730m shown   2.75 1.10
    Nos. 997-1000 (4)   4.45 1.95

A392

1991, Nov. 7   *Perf. 11½*
1001 A392 180m multicolored   .65 .25

Appointment of Pres. Zine El Abidine Ben Ali, 4th anniv.

Tunis-Carthage Center — A393

1991, Nov. 22   **Engr.**   *Perf. 13*
1002 A393 80m red, blue &
           green   1.00 .40

A394

1991, Dec. 12   **Photo.**   *Perf. 14*
1003 A394 450m bright blue   1.60 .55
World Day of the Rights of Man.

A395

1991, Dec. 26   **Engr.**   *Perf. 12½x13*
1004 A395 200m blue   .65 .35
Mahmoud Bayram Et Tounsi (1893-1960), poet.

Expo '92, Seville — A396

1992, Apr. 20   **Photo.**   *Perf. 13½*
1005 A396 180m multicolored   .65 .25

A397

General Post Office, Tunis, Cent. — A397a

    Perf. 13x12½, 12½x13
1992, June 15   **Engr.**
1006 A397 180m red brn, horiz.   .60 .25
1007 A397a 450m dark brown   1.60 .45

"When the Subconscious Awakes," by Moncef ben Amor — A398

1992, July 21   **Litho.**   *Perf. 13½*
1008 A398 500m multicolored   1.90 .50

1992 Summer Olympics, Barcelona A399

1992, Aug. 4
1009 A399 180m Running   1.00 .40
1010 A399 450m Judo, vert.   2.25 .65

Birds — A400

100m, Merops apiaster. 180m, Carduelis carduelis. 200m, Serinus serinus. 500m, Carduelis chloris.

1992, Sept. 22   **Photo.**   *Perf. 11½*
           Granite Paper
1011 A400 100m multicolored   .75 .25
1012 A400 180m multicolored   1.25 .40
1013 A400 200m multicolored   1.50 .50
1014 A400 500m multicolored   3.00 1.00
    Nos. 1011-1014 (4)   6.50 2.15

A401

1992, Oct. 21   *Perf. 11½x12*
           Granite Paper
1015 A401 180m multicolored   .85 .40
UN Conference on Rights of the Child.

African Human Rights Conference, Tunis — A402

1992, Nov. 2   **Photo.**   *Perf. 11½*
           Granite Paper
1016 A402 480m multicolored   2.00 .85

A403   A404

1992, Nov. 7   **Granite Paper**
1017 A403 180m multicolored   .95 .40
1018 A404 730m multicolored   3.00 1.10

Appointment of Pres. Zine El Abidine Ben Ali, 5th anniv.

Arbor Day A405

1992, Nov. 8   *Perf. 11½x12*
           Granite Paper
1019 A405 180m Acacia tortilis   1.00 .50

Intl. Conference on Nutrition, Rome — A406

1992, Dec. 15   **Litho.**   *Perf. 13½*
1020 A406 450m multicolored   2.00 .65

Traditional Costumes — A407

1992, Dec. 23
1021 A407 100m Chemesse   .60 .25
1022 A407 350m Hanifites   1.60 .50

Mosaics A408

1992, Dec. 29
1023 A408 100m Goat   .40 .25
1024 A408 180m Duck   .85 .35
1025 A408 350m Horse   1.40 .50
1026 A408 450m Gazelle   1.50 .90
    Nos. 1023-1026 (4)   4.15 2.00

World Conference on Human Rights, Vienna — A409

1993, June 8   **Litho.**   *Perf. 13½*
1027 A409 450m multi   — —

Arab-African Fair of Tunisia — A410

1993, July 10   **Litho.**   *Perf. 13½x14*
1028 A410 450m multicolored   1.75 .50

Relaxation in the
Patio, by Ali
Guermassi
A411

1993, July 20   Litho.   Perf. 13½
1029 A411 450m multicolored   1.75   .50

Reassembly of the
Democratic
Congress — A412

1993, July 29   Perf. 13½
1030 A412 180m multicolored   .65   .25

A413

A414

1993   Perf. 13
1031 A413 20m Wolf   1.25   .25
1032 A414 60m Hoya carnosa   .75   .25

Appointment of Pres. Zine El Abidine,
6th Anniv.
A414A   A415

1993, Nov. 7   Perf. 13½
1033 A414A 180m multicolored   .75   .25
1034 A415   450m multicolored   1.75   .50

Kairouan
Tapestries — A416

Designs: Various ornate patterns.

1993, Dec. 13   Perf. 13½
1035 A416 100m multicolored   .40   .25
1036 A416 120m multicolored   .75   .25
1037 A416 180m multicolored   1.25   .35
1038 A416 350m multicolored   1.40   .75
        Nos. 1035-1038 (4)   3.80   1.60

Pasteur
Institute
of Tunis,
Cent.
A417

Design: 450m, Charles Nicolle (1866-1936),
bacteriologist, 1928 Nobel medal.

1993, Oct. 12   Litho.   Perf. 13½
1039 A417 450m multicolored   2.00   .65

A418

School
Activities
A419

1993, Dec. 30   Litho.   Perf. 13½
1040 A418 180m Music   .75   .25
1041 A419 180m Art, reading   .75   .25

19th African Cup of Nations Soccer
Tournament — A420

1994, Mar. 26
1042 A420 180m shown   1.00   .25
1043 A420 350m Two players,
              diff.   2.00   .35
1044 A420 450m Map, player   2.75   .65
        Nos. 1042-1044 (3)   5.75   1.25

Presidential and
Legislative
Elections — A421

1994, Mar. 20
1045 A421 180m multicolored   .80   .25

Election of
Pres. Zine El
Abidine ben
Ali — A422

1994, May 15   Photo.   Perf. 11½
              Granite Paper
1046 A422 180m multicolored   .75   .35
1047 A422 350m multicolored   1.25   .75
   a. Souvenir sheet, #1046-1047   3.50   3.50
        No. 1047a exists imperf.

ILO, 75th
Anniv. — A423

1994, May 12   Perf. 13½x14
1048 A423 350m multicolored   1.75   .35

Intl. Year of the
Family — A424

1994, May 15   Litho.   Perf. 14x13½
1049 A424 180m multicolored   .85   .50

Plants — A425

50m, Prunus spinosa. 100m, Xeranthemum
inapertum. 200m, Orchis simia. 1d, Scilla
peruviana.

1994, June 2
1050 A425   50m multicolored   .35   .25
1051 A425 100m multicolored   .35   .25
1052 A425 200m multicolored   1.00   .30
1053 A425   1d multicolored   4.50   1.50
        Nos. 1050-1053 (4)   6.20   2.30

Organization
of African
Unity Summit
Meeting,
Tunis — A426

1994, June 3   Perf. 13½
1054 A426 480m multicolored   2.00   .75

Intl. Olympic
Committee,
Cent.
A427

1994, July 7   Litho.   Perf. 13½
1055 A427 450m multicolored   1.75   .65

Philakorea
'94 — A428

1994, Aug 18   Litho.   Perf. 13¼x13½
1056 A428 450m multi   3.00   .65

A429

Butterflies: 100m, Colias croceus, horiz.
180m, Vanessa atalanta, horiz. 300m, Papilio
podalirius. 350m, Danaus chrysippus, horiz.
450m, Vanessa cardui. 500m, Papilio
machaon.

Perf. 13½x14, 14x13½
1994, Oct. 13   Litho.
1057 A429 100m multicolored   .45   .25
1058 A429 180m multicolored   .70   .35
1059 A429 300m multicolored   1.00   .50
1060 A429 350m multicolored   1.40   .65
1061 A429 450m multicolored   1.75   .85
1062 A429 500m multicolored   2.10   .90
        Nos. 1057-1062 (6)   7.40   3.50

A430

1994, Nov. 16   Perf. 13½
1063 A430 350m Pres. Ali, "7,"
              horiz.   1.25   .50
1064 A430 730m "7," Emblem   2.75   1.00
   Pres. Zine El Abdine, 7th anniv. of taking
office.

41st Military
Boxing World
Championships
A431

1994, Nov. 18   Litho.   Perf. 13½x14
1065 A431 450m multicolored   1.75   .70

Intl. Civil Aviation Organization, 50th
Anniv. — A432

1994, Dec. 7   Litho.   Perf. 13¾x14
1066 A432 450m multi   1.25   .50

Wildlife — A433

180m, Anser anser. 350m, Aythya ferina,
Aythya fuligula. 500m, Bubalus bubalis. 1d,
Lutra lutra, horiz.

1994, Dec. 27   Litho.   Perf. 13½
1067	A433	180m multi	.65	.40
1068	A433	350m multi	1.10	.85
1069	A433	500m multi	1.60	1.25
1070	A433	1d multi	3.00	2.75
	Nos. 1067-1070 (4)		6.35	5.25

"Composition," by Ridha
Bettaieb — A434

1994, Dec. 29   Litho.   Perf. 13
1071 A434 500m multicolored   1.50   .85

Arab League, 50th
Anniv. — A435

1995, May 29   Litho.   Perf. 13½
1072 A435 180m multicolored   1.00   .40

Art of Glass
Blowing — A436

1995, June 29
1073 A436 450m Water bottle   1.50   .90
1074 A436 730m Incense burner   2.25   1.50

Aboulkacem Chebbi (1909-34),
Poet — A437

1995, Aug. 12   Litho.   Perf. 13½
1075 A437 180m multicolored   .85   .40

4th World
Conference on
Women,
Beijing
A438

1995, Sept. 6   Litho.   Perf. 13½
1076 A438 180m multicolored   1.40   .40

FAO, 50th
Anniv.
A439

1995, Oct. 2   Litho.   Perf. 13½x13
1077 A439 350m multicolored   1.40   .65

Hannibal (247-
183BC),
Carthaginian
General — A440

1995, Nov. 14   Engr.   Perf. 14x13½
1078 A440 180m maroon   .65   .40
   a. Souvenir sheet of 1   2.50   2.50
No. 1078a sold for 1d and exists imperf.

United
Nations,
50th
Anniv.
A441

1995, Oct. 24   Litho.   Perf. 14x13½
1079 A441 350m multicolored   1.50   .65

A442   A443

1995, Nov. 7   Litho.   Perf. 13x13½
1080 A442 180m multicolored   .65   .35
1081 A443 350m multicolored   1.25   .65
Appointment of Pres. Zine El Abidine ben
Ali, 8th anniv.

Campaign Against
Desertification — A444

1995, Oct. 31   Litho.   Perf. 13¼
1082 A444 180m multi   .75   .35

Human Rights
Day — A445

1995, Dec. 10   Litho.   Perf. 13x13½
1083 A445 350m multicolored   1.40   .65

Pedestrian
Security
A446

1995, Dec. 19   Perf. 13½x13
1084 A446 350m multicolored   1.10   .65

Flora and
Fauna — A447

Designs: 50m, Ophrys lapethica. 180m,
Gazella dorcas. 300m, Scupellaria cypria.
350m, Chlamydotis undulata.

1995, Dec. 28   Perf. 13½
1085 A447 50m multicolored   .35   .25
1086 A447 180m multicolored   .70   .25
1087 A447 300m multicolored   1.10   .55
1088 A447 350m multicolored   1.25   .75
   Nos. 1085-1088 (4)   3.40   1.80

Traditional
Costumes — A448

1996, Mar.16   Perf. 14x13½
1089 A448 170m Jebra, Khamri   .85   .40
1090 A448 200m Kaftan brode,
      Hammamet   .85   .40

A449

Independence, 40th Anniv.: 390m, Dove,
rainbow, "20, 40."

1996, Mar. 20   Perf. 13x13½
1091 A449 200m multicolored   .75   .30
1092 A449 390m multicolored   1.25   .75

A450

1996, Jan. 20   Litho.   Perf. 13x13½
1093 A450 440m multicolored   1.75   .85
Natl. Trade Union, 50th anniv.

Painting, "Hannana," by Noureddine
Khayachi (1917-87) — A451

1996, Apr. 25   Litho.   Perf. 13½
1094 A451 810m multicolored   2.50   1.60

A451a

1996, June 5   Litho.   Perf. 13x13½
1094A A451a 390m multicolored   1.50   .75
Environment Day.

A452

1996, June 8   Litho.   Perf. 13x13½
1095 A452 200m multicolored   1.10   .35
CAPEX '96.

Insects
A453

200m, Coccinella septempunctata. 810m,
Apis mellifica.

1996, May 23   Litho.   Perf. 14x13½
1096 A453 200m multicolored   1.00   .40
1097 A453 810m multicolored   5.00   2.00

1996
Summer
Olympic
Games,
Atlanta
A455

Olympic emblem, and: 20m, Flags, Olympic
rings, athletic field. 200m, Torch bearer, fireworks, "100," globe, vert. 390m, Early Olympic
wrestlers.

1996, July 19   Litho.   Perf. 13
1099 A455 20m multicolored   .40   .25
1100 A455 200m multicolored   .90   .35
1101 A455 390m multicolored   1.75   .85
   Nos. 1099-1101 (3)   3.05   1.45

Code of Personal Status (Women's Liberation), 40th Anniv. — A456

1996, Aug. 13   **Perf. 14**
1102 A456 200m multicolored   .80   .35

Landmarks — A457

Designs: 20m, Ramparts of Sousse, horiz. 200m, Numidian Mausoleum, Dougga. 390m, Arch of Trajan, Makthar, horiz.

1996, Sept. 16   **Photo.**   **Perf. 11½**
Granite Paper
1103 A457 20m multicolored   .35   .25
1104 A457 200m multicolored   .65   .25
1105 A457 390m multicolored   1.50   .85
    Nos. 1103-1105 (3)   2.50   1.45

Intl. Year to Fight Poverty — A458

1996, Oct. 17   **Litho.**   **Perf. 13x13½**
1106 A458 390m multicolored   1.50   .65

Appointment of Pres. Zine El Abidine, 9th Anniv.
   A459   A460
1996, Nov. 7
1107 A459 200m multicolored   .75   .35
1108 A460 390m multicolored   1.00   .75

National Day of Saharan Tourism — A461

Designs: No. 1109, Camels, oasis, balloon. No. 1110, Decorative designs.

1996, Nov. 12   **Litho.**   **Perf. 13¼x13**
1109 200m multi   .85   .35
1110 200m multi   .85   .35
   a. A461 Horiz. pair, #1109-1110   1.75   1.75

Ezzitouna Mosque, 1300th Anniv. — A462

1996, Nov. 25   **Litho.**   **Perf. 14x13½**
1111 A462 250m multicolored   .85   .40

Natl. Solidarity Day
  A463   A464
1996, Dec. 8   **Perf. 13x13½**
1112 A463 500m multicolored   1.50   .95
1113 A464 500m multicolored   1.50   .95

World Human Rights Day — A465

1996, Dec. 10
1114 A465 500m multicolored   1.75   .90

UNICEF, 50th Anniv. — A466

1996, Dec. 11
1115 A466 810m multicolored   2.75   1.50

Musical Instruments — A467

1996, Dec. 26   **Litho.**   **Perf. 13½**
1116 A467 250m Mezoued   .85   .50
1117 A467 300m Gombri   1.00   .60
1118 A467 350m Tabla   1.60   .65
1119 A467 500m Tar Tounsi
       (Riq)   2.50   .90
    Nos. 1116-1119 (4)   5.95   2.65
    Perf. 13½x13¼
1119A   Vert. strip of 4   —   —
  b.   A467 20m Tabla, 38x25mm   —   —
  c.   A467 30m Mezoued, 38x25mm   —   —
  d.   A467 50m Gombri, 38x25mm   —   —
  e.   A467 100m Tar Tounsi, 38x25mm   —   —

World Book and Copyright Day A468

1997, Apr. 23   **Litho.**   **Perf. 13½**
1120 A468 1d multicolored   3.25   1.75

Marine Life A469

Designs: 50m, Mytilus galloprovincialis. 70m, Tapes decussatus. 350m, Octopus vulgaris. 500m, Sepia officinalis.

1997, May 13
1121 A469 50m multicolored   .30   .25
1122 A469 70m multicolored   .30   .25
1123 A469 350m multicolored   1.10   .65
1124 A469 500m multicolored   1.90   1.25
    Nos. 1121-1124 (4)   3.60   2.40

PACIFIC 97, Intl. Stamp Exhibition, San Francisco — A470

1997, May 29   **Photo.**   **Perf. 11½x12**
Granite Paper
1125 A470 250m multicolored   .85   .40

A471

1997, June 16   **Litho.**   **Perf. 13½**
1126 A471 350m multicolored   1.40   .65
   Mediterranean Games, Bari.

A472

1997, July 15
1127 A472 250m multicolored   .85   .40
   Tunis, 1997 Cultural Capital.

A473

Republic, 40th Anniv. A474

1997, July 25
1128 A473 130m multicolored   .50   .25
1129 A474 500m multicolored   1.50   1.00

Reptiles A475

100m, Uromastix acanthinurus. 350m, Chamaeleo chamaeleon, vert. 500m, Varanus griseus.

1997, Sept. 9   **Litho.**   **Perf. 13½**
1130 A475 100m multicolored   .25   .25
1131 A475 350m multicolored   1.00   .65
1132 A475 500m multicolored   1.25   1.10
    Nos. 1130-1132 (3)   2.50   2.00

Rosa Gallica Flore Pleno — A476

1997, Sept. 23   **Litho.**   **Perf. 13½**
1134 A476 350m multicolored   1.40   .85

Intl. Day for Protection of the Elderly A477

1997, Oct. 1   **Litho.**   **Perf. 13½**
1135 A477 250m multicolored   .85   .40

Tunisian Works of Art — A478

#1136, "L'Automne," by Ammar Farhat. #1137, Sculpture, "Pecheur D'Hommes," by Hedi Selmi. #1138, "Au Cafe-Maure," by Farhat. #1139, "Le Viellard au Kanoun," by Farhat. #1140, "Cafe Des Nattes-Sidi Bou Said," by Hedi Khayachi. #1141, "Le Kouttab," by Yahia Turki. 1000d, "La Fileuse," by Farhat.

1997, Nov. 5
1136 A478 250m multi, vert.   .80   .55
1137 A478 250m multi, vert.   .80   .55
1138 A478 250m multi, vert.   .80   .55
1139 A478 250m multi, vert.   .80   .55
1140 A478 500m multi   1.60   1.10
1141 A478 500m multi   1.60   1.10
1142 A478 1000m multi, vert.   3.50   2.25
   a.   Sheet of 7, #1136-1142, + 3 labels   10.00   10.00
    Nos. 1136-1142 (7)   9.90   6.65
    No. 1142a issued 11/7.

A479

A480

1997, Nov. 7
1143 A479 250m multicolored .75 .40
1144 A480 500m multicolored 1.75 1.10
Pres. Zine El Abdine, 10th anniv. of taking office.

Desert Rose — A481

1997, Nov. 29
1145 A481 250m multicolored 1.10 .40

Intl. Human Rights Day — A482

1997, Dec. 10 Litho. Perf. 13½
1146 A482 500m multicolored 1.50 .90

Horses
A483

Designs: 50m, Arabian. 70m, Barb. 250m, Arabian barb, vert. 500m, Arabian, vert.

1997, Dec. 18 Perf. 12½x13
1147 A483 50m multicolored .35 .25
1148 A483 70m multicolored .35 .25
1149 A483 250m multicolored 1.00 .40
1150 A483 500m multicolored 2.00 .75
Nos. 1147-1150 (4) 3.70 1.65

Bombing of Sakiet Sidi Yoncef, 40th Anniv.
A484

1998, Feb. 8
1151 A484 250m multicolored .85 .30

School Health Week
A485

1998, Feb. 16 Litho. Perf. 12½x13
1152 A485 250m multicolored .85 .30

Bar Assoc. of Tunisia, Cent. — A486

1998, Mar. 27 Perf. 13x12½
1153 A486 250m multicolored .85 .30

Martyr's Day, 60th Anniv.
A487 A488

1998, Apr. 9
1154 A487 250m multicolored .75 .30
1155 A488 520m multicolored 1.60 .55

Okba Ibn Nafaa Mosque, Kairouan — A489

1998, May 28 Litho. Perf. 13
1156 A489 500m multicolored 1.75 .60

1998 World Cup Soccer Championships, France — A490

250m, Tunisian team. 500m Player, trophy.

1998, June 10 Litho. Perf. 13
1157 A490 250m multi .85 .30
1158 A490 500m multi, vert. 1.90 .60

Crustaceans — A491

1998, July 8 Perf. 12½x13
1159 A491 110m Crab .30 .25
1160 A491 250m Shrimp .75 .30
1161 A491 1000m Lobster 3.00 1.10
Nos. 1159-1161 (3) 4.05 1.65

21st Reassembly of the Democratic Congress (RCD) — A492

#1162, Pres. Zine El Abidine ben Ali, flag, emblems. #1163, People holding torches, flag, dove.

1998, July 30 Perf. 13
1162 A492 250m multi .85 .30
1163 A492 250m multi, vert. .85 .30

36th Intl. Congress on the History of Medicine — A493

1998, Sept. 6 Litho. Perf. 13
1164 A493 500m multicolored 1.75 .60

Paintings — A494

#1165, "The Weaver," by Ali Guermassi (1923-92). #1166, "Woman Musician," by Noureddine Khayachi (1917-87). 500m, Still life by Ali Khouja (1947-91).

1998, Oct. 8
1165 A494 250m multi .90 .30
1166 A494 250m multi, vert. .90 .30
1167 A494 500m multi, vert. 1.75 .60
Nos. 1165-1167 (3) 3.55 1.20

Central Bank of Tunisia, 40th Anniv.
A495

1998, Nov. 10 Litho. Perf. 13
1168 A495 250m multicolored .85 .30

A496

1998, Nov. 7
1169 A496 250m multicolored .85 .30
Appointment of Pres. Zine El Abidine ben Ali, 11th anniv.

Universal Declaration of Human Rights, 50th Anniv.
A497

1998, Dec. 10 Litho. Perf. 12½x13
1170 A497 250m multicolored .85 .35

Averroes (Ibn Rushd) (1126-1198), Philosopher — A498

1998, Dec. 12
1171 A498 500m multicolored 1.75 .60

Musicians
A499

1998, Dec. 21 Perf. 12½x13, 13x12½
1172 A499 250m Kaddour Srarfi .85 .30
1173 A499 250m Saliha, vert. .85 .30
1174 A499 500m Ali Riahi, vert. 1.75 .60
Nos. 1172-1174 (3) 3.45 1.20

Boukornine Natl. Park — A500

1998, Dec. 29 Litho. Perf. 13
1175 A500 70m Gazelles .35 .25
1176 A500 110m Rabbit .35 .25
1177 A500 250m Eagles .85 .30
1178 A500 500m Cyclamens 1.75 .60
Nos. 1175-1178 (4) 3.30 1.40

Fruit Trees
A501

1999, Feb. 27 Litho. Perf. 13
1179 A501 250m Orange 1.00 .30
1180 A501 250m Date, vert. 1.00 .30
1181 A501 500m Olive 2.00 .60
Nos. 1179-1181 (3) 4.00 1.20

Archaeological Sites — A502

50m, Gate, Thuburbo Majus. 250m, Thermal baths, Bulla Regia. 500m, Zaghouan Aqueduct.

1999, Mar. 31 Litho. Perf. 13
1182 A502 50m multi, vert. .40 .25
1183 A502 250m multi .95 .30
1184 A502 500m multi 2.10 .60
Nos. 1182-1184 (3) 3.45 1.15

Paintings by Tunisian Artists A503

Designs: No. 1185, "L'Intemporel," by Moncef Ben Amor. No. 1186, "Fiancailles," by Ali Guermassi. No. 1187, "La Poterie," by Ammar Farhat. No. 1188, "Vendeur d'ombrelles et d'eventails," by Yahia Turki.

1999, May 6 Litho. Perf. 13
1185	A503	250m multicolored	.85	.30
1186	A503	250m multicolored	.85	.30
1187	A503	500m multicolored	1.60	.55
1188	A503	500m multicolored	1.60	.55
		Nos. 1185-1188 (4)	4.90	1.70

Constitution, 40th Anniv. — A504

1999, June 1 Litho. Perf. 13
1189	A504	250m multicolored	.85	.40

Flowers — A505

70m, Acacia cyanophilla. #1191, Bouganvillea spectabilis. #1192, Papaver rhoeas. 500m, Dianthus caryophylius.

1999, June 25 Litho. Perf. 12¾
1190	A505	70m multicolored	.35	.25
1191	A505	250m multicolored	.85	.30
1192	A505	250m multicolored	.85	.30
1193	A505	500m multicolored	1.90	.70
a.		Souvenir sheet, #1190-1193, imperf.	8.25	8.25
		Nos. 1190-1193 (4)	3.95	1.55

No. 1193a sold for 1.50d.

Philex France 99 — A506

1999, July 2 Perf. 13x12¾
1194	A506	500m multicolored	2.50	.85

Tahar Haddad (b. 1899), Women's Rights Advocate — A507

1999, Aug. 13 Litho.
1195	A507	500m multicolored	2.50	.85

Marine Life A508

1999, Sept. 22 Perf. 12¾
1196	A508	250m Caretta caretta	.90	.90
1197	A508	500m Epinephelus marginatus	1.75	1.75

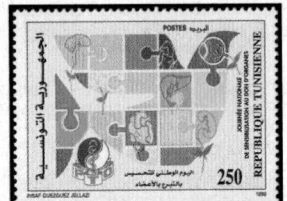

National Organ Donation Day — A509

1999, Oct. 2 Perf. 13x12¾
1198	A509	250m multicolored	1.10	.45

UPU, 125th Anniv. — A510

1999, Oct. 9 Perf. 12¾
1199	A510	500m multicolored	2.00	.75

Elections — A511

1999, Oct. 10 Litho.
1200	A511	500m multicolored	2.25	.85

Tamarisk A512

1999, Oct. 28 Litho. Perf. 12¾x13
1201	A512	250m shown	1.10	.35
1202	A512	500m Dromedary	2.25	.75

Appointment of Pres. Zine El Abidine Ben Ali, 12th Anniv. — A513

1999, Nov. 7 Perf. 13x12¾
1203	A513	250m multi	1.00	.45

Human Rights Day — A514

1999, Dec. 10 Litho. Perf. 13x12¾
1204	A514	250m multi	1.75	.45

Famous Tunisians — A515

No. 1205, Ahmed Ibn Abi Dhiaf (1802-74), historian. No. 1206, Abdelaziz Thaalbi (1876-1944), anti-colonial leader. 500m, Khemaies Tarnane (1894-1964), musician.

1999, Dec. 28 Perf. 12¾x13, 12¾x13
1205	A515	250m multi	.85	.35
1206	A515	250m multi	.85	.35
1207	A515	500m multi, horiz.	1.60	.75
		Nos. 1205-1207 (3)	3.30	1.45

Millennium — A516

1999, Dec. 31 Perf. 13
1208	A516	250m multi	.90	.45

A517

A518

Archaeology A519

Design: 100m, Methred cup. 110m, Aghlabide plate. 250m, Zaghouan water temple. 500m, Ulysses and the Sirens mosaic.

2000, Apr. 22 Litho. Perf. 13x13¼
1209	A517	100m multi	.40	.35
1210	A517	110m multi	.50	.45

Perf. 13¼
1211	A518	250m multi	1.20	1.00
1212	A519	500m multi	2.40	2.00
		Nos. 1209-1212 (4)	4.50	3.80

Ferry Carthage — A520

2000, Apr. 29 Perf. 13¼x13
1213	A520	500m multi	1.90	.80
a.		Souvenir sheet, imperf.	6.00	3.00

No. 1213a sold for 2d.

Expo 2000, Hanover — A521

2000, June 1 Perf. 13¼x13
1214	A521	1d multi	3.50	1.75

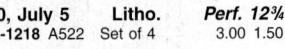

Trees A522

Designs: 50m, Carob. 100m, Apricot. 250m, Avocado, vert. 400m, Apple.

2000, July 5 Litho. Perf. 12¾
1215-1218	A522	Set of 4	3.00	1.50

2001 Mediterranean Games, Tunis — A523

2000, Sept. 2 Litho. Perf. 13
1219	A523	500m multi	1.75	.80
a.		Souvenir sheet of 1, imperf.	3.75	1.90

No. 1219a sold for 1500m.

2000 Summer Olympics, Sydney — A524

2000, Sept. 22 *Perf. 12¾*
1220 A524 500m multi   1.75 .80
Souvenir Sheet
Imperf
1221 A524 1500m multi   6.00 1.90

Flowers — A525

Designs: 110m, Freesias. 200m, Chrysanthemums. No. 1224, 250m, "Golden Times" roses. No. 1225, 250m, Vase with flowers (33x49mm). 500m, "Calibra" roses.

2000, Oct. 21 *Perf. 12¾, 13 (#1225)*
1222-1226 A525   Set of 5   4.75 2.40

Appointment of Pres. Zine El Abidine Ben Ali, 13th Anniv. A526

2000, Nov. 7 *Perf. 13*
1227 A526 250m multi   1.00 .50

Art — A527

Designs: 100m, Still Life, by Hédi Khayachi. No. 1229, 250m, Landscape, by Abdelaziz Berraies. No. 1230, 250m, The Knife Sharpener, by Ali Guermassi. 400m, Date and Milk Seller, by Yahia Turki, vert.

2000, Nov. 18
1228-1231 A527   Set of 4   3.50 1.50

Intl. Human Rights Day — A528

2000, Dec. 10
1232 A528 500m multi   1.75 .85

Shells — A529

Designs: 50m, Neverita josephinia. No. 1234, 250m, Phyllonotus trunculus. No. 1235, 250m, Columbella rustica. 1d, Arca noe.

2000, Dec. 29 *Perf. 13x13¼*
1233-1236 A529   Set of 4   8.00 2.50

A530

Famous Tunisians A531

Designs: No. 1237, 250m, Imam Sahnoun. No. 1238, 250m, Imam Ibn Arafa. No. 1239, 250m, Ali Belhaouane (1909-58), vert. 1d, Mohamed Jamoussi (1910-82), musician.

2000, Dec. 30 *Perf. 12¾*
1237 A530 250m shown   .85 .35
1238 A530 250m multi   .85 .35
1239 A531 250m multi   .85 .35
1240 A531 1d shown   3.50 1.50
   Nos. 1237-1240 (4)   6.05 2.55

Tunisian Presidency of UN Security Council — A532

2001, Feb. 19 *Litho.* *Perf. 13*
1241 A532 250m multi   1.10 .55

World Fund of Solidarity A533

2001, Mar. 29
1242 A533 500m multi   1.75 .80

Year of Digital Culture — A534

2001, May 17 *Perf. 12¾*
1243 A534 250m multi   1.10 .55

Mohamed Dorra, Child Killed in Israeli-Palestinian Violence — A535

2001, May 30
1244 A535 600m multi   2.25 1.10

A536   A537

Designs: No. 1245, 19th cent. ceramic tile, Qallaline. No. 1246, Gigthis, horiz. No. 1247, Tunis City Hall, horiz. 500m, Needles of Tabarka.

2001, Aug. 24
1245 A536 250m multi   .60 .25
1246 A537 250m multi   .60 .25
1247 A537 250m multi   .60 .25
1248 A537 500m multi   1.20 .50
   Nos. 1245-1248 (4)   3.00 1.25

2001 Mediterranean Games, Tunis — A538

Designs: No. 1249, 250m, No. 1251b, Track, stadium. No. 1250, 500m, No. 1251a, Runners, medal.

2001, Sept. 2 *Perf. 12¾*
1249-1250 A538   Set of 2   1.75 .75
Souvenir Sheet
Imperf
1251 A538 750m Sheet of 2, #a-b   3.00 1.50

Paintings — A539

Designs: No. 1252, 250m, Sidi Bou Said, by Pierre Boucherle. No. 1253, 250m, Still Life, by Boucherle. No. 1254, 250m, Dream in Traditional Space, by Aly Ben Salem, vert. 500m, Traditional Open-air Marriage, by Ben Salem.

2001, Sept. 29 *Litho.* *Perf. 13*
1252-1255 A539   Set of 4   3.00 1.40

Year of Dialogue Among Civilizations A540

2001, Oct. 9 *Perf. 12¾x13*
1256 A540 500m multi   2.00 .55

National Employment Fund — A541

2001, Oct. 10
1257 A541 250m multi   .60 .30

Appointment of Pres. Zine El Abidine Ben Ali, 14th Anniv. — A542

2001, Nov. 7 *Perf. 13x12¾*
1258 A542 250m multi   .60 .30

Butterflies — A543

Designs: Nos. 1259, 1263a, 250m, Ariane. No. 1260, 250m, No. 1263c, 500m, Pacha à deux queues. Nos. 1261, 1263b, 250m, Demideuil. Nos. 1262, 1263d, 500m, Grand paon de nuit.

2001, Nov. 15 *Perf. 13x13¼*
1259-1262 A543   Set of 4   3.00 1.50
Souvenir Sheet
Imperf
1263 A543   Sheet of 4, #a-d   3.50 1.75

Birds — A544

Designs: No. 1264, 250m, No. 1268a, 300m, Bec-croise des sapins. 500m, Mesange charbonnière. No. 1266, 600m, Cigogne blanche. No. 1267, 600m, Geai des chenes.

2001, Nov. 22 *Perf. 13*
1264-1267 A544   Set of 4   4.50 2.25
Souvenir Sheet
1268 A544   Sheet, #1265-1267, 1268a   5.50 2.50

Intl. Human Rights Day — A545

2001, Dec. 10 *Perf. 13x12¾*
1269 A545 250m multi   .60 .30

Famous
Men
A546

Designs: No. 1270, 250m, Ibrahim ibn al-Aghlab (757-812), founder of Aghlabid dynasty. No. 1271, 250m, Ibn Rachiq al Kairaouani (1000-71). 350m, Abdelaziz Laroui (1898-1971). 650m, Assad ibn al-Fourat (759-828).

2001, Dec. 29   Perf. 12¾x13
1270-1273 A546   Set of 4   3.25 1.60

Arabic
Calligraphy
A547

Designs: No. 1274, 350m, Shown. No. 1275, 350m, Calligraphy, vert.

2001, Dec. 31   Perf. 12¾x13, 13x12¾
1274-1275 A547   Set of 2   2.00 1.10

Archaeology
A548   A549

Designs: 250m, Kef casbah. 390m, Amphitheater, Oudhna, horiz. No. 1278, Baron of Erlanger Palace. No. 1279, Mosaic of Virgil.

Perf. 13x12¾, 12¾x13
2002, Mar. 26   Litho.
1276 A548 250m multi   .60 .25
1277 A548 390m multi   .95 .40
1278 A549 600m multi   1.40 .60
1279 A549 600m multi   1.40 .60
   Nos. 1276-1279 (4)   4.35 1.85

Animals of Zembra
and Zembretta Natl.
Park — A550

Designs: No. 1280, 250m, No. 1284a, 400m, Ovis musimon. No. 1281, 250m, No. 1284b, 400m, Oryctolagus cuniculus. No. 1282, 600m, Falco peregrinus brookei. No. 1283, 600m, Larus audouinii.

2002, Apr. 10   Perf. 13
1280-1283 A550   Set of 4   4.50 1.75
     Souvenir Sheet
1284 A550   Sheet, #1282-1283,
       1284a-1284b   5.50 1.90

Sahara Desert
Tourism
A551

Designs: No. 1285, 250m, No. 1289a, 400m, Gazella leptoceros. No. 1286, 390m, No. 1289b, 400m, Sahara village. No. 1287, 600m, Horseman. No. 1288, 600m, Tamaghza.

2002, May 22   Perf. 13¼
1285-1288 A551   Set of 4   4.00 1.90

     Souvenir Sheet
1289 A551   Sheet, #1287-1288,
       1289a-1289b, imperf.   5.00 2.00

2002 World Cup Soccer
Championships, Japan and
Korea — A552

World Cup, Emblem of Tunisia and World Cup tournament and: No. 1290, 390m, No. 1292a, 500m, Player, map of Japan and Korea. No. 1291, 600m, 1292b, 1000m, Ball in goal net.

2002, May 29   Perf. 13
1290-1291 A552   Set of 2   2.50 1.00
     Souvenir Sheet
1292 A552   Sheet of 2, #a-b   4.00 1.50

Famous
Men — A553

Designs: 100m, Sheikh Mohamed Senoussi (1851-1900). No. 1294, 250m, Mosbah Jarbou (1914-58). No. 1295, 250m, Mohamed Daghbaji (1885-1924). 1.10d, Abou al-Hassen al-Housri (1029-95).

2002, July 18   Perf. 12¾
1293-1296 A553   Set of 4   4.00 1.75

World Handicapped Games — A554

Tunisian flag and: 100m, Wheelchair racer. 700m, Discus thrower, vert.

2002, July 20
1297-1298 A554   Set of 2   1.75 .85

27th World
Veterinary
Congress,
Tunis
A555

2002, Sept. 25   Litho.   Perf. 12¾
1299 A555 600m multi   1.50 .60

Travel International Club, 20th
Anniv. — A556

2002, Oct. 25   Litho.   Perf. 13x13¼
1300 A556 600m multi   1.50 .60

Appointment of
Pres. Zine El
Abidine Ben Ali,
15th Anniv. — A557

2002, Nov. 7   Perf. 13x12¾
1301 A557 390m multi   .95 .40

Assassination of
Farhat Hached
(1914-52) — A558

2002, Dec. 3   Litho.   Perf. 13x12¾
1302 A558 390m multi   .95 .40

Intl. Human Rights
Day — A559

2002, Dec. 10
1303 A559 700m multi   1.75 .75

     Art Type of 2001

Designs: No. 1304, 250m, Space for Gazelles, by Aly Ben Salem. No. 1305, 250m, Popular Arts, by Ammar Farhat, vert. No. 1306, 250m, Marriage, by Habib Bouabana, vert. 900m, Still Life, by Pierre Boucherle, vert.

2002, Dec. 28   Perf. 13
1304-1307 A539   Set of 4   4.00 1.75

Mosaics
A560

Designs: 390m, Spinner. 600m, Africa.

2003, Feb. 28
1308-1309 A560   Set of 2   2.40 1.00

Scouting in Tunisia, 70th
Anniv. — A561

"70" and scouts: 250m, Reading map, at computer, planting tree. 600m, Saluting flag, at computer, vert.

2003, Mar. 29   Litho.   Perf. 13
1310-1311 A561   Set of 2   1.90 .85

National Book
Year — A562

2003, Apr. 23
1312 A562 390m multi   .95 .40

The Washerwoman, by Yahia
Turki — A563

2003, June 13
1313 A563 1d multi   2.40 1.00

National
Tourism
Day — A564

2003, June 28   Perf. 13¼
1314 A564 600m multi   1.50 .60

Parks — A565

Designs: 200m, Farhat Hached Park, Rades. 250m, Friguia Animal Park. 390m, La Marsa Park. 1d, Ennahli Park.

2003, June 28   Perf. 13
1315-1318 A565   Set of 4   *4.00* 2.00

A566

2003, July 28   Litho.   Perf. 13x12¾
1319 A566 250m multi   .70 .35
     Congress of Ambition.

A567

2003, Aug. 3
1320 A567 390m multi .95 .45
Pres. Habib Bourguiba (1903-2000).

A568

Flora and Fauna — A569

Designs: Nos. 1321a, 50m, 1326, 600m, Oryx dammah. Nos. 1321b, 50m, 1324, 250m, Nyctanthes sambac. Nos. 1321c, 100m, 1323, 250m, Aries. Nos. 1321d, 100m, 1327, 1d, Myrtus communis. Nos. 1321e, 200m, 1325, 390m, Struthio camelus. Nos. 1321f, 200m, 1322, 100m, Rosa canina.

2003, Sept. 25 *Perf. 12¾*
1321 Strip of 6 3.50 .80
a.-b. A568 50m Either single .50 .25
c.-d. A568 100m Either single .50 .25
e.-f. A568 200m Either single .90 .25
1322-1327 A569 Set of 6 5.75 2.75
No. 1321 was issued in a sheet of 6 strips that sold for 4500m.

Appointment of Pres. Zine El Abidine Ben Ali, 16th Anniv. — A570

2003, Nov. 7 *Litho. Perf. 13x12¾*
1328 A570 250m multi .60 .30

First 5+5 Dialogue Summit, Tunis — A571

2003, Dec. 5 *Perf. 13¼*
1329 A571 600m multi 1.40 .60

Universal Declaration of Human Rights — A572

2003, Dec. 10 *Perf. 13x12¾*
1330 A572 350m multi .85 .35

Silver Items
A573

Designs: No. 1331, 600m, Machmoum. No. 1332, 600m, Jewelry.

2003, Dec. 18 *Perf. 12¾x13*
1331-1332 A573 Set of 2 2.75 1.25
1332a Souvenir sheet, #1331-1332 4.50 2.50
No. 1332a sold for 1.50d.

African Soccer Championships — A574

Designs: 250m, Stylized soccer players, African cup, map. 600m, Map of Africa as soccer player.

2004, Jan. 24 *Perf. 13*
1333-1334 A574 Set of 2 1.90 .95
Values are for stamps with surrounding selvage.

Ksar Helal Congress, 70th Anniv. — A575

2004, Mar. 2 *Litho. Perf. 13x12¾*
1335 A575 250m multi .60 .30

Arab League Conference, Tunis
A576

2004, May 22 *Perf. 13*
1336 A576 600m multi 2.50 .60

Copper Handicrafts — A577

Designs: 100m, Water jar, 18th cent. 200m, Ewer, 18th cent. 250m, Bucket, 19th cent. 600m, Brazier, 18th cent. 700m, Amphora, 18th cent. 1000m, Ewer, 19th cent.

2004, June 5 *Perf. 13x13¼*
1337-1342 A577 Set of 6 6.25 3.00
1343 Sheet, 3 each #1337, 1338, 1343a-1343d 7.50 3.75
a. A577 50m Like #1340 .25 .25
b. A577 150m Like #1342 .30 .25
c. A577 250m Like #1341 .60 .30
d. A577 300m Like #1339 .70 .35
No. 1343 sold for 3500m.

Coins and Banknotes
A578

Designs: No. 1344, 250m, Gold coin, 706. No. 1345, 250m, Gold coin, 1767. No. 1346, 600m, Punic silver coin, 300 B.C. No. 1347, 600m, Punic gold coin, 310-290 B.C. 1000m, Banknote, 1847 (65x30mm).

2004, July 23 *Perf. 13¼*
1344-1348 A578 Set of 5 5.75 2.75
1348a Souvenir sheet, #1344-1348 + label 5.75 2.75
No. 1348a sold for 3000m.

African Development Bank, 40th Anniv.
A579

2004, Sept. 10 *Litho. Perf. 13*
1349 A579 700m multi 1.50 .75

Children's Art — A580

2004, Oct. 20
1350 A580 250m multi .60 .30

Presidential and Legislative Elections
A581

2004, Oct. 24
1351 A581 250m multi .60 .30

Appointment of Pres. Zine El Abidine Ben Ali, 17th Anniv.
A582

2004, Nov. 7
1352 A582 250m multi .60 .30

El Abidine Mosque, Carthage — A583

2004, Nov. 11
1353 A583 250m multi .60 .30

Birds — A584

Designs: 100m, Oxyura leucocephala. No. 1355, 600m, Phoenicurus moussieri. No. 1356, 600m, Aythya nyroca. 1000m, Marmaronetta angustirostris.

2004, Nov. 20 *Perf. 13¼*
1354-1357 A584 Set of 4 6.00 2.50

Universal Declaration of Human Rights — A585

2004, Dec. 10 *Perf. 13x12¾*
1358 A585 350m multi .75 .35

Famous People
A586

Designs: 250m, Ibn Chabbat (1221-85), writer. 500m, Ibn Charaf (1000-67), writer. No. 1361, 600m, Princess Elyssa. No. 1362, 600m, Hatem El Mekki (1918-2003), stamp designer, and #580, 619. No. 1363, 600m, Dr. Mongi Ben Hmida (1928-2002), neurologist.

2004, Dec. 18 *Perf. 12¾x13*
1359-1363 A586 Set of 5 6.00 2.75

World Handball
Championships — A587

2005, Jan. 23   **Perf. 13**
1364 A587 600m multi   1.40   .60

Native
Costumes — A588

Designs: 250m, Takhlila, Hammam Sousse.
No. 1366, 390m, Tarf-Ras ceremonial costume, Kerkennah. No. 1367, 390m, Karmas-
soud jebba. 600m, Traditional bridal costume,
Matmata.

2005, Mar. 16   **Perf. 13x12¾**
1365-1368 A588   Set of 4   3.75 1.75

World
Summit on
the
Information
Society,
Tunis
A589

2005, Apr. 7   **Litho.**   **Perf. 13**
1369 A589 600m multi   1.40   .60

Sculptures of
the Punic
and Roman
Eras — A590

Designs: No. 1370, 250m, Victory, 2nd cent.
No. 1371, 250m, Aesculapius, 2nd-3rd cent.
600m, Pottery mask of a woman's face, 4th-
5th cent. B.C. 1000m, Baal Ammon, 1st cent.

2005, May 18   **Perf. 13¼**
1370-1373 A590   Set of 4   5.00 2.25

World No Tobacco Day — A591

2005, May 31   **Perf. 13¼x13**
1374 A591 250m multi   .60   .30

Rotary
International,
Cent. — A592

2005, June 22   **Perf. 13x12¾**
1375 A592 600m multi   1.50   .60

Intl. Year of Sport
and Physical
Education — A593

2005, July 1
1376 A593 600m multi   1.50   .60

World Scout
Conference
A594

2005, Sept. 5
1377 A594 600m multi   1.50   .60

Intl. Year of
Physics
A595

2005, Oct. 15   **Litho.**   **Perf. 13**
1378 A595 2d multi   5.00 2.00

Appointment
of Pres. Zine
El Abidine
Ben Ali, 18th
Anniv.
A596

2005, Nov. 8
1379 A596 250m multi   .60   .25

World Summit on the Information
Society, Tunis — A597

2005, Nov. 12   **Litho.**   **Perf. 13¼x13**
1380 A597 600m multi   .90   .45

Universal
Declaration
of the Rights
of Man, 57th
Anniv.
A598

2005, Dec. 10   **Litho.**   **Perf. 13**
1381 A598 350m multi   1.10   .55

Medicinal
Plants — A599

Designs: 250m, Foeniculum. No. 1383,
600m, Mentha aquatica. No. 1384, 600m,
Lavandula angustifloia. 1000m, Origanum
majorana.

2005, Dec. 22
1382-1385 A599   Set of 4   5.50 2.50
1386   Booklet pane, 2 each
     #1383-1384, 1386a,
     1386b   9.75   —
   a.   A599 600m Like #1382   1.40   .60
   b.   A599 600m Like #1385   1.40   .60
     Complete booklet, #1386   11.00

Ibn Khaldun (1332-
1406), Philosopher
A600

2006, Mar. 15   **Litho.**   **Perf. 13x12¾**
1387 A600 390m multi   1.00   .45

A601

Independence, 50th Anniv. — A602

Designs: No. 1390, Stylized map and flag,
doctor examining child. No. 1391, Bridge and

ship. No. 1392, Stylized woman holding torch.
No. 1393, Woman and book. No. 1394, Computer, man, woman, "@," and stylized dove.

2006, Mar. 18   **Perf. 13x12¾, 12¾x13**
1388 A601 250m shown   .65   .30
1389 A602 250m shown   .65   .30
1390 A601 250m multi   .65   .30
1391 A601 250m multi   .65   .30
1392 A601 390m multi   .85   .40
1393 A601 390m multi   .85   .40
1394 A601 390m multi   .85   .40
   a.   Souvenir sheet, #1388-1394, +
     2 labels   6.00 6.00
     Nos. 1388-1394 (7)   5.15 2.40
     No. 1394a sold for 2.50d.

Dialogue
Among
Civilizations
and Religions
A603

2006, Apr. 26   **Litho.**   **Perf. 13½**
1395 A603 1.35d multi   3.00 1.40

Punic and
Roman Era
Jewelry
A604

Designs: No. 1396, 250m, Gold and garnet
vestment clasps. No. 1397, 250m, Gold-plated
bronze earrings. No. 1398, 250m, Ring depicting god Baal Hammon. No. 1399, 600m, Gold
and amethyst pendants.

2006, May 18   **Litho.**   **Perf. 13¼**
1396-1399 A604   Set of 4   4.25 1.90

Special Handicapped Employment
Program — A605

2006, May 29   **Perf. 13**
1400 A605 2.35d multi   5.50 2.25

National Cleanliness and
Environmental Protection
Program — A606

2006, June 11
1401 A606 250m multi   .85   .30

2006 World Cup Soccer
Championships, Germany — A607

Map, flags of Germany and Tunisia and: 250m, Feet of soccer players. 600m, Soccer player.

2006, June 14
1402-1403 A607   Set of 2   2.10 .95

Tunisian Army, 50th Anniv. A608

2006, June 24
1404 A608 250m multi   .65 .30

Diplomatic Relations Between Tunisia and Japan, 50th Anniv. A609

2006, July 7
1405 A609 700m multi   1.60 .70

Vacation Safety Program — A610

2006, July 31
1406 A610 250m multi   .65 .30

Personal Status Code, 50th Anniv. A611

2006, Aug. 8
1407 A611 2.35d multi   5.25 2.25

Appointment of Pres. Zine El Abidine Ben Ali, 19th Anniv. A612

2006, Nov. 7
1408 A612 250m multi   .75 .30

Universal Declaration of Human Rights — A613

2006, Dec. 10
1409 A613 700m multi   1.60 .70

Traditional Clothing and Textiles A614

Designs: No. 1410, 250m, Jelwa (wedding dress). No. 1411, 250m, Silk jebba. 1.10d, Klim. 1.35d, Woolen blanket from Gafsa.

2007, Mar. 16   Litho.   Perf. 13
1410-1413 A614 Set of 4   8.00 3.25

Independence, 51st Anniv. — A615

2007, Mar. 20
1414 A615 250m multi   .75 .30

Youth and Digital Culture A616

2007, Mar. 21
1415 A616 250m multi   1.25 .30

Natl. Energy Conservation Program A617

2007, Apr. 7
1416 A617 1d multi   3.00 1.00

Dialogue Between Cultures, Civilizations and Religions A618

2007, May 7   Litho.   Perf. 13
1417 A618 600m multi   1.75 .60

Archaeological Sites — A619

Designs: No. 1418, 250m, Baths of Caracalla, Dougga. No. 1419, 250m, Punic city of Kerkouane. No. 1420, 600m, Baths, Makthar. No. 1421, 600m, Capitol, Sbeitla.

2007, May 18   Perf. 13½
1418-1421 A619 Set of 4   4.50 1.90

Carthage Investment Forum — A620

2007, June 21   Perf. 13
1422 A620 600m multi   1.60 .60

National Tourism Day — A621

Designs: No. 1423, 250m, Sahara tourism. No. 1424, 250m, Beach tourism. No. 1425, 600m, Tabarka Jazz Festival. No. 1426, 600m, Golf tourism.

2007, June 28
1423-1426 A621 Set of 4   5.00 1.90

Republic of Tunisia, 50th Anniv. A623

2007, July 25   Litho.   Perf. 13
1427 A622 250m multi   .75 .30
1428 A623 250m multi   .75 .30

Appointment of Pres. Zine El Abidine Ben Ali, 20th Anniv. A624

2007, Nov. 7   Litho.   Perf. 13
1429 A624 250m multi   .75 .30

Friendship Between Germany and Tunisia, 50th Anniv. A625

2007, Dec. 17
1430 A625 600m multi   1.75 .60

Intl. Human Solidarity Day — A626

2007, Dec. 20
1431 A626 1.35d multi   3.50 1.50

French Air Raid on Sakiet Sidi Youssef, 50th Anniv. A627

2008, Feb. 8   Litho.   Perf. 13
1432 A627 250m multi   .75 .30

Government Accounting Board, 40th Anniv. — A628

2008, Mar. 8   Litho.   Perf. 13
1433 A628 250m multi   .60 .25

Universal Declaration of Human Rights, 60th Anniv. — A629

2008, Mar. 10
1434 A629 600m multi   1.25 .55

World Meteorological Day — A630

2008, Mar. 23
1435 A630 250m multi   .75 .25

Terra Cotta Objects — A631

Designs: 250m, Water jug, 19th cent. No. 1437, 600m, Goblet, 3rd cent. B.C. No. 1438, 600m, Plate, 10th cent. B.C. 1.10d, Lamp, 1st cent. B.C.

2008, May 18   Perf. 13x12¾
1436-1439 A631 Set of 4   6.00 3.00

National Day of the Disabled — A632

2008, May 29   Perf. 13
1440 A632 250m multi   .65 .25

Fish — A633

Designs: No. 1441, 250m, Mugil cephalus. No. 1442, 250m, Thunnus thynnus. No. 1443, 600m, Sparus aurata. No. 1444, 600m, Dicentrarchus labrax.

2008, June 5   Litho.   Perf. 13x13¼
1441-1444 A633 Set of 4   4.00 2.00
1444a   As #1444, with incomplete
         frame lines   3.00 .55
1444b   Souvenir sheet #1441-
         1443, 1444a   5.00 5.00

No. 1444b sold for 1.800d.

Democratic Constitutional Rally — A634

2008, July 30   Perf. 13
1445 A634 250m multi   .60 .25

Souvenir Sheet

Arab Post Day — A635

No. 1446 — Emblem and: a, World map, pigeon. b, Camel caravan.

2008, Aug. 3   Perf. 12¾
1446 A635 600m Sheet of 2,
            #a-b   3.50 1.00

2008 Summer Olympics, Beijing A636

Olympic rings, star and crescent, emblem of 2008 Summer Olympics, symbols of athletic events and: No. 1447, 250m, Colored dots and ribbons. No. 1448, 600m, Starbursts.

2008, Aug. 8   Perf. 13½
1447-1448 A636 Set of 2   2.00 1.00
1448a   Souvenir sheet of 2 #1447-
         1448   2.00 2.00

No. 1448a sold for 900m.

Dialogue With Youth A637

2008, Sept. 20   Litho.   Perf. 13¼
1449 A637 250m multi   .75 .40

Appointment of Pres. Zine El Abidine Ben Ali, 21st Anniv. A638

2008, Nov. 7   Perf. 13x13¼
1450 A638 250m multi   .60 .30

University of Tunisia, 50th Anniv. — A639

2008, Nov. 11   Perf. 13¼x13
1451 A639 250m multi   .70 .35

Famous Men A640

Designs: No. 1452, 250m, Ridha El Kalai (1931-2004), musician. No. 1453, 250m, Ammar Farhat (1911-87), painter. No. 1454, 600m, Mahmoud Messadi (1911-2004), writer. No. 1455, 600m, Hedi Jouini (1909-90), musician.

2008, Dec. 20   Perf. 12¾x13, 13x12¾
1452-1455 A640 Set of 4   3.50 1.75

Arab Maghreb Union, 20th Anniv. — A641

2009, Feb. 17   Litho.   Perf. 13
1456 A641 250m multi   .50 .25

Aboul Qasem Chebbi (1909-34), Poet — A642

2009, Feb. 24   Perf. 12¾
1457 A642 250m multi   .50 .25

Kairouan, 2009 Islamic Cultural Capital — A643

Designs: No. 1458, 250m, Mausoleum of Abi Zamaa al-Balawi. No. 1459, 250m, Okba Ibn Nafaa Mosque. 1000m, Emblem.

2009, Mar. 8
1458-1460 A643 Set of 3   3.00 1.50
1460a   Souvenir sheet, #1458-
         1460   3.00 3.00

Woven Fiber Crafts A644

Designs: No. 1461, 250m, Esparto basket and jug holder. No. 1462, 250m, Rattan mat. No. 1463, 600m, Palm fiber fan. No. 1464, 600m, Rattan basket.

2009, Mar. 16   Perf. 13¼
1461-1464 A644 Set of 4   2.50 1.25

Intl. Society for Military Law and the Law of War, 18th Congress A645

2009, May 5   Litho.   Perf. 13
1465 A645 700m multi   1.25 .65

Constitution, 50th Anniv. — A646

2009, June 1
1466 A646 250m multi   .90 .45

Fruit — A647

Designs: 250m, Eryobotrica japonica. No. 1468, 600m, Cerasus spp. No. 1469, 600m, Ficus carica. No. 1470, 600m, Prunus persica.

2009, June 5   Perf. 13¼
1467-1470 A647 Set of 4   3.50 1.75
1470a   Sheet of 4, #1467-1470   3.50 3.50

No. 1470a sold for 2.10d.

16th Mediterranean Games, Pescara, Italy — A648

2009, June 26   **Litho.**   *Perf. 13*
1471 A648 600m multi   1.00 .50

Presidential and Legislative Elections A649

2009, Oct. 25   **Litho.**   *Perf. 13x13¼*
1472 A649 250m multi   .90 .45

Appointment of Pres. Zine El Abidine Ben Ali, 22nd Anniv. A650

2009, Nov. 7
1473 A650 390m multi   .90 .45

Universal Declaration of Human Rights, 61st Anniv. A651

2009, Dec. 10
1474 A651 1.35d multi   2.50 1.25

Tunisian Cuisine A652

Designs: 250m, Tajine à la viande (meat tagine). 700m, Salade mechouia (grilled vegetable salad). 1000m, Poisson grillé (grilled fish). 1100m, Couscous à la viande (couscous with meat).

2009, Dec. 26   *Perf. 13¼*
1475-1478 A652   Set of 4   6.00 3.00
1478a   Souvenir sheet of 4, #1475-1478   7.00 7.00

Arab Women's Day — A653

2010, Feb. 1   *Perf. 13¼x13*
1479 A653 1350m multi   3.00 1.50

Intl. Year of Rapprochement of Cultures — A654

2010, Feb. 6   *Perf. 13x13¼*
1480 A654 2350m multi   5.00 2.50

Intl. Youth Year — A655

2010, Mar. 21   *Perf. 13¼x13*
1481 A655 390m multi   .90 .45

Expo 2010, Shanghai A656

2010, May 1   *Perf. 13¼*
1482 A656 390m multi   .90 .45

Organic Foods and Food Products A657

Designs: No. 1483, 250m, Cynara scolymus. No. 1484, 250m, Prunus dulcis. No. 1485, 250m, Punica granatum. No. 1486, 600m, Capsicum annuum. No. 1487, 600m, Opuntia ficus-indica. No. 1488, 600m, Solanum lycopersicum. No. 1489, 600m, Olea europaea and picher of olive oil. No. 1490, 600m, Phoenix dactylifera.

2010, May 12
1483-1490 A657   Set of 8   7.00 3.50
1490a   Souvenir sheet, #1483-1490   7.00 7.00

Tunisia, a Technological Pole — A658

2010, May 17   *Perf. 13*
1491 A658 390m multi   .90 .45

Year of Peace and Security in Africa A659

2010, June 25
1492 A659 250m multi   .90 .45

Landmarks in Medina of Tunis — A660

Designs: No. 1493, 250m, Bab El Khadra. No. 1494, 250m, Bab Jedid. No. 1495, 250m, Dar Hsine. No. 1496, 250m, Dar Ben Abdallah. 600m, Bab Bhar. 1000m, Bab Saâdoun.

2010, July 2   *Perf. 12¾*
1493-1498 A660   Set of 6   4.00 2.00

2010 Youth Olympics, Singapore A661

2010, Aug. 4   *Perf. 13*
1499 A661 700m multi   1.10 .55

Famous Men — A662

Designs: 250m, Zoubeir Turki (1924-2009), painter. 600m, Jaâfar Majed (1940-2009), poet. 1000m, Ali Ben Salem (1910-2001), painter. 1100m, Mustapha Khraief (1910-67), poet.

2010, Oct. 10   *Perf. 12¾*
1500-1503 A662   Set of 4   4.50 2.25

Third Congress of Organization of Arab Women, Tunis — A663

2010, Oct. 28   *Perf. 13*
1504 A663 1350m multi   2.25 1.00

Appointment of Pres. Zine El Abidine Ben Ali, 23rd Anniv. A664

2010, Nov. 7
1505 A664 390m multi   .90 .45

National Year of Tunisian Cinema A665

2010, Nov. 27   **Litho.**
1506 A665 390m multi   .90 .45

Universal Declaration of Human Rights, 62nd Anniv. A666

2010, Dec. 10
1507 A666 390m multi   .90 .45

A667

A668

A669

Revolution of 2010-11 — A670

2011, Mar. 25   Litho.   *Perf. 13*
1508 A667 250m multi   .65   .35
1509 A668 390m multi   .90   .45
1510 A669 600m multi   1.40   .70
1511 A670 1350m multi   3.00 1.50
    Nos. 1508-1511 (4)   5.95 3.00

World Book and Copyright Day — A671

2011, Apr. 23
1512 A671 2350m multi   4.50 2.25

World Press Freedom Day — A672

2011, May 3
1513 A672 250m multi   1.25   .40

Children's Art — A673

Designs: 700m, I Love My Country, by Syrine Zouari. 1350m, Spring, by Mustapha Gader, vert.

2011, May 20   *Perf. 13*
1514-1515 A673 Set of 2   4.75 2.50

Medicinal Plants A674

Designs: No. 1516, 250m, Allium sativum. No. 1517, 250m, Pimpinella anisum. 600m, Lippia tryphilla. 1000m, Rosemarinus officinalis.

2011, June 28   *Perf. 13¼*
1516-1519 A674 Set of 4   5.25 2.75

Phila Nippon 2011 Intl. Philatelic Exhibition, Yokahama, Japan A675

2011, July 28
1520 A675 250m multi   .65   .30

Human Rights Day — A676

2011, Dec. 10   *Perf. 13*
1521 A676 390m multi   .80   .40

January 14 Revolution, 1st Anniv. A677

2012, Jan. 14
1522 A677 390m multi   1.60   .80

Pottery A678

Designs: Nos. 1523, 1527a, 250m, Maajina plate. Nos. 1524, 1527b, 600m, Borniya jar. Nos. 1525, 1527c, 900m, Charbiya jug. Nos. 1526, 1527d, 1000m, Quallaline receptacle.

2012, Mar. 23   *Perf. 13¼*
Stamps With White Backgrounds
1523-1526 A678 Set of 4   6.75 3.50
Souvenir Sheet
Stamps With Buff Backgrounds
1527 A678 Sheet of 4, #a-d   6.75 3.50

Organic Farming A679

Organic: No. 1528, 250m, Melons. No. 1529, 250m, Strawberries. 600m, Grapes. 1350m, Honey.

2012, May 12   Litho.   *Perf. 13¼*
1528-1531 A679 Set of 4   5.50 2.75
1531a   Souvenir sheet of 4,
    #1528-1531   5.50 2.75

National Army, 56th Anniv. A680

2012, June 24   *Perf. 13*
1532 A680 700m multi   1.40   .70

Fish — A681

Designs: No. 1533, 250m, Saupe (Sarpa salpa). No. 1534, 250m, Marbré (Lithognathus mormyrus). 600m, Sardine (Sardina pilchardus). 1100m, Sparaillon (Diplodus sargus).

2012, Sept. 15   *Perf. 13¼*
1533-1536 A681 Set of 4   5.50 2.75

Arab Post Day — A682

2012, Aug. 3   *Perf. 13*
1537 A682 600m multi   1.40   .70

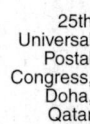 

25th Universal Postal Congress, Doha, Qatar A683

2012, Sept. 24
1538 A683 1000m multi   2.50 1.25

Values are for stamps with surrounding selvage.

Famous Tunisians A684

Designs: No. 1539, 250m, Sheikh Salem Bouhajeb (1827-1926). No. 1540, 250m, Hamda Ben Tijani (1901-83), actor. 390m, Mohamed Bechrouch (1911-44), writer. 600m, Salah Khemissi (1912-58), singer. 900m, Sheikh Mohamed El Fadhel Ben Achour (1909-70), theologian. 1350m, Tawhida Ben Cheikh (1909-2010), physician.

2012, Oct. 16   *Perf. 12¾x13*
1539-1544 A684 Set of 6   9.00 4.50

Intl. Anti-Corruption Day — A685

2012, Dec. 9   *Perf. 13*
1545 A685 700m multi   1.60   .80

World Water Day — A686

2013, Mar. 22   *Perf. 12¾*
1546 A686 2350m multi   4.75 2.50

Train Station, Tozeur A687

Medina, Tozeur — A688

2013, Apr. 26
1547 A687 250m multi   .50   .25
1548 A688 600m multi   1.20   .60

Kairouani Kufic Calligraphy — A689

2013, May 18   *Perf. 13*
1549 A689 250m multi   .50 .25

African Union, 50th Anniv. A690

2013, May 25   *Perf. 13¼*
1550 A690 1100m multi   2.25 1.10

Handcrafted Wood Items — A691

Designs: No. 1551, 250m, Cooking utensils and spice rack (denomination in green). No. 1552, 250m, Rack (denomination in black). 600m, Mortar and pestle. 900m, Clothing box.

2013, June 28   Litho.   *Perf. 13¼*
1551-1554 A691   Set of 4   4.00 2.00

Traffic Accident Prevention A692

2013, Aug. 7   Litho.   *Perf. 13*
1555 A692 1350m multi   2.75 1.50

Lighthouses — A693

Designs: 250m, Cani Island Lighthouse. 600m, Galite Island Lighthouse. 700m, Borj Khadija Lighthouse. 1000m, Borj Jlij Lighthouse.

2013, Sept. 20   Litho.   *Perf. 12¾*
1556-1559 A693   Set of 4   4.75 2.50

Parental Love — A694

2013, Oct. 18   Litho.   *Perf. 13*
1560 A694 250m multi   .50 .25

Intl. Day Against Violence Towards Women — A695

2013, Nov. 25   Litho.   *Perf. 12¾*
1561 A695 600m multi   1.10 .55

Universal Declaration of Human Rights, 65th Anniv. — A696

2013, Dec. 10   Litho.   *Perf. 12¾*
1562 A696 600m multi   1.10 .55

Famous People A697

Designs: No. 1563, 250m, Youssef Rekik (1940-2012), glass painter and playwright. No. 1564, 250m, Ibrahim Dhahhak (1931-2004), painter, vert. 600m, Taher Cheriaa (1927-2010), film maker. 1000m, Zoubeida Bechir (1938-2011), poet.

2013, Dec. 27   Litho.   *Perf. 12¾*
1563-1566 A697   Set of 4   3.50 1.75

Diplomatic Relations Between Tunisia and People's Republic of China, 50th Anniv. A698

2014, Jan. 10   Litho.   *Perf. 13¼*
1567 A698 700m multi   1.25 .60

Adoption of New Constitution — A699

2014, Feb. 7   Litho.   *Perf. 13*
1568 A699 1350m multi   2.25 1.10

Mediterranean Diet — A700

2014, Mar. 25   Litho.   *Perf. 13*
1569 A700 2350m multi   4.00 2.00

Cities — A701

Designs: 250m, Sfax. 600m, Djerba.

2014, Apr. 23   Litho.   *Perf. 13*
1570-1571 A701   Set of 2   1.50 .75
1571a   Souvenir sheet of 2, #1570-1571   1.75 1.75

No. 1571a sold for 1d.

Labor Day — A702

Designs: 250m, Woman's hand, handicrafts. 390m, Books, chemical flasks and beakers.

2014, May 1   Litho.   *Perf. 13*
1572-1573 A702   Set of 2   1.00 .50

A703

National Cleanliness and Environmental Maintenance Day — A704

2014, June 11   Litho.   *Perf. 12¾*
1574 A703 250m multi   .40 .25
1575 A704 1000m multi   1.50 .75

Postal Forum on Electronic Commerce, Hammamet A705

2014, Sept. 22   Litho.   *Perf. 13*
1576 A705 600m multi   .70 .35
a.   Souvenir sheet of 1   1.10 1.10

No. 1576a sold for 1d.

Stamp Day — A706

2014, Oct. 9   Litho.   *Perf. 13*
1577 A706 250m multi   .30 .25

Treaty of Friendship, Commerce and Navigation Between Tunisia and Belgium, 175th Anniv. A707

2014, Oct. 14   Litho.   *Perf. 13*
1578 A707 1000m multi   1.10 .55

World Rural Women's Day — A708

2014, Oct. 15   Litho.   *Perf. 13*
1579 A708 2350m multi   2.60 1.40

Butterflies A710

Designs: No. 1582, 250m, Pyronia cecilia. No. 1583, 250m, Zegris eupheme. No. 1584, 250m, Spialia sertorius. 600m. Pieris brassicae.

2014, Dec. 19   Litho.   *Perf. 13*
1582-1585 A710   Set of 4   1.50 .75
1585a   Souvenir sheet of 4, #1582-1585   1.90 1.90

No. 1585a sold for 1750m.

Traditional Pottery — A711

Designs: Nos. 1586, 1590a, 250m, Djerba jar. Nos. 1587, 1590b, 600m, Sejnane cous-cous pot. Nos. 1588, 1590c, 700m, Jars without decoration. Nos. 1589, 1590d, 1000m, Qalllaline two-handled jar.

2015, Mar. 16 Litho. *Perf. 13x13¼*

Stamps With White Frames

1586-1589	A711	Set of 4	2.75	1.40

Souvenir Sheet

Stamps With Colored Frames

Imperf

1590	A711	Sheet of 4, #a-d	3.25	3.25

No. 1590 sold for 3d. Stamps on No. 1590 have simulated perforations.

SEMI-POSTAL STAMPS

No. 36 Overprinted in Red

1915, Feb. Unwmk. *Perf. 14x13½*

B1	A5	15c vio, *pnksh*	1.40	1.40

No. 32 Overprinted in Red

1916, Feb. 15

B2	A4	5c grn, *grnsh*	2.10	2.10

Types of Regular Issue of 1906 in New Colors and Surcharged

1916, Aug.

B3	A5	10c on 15c brn vio, *bl*	1.40	1.10
B4	A5	10c on 20c brn, *org*	2.10	1.40
B5	A5	10c on 25c bl, *grn*	3.50	3.50
B6	A6	10c on 35c ol grn & vio	10.50	7.00
B7	A6	10c on 40c bis & blk	7.00	4.50
B8	A6	10c on 75c vio brn & grn	14.00	10.50
B9	A7	10c on 1fr red & grn	7.00	7.00
B10	A7	10c on 2fr bis & bl	110.00	110.00
B11	A7	10c on 5fr vio & red	125.00	125.00
		Nos. B3-B11 (9)	280.50	270.00

Nos. B3-B11 were sold at their face value but had a postal value of 10c only. The excess was applied to the relief of prisoners of war in Germany.

Types of Regular Issue of 1906 in New Colors and Surcharged in Carmine

1918

B12	A5	15c on 20c blk, *grn*	2.75	2.75
B13	A5	15c on 25c dk bl, *buff*	2.75	2.75
B14	A6	15c on 35c gray grn & red	3.75	3.75
B15	A6	15c on 40c brn & lt bl	5.00	5.00
B16	A6	15c on 75c red brn & blk	14.00	14.00
B17	A7	15c on 1fr red & vio	32.50	32.50
B18	A7	15c on 2fr bis brn & red	110.00	110.00
B19	A7	15c on 5fr vio & blk	175.00	175.00
		Nos. B12-B19 (8)	345.75	345.75

The different parts of the surcharge are more widely spaced on the stamps of types A6 and A7. These stamps were sold at their face value but had a postal value of 15c only. The excess was intended for the relief of prisoners of war in Germany.

Types of 1906-22 Surcharged

1923

B20	A4	0c on 1c blue	1.10	1.10
B21	A4	0c on 2c ol brn	1.10	1.10
B22	A4	1c on 3c green	1.10	1.10
B23	A4	2c on 5c red vio	1.10	1.10
B24	A9	3c on 10c vio, *bluish*	1.10	1.10
B25	A5	5c on 15c ol grn	1.10	1.10
B26	A5	5c on 20c bl, *pink*	2.10	2.10
B27	A5	5c on 25c vio, *bluish*	2.10	2.10
B28	A9	5c on 30c orange	2.10	2.10
B29	A6	5c on 35c bl & vio	4.25	4.25
B30	A6	5c on 40c bl & brn	4.25	4.25
B31	A9	10c on 50c blk, *bluish*	7.00	5.50
B32	A6	10c on 60c ol brn & bl	10.50	7.75
B33	A6	10c on 75c vio & lt grn	9.00	8.50
B34	A7	25c on 1fr mar & vio	10.50	8.50
B35	A7	25c on 2fr bl & rose	27.50	26.00
B36	A7	25c on 5fr grn & ol brn	70.00	70.00
		Nos. B20-B36 (17)	155.90	147.65

These stamps were sold at their original values but had postal franking values only to the amounts surcharged on them. The difference was intended to be used for the benefit of wounded soldiers.

This issue was entirely speculative. Before the announced date of sale most of the stamps were taken by postal employees and practically none of them were offered to the public.

Mail Delivery — SP1

Type of Parcel Post Stamps, 1906, with Surcharge in Black

1925, June 7 *Perf. 13½x14*

B37	SP1	1c on 5c brn & red, *pink*	.70	.70
a.		Surcharge omitted	140.00	140.00
B38	SP1	2c on 10c brn & bl, *yel*	.70	.70
B39	SP1	3c on 20c red vio & rose, *lav*	1.40	1.40
B40	SP1	5c on 25c sl grn & rose, *bluish*	1.40	1.40
B41	SP1	5c on 40c rose & grn, *yel*	1.40	1.40
B42	SP1	10c on 50c vio & bl, *lav*	2.75	2.75
B43	SP1	10c on 75c grn & ol, *grnsh*	2.75	2.75
B44	SP1	25c on 1fr bl & grn, *bluish*	2.75	2.75
B45	SP1	25c on 2fr rose & vio, *pnksh*	14.00	14.00
B46	SP1	25c on 5fr red & brn, *lem*	50.00	50.00
		Nos. B37-B46 (10)	77.85	77.85

These stamps were sold at their original values but paid postage only to the amount of the surcharged values. The difference was given to Child Welfare societies.

Tunis-Chad Motor Caravan SP2

1928, Feb. Engr. *Perf. 13½*

B47	SP2	40c + 40c org brn	1.40	1.40
B48	SP2	50c + 50c dp vio	1.75	1.75
B49	SP2	75c + 75c dk bl	1.75	1.75
B50	SP2	1fr + 1fr carmine	1.75	1.75
B51	SP2	1.50fr + 1.50fr brt bl	1.75	1.75
B52	SP2	2fr + 2fr dk grn	2.10	2.10
B53	SP2	5fr + 5fr red brn	2.10	2.10
		Nos. B47-B53 (7)	12.60	12.60

The surtax on these stamps was for the benefit of Child Welfare societies.

Nos. 122-135, 137-142 Surcharged in Black

a

b

1938 *Perf. 11, 12½, 12½x13*

B54	A14(a)	1c + 1c	2.75	2.75
B55	A14(a)	2c + 2c	2.75	2.75
B56	A14(a)	3c + 3c	2.75	2.75
B57	A14(a)	5c + 5c	2.75	2.75
B58	A14(a)	10c + 10c	2.75	2.75
B59	A15(a)	15c + 15c	2.75	2.75
B60	A15(a)	20c + 20c	2.75	2.75
B61	A15(a)	25c + 25c	2.75	2.75
B62	A15(a)	30c + 30c	2.75	2.75
B63	A15(a)	40c + 40c	2.75	2.75
B64	A16(a)	50c + 50c	2.75	2.75
B65	A16(a)	75c + 75c	2.75	2.75
B66	A16(a)	90c + 90c	2.75	2.75
B67	A16(a)	1fr + 1fr	2.75	2.75
B68	A17(b)	1.50fr + 1fr	2.75	2.75
B69	A17(b)	2fr + 1.50fr	5.00	5.00
B70	A17(b)	3fr + 2fr	5.50	5.50
B71	A17(b)	5fr + 3fr	21.00	21.00
a.		Perf. 12½	110.00	110.00
B72	A17(b)	10fr + 5fr	45.00	45.00
B73	A17(b)	20fr + 10fr	70.00	70.00
		Nos. B54-B73 (20)	187.75	187.75

50th anniversary of the post office.

Nos. 86, 100-101, 105 Surcharged in Black, Blue or Red

1941 *Perf. 14x13½*

B74	A11	1fr on 45c (Bk)	.55	.55
B75	A13	1.30fr on 1.25fr (Bl)	.55	.55
B76	A13	1.50fr on 1.40fr (Bk)	.55	.55
B77	A13	2fr on 2.25fr (R)	.80	.80
		Nos. B74-B77 (4)	2.45	2.45

The surcharge measures 11x14mm on #B74.

Catalogue values for unused stamps in this section, from this point to the end of the section, are for Never Hinged items.

British, French and American Soldiers SP3

1943 Litho. *Perf. 12*

B78	SP3	1.50fr + 8.50fr crimson	.55	.25

Liberation of Tunisia.

Children — SP3a

1944 Engr. *Perf. 13½*

B78A	SP3a	1.20fr + 1.30fr brown	1.10
B78B	SP3a	1.50fr + 2fr black brown	1.10
B78C	SP3a	2fr + 3fr dark green	1.10
B78D	SP3a	3fr + 4fr red orange	1.10
		Nos. B78A-B78D (4)	4.40

National welfare fund.

Nos. B78A-B78D were issued by the Vichy government in France, but were not issued in Tunisia.

Native Scene — SP4

Surcharged in Black

1944 *Perf. 11½*

B79	SP4	2fr + 48fr red	1.40	1.10

The surtax was for soldiers.

Sidi Mahrez Mosque — SP5

Ramparts of Sfax — SP6

Fort Saint — SP7

Sidi-bou-Said — SP8

1945 Unwmk. Litho. *Perf. 11½*

B80	SP5	1.50fr + 8.50fr choc & red	1.40	1.10
B81	SP6	3fr + 12fr dk bl grn & red	1.40	1.10
B82	SP7	4fr + 21fr brn org & red	1.40	1.10
B83	SP8	10fr + 40fr red & blk	1.40	1.10
		Nos. B80-B83 (4)	5.60	4.40

The surtax was for soldiers.

France No. B193 Overprinted in Black — c

1945 *Perf. 14x13½*

B84	SP147	2fr + 1fr red org	.70	.50

The surtax was for the aid of tuberculosis victims.

Same Overprint on Type of France, 1945

1945   **Engr.**   *Perf. 13*
B85 SP150 2fr + 3fr dk grn   1.10   .55
Stamp Day.

Same Overprint on France No. B192
1945
B86 SP146 4fr + 6fr dk vio brn   .70   .55
The surtax was for war victims of the P.T.T.

Types of 1926 Surcharged in Carmine

1945   **Typo.**   *Perf. 14x13½*
B87 A10   4fr + 6fr on 10c ultra   .70   .35
B88 A12   10fr + 30fr on 80c dk
       grn   .70   .35
The design of type A12 is redrawn, omitting "RF." The surtax was for war veterans.

Tunisian Soldier — SP9

1946   **Unwmk.**   **Engr.**   *Perf. 13*
B89 SP9 20fr + 30fr grn, red &
       blk   1.75   1.40
The surtax aided Tunisian soldiers in Indo-China.

Type of France Overprinted Type "c" in Carmine
1946
B90 SP160 3fr + 2fr dk bl   1.40   1.10
Stamp Day.

Stamps and Types of 1926-46 Surcharged in Carmine and Black

1946   *Perf. 14x13½*
B91 A12   80c + 50c emerald   1.40   1.10
B92 A12   1.50fr + 1.50fr rose lil   1.40   1.10
B93 A12   2fr + 2fr Prus grn   1.40   1.10
B94 A13 2.40fr + 2fr sal pink   1.40   1.10
B95 A13   4fr + 4fr ultra   2.10   1.40
     Nos. B91-B95 (5)   7.70   5.80
The two parts of the surcharge are more widely spaced on stamps of type A13.

Type of France Overprinted Type "c" in Carmine
1947   *Perf. 13*
B96 SP172 4.50fr + 5.50fr sepia   1.40   1.10
On Type of France Surcharged in Carmine with New Value and Bars
B97 SP158   10fr + 15fr on 2fr +
          3fr brt ultra   1.40   1.10

Type of 1926 Surcharged in Carmine

1947   **Typo.**   *Perf. 14x13½*
B98 A13 10fr + 40fr black   1.40   1.10

Feeding Young Bird — SP10

1947   **Engr.**   *Perf. 13*
B99 SP10 4.50fr + 5.50fr dk bl
         grn   1.75   1.40
B100 SP10   6fr + 9fr brt ultra   1.75   1.40
B101 SP10   8fr + 17fr dp car   1.75   1.40
B102 SP10   10fr + 40fr dk pur   1.75   1.40
     Nos. B99-B102 (4)   7.00   5.60
The surtax was for child welfare.

Type of Regular Issue of 1948 Surcharged in Blue

1948
B103 A21 4fr + 10fr ol grn & org   1.40   1.10
The surtax was for anti-tuberculosis work.

Arch of Triumph, Sbeitla SP11

1948
B104 SP11 10fr + 40fr ol grn &
        olive   1.75   1.40
B105 SP11 18fr + 42fr dk bl & in-
        digo   1.75   1.40
Surtax for charitable works of the army.

Arago Type of France Overprinted in Carmine

1948
B106 SP176 6fr + 4fr brt car   1.40   1.10
Stamp Day, Mar. 6-7.

Sleeping Child SP12

1949, June 1
B107 SP12 25fr + 50fr dk grn   2.75   2.10
The surtax was for child welfare.

Neptune Type of 1947 Surcharged in Black with Lorraine Cross and "FFL+15F"
1949, Dec. 8
B108 A20 10fr + 15fr dp ultra &
        car   1.75   1.40
The surtax was for the Tunisian section of the Association of Free French.

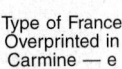 

Type of France Overprinted in Carmine — e

1949, Mar. 26
B109 SP180 15fr + 5fr indigo   2.10   1.40
Stamp Days, Mar. 26-27.

Type of France, 1950, Ovptd. Like No. B106 in Ultramarine

1950, Mar. 11   **Unwmk.**   *Perf. 13*
B110 SP183 12fr + 3fr greenish
         black   2.75   2.10
Stamp Days, Mar. 11-12.

Tunisian and French Woman Shaking Hands SP13

1950, June 5
B111 SP13 15fr + 35fr red   1.75   1.40
B112 SP13 25fr + 45fr dp ultra   1.75   1.40
The surtax was for Franco-Tunisian Mutual Assistance.

Arab Soldier — SP14

1950, Aug. 21   **Engr.**
B113 SP14 25fr + 25fr dp bl   2.75   2.10
The surtax was for old soldiers.

Type of France Overprinted Type "c" in Black
1951, Mar. 10
B114 SP186 12fr + 3fr brnsh gray 2.10 1.40
Stamp Days, Mar. 10-11.

Mother Carrying Child SP15

1951, June 19   **Engr.**   *Perf. 13*
B115 SP15 30fr + 15fr dp ultra   3.50   2.75
The surtax was for child welfare.

National Cemetery of Gammarth SP16

1952, June 15
B116 SP16 30fr + 10fr blue   2.75   2.10
Surtax aided orphans of the military services.

Type of France Overprinted Type "e" in Lilac
1952, Mar. 8   **Unwmk.**
B117 SP190 12fr + 3fr purple   1.75   1.40
Stamp Day, Mar. 8.

Stucco Work, Bardo — SP17

1952, May 5   **Engr.**   *Perf. 13*
B118 SP17 15fr + 1fr ultra & indi-
        go   1.40   1.10
Surtax for charitable works of the army.

Boy Campers — SP18

1952, June 15
B119 SP18 30fr + 10fr dk grn   3.50   2.10
The surtax was for the Educational League vacation camps.

Type of France Surcharged Type "c" and Surtax
1952, Oct. 15
B120 A226 15fr + 5fr bl grn   3.50   2.10
Creation of the French Military Medal, cent.

Type of France Overprinted Type "c"
1953, Mar. 14
B121 SP193 12fr + 3fr vermilion   2.10   1.75
"Day of the Stamp."

Type of France Overprinted Type "c"
1954, Mar. 20
B122 SP196 12fr + 3fr indigo   2.10   1.75
Stamp Day.

Balloon Post, 1870 SP19

1955, Mar. 19
B123 SP19 12fr + 3fr red brown   2.10   1.75
Stamp Days, Mar. 19-20.

Independent Kingdom

Franz von
Taxis
SP20

1956, Mar. 17
B124 SP20 12fr + 3fr dark green 1.25 1.25
Stamp Days, Mar. 17-18

Republic

No. 246
Surcharged
in Red

1957, Aug. 8   **Engr.**
B125 A29 20fr + 10fr dp ultra   .70 .70
15th anniversary of the army.

**Florist Type of 1955 with Added
Inscriptions, Surcharged in Red**
1957, Oct. 19   **Perf. 13**
B126 A34 20fr + 10fr dk vio   .70 .70
No. B126 is inscribed "5e. Foire Internationale" at bottom and lines of Arabic at either
side.

Mailman Delivering
Mail — SP21

1959, May 1   **Engr.**   **Perf. 13**
B127 SP21 20fr + 5fr dk brn &
        org brn   .70 .70
Day of the Stamp. The surtax was for the
Post Office Mutual Fund.

Ornamental
Cock — SP22

1959, Oct. 24   **Litho.**   **Perf. 13**
B128 SP22 10m + 5m yel, lt bl &
        red   .75 .35
Surtax for the Red Crescent Society.

Mailman on Camel
Phoning — SP23

1960, Apr. 16   **Engr.**   **Perf. 13**
B129 SP23 60m + 5m ol, org &
        ultra   1.25 .75
Day of the Stamp.

Dancer of
Kerkennah Holding
Stamp — SP24

Stamp Day: 15m+5m, Mail truck, horiz.
20m+6m, Hand holding magnifying glass and
stamps. 50m+5m, Running boy, symbols of
mail.

1961, May 6   **Unwmk.**   **Perf. 13**
B130 SP24 12m + 4m multi   .60 .60
B131 SP24 15m + 5m multi   .75 .75
B132 SP24 20m + 6m multi   .85 .85
B133 SP24 50m + 5m multi   .95 .95
   Nos. B130-B133 (4)   3.15 3.15

Nos. B130-B133
Overprinted

1963, Oct. 24
B134 SP24 12m + 4m cl, vio & ol   .35 .35
B135 SP24 15m + 5m ol, cl & vio
        bl   .40 .40
B136 SP24 20m + 6m multi   .50 .50
B137 SP24 50m + 5m multi   .85 .85
   Nos. B134-B137 (4)   2.10 2.10
United Nations Day.

Old Man, Red
Crescent — SP25

Tunisian Red Crescent: 75m+10m, Mother,
child and Red Crescent.

1972, May 8   **Engr.**   **Perf. 13**
B138 SP25 10m + 10m pur & dk
        red   .50 .35
B139 SP25 75m + 10m bis brn &
        dl red   .75 .40

Nurse Holding
Bottle of
Blood — SP26

Design: 60m+10m, Red Crescent and
blood donors' arms, horiz.

1973, May 10   **Engr.**   **Perf. 13**
B140 SP26 25m + 10m multi   .60 .40
B141 SP26 60m + 10m gray &
        car   1.00 .40
Red Crescent appeal for blood donors.

Blood
Donors — SP27

Red Crescent Society: 75m+10m, Blood
transfusion, symbolic design.

1974, May 8   **Photo.**   **Perf. 14x13**
B142 SP27 25m + 10m multi   .50 .40
B143 SP27 75m + 10m multi   .75 .50

Man Holding
Scales with
Balanced
Diet — SP28

1975, May 8   **Photo.**   **Perf. 11½**
B144 SP28 50m + 10m multi   .65 .40
Tunisian Red Crescent fighting malnutrition.

Blood Donation,
Woman and
Man — SP29

1976, May 8   **Photo.**   **Perf. 11½**
B145 SP29 40m + 10m multi   1.20 .35
Tunisian Red Crescent Society.

Litter
Bearers
and Red
Crescent
SP30

1977, May 8   **Photo.**   **Perf. 13½x14**
B146 SP30 50m + 10m multi   .65 .40
Tunisian Red Crescent Society.

Blood
Donors — SP31

1978, May 8   **Photo.**   **Perf. 13x14**
B147 SP31 50m + 10m multi   .65 .40
Blood drive of Tunisian Red Crescent
Society.

Hand and Red
Crescent — SP32

1979, May 8   **Photo.**   **Perf. 13½**
B148 SP32 50m + 10m multi   .65 .40
Tunisian Red Crescent Society.

Red Crescent
Society — SP33

1980, May 8   **Photo.**   **Perf. 13½**
B149 SP33 50m + 10m multi   .65 .40

Red Crescent
Society — SP34

1981, May 8   **Perf. 14½x13½**
B150 SP34 50m + 10m multi   .55 .35

Dome of
the Rock,
Jerusalem
SP35

1981, Nov. 29   **Photo.**   **Perf. 13½**
B151 SP35 50m + 5m multi   .55 .35
B152 SP35 150m + 5m multi   1.00 .60
B153 SP35 200m + 5m multi   1.60 .70
   Nos. B151-B153 (3)   3.15 1.65
Intl. Palestinian Solidarity Day.

Red
Crescent
Society
SP36

1982, May 8   **Photo.**   **Perf. 13½**
B154 SP36 80m + 10m multi   .65 .40

Red Crescent
Society — SP37

1983, May 8   **Litho.**   **Perf. 14x13½**
B155 SP37 80m + 10m multi   .75 .35

Sabra and Chatilla Massacre — SP38

1983, Sept. 20   Photo.   Perf. 13
B156 SP38 80m + 5m multi   .75   .50

Red Crescent Society — SP39

1984, May 8   Litho.   Perf. 12½
B157 SP39 80m + 10m First aid   .65   .40

Red Crescent Society — SP40

1985, May 8   Litho.   Perf. 14
B158 SP40 100m + 10m multi   .50   .25

Red Crescent Society — SP41

1986, May 9   Litho.   Perf. 14½x13½
B159 SP41 120m + 10m Map of
         Tunisia   1.10   .40

Red Crescent Society — SP42

1987, May 8   Litho.   Perf. 13x13½
B160 SP42 150m + 10m multi   .75   .45

Intl. Red Cross and Red Crescent
Organizations, 125th Anniv. — SP43

1988, May 9   Photo.   Perf. 14
B161 SP43 150m + 10m multi   .75   .40

Red Crescent Society SP44

1989, May 8   Photo.   Perf. 11½
         Granite Paper
B162 SP44 150m +10m multi   .60   .30

Red Crescent Society — SP45

1990, May 8   Litho.   Perf. 14x13½
B163 SP45 150m +10m multi   .60   .25

Red Crescent Society — SP46

1991, May 8   Litho.   Perf. 13½
B164 SP46 180m +10m multi   .85   .45

Red Crescent Society — SP47

1993, Aug. 17   Litho.   Perf. 14x13½
B165 SP47 120m +30m multi   .85   .30

AIR POST STAMPS

No. 43
Surcharged
in Red

1919, Apr.   Unwmk.   Perf. 14x13½
C1   A6 30c on 35c ol grn &
         brn   1.40   1.40
 a.   Inverted surcharge   160.00
 b.   Double surcharge   160.00
 c.   Double inverted surcharge   190.00
 d.   Double surcharge, one invert-
         ed   160.00

Type A6,
Overprinted
in Rose

1920, Apr.
C2   A6 30c ol grn, bl & rose   1.10   1.10

Nos. 53
and 55
Overprinted
in Red

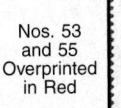

1927, Mar. 24
C3   A7 1fr indigo & ultra   1.10   .70
C4   A7 2fr grn & red, *pink*   3.50   2.10

Nos. 51
and 57
Srchd. in
Black or
Red

C5   A6 1.75fr on 75c (Bk)   1.10   .70
C6   A7 1.75fr on 5fr (R)   3.50   2.10

Type A13 Ovptd. like #C3-C4 in Blue
1928, Feb.
C7   A13 1.30fr org & lt vio   3.50   1.40
C8   A13 1.80fr gray grn & red   4.25   1.10
C9   A13 2.55fr lil & ol brn   3.50   1.10
     Nos. C7-C9 (3)   11.25   3.60

Type A13 Surcharged like #C5-C6 in
         Blue
1930, Aug.
C10 A13 1.50fr on 1.30fr org &
         lt vio   2.75   .85
C11 A13 1.50fr on 1.80fr gray
         grn & red   4.25   .70
C12 A13 1.50fr on 2.55fr lil & ol
         brn   8.50   2.10
     Nos. C10-C12 (3)   15.50   3.65

> **Catalogue values for unused stamps in this section, from this point to the end of the section, are for Never Hinged items.**

UPU Type of Regular Issue
1949, Oct. 28   Engr.   Perf. 13
C13 A23 25fr dk bl, *bluish*   2.50   1.75
UPU, 75th anniv. Exists imperf.; value $40.

Bird from
Antique
Mosaic,
Museum of
Sousse
AP2

1949   Unwmk.
C14 AP2 200fr dk bl & indigo   8.00   2.10

(Arabic on
one
line) — AP3

1950-51
C15 AP3 100fr bl grn & brn   5.00   1.40
C16 AP3 200fr dk bl & ind ('51)   10.50   3.50

Monastir
AP4

Coast at
Korbous
AP5

Design: 1000fr, Air view of Tozeur mosque.

1953-54
C17 AP4 100fr dk bl, ind &
         dk grn ('54)   4.50   1.10
C18 AP4 200fr cl, blk brn &
         red brn
         ('54)   6.25   1.75
C19 AP5 500fr dk brn & ul-
         tra   35.00 12.50
C20 AP5 1000fr dk green   60.00 25.00
     Nos. C17-C20 (4)   105.75 40.35

Imperforates exist.

Independent Kingdom
Types of 1953-54 Redrawn with "RF"
         Omitted
1956, Mar. 1
C21 AP4 100fr slate bl, indigo
         & dk grn   1.50   .70
C22 AP4 200fr multi   3.00   1.40
C23 AP5 500fr dk brn & ultra   6.00   6.00
C24 AP5 1000fr dk green   12.00 12.00
     Nos. C21-C24 (4)   22.50 20.10

Republic

Desert
Swallows — AP6

Birds: #C26, Butcherbird. #C27, Cream-
colored courser. 100m, European chaffinch.
150m, Pink flamingoes. 200m, Barbary partridges. 300m, European roller. 500m,
Bustard.

1965-66   Photo.   Perf. 12½
         Size: 23x31mm
C25 AP6 25m multi   .75   .30
C26 AP6 55m blk & lt bl   1.10   .75
C27 AP6 55m multi ('66)   .90   .55
         Size: 22½x33mm
         Perf. 11½
C28 AP6 100m multi   1.50   .90
C29 AP6 150m multi ('66)   4.75   2.25
C30 AP6 200m multi ('66)   5.75   2.40
C31 AP6 300m multi ('66)   7.50   5.00
C32 AP6 500m multi   11.00   6.00
     Nos. C25-C32 (8)   33.25 18.15

See No. 474.

AIR POST SEMI-POSTAL STAMP

> **Catalogue value for the unused stamp in this section is for a Never Hinged item.**

Window, Great
Mosque of
Kairouan — SPAP1

1952, May 5   Engr.   Perf. 13
CB1 SPAP1 50fr + 10fr blk &
         gray grn   4.25   3.25

Surtax for charitable works of the army.

POSTAGE DUE STAMPS

Regular postage stamps perforated
with holes in the form of a "T," the holes
varying in size and number, were used
as postage due stamps from 1888 to
1901.
For listings, see the *Scott Classic
Specialized Catalogue of Stamps and
Covers.*

D1

Perf. 14x13½
1901-03   Unwmk.   Typo.
J1   D1 1c black   .35   .45
J2   D1 2c orange   .70   .55
J3   D1 5c blue   .70   .45
J4   D1 10c brown   .70   .55

J5	D1	20c blue green	4.25	.85
J6	D1	30c carmine	3.50	.80
J7	D1	50c brown violet	1.75	.85
J8	D1	1fr olive green	1.40	.85
J9	D1	2fr carmine, grn	4.25	1.75
J10	D1	5fr blk, yellow	52.50	35.00
		Nos. J1-J10 (10)	70.10	42.10

No. J10 Surcharged in Blue

1914, Nov.

J11	D1	2fr on 5fr blk, yellow	3.50	3.50

In Jan. 1917 regular 5c postage stamps were overprinted "T" in an inverted triangle and used as postage due stamps.

D2

1922-49

J12	D2	1c black	.35	.30
J13	D2	2c black, yellow	.35	.30
J14	D2	5c violet brown	.70	.30
J15	D2	10c blue	.35	.45
J16	D2	10c yel green ('45)	.25	.25
J17	D2	20c orange, yel	.35	.45
J18	D2	30c brown ('23)	.35	.30
J19	D2	50c rose red	1.05	.50
J20	D2	50c blue vio ('45)	.25	.25
J21	D2	60c violet ('28)	1.05	.50
J22	D2	80c bister ('28)	.70	.55
J23	D2	90c orange red ('28)	1.10	.65
J24	D2	1fr green	.70	.30
J25	D2	2fr olive grn, straw	1.40	.55
J26	D2	2fr car rose ('45)	.30	.30
J27	D2	3fr vio, pink ('29)	.35	.30
J28	D2	4fr grnsh bl ('45)	.35	.45
J29	D2	5fr violet	.70	.55
J30	D2	10fr cerise ('49)	.35	.35
J31	D2	20fr olive gray ('49)	1.40	1.10
		Nos. J12-J31 (20)	12.40	8.50

Inscribed: "Timbre Taxe"

1950   Unwmk.   Perf. 14x13½

J32	D2	30fr blue	1.75	1.50

> Catalogue values for unused stamps in this section, from this point to the end of the section, are for Never Hinged items.

Independent Kingdom

Grain and Fruit — D3

1957, Apr. 1   Engr.   Perf. 14x13

J33	D3	1fr bright green	.25	.25
J34	D3	2fr orange brown	.25	.25
J35	D3	3fr bluish green	.65	.50
J36	D3	4fr indigo	.65	.50
J37	D3	5fr lilac	.65	.50
J38	D3	10fr carmine	.65	.50
J39	D3	20fr chocolate	2.10	1.60
J40	D3	30fr blue	2.75	2.10
		Nos. J33-J40 (8)	7.95	6.20

Republic

Inscribed "Republique Tunisienne"

1960-77

J41	D3	1m emerald	.50	.25
J42	D3	2m red brown	.50	.25
J43	D3	3m bluish green	.50	.25
J44	D3	4m indigo	.50	.25
J45	D3	5m lilac	.50	.25
J46	D3	10m carmine rose	1.00	.50
J47	D3	20m violet brown	1.50	.75
J48	D3	30m blue	1.75	.90
J49	D3	40m lake ('77)	.50	.25
J50	D3	100m blue green ('77)	1.00	.50
		Nos. J41-J50 (10)	8.25	4.15

PARCEL POST STAMPS

Mail Delivery — PP1

1906   Unwmk. Typo.   Perf. 13½x14

Q1	PP1	5c grn & vio brn	.70	.55
Q2	PP1	10c org & red	1.10	.70
Q3	PP1	20c dk brn & org	1.75	.70
a.		Center double	450.00	5,000.
Q4	PP1	25c blue & brn	2.50	.70
Q5	PP1	40c gray & rose	2.75	.70
Q6	PP1	50c vio brn & vio	2.75	.70
Q7	PP1	75c bis brn & bl	3.50	.70
Q8	PP1	1fr red brn & red	2.75	.50
Q9	PP1	2fr carmine & bl	8.50	1.10
Q10	PP1	5fr vio & vio brn	23.00	1.40
		Nos. Q1-Q10 (10)	49.30	7.75

Gathering Dates — PP2

1926

Q11	PP2	5c pale brn & dk bl	.45	.45
Q12	PP2	10c rose & vio	.55	.45
Q13	PP2	20c yel grn & blk	.55	.45
Q14	PP2	25c org brn & blk	.55	.45
Q15	PP2	40c dp rose & dp grn	2.75	.55
Q16	PP2	50c lt vio & blk	1.75	.80
Q17	PP2	60c ol & brn red	1.75	.70
Q18	PP2	75c gray vio & bl grn	1.75	.70
Q19	PP2	80c ver & ol brn	1.75	.70
Q20	PP2	1fr Prus bl & dp rose	2.10	.70
Q21	PP2	2fr vio & mag	4.25	.70
Q22	PP2	4fr red & blk	4.50	.70
Q23	PP2	5fr red brn & dp vio	7.00	1.10
Q24	PP2	10fr dl red & grn, grnsh	14.00	1.10
Q25	PP2	20fr yel grn & dp vio, lav	27.00	1.75
		Nos. Q11-Q25 (15)	70.70	11.30

Parcel post stamps were discontinued July 1, 1940.

TURKEY

ˈtər-kē

LOCATION — Southeastern Europe and Asia Minor, between the Mediterranean and Black Seas
GOVT. — Republic
AREA — 300,947 sq. mi.
POP. — 65,599,206 (1999 est.)
CAPITAL — Ankara

The Ottoman Empire ceased to exist in 1922, and the Republic of Turkey was inaugurated in 1923.

40 Paras = 1 Piaster
40 Paras = 1 Ghurush (1926)
40 Paras = 1 Kurush (1926)
100 Kurush = 1 Lira

Catalogue values for unused stamps in this country are for Never Hinged items, beginning with Scott 817 in the regular postage section, Scott B69 in the semi-postal section, Scott C1 in the air-post section, Scott J97 in the postage due section, Scott O1 in the official section, Scott P175 in the newspaper section, and Scott RA139 in the postal tax section.

Watermarks

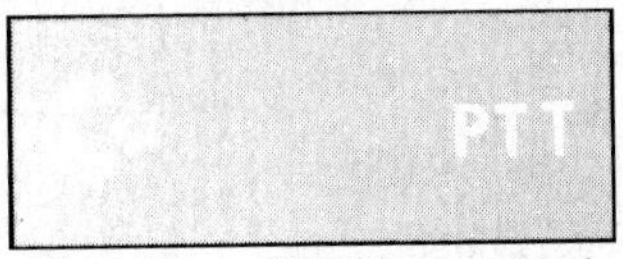

Wmk. 394 — "PTT," Crescent and Star

Wmk. 405

Turkish Numerals

١ ٢ ٣ ٤ ٥
1 2 3 4 5
٦ ٧ ٨ ٩ ٠
6 7 8 9 0

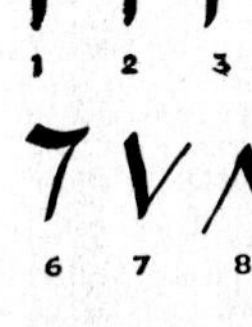 

"Tughra," Monogram of Sultan Abdul-Aziz
A1 A2

A3 A4

1863 Unwmk. Litho. *Imperf.*
Red Band: 20pa, 1pi, 2pi
Blue Band: 5pi
Thin Paper

1 A1 20pa blk, *yellow* 75.00 20.00
a. Tête bêche pair 250.00 200.00
b. Without band 100.00
c. Green band
2 A2 1pi blk, *dl vio* 125.00 20.00
a. 1pi black, *gray* 125.00 21.50
b. Tête bêche pair 400.00 300.00
c. Without band 140.00
d. Design reversed 175.00
e. 1pi blk, *yel* (error) 250.00 150.00
4 A3 2pi blk, *grnsh bl* 115.00 20.00
a. 2pi black, *ind* 115.00 21.50
b. Tête bêche pair 400.00 300.00
c. Without band 140.00
5 A4 5pi blk, *rose* 225.00 45.00
a. Tête bêche pair 500.00 400.00
b. Without band 250.00
c. Green band 275.00
d. Red band 275.00

Thick, Surface Colored Paper

6 A1 20pa blk, *yellow* 250.00 37.50
a. Tête bêche pair 450.00 450.00
b. Design reversed 325.00 325.00
c. Without band 225.00 225.00
d. Paper colored through 225.00 225.00
7 A2 1pi blk, *gray* 300.00 35.00
a. Tête bêche pair 900.00 900.00
b. Design reversed
c. Without band
d. Paper colored through 350.00 225.00
Nos. 1-7 (6) 1,090. 177.50

The 2pi and 5pi had two printings. In the common printing, the stamps are more widely spaced and alternate horizontal rows of 12 are inverted. In the first and rare printing, the stamps are more closely spaced and no rows are tête bêche.
See Nos. J1-J4.

Crescent and Star, Symbols of Turkish Caliphate — A5

Surcharged

The bottom characters of this and the following surcharges denote the denomination. The characters at top and sides translate, "Ottoman Empire Posts."

1865 Typo. *Perf. 12½*

8 A5 10pa deep green 11.00 35.00
c. "1" instead of "10" in each corner 300.00 300.00
9 A5 20pa yellow 7.00 6.00
a. Star without rays 9.00 6.00
10 A5 1pi lilac 12.50 4.00
a. Star without rays 20.00 5.00
11 A5 2pi blue 6.50 4.00
12 A5 5pi carmine 5.50 4.50
d. Inverted surcharge
13 A5 25pi red orange 325.00 250.00

Imperf., Pairs

8b A5 10pa 125.00 125.00
9b A5 20pa 125.00 125.00
10b A5 1pi 100.00 90.00
11a A5 2pi 100.00 90.00
12b A5 5pi 150.00 110.00
13a A5 25pi 900.00 900.00

See Nos. J6-J35. For overprints and surcharges see Nos. 14-52, 64-65, 446-461, 467-468, J71-J77, Eastern Rumelia 1.

Surcharged

1867

14 A5 10pa gray green 9.50
a. Imperf., pair 55.00
15 A5 20pa yellow 15.00
a. Imperf., pair 75.00
16 A5 1pi lilac 20.00
a. Imperf., pair 110.00
b. Imperf., with surcharge of 5pi 200.00
17 A5 2pi blue 5.50 45.00
a. Imperf. 50.00
18 A5 5pi rose 4.50 45.00
a. Imperf. 50.00
19 A5 25pi orange 3,600.
Nos. 14-18 (5) 54.50

Nos. 14, 15, 16 and 19 were never placed in use.

Surcharged

1869 *Perf. 13½*

20 A5 10pa dull violet 100.00 12.00
a. Printed on both sides
b. Imperf., pair 90.00 80.00
c. Inverted surcharge 90.00
d. Double surcharge
e. 10pa yellow (error) 300.00
21 A5 20pa pale green 400.00 14.00
a. Printed on both sides 450.00 275.00
22 A5 1pi yellow 10.00 2.50
c. Inverted surcharge 100.00
d. Double surcharge
e. Surcharged on both sides
f. Printed on both sides
23 A5 2pi orange red 200.00 10.00
b. Imperf., pair 125.00 125.00
c. Printed on both sides 125.00
d. Inverted surcharge 70.00 70.00
e. Surcharged on both sides 140.00
24 A5 5pi blue 5.00 10.00
25 A5 5pi gray 30.00 37.50
26 A5 25pi dull rose 37.50 125.00
Nos. 20-26 (7) 782.50 211.00

Pin-perf., Perf. 5 to 11 and Compound

1870-71

27 A5 10pa lilac 550.00 25.00
28 A5 10pa brown 500.00 15.00
29 A5 20pa gray green 75.00 10.00
a. Printed on both sides
30 A5 1pi yellow 550.00 10.00
a. Inverted surcharge 500.00 80.00
b. Without surcharge
31 A5 2pi red 8.00 5.00
a. Imperf. 20.00 20.00
b. Printed on both sides 40.00
c. Surcharged on both sides
32 A5 5pi blue 5.00 12.50
a. 5pi greenish blue 6.00 8.00
33 A5 5pi slate 40.00 50.00
a. Printed on both sides
b. Surcharged on both sides 80.00
34 A5 25pi dull rose 40.00 75.00
Nos. 27-34 (8) 1,768. 202.50

1873 *Perf. 12, 12½*

35 A5 10pa dark lilac 475.00 25.00
a. Inverted surcharge 90.00
36 A5 10pa olive brown 110.00 17.50
a. 10pa bister 110.00 11.00
37 A5 2pi vermilion 3.50 4.50
a. Surcharged on both sides 22.50 22.50
Nos. 35-37 (3) 588.50 47.00

Surcharged

1874-75 *Perf. 13½*

38 A5 10pa red violet 52.50 7.50
a. Imperf., pair 210.00 50.00
39 A5 20pa yellow green 15.00 5.00
b. Inverted surcharge 30.00 13.00
c. Double surcharge
40 A5 1pi yellow 210.00 30.00
a. Imperf., pair 100.00 80.00

Perf. 12, 12½

41 A5 10pa red violet 25.00 10.00
a. Inverted surcharge 45.00 60.00
Nos. 38-41 (4) 302.50 52.50

Surcharged

1876, Apr. *Perf. 13½*

42 A5 10pa red lilac 2.00 .50
a. Inverted surcharge 70.00
b. Imperf., pair 15.00 15.00
43 A5 20pa pale green 2.00 .50
b. Inverted surcharge 70.00
c. Imperf., pair 15.00 15.00
44 A5 1pi yellow 2.00 .50
a. Imperf., pair 27.50 27.50
46 A5 5pi gray blue 1,700.
47 A5 25pi dull rose 1,700.
Nos. 42-44 (3) 6.00

Nos. 46 and 47 were never placed in use.
See Nos. 64-65.

Surcharged

1876, Jan.

48 A5 ¼pi on 10pa violet 3.00 2.50
49 A5 ½pi on 20pa yel grn 6.25 5.00
50 A5 1¼pi on 50pa rose 2.25 2.50
a. Imperf., pair 60.00
51 A5 2pi on 2pi redsh brn 40.00 7.50
52 A5 5pi on 5pi gray blue 10.00 85.00
Nos. 48-52 (5) 61.50 100.00

The surcharge on Nos. 48-52 restates in French the value originally expressed in Turkish characters.
The vast majority of No. 51 unused are without gum.

A7

1876, Sept. Typo. *Perf. 13½*

53 A7 10pa black & rose lil 2.00 6.25
54 A7 20pa red vio & grn 62.50 5.00
55 A7 50pa blue & yellow 1.25 10.00
56 A7 2pi black & redsh brn 1.60 5.00
57 A7 5pi red & blue 3.00 12.50
b. Cliché of 25pi in plate of 5pi 400.00 375.00
58 A7 25pi claret & rose 15.00 85.00
a. Imperf. 160.00
Nos. 53-58 (6) 85.35 123.75

Nos. 56-58 exist perf. 11½, but were not regularly issued.
See Nos. 59-63, 66-91, J36-J38. For overprints see Nos. 462-466, 469-476, J78-J79, P10-P14, Eastern Rumelia 2-40.

1880-84 *Perf. 13½*

59 A7 5pa black & ol ('81) 3.00 6.50
a. Imperf. 30.00
60 A7 10pa black & grn ('84) 3.00 3.50
61 A7 20pa black & rose 55.00 2.00
62 A7 1pi blk & bl *(piastres)* 75.00 3.00
a. 1pi black & gray blue 85.00
b. Imperf. 60.00
63 A7 1pi blk & bl *(piastre)* ('81) 110.00 5.00
Nos. 59-63 (5) 246.00 20.00

A cliché of No. 63 was inserted in a plate of the Eastern Rumelia 1pi (No. 13). This was found in the remainder stock.
Nos. 60-61 and 63 exist perf. 11½, but were not regularly issued.
See Nos. J36-J38.

1881-82
Surcharged like Apr., 1876 Issue

64 A5 20pa gray 4.25 6.25
a. Inverted surcharge 13.50
b. Imperf., pair 25.00
65 A5 2pi pale salmon 3.00 1.00
a. Inverted surcharge 22.50

1884-86 *Perf. 11½, 13½*

66 A7 5pa lil & pale lil ('86) 200.00 150.00
67 A7 10pa grn & pale grn 1.60 1.25
68 A7 20pa rose & pale rose 2.00 1.25
69 A7 1pi blue & lt blue 2.00 1.25

Perf. 11½

70 A7 2pi ocher & pale ocher 2.25 1.25
71 A7 5pi red brn & pale brn 20.00 25.00
c. 5pi ocher & pale ocher (error) 12.00 12.00

Perf. 11½, 13½

73 A7 25pi blk & pale gray ('86) 300.00 425.00
Nos. 66-73 (7) 527.85 605.00

Imperf

66a A7 5pa 60.00
67a A7 10pa 40.00
68b A7 20pa 40.00
69b A7 1pi 40.00
73a A7 25pi 150.00

1886 *Perf. 13½*

74 A7 5pa black & pale gray 2.00 2.50
75 A7 2pi orange & lt bl 2.00 2.00
76 A7 5pi grn & pale grn 3.00 25.00
77 A7 25pi bis & pale bis 45.00 150.00
Nos. 74-77 (4) 52.00 179.50

Imperf

74a A7 5pa 30.00
75b A7 2pi 40.00
76b A7 5pi 40.00
77a A7 25pi 40.00

Stamps of 1884-86, bisected and surcharged as above, 10pa, 20pa, 1pi and 2pi or surcharged "2" in red are stated to have been made privately and without authority. With the aid of employees of the post office, stamps were passed through the mails.

1888 ***Perf. 13½***
83 A7 5pa green & yellow 2.50 5.00
84 A7 2pi red lilac & bl 1.50 1.50
85 A7 5pi dk brown & gray 5.00 *20.00*
86 A7 25pi red & yellow 30.00 *150.00*
Nos. 83-86 (4) 39.00 *176.50*

Imperf

83a A7 5pa 40.00
84a A7 2pi 40.00
85a A7 5pi 40.00
86a A7 25pi 40.00

Nos. 74-86 exist perf. 11½, but were not regularly issued.

1890 ***Perf. 11½, 13½***
87 A7 10pa green & gray 8.00 1.00
88 A7 20pa rose & gray 1.60 1.00
89 A7 1pi blue & gray 125.00 1.00
90 A7 2pi yellow & gray 2.25 *7.50*
91 A7 5pi buff & gray 5.00 *22.50*
Nos. 87-91 (5) 141.85 *33.00*

Imperf

87a A7 10pa 20.00
88a A7 20pa 20.00
89a A7 1pi 100.00
90b A7 2pi 100.00
91a A7 5pi 25.00

Arms and Tughra of "El Gazi" (The Conqueror) Sultan Abdul Hamid
A10 A11

A12

A13

A14

1892-98 **Typo.** ***Perf. 13½***
95 A10 10pa gray green 2.25 .50
96 A11 20pa violet brn ('98) 1.25 .50
a. 20pa dark pink 7.50 .45
b. 20pa pink 35.00 .45
97 A12 1pi pale blue 110.00 4.00
98 A13 2pi brown org 3.00 1.00
a. Tête bêche pair *30.00 30.00*
99 A14 5pi dull violet 9.00 *15.00*
a. Turkish numeral in upper right corner reads "50" instead of "5" 50.00 45.00
Nos. 95-99 (5) 125.50 *21.00*

See Nos. J39-J42. For surcharges and overprints see Nos. 100, 288-291, 350, 355-359, 477-478, B38, B41, J80-J82, P25-P34, P36, P121-P122, P134-P137, P153-P154.

No. 95 Surcharged in Red

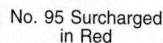

1897
100 A10 5pa on 10pa gray grn 3.00 1.25
a. "Cniq" instead of "Cinq" 20.00 20.00

Turkish stamps of types A11, A17-A18, A21-A24, A26, A28-A39, A41 with or without Turkish overprints and English surcharges with "Baghdad" or "Iraq" are listed under Mesopotamia in Vol. 4.

Turkish stamps of types A19 and A21 with Double-headed Eagle and "Shqipenia" handstamp are listed under Albania in Vol. 1.

A16

1901 **Typo.** ***Perf. 13¼***
For Foreign Postage
102 A16 5pa bister 1.25 .60
103 A16 10pa yellow green 1.25 .60
104 A16 20pa magenta 1.25 .60
a. Perf. 12 2.50 1.00
105 A16 1pi violet blue 1.50 1.00
106 A16 2pi gray blue 2.50 1.00
107 A16 5pi ocher 8.50 3.50
108 A16 25pi dark green 100.00 30.00
109 A16 50pi yellow 250.00 100.00
Nos. 102-109 (8) 366.25 137.30

A17

For Domestic Postage
Perf. 12, 13¼
110 A17 5pa purple 1.25 .50
111 A17 10pa green 1.25 .50
112 A17 20pa carmine 1.25 .50
113 A17 1pi blue 1.25 .50
a. Imperf. 20.00
114 A17 2pi orange 2.00 .50
115 A17 5pi lilac rose 5.75 1.00

Perf. 13½
116 A17 25pi brown 10.00 2.00
a. Perf. 12 25.00 8.50
117 A17 50pi yellow brown 37.50 5.00
a. Perf. 12 55.00 17.00
Nos. 110-117 (8) 60.25 10.50

Nos. 110-113 exist perf. 12x13½.
See Nos. J43-J46.
For overprints and surcharges see Nos. 165-180, 292-303, 340-341, 361-377, 479-493, B19-B20, B37, P37-P48, P69-P80, P123-P126, P138-P146, P155-P164.

A18

1905 ***Perf. 12, 13½ and Compound***
118 A18 5pa ocher 1.00 .50
119 A18 10pa dull green 1.00 .50
a. Imperf. 4.00 3.50
120 A18 20pa carmine 1.00 .50
a. Imperf. 4.00 3.50
121 A18 1pi blue 1.00 .50
122 A18 2pi slate 1.50 .50
123 A18 2½pi red violet 1.50 .50
a. Imperf. 11.00 9.00
124 A18 5pi brown 2.00 .50
125 A18 10pi orange brn 3.75 .50
126 A18 25pi olive green 12.50 15.00
127 A18 50pi deep violet 50.00 30.00

See Nos. J47-J48. For overprints and surcharges see Nos. 128-131, 181-182, 304-314, 351-354, 378-389, 494-508, B1-B3, B21-B23, B39-B40, P49-P54, P127-P129, P147-P150, P165-P171.

Large "Discount" Overprint in Carmine or Blue

1906
128 A18 10pa dull green (C) 3.00 1.00
129 A18 20pa carmine (Bl) 3.00 1.00
130 A18 1pi blue (C) 3.00 1.00
131 A18 2pi slate (C) 17.50 5.00
Nos. 118-131 (14) 101.75 57.00

Stamps bearing this overprint were sold to merchants at a discount from face value to encourage the use of Turkish stamps on foreign correspondence, instead of those of the various European powers which maintained post offices in Turkey. The overprint is the Arab "B," for "Béhié," meaning "discount."

A19

1908
132 A19 5pa ocher 1.25 .50
133 A19 10pa blue green 1.75 .30
134 A19 20pa carmine 40.00 .50
135 A19 1pi bright blue 15.00 .50
a. 1pi ultramarine 50.00 10.00
136 A19 2pi blue black 10.00 .50
137 A19 2½pi violet brown 6.00 .50
138 A19 5pi dark violet 80.00 .50
139 A19 10pi red 70.00 2.50
140 A19 25pi dark green 12.00 5.00
141 A19 50pi red brown 50.00 35.00

See Nos. J49-J50. For overprints and surcharges see Nos. 142-145, 314B-316B, 390-396, 509-516A, B4-B6, B17, B24-B27, P55-P60, P130-P131, P151, P172, Thrace 15.

Small "Discount" Overprint in Carmine or Blue

142 A19 10pa blue green (C) 7.50 2.50
143 A19 20pa carmine (Bl) 7.50 2.50
144 A19 1pi brt blue (C) 15.00 2.50
145 A19 2pi blue black (C) 25.00 12.50
Nos. 132-145 (14) 341.00 65.80

A20

Perf. 12, 13½ & Compound
1908, Dec. 17
146 A20 5pa ocher 1.00 .50
147 A20 10pa blue green 1.50 .50
148 A20 20pa carmine 2.00 1.00
149 A20 1pi ultra 3.00 1.00
150 A20 2pi gray black 12.50 15.00
Nos. 146-150 (5) 20.00 18.00

Imperf

146a A20 5pa 3.00 3.00
147a A20 10pa 4.00 4.00
148a A20 20pa 5.50 5.50
149a A20 1pi 3.00 3.00

Granting of a Constitution, the date of which is inscribed on the banderol: "324 Temuz 10" (July 24, 1908).
For overprints see Nos. 397, 517.

Tughra and "Reshad" of Sultan Mohammed V — A21

1909, Dec.
151 A21 5pa ocher 1.00 .50
152 A21 10pa blue green 1.00 .50
a. Imperf. 3.00 3.00
153 A21 20pa carmine rose 1.00 .50
154 A21 1pi ultra 3.00 .50
a. 1pi bright blue 12.50 .50
155 A21 2pi blue black 3.00 .50
156 A21 2½pi dark brown 90.00 20.00
157 A21 5pi dark violet 12.00 1.00
158 A21 10pi dull red 37.50 1.00
159 A21 25pi dark green 350.00 100.00
160 A21 50pi red brown 150.00 80.00

The 2pa olive green, type A21, is a newspaper stamp, No. P68.
Two types exist for the 10pa, 20pa and 1pi. In the second type, the damaged crescent is restored.
See Nos. J51-J52. For overprints and surcharges see Nos. 161-164, 317-327, 342-343, 398-406, 518-528, 567, B7-B14, B18, B28-B32, P61-P68, P81, P132-P133, P152, P173, Turkey in Asia 67, 72, Thrace 1-4, 13, 13A, 14.

Overprinted in Carmine or Blue

161 A21 10pa blue grn (C) 1.75 .75
a. Imperf.
162 A21 20pa car rose (Bl) 1.75 .75
a. Imperf.
163 A21 1pi ultra (C) 3.50 2.00
a. Imperf. 4.00
b. 1pi bright blue 6.50 3.00
164 A21 2pi blue black (C) 75.00 30.00
a. Imperf.
Nos. 151-164 (14) 730.50 238.00

Stamps of 1901-05 Overprinted in Carmine or Blue

The overprint was applied to 18 denominations in four settings with change of city name, producing individual sets for each city: "MONASTIR," "PRISTINA," "SALONIQUE" and "USKUB."

1911, June 26 ***Perf. 12, 13½***
165 A16 5pa bister 4.50 4.50
166 A16 10pa yel grn 4.50 4.50
167 A16 20pa magenta 9.00 9.00
168 A16 1pi violet blue 9.00 9.00
169 A16 2pi gray blue 9.00 9.00
170 A16 5pi ocher 40.00 60.00
171 A16 25pi dark green 60.00 75.00
172 A16 50pi yellow 100.00 125.00
173 A17 5pa purple 6.00 4.50
174 A17 10pa green 6.00 4.50
175 A17 20pa carmine 9.00 9.00
176 A17 1pi blue 9.00 9.00
177 A17 2pi orange 9.00 9.00
178 A17 5pi lilac rose 40.00 60.00
179 A17 25pi chocolate 85.00 125.00
180 A17 50pi yel brn 100.00 125.00
181 A18 2½pi red violet 65.00 100.00
182 A18 10pi org brn 60.00 60.00
Nos. 165-182 (18) 625.00 802.00

Sultan's visit to Macedonia. The Arabic overprint reads: "Souvenir of the Sultan's Journey, 1329." Values same for all cities. See Nos. P69-P81.

General Post Office, Constantinople
A22

1913, Mar. 14 ***Perf. 12***
237 A22 2pa olive green 1.00 .50
238 A22 5pa ocher 1.00 .50
239 A22 10pa blue green 1.00 .50
240 A22 20pa carmine rose 1.00 .50
241 A22 1pi ultra 1.00 .50
242 A22 2pi indigo 2.00 .50

243 A22	5pi	dull violet	3.50	1.00
244 A22	10pi	dull red	6.00	3.00
245 A22	25pi	gray green	22.50	22.50
246 A22	50pi	orange brown	85.00	125.00

See Nos. J53-J58. For overprints and surcharges see Nos. 247-250, 328-339, 344, 407-414, 529-538, 568, B14-B16, B33-B36, Turkey in Asia 68, Thrace 10, 10A, 11, 11A, 12, N82.

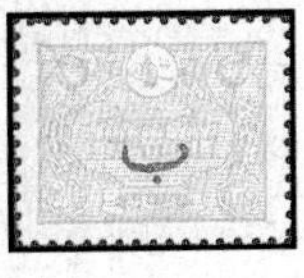

Overprinted in Carmine or Blue

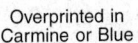

247 A22	10pa	blue green (C)	1.00	.50
248 A22	20pa	car rose (Bl)	1.00	.50
249 A22	1pi	ultra (C)	1.00	.50
250 A22	2pi	indigo (C)	17.50	7.50
		Nos. 237-250 (14)	144.50	163.50

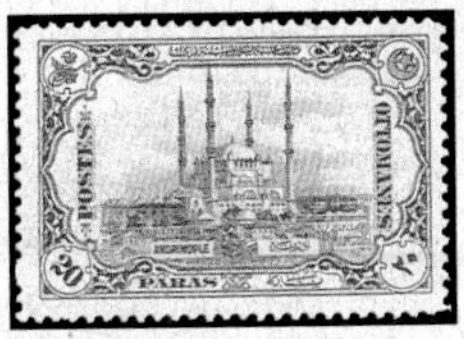

Mosque of Selim, Adrianople — A23

1913, Oct. 23 **Engr.**

251 A23	10pa	green	1.50	1.00
252 A23	20pa	red	2.50	2.00
253 A23	40pa	blue	6.00	3.00
		Nos. 251-253 (3)	10.00	6.00

Recapture of Adrianople (Edirne) by the Turks.

See Nos. 592, J59-J62. For overprints and surcharge see Nos. 415-417, 539-540, J59-J62, J67-J70, J83-J86, Thrace N84.

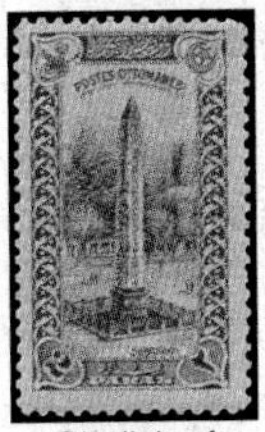

Obelisk of Theodosius in the Hippodrome A24

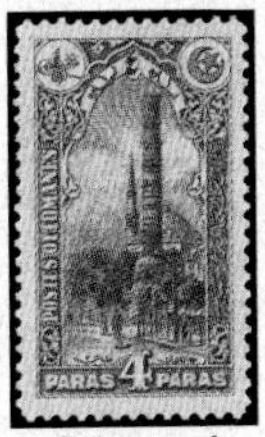

Column of Constantine A25

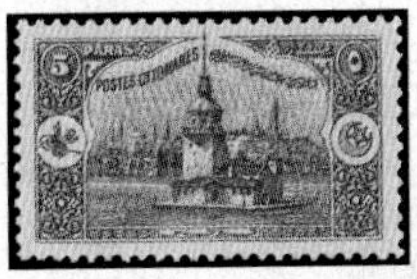

Leander's Tower — A26

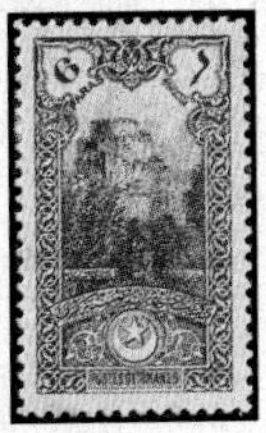

One of the Seven Towers — A27

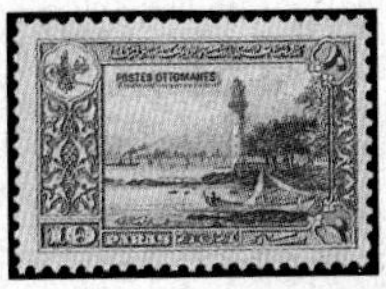

Fener Bahçe (Garden Lighthouse) A28

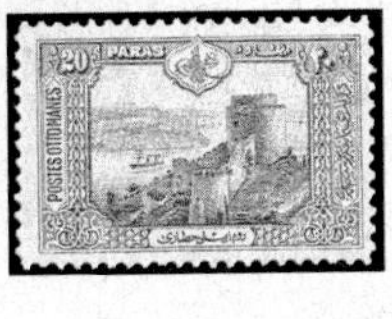

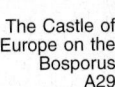

The Castle of Europe on the Bosporus A29

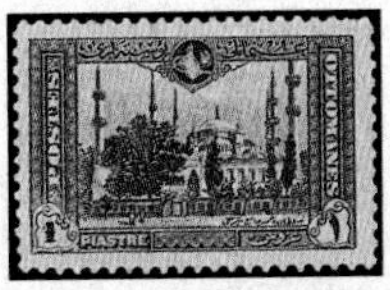

Mosque of Sultan Ahmed — A30

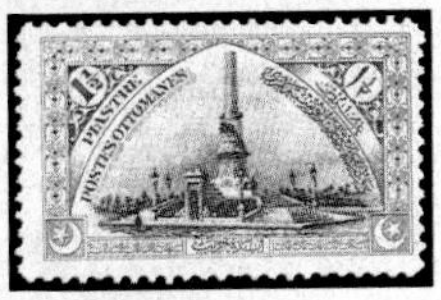

Monument to the Martyrs of Liberty A31

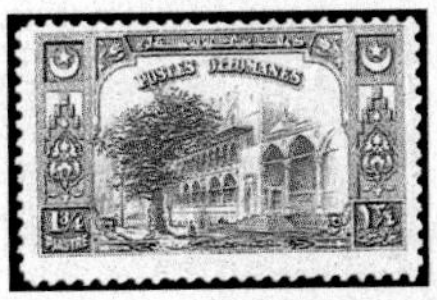

Fountains of Suleiman A32

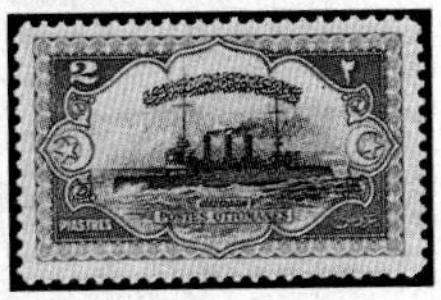

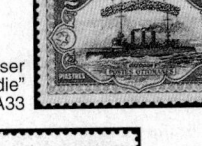

Cruiser "Hamidie" A33

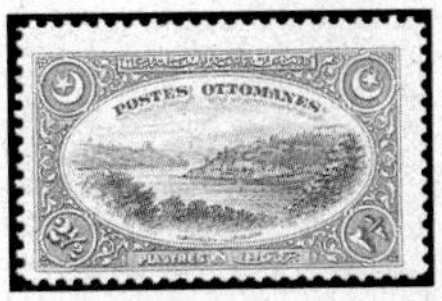

View of Kandili on the Bosporus A34

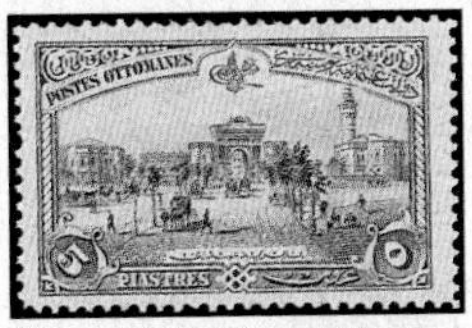

War Ministry (Later Istanbul University) — A35

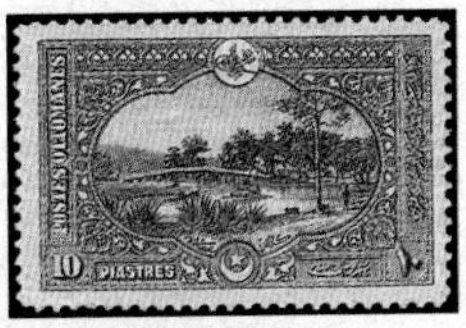

Sweet Waters of Europe Park A36

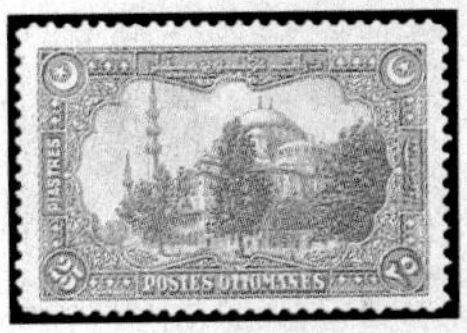

Mosque of Suleiman A37

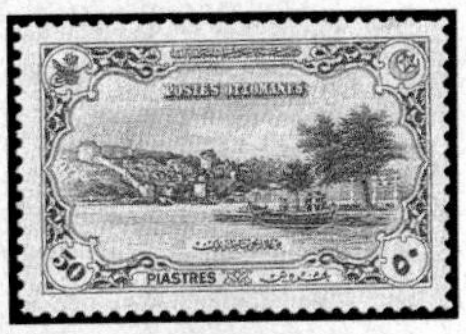

The Bosporus A38

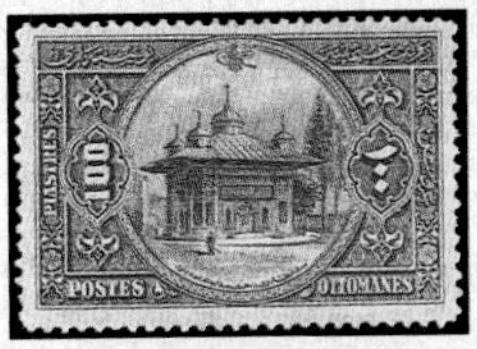

Sultan Ahmed's Fountain A39

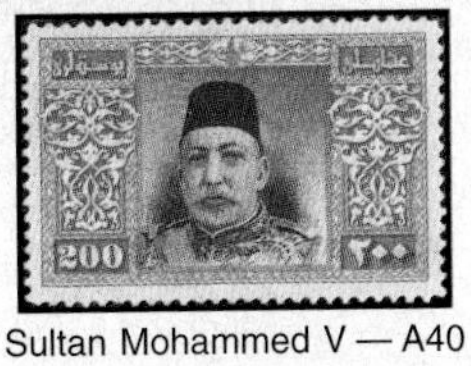

Sultan Mohammed V — A40

Designs A24-A39: Views of Constantinople.

1914, Jan. 14 **Litho.**

254 A24	2pa	red lilac	1.00	.50
255 A25	4pa	dark brown	1.00	.50
256 A26	5pa	violet brown	1.00	.50
257 A27	6pa	dark blue	1.00	.50

Engr.

258 A28	10pa	green	2.00	.40
259 A29	20pa	red	1.75	.40
260 A30	1pi	blue	.75	.50
b.		Booklet pane of 2+2 labels		
261 A31	1 ½pi	car & blk	1.25	.75
262 A32	1 ¾pi	sl & red brn	1.50	1.00
263 A33	2pi	green & blk	2.00	.40
264 A34	2 ½pi	org & ol grn	2.00	.50
265 A35	5pi	dull violet	4.00	1.00
266 A36	10pi	red brown	8.00	1.00
267 A37	25pi	olive green	125.00	5.50
268 A38	50pi	carmine	8.00	3.00
269 A39	100pi	deep blue	75.00	27.50
		Cut cancellation		12.00
270 A40	200pi	green & blk	550.00	*400.00*
		Cut cancellation		25.00
		Nos. 254-270 (17)	785.25	443.95

See Nos. 590-591, 593-598.

For overprints and surcharges see Nos. 271-287, 419, 541, 552-553, 574A, 601, 603-604, P174, Turkey in Asia 1-3, 5-9, 73-74, Thrace N77, N78.

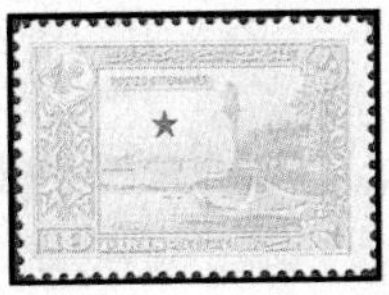

Nos. 258-260, 262-263 Ovptd. in Red or Blue

271 A28	10pa	green (R)	3.00	.75
272 A29	20pa	red (Bl)	10.00	.75
273 A30	1pi	blue (R)	3.00	.75
275 A32	1 ¾pi	sl & red brn (Bl)	4.00	1.25
276 A33	2pi	green & blk (R)	50.00	5.00
		Nos. 271-276 (5)	70.00	8.50

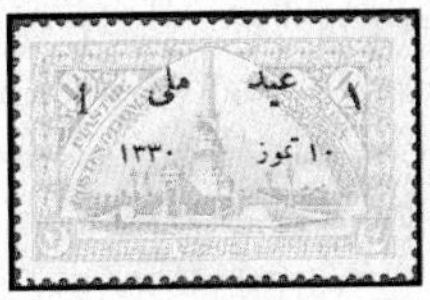

No. 261 Surcharged

1914, July 23

277 A31 1pi on 1 ½pi car & blk		3.25	2.50
a.	"1330" omitted	2.50	1.50
b.	Double surcharge		
c.	Triple surcharge	5.00	5.00

7th anniv. of the Constitution. The surcharge reads "10 July, 1330, National fête" and has also the numeral "1" at each side, over the original value of the stamp.

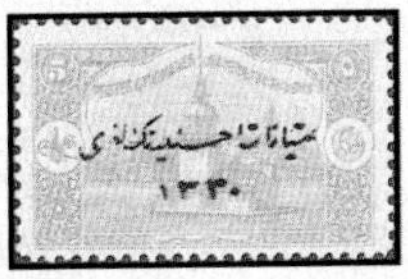

Stamps of 1914 Overprinted in Black or Red

278 A26	5pa	violet brn (Bk)	1.75	.50
279 A28	10pa	green (R)	3.25	.50
280 A29	20pa	red (Bk)	4.00	.50
281 A30	1pi	blue (R)	10.00	1.50
282 A33	2pi	grn & blk (R)	15.00	1.50
283 A35	5pi	dull violet (R)	50.00	4.25
284 A36	10pi	red brown (R)	190.00	65.00
		Nos. 278-284 (7)	274.00	73.75

This overprint reads "Abolition of the Capitulations, 1330".

No. 269 Surcharged

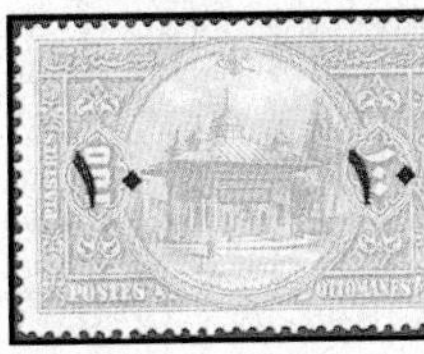

1915

286 A39 10pi on 100pi		62.50	22.50
a.	Inverted surcharge	—	—

No. 270 Surcharged

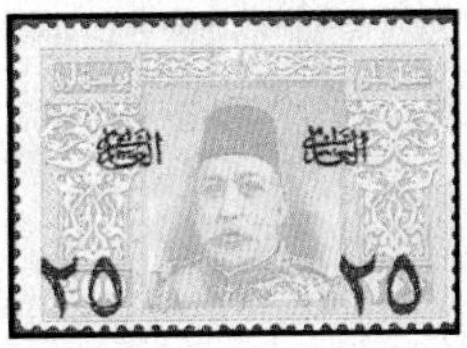

287 A40 25pi on 200pi	25.00	8.00

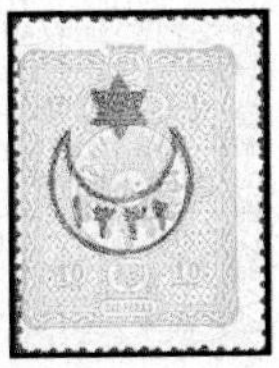

Preceding Issues Overprinted in Carmine or Black

1915 **On Stamps of 1892**

288	A10	10pa gray green	1.00	.50
a.		Inverted overprint	7.50	7.50
289	A13	2pi brown orange	1.50	.50
a.		Inverted overprint	7.50	7.50
290	A14	5pi dull violet	4.00	.50
a.		On No. 99a	17.00	17.00

On Stamp of 1897

291	A10	5pa on 10pa gray grn	1.00	.50
a.		Inverted overprint	5.00	5.00
b.		On No. 100a	10.00	10.00

On Stamps of 1901

292	A16	5pa bister	1.00	.50
293	A16	1pi violet blue	3.00	.50
294	A16	2pi gray blue	2.50	.50
295	A16	5pi ocher	20.00	.50
296	A16	25pi dark green	50.00	20.00
297	A17	5pa purple	1.00	.50
298	A17	10pa green	1.50	.50
299	A17	20pa carmine	1.50	.50
a.		Inverted overprint	7.50	7.50
300	A17	1pi blue	1.50	.50
a.		Inverted overprint	5.00	5.00
301	A17	2pi orange	2.00	.50
a.		Inverted overprint	7.50	7.50
b.		Double ovpt. (R and Bk)	5.00	5.00
302	A17	5pi lilac rose	2.50	.50
303	A17	25pi brown	12.50	2.00

On Stamps of 1905

304	A18	5pa ocher	1.00	.50
305	A18	10pa dull green	1.00	.50
a.		Inverted overprint	5.00	5.00
306	A18	20pa carmine	1.00	.50
a.		Inverted overprint	5.00	5.00
307	A18	1pi brt blue	1.50	.50
a.		Inverted overprint	5.00	5.00
308	A18	2pi slate	2.50	.50
a.		Inverted overprint	10.00	10.00
309	A18	2 ½pi red violet	1.50	.50
310	A18	5pi brown	2.00	.50
a.		Inverted overprint	10.00	10.00
311	A18	10pi orange brown	12.50	.50
312	A18	25pi olive green	50.00	8.00

On Stamps of 1906

313	A18	10pa dull green	2.00	.50
314	A18	2pi slate	5.00	.50
a.		Inverted overprint	5.00	5.00

On Stamps of 1908

314B	A19	2pi blue black	225.00	50.00
315	A19	2 ½pi violet brown	5.00	1.50
315A	A19	5pi dark violet	100.00	35.00
315B	A19	10pi red	15.00	7.50
316	A19	25pi dark green	30.00	5.00
a.		Inverted overprint	17.00	17.00

With Additional Overprint

316B	A19	2pi blue black	15.00	5.00

On Stamps of 1909

317	A21	5pa ocher	1.00	.50
a.		Inverted overprint	10.00	10.00
b.		Double overprint	10.00	5.00
318	A21	20pa car rose	1.25	.75
a.		Inverted overprint	5.00	5.00
319	A21	1pi ultra	2.00	.50
a.		Inverted overprint	5.00	5.00
320	A21	2pi blue blk	2.50	.75
a.		Inverted overprint	5.00	5.00
321	A21	2 ½pi dark brn	67.50	25.00
322	A21	5pi dark violet	1.00	.50
a.		Inverted overprint	6.50	6.50

323 A21 10pi dull red 10.00 .50
324 A21 25pi dark green 1,750. 1,200.

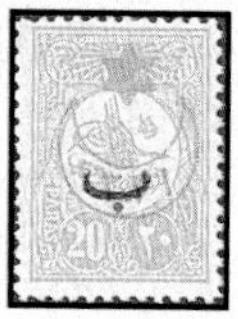

With Additional Overprint

325 A21 20pa carmine rose 2.00 .50
a. Inverted overprint 5.00 5.00
326 A21 1pi ultra 2.00 .50
327 A21 2pi blue black 3.50 .50

On Stamps of 1913

328 A22 5pa ocher 1.00 .50
a. Inverted overprint 7.50 7.50
329 A22 10pa blue green 1.00 .50
a. Inverted overprint 10.00 10.00
330 A22 20pa carmine rose 1.00 .50
a. Inverted overprint 7.50 7.50
331 A22 1pi ultra 1.50 .50
a. Inverted overprint 5.00 5.00
332 A22 2pi indigo 2.00 .50
a. Inverted overprint 5.00 5.00
333 A22 5pi dull violet 3.00 .50
334 A22 10pi dull red 10.00 .50
a. Inverted overprint 10.00 10.00
335 A22 25pi gray green 30.00 20.00

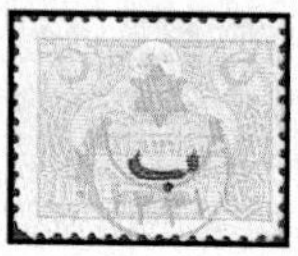

With Additional Overprint

336 A22 10pa blue green 1.00 .50
337 A22 20pa carmine rose 1.00 .50
338 A22 1pi ultra 2.00 .50
339 A22 2pi indigo 7.50 3.00
a. Inverted overprint 10.00 10.00

See Nos. P121-P133.

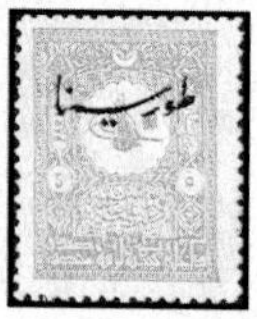

Stamps of 1901-13 Overprinted

1916

340 A17 5pa purple 1.00 .50
a. 5pa purple, #P43 80.00 80.00
341 A17 10pa green 1.50 .50
a. Double overprint 6.50 6.50
b. 10pa yellow green, #103 80.00 80.00
342 A21 20pa car rose, #153 2.00 .75
a. 20pa carmine rose, #162 110.00 110.00
343 A21 1pi ultra 5.50 1.00
344 A22 5pi dull violet 10.00 3.00
Nos. 340-344 (5) 20.00 5.75

Occupation of the Sinai Peninsula.

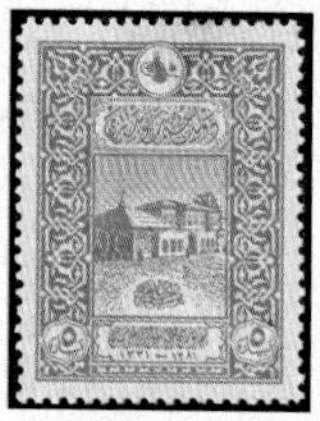

Old General Post Office of Constantinople A41

1916, May 29 Litho. ***Perf. 12½, 13½***

345 A41 5pa green .75 .50
346 A41 10pa carmine .75 .50
347 A41 20pa ultra 1.00 .50
348 A41 1pi violet & blk 1.50 .75
349 A41 5pi yel brn & blk 20.00 2.50
Nos. 345-349 (5) 24.00 4.75

Introduction of postage in Turkey, 50th anniv.
For overprints see Nos. 418, B42-B45.

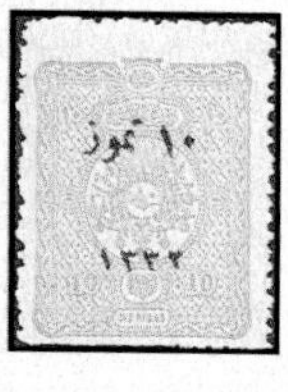

Stamps of 1892-1905 Overprinted

1916

350 A10 10pa gray grn (R) 2.00 2.00
351 A18 20pa carmine (Bl) 3.75 2.50
352 A18 1pi blue (R) 10.00 5.00
353 A18 2pi slate (Bk) 12.50 2.00
354 A18 2½pi red violet (Bk) 20.00 2.25
Nos. 350-354 (5) 48.25 13.75

National Fête Day. Overprint reads "10 Temuz 1332" (July 23, 1916).

Preceding Issues Overprinted or Surcharged in Red or Black

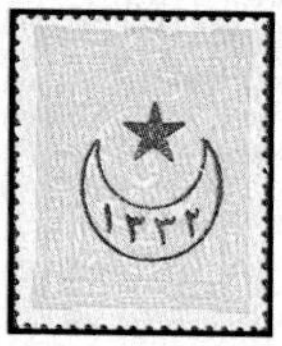

a

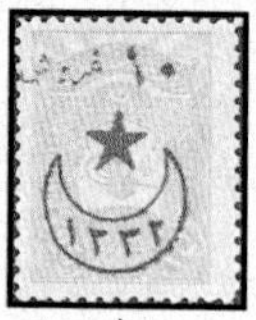

b

1916 **On Stamps of 1892-98**

355 A10(a) 10pa gray green 1.00 .50
355A A11(a) 20pa violet brown 1.00 .50
b. Inverted overprint 10.00 10.00
356 A12(a) 1pi gray blue 50.00 50.00
357 A13(a) 2pi brown org 5.00 1.50
358 A14(a) 5pi dull violet 50.00 50.00

On Stamp of 1897

359 A15(b) 5pa on 10pa gray grn .75 .50

On Stamps of 1901

361 A16(a) 5pa bister .75 .50
a. Double overprint 7.50 7.50
362 A16(a) 10pa yel grn 1.00 .50
363 A16(a) 20pa magenta .75 .50
364 A16(a) 1pi violet blue 1.00 .50
a. Inverted overprint 7.50 7.50
365 A16(a) 2pi gray blue 5.00 1.00
366 A16(b) 5pi on 25pi dk grn 55.00 55.00
367 A16(b) 10pi on 25pi dk grn 55.00 55.00
368 A16(a) 25pi dark green 55.00 55.00
369 A17(a) 5pa purple 75.00 50.00
370 A17(a) 10pa green 2.00 1.50
371 A17(a) 20pa carmine .75 .50
a. Inverted overprint 7.50 7.50
372 A17(a) 1pi blue 1.00 .50
a. Inverted overprint 7.50 7.50
373 A17(a) 2pi orange 1.50 .50
374 A17(b) 10pi on 25pi brown 5.00 1.50
375 A17(b) 10pi on 50pi yel brn 7.50 1.50
376 A17(a) 25pi brown 7.50 1.50
377 A17(a) 50pi yel brn 10.00 2.50

On Stamps of 1905

378 A18(a) 5pa ocher .75 .50
379 A18(a) 20pa carmine 1.00 .50
a. Inverted overprint 10.00 5.00
380 A18(a) 1pi brt blue 2.00 .50
a. Inverted overprint 10.00 5.00
381 A18(a) 2pi slate 1.50 1.00
382 A18(a) 2½pi red violet 7.50 1.50
383 A18(b) 10pi on 25pi ol grn 10.00 3.00
384 A18(b) 10pi on 50pi dp vio 10.00 4.00
385 A18(a) 25pi olive green 10.00 5.00
386 A18(a) 50pi deep violet 7.50 5.00

On Stamps of 1906

387 A18(a) 10pa dull green 1.50 .60
388 A18(a) 20pa carmine 1.50 1.00
389 A18(a) 1pi brt blue 1.50 1.00

On Stamps of 1908

390 A19(a) 2½pi violet brown 67.50 67.50
391 A19(b) 10pi on 25pi dk grn 20.00 12.50
392 A19(b) 10pi on 50pi red brn 67.50 67.50
393 A19(b) 25pi on 50pi red brn 67.50 67.50
394 A19(a) 25pi dark green 15.00 5.00
395 A19(a) 50pi red brown 50.00 50.00

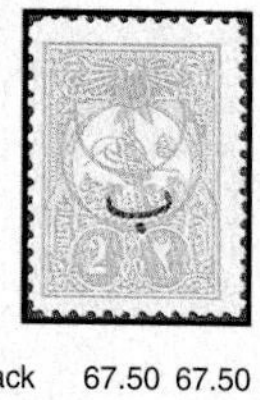

With Additional Overprint

396 A19(a) 2pi blue black 67.50 67.50

On Stamps of 1908-09

397 A20(a) 5pa ocher 67.50 67.50
398 A21(a) 5pa ocher 1.00 2.50
399 A21(a) 10pa blue green 50.00 50.00
400 A21(a) 20pa carmine rose 50.00 50.00
401 A21(a) 1pi ultra 2.00 1.00
402 A21(a) 2pi blue black 4.00 2.00
403 A21(a) 2½pi dark brown 50.00 50.00
404 A21(a) 5pi dark violet 50.00 50.00

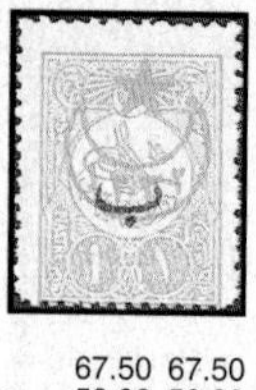

With Additional Overprint

405 A21(a) 1pi ultra 67.50 67.50
406 A21(a) 2pi blue black 50.00 50.00

On Stamps of 1913

407 A22(a) 5pa ocher 1.00 .75
408 A22(a) 20pa carmine rose 1.50 .50
409 A22(a) 1pi ultra 1.50 .50
410 A22(a) 2pi indigo 3.00 1.00
411 A22(b) 10pi on 50pi org brn 12.50 10.00
412 A22(a) 25pi gray green 7.50 5.00
413 A22(a) 50pi orange brown 15.00 12.50

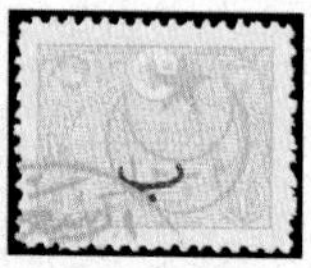

With Additional Overprint

414 A22(a) 1pi ultra 2.00 1.00

On Commemorative Stamps of 1913

415 A23(a) 10pa green 1.25 .50
416 A23(a) 20pa red 2.00 .75
417 A23(a) 40pa blue 6.00 2.50

On Commemorative Stamp of 1916

418 A41(a) 5pi yel brn & blk 1.00 .50

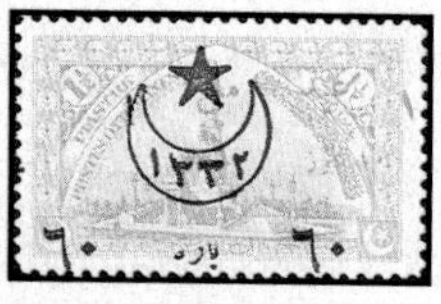

No. 277 Surcharged in Blue

419 A31 60pa on 1pi on 1½pi 3.25 3.50
a. "1330" omitted 40.00 40.00

See Nos. P134-P152, J67-J70.

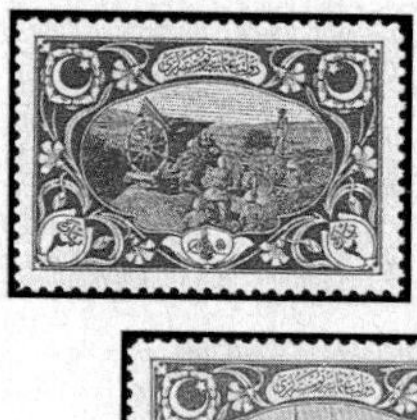

Turkish Artillery A42

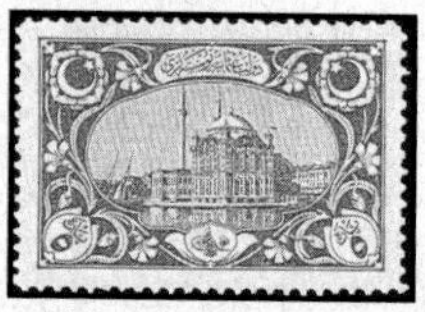

Mosque at Orta Köy, Constantinople — A43

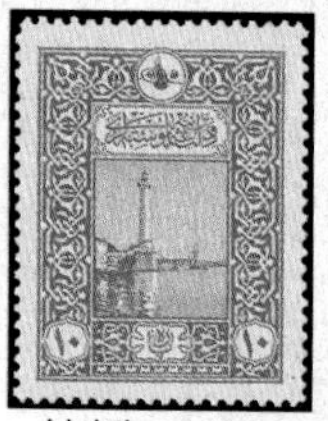

Lighthouse on Bosporus — A44

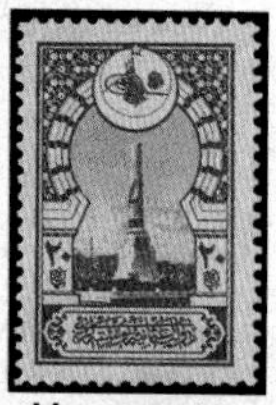

Monument to Martyrs of Liberty — A45

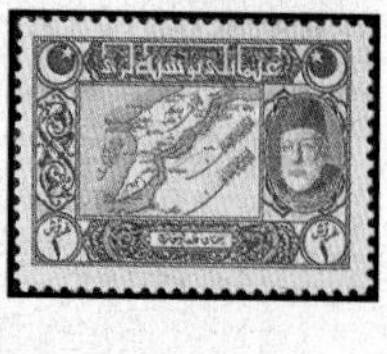

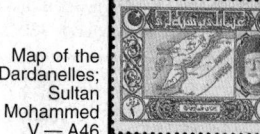

Map of the Dardanelles; Sultan Mohammed V — A46

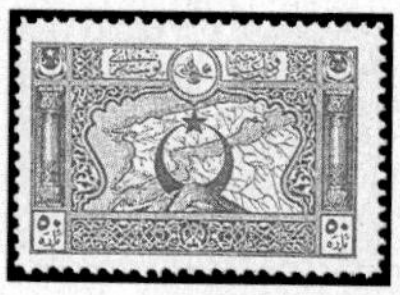

Map of the Dardanelles A47

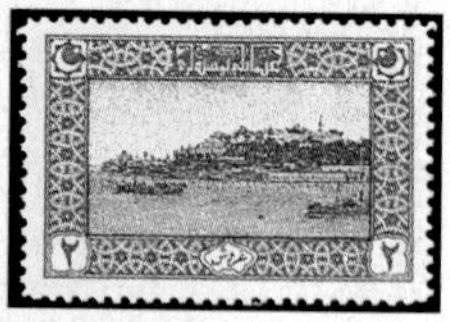

Istanbul Across the Golden Horn A48

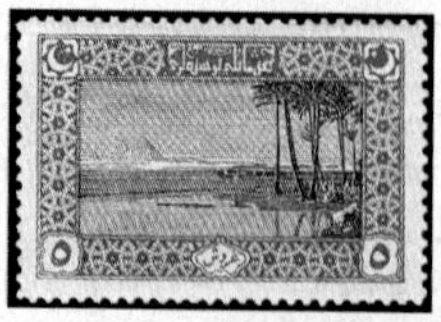

Pyramids of Egypt A49

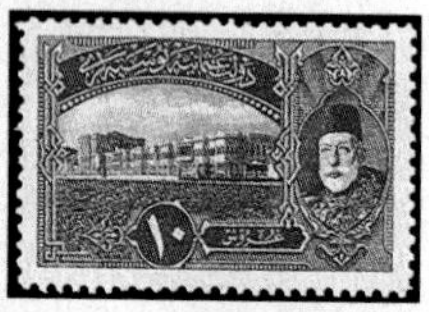

Dolma Bahçe Palace and Mohammed V — A50

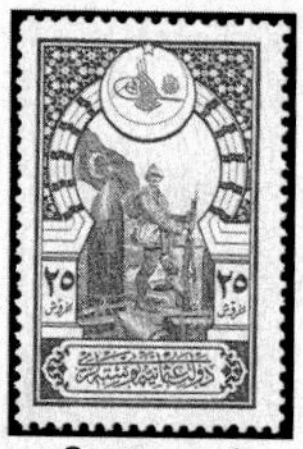

Sentry and Shell — A51

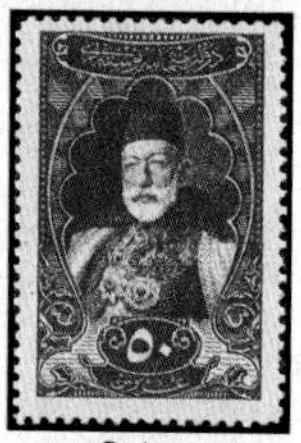

Sultan Mohammed V — A52

1916-18 **Typo.** ***Perf. 11½, 12½***

420 A42 2pa violet 1.50 .75
421 A43 5pa orange 1.00 .75
424 A44 10pa green 1.00 1.00

Engr.

425 A45 20pa deep rose 1.00 .75
426 A46 1pi dull violet 3.00 .50

Typo.

428 A47 50pa ultra 1.50 .50
429 A48 2pi org brn & ind 3.00 .50
430 A49 5pi pale blue & blk 17.50 2.00

Engr.

431 A50 10pi dark green 8.75 5.00
432 A50 10pi dark violet 32.50 2.50
433 A50 10pi dark brown 14.00 2.50
434 A51 25pi carmine, *straw* 2.25 1.50
437 A52 50pi carmine 5.00 5.00
438 A52 50pi indigo 2.00 2.50
439 A52 50pi green, *straw* 2.50 10.00
Nos. 420-439 (15) 96.50 35.75

For overprints and surcharges see Nos. 541B-541E, 554-560, 565-566, 569-574, 575, 577-578, 579A-580, Turkey in Asia 4, 10, 64-66, Thrace N76, N80, N81. Compare designs A42-A43 with A53-A54.

Forgeries of Nos. 446-545 abound.

Preceding Issues Overprinted or Surcharged in Red, Black or Blue

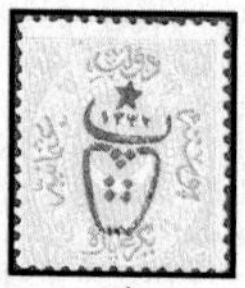

d

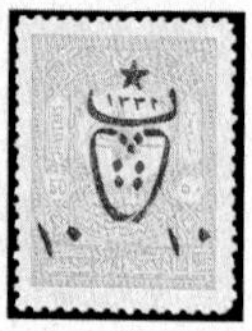

e

f

g

1917   On Stamps of 1865
446 A5(d) 20pa yellow (R)   45.00   67.50
a.   Star without rays (R)   50.00   57.50
447 A5(d) 1pi pearl gray
(R)   45.00   67.50
a.   Star without rays (R)   50.00   57.50
448 A5(d) 2pi blue (R)   45.00   67.50
449 A5(d) 5pi carmine
(Bk)   45.00   67.50

On Stamp of 1867
450 A5(d) 5pi rose (Bk)   45.00   67.50

On Stamps of 1870-71
451 A5(d) 2pi red (Bl)   45.00   67.50
452 A5(d) 5pi blue (Bl)   45.00   67.50
453 A5(d) 25pi dull rose
(Bl)   45.00   67.50

On Stamp of 1874-75
454 A5(d) 10pa red violet
(Bl)   45.00   67.50

On Stamps of April, 1876
455 A5(d) 10pa red lilac (Bl)   45.00   67.50
a.   10pa red violet (Bl)   50.00   67.50
457 A5(d) 20pa pale green
(R)   45.00   67.50
458 A5(d) 1pi yellow (Bl)   45.00   67.50

On Stamps of January, 1876
459 A5(d) ¼pi on 10pa
rose lil (Bl)   45.00   67.50
460 A5(d) ½pi on 20pa yel
grn (R)   45.00   67.50
461 A5(d) 1¼pi on 50pa
rose (Bl)   45.00   67.50

On Stamps of September, 1876
462 A7(d) 50pa blue & yel
(R)   45.00   67.50
463 A7(d) 2pi blk & redsh
brn (R)   45.00   67.50
464 A7(d) 25pi claret &
rose (Bk)   45.00   67.50

On Stamps of 1880-84
465 A7(d) 5pa black & ol
(R)   45.00   67.50
466 A7(d) 10pa black & grn
(R)   45.00   67.50

On Stamps of 1881-82
467 A5(d) 20pa gray (Bl)   45.00   67.50
468 A5(d) 2pi pale sal (Bl)   45.00   67.50

On Stamps of 1884-86
469 A7(d) 10pa grn & pale
grn (Bk)   45.00   67.50
470 A7(d) 2pi ocher &
pale ocher
(Bk)   45.00   67.50
471 A7(d) 5pi red brn &
pale brn
(Bk)   45.00   67.50

On Stamps of 1886
472 A7(d) 5pa blk & pale
gray (R)   4.00   2.25
a.   Inverted overprint   30.00   30.00
473 A7(d) 2pi org & bl
(Bk)   4.50   2.50
a.   Inverted overprint   35.00   35.00
474 A7(d) 5pi grn & pale
grn (R)   45.00   67.50
475 A7(d) 25pi bis & pale
bis (Bk)   45.00   67.50

On Stamp of 1888
476 A7(d) 5pi dk brn &
gray (Bk)   45.00   67.50

On Stamps of 1892-98
477 A11(d) 20pa vio brn
(R)   4.00   3.00
478 A13(d) 2pi brn org
(R)   4.00   3.50
a.   Tête bêche pair   13.50   13.50

On Stamps of 1901
479 A16(d) 5pa bister (R)   3.00   3.00
a.   Inverted overprint   20.00   20.00
480 A16(d) 20pa mag (Bk)   2.00   1.50
a.   Inverted overprint   25.00   25.00
481 A16(d) 1pi vio bl (R)   3.00   3.00
a.   Inverted overprint   20.00   20.00
482 A16(d) 2pi gray bl
(R)   5.00   5.00
483 A16(d) 5pi ocher (R)   32.50   50.00
484 A16(e) 10pi on 50pi
yel (R)   32.50   50.00
485 A16(d) 25pi dk grn (R)   100.00   50.00
486 A17(d) 5pa purple
(Bk)   32.50   50.00
487 A17(d) 10pa green (R)   5.00   5.00

---

488 A17(d) 20pa car (Bk)   2.00   1.50
a.   Inverted overprint   20.00   20.00
489 A17(d) 1pi blue (R)   1.00   .90
490 A17(d) 2pi org (Bk)   3.00   3.00
a.   Inverted overprint   20.00   20.00
491 A17(d) 5pi lil rose
(R)   32.50   50.00
492 A17(e) 10pi on 50pi
yel brn
(R)   45.00   50.00
493 A17(d) 25pi brown (R)   25.00   5.00

On Stamps of 1905
494 A18(d) 5pa ocher (R)   2.00   1.00
a.   Inverted overprint   20.00   20.00
495 A18(d) 10pa dl grn (R)   32.50   50.00
496 A18(d) 20pa car (Bk)   1.00   1.00
a.   Double ovpt., one invtd.   35.00   35.00
b.   Inverted overprint   35.00   35.00
497 A18(d) 1pi blue (R)   1.50   1.00
a.   Inverted overprint   35.00   35.00
498 A18(d) 2pi slate (R)   5.00   5.00
499 A18(d) 2½pi red vio
(Bk)   5.00   5.00
a.   Inverted overprint   20.00   20.00
500 A18(d) 5pi brown (R)   35.00   45.00
501 A18(d) 10pi orange
brn (R)   35.00   50.00
502 A18(e) 10pi on 50pi
dp vio
(R)   35.00   50.00
503 A18(d) 25pi ol grn (R)   35.00   50.00

On Nos. 128-131
504 A18(d) 10pa dl grn (R)   1.50   1.00
a.   Inverted overprint   20.00   20.00
505 A18(d) 20pa car (Bk)   1.00   .75
a.   Double ovpt., one invtd.   20.00   20.00
b.   Inverted overprint   20.00   20.00
506 A18(d) 1pi brt bl (Bk)   1.00   .75
a.   Inverted overprint   20.00   20.00
507 A18(d) 1pi brt bl (R)   1.50   1.25
a.   Inverted overprint   20.00   20.00
508 A18(d) 2pi slate (Bk)   35.00   50.00
    Nos. 494-508 (15)   227.00   311.75

On Stamps of 1908
509 A19(d) 5pa ocher (R)   1.50   1.25
510 A19(d) 10pa bl grn
(R)   20.00   20.00
510A A19(d) 1pi brt blue
(R)   125.00   140.00
511 A19(d) 2pi bl blk (R)   35.00   50.00
512 A19(d) 2½pi violet brn
(Bk)   35.00   35.00
512A A19(d) 10pi red (R)   150.00   225.00
513 A19(e) 10pi on 50pi
red brn
(R)   35.00   50.00
514 A19(d) 25pi dark
green
(R)   35.00   50.00

With Additional Overprint

514A A19(d) 10pa bl grn
(Bk)   150.00   225.00
515 A19(d) 1pi brt bl
(Bk)   35.00   50.00
516 A19(d) 2pi bl blk
(R)   5.00   5.00
516A A19(d) 2pi bl blk
(Bk)   65.00   67.50

On Stamps of 1908-09
517 A20(d) 5pa ocher
(R)   3.00   3.00
518 A21(d) 5pa ocher
(R)   2.00   1.50
a.   Double overprint   20.00   20.00
b.   Dbl. ovpt., one inverted   20.00   20.00
519 A21(d) 10pa bl grn
(R)   2.00   1.50
520 A21(d) 20pa carmine
rose
(Bk)   2.00   1.50
a.   Double overprint   35.00   35.00
521 A21(d) 1pi ultra (R)   1.50   1.00
a.   1p bright blue (R)   30.00   30.00
522 A21(d) 2pi bl blk
(R)   5.00   5.00
523 A21(d) 2½pi dk brn
(Bk)   35.00   50.00
524 A21(d) 5pi dk vio
(R)   35.00   50.00
525 A21(d) 10pi dull red
(R)   35.00   50.00

With Additional Overprint

525A A21(d) 10pa bl grn
(Bk)   175.00   225.00
526 A21(d) 1pi ultra (Bk)   125.00   190.00

---

527 A21(d) 1pi ultra (R)   5.00   4.00
a.   1pi bright blue (R)   125.00   140.00
528 A21(d) 2pi bl blk
(Bk)   35.00   50.00

On Stamps of 1913
529 A22(d) 5pa ocher (R)   2.50   2.00
530 A22(d) 10pa bl grn (R)   35.00   50.00
531 A22(d) 20pa car rose
(Bk)   2.50   2.50
532 A22(d) 1pi ultra (R)   2.50   3.50
533 A22(d) 2pi indigo (R)   3.50   3.50
534 A22(d) 5pi dl vio (R)   35.00   50.00
535 A22(d) 10pi dl red
(Bk)   45.00   50.00

With Additional Overprint

536 A22(d) 10pa bl grn (Bk)   1.50   1.50
a.   Inverted overprint   20.00   20.00
537 A22(d) 1pi ultra (Bk)   3.00   3.00
a.   Inverted overprint   20.00   20.00
538 A22(d) 2pi indigo (Bk)   35.00   100.00

On Commemorative Stamps of 1913
539 A23(d) 10pa green (R)   5.00   5.00
a.   Inverted overprint   20.00   20.00
540 A23(d) 40pa blue (R)   7.00   7.00
a.   Inverted overprint   20.00   20.00

On No. 277, with Addition of New Value
541 A31   60pa on 1pi on
1½pi (Bk)   8.00   5.00
a.   "1330" omitted   45.00   45.00

On Stamps of 1916-18
541B A51(f) 25pi car, straw   5.00   5.00
541C A52(g) 50pi carmine   17.50   17.50
541D A52(g) 50pi indigo   35.00   50.00
541E A52(g) 50pi green,
straw   15.00   27.50

Ovptd. on Eastern Rumelia No. 12
542 A4(d) 20pa blk & rose
(Bl)   35.00   35.00

Ovptd. in Black on Eastern Rumelia #15-17
543 A4(d) 5pa lilac & pale
lilac   45.00   45.00
544 A4(d) 10pa green &
pale
green   45.00   45.00
545 A4(d) 20pa carmine &
pale rose   45.00   45.00

    Some experts question the status of Nos. 510A, 512A and 525A.
    See Nos. J71-J86, P153-P172.

Soldiers in Trench — A52a

1917
545A A52a 5pa on 1pi red   1.25   .75
    It is stated that No. 545A was never issued without surcharge.
    See Nos. 548A, 548Af, 602.

Turkish Artillery A53

1917   Typo.   Perf. 11½, 12½
546 A53 2pa Prussian blue   150.00

    In type A42 the Turkish inscription at the top is in one group, in type A53 it is in two groups. It is stated that No. 546 was never placed in use. Examples were distributed through the Universal Postal Union at Bern.
    For surcharges see Nos. 547-548, Turkey in Asia 69-70.

Surcharged

547 A53 5pi on 2pa Prus bl   15.00   1.75
a.   Inverted surcharge   35.00   15.00
b.   Turkish "5" omitted at lower left

Surcharged

1918
548 A53 5pi on 2pa Prus blue   15.00   2.00
g.   Inverted surcharge   35.00   20.00
    Top line of surcharge on Nos. 547-548 reads "Ottoman Posts."
    For surcharge see Thrace No. N79.

No. 545A
Surcharged

1918
548A A52a 2pa on 5pa on 1pi
red   2.50   1.75
b.   Double surcharge   20.00   20.00
c.   Inverted surcharge   20.00   20.00
d.   Double surcharge inverted   20.00   20.00
e.   Dbl. surch., one inverted   20.00   20.00
f.   In pair with No. 545A   30.00   30.00

Enver Pasha and Kaiser Wilhelm II on Battlefield
A54

St. Sophia and Obelisk of the Hippodrome
A55

1918   Typo.   Perf. 12, 12½
549 A54 5pa brown red   125.00
550 A55 10pa gray green   125.00

    The stamps, of which very few saw postal use, were converted into paper money by pasting on thick yellow paper and reperforating.
    Values are for stamps with original gum. Examples removed from the yellow paper are worth $10 each.

Armistice Issue

Overprinted in Black or Red

1919, Nov. 30
On Stamps of 1913
552 A34 2½pi org & ol grn   125.00   300.00
553 A38 50pi carmine   125.00   300.00
On Stamps of 1916-18
554 A46 1pi dull violet
(R)   7.50   10.00
555 A47 50pa ultra (R),
perf 11½   1.00   1.50
556 A48 2pi org brn &
ind   1.75   2.00
557 A49 5pi pale bl & blk
(R), perf
11½   1.75   2.00
558 A50 10pi dark green
(R)   6.25   10.00
559 A51 25pi carmine,
straw   6.25   10.00

560 A52 50pi grn, *straw*
    (R)   6.25 10.00

Fountain in Desert near Sinai — A56

Sentry at Beersheba — A57

Turkish Troops at Sinai — A58

Typo.

562 A56 20pa claret   1.25 *2.00*
563 A57 1pi blue (R)   125.00 150.00
564 A58 25pi slate blue (R) 125.00 150.00
  Nos. 552-564 (12) 532.00 947.50

The overprint reads: "Souvenir of the Armistice, 30th October 1334." Nos. 562-564 are not known to have been regularly issued without overprint.

See No. J87. For overprints and surcharges see Nos. 576, 579, 582, 583-584, 586, Turkey in Asia 71, Thrace N83.

Stamps of 1911-19 Overprinted in Turkish

"Accession to the Throne of His Majesty, 3rd July 1334-1918," the Tughra of Sultan Mohammed VI and sometimes Ornaments and New Values

Dome of the Rock, Jerusalem — A59

1919

565 A42 2pa violet   1.00 *2.50*
566 A43 5pa orange   .75 .50
567 A21 5pa on 2pa ol grn   .75 .50
  a. Inverted surcharge 10.00 10.00
568 A22 10pa on 2pa ol grn   1.00 .50
569 A44 10pa green   1.25 1.50
  a. Inverted overprint 25.00 25.00
570 A45 20pa deep rose   1.25 .50
  a. Inverted overprint 12.00 12.00
571 A46 1pi dull violet   1.25 1.00
572 A47 60pa on 50pa ultra   1.25 1.00
573 A48 60pa on 2pi org brn & ind   1.00 .50
574 A48 2pi orange brn & ind   1.00 1.00
574A A34 2½pi orange & ol grn   25.00 *37.50*
575 A49 5pi pale blue & blk   1.00 1.00
576 A56 10pi on 20pa cl   1.00 1.00
577 A50 10pi dark brown   2.50 2.50
578 A51 25pi carmine, *straw*   2.00 2.00
579 A57 35pi on 1pi blue   1.50 2.50
579A A52 50pi carmine   25.00 *37.50*
580 A52 50pi green, *straw*   6.00 5.00
581 A59 100pi on 10pa green   6.00 5.00
582 A58 250pi on 25pi sl bl   6.00 5.00
  Nos. 565-582 (20) 86.50 108.50

See note after #586. See #J88-J91.

For overprint and surcharge see Nos. 585, Thrace N82.

Surcharged with Ornaments, New Values and

Perf. 11½, 12½

583 A56 20pa claret   1.75 10.00
584 A57 1pi deep blue   2.50 17.50
585 A59 60pa on 10pa green   1.50 7.50
586 A58 25pi slate blue   9.00 50.00
  a. Inverted overprint   100.00
  Nos. 583-586 (4) 14.75 85.00

#576, 579, 581, 582, 583-586 were prepared in anticipation of the invasion and conquest of Egypt by the Turks. They were not issued at that time but subsequently received various overprints in commemoration of Sultan Mehmet Sadi's accession to the throne (#565-582) and of the 1st anniv. of this event (#583-586).

For surcharge see Thrace No. N83.

Designs of 1913 Modified

1920   **Litho.**   **Perf. 11, 12**
590 A26 5pa brown orange   1.00 .50

Engr.

591 A28 10pa green   1.00 .50
592 A23 20pa rose   1.00 .50
593 A30 1pi blue green   3.75 .50
594 A32 3pi blue   1.00 .50
595 A34 5pi gray   50.00 .50
596 A36 10pi gray violet   12.50 .50
597 A37 25pi dull violet   5.00 2.50
598 A38 50pi brown   5.00 10.00
  Nos. 590-598 (9) 80.25 16.00

On most stamps of this issue the designs have been modified by removing the small Turkish word at right of the tughra of the Sultan. In the 3pi and 5pi the values have been altered, while for the 25pi the color has been changed.

For surcharges see Thrace Nos. N77, N78, N84.

1921-22   **Black Surcharge**
600 SP1 30pa on 10pa red vio   1.50 .50
  a. Double surcharge 37.50 37.50
  b. Imperf.
601 A28 60pa on 10pa green   1.50 .50
  a. Double surcharge 22.50 22.50
602 A52a 4½pi on 1pi red   9.00 4.00
  a. Inverted surcharge 20.00 20.00
603 A32 7½pi on 3pi blue   15.00 2.00
604 A32 7½pi on 3pi bl (R) ('22)   25.00 2.50
  a. Double surcharge 35.00 30.00
  Nos. 600-604 (5) 52.00 9.50

Turkish Stamps of 1916-21 with Greek surcharge as above in blue or black are of private origin.

Issues of the Republic

Crescent and Star — A64

TWO PIASTERS:
Type I — "2" measures 3¼x1¾mm
Type II — "2" measures 2¾x1½mm

FIVE PIASTERS:
Type I — "5" measures 3½x2¼mm
Type II — "5" measures 3x1¾mm

Printed by Ahmed Nazmi, Istanbul

Perf. 13¼x12¾-13¼

1923   **Litho.**   **Thin Paper**
605 A64 10pa gray black   .30 .25
606 A64 20pa olive yellow   .30 .25
607 A64 1pi deep violet   .30 .25
  a. Slanting numeral in lower left corner   .50 .25
608 A64 1½pi emerald   .90 .25
609 A64 2pi bluish grn (I)   .90 .25
  a. 2pi deep green (II)   .90 .25
610 A64 3pi yel brn   .90 .60
611 A64 3¾pi lilac brown   3.00 3.00
612 A64 4½pi carmine   .90 .60
613 A64 5pi deep purple (I)   4.50 1.75
  a. 5pi purple (II)   21.00 1.25
614 A64 7½pi blue   3.00 .60
615 A64 10pi slate   12.00 1.50
  a. 10pi blue   16.00 1.25
616 A64 11¼pi dull rose   3.00 2.50
617 A64 15pi brown   15.00 1.25
618 A64 18¾pi myrtle green   4.25 3.75
619 A64 22½pi orange   12.00 2.50
620 A64 25pi black brown   50.00 3.00
621 A64 50pi gray   125.00 5.00
622 A64 100pi dark violet   250.00 11.00
623 A64 500pi deep green   950.00 275.00
  Cut cancellation   15.00
  Nos. 605-623 (19) 1,436. 313.65
  Set, never hinged 4,250.

Nos. 605-610, 612-617 exist imperf. & part perf.

Printed by Ikdam, Istanbul

1924   **Thick Paper**   **Perf. 11**
605b A64 10pa greenish gray   .90 .25
606b A64 20pa olive yellow   .90 .25
607b A64 1pi deep violet   1.75 .25
  d. Slanting numeral in lower left corner   2.00 .25
609b A64 2pi bluish green (I)   6.00 .90
  d. 2pi bluish green (II)   175.00 2.00
610b A64 3pi yellow brown   150.00 7.50
612b A64 4½pi carmine   1.50 .60
613b A64 5pi purple (II)   3.50 .60
614b A64 7½pi blue   3.50 .60
615b A64 10pi slate   13.00 12.00
617b A64 15pi yellow brown   11.00 12.00
  Set, never hinged 555.00

Printed by Ottoman Public Debt Administration, Istanbul

1924-26   **Thick Paper**   **Perf. 12**
605c A64 10pa black   .30 .25
606c A64 20pa olive yellow   .30 .25
607c A64 1pi violet   .60 .60
609c A64 2pi green (II)   3.00 .60
610c A64 3pi yellow brown   3.50 .60
613c A64 5pi violet   3.50 1.00
615c A64 10pi dark blue   60.00 12.00
  d. 10pi perf. 13¼x12   60.00 12.00
  Set, never hinged 285.00

Bridge of Sakarya and Mustafa Kemal — A65

1924, Jan. 1   **Perf. 12**
625 A65 1½pi emerald   .75 .30
626 A65 3pi purple   .90 .50
627 A65 4½pi pale rose   5.00 2.00
628 A65 5pi yellow brown   4.00 2.00
629 A65 7½pi deep blue   5.00 2.00
630 A65 50pi orange   22.50 10.00
631 A65 100pi brown violet   52.50 20.00
632 A65 200pi olive brown   72.50 35.00
  Nos. 625-632 (8) 163.15 71.80
  Set, never hinged 750.00

Signing of Treaty of Peace at Lausanne.

The Legendary Blacksmith and his Gray Wolf — A66

Sakarya Gorge — A67

Fortress of Ankara — A68

Mustafa Kemal Pasha — A69

1926   **Engr.**
634 A66 10pa slate   .50 .25
635 A66 20pa orange   .50 .25
636 A66 1g brt rose   .50 .25
637 A67 2g green   1.50 .25
638 A67 2½g gray black   2.00 .25
639 A67 3g copper red   2.50 .25
640 A68 5g lilac gray   4.00 .75
641 A68 6g red   1.00 .25
642 A68 10g deep blue   7.50 .50
643 A68 15g deep orange   10.00 .50
644 A69 25g dk green & blk   15.00 1.25
645 A69 50g carmine & blk   20.00 1.50
646 A69 100g olive grn & blk   35.00 2.00
647 A69 200g brown & blk   90.00 5.50
  Nos. 634-647 (14) 190.00 13.75
  Set, never hinged 800.00

Stamps of 1926 Overprinted in Black, Silver or Gold

1927, Sept. 9
648 A66 1g brt rose   .50 .50
649 A67 2g green   .50 1.00
650 A67 2½g gray black   1.50 2.00
651 A67 3g copper red   2.00 2.50
652 A68 5g lilac gray   2.50 4.00
653 A68 6g red   1.50 1.50
654 A68 10g deep blue   3.50 3.50
655 A68 15g deep orange   5.00 5.00
656 A69 25g dk green & blk (S)   15.00 20.00
657 A69 50g car & blk (S)   27.50 37.50
658 A69 100g ol grn & blk (G)   60.00 75.00
  Nos. 648-658 (11) 119.50 152.50
  Set, never hinged 425.00

Agricultural and industrial exhibition at Izmir, Sept. 9-20, 1927.

The overprint reads: "1927" and the initials of "Izmir Dokuz Eylul Sergisi" (Izmir Exhibition, September 9).

Second Izmir Exhibition Issue

Nos. 634-647 Overprinted in Red or Black

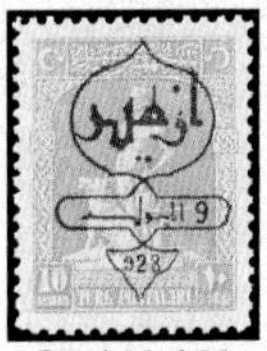

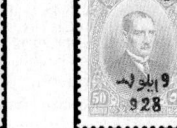

On A66-A68

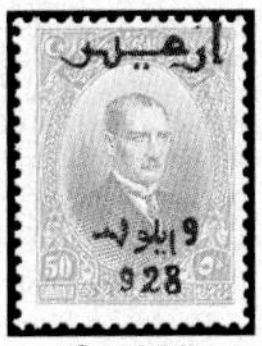
928

On A69

1928, Sept. 9

659	A66	10pa	slate (R)	.50	.40
660	A66	20pa	orange	.50	.40
661	A66	1g	brt rose	1.00	.50
662	A67	2g	green (R)	1.50	1.50
663	A67	2½g	gray blk (R)	1.50	1.50
664	A67	3g	copper red	1.50	1.50
665	A68	5g	lilac gray (R)	2.00	3.00
666	A68	6g	red	.50	.50
667	A68	10g	deep blue	3.50	3.00
668	A68	15g	deep orange	5.00	2.00
669	A69	25g	dk grn & blk (R)	15.00	6.25
670	A69	50g	car & blk	17.50	20.00
671	A69	100g	ol grn & blk (R)	40.00	50.00
672	A69	200g	brn & blk (R)	62.50	62.50
			Nos. 659-672 (14)	152.50	153.05
			Set, never hinged	650.00	

The overprint reads "Izmir, September 9, 1928."

Nos. 636, 652, 654 Surcharged in Black (#673) or Red (#674-675)

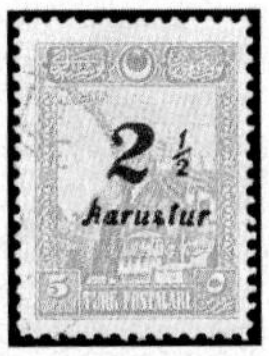
2½
kuruştur

1929

673	A66	20pa	on 1g brt rose	.50	.25
a.			Inverted surcharge	3.50	3.50
674	A68	2½k	on 5g lilac gray	1.00	.50
a.			Inverted surcharge	7.50	7.50
675	A68	6k	on 10g deep blue	6.00	.75
			Nos. 673-675 (3)	7.50	1.50
			Set, never hinged	40.00	

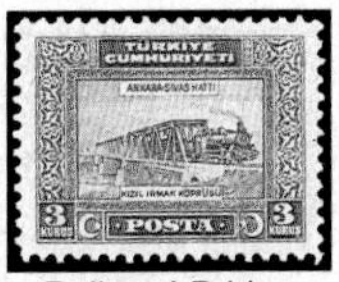
TÜRKİYE CÜMHURİYETİ
POSTA

Railroad Bridge over Kizil Irmak — A70

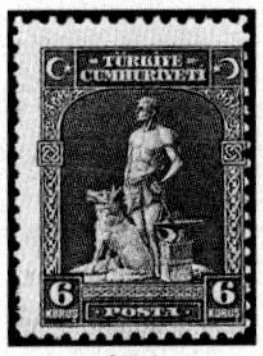
TÜRKİYE CÜMHURİYETİ

A71

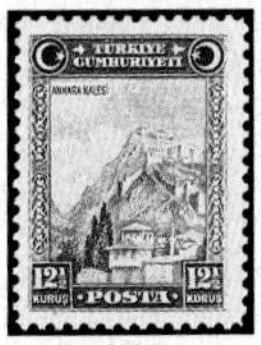
TÜRKİYE CÜMHURİYETİ
POSTA

A72

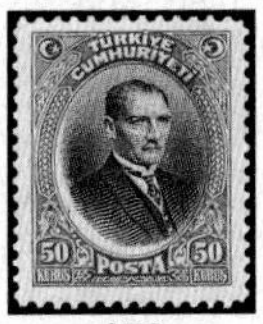
TÜRKİYE CÜMHURİYETİ
POSTA

A73

Latin Inscriptions

Without umlaut over first "U" of "CUMHURIYETI"

1929 **Engr.**

676	A70	2k	gray black	5.00	1.00
677	A70	2½k	green	3.00	1.00
678	A70	3k	violet brown	4.00	1.50
679	A71	6k	dark violet	25.00	1.00
680	A72	12½k	deep blue	35.00	3.75
681	A73	50k	carmine & blk	60.00	8.75
			Nos. 676-681 (6)	132.00	17.00
			Set, never hinged	400.00	

See Nos. 682-691, 694-695, 697, 699. For surcharges & overprints see #705-714, 716-717, 719, 721, 727, 765-766, 770-771, 777, C2, C7.

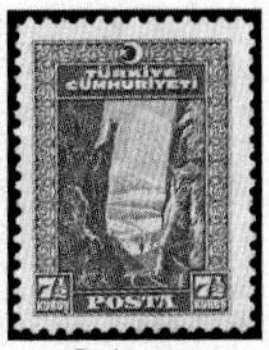
TÜRKİYE CÜMHURİYETİ
POSTA

Sakarya Gorge — A74

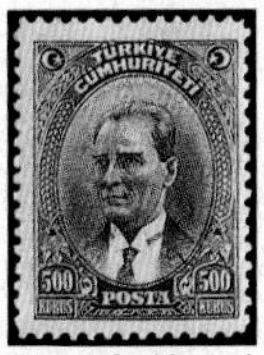
TÜRKİYE CÜMHURİYETİ
POSTA
500

Mustafa Kemal Pasha — A75

With umlaut over first "U" of "CUMHURIYETI"

1930

682	A71	10pa	green	.25	.25
683	A70	20pa	gray violet	.25	.25
684	A70	1k	olive green	.50	.50
685	A71	1½k	olive black	.50	.40
686	A70	2k	dull violet	3.00	.50
687	A70	2½k	deep green	2.00	.50
688	A70	3k	brown orange	20.00	1.50
689	A71	4k	deep rose	7.50	.50
690	A72	5k	rose lake	11.50	.50
691	A71	6k	indigo	7.50	.50
692	A74	7½k	red brown	.25	.25
694	A72	12½k	deep ultra	.75	.25
695	A72	15k	deep orange	.75	.50
696	A74	17½k	dark gray	.75	.50
697	A72	20k	black brown	50.00	2.00
698	A74	25k	olive brown	1.00	1.00
699	A72	30k	yellow brown	1.75	1.00
700	A74	40k	red violet	1.50	1.00
701	A75	50k	red & black	3.50	1.25
702	A75	100k	olive grn & blk	3.50	1.25
703	A75	200k	dk green & blk	3.75	1.50
704	A75	500k	chocolate & blk	17.50	22.50
			Nos. 682-704 (22)	138.00	38.40
			Set, never hinged	600.00	

For surcharges and overprints see Nos. 715, 718, 720, 722-726, 767-769, 772-773, 775-776, 778-780, 823-828, 848-850, C1, C3-C6, C8-C11.

Nos. 682-704 Surcharged in Red or Black

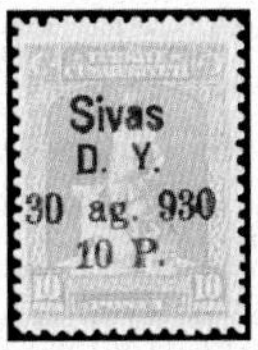
Sivas
D. Y.
30 ag. 930
10 P.

a

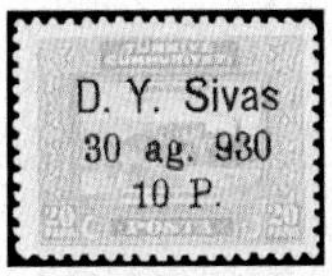
D. Y. Sivas
30 ag. 930
10 P.

b

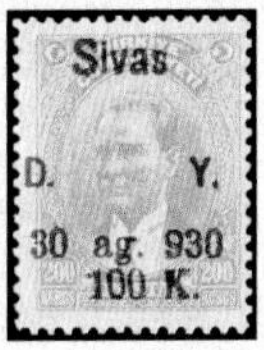
Sivas
D. Y.
30 ag. 930
100 K.

c

1930, Aug. 30

705	A71(a)	10pa	on 10pa (R)	.50	1.25
706	A70(b)	10pa	on 20pa	.50	1.50
707	A70(b)	20pa	on 1ku	1.00	1.50
708	A71(a)	1k	on 1½k (R)	.50	1.25
709	A70(b)	1½k	on 2k	1.00	1.50
710	A70(b)	2k	on 2½k (R)	2.50	2.00
711	A70(b)	2½k	on 3k	2.00	1.50
712	A71(a)	3k	on 4k	2.00	1.00
713	A72(a)	4k	on 5k	2.50	1.00
714	A71(a)	5k	on 6k (R)	3.50	4.00
715	A74(a)	6k	on 7½k	.75	.50
716	A72(a)	7½k	on 12½k (R)	1.25	1.00
717	A72(a)	12½k	on 15k	1.25	1.00
718	A74(b)	15k	on 17½k (R)	5.00	4.00
719	A72(b)	17½k	on 20k (R)	5.00	2.00
720	A74(b)	20k	on 25k (R)	7.50	2.00
721	A72(b)	25k	on 30k	5.00	2.50
722	A74(b)	30k	on 40k	7.50	2.50
723	A75(c)	40k	on 50k	15.00	7.50
724	A75(c)	50k	on 100k (R)	70.00	16.00
725	A75(c)	100k	on 200k (R)	85.00	27.50
726	A75(c)	250k	on 500k (R)	75.00	35.00
			Nos. 705-726 (22)	294.25	118.00
			Set, never hinged	1,200.	

Inauguration of the railroad between Ankara and Sivas.

There are numerous varieties in these settings as: "309," "390," "930" inverted, no period after "D," no period after "Y" and raised period before "Y."

No. 685 Surcharged in Red

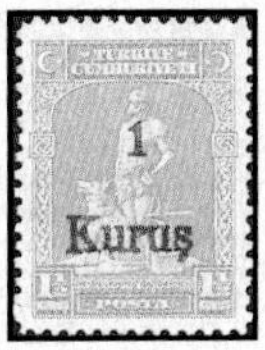
1
Kuruş

1931, Apr. 1

727	A71	1k	on 1½k olive blk	1.75	.30

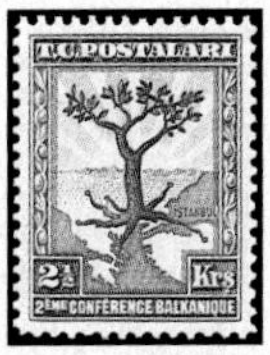
T.C. POSTALARI

Olive Tree with Roots Extending to All Balkan Capitals — A76

1931, Oct. 20 **Engr.** ***Perf. 12***

728	A76	2½k	dark green	.40	.25
729	A76	4k	carmine	.50	.25
730	A76	6k	steel blue	.50	.25
731	A76	7½k	dull red	.50	.25
732	A76	12k	deep orange	1.00	.25
733	A76	12½k	dark blue	1.00	.25
734	A76	30k	dark violet	1.75	1.50
735	A76	50k	dark brown	3.00	.75
736	A76	100k	brown violet	6.25	1.50
			Nos. 728-736 (9)	14.90	5.25
			Set, never hinged	35.00	

Second Balkan Conference.

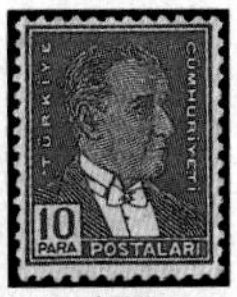
TÜRKİYE CÜMHURİYETİ
POSTALARI

A77

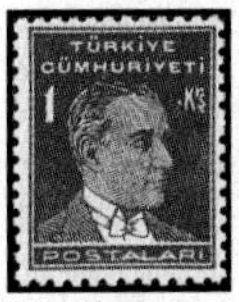
TÜRKİYE CÜMHURİYETİ
POSTALARI

A78

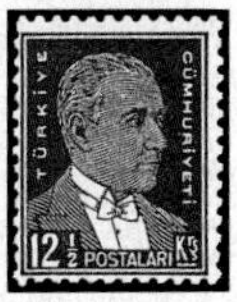
TÜRKİYE CÜMHURİYETİ
POSTALARI

Mustafa Kemal Pasha (Kemal Atatürk) — A79

1931-42 **Typo.** ***Perf. 11½, 12***

737	A77	10pa	blue green	.25	.25
738	A77	20pa	deep orange	.25	.25
739	A77	30pa	brt violet ('38)	.25	.25
740	A78	1k	dk slate green	.25	.25
740A	A77	1½k	magenta ('42)	.55	.25
741	A78	2k	dark violet	.50	.25
741A	A78	2k	yel grn ('40)	.25	.25
742	A77	2½k	green	.50	.25
743	A78	3k	brn org ('38)	1.50	.25
744	A78	4k	slate	2.50	.25
745	A78	5k	rose red	.25	.25
745A	A78	5k	brown blk ('40)	2.00	.50
746	A78	6k	deep blue	3.00	.25
746A	A78	6k	rose ('40)	.80	.30
747	A77	7½k	deep rose ('32)	.50	.25
747A	A78	8k	brt blue ('38)	3.50	.25
b.			8k dark blue ('36)	3.50	.25
748	A77	10k	black brn ('32)	1.00	.25
748A	A77	10k	deep blue ('40)	7.00	.60
749	A77	12k	bister ('32)	1.00	.25
750	A79	12½k	indigo ('32)	1.00	.25
751	A77	15k	org yel ('32)	1.00	.25
752	A77	20k	olive grn ('32)	1.00	.25
753	A77	25k	Prus blue ('32)	2.50	1.00
754	A77	30k	magenta ('32)	7.50	.50
755	A79	100k	maroon ('32)	200.00	5.50
756	A79	200k	purple ('32)	3.75	2.00
757	A79	250k	chocolate ('32)	100.00	11.50
			Nos. 737-757 (27)	342.60	26.65
			Set, never hinged	950.00	

See Nos. 1015-1033, 1117B-1126. For overprints see Nos. 811-816.

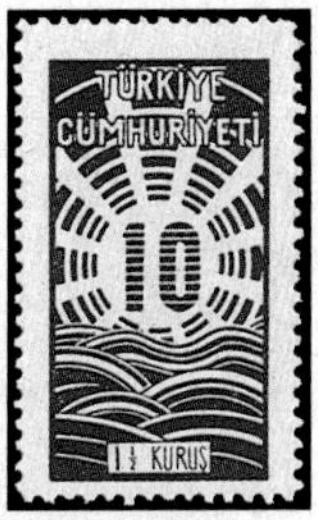
TÜRKİYE CÜMHURİYETİ
10
1½ KURUŞ

Symbolizing 10th Anniversary of Republic — A80

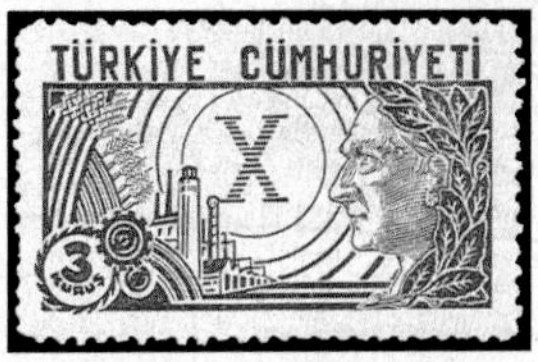
TÜRKİYE CÜMHURİYETİ
X

President Atatürk — A81

1933, Oct. 29 ***Perf. 10***

758	A80	1½k	blue green	1.25	1.00
759	A80	2k	olive brown	1.25	1.00
760	A81	3k	dull red	1.25	1.00
761	A81	6k	deep blue	1.25	1.00
762	A80	12½k	dark blue	3.25	2.50
763	A80	25k	dark brown	8.00	5.00
764	A81	50k	orange brown	20.00	15.00
			Nos. 758-764 (7)	36.25	26.50
			Set, never hinged	90.00	

10th year of the Turkish Republic. The stamps were in use for three days only.

Nos. 682, 685, 692, 694, 696-698, 702 Overprinted or Surcharged in Red

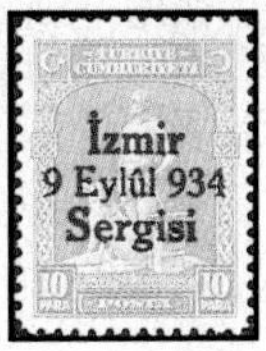
İzmir
9 Eylûl 934
Sergisi

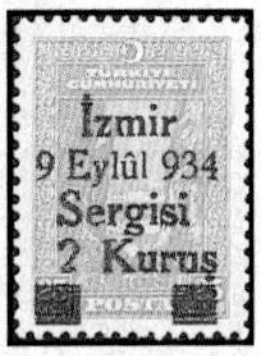
İzmir
9 Eylûl 934
Sergisi
2 Kuruş

1934, Aug. 26 ***Perf. 12***

765	A71	10pa	green	.50	1.00
766	A71	1k	on 1½k	1.00	.75
767	A74	2k	on 25k	1.50	1.25
768	A74	5k	on 7½k	5.00	5.00
769	A74	6k	on 17½k	2.50	2.00
770	A72	12½k	deep ultra	7.50	5.00
771	A72	15k	on 20k	50.00	45.00
772	A74	20k	on 25k	35.00	37.50
773	A75	50k	on 100k	40.00	37.50
			Nos. 765-773 (9)	143.00	135.00
			Set, never hinged	600.00	

Izmir Fair, 1934.

Nos. 696, 698, 701-704 Surcharged in Black

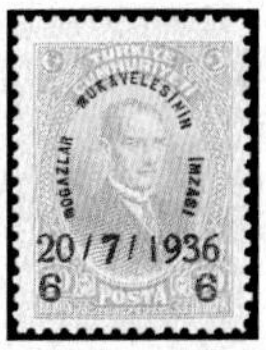
20/7/1936
6 6

1936, Oct. 26

775	A74	4k	on 17½k	1.00	.50
776	A74	5k	on 25k	1.00	.50
777	A73	6k	on 50k	1.00	.50
778	A75	10k	on 100k	1.75	1.00
779	A75	20k	on 200k	5.50	2.00
780	A75	50k	on 500k	10.00	3.25
			Nos. 775-780 (6)	20.25	7.75
			Set, never hinged	75.00	

"1926" in Overprint

775a	A74	4k	on 17½k	6.50	3.75
776a	A74	5k	on 25k	7.00	3.75
777a	A73	6k	on 50k	7.00	3.75
778a	A75	10k	on 100k	9.00	4.50
779a	A75	20k	on 200k	20.00	10.00
780a	A75	50k	on 500k	55.00	27.50
			Nos. 775a-780a (6)	104.50	53.25
			Set, never hinged	250.00	

Re-militarization of the Dardanelles.

Hittite Bronze
Stag — A82

Thorak's Bust
of Kemal
Atatürk — A83

1937, Sept. 20   Litho.   Perf. 12
781	A82	3k light violet	1.75	1.25
782	A83	6k blue	3.00	2.00
783	A82	7½k bright pink	4.75	3.75
784	A83	12½k indigo	10.00	7.50
		Nos. 781-784 (4)	19.50	14.50
		Set, never hinged	40.00	

2nd Turkish Historical Congress, Istanbul,
Sept. 20-30.

Arms of Turkey,
Greece, Romania
and
Yugoslavia — A84

1937, Oct. 29   Perf. 11½
785	A84	8k carmine	6.75	3.50
786	A84	12½k dark blue	15.00	4.75
		Set, never hinged	60.00	

The Balkan Entente.

Street in
Izmir
A85

Fig Tree — A87

30pa, View of Fair Buildings. 3k, Tower,
Government Square. 5k, Olive branch. 6k,
Woman with grapes. 7½k, Woman picking
grapes. 8k, Izmir Harbor through arch. 12k,
Statue of Pres. Atatürk. 12½k, Pres. Atatürk.

1938, Aug. 20   Photo.   Perf. 11½
Inscribed: "Izmir Enternasyonal
Fuari 1938"
789	A85	10pa dark brown	.50	.60
790	A85	30pa purple	.75	.50
791	A87	2½k brt green	1.25	1.00
792	A87	3k brown orange	1.25	.50
793	A87	5k olive green	2.25	.75
794	A85	6k brown	5.00	.40
795	A87	7½k scarlet	5.00	2.50
796	A87	8k brown lake	3.50	1.50
797	A87	12k rose violet	6.25	3.50
798	A87	12½k deep blue	10.00	8.50
		Nos. 789-798 (10)	35.75	19.75
		Set, never hinged	90.00	

Izmir International Fair.

President
Atatürk
Teaching
Reformed
Turkish
Alphabet
A95

1938, Nov. 2
799	A95	2½k brt green	1.00	.55
800	A95	3k orange	1.25	.55
801	A95	6k rose violet	1.50	.65
802	A95	7½k deep rose	1.75	1.00
803	A95	8k red brown	2.00	1.10
804	A95	12½k brt ultra	2.50	1.25
		Nos. 799-804 (6)	10.00	5.10
		Set, never hinged	25.00	

Reform of the Turkish alphabet, 10th anniv.

Army and
Air Force
A96

Atatürk Driving
Tractor — A98

3k, View of Kayseri. 7½k, Railway bridge.
8k, Scout buglers. 12½k, President Atatürk.

1938, Oct. 29
Inscribed: "Cumhuriyetin 15 inc yil
donumu hatirasi"
805	A96	2½k dark green	.60	.35
806	A96	3k red brown	.60	.35
807	A98	6k bister	.90	.35
808	A98	7½k red	2.00	.90
809	A96	8k rose violet	5.00	2.50
810	A98	12½k deep blue	3.75	1.75
		Nos. 805-810 (6)	12.85	6.20
		Set, never hinged	30.00	

15th anniversary of the Republic.

Stamps of 1931-38
Overprinted in Black

1938, Nov. 21   Perf. 11½x12
811	A78	3k brown orange	.75	.35
812	A78	5k rose red	.75	.35
813	A78	6k deep blue	1.00	.50
814	A77	7½k deep rose	1.25	.55
815	A78	8k dark blue	3.00	.75
a.		8k bright blue	225.00	150.00
816	A79	12½k indigo	3.75	1.75
		Nos. 811-816 (6)	10.50	4.25
		Set, never hinged	25.00	

President Kemal Atatürk (1881-1938). The
date is that of his funeral.

> **Catalogue values for unused**
> **stamps in this section, from this**
> **point to the end of the section, are**
> **for Never Hinged items.**

Turkish and
American
Flags — A102

Presidents Inönü and F. D. Roosevelt
and Map of North America
A103

Designs: 3k, 8k, Inonu and Roosevelt. 7½k,
12½k, Kemal Ataturk and Washington.

1939, July 15   Photo.   Perf. 14
817	A102	2½k ol grn, red & bl	.50	.25
818	A103	3k dk brn & bl grn	1.00	.25
819	A102	6k purple, red & bl	1.00	.25
820	A103	7½k org ver & bl grn	2.00	.40
821	A103	8k dp cl & bl grn	1.50	.40
822	A103	12½k brt bl & bl grn	3.50	.85
		Nos. 817-822 (6)	9.50	2.40

US constitution, 150th anniversary.

Nos. 698, 702-704
Surcharged in Black

1939, July 23   Unwmk.   Perf. 13
823	A74	3k on 25k	.40	.25
824	A75	6k on 200k	.65	.50
825	A74	7½k on 25k	.75	.50
826	A75	12k on 100k	1.00	.50
827	A75	12½k on 200k	2.00	.50
828	A75	17½k on 500k	3.00	1.00
		Nos. 823-828 (6)	7.80	3.25

Annexation of Hatay.

Railroad Bridge
A105

Locomotive
A106

Track
Through
Mountain
Pass
A107

Design: 12½k, Railroad tunnel, Atma Pass.

1939, Oct. 20   Typo.   Perf. 11½
829	A105	3k lt orange red	3.50	3.50
830	A106	6k chestnut	4.00	4.00
831	A107	7½k rose pink	6.00	6.00
832	A107	12½k dark blue	9.00	9.00
		Nos. 829-832 (4)	22.50	22.50

Completion of the Sivas to Erzerum link of
the Ankara-Erzerum Railroad.

Atatürk
Residence in
Ankara — A109

Kemal
Atatürk — A110

TÜRKIYE POSTALARI

KEMAL ATATÜRK
1880-1938

A111

Designs: 5k, 6k, 7½k, 8k, 12½k, 17½k, Various portraits of Ataturk, "1880-1938."

1939-40   Photo.
833	A109	2½k brt green	1.00	.50
834	A110	3k dk blue gray	1.00	.50
835	A110	5k chocolate	1.25	.75
836	A110	6k chestnut	1.25	.75
837	A110	7½k rose red	3.75	1.00
838	A110	8k gray green	1.75	1.00
839	A110	12½k brt blue	2.00	1.50
840	A110	17½k brt rose	6.50	2.00
		Nos. 833-840 (8)	18.50	8.00

Souvenir Sheet
841	A111	100k blue black	70.00	100.00

Death of Kemal Ataturk, first anniversary.
Size of No. 841: 90x120mm.
   Issued: 2½k, 6k, 12½k, 11/11/39; others,
1/3/40.

Namik
Kemal — A118

1940, Jan. 3
842	A118	6k chestnut	2.00	.60
843	A118	8k dk olive grn	3.25	1.50
844	A118	12k brt rose red	4.00	2.00
845	A118	12½k brt blue	8.00	3.00
		Nos. 842-845 (4)	17.25	7.10

Birth cent. of Namik Kemal, poet and patriot.

Arms of Turkey,
Greece, Romania
and
Yugoslavia — A119

Perf. 11½
1940, Jan. 1   Typo.   Unwmk.
846	A119	8k light blue	3.50	1.00
847	A119	10k deep blue	7.00	2.25

The Balkan Entente.

Nos. 703-704
Surcharged in Red or
Black

1940, Aug. 20   Perf. 12
848	A75	6k on 200k dk grn &		
		blk (R)	.75	1.00
849	A75	10k on 200k dk grn &		
		blk	1.25	1.50
850	A75	12k on 500k choc & blk	2.00	2.50
		Nos. 848-850 (3)	4.00	5.00

13th International Izmir Fair.

Map of
Turkey
and
Census
Figures
A120

1940, Oct. 1   Typo.   Perf. 11½
851	A120	10pa dark blue green	.50	.25
852	A120	3k orange	1.50	1.25
853	A120	6k carmine rose	2.00	1.50
854	A120	10k dark blue	3.00	2.50
		Nos. 851-854 (4)	7.00	5.50

Census of Oct. 20, 1940.

Runner — A121

Pole Vaulter — A122

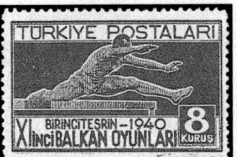

Hurdler A123

Discus Thrower — A124

1940, Oct. 5

855	A121	3k olive green	2.50	2.50
856	A122	6k rose	7.50	3.50
857	A123	8k chestnut brown	3.50	4.00
858	A124	10k dark blue	5.50	10.00
		Nos. 855-858 (4)	19.00	20.00

11th Balkan Olympics.

Mail Carriers on Horseback A125

Postman of 1840 and 1940 — A126

Old Sailing Vessel and Modern Mailboat — A127

Design: 12k, Post Office, Istanbul.

1940, Dec. 31   Typo.   Perf. 10

859	A125	3k gray green	.75	.50
860	A126	6k rose	1.00	.75
861	A127	10k dark blue	1.50	1.00
862	A127	12k olive brown	2.00	1.50
		Nos. 859-862 (4)	5.25	3.75

Centenary of the Turkish post.

Harbor Scene A129

Statue of Atatürk — A132

Designs: 3k, 6k, 17½k, Various Izmir Fair buildings. 12k, Girl picking grapes.

1941, Aug. 20   Litho.   Perf. 11½
Inscribed: "Izmir Enternasyonal Fuari 1941"

863	A129	30pa dull green	.35	.25
864	A129	3k olive gray	.50	.25
865	A129	6k salmon rose	.75	.25
866	A129	10k blue	.95	.30
867	A129	12k dull brown vio	1.10	.45
868	A129	17½k dull brown	1.75	1.25
		Nos. 863-868 (6)	5.40	2.75

Izmir International Fair, 1941.

Tomb of Barbarossa II — A135

Barbarossa's Fleet in Battle — A136

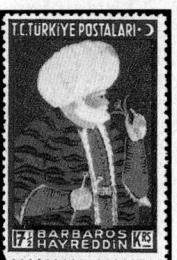

Barbarossa II (Khair ed-Din) — A137

1941

869	A135	20pa dark violet	.25	.25
870	A136	3k light blue	.75	.75
871	A136	6k rose red	1.25	1.25
872	A136	10k deep ultra	1.50	1.50
873	A136	12k dull brn & bis	1.75	1.75
874	A137	17½k multicolored	2.25	2.25
		Nos. 869-874 (6)	7.75	7.75

400th death anniv. of Barbarossa II.

President Inönü
A138   A138a

1942-45   Perf. 11½x11, 11

875	A138	0.25k yellow bis	.25	.25
876	A138	0.50k lt yellow grn	.25	.25
877	A138	1k gray green	.25	.25
877A	A138	1½k brt vio ('45)	.25	.25
878	A138	2k bluish green	.30	.25
879	A138	4k fawn	.30	.30
880	A138	4½k slate	.30	.30
881	A138	5k light blue	.35	.25
882	A138	6k salmon rose	.30	.25
883	A138	6¾k ultra	.80	.25
884	A138	9k brown violet	.80	.25
885	A138	10k dark blue	.30	.25
886	A138	13½k brt pink	.30	.25

887	A138	16k Prus green	.50	.25
888	A138	17½k rose lake	.30	.25
889	A138	20k brown violet	.50	.50
890	A138	27½k orange	.50	.50
891	A138	37k buff	.50	.50
892	A138	50k purple	1.60	.25
893	A138	100k olive bister	5.00	3.00
894	A138a	200k brown	17.50	2.50
		Nos. 875-894 (21)	30.60	11.10

Ankara — A139   Antioch — A141

0.50k, Mohair goats. 1½k, Ankara Dam. 2k, Oranges. 4k, Merino sheep. 4½k, Train. 5k, Tile decorating. 6k, Atatürk statue, Ankara. 6¾k, 10k, Pres. Ismet Inonu. 13½k, Grand National Assembly. 16k, Arnavutkoy, Istanbul. 17½k, Republic monument, Istanbul. 20k, Safety monument, Ankara. 27½k, Post Office, Istanbul. 37k, Monument at Afyon. 50k, "People's House," Ankara. 100k, Atatürk & Inonu. 200k, Pres. Inonu.

1943, Apr. 1   Perf. 11

896	A139	0.25k citron	.25	.25
897	A139	0.50k brt green	.40	.25
898	A141	1k yellow olive	.25	.25
899	A141	1½k deep violet	.25	.25
900	A139	2k brt blue green	.40	.25
901	A139	4k copper red	4.00	1.00
902	A139	4½k black	6.00	2.00
903	A141	5k sapphire	1.25	.50
904	A139	6k carmine rose	.25	.25
905	A139	6¾k brt ultra	.25	.25
906	A139	10k dark blue	.25	.25
907	A141	13½k brt red violet	.30	.25
908	A141	16k myrtle green	3.50	.25
909	A139	17½k brown orange	2.00	.50
910	A139	20k sepia	2.00	.50
911	A139	27½k dk orange	1.50	1.00
912	A139	37k lt yellow brn	2.50	.50
913	A141	50k purple	10.00	.25
914	A139	100k dk olive grn	12.50	2.50
915	A139	200k dark brown	9.00	2.00
a.		Souvenir sheet	70.00	100.00
		Nos. 896-915 (20)	56.85	13.25

No. 915a contains one stamp similar to No. 915, perf. 13½ and printed in sepia. Issued Apr. 20.

For surcharge see No. 928.

Girl with Grapes — A158

Entrance to Izmir Fair A159

Fair Building A160

1943, Aug. 20   Litho.   Perf. 11½

916	A158	4½k dull olive	.25	.25
917	A159	6k carmine rose	.60	.25
918	A160	6¾k blue	.60	.25
919	A159	10k dark blue	.80	.50
920	A158	13½k sepia	1.25	1.00
921	A160	27½k dull gray	1.75	1.75
		Nos. 916-921 (6)	5.25	4.00

Izmir International Fair.

Soccer Team on Parade A161

Turkish Flag and Soldier — A162

Designs: 6¾k, Bridge. 10k, Hospital. 13½k, View of Ankara. 27½k, President Inonu.

1943, Oct. 29   Perf. 11x11½, 11½x11
Inscribed: "Cumhuriyetin 20 nci Yildonomu Hatirasi"

922	A161	4½k lt olive grn	1.50	1.75
923	A162	6k rose red	.75	.25
924	A161	6¾k ultra	.75	.50
925	A161	10k violet blue	.75	.50
926	A161	13½k olive	.75	.25
927	A162	27½k lt brown	.95	.75
		Nos. 922-927 (6)	5.45	4.00

Republic, 20th anniv. Nos. 922-927 exist imperf.

No. 905 Surcharged with New Value in Red

1945   Perf. 11

928	A139	4½k on 6¾k brt ultra	1.00	.45

Recording Census Data — A167

1945, Oct. 21   Litho.   Perf. 11½

929	A167	4½k olive black	.65	.25
930	A167	9k violet	.75	.25
931	A167	10k violet blue	.75	.25
932	A167	18k dark red	1.50	.60
		Nos. 929-932 (4)	3.65	1.35

Souvenir Sheet
Imperf

933	A167	1 l chocolate	75.00	100.00

Census of 1945.

President Ismet Inönü — A169

Perf. 11½ to 12½
1946, Apr. 1   Unwmk.

934	A169	0.25k brown red	.50	.25
935	A169	1k dk slate grn	.50	.25
936	A169	1½k plum	1.00	.25
937	A169	9k purple	1.75	.25
938	A169	10k deep blue	2.00	.75
939	A169	50k chocolate	8.50	.75
		Nos. 934-939 (6)	14.25	2.50

U.S.S. Missouri A170

1946, Apr. 5   **Perf. 11½**
940 A170   9k dark purple   .75   .30
941 A170   10k dk chalky blue   1.25   .60
942 A170   27½k olive green   3.00   3.50
   a.   Imperf., pair   50.00
     Nos. 940-942 (3)   5.00   4.40
Visit of the USS Missouri to Istanbul, 4/5.

Sower — A171

1946, June 16   **Perf. 11½ to 12½**
943 A171   9k violet   .25   .25
944 A171   10k dark blue   .40   .25
945 A171   18k olive green   .65   1.00
946 A171   27½k red orange   1.25   2.50
     Nos. 943-946 (4)   2.55   4.00
Passing of legislation to distribute state lands to poor farmers.

Dove and Flag-Decorated Banderol — A172

1947, Aug. 20   **Photo.**   **Perf. 12**
947 A172   15k violet & dk bl   .40   .25
948 A172   20k blue & dk blue   1.00   .50
949 A172   30k brown & gray blk   .40   .25
950 A172   1 l ol grn & dk grn   .50   .50
     Nos. 947-950 (4)   2.30   1.50
Izmir International Fair.

Victory Monument, Afyon Karahisar A173

Ismet İnönü as General A174

Kemal Atatürk as General — A175

1947, Aug. 30
951 A173   10k dk brn & pale brn   .60   .30
952 A174   15k brt violet & gray   .50   .30
953 A175   20k dp blue & gray   .60   .25
954 A173   30k grnsh blk & gray   1.25   .70
955 A174   60k ol gray & pale brn   1.75   .90
956 A175   1 l dk green & gray   2.75   1.75
     Nos. 951-956 (6)   7.45   4.20
25th anniv. of the Battle of Dumlupinar, Aug. 30, 1922.

Grapes and Istanbul Skyline A176

1947, Sept. 22
957 A176   15k rose violet   .40   .25
958 A176   20k deep blue   .75   .50
959 A176   60k dark brown   1.25   .75
     Nos. 957-959 (3)   2.40   1.50
International Vintners' Congress, Istanbul.

Approaching Train, Istanbul Skyline and Sirkeci Terminus — A177

1947, Oct. 9
960 A177   15k rose violet   .60   .30
961 A177   20k brt blue   1.00   .75
962 A177   60k olive green   2.40   1.90
     Nos. 960-962 (3)   4.00   2.95
International Railroad Congress, Istanbul.

President Ismet İnönü
A178   A179

1948   **Unwmk.**   **Engr.**   **Perf. 12, 14**
963 A178   0.25k dark red   .30   .25
964 A178   1k olive black   .30   .25
965 A178   2k brt rose lilac   .30   .25
966 A178   3k red orange   .30   .25
967 A178   4k dark green   .30   .25
968 A178   5k blue   .30   .25
969 A178   10k chocolate   .75   .50
970 A178   12k deep red   1.25   .30
971 A178   15k violet   .75   .50
972 A178   20k deep blue   1.00   .50
973 A178   30k brown   1.50   .30
974 A178   60k black   4.00   .50
975 A179   1 l olive green   8.00   .50
976 A179   2 l dark brown   30.00   5.00
977 A179   5 l deep plum   17.50   27.50
     Nos. 963-977 (15)   66.55   36.60
For overprints see Nos. O13-O42.

President Ismet İnönü and Lausanne Conference — A180

Conference Building A180a

1948, July 23   **Photo.**   **Perf. 11½**
978 A180   15k rose lilac   .70   .70
979 A180a   20k blue   .90   .90
980 A180a   40k gray green   1.10   1.10
981 A180   1 l brown   1.75   1.75
     Nos. 978-981 (4)   4.45   4.45
25th anniversary of Lausanne Treaty.

Statue of Kemal Atatürk, Ankara — A181

1948, Oct. 29
982 A181   15k violet   .60   .40
983 A181   20k blue   .75   .50
984 A181   40k gray green   1.50   1.10
985 A181   1 l brown   3.25   3.00
     Nos. 982-985 (4)   6.10   5.00
25th anniv. of the proclamation of the republic.

A182   A183

A184

Wrestlers A185

1949, June 3
986 A182   15k rose lilac   2.40   .60
987 A183   20k blue   2.75   1.25
988 A184   30k brown   2.75   .60
989 A185   60k green   4.00   3.50
     Nos. 986-989 (4)   11.90   5.95
5th European Wrestling Championships, Istanbul, June 3-5, 1949.

Ancient Galley A186

Galleon Mahmudiye A187   Monument to Khizr Barbarossa A188

Designs: 15k, Cruiser Hamidiye. 20k, Submarine Sakarya. 30k, Cruiser Yavuz.

1949, July 1
990 A186   5k violet   1.00   1.00
991 A187   10k brown   1.00   1.00
992 A186   15k lilac rose   1.00   1.00
993 A186   20k gray blue   2.50   1.00
994 A186   30k gray   2.50   1.00
995 A188   40k olive gray   4.00   1.75
     Nos. 990-995 (6)   12.00   6.75
Fleet Day, July 1, 1949.

A189

UPU Monument, Bern A190

Perf. 11½
1949, Oct. 9   **Unwmk.**   **Photo.**
996 A189   15k violet   .55   .30
997 A189   20k blue   .55   .30
998 A190   30k dull rose   .55   .30
999 A190   40k green   1.10   .55
     Nos. 996-999 (4)   2.75   1.45
UPU, 75th anniversary.

Istanbul Fair Building A191

1949, Oct. 1   **Litho.**   **Perf. 10**
1000 A191   15k brown   .60   .30
1001 A191   20k blue   .60   .30
1002 A191   30k olive   .80   .60
     Nos. 1000-1002 (3)   2.00   1.20
Istanbul Fair, Oct. 1-31.

Boy and Girl and Globe — A192

1950, Aug. 13   **Perf. 11½**
1003 A192   15k purple   .45   .25
1004 A192   20k deep blue   .90   .60
2nd World Youth Council Meeting, 1950. No. 1004 exists imperf. Value $12.

Aged Woman Casting Ballot — A193

Kemal Atatürk and Map A194

1950, Aug. 30
1005 A193   15k dark brown   .60   .25
1006 A193   20k dark blue   .60   .25
1007 A194   30k dk blue & gray   1.00   .50
     Nos. 1005-1007 (3)   2.20   1.00
Election of May 14, 1950.

Hazel Nuts — A195

Designs: 12k, Acorns. 15k, Cotton. 20k, Symbolical of the fair. 30k, Tobacco.

1950, Sept. 9
1008 A195   8k gray grn & buff   .60   .60
1009 A195   12k magenta   1.25   1.25
1010 A195   15k brn blk & lt brn   .60   .60
1011 A195   20k dk blue & aqua   1.75   1.75
1012 A195   30k brn blk & dull org   1.75   1.75
     Nos. 1008-1012 (5)   5.95   5.95
Izmir International Fair, Aug. 20-Sept. 20.

Symbolical of 1950
Census — A196

1950, Oct. 9   Litho.   Perf. 11½
1013 A196 15k dark brown   .35 .25
1014 A196 20k violet blue   .95 .25

General census of 1950.

Atatürk Types of 1931-42
Perf. 10x11½, 11½x12
1950-51   Typo.
1015 A77 10p dull red brn   .25   .25
1016 A77 10p vermilion ('51)   .35   .50
1017 A77 20p blue green   1.50   .35
1018 A78 1k olive green   .25   .25
1019 A78 2k plum   .25   .25
1020 A78 2k dp yellow
                               .75   .30
1021 A78 3k yellow orange   1.25   .45
1022 A78 3k gray ('51)   .75   .25
1023 A78 4k green ('51)   .75   .25
1024 A78 5k blue   1.25   .45
1025 A78 5k plum ('51)   5.25   .45
1026 A77 10k brown orange   2.25   .25
1027 A77 15k purple   2.75   .45
1028 A77 15k brown car-
          mine   18.00   .35
1029 A77 20k dark blue   30.00   .35
1030 A77 30k pink ('51)   25.50   .75
1031 A79 100k red brown
          ('51)   7.50 1.10
1032 A79 200k dark brown   15.00 1.50
1033 A79 200k rose violet
          ('51)   15.00 2.25
      Nos. 1015-1033 (19)   128.60 10.75

16th Century Flight
of Hezarfen Ahmet
Celebi — A197

Plane over
Istanbul
A198

40k, Biplane over Taurus Mountains.

1950, Oct. 17   Litho.   Perf. 11
1034 A197 20k dk green & blue   .50 .35
1035 A197 40k dk brown & blue   .75 .75
1036 A198 60k purple & blue   1.25 .90
      Nos. 1034-1036 (3)   2.50 2.00

Regional meeting of the ICAO, Istanbul,
Oct. 17.

Farabi
A199

1950, Dec. 1   Unwmk.   Perf. 11½
Multicolored Center
1037 A199 15k blue   .75   .75
1038 A199 20k blue violet   .75   .75
1039 A199 60k red brown   4.25 2.75
1040 A199 1 l gold & bl vio 4.75 4.25
      Nos. 1037-1040 (4)   10.50 8.50

Death millenary of Farabi, Arab philosopher.

Mithat Pasha and Security Bank
Building — A200

Design: 20k, Agricultural Bank.

1950, Dec. 21   Photo.
1041 A200 15k rose violet   2.00 2.00
1042 A200 20k blue   2.00 2.00

3rd Congress of Turkish Cooperatives,
Istanbul, Dec. 25, 1950.

Floating a
Ship
A201

Lighthouse — A202

1951, July 1
1043 A201 15k shown   .75   .75
1044 A201 20k Steamship   .75   .75
1045 A201 30k Diver rising 1.50 1.50
1046 A202 1 l shown   2.75 2.75
      Nos. 1043-1046 (4)   5.75 5.75

25th anniv. of the recognition of coastal
rights in Turkish waters to ships under the
Turkish flag.

Mosque of
Sultan
Ahmed
A203

Henry Carton de
Wiart — A204

Designs: 20k, Dolma Bahce Palace. 60k,
Rumeli Hisari Fortress.

1951, Aug. 31   Photo.   Perf. 13½
1047 A203 15k dark green   .40   .25
1048 A203 20k deep ultra   .60   .30
1049 A204 30k brown   .90   .35
1050 A203 60k purple brown   1.75 1.75
      Nos. 1047-1050 (4)   3.65 2.65

40th Interparliamentary Conf., Istanbul.

Allegory of
Food and
Agriculture
A205

Designs: 20k, Dam. 30k, United Nations
Building. 60k, University, Ankara.

1952, Jan. 3   Unwmk.   Perf. 14
**Inscribed: "Akdeniz Yetistirme
Merkezi. Ankara 1951."**
1051 A205 15k green   1.00   .65
1052 A205 20k blue violet   1.10   .75
1053 A205 30k blue   2.50 2.00
1054 A205 60k red   3.75 3.25
   a. Souvenir sheet of 4 95.00 95.00
      Nos. 1051-1054 (4)   8.35 6.65

UN Mediterranean Economic Instruction
Center.
No. 1054a contains one each of Nos. 1051-
1054, imperf., with inscriptions in dark blue
gray.

Abdulhak Hamid
Tarhan, Poet,
Birth
Cent. — A206

1952, Feb. 5   Photo.   Perf. 13½
1055 A206 15k dark purple   1.00 1.00
1056 A206 20k dark blue   1.00 1.00
1057 A206 30k brown   1.00 1.00
1058 A206 60k dark olive grn 2.75 1.75
      Nos. 1055-1058 (4)   5.75 4.75

Ruins, Bergama
A207

Pavilion, Istanbul
A208

Designs: 1k, Ruins, Bergama. 2k, Ruins,
Milas. 3k, Karatay Gate, Konya. 4k, Kozak pla-
teau. 5k, Urgup. 10k, 12k, 15k, 20k, Kemal
Ataturk. 30k, Mosque, Bursa. 40k, Mosque,
Istanbul. 50, Tarsus Cataract. 75k, Rocks,
Urgup. 1 l, Palace, Istanbul. 5 l, Museum inte-
rior, Istanbul.

1952, Mar. 15   Perf. 13½
1059 A207 1k brown orange   .25   .25
1060 A207 2k olive green   .25   .25
1061 A207 3k rose brown   .40   .25
1062 A207 4k blue green   .70   .70
1063 A207 5k brown   .40   .25
1064 A207 10k dark brown   .25   .25
1065 A207 12k brt rose car   .90   .25
1066 A207 15k purple   .60   .25
1067 A207 20k chalky blue   1.10   .25
1068 A207 30k grnsh gray   .90   .25
1069 A207 40k slate blue   5.50   .90
1070 A208 50k olive   .90   .25
1071 A208 75k slate   .90   .40
1072 A208 1 l deep purple   .70   .25
1073 A208 2 l brt ultra   3.25   .50
1074 A208 5 l sepia   42.50 10.50
      Nos. 1059-1074 (16) 59.50 16.20

Imperfs, value, set $90.
For surcharge & overprint see #1075, 1255.

**No. 1059 Surcharged with New
Value in Black**
1952, June 1
1075 A207 0.50k on 1k brn org   .25 .25

Technical
Faculty
Building
A209

1952, Aug. 20   Perf. 12x12½
1076 A209 15k violet   .65   .65
1077 A209 20k blue   .95   .95
1078 A209 60k brown   1.60 1.60
      Nos. 1076-1078 (3)   3.20 3.20

8th Intl. Congress of Theoretic and Applied
Mechanics.

Turkish
Soldier — A210

20k, Soldier with Turkish flag. 30k, Soldier &
child with comic book. 60k, Raising Turkish
flag.

1952, Sept. 25   Perf. 14
1079 A210 15k Prus blue   .40   .40
1080 A210 20k deep blue   .60   .60
1081 A210 30k brown   .85   .85
1082 A210 60k olive blk & car 1.75 1.75
      Nos. 1079-1082 (4)   3.60 3.60

Turkey's participation in the Korean war.

Pigeons Bandaging
Wounded
Hand — A212

20k, Flag, rainbow and ruined homes.

Dated "1877-1952"
1952, Oct. 29   Perf. 12½x12
1085 A212 15k dk green & red   .80 .40
1086 A212 20k blue & red   2.00 .70

Turkish Red Crescent Society, 75th anniv.

Relief From Panel
of Aziziye
Monument — A213

Aziziye
Monument
A214

Design: 40k, View of Erzerum.

1952, Nov. 9   Perf. 11
1087 A213 15k purple   .60   .30
1088 A214 20k blue   .65   .50
1089 A214 40k olive gray   1.00   .70
      Nos. 1087-1089 (3)   2.25 1.50

75th anniv. of the Battle of Aziziye at
Erzerum.

Rumeli
Hisari
Fortress
A215

Troops Entering Constantinople — A216

Sultan Mohammed II — A217

Designs: 8k, Soldiers moving cannon. 10k, Mohammed II riding into sea, and Turkish armada. 12k, Landing of Turkish army. 15k, Ancient wall, Constantinople. 30k, Mosque of Faith. 40k, Presenting mace to Patriarch Yenadios. 60k, Map of Constantinople, c. 1574. 1 l, Tomb of Mohammed II. 2.50 l, Portrait of Mohammed II.

1953, May 29   Photo.   Perf. 11½
Inscribed: "Istanbulun Fethi 1453-1953"

1090	A215	5k brt blue	1.25 .60
1091	A215	8k gray	1.90 .60
1092	A215	10k blue	.60 .60
1093	A215	12k rose lilac	1.25 .60
1094	A215	15k brown	.90 .30
1095	A216	20k vermilion	1.25 .30
1096	A216	30k dull green	2.40 1.25
1097	A215	40k violet blue	4.25 1.50
1098	A215	60k chocolate	3.00 1.50
1099	A215	1 l blue green	7.25 2.10

Perf. 12

1100	A217	2 l multi	15.00 6.00
1101	A217	2.50 l multi	9.00 9.00
a.		Souvenir sheet	175.00 90.00
		Nos. 1090-1101 (12)	48.05 24.35

Conquest of Constantinople by Sultan Mohammed II, 500th anniv.

Ruins of the Odeon, Ephesus A218

15k, Church of St. John the Apostle. 20k, Shrine of Virgin Mary, Panaya Kapulu. 40k, Ruins of the Double Church. 60k, Shrine of the Seven Sleepers. 1 l, Restored house of the Virgin Mary.

1953, Aug. 16   Litho.   Perf. 13½
Multicolored Center

1102	A218	12k sage green	.50 .50
1103	A218	15k lilac	.50 .50
1104	A218	20k dk slate blue	.60 .60
1105	A218	40k light green	.90 .90
1106	A218	60k violet blue	1.25 1.25
1107	A218	1 l brown red	3.50 2.50
		Nos. 1102-1107 (6)	7.25 6.25

Pres. Celal Bayar, Mithat Pasha. Herman Schulze-Delitzsch and People's Bank — A219

Design: 20k, Pres. Bayar, Mithat Pasha and University of Ankara.

1953, Sept. 2   Photo.   Perf. 10½

1108	A219	15k orange brown	1.00 .50
1109	A219	20k Prus green	1.00 .50

5th Intl. People's Credit Congress, Istanbul, Sept.

Combined Harvester A220

Kemal Atatürk — A221

Designs: 15k, Berdan dam. 20k, Military parade. 30k, Diesel train. 35k, Yesilkoy airport.

1953, Oct. 29   Perf. 14

1110	A220	10k olive bister	.30 .25
1111	A220	15k dark gray	.30 .25
1112	A220	20k rose red	.75 .75
1113	A220	30k olive green	1.25 1.25
1114	A220	35k dull blue	.75 .75
1115	A221	55k dull purple	1.75 1.75
		Nos. 1110-1115 (6)	5.10 5.00

Turkish Republic, 30th anniv.

Kemal Atatürk and Mausoleum at Ankara — A222

1953, Nov. 10

1116	A222	15k gray black	.75 .35
1117	A222	20k violet brown	1.10 .55

15th death anniv. of Kemal Ataturk.

Type of 1931-42
Without umlaut over first "U" of "CUMHURIYETI"
Perf. 11½x12, 10x11½

1953-56   Typo.   Unwmk.

1117B	A77	20p yellow	.30 .25
1118	A78	1k brown orange	.30 .25
1119	A78	2k rose pink ('53)	.50 .25
1120	A78	3k yellow brn ('53)	.50 .25
1120A	A78	4k slate ('56)	1.50 .40
1121	A78	5k blue	2.00 .25
1121A	A78	8k violet ('56)	.50 .25
1122	A77	10k dark olive ('53)	.50 .25
1123	A77	12k brt car rose ('53)	.50 .25
1124	A77	15k fawn	.60 .25
1125	A77	20k rose lilac	3.50 .40
1126	A77	30k lt blue grn ('54)	1.25 .25
		Nos. 1117B-1126 (12)	11.95 3.30

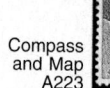

Compass and Map A223

Designs: 20k, Globe, crescent and stars. 40k, Tree symbolical of 14 NATO members.

1954, Apr. 4   Photo.   Perf. 14

1127	A223	15k brown	1.75 1.25
1128	A223	20k violet blue	2.25 1.75
1129	A223	40k dark green	15.50 13.00
		Nos. 1127-1129 (3)	19.50 16.00

NATO, 5th anniv.

Industry, Engineering and Agriculture — A224

Justice and Council of Europe Flag — A225

1954, Aug. 8   Litho.   Perf. 10½

1130	A224	10k brown	3.25 2.40
1131	A225	15k dark green	3.00 1.25
1132	A225	20k blue	3.25 1.25
1133	A224	30k brt violet	14.50 10.00
		Nos. 1130-1133 (4)	24.00 14.90

Council of Europe, 5th anniv.

Flag Signals to Plane — A226

Amaury de La Grange and Plane A227

Design: 45k, Kemal Ataturk and air fleet.

1954, Sept. 20   Perf. 12½

1134	A226	20k black brown	.40 .25
1135	A227	35k dull violet	.60 .25
1136	A227	45k deep blue	1.00 .30
		Nos. 1134-1136 (3)	2.00 .80

47th Congress of the Intl. Aeronautical Federation, Istanbul, 1954.

Souvenir Sheet

A228

1954, Oct. 18   Imperf.

1137	A228	Sheet of 3	16.00 7.00
a.		20k aquamarine	1.25 .85
b.		30k violet blue	1.50 .85
c.		1 l red violet	3.00 1.90

First anniv. of Law of Oct. 17, 1953, reorganizing the Department of Post, Telephone and Telegraph.

Ziya Gokalp — A229

1954, Oct. 25   Perf. 11

1138	A229	15k rose lilac	.50 .50
1139	A229	20k dark green	.60 .60
1140	A229	30k crimson	.90 .90
		Nos. 1138-1140 (3)	2.00 2.00

30th death anniv. of Ziya Gokalp, author and historian.

Kemal Atatürk — A230

1955, Mar. 1   Perf. 12½

1141	A230	15k carmine rose	.60 .60
1142	A230	20k blue	.75 .75
1143	A230	40k dark gray	.90 .90
1144	A230	50k blue green	1.25 1.25
1145	A230	75k orange brown	1.50 1.50
		Nos. 1141-1145 (5)	5.00 5.00

Relief Map of Dardanelles — A231

Artillery Loaders — A232

30k, Minelayer Nusrat. 60k, Col. Kemal Atatürk.

1955, Mar. 18   Perf. 10½

1146	A231	15k green	.25 .25
1147	A232	20k orange brown	.25 .25
1148	A231	30k ultra	.30 .25
1149	A232	60k olive gray	.90 .45
		Nos. 1146-1149 (4)	1.70 1.20

Battle of Gallipoli, 40th anniversary.

Aerial Map A233

1955, Apr. 14   Perf. 11

1150	A233	15k gray	.35 .25
1151	A233	20k aquamarine	.35 .25
1152	A233	30k brown	.60 .25
1153	A233	1 l purple	1.10 .50
		Nos. 1150-1153 (4)	2.40 1.25

City Planning Congress, Ankara, 1955.

Carnation — A234

1955, May 19   Litho.   Perf. 10

1154	A234	10k shown	.55 .55
1155	A234	15k Tulip	.55 .55
1156	A234	20k Rose	.85 .55
1157	A234	50k Lily	2.00 1.10
		Nos. 1154-1157 (4)	3.95 2.75

National Flower Show, Istanbul, May 20-Aug. 20.

Battle First
Aid Station
A235

30k, Gulhane Military Hospital, Ankara.

1955, Aug. 28   Unwmk.   Perf. 12
1158 A235 20k red, lake & gray   .75   .75
1159 A235 30k dp grn & yel grn   1.25 1.25

XVIII Intl. Congress of Military Medicine, Aug. 8-Sept. 1, Istanbul.

Soccer
Game
A236

Emblem and Soccer
Ball — A237

1 l, Emblem with oak & olive branches.

1955, Aug. 30   Perf. 10
1160 A236 15k light ultra   .70   .25
1161 A237 20k crimson rose   .85   .25
1162 A236 1 l light green   1.75 1.10
     Nos. 1160-1162 (3)   3.30 1.60

Intl. Military Soccer Championship games, Istanbul, Aug. 30.

Sureté
Monument,
Ankara
A238

20k, Dolma Bahce Palace. 30k, Police College, Ankara. 45k, Police Martyrs' Monument, Istanbul.

1955, Sept. 5   Perf. 10
Inscribed: "Enterpol Istanbul 1955"
1163 A238 15k blue green   .30   .30
1164 A238 20k brt violet   .45   .45
1165 A238 30k gray black   .55   .40
1166 A238 45k lt brown   1.10 .65
     Nos. 1163-1166 (4)   2.40 1.80

24th general assembly of the Intl. Criminal Police, Istanbul, Sept. 5-9.

Early
Telegraph
Transmitter
A239

Modern
Transmitter
A240

Perf. 13½x14, 14x13½
1955, Sept. 10   Photo.
1167 A239 15k olive   .25   .25
1168 A240 20k crimson rose   .25   .25
1169 A239 45k fawn   .60   .25
1170 A240 60k ultra   .60   .60
     Nos. 1167-1170 (4)   1.70 1.35
Centenary of telecommunication.

Academy of
Science,
Istanbul
A241

Designs: 20k, University. 60k, Hilton Hotel. 1 l, Kiz Kulesi (Leander's Tower).

1955, Sept. 12   Perf. 13½x14
1171 A241 15k yellow orange   .35   .35
1172 A241 20k crimson rose   .35   .35
1173 A241 60k purple   .45   .35
1174 A241 1 l deep blue   .85   .60
     Nos. 1171-1174 (4)   2.00 1.65

10th meeting of the governors of the Intl. Bank of Reconstruction and Development and the Intl. Monetary Fund, Istanbul, Sept. 12-16.

Surlari,
Istanbul
A242

Mosque of Sultan
Ahmed — A243

Designs: 30k, Haghia Sophia. 75k, Map of Constantinople, by Christoforo Buondelmonti, 1422.

1955, Sept. 15   Litho.   Perf. 11½
1175 A242 15k grnsh blk & Prus
           grn   .50   .25
1176 A243 20k vermilion & org .40   .25
1177 A242 30k sepia & vio brn .40   .25
1178 A243 75k ultramarine   1.10 .75
     Nos. 1175-1178 (4)   2.40 1.50

10th Intl. Congress of Byzantine Research, Istanbul, Sept. 15-21, 1955.

Congress
Emblem — A244

30k, Chalet in Istanbul. 55k, Bridges.

**Inscribed: "Beynelmiel X. Vol
Kongresi Istanbul 1955"**

1955, Sept. 26   Perf. 10½x11
1179 A244 20k red violet   .25   .25
1180 A244 30k dk grn & yel grn .25 .25
1181 A244 55k dp bl & brt bl 1.10 .55
     Nos. 1179-1181 (3)   1.60 1.05

10th International Transportation Congress.

Map of
Turkey,
Showing
Population
Increase
A245

1955, Oct. 22   Unwmk.   Perf. 10
Map in Rose
1182 A245 15k lt & dk gray & red .35 .25
1183 A245 20k lt & dk vio & red   .25 .25
1184 A245 30k lt & dk ultra & red .30 .25
1185 A245 60k lt & dk bl grn &
           red   .70 .30
     Nos. 1182-1185 (4)   1.60 1.05
Census of 1955.

Waterfall,
Antalya — A246

Alanya and
Seljukide
Dockyards
A247

Designs: 30k, Theater at Aspendos. 45k, Ruins at Side. 50k, View of Antalya. 65k, St. Nicholas Church at Myra (Demre) and St. Nicholas.

Perf. 14x13½, 13½x14
1955, Dec. 10   Photo.   Unwmk.
1186 A246 18k bl, ol grn & ultra .50 .25
1187 A247 20k blue, ultra & brn   .50 .25
1188 A247 30k dl grn, ol grn &
           grn   .50 .25
1189 A246 45k yel grn & brn   2.25 1.00
1190 A246 50k Prus grn & ol bis   .60 .30
1191 A247 65k orange ver & blk   .80 .40
     Nos. 1186-1191 (6)   5.15 2.45

Kemal Atatürk — A248

1955-56   Litho.   Perf. 12½
1192 A248 0.50k carmine   .25   .25
1193 A248 1k yellow orange   .30   .25
1194 A248 2k brt blue   .40   .25
1195 A248 3k scarlet   .40   .25
1196 A248 5k lt brown   .50   .25
1197 A248 6k lt blue grn   .50   .25
1198 A248 10k blue green   .60   .25
1199 A248 18k rose violet   .60   .25
1200 A248 20k lt violet bl   .75   .25
1201 A248 25k olive green   .75   .25
1202 A248 30k violet   .75   .25
1203 A248 40k fawn   .90   .40
1204 A248 75k slate blue   2.25 1.25
     Nos. 1192-1204 (13)   8.95 4.60

Issue dates: 3k, 1955. Others, 1956.

Tomb at
Nigde — A249

1956, Apr. 12   Perf. 10½
1205 A249 40k violet bl & bl .60   .25

25th anniv. of the Turkish History Society. The tomb of Hüdavent Hatun, a sultan's daughter, exemplifies Seljukian architecture of the 14th century.

Zubeyde
Hanum — A250

1956, May 13   Perf. 11
1206 A250 20k pale brn & dk brn 1.25 1.00

Imperf
1207 A250 20k lt grn & dk grn   1.25 1.75

Mother's Day; Zubeyde Hanum, mother of Kemal Ataturk.

Shah
and
Queen
of Iran
A251

1956, May 15   Unwmk.   Perf. 11
1208 A251 100k grn & pale
            grn   2.50 1.25

Imperf
1209 A251 100k red & pale
            grn   12.00 8.50

Visit of the Shah and Queen of Iran to Turkey, May 15.

Erenkoy
Sanitarium
A252

1956, July 31   Perf. 11
1210 A252 50k dk bl grn & pink .95 .25

Anti-Tuberculosis work among PTT employees.

Symbol of Izmir
Fair — A253

A254

1956, Aug. 20   Perf. 11
1211 A253 45k brt green   .60   .60

Souvenir Sheet
Imperf
1212 A254   Sheet of 2   6.00 5.00
  a.   50k rose red   2.50 .65
  b.   50k bright ultramarine 2.50 .65

25th Intl. Fair, Izmir, 8/20-9/20. See #C28.

Hands Holding
Bottled
Serpent — A255

1956, Sept. 10   Litho.   Perf. 10½
1213 A255 25k multicolored   .30 .30
  a. Tete beche pair   1.25

25th Intl. Anti-Alcoholism Congress, Istanbul Sept. 10-15.
Printed both in regular sheets and in sheets with alternate vertical rows inverted.

Medical Center at Kayseri — A256

1956, Nov. 1   Perf. 12½x12
1214 A256 60k violet & yel   .30 .30

750th anniv. of the first medical school and clinic in Anatolia.

Sariyar Dam — A257

1956, Dec. 2   Litho.   Perf. 10½
1215 A257 20k vermilion   .30 .30
1216 A257 20k bright blue   .30 .30

Inauguration of Sariyar Dam.

Freestyle Wrestling A258

Design: 65k, Greco-Roman wrestling.

1956, Dec. 8   Unwmk.   Perf. 10½
1217 A258 40k brt yel grn & brn   1.00 .40
1218 A258 65k lt bluish gray &
         dp car   1.25 .40

16th Olympic Games, Melbourne, Nov. 22-Dec. 8, 1956.

Mehmet Akif Ersoy — A259

1956, Dec. 26
1219 A259 20k brn & brt yel grn   .25 .25
1220 A259 20k rose car & lt gray   .25 .25
1221 A259 20k vio bl & brt pink   .25 .25
    Nos. 1219-1221 (3)   .75 .75

20th death anniv. of Mehmet Akif Ersoy, author of the Turkish National Anthem.
Each value bears a different verse of the anthem.

Theater in Troy — A260

Trojan Vase — A261

Design: 30k, Trojan Horse.

Perf. 13½x14, 14x13½
1956, Dec. 31   Photo.   Unwmk.
1222 A260 15k green   1.40 .85
1223 A261 20k red violet   1.40 .85
1224 A260 30k chestnut   2.00 .85
    Nos. 1222-1224 (3)   4.80 2.55

Excavations at Troy.

Mobile Chest X-Ray Unit A262

1957, Jan. 1   Litho.   Perf. 12
1225 A262 25k ol brn & red   .45 .30

Fight against tuberculosis.

Kemal Atatürk — A263

1956-57   Perf. 12½
1226 A263 ½k blue green   .25 .25
1227 A263 1k yellow orange   .40 .25
1228 A263 3k gray olive   .40 .25
1229 A263 5k violet   .40 .25
1230 A263 6k rose car ('57)   .50 .25
1231 A263 10k rose violet   .50 .25
1232 A263 12k fawn ('57)   .60 .25
1233 A263 15k lt violet bl   .50 .25
1234 A263 18k carmine ('57)   .60 .25
1235 A263 20k lt brown   .50 .25
1236 A263 25k lt blue green   .50 .25
1237 A263 30k slate blue   .50 .25
1238 A263 40k olive ('57)   .75 .25
1239 A263 50k orange   .60 .25
1240 A263 60k brt blue ('57)   .90 .35
1241 A263 70k Prus green
        ('57)   2.50 1.25
1242 A263 75k brown   1.75 .90
    Nos. 1226-1242 (17)   12.15 6.00

Pres. Heuss of Germany — A264

1957, May 5   Unwmk.   Perf. 10½
1243 A264 40k yellow & brown   .25 .25

Visit of Pres. Theodor Heuss of Germany to Turkey, May 5. See No. C29.

View of Bergama and Ruin A265

40k, Dancers in kermis at Bergama.

1957, May 24
1244 A265 30k brown   .25 .25
1245 A265 40k green   .25 .25

20th anniv. of the kermis at Bergama (Pergamus).

Symbols of Industry and Flags A266

1957, July 1   Photo.   Perf. 13½x14
1246 A266 25k violet   .40 .40
1247 A266 40k gray blue   .40 .40

Turkish-American collaboration, 10th anniv.

Osman Hamdi Bey A267

Hittite Sun Course from Alaça Höyük — A268

1957, July 6   Perf. 10½
1248 A267 20k beige, pale brn &
        blk   .35 .25
1249 A268 30k Prussian green   .40 .25

75th anniv. of the Academy of Art. The 20k exists with "cancellation" omitted.

King of Afghanistan — A269

1957, Sept. 1   Litho.   Perf. 10½
1250 A269 45k car lake & pink   .25 .25

Visit of Mohammed Zahir Shah, King of Afghanistan, to Turkey. See No. C30.

Medical Center, Amasya A270

Design: 65k, Suleiman Medical Center.

1957, Sept. 29   Unwmk.   Perf. 10½
1251 A270 25k vermilion & yellow .25 .25
1252 A270 65k brt grnsh bl & cit-
        ron   .30 .25

11th general meeting of the World Medical Assoc.

Mosque of Suleiman A271

Architect Mimar Koca Sinan (1489-1587) A272

1957, Oct. 18   Perf. 11
1253 A271 20k gray green   .25 .25
1254 A272 100k brown   .60 .40

400th anniv. of the opening of the Mosque of Suleiman, Istanbul.

No. 1073 Surcharged with New Value and "ISTANBUL Filatelik n. Sergisi 1957"
1957, Nov. 11   Photo.   Perf. 13½
1255 A208 50k on 2 l brt ultra   .30 .25

1957 Istanbul Philatelic Exhibition.

Forestation Map of Turkey — A273

25k, Forest & hand planting tree, vert.

1957, Nov. 18   Litho.   Perf. 10½
1256 A273 20k green & brown   .25 .25
1257 A273 25k emerald & bl grn   .25 .25

Centenary of forestry in Turkey.
Nos. 1256-1257 each come with two different tabs attached (four tabs in all) bearing various quotations.

A274

1957, Nov. 23
1258 A274 50k pink, vio, red &
        yel   .50 .25

400th death anniv. of Fuzuli (Mehmet Suleiman Ogiou), poet.

A275

1957, Nov. 28   Photo.   Perf. 14x13½
1259 A275 65k dk Prus blue   .30 .30
1260 A275 65k rose violet   .30 .30

Benjamin Franklin (1706-1790).

Green Dome, Tomb of Mevlana, at Konya — A276

Mevlana — A278

Konya Museum A277

Perf. 11x10½, 10½x11
1957, Dec. 17   Litho.   Unwmk.
1261 A276 50k green, bl & vio   .25 .25
1262 A277 100k dark blue   .75 .25

Miniature Sheet
Imperf
1263 A278 100k multicolored   1.75 1.40

Jalal-udin Mevlana (1207-1273), Persian poet and founder of the Mevlevie dervish order. No. 1263 contains one stamp 32x42mm.

Kemal Atatürk (Double Frame; Serifs) — A279

1957   Unwmk.   Perf. 11½
Size: 18x22mm
1264 A279 ½k lt brown   .25 .25
1265 A279 1k lt violet bl   .40 .25
1266 A279 2k black violet   .40 .25
1267 A279 3k orange   .40 .25
1268 A279 5k blue green   .40 .25
1269 A279 6k dk slate grn   .40 .25
1270 A279 10k violet   .40 .25
1271 A279 12k brt green   .40 .25
1272 A279 15k dk blue grn   .40 .25
1273 A279 18k rose carmine   .40 .25
1274 A279 20k brown   .40 .25
1275 A279 25k brown red   .40 .25
1276 A279 30k brt blue   .40 .25
1277 A279 40k slate blue   .50 .25
1278 A279 50k yellow orange   .50 .25
1279 A279 60k black   .60 .25
1280 A279 70k rose violet   .60 .25
1281 A279 75k gray olive   .75 .30

Size: 21x29mm
1282 A279 100k carmine   1.25 .40
1283 A279 250k olive   2.75 .90
Nos. 1264-1283 (20)   12.00 5.85

College Emblem — A280

1958, Jan. 16   Litho.   Perf. 10½x11
1288 A280 20k bister, ind & org   .25 .25
1289 A280 25k dk blue, bis & org   .25 .25

"Turkiye" on top of 25k. 75th anniv. of the College of Economics and Commerce, Istanbul.

View of Adana — A281

1958   Photo.   Perf. 11½
Size: 26x20½mm
1290 A281 5k Adana   .25 .25
1291 A281 5k Adapazari   .25 .25
1292 A281 5k Adiyaman   .25 .25
1293 A281 5k Afyon   .25 .25
1294 A281 5k Amasya   .25 .25
1295 A281 5k Ankara   .25 .25
1296 A281 5k Antakya   .25 .25
1297 A281 5k Antalya   .25 .25
1298 A281 5k Artvin   .25 .25
1299 A281 5k Aydin   .25 .25
1300 A281 5k Balikesir   .25 .25
1301 A281 5k Bilecik   .25 .25
1302 A281 5k Bingol   .25 .25
1303 A281 5k Bitlis   .25 .25
1304 A281 5k Bolu   .25 .25
1305 A281 5k Burdur   .25 .25
1306 A281 5k Bursa   .25 .25
1307 A281 5k Canakkale   .25 .25
1308 A281 5k Cankiri   .25 .25
1309 A281 5k Corum   .25 .25
1310 A281 5k Denizli   .25 .25
1311 A281 5k Diyarbakir   .25 .25

Size: 32½x22mm
1312 A281 20k Adana   .25 .25
1313 A281 20k Adapazari   .25 .25
1314 A281 20k Adiyaman   .25 .25
1315 A281 20k Afyon   .25 .25
1316 A281 20k Amasya   .25 .25
1317 A281 20k Ankara   .25 .25
1318 A281 20k Antakya   .25 .25
1319 A281 20k Antalya   .25 .25
1320 A281 20k Artvin   .25 .25
1321 A281 20k Aydin   .25 .25
1322 A281 20k Balikesir   .25 .25
1323 A281 20k Bilecik   .25 .25
1324 A281 20k Bingol   .25 .25
1325 A281 20k Bitlis   .25 .25
1326 A281 20k Bolu   .25 .25
1327 A281 20k Burdur   .25 .25
1328 A281 20k Bursa   .25 .25
1329 A281 20k Canakkale   .25 .25
1330 A281 20k Cankiri   .25 .25
1331 A281 20k Corum   .25 .25
1332 A281 20k Denizli   .25 .25
1333 A281 20k Diyarbakir   .25 .25
Nos. 1290-1333 (44)   11.00 11.00

1959   Size: 26x20½mm
1334 A281 5k Edirne   .25 .25
1335 A281 5k Elazig   .25 .25
1336 A281 5k Erzincan   .25 .25
1337 A281 5k Erzurum   .25 .25
1338 A281 5k Eskisehir   .25 .25
1339 A281 5k Gaziantep   .25 .25
1340 A281 5k Giresun   .25 .25
1341 A281 5k Gumusane   .25 .25
1342 A281 5k Hakkari   .25 .25
1343 A281 5k Isparta   .25 .25
1344 A281 5k Istanbul   .25 .25
1345 A281 5k Izmir   .25 .25
1346 A281 5k Izmit   .25 .25
1347 A281 5k Karakose   .25 .25
1348 A281 5k Kars   .25 .25
1349 A281 5k Kastamonu   .25 .25
1350 A281 5k Kayseri   .25 .25
1351 A281 5k Kirklareli   .25 .25
1352 A281 5k Kirsehir   .25 .25
1353 A281 5k Konya   .25 .25
1354 A281 5k Kutahya   .25 .25
1355 A281 5k Malatya   .25 .25

Size: 32½x22mm
1356 A281 20k Edirne   .25 .25
1357 A281 20k Elazig   .25 .25
1358 A281 20k Erzincan   .25 .25
1359 A281 20k Erzurum   .25 .25
1360 A281 20k Eskisehir   .25 .25
1361 A281 20k Gaziantep   .25 .25
1362 A281 20k Giresun   .25 .25
1363 A281 20k Gumusane   .25 .25
1364 A281 20k Hakkari   .25 .25
1365 A281 20k Isparta   .25 .25
1366 A281 20k Istanbul   .25 .25
1367 A281 20k Izmir   .25 .25
1368 A281 20k Izmit   .25 .25
1369 A281 20k Karakose   .25 .25
1370 A281 20k Kars   .25 .25
1371 A281 20k Kastamonu   .25 .25
1372 A281 20k Kayseri   .25 .25
1373 A281 20k Kirklareli   .25 .25
1374 A281 20k Kirsehir   .25 .25
1375 A281 20k Konya   .25 .25
1376 A281 20k Kutahya   .25 .25
1377 A281 20k Malatya   .25 .25
Nos. 1334-1377 (44)   11.00 11.00

1960   Size: 26x20½mm
1378 A281 5k Manisa   .25 .25
1379 A281 5k Maras   .25 .25
1380 A281 5k Mardin   .25 .25
1381 A281 5k Mersin   .25 .25
1382 A281 5k Mugla   .25 .25
1383 A281 5k Mus   .25 .25
1384 A281 5k Nevsehir   .25 .25
1385 A281 5k Nigde   .25 .25
1386 A281 5k Ordu   .25 .25
1387 A281 5k Rize   .25 .25
1388 A281 5k Samsun   .25 .25
1389 A281 5k Siirt   .25 .25
1390 A281 5k Sinop   .25 .25
1391 A281 5k Sivas   .25 .25
1392 A281 5k Tekirdag   .25 .25
1393 A281 5k Tokat   .25 .25
1394 A281 5k Trabzon   .25 .25
1395 A281 5k Tunceli   .25 .25
1396 A281 5k Urfa   .25 .25

1397 A281 5k Usak   .25 .25
1398 A281 5k Van   .25 .25
1399 A281 5k Yozgat   .25 .25
1400 A281 5k Zonguldak   .25 .25

Size: 32½x22mm
1401 A281 20k Manisa   .25 .25
1402 A281 20k Maras   .25 .25
1403 A281 20k Mardin   .25 .25
1404 A281 20k Mersin   .25 .25
1405 A281 20k Mugla   .25 .25
1406 A281 20k Mus   .25 .25
1407 A281 20k Nevsehir   .25 .25
1408 A281 20k Nigde   .25 .25
1409 A281 20k Ordu   .25 .25
1410 A281 20k Rize   .25 .25
1411 A281 20k Samsun   .25 .25
1412 A281 20k Siirt   .25 .25
1413 A281 20k Sinop   .25 .25
1414 A281 20k Sivas   .25 .25
1415 A281 20k Tekirdag   .25 .25
1416 A281 20k Tokat   .25 .25
1417 A281 20k Trabzon   .25 .25
1418 A281 20k Tunceli   .25 .25
1419 A281 20k Urfa   .25 .25
1420 A281 20k Usak   .25 .25
1421 A281 20k Van   .25 .25
1422 A281 20k Yozgat   .25 .25
1423 A281 20k Zonguldak   .25 .25
Nos. 1378-1423 (46)   11.50 11.50
Nos. 1290-1423 (134)   26.80 26.80

Ruins at Pamukkale A282

Designs: 25k, Travertines at Pamukkale.

1958, May 18   Litho.   Perf. 12
1424 A282 20k brown   .25 .25
1425 A282 25k blue   .25 .25

"Industry" — A283

1958, Oct. 10   Unwmk.   Perf. 10½
1426 A283 40k slate blue   .25 .25

National Industry Exhibition.

Europa Issue

Symbolizing New Europe — A284

1958, Oct. 10
1427 A284 25k vio & dull pink   .50 .25
1428 A284 40k brt ultra   .50 .25

Letters A285

1958, Oct. 5
1429 A285 20k orange & blk   .25 .25

Intl. Letter Writing Week, Oct. 5-11.

Atatürk 20th Anniv. Death — A286

1958, Nov. 10   Perf. 12
1430 A286 25k Flame and mausoleum   .25 .25
1431 A286 75k Atatürk   .25 .25
a. A286 Pair, #1430-1431   .65 .60

20th death anniv. of Kemal Ataturk.

Emblem — A288

1959, Jan. 10   Litho.   Perf. 10
1432 A288 25k dk violet & yel   .25 .25

25th anniv. of the Agricultural Faculty of Ankara University.

Blackboard and School Emblem — A289

1959, Jan. 15   Perf. 10½
1433 A289 75k black & yellow   .30 .30

75th anniv. of the establishment of a secondary boys' school in Istanbul.

State Theater, Ankara A290

Design: 25k, Portrait of Sinasi.

1959, Mar. 30   Unwmk.   Perf. 10½
1434 A290 20k red brn & emer   .25 .25
1435 A290 25k Prus grn & org   .25 .25

Centenary of the Turkish theater; Sinasi, writer of the first Turkish play in 1859.

Globe and Stars A291

1959, Apr. 4   Perf. 10
1436 A291 105k red   .25 .25
1437 A291 195k green   1.00 .50

10th anniversary of NATO.

Aspendos Theater A292

1959, May 1   Litho.   Perf. 10½
1438 A292 20k bis brn & vio   .25 .25
1439 A292 20k grn & ol bis   .25 .25
      Aspendos (Belkins) Festival.

No. B70 Surcharged in Ultramarine

1959, May 5
1440 SP25 105k on 15k + 5k org   .55 .25
      Council of Europe, 10th anniversary.

"Karadeniz" — A294

1959, May 21   Perf. 10
1441 A293 25k red org & dk bl   .25 .25
      11th European and Mediterranean Basket-
      ball Championship.

Basketball — A293

Telegraph   Kemal
Mast — A295   Atatürk — A296

Designs: 1k, Turkish Airlines' SES plane.
10k, Grain elevator, Ankara. 15k, Iron and
Steel Works, Karabück. 20k, Euphrates
Bridge, Birecik. 25k, Zonguldak Harbor. 30k,
Gasoline refinery, Batman. 40k, Rumeli Hisari
Fortress. 45k, Sugar factory, Konya. 55k, Coal
mine, Zonguldak. 75k, Railway. 90k, Crane
loading ships. 100k, Cement factory, Ankara.
120k, Highway. 150k, Harvester. 200k, Electric transformer.

Perf. 10½, 11, 11½, 12½, 13½
1959-60   Litho.   Unwmk.
1442 A294   1k indigo   .25 .25
1443 A294   5k brt blue ('59)   .25 .25
1444 A294   10k blue   .25 .25
1445 A294   15k brown   .70 .25
1446 A294   20k slate green   .25 .25
1447 A294   25k violet   .25 .25
1448 A294   30k lilac   .45 .35
1449 A294   40k blue   .70 .25
1450 A294   45k dull violet   .70 .25
1451 A294   55k olive brown   .70 .25
1452 A295   60k green   .95 .25
1453 A295   75k gray olive   3.50 .25
1454 A295   90k dark blue   7.75 .25
1455 A294 100k gray   10.50 .25
1456 A294 120k magenta   3.50 .35
1457 A294 150k orange   3.50 .45
1458 A295 200k yellow green   4.25 .45
1459 A296 250k black brown   4.25 .55
1460 A296 500k dark blue   7.00 .85
      Nos. 1442-1460 (19)   49.70 6.25

Postage Due Stamps of
1936 Surcharged

1959, June 1   Perf. 11½
1461 D6 20k on 20pa brown   .85 .25
1462 D6 20k on 2k lt blue   .35 .25
1463 D6 20k on 3k brt vio   .45 .25
1464 D6 20k on 5k Prus bl   .55 .25
1465 D6 20k on 12k brt rose   .55 .25
      Nos. 1461-1465 (5)   2.75 1.25

Anchor
Emblem — A297

Design: 40k, Sea Horse emblem.

1959, July 4   Perf. 11
1466 A297 30k multicolored   .25 .25
1467 A297 40k multicolored   .25 .25
      50th anniv. of the Merchant Marine College.

11th
Century
Warrior
A298

1959, Aug. 26   Litho.   Perf. 11
1468 A298 2½ l rose lil & lt bl   1.00 .70
      Battle of Malazkirt, 888th anniversary.

A299

Ornament — A300

Design: 40k, Mosque.

1959, Oct. 19   Unwmk.   Perf. 12½
1469 A299 30k black & red   .25 .25
1470 A299 40k lt blue, blk &
            ocher   .25 .25
1471 A300 75k dp blue, yel & red   .50 .25
      Nos. 1469-1471 (3)   1.00 .75
      Turkish Artists Congress, Ankara.

Kemal
Atatürk — A301

Litho.; Center Embossed
1959, Nov. 10   Perf. 14
1472 A301 500k dark blue   3.50 1.00
   a.   Min. sheet of 1, red, imperf.   4.75 2.00

School
of
Political
Science,
Ankara
A302

1959, Dec. 4   Photo.   Perf. 13½
1473 A302 40k green & brown   .25 .25
1474 A302 40k red brown & bl   .25 .25
1475 A303   1 l lt & dk vio & buff   .70 .25
      Nos. 1473-1475 (3)   1.20 .75
      Political Science School, Ankara, cent.

Emblem — A303

Crossed Swords
Emblem — A304

Design: 40k, Bayonet and flame.
**Inscribed: "Kara Harbokulunum 125
Yili"**

1960, Feb. 28   Litho.   Perf. 10½
1476 A304 30k vermilion & org   .25 .25
1477 A304 40k brown, car & yel   .25 .25
      125th anniv. of the Territorial War College.

Window on
World and
WRY Emblem
A305

150k, Symbolic shanties & uprooted oak
emblem.

1960, Apr. 7
1478 A305   90k brt grnsh bl & blk   .25 .25
1479 A305 105k yellow & brown   .30 .25
      World Refugee Year, 7/1/59-6/30/60.

Spring Flower
Festival — A306

1960, June 4   Photo.   Perf. 11½
                   Granite Paper
1480 A306   30k Carnations   .50 .25
1481 A306   40k Jasmine   .70 .25
1482 A306   75k Rose   1.00 .25
1483 A306 105k Tulip   1.40 .50
      Nos. 1480-1483 (4)   3.60 1.25

Atatürk
Square,
Nicosia
A307

Design: 105k, Map of Cyprus.

1960, Aug. 16   Litho.   Perf. 10½
1484 A307   40k blue & pink   .25 .25
1485 A307 105k blue & yellow   .35 .25
      Independence of the Republic of Cyprus.

Women
and Nest
A308

Design: 30k, Globe and emblem.

1960, Aug. 22   Photo.   Perf. 11½
1486 A308 30k lt vio & yel   .25 .25
1487 A308 75k grnsh bl & gray   .35 .25
      16th meeting of the Women's Intl. Council.

Soccer
A309

#1489, Basketball. #1490, Wrestling. #1491,
Hurdling. #1492, Steeplechase.

1960, Aug. 25
1488 A309 30k yellow green   .55 .45
1489 A309 30k black   .55 .45
1490 A309 30k slate blue   .55 .45
1491 A309 30k purple   .55 .45
1492 A309 30k brown   .55 .45
   a.   Sheet of 25, #1488-1492   20.00 11.50
      Nos. 1488-1492 (5)   2.75 2.25
      17th Olympic Games, Rome, 8/25-9/11.
      Printed in sheets of 25 (5x5) with every hori-
      zontal and every vertical row containing one of
      each design. Also printed in normal sheets of
      100.

Common Design Types
pictured following the introduction.

Europa Issue
Common Design Type
1960, Sept. 19   Size: 33x22mm
1493 CD3   75k green & bl grn   .85 .50
1494 CD3 105k dp bl & lt bl   1.25 .85

Agah Efendi
and Front
Page of
Turcamani
Ahval — A310

1960, Oct. 21   Photo.   Perf. 11½
1495 A310 40k brown blk & sl   .25 .25
1496 A310 60k brn blk & bis brn   .25 .25
      Centenary of Turkish journalism.

UN Emblem and
Torch — A311

Design: 105k, UN headquarters building
and UN emblem forming "15," horiz.

1960, Oct. 24   Unwmk.
1497 A311   90k brt bl & dk bl   .30 .30
1498 A311 105k lt bl grn & brn   .30 .30
      15th anniversary of the United Nations.

Army
Emblem
A312

Tribunal
A313

Design: 195k, "Justice," vert.

1960, Oct. 14   Litho.   Perf. 13
1499 A312 40k violet & bister .25 .25
1500 A313 105k red, gray & brn .25 .25
1501 A313 195k grn, rose red &
        brn .45 .25
    Nos. 1499-1501 (3) .95 .75
Trial of ex-President Celal Bayar and ex-Premier Adnan Menderes.

Revolutionaries and Statue — A314

Prancing Horse,
Broken
Chain — A315

Designs: 30k, Ataturk and hand holding torch. 105k, Youth, soldier and broken chain.

1960, Dec. 1   Photo.   Perf. 14½
1502 A314 10k gray & blk .25 .25
1503 A314 30k purple .25 .25
1504 A315 40k brt red & blk .25 .25
1505 A314 105k blue blk & red .40 .25
    Nos. 1502-1505 (4) 1.15 1.00
Revolution of May 27, 1960.

Faculty
Building
A316

Sculptured Head of
Atatürk — A317

Designs: 40k, Map of Turkey and sun disk.

1961, Jan. 9   Litho.   Perf. 13
1506 A316 30k slate grn & gray .30 .25
1507 A316 40k brn blk & bis brn .40 .25
1508 A317 60k dk green & buff .50 .25
    Nos. 1506-1508 (3) 1.20 .75
25th anniv. of the Faculty of Languages, History and Geography, University of Ankara.

Communication and
Transportation — A318

40k, Highway construction, telephone & telegraph. 75k, New parliament building, Ankara.

1961, Apr. 27   Unwmk.   Perf. 13
1509 A318 30k dull vio & blk .25 .25
1510 A318 40k green & black .35 .25
1511 A318 75k dull blue & blk .45 .25
    Nos. 1509-1511 (3) 1.05 .75
9th conference of ministers of the Central Treaty Org. (CENTO), Ankara.

Flag and
People — A319

Legendary
Wolf and
Osman
Warriors
A320

Design: 60k, "Progress" (Atatürk showing youth the way).

1961, May 27   Litho.
1512 A319 30k multicolored .25 .25
1513 A320 40k sl grn & yel .25 .25
1514 A319 60k grn, pink & dk
        red .55 .25
    Nos. 1512-1514 (3) 1.05 .75
First anniversary of May 27 revolution.

Rockets
A321

Designs: 40k, Crescent and star emblem, "50" and Jet. 75k, Atatürk, eagle and jets, vert.

1961, June 1
1515 A321 30k brn, org yel & blk .25 .25
1516 A321 40k violet & red .25 .25
1517 A321 75k slate blk & bis .55 .25
    Nos. 1515-1517 (3) 1.05 .75
50th anniversary of Turkey's air force.

Europa Issue
Common Design Type
1961, Sept. 18   Perf. 13
Size: 32x22mm
1518 CD4 30k dk violet bl .55 .35
1519 CD4 40k gray .65 .35
1520 CD4 75k vermilion 1.25 .60
    Nos. 1518-1520 (3) 2.45 1.30

Tulip and
Cogwheel — A322

Torch,
Hand and
Cogwheel
A323

1961, Oct. 21   Unwmk.   Litho.
1521 A322 30k slate, pink & sil .25 .25
1522 A323 75k ultra, org & blk .35 .25
Technical and professional schools, cent.

Open Book and
Olive
Branch — A324

1961, Oct. 29
1523 A324 30k red, blk & olive .25 .25
1524 A324 75k brt blue, blk & grn .30 .25
Inauguration of the new Parliament.

Kemal Atatürk
A325   A326
1961-62   Litho.   Perf. 10x10½
Size: 20x25mm
1525 A325 1k brown org ('62) .90 .25
1526 A325 5k blue 1.50 .25
1527 A325 10k sepia 2.40 .25
1528 A326 10k car rose 2.40 .25
1529 A325 30k dull grn ('62) 7.00 .30
Size: 21½x31mm
1530 A325 10 l violet ('62) 14.50 1.90
    Nos. 1525-1530 (6) 28.70 3.20

NATO Emblem and
Dove — A327

Design: 105k, NATO emblem, horiz.

1962, Feb. 18   Unwmk.   Perf. 13
1545 A327 75k dl bl, blk & sil .25 .25
1546 A327 105k crimson, blk &
        sil .60 .25
10th anniv. of Turkey's admission to NATO.

Scouts at
Campfire
A328

60k, Scouts with flag. 105k, Scouts saluting.

1962, July 22   Litho.
1547 A328 30k lt grn, blk & red .25 .25
1548 A328 60k gray, blk & red .60 .25
1549 A328 105k tan, blk & red .80 .25
    Nos. 1547-1549 (3) 1.65 .75
Turkish Boy Scouts, 50th anniversary.

Soldier
Statue — A329

Oxcart from
Victory
Monument,
Ankara
A330

Design: 75k, Atatürk.

1962, Aug. 30   Unwmk.   Perf. 13
1550 A329 30k slate green .25 .25
1551 A330 40k gray & sepia .25 .25
1552 A329 75k gray blk & lt gray .80 .25
    Nos. 1550-1552 (3) 1.30 .75
40th anniv. of Battle of Dumlupinar.

Europa Issue
Common Design Type
1962, Sept. 17   Size: 37x23mm
1553 CD5 75k emerald & blk .65 .40
1554 CD5 105k red & blk .85 .50
1555 CD5 195k blue & blk 1.50 .65
    Nos. 1553-1555 (3) 3.00 1.55
Brown imprint.

Virgin Mary's
House,
Ephesus — A331

40k, Inside view after restoration, horiz. 75k, Outside view, horiz. 105k, Statue of Virgin Mary.

1962, Dec. 8   Photo.   Perf. 13½
1556 A331 30k multicolored .25 .25
1557 A331 40k multicolored .25 .25
1558 A331 75k multicolored .35 .25
1559 A331 105k multicolored .45 .25
    Nos. 1556-1559 (4) 1.30 1.00

20pa Stamp of
1863 — A332

Issue of 1863: 30k, 1pi. 40k, 2pi. 75k, 5pi.

1963, Jan. 13   Perf. 13x13½
1560 A332 10k yellow, brn & blk .25 .25
1561 A332 30k rose, lil & blk .25 .25
1562 A332 40k lt bl, bluish grn &
        blk .25 .25
1563 A332 75k red brn, rose &
        blk .45 .25
    Nos. 1560-1563 (4) 1.20 1.00
Centenary of Turkish postage stamps. See No. 1601, souvenir sheet.

Starving
People
A333

Designs: 40k, Sowers. 75k, Hands protecting Wheat Emblem, and globe.

1963, Mar. 21   Unwmk.   Perf. 13
1564 A333 30k dp bl & dk bl .25 .25
1565 A333 40k brn org & brn .25 .25
1566 A333 75k grn & dk grn .55 .25
    Nos. 1564-1566 (3) 1.05 .75
FAO "Freedom from Hunger" campaign.

Julian's Column,
Ankara — A334

Ethnographic
Museum
A335

10k, Ankara Citadel. 30k, Gazi Institute of
Education. 50k, Atatürk's mausoleum. 60k,
President's residence. 100k, Ataturk's home,
Cankaya. 150k, Parliament building.

1963   **Litho.**   *Perf. 13*

1568	A334	1k sl grn & yel grn	.65	.65
1569	A334	1k purple	.25	.25
1570	A335	5k sepia & buff	.65	.65
1571	A335	10k lil rose & pale		
		bl	.65	.25
1573	A335	30k black & violet	.65	.25
1574	A335	50k blue & yellow	.65	.25
1575	A335	60k dk blue gray	4.00	.65
1576	A335	100k olive brown	2.40	.55
1577	A335	150k dull green	12.00	1.60
		Nos. 1568-1577 (9)	21.90	5.10

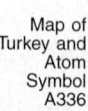 

Map of
Turkey and
Atom
Symbol
A336

Designs: 60k, Symbols of medicine, agriculture, industry and atom. 100k, Emblem of
Turkish Atomic Energy Commission.

1963, May 27   **Unwmk.**   *Perf. 13*

1584	A336	50k red brn & blk	.25	.25
1585	A336	60k grn, dk grn, yel		
		& red	.25	.25
1586	A336	100k violet bl & bl	.55	.30
		Nos. 1584-1586 (3)	1.05	.80

Turkish nuclear research center, 1st anniv.

Meric Bridge
A337

Sultan
Murad I — A338

Designs: 10k, Üçserefeli Mosque. 60k,
Summerhouse, Edirne Palace.

1963, June 17

1587	A338	10k dp bl & yel grn	.25	.25
1588	A337	30k red org & ultra	.25	.25
1589	A337	60k dk bl, red & brn	.25	.25
1590	A338	100k multicolored	1.10	.35
		Nos. 1587-1590 (4)	1.85	1.10

600th anniv. of the conquest of Edirne
(Adrianople).

Soldier
and Rising
Sun
A339

1963, June 28

1591	A339	50k red, blk & gray	.25	.25
1592	A339	100k red, blk & ol	.45	.25

600th anniversary of the Turkish army.

Plowing
A340

Mithat
Pasha — A341

Design: 50k, Agriculture Bank, Ankara.

Perf. 13x13½, 13½x13

1963, Aug. 27   **Photo.**   **Unwmk.**

1593	A340	30k brt yel grn, red		
		brn & grn	.25	.25
1594	A340	50k pale vio & Prus bl	.25	.25
1595	A341	60k gray & green	.30	.25
		Nos. 1593-1595 (3)	.80	.75

Centenary of Agriculture Bank, Ankara.

Sports and
Exhibition
Palace,
Istanbul
and
#5 — A342

Designs: 50k, Sultan Ahmed Mosque & Turkey in Asia #22. 60k, View of Istanbul & Turkey
in Asia #83. 100k, Rumeli Hisari Fortress &
#679. 130k, Ankara Fortress & #C2.

1963, Sept. 7   **Litho.**   *Perf. 13*

1596	A342	10k blk, yel &		
		rose	.25	.25
a.		Rose omitted	37.50	37.50
1597	A342	50k blk, grn &		
		rose lil	.30	.25
1598	A342	60k dk brn, dk bl		
		& blk	.35	.25
1599	A342	100k dk vio & lil		
		rose	.50	.25
1600	A342	130k brn, tan & dp		
		org	.75	.25
		Nos. 1596-1600 (5)	2.15	1.25

"Istanbul 63" Intl. Stamp Exhibition.

**Type of 1963 Inscribed: "F.I.P.
GÜNÜ"**
Souvenir Sheet

Issues of 1863: 10k, 20pa. 50k, 1pi. 60k,
2pi. 130k, 5pi.

Unwmk.

1963, Sept. 13   **Litho.**   *Imperf.*

1601		Sheet of 4	2.00	1.50
a.		A332 10k yel, brown & blk	.25	.25
b.		A332 50k lilac, pink & blk	.25	.25
c.		A332 60k bluish grn, lt bl & blk	.40	.25
d.		A332 130k red brn, pink & blk	.50	.25

Intl. Philatelic Federation.

Europa Issue
Common Design Type

1963, Sept. 16   **Size: 32x24mm**

1602	CD6	50k red & black	.60	.25
1603	CD6	130k bl grn, blk & bl	.80	.35

Atatürk
and First
Parliament
Building
A343

Atatürk and: 50k, Turkish flag. 60k, New
Parliament building.

1963, Oct. 29   **Photo.**   *Perf. 13½*

1604	A343	30k blk, gold, yel &		
		mar	.25	.25
1605	A343	50k dk grn, gold, yel		
		& red	.30	.25
1606	A343	60k dk brn, gold & yel	.40	.25
		Nos. 1604-1606 (3)	.95	.75

40th anniversary of Turkish Republic.

Atatürk, 25th Death
Anniv. — A344

1963, Nov. 10

1607	A344	50k red, gold, grn &		
		brn	.50	.25
1608	A344	60k red, gold, bl &		
		brn	.60	.35

NATO,
15th Anniv.
A346

130k, NATO emblem and olive branch.

1964, Apr. 4   **Litho.**   *Perf. 13*

1610	A346	50k grnsh bl, vio bl		
		& red	.45	.25
1611	A346	130k red & black	.75	.70

12 Stars
and
Europa
with Torch
A347

Design: 130k, Torch and stars.

1964, May 5   **Litho.**   *Perf. 12*

1612	A347	50k red brn, yel &		
		vio bl	.40	.25
1613	A347	130k vio bl, lt bl & org	.80	.50

15th anniversary of Council of Europe.

Hüseyin Rahmi
Gürpinar,
novelist — A348

Portraits: 1k, Hüseyin Rahmi Gürpinar, nov-
elist. 5k, Ismail Hakki Izmirli, scientist. 10k,
Sevket Dag, painter. 50k, Recaizade Mahmut
Ekrem, Writer. 60k, Gazi Ahmet Muhtar
Pasha, commander. 100k, Ahmet Rasim,
writer. 130k, Salih Zeki, mathematician.

1964   **Litho.**   *Perf. 13½x13*

1614	A348	1k red & blk	.25	.25
1615	A348	5k dull grn & blk	.25	.25
1616	A348	10k tan & blk	.25	.25
1617	A348	50k ultra & dk bl	1.25	.25
1618	A348	60k gray & blk	1.40	.25
1619	A348	100k grnsh bl & dk		
		bl	1.50	.25
1620	A348	130k brt grn & dk		
		grn	6.50	.65
		Nos. 1614-1620 (7)	11.40	2.15

Mosque of
Sultan
Ahmed
A349

Kiz Kulesi,
Mersin — A350

Designs: No. 1622, Zeus Temple, Silifke.
No. 1623, View of Amasra. No. 1625, Augustus' Gate and minaret, Ankara.

1964, June 11   **Unwmk.**   *Perf. 13*

1621	A349	50k gray ol & yel grn	.25	.25
1622	A349	50k claret & car	.40	.25
1623	A349	50k dk bl & vio bl	.40	.25
1624	A350	60k sl grn & dk gray	.60	.30
1625	A350	60k dk brn & org brn	.75	.30
		Nos. 1621-1625 (5)	2.40	1.35

Kars
Castle — A351

Alp Arslan,
Conqueror of
Kars,
1064 — A352

1964, Aug. 16   **Unwmk.**   *Perf. 13*

1626	A351	50k blk & pale vio	.40	.40
1627	A352	130k blk, gold, sal &		
		pale vio	1.25	.60

900th anniversary of conquest of Kars.

Europa Issue
Common Design Type

1964, Sept. 14   **Litho.**   *Perf. 13*

Size: 22x33mm

1628	CD7	50k org, ind & sil	.90	.50
1629	CD7	130k lt bl, mag & cit	1.75	.85

Fuat, Resit and Ali Pashas — A353

Design: 60k, Mustafa Resit Pasha, vert.

1964, Nov. 3   *Perf. 13*

**Sizes: 48x33mm (50k, 100k);
22x33mm (60k)**

1630	A353	50k multicolored	.55	.25
1631	A353	60k multicolored	.75	.25
1632	A353	100k multicolored	1.10	.55
		Nos. 1630-1632 (3)	2.40	1.05

125th anniversary of reform decrees.

Parachutist — A354

Designs: 90k, Glider, horiz. 130k, Ataturk
watching squadron in flight.

1965, Feb. 16   **Litho.**   *Perf. 13*

1633	A354	60k lt bl, blk, red &		
		yel	.25	.25
1634	A354	90k bister & multi	.50	.25
1635	A354	130k lt blue & multi	.80	.25
		Nos. 1633-1635 (3)	1.55	.75

Turkish Aviation League, 40th anniv.

Emblem
A355

Designs: 50k, Radio mast and waves, vert.
75k, Hand pressing button.

1965, Feb. 24 Unwmk. *Perf. 13*
1636	A355	30k multicolored	.25	.25
1637	A355	50k multicolored	.25	.25
1638	A355	75k multicolored	.55	.25
	Nos. 1636-1638 (3)		1.05	.75

Telecommunications meeting of the Central Treaty Org., CENTO.

Coast of Ordu — A356

50k, Manavgat Waterfall, Antalya. 60k, Sultan Ahmed Mosque, Istanbul. 100k, Hali Rahman Mosque, Urfa. 130k, Red Tower, Alanya.

1965, Apr. 5 Litho.
1639	A356	30k multicolored	.25	.25
1640	A356	50k multicolored	.35	.25
1641	A356	60k multicolored	.35	.25
1642	A356	100k multicolored	.65	.25
1643	A356	130k multicolored	.95	.25
	Nos. 1639-1643 (5)		2.55	1.25

ITU Emblem, Old and New Communication Equipment — A357

1965, May 17 *Perf. 13*
1644	A357	50k multicolored	.35	.25
1645	A357	130k multicolored	.65	.25

ITU, centenary.

ICY Emblem A358

1965, June 26 Litho. Unwmk.
1646	A358	100k red org, red brn & brt grn	.40	.25
1647	A358	130k gray, lil & ol grn	.65	.35

International Cooperation Year.

Hands Holding Book A358a

Map and Flags of Turkey, Iran and Pakistan A358b

1965, July 21 Unwmk. *Perf. 13*
1648	A358a	50k org brn, yel & dk brn	.30	.25
1649	A358b	75k dl bl, red, grn blk & org	.45	.25

1st anniv. of the signing of the Regional Cooperation Development Pact by Turkey, Iran and Pakistan.
See Iran 1327-1328, Pakistan 217-218.

Kemal Ataturk — A359

1965 Litho. *Perf. 12½*
1650	A359	1k brt green	.40	.25
1651	A359	5k violet blue	.80	.25
1652	A359	10k blue	1.25	.25
1653	A359	25k gray	2.75	.25
1654	A359	30k magenta	2.00	.25
1655	A359	50k brown	3.25	.30
1656	A359	150k orange	11.50	.75
	Nos. 1650-1656 (7)		21.95	2.30

Europa Issue
Common Design Type

1965, Sept. 27 *Perf. 13*
Size: 32x23mm
1665	CD8	50k gray, ultra & grn	1.25	.70
1666	CD8	130k tan, blk & grn	2.25	1.40

Map of Turkey and People A360

Designs: 50k, "1965." 100k, "1965," symbolic eye and man, vert.

Unwmk.
1965, Oct. 24 Litho. *Perf. 13*
1667	A360	10k multicolored	.30	.25
1668	A360	50k grn, blk & lt yel grn	.40	.25
1669	A360	100k orange, sl & blk	.75	.25
	Nos. 1667-1669 (3)		1.45	.75

Issued to publicize the 1965 census.

Plane over Ankara Castle A361

Designs: 30k, Archer and Ankara castle. 50k, Horsemen with spears (ancient game). 100k, Three stamps and medal. 150k, Hands holding book, vert.

1965, Oct. 25
1670	A361	10k brt vio, yel & red	.25	.25
1671	A361	30k multicolored	.25	.25
1672	A361	50k lt gray ol, ind & red	.25	.25
1673	A361	100k gray & multi	.60	.30
	Nos. 1670-1673 (4)		1.35	1.05

Souvenir Sheet
Imperf
1674	A361	150k multicolored	2.75	2.50

1st Natl. Postage Stamp Exhibition "Ankara 65."

Resat Nuri Guntekin, Novelist — A362

Portraits: 5k, Besim Omer Akalin, M.D. 10k, Tevfik Fikret, poet. 25k, Tanburi Cemil, composer. 30k, Ahmet Vefik Pasha, playwright. 50k, Omer Seyfettin, novelist. 60k, Kemalettin Mimaroglu, architect. 150k, Halit Ziya Usakligil, novelist. 220k, Yahya Kemal Beyatli, poet.

1965 Litho. *Perf. 13½x13*
Black Portrait and Inscriptions
1675	A362	1k rose	.25	.25
1676	A362	5k blue	.45	.25
1677	A362	10k buff	.45	.25
1678	A362	25k dull red brn	.75	.25
1679	A362	30k gray	.75	.25
1680	A362	50k orange	1.10	.25
1681	A362	60k red lilac	1.25	.25
1682	A362	150k lt green	1.75	.25
1683	A362	220k tan	3.00	.45
	Nos. 1675-1683 (9)		9.75	2.45

Training Ship Savarona A363

Designs: 60k, Submarine "Piri Reis." 100k, Cruiser "Alpaslan." 130k, Destroyer "Gelibolu." 220k, Destroyer "Gemlik."

1965, Dec. 6 Photo. *Perf. 11½*
1684	A363	50k blue & brown	.35	.25
1685	A363	60k blue & black	.50	.25
1686	A363	100k blue & black	.80	.25
1687	A363	130k blue & vio blk	1.25	.40
1688	A363	220k blue & indigo	1.75	.65
	Nos. 1684-1688 (5)		4.65	1.80

First Congress of Turkish Naval Society.

Kemal Ataturk — A364

Imprint: "Apa Ofset Basimevi"
Black Portrait and Inscriptions

1965 Litho. *Perf. 13½*
1689	A364	1k rose lilac	.60	.25
1690	A364	5k lt green	.80	.25
1691	A364	10k blue gray	1.10	.40
1692	A364	50k olive bister	1.25	.40
1693	A364	150k silver	2.25	.90
	Nos. 1689-1693 (5)		6.00	2.20

See Nos. 1724-1728.

Halide Edip Adivar, Writer — A365

Portraits: 25k, Huseyin Sadettin Arel, writer and composer. 30k, Kamil Akdik, graphic artist. 60k, Abdurrahman Seref, historian. 130k, Naima, historian.

1966 Litho. *Perf. 13½*
1694	A365	25k gray & brn blk	.90	.25
1695	A365	30k rose vio & blk brn	1.10	.25
1696	A365	50k blue & black	1.25	.40
1697	A365	60k lt grn & blk brn	1.40	.25
1698	A365	130k lt vio bl & blk	1.90	.25
	Nos. 1694-1698 (5)		6.55	1.25

Tiles, Green Mausoleum, Bursa — A366

Tiles: 60k, Spring flowers, Hurrem Sultan Mausoleum, Istanbul. 130k, Stylized flowers, 16th century.

1966, May 15 Litho. *Perf. 13½x13*
1699	A366	50k multicolored	.85	.25
1700	A366	60k multicolored	1.40	.50
1701	A366	130k multicolored	2.10	.60
	Nos. 1699-1701 (3)		4.35	1.35

On No. 1700 the black ink was applied by a thermographic process and varnished, producing a shiny, raised effect to imitate the embossed tiles of the design source.

Volleyball — A367

1966, May 20 *Perf. 13x13½*
1702	A367	50k tan & multi	.40	.25

4th Intl. Military Volleyball Championship.

View of Bodrum — A368

Views: 30k, Kusadasi. 50k, Anadolu Hisari, Istanbul. 90k, Marmaris. 100k, Izmir.

1966, May 25 *Perf. 13x13½, 13½x13*
1703	A368	10k multi	.25	.25
1704	A368	30k multi	.65	.25
1705	A368	50k multi, horiz.	.35	.25
1706	A368	90k multi	.35	.25
1707	A368	100k multi, horiz.	.45	.25
	Nos. 1703-1707 (5)		2.05	1.25

Inauguration of Keban Dam — A369

Design: 60k, View of Keban Dam area.

1966, June 10 *Perf. 13½*
1708	A369	50k multicolored	.30	.25
1709	A369	60k multicolored	.50	.25

Visit of King Faisal of Saudi Arabia A370

1966, Aug. 29 Litho. *Perf. 13½x13*
1710	A370	100k car rose & dk car	.75	.30

Symbolic Postmark and Stamp A371

Designs: 60k, Flower made of stamps. 75k, Stamps forming display frames. 100k, Map of Balkan states, magnifying glass and stamp.

1966, Sept. 3 *Perf. 13½x13*
1711	A371	50k multicolored	.25	.25
1712	A371	60k multicolored	.25	.25
1713	A371	75k multicolored	.55	.25
	Nos. 1711-1713 (3)		1.05	.75

Souvenir Sheet
Imperf
1714	A371	100k multicolored	2.50	2.10

2nd "Balkanfila" stamp exhibition, Istanbul.

Sultan Suleiman on Horseback
A372

90k, Mausoleum, Istanbul. 130k, Suleiman.

1966, Sept. 6   **Perf. 13½x13**
1715	A372	60k multicolored	.65	.25
1716	A372	90k multicolored	1.10	.40
1717	A372	130k multicolored	2.25	.65
		Nos. 1715-1717 (3)	4.00	1.30

Sultan Suleiman the Magnificent (1496?-1566). On No. 1717 a gold frame was applied by raised thermographic process.

Europa Issue
Common Design Type
1966, Sept. 26   **Litho.**   **Perf. 13x13½**
Size: 22x33mm
1718	CD9	50k lt bl, vio bl & blk	1.10	.65
a.		Black (inscriptions & imprint) omitted	65.00	
1719	CD9	130k lil, dk red lil & blk	2.25	1.10

Symbols of Education, Science and Culture A373

1966, Nov. 4   **Litho.**   **Perf. 13**
| 1720 | A373 | 130k brn, bis brn & yel | .50 | .25 |

UNESCO, 20th anniversary.

Middle East University of Technology A374

Designs: 100k, Atom symbol. 130k, design symbolizing sciences.

1966, Nov. 15
1721	A374	50k multicolored	.25	.25
1722	A374	100k multicolored	.55	.55
1723	A374	130k multicolored	.85	.55
		Nos. 1721-1723 (3)	1.65	1.05

10th anniv. of the Middle East University of Technology.

Ataturk Type of 1965
Imprint: "Kiral Matbaasi — Ist"
1966   **Litho.**   **Perf. 12½**
Black Portrait and Inscriptions
1724	A364	25k yellow	.35	.25
1725	A364	30k pink	.50	.25
1726	A364	50k rose lilac	1.50	.25
1727	A364	90k pale brown	1.25	.25
1728	A364	100k gray	1.50	.25
		Nos. 1724-1728 (5)	5.10	1.25

Statue of Ataturk, Ankara — A375

Equestrian Statues of Ataturk: No. 1729A, Statue in Izmir. No. 1729B, Statue in Samsun.

Without Imprint
1967   **Litho.**   **Perf. 13x12½**
Size: 23x16mm
| 1729 | A375 | 10k black & yellow | .30 | .25 |

Inscribed "1967"
Imprint: Kiral Matbaasi
Size: 22x15mm
1729A	A375	10k black & salmon	.30	.25
1729B	A375	10k black & lt grn	.30	.25
		Nos. 1729-1729B (3)	.90	.75

Issued for use on greeting cards. See Nos. 1790-1791A, 1911.

Puppets Karagöz and Hacivat — A376

Intl. Tourist Year Emblem and: 60k, Sword and shield game. 90k, Traditional military band. 100k, raised effect.

Perf. 13x13½, 13½x13
1967, Mar. 30   **Litho.**
1730	A376	50k multicolored	.90	.25
1731	A376	60k multicolored	1.25	.25
1732	A376	90k multicolored	1.60	.45
1733	A376	100k multicolored	2.50	.65
		Nos. 1730-1733 (4)	6.25	1.60

Intl. Tourist Year. On No. 1733 the black ink was applied by a thermographic process and varnished, producing a shiny, raised effect.

Woman Vaccinating Child, Knife and Lancet — A377

1967, Apr. 1   **Perf. 13x13½**
| 1734 | A377 | 100k multicolored | .60 | .25 |

250th anniv. of smallpox vaccination (variolation) in Turkey. The gold was applied by a thermographic process and varnished, producing a shiny, raised effect.

Fallow Deer — A378

1967, Apr. 23   **Litho.**   **Perf. 13x13½**
1735	A378	50k shown	.50	.25
1736	A378	60k Wild goat	.65	.25
1737	A378	100k Brown bear	.90	.25
1738	A378	130k Wild boar	1.25	.40
		Nos. 1735-1738 (4)	3.30	1.15

Soccer Players and Emblem with Map of Europe A379

130k, Players at left, smaller emblem.

1967, May 1   **Perf. 13**
| 1739 | A379 | 50k multicolored | 1.00 | .25 |
| 1740 | A379 | 130k yellow & multi | 1.40 | .50 |

20th Intl. Youth Soccer Championships.

Sivas Hospital A380

1967, July 1   **Litho.**   **Perf. 13**
| 1741 | A380 | 50k multicolored | .40 | .25 |

750th anniversary of Sivas Hospital.

Selim Sirri Tarcan A381

60k, Olympic Rings, Baron Pierre de Coubertin.

1967, July 20
1742	A381	50k lt blue & multi	.35	.25
1743	A381	60k lilac & multi	.35	.25
a.		Pair, #1742-1743	.80	.65

1st Turkish Olympic competitions.

Ahmed Mithat, Writer — A382

Portraits: 5k, Admiral Turgut Reis. 50k, Sokullu Mehmet, statesman. 100k, Nedim, poet. 150k, Osman Hamdi, painter.

1967   **Litho.**   **Perf. 12½**
1744	A382	1k green & blk	.65	.25
1745	A382	5k dp bister & blk	1.00	.25
1746	A382	50k brt violet & blk	1.40	.25
1747	A382	100k citron & blk	2.50	.40
1748	A382	150k yellow & blk	4.00	.40
		Nos. 1744-1748 (5)	9.55	1.55

Ruins of St. John's Church, Ephesus A383

Design: 130k, Inside view of Virgin Mary's House, Ephesus.

1967, July 26   **Perf. 13**
| 1749 | A383 | 130k multicolored | .40 | .25 |
| 1750 | A383 | 220k multicolored | .95 | .50 |

Visit of Pope Paul VI to the House of the Virgin Mary in Ephesus, July 26.

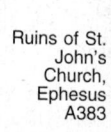

Plate on Firing Grid and Ornaments A384

1967, Sept. 1
| 1751 | A384 | 50k pale lil, blk, ind & bl | .50 | .25 |

5th International Ceramics Exhibition.

View of Istanbul and Emblem A385

1967, Sept. 4   **Litho.**   **Perf. 13**
| 1752 | A385 | 130k dk blue & gray | .80 | .25 |

9th Congress of the Intl. Commission of Large Dams.

Stamps, Ornament and Map of Turkey A386

Design: 60k, Grapes and stamps.

1967
1753	A386	50k multicolored	.35	.25
1754	A386	60k multicolored	.45	.25
a.		Souvenir sheet, #1753-1754	2.50	2.50

Intl. Trade Fair, Izmir.

Kemal Ataturk — A387

1967   **Litho.**   **Perf. 11½x12**
Booklet Stamps
1755	A387	10k black & lt ol grn	3.25	.80
a.		Booklet pane of 10	100.00	
b.		Booklet pane of 25	250.00	
1756	A387	50k black & pale rose	3.25	.80
a.		Booklet pane of 2	40.00	
b.		Bklt. pane, 5 #1755, 4 #1756 + label	35.00	

Symbolic Water Cycle — A388

1967, Dec. 1   **Litho.**   **Perf. 13**
| 1757 | A388 | 90k lt grn, blk & org | .60 | .25 |
| 1758 | A388 | 130k lilac, blk & org | .70 | .60 |

Hydrological Decade (UNESCO), 1965-74.

Child and Angora Cat, Man with Microscope — A389

60k, Horse and man with microscope.

1967, Dec. 23   **Perf. 13**
| 1759 | A389 | 50k multicolored | .50 | .25 |
| 1760 | A389 | 60k multicolored | .70 | .40 |

125th anniv. of Turkish veterinary medicine.

Human Rights Flame — A390

1968, Jan. 1   **Perf. 13x13½**
| 1761 | A390 | 50k rose lil, dk bl & org | .25 | .25 |
| 1762 | A390 | 130k lt bl, dk bl & red org | .75 | .25 |

International Human Rights Year.

Archer on Horseback — A391

Miniatures, 16th Century: 50k, Investiture. 60k, Sultan Suleiman the Magnificent receiving an ambassador, vert. 100k, Musicians.

Perf. 13x13½, 13½x13

1968, Mar. 1			**Litho.**	
1763	A391	50k multicolored	.70	.70
1764	A391	60k multicolored	1.40	1.40
1765	A391	90k multicolored	1.75	1.75
1766	A391	100k multicolored	2.10	2.10
	Nos. 1763-1766 (4)		5.95	5.95

Kemal Ataturk — A392

1968		**Litho.**	**Perf. 12½**	
1767	A392	1k dk & lt blue	.35	.25
1768	A392	5k dk & lt green	.55	.25
1769	A392	50k org brn & yel	2.10	.25
1770	A392	200k dk brown & pink	6.50	.30
	Nos. 1767-1770 (4)		9.50	1.05

Law Book and Oak Branch A393

1968, Apr. 1			**Perf. 13**	
1771	A393	50k multicolored	.35	.35
1772	A394	60k multicolored	.40	.40

Centenary of the Court of Appeal.

Mithat Pasha and Scroll A394

Designs: 50k, Scales of Justice. 60k, Ahmet Cevdet Pasha and scroll.

1968, Apr. 1				
1773	A393	50k multicolored	.30	.25
1774	A394	60k multicolored	.50	.25

Centenary of the Supreme Court.

Europa Issue
Common Design Type

1968, May 6		**Litho.**	**Perf. 13**	
		Size: 31½x23mm		
1775	CD11	100k pck bl, yel & red	1.75	.75
1776	CD11	130k green, yel & red	3.25	1.25

Yacht Kismet — A395

1968, June 15		**Litho.**	**Perf. 13**	
1777	A395	50k lt ultra & multi	.80	.80

Round-the-world trip of the yacht Kismet, Aug. 22, 1965-June 14, 1968.

"Fight Usury" A396

1968, June 19				
1778	A396	50k multicolored	.65	.50

Centenary of the Pawn Office, Istanbul.

Sakarya Battle and Independence Medal — A397

130k, Natl. anthem & reverse of medal.

1968, Aug. 30			**Perf. 13x13½**	
1779	A397	50k gold & multi	.75	.40
1780	A397	130k gold & multi	1.25	.60

Turkish Independence medal. The gold on Nos. 1779-1780 was applied by a thermographic process and varnished, producing a shiny, raised effect.

Ataturk and Galatasaray High School — A398

50k, "100" and old and new school emblems. 60k, Portraits of Beyazit II and Gulbaba.

1968, Sept. 1			**Litho.**	
1781	A398	50k gray & multi	.25	.25
1782	A398	60k tan & multi	.50	.50
1783	A398	100k lt blue & multi	.75	.75
	Nos. 1781-1783 (3)		1.50	1.50

Centenary of Galatasaray High School.

Charles de Gaulle — A399

1968, Oct. 25		**Litho.**	**Perf. 13**	
1784	A399	130k multicolored	1.25	.70

Visit of President Charles de Gaulle of France to Turkey.

Kemal Ataturk — A400

Ataturk and his Speech to Youth — A401

50k, Ataturk's tomb and Citadel of Ankara. 60k, Ataturk looking out a train window. 250k, Framed portrait of Ataturk in military uniform.

1968, Nov. 10				
1785	A400	30k orange & blk	.30	.25
1786	A400	50k brt grn & sl grn	.30	.25
1787	A400	60k bl grn & blk	.35	.25
1788	A401	100k blk, gray & brt grn	.70	.25
1789	A401	250k multicolored	1.25	.40
	Nos. 1785-1789 (5)		2.90	1.40

30th death anniv. of Kemal Ataturk.

Ataturk Statue Type of 1967

Equestrian Statues of Ataturk: No. 1790, Statue in Zonguldak. No. 1791, Statue in Antakya. No. 1791A, Statue in Bursa.

Imprint: Kiral Matbaasi 1968

1968-69		**Litho.**	**Perf. 13x12½**	
		Size: 22x15mm		
1790	A375	10k black & lt blue	.25	.25
1791	A375	10k blk & brt rose lil	.25	.25

Perf. 13½
Imprint: Tifdruk Matbaacilik Sanayii A. S. 1969
Size: 21x16½mm

1791A	A375	10k dk grn & tan ('69)	.30	.25
	Nos. 1790-1791A (3)		.80	.75

Ince Minare Mosque, Konya — A402

Historic Buildings: 10k, Doner Kumbet (tomb), Kayseri. 50k, Karatay Medresse (University Gate), Konya. 100k, Ortakoy Mosque, Istanbul. 200k, Ulu Mosque, Divriki.

1968-69		**Photo.**	**Perf. 13x13½**	
1792	A402	1k dk brn & buff ('69)	.25	.25
1793	A402	10k plum & dl rose ('69)	.50	.25
1794	A402	50k dk ol grn & gray	.65	.25
1795	A402	100k dk & lt grn ('69)	1.75	.40
1796	A402	200k dp bl & lt bl ('69)	2.75	.55
	Nos. 1792-1796 (5)		5.90	1.70

ILO Emblem A403

1969, Apr. 15		**Litho.**	**Perf. 13**	
1797	A403	130k dk red & black	.80	.25

ILO, 50th anniv.

Sultana Hafsa, Medical Pioneer A404

1969, Apr. 26		**Litho.**	**Perf. 13½x13**	
1798	A404	60k multicolored	1.25	1.00

Europa Issue
Common Design Type

1969, Apr. 28			**Perf. 13**	
		Size: 32x23mm		
1799	CD12	100k dull vio & multi	1.60	.65
1800	CD12	130k gray grn & multi	2.25	1.60

Kemal Ataturk — A405

Ataturk and S.S. Bandirma A406

1969, May 19		**Litho.**	**Perf. 13**	
1801	A405	50k multicolored	.40	.25
1802	A406	60k multicolored	.60	.35

50th anniv. of the landing of Kemal Ataturk at Samsun.

Map of Istanbul — A407

1969, May 31				
1803	A407	130k vio bl, lt bl, gold & red	.55	.25

22nd Congress of the Intl. Chamber of Commerce, Istanbul.

Educational Progress A408

Agricultural Progress A409

Designs: 90k, Pouring ladle and industrial symbols. 100k, Road sign (highway construction). 180k, Oil industry chart and symbols.

1969		**Litho.**	**Perf. 13½x13**	
1804	A408	1k black & gray	.25	.25
1805	A408	1k black & bis brn	.25	.25
1806	A408	1k black & lt grn	.25	.25
1807	A408	1k black & lt vio	.25	.25
1808	A408	1k black & org red	.25	.25
1809	A409	50k brown & ocher	.65	.25

1810 A409 90k blk & grnsh gray 1.10 .25
1811 A408 100k black & org red 1.50 .25
1812 A408 180k violet & orange 2.50 .25
Nos. 1804-1812 (9) 7.00 2.25

Issued: 1, 100k, 4/8; 50k, 6/11; 90, 180k, 8/15.

Sultan
Suleiman
Receiving
Sheik Abdul
Latif — A410

Designs: 80k, Lady Serving Wine, Safavi miniature, Iran. 130k, Lady on Balcony, Mogul miniature, Pakistan.

1969, July 21   Litho.   Perf. 13
1813 A410 50k yellow & multi .45 .25
1814 A410 80k yellow & multi .75 .25
1815 A410 130k yellow & multi 1.25 .50
Nos. 1813-1815 (3) 2.45 1.00

5th anniv. of the signing of the Regional Cooperation for Development Pact by Turkey, Iran and Pakistan.
See Iran 1513-1515, Pakistan 274-276.

Kemal
Ataturk — A411

Design: 60k, Ataturk monument and bas-relief showing congress.

1969, July 23
1816 A411 50k black & gray .65 .25
1817 A411 60k black & grnsh
            gray 1.15 .50

50th anniversary, Congress of Erzerum.

Sivas
Congress
Delegates
A412

Design: 50k, Congress Hall.

1969, Sept. 4   Litho.   Perf. 13
1818 A412 50k dk brn & dp rose .35 .35
1819 A412 60k olive blk & yel .45 .45

50th anniv. of the Congress of Sivas (preparation for the Turkish war of independence).

Bar Dance — A413

Folk Dances: 50k, Candle dance (çaydaçira). 60k, Scarf dance (halay). 100k, Sword dance (kiliç-kalkan). 130k, Two male dancers (zeybek), vert.

1969, Sept. 9
1820 A413 30k brown & multi .45 .25
1821 A413 50k multicolored .55 .25
1822 A413 60k multicolored .90 .25
1823 A413 100k yellow & multi 1.00 1.00
1824 A413 130k multicolored 1.60 .55
Nos. 1820-1824 (5) 4.50 2.30

1914
Airplane
"Prince
Celaleddin"
A414

75k, First Turkish letter carried by air.

1969, Oct. 18   Litho.   Perf. 13
1825 A414 60k dk blue & blue .35 .25
1826 A414 75k black & bister .45 .25

55th anniv. of the first Turkish mail transported by air.

"Kutadgu
Bilig"
A415

1969, Nov. 20   Litho.   Perf. 13
1827 A415 130k ol bis, brn &
            gold .55 .25

900th anniv. of "Kutadgu Bilig," a book about the function of the state, compiled by Jusuf of Balasagun in Tashkent, 1069.

Ataturk's Arrival in Ankara, after a
Painting — A416

Design: 60k, Ataturk and his coworkers in automobiles arriving in Ankara, after a photograph.

1969, Dec. 27   Litho.   Perf. 13
1828 A416 50k multicolored .75 .25
1829 A416 60k multicolored 1.25 .30

50th anniv. of Kemal Ataturk's arrival in Ankara, Dec. 27, 1919.

Bosporus Bridge, Map of Europe and
Asia — A417

Design: 60k, View of proposed Bosporus Bridge and shore lines.

1970, Feb. 20   Litho.   Perf. 13
1830 A417 60k gold & multi .75 .30
1831 A417 130k gold & multi 1.50 .65

Foundation ceremonies for the bridge across the Bosporus linking Europe and Asia.

Kemal Ataturk   Kemal Ataturk
and Signature   A419
A418

1970   Litho.   Perf. 13
1832 A418 1k dp orange & brn .25 .25
1833 A419 5k silver & blk .25 .25
1834 A419 30k citron & blk .35 .25
1835 A418 50k lt olive & blk .45 .25
1836 A419 50k pink & blk .75 .25
1837 A419 75k lilac & blk 1.50 .25
1838 A419 100k blue & blk 1.00 .25
Nos. 1832-1838 (7) 4.55 1.75

For surcharge see No. 2078.

Education Year
Emblem — A420

1970, Mar. 16
1839 A420 130k ultra, pink & rose
            lil .80 .25

International Education Year.

Turkish EXPO '70
Emblem — A421

100k, EXPO '70 emblem & Turkish pavilion.

1970, Mar. 27
1840 A421 50k gold & multi .25 .25
1841 A421 100k gold & multi .60 .25

EXPO '70 International Exhibition, Osaka, Japan, Mar. 15-Sept. 13.

Opening of
Grand
National
Assembly
A422

Design: 60k, Session of First Grand National Assembly, 1920.

1970, Apr. 23
1842 A422 50k multicolored .35 .25
1843 A422 60k multicolored .45 .25

Turkish Grand National Assembly, 50th anniv.

Emblem of
Cartographic
Service
A423

Map of Turkey and Gen. Mehmet
Sevki Pasha — A424

Designs: 60k, Plane and aerial mapping survey diagram. 100k, Triangulation point in mountainous landscape.

Perf. 13½x13 (A423), 13x13½ (A424)
1970, May 2   Litho.
1844 A423 50k blue & multi .40 .25
1845 A424 60k blk, gray grn &
            brick red .40 .25
1846 A423 100k multicolored .60 .35
1847 A424 130k multicolored 1.00 .50
Nos. 1844-1847 (4) 2.40 1.35

Turkish Cartographic Service, 75th anniv.

Europa Issue
Common Design Type
1970, May 4   Perf. 13
Size: 37x23mm
1848 CD13 100k ver, blk & org 1.50 .75
1849 CD13 130k dk bl grn, blk &
            org 3.50 1.50

Inauguration of UPU Headquarters,
Bern — A425

1970, May 20
1850 A425 60k blk & dull blue .45 .25
1851 A425 130k blk & dl ol grn .80 .35

Lady with
Mimosa, by
Osman Hamdi
(1842-1910)
A426

Paintings: No. 1853, Deer, by Seker Ahmet (1841-1907). No. 1854, Portrait of Fevzi Cakmak, by Avni Lifij (d. 1927). No. 1855, Sailboats, by Nazmi Ziya (1881-1937); horiz.

1970   Litho.   Perf. 13
Size: 29x49mm
1852 A426 250k multicolored 1.25 .35
1853 A426 250k multicolored 1.25 .35
Size: 32x49mm
1854 A426 250k multicolored 1.25 .35
Size: 73½x33mm
1855 A426 250k multicolored 1.25 .35
Nos. 1852-1855 (4) 5.00 1.40

Issued: #1852-1853, 6/15; #1854-1855, 12/15.

Turkish Folk
Art — A427

1970, June 15
1856 A427 50k multicolored .40 .25

3rd National Stamp Exhibition, ANKARA 70, Oct. 28-Nov. 4. Pane of 50, each stamp setenant with label. This 50k, in pane of 50 without labels, was re-issued Oct. 28 with Nos. 1867-1869.

View of
Fethiye
A428

80k, Seeyo-Se-Pol Bridge, Esfahan, Iran. 130k, Saiful Malook Lake, Pakistan.

1970, July 21   Litho.   Perf. 13
1857 A428 60k multicolored .35 .25
1858 A428 80k multicolored .50 .25
1859 A428 130k multicolored .75 .35
Nos. 1857-1859 (3) 1.60 .85

6th anniv. of the signing of the Regional Cooperation for Development Pact by Turkey, Iran and Pakistan.
See Iran 1558-1560, Pakistan 290-292.

Sultan Balim's
Tomb — A429

Haci Bektas Veli — A430

30k, Tomb of Haci Bektas Veli, horiz.

1970, Aug. 16   Litho.   Perf. 13
1860 A429 30k multicolored   .25   .25
1861 A429 100k multicolored   .70   .25
1862 A430 180k multicolored   1.40 .25
      Nos. 1860-1862 (3)   2.35 .75

700th death anniv. of Haci Bektas Veli, mystic.

Hittite Sun Disk and "ISO" A431

1970, Sept. 15
1863 A431 110k car rose, gold &
                blk   .45   .45
1864 A431 150k ultra, gold & blk   .75   .45

8th General Council Meeting of the Intl. Standardization Org., Ankara.

UN Emblem, People and Globe — A432

100k, UN emblem and propeller, horiz.

1970, Oct. 24   Litho.   Perf. 13
1865 A432 100k gray & multi   .45   .25
1866 A432 220k multicolored   .75   .35

25th anniversary of the United Nations.

Stamp "Flower" and Book — A433

Designs: 60k, Ataturk monument and stamps, horiz. 130k, Abstract flower.

1970, Oct. 28
1867 A433 10k multicolored   .25   .25
1868 A433 60k blue & multi   .40   .25

Souvenir Sheet
1869 A433 130k dk green & org   2.50 1.90

3rd National Stamp Exhibition, ANKARA 70, Oct. 28-Nov. 4. See note below No. 1856.

Inönü Battle Scene — A434

Design: No. 1871, Second Battle of Inönü.

1971   Litho.   Perf. 13
1870 A434 100k multicolored   .80   .25
1871 A434 100k multicolored   .80   .25

1st and 2nd Battles of Inönü, 50th anniv. Issue dates: #1870, Jan. 10; #1871, Apr. 1.

Village on River Bank, by Ahmet Sekür — A435

Painting: No. 1872, Landscape, Yildiz Palace Garden, by Ahmet Ragip Bicakcilar.

1971, Mar. 15   Litho.   Perf. 13
1872 A435 250k multicolored   1.25 .40
1873 A435 250k multicolored   1.25 .40

See #1901-1902, 1909-1910, 1937-1938.

Campaign Against Discrimination A436

1971, Mar. 21   Litho.   Perf. 13
1874 A436 100k multicolored   .45   .25
1875 A436 250k gray & multi   .85   .35

Intl. Year against Racial Discrimination.

Europa Issue
Common Design Type

1971, May 3   Litho.   Perf. 13
Size: 31½x22½mm
1876 CD14 100k lt bl, cl & mag   2.10 1.00
1877 CD14 150k dp org, grn &
                red   3.50 1.50

Kemal Ataturk
A437   A438

1971
1878 A437 5k gray & ultra   .60   .25
1879 A437 25k gray & dk red   .90   .25
1880 A438 25k brown & pink   .60   .25
1881 A437 100k gray & violet   1.25 .25
1882 A438 100k green & salm-
                on   1.25 .35
1883 A438 250k blue & gray   3.00 .60
1884 A438 400k tan & olive
                grn   5.00 .70
      Nos. 1878-1884 (7)   12.60 2.65

Pres. Kemal Gürsel — A439

1971, May 27   Litho.   Perf. 13
1885 A439 100k multicolored   .50   .25

Revolution of May 27, 1960; Kemal Gürsel (1895-1966), president.

Mosque of Selim, Edirne — A440

150k, Religious School, Chaharbagh, Iran. 200k, Badshahi Mosque, Pakistan.

1971, July 21   Litho.   Perf. 13
1886 A440 100k multi   .40   .25
1887 A440 150k multi   .55   .25
1888 A440 200k multi, horiz.   .80   .25
      Nos. 1886-1888 (3)   1.75 .75

Regional Cooperation by Turkey, Iran and Pakistan, 7th anniversary. See Iran 1599-1601, Pakistan 305-307.

Alp Arslan and Battle of Malazkirt — A441

Design: 250k, Archers on horseback.

1971, Aug. 26   Litho.   Perf. 13x13½
1889 A441 100k multicolored   .75   .25
1890 A441 250k red, org & blk   1.20 .40

900th anniversary of the Battle of Malazkirt, which established the Seljuk Dynasty in Asia Minor.

Battle of Sakarya — A442

1971, Sept. 13
1891 A442 100k violet & multi   1.00 .45

50th anniversary of the victory of Sakarya.

Turkey-Bulgaria Railroad — A443

Designs: 110k, Ferry and map of Lake Van. 250k, Turkey-Iran railroad.

1971
1892 A443 100k multicolored   .75   .25
1893 A443 110k multicolored   .75   .25
1894 A443 250k yellow & multi   1.75 .60
      Nos. 1892-1894 (3)   3.25 1.10

Turkish railroad connections with Bulgaria &Iran. Issued: 110, 250k, 9/27; 100k, 10/4.

Soccer and Map of Mediterranean A444

200k, Runner and stadium, vert. 250k, Shot put and map of Mediterranean, vert.

1971, Oct. 6
1895 A444 100k dull vio & blk   .45   .25
1896 A444 200k brn, blk & emer   .80   .35

Souvenir Sheet
Imperf
1897 A444 250k ol bis & slate
                grn   2.00 1.75

Mediterranean Games, Izmir.

Tomb of Cyrus the Great — A445

Designs: 100k, Harpist, Persian mosaic, vert. 150k, Ataturk and Riza Shah Pahlavi.

1971, Oct. 13
1898 A445 25k lt blue & multi   .35   .25
1899 A445 100k multicolored   .80   .25
1900 A445 150k dk brown & buff   1.25 .35
      Nos. 1898-1900 (3)   2.40 .85

2500th anniversary of the founding of the Persian empire by Cyrus the Great.

Painting Type of 1971

No. 1901, Sultan Mohammed I and his Staff. No. 1902, Palace with tiled walls.

1971, Nov. 15   Litho.   Perf. 13
1901 A435 250k multicolored   1.25 .40
1902 A435 250k multicolored   1.25 .40

Yunus Emre — A446

1971, Dec. 27   Litho.   Perf. 13
1903 A446 100k brown & multi   .65   .25

650th death anniv. of Yunus Emre, Turkish folk poet.

First Turkish World Map and Book Year Emblem — A447

1972, Jan. 3   Perf. 13
1904 A447 100k buff & multi   .50   .25

International Book Year.

Doves and NATO Emblem — A448

1972, Feb. 18   Litho.   Perf. 13
1905 A448 100k dull grn, blk &
                gray   1.40 .40
1906 A448 250k dull bl, blk &
                gray   1.75 1.00

Turkey's membership in NATO, 20th anniv.

Europa Issue
Common Design Type
1972, May 2   Litho.   Perf. 13
Size: 22x33mm
1907	CD15	110k blue & multi	3.00	1.00
1908	CD15	250k brown & multi	4.50	2.00

Painting Type of 1971
No. 1909, Forest, Seker Ahmet. No. 1910, View of Gebze, Anatolia, by Osman Hamdi.

1972, May 15   Litho.
1909	A435	250k multicolored	1.25	.35
1910	A435	250k multicolored	1.25	.35

Ataturk Statue Type of 1967
Imprint: Ajans - Turk/Ankara 1972

Design: 25k, Ataturk Statue in front of Ethnographic Museum, Ankara.

Perf. 12½x11½
1972, June 12   Litho.
Size: 22x15½mm
1911	A375	25k black & buff	.25	.25

Fisherman, by Cevat Dereli — A449

Paintings: 125k, Young Man, by Abdur Rehman Chughtai (Pakistan). 150k, Persian Woman, by Behzad.

1972, July 21   Litho.   Perf. 13
1912	A449	100k gold & multi	.90	.25
1913	A449	125k gold & multi	1.50	.40
1914	A449	150k gold & multi	1.60	.55
		Nos. 1912-1914 (3)	4.00	1.20

Regional Cooperation for Development Pact among Turkey, Iran and Pakistan, 8th anniv. See Iran 1647-1649, Pakistan 322-324.

Ataturk and Commanders at Mt. Koca — A450

Designs: No. 1916, Battle of the Commander-in-chief. No. 1917, Turkish army entering Izmir. 110k, Artillery and cavalry.

1972   Litho.   Perf. 13x13½
1915	A450	100k lt ultra & blk	1.00	.25
1916	A450	100k pink & multi	1.00	.25
1917	A450	100k yellow & multi	1.00	.25
1918	A450	110k orange & multi	1.00	.25
		Nos. 1915-1918 (4)	4.00	1.00

50th anniv. of fight for establishment of independent Turkish republic. Issued: #1915, 1918, 8/26; #1916, 8/30; #1917, 9/9.

"Cancer is Curable" A451

1972, Oct. 10   Litho.   Perf. 12½x13
1919	A451	100k blk, brt bl & red	.40	.25

Fight against cancer.

International Railroad Union Emblem — A452

1972, Dec. 31   Litho.   Perf. 13
1920	A452	100k sl grn, ocher & red	.50	.25

Intl. Railroad Union, 50th anniv.

Kemal Ataturk — A453

1972-76   Litho.   Perf. 13½x13
Size: 21x26mm
1921	A453	5k gray & blue	.25	.25
1922	A453	25k orange ('75)	.35	.25
1923	A453	100k buff & red brn ('73)	1.25	.25
1924	A453	100k lt gray & gray ('75)	.45	.25
1925	A453	110k lt bl & vio bl	1.00	.35
1926	A453	125k dull grn ('73)	1.60	.25
1927	A453	150k tan & brown	1.25	.25
1928	A453	150k lt grn & grn ('75)	.35	.25
1929	A453	175k yel & lil ('73)	2.25	.35
1930	A453	200k buff & red	1.60	.25
1931	A453	250k pink & pur ('75)	.40	.25
1931A	A453	400k gray & Prus bl ('76)	.45	.25
1932	A453	500k pink & violet	2.75	.65
1933	A453	500k gray & ultra ('75)	1.00	.30

Size: 22x33mm
Perf. 13
1934	A453	10 l pink & car rose ('75)	2.25	.30
		Nos. 1921-1934 (15)	17.20	4.45

See Nos. 2060-2061. For surcharges see Nos. 2180-2181.

Europa Issue
Common Design Type
1973, Apr. 4   Litho.   Perf. 13
Size: 32x23mm
1935	CD16	110k gray & multi	3.25	1.75
1936	CD16	250k multicolored	6.75	2.75

Painting Type of 1971
Paintings: No. 1937, Beyazit Almshouse, Istanbul, by Ahmet Ziya Akbulut. No. 1938, Flowers, by Suleyman Seyyit, vert.

1973, June 15   Litho.   Perf. 13
1937	A435	250k multicolored	1.25	.50
1938	A435	250k multicolored	1.25	.50

Helmet, Sword and Oak Leaves — A454

Design: 100k, Helmet, sword and laurel.

1973, June 28   Perf. 13x12½
1939	A454	90k brown, gray & grn	.75	.25
1940	A454	100k brown, lem & grn	.95	.40

Army Day.

Mausoleum of Antiochus I — A455

Designs: 100k, Colossal heads, mausoleum of Antiochus I (69-34 B.C.), Commagene, Turkey. 150k, Statue, Shahdad Kerman, Persia, 3000 B.C. 200k, Street, Mohenjo-daro, Pakistan.

1973, July 21   Litho.   Perf. 13
1941	A455	100k lt blue & multi	.35	.25
1942	A455	150k olive & multi	.50	.25
1943	A455	200k brown & multi	.75	.95
		Nos. 1941-1943 (3)	1.60	1.45

Regional Cooperation for Development Pact among Turkey, Iran and Pakistan, 9th anniv. See Iran 1714-1716, Pakistan 343-345.

Minelayer Nusret A456

Designs: 25k, Destroyer Istanbul. 100k, Speedboat Simsek and Naval College. 250k, Two-masted training ship Nuvid-i Futuh.

1973, Aug. 1   Size: 31½x22mm
1944	A456	5k Prus bl & multi	.25	.25
1945	A456	25k Prus bl & multi	.25	.25
1946	A456	100k Prus bl & multi	1.10	.25

Size: 48x32mm
1947	A456	250k blue & multi	2.50	.40
		Nos. 1944-1947 (4)	4.10	1.15

abu-al-Rayhan al-Biruni — A457

1973, Sept. 4   Litho.   Perf. 13x12½
1948	A457	250k multicolored	.80	.80

abu-al-Rayhan al-Biruni (973-1048), philosopher and mathematician.

Emblem of Darussafaka Foundation — A458

1973, Sept. 15   Perf. 13
1949	A458	100k silver & multi	.30	.25

Centenary of the educational and philanthropic Darussafaka Foundation.

BALKANFILA IV Emblem — A459

Designs: 110k, Symbolic view and stamps. 250k, "Balkanfila 4."

1973   Litho.   Perf. 13
1950	A459	100k gray & multi	.35	.25
1951	A459	110k multicolored	.25	.25
1952	A459	250k multicolored	.45	.25
		Nos. 1950-1952 (3)	1.05	.75

BALKANFILA IV, Philatelic Exhibition of Balkan Countries, Izmir, Oct. 26-Nov. 5. Issued: 100k, Sept. 26; 110k, 250k, Oct. 26.

Sivas Shepherd Dog — A460

1973, Oct. 4
1953	A460	25k shown	.25	.25
1954	A460	100k Angora cat	1.00	.25

Kemal Ataturk — A461

1973, Oct. 10   Litho.   Perf. 13
1955	A461	100k gold & blk brn	.40	.25

35th death anniv. of Kemal Ataturk.

Flower and "50" — A462

Ataturk — A463

250k, Torch & "50." 475k, Grain & cogwheel.

1973, Oct. 29
1956	A462	100k purple, red & bl	.25	.25
1957	A462	250k multicolored	.70	.25
1958	A462	475k brt blue & org	1.10	.50
		Nos. 1956-1958 (3)	2.05	1.00

Souvenir Sheet
Imperf
1959	A463	500k multicolored	3.50	2.00

50th anniv. of the Turkish Republic. #1959 contains one stamp with simulated perforations.

Bosporus Bridge A464

150k, Istanbul & Bosporus Bridge. 200k, Bosporus Bridge, children & UNICEF emblem, vert.

1973, Oct. 30 — **Perf. 13**
1960	A464	100k multicolored	.35	.25
1961	A464	150k multicolored	.55	.35
1962	A464	200k multicolored	.60	.35
		Nos. 1960-1962 (3)	1.50	.95

Inauguration of the Bosporus Bridge from Istanbul to Üsküdar, Oct. 30, 1973; UNICEF; children from East and West brought closer through Bosporus Bridge (No. 1962).

Mevlana's Tomb and Dancers — A465

Jalal-udin Mevlana — A466

1973, Dec. 1 — **Perf. 13x12½**
1963	A465	100k blk, lt ultra & grn	.50	.25
1964	A466	250k blue & multi	.80	.35

Jalal-udin Mevlana (1207-1273), poet and founder of the Mevlevie dervish order.

Cotton and Ship — A467

Export Products: 90k, Grapes. 100k, Figs. 250k, Citrus fruits. 325k, Tobacco. 475k, Hazelnuts.

1973, Dec. 10 — **Litho.** — **Perf. 13**
1965	A467	75k black, gray & bl	.25	.25
1966	A467	90k black, olive & bl	.40	.25
1967	A467	100k black, emer & bl	.55	.25
1968	A467	250k blk, brt yel & bl	1.40	.35
1969	A467	325k blk, yel & bl	1.40	.35
1970	A467	475k blk, org brn & bl	2.10	.55
		Nos. 1965-1970 (6)	6.10	2.00

Pres. Inönü — A468

1973, Dec. 25 — **Litho.** — **Perf. 13**
1971	A468	100k sepia & buff	.50	.25

Ismet Inönü, (1884-1973), first Prime Minister and second President of Turkey.

Hittite King, 8th Century B.C. — A469

Europa: 250k, Statuette of a Boy, (2nd millenium B.C.).

1974, Apr. 29 — **Litho.** — **Perf. 13**
1972	A469	110k multicolored	5.50	1.50
1973	A469	250k lt blue & multi	9.50	3.50

Silver and Gold Figure, 3000 B.C. — A470

Archaeological Finds: 175k, Painted jar, 5000 B.C., horiz. 200k, Vessels in bull form, 1700-1600 B.C., horiz. 250k, Pitcher, 700 B.C.

1974, May 24 — **Litho.** — **Perf. 13**
1974	A470	125k multicolored	.35	.25
1975	A470	175k multicolored	.60	.25
1976	A470	200k multicolored	.75	.25
1977	A470	250k multicolored	1.10	.40
		Nos. 1974-1977 (4)	2.80	1.15

Child Care — A471

1974, May 24
1978	A471	110k gray blue & blk	.40	.25

Sisli Children's Hospital, Istanbul, 75th anniv.

Anatolian Rug, 15th Century A472

Designs: 150k, Persian rug, late 16th century. 200k, Kashan rug, Lahore.

1974, July 21 — **Litho.** — **Perf. 12½x13**
1979	A472	100k blue & multi	1.00	.25
1980	A472	150k brown & multi	1.50	.25
1981	A472	200k red & multi	3.00	.25
		Nos. 1979-1981 (3)	5.50	.75

10th anniversary of the Regional Cooperation for Development Pact among Turkey, Iran and Pakistan.
See Iran 1806-1808, Pakistan 365-367.

Dove with Turkish Flag over Cyprus A473

1974, Aug. 26 — **Litho.** — **Perf. 13**
1982	A473	250k multicolored	.95	.45

Cyprus Peace Operation.

Wrestling — A474

90k, 250k, various wrestling holds, horiz.

1974, Aug. 29
1983	A474	90k multicolored	.25	.25
1984	A474	100k multicolored	.40	.25
1985	A474	250k multicolored	.70	.25
		Nos. 1983-1985 (3)	1.35	.75

World Freestyle Wrestling Championships.

Arrows Circling Globe — A475

UPU Emblem and: 110k, "UPU" in form of dove. 200k, Dove.

1974, Oct. 9 — **Litho.** — **Perf. 13**
1986	A475	110k bl, gold & dk bl	.25	.25
1987	A475	200k green & brown	.30	.25
1988	A475	250k multicolored	.55	.30
		Nos. 1986-1988 (3)	1.10	.80

Centenary of Universal Postal Union.

"Law Reforms" A476

"National Economy" A477

"Education" A478

1974, Oct. 29
1989	A476	50k blue & black	.25	.25
1990	A477	150k red & multi	.35	.25
1991	A478	400k multicolored	.80	.40
		Nos. 1989-1991 (3)	1.40	.90

Works and reforms of Kemal Ataturk.

Arrows Pointing Up — A479

Cogwheel and Map of Turkey A480

1974, Nov. 29 — **Litho.** — **Perf. 13**
1992	A479	25k brown & black	.25	.25
1993	A480	100k brown & gray	.45	.25

3rd 5-year Development Program (#1992), and industrialization progress (#1993).

Volleyball — A481

1974, Dec. 30
1994	A481	125k shown	.40	.25
1995	A481	175k Basketball	.75	.25
1996	A481	250k Soccer	1.25	.25
		Nos. 1994-1996 (3)	2.40	.75

Automatic Telex Network A482

Postal Check A483

Radio Transmitter and Waves A484

1975, Feb. 5 — **Litho.** — **Perf. 13**
1997	A482	5k black & yellow	.25	.25
1998	A483	50k ol grn & org	.25	.25
1999	A484	100k blue & black	.30	.25
		Nos. 1997-1999 (3)	.80	.75

Post and telecommunications.

Child Entering Classroom A485

Children's paintings: 50k, View of village. 100k, Dancing children.

1975, Apr. 23 — **Litho.** — **Perf. 13**
2000	A485	25k multicolored	.25	.25
2001	A485	50k multicolored	.25	.25
2002	A485	100k multicolored	.30	.25
		Nos. 2000-2002 (3)	.80	.75

Karacaoglan Monument in Mut, by Huseyin Gezer — A486

1975, Apr. 25
2003	A486	110k dk grn, bis & red	.50	.30

Karacaoglan (1606-1697), musician.

Orange Harvest in Hatay, by Cemal Tollu — A487

Europa: 250k, Yoruk Family on Plateau, by Turgut Zaim.

1975, Apr. 28
2004	A487	110k bister & multi	2.75	1.10
2005	A487	250k bister & multi	4.25	2.00

Porcelain
Vase, Turkey
A488

Designs: 200k, Ceramic plate, Iran, horiz. 250k, Camel leather vase, Pakistan.

Perf. 13½x13, 13x13½

1975, July 21			Litho.	
2006	A488	110k multicolored	1.25	.35
2007	A488	200k multicolored	1.75	.60
2008	A488	250k ultra & multi	1.75	.95
		Nos. 2006-2008 (3)	4.75	1.90

Regional Cooperation for Development Pact among Turkey, Iran and Pakistan. See Iran 1871-1873, Pakistan 383-385.

Horon Folk Dance — A489

Regional Folk Dances: 125k, Kasik. 175k, Bengi. 250k, Kasap. 325k, Kafkas, vert.

1975, Aug. 30			Perf. 13	
2009	A489	100k blue & multi	.55	.25
2010	A489	125k green & multi	.75	.25
2011	A489	175k rose & multi	.90	.25
2012	A489	250k multicolored	1.10	.25
2013	A489	325k orange & multi	1.75	.40
		Nos. 2009-2013 (5)	5.05	1.40

Knight Slaying
Dragon — A490

The Plunder of
Salur Kazan's
House — A491

Design: 175k, Two Wanderers, horiz.

1975, Oct. 15			Litho.	Perf. 13	
2014	A490	90k multicolored	.25	.25
2015	A490	175k multicolored	.40	.30
2016	A491	200k multicolored	.60	.40
		Nos. 2014-2016 (3)	1.25	.95

Illustrations for tales by Dede Korkut.

Common
Carp
A492

1975, Nov. 27			Litho.	Perf. 12½x13	
2017	A492	75k Turbot	1.25	.80
2018	A492	90k shown	1.60	.95
2019	A492	175k Trout	2.40	1.25
2020	A492	250k Red mullet	4.75	1.40
2021	A492	475k Red bream	6.00	2.00
		Nos. 2017-2021 (5)	16.00	6.40

Women's
Participation
A493

Insurance
Nationaliza-
tion — A494

Fine
Arts — A495

1975, Dec. 5			Perf. 12½x13, 13x12½	
2022	A493	100k bis, blk & red	.25	.25
2023	A494	110k violet & multi	.30	.25
2024	A495	250k multicolored	.40	.25
		Nos. 2022-2024 (3)	.95	.75

Works and reforms of Ataturk.

Ceramic
Plate — A496

Europa: 400k, Decorated pitcher.

1976, May 3			Litho.	Perf. 13	
2025	A496	200k purple & multi	5.00	2.00
2026	A496	400k multicolored	10.00	3.00

Sultan Ahmed
Mosque
A497

1976, May 10				
2027	A497	500k gray & multi	.95	.45

7th Islamic Conference, Istanbul.

Lunch in
the Field
A498

Children's Drawings: 200k, Boats on the Bosporus, vert. 400k, Winter landscape.

1976, May 19			Litho.	Perf. 13	
2028	A498	50k multicolored	.25	.25
2029	A498	200k multicolored	.25	.25
2030	A498	400k multicolored	.45	.25
		Nos. 2028-2030 (3)	.95	.75

Samsun 76, First National Junior Philatelic Exhibition, Samsun.

Storks,
Sultan
Marsh
A499

Conservation Emblem and: 200k, Horses, Manyas Lake. 250k, Borabay Lake. 400k, Manavgat Waterfall.

1976, June 5				
2031	A499	150k multicolored	2.50	.80
2032	A499	200k multicolored	.85	.25
2033	A499	250k multicolored	1.40	.25
2034	A499	400k multicolored	1.60	.35
		Nos. 2031-2034 (4)	6.35	1.65

European Wetland Conservation Year.

Nasreddin Hodja
Carrying
Liver — A500

Turkish Folklore: 250k, Friend giving recipe for cooking liver. 600k, Hawk carrying off liver and Hodja telling hawk he cannot enjoy liver without recipe.

1976, July 5			Litho.	Perf. 13	
2035	A500	150k multicolored	.40	.25
2036	A500	250k multicolored	.60	.25
2037	A500	600k multicolored	1.40	.50
		Nos. 2035-2037 (3)	2.40	1.00

Montreal Olympic
Emblem and
Flame — A501

Designs: 400k, "76," Montreal Olympic emblem, horiz. 600k, Montreal Olympic emblem and ribbons.

1976, July 17				
2038	A501	100k red & multi	.25	.25
2039	A501	400k red & multi	.75	.40
2040	A501	600k red & multi	1.40	.60
		Nos. 2038-2040 (3)	2.40	1.25

21st Olympic Games, Montreal, Canada, 7/17-8/1.

Kemal
Ataturk
A502

Designs: 200k, Riza Shah Pahlavi. 250k, Mohammed Ali Jinnah.

1976, July 21			Litho.	Perf. 13½	
2041	A502	100k multicolored	.30	.25
2042	A502	200k multicolored	.50	.25
2043	A502	250k multicolored	.90	.35
		Nos. 2041-2043 (3)	1.70	.85

Regional Cooperation for Development Pact among Turkey, Pakistan and Iran, 12th anniversary. See Iran 1903-1905, Pakistan 412-414.

"Ataturk's
Army"
A503

Ataturk's
Speeches
A504

"Peace at
Home and in
the World"
A505

1976, Oct. 29			Litho.	Perf. 13	
2044	A503	100k black & red	.25	.25
2045	A504	200k gray grn & multi	.30	.25
2046	A505	400k blue & multi	.70	.30
		Nos. 2044-2046 (3)	1.25	.80

Works and reforms of Ataturk.

Hora
A506

1977, Jan. 19			Litho.	Perf. 13	
2047	A506	400k multicolored	.95	.30

MTA Sismik 1 "Hora" geophysical exploration ship.

Keyboard and Violin
Sound Hole — A507

1977, Feb. 24			Litho.	Perf. 13x13½	
2048	A507	200k multicolored	.50	.25

Turkish State Symphony Orchestra, sesquicentennial.

Ataturk and
"100" — A508

Design: 400k, Hand holding ballot.

1977, Mar. 21			Litho.	Perf. 13	
2049	A508	200k black & red	.50	.25
2050	A508	400k black & brown	.95	.50

Centenary of Turkish Parliament.

Hierapolis
(Pamukkale)
A509

Europa: 400k, Zelve (mountains and poppies).

1977, May 2			Litho.	Perf. 13½x13	
2051	A509	200k multicolored	6.00	2.00
2052	A509	400k multicolored	10.00	3.00

Terra
Cotta Pot,
Turkey
A510

Designs: 225k, Terra cotta jug, Iran. 675k, Terra cotta bullock cart, Pakistan.

1977, July 21 **Litho.** **Perf. 13**
2053 A510 100k multicolored .35 .25
2054 A510 225k multicolored 1.10 .35
2055 A510 675k multicolored 2.10 .75
a. Souv. sheet, #2053-2055 11.00 11.00
Nos. 2053-2055 (3) 3.55 1.35

Regional Cooperation for Development Pact among Turkey, Iran and Pakistan, 13th anniv. See Iran 1946-1948, Pakistan 431-433.

Finn-class Yacht — A511

200k, Three yachts. 250k, Symbolic yacht.

1977, July 28
2056 A511 150k lt bl, bl & blk .30 .25
2057 A511 200k ultra & blue .55 .25
2058 A511 250k ultra & black .75 .25
Nos. 2056-2058 (3) 1.60 .75

European Finn Class Sailing Championships, Istanbul, July 28.

Ataturk Type of 1972
1977, June 13 **Litho.** **Perf. 13½x13**
2060 A453 100k olive .75 .25
2061 A453 200k brown 1.00 .25

Kemal Ataturk — A512

Imprint: "GUZEL SANATLAR MATBAASI A.S. 1977"
1977, Sept. 23 **Litho.** **Perf. 13**
Size: 20½x22mm
2062 A512 200k blue .75 .25
2063 A512 250k Prussian blue 1.00 .25

Imprint: "TIFDRUK-ISTANBUL 1978"
1978, June 28 **Photo.** **Perf. 13**
Size: 20x25mm
2065 A512 10k brown .50 .25
2066 A512 50k grnsh gray .75 .25
2067 A512 1 l fawn .75 .25
2068 A512 2½ l purple 1.00 .25
2069 A512 5 l blue 1.25 .25
2072 A512 25 l dl grn & lt bl 3.00 .30
2073 A512 50 l dp org & tan 4.00 .70
Nos. 2065-2073 (7) 11.25 2.25

No. 1832 Surcharged with New Value and Wavy Lines
1977, Aug. 17
2078 A418 10k on 1k dp org & brn .30 .25

"Rationalism" A513 — "National Sovereignty" A514

"Liberation of Nations" — A515

1977, Oct. 29 **Litho.** **Perf. 13**
2079 A513 100k multicolored .25 .25
2080 A514 200k multicolored .25 .25
2081 A515 400k multicolored .80 .25
Nos. 2079-2081 (3) 1.30 .75

Works and reforms of Ataturk.

Mohammad Allama Iqbal — A516

1977, Nov. 9 **Perf. 13x12½**
2082 A516 400k multicolored .80 .25

Mohammad Allama Iqbal (1877-1938), Pakistani poet and philosopher.

Trees and Burning Match — A517

Design: 250k, Sign showing growing tree.

1977, Dec. 15 **Litho.** **Perf. 13**
2083 A517 50k green, blk & red .25 .25
2084 A517 250k gray, grn & blk .60 .25

Forest conservation. See type A542.

Wrecked Car — A518

Passing on Wrong Side — A519 — Traffic Sign, "Slow!" — A520

Two types of 50k:
I — Number on license plate.
II — No number on plate.

Traffic Safety: 250k, Tractor drawing overloaded farm cart. 800k, Accident caused by incorrect passing. 10 l, "Use striped crossings."

1977-78 **Perf. 13½x13, 13x13½**
2085 A518 50k ultra, blk & red, II .60 .55
a. Type I .70 .55
2086 A519 150k red, gray & blk .25 .25
2087 A518 250k ocher, blk & red .50 .25
2088 A520 500k gray, red & blk .50 .25
2089 A520 800k multicolored 1.75 .35
2090 A520 10 l dl grn, blk & brn 1.75 .35
Nos. 2085-2090 (6) 4.70 1.90

Issued: 500k, 1977; others, 1978.
For No. 2089 surcharged, see No. 2182.

Ishak Palace, Dogubeyazit — A521

Europa: 5 l, Anamur Castle.

1978, May 2 **Litho.** **Perf. 13**
2091 A521 2½ l multicolored 7.00 2.50
2092 A521 5 l multicolored 12.00 3.50

Riza Shah Pahlavi — A522

1978, June 16 **Litho.** **Perf. 13x13½**
2093 A522 5 l multicolored .50 .50

Riza Shah Pahlavi (1877-1944) of Iran, birth centenary.

Yellow Rose, Turkey A523

3½ l, Pink roses, Iran. 8 l, Red roses, Pakistan.

1978, July 21 **Litho.** **Perf. 13**
2094 A523 2½ l multi .35 .25
2095 A523 3½ l multi .75 .25
2096 A523 8 l multi 2.00 .45
Nos. 2094-2096 (3) 3.10 .95

Regional Cooperation for Development Pact among Turkey, Iran and Pakistan. See Iran 1984-1986, Pakistan 449-451.

Anti-Apartheid Emblem — A524

1978, Aug. 14 **Litho.** **Perf. 13½x13**
2097 A524 10 l multicolored .85 .25

Anti-Apartheid Year.

View of Ankara — A525

Design: 5 l, View of Tripoli, horiz.

Perf. 13x12½, 12½x13
1978, Aug. 17
2098 A525 2½ l multi .30 .25
2099 A525 5 l multi .75 .25

Turkish-Libyan friendship.

Souvenir Sheet

Bridge and Mosque — A526

1978, Oct. 25 **Imperf.**
2100 A526 15 l multicolored 1.50 1.00

Edirne '78, 2nd Natl. Phil. Youth Exhib.

Independence Medal A527 — Latin Alphabet A529

Speech Reform A528

1978, Oct. 29 **Perf. 13½x13½, 13½x13**
2101 A527 2½ l multi .25 .25
2102 A528 3½ l multi .30 .25
2103 A529 5 l multi .45 .25
Nos. 2101-2103 (3) 1.00 .75

Ataturk's works and reforms.

House on Bosporus, 1699 — A530

Turkish Houses: 2½ l, Izmit, 1774, vert. 3½ l, Kula, 17th cent., vert. 5 l, Milas, 18th-19th cent., vert. 8 l, Safranbolu, 18th-19th cent.

Perf. 13x12½, 12½x13
1978, Nov. 22
2104 A530 1 l multi .40 .25
2105 A530 2½ l multi .60 .25
2106 A530 3½ l multi .60 .40
2107 A530 5 l multi .90 .40
2108 A530 8 l multi 1.50 .45
Nos. 2104-2108 (5) 4.00 1.75

Carrier Pigeon, Plane, Horseback Rider, Train A531

Europa: 5 l, Morse key, telegraph and Telex machine. 7½ l, Telephone dial and satellite.

1979, Apr. 30 **Litho.** **Perf. 13**
2109 A531 2½ l multicolored 3.00 1.00
2110 A531 5 l org brn & blk 5.00 1.00
2111 A531 7½ l brt blue & blk 5.75 1.50
Nos. 2109-2111 (3) 13.75 3.50

Plowing, by Namik Ismail A532

Paintings: 7½ l, Potters, by Kamalel Molk, Iran. 10 l, At the Well, by Allah Baksh, Pakistan.

1979, Sept. 5   Litho.   Perf. 13½x13
2112	A532	5 l	multi	.25	.25
2113	A532	7½ l	multi	.50	.25
2114	A532	10 l	multi	.75	.35
		Nos. 2112-2114 (3)		1.50	.85

Regional Cooperation for Development Pact among Turkey, Pakistan and Iran, 15th anniversary.
See Iran 2020-2022, Pakistan 486-488.

A533

1979, Sept. 17   Perf. 13
2115	A533	5 l	Colemanite	.35	.25
2116	A533	7½ l	Chromite	.50	.25
2117	A533	10 l	Antimonite	.80	.25
2118	A533	15 l	Sulphur	1.00	.30
		Nos. 2115-2118 (4)		2.65	1.05

10th World Mining Congress.

A534

8-shaped road, train tunnel, plane and emblem.

1979, Sept. 24
2119	A534	5 l	multicolored	.40	.25

European Ministers of Communications, 8th Symposium.

Youth — A535

Secularization A536

Design: 5 l, National oath.

1979, Oct. 29   Perf. 13x12½, 12½x13
2120	A535	2½ l	multi	.25	.25
2121	A536	3½ l	multi	.25	.25
2122	A535	5 l	black & orange	.30	.25
		Nos. 2120-2122 (3)		.80	.75

Ataturk's works and reforms.

Poppies — A537

1979, Nov. 26   Litho.   Perf. 13x13½
2123	A537	5 l	shown	.25	.25
2124	A537	7½ l	Oleander	.45	.25
2125	A537	10 l	Late spider orchid	.70	.25
2126	A537	15 l	Mandrake	1.10	.25
		Nos. 2123-2126 (4)		2.50	1.00

See Nos. 2154-2157.

Kemal Ataturk — A538

Perf. 12½x11½, 13x12½(No. 2131)
1979-81   Litho.
2127	A538	50k	olive ('80)	.25	.25
2128	A538	1 l	grn & lt grn	.40	.25
2129	A538	2½ l	purple	.60	.25
2130	A538	2½ l	bl grn & lt bl ('80)	.40	.25
2131	A538	2½ l	orange ('81)	.50	.25
2132	A538	5 l	ultra & gray	.90	.25
a.		Sheet of 8		7.25	6.00
2133	A538	7½ l	brown	.90	.30
2134	A538	7½ l	red ('80)	1.25	.30
2135	A538	10 l	rose carmine	1.50	.40
2136	A538	20 l	gray ('80)	2.25	.50
		Nos. 2127-2136 (10)		8.95	3.00

No. 2132a for Ankara '79 Philatelic Exhibition, Oct. 14-20.
For surcharge see No. 2261.

Kemal Ataturk — A538a

1980-82   Photo.   Perf. 13½
2137	A538a	7½ l	red brown	.50	.25
c.		Sheet of 4		4.00	2.50
2137A	A538a	10 l	brown	1.00	.25
2138	A538a	20 l	lilac	1.00	.25
2138A	A538a	30 l	gray	1.25	.30
2139	A538a	50 l	orange red	2.25	.30
2140	A538a	75 l	brt green	3.00	.75
2141	A538a	100 l	blue	4.00	1.00
		Nos. 2137-2141 (7)		13.00	3.10

No. 2137c for ANTALYA '82 4th Natl. Junior Stamp Show. Exists both perf 13½ and imperf. Same value.
Issued: #2137, 7/15/81; #2137c, 10/3/82; 30 l, 9/23/81; others, 12/10/80.
See Nos. 2164-2169.

Turkish Printing, 250th Anniversary — A539

1979, Nov. 30   Litho.   Perf. 13
2142	A539	10 l	multicolored	.60	.45

2nd International Olive Oil Year — A540

Perf. 12½x13, 13x12½
1979, Dec. 20   Litho.
2143	A540	5 l	shown	.25	.25
2144	A540	10 l	Globe, oil drop, vert.	.45	.25

Uskudarli Hoca Ali Riza Bey (1857-1930), Painter — A541

Europa: 15 l, Ali Sami Boyar (1880-1967), painter. 20 l, Dr. Hulusi Behcet (1889-1948), physician, discovered Behcet skin disease.

1980, Apr. 28   Perf. 13
2145	A541	7½ l	multi	1.75	1.00
2146	A541	15 l	multi	2.50	1.25
2147	A541	20 l	multi	3.25	1.25
		Nos. 2145-2147 (3)		7.50	3.50

Forest Conservation — A542

1980, July 3   Perf. 13½x13
2148	A542	50k	ol grn & red org	.30	.25

See type A517. For surcharge see No. 2262.

Earthquake Destruction — A543

1980, Sept. 8   Perf. 13
2149	A543	7½ l	shown	.30	.25
2150	A543	20 l	Seismograph	.70	.50

7th World Conference on Earthquake Engineering, Istanbul.

Games' Emblem, Sports — A544

1980, Sept. 26   Perf. 13x13½
2151	A544	7½ l	shown	.25	.25
2152	A544	20 l	Emblem, sports, diff.	.70	.25

First Islamic Games, Izmir.

Hegira — A545

1980, Nov. 9
2153	A545	20 l	multicolored	.80	.40

Plant Type of 1979
1980, Nov. 26   Perf. 13
2154	A537	2½ l	Manisa tulip	.25	.25
2155	A537	7½ l	Ephesian bell-flower	.50	.25
2156	A537	15 l	Angora crocus	.75	.25
2157	A537	20 l	Anatolian orchid	1.25	.25
		Nos. 2154-2157 (4)		2.75	1.00

Avicenna Treating Patient A546

Avicenna (Arab Physician), Birth Millenium: 20 l, Portrait, vert.

1980, Dec. 15
2158	A546	7½ l	multi	.40	.25
2159	A546	20 l	multi	.70	.30

Balkanfila VIII Stamp Exhibition, Ankara A547

1981, Jan. 1   Litho.   Perf. 13
2160	A547	10 l	red & black	.75	.25

Kemal Ataturk — A548

1981, Feb. 4   Perf. 13
2163	A548	10 l	lilac rose	.75	.25

Ataturk Type of 1980
1983-84   Perf. 13x13½
2164	A538a	15 l	grnsh blue	.35	.25
2165	A538a	20 l	orange ('84)	.45	.25
2167	A538a	65 l	bluish grn	1.25	.25
2169	A538a	90 l	lilac rose	1.60	.25
		Nos. 2164-2169 (4)		3.65	1.00

Issued: #2164, 2167, 2169, 11/30; #2165, 7/25.

Sultan Mehmet the Conqueror (1432-1481) — A549

1981, May 3   Litho.   Perf. 13x12½
2173	A549	10 l	multicolored	.45	.35
2174	A549	20 l	multicolored	.90	.70

Gaziantep (Folk Dance) A550

Antalya A551

1981, May 4   Litho.   Perf. 13
2175	A550	7½ l	shown	.25	.25
2176	A550	10 l	Balikesir	.35	.25
2177	A550	15 l	Kahramanmaras	1.75	.75
2178	A551	35 l	shown	4.00	1.10
2179	A551	70 l	Burdur	5.00	2.25
		Nos. 2175-2179 (5)		11.35	4.60

Nos. 2178-2179 show CEPT (Europa) emblem.

Nos. C40, 1925, 1931A, 2089
Surcharged in Black with New Value and Wavy Lines

1981, June 3   *Perf. 13½x13*
2179A	AP7	10 l on 60k	.90	.25
2180	A453	10 l on 110k	.90	.25
2181	A453	10 l on 400k	.90	.25
2182	A520	10 l on 800k	.90	.25
	Nos. 2179A-2182 (4)		3.60	1.00

A552

1981, June 22   *Perf. 13x12½*
2183	A552	7 ½ l	Rug, Bilecik	.25	.25
2184	A552	10 l	Embroidery	.35	.25
2185	A552	15 l	Drum, zurna players	.55	.25
2186	A552	20 l	Embroidered napkin	.55	.25
2187	A552	30 l	Rug, diff.	1.10	.25
	Nos. 2183-2187 (5)			2.80	1.25

22nd Intl. Turkish Folklore Congress.

Kemal Ataturk
A553

1981, May 19   Litho.   *Perf. 14x15*
2188	A553	2 ½ l No. 1801	.30	.25
2189	A553	7 ½ l No. 1816	.30	.25
2190	A553	10 l No. 1604	.40	.25
2191	A553	20 l No. 804	.75	.25
2192	A553	25 l No. 777	.90	.30
2193	A553	35 l No. 1959	1.25	.50
	Nos. 2188-2193 (6)		3.90	1.80

Souvenir Sheet
2194		Sheet of 6	20.00	10.00
a.	A553	2 ½ l like 2 ½ l	.25	.25
b.	A553	37 ½ l like 7 ½ l	.50	.25
c.	A553	50 l like 10 l	.75	.25
d.	A553	100 l like 20 l	1.50	.40
e.	A553	125 l like 25 l	2.00	.75
f.	A553	175 l like 35 l	3.00	1.00

Souvenir Sheet

Balkanfila VIII Stamp Exhibition, Ankara — A554

1981, Aug. 8   Litho.   *Perf. 13*
2195	A554	Sheet of 2	6.00	5.00
a.		50 l No. B68	2.75	2.50
b.		50 l No. 733	2.75	2.50

5th General Congress of European Physics Society
A555

1981, Sept. 7   *Perf. 12½x13*
2196	A555	10 l red & multi	.70	.25
2197	A555	30 l blue & multi	1.10	.40

World Food Day
A556

1981, Oct. 16
2198	A556	10 l multicolored	.40	.25
2199	A556	30 l multicolored	.95	.25

Constituent Assembly Inauguration — A557

1981, Oct. 23   *Perf. 13*
2200	A557	10 l multicolored	.55	.25
2201	A557	30 l multicolored	1.25	.25

Ataturk — A558

Portraits of Ataturk.

1981-82   *Perf. 11½x12½, 13 (#2204)*
2202	A558	1 l green	.25	.25
2203	A558	2 ½ l purple	.25	.25
2204	A558	2 ½ l gray & org	.50	.25
2205	A558	5 l blue	.25	.25
2206	A558	10 l orange	.25	.25
2207	A558	35 l brown	.70	.25
	Nos. 2202-2207 (6)		2.20	1.50

Issued: #2204, 12/10/81; others, 1/27/82.

Literacy Campaign — A559

1981, Dec. 24   *Perf. 13½*
2217	A559	2 ½ l Procession	.45	.25

Energy Conservation — A560

1982, Jan. 11   *Perf. 13*
2218	A560	10 l multicolored	.45	.25

Magnolias, by Ibrahim Calli (b. 1882) — A561

1982, Mar. 17   *Perf. 13x13½, 13½x13*
2219	A561	10 l shown	.50	.25
2220	A561	20 l Fishermen, horiz.	.95	.25
2221	A561	30 l Sewing Woman	1.25	.25
	Nos. 2219-2221 (3)		2.70	.75

Europa Issue

Sultanhan Caravanserai
A562

1982, Apr. 26   *Perf. 13x12½*
2222	A562	30 l shown	.75	.25
2223	A562	70 l Silk Route	1.60	.50
a.		Min. sheet, 2 each #2222-2223	7.00	7.00
b.		Pair, #2222-2223	2.50	1.00

1250th Anniv. of Kul-Tigin Monument, Kosu Saydam, Mongolia — A563

10 l, Monument. 30 l, Kul-Tigin (685-732), Gok-Turkish commander.

1982, June 9   *Perf. 13*
2224	A563	10 l multicolored	.25	.25
2225	A563	30 l multicolored	.70	.25

Pendik Shipyard Opening A564

1982, July 1   *Perf. 12½x13*
2226	A564	30 l Ship, emblem	.65	.25

Mountains of Anatolia
A565

1982, July 17   *Perf. 13*
2227	A565	7 ½ l Agri Dagi, vert.	.30	.25
2228	A565	10 l Buzul Dagi	.55	.25
2229	A565	15 l Demirkazik, vert.	.85	.25
2230	A565	20 l Erciyes	1.10	.25
2231	A565	30 l Kackar Dagi, vert.	1.75	.25
2232	A565	35 l Uludag	2.25	.25
	Nos. 2227-2232 (6)		6.80	1.50

Beyazit State Library Centenary A566

1982, Sept. 27
2233	A566	30 l multicolored	.70	.35

Musical Instruments of Anatolia — A567

1982, Oct. 13
2234	A567	7 ½ l Davul	.60	.25
2235	A567	10 l Baglama	.60	.25
2236	A567	15 l shown	.90	.25
2237	A567	20 l Kemence	1.10	.25
2238	A567	30 l Ney	1.50	.25
	Nos. 2234-2238 (5)		4.70	1.25

Roman Temple Columns, Sardis A568

1982, Nov. 3
2239	A568	30 l multi	1.25	.40

Family Planning and Mother-Child Health — A569

1983, Jan. 12   Litho.   *Perf. 13*
2240	A569	10 l Family on map	.25	.25
2241	A569	35 l Mother and child	.75	.25

30th Anniv. of Customs Cooperation Council — A570

1983, Jan. 26
2242	A570	45 l multi	1.10	.25

1982 Constitution — A571

1983, Jan. 27
2243	A571	10 l Ballot box	.50	.25
2244	A571	30 l Open book, scale	.75	.30

Manastirli Bey A572

1983, Mar. 16   Litho.
2245	A572	35 l multi	.90	.25

Manastirli Hamdi Bey (1890-1945), telegrapher of news of Istanbul's occupation to Ataturk, 1920.

Europa Issue

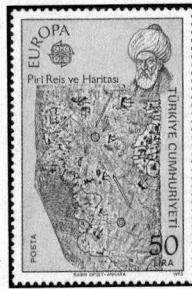

Piri Reis, Geographer A573

100 l, Ulugh Beg (1394-1449), astronomer.

1983, May 5   Litho.   *Perf. 12½x13*
2246	A573	50 l shown	15.00	2.50
2247	A573	100 l multi	35.00	7.50

Youth Week A574

1983, May 16
2248 A574 15 l multi .50 .25

World Communications Year — A575

1983, May 16 **Perf. 13**
2249 A575 15 l Carrier pigeon, vert. .40 .25
2250 A575 50 l Phone lines .80 .25
2251 A575 70 l Emblem, vert. 1.50 .25
Nos. 2249-2251 (3) 2.70 .75

50th Anniv. of State Civil Aviation A576

1983, May 20 **Litho.** **Perf. 13**
2252 A576 50 l Plane, jet 1.10 .25
2253 A576 70 l Airport 1.50 .45

18th Council of Europe Art Exhibition A577

15 l, Eros, 2nd cent. BC, vert. 35 l, Two-headed duck, Hittite, 14th cent BC. 50 l, Zinc jugs, plate, 16th cent., vert. 70 l, Marcus Aurelius and his wife Faustina the Young, 2nd cent.

1983, May 22 **Perf. 13**
2254 A577 15 l multi .60 .25
2255 A577 35 l multi 1.50 .25
2256 A577 50 l multi 1.60 .25
2257 A577 70 l multi 1.75 .25
Nos. 2254-2257 (4) 5.45 1.00

Council of Europe's "The Water's Edge" Campaign — A578

Coastal Views.

1983, June 1 **Litho.** **Perf. 13x12½**
2258 A578 10 l Olodeniz .65 .40
2259 A578 25 l Olympus .65 .40
2260 A578 35 l Kekova 1.40 .80
Nos. 2258-2260 (3) 2.70 1.60

Nos. 2127, 2148 Surcharged
Perf. 12½x11½, 13½x13
1983, June 8
2261 A538 5 l on 50k olive .25 .25
2262 A542 5 l on 50k ol grn & red org .25 .25

Kemal Ataturk — A579

1983, June 22 **Perf. 13**
2263 A579 15 l bl grn & bl .40 .25
  a. Sheet of 5 + label 3.50 2.50
2264 A579 50 l green & blue 1.60 .25
2265 A579 100 l orange & blue 3.50 .55
Nos. 2263-2265 (3) 5.50 1.05
For surcharge see No. 2432.

Aga Khan Architecture Award — A580

1983, Sept. 4 **Photo.** **Perf. 11½**
2266 A580 50 l View of Istanbul 1.10 .25

60th Anniv. of the Republic A582

1983, Oct. 29 **Perf. 13½x13**
2268 A582 15 l multi .30 .25
2269 A582 50 l multi .95 .25

Columns, Aphrodisias — A583

1983, Nov. 2 **Perf. 13**
2270 A583 50 l multi 1.10 .85

UNESCO Campaign for Istanbul and Goreme — A584

1984, Feb. 15 **Litho.** **Perf. 13**
2271 A584 25 l St. Sophia Basilica .50 .25
2272 A584 35 l Goreme .75 .25
2273 A584 50 l Istanbul 1.00 .25
Nos. 2271-2273 (3) 2.25 .75

Natl. Police Org. Emblem A585

1984, Apr. 10 **Litho.** **Perf. 13**
2274 A585 15 l multi .50 .30

Europa (1959-84) A586

1984, Apr. 30 **Perf. 13½x13**
2275 A586 50 l blue & multi 15.00 2.50
2276 A586 100 l gray & multi 26.00 5.00

Mete Khan, Hun Ruler, 204 BC, Flag A587

Sixteen States (Hun Rulers and Flags): 20 l, Panu, Western Hun empire (48-216). 50 l, Attila, 375-454. 70 l, Aksunvar, Ak Hun empire, 420-562.

1984, June 20 **Litho.** **Perf. 13**
2277 A587 10 l multi .75 .25
2278 A587 20 l multi 1.00 .40
2279 A587 50 l multi 2.00 .50
2280 A587 70 l multi 3.50 .50
Nos. 2277-2280 (4) 7.25 1.65
See Nos. 2315-2318, 2349-2352, 2382-2385.

Occupation of Cyprus, 10th Anniv. A588

1984, July 20 **Litho.** **Perf. 13**
2281 A588 70 l Dove, olive branch 1.60 .75

Wild Flowers — A589

1984, Aug. 1 **Perf. 11½x12½**
2282 A589 10 l Marshmallow flower .25 .25
2283 A589 20 l Red poppy .30 .25
2284 A589 70 l Sowbread 1.00 .25
2285 A589 200 l Snowdrop 2.75 .35
2286 A589 300 l Tulip 4.50 .45
Nos. 2282-2286 (5) 8.80 1.55
See Nos. 2301-2308. For surcharges see Nos. 2467, 2479-2480.

Armed Forces Day — A590

20 l, Soldier, dove, flag. 50 l, Sword. 70 l, Arms, soldier, flag. 90 l, Map, soldier.

1984, Aug. 26 **Perf. 13½x13**
2287 A590 20 l multicolored .45 .25
2288 A590 50 l multicolored .90 .25
2289 A590 70 l multicolored 1.40 .25
2290 A590 90 l multicolored 1.75 .25
Nos. 2287-2290 (4) 4.50 1.00

Trees and Wood Products — A591

Seed, Tree and Product: 10 l, Liquidambar, liquidambar grease. 20 l, Oriental spruce, stringed instrument. 70 l, Oriental beech, chair. 90 l, Cedar of Lebanon, ship.

1984, Sept. 19 **Litho.** **Perf. 13x12½**
2291 A591 10 l multi .55 .25
2292 A591 20 l multi .55 .25
2293 A591 70 l multi 1.40 .25
2294 A591 90 l multi 2.00 .25
Nos. 2291-2294 (4) 4.50 1.00

Pres. Ismet Inonu (1884-1973), A592

1984, Sept. 24 **Perf. 13**
2295 A592 20 l Portrait 1.10 .25

First Intl. Turkish Carpet Congress — A593

1984, Oct. 7 **Perf. 13x13½**
2296 A593 70 l Seljukian carpet, 13th cent. 1.10 .75

Ruins of Ancient City of Harran A594

1984, Nov. 7 **Perf. 13½x13**
2297 A594 70 l Columns, arch 1.75 1.25

Turkish Women's Suffrage, 50th Anniv. A595

1984, Dec. 5 **Litho.** **Perf. 13**
2298 A595 20 l Women voting .45 .25

40th Anniv., ICAO — A596

1984, Dec. 7 **Litho.** **Perf. 13**
2299 A596 100 l Icarus, ICAO emblem 1.75 1.40

Souvenir Sheet

No. 1047 — A597

1985, Jan. 13 **Litho.** **Imperf.**
2300 A597 Sheet of 4, 2 each #a.-b. 4.50 3.50
  a.-b. 70 l, any single .55 .55
Istanbul '87. No. 2300b has denomination in lower right.

Flower Type of 1984
1985 **Perf. 11½x12½**
2301 A589 5 l Narcissus .75 .30
Perf. 12½x13
2308 A589 100 l Daisy 1.40 .25
Issue dates: #2301, Feb. 6; #2308, July 31.
For surcharge see No. 2465.

Turkish Aviation League, 60th Anniv. A598

1985, Feb. 16 *Perf. 13*
2310 A598 10 l Parachutist, glider .30 .25
2311 A598 20 l Hot air balloon, vert. .75 .55

INTELSAT, 20th Anniv. — A599

1985, Apr. 3
2312 A599 100 l multi 1.75 .90

Europa Issue

Ulvi Cemal Erkin (1906-1972) and Kosekce — A600

Composers and music: 200 l, Mithat Fenmen (1916-1982) and Concertina.

1985, Apr. 29 *Perf. 13½x13*
2313 A600 100 l multi 25.00 3.50
2314 A600 200 l multi 35.00 5.00

States Type of 1984

Sixteen States (Kagan rulers and flags): 10 l, Bilge, Gokturk Empire (552-743) and Örhon-Turkish alphabet. 20 l, Bayan, Avar Empire (565-803). 70 l, Hazar, Hazar Empire (651-983). 100 l, Kutlug Kul Bilge, Uygur State (774-1335).

1985, June 20
2315 A587 10 l multi .60 .25
2316 A587 20 l multi 1.25 .25
2317 A587 70 l multi 2.40 .25
2318 A587 100 l multi 4.75 .25
Nos. 2315-2318 (4) 9.00 1.00

Intl. Youth Year A601

1985, Aug. 8
2319 A601 100 l multi 1.25 .95
2320 A601 120 l multi 2.00 1.60

Postal Code Inauguration A602

1985, Sept. 4 *Perf. 13*
Background Color
2321 A602 10 l pale yel brn .40 .25
2322 A602 20 l fawn .60 .25
2323 A602 20 l gray green .60 .25
2324 A602 20 l brt blue .60 .25
2325 A602 70 l rose lilac 1.40 .25
2326 A602 100 l gray 1.90 .45
Nos. 2321-2326 (6) 5.50 1.70

Symposium of Natl. Palaces — A603

1985, Sept. 25 *Perf. 13½x13*
2327 A603 20 l Aynalikavak, c. 1703 .50 .25
2328 A603 100 l Beylerbeyi, 1865 1.75 .25

UN, 40th Anniv. A604

1985, Oct. 24
2329 A604 100 l multi 1.25 1.00

Alanya Fortress and City A605

1985, Nov. 7
2330 A605 100 l multi 1.75 .90

A606

1985, Nov. 12 *Perf. 13x13½*
2331 A606 100 l multi 1.75 1.00
Turkish Meteorological Service, 60th anniv.

A607

1985, Dec. 14
2332 A607 20 l multi .50 .25
Isik Lyceum, Istanbul, cent.

Ataturk — A608

Perf. 11½x12½
1985, Dec. 18 **Litho.**
2334 A608 10 l pale bl & ultra .30 .25
2335 A608 20 l beige & brn .40 .25
2336 A608 100 l lt pink & claret 1.50 .25
Nos. 2334-2336 (3) 2.20 .75

For surcharges see Nos. 2433-2434, 2449.

7th Intl. Children's Festival, Ankara A609

Various children's drawings.

1986, Apr. 23 **Litho.** *Perf. 12½x13*
2342 A609 20 l multi .50 .45
2343 A609 100 l multi 1.60 .45
2344 A609 120 l multi 1.90 1.90
Nos. 2342-2344 (3) 4.00 2.80

Europa Issue

Pollution A610

1986, Apr. 28 *Perf. 13*
2345 A610 100 l shown 12.00 2.50
2346 A610 200 l Bandaged leaf 17.50 5.00

1st Ataturk Intl. Peace Prize — A611

1986, May 19 **Litho.** *Perf. 13*
2347 A611 20 l gold & multi .65 .65
2348 A611 100 l silver & multi 1.60 .95

States Type of 1984

Sixteen States (Devleti rulers and flags): 10 l, Bilge Kul Kadir Khan, Kara Khanids State (840-1212). 20 l, Alp-Tekin, Ghaznavids State (963-1183). 100 l, Seldjuk Bey, Seldjuks State (1040-1157). 120 l, Muhammed Harezmsah, Khwarizm-Shahs State (1157-1231).

1986, June 20
2349 A587 10 l multi .50 .25
2350 A587 20 l multi 1.40 .40
2351 A587 100 l multi 2.10 .70
2352 A587 120 l multi 5.00 1.40
Nos. 2349-2352 (4) 9.00 2.75

1st Turkish Submarine, Cent. — A612

1986, June 16 **Litho.** *Perf. 13*
2353 A612 20 l Torpedo sub Abdulhamid 1.00 .50

Kirkpinar Wrestling Matches, Edirne — A613

1986, June 30
2354 A613 10 l Oiling bodies .75 .75
2355 A613 20 l Five wrestlers .75 .75
2356 A613 100 l Two wrestlers 2.10 1.40
Nos. 2354-2356 (3) 3.60 2.90

Organization for Economic Cooperation and Development, 25th Anniv. — A614

1986, Sept. 30 **Litho.** *Perf. 13½x13*
2357 A614 100 l multi 1.40 .45

Automobile, Cent. — A615

10 l, Benz Velocipede, 1886. 20 l, Rolls-Royce Silver Ghost, 1906. 100 l, Mercedes Touring Car, 1928. 200 l, Abstract speeding car.

1986, Oct. 15
2358 A615 10 l multi .90 .60
2359 A615 20 l multi 1.25 .60
2360 A615 100 l multi 2.40 1.25
2361 A615 200 l multi 3.50 1.75
Nos. 2358-2361 (4) 8.05 4.20

Paintings A616

Designs: 100 l, Bouquet with Tulip, by Feyhaman Duran (1886-1970). 120 l, Landscape with Fountain, by H. Avni Lifij (1886-1927), horiz.

1986, Oct. 22 *Perf. 13½x13, 13x13½*
2362 A616 100 l multi 1.00 .60
2363 A616 120 l multi 3.00 .85

Celal Bayar (1883-1986), 3rd President — A617

1986, Oct. 27 *Perf. 13*
2364 A617 20 l shown .70 .25
2365 A617 100 l Profile 1.10 .25

Kubad-Abad Ruins, Beysehir Lake — A618

1986, Nov. 7 *Perf. 13½x13*
2366 A618 100 l multi 1.75 .65

Mehmet Akif Ersoy (1873-1936), Composer of the Turkish National Anthem — A619

1986, Dec. 27 **Litho.** *Perf. 13½x13*
2367 A619 20 l multi .50 .25

Road
Safety — A620

1987, Feb. 4   Litho.   Perf. 13x13½
2368 A620   10 l Use seatbelts   .25   .25
2369 A620   20 l Don't drink alco-
                   hol and drive   .45   .25
2370 A620 150 l Observe speed
                   limit   1.60   .25
      Nos. 2368-2370 (3)   2.30   .75
For surcharges see Nos. 2466, 2477-2478.

Butterflies
A621

10 l, Celerio euphorbiae. 20 l, Vanessa atalanta. 100 l, Euplagia quadripunctaria. 120 l,
Colias crocea.

1987, Feb. 25   Perf. 13½x13
2371 A621   10 l multi   1.00   .25
2372 A621   20 l multi   1.50   .50
2373 A621 100 l multi   5.00 1.75
2374 A621 120 l multi   6.00 2.50
      Nos. 2371-2374 (4)   13.50 5.00

Intl. Year of Shelter
for the
Homeless — A622

1987, Mar. 18   Litho.   Perf. 13x13½
2375 A622 200 l multi   1.25   .75

Karabuk
Iron and
Steel
Works,
50th
Anniv.
A623

1987, Apr. 3   Litho.   Perf. 13½x13
2376 A623   50 l Interior   .65   .25
2377 A623 200 l Exterior   1.60   .25

Natl. Sovereignty — A624

1987, Apr. 23   Perf. 13½x13
2378 A624   50 l multi   .55   .25
Founding of the Turkish state, 67th anniv.

Architecture — A625

Europa: 50 l, Turkish History Institute,
1951-67, designed by Turgut Cansever with
Ertur Yener. 200 l, Social Insurance Institute,
1963, designed by Sedad Hakki Eldem.

1987, Apr. 28   Perf. 13
2379 A625   50 l multi   10.00 2.00
2380 A625 200 l multi   25.00 4.00

92nd Session, Intl.
Olympic Committee,
Istanbul, May 9-
12 — A626

1987, May 9   Litho.   Perf. 13x13½
2381 A626 200 l multi   1.75 1.00

States Type of 1984

Sixteen states (Devleti and Imparatorlugu
rulers and flags): 10 l, Batu Khan, Golden
Horde State (1227-1502). 20 l, Kutlug Timur
Khan, Great Timur Empire (1368-1507). 50 l,
Babur Shah, Babur Empire (1526-1858).
200 l, Osman Bey Gasi, Ottoman Empire
(1299-1923).

1987, June 20   Perf. 12½x13
2382 A587   10 l multi   .60   .30
2383 A587   20 l multi   1.25   .35
2384 A587   50 l multi   1.90   .35
2385 A587 200 l multi   4.00 1.25
      Nos. 2382-2385 (4)   7.75 2.25

Album of the Conqueror, Mehmet II,
15th Cent., Topkapi Palace
Museum — A627

Untitled paintings by Mehmet Siyah Kalem:
10 l, Two warriors, vert. 20 l, Three men, donkey. 50 l, Blackamoor whipping horse. 200 l,
Demon, vert.

Perf. 13½x13, 13x13½
1987, July 1   Litho.
2386 A627   10 l multi   .75   .40
2387 A627   20 l multi   1.00   .40
2388 A627   50 l multi   1.25   .40
2389 A627 200 l multi   2.00 1.00
      Nos. 2386-2389 (4)   5.00 2.20

Natl.
Palaces
A628

1987, Sept. 25   Perf. 13½x13
2390 A628   50 l Ihlamur, c. 1850 1.00   .60
2391 A628 200 l Kucuksu Pavil-
                   ion, 1857   2.00   .75
      See Nos. 2425-2426.

"Tughra," Suleiman's Calligraphic
Signature — A629

Designs: 30 l, Portrait, vert. 200 l, Suleiman
Receiving a Foreign Minister, contemporary
miniature, vert. 270 l, Bust, detail of bas-relief,
The Twenty-Three Law-Givers, entrance to the
gallery of the US House of Representatives.

Litho., Litho. & Engr. (270 l)
1987, Oct. 1   Perf. 13½x13, 13x13½
2392 A629   30 l multi   .50   .35
2393 A629   50 l shown   .75   .45
2394 A629 200 l multi   2.25   .90
2395 A629 270 l multi   2.75 1.25
      Nos. 2392-2395 (4)   6.25 2.95

Suleiman the Magnificent (1494-1566), sultan of the Turkish Empire (1520-1566). On No.
2395, the gold ink was applied by a thermographic process producing a shiny, raised
effect.

A630

Presidents: a, Cemal Gursel (1961-1966). b,
Cevdet Sunay (1966-1973). c, Fahri S.
Koruturk (1973-1980). d, Kenan Evren (1982-
). e, Ismet Inonu (1938-1950). f, Celal Bayar
(1950-1960). g, Mustafa Kemal Ataturk (1923-
1938).

1987, Oct. 29   Litho.   Imperf.
                  Souvenir Sheet
2396 A630   Sheet of 7   6.75 6.75
a.-f.   50 l any single   .65   .65
g.   100 l multi, 26x37mm   .85   .85

A631

200 l, Mosque, architectural elements.

1988, Apr. 9   Litho.   Perf. 13
2397 A631   50 l shown   .75   .50
2398 A631 200 l multi   2.25 1.00
Joseph (Mimar) Sinan (1489-1588), architect.

Health — A632

50 l, Immunization, horiz. 200 l, Fight drug
abuse. 300 l, Safe work conditions, horiz. 600
l, Organ donation.

1988, May 4
2399 A632   50 l multicolored   .25   .25
2400 A632 200 l multicolored   .65   .25
2401 A632 300 l multicolored   .95   .25
2402 A632 600 l multicolored   2.10   .55
      Nos. 2399-2402 (4)   3.95 1.30

Europa Issue

Telecommunications — A633

Transport and communication: 200 l, Modes
of transportation, vert.

1988, May 2   Litho.   Perf. 13, 12½
2403 A633 200 l multi   5.00 2.00
2404 A633 600 l multi   15.00 3.00

Steam,
Electric and
Diesel
Locomotives
A634

50 l, American Standard steam engine, c.
1850. 100 l, Steam engine produced in
Esslingen for Turkish railways, 1913. 200 l,
Henschel Krupp steam engine, 1926. 300 l, E
43001 Toshiba electric engine produced in
Japan, 1987. 600 l, MTE-Tulomsas #24361
diesel-electric high-speed engine, 1984.

1988, May 24   Perf. 13
2405 A634   50 l buff, brn &
                   blk   1.40   .55
2406 A634 100 l buff, brn &
                   blk   2.75 1.10
2407 A634 200 l buff, brn &
                   blk   4.50 1.90
2408 A634 300 l buff, brn &
                   blk   5.50 2.25
2409 A634 600 l buff, brn &
                   blk   7.75 3.50
      Nos. 2405-2409 (5)   21.90 9.30

Court of
Cassation
(Supreme
Court),
120th
Anniv.
A635

1988, July 1   Litho.   Perf. 13½x13
2410 A635   50 l multi   .75   .45

Bridge Openings — A636

Designs: 200 l, Fatih Sultan Mehmet Bridge,
Kavacik-Hisarustu. 300 l, Seto Ohashi (Friendship) Bridges, the Minami and Kita.

1988, July 3   Litho.   Perf. 13x13½
2411 A636 200 l multi   1.90 1.10
2412 A636 300 l multi   3.00 1.50

Telephone
System
A637

1988, Aug. 24   Litho.   Perf. 13½x13
2413 A637 100 l multi   .45   .25

1988
Summer
Olympics,
Seoul
A638

Perf. 12½x13, 13x12½
1988, Sept. 17   Litho.
2414 A638 100 l Running   .60   .25
2415 A638 200 l Archery   1.00   .35
2416 A638 400 l Weight lifting 1.40   .35
2417 A638 600 l Gymnastics,
                   vert.   2.00   .45
      Nos. 2414-2417 (4)   5.00 1.30

Naim Suleymanoglu, 1988 Olympic Gold Medalist, Weight Lifting — A639

1988, Oct. 5   **Litho.**   **Perf. 13x12½**
2418 A639 1000 l multi   8.00 4.00

Aerospace Industries A640

1988, Oct. 28   **Perf. 13½x13, 13x13½**
2419 A640 50 l Gear, aircraft, vert.   .25 .25
2420 A640 200 l shown   .90 .25

Butterflies A641

100 l, Gonepteryx rhamni. 200 l, Chazara briseis. 400 l, Allancastria cerisyi godart. 600 l, Nymphalis antiopa.

1988, Oct. 28   **Perf. 13½x13**
2421 A641 100 l multi   1.60 .85
2422 A641 200 l multi   4.00 1.40
2423 A641 400 l multi   6.50 2.50
2424 A641 600 l multi   8.25 4.00
   a.   Souvenir sheet of 4, #2421-2424   35.00 35.00
   Nos. 2421-2424 (4)   20.35 8.75

ANTALYA '88.

Natl. Palaces Type of 1987
100 l, Maslak Royal Lodge, c. 1890. 400 l, Yildiz Sale Pavilion, 1889.

1988, Nov. 3   **Litho.**   **Perf. 13**
2425 A628 100 l multicolored   .55 .55
2426 A628 400 l multicolored   1.25 1.25

Souvenir Sheet

Kemal Ataturk — A642

1988, Nov. 10   **Perf. 13x13½**
2427 A642 400 l multi   1.75 1.75

Medicinal Plants of Anatolia A643

150 l, Tilia rubra. 300 l, Malva silvestris. 600 l, Hyoscyamus niger. 900 l, Atropa belladonna.

1988, Dec. 14   **Litho.**   **Perf. 13**
2428 A643 150 l multicolored   .55 .25
2429 A643 300 l multicolored   .70 .25
2430 A643 600 l multicolored   1.40 .25
2431 A643 900 l multicolored   2.75 .45
   Nos. 2428-2431 (4)   5.40 1.20

Stamps of 1983-85 Surcharged

Perf. 13, 11½x12½
1989, Feb. 8   **Litho.**
2432 A579 50 l on 15 l No. 2263   .25 .25
2433 A608 75 l on 10 l No. 2334   .45 .25
2434 A608 150 l on 20 l No. 2336   1.10 .25
   Nos. 2432-2434 (3)   1.80 .75

Surcharge on No. 2432 is slightly different.

Artifacts in the Museum of Anatolian Civilizations, Ankara — A644

Designs: 150 l, Seated Goddess with Child, neolithic bisque figurine, Hacilar, 6th millennium B.C. 300 l, Lead figurine, Alisar Huyuk, Assyrian Trading Colonies Era, c. 19th cent. B.C. 600 l, Human-shaped vase, Kultepe, Assyrian Trading Colonies Era, 18th cent. B.C. 1000 l, Ivory mountain god, Bogazkoy, Hittite Empire, 14th cent. B.C.

1989, Feb. 8   **Litho.**   **Perf. 13½x13**
2435 A644 150 l multi   .80 .25
2436 A644 300 l multi   1.25 .80
2437 A644 600 l multi   2.00 1.60
2438 A644 1000 l multi   4.00 2.40
   Nos. 2435-2438 (4)   8.05 5.05

See Nos. 2458-2461, 2495-2498, 2520-2523, 2617-2620.

NATO, 40th Anniv. A645

Wmk. 394
1989, Apr. 4   **Litho.**   **Perf. 13½**
2439 A645 600 l multi   1.75 .25

Europa Issue

Children's Games — A646

600 l, Leapfrog. 1000 l, Open the door, Headbezirgan.

Perf. 13x12½
1989, Apr. 23   **Wmk. 394**
2440 A646 600 l multi   20.00 3.50
2441 A646 1000 l multi   30.00 5.00

Steamships — A647

Perf. 13½x13
1989, July 1   **Litho.**   **Wmk. 394**
2442 A647 150 l Sahilbent   3.00 1.75
2443 A647 300 l Ragbet   4.50 2.50
2444 A647 600 l Tari   6.00 3.00
2445 A647 1000 l Guzelhisar   9.00 4.50
   Nos. 2442-2445 (4)   22.50 11.65

French Revolution, Bicent. — A648

Wmk. 394
1989, July 14   **Litho.**   **Perf. 14**
2446 A648 600 l multi   1.75 .25

Kemal Ataturk — A649

1989, Aug. 16   **Perf. 13x13½**
2447 A649 2000 l gray & bluish gray   3.00 .50
2448 A649 5000 l gray & deep red brn   7.00 2.00

See Nos. 2485-2486, 2538-2541. For surcharge see No. 2656.

No. 2336 Surcharged in Bright Blue
Perf. 11½x12½
1989, Aug. 31   **Litho.**   **Unwmk.**
2449 A608 500 l on 20 l   .70 .25

Photography, 150th Anniv. — A650

1989, Oct. 17   **Perf. 13½x13**
2450 A650 175 l Camera   .40 .25
2451 A650 700 l Shutter   1.40 .25

State Exhibition of Paintings and Sculpture A651

Designs: 200 l, Manzara, by Hikmet Onat. 700 l, Sari Saz, by Bedri Rahmi Eyuboglu. 1000 l, Kadin, by Zuhtu Muridoglu.

Perf. 13½x13
1989, Oct. 30   **Litho.**   **Wmk. 394**
2452 A651 200 l multicolored   .30 .25
2453 A651 700 l multicolored   1.25 .25
2454 A651 1000 l multicolored   1.60 .35
   Nos. 2452-2454 (3)   3.15 .85

Jawaharlal Nehru, 1st Prime Minister of Independent India — A652

1989, Nov. 14   **Perf. 13½x12½**
2455 A652 700 l multicolored   1.10 .25

Sea Turtles A653

1989, Nov. 16   **Perf. 13½x13**
2456 A653 700 l Caretta caretta   4.00 1.25
2457 A653 1000 l Chelonia mydas   8.00 2.50
   a.   Souv. sheet of 2, #2456-2457   24.00 20.00

Artifacts Type of 1989
Perf. 13x12½, 12½x13
1990, Feb. 8   **Litho.**   **Wmk. 394**
2458 A644 100 l Ivory female deity   .30 .30
2459 A644 200 l Ceremonial vessel   .50 .50
2460 A644 500 l Seated goddess pendant   1.00 .75
2461 A644 700 l Carved lion   1.75 1.25
   Nos. 2458-2461 (4)   3.55 2.80

Nos. 2458 and 2460 vert.

Wars of Dardanelles, 1915 — A654

1990, Mar. 18   **Perf. 13**
2462 A654 1000 l multicolored   1.10 .25

EXPO '90 Intl. Garden and Greenery Exposition, Osaka — A655

Perf. 12½x13
1990, Apr. 1   **Litho.**   **Wmk. 394**
2463 1000 l Bridge at left   1.50 .35
2464 1000 l Pavilion at left   1.50 .35
   a.   A655 Pair, #2463-2464   3.25 1.25

Nos. 2301, 2368 and 2284 Surcharged
Perfs. as Before
1990, Apr. 4   **Litho.**
2465 A589 50 l on 5 l #2301   .75 .25
2466 A620 100 l on 10 l #2368   2.00 .25
2467 A589 200 l on 70 l #2284   4.50 .30
   Nos. 2465-2467 (3)   7.25 .80

Grand Natl. Assembly, 70th Anniv. — A657

1990, Apr. 23   **Perf. 13**
2468 A657 300 l multicolored   .50 .50

Europa 1990 — A658

Post offices — 700 l, Ulus, Ankara. 1000 l, Sirkeci, Istanbul, horiz.

1990, May 2
2469 A658 700 l multicolored   7.50 2.75
2470 A658 1000 l multicolored   10.00 3.00

8th European Supreme Courts Conf. A659

1990, May 7   Litho.   Perf. 12½x13
2471 A659 1000 l multicolored   2.25 1.10

Salamandra Salamandra — A660

World Environment Day: No. 2473, Trituras vittatus. No. 2474, Bombina bombina. No. 2475, Hyla arborea, vert.

1990, June 5   Perf. 13½x13
2472 A660 300 l multicolored   .70 .70
2473 A660 500 l multicolored   .70 .70
2474 A660 1000 l multicolored   1.50 1.50
2475 A660 1500 l multicolored   2.50 2.50
       Nos. 2472-2475 (4)   5.40 5.40

Turkey-Japan Relations, Cent. — A661

1990, June 13   Perf. 12½x13
2476 A661 1000 l multicolored   1.75 1.10

Traffic Types of 1987 and Nos. 2283-2284 Surcharged

1990, June 20   Perf. 14
2477 A620 150 l on 10 l   7.00 1.75
2478 A620 300 l on 20 l   11.00 1.75
          Perf. 11½x12½
2479 A589 300 l on 70 l #2284   3.00 .75
2480 A589 1500 l on 20 l #2283   8.75 .75
       Nos. 2477-2480 (4)   29.75 5.00

Boats in Saintes Marines — A662

Paintings by Vincent Van Gogh (1853-1890): 300 l, Self-portrait, vert. 1000 l, Vase with Sunflowers, vert. 1500 l, Road of Cypress and Stars.

Wmk. 394
1990, July 29   Litho.   Perf. 13
2481 A662 300 l multicolored   2.25 1.50
2482 A662 700 l multicolored   4.00 2.25
2483 A662 1000 l multicolored   4.75 3.25
2484 A662 1500 l multicolored   5.25 4.50
       Nos. 2481-2484 (4)   16.25 11.50

Ataturk Type of 1989
1990, Aug. 1   Unwmk.   Perf. 14
2485 A649 500 l gray & olive
                 grn   1.40 .25
2486 A649 1000 l gray & rose vio   1.75 .70

A664

Perf. 13x13½
1990, Aug. 22   Wmk. 394
2487 A664 300 l multicolored   .50 .50
       Intl. Literacy Year.

A665

State exhibition of paintings and sculpture by: 300 l, Nurullah Berk. 700 l, Cevat Dereli. 1000 l, Nijad Sirel.

1990, Oct. 17   Litho.   Perf. 13x13½
2488 A665 300 l multicolored   .45 .25
2489 A665 700 l multicolored   .90 .35
2490 A665 1400 l multicolored   1.40 .50
       Nos. 2488-2490 (3)   2.75 1.10

PTT, 150th Anniv. A666

Past and present communication methods: 200 l, Post rider, truck, train, airplane, ship. 250 l, Telegraph key, computer terminal. 400 l, Telephone switchboard, computerized telephone exchange. 1500 l, Power lines, satellite.

1990, Oct. 23   Perf. 14
2491 A666 200 l multicolored   .25 .25
2492 A666 250 l multicolored   .25 .25
2493 A666 400 l multicolored   .80 .25
2494 A666 1500 l multicolored   3.00 5.75
   a. Souv. sheet of 4, #2491-2494   5.00 3.75
       Nos. 2491-2494 (4)   4.30 6.50

For surcharges see Nos. 2657-2659.

Artifacts Type of 1989

300 l, Figurine of a woman, c. 5000-4500 BC. 500 l, Sistrum, c. 2100-2000 BC. 1000 l, Spouted vessel with 3-footed pedestal, c. 2000-1750 BC. 1500 l, Ceremonial vessel, 1900-1700 BC.

1991, Feb. 8   Litho.   Perf. 13x12½
2495 A644 300 l multi   .40 .25
2496 A644 500 l multi   .75 .45
2497 A644 1000 l multi   1.10 .75
2498 A644 1500 l multi   2.25 1.10
       Nos. 2495-2498 (4)   4.50 2.55

Nos. 2495-2498 are vert.

Lakes of Turkey A667

Wmk. 394
1991, Apr. 24   Litho.   Perf. 13
2499 A667 250 l Abant   .25 .25
2500 A667 500 l Egridir   .75 .25
2501 A667 1500 l Van   2.10 1.10
       Nos. 2499-2501 (3)   3.10 1.60

Europa — A668

Unwmk.
1991, May 6   Litho.   Perf. 13
2502 A668 1000 l multicolored   15.00 3.50
2503 A668 1500 l multi, diff.   22.50 4.00

Natl. Statistics Day — A669

1991, May 9   Perf. 13½x13
2504 A669 500 l multicolored   .45 .25

Eastern Mediterranean Fiber Optic Cable System — A670

1991, May 13
2505 A670 500 l multicolored   .45 .25

European Conf. of Transportation Ministers — A671

1991, May 22   Perf. 13
2506 A671 500 l multicolored   .90 .60

Caricature Art A672

500 l, "Amcabey" by Cemal Nadir Guler. 1000 l, "Abdulcanbaz" by Turhan Selcuk, vert.

Wmk. 394
1991, Sept. 11   Litho.   Perf. 13
2507 A672 500 l multicolored   .70 .25
2508 A672 1000 l multicolored   1.10 .60

Ceramics A673

Wall facings: 500 l, 13th cent. Seljuk bird. 1500 l, 16th cent. Ottoman floral pattern.

1991, Sept. 23   Perf. 13½x13
2509 A673 500 l multicolored   .40 .25
2510 A673 1500 l multicolored   1.40 .65

Symposium on Intl. Protection of Human Rights, Antalya — A674

1991, Oct. 4   Perf. 13x12½
2511 A674 500 l multicolored   .45 .25

Southeastern Anatolia Irrigation and Power Project A675

1991, Oct. 6   Unwmk.   Perf. 13½x13
2512 A675 500 l multicolored   .45 .25

Turkish Fairy Tales — A676

Baldboy: 500 l, With genie. 1000 l, At party. 1500 l, Plowing field.

1991, Oct. 9   Perf. 13x13½
2513 A676 500 l multicolored   .40 .25
2514 A676 1000 l multicolored   .90 .45
2515 A676 1500 l multicolored   1.40 .65
       Nos. 2513-2515 (3)   2.70 1.35

Snakes A677

250 l, Eryx jaculus. 500 l, Elaphe quatuor-lineata. 1000 l, Vipera xanthina. 1500 l, Vipera kaznakovi.

Perf. 12½x13
1991, Oct. 23   Wmk. 394
2516 A677 250 l multi   2.40 .60
2517 A677 500 l multi   3.50 1.25
2518 A677 1000 l multi   7.25 2.40
2519 A677 1500 l multi   9.50 4.25
       Nos. 2516-2519 (4)   22.65 8.50

World Environment Day.

Antiquities Type of 1989

300 l, Statuette of Mother Goddess, Neolithic, 6000 B.C., vert. 500 l, Hasanoglan statuette, Early Bronze Age, 3000 B.C., vert. 1000 l, Inandik vase, Old Hittite, 18th cent. B.C., vert. 1500 l, Lion statuette, Urartian, 8th cent. B.C., vert.

Wmk. 394
1992, Feb. 12   Litho.   Perf. 13
2520 A644 300 l multicolored   .30 .25
2521 A644 500 l multicolored   .45 .25
2522 A644 1000 l multicolored   .90 .45
2523 A644 1500 l multicolored   1.50 .65
       Nos. 2520-2523 (4)   3.15 1.60

Discovery of America, 500th Anniv. A678

Wmk. 394
1992, May 4   Litho.   Perf. 13
2524 A678 1500 l shown   7.00 2.00
2525 A678 2000 l Balloons,
                 vert.   12.50 3.00
       Europa.

Settlement of Jews in Turkey, 500th Anniv. A679

1992, May 15   Perf. 12½x13
2526 A679 1500 l multicolored   1.00 1.00

A681

Wmk. 394
1992, June 1 **Litho.** *Perf. 13*
2529 A681 500 l multicolored .45 .45
Turkish Court of Accounts, 130th anniv.

A682

1992, June 4
2530 A682 1500 l multicolored .90 .90
Economics Congress, Izmir.

World Environment Day — A683

500 l, Vanellus vanellus. 1000 l, Oriolus oriolus. 1500 l, Tadorna tadorna. 2000 l, Halcyon smyrnensis, vert.

1992, June 5 **Litho.** *Perf. 13*
2531 A683 500 l multi .60 .60
2532 A683 1000 l multi .90 .60
2533 A683 1500 l multi 1.25 .60
2534 A683 2000 l multi 1.75 1.25
Nos. 2531-2534 (4) 4.50 3.05

Ataturk Type of 1989 and

Kemal Ataturk — A683a   A683b

10,000 l, Full face. 100,000 l, Facing left.

Perf. 13, 14 (#2539, 2541, 2543-2544A)

1992-96		Litho.	Unwmk.	
2538	A649	250 l gold, brn & org	1.50	.25
2539	A649	5000 l gold & vio	2.00	.40
2540	A649	10,000 l gold & blue	4.50	1.90
2541	A649	20,000 l gold & lil rose	8.00	1.60
2542	A683a	50,000 l multi	4.50	1.75
2543	A683b	50,000 l lake & pink	3.50	.90
2544	A683b	100,000 l grn bl & yel org	4.50	1.75
		Nos. 2538-2544 (7)	28.50	8.55

Issued: 250 l, 10,000 l, 5/28/92; 5000 l, 20,000 l, 9/29/93; #2542, 11/10/94; #2543, 100,000 l, 6/1/96.
For surcharges see Nos. 2655, 2732.

Black Sea Economic Cooperation Summit — A684

Wmk. 394
1992, June 25 **Litho.** *Perf. 13*
2545 A684 1500 l multicolored .90 .45

1992 Summer Olympics, Barcelona A685

1992, July 25 **Wmk. 394**
2546 A685 500 l Doves .45 .25
2547 A685 1000 l Boxing .60 .35
2548 A685 1500 l Weight lifting 1.10 .45
2549 A685 2000 l Wrestling 2.25 .65
Nos. 2546-2549 (4) 4.40 1.70

Anatolian Folktales — A686

Scenes: 500 l, Woman carrying milk to soldiers. 1000 l, Pouring milk into trough. 1500 l, Soldiers dipping into trough.

Perf. 13x12½
1992, Sept. 23 **Litho.** **Wmk. 394**
2550 A686 500 l multicolored .25 .25
2551 A686 1000 l multicolored .60 .25
2552 A686 1500 l multicolored 1.00 .45
Nos. 2550-2552 (3) 1.85 .95

Turkish Handicrafts — A687

500 l, Embroidered flowers. 1000 l, Dolls in traditional costumes, vert. 3000 l, Saddlebags.

1992, Oct. 21 *Perf. 13½x13, 13x13½*
2553 A687 500 l multicolored .25 .25
2554 A687 1000 l multicolored .55 .25
2555 A687 3000 l multicolored 1.50 .80
Nos. 2553-2555 (3) 2.30 1.30
See Nos. 2585-2588, 2611-2612.

Fruits — A688

Wmk. 394
1992, Nov. 25 **Litho.** *Perf. 13*
2556 A688 500 l Cherries .35 .25
2557 A688 1000 l Peaches .70 .25
2558 A688 3000 l Grapes 1.40 .60
2559 A688 5000 l Apples 3.00 1.00
Nos. 2556-2559 (4) 5.45 2.10
See Nos. 2565-2568.

Famous Men — A689

Designs: No. 2560, Sait Faik Abasiyanik (1906-54), writer. No. 2561, Fikret Mualla Saygi (1904-67), artist. No. 2562, Cevat Sakir Kabaagacli (1886-1973), author. No. 2563, Muhsin Ertugrul (1892-1979), actor and producer. No. 2564, Asik Veysel Satiroglu (1894-1973), composer.

Perf. 14, 13½x13 (#2561, 2564)
1992, Dec. 30 **Litho.**
2560 A689 T multicolored 1.10 .25
2561 A689 T multicolored 1.10 .25
2562 A689 M multicolored 1.50 .25
2563 A689 M multicolored 1.50 .25
2564 A689 M multicolored 1.50 .25
Nos. 2560-2564 (5) 6.70 1.25

Value on day of issue: Nos. 2560-2561, 500 l. Nos. 2562-2564, 1000 l.
See Nos. 2577-2581.

Fruit Type of 1992
Wmk. 394
1993, Apr. 28 **Litho.** *Perf. 13*
2565 A688 500 l Bananas .60 .35
2566 A688 1000 l Oranges .60 .60
2567 A688 3000 l Pears 1.25 .95
2568 A688 5000 l Pomegranates 2.50 1.75
Nos. 2565-2568 (4) 4.95 3.65

Europa — A690

Sculptures by: 1000 l, Hadi Bara. 3000 l, Zuhtu Muridoglu.

1993, May 3
2569 A690 1000 l multicolored *1.25* *.60*
2570 A690 3000 l multicolored *2.25* *1.00*

A691

Wmk. 394
1993, July 6 **Litho.** *Perf. 13*
2571 A691 2500 l lt bl, dk bl & gold .90 .60
Economic Cooperation Organization Meeting, Istanbul.

Houses — A692

Various houses from Black Sea region.

1993, July 7
2572 A692 1000 l multicolored .75 .25
2573 A692 2500 l multi, horiz. .75 .60
2574 A692 3000 l multicolored 1.50 .90
2575 A692 5000 l multi, horiz. 1.50 1.25
Nos. 2572-2575 (4) 4.50 3.00
See Nos. 2604-2607, 2631-2634, 2647-2650, 2676-2679.

Hodja Ahmet Yesevi (1093-1166), Poet — A693

1993, July 28
2576 A693 3000 l lt bl, dk bl & gold 1.00 .40

Famous Men Type of 1992
Designs: No. 2577, Haci Arif Bey (1831-84), composer. No. 2578, Neyzen Tevfik Kolayli (1878-1953), poet. No. 2579, Munir Nurettin Selcuk (1900-81), composer, musician. No. 2580, Cahit Sitki Taranci (1910-56), poet. No. 2581, Orhan Veli Kanik (1914-50), writer.

Perf. 14, 13½x13 (2578-2580)
1993, Aug. 4 **Litho.** **Unwmk.**
2577 A689 T brown & red brown 1.10 .25
2578 A689 T brown & red brown 1.10 .25
2579 A689 M brown & red brown 1.50 .25
2580 A689 M brown & red brown 1.50 .25
2581 A689 M brown & red brown 1.50 .25
Nos. 2577-2581 (5) 6.70 1.25

Value on day of issue: Nos. 2577-2578, 500 l. Nos. 2579-2581, 1000 l.

Istanbul, Proposed Site for 2000 Olympics A694

1993, Aug. 11 *Perf. 12½x13*
2582 A694 2500 l multicolored .90 .45

Protection of Mediterranean Sea Against Pollution — A695

Unwmk.
1993, Oct. 12 **Litho.** *Perf. 13*
2583 A695 1000 l Amphora on sea floor .25 .25
2584 A695 3000 l Dolphin jumping 1.60 .65

Handicrafts Type of 1992
Perf. 12½x13, 13x12½
1993, Oct. 21 **Wmk. 394**
2585 A687 1000 l Painted rug .25 .25
2586 A687 2500 l Earrings .95 .25
2587 A687 5000 l Money purse, vert. 2.00 .95
Nos. 2585-2587 (3) 3.20 1.45

Republic, 70th Anniv. — A696

1993, Oct. 29 **Wmk. 394** *Perf. 13*
2588 A696 1000 l multicolored .45 .45

Civil Defence Organization — A697

Perf. 12½x13

1993, Nov. 25   Unwmk.
2589 A697 1000 l multicolored   .45   .45

Turksat
Satellite — A698

Designs: 1500 l, Satellite, globe, map of Turkey. 5000 l, Satellite transmissions to areas in Europe and Asia.

Perf. 13x13½

1994, Jan. 21   Litho.   Wmk. 394
2590 A698 1500 l multicolored   .25   .25
2591 A698 5000 l multicolored   1.10   .25

Natl. Water
Project — A699

1994, Feb. 28   Perf. 13x12½
2592 A699 1500 l multicolored   .45   .35

Native
Cuisine
A700

Perf. 12½x13

1994, Mar. 23   Litho.   Wmk. 394
2593 A700 1000 l Ezogel in
              corbasi   .65   .65
2594 A700 1500 l Mixed dolma   .65   .65
2595 A700 3500 l Shish kebabs   .65   .65
2596 A700 5000 l Baklava   1.25   .65
     Nos. 2593-2596 (4)   3.20 2.60

Europa
A701

1500 l, Marie Curie (1867-1934), chemist, vert. 5000 l, Albert Einstein (1879-1955), physicist.

Unwmk.

1994, May 2   Litho.   Perf. 13
2597 A701 1500 l multicolored   *.50   .50*
2598 A701 5000 l multicolored   *1.50 1.50*

World Environment Day — A703

Views of: 6000 l, Antalya. 8500 l, Mugla, vert.

Wmk. 394

1994, June 5   Litho.   Perf. 13
2602 A703 6000 l multicolored   1.25   .90
2603 A703 8500 l multicolored   1.90 1.25

Houses Type of 1993

2500 l, 2-story housing complex. 3500 l, 3-story home with balconies. 6000 l, Tri-level country home. 8500 l, 2-story home.

1994, July 7
2604 A692 2500 l multi, horiz.   .60   .60
2605 A692 3500 l multi, horiz.   .60   .60
2606 A692 6000 l multi, horiz.   .60   .60
2607 A692 8500 l multi, horiz.   1.75   .60
     Nos. 2604-2607 (4)   3.55 2.40

Tourism
A704

1994, Aug. 3
2608 A704 5000 l Hiking   .75   .45
2609 A704 10,000 l Rafting   1.50   .75

Project of
the Year
2001
A705

1994, Aug. 27
2610 A705 2500 l multicolored   .50   .50

Handicrafts Type of 1992

Designs: 7500 l, Kusak pattern used on 18th cent. clothing, vert. 12,000 l, Pacalik pattern used on 19th cent. clothing.

1994, Oct. 21
2611 A687 7500 l multicolored   1.00   .50
2612 A687 12,500 l multicolored   1.75 1.75

Mushrooms — A706

2500 l, Morchella conica. 5000 l, Agaricus bernardii. 7500 l, Lactarius deliciosus. 12,500 l, Macrolepiota procera.

1994, Nov. 16
2613 A706 2500 l multi   .50   .50
2614 A706 5000 l multi   .90   .90
2615 A706 7500 l multi   1.60 1.60
2616 A706 12,500 l multi   3.25 3.25
     Nos. 2613-2616 (4)   6.25 6.25

See Nos. 2637-2640.

Antiquities Type of 1989

Lydian Treasures, 6th cent. B.C.: 2500 l, Silver pitcher, vert. 5000 l, Silver incense burner, vert. 7500 l, Gold, glass necklace. 12,500 l, Gold brooch.

1994, Dec. 7
2617 A644 2500 l multicolored   .60   .45
2618 A644 5000 l multicolored   .90   .50
2619 A644 7500 l multicolored   1.40   .75
2620 A644 12,500 l multicolored   2.50 1.00
     Nos. 2617-2620 (4)   5.40 2.70

Nevruz,
New Day
A707

1995, Mar. 21
2621 A707 3500 l multicolored   .45   .45

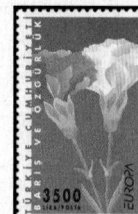

Europa — A708

1995, May 5
2622 A708 3500 l Flowers   *1.00 1.00*
2623 A708 15,000 l Olive branch   *2.00 2.00*

Istanbul '96 World Stamp
Exhibition — A709

a, 7000 l, Buildings. b, 25,000 l, Tower, buildings. c, 7000 l, Mosque, city along harbor. c, 25,000 l, Residential area, mosque, harbor.

1995, May 24
2624 A709 Block of 4, #a.-d.   7.25 3.50
   Nos. 2624a-2624b and 2624c-2624d are each continuous designs.

European Nature Conservation
Year — A710

1995, June 5
2625 A710 5000 l Field of pop-
              pies   .50   .25
2626 A710 15,000 l Trees   1.50   .70
2627 A710 25,000 l Mountain val-
              ley   2.50 1.25
     Nos. 2625-2627 (3)   4.50 2.20

A711

1995, Feb. 1
2628 A711 15,000 l red & blue   1.75 1.75
     Motion Pictures, cent.

A712

1995, Apr. 23
2629 A712 5000 l multicolored   .45   .45
   1sh Conference of the Moslem Women Parliamentaries, Pakistan.

Houses Type of 1993

5000 l, 2-story block house. 10,000 l, Tower of part-stone house. 15,000 l, Interior view of 2-story house, horiz. 20,000 l, Three unit-connecting apartment, horiz.

1995, July 7
2631 A692 5000 l multicolored   .75   .35
2632 A692 10,000 l multicolored   1.10   .40
2633 A692 15,000 l multicolored   1.25   .55
2634 A692 20,000 l multicolored   1.40 1.10
     Nos. 2631-2634 (4)   4.50 2.40

UN, 50th
Anniv. — A713

1995, Oct. 24
2635 A713 15,000 l shown   .80   .40
2636 A713 30,000 l UN emblem,
              "50"   1.60   .80

Mushroom Type of 1994

Designs: 5000 l, Amanita phalloides. 10,000 l, Lepiota helveola. 20,000 l, Gyromitra esculenta. 30,000 l, Amanita gemmata.

1995, Nov. 16
2637 A706 5000 l multicolored   .65   .65
2638 A706 10,000 l multicolored   1.10 1.10
2639 A706 20,000 l multicolored   2.25 2.25
2640 A706 30,000 l multicolored   2.50 2.50
     Nos. 2637-2640 (4)   6.50 6.50

Children's
Rights
A714

6,000 l, Rainbow, hearts, flower, sun in sky. 10,000 l, Child's hand drawing letter "A."

1996, Mar. 13
2641 A714 6,000 l multicolored   .40   .40
2642 A714 10,000 l multicolored   1.10 1.00

Fauna — A715

Designs: a, 5,000 l, Bee. b, 10,000 l, Dog. c, 15,000 l, Rooster. d, 30,000 l, Fish.

1996, Apr. 10   Unwmk.
2643 A715 Sheet of 4, #a.-d.   5.00 5.00
     ISTANBUL '96.

Famous
Women
A716

Perf. 12½x13

1996, May 5   Litho.   Unwmk.
2644 A716 10,000 l Nene Hatun   1.50 1.50
2645 A716 40,000 l Halide Edip
              Adivar   3.00 3.00
     Europa.

World Environment Day — A717

Unwmk.

1996, June 3   **Litho.**   **Perf. 13**
2646 A717 50,000 l multicolored   1.75   .90

Houses Type of 1993

Designs: 10,000 l, Tri-level block house, horiz. 15,000 l, Two story with bay window, gate at entrance to side courtyard, horiz. 25,000 l, Two story townhouse, double wooden doors at bottom. 50,000 l, Flat-roofed, two-story townhouse.

1996, July 7   **Perf. 13**
2647 A692 10,000 l multicolored   .45   .25
2648 A692 15,000 l multicolored   .75   .35
2649 A692 25,000 l multicolored   1.00   .55
2650 A692 50,000 l multicolored   2.10   1.10
    Nos. 2647-2650 (4)   4.30   2.25

1996 Summer Olympic Games, Atlanta — A718

a, 10,000 l, Archery. b, 15,000 l, Wrestling. c, 25,000 l, Weight lifting. d, 50,000 l, Hurdles.

1996, July 19
2651 A718 Sheet of 4, #a.-d.   6.50   6.50
    ISTANBUL '96.

Turkish Press, 50th Anniv. A719

1996, July 24   **Perf. 12½x13**
2652 A719 15,000 l multicolored   .60   .30

Euro '96, European Soccer Championships, Great Britain — A720

1996, June 8   **Perf. 13**
2653 A720 15,000 l Player, vert.   1.10   .45
2654 A720 50,000 l Soccer ball, flags   2.50   1.25

Nos. 2447, 2491, 2493-2494, 2538 Surcharged in Orange or Deep Violet Blue

or

Perfs., Printing Methods as Before
1996, July 22
2655 A649   T on 250 l #2538
      (O)   1.10   .25
2656 A649   T on 2000 l #2447   1.10   .25

2657 A666   M on 200 l #2491   1.75   .25
2658 A666   M on 400 l #2493   1.75   .25
2659 A666   M on 1500 l #2494   1.75   .25
    Nos. 2655-2659 (5)   7.45   1.25

Nos. 2655-2656 and 2657-2659 had face values of 10,000 l and 15,000 l on day of issue.
See No. 2732.

Methods of Transportation — A721

a, 25,000 l, Airplane (b). b, 50,000 l, Helicopter, ship (d). c, 75,000 l, Train. d, 100,000 l, Bus (c).

Unwmk.

1996, Sept. 27   **Litho.**   **Perf. 13**
2660 A721 Sheet of 4, #a.-d.   14.00   10.00
    ISTANBUL '96. Exists imperf. Value, $85.

New Year A722

Unwmk.

1996, Oct. 23   **Litho.**   **Perf. 13**
2661 A722 15,000 l multicolored   .55   .30

Social and Cultural Heritage A723

10,000 l, Public Library, Bayezit, Amasya. 15,000 l, Mosque and hospital, Divrigi.

1996, Dec. 17   **Litho.**   **Perf. 13**
2662 A723 10,000 l multicolored   .35   .35
2663 A723 15,000 l multicolored   .55   .55

Stories and Legends — A724

Europa: 25,000 l, Little children dressed in flowers and leaves riding a giant peacock. 70,000 l, Genie, man being riding a giant bird.

1997, May 5   **Litho.**   **Perf. 13**
2664 A724 25,000 l multicolored   1.25   1.25
2665 A724 70,000 l multicolored   2.50   2.50

White Cat — A725

Designs: a, 25,000 l, Tail, hindquarters. b, 50,000 l, Back legs. c, 75,000 l, Front legs. d, 150,000 l, Face.

1997, Apr. 23
2666 A725 Sheet of 4, #a.-d.   10.00   8.25

Language Day — A726

1997, May 13   **Litho.**   **Perf. 13**
2667 A726 25,000 l multicolored   .50   .50

World Environment Day — A727

1997, June 5
2668 A727 35,000 l multicolored   .90   .90

Orchids — A728

Designs: 25,000 l, Ophrys tenthredinifera. 70,000 l, Ophrys apifera.

1997, May 28
2669 A728 25,000 l multicolored   .80   .25
2670 A728 70,000 l multicolored   1.90   .55

25th Intl. Istanbul Festival A729

1997, June 13   **Perf. 13½**
Background Color
2671 A729   15,000 l blue   .25   .25
2672 A729   25,000 l pink   .65   .65
2673 A729   70,000 l blue green   1.60   1.60
2674 A729   75,000 l purple   2.00   2.00
2675 A729   100,000 l green blue   2.75   2.75
    Nos. 2671-2675 (5)   7.25   7.25

House Type of 1993

Inscribed: 25,000 l, Bir Urfa Evi, vert. 40,000 l, Bir Mardin Evi. 80,000 l, Bir Diyarbakir Evi. 100,000 l, Kemaliye'de Bir Ev, vert.

1997, July 7   **Litho.**   **Perf. 13**
2676 A692   25,000 l multicolored   .50   .50
2677 A692   40,000 l multicolored   .90   .90
2678 A692   80,000 l multicolored   1.75   1.75
2679 A692   100,000 l multicolored   2.25   2.25
    Nos. 2676-2679 (4)   5.40   5.40

A730

Flowers: 40,000 l, Lilium candidum. 100,000 l, Euphorbia pulcherima.

1997, Sept. 8   **Litho.**   **Perf. 13**
2680 A730   40,000 l multicolored   1.10   .25
2681 A730   100,000 l multicolored   2.50   .65

A731

World Air Games: No. 2682, Hang gliding. No. 2683, Sailplane. No. 2684, Man pointing up at biplanes. No. 2685, Hot air balloon.

1997, Sept. 13
2682 A731   40,000 l multi   1.10   1.10
2683 A731   40,000 l multi   1.10   1.10
2684 A731   100,000 l multi   3.25   3.25
2685 A731   100,000 l multi   4.25   4.25
    Nos. 2682-2685 (4)   9.70   9.70

Forestry Congress A732

1997, Oct. 13   **Litho.**   **Perf. 13**
2686 A732 50,000 l multicolored   1.40   1.40

15th European Gymnastics Congress — A733

1997, Oct. 13
2687 A733 100,000 l multicolored   2.75   2.75

Traditional Women's Headcovers A734

1997, Nov. 19   **Litho.**   **Perf. 13**
2688 A734   50,000 l Gaziantep   1.50   .75
2689 A734   50,000 l Canakkale   1.50   .75
2690 A734   100,000 l Isparta   2.50   1.50
2691 A734   100,000 l Bursa   2.50   1.50
    Nos. 2688-2691 (4)   8.00   4.50

See Nos. 2711-2714, 2748-2751, 2765-2768, 2790-2793.

1998 Winter Olympic Games, Nagano — A735

Slalom skiers: No. 2692, #1 on bib. No. 2693, #119 on bib.

1998, Feb. 7   **Litho.**   **Perf. 13**
2692   125,000 l multicolored   2.00   2.00
2693   125,000 l multicolored   2.00   2.00
   a. A735 Pair, #2692-2693   4.25   4.25

Intl. Year of the Ocean — A736

Designs: a, 50,000 l, Turtle, jellyfish. b, 75,000 l, Fish, octopus. c, 125,000 l, Coral, crab. d, 125,000 l, Fish, coral, starfish.

1998, Apr. 18   Litho.   Perf. 13
2694 A736 Sheet of 4, #a.-d.   8.00 8.00

Dardenelles Campaign — A737

Memorial Statues: #2695, "Mother with Children," Natl. War Memorial, Wellington. #2696, "With Great Respect to the Mehmetcik, Gallipoli" (Turkish soldier carrying wounded ANZAC).

1998, Mar. 18   Litho.   Perf. 13
2695 A737 125,000 l multicolored   1.75 1.75
2696 A737 125,000 l multicolored   1.75 1.75

See New Zealand Nos. 1490-1491.

A738

Europa (National Festivals and Holidays): 100,000 l, Kemal Ataturk, natl. flag, people celebrating. 150,000 l, Ataturk, natl. flag, children of different races celebrating together.

1998, May 5
2697 A738 100,000 l multicolored   *1.25 1.25*
2698 A738 150,000 l multicolored   *2.25 2.25*

A739

Tulips: 50,000 l, Sylvestris. 75,000 l, Armena (pink). 100,000 l, Armena (violet). 125,000 l, Saxatilis.

1998, May 1   Litho.   Perf. 13
2699 A739 50,000 l multicolored   .75   .75
2700 A739 75,000 l multicolored   1.60 1.60
2701 A739 100,000 l multicolored 1.90 1.90
2702 A739 125,000 l multicolored 3.00 3.00
    Nos. 2699-2702 (4)   7.25 7.25

Souvenir Sheet

World Environment Day — A740

Owls: a, Two on branches. b, One flying, one standing.

1998, June 5   Litho.   Perf. 13½
2703 A740 150,000 l Sheet of 2,
                #a.-b.   6.25 6.25

Contemporary Arts — A741

75,000 l, Couple dancing. 100,000 l, Man playing cello. 150,000 l, Ballerina.

1998, Aug. 14   Litho.   Perf. 13
2704 A741 75,000 l multi   1.10   .50
2705 A741 100,000 l multi, vert. 1.40   .70
2706 A741 150,000 l multi, vert. 2.10 1.10
    Nos. 2704-2706 (3)   4.60 2.30

Kemal Ataturk — A742

1998, Aug. 20   Litho.   Perf. 13
2707 A742 150,000 l cl & brn   1.60   .65
2708 A742 175,000 l bl & rose
               brn   2.25   .85
2709 A742 250,000 l brn & cl   3.00 1.25
2710 A742 500,000 l brn & dk
               bl   6.50 2.50
    Nos. 2707-2710 (4)   13.35 5.25

Women's Headcovers Type of 1997
1998, Nov. 24   Litho.   Perf. 13
2711 A734 75,000 l Afyon   .85   .40
2712 A734 75,000 l Ankara   .85   .40
2713 A734 175,000 l Mus   1.90   .95
2714 A734 175,000 l Mugla   1.90   .95
    Nos. 2711-2714 (4)   5.50 2.70

Turkish Republic, 75th Anniv. — A743

275,000 l, Flag, silhouette of Ataturk.

1998, Oct. 29   Litho.   Perf. 13
2715 A743 175,000 l shown   1.75   .90
  a.   Souvenir sheet of 1, imperf. 1.75 1.25
2716 A743 275,000 l red & blk   2.75 1.40
  a.   Souvenir sheet of 1, imperf. 2.75 2.00

Nos. 2715a, 2716a have simulated perforations.

Famous People A744

#2717, Ihap Hulusi Görey (1898-1986). #2718, Bedia Muvahhit (1897-1993). No. 2719, Feza Gürsey (1921-92). #2720, Haldun Taner (1915-86). #2721, Vasfi Riza Zobu (1902-92).

1998, Dec. 31   Photo.   Perf. 13
2717 A744 M gray bl, bl & plum   1.50   .30
2718 A744 M lil, dp lil & plum   1.50   .30
2719 A744 T org, brn & plum   2.00   .50
2720 A744 T gray vio, vio &
               plum   2.00   .50
2721 A744 T grn, blk & plum   2.00   .50
    Nos. 2717-2721 (5)   9.00 2.10

On day of issue, Nos. 2717-2718 were valued at 50,000 l each, and Nos. 2719-2721 were valued at 75,000 l each.

NATO, 50th Anniv. A745

1999, Apr. 4   Litho.   Perf. 13
2722 A745 200,000 l multicolored 2.75 2.10

Ottoman Empire, 700th Anniv. A746

Designs: No. 2723, Man on horse surrounded by people in buildings. No. 2724, Man on horse, three men in foreground. No. 2725, Men seated.
No. 2726, Man on white horse, castle. No. 2727, Group of women, horiz.

1999, Apr. 12
2723 A746 175,000 l multicolored 1.75 1.25
2724 A746 175,000 l multicolored 1.75 1.25
2725 A746 175,000 l multicolored 1.75 1.25
    Nos. 2723-2725 (3)   5.25 3.75

Size: 79x119mm, 119x79mm
Imperf
2726 A746 200,000 l multicolored 2.25 2.25
2727 A746 200,000 l multicolored 2.25 2.25

Europa A747

Natl. Parks: 175,000 l, Köprülü Canyon, vert. 200,000 l, Kackarlar.

Perf. 13¼x13, 13x13¼
1999, May 5   Litho.
2728 A747 175,000 l multicolored 2.00 2.00
2729 A747 200,000 l multicolored 2.00 2.00

World Environment Day — A748

No. 2730: a, 100,000 l, Tetrax tetrax. 200,000 l, Hoplopterus spinosus.
No. 2731: a, 100,000 l, Marbled duck. b, 200,000 l, Sitta kruperi.

1999, June 3   Litho.   Perf. 13¼
2730 A748 Sheet of 2, #a.-b.   3.50 3.50
2731 A748 Sheet of 2, #a.-b.   3.50 3.50

See Nos. 2763-2764, 2800-2801.

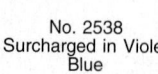

No. 2538 Surcharged in Violet Blue

1999   Litho.   Perf. 13
2732 A649 T on 250 l #2537   .75   .40

No. 2732 sold for 50,000 l on day of issue.

Souvenir Sheet

National Congress During the War for Independence — A749

Designs: a, 100,000 l, Ataturk, two other men, building. b, 100,000 l, Ataturk, two other men seated. c, 200,000 l, Two men standing in front of building. d, 200,000 l, Ataturk standing in front of building.

Perf. 13¼x13
1999, June 22   Litho.   Unwmk.
2733 A749 Sheet of 4, #a.-d.   6.25 6.25

Art — A750

1999, July 8   Litho.   Perf. 13x13¼
2734 A750 250,000 l shown   2.25 1.10
2735 A750 250,000 l multi, diff. 2.25 1.10

Tourism — A751

No. 2736, Temple to Zeus. No. 2737, Antakya Archaeological Museum, horiz. No. 2738, Golf course, Antalya. No. 2739, Sailboat off Bodrum.

Perf. 13x13¼, 13¼x13
1999, Sept. 19   Litho.
2736 A751 125,000 l multi   1.40 1.40
2737 A751 125,000 l multi   1.40 1.40
2738 A751 225,000 l multi   2.10 2.10
2739 A751 225,000 l multi   2.10 2.10
    Nos. 2736-2739 (4)   7.00 7.00

Dams A752

225,000 l, Cubuk 1. 250,000 l, Atatürk.

1999, Sept. 19 Litho. Perf. 13¼x13
2740 A752 225,000 l multi   2.25 2.25
2741 A752 250,000 l multi   2.25 2.25

Kemal Ataturk — A753

1999, Sept. 27   Litho.   Perf. 13¾
2742 A753 225,000 l grn &
               brn   2.50   .55
2743 A753 250,000 l brn & lil   2.50   .65
2744 A753 500,000 l pink &
               grn   3.75 1.40
2745 A753 1,000,000 l bl & red   9.00 4.00
    Nos. 2742-2745 (4)   17.75 6.60

Thanks for Earthquake Rescue
Efforts — A754

Designs: 225,000 l, Hands holding wreckage, flowers, vert. 250,000 l, Rescuers, handclasp.

Perf. 13¼x13, 13x13¼

1999, Oct. 15   **Litho.**
| 2746 | A754 225,000 l multi | 1.40 | .65 |
| 2747 | A754 250,000 l multi | 1.75 | .75 |

Women's Headcovers Type of 1997
1999, Nov. 24   **Litho.**   **Perf. 13¼**
2748	A734 150,000 l Manisa	1.10	.55
2749	A734 150,000 l Nigde	1.10	.55
2750	A734 250,000 l Antalya	2.00	.90
2751	A734 250,000 l Amasya	2.00	.90
	Nos. 2748-2751 (4)	6.20	2.90

Caravansaries — A755

1999, Dec. 24   **Litho.**   **Perf. 13¼x13**
| 2752 | A755 150,000 l Sarapsa | .65 | .25 |
| 2753 | A755 250,000 l Obruk | 1.00 | .45 |

Millennium
A756

Designs: 275,000 l, Earth, brain, satellite. 300,000 l, Monachus monachus.

2000, Feb. 1   **Litho.**   **Perf. 13¼**
| 2754 | A756 275,000 l multi | 2.00 | 2.00 |
| 2755 | A756 300,000 l multi | 2.00 | 2.00 |

Merchant
Ships
A757

125,000 l, Bug. 150,000 l, Gülcemal. 275,000 l, Nusret. 300,000 l, Bandirma.

2000, Mar. 16
2756	A757 125,000 l multi	.65	.65
2757	A757 150,000 l multi	.90	.90
2758	A757 275,000 l multi	2.40	2.40
2759	A757 300,000 l multi	2.75	2.75
	Nos. 2756-2759 (4)	6.70	6.70

See Nos. 2813-2816, 2840-2843.

Grand National
Assembly, 80th
Anniv. — A758

Perf. 13x13¼, 13¼x13
2000, Apr. 23   **Litho.**
| 2760 | A758 275,000 l shown | 1.00 | 1.00 |
| 2761 | A758 300,000 l Sprouts, horiz. | 1.10 | 1.10 |

Europa, 2000
Common Design Type
2000, May 9   **Perf. 13x13¼**
| 2762 | CD17 300,000 l multi | 2.00 | 2.00 |

**World Environment Day Type of
1999**
Souvenir Sheets
No. 2763, 275,000 l: a, Aquila heliaca. b, Picus viridis.
No. 2764, 275,000 l: a, Oxyura leucocephala. b, Recurvirostra avosetta.

2000, June 5   **Litho.**   **Perf. 13¼**
Sheets of 2, #a-b
| 2763-2764 | A748 Set of 2 | 8.00 | 8.00 |

Women's Headcover Type of 1997
Designs: No. 2765, 275,000 l, Trabzon. No. 2766, 275,000 l, Tunceli. No. 2767, 275,000 l, Corum. No. 2768, 275,000 l, Izmir.

2000, July 15   Set of 4
| 2765-2768 | A734 | 7.25 | 7.25 |

Souvenir Sheet

Nomadic Life — A759

a, Woman at loom, woman seated. b, Women & containers. c, Women, 2 goats, carpet on tent rope. d, Woman, children, 6 goats, carpet on rope.

2000
| 2769 | Sheet of 4 | 9.00 | 9.00 |
| a.-d. | A759 300,000 l Any single | 1.60 | 1.60 |

Military
Leaders — A760

Designs: 100,000 l, Gen. Yakup Sevki Subasi. 200,000 l, Lt. Gen. Musa Kazim Karabekir (c. 1882-1948). 275,000 l, Marshal Mustafa Fevzi Cakmak (1876-1950). 300,000 l, Gen. Cevat Cobanli (1871-1938).

2000
| 2770-2773 | A760 Set of 4 | 5.50 | 5.50 |

2000
Summer
Olympics,
Sydney
A761

Designs: 125,000 l, Rhythmic gymnastics. 150,000 l, Swimming. 275,000 l, High jump. 300,000 l, Archery.

2000
| 2774-2777 | A761 Set of 4 | 5.50 | 5.50 |

Crocuses — A762

Designs: 250,000 l, Crocus chrysanthus. 275,000 l, Crocus olivieri. 300,000 l, Crocus biflorus. 1,250,000 l, Crocus sativus.

2000, Oct. 9   **Litho.**   **Perf. 13¾x14**
| 2778-2781 | A762 Set of 4 | 12.00 | 5.50 |

Architecture — A763

Designs: 200,000 l, Arslan Baba. 275,000 l, Karasaç Ana. 300,000 l, Hoca Ahmet Yesevi.

2000, Oct. 19   **Litho.**   **Perf. 13¼x13**
| 2782-2784 | A763 Set of 3 | 8.00 | 8.00 |

Turksat 2A — A764

2001, Jan. 25   **Litho.**   **Perf. 13x13¾**
| 2785 | A764 200,000 l multi | 1.25 | 1.25 |

Women's
Clothing — A765

Designs: No. 2786, 200,000 l, Afyon. No. 2787, 200,000 l, Balikesir. No. 2788, 325,000 l, Kars. No. 2789, 325,000 l, Tokat.

2001, Mar. 19
| 2786-2789 | A765 Set of 4 | 6.25 | 6.25 |

See Nos. 2822-2825, 2757-2760, 2880-2883.

Women's Headcovers Type of 1997
Designs: 200,000 l, Mersin-Silifke. 250,000 l, Sivas. 425,000 l, Aydin. 450,000 l, Hakkari.

2001, Apr. 16   **Litho.**   **Perf. 13¼**
| 2790-2793 | A734 Set of 4 | 7.25 | 7.25 |

Europa — A766

Waterfalls: 450,000 l, Düdenbasi. 500,000 l, Yerköprü.

2001, May 5   **Perf. 13**
| 2794-2795 | A766 Set of 2 | 3.00 | 3.00 |

Aviators
A767

Designs: 250,000 l, Capt. Ismail Hakki Bey. 300,000 l, Lieut. Nuri Bey. 450,000 l, Lieut. Sadik Bey. 500,000 l, Capt. Fethi Bey.

2001, May 15
| 2796-2799 | A767 Set of 4 | 5.00 | 5.00 |

**World Environment Day Type of
1999**
No. 2800, 300,000 l: a, Turdus pilaris. b, Carduelis carduelis.
No. 2801, 450,000 l: a, Merops apiaster. b, Upupa epops.

2001, June 5   **Perf. 13¼**
Sheets of 2, #a-b
| 2800-2801 | A748 Set of 2 | 7.00 | 7.00 |

Kemal
Ataturk — A768

Ataturk (1881-1938) and: 300,000 l, Turkish flag. 450,000 l, Birthplace.

2001, May 19   **Litho.**   **Perf. 13**
| 2802-2803 | A768 Set of 2 | 3.25 | 3.25 |

Medicinal
Plants — A769

Designs: 250,000 l, Myrtus communis. 300,000 l, Achillea millefolium. 450,000 l, Hypericum perforatum. 500,000 l, Rosa moyesii. 1,750,000 l, Crataegus oxyacantha.

2001, June 27   **Perf. 13¾**
| 2804-2808 | A769 Set of 5 | 11.00 | 2.50 |

Horses
A770

Designs: 300,000 l, Horse and foal. No. 2810, 450,000 l, Three horses. No. 2811, 450,000 l, Two horses galloping. 500,000 l, Horse, vert.

2001, July 16   **Perf. 13**
| 2809-2812 | A770 Set of 4 | 5.50 | 5.50 |

Merchant Ships Type of 2000
Designs: 250,000 l, Resitpasa. No. 2814, 300,000 l, Mithatpasa. No. 2815, 300,000 l, Gülnihal, 500,000 l, Aydin.

2001, Sept. 3   **Perf. 13¼**
| 2813-2816 | A757 Set of 4 | 5.00 | 5.00 |

Architecture
A771

Designs: No. 2817, 300,000 l, Sirvansahlar Palace, Baku, Azerbaijan. No. 2818, 300,000 l, Sultan Tekes Mausoleum, Urgench, Uzbekistan. 450,000 l, Timur Mausoleum, Samarkand, Uzbekistan. 500,000 l, While Tlightning Mausoleum, Bursa.

2001, Oct. 15
| 2817-2820 | A771 Set of 4 | 6.25 | 6.25 |

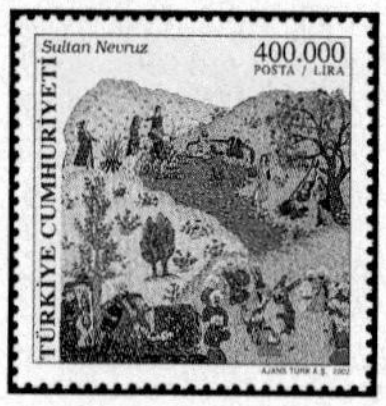

Sultan Nevruz A772

2002, Mar. 21 Litho. *Perf. 13¼*
2821 A772 400,000 l multi 2.25 2.25

Women's Clothing Type of 2001

Designs: 350,000 l, Kastamonu. 400,000 l, Canakkale. 500,000 l, Amasya-Ilisu. 600,000 l, Elazig.

2002, Apr. 16 *Perf. 13x13¼*
2822-2825 A765 Set of 4 7.25 7.25

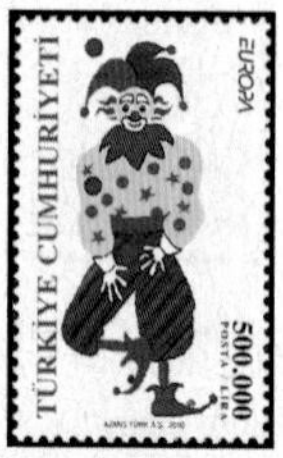

Europa — A773

2002, May 5 Litho. *Perf. 13x13¼*
2826 A773 500,000 l multi 1.50 1.50

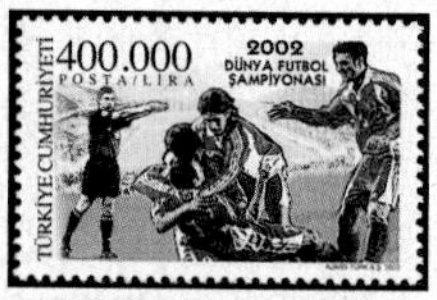

2002 World Cup Soccer Championships, Japan and Korea — A774

Designs: 400,000 l, Players, referee. 600,000 l, Crowd, player making scissors kick.

2002, May 31 Litho. *Perf. 13¼x13*
2827-2828 A774 Set of 2 4.50 4.50

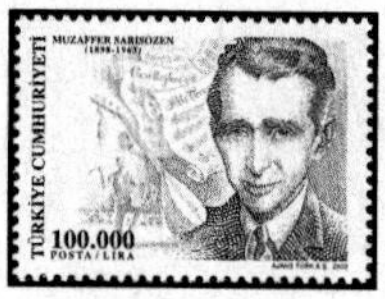

Famous Men — A775

Designs: 100,000 l, Muzaffer Sarisözen (1898-1963), musician. 400,000 l, Arif Nihat Asya (1904-75), writer. 500,000 l, Vedat Tek (1873-1942), architect. 600,000 l, Hilmi Ziya Ulken (1901-74), philosopher. 2,500,000 l, Ibrahim Calli (1882-1960), painter.

2002, June 3 *Perf. 13¾x14*
2829-2833 A775 Set of 5 16.00 5.50

Souvenir Sheet

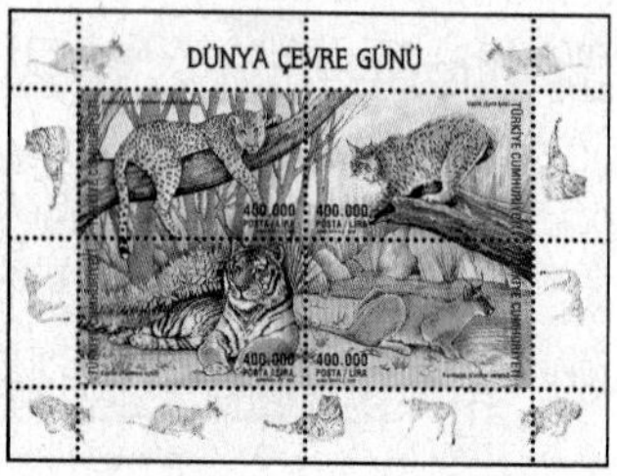

Wild Cats — A776

No. 2834: a, Panthera pardus tulliana. b, Lynx lynx. c, Panthera tigris. d, Caracal caracal.

2002, June 20 *Perf. 13¼x13*
2834 A776 400,000 l Sheet of 4, #a-d 9.00 9.00

Souvenir Sheet

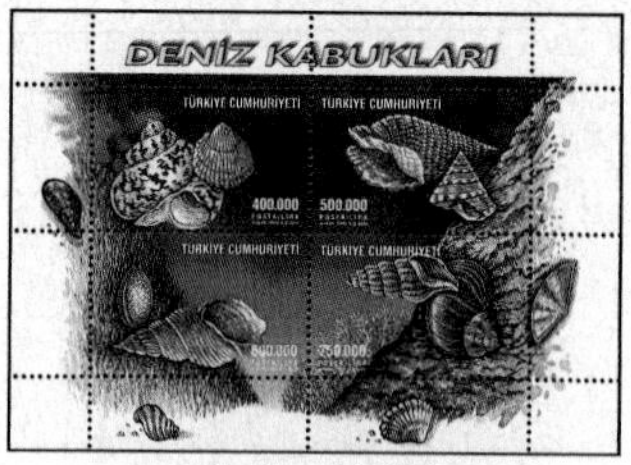

Shells — A777

Various shells: a, 400,000 l. b, 500,000 l. c, 600,000 l. d, 750,000 l.

2002, June 25
2835 A777 Sheet of 4, #a-d 9.00 9.00

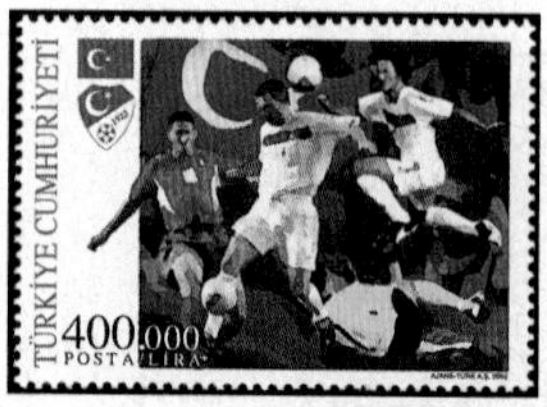

Third Place Finish of Turkish Team in World Cup Soccer Championships — A778

Designs: 400,000 l, Players in action. 700,000 l, Team photo.

2002, July 29 *Perf. 13x13¼*
2836-2837 A778 Set of 2 4.50 4.50

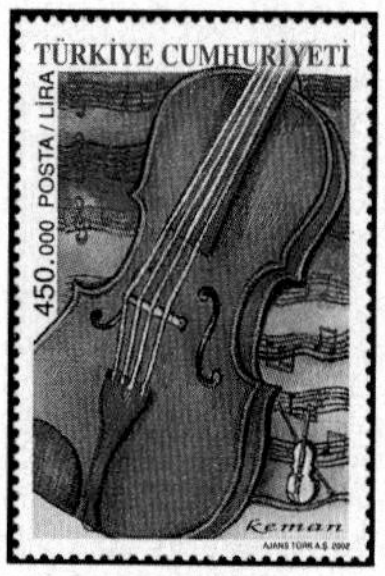

String Instruments A779

Designs: 450,000 l, Violin. 700,000 l, Bass.

2002, Oct. 10 *Perf. 13¼x13*
2838-2839 A779 Set of 2 4.50 4.50

Merchant Ships Type of 2000

Designs: 450,000 l, Ege. 500,000 l, Ayvalik. No. 2842, 700,000 l, Karadeniz. No. 2843, 700,000 l, Marakaz.

2002, Nov. 4 Litho. *Perf. 13*
2840-2843 A757 Set of 4 8.00 8.00

Souvenir Sheet

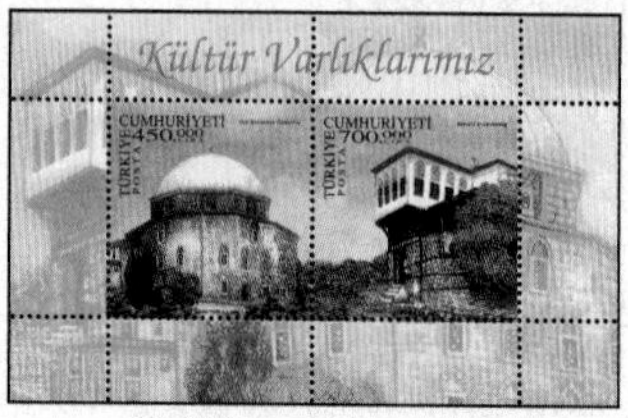

Turkish and Hungarian Buildings — A780

No. 2844: a, 450,000 l, Gazi Kassim Pasha Mosque, Pécs, Hungary. b, 700,000 l, Rakoczi House, Tekirdag, Turkey.

2002, Dec. 2 Litho. *Perf. 13¼*
2844 A780 Sheet of 2, #a-b 4.50 4.50

See Hungary Nos. 3819-3820.

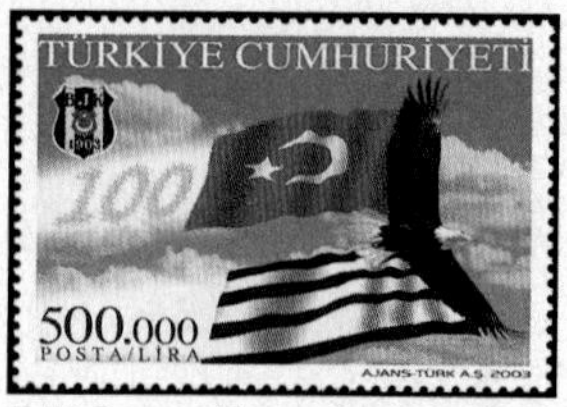

BJK Soccer Team, Cent. — A781

Team emblem and: 500,000 l, Eagle, Turkish and team flags. 700,000 l, Eagle, stadium. 750,000 l, Soccer players. 1,000,000 l, Eagle's head.

2003, Mar. 3 *Perf. 13x13¼*
2845-2848 A781 Set of 4 8.00 8.00

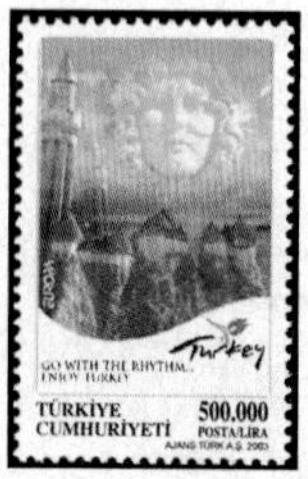

A782

Europa: 500,000 l, Travel poster. 700,000 l, Ankara State Theater poster.

2003, May 9 Litho. *Perf. 13*
2849-2850 A782 Set of 2 3.00 3.00

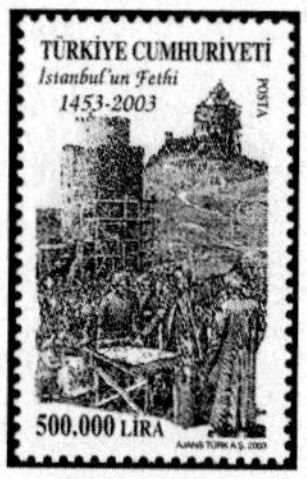

A783

Conquest of Constantinople, 550th Anniv.: No. 2851, 500,000 l, Leaders at table. No. 2852, 500,000 l, Sultan Mehmet II seated. 700,000 l, Robe. 1,500,000 l, Sultan Mehmet II and cartouche.

2003, May 29
2851-2854 A783 Set of 4 7.25 7.25

Souvenir Sheet

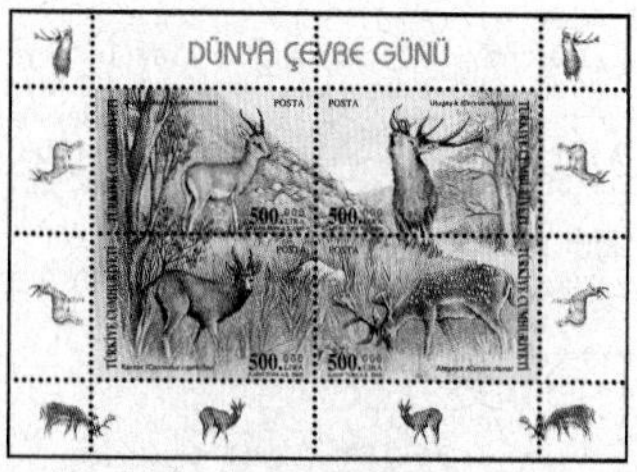

World Environment Day — A784

No. 2855: a, Gazella subgutturosa. b, Cervus elaphus. c, Capreolus capreolus. d, Cervus dama.

2003, June 5
2855 A784 500,000 l Sheet of 4, #a-d 6.25 6.25

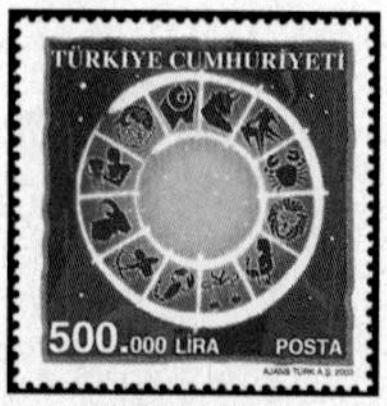

Zodiac A785

2003, June 19 *Perf. 13¼*
2856 A785 500,000 l multi 1.40 1.40

Women's Clothing Type of 2001

Designs: No. 2857, 500,000 l, Sivas. No. 2858, 500,000 l, Gaziantep. No. 2859, 700,000 l, Erzincan. No. 2860, 700,000 l, Ankara-Beypazari.

2003, July 8 *Perf. 13*
2857-2860 A765 Set of 4 7.25 7.25

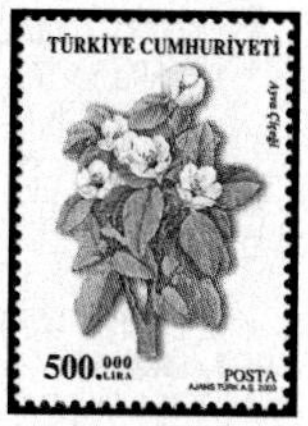

Fruit Blossoms — A786

Blossoms: 500,000 l, Ayva cicegi (quince). 700,000 l, Erik cicegi (plum). 750,000 l, Kiraz cicegi (cherry) . 1,000,000 l, Nar cicegi (pomegranate). 3,000,000 l, Portakal cicegi (orange).

2003, July 25 *Perf. 13¾x14*
2861-2865 A786 Set of 5 13.50 7.25

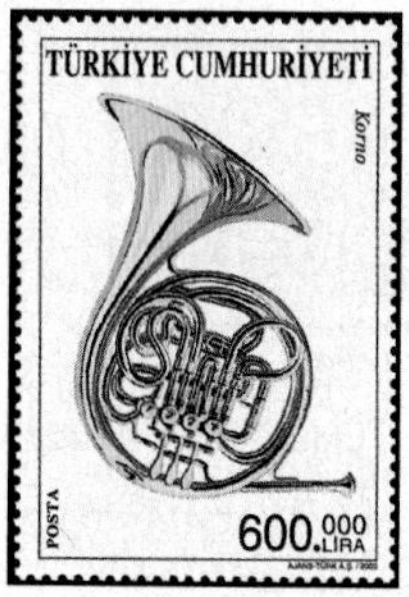

Brass Instruments A787

Designs: 600,000 l, French horn. 800,000 l, Trumpet.

2003, Sept. 23 Litho. *Perf. 13¼x13*
2866-2867 A787 Set of 2 4.50 4.50

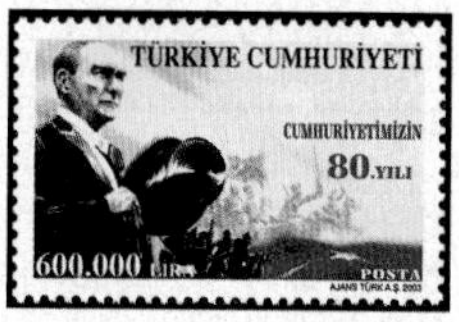

Republic of Turkey, 80th Anniv. A788

Kemal Ataturk, flag and: No. 2868, 600,000 l, Cavalry. No. 2869, 600,000 l, Buildings.

2003, Oct. 29 Litho. *Perf. 13¼x13*
2868-2869 A788 Set of 2 3.50 3.50

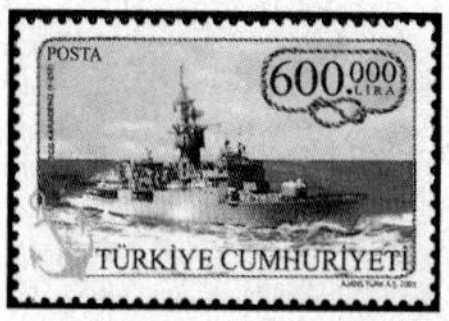

Navy Ships A789

Designs: No. 2870, 600,000 l, Karadeniz. No. 2871, 600,000 l, Gediz. No. 2872, 700,000 l, Salihreis. No. 2873, 700,000 l, Kocatepe.

2003, Nov. 14
2870-2873 A789 Set of 4 9.00 9.00

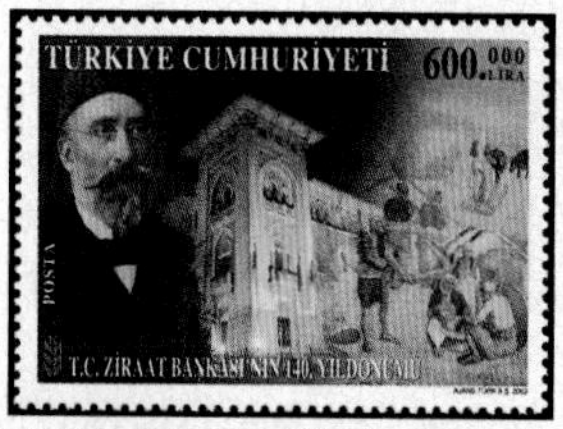

Agriculture Bank, 140th Anniv. — A790

2003, Nov. 20 *Perf. 13x13¼*
2874 A790 600,000 l multi 1.75 1.75

Buildings
Associated with
Kemal
Ataturk — A791

Designs: 600,000 l, House, Trabzon.
700,000 l, Museum, Sakarya. 800,000 l,
House, Selanik. 1,000,000 l, Museum, Ankara.

2003, Dec. 12
2875-2878 A791   Set of 4   7.25 7.25

PTT
Bank — A792

2004, Mar. 3   *Perf. 14*
2879 A792 600,000 l multi   1.75 .80

Women's Clothing Type of 2001
Designs: 600,000 l, Edirne. No. 2881,
700,000 l, Tunceli. No. 2882, 700,000 l,
Burdur. 800,000 l, Trabzon.

2004, Apr. 30   *Perf. 13x13¼*
2880-2883 A765   Set of 4   7.25 7.25

Europa — A793

Designs: 700,000 l, Skier, windsurfer.
800,000 l, Tourist at archaeological ruins,
ships.

2004, May 9
2884-2885 A793   Set of 2   3.00 3.00

Souvenir Sheet

World Environment Day — A794

No. 2886: a, Falco tinnunculus. b, Buteo
buteo. c, Aquila chrysaetos. d, Milvus migrans.

2004, June 5   *Perf. 13¼x13*
2886 A794 700,000 l Sheet of 4,
             #a-d   6.25 6.25

Caravansaries — A795

Designs: 600,000 l, Mamahatun Caravan-
sary, Erzincan. 700,000 l, Cardak Caravasary,
Denizli.

2004, June 7
2887-2888 A795   Set of 2   3.50 3.50

Gendarmerie, 165th
Anniv. — A796

2004, June 14   *Perf. 13x13¼*
2889 A796 600,000 l multi   1.40 .70

Birds — A797

Designs: 100,000 l, Regulus regulus.
250,000 l, Sylvia rueppelli. 600,000 l, Hippo-
lais polyglotta. 700,000 l, Passer domesticus.
800,000 l, Emberiza bruniceps. 1,000,000 l,
Fringilla coelebs. 1,500,000 l, Phoenicurus
phoenicurus. 3,500,000 l, Erithacus rubecula.

2004, July 23   *Perf. 14*
2890 A797 100,000 l multi   .25 .25
2891 A797 250,000 l multi   .35 .25
2892 A797 600,000 l multi   .80 .40
2893 A797 700,000 l multi   1.40 .70
2894 A797 800,000 l multi   1.50 .75
2895 A797 1,000,000 l multi   2.00 1.00
2896 A797 1,500,000 l multi   3.00 1.50
2897 A797 3,500,000 l multi   6.75 3.25
        Nos. 2890-2897 (8)   16.05 8.00

2004
Summer
Olympics,
Athens
A798

Designs: 600,000 l, Wrestling. No. 2899,
700,000 l, Weight lifting. No. 2900, 700,000 l,
Women's track and field, vert. 800,000 l,
Wrestling, diff.

                  Perf. 13¼x13, 13x13¼
2004, Aug. 13
2898-2901 A798   Set of 4   6.25 6.25

Souvenir Sheet

Navy Submarines — A799

No. 2902: a, 600,000 l, 18 Mart. b,
700,000 l, Preveze. c, 700,000 l, Anafartalar.
d, 800,000 l, Atilay.

2004, Sept. 14   *Perf. 13x13¼*
2902 A799   Sheet of 4, #a-d   6.25 6.25

Piri Reis (1465-1554), Admiral and
Map Compiler — A800

2004, Sept. 20
2903 A800 600,000 l multi   1.40 1.40

Waterfalls
A801

Designs: 600,000 l, Kapuzbasi Waterfall.
700,000 l, Sudüsen Waterfall, vert.

2004, Oct. 19   *Perf. 13x13¼, 13¼x13*
2904-2905 A801   Set of 2   3.50 3.50

Buildings Associated With Kemal
Ataturk — A802

Designs: 600,000 l, Ataturk Summer House,
Bursa. No. 2907, 700,000 l, Ataturk House
Museum, Erzurum. No. 2908, 700,000 l, Ata-
turk House, Havza. 800,000 l, State Railways
Director's Building, Ankara.

2004, Nov. 8   Litho.   *Perf. 13¼x13*
2906-2909 A802   Set of 4   6.25 6.25

Souvenir Sheet

Turkish Stars Aerobatics Team — A803

No. 2910: a, 600,000 l, Two airplanes. b,
700,000 l, Five airplanes. c, 800,000 l, Seven
airplanes flying upwards. d, 900,000 l, Seven
airplanes flying left.

2004, Dec. 7   Litho.   *Perf. 13¼x13*
2910 A803   Sheet of 4, #a-d   9.00 9.00

Provinces
A804

2005, Jan. 1   Litho.   *Perf. 14*
2914 A804 1k Adana   .25   .25
2915 A804 5k Adiyaman   .25   .25
2916 A804 10k Afyon   .25   .25
2917 A804 25k Agri   .35   .25
2918 A804 50k Amasya   .70   .35
2919 A804 60k Ankara   .85   .40
2920 A804 60k Bitlis   .85   .40
2921 A804 70k Antalya   1.00   .50
2922 A804 70k Bolu   1.00   .50
2923 A804 80k Artvin   1.10   .55
2924 A804 80k Burdur   1.10   .55
2925 A804 90k Aydin   1.25   .60
2926 A804 1 l Balikesir   1.50   .75
2927 A804 1.50 Bilecik   2.25 1.10
2928 A804 3.50 Bingol   5.00 2.50
2929 A804 3.50 Bursa   5.00 2.50
       Nos. 2914-2929 (16) 22.70 11.70

A805

Designs: 60k, Batiburnu Lighthouse, Canakkale. 70k, Zonguldak Lighthouse, Zonguldak.

2005, Mar. 18   Litho.   *Perf. 13x13¼*
2930-2931 A805   Set of 2   2.75 1.40

A806

Marmaris Intl. Maritime Festival: 70k, Sailboat. 80k, Sailboat, sun on horizon.

2005, Apr. 1
2932-2933 A806   Set of 2   2.75 1.40

A807

2005, Apr. 10
2934 A807 70k multi   1.40 .70

Turkish Police, 160th anniv.

A808

Grand National Assembly, 85th anniv.: 60k,
Torch, star and crescent. 70k, Crescent and
fireworks over Grand National Assembly.

2005, Apr. 23
2935-2936 A808   Set of 2   2.25 1.10

Europa — A809

2005, May 9
2937 A809 70k multi   1.10 .55

Caftans of
Sultans — A810

Caftan of Sultan: No. 2938, 70k, Ahmed I
(shown). No. 2939, 70k, Ahmed I, diff. No.
2940, 70k, Murad III. No. 2941, 70k, Selim.

2005, May 20
2938-2941 A810   Set of 4   5.00 2.50

Souvenir Sheet

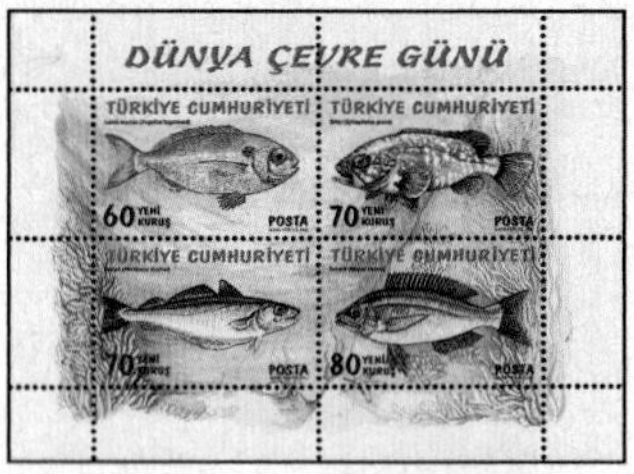

World Environment Day — A811

No. 2942: a, 60k, Pagellus bogaraveo. b, 70k, Epinephelus guaza. c, 70k, Merlanyus euxinus. d, 80k, Maena smaris.

2005, June 5 Litho. ***Perf. 13¼x13***

2942	A811	Sheet of 4, #a-d	5.50	2.75

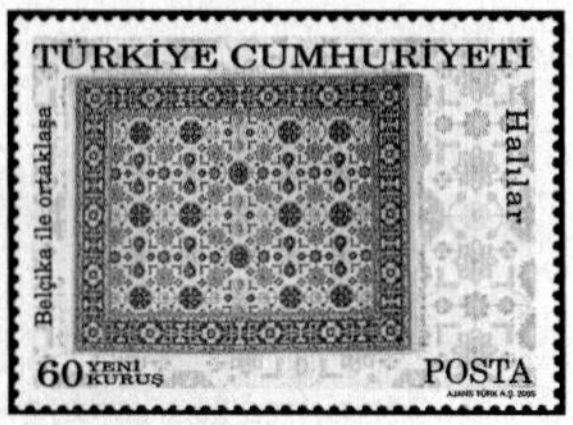

Tapestries & Carpets — A812

Designs: 60k, Carpet from Hereke region, Turkey. 70k, L'humanité Assaillie par les Sept Pechés Capitaux tapestry, Belgium.

2005, June 22 Litho. ***Perf. 13x13¼***

2943-2944	A812	Set of 2	2.25	1.10

See Belgium Nos. 2098-2099.

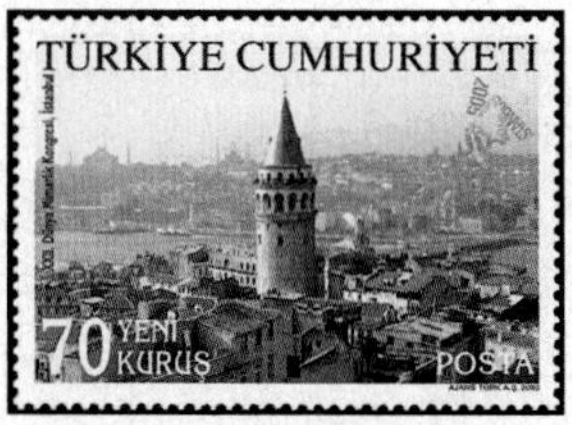

World Architecture Congress, Istanbul — A813

2005, July 3

2945	A813	70k multi	1.40	.70

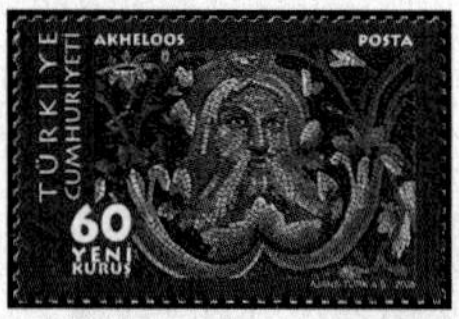

Mosaics A814

Designs: 60k, Akelos. No. 2947, 70k, Oceanos and Tethys. No. 2948, 70k, Achilles. 80k, Menad.

2005, July 5 ***Perf. 13¼x13***

2946-2949	A814	Set of 4	5.50	2.75

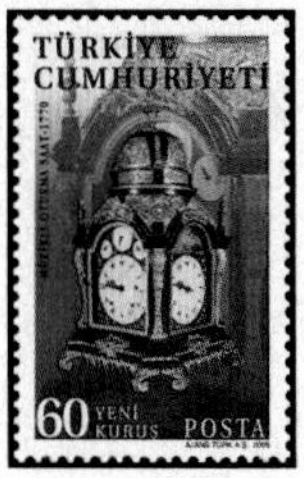

Clocks — A815

Designs: 60k, Musical clock, 1770. 70k, Clock, 1867.

2005, July 20 ***Perf. 13x13¼***

2950-2951	A815	Set of 2	2.25	1.25

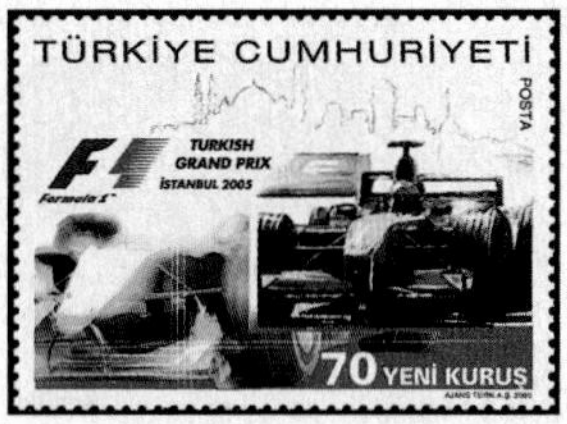

Turkish Grand Prix, Istanbul — A816

2005, Aug. 19 Litho. ***Perf. 13x13¼***

2952	A816	70k multi	1.40	.65

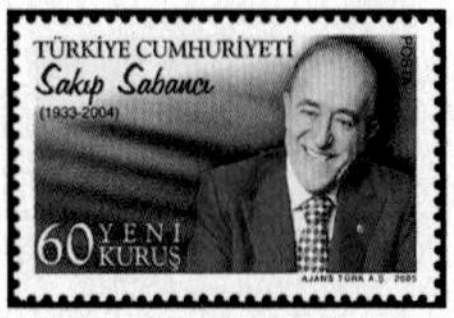

Philanthropic Businessmen — A817

Designs: 60k, Sakip Sabanci (1933-2004). 70k, Vehbi Koç (1901-96).

2005, Sept. 21 Litho. ***Perf. 13¼x13***

2953-2954	A817	Set of 2	2.25	1.25

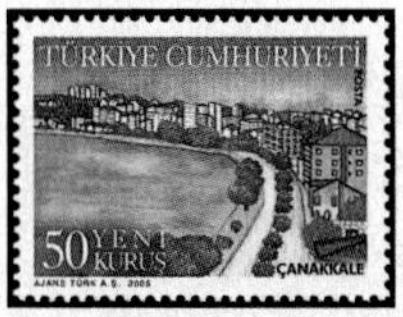

Provinces A818

2005, Sept. 28 ***Perf. 13¾***

2955	A818	50k Canakkale	.75	.35
2956	A818	60k Cankiri	1.00	.50
2957	A818	60k Corum	1.00	.50
2958	A818	60k Denizli	1.00	.50
2959	A818	60k Diyarbakir	1.00	.50
2960	A818	60k Edirne	1.00	.50
2961	A818	60k Elazig	1.00	.50
2962	A818	70k Erzincan	1.25	.60
2963	A818	70k Erzurum	1.25	.60
2964	A818	70k Eskisehir	1.25	.60
2965	A818	70k Gaziantep	1.25	.60
2966	A818	70k Giresun	1.25	.60
2967	A818	70k Gumushane	1.25	.60
2968	A818	1 l Hakkari	1.75	.80
2969	A818	1.50 l Hatay	2.50	1.25
2970	A818	2.50 l Isparta	4.25	2.10
		Nos. 2955-2970 (16)	22.75	11.10

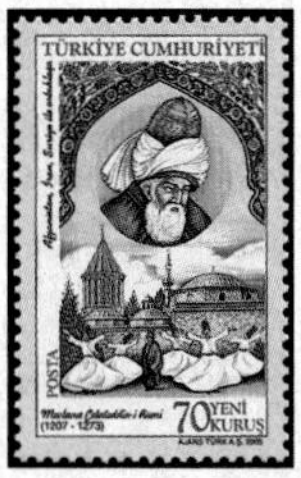

Mevlana Jalal ad-Din ar-Rumi (1207-73), Islamic Philosopher A819

2005, Sept. 30 ***Perf. 13x13¼***

2971	A819	70k multi	1.40	.65

See Afghanistan Nos. 1449-1451, Iran No. 2911 and Syria No. 1574.

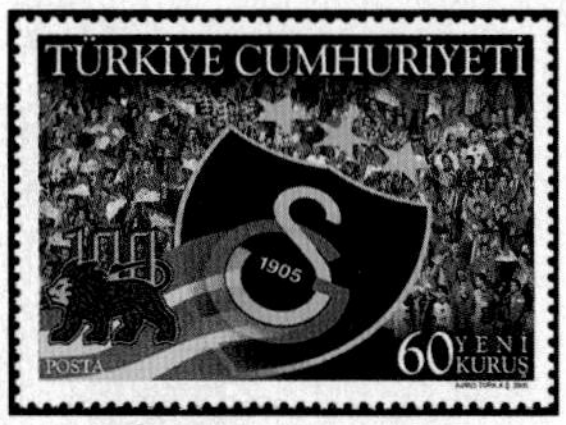

Galatasaray Sports Club, Cent. — A820

Club emblem and: No. 2972, 60k, Soccer stadium crowd, lion and "100." No. 2973, 70k, Soccer stadium, trophy.

No. 2974: a, 60k, Man, lion and "100." b, 70k, Club emblem, building. c, 80k, Soccer players. d, 1 l, Soccer players with trophy.

2005, Oct. 11 ***Perf. 13x13¼***

2972-2973	A820	Set of 2	2.25	1.10

Souvenir Sheet

Perf. 13¼x13

2974	A820	Sheet of 4, #a-d	5.00	2.50

No. 2974 contains four 41x26mm stamps.

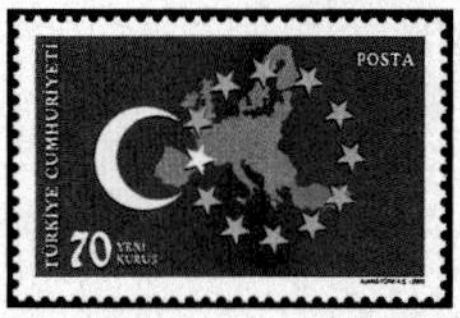

Start of Negotiations for Turkish Admission to European Union — A821

2005, Nov. 3 ***Perf. 13¼x13***

2975	A821	70k multi	1.40	.65

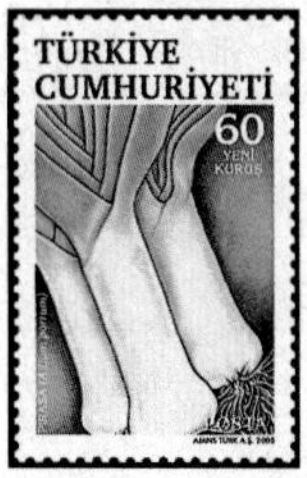

Vegetables — A824

Designs, 60k, Allium porrum (leeks). 70k, Allium sativum (garlic). 80k, Allium cepa (onions).

2005, Nov. 21 Litho. ***Perf. 13x13¼***

2978-2980	A824	Set of 3	3.50	1.75

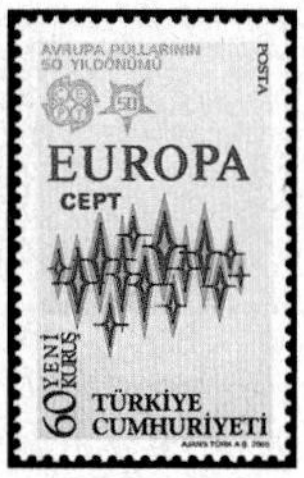

Europa Stamps, 50th Anniv. (in 2006) — A825

Designs: No. 2981, 60k, Vignette of #1907. No. 2982, 70k, Vignette of #1628. 80k, Vignette of #B120. 1 l, Vignette of #1719.

No. 2985, horiz.: a, 10k, #1520. b, 25k, #1800. c, 60k, #1553. d, 70k, #1775.

No. 2986, horiz.: a, 10k, #1493. b, 25k, #1936. c, 60k, #1602. d, 70k, #1876.

2005, Dec. 15 Litho. ***Perf. 13x13¼***

2981-2984	A825	Set of 4	8.00	4.00

Souvenir Sheets

Perf. 13¼x13

2985	A825	Sheet of 4, #a-d	9.00	4.50

Imperf

2986	A825	Sheet of 4, #a-d	13.50	6.75

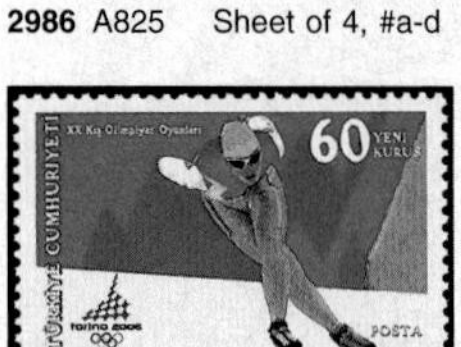

2006 Winter Olympics, Turin A826

Designs: 60k, Speed skating. 70k, Skiing.

2006, Feb. 10 ***Perf. 13¼x13***

2987-2988	A826	Set of 2	2.00	1.00

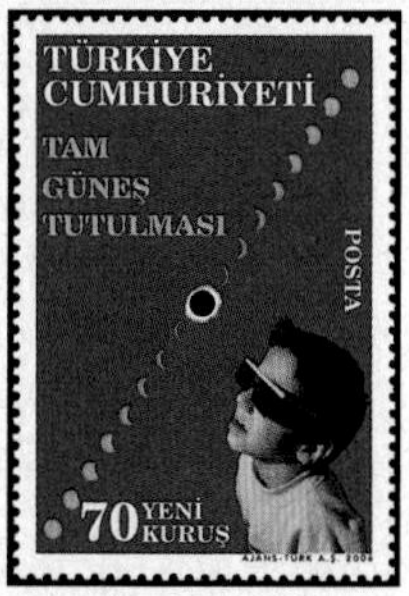

March 29 Total Solar Eclipse A827

2006, Mar. 29 Litho. ***Perf. 13¼x13***

2989	A827	70k multi	1.10	.55

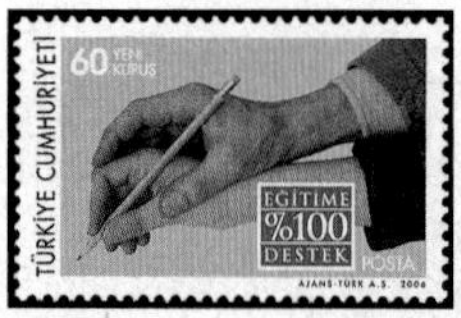

Support for Education A828

2006, Apr. 10

2990	A828	60k multi	.95	.45

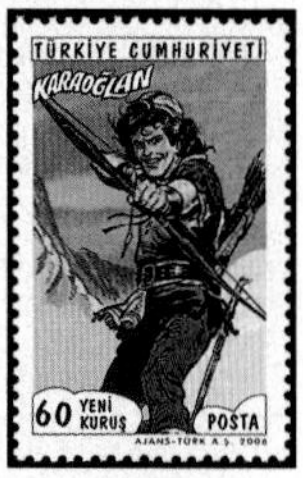

Karaoglan, Cartoon Hero — A829

Karaoglan: 60k, With bow and arrow. No. 2992, 70k, Attacking swordsman. No. 2993, 70k, On horseback. 80k, On horseback, diff.

2006, Apr. 20 ***Perf. 13x13¼***

2991-2994	A829	Set of 4	4.25	2.10

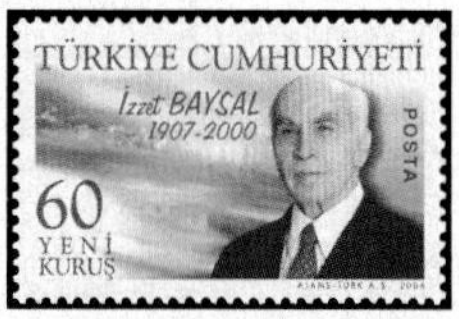

Izzet Baysal (1907-2000), Architect — A830

2006, May 11 Litho. ***Perf. 13¼x13***

2995	A830	60k multi	.85	.45

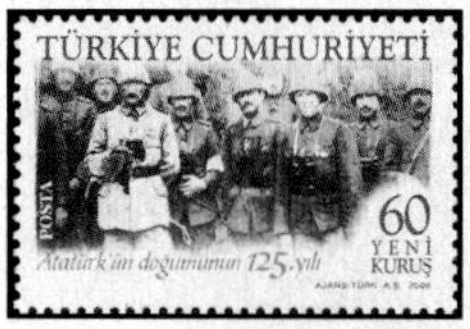

A831

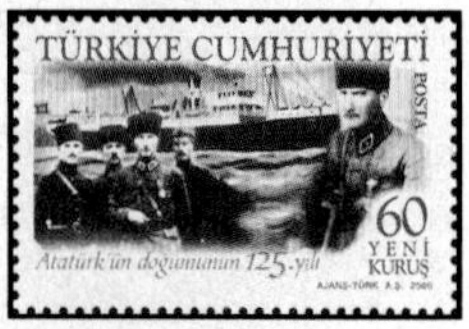

A832

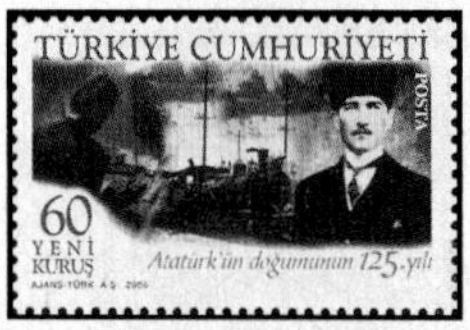

A833

A834

A835

A836

A837

A838

A839

Kemal Ataturk (1881-1938) — A840

2006, May 19

2996		Block of 10	7.50	3.75
a.	A831	60k multi	.75	.35
b.	A832	60k multi	.75	.35
c.	A833	60k multi	.75	.35
d.	A834	60k multi	.75	.35
e.	A835	60k multi	.75	.35
f.	A836	60k multi	.75	.35
g.	A837	60k multi	.75	.35
h.	A838	60k multi	.75	.35
i.	A839	60k multi	.75	.35
j.	A840	60k multi	.75	.35

Europa — A841

2006, May 30   Perf. 13x13¼

2997 A841 70k multi   .90   .45

Miniature Sheet

World Environment Day — A842

No. 2998: a, 25k, Parched earth. b, 50k, Tree. c, 60k, Tree, diff. d, 70k, Forest.

2006, June 5

2998 A842   Sheet of 4, #a-d   2.75 1.40

Intl. Year of Deserts and Desertification.

2006 World Cup Soccer Championships, Germany — A843

Designs: No. 2999, 70k, Player dribbling ball. No. 3000, 70k, Player kicking ball, horiz.

2006, June 9   Perf. 13x13¼, 13¼x13

2999-3000 A843   Set of 2   1.90   .95

Airplanes A844

Designs: 60k, Deperdussin monoplane. No. 3002, 70k, Bleriot monoplane. No. 3003, 70k, R. E. P. monoplane.

2006, June 22   Perf. 13¼x13

3001-3003 A844   Set of 3   2.60 1.40

See Nos. 3034-3036.

Treasures of Karun — A845

Designs: No. 3004, 70k, Bracelet and coins. No. 3005, 70k, Winged sun disc pectoral and bracelet. 80k, Lion's head bracelets.

2006, July 10   Perf. 13x13¼

3004-3006 A845   Set of 3   2.75 1.40

Provinces A846

2006, Sept. 11   Perf. 13¼x13

3007	A846	10k	Kahramanmaras	.25	.25
3008	A846	10k	Manisa	.25	.25
3009	A846	50k	Kirsehir	.70	.35
3010	A846	50k	Kocaeli	.70	.35
3011	A846	60k	Izmir	.80	.40
3012	A846	60k	Konya	.80	.40
3013	A846	60k	Mardin	.80	.40
3014	A846	60k	Mugla	.80	.40
3015	A846	70k	Istanbul	.95	.50
3016	A846	70k	Mersin	.95	.50
3017	A846	1 l	Kastamonu	1.40	.70
3018	A846	1 l	Kirklareli	1.40	.70
3019	A846	1.60 l	Kayseri	2.25	1.10
3020	A846	2 l	Malatya	2.75	1.40
3021	A846	4 l	Kars	5.50	2.75
3022	A846	4 l	Kutahya	5.50	2.75

Nos. 3007-3022 (16)   25.80 13.20

See nos. 3055-3062.

Scenes From Movie, "Selvi Boylum Al Yazmalim" — A847

Various scenes: 60k, 70k.

2006, Sept. 16   Perf. 13x13¼

3023-3024 A847   Set of 2   1.75   .85

Turkish Railroads, 150th Anniv. A848

Designs: 60k, Steam locomotive. 70k, Electric train.

2006, Sept. 23   Perf. 13¼x13

3025-3026 A848   Set of 2   1.75   .85

Central Bank, 75th Anniv. A849

2006, Oct. 3

3027 A849 60k multi   .80   .40

Intl. Telecommunications Union Conference, Antalya — A850

Conference emblem and: 60k, Globe with spotlight on Turkey. 70k, Map with lines drawn to Turkey.

2006, Nov. 6   Perf. 13x13¼

3028-3029 A850   Set of 2   1.90   .95

Middle East Technical University, Ankara, 50th Anniv. — A851

2006, Nov. 15   Litho.   Perf. 13x13¼

3030 A851 60k multi   .85   .40

Turkish Atomic Energy Authority, 50th Anniv. A852

2006, Nov. 22   Litho.   Perf. 13¼x13

3031 A852 60k multi   .85   .40

Geothermal Resources — A853

Designs: 60k, Four steam clouds. 70k, Steam leaving smokestack.

2006, Dec. 11

3032-3033 A853   Set of 2   1.90   .95

Airplanes Type of 2006

Designs: 60k, Breguet XIV B-2. No. 3035, 70k, Albatros C-XV. No. 3036, 70k, Fiat R2.

2007, Mar. 15   Litho.   Perf. 13¼x13

3034-3036 A844   Set of 3   3.00 1.50

A854

A855

KRAL SULUMELI'NIN IBADETI, BAZALT
POSTA 60 YENI KURUS
A856

Hittite Artifacts
A857
MÜHÜR YÜZÜK, ALTIN
POSTA 60 YENI KURUS

2007, Mar. 30
3037 A854 60k multi   .90   .45
3038 A855 60k multi   .90   .45
3039 A856 60k multi   .90   .45
3040 A857 60k multi   .90   .45
      Nos. 3037-3040 (4)   3.60   1.80

Third Meeting of Economic
Cooperation Organization Postal
Authorities, Tehran — A858

2007, Apr. 5   Perf. 13x13¼
3041 A858 60k multi   .90   .45
    See Iran No. 2917, Kazakhstan No. 526 and
Pakistan No. 1101.

Tekirdag as Part of Turkey, 650th Anniv.
A859

2007, Apr. 14   Perf. 13¼x13
3042 A859 60k multi   .90   .45

Fenerbahce Sports Club,
Cent. — A860

Club emblem and: No. 3043, 60k, Men wit-
nessing signing ceremony. No. 3044, 70k,
Quotation and Arabic text.
    No. 3045 — Club emblem and: a, 60k,
Lighthouse. b, 70k, Three men seated at table.
c, 80k, Building, stadium interior. d, 90k, Stadium exterior.

2007, May 3   Perf. 13x13¼
3043-3044 A860 Set of 2   2.00   1.00
            Souvenir Sheet
             Perf. 13¼x13
3045 A860 Sheet of 4, #a-d   4.50   4.50
    No. 3045 contains four 38x23mm stamps.
No. 3045 exists affixed to a booklet cover
which was only sold in a set with an imperforate sheet of eight 41x31mm stamps depicting
various athletes, two first day covers, and a
folder, for 25 l. Value $15.

         Souvenir Sheet

Mevlana Jalal ad-Din ar-Rumi (1207-
73), Islamic Philosopher — A861

    No. 3046: a, 25k, Portrait. b, 50k, Arabic
calligraphy. c, 60k, Dervishes. d, 70k,
Mausoleum.

2007, May 8   Perf. 13x13¼
3046 A861 Sheet of 4, #a-d   3.25   1.60

Europa
A862

    Designs: 60k, Turkish Scouting emblem,
Scout at campfire. 70k, Scouts saluting.

2007, May 9   Perf. 13¼
3047-3048 A862 Set of 2   2.00   1.00
         Scouting, cent.

Mehmetcik Foundation, 25th
Anniv. — A863

2007, May 17 Litho. Perf. 13¼x13
3049 A863 60k multi   .95   .45

         Souvenir Sheet

World Environment Day — A864

    No. 3050: a, 25k, Goats. b, 50k, Cattle. c,
60k, Sheep. d, 70k, Chickens.

2007, June 5 Litho. Perf. 13¼x13
3050 A864 Sheet of 4, #a-d   3.00   1.50

Turkish Cuisine — A865

    Designs: No. 3051, 1 l, Nohutlu Bulgur Pilavi
(chick pea and bulgur pilaf). No. 3052, 1 l,
Yüksük Corbasi (soup). 2 l, Asure
(vegetables).

2007, June 20 Litho. Perf. 13x13¼
3051-3053 A865 Set of 3   6.25   3.25

KEI 15.YIL ZIRVESI
60 YENI KURUS POSTA
Black Sea
Economic
Cooperation
Organization,
15th
Anniversary
Summit
A866

2007, June 25   Perf. 13¼
3054 A866 60k multi   .95   .95

      Provinces Type of 2006
2007, July 10   Perf. 13¼x13
3055 A846 10k Siirt   .25   .25
3056 A846 50k Ordu   .80   .40
3057 A846 60k Rize   .95   .45
3058 A846 1 l Nigde   1.60   .80
3059 A846 2 l Nevsehir   3.25   1.60
3060 A846 2 l Samsun   3.25   1.60
3061 A846 4 l Mus   6.25   3.25
3062 A846 4 l Sakarya   6.25   3.25
      Nos. 3055-3062 (8)   22.60 11.60

Turkish Language Association, 75th
Anniv. — A867

2007, July 12   Perf. 13x13¼
3063 A867 70k multi   1.10   .55

Roses
A869

    Color of rose: No. 3065, 60k, White. No.
3066, 60k, Red. No. 3067, 60k, Yellow.

2007, Aug. 16 Litho. Perf. 13¼
3065-3067 A869 Set of 3   2.75   1.40

Tuzsuz Deli Bekir   Efe
POSTA 60 YENI KURUS
Shadow Play
Characters
A870

    Designs: 60k, Tuzsuz Deli Bekir and Efe.
70k, Hacivat and Karagöz. 80k, Tiryaki and
Celebi.

2007, Sept. 13 Litho. Perf. 13¼x13
3068-3070 A870 Set of 3   3.75   1.90

         Miniature Sheet

Balkanfila XIV Intl. Philatelic Exhibition,
Istanbul — A871

    No. 3071: a, 60k, Blue Mosque, Galata
Tower. b, 70k, Hagia Sophia. c, 80k, City walls
and painting. d, 1 l, Bosporus Bridge.

2007, Oct. 28
3071 A871 Sheet of 4, #a-d   5.25   2.60
    An imperforate sheet containing a 60k dove
and flags stamp, a 70k bridge stamp, 80k flags
stamp and a 1 l flags and map of Turkey stamp
exists. It sold for considerably above face
value.

Mimar Sinan
(1489-1588),
Architect
A873
MIMAR SINAN 1489-1588
BÜYÜKCEKMECE KÖPRÜSÜ
POSTA 60

    Sinan and: 60k, Büyükcekmece Bridge. No.
3074, 70k, Bath of Roxelana (Haseki Hürrem
Sultan Hamami Ayasofya). No. 3075, 70k,
Selimye Mosque, Edirne. 80k, Suleiman
Mosque, Istanbul.

2007, Nov. 14   Perf. 13¼
3073-3076 A873 Set of 4   4.75   2.40

60 YENI KURUS
World Philosophy
Day — A874

2007, Nov. 22   Perf. 13x13¼
3077 A874 60k multi   1.00   .50

posta 60 Yeni Kurus
Cartoon Character "Keloglan" — A875

    Designs: 60k, Keloglan in giant's hand. No.
3079, 70k, Keloglan leaving house. No. 3080,
70k, Keloglan on horse. 80k, Keloglan with
carpet and birds.

2007, Nov. 28
3078-3081 A875 Set of 4   4.75   2.40

      Provinces Type of 2006
2007, Dec. 4   Perf. 13¼x13
3082 A846 5k Tunceli   .25   .25
3083 A846 10k Tokat   .25   .25
3084 A846 65k Sanliurfa   1.10   .55
3085 A846 65k Trabzon   1.10   .55
3086 A846 80k Sivas   1.40   .70
3087 A846 85k Usak   1.50   .75
3088 A846 1 l Tekirdag   1.75   .90
3089 A846 4.50 l Sinop   7.75   4.00
      Nos. 3082-3089 (8)   15.10   7.95

TRT Television, 40th Anniv. A876

Designs: 65k, Emblem. 80k, Emblem and headquarters.

2008, Jan. 31 Litho. Perf. 12¾x13
3090-3091 A876 Set of 2 2.50 1.25

Nasreddin Hoca Fables, 800th Anniv. — A877

Hoca: 25k, And two men at table. 65k, Sitting backward on horse. 80k, Showing two pots to man. 85k, Spooning water into lake.

2008, Feb. 7 Perf. 13x13¼
3092-3095 A877 Set of 4 4.25 2.10

A878

St. Valentine's Day — A879

2008, Feb. 14 Perf. 13
3096 A878 65k multi 1.10 .55
3097 A879 80k multi 1.40 .70

Miniature Sheet

Amasya Medical Center, 700th Anniv. — A880

No. 3098: a, 50k, Building. b, 65k, Six musicians. c, 80k, Seven people. d, 85k, Four people.

2008, Mar. 13 Perf. 13x13¼
3098 A880 Sheet of 4, #a-d 4.50 2.25

Urartian Cultural Artifacts A881

Designs: No. 3099, 65k, Carved ivory spirit figure (Fildisi Kanati Cin). No. 3100, 65k, Gold earring, bronze pin and necklace (Altin küpe, Tunc igne, Boncuk kolye). No. 3101, 80k, Bronze cauldron (Uc ayak uzerinde tunc

kazan). No. 3102, 80k, Harput Castle (Harput Kalesi).

2008, Mar. 27 Perf. 13¼x13
3099-3102 A881 Set of 4 4.50 2.25

Military Aircraft A882

Designs: 65k, Consolidated B24 D. 80k, Curtiss Hawk. 85k, PZL XXIV.

2008, Apr. 25
3103-3105 A882 Set of 3 3.75 1.90
See Nos. 3148-3150.

Europa A883

Designs: 65k, Letter, fingers making heart. 80k, Pen, inkwell.

2008, May 9 Litho. Perf. 13¼
3106-3107 A883 Set of 2 2.40 1.25

Diplomatic Relations Between Turkey and Thailand, 50th Anniv. A884

Designs: 65k, Loha Prasat, Bangkok, Thailand. 80k, Sultan Ahmed Mosque, Istanbul.

2008, May 12 Litho. Perf. 13¼x13
3108-3109 A884 Set of 2 2.40 1.25
See Thailand No. 2359.

National Olympic Committee, Cent. — A885

Olympic Committee emblem and: 65k, Dove and Olympic flag. 80k, Parading athletes. 85k, Stadium. 1 l, Athlete and Olympic flag.

2008, May 26 Perf. 13x13¼
3110-3113 A885 Set of 4 5.25 2.60

Provinces A886

2008, May 28 Perf. 13¼x13
3114 A886 5k Zonguldak .25 .25
3115 A886 50k Yozgat .80 .40
3116 A886 65k Aksaray 1.10 .55
3117 A886 65k Kirikkale 1.10 .55
3118 A886 80k Karaman 1.40 .70
3119 A886 85k Van 1.40 .70

3120 A886 1 l Bayburt 1.60 .80
3121 A886 4.50 l Batman 7.25 3.75
  Nos. 3114-3121 (8) 14.90 7.70
See Nos. 3129-3137.

Miniature Sheet

World Environment Day — A887

No. 3122: a, 25k, Boy and polar bears. b, 65k, Sea ice. c, 80k, Mountains and stream. d, 85k, Girl, flower, parched earth.

2008, June 5 Perf. 13x12¾
3122 A887 Sheet of 4, #a-d 4.25 2.10

Turkish Diplomats Who Saved Jews During World War II — A888

Birds and: 65k, Selehattin Ulkumen (1914-2003). 80k, Necdet Kent (1911-2002).

2008, July 17 Perf. 12¾x13
3123-3124 A888 Set of 2 2.50 1.25

2008 Summer Olympics, Beijing — A889

Designs: 25k, Archery. 65k, Taekwondo, vert. No. 3127, 80k, Weight lifting. No. 3128, 80k, Wrestling.

Perf. 13x13¼, 13¼x13
2008, Aug. 8 Litho.
3125-3128 A889 Set of 4 4.25 2.10

Provinces Type of 2008
Perf. 13¼x13, 13x13¼
2008, Aug. 29
3129 A886 50k Kilis .85 .40
3130 A886 65k Bartin, vert. 1.10 .55
3131 A886 1 l Ardahan 1.75 .85
3132 A886 1 l Igdir 1.75 .85
3133 A886 1.50 l Yalova 2.60 1.25
3134 A886 2 l Karabuk 3.50 1.75
3135 A886 2 l Osmaniye 3.50 1.75
3136 A886 4.50 l Düzce 7.75 3.75
3137 A886 4.50 l Sirnak 7.75 3.75
  Nos. 3129-3137 (9) 30.55 14.90

Glassware — A890

Designs: 65k, Bowl. 80k, Vase.

2008, Sept. 11 Perf. 13x12¾
3138-3139 A890 Set of 2 2.25 1.10

Battle of Preveza, 470th Anniv. — A891

Designs: 65k, Khair ed-Din (Barbarossa), battle, map. 80k, Kemal Ataturk, ships.

2008, Sept. 27 Perf. 13x13¼
3140-3141 A891 Set of 2 2.25 1.10

Miniature Sheet

Friendship Between Turkey and Indonesia — A892

No. 3142: a, 80k Blue Mosque, Turkey. b, 65k Istiqlal Mosque, Indonesia. c, 80k Bosporus Bridge, Turkey. d, 65k Barelang Bridge, Indonesia. e, 80k Whirling dervishes. f, 65k Saman dance. g, 80k Turkish tulip (ters lale). h, 65k Flame of Irian (Mucuna bennettii). i, 80k Turkish Van cat. j, 65k Flat-headed cat (Yassibas kedi).

2008, Oct. 24 Perf. 13x13¼
3142 A892 Sheet of 10, #a-j 9.50 4.75
See Indonesia No. 2167.

Republic of Turkey, 85th Anniv. A893

Kemal Ataturk, Turkish flag and: No. 3143, 80k, Airplane, ship, truck and train. No. 3144, 80k, Computer keyboard, satellite, dish antenna.

2008, Oct. 29 Litho. Perf. 12¾x13
3143-3144 A893 Set of 2 2.10 1.10

Turkish Maritime Enterprises, 160th Anniv. A894

Designs: 65k, Docked ship. No. 3146, 80k, Emblem. No. 3147, 80k, Ship at sea, horiz.

Perf. 13½x13¼, 13¼x13½
2008, Nov. 29 Litho.
3145-3147 A894 Set of 3 3.00 1.50

Military Aircraft Type of 2008
Designs: 65k, C-47 Dakota. 80k, F-100 D Super Sabre. 1 l, F-86 E Sabre.

2009, Mar. 12 Litho. Perf. 13¼x13
3148-3150 A882 Set of 3 3.25 1.60

Miniature Sheet

Fifth World Water Forum,
Istanbul — A895

No. 3151 — Emblem and: a, 25k, Head,
Earth, water. b, 65k, Bosporus Bridge, water
drop. c, 80k, Bosporus Bridge, waterfall. d,
80k, Waterfall, parched land, clay jug pouring
water.

2009, Mar. 16   Perf. 13x13¼
3151 A895   Sheet of 4, #a-d   3.25 1.60

Sultan's Boats — A896

Boats from Istanbul Sea Museum: No. 3152,
80k, Boat with yellow hull and short bowsprit,
gray green sky. No. 3153, 80k, Boat with
brown hull, long bowsprit, blue gray sky.

2009, Apr. 2
3152-3153 A896   Set of 2   2.10 1.10

Council of
Europe,
60th Anniv.
A897

European
Court for
Human
Rights,
50th Anniv.
A898

2009, May 5   Perf. 13¼x13
3154 A897 80k multi   1.10 .55
3155 A898 80k multi   1.10 .55

Mother's
Day — A899

Designs: 65k, Bird, hatchlings in nest
shaped like heart. 80k, Mother's hands holding infant, hearts. No. 3158, 1 l, Mother and
child. No. 3159, 1 l, Hands of mother and
baby, flower.

2009, May 10   Perf. 13¾
3156-3159 A899   Set of 4   4.50 2.25
Nos. 3156-3159 each have perforations in a
heart shape in the vignette.

Ceramics — A900

Designs: 80k, Ceramic pot, Portugal. 85k,
Faience mosque lamp, Turkey.

2009, May 12   Perf. 13x13¼
3160-3161 A900   Set of 2   2.25 1.10
See Portugal Nos. 3111-3112.

Miniature Sheet

Arrival of Kemal Ataturk at Samsun,
90th Anniv. — A901

No. 3162: a, 25k, Congress Building, Sivas.
b, 65k, Congress Building, Erzurum. c, 65k,
Government building, Amasya. d, 80k, Statue
of Ataturk, Samsun.

2009, May 19   Litho.
3162 A901   Sheet of 4, #a-d   3.25 1.60

Ministry of Transport and
Communication, 70th Anniv. — A902

Designs: 50k, Ship, map. 65k, Bridge, highway interchange, bus. 80k, Earth, satellite,
dish antenna, envelopes, computer, cellular
phone. No. 3166, 1 l, Map, train. No. 3167, 1 l,
Postal worker delivering parcel, envelope, airplane, globe.

2009, May 27   Perf. 13¼x13
3163-3167 A902   Set of 5   5.25 2.60

Miniature Sheet

World Environment Day — A903

No. 3168 — Butterflies: a, 25k, Aporia
crataegi. b, 65k, Lasiommate megera. c, 80k,
Plebeius agestis. d, 80k, Gonepteryx rhamni.

2009, June 5   Perf. 13x13¼
3168 A903   Sheet of 4, #a-d   3.25 1.60

Kemal
Ataturk — A904

Various photographs of Ataturk.

2009, June 5   Perf. 13½ Syncopated
3169 A904   5k multi   .25   .25
3170 A904   10k multi   .25   .25
3171 A904   25k multi   .35   .25
3172 A904   50k multi   .65   .35
3173 A904   65k multi   .85   .40
3174 A904   80k multi   1.10   .55
3175 A904   85k multi   1.10   .55
3176 A904   1 l multi   1.40   .70
3177 A904   2 l multi   2.60 1.40
3178 A904 4.50 l multi   6.00 3.00
     Nos. 3169-3178 (10)   14.55 7.70

Europa
A905

Designs: 80k, Cacabey Astronomy
Madrassa, Kirsehir. 1 l, Ali Kuscu (1403-74),
astronomer.

2009, June 16   Perf. 13¼x13
3179-3180 A905   Set of 2   2.40 1.25

Items of the
Phrygians — A906

Designs: 65k, Pitcher. 80k, Clay ceremonial
cup with birds. No. 3183, 1 l, Goose-shaped
clay ceremonial cup. No. 3184, 1 l, Cauldron.

2009, June 25   Perf. 13x13¼
3181-3184 A906   Set of 4   4.50 2.25

Embroidery — A907

Various embroidered pieces with background color of: 75k, Blue. 90k, Pink.

2009, July 2   Perf. 13¼x13
3185-3186 A907   Set of 2   2.25 1.10

Kemal
Ataturk — A908

Various photographs of Ataturk.

2009, July 16   Perf. 13½ Syncopated
3187 A908 75k multi   1.10   .55
3188 A908 90k multi   1.25   .60
3189 A908   5 l multi   7.00 3.50
     Nos. 3187-3189 (3)   9.35 4.65

Miniature Sheet

Haci Bektas Veli (1209-71),
Mystic — A909

No. 3190: a, 75k, Haci Bektas Veli, birds. b,
75k, Birds over town. c, 90k, Dancers. d, 90k,
Haci Bektas Veli, deer, lion, birds.

2009, Aug. 12   Perf. 13x13¼
3190 A909   Sheet of 4, #a-d   4.50 2.25

Postal Cooperation Between Turkey
and Bosnia and Herzegovina — A910

2009, Oct. 9   Litho.
3191 A910 90k multi   1.25   .60
See Bosnia and Herzegovina No. 656.

Namik Kemal Yolga (1914-2001),
Diplomat Who Rescued Jews in World
War II — A911

2009, Oct. 20   Perf. 13¼x13
3192 A911 75k multi   1.00   .50

Castles
A912

Designs: 25k, Kolan Castle, Adana. 75k,
Afyon Castle. 90k, Amasya Castle. 1 l, Ankara
Castle.

2009, Nov. 5
3193-3196 A912   Set of 4   4.00 2.00

Mekteb-i Mülkiye Political Science
Faculty, 150th Anniv.
A913

Designs: 75k, Political Science Faculty
Building, anniversary emblem. 90k, Anniversary emblem.

2009, Dec. 4   Perf. 13¼x13
3197-3198 A913   Set of 2   2.25 1.10

Süleyman Celebi (1351-1422),
Writer — A914

Cengiz Aytmatov (1928-2008),
Writer — A915

2009, Dec. 17
3199 A914 75k multi   1.00   .50
3200 A915 90k multi   1.25   .60

Miniature Sheets

A916

Istanbul, 2010 Capital of European Culture — A917

No. 3201: a, Silhouette of Hagia Sophia, red sky. b, Sculpture. c, Artwork of main dome of Blue Mosque. d, Blue Mosque, blue sky. e, Tower on coastline, blue sky. f, Bread. g, Tram. h, Haydarpasa Station, cloudy sky.
No. 3202: a, Silhouettes of buildings, pink sky. b, Religious painting. c, Fishermen. d, Man in boat, Bosporus Bridge. e, Ship. f, Birds over Bosporus. g, Topkapi Palace. h, Silhouettes of Hagia Sophia and Blue Mosque, orange red sky.

2010, Jan. 7   *Perf. 13x13¼*
3201 A916 75k Sheet of 8, #a-h   8.00 4.00
     Perf. 13¼x13
3202 A917 90k Sheet of 8, #a-h   8.00 4.00

2010 Winter Olympics, Vancouver A918

Designs: 25k, Slalom skier. 75k, Snowboarder. No. 3205, 90k, Cross-country skier. No. 3206, 90k, Speed skater.

2010, Feb. 12   *Perf. 13¼*
3203-3206 A918   Set of 4   3.75 1.90

Military Aircraft A919

Designs: 75k, F-4. 90k, F-16. 1 l, CN-235.

2010, Mar. 18   *Perf. 13x13¼*
3207-3209 A919   Set of 3   3.50 1.75

Early Bronse Age Items — A920

Designs: 75k, Twinned figures. 90k, Ceremonial symbol. No. 3212, 1 l, Necklace. No. 3213, 1 l, Sculpture of nursing woman, vert.

   Perf. 13¼x13½, 13½x13¼
2010, Mar. 31
3210-3213 A920   Set of 4   5.00 2.50

Anatolian News Agency, 90th Anniv, A921

2010, Apr. 6   *Perf. 13¼x13*
3214 A921 75k multi   1.00 .50

A922

National Assembly, 90th Anniv. — A923

2010, Apr. 23   *Perf. 13x13¼*
3215 A922 75k multi   1.00 .50
3216 A923 90k multi   1.25 .60

Sile Lighthouse, 150th Anniv. — A924

2010, May 1
3217 A924 75k multi   1.00 .50

Labor Day — A925

Designs: No. 3218, 80k, Dove with olive branch. No. 3219, 80k, Hands holding globe. No. 3220, 110k, Dove with banner. No. 3221, 110k, Worker.

2010, May 1   *Perf. 13x12¾*
3218-3221 A925   Set of 4   5.00 2.50

Yunus Emre (c. 1240-c. 1321), Poet A926

Emre and: 75k, Tomb, Eskisehir. 90k, Poem, vert.

2010, May 3   *Perf. 13¼x13, 13x13¼*
3222-3223 A926   Set of 2   2.10 1.10

Europe Day A927

2010, May 9   *Perf. 12¾x13*
3224 A927 75k multi   .95 .45

Europa A928

Children's stories: 80k, Balik Cobani (The Fish and the Shepherd). 110k, Book of Dede Korkut.

2010, May 9   *Perf. 13¼x13*
3225-3226 A928   Set of 2   2.40 1.25

RASAT Observational Satellite — A929

2010, May 17   *Perf. 13x13¼*
3227 A929 75k multi   .95 .45

Miniature Sheet

World Environment Day — A930

No. 3228 — Flowers: a, Crocus stevenii. b, Crocus mathewii. c, Astragalus lineatus. d, Erica bocquetii.

2010, June 5
3228 A930 110k Sheet of 4, #a-d 5.75 3.00

Sultan's Boats — A931

Boats from Istanbul Sea Museum: 80k, Boat with red orange and white hull. 110k, Boat with white and gold hull with bird figurehead.

2010, June 14   *Perf. 13x13¼*
3229-3230 A931   Set of 2   2.50 1.25

Kemal Atatürk — A932

Various portraits.

    Perf. 13½ Syncopated
2010, June 24
3231 A932 25k multi   .35 .25
3232 A932 80k multi   1.10 .55
3233 A932 110k multi   1.40 .70
3234 A932 355k multi   4.50 2.25
   Nos. 3231-3234 (4)   7.35 3.75

2010 World Men's Basketball Championships, Turkey
A933   A934

2010, Aug. 28   *Perf. 13x12¾*
     Background Color
3235 A933 80k blue   1.10 .55
3236 A934 80k brown   1.10 .55
3237 A933 110k yellow brown   1.50 .75
3238 A934 110k red   1.50 .75
   Nos. 3235-3238 (4)   5.20 2.60

Miniature Sheet

Japan Year in Turkey — A935

No. 3239: a, 80k, Bridge in Ritsurin Garden, Takamatsu, Japan. b, 80k, Traditional Japanese dancer. c, 80k, Japanese dancers with drums. d, 80k, Tokyo skyline. e, 80k, Noh theater. f, 110k, Samurai headgear. g, 110k, Mt. Fuji. h, 110k, Kokeshi dolls. i, 110k, Turkish frigate Ertugrul. j, 110k, Sushi.

2010, Sept. 2   *Perf. 13x13¼*
3239 A935   Sheet of 10, #a-j   13.00 6.50

Souvenir Sheet

Religious Buildings in Spain and Turkey — A936

No. 3240: a, 80k, Santa María de la Mayor Collegiate Church, Toro, Spain. b, 110k, Ortaköy Mosque, Istanbul.

2010, Oct. 18   *Perf. 12¾x13*
3240 A936   Sheet of 2, #a-b   2.75 1.40
   See Spain No. 3755.

Miniature Sheet

11th Economic Cooperation Orgaization Summit, Istanbul — A937

No. 3241 — Emblem with background color of: a, 90k, Blue. b, 100k, Lilac. c, 130k, Rose. d, 150k, Green

2010, Dec. 20 *Perf. 13x12¾*
3241 A937 Sheet of 4, #a-d 6.25 3.00

Miniature Sheet

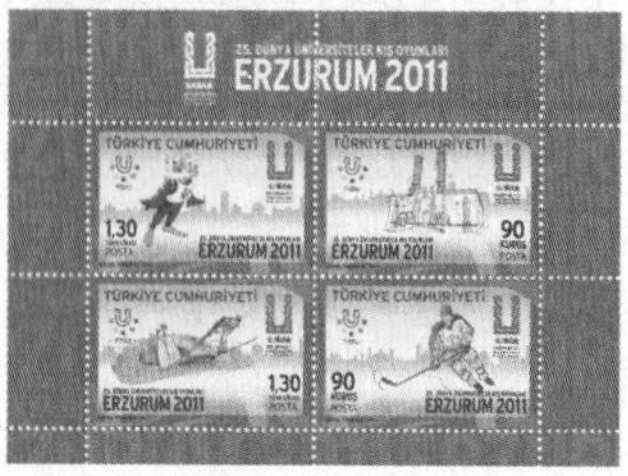

2011 Winter Universiade, Erzurum — A938

No. 3242 — Emblems and: a, 90k, Twin Minaret Madrasa, Erzurum. b, 90k, Ice hockey player. c, 1.30 l, Mascot. d, 1.30 l, Ski jumper.

2011, Jan. 27 *Perf. 13¼x13*
3242 A938 Sheet of 4, #a-d 5.75 2.75

A sheet of four imperforate 1.30 l stamps sold for 30 l.

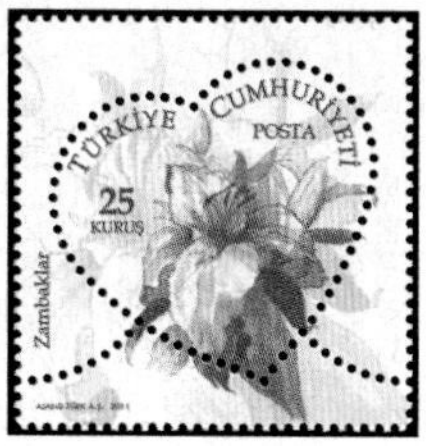

Lilies A939

Various lilies.

2011, Feb. 4 *Perf. 13¾*
3243 A939 25k multi .35 .25
3244 A939 1 l multi 1.25 .65
3245 A939 3.65 l multi 4.75 2.40
3246 A939 6 l multi 7.75 3.75
Nos. 3243-3246 (4) 14.10 7.05

Values are for stamps with surrounding selvage.

Souvenir Sheet

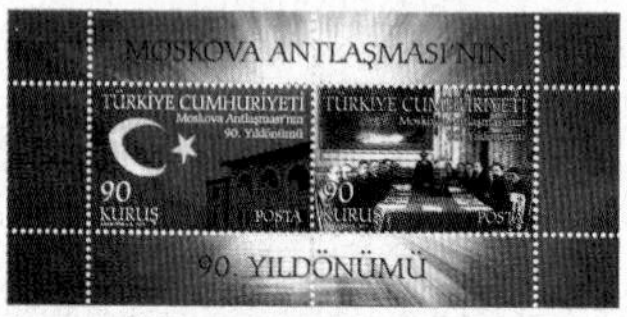

Treaty of Moscow, 90th Anniv. — A940

No. 3247: a, Turkish flag, building. b, Treaty negotiators.

2011, Feb. 4 *Perf. 13¼x13*
3247 A940 90k Sheet of 2, #a-b 2.40 1.25

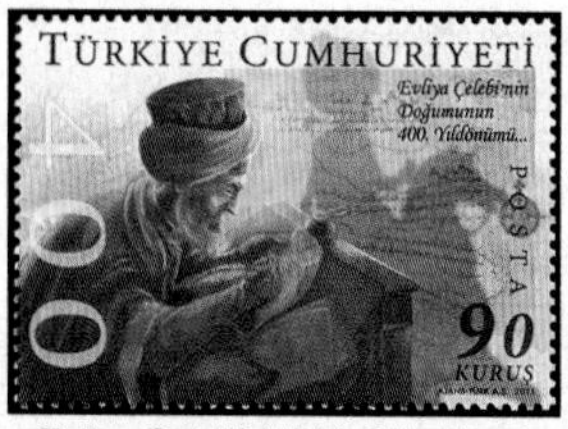

Evliya Celebi (1611-82), Travel Writer — A941

Map and: 90k, Celebi writing, silhouette of Celebi on horse. 1.30 l, Celebi on horse.

2011, Mar. 25 *Perf. 13x13¼*
3248-3249 A941 Set of 2 3.00 1.50

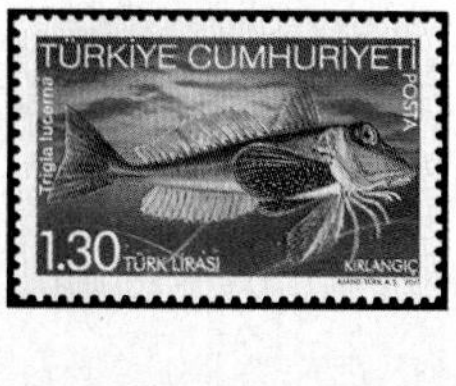

Fish A942

Designs: No. 3250, 1.30 l, Trigla lucerna. No. 3251, 1.30 l, Diplodus vulgaris. No. 3252, 1.30 l, Xiphias gladius.

2011, Apr. 28 *Perf. 13¼x13*
3250-3252 A942 Set of 3 5.25 2.60

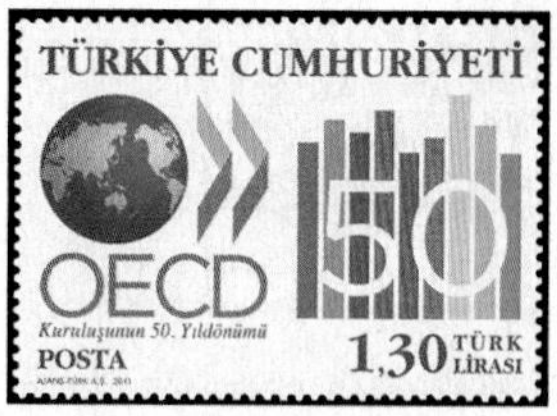

Organization for Economic Cooperation and Development, 50th Anniv. — A943

2011, May 5 *Perf. 13x13¼*
3253 A943 1.30 l multi 1.75 .85

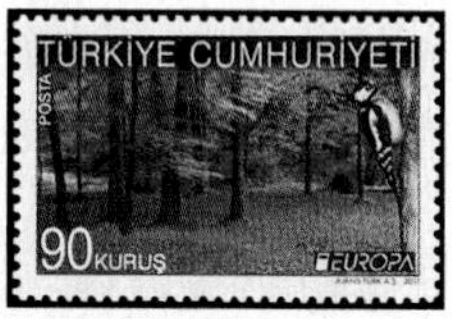

Europa A944

Forest and: 90k, Woodpecker. 1.30 l, Deer.

2011, May 9 *Perf. 13¼x13*
3254-3255 A944 Set of 2 2.75 1.40

Intl. Year of Forests.

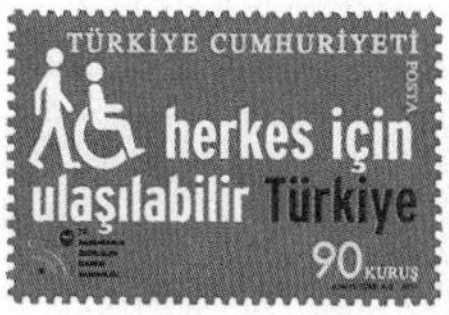

Week of the Disabled A945

Week of the Disabled emblem, stylized person in wheelchair, Turkish text, and: 90k, Stylized person walking. 1.30 l, Hand with blackboard eraser.

2011, May 10 **Litho.**
3256-3257 A945 Set of 2 2.75 1.40

Souvenir Sheet

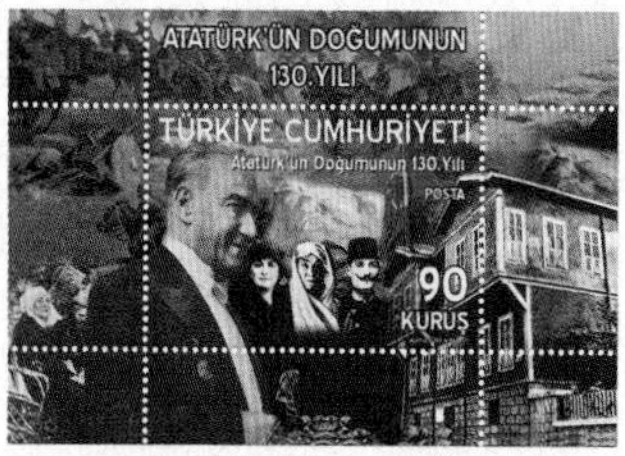

Kemal Atatürk (1881-1938) — A946

2011, May 19 *Perf. 13x13¼*
3258 A946 90k multi 1.25 .60

Miniature Sheet

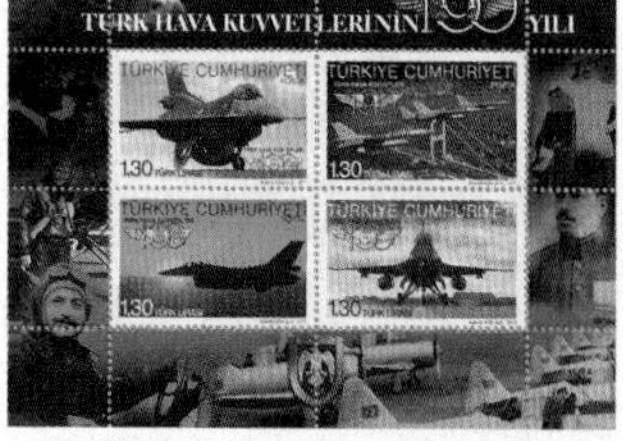

Turkish Air Force, Cent. — A947

No. 3259: a, Jet on ground, blue skies. b, Jets over bridge. c, Jet in flight. d, Jet on runway, gray skies.

2011, June 1 *Perf. 13¼x13*
3259 A947 1.30 l Sheet of 4 #a-d 6.75 3.50

A sheet of four imperforate 1.30 l vertical stamps depicting jets in flight sold for 30 l.

Miniature Sheet

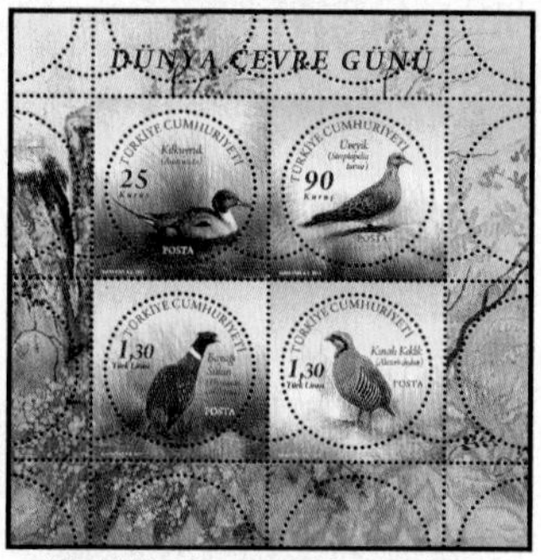

World Environment Day — A948

No. 3260: a, 25k, Anas acuta. b, 90k, Streptopelia turtur. c, 1.30 l, Phasianus colchicus. d, 1.30 l, Alectoris chukar.

2011, June 5 *Perf. 13¾*
3260 A948 Sheet of 4, #a-d 4.75 2.40

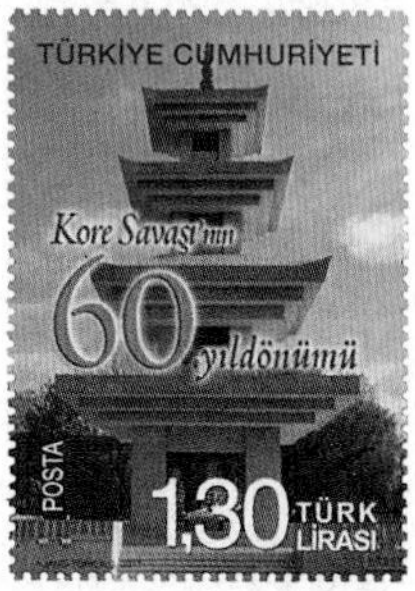

Korean War, 60th Anniv. A949

2011, June 25 *Perf. 13¼x13*
3261 A949 1.30 l multi 1.60 .80

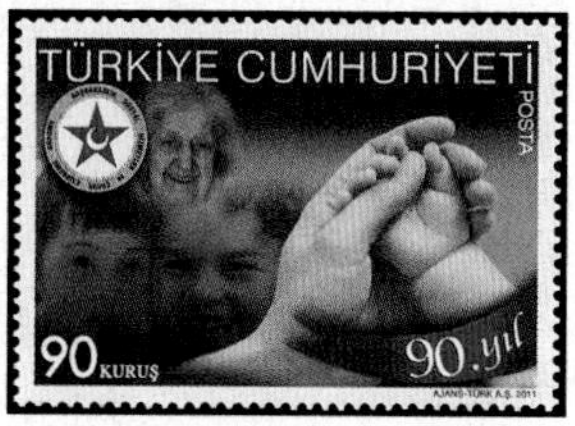

Social Services and Child Protection Agency, 90th Anniv. — A950

2011, June 30 *Perf. 13x13¼*
3262 A950 90k multi 1.10 .55

Miniature Sheet

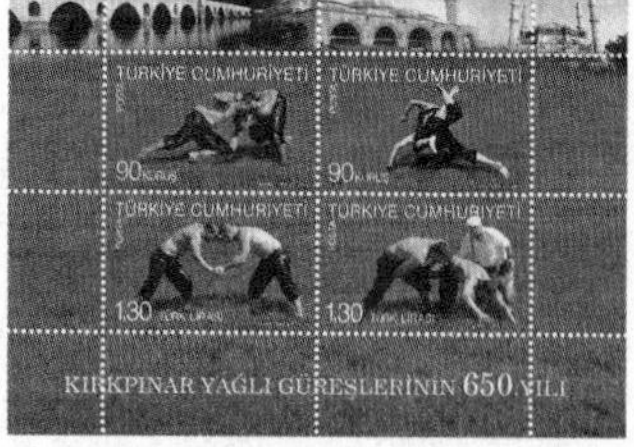

Kirkpinar Oil Wrestling Festival, 650th Anniv. — A951

No. 3263: a, 90k, Two wrestlers, both heads visible. b, 90k, Two wrestlers, heads not visible. c, 1.30 l, Two wrestlers. d, 1.30 l, Two wrestlers and referee.

2011, July 8 *Perf. 13¼x13*
3263 A951 Sheet of 4, #a-d 5.50 2.75

Miniature Sheet

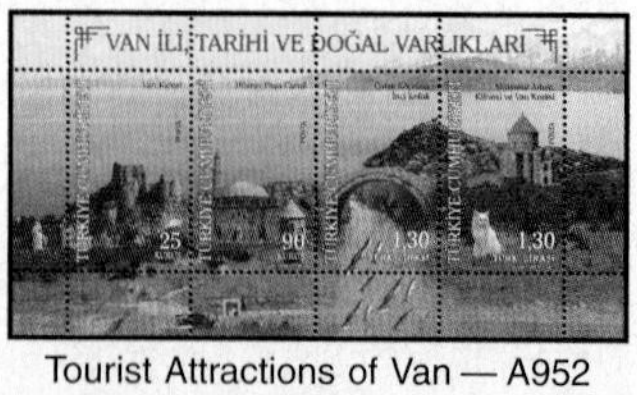

Tourist Attractions of Van — A952

No. 3264: a, 25k, Van Castle. b, 90k, Hüsrev Pasha Mosque. c, 1.30 l, Bridge and fish. d, 1.30 l, Akdamar Church, Van cat.

2011, July 12 *Perf. 13x13¼*
3264 A952 Sheet of 4, #a-d 4.25 2.10

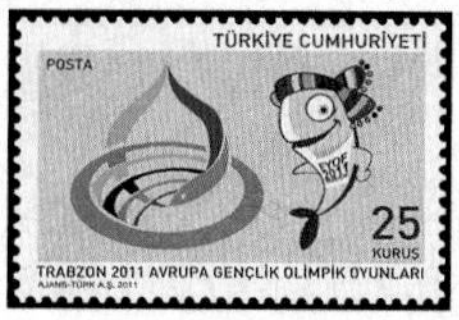

2011 European Youth Summer Olympic Festival, Trabzon A953

Festival mascot and: 25k, Festival emblem. 90k, Festival emblem, diff. No. 3267, 1.30 l, Festival flag and balloons. No. 3268, 1.30 l, Festival emblem, vert.

2011, July 23 *Perf. 13¼x13, 13x13¼*
3265-3268 A953 Set of 4 4.25 2.10

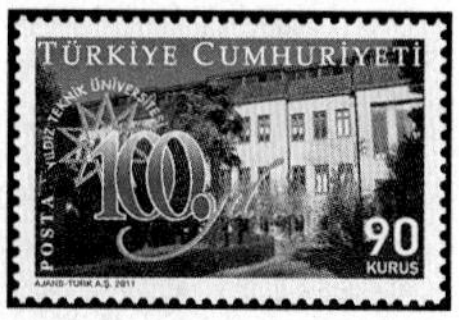

Yildiz Technical University, Cent. A954

Centenary emblem and: 90k, University building. 1.30 l, Star, University building.

2011, Aug. 22 *Perf. 13¼x13*
3269-3270 A954 Set of 2 2.50 1.25

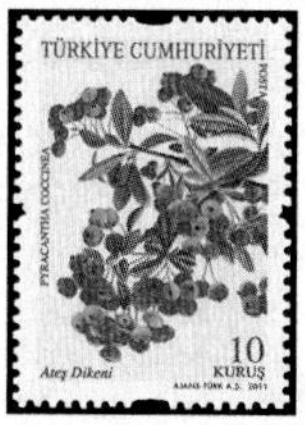

Fruit — A955

Designs: 10k, Pyracantha coccinea. 1 l, Prunus persica. 1.30 l, Prunus avium. 3.65 l, Rubus fruticosus.

Perf. 13½ Syncopated

2011, Aug. 26
3271 A955 10k multi .25 .25
3272 A955 1 l multi 1.10 .55
3273 A955 1.30 l multi 1.50 .75
3274 A955 3.65 l multi 4.25 2.10
Nos. 3271-3274 (4) 7.10 3.65

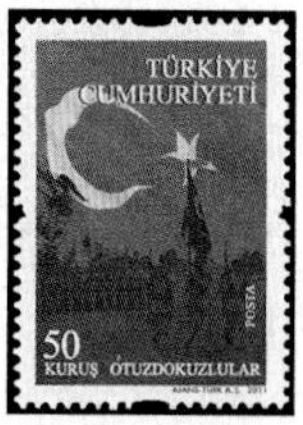

39th Mechanized Infantry Brigade — A956

Designs: 50k, Turkish flag and soldiers carrying flag. 90k, Turkish flag and soldiers. 1.30 l, Soldiers on ship, horiz.

2011, Oct. 6 **Litho.**
3275-3277 A956 Set of 3 3.00 1.50

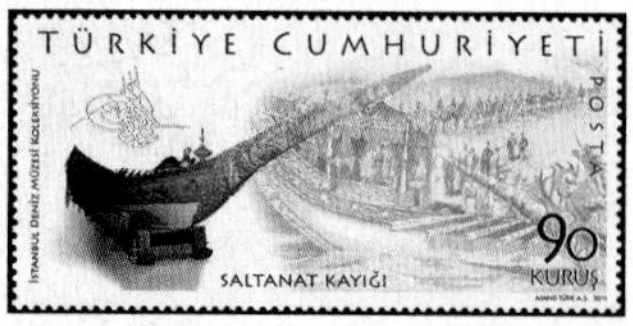

Sultan's Boats — A957

Designs: 90k, Boat with pointed tip. 1.30 l, Boat with white hull and eagle figurehead.

2011, Nov. 28 *Perf. 13x13¼*
3278-3279 A957 Set of 2 2.40 1.25

Photographs of Turkish People and Agriculture — A958

Designs: No. 3280, 50k, Woman and string of pepers. No. 3281, 50k, Workers in field of protected plants. No. 3282, 1 l, Boy swimming in water with livestock, horiz. No. 3283, 1 l, Farm worker in field of plants under protective tents, horiz.

2011, Dec. 28   Perf. 13x13¼, 13¼x13
3280-3283 A958   Set of 4   3.25 1.60

Istanbul, 2012 European Capital of Sports A959

Emblem, Istanbul landmarks and: 50k, Runners, wheelchair racer. No. 3285, 1 l, Sailing. No. 3286, 1 l, Tennis. 2 l, Cycling.

Perf. 13¾ Syncopated
2012, Feb. 15
3284-3287 A959   Set of 4   5.25 2.60

Stylized Man and Woman Holding Up Globe A960

Woman and Flower A961

2012, Mar. 8   Perf. 13½
3288 A960 10k multi + label   .25 .25
3289 A961 1 l multi + label   1.10 .55
3290 A960 2 l multi + label   2.25 1.10
      Nos. 3288-3290 (3)   3.60 1.90
Equality of opportunities for men and women.

Miniature Sheet

2012 World Track and Field Championships, Istanbul — A962

No. 3291 — Bridge and: a, 50k, Female hurdler. b, 1 l, Female long jumper. c, 1 l, Male high jumper. d, 2 l, Male hurdler.

2012, Mar. 9   Perf. 13¾
3291 A962 Sheet of 4, #a-d   5.00 2.50

National History Society Building, Cent. — A963

Perf. 13¾ Syncopated
2012, Mar. 25
3292 A963 1 l multi   1.10 .55

Pertevniyal High School, 140th Anniv. — A964

2012, Apr. 6
3293 A964 1 l multi   1.10 .55

Souvenir Sheet

Morality and Rights — A965

No. 3294: a, Hands and emblem. b, Rose, Arabic inscription.

2012, Apr. 14   Perf. 14 Syncopated
3294 A965 1 l Sheet of 2, #a-b 2.25 1.10

Constitutional Court, 50th Anniv. — A966

Designs: 1 l, 50th anniversary emblem. 2 l, Court and 50th anniversary emblem.

2012, Apr. 25   Perf. 13¾ Syncopated
3295-3296 A966   Set of 2   3.50 1.75

Tourism — A967

Hands and: No. 3297, 2 l, Aspendos (Amphitheater), Antalya. No. 3298, 2 l, Yat Limani (Harbor), Antalya. No. 3299, 2 l, Kiz Kulesi (Leander's Tower), Istanbul. No. 3300, 2 l, Ortaköy, Istanbul. No. 3301, 2 l, Efes (Ephesus), İzmir. No. 3302, 2 l, Saat Kulesi (Clock tower), Izmir. No. 3303, 2 l, Göreme, Nevsehir. No. 3304, 2 l, Zelve Monastery and balloon, Nevsehir.

2012, Apr. 30   Perf. 14 Syncopated
3297-3304 A967   Set of 8   18.50 9.25

Europa A968

Designs: No. 3305, 2 l, Skier and parachute skier. No. 3306, 2 l, Whirling dervishes, sea turtle, tourist attractions.

2012, May 9   Perf. 13¾ Syncopated
3305-3306 A968   Set of 2   4.50 2.25

Union of Chambers and Commodity Excahnges of Turkey, 60th Anniv. A969

2012, May 17
3307 A969 1 l multi   1.10 .55

Treasury and Audit Department, 150th Anniv. — A970

Designs: 1 l, Building and 150th anniversary emblem. 2 l, 150th anniversary emblem.

2012, May 29
3308-3309 A970   Set of 2   3.25 1.60

Miniature Sheet

10th Turkish Olympics — A971

No. 3310: a, 50k, "10 Yasinda." b, 1 l, Globe tethered to map of Turkey with crescent and star. c, 1 l, Flags of various nations around flag of Turkey in oval. d, 2 l, Stylized faces of people of various cultures.

2012, May 30   Perf. 13
3310 A971 Sheet of 4, #a-d   5.00 2.50

Miniature Sheet

World Environment Day — A980

No. 3312 — Dinosaurs: a, 50k, Carnotaurus. b, 1 l, Pteranodon. c, 1 l, Tyrannosaurus rex. d, 2 l, Triceratops.

2012, June 5   Litho.   Perf. 13¼x13
3312 A980 Sheet of 4, #a-d   5.00 2.50

A 46x46mm 3-dimensional 2 l stamp was sold only with a booklet to which the stamp was not attached.

Intl. Year of Cooperatives — A981

Designs: 1 l, Ants carrying Earth. 2 l, Stylized people carrying Turkey.

2012, June 6
3313-3314 A981   Set of 2   3.25 1.60

Istanbul Shopping Festival — A982

Designs: 1 l, Istanbul skyline, woman in red dress. 2 l, Folding fan.

2012, June 9   Perf. 13¾ Syncopated
3315-3316 A982   Set of 2   3.50 1.75

Miniature Sheet

2012 Summer Olympics, London — A983

No. 3317: a, 50k, Volleyball, London Eye. b, 1 l, Hurdles, Tower Bridge. c, 1 l, Wrestling, Regent Street buildings. d, 2 l, Basketball, Buckingham Palace.

2012, July 27   Perf. 13½x14
3317 A983 Sheet of 4, #a-d   5.00 2.50

Souvenir Sheet

European Kick Boxing Championships, Ankara — A984

No. 3318 — Kick boxers and map of: a, Western Europe. b, Central and Eastern Europe.

2012, Oct. 27   Perf. 13¼x13½
3318 A984 1 l Sheet of 2, #a-b 2.25 1.10

Souvenir Sheet

Bridges — A985

No. 3319: a, Bosporus Bridge, Istanbul. b, Yangtze River Bridge, Taizhou, People's Republic of China.

2012, Nov. 26   *Perf. 14x13½*
3319 A985 1 l Sheet of 2, #a-b   2.25 1.10
    See People's Republic of China Nos. 4056-4057.

Souvenir Sheet

Cultural Heritage of Kütahya — A986

No. 3320: a, 1 l, Shaft of light on altar. b, 2 l, Temple of Zeus.

2012, Nov. 29   *Perf. 13¼*
3320 A986   Sheet of 2, #a-b   3.50 1.75

Photographs of Everyday Life — A987

Designs: No. 3321, 50k, Fishermen tending nets. No. 3322, 50k, Hands of goat herder and goat. No. 3323, 1 l, Fisherman casting net. No. 3324, 1 l, Sheep grazing in field. No. 3325, 2 l, Woman with harvesting basket. No. 3326, 2 l, Horses in corral.

2012, Dec. 26   *Perf. 13½x14*
3321-3326 A987   Set of 6   8.00 4.00

A988

Black line and: 20k Flowers. 1.10 l, Tulips. 2.20 l, Flowers, diff. 3.85 l, Decorative circles. 8 l, Flowers, diff.

2013, Jan. 7   *Perf. 13x12½*
3327 A988   20k multi   .25 .25
3328 A988   1.10 l multi   1.25 .65
3329 A988   2.20 l multi   2.50 1.25
3330 A988   3.85 l multi   4.50 2.25
3331 A988   8 l multi   9.25 4.50
    Nos. 3327-3331 (5)   17.75 8.90

Miniature Sheet

Turkish Postage Stamps, 150th Anniv. — A989

No. 3332: a, Emblem of Turkish PTT. b, Leaves, star and crescent. c, Tughra of Sultan Abdul-Aziz. d, Stamp inscribed "150 Yil."

Litho. & Embossed With Foil Application

2013, Jan. 14   *Perf. 14¼*
3332 A989   1.10 l Sheet of 4, #a-
        d, + label   5.00 2.50

Souvenir Sheet

Yildiz Palace, Istanbul — A990

No. 3333: a, Palace and fountain. b, Palace, photograph and tughra of Sultan Abdul Hamid II.

2013, Feb. 27   *Perf. 13½x13¼*
3333 A990   1.10 l Sheet of 2, #a-
        b   2.50 1.25

Miniature Sheet

Eskisehir, 2013 UNESCO Intangible Culture Capital — A991

No. 3334: a, 1.10 l, Train. b, 1.10 l, Meerschaum pipe, spa pool. c, 2.20 l, Porsuk River. d, 2.20 l, Houses in Odupazari District.

2013, Mar. 21 Litho.   *Perf. 13¾x14*
3334 A991   Sheet of 4, #a-d   7.50 3.75

Souvenir Sheet

World Down Syndrome Day — A992

No. 3335 — Face of child with Down Syndrome and: a, 50k, Chromosomes, strand of DNA, heart (40x30mm). b, 1.10 l, Heart (40x30mm). c, 2.20 l, Children in field of flowers, hearts (80x30mm).

    Perf. 13½x13¼
2013, Mar. 21   Litho.
3335 A992   Sheet of 3, #a-c   4.25 2.10

Souvenir Sheet

Expo 2020, Izmir — A993

No. 3336: a, 1.10 l, Izmir tourist attractions, emblem of Expo 2020. b, 1.10 l, Man and woman jogging on waterside path. c, 2.20 l, Emblem of Expo 2020.

2013, Apr. 4   **Litho.**   *Perf. 13½*
3336 A993   Sheet of 3, #a-c   5.00 2.50

Tourist Attractions in Antalya A994

Designs: No. 3337, 2.20 l, Alanya Kalesi (Alanya Castle). No. 3338, 2.20 l, Apollon Tapinagi (Temple of Apollo), Side. No. 3339, 2.20 l, Hadrian Kapisi (Hadrian's Gate). No. 3340, 2.20 l, Kaleiçi (historic city center). No. 3341, 2.20 l, Manavgat Selalesi (Manavgat Waterfalls). No. 3342, 2.20 l, Saat Kulesi ve Yivli Minare (Clock Tower and Yivli Minaret).

    Perf. 13¾ Syncopated
2013, Apr. 12   Litho.
3337-3342 A994   Set of 6   15.00 7.50

Miniature Sheet

Piri Reis Map, 500th Anniv. — A995

No. 3343 — Part of map with: a, 1.10 l, Ship and compass rose. b, 1.10 l, Ship, birds, monkeys. c, 2.20 l, Ships and compass rose. d, 2.20 l, Text and Piri Reis (c.1464-1553).

2013, Apr. 18   **Litho.**   *Perf. 13½*
3343 A995   Sheet of 4, #a-d, +
        label   7.50 3.75

Europa — A996

Designs: 1.10 l, Mailbox, envelope, postal vans and motorcycle. 2.20 l, Postrider, sealed

scroll, horse-drawn carrialge, postal trucks, mailbox.

2013, May 9 Litho.   *Perf. 13½x13¼*
3344-3345 A996   Set of 2   3.50 1.75

Miniature Sheet

Istanbul Technical University, 240th Anniv. — A997

No. 3346: a, Building with eight short pillars. b, Doors and windows. c, Building without pillars. d, Building with four tall pillars.

2013, May 24 Litho.   *Perf. 13¾x14*
3346 A997   1.10 l Sheet of 4, #a-
        d   4.75 2.40

Miniature Sheet

World Environment Day — A998

No. 3347: a, Head and neck with water and dry earth. b, House, stylized globe, flower and trees. c, Farm, tractor, polar bears, map of Northern Africa. d, Family, foxes, rabbit, seal.

2013, June 5 Litho.   *Perf. 14x13¾*
3347 A998   1.10 l Sheet of 4, #a-
        d   4.75 2.40

Miniature Sheet

17th Mediterranean Games, Mersin — A999

No. 3348: a, Shell, track and field athletes, boxer. b, Boxer, weight lifter, yacht. c, Yacht, archer, gymnast. d, Volleyball player, cyclist.

2013, June 10 Litho.   *Perf. 14x13¾*
3348 A999   1.10 l Sheet of 4, #a-
        d   4.75 2.40

A 5 l self-adhesive three-dimensional plastic stamp depicting turtles and the turtle mascot of the Mediterranean Games was produced in a limited quantity and sold only in a folder that also contained No. 3348 and a first day cover of No. 3348.

Public Administration Institute for Turkey and the Middle East, 60th Anniv. — A1000

    Perf. 13¾ Syncopated
2013, June 28   Litho.
3349 A1000 1.10 l multi   1.10 .55

Expo 2016, Antalya — A1001

Designs: No. 3350, 2.20 l, Children, flowers, Yivli Minaret. No. 3351, 2.20 l, Emblem of Expo 2016.

Perf. 13¾ Syncopated
2013, July 25   Litho.
3350-3351 A1001   Set of 2   4.75 2.40

Miniature Sheet

Cuisine of Central Anatolia — A1002

No. 3352: a, Tomato, bread, meat dish, bowl of vegetables and sauce. b, Wheat stalk, three plates of food. c, Scallions, radishes, food in clay pots, rolls. d, Grapes, two plates of food.

2013, Aug. 16   Litho.   **Perf. 14x13¾**
3352 A1002 1.10 l Sheet of 4,
         #a-d   4.50 2.25

Calligraphy A1003

Various depictions of Arabic "w."

Perf. 13¾ Syncopated
2013, Aug. 27   Litho.
3353 A1003   10k lilac & blk   .25 .25
3354 A1003   1 l gray & blk   1.00 .50
3355 A1003   1.10 l blue & blk   1.10 .55
3356 A1003   8 l multi   8.00 4.00
   Nos. 3353-3356 (4)   10.35 5.30

Council of State Building A1004

Council of State 145th Anniv. Emblem A1005

2013, Sept. 2   Litho.   **Perf. 13¾x14**
3357 A1004 1.10 l multi   1.10 .55
3358 A1005 1.10 l multi   1.10 .55

11th Transportation, Maritime Affairs and Communication Forum, Istanbul — A1006

Forum emblem and: No. 3359, 1.10 l, Satellite above Earth. No. 3360, 1.10 l, Airplane over new Istanbul Airport. No. 3361, 2.20 l, Train, Marmaray Tunnel, map of Istanbul. No. 3362, 2.20 l, Yavuz Sultan Selim Bridge, Istanbul.

2013, Sept. 5   Litho.   **Perf. 13¾**
3359-3362 A1006   Set of 4   6.50 3.25

A sheet of four 1.10 l stamps depicting parts of the Izmit Bay Bridge was only offered in a presentation folder that sold for 30 l.

13th Istanbul Biennial Contemporary Art Exhibition — A1007

2013, Sept. 14   Litho.   **Perf. 13¾**
3363 A1007 1.10 l black   1.10 .55

Turkish Language Festival A1008

2013, Sept. 26   Litho.   **Perf. 13¾**
3364 A1008 1.10 l multi   1.10 .55

Souvenir Sheet

King Carol I Mosque, Constanta, Romania — A1009

2013, Oct. 10   Litho.   **Perf. 13½**
3365 A1009 3.85 l multi   4.00 2.00

Diplomatic relations between Turkey and Romania, 135th anniv. See Romania No. 5492.

Turkish Postage Stamp Museum A1010

Designs: 1.10 l, Turkey #3094-3095. 2.20 l, Museum displays.

2013, Oct. 22   Litho.   **Perf. 13¾**
3366-3367 A1010   Set of 2   3.25 1.60

Values for Nos. 3366-3367 are for stamps with surrounding selvage. A 8 l souvenir sheet depicting postal workers, buildings and equipment was only offered in a presentation folder that sold for 30 l.

Souvenir Sheet

Republic of Turkey, 90th Anniv. — A1011

No. 3368 — Bridge and; a, Tank, military jet and helicopter, map of Europe. b, Satellite, train, Kemal Ataturk.

2013, Oct. 29   Litho.   **Perf. 13¼**
3368 A1011 1.10 l   Sheet of 2,
       #a-b   2.25 1.10

Souvenir Sheet

Completion of Marmaray Tunnel Project — A1012

Perf. 13¾ Syncopated
2013, Oct. 29   Litho.
3369 A1012 1.10 l multi   1.10 .55

No. 3369 exists imperforate in a limited printing.

Fifth Izmir Economic Congress A1013

2013, Oct. 30   Litho.   **Perf. 13¾x14**
3370 A1013 1.10 l multi   1.10 .55

Souvenir Sheet

Mosques — A1014

No. 3371: a, 1.10 l, Sultan Ahmed Mosque, Istanbul. b, 2.20 l, Al-Aqsa Mosque, Jerusalem.

Perf. 13½x13¾
2013, Dec. 12   Litho.
3371 A1014   Sheet of 2, #a-b   3.25 1.60

See Palestinian Authority No.

University of Ankara Faculty of Dentistry, 50th Anniv. — A1015

2013, Dec. 14   Litho.   **Perf. 13½**
3372 A1015 1.10 l multi   1.00 .50

Yasar Dogu (1913-61), Wrestler A1016

Perf. 13¾ Syncopated
2013, Dec. 23   Litho.
3373 A1016 50k multi   .45 .25

Turkish Republic of Northern Cyprus Postal Service, 50th Anniv. — A1017

Perf. 14x13¾ Syncopated
2014, Jan. 6   Litho.
3374 A1017 1.10 l multi   1.00 .50

Altay Sports Club, Cent. A1018

Designs: No. 3375, 1.10 l, Basketball. No. 3376, 1.10 l, Soccer. No. 3377, 2.20 l, Swimming. No. 3378, 2.20 l, Handball.

2014, Jan. 16   Litho.   **Perf. 13¾**
3375-3378 A1018   Set of 4   6.00 3.00

Values are for stamps with surrounding selvage.

2014 Winter Olympics, Sochi, Russia A1019

Designs: No. 3379, 1.10 l, Ski jumping. No. 3380, 1.10 l, Pairs figure skating. No. 3381, 2.20 l, Alpine skiing. No. 3382, 2.20 l, Speed skating.

2014, Feb. 7   Litho.   **Perf. 13¾**
3379-3382 A1019   Set of 4   6.00 3.00

Turkish Radio and Television, 50th Anniv. A1020

50th anniv. emblem and: 1.10 l, Text. 2.20 l, Building.

2014, Feb. 20   Litho.   Perf. 13¾
3383-3384 A1020   Set of 2   3.00 1.50

Souvenir Sheet

Topkapi Palace — A1021

No. 3385: a, Tower of Justice and Gate of Salutation, b, Palace interior, Sultan Mehmed II (1432-81) and his monogram.

Litho. With Foil Application
2014, Feb. 27   Perf. 13½x13¼
3385 A1021 1.10 l Sheet of 2,
       #a-b   2.00 1.00

Miniature Sheet

First Deaths of Turkish Military Aviators, Cent. — A1022

No. 3386: a, 50k, Lieutenant Selim Saiq Bey and Captain Mehmet Fethi Bey. b, 1.10 l, Fethi Bey and airplane. c, 1.10 l, Memorial, Haon, Israel. d, 2.20 l, Building and Fethi Bey Monument, Istanbul.

Perf. 13½x13¼
2014, Feb. 27   Litho.
3386 A1022   Sheet of 4, #a-d   4.50 2.25

General Directorate of Hydraulic Works, 60th Anniv. A1023

2014, Mar. 22   Litho.   Perf. 13¾
3387 A1023 1.10 l multi + label 1.10 .55

Souvenir Sheet

Mother's Day — A1024

2014, Apr. 17   Litho.   Perf.
3388 A1024 1.10 l multi + 4 la-
          bels   1.10 .55

Tour of Turkey Bicycle Race, 50th Anniv. — A1025

2014, Apr. 27 Litho.   Perf. 13½x13¼
3389 A1025 1.10 l multi   1.10 .55

A folder containing No. 3389, a first day cover of No. 3389, and a souvenir sheet containing a 2.20 l stamp was produced in limited quantities.

Europa — A1026

Musical instruments: 1.25 l, Kabak kemane. 2.50 l, Ud.

2014, May 9   Litho.   Perf. 13½x13¼
3390-3391 A1026   Set of 2   3.75 1.90

Tourist Attractions — A1027

Attractions in: No. 3392, Erzurum Province. No. 3393, Sanliurfa Province. No. 3394, Izmir Province. No. 3395, Konya Province. No. 3396, Antalya Province. No. 3397, Istanbul Province. 4 l, Trabzon Province. 9 l, Ankara Province.

Perf. 13¾ Syncopated
2014, May 22   Litho.
3392 A1027   35k multi   .35   .25
3393 A1027   35k multi   .35   .25
3394 A1027   1.25 l multi   1.25   .60
3395 A1027   1.25 l multi   1.25   .60
3396 A1027   2.50 l multi   2.40 1.25
3397 A1027   2.50 l multi   2.40 1.25
3398 A1027   4 l multi   3.75 1.90
3399 A1027   9 l multi   8.50 4.25
       Nos. 3392-3399 (8)   20.25 10.35

Souvenir Sheet

World Environment Day — A1028

No. 3400: a, 1.25 l, Bee in flight. b, 1.25 l, Two bees in flight. c, 2.50 l, Bee on flower.

2014, June 5   Litho.   Perf. 13½
3400 A1028   Sheet of 3, #a-c   4.75 2.40

Turkish Gendarmerie, 175th Anniv. — A1030

Perf. 13½x13¼
2014, June 14   Litho.
3405 A1030 1.25 l multi   1.25   .60

Souvenir Sheet

Deer and Mushrooms in National Park — A1031

2014, July 9   Litho.   Perf. 13¼
3406 A1031 2.50 l multi   2.40 1.25

2014 World Cup Soccer Championships, Brazil — A1032

Designs: 1.25 l, World Cup trophy. 2.50 l, Mascot of 2014 World Cup, horiz.

Perf. 14x13¾, 13¾x14
2014, Aug. 6   Litho.
3407-3408 A1032   Set of 2   3.50 1.75

Miniature Sheet

Local Cuisine — A1033

No. 3409: a, 1.25 l, Agzi açik (lamb pies), Sanliurfa Province. b, 1.25 l, Sihilmahsi (stuffed zucchini), Kilis Province. c, 2.50 l, Sogan kebabi (stuffed onions), Mardin Province. d, 2.50 l, Saçma tavasi (stew), Gaziantep Province.

2014, Aug. 15 Litho.   Perf. 14x13¾
3409 A1033   Sheet of 4, #a-d   7.00 3.50

Ottoman Navy Galleon Mahmudiya — A1034

Various depictions of the Mahmudiya, 1.25 l, 2.50 l.

Litho. With Foil Application
Perf. 13¾ Syncopated
2014, Sept. 10
3410-3411 A1034   Set of 2   3.50 1.75

2014 Women's World Basketball Championships, Istanbul and Ankara — A1035

Design: 1.25 l, Emblem. 2.50 l, Emblem and stylized basketball (38x38mm).

Perf. 13¼x13½, 13¼
2014, Sept. 29   Litho.
3412-3413 A1035   Set of 2   3.50 1.75

Souvenir Sheet

Presidential Palace, Ankara — A1036

Litho., Sheet Margin Litho & Embossed With Foil Application
2014, Oct. 29   Perf. 13½x13¼
3414 A1036 1.25 l multi   1.10   .55

Republic of Turkey, 91st anniv. A limited edition packet contained three imperforate souvenir sheets showing different images of the Presidential Palace, with denominations of 1.25 l, 2.50 l, and 4 l, along with first day covers of these items.

SEMI-POSTAL STAMPS

Regular Issues Overprinted in Carmine or Black

Overprint reads: "For War Orphans"
Perf. 12, 13½ and Compound
1915   Unwmk.
       On Stamps of 1905
B1   A18 10pa dull grn (#119)   1.00   .75
B2   A18 10pi orange brown   12.50   .80
       On Stamp of 1906
B3   A18 10pa dull grn (#128) 40.00 25.00
       On Stamps of 1908
B4   A19 10pa blue green   1.50   .75
B5   A19 5pi dark violet   75.00 12.50
       Nos. B1-B5 (5)   130.00 39.80

With Additional "Discount" Overprint on No. B6

B6   A19 10pa blue green   240.00 175.00
       On Stamps of 1909
B7   A21 10pa blue green   1.00   .75
  a.   Inverted overprint   22.50 22.50
  b.   Double overprint, one invtd. 30.00 30.00
B8   A21 20pa carmine rose   1.00   .75
  a.   Inverted overprint   27.50 27.50
B9   A21 1pi ultra   1.00   .75
B10 A21 5pi dark violet   8.75 1.50
       Nos. B7-B10 (4)   11.75 3.75
See note after No. 131.

With Additional Overprint on Nos. B11-B13

B11	A21 10pa blue green	1.00	.75
b.	Double overprint, one inverted	5.00	5.00
B12	A21 20pa carmine rose	1.50	.75
B13	A21 1pi ultra	2.00	.75

On Stamps of 1913

B14	A22 10pa blue green	1.00	.75
a.	Inverted overprint	22.50	22.50
B15	A22 1pi ultra	1.00	.75
a.	Double overprint	5.00	5.00
	Nos. B11-B15 (5)	6.50	3.75

With Additional Overprint on No. B16

B16	A22 10pa blue green	1.75	.75
a.	Inverted overprint	27.50	27.50

On Newspaper Stamp of 1908

B17	A19 10pa blue green	360.00	175.00

On Newspaper Stamp of 1909

B18	A21 10pa blue green	1.75	1.00

Regular Issues Overprinted in Carmine or Black

1916   **On Stamps of 1901**

B19	A17 1pi blue	1.00	.50
B20	A17 5pi lilac rose	10.00	1.50

On Stamps of 1905

B21	A18 1pi brt blue	7.50	2.00
B22	A18 5pi brown	7.50	5.00

On Stamp of 1906

B23	A18 1pi brt blue	1.00	.75

On Stamps of 1908

B24	A19 20pa carmine (Bk)		300.00
B25	A19 10pi red	500.00	200.00

With Additional Overprint on Nos. B26-B27

B26	A19 20pa carmine	8.00	8.00
B27	A19 1pi brt blue (C)	20.00	5.00

On Stamps of 1909

B28	A21 20pa carmine rose	2.00	1.25
B29	A21 1pi ultra	1.50	1.00
B30	A21 10pi dull red	175.00	100.00

With Additional Overprint on Nos. B31-B32

B31	A21 20pa carmine rose	1.50	.75
B32	A21 1pi ultra	2.00	1.00

On Stamps of 1913

B33	A22 20pa carmine rose	2.00	1.50
B34	A22 1pi ultra	2.00	1.00
a.	Inverted overprint	5.00	5.00
B35	A22 10pi dull red	22.50	15.00

With Additional Overprint on No. B36

B36	A22 20pa carmine rose	2.00	1.25

On Newspaper Stamps of 1901

B37	A16 5pi ocher	11.50	6.00
a.	5pa bister, No. P37	150.00	150.00

Regular Issues Surcharged in Black

On Stamp of 1898

B38	A11 10pa on 20pa vio brn	2.00	1.50

On Stamp of 1905

B39	A18 10pa on 20pa carmine	2.00	1.50

On Stamp of 1906

B40	A18 10pa on 20pa carmine	1.50	1.25

On Newspaper Stamp of 1893-99

B41	A11 10pa on 20pa violet brn	2.00	1.50
	Nos. B38-B41 (4)	7.50	5.75

Nos. 346-349 Overprinted

B42	A41 10pa carmine	1.00	.75
a.	Inverted overprint	6.75	6.75
B43	A41 20pa ultra	1.00	.75
a.	Inverted overprint	6.75	6.75
B44	A41 1pi violet & blk	1.00	.90
a.	Inverted overprint	6.75	6.75
B45	A41 5pi yel brn & blk	1.00	.75
a.	Inverted overprint	11.00	11.00
	Nos. B42-B45 (4)	4.00	3.15

Nos. B42-B45 formed part of the Postage Commemoration issue of 1916.

A Soldier's Farewell — SP1

1917, Feb. 20   **Engr.**   **Perf. 12½**

B46	SP1 10pa red violet	1.25	.50

For surcharges see Nos. 600, B47.

Stamp of Same Design Surcharged

B47	SP1 10pa on 20pa car rose	2.00	.50

Badge of the Society — SP9

School Teacher — SP10

Marie Sklodowska Curie — SP16

Kemal Atatürk — SP23

Designs: 2k+2k, Woman farmer. 2½k+2½k, Typist. 4k+4k, Aviatrix and policewoman. 5k+5k, Women voters. 7½k+7½k, Yildiz Palace, Istanbul. 10k+10k, Carrie Chapman Catt. 12½k+12½k, Jane Addams. 15k+15k, Grazia Deledda. 20k+20k, Selma Lagerlof. 25k+25k, Bertha von Suttner. 30k+30k, Sigrid Undset.

1935, Apr. 17   **Photo.**   **Perf. 11½**
Inscribed: "XII Congres Suffragiste International"

B54	SP9 20pa + 20pa brn	.50	.50
B55	SP10 1k + 1k rose car	.75	.50
B56	SP10 2k + 2k sl bl	1.00	.75
B57	SP10 2½k + 2½k yel grn	1.00	.75
B58	SP10 4k + 4k blue	1.50	1.00
B59	SP10 5k + 5k dl vio	2.50	2.00
B60	SP10 7½k + 7½k org red	2.50	2.00
B61	SP16 10k + 10k org	2.50	2.50
B62	SP16 12½k + 12½k dk bl	2.50	2.50
B63	SP16 15k + 15k violet	5.00	5.00
B64	SP16 20k + 20k red org	7.50	6.25
B65	SP16 25k + 25k grn	15.00	14.00
B66	SP16 30k + 30k ultra	90.00	100.00
B67	SP16 50k + 50k dk sl grn	175.00	150.00
B68	SP23 100k + 100k brn car	125.00	140.00
	Nos. B54-B68 (15)	432.25	427.75
	Set, never hinged	750.00	

12th Congress of the Women's Intl. Alliance.

> **Catalogue values for unused stamps in this section, from this point to the end of the section, are for Never Hinged items.**

Katip Chelebi — SP24

Perf. 10½
1958, Sept. 24   **Litho.**   **Unwmk.**

B69	SP24 50k + 10k gray	.35	.25

Mustafa ibn 'Abdallah Katip Chelebi Hajji Khalifa (1608-1657), Turkish author.

Road Building Machine SP25

Kemal Atatürk — SP26

Design: 25k+5k, Tanks and planes.

1958, Oct. 29

B70	SP25 15k + 5k orange	.25	.25
B71	SP26 20k + 5k lt red brn	.25	.25
B72	SP25 25k + 5k brt grn	.25	.25
	Nos. B70-B72 (3)	.75	.75

The surtax went to the Red Crescent Society and to the Society for the Protection of Children.

For surcharge see No. 1440.

Ruins, Göreme SP27

1959, July 8   **Litho.**   **Perf. 10**

B73	SP27 105k + 10k pur & buff	.50	.25

Issued for tourist publicity.

Istanbul SP28

1959, Sept. 11

B74	SP28 105k + 10k lt bl & red	.50	.25

15th International Tuberculosis Congress.

Manisa Asylum SP29

Merkez Muslihiddin SP30

Kermis at Manisa: 90k+5k, Sultan Camil Mosque, Manisa, vert.

1960, Apr. 17   **Unwmk.**   **Perf. 13**

B75	SP29 40k + 5k grn & lt bl	.25	.25
B76	SP29 40k + 5k vio & rose lil	.25	.25
B77	SP29 90k + 5k dp cl & car rose	.60	.25
B78	SP30 105k + 10k multi	.80	.25
	Nos. B75-B78 (4)	1.90	1.00

Census Chart SP31

Census Symbol — SP32

1960, Sept. 23   **Photo.**   **Perf. 11½**
Granite Paper

B79	SP31 30k + 5k bl & rose pink	.25	.25
B80	SP32 50k + 5k grn, dk bl & ultra	.35	.25

Issued for the 1960 Census.

Old Observatory SP33

Fatin Gökmen — SP34

Designs: 30k+5k, Observatory emblem. 75k+5k, Building housing telescope.

1961, July 1   Litho.   Perf. 13
B81 SP33 10k + 5k grnsh bl &
      grn   .25 .25
B82 SP33 30k + 5k vio & blk .75 .75
B83 SP34 40k + 5k brown   .25 .25
B84 SP33 75k + 5k olive grn .75 .75
      Nos. B81-B84 (4)   2.00 2.00

Kandili Observatory, 50th anniversary.

Anti-Malaria Work — SP35

UNICEF, 10th anniv.: 30k+5k, Mother and infant, horiz. 75k+5k, Woman distributing pasteurized milk.

1961, Dec. 11   Unwmk.   Perf. 13
B85 SP35 10k + 5k Prus green .25 .25
B86 SP35 30k + 5k dull violet .30 .25
B87 SP35 75k + 5k dk olive bis .60 .25
      Nos. B85-B87 (3)   1.15 .75

Malaria Eradication Emblem, Map and Mosquito SP36

1962, Apr. 7   Litho.
B88 SP36 30k + 5k dk & lt brn .30 .25
B89 SP36 75k + 5k blk & lil   .35 .25

WHO drive to eradicate malaria.

Poinsettia — SP37

Flowers: 40k+10k, Bird of paradise flower. 75k+10k, Water lily.

1962, May 19   Perf. 12½x13½
Flowers in Natural Colors
B90 SP37 30k + 10k lt bl & blk .25 .25
B91 SP37 40k + 10k lt bl & blk .45 .25
B92 SP37 75k + 10k lt bl & blk .95 .40
      Nos. B90-B92 (3)   1.65 .90

Wheat and Census Chart — SP38

Design: 60k+5k, Wheat and chart, horiz.
Inscribed: "Umumi Ziraat Sayimi"
1963, Apr. 14   Photo.   Perf. 11½
B93 SP38 40k + 5k gray grn & yel .25 .25
B94 SP38 60k + 5k org yel & blk   .25 .25

1961 agricultural census. Two black bars obliterate "Kasim 1960" inscription.

Red Lion and Sun, Red Crescent, Red Cross and Globe SP39

Designs: 60k+10k, Emblems in flowers, vert. 100k+10k, Emblems on flags.

1963, Aug. 1   Perf. 13
B95 SP39 50k + 10k multi .25 .25
B96 SP39 60k + 10k multi .40 .25
B97 SP39 100k + 10k multi .60 .45
      Nos. B95-B97 (3)   1.25 .95

Centenary of International Red Cross.

Angora Goat — SP40

Animals: 10k+5k, Steppe cattle, horiz. 50k+5k, Arabian horses, horiz. 60k+5k, Three Angora goats. 100k+5k, Montofon cattle, horiz.

1964, Oct. 4   Litho.   Perf. 13
B98 SP40 10k + 5k multi   .35 .25
B99 SP40 30k + 5k multi   .35 .25
B100 SP40 50k + 5k multi .60 .25
B101 SP40 60k + 5k multi .85 .25
B102 SP40 100k + 5k multi 1.10 .25
      Nos. B98-B102 (5)   3.25 1.25

Issued for Animal Protection Day.

Olympic Torch Bearer — SP41

Designs: 10k+5k, Running, horiz. 60k+5k, Wrestling. 100k+5k, Discus.

1964, Oct. 10   Unwmk.
B103 SP41 10k + 5k org brn,
       blk & red   .40 .25
B104 SP41 50k + 5k ol, blk &
       red   .40 .25
B105 SP41 60k + 5k bl, blk &
       red   1.00 .25
B106 SP41 100k + 5k vio, blk,
       red & sil   1.40 .40
       Nos. B103-B106 (4) 3.20 1.15

18th Olympic Games, Tokyo, Oct. 10-25.

Map of Dardanelles and Laurel SP42

Designs: 90k+10k, Soldiers and war memorial, Canakkale. 130k+10k, Turkish flag and arch, vert.

1965, Mar. 18   Litho.   Perf. 13
B107 SP42 50k + 10k vio, yel &
       gold   .25 .25
B108 SP42 90k + 10k vio bl, bl,
       yel & grn   .60 .25
B109 SP42 130k + 10k dk brn,
       red & yel   1.10 .90
       Nos. B107-B109 (3) 1.95 1.40

50th anniversary of Battle of Gallipoli.

Tobacco Plant — SP43

50k+5k, Tobacco leaves and Leander's tower, horiz. 100k+5k, Tobacco leaf.

1965, Sept. 16   Unwmk.   Perf. 13
B110 SP43 30k + 5k brn, lt brn
       & grn   .25 .25
B111 SP43 50k + 5k vio bl,
       ocher & pur   .60 .25
B112 SP43 100k + 5k blk, ol grn
       & ocher   1.00 .50
       Nos. B110-B112 (3)   1.85 1.00

Second International Tobacco Congress.

Goddess, Basalt Carving — SP44

Archaeological Museum, Ankara: 30k+5k, Eagle and rabbit, ivory carving, horiz. 60k+5k, Bronze bull. 90k+5k, Gold pitcher.

Perf. 13½x13, 13x13½
1966, June 6   Litho.
B113 SP44 30k + 5k multi   .25 .25
B114 SP44 50k + 5k multi   .55 .25
B115 SP44 60k + 5k multi   .85 .45
B116 SP44 90k + 5k multi 1.10 .60
       Nos. B113-B116 (4)   2.75 1.55

Grand Hotel Ephesus SP45

Designs: 60k+5k, Konak Square, Izmir, vert. 130k+5k, Izmir Fair Grounds.

1966, Oct. 18   Litho.   Perf. 12
B117 SP45 50k + 5k multi   .25 .25
B118 SP45 60k + 5k multi   .45 .25
B119 SP45 130k + 5k multi .95 .55
       Nos. B117-B119 (3)   1.65 1.05

33rd Congress of the Intl. Fair Assoc.

Europa Issue, 1967
Common Design Type
1967, May 2   Litho.   Perf. 13x13½
Size: 22x33mm
B120 CD10 100k + 10k multi 1.00 1.00
a. Dark blue ("Europa") omitted 2.50 1.75
B121 CD10 130k + 10k multi 2.50 1.75
       Nos. B120-B121 (2)   3.50 2.75

Cloverleaf Crossing, Map of Turkey SP46

130k+5k, Highway E5 & map of Turkey.

1967, June 30   Litho.   Perf. 13
B122 SP46 60k + 5k multi   .60 .25
B123 SP46 130k + 5k multi, vert. 1.00 .60

Inter-European Express Highway, E5.

WHO Emblem SP47

1968, Apr. 7   Litho.   Perf. 13
B124 SP47 130k + 10k lt ultra, blk
       & yel   .80 .25

WHO, 20th anniversary.

Efem Pasha, Dr. Marko Pasha and View of Istanbul — SP48

60k+10k, Omer Pasha, Dr. Abdullah Bey & wounded soldiers. 100k+10k, Ataturk & Dr. Refik Saydam in front of Red Crescent headquarters, vert.

1968, June 11   Litho.   Perf. 13
B125 SP48 50k + 10k multi   .45 .25
B126 SP48 60k + 10k multi   .60 .25
B127 SP48 100k + 10k multi .95 .45
       Nos. B125-B127 (3)   2.00 1.00

Centenary of Turkish Red Crescent Society.

NATO Emblem and Dove SP49

NATO, 20th anniv.: 130k+10k, NATO emblem and globe surrounded by 15 stars, symbols of the 15 NATO members.

1969, Apr. 4   Litho.   Perf. 13
B128 SP49 50k + 10k brt grn, blk
       & lt bl   .45 .25
B129 SP49 130k + 10k bluish blk,
       bl & gold   .75 .35

Red Cross, Crescent, Lion and Sun Emblems SP50

Design: 130k+10k, Conference emblem and Istanbul skyline.

1969, Aug. 29   Litho.   Perf. 13
B130 SP50 100k + 10k dk & lt bl
       & red   .50 .30
B131 SP50 130k + 10k red, lt bl
       & blk   .80 .45

21st Intl. Red Cross Conf., Istanbul.

Erosion Control SP51

60k+10k, Protection of flora (dead tree). 130k+10k, Protection of wildlife (bird of prey).

1970, Feb. 9   Litho.   Perf. 13
B132 SP51 50k + 10k multi   .40 .40
B133 SP51 60k + 10k multi   .60 .60
B134 SP51 130k + 10k multi 1.40 1.40
       Nos. B132-B134 (3)   2.40 2.40

1970 European Nature Conservation Year.

Globe and Fencer SP52

Design: 130k+10k, Globe, fencer and folk dancer with sword and shield.

1970, Sept. 13   Litho.   Perf. 13
B135 SP52 90k + 10k bl & blk   .50 .25
B136 SP52 130k + 10k ultra, lt bl,
            blk & org   .70 .25
International Fencing Championships.

"Children's
Protection"
SP53

Designs: 100k+15k, Hand supporting child,
vert. 110k+15k, Mother and child.

1971, June 30   Litho.   Perf. 13
Star and Crescent Emblem in Red
B137 SP53 50k + 10k lil rose &
            blk   .25 .25
B138 SP53 100k + 15k brn, rose
            & blk   .45 .25
B139 SP53 110k + 15k org brn,
            bis & blk   .55 .25
   Nos. B137-B139 (3)   1.25 .75
50th anniv. of the Child Protection Assoc.

UNICEF, 25th
Anniv. — SP54

1971, Dec. 11
B140 SP54 100k + 10k multi   .50 .25
B141 SP54 250k + 15k multi   1.10 .70

"Your Heart is your
Health" — SP55

1972, Apr. 7   Litho.   Perf. 13
B142 SP55 250k + 25k gray, blk &
            red   .80 .60
World Health Day.

Olympic
Emblems,
Runners
SP56

100k+15k, Olympic rings & motion emblem.
250k+25k, Olympic rings & symbolic track
('72).

1972, Aug. 26
B143 SP56 100k + 15k multi   .40 .25
B144 SP56 110k + 25k multi   .50 .25
B145 SP56 250k + 25k multi   .70 .45
   Nos. B143-B145 (3)   1.60 .95
20th Olympic Games, Munich, 8/26-9/11.

Emblem of
Istanbul
Technical
University
SP57

1973, Apr. 21   Litho.   Perf. 13
B146 SP57 100k + 25k multi   .50 .25
Istanbul Technical University, 200th anniv.

Dove and
"50"
SP58

1973, July 24   Litho.   Perf. 12½x13
B147 SP58 100k + 25k multi   .50 .25
Peace Treaty of Lausanne, 50th anniversary.

World
Population
Year — SP59

1974, June 15   Litho.   Perf. 13
B148 SP59 250k + 25k multi   .75 .35

Guglielmo Marconi (1874-1937), Italian
Electrical Engineer and Inventor
SP60

1974, Nov. 15   Litho.   Perf. 13½
B149 SP60 250k + 25k multi   .75 .35

Dr. Albert
Schweitzer — SP61

1975, Jan 14   Litho.   Perf. 13
B150 SP61 250k + 50k multi   .90 .45
Dr. Albert Schweitzer (1875-1965), medical
missionary and music scholar.

Africa with South-
West Africa — SP62

1975, Aug. 26   Litho.   Perf. 13x12½
B151 SP62 250k + 50k multi   .70 .35
Namibia Day (independence for South-West
Africa).

Ziya Gökalp — SP63

1976, Mar. 23   Litho.   Perf. 13
B152 SP63 200k + 25k multi   .55 .25
Ziya Gökalp (1876-1924), philosopher.

Spoonbill — SP64

Birds: 150k+25k, European roller.
200k+25k, Flamingo. 400k+25k, Hermit ibis,
horiz.

1976, Nov. 19   Litho.   Perf. 13
B153 SP64 100k + 25k multi   .65 .25
B154 SP64 150k + 25k multi   .80 .25
B155 SP64 200k + 25k multi   1.25 .35
B156 SP64 400k + 25k multi   2.25 .45
   Nos. B153-B156 (4)   4.95 1.30

Decree by
Mehmet Bey,
and Ongun
Holy
Bird — SP65

1977, May 13   Litho.   Perf. 13
B157 SP65 200k + 25k grn & blk   .50 .25
700th anniv. of Turkish as official language.

10th World
Energy
Conference
SP66

Design: 600k+50k, Conference emblem and
globe with circles.

1977, Sept. 19   Litho.   Perf. 12½
B158 SP66 100k + 25k multi   .40 .25
B159 SP66 600k + 50k multi   1.25 .50

Running
SP67

Designs: 2½ l+50k, Gymnastics. 5 l+ 50k,
Table tennis. 8 l+50k, Swimming.

1978, July 18   Litho.   Perf. 13
B160 SP67 1 l + 50k multi   .30 .25
B161 SP67 2½ l + 50k multi   .40 .30
B162 SP67 5 l + 50k multi   .80 .30
B163 SP67 8 l + 50k multi   1.50 .35
   Nos. B160-B163 (4)   3.00 1.20
GYMNASIADE '78, World School Games,
Izmir.

Ribbon
and Chain
SP68

Design: 5 l+50k, Ribbon and flower, vert.

Perf. 12½x13, 13x12½
1978, Sept. 3   Litho.
B164 SP68 2½ l + 50k multi   .75 .25
B165 SP68 5 l + 50k multi   1.00 .25
European Declaration of Human Rights,
25th anniversary.

Children, Head of
Ataturk — SP69

IYC Emblem and: 5 l+50k, Children with
globe as balloon. 8 l+50k, Kneeling person
and child, globe.

1979, Apr. 23   Litho.   Perf. 13x13½
B166 SP69 2½ l + 50k multi   .35 .25
B167 SP69 5 l + 50k multi   .55 .25
B168 SP69 8 l + 50k multi   .85 .35
   Nos. B166-B168 (3)   1.75 .85
International Year of the Child.

Black
Francolin — SP70

No. B170, Great bustard. No. B171, Crane.
No. B172, Gazelle. No. B173, Mouflon
muffelwild.

1979, Dec. 3   Litho.   Perf. 13x13½
B169 SP70 5 l + 1 l multi   .90 .25
B170 SP70 5 l + 1 l multi   .90 .25
B171 SP70 5 l + 1 l multi   .90 .25
B172 SP70 5 l + 1 l multi   .90 .25
B173 SP70 5 l + 1 l multi   .90 .25
   a. Strip of 5, #B169-B173   6.00 6.00
European Wildlife Conservation Year. No.
B173a has continuous design.

Flowers, Trees and
Sun — SP71

Environment Protection: 7½ l+ 1 l Sun,
water. 15 l+1 l, Industrial pollution, globe.
20 l+1 l, Flower in oil puddle.

1980, June 4   Litho.   Perf. 13
B174 SP71 2½ l + 1 l multi   .25 .25
B175 SP71 7½ l + 1 l multi   .25 .25
B176 SP71 15 l + 1 l multi   .45 .25
B177 SP71 20 l + 1 l multi   .50 .35
   Nos. B174-B177 (4)   1.45 1.10

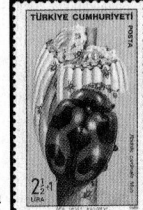

Rodolia
Cardinalis — SP72

Useful Insects: 7½ l+1 l, Bracon hebetor; 15
l+1 l, Calosoma sycophanta; 20 l+1 l, Der-
aeocoris rutilus.

1980, Dec. 3   Litho.   Perf. 13
B178 SP72 2½ l + 1 l multi   .25 .25
B179 SP72 7½ l + 1 l multi   .45 .25
B180 SP72 15 l + 1 l multi   .80 .25
B181 SP72 20 l + 1 l multi   1.00 .25
   Nos. B178-B181 (4)   2.50 1.00

Intl. Year of the
Disabled — SP73

1981, Mar. 25   **Litho.**   ***Perf. 13***
B182 SP73 10 l + 2 ½ l multi   .30 .25
B183 SP73 20 l + 2 ½ l multi   .45 .25

Insects
SP74

Useful Insects: No. B184, Cicindela
campestris. No. B185, Syrphus vitripennis.
No. B186, Ascalaphus macaronius. No. B187,
Empusa fasciata.

1981, Dec. 16   **Litho.**   ***Perf. 13***
B184 SP74 10 l + 2 ½ l multi   .50 .25
B185 SP74 20 l + 2 ½ l multi   .85 .25
B186 SP74 30 l + 2 ½ l multi   1.40 .45
B187 SP74 35 l + 2 ½ l multi   1.75 .60
   Nos. B184-B187 (4)   4.50 1.55

See Nos. B190-B194, B196-B200.

TB Bacillus
Centenary — SP75

Portraits: #B188, Dr. Tevfik Saglam (1882-
1963). #B189, Robert Koch.

1982, Mar. 24   ***Perf. 13x12½***
B188 SP75 10 l + 2 ½ l multi   .50 .25
B189 SP75 30 l + 2 ½ l multi   1.25 .25

Insect Type of 1981

Useful Insects: 10 l+2½ l, Eurydema
spectabile. 15 l+2½ l, Dacus oleae. 20 l+2½ l,
Klapperichicen viridissima. 30 l+2½ l, Lepti-
notarsa decemlineata. 35 l+2½ l, Rhynchites
auratus.

1982, Aug. 18   **Litho.**   ***Perf. 13***
B190 SP74 10 l + 2 ½ l multi   .60 .25
B191 SP74 15 l + 2 ½ l multi   .90 .25
B192 SP74 20 l + 2 ½ l multi   .90 .25
B193 SP74 30 l + 2 ½ l multi   1.00 .25
B194 SP74 35 l + 2 ½ l multi   1.10 .25
   Nos. B190-B194 (5)   4.50 1.25

Richard Wagner (1813-1883),
Composer — SP76

1983, Feb. 13
B195 SP76 30 l + 5 l multi   1.10 1.00

Insect Type of 1981

Harmful Insects: 15 l+5 l, Eurygaster Intergr-
riceps Put. 25 l+5 l, Phyllobius nigrofasciatus
Pes. 35 l+5 l, Cercopis intermedia Kbm.
50 l+10 l, Graphosoma lineatum (L). 75 l+10 l,
Capnodis miliaris (King).

1983, Sept. 14   **Litho.**   ***Perf. 13***
B196 SP74 15 l + 5 l multi   .50 .25
B197 SP74 25 l + 5 l multi   .65 .25
B198 SP74 35 l + 5 l multi   .85 .25
B199 SP74 50 l + 10 l multi   1.25 .25
B200 SP74 75 l + 10 l multi   1.75 .40
   Nos. B196-B200 (5)   5.00 1.40

Topkapi Museum
Artifacts — SP77

1984, May 30   **Litho.**   ***Perf. 13***
B201 SP77   20 l + 5 l Kaftan,
     16th cent.   .60 .25
B202 SP77   70 l + 15 l Ewer   1.90 .75
B203 SP77   90 l + 20 l Swords   3.00 .85
B204 SP77 100 l + 25 l Lock, key   3.50 1.00
   Nos. B201-B204 (4)   9.00 2.85

Surtax was for museum. See Nos. B208-
B211, B213-B216, B218-B221.

1984 Summer
Olympics — SP78

Designs: 20 l+5 l, Banners, horiz. 70 l+15 l,
Medalist. 100 l+20 l, Running, horiz.

1984, July 28
B205 SP78   20 l + 5 l multi   1.10 .70
B206 SP78   70 l + 15 l multi   1.25 1.10
B207 SP78 100 l + 20 l multi   2.10 1.40
   Nos. B205-B207 (3)   4.45 3.20

Artifacts Type of 1984

Ceramicware: 10 l+5 l, Iznik plate.
20 l+10 l, Iznik boza pitcher and mug, 16th
cent. 100 l+15 l, Du Paquier ewer and basin,
1730. 120 l+20 l, Ching dynasty plate, 1522-
1566.

1985, May 30   **Litho.**   ***Perf. 13***
B208 SP77   10 l + 5 l multi   .65 .25
B209 SP77   20 l + 10 l multi   1.10 .50
B210 SP77 100 l + 15 l multi   2.25 1.40
B211 SP77 120 l + 20 l multi   3.25 1.75
   Nos. B208-B211 (4)   7.25 3.90

Rabies Vaccine,
Cent. — SP79

1985, July 16   ***Perf. 13x13½***
B212 SP79 100 l + 15 l Pasteur   1.75 1.10

Artifacts Type of 1984

20 l+5 l, Metal and ceramic incense burner,
c. 17th cent. 100 l+10 l, Jade lidded mug decorated with precious gems, 16th cent.
120 l+15 l, Dagger designed by Mahmut I,
1714. 200 l+30 l, Willow buckler, defensive
shield, undated.

1986, May 30   **Litho.**   ***Perf. 13x12½***
B213 SP77   20 l + 5 l multi   .90 .45
B214 SP77 100 l + 10 l multi   1.75 .70
B215 SP77 120 l + 15 l multi   2.00 .90
B216 SP77 200 l + 30 l multi   4.00 1.40
   Nos. B213-B216 (4)   8.65 3.45

General
Assembly
of NATO
SP80

1986, Nov. 13   **Litho.**   ***Perf. 13½x13***
B217 SP80 100 l + 20 l multi   2.75 .85

Artifacts Type of 1984

Designs: 20 l+5 l, Crystal and gold ewer,
16th cent., vert. 50 l+10 l, Emerald and gold
pendant, 17th cent. 200 l+15 l, Sherbet jug,
19th cent., vert. 250 l+30 l, Crystal and gold
pen box, 16th cent.

1987, May 30   **Litho.**   ***Perf. 13***
B218 SP77   20 l + 5 l multi   .75 .25
B219 SP77   50 l + 10 l multi   1.10 .45
B220 SP77 200 l + 15 l multi   1.40 1.10
B221 SP77 250 l + 30 l multi   2.25 1.40
   Nos. B218-B221 (4)   5.50 3.20

15th Intl. Chemotherapy Congress,
Istanbul — SP81

1987, July 19   **Litho.**   ***Perf. 13***
B222 SP81 200 l + 25 l multi   1.75 .25

Intl. Road
Transport
Union
(IRU) 21st
World
Congress
SP82

1988, June 13   **Litho.**   ***Perf. 12½x13***
B223 SP82 200 l + 25 l multi   .90 .25

European Environmental Campaign
Balancing Nature and
Development — SP83

Designs: 100 l+25 l, Hands, desert reclamation. 400 l+50 l, Eye, road, planted field.

1988, Oct. 19   **Litho.**   ***Perf. 12½x13***
B224 SP83 100 l + 25 l multi   .50 .25
B225 SP83 400 l + 50 l multi   1.75 .40

Silkworm
Industry
SP84

Perf. 13½x13
B226 SP84 150 l + 50 l Silkworm   .50 .25
B227 SP84 600 l + 100 l Cocoon,
     strands   1.75 .40

1989, Apr. 15   **Litho.**   **Wmk. 394**

Council of
Europe,
40th
Anniv.
SP85

1989, May 5   **Litho.**   ***Perf. 13***
B228 SP85 600 l + 100 l multi   1.75 .45

European
Tourism
Year
SP86

1990, Apr. 26   **Wmk. 394**
B229 SP86   300 l + 50 l Antalya   .50 .25
B230 SP86 1000 l + 100 l Istanbul   1.25 .40

Fight Against
Addictions — SP87

Fight Against: No. B231, Smoking. No.
B232, Drugs, horiz.

1990, June 26   **Litho.**   ***Perf. 13***
B231 SP87   300 l +50 l multi   .60 .25
B232 SP87 1000 l +100 l multi   1.60 .75

Yunus Emre (died c.1321), Poet
     SP88   SP89

1991, June 26   **Litho.**   ***Perf. 13***
B233 SP88   500 l +100 l multi   .65 .35
B234 SP89 1500 l +100 l multi   1.60 .75

Wolfgang Amadeus Mozart (1756-
1791), Composer — SP90

1991, July 24
B235 SP90 1500 l +100 l multi   1.75 .90

Turkish
Supreme
Court, 30th
Anniv.
SP91

1992, Apr. 25
B236 SP91 500 l + 100 l multi   .50 .25

Scouts
Planting
Tree
SP92

No. B238 Mountain climber on rope, vert.

1992, Dec. 18
B237 SP92 1000 l +200 l multi   1.00 .60
B238 SP92 3000 l +200 l multi   1.75 1.00

Travertine,
Pamukkale — SP93

Different views of rock formations.

1993, June 6
B239 SP93 1000 l +200 l multi   .75 .25
B240 SP93 3000 l +500 l multi   1.50 .55

Intl. Day
for Natural
Disaster
Reduction
SP94

1993, Oct. 13   *Perf. 12½x13*
B241 SP94 3000 l + 500 l multi   1.40   .75

Intl. Olympic
Committee,
Cent. — SP95

1994, Aug. 17   *Perf. 13*
B242 SP95 12,500 l +500 l multi   1.75 1.10

Trees
SP96

Designs: No. B243, Platanus orientalis. No.
B244, Cupressus sempervirens, vert.

1994, Nov. 30
B243 SP96 7500 l +500 l multi   1.25   .95
B244 SP96 12,500 l +500 l multi   2.40 1.75

TBMM
(Great
Natl.
Assembly),
75th Anniv.
SP97

1995, Apr. 23
B245 SP97 3500 l +500 l multi   .45   .25

The Epic
of Manas
SP98

Designs: No. B246, Lancers charging. No.
B247, Abay Kunanbay (1845-1904), poet, vert.

1995, June 28
B246 SP98 3500 l +500 l multi   .45   .25
B247 SP98 3500 l +500 l multi   .45   .25

For the People of Bosnia-
Herzegovina — SP99

1996, Feb. 28
B248 SP99 10,000 l +2500 l multi .75   .75

Ankara
University,
50th Anniv.
SP100

Unwmk.
1996, Nov. 20   Litho.   *Perf. 13*
B249 15,000 l +2500 l multi   .65   .30

Fight
Against
Cancer,
50th Anniv.
SP101

1997, Feb. 18   Litho.   *Perf. 12½x13*
B250 SP101 25,000 l +5000 l
multi   .65   .30

Pakistan
Independence, 50th
Anniv. — SP102

Mohammed Ali Jinnah (1876-1948).

1997, Mar. 23   Litho.   *Perf. 13*
B251 SP102 25,000 l +5000 l
multi   .60   .30

Universal
Declaration
of Human
Rights
SP103

Stylized designs: 75,000 l, Puzzle piece with
outlines of people's faces. 175,000 l, Heart-
shaped kite with people as tail.

1998, Dec. 10   Litho.   *Perf. 13½*
B252 SP103 75,000 l +25,000 l   1.00   .50
B253 SP103 175,000 l +25,000 l   2.00 1.00

GATA
(Gulhane
Military
Medical
Academy),
Cent.
SP104

1998, Dec. 30   Litho.   *Perf. 13*
B254 SP104 75,000 l +10,000 l
multi   1.40   .70

Kemal Ataturk's
Entry Into War
College,
Cent. — SP105

1999, Mar. 13   Litho.   *Perf. 13*
B255 SP105 75,000 l +5,000 l
multi   .90   .25

Council of
Europe,
50th Anniv.
SP106

1999, Apr. 30   Litho.   *Perf. 13¼*
B256 SP106 175,000 l +10,000 l   2.75 1.40

Church, Mosque and
Synagogue — SP107

Dancers
SP108

2000, May 25   Litho.   *Perf. 13¼*
B257 SP107 275,000 l +10,000 l   2.00 2.00
B258 SP108 300,000 l +10,000 l   2.00 2.00

Tombs and Mausoleums — SP109

150,000 l+25,000 l, Usta Sagirt Kumbeti
Ahlat, vert. 200,000 l+25,000 l, Kocbasli
Mezar Tasi Tunceli. 275,000 l+25,000 l, Isabey
Turbesi, Uskup, vert. 300,000 l+25,000 l, Yusuf
bin Kuseyr Turbesi, Nahcivan, vert.

2000
B259-B262 SP109 Set of 4   7.25 7.25

Coins
SP110

Various coins with background colors of: No.
B263, 300,000 l + 25,000 l, Red. No. B264,
300,000 l + 25,000 l, Blue green. 450,000 l +
25,000 l, Dark carmine. 500,000 l + 25,000 l,
Blue violet.

2001, Oct. 1   Litho.   *Perf. 13*
B263-B266 SP110 Set of 4   6.25 6.25

Caravansaries — SP111

Designs: 300,000 l + 25,000 l, Ashab i Kehf
Han, Afsin. 500,000 l + 25,000 l, Horozlu Han,
Konya.

2001, Nov. 19   Litho.   *Perf. 13*
B267-B268 SP111 Set of 2   4.00 4.00

Turkey's
Admission
to NATO,
50th Anniv.
SP112

2002, Feb. 18
B269 SP112 400,000 l + 25,000 l 2.25 2.25

Trains
SP113

Designs: 500,000 l + 25,000 l, Steam locomotive. 700,000 l + 25,000 l, Electric
locomotive.

2002, Sept. 16   Litho.   *Perf. 13¼x13*
B270-B271 SP113 Set of 2   5.50 5.50

Trains
SP114

Designs: 600,000 l+50,000 l, Trolley.
800,000 l+50,000 l, Subway.

2003, Sept. 9   Litho.   *Perf. 13¼x13*
B272-B273 SP114 Set of 2   3.50 3.50

Ibrahim Hakki
Erzurumlu (1703-
72),
Writer — SP115

2003, Dec. 24   Litho.   *Perf. 13x13¼*
B274 SP115 600,000 l +50,000 l
multi   1.40 1.40

Lighthouses
SP116

Designs: 600,000 l + 50,000 l, Kerempe
Lighthouse, Kastamonu. 700,000 l + 50,000 l,
Taslikburnu Lighthouse, Antalya.

2004, Apr. 5
B275-B276 SP116 Set of 2   4.50 4.50

Scouting — SP117

Designs: 600,000 l + 50,000 l, Girl Scout in
foreground. 700,000 l + 50,000 l, Boy Scout in
foreground.

2004, Sept. 30
B277-B278 SP117 Set of 2   3.50 3.50

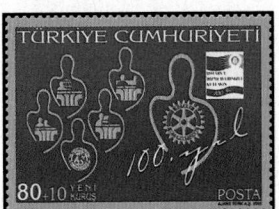

Rotary International, Cent. — SP118

2005, Feb. 23   Litho.   *Perf. 13x13¼*
B279 SP118 80k +10k multi   1.50 1.50

Intl. Year
of Physics
SP119

2005, Sept. 13   Litho.   *Perf. 13¼x13¼*
B280 SP119 70k +10k multi   1.25 1.25

World Forests Day SP120

2006, Mar. 21 Litho. Perf. 13¼x13
B281 SP120 60k +10k multi 1.10 1.10

Mehmet Akif Ersoy (1873-1936), Poet — SP121

Ersoy at: 60k+10k, Left. 70k+10k, Right.

2006, Oct. 13 Litho. Perf. 13¼x13
B282-B283 SP121 Set of 2 2.10 2.10

Coast Guard Command, 25th Anniv. — SP122

2007, July 13 Litho. Perf. 13x13¼
B284 SP122 60k + 10k multi 1.10 1.10

Marbled Art — SP123

Designs: 60k+10k, White flowers. 70k+10k, Red tulips.

2007, Dec. 6 Perf. 13¼x13
B285-B286 SP123 Set of 2 2.60 2.60

Kasgarli Mahmut (1008-1105), Lexicographer — SP124

Kasgarli: 65k+10k, On horseback. 80k+10k, Holding book.

2008, Apr. 10 Litho. Perf. 13¼x13
B287-B288 SP124 Set of 2 2.60 2.60

Railway Terminals in Istanbul — SP125

Designs: 65k+10k, Haydarpasa Terminal. 80k+10k, Sirkeci Terminal.

2008, Oct. 15 Litho. Perf. 13x13¼
B289-B290 SP125 Set of 2 2.25 2.25

Ethics Day SP126

2009, May 25 Perf. 13¼x13
B291 SP126 65k +10k multi 1.00 1.00

Katip Celebi (1609-57), Historian SP127

Celebi, book and: 75k+10k, Quill pen. 90k+10k, Ships.

2009, July 16
B292-B293 SP127 Set of 2 2.60 2.60

Locomotives — SP128

Various locomotives: 80k+10k, 110k+10k.

2010, Aug. 4 Perf. 12¾x13
B294-B295 SP128 Set of 2 3.00 3.00

Rugs SP129

Various rugs: 80k+10k, 110k+10k.

2010, Nov. 17
B296-B297 SP129 Set of 2 3.00 3.00

Hasankeyf — SP130

2011, Sept. 21 Perf. 13x13¼
B298 SP130 130k +10k multi 1.60 1.60

State Personnel Department, 50th Anniv. SP131

2011, Dec. 17 Perf. 13¼x13
B299 SP131 100k +10k multi 1.25 1.25

Souvenir Sheet

Turkish Cuisine — SP132

No. B300: a, 50k+10k, Tursu Kavurma (roasted pickles). b, 1 l+10k, Kara Lahana Dolmasi (stuffed collard greens). c, 1 l+10k, Mihlama (corn meal and cheese fondue). d, 2 l+10k, Hamsi Tava (fried anchovies).

2012, Aug. 16 Perf. 14¼
B300 SP132 Sheet of 4, #a-d + label 5.50 5.50

Karsiyaka Sporting Club, Cent. SP133

Designs: 50k+10k, Bowling, motorcycling, billiards. 1 l+10k, Volleyball, swimming, tennis. 2 l+10k, Basketball, sailing, soccer.

2012, Nov. 1 Litho. Perf. 13¼x13½
B301-B303 SP133 Set of 3 4.25 4.25

Souvenir Sheet

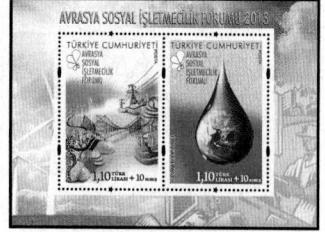

Eurasian Social Business Forum, Erzincan — SP134

No. B304: a, Bridge, roads, wind generators, buildings, power lines. b, Earth in droplet.

Perf. 13¾ Syncopated
2013, May 23 Litho.
B304 SP134 1.10 l +10k Sheet of 2, #a-b 2.60 2.60

Beypazari District, 130th Anniv. — SP135

Designs: No. B305, 1.10 l+10k, Plates of food, carrots, bottle and decorative butterflies. No. B306, 1.10 l+10k, House, vert.

Perf. 13½x13¼, 13¼x13½
2013, May 29 Litho.
B305-B306 SP135 Set of 2 2.60 2.60

Historic Bridges — SP136

Designs: No. B307, 1.10 l +10k, Kesik Bridge, Sivas. No. B308, 1.10 l + 10k, Clandiras Bridge, Usak.

2014, Apr. 10 Litho. Perf. 13½x13¼
B307-B308 SP136 Set of 2 2.25 2.25

Souvenir Sheet

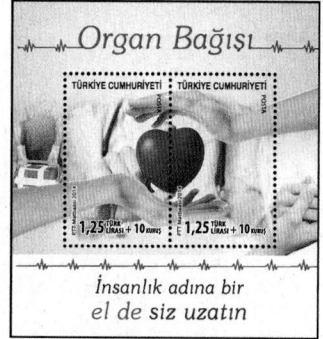

Organ Donation — SP137

Hands and: a, Heart at right. b, Heart at left.

2014, Nov. 3 Litho. Perf. 14x13¾
B309 SP137 1.25 l +10k Sheet of 2, #a-b 2.40 2.40

AIR POST STAMPS

Catalogue values for unused stamps in this section are for Never Hinged items.

Nos. 692, 695, 698, 700 Overprinted or Surcharged in Brown or Blue

1934, July 15 Unwmk. *Perf. 12*
C1 A74 7½k (Br) .75 .25
C2 A72 12½k on 15k (Br) .75 .25
C3 A74 20k on 25k (Br) .75 .25
C4 A74 25k (Bl) 1.00 .40
C5 A74 40k (Br) 2.25 1.25
Nos. C1-C5 (5) 5.50 2.40

Regular Stamps of 1930 Surcharged in Brown

1937
C6 A74 4½k on 7½k red brn 5.00 1.00
C7 A72 9k on 15k dp org 40.00 20.00
C8 A74 35k on 40k red vio 10.00 4.25
Nos. C6-C8 (3) 55.00 25.25

Nos. 698, 703-704 Surcharged in Black

1941, Dec. 18
C9 A74 4½k on 25k 2.00 1.50
C10 A75 9k on 200k 9.75 8.25
C11 A75 35k on 500k 6.25 5.25
Nos. C9-C11 (3) 18.00 15.00

Plane over Izmir AP1

Planes over: 5k, 40k, Izmir. 20k, 50k, Ankara. 30k, 1 l, Istanbul.

1949, Jan. 1 Photo. *Perf. 11½*
C12 AP1 5k gray & vio .25 .25
C13 AP1 20k bl gray & brn .25 .25
C14 AP1 30k bl gray & ol brn 1.00 .25
C15 AP1 40k bl & dp ultra 1.00 1.00
C16 AP1 50k gray vio & red brn 1.00 .25
C17 AP1 1 l gray bl & dk grn 3.00 .65
Nos. C12-C17 (6) 6.50 2.65

For overprints see Nos. C19-C21.

Plane Over Rumeli Hisari Fortress AP2

1950, May 19 Unwmk.
C18 AP2 2½ l gray bl & dk grn 22.50 14.00

Nos. C12, C14 and C16 Overprinted in Red

1951, Apr. 9 *Perf. 11½*
C19 AP1 5k gray & vio 1.50 .50
C20 AP1 30k bl gray & ol brn 2.00 .60
C21 AP1 50k gray vio & red brn 2.50 .70
Nos. C19-C21 (3) 6.00 1.80

Industrial Congress, Ankara, Apr. 9.

Yesilkoy Airport and Plane AP3

Designs: 20k, 45k, Yesilkoy Airport and plane in flight. 35k, 55k, Ankara Airport and plane. 40k, as No. C22.

1954, Nov. 1 *Perf. 14*
C22 AP3 5k red brn & bl 1.00 .25
C23 AP3 20k brn org & bl .65 .25
C24 AP3 35k dk grn & bl .65 .25
C25 AP3 40k dp car & bl .65 .25
C26 AP3 45k violet & bl 1.50 .25
C27 AP3 55k black & bl 4.00 .50
Nos. C22-C27 (6) 8.45 1.75

Symbol of Izmir Fair — AP4

1956, Aug. 20 Litho. *Perf. 10½*
C28 AP4 25k reddish brown .35 .30

25th Intl. Fair at Izmir, Aug. 20-Sept. 20.

Heuss Type of Regular Issue, 1957

1957, May 5
C29 A264 40k sal pink & magenta .35 .30

Zahir Shah Type of Regular Issue, 1957

1957, Sept. 1
C30 A269 25k grn & lt grn .25 .25

Hawk — AP5

Crane — AP6

Birds: 40k, 125k, Swallows. 65k, Cranes. 85k, 195k, Gulls. 245k, Hawk.

1959, Aug. 13 Litho. *Perf. 10½*
C31 AP5 40k bright lilac .50 .25
C32 AP5 65k blue green 3.00 .40
C33 AP5 85k bright blue 1.00 .40
C34 AP5 105k yel & sepia .75 .40
C35 AP6 125k brt violet 1.00 .40
C36 AP6 155k yel green 1.25 .40
C37 AP6 195k violet blue 1.50 .40
C38 AP6 245k brn & brn org 3.50 1.00
Nos. C31-C38 (8) 12.50 3.65

De Havilland Rapide Biplane AP7

Designs: 60k, Fokker Friendship transport plane. 130k, DC9-30. 220k, DC-3. 270k, Viscount 794.

1967, July 13 Litho. *Perf. 13½x13*
C39 AP7 10k pink & blk .40 .25
C40 AP7 60k lt grn, red & blk .65 .25
C41 AP7 130k bl, blk & red .90 .25
C42 AP7 220k lt brn, blk & red 1.40 .35
C43 AP7 270k org, blk & red 2.25 .45
Nos. C39-C43 (5) 5.60 1.55

For surcharge see No. 2179A.

Kestrel — AP8

Birds: 60k, Golden eagle. 130k, Falcon. 220k, Sparrow hawk. 270k, Buzzard.

1967, Oct. 10 Litho. *Perf. 13*
C44 AP8 10k brown & salmon 1.10 .25
C45 AP8 60k brown & yellow .85 .25
C46 AP8 130k brown & lt bl 2.10 .25
C47 AP8 220k brown & lt grn 3.25 .45
C48 AP8 270k org brn & gray 4.75 .65
Nos. C44-C48 (5) 12.05 1.85

F-104 Jet Plane — AP9

Turkish Air Force Emblem and Jets AP10

Designs: 200k, Victory monument, Afyon, and Jets. 325k, F-104 jets and pilot. 400k, Bleriot XI plane with Turkish flag. 475k, Flight of Hezarfen Ahmet Celebi from Galata Tower to Usküdar.

1971, June 1 Litho. *Perf. 13*
C49 AP9 110k multi .90 .25
C50 AP9 200k multi 2.00 .25
C51 AP10 250k multi 2.00 .45
C52 AP9 325k multi 3.10 .45
C53 AP10 400k multi 3.50 .55
C54 AP10 475k multi 4.50 .65
Nos. C49-C54 (6) 16.00 2.60

The gold ink on No. C51 is applied by a thermographic process which gives a raised and shiny effect.

F-28 Plane — AP11

1973, Dec. 11 Litho. *Perf. 13*
C55 AP11 110k shown .65 .25
C56 AP11 250k DC-10 1.10 .30

POSTAGE DUE STAMPS

Same Types as Regular Issues of Corresponding Dates

1863 Unwmk. *Imperf.*

Blue Band

J1 A1 20pa blk, *red brn* 100.00 32.50
 a. Tête bêche pair 225.00 225.00
 b. Without band 50.00
 c. Red band 90.00 45.00
J2 A2 1pi blk, *red brn* 150.00 22.50
 a. Tête bêche pair 225.00 225.00
 b. Without band 50.00
J3 A3 2pi blk, *red brn* 500.00 70.00
 a. Tête bêche pair 650.00 450.00
J4 A4 5pi blk, *red brn* 300.00 80.00
 a. Tête bêche pair 425.00 425.00
 b. Without band 100.00
 c. Red band 150.00
Nos. J1-J4 (4) 1,050. 205.00

1865 *Perf. 12½*
J6 A5 20pa brown 4.00 5.00
J7 A5 1pi brown 4.00 5.00
 b. Half used as 20pa on cover
 c. Printed on both sides 25.00
J8 A5 2pi brown 12.50 25.00
 a. Half used as 1pi on cover
J9 A5 5pi brown 5.00 30.00
 a. Half used as 2½pi on cover
J10 A5 25pi brown 45.00 100.00
Nos. J6-J10 (5) 70.50 165.00

Exist imperf. Values, $60 to $100 each. The 10pa brown is an essay. Value about $2,750.

1867
J11 A5 20pa bister brn 9.00 100.00
J12 A5 1pi bister brn 9.00
 a. With surcharge of 5pi 13.50
 b. Imperf., pair 65.00
J13 A5 2pi fawn 75.00
J14 A5 5pi fawn 17.50
J15 A5 25pi bister brn *21,250.*
Nos. J11-J14 (4) 110.50

Nos. J12-J15 were not placed in use.

1869 *Perf. 13½*

With Yellow-Brown Border

J16 A5 20pa bister brn 10.00 10.00
 a. Without surcharge
J17 A5 1pi bister brn 550.00 20.00
 a. Without surcharge
J18 A5 2pi bister brn 800.00 20.00
J19 A5 5pi bister brn 2.25 12.50
 b. Without border
 c. Printed on both sides 15.00
J20 A5 25pi bister brn — —
Nos. J16-J19 (4) 1,362. 62.50

With Brown Border

Color of border ranges from brown to reddish brown and black brown.

J21 A5 20pa bister brn 125.00 20.00
 a. Inverted surcharge
 b. Without surcharge
J22 A5 1pi bister brn 550.00 12.50
 a. Without surcharge
J23 A5 2pi bister brn 450.00 12.50
 b. Inverted surcharge
J24 A5 5pi bister brn 2.50 15.00
 b. Without surcharge
J25 A5 25pi bister brn 37.50 100.00
Nos. J21-J25 (5) 1,165. 160.00

Pin-perf., Perf. 5 to 11½ and Compound

1871 With Brick Red Border

J26 A5 20pa bister brn 1,250. 50.00
J27 A5 1pi bister brn *5,000.*
J28 A5 2pi bister brn 110.00 140.00
J29 A5 5pi bister brn 7.50 25.00

With Black Brown Border

J31 A5 20pa bister brn 150.00 3.50
 a. Half used as 10pa on cover
 b. Imperf., pair 16.50
 c. Printed on both sides 40.00 40.00
J32 A5 1pi bister brn 225.00 2.50
 a. Half used as 20pa on cover
 c. Inverted surcharge 50.00 35.00
 d. Printed on both sides
J33 A5 2pi bister brn 6.00 9.00
 a. Half used as 1pi on cover
 c. Imperf., pair 16.50
J34 A5 5pi bister brn 2.50 20.00
 a. Half used as 2½pi on cover
 c. Printed on both sides
J35 A5 25pi bister brn 40.00 125.00
 a. Inverted surcharge
Nos. J31-J35 (5) 423.50 *160.00*

1888 *Perf. 11½ and 13½*
J36 A7 20pa black 4.00 12.50
J37 A7 1pi black 4.00 12.50
J38 A7 2pi black 4.00 15.00
 b. Diagonal half used as 1pi
Nos. J36-J38 (3) 12.00 40.00

Imperf

J36a A7 20pa 11.00
J37a A7 1pi 11.00
J38a A7 2pi 11.00

1892 *Perf. 13½*
J39 A11 20pa black 7.00 12.50
J40 A12 1pi black 25.00 12.50
 a. Printed on both sides
J41 A13 2pi black 17.50 12.50
Nos. J39-J41 (3) 49.50 *37.50*

1901
J42 A11 20pa black, *deep rose* 2.50 20.00

1901
J43 A17 10pa black, *deep rose* 4.00 6.00
J44 A17 20pa black, *deep rose* 3.75 8.75
J45 A17 1pi black, *deep rose* 3.00 10.00
J46 A17 2pi black, *deep rose* 2.50 15.00
Nos. J43-J46 (4) 13.25 39.75

1905 *Perf. 12*
J47 A18 1pi black, *deep rose* 3.00 10.00
J48 A18 2pi black, *deep rose* 4.50 20.00

1908, *Perf. 12, 13½ and Compound*
J49 A19 1pi black, *deep rose* 80.00 7.50
J50 A19 2pi black, *deep rose* 12.50 45.00

1909

J51	A21 1pi black, *deep rose*	15.00	*50.00*
J52	A21 2pi black, *deep rose*	*150.00*	*175.00*
a.	Imperf.	65.00	

1913 ***Perf. 12***

J53	A22 2pa black, *deep rose*	1.00	.50
J54	A22 5pa black, *deep rose*	1.00	.50
J55	A22 10pa black, *deep rose*	1.00	.50
J56	A22 20pa black, *deep rose*	1.00	.50
J57	A22 1pi black, *deep rose*	4.50	10.00
J58	A22 2pi black, *deep rose*	8.00	17.50
	Nos. J53-J58 (6)	16.50	29.50

Adrianople Issue

Nos. 251-253 Surcharged in Black, Blue or Red

1913

J59	A23 2pa on 10pa green (Bk)	3.25	.35
J60	A23 5pa on 20pa red (Bl)	3.25	.35
J61	A23 10pa on 40pa blue (R)	10.00	.80
J62	A23 20pa on 40pa blue (Bk)	32.50	11.00
	Nos. J59-J62 (4)	49.00	12.50

For surcharges see Nos. J67-J70, J83-J86.

D1

D2

D3

D4

1914 **Engr.**

J63	D1 5pa claret	1.25	10.00
J64	D2 20pa red	1.25	10.00
J65	D3 1pi dark blue	1.25	10.00
J66	D4 2pi slate	1.25	10.00
	Nos. J63-J66 (4)	5.00	40.00

For surcharges and overprints see Nos. J87-J91.

Nos. J59 to J62 Surcharged in Red or Black

1916

J67	A23 10pa on 2pa on 10pa (R)	55.00	55.00
J68	A23 20pa on 5pa on 20pa	55.00	55.00
J69	A23 40pa on 10pa on 40pa	55.00	55.00
J70	A23 40pa on 20pa on 40pa (R)	55.00	55.00
	Nos. J67-J70 (4)	220.00	220.00

Preceding Issues Overprinted in Red, Black or Blue

1917 **On Stamps of 1865**

J71	A5 20pa red brn (Bl)	45.00	67.50
J72	A5 1pi red brn (Bl)	45.00	67.50
J73	A5 2pi bis brn (Bl)	45.00	67.50
J74	A5 5pi bis brn (Bl)	45.00	67.50
J75	A5 25pi dk brn (Bl)	45.00	67.50
	Nos. J71-J75 (5)	225.00	337.50

On Stamp of 1869

Red Brown Border

J76	A5 5pi bis brn (R)	45.00	67.50

On Stamp of 1871

Black Brown Border

J77	A5 5pi bis brn	75.00	50.00

On Stamps of 1888

J78	A7 1pi black (R)	45.00	67.50
J79	A7 2pi black (R)	45.00	67.50

On Stamps of 1892

J80	A11 20pa black (R)	2.50	2.50
J81	A12 1pi black (R)	2.50	2.50
J82	A13 2pi black (R)	2.50	2.50
	Nos. J80-J82 (3)	7.50	7.50

Adrianople Issue

On Nos. J59 to J62 with Addition of New Value

J83	A23 10pa on 2pa on 10pa (R)	1.25	1.00
J84	A23 20pa on 5pa on 20pa (Bk)	1.50	1.00
J85	A23 40pa on 10pa on 40pa (Bk)	2.00	1.50
a.	"40pa" double		
J86	A23 40pa on 20pa on 40pa (R)	3.75	3.50
	Nos. J83-J86 (4)	8.50	7.00

Nos. J71-J86 were used as regular postage stamps.

Armistice Issue

No. J65 Overprinted

1919, Nov. 30

J87	D3 1pi dark blue	125.00	150.00

Accession to the Throne Issue

Postage Due Stamps of 1914 Overprinted in Turkish "Accession to the Throne of His Majesty. 3rd July, 1334-1918"

1919

J88	D1 10pa on 5pa claret	25.00	37.50
J89	D2 20pa red	25.00	37.50
J90	D3 1pi dark blue	25.00	37.50
J91	D4 2pi slate	25.00	37.50
	Nos. J88-J91 (4)	100.00	150.00

Railroad Bridge over Kizil Irmak — D5

1926 **Engr.**

J92	D5 20pa ocher	1.25	2.50
J93	D5 1g red	2.00	5.00
J94	D5 2g blue green	3.00	5.00
J95	D5 3g lilac brown	3.50	12.50
J96	D5 5g lilac	6.00	20.00
	Nos. J92-J96 (5)	15.75	45.00
	Set, never hinged	30.00	

Catalogue values for unused stamps in this section, from this point to the end of the section, are for Never Hinged items.

Kemal Atatürk — D6

1936 **Litho.** ***Perf. 11½***

J97	D6 20pa brown	.25	.25
J98	D6 2k light blue	.25	.25
J99	D6 3k bright violet	.25	.25
J100	D6 5k Prussian blue	.25	.25
J101	D6 12k bright rose	.35	.25
	Nos. J97-J101 (5)	1.35	1.25

For surcharges see Nos. 1461-1465.

LOCAL ISSUES

Type I

Type II

Type III

Type IV

Type V

Type VI

During 1873//1882 Turkish stamps with the above overprints were used for local postage in Constantinople (types 1-5) and Mount Athos (type 6).

MILITARY STAMPS

For the Army in Thessaly

Tughra and Bridge at Larissa — M1

1898, Apr. 21 **Unwmk.** ***Perf. 13***

M1	M1 10pa yellow green	10.00	7.50
M2	M1 20pa rose	10.00	7.50
M3	M1 1pi dark blue	10.00	7.50
M4	M1 2pi orange	10.00	7.50
M5	M1 5pi violet	10.00	7.50
	Nos. M1-M5 (5)	50.00	37.50

Issued for Turkish occupation forces to use in Thessaly during the Greco-Turkish War of 1897-98.

Forgeries of Nos. M1-M5 are perf. 11½.

OFFICIAL STAMPS

Catalogue values for unused stamps in this section are for Never Hinged items.

O1

Perf. 10 to 12 and Compound

1948 **Typo.** **Unwmk.**

O1	O1 10pa rose brown	.50	.25
O2	O1 1k gray green	.50	.25
O3	O1 2k rose violet	.50	.25
O4	O1 3k orange	.50	.25
O5	O1 5k blue	25.00	.90
O6	O1 10k brown org	7.50	.25
O7	O1 15k violet	2.50	.25
O8	O1 20k dk blue	3.00	.25
O9	O1 30k olive bister	5.00	.80
O10	O1 50k black	5.00	.80
O11	O1 1 l bluish grn	5.00	.80
O12	O1 2 l lilac rose	10.00	1.00
	Nos. O1-O12 (12)	65.00	6.05

Regular Issue of 1948 Overprinted Type "a" in Black

1951

O13	A178 5k blue	.25	.25
O14	A178 10k chocolate	.30	.25
O15	A178 20k deep blue	.60	.25
O16	A178 30k brown	.90	.25
	Nos. O13-O16 (4)	2.05	1.00

Overprint "a" is 15½mm wide. Points of crescent do not touch star. The 0.25k (No. 963) exists with overprint "a" but its status is questionable.

b

c

Overprinted Type "b" in Dark Brown

1953

O17	A178 0.25k dk red	.25	.25
O18	A178 5k blue	.30	.25
O19	A178 10k chocolate	.40	.25
O20	A178 15k violet	1.00	.25
O21	A178 20k deep blue	6.00	1.00
O22	A178 30k brown	1.25	.30
O23	A178 60k black	1.40	.25
	Nos. O17-O23 (7)	10.60	2.55

Overprint "b" is 14mm wide. Lettering thin with sharp, clean corners.

Overprinted Type "c" in Black or Green Black

1953-54

O23A	A178 0.25k dk red (G Bk) ('53)	.25	.25
f.	Black overprint	*4.00*	*4.00*
g.	Violet overprint ('53)	*4.00*	*4.00*
O23B	A178 10k chocolate	12.50	.65
O23C	A178 15k violet	15.00	1.00
O23D	A178 30k brown	6.50	.65
O23E	A178 60k black	8.00	1.00
	Nos. O23A-O23E (5)	42.25	3.55

Lettering of type "c" heavy with rounded corners.

Small Star — d

Large Star — e

Overprinted or Surcharged Type "d" in Black

1955

O24	A178 0.25k dark red	.30	.25
O25	A178 1k olive black	.30	.25
O26	A178 2k brt rose lil	.30	.25
O27	A178 3k red orange	.40	.25
O28	A178 4k dk green	.50	.25
O29	A178 5k on 15k vio	.50	.25
O31	A178 10k on 15k vio	.60	.25
O32	A178 15k violet	.60	.25
O33	A178 20k deep blue	.70	.25
O35	A179 40k on 1 l ol grn	.80	.35
O36	A179 75k on 2 l dk brn	1.10	.80
O37	A179 75k on 5 l dp plum	8.00	8.00
	Nos. O24-O37 (12)	14.10	11.40

Type "d" measures 15x16mm. Overprint on Nos. O35-O37 measures 19x22mm. Nos. O29, O31, O35-O37 have two bars and new value added.

Overprinted or Surcharged Type "e" in Black

1955

O25a	A178 1k olive black	.40	.25
O29a	A178 5k on 15k violet	1.10	.25
O30	A178 5k blue	1.50	.25

O31a	A178	10k on 15k violet	2.50	1.00
c.		"10" without serif	.50	.30
O33a	A178	20k deep blue	.80	.30
O34	A178	30k brown	.50	.30

Heavy
crescent —
f

Thin
crescent —
g

Overprinted or Surcharged Type "f" in Black

1957

O24b	A178	0.25k dark red	.50	.25
O25b	A178	1k olive black	.40	.30
O31b	A178	10k on 15k violet	.80	.30
O35b	A178	75k on 1 l olive grn	1.50	.50
O38b	A178	½k on 1k ol blk	.40	.30
		Nos. O24b-O38b (5)	3.60	1.60

Type "f" crescent is larger and does not touch wavy line. The surcharged "10" on No. O31b exists only without serifs. The overprint on O35b measures 17x22½mm.

Overprinted or Surcharged Type "g" in Black

1957

O38	A178	½k on 1k ol blk	.40	.30
O39	A178	1k ol blk	.40	.30
O40	A178	2k on 4k dk grn	.40	.30
O41	A178	3k on 4k dk grn	.40	.30
O42	A178	10k on 12k dp red	.40	.30
		Nos. O38-O42 (5)	2.00	1.50

The shape of crescent and star on type "g" varies on each value. Overprint measures 14x18mm. The surcharged stamps have two bars and new value added.

O2

1957		**Litho.**	**Perf. 10½**	
O43	O2	5k blue	.25	.25
O44	O2	10k orange brn	.25	.25
O45	O2	15k lt violet	.25	.25
O46	O2	20k red	.25	.25
O47	O2	30k gray olive	.25	.25
O48	O2	40k brown vio	.25	.25
O49	O2	50k grnsh blk	.25	.25
O50	O2	60k lt yel grn	.30	.25
O51	O2	75k yellow org	.50	.25
O52	O2	100k green	.75	.25
O53	O2	200k deep rose	1.25	.50
		Nos. O43-O53 (11)	4.55	3.00

1959		**Unwmk.**	**Perf. 10**	
O54	O2	5k rose	.25	.25
O55	O2	10k ol grn	.25	.25
O56	O2	15k car rose	.25	.25
O57	O2	20k lilac	.25	.25
O58	O2	40k blue	.25	.25
O59	O2	60k orange	.25	.25
O60	O2	75k gray	.50	.25
O61	O2	100k violet	.65	.25
O62	O2	200k red brn	1.10	.65
		Nos. O54-O62 (9)	3.75	2.65

O3

1960		**Litho.**	**Perf. 10½**	
O63	O3	1k orange	.25	.25
O64	O3	5k vermilion	.25	.25
O65	O3	10k gray grn	.35	.25
O67	O3	30k red brn	.25	.25
O70	O3	60k green	.25	.25
O71	O3	1 l rose lilac	.30	.25
O72	O3	1½ l brt ultra	.95	.25
O74	O3	2½ l violet	1.50	.35
O75	O3	5 l blue	3.50	.85
		Nos. O63-O75 (9)	7.60	2.95

For surcharge see No. O83.

O4

1962		**Typo.**	**Perf. 13**	
O76	O4	1k olive bister	.30	.25
O77	O4	5k brt green	.30	.25
O78	O4	10k red brown	.30	.25
O79	O4	15k dk blue	.30	.25
O80	O4	25k carmine	.30	.25
O81	O4	30k ultra	.30	.25
		Nos. O76-O81 (6)	1.80	1.50

For surcharge see No. O82.

Nos. O81 and O70 Surcharged

1963

| O82 | O4 | 50k on 30k ultra | .35 | .25 |

Perf. 10½

Litho.

| O83 | O3 | 100k on 60k green | .50 | .25 |

O5

1963		**Litho.**	**Perf. 12½**	
O84	O5	1k gray	.50	.25
O85	O5	5k salmon	.50	.25
O86	O5	10k green	.50	.25
O87	O5	50k car rose	.50	.25
O88	O5	100k ultra	1.00	.50
		Nos. O84-O88 (5)	3.00	1.50

For surcharge see No. O139.

O6

1964		**Unwmk.**	**Perf. 12½**	
O89	O6	1k gray	.25	.25
O90	O6	5k blue	.25	.25
O91	O6	10k yellow	.25	.25
O92	O6	30k red	.40	.25
O93	O6	50k lt green	.50	.25
O94	O6	60k brown	1.50	.25
O95	O6	80k pale grnsh bl	3.50	.40
O96	O6	130k indigo	3.00	.60
O97	O6	200k lilac	7.50	.80
		Nos. O89-O97 (9)	17.15	3.30

For surcharge see No. O140.

O7

1965		**Litho.**	**Perf. 13**	
O98	O7	1k emerald	.25	.25
O99	O7	10k ultra	.25	.25
O100	O7	50k orange	.35	.25
		Nos. O98-O100 (3)	.85	.75

For surcharge see No. O141.

Carpet Designs — O8

1k, Usak. 50k, Bergama. 100k, Ladik. 150k, Seljuk. 200k, Nomad. 500k, Anatolia.

1966		**Litho.**	**Perf. 13**	
O101	O8	1k orange	.25	.25
O102	O8	50k green	.25	.25
O103	O8	100k brt pink	.30	.25
O104	O8	150k violet blue	.65	.25

O105	O8	200k olive bister	.80	.25
O106	O8	500k lilac	3.00	.25
		Nos. O101-O106 (6)	5.25	1.65

For surcharge see No. O142.

Seljuk Tile, 13th Century — O9

1967		**Litho.**	**Perf. 11½x12**	
O107	O9	1k dk bl & lt bl	.30	.25
O108	O9	50k org & dk bl	.30	.25
O109	O9	100k lil & dk bl	.30	.25
		Nos. O107-O109 (3)	.90	.75

For surcharge see No. O143.

Leaf Design — O10

1968		**Litho.**	**Perf. 13**	
O110	O10	50k brn & lt grn	.25	.25
O111	O10	150k blk & dl yel	.50	.25
O112	O10	500k red brn & lt bl	1.60	.25
		Nos. O110-O112 (3)	2.35	.75

O11

1969, Aug. 25		**Litho.**	**Perf. 13**	
O113	O11	1k lt grn & red	.25	.25
O114	O11	10k lt grn & bl	.25	.25
O115	O11	50k lt grn & brn	.25	.25
O116	O11	100k lt grn & red vio	.40	.25
		Nos. O113-O116 (4)	1.15	1.00

O12

1971, Mar. 1		**Litho.**	**Perf. 11½x12**	
O117	O12	5k brown & blue	.25	.25
O118	O12	10k vio bl & ver	.25	.25
O119	O12	30k org & vio bl	.25	.25
O120	O12	50k Prus bl & sepia	.35	.25
O121	O12	75k yellow & green	.60	.25
		Nos. O117-O121 (5)	1.70	1.25

O13

1971, Nov. 15		**Litho.**	**Perf. 11½x12**	
O122	O13	5k lt bl & gray	.25	.25
O123	O13	25k cit & lt brn	.25	.25
O124	O13	100k org & olive	.25	.25
O125	O13	200k dk brn & bis	.40	.25
O126	O13	250k rose lil & vio	.60	.25
O127	O13	500k dk bl & brt bl	.95	.45
		Nos. O122-O127 (6)	2.70	1.70

O14

1972, Apr. 7		**Litho.**	**Perf. 13**	
O128	O14	5k buff & blue	.25	.25
O129	O14	100k buff & olive	.25	.25
O130	O14	200k buff & carmine	.55	.25
		Nos. O128-O130 (3)	1.05	.75

O15

| **1973, Sept 20** | | **Litho.** | **Perf. 13** | |
| O131 | O15 | 100k violet & buff | .65 | .25 |

O16

1974, June 17		**Litho.**	**Perf. 13½x13**	
O132	O16	10k sal pink & brn	.25	.25
O133	O16	25k blue & dk brn	.25	.25
O134	O16	50k brt pink & brn	.25	.25
O135	O16	150k lt grn & brn	.40	.25
O136	O16	250k rose & brn	.65	.25
O137	O16	500k yellow & brn	1.25	.25
		Nos. O132-O137 (6)	3.05	1.50

O17

| **1975, Nov. 5** | | **Litho.** | **Perf. 12½x13** | |
| O138 | O17 | 100k lt blue & maroon | .25 | .25 |

Nos. O84, O89, O98, O101, O107 Surcharged in Red or Black
Perf. 12½, 13, 11½x12

1977, Aug. 17			**Litho.**	
O139	O5	5k on 1k gray	.25	.25
O140	O6	5k on 1k gray	.25	.25
O141	O7	5k on 1k emer	.25	.25
O142	O8	5k on 1k org (B)	.25	.25
O143	O9	5k on 1k dk & lt bl	.25	.25
		Nos. O139-O143 (5)	1.25	1.25

O18

| **1977, Dec. 29** | | **Litho.** | **Perf. 13½x13** | |
| O144 | O18 | 250k lt bl & grn | .35 | .25 |

O19

1978		**Photo.**	**Perf. 13½**	
O145	O19	50k pink & rose	.25	.25
O146	O19	2½ l buff & grnsh blk	.25	.25
O147	O19	4½ l lil rose & sl grn	.40	.25
O148	O19	5 l lt blue & pur	.40	.25
O149	O19	10 l lt grn & grn	.85	.25
O150	O19	25 l yellow & red	2.25	.25
		Nos. O145-O150 (6)	4.40	1.50

O20

1979		**Litho.**	**Perf. 13½**	
O151	O20	50k dp org & brn	.25	.25
O152	O20	2½ l bl & dk bl	.25	.25

O21

1979, Dec. 20   Litho.   Perf. 13½
O153	O21	50k sal & dk bl	.25	.25
O154	O21	1 l lt grn & red	.25	.25
O155	O21	2 ½ l lil rose & red	.30	.25
O156	O21	5 l lt bl & mag	.30	.25
O157	O21	7 ½ l lt lil & dk bl	.30	.25
O158	O21	10 l yel & dk bl	.40	.25
O159	O21	35 l gray & rose ('81)	1.25	.25
O160	O21	50 l pnksh & dk bl ('81)	1.50	.25
		Nos. O153-O160 (8)	4.55	2.00

O22

1981, Oct. 23   Litho.   Perf. 13½
O161	O22	5 l yel & red	2.00	.25
O162	O22	10 l salmon & red	2.50	.25
O163	O22	35 l gray & rose	3.00	.25
O164	O22	50 l pink & dk bl	3.50	.25
O165	O22	75 l pale grn & grn	6.00	.25
O166	O22	100 l lt bl & dk bl	8.00	.45
		Nos. O161-O166 (6)	25.00	1.70

O23

1983-84   Litho.   Perf. 12½x13
Background Color
O167	O23	5 l yellow	1.00	.25
O168	O23	15 l yellow bister	1.25	.25
O169	O23	20 l gray ('84)	.50	.25
O170	O23	50 l sky blue	3.00	.25
O171	O23	65 l pink	3.75	.25
O172	O23	70 l pale rose ('84)	.75	.25
O173	O23	90 l bister brn	5.50	.25
O174	O23	90 l bl gray ('84)	1.10	.25
O175	O23	100 l lt green ('84)	1.75	.25
O176	O23	125 l lt green	6.00	.50
O177	O23	230 l pale salmon ('84)	3.00	.40
		Nos. O167-O177 (11)	27.60	3.15

For surcharges see Nos. O184, O186-O190.

O24

1986-87
O178	O24	5 l yel & vio	.40	.25
O179	O24	10 l org & vio	.40	.25
O180	O24	20 l gray & vio	.40	.25
O180A	O24	50 l pale blue & dp ultra ('87)	.50	.25
O181	O24	100 l lt yel grn & vio	2.00	.25
O182	O24	300 l pale vio & vio blue ('87)	2.50	.25
		Nos. O178-O182 (6)	6.20	1.50

For surcharges see Nos. O183, O185.

Nos. O179, O168, O180, O172, O173, O177 Surcharged in Dark Orange
1989
O183	O24	500 l on 10 l	2.00	.25
O184	O23	500 l on 15 l	2.00	.25
O185	O24	500 l on 20 l	2.00	.25
O186	O23	1000 l on 70 l	3.00	.25
O187	O23	1000 l on 90 l	3.00	.25
O188	O23	1250 l on 230 l	4.00	.50
		Nos. O183-O188 (6)	16.00	1.75

Issued: #O183, O185-O188, 8/9; #O184, 6/7.

Nos. O171, O173 & O174 Surcharged in Black

1991, Mar. 27
O189	O23	100 l on 65 l	.40	.25
O189A		250 l on 90l (#O173)	—	
O190	O23	250 l on 90 l(#O174)	.80	.25

O25

Perf. 11½x12½
1992, Mar. 24   Litho.
O191	O25	3000 l lt brn & dk brn	2.00	.30
O192	O25	5000 l lt grn & dk grn	6.00	.50

O26

1992, Dec. 2   Litho.   Perf. 12½x13
O193	O26	1000 l bl grn & vio bl	.50	.25
O194	O26	10,000 l vio bl & bl grn	4.50	.50

O27

1993, Sept. 27   Litho.   Perf. 12½x13
O195	O27	1000 l brown & green	1.00	.25
O196	O27	1500 l brown & green	1.50	.25
O197	O27	5000 l green & claret	4.00	.40
		Nos. O195-O197 (3)	6.50	.90

O28

1994, May 9   Litho.   Perf. 11½x12
O198	O28	2500 l pink & violet	1.00	.25
O199	O28	25,000 l yel & brn	2.75	.50

O29

1995, Jan. 25
O200	O29	3500 l violet & lt vio	1.00	.25
O201	O29	17,500 l bl grn & lt grn	4.00	.45

O30

1995, May 17
O202	O30	50,000 l ol & apple grn	3.25	1.60

O31

1995, Nov. 8   Litho.   Perf. 12½x13
O203	O31	5000 l salmon & org	.75	.25

O32   O32a

O32b   O32c

1996, July 10   Litho.   Perf. 11½x12¼
O204	O32	15,000 l bl & red	1.00	.25
O205	O32a	20,000 l grn & pur	1.50	.25
O206	O32b	50,000 l pur & grn	2.00	.40
O207	O32c	100,000 l red & bl	3.00	.75
		Nos. O204-O207 (4)	7.50	1.65

O33

1997, Feb. 5   Litho.   Perf. 12½x13
O208	O33	25,000 l red & blue	.55	.30

O34    O35

1997, Aug. 4   Litho.   Perf. 12½x13
O209	O34	40,000 l multicolored	.55	.30
O210	O35	250,000 l multicolored	3.50	1.75

O36   O37

O38   O39

1998, June 10   Litho.   Perf. 12½x13
O211	O36	40,000 l dk bl & lt bl	.40	.25
O212	O37	100,000 l purple	1.00	.50
O213	O38	200,000 l brn & pale bl grn	1.90	1.00
O214	O39	500,000 l brn & pale bl grn	4.75	2.50
		Nos. O211-O214 (4)	8.05	4.25

O40

1998, July 29   Litho.   Perf. 12½x13
O215	O40	75,000 l multicolored	.75	.30

O41   O42

1999   Litho.   Perf. 11½x12¼
O216	O41	(R) vio & blue grn	2.50	.45
O217	O42	(RT) black & pink	4.50	.45

On day of issue, No. O216 sold for 75,000 l; No. O217, 275,000 l.

O43   O44

O45   O46

2000, Apr. 3   Litho.   Perf. 11½x12¼
O218	O43	50,000 l blue & pink	.40	.25
O219	O44	75,000 l brn & gray	.50	.25
O220	O45	500,000 l red brn & lt bl	3.00	.40
O221	O46	1,250,000 l dk bl & buff	6.00	1.00
		Nos. O218-O221 (4)	9.90	1.90

O46a   O46b

Perf. 11½x12¼
2000, Nov. 20   Litho.
O221A	O46b	R blue & yel grn	—	—
O221B	O46a	RT dk bl & lt bl	—	—

No. O221B sold for 500,000 l on day of issue. No. O221A sold for 300,000 l on day of issue.

O47

Perf. 11½x12¼
2001, Dec. 13   Litho.
O222	O47	R blue & yel org	1.00	.25

Sold for 300,000 l on day of issue.

O48   O49

O50   O51

O52

Perf. 11½x12¼
2002, Dec. 10   **Litho.**
O223 O48   50,000 l multi   .25   .25
O224 O49   100,000 l multi   .25   .25
O225 O50   250,000 l multi   .50   .30
O226 O51   500,000 l multi   1.00   .60
O227 O52 1,500,000 l multi   3.75 1.75
     Nos. O223-O227 (5)   5.75 3.15

O53   O54

O55   O56

Perf. 11½x12¼
2003, Aug. 18   **Litho.**
O228 O53   500,000 l bl & red   1.00   .70
O229 O54   750,000 l bl & yel   1.50   .80
O230 O55 1,000,000 l bl & grn   1.50 1.00
O231 O56 3,000,000 l bl & yel   5.00 2.10
     Nos. O228-O231 (4)   9.00 4.60

O57

2003, Oct. 13 Litho. Perf. 11½x12¼
O232 O57 R pink & purple   1.25   .85
     Sold for 600,000 l on day of issue.

Buildings
O58

Designs: 100,000 l, Hamidiye Etfal Children's Sanitorium. 500,000 l, Heating Plant, Silahtaraga. 600,000 l, PTT Headquarters, Ankara, vert. 1,000,000 l, Finance Ministry building, Ankara, vert. 3,500,000 l, Old Post and Telegraph Ministry building, Istanbul.

2004, Oct. 15   Perf. 13¼x13, 13x13¼
O233 O58   100,000 l multi   .25   .25
O234 O58   500,000 l multi   .75   .50
O235 O58   600,000 l multi   .80   .60
O236 O58 1,000,000 l multi   1.50 1.00
O237 O58 3,500,000 l multi   5.50 2.00
     Nos. O233-O237 (5)   8.80 4.35

Building Type of 2004

Design: 60k, Prime Minister's Building, Ankara.

2005, Jan. 1   Litho.   Perf. 14
O238 O58 60k multi   .90   .90

Buildings
O59

Designs: 10k, Museum of the Republic, Ankara. 25k, Culture and Tourism Ministry, Ankara. 50k, State Guest House, Ankara. 60k, Sculpture Museum, Ankara. 1 l, Ethnographic Museum, Ankara. 3.50 l, National Library, Ankara.

2005, July 4   Litho.   Perf. 13¼x13
Frame Color

O239 O59   10k orange   .25   .25
O240 O59   25k orange   .35   .35
O241 O59   50k yel green .75   .75
O242 O59   60k blue   .90   .90
O243 O59   1 l yellow 1.50 1.50
O244 O59 3.50 l dull org 5.25 5.25
     Nos. O239-O244 (6) 9.00 9.00

Kemal
Ataturk — O60

Various portraits.

2006, Apr. 21   Litho.   Perf. 13x13¼
Background Color

O245 O60   10k blue   .25   .25
O246 O60   50k brown   .75   .75
O247 O60   60k dark red   .95   .95
O248 O60   1 l blue green 1.50 1.50
O249 O60 3.50 l red   5.50 5.50
     Nos. O245-O249 (5)   8.95 8.95

Kemal
Ataturk — O61

Various portraits.

Perf. 13x13½
2007, Feb. 26   **Wmk. 405**
O250 O61 10k multi   .25   .25
O251 O61 50k multi   .70   .70
O252 O61 60k multi   .85   .85
O253 O61 1 l multi 1.40 1.40
O254 O61 4 l multi 5.75 5.75
     Nos. O250-O254 (5) 8.95 8.95

Kemal
Ataturk — O62

2007, Dec. 4   **Wmk. 405**
O255 O62 65k multi   1.10 1.10

 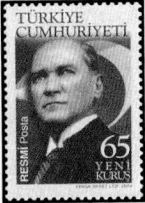

Kemal Ataturk
O63   O64

Various portraits.

Perf. 13x13¼
2008, Feb. 29   **Wmk. 405**
O256 O63   5k multi   .25   .25
O257 O64 65k multi   1.10 1.10
O258 O64 85k multi   1.40 1.40
O259 O64   1 l multi   1.75 1.75
O260 O64 3.35 l multi 5.50 5.50
O261 O64 4.50 l multi 7.50 7.50
     Nos. O256-O261 (6) 17.50 17.50

O65

O66

Kemal Ataturk
O67   O68

Perf. 13x13¼, 13¼x13
2008, Dec. 4   **Wmk. 405**
O262 O65 5k multi   .25   .25
O263 O66 5k multi   .65   .65
O264 O67 65k multi   .85   .85
O265 O68 1 l multi   1.25 1.25
     Nos. O262-O265 (4) 3.00 3.00

Flowers
O69

Designs: 5k, Nergis (daffodils). 10k, Nilüfer (water lily). 25k, Papatya (daisies). 50k, Cigdem (crocuses). 65k, Zambak (lilies). 75k, Yildiz (dahlia). 1 l, Kardelen (snowdrops). 3.35 l, Menekse (violet). 4.50 l, Ortanca (hydrangea). 5 l, Sardunya (geraniums).

2009   **Wmk. 405**   **Perf. 13¾**
O266 O69   5k multi   .25   .25
O267 O69 10k multi   .25   .25
O268 O69 25k multi   .35   .35
O269 O69 50k multi   .65   .65
O270 O69 65k multi   .85   .85
O271 O69 75k multi   1.10 1.10
O272 O69   1 l multi   1.25 1.25
O273 O69 3.35 l multi 4.25 4.25
O274 O69 4.50 l multi 5.75 5.75
O275 O69   5 l multi   7.00 7.00
     Nos. O266-O275 (10) 21.70 21.70
     Issued: 75k, 5 l, 7/16; others, 3/26.

Flowers — O70

Designs: 5k, Ayçiçegi (sunflowers). 10k, Gelincik (poppies). 25k, Carkifelek (passion flower). 80k, Zinya (zinnia). 1 l Gül (rose).

Perf. 13x13¼
2010, Aug. 26   **Wmk. 405**
O276 O70 5k multi   .25   .25
O277 O70 10k multi   .25   .25
O278 O70 25k multi   .35   .35
O279 O70 80k multi   1.10 1.10
O280 O70 1 l multi   1.40 1.40
     Nos. O276-O280 (5) 3.35 3.35

Stylized
Flowers — O71

Various stylized flowers.

2010, Dec. 10   **Wmk. 405**
O281 O71 5k multi   .25   .25
O282 O71 50k multi   .70   .70
O283 O71 80k multi   1.10 1.10
O284 O71 90k multi   1.25 1.25
O285 O71 1 l multi   1.40 1.40
     Nos. O281-O285 (5) 4.70 4.70

Stylized Flowers Type of 2010

Various stylized flowers.

Perf. 13½ Syncopated
2011, Apr. 18   **Wmk. 405**
Inscribed "2011"

O286 O71 10k multi   .25   .25
O287 O71 1 l multi   1.40 1.40
O288 O71 2.80 l multi 3.75 3.75
O289 O71 6 l multi   7.75 7.75
     Nos. O286-O289 (4) 13.15 13.15

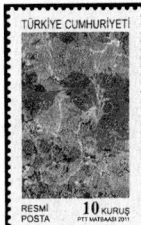

Abstract Art — O72

Various abstract designs.

Perf. 13x13¼
2011, Dec. 19   **Wmk. 405**
O290 O72 10k multi   .25   .25
O291 O72 1 l multi   1.10 1.10
O292 O72 2 l multi   2.25 2.25
O293 O72 7 l multi   7.50 7.50
     Nos. O290-O293 (4) 11.10 11.10

Flowers — O73

Various flowers.

2012, May 2   Perf. 13¾ Syncopated
Background Color
O294 O73 25k dull orange   .30   .30
O295 O73 50k buff   .60   .60
O296 O73 1 l pink   1.10 1.10

O297 O73 3.75 l lilac 4.25 4.25
O298 O73 7 l light blue 8.00 8.00
 Nos. O294-O298 (5) 14.25 14.25

Four Seasons — O74

Designs: 10k, Evergreen branch in winter. 25k, Blossoms on tree in spring. 50k, Cherries on branch in summer. 1k, Brown leaves on tree in autumn.

2012, Sept. 11 **Perf. 14x13¾**
O299 O74 10k multi .25 .25
O300 O74 25k multi .30 .30
O301 O74 50k multi .55 .55
O302 O74 1 l multi 1.10 1.10
 Nos. O299-O302 (4) 2.20 2.20

Carpets — O75

Carpet from: 10k, Balikesir. 25k Kayseri. 1.10 l, Aksaray. 3.85 l, Mugla.

Perf. 13x12½
2013, Feb. 14 **Wmk. 405**
O303 O75 10k multi .25 .25
O304 O75 25k multi .30 .30
O305 O75 1.10 l multi 1.25 1.25
O306 O75 3.85 l multi 4.25 4.25
 Nos. O303-O306 (4) 6.05 6.05

Kemal Ataturk — O76

Various portraits.

Perf. 13¾ Syncopated
2013, Sept. 19 **Litho.** **Unwmk.**
O307 O76 10k multi .25 .25
O308 O76 25k multi .25 .25
O309 O76 1 l multi 1.00 1.00
O310 O76 1.10 l multi 1.10 1.10
O311 O76 8 l multi 8.00 8.00
 Nos. O307-O311 (5) 10.60 10.60

Kemal Ataturk — O77

Various portraits.

Perf. 13¾ Syncopated
2014, Apr. 16 **Litho.** **Unwmk.**
O312 O77 10k multi .25 .25
O313 O77 1 l multi .95 .95
O314 O77 1.10 l multi 1.10 1.10
 Nos. O312-O314 (3) 2.30 2.30

Carpets — O78

Carpet from: 15k, Manisa Province. 1.25 l, Kocaeli Province. 9 l, Konya Province.

Perf. 13¾ Syncopated
2014, May 7 **Litho.**
O315 O78 15k multi .25 .25
O316 O78 1.25 l multi 1.25 1.25
O317 O78 9 l multi 8.50 8.50
 Nos. O315-O317 (3) 10.00 10.00

Tourist Attractions O79

Various tourist attractions.

Perf. 13¾ Syncopated
2014, June 18 **Litho.**
O318 O79 15k multi .25 .25
O319 O79 25k multi .25 .25
O320 O79 1.25 l multi 1.25 1.25
O321 O79 9 l multi 8.50 8.50
 Nos. O318-O321 (4) 10.25 10.25

NEWSPAPER STAMPS

N1

Black Overprint
1879 Unwmk. Perf. 11½ and 13½
P1 N1 10pa blk & rose
 lilac 225.00 225.00

Other stamps found with this "IMPRIMES" overprint were prepared on private order and have no official status as newspaper stamps. Counterfeits exist of No. P1.

The 10pa surcharge, on half of 20pa rose and pale rose was made privately. See note after No. 77.

Regular Issue of 1890 Handstamped in Black, Blue or Red

Nos. P10-P29 were overprinted with a single wooden handstamp. Variations in size are due to inking and pressure.

The handstamps on Nos. P10-P29 are found double, inverted and sideways. Counterfeit overprints comprise most of the examples offered for sale in the marketplace.

1891 **Perf. 13½, 11½**
P10 A7 10pa grn & gray 40.00 12.50
 a. Imperf. 22.50 12.50
P11 A7 20pa rose & gray 75.00 15.00
P12 A7 1pi blue & gray 210.00 150.00
P13 A7 2pi yel & gray 525.00 400.00
P14 A7 5pi buff & gray 1,050. 750.00
 Nos. P10-P14 (5) 1,900. 1,327.

Blue Handstamp
P10b A7 10pa green & gray 210.00 125.00
P11a A7 20pa rose & gray 340.00 250.00
P12a A7 1pi blue & gray 425.00 375.00
 Nos. P10b-P12a (3) 975.00 750.00

This overprint on 2pi and 5pi in blue is considered bogus.

Red Handstamp
P10c A7 10pa green & gray 400.00 325.00
P11b A7 20pa rose & gray 600.00 450.00
P12b A7 1pi blue & gray 900.00 1,000.
 Nos. P10c-P12b (3) 1,900. 1,775.

This overprint in red on 2pi and 5pi is considered bogus.

Excellent forgeries of Nos. P10-P14 exist. Certification by a competant authority is suggested.

Same Handstamp on Regular Issue of 1892

1892 **Perf. 13½**
P25 A10 10pa gray green 500.00 100.00
P26 A11 20pa rose 1,250. 375.00
P27 A12 1pi pale blue 110.00 150.00
P28 A13 2pi brown org 200.00 175.00
P29 A14 5pi pale violet 1,800. 1,250.
 a. On No. 99a 500.00
 Nos. P25-P29 (5) 3,860. 2,050.

Regular Issues of 1892-98 Overprinted in Black

1893-98
P30 A10 10pa gray grn 3.75 2.50
P31 A11 20pa vio brn ('98) 3.00 1.50
 a. 20pa dark pink 2.50 1.25
 b. 20pa pink 325.00 22.50
P32 A12 1pi pale blue 3.00 1.50
P33 A13 2pi brown org 27.50 12.50
 a. Tete beche pair 22.50
P34 A14 5pi pale violet 85.00 75.00
 a. On No. 99a 140.00 65.00
 Nos. P30-P34 (5) 122.25 93.00

For surcharge and overprints see Nos. B41, P121-P122, P134-P136, P153-P154.

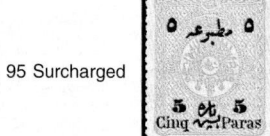

No. 95 Surcharged

1897
P36 A10 5pa on 10pa gray grn 5.00 3.00
 a. "Cniq" instead of "Cinq" 15.00 15.00

For overprint see No. P137.

Nos. 102-107 Overprinted in Black

1901 **Perf. 12, 13½ and Compound**
P37 A16 5pa bister 1.75 1.00
 a. Inverted overprint
P38 A16 10pa yellow grn 6.25 6.25
P39 A16 20pa magenta 32.50 7.50
P40 A16 1pi violet blue 60.00 22.50
P41 A16 2pi gray blue 125.00 37.50
P42 A16 5pi ocher 300.00 90.00
 Nos. P37-P42 (6) 525.50 164.75

For overprints see Nos. B37, P69-P74, P123, P138-P141, P155-P158.

Same Overprint on Nos. 110-115

1901
P43 A17 5pa purple 8.75 2.00
P44 A17 10pa green 32.50 2.50
P45 A17 20pa carmine 8.75 1.50
 a. Overprinted on back
P46 A17 1pi blue 25.00 2.00
P47 A17 2pi orange 87.50 4.00
 a. Inverted overprint
P48 A17 5pi lilac rose 160.00 27.50
 Nos. P43-P48 (6) 322.50 39.50

For overprints see Nos. P75-P80, P124-P126, P142-P146, P159-P164.

Same Overprint on Regular Issue of 1905

1905
P49 A18 5pa ocher 2.50 1.00
P50 A18 10pa dull green 30.00 1.50
P51 A18 20pa carmine 2.50 1.25
P52 A18 1pi pale blue 2.50 1.25
P53 A18 2pi slate 70.00 10.00
P54 A18 5pi brown 175.00 20.00
 Nos. P49-P54 (6) 282.50 35.00

For overprints see Nos. P127-P129, P147-P150, P165-P171.

Regular Issue of 1908 Overprinted in Carmine or Blue

1908
P55 A19 5pa ocher (Bl) 10.00 .50
P56 A19 10pa blue grn (C) 17.50 .50
P57 A19 20pa carmine (Bl) 22.50 1.00
P58 A19 1pi brt blue (C) 100.00 2.50
P59 A19 2pi blue blk (C) 150.00 7.50
P60 A19 5pi dk violet (C) 200.00 17.50
 Nos. P55-P60 (6) 500.00 29.50

For overprints see Nos. B17, P130-P131, P151, P172.

Same Overprint on Regular Issue of 1909

1909
P61 A21 5pa ocher (Bl) 3.50 1.25
 a. Imperf.
P62 A21 10pa blue grn (C) 8.75 1.50
P63 A21 20pa car rose (Bl) 60.00 1.75
 a. Imperf.
P64 A21 1pi brt blue (C) 100.00 5.00
P65 A21 2pi blue blk (C) 250.00 30.00
P66 A21 5pi dk violet (C) 500.00 65.00
 Nos. P61-P66 (6) 922.25 104.50

For surcharge and overprints see Nos. B18, P67-P68, P81, P132-P133, P152.

No. 151 Surcharged in Blue

1910 Perf. 12, 13½ and Compound
P67 A21 2pa on 5pa ocher .75 .75

1911 Perf. 12
P68 A21 2pa olive green 1.00 .50

See No. P173.

Newspaper Stamps of 1901-11 Overprinted in Carmine or Blue

The overprint was applied to 13 denominations in four settings with change of city name, producing individual sets for each city: "MONASTIR," "PRISTINA," "SALONIQUE" and "USKUB."

1911, June 26 **Perf. 12, 13½**
P69 A16 5pa bister 20.00 22.50
P70 A16 10pa yellow grn 20.00 22.50
P71 A16 20pa magenta 20.00 22.50
P72 A16 1pi violet blue 20.00 22.50
P73 A16 2pi gray blue 25.00 30.00
P74 A16 5pi ocher 50.00 60.00
P75 A17 5pa purple 10.00 12.50
P76 A17 10pa green 10.00 12.50
P77 A17 20pa carmine 10.00 12.50
P78 A17 1pi blue 10.00 12.50
P79 A17 2pi orange 12.00 15.00
P80 A17 5pi lilac rose 30.00 30.00
P81 A21 2pa olive green 3.00 3.75
 Nos. P69-P81 (13) 240.00 278.75

Values for each of the 4 city sets of 13 are the same.

The note after No. 182 will also apply to Nos. P69-P81.

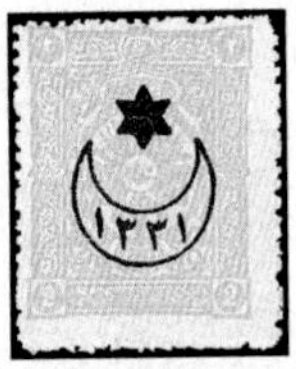

Newspaper Stamps of 1901-11 Overprinted in Carmine or Black

1915 — On Stamps of 1893-98

P121 A10 10pa gray green 6.00 .50
a. Inverted overprint 10.00 10.00
P122 A13 2pi yellow brn 1.50 1.00
a. Inverted overprint 10.00 10.00

On Stamps of 1901

P123 A16 10pa yellow grn 1.00 .50
P124 A17 5pa purple 1.00 1.00
P125 A17 20pa carmine 2.00 1.00
P126 A17 5pi lilac rose 20.00 5.00

On Stamps of 1905

P127 A18 5pa ocher 2.00 1.00
a. Inverted overprint 7.50 7.50
P128 A18 2pi slate 17.50 5.00
P129 A18 5pi brown 10.00 .60

On Stamps of 1908

P130 A19 2pi blue blk *1,375.* *550.00*
P131 A19 5pi dk violet 10.00 1.25

On Stamps of 1909

P132 A21 5pa ocher 1.00 .50
P133 A21 5pi dk violet 100.00 35.00
Nos. P121-P129,P131-P133 (12) 172.00 52.35

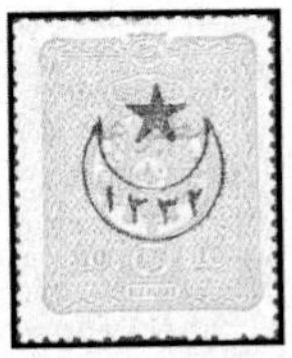

Preceding Newspaper Issues with additional Overprint in Red or Black

1916 — On Stamps of 1893-98

P134 A10 10pa gray green 2.00 .75
P135 A11 20pa violet brn 1.00 .75
P136 A14 5pi dull violet 50.00 50.00

On Stamp of 1897

P137 A10 5pa on 10pa gray grn .60 .50

On Stamps of 1901

P138 A16 5pa bister .50 .30
P139 A16 10pa yellow grn .90 .90
P140 A16 20pa magenta 1.00 .90
a. Inverted overprint 10.00 10.00
P141 A16 1pi violet blue 1.00 1.00
P142 A17 5pa purple 50.00 50.00
P143 A17 10pa green 50.00 50.00
P144 A17 20pa carmine 1.50 .90
P145 A17 1pi blue 1.50 .90
P146 A17 2pi orange 1.50 .90

On Stamps of 1905

P147 A18 5pa ocher 1.00 .75
P148 A18 10pa dull green 50.00 50.00
P149 A18 20pa carmine 50.00 50.00
P150 A18 1pi pale blue 1.75 1.00

On Stamp of 1908

P151 A19 5pa ocher 62.50 62.50

On Stamp of 1909

P152 A21 5pa ocher 62.50 62.50
Nos. P134-P152 (19) 389.25 384.55

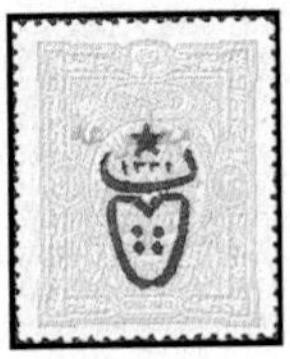

Preceding Newspaper Issues with additional Overprint in Red or Black

1917 — On Stamps of 1893-98

P153 A12 1pi gray (R) 2.50 2.00
P154 A11 20pa vio brn (R) 3.75 3.75

On Stamps of 1901

P155 A16 5pa bister (Bk) 1.50 1.25
a. Inverted overprint 20.00 20.00
P156 A16 10pa yellow grn (R) 1.50 1.25
P157 A16 20pa magenta (Bk) 1.50 1.25
P158 A16 2pi gray blue (R) 40.00 30.00
P159 A17 5pa purple (Bk) 2.25 2.25
a. Inverted overprint 20.00 20.00
b. Double overprint 20.00 20.00
c. Double ovpt., one inverted 25.00 25.00
P160 A17 10pa green (R) 22.50 35.00
P161 A17 20pa carmine (Bk) 1.50 1.25
P162 A17 1pi blue (R) 3.00 3.00
P163 A17 2pi orange (Bk) 2.50 2.50
P164 A17 5pi lilac rose (R) 32.50 50.00

On Stamps of 1905

P165 A18 5pa ocher (R) 2.50 2.00
a. Inverted overprint 10.00 10.00
P166 A18 5pa ocher (Bk) 3.00 2.50
a. Inverted overprint 10.00 10.00
P167 A18 10pa dull green (R) 2.50 2.00
P168 A18 20pa carmine (Bk) 2.50 2.00
a. Double overprint 15.00 15.00
P169 A18 1pi blue (R) 2.50 2.00
a. Inverted overprint 25.00 25.00
P170 A18 2pi slate (R) 32.50 50.00
P171 A18 5pi brown (R) 32.50 50.00

On Stamp of 1908

P172 A19 5pa ocher (R) 32.50 50.00
Nos. P153-P172 (20) *225.50* *294.00*

Nos. P153-P172 were used as regular postage stamps.

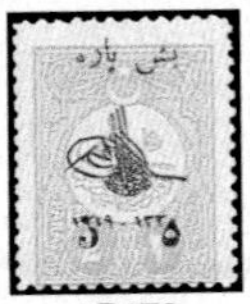

#P173

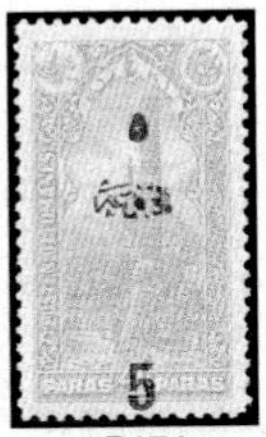

#P174

1919

Blue Surcharge and Red Overprint

P173 A21 5pa on 2pa ol grn 1.25 1.00
a. Red overprint double 12.50 5.00
b. Blue surcharge double 12.50 5.00

1920 — Red Surcharge

P174 A25 5pa on 4pa brn 1.25 .50

Catalogue values for unused stamps in this section, from this point to the end of the section, are for Never Hinged items.

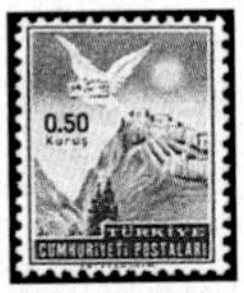

Dove and Citadel of Ankara — N6

1952-55 — Litho. — *Perf. 12½*

P175 N6 0.50k grnsh gray .25 .25
P176 N6 0.50k violet ('53) .25 .25

Perf. 10½, 10

P177 N6 0.50k red org ('54) .25 .25
P178 N6 0.50k brown ('55) .25 .25
Nos. P175-P178 (4) 1.00 1.00

POSTAL TAX STAMPS

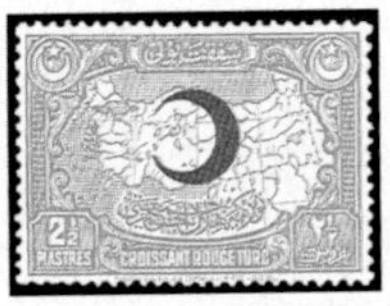

Map of Turkey and Red Crescent PT1

1928 — Unwmk. — Typo. — *Perf. 14*

Crescent in Red

RA1 PT1 ½pi lt brown .30 .25
RA2 PT1 1pi red violet .30 .25
RA3 PT1 2½pi orange .30 .25

Engr.

Various Frames

RA4 PT1 5pi dk brown .60 .45
RA5 PT1 10pi yellow green .75 .55
RA6 PT1 20pi slate 1.25 .60
RA7 PT1 50pi dark violet 3.75 1.40
Nos. RA1-RA7 (7) 7.25 3.75
Set, never hinged 13.00

The use of these stamps on letters, parcels, etc. in addition to the regular postage, was obligatory on certain days in each year.

For surcharges see Nos. RA16, RA21-RA22.

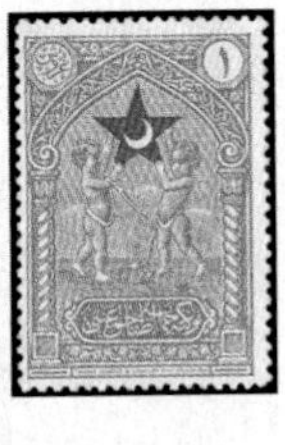

Cherubs Upholding Star — PT2

1932

RA8 PT2 1k ol bis & red 1.00 .30
RA9 PT2 2½k dk brn & red 1.25 .30
RA10 PT2 5k green & red 1.50 .30
RA11 PT2 25k black & red 3.00 1.00
Nos. RA8-RA11 (4) 6.75 1.90
Set, never hinged 9.00

For surcharges and overprints see Nos. RA12-RA15, RA28-RA29, RA36-RA38.

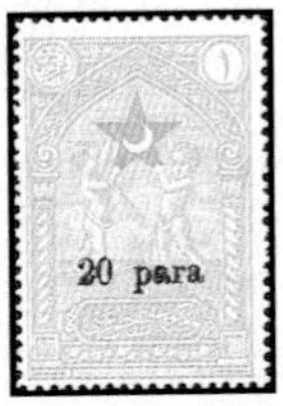

No. RA8 Surcharged

RA12 PT2 20pa on 1k 1.00 .50
RA13 PT2 3k on 1k 1.75 .70
a. 3 "kruus" 2.50 2.50

By a law of Parliament the use of these stamps on letters and telegraph forms, in addition to the regular fees, was obligatory from Apr. 20-30 of each year. The inscription in the tablet at the bottom of the design states that the money derived from the sale of the stamps is devoted to child welfare work.

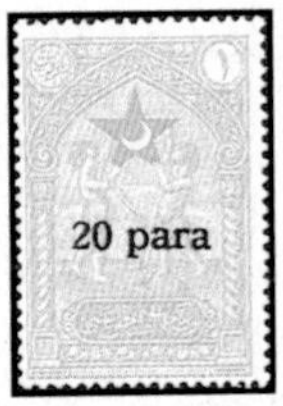

No. RA8 Surcharged

1933

RA14 PT2 20pa on 1k ol bis & red 1.00 .50
RA15 PT2 3k on 1k ol bis & red 1.75 1.00

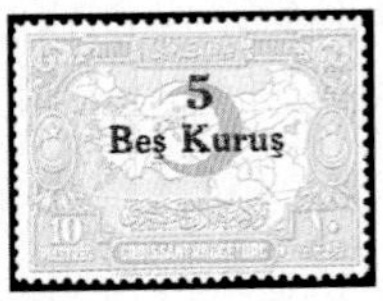

No. RA5 Surcharged

RA16 PT1 5k on 10pi yel grn & red 1.50 .75
Nos. RA14-RA16 (3) 4.25 2.25

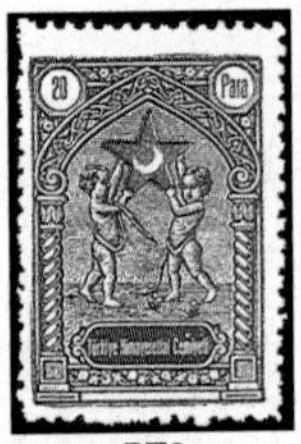

PT3

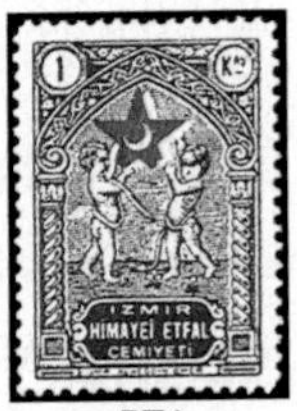

PT4

1933 — *Perf. 11, 11½*

RA17 PT3 20pa gray vio & red 1.00 .50
RA18 PT4 1k violet & red 1.00 .50
RA19 PT4 5k dk brown & red 2.50 .50
RA20 PT3 15k green & red 3.50 .50
Nos. RA17-RA20 (4) 8.00 2.00
Set, never hinged 12.00

Nos. RA17 and RA20 were issued in Ankara; Nos. RA18 and RA19 in Izmir.

For overprint see No. RA27.

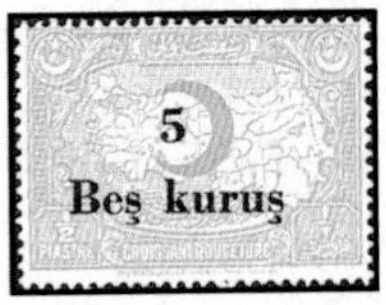

Nos. RA3, RA1 Surcharged in Black

1933-34

RA21 PT1 1k on 2½pi orange .50 .30
RA22 PT1 5k on ½pi lt brown 1.50 .50

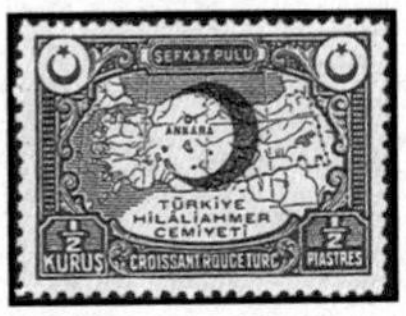

Map of Turkey PT5

1934-35 — Crescent in Red — *Perf. 12*

RA23 PT5 ½k blue ('35) .25 .25
RA24 PT5 1k red brown .25 .25
RA25 PT5 2½k brown ('35) .50 .25
RA26 PT5 5k blue green ('35) 1.25 .25
Nos. RA23-RA26 (4) 2.25 1.00
Set, never hinged 5.00

Frame differs on No. RA26.

See Nos. RA30-RA35B.

Nos. RA17, RA8-RA9 Overprinted "P.Y.S." in Roman Capitals

1936 — *Perf. 11, 14*

RA27 PT3 20pa gray vio & red .40 .25
RA28 PT2 1k ol bis & red .40 .25
RA29 PT2 3k on 2½k dk brn & red .75 .30
Nos. RA27-RA29 (3) 1.55
Set, never hinged 12.00

Type of 1934-35, Inscribed "Türkiye Kizilay Cemiyeti"

1938-46 — *Perf. 8½-11½*

Type I — Imprint, "Devlet Basimevi". Crescent red.

Type II — Imprint, "Alaeddin Kiral Basimevi". Crescent carmine.

Type III — Imprint, "Damga Matbaasi". Crescent red.

Crescent in Red or Carmine

RA30 PT5 ½k blue (I) .50 .25
a. Type II 4.00 1.00
b. Type III .50 .25
RA31 PT5 1k red vio (I) .40 .25
a. Type II 6.50 2.00
b. Type III .50 .25
RA32 PT5 2½k orange (I) .30 .25
a. Type III 2.00 1.00
RA33 PT5 5k blue grn (I) .50 .25
RA33A PT5 5k choc (III) ('42) 1.00 .25
RA34 PT5 10k pale grn (I) 1.50 .30
a. Type III 2.00 1.00
RA35 PT5 20k black (I) 2.50 1.00
RA35A PT5 50k pur (III) ('46) 7.50 1.00
RA35B PT5 1 l blue (III) ('44) 30.00 2.50
Nos. RA30-RA35B (9) 44.20 6.05
Set, never hinged 75.00

For surcharge see No. RA63.

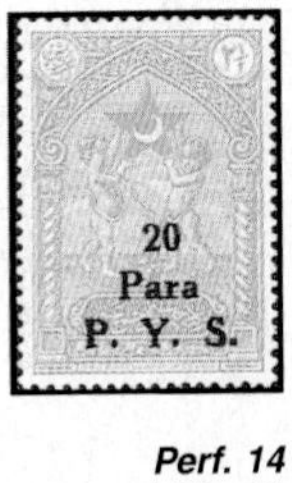

No. RA9 Surcharged in Black

1938 — *Perf. 14*

RA36 PT2 20pa on 2½k 1.00 .50
RA37 PT2 1k on 2½k 1.00 .50

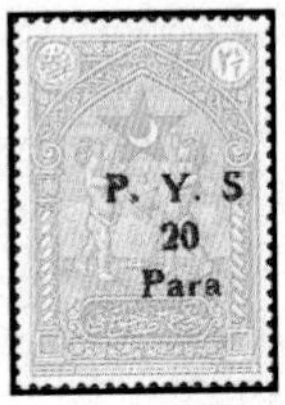

No. RA9 Surcharged in Black

1938 — Unwmk. — *Perf. 14*

RA37A PT2 20pa on 2½k 1.25 .60
RA37B PT2 1k on 2½k 1.50 .75

No. RA9 Surcharged "1 Kurus" in Black

1939			Perf. 14	
RA38	PT2	1k on 2½k dk brn & red	.50	.50

Child — PT6

Nurse with Child — PT7

1940		Typo.	Perf. 12	
		Star in Carmine		
RA39	PT6	20pa bluish grn	.30	.25
RA40	PT6	1k violet	.30	.25
RA41	PT7	1k lt blue	.30	.25
RA42	PT7	2½k pale red lil	.30	.25
RA43	PT6	3k black	.35	.25
RA44	PT6	5k pale violet	.30	.25
RA45	PT7	10k blue green	1.00	.60
RA46	PT6	15k dark blue	.75	.30
RA47	PT7	25k olive bister	2.50	1.25
RA48	PT7	50k olive gray	6.00	2.00
		Nos. RA39-RA48 (10)	12.10	5.95
		Set, never hinged	30.00	

Soldier and Map of Turkey — PT8

1941-44			Perf. 11½	
RA49	PT8	1k purple	.40	.25
RA50	PT8	2k light blue	2.50	.25
RA51	PT8	3k chestnut	2.75	.50
RA51A	PT8	4k mag ('44)	9.50	.35
RA52	PT8	5k brt rose	7.75	2.50
RA53	PT8	10k dk blue	11.00	4.00
		Nos. RA49-RA53 (6)	33.90	7.85
		Set, never hinged	75.00	

The tax was used for national defense.

Baby — PT9

Nurse and Baby — PT13

Nurse and Children PT10

Nurse Feeding Child PT11

Nurse and Child PT12

Nurse and Child — PT14

President Inonu Holding Child — PT15

Children PT16

1942		Unwmk. Typo.	Perf. 11½	
		Star in Red		
RA54	PT9	20pa brt violet	.40	.25
RA55	PT9	20pa chocolate	.40	.25
RA56	PT10	1k dk slate grn	.40	.25
RA57	PT11	2½k yellow grn	.40	.30
RA58	PT12	3k dark blue	.40	.30
RA59	PT13	5k brt pink	.40	.30
RA60	PT14	10k lt blue	.70	.40
RA61	PT15	15k dk red brn	1.10	.70
RA62	PT16	25k brown	1.75	1.00
		Nos. RA54-RA62 (9)	5.95	3.75

See Nos. RA175, RA179-RA180.

No. RA32 Surcharged with New Value in Brown

1942			Perf. 10	
RA63	PT5	1k on 2½k org & red (I)	.25	.25

Child Eating — PT17

Nurse and Child — PT18

Nurse and Child PT19

Child and Red Star — PT20

President Inönü and Child — PT21

Inscribed: "Sefcat Pullari 23 Nisan 1943 Cocuk Esirgeme Kurumu."

1943		Star in Red	Perf. 11	
RA64	PT17	50pa lilac	.25	.25
RA65	PT17	50pa gray green	.25	.25
RA66	PT18	1k lt ultra	.25	.25
RA67	PT19	3k dark red	.30	.25
RA68	PT20	15k cream & blk	1.50	.40
RA69	PT21	100k brt violet blue	2.50	1.60
a.		Souvenir sheet, #RA64-RA69, imperf.	5.50	5.50
		Nos. RA64-RA69 (6)	5.05	3.00

Star and Crescent PT23

Hospital PT24

Nurse and Children PT25

Baby PT26

Nurse Bathing Baby — PT27

Nurse Feeding Child — PT28

Baby with Bottle — PT29

Child — PT30

Hospital — PT31

		Perf. 10 to 12 and Compound		
1943-44			**Star in Red**	
RA71	PT23	20pa deep blue	.40	.30
RA72	PT24	1k gray green	.40	.25
RA73	PT25	3k pale gray brn	.40	.25
RA74	PT26	5k yellow orange	.70	.30
RA75	PT26	5k violet brn	.30	.25
RA76	PT27	10k red	.40	.30
RA77	PT28	15k red violet	.60	.40
RA78	PT29	25k pale violet	.90	.50
RA79	PT30	50k lt blue	2.00	1.00
RA80	PT31	100k lt green	5.00	4.00
		Nos. RA71-RA80 (10)	11.10	7.55
		Set, never hinged	22.00	

For surcharge see No. RA156.

Nurse Holding Baby — PT32

Nurse Feeding Child — PT33

Child — PT34

Star and Crescent PT35

1945-47		Unwmk. Litho.	Perf. 11½	
		Star in Red		
RA81	PT32	1k lilac brn	.40	.25
a.		1k rose violet	.50	.25
RA82	PT33	5k yellow grn	.70	.25
a.		5k green	.70	.25
RA83	PT34	10k red brown	.50	.25
RA84	PT35	250k gray black	9.50	3.50
RA84A	PT35	500k dull vio ('47)	37.50	12.50
		Nos. RA81-RA84A (5)	48.60	16.75
		Set, never hinged	90.00	

Imprint on No. RA82: "Kagit ve Basim isleri A.S. ist." On No. RA82a: "Guzel Sanatlar Matbaasi — Ankara."

Nurse and Wounded Soldier PT36

President Inönü and Victim of Earthquake PT37

Removing Wounded from Hospital Ship — PT38

Nurse and Soldier — PT39

Feeding the Poor — PT40

Wounded Soldiers on Landing Raft — PT41

Symbolical of Red Crescent Relief — PT42

1945			Perf. 12x10, 10x12	
		Crescent in Red		
RA85	PT36	20pa dp bl & brn org	.50	.25
RA86	PT37	1k ol grn & ol bis	.50	.25
RA87	PT38	2½k dp bl & red	1.00	.50
RA88	PT39	5k dp bl & red	2.00	1.00
RA89	PT40	10k dp bl & lt grn	2.00	1.00
RA90	PT41	50k blk & gray grn	4.50	2.00
RA91	PT42	1 l black & yel	15.00	7.50
		Nos. RA85-RA91 (7)	25.50	12.50
		Set, never hinged	45.00	

See Nos. RA181-RA182.

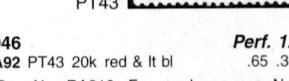

Ankara
Sanatorium
PT43

1946 *Perf. 12*
RA92 PT43 20k red & lt bl .65 .30
 See No. RA210. For surcharge see No.
RA186.

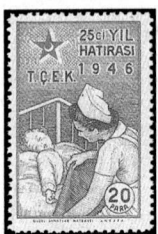

Covering Sleeping
Child — PT44

 Designs: 1k, Mother and child. 2½k, Nurse
at playground. 5k, Doctor examining infant.
15k, Feeding child. 25k, Bathing child. 50k,
Weighing baby. 150k, Feeding baby.

Inscribed: "25ci Yil Hatirasi 1946"
Star in Carmine

1946 **Litho.** *Perf. 12½*
RA93 PT44 20pa brown .35 .25
RA94 PT44 1k blue .35 .25
RA95 PT44 2½k carmine .35 .25
RA96 PT44 5k vio brn .60 .25
RA97 PT44 15k violet .90 .50
RA98 PT44 25k gray grn 1.25 .60
RA99 PT44 50k bl grn 1.75 1.50
RA100 PT44 150k gray brn 3.25 1.75
 Nos. RA93-RA100 (8) 8.80 5.35
 Set, never hinged 15.00

 For surcharge see No. RA155.

Hospital
Ship — PT52

Ambulance
Plane — PT53

Hospital
Train — PT54

Ambulance
PT55

Boy Scout and Red
Crescent
Flag — PT56

Stretcher
Bearers and
Wounded
Soldier
PT57

Nurse and
Hospital — PT58

Sanatorium
PT59

1946 *Perf. 11½*
RA101 PT52 1k multi 1.25 1.25
RA102 PT53 4k multi 1.25 1.25
RA103 PT54 10k multi 3.50 3.50
RA104 PT55 25k multi 4.50 4.50
RA105 PT56 40k multi 8.50 8.50
RA106 PT57 70k multi 6.00 6.00
RA107 PT58 1 l multi 5.50 5.50
RA108 PT59 2½ l multi 12.50 12.50
 Nos. RA101-RA108 (8) 43.00 43.00

 For overprints see Nos. RA139-RA146.

Souvenir Sheet

Pres. Inönü and Child — PT60

1946 **Unwmk. Typo.** *Imperf.*
Without Gum
RA109 PT60 250k slate blk,
 pink & red 20.00 17.50

 Turkish Society for the Prevention of Cruelty
to Children, 25th anniv.

Nurse and
Wounded Soldier
PT61

Pres. Inönü and
Victim of
Earthquake
PT62

Nurse and
Soldier — PT64

Symbolical of
Red Crescent
Relief — PT67

1946-47 **Litho.** *Perf. 11½*
Crescent in Red
RA113 PT61 20pa dk bl vio & ol
 ('47) .25 .25
RA114 PT62 1k dk brn & yel .45 .25
RA115 PT64 5k dp bl & red .45 .25
RA116 PT67 1 l brn blk & yel 1.90 1.25
 Nos. RA113-RA116 (4) 3.05 2.00

PT68

Nurse and
Wounded
Soldier — PT69

Victory and
Soldier — PT70

1947 **Crescent in Red**
RA117 PT68 250k brn blk &
 grn 5.25 2.00
RA118 PT69 5 l sl gray &
 org 8.75 3.50

Booklet Pane of One
Perf. 11½ (top) x Imperf.
RA119 PT70 10 l deep blue 22.50 —

 Black numerals above No. RA119 indicate
position in booklet.

President Inönü
and Victim of
Earthquake
PT71

Nurse and Child
PT72

1947 *Perf. 11½*
RA120 PT71 1k dk brn, pale bl &
 red .25 .25
RA121 PT72 2½k bl vio & car .25 .25
 See Nos. RA221-RA223. For surcharge see
No. RA154.

Nurse Offering
Encouragement
PT73

Plant with Broken
Stem
PT74

Perf. 8½, 11½x10, 11x10½
1948-49 **Typo.** **Unwmk.**
Crescent in Red
RA122 PT73 ½k ultra ('49) .55 .25
RA123 PT73 1k indigo .25 .25
RA124 PT73 2k lilac rose .25 .25
RA125 PT73 2½k org ('49) .25 .25
RA126 PT73 3k bl grn .25 .25
RA127 PT73 4k gray ('49) .35 .25
RA128 PT73 5k blue .70 .25
RA129 PT73 10k pink 1.25 .25
RA130 PT73 25k chocolate 1.60 .25
Perf. 10
RA130A PT74 50k ultra & bl
 gray ('49) 2.25 .75
RA130B PT74 100k grn & pale
 grn ('49) 5.25 1.00
 Nos. RA122-RA130B (11) 12.95 4.00
 Set, never hinged 30.00

 For surcharges see Nos. RA151-RA153,
RA187.

Nurse and
Children — PT75

Various Scenes with Children.

Inscribed: "1948 Cocuk Yili
Hatirasi"

1948 **Litho.** *Perf. 11*
Star in Red
RA131 PT75 20pa dp ultra .30 .25
RA132 PT75 20pa rose lilac .30 .25
RA133 PT75 1k dp Prus bl .50 .30
RA134 PT75 3k dk brn vio .75 .50
RA135 PT75 15k slate black 1.50 1.25
RA136 PT75 30k orange 3.50 3.00
RA137 PT75 150k yellow grn 4.50 4.00
RA138 PT75 300k brown red 7.00 6.50
 Nos. RA131-RA138 (8) 18.35 16.05
 Set, never hinged 30.00

 No. RA136 is arranged horizontally. For
overprints and surcharges see Nos. RA199-
RA206.

 Catalogue values for unused
stamps in this section, from this
point to the end of the section, are
for Never Hinged items.

Nos. RA101
to RA108
Overprinted in
Carmine

1949 *Perf. 11½*
RA139 PT52 1k multi 10.00 10.00
RA140 PT53 4k multi 10.00 10.00
RA141 PT54 10k multi 10.00 10.00
RA142 PT55 25k multi 10.00 10.00
RA143 PT56 40k multi 20.00 20.00
RA144 PT57 70k multi 10.00 10.00
RA145 PT58 1 l multi 10.00 10.00
RA146 PT59 2½ l multi 10.00 10.00
 Nos. RA139-RA146 (8) 90.00 90.00

Ruins and
Tent — PT76

Booklet Panes of One
1949 *Perf. 10 (top) x Imperf.*
RA149 PT76 5k gray, vio gray &
 red 3.00 2.00
RA150 PT76 10k red vio, sal &
 red 3.00 2.00

 Black numerals above each stamp indicate
its position in the booklet.

No. RA124 Surcharged in Black
1950 **Unwmk.** *Perf. 8½*
RA151 PT73 20pa on 2k 1.25 1.00

Postal Tax Stamps of 1944-48
Surcharged with New Value in Black
or Carmine
Perf. 8½ to 12½ and Compound
1952
RA152 PT73 20pa on 3k bl grn .50 .25
RA153 PT73 20pa on 4k gray .75 .25
RA154 PT72 1k on 2½k bl vio
 & car (C) 1.00 1.50
RA155 PT44 1k on 2½k car 2.00 1.00
RA156 PT25 1k on 3k pale
 gray brn 2.00 1.00
 Nos. RA152-RA156 (5) 6.25 4.00

"Protection" PT77

Various Symbolical Designs Inscribed "75 iNCi" etc.

1952	Typo.		Perf. 10	
RA157	PT77	5k bl grn & bl	2.00	1.50
RA158	PT77	15k yel grn, bl & cr	2.00	1.50
RA159	PT77	30k bl, grn & brn	2.00	1.50
RA160	PT77	1k blk, bl & cr	2.00	1.50
a.		Souvenir sheet, #RA157-RA160, imperf.	30.00	30.00
	Nos. RA157-RA160 (4)		8.00	6.00

Printed in sheets of 20 containing one horizontal row of each value.

Nurse and Children PT78

Design: 1k, Nurse and baby.

1954	Litho.		Perf. 10½	
	Star in Red			
RA161	PT78	20pa aqua	.60	.35
RA162	PT78	20pa yellow	.90	.35
RA163	PT12	1k deep blue	1.50	.80
	Nos. RA161-RA163 (3)		3.00	1.50

Globe and Flag — PT79

Designs: 5k, Winged nurse in clouds. 10k, Protecting arm of Red Crescent.

1954				
RA164	PT79	1k multi	.25	.25
RA165	PT79	5k multi	.50	.25
RA166	PT79	10k car, grn & gray	1.00	.25
	Nos. RA164-RA166 (3)		1.75	.75

See Nos. RA208, RA211-RA213. For surcharges see Nos. RA187A-RA187B.

Florence Nightingale — PT80

Selimiye Barracks PT81

30k, Florence Nightingale, full-face.

Crescent in Carmine

1954, Nov. 4				
RA167	PT80	20k gray grn & dk brn	.50	.50
RA168	PT80	30k dl brn & blk	.75	.50
RA169	PT81	50k buff & blk	1.25	.50
	Nos. RA167-RA169 (3)		2.50	1.50

Arrival of Florence Nightingale at Scutari, cent.

Type of 1942 and

Children Kissing — PT82 · Nurse Holding Baby — PT83

1955, Apr. 23			Star in Red	
RA170	PT82	20pa chalky bl	.25	.25
RA171	PT82	20pa org brn	.25	.25
RA172	PT82	1k lilac	.25	.25
RA173	PT82	3k gray bis	.25	.25
RA174	PT82	5k orange	.25	.25
RA175	PT12	10k green	2.50	.75
RA176	PT83	15k dk blue	.25	.25
RA177	PT83	25k brn car	1.50	1.40
RA178	PT83	50k dk gray grn	2.00	1.50
RA179	PT12	2½ l dull brn	375.00	125.00
RA180	PT12	10 l rose lil	875.00	250.00
	Nos. RA170-RA180 (11)		1,257.	380.15

Types of 1945
Inscribed: "Turkiye Kizilay Dernegi"

1955	Litho.	Perf. 10½x11½, 10½		
	Crescent in Red			
RA181	PT36	20pa vio brn & lem	.25	.25
RA182	PT41	1k blk & gray grn	.25	.25

Nurse — PT85

Nurses on Parade PT86

Design: 100k, Two nurses under Red Cross and Red Crescent flags and UN emblem.

	Perf. 10½			
1955, Sept. 5	Unwmk.		Litho.	
	Crescent and Cross in Red			
RA183	PT85	10k blk & pale brn	.75	.35
RA184	PT86	15k dk grn & pale yel grn	.75	.45
RA185	PT85	100k lt ultra	3.50	1.75
	Nos. RA183-RA185 (3)		5.00	2.55

Meeting of the board of directors of the Intl. Council of Nurses, Istanbul, Aug. 29-Sept. 5, 1955.

Nos. RA92 and RA130B Surcharged "20 Para"

1955				
RA186	PT43	20p on 20k	.50	.40
	Typo.			
RA187	PT74	20p on 100k (surch. 11½x2mm)	.60	.40
c.		Surcharge 13½x2½mm	1.00	.75

No. RA164 Surcharged with New Value and Two Bars

1956	Litho.		Perf. 10½	
RA187A	PT79	20p on 1k multi	.25	.25
RA187B	PT79	2.50k on 1k multi	.25	.25

Woman and Children — PT87

Designs: 10k, 25k, 50k, Flag and building. 250k, 5 l, 10 l, Mother nursing baby.

1956	Litho.		Perf. 10½	
	Star in Red			
RA188	PT87	20pa red org	.50	.50
RA189	PT87	20pa gray grn	.50	.50
RA190	PT87	1k purple	.50	.50
RA191	PT87	1k grnsh bl	.50	.50
RA192	PT87	3k lt red brn	1.00	.50
RA193	PT87	10k rose car	2.00	2.00
RA194	PT87	25k brt grn	4.00	2.00
RA195	PT87	50k brt ultra	6.00	2.00
RA196	PT87	250k red lilac	15.00	5.00
RA197	PT87	5 l sepia	35.00	15.00
RA198	PT87	10 l dk sl grn	57.50	30.00
	Nos. RA188-RA198 (11)		122.50	59.00

Nos. RA131-RA138 Overprinted and Surcharged in Black or Red: "IV. DUNYA Cocuk Gunu 1 Ekim 1956"

1956, Oct. 1	Unwmk.		Perf. 11	
RA199	PT75	20pa (R)	12.00	12.00
RA200	PT75	20pa	12.00	12.00
RA201	PT75	1k (R)	12.00	12.00
RA202	PT75	3k (R)	12.00	12.00
RA203	PT75	15k (R)	12.00	12.00
RA204	PT75	25k on 30k	12.00	12.00
RA205	PT75	100k on 150k (R)	12.00	12.00
RA206	PT75	250k on 300k	18.00	18.00
	Nos. RA199-RA206 (8)		102.00	102.00

The tax was for child welfare.

Type of 1954, Redrawn Type of 1946, and

Flower — PT88

Crescent in Red

1957	Unwmk.		Perf. 10½	
RA207	PT88	½k lt ol gray & brn	.50	.25
RA208	PT79	1k ol bis, blk & grn	.50	.25
RA209	PT88	2½k yel grn & bl grn	.50	.25
RA210	PT43	20k red & lt bl	2.75	1.25
RA211	PT79	25k lt gray, blk & grn	2.75	1.25
RA212	PT79	50k bl, dk grn & grn	8.00	1.50
RA213	PT79	100k vio, blk & grn	8.75	3.00
	Nos. RA207-RA213 (7)		23.75	7.75

No. RA210 inscribed "Turkiye Kizilay Cemiyeti." No. RA92 inscribed ". . . . Dernegi."

Children — PT89

1957	Unwmk.		Perf. 10½	
RA214	PT89	20pa car & red	.25	.25
RA215	PT89	20pa grn & red	.25	.25
RA216	PT89	1k ultra & car	.25	.25
RA217	PT89	3k red org & car	1.50	1.50
	Nos. RA214-RA217 (4)		2.25	2.25

"Blood Donor and Recipient" — PT90

Designs: 75k, Figure showing blood circulation. 150k, Blood transfusion symbolism.

1957, May 22		Size: 24x40mm		
RA218	PT90	25k gray, blk & red	.25	.25
		Size: 22½x37½mm		
RA219	PT90	75k grn, blk & red	.50	.30
RA220	PT90	150k yel grn & red	1.25	.60
	Nos. RA218-RA220 (3)		2.00	1.15

Redrawn Type of 1947
Inscribed: "V Dunya Cocuk Gunu"

1957		Star in Red	Perf. 10½	
RA221	PT72	100k blk & bis brn	1.25	.75
RA222	PT72	150k blk & yel grn	1.25	.75
RA223	PT72	250k blk & vio	2.50	1.00
	Nos. RA221-RA223 (3)		5.00	2.50

The tax was for child welfare.

Child and Butterfly — PT91

Various Butterflies. 50k, 75k horiz.

1958	Litho.		Unwmk.	
RA224	PT91	20k gray & red	.75	.75
RA225	PT91	25k multi	.75	.75
RA226	PT91	50k multi	1.50	1.50
RA227	PT91	75k grn, yel & blk	2.00	2.00
RA228	PT91	150k multi	2.50	2.50
	Nos. RA224-RA228 (5)		7.50	7.50

Florence Nightingale — PT92

1958			Crescent in Red	
RA229	PT92	1 l bluish green	.40	.25
RA230	PT92	1½ l red	.60	.50
RA231	PT92	2½ l blue	.80	.60
	Nos. RA229-RA231 (3)		1.80	1.35

Turkey stopped issuing postal tax stamps in June, 1958. Similar stamps of later date are private charity stamps issued by the Red Crescent Society and the Society for the Protection of Children.

POSTAL TAX AIR POST STAMPS

Air Fund Issues

These stamps were obligatory on all air mail for 21 days a year. Tax for the Turkish Aviation Society: 20pa for a postcard, 1k for a regular letter, 2 1/2k for a registered letter, 3k for a telegram, 5k-50k for a package, higher values for air freight. Postal tax air post stamps were withdrawn Aug. 21, 1934 and remainders destroyed later that year.

Biplane
PTAP1

Type PTAP1

Perf. 11, Pin Perf.

1926	Unwmk.		Litho.
	Size: 35x25mm		
RAC1	20pa brn & pale grn	3.00	.30
RAC2	1g blue grn & buff	2.00	.30
	Size: 40x29mm		
RAC3	5g vio & pale grn	8.00	1.00
RAC4	5g car lake & pale grn	35.00	15.00
	Nos. RAC1-RAC4 (4)	48.00	16.60
	Set, never hinged	275.00	

PTAP2

PTAP3

1927-29			Type PTAP2
RAC5	20pa dl red & pale grn	1.50	.50
RAC6	1k green & yel	1.25	.50
			Type PTAP3
	Perf. 11½		
RAC7	2k dp cl & yel grn	1.50	.50
RAC8	2½k red & yel grn	8.00	1.60
RAC9	5k dk bl gray & org	1.25	.50
RAC10	10k dk grn & rose	5.00	1.25
RAC11	15k green & yel	5.00	1.00
RAC12	20k ol brn & yel	7.00	2.00
RAC13	50k dk bl & cob bl	10.00	4.50
RAC14	100k car & lt bl	110.00	80.00
	Nos. RAC5-RAC14 (10)	150.50	92.35
	Set, never hinged	825.00	

#RAC1, RAC5, RAC7 and RAC11 Surcharged in Black (RAC15-RAC16, RAC18-RAC19) or Red (Others)

1930-31			
RAC15	1k ("Bir kurus") on RAC1	200.00	75.00
RAC16	1k ("Bir Kurus") on RAC5	1.50	.50
RAC17	100pa ("Yuz Para") on RAC7	2.00	.75
RAC18	5k ("Bes Kurus") on RAC5	8.00	1.50
RAC19	5k ("5 Kurus") on RAC5	3.00	.75
RAC20	10k ("On kurus") on RAC7	4.00	1.25
RAC21	50k ("Elli kurus") on RAC7	12.00	4.00
RAC22	1 l ("Bir lira") on RAC7	37.50	9.00
RAC23	5 l ("Bes lira") on RAC11	2,000.	400.00
	Nos. RAC15-RAC23 (9)	2,268.	492.75
	Set, never hinged	5,000.	

PTAP4

PTAP5

1931-32	Litho.	*Perf. 11½*	
RAC24	PTAP4 20pa black	5.00	1.75

Typo.

RAC25	PTAP5	1k brown car ('32)	2.00	.50
RAC26	PTAP5	5k red ('32)	4.00	.75
RAC27	PTAP5	10k green ('32)	6.00	1.50
	Nos. RAC24-RAC27 (4)		17.00	4.50

PTAP6

1933		Type PTAP6	
RAC28	10pa ("On Para") grn	3.50	2.00
RAC29	1k ("Bir Kurus") red	8.00	2.75
RAC30	5k ("Bes Kurus") lil	12.00	3.00
	Nos. RAC28-RAC30 (3)	23.50	7.75

TURKEY IN ASIA

'tər-kē in 'ā-zhə

(Anatolia)

40 Paras = 1 Piaster

This designation, which includes all of Turkey in Asia Minor, came into existence during the uprising of 1919, led by Mustafa Kemal Pasha. Actually there was no separation of territory, the Sultan's sovereignty being almost immediately reduced to a small area surrounding Constantinople. The formation of the Turkish Republic and the expulsion of the Sultan followed in 1923. Subsequent issues of postage stamps are listed under Turkey (Republic).

Issues of the Nationalist Government

Turkish Stamps of 1913-18 Surcharged in Black or Red

(The Surcharge reads "Angora 3 Piastres")

1920		Unwmk.	*Perf. 12*	
		On Stamps of 1913		
1	A24	3pi on 2pa red lilac	4.75	5.25
2	A25	3pi on 4pa dk brn	37.50	37.50
3	A27	3pi on 6pa dk bl	250.00	150.00
		On Stamp of 1916-18		
4	A42	3pi on 2pa vio (Bk)	35.00	20.00
		Nos. 1-4 (4)	327.25	212.75

Turkish Stamps of 1913-18 Hstmpd. in Black or Red

(The Srch. reads "Post, Piastre 3")

1921		On Stamps of 1913	*Perf. 12*	
5	A24	3pi on 2pa red lilac	35.00	25.00
a.		On No. 1	47.50	72.50
6	A25	3pi on 4pa dk brown	30.00	30.00
a.		On No. 2	160.00	175.00
7	A25	3pi on 4pa dk brn (R)	150.00	175.00
a.		On No. 2	160.00	175.00
8	A27	3pi on 6pa dk blue	125.00	150.00
9	A27	3pi on 6pa bl (R)	62.50	75.00
a.		On No. 3	110.00	140.00
		On Stamps of 1916-18		
10	A42	3pi on 2pa vio (R)	62.50	75.00
a.		On No. 4	97.50	125.00
		Nos. 5-10 (6)	465.00	530.00

Turkish Revenue Stamps Handstamped in Turkish "Osmanli Postalari, 1336" (Ottoman Post, 1920).

عثمانلی بوستہ کری
١٣٣٦

Type a

Dash at upper left is set high. Bottom (date) line is 8½mm long.

عثمانلی بوستہ لری
١٣٣٦

Type b

Dash at upper left is set lower. Bottom (date) line is 10mm long.

عثمانلی بوستہ لری
١٣٣٦

Type c

Dash at upper left is set lower. Bottom (date) line is 9mm long.

Religious Tribunals Revenue
R1

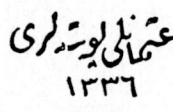

12	R1	1pi grn (a, b, c)	750.00	300.00
13	R1	5pi ultra (a, b)	*16,000.*	*15,500.*
14	R1	50pi gray grn (a, b, c)	25.00	35.00
		Cut cancellation		3.00
15	R1	100pi buff (a)	140.00	97.50
a.		100pi yellow (a)	95.00	72.50
		Cut cancellation		7.50
16	R1	500pi org (a)	225.00	150.00
		Cut cancellation		20.00
17	R1	1000pi brn (a)	3,000.	1,750.
		Cut cancellation		175.00
		See Nos. 29-32.		

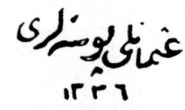

Court Costs Revenue
R2

Black Overprint

18	R2	10pa grn (b, c)	110.00	100.00
19	R2	1pi ultra (a, c)	—	19,000.
20	R2	5pi rose (c)	17,500.	—
21	R2	50pi ocher (a, b, c)	50.00	50.00
a.		50pi yellow (a, b, c)	12.00	17.00
		Cut cancellation, #21, 21a		2.00
22	R2	100pi brown (a)	150.00	100.00
		Cut cancellation		20.00
23	R2	500pi slate (a)	325.00	325.00
		Cut cancellation		20.00
		See Nos. 24, 33-39.		

Notary Public Revenue
R3

Design R2 Overprinted "Katibi Adliye Masus dur" in Red

24	R3	50pi ocher (a)	1,250.	150.00
		Cut cancellation		20.00

Laborer's Passport Tax Stamp — R4

Notary Public Revenue — R5

Black Overprint

25	R4	2pi emerald (a, c)	—	22,000.
26	R5	100pi yellow brn (a)	1,250.	150.00
		Cut cancellation		30.00
		See Nos. 46-48.		

Theater Tax Stamp — R6

Land Registry Revenue — R7

27	R6	20pa black	5,000.	5,000.
28	R7	2pi blue black	6,250.	6,250.
		See Nos. 40, 45.		

Hejaz Railway Tax Stamp — R8

Black Overprint
Perf. 11½

| 28A | R8 | 2pi dk red & bl (b) | 1,750. | 1,750. |

See Nos. 53-57.

Turkish Revenue Stamps Overprinted in Turkish "Osmanli Postalari, 1337" (Ottoman Post, 1921)

On #29-63

Perf. 12

29	R1	10pa slate	20.00	16.00
a.		Handstamped overprint	100.00	50.00
b.		Double overprint		
30	R1	1pi green	32.50	20.00
a.		Inverted overprint	35.00	22.50
b.		Handstamped overprint	3,500.	3,250.
31	R1	5pi ultra	29.00	14.50
a.		"1337" inverted	100.00	90.00
c.		Half used as 2½pi on cover		
		Nos. 29-31 (3)	81.50	50.50

Handstamped Overprint

| 32 | R1 | 50pi green | 7,250. | 7,250. |

Design R2 Overprinted

33	R2	10pa green	24.50	24.50
a.		Handstamped overprint	3,500.	3,500.
34	R2	1pi ultra	50.00	25.00
a.		Handstamped overprint	875.00	875.00
35	R2	5pi red	24.50	25.00
a.		Inverted overprint		
b.		"1337" inverted	100.00	100.00
c.		Half used as 2½pi on cover		
d.		Handstamped overprint	7,500	7,500.
36	R2	50pi ocher, handstamped ovpt.	500.00	100.00
		Cut cancellation		20.00
		Nos. 33-36 (4)	599.00	174.50

Design R3 Overprinted
Additional Turkish Overprint in Red or Black

37	R3	10pa green (R)	100.00	60.00
38	R3	1pi ultra (R)	72.50	50.00
39	R3	5pi rose (Bk)	72.50	50.00
a.		"1337" inverted	200.00	200.00
b.		Handstamped overprint	7,000.	7,000.
		Nos. 37-39 (3)	245.00	160.00

Design R7 Overprinted

| 40 | R7 | 2pi blue black | 125.00 | 110.00 |
| a. | | Handstamped overprint | 5,500. | 5,500. |

R12

1921 Overprinted in Black Perf. 12

41	R12	5pi green	150.00	125.00
		Cut cancellation		17.50
a.		Handstamped overprint	5,500.	5,000.

Museum Tax Stamp R13

Overprinted in Black

42	R13	1pi ultra	475.00	425.00
a.		Handstamped overprint	5,500.	5,500.
43	R13	5pi deep green	525.00	475.00
a.		Handstamped overprint	5,500.	5,500.

Handstamped Overprint

| 44 | R13 | 5pi dark vio | 7,000. | 7,000. |

The overprint variety "337" for "1337" exists on Nos. 42-43.

Design R6 Overprinted

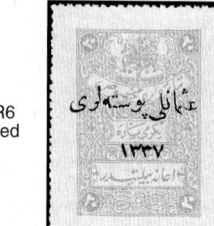

Perf. 12, 12½

45	R6	20pa black	12.50	5.00
a.		Date 4½mm high	15.00	
b.		"337" for "1337"	25.00	

Design R5 Overprinted

46	R5	10pa green	25.00	25.00
a.		Overprint 21mm long		
b.		"131" for "1337"		
47	R5	1pi ultra	37.50	25.00
a.		"13" for "1337"	50.00	50.00
b.		"131" for "1337"	50.00	50.00
c.		Inverted overprint	90.00	90.00
d.		Handstamped overprint	4,500.	4,500.
48	R5	5pi red	62.50	25.00
a.		Inverted overprint	90.00	90.00
b.		"131" for "1337"	85.00	85.00
c.		Handstamped overprint	4,500.	4,400.
		Nos. 46-48 (3)	125.00	75.00

R16

Perf. 11½, 11½x11
Overprinted in Black

49	R16	10pa pink	4.00	1.50
a.		Imperf.		
b.		Date "1237"	5.00	2.00
d.		Inverted overprint	15.00	
e.		Handstamped overprint	1,950.	1,950.
50	R16	1pi yellow	10.00	5.00
a.		Overprint 18mm long	10.00	5.00
b.		Date "1332"	12.00	
c.		Date "1317"		
d.		Inverted overprint	30.00	
e.		Handstamped overprint	1,950.	1,950.
51	R16	2pi yellow grn	12.50	5.00
a.		Date "1237"	15.00	
b.		Date "1317"		
c.		Imperf.		
d.		Inverted overprint	40.00	9.00
e.		Handstamped overprint		
52	R16	5pi red	20.00	1.00
a.		Horiz. pair, imperf. vert.		
b.		Inverted overprint	25.00	7.50
c.		Double overprint	30.00	12.50
d.		Date "1332"	45.00	
e.		Half used as 2½pi on cover		

f.		Overprint 18mm long	20.00	7.50
g.		Handstamped overprint	1,950.	1,950.
		Nos. 49-52 (4)	46.50	12.50

Design R8 Overprinted
Turkish Inscriptions

20 Paras · 1 Piaster

2 Piasters · 5 Piasters

1921 Dark Red & Blue Perf. 11½

53	R8	20pa on 1pi	75.00	75.00
54	R8	1pi on 1pi	7.50	4.00
55	R8	2pi on 1pi	7.50	4.00
a.		Inverted surcharge	25.00	
56	R8	5pi on 1pi	12.00	6.00
		Nos. 53-56 (4)	102.00	89.00

See No. 57.

No. 54 Overprinted

| 57 | R8 | 1pi on 1pi dk red & bl | 50.00 | 50.00 |

Hejaz Railway Tax Stamp — R19

Overprinted in Black

58	R19	1pi grn & brn red	6.00	4.00
a.		Double overprint		
b.		Handstamped overprint		

The errors "1307," "1331" and "2337" occur once in each sheet of Nos. 53-58.

Naval League Labels — R20

Overprinted in Black

1921 Perf. 12x11½

59	R20	1pa orange	11.00	15.00
a.		Date "1327"	30.00	30.00
60	R20	2pa indigo	12.00	15.00
61	R20	5pa green	15.00	17.50
62	R20	10pa brown	30.00	30.00
63	R20	40pa red brown	225.00	190.00
		Nos. 59-63 (5)	293.00	267.50

The error "2337" occurs on all values of this issue.

The Naval League stamps have pictures of three Turkish warships. They were sold for the benefit of sailors of the fleet but did not pay postage until they were overprinted in 1921.

Turkish Stamps of 1915-20 Overprinted

a

b

The overprints on Nos. 64-77 read "Adana December 1st, 1921." This issue commemorated the withdrawal of the French from Cilicia. On No. 71 the lines of the overprint are further apart than on Nos. 68-70 and 73-74.

1921 Perf. 12

64	A44 (a)	10pa grn (424)	10.00	7.00
65	A45 (a)	20pa deep rose (425)	10.00	7.00
a.		Inverted overprint	30.00	
66	A51 (a)	25pi car, straw (434)	20.00	25.00
a.		Double overprint		
b.		Inverted overprint	60.00	37.50
		Nos. 64-66 (3)	40.00	39.00

On Newspaper Stamp of 1915

| 67 | A21 (a) | 5pa och (P132) | 90.00 | 150.00 |

On Stamp of 1915

| 68 | A22 (a) | 5pa och (328) | 350.00 | 400.00 |

On Stamps of 1917-18

| 69 | A53 (b) | 5pi on 2pa (547) | 15.00 | 17.50 |
| 70 | A53 (b) | 5pi on 2pa (548) | 15.00 | 17.50 |

On Stamp of 1919

| 71 | A57 (b) | 35pi on 1pi bl (Bk; 579) | 42.50 | 50.00 |
| a. | | Inverted surcharge | 100.00 | |

On Newspaper Stamp of 1915

| 72 | A21 (b) | 5pa och (P132) | 200.00 | 200.00 |

On No. 72 the overprint is vertical, half reading up and half reading down.

On Stamps of 1920

| 73 | A32 (b) | 3pi blue (594) | 15.00 | 12.50 |
| 74 | A36 (b) | 10pi gray vio (596) | 20.00 | 20.00 |

On Postage Due Stamps of 1914

75	D1 (a)	5pa claret (J63)	350.00	350.00
76	D2 (a)	20pa red (J64)	350.00	400.00
a.		Inverted overprint	750.00	
77	D3 (b)	1pi dk bl (J65)	350.00	400.00
a.		Inverted overprint	750.00	750.00
		Nos. 75-77 (3)	1,050.	1,150.

Withdrawal of the French from Cilicia. Forged overprints exist.

Pact of Revenge, Burning Village at Top — A21

Izmir Harbor — A22

Mosque of Selim, Adrianople A23

Mosque of
Selim,
Konya — A24

Soldier — A25

Legendary
Gray
Wolf — A26

Snake Castle
and Seyhan
River,
Adana — A27

Parliament
Building at
Sivas — A28

A29

Mosque at
Urfa — A30

Map of
Anatolia
A31

Declaration of Faith
from the
Koran — A32

1922

			Litho.	Perf. 11½
78	A21	10pa violet brn	1.00	.25
79	A22	20pa blue grn	1.00	.25
80	A23	1pi dp blue	1.50	.35
81	A24	2pi red brown	3.00	.50
82	A25	5pi dk blue	3.00	.50
83	A26	10pi dk brown	12.50	.75
a.		Vert. pair, imperf between	100.00	
b.		Vert. strip of 3, imperf between	300.00	
84	A27	25pi rose	15.00	2.00
85	A28	50pi indigo	1.50	15.00
86	A29	50pi dk gray	1.50	1.25
87	A30	100pi violet	75.00	8.00
		Cut cancellation		2.00
88	A31	200pi slate	200.00	62.50
		Cut cancellation		10.00
89	A32	500pi green	125.00	27.50
		Cut cancellation		14.00
		Nos. 78-89 (12)	440.00	118.85
		Set, never hinged	2,075.	

Imperf

79a	A22	20pa	25.00	30.00
80a	A23	1pi	15.00	20.00
82a	A25	5pi	15.00	20.00
84a	A27	25pi	35.00	30.00
85a	A28	50pi	27.50	30.00

Stamps of
Type A23
Overprinted

1922

90	A23	1pi deep blue	7.25	15.00
91	A23	5pi deep blue	7.25	20.00
92	A23	10pi brown	7.25	20.00
93	A23	25pi rose	10.00	25.00
94	A23	50pi slate	12.50	25.00
95	A23	100pi violet	17.50	37.50
96	A23	200pi black vio	17.50	50.00
97	A23	500pi blue green	25.00	75.00
		Nos. 90-97 (8)	104.25	267.50
		Set, never hinged	300.00	

Withdrawal of the French from Cilicia and the return of the Kemalist Natl. army. The overprint reads: "Adana, Jan. 5, 1922."

No. 90-97 without overprint were presented to some high government officials.

First
Parliament
House,
Ankara — A33

1922 — Litho.

98	A33	5pa violet	.75	2.50
99	A33	10pa green	1.75	2.50
100	A33	20pa pale red	2.50	2.00
101	A33	1pi brown org	12.00	1.50
102	A33	2pi red brown	20.00	4.25
103	A33	3pi rose	6.00	.70
a.		Arabic "13" in right corner	10.00	7.50
b.		Thin grayish paper	55.00	7.50
		Nos. 98-103 (6)	43.00	13.45
		Set, never hinged	140.00	

Nos. 98-103, 103b exist imperf. In 1923 several stamps of Turkey and Turkey in Asia were overprinted in Turkish for advertising purposes. The overprint reads: "Izmir Economic Congress, 17 Feb., 1339."

POSTAGE DUE STAMPS

D1

1922 — Litho. — Perf. 11½

J1	D1	20pa dull green	1.00	5.00
a.		Imperf.		
J2	D1	1pi gray green	1.00	5.00
J3	D1	2pi red brown	2.50	17.50
J4	D1	3pi rose	4.50	25.00
J5	D1	5pi dark blue	6.00	55.00
		Nos. J1-J5 (5)	15.00	
		Set, never hinged	55.00	

TURKISH REPUBLIC OF NORTHERN CYPRUS

'tər-kish ri-'pə-blik of 'nor-thə̠ r̠n 'sī-prəs

LOCATION — Northern 40% of the Island of Cyprus in the Mediterranean Sea off the coast of Turkey.

Established following Turkish invasion of Cyprus in 1974. On Nov. 15, 1983 Turkey declared the Turkish Republic of Northern Cyprus to be independent. No other country has recognized this country.

1000 Milliemes = 1 Pound

100 Kurus = 1 Turkish Lira (1978)

Catalogue values for all unused stamps in this country are for Never Hinged items.

Letters bearing these stamps enter international mail via the Turkish Post Office.

Watermark

Wmk. 390

Republic of Turkey, 50th Anniv.
A1   A2

Designs: 3m, Woman sentry. 5m, Military parade. 10m, Flag bearers. 15m, Anniversary emblem. 20m, Ataturk statue. 50m, Painting, "The Fallen." 70m, Turkish flag, map of Cyprus.

Perf. 12x11½, 11½x12

1974, July 27 — Litho. — Unwmk.

1	A1	3m multicolored	45.00	37.50
2	A2	5m multicolored	1.00	.50
3	A1	10m multicolored	2.00	.50
4	A2	15m multicolored	1.50	.90
5	A1	20m multicolored	1.25	.70
6	A1	50m multicolored	4.00	2.75
7	A2	70m multicolored	35.00	15.00
		Nos. 1-7 (7)	89.75	57.85

First day covers are dated 1/29/73.

Nos. 5, 3 Surcharged

1975, Mar. 3 — Perf. 12x11½

8	A1	30m on 20m, #5	1.50	1.00
9	A1	100m on 10m, #3	3.00	2.25

Surcharge appears in different positions.

Historical
Sites and
Landmarks
A3

Designs: 3m, Namik Kemal's bust, Famagusta. 5m, 30m, Kyrenia Harbor. 10m, Ataturk Statue, Nicosia. 15m, St. Hilarion Castle. 20m, Ataturk Square, Nicosia. 25m, Coastline, Famagusta. 50m, Lala Mustafa Pasha Mosque, Famagusta vert. 100m, Kyrenia Castle. 250m, Kyrenia Castle, exterior walls. 500m, Othello Tower, Famagusta vert.

1975-76 — Perf. 13

10	A3	3m pink & multi	.40	.30
11	A3	5m bl & multi	.40	.30
12	A3	10m pink & multi	.45	.40
13	A3	15m pink & multi	.50	.40
14	A3	15m bl & multi	.50	.40
15	A3	20m pink & multi	3.00	.40

16	A3	20m bl & multi	.50	.40
17	A3	25m pink & multi	.70	.50
18	A3	30m pink & multi	1.00	.75
19	A3	50m pink & multi	1.50	1.00
20	A3	100m pink & multi	1.75	1.25
21	A3	250m pink & multi	2.50	1.75
22	A3	500m pink & multi	3.50	3.00
		Nos. 10-22 (13)	16.70	10.85

Issued: #10, 12-13, 15, 17-22, 4/21; #11, 14, 16, 8/2/76. #1, 14, 16 have different inscriptions and "1976."

For surcharges see Nos. 28-29.

Peace in
Cyprus — A4

Designs: 50m, Map, olive branch, severed chain. 150m, Map, globe, olive branch, vert.

1975, July 20 — Perf. 13½x13, 13x13½

23	A4	30m multicolored	.40	.25
24	A4	50m multicolored	.50	.35
25	A4	150m multicolored	1.10	1.00
		Nos. 23-25 (3)	2.00	1.60

Europa — A5

Paintings: 90m, Pomegranates by I.V. Guney. 100m, Harvest Time by F. Direkoglu.

1975, Dec. 29 — Perf. 13

26	A5	90m multicolored	2.00	1.00
27	A5	100m multicolored	3.00	1.50

Nos. 19, 20
Surcharged

1976, Apr. 28 — Perf. 13

28	A3	10m on 50m, #19	.50	.50
29	A3	30m on 100m, #20	1.25	1.25

Europa — A6

1976, May 3

30	A6	60m Expectation	1.00	.30
31	A6	120m Man in Meditation	1.25	.65

Fruits — A7

1976, June 28

32	A7	10m Ceratonia siliqua	.25	.25
33	A7	25m Citrus nobilis	.30	.25
34	A7	40m Fragaria vesca	.40	.25
35	A7	60m Citrus sinensis	.50	.30
36	A7	80m Citrus limon	.75	.45
		Nos. 32-36 (5)	2.20	1.50

For surcharges see Nos. 66-69.

Olympic Games, Montreal — A8

Design: 100m, Olympic rings, doves, horiz.

1976, July 17
37	A8	60m multicolored	.75 .25
38	A8	100m multicolored	1.00 .35

Liberation Monument — A9

1976, Nov. 1   *Perf. 13x13½*
39	A9	30m multi	.50 .25
40	A9	150m multi, diff.	.90 .45

Europa — A10

1977, May 2   *Perf. 13*
41	A10	80m Salamis Bay	2.00 .75
42	A10	100m Kyrenia Port	3.00 1.25

Handicrafts A11

1977, June 27
43	A11	15m Pottery	.35 .25
44	A11	30m Gourds, vert.	.55 .30
45	A11	125m Baskets	.95 .30
		Nos. 43-45 (3)	1.85 .80

Landmarks A12

Designs: 20m, Arap Ahmet Pasha Mosque, Nicosia, vert. 40m, Paphos Castle. 70m, Bekir Pasha aqueduct, Larnaca. 80m, Sultan Mahmut library, Nicosia.

1977, Dec. 2   *Perf. 13x13½, 13½x13*
46	A12	20m multicolored	.25 .25
47	A12	40m multicolored	.30 .25
48	A12	70m multicolored	.40 .25
49	A12	80m multicolored	.60 .40
		Nos. 46-49 (4)	1.55 1.15

Namik Kemal (1840-1888), Writer — A13

1977, Dec. 21   *Perf. 13*
50	A13	30m Bust, home	.30 .25
51	A13	140m Portrait, vert.	.90 .50

Social Security — A14

Designs: 275k, Man with sling, crutch. 375k, Woman with children.

1978, Apr. 17   *Perf. 13x13½*
52	A14	150k blk, bl & yel	.30 .25
53	A14	275k blk, grn & red org	.40 .25
54	A14	375k blk, red org & bl	.70 .25
		Nos. 52-54 (3)	1.40 .75

Europa — A15

225k, Oratory in Buyuk Han, Nicosia. 450k, Reservoir, Selimiye Mosque, Nicosia.

1978, May 2   *Perf. 13x13½, 13½x13*
55	A15	225k multi	3.25 1.00
56	A15	450k multi, horiz.	6.50 1.50

Transportation A16

1978, July 10   *Perf. 13½x13*
57	A16	75k Roadway	.30 .25
58	A16	100k Hydrofoil	.40 .25
59	A16	650k Airplane	.70 .70
		Nos. 57-59 (3)	1.40 1.20

National Oath — A17

1978, Sept. 13
60	A17	150k Dove, olive branch	.35 .25
61	A17	225k Stylized pen, vert.	.50 .25
62	A17	725k Stylized dove	.90 .65
		Nos. 60-62 (3)	1.75 1.15

Kemal Ataturk — A18

1978, Nov. 10
63	A18	75k bl grn & lt grn	.50 .25
64	A18	450k brn & buff	.50 .25
65	A18	650k Prus bl & lt bl	.50 .30
		Nos. 63-65 (3)	1.50 .80

Nos. 33-36 Surcharged

1979, June 4
66	A7	50k on 25m	.40 .25
67	A7	1 l on 40m	.50 .25
68	A7	3 l on 60m	.75 .25
69	A7	5 l on 80m	.90 .25
		Nos. 66-69 (4)	2.55 1.00

Souvenir Sheet

Turkish Invasion of Cyprus, 5th Anniv. — A19

1979, July 2   *Imperf.*
70	A19	15 l multicolored	4.00 3.25

Europa A20

Communications: 3 l, Stamps, building, map. 8 l, Early and modern telephones, globe, satellite.

1979, Aug. 20   *Litho.*   *Perf. 13*
71	A20	2 l multicolored	1.50 .40
72	A20	3 l multicolored	2.00 .65
73	A20	8 l multicolored	4.25 1.00
		Nos. 71-73 (3)	7.75 2.05

Intl. Consultative Radio Committee, 50th Anniv. — A21

1979, Sept. 24
74	A21	2 l blue & multi	.25 .25
75	A21	5 l gray & multi	.25 .25
76	A21	6 l green & multi	.35 .30
		Nos. 74-76 (3)	.85 .80

Intl. Year of the Child A22

Childrens' drawings of children.

1979, Oct. 29
77	A22	1½ l multi, vert.	.25 .25
78	A22	4½ l multicolored	.35 .30
79	A22	6 l multi, vert.	.45 .40
		Nos. 77-79 (3)	1.05 .95

Press reports in Jan. 1980 state that the 1979 UPU Congress declared Turkish Cyprus stamps invalid for international mail.

A23

Anniv. and events: 2½ l, Lala Mustafa Pasha Mosque, Famagusta. 10 l, Arap Ahmet Pasha Mosque, Lefkosa. 20 l, Holy Kaaba, Mosque.

1980, Mar. 23
80	A23	2½ l multicolored	.25 .25
81	A23	10 l multicolored	.45 .25
82	A23	20 l multicolored	.70 .70
		Nos. 80-82 (3)	1.40 1.20

1st Islamic Conference in Turkish Cyprus (2½ l). General Assembly of World Islam Congress (10 l). Moslem year 1400 AH (20 l).

Europa — A24

1980, May 23
83	A24	5 l Ebu-Suud Efendi	.75 .40
84	A24	30 l Sultan Selim II	2.50 .80

Historic Landmarks A25

Designs: 2½ l, Omer's Shrine, Kyrenia. 3½ l, Entrance gate, Famagusta. 5 l, Funerary monuments, Famagusta. 10 l, Bella Paise Abbey, Kyrenia. 20 l, Selimiye Mosque, Nicosia.

1980, June 25   *Blue Paper*
85	A25	2½ l buff & Prus bl	.25 .25
86	A25	3½ l pale pink & dk grn	.25 .25
87	A25	5 l pale bl grn & dk car	.25 .25
88	A25	10 l lt grn & red lil	.25 .25
89	A25	20 l buff & dk bl	.40 .35
		Nos. 85-89 (5)	1.40 1.35

For overprints and surcharges see Nos. 198-200.

Cyprus Postage Stamps, Cent. A26

1980, Aug. 16
90	A26	7½ l No. 5, vert.	.25 .25
91	A26	15 l No. 199	.35 .25
92	A26	50 l Social welfare, vert.	.90 .80
		Nos. 90-92 (3)	1.50 1.30

Palestinian Solidarity A27

15 l, Dome of the Rock, entrance, vert.

1980, Mar. 24
93	A27	15 l multicolored	.30 .25
94	A27	35 l multicolored	.75 .60

World Muslim Congress Statement — A28

1981, Mar. 24
95	A28	1 l In Turkish	.35 .25
96	A28	35 l In English	.90 .65

Ataturk by Feyhaman Duran — A29

1981, May 19
97 A29 20 l multicolored   1.50 .75
    Printed with se-tenant label promoting Ataturk Stamp Exhibition.

Europa
A30

    Folk dances.

1981, June 29
98 A30 10 l multicolored   .90 .40
99 A30 30 l multi, diff.   2.25 1.00

Souvenir Sheet

Ataturk, Birth Cent. — A31

1981, July 23   *Imperf.*
100 A31 150 l multicolored   2.25 1.75
    No. 100 has simulated perfs.

Flowers
A32

    Designs: 1 l, Convolvulus althaeoides, vert. 5 l, Cyclamen persicum. 10 l, Mandragora officinarum. 25 l, Papaver rhoeas, vert. 30 l, Arum dioscoridis, vert. 50 l, Chrysanthemum segetum. 100 l, Cistus salviaefolius, vert. 150 l, Ferula communis.

1981-82   *Perf. 13*
101 A32 1 l multicolored   .25 .25
102 A32 5 l multicolored   .25 .25
103 A32 10 l multicolored   .25 .25
104 A32 25 l multicolored   .40 .40
105 A32 30 l multicolored   .45 .45
106 A32 50 l multicolored   .75 .75
107 A32 100 l multicolored   1.50 1.50
108 A32 150 l multicolored   2.25 2.25
    Nos. 101-108 (8)   6.10 6.10
    Issue dates: 1 l, 10 l, 25 l, 150 l, Sept. 28; 5 l, 30 l, 50 l, 100 l, Jan. 22, 1982.
    For surcharge & overprints see #138-141, 201.

Intl. Year for Disabled Persons A33

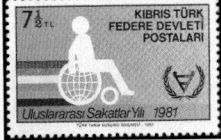

Fight Against Apartheid — A34   World Food Day — A35

1981, Oct. 16
109 A33 7½ l multicolored   .25 .25
110 A34 10 l multicolored   .35 .30
111 A35 20 l multicolored   .65 .50
    Nos. 109-111 (3)   1.25 1.05

Palestinian Solidarity A36

1981, Nov. 29
112 A36 10 l multicolored   .25 .25

Royal Wedding of Prince Charles and Lady Diana Spencer — A37

1981, Nov. 30
113 A37 50 l multicolored   1.00 .70

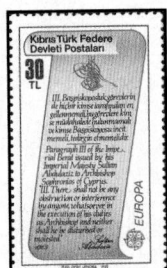

Charter of Cyprus, 1865 — A38

Turkish Forces Landing in Tuzla — A39

1982, July 30
114   Sheet of 4   5.00 5.00
   a. A38 30 l multicolored   1.00 1.00
   b. A39 70 l multicolored   1.00 1.00

    Europa. #114 contains 2 each #114a, 114b.

Buffavento Castle — A40

Windsurfing — A41

Kantara Castle A42

    Tourism: 30 l, Shipwreck museum.

    Perf. 12½x12, 12x12½
1982, Aug. 20
116 A40 5 l multicolored   .25 .25
117 A41 10 l multicolored   .30 .25
118 A42 15 l multicolored   .35 .30
119 A42 30 l multicolored   .60 .40
    Nos. 116-119 (4)   1.50 1.20

Art Treasures — A43

    Designs: 30 l, The Wedding by Aylin Orek. 50 l, Carob Pickers by Ozden Nazim, vert.

1982, Dec. 3   *Perf. 13x13½, 13½x13*
120 A43 30 l multicolored   .50 .30
121 A43 50 l multicolored   .75 .50

Robert Koch, TB Bacillus A44

World Cup Soccer Championships, Spain — A45

Scouting, 75th Anniv. — A46

1982, Dec. 15   *Perf. 12½*
122 A44 10 l multicolored   .25 .25
123 A45 30 l multicolored   .75 .60
124 A46 70 l multicolored   2.00 1.50
    Nos. 122-124 (3)   3.00 2.35

Paintings A47

    30 l, Calloused Hands by Salih Oral. 35 l, Malya-Limassol Bus by Emin Cizenel.

1983, May 16   *Perf. 13½x13*
125 A47 30 l multicolored   .90 .75
126 A47 35 l multicolored   1.25 1.00

Miniature Sheet

Europa — A48

    a, Map by Piri Reis. b, Cyprus seen from Skylab.

1983, June 30   *Perf. 13*
127 A48 Sheet of 2   60.00 30.00
   a.-b. 100 l any single   15.00 15.00

25th Anniv. of Turkish Resistance A49

    Designs: 15 l, No. 3. 20 l, Exploitation, Suppression & Resurrection by Aziz Hasan. 25 l, Resistance by Guner Pir.

1983, Aug. 1   *Perf. 13*
129 A49 15 l multi, vert.   .30 .30
130 A49 20 l multi   .45 .45
131 A49 25 l multi, vert.   .50 .50
    Nos. 129-131 (3)   1.25 1.25

World Communications Year — A50

1983, Aug. 1
132 A50 30 l shown   .60 .60
133 A50 50 l Letters   1.00 1.00

Birds A51

    10 l, Merops apiaster. 15 l, Carduelis carduelis. 50 l, Erithacus rubecula. 65 l, Oriolus oriolus.

1983, Oct. 10
134 A51 10 l multicolored   .25 .25
135 A51 15 l multicolored   .35 .25
136 A51 50 l multicolored   1.00 .70
137 A51 65 l multicolored   1.40 1.00
   a. Block of 4, #134-137   3.50 3.00
    Nos. 134-137 (4)   3.00 2.20

Nos. 103, 108
Ovptd.

Nos. 101,
104
Ovptd. or
Srchd.

1983, Dec. 7
138	A32	10 l multicolored	.25	.25
139	A32	15 l on 1 multi	.25	.25
140	A32	25 l multicolored	.35	.35
141	A32	150 l multicolored	2.00	2.00
		Nos. 138-141 (4)	2.85	2.85

Europa,
25th Anniv.
A52

1984, May 30   *Perf. 12x12½*
142	A52	50 l blk, yel & brn	*1.00*	*.50*
143	A52	100 l blk, bl & ultra	*2.00*	*1.00*
a.		Pair, #142-143	*3.25*	*2.75*

Olympics,
Los
Angeles
A53

Perf. 12½x12, 12x12½
1984, June 19
144	A53	10 l Olympic flame, vert.	.30	.25
145	A53	20 l Olympic rings	.40	.25
146	A53	70 l Judo	.80	.60
		Nos. 144-146 (3)	1.50	1.10

Ataturk
Cultural
Center
A54

Perf. 12x12½
1984, July 20   **Wmk. 390**
147	A54	120 l blk, yel & brn	1.00	.90

Turkish
Invasion of
Cyprus,
10th
Anniv.
A55

1984, July 20
148	A55	20 l shown	.40	.40
149	A55	70 l Map, flag, olive branch	.70	.70

Forest Conservation — A56

1984, Aug. 20
150	A56	90 l multicolored	1.25	.75

Paintings — A57

20 l, Old Turkish Houses in Nicosia by
Cevdet Cagdas. 70 l, Scenery by Olga Rauf.

1984, Sept. 21   *Perf. 13*
151	A57	20 l multicolored	.40	.40
152	A57	70 l multicolored	1.10	1.10

Proclamation of
Turkish Republic of
Northern
Cyprus — A58

Unanimous Vote by Legislative
Assembly — A59

Perf. 12½x12, 12x12½
1984, Nov. 15
153	A58	20 l multicolored	.50	.30
154	A59	70 l multicolored	.95	.70

Independence, 1st Anniv.

European Taekwondo Championship,
Kyrenia — A60

1984, Dec. 10
155	A60	10 l Competitors	.30	.25
156	A60	70 l Flags	.60	.55

Balance of the Spirit — A61

Paintings by Saulo Mercader: 20 l, The
Look, vert.

1984, Dec. 10   *Perf. 12½x13, 13x12½*
157	A61	20 l multicolored	.25	.25
158	A61	70 l multicolored	.50	.50

Visit by
Nuremburg
Chamber
Orchestra
A62

1984, Dec. 10   *Perf. 12½*
159	A62	70 l multicolored	1.00	.50

Dr. Fazil Kucuk
(1906-1984),
Politician — A63

70 l, Kucuk reading newspaper, c. 1970.

1985, Jan.
160	A63	20 l multicolored	.50	.25
161	A63	70 l multicolored	.70	.50

Domestic
Animals
A64

1985, May 29   *Perf. 12x12½*
162	A64	100 l Capra	.55	.55
163	A64	200 l Bos taurus	1.10	1.10
164	A64	300 l Ovis aries	1.60	1.60
165	A64	500 l Equus asinus	2.75	2.75
		Nos. 162-165 (4)	6.00	6.00

Europa — A65

Composers: No. 166, George Frideric Handel (1685-1759). No. 167, Domenico Scarlatti (1685-1757). No. 168, Johann Sebastian Bach (1685-1750). No. 169, Buhurizade Mustafa Itri (1640-1712).

1985, June 26   *Perf. 12½x12*
166	A65	20 l grn & multi	*.30*	*.25*
167	A65	20 l brn lake & multi	*.30*	*.25*
168	A65	100 l bl & multi	1.25	.80
169	A65	100 l brn & multi	1.25	.80
a.		Block of 4, #166-169	3.75	3.75

Printed in sheets of 16, containing 4 No. 169a.

Paintings — A66

Paintings: 20 l, Pastoral Life by Ali Atakan. 50 l, Woman Carrying Water by Ismet V. Guney.

1985, Aug.   *Perf. 12½x13*
170	A66	20 l multicolored	.35	.35
171	A66	50 l multicolored	.55	.55

Intl. Youth
Year
A67

Wmk. 390
1985, Oct. 29   **Litho.**   *Perf. 12½*
172	A67	20 l shown	.40	.25
173	A67	100 l Globe, dove	.90	.60

Northern Cyprus
Air
League — A68

Development of
Rabies Vaccine,
Cent. — A69

Ismet Inonu (1884-
1973), Turkish
Pres. — A70

UN, 40th
Anniv.
A71

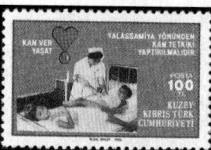

Blood
Donor
Services
A72

1985, Nov. 29
174	A68	20 l multicolored	.25	.25
175	A69	50 l Pasteur	.30	.30
176	A70	100 l brown	.60	.60
177	A71	100 l multicolored	.60	.60
178	A72	100 l multicolored	.60	.60
		Nos. 174-178 (5)	2.35	2.35

Paintings — A73

20 l, House with Arches by Gonen Atakol.
100 l, Ataturk Square by Yalkin Muhtaroglu.

1986, June 20   *Perf. 13*
179	A73	20 l multicolored	.25	.25
180	A73	100 l multicolored	.40	.40

Miniature Sheet

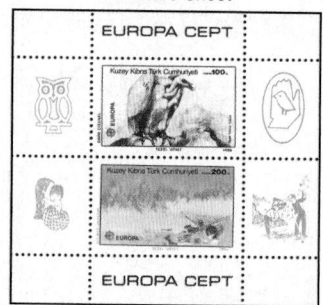

Europa — A74

1986, June 20   *Perf. 12x12½*
181	A74	Sheet of 2	16.00	16.00
a.		100 l Gyps fulvus	4.00	2.00
b.		200 l Roadside litter	8.00	4.00

Karagoz Puppets — A75

1986, July 25   *Perf. 12½x13*
182 A75 100 l multicolored   .90 .40

Anatolian Artifacts A76

Designs: 10 l, Ring-shaped composite pottery, Kernos, Old Bronze Age (2300-1050 B.C.). 20 l, Bird-shaped lidded pot, Skuru Hill tomb, Morphou, late Bronze Age (1600-1500 B.C.), vert. 50 l, Earthenware jug, Vryse, Kyrenia, Neolithic Age (4000 B.C.). 100 l, Terra sigillata statue of Artemis, Sea of Salamis, Roman Period (200 B.C.), vert.

1986, Sept. 15   *Perf. 12½*
183 A76 10 l multicolored   .25 .25
184 A76 20 l multicolored   .25 .25
185 A76 50 l multicolored   .25 .25
186 A76 100 l multicolored   .50 .50
   Nos. 183-186 (4)   1.25 1.25

For surcharge see No. 295A.

Defense Forces, 10th Anniv. — A77   World Food Day — A78

World Cup Soccer Championships, Mexico — A79

Halley's Comet A80

1986, Oct. 13
187 A77 20 l multicolored   .25 .25
188 A78 50 l multicolored   .30 .30
189 A79 100 l multicolored   .35 .35
190 A80 100 l multicolored   .40 .40
   Nos. 187-190 (4)   1.30 1.30

Development Projects — A81

1986, Nov. 17
191 A81 20 l Water resources   .25 .25
192 A81 50 l Housing   .25 .25
193 A81 100 l Airport   .45 .45
   Nos. 191-193 (3)   .95 .95

Royal Wedding of Prince Andrew and Sarah Ferguson — A82

Anniv. and events: No. 195, Queen Elizabeth II, 60th birthday.

1986, Nov. 20   *Perf. 12½x13*   Wmk. 390
194 A82 100 l multicolored   .50 .35
195 A82 100 l multicolored   .50 .35
   a. Pair, #194-195   1.00 .70

Trakhoni Station, 1904 A83

1986, Dec. 31
196 A83 50 l shown   .40 .25
197 A83 100 l Locomotive #1, 1904   1.00 .60

Rail transport, 1904-1951.

Nos. 86, 88-89, 105 Overprinted or Surcharged

a

b

1987, May 18   Unwmk.   *Perf. 13*
198 A25(a) 10 l on #89   .40 .25
199 A25(a) 15 l on 3½ l, #86   .40 .25
200 A25(a) 20 l on #88   .50 .25
201 A32(b) 30 l on #105   .80 .35
   Nos. 198-201 (4)   2.10 1.10

Paintings — A84

Designs: 50 l, Shepherd by Feridun Isiman. 125 l, Pear Woman by Mehmet Uluhan.

Perf. 12½x13
1987, May 27   Wmk. 390
202 A84 50 l multicolored   .35 .25
203 A84 125 l multicolored   .85 .40

Europa A85

Modern architecture: 50 l, Bauhaus-style house, designed by A. Vural Behaeddin, 1973. 200 l, House, designed by Necdet Turgay, 1979.

1987, June 30   *Perf. 12½*
204 A85 50 l multicolored   3.00 .40
205 A85 200 l multicolored   6.00 1.75
   a. Bklt. pane, 2 each #204-205   20.00

No. 205a contains two copies each of Nos. 204-205, printed alternately, with unprinted selvage at each end of the pane, perf between stamps and selvage and imperf on outside edges. Thus, singles from the pane gauge 12½ by imperf.

Folk Dancers — A86

1987, Aug. 20
206 A86 20 l multicolored   .25 .25
207 A86 50 l multi, diff.   .25 .25
208 A86 200 l multi, diff.   .50 .50
209 A86 1000 l multi, diff.   2.50 2.50
   Nos. 206-209 (4)   3.50 3.50

For surcharge see No. 295B.

Infantry Regiment, 1st Anniv. — A87   5th Islamic Summit Conf., Kuwait — A88

Pharmaceutical Federation — A89

1987, Sept. 30
210 A87 50 l multicolored   .25 .25
211 A88 200 l multicolored   .50 .50
212 A89 200 l multicolored   .50 .50
   Nos. 210-212 (3)   1.25 1.25

Ahmet Belig Pasha (1851-1924), Egyptian Judge — A90   Mehmet Emin Pasha (1813-1871), Turkish Grand Vizier — A91

Famous men: 125 l, Mehmet Kamil Pasha (1832-1913), grand vizier.

1987, Oct. 22
213 A90 50 l brn & yel   .25 .25
214 A91 50 l multicolored   .25 .25
215 A91 125 l multicolored   .35 .30
   Nos. 213-215 (3)   .85 .80

Pres. Rauf Denktash, Turkish Prime Minister Turgut Ozal A92

1987, Nov. 2
216 A92 50 l multi   .25 .25

New Kyrenia Harbor A93

   Wmk. 390
1987, Nov. 20   Litho.   *Perf. 12½*
217 A93 150 l shown   .40 .40
218 A93 200 l Eastern Mediterranean University   .55 .55

Chair Weaver, by Osman Guvenir — A94

Paintings: 20 l, Woman Making Pastry, by Ayhan Mentes, vert. 150 l, Woman Weaving a Rug, by Zekai Yesiladali, vert.

   Wmk. 390
1988, May 2   Litho.   *Perf. 13*
219 A94 20 l multi   .25 .25
220 A94 50 l multi   .45 .25
221 A94 150 l multi   .85 .35
   Nos. 219-221 (3)   1.55 .85

Europa A95

200 l, Tugboat Piyale Pasha. 500 l, Satellite dish, broadcast tower, vert.

1988, May 31   *Perf. 12½*
222 A95 200 l multicolored   2.75 1.00
223 A95 500 l multicolored   4.00 1.25

Bayrak Radio and Television Corporation, 25th anniv. (500 l).

Tourism A96

Photographs: 150 l, Nicosia, by Aysel Erduran. 200 l, Famagusta, by Sonia Halliday and Laura Lushington. 300 l, Kyrenia, by Halliday and Lushington.

1988, June 17
224 A96 150 l multi   .25 .25
225 A96 200 l multi   .35 .35
226 A96 300 l multi   .50 .50
   Nos. 224-226 (3)   1.10 1.10

Turkish Prime
Ministers — A97

No. 227, Bulent Ecevit, 1970's. No. 228,
Bulent Ulusu, Sept. 21, 1980-Dec. 13, 1983.
No. 229, Turgut Ozal, from Dec. 13, 1983.

1988, July 20
227 A97 50 l shown .25 .25
228 A97 50 l multi .25 .25
229 A97 50 l multi .25 .25
  Nos. 227-229 (3) .75 .75

Civil
Defense
A98

1988, Aug. 8   *Perf. 12x12½*
230 A98 150 l multicolored .35 .35

Summer
Olympics,
Seoul
A99

1988, Sept. 17   *Perf. 12½*
231 A99 200 l shown .30 .30
232 A99 250 l Women's running .40 .40
233 A99 400 l Seoul .65 .65
  Nos. 231-233 (3) 1.35 1.35

Sedat Simavi (1896-
1953), Turkish
Journalist — A100

Intl. Conferences, Kyrenia — A101

North Cyprus
Intl. Industrial
Fair — A102

Intl. Red. Cross
and Red
Crescent
Organizations,
125th
Anniv. — A103

US-USSR
Summit
Meeting on
Nuclear
Arms
Reduction
A104

WHO, 40th
Anniv. — A105

1988, Oct. 17   *Perf. 12½x12, 12x12½*
234 A100 50 l olive grn .25 .25
235 A101 100 l multi .25 .25
236 A102 300 l multi .55 .55
237 A103 400 l multi .85 .85
238 A104 400 l Gorbachev and
              Reagan .85 .85
239 A105 600 l multi 1.10 1.10
  Nos. 234-239 (6) 3.85 3.85

Miniature Sheet

Portraits and Photographs of Kemal
Ataturk — A106

b, Holding canteen. c, In uniform. d, Facing
left.

1988, Nov. 10   *Perf. 12½*
240 A106 Sheet of 4 3.00 2.00
  a.-d. 250 l any single .50 .40

Souvenir Sheet

Turkish Republic of Northern Cyprus,
5th Anniv. — A107

1988, Nov. 15   *Imperf.*
241 A107 500 l multicolored 3.25 1.75

Dervis Pasha Mansion, 19th Cent.,
Nicosia — A108

Designs: 400 l, Gamblers' Inn, 17th cent.,
Asmaalti Meydani. 600 l, Camii Cedit Mosque,
1902, Paphos, vert.

1989, Apr. 28   *Perf. 13*
242 A108 150 l shown .30 .30
243 A108 400 l multi .80 .80
244 A108 600 l multi 1.25 1.25
  Nos. 242-244 (3) 2.35 2.35

Europa — A109

1989, May 31   *Perf. 12½x12*
245 A109 600 l Girl, doll 3.00 1.00
246 A109 1000 l Flying kite 4.00 1.25
  a. Bklt. pane, 2 each #245-246,
        perf. 12½ 16.00

Geneva
Peace
Summit,
Aug. 24,
1988
A110

1989, June 30   *Perf. 12½*
247 A110 500 l blk & dark red 1.00 1.00

Wildlife
A111

1989, July 31
248 A111 100 l Alectoris chukar .25 .25
249 A111 200 l Lepus cyprius .40 .40
250 A111 700 l Francolinus
                francolinus 1.40 1.40
251 A111 2000 l Vulpes vulpes 4.00 4.00
  Nos. 248-251 (4) 6.05 6.05

Natl. Development Projects — A112

100 l, Road construction. 150 l, Sanitary
water supply. 200 l, Afforestation. 450 l, Telecommunications. 650 l, Power station. 700 l,
Irrigation ponds.

Perf. 12½x12, 12x12½
1989, Sept. 29
252 A112 100 l multicolored .25 .25
253 A112 150 l multicolored .30 .30
254 A112 200 l multicolored .40 .40
255 A112 450 l multicolored .90 .90
256 A112 650 l multicolored 1.25 1.25
257 A112 700 l multicolored 1.40 1.40
  Nos. 252-257 (6) 4.50 4.50

  Nos. 253-256 vert.

Free Port, Famagusta, 15th
Anniv. — A113

Turkish Cypriot
Post, 25th
Anniv. — A114

Saded Newspaper, Cent. — A115

Intl. Marine Organization, 30th
Anniv. — A116

Erenkoy
Uprising,
25th
Anniv.
A117

Perf. 12x12½, 12½x13 (450 l)
1989, Nov. 17
258 A113 100 l multicolored .25 .25
259 A114 450 l multicolored .90 .90
260 A115 500 l multicolored 1.00 1.00
261 A116 600 l multicolored 1.25 1.25
262 A117 1000 l multicolored 2.00 2.00
  Nos. 258-262 (5) 5.40 5.40

Erdal Inonu — A118

1989, Dec. 15   *Perf. 12½x12*
263 A118 700 l multicolored 1.60 1.40

Visit of Inonu, Turkish politician, to northern
Cyprus.

Agriculture — A119

1989, Dec. 25   *Perf. 12x12½, 12½x12*
264 A119 150 l Mule drawn .30 .30
265 A119 450 l Ox drawn .90 .90
266 A119 550 l Millstone, olive
               press 1.10 1.10
  Nos. 264-266 (3) 2.30 2.30

  Nos. 264-265 horiz.

World
Health
Day
A120

Perf. 12x12½
1990, Apr. 19   Litho.   Wmk. 390
267 A120 200 l shown .40 .25
268 A120 700 l Cigarette, heart 1.50 .40

Europa
A121

Post offices.

1990, May 31   Perf. 12x12½
Litho.   Wmk. 390
269 A121 1000 l Yenierenkoy   3.00   1.50
270 A121 1500 l Ataturk
            Meydani   4.50   2.00
a.   Souv. sheet, 2 #269, 2 #270   18.00 16.00

World Cup Soccer Championships,
Italy — A122

300 l, Turkish Cypriot team. 1000 l, Ball,
emblem, globe.

1990, June 8
271 A122   300 l multicolored   .65   .65
272 A122 1000 l multicolored   2.00 2.00

A123

World Environment Day: Birds: 150 l, Turdus
philomelos. 300 l, Sylvia atricapilla. 900 l,
Phoenicurus ochruros. 1000 l, Phyllosopus
collybita.

1990, June 5   Perf. 12
273 A123   150 l multicolored   4.00   .75
274 A123   300 l multicolored   5.75 1.25
275 A123   900 l multicolored   12.00 2.75
276 A123 1000 l multicolored   15.00 5.00
    Nos. 273-276 (4)   36.75 9.75

World Wildlife Fund. For surcharge see No.
386.

A125

Designs: 300 l, Painting by Filiz Ankac. 1000
l, Sculpture by Sinasi Tekman, vert.

1990, July 31   Perf. 13x12½, 12½x13
279 A125   300 l multicolored   .65   .65
280 A125 1000 l multicolored   2.00 2.00

A126

Wmk. 390
1990, Aug. 24   Litho.   Perf. 12½
281 A126   150 l Amphitheater,
                Soli   .35   .35
282 A126 1000 l Mosaic, Soli   2.00 2.00

European Tourism Year.

Visit by
Turkish
President
Kenan
Evren
A127

1990, Sept. 19
283 A127 500 l multicolored   1.00 1.00

Traffic
Safety
A128

150 l, Wear seat belts. 300 l, Obey the
speed limit. 1000 l, Obey traffic signals.

1990, Sept. 21
284 A128   150 l multicolored   .35   .35
285 A128   300 l multicolored   .65   .65
286 A128 1000 l multicolored   2.00 2.00
    Nos. 284-286 (3)   3.00 3.00

A129

1990, Oct. 1
287 A129 1000 l multicolored   2.00 2.00

Visit by Turkish Prime Minister Yildirim
Akbulut.

Flowers — A130

150 l, Rosularia cypria. 200 l, Silene
fraudatrix. 300 l, Scutellaria sibthorpii. 600 l,
Sedum lampusae. 1000 l, Onosma caes-
pitosum. 1500 l, Arabis cypria.

Perf. 12½x12
1990, Oct. 31   Litho.   Wmk. 390
288 A130   150 l multicolored   .35   .25
289 A130   200 l multicolored   .40   .25
290 A130   300 l multicolored   .65   .25
291 A130   600 l multicolored   1.25   .30
292 A130 1000 l multicolored   2.00   .50
293 A130 1500 l multicolored   3.25   .80
    Nos. 288-293 (6)   7.90 2.35

For surcharges see Nos. 295C, 387.

Intl.
Literacy
Year
A131

300 l, Ataturk as teacher. 750 l, A, b, c,
books, map.

1990, Nov. 24   Perf. 12x12½
294 A131   300 l multicolored   .65   .25
295 A131   750 l multicolored   1.60   .40

Nos. 183, 206, 288
Surcharged

1991, June 3
Perfs. & Printing Methods as Before
295A A76   250 l on 10 l #183   .35   .25
295B A86   250 l on 20 l #206   .35   .25
295C A130 500 l on 150 l #288   .45   .25
    Nos. 295A-295C (3)   1.15   .75

    Shape of obliterator varies.

Orchids — A132

Wmk. 390
1991, July 8   Litho.   Perf. 14
296 A132   250 l Ophrys lapethica   .55   .55
297 A132   500 l Ophrys kotschyi   1.60 1.60

See Nos. 303-306.

A133

Europa: a, Hermes space shuttle. b,
Ulysses probe.

Perf. 12½x12
1991, July 29   Litho.   Wmk. 390
Miniature Sheet
298 A133 2000 l Sheet of 2,
              #a.-b.   10.00 8.00

Public
Fountains
A134

250 l, Kuchuk Medrese. 500 l, Djafer Pasha.
1500 l, Sarayonu Square. 5000 l, Arabahmet
Mosque.

Wmk. 390
1991, Sept. 9   Litho.   Perf. 12
299 A134   250 l multicolored   .25   .25
300 A134   500 l multicolored   .35   .35
301 A134 1500 l multicolored   1.10 1.10
302 A134 5000 l multicolored   3.50 3.50
    Nos. 299-302 (4)   5.20 5.20

Orchid Type of 1991

100 l, Serapias levantina. 500 l, Dactylorhiza
romana. 2000 l, Orchis simia. 3000 l, Orchis
sancta.

1991, Oct. 10   Perf. 14
303 A132   100 l multicolored   .25   .25
304 A132   500 l multicolored   .40   .40
305 A132 2000 l multicolored   1.40 1.40
306 A132 3000 l multicolored   2.00 2.00
    Nos. 303-306 (4)   4.05 4.05

Hindiler by Salih M. Cizel — A135

Painting: 500 l, Dusme by Asik Mene.

Wmk. 390
1991, Nov. 5   Litho.   Perf. 13
307 A135   250 l multicolored   .25   .25
308 A135   500 l multicolored   .25   .25

See type A143. For surcharge see No. 381.

World Food Day   Basbakan
A136   Mustafa Cagatay
              (1937-1989)
              A137

Eastern
Mediterranean
University — A138

Wolfgang
Amadeus
Mozart,
Death
Bicent.
A139

1991, Nov. 20   Perf. 12
309 A136   250 l multicolored   .25   .25
310 A137   500 l multicolored   .30   .30
311 A138   500 l multicolored   .30   .30
312 A139 1500 l multicolored   .85   .85
    Nos. 309-312 (4)   1.70 1.70

For surcharge see No. 380.

World
AIDS Day
A140

1991, Dec. 13   Perf. 12
313 A140 1000 l multicolored   .55   .55

Lighthouses — A141

250 l, Canbulat Burcu, Famagusta. 500 l,
Yat Limani, Kyrenia. 1500 l, Turizm Limani,
Kyrenia.

1991, Dec. 16   Perf. 12x12½
314 A141   250 l multicolored   .25   .25
315 A141   500 l multicolored   .30   .30
316 A141 1500 l multicolored   .85   .85
    Nos. 314-316 (3)   1.40 1.40

Tourism A142

Designs: 250 l, Elephant and hippopotamus fossils, Kyrenia. 500 l, Roman fish ponds, Lambusa (58 BC-398 AD). 1500 l, Roman tomb and church, Lambusa (58 BC-1192 AD).

1991, Dec. 27

317	A142	250 l multicolored	.25	.25
318	A142	500 l multicolored	.30	.30
319	A142	1500 l multicolored	.85	.85
		Nos. 317-319 (3)	1.40	1.40

Paintings A143

Designs: 500 l, Ebru, by Arife Kandulu. 3500 l, Nicosia, by Ismet Tartar.

Wmk. 390

1992, Mar. 31 Litho. *Perf. 14*

320	A143	500 l multicolored	.25	.25
321	A143	3500 l multicolored	1.75	1.75

See type A135.

Tourism A144

No. 322, Ancient building, Famagusta. No. 323, Trap shooting range, Nicosia. 1000 l, Salamis Bay resort, Famagusta. 1500 l, Casino, Kyrenia.

1992, Apr. 21 *Perf. 13½x14, 14x13½*

322	A144	500 l multicolored	.25	.25
323	A144	500 l multicolored	.25	.25
324	A144	1000 l multicolored	.50	.50
325	A144	1500 l multi, vert.	.75	.75
		Nos. 322-325 (4)	1.75	1.75

Souvenir Sheet

Discovery of America, 500th Anniv. — A145

Europa: a, 1500 l, Santa Maria, Nina and Pinta. b, 3500 l, Columbus.

1992, May 29 *Perf. 13½x14*

326	A145	Sheet of 2, #a.-b.	*10.00*	*10.00*

Sea Turtles A146

Perf. 13½x14

1992, June 30 Litho. Wmk. 390

327	A146	1000 l Green turtle	*3.00*	*3.00*
328	A146	1500 l Loggerhead turtle	*3.50*	*3.50*
a.		Souv. sheet, 2 ea #327-328	*14.00*	*14.00*

World Wildlife Fund.

1992 Summer Olympics, Barcelona A147

#329: a, Women's gymnastics, vert. b, Tennis, vert. 1000 l, High jump. 1500 l, Cycling.

1992, July 25 *Perf. 14x13½*

329	A147	500 l Pair, #a-b.	.75	.75

Perf. 13½x14

330	A147	1000 l multicolored	.50	.50
331	A147	1500 l multicolored	.75	.75
		Nos. 329-331 (3)	2.00	2.00

Electric Power Plant, Kyrenia A148

Social Insurance, 15th Anniv. A149

Intl. Federation of Women Artists A150

Veterinary Services A151

Perf. 13½x14

1992, Sept. 30 Litho. Wmk. 390

332	A148	500 l multicolored	.25	.25
333	A149	500 l multicolored	.25	.25
334	A150	1500 l multicolored	.75	.75
335	A151	1500 l multicolored	.75	.75
		Nos. 332-335 (4)	2.00	2.00

Civil Aviation Office, 17th Anniv. A152

Meteorology Office, 18th Anniv. — A153

Mapping, 14th Anniv. A154

Perf. 13½x14

1992, Nov. 20 Litho. Wmk. 390

336	A152	1000 l multicolored	.50	.50
337	A153	1000 l multicolored	.50	.50
338	A154	1200 l multicolored	.60	.60
		Nos. 336-338 (3)	1.60	1.60

Native Cuisine A155

Food: 2000 l, Zulbiye (pastry). 2500 l, Cicek Dolmasi (stuffed squash flowers). 3000 l, Tatar Boregi (flaky pastry dish). 4000 l, Seftali kebab (meat dish).

1992, Dec. 14

339	A155	2000 l multicolored	1.00	1.00
340	A155	2500 l multicolored	1.25	1.25
341	A155	3000 l multicolored	1.50	1.50
342	A155	4000 l multicolored	2.00	2.00
		Nos. 339-342 (4)	5.75	5.75

Intl. Conference on Nutrition, Rome. See Nos. 388-390.

Tourism A156

Designs: 500 l, Church and Monastery of St. Barnabas. 10,000 l, Bowl.

Perf. 13½x14

1993, Apr. 1 Litho. Wmk. 390

343	A156	500 l multi	.25	.25
344	A156	10,000 l multi	5.00	5.00

Souvenir Sheet

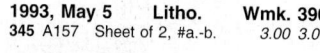

Europa — A157

Contemporary paintings by: a, 2000 l, Turksal Ince. b, 3000 l, Ilkay Onsoy.

Perf. 14x13½

1993, May 5 Litho. Wmk. 390

345	A157	Sheet of 2, #a.-b.	*3.00*	*3.00*

Trees — A158

500 l, Olea europea. 1000 l, Eucalyptus camaldulensis. 3000 l, Platanus orientalis. 4000 l, Pinus brutia tenore.

1993, June 11 *Perf. 14x13½*

346	A158	500 l multicolored	.25	.25
347	A158	1000 l multicolored	.50	.50
348	A158	3000 l multicolored	1.50	1.50
349	A158	4000 l multicolored	2.00	2.00
		Nos. 346-349 (4)	4.25	4.25

Arabahmet Rehabilitation Project — A159

Perf. 13½x14

1993, Sept. 20 Litho. Wmk. 390

350	A159	1000 l shown	.25	.25
351	A159	3000 l Homes, diff.	.50	.50

Creation of Turkish Republic of Northern Cyprus, 10th Anniv. A160

Designs: No. 353, Flags changing to dove, vert. 1000 l, Dove flying from flag. 5000 l, Flowers forming "10," map.

Perf. 13½x14, 14x13½

1993, Nov. 15 Litho. Wmk. 390

352	A160	500 l multicolored	.25	.25
353	A160	500 l multicolored	.25	.25
354	A160	1000 l multicolored	.25	.25
355	A160	5000 l multicolored	.80	.80
		Nos. 352-355 (4)	1.55	1.55

Ataturk, 55th Death Anniv. — A161

State Theaters, 30th Anniv. A162

Turkish Resistance Organization, 35th Anniv. — A163

Turkish News Agency, 20th Anniv. A164

Tchaikovsky, Death Cent. — A165

Perf. 14x13½, 13½x14

1993, Dec. 27 Litho. Wmk. 390

356	A161	500 l multicolored	.25	.25
357	A162	500 l multicolored	.25	.25
358	A163	1500 l multicolored	.30	.30
359	A164	2000 l multicolored	.40	.40
360	A165	5000 l multicolored	1.10	1.10
		Nos. 356-360 (5)	2.30	2.30

Painting by O.
Keten — A295

Painting
by S.
Cavusoglu
A296

2007, July 12 Perf. 14x13¾, 13¾x14
636 A295 50k multi .80 .80
637 A296 70k multi 1.10 1.10

Occupations of the Past — A297

Designs: 40k, Rattan weaver. 65k, Fruit peddler. 70k, Shoemaker. 1 l, Shoeshiner.

2007, Sept. 14 Perf. 13¾x14
638-641 A297 Set of 4 4.75 4.75

Methods of Postal
Transport — A298

Designs: 50k, Carrier pigeons. 60k, Mounted postman, coach, automobile. 1 l, Postman on bicycle, horiz. 1.25 l, Postman on motor scooter, horiz.

Perf. 14x13¾, 13¾x14
2007, Nov. 16
642-645 A298 Set of 4 5.75 5.75

Flowers — A299

Designs: 25k, Asphodelus aestivus. 50k, Ophrys fusca. 60k, Bellis perennis. 70k, Ophrys sphegodes. 80k, Dianthus strictus. 1.60 l, Ophrys argolica. 2.20 l, Crocus cyprius. 3 l, Limodorum abortivum. 5 l, Carlina pygmaea. 10 l, Ophrys kotschyi.

Wmk. 390
2008, Mar. 20 Litho. Perf. 14
646 A299 25k multi .40 .40
647 A299 50k multi .80 .80
648 A299 60k multi .95 .95
649 A299 70k multi 1.10 1.10
650 A299 80k multi 1.25 1.25
651 A299 1.60 l multi 2.50 2.50
652 A299 2.20 l multi 3.50 3.50
653 A299 3 l multi 4.75 4.75
654 A299 5 l multi 7.75 7.75
655 A299 10 l multi 15.50 15.50
Nos. 646-655 (10) 38.50 38.50

Europa — A300

Designs: No. 656, 80k, Woman writing letter. No. 657, 80k, Quill pen, world map.

2008, May 8 Perf. 14x13¾
656-657 A300 Set of 2 2.60 2.60

Souvenir Sheet

2008 Summer Olympics,
Beijing — A301

No. 658: a, Diving. b, Gymnastics.

2008, July 24
658 A301 65k Sheet of 2, #a-b 2.25 2.25
Exists imperf.

Souvenir Sheet

Turkish Resistance Organization, 50th
Anniv. — A302

No. 659: a, Emblem and "50." b, Monument, Lefkosa.

2008, Aug. 1 Imperf.
659 A302 1 l Sheet of 2, #a-b 3.50 3.50

Nicosia
(Lefkosa)
Municipal
Government,
50th Anniv.
A303

Inner Wheel
International
A304

Cyprus
Turkish
Airlines Jet
A305

Civil Defense
Organization
A306

Perf. 14x13¾, 13¾x14
2008, Sept. 18
660 A303 55k multi .85 .85
661 A304 80k multi 1.25 1.25
662 A305 1 l multi 1.60 1.60
663 A306 1.50 l multi 2.40 2.40
Nos. 660-663 (4) 6.10 6.10

Turkish Declaration of Independence
of Northern Cyprus, 25th
Anniv. — A307

2008, Nov. 15 Perf. 14
664 A307 1 l multi 1.25 1.25

Tradesmen — A308

Designs: 60k, Upholsterer. 70k, Miller. 80k, Bicycle mechanic. 2 l, Circumcisor.

2008, Nov. 20 Perf. 13¾x14
665-668 A308 Set of 4 5.25 5.25

Archaeology — A309

Items from Soli archaeological site: 60k, Gold ring. 2 l, Gold crown.

Perf. 13¾x14
2009, Mar. 23 Litho. Wmk. 390
669-670 A309 Set of 2 3.25 3.25

Europa — A310

No. 671: a, Solar system. b, Galaxy and comet.

2009, May 5
671 A310 80k Pair, #a-b 2.10 2.10
Intl. Year of Astronomy.

Medicinal
Plants — A311

Designs: 50k, Cistus creticus. 60k, Capparis spinosa. 70k, Pancratium maritimum. 1 l, Passiflora caerulea.

2009, July 9 Perf. 14x13¾
672-675 A311 Set of 4 3.75 3.75

Reptiles and Amphibians — A312

Designs: 80k, Agama stellio. 1.50 l, Bufo viridis.

2009, Sept. 14 Perf. 13¼
676-677 A312 Set of 2 3.25 3.25

Turkish Cypriot Air Traffic Controllers
Association — A313

Turkish Cypriot
Chamber of
Commerce
A314

Ziya Rizki (1919-
94), Politician
A315

2009, Nov. 12 Perf. 13¾x14
678 A313 65k multi .90 .90
Perf. 14x13¾
679 A314 1 l multi 1.40 1.40
680 A315 1.50 l multi 2.00 2.00
Nos. 678-680 (3) 4.30 4.30

Turkish Cypriot
Representation at
Organization of the
Islamic Conference,
34th Anniv. — A316

Emblem and: 70k, Map of Islamic Conference countries, flag, mosque, arch. 1 l, Mosque, flag, arch.

2010, Mar. 17 Perf. 14x13¾
681-682 A316 Set of 2 2.25 2.25

Europa
A317

2010, May 28   **Perf. 13¾x14**
683 A317   Pair   2.00 2.00
   a.   80k Two faces   1.00 1.00
   b.   80k Girl reading book   1.00 1.00
   c.   As "a," perf. 13¾ horiz.   1.00 1.00
   d.   As "b," perf. 13¾ horiz.   1.00 1.00
   e.   Vert. pair, #683c-683d   2.00 2.00
   f.   Booklet pane, 2 #683e   4.00 —
     Complete booklet, #683f   4.00

Worldwide
Fund for
Nature
(WWF)
A318

Designs: No. 684, 25k, Larus melanocephalus. No. 685, 25k, Larus audouinii. No. 686, 30k, Larus ridibundus. No. 687, 30k, Larus genei.

2010, June 4   **Perf. 14**
684-687 A318   Set of 4   1.40 1.40

2010 World Cup
Soccer
Championships,
South
Africa — A319

2010 World Cup Soccer Championships emblem and: 50k, World Cup trophy, crowd. 2 l, Flag of South Africa, elephants, soccer player, mascot.

2010, July 8   **Perf. 14x13¾**
688-689 A319   Set of 2   3.25 3.25

Foreign Press
Association — A320

Journalists: 60k, Kemal Asik (1925-89). 70k, Abdi Ipekçi (1929-79). 80k, Adem Yavuz (1943-74). 1 l, Sedat Simavi (1896-1953).

2010, Sept. 1   **Perf. 14**
690-693 A320   Set of 4   4.25 4.25

Cruise
Ships and
Tourist
Attractions
A321

Various ships and attractions: 1.50 l, 2 l.

2010, Oct. 20   **Perf. 13¾x14**
694-695 A321   Set of 2   5.00 5.00

Workers for Turkish
Cypriot
Society — A322

Designs: 50k, Ozdemir Sennaroglu (1931-85). 60k, Osman Orek (1925-99). 70k, Salih Miroglu (1953-2005). 80k, Ozker Özgür (1940-2005).

2010, Dec. 24   **Perf. 14x13¾**
696-699 A322   Set of 4   3.50 3.50

American
University,
Girne
(Kyrenia),
25th
Anniv.
A323

2010, Dec. 24   **Perf. 13¾x14**
700 A323   1 l multi   1.40 1.40

Politicians — A324

Designs: 80k, Dr. Niyazi Manyera (1911-99), Republic of Cyprus Minister of Health. 1.10 l, Mustafa Fazil Plümer (1914-2001), Republic of Cyprus Agriculture Minister. 2 l, Osman Orek (1925-99), Prime Minister of Turkish Republic of Northern Cyprus. 2.20 l, Dr. Fazil Küçük (1906-84), Vice-president of Republic of Cyprus.

2011, Mar. 9   **Perf. 14x13¾**
701-704 A324   Set of 4   7.75 7.75

Tourism
A325

Designs: 50k, Ayios Philon Church. 80k, Ayios Trias Basilica, vert. 1.10 l, Aphendrika. 2 l, Apostolos Andreas Monastery, vert.

2011, Apr. 18   **Perf. 13¾x14, 14x13¾**
705-708 A325   Set of 4   5.75 5.75

Europa — A326

Designs: No. 709, 1.50 l, Ladybug, forest on hillside. No. 710, 1.50 l, Pinecone, forest.

Perf. 14x13¾
2011, May 16   **Wmk. 390**
709-710 A326   Set of 2   4.00 4.00
  710a   Souvenir sheet of 2, #a709-710   4.00 4.00

Intl. Year of Forests.

Wedding of Prince
William and
Catherine
Middleton — A327

2011, May 27
711 A327   1 l multi   1.25 1.25

Trees — A328

Designs: 1 l, Quercus infectoria. 2.50 l, Olea europaea.

2011, July 18
712-713 A328   Set of 2   4.00 4.00

Art — A329

Design: 60k, Drawing by Birol Ruhi. 70k, Painting by Kemal Ankaç. 80k, Sculpture by Baki Bogaç. 1 l, Painting by Salih Bayraktar, horiz.

Perf. 14x13¾, 13¾x14
2011, Sept. 14
714-717 A329   Set of 4   3.50 3.50

Flora — A330

Designs: 25k, Ziziphus lotus. 50k, Cynara cardunculus. 60k, Oxalis pes-caprae. 70k, Malva sylvestris. 80k, Rubus sanctus. 1.50 l, Crataegus monogyna.

2011, Nov. 25   **Perf. 13¾**
718-723 A330   Set of 6   4.75 4.75

Miniature Sheet

Rauf Denktash (1924-2012), First
President of Turkish Republic of
Northern Cyprus — A331

No. 724 — Denktash: a, 60k, With dove on arm, flag in background. b, 60k, With flag in background. c, 1 l, At microphone. d, 1 l, Wearing striped tie.

2012, Mar. 16   **Perf. 14**
724 A331   Sheet of 4, #a-d   3.75 3.75

Europa — A332

No. 725 — Birds and various tourist attractions with denomination at: a, Left. b, Right.

Perf. 13¾x14
2012, May 8   **Litho.**   **Wmk. 390**
725 A332   80k Horiz. pair, #a-b   1.75 1.75

Reign of Queen Elizabeth II, 60th
Anniv. — A333

2012, June 1
726 A333   80k multi   .90 .90

2012 European
Soccer
Championships,
Poland and
Ukraine — A334

Emblem of Euro 2012, legs of soccer players, soccer balls and: 70k, Clock tower. 1 l, Stadium.

2012, June 29   **Perf. 14x13¾**
727-728 A334   Set of 2   1.90 1.90

2012 Summer
Olympics,
London — A335

Sites in London and: 2 l, Track. 2.20 l, Sailing.

2012, July 27   **Perf. 13¾**
729-730   A335   Set of 2   4.75 4.75

Motorcycles and Buses — A336

Designs: 60k, 1952 Triumph Tiger Twin motorcycle. 70k, 1948 Ariel Army W110 motorcycle. 80k, 1963 Bedford bus. 1 l, 1960 Fagor bus.

2012, Nov. 22   **Perf. 13¾x14**
731-734   A336   Set of 4   3.50 3.50

Politicians — A337

Designs: 60k, Ahmet Mithat Berberoglu (1921-2002). 70k, Faiz Kaymak (1904-82). 80k, Dr. Mehmet Dervis Manizade (1903-2003). 1 l, Mehmet Zeka (1903-84).

2013, Mar. 12   **Wmk. 390**   **Perf. 14**
735-738   A337   Set of 4   3.50 3.50

Traffic Safety
A338   A339

2013, Apr. 18   **Perf. 14x13¾**
739   A338   1 l multi   1.10 1.10
740   A339   2.20 l multi   2.50 2.50

Europa
A340

Postal vehicles: Nos. 741, 743, Bicycle. Nos. 742, 744, Van.

Perf. 13¾x14
2013, May 6   **Litho.**   **Wmk. 390**
Thick Lettering in Country Name and Bottom Inscriptions
741   A340   80k multi   .85 .85
742   A340   80k multi   .85 .85
Thin Lettering in Country Name and Bottom Inscriptions
743   A340   80k multi   .85 .85
744   A340   80k multi   .85 .85
   Nos. 741-744 (4)   3.40 3.40

Nos. 741 and 742 were each printed in sheets of 15 stamps + label. Each of the 15 stamps on the sheet of No. 741 and 13 of the 15 stamps on the sheet of No. 742 have a gray background design that reproduces the building shown on the label. Values for Nos. 741 and 742 are for any single stamp from the sheets of 15 + label. Nos. 743 and 744 were each printed in sheets of 40 having no gray background design.

A341

Flora and Fauna A342

Designs: 25k, Polyommatus icarus, Iris oratoria. 50k, Upupa epops. 60k, Teucrinum divaricatum ssp.canescens.

Perf. 13¾x14
2013, July 8   **Litho.**   **Wmk. 390**
745   A341   25k multi   .25 .25
Perf. 13½
746   A342   50k multi   .55 .55
747   A342   60k multi   .65 .65
   Nos. 745-747 (3)   1.45 1.45

Islamic Art — A343

Designs: 60k, 18th cent.ceremonial leather shield. 70k, 19th cent. prayer rug. 2 l, 16th cent. candlestick.

Wmk. 390
2013, Sept. 10   **Litho.**   **Perf. 14**
748-750   A343   Set of 3   3.25 3.25

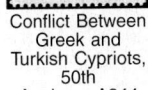

Conflict Between Greek and Turkish Cypriots, 50th Anniv. — A344

Turkish Republic of Northern Cyprus, 30th Anniv. — A345

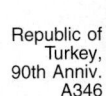

Republic of Turkey, 90th Anniv. A346

Perf. 14x13¾
2013, Nov. 20   **Litho.**   **Wmk. 390**
751   A344   60k black   .60 .60
752   A345   70k multi   .70 .70
Perf. 13¾x14
753   A346   80k red & black   .80 .80
   Nos. 751-753 (3)   2.10 2.10

Turkish Cypriot Post, 50th Anniv. A347

Designs: 50k, Cover bearing Cyprus #227. 60k, Cover bearing Cyprus #230. 1 l, Cover bearing Cyprus #223 and three U.S. #1213.

Perf. 13¾x14
2014, Jan. 6   **Litho.**   **Wmk. 390**
754-756   A347   Set of 3   1.90 1.90

Turkish Education College, 50th Anniv. — A348

Perf. 14x13¾
2014, Jan. 27   **Litho.**   **Wmk. 390**
757   A348   2.20 l multi   2.00 2.00

2014 World Cup Soccer Championships, Brazil — A349

2014 World Cup emblem and various soccer players: 70k, 2 l.

Wmk. 390
2014, Feb. 17   **Litho.**   **Perf. 13¾**
758-759   A349   Set of 2   2.50 2.50

Scenes From *The Only Witness Was the Fig Tree,* Play by Abdullah Oztoprak — A350

Various scenes: 25k, 60k, 70k, 1 l.

Perf. 14x13¾
2014, Mar. 10   **Litho.**   **Wmk. 390**
760-763   A350   Set of 4   2.40 2.40

Europa A351

Musicians and instruments: 80k, Tef (tambourine). 1.80 l, Davul and zurna (drum and reed pipe).

2014, May 23   **Litho.**   **Perf. 13¾**
764-765   A351   Set of 2   2.50 2.50
765a   Souvenir sheet of 2, #764-765   2.50 2.50

Nos. 452 and 461 Surcharged

Methods, Perfs. And Watermarks As Before

2014, July 4
766   A211   30k on 40,000 l #452   .30 .30
767   A214   40k on 90,000 l #461   .40 .40

Erenköy Uprising, 50th Anniv. — A352

Perf. 14x13¾
2014, Aug. 8   **Litho.**   **Wmk. 390**
768   A352   1 l multi   .95 .95

Fruit Blossoms A353

Designs: 60k, Apple blossom. 70k, Orange blossom. 80k, Pomegranate blossom. 1 l, Peach blossom.

Wmk. 390
2014, Sept. 19   **Litho.**   **Perf. 13¾**
769-772   A353   Set of 4   2.75 2.75
   Adjacent stamps in the sheet are rotated 90 degrees.

St. Valentine's Day — A354

Perf. 13¾x14
2015, Feb. 9   **Litho.**   **Wmk. 390**
773   A354   2.20 l multi   1.75 1.75

Naval Battle of the Dardanelles, Cent. — A355

Perf. 14x13¾
2015, Mar. 18   **Litho.**   **Wmk. 390**
774   A355   2 l multi   1.60 1.60

SEMI-POSTAL STAMPS

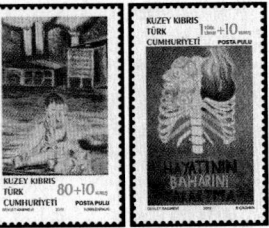

Campaign Against Cancer
SP1   SP2

Perf. 14x13¾
2015, Apr. 1   **Litho.**   **Wmk. 390**
B1   SP1   80k+10k multi   .70 .70
B2   SP2   1 l+10k multi   .85 .85

POSTAL TAX STAMP

Trees — PT1

1995, July 24   **Litho.**   **Perf. 14**
RA1   PT1 1000 l black & green   3.00 1.50

TURKMENISTAN

„tərk-,me-nə-'stan"

LOCATION — Southern Asia, bounded by Kazakhstan, Uzbekistan, Iran and Afghanistan
GOVT. — Independent republic, member of the Commonwealth of Independent States
AREA — 188,417 sq. mi.
POP. — 4,366,383 (1999 est.)
CAPITAL — Ashgabat

With the breakup of the Soviet Union on Dec. 26, 1991, Turkmenistan and ten former Soviet republics established the Commonwealth of Independent States.

100 Kopecks = 1 Ruble
100 Tenge = 1 Manat (1994)

Catalogue values for all unused stamps in this country are for Never Hinged items.

Dagdan Necklace, 19th Century — A1

Designs: No. 3, Girl in traditional costume, horiz. No. 4, Akhaltekin horse and rider in native riding dress. No. 5, Mollanepes Theater, horiz. 15r, National arms. No. 7, Pres. Saparmurad Niyazov at left, national flag, horiz. No. 8, Niyazov at right, flag, horiz. No. 9, Map of Turkmenistan.

1992   **Litho.**   **Perf. 12x12½**
1   A1 50k multicolored   .30 .30

Perf. 12½
2   A1 10r multicolored   .35 .35
3   A1 10r multicolored   .50 .50
4   A1 10r multicolored   .50 .50
5   A1 10r multicolored   .50 .50
6   A1 15r multicolored   1.00 1.00
7   A1 25r multicolored   1.75 1.75
8   A1 25r multicolored   .60 .60
   Nos. 1-8 (8)   5.50 5.50

Size: 112x79mm
Imperf
9   A1 10r multicolored   7.50 7.50

Issued: 50k, 1992; #8, 12/8; others, 8/27.
Nos. 2-8 exist imperf. Value, set $100.

Nos. 4, 6 Overprinted

1992, Dec. 12   **Color of Overprint**
10   A1 10r black   4.50 4.50
11   A1 10r brown   4.50 4.50
12   A1 10r red   4.50 4.50
13   A1 10r vermilion   — —
14   A1 10r carmine   4.50 4.50
15   A1 10r green   4.50 4.50
16   A1 15r black   4.50 4.50
17   A1 15r brown   4.50 4.50
18   A1 15r red   4.50 4.50
19   A1 15r pink   — —
20   A1 15r blue   4.50 4.50
21   A1 15r yellow   — —
   Nos. 10-21 (12)   40.50 40.50

1992 Summer Olympics, Barcelona A2

Designs: a, 1r, Weight lifting. b, 3r, Equestrian. c, 5r, Wrestling. d, 10r, Rowing. e, 15r, Emblem of Turkmenistan Olympic Committee.
No. 23, Flags, symbols for modern pentathlon, weight lifting, rowing, gymnastics.

1992, Dec. 15   **Photo.**   **Perf. 10½x10**
22   A2   Strip of 5, #a.-e.   9.25 9.25
Imperf
Size: 108x82mm
23   A2 15r multicolored   11.00 11.00

For surcharge see No. 33.

Musical Instruments — A3

Photo. & Engr.
1992, Sept. 13   **Perf. 12x11½**
28   A3 35k buff, red brn, gold & black   .30 .30

Horse A4

1992, Aug. 9   **Photo.**   **Perf. 12**
29   A4 20k shown   .25 .25
30   A4 40k Snake, vert.   .25 .25

A5

1992, Nov. 29   **Litho.**   **Perf. 12x11½**
31   A5 1r multicolored   .30 .30

US Pres. Bill Clinton, Pres. Saparmurad Niyazov — A6

Designs dated: a. 21.30.93. b. 22.03.93. c, 23.03.93. d, 24.03.93. e, 25.03.93.

1993, Mar. 21   **Litho.**   **Perf. 10½**
32   A6 100r Strip of 5, #a.-e.   12.00 12.00

Pres. Niyazov's visit to New York City & Washington DC.
Exists imperf. Value, $25.

No. 22 Surcharged

1993, Apr. 1   **Photo.**   **Perf. 10½x10**
33   A2 Strip of 5   7.00 7.00
a.   25r on 1r   1.40 1.40
b.   10r on 3r   .65 .65
c.   15r on 5r   .75 .75
d.   15r on 10r   .75 .75
e.   50r on 15r   2.40 2.40

Size of surcharge varies.

Phoca Caspica — A7

World Wildlife Fund A8

Phoca caspica: #34a, 25r, Facing right. #34b, 500r, Facing left. 15r, Lying in snow. 50r, On rocks. 100r, Mother and young. 150r, Swimming.

1993, Oct. 11   **Litho.**   **Perf. 13½**
34   A7   Pair #a.-b.   4.50 4.50
35   A8 15r multicolored   .60 .60
36   A8 50r multicolored   .95 .95
37   A8 100r multicolored   1.25 1.25
38   A8 150r multicolored   2.75 2.75
a.   Bklt. pane, 2 ea #34-38   28.00 28.00
   Booklet, #38a   32.50
   Nos. 34-38 (5)   10.05 10.05

Formation of Tovarishch Society for Exploitation of Turkmen Oil Fields, 115th Anniv. — A9

Designs: 1m, Two men viewing oil field. 1.5m, Early tanker Turkmen. 2m, Oil well. 3m, Alfred Nobel, Ludwig Nobel, Robert Nobel, Petr Bilderling, vert. 5m, Early oil field.

1994, June 26   **Litho.**   **Perf. 13**
39   A9 1m multicolored   .60 .60
40   A9 1.5m multicolored   .90 .90
41   A9 2m multicolored   1.25 1.25
42   A9 3m multicolored   1.90 1.90
a.   Miniature sheet of 8 + label   17.50 17.50
   Nos. 39-42 (4)   4.65 4.65

Souvenir Sheet
43   A9 5m multicolored   4.50 4.50

See Azerbaijan Nos. 415-418a.

Repetek Natl. Park A10

Designs: 3m, Repetek Institute. No. 45, Desert, camels. No. 46, Echis carinatus. No. 47, Varanus griseus. 20m, Testudo horsfieldi. No. 49, Haloxylon ammodendron.

1994, Dec. 11   **Litho.**   **Perf. 13**
44   A10 3m multicolored   .50 .50
45   A10 5m multicolored   .55 .55
46   A10 5m multicolored   .55 .55
a.   Miniature sheet of 8 + label   10.00 10.00
47   A10 10m multicolored   1.10 1.10
48   A10 20m multicolored   2.00 2.00
   Nos. 44-48 (5)   4.70 4.70

Souvenir Sheet
49   A10 10m multicolored   2.50 2.50

Intl. Olympic Committee, Cent. — A11

1994, Dec. 30   **Litho.**   **Perf. 14**
50   A11 11.25m multicolored   2.75 2.75

Souvenir Sheet
51   A11 20m multicolored   5.00 5.00

Miniature Sheet

Save the Aral Sea — A12

Designs: a, Feis caracal. b, Salmo trutta aralensis. c, Hyaena hyaena. d, Pseudoscaphirhynchus kaufmanni. e, Aspiolucius esocinus.

1996, Apr. 29   **Litho.**   **Perf. 14**
52   A12 100m Sheet of 5, #a.-e.   7.00 7.00

Independence, 5th Anniv. — A13

#53, Map of Turkmenistan on globe, vert. #54, Train pulling into station. #55, Natl. Airport, vert. #56, Iranian Pres. Rafsanjani, Turkmenistan Pres. Saparmurad Niyazov, Turkish Pres. Demirel. 500m, UN Secretary-General Boutros Boutros-Gali, Pres. Niyazov, vert. 1000m, Natl. flag, arms.

1996, Oct. 27   **Litho.**   **Perf. 14**
53   A13 100m multicolored   .50 .50
54   A13 100m multicolored   .60 .60
55   A13 300m multicolored   1.50 1.50
56   A13 300m multicolored   2.00 2.00
57   A13 500m multicolored   2.25 2.25
58   A13 1000m multicolored   4.75 4.75
   Nos. 53-58 (6)   11.60 11.60

1996 Summer Olympic Games, Atlanta A14

1997, May 5	Litho.	Perf. 14x14½
59	A14	100m Judo	.70	.70
60	A14	300m Boxing	1.60	1.60
61	A14	300m Track & field	1.60	1.60
62	A14	300m Wrestling	1.60	1.60
63	A14	500m Shooting	3.25	3.25
		Nos. 59-63 (5)	8.75	8.75

Souvenir Sheet

| 64 | A14 | 1000m Olympic torch | 6.25 | 6.25 |

Items inscribed "Turkmenistan" that were not authorized by Turkmenistan postal officials but which have appeared on the market include:

Single stamps of 100m depicting Princess Diana (3 different stamps), Mother Teresa, Pope John Paul II and Mother Teresa, 50th Anniv. of India, and 50th Anniv. of Pakistan.

Sheets of 4 stamps with denominations of 100m depicting JAPEX 98 / Cats.

Sheets of 9 stamps with denominations of 100m depicting the Titanic, Trains, Golfers, Japanese Armor, Japanese Paper Dolls, and Japanese Art.

Sheets of 6 stamps with denominations of 120m depicting Millennium (8 different sheets).

Sheets of 6 stamps with denominations of 120m depicting Pokémon, and Brad Pitt.

Sheets of 4 stamps with denominations of 195m depicting Greenpeace, Elvis Presley, Birds, Orchids, and Japanese Fashion.

Sheets of 6 stamps with denominations of 195m depicting Marilyn Monroe.

Sheets of 9 stamps with denominations of 195m depicting Cacti, and Minerals.

Sheets of 4 stamps with denominations of 250m depicting Akira Kurosawa.

Sheets of 2 stamps with denominations of 390m depicting Brazilian soccer players from 1998 World Cup.

Sheets of 9 stamps with denominations of 1000m depicting IBRA / Mushrooms (2 different sheets).

Souvenir sheets of 1 stamp with various denominations depicting Hokusai Artwork (2 different sheets), Pope John Paul II (2 different sheets), the Titanic (2 different sheets), 1998 Winter Olympics (2 sheets), Year of the Tiger (2 sheets), 50th Anniv. of Israel, Princess Diana, Queen Mother, Che Guevara, Frank Sinatra, Marilyn Monroe, Elvis Presley, International Year of Older Persons / Bob Hope, 1998 World Cup Soccer Championships, Severiano Ballasteros, Jacques Villeneuve, Leaders of the World / Automobiles, and Maria de Medici / Millennium.

Women's Traditional Clothing — A15

Various costumes.

1999, July 5	Litho.	Perf. 14
65	A15	500m multi	.90	.90
66	A15	1000m multi	1.50	1.50
67	A15	1200m multi	2.10	2.10
68	A15	2500m multi	2.75	2.75
69	A15	3000m multi	3.50	3.50
		Nos. 65-69 (5)	10.75	10.75

Falcons — A16

a, 1000m, Falco tinnunculus. b, 1000m, Falco peregrinus, looking left. c, 1000m, Falco peregrinus, looking right. d, 2500m, Falco tinnunculus, diff. e, 3000m, Falco peregrinus, diff.

2000, Mar. 30	Litho.	Perf. 14
70	A16	Sheet of 5, #a-e	15.00	15.00

Horn — A17

2000, Oct.	Litho.	Imperf.
Self-Adhesive		
71	A17	A multi	1.75	1.75

Sold for 5000m on day of issue.

UN Resolution on the Permanent Neutrality of Turkmenistan, 5th Anniv. — A18

UN emblem, "5," and flags of Turkmenistan and resolution co-sponsors: a, Afghanistan. b, Armenia. c, Azerbaijan. d, Bangladesh. e, Belarus. f, Colombia. g, Czech Republic. h, Egypt. i, France. j, Georgia. k, India. l, Indonesia. m, Iran. n, Kenya. o, Kyrgyzstan. p, Malaysia. q, Mauritius. r, Pakistan. s, Moldova. t, Russia. u, Senegal. v, Tajikistan. w, Turkey. x, Ukraine.

2000, Dec.	Litho.	Perf. 14
72		Sheet of 24 + label	70.00	70.00
a.-x.	A18	3000m Any single	2.75	2.75

Trade Center Building A19

Flag and Arms A20

2001, Apr. 24	Litho.	Imperf.
Self-Adhesive		
73	A19	B multi	1.00	1.00
74	A20	U multi	2.00	2.00

No. 73 sold for 1,200m, No. 74 sold for 3,000m on day of issue.

Horses — A21

No. 75, horiz.: a, Perenli. b, Garader. c, Pyyada. d, Tyllanur. e, Arkadas. f, Yanardag. No. 76, 5000m, Yanardag, diff., horiz. (denomination at LR). No. 77, 5000m, Yanardag, diff., horiz. (denomination at UR). No. 78: a, Bitarap. b, Yanardag, diff.

2001, Aug. 20	Litho.	Perf. 14½x14
75	A21	3000m Sheet of 6, #a-f	9.00	9.00

Size: 116x90mm

Imperf

| 76-77 | A21 | Set of 2 | 10.00 | 10.00 |

Souvenir Sheet

Perf. 14x14½

| 78 | A21 | 5000m Sheet of 2, #a-b | 8.00 | 8.00 |

Items inscribed "Turkmenistan" that were not authorized by Turkmenistan postal officials but which have appeared on the market include:

Sheets of 9 stamps with denominations of 50m depicting Kim Basinger, Matt Damon, and Pope John Paul II.

Sheets of 9 stamps with denominations of 100m depicting Leading Personalities of the 20th Century.

Sheets of 6 stamps with denominations of 120m depicting Leonardo DiCaprio, and Princess Diana.

Sheets of 8 stamps with denominations of 120m and one label depicting scenes and people from the 20th Century (3 different sheets).

Sheets of 9 stamps with denominations of 120m depicting Princess Diana, Musical group V.I.P., Television show "Xena, Warrior Princess," Elizabeth Taylor, Bruce Lee, Jackie Chan, Tiger Woods, Muhammad Ali, Monaco Grand Prix race cars, Auto racer David Coulthard, Soccer player David Beckham, Euro 2000 European Football Championships, Rugby players, Tennis Stars of the Millennium, Sportsmen of the Millennium, Elephants, Cats, Butterflies, and Pokémon.

Sheets of 2 stamps with denominations of 390m depicting Soccer players from the 1998 World Cup (2 different sheets depicting French and Japanese players).

Souvenir sheets of 1 with denominations of 975m depicting the Mona Lisa, Marilyn Monroe, and Lucille Ball.

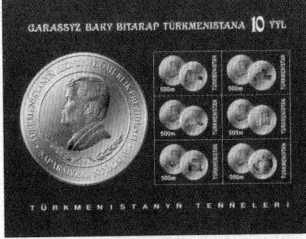

A22

Independence, 10th Anniv. — A23

No. 79 — 500m coins with reverses showing: a, Building with domed roof, coin denomination at right. b, Building with domed roof and tower, coin denomination at left. c, Building with pointed, conical roof. d, Building with archway. e, Building with domed roof on cubic base. f, Statue.

No. 80 — Archaeological sites: a, Soltan Sanjar. b, Nusay. c, Gyz Gala. d, Urgenç. e, Anew. f, Köne Urgenç.

No. 81 — Items in National museum: a, Horn. b, 19th cent. carpet. c, Musical instrument. d, Statue of nude woman. e, Vase. f, 20th cent. decoration.

No. 82, horiz. — Hotels: a, Ahal. b, Gara Altyn. c, Demiryolçy. d, Altyn Suw. e, Köpetdag. f, Aziya.

No. 83 — Buildings: a, Altyn Asyryn Yasayys Jaylary. b, Bitaraplyk Binasy (Arch of Neutrality). c, Türkmendöwletätiyaçlandyrys. d, Random Tower. e, Türkmenbasy Bank. f, Altyn Asyr Söwda Merkezi (Trade Center Building).

No. 84 — Monuments to: a, Oguz Han. b, Seljuk Bay. c, Bayram Han. d, Soltan Sanjar. e, Gorkut Ata. f, Görogly Beg.

No. 85 — Monuments to: a, Sahyrlary Bayram Han. b, Sahyrlary Kemine. c, Sahyrlary Zelili. d, Sahyrlary Seydi. e, Sahyrlary Mollanepes. f, Sahyrlary Mätäji.

2001	Litho.	Imperf.
79	A22	500m Sheet of 6, #a-f	3.00	3.00
80	A23	1000m Sheet of 6, #a-f	5.00	5.00
81	A23	1200m Sheet of 6, #a-f	7.00	7.00
82	A23	1250m Sheet of 6, #a-f	8.00	8.00
83	A23	1250m Sheet of 6, #a-f	8.00	8.00
84	A23	3000m Sheet of 6, #a-f	15.00	15.00
85	A23	3000m Sheet of 6, #a-f	15.00	15.00
		Nos. 79-85 (7)	61.00	61.00

Issued: Nos. 79-80, 10/17; No. 81, 10/19; Nos. 82-83, 10/23; Nos. 84-85, 10/21.

Mohammed Ali Jinnah (1876-1948), First Governor General of Pakistan — A24

2001, Dec. 25	Litho.	Perf. 13
86	A24	500m multi	1.10	1.10

Birds — A25

No. 87, 3000m: a, Motacilla flava. b, Lanius isabellinus. c, Oenanthe oenanthe. d, Corvus monedula. e, Corvus cornix. f, Upupa pyrrhocorax.

No. 88, 3000m: a, Sylvia communis. b, Cuculus canorus. c, Sylvia curruca. d, Corvus pica. e, Corvus frugilegus. f, Corvus corax.

No. 89, 5000m, Anas crecca. No. 90, 5000m, Riparia riparia.

2002, Dec. 1	Litho.	Perf. 14
Sheets of 6, #a-f		
87-88	A25	Set of 2	21.00	21.00
Souvenir Sheets		
89-90	A25	Set of 2	6.50	6.50

Butterflies — A26

No. 91, 3000m, vert.: a, Vanessa indica. b, Cynthia cardui. c, Pararge aegeria. d, Pieris rapae. e, Lysandra bellargus. f, Anthocharis cardamines.

No. 92, 3000m, vert.: a, Pandoriana pandora. b, Chazara briseis. c, Aphantopus hyperantus. d, Iolana iolas. e, Pararge schakra. f, Maniola jurtina.

No. 93, 5000m, Hamearis lucina. No. 94, 5000m, Quercusia quercus.

2002, Dec. 1   Sheets of 6, #a-f
91-92 A26   Set of 2   21.00 21.00
Souvenir Sheets
93-94 A26   Set of 2   6.50 6.50

Mosque — A27

2003, Feb.   Litho.   Imperf.
Self-Adhesive
95 A27 B multi   1.00 .80

Independence and Peace Monument, Ashkhabad — A28

2003, July 25   Self-Adhesive
96 A28 G multi   1.50 1.50

Building and Flags — A29

2004, Feb. 25   Self-Adhesive
97 A29 B multi   1.10 1.10

Dog — A30

2004, Aug. 13   Self-Adhesive
98 A30 A multi   1.60 1.60

Building — A31

2005   Self-Adhesive   Perf. 11¼
99 A31 M multi   1.10 1.10

Souvenir Sheet

Permanent Neutrality of Turkmenistan, 10th Anniv. — A32

No. 100: a, UN Secretary General Kofi Annan and Turkmenistan Pres. Saparmurad Niyazov. b, Sculpture on building, UN emblem.

2005, Dec. 1   Litho.   Perf. 11½
100 A32 5000m Sheet of 2,
#a-b   17.50 17.50

Souvenir Sheets

A33

A34

A35

Akhal-Teke Horses — A36

No. 101: a, Horse's head. b, Horse rearing up.

No. 102: a, Pony nursing. b, Horse walking left.

No. 103: a, Horse facing right. b, Horse facing left.

No. 104: a, Gray horse and mountain. b, Brown horse and mountain.

2005, Dec. 1
101 A33 2500m Sheet of 2,
#a-b   6.25 6.25
102 A34 2500m Sheet of 2,
#a-b   6.25 6.25
103 A35 2500m Sheet of 2,
#a-b   6.25 6.25
104 A36 2500m Sheet of 2,
#a-b   6.25 6.25
Nos. 101-104 (4)   25.00 25.00

Miniature Sheet

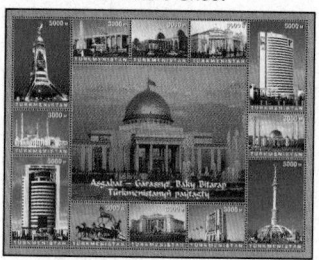

Ashgabat Architecture — A37

No. 105: a, 3000m, Building with dome, fountain at left. b, 3000m, Rukhiyet Palace (building with three green domes, automobiles). c, 3000m, Building with three golden domes and fountain. d, 3000m, Goktepe Mosque (green domes). e, 3000m, Mosque with golden domes. f, 3000m, Statue of Akhal-Teke horses. g, 3000m, Domed building with fence. h, 3000m, Central Bank and flags. i, 5000m, Neutrality Arch at night, vert. j, 5000m, Oil and Gas Ministry Building with flagpoles at right, vert. k, 5000m, President Hotel with flagpoles at left, vert. l, Independence Monument with statues at left and right, vert. Sizes: Nos. 105a-105h, 40x30mm; Nos. 105i-105l, 40x60mm.

2006   Litho.   Perf. 13x12¾
105 A37 Sheet of 12, #a-l, +
label   22.50 22.50

Independence, 15th Anniv. — A38

2006   Litho.   Imperf.
Self-Adhesive
106 A38 multi   1.00 1.00

Miniature Sheets

Pres. Saparmurat Niyazov (1940-2006) — A39

Nos. 108 and 109 — Pres. Niyazov: a, On reviewing stand, tank in background (34x47mm). b, At airplane's door, waving (34x47mm). c, Walking past women in red costumes (34x24mm). d, Wearing suit, seated in chair (34x24mm). e, Lifting girl, helicopter in background (34x24mm). f, Standing with children in front of helicopter (34x24mm). g, Turning key on box on table (34x24mm). h, Waving at crowd (34x24mm). i, Walking from under canopy (34x47mm). j, Seated in front of microphones (34x24mm). k, Standing in farm field (50x24mm). l, Cutting ribbon (34x24mm). m, Standing on red carpet, holding bowl (34x47mm).

Litho. with Foil Application
2007   Perf. 11½
Stamps With Light Blue Panels
107 A39 A Sheet of 13, #a-m 32.50 32.50
Stamps With Green Panels
108 A39 A Sheet of 13, #a-m 32.50 32.50

Leopard — A40

2007   Litho.   Rouletted 8
Self-Adhesive
109 A40 A multi   1.50 1.50

TURKS & CAICOS ISLANDS

ˈtərks ən̦d̦ ˈ kā-kəs ˈī-ləndz

LOCATION — A group of islands in the West Indies, at the southern extremity of the Bahamas
GOVT. — British colony; a dependency of Jamaica until 1959
AREA — 192 sq. mi.
POP. — 16,863 (1999 est.)
CAPITAL — Grand Turk

12 Pence = 1 Shilling
20 Shillings = 1 Pound
100 Cents = 1 US Dollar (1969)

Catalogue values for unused stamps in this country are for Never Hinged items, beginning with Scott 90.

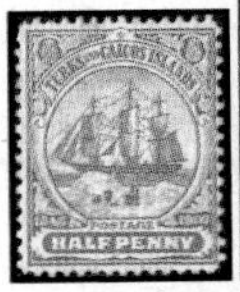
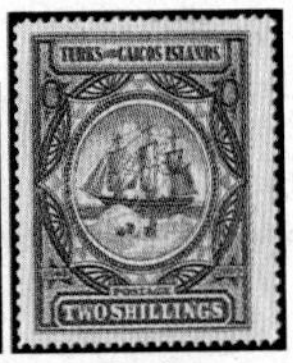

Dependency's Badge
A6 A7

1900-04 Engr. Wmk. 2 *Perf. 14*

1	A6	½p green	3.00	*4.50*
2	A6	1p rose	4.00	.85
3	A6	2p black brown	1.10	*1.40*
4	A6	2½p gray blue ('04)	2.00	1.10
a.		2½p blue ('00)	9.00	*17.50*
5	A6	4p orange	4.25	*8.00*
6	A6	6p violet	2.75	*7.50*
7	A6	1sh purple brn	3.75	*21.00*

Wmk. 1

8	A7	2sh violet	50.00	*80.00*
9	A7	3sh brown lake	80.00	*110.00*
		Nos. 1-9 (9)	150.85	*234.35*

1905-08 Wmk. 3

10	A6	½p green	5.75	.25
11	A6	1p carmine	19.00	.55
12	A6	3p violet, *yel* ('08)	2.50	*7.00*
		Nos. 10-12 (3)	27.25	*7.80*

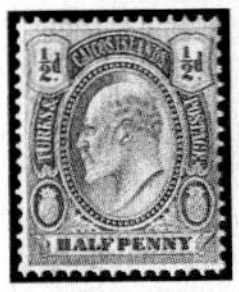

King Edward VII — A8

1909, Sept. 2 *Perf. 14*

13	A8	½p yellow green	.85	.45
14	A8	1p carmine	1.40	.45
15	A8	2p gray	5.50	1.60
16	A8	2½p ultra	8.00	4.25
17	A8	3p violet, *yel*	2.75	2.75
18	A8	4p red, *yel*	3.75	*8.00*
19	A8	6p violet	8.00	7.00
20	A8	1sh black, *green*	8.00	*9.50*
21	A8	2sh red, *grn*	45.00	*60.00*
22	A8	3sh black, *red*	47.50	*45.00*
		Nos. 13-22 (10)	130.75	*139.00*

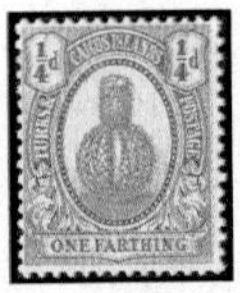

Turk's-Head Cactus — A9

1910-11 Wmk. 3

23	A9	¼p claret	2.00	1.10
24	A9	¼p red ('11)	.70	.50

See Nos. 36, 44.

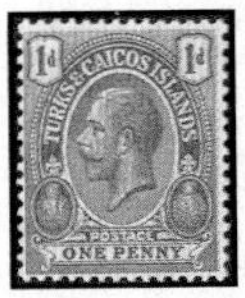

George V — A10

1913-16

25	A10	½p yellow green	.55	*2.00*
26	A10	1p carmine	1.10	*2.50*
27	A10	2p gray	2.50	*4.00*
28	A10	2½p ultra	2.50	*3.50*
29	A10	3p violet, *yel*	2.50	*12.50*
30	A10	4p scarlet, *yel*	1.10	*11.00*
31	A10	5p olive grn ('16)	7.50	*25.00*
32	A10	6p dull violet	2.75	*4.00*
33	A10	1sh orange	1.75	*5.75*
34	A10	2sh red, *bl grn*	18.00	*42.00*
a.		2sh red, *grnsh white* ('19)	30.00	*80.00*
b.		2sh red, *emerald* ('21)	55.00	*80.00*
35	A10	3sh black, *red*	17.50	30.00
		Nos. 25-35 (11)	57.75	142.25

Issued: 5p, 5/18/16; others, 4/1/13.
For overprints see Nos. MR1-MR13.

1921, Apr. 23 Wmk. 4

36	A9	¼p red	4.75	*24.00*
37	A10	½p green	3.00	*6.25*
38	A10	1p scarlet	1.10	*6.25*
39	A10	2p gray	1.10	*21.00*
40	A10	2½p ultra	2.00	*8.50*
41	A10	5p olive green	10.00	*65.00*
42	A10	6p dull violet	7.50	*65.00*
43	A10	1sh brown orange	12.00	*42.50*
		Nos. 36-43 (8)	41.45	*238.50*

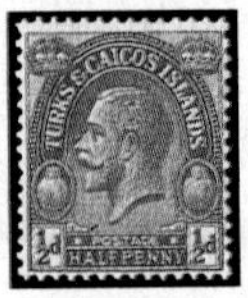

A11

1922-26 Inscribed "Postage"

44	A9	¼p gray black ('26)	1.10	*1.25*
45	A11	½p green	4.75	*4.50*
46	A11	1p brown	.65	*3.75*
47	A11	1½p rose red ('25)	9.00	*21.00*
48	A11	2p gray	.65	*7.00*
49	A11	2½p violet, *yel*	.65	*2.40*
50	A11	3p ultra	.65	*7.00*
51	A11	4p red, *yel*	1.60	*21.00*
52	A11	5p yellow grn	1.25	*30.00*
53	A11	6p dull violet	.95	*12.00*
54	A11	1sh orange	1.10	*25.00*
55	A11	2sh red, *green*	2.75	*12.50*

Wmk. 3

56	A11	2sh red, *green* ('25)	35.00	*95.00*
57	A11	3sh black, *red* ('25)	7.00	*37.50*
		Nos. 44-57 (14)	67.10	*279.90*

Issued: #47, 56-57, 11/24; #44, 10/11; others, 11/20.

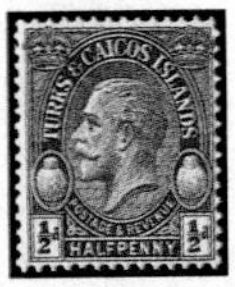

A12

Inscribed "Postage and Revenue"

1928, Mar. 1 Wmk. 4

60	A12	½p green	.95	.60
61	A12	1p brown	.95	.90
62	A12	1½p red	.95	*4.00*
63	A12	2p dk gray	.95	.60
64	A12	2½p vio, *yel*	.95	*6.25*
65	A12	3p ultra	.95	*8.75*
66	A12	6p brown vio	.95	*9.25*
67	A12	1sh brown org	4.50	*9.25*
68	A12	2sh red, *grn*	7.75	*45.00*
69	A12	5sh green, *yel*	13.50	*45.00*
70	A12	10sh violet, *bl*	62.50	*125.00*
		Nos. 60-70 (11)	94.90	*254.60*

Common Design Types pictured following the introduction.

Silver Jubilee Issue
Common Design Type

1935, May 6 *Perf. 11x12*

71	CD301	½p green & blk	.40	1.00
72	CD301	3p ultra & brn	2.75	5.25
73	CD301	6p ol grn & lt bl	2.10	6.00
74	CD301	1sh brn vio & ind	4.00	4.00
		Nos. 71-74 (4)	9.25	16.25
		Set, never hinged	16.00	

Coronation Issue
Common Design Type

1937, May 12 *Perf. 13½x14*

75	CD302	½p deep green	.25	.25
76	CD302	2p gray	.45	.65
77	CD302	3p brt ultra	.60	.65
		Nos. 75-77 (3)	1.30	1.55
		Set, never hinged	1.75	

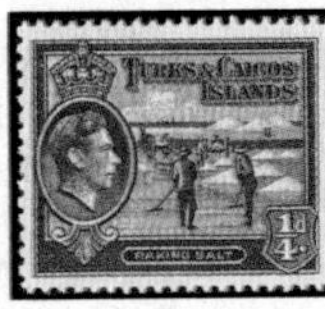

Raking Salt — A13

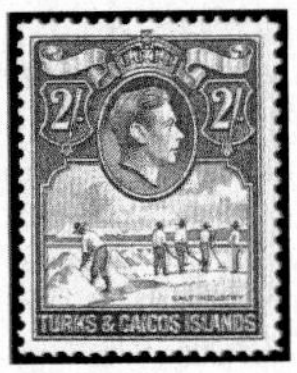

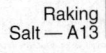

Salt Industry — A14

1938-45 Wmk. 4 *Perf. 12½*

78	A13	¼p black	.25	.25
79	A13	½p green	2.40	.25
80	A13	1p brown	.45	.25
81	A13	1½p carmine	.45	.25
82	A13	2p gray	.70	.30
83	A13	2½p orange	2.50	1.10
84	A13	3p ultra	.30	.30
85	A13	6p rose violet	6.00	3.25
85A	A13	6p blk brn ('45)	.25	.25
86	A13	1sh bister	2.40	*11.00*
86A	A13	1sh dk ol grn ('45)	.25	.25
87	A14	2sh rose car	25.00	17.00
88	A14	5sh green	30.00	25.00
89	A14	10sh dp violet	7.50	*8.50*
		Nos. 78-89 (14)	78.45	67.95
		Set, never hinged	135.00	

Catalogue values for unused stamps in this section, from this point to the end of the section, are for Never Hinged items.

Peace Issue
Common Design Type

1946, Nov. 4 Engr. *Perf. 13½x14*

90	CD303	2p gray black	.25	.25
91	CD303	3p deep blue	.25	.25

Silver Wedding Issue
Common Design Types

1948, Sept. 13 Photo. *Perf. 14x14½*

92	CD304	1p red brown	.25	.30

Perf. 11½x11

Engr.; Name Typo.

93	CD305	10sh purple	15.00	*20.00*

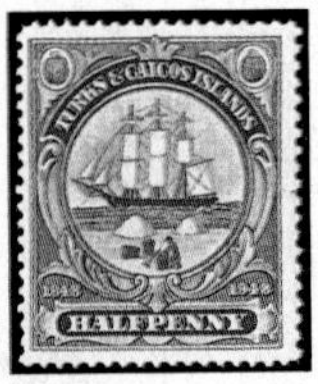

Dependency's Badge — A17

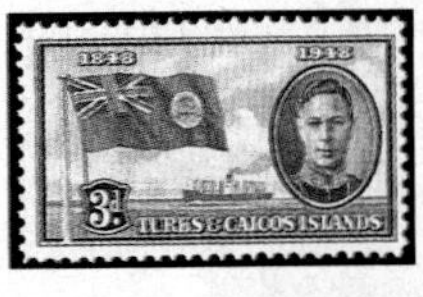

Flag and Merchant Ship — A18

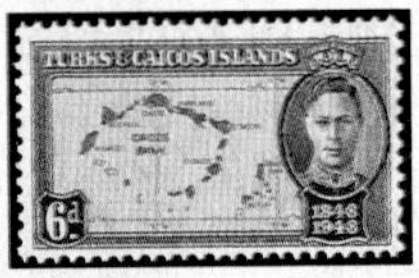

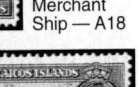

Map of the Islands A19

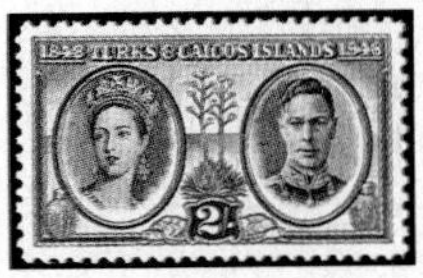

Victoria and George VI A20

1948, Dec. 14 Engr. *Perf. 12½*

94	A17	½p green	.55	.25
95	A17	2p carmine	.95	.25
96	A18	3p deep blue	.70	.25
97	A19	6p violet	.90	.40
98	A20	2sh ultra & blk	1.40	2.25
99	A20	5sh blue grn & blk	4.00	*7.00*
100	A20	10sh chocolate & blk	6.25	*7.00*
		Nos. 94-100 (7)	14.75	*17.40*

Cent. of political separation from the Bahamas.

UPU Issue
Common Design Types

Engr.; Name Typo. on 3p, 6p

Perf. 13½, 11x11½

1949, Oct. 10 Wmk. 4

101	CD306	2½p red orange	.25	*1.50*
102	CD307	3p indigo	1.90	1.25
103	CD308	6p chocolate	.75	.75
104	CD309	1sh olive	.75	.50
		Nos. 101-104 (4)	3.65	4.00

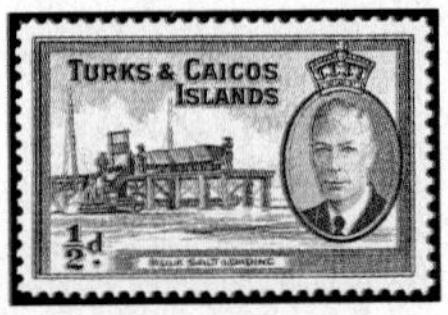

Loading Bulk Salt — A21

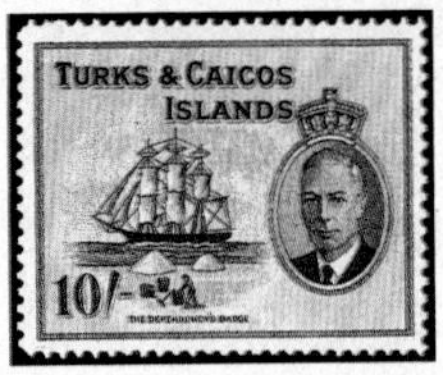

Dependency's Badge — A22

Designs: 1p, Salt Cay. 1½p, Caicos mail. 2p, Grand Turk. 2½p, Sponge diving. 3p, South Creek. 4p, Map. 6p, Grand Turk Light. 1sh, Government House. 1sh6p, Cockburn Harbor. 2sh, Government offices. 5sh, Salt Loading.

1950, Aug. 2 Engr. *Perf. 12½*

105	A21	½p deep green	.95	.60
106	A21	1p chocolate	.80	*1.25*
107	A21	1½p carmine	1.40	.90
108	A21	2p red orange	1.00	.60
109	A21	2½p olive green	1.25	.80
110	A21	3p ultra	.60	*.60*
111	A21	4p rose car & blk	4.00	1.25
112	A21	6p ultra & blk	3.00	.80
113	A21	1sh bl gray & blk	2.50	.60
114	A21	1sh6p red & blk	15.00	5.25
115	A21	2sh ultra & emer	6.50	*5.75*
116	A21	5sh black & ultra	27.50	11.50
117	A22	10sh purple & blk	30.00	*27.50*
		Nos. 105-117 (13)	94.50	*57.40*

Coronation Issue
Common Design Type

1953, June 2 *Perf. 13½x13*

118	CD312	2p red orange & blk	.40	*1.10*

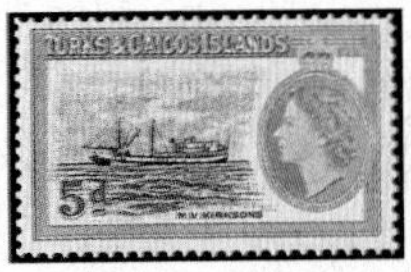

M. S. Kirksons A23

Design: 8p, Flamingos in flight.

1955, Feb. 1 Wmk. 4 *Perf. 12½*

119	A23	5p emerald & blk	.80	.80
120	A23	8p yellow brn & blk	3.25	.80

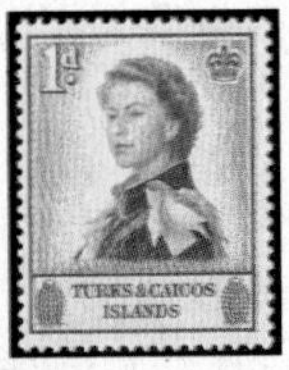

Queen Elizabeth II — A24

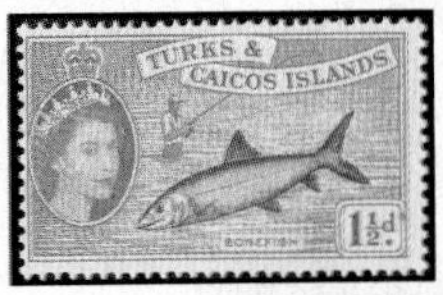

Bonefish A25

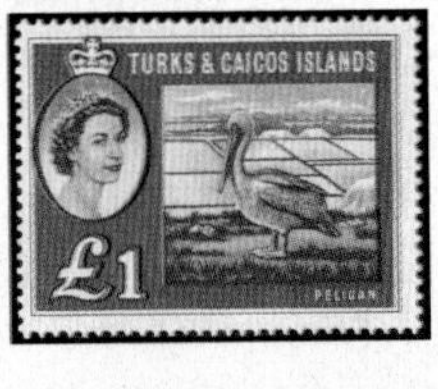

Pelican and Salinas A26

Designs: 2p, Red grouper. 2½p, Spiny lobster. 3p, Albacore. 4p, Muttonfish snapper. 5p,

Permit. 6p, Conch. 8p, Flamingos. 1sh, Spanish mackerel. 1sh6p, Salt Cay. 2sh, Caicos sloop. 5sh, Cable office. 10sh, Dependency's badge.

Perf. 13½x14 (1p), 13½x13

		1957-60	Engr.	Wmk. 314	
121	A24	1p lil rose & dk bl		.25	.25
122	A25	1½p orange & slate		.25	.25
123	A25	2p ol & brn red		.25	.25
124	A25	2½p brt grn & car		.25	.25
125	A25	3p purple & blue		.25	.25
126	A25	4p blk & dp rose		1.25	.25
127	A25	5p brown & grn		1.25	.75
128	A25	6p ultra & car		1.90	.85
129	A25	8p black & ver		3.25	.25
130	A25	1sh blk & dk blue		1.25	.25
131	A25	1sh6p vio bl & dk brn		15.00	2.10
132	A25	2sh lt brn & vio bl		13.00	4.00
133	A25	5sh brt car & blk		7.00	3.00

Perf. 14

134	A26	10sh purple & blk		17.50	13.00

Perf. 14x14½
Photo.

135	A26	£1 dk red & brn		50.00	26.00
		Nos. 121-135 (15)		112.65	51.70

Issued: £1, 11/1/60; others, 11/25/57.

Map of Islands A27

Perf. 13½x14

		1959, July 4	Wmk. 4	Photo.	
136	A27	6p ol grn & salmon		.70	.70
137	A27	8p violet & salmon		.80	.80

Granting of a new constitution.

Freedom from Hunger Issue
Common Design Type
Perf. 14x14½

		1963, June 4		Wmk. 314	
138	CD314	8p carmine rose		.50	.50

Red Cross Centenary Issue
Common Design Type

		1963, Sept. 2	Litho.	Perf. 13	
139	CD315	2p black & red		.25	.40
140	CD315	8p ultra & red		.70	.70

Shakespeare Issue
Common Design Type

		1964, Apr. 23	Photo.	Perf. 14x14½	
141	CD316	8p green		.40	.40

ITU Issue
Common Design Type
Perf. 11x11½

		1965, May 17	Litho.	Wmk. 314	
142	CD317	1p ver & brown		.25	.25
143	CD317	2sh emer & lt blue		.65	.65

Intl. Cooperation Year Issue
Common Design Type

		1965, Oct. 25	Wmk. 314	Perf. 14½	
144	CD318	1p blue grn & claret		.25	.25
145	CD318	8p lt violet & green		.60	.60

Churchill Memorial Issue
Common Design Type

1966, Jan. 24   Photo.   Perf. 14
Design in Black, Gold and Carmine Rose

146	CD319	1p bright blue		.25	.25
147	CD319	2p green		.25	.25
148	CD319	8p brown		.35	.25
a.		Gold impression double		200.00	
149	CD319	1sh6p violet		.75	1.00
		Nos. 146-149 (4)		1.60	1.75

Royal Visit Issue
Common Design Type

1966, Feb. 4   Litho.   Perf. 11x12
Portraits in Black

150	CD320	8p violet blue		.40	.30
151	CD320	1sh6p dk car rose		.80	.40

Andrew Symmer Landing with Union Jack A28

Designs: 8p, Andrew Symmer, his signature, Royal Warrant and Union Jack. 1sh6p, New coat of arms, Royal Cypher and St. Edward's crown.

Perf. 13½

		1966, Oct. 1	Unwmk.	Photo.	
152	A28	1p dk blue & dp org		.25	.25
153	A28	8p dk blue, dl yel & car		.25	.25
154	A28	1sh6p multicolored		.25	.25
		Nos. 152-154 (3)		.75	.75

200th anniv. of the landing of Andrew Symmer, British agent, establishing the ties with Great Britain.

UNESCO Anniversary Issue
Common Design Type
Wmk. 314

		1966, Dec. 1	Litho.	Perf. 14	
155	CD323	1p "Education"		.25	.25
156	CD323	8p "Science"		.30	.30
157	CD323	1sh6p "Culture"		.50	.50
		Nos. 155-157 (3)		1.05	1.05

Turk's-head Cactus — A29

Boat Building A30

Designs: 2p, Donkey cart. 3p, Sisal industry. 4p, Conch industry. 6p, Salt industry. 8p, Skin diving. 1sh, Fishing. 1sh6p, Water skiing. 2sh, Crawfish industry. 3sh, Map of Islands. 5sh, Fishing industry. 10sh, Coat of arms. £1, Queen Elizabeth II.

Perf. 14½x14, 14x14½

		1967, Feb. 1	Photo.	Wmk. 314	
158	A29	1p vio, red & yel		.25	.35
159	A30	1½p choc & org yel		1.10	.35
160	A29	2p gray, yel & sl		.25	.35
161	A29	3p green & dk brn		.25	.35
162	A30	4p grnsh bl, blk & pink		2.50	.35
163	A29	6p blue & dk brn		1.75	.35
164	A29	8p aqua, dk bl & yel		.55	.35
165	A30	1sh grnsh bl & red brn		.25	.35
166	A29	1sh6p brt grnsh bl, yel & brn		.40	.60
167	A30	2sh multicolored		1.10	1.75
168	A30	3sh grnsh bl & mar		1.10	.35
169	A30	5sh sky bl, dk bl & yel		1.50	2.50
170	A30	10sh multicolored		2.75	4.00
171	A29	£1 dk car rose, sil & dk bl		4.00	8.50
		Nos. 158-171 (14)		17.75	20.90

See #181, 217-230. For surcharges see #182-195.

Turks Islands No. 1 A31

Designs: 6p, Turks Islands No. 2 and portrait of Queen Elizabeth on simulated stamp. 1sh, Turks Islands No. 3 (like 1p).

		1967, May 1	Photo.	Perf. 14½	
172	A31	1p lilac rose & blk		.25	.25
173	A31	6p gray & black		.25	.25
174	A31	1sh Prus blue & blk		.40	.40
		Nos. 172-174 (3)		.90	.90

Centenary of Turks Islands stamps.

Human Rights Flame A32

		1968, Apr. 1		Perf. 14x14½	
175	A32	1p lt green & multi		.25	.25
176	A32	8p lt blue & multi		.25	.25
177	A32	1sh6p multicolored		.75	.75
		Nos. 175-177 (3)			

International Human Rights Year.

Martin Luther King, Jr. and Protest March of 1968 A33

		1968, Oct. 1	Photo.	Wmk. 314	
178	A33	2p dk blue, dk & lt brn		.25	.25
179	A33	8p dk car rose, dk & lt brn		.25	.25
180	A33	1sh6p dp vio, dk & lt brn		.25	.25
		Nos. 178-180 (3)		.75	.75

Martin Luther King, Jr. (1929-68), American civil rights leader.

Nos. 158-171 Surcharged

Designs as before and: ¼c, Coat of arms like 10sh.

Perf. 14x14½, 14½x14

		1969, Sept. 8	Photo.	Wmk. 314	
181	A30	¼c lt gray & multi		.25	.25
182	A29	1c on 1p multi		.25	.25
183	A29	2c on 2p multi		.25	.25
184	A29	3c on 3p multi		.25	.25
185	A29	4c on 4p multi		.25	.25
186	A29	5c on 6p multi		.25	.25
187	A29	7c on 8p multi		.25	.25
188	A30	8c on 1½p multi		.25	.25
189	A30	10c on 1sh multi		.25	.25
190	A29	15c on 1sh6p multi		.25	.25
191	A30	20c on 2sh multi		.30	.50
192	A30	30c on 3sh multi		.40	.65
193	A30	50c on 5sh multi		.60	.95
194	A30	$1 on 10sh multi		1.40	2.25
195	A29	$2 on £1 multi		6.00	9.50
		Nos. 181-195 (15)		11.20	16.35

The surcharge is differently arranged on each denomination to fit the design; the old denomination is obliterated with a rectangle on the 8c and 15c.

See Nos. 217-230.

		1969		Wmk. 314 Sideways	
182a	A29	1c on 1p		.25	.30
183a	A29	2c on 2p		.25	.30
184a	A29	3c on 3p		.25	.30
186a	A29	5c on 6p		.25	.30
187a	A29	7c on 8p		.25	.40
190a	A29	15c on 1sh6p		.30	.50
195a	A29	$2 on £1		3.00	5.00
		Nos. 182a-195a (7)		4.55	7.10

Nativity with John the Baptist — A34

Designs from the Book of Hours of Eleanora, Duchess of Tuscany: 3c, 30c, Flight into Egypt.

Perf. 13x12½

		1969, Oct. 20	Litho.	Wmk. 314	
196	A34	1c plum & multi		.25	.25
197	A34	3c dk blue & multi		.25	.25
198	A34	15c olive & multi		.25	.25
199	A34	30c yellow brn & multi		.25	.25
		Nos. 196-199 (4)		1.00	1.00

Christmas.

Coat of Arms — A35

		1970, Feb. 2	Litho.	Perf. 13x12½	
200	A35	7c brown & multi		.25	.25
201	A35	35c violet blue & multi		.75	.75

New Constitution, inaugurated 6/16/69. See No. 769.

Christ Bearing the Cross, by Dürer — A36

Albrecht Dürer Engravings: 7c, Christ on the Cross. 50c, The Lamentation for Christ.

Perf. 13½x14

		1970, Mar. 17	Engr.	Wmk. 314	
202	A36	5c dp blue & blk		.25	.25
203	A36	7c vermilion & blk		.25	.25
204	A36	50c dk brown & multi		.40	1.00
		Nos. 202-204 (3)		.90	1.50

Easter.

Dickens and "Oliver Twist" Scene A37

Charles Dickens and Scene from: 3c, "A Christmas Carol." 15c, "Pickwick Papers." 30c, "The Old Curiosity Shop."

Litho. & Engr.

		1970, June 17		Perf. 13½x13	
205	A37	1c yel, red brn & blk		.25	.25
206	A37	3c sal pink, sl & blk		.25	.25
207	A37	15c salmon, bl & blk		.30	.30
208	A37	30c lt blue, ol & blk		.60	.60
		Nos. 205-208 (4)		1.40	1.40

Charles Dickens (1812-70), English novelist.

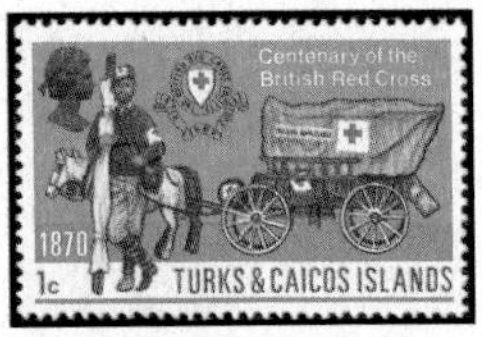

Red Cross Ambulance, 1870 — A38

5c, 30c, Red Cross ambulance, 1970.

1970, Aug. 4 Litho. *Perf. 13½x14*

209 A38 1c orange & multi .25 .25
210 A38 5c ocher & multi .25 .25
211 A38 15c brt pink & multi .25 .25
212 A38 30c multicolored .50 .50
Nos. 209-212 (4) 1.25 1.25

Centenary of British Red Cross Society.

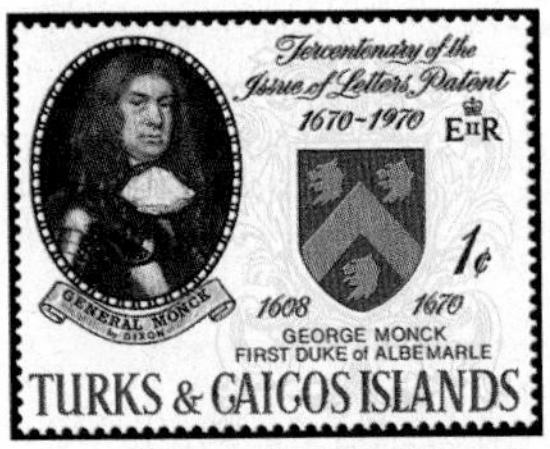

Gen. George Monck, Duke of Albemarle, and his Coat of Arms — A39

Designs: 8c, 35c, Coats of arms of Charles II and Queen Elizabeth II.

1970, Dec. 1 Litho. *Perf. 12½x13½*

213 A39 1c multicolored .25 .25
214 A39 8c multicolored .25 .25
215 A39 10c multicolored .30 .30
216 A39 35c multicolored 1.00 .95
Nos. 213-216 (4) 1.80 1.75

Tercentenary of the issue of Letters Patent to the Six Lords Proprietors.

Types of 1967

Values in Cents and Dollars

Designs: 1c, Turk's-head cactus. 2c, Donkey cart. 3c, Sisal industry. 4c, Conch industry. 5c, Salt industry. 7c, Skin diving. 8c, Boat building. 10c, Fishing. 15c, Water skiing. 20c, Crawfish industry. 30c, Map of Islands. 50c, Fishing industry. $1, Arms of Colony. $2, Queen Elizabeth II.

Perf. 14x14½, 14½x14

1971, Feb. 2 Photo. Wmk. 314

217 A29 1c violet, red & yel .25 .30
218 A29 2c gray, yel & slate .25 .30
219 A29 3c green & dk brn .25 .30
220 A30 4c grnsh bl, blk & pink .25 .30
221 A29 5c blue & dk brown .25 .30
222 A29 7c aqua, dk bl & yel .25 .30
223 A30 8c choc & org yel .25 .30
224 A30 10c grnsh bl & red brn .35 .40
225 A29 15c brt grnsh bl, yel & brn .65 .70
226 A30 20c multicolored .95 1.10
227 A30 30c grnsh bl & mar 1.40 1.60
228 A30 50c sky bl, dk bl & yel 2.25 2.50
229 A30 $1 blue & multi 4.50 4.75
230 A29 $2 dk car rose, sil & dk blue 8.25 9.50
Nos. 217-230 (14) 20.10 22.65

The ¼c, released with this set is a shade of No. 181, the background being a greenish, slightly darker gray.

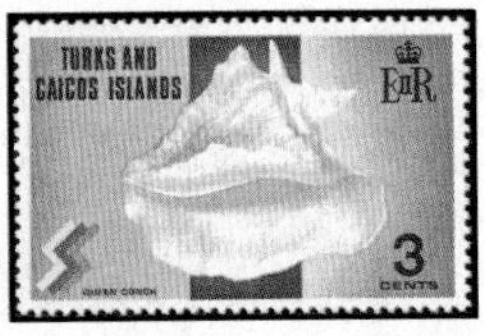

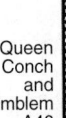

Queen Conch and Emblem A40

Tourist publicity (Sun, Sea and Sand Emblem and): 1c, Seahorse, vert. 15c, American oyster catcher. 30c, Blue Marlin.

Perf. 14½x14, 14x14½

1971, May 2 Litho. Wmk. 314

232 A40 1c multicolored .35 .35
233 A40 3c multicolored .35 .35
234 A40 15c multicolored .55 .55
235 A40 30c multicolored 1.10 1.10
Nos. 232-235 (4) 2.35 2.35

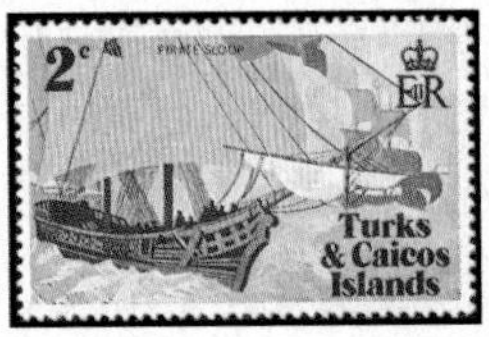

Pirate Sloop A41

Designs: 3c, Pirates burying treasure. 15c, Marooned pirate. 30c, Buccaneers.

1971, July 17 *Perf. 14½x14*

236 A41 2c multicolored .25 .25
237 A41 3c multicolored .25 .25
238 A41 15c multicolored .70 .70
239 A41 30c multicolored 1.40 1.40
Nos. 236-239 (4) 2.60 2.60

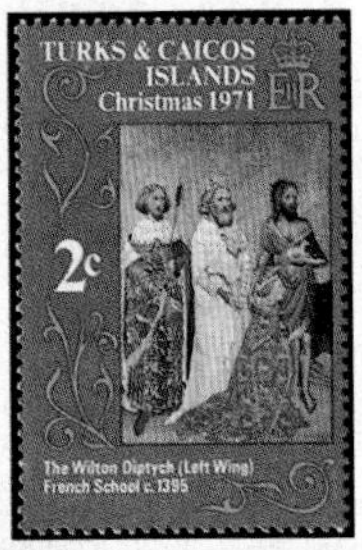

A42

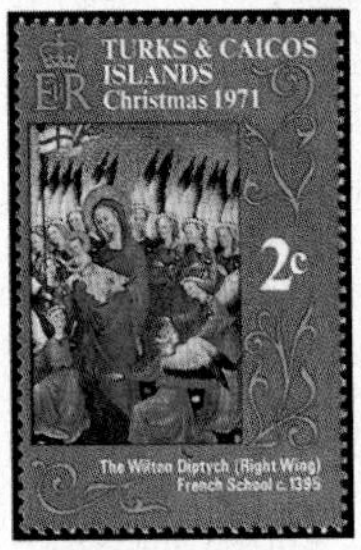

Adoration of the Virgin and Child, from Wilton Diptych, French School, c. 1395 — A43

1971, Oct. 12 Litho. *Perf. 14x13½*

240 A42 2c dull brn & multi .25 .25
241 A43 2c dull brn & multi .25 .25
242 A42 8c green & multi .25 .25
243 A43 8c green & multi .25 .25
244 A42 15c dk blue gray & multi .25 .25
245 A43 15c dk blue gray & multi .25 .25
Nos. 240-245 (6) 1.50 1.50

Christmas.

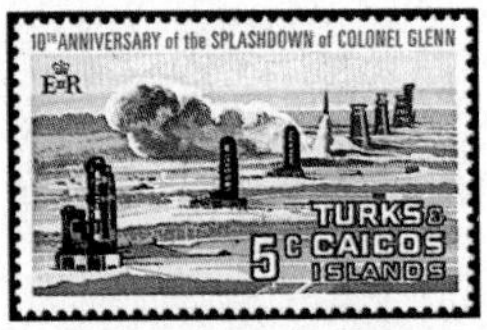

Rocket Launch, Cape Canaveral — A44

10c, Space capsule in orbit around earth. 15c, Map of Turks & Caicos Islands & splashdown. 20c, Distinguished Service Medal, vert.

1972, Feb. 21 *Perf. 13½*

246 A44 5c multicolored .25 .25
247 A44 10c multicolored .25 .25
248 A44 15c lt green & multi .25 .25
249 A44 20c blue & multi .25 .25
Nos. 246-249 (4) 1.00 1.00

First orbital flight by US astronaut Lt. Col. John H. Glenn, Jr., and splashdown off Turks and Caicos Islands, 10th anniversary.

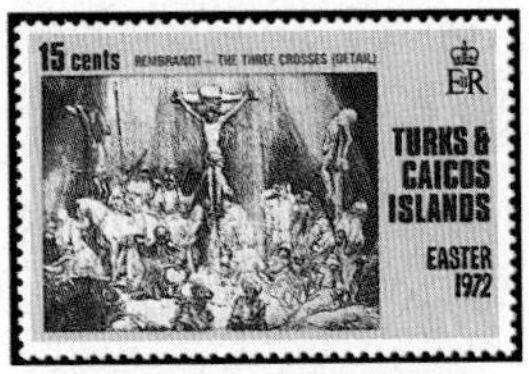

The Three Crosses, by Rembrandt — A45

Details from Etchings by Rembrandt: 2c, Christ Before Pilate, vert. 30c, Descent from the Cross, vert.

1972, Mar. 17 *Perf. 14x13½, 13½x14*

250 A45 2c lilac & black .25 .25
251 A45 15c pink & black .25 .25
252 A45 30c yellow & black .40 .40
Nos. 250-252 (3) .90 .90

Easter.

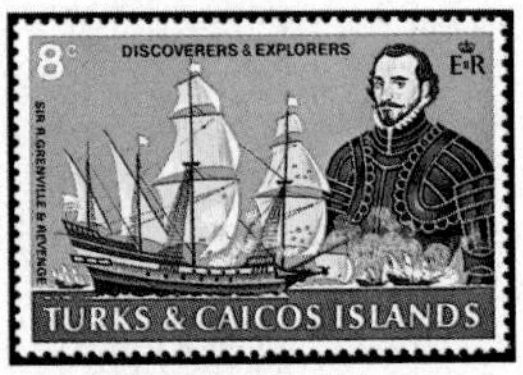

Richard Grenville and "Revenge" — A46

Discoverers and explorers of the Americas: ¼c, Christopher Columbus, Niña, Pinta and Santa Maria, vert. 10c, Capt. John Smith and three-master, vert. 30c, Juan Ponce de León and three-master.

1972, July 4

253 A46 ¼c multicolored .25 .25
254 A46 8c multicolored 1.40 .25
255 A46 10c multicolored 1.40 .35
256 A46 30c multicolored 3.00 1.00
Nos. 253-256 (4) 6.05 1.85

Silver Wedding Issue

Common Design Type

Design: Queen Elizabeth II, Prince Philip, turk's-head cactus and spiny lobster.

Perf. 14x14½

1972, Nov. 20 Photo. Wmk. 314

257 CD324 10c ultra & multi .25 .25
258 CD324 20c multicolored .25 .25

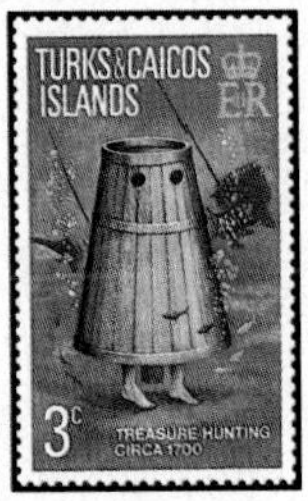

Treasure Hunting, c. 1700 — A47

Designs: 5c, Replica of silver bank medallion, 1687, obverse. 10c, Same, reverse. 30c, Scuba diver, 1973.

Perf. 14x14½

1973, Jan. 18 Litho. Wmk. 314

259 A47 3c Prus blue & multi .25 .25
260 A47 5c plum, silver & blk .25 .25
261 A47 10c brt rose, silver & blk .25 .25
262 A47 30c violet blue & multi .90 .90
a. Souvenir sheet of 4, #259-262 2.25 2.25
Nos. 259-262 (4) 1.65 1.65

Treasure hunting.

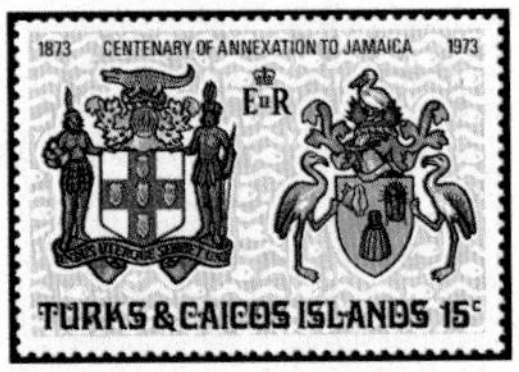

Arms of Jamaica, Turks and Caicos Islands — A48

1973, Apr. 16 Litho. *Perf. 13½x14*

263 A48 15c buff & multi .35 .35
264 A48 35c lt green & multi .75 .75

Centenary of annexation to Jamaica.

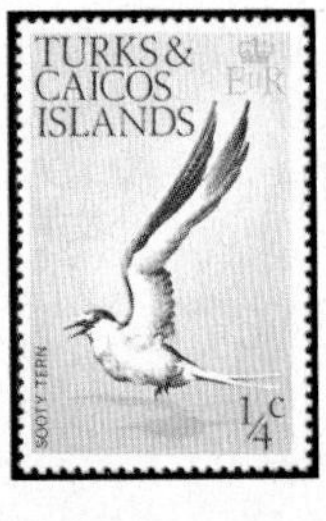

Sooty Tern — A49

Birds: 1c, Magnificent frigate bird. 2c, Noddy tern. 3c, Blue gray gnatcatcher. 4c, Little blue heron. 5c, Catbird. 7c, Black-whiskered vireo. 8c, Osprey. 10c, Flamingo. 15c, Brown pelican. 20c, Parula warbler. 30c, Northern mockingbird. 50c, Ruby-throated hummingbird. $1, Bahama bananaquit. $2, Cedar waxwing. $5, Painted bunting.

Wmk. 314 Sideways

1973, Aug. 1 Litho. *Perf. 14*

265 A49 ¼c yellow & multi .25 .25
266 A49 1c pink & multi .25 .25
267 A49 2c orange & multi .25 .25
268 A49 3c lilac rose & multi .55 .50
269 A49 4c lt blue & multi .25 .25
270 A49 5c lt green & multi .40 .25
271 A49 7c salmon & multi .45 .30
272 A49 8c blue & multi .55 .50
273 A49 10c brt blue & multi .65 .65
274 A49 15c tan & multi 1.00 .90
275 A49 20c brt yel & multi 2.75 2.50
276 A49 30c yellow & multi 2.25 2.10
277 A49 50c yellow & multi 3.50 3.25
278 A49 $1 blue & multi 6.75 6.75
279 A49 $2 gray & multi 15.00 13.50
Nos. 265-279 (15) 34.85 32.20

1974-75 Wmk. 314 Upright

266a A49 1c pink & multi ('75) .60 *.80*
267a A49 2c orange & multi 1.25 *1.60*
268a A49 3c lil rose & multi ('75) 2.00 *2.50*
275a A49 20c brt yel & multi ('75) 6.25 *8.00*
Nos. 266a-275a (4) 10.10 12.90

1976-77 Wmk. 373

265a A49 ¼c yellow & multi ('77) .25 .25
266b A49 1c pink & multi ('77) .25 .25
267b A49 2c orange & multi ('77) .25 .25
268b A49 3c lilac rose & multi .25 .25
269a A49 4c lt bl & multi ('77) .25 .25
270a A49 5c lt grn & multi ('77) .25 .25
273a A49 10c brt bl & multi ('77) .25 .25
274a A49 15c tan & multi ('77) .40 .65
275b A49 20c brt yel & multi .50 .80
276a A49 30c yel & multi ('77) .75 1.25
277a A49 50c yel & multi ('77) 1.25 2.00
278a A49 $1 blue & multi ('77) 2.50 4.00
279b A49 $2 gray & multi ('77) 5.25 8.00
279A A49 $5 yel grn & multi 13.50 21.00
Nos. 265a-279A (14) 25.90 39.45

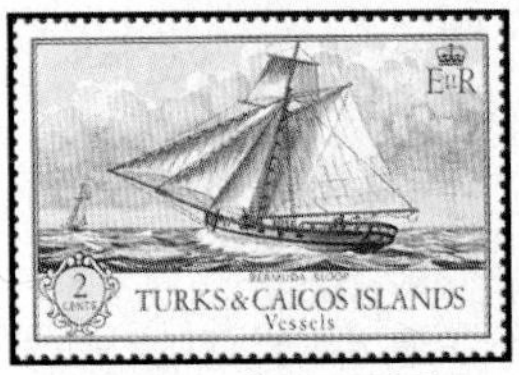

Bermuda Sloop — A50

Old Sailing Ships: 5c, HMS Blanche. 8c, US privateer Grand Turk and packet Hinchinbrooke. 10c, HMS Endymion. 15c, RMS Medina. 20c, HMS Daring.

1973, July 19 Litho. *Perf. 13½*

280 A50 2c multicolored .25 .25
281 A50 5c multicolored .25 .25
282 A50 8c multicolored .25 .25
283 A50 10c multicolored .25 .25
284 A50 15c multicolored .35 .35
285 A50 20c multicolored .50 .50
a. Souvenir sheet of 6, #280-285 2.50 2.50
Nos. 280-285 (6) 1.85 1.85

Princess Anne's Wedding Issue

Common Design Type

1973, Nov. 14 Wmk. 314 *Perf. 14*

286 CD325 12c blue grn & multi .25 .25
287 CD325 18c slate & multi .25 .25
Nos. 286-287 (2) .50 .50

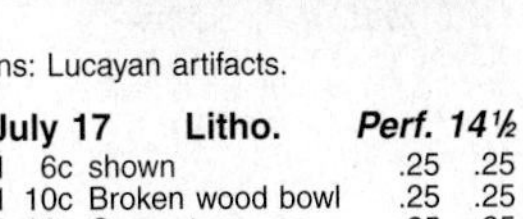

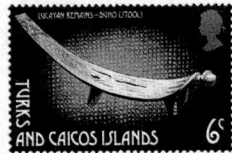

Lucayan Stool A51

Designs: Lucayan artifacts.

1974, July 17 Litho. *Perf. 14½*

288 A51 6c shown .25 .25
289 A51 10c Broken wood bowl .25 .25
290 A51 12c Greenstone axe .25 .25
291 A51 18c Wood bowl .25 .25
292 A51 35c Animal head, fragment of stool .25 .25
a. Souvenir sheet of 5, #288-292 2.50 2.50
Nos. 288-292 (5) 1.25 1.25

Carvings made by Lucayan Indians, first inhabitants of the islands.

Grand Turk G.P.O. A52

UPU Emblem and: 12c, Map of Turks and Caicos Islands and local mail sloop. 18c, "United Service" (globe and "UPU"). 55c, Design symbolic of the Islands joining the UPU in 1881.

1974, Oct. 9   Wmk. 314   Perf. 14

293	A52	4c yellow & multi	.25	.25
294	A52	12c blue & multi	.25	.25
295	A52	18c violet & multi	.25	.25
296	A52	55c lt blue & multi	.55	.55
		Nos. 293-296 (4)	1.30	1.30

Centenary of Universal Postal Union.

"His Finest Hour" A53

12c, Churchill and Franklin D. Roosevelt.

1974, Nov. 30   Wmk. 373

297	A53	12c multicolored	.25	.25
298	A53	18c multicolored	.25	.25
a.		Souvenir sheet of 2, #297-298	.70	.70

Sir Winston Churchill (1874-1965).

Spanish Captain, c. 1492 — A54

Uniforms: 20c, Officer, Royal Artillery, 1783. 25c, Officer, 67th Foot, 1798. 35c, Private, First West India Regiment, 1833.

1975, Mar. 26   Wmk. 314   Perf. 14½

299	A54	5c blue & multi	.25	.25
300	A54	20c blue & multi	.30	.30
301	A54	25c blue & multi	.35	.35
302	A54	35c blue & multi	.50	.50
a.		Souvenir sheet of 4, #299-302	1.60	1.60
		Nos. 299-302 (4)	1.40	1.40

Old Windmill, Salt Cay — A55

Salt industry: 10c, Pink salt pans, horiz. 20c, Salt raking at Salt Cay, horiz. 25c, Unprocessed salt ready for shipment.

1975, Oct. 16   Litho.   Wmk. 373

303	A55	6c violet & multi	.25	.25
304	A55	10c lt brown & multi	.25	.25
305	A55	20c red & multi	.35	.35
306	A55	25c magenta & multi	.45	.45
		Nos. 303-306 (4)	1.30	1.30

Star Coral A56

1975, Dec. 4   Litho.   Wmk. 373

307	A56	6c shown	.30	.30
308	A56	10c Elkhorn coral	.35	.30
309	A56	20c Brain coral	.70	.60
310	A56	25c Staghorn coral	.85	.70
		Nos. 307-310 (4)	2.20	1.90

Schooner A57

American Bicentennial: 20c, Ship of the line. 25c, Frigate Grand Turk. 55c, Ketch.

1976, May 28   Perf. 14x13½

311	A57	6c orange & multi	.25	.25
312	A57	20c violet blue & multi	.40	.30
313	A57	25c brown & multi	.50	.35
314	A57	55c multicolored	.90	.80
a.		Souvenir sheet of 4, #311-314	2.25	2.25
		Nos. 311-314 (4)	2.05	1.70

Turks and Caicos Islands No. 151 A58

25c, Turks and Caicos Islands No. 150.

1976, July 14   Wmk. 373   Perf. 14½

315	A58	20c carmine & multi	.50	.45
316	A58	25c violet blue & multi	.60	.55

Visit of Queen Elizabeth II and Prince Philip to the Caribbean, 10th anniversary.

Virgin and Child, by Carlo Dolci — A59

Christmas: 10c, Virgin and Child with St. John, by Botticelli. 20c, Adoration of the Kings, from Retable by the Master of Paradise. 25c, Adoration of the Kings, illuminated page, French, 15th century.

1976, Nov. 10   Litho.   Perf. 14x13½

317	A59	6c multicolored	.25	.25
318	A59	10c orange & multi	.25	.25
319	A59	20c red lilac & multi	.25	.25
320	A59	25c multicolored	.25	.25
		Nos. 317-320 (4)	1.00	1.00

Queen with Regalia — A60

Designs: 6c, Queen presenting Order of British Empire to E. T. Wood, Grand Turk, 1966. 55c, Royal family on balcony of Buckingham Palace. $5, Portrait of Queen from photograph taken during her 1966 visit to Grand Turk.

1977   Litho.   Perf. 14x13½

321	A60	6c multicolored	.25	.25
322	A60	25c multicolored	.25	.25
323	A60	55c multicolored	.50	.50
		Nos. 321-323 (3)	1.00	1.00

Souvenir Sheet
Perf. 14

324	A60	$5 multicolored	3.00	3.00

25th anniv. of the reign of Elizabeth II. Nos. 322 and 323 were also issued in booklet panes of 2.
Issued: #321-323, Feb. 7; #324, Dec. 6.

Friendship 7 Capsule — A61

Designs: 3c, Lunar rover, vert. 6c, Tracking Station on Grand Turk. 20c, Moon landing craft, vert. 25c, Col. Glenn's rocket leaving launching pad, vert. 50c, Telstar 1 satellite.

Wmk. 373
1977, June 20   Litho.   Perf. 13½

325	A61	1c multicolored	.25	.25
326	A61	3c multicolored	.25	.25
327	A61	6c multicolored	.25	.25
328	A61	20c multicolored	.25	.25
329	A61	25c multicolored	.25	.25
330	A61	50c multicolored	.50	.50
		Nos. 325-330 (6)	1.75	1.75

US Tracking Station on Grand Turk, 25th anniversary.

Adoration of the Kings, 1634 by Rubens — A63

Rubens Paintings: ¼c, Flight into Egypt. 1c, Adoration of the Kings, 1624. 6c, Madonna with Garland. 20c, $1, Virgin and Child Adored by Angels. $2, Adoration of the Kings, 1618.

1977, Dec. 23

331	A63	¼c multicolored	.25	.25
332	A63	½c multicolored	.25	.25
333	A63	1c multicolored	.25	.25
334	A63	6c multicolored	.25	.25
335	A63	20c multicolored	.25	.25
336	A63	$2 multicolored	1.50	1.50
		Nos. 331-336 (6)	2.75	2.75

Souvenir Sheet

337	A63	$1 multicolored	1.90	1.90

Christmas and 400th birth anniversary of Peter Paul Rubens (1577-1640).

Map of Turks Island Passage A64

Designs: 20c, Grand Turk lighthouse and sailboat (LUG cargo vessel). 25c, Deepsea fishing yacht. 55c, S.S. Jamaica Planter.

Wmk. 373, Unwmkd.
1978, Feb. 2   Litho.   Perf. 13½

338	A64	6c multicolored	.30	.30
339	A64	20c multicolored	.50	.40
340	A64	25c multicolored	.60	.50
341	A64	55c multicolored	1.25	1.25
a.		Souv. sheet of 4, #338-341, unwmkd.	2.75	2.75
		Nos. 338-341 (4)	2.65	2.45

Turks Island Passage, a major Caribbean shipping route.
No. 341a exists watermarked. Value $50.

Queen Victoria in Coronation Regalia — A65

British Monarchs in Coronation Regalia: 10c, Edward VII. 25c, George V. $2, George VI. $2.50, Elizabeth II.

1978, June 2   Litho.   Perf. 14

342	A65	6c multicolored	.25	.25
343	A65	10c multicolored	.25	.25
344	A65	25c multicolored	.25	.25
345	A65	$2 multicolored	1.00	1.00
		Nos. 342-345 (4)	1.75	1.75

Souvenir Sheet

346	A65	$2.50 multicolored	1.75	1.75

25th anniversary of coronation of Queen Elizabeth II. Nos. 342-345 also issued in sheets of 3 plus label, perf. 12.

Wilbur Wright and Flyer 3 A66

Aviation Progress: 6c, Cessna 337 and Wright brothers. 10c, Southeast Airlines' Electra and Orville Wright. 15c, C47 cargo plane on South Caicos runway. 35c, Norman-Britten Islander at Grand Turk airport. $1, Orville Wright and Flyer, 1902. $2, Wilbur Wright and Flyer.

1978, June 29   Litho.   Perf. 14½

347	A66	1c multicolored	.25	.25
348	A66	6c multicolored	.25	.25
349	A66	10c multicolored	.25	.25
350	A66	15c multicolored	.25	.25
351	A66	35c multicolored	.60	.60
352	A66	$2 multicolored	1.90	1.90
		Nos. 347-352 (6)	3.50	3.50

Souvenir Sheet

353	A66	$1 multicolored	1.00	1.00

Coronation of Queen Elizabeth II, 25th Anniv. — A67

Designs: 15c, Ampulla and anointing spoon. 25c, St. Edward's crown. $2 Queen Elizabeth II

Imperf. x Roulette 5
1978, July 24   Litho.
Self-adhesive

354		Souvenir booklet	3.75
a.		A67 Bklt. pane of 3, 15c, 25c, $2	2.40
b.		15c value from #354a	.25
c.		25c value from #354a	.25
d.		$2 value from #354a	1.90
e.		A67 Bklt. pane, 3 each, 15c, 25c	1.35

No. 354 contains #354a-354b printed on peelable paper backing with music and text of hymns.

11th Commonwealth Games, Edmonton, Canada, Aug. 3-12 — A68

1978, Aug. 3 Litho. *Perf. 15*

355	A68	6c shown	.25	.25
356	A68	20c Weight lifting	.25	.25
357	A68	55c Boxing	.45	.45
358	A68	$2 Bicycling	1.05	1.05
		Nos. 355-358 (4)	2.00	2.00

Souvenir Sheet

359	A68	$1 Sprinting	1.40	1.40

Fish
A69

1978-79 Litho. *Perf. 14¼*
No Year Imprint Below Design

360	A69	1c Indigo hamlet	.25	.25
361	A69	2c Tobacco fish	.25	.25
362	A69	3c Passing Jack	.25	.25
363	A69	4c Porkfish	.25	.25
364	A69	5c Spanish grunt	.25	.25
365	A69	7c Yellowtail snapper	.25	.25
366	A69	8c Foureye butter-flyfish	.25	.25
367	A69	10c Yellow fin grouper	.25	.25
368	A69	15c Beau Gregory	.30	.30
369	A69	20c Queen angelfish	.40	.40
370	A69	30c Hogfish	.60	.60
371	A69	50c Fairy Basslet	1.00	1.00
372	A69	$1 Clown wrasse	1.90	1.90
373	A69	$2 Stoplight par-rotfish	4.25	4.25
374	A69	$5 Queen triggerfish	10.00	10.00
		Nos. 360-374 (15)	20.45	20.45

Issue dates: 1c, 3c, 5c, 10c, 15c, 20c, Nov. 17, 1978; others Feb. 6, 1979.

1981, Dec. 15 *Perf. 12½x12*
"1981" Imprint Below Design

360a	A69	1c multicolored	.25	.25
364a	A69	5c multicolored	.25	.25
367a	A69	10c multicolored	.25	.25
369a	A69	20c multicolored	.55	.55
371a	A69	50c multicolored	1.25	1.25
372a	A69	$1 multicolored	2.50	2.50
373a	A69	$2 multicolored	5.50	5.50
374a	A69	$5 multicolored	13.00	13.00
		Nos. 360a-374a (8)	23.55	23.55

1983, Jan. 25 *Perf. 14¼x12*
"1983" Imprint Below Design

368b	A69	15c multicolored	1.90	1.00
369b	A69	20c multicolored	1.25	1.25
372b	A69	$1 multicolored	3.00	3.00
373b	A69	$2 multicolored	4.25	4.25
374b	A69	$5 multicolored	10.00	10.00
		Nos. 368b-374b (5)	20.40	19.50

Virgin with the Goldfinch, by Dürer — A70

Dürer Paintings: 20c, Virgin and Child with St. Anne. 35c, Nativity, horiz. $1, Adoration of the Kings, horiz. $2, Praying Hands.

1978, Dec. 11 Litho. *Perf. 14*

375	A70	6c multicolored	.25	.25
376	A70	20c multicolored	.25	.25
377	A70	35c multicolored	.45	.45
378	A70	$2 multicolored	1.75	1.75
		Nos. 375-378 (4)	2.70	2.70

Souvenir Sheet

379	A70	$1 multicolored	2.50	2.50

Christmas and 450th death anniversary of Albrecht Dürer (1471-1528), German painter.

Ospreys
A71

Endangered Species: 20c, Green turtle. 25c, Queen conch. 55c, Rough-toothed dolphin. $1, Humpback whale. $2, Iguana.

1979, May 17 Litho. *Perf. 14*

380	A71	6c multicolored	.30	.30
381	A71	20c multicolored	.90	.40
382	A71	25c multicolored	1.20	.50
383	A71	55c multicolored	2.50	1.20
384	A71	$1 multicolored	4.50	2.25
		Nos. 380-384 (5)	9.40	4.65

Souvenir Sheet

385	A71	$2 multicolored	6.00	5.50

The Beloved, by Dante Gabriel Rossetti
A72

Paintings and IYC Emblem: 25c, Tahitian Girl, by Paul Gauguin. 55c, Calmady Children, by Sir Thomas Lawrence. $1, Mother and Daughter (detail), by Gauguin. $2, Marchesa Elena Grimaldi, by Van Dyck.

1979, July 2 Litho. *Perf. 14*

386	A72	6c multicolored	.25	.25
387	A72	25c multicolored	.25	.25
388	A72	55c multicolored	.35	.35
389	A72	$1 multicolored	.65	.65
		Nos. 386-389 (4)	1.50	1.50

Souvenir Sheet

390	A72	$2 multicolored	1.00	1.00

International Year of the Child.

Stampless Cover and "Medina" — A73

Designs: 20c, Map of Islands and Rowland Hill. 45c, Stamped envelope and "Orinoco." 75c, Paddlewheeler "Shannon" and letter. $1, Royal Packet "Trent," map of Islands. $2, New and old seals.

1979, Sep. 10 Litho. *Perf. 14*

391	A73	6c multicolored	.25	.25
392	A73	20c multicolored	.25	.25
393	A73	45c multicolored	.50	.50
394	A73	75c multicolored	.90	.90
395	A73	$1 multicolored	1.10	1.10

Perf. 12

396	A73	$2 multicolored ('80)	3.25	3.25
a.		Souv. sheet of 1, perf. 14 ('79)	1.75	1.75
		Nos. 391-396 (6)	6.25	6.25

Nos. 391-395 were issued in sheets of 40, and in sheets of 5 stamps plus label, in changed colors, perf. 12.
No. 396 issued May 6, 1980 in sheet of 5 plus label picturing signal flags and map.

No. 396a Overprinted
Souvenir Sheet

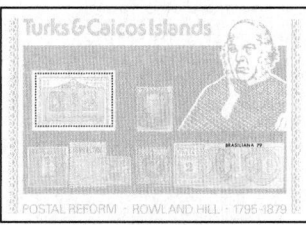

1979, Sept. 10 Litho. *Perf. 14*

397	A73	$2 multicolored	1.25	1.25

Brasiliana 79 Intl. Philatelic Exhibition, Rio de Janeiro, Sept. 15-23.

Cuneiform Script — A74

Designs: 5c, Egyptian papyrus; Chinese writing. 15c, Greek runner; Roman post horse; Roman ship. 25c, Pigeon post; railway post; steamship postal packet. 40c, Balloon post; first airmail plane; supersonic airmail jet. $1, Original stamp press (3 designs each of 5c, 15c, 25c, 40c).

Imperf. x Roulette 5, Imperf. ($1)

1979, Sept. 27 Litho.
Self-adhesive

398		Souvenir booklet	6.00	
a.		A74 Bklt. pane of 1 ($1)		
b.		A74 Bklt. pane, 3 each 5c, 15c		
c.		A74 Bklt. pane, 3 each 25c, 40c		

Sir Rowland Hill (1795-1879), originator of penny postage. No. 398 contains 3 booklet panes on peelable paper backing with descriptions of stamp designs.

International Year of the Child
A74a

Designs: Aquatic scenes — ¼c, Pluto and starfish. ½c, Minnie Mouse. 1c, Mickey Mouse skin-diving. 2c, Goofy riding turtle. 3c, Donald and dolphin. 4c, Mickey Mouse and fish. 5c, Goofy surfing. 25c, Pluto and lobster. $1, Daisy Duck waterskiing. $1.50, Goofy.

1979, Nov. 2 Litho. *Perf. 11*

399	A74a	¼c multicolored	.25	.25
400	A74a	½c multicolored	.25	.25
401	A74a	1c multicolored	.25	.25
402	A74a	2c multicolored	.25	.25
403	A74a	3c multicolored	.25	.25
404	A74a	4c multicolored	.25	.25
405	A74a	5c multicolored	.25	.25
406	A74a	25c multicolored	.60	.25
407	A74a	$1 multicolored	2.40	1.00
		Nos. 399-407 (9)	4.75	3.00

Souvenir Sheet
Perf. 13½x14

408	A74a	$1.50 multicolored	2.10	1.50

St. Nicholas, Icon, 17th Century — A75

Icons or Illuminations: 3c, Emperor Otto II, 10th century. 6c, St. John, Book of Lindisfarne. 15c, Christ and angels. 20c, Christ attended by angels, Book of Kells, 9th century. 25c, St. John the Evangelist. 65c, Christ enthroned, 17th century. $1, St. John, 8th century. $2, St. Matthew, Book of Lindisfarne.

1979, Nov. 26

409	A75	1c multicolored	.25	.25
410	A75	3c multicolored	.25	.25
411	A75	6c multicolored	.25	.25
412	A75	15c multicolored	.25	.25
413	A75	20c multicolored	.25	.25
414	A75	25c multicolored	.25	.25
415	A75	65c multicolored	.25	.25
416	A75	$1 multicolored	.25	.25
		Nos. 409-416 (8)	2.00	2.00

Souvenir Sheet

417	A75	$2 multicolored	1.25	1.25

Christina's World, by Andrew Wyeth — A76

Art Treasures: 10c, Ivory leopards, Benin, 19th century. 20c, The Kiss, by Gustav Klimt, vert. 25c, Portrait of a Lady, by Rogier van der Weyden, vert. 80c, Sumerian bull's head harp, 2600 B.C., vert. $1, The Wave, by Hokusai. $2, Holy Family, by Rembrandt, vert.

1979, Dec. 19 Litho. *Perf. 13½*

418	A76	6c multicolored	.25	.25
419	A76	10c multicolored	.25	.25
420	A76	20c multicolored	.25	.25
421	A76	25c multicolored	.25	.25
422	A76	80c multicolored	.30	.30
423	A76	$1 multicolored	.45	.45
		Nos. 418-423 (6)	1.75	1.75

Souvenir Sheet

424	A76	$2 multicolored	1.75	1.75

Pied-billed Grebe — A77

1980, Feb. 20 Litho. *Perf. 14*

425	A77	20c shown	.75	.40
426	A77	25c Ovenbirds	.90	.45
427	A77	35c Marsh hawks	1.25	.65
428	A77	55c Yellow-bellied sapsucker	2.00	.90
429	A77	$1 Blue-winged teals	3.50	1.75
		Nos. 425-429 (5)	8.40	4.15

Souvenir Sheet

430	A77	$2 Glossy ibis	4.25	4.25

Stamp Under Magnifier, Perforation Gauge, London 1980 Emblem
A78

1980, May 6 Litho. *Perf. 14x14½*

431	A78	25c shown	.25	.25
432	A78	40c Stamp in tongs, gauge	.35	.35

Souvenir Sheet

433	A78	$2 Exhibition Hall	1.10	1.10

London 1980 International Stamp Exhibition, May 6-14.

Trumpet Triton
A79

1980, June 26 Litho. *Perf. 14*

434	A79	15c shown	.25	.25
435	A79	20c Measled cowry	.30	.30
436	A79	30c True tulip	.40	.40
437	A79	45c Lion's paw	.60	.60
438	A79	55c Sunrise tellin	.75	.75
439	A79	70c Grown cone	1.00	1.00
		Nos. 434-439 (6)	3.30	3.30

Queen Mother
Elizabeth, 80th
Birthday — A80

1980, Aug. 4   **Litho.**   **Perf. 14**
440 A80   80c multicolored   .70 .70
Souvenir Sheet
Perf. 12
441 A80 $1.50 multicolored   1.50 1.50

Pinocchio — A81

Christmas: Scenes from Walt Disney's
Pinocchio.

1980, Sept. 25   **Perf. 11**
442 A81   ¼c multicolored   .25 .25
443 A81   ½c multicolored   .25 .25
444 A81   1c multicolored   .25 .25
445 A81   2c multicolored   .25 .25
446 A81   3c multicolored   .25 .25
447 A81   4c multicolored   .25 .25
448 A81   5c multicolored   .25 .25
449 A81   75c multicolored   1.10 1.10
450 A81 $1 multicolored   1.50 1.50
   Nos. 442-450 (9)   4.35 4.35
Souvenir Sheet
451 A81 $2 multi, vert.   4.50 4.50

Medical Examination, Lions — A82

15c, Scholarships, Kiwanis. 45c, Education,
Soroptimists. $1, Lobster boat, Rotary.
$2, Funds for schools, Rotary.

1980, Oct. 8   **Litho.**   **Perf. 14**
452 A82   10c shown   .25 .25
453 A82   15c multicolored   .25 .25
454 A82   45c multicolored   .60 .60
455 A82 $1 multicolored   .90 .90
   Nos. 452-455 (4)   2.00 2.00
Souvenir Sheet
456 A82 $2 multicolored   2.25 2.25

Lions, Rotary, Kiwanis and Soroptimists service organizations; 75th anniv. of Rotary Intl.

Martin Luther King, Jr. (1929-
68) — A83

Human Rights Leaders: 30c, John F. Kennedy. 45c, Roberto Clemente (1934-72),
baseball player. 70c, Frank Worrel (1927-67),
cricket player. $1, Harriet Tubman (1823-
1913), born slave, helped others escape to
freedom. $2, Marcus Garvey (1887-1940),
Jamaican black nationalist leader.

1980, Dec. 22   **Litho.**   **Perf. 14**
457 A83   20c multicolored   .25 .25
458 A83   30c multicolored   .35 .35
459 A83   45c multicolored   .60 .60

460 A83   70c multicolored   .95 .95
461 A83 $1 multicolored   1.35 1.35
   Nos. 457-461 (5)   3.50 3.50
Souvenir Sheet
462 A83 $2 multicolored   2.00 2.00

Racing
Yachts
A84

Designs: Racing yachts.

1981, Jan. 29   **Litho.**   **Perf. 14**
463 A84   6c multicolored   .25 .25
464 A84   15c multicolored   .25 .25
465 A84   35c multicolored   .40 .40
466 A84 $1 multicolored   .85 .85
   Nos. 463-466 (4)   1.75 1.75
Souvenir Sheet
467 A84 $2 multicolored   1.75 1.75

South Caicos Regatta. No. 467 contains
one 28x42mm stamp.

Pluto
Listening to
Sea
Shell — A85

1981, Feb. 16   **Perf. 13½x14**
468 A85   10c shown   .50 .50
469 A85   75c Pluto on raft,
     dolphin   2.00 2.00
Souvenir Sheet
470 A85 $1.50 Pluto   4.25 4.25

50th anniversary of Walt Disney's Pluto.

Night Queen
Cactus — A86

1981, Feb. 10   **Perf. 14**
471 A86   25c shown   .30 .30
472 A86   35c Ripsaw cactus   .40 .40
473 A86   55c Royal strawberry
     cactus   .70 .70
474 A86   80c Caicos cactus   1.10 1.10
   Nos. 471-474 (4)   2.50 2.50
Souvenir Sheet
475 A86 $2 Turks head cactus   2.25 2.25

Donald Duck
and Louie
with Easter
Egg — A87

Easter: Various Disney characters with
Easter eggs.

1981, Mar. 20   **Litho.**   **Perf. 11**
476 A87   10c multicolored   .30 .30
477 A87   25c multicolored   .60 .60
478 A87   60c multicolored   1.60 1.60
479 A87   80c multicolored   2.00 2.00
   Nos. 476-479 (4)   4.50 4.50
Souvenir Sheet
480 A87 $4 multicolored   7.50 7.50

Woman with Fan,
1909 — A88

1981, May 28   **Litho.**   **Perf. 14**
481 A88   20c shown   .25 .25
482 A88   45c Woman with Pears,
     1909   .65 .65
483 A88   80c The Accordionist,
     1911   1.10 1.10
484 A88 $1 The Aficionado,
     1912   1.40 1.40
   Nos. 481-484 (4)   3.40 3.40
Souvenir Sheet
485 A88 $2 Girl with a Mando-
     lin, 1910   3.00 3.00

Pablo Picasso (1881-1973).

Royal Wedding Issue
Common Design Type and

A88a

1981, June 23   **Litho.**   **Perf. 14**
486 CD331a   35c Couple   .25 .25
487 CD331a   65c Kensington
     Palace   .30 .30
488 CD331a   90c Charles   .40 .40
   Nos. 486-488 (3)   .95 .95
Souvenir Sheet
489 CD331 $2 Glass coach   1.25 1.25

***Imperf. x Roulette 5 (20c, $1),
Imperf. ($2)***
1981, July 7   **Self-adhesive**
490   Booklet   4.00
  a.   A88a Pane of 6 (3x20c, Lady Di-
     ana, 3x$1, Charles)   2.25
  b.   A88a Pane of 1, $2, Couple   1.75

Nos. 486-488 also printed in sheets of 5
plus label, perf. 12, in changed colors.

Underwater Marine Biology
Observation — A89

1981, Aug. 21   **Litho.**   **Perf. 14**
491 A89   15c shown   .30 .30
492 A89   40c Underwater photog-
     raphy   .65 .65
493 A89   75c Diving for wreckage   1.10 1.10
494 A89 $1 Diver, dolphins   1.50 1.50
   Nos. 491-494 (4)   3.55 3.55
Souvenir Sheet
495 A89 $2 Diving flag   3.75 3.75

Br'er Rabbit Barricading his
Door — A90

Christmas: Scenes from Walt Disney's
Uncle Remus.

1981, Nov. 2   **Litho.**   **Perf. 14x13½**
496 A90   ¼c multicolored   .30 .30
497 A90   ½c multicolored   .30 .30
498 A90   1c multicolored   .30 .30
499 A90   2c multicolored   .30 .30
500 A90   3c multicolored   .30 .30
501 A90   4c multicolored   .30 .30
502 A90   5c multicolored   .30 .30
503 A90   75c multicolored   1.40 1.40
504 A90 $1 multicolored   1.90 1.90
   Nos. 496-504 (9)   5.40 5.40
Souvenir Sheet
505 A90 $2 multicolored   4.50 4.50

Flags of
Turks and
Caicos
Islands
A91

Maps of Various Islands: a, Grand Turk. b,
Salt Cay. c, South Caicos. d, East Caicos. e,
Middle Caicos. f, North Caicos. g, Caicos
Cays. h, Providenciales. i, West Caicos.

1981, Dec. 1   **Perf. 14**
506   Strip of 10   5.50 5.50
  a.-j.   A91 20c any single   .55 .55

Caribbean
Buckeyes — A92

1982, Jan. 21   **Litho.**   **Perf. 14**
507 A92   20c shown   .40 .40
508 A92   35c Clench's hairstreaks   .75 .75
509 A92   65c Gulf fritillarys   1.25 1.25
510 A92 $1 Bush sulphurs   2.10 2.10
   Nos. 507-510 (4)   4.50 4.50
Souvenir Sheet
511 A92 $2 Turk Isld. leaf but-
     terfly   5.00 5.00

Scouting
Year — A93

1982, Feb. 17   **Litho.**   **Perf. 14**
512 A93   40c Flag ceremony   .90 .90
513 A93   50c Building raft   1.10 1.10
514 A93   75c Cricket match   1.50 1.50
515 A93 $1 Nature study   2.00 2.00
   Nos. 512-515 (4)   5.50 5.50
Souvenir Sheet
516 A93 $2 Baden-Powell, sa-
     lute   4.50 4.50

1982 World Cup Soccer — A94

Designs: Various soccer players.

1982, Apr. 30 Litho. Perf. 14
517 A94 10c multicolored .25 .25
518 A94 25c multicolored .35 .35
519 A94 45c multicolored .60 .60
520 A94 $1 multicolored 1.25 1.25
Nos. 517-520 (4) 2.45 2.45
Souvenir Sheet
521 A94 $2 multi, horiz. 2.25 2.25
#517-520 issued in sheets of 5 + label.

Phillis Wheatley (1753-1784), Poet, and Washington Crossing Delaware — A95

Washington's 250th Birth Anniv. and F.D. Roosevelt's Birth Centenary: 35c, Washington, Benjamin Banneker (1731-1806), astronomer and mathematician, map. 65c, FDR, George Washington Carver (1864-1943). 80c, FDR with stamp collection. $2, FDR examining Washington stamp.

1982, May 3 Litho. Perf. 14
522 A95 20c multicolored .35 .35
523 A95 35c multicolored .70 .70
524 A95 65c multicolored 1.25 1.25
525 A95 80c multicolored 1.75 1.75
Nos. 522-525 (4) 4.05 4.05
Souvenir Sheet
526 A95 $2 multicolored 3.50 3.50

Second Thoughts, by Norman Rockwell — A96

1982, June 23 Litho. Perf. 14x13½
527 A96 8c shown .30 .30
528 A96 15c The Proper Gratuity .30 .30
529 A96 20c Before the Shot .35 .35
530 A96 25c The Three Umpires .45 .45
Nos. 527-530 (4) 1.40 1.40

Princess Diana Issue
Common Design Type

1982 Litho. Perf. 14½x14
530A CD332 8c Sandringham .20 .25
530B CD332 35c Wedding 1.40 .55
530C CD332 $1.10 Diana 4.50 1.75
Nos. 530A-530C (3) 6.20 2.55

1982, July 1 Perf. 14½x14
531 CD332 55c Sandringham 1.50 1.00
532 CD332 70c Wedding 1.50 1.00
533 CD332 $1 Diana 2.75 1.75
Nos. 531-533 (3) 5.75 3.75
Also issued in sheetlets of 5 + label.

Souvenir Sheet
534 CD332 $2 Diana, diff. 5.00 4.00

Skymaster over Caicos Cays — A97

15c, Jetstar, Grand Turk. 65c, Helicopter, South Caicos. $1.10, Seaplane, Providenciales. $2, Boeing 727.

1982, Aug. 26 Litho. Perf. 14
535 A97 8c shown .25 .25
536 A97 15c multicolored .35 .35
537 A97 65c multicolored 1.00 1.00
538 A97 $1.10 multicolored 1.90 1.90
Nos. 535-538 (4) 3.50 3.50
Souvenir Sheet
539 A97 $2 multicolored 3.25 3.25

Christmas — A98

Christmas: Scenes from Walt Disney's Mickey's Christmas Carol.

1982, Dec. 1 Litho. Perf. 13½
540 A98 1c multicolored .25 .25
541 A98 1c multicolored .25 .25
542 A98 2c multicolored .25 .25
543 A98 2c multicolored .25 .25
544 A98 3c multicolored .25 .25
545 A98 3c multicolored .25 .25
546 A98 4c multicolored .25 .25
547 A98 65c multicolored 1.10 1.10
548 A98 $1.10 multicolored 2.50 1.50
Nos. 540-548 (9) 5.35 4.35
Souvenir Sheet
549 A98 $2 multicolored 5.25 5.25

Trams and Locomotives — A99

15c, West Caicos trolley tram. 55c, West Caicos steam locomotive. 90c, Mule-drawn tram, East Caicos. $1.60, Sisal locomotive, East Caicos. $2.50, Steam engine.

1983, Jan. 18 Litho. Perf. 14
550 A99 15c multicolored .30 .30
551 A99 55c multicolored 1.10 1.10
552 A99 90c multicolored 1.60 1.60
553 A99 $1.60 multicolored 3.00 3.00
Nos. 550-553 (4) 6.00 6.00
Souvenir Sheet
554 A99 $2.50 multicolored 4.50 4.50

A99a

1c, Woman crossing guard. 8c, Wind and solar energy sources. 65c, Sailing. $1, Cricket game.

1983, Mar. 14
555 A99a 1c multicolored .35 .35
556 A99a 8c multicolored .35 .35
557 A99a 65c multicolored 1.60 1.60
558 A99a $1 multicolored 2.50 2.50
a. Block or strip of 4, #555-558 5.75 5.75
Commonwealth Day.

Easter — A100

Crucifixion, by Raphael: 35c, Mary Magdalene, St. John. 50c, Mary. 95c, Angel looking to heaven. $1.10, Angel looking to earth. $2.50 shows entire painting.

1983, Apr. 7 Litho. Perf. 14
559 A100 35c multicolored .50 .50
560 A100 50c multicolored .70 .70
561 A100 95c multicolored 1.10 1.10
562 A100 $1.10 multicolored 1.25 1.25
Nos. 559-562 (4) 3.55 3.55
Souvenir Sheet
563 A100 $2.50 multicolored 5.00 5.00

Piked Whale A101

1983 Litho. Perf. 14
564 A101 50c shown 1.60 1.60
565 A101 65c Right whale 2.25 2.25
566 A101 70c Killer whale 2.50 2.50
567 A101 95c Sperm whale 3.50 3.50
568 A101 $1.10 Gooseback whale 4.00 4.00
569 A101 $2 Blue whale 7.00 7.00
570 A101 $2.20 Humpback whale 8.00 8.00
571 A101 $3 Longfin pilot whale 10.50 10.50
Nos. 564-571 (8) 39.35 39.35
Souvenir Sheet
572 A101 $3 Fin whale 15.00 15.00
Issued: 50c, $2.20, #571, 5/16; 70c, 95c, $2, 6/13; others 7/11. Issued in sheets of 4. For overprints see Nos. 637-639.

Manned Flight Bicentenary A102

25c, 1st hydrogen balloon, 1783. 35c, Friendship 7, 1962. 70c, Montgolfiere, 1783. 95c, Columbia space shuttle. $2, Montgolfiere, Columbia.

1983, Aug. 30 Litho. Perf. 14
573 A102 25c multicolored .35 .35
574 A102 35c multicolored .50 .50
575 A102 70c multicolored .90 .90
576 A102 95c multicolored 1.25 1.25
Nos. 573-576 (4) 3.00 3.00
Souvenir Sheet
577 A102 $2 multicolored 3.00 3.00

Ships A103

4c, Dug-out canoe. 5c, Santa Maria. 8c, Spanish treasure galleons. 10c, Bermuda sloop. 20c, Privateer Grand Turk. 25c, Nelson's Frigate Boreas. 30c, Warship Endymion. 35c, Bark Caesar. 50c, Schooner Grapeshot. 65c, Invincible. 95c, Magicienne. $1.10, Durban. $2, Sentinel. $3, Minerva. $5, Caicos sloop.

1983 Litho. Perf. 12½x12
578 A103 4c multicolored .25 .25
579 A103 5c multicolored .25 .25
580 A103 8c multicolored .25 .25
581 A103 10c multicolored .35 .25
582 A103 20c multicolored .90 1.10
583 A103 25c multicolored 1.00 1.40
584 A103 30c multicolored 1.50 2.00
585 A103 35c multicolored 1.75 2.40
586 A103 50c multicolored 2.50 3.00
587 A103 65c multicolored 3.25 4.25
588 A103 95c multicolored 4.50 6.00
589 A103 $1.10 multicolored 5.50 7.00
590 A103 $2 multicolored 9.00 12.00
591 A103 $3 multicolored 14.00 19.00
592 A103 $5 multicolored 22.50 29.00
Nos. 578-592 (15) 67.50 88.15
Issued: 4c, 8c, 10c, 30c, 65c, $1.10, $5, Mar.; 5c, 20c, 25c, 35c, 50c, 95c, $2, Aug. 12; $3, Dec.

1983-84 Perf. 14
578a A103 4c .25 .25
579a A103 5c .25 .25
580a A103 8c .25 .25
581a A103 10c .30 .25
582a A103 20c .90 .95
583a A103 25c 1.10 1.25
584a A103 30c 2.00 1.25
585a A103 35c 1.75 1.60
586a A103 50c 2.25 2.25
587a A103 65c 3.25 3.00
588a A103 95c 4.50 4.00
589a A103 $1.10 5.25 4.75
590a A103 $2 9.00 8.75
591a A103 $3 14.50 13.50
592a A103 $5 21.00 22.50
Nos. 578a-592a (15) 66.55 64.80
Issued: 10c, 30c, 65c, $1.10-$3, 10/5/83; 8c, 25c, 50c, 95c, 12/16/83; 4c, 5c, 20c, 35c, $5, 1/9/84.
For overprints see Nos. 744-746.

Christmas A104

Designs: Scenes from Walt Disney's Oh Christmas Tree.

1983, Nov. Perf. 11
593 A104 1c Fifer Pig .25 .25
594 A104 1c Fiddler Pig .25 .25
595 A104 2c Practical Pig .25 .25
596 A104 2c Pluto .25 .25
597 A104 3c Goofy .25 .25
598 A104 3c Mickey Mouse .25 .25
599 A104 35c Gyro Gearloose .60 .60
600 A104 50c Ludwig Von Drake .80 .80
601 A104 $1.10 Huey, Dewey and Louie 1.90 1.90
Nos. 593-601 (9) 4.80 4.80
Souvenir Sheet
Perf. 13½
602 A104 $2.50 Around the tree 6.50 6.50

John F. Kennedy (1917-1963), 20th Death Anniv. — A105

1983, Dec. 22 Litho. Perf. 14
603 A105 20c multicolored .35 .35
604 A105 $1 multicolored 1.75 1.75

Classic Cars A106

4c, Cadillac V-16, 1933. 8c, Rolls Royce Phantom III, 1937. 10c, Saab 99, 1969. 25c, Maserati Bora, 1973. 40c, Datsun 260Z, 1970. 55c, Porsche 917, 1971. 80c, Lincoln Continental, 1939 . $1, Triumph TR3A, 1957. $2, Daimler, 1886.

1984, Mar. 15 Litho. *Perf. 14*

605 A106 4c multi + label .25 .25
606 A106 8c multi + label .25 .25
607 A106 10c multi + label .25 .25
608 A106 25c multi + label .75 .75
609 A106 40c multi + label 1.25 1.25
610 A106 55c multi + label 1.75 1.75
611 A106 80c multi + label 2.50 2.50
612 A106 $1 multi + label 3.00 3.00
Nos. 605-612 (8) 10.00 10.00

Souvenir Sheet

613 A106 $2 multicolored 3.75 3.75

125th anniv. of first commercially productive oil well, Drake's Rig, Titusville, Pa. Nos. 605-612 se-tenant with labels showing flags and auto museum names. No. 613 for 150th birth anniv. of Gotlieb Daimler, inventor of high-speed internal combustion engine.

Easter — A107

450th death anniv. of Antonio Allegri Correggio (Various cameo portraits of Correggio, paintings): 15c, Rest on the Flight to Egypt with St. Francis. 40c, St. Luke and St. Ambrose. 60c, Diana and her Chariot. 95c, Deposition of Christ. $2, Nativity with St. Elizabeth and the Infant St. John.

1984, Apr. 9

614 A107 15c multicolored .30 .30
615 A107 40c multicolored .95 .95
616 A107 60c multicolored 1.25 1.25
617 A107 95c multicolored 1.75 1.75
Nos. 614-617 (4) 4.25 4.25

Souvenir Sheet

618 A107 $2 multi, horiz. 3.25 3.25

1984 Los Angeles Olympics — A108

Various Disney characters participating in Olympic sports.

1984, Feb. 21 Litho. *Perf. 14*

619 A108 1c 500-meter .30 .30
620 A108 1c Diving .30 .30
621 A108 2c Single kayak .30 .30
622 A108 2c 1000-meter kayak .30 .30
623 A108 3c Highboard diving .30 .30
624 A108 3c Kayak slalom .30 .30
625 A108 25c Freestyle swimming .80 .80
626 A108 75c Water polo 2.25 2.25
627 A108 $1 Yachting 3.00 3.00
Nos. 619-627 (9) 7.85 7.85

Souvenir Sheet

628 A108 $2 Platform diving 6.25 6.25

1984, Apr. *Perf. 12½x12*

Same Designs

619a A108 1c .30 .30
620a A108 1c .30 .30
621a A108 2c .30 .30
622a A108 2c .30 .30
623a A108 3c .30 .30
624a A108 3c .30 .30
625a A108 25c .75 .75
626a A108 75c 2.10 2.10
627a A108 $1 2.75 2.75
Nos. 619a-627a (9) 7.40 7.40

Souvenir Sheet

628a A108 $2 6.50 6.50

Nos. 619a-628a inscribed with Olympic rings emblem. Printed in sheets of 5.

Sir Arthur Conan Doyle (1859-1930) — A109

Scenes from the Adventures of Sherlock Holmes.

1984, July 16 Litho. *Perf. 14*

629 A109 25c Second Stain 3.50 2.10
630 A109 45c Final Problem 4.75 3.50
631 A109 70c Empty House 6.75 5.25
632 A109 85c Greek Interpreter 8.25 6.75
Nos. 629-632 (4) 23.25 17.60

Souvenir Sheet

633 A109 $2 Doyle, vert. 19.00 22.50

Nos. 567-568, 572 Ovptd. with UPU Emblem and "19TH UPU CONGRESS / HAMBURG, WEST GERMANY./ 1874-1984"

1984 Litho. *Perf. 14*

637 A101 95c multicolored 4.50 3.00
638 A101 $1.10 multicolored 4.50 3.50

Souvenir Sheet

639 A101 $3 multicolored 8.00 8.00

AUSIPEX '84 A110

Darwin, Ship, Map of Australia, Fauna.

1984, Aug. 22 *Perf. 14x13½*

640 A110 5c Clown fish 1.05 .85
641 A110 35c Monitor lizard 3.25 3.25
642 A110 50c Rainbow lorikeets 4.50 3.75
643 A110 $1.10 Koalas 6.00 5.00
Nos. 640-643 (4) 14.80 12.85

Souvenir Sheet

644 A110 $2 Grey kangaroo 5.75 5.75

Christmas — A111

Scenes from Walt Disney's The Toy Tinkers.

1984 Litho. *Perf. 14*

645 A111 20c multicolored 1.00 .50
646 A111 35c multicolored 1.40 .70
647 A111 50c multicolored 2.00 1.00
648 A111 75c multicolored 2.75 1.75
649 A111 $1.10 multicolored 3.25 2.50
Nos. 645-649 (5) 10.40 6.45

Souvenir Sheet

650 A111 $2 multicolored 5.00 5.00

No. 648 issued in sheets of 8. Issue dates: 75c, Nov. 26, others, Oct. 8.

Audubon Birth Bicentenary A112

Cameo portrait of Audubon, signature and illustrations from Birds of North America: 25c, Dendroica magnoliae. 45c, Asio flammeus. 70c, Zenaida macroura. 85c, Progne subis. $2, Haematopus ostralegus.

1985, Jan. 28 Litho. *Perf. 14*

651 A112 25c multicolored 2.25 1.10
652 A112 45c multicolored 3.50 2.25
653 A112 70c multicolored 4.25 4.25
654 A112 85c multicolored 4.25 4.75
Nos. 651-654 (4) 14.25 12.35

Souvenir Sheet

655 A112 $2 multicolored 6.75 6.00

Intl. Civil Aviation Org., 40th Anniv. A113

Pioneers & inventions: 8c, Leonardo da Vinci, 15th century glider wing. 25c, Sir Alliott Verdon Roe, 1949 C. 102 Jet. 65c, Robert H. Goddard, first liquid fuel rocket launch, 1926. $1, Igor Sikorsky, 1939 Sikorsky VS300. $2, Aviator Amelia Earhart, 1937 Lockheed 10E Electra.

1985, Feb. 21

656 A113 8c multicolored .85 .45
657 A113 25c multicolored 2.50 .60
658 A113 65c multicolored 4.25 2.25
659 A113 $1 multicolored 6.50 5.25
Nos. 656-659 (4) 14.10 8.55

Souvenir Sheet

660 A113 $2 multicolored 4.75 4.75

Arrival of the Statue of Liberty in New York, Cent. A114

Designs: 20c, Flags of US, France, Franklin, Lafayette. 30c, Designer Frederic A. Bartholdi, engineer Gustave Eiffel, Statue, Eiffel Tower. 65c, Isere, arriving in New York with Statue, 1885. $1.10, Fund raisers Louis Agassiz, H. W. Longfellow, Charles Sumner, Joseph Pulitzer. $2, Dedication day, Oct. 28, 1886.

1985, Mar. 28

661 A114 20c multicolored 1.10 .80
662 A114 30c multicolored 1.60 .95
663 A114 65c multicolored 3.50 2.10
664 A114 $1.10 multicolored 3.75 2.50
Nos. 661-664 (4) 9.95 6.35

Souvenir Sheet

665 A114 $2 multicolored 6.00 6.00

Royal Navy A115

Designs: 20c, Sir Edward Hawke, Royal George. 30c, Lord Nelson, H.M.S. Victory. 65c, Adm. Sir George Cockburn, H.M.S. Albion. 95c, Adm. Sir David Beatty, H.M.S. Indefatigable. $2, 18th century naval gunner, cannons.

1985, Apr. 17

666 A115 20c multicolored 3.25 2.25
667 A115 30c multicolored 3.50 3.25
668 A115 65c multicolored 5.25 4.50
669 A115 95c multicolored 6.50 7.00
Nos. 666-669 (4) 18.50 17.00

Souvenir Sheet

670 A115 $2 multicolored 6.25 6.25

Intl. Youth Year A116

Anniversaries: 25c, Return of Halley's Comet, 1986. 35c, Mark Twain (1835-1910), Mississippi river boat. 50c, Jakob Grimm (1785-1863), Hansel & Gretel, vert. 95c, Grimm, Rumpelstiltskin, vert. $2, Twain, Grimm, portraits.

1985, May 17

671 A116 25c multicolored 1.75 .55
672 A116 35c multicolored 2.75 .70
673 A116 50c multicolored 3.25 1.00
674 A116 95c multicolored 4.50 2.25
Nos. 671-674 (4) 12.25 4.50

Souvenir Sheet

675 A116 $2 multicolored 6.00 6.00

Queen Mother, 85th Birthday — A117

Designs: 30c, Queen Mother outside Clarence House, vert. 50c, Visiting Biggin Hill Airfield by helicopter. $1.10, 80th birthday portrait, vert. $2, With Prince Charles at the 1968 Garter Ceremony, Windsor Castle, vert.

1985, July 15

676 A117 30c multicolored 1.00 1.00
677 A117 50c multicolored 1.50 1.50
678 A117 $1.10 multicolored 3.50 3.50
Nos. 676-678 (3) 6.00 6.00

Souvenir Sheet

679 A117 $2 multicolored 5.00 5.00

George Frideric Handel — A118

Johann Sebastian Bach — A119

Handel or Bach and: 4c, King George II, Zadok the Priest music, 1727. 10c, Queen Caroline, Funeral Anthem, 1737. 15c, Bassoon, Invention No. 3 in D Major. 40c, Natural horn, Invention No. 3 in D Major. 50c, King George I, Water Music, 1714. 60c, Viola d'amore, Invention No. 3 . . . 95c, Clavichord, Invention No. 3 . . . $1.10, Queen Anne, Or la Tromba from Rinaldo. No. 688, Handel, portrait. No. 689, Bach, portrait.

1985, July 17 *Perf. 15*

680 A118 4c multicolored .70 .55
681 A118 10c multicolored 1.10 .55
682 A119 15c multicolored 1.10 .50
683 A119 40c multicolored 2.25 1.00
684 A118 50c multicolored 3.00 2.50
685 A119 60c multicolored 2.75 1.25
686 A119 95c multicolored 3.25 2.50
687 A118 $1.10 multicolored 5.25 5.00
Nos. 680-687 (8) 19.40 13.85

Souvenir Sheets

688 A118 $2 multicolored 7.25 7.25
689 A119 $2 multicolored 5.25 5.00

Motorcycle Centenary — A120

Flag of US, UK, Fed. Rep. of Germany or Japan and: 8c, 1915 dual cylinder Harley-Davidson. 25c, 1950 Thunderbird Triumph. 55c, 1985 BMW K100RS. $1.20, 1985 Honda 1100 Shadow. $2, 1885 Daimler Single Track, vert.

1985, Sept. 4		Perf. 14	
690	A120	8c multicolored	1.00	.40
691	A120	25c multicolored	2.10	1.00
692	A120	55c multicolored	3.25	2.50
693	A120	$1.20 multicolored	5.00	7.75
		Nos. 690-693 (4)	11.35	11.65

Souvenir Sheet

| 694 | A120 | $2 multicolored | 6.25 | 6.25 |

Pirates of the Caribbean — A121

Disneyland, 30th Anniv.: No. 695, Fate of Capt. Kidd. No. 696, Pirates imprisoned. No. 697, Bartholomew Roberts, church-going pirate. No. 698, Buccaneers in battle. No. 699, Bride auction. No. 700, Plunder. No. 701, Singing pirates. No. 702, Blackbeard. No. 703, Henry Morgan. No. 704, Mary Read, Anne Bonney.

1985, Oct. 4		Litho.	Perf. 14	
695	A121	1c multicolored	.35	.35
696	A121	1c multicolored	.35	.35
697	A121	2c multicolored	.35	.35
698	A121	2c multicolored	.35	.35
699	A121	3c multicolored	.35	.35
700	A121	3c multicolored	.35	.35
701	A121	35c multicolored	2.25	.90
702	A121	75c multicolored	4.25	4.75
703	A121	$1.10 multicolored	4.75	5.50
		Nos. 695-703 (9)	13.35	13.25

Souvenir Sheet

| 704 | A121 | $2.50 multicolored | 9.25 | 9.25 |

Girl Guides, 75th Anniv. A122

Uniforms of Turks and Caicos and: 10c, Papua New Guinea and China brownies. 40c, Surinam and Korea brownies. 70c, Australia and Canada girl guides. 80c, West Germany and Israel girl guides.

1985, Nov. 4			
705	A122	10c multicolored	1.10	.75
706	A122	40c multicolored	2.75	2.10
707	A122	70c multicolored	3.75	4.50
708	A122	80c multicolored	3.75	4.75
		Nos. 705-708 (4)	11.35	12.10

Souvenir Sheet

| 709 | A122 | $2 Anniv. emblem | 5.00 | 5.00 |

Grand Turk Chapter, 35th anniv.

World Wildlife Fund A123

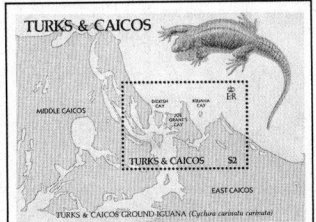

Map of the Islands — A124

Turks & Caicos ground iguanas.

1986, Nov. 20			Perf. 14	
710	A123	8c multicolored	2.50	1.25
711	A123	10c multicolored	2.50	1.25
712	A123	20c multicolored	4.25	2.50
713	A123	35c multicolored	9.75	8.50
		Nos. 710-713 (4)	19.00	13.50

Souvenir Sheet

| 714 | A124 | $2 multicolored | 19.00 | 19.00 |

A125

Wedding pictures.

1986, Dec. 19		Litho.	Perf. 14	
715	A125	35c Couple	1.25	1.25
716	A125	65c Sarah in coach	2.25	2.25
717	A125	$1.10 Couple, close-up	4.00	4.00
		Nos. 715-717 (3)	7.50	7.50

Souvenir Sheet

| 718 | A125 | $2 In Westminster Abbey | 7.00 | 7.00 |

Wedding of Prince Andrew and Sarah Ferguson.

Christmas — A126

Illuminations by miniaturist Giorgio Giulio Clovio (1498-1578) from the Farnese Book of Hours: 35c, Prophecy of the Birth of Christ to King Achaz. 50c, The Annunciation. 65c, The Circumcision. 95c, Adoration of the Kings. $2, The Nativity, from the Townley Lectionary.

1987, Dec. 9		Litho.	Perf. 14	
719	A126	35c multicolored	1.50	.85
720	A126	50c multicolored	2.25	2.10
721	A126	65c multicolored	2.75	2.75
722	A126	95c multicolored	4.00	4.50
		Nos. 719-722 (4)	10.50	10.20

Souvenir Sheet

| 723 | A126 | $2 multicolored | 8.00 | 9.25 |

Accession of Queen Victoria to the Throne of England, 150th Anniv. A127

Ships and memorials: 8c, HMS Victoria, Victoria Cross. 35c, SS Victoria, coin. 55c, Victoria & Albert I, Great Britain No. 1. 95c, Victoria & Albert II, Victoria Public Library, Turks & Caicos. $2, Bark Victoria.

1987, Dec. 24			
724	A127	8c multicolored	3.75	1.60
725	A127	35c multicolored	3.75	3.25
726	A127	45c multicolored	4.25	4.25
727	A127	95c multicolored	5.25	7.00
		Nos. 724-727 (4)	17.00	16.10

Souvenir Sheet

| 728 | A127 | $2 multicolored | 11.00 | 11.00 |

US Constitution Bicentennial — A128

Designs: 10c, NJ state flag. 35c, Freedom of Worship, vert. 65c, US Supreme Court, vert. 80c, John Adams, vert. $2, George Mason, vert.

1987, Dec. 31			
729	A128	10c multicolored	.25	.25
730	A128	35c multicolored	.75	.75
731	A128	65c multicolored	2.00	2.00
732	A128	80c multicolored	3.00	3.00
		Nos. 729-732 (4)	6.00	6.00

Souvenir Sheet

| 733 | A128 | $2 multicolored | 4.00 | 4.50 |

Discovery of America, 500th Anniv. (in 1992) A129

4c, Caravel, first sighting of land, Oct. 12, 1492. 25c, Columbus meets with Indians, Oct. 14. 70c, Fleet anchored in harbor, Oct. 15. $1, Landing, Oct. 16. $2, Nina, Pinta and Santa Maria.

1988, Jan. 20			
734	A129	4c multicolored	.80	.50
735	A129	25c multicolored	1.50	.95
736	A129	70c multicolored	4.50	5.00
737	A129	$1 multicolored	4.50	5.00
		Nos. 734-737 (4)	11.30	11.45

Souvenir Sheet

| 738 | A129 | $2 multicolored | 8.00 | 8.00 |

Sea Scouts Salute Jamboree and Australia A130

Australia Bicent.: 8c, Arawak artifact, scouts exploring cave on Middle Caicos, vert. 35c, Santa Maria, scouts rowing to Hawks Nest. 65c, Scouts diving to explore a sunken Spanish galleon, vert. 95c, Plantation worker cutting sisal, scouts exploring plantation ruins. $2, Splashdown of Friendship 7, piloted by John Glenn, Feb. 20, 1962, vert.

1988, Feb. 12		Litho.	Perf. 14	
739	A130	8c multicolored	.35	.35
740	A130	35c shown	1.00	1.00
741	A130	65c multicolored	1.90	1.90
742	A130	95c multicolored	2.75	2.75
		Nos. 739-742 (4)	6.00	6.00

Souvenir Sheet

| 743 | A130 | $2 multicolored | 5.25 | 5.75 |

Nos. 581, 583 and 590 Ovptd. "40th WEDDING ANNIVERSARY / H.M. QUEEN ELIZABETH II / H.R.H. THE DUKE OF EDINBURGH"

1988, Mar. 14		Litho.	Perf. 14	
744	A103	10c multicolored	.25	.25
745	A103	25c multicolored	.75	.75
746	A103	$2 multicolored	6.00	6.00
		Nos. 744-746 (3)	7.00	7.00

A131

1988, Aug. 29			Litho.	
747	A131	8c Soccer	.75	.40
748	A131	30c Yachting	1.50	1.50
749	A131	70c Cycling	4.75	4.00
750	A131	$1 Running	3.75	4.75
		Nos. 747-750 (4)	10.75	10.65

Souvenir Sheet

| 751 | A131 | $2 Swimming | 5.00 | 5.00 |

1988 Summer Olympics, Seoul.

A132

Billfish Tournament: 8c, Passenger jet, fishing boat and fisherman reeling-in giant swordfish. 10c, Photographing prize catch. 70c, Fishing boat, lighthouse. $1, Blue marlin. $2, Sailfish.

1988, Sept. 5			Litho.	
752	A132	8c multicolored	1.40	.35
753	A132	10c multicolored	.70	.35
754	A132	70c multicolored	3.00	3.25
755	A132	$1 multicolored	3.50	.40
		Nos. 752-755 (4)	8.60	4.35

Souvenir Sheet

| 756 | A132 | $2 multicolored | 6.00 | 6.00 |

Christmas A133

Paintings by Titian: 15c, Madonna and Child with St. Catherine and the Infant John the Baptist, c. 1530. 25c, Madonna with a Rabbit, c. 1526. 35c, Virgin and Child with Sts. Stephen, Jerome and Mauritius, c. 1520. 40c, The Gypsy Madonna, c. 1510. 50c, The Holy Family and a Shepherd, c. 1510. 65c, Madonna and Child, c. 1510. $3, Madonna and Child with St. John the Baptist and St. Catherine, c. 1530. No. 764, Adoration of the Magi, c. 1560. No. 765, The Annunciation, c. 1560.

1988, Oct. 24			Litho.	
757	A133	15c multicolored	.40	.40
758	A133	25c multicolored	.60	.60
759	A133	35c multicolored	.85	.85
760	A133	40c multicolored	.95	.95
761	A133	50c multicolored	1.25	1.25
762	A133	65c multicolored	1.50	1.50
763	A133	$3 multicolored	7.00	7.00
		Nos. 757-763 (7)	12.55	12.55

Souvenir Sheets

| 764 | A133 | $2 multicolored | 5.00 | 5.00 |
| 765 | A133 | $2 multicolored | 5.00 | 5.00 |

Visit of Princess Alexandra, 1st Cousin
of Queen Elizabeth II — A134

Various portraits and: 70c, Government
House. $1.40, Map. $2, Flora, vert.

1988, Nov. 14　　Litho.　　*Perf. 14*
| 766 | A134 | 70c multicolored | 4.50 | 3.75 |
| 767 | A134 | $1.40 multicolored | 10.00 | 10.50 |

Souvenir Sheet
| 768 | A134 | $2 multicolored | 16.00 | 16.00 |

**Arms Type of 1970 Without
Inscription**

Perf. 14½x15
1988, Dec. 15　　Litho.　　Unwmk.
| 769 | A35 | $10 multicolored | 20.00 | 20.00 |

Pre-Columbian Societies and Their
Customs — A135

UPAE and discovery of America anniv.
emblems and: 10c, Hollowing-out tree to make
a canoe, vert. 50c, Body painting and statue.
65c, Three islanders with body paint. $1,
Canoeing, vert. $2, Petroglyph.

1989, May 15　　Litho.　　*Perf. 14*
770	A135	10c multicolored	.40	.40
771	A135	50c multicolored	1.60	1.60
772	A135	65c multicolored	2.00	2.00
773	A135	$1 multicolored	3.25	3.25
		Nos. 770-773 (4)	7.25	7.25

Souvenir Sheet
| 774 | A135 | $2 multicolored | 8.00 | 8.25 |

Discovery of America 500th anniv. (in 1992).

Souvenir Sheet

Lincoln Memorial, Washington,
D.C. — A136

1989, Nov. 17　　Litho.　　*Perf. 14*
| 775 | A136 | $1.50 multicolored | 5.25 | 5.25 |

World Stamp Expo '89.

Miniature Sheets

American Presidential Office, 200th
Anniv. — A137

US presidents, historic events and
monuments.
No. 776: a, Jackson, early train. b, Van
Buren, origins of baseball and Moses Fleet-
wood Walker, 1st black to play professional
baseball. c, Harrison, Harrison's "Keep the
Ball Rollin'" slogan and parade. d, Tyler,
annexation of Texas, 1845. e, Polk, 1st US

postage stamps (#2), 1847, and discovery of
gold in California, 1849. f, Taylor, Mexican-
American War, 1847.
No. 777: a, Hayes, end of Civil War recon-
struction. b, Garfield, Garfield leading Union
soldiers in the Battle of Shiloh. c, Arthur, open-
ing of the Brooklyn Bridge, 1883. d, Cleveland,
Columbian Exposition, 1893 (US #245). e,
Benjamin Harrison, Pan-American Union
building, map. f, McKinley, Spanish-American
War (Rough Riders Monument, by Solon
Borglum).
No. 778: a, Hoover, 1933 Olympic Games,
Los Angeles and Lake Placid (American
sprinter Ralph Metcalf and Norwegian figure
skater Sonja Henie). b, Franklin Delano
Roosevelt, Roosevelt's support of the March of
Dimes (dime, 1946). c, 150th anniv. of inaugu-
ration of Washington, New York World's Fair,
1939. d, Truman, founding of the U.N., 1945.
e, Eisenhower, invasion of Normandy, 1944. f,
Kennedy, Apollo 11 mission, 1969.

1989, Nov. 19　　　　*Perf. 14*
776		Sheet of 6	15.00	15.00
a.-f.	A137 50c any single		2.40	2.40
777		Sheet of 6	15.00	15.00
a.-f.	A137 50c any single		2.40	2.40
778		Sheet of 6	15.00	15.00
a.-f.	A137 50c any single		2.40	2.40

Fraser is incorrectly spelled "Frazer" on No.
778c.

Christmas — A138

Religious paintings by Giovanni Bellini: 15c,
Madonna and Child. 25c, The Madonna of the
Shrubs. 35c, The Virgin and Child. 40c, The
Virgin and Child with a Greek Inscription. 50c,
The Madonna of the Meadow. 65c, The
Madonna of the Pear. 70c, The Virgin and
Child, diff. $1, Madonna and Child, diff. No.
787, The Madonna with John the Baptist and
Another Saint. No. 788, The Virgin and Child
Enthroned.

1989, Dec. 18
779	A138	15c multicolored	.55	.55
780	A138	25c multicolored	.85	.85
781	A138	35c multicolored	1.25	1.25
782	A138	40c multicolored	1.50	1.50
783	A138	50c multicolored	1.75	1.75
784	A138	65c multicolored	2.25	2.25
785	A138	70c multicolored	2.50	2.50
786	A138	$1 multicolored	7.00	7.00
		Nos. 779-786 (8)	17.65	17.65

Souvenir Sheets
| 787 | A138 | $2 multicolored | 8.00 | 8.00 |
| 788 | A138 | $2 multicolored | 8.00 | 8.00 |

Souvenir Sheet

1st Moon Landing, 20th
Anniv. — A139

Designs: a, Liftoff. b, Eagle lunar module on
Moon's surface. c, Aldrin obtaining soil sam-
ples. d, Neil Armstrong walking on Moon. e,
Columbia and Eagle in space.

1990, Jan. 8
| 789 | | Sheet of 5 | 8.50 | 8.50 |
| a.-e. | A139 50c any single | | 1.60 | 1.60 |

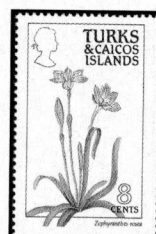

Flowers — A140

8c, Zephyranthes rosea. 10c, Sophora
tomentosa. 15c, Coccoloba uvifera. 20c,
Encyclia gracilis. 25c, Tillandsia streptophylla.
30c, Maurandella antirrhiniflora. 35c, Tillandsia balbisiana. 50c, Encyclia rufa. 65c,
Aechmea lingulata. 80c, Asclepias curassavica. $1, Caesalpinia bahamensis. $1.10,
Capparis cynophallophora. $1.25,
Stachytarpheta jamaicensis. $2, Cassia
biflora. $5, Clusia rosea. $10, Opuntia
bahamana.

1990, Jan. 11　　Litho.　　*Perf. 14*
790	A140	8c multicolored	.25	.25
791	A140	10c multicolored	.25	.25
792	A140	15c multicolored	.35	.35
793	A140	20c multicolored	.50	.50
794	A140	25c multicolored	.60	.60
795	A140	30c multicolored	.70	.70
796	A140	35c multicolored	.85	.85
797	A140	50c multicolored	1.25	1.25
798	A140	65c multicolored	1.50	1.50
799	A140	80c multicolored	1.90	1.90
800	A140	$1 multicolored	2.40	2.40
801	A140	$1.10 multicolored	2.75	2.75
802	A140	$1.25 multicolored	3.00	3.00
803	A140	$2 multicolored	4.75	4.75
804	A140	$5 multicolored	12.00	12.00
805	A140	$10 multicolored	24.00	24.00
		Nos. 790-805 (16)	57.05	57.05

1994　　　　　　*Perf. 12*
790a	A140	8c	.25	.25
791a	A140	10c	.25	.25
792a	A140	15c	.35	.35
793a	A140	20c	.50	.50
794a	A140	25c	.60	.60
795a	A140	30c	.70	.70
796a	A140	35c	.85	.85
797a	A140	50c	1.25	1.25
798a	A140	65c	1.50	1.50
799a	A140	80c	1.90	1.90
800a	A140	$1	2.40	2.40
801a	A140	$1.10	2.75	2.75
802a	A140	$1.25	3.00	3.00
803a	A140	$2	4.75	4.75
804a	A140	$5	12.00	12.00
805a	A140	$10 ('95)	24.00	24.00
		Nos. 790a-805a (16)	57.05	57.05

Birds
A141

10c, Yellow-billed cuckoo. 15c, White-tailed
tropic bird. 20c, Kirtland's warbler. 30c, Yellow-
crowned night heron. 50c, West Indian tree
duck. 80c, Yellow-bellied sapsucker. $1, Amer-
ican kestrel. $1.40, Mockingbird.
No. 814, Osprey. No. 815, Yellow warbler.

1990, Feb. 19
806	A141	10c multicolored	1.40	.80
807	A141	15c multicolored	1.60	.80
808	A141	20c multicolored	2.00	1.10
809	A141	30c multicolored	2.50	1.10
810	A141	50c multicolored	3.50	1.60
811	A141	80c multicolored	4.25	3.50
812	A141	$1 multicolored	5.75	6.50
813	A141	$1.40 multicolored	5.50	4.25
		Nos. 806-813 (8)	26.50	19.65

Souvenir Sheets
| 814 | A141 | $2 multicolored | 12.50 | 12.50 |
| 815 | A141 | $2 multicolored | 12.50 | 12.50 |

Fish
A142

8c, Queen parrotfish. 10c, Queen triggerfish. 25c, Sergeant major. 40c, Spotted goatfish. 50c, Neon goby. 75c, Nassau grouper.
80c, Jawfish. $1, Blue tang.
No. 824, Butter hamlet. No. 825, Queen
angelfish.

1990, Feb. 12　　Litho.　　*Perf. 14*
816	A142	8c multicolored	.30	.30
817	A142	10c multicolored	.30	.30
818	A142	25c multicolored	.70	.70
819	A142	40c multicolored	1.10	1.10
820	A142	50c multicolored	1.40	1.40
821	A142	75c multicolored	2.10	2.10
822	A142	80c multicolored	2.25	2.25
823	A142	$1 multicolored	2.75	2.75
		Nos. 816-823 (8)	10.90	10.90

Souvenir Sheets
| 824 | A142 | $2 multicolored | 9.00 | 9.00 |
| 825 | A142 | $2 multicolored | 9.00 | 9.00 |

Butterflies
A143

15c, White peacock. 25c, Cloudless
sulphur. 35c, Mexican fritillary. 40c, Fiery skipper. 50c, Chamberlain's sulphur. 60c, Pygmy
blue. 90c, Dusky swallowtail. $1, Antillean
dagger wing.
No. 834, Thomas's blue. No. 835, 9 Queen
species.

1990, Mar. 19
826	A143	15c multicolored	1.00	.70
827	A143	25c multicolored	1.25	.90
828	A143	35c multicolored	1.60	1.10
829	A143	40c multicolored	1.75	1.25
830	A143	50c multicolored	1.75	1.50
831	A143	60c multicolored	2.10	2.10
832	A143	90c multicolored	3.50	4.25
833	A143	$1 multicolored	3.50	4.25
		Nos. 826-833 (8)	16.45	16.05

Souvenir Sheets
| 834 | A143 | $2 multicolored | 9.00 | 9.00 |
| 835 | A143 | $2 multicolored | 9.00 | 9.00 |

Nos. 826, 831 and 833 vert.

America
Issue
A144

Fish, UPAE and discovery of America 500th
anniv. emblems: 10c, Rock beauty. 15c,
Coney. 25c, Red hind. 50c, Banded butterflyfish. 60c, French angelfish. 75c, Blackbar
soldierfish. 90c, Stoplight parrotfish. $1,
French grunt.
No. 844, Gray angelfish. No. 845, Blue
chromis.

1990, Apr. 2
836	A144	10c multicolored	.80	.50
837	A144	15c multicolored	.90	.65
838	A144	25c multicolored	1.25	.85
839	A144	50c multicolored	1.75	1.75
840	A144	60c multicolored	2.40	2.10
841	A144	75c multicolored	2.75	3.00
842	A144	90c multicolored	3.00	3.50
843	A144	$1 multicolored	3.25	3.75
		Nos. 836-843 (8)	16.10	16.10

Souvenir Sheets
| 844 | A144 | $2 multicolored | 5.25 | 5.25 |
| 845 | A144 | $2 multicolored | 5.25 | 5.25 |

Penny Black,
150th
Anniv. — A145

British Pillar
Boxes — A146

25c, 1p essay in blue, without letters. 35c, Letter Box #1, 1855. 50c, Penfold Box, 1866. 75c, Great Britain #3, essay. $1, 2p blue essay. $1.25, Air mail box, 1935. #852, Great Britain #1. #853, K type box, 1979.

1990, May 3 Litho. *Perf. 14*

846	A145	25c bluish blk	1.40	.90
847	A146	35c gray & pale brn	1.00	1.00
848	A146	50c gray & dk blue	1.40	1.40
849	A145	75c red brown	3.00	2.25
850	A145	$1 dk blue	3.75	3.75
851	A146	$1.25 gray & blue	3.00	*4.50*
		Nos. 846-851 (6)	13.55	13.80

Souvenir Sheets

852	A145	$2 black	5.75	5.75
853	A146	$2 blk & red brn	7.25	7.25

Stamp World London '90.

Queen Mother, 90th Birthday — A147

1990, Aug. 20 Litho. *Perf. 14*

854	A147	10c multicolored	.55	.50
855	A147	25c multi, diff.	1.10	.80
856	A147	75c multi, diff.	2.00	2.00
857	A147	$1.25 multi, diff.	3.25	*3.75*
		Nos. 854-857 (4)	6.90	7.05

Souvenir Sheet

858	A147	$2 multi, diff.	7.00	7.00

Birds A148

8c, Stripe-headed tanager, vert. 10c, Black-whiskered vireo. 25c, Blue-grey gnatcatcher. 40c, Lesser scaup. 50c, White-cheeked pintail. 75c, Common stilt. 80c, Common oyster-catcher, vert. $1, Tricolored heron.

No. 867, Bahama woodstar. No. 868, American coot.

1990, Sept. 24 Litho. *Perf. 14*

859	A148	8c multicolored	1.25	.90
860	A148	10c multicolored	1.25	.90
861	A148	25c multicolored	1.60	.90
862	A148	40c multicolored	3.25	1.90
863	A148	50c multicolored	3.25	1.90
864	A148	75c multicolored	3.75	3.75
865	A148	80c multicolored	3.75	*4.50*
866	A148	$1 multicolored	4.50	*5.25*
		Nos. 859-866 (8)	22.60	20.00

Souvenir Sheets

867	A148	$2 multicolored	6.25	6.25
868	A148	$2 multicolored	6.25	6.25

Christmas A149

Different details from paintings by Rubens: 10c, 50c, 75c, No. 876, Triumph of Christ over Sin and Death. 35c, 45c, 65c, $1.25, No. 877, St. Theresa Praying for the Souls in Purgatory. Nos. 876-877 show entire painting.

1990, Dec. 17 Litho. *Perf. 14*

869	A149	10c multicolored	.45	.25
870	A149	35c multicolored	1.50	1.25
871	A149	45c multicolored	1.60	1.50
872	A149	50c multicolored	1.90	1.60
873	A149	65c multicolored	2.75	2.10
874	A149	75c multicolored	3.00	2.75
875	A149	$1.25 multicolored	4.50	4.50
		Nos. 869-875 (7)	15.70	13.95

Souvenir Sheets

876	A149	$2 multicolored	9.00	9.00
877	A149	$2 multicolored	9.00	9.00

1992 Summer Olympics, Barcelona — A150

1991, Jan. 17

878	A150	10c Kayaking	.25	.25
879	A150	25c Track	.80	.80
880	A150	75c Pole vault	2.25	2.25
881	A150	$1.25 Javelin	3.75	3.75
		Nos. 878-881 (4)	7.05	7.05

Souvenir Sheet

882	A150	$2 Baseball	10.50	11.50

No. 878 inscribed Canoeing.

Voyages of Discovery A151

Designs: 5c, Henry Hudson, 1611. 10c, Roald Amundsen (airship), 1926. 15c, Amundsen (ship), 1906. 50c, USS Nautilus, 1958. 75c, Robert Scott, 1911. $1, Richard Byrd, Floyd Bennett, 1926. $1.25, Lincoln Ellsworth, 1935. $1.50, Cook, 1772-75. No. 891, The Nina. No. 892, The search for land.

1991, Apr. 15 Litho. *Perf. 14*

883	A151	5c multicolored	1.10	.70
884	A151	10c multicolored	1.10	.70
885	A151	15c multicolored	1.60	1.00
886	A151	50c multicolored	2.10	1.50
887	A151	75c multicolored	3.75	2.75
888	A151	$1 multicolored	4.00	3.50
889	A151	$1.25 multicolored	5.75	*6.75*
890	A151	$1.50 multicolored	6.00	*7.75*
		Nos. 883-890 (8)	25.40	24.65

Souvenir Sheets

891	A151	$2 multicolored	8.00	8.00
892	A151	$2 multicolored	8.00	8.00

Discovery of America, 500th anniv. (in 1992).

Butterflies A152

5c, White peacock. 25c, Orion. 35c, Gulf fritillary. 45c, Caribbean buckeye. 55c, Flambeau. 65c, Malachite. 70c, Florida white. $1, Great southern white.

No. 901, Giant hairstreak. No. 902, Orange-barred sulphur.

1991, May 13 Litho. *Perf. 14*

893	A152	5c multicolored	.35	.35
894	A152	25c multicolored	1.05	1.05
895	A152	35c multicolored	1.40	1.40
896	A152	45c multicolored	1.90	1.90
897	A152	55c multicolored	2.25	2.25
898	A152	65c multicolored	2.60	2.60
899	A152	70c multicolored	3.00	3.00
900	A152	$1 multicolored	4.00	4.00
		Nos. 893-900 (8)	16.55	16.55

Souvenir Sheets

901	A152	$2 multicolored	8.50	8.50
902	A152	$2 multicolored	8.50	8.50

Extinct Animals A153

1991, June 3

903	A153	5c Protohydrochoerus	.35	.35
904	A153	10c Phororhacos	.35	.35
905	A153	15c Prothylacynus	.55	.55
906	A153	50c Borhyaena	1.75	1.75
907	A153	75c Smilodon	2.75	2.75
908	A153	$1 Thoatherium	3.75	3.75
909	A153	$1.25 Cuvieronius	4.75	4.75
910	A153	$1.50 Toxodon	5.75	5.75
		Nos. 903-910 (8)	20.00	20.00

Souvenir Sheets

911	A153	$2 Mesosaurus	9.00	9.00
912	A153	$2 Astrapotherium	9.00	9.00

Royal Family Birthday, Anniversary

Common Design Type

No. 921, Elizabeth, Philip. No. 922, Diana, sons, Charles.

1991 Litho. *Perf. 14*

913	CD347	10c multicolored	.70	.35
914	CD347	25c multicolored	.95	.80
915	CD347	35c multicolored	1.25	.95
916	CD347	45c multicolored	2.75	1.50
917	CD347	50c multicolored	3.00	1.90
918	CD347	65c multicolored	2.25	2.25
919	CD347	80c multicolored	2.75	*3.00*
920	CD347	$1 multicolored	3.50	*4.25*
		Nos. 913-920 (8)	17.15	15.00

Souvenir Sheets

921	CD347	$2 multicolored	6.25	*6.75*
922	CD347	$2 multicolored	8.25	8.25

10c, 45c, 50c, $1, No. 922, Charles and Diana, 10th wedding anniv., issued: July 29. Others, Queen Elizabeth II, 65th birthday, issued: June 8.

For overprints see Nos. 1020-1022.

Mushrooms — A154

10c, Pluteus chrysophlebius. 15c, Leucopaxillus gracillimus. 20c, Marasmius haematocephalus. 35c, Collybia subpruinosa. 50c, Marasmius atrorubens, vert. 65c, Leucocoprinus birnbaumii, vert. $1.10, Trogia cantharelloides, vert. $1.25, Boletellus cubensis, vert. No. 931, Gerronema citrinum. No. 932, Pyrrhoglossum pyrrhum, vert.

1991, June 24 Litho. *Perf. 14*

923	A154	10c multicolored	.35	.35
924	A154	15c multicolored	.55	.55
925	A154	20c multicolored	.70	.70
926	A154	35c multicolored	1.25	1.25
927	A154	50c multicolored	1.75	1.75
928	A154	65c multicolored	2.25	2.25
929	A154	$1.10 multicolored	4.00	4.00
930	A154	$1.25 multicolored	4.50	4.50
		Nos. 923-930 (8)	15.35	15.35

Miniature Sheets

931	A154	$2 multicolored	7.50	*7.75*
932	A154	$2 multicolored	7.50	*7.75*

Paintings by Vincent Van Gogh — A155

Paintings: 15c, Weaver Facing Left, with Spinning Wheel. 25c, Head of a Young Peasant with Pipe, vert. 35c, The Old Cemetery Tower at Nuenen, vert. 45c, Cottage at Nightfall. 50c, Still Life with Open Bible. 65c, Lane at the Jardin du Luxembourg. 80c, The Pont du Carrousel and the Louvre. $1, Vase with Poppies, Cornflowers, Peonies and Chrysanthemums, vert. No. 941, Entrance to the Public Park. No. 942, Plowed Field.

1991, Aug. 26 *Perf. 13*

933	A155	15c multicolored	.65	.65
934	A155	25c multicolored	1.10	1.10
935	A155	35c multicolored	1.50	1.50
936	A155	45c multicolored	2.10	2.10
937	A155	50c multicolored	2.40	2.40
938	A155	65c multicolored	3.00	3.00
939	A155	80c multicolored	3.75	3.75
940	A155	$1 multicolored	4.50	4.50
		Nos. 933-940 (8)	19.00	19.00

Size: 107x80mm

Imperf

941	A155	$2 multicolored	8.50	8.50
942	A155	$2 multicolored	8.50	8.50

Phila Nippon '91 A156

Japanese steam locomotives.

1991, Nov. 4 Litho. *Perf. 14*

943	A156	8c Series 8550	.60	.60
944	A156	10c C 57	.60	.60
945	A156	45c Series 4110	1.90	1.25
946	A156	50c C 55	1.90	1.25
947	A156	65c Series 6250	2.75	2.75
948	A156	80c E 10	3.00	3.00
949	A156	$1 Series 4500	3.25	3.50
950	A156	$1.25 C 11	4.25	4.25
		Nos. 943-950 (8)	18.25	17.20

Souvenir Sheets

951	A156	$2 C 62	6.50	6.50
952	A156	$2 C 58	6.50	6.50

Christmas A157

Details or entire paintings by Gerard David: 8c, Adoration of the Shepherds. 15c, Virgin and Child Enthroned with Two Angels. 35c, The Annunciation (outside wings). 45c, The Rest on the Flight into Egypt. 50c, The Rest on the Flight into Egypt, diff. 65c, Virgin and Child with Angels. 80c, The Adoration of the Shepherds, diff. $1.25, The Perussis Altarpiece. No. 961, The Adoration of the Kings. No. 962, The Nativity.

1991, Dec. 23 *Perf. 12*

953	A157	8c multicolored	.40	.40
954	A157	15c multicolored	.65	.65
955	A157	35c multicolored	1.40	1.40
956	A157	45c multicolored	1.75	1.75
957	A157	50c multicolored	2.10	2.10
958	A157	65c multicolored	3.50	2.50
959	A157	80c multicolored	3.25	3.25
960	A157	$1.25 multicolored	5.00	5.00
		Nos. 953-960 (8)	18.05	17.05

Souvenir Sheets

Perf. 14½

961	A157	$2 multicolored	6.50	6.50
962	A157	$2 multicolored	6.50	6.50

Boy Scouts A160

No. 968, Member of Boy Scout Service Corps at New York World's Fair, 1964-65. No. 969, Lord Robert Baden-Powell, vert. $2, Silver Buffalo Award.

1992, July 6 Litho. *Perf. 14*

968	A160	$1 multicolored	4.50	4.50
969	A160	$1 multicolored	4.50	4.50

Souvenir Sheet

970	A160	$2 multicolored	8.50	8.50

17th World Scout Jamboree, Korea.

Anniversaries and Events — A161

Designs: 25c, Astronaut releasing communications satellite. 50c, Tree with dead side, healthy side. 65c, Emblems, globe, food products. 80c, Fish in polluted, clean water. $1, Runners, Lions Intl. emblem. $1.25, Orbiting quarantine facility modules. No. 977, Planned orbital transfer vehicle for Mars. No. 977A, Industrial pollution, clean beach.

1992-93		Litho.	Perf. 14	
971	A161	25c multicolored	1.50	1.50
972	A161	50c multicolored	1.75	1.75
973	A161	65c multicolored	4.25	4.25
974	A161	80c multicolored	2.50	2.50
975	A161	$1 multicolored	5.00	5.00
976	A161	$1.25 multicolored	7.00	7.00
		Nos. 971-976 (6)	22.00	22.00

Souvenir Sheets

977	A161	$2 multicolored	10.00	10.00
977A	A161	$2 multicolored	10.00	10.00

Intl. Space Year (#971, 976-977). Earth Summit, Rio de Janeiro (#972, 974, 977A). Intl. Conf. on Nutrition, Rome (#973). Lions Intl., 75th anniv. (#975).
Issued: #972, 974, 977A, 1/93; others, 12/92.

Queen Elizabeth II's Accession to the Throne, 40th Anniv.
Common Design Type

1992, Feb. 6		Litho.	Perf. 14	
978	CD348	10c multicolored	.70	.70
979	CD348	20c multicolored	1.40	1.40
980	CD348	25c multicolored	1.50	1.50
981	CD348	35c multicolored	1.50	1.50
982	CD348	50c multicolored	2.25	2.25
983	CD348	65c multicolored	2.75	2.75
984	CD348	80c multicolored	2.75	2.75
985	CD348	$1.10 multicolored	3.25	3.25
		Nos. 978-985 (8)	16.10	16.10

Souvenir Sheets

986	CD348	$2 Queen at left, boat dock	7.50	7.50
987	CD348	$2 Queen at right, shoreline	7.50	7.50

Spanish Art — A162

Paintings: 8c, St. Monica, by Luis Tristan. 20c, 45c, The Vision of Ezekiel: The Resurrection of the Flesh (different details) by Francisco Collantes. 50c, The Martyrdom of St. Philip, by Jose de Ribera. 65c, St. John the Evangelist, by Juan Ribalta. 80c, Archimedes by Jose de Ribera. $1, St. John the Baptist in the Desert by de Ribera. $1.25, The Martyrdom of St. Philip (detail), by de Ribera. No. 996, The Baptism of Christ by Juan Fernandez Navarrete. No. 997, Battle between Christians and Moors at El Sotillo, by Francisco de Zurbaran.

1992, May 26		Litho.	Perf. 13	
988	A162	8c multicolored	.25	.25
989	A162	20c multicolored	.70	.70
990	A162	45c multicolored	1.75	1.75
991	A162	50c multicolored	1.75	1.75
992	A162	65c multicolored	2.25	2.25
993	A162	80c multicolored	3.00	3.00
994	A162	$1 multicolored	3.75	3.75
995	A162	$1.25 multicolored	4.50	4.50
		Nos. 988-995 (8)	17.95	17.95

Size: 95x120mm
Imperf

996	A162	$2 multicolored	8.50	8.50
997	A162	$2 multicolored	8.50	8.50

Granada '92.

Discovery of America, 500th Anniv. A163

Commemorative coins, scenes of first voyage: 10c, Nina, ship. 15c, Pinta, ship. 20c, Santa Maria, Columbus' second coat of arms. 25c, Fleet at sea, ships. 30c, Landfall, sailing ship. 35c, Setting sail, Columbus departing. 50c, Columbus sighting New World, Columbus. 65c, Columbus exploring Caribbean, ship. 80c, Claiming land for Spain, Columbus, priest and cross. $1.10, Columbus exchanging gifts with native, Columbus, native. No. 1008, Coins like #998-1000. No. 1009, Coins like #1004, 1006-1007.

1992, Oct.		Litho.	Perf. 14	
998	A163	10c multicolored	.70	.70
999	A164	15c multicolored	1.10	1.10
1000	A164	20c multicolored	1.10	1.10
1001	A164	25c multicolored	1.50	1.50
1002	A164	30c multicolored	1.50	1.50
1003	A164	35c multicolored	1.75	1.75
1004	A164	50c multicolored	2.00	2.00
1005	A164	65c multicolored	3.00	3.00
1006	A164	80c multicolored	3.00	3.00
1007	A164	$1.10 multicolored	3.25	3.25
		Nos. 998-1007 (10)	18.90	18.90

Souvenir Sheets

1008	A164	$2 multicolored	8.50	8.50
1009	A164	$2 multicolored	8.50	8.50

Christmas A164

Details or entire paintings by Simon Bening: 8c, Nativity. 15c, Circumcision. 35c, Flight to Egypt. 50c, Massacre of the Innocents.
By Dirk Bouts: 65c, The Annunciation. 80c, The Visitation. $1.10, The Adoration of the Angels. $1.25, The Adoration of the Wise Men. No. 1018, The Virgin and Child. No. 1019, The Virgin Seated with the Child.

1992, Nov.		Litho.	Perf. 13½x14	
1010	A164	8c multicolored	.55	.55
1011	A164	15c multicolored	1.10	1.10
1012	A164	35c multicolored	1.60	1.60
1013	A164	50c multicolored	2.00	2.00
1014	A164	65c multicolored	2.75	2.75
1015	A164	80c multicolored	3.25	3.25
1016	A164	$1.10 multicolored	3.75	3.75
1017	A164	$1.25 multicolored	3.75	3.75
		Nos. 1010-1017 (8)	18.75	18.75

Souvenir Sheets

1018	A164	$2 multicolored	8.50	8.50
1019	A164	$2 multicolored	8.50	8.50

Nos. 915, 918 & 921 Ovptd. in Red or Black

1993, Mar. 20		Litho.	Perf. 14	
1020	CD347	35c on #915	2.75	2.75
1021	CD347	65c on #918	5.75	5.75

Souvenir Sheet

1022	CD347	$2 on #921 (Bk)	10.00	10.00

Miniature Sheet

Coronation of Queen Elizabeth II, 40th Anniv. — A165

Designs: a, 15c, Chalice and paten from royal collection. b, 50c, Official coronation photograph. c, $1, Coronation ceremony. d, $1.25, Queen, Prince Philip. $2, New Portrait.

1993, June 2		Litho.	Perf. 13½x14	
1023	A165	Sheet, 2 ea #a.-d.	16.00	16.00

Souvenir Sheet
Perf. 14

1024	A165	$2 multicolored	9.00	9.00

No. 1024 contains one 28x42mm stamp.

Christmas A166

Details or entire woodcut, Mary, Queen of the Angels, by Durer: 8c, 20c, 35c, $1.25.
Details or entire paintings by Raphael: 50c, $1, Virgin and Child with St. John the Baptist. 65c, The Canagiani Holy Family. 80c, The Holy Family with the Lamb.
Each $2: No. 1033, Mary, Queen of the Angels, by Durer. No. 1034, The Canagiani Holy Family, diff., by Raphael.

Perf. 13½x14, 14x13½

1993, Dec.			Litho.	
1025-1032	A166	Set of 8	18.00	18.00

Souvenir Sheets

1033-1034	A166	Set of 2	13.00	13.00

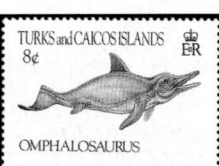

Dinosaurs A167

8c, Omphalosaurus. 15c, Coelophysis. 20c, $2 (#1043), Triceratops. 35c, $2 (#1044), Dilophosaurus. 50c, Pterodactylus. 65c, Elasmosaurus. 80c, Stegosaurus. $1.25, Euoplocephalus.

1993, Nov. 15		Litho.	Perf. 14	
1035-1042	A167	Set of 8	10.00	10.00

Souvenir Sheets

1043-1044	A167	Set of 2	17.00	17.00

Birds A168

Designs: 10c, Killdeer. 15c, Yellow-crowned night heron, vert. 35c, Northern mockingbird. 50c, Eastern kingbird, vert. 65c, Magnolia warbler. 80c, Cedar waxwing, vert. $1.10, Ruby-throated hummingbird. $1.25, Painted bunting, vert. No. 1053, American kestrel. No. 1054, Ruddy duck.

1993, Dec.				
1045	A168	10c multicolored	.50	.50
1046	A168	15c multicolored	.75	.75
1047	A168	35c multicolored	1.90	1.90
1048	A168	50c multicolored	2.50	2.50
1049	A168	65c multicolored	3.50	3.50
1050	A168	80c multicolored	4.00	4.00
1051	A168	$1.10 multicolored	5.50	5.50
1052	A168	$1.25 multicolored	6.25	6.25
		Nos. 1045-1052 (8)	24.90	24.90

Souvenir Sheets

1053	A168	$2 multicolored	8.50	8.50
1054	A168	$2 multicolored	8.50	8.50

Fish A169

Designs: 10c, Bluehead wrasse. 20c, Honeycomb cowfish. 25c, Glasseye snapper. 35c, Spotted drum. 50c, Jolthead porgy. 65c, Smallmouth grunt. 80c, Peppermint bass. $1.10, Indigo hamlet.
Each $2: No. 1063, Bonnethead shark. No. 1064, Sharpnose shark.

1993, Dec. 15				
1055-1062	A169	Set of 8	9.50	9.50

Souvenir Sheets

1063-1064	A169	Set of 2	10.00	10.00

1994 World Cup Soccer Championships, US — A170

Designs: 8c, Segrio Goycochea, Argentina. 10c, Bodo Illgner, Germany. 50c, Nico Claesen, Belgium. 65c, West German team. 80c, Cameroun team. $1, Santin, Francescoli, Uruguay; Cuciuffo, Argentina. $1.10, Sanchez, Mexico.
Each $2: No. 1072, Imre Garaba, Hungary, vert. No. 1073, Pontiac Silverdome.

1994, Sept. 26		Litho.	Perf. 14	
1065-1071	A170	Set of 7	12.50	12.50

Souvenir Sheets

1072-1073	A170	Set of 2	9.00	9.00

Mushrooms — A171

Designs: 5c, Xerocomus guadelupae, vert. 10c, Volvariella volvacea, vert. 35c, Hygrocybe atrosquamosa. 50c, Pleurotus ostreatus. 65c, Marasmius pallescens. 80c, Coprinus plicatilis, vert. $1.10, Bolbitius vitellinus. $1.50, Pyroglossum lilaceipes, vert.
Each $2: No. 1082, Lentinus edodes. No. 1083, Russula cremeolilacina, vert.

1994, Oct. 10				
1074-1081	A171	Set of 8	12.00	12.00

Souvenir Sheets

1082-1083	A171	Set of 2	11.50	11.50

Christmas A172

Illustrations from French Book of Hours:
25c, The Annunciation. 50c, The Visitation.
65c, Annunciation to the Shepherds. 80c, The
Nativity. $1, Flight into Egypt.
$2, The Adoration of the Magi.

1994, Dec. 5   Litho.   Perf. 14
1084-1088 A172 Set of 5   14.00 14.00
Souvenir Sheet
1089 A172 $2 multicolored   8.00 8.00

Butterflies
A173

Designs: 15c, Dryas julia. 20c, Urbanus proteus. 25c, Colobura dirce. 50c, Papilio home-
rus. 65c, Chiodes catilus. 80c, Eurytides
zonaria. $1, Hypolymnas misippus. $1.25,
Phoebis avellaneda.
Each $2: No. 1098, Eurema adamsi. No.
1099, Morpho peleides.

1994, Dec. 12
1090-1097 A173 Set of 8   14.00 14.00
Souvenir Sheets
1098-1099 A173 Set of 2   10.00 10.00

D-Day,
50th
Anniv.
A174

Designs: 10c, Gen. Montgomery, British
landing on Juno Beach. 15c, Adm. Sir Bertram
Ramsay, British commandos at Sword Beach.
35c, Gun crew aboard HMS Belfast. 50c,
Montgomery, Eisenhower, Tedder review battle scene. 65c, Gen. Eisenhower, 101st Airborne Div. paratroopers. 80c, Gen. Omar
Bradley, US landings on Omaha Beach.
$1.10, Second wave of US troops on D-Day.
$1.25, Supreme Commander Eisenhower
presents Operation Overload.
Each $2: No. 1108, Eisenhower, Montgom-
ery seated at table. No. 1109, Beachhead
secured.

1994, Dec. 19
1100-1107 A174 Set of 8   12.00 12.00
Souvenir Sheets
1108-1109 A174 Set of 2   9.50 9.50

Orchids
A175

Designs: 8c, Cattleya deckeri. 20c, Epidendrum carpophorum. 25c, Epidendrum ciliare.
50c, Encyclia phoenicea. 65c, Bletia patula.
80c, Brassia caudata. $1, Brassavola nodosa.
$1.25, Bletia purpurea.
Each $2: No. 1118, Ionopsis utricularioides.
No. 1119, Vanilla planifolia.

1995, Jan. 5
1110-1117 A175 Set of 8   12.00 12.00
Souvenir Sheets
1118-1119 A175 Set of 2   11.00 11.00

Miniature Sheet of 12

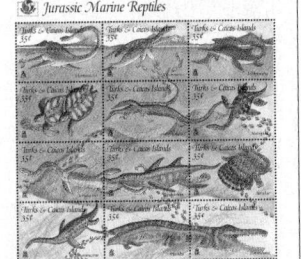

PHILAKOREA '94 — A176

Jurassic marine reptiles: a, Elasmosaurus.
b, Plesiosaurus. c, Ichthyosaurus. d, Arcfielon.
e, Askeptosaurus. f, Macroplata. g, Ceresi-
osaurus. h, Lipoleurodon. i, Henodus. j,
Muraenosaurus. k, Placodus. l, Kronosaurus.

1995, Jan. 23
1120 A176 35c #1120a-1120 l   10.50 10.50

First
Manned
Moon
Landing,
25th
Anniv.
A177

Designs: 10c, Apollo XI in flight. 20c, Simulated moon landing. 25c, Painting, Astronauts
on the Moon, by Kovales. 35c, First foot, footprint on moon. 50c, Aldrin, solar wind experiment. 65c, Armstrong, Aldrin setting up flag on
moon. 80c, Command module Columbia in
Lunar orbit. $1.10, Recovery of Apollo XI in
Pacific.
Each $2: No. 1129, Lift-off at Cape Canav-
eral, vert. No. 1130, Moon rock on display in
Houston.

1995, Jan. 9   Litho.   Perf. 14
1121-1128 A177 Set of 8   9.50 9.50
Souvenir Sheets
1129-1130 A177 Set of 2   9.50 9.50

Intl. Olympic
Committee,
Cent. — A178

Summer, Winter Olympic events: 8c, Fencing. 10c, Speed skating. 15c, Diving. 20c,
Cycling. 25c, Ice hockey. 35c, Figure skating.
50c, Soccer. 65c, Bobsled. 80c, Super giant
slalom. $1.25, Equestrian.
Each $2: #1141, Gymnastics. #1142, Down-
hill skiing.

1995, Feb. 6
1131-1140 A178 Set of 10   17.00 17.00
Souvenir Sheets
1141-1142 A178 Set of 2   11.50 11.50

Domestic
Cats
A179

Various cats, kittens: 15c, 20c, 35c, 50c,
65c, 80c, $1, $1.25.
Each $2: No. 1151, Two sleeping. No. 1152,
Kitten, ladybugs in flowers.

1995, July 3   Litho.   Perf. 14
1143-1150 A179 Set of 8   17.00 17.00
Souvenir Sheets
1151-1152 A179 Set of 2   12.00 12.00

Birds — A180

A180a

10c, Belted kingfisher. 15c, Clapper rail.
20c, American redstart. 25c, Roseate tern.
35c, Purple gallinule. 45c, Ruddy turnstone.
50c, Barn owl. 60c, Brown booby. 80c, Great
blue heron. $1, Antillean nighthawk. $1.25,
Thick-billed vireo. $1.40, American flamingo.
$2, Wilson's plover. $5, Blue-winged teal. $10,
Reddish egret.

1995, Aug. 2   Litho.   Perf. 13
1153 A180 10c multi   .25   .25
1154 A180 15c multi   .40   .40
1155 A180 20c multi   .55   .55
1156 A180 25c multi   .70   .70
1157 A180 35c multi   .95   .95
1158 A180 45c multi   1.25   1.25
1159 A180 50c multi   1.40   1.40
1160 A180 60c multi   1.75   1.75
1161 A180 80c multi   2.25   2.25
1162 A180 $1 multi   2.75   2.75
1163 A180 $1.25 multi   3.50   3.50
1164 A180 $1.40 multi   3.75   3.75
1165 A180 $2 multi   5.50   5.50
1166 A180 $5 multi   13.50 13.50
1166A A180a $10 multi   27.50 27.50
Nos. 1153-1166A (15)   66.00 66.00

Queen
Mother, 95th
Birthday
A181

No. 1167: a, Drawing. b, Wearing crown
jewels. c, Formal portrait. d, Blue dress with
pearls.
$2, Green blue outfit.

1995, Aug. 4   Perf. 13½x14
1167 A181 50c Block or strip of
4, #a.-d.   9.00 9.00
Souvenir Sheet
1168 A181 $2 multicolored   9.00 9.00
No. 1167 was issued in sheets of 8 stamps.

VE Day,
50th
Anniv.
A182

Designs: 10c, "Big Three" meet at Yalta.
15c, Allied war prisoners released. 20c, American, Soviets meet at Elbe River. 25c, Death of
Franklin D. Roosevelt. 60c, US 9th Army con-
firms cease fire. 80c, New York City celebrates
VE Day. $1, Nuremberg War Crimes trials
begin.
$2, Big Ben, US Capitol, St. Basil's
Cathedral.

1995, Aug. 14   Litho.   Perf. 14
1169-1175 A182 Set of 7   11.00 11.00
Souvenir Sheet
1176 A182 $2 multicolored   6.00 6.00

Miniature Sheet of 9

Singapore '95 — A183

Diving equipment, each 60c: No. 1177a,
Wm. James, scuba, 1825. b, Rouquayrol
apparatus, 1864. c, Fluess oxygen rebreathing
apparatus, 1878. d, Armored diving suit, 1900.
e, Jim Janett explores sunken Lusitania in Per-
ess armored diving suit, 1935. f, Cousteau-

Gagnan aqualung, 1943. g, Underwater camera, 1955. h, Sylvia Earle dives to 1,520 ft. in
Jim suit, 1979. i, Spider propeller-driven rigid
suit, 1984.
Each $2: No. 1178, Helmet diver, 1935. No.
1179, Jacques-Yves Cousteau.

1995, Sept. 1   Perf. 14½
1177 A183 Sheet of 9, #a.-i.   15.00 15.00
Souvenir Sheets
1178-1179 A183 Set of 2   10.00 10.00

Christmas
A184

Details or entire paintings, by Piero di
Cosimo (1462-1521): 20c, Madonna and Child
with Young St. John. 25c, Adoration of the
Child. 60c, Madonna and Child with Young St.
John, St. Margaret, and An Angel. $1,
Madonna and Child with An Angel.
$2, Madonna and Child with Angels and
Saints.

1995, Dec. 29   Litho.   Perf. 14
1180-1183 A184 Set of 4   9.00 9.00
Souvenir Sheet
1184 A184 $2 multicolored   10.50 10.50

UN, 50th Anniv. — A185

Designs: 15c, Rights of women and children. 60c, Peace. 80c, Human rights. $1,
Education.
Each $2: No. 1189, Flags of nations forming
"50." No. 1190, Tractor, portions of UN, FAO
emblems.

1996, Feb. 26   Litho.   Perf. 14
1185-1188 A185 Set of 4   6.25 6.25
Souvenir Sheets
1189-1190 A185 Set of 2   10.00 10.00

Queen
Elizabeth II,
70th
Birthday
A186

No. 1191: a, Portrait. b, Wearing blue hat. c,
In uniform, on horseback.
$2, As younger woman wearing white and
yellow hat.

1996, Apr. 21   Litho.   Perf. 13½x14
1191 A186 80c Strip of 3, #a.-c.   5.50 5.50
Souvenir Sheet
1192 A186 $2 multicolored   4.75 4.75
No. 1191 was issued in sheets of 9 stamps.

History of Underwater Exploration
A187

No. 1193, each 55c: a, Glaucus, God of Divers, 2500BC. b, Alexander the Great decends to ocean bottom, 332BC. c, Salvage diver, 1430. d, Borelli's rebreathing device, 1680. e, Edmond Halley's diving bell, 1690. f, John Lethbridge's diving machine, 1715. g, Klingert's diving apparatus, 1789. h, Drieberg's triton, 1808. i, Seibe's diving helmet, 1819.

No. 1194, each 60c: a, Jim Jarrat in "Iron Man" armored diving suit explores Lusitania, 1935. b, Cousteau, team excavate first shipwreck using scuba gear, 1952. c, Oldest shipwreck ever found, coast of Turkey, 1959. d, Swedish warship Vasa raised, 1961. e, Mel Fisher discovers Spanish galleon Atocha, 1971. f, Whydah, first pirate ship found, is discovered by Barry Clifford, 1984. g, Dr. Robert Ballard, using robot sub Argo finds battleship Bismarck, 1989. h, Radeau "Land Tortoise" scuttled in 1758 during French and Indian War found in Lake George, NY, 1991. i, Deep-diving nuclear submarine recovers ancient Roman shipwreck cargo, 1994.

Each $2: No. 1195, Arab diver Issa, 12th cent. No. 1196, Pearl diver in Caribbean, 1498. No. 1197, Diver in Newtsuit investigates Edmund Fitzgerald. No. 1198, Submarine Alvin explores Titanic, 1985.

1996, May 13   Litho.   Perf. 14
1193 A187 Sheet of 9, #a.-i.   16.00 16.00
1194 A187 Sheet of 9, #a.-i.   12.00 12.00
    Souvenir Sheets
1195-1198 A187 Set of 4   20.00 20.00
    CHINA '96 (Nos. 1193, 1195-1196). CAPEX '96 (Nos. 1194, 1197-1198).

1996 Summer Olympics, Atlanta
A188

Olympic gold medals for: No. 1199, Equestrian. No. 1200, Cycling. No. 1201, Fencing. No. 1202, Gymnastics. No. 1203, Hurdles. No. 1204, Pole vault. No. 1205, Sprints. No. 1206, Swimming. No. 1207, Diving. No. 1208, Running.

1996, May 27   Perf. 13½
1199-1208 A188 55c Set of 10   11.50 11.50
1208a   Sheet of 10, #1199-1208   11.50
    Nos. 1199-1208 issued in sheets as well as in No. 1208a.

A189

James A.G.S. McCartney (1945-80), 1st Chief Minister of Turks & Caicos Islands.

1996, July 8   Litho.   Perf. 14
1209 A189 60c multicolored   1.25 1.25
    Ministerial Government, 20th anniv. No. 1209 was issued in sheets of 9.

A190

Working Dogs: No. 1210: a, Space research. b, Racing. c, Rescue. d, Military. e, Sporting. f, Companion. g, Hearing ear. h, Sled. i, Police. j, Guarding. k, Watch. l, Security.
    Each $2: No. 1211, Guide. No. 1212, Sheep dog.

1996, Sept. 8   Litho.   Perf. 14
1210 A190 25c Sheet of 12, #a.-l.   13.00 13.00
    Souvenir Sheets
1211-1212 A190 Set of 2   13.00 13.00

Winnie the Pooh, Christmas
A191

Designs: 15c, Pooh trying to stay awake. 20c, Piglet, star. 35c, Ribbons and bows. 50c, Jingle bells. 60c, "Pooh loves Christmas." 80c, "Big hearts come in bouncy packages." $1, Santa Pooh. $1.25, "My most favorite."
    No. 1221, Piglet, cookie. No. 1222, Piglet placing star atop tree.

1996, Nov. 25   Litho.   Perf. 13½x14
1213-1220 A191 Set of 8   17.00 17.00
    Souvenir Sheets
1221 A191 $2 multicolored   7.50 7.50
1222 A191 $2.60 multicolored   9.50 9.50

Flowers — A192

No. 1223: a, Giant milkweed. b, Geiger tree. c, Passion flower. d, Hibiscus.
    No. 1224: a, Yellow elder. b, Prickly poppy. c, Frangipani. d, Seaside mahoe.
    Each $2: No. 1225, Chain of love. No. 1226, Firecracker.

1997, Feb. 10   Litho.   Perf. 14
1223 A192 20c Strip or block of 4, #a.-d.   3.25 3.25
1224 A192 60c Strip or block of 4, #a.-d.   4.75 4.75
    Souvenir Sheets
1225-1226 A192 Set of 2   9.50 9.50
    Nos. 1223-1224 were each issued in sheets of 8 stamps.

A193

UNICEF, 50th Anniv.: a, Dove flying right. b, Three children. c, Dove flying left. d, Boy with dog, girl holding cat.

1997, Mar. 24   Litho.   Perf. 14
1227 A193 60c Sheet of 4, #a.-d. 8.00 8.00
    Souvenir Sheets

UNESCO, 50th Anniv. — A194

Canterbury Cathedral: No. 1228, View from rear. No. 1229, Interior view.

1997, Mar. 24   Litho.   Perf. 14
1228 A194 $2 multicolored   5.25 5.25
1229 A194 $2 multicolored   5.25 5.25

Queen Elizabeth II, Prince Philip, 50th Wedding Anniv.
A195

Designs: a, Queen waving. b, Royal arms. c, Queen, Prince riding in car. d, Prince, Queen seated. e, Windsor Castle. f, Prince Philip.
    $2, Wedding portrait.

1997, Apr. 21   Litho.   Perf. 14
1230 A195 60c Sheet of 6, #a.-f.   12.00 12.00
    Souvenir Sheet
1231 A195 $2 multicolored   9.00 9.00

Heinrich von Stephan (1831-97), Founder of UPU
A196

Portrait of Von Stephan and: No. 1232: a, British mail coach, 1700's. b, UPU emblem. c, Space shuttle, future transport.
    $2, Von Stephan, Hemerodrome, messenger of ancient Greece.

1997, July 1   Litho.   Perf. 14
1232 A196 50c Sheet of 3, #a.-c. 6.00 6.00
    Souvenir Sheet
1233 A196 $2 multicolored   5.50 5.50
    PACIFIC 97.

Underwater Exploration
A197

No. 1234: a, Edgerton camera taking photos at 6,000 ft., 1954. b, Conshelf Habitat, 1963. c, Sealab II, 1965. d, Research Habitat, Tektite, 1970. e, Discovery of Galapagos Volcanic Rift, 1974. f, Epaulard, robot survey craft, 1979. g, Sea life discovered thriving in undersea oil field, 1995. h, Deep flight, 1996, one-man research vessel. i, Sea ice is studied from above, under sea, Okhotsk Tower, off Japan, 1996.
    Each $2: No. 1235, Coelacanth. No. 1236, John Williamson makes first underwater movies, 1914.

1997, Aug. 21   Litho.   Perf. 14
1234 A197 20c Sheet of 9, #a.-i.   8.00 8.00
    Souvenir Sheets
1235-1236 A197 Set of 2   10.00 10.00
    Stampshow 97.

Christmas
A198

Entire paintings or details: 15c, Adoration of an Angel, by Studio of Fra Angelico. 20c, Scenes from the Life of St. John the Baptist, by Master of Saint Severin. 35c, Archangel Gabriel, by Masolino de Panicale. 50c, 60c, Jeremiah with Two Angels, by Gherardo Starnina (diff. angels). 80c, The Annunciation, by Giovanni di Palo di Grazia. $1, The Annunciation, by Carlo di Bracceso. $1.25, The Nativity, by Benvenuto di Giovanni Guasta.
    Each $2: No. 1245, The Wilton Diptych (right panel), by unknown English or French artist, c. 1395. No. 1246, Adoring Angels, from The Journey of the Magi, by Benozzo Gozzoli.

1997, Dec. 8   Litho.   Perf. 14
1237-1244 A198 Set of 8   12.00 12.00
    Souvenir Sheets
1245-1246 A198 Set of 2   10.50 10.50

World Wildlife Fund — A199

Snapper: a, Blackfin. b, Dog. c, Cubera. d, Mahogany.

1998, Feb. 24   Litho.   Perf. 14
1247 A199 25c Block of 4, #a.-d. 3.75 3.75
    No. 1247 was issued in sheets of 16 stamps. Intl. Year of the Reef.

Marine Life — A200

Underwater photographs: 20c, Spotted flamingo tongue. 50c, Feather duster. 60c, Squirrel fish. 80c, Queen angelfish. $1, Barracuda. $1.25, Fairy basslet.
    Each $2: No. 1254, Rough file clam. No. 1255, Spotted cleaning shrimp.

1998, May 1   Litho.   Perf. 14
1248-1253 A200 Set of 6   13.00 13.00
    Souvenir Sheets
1254-1255 A200 Set of 2   9.50 9.50

A201

Stylized designs showing symbol for earth, water, and — No. 1256: a, Dove. b, Crab. c, Fish. d, Clover leaf.
    $2, Symbol for earth and water.

1998, July 30   **Litho.**   ***Perf. 14***
1256 A201 50c Sheet of 4, #a.-d.   7.00   7.00

Souvenir Sheet
1257 A201 $2 multicolored   6.50   6.50

Intl. Year of the Ocean.

Royal Air Force, 80th Anniv.
Common Design Type Re-Inscribed

Designs: 20c, SE 5A. 50c, Sopwith Camel.
60c, Supermarine Spitfire. 80c, Avro Lancaster. $1, Panavia Tornado. $1.25, Hawker Hurricane.
Each $2: No. 1264, Hawker Siddeley Harrier. No. 1265, Avro Vulcan.

1998, Aug. 18   **Litho.**   ***Perf. 14***
1258-1263 CD350 Set of 6   16.00   16.00

Souvenir Sheets
1264-1265 CD350 Set of 2   16.00   16.00

A202

Anniversaries and Events: 20c, University of the West Indies, 50th anniv. 60c, UNESCO, World Summit Program. 80c, Universal Declaration of Human Rights. $1, John Glenn's return to space.
$2, NASA Space Shuttle leaving launching pad.

1998, July 30   **Litho.**   ***Perf. 14***
1266-1269 A202 Set of 4   6.25   6.25

Souvenir Sheet
1270 A202 $2 multicolored   5.50   5.50

A203

1998, Aug. 31
1271 A203 60c multicolored   2.25   2.25

Diana, Princess of Wales (1961-97). No. 1271 was issued in sheets of 6.

A204

Paintings by Sister Thomasita Fessler — #1272: a, Magi's Visit. b, Flight Into Egypt. c, Wedding Feast. d, Maria. e, Annunciation & Visitation. f, Nativity. $2, Queen of Mothers.

1998, Nov. 30   **Litho.**   ***Perf. 14***
1272 A204 50c Sheet of 6,
   #a.-f.   10.50   10.50

Souvenir Sheet
1273 A204 $2 multicolored   5.50   5.50

Christmas. Nos. 1272e-1272f are each 58x48mm.

Coral Gardens
A205

No. 1274: a, Flamingos in flight. b, Sailboats. c, Seagulls, lighthouse. d, House along shore, seagulls. e, Pillar coral, yellowtail snapper (f). f, Eliptical star coral. g, Porkfish. h, Spotted eagle ray. i, Large ivory coral. j, Mustard hill coral, shy hamlet. k, Blue crust coral. l, Fused staghorn coral. m, Queen angelfish, massive starlet coral. n, Pinnate spiny sea fan. o, Knobby star coral, squirrelfish. p, Lowridge cactus coral, juvenile porkfish. q, Orange telesto coral. r, Spanish hogfish (q), Knobby ten-ray star coral. s, Boulder brain coral, clown wrasse. t, Rainbow parrotfish, regal sea fan. u, Great star coral, bluestriped grunt. v, Stinging coral, blue tang. w, Lavender thin finger coral. x, Juvenile french grunt (w), brilliant sea fingers.
Each $2: No. 1275, Sea fan. No. 1276, Elkhorn coral.

1999, June 7   **Litho.**   ***Perf. 14¼x14½***
1274 A205 20c Sheet of 24,
   #a.-x.   24.00   24.00

Souvenir Sheets
1275-1276 A205 Set of 2   19.00   19.00

Wedding of Prince Edward and Sophie Rhys-Jones — A206

Portraits — #1277: a, Couple facing forward. b, Edward. c, Sophie. d, Couple walking arm in arm.
Each $2: No. 1278, Couple facing forward. No. 1279, Couple facing each other.

1999, June 19   **Litho.**   ***Perf. 14***
1277 A206 60c Sheet of 4,
   #a.-d.   7.50   7.50

Souvenir Sheets
1278-1279 A206 Set of 2   12.00   12.00

Queen Mother (b. 1900)
A207

Designs: a, At age 7. b, At age 19. c, At wedding. d, With daughters. e, With King George VI during World War II. f, In 1958. g, At age 60. h, In 1970. i, With Princes Charles and William, 1983. j, Current photograph.

1999, Aug. 4   **Litho.**   ***Perf. 13½x13¾***
1280 A207 50c Sheet of 10,
   #a.-j.   19.00   19.00

Stamp inscription on No. 1280f is incorrect.
No. 1280 was reissued in 2002 with added inscription in margin, "Good Health and Happiness to her Majesty The Queen Mother on her 101st Birthday." Value, $19.

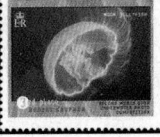

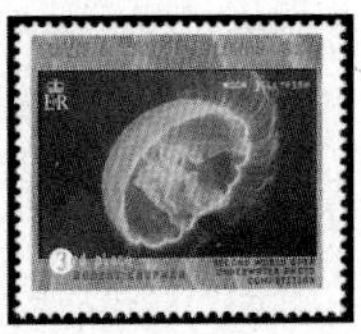

2nd World Underwater Photography Competition Winners
A208

No. 1281: a, 10c, Painted tunicates (8th place). b, 20c, Peacock flounder (7th). c, 50c, Squirt anemone shrimps (6th). d, 60c, Juvenile drum (5th). e, 80c, Batwing coral crab (4th). f, $1, Moon jellyfish (3rd).
Each $2: No. 1282, Christmas tree worms (2nd). No. 1283, Longhorn nudibranch (1st).

1999, Oct. 11   **Litho.**   ***Perf. 14¼x13¾***
1281 A208   Sheet of 6, #a.-f.   11.00   11.00
  g.   As No. 1281, with corrected
     pictures   6.50   6.50

Issued: No. 1281g, 11/6/00.
On No. 1281, the illustrations for the 10c and 20c stamps are incorrect, with the 10c stamp inscribed "Painted tunicates," but depicting a peacock flounder, and the 20c stamp inscribed "Peacock flounder," but depicting painted tunicates. The pictures were switched on No. 1281g, making the inscriptions match the pictures.

Souvenir Sheets
Perf. 13¾
1282-1283 A208   Set of 2   16.00   16.00

Nos. 1282-1283 each contain one 50x38mm stamp.

Christmas
A209

Paintings by Anthony Van Dyck: 20c, The Mystic Marriage of Saint Catherine. 50c, Rest on the Flight into Egypt. No. 1286, $2, Holy Family with Saints John and Elizabeth. No. 1287, The Madonna of the Rosary.

1999, Dec. 7   ***Perf. 13¾***
1284-1286 A209 Set of 3   10.50   10.50

Souvenir Sheet
1287 A209 $2 multicolored   10.50   10.50

Millennium
A210

Perf. 14½x14¼
1999, Nov. 15   **Litho.**
1288 A210 20c silver & multi   .80   .80
1289 A210 $1 gold & multi   4.00   4.00

Millennium
A211

Globe, clock and: No. 1290: a, London. b, Turks & Caicos Islands. c, New York. d, Rome. e, Jerusalem. f, Paris.
Each $2: No. 1291, Flag of Islands. No. 1292, Arms of Islands.

2000, Jan. 18   **Litho.**   ***Perf. 14x13¾***
1290 A211 50c Sheet of 6,
   #a.-f.   12.00   12.00

Souvenir Sheets
1291-1292 A211 Set of 2   18.00   18.00

Mushrooms — A212

No. 1293, vert.: a, Pholiota squarroides. b, Psilocybe squamosa. c, Spathularia velutipes. d, Russula. e, Clitocybe clavipes. f, Boletus frostii.
No. 1294, Strobilurus conigenoides. No. 1295, Stereum ostrea.

2000, July 6   **Litho.**   ***Perf. 14***
1293 A212 50c Sheet of 6, #a-
   f   10.00   10.00

Souvenir Sheets
1294-1295 A212 $2 Set of 2   13.00   13.00

Souvenir Sheet

2000 Summer Olympics,
Sydney — A213

No. 1296: a, Johan Gabriel Oxenstierna. b, Javelin. c, Aztec Stadium, Mexico City and Mexican flag. d, Ancient Greek runners.

2000, Sept. 25
1296 A213 50c Sheet of 4, #a-d   8.00   8.00

Birds
A214

Designs: No. 1297, Chickadee. No. 1298, Scrub turkey. No. 1299, Sickle-bill gull.
No. 1300: a, Egret. b, Tern. c, Osprey. d, Great blue heron. e, Pelican. f, Bahama pintail.
No. 1301, Flamingo, vert. No. 1302, Macaw, vert.

2000, Oct. 2
1297-1299 A214 50c Set of 3   5.50   5.50
1300 A214 60c Sheet of 6, #a-
   f   12.50   12.50

Souvenir Sheets
1301-1302 A214 $2 Set of 2   15.00   15.00

Dogs and Cats — A215

No. 1303, 60c: a, Airedale terrier. b, Beagle. c, Dalmatian. d, Chow chow. e, Chihuahua. f, Pug.
No. 1304, 80c: a, Egyptian mau. b, Manx. c, Burmese. d, Korat. e, Maine coon cat. f, American shorthair.

No. 1305, $2, Collie. No. 1306, $2, Devon rex.

2000, Nov. 13　Litho.　Perf. 14
Sheets of 6, #a-f
1303-1304　A215　Set of 2　24.00　24.00
Souvenir Sheets
1305-1306　A215　Set of 2　12.00　12.00

Battle of Britain, 60th Anniv. A216

Designs: No. 1307, 50c, Douglas Robert Stewart Bader. No. 1308, 50c, Alan Christopher "Al" Deere. No. 1309, 50c, James Edgar "Johnny" Johnson. No. 1310, 50c, Edgar James "Cobber" Kain. No. 1311, 50c, James Harry "Ginger" Lacey. No. 1312, 50c, Air Vice-marshal Trafford Leigh Mallory. No. 1313, 50c, Adolph Gysbert "Sailor" Malan. No. 1314, Air Vice-marshal Keith Park.

No. 1315, each 50c: a, Winston Churchill. b, Barrage balloon. c, Heinkel He-111 Casa 2 111E. d, Soldier's farewell kiss to son. e, Hawker Hurricane. f, Dr, Jocelyn Henry Temple Perkins, clergyman in Home Guard. g, RAF fighter pilots scramble after an alert. h, Civilian volunteers scan the skies.

No. 1316, $2, Churchill, British flag. No. 1317, $2, London children.

2000, Dec. 4　　　　Perf. 14
Stamps + labels
1307-1314　A216　Set of 8　14.00　14.00
1315　A216　Sheet of 8, #a-h　14.00　14.00
Souvenir Sheets
1316-1317　A216　Set of 2　13.00　13.00

Butterflies — A217

No. 1318, 50c: a, Clorinde. b, Blue night. c, Small lace-wing. d, Mosaic. e, Monarch. f, Grecian shoemaker.

No. 1319, 50c: a, Giant swallowtail. b, Common morpho. c, Tiger pierid. d, Banded king shoemaker. e, Figure-of-eight. f, Polydamas swallowtail.

No. 1320, $2, Orange-barred sulphur. No. 1321, $2, White peacock.

2000, Dec. 11　　　　Litho.
Sheets of 6, #a-f
1318-1319　A217　Set of 2　24.00　24.00
Souvenir Sheets
1320-1321　A217　Set of 2　15.00　15.00

Ships A218

Designs: No. 1322, 60c, Neptune. No. 1323, 60c, Eagle. No. 1324, 60c, Gloria. No. 1325, 60c, Clipper ship, vert.

No. 1326, 60c: a, Viking long ship. b, Henri Grace à Dieu. c, Golden Hind. d, Endeavor. e, Anglo-Norman. f, Libertad.

No. 1327, 60c: a, Northern European cog. b, Carrack. c, Mayflower. d, Queen Anne's Revenge. e, Holkar. f, Amerigo Vespucci.

No. 1328, $2, USS Constitution, vert. No. 1329, $2, Denmark, vert.

2001, May 15　Litho.　Perf. 14
1322-1325　A218　Set of 4　9.25　9.25
Sheets of 6, #a-f
1326-1327　A218　Set of 2　27.50　27.50
Souvenir Sheets
1328-1329　A218　Set of 2　18.00　18.00

Whales A219

Designs: No. 1330, 50c, Beluga. No. 1331, 50c, Killer. No. 1332, 50c, Dwarf sperm. No. 1333, 50c, Shortfin pilot.

No. 1334, 50c: a, Bowhead. b, Two killer. c, Pygmy sperm. d, Right. e, Sperm. f, California gray.

No. 1335, 50c: a, Narwhal. b, One killer (in air). c, Bryde's. d, Belugas. e, Sperm (and starfish). f, Pilot.

No. 1336, $2, Cuvier's beaked. No. 1337, $2, Humpback (with calf).

2001, May 15　A219　Set of 4　9.50　9.50
1330-1333　A219　Set of 4　9.50　9.50
Sheets of 6, #a-f
1334-1335　A219　Set of 2　27.00　27.00
Souvenir Sheets
1336-1337　A219　Set of 2　18.00　18.00

UN Women's Human Rights Campaign — A220

Designs: 60c, Woman. 80c, Woman, bird, torch.

2001, June 18　Litho.　Perf. 14
1338-1339　A220　Set of 2　7.00　7.00

Phila Nippon '01 — A221

Designs: No. 1340, 60c, Autumn Moon in Mirror, by Suzuki Harunobu. No. 1341, 60c, Rikaku II as a Fisherman, by Hirosada. No. 1342, 60c, Musical Party, by Hishikawa Moronobu. No. 1343, 60c, Kannon and Four Farmers, by H. Gatto. No. 1344, 60c, Rain in Fifth Month, by Kunisada I. No. 1345, 60c, The Lives of Women, by Kuniyoshi Utagawa.

2001, July 30　　　　Perf. 12x12¼
1340-1345　A221　Set of 6　12.00　12.00

Queen Victoria (1819-1901) — A222

No. 1346, 60c, oval frames: a, Wearing white headcovering. b, Wearing crown as young woman. c, Wearing black hat. d, Wearing crown as old woman.

No. 1347, 60c, rectangular frames: a, Wearing white headcovering. b, Holding flowers. c, Wearing white dress. d, Wearing crown, white dress with blue sash.

No. 1348, $2, Brown orange background. No. 1349, $2, Holding umbrella.

2001, July 2　　　　Perf. 14
Sheets of 4, #a-d
1346-1347　A222　Set of 2　19.00　19.00
Souvenir Sheets
1348-1349　A222　Set of 2　14.00　14.00

Queen Elizabeth II, 75th Birthday — A223

No. 1350: a, In pink hat. b, With crown looking left. c, In green hat. d, With crown looking forward. e, In red orange hat. f, With crown and veil.

$2, Wearing robe.

2001, July 2
1350　A223　60c Sheet of 6, #a-f　14.50　14.50
Souvenir Sheet
1351　A223　$2 multi　8.00　8.00

Butterflies — A224

Designs: 10c, Cuban mimic. 15c, Gundlach's swallowtail, vert. 20c, Graphium androcles. 25c, Eastern black swallowtail. 35c, Papilio velvois, vert. 45c, Schaus swallowtail, vert. 50c, Pipevine swallowtail. 60c, Euploea mniszecki, vert. 80c, Poey's black swallowtail, vert. $1, Graphium encelades, vert. $1.25, Jamaican ringlet. $1.40, Eastern

tiger swallowtail. $2, Graphium milon, vert. $5, Palamedes swallowtail. $10, Zebra swallowtail.

Perf. 14x14¾, 14¾x14
2001, Sept. 27
1352　A224　10c multi　.30　.30
1353　A224　15c multi　.35　.35
1354　A224　20c multi　.45　.45
1355　A224　25c multi　.55　.55
1356　A224　35c multi　.80　.80
1357　A224　45c multi　1.00　1.00
1358　A224　50c multi　1.10　1.10
1359　A224　60c multi　1.40　1.40
1360　A224　80c multi　1.75　1.75
1361　A224　$1 multi　2.25　2.25
1362　A224　$1.25 multi　2.75　2.75
1363　A224　$1.40 multi　3.25　3.25
1364　A224　$2 multi　4.75　4.75
1365　A224　$5 multi　11.00　11.00
1366　A224　$10 multi　22.50　22.50
　　Nos. 1352-1366 (15)　54.20　54.20

25c, 35c, $5, $10 exist dated "2003." Value, set $32.50.

Reign of Queen Elizabeth II, 50th Anniv. — A225

No. 1367: a, Crossing Place Trail, Middle Caicos. b, Wades Green Plantation, North Caicos. c, Underwater scenery, Grand Turk. d, St. Thomas Anglican Church, Grand Turk. e, Ripsaw band, Grand Turk. f, Basketweaving.

No. 1368: a, Visit of Princess Royal, 1960. b, Visit of Queen Elizabeth II, 1966. c, Visit of Princess Alexandra, 1988. d, Visit of Duke of Edinburgh, 1993. e, Visit of Prince Andrew, 2000.

No. 1369: a, Salt Industry, 1952-62. b, Space splashdown, 1962-72. c, Ministerial government system, 1972-82. d, Quincentennial of Columbus' landfall, 1982-92. e, National Museum, 1992-2002.

2002, June 1　Litho.　Perf. 14¼
1367　Sheet of 6　4.25　4.25
　a.-f. A225 25c Any single　.70　.70
Perf. 13¾
1368　Sheet of 5　8.75　8.75
　a.-e. A225 60c Any single　1.75　1.75
Perf. 13¾x14¼
1369　Sheet of 5　11.00　11.00
　a.-e. A225 80c Any single　2.10　2.10

No. 1368 contains five 31x31mm stamps; No. 1369 contains five 30x34mm stamps.

20th World Scout Jamboree, Thailand — A226

No. 1370: a, Scout with mallet and chisel. b, Scout with rifle. c, Scout hanging on rope above water. d, Scouts and lantern.
$2, Handicapped Scouts.

2002, July 15　　　　Perf. 14
1370　A226 80c Sheet of 4, #a-d　9.50　9.50
Souvenir Sheet
1371　A226　$2 multi　6.00　6.00

Intl. Year of Ecotourism — A227

No. 1372, vert.: a, Humpback whale. b, Water sports. c, Regattas. d, Queen angelfish. e, Manta ray. f, Turtle.
$2, Jojo dolphin.

2002, July 15
1372 A227 60c Sheet of 6, #a-f 12.50 12.50
Souvenir Sheet
1373 A227 $2 multi 6.25 6.25

No. 1372 contains six 28x42mm stamps.

Intl. Year of Mountains — A228

No. 1374: a, Devil's Peak, South Africa. b, Mt. Drakensburg, South Africa. c, Mt. Blanc, France. d, Roan Mountain, US. e, Mt. Sefton, New Zealand. f, Mt. Cook, New Zealand.
$2, Northwest Highlands, Scotland.

2002, July 22
1374 A228 80c Sheet of 6, #a-f 14.00 14.00
Souvenir Sheet
1375 A228 $2 multi 6.25 6.25

United We Stand — A229

2002, Aug. 5
1376 A229 50c multi 1.50 1.50
Printed in sheets of 4.

Insects and Birds — A230

No. 1377, 60c: a, Hawk moth. b, Burnet moth. c, Mammoth wasp. d, Branch-boring beetle. e, Flower mantid, Pseudocrebotra species. f, Flower mantid, Creobroter species.
No. 1378, 60c: a, Sooty tern. b, Magnificent frigatebird. c, American white pelican. d, Northern shoveler. e, Baltimore oriole. f, Roseate spoonbill.
No. 1379, $2, Tiphiid wasp. No. 1380, $2, Greater flamingo, vert.

2002, Aug. 12 *Perf. 14*
Sheets of 6, #a-f
1377-1378 A230 Set of 2 22.50 22.50
Souvenir Sheets
1379-1380 A230 Set of 2 12.00 12.00

Queen Mother Elizabeth (1900-2002) — A231

No. 1381: a, Without hat. b, With hat.

2002, Oct. 21
1381 A231 80c Sheet, 2 each #a-b 10.00 10.00

First Nonstop Solo Transatlantic Flight, 75th Anniv. — A232

No. 1382: a, Charles Lindbergh's early exploits as a barnstormer. b, Lindbergh standing in front of Spirit of St. Louis. c, Spirit of St. Louis. d, Take-off from Roosevelt Field. e, Crossing the Atlantic. f, Arrival and welcome in Paris.

2002, Nov. 18 *Litho.* *Perf. 14*
1382 A232 60c Sheet of 6, #a-f 11.50 11.50

Pres. John F. Kennedy (1917-63) — A233

No. 1383 — Portrait color: a, Orange brown. b, Red violet. c, Greenish gray. d, Blue violet. e, Purple. f, Dull brown.

2002, Nov. 18
1383 A233 60c multi 11.50 11.50

Christmas A234

Designs: 20c, Madonna and Child, by Giovanni Bellini, vert. 25c, Adoration of the Magi, by Correggio. 60c, Transfiguration of Christ, by Bellini, vert. 80c, Polyptych of St. Vincent Ferrer, by Bellini, vert. $1, Miraculous Mass, by Simone Martini, vert.
$2, Christ in Heaven with Four Saints, by Domenico Ghirlandaio.

2002, Nov. 25
1384-1388 A234 Set of 5 8.00 8.00
Souvenir Sheet
1389 A234 $2 multi 6.00 6.00

Japanese Art — A235

Designs: 25c, Nagata no Taro Nagamune, by Kuniyoshi Utagawa. 35c, Danjuro Ichikawa VII, by Kunisada Utagawa. 60c, Nagata no Taro Nagamune, by Kuniyoshi Utagawa, diff. $1, Nagata no Taro Nagamune, by Kuniyoshi Utagawa, diff.
No. 1394 — Scroll of Actors, by Chikanobu Toyohara and others: a, Smiling man holding fan. b, Man holding sword at mouth. c, Man holding sword vertically. d, Man with tree branch above head.
$2, Two Women by a River, by Chikanobu Hashimoto.

2003, June 17 *Litho.* *Perf. 14¼*
1390-1393 A235 Set of 4 4.50 4.50
1394 A235 80c Sheet of 4, #a-d 6.50 6.50
Souvenir Sheet
1395 A235 $2 multi 4.00 4.00

Rembrandt Paintings A236

Designs: 25c, Portrait of a Young Man Resting His Chin on His Hand. 50c, A Woman at an Open Door. No. 1398, $1, The Return of the Prodigal Son. No. 1399, $1, Portrait of an Elderly Man.
No. 1400: a, Nicolaas van Bambeeck. b, Agatha Bas, Wife of Nicolaas van Bambeeck. c, Portrait of a Man Holding His Hat. d, Saskia in a Red Hat.
$2, Christ Driving the Money Changers from the Temple.

Perf. 14¼, 13¼ (#1400)
2003, June 17
1396-1399 A236 Set of 4 5.50 5.50
1400 A236 60c Sheet of 4, #a-d 5.00 5.00
Souvenir Sheet
1401 A236 $2 multi 4.00 4.00

Paintings by Joan Miró — A237

Designs: 25c, Portrait of a Young Girl. 50c, Table with Glove. 60c, Self-portrait, 1917. $1, The Farmer's Wife.
No. 1406: a, Portrait of Ramon Sunyer. b, Self-portrait, 1919. c, Portrait of a Spanish Dancer. d, Portrait of Joana Obrador.
No. 1407, Flowers and Butterfly. No. 1408, Still Life of the Coffee Grinder, horiz.

2003, June 17 *Perf. 14¼*
1402-1405 A237 Set of 4 4.75 4.75
1406 A237 80c Sheet of 4, #a-d 6.50 6.50
Imperf
Size: 104x83mm
1407 A237 $2 multi 4.00 4.00
Size: 83x104mm
1408 A237 $2 multi 4.00 4.00

Caribbean Community, 30th Anniv. — A238

2003, July 4 *Perf. 14*
1409 A238 60c multi 1.25 1.25

Tanya Streeter, World Champion Freediver — A239

No. 1410: a, Wearing wetsuit in water. b, Diving underwater, portrait. c, Wearing bathing suit at shore. d, Standing in front of map. e, Holding on to diving apparatus.

2003, July 15
1410 A239 20c Sheet of 5, #a-e 2.00 2.00

Coronation of Queen Elizabeth II, 50th Anniv. — A240

No. 1411: a, Wearing crown and white robe. b, Wearing lilac dress. c, Wearing tiara and red dress.
$2, Wearing hat and blue cape. $5, Profile portrait.

2003, Aug. 25
1411 A240 80c Sheet of 3, #a-
    c   5.00   5.00
    Souvenir Sheets
1412-1413 A240   Set of 2   14.00 14.00

Prince William, 21st Birthday — A241

No. 1414: a, Portrait in blue. b, Pink background. c, Purple background.
$2, Dark blue background.

2003, Aug. 25
1414 A241 $1 Sheet of 3, #a-c   6.00 6.00
    Souvenir Sheet
1415 A241 $2 multi   4.00 4.00

Tour de France Bicycle Race, Cent. — A242

No. 1416: a, Eddy Merckx, 1974. b, Bernard Thévenet, 1975. c, Lucien Van Impe, 1976. d, Thévenet, 1977.
$2, Bernard Hinault, 1979.

2003, Aug. 25   *Perf. 13¾x14¼*
1416 A242 $1 Sheet of 4, #a-d   8.00 8.00
    Souvenir Sheet
1417 A242 $2 multi   4.00 4.00

Powered Flight, Cent. — A243

No. 1418: a, Vought F4U Corsair. b, Messerschmidt Me 262. c, A6M. d, Hawker Hurricane.
$2, Supermarine Spitfire Mk IX.

2003, Aug. 25   *Perf. 14*
1418 A243 60c Sheet of 4, #a-d   5.00 5.00
    Souvenir Sheet
1419 A243 $2 multi   4.00 4.00

German Teddy Bears — A244

No. 1420, vert.: a, Bear with red and yellow uniform. b, Bear with dress. c, Bear with violin case. d, Bear with sword.
$2, Bear on beer mug.

2003, Aug. 25   *Perf. 12x12¼*
1420 A244 50c Sheet of 4, #a-d   4.00 4.00
    Souvenir Sheet
    Perf. 12¼x12
1421 A244 $2 multi   4.00 4.00

Butterflies A245

Designs: 50c, Papilio thersites. 60c, Papilio andraemon. 80c, Papilio pelaus. $1, Consul hippona.
$2, Papilio pelaus, diff.

2003, Nov. 17   *Perf. 14*
1422-1425 A245   Set of 4   6.00 6.00
    Souvenir Sheet
1426 A245 $2 multi   4.00 4.00

Orchids A246

Designs: 50c, Laelia anceps. 60c, Laelia briegeri. 80c, Laelia fidelensis. $1, Laelia cinnabarina.
$2, Laelia rubescens.

2003, Nov. 17
1427-1430 A246   Set of 4   6.00 6.00
    Souvenir Sheet
1431 A246 $2 multi   4.00 4.00

Dogs A247

Designs: 50c, Beagle. 60c, Sabueso Espanol, vert. 80c, Basset hound, vert. $1, Jack Russell terrier, vert.
$2, Dachshund.

2003, Nov. 17
1432-1435 A247   Set of 4   6.00 6.00
    Souvenir Sheet
1436 A247 $2 multi   4.00 4.00

Cats A248

Designs: 50c, Persian. 60c, Cymric. 80c, Main Coon, vert. $1, Tiffany.
$2, Kurile Island bobtail.

2003, Nov. 17
1437-1440 A248   Set of 4   6.00 6.00
    Souvenir Sheet
1441 A248 $2 multi   4.00 4.00

Christmas A249

Paintings: 25c, Madonna of the Harpies, by Andrea del Sarto. 60c, Madonna and Child with St. John, by del Sarto. 80c, Madonna and Child with St. Joseph and St. Peter Martyr, by del Sarto. $1, Madonna and Child with the Angels, by del Sarto.
$2, Montefeltro Altarpiece, by Piero della Francesca.

2003, Nov. 24   *Perf. 14¼*
1442-1445 A249   Set of 4   5.50 5.50
    Souvenir Sheet
1446 A249 $2 multi   4.00 4.00

Marine Life — A250

Photographs from underwater photography contest: Nos. 1447, 1452a, 25c, Golden Rough Head Blennie, by Rand McMeins. Nos. 1448, 1452b, 50c, Octopus at Night, by Marc Van Driessche. Nos. 1449, 1452c, 60c, Sea Turtle, by Mike Nebel. Nos. 1450, 1452d, 80c, Juvenile Octopus, by Amber Blecker. Nos. 1451, 1452e, $1, School of Horse Eye Jacks, by Blecker.
$2, Coral Reef, by Keith Kaplan, vert.

    Perf. 12, 12¾ (#1452)
2006, June 1   *Litho.*
    Stamps With Thin "Shadow" Frame
1447-1451 A250   Set of 5   6.50 6.50

    Miniature Sheet
    Stamps With Thick "Shadow" Frame
1452 A250   Sheet of 5, #a-e   6.50 6.50
    Souvenir Sheet
1453 A250 $2 multi   4.00 4.00

Washington 2006 World Philatelic Exhibition. (Nos. 1452-1453). The perforation tips at the tops of the stamps on Nos. 1452a-1452e are all white, gradiating to blue on the lower halves of the stamps, while the perforation tips on Nos. 1447-1451 show other colors. The shadow frames at the bottom of Nos 1452a-1452e are 1mm thick and about ½mm thick on Nos. 1447-1451. The distances between the bottom of the denomination and the top of the country name differ on Nos. 1452a-1452e from those found on Nos. 1447-1451. No. 1447 has incorrect spelling, "Ruogh," in inscription, while No. 1452a has word correctly spelled as "Rough."

Queen Elizabeth II, 80th Birthday — A251

No. 1454 — Various depictions of Queen Elizabeth II: a, 50c. b, 60c. c, 80c. d, $1.
$6, Wearing crown.

2006, Sept. 12   *Litho.*   *Perf. 13½*
1454 A251   Sheet of 4, #a-d   6.00 6.00
    Souvenir Sheet
1455 A251 $6 multi   12.00 12.00

Christmas — A252

The Birth of Christ and Adoration of the Shepherds, by Peter Paul Rubens: Nos. 1456, 1460a, 25c, Praying shepherd. Nos. 1457, 1460b, 60c, Infant Jesus. Nos. 1458, 1460c, 80c, Heads of two shepherds. Nos. 1459, 1460d, $1, Virgin Mary.
$6, Our Lady, The Christ Child and Saints, by Rubens, vert.

2006, Dec. 27   *Perf. 13¼x13½*
    Stamps With Painting Title
1456-1459 A252   Set of 4   5.50 5.50
    Stamps Without Painting Title
1460 A252   Sheet of 4, #a-d   5.50 5.50
    Souvenir Sheet
    Perf. 13½x13¼
1461 A252 $6 multi   12.00 12.00

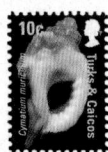

Shells — A253

Designs: 10c, Cymatium muricinum. 15c, Tellina radiata. 20c, Tonna maculosa. 25c, Leucozonia nassa. 35c, Trachycardium magnum. 45c, Papyridea soleniformis. 50c, Epitonium lamellosum. 60c, Astraea brevispina. 80c, Bulla striata. $1, Murex margaritensis. $1.25, Chama macerophylla. $1.40, Vasum capitellum. $2, Coralliophila abbreviata. $5, Trachycardium isocardia. $10, Oliva reticularis.

2007, June 11		Litho.	Perf. 12¾	
1462	A253	10c multi	.30	.30
1463	A253	15c multi	.35	.35
1464	A253	20c multi	.50	.50
1465	A253	25c multi	.60	.60
1466	A253	35c multi	.85	.85
1467	A253	45c multi	1.10	1.10
1468	A253	50c multi	1.20	1.20
1469	A253	60c multi	1.50	1.50
1470	A253	80c multi	1.90	1.90
1471	A253	$1 multi	2.25	2.25
1472	A253	$1.25 multi	3.00	3.00
1473	A253	$1.40 multi	3.50	3.50
1474	A253	$2 multi	4.75	4.75
1475	A253	$5 multi	12.00	12.00
1476	A253	$10 multi	24.00	24.00
	Nos. 1462-1476 (15)		57.80	57.80

Christmas
A254

Paintings: 25c, The Virgin and Child, by Carlo Maratta. 60c, The Adoration of the Magi, by Vincent Malo, horiz. 80c, The Annunciation, by Robert Campin, horiz. $1, The Adoration of the Magi, by Giovanni di Paolo, horiz.
$6, The Adoration of the Magi, by Quentin Massys.

Perf. 14¼x14¾, 14¾x14¼
2007, Dec. 10
1477-1480	A254	Set of 4	5.50	5.50

Souvenir Sheet
Perf. 14
1481	A254	$6 multi	12.00	12.00

No. 1481 contains one 28x42mm stamp.

Worldwide Fund for Nature
(WWF) — A255

No. 1482 — Red-tailed hawk: a, Pair on fenceposts. b, Adults and chicks at nest. c, Adults on hill and in flight. d, Head of hawk.

2007, Dec. 24 **Perf. 13¼**
1482		Horiz. strip of 4	6.00	6.00
a.-d	A255	50c Any single	1.50	1.50
e.		Souvenir sheet, 2 each #a-d	15.00	15.00

Wedding of Queen Elizabeth II and Prince Philip, 60th Anniv. — A256

No. 1483, vert.: a, Couple, country name in purple. b, Queen, country name in purple. c, Queen, country name in blue. d, Couple, country name in blue. e, Couple, country name in black. f, Queen, country name in black.
$6, Couple on balcony.

2007, Dec. 28 **Perf. 13¼**
1483	A256	$1 Sheet of 6, #a-f	12.00	12.00

Souvenir Sheet
1484	A256	$6 multi	12.00	12.00

Princess Diana (1961-97) — A257

No. 1485 — Various photographs as shown.
$6, Princess Diana wearing hat.

2007, Dec. 28
1485	A257	$1 Sheet of 4, #a-d	8.00	8.00

Souvenir Sheet
1486	A257	$6 multi	12.00	12.00

Pope Benedict
XVI — A258

2008, Sept. 15 Litho. **Perf. 13¼**
1487	A258	75c multi	1.50	1.50

Printed in sheets of 8.

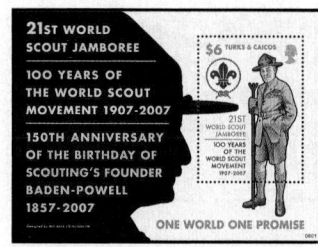

Scouting, Cent. (in 2007) — A259

No. 1488, horiz.: a, Fleur-de-lis, silhouette of Lord Robert Baden-Powell and flags of Tanzania, United States and Colombia on top row. b, Dove, silhouette of fleur-de-lis and green, light green and red national Scouting emblem at UL. c, As "b," with orange, brown and dark green national Scouting emblem at UL. d, As "a," with flags of Israel, Canada, Chile and Macedonia on second row. e, As "a," with flags of Taiwan, Luxembourg and Philippines on top row. f, As "b," with Israel Scouting emblem at UL.
$6, Lord Baden-Powell.

2008, Sept. 23
1488	A259	80c Sheet of 6, #a-f	9.75	9.75

Souvenir Sheet
1489	A259	$6 multi	12.00	12.00

Space Exploration, 50th Anniv. (in 2007) — A260

No. 1490 — International Space Station: a, With solar panels under silhouette of Queen. b, With solar panels touching nose of Queen. c, With solar panels spread horizontally. d, With solar panels running to UL from Queen's chest.
$6, International Space Station, diff.

2008, Sept. 23
1490	A260	$1 Sheet of 4, #a-d	8.00	8.00

Souvenir Sheet
1491	A260	$6 multi	12.00	12.00

Marine
Life
A261

Photographs from underwater photography contest: 25c, Arrow Crab, by Garin Bescoby. 60c, Trumpet Fish, by Karin Nargis. 80c, Sting Ray, by Barbara Shively. $1, Giant Anemone, by Roddy Mcleod.
$6, Red Banded Lobster, by Jayne Baker.

2008, Nov. 25 Litho. **Perf. 13¼**
1492-1495	A261	Set of 4	5.50	5.50
1495a		Souvenir sheet, #1492-1495	5.50	5.50

Souvenir Sheet
1496	A261	$6 multi	12.00	12.00

Christmas
A262

Paintings: 25c, The Nativity, by Philippe de Champaigne. 60c, Mystic Nativity, by Sandro Botticelli. 80c, The Virgin in a Rose Arbor, by Stefan Lochner. $1, The Adoration of the Shepherds, by Francisco Zurbaran.
$6, The Virgin with Angels, by William Bouguereau.

2008, Nov. 25 **Perf. 14x14¾**
1497-1500	A262	Set of 4	5.50	5.50

Souvenir Sheet
1501	A262	$6 multi	12.00	12.00

Souvenir Sheet

New Year 2012 (Year of the Dragon) — A263

2012, July 12 **Perf.**
1502	A263	$3 multi	6.00	6.00

Charles Dickens (1812-70),
Writer — A264

No. 1503: a, Dickens in 1858. b, Illustration from "A Tale of Two Cities." c, Dickens, c. 1860. d, Statue of Dickens in Philadelphia. e, Illustration from "Oliver Twist." f, Illustration from "A Christmas Carol."
$5, Dickens in his study, horiz.

2012, July 12 **Perf. 14**
1503	A264	30c Sheet of 6, #a-f	3.75	3.75

Souvenir Sheet
Perf. 12½
1504	A264	$5 multi	10.00	10.00

No. 1504 contains one 51x38mm stamp.

Flight of John Glenn in Friendship 7, 50th Anniv. — A265

No. 1505: a, Glenn in space helmet. b, Launch of Friendship 7. c, Launch of Space Shuttle (incorrectly identified as launch of Friendship 7). d, Friendship 7 capsule in ocean.
$6, Glenn in space suit, U.S. flags.

2012, July 12 **Perf. 14**
1505	A265	$1.25 Sheet of 4, #a-d	10.00	10.00

Souvenir Sheet
Perf. 12
1506	A265	$6 multi	12.00	12.00

Sinking of the Titanic, Cent. — A266

No. 1507: a, Sky, smokestacks of the Titanic. b, Sky, bow of the Titanic. c, Hull of Titanic at top, waves, smokestacks of Titanic at bottom. d, Hull of Titanic, waves, top of iceberg. e, Titanic at top. f, Prow of Titanic, iceberg. g, Passengers on lifeboat. h, Titanic sinking, lifeboat.
No. 1508, Titanic approaching iceberg. No. 1509, Titanic sinking, lifeboat, diff.

2012, July 12 **Perf. 14**
1507	A266	$1 Sheet of 8, #a-h	16.00	16.00

Souvenir Sheets
1508	A266	$5 multi	10.00	10.00
1509	A266	$5 multi	10.00	10.00

Reign of Queen Elizabeth II, 60th Anniv. — A267

Roses and Queen Elizabeth II wearing: $3.50, Crown. $9, Tiara.

2012, Oct. 10 **Perf. 13¾**
1510	A267	$3.50 multi	7.00	7.00

Souvenir Sheet
1511	A267	$9 multi	18.00	18.00

No. 1510 was printed in sheets of 4.

Souvenir Sheet

Replica of Slave Cabin, Cheshire Hall
Plantation Ruins — A268

2013, Mar. 7   **Perf. 12½x13¼**
1512 A268 $3.50 multi   7.00 7.00
Turks & Caicos National Trust, 20th anniv.

New Year 2013 (Year of the
Snake) — A269

No. 1513: a, Tail of snake. b, Head of snake.
$3.50, Entire snake.

2013, July 12   **Perf. 13¾**
1513 A269 $1.25 Horiz. pair, #a-
b   5.00 5.00
Souvenir Sheet
1514 A269 $3.50 multi   7.00 7.00
No. 1513 was printed in sheets containing
two pairs.

Birth of Prince George of
Cambridge — A270

No. 1515 — Illustrations of characters from
Alice's Adventures in Wonderland, by Lewis
Carroll: a, White Rabbit. b, Knave of Hearts
carrying crown. c, Alice.
$2.50, Playing Card Gardeners and rose
bush.

2013, Oct. 1   **Litho.**   **Perf. 12¾**
1515 A270 $1 Sheet of 3, #a-
c   6.00 6.00
Souvenir Sheet
1516 A270 $2.50 multi   5.00 5.00

A271

Nelson Mandela (1918-2013),
President of South Africa — A272

No. 1517: a, Mandela without hat. b,
Mandela with hat.
No. 1518: a, Mandela casting ballot. b,
Mandela in stadium.
No. 1519, $3.50, Mandela seated, black-
and-white photograph. No. 1520, $3.50,
Mandela seated, color photograph.

2014, Mar. 3   **Litho.**   **Perf. 13¾**
1517 A271 $1 Pair, #a-b   4.00 4.00
1518 A272 $1 Pair, #a-b   4.00 4.00
Souvenir Sheets
1519-1520 A272   Set of 2   14.00 14.00
Nos. 1517-1518 each were printed in sheets
containing two pairs.

Tang Sancai Glazed Horses — A273

No. 1521: a, Brown horse with blue green
saddle. b, Brown horse with white saddle with
gray trim and straps, two ornaments on hindquarters. c, Brown horse with white saddle
with black trim and straps, three ornaments on
hindquarters. d, Light brown horse with red
saddle. e, Brown horse with light brown saddle
and blue pads. f, Black horse with blue green
saddle.
$2.50, Black horse with black saddle, vert.

2014, Mar. 3   **Litho.**   **Perf. 14**
1521 A273   75c Sheet of 6, #a-f 9.00 9.00
Souvenir Sheet
Perf. 12½
1522 A273 $2.50 multi   5.00 5.00
New Year 2014 (Year of the Horse). No.
1522 contains one 38x51mm stamp.

James Alexander
George Smith
McCartney (1945-
80), First Chief
Minister of Turks
& Caicos
Islands — A274

Frame color: 25c, Purple; $10, Red.

2014, May 1   **Litho.**   **Perf. 12x12½**
1523 A274   25c multi   .50 .50
Souvenir Sheet
1524 A274 $10 multi   20.00 20.00
No. 1523 was printed in sheets of 4.

Shells — A275

No. 1525: a, Junonia. b, Channeled duck
clam. c, Zigzag scallop. d, Scotch bonnet.
$4, Queen conch.

2014, Nov. 3   **Litho.**   **Perf. 14**
1525 A275 $1.20 Sheet of 4, #a-
d   9.75 9.75
Souvenir Sheet
Perf. 12¾
1526 A275 $4 multi   8.00 8.00
No. 1526 contains one 51x38mm stamp.

Orchids — A276

No. 1527: a, Oncidium auriferum. b, Oncidium excavatum. c, Oncidium graminifolium. d,
Oncidium altissimum.
No. 1528: a, Oncidium citrinum. b, Oncidium
wentworthianum.

2014, Nov. 3   **Litho.**   **Perf. 12¾**
1527 A276 $1.20 Sheet of 4, #a-
d   9.75 9.75
Souvenir Sheet
1528 A276 $2 Sheet of 2, #a-
b   8.00 8.00

Miniature Sheets

A278

New Year 2015 (Year of the
Ram) — A279

No. 1533 — Chinese character for "ram" on
ram in: a, Green. b, Red. c, Blue. d, Bister.
No. 1534: a, Chinese character for "happiness." b, "Happy New Year." c, Flower and
ram, denomination at right. d, Ram and flower,
denomination at left. e, "2015 Year of the
Ram." f, Chinese character for "ram."

2014, Nov. 24   **Perf. 14**
1533 A278 $1.20 Sheet of 4,
#a-d   9.75 9.75
Perf. 13¾
1534 A279 $1.20 Sheet of 6,
#a-f, + cen-
tral label   14.50 14.50

WAR TAX STAMPS

Regular Issue of 1913-
16 Overprinted

Black Overprint at Bottom of Stamp

1917		**Wmk. 3**	**Perf. 14**	
MR1	A10 1p carmine		.25	1.75
a.	Double overprint		200.00	275.00
b.	"TAX" omitted			
c.	Pair, one without ovpt.		700.00	
MR2	A10 3p violet, yel		1.40	5.75
a.	Double overprint		110.00	

**Black Overprint at Top or Middle of
Stamp**

1917			
MR3	A10 1p carmine	.25	1.40
a.	Inverted overprint	55.00	
b.	Double overprint	65.00	77.50
c.	Pair, one without over-
print	650.00	
MR4	A10 3p violet, yel	.70	2.00
a.	Double overprint	50.00	60.00
b.	Dbl. ovpt., one inverted	375.00	

Same Overprint in Violet or Red

1918-19			
MR5	A10 1p car (V) ('19)	.50	4.50
a.	Double overprint	24.00	
b.	"WAR" omitted	200.00	
MR6	A10 3p violet, yel (R)	15.00	45.00
a.	Double overprint	375.00	

Regular Issue of 1913-
16 Overprinted in Black

1918			
MR7	A10 1p carmine	.25	1.75
MR8	A10 3p violet, yel	4.50	5.00

Same Overprint in Red

1919			
MR9	A10 3p violet, yel	.25	2.75

Regular Issue of 1913-
16 Overprinted in Black

MR10	A10 1p carmine	.25	1.10
a.	Double overprint	160.00	190.00
MR11	A10 3p violet, yel	.35	3.00

Regular Issue of 1913-
16 Overprinted

MR12	A10 1p carmine	.25	2.75
a.	Double overprint	100.00	
MR13	A10 3p violet, yel	.55	3.00

The bottom two rows of this setting show the
words "War" and "Tax" about 1mm farther
apart.

CAICOS

Catalogue values for all unused
stamps in this country are for
Never Hinged items.

**Turks & Caicos Nos. 360, 364, 366,
369, 371-373 Ovptd.**

		Unwmk.		
1981, July 24		**Litho.**	**Perf. 14**	
1	A69	1c Indigo hamlet	.25	.25
2	A69	5c Spanish grunt	.25	.25
3	A69	8c Foureye butter-
flyfish	.25	.25
4	A69	20c Queen angelfish	.40	.40
5	A69	50c Fairy basslet	.85	.85
6	A69	$1 Clown wrasse	1.75	1.75
7	A69	$2 Stoplight parrotfish	3.25	3.25
		Nos. 1-7 (7)	7.00	7.00

Common Design Types
pictured following the introduction.

Royal Wedding Issue
Common Design Type

Turks & Caicos
Nos. 486-489
Overprinted

35c, Charles & Diana. 65c, Kensington Palace. 90c, Prince Charles.
$2, Glass coach.

1981, July 24

8	CD331a	35c multicolored	.30	.30
9	CD331a	65c multicolored	.60	.60
10	CD331a	90c multicolored	.85	.85
		Nos. 8-10 (3)	1.75	1.75

Souvenir Sheet

11	CD331	$2 multicolored	4.50	4.50

*Roulette x Imperf. (#12a), Imperf.
(#12b)*

1981, Oct. 29   **Self-Adhesive**

12	Souvenir booklet	27.50
a.	A88a Pane, 3 each 20c, Diana, $1, Charles)	15.00
b.	A88a Pane of 1 $2, Couple	10.00

Nos. 8-11 exist with overprint in all capital
letters, values about the same. Nos. 8-10, in
both overprint types, also exist in sheets of 5
plus label in changed colors, perf. 12.

Hawksbill
turtle
C1

8c, Diver with lobster and conch shell. 20c,
Stone idol, Arawak Indians. 35c, Sloop construction. 50c, Marine biology. 95c, 707 Jet-
liner. $1.10, 15th cent. Spanish ship. $2, British soldier, Fort St. George. $3, Pirates Anne
Bonny, Calico Jack.

1983-84   **Perf. 14**

13	C1	8c multicolored	.40	.40
14	C1	10c shown	.40	.40
15	C1	20c multicolored	.90	.90
16	C1	35c multicolored	1.40	1.40
17	C1	50c multicolored	2.00	2.00
18	C1	95c multicolored	4.25	4.25
19	C1	$1.10 multicolored	4.75	4.75
20	C1	$2 multicolored	8.50	8.50
21	C1	$3 multicolored	13.00	13.00
		Nos. 13-21 (9)	35.60	35.60

Issued: Nos. 13-19, 6/6/83; Nos. 20-21,
5/18/84.
For overprints see Nos. 47-49.

Christmas Type of Turks and Caicos

Walt Disney characters in Santa Claus is
Coming to Town: No. 22, Chip 'n Dale. No. 23,
Goofy & Patch. No. 24, Morty, Ferdie & Pluto.
No. 25, Morty. No. 26, Donald, Huey, Dewey &
Louie. No. 27, Goofy & Louie. No. 28, Uncle
Scrooge. No. 29, Mickey Mouse & Ferdie. No.
30, Pinocchio, Jiminy Cricket and Figaro.
No. 31, Morty & Ferdie, fireplace.

1983, Nov. 7   **Perf. 11**

22	A104	1c multicolored	.50	.50
23	A104	1c multicolored	.50	.50
24	A104	2c multicolored	.50	.50
25	A104	2c multicolored	.50	.50
26	A104	3c multicolored	.50	.50
27	A104	3c multicolored	.50	.50
28	A104	50c multicolored	3.25	3.25
29	A104	70c multicolored	4.50	4.50
30	A104	$1.10 multicolored	6.25	6.25
		Nos. 22-30 (9)	17.00	17.00

Souvenir Sheet
Perf. 13½x14

31	A104	$2 multicolored	7.50	7.50

Drawings by
Raphael — C2

Designs: 35c, Leda and the Swan. 50c,
Study of Apollo for Parnassus. 95c, Study of
two figures for The Battle of Ostia. $1.10,
Study for the Madonna of the Goldfinch.
$2.50, The Garvagh Madonna.

1983, Dec. 15   **Perf. 14**

32	C2	35c multicolored	1.25	1.25
33	C2	50c multicolored	1.75	1.75
34	C2	95c multicolored	3.25	3.25
35	C2	$1.10 multicolored	3.75	3.75
		Nos. 32-35 (4)	10.00	10.00

Souvenir Sheet

36	C2	$2.50 multicolored	8.00	8.00

500th birth anniv. of Raphael.

1984 Summer
Olympics, Los
Angeles — C3

1984, Mar. 1

37	C3	4c High jump	.25	.25
38	C3	25c Archery	.50	.50
39	C3	65c Cycling	1.40	1.40
40	C3	$1.10 Soccer	2.40	2.40
		Nos. 37-40 (4)	4.55	4.55

Souvenir Sheet

41	C3	$2 Show jumping, horiz.	5.00	5.00

Easter — C4

Walt Disney characters: 35c, Horace Horsecollar, Clarabelle Cow. 45c, Mickey, Minnie
& Chip. 75c, Gyro Gearloose, Chip 'n Dale.
85c, Mickey, Chip 'n Dale. $2.20, Donald sail-
ing with nephews.

1984, Apr. 15   **Perf. 14x13½**

42	C4	35c multicolored	1.40	1.40
43	C4	45c multicolored	1.60	1.60
44	C4	75c multicolored	2.75	2.75
45	C4	85c multicolored	3.50	3.50
		Nos. 42-45 (4)	9.25	9.25

Souvenir Sheet

46	C4	$2.20 mulitcolored	7.00	7.00

Nos. 18-19 Ovptd. in Black

1984, June 19   **Perf. 14**

47	C1	95c multicolored	2.00	2.00
48	C1	$1.10 multicolored	2.50	2.50

No. 20 Overprinted

49ovpt

1984, Aug. 22

49	C1	$2 multicolored	4.75	4.75

Columbus' First Landfall — C5

1984, Sept. 21

50	C5	10c Sighting manatees	1.00	1.00
51	C5	70c Fleet	4.50	4.50
52	C5	$1 West Indies landing	6.50	6.50
		Nos. 50-52 (3)	12.00	12.00

Souvenir Sheet

53	C5	$2 Fleet, map	4.75	4.75

Columbus' first landing, 492nd anniv.

Christmas
C6

Walt Disney characters: 20c, Santa Claus,
Donald and Mickey. 35c, Donald at refrigera-
tor. 50c, Donald, Micky riding toy train. 75c,
Donald carrying presents. $1.10, Huey, Louie,
Dewey and Donald singing carols. $2, Donald
as Christmas tree.

Perf. 13½x14, 12x12½ (75c)

1984, Nov. 26

54	C6	20c multicolored	1.10	1.10
55	C6	35c multicolored	2.00	2.00
56	C6	50c multicolored	2.75	2.75
57	C6	75c multicolored	4.25	4.25
58	C6	$1.10 multicolored	6.25	6.25
		Nos. 54-58 (5)	16.35	16.35

Souvenir Sheet
Perf. 13½x14

59	C6	$2 multicolored	6.25	6.25

No. 57 printed in sheets of 8.

Audubon Birth Bicentenary — C7

1985, Feb. 12   **Perf. 14**

60	C7	20c Thick-billed vireo	1.10	1.10
61	C7	35c Black-faced grass-quit	2.00	2.00
62	C7	50c Pearly-eyed thrash-er	2.75	2.75
63	C7	$1 Greater Antillean bullfinch	5.50	5.50
		Nos. 60-63 (4)	11.35	11.35

Souvenir Sheet

64	C7	$2 Stripe-headed tana-gers	6.25	6.25

No. 64 exists imperf.

Intl. Youth
Year — C8

1985, May 8

65	C8	16c Education	.35	.35
66	C8	35c Health	.80	.80
67	C8	70c Love	1.50	1.50
68	C8	90c Peace	1.90	1.90
		Nos. 65-68 (4)	4.55	4.55

Souvenir Sheet

69	C8	$2 Peace dove, child	5.00	5.00

UN 40th anniv.

Intl. Civil
Aviation
Org., 40th
Anniv.
C9

1985, May 26

70	C9	35c DC-3	2.50	2.50
71	C9	75c Convair 440	5.00	5.00
72	C9	90c TCNA Islander	6.00	6.00
		Nos. 70-72 (3)	13.50	13.50

Souvenir Sheet

73	C9	$2.20 Hang glider	5.75	5.75

Queen Mother, 85th Birthday Type
of Turks & Caicos

1985, July 7

74	A117	35c Wearing green hat	1.25	1.25
75	A117	65c With Princess Anne, horiz.	2.00	2.00
76	A117	95c Wearing white hat	3.25	3.25
		Nos. 74-76 (3)	6.50	6.50

Souvenir Sheet

77	A117	$2 Inspecting guards-men	6.50	6.50

Mark Twain, 150th Birth Anniv. — C10

Walt Disney characters in Tom Sawyer,
Detective (Intl. Youth Year): 8c, Mickey and
Goofy as Tom and Huck reading reward
poster. 35c, Meeting Jake Dunlap. 95c, Spying
on Jubiter Dunlap. $1.10, With Pluto finding
body. No. 86, Unmasking Jubiter Dunlap.
Walt Disney characters portraying Six
Soldiers of Fortune (The Brothers Grimm,
Bicent.): 16c, Donald receiving his meager
pay. 25c, Donald meets Horace Horsecollar as
strong man. 65c, Donald meets Mickey the
marksman. $1.35, Goofy wins footrace against
Princess Daisy. No. 87, Soldiers with sack of
gold.

1985, Dec. 5   **Perf. 14x13½**

78	C10	8c multicolored	.30	.30
79	C10	16c multicolored	.45	.45
80	C10	25c multicolored	.70	.70
81	C10	35c multicolored	1.00	1.00
82	C10	65c multicolored	1.75	1.75
83	C10	95c multicolored	2.60	2.60
84	C10	$1.10 multicolored	3.25	3.25
85	C10	$1.35 multicolored	4.00	4.00
		Nos. 78-85 (8)	14.05	14.05

Souvenir Sheet

86	C10	$2 multicolored	8.00	8.00
87	C10	$2 multicolored	8.00	8.00

Stamps are no longer being produced for
Caicos.

TURKS ISLANDS

ˈtərks ˈī-lənds

LOCATION — West Indies, at the southern extremity of the Bahamas

GOVT. — Former dependency of Jamaica

POP. — 2,000 (approx.)

CAPITAL — Grand Turk

In 1848 the Turks Islands together with the Caicos group, lying to the northwest, were made a British colony. In 1873 the Colony became a dependency under the government of Jamaica although separate stamp issues were continued. Postage stamps inscribed Turks and Caicos Islands have been used since 1900.

12 Pence = 1 Shilling

Values for unused stamps are for examples with original gum as defined in the catalogue introduction. Very fine examples of Nos. 1-42 will have generally rough perforations that cut into the design on one or more sides due to the narrow spacing of the stamps on the plates and imperfect perforating methods. Stamps with perfs clear of the design on all four sides are extremely scarce and will command substantially higher prices.

Because of the printing and imperfect perforating methods, stamps are often found scissor separated. Prices will not be adversely affected on those stamps where the scissor cut does not remove the perforations.

Watermark

Wmk. 5 — Small Star

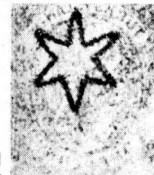

Queen Victoria — A1

Perf. 11½ to 13
1867   **Unwmk.**   **Engr.**

1	A1	1p rose	67.50	67.50
2	A1	6p gray black	110.00	140.00
3	A1	1sh slate blue	105.00	67.50
		Nos. 1-3 (3)	282.50	275.00

Perf. 11 to 13x14 to 15
1873-79   **Wmk. 5**

4	A1	1p lake	57.50	57.50
5	A1	1p dull red ('79)	62.50	67.50
a.		Horiz. pair, imperf. btwn.	26,000.	
b.		Perf. 11-12	1,100.	
6	A1	1sh violet	5,750.	2,250.

Stamps offered as No. 6 are often examples from which the surcharge has been removed.

Stamps of 1867-79 Surcharged in Black

    a    b

---

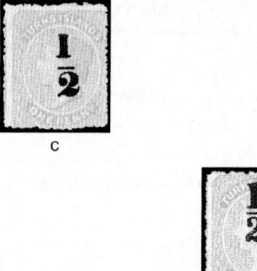
   c    d

      e

12 settings of the ½p, 9 of 2½p, and 6 of 4p.

1881   **Unwmk.**   **Perf. 11 to 13**

7	(a)	½p on 6p gray blk	100.00	170.00
7A	(b)	½p on 6p gray blk	100.00	150.00
8	(b)	½p on 1sh slate bl	140.00	200.00
a.		Double surcharge	8,000.	
8B	(c)	½p on 1sh slate bl	11,000.	
c.		Without fraction bar		
d.		Double surcharge	15,000.	
e.		#8a and #8Bd in pair	27,000.	

Perf. 11 to 13x14 to 15
Wmk. 5

9	(a)	½p on 1p dull red	150.00	200.00
a.		Double surcharge		
10	(b)	½p on 1p dull red	60.00	150.00
11	(c)	½p on 1p dull red	210.00	275.00
a.		Double surcharge	4,250.	
12	(d)	½p on 1p dull red	260.00	
a.		Without fraction bar	1,150.	
b.		Double surcharge		
13	(e)	½p on 1p dull red	600.00	
14	(a)	½p on 1sh violet	175.00	225.00
a.		Double surcharge	4,000.	
15	(b)	½p on 1sh violet	140.00	225.00
a.		Without fraction bar	625.00	
16	(c)	½p on 1sh violet	105.00	190.00

   f   g

    h

Perf. 11 to 13
Unwmk.

17	(f)	2½p on 6p gray blk	16,000.	
18	(g)	2½p on 6p gray blk	425.	600.
a.		Horiz. pair, imperf. between	40,000.	
b.		Double surcharge	17,000.	
19	(h)	2½p on 6p gray blk	250.	425.
a.		Double surcharge	16,000.	

   i   j

Perf. 11 to 13x14 to 15
Wmk. 5

20	(i)	2½p on 1sh violet	4,000.	
21	(h)	2½p on 1sh violet	625.00	950.00
22	(j)	2½p on 1sh violet	9,500.	

   k   l

   m   n

Perf. 11 to 13
Unwmk.

24	(k)	2½p on 6p gray blk	9,500.
25	(k)	2½p on 1sh slate bl	27,000.
26	(l)	2½p on 1sh slate bl	1,500.
27	(m)	2½p on 1sh slate bl	2,200.
a.		Without fraction bar	8,000.
28	(n)	2½p on 1sh slate bl	6,500.

    o

Perf. 11 to 13x14 to 15
Wmk. 5

29	(l)	2½p on 1p dull red	750.00
30	(o)	2½p on 1p dull red	1,500.
31	(l)	2½p on 1sh violet	850.00
a.		Double surcharge of "½"	4,750.
32	(o)	2½p on 1sh violet	1,350.
b.		Double surcharge of "½"	9,000.

   p   q

    r

Perf. 11 to 13
Unwmk.

33	(p)	4p on 6p gray black	110.00	150.00
34	(q)	4p on 6p gray black	400.00	500.00
35	(r)	4p on 6p gray black	750.00	350.00

Examples of No. 33 with top of "4" painted in are sometimes offered as No. 35.

Perf. 11 to 13x14 to 15
Wmk. 5

36	(r)	4p on 1p dull red	950.00	625.00
a.		Inverted surcharge	3,250.	
37	(p)	4p on 1p dull red	850.00	550.00
a.		Inverted surcharge		
38	(p)	4p on 1sh violet	475.00	750.00
39	(q)	4p on 1sh violet	2,750.	

Wmk. Crown and C C (1)
1881   **Engr.**   **Perf. 14**

40	A1	1p brown red	77.50	105.00
a.		Diagonal half used as ½p on cover		
41	A1	6p olive brown	120.00	175.00
42	A1	1sh slate green	190.00	140.00
		Nos. 40-42 (3)	387.50	420.00

    A2

1881   **Typo.**

43	A2	4p ultramarine	170.00	67.50

1882-95   **Engr.**   **Wmk. 2**

44	A1	1p orange brn ('83)	100.00	35.00
a.		Half used as ½p on cover	5,000.	
45	A1	1p car lake ('89)	3.50	2.25
46	A1	6p yellow brn ('89)	4.50	5.00
47	A1	1sh black brn ('87)	6.00	4.50
a.		1sh deep brown	6.00	4.50

Typo.
Die A

48	A2	½p dull green ('85)	6.50	6.00
a.		½p blue green ('82)	29.00	29.00

49	A2	2½p red brown ('82)	40.00	16.00
50	A2	4p gray ('84)	38.00	4.00
a.		Half used as 2p on cover	5,000.	

Die B

51	A2	½p gray green ('94)	3.50	2.00
52	A2	2½p ultra ('93)	3.50	2.75
53	A2	4p dk vio & bl ('95)	11.00	15.00

For descriptions of dies A and B see "Dies of British Colonial Stamps" in table of contents.

1887   **Engr.**   **Perf. 12**

54	A1	1p carmine lake	14.00	3.25

No. 49 Surcharged in Black

1889

55	A2	1p on 2½p red brn	22.00	19.00
a.		Double surcharge		
b.		Double surcharge, one inverted		
c.		"One" omitted	1,800.	
d.		Half used as ½p on cover	5,500.	

No. 55c caused by the misplacement of the surcharge. Stamps also exist from the same sheet reading "Penny One."

No. 50 Surcharged in Black

Two types of surcharge:
Type I — Upper bar continuous across sheet.
Type II — Upper bar breaks between stamps.

1893

56	A2	½p on 4p gray (I)	225.00	180.00
a.		Type II	3,250.	1,450.

This surcharge exists in five settings.

    A3

1894   **Typo.**

57	A3	5p olive grn & carmine	10.00	25.00
a.		Diag. half used as 2½p on cover	5,000.	

TUVALU

tü-'vä-ˌü

LOCATION — A group of islands in the Pacific Ocean northeast of Australia.
GOVT. — Independent state in the British Commonwealth
AREA — 9½ sq. mi.
POP. — 10,588 (1999 est.)
CAPITAL — Fongafale

Tuvalu, formerly Ellice Islands, consists of nine islands.

Australian dollar

Catalogue values for all unused stamps in this country are for Never Hinged items.

Watermark

Wmk. 380 — "POST OFFICE"

Gilbert and Ellice Islands Types of 1971 Overprinted in Violet Blue or Silver (35c)

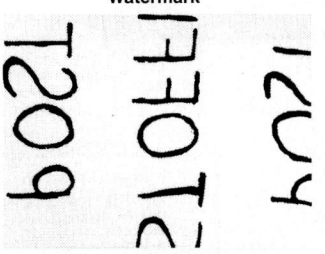

No. 1

No. 12

Wmk. 373

			1976, Jan. 1	Litho.	Perf. 14
1	A18	1c		1.00	.50
2	A19	2c		1.25	.70
a.			Wmk. 314 sideways	200.00	25.00
b.			Wmk. 314 upright	1,400.	140.00
3	A19	3c	Wmk. 314	2.00	1.00
a.			Wmk. 373	.65	.40
4	A19	4c		1.25	.70
5	A19	5c	Wmk. 314	1.25	1.00
6	A18	6c		1.25	.70
7	A18	8c	Wmk. 314	1.25	1.00
8	A18	10c	Wmk. 314	1.25	1.25
9	A18	15c		2.00	.80
10	A19	20c		1.25	1.00
11	A19	25c	Wmk. 314	8.00	2.75
a.			Wmk. 373	.70	.60
12	A19	35c		2.00	1.10
13	A18	50c		1.25	1.00
a.			Wmk. 314	47.50	22.50
14	A18	$1		1.25	1.25
a.			Wmk. 314	110.00	70.00
15	A18	$2		1.60	1.25
			Nos. 1-15 (15)	27.85	16.00

Men from Gilbert and Ellice — A1

Designs: 10c, Map of Gilbert and Ellice Islands, vert. 35c, Gilbert and Ellice canoes.

			1976, Jan. 1		Wmk. 373
16	A1	4c	multicolored	.50	.60
17	A1	10c	multicolored	.65	.70
18	A1	35c	multicolored	.90	1.00
			Nos. 16-18 (3)	2.05	2.30

Separation of the Gilbert and Ellice Islands.

50c Coin and Octopus — A2

New coinage: 10c, 10c-coin and red-dyed crab. 15c, 20c-coin and flyingfish. 35c, $1-coin and green turtle.

Wmk. 373

			1976, Apr. 21	Litho.	Perf. 14
19	A2	5c	bister & multi	.25	.25
20	A2	10c	ultra & multi	.40	.30
21	A2	15c	blue & multi	.60	.40
22	A2	35c	lt green & multi	1.10	.70
			Nos. 19-22 (4)	2.35	1.65

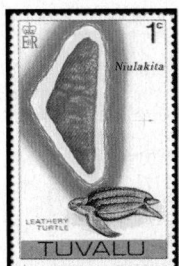

Map of Niulakita, Leathery Turtle — A3

2c, Map of Nukulaelae and sleeping mat. 4c, Map of Nui and talo vegetable. 5c, Map of Nanumanga and grass dancing skirt. 6c, Map of Nukufetau and coconut crab. 8c, Map of Funafuti and banana tree. 10c, Map of Tuvalu Islands. 15c, Map of Niutao and flyingfish. 20c, Map of Vaitupu and maneapa (house). 25c, Map of Nanumea and palu fish hook. 35c, Te Ano Game, horiz. 50c, Canoe pole fishing, horiz. $1, Reef fishing by flare, horiz. $2, House, horiz. $5, Colony Ship M.V. Nivanga, horiz.

1976	Wmk. 373	Litho.	Perf. 13½
23-37	A3	Set of 15	30.00	8.50

Issue dates: $5, Sept. 1; others July 1.
See #58-70. For overprints see #85-91.

New Testament A5

Designs: 20c, Lotolelei Church, Nanumea. 25c, Kelupi Church, Nui. 30c, Mataloa o Tuvalu Church, Vaitupu. 35c, Palataiso o Keliso Church, Nanumanga.

Perf. 14x14½

			1976, Oct. 6	Litho.	Wmk. 373
38-42	A5	Set of 5		6.50	4.00

Christmas 1976. Printed in sheets of 10 stamps and 2 labels.

Prince Philip Carried Ashore at Vaitupu — A6

Designs: 15c, Queen and Prince Philip on Buckingham Palace balcony. 50c, Queen Leaving Buckingham Palace for coronation.

			1977, Feb. 9	Litho.	Perf. 13½x14
43	A6	15c	multicolored	1.25	1.05
44	A6	35c	multicolored	1.60	1.75
45	A6	50c	multicolored	2.50	2.50
a.			Souv. sheet, #43-45, perf. 15	6.50	6.50
			Nos. 43-45 (3)	5.35	5.30

25th anniv. of the reign of Elizabeth II.

Health (Microscope) — A7

20c, Education (blackboard). 30c, Fruit growing (palm). 35c, Map of South Pacific Territory.

			1977, May 4	Litho.	Perf. 13½x14
46	A7	5c	lilac & multi	.50	.30
47	A7	20c	orange & multi	.50	.30
48	A7	30c	yellow grn & multi	.50	.30
49	A7	35c	lt blue & multi	.75	.45
			Nos. 46-49 (4)	2.25	1.35

South Pacific Commission, 30th anniv.

Swearing-in Ceremony and Scout Emblem — A8

Designs (Scout Emblem and): 20c, Scouts in outrigger canoe. 30c, Scouts under sun shelter. 35c, Lord Baden-Powell.

Perf. 13½x14

			1977, Aug. 10	Litho.	Wmk. 373
50	A8	5c	multicolored	.30	.30
51	A8	20c	multicolored	.30	.30
52	A8	30c	multicolored	.50	.50
53	A8	35c	multicolored	.50	.50
			Nos. 50-53 (4)	1.60	1.60

Scouting in Tuvalu (Ellice Islands), 50th anniv.

Hurricane Beach and Coral — A9

Designs: 20c, Boring apparatus on "Porpoise," vert. 30c, Map of islands showing line of dredgings to prove Darwin's theory, vert. 35c, Charles Darwin and "Beagle."

Perf. 13½

			1977, Nov. 2	Unwmk.	Litho.
54	A9	5c	multicolored	.35	.35
55	A9	20c	multicolored	.35	.35
56	A9	30c	multicolored	.55	.45
57	A9	35c	multicolored	.55	.45
			Nos. 54-57 (4)	1.80	1.60

1896-97 Royal Soc. of London Expeditions to explore coral reefs by dredging and boring.

Types of 1976

Designs: 30c, Fatele, local dance. 40c, Screw pine. Others as before.

			1977-78	Unwmk.	Perf. 13½
58	A3	1c	multicolored	.25	.25
59	A3	2c	multicolored	.25	.25
60	A3	4c	multicolored	.25	.25
61	A3	5c	multicolored	.25	.25
62	A3	6c	multicolored	.25	.25
63	A3	8c	multicolored	.25	.25
64	A3	10c	multicolored	.25	.25
66	A3	20c	multicolored	1.25	.85
67	A3	25c	multicolored	.85	.30
68	A3	30c	multi, horiz.	.35	.35
69	A3	40c	multi, horiz.	.45	.50
70	A3	$5	multi, horiz.	3.50	3.50
			Nos. 58-70 (12)	8.15	7.25

Issued: #58, 61, 63-64, 67, 1977; others, 1978.

Pacific Pigeon — A10

Wild Birds of Tuvalu: 20c, Reef heron. 30c, Fairy tern. 40c, Lesser frigate bird.

Perf. 14x13½

			1978, Jan. 25	Litho.	Unwmk.
73	A10	8c	lilac & multi	1.50	.90
74	A10	20c	ocher & multi	1.90	1.25
75	A10	30c	dull green & multi	2.40	1.75
76	A10	40c	brt green & multi	2.40	2.00
			Nos. 73-76 (4)	8.20	5.90

Lawedua — A11

Ships: 20c, Tug Wallacia. 30c, Freighter Cenpac Rounder. 40c, Pacific Explorer.

			1978, Apr. 5	Unwmk.	Perf. 13½x14
77	A11	8c	multicolored	.25	.25
78	A11	20c	multicolored	.35	.35
79	A11	30c	multicolored	.50	.45
80	A11	40c	multicolored	.60	.60
			Nos. 77-80 (4)	1.70	1.65

Canterbury Cathedral — A12

Designs: 30c, Salisbury Cathedral. 40c, Wells Cathedral. $1, Hereford Cathedral.

			1978, June 2	Litho.	Perf. 13½x14
81	A12	8c	multicolored	.25	.25
82	A12	30c	multicolored	.25	.25
83	A12	40c	multicolored	.25	.25
84	A12	$1	multicolored	.25	.25
a.			Souv. sheet, #81-84, perf. 15	.60	.60
			Nos. 81-84 (4)	1.00	1.00

25th anniv. of coronation of Elizabeth II.
#81-84 were also issued in bklt. panes of 2.

Types of 1976 Overprinted "INDEPENDENCE 1ST OCTOBER 1978"

			1978, Oct. 1	Litho.	Perf. 13½
85	A3	8c	multicolored	.25	.25
86	A3	10c	multicolored	.25	.25
87	A3	15c	multicolored	.25	.25
88	A3	20c	multicolored	.25	.25
89	A3	30c	multi, horiz.	.25	.25
90	A3	35c	multi, horiz.	.25	.25
91	A3	40c	multi, horiz.	.25	.25
			Nos. 85-91 (7)	1.75	1.75

Independence, Oct. 1, 1978. Overprint in 3 lines on vert. stamps, 1 line on horiz.

White Frangipani — A13

Wild Flowers: 20c, Zephyrantes rosea. 30c, Gardenia taitensis. 40c, Clerodendron inerme.

1978, Oct. 4   Unwmk.   Perf. 14

92	A13	8c multicolored	.25	.25
93	A13	20c multicolored	.25	.30
94	A13	30c multicolored	.25	.40
95	A13	40c multicolored	.35	.70
		Nos. 92-95 (4)	1.10	1.65

Squirrelfish — A14

Fish: 2c, Yellow-banded goatfish. 4c, Imperial angelfish. 5c, Rainbow butterfly. 6c, Blue angelfish. 8c, Blue striped snapper. 10c, Orange clownfish. 15c, Chevroned coralfish. 20c, Fairy cod. 25c, Clown triggerfish. 30c, Long-nosed butterfly. 35c, Yellowfin tuna. 40c, Spotted eagle ray. 45c, Black-tipped rock cod. 50c, Hammerhead shark. 70c, Lionfish, vert. $1, White-barred triggerfish, vert. $2, Beaked coralfish, vert. $5, Tiger shark, vert.

1979, Jan. 24   Litho.   Perf. 14

96	A14	1c multicolored	.25	.25
97	A14	2c multicolored	.25	.25
98	A14	4c multicolored	.25	.25
99	A14	5c multicolored	.25	.25
100	A14	6c multicolored	.25	.25
101	A14	8c multicolored	.25	.25
102	A14	10c multicolored	.25	.25
103	A14	15c multicolored	.25	.25
104	A14	20c multicolored	.25	.25
105	A14	25c multicolored	.25	.25
106	A14	30c multicolored	.25	.25
107	A14	35c multicolored	.25	.25
108	A14	40c multicolored	.30	.30
108A	A14	45c multicolored	1.50	1.00
109	A14	50c multicolored	.45	.45
110	A14	70c multicolored	.50	.50
111	A14	$1 multicolored	.65	.65
112	A14	$2 multicolored	1.50	1.50
113	A14	$5 multicolored	3.50	3.50
		Nos. 96-113 (19)	11.40	10.90

No. 108A issued June 16, 1981.
#101, 104, 106, 108 and #102, 105, 107, 108A were also issued in booklet panes of 4. For surcharge & overprints see #150, O1-O19.

Capt. Cook A15

Designs: 30c, Flag raising on new island. 40c, Observation of transit of Venus. $1, Death of Capt. Cook.

1979, Feb. 14   Perf. 14x14½

114	A15	8c multicolored	.25	.25
115	A15	30c multicolored	.25	.25
116	A15	40c multicolored	.25	.25
117	A15	$1 multicolored	.30	.30
a.		Strip of 4, #114-117	1.40	1.40

Bicentenary of death of Capt. James Cook (1728-1779). Nos. 114-117 printed se-tenant horizontally in sheets of 12 (4x3) with gutters between horizontal rows.

Grumman Goose over Nukulaelae — A16

Grumman Goose over: 20c, Vaitupu. 30c, Nui. 40c, Funafuti.

1979, May 16   Litho.   Perf. 14x13½

118	A16	8c multicolored	.25	.25
119	A16	20c multicolored	.25	.25
120	A16	30c multicolored	.25	.30
121	A16	40c multicolored	.30	.30
		Nos. 118-121 (4)	1.05	1.10

Inauguration of internal air service.

Hill, Tuvalu No. 16, Letterbox, London, 1855 — A17

Hill, Stamps of Tuvalu and: 40c, No. 17, Penny Black. $1, No. 18, mail coach.

1979, Aug. 16   Litho.   Perf. 13½x14

122	A17	30c multicolored	.25	.25
123	A17	40c multicolored	.25	.25
124	A17	$1 multicolored	.35	.35
a.		Souvenir sheet of 3, #122-124	1.00	1.00
		Nos. 122-124 (3)	.85	.85

Sir Rowland Hill (1795-1879), originator of penny postage.

Boy — A18

Designs: Children of Tuvalu.

1979, Oct. 20   Litho.   Perf. 14

125	A18	8c multicolored	.25	.25
126	A18	20c multicolored	.25	.25
127	A18	30c multicolored	.25	.25
128	A18	40c multicolored	.25	.25
		Nos. 125-128 (4)	1.00	1.00

International Year of the Child.

Cowry Shells A19

1980, Feb.   Litho.   Perf. 14

129	A19	8c Cypraea Argus	.25	.25
130	A19	20c Cypraea scurra	.25	.25
131	A19	30c Cypraea carneola	.30	.30
132	A19	40c Cypraea aurantium	.40	.40
		Nos. 129-132 (4)	1.20	1.20

Philatelic Bureau, Funafuti, Tuvalu No. 28, Arms, London 1980 Emblem — A20

Coat of Arms, London 1980 Emblem and: 20c, Gilbert and Ellice #41, Nukulaelae cancel, Tuvalu #24. 30c, US airmail cover. $1, Map of Tuvalu.

1980, Apr. 30   Litho.   Perf. 13½x14

133	A20	10c multicolored	.25	.25
134	A20	20c multicolored	.25	.25
135	A20	30c multicolored	.30	.30
136	A20	$1 multicolored	.75	.75
a.		Souvenir sheet of 4, #133-136	1.75	1.75
		Nos. 133-136 (4)	1.55	1.55

London 80 Intl. Stamp Exhib., May 6-14.

Queen Mother Elizabeth, 80th Birthday — A21

1980, Aug. 14   Litho.   Perf. 14

137	A21	50c multicolored	.40	.40

Issued in sheets of 10 plus 2 labels.

Aethaloessa Calidalis — A22

1980, Aug. 20   Litho.   Perf. 14

138	A22	8c shown	.25	.25
139	A22	20c Parotis suralis	.25	.25
140	A22	30c Dudua aprobola	.30	.30
141	A22	40c Decadarchis simulans	.40	.40
		Nos. 138-141 (4)	1.20	1.20

Air Pacific Heron (First Regular Air Service to Tuvalu, 1964) — A23

Aviation Anniversaries: 20c, Hawker Siddeley 748 (air service to Tuvalu). 30c, Sunderland Flying Boat (War time service to Funafuti, 1945. 40c, Orville Wright and Flyer (Wright brothers' first flight, 1903).

1980, Nov. 5   Litho.   Perf. 14

142	A23	8c multicolored	.25	.25
143	A23	20c multicolored	.25	.25
144	A23	30c multicolored	.30	.25
145	A23	40c multicolored	.40	.40
		Nos. 142-145 (4)	1.20	1.15

Hypolimnas Bolina Elliciana — A24

1981, Feb. 3   Litho.   Perf. 14½

146	A24	8c shown	.30	.30
147	A24	20c Hypolimnas, diff.	.35	.35
148	A24	30c Hypolimnas, diff.	.40	.40
149	A24	40c Junonia vallida	.65	.65
		Nos. 146-149 (4)	1.70	1.70

No. 109 Surcharged

1981, Feb. 24   Litho.   Perf. 14

150	A14	45c on 50c multicolored	.60	.60

Elizabeth, 1809 A25

Wmk. 373

1981, May 13   Litho.   Perf. 14

151	A25	10c shown	.25	.25
152	A25	25c Rebecca, 1819	.25	.25
153	A25	35c Independence II, 1821	.25	.25
154	A25	40c Basilisk, 1872	.30	.30
155	A25	45c Royalist, 1890	.35	.35
156	A25	50c Olivebank, 1920	.45	.45
		Nos. 151-156 (6)	1.85	1.85

See Nos. 216-221, 353-356, 410-413.

Prince Charles, Lady Diana, Royal Yacht Charlotte A25a

Prince Charles and Lady Diana — A25b

Wmk. 380

1981, July 10   Litho.   Perf. 14

157	A25a	10c Couple, Carolina	.25	.25
a.		Blkt. pane of 4, perf. 12, unwmkd.		.60
158	A25b	10c Couple	.25	.25
159	A25a	45c Victoria and Albert III	.25	.25
160	A25b	45c like #158	.25	.25
a.		Blkt. pane of 2, perf. 12, unwmkd.		1.00
161	A25a	$2 Britannia	.50	.50
162	A25b	$2 like #158	1.40	1.40
		Nos. 157-162 (6)	2.90	2.90

Royal wedding. Issued in sheets of 7 (6 design A25a; 1 design A25b). Set of 3 $12. For surcharges see Nos. B1-B2.

Souvenir Sheet

1981, Dec.   Litho.   Perf. 12

163	A25b	$1.50 Couple	1.00	1.00

Admission to UPU — A26

Wmk. Harrison's, London

1981, Nov. 19   Engr.   Perf. 14½x14

164	A26	70c dark blue	.45	.45
165	A26	$1 dark red brown	.65	.65
a.		Souv. sheet of 2, #164-165, unwmkd.	1.75	1.75

Amatuku Maritime School — A27

1982, Feb. 17   Litho.   Perf. 13½x14
166	A27	10c	Map	.25 .25
167	A27	25c	Motorboat	.25 .25
168	A27	35c	School, dock	.35 .35
169	A27	45c	Flag, ship	.45 .45
			Nos. 166-169 (4)	1.30 1.30

A27a

Wmk. 380

1982, May 19   Litho.   Perf. 14
170	A27a	10c	Caroline of Brandenburg-Ansbach, 1714	.25 .25
171	A27a	45c	Brandenburg-Ansbach arms	.25 .25
172	A27a	$1.50	Diana	.50 .50
			Nos. 170-172 (3)	1.00 1.00

21st birthday of Princess Diana, July 1.

Nos. 170-172 Overprinted "ROYAL BABY"

1982, July 14   Litho.   Perf. 14
173	A27a	10c	multicolored	.30 .30
174	A27a	45c	multicolored	.30 .30
175	A27a	$1.50	multicolored	.40 .40
			Nos. 173-175 (3)	1.00 1.00

Birth of Prince William of Wales, June 21.

Scouting Year — A28

1982, Aug. 18
176	A28	10c	Emblems	.25 .25
177	A28	25c	Campfire	.30 .30
178	A28	35c	Parade	.35 .35
179	A28	45c	Scout	.40 .40
			Nos. 176-179 (4)	1.30 1.30

Visit of Queen Elizabeth II and Prince Philip — A29

25c, Arms, Duke of Edinburgh's Personal Standard. 45c, Flags. 50c, Queen Elizabeth II, maps.

1982, Oct. 26   Litho.   Perf. 14
180	A29	25c	multicolored	.25 .25
181	A29	45c	multicolored	.30 .30
182	A29	50c	multicolored	.35 .35
a.			Souvenir sheet of 3, #180-182	1.25 1.25
			Nos. 180-182 (3)	.90 .90

Handicrafts — A30

1c, Fisherman's hat, lures, hooks. 2c, Cowrie shell handbags. 5c, Wedding & baby food baskets. 10c, Canoe model. 15c, Women's sun hats. 20c, Climbing rope. 25c, Pandanus baskets. 30c, Tray, coconut stands. 35c, Pandanus pillows, shell necklaces. 40c, Round baskets, fans. 45c, Reef sandals, fish trap. 50c, Rat trap, vert. 60c, Waterproof boxes, vert. $1, Pump drill, adze, vert. $2, Fisherman's hat, canoe bailers, vert. $5, Fishing rod, lures, scoop nets, vert.

1983-84   Litho.   Perf. 14
183	A30	1c	multicolored	.30 .25
184	A30	2c	multicolored	.30 .25
185	A30	5c	multicolored	.30 .25
186	A30	10c	multicolored	.30 .25
186A	A30	15c	multicolored	2.25 2.50
187	A30	20c	multicolored	.30 .25
188	A30	25c	multicolored	.30 .25
188A	A30	30c	multicolored	2.00 2.00
189	A30	35c	multicolored	.40 .30
190	A30	40c	multicolored	.30 .45
191	A30	45c	multicolored	.35 .55
192	A30	50c	multicolored	.40 .60
192A	A30	60c	multicolored	2.75 2.00
193	A30	$1	multicolored	.40 .60
194	A30	$2	multicolored	.60 .75
195	A30	$5	multicolored	1.00 1.10
			Nos. 183-195 (16)	12.25 12.35

Issued: 15c, 1984; others, 3/14/83.
For surcharges & overprints see #207, 230, O20-O32.

Commonwealth Day — A31

Wmk. 373

1983, Mar. 14   Litho.   Perf. 14
196	A31	20c	Fishing industry	.25 .25
197	A31	35c	Traditional dancing	.25 .25
198	A31	45c	Satellite view	.25 .25
199	A31	50c	First container ship	.30 .30
			Nos. 196-199 (4)	1.05 1.05

Dragonflies — A32

1983, May 25   Wmk. 380
200	A32	10c	Pantala flavescens	.25 .25
201	A32	35c	Anax guttatus	.50 .50
202	A32	40c	Tholymis tillarga	.60 .60
203	A32	50c	Diplacodes bipunctata	.65 .65
			Nos. 200-203 (4)	2.00 2.00

Boys Brigade Centenary — A33

1983, Aug. 10   Wmk. 373
204	A33	10c	Running, emblem	.25 .25
205	A33	35c	Canoeing	.30 .30
206	A33	$1	Officer, boys	.75 .75
			Nos. 204-206 (3)	1.30 1.30

No. 193 Surcharged in Black

1983, Aug. 26   Wmk. 380
207	A30	60c on $1 multi		1.00 .60

First Manned Flight Bicentenary — A34

25c, Montgolfier balloon, vert. 35c, McKinnon Turbo Goose. 45c, Beechcraft Super King Air 200. 50c, Double Eagle II Balloon, vert.

World Communications Year — A35

1983, Sept. 21   Wmk. 373
208	A34	25c	multicolored	.30 .30
209	A34	35c	multicolored	.40 .40
210	A34	45c	multicolored	.45 .45
211	A34	50c	multicolored	.55 .55
a.			Souvenir sheet of 4, #208-211	2.50 2.50
			Nos. 208-211 (4)	1.70 1.70

25c, Conch Shell Trumpet, vert. 35c, Radio Operator, vert. 45c, Teleprinter. 50c, Transmitting station.

1983, Nov. 18   Wmk. 380
212	A35	25c	multicolored	.25 .25
213	A35	35c	multicolored	.30 .30
214	A35	45c	multicolored	.35 .35
215	A35	50c	multicolored	.40 .40
			Nos. 212-215 (4)	1.30 1.30

Ship Type of 1981

1984, Feb. 16   Wmk. 380
216	A25	10c	Titus, 1897	.25 .25
217	A25	20c	Malaita, 1905	.25 .25
218	A25	25c	Aymeric, 1906	.25 .25
219	A25	35c	Anshun, 1965	.35 .35
220	A25	45c	Beaverbank, 1970	.40 .40
221	A25	50c	Benjamin Bowring, 1981	.55 .55
			Nos. 216-221 (6)	2.05 2.05

Leaders of the World
Large quantities of some Leaders of the World issues were sold at a fraction of face value when the printer was liquidated.

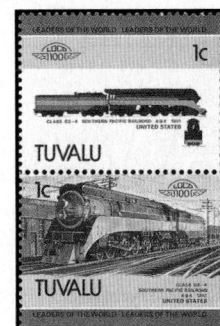

Historic Locomotives — A36

1c, Class GS-4, US, 1941. 15c, AD-60, Australia, 1952. 40c, C38, Australia, 1943. 60c, Achilles England, 1892.

Se-tenant Pairs, #a.-b.
a. — Side and front views.
b. — Action scene.

Perf. 12½x13

1984, Feb. 29   Unwmk.
222	A36	1c	multicolored	.25 .25
223	A36	15c	multicolored	.25 .25
224	A36	40c	multicolored	.50 .50
225	A36	60c	multicolored	.75 .75
			Nos. 222-225 (4)	1.75 1.75

See Nos. 235-246, 291-294, 320-323.

No. 191 Surcharged
Wmk. 380

1984, Feb. 1   Litho.   Perf. 14
230	A30	30c on 45c multi		.40 .40

For overprint see No. O25.

Beach Flowers A38

25c, Ipomoea pes-caprae. 45c, Ipomoea macrantha. 50c, Triumfetta procumbens. 60c, Portulaca quadrifida.

1984, May 30
231	A38	25c	multicolored	.25 .25
232	A38	45c	multicolored	.40 .40
233	A38	50c	multicolored	.50 .50
234	A38	60c	multicolored	.65 .65
			Nos. 231-234 (4)	1.80 1.80

Train Type of 1984

No. 235, Class 9700, Japan, 1897. No. 236, Casey Jones, US, 1896. No. 237, Class 231C/K, France, 1909. No. 238, Triplex, US, 1914. No. 239, Class 370, Gt. Britain, 1981. No. 240, Class 4F, Gt. Britain, 1924. No. 241, Class 640, Italy, 1907. No. 242, Tornado, Gt. Britain, 1888. No. 243, Broadlands, Gt. Britain, 1967. No. 244, Locomotion, Gt. Britain, 1825. No. 245, C57, Japan, 1937. No. 246, Class 4500, France, 1906.

Se-tenant Pairs, #a.-b.
a. — Side and front views.
b. — Action scene.

1984   Litho.   Perf. 12½x13
235	A36	1c	multicolored	.25 .25
236	A36	10c	multicolored	.25 .25
237	A36	15c	multicolored	.25 .25
238	A36	20c	multicolored	.25 .25
239	A36	25c	multicolored	.25 .25
240	A36	25c	multicolored	.25 .25
241	A36	30c	multicolored	.30 .30
242	A36	40c	multicolored	.40 .40
243	A36	50c	multicolored	.50 .50
244	A36	60c	multicolored	.65 .65
245	A36	$1	multicolored	1.00 1.00
246	A36	$1	multicolored	1.00 1.00
			Nos. 235-246 (12)	5.35 5.35

Issued: Nos. 235, 237, 241, 245, 10/4; others, 6/27.

15th South Pacific Forum A38a

1984, Aug. 21   Litho.   Perf. 14
255	A38a	60c	National flag	.55 .55
256	A38a	60c	Tuvalu crest	.55 .55

Ausipex '84 A38b

1984, Aug. 21   Perf. 14
257	A38b	60c	Exhib. emblem	.45 .45
258	A38b	60c	Royal Exhibi. Building	.45 .45

A. Shrewsbury Playing Cricket — A39

Cricket players in action or portrait.

1984, Nov. 5   Litho.   Perf. 12½
Se-tenant Pairs #a.-b.
259	A39	5c	shown	.25 .25
260	A39	30c	H. Verity	.50 .50
261	A39	50c	E.H. Hendren	.50 .50
262	A39	60c	J. Briggs	.60 .60
			Nos. 259-262 (4)	1.85 1.85

Drawings, Christmas 1984 — A40

1984, Nov. 14 Litho. **Perf. 14½x14**
267	A40	15c By Eli Faalata	.25	.25
268	A40	40c By Toakai Niutao	.30	.30
269	A40	50c By Falesa Teuila	.40	.40
270	A40	60c By Piuani Talie	.50	.50
		Nos. 267-270 (4)	1.45	1.45

Classic Automobiles — A41

Sketch listed first followed by angled view:
1c, Morris Minor, 1949. 15c, Studebaker Avanti, 1963. 50c, Chevrolet International Six, 1929. $1, Allard J2, 1950.

Se-tenant Pairs, #a.-b.
a. — Side and front views.
b. — Action scene.

1984, Dec. 7 Litho. **Perf. 12½x13**
271	A41	1c multicolored	.30	.30
272	A41	15c multicolored	.30	.30
273	A41	50c multicolored	.60	.60
274	A41	$1 multicolored	1.25	1.25
		Nos. 271-274 (4)	2.45	2.45

See Nos. 299-302, 332-339, 396-396, 414-425.

John J. Audubon — A42

#279a, Common flicker. #279b, Say's phoebe. #280a, Townsend's warbler. #280b, Bohemian waxwing. #281a, Prothonotary warbler. #281b, Worm-eating warbler. #282a, Broad-winged hawk. #282b, Northern harrier.

1985, Feb. 12 Litho. **Perf. 12½**
279	A42	1c Pair, #a.-b.	.30	.30
280	A42	25c Pair, #a.-b.	.70	.70
281	A42	50c Pair, #a.-b.	1.40	1.40
282	A42	70c Pair, #a.-b.	1.75	1.75
		Nos. 279-282 (4)	4.15	4.15

Birds and Eggs A43

1985, Feb. 27 **Perf. 14**
287	A43	15c Black-naped tern	.50	.35
288	A43	40c Black noddy	1.10	.85
289	A43	50c White-tailed tropic-bird	1.40	.95
290	A43	60c Sooty tern	1.75	1.25
		Nos. 287-290 (4)	4.75	3.40

Train Type of 1984
5c, Churchward, U.K. 10c, Class K.F., China. 30c, Class 99.77, East Germany. $1, Pearson, U.K.

Se-tenant Pairs, #a.-b.
a. — Side and front views.
b. — Action scene.

1985, Mar. 19 **Perf. 12½**
291	A36	5c multicolored	.25	.25
292	A36	10c multicolored	.25	.25
293	A36	30c multicolored	.45	.45
294	A36	$1 multicolored	1.50	1.50
		Nos. 291-294 (4)	2.45	2.45

Automobile Type of 1984
1c, Rickenbacker, 1923. 20c, Detroit-Electric, 1914. 50c, Packard Clipper, 1941. 70c, Audi Quattro, 1982.

Se-tenant Pairs, #a.-b.
a. — Side and front views.
b. — Action scene.

1985, Apr. 3
299	A41	1c multicolored	.30	.30
300	A41	20c multicolored	.30	.30
301	A41	50c multicolored	.65	.65
302	A41	70c multicolored	1.00	1.00
		Nos. 299-302 (4)	2.25	2.25

World War II Aircraft A44

15c, Curtiss P-40N. 40c, Consolidated B-24D Liberator. 50c, Lockheed PV-1 Ventura. 60c, Douglas C-54 Skymaster.

1985, May 29 Litho. **Perf. 14**
307	A44	15c multicolored	1.75	1.00
308	A44	40c multicolored	2.00	1.50
309	A44	50c multicolored	2.00	2.25
310	A44	60c multicolored	2.00	2.25
a.		Souvenir sheet of 4, #307-310	5.50	5.50
		Nos. 307-310 (4)	7.75	7.00

Queen Mother, 85th Birthday — A45

#310a, Facing right. #310b, Facing left. #311a, 317a, Facing right. #311b, 317b, Facing front. #312a, 316a, Waving to crowd. #312b, 316b, Facing front. #313a, Facing front. #313b, Facing left. #314a, As a young woman. #314b, as Queen Consort.

1985-86 Litho. **Perf. 12½**
311	A45	5c Pair, #a.-b.	.30	.30
312	A45	30c Pair, #a.-b.	.35	.35
313	A45	60c Pair, #a.-b.	.70	.70
314	A45	$1 Pair, #a.-b.	1.05	1.05
		Nos. 311-314 (4)	2.40	2.40

Souvenir Sheets
315	A45	$1.20 #a.-b.	1.90	1.90
316	A45	$2 #a.-b.	4.50	4.50
317	A45	$3 #a.-b.	6.50	6.50

Issued: #316-317, 6/10/86; others, 7/4/85.

Train Type of 1984
10c, 1936 Green Arrow, U.K. 40c, 1982 G.M. (EMD) SD-50, US. 65c, 1932 DRG Flying Hamburger, Germany. $1, 1908 JNR Class 1070, Japan.

Se-tenant Pairs, #a.-b.
a. — Side and front views.
b. — Action scene.

1985, Sept. 18
320	A36	10c multicolored	.25	.25
321	A36	40c multicolored	.55	.55
322	A36	65c multicolored	.75	.75
323	A36	$1 multicolored	.80	.80
		Nos. 320-323 (4)	2.35	2.35

Girl Guides, 75th Anniv. — A46

1985, Aug. 28 Litho. **Perf. 15**
328	A46	15c Playing guitar	.25	.25
329	A46	40c Camping	.50	.50
330	A46	50c Flag bearer	.60	.60

331	A46	60c Guides' salute	.70	.70
a.		Souvenir sheet of 4, #328-331	2.00	2.00
		Nos. 328-331 (4)	2.05	2.05

Car Type of 1984
5c, 1929 Cord L-29, US. 10c, 1932 Horch 670 V-12, Germany. 15c, 1901 Lanchester, UK. 35c, 1950 Citroen 2 CV, France. 40c, 1957 MGA, UK. 55c, 1962 Ferrari 250-GTO, Italy. $1, 1932 Ford V-8, US. $1.50, 1977 Aston Martin-Lagonda, UK.

a. — Side and front views.
b. — Action scene.

1985, Oct. 8 **Perf. 12½**
332-339	A41	Set of 8 pairs	4.75	4.75

Crabs A47

1986, Jan. 7 **Perf. 15**
348	A47	15c Stalk-eyed ghost	.35	.35
349	A47	40c Red and white painted	.95	.95
350	A47	50c Red-spotted	1.10	1.10
351	A47	60c Red hermit	1.40	1.40
		Nos. 348-351 (4)	3.80	3.80

Souvenir Sheet of 2

Events — A48

#352a, American and Soviet flags, chess board & knight. #352b, Rotary Intl. emblem.

1986, Mar. 19 Litho. **Perf. 13x12½**
352	A48	$3 #a.-b.	6.50	6.50

Fischer and Karpov, world chess champions; Rotary Intl., 80th anniv.
No. 352 exists with plain or decorated border.

Ship Type of 1981
1986, Apr. 14 **Perf. 15**
353	A25	15c Messenger of Peace	.30	.30
354	A25	40c John Wesley	.80	.80
355	A25	50c Duff	.90	.90
356	A25	60c Triton	1.00	1.00
		Nos. 353-356 (4)	3.00	3.00

Queen Elizabeth II, 60th Birthday — A49

Various portraits.

1986, Apr. 21 **Perf. 12½**
357	A49	10c multicolored	.25	.25
358	A49	90c multicolored	.35	.35
359	A49	$1.50 multicolored	.60	.60
360	A49	$3 multi, vert.	1.10	1.10
		Nos. 357-360 (4)	2.30	2.30

Souvenir Sheet
361	A49	$4 multicolored	3.50	3.50

Peace Corps, 25th Anniv. A50

1986, May 22 **Perf. 14**
362	A50	50c multicolored	.80	.80

For overprint see No. 374.

A51

1986, May 22 **Perf. 14x13½**
363	A51	60c multicolored	.80	.80

AMERIPEX '86.

A52

Players and teams.

1986, June 30 Litho. **Perf. 15**
364	A52	1c So. Korea	.25	.25
365	A52	5c France	.25	.25
366	A52	10c W. Germany, 1974	.25	.25
367	A52	40c Italy	.40	.40

Size: 60x40mm
Perf. 13x12½
368	A52	60c W. Germany vs. Holland, 1974	.50	.50
369	A52	$1 Canada	.80	.80
370	A52	$2 No. Ireland	1.75	1.75
371	A52	$3 England	2.40	2.40
		Nos. 364-371 (8)	6.60	6.60

Souvenir Sheets
372	A52	$1.50 like #369	1.75	1.75
373	A52	$2.50 like #370	3.00	3.00

1986 World Cup Soccer Championships. Nos. 366 and 368 picture emblem; others picture character trademark.

No. 362 Ovptd. with STAMPEX '86 Emblem
1986, Aug. 4 Litho. **Perf. 14**
374	A50	50c multicolored	.70	.70

A53

Wedding of Prince Andrew and Sarah Ferguson — A54

#381a, Andrew, vert. #381b, Couple, vert. #382a, Andrew. #382b, Princess Diana, Sarah.

Perf. 12½

1986, July 18		**Litho.**		**Unwmk.**
381	A53	60c Pair, #a.-b.	.75	.75
382	A53	$1 Pair, #a.-b.	1.25	1.25

Souvenir Sheet
Perf. 13x12½

383	A54	$6 Newlyweds	3.00	3.00

No. 382a pictures Westminster Abbey in LR. For overprints see Nos. 389-390.

Geckos
A55

1986, July 30		**Litho.**		**Perf. 14**
384	A55	15c Mourning gecko	.35	.30
385	A55	40c Oceanic stump-toed	1.15	1.00
386	A55	50c Azure-tailed skink	1.50	1.30
387	A55	60c Moth skink	2.10	1.75
		Nos. 384-387 (4)	5.10	4.35

Souvenir Sheet

South Pacific Forum, 15th Anniv. A56

Flags and maps: a, Australia. b, Cook Islands. c, Micronesia. d, Fiji. e, Kiribati. f, Nauru. g, New Zealand. h, Niue. i, Papua New Guinea. j, Solomon Islands. k, Tonga. l, Tuvalu. m, Vanuatu. n, Western Samoa.

Wmk. 380

1986, Aug. 4		**Litho.**		**Perf. 15**
388		Sheet of 14 + label	9.00	9.00
a.-n.		A56 40c any single	.60	.60

No. 388 has center label picturing Executive Committee headquarters, Suva, Fiji.

Nos. 381-382 Ovptd.
"Congratulations to T.R.H. The Duke & Duchess of York" in Silver

1986		**Unwmk.**		**Perf. 12½**
389	A53	60c Pair, #a.-b.	1.75	1.75
390	A53	$1 Pair, #a.-b.	2.75	2.75

Exist tete-beche.

Car Type of 1984

15c, 1953 Cooper, UK. 40c, 1964 Rover 2000, UK. 50c, 1930 Ruxton, US. 60c, 1950 Jowett Jupiter, UK. 90c, 1964 Cobra Daytona Coupe, US. $1.50, 1903 Packard Model F "Old Pacific," US.

Se-tenant Pairs, #a.-b.
a. — Side and front views.
b. — Action scene.

1986, Oct.		**Litho.**		**Perf. 12½**
391-396	A41	Set of 6 pairs	3.50	3.50

Marine Life A57

1986, Nov. 5		**Unwmk.**		**Perf. 14**
397	A57	15c Sea star	.95	.95
398	A57	40c Pencil urchin	1.60	1.60
399	A57	50c Fragile coral	1.75	1.75
400	A57	60c Pink coral	2.00	2.00
		Nos. 397-400 (4)	6.30	6.30

See Nos. 465-468, 524-527.

Souvenir Sheets

Statue of Liberty, Cent. — A58

Various views of the statue.

1986, Nov. 24				
401	A58	$1.25 multicolored	.65	.65
402	A58	$1.50 multicolored	.90	.90
403	A58	$1.80 multicolored	1.15	1.15
404	A58	$2 multicolored	1.25	1.25
405	A58	$2.25 multicolored	1.50	1.50
406	A58	$2.50 multicolored	1.60	1.60
407	A58	$3 multicolored	2.00	2.00
408	A58	$3.25 multicolored	2.10	2.10
409	A58	$3.50 multicolored	2.50	2.50
		Nos. 401-409 (9)	13.65	13.65

A perforated set of sixteen 65c stamps commemorating the Statue of Liberty centennial in a different design were printed but never issued. The stamps were sold in the liquidation sale of the printer.

Ships Type of 1981

1987, Feb. 4		**Unwmk.**		**Perf. 14**
410	A25	15c Southern Cross IV	.80	.80
411	A25	40c John Williams VI	1.75	1.75
412	A25	50c John Williams IV	2.00	2.00
413	A25	60c M.S. Southern Cross	2.00	2.00
		Nos. 410-413 (4)	6.55	6.55

Car Type of 1984

1c, 1938 Talbot-Lago, France. 2c, 1930 Dupont Model G, US. 5c, 1950 Riley RM, U.K. 10c, 1915 Chevrolet Baby Grand, US. 20c, 1968 Shelby Mustang GT 500 KR, US. 30c, 1952 Ferrari 212 Export Barchetta, Italy. 40c, 1912 Peerless Model 48-Six, US. 50c, 1954 Sunbeam Alpine, U.K. 60c, 1969 Matra-Ford MS80, France. 70c, 1934 Squire 1-Litre, U.K. 75c, 1931 Talbot 105, U.K. $1, 1928 Plymouth Model Q, US.

Se-tenant Pairs, #a.-b.
a. — Side and front views.
b. — Action scene.
Perf. 12½

1987, May 7		**Litho.**		**Unwmk.**
414-425	A41	Set of 12 pairs, #a.-b.	6.50	6.50
425c		Souv. sheet of 2	4.00	4.00

Ferns — A59

1987, July 7		**Wmk. 380**		**Perf. 14**
438	A59	15c Nephrolepis saligna	.25	.25
439	A59	40c Asplenium nidus	.80	.80
440	A59	50c Microsorum scolopendria	1.00	1.00
441	A59	60c Pteris tripartita	1.10	1.10
		Nos. 438-441 (4)	3.15	3.15

Souvenir Sheet

442	A59	$1.50 Psilotum nudum	3.25	3.25

A60

#443a, 444b, 445a, 456b, Flowers, all diff. #443b, 444a, 445b, 456a, Woman wearing fou, all diff.

1987, Aug. 12				**Wmk. 380**
443	A60	15c Pair, #a.-b.	.40	.40
444	A60	40c Pair, #a.-b.	1.00	1.00
445	A60	50c Pair, #a.-b.	1.20	1.20
446	A60	60c Pair, #a.-b.	1.60	1.60
		Nos. 443-446 (4)	4.20	4.20

Crayfish and Coconut Crabs A61

		Wmk. 380		
1987, Nov. 11		**Litho.**		**Perf. 14**
451	A61	40c Coconut crabs	1.20	.90
452	A61	50c Painted crayfish	1.50	1.10
453	A61	60c Ocean crayfish	1.75	1.40
		Nos. 451-453 (3)	4.45	3.40

Photograph of Queen Victoria, 1897, by Downey — A62

60c, Elizabeth and Philip on their wedding day, 1947. 80c, Elizabeth, Charles, Philip, c. 1950. $1, Elizabeth, Anne, 1950. $2, Elizabeth, 1970. $3, Elizabeth, children, 1950.

1987, Nov. 20		**Unwmk.**		**Perf. 15**
454-458	A62	Set of 5	4.75	4.75

Souvenir Sheet

459	A62	$3 red org & blk	3.00	3.00

Accession of Queen Victoria to the throne of England, sesquicentennial; wedding of Queen Elizabeth II and Prince Philip, 40th anniv.

16th World Scout Jamboree, Australia, 1987-88 — A63

Jamboree and Australia bicentennial emblems plus: 40c, Aborigine, Ayer's Rock. 60c, Capt. Cook, by Dance, and HMS Endeavor. $1, Scout and Scout Park Arch. $1.50, Koala and kangaroo. $2.50, Lord and Lady Baden-Powell.

Perf. 13x12½

1987, Dec. 2		**Litho.**		**Unwmk.**
460	A63	40c multicolored	.35	.35
461	A63	60c multicolored	.50	.50
462	A63	$1 multicolored	.85	.85
463	A63	$1.50 multicolored	1.15	1.15
		Nos. 460-463 (4)	2.85	2.85

Souvenir Sheet

464	A63	$2.50 multicolored	2.50	2.50

Marine Life Type of 1986
Unwmk.

1988, Feb. 29		**Litho.**		**Perf. 15**
465	A57	15c Spanish dancer	.55	.35
466	A57	40c Hard corals	1.30	.75
467	A57	50c Feather stars	1.60	.95
468	A57	60c Staghorn corals	1.90	1.10
		Nos. 465-468 (4)	5.35	3.15

Birds
A64

5c, Jungle fowl. 10c, White tern. 15c, Brown noddy. 20c, Phoenix petrel. 25c, Pacific golden plover. 30c, Crested tern. 35c, Sooty tern. 40c, Bristle-thighed curlew. 45c, Eastern bar-tailed godwit. 50c, Reef heron. 55c, Greater frigatebird. 60c, Red-footed booby. 70c, Red-necked stint. $1, New Zealand long-tailed cuckoo. $2, Red-tailed tropicbird. $5, Banded rail.

1988, Mar. 2				**Perf. 15**
469	A64	5c multicolored	.25	.25
470	A64	10c multicolored	.25	.25
471	A64	15c multicolored	.25	.25
472	A64	20c multicolored	.25	.25
473	A64	25c multicolored	.25	.25
474	A64	30c multicolored	.30	.30
475	A64	35c multicolored	.35	.35
476	A64	40c multicolored	.40	.40
477	A64	45c multicolored	.45	.45
478	A64	50c multicolored	.50	.50
479	A64	55c multicolored	.55	.55
480	A64	60c multicolored	.65	.65
481	A64	70c multicolored	.75	.75
482	A64	$1 multicolored	1.25	1.25
483	A64	$2 multicolored	2.25	2.25
484	A64	$5 multicolored	5.50	5.50
		Nos. 469-484 (16)	14.20	14.20

For overprints see Nos. 676-679, 796-799, O33-O48.

Intl. Red Cross and Red Crescent Organizations, 125th Anniv. — A65

15c, Jean-Henri Dunant. 40c, Junior Red Cross. 50c, Care for the handicapped. 60c, First aid training. $1, Lecture.

Perf. 12½

1988, May 9   Litho.   Unwmk.
485	A65	15c multicolored	.25	.25
486	A65	40c multicolored	.25	.25
487	A65	50c multicolored	.25	.25
488	A65	60c multicolored	.30	.30
		Nos. 485-488 (4)	1.05	1.05

Souvenir Sheet
489	A65	$1.50 multicolored	2.25	2.25

A66

Voyages of Capt. Cook — A67

Designs: 20c, HMS *Endeavour* (starboard side). 40c, *Endeavour* (stern). 50c, Landing, Tahiti, 1769, vert. 60c, Maori chief, vert. 80c, *Resolution* and native Hawaiian sail ship. $1, Cook, by Sir Nathaniel Dance-Holland (1735-1811), vert. $2.50, Antarctic icebergs surrounding the *Resolution.*

1988, June 15   Litho.   Perf. 12½
490-495	A66	Set of 6	4.50 4.50

Souvenir Sheet
496	A67	$2.50 shown	10.00 10.00

Fungi — A68

40c, Ganoderma applanatum. 50c, Pseudoepicoccum cocos. 60c, Rigidoporus zonalis. 90c, Rigidoporus microporus.

1988, July 25   Litho.   Perf. 15
497	A68	40c multicolored	1.00	1.00
498	A68	50c multicolored	1.20	1.20
499	A68	60c multicolored	1.40	1.40
500	A68	90c multicolored	2.00	2.00
		Nos. 497-500 (4)	5.60	5.60

See Nos. 520-523.

1988 Summer Olympics, Seoul — A69

Perf. 12½

1988, Aug. 19   Litho.   Unwmk.
501	A69	10c Rifles, target	.30	.30
502	A69	20c Judo	.55	.55
503	A69	40c One-man kayak	1.20	1.20
504	A69	60c Swimming	1.75	1.75
505	A69	80c Yachting	2.25	2.25
506	A69	$1 Balance beam	3.25	3.25
		Nos. 501-506 (6)	9.30	9.30

Natl. Independence, 10th
Anniv. — A70

Wmk. 380

1988, Sept. 28   Litho.   Perf. 14
507	A70	60c Queen Elizabeth in boat	1.00	1.00
a.		Souvenir sheet of 1	1.00	1.00
508	A70	90c In sedan chair	1.50	1.50
a.		Souvenir sheet of 1	1.50	1.50
509	A70	$1 shown	1.75	1.75
a.		Souvenir sheet of 1	1.75	1.75
510	A70	$1.20 Seated at dais	2.10	2.10
a.		Souvenir sheet of 1	2.10	2.10
		Nos. 507-510 (4)	6.35	6.35

Nos. 507-508 and 510 vert.

Christmas — A71

Unwmk.

1988, Dec. 5   Litho.   Perf. 14
511	A71	15c Mary	.35	.35
512	A71	40c Christ child	.90	.90
513	A71	60c Joseph	1.25	1.25
		Nos. 511-513 (3)	2.50	2.50

Souvenir Sheet
514	A71	$1.50 Heraldic angel	2.50	2.50

Palm-frond or Pandanus-leaf
Skirts — A72

1989, Mar. 31   Litho.   Perf. 14
515	A72	40c multi	.80	.80
516	A72	50c multi, diff.	1.00	1.00
517	A72	60c multi, diff.	1.20	1.20
518	A72	90c multi, diff.	1.75	1.75
		Nos. 515-518 (4)	4.75	4.75

Souvenir Sheet
519	A72	$1.50 multi, vert.	3.50	3.50

Fungi Type of 1988

40c, Trametes muelleri. 50c, Pestalotiopsis palmarum. 60c, Trametes cingulata. 90c, Schizophyllum commune.

1989, May 24   Litho.   Perf. 14
520	A68	40c multicolored	1.00	1.00
521	A68	50c multicolored	2.25	2.25
522	A68	60c multicolored	2.75	2.75
523	A68	90c multicolored	4.00	4.00
		Nos. 520-523 (4)	10.00	10.00

Marine Life Type of 1986

40c, Pennant coralfish. 50c, Anemone fish. 60c, Batfish. 90c, Threadfin coralfish.

1989, July 31   Litho.   Perf. 14
524	A57	40c multicolored	1.50	1.50
525	A57	50c multicolored	1.90	1.90
526	A57	60c multicolored	2.25	2.25
527	A57	90c multicolored	4.00	4.00
a.		Miniature sheet of 4, #524-527	9.75	9.75
		Nos. 524-527 (4)	9.65	9.65

Souvenir Sheet

Maiden Voyage of M.V. *Nivaga II*,
1988 — A73

1989, Oct. 9   Litho.   Perf. 14
528	A73	$1.50 multicolored	5.75	5.75

Christmas — A74

Unwmk.

1989, Nov. 29   Litho.   Perf. 14
529	A74	40c Conch shell	.85	.85
530	A74	50c Flower bouquet	1.20	1.20
531	A74	60c Germinated coconut	1.35	1.35
532	A74	90c Shell jewelry	1.90	1.90
		Nos. 529-532 (4)	5.30	5.30

Tropical
Trees — A75

15c, Cocus nucifera. 30c, Rhizophora samoensis. 40c, Messerschmidia argentea. 50c, Pandanus tectorius. 60c, Hernandia nymphaeifolia. 90c, Pisonia grandis.

1990, Feb. 28   Litho.   Perf. 14½
533	A75	15c multicolored	.55	.55
534	A75	30c multicolored	1.00	1.00
535	A75	40c multicolored	1.25	1.25
536	A75	50c multicolored	1.50	1.50
537	A75	60c multicolored	1.90	1.90
538	A75	90c multicolored	3.25	3.25
		Nos. 533-538 (6)	9.45	9.45

Penny
Black,
150th
Anniv.
A76

1990, May 3   Litho.   Perf. 14
539	A76	15c multicolored	.90	.90
540	A76	40c multicolored	2.40	2.40
541	A76	90c multicolored	5.75	5.75
		Nos. 539-541 (3)	9.05	9.05

Souvenir Sheet
542	A76	$2 multicolored	7.50	7.50

Stamp World London '90.

World
War II
Ships
A77

Designs: 15c, Japanese merchant conversion, 1940. 30c, USS Unimak, seaplane tender, 1944. 40c, Amagari, Japanese Hubuki class, 1942. 50c, AO-24 USS Platte, Nov. 1, 1943. 60c, Japanese Shumushu Class (Type A) escort. 90c, CV-22 USS Independence.

1990
543-548	A77	Set of 6	14.50 14.50

Flowers — A78

1990, Sept. 21   Litho.   Perf. 14½
549	A78	15c Erythrina fusca	.30	.30
550	A78	30c Capparis cordifolia	.60	.60
551	A78	40c Portulaca pilosa	.80	.80
552	A78	50c Cordia subcordata	.95	.95
553	A78	60c Scaevola taccada	1.15	1.15
554	A78	90c Suriana maritima	1.75	1.75
		Nos. 549-554 (6)	5.55	5.55

UN Development Program, 40th
Anniv. — A79

40c, Surveyor. 60c, Communications station. $1.20, Fishing boat Te Tautai.

1990, Nov. 20   Litho.   Perf. 14
555	A79	40c multicolored	1.40	1.40
556	A79	60c multicolored	1.90	1.90
557	A79	$1.20 multicolored	3.75	3.75
		Nos. 555-557 (3)	7.05	7.05

Christmas
A80

1990, Nov. 20
558	A80	15c Mary and Joseph	.45	.45
559	A80	40c Nativity	1.25	1.25
560	A80	60c Shepherds	1.90	1.90
561	A80	90c Three Kings	2.75	2.75
		Nos. 558-561 (4)	6.35	6.35

Seashells — A81

40c, Murex ramosus. 50c, Conus marmoreus. 60c, Trochus niloticus. $1.50, Cypraea mappa.

1991, Jan. 18   Litho.   Perf. 14
562	A81	40c multicolored	1.30	1.30
563	A81	50c multicolored	1.75	1.75
564	A81	60c multicolored	1.90	1.90
565	A81	$1.50 multicolored	4.25	4.25
		Nos. 562-565 (4)	9.20	9.20

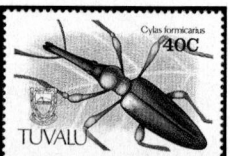

Insects
A82

40c, Cylas formicarius. 50c, Heliothis armiger. 60c, Spodoptera litura. $1.50, Agrius convolvuli.

1991, Mar. 22 Litho. Perf. 14
566	A82	40c multicolored	1.50	1.50
567	A82	50c multicolored	2.00	2.00
568	A82	60c multicolored	2.25	2.25
569	A82	$1.50 multicolored	5.50	5.50
		Nos. 566-569 (4)	11.25	11.25

A83

Endangered marine life.

1991, May 31 Litho. Perf. 14
570	A83	40c Green turtle	1.25	1.25
571	A83	50c Humpback whale	1.50	1.50
572	A83	60c Hawksbill turtle	2.00	2.00
573	A83	$1.50 Sperm whale	4.75	4.75
		Nos. 570-573 (4)	9.50	9.50

A84

1991, July 31 Litho. Perf. 14
574	A84	40c Soccer	1.60	1.60
575	A84	50c Volleyball	2.10	2.10
576	A84	60c Lawn tennis	2.50	2.50
577	A84	$1.50 Cricket	5.75	5.75
		Nos. 574-577 (4)	11.95	11.95

9th South Pacific Games.

World War II Ships A85

1991, Oct. 15 Litho. Perf. 14
578	A85	40c USS Tennessee	3.00	2.25
579	A85	50c IJN Haguro	3.25	3.00
580	A85	60c HMS Achilles	4.00	3.25
581	A85	$1.50 USS North Carolina	8.50	8.50
		Nos. 578-581 (4)	18.75	17.00

A86

Christmas: various traditional dance costumes.

1991, Dec. 13
582	A86	40c multicolored	1.50	1.50
583	A86	50c multicolored	1.90	1.90
584	A86	60c multicolored	2.25	2.25
585	A86	$1.50 multicolored	5.75	5.75
		Nos. 582-585 (4)	11.40	11.40

A87

Constellations.

1992, Jan. 29 Litho. Perf. 14
586	A87	40c Southern Fish	1.60	1.60
587	A87	50c Scorpio	2.00	2.00
588	A87	60c Sagittarius	2.50	2.50
589	A87	$1.50 Southern Cross	6.00	6.00
		Nos. 586-589 (4)	12.10	12.10

British Annexation of the Gilbert & Ellice Islands, Cent. — A88

1992, Mar. 23 Litho. Perf. 14
590	A88	40c King George VI	1.60	1.60
591	A88	50c King George V	1.90	1.90
592	A88	60c King Edward VII	2.50	2.50
593	A88	$1.50 Queen Victoria	6.50	6.50
		Nos. 590-593 (4)	12.50	12.50

Discovery of America, 500th Anniv. A89

Columbus and: 40c, Queen Isabella & King Ferdinand of Spain. 50c, Polynesians. 60c, South American Indians. $1.50, North American Indians.

1992, May 22 Litho. Perf. 14
594	A89	40c black & dk blue	1.10	1.10
595	A89	50c black & dk plum	1.20	1.20
596	A89	60c black & dk green	1.40	1.40
597	A89	$1.50 black & dk purple	3.25	3.25
		Nos. 594-597 (4)	6.95	6.95

World Columbian Stamp Expo '92, Chicago.

Fish A90

Designs: 15c, Bluespot butterflyfish. 20c, Pink parrotfish. 25c, Stripe surgeonfish. 30c, Moon wrasse, 35c, Harlequin filefish. 40c, Bird wrasse. 45c, Black-finned pigfish. 50c, Blue-green chromis. 60c, Hump-headed Maori wrasse. 70c, Ornate coralfish, vert. 90c, Saddled butterflyfish, vert. $1, Vagabond butterflyfish, vert. $2, Longfin bannerfish, vert. $3, Moorish idol, vert.

1992, July 15
598-611	A90	Set of 14	14.50 14.50

For overprints & surcharge see #629-632, 716.

1992 Summer Olympics, Barcelona — A91

1992, July 27 Litho. Perf. 14
612	A91	40c Discus	.90	.90
613	A91	50c Javelin	1.15	1.15
614	A91	60c Shotput	1.60	1.60
615	A91	$1.50 Track & field	4.00	4.00
		Nos. 612-615 (4)	7.65	7.65

Souvenir Sheet
616	A91	$2 Olympic stadium	5.00	5.00

Blue Coral A92

Various views of blue coral.

1992, Sept. 1
617	A92	10c multicolored	1.25	1.25
618	A92	25c multicolored	2.75	2.75
619	A92	30c multicolored	2.75	2.75
620	A92	35c multicolored	3.25	3.25
		Nos. 617-620 (4)	10.00	10.00

World Wildlife Fund.

Christmas — A93

Designs: 40c, Fishermen seeing angel. 50c, Fishermen sailing canoes toward island. 60c, Adoration of the fishermen. $1.50, Flowers, shell necklaces.

1992, Dec. 25 Litho. Perf. 14
621	A93	40c multicolored	.70	.70
622	A93	50c multicolored	.85	.85
623	A93	60c multicolored	.95	.95
624	A93	$1.50 multicolored	2.50	2.50
		Nos. 621-624 (4)	5.00	5.00

Wild Flowers — A94

40c, Calophyllum inophyllum. 50c, Hibiscus tiliaceus. 60c, Lantana camara. $1.50, Plumeria rubra.

1993, Feb. 2 Litho. Perf. 14
625	A94	40c multicolored	.95	.95
626	A94	50c multicolored	1.20	1.20
627	A94	60c multicolored	1.30	1.30
628	A94	$1.50 multicolored	3.00	3.00
		Nos. 625-628 (4)	6.45	6.45

Nos. 601, 603, & 605-606 Ovptd.

1992, Sept. 1 Litho. Perf. 14
629	A90	30c on #601	1.15	1.15
630	A90	40c on #603	1.40	1.40
631	A90	50c on #605	2.10	2.10
632	A90	60c on #606	2.25	2.25
		Nos. 629-632 (4)	6.90	6.90

World War II in the Pacific, 50th Anniv. A95

40c, Japanese bombers. 50c, Anti-aircraft gun, vert. 60c, Using flame thrower. $1.50, Map of Funafuti Atoll, vert.

1993, Apr. 23 Litho. Perf. 14
633	A95	40c multicolored	1.60	1.60
634	A95	50c multicolored	1.90	1.90
635	A95	60c multicolored	2.25	2.25
636	A95	$1.50 multicolored	6.25	6.25
		Nos. 633-636 (4)	12.00	12.00

Souvenir Sheet

Indopex '93 — A96

1993, May 29 Perf. 14x14½
637	A96	$1.50 Cepora perimale	5.75	5.75

Marine Life A97

1993, June 29 Litho. Perf. 14
638	A97	40c Giant clam	.80	.80
639	A97	50c Anemone crab	1.00	1.00
640	A97	60c Octopus	1.25	1.25
641	A97	$1.50 Green turtle	3.00	3.00
		Nos. 638-641 (4)	6.05	6.05

Coronation of Queen Elizabeth II, 40th Anniv. — A98

Queen: 40c, Riding in parade with Prince Phillip. 50c, Drinking coconut milk. 60c, Holding umbrella. $1.50, With natives. $2, Coronation ceremony.

1993, July 5
642	A98	40c multicolored	.70	.70
643	A98	50c multicolored	.90	.90
644	A98	60c multicolored	1.15	1.15
645	A98	$1.50 multicolored	2.75	2.75
		Nos. 642-645 (4)	5.50	5.50

Souvenir Sheet
646	A98	$2 multicolored	7.75	7.75

Souvenir Sheet

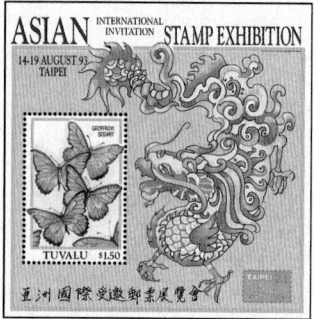

Taipei '93 — A99

Litho. & Typo.
1993, Aug. 14   *Perf. 14½x14*
647 A99 $1.50 Geoffroyi godart   5.25 5.25

Souvenir Sheet

Bangkok '93 — A100

1993, Oct. 1   **Litho.**   *Perf. 14x14½*
648 A100 $1.50 Paradisea staud-
inger   3.50 3.50

Greenhouse
Effect — A101

Beach scene with: 40c, Sun at UR. 50c, Sun
at UL. 60c, Crab on beach. $1.50, Sea gull in
flight.

1993, Nov. 2   **Litho.**   *Perf. 13½*
649 A101 40c multicolored   .65   .65
650 A101 50c multicolored   .85   .85
651 A101 60c multicolored   1.10 1.10
652 A101 $1.50 multicolored   2.60 2.60
   a.   Souvenir sheet of 4, #649-
      652, perf. 14½x14   6.50 6.50
     Nos. 649-652 (4)   5.20 5.20

Christmas — A102

50c, Candle, flowers. 60c, Angel, flowers.
$1.50, Palm tree, candles.

1993, Dec. 6   **Litho.**   *Perf. 13½*
653 A102 40c shown   .75   .75
654 A102 50c multicolored   .90   .90
655 A102 60c multicolored   1.15 1.15
656 A102 $1.50 multicolored   2.75 2.75
     Nos. 653-656 (4)   5.55 5.55

Souvenir Sheet

Hong Kong '94 — A103

1994, Feb. 18   *Perf. 14½x14*
657 A103 $2 Monarch   5.25   5.25

Scenic
Views
A104

1994, Feb. 18   **Litho.**   *Perf. 14*
658 A104 40c shown   .90   .90
659 A104 50c Beach, trees,
     diff.   1.10 1.10
660 A104 60c Boats, ocean   1.25 1.25
661 A104 $1.50 Boats, beach   3.25 3.25
     Nos. 658-661 (4)   6.50 6.50

New Year 1994
(Year of the
Dog) — A105

40c, Irish setter. 50c, Golden retriever. 60c,
West Highland terrier. $1.50, German
shepherd.

1994, Apr. 23   **Litho.**   *Perf. 14*
662 A105 40c multicolored   1.00 1.00
663 A105 50c multicolored   1.10 1.10
664 A105 60c multicolored   1.40 1.40
665 A105 $1.50 multicolored   3.50 3.50
     Nos. 662-665 (4)   7.00 7.00

A106

1994, June 7
666 A106   40c Australia   .60   .60
667 A106   50c England   .80   .80
668 A106   60c Argentina   .90   .90
669 A106 $1.50 Germany   2.40 2.40
     Nos. 666-669 (4)   4.70 4.70

Souvenir Sheet

670 A106 $2 US   6.25 6.25
1994 World Cup Soccer Championships, US.

A107

Seashells.

1994, Aug. 16   **Litho.**   *Perf. 14*
671 A107   40c Umbonium gi-
     ganteum   .90   .90
672 A107   50c Turbo petholatus   1.10 1.10
673 A107   60c Planaxis savignyi   1.35 1.35
674 A107 $1.50 Hydatina physis   3.25 3.25
     Nos. 671-674 (4)   6.60 6.60

Souvenir Sheet

PHILAKOREA '94 — A108

1994, Aug. 16
675 A108 $1.50 Pekinese dog   4.25 4.25

Nos. 469-
470, 476-
477
Ovptd.

1994, Aug. 31   **Litho.**   *Perf. 15*
676 A64   5c multicolored   .30   .30
677 A64 10c multicolored   .30   .30
678 A64 40c multicolored   .90   .90
679 A64 45c multicolored   1.00 1.00
     Nos. 676-679 (4)   2.50 2.50

First Manned Moon Landing, 25th
Anniv. — A109

a, 40c, Saturn V. b, 50c, Apollo 11. c, 60c,
Neil Armstrong. d, $1.50, Splash-down.

1994, Oct. 31   *Perf. 14*
680 A109   Strip of 4, #a.-d.   6.00 6.00

Christmas — A110

40c, Boys playing in water. 50c, Islanders,
fish being gathered. 60c, People seated under
canopy, food. $1.50, Traditional dancers.

1994, Dec. 15   **Litho.**   *Perf. 14*
681 A110   40c multicolored   .80   .80
682 A110   50c multicolored   .90   .90
683 A110   60c multicolored   1.10 1.10
684 A110 $1.50 multicolored   3.00 3.00
     Nos. 681-684 (4)   5.80 5.80

New Year
1995
(Year of
the Boar)
A111

40c, One pig. 50c, Pig, piglet. 60c, Three
pigs. $1.50, Sow nursing litter.

1995, Jan. 30   **Litho.**   *Perf. 14*
685-688 A111   Set of 4   4.75 4.75

FAO,
50th
Anniv.
A112

40c, Men with vegetables in wheelbarrow.
50c, Man with sack of vegetables. 60c, Girl
cleaning vegetables. $1.50, Girl mixing food.

1995, Mar. 31   **Litho.**   *Perf. 14*
689-692 A112   Set of 4   5.75 5.75

Visit
South
Pacific
Year
A113

1995, May 26   **Litho.**   *Perf. 14*
693 A113 40c shown   .65   .65
694 A113 50c Sailboat   .80   .80
695 A113 60c Hut   .95   .95
696 A113 $1.50 Home, beach   2.40 2.40
     Nos. 693-696 (4)   4.80 4.80

Pacific
Coastal
Orchids
A114

40c, Dendrobium comptonii. 50c, Dendrobium aff. involutum. 60c, Dendrobium
rarum. $1.50, Grammatophyllum scriptum.

1995, July 28   **Litho.**   *Perf. 14*
697-700 A114   Set of 4   6.25 6.25

Souvenir Sheet

Jakarta '95, Asian World Stamp
Exhibition — A116

1995, Aug. 19   **Litho.**   *Perf. 12*
702 A116 $1 Traditional dancer   2.50 2.50
     For overprint see No. 715.

Souvenir Sheet

Singapore '95 World Stamp
Exhibition — A117

1995, Sept. 1
703 A117 $1 Phalaenopsis
amabillis 2.75 2.75

End of
World
War II,
50th
Anniv.
A118

40c, Soldier with sub-machine gun, map of
Japan, Tuvalu. 50c, Soldier holding rifle, landing exercise on beach. 60c, US Marine, offshore air and sea battle. $1.50, Soldier firing
rifle, atomic mushroom cloud.

1995, Aug. 19 Litho. **Perf. 14**
704-707 A118 Set of 4 9.50 9.50

Souvenir Sheet

UN, 50th Anniv. — A119

a, Rowing in outrigger canoes. b, UN New
York headquarters.

1995, Oct. 24 **Perf. 14½**
708 A119 $1 Sheet of 2, #a.-b. 4.00 4.00

Christmas — A120

Scores and verses to Christmas carols and:
40c, Map of island, "Silent Night." 50c, Boy
carolers, "O Come All Ye Faithful." 60c, Girl
carolers, "The First Noel." $1.50, Angel, "Hark
the Herald Angels Sing."

1995, Dec. 15 Litho. **Perf. 14**
709-712 A120 Set of 4 5.75 5.75

Miniature Sheet

Independence, First Tuvalu Postage
Stamps, 20th Anniv. — A121

a, 40c, #16. b, 60c, #17. c, $1, #18.

1996, Jan. 1 Litho. **Perf. 14**
713 A121 Sheet of 3, #a.-c. 5.00 5.00

Miniature Sheet

New Year 1996 (Year of the
Rat) — A122

Stylized rats: a, Looking right. b, Facing left,
drinking from container.

1996, Feb. 23 Litho. **Perf. 14x14½**
714 A122 50c Sheet of 2, #a.-b. 5.00 5.00
   c. Ovptd. in sheet margin 5.00 5.00
   d. With added inscription in sheet
      margin 5.00 5.00

No. 714c is overprinted in sheet margin with
exhibition emblem of Hongpex '96.
No. 714d is inscribed in sheet margin with
two exhibition emblems of China '96. Issued:
5/18.

No. 702
Ovptd. in Gold

1996, Mar. 21 Litho. **Perf. 12**
715 A116 $1 multicolored 2.40 2.40

No. 715 also contains same overprint in
sheet margin.

No. 604 Surcharged in Black, Red & Blue

1996, Oct. 21 Litho. **Perf. 14**
716 A90 $1 on 45c multi 2.10 2.10

1996
Summer
Olympic
Games,
Atlanta
A123

1996, Sept. 11 Litho. **Perf. 14**
717 A123 40c Beach volleyball .55 .55
718 A123 50c Swimming .70 .70
719 A123 60c Weight lifting .85 .85
720 A123 $1.50 David Tua, boxer 2.10 2.10
   Nos. 717-720 (4) 4.20 4.20

UNICEF,
50th
Anniv.
A124

1996, Oct. 28
721 A124 40c Immunization .55 .55
722 A124 50c Education for life .65 .65
723 A124 60c Water tank pro-
            ject .80 .80
724 A124 $1.50 Hydroponic farm 2.25 2.25
   Nos. 721-724 (4) 4.25 4.25

Christmas
A125

Designs: 40c, Magi following star. 50c,
Shepherds seeing star. 60c, Adoration of the
Magi. $1.50, Nativity scene.

1996, Nov. 25 **Perf. 14½**
725 A125 40c multicolored .65 .65
726 A125 50c multicolored .75 .75
727 A125 60c multicolored .90 .90
728 A125 $1.50 multicolored 2.25 2.25
   Nos. 725-728 (4) 4.55 4.55

Fish
A126

25c, Bluetail mullet. 30c, Queen fish leather-
skin. 40c, Paddletail. 45c, Long-nose emperor.
50c, Long-snouted unicornfish. 55c, Brigham's
snapper. 60c, Red bass. 70c, Red jobfish.
90c, Leopard flounder. $1, Red snapper. $2,
Longtail snapper. $3, Black trevally.

1997, Mar. 15 **Perf. 14**
729 A126 25c multicolored .35 .35
730 A126 30c multicolored .40 .40
731 A126 40c multicolored .55 .55
732 A126 45c multicolored .65 .70
   Complete bklt., 4 ea #729-
   732 10.00
733 A126 50c multicolored .70 .70
734 A126 55c multicolored .75 .75
735 A126 60c multicolored .85 .85
736 A126 70c multicolored .90 .90
737 A126 90c multicolored 1.25 1.25
738 A126 $1 multicolored 1.30 1.30
739 A126 $2 multicolored 2.60 2.60
   a. Souv. sheet of 1, wmk. 373 4.00 4.00
740 A126 $3 multicolored 4.00 4.00
   Nos. 729-740 (12) 14.30 14.35

No. 739a for return of Hong Kong to China,
July 1, 1997.

Souvenir Sheet

New Year 1997 (Year of the
Ox) — A127

1997, June 20 Litho. **Perf. 14**
741 A127 $2 multicolored 6.00 6.00

Hong Kong '97.

Ducks
and
Drakes
A128

1997, May 29 Litho. **Perf. 14**
742 A128 40c White pekin .60 .60
743 A128 50c Muscovy .75 .75
744 A128 60c Pacific black .90 .90
745 A128 $1.50 Mandarin 2.25 2.25
   Nos. 742-745 (4) 4.50 4.50

PACIFIC 97.

Domestic Cats — A129

40c, Korat king. 50c, Long-haired ginger kitten. 60c, Shaded cameo. $1.50, American
Maine coon.

1997, June 20
746 A129 40c multicolored .70 .70
747 A129 50c multicolored .85 .85
748 A129 60c multicolored 1.00 1.00
749 A129 $1.50 multicolored 2.50 2.50
   Nos. 746-749 (4) 5.05 5.05

Queen Elizabeth II and Prince Philip,
50th Wedding Anniv. — A130

Designs: No. 750, Queen, Prince standing
in open vehicle. No. 751, Queen in yellow hat.
No. 752, Queen holding umbrella. No. 753,
Queen reading, Prince up close. No. 754,
Three pictures of Queen. No. 755, Prince in
top hat, Queen.
$2, Queen, Prince riding in open carriage,
horiz.

Wmk. 373
1997, Oct. 1 Litho. **Perf. 14½**
750 40c multicolored .50 .50
751 40c multicolored .50 .50
   a. A130 Pair, #750-751 1.00 1.00
752 50c multicolored .65 .65
753 50c multicolored .65 .65
   a. A130 Pair, #752-753 1.30 1.30

754		60c multicolored	.75	.75
755		60c multicolored	.75	.75
a.		A130 Pair, #754-755	1.50	1.50
		Nos. 750-755 (6)	3.80	3.80

Souvenir Sheet

756	A130	$2 multicolored	3.00	3.00

No. 756 contains one 38x32mm stamp.

Traditional Activities — A131

Christmas: 40c, Turtle hunting. 50c, Pole fishing. 60c, Canoe racing. $1.50, Traditional dance.

Perf. 13½x13

1997, Nov. 25　Litho.　Wmk. 373

757	A131	40c multicolored	.55	.55
758	A131	50c multicolored	.65	.65
759	A131	60c multicolored	.80	.80
760	A131	$1.50 multicolored	2.00	2.00
		Nos. 757-760 (4)	4.00	4.00

Souvenir Sheet

New Year 1998 (Year of the Tiger) — A132

1998, Feb. 2　Litho.　Perf. 13

761	A132	$1.40 multicolored	4.00	4.00

Diana, Princess of Wales (1961-97)
Common Design Type

Designs: a, Wearing red evening dress. b, Wearing black evening dress. c, Wearing tiara. d, With collar up on coat.

Perf. 14½x14

1998, Mar. 31　Litho.　Wmk. 373

762	CD355	80c Sheet of 4, #a.-d.	4.00	4.00

No. 762 sold for $3.20 + 20c, with surtax from international sales being donated to the Princess Diana Memorial Fund and surtax from national sales being donated to designated local charity.

Royal Air Force, 80th Anniv.
Common Design Type of 1993 Reinscribed

Designs: 40c, Hawker Woodcock. 50c, Vickers Victoria. 60c, Bristol Brigand $1.50, De Haviland DHC 1 Chipmunk.
No. 767: a, Sopwith Pup. b, Armstrong Whitworth FK8. c, North American Harvard. d, Vultee Vengeance.

Wmk. 384

1998, Apr. 1　Litho.　Perf. 13½

763	CD350	40c multicolored	.70	.70
764	CD350	50c multicolored	.80	.80
765	CD350	60c multicolored	1.00	1.00
766	CD350	$1.50 multicolored	2.25	2.25
		Nos. 763-766 (4)	4.75	4.75

Souvenir Sheet

767	CD350	$1 Sheet of 4, #a.-d.	5.00	5.00

Ships A133

Designs: 40c, "Los Reyes," "Santiago," 1567. 50c, "Morning Star," missionary topsail schooner, 1867. 60c, "The Light," brigantine of Church of the Resurrection, 1870. $1.50, New Zealand missionary schooner, 1900.

Wmk. 373

1998, May 19　Litho.　Perf. 14

768	A133	40c multicolored	.50	.50
769	A133	50c multicolored	.60	.60
770	A133	60c multicolored	.75	.75
771	A133	$1.50 multicolored	1.60	1.60
		Nos. 768-771 (4)	3.45	3.45

Dolphins and Porpoises — A134

40c, Bottlenose dolphin. 50c, Dall's porpoise. 60c, Harbor porpoise. $1.50, Common dolphin.

Perf. 13½x13

1998, Aug. 21　Litho.　Wmk. 384

772	A134	40c multicolored	.50	.50
773	A134	50c multicolored	.65	.65
774	A134	60c multicolored	.80	.80
775	A134	$1.50 multicolored	2.00	2.00
		Nos. 772-775 (4)	3.95	3.95

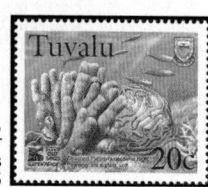

Greenpeace, Save Our Seas A135

Marine life: 20c, Bleached platygyra daedalea, psammocora digitata. 30c, Bleached acropora robusta. 50c, Bleached acropora hyacinthus. $1, Bleached acropora danai, montastrea curta.
$1.50, Bleached seriatopora, bleached stylophora.

Wmk. 373

1998, Nov. 6　Litho.　Perf. 14½

776	A135	20c multicolored	.30	.30
777	A135	30c multicolored	.50	.50
778	A135	50c multicolored	.85	.85
779	A135	$1 multicolored	1.40	1.40
		Nos. 776-779 (4)	3.05	3.05

Souvenir Sheet

780	A135	$1.50 multicolored	2.50	2.50

Intl. Year of the Ocean (#780).

Christmas — A136

40c, Flight into Egypt. 50c, Angel speaking to shepherds. 60c, Nativity. $1.50, Adoration of the Magi.

1998, Nov. 20　Perf. 14½x14

781	A136	40c multicolored	.55	.55
782	A136	50c multicolored	.70	.70
783	A136	60c multicolored	.80	.80
784	A136	$1.50 multicolored	2.00	2.00
		Nos. 781-784 (4)	4.05	4.05

Independence, 20th Anniv. — A137

Stamps on stamps, Prime Ministers: 40c, #722, Bikenibeu Paeniu. 60c, Kamuta Latasi. 90c, Tomasi Puapua. $1.50, Design like #166, Toaripi Lauti.

Wmk. 384

1998, Oct. 1　Litho.　Perf. 14

785	A137	40c multicolored	.55	.55
786	A137	60c multicolored	.85	.85
787	A137	90c multicolored	1.10	1.10

788	A137	$1.50 multicolored	1.75	1.75
a.		Souvenir sheet, #785-788	4.25	4.25
		Nos. 785-788 (4)	4.25	4.25

Souvenir Sheet

New Year 1999 (Year of the Rabbit) — A138

Perf. 14½x14

1999, Feb. 16　Litho.　Wmk. 373

789	A138	$2 multicolored	4.50	4.50

Australia '99, World Stamp Expo A139

Maritime history: 40c, Heemskerck, 1642. 50c, HMS Endeavour, 1769. 90c, PS Sophie Jane, 1831. $1.50, P&O SS Chusan, 1852. $2, HM Brig "Supply."

1999, Mar. 19　Perf. 14

790	A139	40c multicolored	.60	.60
791	A139	50c multicolored	.70	.70
792	A139	90c multicolored	1.40	1.40
793	A139	$1.50 multicolored	2.10	2.10
		Nos. 790-793 (4)	4.80	4.80

Souvenir Sheet

794	A139	$2 multicolored	2.75	2.75

Nos. 472, 475, 479, 482 Ovptd.

1999, June 11　Litho.　Perf. 15

796	A64	20c on #472	.30	.30
797	A64	35c on #475	.50	.50
798	A64	55c on #479	.80	.80
799	A64	$1 on #482	1.40	1.40
		Nos. 796-799 (4)	3.00	3.00

50% of the sales of Nos. 796-799 will be donated to the Kosovo Relief Fund.

1st Manned Moon Landing, 30th Anniv.
Common Design Type

40c, Lift-off. 60c, Lunar module prepares to touchdown. 90c, Ascent stage approaches Command module. $1.50, Recovery. $2, Looking at earth from moon.

Perf. 14x13¾

1999, July 20　Litho.　Wmk. 384

800	CD357	40c multicolored	.60	.60
801	CD357	60c multicolored	.80	.80
802	CD357	90c multicolored	1.40	1.40
803	CD357	$1.50 multicolored	1.90	1.90
		Nos. 800-803 (4)	4.70	4.70

Souvenir Sheet
Perf. 14

804	CD357	$2 multicolored	2.75	2.75

No. 804 contains one circular stamp 40mm in diameter.

Queen Mother's Century
Common Design Type

Queen Mother: 40c, With King George VI inspecting bomb damage. 60c, With daughters at Balmoral. 90c, With Princes Harry and William, 95th birthday. $1.50, As colonel-in-chief of Queen's Dragoon Guards. $2, Age 6 photo, photo of Yuri Gagarin.

Wmk. 384

1999, Aug. 16　Litho.　Perf. 13½

805	CD358	40c multicolored	.55	.55
806	CD358	60c multicolored	.80	.80

807	CD358	90c multicolored	1.30	1.30
808	CD358	$1.50 multicolored	2.00	2.00
		Nos. 805-808 (4)	4.65	4.65

Souvenir Sheet

809	CD358	$2 multicolored	4.00	4.00

Flowers — A141

No. 810: a, Fetai. b, Ateate. c, Portulacacae lueta. d, Tamoloc. e, Beach pea. f, Pomegranate (red letters).
No. 811: a, Cup of gold. b, Rock rose. c, Bower plant. d, Lavender star. e, Hybrid mandevilla. f, Pomegranate (white letters).
No. 812, Scrambled eggs, vert.

Perf. 13¾

1999, Nov. 22　Litho.　Unwmk.

810	A141	90c Sheet of 6, #a.-f.	7.75	7.75
811	A141	90c Sheet of 6, #a.-f.	7.75	7.75

Souvenir Sheet

812	A141	$3 multi	5.50	5.50

A142

Millennium — A143

No. 813, Lady of peace with frame.
No. 814: a, Like No. 813, no frame. b, Olive branch. c, Dove. d, Lion. e, Lamb. f, War crowning peace.
No. 815: Sun on horizon, clock, computer keyboard.

Perf. 14½x14¼

1999, Dec. 31　Litho.

813	A142	90c multi	1.25	1.25
814	A142	90c Sheet of 6, #a.-f.	9.00	9.00

Souvenir Sheet
Perf. 14

815	A143	$2 multi	3.00	3.00

No. 813 printed in sheets of 6.

Worldwide Fund for Nature — A144

Sand tiger shark: a, 10c, Close-up of head. b, 30c, Facing left. c, 50c, Swimming above seaweed. d, 60c, Three sharks.

Perf. 13¼x13½
2000, Feb. 7   **Litho.**   **Unwmk.**
816 A144 Strip of 4, #a.-d.   3.00 3.00
   e.   Souvenir sheet, 2 #816   9.50 9.50
Souvenir Sheet
Stamps Without WWF Emblem
817 A144 Sheet of 4, #a.-d   2.75 2.75

Marine Life and Birds — A145

No. 818, each 90c: a, Common tern. b, White-tailed tropicbird. c, Red emperor snapper. d, Clown triggerfish. e, Longfin bannerfish. f, Harlequin tuskfish.

No. 819, each 90c: a, Wilson's storm petrel. b, Common dolphin. c, Spotted seahorse. d, Threeband demoiselle. e, Coral hind. f, Palette surgeonfish.

No. 820, each 90c: a, Great frigatebird. b, Brown booby. c, Dugong. d, Red knot. e, Common starfish. f, Hawksbill turtle.

No. 821, each 90c: a, Manta ray. b, White shark. c, Hammerhead shark. d, Tiger shark. e, Great barracuda. f, Leatherback turtle.

No. 822, each 90c: a, Whale shark. b, Sixspot grouper. c, Bluestreak cleaner wrasse. d, Lemon shark. e, Spotted trunkfish. f, Longnosed butterflyfish.

No. 823, each 90c: a, Chevroned butterflyfish. b, Mandarinfish. c, Bicolor angelfish. d, Copperbanded butterflyfish. e, Clown anemonefish. f, Lemonpeel angelfish.

Each $3: No. 824, Picassofish. No. 825, Pygmy parrotfish. No. 826, Sailfish.

2000, Mar. 8   **Perf. 14**
Sheets of 6, #a.-f.
818-823 A145 Set of 6   45.00 45.00
Souvenir Sheets
824-826 A145 Set of 3   13.00 13.00

Butterflies — A146

No. 827, each 90c: a, Birdwing. b, Tailed emperor. c, Orchid swallowtail. d, Union Jack. e, Long-tailed blue. f, Common Jezabel.

No. 828, each 90c: a, Caper white. b, Common Indian crow. c, Eastern flat. d, Cairns birdwing. e, Monarch. f, Meadow argus.

No. 829, each 90c, horiz.: a, Glasswing. b, Leftwing. c, Moth butterfly. d, Blue triangle. e, Beak. f, Plane.

Each $3: No. 830, Great egg-fly. No. 831, Palmfly, horiz.

2000, May 1   **Sheets of 6, #a.-f.**
827-829 A146 Set of 3   22.50 22.50
Souvenir Sheets
830-831 A146 Set of 2   7.50 7.50

Birds — A147

#832, each 90c: a, Red-billed leiothrix. b, Gray shrike-thrush. c, Great frigatebird. d, Common kingfisher. e, Chestnut-breasted finch. f, White tern.

#833, each 90c: a, White-collared kingfisher. b, Scaled petrel. c, Superb blue wren. d, Osprey. e, Great cormorant. f, Peregrine falcon.

#834, each 90c: a, Rainbow lorikeet. b, White-throated tree creeper. c, White-tailed kingfisher. d, Golden whistler. e, Black-bellied plover. f, Beach thick-knee.

Each $3: #835, Morepork. #836, Broadbilled prion, horiz.
Illustration reduced.

2000, June 1   **Litho.**   **Perf. 14**
Sheets of 6, #a-f
832-834 A147 Set of 3   22.50 22.50
Souvenir Sheets
835-836 A147 Set of 2   7.50 7.50

Dogs and Cats — A148

No. 837: a, Fox terrier. b, Collie. c, Boston terrier. d, Pembroke Welsh corgi. e, Pointer. f, Dalmatian.

No. 838, vert.: a, Dalmatian. b, Boston terrier. c, Fox terrier. d, Pointer. e, Pembroke Welsh corgi. f, Collie.

No. 839, vert. (denominations in orange): a, Ticked taboy oriental shorthair. b, Balinese. c, Somali. d, Chinchilla Persian. e, Tonkinese. f, Japanese bobtail.

No. 840, vert. (denominations in green): a, Lilac oriental shorthair. b, Balinese. c, Somali. d, Chinchilla Persian. e, Tonkinese. f, Japanese bobtail.

No. 841, Scottish terrier. No. 842, Oriental shorthair, vert.
Illustration reduced.

2000, July 3   **Litho.**   **Perf. 14**
Sheets of 6, #a-f
837-840 A148 90c Set of 4   22.50 22.50
Souvenir Sheets
841-842 A148 $3 Set of 2   7.75 7.75

Birds and Animals — A149

No. 843, horiz.: a, Brown noddy. b, Great frigatebird. c, Emperor angelfish. d, Common dolphin. e, Hermit crab. f, Threadfin butterflyfish.

No. 844, horiz.: a, Red-footed booby. b, Red-tailed tropicbird. c, Black-bellied plover. d, Common tern. e, Ruddy turnstone. f, Sanderling.
$3, Great frigatebird.

2000, Aug. 3   **Sheets of 6, #a-f**
843-844 A149 90c Set of 2   14.50 14.50
Souvenir Sheet
845 A149 $3 Great frigatebird   3.75 3.75

New Year 2000 and 2001 (Years of the Dragon and Snake) A150

Designs: 40c, Dragon. 60c, Snake. 90c, Snake, diff. $1.50, Dragon, diff.

2001, Jan. 15   **Litho.**   **Perf. 13½x13¼**
846-849 A150   Set of 4   8.00 8.00

Motofoua Secondary School Fire, 1st Anniv. A151

Fire trucks: 60c, Anglo specialist rescue uUnit. 90c, Anglo 4800 water/foam tender. $1.50, Bronto 33-2T1 combined telescopic ladder/hydralulic platform. $2, Anglo 450 LRX water tender.
$3, Wormold "Arrestor" ARFFV.

2001, Mar. 9   **Litho.**   **Perf. 13¼**
850-853 A151   Set of 4   14.50 14.50
Souvenir Sheet
854 A151 $3 multi   7.75 7.75

.tv Corporation A152

Palm fronds, satellite dish and: 40c, Woman. 60c, Dancers. 90c, Man. $1.50, Child.
$2, Map.

2001, May 30   **Litho.**   **Perf. 14¼x14½**
855-858 A152   Set of 4   5.75 5.75
Souvenir Sheet
859 A152 $2 multi   4.00 4.00

Souvenir Sheet

Phila Nippon '01 — A153

2001, Aug. 1   **Perf. 13**
860 A153 $3 multi   4.50 4.50

Nos. 806-808 Overprinted in Gold

No. 805 Surcharged in Gold

Wmk. 384
2001, Aug. 4   **Litho.**   **Perf. 13½**
860A CD358 60c multi   .75 .75
860B CD358 90c multi   1.10 1.10
860C CD358 $1.50 multi   1.75 1.75
860D CD358 $2 on 40c multi   2.50 2.50
   Nos. 860A-860D (4)   6.10 6.10

No. 809 Surcharged in Gold

2001, Aug. 4   **Wmk. 384**   **Perf. 13½**
Souvenir Sheet
861 CD358 $5 on $2 multi   6.00 6.00

Fauna A154

Designs: 25c, Mosquito. 30c, Giant African snail. 40c, Cockroach. 45c, Stick insect. 50c, Green stink bug. 55c, Dragonfly. 60c, Monarch caterpillar. 70c, Coconut beetle. 90c, Honeybee. $1, Monarch butterfly. $2, Common eggfly butterfly. $3, Painted lady butterfly.

2001, Oct. 31   **Litho.**   **Unwmk.**   **Perf. 13**
862 A154 25c multi   .40 .40
863 A154 30c multi   .50 .50
864 A154 40c multi   .65 .65
865 A154 45c multi   .75 .75
866 A154 50c multi   .80 .80
867 A154 55c multi   .90 .90
868 A154 60c multi   1.00 1.00
869 A154 70c multi   1.10 1.10
870 A154 90c multi   1.50 1.50
871 A154 $1 multi   1.60 1.60

872	A154	$2 multi	3.25	3.25
873	A154	$3 multi	5.00	5.00
	Nos. 862-873 (12)		17.45	17.45

United We Stand — A155

Statue of Liberty and Tuvalu flag: No. 874, $2, Blue background. No. 875, $2, Yellow background.

2002, Jan. 10   *Perf. 14*

| 874-875 | A155 | Set of 2 | 5.00 | 5.00 |

Paintings Depicting Chapter Scenes From "The Tale of Genji" — A156

No. 876, 40c — Chapter: a, 1. b, 2. c, 3. d, 4. e, 5. f, 6.
No. 877, 60c — Chapter: a, 8, b, 9. c, 10. d, 11. e, 12. f, 13.
No. 878, 90c — Chapter: a, 15. b, 16, c, 17. d, 18. e, 19, f, 20.
No. 879, $4 — Chapter 7. No. 880, $4, Chapter 14. No. 881, $4, Chapter 21.

2002, Apr. 24   *Litho.*   *Perf. 14¼*
Sheets of 6, #a-f

| 876-878 | A156 | Set of 3 | 15.00 | 15.00 |

Imperf

| 879-881 | A156 | Set of 3 | 16.00 | 16.00 |

Nos. 876-878 each contain six 37x50mm stamps.

UN Special Session on Children and Convention on Rights of the Child A157

Designs: 40c, Boy in wheelchair. 60c, Boy and girl sitting near fence. 90c, Nauti Primary School, Funafuti. $4, Mother and child.
No. 886: a, Taulosa Karl. b, Simalua Jacinta Enele.

2002, May 8   *Litho.*   *Perf. 13¼x13½*

| 882-885 | A157 | Set of 4 | 6.50 | 6.50 |

Souvenir Sheet

| 886 | A157 | $1 Sheet of 2, #a-b | 3.50 | 3.50 |

For surcharge, see No. 971A.

Reign of Queen Elizabeth II, 50th Anniv. — A158

No. 887: a, Princes William and Harry. b, Queen in blue green suit. c, Queen and Prince Philip. d, Queen wearing red hat.
$4, Queen on horseback.

2002, June 17   *Perf. 14¼*

| 887 | A158 | $1.50 Sheet of 4, #a-d | 7.75 | 7.75 |

Souvenir Sheet

| 888 | A158 | $4 multi | 5.50 | 5.50 |

2002 World Cup Soccer Championships, Japan and Korea — A159

No. 889: a, Tom Finney. b, Poster from 1974 World Cup. c, Portuguese player and flag. d, Uruguayan player and flag. e, Suwon World Cup Stadium, Seoul (56x42mm).
$4, Johann Cruyff.

2002, July 15   *Perf. 14*

| 889 | A159 | 90c Sheet of 5, #a-e | 6.00 | 6.00 |

Souvenir Sheet

| 890 | A159 | $4 multi | 5.25 | 5.25 |

Queen Mother Elizabeth (1900-2002) — A160

No. 891: a, 60c, Wearing tiara (lilac shading at UL) (26x29mm). b, 60c, Wearing tiara (lilac shading at UR) (26x29mm). c, 90c, In crowd, holding bouquet of flowers (lilac shading at UL) (28x23mm). d, 90c, Receiving flowers from children (lilac shading at UR) (28x23mm). e, 90c, With teddy bear (lilac shading at UL) (28x23mm). f, With man, woman and children (lilac shading at UR) (28x23mm). g, Color photograph (40x29mm).
No. 892, $2, lilac shading at UL: a, As child, with another young girl. b, As older woman.
No. 893, $2, lilac shading at UR: a, Smelling flower. b, Wearing brooch.

***Perf. Compound x14¼ (60c),
13¼x10¾ (90c), 13¼x14¼ ($1.50)***
2002, Aug. 12

| 891 | A160 | Sheet of 7, #a-g | 7.00 | 7.00 |

Souvenir Sheets
Perf. 14¾

| 892-893 | A160 | Set of 2 | 9.00 | 9.00 |

20th World Scout Jamboree, Thailand — A161

No. 894 — Merit badges: a, Citizenship in the World. b, First Aid. c, Personal Fitness. d, Environmental Science.
$5, Lord Robert Baden-Powell.

2002, Oct. 2   *Perf. 14¼*

| 894 | A161 | $1.50 Sheet of 4, #a-d | 7.00 | 7.00 |

Souvenir Sheet

| 895 | A161 | $5 multi | 6.00 | 6.00 |

Intl. Year of Mountains — A162

No. 896, horiz.: a, Mt. Fitzroy, Chile. b, Mt. Foraker, US. c, Mt. Fuji, Japan. d, Mt. Malaku, Nepal and China.
$4, Mt. Godwin Austen, Kashmir.

2002, Oct. 2

| 896 | A162 | $1.50 Sheet of 4, #a-d | 7.00 | 7.00 |

Souvenir Sheet

| 897 | A162 | $4 multi | 5.00 | 5.00 |

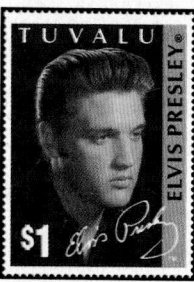

Elvis Presley (1935-77) A163

2002, Dec. 27   *Litho.*   *Perf. 14¼*

| 898 | A163 | $1 multi | 1.75 | 1.75 |

No. 898 was printed in sheets of 6. Value, $12.

Princess Diana (1961-97) — A164

No. 899 — Diana wearing: a, Black dress, no necklace. b, Black dress, choker necklace. c, Blue dress. d, Blue green scarf. e, Pink blouse, hand at chin. f, Pink dress.
$4, Black dress, hand on chin.

2002, Dec. 27   *Perf. 14*

| 899 | A164 | $1 Sheet of 6, #a-f | 7.50 | 7.50 |

Souvenir Sheet

| 900 | A164 | $4 multi | 5.00 | 5.00 |

Year of the Horse (in 2002) — A165

Various horses: 40c, 60c, 90c, $2.
No. 905: a, Head of horse, seahorse. b, Heads of horse, three seahorses.

2003, Jan. 23   **Perf. 13¼**
901-904 A165   Set of 4   7.50 7.50
Souvenir Sheet
905 A165 $1.50 Sheet of 2, #a-b   6.50 6.50

New Year 2003 (Year of the Ram) — A166

No. 906: a, Green and black background. b, White background. c, Blue background.

2003, Feb. 1   **Perf. 14x13¾**
906 A166 75c Vert. strip of 3,
   #a-c   6.00   6.00
No. 906 printed in sheets containing two strips.

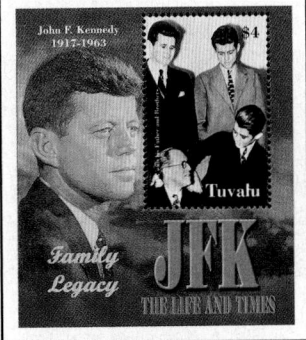

Pres. John F. Kennedy (1917-63) — A167

No. 907: a, In Solomon Islands, 1943. b, On PT 109, 1942. c, Receiving medal for gallantry, 1944. d, Campaigning for Senate, 1952.
$4, With father and brothers.

2003, Mar. 24   **Perf. 14**
907 A167 $1.75 Sheet of 4,
   #a-d   10.00 10.00
Souvenir Sheet
908 A167 $4 multi   6.00 6.00

Powered Flight, Cent. — A168

No. 909, $1.75: a, Orville Wright in early plane, 1903. b, Wilbur Wright and King Alfonso XIII of Spain, 1909. c, Wilbur Wright's plane, 1908. d, Gabriel Voisin's plane piloted by Léon Delagrange, 1907.
No. 910, $1.75: a, Voisin's motor boat powered glider, 1905. b, Trajan Vuia's single winged plane, 1906. c, Santos-Dumont's biplane, 1906. d, Orville Wright circles parade ground, 1908.
No. 911, $4, Wright Brothers biplane in flight, 1908. No. 912, $4, Glenn Curtiss pilots June Bug, 1908.

2003, May 19   **Litho.**   **Perf. 14**
Sheets of 4, #a-d
909-910 A168   Set of 2   21.00 21.00
Souvenir Sheets
911-912 A168   Set of 2   11.50 11.50

Coronation of Queen Elizabeth II, 50th Anniv. — A169

No. 913: a, Wearing gray dress. b, Wearing tiara. c, Wearing yellow hat.
$4, Wearing hat and pearl necklace.

2003, Aug. 11
913 A169 $2 Sheet of 3, #a-c   9.00 9.00
Souvenir Sheet
914 A169 $4 multi   6.25 6.25

Prince William, 21st Birthday — A170

No. 915: a, Wearing school cap. b, Wearing blue shirt. c, Wearing polo helmet.
$4, Wearing suit and tie.

2003, Aug. 11
915 A170 $1.50 Sheet of 3, #a-c   6.50 6.50
Souvenir Sheet
916 A170 $4 multi   5.75 5.75

General Motors Automobiles — A171

No. 917, $1 — Corvettes: a, Yellow 1979. b, Red 1979. c, Silver 1979. d, 1980.
No. 918, $1.50 — Cadillacs: a, 1931 V-16 Sport Phaeton. b, 1959 Eldorado convertible. c, 1979 Seville Elegante. d, 1983 Seville Elegante.
No. 919, $4, 1990 Corvette. No. 920, $4, 1954 Cadillac Coupe de Ville.

2003, Sept. 8   **Perf. 13¾**
Sheets of 4, #a-d
917-918 A171   Set of 2   15.00 15.00
Souvenir Sheets
919-920 A171   Set of 2   11.50 11.50
Corvettes, 50th anniv.; Cadillacs, 100th anniv.

Tour de France Bicycle Race, Cent. — A172

No. 921: a, Gastone Nencini, 1960. b, Jacques Anquetil, 1961. c, Anquetil, 1962. d, Anquetil, 1963.
$4, Jan Janssen, 1968.

2003, Oct. 6   **Perf. 13¾x13¼**
921 A172 $1 Sheet of 4, #a-d   6.50 6.50
Souvenir Sheet
922 A172 $4 multi   6.50 6.50

Butterflies — A173

No. 923, horiz.: a, Malachite. b, White M hairstreak. c, Giant swallowtail. d, Bahamian swallowtail.
$3, Polydamas swallowtail.

2003, Dec. 16   **Perf. 14**
923 A173 $1.25 Sheet of 4, #a-d   8.25 8.25
Imperf
924 A173 $3 multi   5.00 5.00
No. 923 contains four 42x28mm stamps.

Flowers — A174

No. 925: a, Rhododendron. b, Golden Artist tulip. c, Golden Splendor lily. d, Flamingo flower.
$3, Candy Bianca rose.

2003, Dec. 16   **Perf. 14**
925 A174 $1.25 Sheet of 4, #a-d   8.25 8.25
Imperf
926 A174 $3 multi   5.00 5.00
No. 925 contains four 28x42mm stamps.

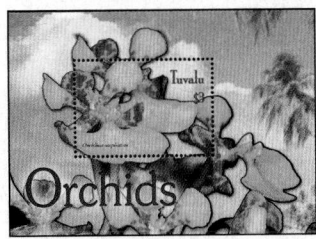

Orchids — A175

No. 927, vert.: a, Dimerandra emarginata. b, Oncidium lanceanum. c, Isochilus linearis. d, Oeceoclades maculata.
$3, Oncidium ampliatum.

2003, Dec. 16   **Perf. 14**
927 A175 $1.25 Sheet of 4, #a-d   8.25 8.25
Souvenir Sheet
928 A175 $3 multi   5.00 5.00

Birds — A176

No. 929: a, Blue-gray gnatcatcher. b, White-eyed vireo. c, Clapper rail. d, Sandhill crane.
$3, Grasshopper sparrow.

2003, Dec. 16
929 A176 $1.25 Sheet of 4, #a-d   8.50 8.50
Souvenir Sheet
930 A176 $3 multi   5.00 5.00

New Year
2004 (Year of
the Monkey)
A177

Paintings by Chang Dai-chen: 75c, Monkey
and Old Tree. $1.50, Two Monkeys.

2004, Jan. 4   **Perf. 13½**
931 A177   75c multi   5.00 5.00
Souvenir Sheet
932 A177 $1.50 multi   6.00 6.00
    No. 931 printed in sheets of 4.

Paintings by Norman Rockwell — A178

No. 933, vert.: a, 100th Year of Baseball. b,
The Locker Room (The Rookie). c, The Dug-
out. d, Game Called Because of Rain.
$3, New Kids in the Neighborhood.

2004, Jan. 30   **Perf. 14¼**
933 A178 $1.25 Sheet of 4, #a-d 8.25 8.25
Souvenir Sheet
934 A178 $3 multi   5.50 5.50
2004 AmeriStamp Expo, Norfolk, Va. (#933).

Paintings by Pablo Picasso (1881-
1973) — A179

No. 935, vert.: a, Seated Woman. b, Woman
in Armchair. c, Bust of Françoise. d, Head of a
Woman.
$4, Françoise Gilot with Paloma and
Claude.

2004, Mar. 1   Litho.   Perf. 14¼
935 A179 $1.50 Sheet of 4,
            #a-d   11.50 11.50
Imperf
936 A179 $4 multi   7.00 7.00
    No. 935 contains four 37x50mm stamps.

Paintings by
Paul
Gauguin
(1848-1903)
A180

Designs: 50c, Les Seins aux Fleurs
Rouges. 60c, Famille Tahitienne. No. 939, $1,
Tahitiennes sur la Plage. $2, Jeune Fille à
L'Eventail.
No. 941, $1: a, Nafea Faa Ipoipo. b, Le Che-
val Blanc. c, Pape Moe. d, Contes Barbares.
$4, Femmes de Tahiti, horiz.

2004, Mar. 1   **Perf. 14¼**
937-940 A180   Set of 4   7.00 7.00
941 A180 $1 Sheet of 4, #a-d   7.00 7.00
Imperf
Size: 93x73mm
942 A180 $4 multi   7.00 7.00

Paintings in
the
Hermitage,
St.
Petersburg,
Russia
A181

Designs: 50c, Philadelphia and Elizabeth
Wharton, by Anthony Van Dyck. 80c, A Glass
of Lemonade, by Gerard Terborch. $1, A Mis-
tress and Her Servant, by Pieter de Hooch.
$1.20, Portrait of a Man and His Three Sons,
by Bartholomaeus Bruyn the Elder.
$4, The Milkmaid's Family, by Louis le Nain,
horiz.

2004, Mar. 1   **Perf. 14¼**
943-946 A181   Set of 4   6.25 6.25
Imperf
Size: 80x68mm
947 A181 $4 multi   7.00 7.00

Fight
Against
HIV and
AIDS
A182

Designs: 60c, Speaker at conference. 90c,
Speaker and dais. $1.50, People standing in
front of banner. $2, People seated at dais.
$3, Conference participants.

2004, May 17   **Perf. 13x13½**
948-951 A182   Set of 4   8.00 8.00
Souvenir Sheet
952 A182 $3 multi   5.25 5.25

Souvenir Sheet

Inauguration of Republic of China
President Chen Shui-bian — A183

No. 953: a, Pres. Chen Shui-bian. b,
Saufatu Sopoanga, Prime Minister of Tuvalu.

2004, May 20   **Perf. 13½x13¼**
953 A183 $2 Sheet of 2, #a-b   6.50 6.50

Souvenir Sheet

Diplomatic Relations Between Tuvalu
and the Republic of China, 25th Anniv.
A183a

2004, Sept. 19   Litho.   Perf. 13¼x13
953C A183a $5 multi   10.00 10.00

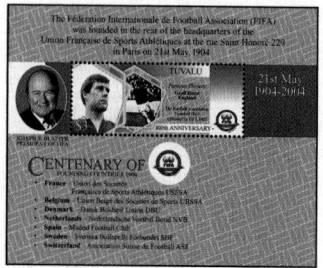

FIFA (Fédération Internationale de
Football Association), Cent. — A184

No. 954: a, Sebastiano Rossi. b, Clarence
Seedorf. c, Zico. d, Jack Charlton.
$3, Geoff Hurst.

Perf. 12¾x12½
2004, Nov. 29   **Litho.**
954 A184 $1 Sheet of 4, #a-d   7.25 7.25
Souvenir Sheet
955 A184 $3 multi   5.75 5.75

Miniature Sheet

World Peace — A185

No. 956: a, Alfred Nobel. b, Doves. c, Nelson Mandela.

2005, Jan. 14   **Perf. 12¾**
956 A185 $1.50 Sheet of 3, #a-c   7.75 7.75

Miniature Sheet

Election of Pope John Paul II, 25th
Anniv. (in 2003) — A186

No. 957: a, With papal arms. b, At
microphone. c, Wearing miter. d, Placing
prayer in Wailing Wall, Jerusalem.

2005, Jan. 14
957 A186 $1.50 Sheet of 4,
            #a-d   11.00 11.00

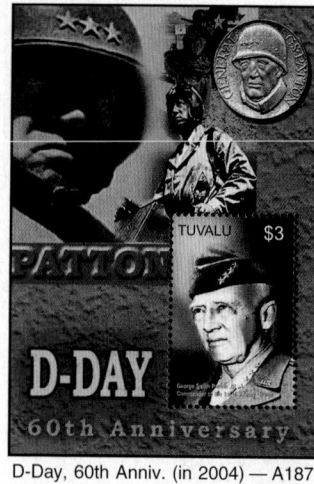

D-Day, 60th Anniv. (in 2004) — A187

No. 958: a, Gen. George C. Marshall. b,
Adm. Sir Ramsay Bertram Home. c, Gen. Wal-
ter Bedell Smith. d, Field Marshal Alan Francis
Brooke.
$3, Gen. George S. Patton.

2005, Jan. 14
958 A187 $1.50 Sheet of 4,
            #a-d   10.00 10.00
Souvenir Sheet
959 A187 $3 multi   5.25 5.25

Dogs — A188

Designs: 20c, Rat terrier. 75c, Large Spanish hound. $1, Lundehund. $2, Beagle harrier.
$3, Old Danish pointer.

2005, Apr. 26   Litho.   Perf. 13¾x13¼
960-963 A188   Set of 4   6.50 6.50
Souvenir Sheet
964 A188 $3 multi   5.00 5.00

Marine Life — A189

No. 965: a, Striped-face unicornfish. b,
Great barracuda. c, Blue-ringed octopus. d,
Giant clam.
$3, Humpback whale.

2005, Apr. 26   **Perf. 13¼x13¾**
965 A189 $1 Sheet of 4, #a-d   8.00 8.00
Souvenir Sheet
966 A189 $3 multi   6.75 6.75

Medicinal Plants — A190

No. 967: a, Common toadflax. b, Pomegranate. c, Black horehound. d, Agnus castus. $3, Black henbane.

2005, Apr. 26   **Perf. 13¾x13¼**
967 A190 $1 Sheet of 4, #a-d   6.75 6.75
Souvenir Sheet
968 A190 $3 multi   5.25 5.25

Insects — A191

No. 969, vert.: a, Louse fly. b, Predacious dung beetle. c, Ladybug. d, Mosquito. $3, House fly.

2005, Apr. 26   **Perf. 13¾x13¼**
969 A191 $1 Sheet of 4, #a-d   6.75 6.75
Souvenir Sheet
Perf. 13¼x13¾
970 A191 $3 multi   5.25 5.25

Pope John Paul II (1920-2005) and Queen Elizabeth II — A192

2005, July 12   **Perf. 13½**
971 A192 $4 multi   10.00 10.00

No. 886 Surcharged

Methods and Perfs As Before
2005, July 17
971A A157   Sheet of 2   7.75 7.75
   b. $2.50 on $1 #886a   3.75 3.75
   c. $2.50 on $1 #886b   3.75 3.75

Battle of Trafalgar, Bicent. — A193

No. 972: a, HMS Victory collides with French ship Redoubtable. b, Admiral Horatio Nelson. c, HMS Victory leads the British fleet. d, Nelson breaths his last breath. $3, Admiral Cuthbert Collingwood.

2005, July 28   **Perf. 12**
972 A193 $1.50 Sheet of 4, #a-d   10.00 10.00
Souvenir Sheet
973 A193 $3 multi   5.25 5.25

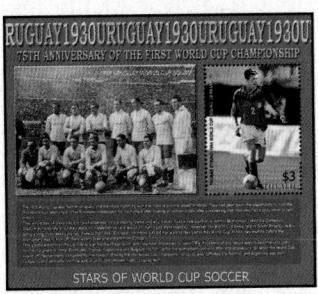

World Cup Soccer Championships, 75th Anniv. — A194

No. 974: a, Thomas Berthold. b, Bobby Charlton. c, Klaus Augenthaler. $3, Thomas Strunz.

2005, July 28   **Perf. 13¼**
974 A194 $2 Sheet of 3, #a-c   10.00 10.00
Souvenir Sheet
Perf. 12
975 A194 $3 multi   5.25 5.25

End of World War II, 60th Anniv. — A195

No. 976, $2: a, Sir Winston Churchill. b, Gen. Charles de Gaulle. c, Newspaper report on death of Adolf Hitler.
No. 977, $2: a, Pres. Harry S. Truman. b, Newspaper report on end of war. c, Gen. Dwight D. Eisenhower.
No. 978, $3, Gen. George S. Patton. No. 979, $3, Brig. Gen. Paul W. Tibbets, Jr. and Enola Gay.

2005, Sept. 21   **Perf. 12¾**
Sheets of 3, #a-c
976-977 A195   Set of 2   20.00 20.00
Souvenir Sheets
978-979 A195   Set of 2   10.00 10.00

Albert Einstein (1879-1955), Physicist — A196

No. 981 — Einstein and: a, Hendrik Lorentz. b, Fritz Haber. c, David Ben-Gurion. $3, Einstein with Thomas Mann.

2005, Sept. 21
980 A196 $2 Sheet of 3, #a-c   10.00 10.00
Souvenir Sheet
981 A196 $3 multi   5.00 5.00

Rotary International, Cent. — A197

No. 982: a, Child. b, Hand holding pills. c, Children. $3, Paul P. Harris, founder.

2005, Nov. 28
982 A197 $2 Sheet of 3, #a-c   10.00 10.00
Souvenir Sheet
983 A197 $3 multi   5.00 5.00

Hans Christian Andersen (1805-75), Author — A198

No. 984: a, Andersen seated. b, Sculpture of Andersen. c, Head of Andersen. $3, Statue of Andersen.

2005, Nov. 28
984 A198 $2 Sheet of 3, #a-c   10.00 10.00
Souvenir Sheet
985 A198 $3 multi   5.00 5.00

A199

Elvis Presley (1935-77) — A200

No. 987 — Presley and: a, Gable and top of column of house. b, Roofline of house. c, Bottom of column of house. d, Archway of house.

2006, Jan. 30   **Perf. 13½**
986 A199 $3 multi   4.50 4.50
987 A200 $3 Sheet of 4, #a-d   18.00 18.00

No. 986 printed in sheets of 4.

National Basketball Association Players and Team Emblems — A201

No. 988, 35c: a, Emblem of Detroit Pistons. b, Chauncey Billups.
No. 989, 35c: a, Emblem of New Jersey Nets. b, Rodney Buford.
No. 990, 35c: a, Emblem of Boston Celtics. b, Ricky Davis.
No. 991, 35c: a, Emblem of Miami Heat. b, Udonis Haslem
No. 992, 35c: a, Emblem of Indiana Pacers, horiz. b, Stephen Jackson.
No. 993, 35c: a, Emblem of Minnesota Timberwolves. b, Wally Szczerbiak.

2006, Jan. 30   **Perf. 13¼**
Sheets of 12, 2 #a, 10 #b
988-993 A201   Set of 6   37.50 37.50

Souvenir Sheet

2006 World Cup Soccer Championships, Germany — A202

No. 994 — Player and uniform for: a, 90c, Spain. b, $1, South Korea. c, $1.50, France. d, $2, United States.

2006, June 9   Litho.   Perf. 13¼
994 A202   Sheet of 4, #a-d   8.25 8.25

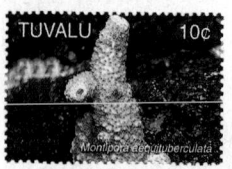

Corals
A203

Designs: 10c, Montipora aequituberculata. 25c, Montipora capricornis. 30c, Montipora verrucosa. 40c, Acropora caroliniana. 50c, Acropora aculeus. 60c, Acropora anthocercis. 65c, Acropora granulosa. 80c, Acropora rosaria. 90c, Acropora cerealis. $1, Acropora yongei. $2, Acropora echinata. $5, Astreopora myriophthalma.

2006, Oct. 12   Perf. 12¾
995   A203 10c multi   .25   .25
996   A203 25c multi   .40   .40
997   A203 30c multi   .45   .45
998   A203 40c multi   .60   .60
999   A203 50c multi   .75   .75
1000 A203 60c multi   .90   .90
1001 A203 65c multi   1.00 1.00
1002 A203 80c multi   1.25 1.25
1003 A203 90c multi   1.40 1.40
1004 A203 $1 multi   1.50 1.50
1005 A203 $2 multi   3.00 3.00
1006 A203 $5 multi   7.50 7.50
     Nos. 995-1006 (12)   19.00 19.00

Miniature Sheets

Pres. John F. Kennedy (1917-63) — A204

No. 1007, $1.30: a, On PT109, 1942. b, Receiving medal for gallantry, 1944. c, Portrait with brown background. d, In Ensign's uniform, 1941.
No. 1008, $1.30: a, Wearing bow tie. b, Wearing tan suit. c, With Eleanor Roosevelt. d, Portrait and U.S. Capitol.

2006, Sept. 21   Litho.   Perf. 13½
       Sheets of 4, #a-d
1007-1008 A204   Set of 2   15.50 15.50

Queen Elizabeth II, 80th Birthday — A205

No. 1009: a, As child holding dog. b, Wearing crown and holding scepter. c, Wearing jacket. d, Wearing sash and tiara.
$3, Wearing crown.

2006, Sept. 21
1009 A205 $1.30 Sheet of 4, #a-d   7.75 7.75
       Souvenir Sheet
1010 A205 $3 multi   4.50 4.50

Space Achievements — A206

No. 1011 — Space Shuttle Discovery's return to space: a, Nose of Shuttle, open cargo doors, text in white reading down. b, Tail of Shuttle, stars, Earth, text in red reading across. c, Tail and wings of Shuttle, open cargo doors, text in red reading down. d, Astronaut on robotic arm. e, Head-on view of Shuttle nose, text in red reading across. f, Robotic arm, text in red and white.
No. 1012 — International Space Station: a, Top of rocket boosters. b, Space Station, text in white reading across. c, Space Shuttle. d, Space Station, text in white reading up.
$3, Calipso Satellite.

2006
1011 A206 $1 Sheet of 6, #a-f   9.50 9.50
1012 A206 $1.30 Sheet of 4, #a-d 7.75 7.75
       Souvenir Sheet
1013 A206 $3 multi   4.50 4.50
     Issued: No. 1011, 12/21; Nos. 1012-1013, 9/21.

Miniature Sheet

Wolfgang Amadeus Mozart (1756-91), Composer — A207

No. 1014: a, Mozart gazing out window. b, Mozart family, 1780. c, Mozart, 1763. d, Art deco illustration of the young Mozart.

2006, Oct. 26
1014 A207 $1.30 Sheet of 4, #a-d 8.00 8.00

Rembrandt (1606-69), Painter
A208

Designs: 10c, Woman in Bed. 20c, The Flight into Egypt. 35c, The Suicide of Lucretia. 95c, Esther Preparing to Intercede with Ahasuerus. $1, Rembrandt's Mother. $2, Child with Dead Peacock.
$3, The Abduction of Ganymede.

2006, Nov. 9   Perf. 14¼
1015-1020 A208   Set of 6   7.25 7.25
                Imperf
              Size: 76x106mm
1021 A208 $3 multi   4.75 4.75

Worldwide Fund for Nature (WWF) — A209

Various Pygmy killer whales.

2006, Nov. 9   Perf. 13½
1022   Horiz. strip of 4   11.00 11.00
  a. A209 40c Four whales   .65   .65
  b. A209 60c Two whales   .95   .95
  c. A209 90c Four whales, diff. 1.40 1.40
  d. A209 $5 Two whales, diff. 8.00 8.00
  e. Miniature sheet, 2 each
      #1022a-1022d   22.00 22.00

Butterflies — A210

No. 1023: a, Tailed jay. b, Ixias undatus. c, Hebomoia leucippe detanii. d, Rajah Brooke's birdwing.
$3, Painted lady.

2006, Nov. 23
1023 A210 $1 Sheet of 4, #a-d 7.00 7.00
       Souvenir Sheet
1024 A210 $3 multi   5.00 5.00

Birds — A211

No. 1025: a, Reed warbler. b, Indian pitta. c, Gurney's pitta. d, Northern shrike.
$3, Black-backed fairy wren.

2006, Nov. 23
1025 A211 $1 Sheet of 4, #a-d 7.00 7.00
       Souvenir Sheet
1026 A211 $3 multi   5.00 5.00

Miniature Sheet

Wedding of Queen Elizabeth II and Prince Philip, 60th Anniv. — A212

No. 1027: a, Photograph, denomination in pink. b, Drawing, denomination in white. c, Photograph, denomination in light green. d, Drawing, denomination in pink. e, Photograph, denomination in white. f, Drawing, denomination in light green.

2007, May 1   Litho.   Perf. 13¼
1027 A212 $1 Sheet of 6, #a-f 10.00 10.00

Princess Diana (1961-97) — A213

No. 1028: a, Wearing black and white hat, pink frame. b, Wearing beige dress, pink frame. c, Wearing pink hat, pink frame. d, Wearing pink hat, lilac frame. e, Wearing beige dress, no frame. f, Wearing black and white hat, lilac frame.
$3, Princess Diana in Tomb of King Seti I, Egypt.

2007, May 1
1028 A213 $1 Sheet of 6, #a-f 10.00 10.00
       Souvenir Sheet
1029 A213 $3 multi   5.00 5.00

Global Warming — A214

No. 1030, $1: a, Windmills. b, Smokestacks, graph of atmospheric carbon dioxide. c, Tree seedling. d, Robotic arm lifting logs, thermometer. e, Recycling emblem. f, Thermometer, graph of global temperatures.
No. 1031, $1 — Text: a, Cause: Deforestation. b, Effect: Melting ice cap. c, Cause: Industrialization. d, Effect: Warmer temperature. e, Cause: Traffic. f, Effect: Extreme weather.
No. 1032, $1 — Text: a, Effect: Habitats destroyed. b, Prevention: Use renewable energy. c, Effect: Coral reef bleaching. d, Prevention: Recycle. e, Effect: Erratic weather patterns. f, Prevention: Plant trees.
No. 1033, $3, Earth on fire, smokestacks, automobile getting fuel. No. 1034, $3, Windmills. No. 1035, $3, Plant in parched soil, vert.

2007, July 21   Litho.
       Sheets of 6, #a-f
1030-1032 A214   Set of 3   32.50 32.50
       Souvenir Sheets
1033-1035 A214   Set of 3   16.00 16.00

First Helicopter Flight, Cent. — A215

Designs: 20c, BO-105. 75c, NH 90, horiz. $1, S-65/RH-53D, horiz. $2, AH 64 Apache, horiz.

No. 1040, horiz.: a, BO-105, diff. b, S-65/RH-53D, diff. c, AH 64 Apache, diff. d, NH 90, diff.

$3, HUP Retriever, horiz.

2007, July 28   *Perf. 13¼*
1036-1039 A215   Set of 4   6.75   6.75
1040 A215 $1.30 Sheet of 4, #a-d   9.00   9.00

Souvenir Sheet
1041 A215 $3 multi   5.25   5.25

Scouting, Cent. A216

Scout: 20c, On bicycle. 75c, At campfire. $1, Playing cricket. $2, Shooting arrow. $3, Dove, Scouting flag, vert.

2007, Aug. 15
1042-1045 A216   Set of 4   6.50   6.50

Souvenir Sheet
1046 A216 $3 multi   5.00   5.00

No. 1046 contains one 37x51mm stamp.

Paintings by Qi Baishi (1864-1957) — A217

No. 1047: a, A Good Wind for Thousands of Miles, top half. b, As "a," bottom half. c, The Yuxia and Lianhua Mountains, top half. d, As "c," bottom half. e, Autumn Landscape with Cormorants, top half. f, As "e," bottom half.

No. 1048: a, Grasshopper on a Branch. b, Fish and Catfish.

$3, Ink Landscape.

2007, Sept. 21
1047 A217 $1 Sheet of 6, #a-f   11.00   11.00
1048 A217 $2.50 Sheet of 2, #a-b   9.00   9.00

Souvenir Sheet
1049 A217 $3 multi   5.50   5.50

Princess Diana (1961-97) — A218

Litho. & Embossed
Serpentine Die Cut
2007, Oct. 1   **Without Gum**
1050 A218 $9 gold & multi   16.50   16.50

Miniature Sheet

Elvis Presley (1935-77) — A219

No. 1051: a, Holding guitar. b, Wearing white shirt. c, Wearing suit and tie. d, Wearing Hawaiian shirt. e, Wearing blue shirt. f, Wearing Army uniform.

2007, Oct. 1   **Litho.**   *Perf. 13¼*
1051 A219 90c Sheet of 6, #a-f   9.75   9.75

Miniature Sheet

Pres. John F. Kennedy (1917-63) — A220

No. 1052 — Kennedy: a, Pointing, text at left. b, Pointing, text at right. c, Not pointing, text at left. d, Not pointing, text at right.

2007, Oct. 15   *Perf. 12¾*
1052 A220 $1 Sheet of 4, #a-d   7.50   7.50

Miniature Sheet

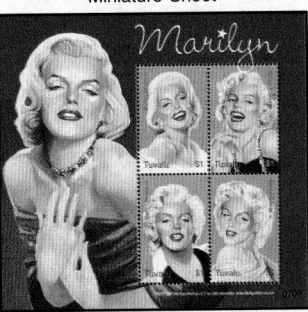

Marilyn Monroe (1926-62), Actress — A221

No. 1053: a, Wearing white boa. b, Wearing black dress, denomination in white. c, Wearing black and white dress, denomination in purple. d, Wearing beige dress.

2007, Oct. 15
1053 A221 $1 Sheet of 4, #a-d   7.50   7.50

Miniature Sheet

Pope Benedict XVI — A222

No. 1054: a, Photomosaic (Pope's ear). b, Photomosaic (Pope's neck and shoulder). c, Photomosaic (Pope's chest). d, Photograph of Pope.

2007, Nov. 11   *Perf. 12¼x12*
1054 A222 $1.30 Sheet of 4, #a-d   9.25   9.25

Christmas — A223

Paintings: 20c, The Adoration of the Shepherds, by Francisco Zurbaran. 75c, Madonna and Child with Angels, by Hans Memling. $1, The Nativity, by Maestro Esiguo. $2, The Nativity, by Philippe de Champaigne.

2007, Dec. 14   *Perf. 14*
1055-1058 A223   Set of 4   7.00   7.00

Miniature Sheet

2008 Summer Olympics, Beijing — A224

No. 1059: a, Baseball. b, Fencing. c, Field hockey. d, Gymnastics.

2008, Jan. 8   **Litho.**   *Perf. 12¾*
1059 A224 60c Sheet of 4, #a-d   4.25   4.25

Miniature Sheet

New Year 2008 (Year of the Rat) — A225

No. 1060 — Rat and Chinese character with yellow background color at: a, LR. b, LL. c, UR. d, UL.

2008, Feb. 28   *Perf. 12*
1060 A225 $1.30 Sheet of 4, #a-d   9.75   9.75

Taiwan Tourist Attractions — A226

No. 1061, horiz.: a, River and Red Suspension Bridge. b, Chinese New Year dragon. c, National Palace Museum. d, Taipei Main Railroad Station. e, Golden Waterfall, Jin Gua Shi. f, National Concert Hall, Taipei.

$2, Buddhist temple.

2008, Mar. 15   *Perf. 13¼*
1061 A226 50c Sheet of 6, #a-f   5.50   5.50

Souvenir Sheet
1062 A226 $2 multi   3.75   3.75

Flowers of the Holy Land — A227

No. 1063: a, Crocuses. b, Aleppo adonis. c, Wild chamomile. d, Fig buttercup. e, Dwarf chicory. f, Queen mallow.

$2, Yellow crocus.

2008, May 14   *Perf. 11½x11¼*
1063 A227 50c Sheet of 6, #a-f   5.75   5.75

Souvenir Sheet
1064 A227 $2 multi   4.00   4.00

2008 World Stamp Championship, Israel.

Cats — A228

No. 1065: a, Siberian. b, California spangled. c, Siamese. d, Burmilla. e, European shorthair. f, Devon rex.

$3, American wirehair.

2008, May 31   *Perf. 13¼*
1065 A228 $1 Sheet of 6, #a-f   11.50   11.50

Souvenir Sheet
1066 A228 $3 multi   5.75   5.75

Miniature Sheet

Orchids — A229

No. 1067: a, Vuylstekeara cambria. b, Dendrobium nobile (pink petals). c, Phalaenopsis nivacolor. d, Cattleya trianae. e, Dendrobium

nobile (purple and green petals). f, Cymbidium alexanderi.

2008, June 15   **Perf. 11½x11¼**
1067 A229 $1 Sheet of 6, #a-f   11.50 11.50

A230

Elvis Presley (1935-77) — A231

No. 1068 — Presley: a, Without microphone. b, Holding microphone in right hand. c, Holding microphone in both hands.

No. 1069 — Presley: a, In white suit, yellow spirals at left and right. b, In leather jacket, yellow spirals at left and right. c, In white suit, yellow spirals at left. d, In white suit, yellow spirals at right. e, In leather jacket, yellow spirals at left. f, In white suit, no yellow spirals.

2008   **Perf. 11½x11¼**
1068   Horiz. strip of 3   5.75 5.75
  a.-c.   A230 $1 Any single   1.90 1.90
    Perf. 13¼
1069 A231 $1 Sheet of 6, #a-f   9.50 9.50

Issued: No. 1068, 7/14; No. 1069, 9/11. No. 1068 was printed in sheets containing two of each stamp.

Miniature Sheet

Birds — A232

No. 1070: a, Magnificent frigatebird. b, Townsend's warbler. c, Sooty tern. d, Common noddy. e, Masked booby. f, Red-tailed tropicbird.

2008, July 25   **Perf. 13¼**
1070 A232 $1 Sheet of 6, #a-f   11.50 11.50

Visit to Lourdes of Pope Benedict XVI — A233

2008, Aug. 31   **Litho.**
1071 A233 $1.30 multi   2.10 2.10
    Printed in sheets of 4.

Miniature Sheets

A234

Space Exploration, 50th Anniv. (in 2007) — A235

No. 1072: a, Saturn V rocket carrying Apollo 11 on launch pad. b, Buzz Aldrin's footprint on Moon. c, Apollo 11 command module. d, Apollo 11 commander Neil A. Armstrong. e, Command module pilot Michael Collins. f, Lunar module pilot Edwin "Buzz" Aldrin.

No. 1073, $1.30 — Chandra X-ray Observatory with: a, Orange nebula at center. b, Stars in background. c, Red background. d, Blue green background.

No. 1074, $1.30 — Sputnik 1: a, Opened up. b, In orbit, satellite above denomination. c, R-7 Senyorka rocket. d, In orbit, with antenna running through denomination.

No. 1075, $1.30 — Cassini-Huygens probe: a, Cassini-Huygens in laboratory. b, Titan !V-B Centaur launch vehicle. c, Cassini-Huygens, Saturn. d, Cassini-Huygens, Saturn and Titan.

No. 1076, $1.30 — Galileo probe: a, Galileo in laboratory. b, Galileo, Europa, Jupiter and Io. c, Galileo probe (orange background). d, Jupiter, Io, Galileo and Ganymede.

2008, Sept. 11   **Perf. 13¼**
1072 A234 $1 Sheet of 6, #a-f   9.50 9.50
    Sheets of 4, #a-d
1073-1076 A235   Set of 4   32.50 32.50

Miniature Sheet

Solo Aerial Circumnavigation of Wiley Post, 75th Anniv. — A236

No. 1077: a, Post wearing pressure suit. b, Post and airplane. c, The Winnie Mae. d, Post atop airplane. e, Post and wife, Mae. f, Harold Gatty, navigator.

2008, Oct. 23   **Perf. 13¼**
1077 A236 $1.30 Sheet of 6, #a-f   10.50 10.50

Miniature Sheet

Princess Diana (1961-97) — A237

No. 1078 — Princess Diana at: a, Left, denomination on lilac background. b, Right (Princess looking to left). c, Left, denomination on white background. d, Right (Princess looking to right).

2008, Nov. 25
1078 A237 $1.30 Sheet of 4, #a-d   6.75 6.75

Christmas A238

Designs: 60c, Holly leaves and berries. 90c, Ornament. $1, Gift. $2.50, Candy cane.

2008, Nov. 25   **Perf. 14¼x14¾**
1079-1082 A238   Set of 4   6.50 6.50

Miniature Sheet

New Year 2009 (Year of the Ox) — A239

No. 1083: a, 60c. b, 90c. d, $1.20. d, $2.50.

2009, Jan. 20   **Litho.**   **Perf. 11½**
1083 A239   Sheet of 4, #a-d   7.00 7.00

Miniature Sheet

Inauguration of US President Barack Obama — A240

No. 1084: a, Pres. Abraham Lincoln. b, Emancipation Proclamation. c, Dr. Martin Luther King, Jr. d, King at March on Washington. e, Pres. Barack Obama. f, Obama giving victory speech.

2009, Jan. 20
1084 A240 $1.30 Sheet of 6, #a-f, + 3 label   10.50 10.50

Miniature Sheet

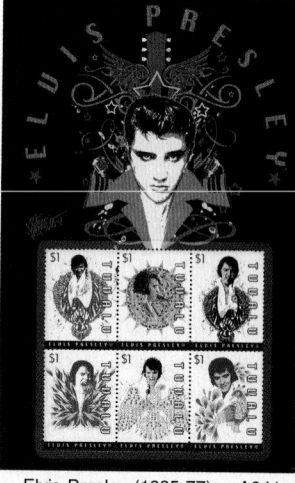

Elvis Presley (1935-77) — A241

No. 1085 — Presley and: a, Red bird. b, Sun. c, Black bird. d, Flames. e, Sequin eagle. f, Peacock.

2009, Mar. 12
1085 A241 $1 Sheet of 6, #a-f   8.75 8.75

Miniature Sheet

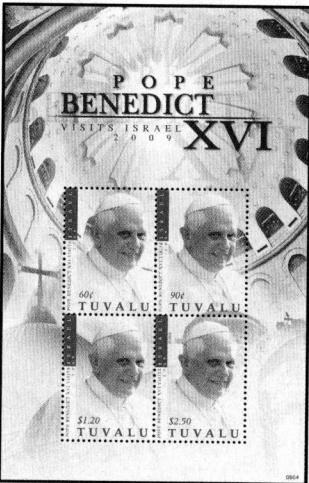

Visit of Pope Benedict XVI to Israel — A242

No. 1086: a, 60c. b, 90c. c, $1.20. d, $2.50.

2009, Apr. 23
1086 A242   Sheet of 4, #a-d   7.50 7.50

Miniature Sheets

A243

Michael Jackson (1958-2009), Singer — A244

No. 1087 — Jackson and stage lighting above country name in: a, Blue. b, White. c, Orange. d, Red, with fireworks.
No. 1088 — Jacskon: a, Wearing jacket and hat, tie above "U." b, Holding microphone. c, Wearing sunglasses. d, Wearing jacket and hat, tie above "L."

2009, July 7   **Perf. 13¼x13**
1087 A243 $1.30 Sheet of 4, #a-d
8.25 8.25

Perf. 13x13¼
1088 A244 $1.30 Sheet of 4, #a-d
8.25 8.25

Miniature Sheet

The Obama Family — A245

No. 1089 — a, First Lady Michelle Obama. b, Pres. Barack Obama. c, Barack Obama and dog, Bo. d, Obama family with dog.

2009, July 13   **Perf. 13½**
1089 A245 $1.30 Sheet of 4, #a-d
8.75 8.75

Miniature Sheet

The Three Stooges — A246

No. 1090 — The Three Stooges in various scenes with country name in: a, Red brown. b, Blue. c, Yellow brown. d, Green.

2009, July 14   **Perf. 11½**
1090 A246 $1.30 Sheet of 4, #a-d
8.75 8.75

Miniature Sheets

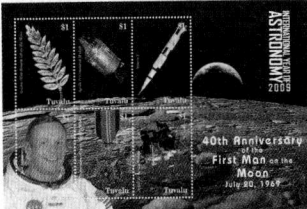

First Man on the Moon, 40th Anniv. — A247

No. 1091: a, Golden olive branch left on Moon. b, Apollo 11 Command Module. c, Saturn V rocket. d, Astronaut Neil Armstrong. e, Congressional Space Medal of Honor. f, Apollo 11 Lunar Module.
No. 1092: a, Buzz Aldrin on Moon. b, Saturn V rocket taking off with Apollo 11. c, Apollo 11 Command Module. d, Apollo 11 crewmen awaiting pickup.

2009, July 20   **Perf. 13½**
1091 A247 $1 Sheet of 6, #a-f
10.00 10.00
1092 A247 $1.30 Sheet of 4, #a-d
8.75 8.75

Miniature Sheet

Visit of Prince Harry to New York — A248

No. 1093: a, Prince Harry and woman at Harlem Children's Zoo. b, Wreath laid by Prince Harry at World Trade Center site. c, Prince Harry playing polo. d, Prince Harry and soldier at Veterans Affairs Medical Center.

2009, Aug. 25   **Perf. 12x11½**
1093 A248 $1.30 Sheet of 4, #a-d
8.75 8.75

Souvenir Sheet

Diplomatic Relations Between Tuvalu and the Republic of China, 30th Anniv. — A249

2009, Sept. 19   **Perf. 13½**
1094 A249 $5 multi
8.75 8.75

Christmas A250

Designs: 60c, Stuffed reindeer, Santa Claus suit and hat with Tuvalu flag. 90c, Bells, Christmas ornament with Tuvalu flag. $1, Cloth Christmas decorations, Tuvalu arms. $2, Santa Claus on cake, bell with Tuvalu flag.

2009, Nov. 25   **Perf. 13½x13**
1095-1098 A250   Set of 4
8.25 8.25

Miniature Sheet

Pres. John F. Kennedy (1917-63) — A251

No. 1099 — Pres. Kennedy: a, Seated at desk. b, With wife, Jacqueline. c, With son, John, Jr. d, At podium.

2009, Nov. 28   **Perf. 12x11½**
1099 A251 $1.30 Sheet of 4, #a-d
9.50 9.50

Butterflies A252

Designs: 60c, Hyposcada kezia. 90c, Heteronympha mirifica. No. 1102, $1, Libythea geoffroy. $2.50, Protographium leosthenes.
No. 1104, $1: a, Horago selina. b, Ornithoptera victoriae. c, Polyura eudamippus. d, Catopsilia scylla. e, Graphium mendana. f, Melanitis amabilis.

2009, Nov. 28   **Perf. 11½**
1100-1103 A252   Set of 4   9.25 9.25
1104 A252 $1 Sheet of 6, #a-f   11.00 11.00

Miniature Sheet

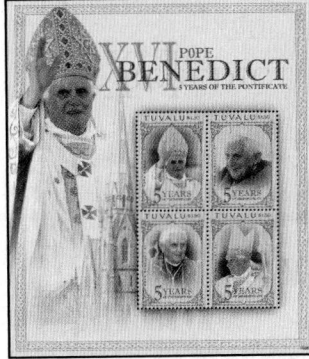

Reign of Pope Benedict XVI, 5th Anniv. — A252a

No. 1104G — Pope Benedict XVI: h, Waving. i, Wearing red vestments, facing left. j, Wearing red vestments, facing right. k, Holding crucifix.

2009, Dec. 10   **Perf. 12x11½**
1104G A252a $1.30 Sheet of 4, #h-k
9.50 9.50

Miniature Sheet

Princess Diana (1961-97) — A252b

No. 1104L: m, Holding infant. b, With arms on hips. c, Wearing face shield. d, Talking with child.

2009, Dec. 20
1104L A252b $1.30 Sheet of 4, #m-p
9.25 9.25

Miniature Sheet

Elvis Presley (1935-77) — A253

No. 1105 — Presley: a, With hands at bottom of guitar. b, With one hand over guitar strings. c, With hand over guitar strings and hand holding neck of guitar. d, Playing guitar and singing.

2010, Jan. 9   **Perf. 13½**
1105 A253 $1.30 Sheet of 4, #a-d
9.25 9.25

Boy Scouts of America, Cent. — A254

No. 1106, $1.30: a, Scout saluting. b, Scout planting tree.
No. 1107, $1.30: a, Scout with backpack and walking stick. b, Scout fishing.

2010, Feb. 1   Pairs, #a-b   Litho.
1106-1107 A254   Set of 2   9.00 9.00
Nos. 1106-1107 were each printed in sheets containing two pairs.

Souvenir Sheet

Elvis Presley (1935-77) — A255

No. 1108: a, Presley facing left. b, Presley and guitar neck.

2010, Jan. 8   **Imperf.**
Without Gum
1108 A255 $6 Sheet of 2, #a-b   21.50 21.50

Miniature Sheet

Earth Day, 40th Anniv. — A256

No. 1109 — Various drawings by children: a, 50c. b, 60c, c, 90c, d, $1.50.

2010, Apr. 22   **Perf. 13¼**
1109 A256   Sheet of 4, #a-d   6.50 6.50

Miniature Sheets

Battle of Britain, 70th Anniv. — A257

No. 1110, $1.30: a, Winston Churchill (black-and-white photograph). b, Coventry Cathedral in ruins. c, London in ruins (bicyclists at left). d, London in ruins (automobiles and trucks on street).
No. 1111, $1.30: a, Winston Churchill (color photograph). b, Messerschmitt BF 109E. c, Emblems of Luftwaffe and Royal Air Force. d, Supermarine Spitfire.

2010, Apr. 23   **Sheets of 4, #a-d**
1110-1111 A257   Set of 2   19.50 19.50

Palaces of the World — A258

No. 1112, horiz.: a, Imperial Palace, Tokyo, Japan. b, Dolmabahçe Palace, Istanbul, Turkey. c, Winter Palace, St. Petersburg, Russia. d, Schönbrunn Palace, Vienna, Austria. e, Summer Palace, Beijing, China. f, Buckingham Palace, London, England.
$3, Palace of Versailles, Versailles, France.

2010, July 28   **Perf. 11½**
1112 A258 $1 Sheet of 6, #a-f   11.00 11.00
Souvenir Sheet
1113 A258 $3 multi   5.50 5.50

Souvenir Sheets

A259

A260

A261

Elvis Presley (1935-77) — A262

2010, July 28   **Perf. 14¼**
1114 A259 $3 multi   5.50 5.50
1115 A260 $3 multi   5.50 5.50
1116 A261 $3 multi   5.50 5.50
1117 A262 $3 multi   5.50 5.50
   Nos. 1114-1117 (4)   22.00 22.00

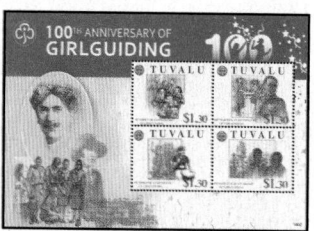

Girl Guides, Cent. — A263

No. 1118 — Drawings of Girl Guides in sepia and: a, Four Girl Guides in blue uniforms. b, Girl Guide wearing red neckerchief. c, Girl Guide with bongo drum. d, Two Girl Guides wearing red neckerchiefs.
$3, Centenary emblem, six Girl Guides, vert.

2010, Aug. 16   **Perf. 12½x12**
1118 A263 $1.30 Sheet of 4, #a-d   9.50 9.50
Souvenir Sheet
Perf. 11¼x11½
1119 A263 $3 multi   5.50 5.50

Miniature Sheets

A264

Pres. Abraham Lincoln (1809-65) — A265

No. 1120 — Lincoln with denomination in: a, Orange. b, Rose. c, Blue. d, Green.
No. 1121: Lincoln with country name in: a, Green. b, Purple. c, Dark red. d, Red brown.

2010, Aug. 21   **Perf. 13¼x13**
1120 A264 $1.30 Sheet of 4, #a-d   9.50 9.50
Perf. 12
1121 A265 $1.30 Sheet of 4, #a-d   9.50 9.50

Souvenir Sheets

Popes and their Coats of Arms — A266

No. 1122, $4: a, Pope John Paul II. b, Arms of Pope John Paul II.
No. 1123, $4: a, Pope Benedict XVI. b, Arms of Pope Benedict XVI.

2010, Aug. 30   **Imperf.**
Sheets of 2, #a-b
Without Gum
1122-1123 A266   Set of 2   30.00 30.00

Election of Pres. John F. Kennedy, 50th Anniv. — A267

No. 1124, $1.30 — Gray frames and blue panels with Kennedy: a, Talking with Tobacco Association representative at Greenbrier Hotel, 1958. b, Signing Cuban quarantine proclamation, 1962. c, Campaigning, 1960. d, At televised debate, 1960.

No. 1125, $1.30 — Olive green frames and brown panels with Kennedy: a, With wife, Jacqueline, on sailboat. b, Reading newspaper on the Honey Fitz, 1963. c, With wife and children, 1962. d, With wife in limousine, 1961.
No. 1126, $1.30 — Bluish black frames and red panels: a, Kennedy with son, John, Jr. b, Crowd at Grand Rapids, Michigan campaign rally, 1960. c, Kennedy debating Richard M. Nixon, 1960. d, Kennedy at lectern at 1960 campaign rally.

2010, Sept. 12   **Perf. 12**
Sheets of 4, #a-d
1124-1126 A267   Set of 3   30.00 30.00

Frédéric Chopin (1810-49), Composer — A268

No. 1127: Various portraits of Chopin facing: a, Left. b, Right. c, Left, diff. d, Right diff.
No. 1128, $3, Chopin, black background.
No. 1129, $3, Chopin, brown background.

2010, Sept. 12
1127 A268 $1.30 Sheet of 4, #a-d   10.00 10.00
Souvenir Sheets
1128-1129 A268   Set of 2   12.00 12.00

Miniature Sheets

A269

Pope Benedict XVI — A270

No. 1130 — Pope Benedict XVI and: a, "XVI" above building at right. b, "I" of "XVI" above building ar right. c, Crowd, window of Vatican City building at UL. d, Crowd, pillars of Vatican City building at UL.
No. 1131 — Pope Benedict XVI and: a, Part of building to left of face. b, No building to left or right of face. c, Purple area to left of face. d, Purple area to left of face with white spot near tip of ear.

2010, Sept. 21   **Perf. 12x12½**
1130 A269 $1.30 Sheet of 4, #a-d   10.00 10.00
1131 A270 $1.30 Sheet of 4, #a-d   10.00 10.00

Miniature Sheets

A271

Pope John Paul II (1920-2005) — A272

No. 1132 — Pope John Paul II waving and: a, "T" of "Tuvalu" on pillar, lower part of first "U" in "Tuvalu" above arch. b, "T" of "Tuvalu" on arc, lower part of first "U" in "Tuvalu" above arc. c, Country name over area with darker gray area near "L" in "Tuvalu." d, Darker gray lines to left of first "U," below "V," to right of "A," and to left of second "U" in "Tuvalu."

No. 1133 — Pope John Paul II holding crucifix and: a, Light area in frame next to lower left corner of photo. b, Blackish brown frame.

2010, Oct. 7
1132	A271	$1.30 Sheet of 4, #a-d	10.50	10.50
1133	A272	$1.30 Sheet of 4, #1133a, 3	10.50	10.50
		#1133b		

Princess Diana (1961-97) — A273

No. 1134 — Princess Diana wearing: a, White jacket and dress, tan background. b, Red and black dress. c, White jacket, black background. d, Red and white tress, tiara.

No. 1135, $3, Strapless white dress. No. 1136, $3, Red and white hat.

2010, Oct. 28   Perf. 12
1134	A273	$1.30 Sheet of 4, #a-d	10.50	10.50
		Souvenir Sheets		
1135-1136	A273	Set of 2	12.50	12.50

Miniature Sheets

A274

Fight Between Muhammad Ali and Joe Frazier, Manila, 35th Anniv. — A275

No. 1137: a, Ali wearing robe encircled by reporters with eight microphones. b, Ali wearing robe, standing. c, Ali, bare-chested, facing right, talking to reporters. d, Ali, bare-chested, looking left, talking to reporters.

No. 1138 — Ali in boxing ring: a, White rope at lower right. b, Frazier at lower left, white and red ropes at lower right. c, Ali with arm extended to right, white rope at bottom. d, Ali with arm extended to left, white and red ropes at bottom.

2010, Nov. 25   Perf. 11¼x11½
1137	A274	$1.30 Sheet of 4, #a-d	10.50	10.50
		Perf. 11½x11¼		
1138	A275	$1.30 Sheet of 4, #a-d	10.50	10.50

Christmas A276

Details of paintings: 60c, Pierre Bladelin Triptych, by Rogier van der Weyden. 90c, Annunciation, by Pietro Cavallini. $1, Altarpiece of the Virgin, by Jacques Daret. $2, Nativity, by Matthias Grunewald.

2010, Nov. 25   Perf. 12
1139-1142	A276	Set of 4	9.00	9.00

Nos. 1139-1142 each were printed in sheets of 4.

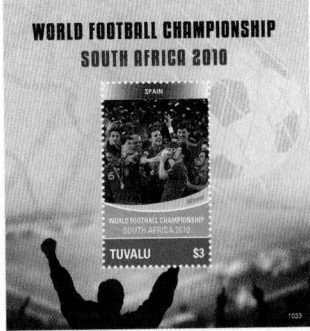

2010 World Cup Soccer Championships, South Africa — A277

No. 1143, $1 — Scenes from June 16, 2010 Spain vs. Switzerland match (Spain in red shirts): a, Spanish player #15 and Swiss goalie. b, Spanish player #22 and Swiss player #17. c, Spanish player #8 and Swiss players #8 and #6. d, Spanish players #15 and #3 and Swiss player #16.

No. 1144, $1 — Scenes from June 21, 2010 Spain vs. Honduras match (Spain in red shirts): a, Spanish players #7 and #8. b, Spanish player #10 and Honduran player #11. c, Spanish player #8 and Honduran player #8. d, Spanish players #11 and #16 and Honduran players #11 and #12.

No. 1145, $1 — Scenes from June 25, 2010 Spain vs. Chile match (Spain in black shirts): a, Spanish players #7 and #10. b, Spanish player #9 and Chilean player #3. c, Spanish players #5, #14 and #16 and Chilean player #10. d, Spanish player #11 and Chilean player #7.

No. 1146, $1 — Scenes from June 29, 2010 Spain vs. Portugal match (Spain in red shirts): a, Spanish goalie leaping into arms of Spanish player #19. b, Spanish player #16 and Portuguese player #23. c, Spanish player #7. d, Spanish player falling and Portuguese player #23.

No. 1147, $1 — Scenes from July 3, 2010 Spain vs. Paraguay match (Spain in black shirts): a, Spanish players #8 and #10 and Paraguayan player #16. b, Spanish goalie (player #1). c, Spanish player #16 and Paraguayan player #3. d, Spanish player #15 and Paraguayan player #21.

No. 1148, $1 — Scenes from July 7, 2010 Spain vs. Germany match (Spain in red shirts): a, Spanish player #11 and German player #15 (with hand on Spanish player's back). b, Spanish player #8 and German player #7. c, Spanish player #6 and German player #6. d, Spanish player #11 and German player #15 (both players with arms extended).

No. 1149, $1 — Scenes from July 11, 2010 Spain vs. Netherlands match (Spain in black shirts): a, Spanish player #15 and Netherlands player #4. b, Spanish player #15 on knees and Netherlands player #10. c, Spanish player #7 and Netherlands player #4. d, Spanish player #10 and Netherlands player #9.

$3, Spanish team celebrating championship.

2010, July 11
		Sheets of 4, #a-d		
1143-1149	A277	Set of 7	52.50	52.50
		Souvenir Sheet		
1150	A277	$3 multi	5.50	5.50

Nos. 1143-1150 could not have been issued on the stated day of issue as Nos. 1149 and 1150 depict photographs taken that day.

Miniature Sheet

Expo 2010, Shanghai — A278

No. 1151 — Expo 2010 emblem and various views of Green Island: a, 60c. b, 90c. c, $1.50. d, $2.

2010, Aug. 25   Perf. 13¼
1151	A278	Sheet of 4, #a-d	9.25	9.25

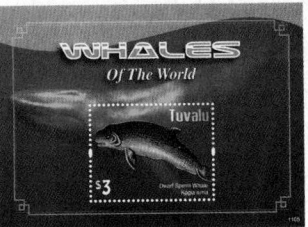

Whales — A279

No. 1152: a, Orca. b, Short-finned pilot whale. c, Melon-headed whale. d, Pygmy killer whale. e, False killer whale. f, Sperm whale. $3, Dwarf sperm whale.

2011, Jan. 30   Perf. 13 Syncopated
1152	A279	$1 Sheet of 6, #a-f	12.50	12.50
		Souvenir Sheet		
1153	A279	$3 multi	6.25	6.25

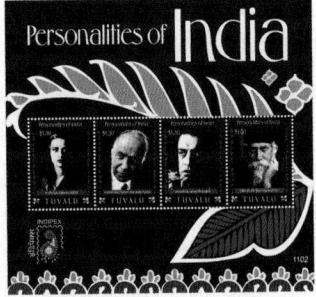

Famous Indians — A280

No. 1154: a, Amrita Sher-Gil (1913-41), painter. b, Subrahmanyan Chandrasekhar (1910-95), astrophysicist. c, Satyajit Ray (1921-92), filmmaker. d, Rabindranath Tagore (1861-1941), writer.

$3, Mohandas K. Gandhi (1869-1948), nationalist leader.

2011, Feb. 12   Perf. 12¾x12½
1154	A280	$1.30 Sheet of 4, #a-d	10.50	10.50
		Souvenir Sheet		
		Perf. 13¼		
1155	A280	$3 multi	6.25	6.25

Indipex 2011 Intl. Philatelic Exhibition, New Delhi. No. 1155 contains one 38x50mm stamp.

Miniature Sheets

A281

Elvis Presley (1935-77) — A282

No. 1156 — Presley: a, Standing, with arm extended. b, With both hands near microphone. c, Holding microphone with arm at side. d, With bent knees and arm extended.

No. 1157 — Presley: a, Standing in front of man on stage. b, With guitar, audience in background. c, Playing guitar. d, Holding microphone.

2011, Feb. 15   *Perf. 13 Syncopated*
1156 A281 $1.30 Sheet of 4,
          #a-d   10.50 10.50
          Perf. 12
1157 A282 $1.30 Sheet of 4,
          #a-d   10.50 10.50

Personalities of the U.S. Civil
War — A283

No. 1158: a, Head of Pres. Abraham Lincoln. b, Lieutenant General Ulysses S. Grant.
c, Major General George G. Meade. d, Lincoln, standing.
No. 1159, horiz.: a, Lincoln, no hands visible. b, Lincoln, with hand on chin.

2011, Feb. 28   *Perf. 13 Syncopated*
1158 A283 $1.30 Sheet of 4,
          #a-d   10.50 10.50
          Souvenir Sheet
          Perf. 12
1159 A283 $3 Sheet of 2,
          #a-b   12.50 12.50

A284

Statue of Liberty, 125th Anniv. — A285

No. 1160 — Statue of Liberty and: a, Gray
background, "86" at left. b, Blue background,
denomination at LL. c, Gray and purple background, denomination at UL. d, Gray background, "20" at right.
No. 1161: a, Side view of statue. b, Head of
statue.

2011, Mar. 15   *Perf. 13 Syncopated*
1160 A284 $1.30 Sheet of 4,
          #a-d   11.00 11.00
          Souvenir Sheet
1161 A285 $1.50 Sheet of 2,
          #a-b   6.50 6.50

Beatification of Pope John Paul
II — A286

Pope John Paul II: No. 1162, $1, Greeting
crowd. No. 1163, $1, With mass attendants,
reading. $3, Pope John Paul II in crowd, diff.

2011, Apr. 15   *Perf. 13 Syncopated*
1162-1163 A286 Set of 2   4.25 4.25
          Souvenir Sheet
          Perf. 12
1164 A286 $3 multi   6.50 6.50
Nos. 1162 and 1163 were printed in a sheet
of six containing three of each stamp.

Wedding of Prince William and
Catherine Middleton — A287

No. 1165, $1.30: a, Couple, facing forward.
b, Bride.
No. 1166, $1.30: a, Groom waving. b,
Couple, looking at each other.
$3, Couple, kissing.

2011, Apr. 29   *Perf. 12*
          Pairs, #a-b
1165-1166 A287 Set of 2   11.50 11.50
          Souvenir Sheet
          Perf. 11¼x11½
1167 A287 $3 multi   6.50 6.50
Nos. 1165-1166 each were printed in sheets
containing two pairs. No. 1167 contains one
30x79mm stamp. Nos. 1165-1167 could not
have been issued on the stated day of issue
because stamps have photographs taken that
day, which was the day of the wedding.

Parrots — A288

No. 1168: a, Western rosella. b, Australian
ringneck. c, Budgerigar. d, Northern rosella. e,
Red-capped parrot. f, Regent parrot.
$3, Red-winged parrot.

2011, June 6   *Perf. 12*
1168 A288 $1 Sheet of 6, #a-f   13.00 13.00
          Souvenir Sheet
1169 A288 $3 multi   6.50 6.50

Personalizable
Stamp — A289

2011, June 15   *Perf. 14¼x14¾*
1170 A289 20c multi   .45   .45

A290

Meeting of U.S. Pres. Barack Obama
and Australian Prime Minister Julia
Gillard — A291

No. 1171: a, Prime Minister Gillard and
Pres. Obama, no hands visible. b, Obama. c,
Gillard and Obama shaking hands. d, Gillard.
No. 1172: a, Gillard. b, Obama.

2011, June 15   *Perf. 11½x12*
1171 A290 $1.30 Sheet of 4,
          #a-d   11.50 11.50
          Souvenir Sheet
1172 A291 $1.25 Sheet of 2,
          #a-b   5.50 5.50

First Man in Space, 50th
Anniv. — A292

No. 1173, $1.30, horiz.: a, Sergei Korolev
(1907-66), spacecraft designer, and rocket. b,
Yuri Gagarin, first man in space, with helmet.
c, Erecting rocket from train. d, John Glenn,
U.S. astronaut.
No. 1174, $1.30, horiz.: a, Vostok capsule.
b, Vostok 1A rocket. c, Vostok Memorial. d,
Virgil Grissom, U.S. astronaut.
No. 1175, $3, Gagarin wearing brown uni-
form. No. 1176, $3, Gagarin wearing white
uniform and medal.

2011, June 27   *Perf. 12½x12*
          Sheets of 4, #a-d
1173-1174 A292 Set of 2   22.50 22.50
          Souvenir Sheets
          Perf. 11¼x11½
1175-1176 A292 Set of 2   13.00 13.00

U.S. Pres. Ronald Reagan (1911-
2004) — A293

No. 1177 — Pres. Reagan: a, Wearing red
and blue striped tie. b, Wearing overcoat,
striped shirt and polka dot tie. c, Wearing

black suit. d, With American flag in
background.
No. 1178 — Pres. Reagan: a, Wearing
maroon patterned tie. b, Wearing striped tie,
American flag in background.

2011, June 30   Litho.   Perf.
1177 A293 $1 Sheet of 4, #a-d   8.50 8.50
          Souvenir Sheet
1178 A293 $3 Sheet of 2, #a-b   13.00 13.00

Miniature Sheets

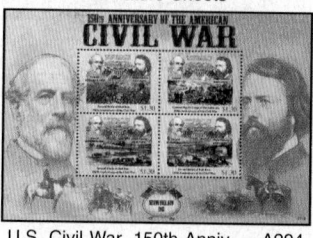

U.S. Civil War, 150th Anniv. — A294

No. 1179, $1.30 — Eagle, shield, Union and
Confederate flags, General Robert E. Lee,
Major General John Pope, and scenes from
Second Battle of Bull Run, Aug. 28-30, 1862:
a, Soldiers carrying Union flag at center. b,
General Sigel's Corps at the battle site. c,
Soldiers marching, green background. d, Bat-
tle scene, horses and building at right.
No. 1180, $1.30 — Eagle, shield, Union and
Confederate flags, General Braxton Bragg,
Major General William S. Rosecrans, and
scenes from Battle of Stones River, Dec. 31,
1862-Jan. 2, 1863: a, Gen. Rosecrans rallies
troops at Stones River. b, Union Army flees a
Confederate onslaught. c, Confederates fron-
tal attack on the Union. d, General Rosecrans
tries to save his army.
No. 1181, $1.30 — Eagle, shield, Union and
Confederate flags, General Robert E. Lee,
General Ulysses S. Grantm and scenes from
the Battle of the Wilderness, May 5-7, 1864: a,
Battle near Orange Court House Plank Road.
b, The gloom at the outset in dense woods. c,
Army of the Potomac charging the enemy. d,
Carrying a wounded soldier to safety.

2011, July 4   *Perf. 12½x12*
          Sheets of 4, #a-d
1179-1181 A294 Set of 3   34.00 34.00

Miniature Sheets

Mother Teresa (1910-97),
Humanitarian — A295

No. 1182, $1.30 — Mother Teresa: a, Hold-
ing child, children in background. b, With wall
inscribed "Peace" in background. c, With
hands held together. d, Holding Nobel Peace
Prize diploma and medal box.
No. 1183, $1.30 — Mother Teresa: a, Black-
and-white photograph of head. b, With Pres.
Ronald Reagan and wife, Nancy. c, Holding
baby, door in background. d, Under umbrella.

          Perf. 12x12½, 11¼ (#1183)
2011, July 5   Sheets of 4, #a-d
1182-1183 A295 Set of 2   22.50 22.50

Miniature Sheets

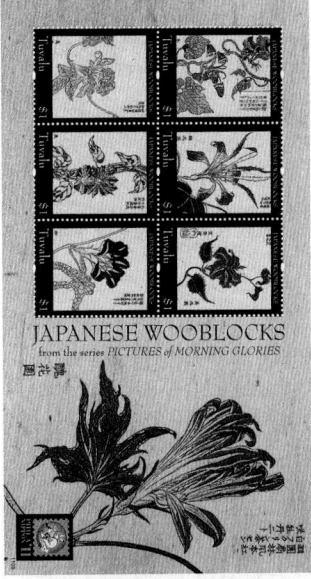

JAPANESE WOOBLOCKS
from the series *PICTURES of MORNING GLORIES*

Woodblock Prints of Morning
Glories — A296

Woodblock Prints of Mount Fuji, by
Hiroshige — A297

No. 1184: a, Unopened buds on vine. b, Brownish purple flower with thin, spiked leaves, three Japanese characters at LL. c, Red flower on vine. d, Pink flowers on thin vine running horizontally. e, Pink flower on thick vine running vertically. f, Dark red and black flower on thin vine, one Japanese character at LL.

No. 1185: a, Mount Fuji above village. b, Mount Fuji with hill in foreground. c, Reflection of Mount Fuji in lake. d, Ocean wave and Mount Fuji.

2011, July 28   Perf. 13 Syncopated
1184 A296 $1 Sheet of 6,
    #a-f   12.50 12.50
    Perf. 12
1185 A297 $1.30 Sheet of 4,
    #a-d   11.00 11.00

PhilaNippon '11 Intl. Philatelic Exhibition, Yokohama.

Princess Diana (1961-97) — A298

No. 1186 — Princess Diana wearing: a, Tiara. b, Dark dress. c, Pearl necklace and hat with striped ribbon. d, Dress with ruffled collar.
    $3, Princess Diana wearing pearl necklace and hat with black ribbon.

2011, Aug. 1   Perf. 12½x12
1186 A298 $1.30 Sheet of 4,
    #a-d   11.00 11.00
    Souvenir Sheet
    Perf. 11½
1187 A298 $3 multi   6.25 6.25

Souvenir Sheets

War Horses — A299

Carriage Horses — A300

Race Horses — A301

No. 1188: a, Denomination at LR. b, Denomination at LL.
No. 1189: a, White horse pulling man and woman in carriage. b, Silhouette of horse and carriage.
No. 1190: a, Three horses. b, Four horses.

2011, Aug. 31   Litho.   Perf. 12
1188 A299 $3 Sheet of 2, #a-b 12.50 12.50
1189 A300 $3 Sheet of 2, #a-b 12.50 12.50
1190 A301 $3 Sheet of 2, #a-b 12.50 12.50
    Nos. 1188-1190 (3)   37.50 37.50

Miniature Sheet

2011 Women's World Cup Soccer
Championships, Germany — A302

No. 1191: a, Japanese team captain Homare Sawa. b, Japanese Team. c, U.S. team. d, U.S. team captain Christie Rampone.

2011, Sept. 21   Perf. 12x12½
1191 A302 $1.30 Sheet of 4,
    #a-d   10.50 10.50

Marine Fauna — A303

No. 1192: a, Christmas shearwater. b, Flying fish. c, Albacore tuna. d, Pantropical spotted dolphin. e, Pygmy killer whale.
    $3, Parrotfish.

2012, Jan. 1   Perf. 13x13¼
1192 A303 $1 Sheet of 5, #a-e 10.50 10.50
    Souvenir Sheet
    Perf. 13¼
1193 A303 $3 multi   6.25 6.25
No. 1192 contains five 40x30mm stamps.

Disappearance of Amelia Earhart, 75th
Anniv. — A304

No. 1194 — Earhart: a, Wearing leather pilot's helmet, brick wall in background. b, Without pilot's helmet, airplane fuselage in background. c, Wearing leather pilot's helmet, airplane propeller in background. d, Without pilot's helmet, airplane propeller in background.
    $3.50, Earhart on side of airplane.

2012, Feb. 6   Perf. 13
1194 A304 $1.25 Sheet of 4,
    #a-d   11.00 11.00
    Souvenir Sheet
1195 A304 $3.50 multi   7.75 7.75

Miniature Sheet

Sinking of the Titanic, Cent. — A305

No. 1196: a, Smokestacks. b, Mast and aft deck. c, Flagpole and ship's stern.
    $3.50, Flagpole and ship's stern, diff.

2012, Apr. 15   Perf. 13 Syncopated
1196 A305 $1.50 Sheet of 3, #a-
    c   9.25 9.25
    Souvenir Sheet
1197 A305 $3.50 multi   7.25 7.25

Climate Change Awareness — A306

Inscriptions: No. 1198, $1, Plant a tree to help reduce greenhouse gases. No. 1199, $1, Turning off lights to save energy. No. 1200, $1, Distillation plants turn seas into clean drinking water. No. 1201, $1, Crops that are genetically enhanced to grow near salt water. No. 1202, $1, Mangrove trees encourage new land formation.

2012, May 1   Perf. 14
1198-1202 A306   Set of 5   10.50 10.50
    Expo 2012, Yeosu, South Korea.

Souvenir Sheets

Elvis Presley (1935-77) — A307

Designs: No. 1203, $3.50, Red background, Presley on stage. No. 1204, $3.50, Red background, close-up of Presley. No. 1205, $3.50, Red background, two photographs of Presley. No. 1206, $3.50, Light blue background, black-and-white photograph of Presley. No. 1207, $3.50, Light blue background, color photograph of Presley.

2012, May 14   Perf. 12¾
1203-1207 A307   Set of 5   35.00 35.00

2012 Summer Olympics,
London — A308

No. 1208 — British flag on simulated Olympic medals in: a, Bronze. b, Silver. c, Gold.
    $1.50, Olympic rings, colored stripes, London landmarks, vert.

2012, May 30   Perf.
1208 A308   50c Sheet of 3, #a-
    c   3.00 3.00
    Souvenir Sheet
    Perf. 12¼x12
1209 A308 $1.50 multi   3.00 3.00
No. 1209 contains one 30x50mm stamp.

Souvenir Sheets

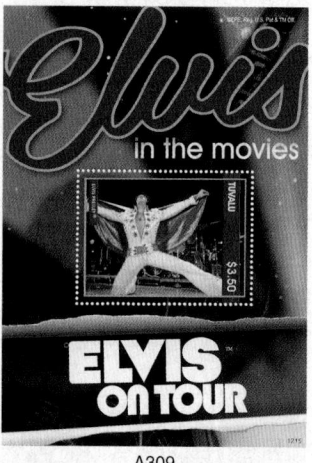

A309

A310

A311

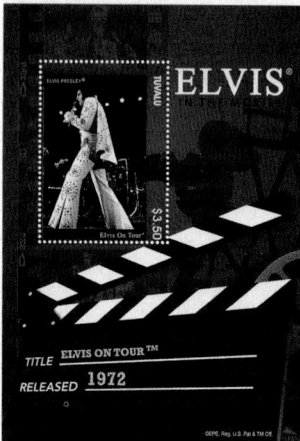

TITLE ELVIS ON TOUR ™

RELEASED 1972

Elvis Presley (1935-77) — A312

2012, June 27   *Perf. 13¼*
1210 A309 $3.50 multi   7.25   7.25
1211 A310 $3.50 multi   7.25   7.25
1212 A311 $3.50 multi   7.25   7.25
1213 A312 $3.50 multi   7.25   7.25
     Nos. 1210-1213 (4)   29.00   29.00

Fish — A313

Designs: 10c, Epibulus insidiator. 40c, Zanclus cornutus. 60c, Anampses cuvier. 90c, Rhinecanthus verrucosus. $1, Lactoria fornasini. $1.25, Enchelycore pardalis. $1.50, Diodon liturosus. $1.75, Anampses elegans. $2, Thalassoma trilobatum. $2.75, Pomacanthus imperator. $3.25, Pomacanthus semicirculatus. $5, Cheilinus fasciatus.

2012, July 15   *Perf. 13¾*
1214 A313   10c multi   .25   .25
1215 A313   40c multi   .85   .85
1216 A313   60c multi   1.25   1.25
1217 A313   90c multi   1.90   1.90
1218 A313 $1 multi   2.10   2.10
1219 A313 $1.25 multi   2.75   2.75
1220 A313 $1.50 multi   3.25   3.25
1221 A313 $1.75 multi   3.75   3.75
1222 A313 $2 multi   4.25   4.25
1223 A313 $2.75 multi   6.00   6.00
1224 A313 $3.25 multi   7.00   7.00
1225 A313 $5 multi   10.50   10.50
     Nos. 1214-1225 (12)   43.85   43.85

Dogs
A314

No. 1226: a, Duck tolling retriever. b, Berger Picard. c, Chow chow. d, Great Dane. e, Labrador retriever.

2012, July 15   *Perf. 14*
1226   Sheet of 5   10.50   10.50
a.-e. A314 $1 Any single   2.10   2.10

Miniature Sheet

Cats — A315

No. 1227: a, Siamese. b, Devon Rex. c, American wirehair. d, Cornish Rex. e, Burmese.

2012, Aug. 7
1227 A315 80c Sheet of 5, #a-e   8.50   8.50

Beetles — A316

No. 1228: a, Asian lady beetle. b, Blister beetle. c, Water beetle. d, Clytus arietis. $3, Firefly.

2012, Sept. 5
1228 A316 $1.25 Sheet of 4,
     #a-d   10.50   10.50
     Souvenir Sheet
     Perf. 12
1229 A316 $3 multi   6.25   6.25

Paintings by Raphael — A317

No. 1230: a, St. Margaret. b, Saint Michael Vanquishing Satan. c, Portrait of Elisabetta Gonzaga. d, The Holy Family. $3, St. Margaret, diff.

2012, Sept. 5   *Perf. 12¾*
1230 A317 $1 Sheet of 4, #a-d   8.50   8.50
     Souvenir Sheet
1231 A317 $3 multi   6.25   6.25

Visit of Duke and Duchess of
Cambridge to Tuvalu — A318

No. 1232: a, Duchess of Cambridge. b, Crest of Tuvalu. c, Duke and Duchess of Cambridge. d, Queen Elizabeth II visiting Tuvalu, 1982. e, Duke of Cambridge.
$3.50, Duke and Duchess of Cambridge, horiz.

2012, Oct. 1   *Perf. 14*
1232 A318 $1.25 Sheet of 5,
     #a-e   13.00   13.00
     Souvenir Sheet
     Perf. 12
1233 A318 $3.50 multi   7.25   7.25
No. 1233 contains one 50x30mm stamp. No. 1232 exists imperf.

Reign of Queen Elizabeth II, 60th
Anniv. — A319

No. 1234 — Queen Elizabeth II and: a, Prince Philip on Great Wall of China, 1986. b, Park ranger with hat at Yosemite National Park, 1983. c, Emperor Haile Selassie at Tissial Falls, Ethiopia, 1965. d, Prince Philip at Taj Mahal, 1961.
$3.50, Queen Elizabeth II and sailor in Tuvalu, 1982, vert.

2012, Dec. 31   *Perf. 13 Syncopated*
1234 A319 $1.25 Sheet of 4,
     #a-d   10.50   10.50
     Souvenir Sheet
1235 A319 $3.50 multi   7.50   7.50

World Humanitarian Day — A320

No. 1236: a, Earth. b, Dove with olive branch. c, Peace symbol. d, Red cross. $3.50, Heart.

2013, Mar. 21   *Perf. 13¾*
1236 A320 $1.20 Sheet of 4,
     #a-d   10.00   10.00
     Souvenir Sheet
1237 A320 $3.50 multi   7.50   7.50

Mushrooms — A321

No. 1238: a, Devil's bolete. b, Shaggy mane. c, Black trumpet. d, Chantarelle. $3.50, Entoloma clypeatum, vert.

2013, Apr. 29   *Perf. 12*
1238 A321 $1.20 Sheet of 4,
     #a-d   10.00   10.00
     Souvenir Sheet
1239 A321 $3.50 multi   7.25   7.25

A322

Flowers — A323

No. 1240: a, Medinilla magnifica. b, Alpinia purpurata. c, Nymphaea rubra. d, Crotalaria retusa.
No. 1241: a, Hibiscus rosa-sinensis. b, Gardenia taitensis. c, Hibiscus brackenridgei. d, Ranunculus lyallii.
No. 1242, Etlingera elatior. No. 1243, Tecomanthe speciosa, vert.

2013, Apr. 29   *Perf. 14*
1240 A322 $1.20 Sheet of 4,
     #a-d   10.00   10.00
     Perf. 12
1241 A323 $1.20 Sheet of 4,
     #a-d   10.00   10.00
     Souvenir Sheet
1242 A322 $3.50 multi   7.25   7.25
1243 A323 $3.50 multi   7.25   7.25

A324

Election of Pope Francis — A325

No. 1244: a, White smoke rising from chimney of Sistine Chapel. b, Pope Francis waving and holding crucifix. c, Pope Francis in window. d, Head of Pope Francis.
$8, Pope Francis waving.

2013, June 3   Litho.   Perf. 14
1244 A324 $1.20 Sheet of 4, #a-d   9.25 9.25

Souvenir Sheet
Without Gum
Litho., Margin Embossed With Foil Application
Imperf
1245 A325 $8 multi   15.50 15.50

Miniature Sheet

Seashells — A326

No. 1246: a, Depressed cowry. b, Japanese wonder shell. c, Fluted giant clam. d, Chambered nautilus. e, Precious wentletrap.

Perf. 13 Syncopated
2013, June 3   Litho.
1246 A326 $1 Sheet of 5, #a-e   9.50 9.50
Tel Aviv 2013 International Stamp Exhibition.

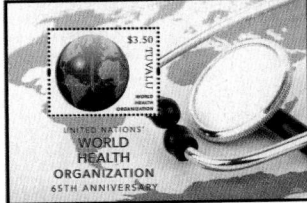

World Health Organization, 65th Anniv. — A327

No. 1247 — Globe and inscription: a, World Tuberculosis Day. b, World Immunization Week. c, World Health Day. d, World AIDS Day. e, World No Tobacco Day. f, World Blood Donor Day.
$3.50, Globe and inscription "World Health Organization."

2013, June 25
1247 A327 90c Sheet of 6, #a-f   10.00 10.00
Souvenir Sheet
1248 A327 $3.50 multi   6.50 6.50

Dolphins — A328

No. 1249: a, Short-finned pilot whale. b, Risso's dolphin. c, Pacific white-sided dolphin. d, Northern right whale dolphin.
$3.50, Melon-headed whale.

2013, July 24   Perf. 12
1249 A328 $1.25 Sheet of 4, #a-d   9.00 9.00
Souvenir Sheet
1250 A328 $3.50 multi   6.50 6.50

Miniature Sheets

Fish — A329

No. 1251, $1.25: a, Blue-head fairy wrasse. b, Clownfish. c, Clown triggerfish. d, Copperband butterflyfish.
No. 1252, $1.25: a, Scribbled angelfish. b, Flame angelfish. c, Harlequin tuskfish. d, Flameback angelfish.

2013, July 24   Perf. 13¾
Sheets of 4, #a-d
1251-1252 A329 Set of 2   18.00 18.00

Temples of Thailand — A330

No. 1253: a, Wat Pha Sorn Kaew. b, Wat Pho. c, Wat Phra Kaew. d, Wat Phra Singh.
$3.50, Wat Suthat.

2013, July 30   Litho.
1253 A330 $1.20 Sheet of 4, #a-d   8.75 8.75
Souvenir Sheet
1254 A330 $3.50 multi   6.50 6.50
Thailand 2013 World Stamp Exhibition, Bangkok.

Coronation of Queen Elizabeth II, 60th Anniv. — A331

No. 1255 — Queen Elizabeth II: a, Waving. b, Wearing tiara. c, Wearing white hat. d, Watching young Prince Charles at play.
$3.50, Queen Elizabeth II, diff.

2013, Oct. 7   Litho.   Perf. 13¾
1255 A331 $1.20 Sheet of 4, #a-d   9.25 9.25
Souvenir Sheet
1256 A331 $3.50 multi   6.75 6.75

Birth of Prince George of Cambridge — A332

No. 1257: a, Duke and Duchess of Cambridge, Prince George. b, Prince Charles, Princess Diana, Prince William. c, Princess Diana holding Prince William. d, Duchess of Cambridge holding Prince George.
$3.50, Duke and Duchess of Cambridge, Prince George, diff.

2013, Oct. 7   Litho.   Perf. 14
1257 A332 $1.20 Sheet of 4, #a-d   9.25 9.25
Souvenir Sheet
Perf. 12
1258 A332 $3.50 multi   6.75 6.75

Miniature Sheet

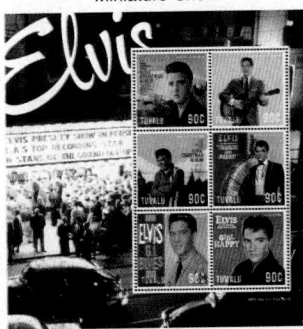

Elvis Presley (1935-77) — A333

No. 1259: a, Album cover for Elvis' Christmas Album, Presley to right of text. b, Presley playing guitar. c, Album cover for Elvis' Christmas Album, Presley to left of text. d, Frankie and Johnny album cover. e, G.I. Blues album cover. f, Girl Happy album cover.

2013, Dec. 2   Litho.   Perf. 13¾
1259 A333 90c Sheet of 6, #a-f   9.75 9.75

Orange Blossom Special — A334

2013, Dec. 9   Litho.   Perf. 12½
1260 A334 60c multi   1.10 1.10

Souvenir Sheet
Perf. 13½
1261 A334 $3.50 multi   6.25 6.25
No. 1260 was printed in sheets of 9. No. 1261 contains one 38x51mm stamp.

Meeting of Pres. Barack Obama and Queen Elizabeth II — A335

No. 1262: a, Queen Elizabeth II. b, Pres. Barack Obama. c, Michelle Obama. d, Prince Philip.
No. 1263, horiz.: a, Pres. Obama. b, Michelle Obama.
$3.50, Queen Elizabeth II and Pres. Obama.

Perf. 12½, 13½ (#1263)
2013, Dec. 9   Litho.
1262 A335 $1.20 Sheet of 4, #a-d   8.75 8.75
1263 A335 $1.75 Sheet of 2, #a-b   6.25 6.25
Souvenir Sheet
1264 A335 $3.50 multi   6.25 6.25
No. 1263 contains two 51x38mm stamps.

A336

Nelson Mandela (1918-2013), President of South Africa — A337

No. 1266 — South African flag and Mandela: a, With fist raised, sign at right. b, With fist raised, standing at lectern. c, Wearing suit and tie. d, Standing in crowd with fist raised, man to Mandela's right. e, Waving at crowd, wife, Winnie, to Mandela's right. f, Holding on to railing.

2013, Dec. 15   Litho.   Perf. 13¾
1265 A336 $1 multi   1.90 1.90
1266 A337 $1 Sheet of 6, #a-f   11.00 11.00
No. 1265 was printed in sheets of 6.

Pope John Paul II (1920-
2005) — A338

No. 1267 — Pope John Paul II with denomination in: a, Black. b, White.
$3.50, Pope John Paul II, horiz.

2013, Dec. 23   Litho.   Perf. 14
1267 A338 $1.20 Horiz. pair, #a-
          b   4.25 4.25
Souvenir Sheet
1268 A338 $3.50 multi   6.25 6.25
No. 1267 was printed in sheets containing two pairs.

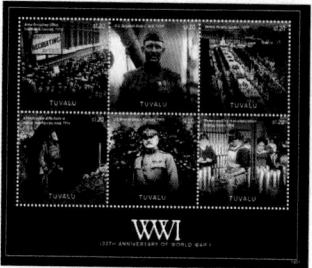

World War I, Cent. — A339

No. 1269: a, Army Recruiting Office, Southwark, London, England, 1915. b, U.S. Sergeant Alvin C. York, 1919. c, Victory parade, London, 1919. d, French soldier at Battle of Verdun wearing gas mask, 1916. e, U.S. General John J. Pershing, 1918. f, Women working in ammunition factory, France, 1914.
$4, U.S. Army recruiting poster, vert.

2014, Mar. 5   Litho.   Perf. 13¾
1269 A339 $1.20 Sheet of 6,
          #a-f   13.50 13.50
Souvenir Sheet
Perf. 12½
1270 A339 $4 multi   7.50 7.50
No. 1270 contains one 38x51mm stamp.

Characters From *Downton Abbey*
Television Series — A340

No. 1271: a, Sir Richard Carlisle. b, Lady Mary Crawley. c, Matthew Crawley. d, Dr. Richard Clarkson.
$3.50, Matthew Crawley and Lady Mary Crawley, horiz.

2014, Mar. 5   Litho.   Perf. 14
1271 A340 $1.20 Sheet of 4, #a-
          d   9.00 9.00
Souvenir Sheet
1272 A340 $3.50 multi   6.50 6.50

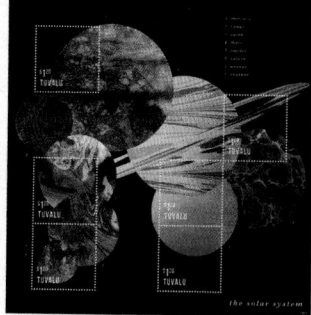

Solar System — A341

No. 1273: a, Jupiter. b, Neptune, rings of Saturn. c, Earth and Venus. d, Saturn and Uranus. e, Venus and Mercury. f, Uranus.
$4.50, Sun.

2014, Mar. 24   Litho.   Perf. 13¾
1273 A341 $1.20 Sheet of 6,
          #a-f   13.50 13.50
Souvenir Sheet
1274 A341 $4.50 multi   8.50 8.50

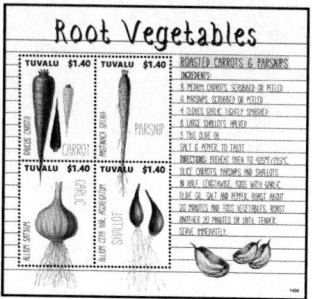

Vegetables — A342

No. 1275, $1.40: a, Carrots. b, Parsnip. c, Garlic. d, Shallots.
No. 1276, $1.40: a, Kohlrabi. b, Turnip. c, Sweet potato. d, Onion.
No. 1277, $2.25, horiz.: a, Radishes. b, Fennel.
No. 1278, $2.25, horiz.: a, Potato. b, Leek.

2014, Apr. 23   Litho.   Perf. 14
Sheets of 4, #a-d
1275-1276 A342 Set of 2   21.00 21.00
Souvenir Sheets of 2, #a-b
1277-1278 A342 Set of 2   17.00 17.00

Giant Pacific Octopus — A343

No. 1279: Various photographs of octopus, as shown.
$4.50, Octopus, vert.

2014, May 8   Litho.   Perf. 13¾
1279 A343 50c Block of 4, #a-d 3.75 3.75
Souvenir Sheet
Perf. 12¾
1280 A343 $4.50 multi   8.50 8.50
No. 1280 contains one 38x51mm stamp.

Meeting of
Queen
Elizabeth II
and Pope
Francis
A344

Designs: No. 1281, Queen Elizabeth II and Pope Francis shaking hands, orange yellow frame.
No. 1282: a, Queen Elizabeth II, Prince Philip and Pope Francis shaking hands, tan frame. b, Queen Elizabeth II and Pope Francis, flowers in background, green frame. c, Queen Elizabeth II and Pope Francis seated, green frame. d, Queen Elizabeth II, Prince Philip, Pope Francis and other men, tan background.
$3.50, Queen Elizabeth II and Pope Francis, vert.

2014, July 21   Litho.   Perf. 14
1281 A344 $1.20 multi   2.25 2.25
1282 A344 $1.20 Sheet of 4, #a-
          d   9.00 9.00
Souvenir Sheet
Perf. 12¾
1283 A344 $3.50 multi   6.50 6.50
No. 1281 was printed in sheets of 4. No. 1283 contains one 38x51mm stamp.

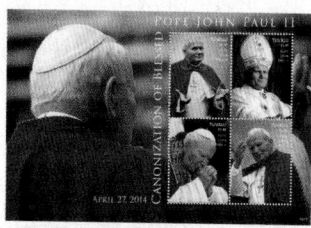

A345

A346

A347

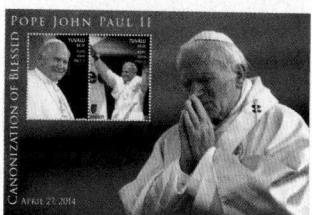

Canonization of Pope John Paul
II — A348

Various photographs of Pope John Paul II, as shown.

2014, July 21   Litho.   Perf. 14
1284 A345 $1.40 Sheet of 4,
          #a-d   10.50 10.50
1285 A346 $1.40 Sheet of 4,
          #a-d   10.50 10.50
Souvenir Sheets
1286 A347 $2.25 Sheet of 2,
          #a-b   8.50 8.50
1287 A348 $2.25 Sheet of 2,
          #a-b   8.50 8.50

Ducks — A349

No. 1288, $1.40: a, Mandarin duck facing right. b, Mandarin duck facing left. c, Mandarin duck with wing extended. d, Mandarin duck in water.
No. 1289, $1.40: a, Female wood duck. b, Mallard. c, Male wood duck. d, Mandarin duck facing left, diff.
No. 1290, $2.25: a, Wood duck, diff. b, Mandarin duck, diff.
No. 1291, $2.25, vert.: a, Mallard. b, Mandarin duck, diff.

2014, July 21   Litho.   Perf. 14
Sheets of 4, #a-d
1288-1289 A349 Set of 2   21.00 21.00
Souvenir Sheets of 2, #a-b
1290-1291 A349 Set of 2   17.00 17.00

Fall of the Berlin Wall, 25th
Anniv. — A350

No. 1292 — Berlin Wall graffiti depicting: a, Red bear. b, Animal with boxing gloves, graffiti artist. c, Stylized flower and cartoon balloon. d, Woman wearing cap.
$5, "Change Your Life."

2014, Aug. 14   Litho.   Perf. 14
1292 A350 $1.40 Sheet of 4,
          #a-d   10.50 10.50
Souvenir Sheet
Perf. 12¾
1293 A350 $5 multi   9.25 9.25
No. 1293 contains one 38x51mm stamp.

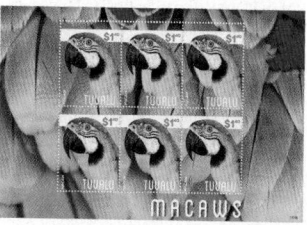

A351

Macaws — A352

Nos. 1294 and 1295: a-f, Macaw with different feather lines and colors in background, as shown.
No. 1296, horiz. — Macaw with denomination at: a, Right. b, Left.
$4.50, Macaw, diff.

2014, Aug. 14   Litho.   Perf. 14
1294 A351 $1.40 Sheet of 6,
          #a-f   15.50 15.50
1295 A352 $1.40 Sheet of 6,
          #a-f   15.50 15.50

Souvenir Sheets
Perf. 12¾

1296	A352	$2.25 Sheet of 2,		
		#a-b	8.50	8.50
1297	A352	$4.50 multi	8.50	8.50

No. 1296 contains two 51x38mm stamps.
No. 1297 contains one 38x51mm stamp.

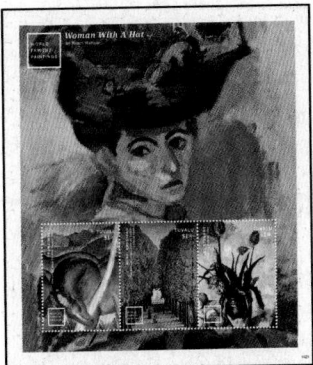

Paintings — A353

No. 1298, $1.50: a, The Large Blue Horses, by Franz Marc. b, The Avenue in the Port at Saint-Cloud, by Henri Rousseau. c, Tulips in a Vase, by Paul Cézanne.

No. 1299, $1.50: a, Woman Reading, by Henri Matisse. b, Pyramid of Skulls, by Cézanne. c, Self-portrait with Pipe, by Vincent van Gogh.

No. 1300, $4.50, Nighthawks, by Edward Hopper. No. 1301, $4.50, Portrait of Père Tanguy, by van Gogh.

2014, Aug. 14   Litho.   Perf. 12¾
Sheets of 3, #a-c

1298-1299	A353	Set of 2	17.00	17.00

Imperf
Size: 100x100mm

1300-1301	A353	Set of 2	17.00	17.00

Sharks — A354

No. 1302, $1.40: a, Whale shark. b, Hammerhead shark. c, Caribbean reef shark. d, Great white shark.

No. 1303, $1.40: a, Whitetip shark. b, Gray reef shark. c, Leopard shark. d, Tiger shark.

No. 1304: a, Whale shark, diff. b, Gray reef shark, diff.

$4.50, Blacktip reef shark.

Perf. 14, 12¾ (#1303, 1305)
2014, Sept. 3   Litho.
Sheets of 4, #a-d

1302-1303	A354	Set of 2	20.00	20.00

Souvenir Sheets

1304	A354	$2.25 Sheet of 2,		
		#a-b	8.00	8.00
1305	A354	$4.50 multi	8.00	8.00

No. 1303 contains four 51x38mm stamps.
No. 1305 contains one 51x38mm stamp.

A355

A356

A357

Sea Turtles — A358

Various sea turtles, as shown.

2014, Sept. 3   Litho.   Perf. 12

1306	A355	$1.40 Sheet of 4,		
		#a-d	10.00	10.00
1307	A356	$1.40 Sheet of 4,		
		#a-d	10.00	10.00

Souvenir Sheets
Perf. 12¾

1308	A357	$2.25 Sheet of 2,		
		#a-b	8.00	8.00
1309	A358	$2.25 Sheet of 2,		
		#a-b	8.00	8.00

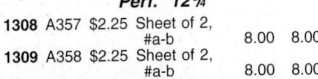

Surfing — A360

No. 1314, $1.40 — Various silhouettes of surfers with central background color of: a, Light blue green. b, Blue violet. c, Red. d, Bister.

No. 1315, $1.40, horiz. — Surfboards decorated with: a, Palm tree and sun. b, Flowers and wave. c, Vine and stripes. d, Waves.

No. 1316, $2.25, horiz. — Various silhouettes of surfers with central background color of: a, Light blue green (surfer's hands visible). b, Blue (surfer's hands not visible).

No. 1317, $2.25, horiz. — Surfboards decorated with: a, Waves, diff. b, Vine.

Perf. 13¾, 12 (#1315, 1317)
2014, Dec. 16   Litho.
Sheets of 4, #a-d

1314-1315	A360	Set of 2	18.50	18.50

Souvenir Sheets of 2, #a-b

1316-1317	A360	Set of 2	15.00	15.00

Nos. 1316 and 1317 each contain two 50x30mm stamps.

Inaugural Mass of Pope Benedict XVI — A361

No. 1318 — Pope Benedict XVI: a, On steps. b, Wearing zucchetto, waving. c, Swinging censer. d, Wearing miter, waving.

$4.50, Pope Benedict XVI waving, diff.

2014, Dec. 31   Litho.   Perf. 14

1318	A361	$1.40 Sheet of 4, #a-		
		d	9.25	9.25

Souvenir Sheet
Perf. 12

1319	A361	$4.50 multi	7.25	7.25

No. 1319 contains one 30x50mm stamp.

Souvenir Sheet

St. John Paul II (1920-2005) — A362

2015, Feb. 2   Litho.   Perf. 14

1320	A362	$3.50 multi	5.50	5.50

Corals — A363

No. 1321: a, Bubble coral. b, Frogspawn coral. c, Mushroom coral. d, Brain coral.

$4.50, Coral on giant clam.

2015, Feb. 2   Litho.   Perf. 14

1321	A363	$1.40 Sheet of 4, #a-		
		d	8.75	8.75

Souvenir Sheet
Perf. 12

1322	A363	$4.50 multi	7.00	7.00

Tropical Fish — A364

No. 1323, $1.75: a, Flame angelfish. b, Passer angelfish. c, Palette surgeonfish. d, Scribbled angelfish.

No. 1324, $1.75: a, Clown triggerfish. b, Powder blue surgeonfish. c, Clown anemonefish. d, Emperor angelfish.

No. 1325, $2.25: a, Southern orange-lined cardinalfish. b, Yellow tang.

No. 1326, $2.25: a, Coral grouper. b, Fire clownfish.

2015, Mar. 2   Litho.   Perf. 14
Sheets of 4, #a-d

1323-1324	A364	Set of 2	22.00	22.00

Souvenir Sheets of 2, #a-b
Perf. 12¾

1325-1326	A364	Set of 2	14.00	14.00

Nos. 1325-1326 each contain two 51x38mm stamps.

SEMI-POSTAL STAMPS

Nos. 159-160 Srchd. and Ovptd. "TONGA CYCLONE / RELIEF / 1982" in 1 or 3 Lines
Wmk. 380

1982, May 20   Litho.   Perf. 14

B1	A25a	45c + 20c multi	.35	.35
B2	A25b	45c + 20c multi	.35	.35

POSTAGE DUE STAMPS

Arms of Tuvalu — D1

1981, May 13   Litho.   Perf. 14

J1	D1	1c brt rose lil & blk	.25	.25
J2	D1	2c grnsh bl & blk	.25	.25
J3	D1	5c yellow brn & blk	.25	.25
J4	D1	10c blue grn & blk	.25	.25
J5	D1	20c chocolate & blk	.25	.25
J6	D1	30c orange & blk	.25	.25
J7	D1	40c ultra & blk	.25	.25
J8	D1	50c yellow grn & blk	.30	.30
J9	D1	$1 brt lilac & blk	.55	.55
		Nos. J1-J9 (9)	2.60	2.60

1982-83			**Perf. 14x15**	
J1a	D1	1c bright rose lilac & black	.25	.25
J2a	D1	2c greenish blue & black	.25	.25
J3a	D1	5c yellow brown & black	.25	.25
J4a	D1	10c blue green & black	.25	.25
J5a	D1	20c chocolate & black	.25	.25
J6a	D1	30c orange & black	.35	.30
J7a	D1	40c ultra & black	.45	.35
J8a	D1	50c yellow green & black	.55	.45
J9a	D1	$1 bright lilac & black	.90	.65
		Nos. J1a-J9a (9)	3.50	3.00

Issued: 1c-20c, 11/25/82 (inscribed "1982"); 30c-$1, 5/25/83 (inscribed "1983").

OFFICIAL STAMPS

Nos. 96-113 Overprinted "OFFICIAL"

1981 Litho. Unwmk. *Perf. 14*

O1	A14	1c multicolored	.25	.25
O2	A14	2c multicolored	.25	.25
O3	A14	4c multicolored	.25	.25
O4	A14	5c multicolored	.25	.25
O5	A14	6c multicolored	.25	.25
O6	A14	8c multicolored	.25	.25
O7	A14	10c multicolored	.25	.25
O8	A14	15c multicolored	.25	.25
O9	A14	20c multicolored	.25	.25
O10	A14	25c multicolored	.25	.25
O11	A14	30c multicolored	.30	.30
O12	A14	35c multicolored	.35	.35
O13	A14	40c multicolored	.45	.45
O14	A14	45c multicolored	.50	.50
O15	A14	50c multicolored	.55	.55
O16	A14	70c multicolored	.70	.70
O17	A14	$1 multicolored	.90	.90
O18	A14	$2 multicolored	2.00	2.00
O19	A14	$5 multicolored	4.50	4.50
		Nos. O1-O19 (19)	12.75	12.75

No. 193 Srchd. and Ovptd. "OFFICIAL"

Wmk. 380

1983, Aug. Litho. *Perf. 14*

O20	A30	60c on $1 multi	.75	.75

Nos. 185-186A, 188, 230, 188A-195 Ovptd. "OFFICIAL"

1984 Litho. Wmk. 380 *Perf. 14*

O21	A30	5c multicolored	.25	.35
O22	A30	10c multicolored	.25	.35
O23	A30	15c multicolored	.25	.65
O24	A30	25c multicolored	.30	.55
O25	A30	30c on 45c multi	.65	.65
O25A	A30	30c multicolored	.40	.65
O26	A30	35c multicolored	.50	.70
O27	A30	40c multicolored	.55	.70
O28	A30	45c multicolored	.65	.70
O29	A30	50c multicolored	.65	.65
O29A	A30	60c multicolored	.75	.90
O30	A30	$1 multicolored	.95	.90
O31	A30	$2 multicolored	1.50	1.00
O32	A30	$5 multicolored	3.50	2.25
		Nos. O21-O32 (14)	11.15	11.00

Issued: #O23, O29A, Apr. 30; others Feb. 1.

Nos. 469-484 Overprinted "OFFICIAL"

1989, Feb. 22 Litho. *Perf. 15*

O33	A64	5c multicolored	.25	.25
O34	A64	10c multicolored	.25	.25
O35	A64	15c multicolored	.25	.25
O36	A64	20c multicolored	.25	.25
O37	A64	25c multicolored	.30	.30
O38	A64	30c multicolored	.40	.40
O39	A64	35c multicolored	.45	.45
O40	A64	40c multicolored	.50	.50
O41	A64	45c multicolored	.60	.60
O42	A64	50c multicolored	.65	.65
O43	A64	55c multicolored	.70	.70
O44	A64	60c multicolored	.75	.75
O45	A64	70c multicolored	.90	.90
O46	A64	$1 multicolored	1.25	1.25
O47	A64	$2 multicolored	2.50	2.50
O48	A64	$5 multicolored	6.50	6.50
		Nos. O33-O48 (16)	16.50	16.50

For the following islands all are types of Tuvalu unless otherwise specified.

See note following Tuvalu No. 221.

Leaders of the World

Large quantities of some Leaders of the World sets, including unissued stamps, were sold at a fraction of face value when the printer was liquidated.

FUNAFUTI

Catalogue values for all unused stamps in this country are for Never Hinged items.

Locomotive Type of 1984

No. 1, 1919 Class C51, Japan. No. 2, 1935 F.C.C. Andes Class, Peru. No. 3, 1934 Kolhapur Class, UK. No. 4, 1941 V.R. Class H, Australia. No. 5, 1885 S.A.R. Class Y, Australia. No. 6, 1951 Class 4, UK. No. 7, 1928 Class U, UK. No. 8, 1923 Eryri Cog, UK. No. 9, 1927 Royal Scot Class, UK. No. 10, 1828 Lancashire Witch, UK. No. 11, 1906 NY, NH & H RR Class EP-1, US. No. 12, 1942 Springbok Class B1, UK. No. 13, 1827 Royal George, UK. No. 14, 1926 Northern Pacific Class A5, US. No. 15, 1900 Aberdare Class 2600, UK. No. 16, 1829 Sans Pareil, UK. No. 17, 1924 EST Class 241A, France. No. 18, 1911 Class 8K, UK. No. 19, 1913 Sir Gilbert Claughton, UK. No. 20, 1920 Sherlock Holmes, UK. No. 21, 1949 Class K1, UK. No. 22, 1925 Class P1, UK. No. 23, 1940 SNCF Class 232R, France. No. 24, 1904 B&O Class DD-1.

Se-tenant Pairs, #a.-b.

a. — Side and front views.

b. — Action scene.

Perf. 12½x13

1984-86 Litho. Unwmk.

1	A36	5c multicolored	.25	.25
2	A36	5c multicolored	.25	.25
3	A36	15c multicolored	.25	.25
4	A36	15c multicolored	.25	.25
5	A36	15c multicolored	.25	.25
6	A36	20c multicolored	.25	.25
7	A36	20c multicolored	.25	.25
8	A36	25c multicolored	.25	.25
9	A36	30c multicolored	.30	.30
10	A36	35c multicolored	.35	.35
11	A36	35c multicolored	.35	.35
12	A36	40c multicolored	.35	.35
13	A36	40c multicolored	.35	.35
14	A36	40c multicolored	.35	.35
15	A36	40c multicolored	.35	.35
16	A36	50c multicolored	.55	.55
17	A36	50c multicolored	.55	.55
18	A36	55c multicolored	.55	.55
19	A36	60c multicolored	.60	.60
20	A36	60c multicolored	.60	.60
21	A36	60c multicolored	.60	.60
22	A36	$1 multicolored	1.00	1.00
23	A36	$1 multicolored	1.00	1.00
24	A36	$1.50 multicolored	1.50	1.50
		Nos. 1-24 (24)	11.35	11.35

Issued: #3, 6, 9, 12, 16, 19, 4/16/84; 1, 4, 8, 10, 13, 18, 20, 22, 12/24/84; 2, 5, 11, 14, 17, 23, 4/29/85; 7, 15, 21, 24, 12/30/86.

1986 stamps not inscribed "Leaders of the World."

Automobile Type of 1984

No. 25, 1957 Triumph TR3A, UK. No. 26, 1932 Nash Special 8 Convertible, US. No. 27, 1937 Cord 812 Supercharged, US. No. 28, 1925 AC Six, UK. No. 29, 1924 Alfa Romeo P2, Italy. No. 30, 1935 Aston Martin Ulster, UK. No. 31, 1948 Morgan 4+4, UK. No. 32, 1906 Renault GP, France. No. 33, 1903 Cadillac Model A. No. 34, 1971 Porsche 917K, Germany. No. 35, 1913 Simplex 75HP, US. No. 36, 1939 Delahaye Type 165, France. No. 37, 1938 Opel Admiral, Germany. No. 38, 1936 Jaguar SS 100, UK. No. 39, 1965 Aston Martin DB5, UK. No. 40, 1977 Porsche 935.

Se-tenant Pairs, #a.-b.

a. — Side and front views.

b. — Action scene.

1984-87

25	A41	1c multicolored	.25	.25
26	A41	1c multicolored	.25	.25
27	A41	10c multicolored	.25	.25
28	A41	10c multicolored	.25	.25
29	A41	20c multicolored	.25	.25
30	A41	30c multicolored	.30	.30
31	A41	40c multicolored	.40	.40
32	A41	40c multicolored	.40	.40
33	A41	55c multicolored	.55	.55
34	A41	60c multicolored	.60	.60
35	A41	60c multicolored	.60	.60
36	A41	75c multicolored	.75	.75
37	A41	80c multicolored	.80	.80
38	A41	$1 multicolored	1.00	1.00
39	A41	$1 multicolored	1.00	1.00
40	A41	$1.50 multicolored	1.60	1.60
		Nos. 25-40 (16)	9.25	9.25

Issued: #25, 27, 31, 38, 9/13/84; 26, 30, 33, 34, 2/8/85; 28-29, 32, 35-37, 39-40, 8/27/87.

1987 stamps not inscribed "Leaders of the World."

Queen Mother Type of 1985

Hats: #45a, Blue feathered. #45b, White. #46a, 50a, Pink. #46b, 50b, Tiara. #47a, 51a, Blue. #47b, 51b, Blue with veil covering face. #48a, Blue. #48b, Tiara. #49a, Headband. #49b, Hat.

1985-86 *Perf. 13x12½*

45	A45	5c Pair, #a.-b.	.30	.30
46	A45	25c Pair, #a.-b.	.40	.40
47	A45	80c Pair, #a.-b.	1.20	1.20
48	A45	$1.05 Pair, #a.-b.	1.40	1.40
		Nos. 45-48 (4)	3.30	3.30

Souvenir Sheets of 2

49	A45	$1.05 #a.-b.	2.50	2.50
50	A45	$2 #a.-b.	2.75	2.75
51	A45	$3 #a.-b.	4.75	4.75

Issued: #45-49, 8/26; #50-51, 1/3/86.

Elizabeth II 60th Birthday Type

1986, Apr. 21 *Perf. 13x12½, 12½x13*

52	A49	10c Trooping the colors	.25	.25
53	A49	50c Tiara	.35	.35
54	A49	$1.50 As young woman, 1952	1.10	1.10
55	A49	$3.50 Tiara, diff., vert.	2.75	2.75
		Nos. 52-55 (4)	4.45	4.45

Souvenir Sheet

56	A49	$5 Scarf	4.00	4.00

Royal Wedding Type of 1986

#59a, Andrew holding rifle, vert. #59b, Sarah Ferguson, vert. #60a, Couple. #60b, Prince Philip and Andrew.

1986, July 23

59	A53	60c Pair, #a.-b.	1.25	1.25
60	A53	$1 Pair, #a.-b.	2.00	2.00

Souvenir Sheet

61	A56	$4 Newlyweds	4.75	4.75

Nos. 59-60 Ovptd. in Silver "Congratulations to T.R.H. The Duke & Duchess of York"

1986, July 23

62	A53	60c Pair, #a.-b.	2.00	2.00
63	A53	$1 Pair, #a.-b.	3.75	3.75

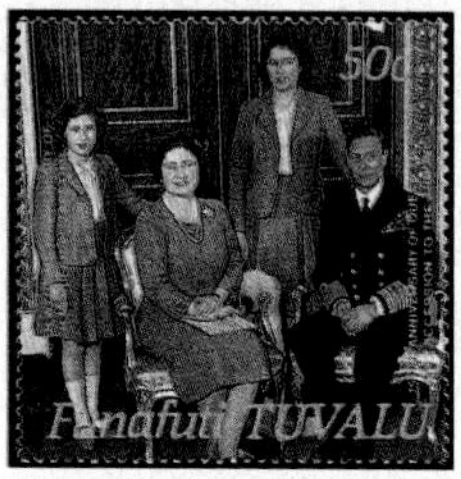

Royal Anniversaries — A1

1987 *Perf. 15*

66	A1	20c Queen Victoria	.30	.30
67	A1	50c George VI, Family	.65	.65
68	A1	75c Elizabeth	1.05	1.05
69	A1	$1.20 Elizabeth, Philip	1.75	1.75
70	A1	$1.75 Elizabeth, diff.	2.50	2.50
		Nos. 66-70 (5)	6.25	6.25

Souvenir Sheet

71	A1	$3 Elizabeth, Family	5.50	5.50

Elizabeth's 40th wedding anniv., Queen Victoria's accession to the throne, sesquicentennial.

Summer Olympics Type of 1988

1988, Aug. 19 *Perf. 13x12½*

72	A69	10c Hurdles	.25	.25
73	A69	20c High jump	.25	.25
74	A69	40c Running	.50	.50
75	A69	50c Discus	.60	.60
76	A69	80c Pole vault	1.00	1.00
77	A69	90c Javelin	1.10	1.10
		Nos. 72-77 (6)	3.70	3.70

NANUMAGA

Automobile Type of 1984

No. 1, 1903 De Dion-Bouton Single Cylinder. No. 2, 1955 Ford Thunderbird. No. 3, 1966 Lotus Elan, UK. No. 4, 1915 Stutz Bearcat. No. 5, 1915 Dodge 4-Cylinder Touring Car. No. 6, 1976 Jaguar XJ-S, UK. No. 7, 1928 Morgan Super Sports, UK. No. 8, 1906 Spyker, Holland. No. 9, 1957 Dual-Ghia, US. No. 10, 1966 Lamborghini P400 Miura Coupe, Italy. No. 11, 1947 Kaiser Traveler, US. No. 12, 1951 Lancia Aurelia, Italy. No. 13, 1963 Chevrolet Corvette Coupe. No. 14, 1949 Jaguar XK 120, UK. No. 15, 1930 Renault Reinastella, France. No. 16, 1938 Alvis Speed 25, UK. No. 17, 1956 Studebaker Golden Hawk. No. 18, 1909 Alco, US. No. 19, 1966 Shelby GT-350 Coupe, US. No. 20, 1968 Mercedes 300 SEL, Germany. No. 21, 1953 BRM V-16, UK. No. 22, 1910 Lozier Briarcliff, US.

Se-tenant Pairs, #a.-b.

a. — Side and front views.

b. — Action scene.

Perf. 12½x13

1984-87 Litho. Unwmk.

1	A41	5c multicolored	.25	.25
2	A41	5c multicolored	.25	.25
3	A41	5c multicolored	.25	.25
4	A41	10c multicolored	.25	.25
5	A41	10c multicolored	.25	.25
6	A41	10c multicolored	.25	.25
7	A41	10c multicolored	.25	.25
8	A41	15c multicolored	.25	.25
9	A41	20c multicolored	.25	.25
10	A41	25c multicolored	.35	.35
11	A41	25c multicolored	.35	.35
12	A41	25c multicolored	.35	.35
13	A41	30c multicolored	.40	.40
14	A41	40c multicolored	.55	.55
15	A41	40c multicolored	.55	.55
16	A41	50c multicolored	.60	.60
17	A41	60c multicolored	.80	.80
18	A41	75c multicolored	1.00	1.00
19	A41	$1 multicolored	1.50	1.50
20	A41	$1 multicolored	1.50	1.50
21	A41	$1 multicolored	1.50	1.50
22	A41	$1 multicolored	1.50	1.50
		Nos. 1-22 (22)	13.20	13.20

Issued: #1, 4, 10, 14, 19, 6/11/84; #2, 5, 16, 20, 12/24/84; #6, 11, 18, 21, 7/23/85; #3, 7-9, 12, 15, 17, 22, 8/6/87.

1987 stamps not inscribed "Leaders of the World."

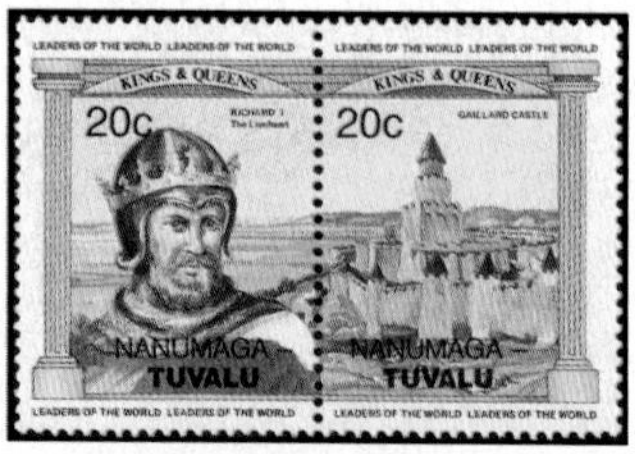

British Monarchs — A2

Se-tenant Pairs, #a.-b.

a. — Left stamp.

b. — Right stamp.

1984, Nov. 27 *Perf. 13x12½*

23	A2	10c Richard I	.25	.25
24	A2	20c Richard I, diff.	.25	.25
25	A2	30c Third Crusade	.35	.35
26	A2	40c Alfred the Great	.45	.45
27	A2	50c Alfred, diff.	.55	.55
28	A2	$1 Battle of Edington	1.10	1.10
		Nos. 23-28 (6)	2.95	2.95

Locomotive Type of 1984

10c, 1906 NYC & HR Class S. 25c, 1884 T.R. Class B, Australia. 50c, 1902 Decapod, UK. 60c, 1846 Coppernob, UK.

Se-tenant Pairs, #a.-b.

a. — Side and front views.

b. — Action scene.

1985, Apr. 3 *Perf. 12½x13*

29	A36	10c multicolored	.25	.25
30	A36	25c multicolored	.50	.50
31	A36	50c multicolored	.90	.90
32	A36	60c multicolored	1.10	1.10
		Nos. 29-32 (4)	2.75	2.75

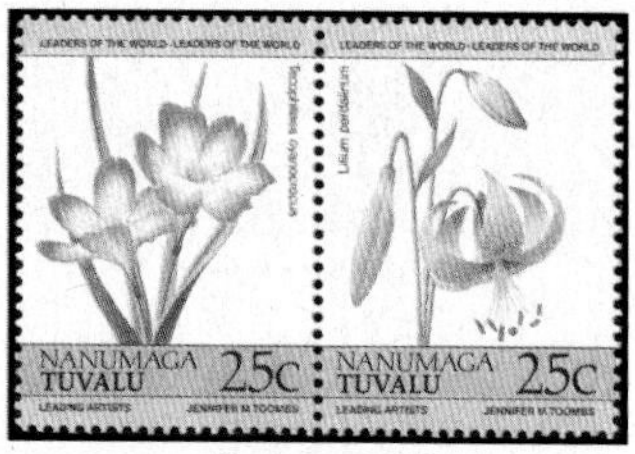

Flowers — A3

#33a, Tecophilaea cyanocrocus. #33b, Lilium pardalinum. #34a, Canarina abyssinica. #34b, Vanda coerulea. #35a, Lathyrus maritimus. #35b, Narcissus tazetta. #36a, Bauera sessiflora. #36b, Thelymitra venosa.

1985, May 3 *Perf. 13x12½*

33	A3	25c Pair, #a.-b.	.60	.60
34	A3	30c Pair, #a.-b.	.70	.70
35	A3	40c Pair, #a.-b.	1.00	1.00
36	A3	50c Pair, #a.-b.	1.25	1.25
		Nos. 33-36 (4)	3.55	3.55

Queen Mother Type of 1985

Hats: #45a, White. #45b, Blue feathered. #46a, 50a, Violet blue wide-brimmed. #46b, 50b, Blue green wide-brimmed. #47a, 51a, Tiara. #47b, 51b, Light blue. #48a, Dark blue. #48b, Black.

#49a, As young girl. #49b, As young woman.

1985-86

45	A45	15c Pair, #a.-b.	.30	.30
46	A45	55c Pair, #a.-b.	1.00	1.00
47	A45	65c Pair, #a.-b.	1.10	1.10
48	A45	90c Pair, #a.-b.	1.60	1.60
		Nos. 45-48 (4)	4.00	4.00

Souvenir Sheets of 2

49	A45	$1.15 #a.-b.	1.75	1.75
50	A45	$2.10 #a.-b.	2.50	2.50
51	A45	$2.50 #a.-b.	3.00	3.00

Issued: #41-49, 9/5; 50-51, 1/3/86.

Elizabeth II 60th Birthday Type

1986, Apr. 21 *Perf. 13x12½, 12½x13*

52	A49	5c White hat	.25	.25
53	A49	$1 As young woman	.40	.40
54	A49	$1.75 Tam	.75	.75
55	A49	$2.50 Tiara, vert.	.95	.95
		Nos. 52-55 (4)	2.35	2.35

Souvenir Sheet

56	A49	$4 Portrait	3.00	3.00

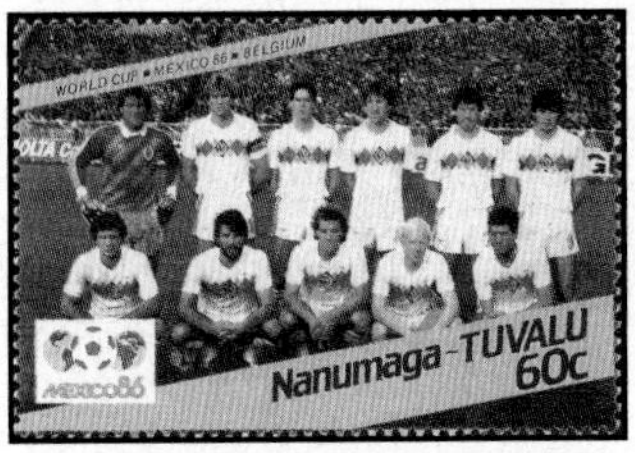

World Cup Soccer Championships, Mexico — A4

Players and teams from participating countries.

Perf. 12½x13, 13x12½

1986, June 30

57	A4	1c Uruguay, vert.	.25	.25
58	A4	5c Morocco, vert.	.25	.25
59	A4	5c Hungary, vert.	.25	.25
60	A4	10c Poland, vert.	.25	.25
61	A4	20c Argentina, vert.	.25	.25
62	A4	35c Bulgaria	.25	.25
63	A4	50c Portugal, vert.	.25	.25
64	A4	60c Belgium	.35	.35
65	A4	75c France	.35	.35
66	A4	$1 Canada, vert.	.55	.55
67	A4	$2 Germany	.85	.85
68	A4	$4 Scotland, vert.	1.75	1.75
		Nos. 57-68 (12)	5.60	5.60

Royal Wedding Type of 1986

#71a, Prince Andrew, vert. #71b, Sarah Ferguson, vert. #72a, Prince Philip, Andrew. #72b, Prince Andrew.

1986, July 23

71	A53	60c Pair, #a.-b.	1.10	1.10
72	A53	$1 Pair, #a.-b.	1.90	1.90

Souvenir Sheet

73	A56	$4 Couple	5.25	5.25

Nos. 71-72 Ovptd. in Silver "Congratulations to T.R.H. The Duke & Duchess of York"

1986, Oct. 26

74	A53	60c Pair, #a.-b.	2.00	2.00
75	A53	$1 Pair, #a.-b.	3.75	3.75

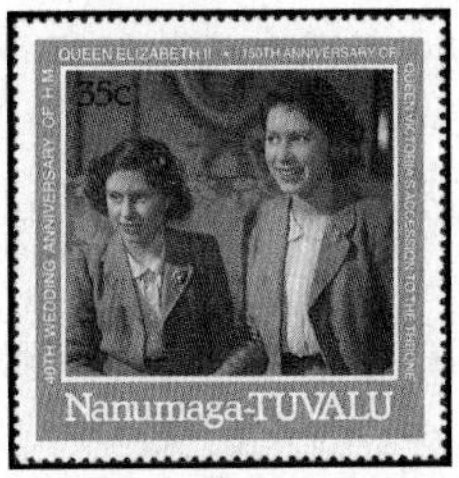

Royal Anniversaries — A5

15c, Queen Victoria. 35c, Princesses Margaret and Elizabeth. 60c, Elizabeth holding Princess Anne. $1.50, Elizabeth, Philip. $1.75, Elizabeth wearing tiara.
$3, Elizabeth.

1987, Oct. 15 *Perf. 15*

78	A5	15c multicolored	.25	.25
79	A5	35c multicolored	.40	.40
80	A5	60c multicolored	.65	.65
81	A62	$1.50 multicolored	1.60	1.60
82	A62	$1.75 multicolored	1.75	1.75
		Nos. 78-82 (5)	4.65	4.65

Souvenir Sheet

83	A5	$3 multicolored	3.50	3.50

Elizabeth's 40th wedding anniv.; Victoria's accession to the throne, sesquicentennial.

NANUMEA

Locomotive Type of 1984

No. 1, 1940 Class E94, Germany. No. 2, 1946 Class 2251, UK. No. 3, 1941 Bantam Cock Class V4, UK. No. 4, 1902 Class C1, UK. No. 5, 1952 S.N.C.F. CC 7121, France. No. 6, 1903 La France Frenchmen Class, UK. No. 7, 1929 5700 Class, UK. No. 8, 1954 S.N.C.F. Class BB 1200, France. No. 9, 1881 Fairlight Class G, UK. No. 10, 1928 V.R. Class S, Australia.

Se-tenant Pairs, #a.-b.

a. — Side and front views.

b. — Action scene.

Perf. 12½x13

1984-85 Litho. Unwmk.

1	A36	1c multicolored	.25	.25
2	A36	15c multicolored	.35	.35
3	A36	20c multicolored	.50	.50
4	A36	30c multicolored	.55	.55
5	A36	35c multicolored	.75	.75
6	A36	40c multicolored	.85	.85
7	A36	50c multicolored	1.00	1.00
8	A36	50c multicolored	1.00	1.00
9	A36	60c multicolored	1.10	1.10
10	A36	60c multicolored	1.10	1.10
		Nos. 1-10 (10)	7.45	7.45

Issued: Nos. 2-4, 6-7, 9, 4/30; others, 2/8/85.

Cricket Players Type of 1984

1c, J.A. Snow. 10c, C.J. Tavare. 40c, G.B. Stevenson. $1, P. Carrick.

Se-tenant Pairs, #a.-b.

1984, Oct. 9 *Perf. 13x12½*

11	A39	1c multicolored	.30	.30
12	A39	10c multicolored	.30	.30
13	A39	40c multicolored	.80	.80
14	A39	$1 multicolored	1.90	1.90
		Nos. 11-14 (4)	3.30	3.30

Automobile Type of 1984

No. 15, 1965 Humber Supersnipe, UK. No. 16, 1934 Singer 9, UK. No. 17, 1948 Holden FX 2.1 Liter Sedan, Australia. No. 18, 1953 Buick Skylark. No. 19, 1951 Simca Aronde, France. No. 20, 1967 Toyota 2000 GT, Japan. No. 21, 1960 Elva Courier, UK. No. 22, 1952 Bentley Continental, UK. No. 23, 1938 Hispano-Suiza V12 Saoutchik Cabriolet, Spain/France. No. 24, 1913 Peugeot Bebe, France. No. 25, 1935 Bluebird V (LSR), UK. No. 26, 1978 Mazda RX7, Japan. No. 27, 1970 Lola T70, UK. No. 28, 1908 Locomobile, US.

Se-tenant Pairs, #a.-b.

a. — Side and front views.

b. — Action scene.

1985-86 *Perf. 12½x13*

15	A41	5c multicolored	.25	.25
16	A41	10c multicolored	.25	.25
17	A41	15c multicolored	.25	.25
18	A41	20c multicolored	.30	.30
19	A41	20c multicolored	.30	.30
20	A41	35c multicolored	.45	.45
21	A41	40c multicolored	.50	.50
22	A41	50c multicolored	.60	.60
23	A41	50c multicolored	.60	.60
24	A41	50c multicolored	.60	.60
25	A41	60c multicolored	.70	.70
26	A41	60c multicolored	.70	.70
27	A41	75c multicolored	.80	.80
28	A41	$2 multicolored	2.50	2.50
		Nos. 15-28 (14)	8.80	8.80

Issued: Nos. 15, 21-22, 25, 1/14; Nos. 17-18, 23, 26, 2/22; Nos. 16, 19-20, 24, 27-28, 12/30/86.

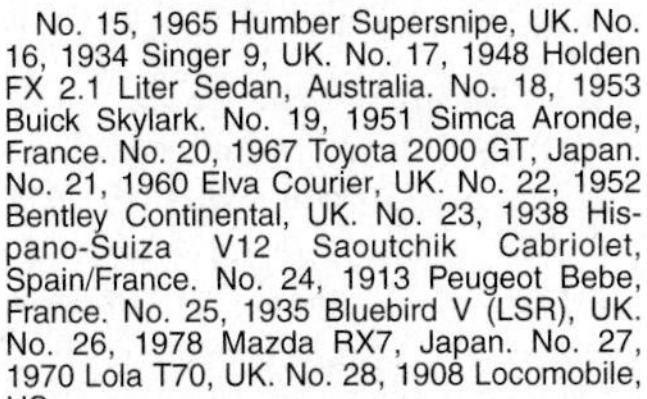

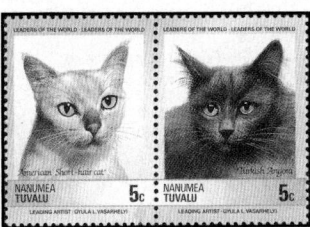

Cats — A6

#29a, American short-hair. #29b, Turkish Angora. #30a, Korat. #30b, American Maine Coon. #31a, Himalayan. #31b, Shaded Cameo. #32a, Long-haired ginger. #32b, Siamese Seal Point.

1985, May 28 *Perf. 13x12½*

29	A6	5c Pair, #a.-b.	.25	.25
30	A6	30c Pair, #a.-b.	.65	.65
31	A6	50c Pair, #a.-b.	1.00	1.00
32	A6	$1 Pair, #a.-b.	2.00	2.00
		Nos. 29-32 (4)	3.90	3.90

Queen Mother Type of 1985

Hats: #41a, 47a, Light gray. #41b, 47b, Light blue. #42a, Lavender. #42b, Blue. #43a, Purple. #43b, Pink. #44a, 46a, Blue. #44b, 46b, Blue flowered. #45a, Feathered. #45b, Veiled.

1985-86

41	A45	5c Pair, #a.-b.	.25	.25
42	A45	30c Pair, #a.-b.	.45	.45
43	A45	75c Pair, #a.-b.	1.40	1.40
44	A45	$1.05 Pair, #a.-b.	1.75	1.75
		Nos. 41-44 (4)	3.85	3.85

Souvenir Sheets of 2

45	A45	$1.20 #a.-b.	2.25	2.25
46	A45	$1 #a.-b.	1.00	1.00
47	A45	$4 #a.-b.	4.00	4.00

Issued: #41-45, 9/5; 46-47, 1/10/86.

Elizabeth II 60th Birthday Type

1986, Apr. 21 *Perf. 13x12½, 12½x13*

48	A49	10c As teenager	.25	.25
49	A49	80c As young woman	.30	.30
50	A49	$1.75 Red hat	.75	.75
51	A49	$3 Tiara, vert.	1.35	1.35
		Nos. 48-51 (4)	2.65	2.65

Souvenir Sheet

52	A49	$4 Green print hat	4.00	4.00

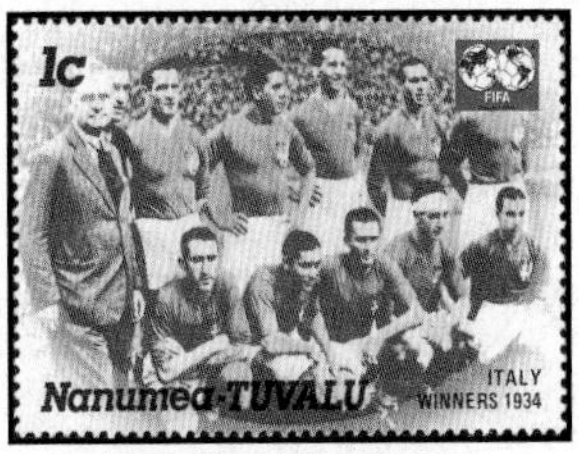

1986 World Cup Soccer Championships, Mexico — A7

1c, Italy, 1934. 2c, Italy, 1938. 5c, Uruguay, 1950. 10c, Brazil, 1958. 25c, Argentina vs. Holland, 1978. 40c, Brazil vs. Czechoslovakia, 1962. 50c, Uruguay vs. Argentina, 1930. 75c, West Germany vs. Hungary, 1954. 90c, Brazil, 1970. $1, West Germany, 1974. $2.50, Italy vs. West Germany, 1982. $4, England, 1966.

1986, June 10 *Perf. 13x12½*

53	A7	1c multicolored	.25	.25
54	A7	2c multicolored	.25	.25
55	A7	5c multicolored	.25	.25
56	A7	10c multicolored	.25	.25
57	A7	25c multicolored	.25	.25
58	A7	40c multicolored	.25	.25
59	A7	50c multicolored	.30	.30
60	A7	75c multicolored	.40	.40
61	A7	90c multicolored	.50	.50
62	A7	$1 multicolored	.55	.55
63	A7	$2.50 multicolored	1.30	1.30
64	A7	$4 multicolored	1.90	1.90
		Nos. 53-64 (12)	6.45	6.45

Royal Wedding Type of 1986

No. 65, Prince Andrew in jeep, vert. No. 66, Sarah Ferguson, vert. No. 67, Couple. No. 68, Prince Andrew, Princess Anne and parents.
No. 69, Newlyweds.

1986, July 23 *Perf. 13x12½, 12½x13*

65	A53	60c multicolored	.40	.40
66	A53	60c multicolored	.40	.40
67	A53	$1 multicolored	.65	.65
68	A53	$1 multicolored	.65	.65
		Nos. 65-68 (4)	2.10	2.10

Souvenir Sheet

69	A56	$4 multicolored	3.50	3.50

Nos. 65-68 Ovptd. in Silver "Congratulations to T.R.H. The Duke & Duchess of York"

#70a, Prince Andrew in jeep. #70b, Sarah Ferguson. #71a, Couple. #71b, Prince Andrew, Princess Anne and parents.

1986, Oct. 28

70	A53	60c Pair, #a.-b.	2.00	2.00
71	A53	$1 Pair, #a.-b.	3.75	3.75

Elizabeth 40th Wedding Anniv. Type

40c, Victoria. 60c, Elizabeth & Philip, wedding portrait. 80c, Elizabeth, Philip & Prince Charles. $1, Elizabeth, Princess Anne. $2, Elizabeth.
$3, Royal family, diff.

1987, Oct. 15 *Perf. 15*

74	A62	40c multicolored	.40	.40
75	A62	60c multicolored	.65	.65
76	A62	80c multicolored	.85	.85
77	A62	$1 multicolored	1.00	1.00
78	A62	$2 multicolored	2.10	2.10
		Nos. 74-78 (5)	5.00	5.00

Souvenir Sheet

79	A62	$3 multicolored	4.75	4.75

Queen Victoria's accession to the throne, 150th anniv.

NIUTAO

Automobile Type of 1984

No. 1, 1930 Bentley 4½ Liter Supercharged, UK. No. 2, 1935 Wolseley Hornet Special, UK. No. 3, 1920 Crossley 25/30HP, UK. No. 4, 1976 Cadillac Eldorado 7-Liter V-8. No. 5, 1968 Austin Mini Cooper, UK. No. 6, 1958 BMW 507 Cabriolet, W. Germany. No. 7, 1963 Porsche 365C Cabriolet, W. Germany. No. 8, 1971 Tyrrell Ford 001, UK.

Se-tenant Pairs, #a.-b.

a. — Side and front views.

b. — Action scene.

Perf. 12½x13

1984-85 Litho. Unwmk.

1	A41	15c multicolored	.25	.25
2	A41	20c multicolored	.40	.40
3	A41	25c multicolored	.50	.50
4	A41	30c multicolored	.65	.65
5	A41	40c multicolored	.85	.85
6	A41	40c multicolored	.85	.85
7	A41	50c multicolored	1.05	1.05
8	A41	60c multicolored	1.20	1.20
		Nos. 1-8 (8)	5.75	5.75

Issued: Nos. 1, 4-5, 7, 4/16; Nos. 2-3, 6, 8, 5/2/85.

Locomotive Type of 1984

No. 9, 1830 Planet, UK. No. 10, 1863 Prince, UK. No. 11, 1943 Gordon Austerity Class, UK. No. 12, 1830 Northumbrian, UK. No. 13, 1879 Merddin Emrys, UK. No. 14, 1829 Agenoria, UK. No. 15, 1909 Atchison, Topeka & Santa Fe, 1301. No. 16, 1897 Class 6200, Japan. No. 17, 1938 F.M.S.R. Class O, Malaya. No. 18, 1880 1F, UK. No. 19, 1908 Class E550, Italy. No. 20, 1914 J.N.R. Class 6760, Japan.

Se-tenant Pairs, #a.-b.

a. — Side and front views.

b. — Action scene.

1984-85

9	A36	5c multicolored	.25	.25
10	A36	10c multicolored	.25	.25
11	A36	10c multicolored	.25	.25
12	A36	20c multicolored	.35	.35
13	A36	30c multicolored	.50	.50
14	A36	40c multicolored	.70	.70
15	A36	45c multicolored	.75	.75
16	A36	50c multicolored	.85	.85
17	A36	60c multicolored	.85	.85
18	A36	75c multicolored	1.20	1.20
19	A36	$1 multicolored	1.75	1.75
20	A36	$1.20 multicolored	2.10	2.10
		Nos. 9-20 (12)	9.80	9.80

Issue dates: Nos. 9-10, 12, 14, 16, 19, Sept. 17; Nos. 11, 13, 15, 18, 20, Aug. 21, 1985.

Cricket Players Type of 1984

1c, S.G. Hinks. 15c, C. Penn. 50c, T.M. Alderman. $1, K.B.S. Jarvis.

Se-tenant Pairs, #a.-b.

a. — Head.

b. — Action scene.

1985, Jan. 7 *Perf. 13x12½*

21	A39	1c multicolored	.25	.25
22	A39	15c multicolored	.40	.40
23	A39	50c multicolored	1.60	1.60
24	A39	$1 multicolored	3.00	3.00
		Nos. 21-24 (4)	5.25	5.25

Audubon Bicentennial Type

#25a, Purple finch. #25b, White-throated sparrow. #26a, Anna's hummingbird. #26b, Smith's longspur. #27a, White-tailed kite. #27b, Harris' hawk. #28a, Northern oriole. #28b, Great crested flycatcher.

1985, Apr. 4

25	A42	5c Pair, #a.-b.	.25	.25
26	A42	15c Pair, #a.-b.	.40	.40
27	A42	25c Pair, #a.-b.	.65	.65
28	A42	$1 Pair, #a.-b.	2.75	2.75
		Nos. 25-28 (4)	4.05	4.05

Queen Mother Type of 1985

Hat: #37a, Light blue. #37b, Yellow. #38a, 43a, Black. #38b, 43b, Blue. #39a, Tiara. #39b, Pink. #40a, 42a, White. #40b, 42b, Blue. #41a, As young woman. #41b, Feathered.

1985-86

37 A45 15c Pair, #a.-b. .25 .25
38 A45 35c Pair, #a.-b. .75 .75
39 A45 70c Pair, #a.-b. 1.60 1.60
40 A45 95c Pair, #a.-b. 2.10 2.10
Nos. 37-40 (4) 4.70 4.70

Souvenir Sheets

41 A45 $1.05 #a.-b. 1.05 1.05
42 A45 $1.50 #a.-b. 1.50 1.50
43 A45 $4 #a.-b. 3.75 3.75

Issued: #37-41, 9/4; #42-43, 1/10/86.

Elizabeth II 60th Birthday Type

1986, Apr. 21 ***Perf. 13x12½, 12½x13***

44 A49 5c White & gray hat .25 .25
45 A49 60c Infant .30 .30
46 A49 $1.50 Flowered white hat .75 .75
47 A49 $3.50 Tiara, vert. 1.75 1.75
Nos. 44-47 (4) 3.05 3.05

Souvenir Sheet

48 A49 $5 With tiara, diff. 4.75 4.75

For overprints see Nos. 58-62.

Royal Wedding Type

#51a, Couple, vert. #51b, Sarah Ferguson, vert. #52a, Prince Andrew. #52b, Sarah in evening gown.

1986, July 23 ***Perf. 12½x13, 13x12½***

51 A53 60c Pair, #a.-b. .75 .75
52 A53 $1 Pair, #a.-b. 1.75 1.75

Souvenir Sheet

53 A56 $4 Newlyweds 3.25 3.25

Nos. 51-52 Ovptd. in Silver "Congratulations to T.R.H. The Duke & Duchess of York"

1986, Oct. 28

54 A53 60c Pair, #a.-b. 2.00 2.00
55 A53 $1 Pair, #a.-b. 3.75 3.75

Nos. 44-48 Ovptd. in Gold "40th WEDDING ANNIVERSARY OF H.M. QUEEN ELIZABETH II"

1987, Mar. ***Perf. 13x12½, 12½x13***

58 A49 5c multicolored .25 .25
59 A49 60c multicolored .75 .75
60 A49 $1.50 multicolored 1.90 1.90
61 A49 $3.50 multicolored 4.50 4.50
Nos. 58-61 (4) 7.40 7.40

Souvenir Sheet

62 A49 $5 multicolored 6.00 6.00

NUI

Locomotives Type of 1984

No. 1, 1911 Class 8800, Japan. No. 2, 1932 Soviet Union Railways Class SU. No. 3, 1847 Jenny Lind Type, UK. No. 4, 1907 Victorian Government Railways Class A2, Australia. No. 5, same, 1950 Class R. No. 6, 1913 Class 9600, Japan. No. 7, 1934 LMS Stanier Tilbury Class 4P, UK. No. 8, 1924 Jinty Class 3, UK. No. 9, 1928 Boston & Albany Class D12. No. 10, 1847 Iron Duke Class, UK. No. 11, 1917 Wabash Railroad Class L. No. 12, 1943 South Australian Government Railways 520 Class. No. 13, 1885 Tennant Class 1463, UK. No. 14, 1947 No. 10000, UK. No. 15, 1848 Padarn Railway Fire Queen, UK. No. 16, 1935 Princess Margaret Rose Class 8P, UK. No. 17, 1932 Soviet Union Railways Class IS. No. 18, 1973 D.B. Class ET403, W. Germany. No. 19, 1916 E. Tenn. & W. N. Carolina R.R. No. 10. No. 20, 1973 D.B. Class 151, W. Germany. No. 21, 1909 Tasmanian Goverment Railways Class K Garratt. No. 22, 1927 B&O President Class. No. 23, 1832 Mohawk & Hudson Railroad Experiment. No. 24, 1934 Union Pacific Railroad, M-10000 Streamliner.

Se-tenant Pairs, #a.-b.

a. — Side and front views.

b. — Action scene.

1984-88 **Litho.** ***Perf. 12½x13***

1 A36 5c multicolored .25 .25
2 A36 5c multicolored .25 .25
3 A36 10c multicolored .25 .25
4 A36 10c multicolored .25 .25
5 A36 15c multicolored .25 .25
6 A36 15c multicolored .25 .25
7 A36 20c multicolored .25 .25
8 A36 25c multicolored .30 .30
9 A36 25c multicolored .30 .30
10 A36 25c multicolored .30 .30
11 A36 25c multicolored .30 .30
12 A36 30c multicolored .35 .35
13 A36 35c multicolored .40 .40
14 A36 40c multicolored .45 .45
15 A36 40c multicolored .45 .45
16 A36 50c multicolored .55 .55
17 A36 50c multicolored .55 .55
18 A36 60c multicolored .60 .60
19 A36 60c multicolored .60 .60
20 A36 75c multicolored .80 .80
21 A36 75c multicolored .80 .80
22 A36 $1 multicolored 1.10 1.10
23 A36 $1 multicolored 1.10 1.10
24 A36 $1.25 multicolored 1.40 1.40
Nos. 1-24 (24) 12.10 12.10

Issued: Nos. 5, 8, 12, 16, 3/19; Nos. 1, 6, 9, 22, 2/22/85; Nos. 3, 10, 13, 14, 18, 20, 23, 24, 8/7/87; Nos. 2, 4, 7, 11, 15, 17, 19, 21, 1/29/88.

1987 and 1988 stamps not inscribed "Leaders of the World."

British Monarchs Type of Nanumaga

1984, July 18 ***Perf. 13x12½***

Se-tenant Pairs, #a.-b.

25 A2 1c Queen Anne .25 .25
26 A2 5c Henry V .25 .25
27 A2 15c Henry V, diff. .25 .25
28 A2 40c Queen Anne, diff. .45 .45
29 A2 50c Queen Anne, diff. .60 .60
30 A2 $1 Henry V, diff. 1.00 1.00
Nos. 25-30 (6) 2.80 2.80

Automobile Type of 1984

No. 31, 1909 Buick. No. 32, 1966 Oldsmobile Toronado. No. 33, 1947 Railton Mobil Special, UK. No. 34, 1924 Opel Laubfrosch, Germany. No. 35, 1966 Jensen FF, UK. No. 36, 1963 Lotus-Climax GP MK 25, UK. No. 37, 1910 Delaunay Belleville, France. No. 38, 1956 Jensen 541, UK. No. 39, 1924 Hispano-Suiza H6 Boulogne, France. No. 40, 1972 Citroen-Maserati S.M. Coupe, France.

Se-tenant Pairs, #a.-b.

a. — Side and front views.

b. — Action scene.

1985 ***Perf. 12½x13***

31 A41 5c multicolored .25 .25
32 A41 15c multicolored .35 .35
33 A41 25c multicolored .70 .70
34 A41 30c multicolored .75 .75
35 A41 40c multicolored 1.00 1.00
36 A41 40c multicolored 1.00 1.00
37 A41 50c multicolored 1.40 1.40
38 A41 60c multicolored 1.50 1.50
39 A41 90c multicolored 2.25 2.25
40 A41 $1.10 multicolored 2.75 2.75
Nos. 31-40 (10) 11.95 11.95

Issued: #33-35, 37, 4/2; #31-32, 36, 38-40, 10/9.

Cricket Players Type of 1984

1c, S.C. Goldsmith. 40c, S.N.V. Waterton. 60c, A. Sidebottom. 70c, A.A. Metcalfe.

Se-tenant Pairs, #a.-b.

1985, May 27 ***Perf. 13x12½***

41 A39 1c multicolored .25 .25
42 A39 40c multicolored .65 .65
43 A39 60c multicolored .95 .95
44 A39 70c multicolored 1.25 1.25
Nos. 41-44 (4) 3.10 3.10

Queen Mother Type of 1985

#49a, 54a, Purple. #49b, 54b, Tiara. #50a, Light blue. #50b, Lavender. #51a, Violet. #51b, White. #52a, 55a, Light blue. #52b, 55b, Tiara. #53a, White. #53b, Black.

1985-86

49 A45 5c Pair, #a.-b. .25 .25
50 A45 50c Pair, #a.-b. .90 .90
51 A45 75c Pair, #a.-b. 1.40 1.40
52 A45 85c Pair, #a.-b. 1.60 1.60
Nos. 49-52 (4) 4.15 4.15

Souvenir Sheets of 2

53 A45 $1.15 #a.-b. 2.50 2.50
54 A45 $1.50 #a.-b. 2.00 2.00
55 A45 $3.50 #a.-b. 4.50 4.50

Issued: #49-53, 9/4; 54-55, 1/8/86.

Elizabeth II 60th Birthday Type

1986, Apr. 21 ***Perf. 13x12½, 12½x13***

56 A49 10c Feathered hat .25 .25
57 A49 80c As young woman .55 .55
58 A49 $1.75 Tiara 1.05 1.05
59 A49 $3 Tiara, diff., vert. 1.90 1.90
Nos. 56-59 (4) 3.75 3.75

Souvenir Sheet

60 A49 $4 Portrait 4.00 4.00

Royal Wedding Type of 1986

#63a, Couple, vert. #63b, Prince Andrew, vert. #64a, Couple, Queen Elizabeth II. #64b, Andrew as young boy.

1986, July 23 ***Perf. 12½x13, 13x12½***

63 A53 60c Pair, #a.-b. .85 .85
64 A53 $1 Pair, #a.-b. 1.15 1.15

Souvenir Sheet

65 A56 $4 Sarah in wedding dress 4.00 4.00

Nos. 63-64 Ovptd. in Silver "Congratulations to T.R.H. The Duke & Duchess of York"

1986, Oct. 28

66 A53 60c Pair, #a.-b. 1.90 1.90
67 A53 $1 Pair, #a.-b. 3.50 3.50

Elizabeth 40th Wedding Anniv. Type of Funafuti

1987, Oct. 15 ***Perf. 15***

70 A1 20c Queen Victoria .25 .25
71 A1 50c George VI, Family .60 .60
72 A1 75c Elizabeth .85 .85
73 A1 $1.20 Elizabeth, Philip 1.40 1.40
74 A1 $1.75 Elizabeth, diff. 2.00 2.00
Nos. 70-74 (5) 5.10 5.10

Souvenir Sheet

75 A1 $3 Elizabeth, Family 4.00 4.00

Queen Victoria's accession to the throne, sesquicentennial.

NUKUFETAU

Automobile Type of 1984

No. 1, 1904 Mercedes 28 PS, Germany. No. 2, 1966 Ford GT40 Mark II. No. 3, 1911 Vauxhall Prince Henry, UK. No. 4, 1956 Lincoln Continental Mark II. No. 5, 1950 Bristol 400, UK. No. 6, 1913 Morris Oxford "Bullnose," UK. No. 7, 1923 Austin Seven Tourer. No. 8, 1921 Bugatti Type 13 "Brescia," France. No. 9, 1967 Monteverdi, Switzerland. No. 10, 1925 Lancia Lambda, Italy. No. 11, 1938 Panhard Dynamic, France. No. 12, 1960 A.C. Ace, UK. No. 13, 1950 Land Rover Model 80, UK.

Se-tenant Pairs, #a.-b.

a. — Side and front views.

b. — Action scene.

Perf. 12½x13

1984-85 **Litho.** **Unwmk.**

1 A41 5c multicolored .25 .25
2 A41 10c multicolored .25 .25
3 A41 10c multicolored .25 .25
4 A41 15c multicolored .25 .25
5 A41 20c multicolored .30 .30
6 A41 25c multicolored .50 .50
7 A41 30c multicolored .55 .55
8 A41 50c multicolored 1.00 1.00
9 A41 50c multicolored 1.00 1.00
10 A41 60c multicolored 1.00 1.00
11 A41 60c multicolored 1.00 1.00
12 A41 75c multicolored 1.15 1.15
13 A41 $1.50 multicolored 2.75 2.75
Nos. 1-13 (13) 10.25 10.25

Issued; #2, 6-8, 10, 5/23; others, 6/26/85.

British Monarchs Type of Nanumaga

1984, Nov. 27 ***Perf. 13x12½***

Se-tenant Pairs, #a.-b.

14 A2 1c Mary II .30 .30
15 A2 10c Mary II, diff. .30 .30
16 A2 30c Mary II, diff. .50 .50
17 A2 50c Henry IV .90 .90
18 A2 60c Henry IV, diff. 1.00 1.00
19 A2 $1 Henry IV, diff. 1.60 1.60
Nos. 14-19 (6) 4.60 4.60

Cricket Players Type of 1984

1985, Jan. 7

Se-tenant Pairs, #a.-b.

20 A39 1c D.G. Aslett .25 .25
21 A39 10c N.R. Taylor .25 .25
22 A39 55c S. Oldham .90 .90
23 A39 $1 C.W.J. Athey 1.90 1.90
Nos. 20-23 (4) 3.30 3.30

Locomotive Type of 1984

No. 24, 1900 Class XV, Germany. No. 25, 1859 ECR Class Y, UK. No. 26, 1923 Nord Super Pacific, France. No. 27, 1905 LNWR Experiment Class, UK. No. 28, 1941 SR Merchant Navy Class, UK. No. 29, 1830 S. Carolina Railroad Best Friend of Charleston. No. 30, 1941 SR No. 1, UK. No. 31, 1987 Class 89, UK. No. 32, 1923 Southern Pacific Railroad Class 4300, US. No. 33, 1956 New South Wales Government Railways Class 46. No. 34, 1953 D.B. Class V200, Germany. No. 35, 1936 Union Railroad Class S-7, US. No. 36, 1877 Phildelphia & Reading Railroad Camelback. No. 37, 1968 J.N.R. Class 381, Japan. No. 38, 1933 Rio Grande Southern Railroad Galloping Goose Railcar, US. No. 39, 1935 Chicago, Milwaukee, St. Paul & Pacific Class A.

Se-tenant Pairs, #a.-b.

a. — Side and front views.

b. — Action scene.

1985-88

24 A36 1c multicolored .25 .25
25 A36 5c multicolored .25 .25
26 A36 10c multicolored .25 .25
27 A36 10c multicolored .25 .25
28 A36 15c multicolored .30 .30
29 A36 20c multicolored .40 .40
30 A36 25c multicolored .55 .55
31 A36 30c multicolored .65 .65
32 A36 40c multicolored .85 .85
33 A36 50c multicolored 1.10 1.10
34 A36 60c multicolored 1.25 1.25
35 A36 60c multicolored 1.25 1.25
36 A36 60c multicolored 1.25 1.25
37 A36 70c multicolored 1.50 1.50
38 A36 $1 multicolored 2.25 2.25
a. Souvenir sheet of 2 2.50 2.50
39 A36 $1.50 multicolored 3.25 3.25
Nos. 24-39 (16) 15.60 15.60

Issued: Nos. 24, 26, 34, 37, 4/2/85; Nos. 29, 32, 35, 39, 3/20/86; Nos. 25, 27-28, 30-31, 33, 36, 38, 38a, 9/10/87.

1986 and 1987 stamps not inscribed "Leaders of the World."

Queen Mother Type of 1985

Hat: #44a, Wide-brimmed blue. #44b, Tiara. #45a, Tiara. #45b, Lavender. #46a, Blue. #46b, White stole. #47a, 50a, White. #47b, 50b, Blue. #48a, 49a, White. #48b, 49b, Wide-brimmed.

1985, Sept. 5 ***Perf. 13x12½***

44 A45 10c Pair, #a.-b. .25 .25
45 A45 45c Pair, #a.-b. .80 .80
46 A45 65c Pair, #a.-b. 1.10 1.10
47 A45 $1 Pair, #a.-b. 1.75 1.75
Nos. 44-47 (4) 3.90 3.90

Souvenir Sheets of 2

48 A45 $1.10 #a.-b. 2.00 2.00
49 A45 $1.75 #a.-b. 2.25 2.25
50 A45 $3 #a.-b. 3.25 3.25

Elizabeth II 60th Birthday Type

1986, Apr. 21 ***Perf. 13x12½, 12½x13***

51 A49 5c Scarf .25 .25
52 A49 40c Tiara .25 .25
53 A49 $2 Bareheaded .70 .70
54 A49 $4 Tiara, vert. 1.75 1.75
Nos. 51-54 (4) 2.95 2.95

Souvenir Sheet

55 A49 $5 Blue hat 4.00 4.00

For overprints see Nos. 65-69.

Royal Wedding Type of 1986

#58a, Couple, vert. #58b, Andrew, vert. #59a, Andrew, parents. #59b, Andrew.

1986, July 22

58 A53 60c Pair, #a.-b. 1.00 1.00
59 A53 $1 Pair, #a.-b. 1.50 1.50

Souvenir Sheet

60 A56 $4 Wedding ceremony 4.00 4.00

Nos. 58-59 Ovptd. in Silver "Congratulations to T.R.H. The Duke & Duchess of York"

1986, Oct. 28

61 A53 60c Pair, #a.-b. 2.00 2.00
62 A53 $1 Pair, #a.-b. 3.50 3.50

Nos. 51-55 Ovptd. in Gold "40th WEDDING ANNIVERSARY OF H.M. QUEEN ELIZABETH II"

1987, Oct. 15

65 A49 5c multicolored .25 .25
66 A49 40c multicolored .35 .35
67 A49 $2 multicolored 1.75 1.75
68 A49 $4 multicolored 3.50 3.50
Nos. 65-68 (4) 5.85 5.85

Souvenir Sheet

69 A49 $5 multicolored 5.50 5.50

NUKULAELAE

Locomotive Type of 1984

No. 1, 1891 Calbourne Class 02, UK. No. 2, 1912 K.P.E.V. Class T18, Germany. No. 3, 1942 SNCF Class 141P, France. No. 4, 1962 Class 47, UK. No. 5, 1941 Union Pacific Big Boy, US. No. 6, 1955 DRB 83-10, Germany. No. 7, 1940 S.N.C.F. 160-A-1, France. No. 8, 1901 Class AEG High Speed Railcar, Germany. No. 9, 1839 Albion Railroad Samson, Canada. No. 10, 1907 Saint Class, UK. No. 11, 1900 Nord De Glehn Atlantic, France. No.

12, 1851 Folkstone Class, UK. No. 13, 1914 J.N.R. Class 8620, Japan. No. 14, 1936 Class 8F, UK. No. 15, 1857 Shannon, UK. No. 16, 1948 Class A1, UK. No. 17, 1955 E.A.R. Class 59, Kenya. No. 18, 1897 V.R. Class Na, Australia. No. 19, 1859 Undine Class, UK. No. 20, 1935 Turbomotive, UK.

Se-tenant Pairs, #a.-b.
a. — Side and front views.
b. — Action scene.

Perf. 12½x13

1984-86 Litho. Unwmk.

1 A36 5c multicolored .25 .25
2 A36 5c multicolored .25 .25
3 A36 10c multicolored .25 .25
4 A36 10c multicolored .25 .25
5 A36 15c multicolored .25 .25
6 A36 15c multicolored .25 .25
7 A36 20c multicolored .25 .25
8 A36 25c multicolored .25 .25
9 A36 25c multicolored .25 .25
10 A36 40c multicolored .45 .45
11 A36 40c multicolored .45 .45
12 A36 40c multicolored .45 .45
13 A36 50c multicolored .55 .55
14 A36 50c multicolored .55 .55
15 A36 80c multicolored .95 .95
16 A36 $1 multicolored 1.20 1.20
17 A36 $1 multicolored 1.20 1.20
18 A36 $1 multicolored 1.20 1.20
19 A36 $1 multicolored 1.20 1.20
20 A36 $1.50 multicolored 1.75 1.75
Nos. 1-20 (20) 12.20 12.20

Issued: Nos. 1, 5, 10, 16, 5/23; Nos. 2, 7, 11, 17, 12/12; Nos. 3, 8, 13, 18, 3/24/85; Nos. 4, 6, 9, 12, 14, 15, 19-20, 7/11/86.

1986 stamps not inscribed "Leaders of the World."

Cricket Players Type of 1984

1984, Aug. 8 ***Perf. 13x12½***

Se-tenant Pairs, #a.-b.

21 A39 5c D.B. Close .25 .25
22 A39 15c G. Boycott .25 .25
23 A39 30c D.L. Bairstow .65 .65
24 A39 $1 T.G. Evans 1.90 1.90
Nos. 21-24 (4) 3.05 3.05

Automobile Type of 1984

No. 25, 1924 Bugatti Type 35, France. No. 26, 1908 Sizaire-Naudin, France. No. 27, 1965 Sunbeam Tiger, UK. No. 28, 1907 Napier 60HP Touring Car, UK. No. 29, 1975 BMW 2002 TII, Germany. No. 30, 1910 Austro-Daimler Prince Henry, Austria. No. 31, 1927 La Salle, US. No. 32, 1901 Oldsmobile Curved Dash Buckboard. No. 33, 1955 Rover 90, UK. No. 34, 1948 Chrysler Town & Country.

Se-tenant Pairs, #a.-b.
a. — Side and front views.
b. — Action scene.

1985 ***Perf. 12½x13***

25 A41 5c multicolored .25 .25
26 A41 10c multicolored .25 .25
27 A41 25c multicolored .45 .45
28 A41 35c multicolored .65 .65
29 A41 35c multicolored .65 .65
30 A41 50c multicolored .95 .95
31 A41 50c multicolored .95 .95
32 A41 70c multicolored 1.25 1.25
33 A41 75c multicolored 1.40 1.40
34 A41 $1 multicolored 1.60 1.60
Nos. 25-34 (10) 8.40 8.40

Issue dates: Nos. 25, 28, 30, 32, Feb. 8; Nos. 26-27, 29, 31, 33-34, July 23.

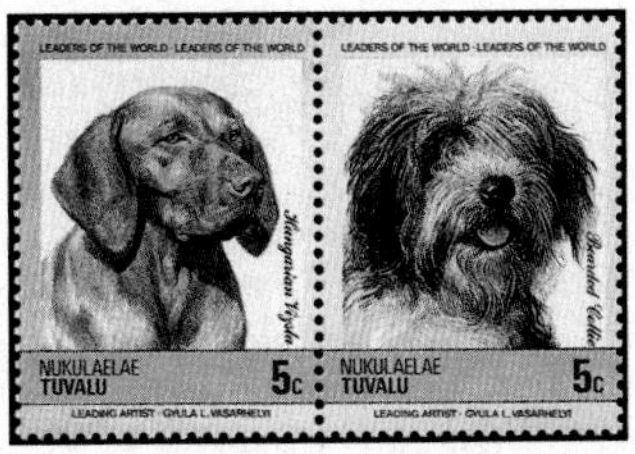

Dogs — A8

#35a, Hungarian vizsla. #35b, Bearded collie. #36a, Bernese mountain dog. #36b, Boxer. #37a, Labrador retriever. #37b, Shetland sheepdog. #38a, Welsh springer spaniel. #38b, Scottish terrier.

1985, Apr. 30

35 A8 5c Pair, #a.-b. .25 .25
36 A8 20c Pair, #a.-b. .35 .35
37 A8 50c Pair, #a.-b. .90 .90
38 A8 70c Pair, #a.-b. 1.25 1.25
Nos. 35-38 (4) 2.75 2.75

Queen Mother Type of 1985

Hat: #47a, Purple. #47b, Blue. #48a, 52a, Tiara. #48b, 52b, Lavender. #49a, 53a, Pink. #49b, 53b, Dark blue. #50a, Light purple. #50b, Light blue. #51a, As young girl. #51b, Lace.

1985-86

47 A45 5c Pair, #a.-b. .25 .25
48 A45 25c Pair, #a.-b. .45 .45
49 A45 85c Pair, #a.-b. 1.60 1.60
50 A45 $1 Pair, #a.-b. 2.00 2.00
Nos. 47-50 (4) 4.30 4.30

Souvenir Sheets of 2

51 A45 $1.20 #a.-b. 1.75 1.75
52 A45 $1.20 #a.-b. 1.50 1.50
53 A45 $3.50 #a.-b. 4.75 4.75

Issued: #46-51, 9/4; #52-53, 1/8/86.

Elizabeth II 60th Birthday Type

1986, Apr. 21 ***Perf. 13x12½, 12½x13***

54 A49 10c White hat .25 .25
55 A49 $1 As young woman .55 .55
56 A49 $1.50 In orange dress .85 .85
57 A49 $3 Tiara, vert. 1.50 1.50
Nos. 54-57 (4) 3.15 3.15

Souvenir Sheet

58 A49 $4 In brown dress 3.00 3.00

Royal Wedding Type of 1986

#61a, Andrew, vert. #61b, Couple, vert. #62a, Sarah Ferguson and Princess Diana. #62b, Andrew.

1986, July 23 ***Perf. 12½x13, 13x12½***

61 A53 60c Pair, #a.-b. 1.10 1.10
62 A53 $1 Pair, #a.-b. 1.75 1.75

Souvenir Sheet

63 A56 $4 Sarah in wedding dress 4.50 4.50

Nos. 61-62 Ovptd. in Silver "Congratulations to T.R.H. The Duke & Duchess of York"

1986, Oct. 28

64 A53 60c Pair, #a.-b. 2.00 2.00
65 A53 $1 Pair, #a.-b. 3.25 3.25

Queen Elizabeth II 40th Wedding Anniv. Type of Nanumaga

15c, Queen Victoria. 35c, Princesses Margaret and Elizabeth. 60c, Elizabeth holding Princess Anne. $1.50, Elizabeth, Philip. $1.75, Elizabeth wearing tiara.
$3, Elizabeth.

1987, Oct. 15 ***Perf. 15***

68 A5 15c multicolored .25 .25
69 A5 35c multicolored .50 .50
70 A5 60c multicolored .75 .75
71 A5 $1.50 multicolored 2.10 2.10
72 A5 $1.75 multicolored 2.40 2.40
Nos. 68-72 (5) 6.00 6.00

Souvenir Sheet

73 A5 $3 multicolored 4.00 4.00

Queen Victoria's accession to the throne, sesquicentennial.

VAITUPU

Automobile Type of 1984

No. 1, 1961 Lotus Elite, UK. No. 2, 1950 MG TD Midget, UK. No. 3, 1932 Hillman Minx, UK. No. 4, 1905 White Model E Steam Car, US. No. 5, 1935 Auburn Supercharged 851, US. No. 6, 1981 Renault RE20, France. No. 7, 1928 Lea-Francis Hyper. No. 8, 1940 Packard Darrin. No. 9, 1938 Graham, US. No. 10, 1968 Chevrolet Camaro. No. 11, 1957 Renault Dauphine-Gordini, France. No. 12, 1930 Packard Eight. No. 13, 1926 Miller Special, US. No. 14, 1950 Healey Silverstone, UK. No. 15, 1970 De Tomaso Pantera, Italy. No. 16, 1927 Bentley 3-Liter, UK.

Se-tenant Pairs, #a.-b.
a. — Side and front views.
b. — Action scene.

Perf. 12½x13

1984-85 Litho. Unwmk.

1 A41 5c multicolored .25 .25
2 A41 15c multicolored .25 .25
3 A41 15c multicolored .25 .25
4 A41 15c multicolored .25 .25
5 A41 25c multicolored .25 .25
6 A41 25c multicolored .25 .25
7 A41 30c multicolored .25 .25
8 A41 30c multicolored .25 .25
9 A41 30c multicolored .25 .25
10 A41 40c multicolored .35 .35
11 A41 40c multicolored .35 .35
12 A41 50c multicolored .45 .45
13 A41 50c multicolored .45 .45
14 A41 60c multicolored .55 .55
15 A41 60c multicolored .55 .55
16 A41 $1 multicolored .90 .90
Nos. 1-16 (16) 5.85 5.85

Issued: Nos. 2, 5, 7, 12, Mar. 19; Nos. 1, 3, 6, 8, 10, 13-14, 16, Dec. 12; Nos. 4, 9, 11, 15, Apr. 4, 1985.

British Monarchs Type of Nanumaga

1984, July 18 ***Perf. 13x12½***

Se-tenant Pairs, #a.-b.

17 A2 1c Richard III .25 .25
18 A2 5c Charles I .25 .25
19 A2 15c Charles I, diff. .25 .25
20 A2 40c Richard III, diff. .50 .50
21 A2 50c Richard III, diff. .60 .60
22 A2 $1 Charles I, diff. 1.15 1.15
Nos. 17-22 (6) 3.00 3.00

Locomotive Type of 1984

No. 23, 1929 D.R.G. V3201, Germany. No. 24, 1841 G.W.R. Leo Class, UK. No. 25, 1937 New York Central Railroad Class J3a. No. 26, 1949 Richmond, Fredericksburg & Potomac Railroad Class E8. No. 27, 1845 Columbine, UK. No. 28, 1954 BR Class 2MT, UK. No. 29, 1980 Amtrak Class AEM-7. No. 30, 1981 Via Rail LRC Class MPA-27a, Canada. No. 31, 1983 British Columbia Railway Class GF6C. No. 32, 1888 D&H Class B, India. No. 33, 1936 D.R. Class 45, Germany. No. 34, 1904 Northern Pacific Railway Class W, US. No. 35, 1855 W. & A. R.R. General, US. No. 36, 1938 Chicago & North Western Railway Class E-4. No. 37, 1911 J.N.R. Class 9020 Mallet, Japan. No. 38, 1977 Chicago Regional Transportation Authority Class F40.

Se-tenant Pairs, #a.-b.
a. — Side and front views.
b. — Action scene.

1985-87 ***Perf. 12½x13***

23 A36 5c multicolored .25 .25
24 A36 10c multicolored .25 .25
25 A36 10c multicolored .25 .25
26 A36 15c multicolored .30 .30
27 A36 25c multicolored .55 .55
28 A36 25c multicolored .55 .55
29 A36 25c multicolored .55 .55
30 A36 35c multicolored .75 .75
31 A36 45c multicolored .95 .95
32 A36 50c multicolored 1.10 1.10
33 A36 60c multicolored 1.25 1.25
34 A36 65c multicolored 1.40 1.40
35 A36 80c multicolored 1.75 1.75
36 A36 85c multicolored 1.90 1.90
37 A36 $1 multicolored 2.25 2.25
38 A36 $1 multicolored 2.25 2.25
Nos. 23-38 (16) 16.30 16.30

Issued: Nos. 24, 27, 32-33, 3/7/85; Nos. 23, 28, 35, 37, 1/16/86; Nos. 25-26, 29-31, 34, 36, 38, 9/10/87.

1986 and 1987 stamps not inscribed "Leaders of the World."

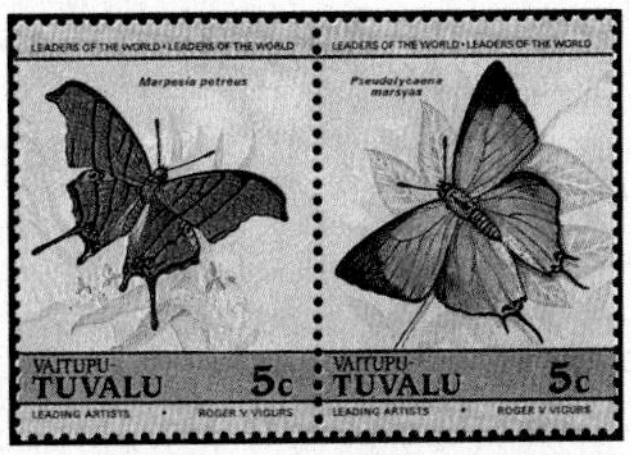

A9

Butterfly illustrations by Roger V. Vigurs: #39a, Marpesia petreus. #39b, Pseudolycaena marsyas. #40a, Charaxes jasius. #40b, Junonia coenia. #41a, Palaeochrysophanus hippothoe. #41b, Sticopthalma camadeva. #42a, Phoebis avellaneda. #42b, Apatura iris.

1985, Mar. 12 ***Perf. 13x12½***

39 A9 5c Pair, #a.-b. .25 .25
40 A9 15c Pair, #a.-b. .30 .30
41 A9 50c Pair, #a.-b. 1.00 1.00
42 A9 75c Pair, #a.-b. 1.60 1.60
Nos. 39-42 (4) 3.15 3.15

Queen Mother Type of 1985

Hat: #51a, 57a, Light blue. #51b, 57b, White. #52a, Tiara. #52b, Lavender. #53a, 56a, Violet. #53b, 56b, Green. #54a, Blue. #54b, Pink. #55a, Looking up. #55b, Looking forward.

1985-86

51 A45 15c Pair, #a.-b. .25 .25
52 A45 40c Pair, #a.-b. .75 .75
53 A45 65c Pair, #a.-b. 1.10 1.10
54 A45 95c Pair, #a.-b. 1.90 1.90
Nos. 51-54 (4) 4.00 4.00

Souvenir Sheets of 2

55 A45 $1.10 #a.-b. 2.10 2.10
56 A45 $2 #a.-b. 2.25 2.25
57 A45 $2.50 #a.-b. 3.00 3.00

Issued: #51-55, 8/28; 56-57, 1/8/86.

Elizabeth II 60th Birthday Type

1986, Apr. 21 ***Perf. 13x12½, 12½x13***

58 A49 5c Green hat .25 .25
59 A49 60c As young woman .25 .25
60 A49 $2 Flowered hat .65 .65
61 A49 $3.50 Tiara, vert. 1.05 1.05
Nos. 58-61 (4) 2.20 2.20

Souvenir Sheet

62 A49 $5 Straw hat 4.25 4.25

For overprints see Nos. 72-76.

Royal Wedding Type of 1986

#65a, Andrew, vert. #65b, Sarah Ferguson, vert. #66a, Charles, Andrew. #66b, Couple.

1986, July 18 ***Perf. 12½x13, 13x12½***

65 A53 60c Pair, #a.-b. 1.10 1.10
66 A53 $1 Pair, #a.-b. 1.75 1.75

Souvenir Sheet

67 A56 $4 Newlyweds 4.00 4.00

Nos. 65-66 Ovptd. in Silver "Congratulations to T.R.H. The Duke & Duchess of York"

1986, Oct. 28

68 A53 60c Pair, #a.-b. 2.25 2.25
69 A53 $1 Pair, #a.-b. 3.50 3.50

Nos. 58-62 Ovptd. in Gold "40th WEDDING ANNIVERSARY OF H.M. QUEEN ELIZABETH II"

1987, Oct. 15 ***Perf. 13x12½, 12½x13***

72 A49 5c multicolored .25 .25
73 A49 60c multicolored .75 .75
74 A49 $2 multicolored 2.50 2.50
75 A49 $3 multicolored 3.75 3.75
Nos. 72-75 (4) 7.25 7.25

Souvenir Sheet

76 A49 $5 multicolored 5.75 5.75

UBANGI-SHARI

ü-'baŋ,gē 'shär-ē

(Ubangi-Shari-Chad)

LOCATION — In Western Africa, north of the equator
GOVT. — French Colony
AREA — 238,767 sq. mi.
POP. — 833,916
CAPITAL — Bangui

In 1910 French Congo was divided into the three colonies of Gabon, Middle Congo and Ubangi-Shari and officially named "French Equatorial Africa." Under that name in 1934 the group, with the territory of Chad included, became a single administrative unit. See Gabon.

100 Centimes = 1 Franc

Stamps of Middle Congo Ovptd. in Black

1915-22		**Unwmk.**	**Perf. 14x13½**	
		Chalky Paper		
1	A1	1c ol gray & brn	.35	.35
a.		Double overprint	225.00	
b.		Imperf.	67.50	
2	A1	2c violet & brn	.35	.70
3	A1	4c blue & brn	.70	.70
4	A1	5c dk grn & bl	.70	1.00
5	A1	5c yel & bl ('22)	1.00	1.40
6	A1	10c carmine & bl	1.40	
7	A1	10c dp grn & bl grn ('22)	1.00	1.40
8	A1	15c brn vio & rose	1.75	2.10
9	A1	20c brown & blue	3.50	4.25

No. 8 is on ordinary paper

Overprinted

10	A2	25c blue & grn	2.10	2.10
11	A2	25c bl grn & gray ('22)	1.40	1.40
12	A2	30c scarlet & grn	2.10	2.10
13	A2	30c dp rose & rose ('22)	1.00	1.40
14	A2	35c vio brn & bl	5.50	5.50
15	A2	40c dl grn & brn	5.50	7.00
16	A2	45c vio & red	5.50	7.00
17	A2	50c bl grn & red	7.00	7.00
18	A2	50c blue & grn ('22)	1.00	1.40
19	A2	75c brown & bl	14.00	14.00
20	A1	1fr dp grn & vio	14.00	14.00
21	A3	2fr vio & gray grn	14.00	17.50
22	A3	5fr blue & rose	42.50	42.50
		Nos. 1-22 (22)	126.35	135.80

For surcharges see Nos. B1-B2.

Middle Congo of 1907-22 Ovptd. in Black or Red

1922				
23	A1	1c violet & grn	.70	1.00
a.		Overprint omitted	170.00	190.00
b.		Imperf.	40.00	
24	A1	2c grn & salmon	.70	1.00
25	A1	4c ol brn & brn	1.00	1.40
a.		Overprint omitted	200.00	225.00
26	A1	5c indigo & rose	1.00	1.40
27	A1	10c dp grn & gray grn	1.75	2.10
28	A1	15c lt red & dl bl	1.75	2.10
29	A1	20c choc & salmon	5.00	5.50

Overprinted

30	A2	25c vio & salmon	7.00	8.50
31	A2	30c rose & pale rose	2.75	3.50
32	A2	35c vio & grn	4.75	5.00
33	A2	40c ind & vio (R)	4.75	5.00
34	A2	45c choc & vio	4.75	5.00
35	A2	50c dk bl & pale bl	2.75	3.50
36	A2	60c on 75c vio, pnksh	3.50	4.25
37	A2	75c choc & sal	5.00	6.25
38	A3	1fr grn & dl bl (R)	10.50	11.00
a.		Overprint omitted	275.00	
39	A3	2fr grn & salmon	14.00	14.00
40	A3	5fr grn & ol brn	21.00	25.00
		Nos. 23-40 (18)	92.65	105.50

Nos. 23-29 with Additional Ovpt. in Black, Blue or Red

1924-33				
41	A1	1c vio & grn (Bl)	.35	.50
a.		"OUBANGUI CHARI" omitted	140.00	140.00
42	A1	2c grn & sal (Bl)	.35	.55
a.		"OUBANGUI CHARI" omitted	140.00	140.00
b.		Double overprint	150.00	
43	A1	4c ol brn & brn (Bl)	.35	.55
a.		Double overprint (Bl + Bk)	175.00	
b.		"AEF" omitted	160.00	
44	A1	5c ind & rose	.35	.55
a.		"OUBANGUI CHARI" omitted	130.00	
45	A1	10c dp grn & gray grn	.70	.85
46	A1	10c red org & bl ('25)	.70	.70
47	A1	15c sal & dl bl	.80	.85
48	A1	15c sal & dl bl (Bl) ('26)	1.00	1.40
49	A1	20c choc & salmon (Bl)	1.25	1.40

On Nos. 41-49 the color in ( ) refers to the overprint "Afrique Equatoriale Francaise."

Overprinted

50	A2	25c vio & salmon (Bl)	.70	.70
a.		Imperf.		
51	A2	30c rose & pale rose (Bl)	.70	1.00
52	A2	30c choc & red ('25)	.70	1.00
a.		"OUBANGUI CHARI" omitted	140.00	
53	A2	30c dk grn & grn ('27)	1.40	1.75
54	A2	35c vio & grn (Bl)	.70	1.00
a.		"OUBANGUI CHARI" omitted	275.00	
55	A2	40c ind & vio (Bl)	.70	1.00
56	A2	45c choc & vio (Bl)	1.00	1.40
57	A2	50c dk bl & pale bl (R)	.70	.70
58	A2	50c gray & bl vio ('25) (R)	1.40	1.40
59	A2	60c on 75c dk vio, pnksh (R)	.70	.55
60	A2	65c org brn & bl ('28)	1.40	1.75
61	A2	75c choc & sal (Bl)	1.75	2.10
62	A2	75c dp bl & lt bl ('25) (R)	1.40	1.40
a.		"OUBANGUI CHARI" omitted	140.00	
63	A2	75c rose & dk brn ('28)	2.10	2.50
64	A2	90c brn red & pink ('30)	4.25	5.00
65	A3	1fr grn & ind (Bk + Bl) ('25)	.70	1.00
66	A3	1fr grn & ind (R + Bl)	1.40	2.10
67	A3	1.10fr bister & bl ('28)	3.50	3.50
68	A3	1.25fr mag & lt grn ('33)	10.50	10.50
69	A3	1.50fr ultra & bl ('30)	7.00	7.00
70	A3	1.75fr dk brn & dp buff ('33)	10.50	14.00

71	A3	2fr grn & red	1.40	2.10
a.		"OUBANGUI CHARI" omitted	1,250.	1,050.
a.		"OUBANGUI CHARI" double	1,200.	
72	A3	3fr red vio ('30)	5.00	5.50
73	A3	5fr grn & ol brn (Bl)	4.50	5.50
		Nos. 41-73 (33)	69.95	81.80

On Nos. 65, 66 the first overprint color refers to OUBANGUI CHARI.
For surcharges see Nos. 74-81.

Types of 1924 Issue Surcharged with New Values in Black or Red

1925-26				
74	A3	65c on 1fr vio & ol	2.10	2.10
a.		"65" omitted	140.00	
75	A3	85c on 1fr vio & ol	2.10	2.10
a.		"AFRIQUE EQUATORIALE FRANCAISE" omitted	140.00	160.00
b.		Double surcharge	160.00	
76	A3	1.25fr on 1fr dk bl & ultra (R) ('26)	1.40	2.25
a.		"1f25" omitted	165.00	

Bars cover old denomination on No. 76.

Types of 1924 Issue Surcharged with New Values and Bars

1927				
77	A2	90c on 75c brn red & rose red	2.10	2.75
78	A3	1.50fr on 1fr ultra & bl	2.10	2.75
79	A3	3fr on 5fr org brn & dl red	3.50	3.50
80	A3	10fr on 5fr ver & vio	17.50	19.00
81	A3	20fr on 5fr vio & gray	27.50	29.00
		Nos. 77-81 (5)	52.70	57.00

Common Design Types pictured following the introduction.

Colonial Exposition Issue
Common Design Types

1931		**Engr.**	**Perf. 12½**	
Name of Country Typo. in Black				
82	CD70	40c deep green	5.00	5.00
83	CD71	50c violet	5.00	5.00
84	CD72	90c red orange	5.50	5.50
a.		Imperf.	120.00	
85	CD73	1.50fr dull blue	5.50	5.50
		Nos. 82-85 (4)	21.00	21.00

SEMI-POSTAL STAMPS

Regular Issue of 1915 Surcharged

1916		**Unwmk.**	**Perf. 14x13½**	
		Chalky Paper		
B1	A1	10c + 5c car & blue	2.75	3.25
a.		Inverted surch.	160.00	
b.		Double surcharge	160.00	
c.		Double surch., one invtd.	125.00	125.00
d.		Vertical surcharge	140.00	140.00
e.		No period under "C"	17.50	17.50

Regular Issue of 1915 Surcharged in Carmine

B2	A1	10c + 5c car & blue	1.75	2.10

POSTAGE DUE STAMPS

Postage Due Stamps of France Overprinted

1928		**Unwmk.**	**Perf. 14x13½**	
J1	D2	5c light blue	1.40	2.10
J2	D2	10c gray brown	1.75	2.10
J3	D2	20c olive green	1.75	2.10
J4	D2	25c bright rose	1.75	2.10
J5	D2	30c light red	1.75	2.10
J6	D2	45c blue green	1.75	2.10
J7	D2	50c brown violet	2.50	3.50
J8	D2	60c yellow brown	2.75	3.50
J9	D2	1fr red brown	3.50	5.00
J10	D2	2fr orange red	7.00	7.00
J11	D2	3fr bright violet	7.00	7.00
		Nos. J1-J11 (11)	32.90	38.60

Landscape D3

Emile Gentil — D4

1930				**Typo.**
J12	D3	5c dp bl & olive	.70	1.05
J13	D3	10c dk red & brn	1.05	1.40
J14	D3	20c green & brn	1.05	1.40
J15	D3	25c lt bl & brn	1.40	1.75
J16	D3	30c bis brn & Prus bl	2.50	2.75
J17	D3	45c Prus bl & ol	3.25	3.50
J18	D3	50c red vio & brn	5.25	6.00
J19	D3	60c gray lil & bl blk	5.50	5.50
J20	D4	1fr bis brn & bl blk	5.25	6.00
J21	D4	2fr violet & brown	5.50	7.00
J22	D4	3fr dp red & brn	7.00	8.50
		Nos. J12-J22 (11)	38.45	44.85

Stamps of Ubangi-Shari were replaced in 1936 by those of French Equatorial Africa.

UGANDA

ü-'gan-də

LOCATION — East Africa, at the Equator and separated from the Indian Ocean by Kenya and Tanzania
GOVT. — Independent state
AREA — 91,343 sq. mi.
POP. — 21,619,700 (1999 est.)
CAPITAL — Kampala

Stamps of 1898-1902 were replaced by those issued for Kenya, Tanganyika and Uganda. Uganda became independent October 9, 1962.

Cowries (50 = 4 Pence)
16 Annas = 1 Rupee (1896)
100 Cents = 1 Shilling (1962)

Catalogue values for unused stamps in this country are for Never Hinged items, beginning with Scott 79 in the regular postage section and Scott J1 in the postage due section.

Unused values for Nos. 2-68 are for stamps without gum. Very fine examples will be evenly cut and will show at least two full typewritten framelines.

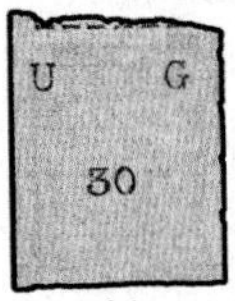

A1

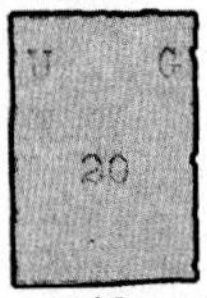

A2

Nos. 1-53 were produced with a typewriter by Rev. Ernest Millar of the Church Missionary Society. They were 20-26mm wide, with nine stamps in a horizontal row. Later two more were added to each row, and the stamps became narrower, 16-18mm.

Rev. Millar got a new typewriter in 1895, and the stamps he typed on it have a different appearance. A violet ribbon in the machine, inserted late in 1895, resulted in Nos. 35-53.

Nos. 1-53 are on thin, tough, white paper, laid horizontally with traces of a few vertical lines.

Forgeries of Nos. 1-53 are known.

Without Gum
Wide Letters
Typewritten on Thin Laid Paper
Stamps 20 to 26mm wide

1895 Unwmk. *Imperf.*

1	A1	10(c) black	*5,750.*	3,750.
2	A1	20(c) black	*9,600.*	*2,350.*
a.		"U A" instead of "U G"		*7,750.*
3	A1	30(c) black	*2,500.*	*2,000.*
4	A1	40(c) black	*7,750.*	2,850.
5	A1	50(c) black	*1,800.*	*1,400.*
a.		"U A" instead of "U G"		*10,000.*
6	A1	60(c) black	*3,250.*	2,850.

Surcharged with New Value in Black, Pen-written

9	A1	10 on 30(c) black		*85,000.*
10	A1	10 on 50(c) black		*85,000.*
11	A1	15 on 10(c) black		*85,000.*
12	A1	15 on 20(c) black		*65,000.*
13	A1	15 on 40(c) black		*85,000.*
14	A1	15 on 50(c) black		*80,000.*
15	A1	25 on 50(c) black		*85,000.*
16	A1	50 on 60(c) black		*85,000.*

Stamps 16 to 18mm wide

17	A1	5(c) black	4,000.	*1,650.*
18	A1	10(c) black	4,000.	*2,000.*
19	A1	15(c) black	2,500.	*1,900.*
a.		Verticaly laid paper		6,500.
20	A1	20(c) black	4,000.	*1,900.*
a.		Vertically laid paper		*8,250.*
21	A1	25(c) black	*2,000.*	*2,000.*
22	A1	30(c) black	*10,500.*	*10,000.*
23	A1	40(c) black	*10,000.*	*10,000.*
24	A1	50(c) black	*4,750.*	*5,750.*
25	A1	60(c) black	*10,000.*	*10,000.*

Narrow Letters
Stamps 16 to 18mm wide

26	A2	5(c) black	*2,000.*	
27	A2	10(c) black	*2,150.*	
28	A2	15(c) black	*2,150.*	
29	A2	20(c) black	*1,800.*	
30	A2	25(c) black	*2,000.*	
31	A2	30(c) black	*2,250.*	
32	A2	40(c) black	*2,000.*	
33	A2	50(c) black	*2,150.*	
34	A2	60(c) black	*3,200.*	
35	A2	5(c) violet	*900.*	*825.*
36	A2	10(c) violet	*825.*	*825.*
37	A2	15(c) violet	*1,400.*	*750.*
38	A2	20(c) violet	*600.*	*375.*
a.		"G A" instead of "U G"		
b.		Vertically laid paper	3,850.	
39	A2	25(c) violet	*2,300.*	*2,000.*
40	A2	30(c) violet	*2,850.*	*1,400.*
41	A2	40(c) violet	*2,800.*	*1,900.*
42	A2	50(c) violet	*2,500.*	1,900.
43	A2	100(c) violet	*3,250.*	3,750.

As a favor to a philatelist, 35c and 45c denominations were made in black and violet. They were not intended for postal use and no rate called for those denominations.

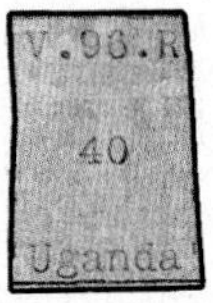

A3

1896

44	A3	5(c) violet	*950.*	*1,250.*
45	A3	10(c) violet	*1,050.*	*825.*
46	A3	15(c) violet	*950.*	*950.*
47	A3	20(c) violet	*500.*	*275.*
48	A3	25(c) violet	*875.*	*1,150.*
49	A3	30(c) violet	*950.*	*1,050.*
50	A3	40(c) violet	*1,100.*	*1,150.*
51	A3	50(c) violet	*950.*	*1,000.*
52	A3	60(c) violet	*2,000.*	*2,500.*
53	A3	100(c) violet	*1,900.*	2,500.

A4

Overprinted "L" in Black

1896 Typeset White Paper

54	A4	1a black (thin "1")	210.	190.
a.		Small "O" in "POSTAGE"	1,550.	1,300.
55	A4	2a black	135.	*140.*
a.		Small "O" in "POSTAGE"	615.	*675.*
56	A4	3a black	300.	*375.*
a.		Small "O" in "POSTAGE"	1,900.	*2,250.*
57	A4	4a black	135.	*180.*
a.		Small "O" in "POSTAGE"	625.	

Yellowish Paper

58	A4	8a black	225.	*340.*
a.		Small "O" in "POSTAGE"	1,675.	*2,100.*
59	A4	1r black	425.	*500.*
a.		Small "O" in "POSTAGE"	2,250.	
60	A4	5r black	37,500.	37,500.

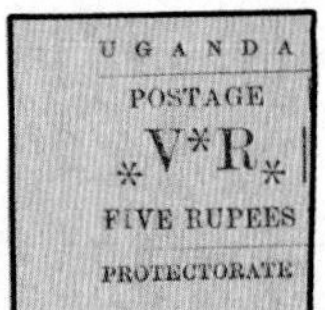

A4a

Without Overprint
White Paper

61	A4a	1a black (thin "1")	125.00	110.00
a.		Small "O" in "POSTAGE"	700.00	675.00
62	A4a	1a black (thick "1")	26.00	*30.00*
a.		Small "O" in "POSTAGE"	95.00	*110.00*
63	A4a	2a black	32.50	*40.00*
a.		Small "O" in "POSTAGE"	110.00	*140.00*
64	A4a	3a black	32.50	*50.00*
a.		Small "O" in "POSTAGE"	135.00	*200.00*
65	A4a	4a black	35.00	*42.50*
a.		Small "O" in "POSTAGE"	125.00	*140.00*

Yellowish Paper

66	A4a	8a black	42.50	*50.00*
a.		Small "O" in "POSTAGE"	155.00	*200.00*
67	A4a	1r black	95.00	*110.00*
a.		Small "O" in "POSTAGE"	400.00	*475.00*
68	A4a	5r black	300.00	*400.00*
a.		Small "O" in "POSTAGE"	1,000.	*1,250.*

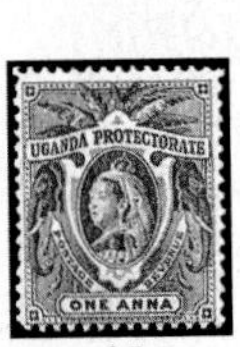

A5

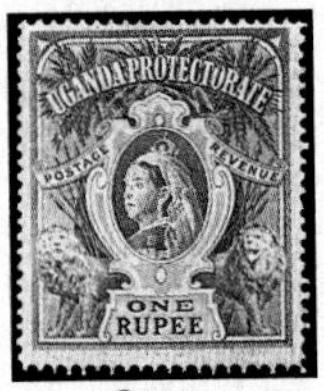

Queen Victoria — A6

1898-1902 Engr. Wmk. 2 *Perf. 14*

69	A5	1a red	5.00	4.50
70	A5	1a car rose ('02)	2.50	2.00
71	A5	2a brown	9.25	*11.00*
72	A5	3a gray	20.00	*50.00*
73	A5	4a dark green	13.00	*16.00*
74	A5	8a olive gray	15.00	*32.50*

Wmk. 1

75	A6	1r ultra	60.00	*60.00*
76	A6	5r brown	110.00	*130.00*
		Nos. 69-76 (8)	234.75	*306.00*

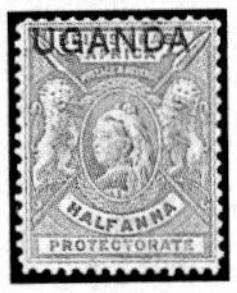

A7

1902 Wmk. 2 Black Overprint

77	A7	½a yellow green	3.25	1.90
a.		Inverted overprint	*2,200.*	
b.		Double overprint	*2,500.*	
c.		Pair, one without overprint	*5,250.*	

Red Overprint

78	A7	2½a dark blue	5.00	3.50
a.		Double overprint	650.00	

Catalogue values for unused stamps in this section, from this point to the end of the section, are for Never Hinged items.

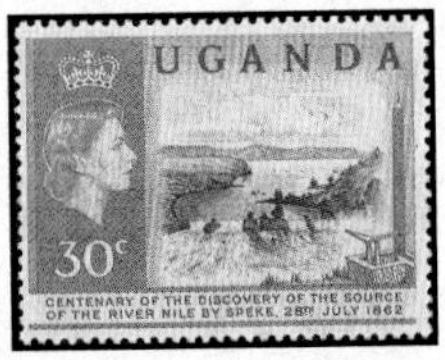

Ripon Falls and Speke Monument A8

Wmk. 314

1962, July 28 Engr. *Perf. 14*

79	A8	30c vermilion & blk	.30	.30
80	A8	50c violet & blk	.30	.30
81	A8	1.30sh green & blk	.55	.55
82	A8	2.50sh ultra & blk	2.00	2.00
		Nos. 79-82 (4)	3.15	3.15

Cent. of the discovery of the source of the Nile by John Hanning Speke.

Independent State

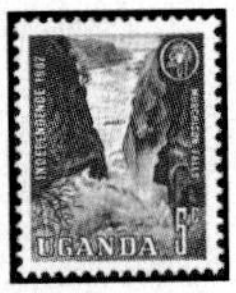

Murchison Falls — A9

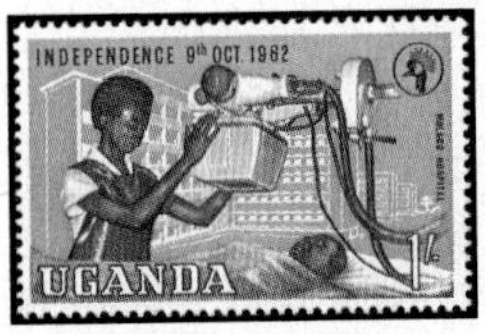

Mulago Hospital, X-Ray Service A10

Designs: 10c, Tobacco growing. 15c, Coffee growing. 20c, Ankole cattle. 30c, Cotton growing. 50c, Mountains of the Moon. 1.30sh, Rubaga and Namirembe Cathedrals and Kibuli Mosque. 2sh, Makerere College and students. 5sh, Copper mining. 10sh, Cement factory. 20sh, Parliament.

Perf. 14½x14, 14x14½

1962, Oct. 9 Photo. Unwmk.

83	A9	5c	Prus green	.25	.25
84	A9	10c	red brown	.25	.25
85	A9	15c	grn, blk & car	.25	.25
86	A9	20c	bister & pur	.25	.25
87	A9	30c	brt blue	.25	.25
88	A9	50c	bluish grn & blk	.25	.25
89	A10	1sh	bl grn, sep & red	.75	.65
90	A10	1.30sh	pur & ocher	.30	.65
91	A10	2sh	grnsh bl, blk & dk car	.50	.80
92	A10	5sh	dk green & red	6.00	1.60
93	A10	10sh	red brn & slate	4.00	3.75
94	A10	20sh	blue & pale brn	5.50	*17.50*
			Nos. 83-94 (12)	18.55	26.45

Uganda's independence, Oct. 9, 1962.

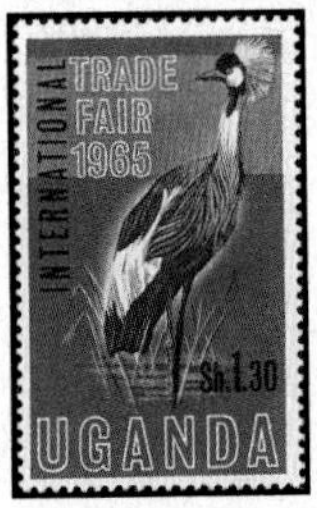

Crowned Crane — A11

1965, Feb. 20 Photo. *Perf. 14½*

95	A11	30c bl grn, blk, yel & red	.30	.25
96	A11	1sh30c ultra, blk, yel & red	.90	.70

Intl. Trade Fair at Lugogo Stadium, Kampala, Feb. 20-28.

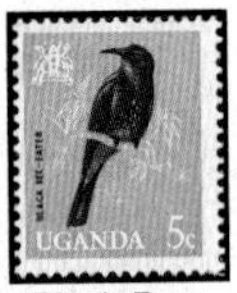

Black Bee-eater A12

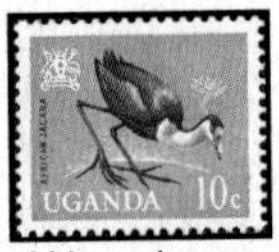

African Jacana A13

Arms of Uganda and Birds: 15c, Orange weaver. 20c, Narina trogon. 30c, Sacred ibis. 40c, Blue-breasted kingfisher. 50c, Whale-headed stork. 65c, Black-winged red bishop. 1sh, Ruwenzori turaco. 1.30sh, African fish eagle. 2.50sh, Great blue turaco. 5sh, Lilac-breasted roller. 10sh, Black-collared lovebird. 20sh, Crowned crane.

Perf. 14½x14, 14x14½

1965, Oct. 9 Photo. Unwmk.

Birds in Natural Colors

Size: 17x21mm, 21x17mm

97	A12	5c	lt vio bl & blk	.30	.40
98	A13	10c	dull blue & red	.30	.40
99	A12	15c	dk brown & org	.30	.40
100	A12	20c	bister & brt grn	.30	.40
101	A13	30c	hn brn & blk	2.00	.40
102	A12	40c	lt yel grn & red	1.25	.60
103	A12	50c	dp pur & gray	.35	.40
104	A13	65c	gray & brick red	2.75	2.00

Perf. 14½

Size: 41x25mm, 25x41mm

105	A13	1sh	lt blue & blk	.70	.40
106	A12	1.30sh	yel & red brn	7.00	.40
107	A13	2.50sh	brt yel grn & blk	5.50	.60
108	A12	5sh	lil gray & vio bl	8.50	4.00
109	A13	10sh	lt brown & blk	13.50	10.50
110	A13	20sh	olive grn & blk	25.00	34.00
			Nos. 97-110 (14)	67.75	54.90

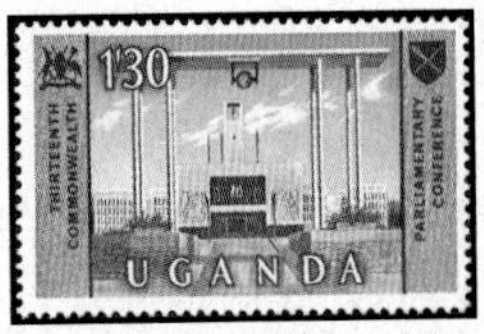

Parliament Building — A14

13th Commonwealth Parliamentary Assoc. Conf.: 30c, Animal carvings from entrance hall of Uganda Parliament. 50c, Arms of Uganda. 2.50sh, Parliament Chamber.

1967, Oct. 26 Photo. *Perf. 14½*

111	A14	30c	multicolored	.25	.25
112	A14	50c	multicolored	.25	.25
113	A14	1.30sh	multicolored	.25	.25
114	A14	2.50sh	multicolored	.50	1.25
			Nos. 111-114 (4)	1.25	2.00

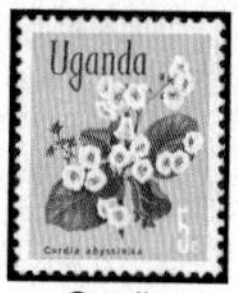

Cordia Abyssinica
A15

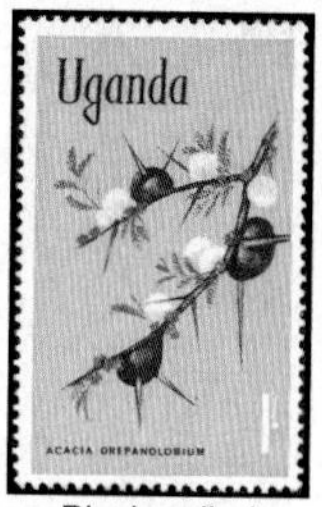

Black-galled Acacia
A16

Flowers: 10c, Grewia similis. 15c, Cassia didymobotrya. 20c, Coleus barbatus. 30c, Ochna ovata. 40c, Ipomoea spathulata (morning glory). 50c, Spathodea nilotica (flame tree). 60c, Oncoba spinosa. 70c, Carissa edulis. 1.50sh, Clerodendrum myricoides (blue butterfly bush). 2.50sh, Acanthus arboreus. 5sh, Kigelia aethiopium (sausage tree). 10sh, Erythrina abyssinica (Uganda coral). 20sh, Monodora myristica.

Perf. 14½x14

1969, Oct. 9 Photo. Unwmk.

115	A15	5c multicolored	.25	.25
116	A15	10c multicolored	.25	.25
117	A15	15c multicolored	.25	.25
118	A15	20c multicolored	.25	.25
119	A15	30c multicolored	.25	.25
120	A15	40c gray & multi	.25	.25
121	A15	50c tan & multi	.25	.25
122	A15	60c multicolored	.25	.25
123	A15	70c multicolored	.25	.25

Perf. 14

124	A16	1sh multicolored	.35	*.25*
125	A16	1.50sh multicolored	.55	*.25*
126	A16	2.50sh multicolored	.70	*.25*
127	A16	5sh multicolored	1.25	*.25*
128	A16	10sh multicolored	3.00	*.55*
129	A16	20sh tan & multi	7.75	*1.25*
		Nos. 115-129 (15)	15.85	*5.05*

Values of Nos. 124-129 are for canceled-to-order stamps. Cancellations were printed on Nos. 128-129. Postally used examples sell for higher prices.

Nos. 125-126, 129 Surcharged

1975, Sept. 29 Photo. *Perf. 14*

130	A16	2sh on 1.50sh multi	.90	1.75
131	A16	3sh on 2.50sh multi	17.50	37.50
132	A16	40sh on 20sh multi	7.00	15.00
		Nos. 130-132 (3)	25.40	54.25

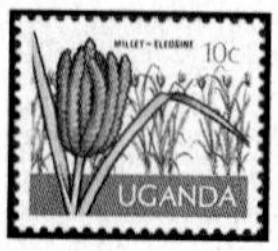

Millet — A17

Ugandan Crops: 20c, Sugar cane. 30c, Tobacco. 40c, Onions. 50c, Tomatoes. 70c, Tea. 80c, Bananas. 1sh, Corn. 2sh, Pineapple. 3sh, Coffee. 5sh, Oranges. 10sh, Peanuts. 20sh, Cotton. 40sh, Beans.

1975, Oct. 9 Photo. *Perf. 14x14½*
Size: 21x17mm
Multicolored, Name Panel as follows

133	A17	10c lt brown	.25	.25
134	A17	20c blue	.25	.25
135	A17	30c vermilion	.25	.25
136	A17	40c lilac	.25	.25
137	A17	50c olive	.25	.25
138	A17	70c brt green	.25	.25
139	A17	80c purple	.25	.25

Perf. 14½
Size: 41x25mm

140	A17	1sh ocher	.25	.25
141	A17	2sh slate	.25	.25
142	A17	3sh blue	.30	.40
143	A17	5sh yellow green	.35	.55
144	A17	10sh brown red	.70	1.10
145	A17	20sh rose lilac	1.50	2.25
146	A17	40sh orange	2.75	4.25
		Nos. 133-146 (14)	7.85	10.80

See #195-198. For surcharge & overprints see #175, 203-206, 227-244, 253-257.

Communications Type of Tanzania 1976

Designs: 50c, Microwave tower. 1sh, Cordless switchboard and operators, horiz. 2sh, Telephones of 1880, 1930 and 1976. 3sh, Message switching center, horiz.

1976, Apr. 15 Litho. *Perf. 14½*

147	A6a	50c blue & multi	.25	.25
148	A6a	1sh red & multi	.25	.25
149	A6a	2sh yellow & multi	.25	.25
150	A6a	3sh multicolored	.35	.35
a.		Souvenir sheet of 4	1.40	1.40
		Nos. 147-150 (4)	1.10	1.10

Telecommunications development in East Africa. No. 150a contains 4 stamps similar to Nos. 147-150 with simulated perforations.

Olympics Type of Tanzania 1976

Designs: 50c, Akii Bua, Ugandan hurdler. 1sh, Filbert Bayi, Tanzanian runner. 2sh, Steve Muchoki, Kenyan boxer. 3sh, Olympic torch, flags of Kenya, Tanzania and Uganda.

1976, July 5 Litho. *Perf. 14½*

151	A6b	50c blue & multi	.25	.25
152	A6b	1sh red & multi	.25	.25
153	A6b	2sh yellow & multi	.30	.30
154	A6b	3sh blue & multi	.50	.40
a.		Souv. sheet of 4, #151-154, perf. 13	6.00	5.00
		Nos. 151-154 (4)	1.30	1.20

21st Olympic Games, Montreal, Canada, July 17-Aug. 1.

Railway Type of Tanzania 1976

Designs: 50c, Tanzania-Zambia Railway. 1sh, Nile Bridge, Uganda. 2sh, Nakuru Station, Kenya. 3sh, Class A locomotive, 1896.

1976, Oct. 4 Litho. *Perf. 14*

155	A6c	50c lilac & multi	.25	.25
156	A6c	1sh emerald & multi	.35	.25
157	A6c	2sh brt rose & multi	.65	.45
158	A6c	3sh yellow & multi	1.00	.65
a.		Souv. sheet, #155-158, perf 13	3.25	3.25
		Nos. 155-158 (4)	2.25	1.60

Rail transport in East Africa.

Fish Type of Tanzania 1977

1977, Jan. 10 Litho. *Perf. 14½*

159	A6d	50c Nile perch	.25	.25
160	A6d	1sh Tilapia	.30	.25
161	A6d	3sh Sailfish	.80	.60
162	A6d	5sh Black marlin	1.10	1.00
a.		Souvenir sheet of 4, #159-162	5.50	5.50
		Nos. 159-162 (4)	2.45	2.10

Festival Type of Tanzania 1977

Festival Emblem and: 50c, Masai tribesmen bleeding cow. 1sh, Dancers from Uganda. 2sh, Makonde sculpture, Tanzania. 3sh, Tribesmen skinning hippopotamus.

1977, Jan. 15 *Perf. 13½x14*

163	A6e	50c multicolored	.25	.25
164	A6e	1sh multicolored	.25	.25
165	A6e	2sh multicolored	.40	.35
166	A6e	3sh multicolored	.60	.60
a.		Souvenir sheet of 4, #163-166	2.25	2.25
		Nos. 163-166 (4)	1.50	1.45

2nd World Black and African Festival, Lagos, Nigeria, Jan. 15-Feb. 12.

Rally Type of Tanzania 1977

Safari Rally Emblem and: 50c, Automobile passing through village. 1sh, Winner at finish line. 2sh, Car passing through washout. 5sh, Car, elephants and Mt. Kenya.

1977, Apr. 5 Litho. *Perf. 14*

167	A6f	50c multicolored	.25	.25
168	A6f	1sh multicolored	.25	.25
169	A6f	2sh multicolored	.35	.25
170	A6f	5sh multicolored	.85	.75
a.		Souvenir sheet of 4, #167-170	2.25	2.25
		Nos. 167-170 (4)	1.70	1.50

25th Safari Rally, Apr. 7-11.

Church Type of Tanzania 1977

Designs: 50c, Rev. Canon Apolo Kivebulaya. 1sh, Uganda Cathedral. 2sh, Early grass-topped Cathedral. 5sh, Early tent congregation, Kigezi.

1977, June 30 Litho. *Perf. 14*

171	A6g	50c multicolored	.25	.25
172	A6g	1sh multicolored	.25	.25
173	A6g	2sh multicolored	.25	.25
174	A6g	5sh multicolored	.60	.60
a.		Souvenir sheet of 4, #171-174	1.50	1.50
		Nos. 171-174 (4)	1.35	1.35

Church of Uganda, centenary.

Type of 1975 Surcharged with New Value and 2 Bars

1977, Aug. 22 Photo. *Perf. 14x14½*

175	A17	80c on 60c bananas	.40	.25

No. 175 was not issued without surcharge.

Wildlife Type of Tanzania 1977

Wildlife Fund Emblem and: 50c, Pancake tortoise. 1sh, Nile crocodile. 2sh, Hunter's hartebeest. 3sh, Red colobus monkey. 5sh, Dugong.

1977, Sept. 26 Litho. *Perf. 14x13½*

176	A6h	50c multicolored	.30	.25
177	A6h	1sh multicolored	.50	.40
178	A6h	2sh multicolored	2.25	1.00
179	A6h	3sh multicolored	3.25	1.40
180	A6h	5sh multicolored	3.25	2.50
a.		Souvenir sheet of 4, #177-180	8.50	6.00
		Nos. 176-180 (5)	9.55	5.55

Endangered species.

Soccer Type of Tanzania

Soccer Cup and: 50c, Soccer scene and Joe Kadenge. 1sh, Mohammed Chuma receiving trophy, and his portrait. 2sh, Shot on goal and Omari S. Kidevu. 5sh, Backfield defense and Polly Ouma.

1978, May 3 Litho. *Perf. 14x13½*

181	A8a	50c green & multi	.25	.25
182	A8a	1sh lt brown & multi	.25	.25
183	A8a	2sh lilac & multi	.30	.30
184	A8a	5sh dk blue & multi	.90	.90
a.		Souvenir sheet of 4, #181-184	2.00	2.00
		Nos. 181-184 (4)	1.70	1.70

World Soccer Cup Championships, Argentina, June 1-25.
See Nos. 203-206.

Crop Type of 1975

Designs as before.

1978, June Litho. *Perf. 14½*
Size: 41x25mm
Multicolored, Name Panel as follows

195	A17	5sh blue	.25	.25
196	A17	10sh rose lilac	.45	.45
197	A17	20sh brown	.90	.90
198	A17	40sh deep orange	1.90	1.90
		Nos. 195-198 (4)	3.50	3.50

For overprint see Nos. 241-244.

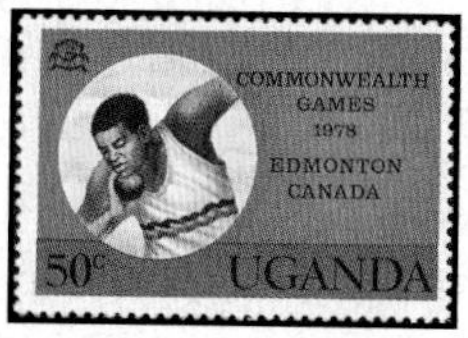

Shot Put
A18

1978, July 10 Litho. *Perf. 14*

199	A18	50c shown	.25	.25
200	A18	1sh Broad jump	.25	.25
201	A18	2sh Running	.25	.25
202	A18	5sh Boxing	.55	1.00
a.		Souv. sheet, #199-202, perf 12	2.75	2.75
		Nos. 199-202 (4)	1.30	1.75

Commonwealth Games, Edmonton, Canada, Aug. 3-12.
For overprints see Nos. 249-252.

Soccer Type of Tanzania 1978 Inscribed "WORLD CUP 1978"

Designs: 50c, Backfield defense and Polly Ouma. 2sh, Shot on goal and Omari S. Kidevu. 5sh, Soccer scene and Joe Kadenge. 10sh, Mohammed Chuma receiving trophy, and his portrait.

1978, Sept. 11 *Perf. 14x13½*

203	A8a	50c dk blue & multi	.25	.25
204	A8a	2sh lilac & multi	.30	.25
205	A8a	5sh green & multi	.70	.90
206	A8a	10sh lt brown & multi	1.35	1.75
a.		Souv. sheet of 4, #203-206, perf. 12	3.50	3.50
		Nos. 203-206 (4)	2.60	3.15

World Cup Soccer Championship winners.
For overprint see Nos. 253-257.

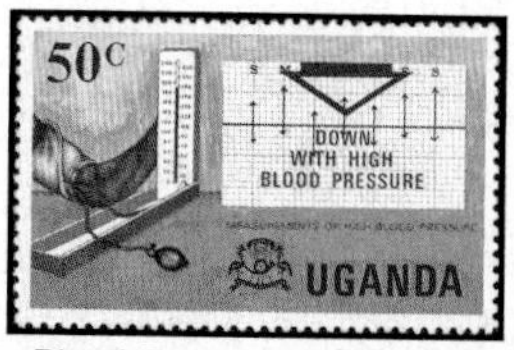

Blood Pressure Gauge and Chart — A19

1978, Sept. 25 Litho. *Perf. 14*

207	A19	50c shown	.25	.25
208	A19	1sh Heart	.25	.25
209	A19	2sh Retina	.35	.30
210	A19	5sh Kidneys	.80	1.10
a.		Souvenir sheet of 4, #207-210	2.75	2.75
		Nos. 207-210 (4)	1.65	1.90

World Health Day and Hypertension Month.

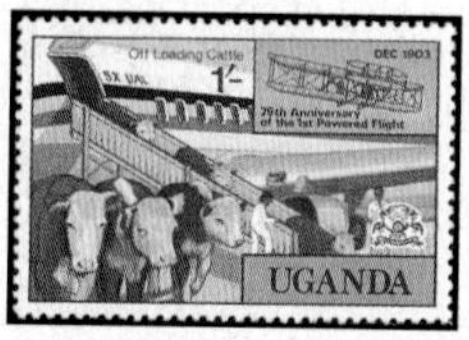

Cattle Unloaded from Plane
A20

Flyer 1 and: 1.50sh, "Islander" on runway, Kampala. 2.70sh, Coffee loaded on transport jet. 10sh, Concorde.

1978, Dec. 16

211	A20	1sh multicolored	.25	.25
212	A20	1.50sh multicolored	.25	.25
213	A20	2.70sh multicolored	.45	.40
214	A20	10sh multicolored	1.90	1.40
a.		Souvenir sheet of 4, #211-214	3.00	3.00
		Nos. 211-214 (4)	2.85	2.30

75th anniversary of 1st powered flight.
For overprints see Nos. 258-261.

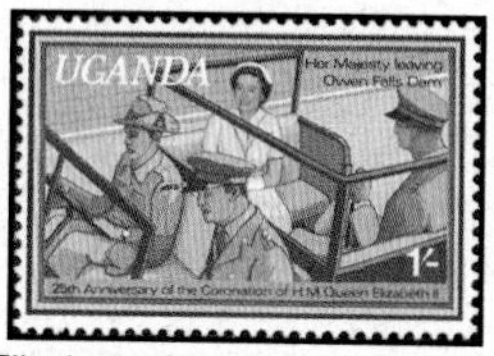

Elizabeth II Leaving Owen Falls Dam — A21

Designs: 1.50sh, Coronation regalia. 2.70sh, Coronation ceremony. 10sh, Royal family on balcony of Buckingham Palace.

1979, Mar. 1 Litho. *Perf. 12½x12*

215	A21	1sh multicolored	.25	.25
216	A21	1.50sh multicolored	.25	.25
217	A21	2.70sh multicolored	.25	.25
218	A21	10sh multicolored	.65	1.25
a.		Souvenir sheet of 4, #215-218	2.40	2.40
		Nos. 215-218 (4)	1.40	2.00

25th anniv. of coronation of Elizabeth II.
For overprints see Nos. 245-248.

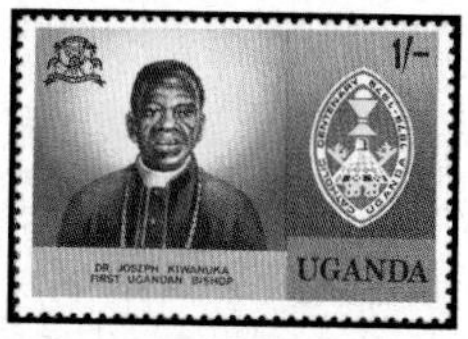

Bishop Joseph Kiwanuka
A22

Designs: 1.50sh, Lubaga Cathedral. 2.70sh, Ugandan pilgrims and St. Peter's, Rome. 10sh, Friar Lourdel-Mapeera, missionary.

1979, Feb. 15 *Perf. 14*

219	A22	1sh multicolored	.25	.25
220	A22	1.50sh multicolored	.25	.25
221	A22	2.70sh multicolored	.25	.25
222	A22	10sh multicolored	.70	.90
a.		Souvenir sheet of 4, #219-222	2.00	2.00
		Nos. 219-222 (4)	1.45	1.65

Ugandan Catholic Church, centenary.
See No. 274. For overprints see Nos. 262-265.

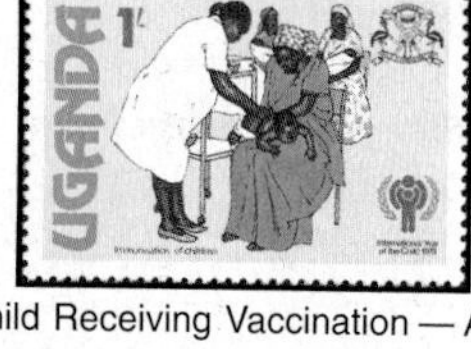

Child Receiving Vaccination — A23

IYC Emblem and: 1.50sh, Handicapped children playing. 2.70sh, Ugandan IYC emblem. 10sh, Teacher and pupils.

1979, July 16 Litho. *Perf. 14*

223	A23	1sh multicolored	.25	.25
224	A23	1.50sh multicolored	.25	.25
225	A23	2.70sh multicolored	.25	.30
226	A23	10sh multicolored	.50	.90
a.		Souvenir sheet of 4, #223-226	2.00	2.00
		Nos. 223-226 (4)	1.25	1.70

International Year of the Child.
For overprints see Nos. 266-269.

Nos. 133-146, 195-198, 215-218 Overprinted "UGANDA / LIBERATED / 1979"

1979, July 12 Photo. *Perf. 14x14½*

Size: 21x17mm

227	A17	10c multicolored	.25	.25
228	A17	20c multicolored	.25	.25
229	A17	30c multicolored	.25	.25
230	A17	40c multicolored	.25	.25
231	A17	50c multicolored	.25	.25
232	A17	70c multicolored	.25	.25
233	A17	80c multicolored	.25	.25

Perf. 14½

Size: 41x25mm

234	A17	1sh multicolored	.25	.25
235	A17	2sh multicolored	.25	.25
236	A17	3sh multicolored	.25	.25
237	A17	5sh multicolored	.35	.30
238	A17	10sh multicolored	.70	.60
239	A17	20sh multicolored	1.50	1.50
240	A17	40sh multicolored	3.00	3.00
		Nos. 227-240 (14)	8.05	7.90

1979 Litho. *Perf. 14½*

Multicolored, name panel as follows

241	A17	5sh blue	.45	.35
242	A17	10sh rose lilac	.85	.70
243	A17	20sh brown	1.60	1.40
244	A17	40sh deep orange	3.25	2.75
		Nos. 241-244 (4)	6.15	5.20

1979, July 12 Litho. *Perf. 12½x12*

245	A21	1sh multicolored	.25	.25
246	A21	1.50sh multicolored	.25	.25
247	A21	2.70sh multicolored	.25	.25
248	A21	15sh on 10sh multi	1.40	1.10
a.		Souvenir sheet of 4	2.50	
		Nos. 245-248 (4)	2.15	1.85

No. 248a contains Nos. 245-247 and a 15sh in design of No. 218. Issued Aug. 1.

Nos. 199-202, 203-206, 211-214, 219-222, 223-226 Overprinted "UGANDA LIBERATED 1979"

1979, Aug. 1 Litho. *Perf. 14*

249	A18	50c multicolored	.25	.25
250	A18	1sh multicolored	.25	.25
251	A18	2sh multicolored	.25	.25
252	A18	5sh multicolored	.40	.35

1979, Aug. 1 *Perf. 14x13½*

253	A8a	50c multi	.25	.25
255	A8a	2sh multi (#204)	.25	.25
256	A8a	5sh multi	.40	.35
257	A8a	10sh multi	.85	.70

Overprint exists on No. 183.

1979, Aug. 1 *Perf. 14*

258	A20	1sh multicolored	.25	.25
259	A20	1.50sh multicolored	.25	.25
260	A20	2.70sh multicolored	.30	.25
261	A20	10sh multicolored	1.05	.85

1979, Aug. 1

262	A22	1sh multicolored	.25	.25
263	A22	1.50sh multicolored	.25	.25
264	A22	2.70sh multicolored	.25	.25
265	A22	10sh multicolored	.80	.70

1979, Aug. 16

266	A23	1sh multicolored	.25	.25
267	A23	1.50sh multicolored	.25	.25
268	A23	2.70sh multicolored	.25	.25
269	A23	10sh multicolored	.85	.80
a.		Souvenir sheet of 4, #266-269	2.25	2.25
		Nos. 249-269 (20)	7.90	7.25

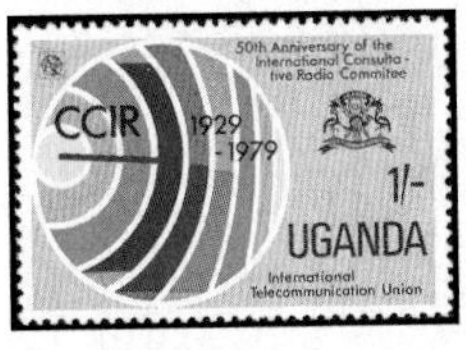

ITU Emblem, Radio Waves A24

1979, Sept. 11

270	A24	1sh lt gray & multi	.25	.25
271	A24	1.50sh orange & multi	.25	.25
272	A24	2.70sh yellow & multi	.25	.25
273	A24	10sh blue & multi	.35	.90
		Nos. 270-273 (4)	1.10	1.65

50th anniv. of Intl. Radio Consultative Committee (CCIR) of the ITU.

No. 222a Redrawn and Inscribed FREEDOM OF WORSHIP DECLARED

Souvenir Sheet

1979, Sept. *Perf. 12*

274	Sheet of 4	2.00	2.00
a.	A22 1sh No. 219	.25	.25
b.	A22 1.50sh No. 220	.25	.25
c.	A22 2.70sh No. 221	.25	.25
d.	A22 10sh No. 222	1.25	1.25

In top panel of margin scrolls and coat of arms have been replaced by inscription.

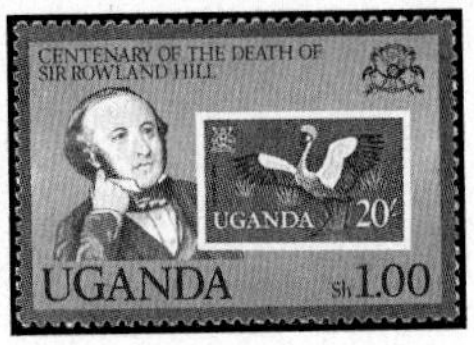

A25

1979, Nov. 12 Litho. *Perf. 14*

275	A25	1sh #110	.25	.25
276	A25	1.50sh #112	.25	.25
277	A25	2.70sh #94	.25	.30
278	A25	10sh #69	.40	1.00
a.		Souvenir sheet of 4, #275-278	2.00	2.00
		Nos. 275-278 (4)	1.15	1.80

Sir Rowland Hill (1795-1879), originator of penny postage.

For overprints see Nos. 293-296.

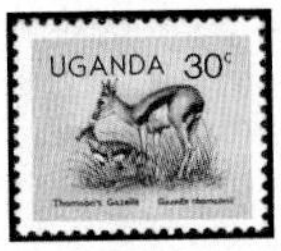

Thomson's Gazelle — A26

Designs: 10c, Impalas. 20c, Large-spotted genet. 50c, Bush babies. 80c, Wild hunting dogs. 1sh, Lions. 1.50sh, Mountain gorillas. 2sh, Zebras. 2.70sh, Leopards. 3.50sh, Black rhinoceroses. 5sh, Defassa waterbucks. 10sh, African black buffaloes. 20sh, Hippopotami. 40sh, African elephants.

1979, Dec. 3 Litho. *Perf. 14*

No Date Imprint Below Design

Size: 21x17mm

279	A26	10c multicolored	.25	.25
280	A26	20c multicolored	.25	.25
281	A26	30c multicolored	.25	.25
282	A26	50c multicolored	.25	.25
283	A26	80c multicolored	.25	.25

Size: 39x25mm

284	A26	1sh multicolored	.25	.25
a.		Imprint "1982"	.45	.25
285	A26	1.50sh multicolored	.25	.25
286	A26	2sh multicolored	.25	.25
a.		Imprint "1982"	.60	.30
287	A26	2.70sh multicolored	.25	.25
288	A26	3.50sh multicolored	.30	.25
289	A26	5sh multicolored	.45	.40
a.		Imprint "1982"	.60	.60
290	A26	10sh multicolored	.85	.85
291	A26	20sh multicolored	1.90	1.90
292	A26	40sh multicolored	4.00	4.00
		Nos. 279-292 (14)	9.75	9.65

Nos. 284, 286, 289 reissued inscribed 1982. See Nos. 400-406. For surcharges see Nos. 386-392.

Nos. 275-278a Overprinted: "LONDON 1980"

1980, May 6 Litho. *Perf. 14*

293	A25	1sh multicolored	.25	.25
294	A25	1.50sh multicolored	.25	.25
295	A25	2.70sh multicolored	.30	.25
296	A25	10sh multicolored	1.10	1.10
a.		Souvenir sheet of 4, #293-296	2.00	2.00
		Nos. 293-296 (4)	1.90	1.85

London 80 Intl. Stamp Exhib., May 6-14.

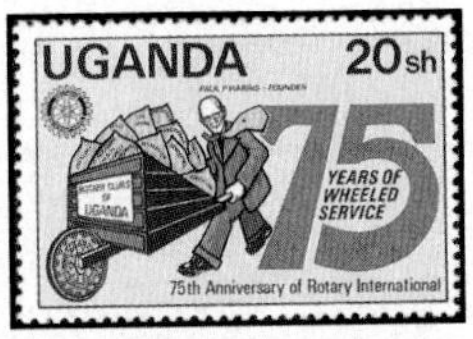

Paul Harris Wheeling Rotary Cart A27

1980, Aug. Litho. *Perf. 14*

297	A27	1sh Rotary emblem, vert.	.25	.25
298	A27	20sh shown	1.60	1.60
a.		Souvenir sheet of 2, #297-298	2.75	2.75

Rotary International, 75th anniversary.

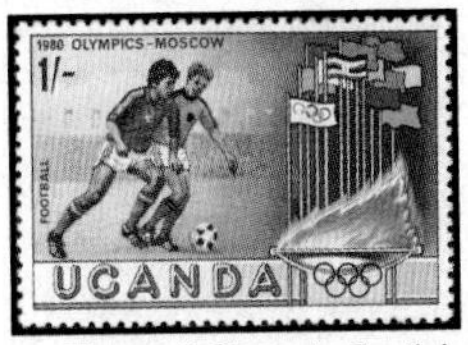

Soccer, Flags of Olympic Participants, Flame — A28

1980, Dec. 29 Litho. *Perf. 14*

299	A28	1sh shown	.25	.25
300	A28	2sh Relay race	.25	.25
301	A28	10sh Hurdles	.50	.50
302	A28	20sh Boxing	1.00	1.00
		Nos. 299-302 (4)	2.00	2.00

Souvenir Sheet

303	Sheet of 4	2.50	2.50
a.	A28 2.70sh like #299	.25	.25
b.	A28 3sh like #300	.25	.25
c.	A28 5sh like #301	.35	.30
d.	A28 25sh like 302	1.60	1.40

22nd Summer Olympic Games, Moscow, July 19-Aug. 3.

Nos. 299-303 Overprinted with Sport, Winner and Country

1980, Dec. 29

304	A28	1sh multicolored	.25	.25
305	A28	2sh multicolored	.25	.25
306	A28	10sh multicolored	.50	.50
307	A28	20sh multicolored	1.00	1.00
		Nos. 304-307 (4)	2.00	2.00

Souvenir Sheet

308	Sheet of 4	2.50	2.50
a.	A28 2.70sh like #304	.25	.25
b.	A28 3sh like #305	.25	.25
c.	A28 5sh like #306	.35	.30
d.	A28 25sh like #307	1.60	1.40

Souvenir Sheet

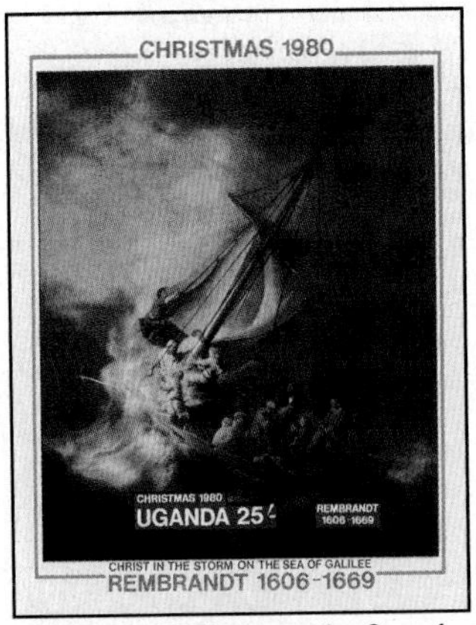

Christ in the Storm on the Sea of Galilee, by Rembrandt — A29

1980, Dec. 31 *Imperf.*

309	A29	25sh multicolored	6.50	5.50

Christmas 1980.

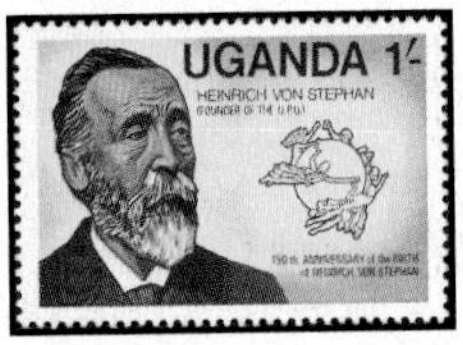

Heinrich von Stephan and UPU Emblem A30

1981, June 2 Litho. *Perf. 14*

310	A30	1sh shown	.25	.25
311	A30	2sh UPU headquarters	.35	.25
312	A30	2.70sh Mail plane, 1935	.45	.35
313	A30	10sh Mail train, 1927	1.40	1.25
a.		Souvenir sheet of 4, #310-313	3.75	3.75
		Nos. 310-313 (4)	2.45	2.10

Von Stephan (1831-97), UPU founder.

Common Design Types pictured following the introduction.

Royal Wedding Issue

Common Design Type

1981 Litho. *Perf. 14*

314	CD331a	10sh Couple	.25	.25
a.		10sh on 1sh	.25	.25
315	CD331a	50sh Tower of London	.30	.25
a.		50sh on 5sh	.30	.25
316	CD331a	200sh Prince Charles	1.50	1.25
a.		200sh on 20sh	1.50	1.25
		Nos. 314-316 (3)	2.05	1.75
		Nos. 314a-316a (3)	2.05	1.75

Souvenir Sheet

317	CD331	250sh Royal mews	1.25	1.25
a.		250sh on 25sh, light orange	1.25	1.25

Royal wedding. Issue dates: surcharges, July 13; others, July 29. Nos. 314-316 also issued in sheets of 5 plus label, perf. 12, in changed colors.

For overprints see Nos. 342-345.

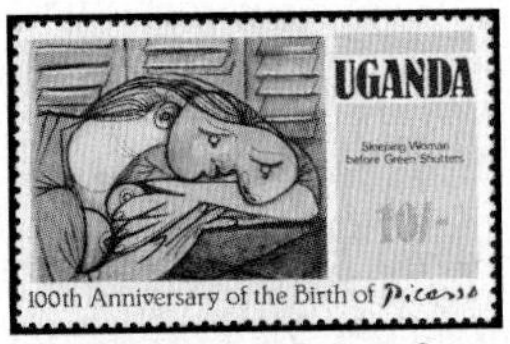

Sleeping Woman Before Green Shutters, by Picasso — A31

Picasso Birth Centenary: 20sh, Bullfight. 30sh, Nude Asleep on a Landscape. 200sh, Interior with a Girl Drawing. 250sh, Minotaur.

1981, Sept. 21 Litho. *Perf. 14*

318	A31	10sh multicolored	.25	.25
319	A31	20sh multicolored	.30	.25
320	A31	30sh multicolored	.40	.30
321	A31	200sh multicolored	2.00	2.75

Size: 120x146mm

Imperf

322	A31	250sh multicolored	2.50	4.00
		Nos. 318-322 (5)	5.45	7.55

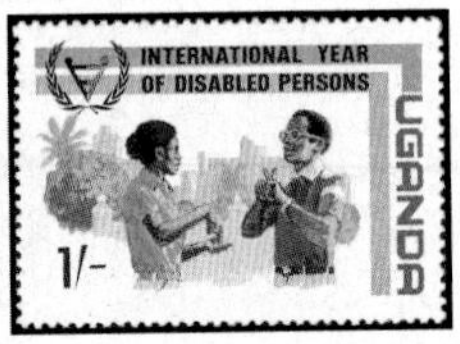

Intl. Year of the Disabled A32

1981, Dec. *Perf. 15*

323	A32	1sh Sign language	.25	.25
324	A32	10sh Teacher in wheelchair	.25	.25
325	A32	50sh Retarded children	.80	.65
326	A32	200sh Blind man	1.75	2.00
a.		Souvenir sheet of 4, #323-326	4.50	4.50
		Nos. 323-326 (4)	3.05	3.15

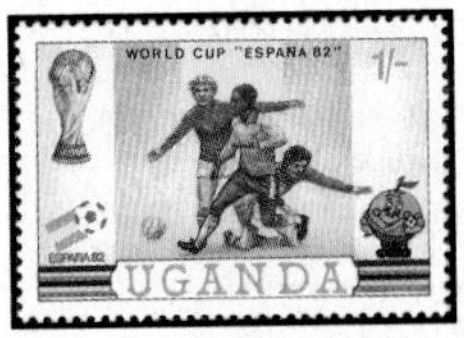

1982 World Cup Soccer A33

Designs: Various soccer players.

1982, Jan. 11 Litho. *Perf. 14*

327	A33	1sh multicolored	.25	.25
328	A33	10sh multicolored	.25	.25
329	A33	50sh multicolored	.75	.75
330	A33	200sh multicolored	2.75	2.25
		Nos. 327-330 (4)	4.00	3.50

Souvenir Sheet

331	A33	250sh World Cup	4.00	4.00

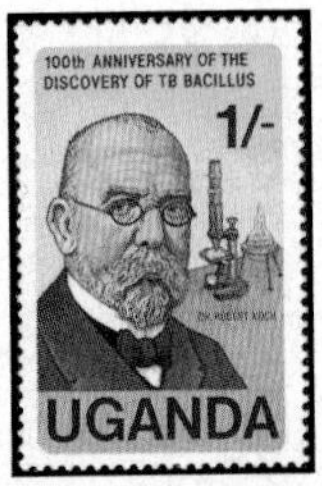

TB Bacillus Centenary — A34

1982, June 14 Litho.

332	A34	1sh Koch	.30	.30
333	A34	10sh Microscope	.50	.35
334	A34	50sh Inoculation	2.25	1.60
335	A34	100sh Bacteria under microscope	4.50	3.25
		Nos. 332-335 (4)	7.55	5.50

Souvenir Sheet

336	A34	150sh Medical School	6.00	3.50

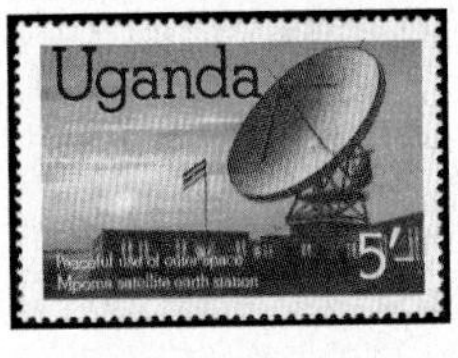

Peaceful Uses of Outer Space A35

5sh, Mpoma Satellite Earth Station. 10sh, Pioneer II. 50sh, Columbia space shuttle. 100sh, Voyager II, Saturn. 150sh, Columbia shuttle.

1982, May 17		Litho.	Perf. 15	
337	A35	5sh multicolored	.35	.35
338	A35	10sh multicolored	.35	.35
339	A35	1.60 multicolored	1.60	1.40
340	A35	100sh multicolored	3.25	2.75
		Nos. 337-340 (4)	5.55	4.85

Souvenir Sheet

341	A35	150sh multicolored	5.25	4.50

Nos. 314-317 Overprinted: "21st BIRTHDAY / HRH Princess of Wales / JULY 1 1982"

1982, July 7			Perf. 14	
342	CD331	10sh multicolored	.25	.25
343	CD331	50sh multicolored	.40	.40
344	CD331	200sh multicolored	1.90	1.50
		Nos. 342-344 (3)	2.55	2.15

Souvenir Sheet

345	CD331	250sh multicolored	3.00	2.50

Also issued in sheets of 5 + label in changed colors, perf. 12x12½.

20th Anniversary of Independence
A 150sh souvenir sheet showing the Coat of Arms was not issued.

Hornbill — A36

1982, July 12				
346	A36	1sh shown	.25	.25
347	A36	20sh Superb starling	.70	.60
348	A36	50sh Bateleur eagle	1.60	1.40
349	A36	100sh Saddle-bill stork	3.50	2.90
		Nos. 346-349 (4)	6.05	5.15

Souvenir Sheet

350	A36	200sh Laughing dove	11.50	10.00

Scouting Year A37

5sh, Scouts. 20sh, Trophy presentation. 50sh, Helping disabled. 100sh, First aid instruction. 150sh, Baden-Powell.

1982, Aug. 23				
351	A37	5sh multicolored	.30	.30
352	A37	20sh multicolored	.75	.60
353	A37	50sh multicolored	1.90	1.60
354	A37	100sh multicolored	3.75	3.25
		Nos. 351-354 (4)	6.70	5.75

Souvenir Sheet

355	A37	150sh multicolored	4.50	4.00

For overprints see Nos. 376-380.

Franklin D. Roosevelt (1882-1945) — A38

Roosevelt and Washington: 50sh, 200sh, Inaugurations. No. 358, Mount Vernon. No. 359, Hyde Park.

1982, Sept.			Litho.	
356	A38	50sh multicolored	.60	.50

357	A38	200sh multicolored	2.50	2.25

Souvenir Sheets

358	A38	150sh multicolored	1.75	1.75
359	A38	150sh multicolored	1.75	1.75

Italy's Victory in 1982 World Cup A39

1982, Oct.		Litho.	Perf. 14½	
359A	A39	10sh Players	.25	.25
359B	A39	200sh Team	2.50	2.50

Souvenir Sheet

359C	A39	250sh Globe	2.50	2.50

A39a

5sh, Dancers. 20sh, Traditional currency. 50sh, Village. 100sh, Drums.

1983, Mar. 14		Litho.	Perf. 14	
360	A39a	5sh multicolored	.25	.25
361	A39a	20sh multicolored	.25	.25
362	A39a	50sh multicolored	.50	.50
363	A39a	100sh multicolored	.70	.70
		Nos. 360-363 (4)	1.70	1.70

Commonwealth Day.

St. George and the Dragon, by Raphael A40

20sh, St. George and the Dragon, 1505. 50sh, Moses Parts the Red Sea. 200sh, Expulsion of Heliodorus. 250sh, Leo the Great and Attila, 1513.

1983, Apr.				
364	A40	5sh multicolored	.25	.25
365	A40	20sh multicolored	.30	.30
366	A40	50sh multicolored	.75	.75
367	A40	200sh multicolored	2.00	2.00
		Nos. 364-367 (4)	3.30	3.30

Souvenir Sheet

368	A40	250sh multicolored	2.75	2.75

A41

7th Non-aligned Summit Conference — A42

1983, Aug. 15		Litho.	Perf. 14½	
369	A41	5sh multicolored	.25	.25
370	A42	200sh multicolored	2.00	2.00

African Elephants and World Wildlife Emblem A43

5sh, Three adults with elephant bones. 10sh, Three adults walking. 30sh, Elephants standing in water hole. 70sh, Adults with calf.

1983, Aug. 22			Perf. 15	
371	A43	5sh multicolored	1.10	1.10
372	A43	10sh multicolored	1.75	1.75
373	A43	30sh multicolored	4.25	4.25
374	A43	70sh multicolored	11.00	11.00
		Nos. 371-374 (4)	18.10	18.10

Nos. 371-374 were reprinted in 1990, perf. 14. Value $25.

Souvenir Sheet

375	A43	300sh Zebras, vert.	6.25	5.25

No. 375 does not have the WWF emblem. See Nos. 948-953.

Nos. 351-355 Ovptd. or Srchd. "BOYS BRIGADE CENTENARY 1883-1983"

1983, Sept. 19		Litho.	Perf. 14	
376	A37	5sh multicolored	.25	.25
377	A37	20sh multicolored	.25	.25
378	A37	50sh multicolored	.40	.40
379	A37	400sh on 100sh multi	2.50	2.50
		Nos. 376-379 (4)	3.40	3.40

Souvenir Sheet

380	A37	150sh multicolored	1.75	1.75

World Communications Year — A44

Designs: 20sh, Mpoma Satellite Earth Station. 50sh, Railroad, Computer Operator. 70sh, Filming Lions. 100sh, Pilots, Radio Communications. 300sh, Communications Satellite.

1983, Oct. 3		Litho.	Perf. 15	
381	A44	20sh multicolored	.25	.25
382	A44	50sh multicolored	.65	.65
383	A44	70sh multicolored	.85	.85
384	A44	100sh multicolored	1.25	1.25
		Nos. 381-384 (4)	3.00	3.00

Souvenir Sheet

385	A44	300sh multicolored	2.50	2.50

Nos. 279, 281-285, 289 Surcharged

1983, Nov. 7		Litho.	Perf. 14	
386	A26	100sh on 10c multi	.70	.70
387	A26	135sh on 1sh multi	.85	.85
388	A26	175sh on 30c multi	1.00	1.00
389	A26	200sh on 50c multi	1.40	1.40
390	A26	400sh on 80c multi	3.00	3.00
391	A26	700sh on 5sh multi	4.75	4.75
392	A26	1000sh on 1.50sh	6.50	6.50
		Nos. 386-392 (7)	18.20	18.20

World Food Day A45

1984, Jan. 12		Litho.	Perf. 14	
393	A45	10sh Plowing	.50	.50
394	A45	300sh Banana crop	3.75	3.75

Christmas — A46

10sh, Nativity. 50sh, Sheperds and Angel. 175sh, Flight into Egypt. 400sh, Angels Blowing Trumpets.

300sh, Three Kings.

1983, Dec. 12		Litho.	Perf. 14	
395	A46	10sh multicolored	.25	.25
396	A46	50sh multicolored	.30	.30
397	A46	175sh multicolored	.70	.70
398	A46	400sh multicolored	1.75	1.75
		Nos. 395-398 (4)	3.00	3.00

Souvenir Sheet

399	A46	300sh multicolored	2.25	2.25

Animal Type of 1979

1983, Dec. 19				
400	A26	100sh like No. 284	.70	.70
401	A26	135sh like No. 285	.85	.85
402	A26	175sh like No. 286	1.00	1.00
403	A26	200sh like No. 287	1.40	1.40
404	A26	400sh like No. 288	3.00	3.00
405	A26	700sh like No. 292	4.75	4.75
406	A26	1000sh like No. 291	6.50	6.50
		Nos. 400-406 (7)	18.20	18.20

1984 Summer Olympics A48

1983			Perf. 14½	
417	A48	5sh Ruth Kyalisiima	.25	.25
418	A48	115sh Javelin	.50	.50
419	A48	155sh Wrestling	.65	.65
420	A48	175sh Rowing	.85	.85
		Nos. 417-420 (4)	2.25	2.25

Souvenir Sheet

421	A48	500sh Akii-Bua	2.10	2.10

For overprints see Nos. 458-462.

Intl. Civil Aviation Org., 40th Anniv. A49

1984, Sept.				
422	A49	5sh Passenger service	.45	.45
423	A49	115sh Cargo service	1.75	1.75
424	A49	155sh Police airwing	2.50	2.50
425	A49	175sh Soroti Flying School plane	3.50	3.50
		Nos. 422-425 (4)	8.20	8.20

Souvenir Sheet

426	A49	250sh Hot air balloon	4.00	4.00

Butterflies A50

5sh, Silver-barred Charaxes. 115sh, Western Emperor Swallowtail. 155sh, African Giant Swallowtail. 175sh, Blue Salamis. 250sh, Veinted Yellow.

1984, Oct.		Litho.	Perf. 14½	
427	A50	5sh multi	.35	.35
428	A50	115sh multi	2.50	2.50
429	A50	155sh multi	3.50	3.50
430	A50	175sh multi	4.00	4.00
		Nos. 427-430 (4)	10.35	10.35

Souvenir Sheet

431	A50	250sh multi	4.50	4.00

Freshwater Fish — A51

5sh, Nothobranchius taeniopygus. 10sh, Bagrus dogmac. 50sh, Polypterus senegalus. 100sh, Clarias. 135sh, Mormyrus kannume. 175sh, Synodontis victoriae. 205sh, Haplochromis brownae. 400sh, Lates niloticus. 700sh, Protopterus aethiopicus.

1000sh, Barbus radcliffii. 2500sh, Malapterus electricus.

1985 Litho. *Perf. 15*

432	A51	5sh multicolored	.55	.55
433	A51	10sh multicolored	.80	.55
434	A51	50sh multicolored	1.50	.45
435	A51	100sh multicolored	1.50	.45
436	A51	135sh multicolored	2.50	1.40
437	A51	175sh multicolored	2.50	2.40
438	A51	205sh multicolored	2.50	*2.75*
439	A51	400sh multicolored	2.50	*3.00*
440	A51	700sh multicolored	2.50	*3.50*
441	A51	1000sh multicolored	2.50	*3.50*
442	A51	2500sh multicolored	3.00	*4.75*
		Nos. 432-442 (11)	22.35	23.30

Issued: #432-435, 437-441, 4/1; #436, 442, 6/10.

For overprints see Nos. 490-494.

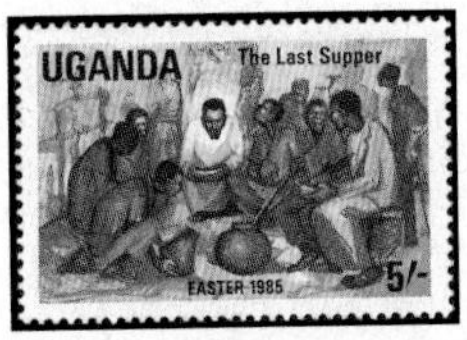

Easter A52

5sh, The Last Supper. 115sh, Jesus confronts doubting Thomas. 155sh, Crucifixion. 175sh, Pentecost.
250sh, Last prayer in garden.

1985, May 13 Litho. *Perf. 14*

443	A52	5sh multicolored	.50	.50
444	A52	115sh multicolored	1.60	1.60
445	A52	155sh multicolored	1.75	*2.50*
446	A52	175sh multicolored	2.25	*3.25*
		Nos. 443-446 (4)	6.10	7.85

Souvenir Sheet

447	A52	250sh multicolored	1.25	1.25

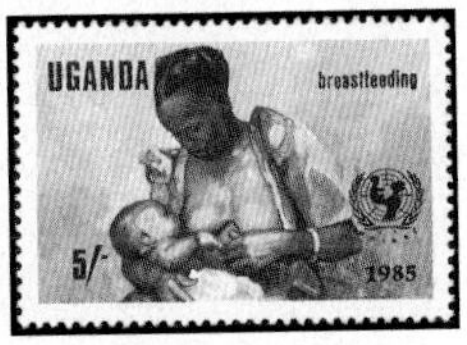

UN Child Survival Campaign A53

5sh, Mother breastfeeding. 115sh, Growth monitorization. 155sh, Immunization. 175sh, Oral rehydration therapy.
500sh, Expectant Mother, food.

1985, July 1

448	A53	5sh multi	.35	.35
449	A53	115sh multi	1.90	1.90
450	A53	155sh multi	2.50	2.50
451	A53	175sh multi	3.00	3.00
		Nos. 448-451 (4)	7.75	7.75

Souvenir Sheet

452	A53	500sh multi	5.25	5.25

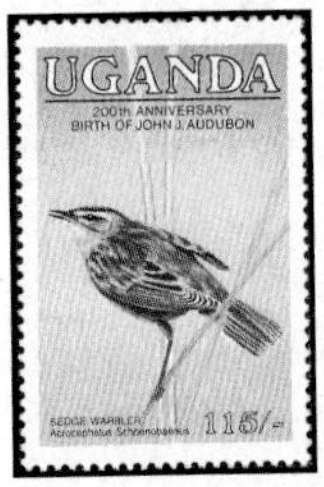

Audubon Birth Bicent. — A54

115sh, Acrocephalus schoenobaenus. 155sh, Ardeola ibis. 175sh, Galerida gristata. 500sh, Aythya fuligula.
1000sh, Strix aluco.

1985, July

453	A54	115sh multi	1.90	1.75
454	A54	155sh multi	2.25	1.90
455	A54	175sh multi	1.90	2.25
456	A54	500sh multi	3.00	*4.75*
		Nos. 453-456 (4)	9.05	10.65

Souvenir Sheet

457	A54	1000sh multi	10.00	10.00

See Nos. 469-473.

Nos. 417-421 Ovptd. or Srchd. with Winners Names, Medals and Countries in Gold

Gold medalists: 5sh, Benita Brown-Fitzgerald, US, 100-meter hurdles. 115sh, Arto Haerkoenen, Finland, javelin. 155sh, Atsuji Miyahara, Japan, 115-pound Greco-Roman wrestling. 100sh, West Germany, quadruple sculls. 1200sh, Edwin Moses, US, 400-meter hurdles.

1985, July *Perf. 15*

458	A48	5sh multicolored	.25	.25
459	A48	115sh multicolored	.35	.35
460	A48	155sh multicolored	.50	.50
461	A48	1000sh on 175sh multi	3.00	3.00
		Nos. 458-461 (4)	4.10	4.10

Souvenir Sheet

462	A48	1200sh on 500sh multi	3.50	3.50

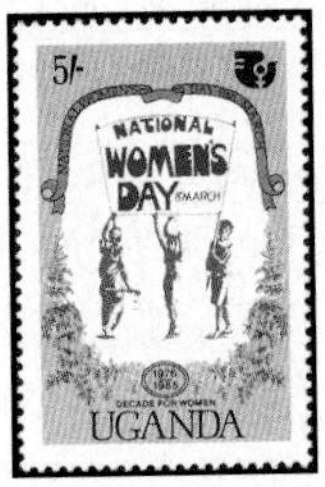

UN Decade for Women — A56

5sh, Natl. Women's Day, Mar. 8. 115sh, Girl Guides 75th anniv., horiz. 155sh, Mother Theresa, 1979 Nobel Peace Prize laureate. 1000sh, Queen Mother. #467, Queen Mother inspecting troops. #468, like 115sh, horiz.

1985 Litho. *Perf. 14*

463	A56	5sh multicolored	.25	.25
464	A56	115sh multicolored	1.75	1.60
465	A56	155sh multicolored	2.90	2.50
466	A56	1000sh multicolored	1.40	1.75
		Nos. 463-466 (4)	6.30	6.10

Souvenir Sheets

467	A56	1500sh multicolored	3.00	3.00
468	A56	1500sh multicolored	4.50	4.50

Issued: #466-467, Aug. 21; others, Nov. 1.

Audubon Type of 1985

5sh, Rock ptarmigan. 155sh, Sage grouse. 175sh, Lesser yellowlegs. 500sh, Brown-headed cowbird.
1000sh, Whooping crane.

1985, Dec. 23 *Perf. 12½x12*

469	A54	5sh multi	.50	.40
470	A54	155sh multi	2.00	2.00
471	A54	175sh multi	2.00	*2.50*
472	A54	500sh multi	3.50	*4.50*
		Nos. 469-472 (4)	8.00	9.40

Souvenir Sheet
Perf. 14

473	A54	1000sh multi	9.50	9.50

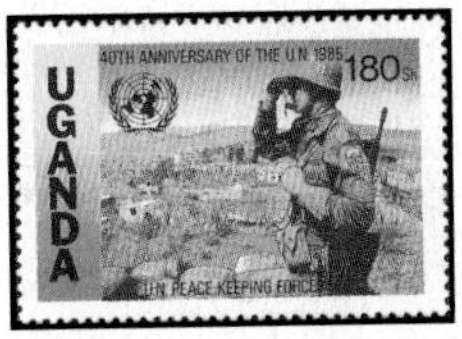

UN, 40th Anniv. A57

Designs: 10sh, Forest resources, vert. 180sh, UN Peace-keeping Force. 200sh, Emblem, UN Development Project. 250sh, Intl. Peace Year. 2000sh, Natl., UN flags, vert. 2500sh, Flags, UN Building, New York, vert.

1986, Feb. *Perf. 15*

474	A57	10sh multicolored	.25	.25
475	A57	180sh multicolored	.35	.35
476	A57	200sh multicolored	.45	.45
477	A57	250sh multicolored	.55	.55
478	A57	2000sh multicolored	4.25	4.25
		Nos. 474-478 (5)	5.85	5.85

Souvenir Sheet

479	A57	2500sh multicolored	3.25	3.25

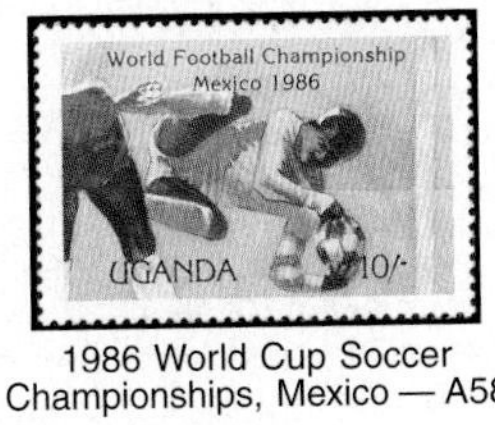

1986 World Cup Soccer Championships, Mexico — A58

Various soccer plays.

1986, Mar. *Perf. 14*

480	A58	10sh multicolored	.30	.30
481	A58	180sh multicolored	.90	.60
482	A58	250sh multicolored	1.00	.75
483	A58	2500sh multicolored	5.75	*6.50*
		Nos. 480-483 (4)	7.95	8.15

Souvenir Sheet

484	A58	3000sh multicolored	5.50	5.50

No. 484 contains vert. stamp.
For overprints see Nos. 514-518.

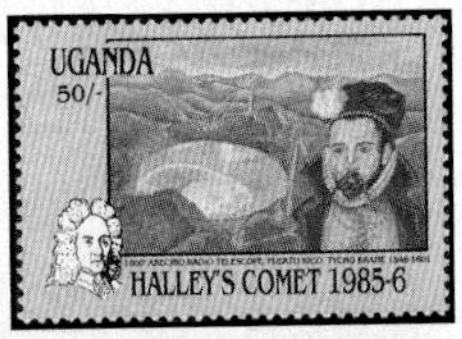

A59

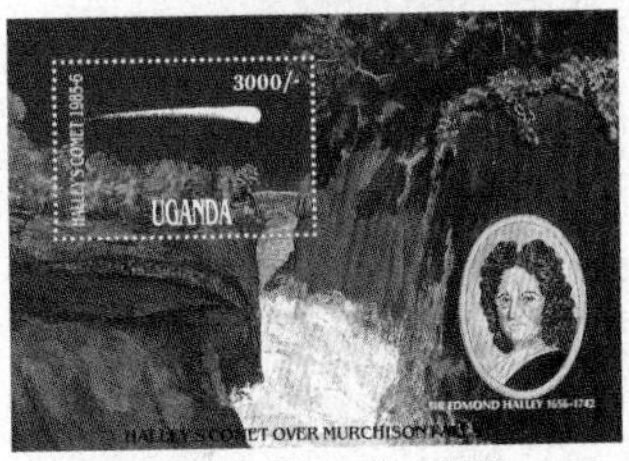

Halley's Comet — A60

Designs: 50sh, Arecibo radio telescope, Puerto Rico, and Tycho Brahe (1546-1601), Danish astronomer. 100sh, Recovery of Astronaut John Glenn, US space capsule, Caribbean, 1962. 140sh, Adoration of the Magi, 1301, by Giotto (1276-1337). 2500sh, Sighting, 1835, Davy Crockett at The Alamo.

1986, Mar. Litho. *Perf. 14*

485	A59	50sh multicolored	.30	.25
486	A59	100sh multicolored	.40	.25
487	A59	140sh multicolored	.60	.45
488	A59	2500sh multicolored	5.25	*6.25*
		Nos. 485-488 (4)	6.55	7.20

Souvenir Sheet

489	A60	3000sh multicolored	7.50	7.50

For overprints see Nos. 519-523.

Nos. 437, 439-442 and 468 Ovptd. "NRA LIBERATION / 1986" in Silver or Black

1986, Apr. *Perf. 15*

490	A51	175sh multi	1.25	1.10
490A	A51	400sh multi	2.50	2.50
491	A51	700sh multi	3.75	3.75
492	A51	1000sh multi (Bk)	4.00	4.00
493	A51	2500sh multi (Bk)	6.50	*7.75*
		Nos. 490-493 (5)	18.00	19.10

Souvenir Sheet
Perf. 14

494	A56	1500sh multi (Bk)	6.25	4.75

No. 494 ovptd. in one line in margin. A 400sh also exists with silver overprint. All stamps exist with overprint colors transposed.

Queen Elizabeth II, 60th Birthday
Common Design Type

100sh, At London Zoo, c. 1938. 140sh, At the races, 1970. 2500sh, Sandringham, 1982.
3000sh, Engagement, 1947.

1986, Apr. 21 *Perf. 14*

495	CD339	100sh multi	.25	.25
496	CD339	140sh multi	.25	.25
497	CD339	2500sh multi	3.75	3.75
		Nos. 495-497 (3)	4.25	4.25

Souvenir Sheet

498	CD339	3000sh multi	4.25	4.25

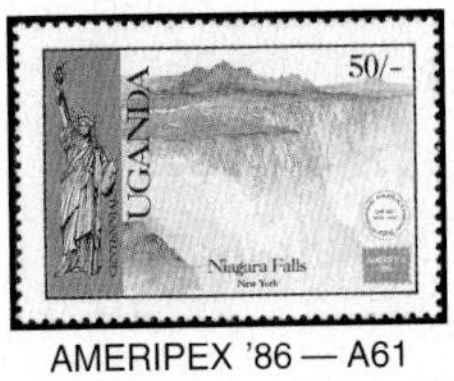

AMERIPEX '86 — A61

50sh, Niagara Falls. 100sh, Jefferson Memorial. 250sh, Liberty Bell. 1000sh, The Alamo. 2500sh, George Washington Bridge.
3000sh, Grand Canyon.

1986, May 22 *Perf. 15*

499	A61	50sh multicolored	.30	.30
500	A61	100sh multicolored	.30	.30
501	A61	250sh multicolored	.50	.50
502	A61	1000sh multicolored	1.90	1.90
503	A61	2500sh multicolored	4.50	4.50
		Nos. 499-503 (5)	7.50	7.50

Souvenir Sheet

504	A61	3000sh multicolored	3.75	3.75

Statue of Liberty, cent.

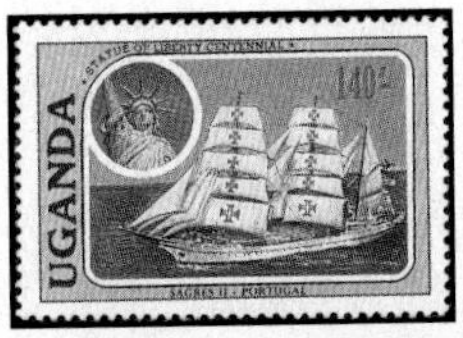

A62

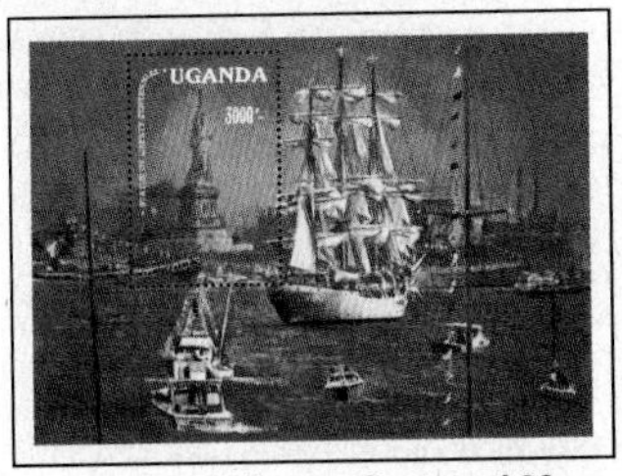

Statue of Liberty, Cent. — A63

Tall ships, Operation Sail: 50sh, Gloria, Colombia, vert. 100sh, Mircea, Romania, vert. 140sh, Sagres II, Portugal. 2500sh, Gazela Primero, US.

1986, July *Perf. 14*

505	A62	50sh multicolored	.75	.60
506	A62	100sh multicolored	1.00	.60
507	A62	140sh multicolored	1.75	1.25
508	A62	2500sh multicolored	7.75	*10.00*
		Nos. 505-508 (4)	11.25	12.45

Souvenir Sheet

509	A63	3000sh multicolored	4.50	4.50

Royal Wedding Issue, 1986
Common Design Type

Designs: 50sh, Prince Andrew and Sarah Ferguson. 140sh, Andrew and Princess Anne. 2500sh, At formal affair. 3000sh, Couple diff.
Nos. 510-512 horiz.

1986, July 23

510	CD340	50sh multicolored	.25	.25
511	CD340	140sh multicolored	.25	.25
512	CD340	2500sh multicolored	3.75	*4.50*
		Nos. 510-512 (3)	4.25	5.00

Souvenir Sheet

513	CD340	3000sh multicolored	5.00	5.00

Nos. 480-484 Ovptd. or Surcharged "WINNERS Argentina 3 W. Germany 2" in Gold in 2 or 3 Lines

1986, Sept. 15 Litho. *Perf. 14*

514	A58	50sh on 10sh multi	.25	.25
515	A58	180sh multicolored	.25	.25
516	A58	250sh multicolored	.30	.30
517	A58	2500sh multicolored	3.25	*3.75*
		Nos. 514-517 (4)	4.05	4.55

Souvenir Sheet

518	A58	3000sh multicolored	6.00	6.00

Nos. 485-489 Ovptd. with Halley's Comet Emblem

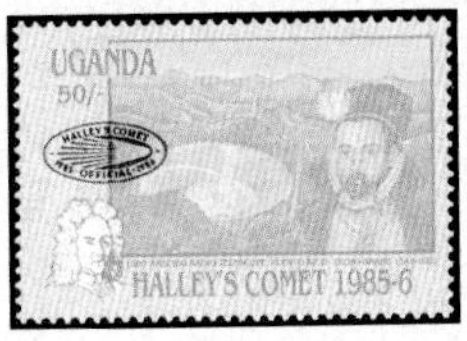

1986, Oct. 15 Litho. *Perf. 14*

519	A59	50sh multicolored	.35	.35
520	A59	100sh multicolored	.60	.40
521	A59	140sh multicolored	.80	.70
522	A59	2500sh multicolored	6.75	*8.00*
		Nos. 519-522 (4)	8.50	9.45

Souvenir Sheet

523	A60	3000sh multicolored	6.50	6.50

Christian
Martyrs
A64

Designs: 50sh, St. Kizito. 150sh, St. Kizito educating Ganda converts. 200sh, Execution of Bishop James Hannington. 1000sh, Mwanga's execution of converts, cent. 1500sh, King Mwanga sentencing Christians to death.

1986, Oct. 15

524	A64	50sh multicolored	.25	.25
525	A64	150sh multicolored	.25	.25
526	A64	200sh multicolored	.50	.50
527	A64	1000sh multicolored	2.00	3.00
		Nos. 524-527 (4)	3.00	4.00

Souvenir Sheet

528	A64	1500sh multicolored	2.25	2.25

A65

Christmas — A66

Paintings by Albrecht Dürer and Titian: 50sh, Madonna of the Cherries. 150sh, Madonna and Child, vert. 200sh, Assumption of the Virgin, vert. 2500sh, Praying Hands, vert. No. 533, Adoration of the Magi. No. 534, Presentation of the Virgin in the Temple.

1986, Nov. 26   Litho.   Perf. 14

529	A65	50sh multicolored	.25	.25
530	A65	150sh multicolored	.55	.25
531	A65	200sh multicolored	.75	.30
532	A65	2500sh multicolored	5.50	7.00
		Nos. 529-532 (4)	7.05	7.80

Souvenir Sheets

533	A66	3000sh multicolored	5.00	5.00
534	A66	3000sh multicolored	5.00	5.00

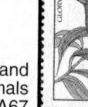

Birds and
Animals
A67

2sh, Red-billed firefinch. 5sh, African pygmy kingfisher. 10sh, Scarlet-chested sunbird. 25sh, White rhinoceros. 35sh, Lion. 45sh, Cheetahs. 50sh, Cordon bleu. 100sh, Giant eland. No. 543, Carmine bee-eaters. No. 544, Cattle egret, zebra.

1987   Perf. 15

535	A67	2sh multi	.40	.35
536	A67	5sh multi	.55	.35
537	A67	10sh multi	.80	.35
538	A67	25sh multi	1.25	.95
539	A67	35sh multi	1.25	1.25
540	A67	45sh multi	1.50	1.75
541	A67	50sh multi	1.75	2.10
542	A67	100sh multi	2.75	3.75
		Nos. 535-542 (8)	10.25	10.85

Souvenir Sheets

543	A67	150sh multi	4.50	4.50
544	A67	150sh multi	4.50	4.50

Issue dates: Nos. 535-537, 541, 543, Nov. 2; Nos. 538-540, 542-544, July 22.

Transportation Innovations — A68

2sh, Eagle, 1987. 3sh, Bremen, 1928. 5sh, Winnie Mae, 1933. 10sh, Voyager, 1986. 15sh, Chanute biplane glider, 1896. 25sh, Norge, 1926. 35sh, Curtis biplane, USS Pennsylvania, 1911. 45sh, Freedom 7, 1961. 100sh, Concorde, 1976.

1987, Aug. 14

545	A68	2sh multicolored	.30	.30
546	A68	3sh multicolored	.30	.30
547	A68	5sh multicolored	.35	.35
548	A68	10sh multicolored	.50	.50
549	A68	15sh multicolored	.80	.80
550	A68	25sh multicolored	1.10	1.10
551	A68	35sh multicolored	1.75	1.75
552	A68	45sh multicolored	2.00	2.00
553	A68	100sh multicolored	5.75	6.75
		Nos. 545-553 (9)	12.85	13.85

1988
Summer
Olympics,
Seoul
A69

Flags and athletes.

1987, Oct. 5   Perf. 14½x14

554	A69	5sh Torch bearer	.25	.25
555	A69	10sh Swimming	.30	.30
556	A69	15sh Cycling	1.25	1.25
557	A69	100sh Gymnastic rings	2.50	2.50
		Nos. 554-557 (4)	4.30	4.30

Souvenir Sheet

558	A69	150sh Boxing	4.00	4.50

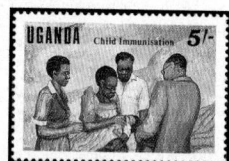

A70

Natl. Independence, 25th
Anniv. — A71

1987, Oct. 8

559	A70	5sh shown	.25	.25
560	A70	10sh Mulago Hospital	.45	.45
561	A70	25sh Independence Monument	.90	.90
562	A70	50sh High Court	1.75	1.75
		Nos. 559-562 (4)	3.35	3.35

Souvenir Sheet

563	A71	100sh shown	3.25	3.25

A72

Science and Space — A73

Designs: 5sh, Hippocrates, father of modern medicine, caduceus and surgeons. 25sh, Albert Einstein and Theory of Relativity equation. 35sh, Sir Isaac Newton and Optics Theory. 45sh, Karl Benz (1844-1929), German engineer, automobile pioneer, and the Velocipede, Mercedes-Benz sports coupe and manufacturers' emblems.

1987, Nov. 2   Perf. 14½x14

564	A72	5sh multicolored	.60	.60
565	A72	25sh multicolored	2.50	2.50
566	A72	35sh multicolored	3.00	3.00
567	A72	45sh multicolored	3.75	3.75
		Nos. 564-567 (4)	9.85	9.85

Souvenir Sheet
Perf. 14x14½

568	A73	150sh shown	5.75	5.75

Birds — A74

5sh, Golden-backed weaver. 10sh, Hoopoe. 15sh, Red-throated bee-eater. 25sh, Lilac-breasted roller. 35sh, Pygmy goose. 45sh, Scarlet-chested sunbird. 50sh, Crowned crane. 100sh, Long-tailed fiscal shrike. No. 577, African barn owl, horiz. No. 578, African fish-eagle, horiz.

1987, Nov. 2   Litho.   Perf. 14

569	A74	5sh multicolored	.75	.75
570	A74	10sh multicolored	1.60	1.40
571	A74	15sh multicolored	1.75	1.40
572	A74	25sh multicolored	2.25	1.90
573	A74	35sh multicolored	2.50	2.10
574	A74	45sh multicolored	2.75	2.75
575	A74	50sh multicolored	2.75	2.75
576	A74	100sh multicolored	5.00	5.00
		Nos. 569-576 (8)	19.35	18.05

Souvenir Sheets

577	A74	150sh multicolored	4.25	4.25
578	A74	150sh multicolored	4.25	4.25

14th World Boy Scout Jamboree,
Australia, 1987-88 — A75

Activities: 5sh, Stamp collecting, Uganda Nos. 84 and 116. 25sh, Planting trees, Natl. flag. 35sh, Canoeing on Lake Victoria. 45sh, Hiking and camping. 150sh, Logo of 1987 jamboree and natl. Boy Scout organization emblem.

1987, Nov. 20

579	A75	5sh multicolored	.30	.30
580	A75	25sh multicolored	1.10	1.10
581	A75	35sh multicolored	1.60	1.60
582	A75	45sh multicolored	1.90	1.90
		Nos. 579-582 (4)	4.90	4.90

Souvenir Sheet

583	A75	150sh multicolored	4.75	4.75

Christmas
A76

The life of Christ and the Virgin pictured on bas-reliefs, c. 1250, and a tapestry from France: 5sh, The Annunciation. 10sh, The Nativity. 50sh, Flight into Egypt. 100sh, The Adoration of the Magi. 150sh, The Mystic Wine Tapestry.

1987, Dec. 18

584	A76	5sh multicolored	.25	.25
585	A76	10sh multicolored	.25	.25
586	A76	50sh multicolored	1.40	1.75
587	A76	100sh multicolored	2.60	3.00
		Nos. 584-587 (4)	4.50	5.25

Souvenir Sheet

588	A76	150sh multicolored	4.75	4.75

Locomotives — A77

Designs: 5sh, Class 12 2-6-2T light shunter. 10sh, Class 92 1Co-Co1 diesel electric. 15sh, Class 2-8-2. 25sh, Class 2-6-2T light shunter. 35sh, Class 4-8-0. 45sh, Class 4-8-2. 50sh, Class 4-8-4+4-8-4 Garratt. 100sh, Class 87 1Co-Co1 diesel electric. No. 597, Class 59 4-8-2+2-8-4 Garratt. No. 598, Class 31 2-8-4.

1988, Jan. 18

589	A77	5sh multicolored	.25	.25
590	A77	10sh multicolored	.45	.45
591	A77	15sh multicolored	.70	.65
592	A77	25sh multicolored	1.00	1.00
593	A77	35sh multicolored	1.60	1.25
594	A77	45sh multicolored	2.00	1.75
595	A77	50sh multicolored	2.10	1.90
596	A77	100sh multicolored	4.25	2.75
		Nos. 589-596 (8)	12.35	10.00

Souvenir Sheets

597	A77	100sh multicolored	5.00	5.00
598	A77	150sh multicolored	5.00	5.00

Minerals — A78

1988, Jan. 18

599	A78	1sh Columbite-tantalite	.25	.25
600	A78	2sh Galena	.25	.25
601	A78	5sh Malachite	.25	.25
602	A78	10sh Cassiterite	.35	.35
603	A78	35sh Ferberite	1.50	1.50
604	A78	50sh Emerald	2.00	2.00
605	A78	100sh Monazite	3.50	3.50
606	A78	150sh Microcline	5.25	5.25
		Nos. 599-606 (8)	13.35	13.35

1988
Summer
Olympics,
Seoul
A79

1988, May 16   Litho.   Perf. 14

607	A79	5sh Hurdles	.30	.30
608	A79	25sh High jump	.55	.75
609	A79	35sh Javelin	.60	.75
610	A79	45sh Long jump	.85	1.00
		Nos. 607-610 (4)	2.30	2.80

Souvenir Sheet

611	A79	150sh Medals, five-ring emblem	2.25	2.25

For overprints see Nos. 651-655.

Flowers
A80

5sh, Spathodea campanulata. 10sh, Gloriosa simplex. 20sh, Thevetica peruviana, vert. 25sh, Hibiscus schizopetalus. 35sh, Aframomum sceptrum. 45sh, Adenium obesum. 50sh, Kigelia africana, vert. 100sh, Clappertonia ficifolia.
No. 620, Costus spectabiis. No. 621, Canarina abyssinica, vert.

1988, July 28   Litho.   Perf. 15
612 A80 5sh multicolored   .60 .25
613 A80 10sh multicolored   .60 .25
614 A80 20sh multicolored   .80 .60
615 A80 25sh multicolored   .80 .80
616 A80 35sh multicolored   .80 .85
617 A80 45sh multicolored   .80 1.10
618 A80 50sh multicolored   1.00 1.40
619 A80 100sh multicolored 1.50 2.25
    Nos. 612-619 (8)   6.90 7.50

Souvenir Sheets
620 A80 150sh multicolored 3.50 3.50
621 A80 150sh multicolored 3.50 3.50

Intl. Red Cross, 125th Anniv. A81

10sh, "AIDS". 40sh, Immunize children. 70sh, Relief distribution. 90sh, First aid. 150sh, Jean-Henri Dunant, vert.

1988, Oct. 28   Litho.   Perf. 14
622 A81 10sh multicolored   .30 .30
623 A81 40sh multicolored   1.00 1.00
624 A81 70sh multicolored   2.00 2.00
625 A81 90sh multicolored   2.50 2.50
    Nos. 622-625 (4)   5.80 5.80

Souvenir Sheet
626 A81 150sh multicolored 3.00 3.00

Paintings by Titian — A82

Designs: 10sh, Portrait of a Lady, c. 1508. 20sh, Portrait of a Man, 1507. 40sh, Portrait of Isabella d'Este, c. 1534. 50sh, Portrait of Vincenzo Mosti, 1520. 70sh, Pope Paul III Farnese, c. 1545. 90sh, Violante, 1515. 100sh, Lavinia, Titian's Daughter, c. 1565. 250sh, Portrait of Dr. Parma, c. 1515. No. 635, The Speech of Alfonso D'Avalos, c. 1540. No. 636, Cain and Abel.

1988, Oct. 31   Perf. 14
627 A82 10sh multicolored   .25 .25
628 A82 20sh multicolored   .40 .40
629 A82 40sh multicolored   .60 .60
630 A82 50sh multicolored   .75 .75
631 A82 70sh multicolored   .85 .85
632 A82 90sh multicolored   .90 .90
633 A82 100sh multicolored 1.10 1.10
634 A82 250sh multicolored 2.10 2.10
    Nos. 627-634 (8)   6.95 6.95

Souvenir Sheets
635 A82 350sh multicolored 3.50 3.50
636 A82 350sh multicolored 3.50 3.50

Game Preserves — A83

Designs: 10sh, Giraffes, Kidepo Valley Natl. Park. 25sh, Zebras, Lake Mburo Natl. Park. 100sh, African buffalo, Murchison Falls Natl. Park. 250sh, Pelicans, Queen Elizabeth Natl. Park. 350sh, Roan antelopes, Lake Mburo Natl. Park.

1988, Nov. 18   Litho.   Perf. 14
637 A83 10sh multicolored   .45 .25
638 A83 25sh multicolored   1.60 .65
639 A83 100sh multicolored 3.25 3.25
640 A83 250sh multicolored 9.00 9.00
    Nos. 637-640 (4)   14.30 13.15

Souvenir Sheet
641 A83 350sh multicolored 4.25 4.25

WHO 40th Anniv., Alma Ata Declaration 10th Anniv. — A84

1988, Dec. 1
642 A84 10sh Primary health care   .25 .25
643 A84 25sh Mental health   .45 .45
644 A84 45sh Rural health care   .75 .75
645 A84 100sh Dental care   1.60 1.60
646 A84 200sh Postnatal care   3.00 3.00
    Nos. 642-646 (5)   6.05 6.05

Souvenir Sheet
647 A84 350sh Conference Hall, Alma-Ata, USSR 4.25 4.25

Miniature Sheet

Christmas, Mickey Mouse 60th Birthday — A85

Walt Disney characters: No. 648a, Santa Claus. b, Goofy. c, Mickey Mouse. d, Huey at conveyor belt. e, Dewey packing building blocks. f, Donald Duck. g, Chip-n-Dale. h, Louie at conveyor belt controls. No. 649, Preparing reindeer for Christmas eve flight. No. 650, Mickey loading sleigh with toys, horiz.

1988, Dec. 2   Perf. 13½x14, 14x13½
648   Sheet of 8   10.00 10.00
a.-h. A85 50sh any single   .80 .80

Souvenir Sheets
649 A85 350sh multicolored 5.25 5.25
650 A85 350sh multicolored 5.25 5.25

Nos. 607-611 Ovptd. or Surcharged to Honor Olympic Winners

5sh: "110 M HURDLES / R. KINGDOM / USA"
25sh: "HIGH JUMP / G. AVDEENKO / USSR"
35sh: "JAVELIN / T. KORJUS / FINLAND"
300sh: "LONG JUMP / C. LEWIS / USA"

1989, Jan. 30   Litho.   Perf. 14
651 A79 5sh multicolored   .25 .25
652 A79 25sh multicolored   .30 .30
653 A79 35sh multicolored   .35 .35
654 A79 300sh on 45sh multi 3.25 3.25
    Nos. 651-654 (4)   4.15 4.15

Souvenir Sheet
655 A79 350sh on 150sh multi 5.00 5.00

1990 World Cup Soccer Championships, Italy — A86

Various action scenes.

1989, Apr. 24   Litho.   Perf. 14
656 A86 10sh multi, vert.   .35 .35
657 A86 25sh multicolored   .55 .55
658 A86 75sh multicolored   1.25 1.25
659 A86 200sh multi, vert. 2.25 2.25
    Nos. 656-659 (4)   4.40 4.40

Souvenir Sheet
660 A86 300sh multicolored 3.75 3.75

Mushrooms — A87

10sh, Suillus granulatus. 15sh, Omphalotus olearius. 45sh, Oudemansiella radicata. 50sh, Clitocybe nebularis. 60sh, Macrolepiota rhacodes. 75sh, Lepista nuda. 150sh, Suillus luteus. 200sh, Agaricus campestris.
No. 669, Schizophyllum commune. No. 670, Bolbitius vitellinus.

1989, Aug. 14   Litho.   Perf. 14
661 A87 10sh multicolored   .45 .45
662 A87 15sh multicolored   .55 .55
663 A87 45sh multicolored   1.15 1.15
664 A87 50sh multicolored   1.15 1.15
665 A87 60sh multicolored   1.20 1.20
666 A87 75sh multicolored   1.40 1.40
667 A87 150sh multicolored 2.60 2.60
668 A87 200sh multicolored 2.75 2.75
    Nos. 661-668 (8)   11.25 11.25

Souvenir Sheets
669 A87 350sh multicolored 6.00 6.00
670 A87 350sh multicolored 6.00 6.00

"The Thirty-six Views of Mt. Fuji" — A88

Prints by Hokusai (1760-1849): 10sh, Fuji and the Great Wave off Kanagawa. 15sh, Fuji from Lake Suwa. 20sh, Fuji from Kajikazawa. 60sh, Fuji from Shichirigahama. 90sh, Fuji from Ejiri in Sunshu. 120sh, Fuji Above Lightning. 200sh, Fuji from Lower Meguro in Edo. 250sh, Fuji from Edo. No. 679, The Red Fuji from the Foot. No. 680, Fuji from Umezawa.

1989, May 15   Litho.   Perf. 14x13½
671 A88 10sh multicolored   .35 .35
672 A88 15sh multicolored   .35 .35
673 A88 20sh multicolored   .35 .35
674 A88 60sh multicolored   .90 .90
675 A88 90sh multicolored   1.40 1.40
676 A88 120sh multicolored 2.00 2.00
677 A88 200sh multicolored 2.75 2.75
678 A88 250sh multicolored 3.00 3.00
    Nos. 671-678 (8)   11.10 11.10

Souvenir Sheets
679 A88 500sh multicolored 5.25 5.25
680 A88 500sh multicolored 5.25 5.25

Hirohito (1901-1989), Showa emperor, and Akihito, Heisei emperor of Japan.

PHILEXFRANCE '89 — A89

1989, July 7   Litho.   Perf. 14
681 A89 20sh No. 1   .60 .60
682 A89 70sh No. 10   1.50 1.50
683 A89 100sh No. 48 1.75 1.75
684 A89 250sh No. 67 3.50 3.50
a.   Souvenir sheet of 4, #681-684 10.00 10.00
    Nos. 681-684 (4)   7.35 7.35

No. 684a sold for 500sh.

2nd All African Scout Jamboree, Aug. 3-15 — A90

1989, Aug. 3   Litho.   Perf. 14
685 A90 10sh Fatal child ailments .35 .35
686 A90 70sh Raising poultry 1.50 1.50
687 A90 90sh Immunization   1.90 1.90
688 A90 100sh Brick-making 1.90 1.90
    Nos. 685-688 (4)   5.65 5.65

Souvenir Sheet
689 A90 500sh Natl. emblem, vert. 5.25 5.25

Scouting, 75th anniv.
For surcharges see Nos. 1301-1304.

Miniature Sheet

Wildlife at Waterhole — A91

Designs: a, Saddle-billed stork. b, White pelican. c, Marabou stork. d, Egyptian vulture, giraffes. e, Bateleur eagle, antelope. f, African elephant. g, Giraffe. h, Goliath heron. i, Black rhinoceros, zebras. j, Zebras, oribi. k, African fish eagle. l, Hippopotamus. m, Black-backed jackal, white pelican. n, Cape buffalo. o, Olive baboon. p, Bohor reedbuck. q, Lesser flamingo, serval. r, Shoebill stork. s, Crowned crane. t, Impala. No. 691, Lion. No. 692, Longcrested eagle.

1989, Sept. 12   Perf. 14½x14
690   Sheet of 20   22.00 22.00
a.-t. A91 30sh any single   .60 .60

Souvenir Sheets
691 A91 500sh multicolored 5.25 5.25
692 A91 500sh multicolored 5.25 5.25

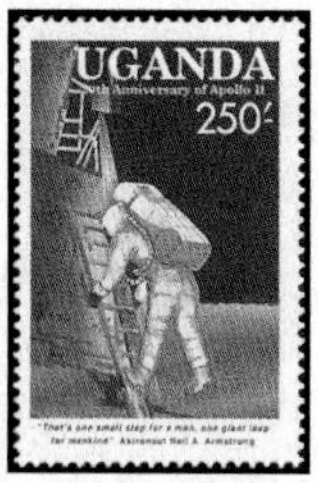

1st Moon Landing, 20th Anniv. — A92

Quotations and scenes from the Apollo 11 mission: 10sh, Launch vehicle, Moon. 20sh, Eagle lower stage on Moon. 30sh, Columbia. 50sh, Eagle landing. 70sh, Aldrin on Moon. 250sh, Armstrong on ladder. 300sh, Eagle ascending. 350sh, Aldrin, diff.
No. 701, Liftoff. No. 702, Parachute landing.

1989, Oct. 20 Litho. *Perf. 14*

693	A92	10sh multicolored	.35	.35
694	A92	20sh multicolored	.35	.35
695	A92	30sh multicolored	.65	.65
696	A92	50sh multicolored	.90	.90
697	A92	70sh multicolored	1.30	1.30
698	A92	250sh multicolored	4.50	4.50
699	A92	300sh multicolored	5.00	5.00
700	A92	350sh multicolored	6.00	6.00
		Nos. 693-700 (8)	19.05	19.05

Souvenir Sheets

701	A92	500sh multicolored	4.50	4.50
702	A92	500sh multicolored	4.50	4.50

Nos. 693-697 and 699 horiz.

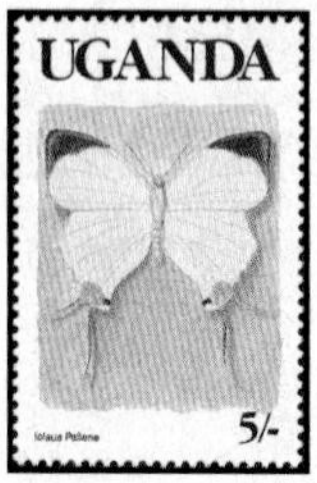

Butterflies — A93

5sh, Ioalus pallene. 10sh, Hewitsonia boisduvali. 20sh, Euxanthe wakefeildi. 30sh, Papilio echerioides. 40sh, Acraea semivitrea. 50sh, Colotis antevippe. 70sh, Acraea perenna. 90sh, Charaxes cynthia. 100sh, Euphaedra neophroa. 150sh, Cymothoe beckeri. 200sh, Vanessula milca. 400sh, Mimacraea marshalli. 500sh, Axiocerses amanga. 1000sh, Precis hierta.

1989, Nov. 13 "UGANDA" in Black

703	A93	5sh multicolored	.65	.65
704	A93	10sh multicolored	.70	.70
705	A93	20sh multicolored	1.10	1.10
706	A93	30sh multicolored	1.25	1.25
707	A93	40sh multicolored	1.40	1.40
708	A93	50sh multicolored	1.40	1.40
709	A93	70sh multicolored	1.75	1.75
710	A93	90sh multicolored	1.75	1.75
711	A93	100sh multicolored	1.75	1.75
712	A93	150sh multicolored	2.25	2.25
713	A93	200sh multicolored	2.25	2.25
714	A93	400sh multicolored	3.25	3.25
715	A93	500sh multicolored	3.50	3.50
716	A93	1000sh multicolored	4.50	4.50
		Nos. 703-716 (14)	27.50	27.50

See Nos. 826-839 for "UGANDA" in blue.

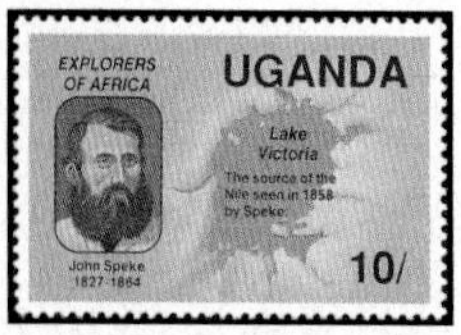

Explorers of Africa A94

Designs: 10sh, John Speke (1827-64), satellite view of Lake Victoria. 25sh, Sir Richard Burton (1821-90), satellite view of Lake Tanganyika. 40sh, Richard Lander (1804-34), bronze ritual figure of the Bakota tribe. 90sh, Rene Caillie (1799-1838), mosque. 125sh, Dorcas gazelle and Sir Samuel Baker (1821-93), discoverer of Lake Albert. 150sh, Phoenician galley and Necho II (d. 595 B.C.), king of Egypt credited by Herodotus with sending an expedition to circumnavigate Africa. 250sh, Vasco da Gama (c. 1460-1524), 1st European to sail around the Cape of Good Hope, and caravel. 300sh, Sir Henry Stanley (1841-1904), discoverer of Lake Edward, and Lady Alice . No. 725, Dr. David Livingstone (1813-73), discoverer of Victoria Falls, and steam launch Ma-Robert. No. 726, Mary Kingsley (1862-1900), ethnologist, and tail-spot climbing perch.

1989, Nov. 15 Litho. *Perf. 14*

717	A94	10sh multicolored	.30	.30
718	A94	25sh multicolored	.35	.35
719	A94	40sh multicolored	.55	.55
720	A94	90sh multicolored	1.10	1.10
721	A94	125sh multicolored	1.60	1.60
722	A94	150sh multicolored	1.90	1.90
723	A94	250sh multicolored	3.25	3.25
724	A94	300sh multicolored	3.75	3.75
		Nos. 717-724 (8)	12.80	12.80

Souvenir Sheets

725	A94	500sh multicolored	5.25	5.25
726	A94	500sh multicolored	5.25	5.25

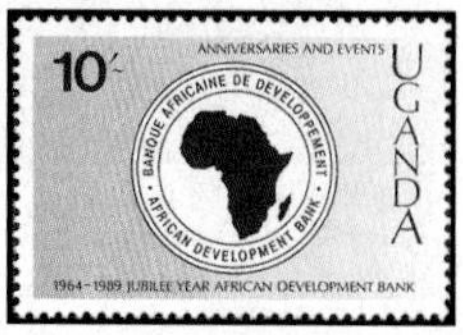

Anniversaries and Events — A95

10sh, Bank emblem. 20sh, Satellite dishes, arrows. 75sh, Nehru. 90sh, Pan-American Dixie Clipper. 100sh, Locomotion, Stephenson. 150sh, Concorde cockpit. 250sh, Wapen von Hamburg, Leopoldus Primus. 300sh, Concorde cockpit, crew.
No. 735, Storming of the Bastille. No. 736, Emperor Frederick I Barbarossa, charter.

1989, Dec. 12

727	A95	10sh multicolored	.30	.30
728	A95	20sh multicolored	.30	.30
729	A95	75sh multicolored	2.40	2.40
730	A95	90sh multicolored	2.40	2.40
731	A95	100sh multicolored	2.40	2.40
732	A95	150sh multicolored	3.75	3.50
733	A95	250sh multicolored	3.75	3.50
734	A95	300sh multicolored	4.75	4.75
		Nos. 727-734 (8)	20.05	19.55

Souvenir Sheets

735	A95	500sh multicolored	5.25	5.25
736	A95	500sh multicolored	5.25	5.25

African Development Bank 25th anniv. (10sh); World Telecommunications Day, May 17 (20sh); Birth cent. of Jawaharlal Nehru, 1st prime minister of independent India (75sh); 1st scheduled transatlantic airmail flight, 50th anniv. (90sh); 175th anniv. of the invention of the 1st steam locomotive by George Stephenson and opening of the Stockton & Darlington Railway in 1825 (100sh); 1st test flight of the Concorde, 20th anniv. (150sh, 300sh); Port of Hamburg, 800th anniv. (250sh, No. 736); and French revolution bicent. (No. 735).

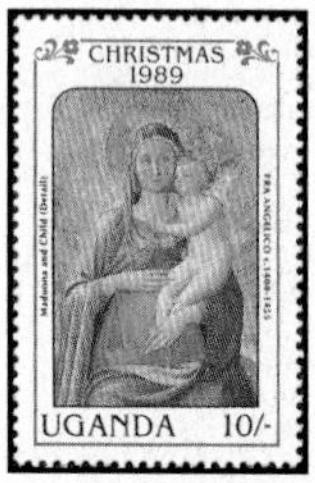

Christmas — A96

Religious paintings by Fra Angelico: 10sh, Madonna and Child. 20sh, Adoration of the Magi. 40sh, Virgin and Child Enthroned with Saints. 75sh, The Annunciation. 100sh, St. Peter Martyr triptych center panel. 150sh, Virgin and Child Enthroned with Saints, diff. 250sh, Virgin and Child Enthroned. 350sh, Annalena Altarpiece. No. 745, Bosco ai Frati Altarpiece. No. 746, Madonna and Child with Twelve Angels.

1989, Dec. 18

737	A96	10sh multicolored	.25	.25
738	A96	20sh multicolored	.25	.25
739	A96	40sh multicolored	.50	.50
740	A96	75sh multicolored	.85	.85
741	A96	100sh multicolored	1.00	1.00
742	A96	150sh multicolored	1.40	1.40
743	A96	250sh multicolored	2.00	2.00
744	A96	350sh multicolored	2.25	2.25
		Nos. 737-744 (8)	8.50	8.50

Souvenir Sheets

745	A96	500sh multicolored	3.00	3.00
746	A96	500sh multicolored	3.00	3.00

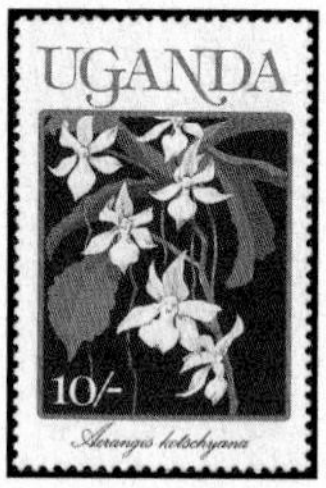

Orchids — A97

10sh, Aerangis kotschyana. 15sh, Angraecum infundibulare. 45sh, Cyrtorchis chailluana. 50sh, Aerangis rhodosticta. 100sh, Eulophia speciosa. 200sh, Calanthe sylvatica. 250sh, Vanilla imperialis. 350sh, Polystachya vulcanica.
No. 755, Ansellia africana. No. 756, Ancistrochilus rothschildianus.

1989, Dec. 18

747	A97	10sh multicolored	.30	.30
748	A97	15sh multicolored	.30	.30
749	A97	45sh multicolored	.70	.70
750	A97	50sh multicolored	.75	.75
751	A97	100sh multicolored	1.40	1.40
752	A97	200sh multicolored	3.00	3.00
753	A97	250sh multicolored	3.50	3.50
754	A97	350sh multicolored	5.00	5.00
		Nos. 747-754 (8)	14.95	14.95

Souvenir Sheets

755	A97	500sh multicolored	6.75	6.75
756	A97	500sh multicolored	6.75	6.75

For overprints see Nos. 782-786A.

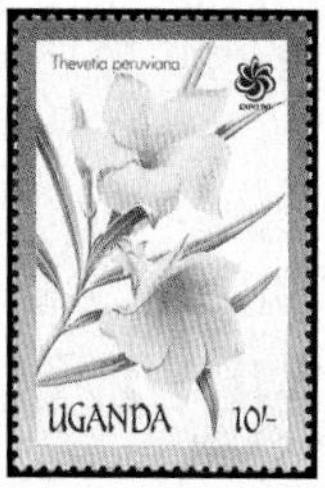

EXPO '90, Osaka — A98

Flowering trees — 10sh, Thevetia peruviana. 20sh, Acanthus eminens. 90sh, Gnidia glauca. 150sh, Oncoba spinosa. 175sh, Hibiscus rosa-sinensis. 400sh, Jacaranda mimosifolia. 500sh, Erythrina abyssinica. 700sh, Bauhinia purpurea.
No. 765, Delonix regia. No. 766, Cassia didymobatrya.

1990, Apr. 17 Litho. *Perf. 14*

757	A98	10sh multi	.30	.30
758	A98	20sh multi	.30	.30
759	A98	90sh multi	.70	.70
760	A98	150sh multi	1.00	1.00
761	A98	175sh multi	1.10	1.10
762	A98	400sh multi	1.75	1.75
763	A98	500sh multi	2.00	2.00
764	A98	700sh multi	2.25	2.25
		Nos. 757-764 (8)	9.40	9.40

Souvenir Sheets

765	A98	1000sh multi	5.50	5.50
766	A98	1000sh multi	5.50	5.50

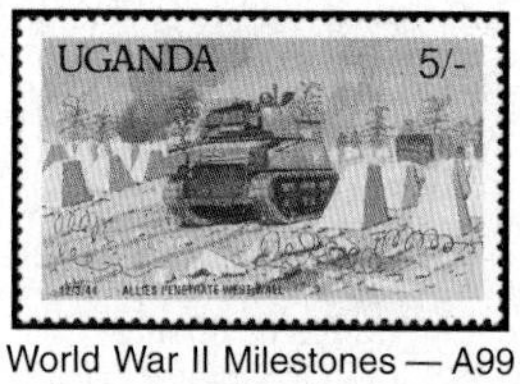

World War II Milestones — A99

Designs: 5sh, Allies penetrate west wall, Dec. 3, 1944. 10sh, VE Day, May 8, 1945. 20sh, US forces capture Okinawa, June 22, 1945. 75sh, DeGaulle named commander of all Free French forces, Apr. 4, 1944. 100sh, US troops invade Saipan, June 15, 1944. 150sh, Allied troops launch Operation Market Garden, Sept. 17, 1944. 200sh, Gen. MacArthur returns to Philippines, Oct. 20, 1944. 300sh, US victory at Coral Sea, May 8, 1942. 350sh, First battle of El Alamein, July 1, 1942. 500sh, Naval battle at Guadalcanal, Nov. 12, 1942. 1000sh, Battle of Britain.

1990, June 8 Litho. *Perf. 14*

767	A99	5sh multicolored	.30	.30
768	A99	10sh multicolored	.30	.30
769	A99	20sh multicolored	.30	.30
770	A99	75sh multicolored	.60	.60
771	A99	100sh multicolored	.80	.80
772	A99	150sh multicolored	1.15	1.15
773	A99	200sh multicolored	1.40	1.40
774	A99	300sh multicolored	2.50	2.50
775	A99	350sh multicolored	3.00	3.00
776	A99	500sh multicolored	4.00	4.00
		Nos. 767-776 (10)	14.35	14.35

Souvenir Sheet

777	A99	1000sh multicolored	7.50	7.50

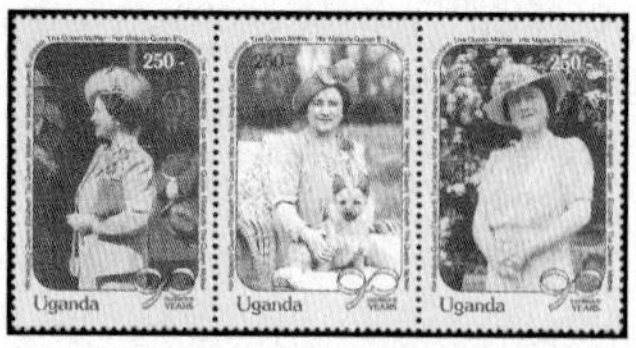

Queen Mother, 90th Birthday — A100

1990, July 5

778		250sh Hands clasped	1.00	1.00
779		250sh Facing left	1.00	1.00
780		250sh Holding dog	1.00	1.00
a.	A100	Strip of 3, #778-780	4.25	4.25
		Nos. 778-780 (3)	3.00	3.00

Souvenir Sheet

781	A100	1000sh like No. 778	4.00	4.00

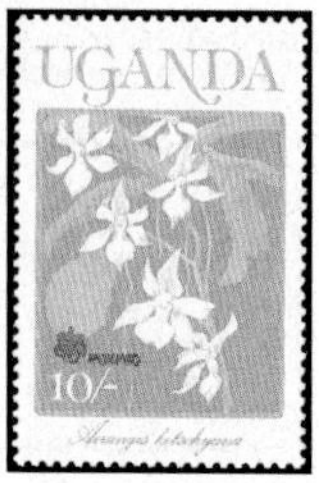

Nos. 747-754 Ovptd. in Silver

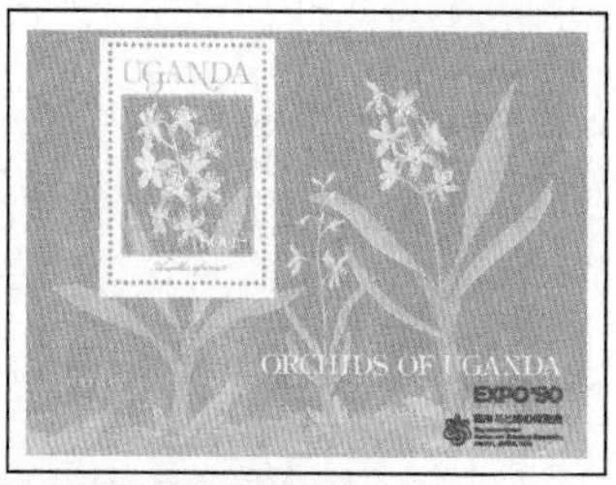

Nos. 755-756 Ovptd. in Silver in Sheet Margin

1990 Litho. *Perf. 14*

782	A97	10sh on No. 747	1.00	1.00
782A	A97	15sh on No. 748	1.00	1.00
782B	A97	45sh on No. 749	1.50	1.50
783	A97	50sh on No. 750	1.50	1.50
783A	A97	100sh on No. 751	1.90	1.90
784	A97	200sh on No. 752	2.50	2.50
785	A97	250sh on No. 753	2.50	2.50
785A	A97	350sh on No. 754	3.00	3.00
		Nos. 782-785A (8)	14.90	14.90

Souvenir Sheet

786	A97	500sh on No. 755	5.00	5.00
786A	A97	500sh on No. 756	5.00	5.00

Issue dates: 15sh, 45sh, 100sh, 350sh, No. 786A, Nov.; others, July 30.

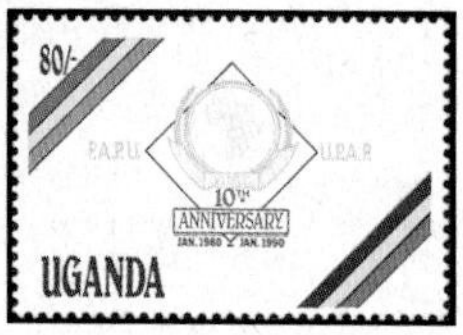

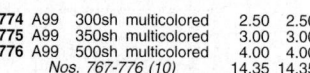

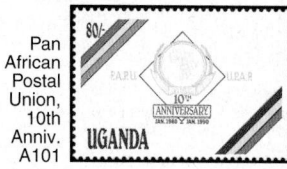

Pan African Postal Union, 10th Anniv. A101

Designs: 750sh, UN Conference on the least developed countries, Paris, Sept. 3-14.

1990, Aug. 3 Litho. *Perf. 14*

787	A101	80sh multicolored	1.25	1.25

Souvenir Sheet

788	A101	750sh multicolored	3.75	3.75

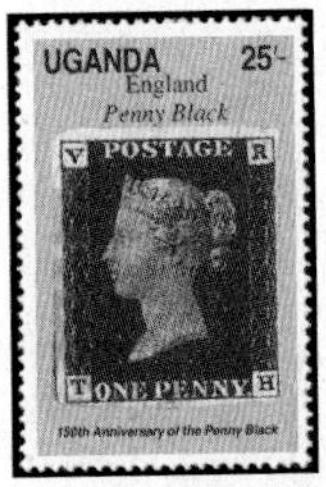

Great Britain No. O1 — A102

Designs: 50sh, Canada #12. 100sh, Baden #4b. 150sh, Switzerland #3L1. 200sh, US #C3a. 300sh, Western Australia #1. 500sh, Uganda #29. 600sh, Great Britain #2. No. 797, Uganda #29. No. 798, Sir Rowland Hill.

1990, Aug. 6 Litho. *Perf. 14*

789	A102	25sh multicolored	.35	.35
790	A102	50sh multicolored	.65	.65
791	A102	100sh multicolored	1.25	1.25
792	A102	150sh multicolored	1.50	1.50
793	A102	200sh multicolored	1.75	1.75
794	A102	300sh gray & black	2.25	2.25
795	A102	500sh multicolored	2.50	2.50
796	A102	600sh multicolored	2.50	2.50
		Nos. 789-796 (8)	12.75	12.75

Souvenir Sheets

Size: 108x77mm

797	A102	1000sh multicolored	5.75	5.75

Size: 119x85mm

798	A102	1000sh scarlet & blk	5.75	5.75

Penny Black, 150th anniversary. Nos. 797-798, Stamp World London '90.

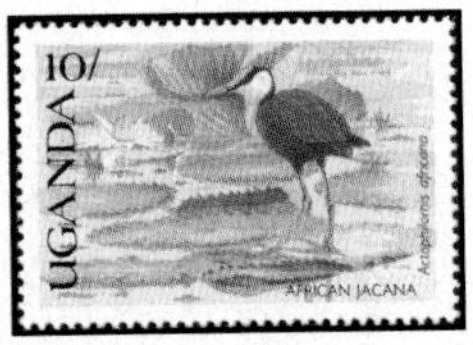

Birds A103

10sh, African jacana. 15sh, Ground hornbill. 45sh, Kori bustard, vert. 50sh, Secretary bird. 100sh, Egyptian geese. 300sh, Goliath heron, vert. 500sh, Ostrich, vert. 650sh, Saddlebill stork, vert.

No. 807, Volturine guinea fowl, vert. No. 808, Lesser flamingo, vert.

1990, Sept. 3 Litho. *Perf. 14*

799	A103	10sh multicolored	.90	.90
800	A103	15sh multicolored	.90	.90
801	A103	45sh multicolored	1.10	1.10
802	A103	50sh multicolored	1.10	1.10
803	A103	100sh multicolored	1.75	1.75
804	A103	300sh multicolored	3.00	3.00
805	A103	500sh multicolored	4.00	4.00
806	A103	650sh multicolored	4.25	4.25
		Nos. 799-806 (8)	17.00	17.00

Souvenir Sheets

807	A103	1000sh multicolored	5.75	5.75
808	A103	1000sh multicolored	5.75	5.75

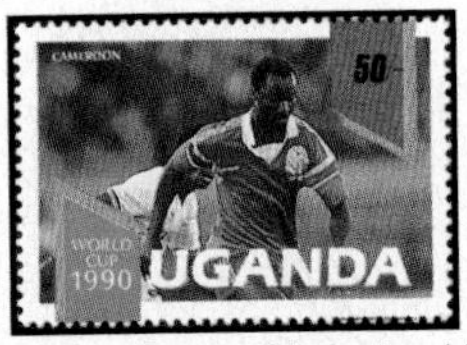

World Cup Soccer Championships, Italy — A104

Players from various national teams.

1990, Sept. 24

809	A104	50sh Cameroun	.25	.25
810	A104	100sh Egypt	.50	.50
811	A104	250sh Ireland	1.25	1.25
812	A104	600sh West Germany	3.25	3.25
		Nos. 809-812 (4)	5.25	5.25

Souvenir Sheets

813	A104	1000sh Sweden	5.25	5.25
814	A104	1000sh Scotland	5.25	5.25

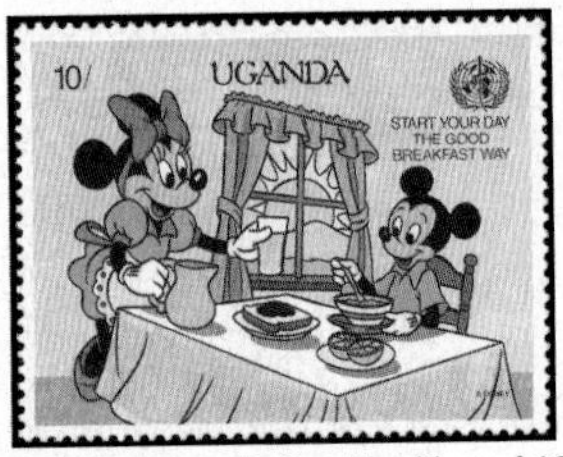

WHO, Promote Better Health — A105

Walt Disney characters in scenes promoting improved health: 10sh, Mickey, Minnie Mouse having a good breakfast. 20sh, Huey, Dewey and Louie looking before crossing street. 50sh, Mickey, Donald Duck against smoking. 90sh, Mickey saving Donald from choking. 100sh, Mickey, Goofy using seat belts. 250sh, Mickey, Minnie avoiding drugs. 500sh, Donald, Daisy exercising. 600sh, Mickey showing bicycle safety. No. 823, Mickey, friends at doctor's office. No. 824, Mickey, friends walking.

1990, Oct. 19 Litho. *Perf. 13½x13*

815	A105	10sh multicolored	.30	.30
816	A105	20sh multicolored	.30	.30
817	A105	50sh multicolored	.45	.45
818	A105	90sh multicolored	.75	.75
819	A105	100sh multicolored	.85	.85
820	A105	250sh multicolored	1.75	1.75
821	A105	500sh multicolored	4.00	4.00
822	A105	600sh multicolored	4.50	4.50
		Nos. 815-822 (8)	12.90	12.90

Souvenir Sheets

823	A105	1000sh multicolored	6.00	6.00
824	A105	1000sh multicolored	6.00	6.00

Butterfly Type of 1989

3000sh, Euphaedra eusemoides. 4000sh, Acraea natalica. 5000sh, Euphaedra themis.

"Uganda" in Blue

1990-92 Litho. *Perf. 14*

826	A93	10sh like #704	.65	.65
827	A93	20sh like #705	.75	.75
a.		Imprint "1991"	.85	.75
828	A93	30sh like #706	.75	.75
829	A93	40sh like #707	.75	.75
830	A93	50sh like #708	1.00	1.00
831	A93	70sh like #709	1.00	1.00
832	A93	90sh like #710	1.10	1.10
833	A93	100sh like #711	1.10	1.10
a.		Imprint "1991"	1.20	1.10
834	A93	150sh like #712	1.50	1.50
835	A93	200sh like #713	1.90	1.90
a.		Imprint "1991"	1.90	1.90
836	A93	400sh like #714	2.25	2.25
837	A93	500sh like #715	2.25	2.25
838	A93	1000sh like #716	4.50	4.50
839	A93	2000sh like #716	11.00	11.00
a.		Imprint "1991"	5.50	5.50
840	A93	3000sh multi	13.50	13.50
841	A93	4000sh multi	14.50	14.50
842	A93	5000sh multi	14.50	14.50
		Nos. 826-842 (17)	73.00	73.00

Issue dates: 10sh, 20sh, 30sh, 40sh, 70sh, 90sh, 100sh, 150sh, 200sh, 2000sh, 11/90. 50sh, 400sh, 500sh, 1000sh, 11/4/91. 3000sh, 4000sh, 10/9/92.

Nos. 826-829, 831-835, 839-842 do not have a year date imprint below design. Nos. 830, 836-838 are inscribed "1991" below design.

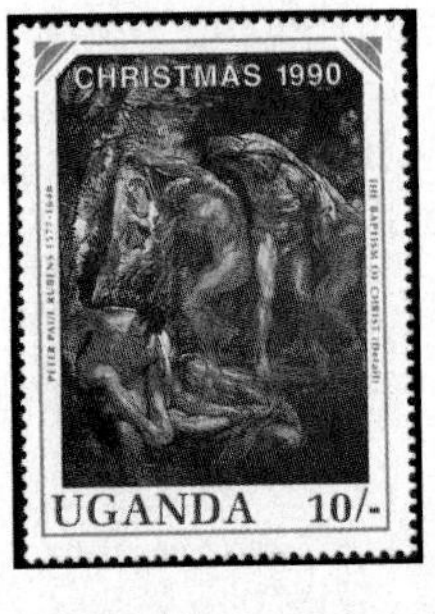

Christmas A106

Details from paintings by Rubens: 10sh, 500sh, The Baptism of Christ. 20sh, 150sh, 400sh, 600sh, St. Gregory the Great and Other Saints. 100sh, Saints Nereus, Domitilla and Achilleus. 300sh, Saint Augustine. No. 853, Victory of Eucharistic Truth Over Heresy, horiz. No. 854, Triumph of Faith, horiz.

1990, Dec. 17 Litho. *Perf. 14*

845	A106	10sh multicolored	.25	.25
846	A106	20sh multicolored	.25	.25
847	A106	100sh multicolored	.80	.80
848	A106	150sh multicolored	1.10	1.10
849	A106	300sh multicolored	1.75	1.75
850	A106	400sh multicolored	1.90	1.90
851	A106	500sh multicolored	2.00	2.00
852	A106	600sh multicolored	2.25	2.25
		Nos. 845-852 (8)	10.30	10.30

Souvenir Sheets

853	A106	1000sh multicolored	5.25	5.25
854	A106	1000sh multicolored	5.25	5.25

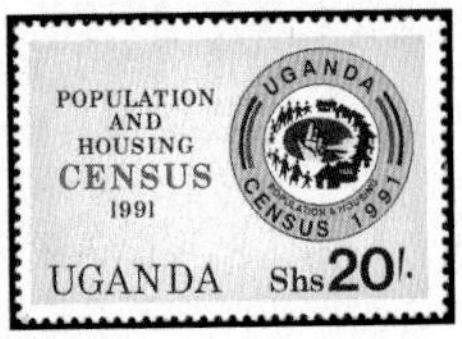

Natl. Census A107

Design: 1000sh, Counting on fingers, houses, people.

1990, Dec. 28 Litho. *Perf. 14*

855	A107	20sh multicolored	1.00	1.00

Souvenir Sheet

856	A107	1000sh multicolored	5.00	5.00

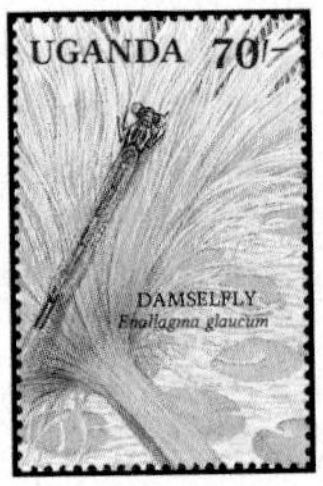

Wetlands Fauna — A108

No. 857: a, Damselfly. b, Purple gallinule. c, Sitatunga. d, Purple heron. e, Bushpig. f, Vervet monkey. g, Long reed frog. h, Malachite kingfisher. i, Marsh mongoose. j, Painted reed frog. k, Jacana. l, Charaxes butterfly. m, Nile crocodile. n, Herald snake. o, Dragonfly. p, Lungfish.

No. 858, Nile monitor, horiz.

1991, Jan. 1 Litho. *Perf. 14*

857	A108	70sh Sheet of 16, #a.-p.	21.00	21.00

Souvenir Sheet

858	A108	1000sh multi	11.50	11.50

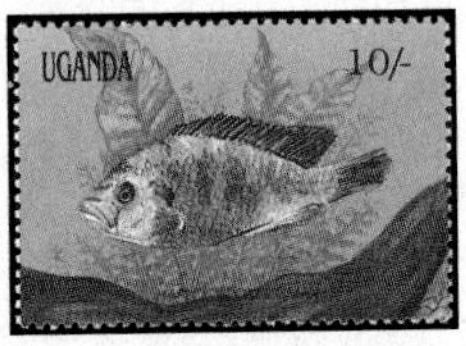

Fish A109

Designs: 10sh, Haplochromis limax. 20sh, Notobranchius palmqvisti. 40sh, Distichodus affinis. 90sh, Haplochromis sauvagei. 100sh, Aphyosemion calliurum. 350sh, Haplochromis johnstoni. 600sh, Haplochromis dichrourus. 800sh, Hemichromis bimaculatus. No. 867, Haplochromis sp. No. 868, Aphyosemion striatum.

1991, Jan. 18 Litho. *Perf. 14*

859	A109	10sh multicolored	.30	.30
860	A109	20sh multicolored	.30	.30
861	A109	40sh multicolored	.30	.30
862	A109	90sh multicolored	.55	.55
863	A109	100sh multicolored	.65	.65
864	A109	350sh multicolored	1.60	1.60
865	A109	600sh multicolored	3.25	3.25
866	A109	800sh multicolored	4.00	4.00
		Nos. 859-866 (8)	10.95	10.95

Souvenir Sheets

867	A109	1000sh multicolored	6.50	6.50
868	A109	1000sh multicolored	6.50	6.50

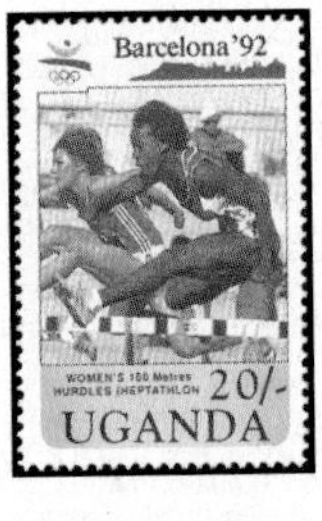

1992 Summer Olympics, Barcelona — A110

20sh, Women's hurdles. 40sh, Long jump. 125sh, Table tennis. 250sh, Soccer. 500sh, 800-meter race.

No. 874 Women's 4x100-meter relay, horiz. No. 875, Opening ceremony, horiz.

1991, Feb. 25 Litho. *Perf. 14*

869	A110	20sh multicolored	.25	.25
870	A110	40sh multicolored	.25	.25
871	A110	125sh multicolored	.80	.80
872	A110	250sh multicolored	1.75	1.75
873	A110	500sh multicolored	3.25	3.25
		Nos. 869-873 (5)	6.30	6.30

Souvenir Sheets

874	A110	1200sh multicolored	5.00	5.00
875	A110	1200sh multicolored	5.00	5.00

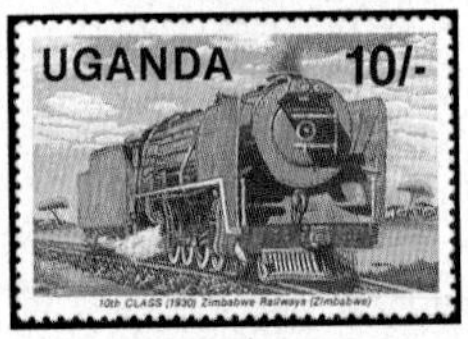

Trains A111

Designs: 10sh, 10th Class, Zimbabwe. 20sh, 12th Class, Zimbabwe. 80sh, Tribal class, Tanzania and Zambia. 200sh, 4-6-0 Type, Egypt. 300sh, Mikado, Sudan. 400sh, Mountain class Garrat, Uganda. 500sh, Mallet Type, Uganda. 1000sh, 5 F 1 Electric locomotive, South Africa. No. 884, 4-8-2 Type, Zimbabwe. No. 885, Atlantic type, Egypt. No. 886, 4-8-2 Type, Angola. No. 887, Mallet Compound Type, Natal.

1991, Apr. 2 Litho. *Perf. 14*

876	A111	10sh multicolored	.30	.30
877	A111	20sh multicolored	.30	.30
878	A111	80sh multicolored	.45	.45
879	A111	200sh multicolored	1.30	1.30
880	A111	300sh multicolored	1.75	1.75
881	A111	400sh multicolored	2.40	2.40
882	A111	500sh multicolored	3.00	3.00
883	A111	1000sh multicolored	5.75	5.75
		Nos. 876-883 (8)	15.25	15.25

Souvenir Sheets

884	A111	1200sh multicolored	4.50	4.50
885	A111	1200sh multicolored	4.50	4.50
886	A111	1200sh multicolored	4.50	4.50
887	A111	1200sh multicolored	4.50	4.50

Even though Nos. 886-887 have the same issue date as Nos. 876-885, their dollar value was lower when they were released.

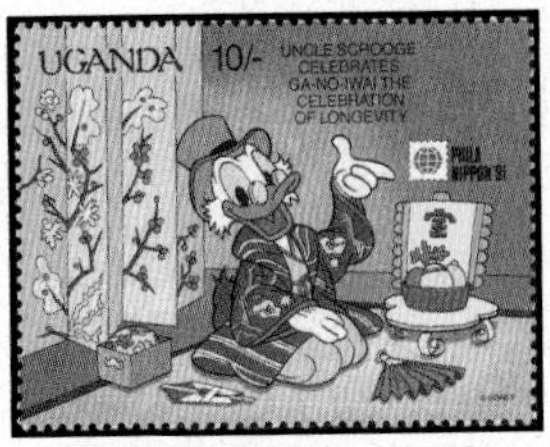

Phila Nippon '91 — A112

Walt Disney characters in Japan: 10sh, Scrooge McDuck celebrating Ga-No-Iwai. 20sh, Mickey removes shoes before entering Minnie's home. 70sh, Cartman Goofy leading horse. 80sh, Daisy, Minnie exchange gifts. 300sh, Minnie kneels at entrance to home. 400sh, Mickey, Donald in volcanic sand bath. 500sh, Clarabelle Cow enjoys incense burning. 1000sh, Mickey, Minnie writing New Year cards. No. 896, Mickey, Donald and Goofy in public bath. No. 897, Mickey and friends playing Japanese music.

1991, May 29 Litho. *Perf. 14x13½*

888	A112	10sh multicolored	.25	.25
889	A112	20sh multicolored	.25	.25
890	A112	70sh multicolored	.45	.45
891	A112	80sh multicolored	.50	.50
892	A112	300sh multicolored	1.90	1.90
893	A112	400sh multicolored	2.40	2.40
894	A112	500sh multicolored	3.25	3.25
895	A112	1000sh multicolored	6.00	6.00
		Nos. 888-895 (8)	15.00	15.00

Souvenir Sheets

896	A112	1200sh multicolored	7.50	7.50
897	A112	1200sh multicolored	7.50	7.50

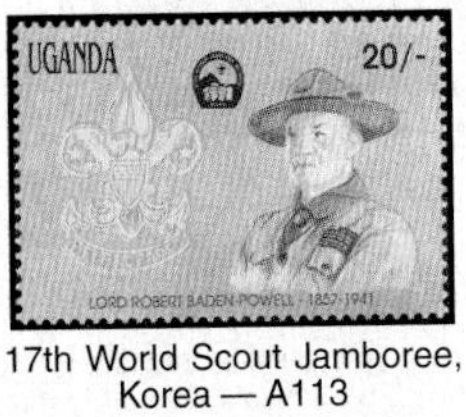

17th World Scout Jamboree, Korea — A113

Designs: 20sh, Lord Baden-Powell. 80sh, Scouts collecting stamps. 100sh, Scout encampment, NY World's Fair, 1939. 150sh, Cover of 1st Scout Handbook. 300sh, Cooking over campfire. 400sh, Neil Armstrong, Edwin Aldrin, 1st scouts on moon. 500sh, Hands raised for Scout Pledge. 1000sh, Statue to Unknown Scout, Gilwell Park, England. No. 906, William D. Boyce, Lord Baden-Powell, Rev. L. Hadley. No. 907, 17th Jamboree Emblem.

1991, May 27 *Perf. 14*

898	A113	20sh multicolored	.30	.30
899	A113	80sh multicolored	.45	.45
900	A113	100sh multicolored	.55	.55
901	A113	150sh grn & blk	.80	.80
902	A113	300sh multicolored	1.50	1.50
903	A113	400sh multicolored	2.10	2.10
904	A113	500sh multicolored	2.50	2.50
905	A113	1000sh multicolored	4.75	4.75
		Nos. 898-905 (8)	12.95	12.95

Souvenir Sheets

906	A113	1200sh multicolored	6.25	6.25
907	A113	1200sh cream & blk	6.25	6.25

For surcharge see No. 1305.

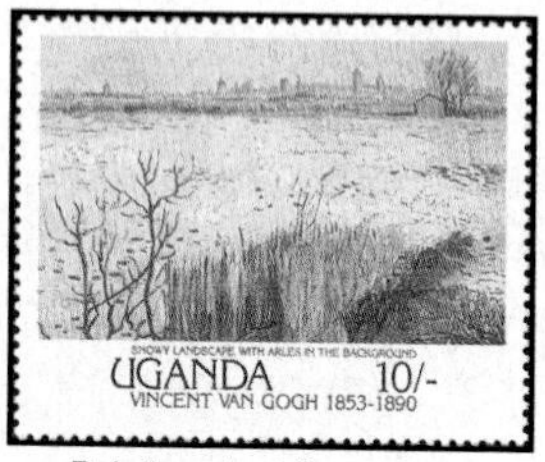

Paintings by Vincent Van Gogh — A114

Paintings: 10sh, Snowy Landscape with Arles in the Background. 20sh, Peasant Woman Binding Sheaves, vert. 60sh, The Drinkers. 80sh, View of Auvers. 200sh, Mourning Man, vert. 400sh, Still Life: Vase with Roses. 800sh, The Raising of Lazarus. 1000sh, The Good Samaritan, vert. No. 916, First Steps. No. 917, Village Street and Steps in Auvers with Figures.

1991, June 26 **Litho.** *Perf. 13½*

908	A114	10sh multicolored	.25	.25
909	A114	20sh multicolored	.25	.25
910	A114	60sh multicolored	.30	.30
911	A114	80sh multicolored	.40	.40
912	A114	200sh multicolored	1.00	1.00
913	A114	400sh multicolored	2.00	2.00
914	A114	800sh multicolored	4.00	4.00
915	A114	1000sh multicolored	5.00	5.00
		Nos. 908-915 (8)	13.20	13.20

Size: 102x76mm

Imperf

916	A114	1200sh multicolored	7.00	7.00
917	A114	1200sh multicolored	7.00	7.00

Royal Family Birthday, Anniversary

Common Design Type

No. 926, Elizabeth, Philip. No. 927, Sons, Diana, Charles.

1991, July 5 **Litho.** *Perf. 14*

918	CD347	20sh multi	.25	.25
919	CD347	70sh multi	.40	.40
920	CD347	90sh multi	.60	.60
921	CD347	100sh multi	.65	.65
922	CD347	200sh multi	1.20	1.20
923	CD347	500sh multi	2.75	2.75
924	CD347	600sh multi	3.50	3.50
925	CD347	1000sh multi	5.75	5.75
		Nos. 918-925 (8)	15.10	15.10

Souvenir Sheets

926	CD347	1200sh multi	5.00	5.00
927	CD347	1200sh multi	6.50	6.50

20sh, 100sh, 200sh, 1000sh, No. 927, Charles and Diana, 10th wedding anniversary. Others, Queen Elizabeth II, 65th birthday.

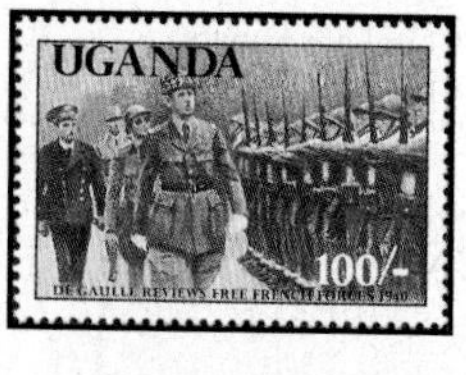

Charles de Gaulle, Birth Cent. A115

Designs: 20sh, Portrait, vert. 70sh, Liberation of Paris, 1944, vert. 90sh, With King George VI, 1940, vert. 100sh, Reviewing Free French forces, 1940. 200sh, Making his appeal on BBC, 1940. 500sh, In Normandy, 1944. 600sh, At Albert Hall, 1940. 1000sh, Becoming President of France, 1959, vert. No. 936, Entering Paris, 1944, vert. No. 937, With Eisenhower, 1942.

1991, July 15 *Perf. 14*

928	A115	20sh multicolored	.25	.25
929	A115	70sh multicolored	.30	.30
930	A115	90sh multicolored	.40	.40
931	A115	100sh multicolored	.45	.45
932	A115	200sh multicolored	.85	.85
933	A115	500sh multicolored	2.10	2.10
934	A115	600sh multicolored	2.50	2.50
935	A115	1000sh multicolored	4.25	4.25
		Nos. 928-935 (8)	11.10	11.10

Souvenir Sheets

936	A115	1200sh multicolored	6.00	6.00
937	A115	1200sh multicolored	6.00	6.00

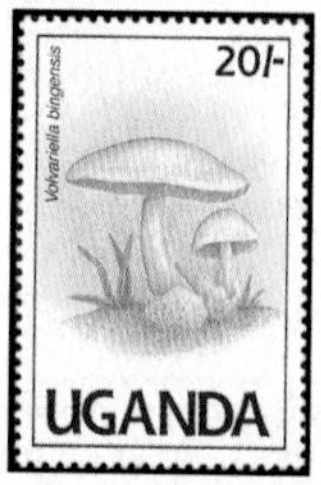

Mushrooms A116

Designs: 20sh, Volvariella bingensis. 70sh, Agrocybe broadwayi. 90sh, Camarophyllus olidus. 140sh, Marasmius arborescens. 180sh, Marasmiellus subcinereus. 200sh, Agaricus campestris. 500sh, Chlorophyllum molybdites. 1000sh, Agaricus bingensis. No. 946, Leucocoprinus cepaestipes, horiz. No. 947, Laccaria lateritia, horiz.

1991, July 19 **Litho.** *Perf. 14*

938	A116	20sh multicolored	.30	.30
939	A116	70sh multicolored	.50	.50
940	A116	90sh multicolored	.65	.65
941	A116	140sh multicolored	1.00	1.00
942	A116	180sh multicolored	1.25	1.25
943	A116	200sh multicolored	1.40	1.40
944	A116	500sh multicolored	4.00	4.00
945	A116	1000sh multicolored	8.00	8.00
		Nos. 938-945 (8)	17.10	17.10

Souvenir Sheets

946	A116	1200sh multicolored	5.50	5.50
947	A116	1200sh multicolored	5.50	5.50

World Wildlife Type of 1983

1991, Aug. 1

948	A43	100sh as No. 371	1.00	1.00
949	A43	140sh as No. 372	1.40	1.40
950	A43	200sh as No. 373	1.90	1.90
951	A43	600sh as No. 374	5.50	5.50
		Nos. 948-951 (4)	9.80	9.80

Souvenir Sheets

Perf. 13x12½

952	A43	1200sh Giraffe	8.00	8.00
953	A43	1200sh Rhinoceros	8.00	8.00

World Wildlife Fund. Nos. 952-953 do not have the WWF emblem.

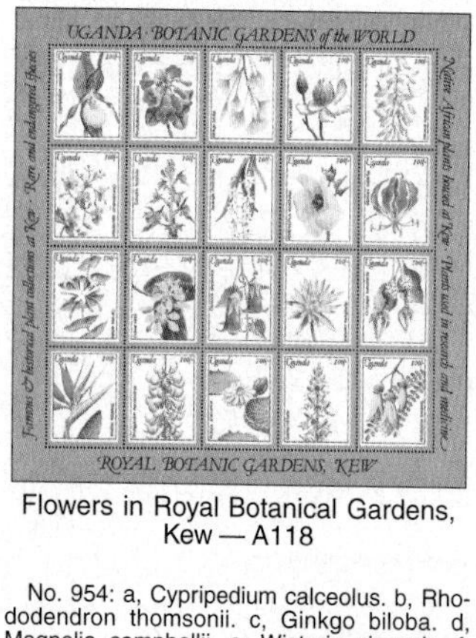

Flowers in Royal Botanical Gardens, Kew — A118

No. 954: a, Cypripedium calceolus. b, Rhododendron thomsonii. c, Ginkgo biloba. d, Magnolia campbellii. e, Wisteria sinensis. f, Clerodendrum ugandense. g, Eulophia horsfallii. h, Aerangis rhodosticta. i, Abelmoschus moschatus. j, Gloriosa superba. k, Carissa edulis. l, Ochna kirkii. m, Canarina abyssinica. n, Nymphaea caerulea. o, Ceropegia succulenta. p, Strelitzia reginae. q, Strongylodon macrobotrys. r, Victoria amazonica. s, Orchis militaris. t, Sophora microphylla.

No. 955 — Royal Botanic Gardens, Melbourne, Australia: a, Anigozanthos manglesii. b, Banksia grandis. c, Clianthus formosus. d, Gossypium sturtianum. e, Callistemon lanceolatus. f, Saintpaulia ionantha. g, Calodendrum capense. h, Aloe ferox. i, Bolusanthus speciousus. j, Lithops schwantesii k, Protea repens. l, Plumbago capensis. m, Clerodendrum thomsoniae. n, Thunbergia alata. o, Schotia latifolia. p, Epacris impressa. q, Acacia pycnantha. r, Telopea speciosissima. s, Wahlenbergia gloriosa. t, Eucalyptus globulus.

No. 956, The Pagoda, Kew. No. 957, Temple of the Winds, Melbourne.

1991, Nov. 25 **Litho.** *Perf. 14½*

954	A118	100sh Sheet of 20, #a.-t.	12.00	12.00
955	A118	90sh Sheet of 20, #a.-t.	8.00	8.00

Souvenir Sheets

956	A118	1400sh multicolored	8.00	8.00
957	A118	1400sh multicolored	5.50	5.50

No. 956 contains one 30x38mm stamp.

While Nos. 955 and 957 have the same issue date as Nos. 954 and 956, their dollar value was lower when released.

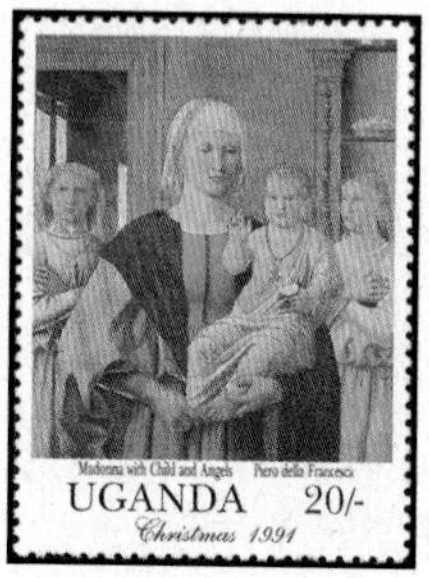

Christmas A120

Paintings by Piero Della Francesca: 20sh, Madonna with Child and Angels. 50sh, The Baptism of Christ. 80sh, Polyptych of Mercy. 100sh, The Madonna of Mercy. 200sh, The Legend of the True Cross: The Annunciation. 500sh, Pregnant Madonna. 1000sh, Polyptych of St. Anthony: The Annunciation. 1500sh, The Nativity. No. 968, The Brera Altarpiece. No. 969, Polyptych of St. Anthony.

1991, Dec. 18 **Litho.** *Perf. 12*

960	A120	20sh multicolored	.25	.25
961	A120	50sh multicolored	.25	.25
962	A120	80sh multicolored	.35	.35
963	A120	100sh multicolored	.45	.45
964	A120	200sh multicolored	.85	.85
965	A120	500sh multicolored	2.10	2.10
966	A120	1000sh multicolored	4.25	4.25
967	A120	1500sh multicolored	6.50	6.50
		Nos. 960-967 (8)	15.00	15.00

Souvenir Sheets

Perf. 14½

968	A120	1800sh multicolored	7.50	7.50
969	A120	1800sh multicolored	7.50	7.50

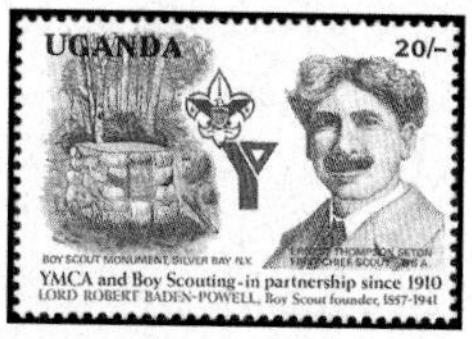

Boy Scouts A121

Designs: 20sh, Boy Scout Monument, Silver Bay, NY and Ernest Thompson Seton, first chief scout. 50sh, Tree house and Daniel Beard, Boy Scout pioneer, vert. 1500sh, Boy Scout emblem.

1992, Jan. 6 **Litho.** *Perf. 14*

970	A121	20sh multicolored	.90	.90
971	A121	50sh multicolored	1.25	1.25

Souvenir Sheet

972	A121	1500sh multicolored	7.00	7.00

YMCA-Boy Scouts partnership, Lord Robert Baden-Powell, 50th death anniv. in 1991 (#970) and 17th World Scout Jamboree, Korea (#971-972).

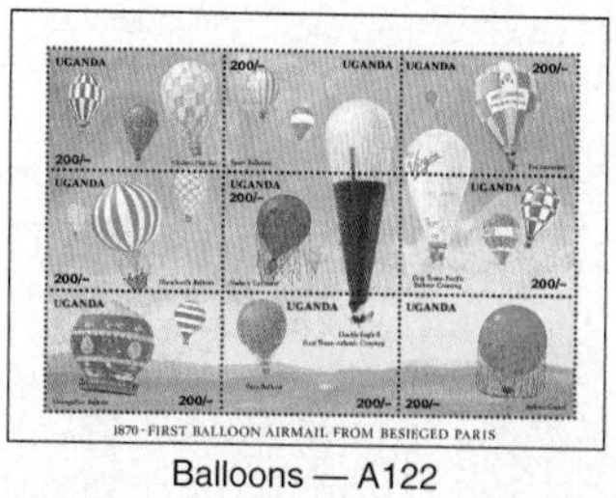

Balloons — A122

Balloons: a, Modern Hot Air. b, Sport. c, Pro Juventute. d, Blanchard's. e, Nadar's Le Geant. f, First trans-Pacific balloon crossing. g, Montgolfier's. h, Paris, Double Eagle II, used in first trans-Atlantic balloon crossing. i, Tethered.

1992, Jan. 6 **Litho.** *Perf. 14*

974	A122	200sh Sheet of 9, #a.-i.	9.50	9.50

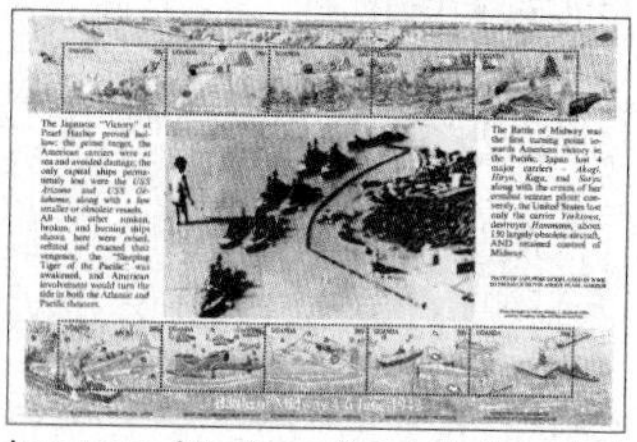

Japanese Attack on Pearl Harbor, 50th Anniv. (in 1991) — A123

Designs: a, Japanese bombers attack USS Vestal. b, Japanese Zero fighter. c, Zeros over burning USS Arizona. d, Battleship Row, USS Nevada under way. e, Japanese Val dive bomber. f, US Dauntless dive bomber attacking Hiryu. g, Japanese planes over Midway Island. h, US Buffalo fighter plane. i, US Wildcat fighters over carrier. j, USS Yorktown and Hammann torpedoed by Japanese submarine.

1992, Jan. 6 *Perf. 14½x15*

975	A123	200sh Sheet of 10, #a.-j.	12.50	12.50

Battle of Midway, 50th anniv. (#975f-975j). Inscription for No. 975i incorrectly describes fighters as Hellcats.

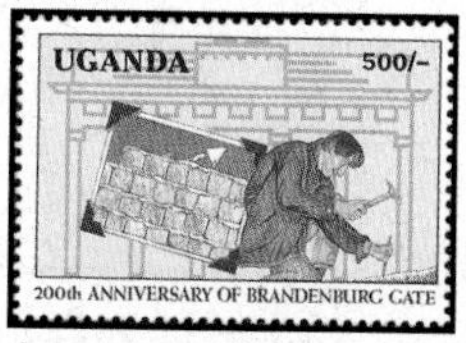

Anniversaries and Events — A124

Designs: 400sh, Glider No. 8. 500sh, Man breaking pieces from Berlin Wall. 700sh, Portrait of Mozart and scene from "The Magic Flute." 1200sh, Electric locomotive.

1992, Jan. 6 **Litho.** *Perf. 14*

976	A124	400sh multicolored	1.60	1.60
977	A124	500sh multicolored	2.00	2.00
978	A124	700sh multicolored	6.50	6.50
		Nos. 976-978 (3)	10.10	10.10

Souvenir Sheet

979	A124	1200sh multicolored	5.75	5.75

Otto Lillienthal, hang glider, cent. (in 1991) (#976). Brandenburg Gate, Bicent. (#977), Wolfgang Amadeus Mozart, death bicent. (#978), Trans-Siberian Railway, cent. (#979).

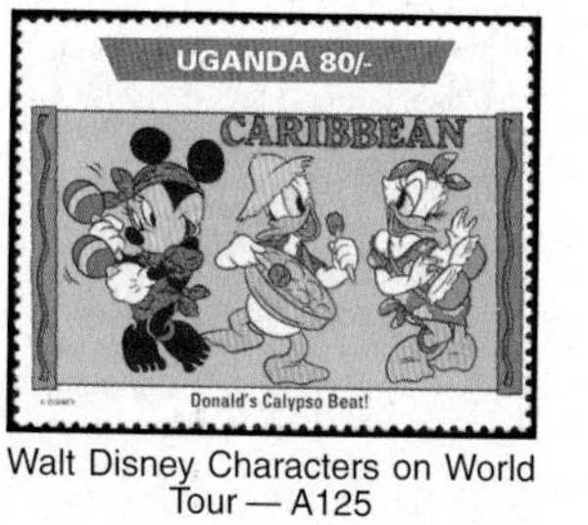

Walt Disney Characters on World Tour — A125

Designs: 20sh, Safari surprise in Africa. 50sh, Pluto's tail of India. 80sh, Donald's calypso beat in Caribbean. 200sh, Goofy pulling rickshaw in China. 500sh, Minnie, Mickey on camel in Egypt. 800sh, Wrestling, Japanese style. 1000sh, Goofy bullfighting in Spain. 1500sh, Mickey scoring in soccer game. No. 988, Daisy singing opera in Germany. No. 989, Mickey and Pluto as Cossack dancers in Moscow.

1992, Feb. *Perf. 13*

980	A125	20sh multi	.30	.30
981	A125	50sh multi	.30	.30
982	A125	80sh multi	.30	.30
983	A125	200sh multi	.70	.70
984	A125	500sh multi	1.75	1.75
985	A125	800sh multi	3.00	3.00
986	A125	1000sh multi	3.50	3.50
987	A125	1500sh multi	5.25	5.25
		Nos. 980-987 (8)	15.10	15.10

Souvenir Sheets

988	A125	2000sh	multi, vert.	7.50	7.50
989	A125	2000sh	multi, vert.	7.50	7.50

Queen Elizabeth II's Accession to the Throne, 40th Anniv.

Common Design Type

No. 994, Queen, waterfalls. No. 995, Queen, dam.

1992, Feb. 6 Litho. *Perf. 14*

990	CD348	100sh	multi	.50	.50
991	CD348	200sh	multi	.75	.75
992	CD348	500sh	multi	2.00	2.00
993	CD348	1000sh	multi	4.25	4.25
		Nos. 990-993 (4)		7.50	7.50

Souvenir Sheets

994	CD348	1800sh	multi	6.00	6.00
995	CD348	1800sh	multi	6.00	6.00

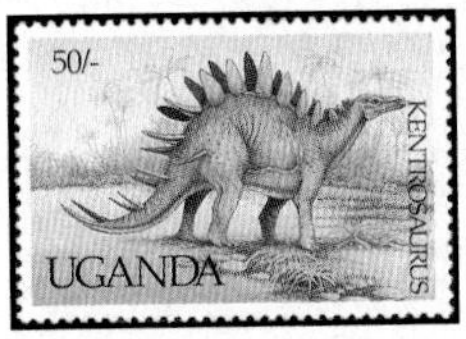

Dinosaurs A126

50sh, Kentrosaurus. 200sh, Iguanodon. 250sh, Hypsilophodon. 300sh, Brachiosaurus. 400sh, Peloneustes. 500sh, Pteranodon. 800sh, Tetra- lophodon. 1000sh, Megalosaurus.

1992, Apr. 8 Litho. *Perf. 14*

996	A126	50sh	multi	.35	.35
997	A126	200sh	multi	.65	.65
998	A126	250sh	multi	1.25	1.25
999	A126	300sh	multi	1.00	1.00
1000	A126	400sh	multi	1.75	1.75
1001	A126	500sh	multi	1.60	1.60
1002	A126	800sh	multi	2.50	2.50
1003	A126	1000sh	multi	4.50	4.50
		Nos. 996-1003 (8)		13.60	13.60

Souvenir Sheets

1004	A126	2000sh	like #1003	6.50	6.50
1005	A126	2000sh	like #998	6.50	6.50

Nos. 1004-1005 printed in continuous design.

While Nos. 997, 999, 1001-1002, 1005 have the same release date as Nos. 996, 998, 1000, 1003-1004, their value in relation to the dollar was lower when they were released.

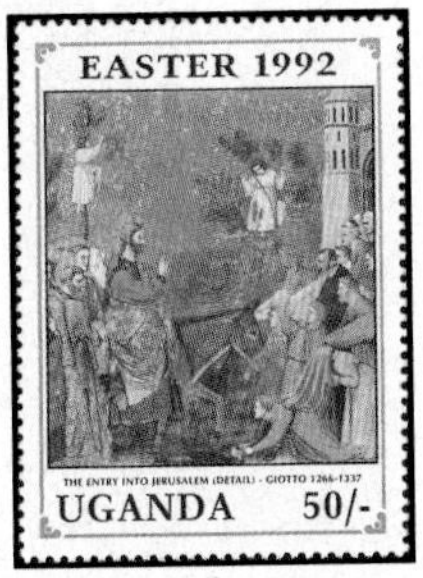

Easter A127

Paintings: 50sh, The Entry into Jerusalem (detail), by Giotto. 100sh, Pilate and the Watch from psalter of Robert de Lisle. 200sh, The Kiss of Judas (detail), by Giotto. 250sh, Christ Washing the Feet of the Disciples, illumination from Life of Christ. 300sh, Christ Seized in the Garden from Melissande Psalter. 500sh, Doubting Thomas, illumination from Life of Christ. 1000sh, The Marys at the Tomb (detail), artist unknown. 2000sh, The Ascension, from 14th century Florentine illuminated manuscript.

Limoge enamels: No. 1014, Agony at Gethsemane. No. 1015, The Piercing of Christ's Side.

1992 Litho. *Perf. 13½x14*

1006	A127	50sh	multi	.25	.25
1007	A127	100sh	multi	.30	.30
1008	A127	200sh	multi	.70	.70
1009	A127	250sh	multi	.75	.75
1010	A127	300sh	multi	.90	.90
1011	A127	500sh	multi	1.50	1.50
1012	A127	1000sh	multi	3.00	3.00
1013	A127	2000sh	multi	6.25	6.25
		Nos. 1006-1013 (8)		13.65	13.65

Souvenir Sheets

1014	A127	2500sh	multi	7.00	7.00
1015	A127	2500sh	multi	7.00	7.00

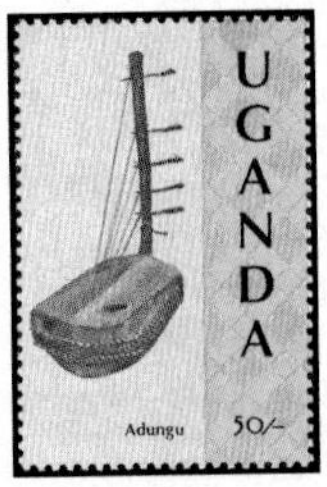

Musical Instruments A128

1992, July 20 Litho. *Perf. 14*

1016	A128	50sh	Adungu	.25	.25
1017	A128	100sh	Endingidi	.30	.30
1018	A128	200sh	Akogo	.65	.65
1019	A128	250sh	Nanga	.75	.75
1020	A128	300sh	Engoma	.90	.90
1021	A128	400sh	Amakondere	1.25	1.25
1022	A128	500sh	Akaky-enkye	1.50	1.50
1023	A128	1000sh	Ennanga	3.00	3.00
		Nos. 1016-1023 (8)		8.60	8.60

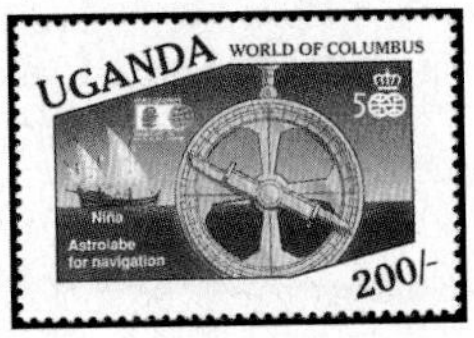

Discovery of America, 500th Anniv. A129

Designs: 50sh, World map, 1486. 100sh, Map of Africa, 1508. 150sh, New World, 1500. 200sh, Nina, astrolabe. 600sh, Quadrant, Pinta. 800sh, Hour glass. 900sh, 15th century compass. 2000sh, World map, 1492. No. 1032, 1490 Map by Henricus Martellus, 1490. No. 1033, Sections of 1492 globe.

1992, July 24 Litho. *Perf. 14*

1024	A129	50sh	multi	.25	.25
1025	A129	100sh	multi	.25	.25
1026	A129	150sh	multi	.25	.25
1027	A129	200sh	multi	.70	.70
1028	A129	600sh	multi	2.00	2.00
1029	A129	800sh	multi	2.60	2.60
1030	A129	900sh	multi	2.75	2.75
1031	A129	2000sh	multi	2.25	2.25
		Nos. 1024-1031 (8)		11.05	11.05

Souvenir Sheets

1032	A129	2500sh	multi, vert.	6.50	6.50
1033	A129	2500sh	multi	4.50	4.50

World Columbian Stamp Expo '92, Chicago.

While Nos. 1024-1026, 1031 and 1033 have the same issue date as Nos. 1027-1030 and 1032, their value in relation to the dollar was lower when they were released.

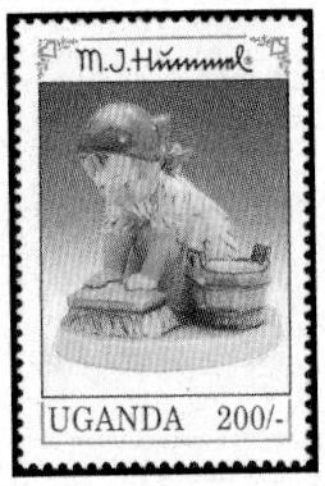

Hummel Figurines — A130

No. 1034, Little Laundry Girl. No. 1035, Scrub Girl. No. 1036, Sweeper Girl. No. 1037, Little Mother. No. 1038, Little Mountaineer. No. 1039, Little Knitter. No. 1040, Little Cowboy. No. 1041, Little Astronomer.

No. 1042: a, Like #1034. b, Like #1035. c, Like #1036. d, Like #1037.

No. 1043: a, Like #1039. b, Like #1038. c, Like #1040. d, Like #1041.

1992, Aug. 28 Litho. *Perf. 14*

1034	A130	50sh	multi	.25	.25
1035	A130	200sh	multi	.65	.65
1036	A130	250sh	multi	.70	.70
1037	A130	300sh	multi	.90	.90
1038	A130	600sh	multi	1.30	1.30
1039	A130	900sh	multi	1.75	1.75
1040	A130	1000sh	multi	2.25	2.25
1041	A130	1500sh	multi	4.50	4.50
		Nos. 1034-1041 (8)		12.30	12.30

Souvenir Sheets

1042	A130	500sh	Sheet of 4, #a.-d.	6.75	6.75
1043	A130	500sh	Sheet of 4, #a.-d.	6.75	6.75

While Nos. 1034, 1038-1040, 1043 have the same release date as Nos. 1035-1037, 1041-1042, their value in relation to the dollar was lower when they were released.

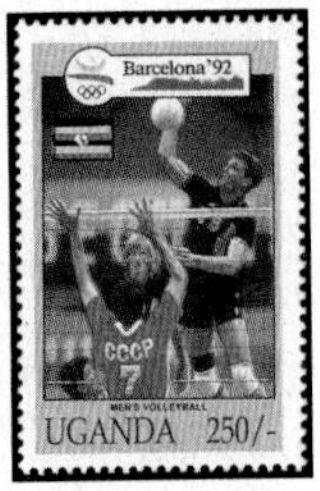

1992 Summer Olympics, Barcelona — A131

50sh, Javelin. 100sh, High jump, horiz. 200sh, Pentathlon (Fencing). 250sh, Volleyball. 300sh, Women's platform diving. 500sh, Team cycling. 1000sh, Tennis. 2000sh, Boxing, horiz.

No. 1052, Baseball. No. 1053, Basketball.

1992 Litho. *Perf. 14*

1044	A131	50sh	multi	.35	.35
1045	A131	100sh	multi	.35	.35
1046	A131	200sh	multi	.55	.55
1047	A131	250sh	multi	.65	.65
1048	A131	300sh	multi	.80	.80
1049	A131	500sh	multi	1.30	1.30
1050	A131	1000sh	multi	2.75	2.75
1051	A131	2000sh	multi	5.25	5.25
		Nos. 1044-1051 (8)		12.00	12.00

Souvenir Sheets

1052	A131	2500sh	multi	5.75	5.75
1053	A131	2500sh	multi	5.75	5.75

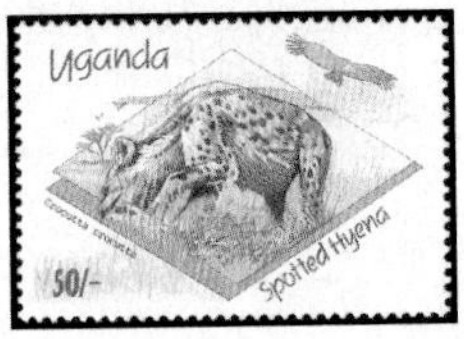

Wild Animals A132

50sh, Spotted hyena. 100sh, Impala. 200sh, Giant forest hog. 250sh, Pangolin. 300sh, Golden monkey. 800sh, Serval. 1000sh, Bush genet. 3000sh, Defassa waterbuck.

No. 1062, Mountain gorilla. No. 1063, Hippopotamus.

1992, Sept. 25 Litho. *Perf. 14*

1054	A132	50sh	multi	.25	.25
1055	A132	100sh	multi	.25	.25
1056	A132	200sh	multi	.45	.45
1057	A132	250sh	multi	.55	.55
1058	A132	300sh	multi	.70	.70
1059	A132	800sh	multi	1.75	1.75
1060	A132	1000sh	multi	2.25	2.25
1061	A132	3000sh	multi	6.75	6.75
		Nos. 1054-1061 (8)		12.95	12.95

Souvenir Sheets

1062	A132	2500sh	multi	5.50	5.50
1063	A132	2500sh	multi	5.50	5.50

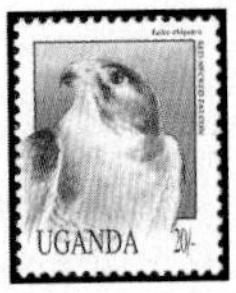

Birds — A133

Designs: 20sh, Red necked falcon. 30sh, Yellow-billed hornbill. 50sh, Purple heron. 100sh, Regal sunbird. 150sh, White-brown robin chat. 200sh, Shining-blue kingfisher. 250sh, Great blue turaco. 300sh, Emerald cuckoo. 500sh, Abyssinian roller. 800sh, Crowned crane. 1000sh, Doherty's bush shrike. 2000sh, Splendid glossy starling. 3000sh, Little bee eater. 4000sh, Red-headed lovebird.

1992, Aug. Litho. *Perf. 15x14*

1064	A133	20sh	multi	.35	.35
1065	A133	30sh	multi	.35	.35
1066	A133	50sh	multi	.35	.35
1067	A133	100sh	multi	.35	.35
1068	A133	150sh	multi	.40	.40
1069	A133	200sh	multi	.55	.55
1070	A133	250sh	multi	.70	.70
1071	A133	300sh	multi	.75	.75
1072	A133	500sh	multi	1.40	1.40
1073	A133	800sh	multi	2.25	2.25
1074	A133	1000sh	multi	2.75	2.75
1075	A133	2000sh	multi	5.50	5.50
1076	A133	3000sh	multi	8.50	8.50
1076A	A133	4000sh	multi	11.00	11.00
		Nos. 1064-1076A (14)		35.20	35.20

Issued: 3000sh, Oct.; others, Aug.?

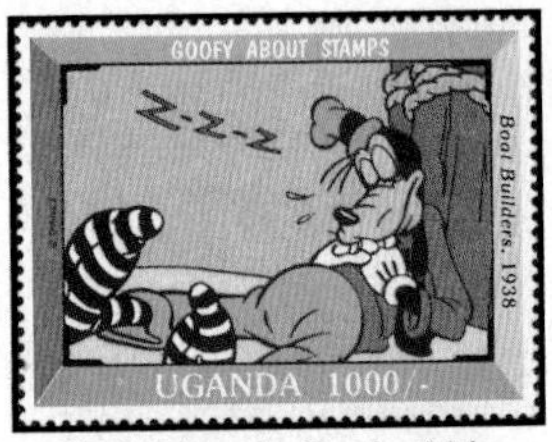

Walt Disney's Goofy, 60th Anniv. — A134

Scenes from Disney animated films: 50sh, Hawaiian Holiday, 1937, vert. 100sh, The Nifty Nineties, 1941, vert. 200sh, Mickey's Fire Brigade, 1935, vert. 250sh, The Art of Skiing, 1941. 300sh, Mickey's Amateurs, 1937. 1000sh, Boat Builders, 1938. 1500sh, The Olympic Champ, 1942, vert. 2000sh, The Olympic Champ, 1942, vert. No. 1085, Goofy and Wilbur, 1939. No. 1086, Goofy's family tree, vert.

Perf. 13½x14, 14x13½

1992, Nov. 2 Litho.

1077	A134	50sh	multi	.25	.25
1078	A134	100sh	multi	.25	.25
1079	A134	200sh	multi	.50	.50
1080	A134	250sh	multi	.65	.65
1081	A134	300sh	multi	.80	.80
1082	A134	1000sh	multi	2.50	2.50
1083	A134	1500sh	multi	4.00	4.00
1084	A134	2000sh	multi	5.25	5.25
		Nos. 1077-1084 (8)		14.20	14.20

Souvenir Sheets

1085	A134	3000sh	multi	7.50	7.50
1086	A134	3000sh	multi	7.50	7.50

Souvenir Sheet

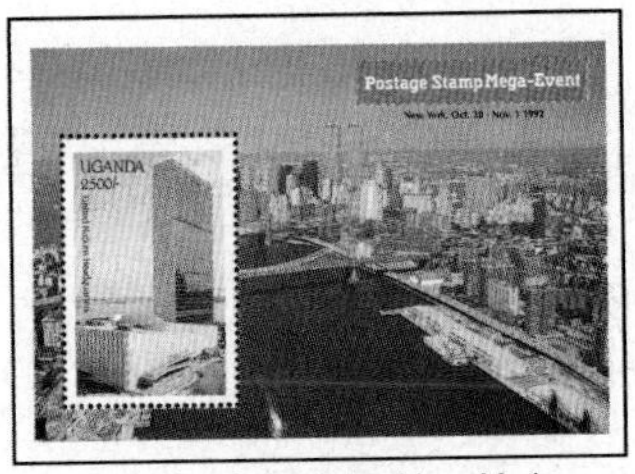

UN Headquarters, New York City — A135

1992, Oct. 28 Litho. *Perf. 14*

1087	A135	2500sh	multi	7.50	7.50

Postage Stamp Mega Event '92, NYC.

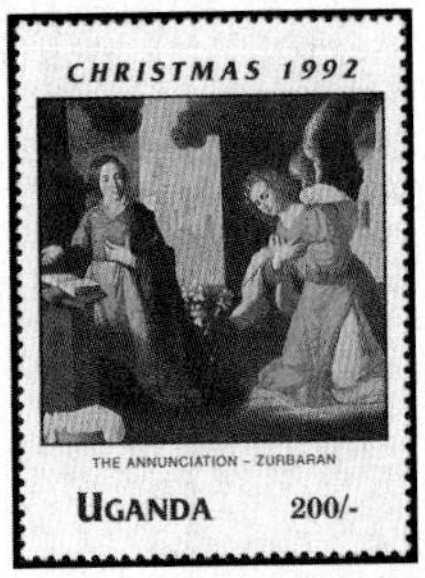

Christmas A136

Details or entire paintings by Zurbaran: 50sh, The Annunciation (angel at left). 200sh, The Annunciation (angel at right). 250sh, The Virgin of the Immaculate Conception. 300sh, The Virgin of the Immaculate Conception (detail). 800sh, 900sh, The Holy Family with Saints Anne, Joachim and John the Baptist (800sh, entire, 900sh, detail). 1000sh, Adoration of the Magi (entire). 2000sh, Adoration of the Magi. No. 1096, The Virgin of the Immaculate Conception (Virgin with arms outstretched). No. 1097, The Virgin of the Immaculate Conception (Virgin with arms folded).

1992, Nov. 16 Litho. *Perf. 13½x14*

1088	A136	50sh	multi	.25	.25
1089	A136	200sh	multi	.45	.45
1090	A136	250sh	multi	.60	.60
1091	A136	300sh	multi	.75	.75
1092	A136	800sh	multi	2.00	2.00
1093	A136	900sh	multi	2.25	2.25
1094	A136	1000sh	multi	2.40	2.40
1095	A136	2000sh	multi	4.75	4.75
		Nos. 1088-1095 (8)		13.45	13.45

Souvenir Sheets

1096	A136	2500sh	multi	7.00	7.00
1097	A136	2500sh	multi	7.00	7.00

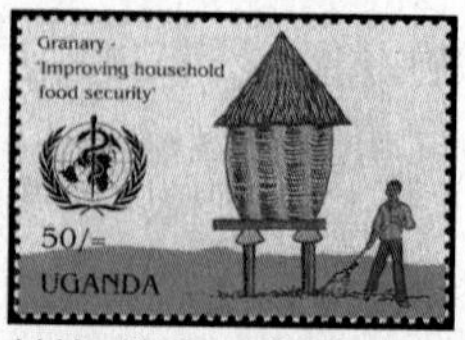

World Health Organization — A137

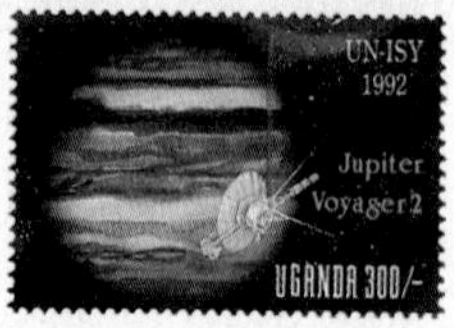

Anniversaries and Events — A138

Designs: 50sh, Improving household food security. 200sh, Continue to breastfeed. 250sh, At four months old, give breast milk and soft food. No. 1101, Drink water from a safe and protected source. No. 1102, Jupiter, Voyager 2. No. 1103, Mother holding baby. No. 1104, Impala. No. 1105, Zebra. No. 1106, Count Ferdinand von Zeppelin, zeppelin. 2000sh, Neptune, Voyager 2. 3000sh, Count Zeppelin, zeppelin, diff. No. 1109, Voyager 2, Jupiter, diff. No. 1110, Wart hog. No. 1111, Doctor examining child, Lions Intl. emblem. No. 1112, Count Zeppelin, balloon.

1992 Litho. *Perf. 14*

1098	A137	50sh multi	.25	.25
1099	A137	200sh multi	.40	.40
1100	A137	250sh multi	.50	.50
1101	A137	300sh multi	.60	.60
1102	A138	300sh multi	1.40	1.40
1103	A137	800sh multi	1.60	1.60
1104	A138	800sh multi	3.25	3.25
1105	A138	1000sh multi	3.75	3.75
1106	A138	1000sh multi	2.00	2.00
1107	A138	2000sh multi	9.75	9.75
1108	A138	3000sh multi	6.00	6.00
		Nos. 1098-1108 (11)	29.50	29.50

Souvenir Sheets

1109	A138	2500sh multi	7.75	7.75
1110	A138	2500sh multi	7.75	7.75
1111	A138	2500sh multi	7.75	7.75
1112	A138	2500sh multi	7.75	7.75

WHO (#1098-1101, 1103). Intl. Space Year (#1102, 1107, 1109). Earth Summit, Rio de Janeiro (#1104-1105, 1110). Count Zeppelin, 75th anniv. of death (#1106, 1108, 1112). Lions Intl., 75th anniv. (#1111).

Issue dates: Nos. 1098-1103, 1106, 1109, 1112, Nov.; others, Dec.

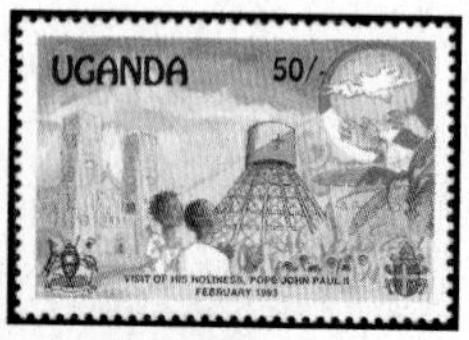

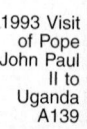

1993 Visit of Pope John Paul II to Uganda A139

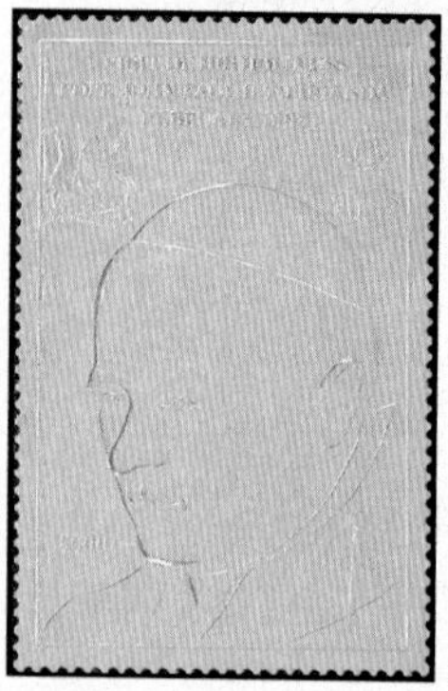

A139a

Designs: 50sh, Cathedral in Kampala, site of Papal Mass, Kampala, hands releasing doves. 200sh, Site of Papal Mass, Pope. 250sh, Ugandan man, Pope. 300sh, Three Ugandan Catholic leaders, Pope. 800sh, Pope waving, Ugandan map and flag. 900sh, Ugandan woman, Pope wearing mitre. 1000sh, Pope, Ugandan flag, site of Papal Mass. 2000sh, Ugandan flag, Pope waving.

No. 1121, Pope at door of airplane, vert. No. 1122, Pope delivering message at podium, vert.

No. 1123, Pope John Paul II. No. 1124, Pope with hands raised.

1993, Feb. 1 Litho. *Perf. 14*

1113	A139	50sh multi	.30	.30
1114	A139	200sh multi	.50	.50
1115	A139	250sh multi	.60	.60
1116	A139	300sh multi	.70	.70
1117	A139	800sh multi	1.75	1.75
1118	A139	900sh multi	1.90	1.90
1119	A139	1000sh multi	2.25	2.25
1120	A139	2000sh multi	4.50	4.50
		Nos. 1113-1120 (8)	12.50	12.50

Souvenir Sheets

1121	A139	3000sh multi	6.25	6.25
1122	A139	3000sh multi	6.25	6.25

Embossed

Perf. 12

1123	A139a	5000sh gold	30.00	30.00

Souvenir Sheet

Imperf

1124	A139a	5000sh gold	30.00	30.00

Miniature Sheet

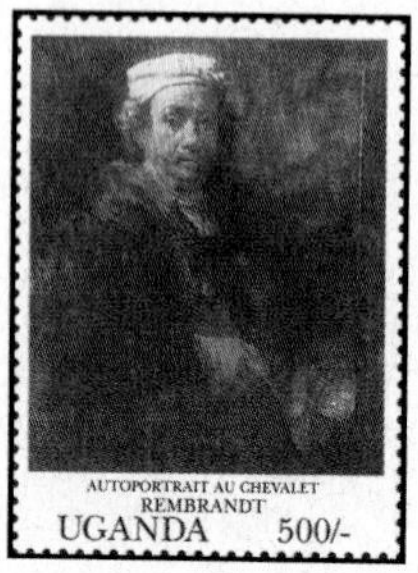

Louvre Museum, Bicent. A140

Details or entire paintings by Rembrandt: No. 1125a, Self-Portrait with an Easel. b, Birds of Paradise. c, The Beef Carcass. d, The Supper at Emmaus. e, Hendrickje Stoffels. f, Titus, Son of the Artist. g, The Holy Family (left). h, The Holy Family (right).

2500sh, Philosopher in Meditation, horiz.

1993, Apr. 5 Litho. *Perf. 12*

1125	A140	500sh Sheet of 8, #a.-h. + label	10.00	10.00

Souvenir Sheet

Perf. 14½

1126	A140	2500sh multi	6.50	6.50

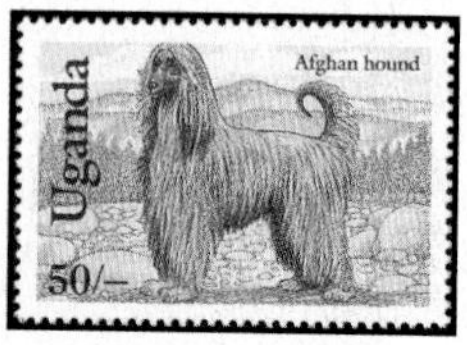

Dogs A141

50sh, Afghan hound. 100sh, Newfoundland. 200sh, Siberian huskies. 250sh, Briard. 300sh, Saluki. 800sh, Labrador retriever, vert. 1000sh, Greyhound. 1500sh, Pointer.

No. 1135, Cape hunting dog. No. 1136, Norwegian elkhound.

1993, May 28 Litho. *Perf. 14*

1127	A141	50sh multi	.45	.45
1128	A141	100sh multi	.45	.45
1129	A141	200sh multi	.80	.80
1130	A141	250sh multi	1.00	1.00
1131	A141	300sh multi	1.40	1.40
1132	A141	800sh multi	3.50	3.50
1133	A141	1000sh multi	4.00	4.00
1134	A141	1500sh multi	6.50	6.50
		Nos. 1127-1134 (8)	18.10	18.10

Souvenir Sheets

1135	A141	2500sh multi	11.00	11.00
1136	A141	2500sh multi	11.00	11.00

Miniature Sheet

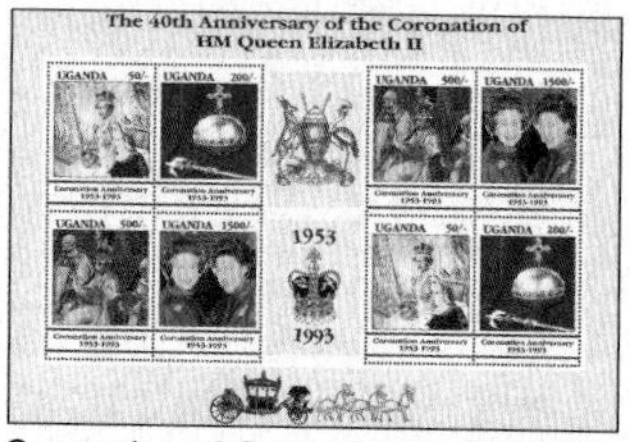

Coronation of Queen Elizabeth II, 40th Anniv. — A142

No. 1137: a, 50sh, Official coronation photograph. b, 200sh, Orb, Rod of Equity & Mercy. c, 500sh, Queen during coronation ceremony. d, 1500sh, Queen Elizabeth II, Princess Margaret.

2500sh, The Crown, by Grace Wheatley, 1959.

1993, June 2 Litho. *Perf. 13½x14*

1137	A142	Sheet, 2 each #a.-d.	12.50	12.50

Souvenir Sheet

Perf. 14

1138	A142	2500sh multicolored	7.00	7.00

No. 1138 contains one 28x42mm stamp.

Miniature Sheet

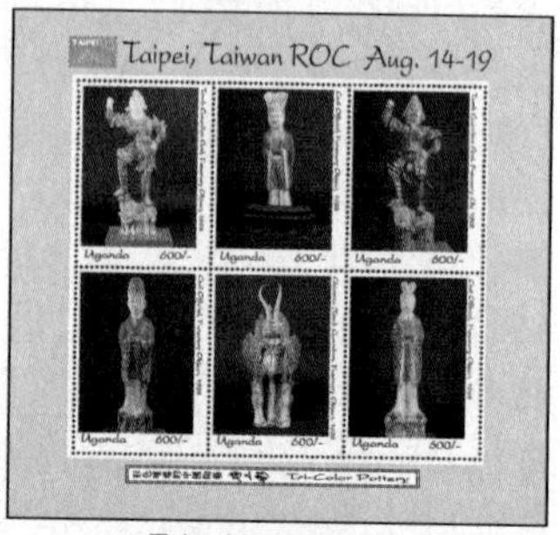

Taipei '93 — A143

Funerary objects: No. 1139a, Tomb guardian god. b, Civil official. c, Tomb guardian god, diff. d, Civil official, diff. e, Chimera. f, Civil official, diff.

2500sh, Statue of Sacred Mother, Ceremonial Hall, Taiyuan, Shanxi.

1993, Sept. 22 Litho. *Perf. 14x13½*

1139	A143	600sh Sheet of 6, #a.-f.	7.50	7.50

Souvenir Sheet

1140	A143	2500sh multicolored	7.00	7.00

With Bangkok '93 Emblem

Thai sculpture: No. 1141a, Standing Buddha, 13th-15th cent. b, Crowned Buddha, 13th cent. c, Thepanom, 15th cent. d, Crowned Buddha, 12th cent. e, Four-armed Avalokitesvara, 9th cent. f, Lop Buri standing Buddha, 13th cent.

2500sh, Buddha, interior of Wat Mahathat.

1993, Sept. 22

1141	A143	600sh Sheet of 6, #a.-f.	7.50	7.50

Souvenir Sheet

1142	A143	2500sh multicolored	7.00	7.00

With Indopex '93 Emblem

Japanese Wayang Puppets, Indonesia: No. 1143a, Bupati karma, Prince of Wangga. b, Rahwana. c, Sondjeng Sandjata. d, Raden Damar Wulan. e, Klitik figure. f, Hanaman.

2500sh, Candi Mendut in Kedu Plain, Java, Indonesia.

1993, Sept. 22 Litho. *Perf. 13½x14*

1143	A143	600sh Sheet of 6, #a.-f.	7.50	7.50

Souvenir Sheet

1144	A143	2500sh multicolored	7.00	7.00

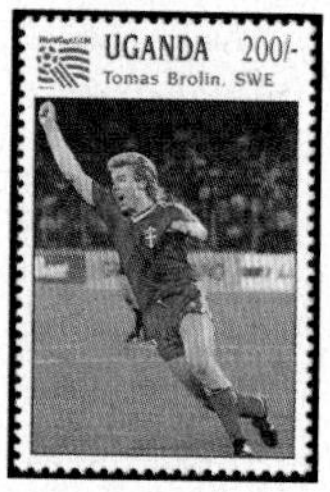

A144

50sh, Gutierrez, Voeller. 200sh, Tomas Brolin. 250sh, Gary Lineker. 300sh, Munoz, Butragueno. 800sh, Carlos Valderrama. 900sh, Diego Maradona. 1000sh, Pedro Troglio. 2000sh, Enzo Scifo.

No. 1153, Brazil coaches. No. 1154, De Napoli, Skuhravy, horiz.

1993, Oct. 1 Litho. *Perf. 14*

1145	A144	50sh multi	.35	.35
1146	A144	200sh multi	.60	.60
1147	A144	250sh multi	.75	.75
1148	A144	300sh multi	.85	.85
1149	A144	800sh multi	2.40	2.40
1150	A144	900sh multi	2.55	2.55
1151	A144	1000sh multi	3.00	3.00
1152	A144	2000sh multi	6.00	6.00
		Nos. 1145-1152 (8)	16.50	16.50

Souvenir Sheets

1153	A144	2500sh multi	7.25	7.25
1154	A144	2500sh multi	7.25	7.25

1994 World Cup Soccer Championships, US.

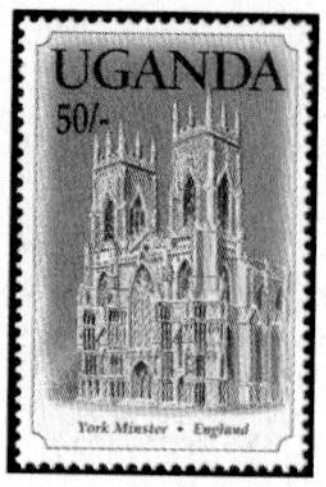

A145

Cathedrals of the World: 50sh, York Minster, England. 100sh, Notre Dame, Paris. 200sh, Little Metropolis, Athens. 250sh, St. Patrick's, New York. 300sh, Ulm, Germany. 800sh, St. Basil's, Moscow. 1000sh, Roskilde, Denmark. 2000sh, Seville, Spain. No. 1163, Namirembe, Uganda. No. 1163A, St. Peter's, Vatican City.

1993, Nov. 3 *Perf. 14*

1155	A145	50sh multi	.35	.35
1156	A145	100sh multi	.35	.35
1157	A145	200sh multi	.65	.65
1158	A145	250sh multi	.70	.70
1159	A145	300sh multi	.95	.95
1160	A145	800sh multi	2.25	2.25
1161	A145	1000sh multi	3.00	3.00
1162	A145	2000sh multi	5.75	5.75
		Nos. 1155-1162 (8)	14.00	14.00

Souvenir Sheets

1163	A145	2500sh multi	7.50	7.50
1163A	A145	2500sh multi	7.50	7.50

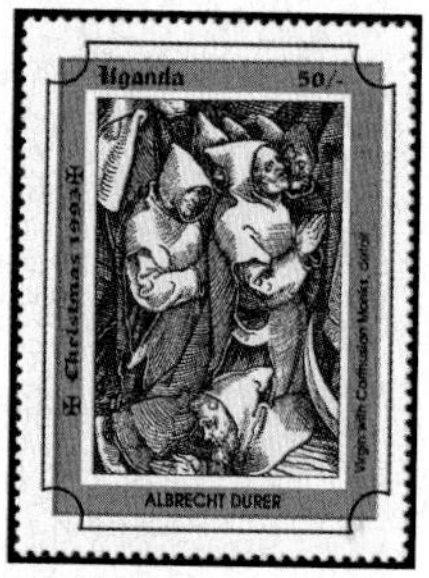

Christmas A146

Details or entire woodcut, The Virgin with Carthusian Monks, by Durer: 50sh, 200sh, 300sh, 2000sh.

Details or entire paintings by Raphael: 100sh, 800sh, Sacred Family. 250sh, The Virgin of the Rose. 1000sh, Holy Family (Virgin with Beardless Joseph).

No. 1172, 2500sh, The Virgin with Carthusian Monks, by Durer. No. 1173, 2500sh, Sacred Family, by Raphael.

1993, Nov. 19 Litho. *Perf. 13½x14*

1164-1171	A146	Set of 8	13.50	13.50

Souvenir Sheets

1172-1173	A146	Set of 2	15.00	15.00

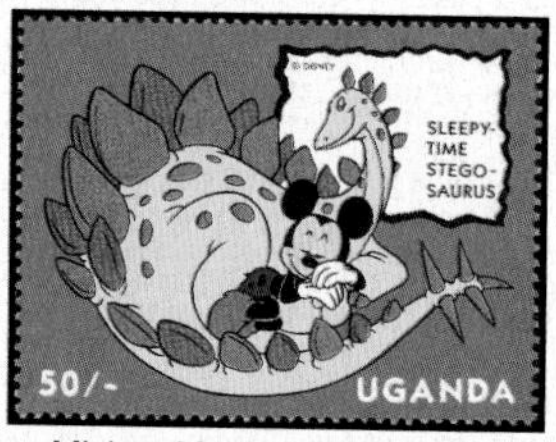

Mickey Mouse, Friends with Dinosaurs — A147

Disney characters depicted with: 50sh, Stegosaurus. 100sh, Pterandom. 200sh, Mamenchisaurus. 250sh, Rock painting. 300sh, Dino "sails." 500sh, Diplodocus. 800sh, Mamenshisaurus, diff. 1000sh, Triceratops.

No. 1182, 2500sh, Tyrannosaurus rex, Mickey. No. 1183, 2500sh, Minnie, Mickey, mamenchisaurus, diff.

1993, Dec. 22 Litho. *Perf. 14x13½*

1174-1181	A147	Set of 8	13.00	13.00

Souvenir Sheets

1182-1183	A147	Set of 2	13.00	13.00

Rinderpest Campaign — A148

1993, Dec. 29   **Perf. 14**
1184 A148 200sh multicolored   1.00 1.00

Picasso (1881-1973) A149

Paintings: 100sh, Woman in Yellow, 1907. 250sh, Gertrude Stein, 1906. 2500sh, Woman by a Window, 1956.

1993, Dec. 29
1185-1186 A149 Set of 2   1.50 1.50
Souvenir Sheet
1187 A149 2500sh multicolored   7.50 7.50

Copernicus (1473-1543) — A150

Telescopes: 500sh, Early. 1000sh, Modern. 2500sh, Copernicus.

1993, Dec. 29
1188-1189 A150 Set of 2   4.50 4.50
Souvenir Sheet
1190 A150 2500sh multicolored   7.50 7.50

Polska '93 — A151

Paintings: 800sh, Creation of the World, by S. I. Witkiewicz par J. Gloqowski, 1921. 1000sh, For the Right to Work, by Andrezej Strumillo, 1952. 2500sh, Temptation of St. Anthony I, by S. I. Witkiewicz (1908-21), horiz.

1993, Dec. 29
1191-1192 A151 Set of 2   5.75 5.75
Souvenir Sheet
1193 A151 2500sh multicolored   7.00 7.00

World Meteorological Day — A152

Designs: 50sh, Weather station, horiz. 200sh, Observatory at Meteorological Training School, Entebbe. 250sh, Satellite receiver at National Meteorological Center, horiz. 300sh, Reading temperatures, National Center,

Entebbe, horiz. 400sh, Automatic weather station. 800sh, Destruction by hail storm, horiz. 2500sh, Barograph, horiz.

1993, Dec. 29
1194-1199 A152 Set of 6   10.50 10.50
Souvenir Sheet
1200 A152 2500sh multicolored   8.25 8.25

Fruits and Crops — A153

Designs: 50sh, Passiflora edulis. 100sh, Helianthus annus. 150sh, Musa sapientum. 200sh, Vanilla fragrans. 250sh, Ananas comosus. 300sh, Artocarpus heterophyllus. 500sh, Sorghum bicolor. 800sh, Zea mays. No. 1209, 2000sh, Sesamum indicum. No. 1210, 2000sh, Coffea canephora.

1993, Dec. 29
1201-1208 A153 Set of 8   7.50 7.50
Souvenir Sheets
1209-1210 A153 Set of 2   10.00 10.00

Automotive Anniversaries — A154

No. 1211: a, 1903 Model A Ford, Henry Ford. b, Model T Snowmobile at 1932 Winter Olympics, Jack Shea. c, Lee Iacocca, Ford Mustang at New York World's Fair. d, Jim Clark, Lotus-Ford winning 1965 Indianapolis 500 race.
No. 1212: a, 1994 Mercedes Benz S600 Coupe. b, 1955 Mercedes Benz W196 Grand Prix Champion car, Juan Manuel Fangio. c, 1938 Mercedes Benz W125 road speed record holder, Rudolph Caracciola. d, Carl Benz, 1893 Benz Viktoria.
No. 1213, Carl Benz, vert. No. 1214, Henry Ford, vert.

1994, Jan. 18   Litho.   Perf. 14
1211 A154 700sh Strip of 4,
               #a.-d.   5.75 5.75
1212 A154 800sh Strip of 4,
               #a.-d.   6.75 6.75
Souvenir Sheets
1213 A154 2500sh multicolored   6.00 6.00
1214 A154 2500sh multicolored   6.00 6.00

First Ford motor, cent. (#1211, #1214). First Benz four-wheel car, cent. (#1212, #1213).

A155

Hong Kong '94 — A156

Stamps, religious shrines, Repulse Bay: No. 1215, Hong Kong #531. No. 1216, #1163.
Snuff boxes, Qing Dynasty: No. 1217a, Glass painted enamel with pavilion. b, Porcelain with floral design. c, Porcelain with quail design. d, Porcelain with openwork design. e, Agate with pair of dogs. f, Agate with man on donkey.

1994, Feb. 18   Litho.   Perf. 14
1215 A155 500sh multicolored   .90   .90
1216 A155 500sh multicolored   .90   .90
   a.   Pair, #1215-1216   1.75 1.75
Miniature Sheet
1217 A156 200sh Sheet of 6,
               #a.-f.   3.75 3.75

Nos. 1215-1216 issued in sheets of 5 pairs. No. 1216a is continuous design.
New Year 1994 (Year of the Dog) (#1217e).

Miniature Sheet

1994 World Cup Soccer Championships, US — A157

Designs: No. 1218a, Georges Grun, Belgium. b, Oscar Ruggeri, Argentina. c, Frank Rijkaard, Holland. d, Magid "Tyson" Musisi, Uganda. e, Donald Keeman, Holland. f, Igor Shallmov, Russia.
No. 1219, 2500sh, RFK Stadium, Washington DC. No. 1220, 2500sh, Ruud Gullit, Holland.

1994, June 27   Litho.   Perf. 14
1218 A157 500sh Sheet of 6,
               #a.-f.   10.50 10.50
Souvenir Sheets
1219-1220 A157 Set of 2   12.00 12.00

Heifer Project Intl., 50th Anniv. A158

1994, June 29   Litho.   Perf. 14
1221 A158 100sh multicolored   2.25 2.25

Moths — A159

Designs: 100sh, Lobobunaea goodii. 200sh, Bunaeopsis hersilia. 300sh, Rufoglanis rosea. 350sh, Acherontia atropos. 400sh, Rohaniella pygmaea. 450sh, Euchloron megaera. 500sh, Epiphora rectifascia. 1000sh, Polyphychus coryndoni.
Lobobunaea goodii: No. 1230, 2500sh, Wings down. No. 1231, 2500sh, Wings extended.

1994, July 13
1222-1229 A159 Set of 8   8.75 8.75
Souvenir Sheets
1230-1231 A159 Set of 2   12.00 12.00

Native Crafts — A160

Designs: 100sh, Wood stool. 200sh, Wood & banana fiber chair. 250sh, Raffia & palm leaves basket. 300sh, Wool tapestry showing tree planting. 450sh, Wool tapestry showing hair grooming. 500sh, Wood sculpture, drummer. 800sh, Decorated gourds. 1000sh, Lady's bag made from bark cloth.
No. 1240, 2500sh, Raffia baskets. No. 1241, 2500sh, Papyrus hats.

1994, July 18
1232-1239 A160 Set of 8   8.25 8.25
Souvenir Sheets
1240-1241 A160 Set of 2   11.00 11.00

Cats — A161

Cat, historic landmark: 50sh, Turkish angora, Blue Mosque, Turkey, horiz. 100sh, Japanese bobtail, Mt. Fuji, Japan, horiz. 200sh, Norwegian forest cat, windmill, Holland, horiz. 300sh, Egyptian mau, pyramids, Egypt. 450sh, Rex, Stonehenge, England. 500sh, Chartreux, Eiffel Tower, France, horiz. 1000sh, Burmese, Shwe Dagon Pagoda, Burma. 1500sh, Maine coon, Pemaquid Point Lighthouse, Maine.
No. 1250, 2500sh, Russian blue, horiz. No. 1251, 2500sh, Manx, horiz.

1994, July 22
1242-1249 A161 Set of 8   14.00 14.00
Souvenir Sheets
1250-1251 A161 Set of 2   15.00 15.00

ILO, 75th Anniv. — A162

1994, July 29
1252 A162 350sh multicolored   1.25 1.25

PHILAKOREA '94 — A163

Designs: 100sh, Eight story Sari pagoda, Paekyangsa. 350sh, Ch'omsongdae (Natl. treasure). 1000sh, Pulguksa Temple exterior. 2500sh, Bronze mural, Pagoda Park, Seoul.

1994, Aug. 8
1253-1255 A163 Set of 3   2.75 2.75
Souvenir Sheet
1256 A163 2500sh multicolored   4.75 4.75

Intl. Year of the Family A164

1994, Aug. 11
1257 A164 100sh multicolored   1.10 1.10

D-Day, 50th Anniv. A165

Designs: 300sh, Mulberry Harbor pierhead moves into position. 1000sh, Mulberry Harbor floating bridge lands armor. 2500sh, Ships, Mulberry Harbor.

1994, Aug. 11
1258	A165	300sh multicolored	.85	.85
1259	A165	1000sh multicolored	2.75	2.75

Souvenir Sheet
1260	A165	2500sh multicolored	7.50	7.50

A166

Intl. Olympic Committee,
Cent. — A167

Designs: 350sh, John Akii-bua, Uganda, 100-meter hurdles, 1972. 900sh, Heike Herkel, Germany, high jump, 1992.
2500sh, Aleksei Urmanov, Russia, figure skating, 1994.

1994, Aug. 11
1261	A166	350sh multicolored	.70	.70
1262	A167	900sh multicolored	1.75	1.75

Souvenir Sheet
1263	A166	2500sh multicolored	5.50	5.50

First Manned Moon Landing, 25th
Anniv. — A168

No. 1264 — Project Mercury astronauts: a, 50sh, Alan B. Shepard, Jr., Freedom 7. b, 100sh, M. Scott Carpenter, Aurora 7. c, 200sh, Virgil I. Grissom, Liberty Bell 7. d, 300sh, L. Gordon Cooper, Jr., Faith 7. e, 400sh, Walter M. Schirra, Jr., Sigma 7. f, 500sh, Donald K. Slayton, Apollo-Soyuz, 1975. g, John H. Glenn, Jr., Friendship 7.
3000sh, Apollo 11 anniv. emblem.

1994, Aug. 11
1264	A168	Sheet of 7, #a.-g, + 2 labels	10.50	10.50

Souvenir Sheet
1265	A168	3000sh multi	10.50	10.50

A169

Disney's The Lion King — A169a

No. 1266: a, Baby Simba. b, Mufasa, Simba, Sarabi. c, Young Simba, Nala. d, Timon. e, Rafiki. f, Pumbaa. g, Hyenas. h, Scar. i, Zazu.
No. 1267: a, Rafiki, Mufasa. b, Rafiki, Mufasa, Sarabi. c, Rafiki, Simba. d, Scar, Zazu. e, Rafiki seeing vision. f, Simba, Scar. g, Simba, Nala. h, Simba trying on mane. i, Simba, Nala, Zazu.
No. 1268: a, Scar plots evil plan. b, Mufasa rescues Simba. c, Destroying Mufasa. d, Simba escaping hyenas. e, Timon, Pumbaa, Simba. f, Simba, Timon, Pumbaa sing Hakuna Matata. g, Rafiki. h, Simba, Nala. i, Simba seeing reflection.
No. 1269, 2500sh, Simba, Timon. No. 1270, 2500sh, Characters of the Lion King, vert. No. 1271, 2500sh, Simba's colorful animal kingdon.
No. 1271A, Mufasa, Simba. No. 1271B, Mufasa, Simba on back, standing on rock.
Illustration A169a reduced.

Perf. 14x13½, 13½x14

1994, Sept. 30
1266	A169	100sh Sheet of 9, #a.-i.	2.75	2.75
1267	A169	200sh Sheet of 9, #a.-i.	5.75	5.75
1268	A169	250sh Sheet of 9, #a.-i.	7.50	7.50
		Nos. 1266-1268 (3)	16.00	16.00

Souvenir Sheets
1269-1271	A169	Set of 3	24.00	24.00

Litho. & Embossed
Perf. 11½
1271A	A169a	5000sh gold	
1271B	A169a	5000sh gold	

Sierra Club,
Cent. — A170

No. 1272, horiz.: a, 200sh, Cheetahs. b, 250sh, Cheetah kittens. c, 300sh, African wild dog. d, 500sh, African wild dog. e, 600sh, Grevy's zebra. f, 800sh, Chimpanzee. g, 1000sh, Grevy's zebra.
No. 1273: a, 100sh, Chimpanzee. b, 200sh, Chimpanzee. c, 250sh, African wild dog. d, 300sh, Cheetah. e-f, 500sh, 600sh, Gelada baboon. g, 800sh, Grevy's zebra. h, 1000sh, Gelada baboon.

1994, Nov. 9
1272	A170	Sheet of 7, #a.-g. + label	8.50	8.50
1273	A170	Sheet of 8, #a.-h.	8.75	8.75

ICAO,
50th
Anniv.
A171

Designs: 100sh, Entebbe Intl. Airport terminal building. 250sh, Entebbe control tower.

1994, Nov. 14   Litho.   Perf. 14
1274	A171	100sh multicolored	.90	.90
1275	A171	250sh multicolored	1.60	1.60

Environmental
Protection — A172

Designs: 100sh, Stop poaching. 250sh, Waste disposals. 350sh, Overfishing is a threat. 500sh, Deforestation.

1994, Nov. 15
1276-1279	A172	Set of 4	4.00	4.00

Christmas
A173

Paintings: 100sh, Adoration of the Christ Child, by Fillipino Lippi. 200sh, The Holy Family Rests on the Flight into Egypt, by Annibale Carracci. 300sh, Madonna with Christ Child ant St. John, by Piero di Cosimo. 350sh, The Conestabile Madonna, by Raphael. 450sh, Madonna and Child with Angels, after Antonio Rossellino. 500sh, Madonna and Child with St. John, by Raphael. 900sh, Madonna and Child, by Luca Signorelli. 1000sh, Madonna with the Child Jesus, St. John and an Angel, in style of Pier Francesco Fiorentino.
No. 1288, 2500sh, The Madonna of the Magnificat, by Sandro Botticelli. No. 1289, 2500sh, Adoration of the Magi, by Fra Angelico & Filippo Lippi.

1994, Dec. 5   Litho.   Perf. 13½x14
1280-1287	A173	Set of 8	10.00	10.00

Souvenir Sheets
1288-1289	A173	Set of 2	11.00	11.00

Tintoretto
(1518-94)
A174

Details or entire paintings: 100sh, Self-portrait. 300sh, A Philosopher. 400sh, The Creation of the Animals, horiz. 450sh, The Feast of Belshazzar, horiz. 500sh, The Raising of the Brazen Serpent. 1000sh, Elijah Fed by the Angel.
No. 1296, 2000sh, Finding of Moses. No. 1297, 2000sh, Moses Striking Water from a Rock.

1995, Feb. 7   Litho.   Perf. 13½
1290-1295	A174	Set of 6	7.00	7.00

Souvenir Sheets
1296-1297	A174	Set of 2	10.50	10.50

Birds
A175

No. 1298: a, White-faced tree duck. b, European shoveler. c, Hartlaub's duck. d, Milky eagle-owl. e, Avocet. f, African fish eagle. g, Spectacled weaver. h, Black-headed gonolek. i, Great crested grebe. j, Red-knobbed coot. k,

Woodland kingfisher. l, Pintail. m, Squacco heron. n, Purple gallinule. o, African darter. p, African jacana.
No. 1299, 2500sh, Fulvous tree duck. No. 1300, 2500sh, Pygmy goose.

1995, Apr. 24   Litho.   Perf. 14
1298	A175	200sh Sheet of 16, #a.-p.	14.00	14.00

Souvenir Sheets
1299-1300	A175	Set of 2	11.00	11.00

Nos. 685-688, 906 Surcharged

1995, June 1   Litho.   Perf. 14
1301	A90	100sh on #688 multi	.25	.25
1302	A90	450sh on 70sh #686	1.25	1.25
1303	A90	800sh on 90sh #687	2.00	2.00
1304	A90	1500sh on 10sh #685	3.75	3.75
		Nos. 1301-1304 (4)	7.25	7.25

Souvenir Sheet
1305	A113	2500sh on 1200sh multi	6.00	6.00

UN, 50th
Anniv. — A176

Designs: 1000sh, Hands releasing butterflies, dragonfly, dove.
No. 1308, Infant's hand holding adult's finger.

1995, July 6   Litho.   Perf. 14
1306	A176	450sh shown	1.00	1.00
1307	A176	1000sh multicolored	2.25	2.25

Souvenir Sheet
1308	A176	2000sh multicolored	4.00	4.00

FAO, 50th Anniv. — A177

No. 1309 — Corn huskers: a, 350sh, Young woman. b, 500sh, Old woman, girl. c, 1000sh, Woman with baby on back.
2000sh, Boy beside bore well for livestock, irrigation.

1995, July 6
1309	A177	Strip of 3, #a.-c.	3.00	3.00

Souvenir Sheet
1310	A177	2000sh multicolored	4.00	4.00

A178

End of
World
War II,
50th
Anniv.
A179

No. 1311: a, Russian 152mm gun fires into center of Berlin. b, Soviets capture Moltke Bridge. c, Emperor William Memorial Church.

now war memorial. d, Brandenburg Gate falls to Russian tanks. e, US B-17's continue to devastate industrial Germany. f, Soviet tanks enter Berlin. g, Hitler's chancellery lies in ruins. h, Reichstag burns.

Flags of countries each forming "VJ:" No. 1312a, Australia. b, Great Britain. c, New Zealand. d, US. e, China. f, Canada.

No. 1313, Waving Soviet flag from atop building in Berlin. No. 1314, US flag, combat soldier.

1995, July 6

1311 A178 500sh Sheet of 8, #a.-h. + label 11.00 11.00
1312 A179 600sh Sheet of 6, #a.-f. + label 8.75 8.75

Souvenir Sheets

1313 A178 2500sh multi 7.00 7.00
1314 A179 2500sh multi 7.50 7.50

No. 1313 contains one 56x42mm stamp.

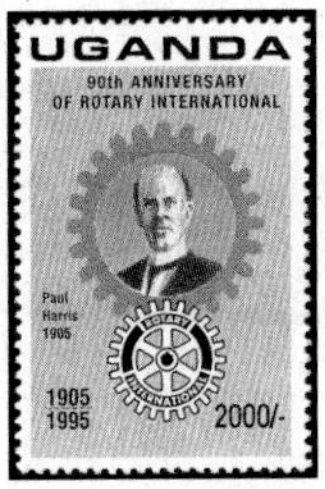

Rotary Intl., 90th Anniv. — A180

Rotary emblem and: No. 1315, Paul Harris. No. 1316, Natl. flag.

1995, July 6 Litho. *Perf. 14*

1315 A180 2000sh multicolored 4.00 4.00

Souvenir Sheet

1316 A180 2000sh multicolored 4.00 4.00

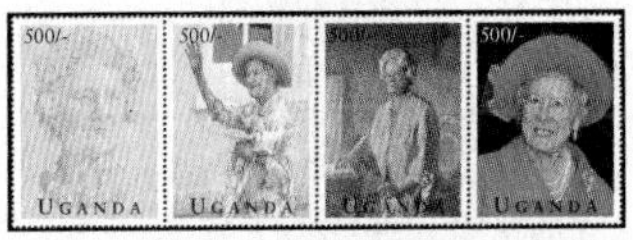

Queen Mother, 95th Anniv. — A181

No. 1317: a, Drawing. b, Waving. c, Formal portrait. d, Green blue outfit.
2500sh, Pale blue outfit.

1995, July 6 *Perf. 13½x14*

1317 A181 500sh Block or strip of 4, #a.-d. 7.50 7.50

Souvenir Sheet

1318 A181 2500sh multicolored 7.25 7.25

No. 1317 was issued in sheets of 8 stamps.
Sheets of Nos. 1317-1318 exist with with black border and text "In Memoriam/1900-2002" in sheet margins.

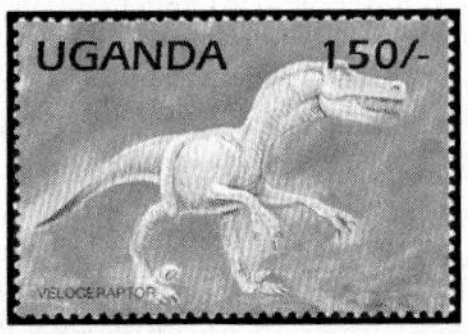

Dinosaurs A182

Designs: 150sh, Velociraptor. 200sh, Psittacosaurus. 350sh, Dilophosaurus. 400sh, Kentrosaurus. 500sh, Stegosaurus. 1500sh, Pterodaustro.

No. 1325, vert: a, Archaeopteryx. b, Quetzalcoatlus. c, Pteranodon (b, d). d, Brachiosa (g, h). e, Tsintaosaur. f, Allosaur (g-h). g, Tyranosaur (f, i-k). h, Apatosaur (l). i, Giant dragonfly. j, Dimorphodon. k, Triceratops (l). l, Compsognathus.

No. 1326, 2000sh, Parasaurolophus. No. 1327, 2000sh, Shunosaurus.

1995, July 15 *Perf. 14*

1319-1324 A182 Set of 6 9.00 9.00
1325 A182 300sh Sheet of 12, #a.-l. 11.00 11.00

Souvenir Sheets

1326-1327 A182 Set of 2 9.50 9.50

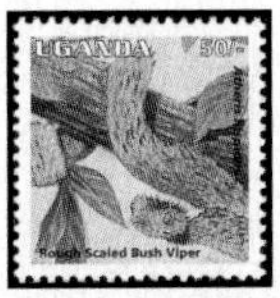

Reptiles — A183

50sh, Rough scaled bush viper. 100sh, Pygmy python. 150sh, Three horned chameleon. 200sh, African rock python. 350sh, Nile monitor. 400sh, Savannah monitor. 450sh, Bush viper. 500sh, Nile crocodile. 700sh, Bell's hinged tortoise. 900sh, Rhinoceros viper. 1000sh, Gaboon viper. 2000sh, Spitting cobra. 3000sh, Leopard tortoise. 4000sh, Puff adder. 5000sh, Common house gecko. 6000sh, Dwarf chameleon. 10,000sh, Boomslang.

1995 Litho. *Perf. 14x15*

1328	50sh	multicolored	.25	.25
1329	100sh	multicolored	.25	.25
1330	150sh	multicolored	.30	.30
1331	200sh	multicolored	.40	.40
1332	350sh	multicolored	.70	.70
1333	400sh	multicolored	.85	.85
1334	450sh	multicolored	.95	.95
1335	500sh	multicolored	1.00	1.00

Size: 38x24mm

Perf. 14

1336	700sh	multicolored	1.40	1.40
1337	900sh	multicolored	1.90	1.90
1338	1000sh	multicolored	2.00	2.00
1339	2000sh	multicolored	4.00	4.00
1340	3000sh	multicolored	6.25	6.25
1341	4000sh	multicolored	8.25	8.25
1341A	5000sh	multicolored	10.00	10.00
1341B	6000sh	multicolored	12.00	12.00
1341C	10,000sh	multicolored	20.00	20.00
	Nos. 1328-1341C (17)		70.50	70.50

Issued: 5000sh, 6000sh, 10,000sh, 11/20; others, 8/21.
Compare with Nos. 1550-1552.

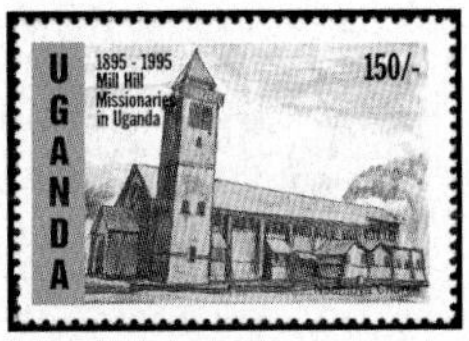

Nsambya Church A184

Designs: 450sh, Namilyango College. 500sh, Intl. Cooperative Alliance, cent. 1000sh, UN Volunteers, 25th anniv.

1995, Sept. 7 Litho. *Perf. 14*

1342-1345 A184 Set of 4 4.00 4.00

Mill Hill Missionaries in Uganda, cent. (#1342-1343).

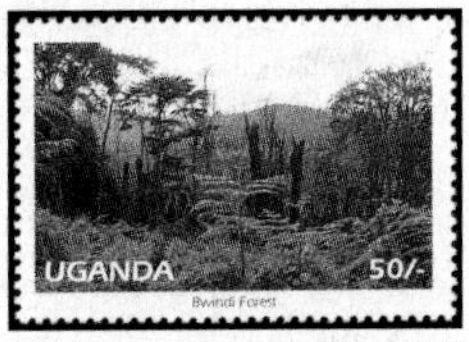

Scenic Landscapes & Waterfalls of Uganda — A185

Designs: No. 1346, 50sh, Bwindi Forest. No. 1347, 50sh, Sipi Falls, vert. No. 1348, 100sh, Karamoja. No. 1349, 100sh, Murchison Falls. No. 1350, 450sh, Sunset, Lake Mburo Natl. Park. No. 1351, 450sh, Bujagali Falls. No. 1352, 500sh, Sunset, Gulu District. No. 1353, 500sh, Two Falls, Murchison. No. 1354, 900sh, Kabale District. No. 1355, 900sh, Falls, Rwenzoris, vert. No. 1356, 1000sh, Rwenzori Mountains. No. 1357, 1000sh, Falls, Rwenzoris, diff., vert.

1995, Sept. 14

1346-1357 A185 Set of 12 12.50 12.50

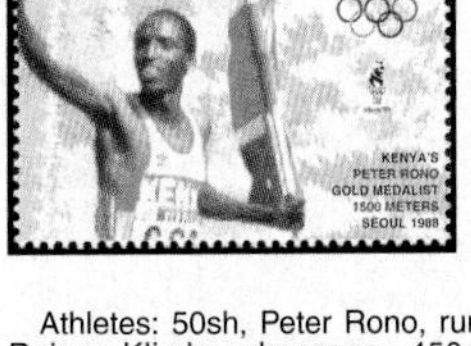

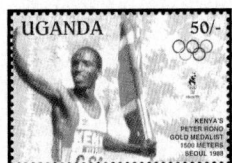

1996 Summer Olympics, Atlanta A186

Athletes: 50sh, Peter Rono, runner. 350sh, Reiner Klimke, dressage. 450sh, German cycling team. 500sh, Grace Birungi, runner. 900sh, Francis Ogola, track. 1000sh, Nyakana Godfrey, welter-weight boxer.

No. 1364, 2500sh, Rolf Dannenberg, discus, vert. No. 1365, 2500sh, Sebastian Coe, runner.

1995, Sept. 21

1358-1363 A186 Set of 6 7.25 7.25

Souvenir Sheets

1364-1365 A186 Set of 2 9.50 9.50

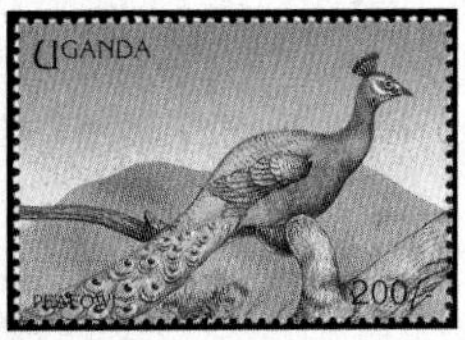

Domestic Animals A187

No. 1366: a, Peafowl (e). b, Pouter pigeon. c, Rock dove. d, Rouen duck. e, Guinea fowl. f, Donkey. g, Shetland pony. h, Palomino. i, Pigs. j, Border collie. k, Merino sheep. l. Milch goat. m, Black dutch rabbit. n, Lop rabbit. o, Somali cat (p). p, Asian cat.

No. 1367, 2500sh, Saddle bred horses. No. 1368, 2500sh, Oxen.

1995, Oct. 2

1366 A187 200sh Sheet of 16, #a.-p. 12.50 12.50

Souvenir Sheets

1367-1368 A187 Set of 2 12.00 12.00

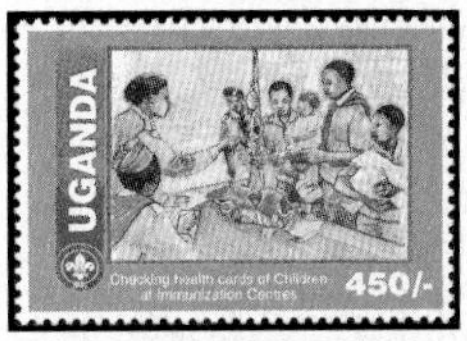

Boy Scouts at Immunization Centers — A188

Designs: 150sh, Dressing children for weighing, vert. 350sh, Helping mothers carry children, vert. 450sh, Checking health cards. 800sh, Assisting in immunization. 1000sh, Weighing children, vert.

1995, Oct. 18 Litho. *Perf. 14*

1369-1373 A188 Set of 5 6.00 6.00

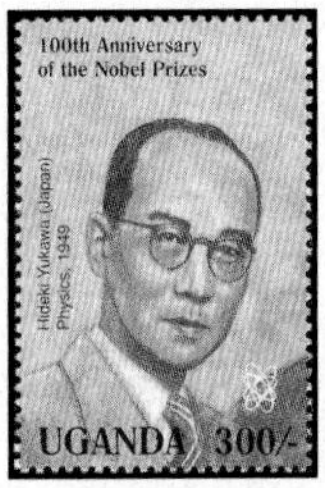

Establishment of Nobel Prize Fund, Cent. — A189

No. 1374, 300sh: a, Hideki Yukawa, physics, 1949. b, F.W. DeKlerk, peace, 1993. c, Nelson Mandela, peace, 1993. d, Odysseus Elytis, literature, 1979. e, Ferdinand Buisson, peace, 1927. f, Lev Landau, physics, 1962. g, Halldor Laxness, literature, 1955. h, Wole Soyinka, literature, 1986. i, Desmond Tutu, peace, 1984. j, Susumu Tonegawa, physiology or medicine, 1987. k, Louis de Broglie, physics, 1929. l, George Seferis, literature, 1963.

No. 1375, 300sh: a, Hermann Staudinger, chemistry, 1953. b, Fritz Haber, chemistry, 1918. c, Bert Sakmann, physiology or medicine, 1991. d, Adolf O.R. Windaus, chemistry, 1928. e, Wilhelm Wien, physics, 1911. f, Ernest Hemingway, literature, 1954. g, Richard M. Willstätter, chemistry, 1915. h, Stanley Cohen, physiology or medicine, 1986. i, J. Hans D. Jensen, physics, 1963. j, Otto H. Warburg, physiology or medicine, 1931. k, Heinrich O. Wieland, chemistry, 1927. l, Albrecht Kossel, physiology or medicine, 1910.

No. 1376, 2000sh, Werner Forssmann, physiology or medicine, 1956. No. 1377, 2000sh, Nelly Sachs, literature, 1966.

1995, Oct. 31 Sheets of 12, #a-l

1374-1375 A189 Set of 2 20.00 20.00

Souvenir Sheets

1376-1377 A189 Set of 2 10.50 10.50

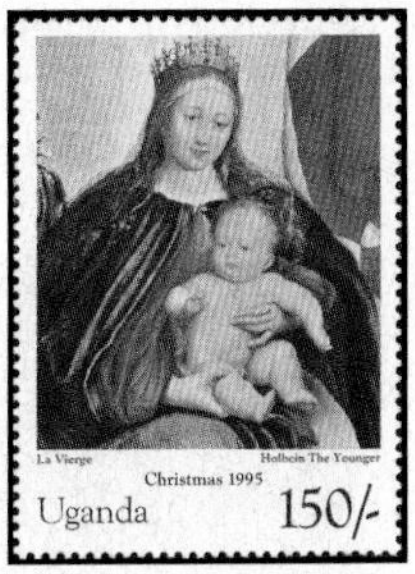

Christmas A190

Details or entire paintings of the Madonna and Child, by: 150sh, Hans Holbein the Younger. 350sh, Procaccini. 500sh, Pisanello. 1000sh, Crivelli. 1500sh, Le Nain.

No. 1383, 2500sh, The Holy Family, by Andrea Del Sarto. No. 1384, 2500sh, Madonna and Child, by Bellini.

1995, Nov. 30 Litho. *Perf. 13½x14*

1378-1382 A190 Set of 5 7.50 7.50

Souvenir Sheets

1383-1384 A190 Set of 2 11.00 11.00

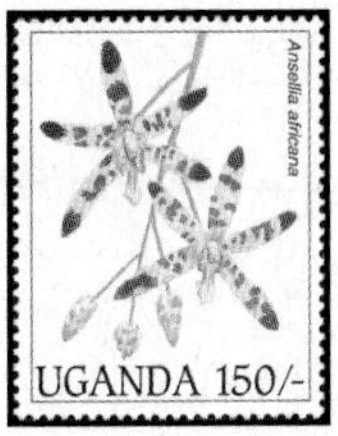

Orchids — A191

Designs: 150sh, Ansellia africana. 450sh, Satyricum crassicaule. 500sh, Polystachya cultriformis. 800sh, Disa erubescens.

No. 1389: a, Aerangis iuteoalba. b, Satyrium sacculatum. c, Bolusiella maudiae. d, Habenaria attenuata. e, Cyrtorchis arcuata. f, Eulophia angolensis. g, Tridactyle bicaudata. h, Eulophia horsfallii. i, Diaphananthe fragrantissima.

No. 1390, 2500sh, Diaphananthe pulchella. No. 1391, 2500sh, Rangaeris amaniensis.

1995, Dec. 8 *Perf. 14*

1385-1388 A191 Set of 4 6.00 6.00

Miniature Sheet

1389 A191 350sh Sheet of 9, #a.-i. 14.00 14.00

Souvenir Sheets

1390-1391 A191 Set of 2 12.00 12.00

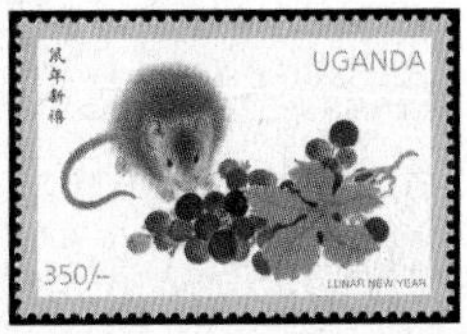

New Year 1996 (Year of the Rat) A192

Rat eating: a, Purple grapes. b, Radishes. c, Corn. d, Squash.
2000sh, Green grapes.

1996, Jan. 29 Litho. *Perf. 14*

1392 A192 350sh Block of 4, #a.-d. 2.50 2.50
e. Miniature sheet, No. 1392 2.50 2.50

Souvenir Sheet

1393 A192 2000sh multicolored 3.00 3.00

No. 1392 issued in sheets of 16 stamps.

Miniature Sheet

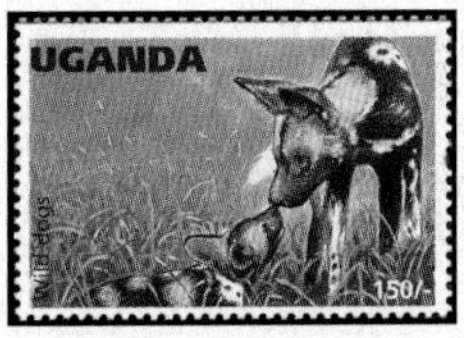

Wildlife A193

No. 1394: a, 150sh, Wild dogs. b, 200sh, Fish eagle. c, 250sh, Hippopotamus. d, 350sh, Leopard. e, 400sh, Lion. f, 450sh, Lioness. g, 500sh, Meerkat. h, 550sh, Black rhinoceros.

No. 1395: a, 150sh, Gorilla. b, 200sh, Cheetah. c, 250sh, Elephant. d, 350sh, Thomson's gazelle. e, 400sh, Crowned crane. f, 450sh, Sattlebill. g, 500sh, Vulture. h, 550sh, Zebra.

No. 1396, 2000sh, Giraffe, vert. No. 1397, 2000sh, Gray heron.

1996, Mar. 27   Litho.   Perf. 14
1394 A193 Sheet of 8, #a.-h.   6.25 6.25
1395 A193 Sheet of 8, #a.-h.   6.75 6.75
Souvenir Sheets
1396-1397 A193 Set of 2   9.00 9.00

Disney Characters on the Orient Express — A194

Designs: 50sh, From London to Constantinople via Calais. 100sh, From Paris to Athens. 150sh, Ticket for the Pullman. 200sh, Pullman Corridor. 250sh, Dining car. 300sh, Staff beyond reproach. 600sh, Fun in the Pullman. 700sh, 1901 Unstoppable train enters the buffet in Frankfurt station. 800sh, 1929 passage detained five days by snowstorm. 900sh, Filming "Murder on the Orient Express."
No. 1408, 2500sh, Donald Duck in engine. No. 1409, 2500sh, Mickey, Goofy, Minnie waving from back of train.

1996, Apr. 15   Perf. 14x13½
1398-1407 A194 Set of 10   12.50 12.50
Souvenir Sheets
1408-1409 A194 Set of 2   13.00 13.00

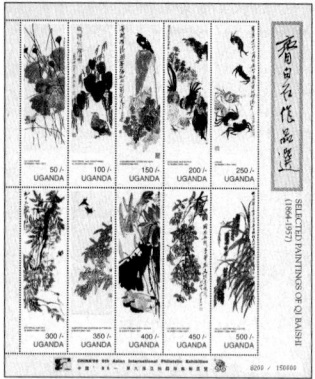

Paintings by Qi Baishi (1864-1957) — A195

No. 1410: a, 50sh, Autumn Pond. b, 100sh, Partridge and Smartweed. c, 150sh, Begonias and Mynah. d, 200sh, Chrysanthemums, Cocks and Hens. e, 250sh, Crabs. f, 300sh, Wisterias and Bee. g, 350sh, Smartweed and Ink-drawn Butterflies. h, 400sh, Lotus and Mandarin Ducks. i, 450sh, Lichees and Locust. j, 500sh, Millet and Preying Mantis.
No. 1411: a, Locust, flowers. b, Crustaceans.

1996, May 8   Litho.   Perf. 15x14
1410 A195 Sheet of 10, #a.-j.   8.00 8.00
Souvenir Sheet
Perf. 14
1411 A195 800sh Sheet of 2, #a.-b.   7.50 7.50

No. 1411 contains two 48x34mm stamps. The captions on Nos. 1410c and 1410d are transposed.
CHINA '96, 9th Asian Intl. Philatelic Exhibition.
See Nos. 1475-1476.

Queen Elizabeth II, 70th Birthday — A196

No. 1412: a, Portrait. b, As young woman, wearing crown jewels. c, Wearing red hat, coat.
2000sh, Portrait, diff.

1996, July 10   Perf. 13½x14
1412 A196 500sh Strip of 3, #a.-c.   4.00 4.00
Souvenir Sheet
1413 A196 2000sh multicolored   4.00 4.00
No. 1412 was issued in sheets of 9 stamps.

Jerusalem, 3000th Anniv. — A197

No. 1414: a, 300sh, Knesset Menorah. b, 500sh, Jerusalem Theater. c, 1000sh, Israel Museum.
2000sh, Grotto of the Nativity.

1996, July 10   Perf. 14
1414 A197 Sheet of 3, #a.-c.   4.75 4.75
Souvenir Sheet
1415 A197 2000sh multicolored   4.75 4.75
For overprint see Nos. 1556-1557.

Radio, Cent. A198

Entertainers: 200sh, Ella Fitzgerald. 300sh, Bob Hope. 500sh, Nat "King" Cole. 800sh, Burns & Allen.
2000sh, Jimmy Durante.

1996, July 10   Perf. 13½x14
1416-1419 A198 Set of 4   3.75 3.75
Souvenir Sheet
1420 A198 2000sh multicolored   4.00 4.00

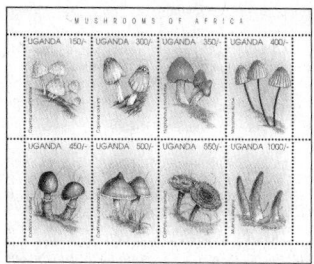

Mushrooms — A199

No. 1421: a, 150sh, Coprinus disseminatus. b, 300sh, Caprinus radians. c, 350sh, Hygrophorus coccineus. d, 400sh, Marasmius siccus. e, 450sh, Cortinarius collinitus. f, 500sh, Cortinarius cinnabarinus. g, 550sh, Coltricia cinnamomea. h, 1000sh, Mutinus elegans.
No. 1422, 2500sh, Inocybe soroia. No. 1423, 2500sh, Flammulina velutipes.

1996, June 24   Perf. 14
1421 A199 Sheet of 8, #a.-h.   6.50 6.50
Souvenir Sheets
1422-1423 A199 Set of 2   9.00 9.00

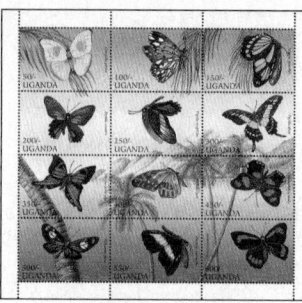

Butterflies — A200

No. 1424: a, 50sh, Catopsilia philea. b, 100sh, Dione vanillae. c, 150sh, Metemorpha dido. d, 200sh, Papilio sesostris. e, 250sh, Papilio neophilus. f, 300sh, Papilio thoas. g, 350sh, Diorina periander. h, 400sh, Morpho cipris. i, 450sh, Catonephele numilia. j, 500sh, Heliconius doris. k, 550sh, Prepona antimache. l, 600sh, Eunica alcmena.
No. 1425, 2500sh, Caligo martia. No. 1426, 2500sh, Heliconius doris.

1996, June 26
1424 A200 Sheet of 12, #a.-l.   9.00 9.00
Souvenir Sheets
1425-1426 A200 Set of 2   10.00 10.00

UNICEF, 50th Anniv. A201

Designs: 450sh, Two children. 500sh, Two children wearing hats. 550sh, Boy in classroom.
2000sh, Mother and child, vert.

1996, July 10   Litho.   Perf. 14
1427-1429 A201 Set of 3   4.00 4.00
Souvenir Sheet
1430 A201 2000sh multicolored   4.00 4.00

UNESCO, 50th Anniv. — A202

Natl. Parks: 450sh, Darien, Panama. 500sh, Los Glaciares, Argentina. 550sh, Tubbatha Reef Marine Park, Philippines.
2500sh, Rwenzori Mountains, Uganda.

1996, July 10
1431-1433 A202 Set of 3   4.75 4.75
Souvenir Sheet
1434 A202 2500sh multicolored   6.25 6.25

Trains — A203

No. 1435: a, Loco Type B.B.B., Japan, 1968. b, Stephenson's "Rocket," 1829. c, "Austria," 1843. d, 19th cent. type. e, Loco Anglo-Indian, India, 1947. f, Type CoCo DB, Germany.
No. 1436: a, "Lady of Lynn," Great Western, England. b, Chinese type, 1930. c, Meyer-Ritson, Chile. d, Union Pacific "Centennial," US. e, "581" Japanese Natl. Railway, Japan, 1968. f, Co.Co. Series "120" DB, Germany.
No. 1437, 2500sh, Mallard, Great Britain. No. 1438, 2500sh, "99" Type 1-5-0, Germany.

1996, July 25
1435 A203 450sh Sheet of 6, #a.-f.   5.50 5.50
1436 A203 550sh Sheet of 6, #a.-f.   6.50 6.50
Souvenir Sheets
1437-1438 A203 Set of 2   10.00 10.00

Uganda Post Office, Cent. A204

Designs: 150sh, Emblem. 450sh, Post bus service. 500sh, Modern mail transportation means. 550sh, "100," #48, #59.

1996, Aug. 30   Litho.   Perf. 14
1439-1442 A204 Set of 4   6.00 6.00

Fruits A205

Designs: 150sh, Mango, vert. 350sh, Orange, vert. 450sh, Paw paw, vert. 500sh, Avocado, vert. 550sh, Watermelon.

1996, Oct. 8   Litho.   Perf. 14
1443-1447 A205 Set of 5   6.00 6.00

Christmas A206

Details or entire paintings: 150sh, Annunciation, by Lorenzo Di Credi. 350sh, Madonna of the Loggia (detail), by Botticelli. 400sh, Virgin in Glory with Child and Angels, by Lorenzetti P. 450sh, Adoration of the Child, by Filippino Lippi. 500sh, Madonna of the Loggia, by Botticelli. 550sh, The Strength, by Bottticelli.
No. 1454, 2500sh, Holy Allegory, by Giovanni Bellini, horiz. No. 1455, 2500sh, The Virgin on the Throne with Child and Saints, by Ghirlandaio, horiz.

1996, Nov. 18   Perf. 13½x14
1448-1453 A206 Set of 6   5.75 5.75
Souvenir Sheets
Perf. 14x13½
1454-1455 A206 Set of 2   10.00 10.00

Sylvester Stallone in Movie, "Rocky III" — A207

1996, Nov. 21   Litho.   Perf. 14
1456 A207 800sh Sheet of 3   5.50 5.50

1996 Summer Olympic Games, Atlanta A208

Scenes from first Olympic Games in US, St. Louis, 1904: 350sh, Steamboat race, stadium. 450sh, Boxer George Finnegan. 500sh, Quadriga race (ancient games). 800sh, John Flanagan, hammer throw, vert.

1996, Dec. 8
1457-1460 A208 Set of 4   4.75 4.75

Traditional Attire — A209

Designs: 150sh, Western region, vert. 350sh, Karimo Jong women, vert. 450sh, Ganda. 500sh, Acholi.

No. 1465. — Headdresses: a, Acholi. b, Alur. c, Bwola dance. d, Madi. e, Karimojong. f, Karimojong with feathers.

1997, Jan. 2
1461-1464 A209 Set of 4   4.00 4.00
1465 A209 300sh Sheet of 6,   5.00 5.00
     #a.-f.

New Year 1997 (Year of the Ox) A210

Paintings of oxen: Nos. 1466a, 1467b, Walking left. Nos. 1466b, 1467b, Calf nursing. Nos. 1466c, 1467d, Calf lying down, adult. Nos. 1466d, 1467c, Adult lying down. 1500sh, Calf, vert.

1997, Jan. 24   Litho.   Perf. 14
1466 A210 350sh Strip of 4,   4.25 4.25
     #a.-d.
1467 A210 350sh Sheet of 4,   4.25 4.25
     #a.-d.
Souvenir Sheet
1468 A210 1500sh multicolored   4.25 4.25
No. 1466 was issued in sheets of 4 vert. strips.

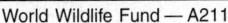

World Wildlife Fund — A211

No. 1469 — Rothschild's giraffe: a, Running. b, One bending neck across another's back. c, Head up close. d, Young giraffe, adult facing opposite directions.
2500sh, like #1469d, horiz.

1997, Feb. 12
1469 A211 300sh Strip of 4,   4.00 4.00
     #a.-d.
Souvenir Sheet
1470 A211 2500sh multicolored   6.50 6.50
No. 1469 was issued in sheets of 4 strips with each strip in a different order.

No. 1470 does not have the WWF emblem.

Souvenir Sheet

Mural from an Ancient Tomb in Xian — A212

1996, May 8   Litho.   Perf. 14
1471 A212 500sh multicolored   3.00 3.00
China '96. No. 1471 was not available until March 1997.

Promulgation of the Constitution, Oct. 8, 1995 — A213

Designs: 150sh, shown. 350sh, Scroll. 550sh, Closed book, vert.

1997, Feb. 25   Perf. 14x13½
1472-1474 A213 Set of 3   3.25 3.25

Paintings Type of 1996

No. 1475 — Paintings by Wu Changshuo (1844-1927): a, 50sh, Red Plum Blossom and Daffodil. b, 100sh, Peony. c, 150sh, Rosaceae. d, 200sh, Pomegranate. e, 250sh, Peach, Peony, and Plum Blossom. f, 300sh, Calyx canthus. g, 350sh, Chrysanthemum. h, 400sh, Calabash. i, 450sh, Chrysanthemum, diff. j, 500sh, Cypress tree.
No. 1476: a, 550sh, Litchi. b, 1000sh, Water lily.

1997, Mar. 5   Perf. 14x15
1475 A195 Sheet of 10, #a.-j.   6.50 6.50
Souvenir Sheet
Perf. 14
1476 A195 Sheet of 2, #a.-b.   3.50 3.50
Hong Kong '97. No. 1476 contains two 51x38mm stamps.

Summer Olympic Winners — A214

No. 1477: a, 150sh, Sohn Kee-chung, marathon, 1936. b, 200sh, Walter Davis, high jump, 1952. c, 250sh, Roland Matthes, swimming, 1968. d, 300sh, Akii Bua, 400m hurdles, 1972. e, 350sh, Wolfgang Nordwig, pole vault, 1972. f, 400sh, Wilma Rudolph, 4x100m relay, 1960. g, 450sh, Abebe Bikila, marathon, 1964. h, 500sh, Edwin Moses, 400m hurdles, 1984. i, 550sh, Randy Williams, long jump, 1972.
No. 1478: a, 150sh, Bob Hayes, 100m, 1964. b, 200sh, Rod Milburn, 110m hurdles, 1972. c, 250sh, Filbert Bayi, running, 1976. d, 300sh, H. Kipchoge Keino, steeple chase, 1972. e, 350sh, Ron Ray, running, 1976. f, 400sh, Joe Frazier, boxing, 1976. g, 450sh, Carl Lewis, 100m race, 1984. h, 500sh, Gisela Mauermayer, discus, 1936. i, 550sh, Dietmar Mogenburg, high jump, 1984.

1997, Mar. 3   Litho.   Perf. 14
Sheets of 9, #a-i
1477-1478 A214 Set of 2   15.00 15.00
No. 1478h is inscribed shot put in error.

Disney's "Toy Story" — A215

No. 1479, vert.: a, Woody. b, Buzz Lightyear. c, Bo Peep. d, Hamm. e, Slinky. f, Rex.
No. 1480: a, Woody on Andy's bed. b, "Get this wagon train a-movin." c, Bo Peep, blocks. d, Buzz Lightyear. e, Slinky, Rex. f, Woody hides. g, Buzz, Woody. h, Rex, Slinky, Buzz. i, Buzz, Woody on bed.
No. 1481: a, Woody telling Buzz he's sheriff. b, Green Army on alert. c, Woody, Buzz compete. d, Woody sights alien. e, Buzz ponders fate. f, "The Cla-a-a-a-a-w." g, Intergalactic emergency. h, Buzz, Woody argue at gas station. i, Buzz, Woody give chase.
No. 1482, 2000sh, Woody spots an intruder, vert. No. 1483, 2000sh, Andy's toys, vert. No. 1484, 2000sh, Buzz Lightyear in space, vert.

1997, Apr. 2   Perf. 14x13½, 13½x14
1479 A215 100sh Sheet of 6,   2.75 2.75
     #a.-f.
1480 A215 150sh Sheet of 9,   6.00 6.00
     #a.-i.
1481 A215 200sh Sheet of 9,   7.25 7.25
     #a.-i.
Souvenir Sheets
1482-1484 A215 Set of 3   21.00 21.00

Man in Space A216

No. 1484A: b, Pioneer 10. c, Voyager 1. d, Viking Orbiter. e, Pioneer, Venus 1. f, Mariner 9. g, Galileo Entry Probe. h, Mariner 10. i, Voyager 2.
No. 1485: a, Sputnik 1. b, Apollo. c, Soyuz. d, Intelsat 1. e, Manned maneuvering unit. f, Skylab. g, Telstar 1. h, Hubble telescope.
No. 1486, Space shuttle Challenger. No. 1486A, Mars Viking Lander Robot.

1997, Apr. 16   Litho.   Perf. 14
1484A A216 250sh Sheet of 8,   5.00 5.00
     #b.-i.
1485 A216 300sh Sheet of 8,   5.50 5.50
     #a.-h.
Souvenir Sheet
1486 A216 2000sh multicolored 4.75 4.75
1486A A216 2000sh multicolored 5.00 5.00
No. 1486 contains one 34x61mm stamp, No. 1486A one 61x35mm stamp.

Deng Xiaoping (1904-97), Chinese Leader — A217

Designs: a, 500sh. b, 550sh. c, 1000sh. 2000sh, Portrait, diff.

1997, May 9
1487 A217 Sheet of 3, #a.-c.   5.50 5.50
Souvenir Sheet
1488 A217 2000sh multicolored   4.75 4.75

Environmental Protection — A218

No. 1489: a-d, Various water hyacinths.
No. 1490: a, Buffalo. b, Uganda kob. c, Guinea fowl. d, Malibu stork.
2500sh, Gorilla.

1997, May 14
1489 A218 500sh Sheet of 4,   3.75 3.75
     #a.-d.
1490 A218 550sh Sheet of 4,   4.25 4.25
     #a.-d.
Souvenir Sheet
1491 A218 2500sh multicolored   5.25 5.25

Queen Elizabeth II, Prince Philip, 50th Wedding Anniv. A219

No. 1492: a, Queen. b, Royal arms. c, Queen in purple outfit, Prince. d, Prince, Queen in white hat. e, Buckingham Palace. f, Prince Philip.
2000sh, Queen in wedding dress.

1997, June 2   Litho.   Perf. 14
1492 A219 200sh Sheet of 6,   7.00 7.00
     #a.-f.
Souvenir Sheet
1493 A219 2000sh multicolored   4.75 4.75

Paul E. Harris (1868-1947), Founder of Rotary, Intl. — A220

Designs: 1000sh, Combating hunger, Harris. 2500sh, First Rotarians, Gustavus H. Loehr, Sylvester Schiele, Hiram E. Shorey, Paul E. Harris.

1997, June 2
1494 A220 1000sh multicolored   3.00 3.00
Souvenir Sheet
1495 A220 2500sh multicolored   4.50 4.50

Heinrich von Stephan (1831-97) A221

No. 1496 — Portrait of Von Stephan and: a, Chinese post boat. b, UPU emblem. c, Russian special post.
2500sh, Von Stephan, French postman on stilts.

1997, June 2
1496 A221 800sh Sheet of 3,   4.50 4.50
     #a.-c.
Souvenir Sheet
1497 A221 2500sh multicolored   4.50 4.50
PACIFIC 97.

Chernobyl Disaster, 10th Anniv. A222

Designs: 500sh, UNESCO. 700sh, Chabad's Children of Chernobyl.

1997, May 21   Litho.   Perf. 14x13½
1498 A222 500sh multicolored   1.50 1.50
1499 A222 700sh multicolored   2.00 2.00

1998 Winter Olympic Games, Nagano A223

Designs: 350sh, Men's slalom, vert. 450sh, Two-man bobsled, vert. 800sh, Women's slalom. 2000sh, Men's speed skating.
No. 1504: a, Ski jumping. b, Giant slalom. c, Cross-country skiing. d, Ice hockey. e, Man, pairs figure skating. f, Woman, pairs figure skating.
No. 1505, 2500sh, Downhill skiing. No. 1506, 2500sh, Women's figure skating.

1997, June 23		**Litho.**		**Perf. 14**
1500-1503	A223	Set of 4	7.25	7.25
1504	A223	500sh Sheet of 6, #a.-f.	6.25	6.25

Souvenir Sheets

1505-1506	A223	Set of 2	9.00	9.00

Makerere University, 75th Anniv. — A224

Designs: 150sh, Main building, administration block. 450sh, East African School of Librarianship, vert. 500sh, Buyana stock farm. 550sh, Ceramic dish, School of Architectural and Fine Arts.

1997, July 31		**Perf. 14x13½, 13½x14**		
1507-1510	A224	Set of 4	3.50	3.50

Mahatma Gandhi (1869-1948) A225

Various portraits.

1997, Oct. 5		**Litho.**		**Perf. 14**
1511	A225	600sh multicolored	2.50	2.50
1512	A225	700sh multicolored	2.75	2.75

Souvenir Sheet

1513	A225	1000sh multicolored	4.50	4.50

1998 World Cup Soccer Championships, France — A226

No. 1514, vert: a, 200sh, Fritz Walter, Germany. b, 300sh, Daniel Passarella, Argentina. c, 450sh, Dino Zoff, Italy. d, 500sh, Bobby Moore, England. e, 600sh, Diego Maradona, Argentina. f, 550sh, Franz Beckenbauer, West Germany.
No. 1515 — Argentina vs. West Germany, Mexico City, 1986: a, d, e, f, h, Action scenes. b, Azteca Stadium. c, Argentine player holding World Cup. g, Argentina team picture.
No. 1516 — Top tournament scorers: a, Paulo Rossi. b, Mario Kempes. c, Gerd Muller. d, Grzegorz Lato. e, Ademir. f, Eusebio Ferreica da Silva. g, Salvatore (Toto) Schillaci. h, Leonidas da Silva. i, Gary Lineker.

No. 1517, 2000sh, England, 1966. No. 1518, 2000sh, W. Germany, 1990.

1997, Oct. 3		**Litho.**		**Perf. 14**
1514	A226	Sheet of 6, #a.-f.	5.50	5.50
1515	A226	250sh Sheet of 8, #a.-h.	5.00	5.00
1516	A226	250sh Sheet of 9, #a.-i. + label	5.00	5.00

Souvenir Sheets

1517-1518	A226	Set of 2	8.50	8.50

Diana, Princess of Wales (1961-97) A227

1997, Dec. 1

1519	A227	60sh multicolored	2.00	2.00

No. 1519 was issued in sheets of 6.

Christmas A228

Sculpture, entire paintings or details: 200sh, Putto and Dolphin, by Andrea del Verrocchio. 300sh, The Fall of the Rebel Angels, by Pieter Bruegel the Elder. 400sh, The Immaculate Conception, by Murillo. 500sh, Music-making Angel, by Rosso Fiorentino. 600sh, Cupid and Psyche, by Adolphe-William Bouguereau. 700sh, Cupid and Psyche, by Antonio Canova.
No. 1526, 2500sh, Virgin, Angels from The Assumption of the Virgin, by El Greco. No. 1527, 2500sh, Angel from The Assumption of the Virgin, by El Greco.

1997, Dec. 1				
1520-1525	A228	Set of 6	5.75	5.75

Souvenir Sheets

1526-1527	A228	Set of 2	8.50	8.50

New Year 1998 (Year of the Tiger) A229

Various paintings of tigers: No. 1528: a, Looking backward. b, Jumping. c, Lying, looking forward. d, Lying, mouth open.
1500sh, On cliff.

1998, Jan. 16		**Litho.**		**Perf. 13½**
1528	A229	350sh Sheet of 4, #a.-d.	3.25	3.25

Souvenir Sheet

1529	A229	1500sh multicolored	3.00	3.00

Tourist Attractions — A230

Designs: 300sh, Namugongo Martyrs Shrine, vert. 400sh, Kasubi Tombs. 500sh,

Tourist boat, Kazinga Channel. 600sh, Elephant. 700sh, Bujagali Falls, Jinja.

1998, Feb. 6		**Litho.**		**Perf. 14**
1530-1534	A230	Set of 5	6.25	6.25

Mother Teresa (1910-97) — A231

No. 1535: a-h, Various portraits. 2000sh, With Diana, Princess of Wales (1961-97).

1998, Feb. 9		**Litho.**		**Perf. 14**
1535	A231	300sh Sheet of 8, #a.-h.	7.00	7.00

Souvenir Sheet

1536	A231	2000sh multicolored	6.50	6.50

Nos. 1535a, 1535d-1535e, 1535h are each 22x36mm.

UNICEF in Uganda, 30th Anniv. A232

Designs: 300sh, "Support for children with disabilities." 400sh, "Safeguard children against polio." 600sh, "Sanitation... responsibility for all." 700sh, "Children's right to basic education."

1998, Mar. 6				**Perf. 13½x14**
1537-1540	A232	Set of 4	6.00	6.00

Dinosaurs — A233

Designs, horiz: 300sh, Pteranodon. 400sh, Diplodocus. 500sh, Lambeosaurus. 600sh, Centrosaurus. 700sh, Parasaurolophus.
No. 1546: a, Cetiosaurus. b, Brontosaurus. c, Brachiosaurus. d, Deinonychus. e, Dimetrodon. f, Megalosaurus.
No. 1547, 2500sh, Tyrannosaurus. No. 1548, 2500sh, Iguanodon.

1998, Mar. 24		**Litho.**		**Perf. 14**
1541-1545	A233	Set of 5	5.50	5.50
1546	A233	600sh Sheet of 6, #a.-f.	8.00	8.00

Souvenir Sheets

1547-1548	A233	Set of 2	12.00	12.00

Nos. 1547-1548 each contain one 43x57mm stamp.

Writers — A234

No. 1549: a, Rita Dove. b, Mari Evans. c, Sterling A. Brown. d, June Jordan. e, Stephen Henderson. f, Zora Neale Hurston.

1998, Apr. 6

1549	A234	300sh Sheet of 6, #a.-f.	4.25	4.25

Reptiles — A235

Designs: 300sh, Armadillo girdled lizard. 600sh, Spotted sandveld lizard. 700sh, Bell's ringed tortoise.

1998, Apr. 21				**Perf. 13½**
1550	A235	300sh multicolored	.75	.75
1551	A235	600sh multicolored	1.50	1.50
1552	A235	700sh multicolored	1.75	1.75
		Nos. 1550-1552 (3)	4.00	4.00

Compare with Nos. 1328-1335.

Mickey Mouse, 70th Birthday — A236

No. 1553 — Scenes from cartoon, "Runaway Brain:" a, Mickey afraid of shadow. b, Mickey petting Pluto, newspaper. c, Mickey playing computer game, Pluto. d, Mickey, Minnie running. e, Mickey as target of experiment. f, Minnie being held captive by Pete on top of skyscraper. g, Mickey throwing lasso. h, Mickey surrounding Pete with rope. i, Mickey, Minnie holding onto rope above skyscrapers.
No. 1554, 3000sh, Mickey, Minnie embracing on top of skyscraper. No. 1555, 3000sh, Mickey, Minnie kissing on raft, vert.

1998, May 4		**Litho.**		**Perf. 14x13½**
1553	A236	400sh Sheet of 9, #a.-i.	9.75	9.75

Souvenir Sheets

1554-1555	A236	Set of 2	13.50	13.50

Nos. 1414-1415 Ovptd.

1998, May 13		**Litho.**		**Perf. 14**
1556	A197	Sheet of 3, #a.-c. (#1414)	3.75	3.75

Souvenir Sheet

1557	A197	2000sh multi (#1415)	4.00	4.00

Sheet margins of Nos. 1556-1557 each contain additional overprint, "ISRAEL 98 — WORLD STAMP EXHIBITION/TEL-AVIV 13-21 MAY 1998."

Sailing Ships A237

No. 1558, 1000sh: a, Fishing schooner. b, Chesapeake oyster boat. c, Java Sea schooner.
No. 1559, 1000sh: a, Santa Maria, 15th cent. galleon. b, Mayflower, 15th cent. galleon. c, Bark.
No. 1560, 3000sh, Boat with lateen sails. No. 1561, 3000sh, Thames River barge, vert.

1998, June 2 Litho. Perf. 13x13½
Sheets of 3, #a-c + Label
1558-1559 A237 Set of 2 12.00 12.00
Souvenir Sheets
1560-1561 A237 Set of 2 12.00 12.00

Nos. 1560-1561 are continuous designs.

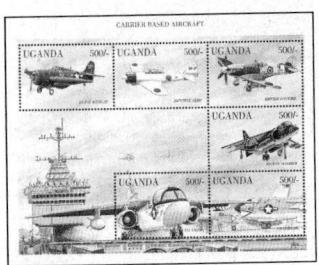

Aircraft — A238

No. 1562: a, US F4F Wildcat. b, Japanese Zero. c, British Spitfire. d, British Harrier. e, S3A Viking. f, US Corsair.
No. 1563: a, Dornier Do-X transatlantic flyer, 1929. b, German Zucker mail rocket, 1930. c, X-15 Rocket Plane, 1955. d, Goddard's Rocket, 1930's. e, Wright brothers' flight, 1903. f, 160R Sikorsky helicopter, 1939.
No. 1564, 2500sh, P40 Tomahawk. No. 1565, 2500sh, SH346 Seabat.

1998, July 24 Litho. Perf. 14
1562 A238 500sh Sheet of 6,
#a.-f. 7.00 7.00
1563 A238 600sh Sheet of 6,
#a.-f. 8.25 8.25
Souvenir Sheets
1564-1565 A238 Set of 2 11.00 11.00

Flowers of the Mediterranean — A239

No. 1566, vert: a, Onosma. b, Rhododendron luteum. c, Paeonia mascula. d, Geranium macorrhizum. e, Cyclamen graecum. f, Lilium rhodopaedum. g, Narcissus pseudonarcissus. h, Paeonia rhodia. i, Aquilegia amaliae.
No. 1567: a, Paeonia peregrina. b, Muscari comutatum. c, Sternbergia. d, Dianthus. e, Verbascum. f, Aubrieta gracilis. g, Galanthus nivalis. h, Campanula incurva. i, Crocus sieberi.
No. 1568, 2000sh, Paeonia parnassica, vert. No. 1569, 2000sh, Pancratium maritimum, vert.

1998, Sept. 23 Litho. Perf. 14
1566 A239 300sh Sheet of 9,
#a.-i. 5.00 5.00
1567 A239 600sh Sheet of 9,
#a.-i. 9.00 9.00
Souvenir Sheets
1568-1569 A239 Set of 2 10.00 10.00

Christmas
A240

Birds: 300sh, Bohemian waxwing. 400sh, House sparrow. 500sh, Black-capped chickadee. 600sh, Eurasian bullfinch. 700sh, Painted bunting. 1000sh, Northern cardinal.
No. 1576, 2500sh, Winter wren, vert. No. 1577, 2500sh, Red-winged blackbird, vert.

1998, Dec. 3 Litho. Perf. 14
1570-1575 A240 Set of 6 7.00 7.00
Souvenir Sheets
1576-1577 A240 Set of 2 11.00 11.00

Diana, Princess of Wales (1961-97)
A241

1998, Dec. 28 Litho. Perf. 14½
1578 A241 700sh multicolored 2.00 2.00

Picasso
A242

Paintings: 500sh, Woman Reading, 1935, vert. 600sh, Portrait of Dora Maar, 1937, vert. 700sh, Des Moiselles D'Avignon, 1907.
2500sh, Night Fishing at Antibes, 1939, vert.

1998, Dec. 28 Perf. 14½x13, 13x14½
1579-1581 A242 Set of 3 4.00 4.00
Souvenir Sheet
1582 A242 2500sh multicolored 4.75 4.75

Gandhi — A243

1998, Dec. 28 Perf. 14
1583 A243 600sh Portrait 5.50 5.50
Souvenir Sheet
1584 A243 2500sh Family portrait, horiz. 7.00 7.00

No. 1583 was issued in sheets of 4.

1998 World Scouting Jamboree, Chile — A244

No. 1585: a, Cub Scouts greet Pres. Eisenhower, Georgia, 1956. b, Uncle Dan Beard at 90th birthday party, 1990. c, Future Vice President Hubert Humphrey leads South Dakota troop, 1934.
2000sh, Young scout, tamed beaver, vert.

1998, Dec. 28
1585 A244 700sh Sheet of 3,
#a.-c. 6.00 6.00
Souvenir Sheet
1586 A244 2000sh multicolored 4.00 4.00

New Year 1999 (Year of the Rabbit)
A245

No. 1587 — Rabbits: a, White. b, With carrot. c, Brown & white. e, Black & white.

1999, Jan. 4
1587 A245 350sh Sheet of 4,
#a.-d. 4.00 4.00
Souvenir Sheet
1588 A245 1500sh Rabbit, diff. 4.00 4.00

Uganda Post Office
A246

1999, Jan. 18
1589 A246 300sh multicolored 1.75 1.75

Traditional Hairstyles — A247

Hairstyle, region: 300sh, Iru, Bairu. 500sh, Enshunju, Bahima. 550sh, Elemungole, Karamojong. 600sh, Longo, Langi. 700sh, Ekikuura, Bahima.

1999, Feb. 1
1590-1594 A247 Set of 5 6.25 6.25

Marine Life
A248

No. 1595: a, Wolffish. b, Equal sea star. c, Purple sea urchin. d, Mountain crab.
No. 1596: a, Blue marlin. b, Arctic tern. c, Common dolphin. d, Blacktip shark. e, Manta ray. f, Blackedge moray. g, Loggerhead turtle. h, Sailfin tang. i, Two-spotted octopus.
No. 1597, 2500sh, Sea nettle jellyfish. No. 1598, 2500sh, Decatopecten striatus.

1999, Mar. 15 Litho. Perf. 14
1595 A248 500sh Sheet of 4,
#a.-d. 3.50 3.50
1596 A248 500sh Sheet of 9,
#a.-i. 9.00 9.00
Souvenir Sheets
1597-1598 A248 each 9.50 9.50

Intl. Year of the Ocean.

Intl. Year of the Elderly
A249

Designs: 300sh, Income generating activity. 500sh, Learning from each other. 600sh, Leisure time for the aged. 700sh, Distributing food to the aged.

1999, July 19 Litho. Perf. 13x13½
1599-1602 A249 Set of 4 5.50 5.50

First Manned Moon Landing, 30th Anniv. — A250

No. 1603: a, Apollo 11 launch. b, Apollo 11 command and service modules. c, Edwin E. Aldrin, Jr. on lunar module ladder. d, Saturn V ready to launch. e, Lunar module descending. f, Aldrin on moon.
No. 1604: a, Freedom 7. b, Gemini 4. c, Apollo 11 command and service modules, diff.

d, Vostok 1. e, Saturn V. f, Lunar module on moon.
No. 1605, 3000sh, Aldrin with scientific experiment. No. 1606, 3000sh, Command module re-entry.

1999, Nov. 24 Litho. Perf. 13¾
1603 A250 600sh Sheet of 6,
#a.-f. 7.00 7.00
1604 A250 700sh Sheet of 6,
#a.-f. 8.00 8.00
Souvenir Sheets
1605-1606 A250 Set of 2 14.00 14.00

Queen Mother (b. 1900) — A251

No. 1607: a, With stole. b, At wedding. c, With tiara (black and white photo). d, With tiara (color photo).
3000sh, Visiting Cambridge, 1961.

1999, Nov. 24 Perf. 14
1607 A251 1200sh Sheet of 4,
#a.-d. 10.00 10.00
Souvenir Sheet
Perf. 13¾
1608 A251 3000sh multi 8.00 8.00

No. 1608 contains one 38x51mm stamp.

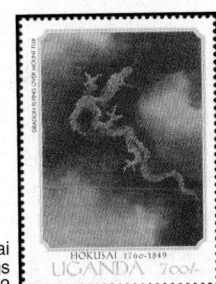

Hokusai Paintings
A252

No. 1609: a, Dragon Flying Over Mount Fuji (dragon). b, Famous Poses From the Kabuki Theater (one figure). c, Kitsune No Yomeiri. d, Dragon Flying Over Mount Fuji (Mount Fuji). e, Famous Poses From the Kabuki Theater (two figures). f, Girl Holding Cloth.
3000sh, Japanese Spaniel.

1999, Nov. 24 Litho. Perf. 13¾
1609 A252 700sh Sheet of 6,
#a.-f. 8.00 8.00
Souvenir Sheet
1610 A252 3000sh multicolored 6.25 6.25

Birds — A253

Designs: 300sh, African penduline tit. 1000sh, Yellow-fronted tinkerbird. 1200sh, Zebra waxbill. 1800sh, Sooty anteater chat.
No. 1615: a, Gray-headed kingfisher. b, Green-headed sunbird. c, Speckled pigeon. d, Gray parrot. e, Barn owl. f, Gray crowned crane. g, Shoebill. h, Black heron.
No. 1616: a, Scarlet-chested sunbird. b, Lesser honeyguide. c, African palm swift. d, Swamp flycatcher. e, Lizard buzzard. f, Osprey. g, Cardinal woodpecker. h, Pearl-spotted owlet.
No. 1617: a, Fox's weaver. b, Chin-spot flycatcher. c, Blue swallow. d, Purple-breasted sunbird. e, Knob-billed duck. f, Red-collared widowbird. g, Ruwenzori turaco. h, African cuckoo hawk.
No. 1618, 3000sh, Four-banded sandgrouse. No. 1619, 3000sh, Paradise whydah.

1999, Dec. 6   **Perf. 14**
1611-1614 A253 Set of 4   9.75 9.75
1615 A253 500sh Sheet of 8,
    #a.-h.   9.00 9.00
1616 A253 600sh Sheet of 8,
    #a.-h.   10.50 10.50
1617 A253 700sh Sheet of 8,
    #a.-h.   12.50 12.50
    Souvenir Sheets
1618-1619 A253 Set of 2   14.50 14.50

Primates — A254

Designs: 300sh, L'hoesti monkey. 400sh, Blue monkey. 500sh, Patas monkey. 600sh, Red-tailed monkey. 700sh, Black and white colobus. 1000sh, Mountain gorilla.
2500sh, Olive baboon.

1999, Nov. 19   **Litho.**   **Perf. 13½x14**
1620-1625 A254 Set of 6   7.00 7.00
    Souvenir Sheet
1626 A254 2500sh multicolored   5.50 5.50

Butterflies A255

Designs: 300sh, Epiphora bauhiniae, vert. 400sh, Phylloxiphia formosa. 500sh, Bunaea alcinoe, vert. 600sh, Euchloron megaera. 700sh, Argema mimosae, vert. 1800sh, Denephila nerii.
3000sh, Lobobunaea angasana.

Perf. 13½x13¼, 13¼x13½
2000, Jan. 19   **Litho.**
1627-1632 A255 Set of 6   9.25 9.25
    Souvenir Sheet
1633 A255 3000sh multi   7.75 7.75

A256

UPU, 125th anniv. (in 1999): 600sh, Postman, two women, girl. 700sh, Woman, girl, mail box. 1200sh, Postman in horse-drawn wagon.

2000, Jan. 28   **Litho.**   **Perf. 14**
1634-1636 A256 Set of 3   5.50 5.50

A257

No. 1637, 600sh — Orchids: a, Angraecum eichcerianum. b, Angraecum leonis. c, Arpophyllum giganteum. d, Bulbophyllum barbigerum. e, Angraecum ciryamae. f, Aerangis ellisii. g, Disa umiflora. h, Eulophia alta. i, Ancistrochilius stylosa.
No. 1638, 600sh: a, Eulophia paivenna. b, Ansellia gigantea. c, Anglaecopsis gracillima. d, Bonatea steudneri. e, Bulbophyllum falcatum. f, Aerangis citrata. g, Eulophiella

elisabethae. h, Aerangis rhodosticta. i, Angraecum scottianum.
No. 1639, 700sh: a, Grammangis ellisii. b, Eulophia stenophylia. c, Oeoniella polystachys. d, Cymbidiella humblotti. e, Polystachya bella. f, Vanilla polycepis. g, Eulophileea roemplerana. h, Habenaria englerana. i, Ansellia frallana.
No. 1640, 700sh: a, Eulophia orthoplectra. b, Cirrhopetalum umbellatum. c, Eulophiella rolfei. d, Eulophia porphyroglossa. e, Eulopia petersii. f, Cyrtorchis arcuata. g, Eurychone rothschildiana. h, Eulophia quartiniana. i, Eulophia stenophylia (one flower).
No. 1641, 3000sh, Polystachya tayloriana, horiz. No. 1642, 3000sh, Ancistrochilus rothschildianus, horiz. No. 1643, 3000sh, Calanthe corymbosa, horiz. No. 1644, 3000sh, Cymbidiella rhodochila, horiz.

2000, Feb. 18   **Sheets of 9, #a.-i.**
1637-1638 A257 Set of 2   20.00 20.00
1639-1640 A257 Set of 2   25.00 25.00
    Souvenir Sheets
1641-1644 A257 Set of 4   21.00 21.00

Butterflies — A258

Designs: 300sh, Short-tailed admiral. 400sh, Guineafowl. 1200sh, Club-tailed charaxes. 1800sh, Cymothoe egesta.
No. 1649: a, Charaxes anrticlea. b, Epitola posthumus. c, Beautiful monarch. d, Blue-banded nymph. e, Euxanthe crossleyi. f, African map. g, Western blue charaxes. h, Noble.
No. 1650: a, Green-veined charaxes. b, Ansorge's leaf butterfly. c, Crawshay's sapphire blue. d, Palla ussheri. e, Friar. f, Blood-red cymothoe. g, Mocker. h, Charaxes eupale.
No. 1651: a, Aeraea pseudolycia. b, Veined yellow. c, Buxton's hairstreak. d, Iolaus isomenias. e, Veined swallowtail. f, Figtree blue. g, Scarlet tip. h, Precis octavia.
No. 1652, 3000sh, African monarch. No. 1653, 3000sh, Kigezi swordtail.

2000, May 24   **Litho.**   **Perf. 14**
1645-1648 A258 Set of 4   7.75 7.75
1649 A258 500sh Sheet of 8,
    #a-h   8.00 8.00
1650 A258 600sh Sheet of 8,
    #a-h   8.00 8.00
1651 A258 700sh Sheet of 8,
    #a-h   9.00 9.00
    Souvenir Sheets
1652-1653 A258 Set of 2   11.00 11.00
The Stamp Show 2000, London (Nos. 1649-1653).

Popes — A259

No. 1654: a, Agapetus II (946-55). b, Alexander II (1061-73). c, Anastasius IV (1153-54). d, Benedict VIII (1012-24). e, Benedict VII (974-83). f, Calixtus II (1119-24).
No. 1655, Celestine III (1191-98).

2000, June 28   **Perf. 13¾**
1654 A259 900sh Sheet of 6,
    #a-f   14.00 14.00
    Souvenir Sheet
1655 A259 3000sh multi   7.00 7.00

Monarchs — A260

No. 1655A: b, Philip II of France (1180-1223). c, Richard I of England (1189-99). d, William I of England (1066-87).
No. 1656: a, Boris III of Bulgaria (1918-43). b, Holy Roman Emperor Charles V (1519-58). c, Pedro II of Brazil (1831-89). d, Empress Elizabeth of Austria (1854-98). e, Francis Joseph of Austria (1848-1916). f, Frederick I of Bohemia (1619-20).
No. 1657, Mutesa I of Buganda (1191-98). No. 1657A, Cwa II Kabaleega.

2000, June 28   **Perf. 13¾**
1655A A260 900sh Sheet of 3,
    #b-d   5.00 5.00
1656 A260 900sh Sheet of 6,
    #a-f   9.00 9.00
    Souvenir Sheets
1657 A260 3000sh multi   5.50 5.50
1657A A260 3000sh multi   5.50 5.50

Millennium — A261

No. 1658 — Highlights of 1850-1900: a, Opening of Japan. b, First safe elevator. c, Bessemer process of steel production. d, Florence Nightingale establishes nursing as a professsion. e, Louis Pasteur proposes germ theory of disease. f, First oil well drilled. g, Charles Darwin publishes *The Origin of Species*. h, Gregor Mendel discovers laws of heredity. i, Alfred Nobel invents dynamite. j, Suez Canal opens. k, Invention of the telephone. l, Invention of the electric light. m, World's time zones established. n, Invention of the electric motor. o, Motion pictures appear. p, US Civil War (57x37mm). q, Restoration of the Olympic Games.
Illustration reduced.

2000, June 28   **Perf. 12¾x12½**
1658 A261 300sh Sheet of 17,
    #a-q + label   8.00 8.00

Millennium — A262

Designs: 300sh, Education for all. 600sh, Nile River. 700sh, Non-traditional exports. 1800sh, Tourism.

2000, July 24   **Perf. 14½**
1659-1662 A262 Set of 4   6.00 6.00

Common Market for Eastern and Southern Africa A263

Designs: 500sh, Border checkpoint before and after COMESA treaty. 1400sh, Open border checkpoint.

2000, July 24
1663-1664 A263 Set of 2   2.50 2.50

Modern British Commonwealth, 50th Anniv. — A264

Designs: 600sh, Flags. 1200sh, Map.

2000, July 24
1665-1666 A264 Set of 2   2.25 2.25

Trains A265

Designs: 300sh, Kenya Railways A 60 Class 4-8-2+2-8-4. 400sh, Mozambique Railways Baldwin 2-8-0. 600sh, Uganda Railways 73 Class German locomotive. 700sh, South Africa Railways Baby Garratt. 1200sh, Uganda Railways 82 Class French locomotive. 1400sh, East Africa Railway Beyer Garratt 4-8-2+2-8-4. 1800sh, Rhodesian Railways 2-8-2+2-8-2 Beyer Garratt. 2000sh, East African Railways Garratt.
No. 1675, 700sh: a, Uganda Railways 36 Class German locomotive. b, South African Railways Class 19D 4-8-2. c, Algeria Railways Garratt 4-8-2+2-8-4. d, Cameroon Railways French locomotive. e, South Africa railways electric freight locomotive. f, Rhodesia Railways 14A Class 2-8-2. g, British-built Egyptian railways locomotive. h, Uganda Railways 73 Class German locomotive, diff.
No. 1676, 700sh: a, 36 Class German locomotive (no counrrtry specified). b, Rhodesian Railways 12th Class locomotive. c, Rhodesian Railways Garratt. d, 62 Class German locomotive. e, South Africa Railways Beyer Garratt. f, Sudan Railways locomotive. g, Nigerian Railways locomotive. h, 4-8-0 South Africa Railways.
No. 1677, 3500sh, East African Railways locomotive. No. 1678, 3500sh, Rhodesian Railways Alco 2-8-0. No. 1679, 3500sh, Egyptian State Railways 4-8-2.

2000, Aug. 14   **Perf. 14**
1667-1674 A265 Set of 8   11.00 11.00
    Sheets of 8, #a-h
1675-1676 A265 Set of 2   14.00 14.00
    Souvenir Sheets
1677-1679 A265 Set of 3   13.50 13.50
Nos. 1677-1679 each contain one 56x42mm stamp.

Christmas — A266

Artwork by: 300sh, Drateru Fortunate Oliver, vert. 400sh, Brenda Tumwebaze. 500sh, Joseph Mukiibi, vert. 600sh, Paul Serunjogi.

700sh, Edward Maswere. 1200sh, Ndeba Harriet. 1800sh, Jude Kasagga, vert.
No. 1687, 3000sh, Nicole Kwiringira, vert. No. 1688, 3000sh, Michael Tinkamanyire, vert.

2000, Dec. 14   Litho.   Perf. 14
1680-1686 A266   Set of 7   7.00 7.00
Souvenir Sheets
1687-1688 A266   Set of 2   7.50 7.50

New Year 2001 (Year of the Snake) — A267

No. 1689: a, Snake with tongue out. b, Snake wrapped around person. c, Snake with open mouth. d, Snake hanging from branch.

2001, Jan. 5
1689 A267   600sh Sheet of 4, #a-d   3.00 3.00
Souvenir Sheet
1690 A267 2500sh shown   3.25 3.25

Wildlife — A268

No. 1691: a, Bongo, horiz. b, Black rhinoceros, horiz. c, Leopard.
No. 1692, 3000sh, Parrot. No. 1693, 3000sh, Mountain gorillas, horiz.

Perf. 13¼x13¾, 13¾x13¼
2001, Feb. 5
1691 A268   600sh Strip of 3, #a-c   2.25 2.25
Souvenir Sheets
1692-1693 A268   Set of 2   7.50 7.50

Holy Year 2000 — A269

Designs: 300sh, Holy Family. 700sh, Madonna and Child. 1200sh, Nativity, horiz.

2001, Apr. 4   Litho.   Perf. 13¼
1694-1696 A269   Set of 3   2.75 2.75

East African School of Library and Information Science, Makerere University, Kampala — A270

Nairobi University, Kenya — A271

Universities and Flags on Map — A272

Design: 1200sh, Nkrumah Hall, University of Dar es Salaam, Tanzania.

2001, Apr. 23
1697 A270   300sh multi   .40 .40
1698 A271   400sh multi   .50 .50
1699 A270   1200sh multi   1.50 1.50
1700 A272   1800sh multi   2.25 2.25
    Nos. 1697-1700 (4)   4.65 4.65

World Meteorological Organization, 50th Anniv. (in 2000) — A273

Designs: 300sh, Anemometer, vert. 2000sh, Tropical sun recorder.

2001, May 28
1701-1702 A273   Set of 2   3.00 3.00

UN High Commissioner for Refugees — A274

Designs: 300sh, Ensure crop production. 600sh, Ensure community participation. 700sh, Ensure improved skills. 1800sh, Ensure improved health and water services.

2001, June 15
1703-1706 A274   Set of 4   4.25 4.25

Phila Nippon '01, Japan — A275

Designs: 600sh, Kikunojo Segawa I and Danjuro Ichikawa as Samurai, by Kiyonobu II. 700sh, Kamezo Tchimura as a Warrior, by Kiyohiro. 1000sh, Danjuro Ichikawa as Shirobei, by Kiyomitsu. 1200sh, Actor Sangoro

Arashi, by Shunsho. 1400sh, Koshiro Matsumoto IV as Sukenari Juro, by Kiyonaga. 2000sh, Pheasant on Pine Branch, by Kiyomasu II.
3500sh, Tale of Ise, by Eishi.

2001, Aug. 1   Litho.   Perf. 14
1707-1712 A275   Set of 6   8.75 8.75
Souvenir Sheet
1713 A275 3500sh multi   4.50 4.50

Cats and Dogs — A276

Designs: 400sh, Tabby British shorthair. 900sh, Turkish cat.
No. 1716, 600sh, horiz.: a, Blue and cream shorthair. b, Manx. c, Angora. d, Red and white British shorthair. e, Turkish cat, diff. f, Egyptian mau.
No. 1717, 1400sh, horiz.: a, Red tabby shorthair. b, Japanese bobtail. c, Siamese. d, Tabby Persian. e, Black and white Persian. f, Blue Russian.
No. 1718, 3500sh, Blue-eyed British shorthair. No. 1719, 3500sh, Calico American shorthair.

2001, Aug. 23
1714-1715 A276   Set of 2   1.60 1.60
Sheets of 6, #a-f
1716-1717 A276   Set of 2   15.00 15.00
Souvenir Sheets
1718-1719 A276   Set of 2   9.00 9.00

2001, Aug. 23
Designs: 1100sh, German shepherd. 1200sh, Irish setter.
No. 1722, 700sh, horiz.: a, Rottweiler. b, Flat-coated retriever. c, Samoyed. d, Poodle. e, Maltese. f, Irish terrier.
No. 1723, 1300sh, horiz: a, English sheepdog. b, German shepherd, diff. c, Great Dane. d, Boston terrier. e, Bull terrier. f, Australian terrier.
No. 1724, 3500sh, Bloodhound. No. 1725, 3500sh, Pointer, horiz.

1720-1721 A276   Set of 2   3.00 3.00
Sheets of 6, #a-f
1722-1723 A276   Set of 2   15.00 15.00
Souvenir Sheets
1724-1725 A276   Set of 2   9.00 9.00
    APS Stampshow, Chicago (#1723).

Royal Navy Submarines, Cent. — A277

No. 1726, vert.: a, HMS Tribune. b, HMS Royal Oak. c, HMS Invincible. d, HMS Dreadnought. e, HMS Ark Royal. f, HMS Cardiff.

2001, Aug. 27
1726 A277   1000sh Sheet of 6, #a-f   7.50 7.50
Souvenir Sheet
1727 A277 3500sh HMS Triad   4.50 4.50

Queen Victoria (1819-1901) — A278

No. 1728: a, Wearing tiara. b, Wearing white head covering, looking right. c, Wearing black hat. d, Wearing red dress with blue sash. e, Wearing white head covering, looking left. f, With hand on chin.
3500sh, Wearing black, hat, diff.

2001, Aug. 27
1728 A278   1000sh Sheet of 6, #a-f   7.50 7.50
Souvenir Sheet
1729 A278 3500sh multi   4.50 4.50

Queen Elizabeth II, 75th Birthday — A279

No. 1730: a, In 1926. b, In 1931. c, In 1939. d, In 1955. e, In 1963. f, In 1999.
3500sh, Wearing cap.

2001, Aug. 27
1730 A279   1000sh Sheet of 6, #a-f   7.50 7.50
Souvenir Sheet
1731 A279 3500sh multi   4.50 4.50

Toulouse-Lautrec Paintings — A280

No. 1732: a, Woman Combing Her Hair. b, The Toilette. c, The English Girl at the Star in Le Havre.
3500sh, Ambassadeurs: Aristide Bruant.

2001, Aug. 27   Litho.   Perf. 13¾
1732 A280   1500sh Sheet of 3, #a-c   5.75 5.75
Souvenir Sheet
1733 A280 3500sh multi   4.50 4.50

Monet Paintings — A281

No. 1734, horiz.: a, Storm, Belle-Ile Coast. b, The Manneporte, Etretat. c, The Rocks at Pourville, Low Tide. d, The Wild Sea. 3500sh, Sunflowers.

2001, Aug. 27
1734 A281 1200sh Sheet of 4,
    #a-d   6.00 6.00
Souvenir Sheet
1735 A281 3500sh multi   4.50 4.50

Year of Dialogue Among Civilizations A282

Perf. 13¾x13¼
2001, Nov. 16   **Litho.**
1736 A282 3000sh multi   3.75 3.75

Intl. Volunteers Year A283

Designs: 300sh, Ebola outbreak. 700sh, Save life, donate blood. 2000sh, Collective effort for clean water.

2001, Nov. 16   **Perf. 13¼x13¾**
1737-1739 A283   Set of 3   3.75 3.75

Mushrooms — A284

Designs: 300sh, Amanita excelsa. 500sh, Coprinus cinereus. 600sh, Scleroderma aurantium. 700sh, Armillaria mellea. 1200sh, Leopiota procera. 2000sh, Flammulina velutipes. 3000sh, Amanita phalloides.

2001, Nov. 26   **Perf. 14½**
1740-1745 A284   Set of 6   6.75 6.75
Souvenir Sheets
1746 A284 3000sh multi   3.75 3.75
1746A A284 3000sh multi   3.75 3.75

Christmas — A285

Musical instruments: 400sh, Single skin long drum. 800sh, Animal horn trumpet, horiz. 1000sh, Bugisu clay drum. 1200sh, Musical bow. 1400sh, Pan pipes. 2000sh, Log xylophones, horiz.

No. 1753, 3500sh, Eight-stringed giant bow harp. No. 1754, Nativity scene, horiz.

2001   **Perf. 13¾x13¼, 13¼x13¾**
1747-1752 A285   Set of 6   8.50 8.50
Souvenir Sheets
1753-1754 A285   Set of 2   9.00 9.00

New Year 2002 (Year of the Horse) — A286

No. 1755: a, White horse facing left. b, Dark brown and gray brown horse facing right with all feet on ground. c, Tan and brown horse facing right, with two feet raised. 3000r, Rearing horse.

2002, May 8 **Litho.**   **Perf. 14x14¼**
1755 A286 1200sh Sheet of 3,
    #a-c   4.50 4.50
Souvenir Sheet
1756 A286 3000sh multi   3.75 3.75

Historic Sites of East Africa A287

Designs: 400sh, Namugongo Shrine Church, Uganda. 800sh, Maruhubi Palace Ruins, Zanzibar, Tanzania. 1200sh, Kings' Burial Grounds, Mparo, Uganda. 1400sh, Old Law Courts, Mombasa, Kenya, vert.

2002, May 8   **Perf. 14½**
1757-1760 A287   Set of 4   4.75 4.75

Reign of Queen Elizabeth II, 50th Anniv. — A288

No. 1761: a, Wearing blue dress. b, Wearing blue and red hat. c, Without hat. d, Wearing blue hat. 3500sh, Wearing brown hat.

2002, June 17   **Perf. 14¼**
1761 A288 1500sh Sheet of 4,
    #a-d   7.50 7.50
Souvenir Sheet
1762 A288 3500sh multi   4.50 4.50

8th Intl. Interdisciplinary Congress on Women, Kampala — A289

Designs: 400sh, Women, building. 1200sh, Makerere University arms, vert.

Perf. 13¼x13¾, 13¾x13¼
2002, July 8
1763-1764 A289   Set of 2   2.00 2.00

United We Stand — A290

2002, July 15   **Perf. 13¾x13¼**
1765 A290 1500sh multi   1.90 1.90
Printed in sheets of 4.

Intl. Year of Mountains — A291

No. 1766: a, Tateyama, Japan. b, Mt. Nikko, Japan. c, Mt. Hodaka, Japan. 3500sh, Mt. Fuji, Japan.

2002, July 15   **Perf. 13¼x13¾**
1766 A291 2000sh Sheet of 3,
    #a-c   7.50 7.50
Souvenir Sheet
1767 A291 3500sh multi   4.50 4.50

2002 Winter Olympics, Salt Lake City — A292

Designs: No. 1768, 1200sh, Cross-country skiing. No. 1769, 1200sh, Ski jumping.

2002, July 15   **Perf. 13¾x13¼**
1768-1769 A292   Set of 2   3.00 3.00
1769a   Souvenir sheet, #1768-
    1769   3.00 3.00

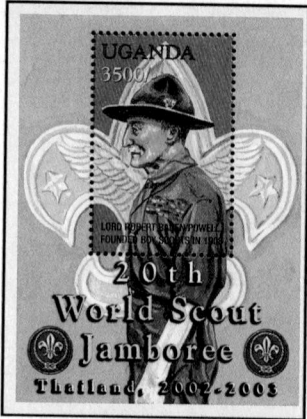

20th World Scout Jamboree, Thailand — A293

No. 1770: a, Scout in forest, 1930s. b, Scout saluting. c, Scouts hiking. d, Scout badge. 3500sh, Lord Robert Baden-Powell.

2002   **Perf. 13¼x13¾**
1770 A293 1400sh Sheet of 4,
    #a-d   7.00 7.00
Souvenir Sheet
Perf. 13¾x13¼
1771 A293 3500sh multi   4.50 4.50

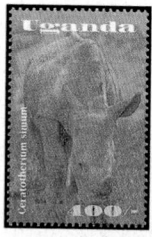

Mammals, Insects, Flowers and Mushrooms — A294

Designs: 400sh, Ceratotherium simum. 800sh, Macrotermes subhyalinus. No. 1774, 1200sh, Gloriosa superba. 1400sh, Cyptotrama asprata.
No. 1776, 1000sh, horiz. — Insects: a, Nudaurelia cytherea. b, Locusta migratoria. c, Anacridium aegyptium. d, Sternotomis bohemanni. e, Papilio dardanus. f, Mantis polyspilota.
No. 1777, 1000sh, horiz. — Mushrooms: a, Termitomyces microcarpus. b, Agaricus trisulphuratus. c, Macrolepiota zeyheri. d, Lentinus stupeus. e, Lentinus sajor-caju. f, Lentinus velutinus.
No. 1778, 1200sh, horiz. — Flowers: a, Canarina eminii. b, Vigna unguiculata. c, Gardenia ternifolia. d, Canavalia rosea. e, Hibiscus calyphyllus. f, Nymphaea lotus.
No. 1779, 1200sh, horiz. — Mammals: a, Kobus kob. b, Alcelaphus buselaphus. c, Damaliiscus lunatus. d, Papio anubis. e, Panthera leo. f, Phacochoerus africanus.
No. 1780, 4000sh, Glossina austeni, horiz. No. 1781, 4000sh, Podoscypha parvula, horiz. No. 1782, 4000sh, Abutilon grandiflorum, horiz. No. 1783, 4000sh, Kobus ellipsiprymnus.

2002, Nov. 6 **Litho.**   **Perf. 14**
1772-1775 A294   Set of 4   4.75 4.75
Sheets of 6, #a-f
1776-1779 A294   Set of 4   35.00 35.00
Souvenir Sheets
1780-1781 A294   Set of 4   20.00 20.00

A295

Pres. John F. Kennedy (1917-63) — A296

Various photos.

2002, Dec. 30
1784 A295 1200sh Sheet of 4,
#a-d   6.00 6.00
1785 A296 1400sh Sheet of 4,
#a-d   7.00 7.00

A297

Pres. Ronald Reagan — A298

Various photos.

2002, Dec. 30
1786 A297 1200sh Sheet of 4,
#a-d   6.00 6.00
1787 A298 1400sh Sheet of 4,
#a-d   7.00 7.00

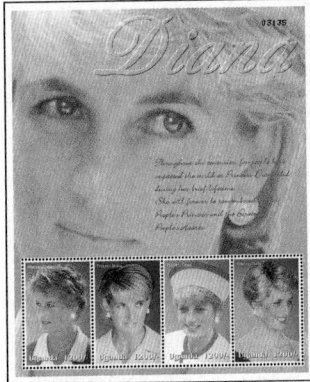

A299

Princess Diana (1961-97) — A300

2002, Dec. 30
1788 A299 1200sh Sheet of 4,
#a-d   6.00 6.00
1789 A300 2000sh Sheet of 4,
#a-d   10.00 10.00

New Year 2003 (Year of the Ram) — A301

No. 1790: a, Ram on stage. b, Ram on hill. c, Ram on hill, six ram's heads. d, Six rams. e, Ram in field. f, Ram on mountainside.

2003, Feb. 1   *Perf. 14¼x14*
1790 A301 1000sh Sheet of 6,
#a-f   7.50 7.50

Japanese Art — A302

Designs: 400sh, Beauty Arranging Her Hair, by Eisen Keisai. 1000sh, Geishas, by Tsukimaro Kitagawa. 1200sh, Woman Behind a Screen, by Chikanobu Toyohara. 1400sh, Geishas, by Kitagawa, diff.
No. 1795: a, Scene in a Villa (basin in foreground), by Kinichika Toyohara. b, Scene in a Villa (screen at left), by Kunichika Toyohara. c, Visiting a Flower Garden (two people), by Kunisada Utagawa. d, Visiting a Flower Garden (one person), by Utagawa.
5000sh, Woman and Children, by Chikakazu.

2003, May 26   Litho.   Perf. 14¼
1791-1794 A302   Set of 4   5.00 5.00
1795 A302 1200sh Sheet of 4,
#a-d   6.00 6.00
Souvenir Sheet
1796 A302 5000sh multi   6.25 6.25

Rembrandt Paintings A303

Designs: 400sh, Jacob Blessing the Sons of Joseph. 1000sh, A Young Woman in Profile With Fan. 1200sh, The Apostle Peter Kneeling. 1400sh, The Painter Hendrick Martensz Sorgh.
No. 1801: a, Portrait of Margaretha de Geer. b, Portrait of a White Haired Man. c, Portrait of Nicolaes Ruts. d, Portrait of Catrina Hooghsaet.
5000sh, Joseph Accused by Potiphar's Wife.

2003, May 26
1797-1800 A303   Set of 4   5.00 5.00
1801 A303 1400sh Sheet of 4,
#a-d   7.00 7.00
Souvenir Sheet
1802 A303 5000sh multi   6.25 6.25

Paintings of Joan Miró — A304

Designs: 400sh, Group of Personages in the Forest. 800sh, Nocturne. 1200sh, The Smile of a Tear. 1400sh, Personage Before the Sun.
No. 1807, vert: a, Man's Head III. b, Catalan Peasant by Moonlight. c, Woman in the Night. d, Seated Woman.
No. 1808, 3500sh, Self-portrait II. No. 1809, 3500sh, Woman with Three Hairs, Birds and Constellations.

2003, May 26   *Perf. 14¼*
1803-1806 A304   Set of 4   4.75 4.75
1807 A304 1400sh Sheet of 4,
#a-d   7.00 7.00
Imperf
Size: 103x82mm
1808-1809 A304   Set of 2   8.75 8.75

Buganda Princess Katrina-Sarah Ssangalyambogo, 2nd Birthday — A305

Princess and: 400sh, Bulange (government office building). 1200sh, Twekobe (palace), vert. 1400sh, Drummer, vert.

Perf. 13x13¼, 13¼x13
2003, June 16
1810-1812 A305   Set of 3   3.75 3.75

Coronation of Queen Elizabeth II, 50th Anniv. — A306

No. 1813: a, As toddler. b, As young woman, wearing flowered hat. c, Wearing robe and feathered hat.
3500sh, Wearing crown.

2003, July 15   *Perf. 14*
1813 A306 2000sh Sheet of 3,
#a-c   7.50 7.50
Souvenir Sheet
1814 A306 3500sh multi   4.50 4.50

Prince William, 21st Birthday — A307

No. 1815: a, Wearing cap. b, Wearing blue striped shirt. c, Wearing white shirt.
5000sh, With hand on chin.

2003, July 15
1815 A307 2000sh Sheet of 3,
#a-c   7.50 7.50
Souvenir Sheet
1816 A307 5000sh multi   6.25 6.25

General Motors Automobiles — A308

No. 1817, 1200sh — Cadillacs: a, 1979 Seville Elegante. b, 1998 Eldorado Touring Coupe. c, 2002 Escalade. d, 1983 Seville Elegante.
No. 1818, 1400sh — Corvettes: a, 1970. b, 1972. c, 1982 Collector Edition. d, 1977.
No. 1819, 3500sh, Cadillac Eldorado convertible, 1950s. No. 1820, 3500sh, 1982 Collector Edition Corvette, diff.

2003, July 15   *Perf. 14¼*
Sheets of 4, #a-d
1817-1818 A308   Set of 2   13.00 13.00
Souvenir Sheets
1819-1820 A308   Set of 2   8.75 8.75

Millennium Development Goals — A309

Designs: No. 1821, 400sh, Promote gender equity and empower women. No. 1822, 400sh, Improve maternal health. 600sh, Ensure environmental sustainability. 1000sh, Reduce child mortality. No. 1825, 1200sh, Eradicate extreme poverty and hunger. No. 1826, 1200sh, Combat HIV, AIDS, malaria and other diseases. 1400sh, Achieve universal primary education. 2000sh, Develop a global partnership for development.

2003, Oct. 24   *Perf. 14½*
1821-1828 A309   Set of 8   10.50 10.50

Dances and
Costumes — A310

Dances: 400sh, Entogoro. 800sh,
Karimojong. 1400sh, Teso.
No. 1832 — Costumes: a, Kiga. b, Acholi. c,
Karimojong. d, Ganda.

2003, Nov. 10   *Perf. 14*
1829-1831 A310   Set of 3   3.25 3.25
1832 A310 1200sh Sheet of 4,
                             #a-d   6.00 6.00

Christmas — A311

Dances: 300sh, Journey to Bethlehem.
400sh, Shepherds and angels. 1200sh, Nativity. 1400sh, Adoration of the Magi.
3000sh, Holy Family.

2003, Nov. 10
1833-1836 A311   Set of 4   4.25 4.25
Souvenir Sheet
1837 A311 3000sh multi   3.75 3.75

All-Africa Conference on Assuring
Food and Nutrition Security in Africa
by 2020, Kampala — A312

Map of Africa, food basket, Intl. Food Policy
Research Institute emblem and: 400sh, Boy.
1400sh, Boy, diff.

2004, Aug. 31   Litho.   Perf. 14¼
1838-1839 A312   Set of 2   2.25 2.25

Straight Talk Foundation — A313

Child and: 400sh, "Pioneers in Adolescent
Health Communication." 1200sh, "Communication for Better Adolescent Health," vert.

2004, Sept. 22
1840-1841 A313   Set of 2   2.00 2.00

Campaign Against Child
Labor — A314

Inscriptions: 400sh, "Stop Child Domestic
Labor." 2000sh, "Keep the Community
Informed."

2004, Sept. 22
1842-1843 A314   Set of 2   3.00 3.00

Rotary International, Cent. (in
2005) — A315

Rotary emblem and: 400sh, "Celebrate
Rotary." 1200sh, "A Century of Service / A
New Century of Success," vert.

2004, Sept. 22
1844-1845 A315   Set of 2   2.00 2.00

New Year 2005 (Year of the
Rooster) — A316

No. 1846 — Rooster shades: a, Blue. b,
Orange. c, Purple. d, Red.
5000sh, Yellow.

2005, Apr. 4   Litho.   Perf. 14
1846 A316 1200sh Sheet of 4,
                             #a-d   6.00 6.00
Souvenir Sheet
1847 A316 5000sh multi   6.25 6.25

Fight Against
Tuberculosis,
HIV and
Leprosy — A317

WHO emblem and: No. 1848, 400sh, Ill man
in blanket. No. 1849, 400sh, Doctor holding
arm of ill man. No. 1850, 400sh, Mother and
infant. No. 1851, 400sh, Infant in blanket. No.
1852, 400sh, Leper with artificial leg. No.
1853, 400sh, Leper wearing crucifix.

2005, May 31   *Perf. 13x12¾*
1848-1853 A317   Set of 6   3.00 3.00

Flowering
Plants — A318

Designs: 100sh, Clerodendrum sp. 400sh,
Calliandra haematocephala. 600sh, Astera-
ceae compositae. 850sh, Angraecum sp.
900sh, Delonix regia. 1100sh, Bidens grantii.
1200sh, Musa sapientum. 1400sh, Begonia
coccinea. 1600sh, Impatiens walleriana.
2000sh, Strelitzia reginae. 5000sh, Tecomaria
capensis. 6000sh, Ixora hybrida. 10,000sh,
Datura suaveolens. 20,000sh, Cucurbita pepo.

Perf. 12¾x13½
2005, June 22   *Litho.*
1854 A318   100sh multi   .25   .25
1855 A318   400sh multi   .45   .45
1856 A318   600sh multi   .70   .70

1857 A318   850sh multi   1.00 1.00
1858 A318   900sh multi   1.10 1.10
1859 A318 1100sh multi   1.25 1.25
1860 A318 1200sh multi   1.40 1.40
1861 A318 1400sh multi   1.60 1.60
1862 A318 1600sh multi   1.90 1.90
1863 A318 2000sh multi   2.40 2.40
1864 A318 5000sh multi   5.75 5.75
1865 A318 6000sh multi   7.00 7.00
1866 A318 10,000sh multi   11.50 11.50
1867 A318 20,000sh multi   23.00 23.00
    Nos. 1854-1867 (14)   59.30 59.30

Fish
A319

Designs: 400sh, Synodontis afrofischeri.
600sh, Protopterus aethiopicus. 1100sh,
Clarias gariepinus. 1200sh, Rastrineobola
agentea. 1600sh, Bagrus docmac. 2000sh,
Schilbe mystus.
No. 1874: a, Mormyrus kannume. b, Barbus
jacksonni. c, Bagrus docmac, diff. d, Labeo
victorianus.

2005, Oct. 6   Litho.   Perf. 13¼
1868-1873 A319   Set of 6   8.75 8.75
Souvenir Sheet
1874 A319 1000sh Sheet of 4,
                             #a-d   5.00 5.00

Western Union in Africa, 10th
Anniv. — A320

Designs: 400sh, Map of Africa, olive
branches. 1600sh, Globe. 2000sh, Globe and
flags, vert.

2006, July 20   Litho.   Perf. 14¼
1875-1877 A320   Set of 3   5.00 5.00

Bank of Uganda,
40th
Anniv. — A321

Designs: 400sh, Bank emblem. 600sh,
Bank emblem, building, wildlife. 1600sh, Bank
emblem, Tilapia nilotica. 2000sh, Bank
emblem, mountain gorilla.

2006, Oct. 3   *Perf. 13¼*
1878-1881 A321   Set of 4   5.75 5.75

Wetlands
A322

Designs: 400sh, Cattle and herdsman at
water, Ramsar Convention emblem. 1600sh,
People and birds near stream. 2000sh, Fishermen at Lake George.

2006   *Perf. 13x13½*
1882-1884 A322   Set of 3   5.00 5.00

2007 Commonwealth Heads of
Government Meeting,
Kampala — A323

Flag of Uganda and: 400sh, Commonwealth
Heads of Government Meeting emblem.
1600sh, Boniface Kiprop, runner. 2000sh,
Dorcas Inzikuru, runner. 5000sh, Arms of
Uganda, vert.

2007, Nov. 27   Litho.   Perf. 13x13½
1885-1888 A323   Set of 4   10.50 10.50

24th UPU
Congress,
Geneva — A324

People in native costumes: No. 1889,
Karimojong man.
No. 1890: a, Omwenda women. b,
Ebibaraho man. c, Kikoyi women. d, Kanzu
men. e, Gomesi women.

2007, Dec. 7   Litho.   Perf. 13¼x13
1889 A324 1600sh multi   1.90 1.90
1890 A324 1600sh Horiz. strip of
                             5, #a-e   9.50 9.50
The UPU Congress was moved from Nai-
robi, Kenya, to Geneva because of political
unrest.

Miniature Sheet

2008 Summer Olympics,
Beijing — A325

No. 1891: a, Javelin. b, Running. c, Boxing.
d, Swimming.

2008, June 18   *Perf. 12*
1891 A325 1000sh Sheet of 4,
                             #a-d   5.00 5.00

Worldwide Fund for Nature
(WWF) — A326

No. 1892 — Spotted hyena: a, Running. b,
With pack, devouring prey. c, Adult and
juveniles. d, Two juveniles.

2008, June 18   *Perf. 13¼*
1892   Strip of 4   5.00 5.00
a.-d. A326 1000sh Any single   1.25 1.25
e. Sheet of 8, 2 each #1892a-
    1892d   10.00 10.00

Reign of
Aga
Khan,
50th
Anniv.
(in 2007)
A327

Designs: No. 1893, 400sh, Diamond Trust Building. No. 1894, 400sh, Kampala Serena Hotel. No. 1895, 400sh, Jubilee Insurance Company Building.

No. 1896: a, School children (madrasa program). b, Ismaili Jamatkhana, Kampala. c, Aga Khan High School (educational services). d, Air Uganda airplane. e, Dam (Bujagali hydropower project).

2008, Sept. 30   **Litho.**   **Perf. 14½**
1893-1895 A327   Set of 3   1.50 1.50
1896 A327 1100sh Horiz. strip of 5, #a-e   6.50 6.50

Peony
A328

2009, Apr. 10   **Litho.**   **Perf. 13¼**
1897 A328 1600sh multi   1.50 1.50

Printed in sheets of 8 + central label.

Miniature Sheet

China 2009 World Stamp Exhibition, Luoyang — A329

No. 1898 — Tourist attractions in China: a, Longmen Grottoes, Luoyang. b, Bridge over Pearl River, Guangzhou. c, Twin Temples on Fir Lake, Guilin. d, Yu Yuan Garden, Shanghai.

2009, Apr. 10   **Perf. 12**
1898 A329 1000sh Sheet of 4, #a-d   3.75 3.75

Miniature Sheet

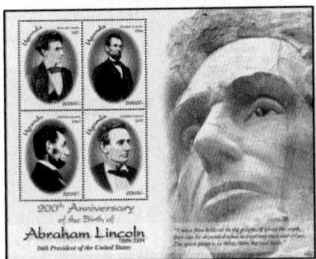

Pres. Abraham Lincoln (1809-65) — A330

No. 1899 — Photographs of Lincoln taken in: a, 1857 (wearing vest). b, 1864. c, 1863. d, 1857 (without vest).

2009, Apr. 10   **Perf. 13¼**
1899 A330 2000sh Sheet of 4, #a-d   7.50 7.50

Miniature Sheet

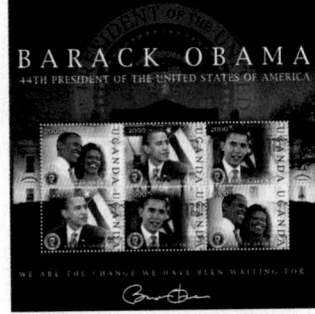

Inauguration of US Pres. Barack Obama — A331

No. 1900: a, Pres. Obama and wife, Michelle, balustrade over heads. b, Pres. Obama with blue striped tie, window at left. c, Pres. Obama with red and gold tie, balustrade above head. d, As "b," window above head. e, As "c," White House portico lamp above head. f, As "a," windows over heads.

2009, Apr. 10   **Perf. 11½x11¼**
1900 A331 2000sh Sheet of 6, #a-f   11.00 11.00

Miniature Sheets

A332

Michael Jackson (1958-2009), Singer — A333

No. 1901: a, Wearing tan jacket, no microphone shown. b, Wearing blue and white shirt, no microphone shown. c, Wearing blue jacket, with microphone. d, Wearing tan jacket, with microphone.

No. 1902: a, Facing right, microphone at mouth. b, Holding microphone on stand. c, Behind microphone on stand. d, Facing left, microphone at mouth.

2009   **Perf. 13¼x13**
1901 A332 2000sh Sheet of 4, #a-d   8.50 8.50
1902 A333 2000sh Sheet of 4, #a-d   8.50 8.50

The printer of Nos. 1901-1902 claims the stamps were issued June 25, the day Michael Jackson died. The editors doubt this claim.

Chinese Aviation, Cent. — A334

No. 1903: a, Q-5. b, Q-5C. c, JH-7A. d, JH-7 on ground. 4000sh, JH-7 in flight.

2009, Nov. 12   **Perf. 14¼**
1903 A334 2000sh Sheet of 4, #a-d   8.50 8.50
Souvenir Sheet
1904 A334 4000sh multi   4.25 4.25

Aeropex 2009, Beijing. No. 1903 contains four 42x33mm stamps.

Miniature Sheet

Princess Diana (1961-97) — A335

No. 1905 — Princess Diana: a, Wearing black and white hat. b, Wearing pink hat. c, Wearing white blouse. d, Holding flowers.

2010, Feb. 15   **Perf. 11½**
1905 A335 2000sh Sheet of 4, #a-d   8.00 8.00

Miniature Sheet

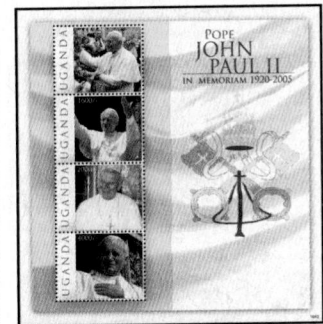

Pope John Paul II (1920-2005) — A336

No. 1906 — Pope John Paul II: a, 400sh, Greeting crowd. b, 1600sh, With arms raised. c, 2000sh, Standing in front of painting. d, 4000sh, With hand on chest.

2010, June 24
1906 A336   Sheet of 4, #a-d   7.25 7.25

Souvenir Sheet

Boy Scouts of America, Cent. — A337

No. 1907 — Emblem of: a, National Scout Jamboree. b, Philmont Scout Ranch, Cimarron, New Mexico. c, Florida High Adventure Sea Base.

2010, Oct. 14   **Perf. 13½**
1907 A337 3000sh Sheet of 3, #a-c   8.00 8.00

Miniature Sheets

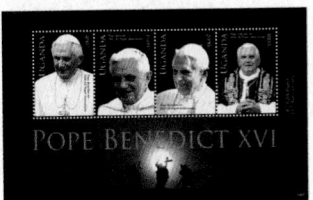

A338

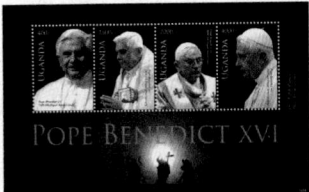

Pope Benedict XVI — A339

No. 1908 — Various photographs of Pope Benedict XVI with denomination at upper right: a, 400sh. b, 1600sh. c, 2000sh. d, 4000sh.
No. 1909 — Various photographs of Pope Benedict XVI with denomination at upper left: a, 400sh. b, 1600sh. c, 2000sh. d, 4000sh.

2011, Feb. 25   **Perf. 12**
1908 A338   Sheet of 4, #a-d   6.75 6.75
1909 A339   Sheet of 4, #a-d   6.75 6.75

Miniature Sheets

2010 World Cup Soccer Championships, South Africa — A340

No. 1910 — Team from: a, 400sh, Algeria. b, 400sh, South Africa. c, 1600sh, Ghana. d, 1600sh, Nigeria. e, 3000sh, Ivory Coast. f, 3000sh, Cameroun.
No. 1911 — Team from: a, 900sh, Italy. b, 900sh, Brazil. c, 1100sh, Japan. d, 1100sh, New Zealand. e, 4000sh, Australia. f, 4000sh, United States.

2011, Feb. 25   **Litho.**   **Perf. 12**
Sheets of 6, #a-f
1910-1911 A340   Set of 2   18.50 18.50

Disease Prevention
A341

Inscriptions: 400sh, Treat livestock against nagana. 900sh, Treat humans against sleeping sickness, horiz. 1600sh, War against tsetse flies in Uganda, horiz. 3000sh, Empower communities against trypanosomiasis, horiz.

2011, Jan. 18   **Perf. 13x13½, 13½x13**
1912-1915 A341   Set of 4   5.25 5.25

Souvenir Sheet

New Year 2011 (Year of the Rabbit) — A342

No. 1916: a, Rabbit standing on hind legs. b, Rabbit leaping.

2011, Feb. 1　　　　　　　**Perf. 12**
1916 A342 2000sh Sheet of 2,
　　　　　#a-b　　　　　　3.50　3.50

Wedding of Prince William and Catherine Middleton — A343

No. 1917 — Stamps with blue panels: a, 600sh, Bride standing. b, 2500sh, Couple.

No. 1918 — Stamps with red panels: a, 600sh, Bride in coach. b, 2500sh, Couple waving.

2011, Apr. 29　　　　**Perf. 13¼x13**
　　　　　Pairs, #a-b
1917-1918 A343　Set of 2　　5.25　5.25

Nos. 1917-1918 each were printed in sheets containing two pairs. Nos. 1917-1918 could not have been issued on the stated day of issue, as the stamps show photographs of the wedding that day.

A344

A345

A346

A347

A348

A349

A350

A351

A352

A353

A354

A355

A356

Gorillas
A363

2011, June 18　　　　　　**Perf. 14½**
1919　　　　Block of 10　　　3.00　3.00
　a.　A344 400sh multi　　　　.30　.30
　b.　A345 400sh multi　　　　.30　.30
　c.　A346 400sh multi　　　　.30　.30
　d.　A347 400sh multi　　　　.30　.30
　f.　A348 400sh multi　　　　.30　.30
　f.　A349 400sh multi　　　　.30　.30
　g.　A350 400sh multi　　　　.30　.30
　h.　A351 400sh multi　　　　.30　.30
　i.　A352 400sh multi　　　　.30　.30
　j.　A352 400sh multi　　　　.30　.30
1920　　　Vert. strip of 5　　4.00　4.00
　a.　A354 1000sh multi　　　.80　.80
　b.　A355 1000sh multi　　　.80　.80
　c.　A356 1000sh multi　　　.80　.80
　d.　A357 1000sh multi　　　.80　.80
　e.　A358 1000sh multi　　　.80　.80
1921　　　Vert. strip of 5　　6.25　6.25
　a.　A359 1600sh multi　　1.25　1.25
　b.　A360 1600sh multi　　1.25　1.25
　c.　A361 1600sh multi　　1.25　1.25
　d.　A362 1600sh multi　　1.25　1.25
　e.　A363 1600sh multi　　1.25　1.25
　　Nos. 1919-1921 (3)　13.25 13.25

Pan-African Postal Union, 30th anniv. (in 2010).

A357

A358

A359

A360

A361

A362

AIDS Prevention
A364

Emblems and: 700sh, Philly Bongoley Lutaaya (1951-89), musician. 1500sh, Man and woman receiving information about AIDS at clinic, horiz. 1800sh, Medical workers in laboratory, horiz. 1900sh, People holding candles, horiz. 2700sh, AIDS ribbon within frame with simulated perforations and cancel. 3400sh, Family at home, horiz.

Perf. 13¼x13, 13x13¼
2012, Mar. 29　　　　　　**Litho.**
1922-1927 A364　Set of 6　　9.75　9.75

Discovery of human immunodeficiency virus, 30th anniv.

Wildlife — A365

No. 1928 — Primates: a, 3400sh, De Brazza's monkey. b, 3400sh, Brown greater galago. c, 4100sh, Patas monkey. d, 4100sh, L'Hoest's monkey.

No. 1929 — Wildcats: a, 3400sh, Cheetah chasing Thomson's gazelle. b, 3400sh, Lions. c, 4100sh, Leopards. d, 4100sh, Caracals.

No. 1930 — Two African bush elephants: a, 3400sh, Elephant at right facing left. b, 3400sh, Elephant at right facing forward. c, 4100sh, Elephant at right facing left. d, 4100sh, Elephant at right facing forward.

No. 1931 — Owls: a, 3400sh, Pel's fishing owls. b, 3400sh, African wood owls. c, 4100sh, Spotted eagle-owls. d, 4100sh, Cape eagle-owls.

No. 1932 — Kingfishers: a, 3400sh, Pied kingfisher. b, 3400sh, Gray-headed kingfishers. c, 4100sh, Malachite kingfishers. d, 4100sh, Malachite kingfisher, Pied kingfisher.

No. 1933 — Birds of prey: a, 3400sh, Tawny eagle. b, 3400sh, Bateleurs. c, 4100sh, Osprey. d, 4100sh, Rüppell's vulture.

No. 1934 — Butterflies: a, 3400sh, Silverbarred charaxes. b, 3400sh, Green-banded swallowtail. c, 4100sh, Crossley's forest queen. d, 4100sh, Acraea swordtail.

No. 1935 — Fish: a, 3400sh, Haplochromis katonga. b, 3400sh, Haplochromis nyererei. c, 4100sh, Lates niloticus. d, 4100sh, Mormyrus macrocephalus.

No. 1936 — Reptiles: a, 3400sh, Graceful chameleon. b, 3400sh, Leopard tortoise. c, 4100sh, Gaboon viper. d, 4100sh, Nile crocodile.

No. 1937 — Endangered species: a, 3400sh, Beaudoin's snake eagles. b, 3400sh, African golden cats. c, 4100sh, Cheetahs. d, 4100sh, Checkered elephant shrews.

No. 1938, 8300sh, Blue monkeys. No. 1939, 8300sh, Leopards, diff. No. 1940, 8300sh, Two African bush elephants, diff. No. 1941, 8300sh, Verreaux's eagle-owl. No. 1942, 8300sh, Gray-headed kingfishers, diff. No. 1943, 8300sh, Western marsh harriers. No. 1944, 8300sh, Two Precis octavia. No. 1945, 8300sh, Haplochromis petronius. No. 1946, 8300sh, Gaboon viper, diff. No. 1947, 8300sh, Black-crowned crane.

2012, Mar. 30　Litho.　Perf. 13¼
　　　　Sheets of 4, #a-d
1928-1937 A365　Set of 10　120.00 120.00
　　　　Souvenir Sheets
1938-1947 A365　Set of 10　62.50 62.50

Miniature Sheets

A366

Chimpanzees — A367

Various photographs of chimpanzees, as shown.

2012, Apr. 11		**Litho.**	**Perf. 12**	
1948	A366	3500sh Sheet of 4, #a-d		11.50 11.50
1949	A367	3500sh Sheet of 4, #a-d		11.50 11.50

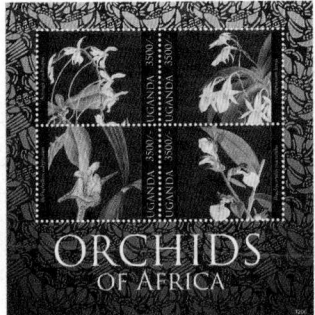

Orchids — A368

No. 1950: a, Aerangis arachnopus. b, Angraecum leonis. c, Bulbophyllum calyptratum. d, Brachycorythis macrantha.
10,000sh, Bulbophyllum sandersonii, vert.

2012, Apr. 11		**Litho.**	**Perf. 12**	
1950	A368	3500sh Sheet of 4, #a-d		11.50 11.50
Souvenir Sheet				
Perf. 12½				
1951	A368	10,000sh multi		8.25 8.25

No. 1951 contains one 38x51mm stamp.

Endangered Animals — A369

No. 1952: a, Addax. b, Cheetah. c, Western lowland gorilla. d, Mountain zebra. e, Dama gazelle.
10,000sh, Ostrich.

2012, Apr. 11		**Litho.**	**Perf. 14**	
1952	A369	3000sh Sheet of 5, #a-e		12.50 12.50
Souvenir Sheet				
Perf. 12½				
1953	A369	10,000sh multi		8.25 8.25

No. 1953 contains one 51x38mm stamp.

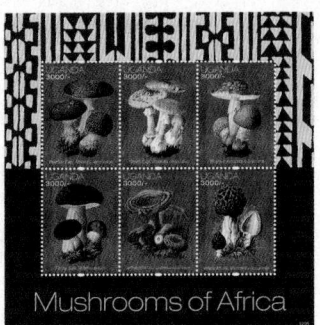

Mushrooms — A370

No. 1954: a, Panther cap. b, Death cap. c, Blusher. d, Penny bun. e, Saffron milk cap. f, Yellow morel.
No. 1955: a, Amethyst deceiver. b, Mica cap.

Perf. 13 Syncopated			
2012, Apr. 11		**Litho.**	
1954	A370	3000sh Sheet of 6, #a-f	15.00 15.00
Souvenir Sheet			
1955	A370	5000sh Sheet of 2, #a-b	8.25 8.25

Sinking of the Titanic, Cent. — A371

No. 1956: a, Titanic under construction. b, Stern of Titanic. c, Table and chairs. d, Deck. e, Bow of Titanic. f, Lifeboats.
10,000d, Titanic, diff.

Perf. 13 Syncopated			
2012, Apr. 11		**Litho.**	
1956	A371	3000sh Sheet of 6, #a-f	15.00 15.00
Souvenir Sheet			
1957	A371	10,000sh multi	8.25 8.25

American Civil War, 150th Anniv. — A372

No. 1958 — Abraham Lincoln and detail from Battle of Chattanooga print published by Kurz and Allison: a, Red panel at top. b, White panel at top, no flag. c, Blue panel at top. d, White panel at top, flag visible.
10,000sh, Lincoln, Battle of Spotsylvania print by Kurz and Allison.

Perf. 13 Syncopated			
2012, Apr. 11		**Litho.**	
1958	A372	3500sh Sheet of 4, #a-d	11.50 11.50
Souvenir Sheet			
1959	A372	10,000sh multi	8.25 8.25

Inauguration of Pres. John F. Kennedy, 50th Anniv. (in 2011) — A373

No. 1960 Pres. Kennedy: a, With Vice President Lyndon B. Johnson. b, With wife, Jacqueline. c, Taking oath of office. d, Delivering inaugural speech.
10,000sh, Pres. Kennedy speaking, vert.

2012, Apr. 11		**Litho.**	**Perf. 12**	
1960	A373	3500sh Sheet of 4, #a-d		11.50 11.50
Souvenir Sheet				
1961	A373	10,000sh multi		8.25 8.25

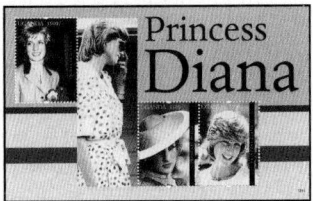

Princess Diana (1961-97) — A374

No. 1962 — Princess Diana: a, Holding flowers. b, Wearing hat. c, Without hat.
10,000sh, Princess Diana wearing hat, diff.

Perf. 13 Syncopated			
2012, Apr. 11		**Litho.**	
1962	A374	3500sh Sheet of 3, #a-c	8.50 8.50
Souvenir Sheet			
Perf. 12			
1963	A374	10,000sh multi	8.25 8.25

No. 1963 contains one 30x50mm stamp.

Paintings by Peter Paul Rubens (1577-1640) — A375

No. 1964: a, 3400sh, The Deposition. b, 3400sh, The Martyrdom of St. Stephen. c, 4100sh, The Last Judgment. d, 4100sh, Christ and Mary Magdalene.
8300sh, Christ at Simon the Pharisee, horiz.

2012, July 26		**Litho.**	**Perf. 13¼**	
1964	A375	Sheet of 4, #a-d		12.00 12.00
Souvenir Sheet				
1965	A375	8300sh multi		6.75 6.75

Yuri Gagarin (1934-68), First Man in Space — A376

No. 1966: a, 3400sh, Gagarin, Vostok 1 in orbit. b, 3400sh, Gagarin, MiG-15. c, 4100sh, Monuments to Gagarin. d, 4100sh, Gagarin in helmet, launch of Vostok 1.
8300sh, Gagarin, launch of Vostok 1, diff.

2012, July 26		**Litho.**	**Perf. 13¼**	
1966	A376	Sheet of 4, #a-d		12.00 12.00
Souvenir Sheet				
1967	A376	8300sh multi		6.75 6.75

Chess Match Between Deep Blue Computer and Garry Kasparov, 15th Anniv. — A377

No. 1968: a, 3400sh, Kasparov standing at right, television screens at left. b, 3400sh, Kasparov and flags. c, 4100sh, Kasparov seated, computer display of chess board. d, 4100sh, Kasparov seated, television screens at left.
8300sh, Kasparov, chess board, arm of human and mechanical arm wrestling.

2012, July 26		**Litho.**	**Perf. 13¼**	
1968	A377	Sheet of 4, #a-d		12.00 12.00
Souvenir Sheet				
1969	A377	8300sh multi		6.75 6.75

Whitney Houston (1963-2012), Singer — A378

No. 1970 — Two images of Houston with larger image of Houston (without microphone) with: a, 3400sh, Hand on cheek. b, 3400sh, Eyes shut. c, 4100sh, Strapless gown. d, 4100sh, Dress with zipper, with hand touching side of head.
8300sh, Houston, diff.

2012, July 26		**Litho.**	**Perf. 13¼**	
1970	A378	Sheet of 4, #a-d		12.00 12.00
Souvenir Sheet				
1971	A378	8300sh multi		6.75 6.75

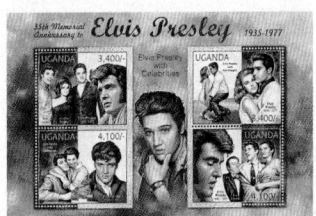

Elvis Presley (1935-77) — A379

No. 1972 — Presley with: a, 3400sh, Wife, Priscilla, and Tom Jones. b, 3400sh, Ann-Margret. c. 4100sh, Sophia Loren. d, 4100sh, Lou Costello and Jane Russell.
8300sh, Presley with Muhammad Ali.

2012, July 26	Litho.	Perf. 13¼
1972 A379	Sheet of 4, #a-d	12.00 12.00

Souvenir Sheet

| 1973 A379 | 8300sh multi | 6.75 6.75 |

Elvis Presley (1935-77) — A380

No. 1974 — Presley with guitar, with frame color of: a, Dark blue green. b, Light blue green. c, Blue green.
10,000sh, Presley holding microphone.

2012, July 26	Litho.	Perf. 12
1974 A380	3500sh Sheet of 4, #1974a, 1974b, 2 #1974c	11.50 11.50

Souvenir Sheet

| 1975 A380 | 10,000sh multi | 8.00 8.00 |

Olympic Rings and Stylized Torch — A381

Stadia for the 2012 Summer Olympics, London A382

No. 1977: a, Olympic Stadium. b, Wembley Stadium. c, Old Trafford Stadium.

2012, Aug. 3	Litho.	Perf. 13¼x13
1976 A381	1500sh multi	1.25 1.25
	Perf. 13¼	
1977	Vert. strip of 3	2.60 2.60
a.-c.	A382 1050sh Any single	.85 .85

Independence, 50th Anniv. — A383

Designs: 700sh, 50th anniv. emblem. 1800sh, Independence Monument. 2700sh, Flag of Uganda.

2012, Oct. 9	Litho.	Perf. 14
1978-1980 A383	Set of 3	4.00 4.00

Transportation — A385

No. 1983 — Sailboats, with inscriptions: a, 3400sh, "2010 Extreme Sailing Series, skipper of The Wave, Muscat." b, 3400sh, "McDougall at PUMA Moth Worlds, 2010." c, 4100sh, "Tom Slingsby, ISAF World Sailor of the Year, 2010." d, 4100sh, "Bahrain Pindar Team, Langenargen, World Match Racing Tour 2009."

No. 1984 — Steam trains: a, 3400sh, Tornado 60163. b, 3400sh, Furness Railway No. 20. c, 4100sh, Terrier 32662. d, 4100sh, Brighton Works DS 377.

No. 1985 — High-speed trains: a, 3400sh, Transrapid TR-09, "2012" at LL. b, 3400sh, Transrapid TR-09, "2012" at UR. c, 4100sh, CR380A, black denomination at LL. d, 4100sh, CR380A, white denomination at UR.

No. 1986 — Airplanes: a, 3400sh, Airbus A380. b, 3400sh, Boeing 747-8. c, 4100sh, Aerospatiale BAC Concorde. d, 4100sh, Boeing 777-300.

No. 1987 — Airships: a, 3400sh, LZ-127. b, 3400sh, Hindenburg (LZ-129). c, 4100sh, USS Macon (ZRS-5). d, 4100sh, LZ-17 Sachsen.

No. 1988 — Formula 1 race cars and drivers: a, 3400sh, McLaren-Mercedes car, Lewis Hamilton. b, 3400sh, Lotus-Renault car, Kimi Räikkönen. c, 4100sh, Mercedes car, Michael Schumacher. d, 4100sh, Red Bull Racing-Renault car, Sebastian Vettel.

No. 1989 — Motorcycles: a, 3400sh, Kawasaki VERSYS 650. b, 3400sh, Ferrari V4 Superbike Concept. c, 4100sh, Honda V4 Concept. d, 4100sh, Yamaha YZF R1 1000.

No. 1990 — Unmotorized vehicles: a, 3400sh, Horse and cart. b, 3400sh, Paddleboat. c, 4100sh, Velomobile. d, 4100sh, Skateboard.

No. 1991 — Special transport vehicles: a, 3400sh, 1964 Ford F-600 Young fire truck. b, 3400sh, 1975 Plymouth Grand Fury and 1999 Ford Crown Victoria police cars, 1970 Harley-Davidson FLH police motorcycle. c, 4100sh, 1968 Citroen DS and 2008 Ford E450 Horton Type III ambulances. d, 4100sh, 2010 Ford F550 Gurkha MAPV police vehicle, 1970 Harley-Davidson FLH police motorcycle.

No. 1992 — Futuristic concept cars: a, 3400sh, Audi A9 concept car. b, 3400sh, Peugeot Touch concept car. c, 4100sh, Lotus Esquive concept car. d, 4100sh, Honda 3R-C concept car.

No. 1993, 8300sh, Extreme Sailing Series, Boston, 2011. No. 1994, 8300sh, Brighton Blue Bell steam train, clock. No. 1995, 8300sh, Bombardier Zefiro 380. No. 1996, 8300sh, Boeing 747-8, diff. No. 1997, 8300sh, Hindenburg (LZ-129), diff. No. 1998, 8300sh, Ferrari car, Fernando Alonso. No. 1999, 8300sh, Suzuki Biplane concept motorcycle. No. 2000, 8300sh, Hang glider. No. 2001, 8300sh, 1949 Mack L Model fire trucks. No. 2002, 8300sh, Lotus Hot Wheels concept car.

2012, Oct. 22	Litho.	Perf. 13¼

Sheets of 4, #a-d

| 1983-1992 A385 | Set of 10 | 120.00 120.00 |

Souvenir Sheets

| 1993-2002 A385 | Set of 10 | 65.00 65.00 |

Endangered Animals — A386

No. 2003 — Chimpanzees: a, 3400sh, Adult and juvenile. b, 3400sh, Adult. c, 4100sh, Adult, diff. d, 4100sh, Adult on tree branch.

No. 2004 — Gorillas: a, 3400sh, Two adult Gorilla gorilla facing right, denomination at top center. b, 3400sh, Gorilla gorilla and Gorilla beringei facing left, denomination at UL. c, 4100sh, Gorilla gorilla and Gorilla beringei. d, 4100sh, Two adult Gorilla beringei beringei and juvenile.

No. 2005 — Lions: a, 3400sh, Female on rock. b, 3400sh, Male and female, animal name at UR. c, 4100sh, Female stalking. d, 4100sh, Male.

No. 2006 — Lions: a, 3400sh, Head of male, female looking left, animal name at top center. b, 3400sh, Two males and one female. c, 4100sh, Female and cub. d, 4100sh, Female and head of cub.

No. 2007 — Cheetahs: a, 3400sh, Running left. b, 3400sh, Standing. c, 4100sh, Walking right. d, 4100sh, Resting.

No. 2008 — Elephants: a, 3400sh, Two animals, animal name above country name. b, 3400sh, Two animals, front animal facing left, animal name at UL. c, 4100sh, Four animals, animal name at UL. d, 4100sh, Two animals, animal name above country name.

No. 2009 — Elephants: a, 3400sh, One animal. b, 3400sh, Two animals walking side-by-side, animal name at UL. c, 4100sh, Adult and juvenile. d, 4100sh, One animal.

No. 2010 — Birds of prey: a, 3400sh, Neophron percnopterus in flight. b, 3400sh, Gyps rueppellii on branch. c, 4100sh, Gyps rueppellii facing right. d, 4100sh, Neophron percnopterus on rock.

No. 2011 — Secretary bird: a, 3400sh, Facing right, in flight. b, 3400sh, Facing left, in flight. c, 4100sh, Head of bird facing right and bird facing left. d, 4100sh, Two birds facing left.

No. 2012, 8300sh, Pan troglodytes (chimpanzee). No. 2013, 8300sh, Gorilla beringei, Gorilla beringei beringei (gorillas). No. 2014, 8300sh, Male and female Panthera leo (lions). No. 2015, 8300sh, Male Panthera leo (lion). No. 2016, 8300sh, Acinonyx jubatus (cheetah). No. 2017, 8300sh, One Loxodonta africana (elephant). No. 2018, 8300sh, Three Loxodonta africana (elephants). No. 2019, 8300sh, Gyps rueppellii (bird of prey), diff. No. 2020, 8300sh, Two Sagittarius serpentarius facing left (secretrary birds).

2012, Nov. 8	Litho.	Perf. 13¼

Sheets of 4, #a-d

| 2003-2011 A386 | Set of 9 | 100.00 100.00 |

Souvenir Sheets

| 2012-2020 A386 | Set of 9 | 55.00 55.00 |

Compare No. 2020 with No. 2022.

A387

A388

A389

Worldwide Fund for Nature (WWF) A390

Secretary Bird — A391

2012, Nov. 8	Litho.	Perf. 13x13¼
2021	Horiz. strip of 4	12.00 12.00
a.	A387 4100sh multi	3.00 3.00
b.	A388 4100sh multi	3.00 3.00
c.	A389 4100sh multi	3.00 3.00
d.	A390 4100sh multi	3.00 3.00
e.	Souvenir sheet of 4, #2021a-2021d	12.00 12.00
f.	Souvenir sheet of 8, 2 each #2021a-2021d	24.00 24.00

Souvenir Sheet
Perf. 12¾x13¼

| 2022 A391 | 8300sh multi | 6.25 6.25 |

Compare No. 2022 with No. 2020.

SEMI-POSTAL STAMPS

> Catalogue values for all unused stamps in this section are for never Hinged items.

PAPU (Pan African Postal Union), 18th Anniv. — SP1

No. B1, Mountain gorilla.

1998, Jan. 18	Litho.	Perf. 14
B1	SP1 300sh +150sh multi	1.10 1.10

POSTAGE DUE STAMPS

> Catalogue values for unused stamps in this section are for Never Hinged items.

Type of Kenya, 1967
Perf. 14x13½

1967, Jan. 3		Litho.	Unwmk.	
J1	D1	5c red	.25	4.25
J2	D1	10c green	.25	4.25
J3	D1	20c dark blue	.25	5.50
J4	D1	30c reddish brown	.40	7.25
J5	D1	40c red lilac	.60	8.00
J6	D1	1sh orange	1.75	20.00
		Nos. J1-J6 (6)	3.50	49.25

1970, Mar. 31			Perf. 14x15	
J1a	D1	5c red	.25	1.25
J2a	D1	10c green	.25	1.25
J3a	D1	20c dark blue	.30	4.25
J4a	D1	30c reddish brown	.40	5.25
J5a	D1	40c red lilac	.60	6.25
		Nos. J1a-J5a (5)	1.80	18.25

1973			Perf. 15	
J1b	D1	5c red	.25	2.25
J2b	D1	10c green	.25	2.25
J3b	D1	20c dark blue	.70	6.00
J4b	D1	30c reddish brown	.95	9.00
J5b	D1	40c red lilac	1.60	13.50
J6b	D1	1sh orange	4.00	24.00
		Nos. J1b-J6b (6)	7.75	57.00

Nos. J1-J6 Overprinted in Black "LIBERATED / 1979"

1979, Dec.		Litho.	Perf. 14	
J7	D1	5c red	.25	.70
J8	D1	10c green	.25	.70
J9	D1	20c violet blue	.25	.70
J10	D1	30c reddish brown	.25	1.00
J11	D1	40c red lilac	.25	1.00
J12	D1	1sh orange	.60	1.25
		Nos. J7-J12 (6)	1.85	5.35

Wildlife — D2

1985, Mar. 11   Litho.   Perf. 15x14

J13	D2	5sh Lion	.25	.95
J14	D2	10sh African buffalo	.25	.95
J15	D2	20sh Kob antelope	.60	1.40
J16	D2	40sh Elephant	1.25	2.10
J17	D2	50sh Zebra	1.25	2.10
J18	D2	100sh Rhinoceros	1.75	3.50
		Nos. J13-J18 (6)	5.35	11.00

UKRAINE

yü-'krän

LOCATION — In southeastern Europe, bordering on the Black Sea
GOVT. — Republic
AREA — 231,900 sq. mi.
POP. — 48,760,474 (2001)
CAPITAL — Kyiv

Following the collapse of the Russian Empire, a national assembly met at Kyiv and declared the Ukrainian National Republic on Jan. 22, 1918. During three years of civil war, the Ukrainian army, as well as Bolshevik, White Russian, Allied and Polish armies, fought back and forth across the country. By November, 1920, Ukraine was finally occupied by Soviet forces, and Soviet stamps were used from that time, until the recreation of the independent Ukraine on Aug. 24, 1991.

200 Shahiv = 100 Kopiyok (Kopecks)
= 1 Karbovanets (Ruble)

100 Shahiv = 1 Hryvnia

100 Kopiyok = 1 Karbovanets (1992)

100 Kopiyok = 1 Hryvnia (1996)

> Catalogue values for unused stamps in this country are for Never Hinged stamps, beginning with Scott 100 in the regular postage section, Scott B9 in the semipostal section, and Scott F1 in the registration section.

Watermarks

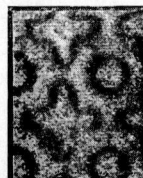

Wmk. 116 —
Crosses and
Circles

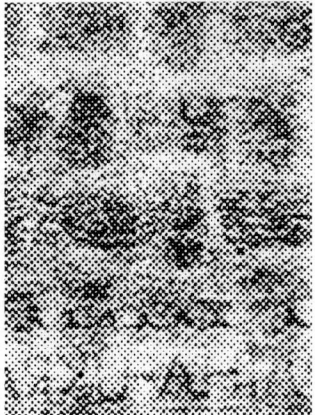

Wmk. 399

Republic's
Trident
Emblem — A1

Allegorical
Ukraine — A3

Ukrainian
Peasant — A2

Trident — A4

Inscription of
Value — A5

1918, July   Typo.   Imperf.
Thin Paper

1	A1	10sh buff	.35	.40
2	A2	20sh brown	.35	.40
3	A3	30sh ultra	.35	.40
a.		30sh blue	2.75	6.50
4	A4	40sh green	.35	.40
5	A5	50sh red	.35	.40
		Nos. 1-5 (5)	1.75	2.00

The stamps of this issue exist perforated or pin-perforated unofficially.

Forgeries of this set exist on a very thin, glossy paper.

These designs were earlier (April, 1918) utilized for money tokens, printed on thin cardboard, perforated 11 ½, and bearing an inscription on the reverse "Circulates on par with coins" in Ukrainian. These tokens exist favor canceled but were not postage stamps. Value uncanceled, $6 each.

Stamps of Russia
Overprinted in Violet,
Black, Blue, Red, Brown
or Green

This trident-shaped emblem was taken from the arms of the Grand Prince Volodymyr and adopted as the device of the Ukrainian Republic.

In the early months of independence, Russian stamps were commonly used, but the influx of large quantities of stamps from Russia made it necessary to take measures to protect postal revenue. In August, 1918, local post offices were ordered to send their existing stocks of Russian stamps to regional centers, where they were overprinted with the trident arms. Unoverprinted Russian stamps were declared invalid after October 1, although they were often accepted for use.

This overprint was handstamped, typographed or lithographed. It was applied in various cities in the Ukraine and there are numerous types.

> Nos. 6-47 represent the basic Russian stamps that received these overprints. Values are for the most common overprint variety.
> For a detailed listing of these overprints, see the *Scott Classic Specialized Catalogue of Stamps and Covers 1840-1940*.

The basic Russian stamps to which Trident overprints were applied:

A8

A9

A11

A12

A13

A14

A15

On Stamps of 1902-03

1918		Wmk. 168	Perf. 13½	
6	A12	3½r black & gray	100.00	75.00
7	A12	7r black & yellow	100.00	75.00

On Stamps of 1909-18
Lozenges of Varnish on Face
Perf. 14, 14½x15
Unwmk.

8	A14	1k orange	.25	.35
9	A14	2k green	.25	.35
10	A14	3k red	.25	.35
11	A15	4k carmine	.25	.35
12	A14	5k claret	.25	.35
13	A14	7k light blue	.25	.35
14	A15	10k dark blue	.25	.35
15	A11	14k blue & rose	.25	.35
16	A11	15k red brn & bl	.25	.35
17	A8	20k blue & car	.25	.35
18	A11	25k grn & gray vio	.40	.50
19	A11	35k red brn & grn	.25	.35
20	A8	50k violet & grn	.25	.35
21	A11	70k brown & org	.25	.35

Perf. 13½

22	A9	1r lt brn, brn & org	.55	.75
23	A12	3½r mar & lt grn	1.25	2.50
24	A13	5r dk bl, grn & pale bl	7.50	11.00
25	A12	7r dk grn & pink	9.00	12.00
26	A13	10r scar, yel & gray	13.00	18.00
		Nos. 6-26 (21)	234.95	199.30

On Stamps of 1917
Perf. 14, 14½x15

27	A14	10k on 7k light blue	.75	1.00
28	A11	20k on 14k bl & rose	.75	1.00

On Stamps of 1917-18
Imperf

29	A14	1k orange	.25	.35
30	A14	2k gray green	.25	.35
31	A14	3k red	.25	.35
32	A15	4k carmine	.25	.35
33	A14	5k claret	.90	1.50
34	A11	15k red brn & bl	.25	.35
35	A8	20k bl & car	.75	1.50
36	A11	25k grn & gray vio	60.00	—
37	A11	35k red brn & grn	.25	.35
38	A8	50k violet & grn	.30	.35
39	A11	70k brown & org	.25	.35
40	A9	1r pale brn, brn & red org	.25	.60
41	A12	3½r mar & lt grn	1.00	2.50
42	A13	5r dk bl, grn & pale bl	1.50	3.00
43	A12	7r dk grn & pink	2.50	4.00
44	A13	10r scar, yel & gray	70.00	85.00
		Nos. 29-44 (16)	138.95	100.90

PF1

Russian Stamps AR1-AR3.

Wmk. 171   Litho.
Perf. 14, 14½x14¾

45	PF1	1k red, buff	5.00	25.00
46	PF1	5k green, buff	20.00	120.00
47	PF1	10k brown, buff	35.00	350.00
		Nos. 45-47 (3)	60.00	495.00

Nos. 45-47 were used and accepted as postage stamps during stamp shortages.

The trident overprint was applied by favor to Russia Nos. 88-104, 110-111, the Romanov issue.

For surcharges see Russian Offices in the Turkish Empire Nos. 320-339.

A6

1919, Jan.   Litho.

48	A6	20h red & green	10.00	25.00

Because of its high face value, No. 48 was used primarily on money transfer forms or parcel receipts. Used value is for a postally used example.

Nos. 1 and 5
Surcharged

1919, Feb.   Unwmk.   Imperf.

49	A1	35k on 10sh buff	9.00	20.00
50	A5	70k on 50sh red	70.00	50.00
a.		Surcharge inverted		60.00

Nos. 49 and 50 were originally believed to have been created by the Soviets in the Ukraine in April, 1919, but more recent research seems to indicate that they were created by the White (Don) Army operating in eastern Ukraine at the request of the Ukrainian government. Correctly franked covers have been recorded from the February-June 1919 period.

Excellent forged surcharges exist.

Ukrainian Soviet Socialist Republic

During 1920/1921, hyperinflation of the ruble created a desperate need for stamps to pay ever-rising postal rates. Many Russian cities and districts surcharged existing stocks of Russian stamps in needed denominations for provisional use.

In June 1920 the national government of the Soviet Ukrainian Republic authorized the Kharkiv post office to create such surcharges for use in the Kharkiv region and in adjacent oblasts. Both unoverprinted Russian stamps and stamps bearing the regional trident overprints of Katerynoslav, Kharkiv and Kyiv were surcharged to raise their face value 100-fold. They were sold at 236 post offices in the Ukraine from June 1920 through Feb. 1921.

In Feb. 1922 three Russian postal savings stamps were surcharged for provisional use by the Kyiv post office, at the direction of the central government. As with the Kharkiv surcharges, these stamps were distributed over a wide area within the country.

KHARKIV ISSUE
Ukrainian and Russian Stamps
Handstamp Surcharged

Ukrainian trident overprinted issues and unoverprinted Russian stamps revalued 100-

fold by changing denominations from kopecks to rubles.

Two types of overprint: type I, Cyrillic RUB (not including periods) 9.5mmx6.5mm; type II, 8.5mmx6.5mm.

Number of basic Ukrainian or Russian stamp shown in parentheses.

On Katerynoslav Trident Ovpt. Issue of 1918

Type I Reading Upward

1920, June

51	A11	15k red brown & blue (#16a)	75.00	75.00

Kharkiv Trident Ovpt.
Issue of 1918

52	A14	1k orange (#8b)	100.00	60.00
a.		Surcharge reading downward	150.00	150.00
53	A14	2k green (#9b)	100.00	65.00
54	A14	3k red (#10b)	80.00	40.00
55	A11	15k red brn & blue (#16b)	40.00	35.00
56	A8	20k blue & car (#17b)	200.00	175.00
a.		Surcharge reading downward	300.00	300.00
57	A11	20k on 14k blue & rose (#28b)	170.00	190.00

Imperf

58	A14	1k orange (#29b)	75.00	75.00
a.		Surcharge reading downward	120.00	120.00
59	A14	2k green (#30b)	250.00	250.00
60	A14	3k red (#31b)	40.00	40.00

On Kyiv Trident Ovpt. Issue of 1918

No. 61   No. 63

On Kyiv II Overprint

61	A14	1k orange (#8f)	40.00	40.00

Imperf

62	A14	1k orange (#29f)	40.00	50.00
a.		Surcharge reading downward		

On Kyiv III Overprint

63	A14	3k red (#31g)	15.00	20.00

On Russian Arms Issue of 1909-18

No. 64

64	A14	1k orange (#73)	50.00	50.00
65	A14	2k green (#74)	10.00	15.00
a.		Surcharge reading downward	15.00	20.00
66	A14	3k red (#75)	10.00	15.00
a.		Surcharge reading downward	25.00	20.00
67	A15	4k red (#76)	325.00	
68	A14	5k claret (#77)	7.00	6.00
a.		Surcharge reading downward	20.00	20.00
69	A15	10k dk blue (#79)	15.00	15.00
a.		Surcharge reading downward	90.00	100.00
70	A11	15k red brn & blue (#81)	7.00	6.00
a.		Surcharge reading downward	10.00	10.00
71	A8	20k blue & car (#82)	10.00	6.00
a.		Surcharge reading downward	15.00	12.00

Imperf

72	A14	1k orange (#119)	50.00	36.00
a.		Surcharge reading downward	100.00	100.00
73	A14	2k green (#120)	45.00	55.00
74	A14	3k red (#121)	30.00	36.00
75	A14	5k claret (#123)	9.00	7.00
a.		Surcharge reading downward	25.00	25.00
76	A11	15k red brn & blue (#125)	120.00	130.00
a.		Surcharge reading downward	—	—

Type II Reading Upward
On Kharkiv Trident Ovpt. Issue of 1918

No. 79a

77	A14	3k red (#31b)	35.00	40.00

On Kyiv Trident Ovpt. Issue of 1918

78	A14	1k orange (#29f)	20.00	25.00

On Russian Arms Issue of 1919-18
Perf. 14x14½

79	A14	2k green (#74)	6.00	7.00
a.		Surcharge reading downward	12.00	12.00
80	A14	5k claret (#77)	8.00	7.00
a.		Surcharge reading downward	15.00	12.00
81	A15	10k dk blue (#79)	18.00	18.00
a.		Surcharge reading downward	100.00	115.00
82	A11	15k red brn & blue (#81)	8.00	7.00
a.		Surcharge reading downward	12.00	10.00
83	A8	20k blue & car (#82)	8.00	7.00

Imperf

84	A14	2k green (#120)	50.00	60.00

KYIV ISSUE

Russian Postal Savings
Stamps Handstamp
Surcharged

1922, Feb.   **Wmk. 171**

85	7500 (r) on 5k, green, buff		50.00	50.00
a.	Surcharge reading downward		60.00	55.00
86	8000 (r) on 5k, green, buff		150.00	90.00
a.	Surcharge reading downward		180.00	150.00
87	15000 (r) on 10k, brown, buff		300.00	150.00
a.	Surcharge reading downward		450.00	250.00

Nos. 85-87 are normally found on stamps watermarked with a vertical diamond pattern (Wmk. 171) but also exist on paper watermarked sideways, with both upward and downward-reading surcharges. These are rare and are worth approximately 8 times the values shown.

Nos. 1-5 surcharged in grivni (hryven) with the Polish eagle were sold as Polish occupation issues. They are of private origin.

Nos. 1-3 and 5 overprinted diagonally as above ("South Russia") are believed to be of private origin.

A lithographed set of 14 stamps (1h-200h) of these types, perf. 11½, was prepared in 1920, but never placed in use. Value, set $5.

All values exist imperf., some with inverted centers. Trial printings exist on various papers, including inverted, multiple, omitted and misaligned center vignettes. These are from the printer's waste.

This set handstamped "VILNA UKRAINA / 1921" and 6 values additionally overprinted "DOPLATA" are of private origin.

In 1923 the Ukrainian government-in-exile in Warsaw prepared an 11-value set, consisting of the 10h, 20h and 40h denominations of the unissued 1920 set surcharged and overprinted with the Cyrillic "UPP," supposedly intended as a Field Post issue for a planned invasion of the Ukraine. The invasion never occurred, and the stamps were never issued. Value $15.

For German stamps overprinted "Ukraine" see Russia Nos. N29-N48.

> **Catalogue values for unused stamps in this section, from this point to the end of the section, are for Never Hinged items.**

Cossacks in Ukraine, 500th Anniv. — A20

Design: No. 101, Ukrainian emigrants to Canada.

1992, Mar. 1   Litho.   Perf. 12

100	A20	15k multicolored	1.25	1.25
101	A20	15k multicolored	1.25	1.25

Ukrainian emigration to Canada, centennial (No. 101). Dated 1991.

Mykola V. Lysenko (1842-1912),
Composer — A21

1992, Mar. 22   Perf. 13

102	A21	100k multicolored	1.25	1.25

Numerous trident overprints on Soviet stamps exist. Many of them are legitimate local issues and were in official use. Locally produced stamps also exist.

Ukrainian Girl — A22

1992   Litho.   Perf. 12x12½

118	A22	50k bright blue	.25	.25
119	A22	70k bister	.25	.25
121	A22	1kb yellow green	.25	.25
122	A22	2kb purple	.25	.25
124	A22	5kb blue	.25	.25
126	A22	10kb red	.50	.50
128	A22	20kb green	2.50	2.50
130	A22	50kb brown	3.00	3.00
		Nos. 118-130 (8)	7.25	7.25

Issued: Nos. 124, 126, 128, 130, 5/16; 118-119, 121-122, 6/17.

Mykola I. Kostomarov (1817-1885), Writer — A23

1992, May 16   Photo.   Perf. 12x11½

133	A23	20k olive green	1.25	1.25

1992 Summer Olympics, Barcelona

A24   A25

1992, July 25   Litho.   Perf. 13

134	A24	3kb yel green & multi	.65	.65
135	A25	4kb multicolored	.85	.85
136	A24	5kb buff & multi	1.10	1.10
		Nos. 134-136 (3)	2.60	2.60

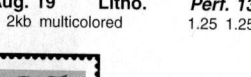

World Forum of Ukrainians, Kyiv — A26

1992, Aug. 19   Litho.   Perf. 13

137	A26	2kb multicolored	1.25	1.25

Declaration of Independence from the Soviet Union — A27

1992, Aug. 19   Perf. 13½x13

138	A27	2kb multicolored	1.25	1.25

Souvenir Sheet

Union of Ukrainian Philatelists, 25th Anniv. — A28

1992, Aug. 19   *Perf. 12*
139 A28 2kb multicolored   2.10 2.10

Intl. Letter Writing Week A29

1992, Oct. 4   *Perf. 13x13½*
140 A29 5kb multicolored   .70 .70

World Congress of Ukrainian Lawyers, Kyiv — A30

1992, Oct. 18   **Litho.**   *Perf. 13*
141 A30 15kb multicolored   1.25 1.25

Ukrainian Diaspora in Austria A31

Perf. 13½x14½
1992, Nov. 27   **Litho.**
142 A31 5kb multicolored   1.40 1.40

Embroidery A32

1992, Nov. 16   **Litho.**   *Perf. 11½x12*
143 A32 50k black & orange   1.40 1.40

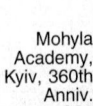 

Mohyla Academy, Kyiv, 360th Anniv. A33

1992, Nov. 27   **Litho.**   *Perf. 12x12½*
144 A33 1.50kb multicolored   1.40 1.40

Souvenir Sheet

Ukrainian Medal Winners, 1992 Summer Olympics, Barcelona — A34

1992, Dec. 14   **Litho.**   *Perf. 14*
145 A34 10kb multicolored   4.00 4.00

Coats of Arms — A35

1993, Feb. 15   **Litho.**   *Perf. 14x13½*
148 A35 3kb Lviv   1.75 1.75
150 A35 5kb Kyiv   2.75 2.75
See No. 292.

Cardinal Joseph Slipyj (1892-1984) A36

1993, Feb. 17   **Litho.**   *Perf. 14x13½*
166 A36 15kb multicolored   3.00 3.00

1st Vienna-Cracow-Lviv-Kyiv Air Mail Flight, 75th Anniv. — A37

1993, Mar. 31   *Perf. 13½x14*
167 A37 35kb Biplane   1.30 1.30
168 A37 50kb Jet   1.90 1.90

Easter A39

1993, Apr. 18   **Litho.**   *Perf. 13½*
169 A39 15kb multicolored   1.25 1.25

UN Declaration of Human Rights, 45th Anniv. — A40

Design: 5kb, Country Wedding in Lower Austria, by Ferdinand Georg Waldmuller.

Perf. 14½x13½
1993, June 11   **Litho.**
170 A40 5kb multicolored   3.00 3.00

 A41   A41a

 A41b   A41c

 A41d   A41e

 A41f   A41g

 A41h

Villagers at Work: 50kb, No. 177, Reaper with scythe. 100kb, No. 183, Ox carts. No. 173, 200kb, 500kb, Reapers with sickles. No. 174, Farmer with oxen. 150kb, 300kb, No. 181, Shepherd. No. 180, Bee keeper. No. 182, Fisherman. No. 185, Potter. (Illustrations A41a-A41h help identify the Cyrillic characters, not the designs.)

Perf. 12x12½, 14 (#174, 180, 182, 184)

1993-98			**Litho.**	
171 A41	50kb	green	.40	.40
172 A41	100kb	blue	.40	.40
173 A41c	(100kb)	brown	.50	.50
174 A41e	(100kb)	magenta	.60	.60
175 A41	150kb	red	.40	.40
176 A41	200kb	orange	.50	.50
177 A41d	(250kb)	green	.50	.50
178 A41	300kb	violet	.50	.50
179 A41	500kb	brown	.50	.50
180 A41f	(1800kb)	org brn	.50	.50
181 A41a	(5000kb)	red	2.50	2.50
182 A41g	(5300kb)	blue	1.25	1.25
183 A41b	(10,000kb)	blue	1.00	.50
a.	Perf. 14		7.00	7.00
184 A41h	(17,000kb)	red brn	2.25	2.25
	Nos. 171-184 (14)		11.80	11.30

Nos. 174, 181 issued for domestic letter rate; Nos. 177, 180 for letters within the Commonwealth of Independent States; Nos. 183-184 for mail abroad, surface and airmail. Actual amounts sold for varied with inflation. No. 183a sold for 30k on date of issue and was used for the domestic rate.

Issued: 50, 100, 150, 200, 300, 500kb, 12/18/93; #181, 183a, 5/28/94; #173, 177, 7/2/94; #174, 182, 10/15/94; #180, 184, 11/12/94; #183, 12/30/98.

Famine Deaths, 60th Anniv. — A42

1993, Sept. 12   **Litho.**   *Perf. 12*
188 A42 75kb brown   1.40 1.40

First Ukrainian Postage Stamp, 75th Anniv. A43

1993, Oct. 9
189 A43 100kb blue & brown   1.40 1.40
Stamp Day.

Liberation of Kyiv, 50th Anniv. A44

1993, Nov. 6   **Litho.**   *Perf. 12*
190 A44 75kb multicolored   1.25 1.25

A45

1994, Jan. 15   **Litho.**   *Perf. 12*
191 A45 200kb black & red   1.25 1.25
Agapit, Kyivan Rus physician, Middle Ages.

A46

Endangered species: No. 192, Erythronium dens, canis. No. 193, Cypripedium calceolus.

1994, Feb. 19   *Perf. 12x12½*
192 A46 200kb multicolored   1.30 1.30
193 A46 200kb multicolored   1.30 1.30

Independence Day — A47

1994, Sept. 3   Litho.   Imperf.
194 A47 5000kb multicolored   1.50 1.50
No. 194 has simulated perforations.

Kyiv University A47a

Litho. & Engr.
1994, Sept. 24   Perf. 13x13½
194A A47a 10,000kb multi   1.00 1.00
Souvenir Sheet
Perf. 12½x13
194B A47a 25,000kb multi   2.50 2.50
No. 194B contains one 40x27mm stamp.

Liberation of Soviet Areas, 50th Anniv. — A48

Battle maps and: a, Katyusha rockets, liberation of Russia. b, Fighter planes, liberation of Ukraine. c, Combined offensive, liberation of Belarus.

1994, Oct. 8   Litho.   Perf. 12½x12
195 A48 500kb Block of 3, #a.-c.,
    + label   1.50 1.50
See Russia No. 6213, Belarus No. 78.

Excavation of Trypillia culture, Cent. — A49

1994, Dec. 17   Litho.   Perf. 12x12½
196 A49 4000kb multicolored   .50 .50

1st Books Printed in Ukrainian, 500th Anniv. — A50

1994, Dec. 17   Perf. 13½
197 A50 4000kb multicolored   .50 .50

Sofiyivka Natural Park, Bicent. A51

1994, Dec. 17   Perf. 12½x12
198 A51 5000kb multicolored   .75 .75

Ilya Y. Repin (1844-1930), Painter — A52

1994, Dec. 17   Perf. 12x12½
199 A52 4000kb multicolored   .50 .50

City of Uzhhorod, 1100th Anniv. — A53

1995, Jan. 28   Litho.   Perf. 12
200 A53 5000kb multicolored   .60 .60

Ivan Franko (1856-1916), Writer — A54

Ivan Puliuj (1845-1918), Physicist — A55

No. 203, Lesia Ukrainka (1871-1913), poet.

1995, Feb. 2   Perf. 13½
201 A54 3000kb multicolored   .70 .70
202 A55 3000kb multicolored   .80 .80
203 A54 3000kb multicolored   .70 .70
    Nos. 201-203 (3)   2.20 2.20

Falco Peregrinus — A56

1995, Apr. 15   Litho.   Perf. 12
204 A56 5000kb shown   .50 .50
205 A56 10,000kb Grus grus   1.00 1.00

Maksym T. Rylskyi (1895-1964), Writer — A57

1995, Apr. 15   Perf. 13½x14
206 A57 50,000kb multicolored   2.00 2.00

End of World War II, 50th Anniv. — A58

1995, May 9   Litho.   Perf. 13½
207 A58 100,000kb multicolored   2.25 2.25

Artek, Intl. Children's Camp A59

1995, June 16   Litho.   Perf. 13½
208 A59 5000kb multicolored   .75 .75

Famous Writers A60

Design: 1000kb, Ivan Kotliarevskyi (1769-1838), depiction of his poem, "Eneida." 3000kb, Taras Shevchenko (1814-61), his book, "Kobzar."

1995, July 8
209 A60 1000kb multicolored   .50 .50
210 A60 3000kb multicolored   .50 .50

Hetman Petro Konashevych-Sahaidachny — A61

1995, July 22   Litho.   Perf. 13½
211 A61 30,000kb multicolored   1.00 1.00

Arms of Luhansk — A62

1995   Litho.   Perf. 13½
212 A62 10,000kb shown   .50 .50
213 A62 10,000kb Chernihiv   1.50 1.50
Issued: No. 212, 9/15; No. 213, 10/22.

Hetman Bohdan Khmelnytsky (Khmelnytskyi; 1593?-1657) — A63

1995, Sept. 23   Litho.   Perf. 12½x12
214 A63 40,000kb multi   1.10 1.10

Hetman Ivan Mazepa (1640?-1709) — A64

1995, Oct. 14   Perf. 13½
215 A64 30,000kb multi   1.60 1.60

A65

1995, Oct. 14
216 A65 50,000kb multi   2.00 2.00
European Nature Protection Year.

A66

1995, Oct. 22
217 A66 50,000kb multi   1.60 1.60
Intl. Children's Day.

UN, 50th Anniv. A67

1995, Oct. 24   Perf. 12x12½
218 A67 50,000kb multi   1.60 1.60

A68

1995, Dec. 9   **Perf. 13½**
219 A68 50,000kb multi   1.40 1.40

Ivan Karpenko-Karyi, playwright, actor.

A69

1995, Dec. 9
220 A69 50,000kb multi   1.75 1.75

Mikhailo Hrushevskyi, 1st Ukrainian president.

P. Safarik (1795-1861), Writer — A70

1995, Dec. 27
221 A70 30,000kb green   1.40 1.40

Trolleybus   Streetcar
A71   A72

City Bus — A73

1995, Dec. 27   Litho.   Perf. 14
No Year Date

222 A71 (1000kb) blue violet   .25   .25
  a.   Imprint "2003"   1.25 1.25
  b.   Imprint "2005"   1.25 1.25
  c.   Imprint "2006"   1.25 1.25
223 A72 (2000kb) green   2.75 2.75
224 A73 (3000kb) red   1.00   .80
  a.   Imprint "2006"   .25   .25
      Nos. 222-224 (3)   4.00 3.80

The postal rate that No. 223 paid was sharply increased greatly affecting the cost of the stamp at the post offices.
Imprinted values issued: #222a, 2003; #222b, 12/1/05; #222c, 2/3/06. #224a, 9/28/06.

Taras Shevchenko University Astronomical Observatory, Kyiv, 150th Anniv. — A74

a, 20,000 l, Early astronomical instruments. b, 30,000 l, Telescope. c, 50,000 l, Observatory, sun.

1996, Jan. 13   Perf. 12
225 A74 Strip of 3, #a.-c.   2.40 2.40

Souvenir Sheet

1994 Winter Olympics, Lillehammer — A75

Medalists: a, 40,000kb, Valentina Tserbe, bronze, biathlon. b, 50,000kb, Oksana Bayul, gold, figure skating.

1996, Jan. 13
226 A75 Sheet of 2, #a.-b.   2.25 2.50

Ahatanhel Krymskyi (1871-1942), Writer — A76

1996, Jan. 15   Perf. 13½
227 A76 20,000kb bister & brown   .90   .90

Kharkiv Zoo, Cent. — A77

1996, Mar. 23   Perf. 12½x12
228 A77 20,000kb multicolored   .80   .80

Ivan S. Kozlovskyi (1900-93), Opera Singer — A78

1996, Mar. 23   Perf. 13½
229 A78 20,000kb multicolored   .50   .50

Motion Pictures, Cent. A79

Oleksandr Dovzhenko, film maker, house.

1996, Mar. 23   Perf. 12½x12
230 A79 4000kb multicolored   .90   .90

No. 230 was issued se-tenant with two labels showing scenes from films.

Chernobyl Nuclear Disaster, 10th Anniv. — A80

1996, Apr. 26   Litho.   Perf. 13½
231 A80 20,000kb multicolored   .90   .90

Symyrenko Family A81

Vasyl Fedorovych (1835-1915), Volodymyr Levkovych (1891-1938), Levko Platonovych (1855-1920).

1996, May 25
232 A81 20,000kb multicolored   .90   .90

Vasil Stefanyk (1871-1936), Writer — A82

1996, June 29
233 A82 20,000kb multicolored   .90   .90

Mykola M. Myklukho-Maklai (1846-88), Explorer, Philologist — A83

Litho. & Engr.
1996, July 17   Perf. 13½
234 A83 40,000kb multicolored   1.50 1.50

1996 Summer Olympic Games, Atlanta — A84

Modern Olympic Games, Cent. A85

1996, July 19   Litho.   Perf. 13½
235 A84 20,000kb Wrestling   .60   .60
236 A84 40,000kb Handball   1.25 1.25
237 A85 40,000kb Greek athletes 1.75 1.75
      Nos. 235-237 (3)   3.60 3.60
Souvenir Sheet
Perf. 12
238 A84 100,000kb Gymnast   2.25 2.25

Independence, 5th Anniv. — A86

1996, Aug. 24   Perf. 13½
239 A86 20,000kb multicolored   .70   .70

First Ukrainian Satellite, "Sich-1" — A87

1996, Aug. 31
240 A87 20,000kb multicolored   .80   .80

Locomotives — A88

Designs: 20,000kb, Steam, class OD. 40,000kb, Diesel class 2 TE-116.

1996, Aug. 31
241 A88 20,000kb multicolored   .80   .80
242 A88 40,000kb multicolored   1.50 1.50
  a.   Pair, #241-242   2.75 2.75

Airplanes Designed by O.K. Antonov (1906-84) A89

No. 243, Glider A-15, portrait of Antonov. No. 244, AN-2. No. 245, AN-124. No. 246, AN-225.

1996, Sept. 14
243 A89 20,000kb multicolored   1.00 1.00
244 A89 20,000kb multicolored   1.00 1.00
245 A89 40,000kb multicolored   1.00 1.00
246 A89 40,000kb multicolored   1.00 1.00
  a.   Block of 4, #243-246   4.00 4.00

Ivan Piddubnyi (1871-1949), Wrestler — A90

1996, Nov. 16
247 A90 40k multicolored   1.20 1.20

First Ukrainian Antarctic Expedition A91

1996, Nov. 23
248 A91 20k multicolored   3.25 3.25

A92

Flowers: 20k, Leontopodium alpinum. 40k, Narcissus anqustifolius.

1996, Nov. 23
249 A92 20k multicolored .75 .75
250 A92 40k multicolored 1.10 1.10
a. Pair, #249-250 + label 2.10 2.10

A93

1996, Dec. 7 Litho. Perf. 13½
251 A93 20k multicolored .80 .80
UNESCO, 50th anniv.

Viktor S. Kosenko, Composer, Birth Cent. A94

1996, Dec. 21 Litho. Perf. 13½
252 A94 20k multicolored .60 .60

St. Sophia's Cathedral, Kyiv — A95

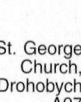 

Illinska (St. Elijah) Church, Subotiv A96

St. George Church, Drohobych A97

#256, Troitska Cathedral, Novomoskovsk.

1996, Dec. 25
253 A95 20k multicolored .50 .50
254 A96 20k multicolored .50 .50
255 A97 20k multicolored .50 .50
256 A97 20k multicolored .50 .50
a. Block of 4, #253-256 2.50 2.50

UNICEF, 50th Anniv. A98

1996, Dec. 31
257 A98 20k multicolored .75 .75

Petro Mohyla (1596-1647), Metropolitan of Kyiv — A99

1996, Dec. 31
258 A99 20k multicolored .75 .75

Wild Animals — A100

1997, Mar. 22 Litho. Perf. 13½
259 A100 20k Lynx lynx 1.00 1.00
260 A100 20k Ursos arctos 1.00 1.00
a. Pair, #259-260 + label 3.00 3.00

Cathedral of the Exaltation of the Holy Cross, Poltava, 17th Cent. A101

Designs: No. 262, St. George's Cathedral, Lviv, 18th cent. No. 263, Protection Fortified Church, Sutkivtsi, 14-15th cent.

1997, Apr. 19 Perf. 13½
261 A101 20k multicolored 1.00 1.00
262 A101 20k multicolored 1.00 1.00
263 A101 20k multicolored 1.00 1.00
Nos. 261-263 (3) 3.00 3.00

Legendary Founders of Kyiv — A101a

Europa: a, Kyi (holding staff and shield) and Shchek (holding sword). b, Khoriv (holding sword, leaning on shield) and sister, Lybid.

1997, May 6 Litho. & Engr. Perf. 13
264 A101a 40k Sheet of 2, #a.-b. 10.00 10.00

4th Natl. Philatelic Exhibition, Cherkasy A102

Design: Statue of Taras Shevchenko, stamps, exhibition hall.

1997, May 17 Litho. Perf. 13½
265 A102 10k multicolored .90 .90

Yurii V. Kondratiuk (1897-1942), Space Pioneer — A103

1997, June 21 Perf. 12½x12
266 A103 20k multicolored .90 .90

Constitution, 1st Anniv. — A104

1997, June 28 Perf. 13½
267 A104 20k multicolored .80 .80

Midsummer Festival of Ivan Kupalo — A104a

1997, July 5 Litho. Perf. 13½
268 A104a 20k multicolored .75 .75

Princess Olha A105

Sultana Roksoliana A106

1997, July 12 Litho. Perf. 13½
269 A105 40k multicolored 1.40 1.25
270 A106 40k multicolored 1.40 1.25

First Ukrainian Emigration to Argentina, Cent. A107

Design: Monument to poet Taras Shevchenko, Buenos Aires.

1997, Aug. 16 Litho. Perf. 13½
271 A107 20k multicolored .90 .90

For Exceptional Service — A108

Order of Yaroslav the Wise — A109

Medals for: No. 273, Military Service. 30k, Bravery. 40k, Order of Bohdan Khmelnytsky. No. 276, Honored Service.
No. 277: a, Medal hanging from chain. b, 8-point star.

Litho. & Engr.
1997, Aug. 20 Perf. 13½
272 A108 20k multicolored 1.40 1.40
273 A108 20k multicolored 1.40 1.40
274 A108 30k multicolored 2.10 2.10
275 A108 40k multicolored 2.75 2.75
276 A108 60k multicolored 4.00 4.00
a. Strip of 5, #272-276 15.00 15.00

Souvenir Sheet
Perf. 13
277 A109 60k Sheet of 2, #a.-b. 9.00 9.00
Nos. 277a-277b are each 35x50mm.

Hetman — A110

No. 278, Dmytro "Baida" Vyshnevetskyj (?-1563), boats, archers. No. 279, Pylyp Orlyk (1672-1742), Stockholm harbor, crowd in Thessaloniki street.

1997, Sept. 13 Litho. Perf. 12½x12
278 A110 20k multicolored 1.10 1.10
279 A110 20k multicolored 1.10 1.10

See Nos. 357-358, 376-377, 412-413, 449-451, 510-511.

Solomiia Krushelnytska (Salomea Krusceniski, 1872-1952), Actress, Singer — A111

1997, Sept. 23 Litho. Perf. 13½
280 A111 20k multicolored .95 .95

Airplanes A112

Designs: 20k, Antonov An-74 TK-200. 40k, Antonov An-38-100.

1997, Oct. 30
281 A112 20k multicolored .60 .60
282 A112 40k multicolored 1.40 1.40

Ships A113

20k, Zavyietnyj, 1903. 40k, Serhii Korolev, 1970, Academician.

1997, Dec. 6   Litho.   Perf. 13½
283 A113 20k multicolored   .60   .60
284 A113 40k multicolored   1.40 1.40

A114

1997, Dec. 6   Litho.   Perf. 12x12½
285 A114 40k multi + label   1.75 1.75

Participation of Ukrainian astronaut in US space shuttle mission.

A115

Vasyl Krychevskyi (1872-1952), painter, architect.

1997, Dec. 20   Perf. 13½
286 A115 10k multicolored   .75   .75

Christmas — A116

1997, Dec. 20
287 A116 20k multicolored   1.00 1.00

Traditional Handicrafts A117

Region: #288, Rooster, Dnipropetrovsk. #289, Vest, Chernivtsi. #290, Ram, Poltava. #291, Molded design, Ivano-Frankivsk.

1997, Dec. 20
288 A117 20k multicolored   .75   .75
289 A117 20k multicolored   .75   .75
290 A117 40k multicolored   1.25 1.25
291 A117 40k multicolored   1.25 1.25
     Nos. 288-291 (4)   4.00 4.00

Perf. 11½
288a   20k   .75   .75
289a   20k   .75   .75
290a   40k   1.25 1.25
291a   40k   1.25 1.25
     b. Sheet, 2 each #288a-291a   8.00 8.00

Nos. 288-291 have colored border. Nos. 288a-291a do not.

Arms Type of 1993

Arms of Transcarpathia (Zakarpattya).

1997, Dec. 30   Litho.   Perf. 13½
292 A35 20k multicolored   .90   .90

A118

Wildlife: a, 20k, Skylark. b, 40k, White-tailed eagle. c, 20k, Black stork. d, 40k, Long-eared hedgehog. e, 20k, Garden dormouse. f, 40k, Wild boar.

1997, Dec. 30   Litho.   Perf. 11½
293 A118 Sheet of 6, #a.-f.   5.00 5.00

A119

Litho. & Engr.
1997, Dec. 27   Perf. 13½
294 A119 60k multicolored   1.10 1.10

Hryhorii Skovoroda (1722-94), philosopher.

A120

1998, Jan. 6   Litho.   Perf. 13½
295 A120 20k multicolored   1.50 1.00

Volodymyr Sosiura (1898-1965), poet.

A121

1998, Feb. 14   Litho.   Perf. 13½
296 A121 20k Figure skating   .75   .75
297 A121 20k Biathlon   .75   .75

1998 Winter Olympic Games, Nagano.

Bilhorod Dnistrovskyi Fortress, 2500th Anniv. — A122

1998, Apr. 21   Litho.   Perf. 13½
298 A122 20k multicolored   .90   .90

UKRFILEKS 98 Natl. Philatelic Exhibition, Sevastopol — A123

Design: Frigate, "Hetman Sahaidachnyi."

1998, Apr. 28   Litho.   Perf. 13½
299 A123 30k multi + label   .90   .90

European Bank of Reconstruction and Development — A124

Obverse, reverse of Ukrainian coins: a, 1k, Gold, 11th cent. b, 1k, Silver, 11th cent. c, 60k, 500h St. Sophia Cathedral gold coin. d, 60k, 200h Taras Shevchenko gold coin. e, 30k, 1,000,000k Bohdan Khmelnytsky silver coin. f, 30k, 10h Petro Mohyla silver coin.

Litho. & Engr.
1998, May 8   Perf. 13½
300 A124 Sheet of 6, #a.-f.   11.00 11.00

Ivan Kupalo Natl. Festival — A125

1998, May 16   Litho.   Perf. 13½
301 A125 40k multicolored   2.50 2.50

Europa.

Souvenir Sheet

Askania Nova Nature Preserve, Cent. — A126

a, 40k, Deer. b, 60k, Przewalski horses.

1998, May 16   Litho.   Perf. 11½
302 A126 Sheet of 2, #a.-b.   4.00 4.00

Paintings from Lviv Picture Gallery — A127

Designs: No. 303, Portrait of Maria Theresa, by J.E. Liotard. No. 304, Man with a Cello, by Gerard von Honthorst. 40k, Madonna and Child, 17th cent. Lviv School. 1.20h, Madonna and Child and Two Saints, by 16th cent. Italian school.

1998, June 20   Perf. 13½
303 A127 20k multicolored   .40   .40
304 A127 20k multicolored   .40   .40
305 A127 40k multicolored   .80   .80
  a.   Strip of 3, #303-305   2.00 2.00

Souvenir Sheet
306 A127 1.20h multicolored   2.25 2.25

Souvenir Sheet

Polytechnical Institute, Kyiv, Cent. — A128

1998, June 27   Litho.   Perf. 11½
307 A128 1h multicolored   4.00 4.00

Askold & Dyr A129

Litho. & Engr.
1998, July 4   Perf. 13½
308 A129 3h multi + label   5.00 5.00

Hetman Bohdan Khmelnytsky — A130

Designs: a, 30k, Battle scene, denomination LR. b, 2k, Portrait of Khmelnytsky. c, 30k, Battle scene, denomination LL. d, 40k, denomination LR. e, 60k, Battle scene. f, 40k, Battle scene, denomination LL.

1998, July 25   Litho. & Engr.
309 A130 Sheet of 6, #a.-f.   8.00 8.00

Ukrainian uprising, 350th anniv.

Town of Halych, 1100th Anniv. A131

1998, Aug. 1   Litho.
310 A131 20k multicolored   .70   .70

Queen Anna Yaroslavna (1024?-75) A132

1998, Aug. 8
311 A132 40k multicolored   1.00 1.00

Yurii Lysianskyi (1773-1837),
Explorer — A133

1998, Aug. 13
312 A133 40k multicolored 1.40 1.40

Natalia Uzhvii (1898-1986), Stage
Actress — A134

1998, Sept. 8 Litho. Perf. 13½
313 A134 40k multicolored 1.25 1.25

Polytechnical Institute, Kyiv,
Cent. — A135

Designs: 10k, W.L. Kirpichov, first president.
No. 315, E.O. Paton, bridge. No. 316, S.P.
Timoschenko, mathematical formula. 30k, Igor
I. Sikorsky, biplane. 40k, Sergei P. Korolev,
rocket, satellite.

1998, Sept. 10 Perf. 12½x12
314 A135 10k multicolored .60 .60
315 A135 20k multicolored .60 .60
316 A135 20k multicolored .60 .60
317 A135 30k multicolored 1.10 1.10
318 A135 40k multicolored 1.25 1.25
a. Strip of 5, #314-318 4.75 4.75

A136

1998, Sept. 19 Litho. Perf. 13½
319 A136 10k multicolored .75 .75
World Post Day.

A137

1998, Sept.19
320 A137 20k multicolored .75 .75
Ukrainian book, 1000th anniv.

Church
Architecture
A138

Designs: No. 321, Church of the Transfiguration, Chernihiv, 11th cent. No. 322, Church of
the Holy Protection, Kharkiv, 17th cent.

1998, Sept. 21
321 A138 20k multicolored .90 .70
322 A138 20k multicolored .90 .70

World Wildlife Fund — A139

Branta ruficollis: a, f, 20k, Adults. b, g, 30k,
Female on nest. c, h, 40k, Female with goslings. d, i, 60k, Adults, goslings.

1998, Oct. 10 Litho. Perf. 13½
323 A139 Block of 4, #a.-d. 3.00 3.00
e. Block of 4, perf. 11½, #f.-i. 3.50 3.50
j. Sheet of 2, #323e 7.00 7.00

Antonov
Airplanes
A140

1998, Nov. 28 Litho. Perf. 13½
324 A140 20k Antonov 140 .65 .65
325 A140 40k Antonov 70 .85 .85

Hetman Type of 1997
Design: Petro Doroshenko (1627-98).

1998, Nov. 28 Litho. Perf. 12½x12
326 A141 20k multicolored .80 .80

Borys D. Hrinchenko (1863-1910),
Writer — A142

1998, Dec. 4 Litho. Perf. 13½
327 A142 20k multicolored 1.50 1.50

Christmas — A143

1998, Dec. 11
328 A143 30k multicolored 1.50 1.00

Ukrainians
in Australia,
50th Anniv.
A144

1998, Dec. 20
329 A144 40k multicolored 1.00 1.00

Illintsi
Meteor
Impact
Area
A145

1998, Dec. 25
330 A145 40k multicolored 1.25 1.25

Universal
Declaration of
Human Rights,
50th
Anniv. — A146

Paintings of various flowers by Kateryna
Bilokur (1900-61): 30k, 1940. 50k, 1959.

1998, Dec. 25
331 A146 30k multicolored .75 .75
332 A146 50k multicolored 1.20 1.20
a. Pair, #331-332 +label 2.00 2.00

Serhii Paradzhanov (1924-90), Film
Director — A147

1999, Feb. 27 Litho. Perf. 13½
333 A147 40k multi + label 1.30 1.30

Volodymyr
Ivasiuk
(1949-79),
Composer
A148

1999, Mar. 4
334 A148 30k multicolored .50 .50

Scythian
Gold
A149

1999, Mar. 20
335 A149 20k Clasp .40 .40
336 A149 40k Boar .65 .65
337 A149 50k Young elk .85 .85
338 A149 1h Necklace 1.40 1.40
a. Block of 4, #335-338 3.50 3.50

Spring Easter
Dance — A150

1999, Apr. 7
339 A150 30k multicolored .50 .50

A151

Synevyr Natl. Park: a, 50k, Wooden monuments on bank of Tereblyia River. b, 1h,
Thymallus thymallus, river scene.

1999, Apr. 24
340 A151 Pair, #a.-b. 3.00 3.00
Europa.

A152

1999, May 13
341 A152 40k multicolored .80 .80
Panas Myrnyi (1849-1920), writer.

Honoré de Balzac (1799-1850),
Writer — A153

1999, May 20
342 A153 40k multicolored .80 .80

Council of
Europe,
50th Anniv.
A154

1999, May 22
343 A154 40k multicolored .80 .80

Aleksandr Pushkin (1799-1837),
Poet — A155

1999, June 6
344 A155 40k + label .80 .80

Sailboats — A156

No. 345: a, Bark (Baidak), double sails, one
man at tiller. b, Cossack (Chaika), single sail,
rowers.

1999, June 26
345 A156 30k Pair, #a.-b. 1.25 1.25

Souvenir Sheet

Yaroslav the Wise — A157

1999, July 2   **Litho.**   **Perf. 11½**
346 A157 1.20h multicolored   2.50 2.50

Principality of Halytsko-Volynskyi,
800th Anniv. — A158

1999, July 27   **Perf. 13½**
347 A158 50k multicolored   1.50 1.00

A159

Designs: a, 30k, Icon of St. George. b, 60, Girl in a Red Hat, by O.O. Murashko.

1999, July 27
348 A159 Pair, #a.-b. + label   2.00 1.50
Natl. Museum of Art, Cent.

A160

1999, Aug. 7
349 A160 30k Bee on flower   1.00 1.00
Bee keeping in Ukraine.

A161

1999, Aug. 14   **Litho.**   **Perf. 13½**
350 A161 30k multicolored   .65 .65
UPU, 125th anniv.

A162

1999, Aug. 14
351 A162 30k multicolored   .80 .80
Poltava, 1100th anniv.

Presidential
Medals — A163

Designs: 30k, Order of Princess Olga.
No. 353: a, Medal with trident. b, Medal with star.

1999, Aug. 17   **Litho. & Engr.**
352 A163 30k multicolored   .80 .80

Souvenir Sheet of 2
353 A163 2.50h #a.-b.   8.00 8.00
No. 353 contains two 35x50mm stamps.

Polish-Ukrainian Cooperation in Nature
Conservation — A164

a, Cervus elaphus. b, Felis silvestris.

1999, Sept. 22   **Litho.**   **Perf. 13½**
354 A164 1.40h Pair, #a.-b.   3.50 2.00
See Poland Nos. 3477-3478.

National
Bank — A165

1999, Sept. 28   **Litho. & Engr.**
355 A165 3h multicolored   4.00 3.00

Souvenir Sheet
356 A165 5h multicolored   6.75 5.50

Hetman Type of 1997

Designs: No. 357, Ivan Vyhovskyi (d. 1664), cavalry in water. No. 358, Pavlo Polubotok (1660-1724), ships in water.

1999   **Litho.**   **Perf. 12¼x12**
357 A110 30k multi   .90 .90
358 A110 30k multi   .90 .90
Issued: No. 357, 11/20; No. 358, 12/22.

A166

Christmas
A167

1999, Nov. 26   **Wmk. 399**   **Perf. 13½**
359 A166 30k multi   .50 .50
Unwmk.
360 A167 60k multi   1.00 1.00

Children's Art — A168

a, Spacecraft, alien creatures. b, Elephant in space. c, Rocket and space car on planet.

1999, Nov. 30   **Unwmk.**   **Perf. 11½**
361 A168 10k Strip of 3, #a.-c.   3.00 3.00

Fauna
A169

Designs: a, 40k, Desmana moschata. b, 60k, Gyps fulvus. c, 40k, Lucanus cervus.

1999, Dec. 9   **Perf. 13½**
362 A169 Strip of 3, #a.-c.   2.25 2.25

Church of St. Andrew, Kyiv — A170

1999, Dec. 12
363 A170 60k multi + label   2.00 2.00

Mushrooms
A171

Designs: a, 30k, Armillariella mellea. b, 30k, Paxillus atrotomentosus. c, 30k, Pleurotus ostratus. d, 40k, Cantharellus cibarius. e, 60k, Agaricus campester.

1999, Dec. 15   **Perf. 11½**
364 A171 Sheet of 5, #a.-e., +
     label   4.00 4.00

New Year 2000 — A172

1999, Dec. 18   **Perf. 13½**
365 A172 50k multi + label   2.00 2.00

Motor Vehicles — A173

a, Kraz-65032 truck. b, Tavriia Nova car.

1999, Dec. 18   **Litho.**
366 A173 30k Pair, #a.-b.   1.50 1.00

Works of Maria Prymachenko — A174

Denomination colors: a, Green. b, Violet.

1999, Dec. 22
367 A174 30k Pair, #a.-b., + cen-
     tral label   1.50 1.00

Halshka
Hulevychivna,
Philanthropist
A175

1999, Dec. 25   **Perf. 13½**
368 A175 30k multi   .80 .80

Zoogeographic Endowment
Fund — A176

Animals from: a, 10k, Carpathian Reserve. b, 30k, Polissia Reserve. c, 40k, Kaniv Reserve. d, 60k, Trakhtemyriv Reserve. e, 1h, Askaniia-Nova Reserve (ram, birds). f, 1h, Kara-Dag Reserve (birds).

1999, Dec. 28   **Perf. 11½**
369 A176 Sheet of 6, #a.-f.   5.50 *4.00*

Christianity, 2000th Anniv. — A177

Designs: a, Mother of God mosaic, St. Sofia Cathedral, Kyiv, 11th cent. b, Christ Pantocrator fresco, Church of the Savior's Transfiguration, Polotsk, Belarus, 12th cent. c, Volodymyr Madonna, Tretiakov Gallery, Moscow, 12th cent.

2000, Jan. 5   **Litho.**   **Perf. 11½**
370 A177 80k Sheet of 3, #a.-c.   5.00 *4.25*

Souvenir Sheet

Opera and Ballet Theaters — A178

No. 371: a, National Academic, Kyiv. b, Odessa State, Odessa. c, Kharkov State Academic, Kharkov. d, Ivan Franko State Academic, Lviv.

2000, Jan. 29   Litho.   Perf. 11½
371   A178   40k   Sheet of 4, #a.-d.   5.00   5.00

Kyiv Bridges — A179

No. 372: a, 10k, Moscow Bridge. b, 30k, Y. O. Paton Bridge. c, 40k, Pedestrian park bridge. d, 60k, Subway bridge.

2000, Jan. 29   Perf. 12¼x12
372   A179   Block of 4, #a.-d.   3.00   3.00

Souvenir Sheet

Peresopnytsia Gospel — A180

2000, Feb. 8   Perf. 11½
373   A180   1.50h   multi   2.50   2.40

   A181

2000, Feb. 11   Perf. 13½
374   A181   30k   multi   1.50   .60
Oksana Petrusenko (1900-40), opera singer

A182

2000, Feb. 18
375   A182   40k   multi   1.25   1.25
Marusia Churai, 17th cent. singer

Hetman Type of 1997

Designs: No. 376, Danylo Apostol (1654-1734), church, burning castle. No. 377, Ivan Samoylovych (d. 1690), tent, winter scene.

2000   Perf. 12¼x12
376   A110   30k   multi   1.00   1.00
377   A110   30k   multi   1.00   1.00
    Issued: No. 376, 2/22; No. 377, 3/3.

 World Meteorological Organization, 50th Anniv. — A183

2000, Mar. 10   Litho.   Perf. 13½
378   A183   30k   multi   1.00   1.00

Europa Issue
Common Design Type
2000, Mar. 29   Litho.   Perf. 13½
379   CD17   3h   multi   *4.50*   3.00

Souvenir Sheets

Easter Eggs — A184

No. 380: a, 30k, Egg with black and red star design, Podillia region. b, 30k, Flower egg, Chernihiv region. c, 30k, Egg with leaf design, Kyiv region. d, 30k, Egg with green, white and yellow geometric design, Odesa region. e, 70k, Egg with reindeer design, Hutsulschyna region. f, 70k, Egg with cross design, Volyn region.

2000, Apr. 28   Perf. 11½
380   A184   Sheet of 6, #a-f   5.25   3.50

Stamp Exhibitions — A185

No. 381: a, Woman in native costume, Austria #2. b, Man in native costume, Great Britain #1.

2000, May 20
381   A185   80k   Sheet of 2, #a-b   3.00   2.50
    WIPA 2000 Stamp Exhibition, Vienna; The Stamp Show 2000, London.

Donetsk Oblast — A186

City of Kyiv — A187

2000   Perf. 12¼x12
382   A186   30k   multi   .80   .80
383   A187   30k   multi   .80   .80
    Regional and administrative areas.
    Issued: No. 382, 5/26; No. 383, 5/28.

6th Natl. Philatelic Exhibition, Donetsk — A188

2000, May 28   Litho.   Perf. 12¼x12
384   A188   30k   multi   .80   .80

 City of Ostroh, 900th Anniv. — A189

2000, June 16   Litho.   Perf. 13½
385   A189   30k   multi   .80   .80

 2000 Summer Olympics, Sydney — A190

2000, June 26
386   A190   30k   High jump   .50   .50
387   A190   30k   Boxing   .50   .50
388   A190   70k   Yachting   .85   .85
389   A190   1h   Rhythmic gymnastics   1.50   1.50
    Nos. 386-389 (4)   3.35   3.35

Petro Prokopovych (1775-1850), Apiarist — A191

2000, July 12   Litho.   Perf. 13½
390   A191   30k   multi   .70   .70

Shipbuilding — A192

2000, July 14
391   A192   Pair   1.75   1.75
  a.   40k   Ship St. Paul   .65   .65
  b.   70k   Ship St. Nicholas   1.00   1.00

Tetiana Pata (1884-1976), Artist — A193

No. 392: a, Leafy Plants with Flowers, 1950s. b, Viburnum Berries and Bird, 1957.

2000, July 21
392   A193   Horiz. pair, #a-b + central label   1.00   1.00
  a.-b.   40k   Any single   .45   .45

 Dubno, 900th Anniv. — A194

2000, July 28
393   A194   30k   multi   .60   .60

 Harvest Festival — A195

2000, Aug. 4
394   A195   30k   multi   .65   .65

Souvenir Sheet

Presidential Symbols — A196

Designs: a, Flag. b, Mace. c, Seal. d, Badge.

2000, Aug. 18   Litho.   Perf. 11½
395   A196   60k   Sheet of 4, #a-d   5.00   4.00

Regional and Administrative Areas

Volynska Oblast — A197

Autonomous Republic of
Crimea — A198

2000 **Perf. 12¼x12**
396 A197 30k multi .55 .55
397 A198 30k multi .65 .65
Issued: No. 396, 8/23; No. 397, 10/20.

Kyiv Post Office, 225th Anniv. — A199

2000, Sept. 3 **Perf. 11½**
398 A199 30k multi .60 .60

Endangered Amphibians — A200

No. 399: a, 30k, Triturus vulgaris. b, 70k,
Salamandra salamandra.

2000, Sept. 8 **Perf. 13½**
399 A200 Pair, #a-b 1.75 1.40

Yurij
Drohobych
(1450-94),
Writer
A201

2000, Sept. 12
400 A201 30k multi .70 .70

Souvenir Sheet

Carpathian National Park — A202

No. 401: a, Mt. Breskul, 1911 meters. b, Mt.
Hoberla, 2061 meters.

2000, Sept. 15 **Perf. 11½**
401 A202 80k Sheet of 2, #a-b 5.00 4.00

Flowers — A203

Designs: a, Marigolds. b, Chamomiles. c,
Hollyhocks. d, Poppies. e, Periwinkles. f, Cornflowers. g, Morning glories. h, Martagon lilies.
i, Peonies. j, Bluebells.

2000, Oct. 6
402 A203 30k Sheet of 10, #a-j 7.50 6.00

Children's Folk Tales — A204

Designs: a, "Ivasyk and Telesyk," (boy in
boat, witch). b, "The Crooked Duck," (couple
with duck). c, "The Cat and the Rooster."

2000, Nov. 3
403 30k Horiz. strip of 3 2.00 1.60
a.-c. A204 Any single .50 .50

New
Year
2001
A205

2000, Nov. 24
404 A205 30k multi .70 .70

St. Onufrius
Church,
Lviv — A206

Church of Christ's
Birth,
Velyke — A207

Design: 70k, Church of the Resurrection,
Sumy.

2000, Dec. 8 **Perf. 13½**
405 A206 30k multi .55 .55
406 A207 30k multi .55 .55
407 A207 70k multi 1.10 1.10
Nos. 405-407 (3) 2.20 2.20

Souvenir Sheet

St. Vladimir (c. 956-1015), Kyivan
Prince — A208

2000, Dec. 15 **Perf. 11½**
408 A208 2h multi 4.50 3.00

Dmytro Rostovskyi (1651-1709),
Religious Leader — A209

2001, Jan. 16 **Litho.** **Perf. 13½**
409 A209 75k multi 1.40 1.00

Love — A210

2001, Jan. 26
410 A210 30k multi .80 .80

Souvenir Sheet

Prince Danylo Romanovych (1201-
64) — A211

2001, Feb. 1 **Perf. 11½**
411 A211 3h multi 5.00 4.00

Hetman Type of 1997

Designs: 30k, Yuryi Khmelnytski (1641-85),
as monk in Turkish prison, Kamianets-Podilskyi fortifications. 50k, Mykhailo Khanenko
(1620-80), leading troops, relinquishing power.

2001, Feb. 20 **Perf. 12¼x12**
412-413 A110 Set of 2 1.25 1.25

Invention of
the
Telephone,
125th
Anniv.
A212

2001, Mar. 6 **Perf. 13½**
414 A212 70k multi 1.00 1.00

Children's
Art — A213

Art by: 10k, Alyna Nochvaj. 30k, Olyia
Pynych. 40k, Dasha Chemberzhi.

2001, Mar. 7 **Perf. 11½**
415-417 A213 Set of 3 1.60 1.60

Hollyhocks
A214

Marigolds
A215

Sunflower
A216

Viburnum
Opulus
Berries
A217

Wheat — A218

2001, Apr. 4 **Litho.** **Perf. 13¾**
418 A214 (10k) multi .25 .25
419 A215 (30k) multi .25 .25
420 A216 (71k) multi .50 .50
b. Imprint "2003" 3.00 3.00
c. Imprint "2004" 2.50 2.50
421 A217 (2.66h) multi 1.75 .85
b. Imprint "2003" 2.50 2.50
c. Imprint "2005" 2.00 2.00
d. Imprint "2006" 2.50 2.50
422 A218 (3.65h) multi 2.50 1.00
b. Imprint "2003" 3.75 3.75
c. Imprint "2004" 3.75 3.75
d. Imprint "2005" 2.50 2.50
e. Imprint "2006" 2.50 2.50
Nos. 418-422 (5) 5.25 2.85

2006, Oct. 9 **Perf. 11½**
Dated 2006
418a A214 (10k) multi 1.10 1.10
419a A215 (30k) multi 1.10 1.10
420a A216 (71k) multi 1.25 1.25
421a A217 (2.66h) multi 4.50 4.50
422a A218 (3.65h) multi 6.00 6.00
Nos. 418a-422a (5) 13.95 13.95

Nos. 418a-422a were issued only in No. F2b.
See Nos. 453-454, 466-468, 515, 572, 606-
609.

Folktales — A219

No. 423: a, The Fox and Wolf (fox on sleigh,
fish). b, The Mitten (bear, fox, wolf, rabbit
mouse, frog). c, Sirko the Dog (wolf with bottle,
dog).

2001, Apr. 14 **Perf. 13½**
423 A219 30k Horiz. strip of 3,
#a-c 1.40 1.40

Ships — A220

No. 424: a, 20k, Twelve Apostles. b, 30k,
Three Priests.

2001, Apr. 20
424 A220 Horiz. pair, #a-b 1.25 1.25

Europa — A221

Fish, jellyfish, seaweed: a, 28x40mm. b, 56x40mm.

2001, Apr. 27
425 A221 1h Horiz. pair, #a-b   3.00 3.00

Holy Trinity
A222

2001, May 15
426 A222 30k multi   .70 .70

Souvenir Sheet

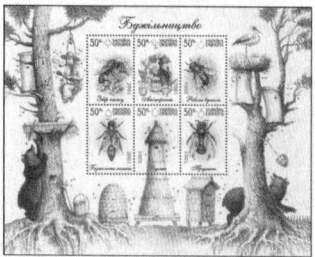

Apiculture — A223

No. 427: a, Bee on flower. b, Plant cutting, jar of honey, bowl of pollen, jars. c, Worker on honeycomb. d, Queen. e, Hive. f, Drone.

2001, May 22   Perf. 11½
427 A223 50k Sheet of 6, #a-f   6.50 6.00

Souvenir Sheet

Kyievo-Pecherska Monastery, 950th Anniv. — A224

2001, May 25
428 A224 1.50h multi   2.25 2.25

Visit of Pope John Paul II, June 23-27
A225

2001, June 15   Perf. 13½
429 A225 3h multi   2.75 2.50

Regional and Administrative Areas

Zakarpatska Oblast — A226

Kharkivska Oblast — A227

Chernihivska Oblast — A228

Kirovohradska Oblast — A229

2001   Litho.   Perf. 12¼x12
430 A226 30k multi   .70 .70
431 A227 30k multi   .70 .70
432 A228 30k multi   .70 .70
433 A229 30k multi   .70 .70

Issued: No. 430, 6/29; No. 431, 8/18; No. 432, 9/21; No. 433, 9/22.

Souvenir Sheet

Icons From Khanenko Art Museum — A230

No. 434: a, 20k, Virgin and Child, 28x40mm. b, 30k, St. John the Baptist, 28x40mm. c, Saints Serhyi and Bacchus, 56x40mm.

2001, July 12   Litho.   Perf. 11½
434 A230 Sheet of 3, #a-c   2.25 1.90

Endangered Species A231

No. 435: a, Milvus milvus. b, Scirtopoda telum.

2001, July 24   Perf. 13
435 A231 1h Vert. pair, #a-b   1.75 1.75

Dmytro Bortnianskyi (1751-1825), Composer — A232

2001, July 26
436 A232 20k multi   .50 .50

Soccer — A233

2001, Aug. 10
437 A233 50k multi   .70 .70

Souvenir Sheet

Independence, 10th Anniv. — A234

2001, Aug. 15   Perf. 11½
438 A234 3h multi   3.25 3.25

7th Natl. Philatelic Exhibition, Dnipropetrovsk — A235

2001, Oct. 7   Litho.   Perf. 12¼x12
439 A235 30k multi   .65 .65

Year of Dialogue Among Civilizations A236

2001, Oct. 9   Perf. 13
440 A236 70k multi   1.25 1.25

Souvenir Sheet

Black Sea Marine Life — A237

No. 441: a, 30k, Seahorses. b, 70k, Dolphins, birds.

2001, Oct. 19   Perf. 11½
441 A237 Sheet of 2, #a-b   2.40 2.40

Christmas — A238

2001, Nov. 9   Perf. 12¼x12
442 A238 30k multi   .85 .85

St. Nicholas A239

2001, Nov. 16   Perf. 13
443 A239 30k multi   .75 .75

Happy New Year — A240

2001, Nov. 23
444 A240 30k multi   .75 .75

Poets — A241

No. 445: a, Taras Shevchenko (1814-61), Ukrainian poet. b, Akakii Tsereteli (1840-1915), Georgian poet.

2001, Dec. 19
445 A241 40k Horiz. pair, #a-b   1.00 1.00
See Georgia No. 276.

Regional Costumes

Kyivshchyna Region — A242

Chernihivshchyna Region — A243

Poltavshchyna Region — A244

No. 446: a, 20k, Two women. b, 50k, Man and woman.
No. 447: a, 20k, Musicians and girl. b, 50k, Bride and groom, boy.
No. 448: a, 20k, Priest and family. b, 50k, Two women.

2001, Dec. 20   Perf. 13¼
446 A242 Horiz. pair, #a-b   .60 .60
447 A243 Horiz. pair, #a-b   .60 .60
448 A244 Horiz. pair, #a-b   .60 .60
  c.   Souvenir sheet, #446-448, perf. 11½   2.00 2.00
  Nos. 446-448 (3)   1.80 1.80

Hetman Type of 1997

Designs: No. 449, 40k, Pavlo Teteryia (d. 1670) holding scepter, people in town, horsemen and carriage heading for town. No. 450, 40k, Demyian Mnohohrishnyi, receiving scepter, boats in river. No. 451, 40k, Ivan Briukhovetskyi (d. 1668), battle scenes.

2002, Jan. 17   Perf. 12¼x12
449-451 A110 Set of 3   1.60 1.60

Scythian Military History — A245

No. 452: a, Archer on horseback. b, Swordsman in battle. c, Commander on horseback, warrior. d, Female warrior.

2002, Jan. 29   *Perf. 13*
452 A245 40k Block of 4, #a-d   1.50 1.50

Flower Type of 2001 and

Periwinkle — A246

2002		Litho.	*Perf. 13¾*
		Year imprint	
453	A246	5k multi, "2002"	.50 .50
a.		Perf. 11½, dated "2006"	1.50 1.50
b.		As #453, dated "2004"	.75 .75
c.		As #453, dated "2005"	.75 .75
d.		As #453, dated "2006"	.75 .75
454	A214	10k multi, "2002"	.50 .50
a.		Perf. 11½, dated "2006"	1.50 1.50
b.		As #454, dated "2003"	.75 .75
c.		As #454, dated "2005"	.75 .75
d.		As #454, dated "2006"	.75 .75

Issued: #453, 2/1; #453b, 7/19/04; #453c, 2005; #453d, 12/1/05. #454, 2/26; #454b, 2003; #454c, #2005; #454d, 12/1/05. Nos. 453a-454a, 10/9/06. Nos. 453a-454a were issued only in No. F2b.

Sporting Achievements — A247

Designs: No. 455, 40k, Zhanna Pintusevich-Block winning 100-meter dash at 2001 World Track and Field Championships. No. 456, 40k, Swimmer at 2000 Summer Olympics.

2002, Feb. 15   *Perf. 13*
455-456 A247   Set of 2   .90 .90

Regional and Administrative Areas

Kyivska Oblast — A248

2002, Feb. 18   *Perf. 12¼x12*
457 A248 40k multi   .50 .50

Shipbuilding — A249

No. 458: a, Frigate Sizopol and coast. b, Brigantine Perseus.

2002, Feb. 22   *Perf. 13½*
458 A249 40k Horiz. pair, #a-b   .80 .80

Issuance of First Stamp After Independence, 10th Anniv. — A250

2002, Mar. 1
459 A250 40k No. 100   .80 .80

Leonid Hlibov (1827-93), Writer — A251

2002, Mar. 4   Litho.   *Perf. 13¼*
460 A251 40k multi   .50 .50

Ruslan Ponomariov, Winner of 16th World Chess Championships — A252

2002, Mar. 29   *Perf. 13½*
461 A252 3.50h multi   2.00 2.00

Souvenir Sheet

Europa — A253

No. 462: a, Lion. b, Tiger, horiz.

2002, Apr. 4   *Perf. 11½*
462 A253 1.75h Sheet of 2, #a-b   4.25 4.25

Palm Sunday — A254

2002, Apr. 19   *Perf. 13½*
463 A254 40k multi   .45 .45

Worldwide Fund for Nature (WWF) — A255

Various views of Elaphe situla: a, 40k. b, 70k. c, 80k. d, 2.50h.

2002, May 25   *Perf. 13½*
464 A255   Block of 4, #a-d   2.50 2.50
e.   Perf. 11½   3.50 3.50

Souvenir Sheet

Opera and Ballet Theaters — A256

No. 465: a, Donetsk (tree at center). b, Dnipropetrovsk (trees at side).

2002, May 31   *Perf. 11½*
465 A256 1.25h Sheet of 2, #a-b   2.25 2.25

Flower Type of 2001 and

Blue Cornflower A257   Lilac A258

2002		Litho.	*Perf. 13¾*
		Year Imprint	
466	A215	30k multi, "2002"	.50 .50
a.		Perf. 11½, dated "2006"	1.75 1.75
b.		As #466, dated "2003"	.70 .70
c.		As #466, dated "2004"	.70 .70
d.		As #466, dated "2005"	.70 .70
e.		As #466, dated "2006"	.70 .70
467	A257	45k multi, "2002"	.50 .50
a.		Perf. 11½, dated "2006"	1.75 1.75
b.		As #467, dated "2003"	.70 .70
c.		As #467, dated "2004"	.70 .70
d.		As #467, dated "2005"	.70 .70
e.		As #467, dated "2006"	.70 .70
468	A258	(80k) multi, "2002"	.80 .80
a.		Perf. 11½, dated "2006"	2.50 2.50
b.		As #468, dated "2003"	1.00 1.00
c.		As #468, dated "2004"	1.00 1.00

Issued: Issued: #466, 6/1/02; #466b4/17/03; #466c, 1/22/04; #466d, 2/3/05; #466e, 12/1/05. #467, 9/19/02; #467b, 4/17/03; #467c, 2/6/04; #467d, 4/29/05; #467e, 3/3/06. #468, 7/5/02; #468b, 2003; #468c, 7/19/04. Nos. 466a-468a issued 10/9/06. Nos. 466a-468a were issued only in No. F2b.

Regional and Administrative Areas

Luhanska Oblast — A259

Chernivetska Oblast — A260

Odeska Oblast — A261

Cherkaska Oblast — A262

Sumska Oblast — A263

2002			*Perf. 12¼x12*
469	A259	40k multi	.50 .50
470	A260	40k multi	.50 .50
471	A261	45k multi	.50 .50
472	A262	45k multi	.50 .50
473	A263	45k multi	.50 .50
		Nos. 469-473 (5)	2.50 2.50

Issued: No. 469, 6/2; No. 470, 6/27; No. 471, 9/20. No. 472, 10/9; No. 473, 10/21.

Endangered Species A264

No. 474: a, Phalacrocorax aristotelis. b, Phocoena phocoena.

2002, June 14   Litho.   *Perf. 13*
474 A264 70k Pair, #a-b   1.10 1.10

Mykola Leontovich (1877-1921), Composer — A265

2002, June 21   *Perf. 13½*
475 A265 40k multi   .50 .50

Souvenir Sheet

Black Sea Nature Reserve — A266

No. 476: a, Haematopus ostralegus (40x28mm). b, Larus genei (40x28mm). c, Iris pumila (22x26mm). d, Numenius arquata (26x22mm). e, Charadrius alexandrinus (26x22mm).

2002, July 13   *Perf. 11½*
476 A266 50k Sheet of 5, #a-e   3.00 2.50

Folk Tales — A267

No. 477: a, Fox and Pancake. b, Mr. Cat. c, Speckled Chicken.

2002, July 19   *Perf. 14¼x14*
477 A267 40k Horiz. strip of 3,
     #a-c   .80   .80

Art of Hanna Sobachko-
Shostak — A268

No. 478: a, Cage for Starlings, 1963 (peach
background). b, Vase with Flowers, 1964 (red
background). c, Chamomile Flowers, 1964
(yellow background).

2002, Aug. 9   *Perf. 14x14¼*
478   Horiz. strip of 3   .90   .90
a.-c. A268 45k Any single   .30   .30

Space Pioneers — A269

Designs: 40k, Yurii V. Kondratiuk (1897-
1942). 45k, Mykhailo Yianhel (1911-71). 50k,
Mykola Kybalchych (1853-81). 70k, Serhii
Korolov (1907-66).

2002, Aug. 23   *Perf. 12¼x12*
479-482 A269   Set of 4   1.60   1.60
See Nos. 500-503.

Marine Life — A270

No. 483: a, Phoca caspica. b, Huso huso
ponticus.

2002, Sept. 6   *Perf. 14x14¼*
483 A270 75k Horiz. pair, #a-b   1.25   1.25
See Kazakhstan No. 386.

Khotyn, 1000th Anniv. — A271

2002, Sept. 21   *Perf. 12¼x12*
484 A271 40k multi   .55   .55

Odesaphil 2002
Stamp Exhibition,
Odesa — A272

2002, Oct. 5   Litho.   *Perf. 14¼x14*
485 A272 45k multi   .50   .50

Paintings of Kyiv by Taras Shevchenko
(1814-61) — A273

Designs: 45k, Askold's Tomb. 75k, Dnieper
River Shoreline. 80k, St. Alexander's Church.

   Perf. 13¾x14½
2002, Nov. 15   Litho.
486-488 A273   Set of 3   1.40   1.40
See Nos. 516-519, 548-551, 590-593

Happy New
Year
A274

2002, Nov. 22   *Perf. 14x14¼*
489 A274 45k multi   .70   .70

Regional Costumes

Vinychyna Region — A275

Cherkashchyna Region — A276

Ternopilska Region — A277

No. 490: a, Family, rainbow. b, Family, fruit
tree.
No. 491: a, Four girls holding hands. b,
Couple gathering crops.
No. 492: a, Priest blessing family. b, People
with Easter baskets.

2002, Dec. 6   *Perf. 13¼*
490 A275 45k Horiz. pair, #a-b   .55   .55
491 A276 45k Horiz. pair, #a-b   .55   .55
492 A277 45k Horiz. pair, #a-b   .55   .55
c.   Souvenir sheet, #490-492, perf.
     11½   1.75   1.75
     Nos. 490-492 (3)   1.65   1.65

Folk Tales — A278

No. 493: a, Koza-Dezera (cow on bridge). b,
The Straw Bull. c, The Fox and Crane.

2003, Jan. 17   Litho.   *Perf. 14¼x14*
493 A278 45k Horiz. strip of 3,
     #a-c   .75   .75

Speed
Skating
A279

2003, Jan. 24   *Perf. 14x14¼*
494 A279 65k multi   .60   .60

Military History — A280

No. 495: a, War with Goths, 4th cent. (soldier with spear and shield) b, Battles with
Huns, 5th cent. (archer). c, Balkan campaigns,
6th cent. (soldier with hatchet). d, Battles with
the Avars, 6th cent. (soldier with spears).

2003, Feb. 7
495 A280 45k Block of 4, #a-d   1.10   1.10

Shipbuilding — A281

No. 496: a, Steamship Grozny (denomination at left. b, Steamship Odessa (denomination at right).

2003, Feb. 14
496 A281 1h Horiz. pair, #a-b   1.25   1.25

Mikola Arkas (1853-1909),
Composer — A282

2003, Feb. 21
497 A282 45k multi   .50   .50

Souvenir Sheet

Javorivsky National Nature
Park — A283

No. 498: a, 1h, Alcede atthis (32x44mm). b,
1h, Cypripedium calceolus (36x41mm). c,
1.50h, Eudia pavonia, horiz. (44x32mm)

2003, Mar. 3   *Perf. 11½*
498 A283   Sheet of 3, #a-c   3.00   3.00

Europa — A284

Poster by Oleksiy Shtanko: a, Virgin Mary
with dove. b, Guardian angel.

2003, Mar. 21   *Perf. 11½*
499 A284 1.75h Horiz. pair, #a-b   3.50   3.50
c.   Booklet pane, 2 #499 + central
     label   6.25   —
     Complete booklet, #499c   6.25

Space Pioneers Type of 2002

Designs: 45k, Olkeksandr Zasiadko (1779-
1837). 65k, Kostyantin Konstantinov (1817-
71). 70k, Valyntyn Hlushko (1908-89). 80k,
Volodymyr Chelomei (1914-84).

2003, Apr. 11   Litho.   *Perf. 13¾x14½*
500-503 A269   Set of 4   1.60   1.60

Ukrainian Red Cross Society, 85th
Anniv. — A285

2003, Apr. 18
504 A285 45k multi   .50   .50

Regional and Administrative Areas

Dnipropetrovska Oblast — A286

Lvivska Oblast — A287

Khmelnytska Oblast — A288

Mykolayivska Oblast — A289

Zaporizhiya Oblast — A290

2003
505 A286 45k multi   .50   .50
506 A287 45k multi   .50   .50
507 A288 45k multi   .50   .50
508 A289 45k multi   .50   .50
509 A290 45k multi   .50   .50
     Nos. 505-509 (5)   2.50   2.50

Issued: No. 505, 4/21; No. 506, 5/8; No.
507, 9/26; No. 508, 10/4; No. 509, 10/11.

Hetman Type of 1997

Designs: No. 510, 45k, Ivan Skoropadskiy
(1646-1722) wearing robe, serfs in field, subjects bowing. No. 511, 45k, Kyrylo Rozumov-
skiy (1728-1803) holding scepter, attack of
palace, palace ruins.

2003, May 22
510-511 A110   Set of 2   .75   .75

Souvenir Sheet

Volodymyr Monomakh (1053-1125), Grand Prince of Kyiv — A291

2003, May 28　　**Perf. 11½**
512 A291 3.50h multi　　1.90 1.90

Owls — A292

No. 513: a, Bubo bubo. b, Strix uralensis. c, Strix aluco. d, Strix nebulosa. e, Glaucidium passerinum. f, Aegolius funereus. g, Otus scops. h, Athene noctua. i, Tyto alba. j, Asio otus. k, Asio flammeus. l, Surnia ulula. Size of # 513e-513h: 25x27mm; others: 25x36mm.

2003, June 14
513 A292 45k Sheet of 12, #a-l　7.00 3.50

Oleksandr Myshuha (1853-1922), Opera Singer — A293

2003, June 20　　**Perf. 13¼**
514 A293 45k multi　　.55 .55

Sweet Pea — A294

2003, July 4　　**Perf. 13¾**
Year Imprint
515 A294 65k multi, "2003"　　.90 .90
a.　Perf. 11½, dated "2006"　2.50 2.50
b.　As #515, dated "2004"　2.00 2.00
c.　As #515, dated "2005"　1.25 1.25

Issued: #515b, 2/6/04; #515c, 2/1/05.
No. 515a issued 10/9/06. No. 515a was issued only in No. F2b.

Paintings Type of 2002

Paintings of Kyiv: No. 516, 45k, Podil, by Mykhailo Sazhyn, 1840. No. 517, 45k, Kyiv-Pecherska Monastery, by Vasyl Timm, 1857. No. 518, 45k, Ruins of St. Irene Monastery, by Sazhyn, 1846. No. 519, 45k, View of Old City from Yaroslav Embankment, by Timm, 1854.

2003, July 18　　**Perf. 13¾x14½**
516-519 A273　Set of 4　　1.40 1.40

Customs and Traditions — A295

No. 520: a, Celebration of the Harvest (Church, flowers and insects). b, Ascension (Church, fruit).

2003, July 25　　**Perf. 14¼x14**
520 A295 45k Horiz. pair, #a-b　　.55 .55

Borys Hmyryia (1903-69), Composer A296

2003, Aug. 5　　**Perf. 14x14¼**
521 A296 45k multi　　.55 .55

Souvenir Sheet

Manyiavskyi Monastery — A297

No. 522: a, Denomination at LL. b, Denomination at LR.

2003, Aug. 15　　**Perf. 11x11½**
522 A297 1.25h Sheet of 2, #a-b　1.40 2.00

Yevpatoriya, 2500th Anniv. — A298

2003, Aug. 29　　**Perf. 13¾x14½**
523 A298 45k multi　　.55 .55

Ancient Trade Routes — A299

No. 524: a, Arrival of Scandinavian seamen in rowboat, coin of Danish King Svend Estridsen. b, Silver coin of Prince Volodymyr Sviatoslavovych, Slavic warship with sail.

2003, Sept. 17　　**Perf. 11½**
524 A299 80k Vert. pair, #a-b, +　　.90　.90
　　central label
c.　Booklet pane, #524　3.75　—
d.　Booklet pane, #524a　2.50　—

e.　Booklet pane, #524b　2.50　—
　　Complete booklet, #524c, 524d,　9.00
　　524e

Hryhoryi Kvitka-Osnovyianenko (1778-1843), Writer — A300

2003, Nov. 14 Litho.　　**Perf. 14¼x14**
525 A300 45k multi　　.55 .55

Famine of 1932-33 — A301

2003, Nov. 21　　**Perf. 13¾x14½**
526 A301 45k multi　　.40 .40

Christmas A302

Litho. with Foil Application
2003, Nov. 25　　**Perf. 13¼x13½**
527 A302 45k multi　　1.00 1.00

New Year's Greetings A303

2003, Nov. 25 Litho.　　**Perf. 13½**
528 A303 45k multi　　1.00 1.00

Regional Costumes

Kharkiv Region — A304

Sumy Region — A305

Donetsk Region — A306

No. 529: a, Women, religious icons. b, Family, lute.
No. 530: a, Woman, men. b, Group of women.
No. 531: a, Family, sled. b, Workers in field.

2003, Dec. 19　　**Perf. 13¼**
529 A304 45k Horiz. pair, #a-b　1.00 1.00
530 A305 45k Horiz. pair, #a-b　1.00 1.00
531 A306 45k Horiz. pair, #a-b　1.00 1.00
c.　Souvenir sheet, #529-531, perf.　3.00 3.00
　　11½

Unification of Ukraine and Western Ukraine, 85th Anniv. — A307

2004, Jan. 22 Litho.　**Perf. 13¾x14½**
532 A307 45k multi　　.40 .40

Stanislav Ludkevych (1879-1979), Composer A308

2004, Jan. 24　　**Perf. 13¼**
533 A308 45k multi　　.40 .40

Possessions of Hetman Bohdan Khmelnytsky — A309

No. 534: a, Flag. b, Mace. c, Cap. d, Chalice decorated with leaves. e, Tankard. f, Sword.

Litho. With Foil Application
2004, Jan. 29　　**Perf. 11½**
534 A309 45k Sheet of 6, #a-f　2.50 2.50

Shipbuilding — A310

No. 535: a, 1h, Oil tanker Kriti Amber (55x26mm). b, 2.50h, Anti-submarine ship Mikolayiv (55x29mm). c, 3.50h Aircraft carrier Admiral Kuznetzov (55x40mm).

2004, Feb. 21	Litho.	Perf. 11½
535 A310	Sheet of 3, #a-c	5.00 5.00

Regional and Administrative Areas

Ternopilska Oblast — A311

2004, Mar. 3		Perf. 13¾x14½
536 A311	45k multi	.50 .50

Membership in UNESCO, 50th Anniv. — A312

2004, Mar. 19		Perf. 14¼x14
537 A312	45k multi	.50 .50

Butterflies — A313

No. 538: a, 45k, Endromis versicolora. b, 75k, Smerinthus ocellatus. c, 80k, Catocala fraxini. d, 2.60h, Apatura ilia. e, 3.50h, Papilio machaon.

2004, Mar. 26		Perf. 8
538 A313	Sheet of 5, #a-e	4.50 7.00

Famous Ukrainians A314

Designs: No. 539, 45k, Serhyi Lyfar (1904-86), ballet dancer and choreographer. No. 540, 45k, Maria Zankovetska (1854-1934), actress. No. 541, 45k, Mykhaylo Maksymovych (1804-73), historian.

2004	Litho.	Perf. 14x14¼
539-541 A314	Set of 3	1.25 1.25

Issued: No. 539, 4/2, Nos. 540-541, 7/23.
See Nos. 574-575, 613-614, 641, 655-656, 750-751, 757-758.

Zenit-1 Rocket A315

2004, Apr. 14		
542 A315	45k multi	.55 .55

European Weight Lifting Championships, Kyiv — A316

2004, Apr. 20		
543 A316	65k multi	.60 .60

Miniature Sheet

Europa — A317

No. 544: a, 45k, Lastivchyne Hnizdo (22x33mm). b, 75k, Carpathian Mountains (22x33mm). c, 2.61h, Khotyn Castle (29x33mm). d, 3.52h, Pecherska Lavra (39x28mm).

2004, Apr. 23		Perf. 11½
544 A317	Sheet of 4, #a-d	6.50 6.50

UEFA (European Football Union), 50th Anniv. — A318

2004, May 17		Perf. 14¼x14
545 A318	3.52h multi	2.00 2.00

FIFA (Fédération Internationale de Football Association), Cent. — A319

No. 546: a, 45k, Player #11. b, 75k, Player #6. c, 80k, Fan. d, 2.61h, Two women players.

2004, May 17		Perf. 13¼
546 A319	Block of 4, #a-d	2.50 2.50

Symon Petlura (1879-1926), Political Leader — A320

2004, May 21
547 A320 45k multi   .50 .50

Painting Type of 2002

Designs: No. 548, 45k, Kiev with St. Andrew's Church, by unknown artist, 1889. No. 549, 45k, Fountain Near the Golden Gate, by Petro Levchenko, 1910. No. 550, 45k, Spring in Kurenivka, by Abram Manevych, 1914-15. No. 551, 45k, St. Michael's Cathedral From the South, by Mykola Burachek, 1919.

2004, June 11		Perf. 13¾x14½
548-551 A273	Set of 4	1.25 1.25

Folktales — A321

No. 552: a, The Cat. b, Ivasyk Telesyk. c, The Fat Man.

2004, June 18		Perf. 14¼x14
552 A321	45k Horiz. strip of 3, #a-c	.90 .90

2004 Summer Olympics, Athens A322

2004, June 26		Perf. 14x14¼
553 A322	2.61h multi	1.40 1.40

Regional and Administrative Areas

Rovenska Oblast — A323

Khersonska Oblast — A324

Poltavska Oblast — A325

2004		Perf. 13¾x14½
554 A323	45k multi	.55 .55
555 A324	45k multi	.55 .55
556 A325	45k multi	.55 .55

Issued: No. 554, 7/16; No. 555, 8/20; No. 556, 9/22.

Balaklava, 2500th Anniv. — A327

		Perf. 13¾x14½
2004, Aug. 14		Litho.
557 A327	45k multi	.55 .55

Kharkiv, 350th Anniv. — A328

2004, Aug. 20		Perf. 14¼x14
558 A328	45k multi	.55 .55

Bridges — A329

No. 559: a, Inhulskyi Bridge (open drawbridge). b, Darnytska Bridge (three arches above roadway). c, B. M. Preobrazhenskoho Bridge (arches below roadway). d, Southern Buh Bridge (swing bridge).

2004, Aug. 25		Perf. 13¾x14½
559 A329	45k Block of 4, #a-d	1.25 1.25

No. 194B Surcharged

	Litho. & Engr.
2004, Sept. 15	Perf. 12½x13
560 A47a	2.61h on 25,000kb multi	1.50 1.50

Taras Shevchenko University, 170th anniv.

Kirovohrad, 250th Anniv. — A330

		Perf. 13¾x14¼
2004, Sept. 17		Litho.
561 A330	45k multi	.55 .55

Military History — A331

No. 562: a, Infantryman of Prince Oleg, 10th cent. b, National militia, 11th-12th cent. c, Archer on horseback, 12th cent. d, Cavalryman for Danylo Halyts, 13th cent.

2004, Oct. 15		Perf. 14x14¼
562 A331	45k Block of 4, #a-d	1.50 1.50

Miniature Sheet

Birds of the Danube Nature Reserve — A332

No. 563: a, 45k, Cygnus olor. b, 75k, Phalacrocorax pygmaeus. c, 80k, Egretta alba. d, 2.61h, Anser anser. e, 3.52h, Platalea leucordia.

2004, Oct. 26   **Perf. 11½**
563 A332   Sheet of 5, #a-e   4.50   6.00

Khartron Control Systems in Space A333

1516 Battle Between Cossacks and Tartars Using Fiery Projectiles A334

2004, Nov. 12   **Perf. 14x14¼**
564 A333   45k multi   .55   .55
565 A334   45k multi   .55   .55

Christmas A335

No. 566: a, Magi facing right ("2" in background). b, Magi facing left ("5" in background). c, Nativity ("0" in background).

Litho. With Foil Application
2004, Nov. 26   **Perf. 13¼**
566   Horiz. strip of 4, #a-b, 2 #c   1.00   1.00
a.-c.   A335 45k Any single, gold & multi   .25   .25

Numbers in background of strip of 4 read "2005."

New Year's Greetings A336

No. 567: a, Santa Claus, large trees at left ("2" in background). b, Santa Claus, large trees at right ("5" in background). c, Tree and gifts ("0" in background).

2004, Nov. 26
567   Horiz. strip of 4, #a-b, 2 #c   1.00   1.00
a.-c.   A336 45k Any single, silver & multi   .25   .25

Numbers in background of strip of 4 read "2005."

Ukrainian and Iranian Aircraft — A337

No. 568: a, Antonov-140, Ukraine (denomination at left). b, Iran-140, Iran (denomination at right).

2004, Nov. 30   **Litho.**   **Perf. 11½**
568   Horiz. pair + central label   1.10   1.00
a.-b.   A337 80k Either single   .50   .50
See Iran No.

Regional Costumes

Lvivshchyna Region — A338

Ivano-Frankivshchyna Region — A339

Hutsulshchyna Region — A340

No. 569: a, Family, rooster. b, Family, pitcher.
No. 570: a, Musicians. b, Dancers at wedding.
No. 571: a, Men, child, lamb. b, Family, cradle.

2004, Dec. 10   **Perf. 13¼**
569 A338   60k Horiz. pair, #a-b   .70   .70
570 A339   60k Horiz. pair, #a-b   .70   .70
571 A340   60k Horiz. pair, #a-b   .70   .70
c.   Miniature sheet, #569-571, perf. 11½   2.10   2.10

Poppy — A341

2005, Jan. 14   **Litho.**   **Perf. 13¾**
Date Imprint
572 A341 1h multi, "2005"   1.00   1.00
a.   Perf. 11½, dated "2006"   2.50   2.50
b.   As #572, dated "2006"   1.00   1.00
No. 572b issued 5/23/06.
No. 572a issued 10/9/06. No. 572a was issued only in No. F2b.

November - December 2004 Protests Against Rigged Elections — A342

2005, Jan. 23   **Perf. 11½**
573 A342   45k multi   .45   .45
Printed in sheets of 7 + label.

Famous Ukrainians Type of 2004

Design: No. 574, Pavlo Virskyi (1905-75), choreographer. No. 575, Volodymyr Vynnychenko (1880-1951), writer and statesman.

2005   **Litho.**   **Perf. 14x14¼**
574 A314   45k multi   .45   .45
575 A314   45k multi   .45   .45
Issued: No. 574, 2/4; No. 575, 7/15.

Miniature Sheet

Moths — A343

No. 576: a, 45k, Acherontia atropos. b, 75k, Catocala sponsa. c, 80k, Staurophora celsia. d, 2.61h, Marumba quercus. e, 3.52h, Saturnia pyri.

2005, Feb. 11   **Perf. 11½**
576 A343   Sheet of 5, #a-e   4.50   4.50

Regional and Administrative Areas

Vinnytska Oblast — A344

Sevastopol City — A345

Ivano-Frankivska Oblast — A346

Zhitomyrska Oblast — A347

2005   **Perf. 13¾x14½**
577 A344   45k multi   .45   .45
578 A345   45k multi   .45   .45
579 A345   45k multi   .45   .45
580 A347   70k multi   .55   .55
    Nos. 577-580 (4)   1.90   1.90
Issued: No. 577, 2/23; No. 578, 6/11; No. 579, 7/16; 70k, 9/10.

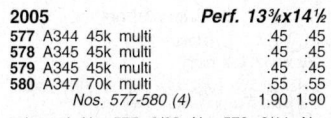

Paintings by Ivan Aivazovskyi — A348

No. 581: a, Sea — Koktebel, 1853. b, Towers on the Rock Near the Bosporus, 1859.

2005, Mar. 4   **Litho.**   **Perf. 14x14¼**
581   Horiz. pair, #a-b, + central label   .90   .90
a.-b.   A348 45k Either single   .45   .45

The Shepherd, by Heorhyi Yakutovych (1930-2000) — A349

Litho. & Engr.
2005, Mar. 26   **Perf. 11½**
582 A349   3.52h silver & gray blue   2.00   2.00

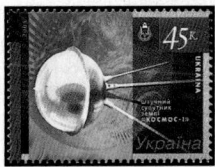

Cosmos-1 Satellite A350

Zenit-2 Rocket A351

Designs: No. 585, Dnepr rocket. No. 586, Cyclone-3 rocket.

2005, Apr. 12   **Litho.**   **Perf. 14x14¼**
583 A350   45k shown   .45   .45
584 A351   45k shown   .45   .45
585 A351   45k multi   .45   .45
586 A351   45k multi   .45   .45
    Nos. 583-586 (4)   1.80   1.80

A352

End of World War II, 60th Anniv. — A353

2005   **Perf. 14x14¼**
587 A352   45k multi   .45   .45

Souvenir Sheet
Perf. 11½
588 A353 80k multi   .80   .80

Issued: 45k, 4/22; 80k, 5/7. No. 587 issued in sheets of 8 + central label.

Ninth Intl. Philatelic Exhibition,
Kyiv — A354

2005, May 17   Perf. 13¾x14½
589 A354 45k multi   .45   .45

Painting Type of 2002

Paintings of Kyiv: 45k, New Street, by Serhyi Shyshko, 1966. 75k, Park in Winter, by Shyshko, 1960. 80k, Sacred Sophia, by Yuryi Khymych, 1965. 1h, Khreshchatyk Boulevard, by Khymych, 1967, vert.

Perf. 13¾x14½, 14½x13¾
2005, May 18
590-593 A273 Set of 4   2.50 2.50

Ruslana, Winner of 2004 Eurovision
Song Contest — A355

Logo for 2005
Eurovision Song
Contest — A356

2005, May 19   Perf. 11½
594 A355 45k multi   .45   .45
595 A356 2.50h multi   1.75 1.75

Europa — A357

Nos. 596 and 597: a, 2.61h, Bowl of borscht, beets, onions, garlic, tomatoes, pepper, beans, lard, parsley and dill. b, 3.52h, Lidded tureen, cabbage, carrots, onion, garlic, pepper.

2005, May 20   Perf. 11½
Stamp Size: 45x32mm
596 A357   Horiz. pair, #a-b   3.50 3.50
Booklet Stamps
Stamp Size: 40x27mm
Perf. 14x14¼
597 A357   Horiz. pair, #a-b   6.00 6.00
  c.   Booklet pane, 2 #597   12.00   —
        Complete booklet, #597c   12.00

Complete booklet sold for 19.38h.

Development of
the Cyrillic
Alphabet — A358

Litho. & Embossed
2005, May 21   Perf. 14¼x14
598 A358 45k multi   .45   .45

Souvenir Sheet

Flora and Fauna in Karadazkyi Nature
Reserve — A359

No. 599: a, 45k, Falco cherrug (33x40mm). b, 70k, Ascalaphus macaronius (29x35mm). c, 2.50h, Tursiops truncatus ponticus (33x33mm). d, 3.50h, Martes foina (49x33mm).

2005, July 28   Litho.   Perf. 11½
599 A359 Sheet of 4, #a-d   4.25 4.25

World
Summit on
the
Information
Society,
Tunis
A360

2005, Aug. 12   Perf. 14x14¼
600 A360 2.50h multi   1.40 1.40

Series Ov Locomotive — A361

Series C Locomotive — A362

Series Shch Locomotive — A363

Series Ye Locomotive — A364

2005, Aug. 31
601 A361 70k multi   .50   .50
602 A362 70k multi   .50   .50
603 A363 70k multi   .50   .50
604 A364 70k multi   .50   .50
        Nos. 601-604 (4)   2.00 2.00

Nos. 601-604 were each printed in sheets of 11 + label.

Sumy, 350th Anniv. — A365

2005, Sept. 2
605 A365 45k multi   .45   .45

Nasturtium
A366

Water Lily
A367

Violets — A368

Wild
Rose — A369

2005   Date imprint   Perf. 13¾
606 A366   25k multi   .45   .45
  a.   Perf. 11½, dated "2006"   .75   .75
  b.   As #606, dated "2006"   1.00 1.00
607 A367   70k multi   .90   .90
  a.   Perf. 11½, dated "2006"   1.00 1.00
  b.   As #607, dated "2006"   .90   .90
608 A368 (1.53h) multi   1.50 1.50
  a.   Perf. 11½, dated "2006"   4.00 4.00
  b.   As #608, dated "2006"   1.50 1.50
609 A369 (2.55h) multi   2.50 2.50
  a.   Perf. 11½, dated "2006"   5.00 5.00
  b.   As #609, dated "2006"   2.50 2.50
        Nos. 606-609 (4)   5.35 5.35

Issued: #606, 9/8/05; #606b, 2/7/06. #607, 9/12/05; #607b, 2/7/06. #608, 12/16/05; #608b, 9/28/06. #609,11/25/05; 609a, 6/5/06. Nos. 606a-609a issued 10/9/06. Nos. 606a-609a were issued only in No. F2b.

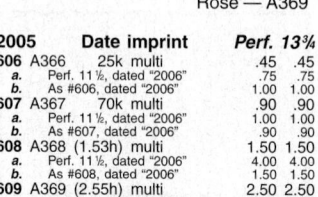

Horses — A370

No. 610: a, Novoolexandrivskyi heavy draft horse (brown horse facing left with four-line inscription). b, Orlov-Rostopchin (white horse). c, Ukrainian riding horse (brown horse facing left with three-line inscription). d, Thoroughbred (brown horse facing right).

2005, Sept. 15   Perf. 11½
610 A370 70k Block of 4, #a-d   1.60 1.60

"Safety -
Green
Light"
A371

"Give a
Helping
Hand"
A372

"No to
Drugs"
A373

2005, Oct. 14   Perf. 14x14¼
611   Horiz. strip of 3   1.60 1.60
  a.   A371 70k multi   .50   .50
  b.   A372 70k multi   .50   .50
  c.   A373 70k multi   .50   .50

Military History — A374

No. 612: a, Commander Bobrok Volnyets at Battle of Kulikovo, 1380. b, Artillerymen and riflemen, 14th-15th cent. c, Knight Ivanko Sushyk at Grunwald, 1410. d, Prince Konstiantyn Ostrozkyi at Orsha, 1512.

2005, Oct. 22
612 A374 70k Block of 4, #a-d   1.60 1.60

Famous Ukrainians Type of 2004

Designs: No. 613, Dmytro Yiavornytskyi (1855-1940), historian. No. 614, Oleg Antonov (1906-84), aircraft designer.

2005-06   Litho.
613 A314 70k multi   .60   .60
614 A314 70k multi   .60   .60

Issued: #613, 11/7; #614, 2/7/06.

Christmas
A375

Litho. With Foil Application
2005, Nov. 11   Perf. 13¼
615 A375 70k multi   .55   .55

New Year's
Day — A376

2005, Nov. 11   Litho.
616 A376 70k multi   .55   .55

St. Barbara's Church, Vienna,
Austria — A377

2005, Dec. 9   Perf. 14¼x14
617 A377 75k multi + label   .75   .75

Lviv National Museum, Cent. — A378

No. 618: a, Archangel Michael, by unknown artist (denomination at right). b, Dalmatynka, by Teofil Kopystynskyi (denomination at left).

2005, Dec. 13   Litho.
618 A378 70k Horiz. pair, #a-b, +
        central label   1.10 1.10

Regional Costumes

Zhytomyrshchyna Region — A379

Rivnenshchyna Region — A380

Volyn Region — A381

No. 619: a, Family and dog, St. Basil's Day. b, Man and woman, St. Zosyma's Day.
No. 620: a, People with animals, St. George's Day. b, Men, women and musician, Sts. Peter and Paul's Day.
No. 621: a, People with buckets, Annunciation Day. b, Family and cat, St. Nicholas's Day.

2005, Dec. 20   *Perf. 13¼*
619 A379 70k Horiz. pair, #a-b   .85 .85
620 A380 70k Horiz. pair, #a-b   .85 .85
621 A381 70k Horiz. pair, #a-b   .85 .85
   c.   Miniature sheet, #619-621, perf. 11½   3.75 3.75

Europa Stamps, 50th Anniv. — A382

Designs: Nos. 622a, 623a, 1.30h, 50th anniversary emblem. Nos. 622a, 622b, 2.50h, CEPT emblem.

2006, Jan. 5   Litho.   *Perf. 13¼*
With Names of Designers at Right of Stamps
622 A382 Vert. pair, #a-b   2.25 2.25
Souvenir Sheet
Without Names of Designers at Right of Stamps
Perf. 11½
623 A382 Sheet of 2, #a-b   2.25 2.25

Art by Hryhoryi Narbut (1886-1920) — A383

Litho. & Engr.
2006, Mar. 10   *Perf. 11½*
624 A383 3.33h multi   2.10 2.10
Printed in sheets of 11 + label.

Miniature Sheet

Traditional Women's Headdresses — A384

No. 625: a, Drawing of woman wearing fur hat. b, Woman, facing left, wearing black hat with brown ribbon. c, Drawing of woman facing left, wearing undecorated head covering. d, Woman wearing large floral head covering. e, Woman wearing red kerchief. f, Woman wearing small floral head covering. g, Woman wearing white kerchief with red dots. h, Woman wearing brown kerchief with knot in front. i, Drawing of woman, facing right, wearing undecorated head covering. j, Woman wearing floral headcovering with thin black edge. k, Woman wearing kerchief with floral pattern. l, Woman wearing small floral head covering with ribbon.

2006, Mar. 30   Litho.   *Perf. 11½*
625 A384 70k Sheet of 12, #a-l   5.00 5.00

Coronas-1 Satellite A385

Designs: No. 627, Welding in space. No. 628, International observation of Halley's Comet.

2006, Apr. 12   *Perf. 14x14¼*
Color of Panel Denomination Panel
626 A385 85k gray   .80 .80
627 A385 85k red brown   .80 .80
628 A385 85k dull brown   .80 .80
   Nos. 626-628 (3)   2.40 2.40

Europa — A386

Designs: Nos. 629a, 630a, 2.50h, Earth and Saturn. Nos. 629b, 630b, 3.50h, Earth and Jupiter.

2006, Apr. 28   *Perf. 11½*
Top Cyrillic Inscription in Black
629 A386   Horiz. pair, #a-b   3.50 3.50
Top Cyrillic Inscription in Red
630 A386   Booklet pane of 2, #a-b + 2 labels   8.00 8.00
   Complete booklet, #630   8.00
Nos. 630a-630b are 52x26mm. No. 630 sold for 11.52h.

2006 World Cup Soccer Championships, Germany — A387

Designs: 2.50k, Ukrainian soccer players. 3.50k, Soccer ball.

2006, May 4
631-632 A387   Set of 2   4.50 4.50

Georgia, Ukraine, Azerbaijan and Moldova Summit, Kiev A388

2006, May 23   *Perf. 14x14¼*
633 A388 70k multi   .65 .65

Paintings of Kiev — A389

Designs: No. 634, 70k, Zaborovskyi Gate, by Boris Tulin, 1987 (shown). No. 635, 70k, Olha Basystiuk Sings, by Tulin, 1987. No. 636, 70k, Kiev-Peherska Lavra, by Oleksandr Hubarev, 1990. No. 637, 70k, Andrew's Alley, by Hubarev, 1983.

2006, May 24   *Perf. 13¾x14¼*
634-637 A389   Set of 4   2.40 2.40

Souvenir Sheet

Lviv, 750th Anniv. — A390

No. 638 — View of Lviv, 1618 and: a, 70k, Coat of arms (38x31mm). b, 2.50h, Coin (69x31mm).

2006, June 16   *Perf. 11½*
638 A390   Sheet of 2, #a-b   2.10 2.10

Miniature Sheet

Fauna of Shatskyi National Park — A391

No. 639: a, Lanius excubitor (28x40mm). b, Lynx lynx (33x35mm). c, Anguilla anguilla (41x29mm). d, Bufo calamita (28x29mm). e, Mustela erminea (45x29mm).

2006, July 14
639 A391 70k Sheet of 5, #a-e   3.25 3.25

Miniature Sheet

Cossack Leaders — A392

No. 640: a, Ivan Bohun (denomination at UL). b, Ivan Honta (denomination at UR). c, Ivan Pidkova (denomination at LL). d, Ivan Sirko (denomination at LR).

Litho. & Engr. With Foil Application
2006, Aug. 18
640 A392 3.50h Sheet of 4, #a-d   8.50 8.50

Famous Ukrainians Type of 2004
Design: Ivan Franko (1856-1916), writer.

2006, Aug. 27   Litho.   *Perf. 14x14¼*
641 A314 70k multi   .65 .65

Series L Locomotive — A393

Series SO Locomotive — A394

Series YS Locomotive — A395

Series FD Locomotive — A396

2006, Sept. 15
642 A393 70k multi   .65 .65
643 A394 70k multi   .65 .65
644 A395 70k multi   .65 .65
645 A396 70k multi   .65 .65
   Nos. 642-645 (4)   2.60 2.60
Each stamp printed in sheets of 11 + label.

Tenth Natl. Philatelic Exhibition, Lviv — A397

2006, Oct. 6   Litho. & Embossed
646 A397 70k multi   .65 .65

Military History — A398

No. 647: a, Cossack-siroma, 16th-17th cent. b, Naval campaigns of 16th-18th cents. c, Khmelnychna national liberation movement (soldiers aiming guns), 17th cent. d, Haidamachnya national liberation movement (soldier with sword), 17th cent.

2006, Nov. 3 Litho. ***Perf. 14x14¼***

647 A398 70k Block of 4, #a-d 2.60 2.60

Horses in Sports — A399

No. 648: a, Dressage. b, Horse racing. c, Harness racing. d, Show jumping.

2006, Nov. 17 ***Perf. 11½***

648 A399 70k Block of 4, #a-d 2.60 2.60

Printed in sheets containing two each of Nos. 648a-648d.

St. Nicholas's Day — A400

No. 649: a, Children following angel. b, Angel and St. Nicholas.

Litho. With Foil Application

2006, Nov. 17 ***Perf. 13¼***

649 A400 70k Horiz. pair, #a-b 1.00 1.00

Christmas — A401

2006, Nov. 24 ***Perf. 14¼x14***

650 A401 70k multi .65 .65

Lviv, 750th Anniv. A402

Litho. & Engr.

2006, Dec. 1 ***Perf. 14x13¾***

651 A402 3.50h multi 2.75 2.75

Printed in sheets of 10 + 5 labels. See Austria No. 2075.

Regional Costumes

Zaporizhzha Region — A403

Khersonshchyna Region — A404

Odeshchyna Region — A405

No. 652: a, People with flags, candle, and swords, St. Michael's Day. b, People and horses, Assumption Day.

No. 653: a, Women and spinning wheel, St. Catherine's Day. b, Men and oxen, St. Elias's Day.

No. 654: a, People and pig, St. Barbara and St. Sava's Day. b, People and fish, St. Boris and St. Hlib's Day.

2006, Dec. 15 Litho. ***Perf. 13¼***

652 A403 70k Horiz. pair, #a-b .75 .75
653 A404 70k Horiz. pair, #a-b .75 .75
654 A405 70k Horiz. pair, #a-b .75 .75
c. Miniature sheet, #652-654, perf. 11½ 2.25 2.25

Famous Ukrainians Type of 2004

Designs: No. 655, 70k, Metropolitan Ivan Ohienko (1882-1972). No. 656, 70k, Igor Stravinsky (1882-1971), composer.

2007 Litho. ***Perf. 14x14¼***

655-656 A314 Set of 2 1.40 1.40

Issued: No. 655, 1/12; No. 656, 6/8.

Conjoined Pots A406

Candelabra A407

Clay Bull A408

Inkwell A409

Mug — A410

Rag Doll — A411

Folk decorative art: 3k, Horse figurine. 5k, Whistle. 10k, Jug. 50k, Spinning wheel. 60k, Demijohn. 70k, Circular water container. 85k, Ladle. 1h, Decorated cup with handle. 2h, Pitcher with handle.

2007 Litho. ***Perf. 13¾***

Date Imprint

657 A406 1k multi, "2007" .25 .25
a. Imprint "2007-II" .25 .25
658 A406 3k multi, "2007" .25 .25
a. Imprint "2007-II" .25 .25
b. Imprint "2008" .50 .50
659 A406 5k multi, "2007" .25 .25
a. Imprint "2007-II" .25 .25
b. Imprint "2008" .25 .25
c. Imprint "2008-II" .50 .50
d. Imprint "2008-III" .50 .50
e. Imprint "2010" .40 .40
f. Imprint "2010-II" .25 .25
g. Imprint "2011" .25 .25
660 A406 10k multi, "2007" .25 .25
a. Imprint "2007-II" .25 .25
b. Imprint "2008" .50 .50
c. Imprint "2008-II" .50 .50
d. Imprint "2008-III" .50 .50
e. Imprint "2008-IV" .50 .50
f. Imprint "2009" .25 .25
g. Imprint "2010" .50 .50
h. Imprint "2010-II" .50 .50
i. Imprint "2011" .25 .25
j. Imprint "2011-II" .25 .25
661 A406 50k multi, "2007" .40 .40
a. Imprint "2007-II" .40 .40
b. Imprint "2008" .50 .50
c. Dated "2009" .50 .50
d. Imprint "2009-II" .50 .50
e. Imprint "2010" .75 .75
f. Imprint "2010-II" .75 .75
g. Imprint "2011" .25 .25
h. Imprint "2011-II" .25 .25
i. Imprint "2012" .25 .25
662 A406 60k multi, "2007" .50 .50
a. Imprint "2008" .50 .50
b. Imprint "2008-II" .75 .75
663 A406 70k multi, "2007" .50 .50
a. Imprint "2007-II" .50 .50
b. Imprint "2008" .75 .75
c. Imprint "2008-II" .75 .75
d. Imprint "2008-III" .75 .75
664 A406 85k multi, "2007" .75 .75
a. Imprint "2007-II" .75 .75
b. Imprint "2008" .90 .90
665 A406 1h multi, "2007" .75 .75
a. Imprint "2007-II" .75 .75
b. Imprint "2008" .80 .80
c. Imprint "2008-II" .80 .80
d. Imprint "2009" .80 .80
e. Imprint "2009-II" .80 .80
f. Imprint "2010" .85 .85
g. Imprint "2010-II" .85 .85
h. Imprint "2011" .25 .25
i. Imprint "2011-II" .25 .25
666 A407 (1.52h) multi, "2007" .80 .80
a. Imprint "2007-II" .80 .80
b. Imprint "2008" 1.00 1.00
c. Imprint "2010" .75 .75
d. Imprint "2011" .60 .60
667 A406 2h multi, "2007" 1.40 1.40
a. Imprint "2007-II" 1.40 1.40
b. Imprint "2008" 1.40 1.40
c. Imprint "2008-II" 2.00 2.00
d. Dated "2009" 1.40 1.40
e. Imprint "2009-II" 1.50 1.50
f. Imprint "2010" 1.50 1.50
g. Imprint "2010-II" 1.50 1.50
h. Imprint "2010-III" 1.50 1.50
i. Imprint "2011" .75 .75
j. Imprint "2011-II" .75 .75
k. Imprint "2011-III" .50 .50
l. Imprint "2012" .50 .50
668 A408 (2.48h) multi, "2007" 1.25 1.25
a. Imprint "2007-II" 1.25 1.25
b. Imprint "2008" 1.25 1.25
669 A409 (3.33h) multi, "2007" 1.75 1.75
a. Imprint "2007-II" 1.75 1.75
b. Imprint "2008" 1.75 1.75
670 A410 (3.79h) multi, "2007" 2.00 2.00
a. Imprint "2008" 2.00 2.00
b. Imprint "2011" 2.00 2.00
671 A411 (10.10h) multi, "2007" 5.25 5.25
a. Imprint "2007-II" 5.25 5.25
b. Imprint "2008" 5.25 5.25
c. Imprint "2011" 5.25 5.25
Nos. 657-671 (15) 16.35 16.35

Issued: No. 657, 4/14/07, No. 657a, 12/07. No. 658, 4/14/07; No. 658a,9/6/07; No. 658b, 2008. No. 659, 3/16/07; No. 659a, 9/8/07; No. 659b, 2/08; No. 659c, 9/27/08; No. 659d, 10/27/08; No. 659e, 3/24/10; No. 659f, 8/13/10; No. 659g, 6/7/11. No. 660, 4/14/07; No. 660a, 11/16/07; No. 660b, 4/18/08; No. 660c, 5/30/08; No. 660d, 9/5/08; No. 660e, 2008; No. 660f, 9/7/09; No. 660g, 2/8/10; No. 660h, 8/13/10; Nos. 660i-660j, 6/7/11. No. 661, 1/26/07; No. 661a, 5/07; No. 661b, 8/22/08; No. 661c, 6/10/09; No. 661d, 9/7/09; No. 661e, 2/8/10; No. 661f, 8/13/10; Nos. 661g-661h, 6/7/11; No. 661i, 2012. No. 662, 1/26/07; No. 662a, 6/18/08; No. 662b, 8/22/08. No. 663, 1/26/07; No. 663a, 9/6/07; No. 663b, 4/11/08; No. 663c, 5/30/08; No. 663d, 7/28/08. No. 664, 1/26/07; No. 664a, 8/13/07; No. 664b, 8/22/08. No. 665, 4/6/07; No. 665a, 12/07; No. 665b, 7/26/08; No. 665c, 2008; Nos. 665d, 665e, 2009; No. 665f, 2/8/10; No. 665g, 8/13/10; Nos. 665h-665i, 6/7/11. No. 666, 4/6/07; No. 666a, 10/24/07; No. 666b, 10/21/08; No. 666c, 8/13/10; No. 666d, 6/7/11. No. 667, 3/16/07; No. 667a, 10/24/07; Nos. 667b, 667c, 9/27/08; No. 667d, 7/16/09; No. 667e, 9/7/09; No. 667f, 2/8/10; No. 667g, 3/24/10; No. 667h, 2010; Nos. 667i-667k, 6/7/11, No. 667l, 2012. No. 668, 4/6/07; No. 668a, 11/16/07; No. 668b, 10/17/08. No. 669, 4/14/07; No. 669a, 12/07; No. 669b, 11/08. No. 670, 3/16/07; No. 670a, 11/8/08; No. 670b, 6/7/11. NO. 671, 3/16/07; No. 671a, 11/16/07; No. 671b, 11/8/08; No. 671c, 6/7/11.

For surcharges, see Nos. 803-804.

See Nos. 720, 764, 817-820.

St. Michael's Cathedral, Adelaide, Australia — A412

2007, Feb. 9 ***Perf. 13¼***

672 A412 3.35k multi + label 1.75 1.75

Souvenir Sheet

Taras Shevchenko (1814-61), Poet — A413

No. 673: a, 2.50h, Drawing of Shevchenko's house, poem (66x40mm). b, 3.35k, Shevchenko (36x40mm).

Litho. With Foil Application

2007, Feb. 23 ***Perf. 11½***

673 A413 Sheet of 2, #a-b 3.75 3.75

Wedding Rings — A414

Flowers — A415

Pechersk Lavra Monastery, Kiev — A416

Oranta Monument — A417

2007, Mar. 1 Litho. ***Perf. 11½***

674 A414 70k multi + label 1.75 1.75
675 A415 70k multi + label 1.75 1.75
676 A416 70k multi + label 1.75 1.75
677 A417 70k multi + label 1.75 1.75
Nos. 674-677 (4) 7.00 7.00

Nos. 674-676 were printed in sheets of 22 stamps + 22 labels that could be personalized, and sold for 60.60h per sheet. No. 677 was printed in sheets of 18 stamps + 18 labels that

could be personalized, and sold for 54.60h per sheet. Labels shown are generic.

Space Exploration
A418

Designs: No. 678, 70k, Leonid Kadeniuk, first Ukrainian cosmonaut. No. 679, 70k, Sea Launch rocket lifting off.

2007, Apr. 12 Perf. 14x14¼
678-679 A418 Set of 2 .80 .80

Europa — A419

Nos. 680 and 681: a, 2.50h, Scout emblem, neckerchief and "100." b, 3.35h, Scouts.

2007, Apr. 28 Perf. 14x14¼
Stamp Size: 40x28mm
680 A419 Horiz. pair, #a-b 3.50 3.50
Stamp Size: 45x33mm
Perf. 11½
681 A419 Booklet pane of 2, #a-b 7.50 —
      Complete booklet, #681 7.50

Scouting, cent. No. 681 sold for 11.52h.

Paintings of Kiev — A420

Designs: No. 682, 70k, Sunny Day, Yaroslaviv Val, by Vitalii Petrovskyi, 1997. No. 683, 70k, Street of Recollections, by Tetiana Kuhai, 2004 (red panel), vert. No. 684, 70k, Kiev Walk, by Yulia Kuznietsova, 2004 (lilac panel), vert. No. 685, 70k, Snowing, by Maria Lashkevych, 2007.

Perf. 13¾x14½, 14½x13¾
2007, May 18
682-685 A420 Set of 4 2.60 2.60

Miniature Sheets

Dogs — A421

Cats — A422

No. 686: a, Pug. b, Irish setter. c, Alaskan malamute. d, Basset hound. e, Bull mastiff. f, American cocker spaniel.
No. 687: a, American shorthair. b, Sphynx. c, Scottish fold. d, Snowshoe. e, Russian blue. f, Somali.

2007, June 15 Perf. 11½
686 A421 70k Sheet of 6, #a-f 3.25 3.25
687 A422 70k Sheet of 6, #a-f 3.25 3.25

Roman Shukhevych (1907-50), Military Leader — A423

2007, June 29 Perf. 14x14¼
688 A423 70k multi .65 .65

TE1 Diesel Locomotive — A424

TE2 Diesel Locomotive — A425

TE3 Diesel Locomotive — A426

TE7 Diesel Locomotive — A427

2007, July 13 Litho. Perf. 14x14¼
689 A424 70k multi .65 .65
690 A425 70k multi .65 .65
691 A426 70k multi .65 .65
692 A427 70k multi .65 .65
      Nos. 689-692 (4) 2.60 2.60

Each stamp printed in sheets of 11 + label.

Miniature Sheet

Wedding Headdresses — A428

No. 693: a, Woman facing right wearing floral headdress with gray ribbon behind head. b, Woman facing left wearing gathered fabric headdress with broad red headband. c, Woman facing left wearing floral headdress with broad red ribbon at back. d, Woman facing right wearing ribboned floral headdress. e, Woman facing forward wearing tall red headdress with black and white spots. f, Woman wearing fabric headdress. g, Woman wearing headdress with wide floral ring above smaller floral rings. h, Man wearing hat and jacket with high collar. i, Woman facing left wearing tall floral headdress covering ear. j, Man wearing tall hat and collarless shirt with decorated front. k, Woman wearing headdress with one floral ring above broad red headband. l, Man wearing hat with chinstrap.

2007, Aug 23 Litho. Perf. 11½
693 A428 70k Sheet of 12, #a-l 5.75 5.75

Dnieper River Fish Preservation — A429

No. 694: a, Acipenser gueldenstaedtii. b, Zingel zingel.

2007, Sept. 6
694 Horiz. pair + central label 2.50 2.50
a. A429 1.50h multi 1.00 1.00
b. A429 2.50h multi 1.50 1.50

See Moldova No. 569.

Pereyaslav Khmelnytskyi, 1100th Anniv. — A430

2007, Sept. 16 Perf. 14x14¼
695 A430 70k multi .65 .65

Worldwide Fund for Nature (WWF) — A431

No. 696 — Pelecanus onocrotalus: a, 70k, In flight. b, 1.50h, In water. c, 2.50h, Two birds. d, 3.50h, One bird standing.

2007, Sept. 20 Perf. 14x14¼
696 A431 Block of 4, #a-d 4.25 4.25
e. Miniature sheet, 4 each #696a-696d, perf. 11½, + 4 labels 17.00 17.00

Souvenir Sheet

Launch of Sputnik 1, 50th Anniv. — A432

2007, Oct. 4 Perf. 11½
697 A432 3.33h multi 2.00 2.00

Miniature Sheets

A433

Peasant Houses — A434

No. 698 — House from: a, Podillya, with ox cart in front. b, Kiev, with couple, cat and pumpkins in front. c, Lemkivschyna, with horse and ducks in front. d, Hutsulschyna, with horse in front. e, Volyn, with wheat sheaves in front. f, Slobozhanschyna, with sunflowers at sides of house.
No. 699 — House from: a, Polissya, with basket weavers and horse in front. b, Khorolschyna, with children rolling hoop in front. c, Bukovyna, with couple in doorway. d, Boikivschyna, with dog and people carrying bundles of sticks in front. e, Poltava, people threshing grain in front. f, Lower Dnieper area, with man with fishing net in front.

2007, Oct. 24
698 A433 70k Sheet of 6, #a-f 3.75 3.75
699 A434 70k Sheet of 6, #a-f 3.75 3.75

Christmas and New Year's Day — A435

No. 700: a, Angels in sled. b, Angels with Christmas tree.

Litho. With Foil Application
2007, Nov. 16 Perf. 13½
700 A435 70k Horiz. pair, #a-b .85 .85

Christmas and New Year's Day — A436

2007, Nov. 23 Perf. 11½
701 A436 1h multi + label 2.75 2.75

Printed in sheets of 18 stamps + 18 labels that could be personalized.

2012 European Soccer Championships, Poland and Ukraine — A437

2007, Dec. 22
702 A437 3.33h multi 2.10 2.10

Regional Costumes

Khmelnytska Region — A438

Bukovyna Region — A439

Zakarpatyia Region — A440

No. 703: a, Potter and carolers, Christmas. b, People celebrating St. Simeon's Day, horses.

No. 704: a, Woman holding cross, man, woman, fruit basket, St. Ephrosinia's Day. b, Man holding violin, women and children, Ascension Day.

No. 705: a, Men and blacksmith holding mugs, Kuzma and Demyan Day. b, People near cross and candle, Easter.

2007, Dec. 22   Litho.   Perf. 13¼

703	A438	70k Horiz. pair, #a-b	.80	.80
704	A439	70k Horiz. pair, #a-b	.80	.80
705	A440	70k Horiz. pair, #a-b	.80	.80
c.		Miniature sheet, #703-705, perf. 11½	2.40	2.40

Aries — A441    Taurus — A442

Gemini — A443   Cancer — A444

Leo — A445   Virgo — A446

Libra — A447   Scorpio — A448

Sagittarius   Capricorn
A449   A450

Aquarius — A451   Pisces — A452

2008, Jan. 18   Perf. 14¼x14

706	A441	1h multi	.90	.90
707	A442	1h multi	.90	.90
708	A443	1h multi	.90	.90
709	A444	1h multi	.90	.90
710	A445	1h multi	.90	.90
711	A446	1h multi	.90	.90
712	A447	1h multi	.90	.90
713	A448	1h multi	.90	.90
714	A449	1h multi	.90	.90
715	A450	1h multi	.90	.90
716	A451	1h multi	.90	.90
717	A452	1h multi	.90	.90
		Nos. 706-717 (12)	10.80	10.80

2008 Summer Olympics,
Beijing — A453

No. 718: a, 1h, Archery. b, 1.30h, Fencing. c, 2.47h, Cycling. d, 3.33h, Rowing.

Litho. With Foil Application

2008, Jan. 26   Perf. 11½

718	A453	Block of 4, #a-d	4.50	4.50

Roses and Hearts — A454

2008, Feb. 6   Litho.   Perf. 11½

719	A454	1h multi + label	2.00	2.00

Printed in sheets of 22 stamps + 22 labels that could be personalized that sold for 69.90h. Label shown is generic.

Folk Decorative Art Type of 2007

Design: Carved pipe.

2008, Feb. 15   Litho.   Perf. 13¾

720	A406	30k multi, "2008"	.25	.25
a.		Imprint "2008-II"	.25	.25
b.		Imprint "2009"	.50	.50
c.		Imprint "2009-II"	.50	.50
d.		Imprint "2010"	.75	.75

e.	Imprint "2010-II"		.90	.90
f.	Imprint "2011"		.25	.25
g.	Imprint "2012"		.25	.25

Issued: No. 720a, 7/26/08; No. 720b, 7/16/09; No. 720c, 2009; No. 720d, 2/1/10; No. 720e, 8/13/10. No. 720f, 6/7/11. No. 720g, 2012.

Paintings by
Taras
Shevchenko
(1814-61)
A455

Designs: 1h, Gypsy Fortune Teller. 1.52h, Kateryna. 2.47h, Self-portrait.

Litho. With Foil Application

2008, Feb. 23   Perf. 11½

721-723	A455	Set of 3	3.00	3.00

Europa — A456

No. 724 — Letter writers with: a, 2.47h, Quill pen. b, 3.33h, Computer.

2008, Mar. 12   Litho.   Perf. 13¼

724	A456	Horiz. pair, #a-b	3.50	3.50

A booklet containing two 37x30mm perf. 11½ stamps like Nos. 724a-724b sold for 12.84h.

Nicolay Gogol (1809-52),
Writer — A457

No. 725: a, 1.52h, Gogol, gun, quill pen and inkwell, pipe. b, 2.47h, Taras Bulba on horseback.

2008, Mar. 21   Perf. 14x14¼

725	A457	Pair, #a-b	2.50	2.50

Easter — A458

Litho. With Foil Application

2008, Apr. 11   Perf. 13¼

726	A458	1h multi	.90	.90

Miniature Sheet

18th and 19th Century Decorative
Clocks — A459

No. 727: a, French mantle clock with clock as chariot wheel, 19th cent. (33x33mm). b, Russian mantle clock with nymphs, 19th cent. (33x33mm). c, French mantle clock with nude woman and nymphs on goats, 19th cent. (33x33mm). d, French clock by Charles Baltazar with blue green frame and nymph on top, 18th cent. (33x45mm). e, French clock with woman with shield on top, 18th cent. (33x45mm). f, German clock with woman trumpeter on top, 18th cent. (33x45mm). g, English clock with landscape above face, 18th cent. (33x45mm). h, Austrian clock with pillars at sides, 19th cent. (33x45mm). i, French mantle clock with birds at top, 19th cent. (33x45mm).

Litho. With Foil Application

2008, Apr. 18   Perf. 11½

727	A459	1h Sheet of 9, #a-i	5.50	5.50

Miniature Sheets

Dogs — A460

Cats — A461

No. 728: a, Smooth-haired dachshund. b, American bulldog. c, Rottweiler. d, Chow chow. e, Schnauzer. f, German shepherd.

No. 729: a, Persian. b, Selkirk Rex. c, Exotic shorthair. d, Burmese. e, Siamese. f, Kuril Island bobtail.

2008, May 16   Litho.

728	A460	1r Sheet of 6, #a-f	3.75	3.75
729	A461	1r Sheet of 6, #a-f	3.75	3.75

Miniature Sheet

Crimean Nature Reserve — A462

No. 730: a, Aegypius monachus (31x38mm). b, Cranes and swans (36x31mm). c, Cervus elaphus (47x31mm). d, Silene jailensis and insect (31x31mm).

2008, June 18
730 A462 1h Sheet of 4, #a-d   2.60 2.60

Souvenir Sheets

Ukrainian Postage Stamps, 90th Anniv. — A463

No. 731: a, 2.47h, Ukraine #1. b, 3.33h, Ukraine #2.
No. 732: a, 1h, Ukraine #4. b, 2.47h, Ukraine #5. c, 3.33j, Ukraine #3.

2008, July 4
| 731 | A463 | Sheet of 2, #a-b, + 2 labels | 3.50 | 3.50 |
| 732 | A463 | Sheet of 3, #a-c, + label | 4.25 | 4.25 |

Souvenir Sheet

Myhailivskyi Monastery, 900th Anniv. — A464

2008, July 11
733 A464 3.33h multi   2.10 2.10

TEP10 Diesel Locomotive — A465

2TE10L Diesel Locomotive — A466

M62 Diesel Locomotive — A467

TE109 Diesel Locomotive — A468

2008, Aug. 8   *Perf. 14x14¼*
734	A465	1h multi	.60	.60
735	A466	1h multi	.60	.60
736	A467	1h multi	.60	.60
737	A468	1h multi	.60	.60
		Nos. 734-737 (4)	2.40	2.40

Each stamp printed in sheets of 11 + label.

Christmas Carols — A469

Songs of Spring — A470

Songs of the Cossacks A471

Songs of the Chumaks A472

2008, Sept. 5   *Perf. 13½*
738	A469	1h multi	.60	.60
739	A470	1h multi	.60	.60
740	A471	1h multi	.60	.60
741	A472	1h multi	.60	.60
		Nos. 738-741 (4)	2.40	2.40

Ukrainian musical heritage.

Jewelry — A473

No. 742: a, 2.47h, Earring, 12th-13th cent. b, 3.33h, Pendant, 19th cent.

2008, Sept. 18   *Perf. 11½*
742 A473 Horiz. pair, #a-b, + central label   3.50 3.50

See Azerbaijan No. 885.

Ukrainian and Swedish Military and Political Alliances of 17th and 18th Centuries A474

Litho. With Foil Application
2008, Oct. 1
743 A474 1h multi   .80 .80

A475

Ninth Natl. Philatelic Exhibition, Chernivtsi — A476

2008, Oct. 3   Litho.   *Perf. 14x14¼*
744 A475 1h multi   .80 .80

Perf. 11½
745 A476 1h multi + label   4.50 4.50

No. 745 was printed in sheets of 10 stamps + 10 labels that could be personalized that sold for 88.38h. Label shown is generic.

Chernivtsi, 600th Anniv. A477

2008, Oct. 4   *Perf. 14x14¼*
746 A477 1h multi   .80 .80

Sacking of Baturyn, 300th Anniv. — A478

2008, Oct. 24   *Perf. 14¼x14*
747 A478 1h multi   .80 .80

Christmas — A479

New Year's Day — A480

Litho. With Foil Application
2008, Nov. 21   *Perf. 11½*
| 748 | A479 | 1h multi | .80 | .80 |
| 749 | A480 | 1h multi | .80 | .80 |

Famous Ukrainians Type of 2004
Designs: No. 750, 1h, Marko Vovchok (1833-1907), writer. No. 751, 1h, Vyachyslav Chornovil (1937-99), politician.

2008   Litho.   *Perf. 14x14¼*
750-751 A314 Set of 2   1.60 1.60

Issued: No. 750, 11/28; No. 751, 12/24.

Miniature Sheet

Headdresses — A481

No. 752: a, Woman facing right wearing brown and red headdress and red necklace. b, Woman facing forward wearing white headdress wrapping under chin. c, Woman facing left with headdress with blue-tipped tassels above eyes. d, Woman facing right wearing white headdress. e, Woman facing forward wearing brown, red and green headdress and red necklace. f, Woman facing forward wearing white, red and green headdress, denomination in white. g, Woman wearing white headdress and laurel wreath. h, Woman wearing white, gray and red headdress. i, Woman facing left wearing white, red and green headdress with floral pattern over red striped forehead band. j, Man wearing brown hat. k, Woman facing forward wearing headdress with lace trim on forehead. l, Man wearing black and red hat.

2008, Dec. 10   *Perf. 11½*
752 A481 1h Sheet of 12, #a-l   7.75 7.75

Regional Costumes

Crimea Region — A482

Dnipropetrovshchyna Region — A483

Luhanshchyna Region — A484

No. 753: a, People with grapes, Feast of the Transfiguration. b, Baby being christened.
No. 754: a, Bride and groom receiving crowns. b, Three women at Harvest Festival.
No. 755: a, Musicians, Feast of Saints Cyril and Methodius. b, People and church on hill, Feast of the Miracle Worker.

2008, Dec. 25　Litho.　Perf. 13¼

753	A482	1h Horiz. pair, #a-b	.80	.80
754	A483	1h Horiz. pair, #a-b	.80	.80
755	A484	1h Horiz. pair, #a-b	.80	.80
c.		Miniature sheet, #753-755, perf. 11½	2.40	2.40
		Nos. 753-755 (3)	2.40	2.40

Stephan Bandera (1909-59), Nationalist Leader — A485

2009, Jan. 1

756	A485	1h multi	.65	.65

Famous Ukrainians Type of 2004

Designs: 1h, Stepan Rudanskyi (1834-73), poet. 2.20h, Sholem Aleichem (1859-1916), writer.

2009　　　　　　　　Perf. 14x14¼

757-758	A314	Set of 2	1.40	1.40

Issued: No. 757, 1/17; No. 758, 2/18.

Souvenir Sheet

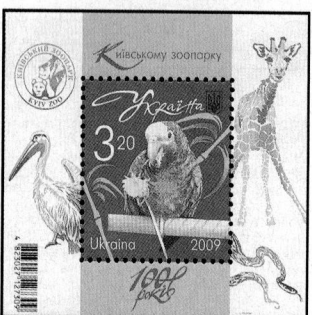

Kiev Zoo, Cent. — A486

2009, Feb. 20　Litho.　Perf. 11½

759	A486	3.20h multi	1.40	1.40

Paintings by Taras Shevchenko A487

Designs: No. 760, 1.50h, Portrait of I. I. Lyzohub, 1846-47. No. 761, 1.50h, Portrait of E. V. Keikuatova, 1847. No. 762, 1.50h, Village Family, 1843, horiz.

Litho. With Foil Application

2009, Mar. 9

760-762	A487	Set of 3	1.75	1.75

Nos. 760-762 each were printed in sheets of 11 + label.

Preservation of Polar Regions — A488

No. 763: a, Academician Vernadskiy Antarctic Station. b, Iceberg.

2009, Mar. 18

763	A488	3.30h Pair, #a-b	2.75	2.75

Printed in sheets containing 4 of each stamp and a central label.

Folk Art Type of 2007

Designs: Tile depicting Cossack on horse.

2009, Mar. 25　Litho.　Perf. 13¾

764	A406	1.50h multi	.60	.60
a.		Imprint "2009-II"	.75	.75
b.		Imprint "2010"	.75	.75
c.		Imprint "2010-II"	.75	.75
d.		Imprint "2011"	.55	.55
e.		Imprint "2011-II"	.55	.55
f.		Imprint "2011-III"	.40	.40

Issued: No. 764a, 7/16; Nos. 764b, 764c, 2010. Nos. 764d, 764e, 6/7/11. No. 764f, 6/7/11.

Souvenir Sheet

Nikolai Gogol (1809-52), Writer — A489

No. 765: a, 1.50h, Scene from "Night Before Christmas." b, 2.20h, Gogol.

Litho. With Foil Application

2009, Apr. 1　　　　Perf. 11½

765	A489	Sheet of 2, #a-b	1.50	1.50

Europa — A490

No. 766: a, Telescope and star chart. b, Map of solar system, Galileo Galilei and his telescope.

2009, Apr. 17　Litho.　Perf. 13¾x14¼
Size: 52x25mm

766		Horiz. pair	3.00	3.00
a.	A490	3.75h multi	1.25	1.25
b.	A490	5.25h multi	1.75	1.75

Intl. Year of Astronomy. A booklet containing a pane with a pair of 57x28mm perf. 11½ stamps like Nos. 766a-766b sold for 18.42h. Value, $8.

Architecture in China and Ukraine A491

No. 767: a, Stork Tower, Shanghai. b, Golden Gate, Kiev.

2009, Aug. 14　　　　Perf. 11½

767		Horiz. pair + central label	3.75	3.75
a.	A491	3.85h multi	1.60	1.60
b.	A491	5.40h multi	2.00	2.00

Miniature Sheet

Gorgany Game Reserve — A492

No. 768: a, Tetrao urogallus (40x37mm). b, Pinus cembra (30x47mm). c, Arnica montana (40x40mm). d, Felis silvestris (57x30mm).

2009, Sept. 29

768	A492	1.50h Sheet of 4, #a-d	2.50	2.50

Electric Locomotive VL26 — A493

Electric Locomotive VL41 — A494

Diesel Locomotive 2TE116 — A495

Diesel Locomotive 2TE121 — A496

2009, Oct. 22　　　　Perf. 13¾x14¼

769	A493	1.50h multi	.60	.60
770	A494	1.50h multi	.60	.60
771	A495	1.50h multi	.60	.60
772	A496	1.50h multi	.60	.60
		Nos. 769-772 (4)	2.40	2.40

Miniature Sheet

Lighthouses — A497

No. 773: a, Kyz-Aulskyi Lighthouse (blue top). b, Luparivskyi Front Lighthouse (base with vertical red and white stripes). c, Yaltinskyi Lighthouse (white, with hexagonal base). d, Vorontsovskyi Lighthouse (red top). e, Sarych Lighthouse (white, with circular base). f, Berdianskyi Lower Lighthouse (base with horizontal red and white stripes).

2009, Oct. 30　　　　Perf. 11½

773	A497	1.50h Sheet of 6, #a-f	3.75	3.75

Ukrainian Supreme Liberation Council, 65th Anniv. — A498

2009, Nov. 27　　　　Perf. 14¼x14

774	A498	1.50h multi	.65	.65

A499

A500

A501

Songs — A502

2009, Nov. 27　　　　Perf. 11½

775	A499	1.50h multi	.75	.75
776	A500	1.50h multi	.75	.75
777	A501	2h multi	.90	.90
778	A502	2h multi	.90	.90
		Nos. 775-778 (4)	3.30	3.30

Christmas A503

New Year 2010 — A504

Litho. With Foil Application

2009, Dec. 9　　　　Perf. 11½

779	A503	1.50h multi	.65	.65

Perf. 13¾x14¼

780	A504	1.50h multi	.65	.65

White Sukholimanskiy Grapes and Vineyard — A505

White Muscat Grapes, Sailboat and
Vineyard — A506

2009, Dec. 15 Litho. Perf. 11½
781 A505 1.50h multi .65 .65
782 A506 1.50h multi .65 .65

Narodny Rukh
(People's
Movement) Party,
20th Anniv. — A507

2009, Dec. 19 Perf. 13¾
783 A507 1.50h multi .65 .65

Miniature Sheet

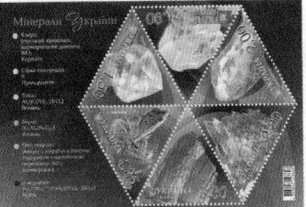

Minerals — A508

No. 784: a, 1.50h, Quartz. b, 1.90h, Native
sulphur. c, 2h, Topaz. d, 2.20h, Beryl. e, 3.30h,
Tiger's eye. f, 4.85h, Kertschenite.

Litho. & Embossed
2009, Dec. 23 Perf. 11½
784 A508 Sheet of 6, #a-h 7.00 7.00

2010 Winter Olympics,
Vancouver — A509

No. 785: a, 1.50h, Cross-country skiing. b,
1.50h, Biathlon. c, 2h, Freestyle skiing. d, 2h,
Luge.

Litho. With Foil Application
2010, Feb. 5 Perf. 11½
785 A509 Horiz. strip of 4, #a-d 3.50 3.50

Souvenir Sheet

Taras Shevchenko (1814-61),
Poet — A510

No. 786: a, 1.50h, Woman at butter churn,
poem (66x40mm). b, 2h, Self-portrait
(36x40mm).

2010, Mar. 9
786 A510 Sheet of 2, #a-b 1.75 1.75

Souvenir Sheet

Constitution of Pylyp Orlik, 300th
Anniv. — A511

2010, Mar. 29 Litho.
787 A511 1.50h multi .85 .85

Victory in World
War II, 65th
Anniv. — A512

2010, Apr. 15 Perf. 13¼
788 A512 1.50h multi .85 .85

Souvenir Sheets

Prepared But Unissued Postage
Stamps of Ukrainian National
Republic, 90th Anniv. — A513

No. 789: a, 1.50h, Unissued 1h stamp. b,
1.50h, Unissued 10h stamp. c, 2h, Unissued
2h stamp. d, 2h, Unissued 15h stamp.
No. 790: a, 1.50h, Unissued 20h stamp. b,
1.50h, Unissued 40h stamp. c, 2h, Unissued
30h stamp. d, 2h, Unissued 50h stamp.

2010, Apr. 22 Perf. 11½
Sheets of 4, #a-d, + Label
789-790 A513 Set of 2 6.50 6.50

Europa — A514

Nos. 791 and 792 — Scenes from children's
books: a, 2.20h, Mare's Head. b, 3.30h, Gold
Shoe.

Litho. With Foil Application
2010, Apr. 30 Perf. 13¼
791 A514 Horiz. pair, #a-b 2.50 2.50
Perf. 11½
792 A514 Booklet pane of 2,
#a-b, + central label 5.00 —
Complete booklet, #792 5.00

Nos. 792a and 792b are 43x41mm. No. 792
sold for 10.50h.

Famous Ukrainians Type of 2004

Designs: 1h, Oleksandr Potebnia (1835-91),
linguist. 1.50h, Mykola Pyrohov (1810-81),
surgeon.

2010 Litho. Perf. 14x14¼
793 A314 1h multi .65 .65
794 A314 1.50h multi .85 .85

Issued: No. 793, 9/10; No. 794, 6/2.

Wladimir
and Vitali
Klitschko,
Boxers
A515

2010, June 8
795 A515 1.50h multi .85 .85

Flowers — A516

Litho. With Foil Application
2010, Aug. 11 Perf. 13¼x13½
796 A516 (1.50h) multi + label 3.75 3.75

No. 796 was printed in sheets of 10 stamps
+ 10 labels that could be personalized that
sold for 105h. The label shown is generic.

DE1 Electric Locomotive — A517

DC3 Electric Locomotive — A518

TEM103 Diesel Locomotive — A519

TEP150 Diesel Locomotive — A520

2010, Sept. 4 Litho. Perf. 14x14¼
797 A517 1h multi .45 .45
798 A518 1.50h multi .60 .60
799 A519 2h multi .85 .85
800 A520 2h multi .85 .85
Nos. 797-800 (4) 2.75 2.75

Nos. 797-800 each printed in sheets of 11 +
label.

Sculptures by Johann Georg
Pinsel — A521

No. 801: a, 1.50h, Mother of God. b, 2h,
Angel.

2010, Sept. 8 Perf. 13¼
801 A521 Horiz. pair, #a-b 1.40 1.40

Miniature Sheet

National Technical University Kharkhiv
Polytechnical Institute, 125th
Anniv. — A522

No. 802: a, 1.50h, O. M. Beketov (1862-
1941), architect. b, 1.50h, P. P. Kopniaev
(1867-1932), electrical engineer. c, 1.50h, O.
M. Liapunov (1857-1918), mathematician. d,
1.50h, E. I. Orlov (1865-1944), chemical engineer. e, 1.50h, M. D. Pylchykov (1857-1908),
physicist. f, 1.50h, V. M. Khrushchov (1882-
1941), electrical engineer. g, 2h, V. L.
Kyrpychov (1845-1913), mechanical engineer.
h, 2h, M. M. Beketov (1827-1911), chemist. i,
2h, L. D. Landau (1908-68), theoretical physicist. j, 2m, P. M. Mukhachov (1861-1935),
engineer. k, 2h, V. A. Stieklov (1863-1926),
mathematician.

2010, Sept. 16 Perf. 11½
802 A522 Sheet of 11, #a-k, +
label 8.00 8.00

Nos. 657a, 658a, 658b
Surcharged

Methods and Perfs As Before
2010, Oct. 6
803 A406 1.50h on 3k #658a 1.25 1.25
a. A406 1.50h on 3k #658b 1.25 1.25
804 A406 2h on 1k #657a 1.75 1.75

Miniature Sheet

Lighthouses — A523

No. 805: a, 1.50h, Tendrivskyi Lighthouse
(with two horizontal black bands). b, 1.50h,
Pavlovskyi Fort Lighthouse (hexagonal with
brown vertical stripe). c, 1.50h, Khersoneskyi
Lighthouse (round white lighthouse with ten
windows). d, 2h, Sanzhiiskyi Lighthouse (hexagonal white lighthouse with two windows). e,
2h, Tarkhankutskyi Lighthouse (round white
lighthouse with four windows). f, 2h, Illichivskyi
Lighthouse (with horizontal red bands).

2010, Oct. 8 Litho. Perf. 11½
805 A523 Sheet of 6, #a-f 4.50 4.50

Leaders of Cossack
Rebellions — A524

No. 806: a, 1.50h, Kryshtof Kosynskyi
(1545-93). b, 2h, Bohdan Mykoshynskyi.

2010, Oct. 15 Perf. 14x14¼
806 A524 Block of 2, #a-b, + 2
labels 1.40 1.40

Military History — A525

No. 807: a, 1.50h, Danubian Sich (country name in brown). b, 1.50h, Cossack regiments of 1812 (country name in blue). c, 2h, Defense of Sevastopol (country name in blue). d, 2h, Ataman Yakiv Kukharenko on horse (country name in brown).

2010, Oct. 29
807   A525   Block of 4, #a-d   3.00 3.00

Hetman Pavlo Polubotok (1660-1724) — A526

Litho. With Foil Application
2010, Oct. 29
808   A526   1.50h multi   .65   .65

Miniature Sheet

Kiev Metro, 50th Anniv. — A527

No. 809: a, 1.50h, Dorohzhychi Station escalators. b, 1.50h, Train. c, 2h, Lukianivska Station exterior. d, 2h, Tunnel under construction.

2010, Nov. 3   Litho.   Perf. 11½
809   A527   Sheet of 4, #a-d   3.00 3.00

Cabernet Sauvignon Grapes and Estate — A528

2010, Dec. 17
810   A528   1.50h multi   .65   .65

Miniature Sheet

Fauna of Sviati Hory National Park — A529

No. 811: a, 1h, Zerynthia polyxena (38x30mm). b, 1.50h, Luscinia svecica

(38x30mm). c, 1.50h, Lutra lutra (38x37mm). d,2h, Emys orbicularis (38x37mm).

2010, Dec. 28
811   A529   Sheet of 4, #a-d   2.50 2.50

Signing of the Universal Declaration of Human Rights, 60th Anniv. A530

2010, Dec. 31   Perf. 14x14¼
812   A530   1.50h multi   .65   .65

Miniature Sheet

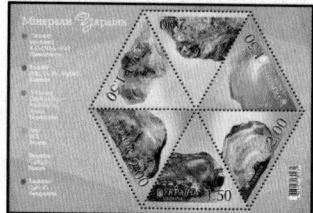

Minerals — A531

No. 813: a, 1.50h, Syngenite (brown mineral). b, 1.50h, Amber. c, 1.50h, Labradorite (black and red mineral). d, 2h, Carpathite (black arnd brown mineral). e, 2h, Agate (mineral with rings). f, 2h, Rhodonite (red and gray mineral).

Litho. & Embossed
2010, Dec. 31   Perf. 11½
813   A531   Sheet of 6, #a-f   4.50 4.50

First Man in Space, 50th Anniv. — A532

2011, Apr. 12   Litho.   Perf. 14x14¼
814   A532   6h multi   2.25 2.25

Georgy Beregovoi (1921-95), Cosmonaut — A533

2011, Apr. 16   Perf. 14¼x14
815   A533   2.20h multi   .75   .75

Kazashka Katya, Painting by Taras Shevchenko (1814-61) A534

Litho. With Foil Application
2011, May 21   Perf. 11½
816   A534   1.50h multi   .60   .60

Folk Decorative Art Type of 2007

Designs: 1.90h, Tobacco pouch. 2.20h, Powder flask. 6h, Bandura. 7h, Bowl with lid.

2011   Litho.   Perf. 13¾
817   A406   1.90h multi   .75   .75
    a.   Imprint "2011-II"   .50   .50
818   A406   2.20h multi   .85   .85
    a.   Imprint "2011-II"   .55   .55
819   A406   6h multi   2.40 2.40
820   A406   7h multi   2.75 2.75
        Nos. 817-820 (4)   6.75 6.75
    Issued: Nos. 817-820, 6/7. Nos. 817a, 818a, 6/7.

Leaders of Cossack Rebellions — A535

No. 821: a, 1.50h, Hryhorii Loboda. b, 2h, Severyn Nalyvaiko.

2011, June 9   Perf. 14x14¼
821   A535   Block of 2, #a-b, + 2
             labels   1.40 1.40

Ukrainian Constitution, 15th Anniv. — A536

Litho. & Embossed With Foil Application
2011, June 17   Perf. 11½
822   A536   6h multi   2.25 2.25

Miniature Sheet

Farmhouse and Animals — A537

No. 823: a, 1.50h, Cat. b, 1.50h, Birds. c, 1.50h, Pig. d, 2h, Cow. e, 2h, Dog.

2011, June 25   Litho.
823   A537   Sheet of 5, #a-e   3.50 3.50

Personalized Stamp — A538

Litho. With Foil Application
2011, June 25   Perf. 11½
824   A538   (1.50h) multi + label 3.00 3.00

No. 824 was printed in sheets of 18 + 18 labels that could be personalized. The label shown, depicting the national arms and posthorns, is the generic label image.
Compare with type A552.

Trains — A539

Designs: 1.50h, Diesel train DPL1. 1.90h, Diesel train, DEP 02. 2.20h, Electric train EPL 2T. 6h, Electric train EPL 9T.

2011, July 5   Litho.   Perf. 14x14¼
825-828   A539   Set of 4   4.50 4.50

First Flight of Dirigible "Kiev," Cent. — A540

2011, Aug. 5
829   A540   2.20h multi   .90   .90

Emigration of Ukrainians to Brazil, 120th Anniv. — A541

2011, Aug. 24   Perf. 14¼x14
830   A541   2.20h multi   .90   .90

Independence, 20th Anniv. — A542

Litho. With Foil Application
2011, Aug. 24   Perf. 14x14¼
831   A542   2.20h multi   .90   .90

"The Snow Queen" Fairy Tale — A543

No. 832: a, 1.50h, Snow Queen in horse-drawn sleigh flying above town (43x26mm). b, 6h, Crow and girl (26x26mm).

2011, Sept. 1   Litho.   Perf. 11½
832   A543   Horiz. pair, #a-b   2.75 2.75

12th Natl. Philatelic Exhibition, Odessa A544

2011, Sept. 9   Perf. 14x14¼
833   A544   4.30h multi   1.75 1.75

Miniature Sheet

Prepared but Unissued Ukrainian National Republic Stamps, 90th Anniv. — A545

No. 834: a, 1.50h, Unissued 5h stamp. b, 1.50h, Unissued 3h stamp. c, 2h, Unissued 60h stamp. d, 2h, Unissued 80h stamp. e, 6h, Unissued 100h stamp. f, 7h, Unissued 200h stamp.

2011, Sept. 12   *Perf. 11½*
834   A545   Sheet of 6, #a-f   7.50   7.50

Tetiana Markus (1921-43), Anti-Nazi Resistance Fighter — A546

2011, Sept. 21   *Perf. 14x14¼*
835   A546   1.50h multi   .55   .55

Babi Yar Massacres, 70th Anniv. — A547

2011, Sept. 29   *Perf. 13¼*
836   A547   2.20h multi   .90   .90

Motion Picture *Natalka Poltavka,* 75th Anniv. — A548

No. 837: a, 1.50h, People. b, 6h, Woman.

Litho. With Foil Application
2011, Sept. 30   *Perf. 14x14¼*
837   A548   Horiz. pair, #a-b   2.75   2.75

Lvov National University, 350th Anniv. — A549

2011, Oct. 11   **Litho.**   *Perf. 11½*
838   A549   1.50h multi   .55   .55

Regional Communications Commonwealth, 20th Anniv. — A550

2011, Oct. 14
839   A550   1.90h multi   .75   .75

Mykhailo Yanhel (1911-71), Missile Designer A551

2011, Oct. 25   *Perf. 13¼*
840   A551   1.50h multi   .55   .55

Personalized Stamp — A552

Litho. With Foil Application
2011, Nov. 1   *Perf. 11½*
841   A552   (1.80h) multi + label   3.00   3.00

No. 841 was printed in sheets of 12 + 12 labels that could be personalized. The label shown, depicting the national arms and post-thorns, is the generic label image.
Compare with type A538.

St. Sophia's Cathedral, Kyiv, 1000th Anniv. A553

No. 842: a, Painting above three arches. b, Round ceiling painting.

2011, Nov. 18
842   Horiz. pair + central label   3.00   3.00
a.   A553 1.90h multi   .75   .75
b.   A553 6h multi   2.25   2.25

Miniature Sheet

Amphibians — A554

No. 843: a, 1.80h, Pelophylax esculentus. b, 1.80h, Hyla arborea. c, 2.20h, Pelophylax lessonae. d, 2.20h, Rana dalmantina. e, 4.30h, Pelophylax ridibundus.

2011, Nov. 22   **Litho.**
843   A554   Sheet of 5, #a-e   4.50   4.50

Miniature Sheet

Spring — A555

No. 844: a, 1.80h, Bird on flower branch held by woman (30x40mm). b, 1.80h, Bare trees, white flowers and pond (30x21mm). c, 1.80h, Purple and yellow flowers (24x32mm). d. 1.90h, Cut flowers held by woman (30x40mm). e, 2.20h, Purple flowers (30x40mm). f, 6h, White flowers (30x40mm).

Litho. With Foil Application
2011, Nov. 25
844   A555   Sheet of 6, #a-f   5.75   5.75

Traminer Grapes and Vineyard — A556

Aligoté Grapes and Vineyard — A557

2011, Nov. 30   **Litho.**
845   A556   1.90h multi   .70   .70
846   A557   4.30h multi   1.60   1.60

Campaign Against AIDS, 30th Anniv. — A558

2011, Dec. 1   *Perf. 13¼*
847   A558   1.80h multi   .65   .65

Commonwealth of Independent States, 20th Anniv. — A559

2011, Dec. 8   *Perf. 13½*
848   A559   2.20h multi   .90   .90

Miniature Sheet

Natural Wonders of Ukraine — A560

No. 849: a, Lake Svityaz (dark blue denomination). b, Lake Synevir (light blue denomination). c, Bug River rapids (red denomination). d, Hill near Dniester River (red denomination). e, Deer in Askania-Nova Nature Reserve (white denomination). f, Podilsky Tovtry Park (orange denomination). g, Marble Cave of the Crimea (white denomination).

2011, Dec. 19   *Perf. 11½*
849   A560   2.20h Sheet of 7, #a-g   5.75   5.75

Europa — A561

No. 850: a, 2.20h, Bird-shaped opening in forest canopy. b, 4.30h, Star in opening in snow-covered forest canopy.

2011, Dec. 20   *Perf. 13¼*
850   A561   Horiz. pair, #a-b   2.40   2.40

     Intl. Year of Forests.

Christmas and New Year's Greetings — A562

No. 851: a, Grandfather Frost with bag of toys. b, People outside of church.

2011, Dec. 23   *Perf. 11½*
851   A562   1.80h Horiz. pair, #a-b   1.40   1.40

Miniature Sheet

Water Mills — A563

No. 852 — Various mills: a, 1.80h. b, 2.20h. c, 6.50h. d, 7.70h.

2011, Dec. 28
852   A563   Sheet of 4, #a-d   6.75   6.75

Tree Leaves and Fruit — A564

Designs: 5k, Sorbus aucuparia. 20k, Robinia pseudoacacia. 30k, Fraxinus excelsior. 40k, Juglans regia. 50k, Aesculus hippocastanum. 70k, Betula pendula. 2h, Quercus robur. 2.50h, Acer platanoides. 3h, Tilia cordata. 4h, Fagus sylvatica. 5h, Alnus incana. 8h, Ulmus laevis. 10h, Populus tremula.

2012		**Litho.**	**Perf. 13¾**	
853	A564	5k multi	.25	.25
a.		Imprint "2012-II"	.25	.25
b.		Imprint "2012-III"	.25	.25
c.		Imprint "2013"	.25	.25
d.		Imprint "2014"	.25	.25
e.		Imprint "2014-II"	.25	.25
854	A564	20k multi	.25	.25
a.		Imprint "2012-II"	.25	.25
b.		Imprint "2012-III"	.25	.25
c.		Imprint "2013"	.25	.25
d.		Imprint "2014"	.25	.25
855	A564	30k multi	.25	.25
a.		Imprint "2012-II"	.25	.25
b.		Imprint "2012-III"	.25	.25
c.		Imprint "2013"	.25	.25
d.		Imprint "2013-II"	.25	.25
e.		Imprint "2013-III"	.25	.25
f.		Imprint "2014"	.25	.25
856	A564	40k multi	.25	.25
a.		Imprint "2012-II"	.25	.25
b.		Imprint "2012-III"	.25	.25
c.		Imprint "2013"	.25	.25
d.		Imprint "2014"	.25	.25
857	A564	50k multi	.25	.25
a.		Imprint "2012-II"	.25	.25
b.		Imprint "2012-III"	.25	.25
c.		Imprint "2013"	.25	.25
d.		Imprint "2013-II"	.25	.25
e.		Imprint "2013-III"	.25	.25
f.		Imprint "2014"	.25	.25
g.		Imprint "2014-II"	.25	.25
h.		Imprint "2014-III"	.25	.25
858	A564	70k multi	.25	.25
a.		Imprint "2012-II"	.25	.25
b.		Imprint "2013"	.25	.25
c.		Imprint "2014"	.25	.25
859	A564	2h multi	.75	.75
a.		Imprint "2012-II"	.75	.75
b.		Imprint "2012-III"	.75	.75
c.		Imprint "2013"	.75	.75
d.		Imprint "2013-II"	.75	.75
e.		Imprint "2014"	.70	.70
f.		Imprint "2014-II"	.70	.70
g.		Imprint "2014-III"	.70	.70
860	A564	2.50h multi	.90	.90
a.		Imprint "2012-II"	.90	.90
b.		Imprint "2012-III"	.90	.90
c.		Imprint "2013"	.90	.90
d.		Imprint "2013-II"	.90	.90
861	A564	3h multi	1.10	1.10
a.		Imprint "2012-II"	1.10	1.10
b.		Imprint "2013"	1.10	1.10
c.		Imprint "2014"	1.00	1.00
862	A564	4.80h multi	1.75	1.75
a.		Imprint "2012-II"	1.75	1.75
b.		Imprint "2012-III"	1.75	1.75
c.		Imprint "2013"	1.75	1.75
d.		Imprint "2013-II"	1.75	1.75
863	A564	5h multi	1.90	1.90
a.		Imprint "2013"	1.90	1.90
b.		Imprint "2014"	1.75	1.75
c.		Imprint "2014-II"	1.75	1.75
864	A564	8h multi	3.00	3.00
a.		Imprint "2013"	3.00	3.00
b.		Imprint "2014"	2.75	2.75
865	A564	10h multi	3.75	3.75
		Nos. 853-865 (13)	14.65	14.65

Issued: 5k, 30k, 50k, 2h, 2/3; 20k, 40k, 70k, 2.50h, 1/14; 3h, 4.80h, 5h, 8h, 10h, 1/24. Nos. 853c, 857c, 1/11/13.

See Nos. 882-883, 909, 942-943.

A565

A566

A567

Personalized Stamps — A568

2012, Feb. 20   Litho.   Perf. 11½
Background Color
Cyrillic Country Name in Yellow
866 A565 (1.80h) violet blue + label   3.50 3.50
867 A566 (1.80h) blue + label   3.50 3.50
Cyrillic Country Name in Blue
868 A567 (1.80h) blue + label   3.50 3.50
Cyrillic Country Name in Pink
869 A568 (1.80h) blue + label   3.50 3.50
    Nos. 866-869 (4)   14.00 14.00

Nos. 866-869 were each printed in sheets of 14 + 14 labels that could be personalized. The labels shown, depicting a soccer ball and various stadiums used for the 2012 European Soccer Championships, are generic.

Paintings by Taras Shevchenko (1814-61) — A569

Designs: 2h, Fortification at Raim, 1848. 2.50h, Moonlit Night on Kos-Aral, 1849 (49x28mm).

Litho. With Foil Application
2012, Mar. 9
870-871 A569   Set of 2   1.75 1.75

Souvenir Sheet

National Arms and Flag, 20th Anniv. — A570

No. 872: a, 2h, Arms. b, 3h, Flag.

2012, Mar. 23   Perf. 11½
872 A570   Sheet of 2, #a-b   1.90 1.90

Ivano-Frankivsk, 350th Anniv. — A571

2012, May 7   Litho.   Perf. 13¾x14¼
873 A571   2h multi   .80 .80

Mykhailo Stelmakh (1912-83), Writer — A572

2012, May 24   Perf. 13¼
874 A572   2h multi   .80 .80
Printed in sheets of 11 + label.

A573

A574

A575

A576

A577

2012 UEFA European Soccer Championships, Poland and Ukraine — A578

No. 878 — Buildings in: a, Lviv (country name in purple). b, Kyiv (country name in yellow green). c, Kharkiv (country name in yellow). d, Donetsk (country name in red).
No. 879: a, Lviv Stadium (country name in purple). b, Olympic Stadium, Kyiv (country name in yellow green). c, Metalist Stadium, Kharkiv (country name in yellow). d, Donbass Stadium, Donetsk (country name in red).
No. 880: a, Emblem of 2012 tournament. b, Soccer ball, crowd.

2012			**Perf. 14x14¼**	
875	A573	4.80h multi	1.90	1.90
876	A574	12h multi	4.50	4.50
877	A575	27.60h multi	10.00	10.00
878	A576	4.80h Block of 4,		
		#a-d	7.25	7.25
879	A577	4.80h Block of 4,		
		#a-d	7.25	7.25
		Nos. 875-879 (5)	30.90	30.90

Souvenir Sheet
Perf. 11½
880 A578 27.60h Sheet of 2, #a-b   20.00 20.00

Issued: No. 875, 6/1; No. 876, 6/8; No. 877, 6/8; Nos. 878-879, 5/28; No. 880, 6/11.

The souvenir sheet containing three 13.80h stamps was issued on June 25 and sold for 300h. The souvenir sheet containing one 62.55h stamp was issued on May 11 and sold for 360h.

Europa — A579

No. 881: a, 4h, Musicians in costume. b, 5.60h, Mountain and direction post.

2012, June 13   Perf. 14xx14¼
881 A579   Horiz. pair, #a-b   3.75 3.75
c.   Booklet pane of 2, #881a-881b, perf. 11½   6.75
    Complete booklet, #881c   6.75

No. 881 was printed in sheets of 5 pairs + 2 labels. Complete booklet sold for 17.10h.

Tree Leaves and Fruit
A580   A581

Designs: (4.30h), Acer pseudoplatanus. (8.10h), Salix alba.

2012, July 25   Perf. 13¾
882 A580 (4.30h) multi   1.60 1.60
883 A581 (8.10h) multi   3.00 3.00

A582

A583

Railway Passenger Cars — A584

2012, July 27   *Perf. 14x14¼*
884 A582 2h multi   .75 .75
885 A583 2h multi   .75 .75
886 A584 2h multi   .75 .75
Nos. 884-886 (3)   2.25 2.25

Nos. 884-886 each were printed in sheets of 11 + label.

2012 Summer Olympics, London — A585

No. 887: a, 2h, Canoeing. b, 2h, High jump. c, 2.50h, Running. d, 5.30h, Shot put.

Litho. With Foil Application
2012, July 27   *Perf. 11½*
887 A585 Block of 4, #a-d   4.50 4.50

13th National Philatelic Exhibition, Odessa — A586

2012, Aug. 10   *Perf. 13¼*
888 A586 2h multi   .80 .80

Miniature Sheet

Ukrainian Soviet Socialist Republic Semi-Postal Stamps of 1923, 89th Anniv. — A587

No. 889: a, 2h, #B4. b, 2.50h, #B1. c, 4.30h, #B3. d, 4.80h, #B2.

2012, Aug. 13   **Litho.**   *Perf. 11½*
889 A587 Sheet of 4, #a-d, + label   5.25 5.25

Pavel Popovich (1930-2009), Cosmonaut — A588

2012, Aug. 15   *Perf. 14x14¼*
890 A588 2k multi   .75 .75

Miniature Sheet

Farm Animals — A589

No. 891: a, 2h, Horse. b, 2h, Goat. c, 2h, Ducks. d, 2.50h, Chicken. e, 2.50h, Rabbit.

2012, Aug. 18   *Perf. 11½*
891 A589 Sheet of 5, #a-e   4.25 4.25

Personalized Stamp — A590

2012, Aug. 23
892 A590 (2h) multi + label   3.00 3.00

No. 892 was printed in sheets of 18 + 18 labels that could be personalized. The label shown, depicting the national arms and posthorns, is the generic label image.

Fairy Tale "Zaliznonosa Bosorkania" — A591

No. 893: a, 2h, Man, man with long nose, cat (43x26mm). b, 2.50h, Men on horse (26x26mm).

2012, Sept. 1   *Perf. 11½*
893 A591 Horiz. pair, #a-b   1.75 1.75

Miniature Sheet

Fruits and Flowers — A592

No. 894: a, 2h, Cerasus vulgaris (30x45mm). b, 2h, Tagetes patula (30x50mm).

c, 2.50h, Alcea rosea (30x50mm). d, 3.30h, Fragaria vesca (30x50mm).

Litho. With Foil Application
2012, Sept. 1
894 A592 Sheet of 4, #a-d   3.75 3.75

Ginsburg Apartment House, Kyiv, Cent. — A593

2012, Sept. 14   **Litho.**   *Perf. 14x14¼*
895 A593 2h multi   .80 .80

Sudak, 1800th Anniv. — A594

2012, Sept. 20   *Perf. 11½*
896 A594 2h multi   .80 .80

Souvenir Sheet

Donetsk Region, 80th Anniv. — A595

2012, Sept. 25
897 A595 2h multi   .80 .80

Miniature Sheet

Nikita Botanical Gardens, 200th Anniv. — A596

No. 898: a, 2h, Gazebo (38x31mm). b, 2h, Administration Building (45x31mm). c, 2.50h, Arbor and steps (50x33mm). d, 5.30h, Echinocereus (50x33mmm).

Litho. With Foil Application
2012, Oct. 4
898 A596 Sheet of 4, #a-d   4.50 4.50

Sun and Flowers, by Aliona Panasiuk, Winning Design in Children's Stamp Designing Contest — A597

2012, Oct. 9   **Litho.**   *Perf. 13¼*
899 A597 2h multi   .80 .80

Chyhyryn, 500th Anniv. — A598

2012, Oct. 14   *Perf. 14x14¼*
900 A598 2h multi   .80 .80

Battle of Blue Waters, 650th Anniv. — A599

2012, Oct. 24
901 A599 2h multi   .80 .80

Miniature Sheet

Windmills — A600

No. 902: a, 2h, Four-bladed windmill in winter. b, 2.50h, Six-bladed windmill. c, 3.30h, Six-bladed windmill, diff. d, 4.80h, Four-bladed windmill, diff.

2012, Nov. 9   *Perf. 11½*
902 A600 Sheet of 4, #a-d   4.75 4.75

Andrii Malyshko (1912-70), Poet — A601

2012, Nov. 14   *Perf. 13¼*
903 A601 2h multi   .80 .80

No. 903 was printed in sheets of 11 + label.

Miniature Sheet

Seven Wonders of Ukraine — A602

No. 904: a, Akkerman Fortress (name in light blue). b, Khotyn Fortress (name in light green). c, Vorontsov Palace (wall in front). d, Lutsk Castle (name in red). e, Mytropolychyi Palace (diamonds on roof). f, Kamianets-Podilskyi Fortress (with curving road). g, Kachanivka Palace (with cupola and pillars).

2012, Nov. 29   *Perf. 11½*
904 A602 2.50h Sheet of 7, #a-g   6.75 6.75

Christmas and New Year's Day — A603

No. 905: a, Tree, angel, bird, sleigh, candle, house. b, Decoration, grain, bowl and spoon, church and house.

Litho. With Foil Application
2012, Dec. 8
905 A603 2h Horiz. pair, #a-b   1.60 1.60
No. 905 was printed in sheets containing 6 pairs and 3 labels

Miniature Sheet

Frogs and Toads — A604

No. 906: a, 2h, Bufo bufo. b, 2h, Bombina variegata. c, 4.30h, Bufo viridis. d, 5.40h, Pelobates fuscus. e, 5.40h, Rana temporaria.

2012, Dec. 17   **Litho.**
906 A604 Sheet of 5, #a-e   7.25 7.25

Traditional Women's Costume — A605

2012, Dec. 28   **Perf. 13¼**
907 A605 2h multi   .80 .80

Film, *Man with a Movie Camera,* by Dziga Vertov, 83rd Anniv. — A606

No. 908: a, Lens and eye. b, Camera.

2012, Dec. 29
908 A606 2h Horiz. pair, #a-b   1.60 1.60

Morus Alba Leaf and Fruit — A607

2013, Jan. 11   **Perf. 13¾**
909 A607 (4k) multi   1.60 1.60
a.   Imprint "2013-II"   1.60 1.60

Souvenir Sheet

Charter of Volodymyr II Monomakh, 900th Anniv. — A608

2013, Feb. 22   **Perf. 11½**
910 A608 6.40h multi   2.50 2.50

Vladimir Vernadsky (1863-1945), Mineralogist A609

2013, Feb. 28   **Perf. 13¼**
911 A609 2h multi   .80 .80
No. 911 was printed in sheets of 11 + label.

Honta and Zalizniak, by Mykola Storozhenko A610

Fate, by Oleksandr Ivakhnenko A611

Litho. With Foil Application
2013, Mar. 9   **Perf. 11½**
912 A610 3.30h multi   1.25 1.25
913 A611 4.80h multi   1.90 1.90
Nos. 912-913 each were printed in sheets of 11 + label.

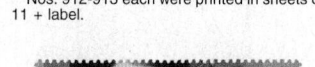

Semen Hulak-Artemovskyi (1813-73), Composer — A612

2013, Mar. 25 Litho. Perf. 14x14¼
914 A612 2h multi   .80 .80

12-791 Rail Car — A613

15-1547-03 Rail Tanker — A614

19-7017-01 Rail Tanker — A615

20-7032 Rail Car — A616

2013, Mar. 27
915 A613   2h multi   .80   .80
916 A614   2h multi   .80   .80
917 A615 2.50h multi   .95   .95
918 A616 2.50h multi   .95   .95
   Nos. 915-918 (4)   3.50 3.50
Nos. 915-918 each were printed in sheets of 11 + label.

Boryspil International Airport, Kyiv — A617

2013, Apr. 2
919 A617 2h multi   .80   .80

Khan's Palace, Bakhchisaray — A618

Ayu-Dag Mountain A619

Crimean Tourist Attractions — A620

No. 922: a, 2h, Valley of Ghosts, near Alushta (26x40mm). b, 2h, St. John's Cathedral, Kerch (37x26mm). c, 2.50h, Wine barrels and grapes, Masandra (37x26mm). d, 2.50h, Urn (26x40mm). e, 4.80h, Southern coast (56x26mm).

2013, Apr. 24   **Perf. 14x14¼**
920 A618   2h multi   .80   .80
921 A619 2.50h multi   .95   .95
Miniature Sheet
Perf. 11½
922 A620   Sheet of 5, #a-e   5.25 5.25

Easter A621

2013, Apr. 30   **Perf. 14x14¼**
923 A621 2h multi   .80 .80

Saints Cyril and Methodius — A622

2013, May 22   **Perf. 14¼x13¾**
924 A622 2.50h multi   1.10 1.10
Slavic writing, 1150th anniv.

Souvenir Sheet

Medals for First All-Russian Olympiad, Kyiv, Cent. — A623

2013, May 25   **Perf. 11½**
925 A623 4.80h multi   1.90 1.90

Europa — A624

No. 926 — Postal vehicles: a, 4h, 1953 Moskvich 400. b, 5.60h, 2013 MAZ-5440 truck.

2013, May 29   **Perf. 14x14¼**
926 A624   Pair, #a-b   3.75 3.75
c.   Booklet pane of 2, #926a-926b,
        perf. 11½   5.00   —
        Complete booklet, #926c   5.00
Complete booklet sold for 12.12h.

Children's Day — A625

No. 927: a, Rainbow, boy on one knee giving heart to girl in wheelchair. b, Children and balloons.

2013, May 31   **Perf. 13¼**
927 A625 2h Pair, #a-b   1.60 1.60

St. Volodymyr's Cathedral, Sevastopol
A626

2013, June 27 Litho. Perf. 14x14¼
928 A626 3.30h multi   1.50 1.50

Souvenir Sheet

Tale of Bygone Years (History of Kievan Rus), by Nestor, 900th Anniv. — A627

Litho. With Foil Application
2013, July 26   Perf. 11½
929 A627 5.70h multi   2.50 2.50

Souvenir Sheet

Christianization of Kievan Rus, 1025th Anniv. — A628

Litho., Margin Litho. With Foil Application
2013, July 28   Perf. 11½
930 A628 5.40h multi   2.40 2.40

See Belarus No. 870, Russia No. 7466.

Personalized Stamp — A629

2013, Aug. 19 Litho. Perf. 11½
931 A629 (2h) blk & sil + label   2.40 2.40

No. 931 was printed in sheets of 28 stamps + 28 labels that could be personalized. The label shown, deptincting the national arms and posthorns, is the generic label image.

Miniature Sheet

Breads — A630

No. 932: a, 2h, Loaf of white bread. b, 2h, Kolache with hole in middle. c, 2.50h, Loaf of black bread. d, 2.50h, Three bubliks. e, 4.80h, Decorated korovai.

2013, Aug. 20 Litho. Perf. 11½
932 A630   Sheet of 5, #a-e, + 4
            labels   6.00 6.00

Dnepropetrovsk Skyline — A631

2013, Aug. 23 Litho. Perf. 14x14¼
933 A631 2h multi   .95 .95

Miniature Sheet

Dnepropetrovsk Oblast — A632

No. 934: a, 2h, Trinity Cathedral (35x26mm). b, 2h, Dnepropetrovsk skyline (35x26mm). c, 2.50h, Zenit-3SLB rocket (35x26mm). d, 3.30h, Painting of rooster and flowers from Petrekivka area (43x52mm).

2013, Aug. 23 Litho. Perf. 11½
934 A632   Sheet of 4, #a-d   4.50 4.50

Pumpkins, by Evdokim Voloshinov (1824-1913) A633

2013, Aug. 24 Litho. Perf. 14x14¼
935 A633 2h multi   .95 .95

Antonov AN-158 — A634

2013, Aug. 31 Litho. Perf. 14x14¼
936 A634 2h multi   .95 .95

Water Tower, Vinnitsa — A635

2013, Sept. 5 Litho. Perf. 14¼x14
937 A635 2h multi   .95 .95

Miniature Sheet

Vinnitsa Oblast — A636

No. 938: a, 2h, Dniester River (26x36mm). b, 2h, Trinity Monastery, Brailov (26x36mm). c, 2.50h, Shcherbatov Palace, Nemyriv (45x23mm). d, 4.80h, Roshen Fountain, Vinnitsa (56x30mm).

2013, Sept. 9 Litho. Perf. 11½
938 A636   Sheet of 4, #a-d   5.00 5.00

Souvenir Sheet

Beheading of St. John the Baptist Monastery, Lyadova, 1000th Anniv. — A637

Litho. With Foil Application
2013, Sept. 15   Perf. 11½
939 A637 4.30h multi   2.00 2.00

Post Rider — A638

2013, Oct. 9 Litho. Perf. 13½
940 A638 2h multi   .95 .95

Miniature Sheet

Autumn — A639

No. 941: a, 2h, Sorbus aucuparia (30x45mm). b, 2h, Citrullus lanatus (30x50mm). c, 2.50h, Dahlia (30x50mm). d, 3.30h, Boletus edulis (30x50mm).

Litho. With Foil Application
2013, Oct. 14   Perf. 11½
941 A639   Sheet of 4, #a-d   4.50 4.50

Hippophae Rhamnoides Leaf and Fruit — A640   Pyris Communis Leaf and Fruit — A641

2013   Litho.   Perf. 13¾
942 A640 (5.60h) multi   2.60 2.60
943 A641 (6.40h) multi   3.00 3.00

Issued: No. 942, 11/5; No. 943, 10/22.

Vera Kholodnaya (1893-1919), Film Actress — A642

2013, Oct. 31 Litho. Perf. 14x14¼
944 A642 2h multi   .95 .95

Kyiv Is Ours, by Georgy Malakov (1928-79) A643

2013, Nov. 6 Litho. Perf. 13¼
945 A643 2h multi   .95 .95

Liberation of Kyiv, 70th anniv.

Miniature Sheet

Winter on the Farm — A644

No. 946: a, 2h, Squirrel in tree (32x24mm). b, 2h, Birds in tree (32x24mm). c, 2.50h, Children with Christmas decoration (32x48mm). d, 2.50h, Turkey (32x24mm).

2013, Nov. 22 Litho. Perf. 11½
946 A644   Sheet of 4, #a-d   4.00 4.00

Olha Kobylianska (1863-1942), Writer — A645

2013, Nov. 27 Litho. Perf. 14x14¼
947 A645 2h multi   .95 .95

Christmas A646

Litho. With Foil Application
2013, Dec. 6   **Perf. 13½**
948 A646 2h multi   .95 .95

Mykola Amosov (1913-2002), Surgeon — A647

2013, Dec. 6   Litho.   Perf. 13¼
949 A647 2h multi   .95 .95

Printed in sheets of 11 + label.

Miniature Sheet

Pectoral, 4th Cent. — A648

No. 950 — Part of pectoral with denomination at: a, 4h, LL (33x29mm). b, 4h, LR (33x29mm). c, 5.60h, UL (40x29mm). d, 5.60h, LL (40x29mm).

Litho. & Embossed With Foil Application
2013, Dec. 12   **Perf. 11½**
950 A648   Sheet of 4, #a-d   8.50 8.50

Ports of Ukraine and Morocco — A649

No. 951: a, 2h, Odessa, Ukraine. b, 3.30h, Tangiers, Morocco.

2013, Dec. 18   Litho.   Perf. 11½
951 A649   Horiz. pair, #a-b   2.40 2.40

See Morocco No.

Churches in Ukraine and Romania — A650

No. 952: a, 2h, Church of the Savior, Berestovo, Ukraine. b, 3.30h, Church of the Sucevita Monastery, Romania.

Litho. With Foil Application
2013, Dec. 21   **Perf. 11½**
952 A650   Horiz pair, #a-b, + central label   2.40 2.40

See Romania Nos. 5509-5510.

Miniature Sheets

A651

Chinese Zodiac Animals — A652

No. 953: a, Rat. b, Ox. c, Tiger. d, Rabbit. e, Dragon. f, Snake.
No. 954: a, Horse. b, Goat. c, Monkey. d, Rooster. e, Dog. f, Pig.

Litho. With Foil Application
2013, Dec. 25   **Perf. 13½**
953 A651 2.50h Sheet of 6, #a-f   6.50 6.50
954 A652 2.50h Sheet of 6, #a-f   6.50 6.50

Bunch of Daisies, by Andrey Guk — A653

2014, Jan. 24   Litho.   Perf. 13¼
955 A653 2h multi   .90 .90

Leonid Kravchuk, First President of Ukraine, 80th Birthday A654

2014, Jan. 31   Litho.   Perf. 14x14¼
956 A654 2h multi   .90 .90

Ukrainian Women's Biathlon Relay Team for 2014 Winter Olympics A655

2014, Jan. 31   Litho.   Perf. 14x14¼
957 A655 3.30h multi   1.40 1.40

No. 957 was printed in sheets of 16 + 4 labels. On Apr. 15, No. 957 was overprinted in gold Cyrillic text to commemorate the victory of the biathlon team at the Winter Olympics. It was produced in limited quantities.

Miniature Sheet

Architecture in Kyiv of Wladislaw Horodecki (1863-1930) — A656

No. 958: a, 2h, Sculpture of lion from House of Chimeras (33x30mm). b, 2h, Sculpture of woman and frogs from House of Chimeras (33x30mm). c, 2h, Karaite Kenesa (33x30mm). d, 3.30h, National Art Museum (40x30mm). e, 4.80h, St. Nicholas Cathedral (33x60mm). f, 5.60h, House of Chimeras (40x30mm).

Litho. & Engr.
2014, Feb. 14   **Perf. 11½**
958 A656   Sheet of 10, #958a, 958b, 2 each #958c-958f   14.00 14.00

Icon Depicting Archangel Gabriel — A657

2014, Feb. 18   Litho.   Perf. 13½
959 A657 4.80h multi   1.90 1.90

No. 959 was printed in sheets of 8 + central label.

Art School, Kirovohrad — A658

2014, Feb. 27   Litho.   Perf. 14x14¼
960 A658 2h multi   .80 .80

Miniature Sheet

Kirovohrad Oblast — A659

No. 961: a, 2h, Ascension Cathedral (30x37mm). b, 2h, Scythian stele (30x37mm). c, 2.50h, Kropivnitsky Theater (35x26mm). d, 4.80h, Dancers (52x47mm).

2014, Feb. 27   Litho.   Perf. 11½
961 A659   Sheet of 4, #a-d   4.25 4.25

Ukrposhta (Ukrainian Postal Service), 20th Anniv. — A660

Litho. & Embossed With Foil Application
2014, Mar. 25   **Perf. 14¼x14**
962 A660 2h multi   .80 .80

Metropolitan Vasily Lipkivski (1864-1937) A661

2014, May 8   Litho.   Perf. 13¼
963 A661 2h multi   .80 .80

Maria Kapnist (1914-93), Actress A662

2014, May 16   Litho.   Perf. 14x14¼
964 A662 2h multi   .80 .80

Children Playing and UNICEF Emblem A663

2014, May 29   Litho.   Perf. 13½
965 A663 2h multi   .80 .80

Still Life with a Chocolate Mill, by Juan de Zurbarán A664

2014, May 29   Litho.   Perf. 14x14¼
966 A664 5.70h multi   2.25 2.25

No. 966 was printed in sheets of 8 + central label.

Sikorsky Ilya Muromets Airplane — A665

2014, June 17   Litho.   Perf. 14x14¼
967 A665 2h multi   .80 .80

Europa — A666

Designs: 4.80h, Painting depicting Cossack Mamay playing kobza. 5.70h, Kobza.

2014, July 25   **Litho.**   **Perf. 11½**
968 A666 4.80h multi   1.50 1.50
   a.   Booklet pane of 1   1.50
969 A666 5.70h multi   1.90 1.90
   a.   Booklet pane of 1   1.90 —
    Complete booklet, #968a, 969a   3.50

Reply of the Zaporozhian Cossacks to Sultan Mehmed IV of the Ottoman Empire, by Ilya Y. Repin (1840-1930) — A667

2014, July 29   **Litho.**   **Perf. 11½**
970 A667 3.30h multi   1.10 1.10
   No. 970 was printed in sheets of 8 + central label.

Cacti — A668

Designs: 2h, Gymnocalycium anisitsii. 2.50h, Opuntia microdasys. 3.30h, Pilosocereus palmeri. 4.80h, Graptopetalum bellum.

Perf. 13½x13¼
2014, Aug. 15   **Litho.**
971 A668   2h multi   .70 .70
972 A668   2.50h multi   .90 .90

Perf. 14¼x14
Size: 25x52mm
973 A668   3.30h multi   1.10 1.10
Size: 28x40mm
974 A668   4.80h multi   1.75 1.75
    Nos. 971-974 (4)   4.45 4.45

2013 Euromaidan Demonstrations — A669

2014, Aug. 22   **Litho.**   **Perf. 11½**
975 A669 2h multi   .80 .80

Statue of Sailor's Wife and Child, Odessa A670

2014, Sept. 2   **Litho.**   **Perf. 13½**
976 A670 2h multi   .80 .80

Miniature Sheet

Odessa Oblast — A671

No. 977: a, 2h, Akkerman Fortress (53x25mm). b, 2.50h, Port of Odessa (40x30mm). c, 2.50h, St. Nikolai Church, Vilkove (40x30mm). d, 5.70h, Ilyichevsk Lighthouse and ship (58x45mm).

2014, Sept. 2   **Litho.**   **Perf. 11½**
977 A671   Sheet of 4, #a-d   4.75 4.75

Monument to Shipbuilders, Mykolaiv — A672

2014, Sept. 13   **Litho.**   **Perf. 13½**
978 A672 2h multi   .80 .80

Miniature Sheet

Mykolaiv Oblast — A673

No. 979: a, 2h, Traffic circles and bridges (26x37mm). b, 2.50h, Kasperovskaya Cathedral of Our Lady, Mykolaiv (37x26mm). c, 2.50h, Buzky Gard National Park (37x26mm). d, 5.70h, Ship factory (51x52mm).

2014, Sept. 13   **Litho.**   **Perf. 11½**
979 A673   Sheet of 4, #a-d   4.75 4.75

Portrait of V. L. Kochubey, by Taras Shevchenko (1814-61) — A674

Gifts in Chigrin, 1644, Etching by Shevchenko — A675

A676

No. 982: a, 3.30h, Portraits of Lusha Polusmak and Kobza player (56x35mm). b, 5.70h, Self-portrait of Shevchenko (36x35mm).

Litho. With Foil Application
2014, Sept. 26   **Perf. 11½**
980 A674   2h multi   .80 .80
981 A675   2.50h multi   1.00 1.00

Souvenir Sheet
982 A676   Sheet of 2, #a-b   3.50 3.50
   Nos. 980-981 were each printed in sheets of 11 + label.

A Lady in Black, by Boris Grigoriev (1886-1939) A677

2014, Oct. 6   **Litho.**   **Perf. 13½**
983 A677 2h multi   .80 .80
   No. 983 was printed in sheets of 8 + central label.

Pigeons A678

Designs: No. 984, 2h, Kryukovsky pigeon (white bird). No. 985, 2h, Odessa Turman pigeon (brown and white bird). 2.50h, Kiev Tumbler pigeon. 3.30h, Micholaivsky Shield Tumbler pigeon.

2014, Oct. 10   **Litho.**   **Perf. 14x14¼**
984-987 A678   Set of 4   3.25 3.25

World War II Liberation of Ukraine, 70th Anniv. — A679

Litho. With Foil Application
2014, Oct. 28   **Perf. 11½**
988 A679 2h multi   .80 .80

Chernivtsi Post Office, 125th Anniv. A680

Perf. 14x14¼ Syncopated
2014, Oct. 31   **Litho.**
989 A680 2h multi   .80 .80

Self-Adhesive

Tereshchenko Family — A681

No. 990: a, 4.80h, Tereshchenko coat of arms. b, 5.70h, Artemi Tereshchenko (1794-1877), industrialist.

Litho. With Foil Application
2014, Nov. 14   **Perf. 11½**
990 A681   Sheet of 2, #a-b   3.00 3.00

Christmas and New Year's Day — A682

Litho. With Foil Application
2014, Nov. 14   **Perf. 14¼x14**
991 A682 2h multi   .65 .65

Railroad Station, Lutsk A683

2014, Dec. 4   **Litho.**   **Perf. 14¼x14**
992 A683 2h multi   .65 .65

Miniature Sheet

Volynska Oblast — A684

No. 993: a, Statue of Lesya Ukrainka, Lutsk (27x41mm). b, 2h, Lake, Okonsk (27x28mm). c, 2.50h, Angel (30x28mm). d, 4.20h, Monastery, Zimne (56x39mm).

2014, Dec. 4   **Litho.**   **Perf. 11½**
993 A684   Sheet of 4, #a-d   3.25 3.25

Army Day A685

Perf. 14x14¼ Syncopated
2014, Dec. 5   **Litho.**
994 A685 2h multi   .65 .65

SEMI-POSTAL STAMPS

Ukrainian Soviet Socialist Republic

"Famine" — SP1

Taras H. Shevchenko SP2

"Death" Stalking Peasant — SP3

"Ukraine" Distributing Food — SP4

Perf. 14½x13½, 13½x14½

1923, June   Litho.   Unwmk.

B1	SP1	10k + 10k gray bl & blk	1.00	5.50
B2	SP2	20k + 20k vio brn & org brn	1.00	5.50
B3	SP3	90k + 30k db & blk, straw	1.00	5.50
B4	SP4	150k + 50k red brn & blk	1.00	5.50
		Nos. B1-B4 (4)	4.00	22.00

Imperf., Pairs

B1a	SP1	10k + 10k	100.00	120.00
B2a	SP2	20k + 20k	100.00	120.00
B3a	SP3	90k + 30k	100.00	120.00
B4a	SP4	150k + 50k	100.00	120.00

The values of these stamps are in karbovanets, which by 1923 converted to rubles at 100 to 1.

Wmk. 116

Same Colors

B5	SP1	10k + 10k	50.00	70.00
B6	SP2	20k + 20k	50.00	70.00
a.		Imperf., pair	2.500.	
B7	SP3	90k + 30k	50.00	70.00
B8	SP4	150k + 50k	50.00	70.00
		Nos. B5-B8 (4)	200.00	280.00

Catalogue values for unused stamps in this section, from this point to the end of the section, are for Never Hinged items.

Charity and Health Fund — SP5

1994, Jan. 15   Litho.   Perf. 12

B9	SP5	150kb +20kb multi	1.25	.65

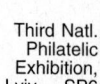 

Third Natl. Philatelic Exhibition, Lviv — SP6

1995, Sept. 23   Litho.   Perf. 13½

B10	SP6	50,000kb +5000kb multi	1.50	1.50

Souvenir Sheet

Zymnenska Icon of Madonna and Child — SP7

1999, Sept. 4   Litho.   Perf. 11½

B11	SP7	1.20h +10k multicolored	3.50	3.50

Intl. Year of the Elderly.

REGISTRATION STAMPS

Catalogue values for unused stamps in this section are for Never Hinged items.

Trident — R1

2001, Apr. 1   Litho.   Perf. 13¾

F1	R1	(10.84h) multi	8.00	7.25
a.		Imprint "2003"	9.00	7.25
b.		Perf. 11½, dated "2006"	7.25	7.25

Issued: No. F1a, 1/28/03; No. F1b, 10/9/06. No. F1b was issued only in No. F2c.

Trident With Frame — R2

2005-06   Litho.   Perf. 13¾

F2	R2	(10.10h) multi	7.00	7.00
a.		Imprint "2006"	7.00	7.00
b.		Perf. 11½, dated "2006"	7.00	7.00
c.		Sheet of 18, #418a-422a, 453a-454a, 466a-468a, 515a, 572a, 606a-609a, F1b, F2b	25.00	25.00

Issued: No. F2, 10/28/05; No. F2a, 2/7/06; No. F2b, 10/9/06. No. F2b was issued only in No. F2c. No. F2c sold for 35.41h and exists imperf.

MILITARY STAMPS

COURIER FIELD POST ISSUE

Nos. 1-5, 48 Surcharged

Кур'єрсько-польова Пошта
10 Гривень

1920, Aug. 26

M1	A1	10h on 10sh buff	20.00	—
a.		Inverted surcharge	80.00	
M2	A2	10h on 20sh brown	40.00	—
M3	A3	10h on 30sh ultramarine	50.00	—
M4	A4	10h on 40sh green	55.00	—
a.		Inverted surcharge	215.00	
M5	A5	10h on 50sh red	50.00	—
M6	A1	20h on 10sh buff	55.00	—
M7	A2	20h on 20sh brown	15.00	—
a.		Inverted surcharge	60.00	
M8	A3	20h on 30sh ultramarine	40.00	—
a.		Inverted surcharge	160.00	
M9	A4	20h on 40sh green	40.00	—
M10	A5	20h on 50sh red	40.00	—
a.		Inverted surcharge	160.00	
M11	A1	40h on 10sh buff	200.00	—
M12	A2	40h on 20sh brown	100.00	—

M13	A3	40h on 30sh ultramarine	400.00	—
M14	A4	40h on 40sh green	200.00	—
M15	A5	40h on 50sh red	400.00	—
M16	A6	40h on 20hr red & green		—

Nos. M1-M16 were prepared to facilitate communications between the Ukrainian government-in-exile at Tarnow, Poland, and its military units in the field.

Only two examples of No. M16 are known, one unused and one used on cover.

Forged surcharges and cancellations exist.

UMM AL QIWAIN

'um-al-kï-'wïn

LOCATION — Oman Peninsula, Arabia, on Arabian Gulf
GOVT. — Sheikdom under British protection
AREA — 300 sq. mi.
POP. — 5,700

Umm al Qiwain is one of six Persian Gulf sheikdoms to join the United Arab Emirates which proclaimed independence Dec. 2, 1971. See United Arab Emirates.

100 Naye Paise = 1 Rupee
100 Dirham = 1 Riyal (1967)

Catalogue values for all unused stamps in this country are for Never Hinged items.

Sheik Ahmed bin Rashid al Mulla and Gazelles — A1

Photogravure and Lithographed

1964, June 29   Unwmk.   Perf. 14

Size: 35x22mm

1	A1	1np shown	.25	.25
2	A1	2np Snake	.25	.25
3	A1	3np Hyena	.25	.25
4	A1	4np Conspicuous triggerfish	.25	.25
5	A1	5np Fish	.25	.25
6	A1	10np Silver angelfish	.30	.25
7	A1	15np Palace	.30	.25
8	A1	20np Umm al Qiwain	.30	.25
9	A1	30np Tower	.35	.30

Size: 42x26mm

10	A1	40np as 1np	.35	.30
11	A1	50np as 2np	.45	.35
12	A1	70np as 3np	.75	.40
13	A1	1r as 4np	1.00	.50
14	A1	1.50r as 4np	1.25	.65
15	A1	2r as 10np	1.75	.90

Size: 52x33mm

16	A1	3r as 15np	3.00	2.00
17	A1	5r as 20np	5.25	3.25
18	A1	10r as 30np	9.00	6.00
		Nos. 1-18 (18)	25.30	16.65

National Stadium, Tokyo, and Discobolus — A2

Designs: 1r, 2r, National Stadium, Tokyo. 1.50r, Indoor swimming arena. 3r, Komazawa Gymnasium. 4r, Stadium entrance.

1964, Nov. 25   Photo.   Perf. 14

19	A2	50np multi	.30	.25
20	A2	1r multi	.50	.25
21	A2	1.50r multi	.65	.25
22	A2	2r multi	1.00	.25
23	A2	3r multi	1.25	.45

24	A2	4r multi	2.50	.85
25	A2	5r multi	3.25	1.00
		Nos. 19-25 (7)	9.45	3.30

18th Olympic Games, Tokyo, Oct. 10-25, 1964. Perf. and imperf. souvenir sheets contain 4 stamps similar to #22-25 in changed colors. Size: 145x115mm.

A3

Designs: 10np, Pres. Kennedy's funeral cortege leaving White House. 15np, Mrs. Kennedy with children, and Robert Kennedy following coffin. 50np, Horse-drawn caisson. 1r, Presidents Truman and Eisenhower, and Margaret Truman Daniels. 2r, Pres. Charles de Gaulle, Emperor Haile Selassie, Chancellor Ludwig Erhart, Sir Alec Douglas-Home and King Frederick IX. 3r, Kennedy family on steps of St. Matthew's Cathedral. 5r, Honor guard at tomb. 7.50r, Portrait of Pres. John F. Kennedy.

Perf. 14½

1965, Jan. 20   Unwmk.   Photo.

Black Design with Gold Inscriptions

Size: 29x44mm

26	A3	10np pale blue	.25	.25
27	A3	15np pale yellow	.25	.25
28	A3	50np pale green	.30	.25
29	A3	1r pale pink	.60	.45
30	A3	2r pale green	1.00	.45

Size: 33x51mm

31	A3	3r pale gray	1.75	.65
32	A3	5r pale blue	3.00	.90
33	A3	7.50r pale yellow	4.00	1.50
		Nos. 26-33 (8)	11.15	4.60

Pres. John F. Kennedy. A souvenir sheet contains 2 stamps similar to Nos. 32-33 with pale green (5r) and pale salmon (7.50r) backgrounds, size: 29x44mm. Size of sheet: 114x70mm.

A4

Designs: 10d, Astronaut on Moon. 20d, Landing module approaching moon. 30d, Apollo XII on launching pad. 50d, Commanders Charles Conrad, Jr., Alan L. Bean, Richard F. Gordon, Jr., earth and moon, horiz. 75d, Earth and Apollo XII, horiz. 1r, Sheik Ahmed, rocket and lunar landing module, horiz.

1969, Nov. 19   Litho.   Perf. 14½

34	A4	10d multi	.25	
35	A4	20d multi	.35	
36	A4	30d multi	.45	
37	A4	50d emerald & multi	.55	
38	A4	75d purple & multi	1.00	
39	A4	1r dk bl & multi	1.75	
		Nos. 34-39 (6)	4.35	

US Apollo XII moon landing mission, 11/14-24/69.

Two imperf. souvenir sheets of 3 exist, containing stamps similar to Nos. 34-36 and Nos. 37-39.

A5

1970, May 29   Litho.   Perf. 14

40	A5	10d James A. Lovell	.25	
41	A5	30d Fred W. Haise, Jr.	.40	
42	A5	50d John L. Swigert, Jr.	.90	
a.		Souv. sheet of 3, #40-42	2.00	
		Nos. 40-42 (3)	1.55	

Safe return of the crew of Apollo 13.

A6

Designs: 5d, 1.25r, EXPO '70 Emblem. 10d, 20d, Japanese Pavilion.

1970, Aug. 14   Litho.   Perf. 13½x14

43	A6	5d yellow & multi	.25	
44	A6	10d blue & multi	.35	
45	A6	20d red & multi	.45	
48	A6	1.25r red & multi	.90	
		Nos. 43-48 (4)	1.95	

EXPO '70 Intl. Exhib., Osaka, Japan, Mar. 15-Sept. 13, 1970.

A 40d and 1r, showing the Emperor and Empress of Japan, and a souvenir sheet containing these and Nos. 43-45, 48 were prepared, but not issued.

A7

Uniforms: 10d, Private, North Lancashire Regiment. 20d, Royal Navy seaman. 30d, Officer, North Lancashire (Loyal) Regiment. 50d, Private, York and Lancaster Regiment. 75d, Royal Navy officer. 1r, Officer, York and Lancaster Regiment.

1970, Oct. 12   Litho.   Perf. 14½x14

49	A7	10d multi	.25	
50	A7	20d multi	.35	
51	A7	30d multi	.55	
a.		Souv. sheet of 3, #49-51	2.75	
52	A7	50d buff & multi	.90	
53	A7	75d multi	1.25	
54	A7	1r buff & multi	1.75	
a.		Souv. sheet of 3, #52-54	4.00	
		Nos. 49-54 (6)	5.05	

British landings on the Trucial Coast, 150th anniv.

Stamps of Umm al Qiwain were replaced in 1972 by those of United Arab Emirates.

AIR POST STAMPS

Type of Regular Issue, 1964

Photogravure and Lithographed

1965   Unwmk.   Perf. 14

Size: 42x26mm

C1	A1	15np as #1	.25	.25
C2	A1	25np as #2	.25	.25
C3	A1	35np as #3	.25	.25
C4	A1	50np as #4	.60	.25
C5	A1	75np as #5	1.10	.30
C6	A1	1r as #6	1.40	.40

Size: 52x33mm

C7	A1	2r as #7	2.25	.55
C8	A1	3r as #8	3.25	.75
C9	A1	5r as #9	4.50	1.25
		Nos. C1-C9 (9)	13.85	4.25

Issued: #C7-C9, Nov. 6; others, Oct. 18.

AIR POST OFFICIAL STAMPS

Type of Regular Issue, 1964
Size: 42x26mm

Photogravure and Lithographed

1965, Dec. 22   Unwmk.   Perf. 14

| CO1 | A1 | 75np as #6 | 1.00 | .30 |

Size: 52x33mm

CO2	A1	2r as #7	2.50	.75
CO3	A1	3r as #8	3.75	1.00
CO4	A1	5r as #9	5.00	1.50
		Nos. CO1-CO4 (4)	12.25	3.55

OFFICIAL STAMPS

Type of Regular Issue, 1964
Size: 42x26mm

Photogravure and Lithographed

1965, Dec. 22   Unwmk.   Perf. 14

O1	A1	25np as #1	.35	.25
O2	A1	40np as #2	.45	.25
O3	A1	50np as #3	.75	.25
O4	A1	75np as #4	1.00	.30
O5	A1	1r as #5	1.25	.35
		Nos. O1-O5 (5)	3.80	1.40

UNITED ARAB EMIRATES

yu-ˌnī-təd ˈar-əb i-ˈmiˌə r-əts

(Trucial States)

LOCATION — Arabia, on Arabian Gulf
GOVT. — Federation of sheikdoms
AREA — 32,300 sq. mi.
POP. — 2,377,453 (1995)
CAPITAL — Abu Dhabi

The UAE was formed Dec. 2, 1971, by the union of Abu Dhabi, Ajman, Dubai, Fujeira, Sharjah and Umm al Qiwain. Ras al Khaima joined in Feb. 1972.

1,000 Fils = 1 Dinar
100 Fils = 1 Dirham (1973)

> **Catalogue values for all unused stamps in this country are for Never Hinged items.**

Abu Dhabi Nos. 56-67 Overprinted

1972, Aug.   Litho.   Unwmk.   Perf. 14

1	A10	5f multicolored	3.25	3.25
2	A10	10f multicolored	3.25	3.25
3	A10	25f multicolored	5.00	5.00
4	A10	35f multicolored	6.50	6.50
5	A10	50f multicolored	11.00	11.00
6	A10	60f multicolored	12.00	12.00
7	A10	70f multicolored	16.00	16.00
8	A10	90f multicolored	20.00	20.00
9	A11	125f multicolored	65.00	65.00
10	A11	150f multicolored	90.00	90.00
11	A11	500f multicolored	210.00	210.00
12	A11	1d multicolored	400.00	400.00
		Nos. 1-12 (12)	842.00	842.00

The overprint differs.
#1-12 were used in Abu Dhabi. #2-3 were placed on sale later in Dubai & Sharjah.

Map and Flag of UAE
A1

Almagta Bridge, Abu Dhabi — A2

Designs: 10f, Like 5f. 15f, 35f, Coat of arms of UAE (eagle). 75f, Khor Fakkan, Sharjah. 1d, Steel Clock Tower, Dubai. 1.25d, Buthnah Fort, Fujeira. 2d, Alfalaj Fort, Umm al Qiwain. 3d, Khor Khwair, Ras al Khaima. 5d, Palace of Sheik Rashid bin Humaid al Nuaimi, Ajman. 10d, Sheik Zaid bin Sultan al Nahayan, Abu Dhabi.

1973, Jan. 1   Unwmk.   Perf. 14½

Size: 41x25mm

13	A1	5f multicolored	.25	.25
14	A1	10f multicolored	.25	.25
15	A1	15f blue & multi	.50	.25
16	A1	35f olive & multi	.75	.30

Perf. 14x15

Size: 45x29½mm

17	A2	65f multicolored	1.25	1.25
18	A2	75f multicolored	1.75	1.25
19	A2	1d multicolored	2.00	1.25
20	A2	1.25d multicolored	4.25	2.00
21	A2	2d multicolored	50.00	12.50
22	A2	3d multicolored	10.00	7.25
23	A2	5d multicolored	11.00	7.50
24	A2	10d multicolored	25.00	16.00
		Nos. 13-24 (12)	107.00	50.05

For surcharge see No. 68.

Festival Emblem
A3

1973, Mar. 27   Litho.   Perf. 13½x14

| 25 | A3 | 10f shown | 7.50 | .35 |
| 26 | A3 | 1.25d Trophy | 18.50 | 11.00 |

National Youth Festival, Mar. 27.

Pedestrian Crossing in Dubai — A4

35f, Traffic light school crossing sign, vert. 1.25d, Traffic policemen with car & radio, vert.

1973, Apr. 1   Perf. 13½x14, 14x13½

27	A4	35f green & multi	4.00	1.75
28	A4	75f blue & multi	7.50	3.50
29	A4	1.25d violet & multi	13.00	6.00
		Nos. 27-29 (3)	24.50	11.25

Traffic Week, Apr. 1-7.

Human Rights Flame and People — A5

1973, Dec. 10   Litho.   Perf. 14½x14

30	A5	35f blue, blk & org	1.50	.95
31	A5	65f red, blk & org	5.25	2.00
32	A5	1.25d olive, blk & org	9.75	4.00
		Nos. 30-32 (3)	16.50	6.95

25th anniversary of the Universal Declaration of Human Rights.

UPU and Arab Postal Union Emblems — A6

1974, Aug. 5   Litho.   Perf. 14x14½

33	A6	25f multicolored	2.00	1.00
34	A6	60f emerald & multi	3.25	1.75
35	A6	1.25d lt brown & multi	6.75	4.50
		Nos. 33-35 (3)	12.00	7.25

Centenary of Universal Postal Union.

Health Care — A7

Education — A8

Designs: 65f, Construction. 1.25d, UAE flag, UN and Arab League emblems.

1974, Dec. 2   Litho.   Perf. 13½

36	A7	10f multicolored	1.10	.40
37	A8	35f multicolored	3.00	1.00
38	A8	65f blue & brown	3.25	1.50
39	A8	1.25d multicolored	7.00	3.25
		Nos. 36-39 (4)	14.35	6.15

Third National Day.

Arab Man and Woman Holding Candle over Book — A9

Man and Woman Reading Book — A10

1974, Dec. 27   Perf. 14x14½, 14½x14
40	A9	35f deep ultra & multi	2.75	.60
41	A10	65f orange brn & multi	3.25	1.25
42	A10	1.25d gray & multi	6.75	2.50
		Nos. 40-42 (3)	12.75	4.35

World Literacy Day.

Oil De-gassing Station — A11

50f, Off-shore drilling platform. 100f, Underwater storage tank. 125f, Oil production platform.

1975, Mar. 10   Litho.   Perf. 13x13½
43	A11	25f multicolored	1.50	.55
44	A11	50f multicolored	3.25	1.00
45	A11	100f multicolored	8.00	2.50
46	A11	125f multicolored	11.00	3.00
a.		Souvenir sheet of 4, #43-46	40.00	30.00
		Nos. 43-46 (4)	23.75	7.05

9th Arab Petroleum Conference.

Three stamps to commemorate the 2nd Gulf Long Distance Swimming Championship were prepared in June, 1975, but not issued. Value $500.

Jabal Ali Earth Station — A12

Jabal Ali Earth Station: 35f, 65f, Communications satellite over globe.

1975, Nov. 8   Litho.   Perf. 13
47	A12	15f multicolored	1.25	.35
48	A12	35f multicolored	3.00	.65
49	A12	65f multicolored	5.00	1.10
50	A12	2d multicolored	11.00	4.00
		Nos. 47-50 (4)	20.25	6.10

Various Scenes — A13

Sheik Hamad, Fujeira Ruler — A14

Supreme Council Members (Sheikdom rulers): 60f, Sheik Rashid bin Humaid al Naimi, Ajman. 80f, Sheik Ahmed bin Rashid al Mulla, Umm al Qiwain. 90f, Sheik Sultan bin Mohammed al Qasimi, Sharjah. 1d, Sheik Saqr bin Mohammed al Qasimi, Ras al Khaima. 140f, Sheik Rashid bin Said al Maktum, Dubai. 5d, Sheik Zaid bin Sultan al Nahayan, Abu Dhabi.

1975, Dec. 2   Litho.   Perf. 14
51	A13	10f multicolored	.85	.25
52	A14	35f multicolored	2.25	.90
53	A14	60f multicolored	3.25	1.75
54	A14	80f multicolored	4.50	2.75
55	A14	90f multicolored	5.25	3.00
56	A14	1d multicolored	5.50	3.50
57	A14	140f multicolored	7.75	4.50
58	A14	5d multicolored	32.50	18.00
		Nos. 51-58 (8)	61.85	34.65

Fourth National Day.

Students and Lamp of Learning — A15

Arab Literacy Day: 15f, Lamp of learning.

1976, Feb. 8   Litho.   Perf. 14
59	A15	15f orange & multi	.75	.35
60	A15	50f ultra & multi	2.50	1.00
61	A15	3d multicolored	12.00	7.75
		Nos. 59-61 (3)	15.25	9.10

Children Crossing Street — A16

Traffic Week: 15f, Traffic lights and signals, vert. 80f, Road and traffic lights.

Perf. 14½x14, 14x14½
1976, Apr. 1   Litho.
62	A16	15f brt blue & multi	2.50	1.25
63	A16	80f blue & multi	9.25	4.50
64	A16	140f ocher & multi	18.00	10.00
		Nos. 62-64 (3)	29.75	15.75

Waves and Ear Phones, ITU Emblem, Coat of Arms — A17

1976, May 17   Litho.   Perf. 14
65	A17	50f gray grn & multi	1.50	.65
66	A17	80f pink & multi	3.00	1.25
67	A17	2d tan & multi	6.50	3.25
		Nos. 65-67 (3)	11.00	5.15

International Telecommunications Day.

No. 18 Surcharged

1976   Litho.   Perf. 14x15
68	A2	50f on 75f multi	75.00	24.00

Coat of Arms — A18

1976, Aug. 15   Litho.   Perf. 11½
69	A18	5f dull rose	.35	.25
70	A18	10f golden brown	.35	.25
71	A18	15f orange	.50	.40
72	A18	35f dull red brn	.75	.25
73	A18	50f bright lilac	1.00	.50
74	A18	60f bister	1.25	.60
75	A18	80f yellow green	1.50	.70
76	A18	90f ultra	2.00	.90
77	A18	1d blue	2.25	.80
78	A18	140f olive green	3.50	1.50
79	A18	150f rose violet	5.25	2.00
80	A18	2d slate	5.50	2.25
81	A18	5d blue green	13.00	6.25
82	A18	10d lilac rose	24.00	14.00
		Nos. 69-82 (14)	61.20	30.55

See Nos. 91-104.

Sheik Zaid — A19

1976, Dec. 12   Litho.   Perf. 13
83	A19	15f rose & multi	6.00	.60
84	A19	140f blue & multi	12.00	5.00

5th National Day.

Symbolic Falcon and Globe — A20

1976, Dec. 15   Litho.   Perf. 14x13½
85	A20	80f yellow & multi	6.00	1.50
86	A20	2d red & multi	11.00	6.00

International Falconry Congress, Abu Dhabi, Dec. 1976.

A21

1976, Dec. 30   Litho.   Perf. 13
87	A21	50f multicolored	5.00	1.50
88	A21	80f multicolored	10.00	3.00

Mohammed Ali Jinnah (1876-1948), 1st Governor General of Pakistan.

A22

APU emblem, members' flags.

1977, Apr. 12   Litho.   Perf. 13½x14
89	A22	50f multicolored	6.00	1.50
90	A22	80f multicolored	9.00	3.50

Arab Postal Union, 25th anniversary.

Arms Type of 1976

1977, July 25   Litho.   Perf. 11½
91	A18	5f dull rose & blk	.40	.35
92	A18	10f gldn brn & blk	.40	.35
93	A18	15f dull org & blk	.55	.45
94	A18	35f lt brown & blk	1.40	.50
95	A18	50f brt lilac & blk	1.60	.55
96	A18	60f bister & blk	1.75	.60
97	A18	80f yel grn & blk	1.75	.60
98	A18	90f ultra & blk	2.75	.95
99	A18	1d blue & blk	4.00	1.40
100	A18	140f ol grn & blk	6.00	1.90
101	A18	150f rose vio & blk	6.50	2.25
102	A18	2d slate & blk	10.00	3.25
103	A18	5d blue grn & blk	22.50	8.25
104	A18	10d lil rose & blk	37.50	24.50
		Nos. 91-104 (14)	97.10	45.90

Man Reading Book, UAE Arms, UN Emblem A23

1977, Sept. 8   Litho.   Perf. 14x13½
105	A23	50f green, brn & gold	3.50	.80
106	A23	3d blue & multi	12.50	5.50

International Literacy Day.

A set of three stamps for the 6th Natl. Day was withdrawn from sale on the day of issue, Dec. 2, 1977. Value, $850.

Post Horn and Sails — A24

1979, Apr. 14   Photo.   Perf. 12x11½
107	A24	50f multicolored	1.25	1.00
108	A24	5d multicolored	8.50	6.00

Gulf Postal Organization, 2nd Conf., Dubai.

Arab Achievements — A25

1980, Mar. 22   Litho.   Perf. 14x14½
109	A25	50f multicolored	.75	.50
110	A25	140f multicolored	2.25	1.25
111	A25	3d multicolored	4.50	2.75
		Nos. 109-111 (3)	7.50	4.50

9th National Day — A26

1980, Dec. 2   Litho.   Perf. 13½
112 A26 15f multicolored .60 .35
113 A26 50f multicolored 2.00 1.00
114 A26 80f multicolored 2.50 1.50
115 A26 150f multicolored 3.75 2.25
    Nos. 112-115 (4) 8.85 5.10
Souvenir Sheet
Perf. 13½x14
116 A26 3d multicolored 15.00 15.00

Family on
Graph — A27

1980, Dec. 15
117 A27 15f shown .80 .35
118 A27 80f Symbols 2.75 1.25
119 A27 90f like #118 3.50 2.25
120 A27 2d like #117 7.25 5.00
    Nos. 117-120 (4) 14.30 8.85

1980 population census.

Hegira
(Pilgrimage
Year) — A28

1980, Dec. 18   Perf. 14x13½
121 A28 15f multicolored .50 .25
122 A28 80f multicolored 2.00 1.25
123 A28 90f multicolored 2.75 1.50
124 A28 140f multicolored 4.25 2.50
    Nos. 121-124 (4) 9.50 5.50
Souvenir Sheet
125 A28 2d multicolored 11.50 11.50

No. 125 contains one 36x57mm stamp.

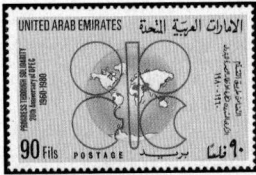

OPEC Emblem — A29

1980, Dec. 21   Perf. 14
126 A29 50f Men holding
        OPEC emblem,
        vert. 1.25 .50
127 A29 80f like #126 2.00 1.25
128 A29 90f shown 2.25 1.50
129 A29 140f like #128 4.00 2.25
    Nos. 126-129 (4) 9.50 5.50
Souvenir Sheet
130 A29 3d like #128 18.00 18.00

Traffic Week — A30

15f, 80f, Crossing guard, students, traffic
light. 50f, 5d, Crossing guard, traffic light and
signs.

1981, Mar. 26   Litho.   Perf. 14½
131 A30 15f multicolored .65 .30
132 A30 50f multicolored 1.25 .75
133 A30 80f multicolored 2.50 1.50
134 A30 5d multicolored 11.00 7.50
    Nos. 131-134 (4) 15.40 10.05

Size of Nos. 131 and 133: 25½x35mm.

10th Natl.
Day — A31

1981, Dec. 2   Litho.   Perf. 15x14
135 A31 25f Cogwheel .75 .40
136 A31 150f Soldiers 5.00 2.50
137 A31 2d UN emblem 6.50 3.00
    Nos. 135-137 (3) 12.25 5.90

Intl. Year of the
Disabled — A32

Perf. 14½x14, 14x14½
1981, Dec. 26   Litho.
138 A32 25f Couple .75 .35
139 A32 45f Man in wheel-
        chair, vert. 1.50 1.10
140 A32 150f like #139 5.00 2.50
141 A32 2d like #138 7.50 3.25
    Nos. 138-141 (4) 14.75 7.20

Natl. Arms — A33

1982-86
142 A33 5f multicolored .25 .25
143 A33 10f multicolored .25 .25
144 A33 15f multicolored .25 .25
145 A33 25f multicolored .25 .25
145A A33 35f multicolored .25 .25
146 A33 50f lt. blue &
        multi .40 .40
146A A33 50f dark blue &
        multi 3.00 1.50
147 A33 75f multicolored .60 .60
148 A33 100f multicolored .90 .90
149 A33 110f multicolored 1.00 1.00
150 A33 125f multicolored 1.50 1.40
151 A33 150f multicolored 1.75 1.25
151A A33 175f multicolored 2.00 1.25
Size: 23x27mm
Perf. 13
152 A33 2d multicolored 2.25 1.60
152A A33 250f multicolored 2.40 1.40
153 A33 3d multicolored 3.50 1.90
154 A33 5d multicolored 6.00 3.25
155 A33 10d multicolored 13.00 8.25
156 A33 20d multicolored 24.50 13.50
157 A33 50d multicolored 50.00 24.50
    Nos. 142-157 (20) 114.05 63.95

Issued: 35f, 175f, 250f, 12/15/84; 50d,
2/6/86; others, 3/7/82.

6th Arab Gulf Soccer
Championships — A34

1982, Apr. 4   Litho.   Perf. 14
167 A34 25f Emblem, flags 1.25 .60
168 A34 75f Eagle, soccer
        ball, stadium,
        vert. 3.25 2.40
169 A34 125f Players, vert. 4.25 3.00
170 A34 3d like 75f, vert. 9.25 7.75
    Nos. 167-170 (4) 18.00 13.75

2nd
Disarmament
Meeting
A35

1982, Oct. 24   Litho.   Perf. 13x13½
171 A35 25f multicolored .65 .30
172 A35 75f multicolored 2.00 2.25
173 A35 125f multicolored 3.50 2.40
174 A35 150f multicolored 4.00 3.00
    Nos. 171-174 (4) 10.15 7.95

11th Natl.
Day — A36

Designs: 25f, 150f, Skyscraper, communications tower, natl. crest, castle turret, open
book, flag. 75f, 125f, Sun, bird, vert.

1982, Dec. 2   Litho.   Perf. 14½
175 A36 25f multicolored .60 .40
176 A36 75f multicolored 2.40 1.60
177 A36 125f multicolored 3.25 2.25
178 A36 150f multicolored 3.75 2.75
    Nos. 175-178 (4) 10.00 7.00

A37

1983, Dec. 20   Litho.   Perf. 14x14½
179 A37 25f multicolored .80 .30
180 A37 150f multicolored 3.50 1.60
181 A37 2d multicolored 5.00 3.00
182 A37 3d multicolored 7.00 3.75
    Nos. 179-182 (4) 16.30 8.65

World Communications Year.

A38

Arab Literacy Day: 25f, 75f, Oil lamp, open
Koran. 35f, 3d, Scribe.

1983, Jan. 8   Litho.   Perf. 14½
183 A38 25f multicolored *42.50* 60.00
184 A38 35f multicolored 1.50 .80
185 A38 75f multicolored *42.50* 55.00
186 A38 3d multicolored 10.00 5.00

Nos. 183 and 185 withdrawn from sale on
day of issue because of an error in Koranic
inscription.

INTELSAT, 20th Anniv. — A39

1984, Nov. 24   Litho.   Perf. 14½
187 A39 2d multicolored 5.50 5.00
188 A39 2.50d multicolored 8.00 7.00

13th Natl.
Day
A40

Flag, portrait of an Emir and building or view
from each capital.

1984, Dec. 2   Perf. 14½x13½
189 A40 1d Building, pavilion 2.50 1.50
190 A40 1d Fortress, cannon 2.50 1.50
191 A40 1d Port, boats 2.50 1.50
192 A40 1d Fortress 2.50 1.50
193 A40 1d Oil refinery 2.50 1.50
194 A40 1d Building, garden 2.50 1.50
195 A40 1d Oil well, palace 2.50 1.50
    Nos. 189-195 (7) 17.50 10.50

Tidy Week — A41

1985, Mar. 15   Perf. 12½
196 A41 5d multicolored 11.50 10.00

A42

1985, Sept. 10   Perf. 13½x14½
197 A42 2d multicolored 7.00 4.50
198 A42 250f multicolored 10.00 6.50

World Junior Chess Championships,
Sharjah, Sept. 10-27.

14th Natl.
Day — A43

1985, Dec. 2   Perf. 14x13½
199 A43 50f multicolored .75 .55
200 A43 3d multicolored 7.00 4.50

Population
Census — A44

1985, Dec. 16
201 A44 50f multicolored 1.10 .55
202 A44 1d multicolored 3.00 1.40
203 A44 3d multicolored 7.75 3.50
    Nos. 201-203 (3) 11.85 5.45

Intl.
Youth
Year
A45

50f, Silhouettes, sapling, vert. 175f, Globe,
open book. 2d, Youth carrying world, vert.

1985, Dec. 23   **Perf. 14½**
204 A45 50f multicolored   1.00 .65
205 A45 175f multicolored   3.00 1.60
206 A45 2d multicolored   3.75 2.25
   Nos. 204-206 (3)   7.75 4.50

Women and
Family
Day — A46

1986, Mar. 21   **Perf. 13½**
207 A46 1d multicolored   1.50 1.00
208 A46 3d multicolored   4.50 3.25

General
Postal
Authority,
1st Anniv.
A47

Designs: 50f, 250f, Posthorn, map, natl.
flag, globe. 1d, 2d, Emblem, globe, vert.

1986, Apr. 1
209 A47 50f multicolored   .60 .50
210 A47 1d multicolored   1.25 .80
211 A47 2d multicolored   3.25 2.25
212 A47 250f multicolored   3.50 2.75
   Nos. 209-212 (4)   8.60 6.30

United
Arab
Shipping
Co., 10th
Anniv.
A48

1986, Aug. 20   **Perf. 13x13½**
213 A48 2d shown   4.50 2.75
214 A48 3d Ship's bow, vert.   5.50 3.75

A49

1986, Sept. 1   **Perf. 13½x13**
215 A49 250f multicolored   4.25 1.65
216 A49 3d multicolored   5.25 1.90

Emirates Telecommunications Corp., Ltd.,
10th anniv.

Hawk — A50

1986, Sept. 9   **Photo.**   **Perf. 15x14**
Booklet Stamps
Background Color
217 A50 50f pale green   .75 .75
218 A50 75f pink   1.25 1.25
219 A50 125f gray   2.00 2.00
   a. Bklt. pane, 75f, 125f, 2 50f   8.00
   Nos. 217-219 (3)   4.00 4.00

A51

1986, Oct. 25   **Perf. 13½**
220 A51 50f Jet, camel   1.75 1.25
221 A51 175f Jet   5.50 4.25

Emirates Airlines, 1st anniv.

State
Crests,
GCC
Emblem
A52

1986, Nov. 2   **Perf. 13**
222 A52 50f shown   .80 .60
222A A52 175f like no. 223   2.75 2.25
223 A52 3d Tree, emblem   4.50 4.25
   Nos. 222-223 (3)   8.05 7.10

Gulf Cooperation Council supreme council
7th session, Abu Dhabi, Nov. 1986. No. 222A
incorrectly inscribed "1.75f."

15th Natl.
Day — A53

1986, Dec. 2   **Litho.**   **Perf. 13½**
224 A53 50f shown   1.10 .55
225 A53 1d like 50f   2.50 1.60
226 A53 175f Flag, emblem   4.50 2.75
227 A53 2d like 175f   4.50 3.25
   Nos. 224-227 (4)   12.60 8.15

27th Chess Olympiad, Dubai — A54

1986, Nov. 14   **Perf. 12½**
228 A54 50f Skyscraper, vert.   1.40 .80
229 A54 2d shown   5.50 4.50
230 A54 250f Tapestry, diff.   7.00 5.50
   a. Souv. sheet, #228-230, perf 13   22.50 22.50
   Nos. 228-230 (3)   13.90 10.80

No. 230a exists imperf. Value, $35.

Arab Police
Day — A55

1986, Dec. 18   **Perf. 13½**
231 A55 50f multicolored   1.75 1.00
232 A55 1d multicolored   3.00 2.50

A56

1987, Mar. 15
233 A56 50f multicolored   1.75 1.00
234 A56 1d multicolored   3.00 2.50

Municipalities and Environment Week.

A57

1987, Apr. 10
235 A57 200f multicolored   3.50 3.50
236 A57 250f multicolored   4.00 4.00

UAE Flight Information Region, 1st anniv.

A58

50f, Water. 2d, Solar energy, oil well.

1987, May 25
237 A58 50f multicolored   1.00 1.00
238 A58 2d multicolored   8.50 8.50

Conservation.

A59

1987, June 23
239 A59 1d multicolored   1.75 1.75
240 A59 3d multicolored   4.50 4.50

United Arab Emirates University, 10th anniv.

1st Shipment of Crude Oil from Abu
Dhabi, 25th Anniv. — A60

1987, July 4   **Perf. 13**
241 A60 50f Oil rig   .80 .80
242 A60 1d Drilling well, vert.   1.90 1.90
243 A60 175f Crew, drill   3.00 3.00
244 A60 2d Oil tanker   3.25 3.25
   Nos. 241-244 (4)   8.95 8.95

Arab Palm Tree
and Date
Day — A61

1987, Sept. 15   **Litho.**   **Perf. 14x15**
245 A61 50f shown   .90 .90
246 A61 1d Tree, fruit, diff.   1.60 1.60

A62

1987, Nov. 21   **Litho.**   **Perf. 13x13½**
247 A62 2d multicolored   3.00 3.00
248 A62 250f multicolored   3.50 3.50

Intl. Year of Shelter for the Homeless.

A63

1987, Dec. 15   **Perf. 13½**
249 A63 1d multicolored   2.00 2.00
250 A63 2d multicolored   4.50 4.50

Salim Bin Ali Al-Owais (b. 1887), poet.

UN Child Survival
Campaign — A64

50f, Growth monitoring. 1d, Immunization.
175f, Oral rehydration therapy. 2d, Breast
feeding, horiz.

1987, Oct. 25   **Litho.**   **Perf. 13**
251 A64 50f multicolored   .60 .50
252 A64 1d multicolored   1.25 1.00
253 A64 175f multicolored   2.00 1.75
254 A64 2d multicolored   2.25 1.90
   Nos. 251-254 (4)   6.10 5.15

Abu Dhabi Intl. Airport, 6th Anniv. — A65

1988, Jan. 2
255	A65	50f Control tower	.85	.85
256	A65	50f Terminal interior	.85	.85
257	A65	100f Aircraft over airport	2.00	2.00
258	A65	100f Aircraft at gates	2.00	2.00
		Nos. 255-258 (4)	5.70	5.70

Natl. Arts Festival A66

1988, Mar. 21   Litho.   Perf. 13½
259	A66	50f multicolored	1.25	1.25
260	A66	250f multicolored	3.75	3.75

Youth Cultural Festival A67

Winning children's drawings of a design contest sponsored by the Ministry of Education and the Sharjah Cultural and Information Department.

Perf. 13x13½, 13½x13
1988, May 25   Litho.
261	A67	50f Net fisherman	.75	.50
262	A67	1d Woman	1.40	1.25
263	A67	1.75d Youth as flower	2.25	2.00
264	A67	2d Recreation	2.75	2.50
		Nos. 261-264 (4)	7.15	6.25

Palestinian Uprising — A68

1988, June 28   Litho.   Perf. 13½
265	A68	2d multicolored	2.75	2.25
266	A68	250f multicolored	3.50	2.75

A69

Banks — A70

1988, July 16   Litho.   Perf. 13½
267	A69	50f multicolored	2.50	2.50
268	A70	50f multicolored	2.50	2.50

Abu Dhabi Natl. Bank, Ltd., 20th anniv. (No. 267); Natl. Bank of Dubai, Ltd., 25th anniv. (No. 268).

Port Rashid, Dubai, 16th Anniv. — A71

1988, Aug. 31   Litho.   Perf. 13½
269	A71	50f Ground transportation	.60	.60
270	A71	1d Piers	1.25	1.25
271	A71	175f Ship at dock	2.50	2.50
272	A71	2d Ship, unloading cranes	2.75	2.75
		Nos. 269-272 (4)	7.10	7.10

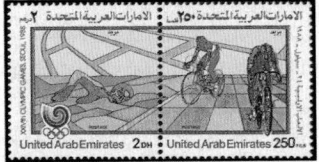

1988 Summer Olympics, Seoul — A72

1988, Sept. 17   Perf. 15x14½
273		2d Swimming	3.25	3.25
274		250f Cycling	4.00	4.00
	a.	A72 Pair, #273-274	7.50	7.50

Ras Al Khaima Natl. Museum, 1st Anniv. — A74

1988, Nov. 19   Litho.   Perf. 14
275	A74	50f Vase, vert.	.75	.55
276	A74	3d Gold crown	3.25	2.25

18th Arab Scout Conference, Nov. 29-Dec. 3, Abu Dhabi — A75

1988, Nov. 29   Perf. 12½
277	A75	1d multicolored	1.20	1.20

10th Arbor Day — A76

Perf. 13½x13, 13x13½
1989, Mar. 6   Litho.
278	A76	50f Ghaf, vert.	.60	.60
279	A76	100f Palm	1.25	1.25
280	A76	250f Dahlia blossom	2.75	2.75
		Nos. 278-280 (3)	4.60	4.60

Sharjah Intl. Airport, 10th Anniv. A77

1989, Apr. 21   Litho.   Perf. 13½
281	A77	50f multicolored	.90	.90
282	A77	100f multicolored	2.10	2.10

Postal Service, 80th Anniv. A78

1989, Aug. 19   Litho.   Perf. 13x13½
283	A78	50f Seaplane	1.00	1.00
284	A78	3d Ship	6.50	6.50

Al-Ittihad Newspaper, 20th Anniv. — A79

1989, Oct. 20   Litho.   Perf. 13½
285	A79	50f shown	.75	.75
286	A79	1d Al Ittihad Press	1.25	1.25

Gulf Investment Corporation, 5th Anniv. — A80

1989, Nov. 25
287	A80	50f multicolored	.75	.75
288	A80	2d multicolored	3.25	3.25

Child on Crutches, Hands — A81

Designs: 2d, Crouched youth, cracked earth, bread in hand, horiz.

1989, Dec. 5   Perf. 15x14, 14x15
289	A81	2d multicolored	2.75	2.75
290	A81	250f shown	3.25	3.25

Intl. Volunteer's Day, Red Crescent Soc.

Bank Building — A82

50f, Emblem, architecture.

1989, Dec. 20   Perf. 13½
291	A82	50f multicolored	.75	.75
292	A82	1d shown	1.25	1.25

Commercial Bank of Dubai, Ltd., 20th Anniv.

Astrolabe, Manuscript Page and Ship of Bin Majid, 15th Cent. Navigator and Writer A83

1989, Dec. 25   Perf. 13x13½, 13½x13
293	A83	1d shown	1.25	1.25
294	A83	3d Ship, page, vert.	4.25	4.25

Heritage revival.

A84

1990, Jan. 17   Perf. 13½
295	A84	50f multicolored	.75	.75
296	A84	1d multicolored	1.90	1.90

3rd Al Ain festival.

Falcon — A85

1990, Feb. 17   Litho.   Perf. 11½
Granite Paper
297	A85	5f multicolored	.25	.25
298	A85	20f multicolored	.25	.25
299	A85	25f multicolored	.25	.25
301	A85	50f multicolored	.45	.40
302	A85	100f multicolored	2.25	1.25
303	A85	150f multicolored	3.75	1.75
304	A85	175f multicolored	4.00	2.00

Size: 21x26mm
Perf. 11½x12
306	A85	2d multicolored	5.50	3.00
307	A85	250f multicolored	6.00	3.25
309	A85	3d multicolored	7.75	3.75
310	A85	5d multicolored	11.00	6.50
311	A85	10d multicolored	22.50	13.00
312	A85	20d multicolored	37.50	22.50
313	A85	50d multicolored	100.00	60.00
		Nos. 297-313 (14)	201.45	118.15

See also Nos. 726A-726G.

A86

1990, Mar. 10   Litho.   Perf. 13½
316	A86	50f multicolored	.60	.60
317	A86	250f multicolored	2.50	2.50

Children's cultural festival.

A87

1990, Aug. 5   Litho.   Perf. 14x15
318 A87 175f shown   1.90 1.90
319 A87   2d Starving child   2.50 2.50

Red Crescent Society.

Dubai Chamber of Commerce and Industry, 25th Anniv. A88

1990, July 1   Perf. 13
320 A88 50f multicolored   .75   .75
321 A88   1d multicolored   1.50 1.50

World Cup Soccer Championships, Italy — A89

UAE emblem, character trademark and: 1d, Leaning Tower of Pisa, desert, vert. 2d, Soccer ball, vert. 250f, Circle of flags. 3d, Map, vert.

1990, June 8   Perf. 13½
322 A89 50f multicolored   .75   .75
323 A89   1d multicolored   1.50 1.50
324 A89   2d multicolored   3.00 3.00
325 A89 250f multicolored   4.00 4.00
     Nos. 322-325 (4)   9.25 9.25

Souvenir Sheet
Perf. 12½
326 A89   3d multicolored   7.00 7.00

A90

1990, Sept. 22   Litho.   Perf. 13½
327 A90 50f shown   .75   .75
328 A90   1d Emblem, 30 years   2.25 2.25
329 A90 175f Emblem, drop of oil   3.50 3.50
     Nos. 327-329 (3)   6.50 6.50

Organization of Petroleum Exporting Countries (OPEC), 30th anniv.

A91

Flowers: No. 330, Argyrolobeum roseum. No. 331, Lamranthus roseus. No. 332, Centavrea pseudo sinaica. No. 333, Calotropis procera. No. 334, Nerium oleander. No. 335, Catharanthus roseus. No. 336, Hibiscus rosa sinensis. No. 337, Bougainvillea glabra.

1990, Aug. 25   Perf. 14x14½
330 A91 50f multicolored   .90   .90
331 A91 50f multicolored   .90   .90
332 A91 50f multicolored   .90   .90
333 A91 50f multicolored   .90   .90
 a.   Souvenir sheet of 4, #330-333   4.50 4.50
334 A91 50f multicolored   .90   .90
335 A91 50f multicolored   .90   .90
336 A91 50f multicolored   4.00 4.00

337 A91 50f multicolored   4.00 4.00
 a.   Souvenir sheet of 4, #334-337   17.00 17.00
     Nos. 330-337 (8)   13.40 13.40

A92

1990, Oct. 8   Litho.   Perf. 13
338 A92 50f Water pollution   .50   .50
339 A92   3d Air pollution   3.25 3.25

Environmental pollution.

A93

1990, Dec. 2   Perf. 13½
340 A93 50f shown   .50   .50
341 A93 175f Bank building,
              horiz.   3.25 3.25

Central Bank, 10th anniv.

Intl. Conference on High Salinity Tolerant Plants — A94

1990, Dec. 8   Perf. 13x13½
342 A94 50f Tree   .50   .50
343 A94 250f Water, trees   2.75 2.75

Grand Mosque, Abu Dhabi — A95

2d, Al Jumeirah Mosque, Dubai, vert.

Perf. 13½x13, 13x13½
1990, Nov. 26
344 A95   1d multicolored   1.10 1.10
345 A95   2d multicolored   4.50 4.50

A96

1991, Jan. 16   Litho.   Perf. 13x13½
346 A96 50f multicolored   1.00 1.00
347 A96   2d multicolored   2.50 2.50

Abu Dhabi Intl. Fair.

A97

1991, May 17   Litho.   Perf. 14x13½
348 A97   2d multicolored   3.00 3.00
349 A97   3d multicolored   4.50 4.50

World Telecommunications Day.

A98

1991, June 18   Perf. 13½
350 A98   1d Sheikh Saqr Mosque   1.50 1.50
351 A98   2d King Faisal Mosque   3.25 3.25

Children's Paintings A99

Designs: 50f, Celebration. 1d, Women waving flags. 175f, Women playing blind-man's buff. 250f, Women dancing for men.

1991, July 15   Litho.   Perf. 14x13½
352 A99 50f multicolored   .60   .45
353 A99   1d multicolored   1.40 1.00
354 A99 175f multicolored   2.50 2.25
355 A99 250f multicolored   3.00 2.50
     Nos. 352-355 (4)   7.50 6.20

Fish A100

1991, Aug. 5   Litho.   Perf. 13½x14
356 A100 50f Yellow marked but-
                terflyfish   .60   .60
357 A100 50f Golden trevally   .60   .60
358 A100 50f Two banded porgy   .60   .60
359 A100 50f Red snapper   .60   .60
360 A100   1d Three banded
                grunt   1.25 1.25
361 A100   1d Rabbit fish   1.25 1.25
362 A100   1d Black bream   1.25 1.25
363 A100   1d Greasy grouper   1.25 1.25
 a.   Min. sheet of 8, #356-363   8.50 8.50
     Nos. 356-363 (8)   7.40 7.40

A101

Intl. Aerospace Exhibition, Dubai: 175f, Jet fighter over Dubai Intl. Airport. 2d, Fighter silhouette over airport.

1991, Nov. 3   Litho.   Perf. 13½
364 A101 175f multicolored   2.25 2.25
365 A101   2d multicolored   2.50 2.50

A102

Sheikh Rashid Bin Said Al Maktum (1912-90), Ruler of Dubai and: 50f, Airport, vert. 175f, City skyline, vert. 2d, Waterfront, satellite dish.

1991, Oct. 7   Perf. 13
366 A102 50f multicolored   .50   .50
367 A102   1d multicolored   1.10 1.10
368 A102 175f multicolored   2.00 2.00
369 A102   2d multicolored   2.25 2.25
     Nos. 366-369 (4)   5.85 5.85

A103

1991, Oct. 8   Litho.   Perf. 13½
370 A103 50f multicolored   .75   .75
371 A103   1d multicolored   1.75 1.75

Civil Defense Day.

A104

A105

A106

20th Natl. Day — A107

#374, Emir at left, fortress, cannon. #377, Fortress on rocky outcropping. #378, Emir at right, fortress, cannon. 3d, Sheikh Said bin Sultan al Nahayan, Defense Forces.

1991, Dec. 2   Litho.   Perf. 13
372 A104 75f multicolored   1.20 1.20
373 A105 75f multicolored   1.20 1.20
374 A105 75f multicolored   1.20 1.20
375 A106 75f multicolored   1.20 1.20
376 A107 75f multicolored   1.20 1.20
377 A107 75f multicolored   1.20 1.20
378 A107 75f multicolored   1.20 1.20

Imperf
Size: 70x90mm
378A A107 3d multicolored   8.00 8.00
     Nos. 372-378A (8)   16.40 16.40

On Nos. 372-378 portions of the design were applied by a thermographic process producing a shiny, raised effect.

A108

1991, Nov. 16   **Perf. 13½**
379 A108 50f lt green & multi .45 .45
380 A108 3d orange & multi 3.75 3.75
Gulf Cooperaton Council, 10th anniv.

A109

1992, Jan. 15   **Litho.**   **Perf. 13½**
381 A109 175f pink & multi 2.20 2.20
382 A109 250f lt blue & multi 2.50 2.50
Abu Dhabi National Oil Co., 20th anniv.

Al-Jahli Castle Al-Ain
A110

1992, Apr. 20   **Litho.**   **Perf. 13½**
383 A110 2d multicolored 2.00 2.00
384 A110 250f multicolored 60.00 60.00
Expo '92, Seville.
No. 384 was withdrawn because of poor rendition of Arabic word for "postage."

A111

Mosques: 50f, Sheikh Rashid bin Humaid al Nuaimi, Ajman. 1d, Sheikh Ahmed Bin Rashid Al Mualla, Umm Al Quwain.

1992, Mar. 26   **Perf. 14x13½**
385 A111 50f multicolored .80 .80
386 A111 1d multicolored 1.60 1.60
See Nos. 417-418.

A112

1992, Apr. 20   **Perf. 13½x13**
387 A112 1d shown 1.75 1.75
388 A112 3d Ear with hearing aid 4.00 4.00
Week of the deaf child.

Zayed Seaport, 20th Anniv. — A113

1992, June 28   **Litho.**   **Perf. 13½**
389 A113 50f Aerial view .50 .50
390 A113 1d Cargo transport 1.25 1.25
391 A113 175f Ship docked 2.25 2.25
392 A113 2d Map 2.50 2.50
Nos. 389-392 (4) 6.50 6.50

1992 Summer Olympics, Barcelona
A114

1992, July 25   **Litho.**   **Perf. 14x13½**
393 A114 50f Yachting .50 .50
394 A114 1d Running 1.00 1.00
395 A114 175f Swimming 2.00 2.00
396 A114 250f Cycling 2.25 2.25
Nos. 393-396 (4) 5.75 5.75

Souvenir Sheet
396A A114 3d Equestrian 5.75 5.75

Children's Paintings
A115

1992, Aug. 15   **Perf. 13½x14**
397 A115 50f Playing soccer .50 .50
398 A115 1d Playing in field 1.00 1.00
399 A115 2d Playground 2.25 2.25
400 A115 250f Children among trees 3.00 3.00
Nos. 397-400 (4) 6.75 6.75

Intl. Bank of United Arab Emirates, 15th Anniv. — A116

Design: 175f, Bank emblem.

Litho. & Embossed
1992, Sept. 9   **Perf. 11**
401 A116 50f gold & multi .75 .75
Size: 35x41mm
Perf. 11½
402 A116 175f lake, gold & vio 2.25 2.25

Traditional Musical Instruments — A116a

No. 402A, Tambourah, vert. No. 402B, Oud, vert. No. 402C, Rababah, vert. No. 402D, Mizmar, shindo. No. 402E, Tabel, hibban. No. 402F, Marwas, duff.

1992, Oct. 17   **Litho.**   **Perf. 13½**
402A A116a 50f multicolored .60 .60
402B A116a 50f multicolored .60 .60
402C A116a 50f multicolored 1.25 1.25
  g. Sheet, #402A-402C, perf. 12¾ 3.50 3.50
402D A116a 1d multicolored 2.50 2.50
402E A116a 1d multicolored 2.50 2.50
402F A116a 1d multicolored 2.50 2.50
  h. Sheet, #402D-402F, perf. 12¾ 7.25 7.25
Nos. 402A-402F (6) 9.95 9.95

Camels
A117

Designs: 50f, Race. 1d, Used for transportation, vert. 175f, Harnessed for obtaining water from well. 2d, Roaming free, vert.

1992, Dec. 23   **Litho.**   **Perf. 13½**
403 A117 50f multicolored .50 .30
404 A117 1d multicolored 1.25 .70
405 A117 175f multicolored 2.50 1.25
406 A117 2d multicolored 2.75 1.50
Nos. 403-406 (4) 7.00 3.75

A118

1992, Dec. 21
407 A118 50f multicolored 1.25 1.25
408 A118 2d yellow & multi 5.50 5.50
Gulf Cooperation Council, 13th session.

A119

1993, Jan. 28   **Litho.**   **Perf. 13½**
409 A119 2d shown 2.50 2.50
410 A119 250f Building, fishing boat 4.25 4.25
Dubai Creek Golf and Yacht Club.

A120

1993, Jan. 16
411 A120 50f Golf, horiz. .75 .75
412 A120 1d Fishing 1.50 1.50
413 A120 2d Boating, horiz. 3.00 3.00
414 A120 250f Motor vehicle touring, horiz. 3.75 3.75
Nos. 411-414 (4) 9.00 9.00
Tourism.

A121

1993, Mar. 27   **Litho.**   **Perf. 14x13½**
415 A121 50f violet & multi 1.00 1.00
416 A121 3d red brown & multi 4.00 4.00
Natl. Youth Festival.

Mosque Type of 1992
50f, Thabit bin Khalid Mosque, Fujeira. 1d, Sharq al Morabbah Mosque, Al Ain.

1993, Feb. 16   **Perf. 13½**
417 A111 50f multicolored 1.25 1.25
418 A111 1d multicolored 2.50 2.50

Shells
A122

25f, Conus textile. 50f, Pinctada radiata. 100f, Murex scolopax. 150f, Natica pulicaris. 175f, Lambis truncata sebae. 200f, Cardita bicolor. 250f, Cypraea grayana. 300f, Cymatium trilineatum.

1993, Apr. 3   **Litho.**   **Perf. 13**
419 A122 25f multicolored .35 .35
420 A122 50f multicolored .50 .50
421 A122 100f multicolored 1.00 1.00
422 A122 150f multicolored 1.50 1.50
423 A122 175f multicolored 2.25 2.25
424 A122 200f multicolored 2.50 2.50
425 A122 250f multicolored 3.00 3.00
426 A122 300f multicolored 4.00 4.00
Nos. 419-426 (8) 15.10 15.10

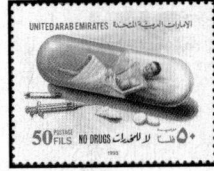

Campaign Against Drugs
A123

Design: 1d, Skull, drugs, vert.

1993, Aug. 21   **Litho.**   **Perf. 13½**
427 A123 50f multicolored 1.60 1.60
428 A123 1d multicolored 2.25 2.25

A124

Natl. Bank of Abu Dhabi, 25th Anniv.: 50f, Abu Dhabi skyline, bank emblem. 1d, Bank emblem. 175f, Bank building, emblem. 2d, Skyline, emblem, diff.

Litho. & Typo.
1993, Sept. 15   **Perf. 11½**
429 A124 50f silver & multi .55 .55
430 A124 1d silver & multi 1.10 1.10
431 A124 175f silver & multi 2.50 2.50
432 A124 2d silver & multi 2.75 2.75
Nos. 429-432 (4) 6.90 6.90

A125

Dubai Ports Authority: 50f, Aerial view of port. 1d, Loading cargo. 2d, Aerial view, diff. 250f, Globe.

1993, Nov. 10   Litho.   Perf. 13½
433 A125 50f purple & multi   .60   .60
434 A125 1d green & multi   1.50   1.50
435 A125 2d orange & multi   3.00   3.00
436 A125 250f pink & multi   3.75   3.75
            Nos. 433-436 (4)   8.85   8.85

Natl. Day
A126

Children's paintings: 50f, Soldiers saluting flag. 1d, Two women sitting, one standing, flag, vert. 175f, Flag, boat. 2d, Flags atop castle tower.

1993, Dec. 2   Litho.   Perf. 13½
437 A126 50f multicolored   .60   .60
438 A126 1d multicolored   1.50   1.50
439 A126 175f multicolored   2.75   2.75
440 A126 2d multicolored   3.00   3.00
            Nos. 437-440 (4)   7.85   7.85

Archaeological Discoveries — A127

Designs: 50f, Tomb. 1d, Rectangular artifact. 175f, Animal-shaped artifact. 250f, Bowl.

1993, Dec. 15   Perf. 14x13½
441 A127 50f multicolored   .60   .60
442 A127 1d multicolored   1.40   1.40
443 A127 175f multicolored   2.50   2.50
444 A127 250f multicolored   3.25   3.25
            Nos. 441-444 (4)   7.75   7.75

10th Childrens' Festival, Sharjah A128

Children's paintings: 50f, Children with balloons, flags. 1d, Children playing, three trees. 175f, Child with picture, girls with balloons. 2d, House, children playing outdoors.

1994, Mar. 19   Litho.   Perf. 13x13½
445 A128 50f green & multi   .60   .60
446 A128 1d blue & multi   1.50   1.50
447 A128 175f red violet & multi   2.50   2.50
448 A128 2d carmine & multi   2.75   2.75
            Nos. 445-448 (4)   7.35   7.35

Arabian Horses
A129

50f, Brown horse on hind feet, vert. 1d, White horse. 175f, Head of brown horse, vert. 250f, Head of white and brown horse.

1994, Jan. 25   Perf. 13x13½, 13½x13
449 A129 50f multicolored   .60   .60
450 A129 1d multicolored   1.50   1.50
451 A129 175f multicolored   2.50   2.50
452 A129 250f multicolored   3.25   3.25
            Nos. 449-452 (4)   7.85   7.85

10th Conference of Arab Towns, Dubai A130

Perf. 13x13½, 13½x13
1994, May 15   Litho.
453 A130 50f Map, city, vert.   .55   .55
454 A130 1d shown   2.25   2.25

Pilgrimage to Mecca — A131

1994, Apr. 29   Litho.   Perf. 13x13½
455 A131 50f shown   .75   .75
456 A131 2d Holy Ka'aba   3.00   3.00

Intl. Year of the Family A132

Intl. Olympic Committee, Cent. A133

Arab Housing Day — A134

Writers Assoc., 10th Anniv. — A135

1994, June 15   Perf. 13x13½
457 A132 1d multicolored   1.40   1.40
458 A133 1d multicolored   1.40   1.40
Perf. 13½x13
459 A134 1d multicolored   1.40   1.40
460 A135 1d multicolored   1.40   1.40
            Nos. 457-460 (4)   5.60   5.60

Archaeological Finds, Al Qusais, Dubai — A136

Designs: 50f, Lidded pitcher, vert. 1d, Pointed-handle pitcher. 175f, Pitcher, arm-shaped handle. 250f, Short round vase.

1994, Aug. 16   Litho.   Perf. 13½
461 A136 50f multicolored   .55   .55
462 A136 1d multicolored   1.30   1.30
463 A136 175f multicolored   2.20   2.20
464 A136 250f multicolored   3.00   3.00
            Nos. 461-464 (4)   7.05   7.05

Environmental Protection — A137

Designs: 50f, Arabian leopard. 1d, Gordon's wildcat. 2d, Caracal. 250f, Sand cat.

1994, Oct. 10   Litho.   Perf. 13½
465 A137 50f multicolored   .60   .60
466 A137 1d multicolored   1.60   1.60
467 A137 2d multicolored   3.50   3.50
468 A137 250f multicolored   4.25   4.25
            Nos. 465-468 (4)   9.95   9.95

12th Arab Gulf Soccer Championships, Abu Dhabi — A138

1994, Nov. 3   Litho.   Perf. 13½
469 A138 50f Ball, emblem, vert.   .55   .55
470 A138 3d Soccer players   3.75   3.75

Birds A139

50f, Merops orientalis. 175f, Halcyon chloris. 2d, Dromas ardeola. 250f, Coracias benghalensis. 3d, Phoenicopterus ruber.

1994, Dec. 12
471 A139 50f multicolored   .60   .60
472 A139 175f multicolored   3.25   3.25
473 A139 2d multicolored   3.50   3.50
474 A139 250f multicolored   5.50   5.50
            Nos. 471-474 (4)   12.85 12.85
Souvenir Sheet
475 A139 3d multi, vert.   8.00   8.00

Archaeological Finds, Mulaiha, Sharjah — A140

Designs: 50f, Front of carved horse, vert. 175f, Ancient coin, vert. 2d, Inscription on metal, vert. 250f, Inscription on stone.

1995, Jan. 25   Litho.   Perf. 13½
476 A140 50f multicolored   .55   .55
477 A140 175f multicolored   2.25   2.25
478 A140 2d multicolored   3.00   3.00
479 A140 250f multicolored   3.25   3.25
            Nos. 476-479 (4)   9.05   9.05

Natl. Dances A141

1995, Feb. 14
480 A141 50f Al-Naashat   .50   .50
481 A141 175f Al-Ayaalah   2.10   2.10
482 A141 2d Al-Shahhoh   2.40   2.40
            Nos. 480-482 (3)   5.00   5.00

A142

1995, Mar. 19   Litho.   Perf. 13½
483 A142 50f Helicopters   .50   .50
484 A142 1d Emblem   1.50   1.50
485 A142 175f Warships, horiz.   2.75   2.75
486 A142 2d Artillery, horiz.   3.25   3.25
            Nos. 483-486 (4)   8.00   8.00

Intl. Defense Exhibition & Conf., Abu Dhabi.

A143

1d, Arab League emblem. 2d, FAO emblem. 250f, UN emblem.

1995, Mar. 22
487 A143 1d multicolored   1.25   1.25
488 A143 2d multicolored   2.75   2.75
489 A143 250f multicolored   3.50   3.50
            Nos. 487-489 (3)   7.50   7.50

50th Anniv. of Arab League, FAO & UN.

General Post Office Authority, 10th Anniv. — A144

1995, Apr. 1
490 A144 50f multicolored   .75   .75

First Gulf Cooperation Council Philatelic Exhibition, Abu Dhabi — A145

1995, Apr. 11   Litho.   Perf. 13½
491 A145 50f multicolored   .75   .75

Traditional
Games, Ajman
Museum — A146

50f, Boy with hoop, stick. 175f, Girl on
swing. 2d, Boy, girl playing stick game within
marked boundary. 250f, Two girls playing
game with stones.

1995, Aug. 28   Litho.   Perf. 13½x13
492 A146   50f multicolored   .45   .45
493 A146   175f multicolored   1.90 1.90
494 A146   2d multicolored   2.25 2.25
495 A146   250f multicolored   2.50 2.50
    Nos. 492-495 (4)   7.10 7.10

A147

Birds: 50f, Falco naumanni. 175f,
Phalacrocorax nigrogularis. 2d, Cursorius cur-
sor. 250f, Upupa epops.

1995, Sept. 25
496 A147   50f multicolored   .55   .55
497 A147   175f multicolored   2.10 2.10
498 A147   2d multicolored   2.50 2.50
499 A147   250f multicolored   2.75 2.75
    Nos. 496-499 (4)   7.90 7.90

See Nos. 528-532.

A148

Natl. Census: 50f, Stylized family, building.
250f, Mosque, skyscrapers, stylized family.

1995, Nov. 20
500 A148   50f multicolored   .50   .50
501 A148   250f multicolored   2.50 2.50

National
Day
A149

Children's paintings: 50f, People wearing
feathered headdresses, palm trees, building.
175f, Girls with flags, balloons, flowers. 2d,
Trees, family in front of house holding balloons, flags. 250f, Groups of children along
street watching parade of cars.

1995, Dec. 2   Perf. 13x13½
502 A149   50f multicolored   .45   .45
503 A149   175f multicolored   1.25 1.25
504 A149   2d multicolored   1.40 1.40
505 A149   250f multicolored   1.75 1.75
    Nos. 502-505 (4)   4.85 4.85

Environmental Protection — A150

50f, Dugong dugon. 2d, Delphinus delphis.
3d, Delphinus delphis.

1996, Jan. 25   Litho.   Perf. 13x13½
506 A150   50f multicolored   .50   .50
507 A150   2d multicolored   1.50 1.50
508 A150   3d Megaptera novae-
            angliae   2.25 2.25
  a. Souvenir sheet, #506-508   4.75 4.75
    Nos. 506-508 (3)   4.25 4.25

A151

1996, Feb. 27   Perf. 13½
509 A151   50f shown   .50   .50
510 A151   3d Building, beach   2.75 2.75

Hobie Cat 16 World Sailing Championships.

A152

Archaeological Finds, Fujeira Museum: 50f,
Two-handled pitcher. 175f, Kettle. 250f, Bracelet. 3d, Metal ornament, horiz.

1996, Apr. 15
511 A152   50f multicolored   .50   .50
512 A152   175f multicolored   1.25 1.25
513 A152   250f multicolored   2.25 2.25
514 A152   3d multicolored   2.75 2.75
    Nos. 511-514 (4)   6.75 6.75

1996
Summer
Olympic
Games,
Atlanta
A153

Perf. 13½x14, 14x 13½
1996, July 19   Litho.
515 A153   50f Shooting   .50   .50
516 A153   1d Cycling, vert.   .80   .80
517 A153   250f Running, vert.   2.00 2.00
518 A153   350f Swimming   2.50 2.50
    Nos. 515-518 (4)   5.80 5.80

Women's
Union, 21st
Anniv.
A154

Perf. 14x13½, 13½x14
1996, Aug. 15
519 A154   50f Emblem, vert.   .50   .50
520 A154   3d shown   2.75 2.75

A155

1996, Sept. 15   Perf. 14x13½
521 A155   1d shown   .75   .75
522 A155   250f Soccer player   2.00 2.00

11th Asian Soccer Cup Championship.

A156

UN Campaign Against Illegal Use of Drugs:
50f, World with snake around it. 3d, Half of
man's face, half of skull, hypodermic needle,
pills.

1996, Oct. 15   Perf. 13½
523 A156   50f multicolored   .75   .75
524 A156   3d multicolored   2.75 2.75

Sheikh Saeed Al-Maktoum House,
Cent. — A157

Designs: 250f Sheikh Saeed, close-up view
of house. 350f, Overall view of house.

1996, Nov. 12   Litho.   Perf. 13x13½
525 A157   50f multicolored   .50   .50
526 A157   250f multicolored   1.75 1.75
527 A157   350f multicolored   2.50 2.50
    Nos. 525-527 (3)   4.75 4.75

Bird Type of 1995

Designs: 50f, Pterocles exustus. 150f, Otus
brucei. 250f, Hypocolus ampelinus. 3d, Irania
gutturalis. 350f, Falco concolor.

1996, Nov. 18   Perf. 14x13½
528 A147   50f multicolored   .35   .35
529 A147   150f multicolored   1.25 1.25
530 A147   250f multicolored   2.25 2.25
531 A147   3d multicolored   3.00 3.00
532 A147   350f multicolored   3.25 3.25
    Nos. 528-532 (5)   10.10 10.10

Children's
Paintings
A158

50f, Face. 1d, Boats. 250f, Flowers. 350f,
Woman in long dress, palm tree, tent.

Perf. 14x13½, 13½x14
1996, Nov. 19
533 A158   50f multi, vert.   .35   .35
534 A158   1d multi   .80   .80
535 A158   250f multi, vert.   2.25 2.25
536 A158   350f multi, vert.   2.75 2.75
    Nos. 533-536 (4)   6.15 6.15

Sheik Zaid
bin Sultan
al
Nahayan,
Accession
to the
Throne of
Abu
Dhabi,
30th
Anniv. —
A158a

A159

Sheik and: 50f, 250f, Flowers. 1d, 350f,
Date palm.

1996, Dec. 2   Photo.   Perf. 12
537 A158a   50f red & multi   .40   .40
538 A158a   1d olive & multi   .65   .65
539 A158a   250f purple & multi   1.60 1.60
540 A158a   350f gray & multi   2.25 2.25
    Nos. 537-540 (4)   4.90 4.90

Photo. & Embossed
Imperf
Size: 90x70mm
541 A159   5d On horseback,
            gazelles   5.00 5.00

Anniversaries
A160

Photo. & Embossed
1996, Dec. 2   Perf. 12
542 A160   50f red violet & multi   .30   .30
543 A160   1d silver & multi   1.40 1.40

Sheik Zaid bin Sultan al Nahayan's accession to the throne of Abu Dhabi, 30th anniv.,
Creation of United Arab Emirates, 25th anniv.

Natl. Day, 25th
Anniv. — A161

50f, 150f, Seven rulers of United Arab Emirates. 1d, 3d, Heraldic eagle, national flag. 5d,
Score of Natl. Anthem.

1996, Dec. 2   Granite Paper
544 A161   50f green & multi   .70   .70
545 A161   1d multicolored   1.25 1.25
546 A161   150f tan & multi   1.60 1.60
547 A161   3d multicolored   3.25 3.25
    Nos. 544-547 (4)   6.80 6.80

Photo. & Embossed
Imperf
Size: 70x90mm
547A A161   5d multicolored   5.50 5.50

Butterflies
A162

1997, Jan. 28   Litho.   Perf. 14x13½
548 A162   50f Agrodiaetus
            loewii   .60   .60
549 A162   1d Papilio machaon   1.25 1.25
550 A162   150f Orithya   1.90 1.90
551 A162   250f Chrysippus   3.25 3.25
    Nos. 548-551 (4)   7.00 7.00

Dubai Shopping Festival
A163

Perf. 13¼x13¾, 13¾x13¼
1997, Feb. 22   **Litho.**
552 A163 50f shown   .50 .50
553 A163 250f Shopping bag, vert.   2.50 2.50

Intl. Defense Exhibition & Conference A164

50f, Helicopter airlifting jeep. 1d, Emblem. 250f, Artillery, emblem. 350f, Ships, emblem.

1997, Mar. 16   **Litho.**   **Perf. 13½**
554 A164 50f multicolored   .50 .50
555 A164 1d multicolored   .85 .85
556 A164 250f multicolored   2.25 2.25
557 A164 350f multicolored   3.25 3.25
    Nos. 554-557 (4)   6.85 6.85

Emirates Bank Group, 20th Anniv. — A165

Perf. 13¾x13¼
1997, Mar. 23   **Litho.**
568 A165 50f multi   .55 .55
569 A165 1d buff & multi   1.20 1.20
  a.   Souv. sheet, #568-569, imperf.   6.00 6.00
    No. 569a sold for 5d.

Technical Education and National Development Conference A166

1997, Apr. 6   **Perf. 13¾x13¼**
570 A166 50f shown   .75 .75
571 A166 250f Emblem   2.75 2.75

Sharjah Heritage A167

Designs: 50f, Coins. 3d, Museum.

1997, June 17   **Litho.**   **Perf. 13½**
572 A167 50f multicolored   .75 .75
573 A167 3d multicolored   3.25 3.25

Emirates Philatelic Association A168

Perf. 13¾x13¼, 13¼x13¾
1997, June 24   **Litho.**
574 A168 50f shown   .50 .50
575 A168 250f Stamps, horiz.   2.50 2.50

Children's Paintings A169

50f, Cats. 1d, Children playing. 250f, Children, moon, vert. 3d, Abstract.

1997, Sept. 15   **Litho.**   **Perf. 13½**
576 A169 50f multicolored   .55 .55
577 A169 1d multicolored   .95 .95
578 A169 250f multicolored   2.25 2.25
579 A169 3d multicolored   3.00 3.00
    Nos. 576-579 (4)   6.75 6.75

Reunion, by Sheikha Hassan Maktoum al Maktoum — A170

Mindscape, by Sarah Majid al Futtaim A170a

Blue Musings, by Maha Abdulla Al Mazroui — A170b

The Pause, by Khulood Mattar Rashid A170c

The Seas I, by Sheikha Sawsan Abdulaziz Al Qasimi — A170d

Still Life, by Sheikha Bodour Sultan Al Qasimi A170e

The Opening, by Tina Ahmed and Others — 170f

1997, Oct. 25   **Litho.**   **Perf. 13¾**
580 A170 50f multi   .65 .65
581 A170a 50f multi   .65 .65
582 A170b 50f multi   .65 .65
583 A170c 50f multi   .65 .65
584 A170d 50f multi   .65 .65
585 A170e 50f multi   .65 .65
    Nos. 580-585 (6)   3.90 3.90

Imperf
586 A170f 5d multi   7.50 7.50

Intl. Aerospace Exhibition, Dubai A171

1997, Nov. 16   **Litho.**
587 A171 250f Jet fighter   3.00 3.00
588 A171 3d VTOL airplane   3.75 3.75

26th National Day A172

Sheikh Zaid bin Sultan al Nahayan and: 50f, Gardens. 1d, Trees and mountains. 150f, Water, trees and mountains. 250f, Roadway.

1997, Dec. 2   **Litho.**   **Perf. 13½x13¾**
589 A172 50f multi   .45 .45
590 A172 1d multi   .75 .75
591 A172 150f multi   1.20 1.20
592 A172 250f multi   1.75 1.75
    Nos. 589-592 (4)   4.15 4.15

3rd Afro-Arab Trade Fair A173

Perf. 13x13¼, 13¼x13
1997, Dec. 6   **Litho.**
593 A173 150f Emblem, vert.   1.25 1.25
594 A173 350f Handshake   2.75 2.75

Arthropods A174

50f, Blepharopsis mendica. 150f, Galeodes sp. 250f, Crocothemis arythraea. 350f, Xylocopa aestuans.

1998, Feb. 25   **Litho.**   **Perf. 13¼**
595 A174 50f multicolored   .55 .55
596 A174 150f multicolored   1.50 1.50
597 A174 250f multicolored   2.50 2.50
598 A174 350f multicolored   3.25 3.25
    Nos. 595-598 (4)   7.80 7.80

ISAF World Sailing Championship — A175

Various sailboats.

Perf. 13¼x13, 13x13¼
1998, Mar. 2   **Litho.**
599 A175 50f multi, vert.   .45 .45
600 A175 1d multi   1.25 1.25
601 A175 250f multi   2.10 2.10
602 A175 3d multi, vert.   3.00 3.00
    Nos. 599-602 (4)   6.80 6.80

A176

Triple Intl. Defense Exhibition & Conf., Abu Dhabi: 50f, Combat soldiers in protective gear, horiz. 1d, Emblem over world map, skyline of Abu Dhabi. 150f, Electronic gear. 350f, Missile battery, electronic warfare components.

1998, Mar. 15   **Litho.**   **Perf. 13½**
603 A176 50f multicolored   .45 .45
604 A176 1d multicolored   1.25 1.25
605 A176 150f multicolored   2.10 2.10
606 A176 350f multicolored   3.00 3.00
    Nos. 603-606 (4)   6.80 6.80

A177

1998, Apr. 20   **Litho.**   **Perf. 13½**
607 A177 50f shown   .50 .50
608 A177 3d Emblem, monument   3.75 3.75

Sharjah, 1998 Arab cultural capital.

World Environment Day — A178

1998, May 17   **Litho.**   **Perf. 13½**
609 A178 1d Landscape, oryx   1.75 1.75
610 A178 350f multicolored   3.00 3.00

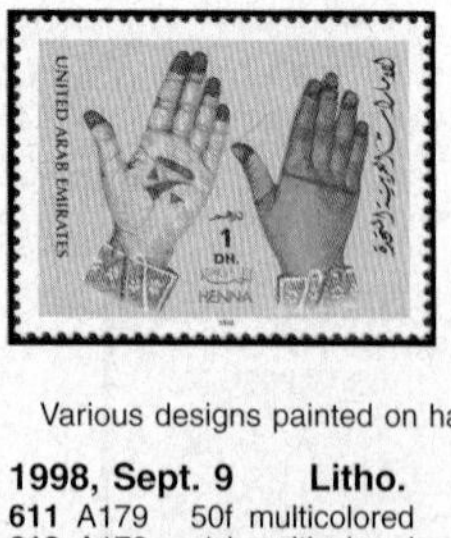

Henna A179

Various designs painted on hands.

1998, Sept. 9   **Litho.**   **Perf. 13½**
611 A179 50f multicolored   .60 .60
612 A179 1d multicolored   .90 .90
613 A179 150f multicolored   1.40 1.40
614 A179 2d multicolored   1.75 1.75

615 A179 250f multicolored   2.25   2.25
616 A179 3d multicolored   2.75   2.75
Nos. 611-616 (6)   9.65   9.65

Art — A180

50f, Fish. 250f, Mosque, palm trees, vert. 350f, Door, jar.

1998, Oct. 20   **Litho.**   **Perf. 13½**
617 A180 50f multicolored   .50   .50
618 A180 1d shown   .95   .95
619 A180 250f multicolored   2.25   2.25
620 A180 350f multicolored   3.25   3.25
Nos. 617-620 (4)   6.95   6.95

27th National Day A181

1998, Dec. 2   **Litho.**   **Perf. 13x13¼**
621 A181 50f Mountain road   .45   .45
622 A181 350f Boat, city skyline   4.25   4.25

Flowers — A182

Designs: 25f, Indigofera arabica. 50f, Centaureum pulchellum. 75f, Lavandula citriodora. 1d, Taverniera glabra. 150f, Convolvulus deserti. 2d, Capparis spinosa. 250f, Rumex vesicrius. 3d, Anagallis arvensis. 350f, Tribulus arabicus. 5d, Reichardia tinitana.

1998, Dec. 8   **Litho.**   **Perf. 13¼x13¾**
623 A182 25f multicolored   .25   .25
624 A182 50f multicolored   .45   .45
625 A182 75f multicolored   .60   .60
626 A182 1d multicolored   .80   .80
627 A182 150f multicolored   1.25   1.25
628 A182 2d multicolored   1.60   1.60
629 A182 250f multicolored   2.10   2.10
630 A182 3d multicolored   2.50   2.50
631 A182 350f multicolored   2.75   2.75
632 A182 5d multicolored   4.00   4.00
Nos. 623-632 (10)   16.30   16.30

Arthropods A183

50f, Anthia duodecimguttata. 150f, Daphnis nerii. 250f, Acorypha glaucopsis. 350f, Androctonus crassicauda.

1999, Mar. 15   **Litho.**   **Perf. 13½x14**
633 A183 50f multicolored   .60   .60
634 A183 150f multicolored   1.40   1.40
635 A183 250f multicolored   2.75   2.75
636 A183 350f multicolored   4.25   4.25
Nos. 633-636 (4)   9.00   9.00

Intl. Day for Monuments and Sites A184

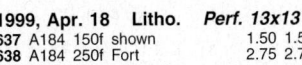

1999, Apr. 18   **Litho.**   **Perf. 13x13½**
637 A184 150f shown   1.50   1.50
638 A184 250f Fort   2.75   2.75

UPU, 125th Anniv. — A185

1999   **Litho.**   **Perf. 13½x13**
639 A185 50f shown   1.00   1.00
640 A185 350f Emblem, "125"   2.75   2.75

Imperf

Size: 90x70mm
641 A185 5d Hemispheres   6.00   6.00

Environmental Protection — A186

Marine life: 50f, Lamprometra klunzingeri. 150f, Pelagia noctiluca. 250f, Hexabranchus sanguineus. 3d, Siphonochalina siphonella.

1999, Nov. 3   **Litho.**   **Perf. 13½x14**
642 A186 50f multi   .60   .60
643 A186 150f multi   2.00   2.00
644 A186 250f multi   3.25   3.25
645 A186 3d multi   3.75   3.75
Nos. 642-645 (4)   9.60   9.60

Handicrafts A187

Designs: 50f, Lacemaking. 1d, Embroidery. 250f, Woman with wickerwork. 350f, Finished wickerwork.

1999, Nov. 8   **Perf. 14x13½**
646 A187 50f multi   .60   .60
647 A187 1d multi   1.40   1.40
648 A187 250f multi   3.50   3.50
649 A187 350f multi   5.50   5.50
Nos. 646-649 (4)   11.00   11.00

14th Pro World Ten-pin Bowling Championships A188

Designs: 50f, Emblem. 250f, Bowler, pins, Abu Dhabi skyline.

1999, Nov. 16   **Litho.**   **Perf. 14x13½**
650-651 A188 Set of 2   3.25   3.25

Children's Art — A189

Art by: 50f, Nooran Khaleefa. 1d, Khawla Al Hawal. 150f, Khawla Salem. 250f, Fatimah Ibrahim.

1999, Dec. 15   **Perf. 13x13½**
652-655 A189 Set of 4   5.75   5.75

Millennium A190

Falcon and "2000" in: 50f, Gray and silver. 250f, Blue and gold.

1999, Dec. 22   **Perf. 13½x13**
656-657 A190 Set of 2   2.75   2.75

Dubai Ports and Customs, Cent. A191

50f, Old building. 3d, Modern building.

2000, Jan. 26   **Perf. 13x13½**
658-659 A191 Set of 2   3.75   3.75

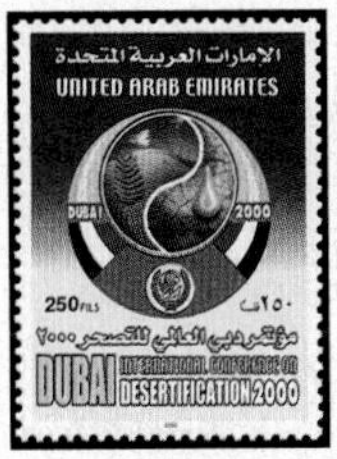

Intl. Desertification Conference, Dubai — A192

2000, Feb. 12   **Perf. 13½x13**
660 A192 250f multi   2.50   2.50

Environmental Protection — A193

Designs: 50f, Palm trees, Al Gheel. 250f, Aggah Beach.

2000, Feb. 29   **Litho.**   **Perf. 13x13½**
661 A193 50f multi   .50   .50
662 A193 250f multi   2.25   2.25

2000 Summer Olympics, Sydney A194

Emblem and: 50f, Swimmer. 2d, Runner. 350f, Shooter.

2000, Sept. 16   **Litho.**   **Perf. 13x13½**
663-665 A194 Set of 3   4.25   4.25

Dubai Intl. Holy Koran Award — A195

50f, Medal on ribbon of flags. 250f, Sheikh Zaid bin Sultan al Nahayan and UAE flag.

2000, Sept. 23   **Perf. 13½x13**
666-667 A195 Set of 2   4.25   4.25

World Meteorological Organization, 50th Anniv. — A196

Designs: 50f, Barometer and modern map. 250f, Gauge's pointer and old map.

2000
668-669 A196 Set of 2   4.25   4.25

Expansion of Dubai Intl. Airport A197

Denominations: 50f, 350f.

2000, Nov. 4   **Litho.**   **Perf. 13x13½**
670-671 A197 Set of 2   5.75   5.75

Development and Environment A198

Designs: 50f, Smile. 250f, Flower. 3d, Heart as leaf. 350f, Heart as globe.

2001, Mar. 20   **Litho.**   **Perf. 13¼x13**
672-675 A198 Set of 4   10.00   10.00

Dubai Millennium, Winner of 2000 Dubai World Cup A199

Designs: 3d, Horse's head. 350f, Horse at track.

2001, Mar. 24   **Perf. 13x13¼**
676-677 A199 Set of 2   9.50   9.50

Sultan Bin Ali Al Owais (1925-2000), Poet — A200

Designs: 50f, Calligraphy. 1d, Portrait.

2001, Apr. 30   **Perf. 13¼x13**
678-679 A200   Set of 2   3.75 3.75

Arab Bank for Investment and Foreign Trade, 25th Anniv. — A201

Designs: 50f, Emblem. 1d, Emblem, diff.

2001, July 7   **Litho.**   **Perf. 13¼x13**
680-681 A201   Set of 2   2.75 2.75

7th GCC Postage Stamp Exhibition, Dubai — A202

2001, July 10
682 A202 50f multi   1.75 1.75

Traditional Boats A203

Designs: 50f, Shahoof. 250f, Bagarah. 3d, Sam'aa. 350f, Jalboot.

2001, Aug. 25   **Perf. 14x13¼**
683-686 A203   Set of 4   10.00 10.00

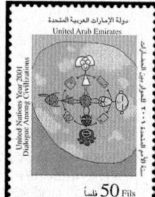

Year of Dialogue Among Civilizations A204

Designs: 50f, Emblem. 250f, Branch with multicolored leaves.

2001, Oct. 9   **Perf. 13¼x13**
687-688 A204   Set of 2   3.75 3.75

Emirates Post A205

Falcons and inscription: 50f, Changing. 250f, Growing. 3d, Achieving.

2001, Sept. 15   **Perf. 13x13¼**
689-691 A205   Set of 3   7.50 7.50

Children's Art — A206

Designs: 1d, Mosque. 250f, Boatbuilding. 3d, Man pouring coffee, vert. 350f, Falconry.

Perf. 14x13¼, 13¼x14
2001, Nov. 12   **Litho.**
692-695 A206   Set of 4   10.50 10.50

Unification of Armed Forces, 25th Anniv. — A207

2001, Dec. 30   **Perf. 13¼x13**
696 A207 1d multi   2.75 2.75

Intl. Water Resources and Management Conference, Dubai — A208

2002, Feb. 2
697 A208 50f multi   2.00 2.00

UAE University, 25th Anniv. — A209

Background colors: 50f, Blue. 1d, Red.

2002, Mar. 25   **Perf. 13¼x14**
698-699 A209   Set of 2   2.75 2.75

Arabian Saluki A210

Various salukis: 50f, 150f, 250f, 3d.

2002, Apr. 29   **Litho.**   **Perf. 13½x13¼**
700-703 A210   Set of 4   14.00 14.00

Emirates Post, 1st Anniv. — A211

"1" and: 50f, Ring of text. 3d, Emblem.

2002, May 29   **Perf. 13¼x13**
704 A211 50f blue   2.00 2.00

Souvenir Sheet
Perf. 14¼
705 A211 3d multi   11.50 11.50
No. 705 contains one 45x35mm stamp.

Rashid Bin Salim Al-Suwaidi Al-Khadhar (1905-80), Poet A212

Designs: 50f, Text. 250f, Portrait.

2002, July 17   **Litho.**   **Perf. 13½x13¼**
706-707 A212   Set of 2   6.50 6.50

Children's Creativity A213

Designs: 50f, Antelope and boat, by Amna al-Bloushi. 1d, Children, by Fahd al-Habsi. 2d, Earth holding flower, by Hana Mohammed. 250f, Fish, by Hatem al-Dhaheri. 3d, Child holding Earth, by Abdulla Ridha. 350f, Stick figures, by Yousef al-Sind. 5d, Emblem of Latifa Bint Mohammed Award for Childhood Creativity (29x39mm).

Perf. 13x13¼, 13¼x13 (5d)
2002, Oct. 9
708-714 A213   Set of 7   17.50 17.50

Sheikh Hamdan Bin Rashid Al-Maktoum Award for Medical Sciences A214

Designs: 50f, Award, emblem, sand dunes. 250f, Caduceus, map.

2002, Oct. 21   **Perf. 13x13¼**
715-716 A214   Set of 2   4.75 4.75

31st National Day — A215

Landmarks in the Emirates: Nos. 717, 724a, 50f, Ajman. Nos. 718, 724b, 50f, Sharjah. Nos. 719, 724c, 50f, Dubai. Nos. 720, 724d, 50f, Abu Dhabi. Nos. 721, 724e, 50f, Ras al Khaima. Nos. 722, 724f, Fujeira. Nos. 723, 724g, Umm al Qiwain.

2002, Dec. 2   **Litho.**   **Perf. 13¼x14**
717-723 A215   Set of 7   7.50 7.50
Souvenir Sheet
Litho. & Embossed
Imperf
724   Sheet of 7   7.50 7.50
a.-g.   A215 50f Any single   1.00 1.00
No. 724 sold for 5d.

Thuraya Satellite Communications A216

Denominations: 25f, 250f.

2002   **Litho.**   **Perf. 14**
725-726 A216   Set of 2   2.75 2.75
Issued: 25f, 1/27; 250f, 1/6.

Falcon Type of 1990
2003-04   **Litho.**   **Perf. 11½**
Granite Paper
726A   A85 125f multi   .90 .90

Size: 21x26mm
Perf. 11½x11¾
726B   A85 225f multi   1.50 1.50
726C   A85 275f multi   2.00 2.00
726D   A85 325f multi   2.75 2.75
726E   A85 375f multi   1.90 1.90
726F   A85   4d multi   2.25 2.25
726G   A85   6d multi   3.00 3.00
    Nos. 726A-726G (7)   14.30 14.30
Issued: 125f, 2/23; 225f, 11/24/04; 275f, 325f, 375f, 4/13; 4d, 6d, 9/16.

Items in Al Ain National Museum A217

Designs: 50f, Jar from Hili tombs. 275f, Pottery from Umm an-Nar tombs. 4d, Bronze axe. 6d, Soapstone vessel.

2003, Feb. 25   **Perf. 14x13½**
727-730 A217   Set of 4   11.50 11.50

National Bank of Dubai, 40th Anniv. A218

Panel color: 50f, Blue. 4d, Orange. 6d, Red.

2003, Apr. 15   **Litho.**   **Perf. 14x13¼**
731-733 A218   Set of 3   10.50 10.50

Miniature Sheet

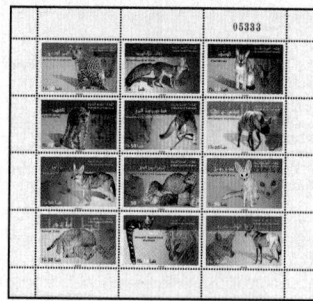

Wildlife — A218a

No. 733A: b, Arabian leopard. c, Blanford's fox. d, Caracal. e, Cheetah. f, Gordon's wild cat. g, Striped hyena. h, Jackal. i, White-tailed mongoose. j, Ruppell's fox. k, Sand cat. l, Small spotted genet. m, Arabian wolf.

2003, June 10   **Litho.**   **Perf. 14½**
733A A218a 50f Sheet of 12, #b-m   8.00 8.00

Coins A219

Designs: 50f, Dirham of Caliph Al Walid bin Abdul Malik. 125f, Arab Sasanian Dirham of Caliph Abdul Malik Bin Marwan. 275f, Dinar of Al Mustansir Billah Al Fatimi. 375f, Dinar of Caliph Abdul Malik bin Marwan.
5d, Dirham of Caliph Muhammed Al Ameen to mark election of Mousa Al Natiq Bilhaq.

2003, July 20   **Litho.**   **Perf. 13¼x13¾**
734-737 A219   Set of 4   7.50 7.50
Size: 106x73mm
Imperf
738   A219 5d multi   20.00 20.00

Sheikh Zaid bin Sultan al Nahayan, 37th Anniv. of Accession as Ruler of Abu Dhabi A220

Sheikh Zaid and: 50f, Camel and sand dune. 175f, Modern buildings.

2003, Aug. 6 Litho. *Perf. 13*
739-740 A220 Set of 2 2.75 2.75

World Youth Soccer Championships, United Arab Emirates — A221

2003, Sept. 7 *Perf. 13x13¼*
741 A221 375f multi 3.75 3.75

World Bank Boards of Governors Annual Meetings, Dubai — A222

Emblem and: 50f, Emirates Tower. 175f, Falcon. 275f, Mosque domes, horiz. 375f, Dhow. 5d, English and Arabic text.

Perf. 13¼x13, 13x13¼
2003, Sept. 23 Litho.
742-745 A222 Set of 4 8.50 8.50
Imperf
Size: 118x74mm
746 A222 5d multi 6.75 6.75

Peace A223

Dove and: 50f, Zakharafs. 225f, Door and wind tower. 275f, Columns. 325f, Water taxi.

2003, Oct. 1 *Perf. 13x13¼*
747-750 A223 Set of 4 9.50 9.50

Traditional Housing A224

Designs: 50f, Palm frond house. 175f, Mud house. 275f, Stone house. 325f, Tent.

2003, Oct. 20 *Perf. 13½x14*
751-754 A224 Set of 4 10.00 10.00

Falcons — A225

Designs: 50f, Peregrine falcon. 125f, Hybrid gyr-peregrine falcon. 275f, Gyrfalcon. 375f, Saker falcon.

2003, Nov. 17 *Perf. 13¼x14*
755-758 A225 Set of 4 5.75 5.75

Poetry of Saeed Bin Ateej Al Hamli (1875-1919) A226

Poetry: 125f, Four short lines. 175f, Four long lines.

2003, Dec. 29 *Perf. 13x13¼*
759-760 A226 Set of 2 3.25 3.25

Mohammed Bin Saeed Bin Ghubash (1899-1969), Religious Scholar — A227

Designs: 50f, Portrait. 175f, Books.

2004, Apr. 5 Litho. *Perf. 13¼x14*
761-762 A227 Set of 2 3.25 3.25

Fourth Family Meeting — A228

Color of hands: 375f, Orange. 4d, Purple.

2004, Apr. 19
763-764 A228 Set of 2 5.25 5.25

FIFA (Fédération Internationale de Football Association), Cent. — A229

2004, May 21 Litho. *Perf. 13x13¼*
765 A229 375f multi 2.75 2.75

Handicrafts by Special Needs Persons — A230

Designs: 50f, Handcrafted vase. 125f, Painting. 275f, Framed branch. 5d, Pottery artwork.

2004, June 29 *Perf. 13¼x13*
766-769 A230 Set of 4 5.25 5.25

2004 Summer Olympics, Athens A231

Olympic rings and: 50f, Track athlete. 125f, Rifle shooter. 275f, Swimmer. 375f, 2004 Athens Olympics emblem, torch bearer.

2004, Aug. 13 Litho. *Perf. 13x13¼*
770-773 A231 Set of 4 4.50 4.50

Endangered or Extinct Persian Gulf Marine Life — A232

Designs: 50f, Black finless porpoise. 175f, Serranidae. 275f, Whale shark. 375f, Dugongidae.

2004, Sept. 26 *Perf. 14*
774-777 A232 Set of 4 4.75 4.75
777a Booklet pane, 2 each #774- —
777 9.50
Complete booklet, #777a 9.50

Operation Emirates Solidarity for Mine Clearance in South Lebanon — A233

Flags and: 275f, Person clearing mines. 375f, Map, people clearing mines, horiz.

2004, Oct. 25 *Perf. 13x12¾, 12¾x13*
778-779 A233 Set of 2 3.50 3.50

Sheik Dr. Sultan bin Mohammed al-Qassimi, Ruler of Sharjah — A234

Color of denomination: 50f, Orange brown. 125f, Green. 275f, Red brown. 4d, Blue.

2004, Nov. 30 *Perf. 13½x14*
780-783 A234 Set of 4 4.75 4.75

Traditional Women's Clothing — A235

Designs: 50f, Drawers. 125f, Robe. 175f, Gown. 225f, Jalabia. 275f, Scarf. 375f, Yashmak.

Dubai Aluminum, 25th Anniv. A236

Designs: 50f, Smelting complex. 275f, Smelting complex, sheikhs (brown background). 375f, Like 275f, blue background.

2005, Jan. 8 *Perf. 13*
790-792 A236 Set of 3 4.00 4.00

10th Dubai Shopping Festival — A237

Designs: 50f, Emblem. 125f, Emblem, diff. 275f, Emblem and "10," green background. 375f, Emblem and "10," red background.

2005, Jan. 12 *Perf. 13¼x13*
793-796 A237 Set of 4 4.50 4.50

2nd Intl. Gathering of Scouting and Belonging, Sharjah — A238

Designs: 50f, Emblem. 375f, Scouts and truck.

2005, Apr. 1 Litho. *Perf. 13¼x14*
797-798 A238 Set of 2 2.40 2.40

Shaikha Fatima Bint Mubarak, Women's Rights Activist — A239

2005, Apr. 10 *Perf. 14½*
799 A239 50f multi .30 .30

Al Majedi Bin Dhaher, 17th Century Poet A240

Poetry and: 50f, Sand. 175f, Bricks.

2005, May 30 Litho. *Perf. 14½*
800-801 A240 Set of 2 1.25 1.25

2004, Dec. 29 Litho. *Perf. 14*
784-789 A235 Set of 6 6.75 6.75
789a Booklet pane, #784-789 6.75 6.75
Complete booklet, #789a 6.75

Reptiles
A241

Designs: 50f, Agama. 125f, Desert monitor. 225f, Sand lizard. 275f, Dune sand gecko. 375f, Spiny-tailed lizard. 5d, Sand skink.

2005, Aug. 2		Perf. 13¾	
802-807	A241	Set of 6	8.50 8.50
807a		Booklet pane, #802-807	8.50 —
		Complete booklet, #807a	8.50

Accession of Sheik Khalifa Bin Zayed Al Nahyan, 1st Anniv. — A242

Sheik Khalifa: 50f, With a child. 175f, With another sheik. 275f, With another sheik, diff. 375f, Kissing sheik.

2005, Nov. 3		Litho.	Perf. 14x13¼	
808-811	A242	Set of 4	4.75 4.75	
811a		Sheet of 4, #808-811	5.50 5.50	

No. 811a sold for 10d.

2005
Census — A243

Emblem at: 50f, Bottom. 375f, Left, horiz.

Perf. 13¼x13, 13x13¼

2005, Nov. 10			
812-813	A243	Set of 2	2.40 2.40

Desert
Plants
A244

Designs: 50f, Leptadenia pyrotechnica. 125f, Lycium shawii. 225f, Calotropis procera. 275f, Prosopis cineraria. 325f, Zizyphus spinachristi. 375f, Acacia tortilis.

2005, Nov. 27		Litho.	Perf. 13½	
814-819	A244	Set of 6	7.50 7.50	
819a		Booklet pane, #814-819	7.50	—
		Complete booklet, #819a	7.50	

34th National
Day — A245

Children's art: 50f, Flower in Arabic script, by Shaimaa Mohammed Al Halabi. 125f, Ring of children, by Muaz Jamal Ahmed Hassan, horiz. 275f, Hands, by Pithani Srinidhi. 375f,

Doves, flag and plants, by Lina Abu Baker Mukhtar, horiz.

2005, Dec. 2		Perf. 14¼	
820-823	A245	Set of 4	4.50 4.50

Pearl
Diving
Tools
A246

Designs: 50f, F'ttam (nose clip). 125f, Al Khabet (finger protectors). 175f, Al Dayeen (basket). 275f, Sea rock (diver's weight). 375f, Diver's outfit.

2005, Dec. 21		Perf. 14	
824-828	A246	Set of 5	5.50 5.50

A souvenir sheet containing Nos. 824-828 with pearl halves affixed to each stamp sold for 100d.

Gulf Cooperation Council Day for Autistic Children — A247

2006, Apr. 4		Litho.	Perf. 13	
829	A247	4d multi	2.25 2.25

Souvenir Sheet

Hamad Bin Khalifa Abu Shehab (1932-2002), Poet — A248

No. 830: a, 1d, Head. b, 2d, Hands, poetry in Arabic text.

2006, Apr. 26		Perf. 14¼	
830	A248	Sheet of 2, #a-b	1.75 1.75

A249

Gulf Cooperation Council, 25th Anniv. — A250

Litho. with Foil Application

2006, May 25		Perf. 14	
831	A249	1d multi	.55 .55

Imperf
Size: 165x105mm

832	A250	5d multi	2.75 2.75

See Bahrain Nos. 628-629, Kuwait Nos. 1646-1647, Oman Nos. 477-478, Qatar Nos. 1007-1008, and Saudi Arabia No. 1378.

Dubai Police, 50th Anniv. — A251

2006, June 1		Perf. 13¼x13	
833	A251	1d multi	.55 .55

19th Asian Stamp Exhibition, Dubai A252

Designs: 1d, shown. 4d, Four towers.

Litho. With Foil Application

2006, June 24		Perf. 13¾	
834-835	A252	Set of 2	2.75 2.75

Dubai Intl. Holy Koran Award, 10th Anniv. A253

2006, July 24		Litho.	Perf. 14x13½	
836	A253	1d multi	.55 .55

Al Raha Beach Developments — A254

Designs: 1d, Khor Al Raha. 2d, Al Lissaily. 350f, Al Wateed (40x40mm). 4d, Al Bandar (40x40mm).

2006, Sept. 18		Litho.	Perf. 13	
837-840	A254	Set of 4	5.75 5.75

UPU Strategy Conference, Dubai — A255

Designs: 1d, Green arrows. 4d, Blue and green arrows.

Litho. & Embossed

2006, Sept. 27		Perf. 14x13½	
841-842	A255	Set of 2	2.75 2.75

12th Gulf Cooperation Council Postage Stamp Exhibition A256

2006, Nov. 13		Litho.	Perf. 13¼x13	
843	A256	1d multi	.55 .55

35th National Day — A257

2006, Dec. 1			
844	A257	1d multi	.55 .55

A souvenir sheet containing one stamp sold for 10d.

Sheikh Mohammed bin Rashid al Maktoum, Prime Minister — A258

Sheikh Mohammed: 1d, Wearing kaffiyeh. 4d, Wearing polo helmet (44x53mm).

Litho. With 3-Dimensional Plastic Affixed

2006, Dec. 2		*Serpentine Die Cut 9*	
		Self-Adhesive	
845-846	A258	Set of 2	2.75 2.75

Gazelles
A259

Designs: 1d, Tahr. 2d, Sand gazelle. 3d, Mountain gazelle. 350f, Arabian oryx.

2006, Nov. 29   Litho.   Perf. 14

847-850	A259	Set of 4	5.25	5.25
850a		Souvenir sheet, #847-850	5.25	5.25

Intl. Volunteers Day A260

Man giving items to: 2d, Two children. 4d, Three children.

2006, Dec. 5   Perf. 13x13¼

851-852	A260	Set of 2	3.25	3.25

Women's Jewelry A261

Designs: 1d, Mariya um alnairat. 150f, Mortasha. 2d, Shaghab bu shouk. 3d, Shahid ring. 350f, Bushuq. 4d, Tassah.

2006, Dec. 31   Perf. 13x13¼

853-858	A261	Set of 6	8.25	8.25
858a		Booklet pane, #853-858	8.25	—
		Complete booklet, #858a	8.25	

Falcon — A262

2007, Jan. 31   Perf. 13¼x13

Background Color

859	A262	1d buff	.55	.55
860	A262	150f gray	.85	.85
861	A262	2d lilac	1.10	1.10
862	A262	3d yellow	1.60	1.60
863	A262	350f yel green	1.90	1.90
864	A262	4d pink	2.25	2.25
865	A262	5d blue vio	2.75	2.75
		Nos. 859-865 (7)	11.00	11.00

Booklet Stamps
Self-Adhesive
Serpentine Die Cut 12½
Background Color

865A	A262	1d buff	.55	.55
865B	A262	150f gray	.85	.85
865C	A262	2d lilac	1.10	1.10
865D	A262	3d yellow	1.60	1.60
865E	A262	350f yel green	1.90	1.90
865F	A262	4d pink	2.25	2.25
865G	A262	5d blue vio	2.75	2.75
h.		Booklet pane, #865A-865G	11.00	—
		Complete booklet, #865Gh	11.00	
		Nos. 865A-865G (7)	11.00	11.00

See Nos. 937, 959-965, 1081-1085.

Dubai Tennis Championships A263

Background colors: 1d, Orange. 3d, Red violet.

2007, Feb. 19   Perf. 14

866-867	A263	Set of 2	2.25	2.25

18th Arabian Gulf Soccer Cup Championships, Abu Dhabi — A264

Arabian Gulf Cup with frame in: 1d, Red. 3d, Green.

2007, May 9   Litho.   Perf. 14x13¾

868-869	A264	Set of 2	2.25	2.25
869a		Souvenir sheet, #868-869	5.50	5.50

No. 869a sold for 10d.

Etisalat (Telecommunications Company), 30th Anniv. — A265

Denomination color: 1d, Blue. 3d, Orange red. 350f, Purple. 4d, Red.

2007, May 17   Perf. 13x13¼

870-873	A265	Set of 4	6.25	6.25

Each stamp has a die cut opening.

Souvenir Sheet

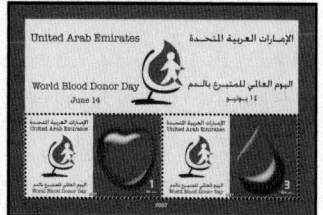

World Blood Donor Day — A266

No. 874 — World Blood Donor Day emblem and: a, 1d, Heart. b, 3d, Blood drop.

2007, June 14   Perf. 13

874	A266	Sheet of 2, #a-b	2.25	2.25

Sheikh Ahmed Mohamed Hasher Al Maktoum, UAE's First Olympic Gold Medalist — A267

2007, July 17   Perf. 14x13½

875	A267	3d multi	1.75	1.75

A268

Emirates Bank, 30th Anniv. A269

Perf. 14x13¾ (A268), 14 (A269)

2007, Aug. 28

876	A268	1d blue & multi	.55	.55
877	A269	150f blue & multi	.85	.85
878	A268	3d brn & multi	1.75	1.75
879	A269	350f brn & multi	1.90	1.90
a.		Souvenir sheet, #876-879	8.25	8.25
		Nos. 876-879 (4)	5.05	5.05

No. 879a sold for 15d.

Emirates Banks Association, 25th Anniv. — A270

2007, Oct. 4   Perf. 13¾

880	A270	1d red & bis brn	.55	.55

Abu Dhabi Islamic Bank, 10th Anniv. — A271

Differing backgrounds with denominations of: 1d, 150f, 2d, 3d.

2007, Nov. 8   Litho.   Perf. 14¼

881-884	A271	Set of 4	4.25	4.25
884a		Souvenir sheet, #881-884	4.25	4.25

Abu Dhabi Police, 50th Anniv. — A272

Litho. With Foil Application
2007, Nov. 14   Perf. 13¼x14

885	A272	1d multi	.55	.55

Children's Art — A273

Designs: Nos. 886, 892, Woman and two men in prayer. Nos. 887, 893, Woman presenting gift to another woman, vert. Nos. 888, 894, Children facing mosque. Nos. 889, 895, Hands holding child giving item to woman, vert. Nos. 890, 896, Child helping man across street. Nos. 891, 897, Child helping handicapped person, vert.

2007, Nov. 29   Litho.   Perf. 14

886	A273	1d multi	.55	.55
887	A273	150f multi	.85	.85
888	A273	2d multi	1.10	1.10
889	A273	3d multi	1.75	1.75

890	A273	350f multi	1.90	1.90
891	A273	4d multi	2.25	2.25
		Nos. 886-891 (6)	8.40	8.40

Booklet Stamps
Self-Adhesive
Die Cut Perf. 11¼x12, 12x11¼

892	A273	1d multi	.55	.55
893	A273	150f multi	.85	.85
894	A273	2d multi	1.10	1.10
895	A273	3d multi	1.75	1.75
896	A273	350f multi	1.90	1.90
897	A273	4d multi	2.25	2.25
a.		Complete booklet, #892-897	8.50	
		Nos. 892-897 (6)	8.40	8.40

Complete booklet is stapled in center with one stamp per page and with the center leaf of the booklet having stamps on both sides.

Souvenir Sheet

Sheikh Mohammed Al Khazraji (1919-2006), Chief Justice — A274

No. 898: a, 1d, Facing right. b, 3d, Facing forward.

2007, Dec. 9   Perf. 13½x13¾

898	A274	Sheet of 2, #a-b	2.25	2.25

Al Abbas Group, 40th Anniv. A275

Denominations: 1d, 150f, 2d, 3d.

2007, Dec. 16   Perf. 14¼

899-902	A275	Set of 4	4.25	4.25

Al Rostamani Group, 50th Anniv. A276

Background colors: 1d, Gray. 150f, Prussian blue.

2007, Dec. 23   Perf. 13x13¼

903-904	A276	Set of 2	1.40	1.40

Union Properties, 20th Anniv. A277

Designs: 1d, Emblem. 150f, F1 Theme Park, Dubai, horiz. 2d, Uptown. 3d, Green community, horiz.

Perf. 13¼x13½, 13½x13¼

2007, Dec. 27

905-908	A277	Set of 4	4.25	4.25
908a		Souvenir sheet, #905-908	8.50	8.50

No. 908a sold for 15d.

Federal National Council, 36th Anniv. A278

2008, Feb. 12   *Perf. 13¼*
909 A278 1d multi   .55 .55

National Bank of Abu Dhabi, 40th Anniv. A279

"40" and: 1d, Yellow panel at top. 150f, Yellow panel at top. 225d, White panel at top. 4d, White panel at top.

2008, Feb. 13   *Perf. 13*
910-913 A279   Set of 4   4.75 4.75
913a   Souvenir sheet, #910-913   8.25 8.25
No. 913a sold for 15d.

Municipality and Planning Department of Ajman — A280

Emblems of: 1d, Municipality and Planning Department. 150f, Ajman Urban Planning Conference. 2d, E-services. 4d, Geographic Information Systems.

2008, Mar. 24   Litho.   Perf. 13¼
914-917 A280   Set of 4   4.75 4.75
917a   Souvenir sheet, #914-917,
        perf. 13¼x14¼   8.25 8.25
No. 917a sold for 15d.

Souvenir Sheet

Hamdan Bin Rashid Al Maktoum Award for Distinguished Academic Performance — A281

No. 918: a, 1d, Emblem and "10." b, 2d, Rashid Al Maktoum, emblem.

2008, Apr. 1   *Perf. 13¼*
918 A281   Sheet of 2, #a-b   1.75 1.75

Traditional Souqs — A282

Marketplaces: 1d, Spice Souq, Dubai. 150f, Al Arsa Souq, Sharjah. 2d, Gold Souq, Dubai. 3d, Old Souq, Abu Dhabi.

Litho. & Embossed
2008, Apr. 20   *Perf. 13½x13¼*
919-922 A282   Set of 4   4.25 4.25

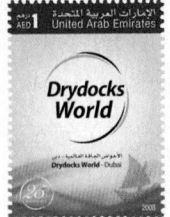

Drydocks World, 25th Anniv. — A283

Designs: 1d, Shown. 4d, Emblem, dhow, horiz.

Perf. 13¼x13, 13x13¼
2008, June 4   Litho.
923-924 A283   Set of 2   2.75 2.75

Sharjah Intl. Airport, 75th Anniv. — A284

2008, July 7   *Perf. 13½*
925 A284 1d multi   .55 .55

2008 Summer Olympics, Beijing A285

Emblem of Beijing Olympics, emblems of five sports and: 1d, Yellow orange background. 4d, Olympic torch, vert. 475f Olympic torch, diff., vert. 550f, Red violet background. 10d, Olympic torch, vignettes of Nos. 926-929.

2008, Aug. 4   Perf. 14x13¼, 13¼x14
926-929 A285   Set of 4   8.50 8.50
Size: 120x120mm
Imperf
930 A285 10d multi   5.50 5.50

Gulf News, 30th Anniv. — A286

Background color: 1d, Blue. 150f, Maroon. 225f, Orange.

2008, Sept. 30   *Perf. 13½x13¼*
Granite Paper
931-933 A286   Set of 3   2.60 2.60
A souvenir sheet containing Nos. 931-933 sold for 15d.

Souvenir Sheet

Arab Postal Day — A287

No. 934 — Emblem and: a, 1d, World map, pigeon. b, 225f, Camel caravan.

Litho. & Silkscreened With Foil Application
2008, Oct. 10
934 A287   Sheet of 2, #a-b   1.75 1.75

Miniature Sheets

Date Varieties — A288

No. 935: a, Abuman. b, Jash Hamad. c, Msalli.
No. 936, vert.: a, Farth. b, Mirzaban. c, Abukibal. d, Salani.

2008, Oct. 22   Litho.   Perf. 13x13¼
935 A288 1d Sheet of 3, #a-c   1.75 1.75
Perf. 13¼x13
936 A288 1d Sheet of 4, #a-d   2.25 2.25

Falcon Type of 2007 Inscribed "Priority"
Litho. & Embossed
2008, Dec. 2   *Perf. 13¼x14*
Background Color
937 A262 2d vermilion   1.10 1.10

Center for Documentaion and Research, 40th Anniv. — A289

Designs: 1d, Building. 4d, Sheikhs and crowd of people. 10d, Sheikhs, vert.

2008, Dec. 2   Litho.   Perf. 14¼
939 A289 1d multi   .55 .55
940 A289 4d multi   2.25 2.25

Miniature Sheet
Litho With 3-Dimensional Plastic Affixed
Self-Adhesive
Serpentine Die Cut 9
941 A289 10d multi   5.50 5.50

Eid Al Adha — A290

Designs: 1d, Al Eidiya. 3d, Eid prayers.

Litho. With Foil Application
2008, Dec. 6   *Perf. 13¾*
942-943 A290   Set of 2   2.25 2.25
943a   Souvenir sheet, #942-943   3.25 3.25
No. 943a sold for 6d.

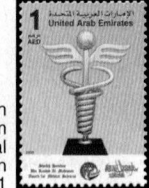

Sheikh Hamdan Bin Rashid Al Maktoum Award for Medical Science, 10th Anniv. — A291

Designs: 1d, Award. 2d, Special Recognition Award. 3d, Sheikh Hamdan Bin Rashid Al Maktoum, award. 4d, 10th anniversary emblem.

2008, Dec. 15   Litho.   Perf. 13¼
944-947 A291   Set of 4   5.50 5.50
947a   Souvenir sheet, #944-947   8.25 8.25
No. 947a sold for 15d.

Dubai Duty Free, 25th Anniv. — A292

Designs: 1d, 25th anniversary emblem in gray. 2d, 25th anniversary emblem in red. 3d, Dubai Duty Free shop. 4d, Shop, diff.

2008, Dec. 20   Litho.   Perf. 13¼x13
948-951 A292   Set of 4   5.50 5.50
951a   Souvenir sheet, #948-951   5.50 5.50

Universal Declaration of Human Rights, 60th Anniv. — A293

Color of top panel: 1d, Red brown. 4d, Orange and yellow.

Perf. 13¾x13½
2008, Dec. 31   Litho.
952-953 A293   Set of 2   2.75 2.75
953a   Souvenir sheet, #952-953   3.25 3.25
No. 953a sold for 6d.

Second Arab Stamp Exhibition, Dubai — A294

Serpentine Die Cut 12½
2009, Mar. 5   Litho. & Embossed
Self-Adhesive
Printed on Clear Plastic Film
954 A294 1d multi   .55 .55
No. 954 has white backing paper.

Emirates Center for Strategic Studies and Research (ECSSR), 15th Anniv. A295

Designs: 1d, Books published by ECSSR. 150f, UAE Federation Library. 2d, Media monitoring room. 4d, ECSSR Building.

2009, Mar. 26   Litho.   Perf. 13¼
Granite Paper

955-958	A295	Set of 4	4.75	4.75
958a		Souvenir sheet, #955-958	5.50	5.50

No. 958a sold for 10d.

Falcon Type of 2007 Redrawn
2009, Apr. 2   Litho.   Perf. 13¼x13
Background Color

959	A262	25f black	.25	.25
960	A262	1d dark buff	.55	.55
961	A262	150f brownish gray	.80	.80
962	A262	2d gray lilac	1.10	1.10
963	A262	10d orange	5.50	5.50
964	A262	20d lt greenish blue	11.00	11.00
965	A262	50d dark green	27.50	27.50
		Nos. 959-965 (7)	46.70	46.70

Nos. 959-965 are dated 2009 and lack the buff curved line to the left of the Arabic country name found on Nos. 859-865. Denominations for Nos. 960 and 962 use "AED" rather than the "Dh." or "Dhs." used on Nos. 859 and 861.

Rashid Bin Tannaf (1910-99), Poet — A296

Rashid Bin Tannaf: 1d, Wearing kaffiyeh. 4d, Without kaffiyeh.

2009, Apr. 30   Perf. 13¼
Granite Paper

966-967	A296	Set of 2	2.75	2.75

A souvenir sheet containing Nos. 966-967 sold for 15d.

Discovery of Umm An Nar Culture, 50th Anniv. A297

Umm An Nar tomb with background color of: 1d, Red brown. 150f, Brown. 4d, Olive green.

2009, June 28   Perf. 13x13¼

968-970	A297	Set of 3	3.75	3.75

Jerusalem, Capital of Arab Culture — A298

2009, Aug. 3   Perf. 13¼x13

971	A298	2d multi	1.10	1.10

Postal Services in the Emirates, Cent. — A299

Covers bearing: 1d, Pakistan Nos. 1, 2, 5 and 12. 150f, Trucial States No. 4, Oman Nos. 21 and 52. 4f, United Arab Emirates No. 3, Dubai Nos. 80 and 83, and Sharjah stamp. 5d, Withdrawn United Arab Emirates National Day stamp of 1977. 10d, Various India stamps.

2009, Aug. 19   Perf. 13¼
Granite Paper

972-975	A299	Set of 4	6.25	6.25

Souvenir Sheet

976	A299	10d multi	5.50	5.50

38th National Day A300

2009, Dec. 2   Perf. 13

977	A300	1d multi	.55	.55

FIFA 2009 Club World Cup Soccer Championships, Abu Dhabi — A301

Designs: 1d, Shown. 10d, Similar to 1d, with United Arab Emirates flag at right.

2009, Dec. 19   Perf. 13¾

978	A301	1d multi	.55	.55

Souvenir Sheet
Perf. 13

979	A301	10d multi	5.50	5.50

No. 979 contains one 40x40mm stamp.

Securities and Commodities Authority, 10th Anniv. — A302

Emblem and: 1d, Numerals and squares. 2d, Text on computer screen, graphs. 3d, Emirates Securities Market trading board. 5d, Falcon and numerals.

2010, Feb. 1   Perf. 13
Granite Paper

980-983	A302	Set of 4	6.00	6.00

A souvenir sheet containing No. 983 sold for 15d.

Emirates Aluminum, 3rd Anniv. A303

Designs: 1d, Emblem. 2d, Hand holding frame with picture of smelting complex. 3d, Falcon, horse. 5d, United Arab Emirates flag.

2010, Feb. 24   Perf. 13x14¼

984-987	A303	Set of 4	6.00	6.00
987a		Souvenir sheet, #984-987, perf. 14¼	8.25	8.25

No. 987a sold for 15d.

United Arab Emirates Pavilion, Expo 2010, Shanghai A304

Pavilion: 1d, In daylight. 550f, At dusk.

Litho. With Foil Application
2010, May 13   Perf. 13¼x13

988-989	A304	Set of 2	3.75	3.75

Diplomatic Relations Between United Arab Emirates and Republic of Korea, 30th Anniv. — A305

No. 990: a, 1d, Flag of United Arab Emirates and air-conditioning tower. b, 550f, Flag of South Korea and Mt. Amisan Chimney, Gyeongbokgung Palace.

2010, June 17   Litho.   Perf. 13x13¼

990	A305	Horiz. pair, #a-b	3.75	3.75

See South Korea No. 2337.

Jebel Ali Free Zone, 25th Anniv. — A306

Designs: 1d, Zone in 1986. 2d, Zone in 1997. 3d, Zone in 2009. 4d, 25th anniversary emblem.

2010, June 30   Perf. 13¼x13½

991-994	A306	Set of 4	5.50	5.50
994a		Sheet of 4, #991-994, perf. 14¼x13½	8.25	8.25

No. 994a sold for 15d.

2010 Youth Olympics, Singapore — A307

2010, Aug. 19   Perf. 13¾

995	A307	475f multi	2.60	2.60

Sheikh Zayed Grand Mosque — A308

Designs: 1d, Mosque. 5d, Mosque, horiz. 25d, Mosque, diff., horiz.

Perf. 13½x13¼, 13¼x13½
2010, Aug. 29   Litho.

996-997	A308	Set of 2	3.25	3.25

Litho. & Embossed With Foil Application
Imperf
Size:145x110mm

998	A308	25d gold & multi	14.00	14.00

Old Schools — A309

Designs: 1d, Al Nehyania School, Abu Dhabi. 150f, Al Ahmadiya School, Dubai. 4d, Al Eslah School, Sharjah.

Perf. 13½x13¾
2010, Sept. 19   Litho.

999-1001	A309	Set of 3	3.75	3.75

A souvenir sheet containing Nos. 999-1001 sold for 15d.

Organization of the Petroleum Exporting Countries, 50th Anniv. — A310

2010, Sept. 27   Perf. 13

1002	A310	1d multi	.55	.55

World Post Day
A311

Designs: 1d, Dove holding envelope. 550f, Universal Postal Union emblem.

2010, Oct. 9   Perf. 13¼x13
1003-1004 A311 Set of 2   3.75 3.75

Miniature Sheet

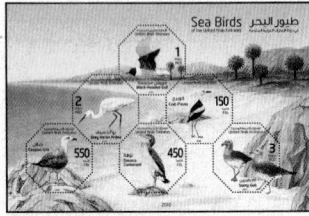

Sea Birds — A312

No. 1005: a, 1d, Black-headed gull. b, 150f, Crab plover. c, 2d, Gray heron ardea. d, 3d, Sooty gull. e, 450f, Socotra cormorant. f, 550f, Caspian gull.

2010, Nov. 4   Litho.   Perf. 13
Granite Paper
1005 A312 Sheet of 6, #a-f, +
            label   9.50 9.50

DP World Marine Terminal Operators A313

DP World emblem and various port scenes: 1d, 2d, 3d, 4d.

2010, Nov. 9   Perf. 14¼x13¾
Granite Paper
1006-1009 A313 Set of 4   5.50 5.50
1009a   Sheet of 4, #1006-1009   8.25 8.25
  No. 1009a sold for 15d.

Yas Marina Racing Circuit, Abu Dhabi — A314

Designs: 1d, Race car on track. 550f, Grandstands.

2010, Nov. 14   Perf. 13¼x13
1010-1011 A314 Set of 2   3.75 3.75

Watani (National Identity) A315

Designs: 1d, Four stylized fingerprints. 150f, Map of United Arab Emirates composed of fingerprints, vert.

2010, Dec. 2 Perf. 13x13½, 13½x13
1012-1013 A315 Set of 2   1.40 1.40

39th National Day — A316

Nos. 1014 and 1015 — Winning designs in children's stamp design contest: a, Four automobiles, people waving flags and signs. b, Children with flags around grills. c, Flag of United Arab Emirates, tower. d, Four people, flags, towers. e, Children with balloons. f, Flag and "December 2."

2010, Dec. 2   Perf. 13
1014 A316 1d Sheet of 6, #a-f   3.25 3.25
Stamp Size: 35x26mm
Self-Adhesive
Serpentine Die Cut 12¾
1015 A316 1d Booklet pane of
            12, 2 each #a-f   6.50 6.50

Ghaf Tree — A317

2011, Mar. 31   Perf. 13¼
1016 A317 1d green   .55 .55
  A souvenir sheet containing No. 1016 and a 4d stamp with a ghaf tree seed and a plastic netting affixed to it sold for 40d.

17th Gulf Cooperation Council Postage Stamp Exhibition, Abu Dhabi — A318

2011, Apr. 4   Perf. 13
1017 A318 150f multi   .85 .85

Miniature Sheet

31st Session of the Gulf Cooperation Council Supreme Council, Abu Dhabi — A319

No. 1018 — Various buildings and: a, King Abdullah, flag of Saudi Arabia. b, Sheikh Khalifa, flag of United Arab Emirates. c, Sheikh Sabah, flag of Kuwait. d, King Hamad, flag of Bahrain. e, Sheikh Hamad, flag of Qatar. f, Sultan Qaboos, flag of Oman.

2011, Apr. 5   Perf. 13½x13¾
1018 A319 150f Sheet of 6, #a-f   5.00 5.00

Fifth Gulf Federation for Cancer Control Conference, Sharjah — A320

2011, May 31 Litho. Perf. 14x13½
Granite Paper
1019 A320 1d multi   .55 .55

Emblem of Sheikha Fatima Bint Mubarak A321

Litho. With Foil Application
2011, July 24   Perf. 13
1020 A321 1d multi   .55 .55

Al Bidyah Mosque, Fujeira — A322

Designs: 1d, Archway. 150f, Mosque exterior.
15d, Mosque exerior, wall carving.

2011, Aug. 27 Litho. Perf. 14x14¼
1021 A322 1d multi   .55 .55
1022 A322 150f multi   .85 .85
Litho. & Embossed
Imperf
Size: 130x80mm
1023 A322 15d multi   8.25 8.25
  No. 1023 contains one 40x40mm perforated label.

Fauna of Bu Tinah Island — A323

Designs: No. 1024, 1d, Dugong (35x35mm). No. 1025, 1d, One fish (35x35mm). No. 1026, 1d, Three fish (35x35mm). No. 1027, 1d, Crab (35x35mm). No. 1028, 1d, Bird (35x35mm). No. 1029, 1d, Coral (35x35mm). No. 1030, 1d, Coral (48x30mm). No. 1031, 1d, Dolphin (48x30mm). No. 1032, 1d, Flamingos (48x30mm). No. 1033, 1d, Sea turtle (48x30mm).
15d, Sea turtle, dugong, dolphins, coral, crab, birds.

Perf. 13¼, 13¼x13½ (#1030-1033)
2011, Nov. 30   Litho.
1024-1033 A323 Set of 10   5.50 5.50
Size: 120x70mm
Imperf
1034 A323 15d multi   8.25 8.25

40th National Day — A324

2011, Dec. 2   Perf. 13½x13¾
Granite Paper
1035 A324 1d multi   .55 .55

Winter Plants — A325

Designs: No. 1036, 1d, Bladder dock. No. 1037, 1d, Cart-track plant. No. 1038, 1d, Arta. No. 1039, 1d, Hawa. No. 1040, 150f, Rohida tree. No. 1041, 150f, Puncturevine.

2011, Dec. 26   Perf. 14x13
1036-1041 A325 Set of 6   4.00 4.00

Camels — A326

Designs: 1d, Four camels. 4d, One camel.

2011, Dec. 29   Perf. 13¾
1042-1043 A326 Set of 2   2.75 2.75
  A souvenir sheet containing one each of Nos. 1042-1043 sold for 15d.

Sultan Bin Ali Al Owais Culturan Foundation, 25th Anniv. — A327

Designs: 1d, Sultan and "25." 15d, Sultan and "25," diff.

**   Perf. 13¾x13½**
2012, Mar. 14   Litho.
1044 A327 1d multi   .55 .55
Litho. With Foil Application
Size: 100x120mm
Imperf
1045 A327 15d multi + label   8.25 8.25

22nd Al Gaffal 60-Foot Traditional
Dhow Sailing Race — A328

No. 1046: a, 1d, View of dhow from air. b,
5d, View of dhow from surface of water.
15d, Various dhows.

2012, May 26 Litho. Perf. 13¼x13½
1046 A328   Horiz. pair, #a-b   3.25 3.25
Size: 185x85mm
Imperf
1047 A328 15d multi + 5 labels   8.25 8.25

First Shipment of
Crude Oil, 50th
Anniv. — A329

Designs: 1d, Abu Dhabi Marine Operating
Company Building. 150f, Offshore oil rig and
birds. 3d, Oil platforms and dolphins, horiz. 4d,
Oil tanker and tanks, horiz.
15d, Emblem of Abu Dhabi Marine Operating Company, vignettes of Nos. 1048-1051.

Litho. With Foil Application
Perf. 13¼x13½, 13½x13¼
2012, July 4
1048-1051 A329   Set of 4   5.25 5.25
Size: 120x95mm
Imperf
1052 A329 15d multi + 5 labels   8.25 8.25

Liwa Date
Festival — A330

Designs: 1d, Bowl of dates, palm frond. 5d,
Dates, palm frond.
15d, Dates, trees, rug, horiz.

2012, July 17   **Perf. 14**
1053-1054 A330   Set of 2   3.25 3.25
Size: 120x80mm
Imperf
1055 A330 15d multi   8.25 8.25

Arab
Post
Day
A331

Perf. 13½x13¼
2012, Aug. 15   **Litho.**
1056 A331 225f multi   1.25 1.25

World
Energy
Forum
2012,
Dubai
A332

Emblems of World Energy Forum and
Supreme Council of Energy and: 1d,
"E=WEF." 2d, Building in Dubai. 3d, Solar
energy collector. 4d, Sheikhs Khalifa Bin
Zayed Al Nahyan and Mohammed bin Rashid
al Maktoum.

2012, Oct. 22   **Perf. 14**
1057-1060 A332   Set of 4   5.50 5.50
1060a   Souvenir sheet of 4,
           #1057-1060   8.25 8.25
No. 1060a sold for 15d.

Snakes
A333

No. 1061: a, Arabian horned viper. b, Carpet viper. c, Arabian rearfang. d, Sochurek's
saw-scaled viper. e, Sand boa.
25d, Snakes depicted on Nos. 1061a-
1061e.

2012, Nov. 1   **Perf. 14x13½**
1061   Vert. strip of 5   8.50 8.50
a. A333 1d multi   .55   .55
b. A333 150f multi   .85   .85
c. A333 3d multi   1.75   1.75
d. A333 4d multi   2.25   2.25
e. A333 550f multi   3.00   3.00
Size: 130x100mm
Imperf
1062 A333 25d multi + 5 perf.
           14x13½ la-
           bels   14.00 14.00

A334

Ruler and scene from: No. 1064, 4d, Abu
Dhabi. No. 1065, 4d, Ajman. No. 1066, 4d,
Dubai. No. 1067, 4d, Fujeira. No. 1068, 4d,
Ras al Khaima. No. 1069, 4d, Sharjah. No.
1070, 4d, Umm al Qiwain.

**Litho. & Embossed With Foil
Application**
2012, Nov. 29   **Perf. 14¼**
1063 A334 1d multi   .55   .55
Imperf
1064-1070 A335   Set of 7   15.50 15.50

Al Ahmadiya School, Dubai,
Cent. — A336

No. 1071: a, School room, sheikh and student. b, School building.
6d, Sheikh, various pictures of school.

2012, Dec. 12 Litho. Perf. 13¼
1071   Horiz. pair   1.40 1.40
a. A336 1d multi   .55   .55
b. A336 150f multi   .85   .85

United Arab Emirates Soccer Team,
Champions of 21st Gulf Cup
Tournament — A337

Designs: 2d, Team. 6d, Gulf Cup, vert.

2013, Feb. 10 Litho. Perf. 13¼
1073 A337 2d multi   1.10 1.10
Souvenir Sheet
Perf. 13¼x12¾
1074 A337 6d multi   3.25 3.25
No. 1074 contains one 30x50mm stamp.

Mother's
Day — A338

Litho. With Foil Application
2013, Mar. 21   **Perf. 13**
1075 A338 3d red vio & gold   1.75 1.75

Postal Services in Abu Dhabi, 50th
Anniv. — A339

50th anniv. emblem and: 1d, Abu Dhabi
#26, 80 on covers. 150f, Abu Dhabi #62 on
cover, block of Abu Dhabi #10. 3d, Abu Dhabi
#42 on cover, block of Abu Dhabi #14. 4d, Abu
Dhabi #39, 46 on cover, Abu Dhabi #80, pair
of Abu Dhabi #18.
10d, Photographs of various post offices in
Abu Dhabi from 1963, 1968, 1975 and 1993,
various stamps.

2013, Mar. 30 Litho. Perf. 14xx13¼
1076-1079 A339   Set of 4   5.25 5.25
Imperf
Size: 100x100mm
1080 A339 10d multi   5.50 5.50
No. 1080 contains four labels showing the
various post offices.

**Falcon Type of 2007 Redrawn With
Area Inside Falcon Shaded**
2013, Apr. 7   **Perf. 14**
Dated "2013"
Background Color
1081 A262   1d yellowish buff   .55   .55
1082 A262   150f grayish sepia   .80   .80
1083 A262   3d dull yellow   1.75   1.75
1084 A262   5d violet blue   2.75   2.75
1085 A262   6d white   3.25   3.25
           Nos. 1081-1085 (5)   9.10   9.10
Denominations on Nos. 1081, 1083-1084
use "AED" instead of "Dh." or "Dhs." used on
Nos. 859, 862 and 865. Background colors
and color of shading within falcon differ on
Nos. 860, 961 and 1082.

Size: 144x94mm
Litho. With Foil Application
Imperf
1072 A336 6d multi   3.25 3.25

Yahsat,
Communications
Satellite of United
Arab
Emirates — A340

2013, May 13   **Perf. 14**
1086 A340 4d multi   2.25 2.25

Fazza Heritage
Championships — A341

Designs: 1d, Diver in free diving competition. 150f, Yola (traditional dance) competition.

2013, July 28 Litho. Perf. 13½
1087-1088 A341   Set of 2   1.40 1.40

Oryxes — A342

Designs: 1d, Oryxes standing and on
ground. 150f, Oryxes battling. 3d, Four oryxes
running.
15d, Oryxes.

2013, Aug. 26 Litho. Perf. 13
1089-1091 A342   Set of 3   3.00 3.00
Size: 180x100mm
Imperf
1092 A342 15d multi + 3 labels   8.25 8.25

Abu Dhabi International
Triathlon — A343

2013, Oct. 31 Litho. Perf. 12¾x13¼
1093 A343 3d multi   1.75 1.75

Qasr al-Hosn, Oldest Stone Building in
Abu Dhabi — A344

Designs: 1d, Aerial view, desert in background. 150f, Man in doorway (40x30mm). 2d,
Gate. 3d, Aerial view, skyscrapers in background (40x30mm).
8d, Colorized aerial view denoting additions
to building.

Perf. 12¾x13¼, 14 (150f, 3d)
Litho. With Foil Application
2013, Nov. 25
1094-1097 A344   Set of 4   4.25 4.25
Size: 131x81mm
Imperf
1098 A344 8d multi   4.50 4.50

10th Dubai International Film Festival — A345

No. 1099 — Horse's head and: a, Top of "1" in "10." b, Top of "0" in "10." c, Bottom of "1" in "10." d, Bottom of "0" in "10."

Litho. With Foil Application
2013, Dec. 3   Perf. 13¼x13¾
1099 A345 3d Block of 4, #a-d   6.50 6.50

Emirates National Bank of Dubai, 50th Anniv. A346

Designs: 1d, Orange and white arcs from bank's emblem. 2d, Bank's emblem and 50th anniv. ribbon. 3d, 50th anniv. ribbon. 4d, Arabic text in circle.

2013, Dec. 18   Litho.   Perf. 13
1100-1103 A346 Set of 4   5.50 5.50
1103a   Souvenir sheet of 4,
               #1100-1103   5.50 5.50

Coffee Tools A347

Designs: 1d, Al Tawa and Al Mehmas (roasting pan and mixer). 150f, Al Menhaz and Al Rashad (mortar and pestle). 3d, Al Dallah (coffee pot). 4d, Al Fenjan (coffee cup).
10d, Man roasting coffee beans, labels without denominations, similar to Nos.1104-1107.

2013, Dec. 24   Litho.   Perf. 13x13¼
1104-1107 A347 Set of 4   5.25 5.25
Souvenir Sheet
Imperf
1108 A347 10d multi + 4 labels   5.50 5.50

Parts of the design of No. 1108 have a scratch-and-sniff sandalwood scent.

Jumeirah Islamic Archaeological Site — A348

Designs: 1d, Walls and pillars. 150f, Walls.

2013, Dec. 30   Litho.   Perf. 14x14¼
1109-1110 A348 Set of 2   1.40 1.40

Emirates Center for Strategic Studies and Research, 20th Anniv. A349

Building, stylized globe emblem and background color of: 1d, Gray. 150f, Purple. 2d, Green. 4d, Brown.
10d, Stylized globe emblem and labels without denominations similar to Nos. 1111-1114.

2014, Jan. 2   Litho.   Perf. 13
1111-1114 A349 Set of 4   4.75 4.75
Souvenir Sheet
Imperf
1115 A349 10d multi + 4 labels   5.50 5.50

Souvenir Sheet

Crown Prince Hamdan, Sixth Anniv. of Accession — A350

Litho. With Foil Application
2014, Feb. 1   Perf. 14½
1116 A350 3d multi   1.75 1.75

Sharjah, 2014 Islamic Cultural Capital — A351

2014, Apr. 15   Litho.   Perf. 14
1117 A351 3d multi   1.75 1.75

Miniature Sheet

Union Supreme Court, 40th Anniv. — A352

No. 1118 — Anniversary emblem and background color of: a, Red. b, Green. c, White. d, Blue.

2014, May 8   Litho.   Perf. 13¼x13½
1118 A352 1d Sheet of 9, 3
            #1118a, 2 each
            #1118b-1118d   5.00 5.00

Zayed Humanitarian Day — A353

2014, July 17   Litho.   Perf. 14¼
1119 A353 1d multi   .55   .55

Expo 2020, Dubai — A354

No. 1120: a, Denomination at left. b, Denomination at right.
10d, Emblem and perforated labels without denominations similar to Nos. 1120a-1120b.

2014, Sept. 30   Litho.   Perf. 13x13½
1120 A354 3d Horiz. pair, #a-b   3.25 3.25
Size: 160x90mm
Imperf
1121 A354 10d multi + 2 labels   5.50 5.50

Flag Day — A355

Litho. With Foil Application
2014, Nov. 3   Perf. 14
1122 A355 3d multi   1.75 1.75

43rd National Day A356

Litho. & Embossed
2014, Dec. 2   Perf. 14¼
1123 A356 1d multi   .55   .55

History of Civil Aviation in Dubai — A357

Designs: 1d, Airplane, Sheikh Sa'id bin Maktum, 1937 agreement to build airport. 3d, Airport, Sheikh Rashid, text of 1966 decree creating Department of Civil Aviation. 5d, Sheikh Mohammed, airplanes and airport.

2014, Dec. 7   Litho.   Perf. 13¼
1124-1126 A357 Set of 3   5.00 5.00

Miniature Sheets

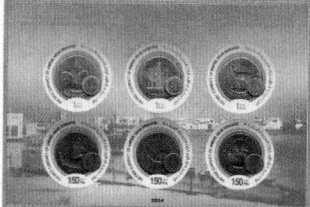

First United Arab Emirates Currency — A358

No. 1127 — Obverse and reverse of 1973 coins: a, 1-dirham coin depicting pitcher. b, 50-fils coin depicting oil derricks. c, 25-fils coin depicting gazelle. d, 10-fils coin depicting dhow. e, 5-fils coin depicting fish. f, 1-fils coin depicting date palms.
No. 1128 — Fronts and backs of banknotes: a, 1973 1-dirham note. b, 1973 50-dirham note. c, 1973 5-dirham note. d, 1973 100-dirham note. e, 1973 10-dirham note. f, 1976 1000-dirham note.

Litho. & Embossed
2014, Dec. 25   Serpentine Die Cut
Self-Adhesive
1127 A358 Sheet of 6   4.25
a.-c.   1d Any single   .55   .55
d.-f.   150f Any single   .85   .85
Litho. & Embossed With Foil Application
Serpentine Die Cut 13
1128 A358 Sheet of 6   10.50
a.-b.   2d Either single   1.10 1.10
c.-d.   3d Either single   1.75 1.75
e.-f.   4d Either single   2.25 2.25

History of Civil Aviation in Abu Dhabi — A359

Abu Dhabi Intl. Airport: 1d, Control tower and airplane in flight. 150f, Interior of terminal.

2014, Dec. 31   Litho.   Perf. 13¼
1129-1130 A359 Set of 2   1.40 1.40

UPPER SENEGAL & NIGER

'ə-pər ˌse-nə-gäl and 'nī-jər

LOCATION — In Northwest Africa, north of French Guinea and Ivory Coast

GOVT. — A former French Colony

AREA — 617,600 sq. mi.

POP. — 2,474,142

CAPITAL — Bamako

In 1921 the name of this colony was changed to French Sudan and postage stamps so inscribed were placed in use.

100 Centimes = 1 Franc

Gen. Louis Faidherbe A1

Oil Palms — A2

Dr. N. Eugène Ballay A3

Perf. 14x13½
1906-07 Unwmk. Typo.
Name of Colony in Red or Blue

1	A1	1c slate	1.40	1.75
2	A1	2c brown	1.75	2.10
3	A1	4c brn, *gray bl*	2.50	2.50
4	A1	5c green	5.50	2.75
5	A1	10c car (B)	6.25	2.75
6	A1	15c vio ('07)	4.25	5.00
7	A2	20c black & red, *azure*	5.50	5.50
8	A2	25c bl, *pnksh*	17.50	4.25
9	A2	30c vio brn, *pnksh*	7.00	5.50
10	A2	35c blk, *yellow*	5.50	5.00
11	A2	40c car, *az* (B)	9.00	9.00
12	A2	45c brn, *grnsh*	10.50	11.00
13	A2	50c dp vio	10.50	11.00
14	A2	75c bl, *org*	10.50	12.00
15	A3	1fr blk, *azure*	25.00	27.50
16	A3	2fr bl, *pink*	45.00	52.50
17	A3	5fr car, *straw* (B)	95.00	105.00
		Nos. 1-17 (17)	262.65	265.10

Camel with Rider — A4

1914-17   Perf. 13½x14

18	A4	1c brn vio & vio	.35	.45
19	A4	2c gray & brn vio	.35	.45
20	A4	4c black & blue	.35	.45
21	A4	5c yel grn & bl grn	1.05	.50
22	A4	10c red org & rose	2.50	2.00
23	A4	15c choc & org ('17)	2.10	1.05
24	A4	20c brn vio & blk	2.10	2.10
25	A4	25c ultra & bl	2.10	1.40
26	A4	30c ol brn & brn	2.10	2.10
27	A4	35c car rose & vio	3.50	2.50
28	A4	40c gray & car rose	2.10	1.40
29	A4	45c bl & ol brn	2.10	2.10
30	A4	50c black & green	2.75	2.75
31	A4	75c org & ol brn	2.75	2.75
32	A4	1fr brown & brn vio	2.75	3.50

33	A4	2fr green & blue	3.50	3.50
34	A4	5fr violet & black	12.40	14.00
		Nos. 18-34 (17)	44.85	43.00

See Burkina Faso for types of this issue that escaped overprinting.
For surcharge see No. B1.

SEMI-POSTAL STAMP

Regular Issue of 1914 Surcharged in Red

1915   Unwmk.   Perf. 13½x14
B1	A4	10c + 5c red orange & rose	2.10	2.10

POSTAGE DUE STAMPS

Natives — D1

1906 Unwmk. Typo.   Perf. 14x13½

J1	D1	5c green, *greenish*	3.50	3.50
J2	D1	10c red brown	7.00	7.00
J3	D1	15c dark blue	10.50	10.50
J4	D1	20c black, *yellow*	14.00	7.00
J5	D1	50c violet	27.50	27.50
J6	D1	60c black, *buff*	21.00	21.00
J7	D1	1fr black, *pinkish*	35.00	37.50
		Nos. J1-J7 (7)	118.50	114.00

D2

1914
J8	D2	5c green	1.05	1.40
J9	D2	10c rose	1.40	1.75
J10	D2	15c gray	1.40	1.75
J11	D2	20c brown	1.40	1.75
J12	D2	30c blue	2.10	2.50
J13	D2	50c black	1.75	2.10
J14	D2	60c orange	6.25	7.00
J15	D2	1fr violet	6.25	7.00
		Nos. J8-J15 (8)	21.60	25.25

Stamps of Upper Senegal and Niger were superceded in 1921 by those of French Sudan.

UPPER SILESIA

'ə-pər sī'lē-zhē-ə

LOCATION — Formerly in eastern Germany and prior to World War I a part of Germany.

A plebiscite held under the terms of the Treaty of Versailles failed to determine the status of the country, the voting resulting about equally in favor of Germany and Poland. Accordingly, the League of Nations divided the territory between Germany and Poland.

100 Pfennig = 1 Mark
100 Fennigi = 1 Marka

Plebiscite Issues

A1

Perf. 14x13½
1920, Feb. 20   Typo.   Unwmk.

1	A1	2½pf slate	.40	.80
2	A1	3pf brown	.40	.85
3	A1	5pf green	.30	.80
4	A1	10pf dull red	.40	.90
5	A1	15pf violet	.25	.80
6	A1	20pf blue	.25	.80
a.		Imperf., pair	275.00	
b.		Half used as 10pf on cover		110.00
7	A1	50pf violet brn	4.75	8.00
8	A1	1m claret	5.00	11.00
9	A1	5m orange	5.00	11.00
		Nos. 1-9 (9)	16.75	34.95
		Set, never hinged	55.00	

Black Surcharge

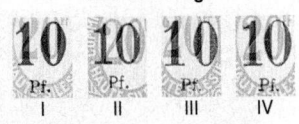

	5 Pf.	5 Pf.	5 Pf.	5 Pf.	
	I	II	III	IV	

10	A1	5pf on 15pf vio (I)	160.00	525.00
		Never hinged	450.00	
a.		Type II		
b.		Type III		
c.		Type IV		
11	A1	5pf on 20pf blue (I)	1.10	3.25
		Never hinged	3.00	
a.		Type II	1.25	3.75
b.		Type III	1.60	4.00
c.		Type IV	2.00	5.00

Red Surcharge

	10 Pf.	10 Pf.	10 Pf.	10 Pf.	
	I	II	III	IV	

12	A1	10pf on 20pf bl (I)	1.10	3.25
		Never hinged	3.00	
a.		Type II	1.10	3.25
b.		Type III	1.10	3.25
c.		Type IV	1.10	3.25
d.		Imperf.	60.00	240.00

Black Surcharge

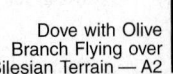

50 Pf.	50 Pf.	50 Pf.	50 Pf.	50 Pf.	
Type I	Type II	Type III	Type IV	Type V	

13	A1	50pf on 5m org (I), shiny ovpt.	27.50	52.50
		Never hinged	200.00	
a.		Type II	29.00	55.00
b.		Type III	30.00	87.50
c.		Type IV	30.00	87.50
d.		Type V	42.50	120.00
e.		Type I, matte ovpt.	37.50	87.50

Nos. 10-13 are found with many varieties including surcharges inverted, double and double inverted.

Dove with Olive Branch Flying over Silesian Terrain — A2

A3

1920, Mar. 26   Typo.   Perf. 13½x14
15	A2	2½pf gray	.55	.80
16	A2	3pf red brown	.55	.80
17	A2	5pf green	.55	.80
18	A2	10pf dull red	.55	.80
19	A2	15pf violet	.55	.80
20	A2	20pf blue	.80	2.00
21	A2	25pf dark brown	.55	.80
22	A2	30pf orange	.55	.80
23	A2	40pf olive green	.55	2.00

Perf. 14x13½
24	A3	50pf gray	1.00	.80
25	A3	60pf blue	.55	1.60
26	A3	75pf deep green	1.60	2.00
27	A3	80pf red brown	1.60	1.10
28	A3	1m claret	1.60	.80
29	A3	2m dark brown	1.40	.80
30	A3	3m violet	1.40	.80
31	A3	5m orange	4.00	4.50
		Nos. 15-31 (17)	18.35	22.00
		Set, never hinged	67.50	

Nos. 18-28 Overprinted in Black or Red

1921, Mar. 20
32	A2	10pf dull red	4.00	10.00
33	A2	15pf violet	4.00	10.00
34	A2	20pf blue	5.50	14.00
35	A2	25pf dk brn (R)	12.00	32.50
36	A2	30pf orange	10.00	20.00
37	A2	40pf olive grn (R)	11.00	20.00

Overprinted

38	A3	50pf gray (R)	11.00	27.50
39	A3	60pf blue	12.00	22.50
40	A3	75pf deep green	12.00	27.50
a.		75pf blue green	1,650.	1,850.
41	A3	80pf red brown	20.00	35.00
42	A3	1m claret	24.00	65.00
		Nos. 32-42 (11)	125.50	284.00
		Set, never hinged	700.00	

Inverted or double overprints exist on Nos. 32-33, 35-40. Counterfeit overprints exist.

Type of 1920 and Surcharged

1922, Mar.
45	A3	4m on 60pf ol grn	.80	2.00
46	A3	10m on 75pf red	1.25	2.75
47	A3	20m on 80pf orange	6.50	16.00
		Nos. 45-47 (3)	8.55	20.75
		Set, never hinged	32.00	

Stamps of the above design were a private issue not recognized by the Inter-Allied Commission of Government. Value, set of 7, $65 unused, $225 never hinged, $225 used.

OFFICIAL STAMPS

German Stamps of 1905-20 Handstamped in Blue

1920, Feb.   Wmk. 125   Perf. 14, 14½
On Stamps of 1906-19

O1	A22	2pf gray	1.10	1.25
O3	A22	2½pf gray	.55	.65
O4	A16	3pf brown	.55	.65
O5	A16	5pf green	.55	.65
O6	A22	7½pf orange	.55	.65
O7	A16	10pf car rose	.55	.65
O8	A22	15pf dk violet	.55	.65
O9	A16	20pf blue violet	.55	.65
O10	A16	25pf org & blk, *yel*	8.00	6.50

O11	A16	30pf org & blk, *buff*	.55	.65
O12	A22	35pf red brown	.55	.65
O13	A16	40pf lake & blk	.55	.65
O14	A16	50pf vio & blk, *buff*	.55	.65
O15	A16	60pf magenta	.55	.65
O16	A16	75pf green & blk	.55	.65
O17	A16	80pf lake & blk, *rose*	6.50	8.00
O18	A17	1m car rose	1.10	1.25
O19	A21	2m gray blue	5.25	6.50

On National Assembly Stamps of 1919-20

O25	A23	10pf car rose	.90	1.10
O26	A24	15pf choc & bl	1.60	2.00
O27	A25	25pf green & red	3.25	4.00
O28	A25	30pf red vio & red	2.50	3.00

On Semi-Postal Stamps of 1919

O30	A16	10pf + 5pf carmine	6.50	8.00
O31	A22	15pf + 5pf dk vio	6.50	8.00
		Nos. O1-O31 (24)	50.35	58.05

Red Handstamp

O5a	A16	5pf	10.00	14.00
O8a	A22	15pf	6.50	10.00
O9a	A16	20pf	6.50	10.00
O13a	A16	40pf	20.00	30.00
O16a	A16	75pf	20.00	30.00
O26a	A24	15pf	1.10	1.25
		Nos. O5a-O26a (6)	64.10	95.25

Values of Nos. O1-O31 are for reprints made with a second type of handstamp differing in minor details from the original (example: period after "S" is round instead of the earlier triangular form). Originals are scarce. Counterfeits exist.

Germany No. 65C with this handstamp is considered bogus by experts.

Local Official Stamps of Germany, 1920, Overprinted

1920, Apr.			**Perf. 14**	
O32	LO2	5pf green	.30	1.00
O33	LO3	10pf carmine	.30	1.00
O34	LO4	15pf violet brn	.30	1.00
O35	LO5	20pf deep ultra	.30	1.00
O36	LO6	30pf orange, *buff*	.30	1.00
O37	LO7	50pf violet, *buff*	.80	3.00
O38	LO8	1m red, *buff*	6.50	15.00
		Nos. O32-O38 (7)	8.80	23.00

Same Overprint on Official Stamps of Germany, 1920-21

1920-21				
O39	O1	5pf green	1.00	8.00
O40	O2	10pf carmine	.25	1.00
O41	O3	15pf violet brn	.25	1.00
O42	O4	20pf deep ultra	.25	1.00
O43	O5	30pf orange, *buff*	.25	1.00
O44	O6	40pf carmine rose	.25	1.00
O45	O7	50pf violet, *buff*	.25	1.00
O46	O8	60pf red brown	.25	1.00
O47	O9	1m red, *buff*	.25	1.00
O48	O10	1.25m dk blue, *yel*	.25	1.00
O49	O11	2m dark blue	7.25	12.00
O50	O12	5m brown, *yel*	.25	1.00
1922, Feb.			**Wmk. 126**	
O51	O11	2m dark blue	.25	1.00
		Nos. O39-O51 (13)	11.00	31.00

This overprint is found both horizontal, reading upright or inverted, and vertical, reading up or down. These variations generally command no premium over the values above.

The overprint also exists on most values double and double, one inverted, in the above formats, as well as at a 45 degree angle, upreading and downreading, either upright or inverted. These varieties generally sell for 25-100 percent over the value of normal examples.

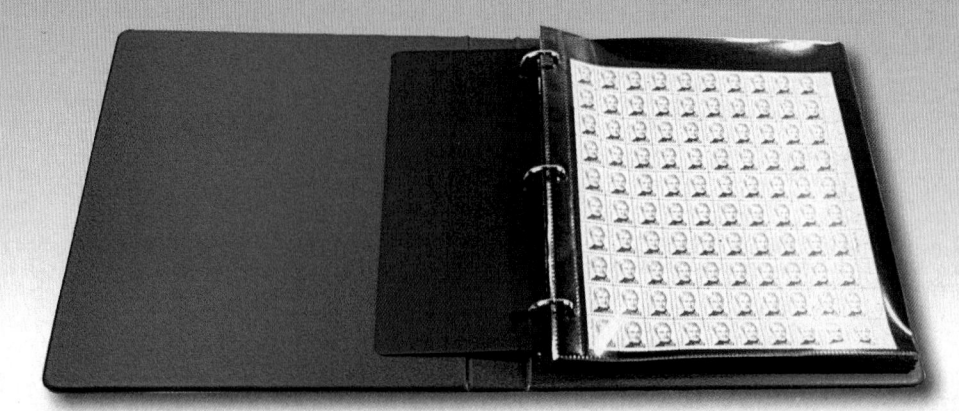

Mint Sheet Binders & Pages

Keep those mint sheets intact in a handsome, 3-ring binder. Just like the cover album, the Mint Sheet album features the "D" ring mechanism on the right-hand side of binder so you don't have to worry about damaging your stamps when turning the pages.

MINT SHEET BINDERS

Item	Description	Retail	AA*
MBRD	Red (Burgundy)	$18.99	$15.25
MBBL	Blue	$18.99	$15.25
MBGY	Gray	$18.99	$15.25
MBBK	Black	$18.99	$15.25

MINT SHEET PAGES

Item	Description	Retail	AA*
MS1	Black, 25 per pack	$14.99	$11.99
SSMP3C	Clear, 12 per pack	$9.95	$8.95

Save more when you buy in sets!

Item	Description	Retail	AA*
MBBK3PB	Black Binder with Black Pages (25 per pack)	$32.99	$24.99
MBBK3PC	Black Binder with Clear Pages (24 per pack)	$35.99	$29.99
MBBL3PB	Blue Binder with Black Pages (25 per pack)	$32.99	$24.99
MBBL3PC	Blue Binder with Clear Pages (24 per pack)	$35.99	$29.99
MBRD3PB	Burgundy Binder with Black Pages (25 per pack)	$32.99	$24.99
MBRD3PC	Burgundy Binder with Clear Pages (24 per pack)	$35.99	$29.99
MBGY3PB	Gray Binder with Black Pages (25 per pack)	$32.99	$24.99
MBGY3PC	Gray Binder with Clear Pages (25 per pack)	$35.99	$29.99

AMOS ADVANTAGE

URUGUAY

'yur-ə-,gwā

LOCATION — South America, between Brazil and Argentina and bordering on the Atlantic Ocean
GOVT. — Republic
AREA — 68,037 sq. mi.
POP. — 3,137,668 (1996)
CAPITAL — Montevideo

120 Centavos = 1 Real
8 Reales = 1 Peso
100 Centesimos = 1 Peso (1859)
1000 Milesimos = 1 Peso (1898)

Watermarks

Wmk. 90 — Large Sun and RA

Wmk. 187 — R O in Diamond

Wmk. 188 — REPUBLICA O. DEL URUGUAY

Wmk. 189 — Caduceus

Wmk. 227 — Greek Border and REPUBLICA O. DEL URUGUAY in Alternate Curved Lines

Wmk. 327 — Coat of Arms

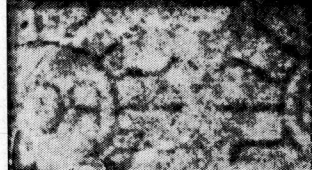

Wmk. 332 — Large Sun and R O U

Catalogue values for unused stamps in this country are for Never Hinged items, beginning with Scott 534 in the regular postage section, Scott B5 in the semi-postal section, Scott C113 in the airpost section, Scott CB1 in the airpost semi-postal section, Scott E9 in the special delivery section, and Scott Q64 in the parcel post section.

CARRIER ISSUES

Issued by Atanasio Lapido, Administrator-General of Posts

A1   A1a
"El Sol de Mayo"

Unwmk.

1856, Oct. 1		**Litho.**		***Imperf.***
1	A1	60c blue	450.	450.
2	A1	80c green	500.	500.
3	A1	1r vermilion	400.	400.

1857, Oct. 1
3B   A1a 60c blue   2,750.   —

Nos. 1-3B were spaced very closely on the stone. Very fine examples will have clear margins on three sides and touching or slightly cut into the frames on the fourth (consult the grading illustrations in the catalogue introduction). All genuinely used examples are pen canceled. Certification by a recognized authority is recommended.

Stamps with tiny faults, such as small thin spots, sell for about 75% of the values of sound examples.

See Nos. 410-413, 771A.

A2

1858, Mar.				
4	A2	120c blue	575.00	650.00
c.		Tête bêche pair		—
5	A2	180c green	150.00	200.00
c.		Thick paper	500.00	
d.		Tête bêche pair		—
6	A2	240c dull ver	150.00	1,200.
c.		180c in stone of 240c		—
d.		Thick paper (dull ver)		—
e.		240c setenant with a vacant space	5,000.	
		Nos. 4-6 (3)	875.00	2,050.

Nos. 4-6e have been extensively forged. Certification by a recognized authority is recommended.

GOVERNMENT ISSUES

A3   A4

1859, June 26		**Thin Numerals**		
7	A3	60c lilac	50.00	40.00
a.		60c gray lilac	50.00	35.00
8	A3	80c orange	325.00	65.00
a.		80c yellow	450.00	75.00
9	A3	100c brown lake	110.00	75.00
a.		100c brown rose	120.00	100.00
10	A3	120c blue	65.00	30.00
a.		120c slate blue	75.00	25.00
11	A3	180c green	25.00	30.00
12	A3	240c vermilion	90.00	90.00
		Nos. 7-12 (6)	665.00	330.00

1860		**Thick Numerals**		
13	A4	60c dull lilac	30.00	15.00
a.		60c gray lilac	30.00	15.00
b.		60c brown lilac	30.00	18.00
c.		60c red lilac	120.00	60.00
d.		As "a", fine impression (1st printing)	125.00	45.00
14	A4	80c yellow	50.00	25.00
a.		80c orange	100.00	27.50
15	A4	100c rose	100.00	55.00
a.		100c carmine	110.00	55.00
16	A4	120c blue	45.00	25.00
17	A4	180c yellow grn	425.00	375.00
a.		180c deep green	425.00	450.00
		Nos. 13-17 (5)	650.00	495.00

No. 13 was first printed (1860) in sheets of 192 (16x12) containing 24 types. The impressions are very clear; paper is whitish and of better quality than that of the later printings. In the 1861-62 printings, the layout contains 12 types and the subjects are spaced farther apart.

Coat of Arms — A5

1864, Apr. 13				
18	A5	6c rose	18.00	12.00
a.		6c carmine	40.00	30.00
b.		6c red	40.00	30.00
c.		6c brick red	45.00	30.00
20	A5	6c salmon	500.00	500.00
21	A5	8c green	25.00	25.00
a.		Tête bêche pair	775.00	
22	A5	10c yellow	32.50	25.00
a.		10c ocher	35.00	25.00
23	A5	12c blue	15.00	12.00
a.		12c dark blue	25.00	18.00
b.		12c slate blue	30.00	20.00

No. 20, which is on thicker paper, was never placed in use.

Stamps of 1864
Surcharged in Black

1866, Jan. 1				
24	A5	5c on 12c blue	30.00	55.00
a.		5c on 12c slate blue	30.00	60.00
b.		Inverted surcharge	150.00	
c.		Double surcharge	150.00	
d.		Pair, one without surcharge		
e.		Triple surcharge	55.00	
25	A5	10c on 8c brt grn	30.00	55.00
a.		10c on 8c dl grn	30.00	55.00
b.		Tête bêche pair	300.00	
c.		Double surcharge	150.00	
26	A5	15c on 10c ocher	35.00	90.00
a.		15c on 10c yellow	35.00	90.00
b.		Inverted surcharge	150.00	
c.		Double surcharge	150.00	
27	A5	20c on 6c rose	40.00	80.00
a.		20c on 6c rose red	37.50	75.00
b.		Inverted surcharge	150.00	
c.		Double surcharge	150.00	
d.		Pair, one without surcharge		
28	A5	20c on 6c brick red	400.00	
a.		Double surcharge	500.00	
		Nos. 24-27 (4)	135.00	280.00

Many counterfeits exist.
No. 28 was not issued.

Coat of Arms and Numeral of Value — A7

A8   A8a

A8b   A8c

Type I

Type II

ONE CENTESIMO:
Type I — The wavy lines behind "CENTESIMO" are clear and distinct. Stamps 4mm apart.
Type II — The wavy lines are rough and blurred. Stamps 3mm apart.

1866, Jan. 10				***Imperf.***
29	A7	1c black (type II)	5.00	7.50
a.		1c black (type I)	5.00	7.50
30	A8	5c blue	6.00	4.00
a.		5c dull blue	5.00	2.50
b.		5c ultramarine	32.50	7.50
c.		Numeral with white flag	25.00	12.00
d.		"ENTECIMOS"	25.00	12.00
e.		"CENTECIMO"	25.00	12.00
f.		"CENTECIMOS" with small "S"	25.00	12.00
g.		Pelure paper	100.00	100.00
h.		Thick paper		
31	A8a	10c yellow green	20.00	7.00
a.		10c blue green	20.00	7.00
b.		"I" of "CENTECIMOS" omitted	27.50	14.00
c.		"CENIECIMOS"	27.50	14.00
d.		"CENTRCIMOS"	27.50	14.00
32	A8b	15c orange yel	30.00	15.00
a.		15c yellow	30.00	15.00
33	A8c	20c rose	35.00	15.00
a.		20c lilac rose	35.00	15.00
b.		Thick paper	37.50	16.00
		Nos. 29-33 (5)	96.00	48.50

See Nos. 34-38. For overprint see No. O11.
Engraved plates were prepared for Nos. 30 to 33 but were not put in use. The stamps were printed from lithographic transfers from the plate. In 1915 a few reprints of the 15c were made from the engraved plate by a California philatelic society, each sheet being numbered and signed by officers of the society; then the plate was defaced.

1866-67			***Perf. 8½ to 13½***	
34	A7	1c black	6.50	20.00
35	A8	5c blue	5.00	2.50
a.		5c dark blue	5.00	1.00
b.		Numeral with white flag	25.00	12.00
c.		"ENTECIMOS"	25.00	12.00
d.		"CENTECIMO"	25.00	12.00
e.		"CENTECIMOS" with small "S"	15.00	8.00
f.		Pelure paper	90.00	20.00
36	A8a	10c green	12.00	4.00
a.		10c yellow green	14.00	4.00
b.		"CENIECIMOS"	35.00	14.00
c.		"I" of "CENTECIMOS" omitted	35.00	14.00
d.		"CENTRCIMOS"	35.00	14.00
e.		Pelure paper	90.00	20.00
37	A8b	15c orange yel	21.00	6.00
a.		15c yellow	21.00	6.00
b.		Thin paper	25.00	10.00
38	A8c	20c rose	25.00	10.00
a.		20c brown rose	25.00	10.00
b.		Thin paper	30.00	15.00
c.		Thick paper	30.00	15.00
		Nos. 34-38 (5)	69.50	42.50

A9

A10

A11

A12

1877-79 Engr. *Rouletted 8*

39	A9	1c red brown	.80	.50
40	A10	5c green	1.00	.50
a.		Thick paper	5.00	2.50
41	A11	10c vermilion	2.00	.80
42	A11	20c bister	3.50	1.25
43	A11	50c black	12.50	3.50
43A	A12	1p blue ('79)	50.00	22.50
		Nos. 39-43A (6)	69.80	29.05

The first printing of the 1p had the coat of arms smaller with quarterings reversed. These "error" stamps were not issued, and all were ordered burned. One example is known to have been in a celebrated Uruguayan collection and a few others exist.

See No. 44. For overprints and surcharges see Nos. 52-53, O1-O8, O10, O19.

1880, Nov. 10 Engr. *Rouletted 6*

44	A9	1c brown	.50	.50
a.		Imperf., pair	10.00	
b.		Rouletted 12½	2.50	

Joaquin Suárez — A13

1881, Aug. 25 *Perf. 12½*

45	A13	7c blue	2.50	2.50
a.		Imperf., pair	9.00	9.00

For overprint see No. O9.

A14

Devices from Coat of Arms — A14a

1882, May 15

46	A14	1c green	1.50	1.50
a.		1c yellow green	4.00	2.00
b.		Imperf., pair	13.00	
47	A14a	2c rose	1.25	1.00
a.		Imperf., pair	15.00	

These stamps bear numbers from 1 to 100 according to their position on the sheet.

Counterfeits of Nos. 46 and 47 are plentiful.

See Nos. 1132-1133. For overprints see Nos. 54, O12-O13, O20.

Coat of Arms
A15 A16

Gen. Máximo Santos — A17

General José Artigas — A18

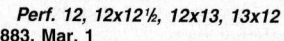

Perf. 12, 12x12½, 12x13, 13x12

1883, Mar. 1

48	A15	1c green	1.50	1.00
49	A16	2c red	2.50	1.50
50	A17	5c blue	2.75	1.75
51	A18	10c brown	5.00	2.50
		Nos. 48-51 (4)	11.75	6.75

Imperf., Pairs

48a	A15	1c	7.00
49a	A16	2c	7.00
50a	A17	5c	6.50
51a	A18	10c	11.00

For overprints see Nos. O14-O18.

No. 40 Overprinted in Black

1883, Sept. 24 *Rouletted 8*

52	A10	5c green	1.00	.75
a.		Double overprint	15.00	15.00
b.		Overprint reading down	6.00	6.00
c.		"Provisorio" omitted	7.00	7.00
d.		"1883" omitted	4.50	4.50

No. 52 with overprint in red is a color essay.

No. 41 Surcharged in Black

1884, Jan. 15

53	A11	1c on 10c ver	.50	.50
a.		Small figure "1"	4.25	4.25
b.		Inverted surcharge	4.25	4.25
c.		Double surcharge	8.00	5.00

No. 47 Overprinted in Black

Perf. 12½

54	A14a	2c rose	.75	.75
a.		Double overprint	14.00	
b.		Imperf., pair	40.00	

A22

A23

Thick Paper

1884, Jan. 25 Litho. Unwmk.

55	A22	5c ultra	2.00	1.00
a.		Imperf., pair	7.50	4.00

Thin Paper

Perf. 12½, 13 and Compound

56	A23	5c blue	1.50	.70
a.		Imperf., pair	14.00	

For overprints see Nos. O21-O22.

A24

A24a

A24b

Artigas — A25

Santos — A26

A27

A28

1884-88 Engr. *Rouletted 8*

57	A24	1c gray	.80	.50
58	A24	1c olive	.75	.40
59	A24	1c green	.65	.40
60	A24a	2c vermilion	.40	.25
60A	A24a	2c rose ('88)	.40	.25
61	A24b	5c deep blue	.80	.30
61A	A24b	5c blue, *blue*	2.00	.85
62	A24b	5c violet ('86)	.50	.25
63	A24b	5c lt bl ('88)	.50	.25
64	A25	7c dk brown	2.00	.85
65	A25	7c org ('88)	2.00	.75
66	A26	10c olive brn	.80	.35
67	A27	20c red violet	2.00	1.00
68	A27	20c bis brn ('88)	2.00	1.00
69	A28	25c gray violet	4.00	1.50
70	A28	25c ver ('88)	3.00	1.00
		Nos. 57-70 (16)	22.60	9.90

Water dissolves the blue in the paper of No. 61A.

For overprints see Nos. 73, 98-99, O23-O34, O36-O39, O61.

A29

1887, Oct. 17 Litho. *Rouletted 9*

71	A29	10c lilac	2.50	1.25
a.		10c gray lilac	3.00	1.25

For overprint see No. O40.

A30

1888, Jan. 1 Engr. *Rouletted 8*

72	A30	10c violet	.60	.25

For overprint see No. O35.

No. 62 Overprinted in Black

1889, Oct. 14

73	A24b	5c violet	.40	.40
a.		Inverted overprint	8.00	6.00
b.		Inverted "A" for "V" in "Provisorio"	4.00	4.00

No. 73 with overprint in red is a color essay.

Coat of Arms — A32

Numeral of Value — A33

A34

A35

A36

A37

Justice
A38

Mercury
A39

A40

Perf. 12½ to 15½ and Compound

1889-1901 Engr.

74	A32	1c green	.50	.25
a.		Imperf., pair	13.00	
75	A32	1c dull bl ('94)	.50	.25
76	A33	2c rose	.50	.25
77	A33	2c red brn ('94)	.55	.25
78	A33	2c org ('99)	.55	.25
79	A34	5c dp blue	.50	.25
80	A34	5c rose ('94)	.55	.25
81	A35	7c bister brn	1.00	.30
82	A35	7c green ('94)	4.75	2.75
83	A35	7c car ('00)	4.00	1.75
84	A36	10c blue grn	3.50	.85
a.		Printed on both sides	20.00	
85	A36	10c org ('94)	3.25	.60
86	A37	20c orange	2.50	.60
87	A37	20c brown ('94)	4.75	1.75
88	A37	20c lt blue ('00)	2.75	.40
a.		20c greenish blue	3.00	.40
89	A38	25c red brown	3.25	.85
90	A38	25c ver ('94)	6.75	3.50
91	A38	25c bis brn ('01)	3.75	.50
92	A39	50c lt blue	7.50	5.00
93	A39	50c lilac ('94)	11.00	5.50
94	A39	50c car ('01)	6.75	1.00
95	A40	1p lilac	18.00	5.00
96	A40	1p lt blue ('94)	25.00	7.00
97	A40	1p dp grn ('01)	20.00	2.25
a.		Imperf., pair	30.00	
		Nos. 74-97 (24)	132.15	41.35

For surcharges and overprints see Nos. 100-101, 142, 180, 185, C1-C3, O41-O60, O89-O91, O108-O109.

Nos. 59 and 62 Overprinted in Red

a

b

1891-92 *Rouletted 8*

98	A24 (a)	1c green ('92)	.40	.40
a.		Inverted overprint	6.00	6.00
b.		Double overprint	7.75	7.75
c.		Double ovpt., one invtd.	3.00	2.50
d.		"PREVISORIO"	4.00	4.00
99	A24b (b)	5c violet	.25	.25
a.		"1391"	4.00	2.75
b.		Double overprint	4.00	2.75
c.		Inverted overprint	4.00	2.75
d.		Double ovpt., one invtd.	5.00	3.00

Nos. 86 and 81 Surcharged in Black or Red

c

d

Perf. 12½ to 15½ and Compound

1892

100 A37 (c) 1c on 20c org (Bk) .40 .40
a. Inverted surcharge 6.00 6.00
101 A35 (d) 5c on 7c bis brn (R) .40 .40
a. Inverted surcharge 1.00 1.00
b. Double surcharge, one invtd. 3.00 3.00
c. Double surcharge 3.00 3.00
d. Vertical surcharge 10.00
e. "PREVISORIO" 3.00 3.00
f. "Cinco" omitted 4.50

No. 101 with surcharge in green is a color essay.

Several surcharge errors of date and misspelling of "Centésimos" exist. Value $15.

A45

A46

Arms
A47

Peace
A48

1892 **Engr.**

102 A45 1c green .50 .25
103 A46 2c rose .50 .25
104 A47 5c blue .50 .25
105 A48 10c orange 2.00 .85
Nos. 102-105 (4) 3.50 1.60

Issued: 1c, 2c, 3/9; 5c, 4/19; 10c, 12/15.

Liberty
A49

Arms
A50

1894, June 2

106 A49 2p carmine 30.00 17.50
107 A50 3p dull violet 30.00 17.50

Gaucho
A51

Solis Theater
A52

Locomotive
A53

Bull's Head
A54

Ceres — A55

Sailing Ship — A56

Liberty — A57

Mercury — A58

Coat of Arms — A59

Montevideo Fortress — A60

Cathedral in Montevideo
A61

Perf. 12 to 15½ and Compound

1895-99

108 A51 1c bister .50 .25
109 A51 1c slate bl ('97) .50 .25
a. Printed on both sides 14.00
110 A52 2c blue .50 .25
111 A52 2c claret ('97) .50 .25
112 A53 5c red .50 .25
113 A53 5c green ('97) .65 .25
a. Imperf., pair 3.50
114 A53 5c grnsh bl ('99) 1.00 .40
115 A54 7c deep green 7.75 2.50
116 A54 7c orange ('97) 3.50 1.25
117 A55 10c brown 2.00 .50
118 A56 20c green & blk 7.00 .85
119 A56 20c cl & blk ('97) 4.75 .60
120 A57 25c red brn & blk 5.50 1.50
a. Center inverted 2,000.
121 A57 25c pink & bl ('97) 3.50 .60
122 A58 50c blue & blk 7.00 3.50
123 A58 50c grn & brn ('97) 5.00 1.25
124 A59 1p org brn & blk 14.00 5.50
125 A59 1p yel brn & bl ('97) 9.50 3.50
126 A60 2p violet & grn 32.50 20.00
127 A60 2p bis & car ('97) 9.50 2.00
128 A61 3p carmine & blue 32.50 20.00
129 A61 3p lil & car ('97) 12.50 2.50
Nos. 108-129 (22) 160.65 67.95

All values of this issue exist imperforate but they were not issued in that form.

For overprints and surcharges see Nos. 138-140, 143, 145, 147, O62-O78.

President Joaquin Suárez
A62 A63

Statue of President Suárez — A64

Perf. 12½ to 15 and Compound

1896, July 18

130 A62 1c brown vio & blk .25 .25
131 A63 5c pale bl & blk .25 .25
132 A64 10c lake & blk 1.00 .30
Nos. 130-132 (3) 1.50 .80

Dedication of Pres. Suárez statue.

For overprints and surcharge see Nos. 133-135, 144, 146, 152, O79-O81.

Same Overprinted in Red

e

f

1897, Mar. 1

133 A62 (e) 1c brn vio & blk .40 .40
a. Inverted overprint 6.00 6.00
134 A63 (e) 5c pale blue & blk .50 .40
a. Inverted overprint 9.50 6.00
135 A64 (f) 10c lake & blk 1.00 .60
a. Inverted overprint 12.00 9.50
b. Double overprint 7.50
Nos. 133-135 (3) 1.90 1.40

"Electricity" — A68

1897-99 **Engr.**

136 A68 10c red 1.75 .40
137 A68 10c red lilac ('99) .75 .50

For overprints see Nos. 141, O82-O83.

Regular Issues Overprinted in Red or Blue

1897, Sept. 26

138 A51 1c slate bl (R) .80 .60
a. Inverted overprint 4.75 4.75
139 A52 2c claret (Bl) 1.25 1.25
a. Inverted overprint 4.75 4.75
140 A53 5c green (Bl) 1.75 1.60
a. Inverted overprint 7.75 7.75
b. Double overprint
141 A68 10c red (Bl) 2.75 2.75
a. Inverted overprint 17.00 17.00
Nos. 138-141 (4) 6.55 6.20

Commemorating the Restoration of Peace at the end of the Civil War.

Issue for use only on the days of the National Fête, Sept. 26-28, 1897.

Regular Issues Surcharged in Black, Blue or Red

1898, July 25

142 A32 ½c on 1c bl (Bk) .40 .40
a. Inverted surcharge 3.00 3.00
143 A51 ½c on 1c bis (Bl) .40 .40
a. Inverted surcharge 3.00
b. Double surcharge 2.50
144 A62 ½c on 1c brn vio & blk (R) .40 .40
145 A52 ½c on 2c blue (Bk) .40 .40
146 A63 ½c on 5c pale bl & blk (R) .40 .40
a. Double surcharge 6.25
147 A54 ½c on 7c dp grn (R) .40 .40
Nos. 142-147 (6) 2.40 2.40

The 2c red brown of 1894 (#77) was also surcharged like #142-147 but was not issued. Value $12.

Liberty — A69

1898-99 **Litho.** ***Perf. 11, 11½***

148 A69 5m rose .25 .25
149 A69 5m purple ('99) .25 .25

Statue of Artigas — A70

1899-1900 **Engr.** ***Perf. 12½, 14, 15***

150 A70 5m lt blue .25 .25
151 A70 5m orange ('00) .25 .25

No. 135 With Additional Surcharge in Black

1900, Dec. 1

152 A64 5c on 10c lake & blk .50 .25
a. Black bar covering "1897" omitted 15.00

Cattle — A72

Girl's Head — A73

Shepherdess — A74

Perf. 13½ to 16 and Compound

1900-10 **Engr.**

153 A72 1c yellow green .40 .25
154 A73 5c dull blue .80 .25
155 A73 5c slate grn ('10) .80 .25
156 A74 10c gray violet 1.00 .25
Nos. 153-156 (4) 3.00 1.00

For surcharges and overprints see Nos. 179, 184, O84, O86, O88, O106-O107.

Eros and Cornucopia
A75

Basket of Fruit
A76

1901, Feb. 11

157 A75 2c vermilion .50 .25
158 A76 7c brown orange 1.75 .25

For surcharges and overprints see Nos. 197-198, O85, O87, O105.

General Artigas — A78

Cattle — A79

Eros — A80

Cow — A81

Shepherdess
A82

Numeral
A83

Justice — A84

1904-05   Litho.   Perf. 11½
160 A78 5m orange   .40   .25
　a.   5m yellow   .40   .25
161 A79 1c green   .50   .25
162 A80 2c dp orange   .25   .25
　a.   2c orange red   .25   .25
　b.   Imperf., pair   3.00
163 A81 5c blue   .80   .25
　a.   Imperf., pair   3.50
164 A82 10c dk violet ('05)   .50   .25
165 A83 20c gray grn ('05)   2.50   .50
166 A84 25c olive bis ('05)   3.25   .25
　　Nos. 160-166 (7)   8.20 2.55

Design of No. 163 measures 17mm by 23mm. See No. 170.
For overprints see Nos. 167-169, O92-O98, O101-O103.

Overprinted Diagonally in Carmine or Black

1904, Oct. 15
167 A79 1c green (C)   .40   .40
168 A80 2c deep orange (Bk)   .65   .40
169 A81 5c dark blue (C)   1.25   .60
　　Nos. 167-169 (3)   2.30 1.40

End of the Civil War of 1904. In the first overprinting, "Paz 1904" appears at a 50-degree angle; in the second, at a 63-degree angle.

A85

1906, Feb. 23   Litho.   Unwmk.
170 A85 5c dark blue   1.10   .25
　a.   Imperf., pair   6.00

Design of No. 170 measures 19¼mm by 25½mm. See No. 163.

A86

1906-07
171 A86 5c deep blue   .30   .30
172 A86 7c orange brn ('07)   .70   .50
173 A86 50c rose   5.00 1.25
　　Nos. 171-173 (3)   6.00 2.05

Cruiser "Montevideo" — A87

1908, Aug. 23   Typo.   Rouletted 13
174 A87 1c car & dk grn   2.00 1.50
175 A87 2c green & dk grn   2.00 1.50
176 A87 5c org & dk grn   2.00 1.50
　　Nos. 174-176 (3)   6.00 4.50

Center Inverted
174a A87 1c   300.00 300.00
175a A87 2c   300.00 300.00
176a A87 5c   300.00 300.00
　　Nos. 174a-176a (3)   900.00 900.00

Imperf., Pairs
174b A87 1c   30.00
175b A87 2c   30.00
176b A87 5c   30.00

Independence of Uruguay, declared Aug. 25, 1825. Counterfeits exist.
For surcharges and overprints see Nos. 186, O99-O100, O104, O110.

View of the Port of Montevideo — A88

Wmk. 187
1909, Aug. 24   Engr.   Perf. 11½
177 A88 2c lt brown & blk   1.25 1.20
178 A88 5c rose red & blk   1.25 1.20

Issued to commemorate the opening of the Port of Montevideo, Aug. 25, 1909.

Nos. 156, 91 Surcharged

Perf. 14 to 16
1909, Sept. 13   Unwmk.
179 A74 8c on 10c dull vio   .75   .25
　a.   "Contesimos"   4.00 2.00
180 A38 23c on 25c bis brn   1.75   .60

Centaur — A89

Wmk. 187
1910, May 22   Engr.   Perf. 11½
182 A89 2c carmine red   .60   .40
183 A89 5c deep blue   .60   .40

Cent. of Liberation Day, May 25, 1810.
The 2c in deep blue and 5c in carmine red were prepared for collectors.

Stamps of 1900-06 Surcharged

g   h

i

Perf. 14 to 16, 11½
1910, Oct. 6   Unwmk.
Black Surcharge
184 A72 (g) 5m on 1c yel grn   .25   .25
　a.   Inverted surcharge   4.50 3.75
Dark Blue Surcharge
185 A39 (h) 5c on 50c dull
　　 red   .40   .25
　a.   Inverted surcharge   4.50 4.50
Blue Surcharge
186 A86 (i) 5c on 50c rose   .80   .45
　a.   Double surcharge   20.00
　b.   Inverted surcharge   10.00 8.75
　　Nos. 184-186 (3)   1.45   .95

Artigas   "Commercial
A90   Progress"
                 A91

1910, Nov. 21   Engr.   Perf. 14, 15
187 A90 5m dk violet   .25   .25
188 A90 1c dp green   .25   .25
189 A90 2c orange red   .25   .25
190 A90 5c dk blue   .25   .25
191 A90 8c gray blk   .40   .25
192 A90 20c brown   .60   .25
193 A91 23c dp ultra   2.75   .40
194 A91 50c orange   4.00 1.25
195 A91 1p scarlet   7.50 1.25
　　Nos. 187-195 (9)   16.25 4.40

See Nos. 199-210. For overprints see Nos. 211-213, O118-O124.

Symbolical of the Posts — A92

1911, Jan. 6   Wmk. 187   Perf. 11½
196 A92 5c rose car & blk   .80   .60

1st South American Postal Cong., at Montevideo, Jan. 1911.

No. 158 Surcharged in Red or Dark Blue

Perf. 14 to 16
1911, May 17   Unwmk.
197 A76 2c on 7c brn org (R)   .40   .40
198 A76 2c on 7c brn org (Bl)   .40   .25
　a.   Inverted surcharge   8.50 8.50

Centenary of the battle of Las Piedras, won by the forces under Gen. Jose Gervasio Artigas, May 8, 1811.

Types of 1910

FOUR AND FIVE CENTESIMOS:
Type I — Large numerals about 3mm high.
Type II — Small numerals about 2¼mm high.

1912-15   Typo.   Perf. 11½
199 A90 5m violet   .25   .25
　a.   5m purple   .25   .25
200 A90 5m magenta   .25   .25
　a.   5m dull rose   .25   .25
201 A90 1c green ('13)   .25   .25
202 A90 2c brown org   .25   .25
203 A90 2c rose red ('13)   .25   .25
　a.   2c deep red ('14)   .25   .25
204 A90 4c org (I) ('14)   .25   .25
　a.   4c orange (II) ('15)   .25   .25
　b.   4c yellow (II) ('13)   .25   .25
205 A90 5c dull bl (I)   .40   .25
　a.   5c blue (II)   .40   .25
206 A90 8c ultra ('13)   .50   .25
207 A90 20c brown ('13)   1.40   .25
　a.   20c chocolate   1.40   .25
208 A91 23c dk blue ('15)   3.50   .60
209 A91 50c orange ('14)   3.50 1.50
210 A91 1p vermilion ('15)   10.50 1.25
　　Nos. 199-210 (12)   21.30 5.60

Stamps of 1912-15 Overprinted

1913, Apr. 4
211 A90 2c brown orange   .85   .50
　a.   Inverted overprint   5.00 4.50

---

212 A90 4c yellow   .85   .50
213 A90 5c blue   .85   .50
　　Nos. 211-213 (3)   2.55 1.50
Cent. of the Buenos Aires Cong. of 1813.

Liberty Extending Peace to the Country — A93

1918, Jan. 3   Litho.
214 A93 2c green & red   .85   .50
215 A93 5c buff & blue   .85   .50

Promulgation of the Constitution.

Statue of Liberty, New York Harbor — A94

Perf. 14, 15, 13½
1919, July 15   Engr.
217 A94 2c carmine & brn   .55   .25
218 A94 4c orange & brn   .55   .25
219 A94 5c blue & brn   .80   .40
220 A94 8c org brn & ind   .80   .40
221 A94 20c ol bis & blk   2.00   .80
222 A94 23c green & blk   4.00 1.25
　　Nos. 217-222 (6)   8.70 3.35

Peace at end of World War I.
Perf 13½ used only on 2c, 20c, 23c.

Harbor of Montevideo — A95

1919-20   Litho.   Perf. 11½
225 A95 5m violet & blk   .25   .25
226 A95 1c green & blk   .25   .25
227 A95 2c red & blk   .25   .25
228 A95 4c orange & blk   .35   .25
229 A95 5c ultra & slate   .40   .25
230 A95 8c gray bl & lt brn   .50   .25
231 A95 20c brown & blk   1.60   .35
232 A95 23c green & brn   2.75   .65
233 A95 50c brown & blue   5.00 2.00
234 A95 1p dull red & bl   10.00 3.00
　　Nos. 225-234 (10)   21.35 7.50

For overprints see Nos. O125-O131.

José Enrique Rodó — A96

1920, Feb. 28   Engr.   Perf. 14, 15
235 A96 2c car & blk   .55   .40
236 A96 4c org & bl   .65   .50
237 A96 5c bl & brn   .75   .55
　　Nos. 235-237 (3)   1.95 1.45

Issued to honor José Enrique Rodó, author.
For surcharges see Nos. P2-P4.

Mercury — A97

1921-22   Litho.   Perf. 11½
238 A97 5m lilac   .25   .25
239 A97 5m gray blk ('22)   .25   .25
240 A97 1c lt grn   .25   .25
241 A97 1c vio ('22)   .25   .25

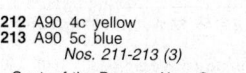

242	A97	2c fawn	.40	.25
243	A97	2c red ('22)	.40	.25
244	A97	3c bl grn ('22)	.60	.25
245	A97	4c orange	.40	.25
246	A97	5c ultra	.50	.25
247	A97	5c choc ('22)	.60	.25
248	A97	12c ultra ('22)	2.40	.60
249	A97	36c ol grn ('22)	7.75	2.75
		Nos. 238-249 (12)	14.05	5.85

See Nos. 254-260. For overprint and surcharge see Nos. E1, P1.

Dámaso A. Larrañaga (1771-1848), Bishop, Writer, Scientist and Physician — A98

1921, Dec. 10 **Unwmk.**

250	A98	5c slate	1.25	1.00

Mercury Type of 1921-22

1922-23 **Wmk. 188**

254	A97	5m gray blk	.25	.25
255	A97	1c violet ('23)	.25	.25
a.		1c red violet	.25	.25
256	A97	2c pale red	.25	.25
257	A97	2c deep rose ('23)	.30	.25
259	A97	5c yel brn ('23)	.65	.25
260	A97	8c salmon pink ('23)	1.00	.90
		Nos. 254-260 (6)	2.70	2.15

Equestrian Statue of Artigas — A99

Unwmk.

1923, Feb. 26 **Engr.** ***Perf. 14***

264	A99	2c car & sepia	.40	.25
265	A99	5c vio & sepia	.40	.25
266	A99	12c blue & sepia	.40	.25
		Nos. 264-266 (3)	1.20	.75

Southern Lapwing — A100

Perf. 12½, 11½x12½

1923, June 25 **Litho.** **Wmk. 189**

Size: 18x22½mm

267	A100	5m gray	.25	.25
268	A100	1c org yel	.25	.25
269	A100	2c lt vio	.25	.25
270	A100	3c gray grn	.40	.25
271	A100	5c lt bl	.40	.25
272	A100	8c rose red	.80	.50
273	A100	12c dp bl	.80	.50
274	A100	20c brn org	2.00	.50
275	A100	36c emerald	4.00	1.75
276	A100	50c orange	6.75	2.75
277	A100	1p brt rose	32.50	20.00
278	A100	2p lt grn	47.50	20.00
		Nos. 267-278 (12)	95.90	47.25

See #285-298, 309-314, 317-323, 334-339. For surcharges and overprints see Nos. 345-348, O132-O148, P5-P7.

Battle Monument A101

1923, Oct. 12 **Wmk. 188** ***Perf. 11½***

279	A101	2c dp grn	.55	.40
280	A101	5c scarlet	.55	.40
281	A101	12c dk bl	.55	.40
		Nos. 279-281 (3)	1.65	1.20

Unveiling of the Sarandi Battle Monument by José Luis Zorrilla, Oct. 12, 1923.

"Victory of Samothrace" — A102

Unwmk.

1924, July 29 **Typo.** ***Perf. 11***

282	A102	2c rose	20.00	10.00
283	A102	5c mauve	20.00	10.00
284	A102	12c brt bl	20.00	10.00
		Nos. 282-284 (3)	60.00	30.00

Olympic Games. Sheets of 20 (5x4).

Five hundred sets of these stamps were printed on yellow paper for presentation purposes. They were not on sale at post offices. Value for set, $650.

Lapwing Type of 1923
First Redrawing

Imprint: "A. BARREIRO Y RAMOS"

1924, July 26 **Litho.** ***Perf. 12½, 11½***

Size: 17¼x21½mm

285	A100	5m gray blk	.25	.25
286	A100	1c fawn	.25	.25
287	A100	2c rose lil	.30	.25
288	A100	3c gray grn	.25	.25
289	A100	5c chalky blue	.25	.25
290	A100	8c pink	.50	.25
291	A100	10c turq blue	.40	.25
292	A100	12c slate blue	.50	.25
293	A100	15c lt vio	.50	.25
294	A100	20c brown	.75	.30
295	A100	36c salmon	3.00	.70
296	A100	50c greenish gray	5.00	2.00
297	A100	1p buff	12.00	4.00
298	A100	2p dl vio	20.00	10.00
		Nos. 285-298 (14)	43.95	19.25

Landing of the 33 "Immortals" Led by Juan Antonio Lavalleja — A103

Perf. 11, 11½

1925, Apr. 19 **Wmk. 188**

300	A103	2c salmon pink & blk	1.40	.80
301	A103	5c lilac & blk	1.40	.80
302	A103	12c blue & blk	1.40	.80
		Nos. 300-302 (3)	4.20	2.40

Cent. of the landing of the 33 Founders of the Uruguayan Republic.

Legislative Palace — A104

Perf. 11½

1925, Aug. 24 **Unwmk.** **Engr.**

303	A104	5c vio & blk	1.25	.80
304	A104	12c bl & blk	1.25	.80

Dedication of the Legislative Palace.

General Fructuoso Rivera — A105

Wmk. 188

1925, Sept. 24 **Litho.** ***Perf. 11***

305	A105	5c light red	.50	.40

Centenary of Battle of Rincón. See No. C9.

Battle of Sarandí A106

1925, Oct. 12 ***Perf. 11½***

306	A106	2c bl grn	1.25	1.00
307	A106	5c dl vio	1.25	1.00
308	A106	12c dp bl	1.25	1.00
		Nos. 306-308 (3)	3.75	3.00

Centenary of the Battle of Sarandi.

Lapwing Type of 1923
Second Redrawing

Imprint: "Imprenta Nacional"

1925-26 ***Perf. 11, 11½, 10½***

Size: 17½x21¾mm

309	A100	5m gray blk	1.00	.25
310	A100	1c dl vio	1.25	.25
311	A100	2c brt rose	1.60	.25
312	A100	3c gray grn	1.25	.40
313	A100	5c dl bl ('26)	2.00	.25
314	A100	12c slate blue	4.00	.40
		Nos. 309-314 (6)	11.10	1.80

The design differs in many small details from that of the 1923-24 issues. These stamps may be readily identified by the imprint and perforation.

Lapwing Type of 1923
Third Redrawing

Imprint: "Imp. Nacional" at center

1926-27 ***Perf. 11, 11½, 10½***

Size: 17½x21¾mm

317	A100	5m gray	.40	.25
318	A100	1c lt vio ('27)	2.40	.55
319	A100	2c red	1.75	.40
320	A100	3c gray grn	2.40	.65
321	A100	5c lt bl	.75	.25
322	A100	8c pink ('27)	3.50	.80
323	A100	36c rose buff	8.00	4.00
		Nos. 317-323 (7)	19.20	6.90

These stamps may be distinguished from preceding stamps of the same design by the imprint.

Philatelic Exhibition Issue

Post Office at Montevideo A107

Unwmk.

1927, May 25 **Engr.** ***Imperf.***

330	A107	2c green	4.75	3.50
a.		Sheet of 4	20.00	20.00
331	A107	5c dull red	4.75	3.50
a.		Sheet of 4	20.00	20.00
332	A107	8c dark blue	4.75	3.50
a.		Sheet of 4	20.00	20.00
		Nos. 330-332 (3)	14.25	10.50

Printed in sheets of 4 and sold at the Montevideo Exhibition. Lithographed counterfeits exist.

Lapwing Type of 1923
Fourth Redrawing

Imprint: "Imp. Nacional" at right

Perf. 11, 11½

1927, May 6 **Litho.** **Wmk. 188**

Size: 17¾x21¾mm

334	A100	1c gray vio	.40	.25
335	A100	2c vermilion	.40	.25
336	A100	3c gray grn	.80	.35
337	A100	5c blue	.40	.25
338	A100	8c rose	3.00	.80
339	A100	20c gray brn	4.00	1.60
		Nos. 334-339 (6)	9.00	3.50

The design has been slightly retouched in various places. The imprint is in italic capitals and is placed below the right numeral of value.

No. 292 Surcharged in Red

1928, Jan. 13 **Unwmk.** ***Perf. 11½***

345	A100	2c on 12c slate blue	2.00	2.00
346	A100	5c on 12c slate blue	2.00	2.00
347	A100	10c on 12c slate blue	2.00	2.00
348	A100	15c on 12c slate blue	2.00	2.00
		Nos. 345-348 (4)	8.00	8.00

Issued to celebrate the inauguration of the railroad between San Carlos and Rocha.

General Rivera — A108

1928, Apr. 19 **Engr.** ***Perf. 12***

349	A108	5c car rose	.50	.35

Centenary of the Battle of Las Misiones.

Artigas (7 dots in panels below portrait.) — A109

Imprint: "Waterlow & Sons. Ltd., Londres"

Perf. 11, 12½, 13x13½, 12½x13, 13x12½

1928-43 **Size: 16x19½mm**

350	A109	5m black	.25	.25
350A	A109	5m org ('43)	.25	.25
351	A109	1c dk vio	.25	.25
352	A109	1c brn vio ('34)	.25	.25
352A	A109	1c vio bl ('43)	.25	.25
353	A109	2c dp grn	.25	.25
353A	A109	2c brn red ('43)	.25	.25
354	A109	3c bister	.25	.25
355	A109	3c dp grn ('32)	.25	.25
355A	A109	3c brt grn ('43)	.25	.25
356	A109	5c red	.25	.25
357	A109	5c ol grn ('33)	.25	.25
357A	A109	5c dl pur ('43)	.25	.25
358	A109	7c car ('32)	.25	.25
359	A109	8c dk bl	.25	.25
360	A109	8c brn ('33)	.25	.25
361	A109	10c orange	.25	.25
362	A109	10c red org ('32)	.60	.40
363	A109	12c dp bl ('32)	.40	.25
364	A109	15c dl bl	.40	.25
365	A109	17c dk vio ('32)	.80	.25
366	A109	20c ol brn	.65	.25
367	A109	20c red brn ('33)	1.25	.50
368	A109	24c car rose	.90	.35
369	A109	24c yel ('33)	.80	.40
370	A109	36c ol grn ('33)	1.40	.50
371	A109	50c gray	2.40	1.25
372	A109	50c blk ('33)	3.50	1.60
373	A109	50c blk brn ('33)	3.00	1.25
374	A109	1p yel grn	7.00	4.00
		Nos. 350-374 (30)	27.35	15.50

1929-33 ***Perf. 12½***

Size: 22 to 22½x28½ to 29½mm

375	A109	1p ol brn ('33)	6.00	4.00
376	A109	2p dk grn	17.00	9.00
377	A109	2p dl red ('32)	20.00	16.00
378	A109	3p dk bl	25.00	17.00
379	A109	3p blk ('32)	23.00	20.00
380	A109	4p violet	28.00	17.00
381	A109	4p dk ol grn ('32)	23.00	20.00
382	A109	5p car brn	32.50	23.00
383	A109	5p red org ('32)	30.00	20.00
384	A109	10p lake ('33)	92.50	70.00
385	A109	10p dp ultra ('33)	92.50	70.00
		Nos. 375-385 (11)	389.50	286.00

See Nos. 420-423, 462. See type A135.

Equestrian Statue of Artigas — A110

1928, May 1

386	A110	2p Prus bl & choc	16.00	7.75
387	A110	3p dp rose & blk	23.00	12.00

Symbolical of Soccer Victory — A111

1928, July 29

388	A111	2c brn vio	16.00	9.25
389	A111	5c dp red	16.00	9.25
390	A111	8c ultra	16.00	9.25
		Nos. 388-390 (3)	48.00	27.75

Uruguayan soccer victories in the Olympic Games of 1924 and 1928. Printed in sheets of 20, in panes of 10 (5x2).

Gen. Eugenio Garzón — A112

1928, Aug. 25 *Imperf.*

391	A112	2c red	1.40	1.40
a.		Sheet of 4	6.50	6.50
392	A112	5c yel grn	1.40	1.40
a.		Sheet of 4	6.50	6.50
393	A112	8c dp bl	1.40	1.40
a.		Sheet of 4	6.50	6.50
		Nos. 391-393 (3)	4.20	4.20

Dedication of monument to Garzon. Issued in sheets of 4. Lithographed counterfeits exist.

Black River Bridge A113

Gauchos Breaking a Horse — A114

Peace A115

Montevideo A116

Liberty and Flag of Uruguay A117

Liberty with Torch and Caduceus A118

Statue of Artigas A124

Artigas Dictating Instructions for 1813 Congress A119

Seascape A120

Montevideo Harbor, 1830 — A121

Liberty and Coat of Arms A122

Montevideo Harbor, 1930 — A123

1930, June 16 *Perf. 12½, 12*

394	A113	5m gray blk	.25	.25
395	A114	1c dk brn	.25	.25
396	A115	2c brn rose	.25	.25
397	A116	3c yel grn	.25	.25
398	A117	5c dk bl	.25	.25
399	A118	8c dl red	.35	.25
400	A119	10c dk vio	.50	.35
401	A120	15c bl grn	.65	.50
402	A121	20c indigo	.80	.65
403	A122	24c red brn	1.10	.80
404	A123	50c org red	3.00	2.00
405	A124	1p black	6.00	3.00
406	A124	2p bl vio	14.00	8.50
407	A124	3p dk red	20.00	14.00
408	A124	4p red org	23.00	19.00
409	A124	5p lilac	35.00	22.50
		Nos. 394-409 (16)	105.65	72.80

Cent. of natl. independence and the promulgation of the constitution.

Type of 1856 Issue
Values in Centesimos
Wmk. 227

1931, Apr. 11 **Litho.** *Imperf.*

410	A1	2c gray blue	3.00	2.00
a.		Sheet of 4	15.00	15.00
411	A1	8c dull red	3.00	2.00
a.		Sheet of 4	15.00	15.00
412	A1	15c blue black	3.00	2.00
a.		Sheet of 4	15.00	15.00

Wmk. 188

413	A1	5c light green	3.00	2.00
a.		Sheet of 4	15.00	15.00
		Nos. 410-413 (4)	12.00	8.00

Sold only at the Philatelic Exhibition, Montevideo, Apr. 11-15, 1931. Issued in sheets of 4.

Juan Zorrilla de San Martin, Uruguayan Poet — A125

1932, June 6 **Unwmk.** *Perf. 12½*

414	A125	1½c brown violet	.25	.25
415	A125	3c green	.25	.25
416	A125	7c dk blue	.25	.25
417	A125	12c lt blue	.40	.25
418	A125	1p deep brown	20.00	13.00
		Nos. 414-418 (5)	21.15	14.00

Semi-Postal Stamp No. B2 Surcharged

1932, Nov. 1 *Perf. 12*

419	SP1	1½c on 2c + 2c dp grn	.35	.35

Artigas Type of 1928
Imprint: "Imprenta Nacional" at center

1932-35 **Litho.** *Perf. 11, 12½*
Size: 15¾x19¼mm

420	A109	5m lt brown ('35)	.25	.25
421	A109	1c pale violet ('35)	.25	.25
422	A109	15m black	.25	.25
423	A109	5c bluish grn ('35)	.50	.25
		Nos. 420-423 (4)	1.25	1.00

Gen. J. A. Lavalleja — A126

1933, July 12 **Engr.** *Perf. 12½*

429	A126	15m brown lake	.25	.25

Flag of the Race and Globe — A127

Perf. 11, 11½, 11x11½

1933, Aug. 3 **Litho.**

430	A127	3c blue green	.50	.25
431	A127	5c rose	.50	.25
432	A127	7c lt blue	.50	.25
433	A127	8c dull red	1.00	.55
434	A127	12c deep blue	.65	.25
435	A127	17c violet	1.75	.80
436	A127	20c red brown	3.50	1.60
437	A127	24c yellow	3.50	1.75
438	A127	36c orange	5.00	2.40
439	A127	50c olive gray	5.50	3.00
440	A127	1p bister	13.00	6.25
		Nos. 430-440 (11)	35.40	17.35

Raising of the "Flag of the Race" and of the 441st anniv. of the sailing of Columbus from Palos, Spain, on his first voyage to America.

Sower — A128

1933, Aug. 28 **Unwmk.** *Perf. 11½*

441	A128	3c blue green	.25	.25
442	A128	5c dull violet	.40	.25
443	A128	7c lt blue	.40	.25
444	A128	8c deep red	.80	.50
445	A128	12c ultra	2.00	1.00
		Nos. 441-445 (5)	3.85	2.25

3rd Constituent National Assembly.

Juan Zorrilla de San Martin — A129

1933, Nov. 9 **Engr.** *Perf. 12½*

446	A129	7c slate	.25	.25

Albatross Flying over Map of the Americas — A130

1933, Dec. 3 **Typo.** *Perf. 11½*

447	A130	3c green, blk & brn	2.75	2.00
448	A130	7c turq bl, brn & blk	1.60	.80
449	A130	12c dk bl, gray & ver	2.40	1.60
450	A130	17c ver, gray & vio	5.00	2.75
451	A130	20c yellow, bl & grn	6.00	3.50
452	A130	36c red, blk & yel	7.75	5.50
		Nos. 447-452 (6)	25.50	16.15

7th Pan-American Conf., Montevideo. Issued in sheets of 6. Value $200. For overprints see Nos. C61-C62.

General Rivera — A131

1934, Feb. **Engr.** *Perf. 12½*

453	A131	3c green	.25	.25

Stars Representing the Three Constitutions — A132

1934, Mar. 23 **Typo.**

454	A132	3c yellow grn & grn	.60	.40
455	A132	7c org red & red	.60	.40
456	A132	12c ultra & blue	2.00	.80

Perf. 11½

457	A132	17c brown & rose	2.50	1.25
458	A132	20c yellow & gray	3.50	1.60
459	A132	36c dk vio & bl grn	3.50	1.60
460	A132	50c black & blue	7.00	3.25
461	A132	1p dk car & vio	16.00	6.75
		Nos. 454-461 (8)	35.70	16.05

First Year of Third Republic.

Artigas Type of 1928
Imprint: "Barreiro & Ramos S. A."

1934, Nov. 28 **Litho.**

462	A109	50c brown black	6.00	2.50

"Uruguay" and "Brazil" Holding Scales of Justice — A133

1935, May 30 **Unwmk.** *Perf. 11*

463	A133	5m brown	.80	.40
464	A133	15m black	.40	.25
465	A133	3c green	.40	.25
466	A133	7c orange	.40	.25
467	A133	12c ultra	.80	.60
468	A133	50c brown	4.00	2.50
		Nos. 463-468 (6)	6.80	4.25

Visit of President Vargas of Brazil.

Florencio Sánchez — A134

1935, Nov. 7

469	A134	3c green	.25 .25
470	A134	7c brown	.25 .25
471	A134	12c blue	.55 .35
	Nos. 469-471 (3)		1.05 .85

Florencio Sanchez (1875-1910), author.

Artigas (6 dots in panels below portrait) — A135

Imprint: "Imprenta Nacional" at center

1936-44   *Perf. 11, 12½*

474	A135	5m org brn ('37)	.25 .25
475	A135	5m lt brown ('39)	.25 .25
476	A135	1c lt violet ('37)	.25 .25
477	A135	2c dk brown ('37)	.25 .25
478	A135	2c green ('39)	.25 .25
479	A135	5c brt blue ('37)	.25 .25
480	A135	5c bluish grn ('39)	.40 .25
481	A135	12c dull blue ('38)	.40 .25
482	A135	20c fawn	1.40 .35
482A	A135	20c rose ('44)	1.00 .40
483	A135	50c brown black	3.00 .80

Size: 21½x28½mm

483A	A135	1p brown	8.50 3.00
483B	A135	2p blue	14.00 12.00
483C	A135	3p gray black	20.00 16.00
	Nos. 474-483C (14)		50.20 34.55

See Nos. 488, and 576. See type A109.

Power Dam on Black River — A136

1937-38

484	A136	1c dull violet	.25 .25
485	A136	10c blue	.50 .25
486	A136	15c rose	1.25 .65
487	A136	1p choc ('38)	6.25 2.50
	Nos. 484-487 (4)		8.25 3.65

Imprint: "Imprenta Nacional" at right

1938

488	A135	1c bright violet	.40 .25

International Law Congress, 1889 — A137

1939, July 16   Litho.   *Perf. 12½*

489	A137	1c brown orange	.25 .25
490	A137	2c dull green	.25 .25
491	A137	5c rose ver	.25 .25
492	A137	12c dull blue	.65 .40
493	A137	50c lt violet	2.50 1.50
	Nos. 489-493 (5)		3.90 2.65

50th anniversary of the Montevideo Congress of International Law.

Artigas — A138

1939-43   Litho.   Unwmk.
Size: 15¾x19mm

494	A138	5m dl brn org ('40)	.25 .25
495	A138	1c lt blue	.25 .25
496	A138	2c lt violet	.25 .25
497	A138	5c violet brn	.25 .25
498	A138	8c rose red	.25 .25
499	A138	10c green	.50 .25
500	A138	15c dull blue	1.25 .60

Size: 24x29½mm

501	A138	1p dull brn ('41)	2.50 1.00
502	A138	2p dl rose vio ('40)	7.00 3.00
503	A138	4p orange ('43)	9.25 4.00
504	A138	5p ver ('41)	14.00 6.00
	Nos. 494-504 (11)		35.75 16.10

See No. 578.

Artigas —A138a

Redrawn: Horizontal lines in portrait background

1940-44   Size: 17x21mm

505	A138a	5m brn org ('41)	.25 .25
506	A138a	1c lt blue	.25 .25
507	A138a	2c lt violet ('41)	.25 .25
508	A138a	5c violet brn	.25 .25
509	A138a	8c sal pink ('44)	.25 .25
510	A138a	10c green ('41)	.25 .25
511	A138a	50c olive bis ('42)	6.25 1.75
511A	A138a	50c yel grn ('44)	4.75 1.75
	Nos. 505-511A (8)		12.65 5.00

See Nos. 568-575, 577, 601, 632, 660-661. For surcharges see Nos. 523, 726.

Juan Manuel Blanes, Artist — A139

1941, Aug. 11   Engr.   *Perf. 12½*

512	A139	5m ocher	.25 .25
513	A139	1c henna brown	.25 .25
514	A139	2c green	.25 .25
515	A139	5c rose carmine	.60 .25
516	A139	12c deep blue	1.25 .60
517	A139	50c dark violet	4.75 3.25
	Nos. 512-517 (6)		7.35 4.85

Francisco Acuna de Figueroa — A140

1942, Mar. 18   Unwmk.

518	A140	1c henna brown	.25 .25
519	A140	2c deep green	.25 .25
520	A140	5c rose carmine	.25 .25
521	A140	12c deep blue	1.00 .40
522	A140	50c dark violet	3.25 2.50
	Nos. 518-522 (5)		5.00 3.65

Issued in honor of Francisco Acuna de Figueroa, author of the National anthem.

No. 506 Surcharged in Red

1943, Jan. 27

523	A138a	5m on 1c lt bl	.25 .25

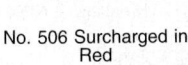

Coat of Arms — A141

1943, Mar. 12   Litho.

524	A141	1c on 2c dl vio brn (R)	.25 .25
525	A141	2c on 2c dl vio brn (V)	.25 .25
a.	Inverted surcharge		20.00 20.00

Nos. 524-525 are unissued stamps surcharged. See Nos. 546-555, Q67, Q69, Q74-Q76.

Clio — A142

Artigas —A138a

1943, Aug. 24

526	A142	5m lt violet	.25 .25
527	A142	1c lt ultra	.25 .25
528	A142	2c brt rose	.50 .25
529	A142	5c buff	.50 .25
	Nos. 526-529 (4)		1.50 1.00

100th anniversary of the Historic and Geographic Institute of Uruguay.

Swiss Colony Monument — A143

Overprinted and Surcharged in Various Colors

1944, May 18   *Perf. 11, 12½*

530	A143	1c on 3c dull grn (R)	.25 .25
531	A143	5c on 7c brn red (B)	.25 .25
532	A143	10c on 12c dk bl (Br)	.65 .25
	Nos. 530-532 (3)		1.15 .75

Founding of the Swiss Colony, 50th anniv. Nos. 530-532 are unissued stamps surcharged.

YMCA Seal — A144

1944, Sept. 8   *Perf. 12½*

533	A144	5c blue	.25 .25

100th anniv. of the YMCA.

> **Catalogue values for unused stamps in this section, from this point to the end of the section, are for Never Hinged items.**

"La Educación del Pueblo" A145

José Pedro Varela A146

A147

Monument A148

Perf. 11½
1945, June 13   Litho.   Unwmk.

534	A145	5m brt green	.25 .25
535	A146	1c dp brown	.25 .25

Perf. 12½

536	A147	2c rose red	.25 .25
537	A148	5c blue	.25 .25
a.	Perf. 11½		1.00 1.00
	Nos. 534-537 (4)		1.00 1.00

José Pedro Varela, author, birth cent.

Santiago Vazquez A149

Silvestre Blanco A150

Eduardo Acevedo A151

Bruno Mauricio de Zabala A152

Bruno Mauricio de Zabala A152

José Pedro Varela — A153

José Ellauri — A154

Gen. Luis de Larrobla — A155

Engraved (5m, 5c, 10c); Lithographed

1945-47   *Perf. 10½, 11, 11½, 12½*

538	A149	5m purple ('46)	.25 .25
539	A150	1c yel brn ('46)	.25 .25
540	A151	2c brown vio	.25 .25
541	A152	3c grn & dp grn ('47)	.25 .25
542	A153	5c brt carmine	.25 .25
543	A154	10c ultra	.40 .25
544	A155	20c dp grn & choc ('47)	1.25 .50
	Nos. 538-544 (7)		2.90 2.00

No. C86A Surcharged in Blue

1946, Jan. 9   *Perf. 12½*

545	AP7	20c on 68c pale vio brn	1.25 .60

Inauguration of the Black River Power Dam. See No. C120.

Type A141 Overprinted

1946-51   Unwmk.   Litho.   *Perf. 12½*

546	A141	5m orange ('49)	.25 .25
a.	Inverted overprint		
547	A141	2c dl vio brn ('47)	.25 .25
548	A141	3c green	.25 .25
549	A141	5c ultra ('51)	.25 .25
550	A141	10c orange brn	.35 .25
551	A141	20c dk green	.65 .25
552	A141	50c brown	2.00 1.00
553	A141	3p lilac rose	7.00 4.50
	Nos. 546-553 (8)		11.00 7.00

Type A141 Surcharged

1947-48

554	A141	2c on 5c ultra ('48)	.25 .25
555	A141	3c on 5c ultra	.25 .25

Statue of Ariel — A158

Bust of José Enrique Rodó — A159

Bas-relief A160

Bas-relief A161

Perf. 12½
1948, Jan. 30   Unwmk.   Engr.
Center in Orange Brown

556	A158	1c grnsh gray	.25	.25
557	A159	2c purple	.25	.25
558	A160	3c green	.25	.25
559	A161	5c red violet	.25	.25
560	A160	10c dp orange	.35	.25
561	A161	12c ultra	.40	.25
562	A158	20c rose violet	.80	.25
563	A159	50c dp carmine	2.50	.90
		Nos. 556-563 (8)	5.05	2.65

Dedication of the Rodó monument.

View of the Port, Paysandú — A162

Arms of Paysandú A163

1948, Oct. 9   Litho.

564	A162	3c blue green	.25	.25
565	A163	7c ultra	.40	.25

Exposition of Industry and Agriculture, Paysandú, October-November 1948.

Santa Lucia River Highway Bridge A164

1948, Dec. 10

566	A164	10c dark blue	.80	.25
567	A164	50c green	2.50	1.00

Redrawn Artigas Types of 1940, 1936, 1939

1948-51   Litho.   Perf. 12½

568	A138a	5m gray ('49)	.25	.25
569	A138a	1c rose vio ('50)	.25	.25
570	A138a	2c orange	.25	.25
571	A138a	2c choc ('50)	.25	.25
572	A138a	3c blue green	.25	.25
572A	A138a	7c violet blue	.25	.25
573	A138a	8c rose car ('49)	.25	.25
574	A138a	10c orange brn ('51)	.25	.25
575	A138a	12c blue ('51)	.25	.25
576	A135	20c violet	.30	.25
577	A138a	20c rose pink ('51)	.55	.25

Size: 18x21¾mm

578	A138	1p lilac rose ('51)	1.10	.25
		Nos. 568-578 (12)	4.20	3.00

Nos. 571-572A also exist perf. 11.

Plowing A165

Mounted Cattle Herder A166

1949, Apr. 29   Unwmk.   Perf. 12½

579	A165	3c green	.25	.25
580	A166	7c blue	.40	.25

4th Regional American Conf. of Labor, 1949.

Cannon, Rural and Urban Views — A167

1950, Oct. 11   Litho.

581	A167	1c lilac rose	.25	.25
582	A167	3c green	.25	.25
583	A167	7c deep blue	.25	.25
		Nos. 581-583 (3)	.75	.75

200th anniv. of the founding of Cordón, a district of Montevideo.

Symbolical of Soccer Matches — A168

1951, Mar. 20   Perf. 12½, 11

584	A168	3c green	1.00	.25
585	A168	7c violet blue	2.25	.80

4th World Soccer Championship, Rio de Janeiro.

Gen. José Artigas — A169

Flight of the People A170

1c, 2c, 5c, Various equestrian portraits of Artigas. 7c, Dictating instructions. 8c, In congress. 10c, Artigas' flag. 14c, At the citadel. 20c, Arms of Artigas. 50c, In Paraguay. 1p, Bust.

Engraved and Photogravure
1952, Jan. 7   Unwmk.   Perf. 13½

586	A169	5m slate	.25	.25
587	A169	1c bl & blk	.25	.25
588	A169	2c pur & red brn	.25	.25
589	A170	3c aqua & dk brn	.25	.25
590	A169	5c red org & blk	.25	.25

591	A170	7c ol & blk	.30	.25
592	A170	8c car & blk	.40	.25
593	A170	10c choc, brt ultra & crim	.40	.25
594	A169	14c dp bl	.40	.25
595	A169	20c org yel, dp ultra & car	.90	.25
596	A169	50c org brn & blk	1.75	.40
597	A169	1p bl gray & cit	3.25	1.25
		Nos. 586-597 (12)	8.65	4.15

Centenary (in 1950) of the death of Gen. José Artigas.

Plane and Stagecoach A171

1952, Oct. 9   Photo.   Perf. 13½x13

598	A171	3c bl grn	.25	.25
599	A171	7c blk brn	.25	.25
600	A171	12c ultra	.30	.25
		Nos. 598-600 (3)	.80	.75

75th anniv. (in 1949) of the UPU.

Redrawn Artigas Type of 1940-44
1953, Feb. 23   Litho.   Perf. 11
Size: 24x29½mm

601	A138a	2p fawn	11.00	8.50

Franklin D. Roosevelt — A172

1953, Apr. 9   Engr.   Perf. 13½

602	A172	3c green	.25	.25
603	A172	7c ultra	.25	.25
604	A172	12c blk brn	.40	.25
		Nos. 602-604 (3)	.90	.75

5th Postal Cong. of the Americas & Spain.

Ceibo, Natl. Flower — A173

Horse Breaking — A174

Legislature Building A175

"Island of Seals" (Southern Sea Lions) — A176

Designs: 2c, 10c, 5p, Ombu tree. 3c, 50c, Passion Flower. 7c, 3p, Montevideo fortress. 12c, 2p, Outer gate, Montevideo.

Perf. 13x13½, 13½x13, 12½x13, 13x12½
Photo. (5m, 3c, 20c, 50c); Engr.
1954, Jan. 14   Unwmk.

605	A173	5m multi	.25	.25
606	A174	1c car & blk	.25	.25
607	A174	2c brn & grn	.25	.25
608	A173	3c multi	.25	.25
609	A175	5c pur & red brn	.25	.25
610	A173	7c brn & grn	.25	.25

611	A176	8c car & ultra	.50	.25
612	A174	10c org & grn	.40	.25
613	A175	12c dp ultra & dk brn	.30	.25
614	A174	14c rose lil & blk	.30	.25
615	A173	20c grn, brn, gray & car	.95	.25
616	A173	50c car & multi	2.40	.25
617	A175	1p car & red brn	2.75	1.00
618	A175	2p car & blk brn	4.75	1.60
619	A173	3p lil & grn	5.50	2.00
620	A176	4p dp brn & dp ultra	16.00	5.00
621	A174	5p vio bl & grn	12.00	4.00
		Nos. 605-621 (17)	47.35	16.60

For surcharges see Nos. 637-639, 750, C299.

Fair Entrance — A177

1956, Jan. 19   Litho.   Perf. 11

622	A177	3c pale olive green	.25	.25
623	A177	7c blue	.25	.25
		Nos. 622-623,C166-C168 (5)	3.00	1.60

First Exposition of National Products.

José Batlle y Ordonez, Birth Centenary A178

Design: 7c, Full length portrait.

Perf. 13½
1956, Dec. 15   Wmk. 90   Photo.

624	A178	3c rose red	.25	.25
625	A178	7c sepia	.25	.25
		Nos. 624-625,C169-C172 (6)	3.10	1.90

No. 624 Surcharged

No. 625 Surcharged

1957-58

626	A178	5c on 3c ('58)	.25	.25
627	A178	10c on 7c	.25	.25
a.		Surcharge inverted	25.00	25.00

Diver — A179

Design: 10c, Swimmer at start, horiz.

Perf. 10½, 11½

1958, Feb. 15   Litho.   Unwmk.
628 A179   5c brt bl grn   .25   .25
629 A179   10c brt bl   .35   .25

14th South American swimming meet, Montevideo.

Eduardo Acevedo — A180

1958, Mar. 19   Perf. 11½, 10½
630 A180   5c lt ol grn & blk   .25   .25
631 A180   10c ultra & blk   .25   .25

Eduardo Acevedo (1856-1948), lawyer, legislator, minister of foreign affairs, birth cent.

Redrawn Artigas Type of 1940-44
1958, Sept. 25   Litho.   Perf. 11
632 A138a 5m blue   .25   .25

Baygorria Hydroelectric Works — A181

1958, Oct. 30   Unwmk.   Perf. 11
633 A181   5c yel grn & blk   .25   .25
634 A181   10c brn org & blk   .25   .25
635 A181   1p bl gray & blk   1.25   .25
636 A181   2p rose & blk   2.50   .55
     Nos. 633-636 (4)   4.25 1.30

Nos. 608, 610 and 605 Surcharged Similarly to

Photogravure and Engraved
1958-59   Perf. 13x13½
637 A173   5c on 3c multi ('59)   .30   .25
638 A173   10c on 7c brn & grn   .30   .25
639 A173   20c on 5m multi   .30   .25
     Nos. 637-639 (3)   .90   .75

Gabriela Mistral — A182

Wmk. 327
1959, July 6   Litho.   Perf. 11½
640 A182   5c green   .25   .25
641 A182   10c dark blue   .30   .25
642 A182   20c red   .40   .25
     Nos. 640-642 (3)   .95   .75

Gabriela Mistral, Chilean poet and educator.

Carlos Vaz Ferreira — A183

1959, Sept. 3   Perf. 11
643 A183   5c blk & lt bl   .25   .25
644 A183   10c blk & ocher   .25   .25
645 A183   20c blk & ver   .25   .25
646 A183   50c blk & vio   .35   .25
647 A183   1p blk & grn   .55   .25
     Nos. 643-647 (5)   1.65 1.25

Ferreira (1872-1958), educator and author.

A184

Wmk. 332
1960, May 16   Litho.   Perf. 12
648 A184   3c red lil & blk   .25   .25
649 A184   5c dp vio & blk   .25   .25
650 A184   10c brt bl & blk   .25   .25
651 A184   20c chocolate & blk   .30   .25
652 A184   1p gray & blk   .45   .25
653 A184   2p org & blk   1.10   .25
654 A184   3p olive grn & blk   1.75   .40
655 A184   4p yel brn & blk   2.25   .75
656 A184   5p brt red & blk   2.75   .75
     Nos. 648-656 (9)   9.35 3.40

Dr. Martin C. Martinez (1859-1940), statesman.

A185

1960, June 6   Wmk. 332   Perf. 12
657 A185   10c Uprooted oak emblem   .25   .25

Issued to publicize World Refugee Year, July 1, 1959-June 30, 1960. See No. C207.

Revolutionists and Cabildo, Buenos Aires — A186

1960, Nov. 4   Litho.   Perf. 12
658 A186   5c bl & blk   .25   .25
659 A186   10c bl & ocher   .25   .25
     Nos. 658-659,C208-C210 (5)   1.50 1.25

150th anniv. of the May Revolution of 1810.

Redrawn Artigas Type of 1940-44
1960-61   Wmk. 332   Perf. 11
660 A138a 2c gray   .25   .25
661 A138a 50c brn ('61)   .25   .25

Gen. Manuel Oribe (1796?-1857), Revolutionary Leader, Pres. of Uruguay (1835-38) — A187

1961, Mar. 4   Litho.   Perf. 12
671 A187   10c brt bl & blk   .25   .25
672 A187   20c bis & blk   .30   .25
673 A187   40c grn & blk   .30   .25
     Nos. 671-673 (3)   .85   .75

Cavalry Charge A188

1961, June 12   Wmk. 332   Perf. 12
674 A188   20c bl & blk   .25   .25
675 A188   40c emer & blk   .40   .25

150th anniversary of the revolution.

Welfare, Justice and Education A189

1961, Aug. 14   Wmk. 322   Perf. 12
676 A189   2c bister & lilac   .40   .25
677 A189   5c bister & orange   .40   .25
678 A189   10c bister & scarlet   .40   .25
679 A189   20c bister & yel grn   .40   .25
680 A189   50c bister & light vio .40   .25
681 A189   1p bister & blue   .40   .25
682 A189   2p bister & citron   1.10   .25
683 A189   3p bister & gray   1.50   .65
684 A189   4p bister & light bl 2.50   .80
685 A189   5p bister & chocolate 2.75 1.25
     Nos. 676-685 (10)   10.25 4.45

Inter-American Economic and Social Conference of the Organization of American States, Punta del Este, August, 1961. See Nos. C233-C244.

Gen. José Fructuoso Rivera — A190

Wmk. 332
1962, May 29   Litho.   Perf. 12
686 A190   10c brt red & blk   .25   .25
687 A190   20c bis & blk   .25   .25
688 A190   40c grn & blk   .25   .25
     Nos. 686-688 (3)   .75   .75

Issued to honor Gen. José Fructuoso Rivera (1790-1854), first President of Uruguay.

Spade, Grain, Swiss "Scarf" and Hat — A191

1962, Aug. 1   Wmk. 332   Perf. 12
689 A191   10c bl, blk & car   .25   .25
690 A191   20c lt grn, blk & car .25   .25
     Nos. 689-690,C245-C246 (4)   1.30 1.10

Swiss Settlement in Uruguay, cent.

Bernardo Prudencio Berro — A192

1962, Oct. 22   Litho.   Perf. 12
691 A192   10c grnsh bl & blk   .25   .25
692 A192   20c yel brn & blk   .25   .25

Pres. Bernardo P. Berro (1803-1868).

Damaso Larrañaga A193

1963, Jan. 24   Wmk. 332   Perf. 12
693 A193   20c lt bl grn & dk brn .25   .25
694 A193   40c tan & dk brn   .25   .25

Damaso Antonio Larranaga (1771-1848), teacher, writer and founder of National Library.

Rufous-bellied Thrush — A194

Birds: 50c, Rufous ovenbird. 1p, Chalk-browed mockingbird. 2p, Rufous-collared sparrow.

1963, Apr. 1   Wmk. 332   Perf. 12
695 A194   2c rose, brn & blk   .25   .25
696 A194   50c lt brn & blk   .85   .25
697 A194   1p tan, brn & blk   2.10   .25
698 A194   2p lt brn, blk & gray 4.00   .80
     Nos. 695-698 (4)   7.20 1.55

Thin frame on No. 696, no frame on No. 698.

UPAE Emblem A195

1963, May 31   Litho.
699 A195   20c ultra & blk   .50   .25
     Nos. 699,C252-C253 (3)   1.15   .75

50th anniv. of the founding of the Postal Union of the Americas and Spain, UPAE. For surcharge see No. C321.

Wheat Emblem — A196

1963, July 8   Wmk. 332   Perf. 12
700 A196   10c grn & yel   .25   .25
701 A196   20c brn & yel   .30   .25
     Nos. 700-701,C254-C255 (4)   1.30 1.25

FAO "Freedom from Hunger" campaign.

Anchors — A197

1963, Aug. 16
702 A197 10c org & vio .25 .25
703 A197 20c dk red & gray .30 .25
　Nos. 702-703,C256-C257 (4) 1.55 1.20

Voyage around the world by the Uruguayan sailing vessel "Alferez Campora," 1960-63.

Large Intestine, Congress Emblem A198

1963, Dec. 9 Litho.
704 A198 10c lt grn, blk & dk car .25 .25
705 A198 20c org, yel, blk & dk car .30 .25

1st Uruguayan Proctology Cong., Montevideo, Dec. 9-15.

Red Cross Centenary Emblem A199

Imprint: "Imp. Nacional"

1964, June 5 Wmk. 332 Perf. 12
706 A199 20c blue & red .25 .25
707 A199 40c gray & red .25 .25

Centenary of International Red Cross. No. 706 exists with imprint missing. Value $4.

Luis Alberto de Herrera A200

1964, July 22 Litho. Unwmk.
708 A200 20c dl grn, bl & blk .25 .25
709 A200 40c lt bl, bl & blk .25 .25
710 A200 80c yel org, bl & blk .25 .25
711 A200 1p lt vio, bl & blk .45 .25
712 A200 2p gray, bl & blk .65 .50
　Nos. 708-712 (5) 1.85 1.50

Herrera (1873-1959), leader of Herrerista party and member of National Government Council.

Nile Gods Uniting Upper and Lower Egypt (Abu Simbel) A201

1964, Oct. 30 Wmk. 332 Perf. 12
713 A201 20c multi .25 .25
　Nos. 713,C266-C267 (3) 1.80 1.00

UNESCO world campaign to save historic monuments in Nubia. See No. C267a.

Pres. John F. Kennedy A202

1965, Mar. 5 Wmk. 327 Perf. 11½
714 A202 20c gold, emer & blk .25 .25
　a.　Gold omitted
715 A202 40c gold, redsh brn & blk .30 .25
　a.　Gold omitted
　Nos. 714-715,C269-C270 (4) 1.55 1.50

Tete Beche Pair of 1864, No. 21a A203

1965, Mar. 19 Wmk. 332 Perf. 12
716 A203 40c black & green .25 .25

1st Rio de la Plata Stamp Show, sponsored jointly by the Argentine and Uruguayan philatelic associations, Montevideo, Mar. 19-28. See No. C271. For overprint see No. 736.

Benito Nardone A204

40c, Benito Nardone before microphone.

1965, Mar. 25 Litho.
717 A204 20c blk & emer .30 .25
718 A204 40c blk & emer, vert. .35 .25

1st anniversary of the death of Benito Nardone, president of the Council of Government.

Artigas Quotation — A205

40c, Artigas bust, quotation. 80c, José Artigas.

Perf. 12x11½
1965, May 17 Litho. Wmk. 327
719 A205 20c bl, yel & red .25 .25
720 A205 40c vio bl, cit & blk .25 .25
721 A205 80c brn, yel, red & bl .35 .25
　Nos. 719-721,C273-C275 (6) 2.50 1.75

José Artigas (1764-1850), leader of the independence revolt against Spain.

Soccer A206

Designs: 40c, Basketball. 80c, Bicycling. 1p, Woman swimmer.

1965, Aug. 3 Litho. Wmk. 327
722 A206 20c grn, org & blk .30 .25
723 A206 40c hn brn, cit & blk .30 .25
724 A206 80c gray, red & blk .30 .25
725 A206 1p bl, yel grn & blk .30 .25
　Nos. 722-725,C276-C281 (10) 5.50 3.45

18th Olympic Games, Tokyo, 10/10-25/64.

No. 572A Surcharged in Red

1965 Unwmk. Perf. 12½
726 A138a 10c on 7c vio bl .25 .25

No. B5 Srchd.

1966, Jan. 25 Wmk. 327 Perf. 11½
727 SP2 4c on 5c + 10c grn & org .25 .25

Association of Uruguayan Architects, 50th anniv.

Winston Churchill A207

Wmk. 332
1966, Apr. 29 Litho. Perf. 12
728 A207 40c car, dp ultra & brn .25 .25

Sir Winston Spencer Churchill, statesman and World War II leader. See No. C284.

Arms of Rio de Janeiro and Sugar Loaf Mountain A208

1966, June 9 Litho. Wmk. 332
729 A208 40c emer & brn .25 .25

400th anniversary of the founding of Rio de Janeiro. See No. C285.

Army Engineer — A209

1966, June 17 Litho.
730 A209 20c blk, red, vio bl & yel .25 .25

50th anniversary of the Army Engineers Corps.

Daniel Fernandez Crespo — A210

Portraits: No. 732, Washington Beltran. No. 733, Luis Batlle Berres.

1966, Sept. 16 Wmk. 332 Perf. 12
731 A210 20c lt bl & blk .25 .25
732 A210 20c lt bl & dk brn .25 .25
733 A210 20c brick red & blk .25 .25
　Nos. 731-733 (3) .75 .75

Issued to honor political leaders.

Old Printing Press — A211

1966, Oct. 14 Photo. Perf. 12
734 A211 20c tan, grnsh gray & dk brn .25 .25

50th anniversary of State Printing Office.

Fireman A212

1966, Oct. 21 Litho.
735 A212 20c red & blk .50 .25

Issued to publicize fire prevention. Printed with alternating red and black labels inscribed: "Prevengase del fuego! Del pueblo y para el pueblo."

No. 716 Overprinted in Red

1966, Nov. 4
736 A203 40c blk & grn .25 .25

2nd Rio de la Plata Stamp Show, Buenos Aires, Apr. 1966, and cent. of Uruguay's 1st surcharged issue. See No. C298.

General Leandro Gomez — A213

#738, Gen. Juan Antonio Lavalleja. #739, Aparicio Saravia, revolutionary, on horseback.

Wmk. 332
1966, Nov. 24 Litho. Perf. 12
737 A213 20c slate, blk & dp bl .30 .25
738 A213 20c red, blk & bl .30 .25
739 A213 20c blue & blk, horiz. .30 .25
　Nos. 737-739 (3) .90 .75

Montevideo Planetarium A214

1967, Jan. 13 Wmk. 332 Perf. 12
740 A214 40c pink & blk .30 .25

10th anniv. of the Montevideo Municipal Planetarium. See No. C301.

Sunflower, Cow and Emblem — A215

1967, Jan. 13   **Litho.**
741 A215 40c dk brn & yel   .30 .25
    Young Farmers' Movement, 20th anniv.

Church of San Carlos — A216

1967, Apr. 17   **Wmk. 332**   *Perf. 12*
742 A216 40c lt bl, blk & dk red   .40 .25
    Bicentenary of San Carlos.

Eduardo Acevedo A217

1967, Apr. 17
743 A217 20c grn & brn   .25 .25
744 A217 40c org & grn   .30 .25
    Issued to honor Eduardo Acevedo, lawyer, legislator and Minister of Foreign Affairs.

Arms of Carmelo — A218

1967, Aug. 11   **Litho.**   *Perf. 12*
745 A218 40c lt & dk bl & ocher   .30 .25
    Founding of Carmelo, 150th anniv.

José Enrique Rodó — A219

   2p, Portrait of Rodó and sculpture, horiz.

1967, Oct. 6   **Wmk. 332**   *Perf. 12*
746 A219 1p gray, brn & blk   .30 .25
747 A219 2p rose claret, blk & tan   .30 .25
    50th anniversary of the death of José Enrique Rodó, author.

Senen M. Rodriguez and Locomotive A220

1967, Oct. 26   **Litho.**   *Perf. 12*
748 A220 2p ocher & dk brn   .40 .25
    Centenary of the founding of the first national railroad company.

Child and Map of Americas — A221

1967, Nov. 10   **Wmk. 332**   *Perf. 12*
749 A221 1p vio & red   .30 .25
    Inter-American Children's Institute, 40th anniv.

No. 610 Surcharged in Red

       Perf. 13x13½
1967, Nov. 10   **Engr.**   **Unwmk.**
750 A173 1p on 7c brn & grn   .25 .25

Cocoi Heron — A222

   Birds: 1p, Great horned owl. 3p, Brown-headed gull, horiz. No. 754, White-faced tree duck, horiz. No. 754A, Black-tailed stilts. 5p, Wattled jacanas, horiz. 10p, Snowy egret, horiz.

1968-70   **Wmk. 332**   **Litho.**   *Perf. 12*
751   A222   1p dl yel & brn   2.00 .40
752   A222   2p bl grn & blk   2.00 .40
753   A222   3p org, gray & blk ('69)   1.50 .35
754   A222   4p brn, tan & blk   3.25 .60
754A A222   4p ver & blk ('70)   1.50 .35
755   A222   5p lt red brn, blk & yel   3.75 .60
756   A222   10p lil & blk   6.75 .80
     Nos. 751-756 (7)   20.75 3.50

Concord Bridge, Presidents of Uruguay, Brazil A223

1968, Apr. 3
757 A223 6p brown   .30 .25
    Opening of Concord Bridge across the Uruguay River by Presidents Jorge Pacheco Areco of Uruguay and Arthur Costa e Silva of Brazil.

Soccer Player and Trophy — A224

1968, May 29   **Litho.**
758 A224 1p blk & yel   .30 .25
    Victory of the Penarol Athletic Club in the Intercontinental Soccer Championships of 1966.

St. John Bosco, Symbols of Education and Industry A225

1968, July 31   **Wmk. 332**   *Perf. 12*
759 A225 2p brn & blk   .25 .25
    75th anniv. of the Don Bosco Workshops of the Salesian Brothers.

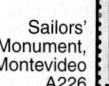 

Sailors' Monument, Montevideo A226

   Designs: 6p, Lighthouse and buoy, vert. 12p, Gunboat "Suarez" (1860).

1968, Nov. 12   **Litho.**   *Perf. 12*
760 A226 2p gray ol & blk   .25 .25
761 A226 6p lt grn & blk   .25 .25
762 A226 12p brt bl & blk   .25 .25
     Nos. 760-762,C340-C343 (7)   2.15 1.75
    Sesquicentennial of National Navy. For surcharge see No. Q101.

Oscar D. Gestido A227

1968, Dec. 6   **Wmk. 332**   *Perf. 12*
763 A227 6p brn, dp car & bl   .25 .25
    First anniversary of the death of President Oscar D. Gestido.

Gearwheel, Grain and Two Heads A228

1969, Mar. 17   **Litho.**   *Perf. 12*
764 A228 2p blk & ver   .25 .25
    25th anniversary of Labor University.

Bicyclists A229

1969, Mar. 21   **Wmk. 332**
765 A229 6p dk bl, org & emer   .30 .25
    1968 World Bicycle Championships. See No. C347.

Gymnasts and Club Emblem A230

1969, May 8   **Wmk. 332**   *Perf. 12*
766 A230 6p blk & ver   .30 .25
    75th anniversary of L'Avenir Athletic Club.

Baltasar Brum (1883-1933) A231

   Former presidents: No. 768, Tomas Berreta (1875-1947).

1969   **Litho.**   *Perf. 12*
767 A231 6p rose red & blk   .25 .25
768 A231 6p car rose & blk   .25 .25

Fair Emblem — A232

1969, Aug. 15   **Wmk. 332**   *Perf. 12*
769 A232 2p multi   .25 .25
    Issued to publicize the 2nd Industrial World's Fair, Montevideo, 1970.

Diesel Locomotive A233

   Design: No. 771, Old steam locomotive and modern railroad cars.

1969, Sept. 19   **Litho.**   **Wmk. 332**
770 A233 6p car, blk & ultra   .40 .25
771 A233 6p car, blk & ultra   .40 .25
   e.   Pair, #770-771
    Centenary of Uruguayan railroads. No. 771e has continuous design and label between pairs.
    For surcharges see Nos. Q102-Q103.

Souvenir Sheet

Diligencia Issue, 1856 — A233a

1969, Oct. 1   *Imperf.*
771A A233a Sheet of 3   10.00 10.00
   b.   60p blue   2.50 2.50
   c.   80p green   3.25 3.25
   d.   100p red   3.75 3.75
    Stamp Day 1969. No. 771A contains stamps similar to No. 1-3, with denominations in pesos.
    No. 771A was re-issued Apr. 15, 1972, with black overprint for 15th anniv. of 1st Lufthansa flight from Uruguay to Germany and the Munich Olympic Games. Value $30.

"Combat" and Sculptor Belloni — A234

1969, Oct. 22   Wmk. 332   Perf. 12
772 A234 6p olive, slate grn & blk   .40   .25

José L. Belloni (1882-), sculptor.

Reserve Officers' Training Center Emblem A235

Design: 2p, Training Center emblem, and officer in uniform and as civilian.

1969, Nov. 5   Litho.
773 A235 1p yel & dk bl   .25   .25
774 A235 2p dk brn & lt bl   .25   .25

Reserve Officers' Training Center, 25th anniv.

Map of Americas and Sun — A236

1970, Apr. 20   Wmk. 332   Perf. 12
775 A236 10p dp bl & gold   .40   .25

11th meeting of the governors of the Inter-American Development Bank, Punta del Este.

Stylized Pine — A237

1970, May 14
776 A237 2p red, blk & brt grn   .35   .25
2nd National Forestry and Wood Exhibition.

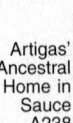 

Artigas' Ancestral Home in Sauce A238

1970, June 18   Wmk. 332   Perf. 12
777 A238 15p ver, ultra & blk   .40   .25

Map of Uruguay, Sun and Sea A239

1970, July 8   Litho.
778 A239 5p greenish blue   .35   .25
Issued for tourist publicity.

EXPO '70 Emblem, Mt. Fuji and Uruguay Coat of Arms A240

EXPO '70 Intl. Exhibition, Osaka, Japan, 3/15-9/13: No. 780, Geisha. No. 781, Sun Tower. No. 782, Youth pole.

1970, Aug. 5   Wmk. 332   Perf. 12
779 A240 25p grn, slate bl & yel   .40   .40
780 A240 25p org, slate bl & grn   .40   .40
781 A240 25p yel, slate bl & pur   .40   .40
782 A240 25p pur, slate bl & org   .40   .40
   a.   Block of 4, #779-782   1.90   1.90

Cobbled Street in Colonia del Sacramento A241

1970, Oct. 21   Litho.   Perf. 12
783 A241 5p blk & multi   .35   .25

290th anniv. of the founding of Colonia del Sacramento, the 1st European settlement in Uruguay.

Mother and Son by Edmundo Prati in Salto — A242

1970, Nov. 4   Litho.
784 A242 10p grn & blk   .45   .30
Issued to honor mothers.

URUEXPO Emblem A243

1970, Dec. 9   Wmk. 332   Perf. 12
785 A243 15p bl, brn org & vio   .40   .40

URUEXPO '70, National Philatelic Exposition, Montevideo, Sept. 26-Oct. 4.

Children Holding Hands, and UNESCO Emblem — A244

Children's Drawings: No. 786, Two girls holding hands, vert. No. 788, Boy sitting at school desk, vert. No. 789, Astronaut and monster.

1970, Dec. 29   Litho.   Perf. 12½
786 A244 10p multi   .35   .35
787 A244 10p multi   .35   .35
788 A244 10p dp car & multi   .35   .35
789 A244 10p bl & multi   .35   .35
   a.   Block of 4, #786-789 + 2 labels   1.60   1.60
International Education Year.

Alfonso Espinola (1845-1905), Physician, Professor and Philanthropist A245

1971, Jan. 13   Wmk. 332   Perf. 12
790 A245 5p dp org & blk   .35   .25

Exposition Poster — A246

1971   Litho.   Perf. 12
791 A246 15p multi   .35   .25

Uruguay Philatelic Exposition, 1971, Montevideo, March 26-Apr. 19.

5c Coin of 1840, Obverse A247

Design: #793, 1st coin of Uruguay, reverse.

1971, Apr. 16   Wmk. 332   Perf. 12
792 A247 25p bl, brn & blk   .60   .60
793 A247 25p bl, brn & blk   .50   .50
   a.   Pair, #792-793   1.40   1.40

Numismatists' Day.

Domingo Arena, Lawyer and Journalist — A248

1971, May 3   Wmk. 332   Perf. 12
794 A248 5p dk car   .30   .25

National Anthem A249

1971, May 19   Litho.
795 A249 15p bl, blk & yel   .40   .40

José F. Arias, Physician — A250

1971, May 25   Wmk. 332   Perf. 12
796 A250 5p sepia   .45   .25

Eduardo Fabini, Bar from "Campo" A251

1971, June 2   Litho.
797 A251 5p dk car rose & blk   .65   .40

Eduardo Fabini (1882-1950), composer, and 40th anniversary of first radio concert.

José E. Rodó, UPAE Emblem A252

1971, July 15   Wmk. 332   Perf. 12
798 A252 15p ultra & blk   .50   .25

José Enrique Rodó (1871-1917), writer, first Uruguayan delegate to Congress of the Postal Union of the Americas and Spain.

Water Cart and Faucet A253

1971, July 17
799 A253 5p ultra & multi   .35   .25
Centenary of Montevideo's drinking water system.

Sheep and Cloth A254

Design: 15p, Sheep, cloth and bale of wool.

1971, Aug. 7
800 A254   5p grn & gray   .25   .25
801 A254 15p dk bl, grnsh bl & gray   .30   .25
Wool Promotion.

José Maria Elorza and Merilin Sheep A255

1971, Aug. 10
802 A255 5p lt bl, grn & blk   .30   .25
José Maria Elorza, developer of the Merilin sheep.

Criollo Horse A256

1971, Aug. 11
803 A256 5p blk, gray bl & org   .80   .25

Bull and
Ram
A257

1971, Aug. 13
804 A257 20p red, grn, blk & gold   .45 .35
Centenary of Rural Association of Uruguay;
19th International Cattle Breeding Exposition,
and 66th National Cattle Championships at
Prado, Aug. 1971.

Symbol of
Liberty
and Order
A258

20p, Policemen, flag of Uruguay and
emblem.

1971
805 A258 10p gray, blk & bl   .30 .25
806 A258 20p dk bl, blk, lt bl &
       gold   .35 .25
To honor policemen killed on duty. Issue
dates: 10p, Sept. 9; 20p, Nov. 4.

10p Banknote of 1896 — A259

Design: No. 808, Reverse of 10p note.

1971, Sept. 23
807 A259 25p dl grn, gold & blk   .50 .50
808 A259 25p dl grn, gold & blk   .50 .50
 a.   Pair, #807-808 + label   1.25 1.25
75th anniversary of Bank of the Republic.

Farmer
and Arms
of
Durazno
A260

1971, Oct. 11
809 A260 20p gold, bl & blk   .50 .25
Sesquicentennial of the founding of Durazno.

Emblem and Laurel — A261

1971, Oct. 20
810 A261 10p vio bl, gold & red   .50 .25
Winners of Liberator's Cup, American Soccer Champions, 1971.
For surcharge see No. 825.

Voter Casting
Ballot — A262

Design: 20p, Citizens voting, horiz.

1971, Nov. 22   Wmk. 332   Perf. 12
811 A262 10p bl & blk   .30 .25
812 A262 20p bl & blk   .30 .25
Universal, secret and obligatory franchise.

Map of
Uruguay on
Globe
A263

1971, Dec. 23
813 A263 20p lt bl & vio brn   .50 .25
7th Littoral Expo., Paysandu, 3/26-4/11.

Juan Lindolfo
Cuestas — A264

No. 815, Julio Herrera y Obes. No. 816,
Claudio Williman. No. 817, José Serrato. No.
818, Andres Martinez Truebá.

1971, Dec. 27
814 A264 10p shown   .25 .25
815 A264 10p multicolored   .25 .25
816 A264 10p multicolored   .25 .25
817 A264 10p multicolored   .25 .25
818 A264 10p multicolored   .25 .25
 a.   Horiz. strip of 5, #814-818 1.50 1.50
Presidents of Uruguay.

Souvenir Sheet

Uruguay No. 4, Cathedral of
Montevideo and Plaza de la
Constitucion — A265

1972, Jan. 17   Imperf.
819 A265 120p brn, bl & dp rose   1.25 1.00
Stamp Day 1971 (release date delayed).
See Nos. 834-835, 863.

Bartolomé
Hidalgo — A266

1972, Feb. 28   Perf. 12
820 A266 5p lt brn, blk & red   .55 .25
Bartolomé Hidalgo (1788-1822), Uru-
guayan-Argentine poet.

Missa Solemnis, by
Beethoven — A267

1972, Apr. 20   Litho.   Wmk. 332
822 A267 20p lil, emer & blk   .40 .25
12th Choir Festival of Eastern Uruguay.

Dove and
Wounded
Bird — A268

1972, May 9
823 A268 10p ver & multi   .40 .25
To honor Dionision Disz (age 9), who died
saving his sister.

Columbus Arch,
Colon — A269

1972, June 21
824 A269 20p red, bl & blk   .40 .25
Centenary of Colon, now suburb of
Montevideo.

No. 810 Surcharged in Silver

(Surcharge 69mm wide)

1972, June 30
825 A261 50p on 10p multi   .50 .25
Winners of the 1971 Intl. Soccer Cup.

Tree
Planting — A270

1972, Aug. 5   Wmk. 332   Perf. 12
826 A270 20p grn & blk   .35 .25
Afforestation program.

"Collective
Housing" — A271

1972, Sept. 30   Litho.
827 A271 10p dp bl & multi   .35 .25
Publicity for collective housing plan.

Amethyst
A272

Uruguayan Gem Stones: 9p, Agate. 15p,
Chalcedony.

1972, Oct. 7
828 A272 5p gray & multi   .50 .50
829 A272 9p gray bl & multi   .50 .50
830 A272 15p gray grn & multi   .60 .60
      Nos. 828-830 (3)   1.60 1.60

Uniform of
1830 — A273

Design: 20p, Lancer.

1972, Nov. 21   Litho.
831 A273 10p multi   .35 .25
832 A273 20p rose red & multi   .35 .25

Red
Cross and
Map of
Uruguay
A274

1972, Dec. 11   Wmk. 332   Perf. 12
833 A274 30p multi   .40 .25
75th anniv. of the Uruguayan Red Cross.

Stamp Day Type of 1972
Souvenir Sheets

Designs: 200p, Coat of arms type of 1864
similar to Nos. 18, 20-21, but 60p, 60p and
80p. 220p, Similar to Nos. 22-23, but 100p and
120p.

1972, Dec. 20   Imperf.
834 A265 200p multi   1.25 .60
835 A265 220p multi   1.50 .75
Stamp Day 1972. 1st printed cancellations,
200th anniv., #834; Decree establishing regular postal service, cent., #835.

Scales of
Justice,
Olive
Branch
A275

1972, Dec. 27   Wmk. 332   Perf. 12
836 A275 10p gold, dk & lt bl   .30 .25
Civil Rights Law for Women, 25th anniv.

Gen. José Artigas — A276

1972-74   Wmk. 332   Litho.   *Perf. 12*
837	A276	5p yel ('74)	.25	.25
838	A276	10p dk bis ('74)	.25	.25
839	A276	15p emer ('74)	.25	.25
840	A276	20p lilac ('73)	.25	.25
841	A276	30p lt bl ('73)	.25	.25
842	A276	40p dp org ('73)	.25	.25
843	A276	50p ver ('73)	.25	.25
844	A276	75p ap grn ('73)	.25	.25
845	A276	100p emerald	.25	.25
846	A276	150p choc ('73)	.25	.25
847	A276	200p dk bl ('73)	.45	.30
848	A276	250p pur ('73)	.50	.35
849	A276	500p gray ('73)	1.25	.60
849A	A276	1000p blue ('73)	2.50	1.25
	Nos. 837-849A (14)		7.20	5.00

For surcharges see Nos. 929-932.

Hand Holding Cup; Grain, Map of Americas — A277

1973, Jan. 9
850   A277   30p rose red, yel & blk   .30   .25
Intl. Institute for Agricultural Research, 39th anniv.

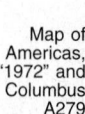

Elbio Fernandez and José P. Varela — A278

1973, Jan. 16
851   A278   10p dl grn, gold & blk   .30   .25
Society of Friends of Public Education, cent.

Map of Americas, "1972" and Columbus A279

1973, Jan. 30
852   A279   50p purple   .30   .25
Tourist Year of the Americas 1972.

Carlos Maria Ramirez, Scales and Books A280

No. 854, Justino Jimenez de Arechaga. No. 855, Juan Andres Ramirez. No. 856, Justino E. Jimenez de Arechaga.

1973, Feb. 15
853	A280	10p shown	.25	.25
854	A280	10p multicolored	.25	.25
855	A280	10p multicolored	.25	.25
856	A280	10p multicolored	.25	.25
a.	Horiz. strip, #853-856 + label		1.25	1.25

Professorship of Constitutional Rights, cent.

Provincial Map of Uruguay A281

1973, Feb. 27   Litho.   *Perf. 12½x12*
857   A281   20p bl & multi   .40   .25
See No. 1167.

Francisco de los Santos A282

1973, May 16   Wmk. 332   *Perf. 12*
858   A282   20p grn & blk   .35   .25
Soldiers' Day and Battle of Piedras. Santos was a courier who went through enemy lines.

No. C319 Srchd. with New Value and "HOMENAJE AL 4 CENTENARIO DE CORDOBA . ARGENTINA . 1973"

1973, May 9   Litho.   *Imperf.*
Souvenir Sheet
859   AP57   100p on 5p multi   1.25   1.00
Founding of Cordoba in Argentina, 400th anniv.

Friar, Indians, Church — A283

1973, July 25   *Perf. 12*
860   A283   20p lt ultra, pur & blk   .30   .25
Villa Santo Domingo Soriano, first Spanish settlement in Uruguay.

Symbolic Fish A284

1973, Aug. 15
861   A284   100p bl & multi   .50   .25
First station of Oceanographic and Fishery Service, Montevideo.

A285

Sun over flower in Italian colors.

1973, Sept.
862   A285   100p multi   .30   .25
Italian Chamber of Commerce of Uruguay.

Stamp Day Type of 1972
Souvenir Sheet
Design: 240p, Thin numeral sun type of 1859 and street scene.

Wmk. 332
1973, Oct. 1   Litho.   *Imperf.*
863   A265   240p grn, org & blk   1.50   1.50
Stamp Day 1973.

Herrera — A286

1973, Nov. 12   *Perf. 12*
866   A286   50p gray, brn & dk brn   .30   .25
Centenary of the birth of Luis Alberto de Herrera.

Emblem of Social Coordination Volunteers A287

Wmk. 352
1973, Nov. 19   Litho.   *Perf. 12*
867   A287   50p bl & multi   .35   .25
Festival of Nations, Montevideo.

Arm with Arteries and Heart A288

1973, Nov. 22
868   A288   50p blk, red & pink   .30   .25
3rd Cong. of the Pan-American Federation of Blood Donors, Montevideo, Nov. 23-25.

Madonna, by Rafael Perez Barradas — A289

1973, Dec. 10   Litho.   Wmk. 332
869   A289   50p grn, gray & yel grn   .40   .25
Christmas 1973.

Nicolaus Copernicus — A290

1973, Dec. 26   Litho.
870   A290   50p grn & multi   .45   .25
500th anniversary of the birth of Nicolaus Copernicus (1473-1543), Polish astronomer.

Praying Hands and Andes — A291

75p, Statue of Christ on mountain, and flower.

1973, Dec. 26   Litho.
871   A291   50p blk, lt grn & ultra   .25   .25
872   A291   75p bl, blk & org   .30   .25
Survival and rescue of victims of airplane crash.

OAS Emblem and Map of Americas A292

1974, Jan. 14   Wmk. 332   *Perf. 12*
873   A292   250p gray & multi   .85   .40
25th anniversary of the Organization of American States (OAS).

Scout Emblems and Flame A293

1974, Jan. 21
874   A293   250p multi   .85   .40
1st Intl. Boy Scout Games, Montevideo, 1974.

Hector Suppici Sedes and Car — A294

1974, Jan. 28   *Perf. 12*
875   A294   50p sep, grn & blk   .50   .25
70th anniversary of the birth of Hector Suppici Sedes (1903-1948), automobile racer.

Three Gauchos — A295

1974, Mar. 20   Litho.   Wmk. 332
876   A295   50p multi   .60   .25
Centenary of the publication of "Los Tres Gauchos Orientales" by Antonio D. Lussich.

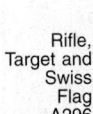

Rifle, Target and Swiss Flag A296

1974, Apr. 2
877 A296 100p multi   .45 .25
Centenary of the Swiss Rifle Association.

Old and New School and Founders A300

1974, May 21
883 A300 75p black & bister   .40 .25
Centenary of the Osimani-Llerena Technical School at Salto, founded by Gervasio Osimani and Miguel Llerena.

Map of Uruguay and Compass Rose A297

1974, Apr. 23   **Litho.**
878 A297 50p multi   .40 .25
Military Geographical Service.

Gardel and Score — A301

  Wmk. 332
1974, June 24 **Litho.** **Perf. 12**
884 A301 100p multi   .60 .25
Carlos Gardel (1887-1935), singer and motion picture actor. See No. 1173.

Montevideo Stadium Tower — A298

Design: 75p, Soccer player, Games' emblem, horiz. 1000p, similar to 75p.

1974, May 7 **Wmk. 332** **Perf. 12**
879 A298 50p multi   .25 .25
880 A298 75p multi   .25 .25
881 A298 1000p multi   22.50 8.50
World Cup Soccer Championship, Munich, June 13-July 7.
No. 881 had limited distribution. A souvenir sheet of one No. 881 was not valid for postage.

Volleyball and Net — A302

1974, July 11 **Wmk. 332** **Perf. 12**
885 A302 200p lil, yel & blk   .50 .25
First anniversary of Women's Volleyball championships, Montevideo, 1973.

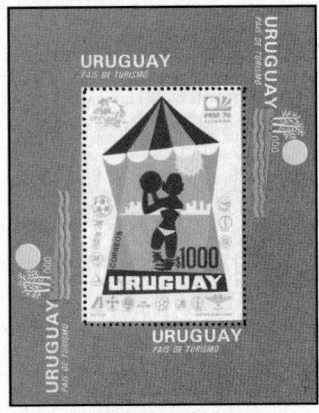

Tourism — A299

  Wmk. 332
1974, June 6 **Litho.** **Perf. 12**
882 A299 1000p multicolored 35.00 35.00
No. 882 had limited distribution.

"Protect your Heart" — A303

1974, July 24   **Litho.**
886 A303 75p ol grn, yel & red   .45 .25
Heart Foundation publicity.

Portrait and Statue — A304

1974, Aug. 5
887 A304 75p dk & lt bl   .40 .25
Centenary (in 1973) of the founding of San José de Mayo by Eusebio Vidal.

A305

Artigas statue, Buenos Aires, flags of Uruguay and Argentina.

1974, Aug. 13   **Perf. 12½**
888 A305 75p multicolored   .45 .25
Unveiling of Artigas monument, Buenos Aires.

A306

1974, Sept. 24 **Wmk. 332** **Perf. 12**
889 A306 100p Radio tower and waves   .40 .25
50th anniv. of Broadcasting in Uruguay.

URUEXPO 74 Emblem — A307

URUEXPO Emblem and Old Map of Montevideo Bay — A308

1974
890 A307 100p blk, dk bl & red   .25 .25
891 A308 300p sepia, red & grn   .60 .60
URUEXPO 74 Philatelic Exhibition, 10th anniversary of Philatelic Circle of Uruguay (100p) and 250th anniversary of fortification of Montevideo.
Issue dates: 100p, Oct. 1; 300p, Oct. 19.

Letters and UPU Emblem A309

UPU Cent.: 200p, UPU emblem, letter, and globe.

1974, Oct. 9
892 A309 100p lt bl & multi   .25 .25
893 A309 200p lil, blk & gold   .35 .25
  Nos. 892-893,C395-C396 (4) 2.60 2.50
A 1000p souvenir sheet was not valid for postage. Value $45.

Artigas Statue and Map of Lavalleja A310

1974, Oct. 17   **Perf. 12**
894 A310 100p ultra & multi   .45 .25
Unveiling of Artigas statue in Minas, Lavalleja.

Ship in Dry Dock, Arsenal's Emblem A312

1974, Nov. 15 **Litho.** **Wmk. 332**
896 A312 200p multi   .45 .30
Centenary of Naval Arsenal, Montevideo.

Globe Hydrogen Balloon — A313

No. 898, Farman biplane. No. 899, Castaibert monoplane. No. 900, Bleriot monoplane. No. 901, Military and civilian pilots' emblems. No. 902, Nieuport biplane. No. 903, Breguet-Bidon fighter. No. 904, Caproni bomber.

1974, Nov. 20
897 A313 100p shown   .55 .35
898 A313 100p multicolored   .55 .35
899 A313 100p multicolored   .55 .35
900 A313 100p multicolored   .55 .35
  a. Strip of 4, #897-900 2.25 2.25
901 A313 150p multicolored   .55 .35
902 A313 150p multicolored   .55 .35
903 A313 150p multicolored   .55 .35
904 A313 150p multicolored   .55 .35
  a. Strip of 4, #901-904 2.25 2.25
  Nos. 897-904 (8) 4.40 2.80
Aviation pioneers.

Sugar Loaf Mountain and Summit Cross — A314

1974, Nov. 30
905 A314 150p multicolored   .45 .25
Cent. of the founding of Sugar Loaf City.

Adoration of the Kings — A315

1974   **Perf. 12**
906 A315 100p shown   .30   .25
907 A315 150p Three Kings   .30   .25
    Nos. 906-907,C400 (3)   1.20   .75

Christmas 1974. See No. C401. Issue dates: 100p, Dec. 17; 150p, Dec. 19.

Nike, Fireworks, Rowers and Club Emblem — A316

1975, Jan. 27   Litho.   Wmk. 332
908 A316 150p gray & multi   .45   .25
    Centenary of Montevideo Rowing Club.

Treaty Signing, by José Zorilla de San Martin — A317

1975, Feb. 12   **Perf. 12**
909 A317 100p multi   .45   .25
    Commercial Treaty between Great Britain and Uruguay, 1817.

Rose — A318

1975, Mar. 18   Litho.   Wmk. 332
910 A318 150p multicolored   .70   .40
    Bicentenary of city of Rosario.

"The Oath of the 33," by Juan M. Blanes — A319

1975, Apr. 16   **Perf. 12**
911 A319 150p gold & multi   .45   .25
    Sesquicentennial of liberation movement.

Ship, Columbus and Ancient Map — A320

1975, Oct. 9   Litho.   Wmk. 332
912 A320 1p gray & multi   1.60 1.00
    Hispanic Stamp Day.

Leonardo Olivera and Santa Teresa Fort — A321

Artigas as Young and Old Man A322

1975   Litho.   Wmk. 332   Perf. 12
913 A321 10c org & multi   .30   .25
914 A322 50c vio bl & multi   .70   .40
    Sesquicentennial of the capture of Fort Santa Teresa (10c) and of Uruguay's declaration of independence (50c).
    Issue dates: 10c, Oct. 20; 50c, Oct. 17.

Battle of Rincon, by Diogenes Hequet — A323

#916, Artigas' Home, Ibiray, Paraguay. 25c, Battle of Sarandi, by J. Manuel Blanes.

1975   Litho.
915 A323 15c gold & blk   .30   .25
916 A323 15c gold & multi   .30   .25
917 A323 25c gold & multi   .50   .30
    Nos. 915-917 (3)   1.10   .80
    Uruguayan independence. Nos. 915 and 917, 150th anniversary of Battles of Rincon and Sarandi. No. 916, 50th anniversary of school at Artigas mansion.
    Issued: #915, 10/23; #916, 11/18; #917, 11/28.

"En Familia," by Sanchez A324

Florencio Sanchez A325

Plays by Sanchez: #919, Barranca Abajo. #920, M'Hijo el Doctor. #921, Canillita.

1975, Oct. 31   Wmk. 332   Perf. 12
918 A324 20c gray, red & blk   .35   .25
919 A324 20c bl, grn & blk   .35   .25
920 A324 20c red, bl & blk   .35   .25
921 A324 20c grn, gray & blk   .35   .25
922 A325 20c multi   .35   .25
  a.   Block of 5 stamps + 4 labels   2.75 2.75
    Florencio Sanchez (1875-1910), dramatist, birth centenary. Nos. 918-922 printed se-tenant in sheets of 30 stamps and 20 labels.

Maria Eugenia Vaz Ferreira A326

Design: No. 924, Julio Herrera y Reissig.

1975
923 A326 15c yel, blk & brn   .35   .25
924 A326 15c org, blk & maroon   .35   .25
    Maria Eugenia Vaz Ferreira (1875-1924), poetess, and Julio Herrera y Reissig (1875-1910), poet, birth anniversaries.
    Issue dates: #923, Dec. 9; #924, Dec. 29.

A327

Virgin and Child — A328

Fireworks — A329

1975
925 A327 20c bl & multi   .35   .35
926 A328 30c blk & multi   .60   .60
927 A329 60c multi   .75   .75
    Nos. 925-927 (3)   1.70 1.70
    Christmas 1975.
    Issued: 20c, 12/16; 30c, 12/15; 60c, 12/11.

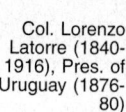

Col. Lorenzo Latorre (1840-1916), Pres. of Uruguay (1876-80) A330

1975, Dec. 30   **Perf. 12**
928 A330 15c multicolored   .35   .25

Nos. 840, 842-843, 849A Surcharged

1975
929 A276 10c on 20p lilac   .25   .25
930 A276 15c on 40p orange   .25   .25
931 A276 50c on 50p ver   .45   .45
932 A276 1p on 1000p blue   .95   .95
    Nos. 929-932 (4)   1.90 1.90
    There are two surcharge types for Nos. 929 and 930. Values are the same.

Ariel, Stars, Book and Youths A331

1976, Jan. 12   Litho.   Wmk. 332
933 A331 15c grn & multi   .35   .25
    75th anniversary of publication of "Ariel," by Jose Enrique Rodo (1872-1917), writer.

Water Sports — A332

1976, Mar. 12   Litho.   Wmk. 332
934 A332 30c multicolored   .45   .25
    23rd South American Swimming, Diving and Water Polo Championships.

Telephone A333

1976, Apr. 9   **Perf. 12**
935 A333 83c multicolored   .60   .30
    Centenary of first telephone call by Alexander Graham Bell, Mar. 10, 1876.

"Plus Ultra" and Columbus' Ships — A334

Wmk. 332
1976, May 10   Litho.   Perf. 12
936 A334 63c gray & multi   .50   .30
    Flight of Dornier "Plus Ultra" from Spain to South America, 50th anniversary.

Dornier "Wal" and Boeing 727, hourglass.

1976, May 24
937 A335 83c gray & multi .50 .30
Lufthansa German Airline, 50th anniv.

A336

Designs: 10c, Olympics. 15c, Telephone, cent. 25c, UPU, cent., UN #2. 50c, World Cup Soccer Championships, Argentina, 1978.

1976, June 3 *Perf. 11½*
938 A336 10c shown 1.75 .60
939 A336 15c multicolored 1.75 .60
940 A336 25c multicolored 1.75 .60
941 A336 50c multicolored 1.75 .60
Nos. 938-941 (4) 7.00 2.40

Nos. 938-941 had limited distribution.
A souvenir sheet containing one each, Nos. 938-941, was not valid for postage. Value $45.

Louis Braille A340

1976, June 7
942 A340 60c blk & brn 1.00 .40
Sesquicentennial of the invention of the Braille system of writing for the blind by Louis Braille (1809-1852).

Signing of US Declaration of Independence A341

1976, June 21
943 A341 1.50p multicolored 2.75 2.25
American Bicentennial.

The Candombe, by P. Figari — A342

Wmk. 332
1976, July 29 *Litho.* *Perf. 12*
944 A342 30c ultra & multi .45 .25
Abolition of slavery, sesquicentennial.

Gen. Fructuoso Rivera Statue A343

1976, Aug. 2
945 A343 5p on 10p multi 4.50 2.25
No. 945 was not issued without surcharge.

General Accounting Office — A344

Wmk. 332
1976, Aug. 24 *Litho.* *Perf. 12*
946 A344 30c bl, blk & brn .35 .25
National General Accounting Office, sesquicentennial.

Old Pump, Emblem and Flame — A345

1976, Sept. 6
947 A345 20c red & blk 1.00 .25
First official fire fighting service, centenary.

Southern Lapwing A346

Mburucuya Flower A347

Spearhead A348

Figurine A349

La Yerra, by J. M. Blanes A350

The Gaucho, by Blanes A351

Artigas — A352

Designs: 15c, Ceibo flower.

1976-79 *Litho.* *Wmk. 332* *Perf. 12*
948 A346 1c violet .25 .25
949 A347 5c lt grn .25 .25
950 A347 15c car rose .25 .25
951 A348 20c gray .25 .25
952 A349 30c gray blue .25 .25
953 A352 45c brt bl ('79) .25 .25
954 A350 50c grnsh bl ('77) .25 .25
955 A351 1p dk brn ('77) .50 .25
956 A352 1p brt yel ('79) .25 .25
957 A352 1.75p bl grn ('79) .40 .30
958 A352 1.95p gray ('79) .40 .30
959 A352 2p dl grn ('77) 1.10 .60
960 A352 2p lil rose ('79) .50 .35
961 A352 2.65p vio ('79) .50 .40
962 A352 5p dk bl 3.50 2.00
963 A352 10p brn ('77) 6.75 2.00
Nos. 948-963 (16) 15.65 8.00

"Diligencia" Uruguay No. 1 — A353

Wmk. 332
1976, Sept. 26 *Litho.* *Perf. 12*
964 A353 30c bister, red & blue .45 .25
Philatelic Club of Uruguay, 50th anniv.

Games' Emblem — A354

1976, Oct. 26 *Litho.* *Perf. 12*
965 A354 83c gray & multi 1.00 .50
5th World University Soccer Championships.

World Cup Soccer Championships, Argentina — A355

Anniversaries and Events: 30c, 1976 Summer Olympics, Montreal. 50c, Viking spacecraft. 80c, Nobel prizes, 75th anniv.

1976, Nov. 12 *Perf. 12*
966 A355 10c multicolored 1.75 .85
967 A355 30c multicolored 1.75 .85
968 A355 50c multicolored 1.75 .85
969 A355 80c multicolored 1.75 .85
Nos. 966-969 (4) 7.00 3.40

Nos. 966-969 had limited distribution.
See Nos. C424-C425.

Eye and Spectrum A356

1976, Nov. 24
970 A356 20c blk & multi .50 .25
Foresight prevents blindness.

Map of Montevideo, 1748 — A357

45c, Montevideo Harbor, 1842. 70c, First settlers, 1726. 80c, Coin with Montevideo

arms, vert. 1.15p, Montevideo's first coat of arms, vert.

Wmk. 332
1976, Dec. 30 *Litho.* *Perf. 12*
971 A357 30c multi .40 .25
972 A357 45c multi .55 .25
973 A357 70c multi .70 .35
974 A357 80c multi 1.00 .35
975 A357 1.15p multi 1.60 .45
Nos. 971-975 (5) 4.25 1.65
Founding of Montevideo, 250th anniversary.

Symbolic of Flight A358

1977, May 7 *Litho.* *Perf. 12*
976 A358 80c multicolored .75 .50
50th anniversary of Varig airlines.

Artigas Mausoleum — A359

1977, June 17 *Litho.* *Perf. 12*
977 A359 45c multicolored .50 .30

A360

1977, July 5 *Wmk. 332*
978 A360 45c Map of Uruguay, arch .45 .25
Centenary of Salesian Brothers' educational system in Uruguay.

A361

Anniversaries and events: 20c, Werner Heisenberg, Nobel Prize for Physics. 30c, World Cup Soccer Championships, Uruguay Nos. 282, 390. 50c, Lindbergh's trans-Atlantic flight, 50th anniv. 1p, Rubens 400th birth anniv.

1977, July 21
979 A361 20c shown 2.25 1.40
980 A361 30c multicolored 2.25 1.40
981 A361 50c multicolored 2.25 1.40
982 A361 1p multicolored 2.25 1.40
a. Strip, 2 ea #979-982 + 2 labels —
Nos. 979-982 (4) 9.00 5.60

Nos. 979-982 had limited distribution.
A souvenir sheet containing Nos. 979-982, imperf., was not valid for postage. It sold for 8p. See Nos. C426-C427.

Children — A362

1977, Aug. 10   Litho.   Perf. 12
983 A362 45c multi   .50 .30
Interamerican Children's Inst., 50th anniv.

"El Sol de
Mayo"
A363

1977, Oct. 1   Litho.   Perf. 12
984 A363 45c multi   .60 .60
Stamp Day 1977.

Windmills — A364

1977, Sept. 29   Wmk. 332
985 A364 70c yel, car & blk   .75 .35
Spanish Heritage Day.

Souvenir Sheet

View of Sans (Barcelona), by
Barradas — A365

1977, Oct. 7   Litho.   Perf. 12
986 A365 Sheet of 2   6.50 6.50
a.-b.   5p, single stamp   3.00 3.00
ESPAMER '77 Philatelic Exhibition, Barcelona, Oct. 7-13.

Planes,
UN
Emblem,
Globe
A366

1977, Oct. 17
987 A366 45c multi   .45 .25
30th anniv. of Civil Aviation Organization.

Holy
Family — A367

Santa Claus — A368

1977, Dec. 1   Wmk. 332
988 A367 45c multi   .25 .25
989 A368 70c blk, yel & red   .25 .25
Christmas 1977.

Map of
Rio Negro
Province
A369

1977, Dec. 16
990 A369 45c multi   1.00   .30
Rio Negro Dam; development of argiculture,
livestock and beekeeping. See Nos. 1021-
1033.

Mail Collection
A370

No. 992, Mail truck. No. 993, Post office
counter. No. 994, Postal boxes. No. 995, Mail
sorting. No. 996, Pigeonhole sorting. No. 997,
Route sorting (seated carriers). No. 998,
Home delivery. No. 999, Special delivery
(motorcyclists). No. 1000, Airport counter.

1977, Dec. 21
991   A370 50c shown   .40   .25
992   A370 50c multicolored   .40   .25
993   A370 50c multicolored   .40   .25
994   A370 50c multicolored   .40   .25
995   A370 50c multicolored   .40   .25
996   A370 50c multicolored   .40   .25
997   A370 50c multicolored   .40   .25
998   A370 50c multicolored   .40   .25
999   A370 50c multicolored   .40   .25
1000 A370 50c multicolored   .40   .25
a.   Strip of 10, #991-1000   7.50 7.50
Uruguayan postal service, 150th anniv.

Edison's Phonograph, 1877 — A371

1977, Dec. 30
1001 A371 50c vio brn & yel   .75   .30
Centenary of invention of the phonograph.

"R",
Rainbow
and
Emblem
A372

1977, Dec. 30   Wmk. 332
1002 A372 50c multi   .40 .25
World Rheumatism Year.

Emblem
and
Diploma
A373

1978, Mar. 27   Litho.   Perf. 12
1003 A373 50c multi   .40 .25
50th anniversary of Military College.

Erhard Schon by Albrecht Durer
(1471-1528) — A374

Painting: 50c, Self-Portrait by Peter Paul
Rubens (1577-1640).

1978, June 13   Perf. 12½
1004 A374 25c blk & brn   1.25 1.00
1005 A374 50c brn & blk   2.00 1.50
Nos. 1004-1005 had limited distribution.
See Nos. C430-C432.

Map and Arms of Artigas
Department — A375

Wmk. 332
1978, June 16   Litho.   Perf. 12
1006 A375 45c multi   .45 .25

Souvenir Sheet

Anniversaries — A376

Designs: 2p, Papilio thoas. No. 1007b,
"100." No. 1007c, Argentina '78 emblem and
globes. 5p, Model T Ford.

Wmk. 332
1978, Aug. 24   Litho.   Perf. 12
1007 A376 Sheet of 4   18.00 18.00
a.   2p multi   1.75 1.75
b.   4p multi   3.50 3.50
c.   4p multi   3.50 3.50
d.   5p multi   4.25 4.25
75th anniv. of 1st powered flight; URUEXPO
'78 Phil. Exhib.; Parva Domus social club,
cent.; 11th World Cup Soccer Championship,
Argentina, June 1-25; Ford motor cars, 75th
anniv.

Visiting Angels, by Solari — A377

Designs (Details from No. 1008b): No.
1008a, Second angel. No. 1008c, Third angel.

1978, Sept. 13   Unwmk.
1008 Strip of 3   2.00 2.00
a.   A377 1.50p, 19x30mm   .40   .40
b.   A377 1.50p, 38x30mm   .40   .40
c.   A377 1.50p, 19x30mm   .40   .40
Solari, Uruguayan painter.

Bernardo
O'Higgins
A378

#1010, José de San Martin and monument.

1978   Wmk. 332
1009 A378 1p multi   .50 .25
1010 A378 1p multi   .50 .25
Benardo O'Higgins (1778-1842 and José de
San Martin (1778-1850), South American
liberators.
Issued: #1009, Sept. 13; #1010, Oct. 10.

Telephone
Dials
A379

1978, Sept. 25
1011 A379 50c multi   .50 .25
Automation of telephone service.

Symbolic
Stamps
A380

Iberian Tile
Pattern — A381

1978, Oct. 31
1012 A380 50c multi   .40 .25
1013 A381 1p multi   .50 .25
Stamp Day (50c) and Spanish heritage (1p).

Boeing 727
A382

1978, Nov. 27
1014 A382 50c multi .60 .25
Inauguration of Boeing 727 flights by PLUNA Uruguayan airlines, Nov. 1978.

Angel Blowing Horn — A383

1978, Dec. 7
1015 A383 50c multi .25 .25
1016 A383 1p multi .35 .25
Christmas 1978.

A384

1978, Dec. 15 *Perf. 12½*
1017 A384 1p Flag flying on Plaza of the Nation .50 .25

A385

Wmk. 332
1978, Dec. 27 **Litho.** *Perf. 12*
1018 A385 1p blk, red & yel .50 .25
Horacio Quiroga (1868-1928), short story writer.

Arch, Olympic Rings, Lake Placid and Moscow Emblems A386

7p, Olympic Rings, Lake Placid '80 emblem.

1979, Apr. 28 **Litho.** *Perf. 12*
1019 A386 5p multi 2.00 1.40
1020 A386 7p multi 2.25 1.00
81st Session of Olympic Organizing Committee, Apr. 3-8 (5p), and 13th Winter Olympic Games, Lake Placid, NY, Feb. 12-24.

Souvenir Sheets
1021 Sheet of 4 35.00 35.00
  a. A386 3p similar to #1019
  b. A386 5p Olympic rings
  c. A386 7p Rider looking back
  d. A386 10p Rider facing forward
1022 Sheet of 4 35.00 35.00
  a. A386 3p similar to #1020
  b. A386 5p Uruguay '79
  c. A386 7p World Chess Olympics '78
  d. A386 10p Sir Rowland Hill, Great Britain stamp
No. 1022d shows Great Britain No. 836, but with 11p denomination. No. 1021c-1021d have continuous design.
Nos. 1021-1022 had limited distribution. Except for No. 1022d, singles were sold for postal use in 1980. Nos. 1021-1022 exist imperf.

Map and Arms of Paysandu A387

Map and Arms of Maldonado A388

1979-81
1023 A387 45c shown .50 .40
1024 A387 45c Salto .50 .40
1025 A388 45c shown .50 .40
1026 A387 45c Cerro Largo .50 .40
1027 A387 50c Treinta y Tres .50 .40
1028 A387 50c Durazno ('80) .50 .40
1029 A388 2p Rocha ('81) .50 .40
1030 A388 2p Flores .50 .40
  Nos. 1023-1030 (8) 4.00 3.20
See No. 990.

Sapper with Pickax, 1837 — A389

Army Day: No. 1039, Artillery man with cannon, 1830.

1979, May 18 **Litho.** *Perf. 12*
1038 A389 5p multi 1.90 1.00
1039 A389 5p multi 1.90 1.00

Madonna and Child by Durer A390

Anniversaries and events: 80c, World Cup Soccer Championships, Spain. 1.30p, Sir Rowland Hill, Greece No. 117.

1979, June 18 *Perf. 12*
1040 A390 70c brn & gray 6.50 3.25
1041 A390 80c multicolored 5.00 2.75
1042 A390 1.30p multicolored 5.00 2.75
  Nos. 1040-1042 (3) 16.50 8.75
Nos. 1040-1042 had limited distribution.
Issued in sheets of 24 containing 6 blocks of 4 with margin around. See #C437-C438.

Salto Dam A391

1979, June 19
1043 A391 2p multi .75 .30

Crandon Institute Emblem, Grain A392

1979, July 19
1044 A392 1p vio bl & bl .30 .25
Crandon Institute (private Methodist school), centenary.

IYC Emblem, Smiling Kites — A393

Cinderella A394

1979
1045 A393 2p multi .60 .25
1046 A394 2p multi .60 .25
International Year of the Child. Issue dates: No. 1045, July 23; No. 1046, Aug. 29.

Uruguay Coat of Arms 150th Anniversary — A395

1979, Sept. 6
1047 A395 8p multi 3.00 1.40

Virgin and Child — A396

Wmk. 332
1979, Nov. 19 **Litho.** *Perf. 12*
1048 A396 10p multi 2.75 1.60
Christmas 1979; Intl. Year of the Child.

Symbols, by Torres-Garcia A397

1979, Nov. 12
1049 A397 10p yel & blk 3.00 1.60
J. Torres-Garcia (1874-1948), painter.

UPU and Brazilian Postal Emblems — A398

1979, Oct. 11
1050 A398 5p multi 1.25 .80
18th UPU Congress, Rio, Sept.-Oct.

Dish Antenna and Sun — A400

Perf. 12x11½
1979, Nov. 26 **Litho.** **Wmk. 332**
1052 A400 10p multi 3.00 1.25
Telecom '79, 3rd World Telecommunications Exhibition, Geneva, Sept. 20-26.

Spanish Heritage Day — A401

1979, Dec. 3 *Perf. 12*
1053 A401 10p multi 2.00 1.50

Silver Coin Centenary A402

Designs: Obverse and reverse of coins in denominations matching stamps.

1979, Dec. 26
1054 A402 10c multi .25 .25
1055 A402 20c multi .25 .25
1056 A402 50c multi .25 .25
1057 A402 1p multi .45 .25
  Nos. 1054-1057 (4) 1.20 1.00

Souvenir Sheet

A403

1980, Jan. 10
1058 Sheet of 4   3.50 3.50
  a. A403 1p Police emblem   .30 .30
  b. A403 2p Security Agent   .50 .50
  c. A403 3p Policeman, 1843   .75 .75
  d. A403 4p Cadet, 1979   1.00 1.00
    Police force sesquicentennial.

Light Bulb, Thomas Edison — A404

1980, Jan. 18
1059 A404 2p multi   1.00 .35
    Centenary of electric light (1979).

Bass and
Singer — A405

1980, Jan. 30
1060 Sheet of 4   3.00 3.00
  a. A405 2p Radio waves   .65 .65
  b. A405 2p shown   .65 .65
  c. A405 2p Ballerina   .65 .65
  d. A405 2p Television waves   .65 .65
    Performing Arts Society, 50th anniversary.

Stamp
Day — A406

1980, Feb.
1061 A406 1p multi   .60 .25

La Leyenda
Patria — A407

1980, Feb. 26
1062 A407 1p multi   .50 .25

Printers'
Association,
50th
Anniversary
A408

1980, Feb.
1063 A408 1p multi   .35 .25

Lufthansa Cargo Container Service
Inauguration — A409

1980, Apr. 12   Unwmk.   Perf. 12½
1064 A409 2p multi   .60 .25

Conf. Emblem,
Banners — A410

1980, Apr. 28   Wmk. 332   Perf. 12
1065 A410 2p multi   .50 .25
    8th World Hereford Conf., Punta del Este
and Livestock Exhib., Prado/Montivideo.

Man, Woman and
Birds — A411

1980   Litho.   Perf. 12
1066 A411 1p multi   .65 .25
    International Year of the Child (1979).

Latin-American Lions, 9th
Forum — A412

1980, May 6   Wmk. 332   Perf. 12
1067 A412 1p multi   .65 .25

Souvenir Sheet

Army Day, May 18 — A413

1980, May 16
1068 Sheet of 4   5.00 5.00
  a. A413 2p Rifleman, 1814   1.00 1.00
  b. A413 2p Cavalry officer, 1830   1.00 1.00
  c. A413 2p Private Liberty Dragoons,
    1826   1.00 1.00
  d. A413 2p, Artigas Militia officer,
    1815   1.00 1.00

Arms of
Colonia — A414

Colonia,
1680
A415

1980, June 17   Litho.   Perf. 12
1069 A414 50c multi   1.50 .25

Souvenir Sheet

1070 Sheet of 4   4.00 4.00
  a. A415 1p shown   1.00 1.00
  b. A415 1p 1680, diff.   1.00 1.00
  c. A415 1p 1980   1.00 1.00
  d. A415 1p 1980, diff.   1.00 1.00
    Colonia, 300th anniversary.

Rotary Emblem
on Globe — A416

1980, July 8
1071 A416 5p multi   1.50 .90
    Rotary International, 75th anniversary.

Hand Putting Out
Cigarette — A417

1980, Sept. 8   Photo.
1072 A417 1p multi   .60 .25
    World Health Day and anti-smoking
campaign.

Artigas — A418

		Wmk. 332		
1980-85		**Litho.**	**Perf. 12½**	
1073	A418	10c blue ('81)	.25	.25
1074	A418	20c orange	.25	.25
1075	A418	50c red	.25	.25
1076	A418	60c yellow	.25	.25
1077	A418	1p gray	.55	.25
1078	A418	2p brown	1.00	.30
1079	A418	3p brt grn	1.75	.35
1080	A418	4p brt bl ('82)	2.10	.45
1081	A418	5p green ('82)	1.10	.25
1082	A418	6p brt org ('85)	.40	.25
1083	A418	7p lil rose ('82)	5.00	.75
1084	A418	10p blue ('82)	2.00	.35
1085	A418	12p blk ('85)	1.10	.25
1086	A418	15.50p emer ('85)	1.50	.30
1087	A418	20p dk vio ('82)	4.25	.75
1088	A418	30p lt brn ('82)	6.50	.75
1089	A418	50p gray bl ('82)	11.00	1.90
	Nos. 1073-1089 (17)		39.25	7.90

Christmas
1980
A419

1980, Dec. 15   Litho.   Perf. 12
1090 A419 2p multi   .75 .25

Constitution Title Page — A420

1980, Dec. 23   Perf. 12½
1091 A420 4p brt bl & gold   1.25 .65
    Sesquicentennial of Constitution.

A421

    No. 1092, Montevideo Stadium. No. 1093,
Soccer gold cup. No. 1094, Flags.

1980, Dec. 30   Perf. 12
1092 A421 5p multicolored   2.00 1.00

1093 A421 5p multicolored 2.00 1.00
Size: 25x79mm
1094 A421 10p multicolored 2.00 1.00
 a. Souv. sheet of 3, #1092-1094 10.50 10.50
 Nos. 1092-1094 (3) 6.00 3.00
Soccer Gold Cup Championship, Montevideo.

A422

1981, Jan. 27
1095 A422 2p multi .70 .25
Spanish Heritage Day.

UPU Membership Centenary — A423

1981, Feb. 6
1096 A423 2p multi .70 .25

Alexander von Humboldt (1769-1859), German Explorer and Scientist — A424

1981, Feb. 19
1097 A424 2p multi 1.25 .25

Intl. Education Congress and Fair, Montevideo (1980) — A425

1981, Mar. 31
1098 A425 2p multi .60 .25

Hand Holding Gold Cup — A426

1981, Apr. 8
1099 A426 2p multi .60 .25
1100 A426 5p multi 1.40 .50
 1980 victory in Gold Cup Soccer Championship.

Eighth Notes on Map of Americas — A427

1981, Apr. 28
1101 A427 2p multi .60 .25
Inter-American Institute of Musicology, 40th anniv.

World Tourism Conference, Manila, Sept. 27, 1980 — A428

Wmk. 332
1981, June 1 Litho. Perf. 12
1102 A428 2p multi .60 .25

Inauguration of PLUNA Flights to Madrid — A429

1981, May 12
1103 A429 2p multi .40 .25
1104 A429 5p multi .95 .45
1105 A429 10p multi 1.90 .95
 Nos. 1103-1105 (3) 3.25 1.65

Army Day — A430

No. 1106, Cavalry soldier, 1843. No. 1107, Infantryman, 1843.

Wmk. 332
1981, May 18 Litho. Perf. 12
1106 A430 2p multicolored .70 .25
1107 A430 2p multicolored .70 .25

Natl. Atomic Energy Commission, 25th Anniv. — A431

1981, July 20
1108 A431 2p multi .70 .25

Europe-South American Soccer Cup — A432

1981, Aug. 4
1109 A432 2p multi .90 .25

Stone Tablets, Salto Grande Excavation — A433

1981, Sept. 10
1110 A433 2p multi 1.25 .25

10th Lavalleja Week — A434

1981, Oct. 3
1111 A434 4p multi 1.40 .45

Intl. Year of the Disabled A435

Wmk. 332
1981, Oct. 26 Litho. Perf. 12
1112 A435 2p multi .60 .25

UN Environmental Law Meeting Montevideo, Oct. 28-Nov. 6 — A436

1981, Oct. 28
1113 A436 5p multi 1.40 .45

A437

1981, Oct. 13
1114 A437 2p multi .70 .25
 50th anniv. of ANCAP (Natl. Administration of Combustible Fuels, Alcohol and Cement).

Souvenir Sheets

Uruguay 81 Intl. Philatelic Exhibition — A438

No. 1114A: b, Copa de Oro trophy. c, Soccer player kicking ball.
No. 1115: a, Chess pieces. b, Prince Charles and Lady Diana, flags of Uruguay and Great Britain.

Wmk. 332
1981, Nov. 23 Litho. Perf. 12
1114A A438 5p Sheet of 2, #b-c 23.00 23.00
1115 A438 5p Sheet of 2, #a-b 25.00 25.00

 1982 World Cup Soccer Championships, Spain (No. 1114Ac), World Chess Championships, Atlanta (No. 1115a); Wedding of Prince Charles and Lady Diana (No. 1115b). Nos. 1114A-1115 exist imperf., which were not valid for postage.

Topographical Society Sesequicentennial — A439

1981, Dec. 5 Perf. 12
1116 A439 2p multi 1.00 .25
See No. 1407.

Bank of Uruguay, 85th Anniv. — A440

1981, Dec. 17 Perf. 12½
1117 A440 2p multi .60 .25

Palmar Dam — A441

1981, Dec. 22 Perf. 12
1118 A441 2p multi 1.00 .25

Christmas
1981
A442

1981, Dec. 23
1119 A442 2p multi　　　　　　　.60　.25

Pres. Joaquin
Suarez
Bicentenary
A443

1982, Mar. 15
1120 A443 5p multi　　　　　1.50　.50

Artillery Captain,
1872, Army
Day — A444

Wmk. 332
1982, May 18　Litho.　Perf. 12
1121 A444 3p shown　　　　　1.00　.25
1122 A444 3p Florida Battalion,
　　　　　1865　　　　　　1.00　.25
　　See Nos. 1136-1137.

Cent. (1981) of
Pinocchio, by
Carlo
Collodi — A445

1982, June 17
1123 A445 2p multi　　　　　　.70　.25

2nd UN
Conference on
Peaceful Uses
of Outer
Space,
Vienna, Aug.
9-21 — A446

1982, June 3
1124 A446 3p multi　　　　　1.25　.70

World
Food Day
A447

1982
1125 A447 2p multi　　　　　　.65　.25

25th Anniv. of Lufthansa's Uruguay-
Germany Flight — A448

3p, Lockheed L-1049-G Super Constellation. 7p, Boeing 747.

1982, Apr. 14　Unwmk.　Perf. 12½
1126 A448 3p multicolored　　1.00　.40
1127 A448 7p multicolored　　2.25　.80

American Air
Forces
Cooperation
System — A449

1982, Apr. 14　Wmk. 332　Perf. 12
1128 A449 10p Emblem　　　2.75　.80

Juan Zorilla de San Martin (1855-
1931), Painter — A450

1982, Aug. 18　　　　Perf. 12½
1129 A450 3p Self-portrait　　.80　.40

165th Anniv. of Natl. Navy — A451

1982, Nov. 15　　　　Perf. 12
1130 A451 3p Navy vessel
　　　　Capitan Miranda　1.00　.40

Natl. Literacy
Campaign
A452

1982, Nov. 30
1131 A452 3p multi　　　　　　.80　.35

Stamp Day — A453

1982, Dec. 23　　　　Perf. 12½
1132 A453 3p like #46　　　　.40　.25
1133 A453 3p like #47　　　　.40　.25
　a.　Pair, #1132-1133　　　1.40　1.40
These stamps bear numbers from 1 to 100
according to their position on the sheet.

Christmas 1982 — A454

1983, Jan. 4　　　　　Perf. 12
1134 A454 3p multi　　　　　　.60　.25

Eduardo Fabini (1882-1950),
Composer — A455

1983, May 10
1135 A455 3p gold & brn　　　.65　.25

Army Day Type of 1982
1983, May 18
1136 A444 3p Military College
　　　　cadet, 1885　　　　.60　.25
1137 A444 3p 2nd Cavalry Regi-
　　　　ment officer,
　　　　1885　　　　　　　.60　.25

Visit of King Juan Carlos and Queen
Sofia of Spain, May — A456

1983, May 20　　　　　Unwmk.
1138 A456 3p Santa Maria, globe　.75　.40
1139 A456 7p Profiles, flags　　1.75　.80
　　Size of No. 1138: 29x39mm.

Brasiliana '83
Emblem — A457

80th Anniv. of
First Automobile
in
Uruguay — A458

Opening of UPAE
Building,
Montevideo
A459

Jose Cuneo
(1887-1977),
Painter — A460

1982
World
Cup
A461

Graf Zeppelin Flight Over Montevideo,
50th Anniv. (1984) — A462

J.W. Goethe (1749-1832), 150th
Death Anniv. — A463

First
Space
Shuttle
Flight
A464

1983　Litho.　Wmk. 332　Perf. 12
1140 A457 3p multi　　　　　1.00　1.00
1141 A458 3p multi　　　　　1.00　1.00
1142 A459 3p multi　　　　　1.00　1.00
1143 A460 3p multi　　　　　1.00　1.00
　a.　Souvenir sheet of 4　　　6.00　6.00

1144	A461 7p multi	1.50	1.50
1145	A462 7p multi	1.50	1.50
1146	A463 7p multi	1.50	1.50
1147	A464 7p multi	1.50	1.50
a.	Souvenir sheet of 4	10.00	10.00
	Nos. 1140-1147 (8)	10.00	10.00

No. 1143a contains stamps similar to Nos. 1140-1143. No. 1147a stamps similar to Nos. 1144-1147. Nos. 1143a and 1147a for URUEXPO '83 and World Communications Year.

Issued: #1142, 6/8; #1143, 1146, 9/29; #1143a, 1147a, 6/9; #1140, 7/22; #1144, 12/13; #1146, 9/20; #1145, 12/8.

Bicentenary of City of Minas — A465

Wmk. 332
1983, Oct. 17   Litho.   Perf. 12
1148 A465 3p Founder   .75   .25

World Communications Year — A466

1983, Nov. 30
1149 A466 3p multi   .60   .25

Garibaldi Death Centenary A467

1983, Dec. 5
1150 A467 7p multi   1.00   .40

Christmas 1983 A468

Lithographed and Embossed (Braille)
1983, Dec. 21   Perf. 12½
1151 A468 4.50p multi   .75   .25

50th Anniv. of Automatic Telephones — A469

1983, Dec. 27   Perf. 12
1152 A469 4.50p multi   .60   .25

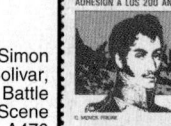

Simon Bolivar, Battle Scene A470

Wmk. 332
1984, Mar. 28   Litho.   Perf. 12
1153 A470 4.50p brn & gldn brn 1.25 .40

Gen. Leandro Gomez — A471

1984, Jan. 2
1154 A471 4.50p multi   .60   .25

American Women's Day — A472

1984, Feb. 18
1155 A472 4.50p Flags, emblem   .60   .25

Reunion Emblem A473

1984, Mar. 23
1156 A473 10p multi   1.25   .45
Intl. Development Bank Governors, 25th annual reunion, Punta del Este.

50th Anniv. of Radio Club of Uruguay (1983) A474

1984, Apr. 11
1157 A474 7p multi   .75   .30

A475

1984, Feb. 7   Litho.   Perf. 12
1158 A475 4.50p multi   .60   .25
Intl. Maritime Org., 25th anniv.

A476

1984, May 2   Litho.   Perf. 12
1159 A476 4.50p multi   .60   .25
1930 World Soccer Championships, Montevideo.

Department of San Jose de Mayo, 200th Anniv. — A477

1984, May 9   Litho.   Perf. 12
1160 A477 4.50p multi   .60   .25

Tourism, 50th Anniv. A478

1984, May 15   Litho.   Perf. 12
1161 A478 4.50p multi   .60   .25

Military Uniforms — A479

No. 1162, Artillery Regiment, 1895. No. 1163, Cazadores, 2nd battalion.

1984, June 19   Litho.   Perf. 12
1162 A479 4.50p multicolored   .60   .25
1163 A479 4.50p multicolored   .60   .25

Artigas on the Plains — A480

1984, July 2   Litho.   Perf. 12
1164 A480 4.50p bl & blk   .50   .25
1165 A480 8.50p bl & redsh brn .95   .40

A. Penarol Soccer Club A481

1984, Aug. 21   Litho.   Perf. 12
1166 A481 4.50p Championship trophy .60 .25

1984, Sept. 21   Litho.   Perf. 12
1167 A281 4.50p multi   .60   .25

Childrens Council, 50th Anniv. A482

1984, Oct. 11   Litho.   Perf. 12
1168 A482 4.50p multi   .50   .25

Christmas A483

1984   Litho.   Perf. 12
1169 A483 6p multi   .70   .30

A484

1985, Feb. 13   Litho.   Perf. 12
1170 A484 4.50p multi   .60   .25
1st Jr. World Jai Alai Championships.

Don Bruno Mauricio de Zabala, 300th Birth Anniv. — A485

1985, Apr. 16   Litho.   Perf. 12
1171 A485 4.50p multi   .60   .25

Intl. Olympic Committee, 90th Anniv. — A486

Design: Olympic rings, Los Angeles and Sarajevo 1984 Games emblems.

1985, May 22   Perf. 12½
1172 A486 12p multi   1.00 .50

Carlos Gardel,
(1890-1935),
Entertainer
A487

1985, June 21   *Perf. 12*
1173 A487 6p lt gray, red brn &
bl   .60 .25

Catholic Circle of
Workers,
Cent. — A488

       Wmk. 332
1985, June 21   **Litho.**   *Perf. 12*
1174 A488 6p Cross, clasped
hands   .30 .25

Icarus, by Hans Erni — A489

1985, July   **Photo.**   **Wmk. 332**
1175 A489 4.50p multi   .60 .25
Intl. Civil Aviation Org., 40th anniv.

American Air
Forces
Cooperation
System, 25th
Anniv. — A490

1985, July
1176 A490 12p Emblem, flags   .60 .25

FUNSA, Natl. Investment Funds Corp.,
50th Anniv. — A491

1985, July 31   **Litho.**   **Wmk. 332**
1177 A491 6p multi   .60 .25

Intl. Youth
Year
A492

1985, Aug. 28
1178 A492 12p mar & blk   .40 .25

Installation of Democratic
Government — A493

1985, Aug. 30
1179 A493 20p brt pur, yel ocher
& dk grnsh bl   1.20 .45

Intl. Book
Fair — A494

1985
1180 A494 20p multi   .80 .35

Military
School,
Cent.
A495

1985, Nov. 29   **Litho.**   *Perf. 12*
1181 A495 10p multi   .40 .25

Department of
Flores,
Cent. — A496

1985, Dec. 9
1182 A496 6p Map, arms   .40 .25

Christmas
1985
A497

1985, Dec. 23
1183 A497 10p multi   .40 .25
1184 A497 22p multi   .60 .30

Day of Hispanic
Solidarity — A498

1985, Dec. 27
1185 A498 12p Isabel Monument   .50 .25

3rd Inter-American Agricultural
Congress — A499

       Wmk. 332
1986, Jan. 7   **Photo.**   *Perf. 12*
1186 A499 12p blk, dl yel & red   .75 .30

UPU Day
A500

1986, Jan. 14   **Litho.**   *Perf. 12*
1187 A500 15.50p multi   .60 .25

1985
Census
A501

1986, Jan. 21
1188 A501 10p multi   .40 .25

Conaprole, 50th Anniv. — A502

1986, Jan. 25
1189 A502 10p gold, brt ultra &
bl   .50 .25

UN, 40th
Anniv.
A503

       Wmk. 332
1986, Feb. 26   **Litho.**   *Perf. 12*
1190 A503 20p multi   .60 .25

Brokers and
Auctioneers
Assoc., 50th
Anniv. — A504

1986, Mar. 19
1191 A504 10p multi   .40 .25

Gen. Manuel Ceferino
Oribe (1792-1857),
President — A505

Portraits: Nos. 1196, 1200, 2p, 7p, 15p, 20p,
Oribe. Nos. 1195, 1209, 1211, 3p, Lavalleja.

Nos. 1199, 1208, 1210, 30p, 100p, 200p, Artigas. No. 1198, 17p, 22p, 26p, 45p, 75p,
Rivera.

1986-89   *Perf. 12½*

1192	A505	1p dl grn	.25	.25
1193	A505	2p scarlet	.25	.25
1194	A505	3p ultra	.25	.25
1195	A505	5p dark blue	.25	.25
1196	A505	5p violet blue	.25	.25
1197	A505	7p tan	.25	.25
1198	A505	10p lilac rose	.30	.25
1199	A505	10p brt green	.25	.25
1200	A505	10p bluish grn	.25	.25
1201	A505	15p dull blue	.25	.25
1202	A505	17p deep blue	.30	.25
1203	A505	20p light brown	.25	.25
1204	A505	22p violet	.25	.25
1205	A505	26p olive blk	.35	.25
1206	A505	30p pale org	.35	.25
1207	A505	45p dark red	.35	.25
1208	A505	50p dp bis	.65	.45
1209	A505	50p bright pink	.25	.25
1210	A505	60p dark gray	.90	.45
1211	A505	60p orange	.25	.25
1211A	A505	75p red orange	.35	.25
1211B	A505	100p dl red brn	1.40	.60
1211C	A505	200p brt yel grn	2.00	.75
	Nos. 1192-1211C (23)		10.20	7.00

The 22p is airmail.
Issued: 1p, 7p, 4/18; #1195, 30p, 6/16;
#1198, 22p, 9/24; #1208, 8/5; 100p, 7/2; 2p,
6/16/87; 3p, #1210, 8/14/87; #1199, 17p,
8/4/87; 26p, 9/2/87; 15p, 9/9/88; 45p,
12/20/88; 200p, 10/19/88; #1211A, 5/19/89;
#1211, 7/27/89; #1196, 1203, 8/15/89; #1209,
12/12/89; #1200, 1989.
See Nos. 1321-1329.

Italian Chamber of Commerce in
Uruguay — A506

1986, May 5   *Perf. 12*
1212 A506 20p multi   .75 .25

A507

1986, May 28   **Photo.**   *Perf. 12*
1213 A507 20p multi   .60 .30
1986 World Cup Soccer Championships,
Mexico.

A508

       Wmk. 332
1986, May 19   **Litho.**   *Perf. 12*
1214 A508 10p multi   .60 .30
Genocide of the Armenian people, 71st
anniv.

A509

1986, June 16
1215 A509 10p multi .45 .25
El Dia Newspaper, cent.

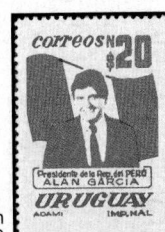

Garcia, Peruvian Flag — A510

1986, July 14
1216 A510 20p multi .40 .25
State visit of Pres. Alan Garcia of Peru.

Simon Bolivar, Gen. Sucre, Map A511

1986, July 24
1217 A511 20p multi .65 .25
State visit of Pres. Jaime Lusinchi of Venezuela.

State Visit of Pres. Jose Sarney of Brazil — A512

1986, July 31
1218 A512 20p multi .60 .25

Zelmar Michelini, Assassinated Liberal Senator — A513

1986, Aug. 21
1219 A513 10p vio bl & rose lake .45 .25

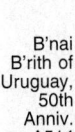 

B'nai B'rith of Uruguay, 50th Anniv. A514

1986, Sept. 10
1220 A514 10p red, gold & red brn .70 .30

General Agreement on Tariffs & Trade (GATT) Committee Meeting, Punta del Este — A515

1986, Sept. 15
1221 A515 10p multi .50 .25

Scheduled Flights between Uruguay and Spain, 40th Anniv. — A516

1986, Sept. 22
1222 A516 20p multi .60 .30

Fish Exports A517

1986, Oct. 1
1223 A517 20p multi .60 .30

Wool Exports A518

1986, Oct. 15
1224 A518 20p multi .60 .30

Pres. Blanco, Natl. and Dominican Flags A519

1986, Oct. 29
1225 A519 20p multi .60 .25
State visit of Pres. Salvador Jorge Blanco of the Dominican Republic.

State Visit of Pres. Sandro Pertini of Italy — A520

1986, Oct. 31
1226 A520 20p grn & buff .60 .25

State Visit of Pres. Raul Alfonsin of Argentina A521

1986, Nov. 10
1227 A521 20p multi .60 .25

Hispanic Solidarity Day A522

Design: Felipe and Santiago, the patron saints of Montevideo, and cathedral.

Wmk. 332
1987, Jan. 12   Litho.   Perf. 12
1228 A522 10p rose lake & blk .60 .30

JUVENTUS, 50th Anniv. (in 1986) — A523

1987, Jan. 28
1229 A523 10p brt yel, blk & ultra .45 .25
Juventus, a Catholic sports, culture and leisure organization.

Hector Gutierrez Ruiz (1934-1976), Politician — A524

Intl. Symposium on Science and Technology A525

1987, Feb. 23
1230 A524 10p brn & deep mag .45 .25
1231 A525 20p multi .60 .25
Ruiz represented Uruguay at an earlier science and technology symposium.

Visit of Pope John Paul II to La Plata Region — A526

1987, Mar. 31
1232 A526 50p blk & deep org 1.00 .50

Dr. Jose F. Arias (1885-1965), Founder of the University of Crafts — A527

1987, Apr. 28
1233 A527 10p multi .45 .25

Jewish Community in Uruguay, 70th Anniv. — A528

1987, July 8
1234 A528 10p blk, org & brt bl .60 .30

Pluna Airlines, 50th Anniv. (in 1986) A529

1987, Sept. 16
1235 A529 10p Dragon Fly .40 .25
1236 A529 20p Douglas DC-3 .50 .25
1237 A529 25p Vickers Viscount .60 .25
1238 A529 30p Boeing 707 .80 .30
Nos. 1235-1238 (4) 2.30 1.05

Artigas Antarctic Station A530

1987, Sept. 28
1239 A530 20p multi 1.00 .30

Uruguay Mortgage Bank, 75th Anniv. A531

1987, Oct. 14
1240 A531 26p multi .60 .25

Exports — A532

1987, Oct. 28
1241 A532 51p Beef .85 .40
1242 A532 51p Milk products .85 .40

Christmas 1987 — A533

1987, Dec. 21
1243	A533	17p Nativity, vert.	.45	.25
1244	A533	66p shown	.85	.50

State Visit of Jose Napoleon Duarte, President of El Salvador — A534

1988, Jan. 12
1245	A534	20p brt olive grn & Prus blue	.60	.25

VARIG Airlines, 60th Anniv. (in 1987) — A535

1988, Feb. 9
1246	A535	66p blk, blue & brt yel	1.10	1.10

Post Office Stamp Foundation A536

Wmk. 332
1988, Feb. 9   Litho.   Perf. 12
1247	A536	30p on 10+5p brt blue, blk & yel	1.10	.30

No. 1247 not issued without surcharge.

Intl. Peace Year A537

1988, Feb. 11
1248	A537	10p multi	.30	.25

Euskal Erria, 75th Anniv. (in 1987) — A538

1988, Mar. 9
1249	A538	66p multi	.70	.40

Basque-Uruguayan diplomatic relations.

Air Force, 75th Anniv. A539

1988, Mar. 11
1250	A539	17p multi	.40	.25

Interamerican Children's Institute, 60th Anniv. — A540

Wmk. 332
1988, Mar. 28   Litho.   Perf. 12
1251	A540	30p apple grn, blk & grn	.70	.30

State Hydroelectric Works (UTE), 75th Anniv. — A541

1988, Apr. 20
1252	A541	17p shown	.25	.25
1253	A541	17p Baygorria Dam	.25	.25
1254	A541	51p Gabriel Terra Dam	.70	.30
1255	A541	51p Constitucion Dam	.70	.30
1256	A541	66p Dams on map	1.00	.45
		Nos. 1252-1256 (5)	2.90	1.55

Dated 1987.

Postal Union of America and Spain (UPAE), 75th Anniv. (in 1987) A542

1988, May 10
1257	A542	66p multi	.65	.45

Israel, 40th Anniv. A543

1988, May 17
1258	A543	66p lt ultra & blk	1.00	.35

Postal Messenger of Peace — A544

1988, May 24
1259	A544	66p multi	.65	.35

Portrait, *La Cumparsita* Tango — A545

1988, June 7
1260	A545	17p Parade, horiz.	.45	.25
1261	A545	51p Score	1.40	.55

Gerardo H. Matos Rodrigues, composer.

Firemen, Cent. — A546

17p, Pablo Banales, founder. 26p, Fireman, 1900. 34p, Emblem, horiz. 51p, Merry Weather fire engine, 1907, horiz. 66p, Fire pump, 1888, horiz. 100p, Ladder truck, 1921.

1988, June 21
1262	A546	17p multi	.40	.25
1263	A546	26p multi	.45	.25
1264	A546	34p multi	.60	.30
1265	A546	51p multi	.90	.45
1266	A546	66p multi	1.40	.65

Size: 44x24½mm
1267	A546	100p multi	2.25	1.10
		Nos. 1262-1267 (6)	6.00	3.00

Capitan Miranda Trans-world Voyage, Cent. — A547

1988, July 28
1268	A547	30p multi	.40	.25

Exports A548

1988
1269	A548	30p Citrus fruit	.35	.25
1270	A548	45p Rice	.70	.25
1271	A548	55p Footwear	.80	.30
1272	A548	55p Leather and furs	.80	.35
		Nos. 1269-1272 (4)	2.65	1.15

Issued: 30p, #1272, 9/14; 45p, #1271, 8/23.

Natl. Museum of Natural History, 150th Anniv. — A549

30p, Usnea densirostra fossil. 90p, Toxodon platensis bone, Quaternary period.

1988, Sept. 20
1273	A549	30p blk, yel & red brn	.60	.30
1274	A549	90p blk, ultra & beige	1.40	.65
a.		Pair, #1273-1274	3.00	3.00

Battle of Carpinteria, 150th Anniv. (in 1986) — A550

1988, Nov. 23
1275	A550	30p multi	.30	.25

Horiz. row contains two stamps, label, then two more stamps.

A551

1988, Dec. 21
1276	A551	115p multi	1.00	1.00

Christmas.

A552

Paintings: a, Manolita Pina, 1920, by J. Torres Garcia. b, 78 Squares and Rectangles, by J.P. Costigliolo. c, Print publicizing an exhibition of works by Pedrero Figari, 1945. d, Self-portrait, 1947, by J. Torres Garcia.

1988, Dec. 27
1277		Block or strip of 4 + label	4.50	4.50
a.-d.	A552	115p any single	1.00	.65

No. 1277 can be collected as a vert. or horiz. strip of 4, or block of 4, with label.

Spanish Heritage Day A553

1989, Jan. 9
1278	A553	90p multi	.75	.40
1279	A553	115p multi	1.10	.50

Armenian Organization Hnchakian, Cent. — A554

1989, June 7 Litho. *Perf. 12*
1280 A554 210p red, yel & blue 1.75 .70

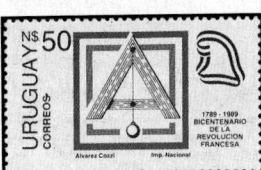

French Revolution,
Bicentennial — A555

No. 1281, Plumb line, frame. No. 1282, Liberty tree. No. 1283, Eye in sunburst. No. 1284, Liberty.

1989, July 3
1281 A555 50p multi .35 .25
1282 A555 50p multi .35 .25
1283 A555 210p multi 1.40 .45
1284 A555 210p multi 1.40 .45
Nos. 1281-1284 (4) 3.50 1.40

Use Postal Codes — A556

50p, Montevideo Dept. map. 210p, National map, vert.

1989, July 25
1285 A556 50p multi .35 .25
1286 A556 210p multi 1.10 .40

3rd Pan
American Milk
Congress
A557

1989, Aug. 24
1287 A557 170p sky blue & ultra 1.20 .45

A558

Wmk. 332
1989, Aug. 29 Photo. *Perf. 12*
1288 A558 170p multicolored .85 .30

Joaquin Jose da Silva Xavier.

A559

1989, Aug. 31
1289 A559 210p blk, red & bl 1.00 .35

Inter-Parliamentary Union Conf., London.

FAO Emblem, Map, Citrus
Slice — A560

1989, Sept. 11
1290 A560 180p multicolored .80 .35

8th Conf., Intergovernmental Group on Citrus Fruits.

UN Decade for the Disabled — A561

1989, Oct. 4
1291 A561 50p shown .35 .25
1292 A561 210p Disabled people .95 .40

America
Issue — A562

Nacurutu artifact and UPAE emblem.

1989, Oct. 11 *Perf. 12½*
1293 A562 60p multicolored 1.25 .40
1294 A562 180p multicolored 2.75 1.10

City of Pando, Bicentennial — A563

1989, Dec. 27 Litho. *Perf. 12*
1295 A563 60p multicolored .30 .25

Christmas
A564

70p, Virgin of Trienta y Tres. 210p, Barradas, horiz.

1989, Dec. 19
1296 A564 70p multi .45 .25
1297 A564 210p multi 1.10 .45

Charity Hospital, Bicent. (in 1988) — A565

1990, Jan. 23 **Wmk. 332**
1298 A565 60p multicolored .70 .70

Provincial
Arms and
Maps
A566

1990
1299 A566 70p Soriano .40 .40
1300 A566 70p Florida, vert. .45 .45
1301 A566 90p Canelones .50 .50
1302 A566 90p Lavalleja, vert. .50 .50
1303 A566 90p San Jose, vert. .50 .50
1304 A566 90p Rivera .50 .50
Nos. 1299-1304 (6) 2.85 2.85

Dated 1989.

Writers — A567

Designs: a, Luisa Luisi (1883-1940). b, Javier de Viana (1872-1926). c, Delmira Agustini (1886-1914). d, J. Zorrilla de San Martin (1855-1931). e, Alfonsina Storni (1892-1938). f, Julio Casal (1889-1954). g, Juana de Ibarbourou (1895-1979). h, Carlos Roxlo (1861-1926).

1990, Mar. 20
1320 Block of 8 + 2 labels 6.00 6.00
a.-b. A567 60p any single .35 .35
c.-d. A567 75p any single .40 .40
e.-f. A567 170p any single 1.00 1.00
g.-h. A567 210p any single 1.25 1.25

Printed in sheets of 4 blocks of 4 separated by vert. and horiz. rows of 5 labels. Position of denomination varies to form border around each block.
Dated 1989.

Portraits Type of 1986

25p, 30p, Lavalleja. 60p, 90p, Rivera. 100p, 150p, 300p, 500p, 1000p, Artigas.

1990 Litho. **Wmk. 332** *Perf. 12½*
1321 A505 25p orange .30 .25
1322 A505 30p ultra .30 .25
1323 A505 60p purple .30 .25
1324 A505 90p org red .60 .30
1325 A505 100p brown 1.50 .35
1326 A505 150p dk blue green .90 .50
1327 A505 300p blue 1.50 1.00
1328 A505 500p orange red 2.50 1.00
1329 A505 1000p red 5.00 3.00
Nos. 1321-1329 (9) 12.90 6.90

Issued: 30p, 60p, 7/17; 90p, 3/24; 150p, 6/22; 300p, 7/5; 500p, 3/22; 1000p, 7/24.

A568

1990, Apr. 3 *Perf. 12*
1346 A568 70p multicolored .40 .40

City of Mercedes, bicent. Dated 1989.

A569

1990, Apr. 24
1347 A569 210p multicolored 1.25 1.25

Intl. Agricultural Development Fund, 10th anniv. Dated 1989.

Traffic Safety — A570

Designs: a, Bus, car. b, Don't drink and drive. c, Cross on the green light. d, Obey traffic signs.

1990, May 28
1348 A570 70p Block of 4, #a.-d. 1.50 1.50

General
Artigas
A571

1990, June 18
1349 A571 60p red & blue .45 .45

A572

1990, June 26
1350 A572 70p multicolored   .40   .40
Intl. Mothers' Day. Dated 1989.

A573

Treaty of Montevideo, 1889: a, Gonzalo Ramirez. b, Ildefonso Garcia. c, Flags at left. d, Flags at right.

1990, July 10
1351 A573 60p Block of 4, #a.-d. 1.40 1.40
Nos. 1351c-1351d printed in continuous design. Dated 1989.

Microphone, Tower — A574

b, Newspaper boy. c, Television camera. d, Books.

1990, Sept. 26
1352 A574 70p Block of 4, #a.-d. 2.00 2.00

Carlos Federico Saez (1878-1901) — A575

Portraits: b, Pedro Blanes Viale (1879-1926). c, Edmundo Prati (1889-1970). d, Jose L. Zorrilla de San Martin (1891-1975).

1990, Dec. 26
1353   Block of 4   3.50 3.50
a.-b. A575 90p any single   .50   .50
c.-d. A575 210p any single   1.10 1.10

Prevent Forest Fires — A576

Wmk. 332
1990, Oct. 26   Litho.   Perf. 12
1354 A576 70np multicolored   2.00 2.00

America Issue — A577

1990, Nov. 6
1355 A577 120p Odocoileus
              bezoarticus   1.00 1.00
1356 A577 360p Peltophorum
              dubium, vert.   3.50 3.50

Army Corps of Engineers, 75th Anniv. — A578

1991, Jan. 21
1357 A578 170p multicolored   1.00 1.00

The Nativity by Brother Juan B. Maino — A579

1990, Dec. 24
1358 A579 170p bister & multi   1.00 1.00
1359 A579 830p silver & multi   4.75 4.75

Organization of American States, Cent. (in 1989) A580

Wmk. 332
1991, Mar. 21   Litho.   Perf. 12
1360 A580 830p bl, blk & yel   4.50 4.50

Prevention of AIDS — A581

1991, Mar. 8
1361 A581 170p bl & multi   1.00 1.00
1362 A581 830p grn & multi   4.75 4.75

Carnival — A582

1991, Feb. 19
1363 A582 170p multicolored   1.00 1.00

Education — A583

Expanding youth's horizons: a, Stone ax, megalithic monument. b, Wheel, pyramids. c, Printing press, solar system. d, Satellite, diagram.

Wmk. 332
1991, Apr. 23   Litho.   Perf. 12
1364   Block of 4   3.00 3.00
a.-b. A583 120p any single   .40   .40
c.-d. A583 330p any single   1.25 1.25

Natl. Cancer Day — A584

1991, June 17
1365 A584 360p red & black   1.10 1.10

A585

Exports of Uruguay — A586

Perf. 12½x13, 13x12½
1991   Litho.   Wmk. 332
1366 A585 120p Textiles   .40   .40
1367 A586 120p Clothing   .50   .35
1368 A585 400p Semiprecious
              stones, granite   1.40 1.40
Nos. 1366-1368 (3)   2.30 2.15
Issued: #1366, 400p, 4/23; #1367, 6/26.

7th Pan American Maccabiah Games — A587

1991, July 4   Perf. 12½x13
1369 A587 1490p multicolored   6.00 6.00

Dornier Wal, Route Map — A588

1991, July 5   Perf. 12
1370 A588 1510p multicolored   5.00 5.00
Espamer '91.

Entrance to Sacramento Colony A589

Railroads and Trains: 540p, 825p, First locomotive, 1869. 600p, like 360p. 800p, Entrance to Sacramento Colony. 1510p, 2500p, Horse-drawn streetcar.

Wmk. 332
1991-2002   Litho.   Perf. 12
1378   A589 360p ol bis & yel   .95   .60
1378A A589 540p dk bl &
                  gray   1.40   .95
1379   A589 600p brn, yel &
                  blk   .95   .85
1379A A589 800p grn & yel
                  grn   .95   .95
1379B A589 825p bl, gray &
                  blk   1.40 1.25
1380   A589 1510p ol bis &
                  emer   4.25 3.00
1382   A589 2500p ol bis, em-
                  er & blk   3.50 3.00
Nos. 1378-1382 (7)   13.40 10.60

Issued: 360p, 540p, 1510p, July 19; 825p, Feb. 11, 1992; 2500p, May 29, 2002; 600p, June 18, 1992; 800p, Feb. 9, 1993.
For surcharges, see Nos. 2011B, 2057-2059.

Sagrada Family College, Cent. — A590

College of the Immaculate Heart of Mary, Cent. — A591

Wmk. 332
1991, June 26   Litho.   Perf. 12
1383 A590 360p multicolored   .75   .75
1384 A591 1370p multicolored   3.00 3.00

Constitutional Oath — A592

1991, July 17
1385 A592 360p multicolored .90 .90

Swiss Confederation, 700th Anniv. — A593

1991, Aug. 1 Perf. 13x12½
1386 A593 1510p multicolored 5.25 5.25
Souvenir Sheet
Perf. 12
1387 A593 3000p multicolored 11.00 11.00

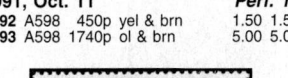

Photography, 150th Anniv. — A594

Perf. 12½x13
1991, Sept. 12 Litho. Wmk. 332
1388 A594 1370p multi 3.50 3.50

Actors Society of Uruguay, 50th Anniv. — A595

1991, Aug. 24 Perf. 12
1389 A595 450p blk & red 1.25 1.25

CREA (Agriculture Association), 25th Anniv. — A596

1991, Sept. 14 Perf. 12½x13
1390 A596 450p multicolored 1.25 1.25

Whitbread Around the World Race — A597

1991, Aug. 20 Perf. 13x12½
1391 A597 1510p multicolored 4.00 4.00

Amerigo Vespucci (1454-1512) — A598

America Issue: 450p, First landing at River Plate, 1602, vert.

1991, Oct. 11 Perf. 12
1392 A598 450p yel & brn 1.50 1.50
1393 A598 1740p ol & brn 5.00 5.00

Automobiles — A599

Designs: 350p, Gladiator, 1902. 1370p, E.M.F., 1909. 1490p, Renault, 1912. 1510p, Clement-Bayard, 1903, vert.

1991, Oct. 18 Perf. 12½x13, 13x12½
1394 A599 360p multicolored .90 .90
1395 A599 1370p multicolored 3.50 3.50
1396 A599 1490p multicolored 3.50 3.50
1397 A599 1510p multicolored 3.50 3.50
Nos. 1394-1397 (4) 11.40 11.40

Team Nacional Montevideo, Winners of Toyota and Europe-South America Soccer Cups — A600

Wmk. 332
1991, Nov. 8 Litho. Perf. 12
1398 A600 450p shown 1.25 1.25
1399 A600 450p Emblem, trophy, vert. 1.25 1.25

Margarita Xirgu (1888-1969), Actress — A601

1991, Oct. 4
1400 A601 360p yel & brn 1.00 1.00

INTERPOL, 60th Congress A602

1991, Oct. 30
1401 A602 1740p multicolored 3.50 3.50

Maria Auxiliadora Institute, Cent. — A603

1991, Nov. 11
1402 A603 450p multicolored 1.25 1.25

Technological Laboratory, 25th Anniv. — A604

1991, Nov. 11
1403 A604 1570p dk bl & lt bl 3.00 3.00

The Table by Zoma Baitler — A605

1991, Oct. 18
1404 A605 360p multicolored 1.25 1.25

World Food Day A606

1991,Oct. 16 Perf. 12½x13
1405 A606 1740p multicolored 4.00 4.00

Ships A607

Designs: a, Steam yacht, Gen. Rivera. b, Coast Guard cutter, Salto. c, Cruiser, Uruguay. d, Tanker, Pte. Oribe.

Wmk. 332
1991, Oct. 4 Litho. Perf. 12
1406 Block of 4 10.00 10.00
a.-b. A607 450p any single 1.25 1.25
c.-d. A607 1570p any single 3.50 3.50

Topographical Society Type of 1981
1991, Dec. 3 Perf. 12½
1407 A439 550p multi .85 .85
Topographical Society, 160th anniv.

World AIDS Day — A608

1991, Dec. 1
1408 A608 550p bl, blk & brt yel 1.10 1.10
1409 A608 2040p lt grn, blk & lil 3.75 3.75

Export Industries A609

Wmk. 332
1991, Mar. 20 Litho. Perf. 12½
1410 A609 120p multicolored .40 .40

Christmas A610

1991, Dec. 24 Perf. 12
1411 A610 550p Angel .90 .90
1412 A610 2040p Adoration of the Angels 3.00 3.00

Muscians — A611

Designs: a, Juan de Dios Filiberto. b, Pintin Castellanos. c, Francisco Canaro. d, Anibal Troilo.

Wmk. 332
1992, Jan. 20 Photo. Perf. 12
1413 A611 450p Block of 4, #a-d 3.50 3.50

Patricio Aylwin, Pres. of Chile — A612

Perf. 11½x12
1992, Mar. 23 Litho. Unwmk.
1415 A612 550p multicolored .85 .85

Penarol, Winners of Liberator's Cup in Club Soccer — A612a

Perf. 13x12½
1992, May 29   Litho.   Wmk. 332
1415A   A612a   600p yel & blk   1.25 1.25

Souvenir Sheet
Perf. 12
1415B   A612a   3000p yel & blk   5.00 5.00

La Paz City, 120th Anniv. — A612b

1992, May 25   Perf. 13x12½
1415C   A612b   550p multicolored   .85   .85

World No-Smoking Day — A613

Wmk. 332
1992, May 31   Litho.   Perf. 12
1416   A613   2500p multicolored   3.75 3.75

United Nations World Health Day A614

Wmk. 332
1992, July 28   Litho.   Perf. 13
1417   A614   2500p bl, lt bl & red   3.75 3.75

Mercosur A615

1992, Aug. 5   Photo.   Perf. 12
1418   A615   2500p multicolored   3.75 3.75

Olymphilex '92, Barcelona — A616

Wmk. 332
1992, Aug. 8   Photo.   Perf. 12
1419   A616   2900p multicolored   4.50 4.50

Discovery of America, 500th Anniv. — A617

Perf. 11½x12, 12x11½
1992, Oct. 10   Litho.   Unwmk.
1420   A617   700p Ship, masts, vert.   1.25 1.25
1421   A617   2900p Globe, ship   4.00 4.00

Jose Pedro Varela Natl. Teachers College, 50th Anniv. A618

1992, Oct. 22   Perf. 12x11½
1422   A618   700p multicolored   .85   .85

22nd Regional FAO Conference — A619

Designs: 2500p, Emblems. 2900p, Emblems, children with food basket.

1992, Sept. 28
1423   A619   2500p multicolored   3.00 3.00
1424   A619   2900p multicolored   3.75 3.75
Intl. Conf. on Nutrition, Rome, Italy (#1424).

Cesar Vallejo (1892-1938), Poet — A620

1992, Sept. 30
1425   A620   2500p brn & dk brn   3.25 3.25

A621

1992, Oct. 26   Perf. 11½x12
1426   A621   700p gray, red & blk   .85   .85
Assoc. of Wholesalers and Retailers, cent.

A622

Perf. 11½x12
1992, Oct. 10   Unwmk.
1427   A622   700p black, blue & grn   1.00 1.00
Monument to Columbus, cent.

A623

Ruins and lighthouse, Colonia del Sacramento.

1992, Oct. 10
1428   A623   700p multicolored   1.25 1.25
Discovery of America, 500th anniv.

A624

1992, Oct. 19
1429   A624   700p red lil, rose lil & blk   1.25 1.25
Columbus Philanthropic Society, cent.

A625

1992, Oct. 19
1430   A625   2900p multicolored   3.75 3.75
Judaism in the Americas, 500th anniv.

A626

1992, Oct. 30
1431   A626   2900p multicolored   3.75 3.75
Lebanon Society of Uruguay, 50th anniv.

Pan American Health Organization, 90th Anniv. — A627

22nd Lions Club Forum for Latin America and the Caribbean — A628

1992, Dec. 2
1433   A628   2700p multicolored   3.00 3.00

Christmas A629

1992, Dec. 1   Perf. 11½x12
1434   A629   800p Nativity scene   1.00 1.00
1435   A629   3200p Star in sky   3.50 3.50

General Manuel Oribe, Birth Bicent. A630

Designs: No. 1436, Oribe, Oriental College. No. 1437, Oribe in military dress uniform, vert.

Perf. 12x11½, 11½x12
1992, Dec. 8   Litho.   Unwmk.
1436   A630   800p multicolored   1.00 1.00
1437   A630   800p multicolored   1.00 1.00

Logosofia, 60th Anniv. — A631

1992, Dec. 29   Perf. 12x11½
1438   A631   800p blue & yellow   1.00 1.00

Immigrants' Day — A632

1992, Dec. 4   Perf. 11½x12
1439   A632   800p black & green   1.00 1.00

ANDEBU, 70th Anniv. — A633

Perf. 12x11½
1992, Dec. 15   Litho.   Unwmk.
1432   A627   3200p blk, bl & yel   3.75 3.75

Caritas
of Uruguay,
30th
Anniv.
A634

1992, Dec. 22 Photo. Perf. 12x11½
1440 A633 2700p Satellite 3.00 3.00
1441 A634 3200p Map, huts by
water 3.75 3.75

A635

1992, Dec. 18 Perf. 11½x12
1442 A635 800p brown & yellow 1.00 1.00
Jose H. Molaguero S. A., 50th anniv.

A636

Perf. 11½x12
1993, Mar. 1 Litho. Unwmk.
1443 A636 80c multicolored .90 .90
Wilson Ferreira Aldunate.

Economic Science and Accountancy
College, Cent. — A637

Perf. 12x11½
1993, Apr. 15 Photo. Unwmk.
1444 A637 1p multicolored 1.10 1.10

Souvenir Sheet

Polska '93, Intl. Philatelic
Exhibition — A638

a, Lech Walesa. b, Pope John Paul II.

1993, May 3 Perf. 11½x12
1445 A638 2p Sheet of 2, #a.-b. 6.00 6.00

A639

A639a

A639b

A639c

A639d

A639e

A639f

A639g

A639h

Design A639g shows the Postal Administration Tower.

ONE PESO (Letter Box — A639):
Type I — "Bugon vecinal 1879" 21½mm, letter box 23½mm high.
Type II — "Bugon vecinal 1879" 22mm, letter box 22½mm high.
Type III — "Bugon vecinal 1879" 19½mm, letter box 21mm high.
There are other differences among the three types.

Perf. 12½, 12 (#1449, 1465)
1993-99 Litho. Wmk. 332
1446	A639	50c gray ol & yel	.30	.30
1447	A639	1p lt brn & yel (I)	.50	.50
a.		Type II	.60	.60
b.		Type III, unwatermarked	.35	.35
c.		Type III, photo., unwmkd.	.35	.35
1448	A639a	1p org yel & bl	1.00	1.00
1449	A639b	1p org & bl	.65	.65
1450	A639c	(1.20p) blue	.70	.70
1451	A639c	(1.40p) green	.75	.75
1452	A639d	1.40p yel & bl	.75	.75
1453	A639c	(1.60p) red	1.25	1.25
1454	A639	1.80p bl & yel	1.40	1.40
1455	A639c	(1.80p) brown	1.25	1.25
1456	A639c	(2p) gray	1.25	1.25
1457	A639c	(2.30p) lilac	1.60	1.60
1458	A639	2.60p bl, yel & grn	1.60	1.60
1459	A639e	(2.60p) grn & yel	1.60	1.60
1460	A639e	(2.90p) bl & yel	1.60	1.60
1460A	A639e	(3p) gray & brt yel grn	1.00	1.00
b.		Unwmkd.	1.00	1.00
1461	A639e	(3.10p) red & pink	1.10	1.10
1462	A639e	(3.20p) rose brn & lt brn	5.00	5.00
1462A	A639e	(3.50p) pur & lt bl	—	—
1462B	A639e	(3.80p) brt blue	1.60	1.60
1463	A639e	(4p) bis & yel, litho.	1.25	1.25
1464	A639f	5p bl & yel, perf. 12½	3.00	3.00
1465	A639g	6p blue & blk	1.75	1.75
1465A	A639f	7p blue & blk	3.75	3.75
1465B	A639	7.50p vio & yel	4.00	4.00
1465C	A639h	8p bl & yel	4.00	4.00
		Nos. 1446-1462,1463-1465C (24)	41.05	41.05

The design of Nos. 1460A, 1462-1463 does not include "PORTE MINIMO." There are minor design differences between #1464 and 1465A.

Issued: #1448, 4/15/93; #1450, 8/2/93; #1451, 12/1/93; #1452, 1/4/94; #1453, 4/4/94; #1455, 8/1/94; #1454 8/9/94; #1449, 10/3/94; 1456, 12/1/94. #1457, 4/1/95; #1458, (2.60p), 8/10/95; 50c, #1447, 8/27/96; #1460, (3.10p), (3.50p), 4/1/96; 7.50p, 5/21/96; 5p, 1997; (3.80p), 5/9/97; #1463, 8/1/97; 6p, 8/13/97; (3.50p), 7/28/98; (3p), 2/1/99. #1460Ab, 1999. For surcharges, see Nos. 2056, 2106, 2186, 2269

Interior Fire
Service, 50th
Anniv. — A640

Perf. 11½x12
1993, May 28 Litho. Unwmk.
1466 A640 1p multicolored 1.00 1.00

15th Congress of
UPAEP — A641

1993, June 21
1467 A641 3.50p multicolored 3.75 3.75

Uruguayan Navy, 175th Anniv. — A642

Sailing ship, Pedro Campbell, first admiral.

Perf. 12x11½
1993, June 28 Litho. Wmk. 332
1468 A642 1p multicolored 1.25 1.25

Intl. University Society, 25th
Anniv. — A643

1993, July 2
1469 A643 1p multicolored 1.10 1.10

Automobile Club of Uruguay, 75th
Anniv. — A644

1993, July 19 Photo. Unwmk.
1470 A644 3.50p 1910
Hupmobile 3.75 3.75

Uruguay Battalion in UN Peacekeeping
Force, Cambodia — A645

Perf. 12x11½
1993, Aug. 6 Litho. Unwmk.
1471 A645 1p multicolored 1.25 1.25

Souvenir Sheet

Brasiliana '93 — A646

World Cup Soccer Champions: a, Uruguay, 1930, 1950. b, Brazil, 1958, 1962, 1970.

1993, July 28 Perf. 11½x12
1472 A646 2.50p Sheet of 2, #a.-
b. 9.00 9.00

State Television Channel 5, 30th
Anniv. — A647

1993, Aug. 19 Perf. 12x11½
1473 A647 1.20p multicolored 1.25 1.25

ANDA,
60th
Anniv.
A648

Perf. 12½
1993, Sept. 24 Litho. Unwmk.
1474 A648 1.20p multicolored 1.25 1.25

Natl.
Police
Academy,
50th
Anniv.
A649

1993, Sept. 24
1475 A649 1.20p multicolored 1.40 1.40

Newspaper Diario
El Pais, 75th
Anniv. — A650

Perf. 12½
1993, Sept. 30 Litho. Unwmk.
1476 A650 1.20p multicolored 1.40 1.40

Latin American Conference on Rural Electrification — A651

1993, Oct. 11
1477 A651 3.50p multicolored   3.75 3.75

B'nai B'rith, 150th Anniv. A652

1993, Oct. 13
1478 A652 3.70p multicolored   3.75 3.75

A653   Fauna — A654

1993 Photo. Wmk. 332 Perf. 12½
1482 A653   20c Seriema bird   .55 .25
1484 A653   30c Dragon bird   1.00 .25
1486 A653   50c Anteaters, horiz.   2.00 .40
1492 A654   1.20p Giant armadillo   2.50 1.25
   Nos. 1482-1492 (4)   6.05 2.15

Issued: 1.20p, 8/3/93; 20c, 30c, 50c, 10/22/93.
For surcharges, see Nos. 2011A, 2055, 2150, 2185.

America Issue A655

1.20p, Caiman latirostris. 3.50p, Athene cunicularia, vert.

Perf. 12½
1993, Oct. 6   Litho.   Unwmk.
1504 A655 1.20p multicolored   1.50 1.50
1505 A655 3.50p multicolored   4.25 4.25

Souvenir Sheet

Whitbread Trans-Global Yacht Race — A656

1993, Oct. 22   Perf. 11½x12
1506 A656 5p multicolored   5.00 5.00

Beatification of Mother Francisca Rubatto — A657

1993, Oct. 29   Wmk. 332   Perf. 12
1507 A657 1.20p multicolored   1.25 1.25

Intl. Year of Indigenous People — A658

Perf. 13x12½
1993, Oct. 29   Unwmk.
1508 A658 3.50p multicolored   3.25 3.25

Rotary Club of Montevideo, 75th Anniv. — A658a

Perf. 12½
1993, Nov. 10   Litho.   Unwmk.
1508A A658a 3.50p dk bl & bis   3.50 3.50

Rhea Americana A659

1993, Dec. 20   Litho.   Perf. 12
1509 A659   20c shown   .80 .35
1510 A659   20c With chicks   .90 .40
1511 A659   50c Head   1.40 .75
1512 A659   50c Two walking   1.40 .75
   Nos. 1509-1512 (4)   4.50 2.25

World Wildlife Fund.

Children's Rights Day A660

1994, Jan. 4   Perf. 12½
1513 A660 1.40p multicolored   1.25 1.25

Independence of Lebanon, 50th Anniv. — A661

1993, Nov. 22
1514 A661 3.70p multicolored   3.25 3.25

Eduardo Victor Haedo — A662

1993, Nov. 24
1515 A662 1.20p multicolored   1.20 1.20

Christmas A663

1993, Dec. 7
1516 A663 1.40p shown   1.25 1.25
1517 A663   4p Nativity, diff.   3.50 3.50

Intl. AIDS Day — A664

1993, Dec. 1
1518 A664 1.40p multicolored   2.00 2.00

Souvenir Sheets

Anniversaries & Events — A665

Designs: No. 1519a, Switzerland #3L1, 1913 Swiss private air mail stamp. b, Germany #C39, Uruguay #C426c. c, Uruguay #C372, US #C76. d, Uruguay #C282a, US #C104. No. 1520a, Switzerland Types A1, A2. b, Switzerland #B541.

1993, Nov. 18
1519 A665   1p #a.-d.   11.00 11.00
1520 A665 2.50p #a.-b.   11.00 11.00

Swiss postage stamps, 150th anniv. (#1519a, 1520). Dr. Hugo Eckener, 125th anniv. of birth (#1519b). First man on moon, 25th anniv. (#1519c). 1994 World Cup Soccer Championships, US (#1519d).
Nos. 1519-1520 exist imperf. Value $30.

17th Inter-American Naval Conference — A666

1994, Mar. 21   Litho.   Perf. 12½
1521 A666 3.70p multicolored   3.25 3.25

A667

1994, Mar. 11   Perf. 12½
1522 A667 4p multicolored   3.75 3.75

5th World Sports Congress, Punta del Este.

A668

Unwmk.
1994, Apr. 4   Litho.   Perf. 12
1523 A668 3.90p multicolored   2.75 2.75

Latin America Youth Organization, 7th conference.

A669

1994, Apr. 18
1524 A669 4.30p multicolored   3.75 3.75

4th World Congress on Merino Wool.

A670

1994, Apr. 28   Perf. 12½
1525 A670 4.30p multicolored   3.25 3.25

ILO, 75th anniv.

Miniature Sheet

1994 Winter Olympic Medal Winners — A671

Designs: a, Katja Seizinger. b, Markus Wasmeier. c, Vreni Schneider. d, Gustav Weder.

1994, May 6   *Perf. 12*
1526 A671 1.25p Sheet of 4,
   #a.-d.   10.00 10.00

No. 1526 exists demonetized and imperf on paper with watermark 322. This item was sold with No. 1526 and has a matching serial number.

Miniature Sheet

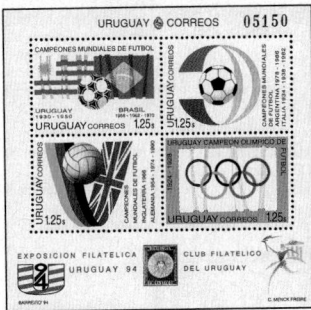

1994 World Cup Soccer
Championships, US — A672

a, Soccer ball, flags of Uruguay, Brazil. b, Ball, flags of Italy, Argentina. c, Ball, flags of Germany, Great Britain. d, Olympic Rings.

1994, May 16
1527 A672 1.25p Sheet of 4,
   #a.-d.   10.00 10.00

Uruguay, Olympic soccer gold medalists, 1924-1928 (#1527d).
See note after No. 1526.

Clemente Estable (1894-1976),
Biologist — A673

1994, May 23   Litho.   *Perf. 12½*
1528 A673 1.60p olive & black   1.40 1.40

Electoral Court,
70th
Anniv. — A674

1994, June 7
1529 A674 1.60p multicolored   1.40 1.40

Natl. Commission to Prevent
Tapeworms — A675

      Perf. 12½
1994, June 17   Litho.   Unwmk.
1530 A675 1.60p multicolored   2.00 2.00

Souvenir Sheet

Cesareo L. Berisso, First Aviator to
Land at Natl. Airport,
Carrasco — A676

1994, June 21   *Perf. 12*
1531 A676 5p multicolored   4.00 4.00

Intl. Cooperatives, 150th
Anniv. — A677

1994, July 1   *Perf. 12½*
1532 A677 4.30p multicolored   3.00 3.00

Commission on
Integration of
Regional
Electricity, 30th
Anniv. — A678

1994, July 8
1533 A678 1.60p multicolored   1.25 1.25

Abate
Pierre
A679

      Perf. 12½
1994, Aug. 5   Litho.   Unwmk.
1534 A679 4.80p multicolored   3.75 3.75

Intl. Year
of the
Family
A680

1994, July 28
1535 A680 4.80p multicolored   3.75 3.75

The Man of Lugano, by Goffredo
Sommavilla (1850-1944) — A681

      Perf. 12½
1994, Aug. 15   Litho.   Unwmk.
1536 A681 4.80p multicolored   3.25 3.25

First
Manned
Moon
Landing,
25th
Annvi.
A682

1994, July 20
1537 A682 3p multicolored   3.00 3.00

Intl. Olympic
Committee,
Cent. — A683

1994, Aug. 23
1538 A683 4.80p multicolored   3.75 3.75

Elbio
Fernandez
School,
125th
Anniv.
A684

      Perf. 12½
1994, Aug. 29   Litho.   Unwmk.
1539 A684 1.80p multicolored   1.25 1.25

Gral. Aparicio Saravia, 90th Death Anniv.

A685

1994, Sept. 10   *Perf. 12*
1540 A685 1.80p black & blue   1.25 1.25
Gral. Aparicio Saravia, 90th Death Anniv.

A686

1994, Sept. 30   *Perf. 12½*
1541 A686 4.80p multicolored   3.75 3.75
6th Latin American Urban Congress.

General Assoc.
of Uruguayan
Authors, 65th
Anniv. — A687

      Perf. 12½
1994, Sept. 26   Litho.   Unwmk.
1542 A687 1.80p multicolored   1.25 1.25

America
Issue
A688

1994, Oct. 10
1543 A688 1.80p Stagecoach   2.00 2.00
1544 A688 4.80p Paddle steamer   5.00 5.00

A689

      Perf. 12½
1994, Oct. 28   Litho.   Unwmk.
1545 A689 2p multicolored   1.25 1.25
Assoc. of Directors of Marketing, 50th anniv.

A690

1994, Nov. 25
1546 A690 2p multicolored   1.75 1.75
YMCA in Uruguay, 85th anniv.

Lottery,
55th
Anniv.
A691

1994, Nov. 21
1547 A691 2p multicolored   1.75 1.75

First Intl.
Seminar
to
Promote
Roads in
Uruguay,
Punta del
Este
A692

1994, Oct. 14
1548 A692 2p multicolored   1.60 1.60

Uruguayan Press Assoc., 50th
Anniv. — A693

1994, Oct. 24
1549 A693 2p multicolored   1.75 1.75

Miniature Sheet

Natl. Mint, 150th Anniv. — A694

Portions of old coin press and: a, Mint building. b, 1844 Copper coin. c, 1844 Silver coin. d, Montevideo silver peso.

1994, Oct. 17   **Perf. 12**
1550 A694 1.50p Sheet of 4, #a.-
d.   9.00 9.00

No. 1550 exists demonitized and imperf. on paper with watermark 332. This item was sold with No. 1550 and has matching serial numbers.

Miniature Sheet

Natl. Navy — A695

Ships: a, ROU Uruguay, ROU Artigas. b, ROU Fortuna. c, ROU Uruguay. d, ROU Cte. Pedro Campbell.

1994, Nov. 15
1551 A695 1.50p Sheet of 4, #a.-
d.   8.00 8.00

Latin American Peace Movement, 25th Anniv. — A696

1994, Nov. 15   **Perf. 12½**
1552 A696 4.30p multicolored   3.00 3.00

4th Conference of the Latin American and Caribbean Organization of High Fiscal Entities, Montevideo — A697

1994, Dec. 5
1553 A697 5.50p multicolored   3.50 3.50

Christmas
A698

1994, Dec. 2
1554 A698   2p shown   1.25 1.25
1555 A698 5.50p Star, tree,
house   3.25 3.25

Uruguayan Red Cross & Red Crescent Societies, 75th Anniv. — A699

Perf. 12½
1994, Dec. 20   Litho.   Unwmk.
1556 A699 5p multicolored   2.75 2.75

City Post
Office — A700

1995-97 Litho. Wmk. 332 Perf. 12
1557 A700 20c yellow green   .50 .50
1565 A700 10p brown   6.75 6.75
1566 A700 10p dark brown   3.75 3.75
Unwmk.
1566A A700 10p claret &
black   3.75 3.75
Nos. 1557-1566A (4)   14.75 14.75

Issued: 20c, 1/11/95; 10p, 5/21/96; #1566, 1566A, 1997.
Denomination has no decimal places on Nos. 1566-1566A.
This is an expanding set. Number may change.

Naval
Aviation,
70th
Anniv.
A704

Perf. 12½
1995, Feb. 7   Litho.   Unwmk.
1567 A704 2p multicolored   1.50 1.50

World Tourism Organization — A705

Designs: No. 1568, Ranch house, sheep herders. No. 1569, Water recreation park. No. 1570, Native wildlife. No. 1571, Beach resort.

1995, Feb. 13
1568 A705 5p multicolored   3.25 3.25
1569 A705 5p multicolored   3.25 3.25
1570 A705 5p multicolored   3.25 3.25
1571 A705 5p multicolored   3.25 3.25
Nos. 1568-1571 (4)   13.00 13.00

17th World
Conference of
Lifeguard
Services — A706

1995, Feb. 15
1572 A706 5p multicolored   3.25 3.25

Rotary
Intl., 90th
Anniv.
A707

1995, Feb. 22
1573 A707 5p multicolored   3.00 3.00

ICAO,
50th
Anniv.
A708

1995, Mar. 14
1574 A708 5p multicolored   3.25 3.25

Pietro Mascagni (1863-1945),
Composer — A709

Perf. 12½
1995, Mar. 30   Litho.   Unwmk.
1575 A709 5p multicolored   3.50 3.50

Miniature Sheet

Butterflies — A710

Designs: a, Phoebis neocypris. b, Diogas erippus. c, Euryades duponcheli. d, Automeris coresus.

1995, June 15   Litho.   Perf. 12½
1576 A710 5p Sheet of 4, #a.-
d.   12.00 12.00

Wild Dog
A711

1995, May 17   Litho.   Perf. 12½
1577 A711 2.30p multicolored   2.00 2.00

America Cup
Soccer
Championships
A712

Game scenes, flags of participating countries, match sites: a, Paysandu. b, Rivera. c, Ball (no site). d, Montevideo. e, Maldonado.

1995, July 4
1578 A712 2.30p Strip of 5, #a.-
e.   6.50 6.50

No. 1578 is a continuous design.

FAO, 50th
Anniv. — A713

1995, July 7
1579 A713 5.50p multicolored   3.25 3.25

UN Peace-Keeping Missions — A714

1995, July 14   Litho.   Perf. 12½
1580 A714 2.30p multicolored   1.75 1.75

Visit of
Italy's
Pres.
Oscar
Luigi
Scalfaro
A715

1995, July 21
1581 A715 5.50p multicolored   3.00 3.00

A716

1995, July 24
1582 A716 5p multicolored   3.00 3.00
Rotary Intl., 90th anniv.

A717

1995, Sept. 22
1583 A717 2.60p multicolored 1.60 1.60
Jose Pedro Varela, 150th birth anniv.

Miniature Sheet

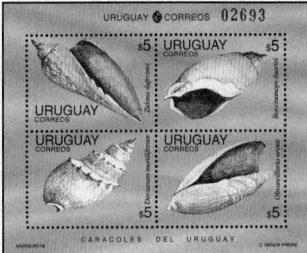

Shells — A718

a, Zidona dufresnei. b, Boccinanops duartei.
c, Dorsanum moniliferum. d, Olivancillaria
uretai.

1995, Aug. 4
1584 A718 5p Sheet of 4, #a.-
d. 20.00 20.00

America
Issue
A719

Designs: 3p, Dicksonia sellowiana, vert. 6p,
Chrysocyon brachyurus.

Unwmk.
1995, Oct. 10   Litho.   Perf. 12
1585 A719 3p multicolored 2.00 2.00
1586 A719 6p multicolored 3.50 3.50

Carlos
Gardel,
Musician
A720

1995, Sept. 4   Perf. 12½
1587 A720 5.50p blue & black 3.25 3.25

Flowers — A721

Designs: a, Notocactus roseinflorus. b, Verbena chamaedryfolia. c, Bauhinia candicans.
d, Tillandsia aeranthos. e, Eichhornia
crassipes.

1995, Sept. 12
1588 A721 3p Strip of 5, #a.-e. 10.00 10.00

Miniature Sheet

Uruguay's Artigas Antarctic Scientific
Research Base, 10th Anniv. — A722

Designs: a, 2.50p, Albatross. b, 4p, Fairchild
FAU572. c, 4p, ROU Vanguard. d, 2.50p,
PTS/M Amphibian transporter.

1995, Oct. 13
1589 A722 Sheet of 4, #a.-d. 12.00 12.00
Uruguayan Antarctic Institute, 20th anniv.
No. 1589 exists demonitized and imperf. on
paper with watermark 332. This item was sold
with No. 1589 and has matching serial
numbers.

Holocaust
Memorial — A723

1995, Sept. 27   Litho.   Perf. 13x12½
1590 A723 6p multicolored 6.00 6.00

UN, 50th
Anniv. — A724

1995, Oct. 24   Litho.   Perf. 12
1591 A724 6p multicolored 3.75 3.75

Early Locomotives — A725

No. 1592, Beyer & Peacock, 1876. No.
1593, Criollo, 1895. No. 1594, Beyer & Peacock, 1910.

1995, Nov. 7
1592 A725 3p multicolored 2.00 2.00
1593 A725 3p multicolored 2.00 2.00
1594 A725 3p multicolored 2.00 2.00
  Nos. 1592-1594 (3) 6.00 6.00

Uruguayan Navy, 178th Anniv. — A726

No. 1595, Sailing ship, Artiguista. No. 1596,
ROU Pte. Rivera. No. 1597, ROU Montevideo.

1995, Nov. 15   Perf. 12½
1595 A726 3p multicolored 2.00 2.00
1596 A726 3p multicolored 2.00 2.00
1597 A726 3p multicolored 2.00 2.00
  Nos. 1595-1597 (3) 6.00 6.00

Motion
Pictures,
Cent.
A727

1995, Dec. 13
1598 A727 6p Lumiere Brothers 4.00 4.00

A728

Christmas
A729

1995, Dec. 15
1599 A728 2.90p multicolored 1.50 1.50
1600 A729 6.50p multicolored 3.50 3.50

Modern Olympic Games,
Cent. — A730

Designs: a, Equestrian event, Atlanta 1996.
b, Ski jumper, Nagano 1998. c, Torch bearer,
Sydney 2000. d, Skier, Salt Lake City 2002.

1996, Jan. 30   Litho.   Perf. 12½
1601 A730 2.50p Sheet of 4, #a.-
d. 9.50 9.50

Latin America Philatelic Exposition.
No. 1601 exists demonitized and imperf. on
paper with watermark 332. This item was sold
with No. 1601 and has matching serial
numbers.

Carnival
Personalities
A732

1996, Feb. 16   Litho.   Perf. 12½
1603 A732 2.90p Rosa Luna 2.00 2.00
1604 A732 2.90p Pepino 2.00 2.00
1605 A732 2.90p Santiago Luz 2.00 2.00
  Nos. 1603-1605 (3) 6.00 6.00

Golf in
Uruguay
A733

Designs: a, Cantegril Country Club. b, Cerro
Golf Club. c, Fay Crocker. d, Lago Golf Club.
e, Golf Club of Uruguay.

1996, Feb. 27
1606 A733 2.90p Strip of 5,
  #a.-e. 12.00 12.00
No. 1606 was issued in sheets of 25 stamps.

Famous People, Events — A734

Designs: a, Statue, Cardinal Barbieri (1892-
1979). b, Yitzhak Rabin (1922-95), Nobel
Peace Prize. c, Soccer players, First World
Cup Soccer Championship, Grand Park Central, July 13, 1930. d, Robert Stolz (1880-
1975), composer.

1996, Mar. 8
1607 A734 2.50p Sheet of 4, #a.-
d. 7.00 7.00
Philatelic Academy of Uruguay. The Stamp
of Today, SODRE Chanel 5, 10th anniv.

Montevideo, Capital of Latin American
Culture — A735

1996, Mar. 5
1608 A735 2.90p Solis Theater,
  1837 1.75 1.75
  a. Booklet pane of 3 7.00
      Complete booklet, #1608a 7.00

General
Census
A736

1996, Apr. 29
1609 A736 3.20p multicolored 1.50 1.50

1998 World Cup Soccer
Championships, France — A737

a, Player in early uniform, Olympic champions, 1924-28, world cup champions, 1930-50, older trophy. b, Trophy, player. d, Two children playing, UNICEF emblem, soccer emblems. e, Olympic rings, two players, eliminations for Atlanta '96.

1996, Apr. 10
1610 A737 2.50p Sheet of 4, #a.-
　　　　　　d.　　　　　　7.50 7.50

Latin America Philatelic Exposition.
No. 1610 exists demonitized and imperf. on paper with watermark 332. This item was sold with No. 1610 and has matching serial numbers.

Bones from Indian Burial Grounds — A738

1996, Apr. 18
1611 A738 3.20p multicolored　　1.75　1.75

Alfredo Zitarrosa (1936-89), Guitarist A739

1996, Mar. 15　　　　　**Perf. 12**
1612 A739 3p multicolored　　2.00　2.00

Prehistoric Animals — A740

Designs: a, Glyptodon claripes. b, Macrauchenia patachonica. c, Toxodon platensis. d, Glossotherium robustum. e, Titanosaurus.

1996, Apr. 18　　　　　**Perf. 12½**
1613 A740 3.20p Strip of 5,
　　　　#a.-e.　　　　10.00 10.00

No. 1613 was issued in sheets of 25 stamps.

Taking Care of Planet Earth, Everyone's Responsibility, by Soraya Campanella — A741

Unwmk.
1996, June 5　　Litho.　　Perf. 12
1614 A741 3.20p multicolored　　1.75　1.75

Souvenir Sheet

Calidris Canutus — A742

1996, May 28　　　　　**Perf. 12½**
1615 A742 12p multicolored　　11.00 11.00
CAPEX '96.

Early Methods of Transportation — A743

Designs: a, 1912 Dion-Buton omnibus. b, 1928 Ford Model A. c, 1940 Raleigh bicycle. d, 1926 Magirus firetruck. e, 1917 Hotchkiss ambulance.

1996, May 21
1616 A743 3.20p Strip of 5,
　　　　#a.-e.　　　　10.00 10.00

No. 1616 was issued in sheets of 25 stamps.

Sailing Ships A744

Designs: a, Our Lady of Encina, 1726. b, San Francisco. c, Ships of E. Moreau. d, Bold Lady. e, Our Lady of the Light.

1996, June 17　　Litho.　　Perf. 12½
1617 A744 3.20p Strip of 5, #a.-
　　　　e.　　　　8.50　8.50

No. 1617 was issued in sheets of 25 stamps.

Landscape in Las Flores, by Carmelo de Arzadun — A745

1996, July 15　　Litho.　　Perf. 12½
1618 A745 3.50p multicolored　　1.50　1.50

Jewish Community in Uruguay, 80th Anniv. — A746

1996, July 29
1619 A746 7.50p multicolored　　4.00　4.00

A747

Scientists from Uruguay A748

No. 1620, Enrique Legrand (1861-1939). No. 1621, Victor Bertullo (1919-79). No. 1622, Tomas Beno Hirschfeld (1939-86). No. 1623, Miguel C. Rubino (1886-1945).

1996, July 30
1620 A747 3.50p multicolored　　1.90　1.90
1621 A747 3.50p multicolored　　1.90　1.90
1622 A748 3.50p multicolored　　1.90　1.90
1623 A748 3.50p multicolored　　1.90　1.90
　　Nos. 1620-1623 (4)　　7.60　7.60

Bank of Uruguay, Cent. — A749

1996, Sept. 9　　　　　**Perf. 12**
1624 A749 3.50p 10p note　　2.00　2.00
　a.　　Booklet pane, #1624　　3.00
1625 A749 3.50p 500p note　　2.00　2.00
　a.　　Booklet pane, #1625　　3.00
　　　Complete bklt., #1624a, 1625a　6.00

Souvenir Sheet

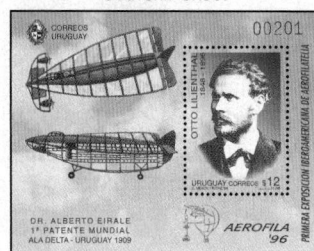

Otto Lilienthal (1848-1896) — A750

1996, Aug. 30
1626 A750 12p multicolored　　6.50　6.50
AEROFILA '96.

Scientists A751

No. 1627, Albert Einstein. No. 1628, Aristotle. No. 1629, Isaac Newton.

1996, Sept. 3　　　　　**Perf. 12½**
1627 A751 7.50p multicolored　　4.00　4.00
1628 A751 7.50p multicolored　　4.00　4.00
1629 A751 7.50p multicolored　　4.00　4.00
　　Nos. 1627-1629 (3)　　12.00 12.00

National Heritage — A752

Designs: No. 1630, Map of Gorriti Island showing locations of Spanish forts, 18th cent. No. 1631, Narbona Church, 18th cent.

Perf. 13x12½
1996, Sept. 12　　Litho.　　Unwmk.
1630 A752 3.50p multicolored　　1.60　1.60
1631 A752 3.50p multicolored　　1.60　1.60

Rural Assoc., 125th Anniv. A753

1996, Sept. 20　　　　　**Perf. 12½x13**
1632 A753 3.50p multicolored　　1.75　1.75

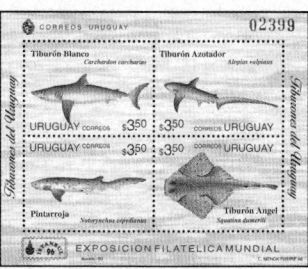

Marine Life — A754

a, Carchardon carcharias. b, Alopias vulpinus. c, Notorynchus cepedianus. d, Squatina dumerili.

1996, Sept. 23
1633 A754 3.50p Sheet of 4, #a.-
　　　　　　d.　　　　　　8.00　8.00
Istanbul '96.

Sports Champions from Uruguay — A755

Designs: a, Angel Rodriguez, boxing, 1917. b, Leandro Noli, cycling, 1939. c, Eduardo G. Risso, rowing, 1948. d, Estrella Puente, javelin, 1949. e, Oscar Moglia, basketball, 1956.

1996, Oct. 1
1634 A755 3.50p Strip of 5, #a.-
　　　　e.　　　　9.50　9.50

Traditional Costumes A756

America issue: 3.50p, Gaucho. 7.50p, Woman of the campana.

1996, Oct. 11　　　　　**Perf. 13x12½**
1635 A756 3.50p multicolored　　2.00　2.00
1636 A756 7.50p multicolored　　3.75　3.75

3rd Space Conference of the
Americas — A757

1996, Nov. 4   Wmk. 332   *Perf. 12*
1637 A757 3.50p multicolored   2.10 2.10

Comic
Strips,
Cent.
A758

"Peloduro," by Julio E. Suarez.

1996, Nov. 7
1638 A758 4p multicolored   2.40 2.40

Health
Institute,
Cent.
A759

1996, Nov. 20
1639 A759 4p multicolored   1.75 1.75

Church of the 7th
Day Adventists in
Uruguay,
Cent. — A760

Wmk. 332
1996, Nov. 26   Litho.   *Perf. 12½*
1640 A760 3.50p multicolored   1.75 1.75

Felix de Azara (1746-1811),
Naturalist — A761

1996, Nov. 20   *Perf. 12*
1641 A761 4p multicolored   2.50 2.50

Fish
A762

Designs: No. 1642, Cynolebia nigripinnis.
No. 1643, Cynolebia viarius.

Unwmk.
1997, Feb. 24   Litho.   *Die Cut*
Self-Adhesive
1642 A762 4p multicolored   2.00 2.00
1643 A762 4p multicolored   2.00 2.00

Popular
Festivals
A763

#1644, Natl. Folklore Festival, Durazno.
#1645, Traditional Gaucho Festival,
Tacuarembo.

1997   Wmk. 332   *Perf. 12½*
1644 A763 4p multi   2.25 2.25
1645 A763 4p multi, vert.   2.25 2.25

Issued: #1644, 1/30; #1645, 3/10.
See Nos. 1653-1656.

Mushrooms — A764

Designs: a, Tricholoma nudum. b, Agaricus
xanthodermus. c, Russula sardonia. d,
Microsporum canis. e, Polyporus versicolor.

1997, Feb. 7
1646 A764 4p Strip of 5, #a.-e.   12.00 12.00
No. 1646 was issued in sheets of 25 stamps.

Ports
A765

No. 1647, Colonia. No. 1648, Punta del
Este. No. 1649, Santiago Vázquez. No. 1650,
Buceo.

1997, Feb. 28   Litho.   *Die Cut*
Self-Adhesive
1647 A765 4p multicolored   2.00 2.00
1648 A765 4p multicolored   2.00 2.00
1649 A765 4p multicolored   2.00 2.00
1650 A765 4p multicolored   2.00 2.00
     Nos. 1647-1650 (4)   8.00 8.00

Artigas'
Lancers,
Bicent.
A766

1997, Mar. 10   Wmk. 332   *Perf. 12½*
1651 A766 4p multicolored   2.00 2.00

Military Academy,
50th
Anniv. — A767

1997, Mar. 13
1652 A767 4p multicolored   2.00 2.00

Popular Festivals Type of 1997

Coat of arms and: No. 1653, Performers
under outdoor pavilion, Beer Week. No. 1654,
Ruben Lena, bridge, river, Olimar River Festival, vert. No. 1655, Guitar, man on horse, Festival de Minas Y Abril. No. 1656, Family
around person on horseback, Roosevelt Park.

1997   Litho.
1653 A763 5p multicolored   3.25 3.25
1654 A763 5p multicolored   3.25 3.25
1655 A763 5p multicolored   3.25 3.25
Die Cut
Unwmk.
Self-Adhesive
1656 A763 5p multicolored   3.25 3.25
     Nos. 1653-1656 (4)   13.00 13.00
  Lions Intl. (#1656). Issued: #1653, 3/23;
#1654, 3/24; #1655, 4/26; #1656, 3/21.

United
Mobile
Coronary
Unit
(UCM),
20th
Anniv.
A768

1997, Apr. 4   Unwmk.   *Die Cut*
Self-Adhesive
1657 A768 5p multicolored   3.25 3.25

UNICEF, 50th
Anniv. — A769

1997, Apr. 8   *Die Cut*
Self-Adhesive
1658 A769 5p multicolored   3.25 3.25

Lighthouses
A770

Various birds and: a, Anchorena Tower,
1920. b, Farallón Lighthouse, 1870. c, José
Ignacio Lighthouse, 1874. d, Santa Maria
Lighthouse, 1874. e, Vigía Tower, 18th cent.

1997, Apr. 22   *Die Cut*
Self-Adhesive
1659 A770 5p Strip of 5, #a.-e.   15.00 15.00

Prehistoric
Animals
A771

Designs: a, Devincenzia gallinali. b,
Smilodon populator. c, Mesosaurus tenuidens.
d, Doedicurus clavicaudatus. e, Artigasia
magna.

1997, May 5   *Die Cut*
Self-Adhesive
1660 A771 5p Strip of 5, #a.-e.   15.00 15.00

A772

Ecclesiastical Provinces — A772a

#1661, Church, diocese of Salto. #1662,
Church, diocese of Melo. #1663, Bishop
Jacinto Vera, 1st bishop of Montevideo.
#1664, Msgr. Mariano Soler, 1st archbishop of
Montevideo.

Wmk. 332
1997, May 9   Litho.   *Perf. 12½*
1661 A772   5p multicolored   3.00 3.00
1662 A772   5p multicolored   3.00 3.00
1663 A772a 5p multicolored   3.00 3.00
1664 A772a 5p multicolored   3.00 3.00
     Nos. 1661-1664 (4)   12.00 12.00

Youth
Stamp
Collecting
A773

Designs: a, 2p, Boy, "Philately?" b, 2p, Boy
thinking of stamps. c, 2p, Girl with soccer ball,
boy. d, 1p, Boy looking at stamps in album. e,
1p, Boy with tongs and magnifying glass.

1997, May 25   Unwmk.
1665 A773 Strip of 5, #a.-e.   5.00 5.00

PACIFIC 97 — A774

1997, May 29   *Perf. 12*
1666 A774 10p Rynchops niger   5.00 5.00

Maccio
Theater of
San Jose,
85th
Anniv.
A775

1997, June 5   Wmk. 332   *Perf. 12½*
1667 A775 5p multicolored   2.50 2.50

Inter-American Institute of Children,
70th Anniv. — A776

1997, June 9   Unwmk.
1668 A776 5p multicolored   2.50 2.50

Colony of Sacramento — A777

1997, July 4
1669 A777 5p multicolored   2.50 2.50

Punta del Este, 90th Anniv. A778

1997, July 1
1670 A778 5p multicolored   2.50 2.50

Uruguayan Comics — A779

Scenes from comics by: No. 1671, Julio E. Suarez (Peloduro). No. 1672, Geoffrey Foladori.

Perf. 12½
1997, June 30   Litho.   Unwmk.
1671 A779 5p multicolored   2.00 2.00
1672 A779 5p multicolored   2.00 2.00

Zionism, Cent. A780

Design: Theodor Herzl (1860-1904), founder of Zionist movement.

1997, July 17
1673 A780 5p multicolored   3.00 3.00

Children's Painting A781   Geranoaetus Melanoleucus A782

1997, July 21   Litho.   Die Cut
Self-Adhesive
1674 A781 15p multicolored   10.00 10.00
1675 A782 25p multicolored   16.00 16.00
   a.   Type II ('04)   4.50 4.50

Type I stamps have printer's name at right, designer's name at left, and have an eagle's head that is rounder, with its edge making a sharper angle with the right margin than on type II. Type II stamps have the printer's name at left and the designer's name at right.
No. 1675a issued 2004. No. 1675a also exists dated "2005."
Nos. 1674, 1675 exist dated 1999.
See Nos. 1840, 1850, 1853, 1855.

Isolation of Acetylsalicylic Acid from Willow Trees, Cent. — A783

1997, Aug. 12   Litho.   Perf. 12½
1676 A783 6p multicolored   2.00 2.00
   a.   Booklet pane of 2   6.50
     Complete booklet, #1676a   6.50

Department of Salto — A784

1997, Aug. 26
1677 A784 6p multicolored   2.00 2.00

Felix Mendelssohn (1809-47) — A785

No. 1679, Johannes Brahms (1833-97).

1997, Sept. 1
1678 A785 6p multicolored   1.90 1.90
1679 A785 6p multicolored   1.90 1.90
   a.   Pair, #1678-1679   4.25 4.25

Natural History Museum of Montevideo, 160th Anniv. — A786

Designs: a, Lucas Kraguevich, paleontologist. b, Jose Arechavaleta, botanist. c, Garibaldi J. Devincenzi, zoologist. d, Antonio Taddei, archaelogist.

1997, Sept. 3
1680 A786 6p Strip of 4, #a.-d.   7.50 7.50

Mercosur (Common Market of Latin America) A787

1997, Sept. 26   Perf. 12
1681 A787 11p multicolored   3.75 3.75

See Argentina, No. 1975; Bolivia No. 1019; Brazil, No. 2646; Paraguay, No. 2564.

Souvenir Sheet

Passiflora Coerulea — A788

1997, Sept. 26   Perf. 12½
1682 A788 15p multicolored   5.00 5.00
1st Philatelic Exhibition of Mercosur countries.

Heinrich von Stephan (1831-97) A789

1997, Oct. 9
1683 A789 11p multicolored   3.75 3.75

Souvenir Sheet

Spanish-Uruguayan Monument — A790

1997, Oct. 9
1684 A790 15p Monument   5.00 5.00
Philatelic Exhibition, Spain 1997.

America Issue — A791

Designs: 6p, Woman carrying mail. 11p, Man delivering letters.

1997, Oct. 10
1685 A791   6p multicolored   2.00 2.00
1686 A791 11p multicolored   3.75 3.75

Artigas Scientific Base, Antarctica — A792

1997, Oct. 15   Perf. 12
1687 A792 6p Pygoscelis papua   3.50 3.50

Painting, by Domingo Laporte (1855-1928) — A793

1997, Oct. 21   Perf. 12½
1688 A793 6p multicolored   2.00 2.00

Galicia House, 80th Anniv. A794

1997, Oct. 24
1689 A794 6p multicolored   2.00 2.00

3rd Intl. Congress of Aeronautical and Space History, Montevideo — A795

Perf. 12½
1997, Oct. 27   Litho.   Unwmk.
1690 A795 6p Arme 2 Biplane   2.00 2.00

1st Biennial Interparliamentary Exhibition of MERCOSUR Paintings, Montevideo — A796

1997, Oct. 28
1691 A796 11p multicolored   3.50 3.50

Souvenir Sheet

Pope John Paul II, Holy Year 2000 — A797

1997, Nov. 7
1692 A797 10p multicolored   8.00 8.00

Third Intl. Assembly Punta del Este, and of arrival of first Polish colonists at River Plate, cent.

Uruguayan Navy, 180th Anniv. — A798

1997, Nov. 14
1693 A798 6p multicolored   2.00 2.00

Shanghai '97 Intl. Stamp and Coin Exhibition — A799

No. 1694: a, 3.50p, Front and back of 1 peso coin. b, 3.50p, Chinese flag, Hong Kong harbor, flower, junk. c, 4p, Michael Schumacher, Formula 1 driving champion, Ferrari. d, 4p, Sojourner on Mars, Pathfinder Mission.
No. 1695: a, 3.50p, Martina Hingis, 1997 Wimbledon Ladies' champion. b, 3.50p, Jan Ullrich, 1997 Tour de France winner. c, 4p, Soccer players, 1998 World Cup Soccer Championship, France. d, 4p, Ski jumper, 1998 Winter Olympic Games, Nagano.

1997, Nov. 19
1694	A799	Sheet of 4, #a.-d.	6.00	6.00
1695	A799	Sheet of 4, #a.-d.	6.00	6.00

Christmas
A800

1997, Nov. 20
1696	A800	6p Magi	2.00	2.00
1697	A800	11p Madonna & Child	3.50	3.50

Uruguayan Sportsmen — A801

Designs: a, Adesio Lombardo, Olympic bronze medalist, basketball, Helsinki, 1952. b, Guillermo Douglas, Olympic bronze medalist, single sculls, Rome, 1932. c, Obdulio Varela, soccer player on 1950 World Cup championship team. d, Atilio Francois, silver medalist, 1947 World Cycling Championships, Paris. e, Juan López Testa, South American 100 meters champion, 1947.

1997, Nov. 26
1698	A801	6p Strip of 5, #a.-e.	10.00	10.00

Mevifil '97, 1st Intl. Exhibition of Philatelic Audio-Visual and Computer Systems — A802

1997, Dec. 1 *Perf. 12*
1699	A802	11p multicolored	3.50	3.50

INDEPEX '97 — A803

Early vehicles, inventors: a, 1st Land Rover, 1947. b, Henry Ford (1863-1947), Model A. c, Robert Bosch (1861-1942), inventor of automotive components. d, Rudolf Diesel (1858-1913), patented first diesel engine, 1897.

1997, Dec. 8 *Perf. 12½*
1700	A803	6p Strip of 4, #a.-d.	8.00	8.00

Naval Academy of Uruguay, 90th Anniv. A804

1997, Dec. 12
1701	A804	6p multicolored	2.00	2.00

Supreme Court of Uruguay, 90th Anniv. A805

1997, Dec. 12
1702	A805	6p multicolored	2.00	2.00

Uruguayan Post Office, 170th Anniv. — A806

1997, Dec. 19
1703	A806	6p multicolored	2.00	2.00

MEVIR (Movement for Eradication of Unsanitary Rural Housing), 90th Anniv. — A807

Design: Homes, Dr. A. Gallinal, logo.

1997, Dec. 26
1704	A807	6p multicolored	2.00	2.00

Construction Projects — A808

a, Preparation. b, Planning. c, Execution.

1997, Dec. 29 *Perf. 12*
1705	A808	6p Strip of 3, #a.-c.	6.00	6.00
d.		Booklet pane, #1705	7.25	
		Complete booklet, #1705d	7.25	

Souvenir Sheet

1897 Revolution, Cent. — A809

Design: Gen. Antonio "Chiquito" Saravia and Col. Diego Lamas.

1997, Dec. 30 *Perf. 12½*
1706	A809	15p multicolored	5.00	5.00

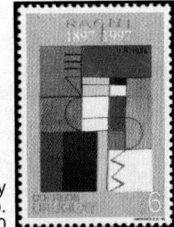

Painting by Héctor Ragni (b. 1898) — A810

1998, Feb. 6
1707	A810	6p multicolored	2.00	2.00

Naval Station, Montevideo — A811

1998, Feb. 13
1708	A811	6p multicolored	2.00	2.00

Native Trees — A812

a, Butia capitata. b, Grove of butia capitata. c, Grove of phytolacca dioica. d, Phytolacca dioica.

1998, Mar. 20 *Perf. 12*
1709	A812	6p Block of 4, #a.-d.	7.50	7.50

Museum of Humor — A813

Cartoons: No. 1710, by Oscar Abín. No. 1711, by Emilio Cortinas.

1998, Mar. 13 *Perf. 12½*
1710	A813	6p multicolored	2.00	2.00
1711	A813	6p multicolored	2.00	2.00
a.		Pair, #1710-1711	4.00	4.00

Wilson Ferreira Aldunate (1919-88) A814

1998, Mar. 17 *Perf. 12*
1712	A814	6p multicolored	2.00	2.00

Fossilized Animals — A815

Designs: a, Testudinites sellowi. b, Proborhyaena gigantea. c, Propachyrucos schiaffinos. d, Stegomastodon platensis.

1998, Mar. 26
1713	A815	6p Block of 4, #a.-d.	8.00	8.00

Israel '98, State of Israel, 50th Anniv. — A816

1998, Mar. 31 *Perf. 12*
1714	A816	12p multicolored	5.00	5.00

Birds — A820

a, Plyborus plancus. b, Cygnus melancoryphus. c, Platalea ajaja. d, Theristicus caudatus.

1998, Apr. 30
1718	A820	6p Block of 4, #a.-d.	9.00	9.00

Organization of
American States,
50th
Anniv. — A821

1998, Apr. 14   Litho.   Perf. 12¾x12½
1719 A821 12p multi   4.25 4.25

61st World
Congress of
Sports
Journalism
A822

1998, Apr. 21   Litho.   Perf. 12
1720 A822 6p multicolored   2.00 2.00

Land Settlement
Institute, 50th
Anniv. — A823

1998, Apr. 22   Litho.   Perf. 12¾x12½
1721 A823 6p multi   2.00 2.00

Souvenir Sheet

Intl. Topical Philatelic Exhibition, Nueva
Helvecia — A824

Cross and: a, 3.50p, Switzerland #5, Uruguay #1. b, 3.50p, Obverse and reverse of
Euro coin. c, 4p, Olympic rings and mountain.
d, 4p, Space station.

1998, May 12   Perf. 12½x12¾
1722 A824 Sheet of 4, #a.-d.   6.00 6.00
    Swiss Republic, bicent.

Souvenir Sheet

Whales — A825

a, 3.50p, Balaeneoptera physalus (b). b,
3.50p, Balaeneoptera acutorostrata. c, 4p,
Megaptera novaeangliae (d). d, 4p, Eubalaena
australis (c).

1998, May 15   Litho.   Perf. 12½
1723 A825 Sheet of 4, #a.-d.   7.50 7.50
    Ambiente '98, Maia, Portugal; Intl. Year of
the Ocean; Expo '98, Lisbon.

1983 Labor Day Democracy
Demonstrations — A826

Perf. 12¼x12¾
1998, May 27   Litho.   Wmk. 332
1724 A826 6p brn & blk   1.75 1.75
    See Nos. 1740, 1775.

Street Cars — A827

Historic Montevideo trams: a, English "La
Comercial," 1906. b, German Transatlantica
Co., 1907. c, Transatlantica, 1908. d, Tran-
satlantica double decker, 1916.

1998, May 29   Litho.   Perf. 12
1725 A827 6p Block of 4, #a.-d.   7.50 7.50

Juvalux '98 — A828

Wildcats: a, Felis colocola. b, Felis pardalis.
c, Felis wiedil. d, Panthera onca.

Unwmk.
1998, June 18   Litho.   Perf. 12
1726 A828 6p Block of 4, #a.-d.   8.50 8.50

Ships — A829

a, "Sirus." b, Gunboat "18 de Julio." c, Transport, "Maldonado." d, "Instituto de Pesca No.
1."

1998, June 25   Litho.   Perf. 12
1727 A829 6p Block of 4, #a.-d.   7.50 7.50

Jesuit
Mission
Church,
Calera de
las
Huérfanas
A830

Perf. 12½x12¾
1998, July 24   Litho.   Unwmk.
1728 A830 12p multi   3.50 3.50

Monument to the
Peace of 1872,
San José de
Mayo, 125th
Anniv. — A831

1998, July 31   Perf. 12¾x12½
1729 A831 6p multi   2.00 2.00

155mm
Artillery
Unit No.
5, Cent.
A832

1998, Aug. 7   Perf. 12½x12¾
1730 A832 6p multi   2.00 2.00

Butterflies — A833

1998, Aug. 14   Litho.   Perf. 12
1731 A833 6p Eacles imperialis   3.00 3.00
1732 A833 6p Protoparce luceti-
            us   3.00 3.00
   a.   Pair, #1731-1732   6.00 6.00

First Monument
to José Artigas,
San José de
Mayo,
Cent. — A834

Perf. 12¾x12½
1998, Aug. 24   Litho.
1733 A834 6p multi   2.00 2.00

A835

1998, Aug. 28
1734 A835 6p multi   2.00 2.00
    Dr. Mauricio López Lombo (1918-93), zoo
founder.

A836

1998, Aug. 31
1735 A836 6p multi   2.00 2.00
    Falleri-Balzo Music Conservatory, Monte-
video, cent.

José Fernández
Vergara (1810-
1906), Founder of
Pueblo
Vergara — A837

1998, Sept. 8
1736 A837 6p multi   2.00 2.00

Souvenir Sheet

El Pais Newspaper, 80th
Anniv. — A838

1998, Sept. 14   Perf. 12½x12¾
1737 A838 12p multi   4.50 4.50

Collective Medical
Assistance
Institute, 145th
Anniv. — A839

1998, Sept. 24   Perf. 12¾x12½
1738 A839 6p multi   2.00 2.00

Postal Link Between Montevideo and Corunna, Spain, 230th Anniv. — A840

1998, Sept. 24
1739 A840 12p multi 4.50 4.50

Espamer '98, Buenos Aires.

Labor Day Type

6p, March of the Social and Cultural Assoc. of Public School Students, 9/25/83.

Perf. 12½x12¾
1998, Sept. 25 **Wmk. 332**
1740 A826 6p brn & blk 2.00 2.00

Iberoamericana '98 Philatelic Exhibition, Maia, Portugal — A841

Airplanes: a, Junkers J52. b, Spad VII. c, Ansaldo SVA-10. d, Neybar.

Unwmk.
1998, Oct. 2 **Litho.** *Perf. 12*
1741 A841 6p Block of 4, #a.-d. 7.50 7.50

Death of Chilean Pres. Salvador Allende, 25th Anniv. A842

Perf. 12¼x12¾
1998, Oct. 2 **Litho.** **Unwmk.**
1742 A842 12p multi 3.75 3.75

50th Anniv. of Enrique Rodríguez Fabregat (1885-1976) as UN Commissioner for Palestine — A843

1998, Oct. 5 *Perf. 12¾x12½*
1743 A843 6p multi 2.00 2.00

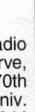

Radio Carve, 70th Anniv. A844

1998, Oct. 7 **Litho.** *Perf. 12½x12¾*
1744 A844 6p multi 2.00 2.00

World Post Day A845

1998, Oct. 9 **Litho.** *Perf. 12½x12¾*
1745 A845 12p multi 3.75 3.75

Ilsapex '98, Johannesburg.

America Issue — A846

Famous women: 6p, Julia Guarino (1897-1985), first woman architect in South America. 12p, Dr. Paulina Luisi (1875-1950).

1998, Oct. 9 **Litho.** *Perf. 12*
1746 A846 6p multi 2.00 2.00
1747 A846 12p multi 4.00 4.00

Assoc. of Inland Pharmacies, 50th Anniv. — A847

1998, Oct. 10 *Perf. 12½x12¾*
1748 A847 6p multi 2.00 2.00

Postal Services A847a

Serpentine Die Cut 11¼
1998, Oct. 15 **Litho.** **Unwmk.**
Self-Adhesive
1748A A847a 25p multi 7.50 7.50

Exists dated 1999.

Classic Vehicles — A848

Designs: a, 1950 Lancia fire engine. b, 1946 Maserati San Remo. c, 1954 Alfa Romeo trolley bus. d, 1936 Fiat Topolino.

1998, Oct. 23 **Litho.** *Perf. 12*
1749 A848 6p Block of 4, #a.-d. 8.50 8.50

Italia'98.

Artists A849

Designs: No. 1750, Sculpture, "Motherhood," and self-portrait of Nerses Ounanian (1920-57). No. 1751, Illustrations from book "Piquín y Chispita," by Serafin J. Garcia (1905-85), vert. No. 1752, Musical score by Héctor M. Artola (1903-82), vert.

Perf. 12½x12¾, 12¾x12½
1998, Oct. 27 **Litho.**
1750 A849 6p multi 1.90 1.90
1751 A849 6p multi 1.90 1.90
1752 A849 6p multi 1.90 1.90
Nos. 1750-1752 (3) 5.70 5.70

Juvenalia '98 — A850

1998, Oct. 30 **Litho.** *Perf. 12¾x12½*
1753 A850 6p multi 2.00 2.00

Souvenir Sheet

Uruguay-Germany Philatelic Exhibition, Montevideo — A851

Designs: a, 3.50p, Zeppelin cover, Zeppelin NT. b, 3.50p, Germany #1592, Germany Berlin #9N584, German Democratic Republic #2791, mail box. c, 4p, Brandenburg Gate, Volkswagen Beetle, Konrad Adenauer. d, 4p, Airplane, German mark note and coin.

1998, Nov. 6 **Litho.** *Perf. 12½x12¾*
1754 A851 Sheet of 4, #a.-d. 4.50 4.50

IBRA '99, 150th anniv. of German stamps (#1754a, 1754b), 50th anniv. of Federal Republic of Germany (#1754c), 50th anniv. of German mark (#1754d).

16th Congress of Expenditure Control Boards — A852

1998, Nov. 9
1755 A852 12p blue & silver 3.75 3.75

Uruguayan Chamber of Industries, Cent. — A853

1998, Nov. 9
1756 A853 6p multi 2.00 2.00

Flowers A854

1p, Oxalis pudica. 4p, Oxalis pudica (white). 5p, Oxalis pudica (purple). 6p, Eugenia uniflora. 7p, Eugenia uniflora. 9p, Eugenia uniflora. 10p, Aechmea recurvata. 14p, Acca sellowiana. 50p, Acca sellowiana.

Serpentine Die Cut 11¼
1998-99 **Self-Adhesive** **Litho.**
1757 A854 1p "98" date .40 .30
 a. "99" in inscription .40 .30
 b. "2000" in inscription .40 .30
 c. "2001" in inscription .40 .30
 d. "2002" in inscription .40 .30
1760 A854 4p multi 1.00 1.00
1761 A854 5p multi .80 .80
1762 A854 6p multi 1.75 1.75
1763 A854 7p multi 1.75 1.75
1765 A854 9p multi 5.50 5.50
1766 A854 10p "98" date 2.75 2.75
 a. "99" in inscription 2.75 2.75
 b. "2002" in inscription 2.75 2.75
1770 A854 14p multi 3.75 3.75
1771 A854 50p multi 9.50 9.50
Nos. 1757-1771 (9) 27.20 27.10

Issued: 7p, 2/4/99; 4p, 12/23/99; 14p, 8/6/99; 1p, 6p, 10p, 50p, 1998. 9p, 1999. 5p, 2/19/02.
Reprints issued: #1757a, 12/7/99; #1757b, 12/15/00; #1757c, 2/24/01; #1757d, 5/22/02. #1766a, 12/7/99; #1766b, 2/8/02.

Christmas — A855

Designs: 6p, The Virgin's Descent to Reward St. Ildefons' Writings (detail), by El Greco. 12p, St. Peter's Tears (detail), by Bartolomé Esteban Murillo.

1998, Nov. 23 **Litho.** *Perf. 12*
1772 A855 6p multi 1.75 1.75
1773 A855 12p multi 3.50 3.50

Paso Del Molina Neighborhood of Montevideo, 250th Anniv. — A856

1998, Nov. 26 *Perf. 12½x12¾*
1774 A856 6p multi 2.00 2.00

Labor Day Type

6p, Proclamation at the Obelisk, 11/27/83.

Perf. 12¼x12¾
1998, Nov. 27 **Litho.** **Wmk. 332**
1775 A826 6p brn & blk 2.00 2.00

Morosoli Cultural Awards — A857

Perf. 12¾x12½
1998, Nov. 27 **Litho.** **Unwmk.**
1776 A857 6p multi 2.00 2.00

Universal Declaration of Human Rights, 50th Anniv. — A858

1998, Dec. 10   *Perf. 12½x12¾*
1777 A858 6p multi   2.00 2.00

Uruguayan Olympic Committee, 75th Anniv. — A859

1998, Dec. 15   *Perf. 12*
1778 A859 6p multi   2.00 2.00

Uruguayan Sportsmen A860

Designs: a, Juan Lopez (1907-83), soccer coach. b, Hector Scarone (1899-1967), soccer player. c, Leandro Gomez Harley (1902-79), basketball player, hurdler. d, Liberto Corney (1905-55), boxer.

1998, Dec. 15   *Perf. 12¾x12½*
1779 A860 6p Block of 4, #a.-d.   7.50 7.50

Famous Uruguayans — A861

Designs: No. 1780: Dr. Roberto Caldeyro Barcia (1921-96), physiologist. No. 1781, Dr. José Verocay (1876-1923), pathologist. No. 1782, Dr. José L. Duomarco (1905-85), medical researcher.

    Perf. 12¼x12¾
1998, Dec. 18   **Litho.**   **Unwmk.**
1780 A861 6p multi   1.75 1.75
1781 A861 6p multi   1.75 1.75
1782 A861 6p multi   1.75 1.75
    Nos. 1780-1782 (3)   5.25 5.25

Emile Zola's "J'accuse" Letter, Cent. (in 1998) A862

1999, Jan. 4   **Litho.**   *Perf. 12½x12¾*
1783 A862 14p multicolored   4.00 4.00

Las Cañas Resort, Fray Bentos A863

1999, Feb. 26
1784 A863 7p multicolored   2.25 2.25

Rio de la Plata Boundary Treaty, 25th Anniv. A864

1999, Mar. 15
1785 A864 7p multicolored   2.25 2.25

Famous Uruguayans — A865

Designs: No. 1786, Joaquin Torres Garcia (1874-1949), painter. No. 1787, Luis Ernesto Aroztegui (1930-94), textile artist. No. 1788, Juan José Morosoli (1899-1957), writer.

1999, Mar. 26
1786 A865 7p multicolored   2.50 2.50
1787 A865 7p multicolored   2.50 2.50
1788 A865 7p multicolored   2.50 2.50
    Nos. 1786-1788 (3)   7.50 7.50

Birds and Flowering Trees A866

a, Psidium cattleianum, Pipraeidea melanonota. b, Tabebuia ipe, Chlorostilbon aureoventris. c, Duranta repens, Tangara preciosa. d, Citharexylum montevidense, Tachuris rubigastra.

1999, Apr. 14 Litho.   *Perf. 12¼x12¾*
1789 A866 7p Block of 4, #a.-d.   7.50 7.50

Carriages A867

Designs: a, Break de chasse. b, Mylord. c, Coupé trois quarts. d, Break de champ.

1999, Apr. 29 Litho.   *Perf. 12½x12¾*
1790 A867 7p Block of 4, #a.-d.   7.50 7.50

National Soccer Team, Cent. — A868

Designs: a, B. Céspedes, M. Nebel, C. Céspedes, team's first field. b, H. Castro, P. Cea, A. Ciocca, team flag. c, R. Porta, A García, S. Gambetta, team headquarters.

1999, May 5   **Litho.**   *Perf. 12*
1791 A868 7p Strip of 3, #a.-c.   6.25 6.25
    Complete booklet, #1791   7.25

Children's Millennium Stamp Design Contest Winners A869

Designs: a, By Stefani Andrea Furtado. b, By Pilar Trujillo. c, By Lucia Lavie. d, By Cecilia Chopitea.

1999, May 6 Litho.   *Perf. 12½x12¾*
1792 A869 7p Block of 4, #a.-d.   7.50 7.50

Jorge Chebataroff (1909-84), Geographer, Botanist — A870

1999, May 14
1793 A870 7p multicolored   2.00 2.00

Formation of Infantry Brigade No. 1, 60th Anniv. A871

Paintings: No. 1794, Infantry Battalion No. 2 at Battle of Montecaseros, 1852. No. 1795, Infantry Brigade No. 1 at Battle of Estero Bellaco, 1866. No. 1796, Infantry Battalion No. 1 at Battle of Boquerón, 1866.

1999, May 18
1794 A871 7p multicolored   1.90 1.90
1795 A871 7p multicolored   1.90 1.90
1796 A871 7p multicolored   1.90 1.90
    Nos. 1794-1796 (3)   5.70 5.70

Villa de la Restauracion, 150th Anniv. — A872

1999, May 24   *Perf. 12¾x12½*
1797 A872 7p multicolored   2.00 2.00

Souvenir Sheet

Barcelona, Spain Soccer Team, Cent. — A873

1999, May 28 Litho.   *Perf. 12½x12¾*
1798 A873 15p multi   4.25 4.25

1st Festival of Film Critics, Montevideo A874

1999, June 2   *Perf. 12¾x12¼*
    Booklet Stamp
1799 A874 7p multi   2.00 2.00
    a.   Booklet pane, 2 #1799   4.00
       Complete booklet, #1799a   4.00

Philex France 99 A875

Horses: a, Arabian. b, Quarter horse. c, Thoroughbred. d, Shetland pony.

    Perf. 12½x12¾
1999, June 10   **Litho.**
1800 A875 7p Block of 4, #a.-d.   7.50 7.50

Publication "Marcha," 60th Anniv. — A876

    Perf. 12¼x12¾
1999, June 23   **Litho.**
1801 A876 7p multi   2.00 2.00

Permanent Home for "Espacio Ciencia" Science Exhibits — A877

1999, July 2   *Perf. 12¾x12¼*
1802 A877 7p multi   2.00 2.00

Artigas Antarctic Scientific Base, 25th Anniv. A878

1999, July 12   *Perf. 12¼x12¾*
1803 A878 7p multi   2.50 2.50

Republic of Uruguay University, 150th Anniv. A879

1999, July 19
1804 A879 7p yel & blk   2.00 2.00

UNESCO Regional Office, 50th Anniv. — A880

1999, July 20   **Perf. 12¾x12¼**
1805 A880 7p multi   2.00 2.00

The Last Charruas — A881

a, One seated, one standing. b, Two seated.

1999, July 22 Litho.   **Perf. 12¾x12½**
1806 A881 7p Pair, #a.-b.   4.25 4.25

Souvenir Sheet

Millennium — A882

a, 3.50p, Apollo space program. b, 3.50p, Soccer players, 2000 Olympic Games, Sydney. c, 4p, Centenary of Zeppelins. d, 4p, #C60.

1999, July 30 Litho.   **Perf. 12½x12¾**
1807 A882 Sheet of 4, #a.-d.   7.50 7.50

UPU, 125th anniv., Bangkok 2000, Espana 2000, WIPA 2000, Hanover World's Fair.

El Galpón Theater, Montevideo, 50th Anniv. — A883

1999, Aug. 3   **Perf. 12¾x12¼**
1808 A883 7p multi   2.00 2.00

China 1999 World Philatelic Exhibition — A884

Sea planes: a, Piper J-3. b, Short Sunderland.

1999, Aug. 18   **Perf. 12¼x12¾**
1809 A884 7p Pair, #a.-b.   4.00 4.00

Dogs — A885

Designs: a, Cocker spaniel. b, German shepherd. c, Dalmatian. d, Basset hound.

Perf. 12¾x12½
1999, Aug. 24   **Litho.**
1810 A885 7p Block of 4, #a.-d.   7.50 7.50

Insects & Flowers A886

a, Halictidae, Oxalis sp. b, Apanteles sp., Epidendrum paniculosum. c, Metabolosia univita, Baccharis trimera. d, Compositae, Cantarido.

Perf. 12½x12¾
1999, Sept. 10   **Litho.**
1811 A886 7p Block of 4, #a.-d.   7.50 7.50

A887

Uruguayan Artists: No. 1812, Orlando Aldama (1904-87), writer. No. 1813, Julio Martínez Oyanguren (1901-73), guitarist.

Perf. 12¾x12½
1999, Sept. 13   **Litho.**
1812 A887 7p multi   1.90 1.90
1813 A887 7p multi   1.90 1.90

A888

Perf. 12¾x12¼
1999, Sept. 18   **Litho.**
1814 A888 7p multi   1.90 1.90
Cultural heritage of Mercosur countries.

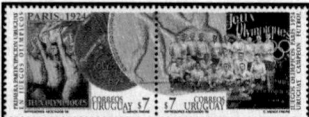

First Uruguayan Participation in Olympics, Paris, 1924 — A889

Designs: a, Poster, medal. b, Medal, medal-winning soccer team.

1999, Sept. 30   **Perf. 12¼x12¾**
1815 A889 7p Pair, #a.-b.   4.00 4.00

Intl. Year of Older Persons A890

1999, Oct. 1 Litho.   **Perf. 12¼x12¾**
1816 A890 7p multi   2.00 2.00

Philatelic Witches Sabbath, by Mariano Barbasán — A891

1999, Oct. 1   **Perf. 12**
1817 A891 7p multi   2.00 2.00
Stamp Day.

America Issue, A New Millennium Without Arms — A892

7p, Arms in trash can. 14p, Earth, satellites.

1999, Oct. 6   **Perf. 13¾x12¼**
1818 A892 7p multi   2.00 2.00
1819 A892 14p multi   4.00 4.00

Inter-American Development Bank, 40th Anniv. — A893

1999, Oct. 6   **Perf. 12¼x12¾**
1820 A893 7p multi   2.00 2.00

Winner of Older Person's Stamp Design Contest A894

1999, Oct. 8
1821 A894 7p multi   2.00 2.00

El Ceibo Society, 50th Anniv. A895

1999, Oct. 8
1822 A895 7p multi   2.00 2.00

Third Intl. Conference of Ministers for Sports, Punta del Este — A896

1999, Oct. 13   **Perf. 12**
1823 A896 7p multi   2.00 2.00

Souvenir Sheets

Official Service of Broadcasting, Television and Entertainment — A897

No. 1824: a, 4p, Television cameraman. b, 4p, Building. c, 3p, Radio studio. d, 3p, Film cameraman.
No. 1825: a, 4p, Symphony orchestra. b, 4p, Chamber music group. c, 3p, Chorus. d, 3p, Ballet dancers.

1999, Oct. 22   **Perf. 12¼x12¾**
1824 A897 Sheet of 4, #a.-d.   4.25 4.25
1825 A897 Sheet of 4, #a.-d.   4.25 4.25

Uruguayan Standards Institute, 60th Anniv. — A898

1999, Nov. 3
1826 A898 7p multi   2.00 2.00

A899

1999, Nov. 3   **Perf. 12¾x12¼**
1827 A899 7p multi   2.00 2.00
Vice-President Hugo Batalla (1926-98).

A900

Cover of 4/29/29 Mundo Uruguayo magazine.

1999, Nov. 12
1828 A900 7p multi   2.00 2.00

Exhibition of art and design from the 1920s, Blanes Museum, Montevideo.

Millennium — A901

No. 1829 — Various buildings and: a, "1999." b, "2000."

1999, Nov. 23   Litho.   Perf. 12
1829 A901 3.50p Pair, #a.-b.   2.00 2.00

Celmar Poumé (1924-83), Cartoonist A902

1999, Nov. 26   Perf. 12¾x12¼
1830 A902 7p multi   2.00 2.00

Christmas A903

9p, Tree with ornaments. 18p, Carolers.

Perf. 12¼x12¾, 12¾x12¼
1999, Dec. 3
1831 A903 9p multi   2.25 2.25
1832 A903 18p multi, vert.   4.50 4.50

Tannat Wines, 20th Anniv. — A904

1999, Dec. 9   Perf. 12
1833 A904 9p shown   3.00 3.00
1834 A904 9p Wine drinker   3.00 3.00

New Maldonado Department Governmental Building — A905

1999, Dec. 11   Perf. 12¼x12¾
1835 A905 9p multi   3.00 3.00

Types of 1997 and

Crow's Gorge Nature Reserve A907

Chilean Lapwing — A908

Design: 2p, Penitente Waterfall, vert. 5p, Chilean Lapwing (Vanellus chilensis). 10p, Crow's Gorge Nature Reserve. No. 1841, Gruta del Palacio, vert. 100p, Sierra de los Caracoles.

Serpentine Die Cut 11¼, Die Cut (#1836A, 1840, 1850, 1853)

2000-06		**Self-Adhesive**		**Litho.**
1836	A907	2p multi, "2001"	.30	.30
b.		Dated "2002"	.30	.30
1836A	A908	5p multi	.45	.45
1837	A907	10p multi	.85	.85
1838	A907	11p multi	2.00	2.00
1840	A781	20p multi, "2000"	4.50	4.50
a.		Dated "2001"	4.50	4.50
1841	A907	20p multi, "2001"	5.00	5.00
a.		Dated "2006"	5.00	5.00
1850	A782	32p multi	7.25	7.25
1853	A782	80p multi	18.00	18.00
1854	A907	100p multi	14.00	14.00
1855	A782	100p multi	7.50	7.50
1855A	A782	100p multi	7.50	7.50
		Nos. 1836-1855A (11)	67.35	67.35

Issued: 32p, 1/20. No. 1840, 80p, 12/12. 11p, 3/16/01. No. 1841, 4/26/01. 2p, 8/1/01. No. 1854, 2/13/02. No. 1855, 10/5/04. 5p, 12/1/06; 10p, 10/18/06; No. 1855A, 9/26/06. No. 1855 has straight numerals in denomination. No. 1855A has slanted numerals.

50th Anniv of Artistic Career of Carlos Páez Vilaró — A916

2000, Jan. 15   Litho.   Perf. 12
1856 A916 9p multi   3.00 3.00

Orchids — A917

No. 1857: a, 5p, Laelia purpurata. b, 4p, Cattleya corcovado. c, 4p, Cattleya sp. "hybrid." d, 5p, Laelia tenebrosa.

2000, Mar. 3
1857 A917 Block of 4, #a.-d.   6.50 6.50

Lighthouses — A918

No. 1858: a, 5p, Isla de Flores, 1828. b, 4p, Punta del Este, 1860. c, 4p, Cabo Polonio, 1881. d, 5p, Punta Brava, 1876.

2000, Mar. 14
1858 A918 Block of 4, #a.-d.   7.50 7.50

Carlos Quijano (1900-84), Economics Journalist — A919

2000, Mar. 30   Perf. 12¼x12¾
1859 A919 9p multi   3.00 3.00

The Gold Rush, Starring Charlie Chaplin, 75th Anniv. A920

2000, Apr. 7   Litho.   Perf. 12¼x12¾
1860 A920 18p multi   5.75 5.75

Lubrapex 2000 Stamp Show, Brazil.

El Cordón Neighborhood of Montevideo, 250th Anniv. — A921

2000, Apr. 10   Litho.   Perf. 12¼x12¾
1861 A921 9p multi   3.00 3.00

Mural "Espina de la Cruz," by Children of Mercedes — A922

a, 5p, Branches. b, 4p, Two red flowers.

2000, Apr. 26   Perf. 12¼x12
1862 A922 Pair, #a-b   3.00 3.00

Francisco García y Santos (1856-1921), Government Official — A923

2000, May 2   Perf. 12¾x12¼
1863 A923 9p multi   3.00 3.00

Uruguayan Notaries Assoc., 125th Anniv. — A924

2000, May 9   Litho.   Perf. 12¾x12¼
1864 A924 9p multi   3.00 3.00

Intl. Museum Day — A925

2000, May 18   Litho.   Perf. 12¾x12¼
1865 A925 9p multi   3.00 3.00

Stampin' the Future Children's Stamp Design Contest Winners — A926

Artwork by: a, 5p, Helena Perez. b, 4p, Maria Pia Pereyra. c, 4p, Virginia Regueiro. d, 5p, Blanca E. Lima.

2000, June 2   Litho.   Perf. 12
1866 A926 Block of 4, #a-d   5.75 5.75

Club Soriano, 90th Anniv. A927

2000, June 9   Litho.   Perf. 12¼x12¾
1867 A927 9p multi   3.00 3.00

Antonio Rupenian, Founder of Radio Armenia — A928

2000, June 16   Perf. 12¾x12¼
1868 A928 18p multi   5.25 5.25

"1900 Generation" Writers, Cent. — A929

Perf. 12¾x12¼

2000, June 22 Litho.
1869 A929 9p multi 3.00 3.00

Cacti — A930

No. 1870: a, 5p, Notocactus ottonis. b, 4p, Echinopsis multiplex.

2000, July 4 **Perf. 12¼**
1870 A930 Horiz. pair, #a-b 3.00 3.00

Uruguayan Soccer Association, Cent. — A931

No. 1871: a, 5p, Players marching. b, 4p, Team photo. c, 4p, Stadium, World Cup. d, 5p, Players in action, World Cup.

2000, July 14 Litho. **Perf. 12¼x12**
1871 A931 Block of 4, #a-d 8.75 8.75

Opera Anniversaries — A932

No. 1872: a, 9p, Scene from Carmen, composer Georges Bizet. b, 9p, Scene from Tosca, composer Giacomo Puccini.

2000, July 20
1872 A932 Pair, #a-b 5.75 5.75

Carmen, 125th anniv.; Tosca, cent.

Latin American Integration Association, 20th Anniv. — A933

2000, Aug. 11 **Perf. 12¾x12¼**
1873 A933 18p multi 5.75 5.75

Naval Aviation, 75th Anniv. A934

2000, Aug. 18 **Perf. 12¼x12¾**
1874 A934 9p multi 3.00 3.00

ORT, 120th Anniv. A935

2000, Aug. 28
1875 A935 9p multi 3.00 3.00

Luis de la Robla (1780-1844), First Postmaster General — A936

2000, Aug. 28 **Perf. 12¾x12¼**
1876 A936 9p multi 3.00 3.00

Gonzalo Rodriguez (1971-99), Race Car Driver — A937

a, 9p, Rodriguez, dark blue car. b, 9p, Rodriguez holding trophy, light blue car.

2000, Sept. 11 **Perf. 12x12¼**
1877 A937 Pair, #a-b 6.25 6.25

Gen. José Artigas (1764-1850) A938

2000, Sept. 22 Litho. **Perf. 12¼**
1878 A938 9p multi + label 3.00 3.00

España 2000 Intl. Philatelic Exhibition — A939

Birds: a, 5p, Donacospiza albifrons. b, 4p, Geositta cunicularia. c, 4p, Phacellodomus striaticollis. d, 5p, Cacicus chrysopterus.

2000, Sept. 27 **Perf. 12**
1879 A939 Block of 4, #a-d 7.00 7.00

Soka Gakkai International, 25th Anniv. — A940

2000, Oct. 2 **Perf. 12¼x12¾**
1880 A940 18p multi 6.00 6.00

America Issue, Fight Against AIDS — A941

No. 1881: a, 9p, Tic-tac-toe game with condoms and crosses. b, 18p, Syringe and red ribbon.

2000, Oct. 10 **Perf. 12¼**
1881 A941 Horiz. pair, #a-b 8.00 8.00

Mercosur Cultural Heritage Day — A942

2000, Oct. 14 **Perf. 12¾x12¼**
1882 A942 18p multi 6.00 6.00

Dragon, by Luis Mazzey (1895-1983) — A943

2000, Oct. 19 **Perf. 12¼x12¾**
1883 A943 9p multi 3.00 3.00

Fire Fighters A944

Designs: No. 1884, 9p, At car crash. No. 1885, 9p, Searching for victims, vert.

Perf. 12¼x12¾, 12¾x12¼
2000, Oct. 26
1884-1885 A944 Set of 2 8.00 8.00

Prof. Julio Ricaldoni (1906-93), Structural Engineer A945

2000, Nov. 13 **Perf. 12¼x12¾**
1886 A945 9p multi 3.00 3.00

29th Conference on Structural Engineering, Punta del Este.

Training Ship "Capitan Miranda," 70th Anniv. A946

2000, Nov. 15
1887 A946 9p multi 3.00 3.00

Holy Roman Emperor Charles V (1500-58) A947

2000, Nov. 22 Litho.
1888 A947 22p multi 6.00 6.00

Christmas A948

Designs: 11p, Fireworks. 22p, Holy Family.

2000, Dec. 1
1889-1890 A948 Set of 2 9.00 9.00

Sarandi del Yi, 125th Anniv. — A949

2000, Dec. 14 **Perf. 12¾x12¼**
1891 A949 11p multi 3.25 3.25

Forest Fire Prevention Service A950

2001, Feb. 9 Litho. **Perf. 12½x12¾**
1892 A950 11p multi 3.50 3.50

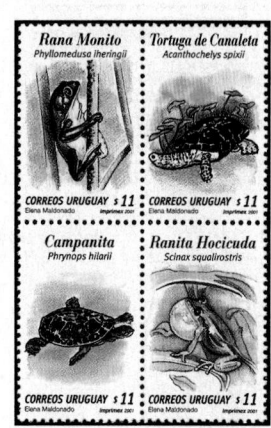

Amphibians and Reptiles — A951

No. 1893: a, Phyllomedusa iheringii. b, Acanthochelys spixii. c, Phrynops hilarii. d, Scinax sqalirostris.

2001, Feb. 15
1893 A951 11p Block of 4, #a-d **Perf. 12**
14.00 14.00

Paysandú Rowing Club, Cent. A952

2001, Feb. 28   **Perf. 12½x12¾**
1894 A952 11p multi   3.25 3.25

17th Congress of Latin American Confederation of Congress Organizers A953

2001, Mar. 2   **Perf. 12¾x12½**
1895 A953 11p multi   3.00 3.00

City of Belén, Bicent. — A954

2001, Mar. 14
1896 A954 11p multi   2.75 2.75

David, by Michelangelo, 500th Anniv. — A955

2001, Mar. 22
1897 A955 22p multi   6.00 6.00

Uruguayan Society of Performers, 50th Anniv. — A956

2001, Mar. 26   **Perf. 12½x12¾**
1898 A956 11p multi   3.00 3.00

Casal Catalá, 75th Anniv. — A957

2001, Apr. 20   **Perf. 12¾x12½**
1899 A957 11p multi   3.00 3.00

Universidad Mayor de la República Engineering Faculty, 85th Anniv. — A958

2001, Apr. 30
1900 A958 11p blue   3.25 3.25

Rodolfo V. Tálice (1899-1999), Biologist — A959

2001, May 2   **Perf. 12½x12¾**
1901 A959 11p multi   3.50 3.50

Montevideo Lions Club, 50th Anniv. — A960

2001, May 14   **Perf. 12¾x12½**
1902 A960 11p multi   3.50 3.50

Invention of the Telephone, 125th Anniv. A961

2001, May 22   **Perf. 12½x12¾**
1903 A961 22p multi   6.00 6.00

Snakes — A962

No. 1904: a, Philodryas olfersii. b, Bothrops alternatus.

2001, May 28   **Perf. 12**
1904 A962 11p Horiz. pair, #a-b 7.00 7.00

Juan Manuel Blanes (1830-1901), Painter — A963

2001, June 8 Litho. Perf. 12½x12¾
1905 A963 11p multi   2.75 2.75

Start of Pediatrics Teaching by Dr. Luis Morquio, Cent. — A964

2001, June 15   **Perf. 12¾x12½**
1906 A964 11p multi   2.75 2.75

The Ring of the Nibelung, by Richard Wagner — A965

No. 1907: a, The Rhinegold (El Oro del Rin). b, The Valkyrie (La Walquiria). c, Siegfried (Sigfrido). d, The Twilight of the Gods (El Ocaso de los Dioses).

2001, June 29   **Perf. 12**
1907 A965 11p Block of 4, #a-d 8.50 8.50

Intl. Organization for Migration, 50th Anniv. — A966

2001, July 5   **Perf. 12¾x12½**
1908 A966 22p blue & black   5.00 5.00

Thomas Alva Edison (1847-1931) A967

2001, July 12
1909 A967 22p multi   5.00 5.00

Laying of Foundation Stone for Montevideo Port, Cent. — A968

2001, July 18   **Perf. 12½x12¾**
1910 A968 11p multi   3.00 3.00

Fowl — A969

No. 1911: a, New Hampshire. b, Orpington-Buff. c, Araucanas. d, Leghorn-Light brown.

2001, July 30   **Perf. 12**
1911 A969 11p Block of 4, #a-d 8.00 8.00

Moby Dick, by Herman Melville, 150th Anniv. — A970

2001, Aug. 2   **Perf. 12¾x12½**
1912 A970 22p multi   5.00 5.00

Bernardo González Pecotche (1901-63), Founder of Logosophy A971

2001, Aug. 7   **Perf. 12**
1913 A971 11p multi   3.00 3.00

First Concorde Flight, 25th Anniv. A972

2001, Aug. 10   **Perf. 12½x12¾**
1914 A972 22p multi   6.00 6.00

Rose Varieties — A973

No. 1915: a, Louis Philippe. b, Souvenir de Mme. Léonie Viennot. c, Kronenbourg. d, Lady Hillingdon.

2001, Aug. 16   **Perf. 12**
1915 A973 11p Block of 4, #a-d
10.00 10.00

Apiculture — A974

No. 1916: a, Apiculturists. b, Bee on flower.

2001, Sept. 12
1916 A974 12p Horiz. pair, #a-b   7.00 7.00

Town of Dolores, Bicent. — A975

2001, Sept. 21   *Perf. 12¾x12½*
1917 A975 12p multi   2.75 2.75

Uruguay Philatelic Club, 75th Anniv. A976

Sun and inscription: No. 1918, 12p, "75 Años." No. 1919, 12p, "1er Presidente / Dr. Miguel A. Paez Formoso."

2001, Sept. 26   *Perf. 12½x12¾*
1918-1919 A976   Set of 2   6.50 6.50

America Issue - UNESCO World Heritage Sites — A977

Buildings from Historic Quarter of Colonia del Sacramento: a, 12p, Basilica del Santisimo. b, 24p, San Benito de Palermo Chapel.

2001, Sept. 28   *Perf. 12*
1920 A977   Horiz. pair, #a-b   9.50 9.50

Carlos Amoretti, 50th Anniv. as Artist A978

2001, Oct. 2   *Perf. 12½x12¾*
1921 A978 12p multi   3.00 3.00

Town of Sauce, 150th Anniv. — A979

2001, Oct. 12   *Perf. 12¾x12½*
1922 A979 12p multi   5.00 5.00

Uruguay - Japan Diplomatic Relations, 80th Anniv. A980

2001, Sept. 24   *Perf. 12¼x12¾*
1923 A980 24p multi   6.00 6.00

Prevention of Illegal Drug Use A981

2001, Oct. 16
1924 A981 12p multi   3.00 3.00

Year of Dialogue Among Civilizations A982

2001, Oct. 23   *Perf. 12¾x12¼*
1925 A982 24p multi   7.00 7.00

Honorary Committee for Fighting Cancer — A983

2001, Oct. 29
1926 A983 12p multi   3.00 3.00

Ultimas Noticias Newspaper, 20th Anniv. — A984

2001, Oct. 31
1927 A984 12p multi   2.75 2.75

Sauce Basketball Club, 50th Anniv. A985

2001, Nov. 9   *Perf. 12¼x12¾*
1928 A985 12p multi   3.75 3.75

Blood Donor's Day — A986

2001, Nov. 12   *Perf. 12¾x12¼*
1929 A986 12p multi   2.75 2.75

Juan Zorrilla de San Martín (1855-1931), Writer — A987

2001, Nov. 13   *Perf. 12¼x12¾*
1930 A987 12p multi   2.75 2.75

Uruguayan Navy's Hydrographic Ship "Oyarvide" — A988

2001, Nov. 14
1931 A988 12p multi   3.25 3.25

Uruguayan Visit of Rotary Intl. President Richard King and Wife Cherie — A989

2001, Nov. 20   *Perf. 12¾x12¼*
1932 A989 24p multi   5.00 5.00

Peñarol Athletic Club, 110th Anniv. — A990

2001, Nov. 22   *Perf. 12*
1933 A990 12p multi   2.75 2.75

Julio Sosa (1926-64), Tango Singer — A991

2001, Nov. 26   *Perf. 12¾x12¼*
1934 A991 12p multi   2.75 2.75

José Nasazzi (1901-68), Soccer Player — A992

2001, Nov. 29
1935 A992 12p multi   2.75 2.75

Christmas — A993

Paintings of Adoration of the Shepherds, by: 12p, José Ribera. 24p, Anton Raphael Mengs.

2001, Dec. 6
1936-1937 A993   Set of 2   7.00 7.00

Church of San Carlos, Bicent. — A994

2001, Dec. 7
1938 A994 12p multi   2.75 2.75

National Museum of Visual Arts, 90th Anniv. — A995

2001, Dec. 12   *Perf. 12*
1939 A995 12p multi   3.50 3.50

State Insurance Bank, 90th Anniv. — A996

2001, Dec. 20   *Perf. 12¾x12¼*
1940 A996 12p multi   2.75 2.75

Guettarda Uruguensis — A997

2001, Dec. 21   *Perf. 12¼x12¾*
1941 A997 24p multi   5.00 5.00

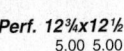

St. Josemaría Escrivá de Balaguer
(1902-75) — A998

Balaguer and quotes: a, "El trabajo es. . ." b,
"Quieres de verdad. . ." c, "La santidad. . ." d,
"Que busques. . ."

2002, Jan. 9   **Perf. 12**
1942 A998 12p Block of 4, #a-
     d   10.00 10.00

Uruguayan Association of Directors of
Carnivals and Folk Festivals, 50th
Anniv. — A999

Feet of: a, Ringmaster. b, Clown. c, Acrobat.

2002, Mar. 8   **Litho.**   **Perf. 12½**
            Self-Adhesive
1943   Booklet pane of 3   5.00 5.00
  a.-b.   A999 6p Either single   1.25 1.25
    c.   A999 12p black   2.50 2.50
       Booklet, #1943   6.00 6.00

Christianity in
Armenia,
1700th Anniv.
A1000

2002, Apr. 23   **Perf. 12**
1944 A1000 12p multi   2.50 2.50

New Year 2003
(Year of the
Horse) — A1001

2002, May 14   **Perf. 12¾x12¼**
1945 A1001 24p multi   4.50 4.50

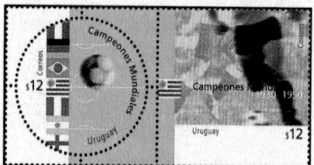

2002 World Cup Soccer
Championships, Japan and
Korea — A1002

No. 1946: a, Flags, soccer ball, and field
(38mm diameter). b, Soccer players, years of
Uruguayan championships.

2002, May 21   **Perf. 12¾**
1946 A1002 12p Horiz. pair, #a-b 4.00 4.00
    See Argentina No. 2184, Brazil No. 2840,
France No. 2891, Germany No. 2163 and Italy
No. 2526.

Book
Day — A1003

2002, May 24   **Perf. 12¾x12¼**
1947 A1003 12p multi
                    2.25 2.25

Inter-American Children's Institute,
75th Anniv. — A1004

2002, June 10   **Perf. 12¼x12¾**
1948 A1004 12p multi   2.25 2.25

Department of Tacuarembó, 165th
Anniv. — A1005

2002, June 14
1949 A1005 12p multi   2.25 2.25

Cerro de Montevideo Lighthouse,
Bicent. — A1006

Designs: 12p, Old lighthouse. 24p, New
lighthouse, vert.

    Perf. 12¼x12¾, 12¾x12¼
2002, June 24
1950-1951 A1006   Set of 2   5.00 5.00

Villa Constitución, 150th
Anniv. — A1007

2002, July 11   **Perf. 12¼x12¾**
1952 A1007 12p multi   2.00 2.00

"We Are
United"
A1008

2002, July 17
1953 A1008 6p multi   1.00 1.00
    Printed in sheets of 3 + label. Value $4.

Natural
Uruguay
A1009

2002, July 22   **Litho.**
1954 A1009 24p blue & orange   3.25 3.25

Montevideo Botanical
Gardens,
Cent. — A1010

No. 1955: a, Botanical Gardens building,
Erythrina cristigalli. b, Rhodophiala bifida. c,
Prof. Atilio Lombardo and Tillandsia arequitae.
d, Heteropterys dumetorum.

2002, July 31   **Perf. 12**
1955   Horiz. strip of 4   7.00 7.00
  a.-d.   A1010 12p Any single   1.60 1.60

Montevideo
Wanderers Soccer
Team,
Cent. — A1011

2002, Aug. 1   **Perf. 12¾x12¼**
1956 A1011 12p black   2.00 2.00

Sportsmen — A1012

Designs: No. 1957, 12p, Lorenzo Fernán-
dez, soccer player. No. 1958, 12p, Josè Lean-
dro Andrade, soccer player. No. 1959, 12p,
Alvaro Gestido, soccer player. No. 1960, 12p,
César L. Gallardo, fencer. No. 1961, 12p,
Pedro Petrone, soccer player.

2002, Aug. 16   **Perf. 12¼x12¾**
1957-1961 A1012   Set of 5   8.50 8.50

Elvis Presley
(1935-77)
A1013

2002, Aug. 19   **Perf. 12¾x12¼**
1962 A1013 24p multi   3.00 3.00

Agustín Bisio
(1894-1952),
Poet — A1014

2002, Aug. 30   **Perf. 12¾x12¼**
           Self-Adhesive
1963 A1014 12p multi   2.00 2.00

City of Artigas,
150th
Anniv. — A1015

2002, Sept. 12   **Perf. 12¾x12¼**
           Self-Adhesive
1964 A1015 12p multi   2.00 2.00

Uruguayan Cooperative Society of Bus
Services, 65th Anniv. — A1016

2002, Sept. 16   **Perf. 12¼x12¾**
1965 A1016 12p multi   2.00 2.00

Psychoanalysis, Cent. — A1017

2002, Sept. 20   **Perf. 12**
1966 A1017 12p multi   2.00 2.00
    24th Latin American Psychoanalysis Con-
gress, Montevideo.

Horacio Arredondo (1888-1967),
Historical Preservationist, and San
Miguel Fort — A1018

2002, Sept. 20   **Perf. 12¼x12¾**
1967 A1018 12p multi   2.00 2.00

Paso del Rey Barracks Natl. Historic
Monument — A1019

2002, Sept. 23   **Perf. 12**
1968 A1019 12p multi   2.00 2.00

Intl. Year of Ecotourism — A1020

2002, Sept. 24   **Litho.**
1969 A1020 12p multi   2.00 2.00

Uruguayan Postal Services, 175th Anniv. — A1021

Designs: No. 1970, Postal Services head-quarters, Montevideo. No. 1971, Letter box.

2002, Oct. 9   **Perf. 12¾x12¼**
1970 A1021 12p multi   2.00 2.00

Souvenir Sheet
Imperf
1971 A1021 12p multi   2.00 2.00

First Equestrian Statue of Brig. Gen. Juan Antonio Lavalleja, Cent. — A1022

2002, Oct. 11   **Perf. 12¾x12¼**
1972 A1022 12p multi   2.00 2.00

America Issue — Youth, Education and Literacy A1023

"ANALFABETISMO" in: 12p, Word search puzzle. 24p, Bowl of alphabet soup.

2002, Oct. 16   **Perf. 12¼x12¾**
1973-1974 A1023   Set of 2   5.00 5.00

Christmas A1024

2002, Nov. 4   **Perf. 12¾x12¼**
1975 A1024 12p multi   2.00 2.00

Association of Uruguayan Pharmacies, 65th Anniv. — A1025

2002, Nov. 8   **Litho.**
1976 A1025 12p multi   2.00 2.00

Tannat Wine — A1026

2002, Nov. 13
1977 A1026 12p multi   2.00 2.00

Uruguayan Navy, 185th Anniv. — A1027

2002, Nov. 13   **Perf. 13½**
1978 A1027 12p multi   2.00 2.00

National Organ and Tissue Bank, 25th Anniv. A1028

2002, Nov. 15
1979 A1028 12p multi   2.00 2.00

Taxis in Uruguay, Cent. A1029

2002, Nov. 25   **Perf. 12¼x12¾**
1980 A1029 12p multi   2.00 2.00

Brig. Gen. Manuel Oribe (1792-1857) A1030

2002, Nov. 28   **Perf. 12¾x12¼**
1981 A1030 12p multi   2.00 2.00

George Harrison (1943-2001), Rock Musician A1031

2002, Nov. 29   **Perf. 13½**
1982 A1031 24p multi   4.50 4.50

Pan-American Health Organization, Cent. — A1032

2002, Dec. 2
1983 A1032 12p multi   2.00 2.00

Uruguayan Participation in U.N. Peace Keeping Missions, 50th Anniv. — A1033

2002, Dec. 6   **Perf. 12¼x12¾**
1984 A1033 12p multi   2.00 2.00

Alfredo Testoni (1919-2000), Artist — A1034

2002, Dec. 9   **Perf. 13½**
1985 A1034 12p multi   2.00 2.00

Mercosur A1035

Designs: 12p, Ship and coastline. 24p, Beach.

2002, Dec. 12
1986-1987 A1035   Set of 2   5.00 5.00

Battle of Ituzaingó, 175th Anniv. A1036

2002, Dec. 17   **Litho.**
1988 A1036 12p multi   2.00 2.00

Battle of Juncal, 175th Anniv. A1037

2002, Dec. 17
1989 A1037 12p multi   2.00 2.00

Town of Juanicó, 130th Anniv. A1038

2002, Dec. 23   **Perf. 12¼x12¾**
1990 A1038 12p multi   2.00 2.00

Uruguay on World Map A1039

2003, Jan. 17   **Litho.**   **Perf. 12¼x12¾**
1991 A1039 12p multi   2.00 2.00

Busqueda Weekly, 30th Anniv. A1040

2003, Jan. 29
1992 A1040 12p multi   2.00 2.00

Water Goddess Iemanja — A1041

2003, Jan. 29   **Perf. 12¾x12¼**
1993 A1041 12p multi   2.00 2.00

Uruguay - People's Republic of China Diplomatic Relations, 15th Anniv. — A1042

2003, Jan. 31   **Perf. 12**
1994 A1042 12p multi   2.00 2.00

New Year 2003
(Year of the
Ram) — A1043

2003, Feb. 7   *Perf. 12¾x12¼*
1995 A1043 5p multi   .75   .75

Explorers
A1044

Explorers and maps of their voyages: a, Christopher Columbus, 4th voyage, 1502. b, Juan Díaz de Solís, 1516. c, Sebastian Cabot, 1526-30. d, Hernando Arias de Saavedra, 1597-1618.

2003, Feb. 14   *Perf. 12*
1996   Horiz. strip of 4   5.25   5.25
a.-d.   A1044 12p Any single   1.25   1.25

Communications Services Regulatory
Union, 2nd Anniv. — A1045

2003, Feb. 21   *Perf. 12¼x12¾*
1997 A1045 12p multi   1.75 1.75

Intl. Women's
Day — A1046

2003, Mar. 7   *Perf. 12¾x12¼*
1998 A1046 12p multi   1.75 1.75

City of
Treinta y
Tres, 150th
Anniv.
A1047

2003, Mar. 10   *Perf. 12¼x12¾*
1999 A1047 12p multi   1.75 1.75

Butterflies — A1048

No. 2000: a, Heliconius erato. b, Junonia evarete. c, Dryadula phaetusa. d, Parides perrhebus.

2003, Mar. 18   *Perf. 12*
2000 A1048 12p Block of 4, #a-d   9.00 9.00

First
Presidency of
José Batlle y
Ordóñez,
Cent. — A1049

No. 2001 — Batlle y Ordóñez: a, Wearing overcoat. b, Wearing presidential sash. c, With head on hand. d, Wearing white jacket.

2003, Mar. 25   *Perf. 12*
2001   Horiz. strip of 4   4.00 4.00
a.-d.   A1049 12p Any single   1.00 1.00

Rural
Women's
Crafts
A1050

No. 2002: a, Basket weaving. b, Knitting. c, Pottery making. d, Food canning. e, Jewelry making.

2003, Mar. 23   *Litho.*   *Perf. 12*
2002   Horiz. strip of 5   6.50 6.50
a.-e.   A1050 12p Any single   1.25 1.25

Farruco's
Chapel — A1051

2003, Apr. 4   *Litho.*   *Perf. 12¾x12¼*
2003 A1051 12p multi   1.75 1.75

Natural
Foods
A1052

2003, Apr. 9   *Perf. 12¼x12¾*
2004 A1052 12p multi   1.75 1.75

Cerros
Azules
Caiman
Farm
A1053

Serpentine Die Cut 11¼
2003, Apr. 10
Self-Adhesive
2005 A1053 12p multi   1.75 1.75

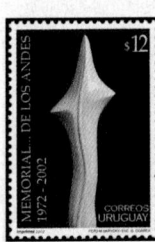

Memorial to 1972
Airplane Crash in
the
Andes — A1054

2003, Apr. 22   *Perf. 12¾x12¼*
2006 A1054 12p multi   1.75 1.75

Military
Center — A1055

2003, May 21
2007 A1055 12p multi   1.75 1.75

May 18,
1811
Military
Museum,
150th
Anniv.
A1056

2003, May 26   *Perf. 12*
2008 A1056 12p multi   1.75 1.75

Casa de Ximénes and Las Bóvedas,
Montevideo Historical District — A1057

2003, May 30   *Perf. 12¼*
2009 A1057 14p multi   2.00 2.00

Wilson Ferreira Aldunate (1919-88),
Politician — A1058

No. 2010: a, Brown background. b, Green background. c, Dark violet background, text at right. d, Light violet background, text at left.

2003, June 16   *Litho.*   *Perf. 12*
2010 A1058 14p Block of 4, #a-d   6.25 6.25

Olympic
Soccer
Gold
Medal,
75th
Anniv.
A1059

2003, June 18
2011 A1059 14p multi   1.60 1.60

Nos. 1382, 1492 Overprinted in Gold

**Methods, Perfs and Watermarks as
Before**
2003, June 18
2011A A654 (14p) on 1.20p
       #1492   1.50 1.50
       Complete booklet of 10   15.00
2011B A589 (36p) on 2500p
       #1382   4.50 4.50
       Complete booklet of 10   45.00

Compare No. 2011A with No. 2055.

Richard
Anderson
College, 70th
Anniv. — A1060

2003, July 15
2012 A1060 14p multi   1.75 1.75

Santa Isabel del Paso de los Toros,
Cent. — A1061

2003, July 17
2013 A1061 14p multi   1.75 1.75

National Association of Affiliates, 70th
Anniv. — A1062

2003, July 24
2014 A1062 14p multi   1.75 1.75

Jesús María College, Carrasco, 50th Anniv. — A1063

2003, Aug. 4
2015 A1063 14p multi   1.75 1.75

Philatelic Academy of Uruguay, 25th Anniv. A1064

2003, Aug. 5
2016 A1064 14p multi   1.75 1.75

Palacio Heber A1065

2003, Aug. 14
2017 A1065 14p multi   1.75 1.75

Parva Domus Magna Quies, 125th Anniv. — A1066

2003, Aug. 15
2018 A1066 14p multi   1.75 1.75

Security Dept. Commission of Interior Ministry, 4th Anniv. — A1067

2003, Aug. 18
2019 A1067 14p multi   1.75 1.75

First International Victory of Uruguayan Soccer Team, Cent. — A1068

2003, Sept. 12   *Perf. 12½x12¾*
2020 A1068 14p multi   1.75 1.75

Lauro Ayestarán (1913-66), Musicologist — A1069

2003, Sept. 19   *Perf. 12*
2021 A1069 14p multi   1.75 1.75

Asociacion Española Primera de Socorros Mutuos Hospital, 150th Anniv. A1070

2003, Sept. 19   *Perf. 12½x12¾*
2022 A1070 14p multi   1.75 1.75

Dr. Manuel Quintela Clinical Hospital, 50th Anniv. A1071

2003, Sept. 23   *Perf. 12*
2023 A1071 14p multi   1.75 1.75

Society of Friends of Public Education, 135th Anniv. — A1072

2003, Sept. 24
2024 A1072 14p multi   1.75 1.75

Association of Uruguayan Newspaper Reporters, 45th Anniv. — A1073

2003, Sept. 29   *Perf. 12½x12¾*
2025 A1073 14p multi   1.75 1.75

Pres. Fructuoso Rivera (c. 1788-1854) A1074

2003, Oct. 1   *Perf. 12*
2026 A1074 14p multi   2.50 2.50

Naval Club, 75th Anniv. A1075

2003, Oct. 1   *Perf. 12½x12¾*
2027 A1075 14p multi   1.75 1.75

Malos Pensamientos Radio Program — A1076

2003, Oct. 3
2028 A1076 14p multi   1.75 1.75

Successes in Intl. Events by Milton Wynants, Cyclist — A1077

2003, Oct. 7   *Perf. 12¾x12½*
2029 A1077 14p multi   1.75 1.75

Ente Nazionale Assistenza Sociale in Uruguay, 50th Anniv. — A1078

2003, Oct. 9   *Perf. 12½x12¾*
2030 A1078 14p multi   1.75 1.75

City of Cardona, Cent. — A1079

2003, Oct. 10   *Perf. 12*
2031 A1079 14p multi   1.75 1.75

Construction League of Uruguay, 84th Anniv. — A1080

2003, Oct. 14   *Perf. 12¾x12½*
2032 A1080 14p multi   1.75 1.75

María Tsakos Foundation, 25th Anniv. — A1081

2003, Oct. 15
2033 A1081 14p multi   1.75 1.75

America Issue — Flora and Fauna A1082

Designs: 14p, Prosopis affinis. 36p, Agouti paca paca.

2003, Oct. 22   *Perf. 12½x12¾*
2034-2035 A1082   Set of 2   5.25 5.25

Independence of Lebanon, 60th Anniv. — A1083

2003, Oct. 24
2036 A1083 14p olive grn & red   1.75 1.75

Souvenir Sheet

Masons in Uruguay, 147th Anniv. — A1084

2003, Oct. 29   *Perf. 12¾x12½*
2037 A1084 14p multi   1.75 1.75

Cacho Bochinche Television Show, 30th Anniv. A1085

2003, Oct. 29   *Perf. 12½x12¾*
2038 A1085 14p multi   1.75 1.75

Morenada, 50th Anniv. — A1086

2003, Oct. 29
2039 A1086 14p multi   1.75 1.75

Brig. Gen.
Juan A.
Lavalleja (c.
1786-1853)
A1087

2003, Oct. 30   *Perf. 12*
2040 A1087 14p multi   1.75 1.75

Souvenir Sheet

Election of Pope John Paul II, 25th
Anniv. — A1088

No. 1089 — Uruguayan flag and: a, Pope
John Paul II, Vatican arms. b, Polish eagle,
map of Latin America.

2003, Oct. 31
2041 A1088 12p Sheet of 2, #a-b 3.50 3.50
Union of Latin American Polish Societies
and Organizations, 10th anniv. (#2041b).

Souvenir Sheet

2006 World Cup Soccer
Championships, Germany — A1089

No. 2042 — World Cup trophy and: a, Uruguayan flag, J. A. Schiaffino. b, German flag,
Fritz Walter.

2003, Oct. 31
2042 A1089 12p Sheet of 2, #a-b 3.50 3.50

Christmas
A1090

2003, Nov. 7   *Perf. 12¾x12½*
2043 A1090 14p multi   1.75 1.75

Italian Chamber of Commerce of
Uruguay, 120th Anniv.
A1091

2003, Nov. 10   *Perf. 12½x12¾*
2044 A1091 14p multi   1.75 1.75

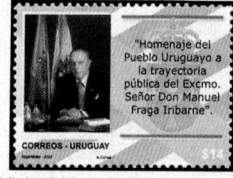

Visit of Manuel Fraga Iribarne,
President of Spanish Autonomous
Community of Galicia — A1092

2003, Nov. 10
2045 A1092 14p multi   1.75 1.75

San
Gregorio
de
Polanco,
150th
Anniv.
A1093

2003, Nov. 14
2046 A1093 14p multi   1.75 1.75

United
Biblical
Society,
Bicent.
A1094

2003, Nov. 24
2047 A1094 14p multi   1.75 1.75

R.O.U.
Paysandu
A1095

2003, Nov. 25   *Perf. 12*
2048 A1095 14p multi   1.75 1.75

University Culture
Foundation, 35th
Anniv. — A1096

2003, Nov. 28
2049 A1096 14p multi   1.75 1.75

Uruguayan
Air Force,
50th Anniv.
A1097

2003, Dec. 4
2050 A1097 14p multi   1.75 1.75

Visit of Mirko
Tremaglia, Italian
Minister for
Italians
Abroad — A1098

2003, Dec. 15
2051 A1098 14p multi   1.75 1.75

Mercosur
A1099

Designs: 14p, Horn. 36p, Silver stirrup.

2003, Dec. 16
2052-2053 A1099   Set of 2   7.00 7.00

Powered
Flight,
Cent.
A1100

2003, Dec. 19
2054 A1100 14p multi   1.75 1.75

**Nos. 1378, 1382, 1458 and 1492
Surcharged in Black or Blue Violet**

j

k

Methods and Perfs. as Before
2004   **Wmk. 332**
2055 A654(j)   1p on 1.20p
                    #1492   .40   .40
2056 A639(j)   2p on 2.60p
                    #1458 (BV)   .40   .40
2057 A589(k)   5p on 2500p
                    #1382   .60   .60
2058 A589(k) 10p on 360p #1378 1.00 1.00
2059 A589(k) 50p on 825p
                    #1379B   5.00 5.00
   Nos. 2055-2059 (5)   7.40 7.40

Issued: Nos. 2055-2056, 1/19; Nos. 2057-
2058, 2/16; No. 2059, 3/23. Obliterator on
Nos. 2055 and 2056 covers the centesimos
portion of the denomination.
Compare No. 2055 with No. 2011A.

Birds — A1101

No. 2060: a, Puffinus gravis. b, Macronectes
halli. c, Daption capense. d, Diamedea
melanophrys.

Unwmk.
2004, Jan. 22   Litho.   *Perf. 12*
2060 A1101 14p Block of 4, #a-d 8.25 8.25

Isla de Lobos
Lighthouse
A1102

No. 2061: a, Isla de Flores Lighthouse. b,
Farallon Lighthouse. c, La Panela Lighthouse.
d, Banco Ingles Floating Lighthouse.

2004, Feb. 10   Litho.   *Perf. 12*
2061 A1102 10p Block of 4, #a-d 4.00 4.00
2062 A1102 14p shown   1.50 1.50

Abitab, 10th
Anniv. — A1103

Unwmk.
2004, Feb. 12   Litho.   *Perf. 12*
2063 A1103 14p multi   1.60 1.60

National Naval Prefecture, 175th
Anniv. — A1104

2004, Feb. 20   Litho.   *Perf. 12*
2064 A1104 14p multi   1.60 1.60

Maté Containers — A1105

No. 2065: a, Maté de Cáliz. b, Maté de Plata Colonial. c, Maté de Calabaza.

2004, Mar. 4
2065 A1105 5p Strip of 3, #a-c 1.75 1.75

33 Orientales Mechanized Infantry Battalion No. 10, Cent. — A1106

2004, Mar. 12
2066 A1106 14p multi 1.60 1.60

Intl. Water Day A1107

2004, Mar. 25
2067 A1107 14p multi 1.60 1.60

Regional Energy Integration Commission, 40th Anniv. — A1108

2004, Mar. 25
2068 A1108 14p multi 1.60 1.60

Grenadier Guards, 80th Anniv. — A1109

2004, Apr. 1
2069 A1109 14p multi 1.60 1.60

Expansion of La Teja Refinery — A1110

2004, Apr. 2
2070 A1110 14p multi 1.60 1.60

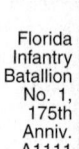

Florida Infantry Batallion No. 1, 175th Anniv. A1111

2004, Apr. 16
2071 A1111 14p multi 1.60 1.60

Tribute to Servicemen — A1112

2004, May 26
2072 A1112 14p multi 1.60 1.60

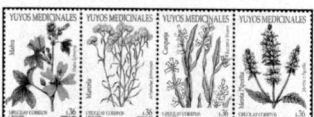

Medicinal Plants — A1113

No. 2073: a, Malva sylvestris. b, Achyrocline satureiodes. c, Baccharis trimera. d, Mentha x piperita.

2004, June 3
2073 Strip of 4 11.00 11.00
a.-d. A1113 36p Any single 2.75 2.75

Map and Arms of Montevideo Department — A1114

2004, June 17
2074 A1114 14p multi 1.60 1.60
a. Booklet pane of 2 3.50 —
  Complete booklet, #2074a 3.50

No. 2074a sold for 35p.

Carlos Gardel (1890-1935), Singer — A1115

2004, June 24 Litho. Perf. 12
2075 A1115 14p multi 1.60 1.60

Campaign Against Illegal Drugs — A1116

2004, June 25 Litho. Perf. 12
2076 A1116 14p multi 1.60 1.60

Renán Rodríguez, Politician — A1117

2004, Aug. 10
2077 A1117 14p multi 1.60 1.60

Maimonides (1135-1204), Philosopher A1118

2004, Aug. 12
2078 A1118 16p multi 1.75 1.75

Galician Center, Montevideo, 125th Anniv. — A1119

2004, Aug. 30
2079 A1119 16p multi 1.75 1.75

1904 Battles of Gen. Aparicio Saravia — A1120

No. 2080 — Battle of: a, Illescas. b, Fray-Marcos. c, Paso del Parque. d, Masoller.

2004, Sept. 8
2080 Block of 4 4.00 4.00
a.-d. A1120 10p Any single 1.00 1.00

Highway Patrol, 50th Anniv. A1121

2004, Sept. 15 Perf. 12½x12¾
2081 A1121 16p multi 1.75 1.75

Joaquín Torres García (1874-1949), Painter — A1122

2004, Sept. 19
2082 A1122 16p multi 1.75 1.75

Magisterial Cooperative, 75th Anniv. — A1123

2004, Sept. 22
2083 A1123 16p multi 1.75 1.75

Army Administrative Corps, Cent. — A1124

2004, Sept. 22
2084 A1124 16p multi 1.75 1.75

FIFA (Fédération Internationale de Football Association), Cent. — A1125

2004, Oct. 5 Perf. 12
2085 A1125 37p multi 3.75 3.75

Uruguay - Republic of Korea Diplomatic Relations, 40th Anniv. — A1126

2004, Oct. 7
2086 A1126 16p multi 1.75 1.75

Montevideo Cathedral, Bicent. — A1127

2004, Oct. 19 Litho. Perf. 12
2087 A1127 16p multi 1.75 1.75

Montevideo Council Building — A1128

2004, Oct. 22 Litho. Perf. 12
2088 A1128 16p multi 1.75 1.75

Tomás Toribio House — A1129

2004, Oct. 22
2089 A1129 16p multi 1.75 1.75

America Issue - Environmental
Protection — A1130

Dirty and clean: 16p, Water. 37p, Birds.

2004, Oct. 26
2090-2091 A1130 Set of 2   5.75 5.75

Armored Infantry Batallion No. 13,
Cent. — A1131

2004, Nov. 16
2092 A1131 16p multi   1.75 1.75

Corner
Store,
18th
Cent.
A1132

2004, Nov. 22
2093 A1132 16p multi   1.75 1.75

PriceWaterhouseCoopers in Uruguay,
85th Anniv. — A1133

2004, Dec. 7
2094 A1133 16p multi   1.75 1.75

Review of Court
Clerks,
Cent. — A1134

2004, Dec. 8
2095 A1134 16p multi   1.75 1.75

Christmas
A1135

2004, Dec. 14
2096 A1135 16p multi   1.75 1.75

Water
Conservation
A1136

2004, Dec. 21
2097 A1136 37p multi   4.00 4.00

Souvenir Sheet

Punta del Este — A1137

2004, Dec. 27
2098 A1137 16p multi   1.75 1.75

1912 Orenstein & Kopell
Locomotive — A1138

Serpentine Die Cut 11¼
2004, Dec. 28   **Self-Adhesive**
2099 A1138 30p multi   3.50 3.50

Rotary
International,
Cent. — A1139

2005, Feb. 23 **Litho.** ***Perf. 12***
2100 A1139 37p multi   6.00 6.00

Bridges — A1140

No. 2101: a, Chuy del Tacuari Bridge. b,
Barra Bridge, Maldonado. c, Mauá Bridge
Yaguarón River. d, Castells Bridge, Víboras.

2005, Mar. 18
2101 A1140 16p Block of 4, #a-d 8.25 8.25

Ninth Meeting of Latin American
Energy Regulators — A1141

2005, Apr. 5
2102 A1141 16p multi   1.75 1.75

"Liberating Dragoons" Ninth
Mechanized Cavalry Regiment,
Cent. — A1142

2005, Apr. 11
2103 A1142 16p multi   1.75 1.75

Armenian
Genocide, 90th
Anniv. — A1143

2005, Apr. 25
2104 A1143 16p multi   1.75 1.75

Fingerprint Analysis in Uruguay,
Cent. — A1144

2005, Apr. 26
2105 A1144 16p multi   1.75 1.75

No. 1446 Surcharged

Wmk. 332
2005, May 27 **Litho.** ***Perf. 12½***
2106 A639 2p on 50c #1446   .35 .35

Fountains
A1145

Designs: No. 2107, 10p, Constitution Plaza
Fountain. No. 2108, 10p, Botanical Garden
Fountain. No. 2109, 10p, Athlete's Fountain,
Rodó Park. 37p, Cordier Fountain, Prado,
horiz.

2005, June 8 **Litho.** ***Perf. 12***
2107-2110 A1145 Set of 4   7.00 7.00

Catholic
Circle,
120th
Anniv.
A1146

2005, June 9
2111 A1146 16p multi   2.00 2.00

SOS
Children's
Villages,
45th
Anniv.
A1147

2005, June 23
2112 A1147 16p multi   2.00 2.00

St. John
the
Baptist
College,
75th
Anniv.
A1148

2005, June 24
2113 A1148 16p multi   2.00 2.00

Souvenir Sheet

Death of Pope John Paul II and
Election of Pope Benedict
XVI — A1149

No. 2114: a, Cross and statue of Pope John
Paul II, Montevideo. b, Pope Benedict XVI.

Perf. 12x11¾
2005, July 15 **Litho.** **Unwmk.**
2114 A1149 10p Sheet of 2, #a-b 2.50 2.50

Medical
Association
Assistance
Center, 70th
Anniv. — A1150

2005   ***Perf. 12***
2115 A1150 16p multi   2.00 2.00

**Inscribed "Correos Uruguay" at
Right**
Perf. 12¾x12½
2116 A1150 16p multi   2.00 2.00
Issued: No. 2115, 7/19; No. 2116, 8/4.

Seminary
College,
125th
Anniv.
A1151

Designs: No. 2117, 16p, St. Ignatius of Loyola, college building. No. 2118, 16p, College building.

2005, July 29 — *Perf. 12*
2117-2118 A1151 Set of 2   3.50 3.50

General Liber Seregni (1916-2004) — A1152

No. 2119 — Inscriptions: a, Vocacion. b, Comienzo. c, Liberacion. d, Reconocimiento.

2005
2119 A1152 16p Block of 4, #a-d   8.00 8.00
   e.   Booklet pane, #2119   8.50
     Complete booklet, #2119e   10.00

Issued: No. 2119, 8/1; No. 2119e, 10/11.

Pope John Paul II (1920-2005) A1153

2005, Aug. 11 — *Perf. 13½x13¾*
2120 A1153 37p multi   4.25 4.25

Europa Stamps, 50th Anniv. A1154

Designs: 16p, Landscape, by C. De Arzadun, Spain #1263. 37p, The Emus, by De Arzadun, Spain, #1126, vert.

Perf. 13¾x13½, 13½x13¾
2005, Aug. 11 — *Litho.*
2121-2122 A1154 Set of 2   6.00 6.00

Urutem 2005 Philatelic Exhibition A1155

2005, Aug. 15 — *Litho.* — *Perf. 12*
2123 A1155 16p multi   2.00 2.00

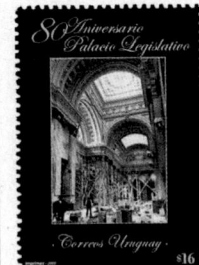

Legislative Palace, 80th Anniv. A1156

2005, Aug. 24 — *Litho.* — *Perf. 12*
2124 A1156 16p multi   2.00 2.00

Estadio Centenario, 75th Anniv. — A1157

Children's art: No. 2125, $16, Stadium, by Jonatan Belón. No. 2126, 16p, "75" made with flag and soccer field, by Sofia Arca.

2005, Aug. 30
2125-2126 A1157 Set of 2   3.25 3.25

Carlos Solé, Soccer Broadcaster — A1158

2005, Sept. 20
2127 A1158 16p multi   2.00 2.00

World Cup Soccer Championships, 75th Anniv. — A1159

Designs: No. 2128, 16p, Parade of athletes. No. 2129, 16p, Handshake before match. No. 2130, 16p, Awarding of World Cup. 37p, Flags of Germany and Uruguay, emblem of 2006 World Cup Soccer Championships, Germany.

2005, Oct. 3
2128-2131 A1159 Set of 4   8.50 8.50

44th Congress of Intl. Congress and Convention Association, Montevideo — A1160

No. 2132: a, Fish sun and buildings. b, Association emblem.

2005, Nov. 4 — *Litho.* — *Perf. 12*
2132 A1160 8p Horiz. pair, #a-b   2.00 2.00

Uruguay River Fish — A1161

No. 2133: a, Rhamdia sapo. b, Odontesthes bonariensis. c, Hoplias malabaricus. d, Pygocentrus nattereri.

2005, Nov. 22
2133 A1161 16p Block of 4, #a-d   6.75 6.75

El Escolar Magazine, 50th Anniv. — A1162

2005, Nov. 23
2134 A1162 16p multi   2.00 2.00

Customhouse Brokers Association, 70th Anniv. — A1163

2005, Nov. 25
2135 A1163 16p multi   2.00 2.00

Detail From Mural, *Oficios,* by Julio Alpuy — A1164

2005, Dec. 1
2136 A1164 16p multi   2.00 2.00

Writers — A1165

Designs: 16p, Juan Zorrilla de San Martin (1855-1931). 37p, Constancio C. Vigil (1876-1954).

2005, Dec. 9
2137-2138 A1165 Set of 2   5.50 5.50

Commercial and Industrial Center of Salto, Cent. — A1166

2005, Dec. 12
2139 A1166 16p multi   2.00 2.00

Central Español Soccer Team, Cent. A1167

2005, Dec. 12
2140 A1167 16p multi   2.00 2.00

Christmas — A1168

2005, Dec. 12
2141 A1168 16p multi   2.00 2.00

Montevideo Atheneum, 137th Anniv. — A1169

2005, Dec. 14 — *Litho.*
2142 A1169 16p multi   2.00 2.00

1924 Paris Olympics, 80th Anniv. (in 2004) A1170

Designs: No. 2143, 16p, Andrés Mazali, soccer gold medalist. No. 2144, 16p, Juan Pedro Cea, soccer gold medalist. No. 2145, 16p, Alfredo Ghierra, soccer gold medalist. 37p, Urn showing soccer players, vert.

2005, Dec. 20 — *Perf. 12*
2143-2146 A1170 Set of 4   8.75 8.75

America Issue, Fight Against Poverty — A1171

Designs: 16p, Children, teacher and school. 37p, Men with shovel.

2005, Dec. 22
2147-2148 A1171 Set of 2   5.50 5.50

Capitán Miranda, 75th Anniv. — A1172

No. 2149: a, Capitán Miranda in 1930. b, Capitán Miranda in 2005. c, Capt. Francisco P. Miranda (1869-1925). d, Crests of ships Capitán Miranda, Cádiz, and Montevideo.

2005, Dec. 28
2149 A1172 16p Block of 4, #a-d   7.00 7.00

No. 1492
Surcharged in
Brown

2005? Photo. Wmk. 332 Perf. 12½
2150 A654 1p on 1.20p #1492   .50 .50

Obliterator on No. 2150 covers the "20" of original denomination. Compare with Nos. 2055 and 2011A.

Maldonado, 250th Anniv. — A1173

Designs: No. 2151, 16p, San Fernando Cathedral. No. 2152, 16p, Dragoon Quarters.

2006, Feb. 22   Litho.   Perf. 12
2151-2152 A1173   Set of 2   3.50 3.50

Alfredo Zitarrosa (1936-89),
Singer — A1174

Zitarrosa and: No. 2153, 16p, Guitar, violin. No. 2154, 16p, Guitar, violin, vert.

2006, Mar. 10
2153-2154 A1174   Set of 2   3.50 3.50

Solís Theater, 150th Anniv. — A1175

2006, Mar. 28
2155 A1175 16p multi   2.00 2.00

Diario Español
Newspaper,
Cent. — A1176

2006, May 15
2156 A1176 16p multi   2.00 2.00

Public Enterprise Day — A1177

2006, May 19
2157 A1177 16p black   2.00 2.00

Assassinated Politicians — A1178

Designs: No. 2158, 16p, Héctor Gutiérrez Ruiz (1934-76). No. 2159, 16p, Zelmar Michelini (1924-76). No. 2160, 16p, Michelini and Gutiérrez Ruiz.

2006, June 1
2158-2160 A1178   Set of 3   5.00 5.00

SODRE Symphonic Orchestra, 75th
Anniv. — A1179

2006, June 20
2161 A1179 16p black   2.00 2.00

Masons in
Uruguay, 150th
Anniv. — A1180

2006, Aug. 15
2162 A1180 16p multi   2.00 2.00

Horse Breeds — A1181

No. 2163: a, Appaloosa. b, Percheron. c, Belgian Heavy Draft. d, Criollo.

2006, Aug. 18
2163 A1181 16p Block of 4, #a-d 6.75 6.75

First Uruguayan Postage Stamps,
150th Anniv. — A1182

2006, Sept. 29
2164 A1182 16p multi   2.00 2.00

Eladio Dieste (1917-2000),
Architect — A1183

2006, Oct. 3
2165 A1183 16p multi   2.00 2.00

Syndical Unification Congress, 40th
Anniv. — A1184

No. 2166: a, Marchers with banner. b, Marchers with flag.

2006, Oct. 3
2166 A1184 16p Horiz. pair, #a-b 3.50 3.50

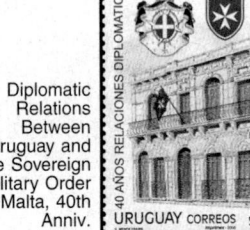

Diplomatic
Relations
Between
Uruguay and
the Sovereign
Military Order
of Malta, 40th
Anniv.
A1185

2006, Oct. 4
2167 A1185 16p multi   2.00 2.00

Paysandú, 250th Anniv. — A1186

2006, Oct. 12
2168 A1186 16p multi   2.00 2.00

Dr. Washington
Beltrán (1914-
2003), Politician
A1187

2006, Oct. 25
2169 A1187 16p multi   2.00 2.00

16th Ibero-American Summit,
Montevideo — A1188

2006, Nov. 1   Litho.   Perf. 12
2170 A1188 37p multi   4.25 4.25

Salto,
250th
Anniv.
A1189

2006, Nov. 7   Litho.   Perf. 12
2171 A1189 16p multi   2.00 2.00

Channel 10, 50th Anniv. — A1190

2006, Nov. 8   Litho.   Perf. 12
2172 A1190 16p multi   2.00 2.00

America Issue, Energy
Conservation — A1191

No. 2173: a, 16p, Screw-in fluorescent light bulbs. b, 37p, Solar panels.

2006, Nov. 17   Litho.   Perf. 12
2173 A1191   Horiz. pair, #a-b   6.00 6.00

Sports
A1192

Designs: No. 2174, 16p, Indoor soccer. No. 2175, 16p, Handball. No. 2176, 16p, Rugby. No. 2177, 16p, Tennis.

2006, Nov. 30
2174-2177 A1192   Set of 4   6.75 6.75

Christmas
A1193

2006, Dec. 7
2178 A1193 37p multi   4.00 4.00

Musical
Instruments
A1194

Designs: 15p, Guitar. 37p, Drum, horiz.

2006, Dec. 11
2179-2180 A1194   Set of 2   5.50 5.50

Ocean Liners and Ports — A1195

No. 2181: a, Queen Mary 2, Montevideo. b,
Costa Fortuna, Montevideo. c, Zuiderman,
Montevideo. d, Star Princess, Punta del Este.

2006, Dec. 18
2181 A1195 37p Block of 4,
       #a-d   18.00 18.00

Uruguayan Lottery, 150th
Anniv. — A1196

2006, Dec. 22   **Litho.**   **Perf. 12**
2182 A1196 15p multi   1.75 1.75

Optimist Class Yacht World
Championships — A1197

2006, Dec. 28   **Litho.**   **Perf. 12**
2183 A1197 37p multi   4.50 4.50

Uruguay
Post
Emblem
A1198

Serpentine Die Cut 11¼
2006, Dec. 29   **Litho.**
     Self-Adhesive
2184 A1198 15p multi   1.75 1.75

No. 1492
Surcharged in
Golden Brown

No. 1454 Surcharged in
Black and Silver

**Methods, Perfs, and Watermarks As
Before**
2007, Jan. 24
2185 A654 1p on 1.20p #1492   .60 .60
2186 A639 2p on 1.80p #1454   .60 .60
   Compare No. 2185 with Nos. 2011A, 2055
and 2150.

Punta del Este, Cent. — A1199

           Unwmk.
2007, Jan. 26   **Litho.**   **Perf. 12**
2187 A1199 37p multi   4.25 4.25

José Nasazzi
Children's
Soccer
Cup — A1200

2007, Feb. 5   **Litho.**   **Perf. 12**
2188 A1200 15p multi   1.75 1.75

Julia Arévalo (1898-1985),
Politician — A1201

2007, Mar. 8   **Litho.**   **Perf. 12**
2189 A1201 15p multi   1.75 1.75

Souvenir Sheet

Ministry of Transportation and Public
Works, Cent. — A1202

No. 2190: a, 5p, Highway construction crew.
b, 10p, Airplanes at airport. c, 15p, Bridge.

2007, Mar. 12   **Litho.**   **Perf. 12¼**
2190 A1202   Sheet of 3, #a-c   2.50 2.50

Colón
Soccer
Club,
Cent.
A1203

2007, Mar. 12   **Litho.**   **Perf. 12**
2191 A1203 15p multi   1.75 1.75

Campaign
Against Dengue
Fever — A1204

Serpentine Die Cut 11¼
2007, Mar. 28   **Self-Adhesive**
2192 A1204 15p multi   1.75 1.75

National
Cadastre,
Cent.
A1205

2007, Apr. 12   **Perf. 12**
2193 A1205 15p multi   1.75 1.75

Regional Art
Meeting
A1206

2007, June 8
2194 A1206 15p multi   1.75 1.75

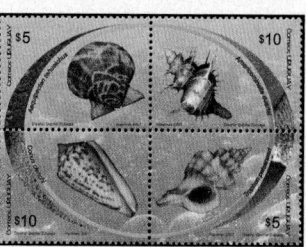

Shells — A1207

No. 2195: a, 5p, Aequipecten tehuelchus. b,
5p, Trophon pelseneeri. c, 10p, Amer-
icominella duartei. d, 10p, Conus clenchi.

2007, June 26
2195 A1207   Block of 4, #a-d   4.00 4.00

Giuseppe Garibaldi (1807-82), Italian
Leader — A1208

Designs: 15p, Ship, Garibaldi on horseback.
37p, Garibaldi, ship.

2007, July 4
2196-2197 A1208   Set of 2   6.00 6.00
   See Brazil Nos. 3021-3022.

Guichón,
Cent. — A1209

2007, July 13
2198 A1209 15p multi   2.00 2.00

Souvenir Sheet

La Estrella del Sur Publication,
Bicent. — A1210

2007, July 19   **Perf. 12½x12¾**
2199 A1210 15p multi   2.00 2.00

Agronomy Faculties, Cent. — A1211

2007, July 30
2200 A1211 15p multi   2.00 2.00

Scouting, Cent. — A1212

Children's drawings: No. 2201, 15p, Scout emblem, by Victoria Ferrer. No. 2202, 15p, Scouts at Flag Ceremony, by Paula Barrios. No. 2203, horiz.: a, Knot, Lord Robert Baden-Powell and Duke of Connaught. b, Knot, International Scout emblem patch.

2007, Aug. 9   **Perf. 12**
2201-2202 A1212 Set of 2   3.75 3.75
     Souvenir Sheet
2203 A1212 25p Sheet of 2, #a-b 6.00 6.00

Three Musicians in Primary Colors, by José Gurvich (1927-74) A1213

2007, Aug. 17
2204 A1213 15p multi   1.75 1.75

Diplomatic Relations Between Uruguay and Guatemala, Cent. — A1214

No. 2205: a, 15p, Santa Catarina Arch, Antigua, Guatemala. b, 37p, City gate, Colonia del Sacramento, Uruguay.

2007, Sept. 3 Litho. Perf. 12½x12¾
2205 A1214   Horiz. pair, #a-b   6.00 6.00
     See Guatemala No. 583.

German College and High School, Montevideo, 150th Anniv. A1215

No. 2206: a, Anniversary emblem. b, Children's drawing of girl and colors of flags of Germany and Uruguay.

2007, Sept. 5   **Perf. 12**
2206   Horiz. pair + central label   3.50 3.50
   a.-b. A1215 15p Either single 1.75 1.75

Occupations — A1216

Designs: 1p, Peanut vendor. 7p, Knife grinder, vert. 10p, Organ grinder, vert. 25p, Barber, vert. 50p, Druggist, vert.

Serpentine Die Cut 11¼
2007, Oct. 6   **Self-Adhesive**
2207 A1216   1p multi   .25   .25
2208 A1216   7p multi   .80   .80
2209 A1216 10p multi   1.10 1.10
2210 A1216 25p multi   2.75 2.75
2211 A1216 50p multi   5.50 5.50
   Nos. 2207-2211 (5)   10.40 10.40
     See Nos. 2253, 2282, 2290, 2292-2295, B13.

Marine Mammal Conservation — A1217

2007, Oct. 12   *Die Cut*
     Self-Adhesive
2212 A1217 37p multi   4.50 4.50

Butterflies — A1218

No. 2213: a, 5p, Eurybia lycisca. b, 10p, Catagramma excelsior pastazza. c, 15p, Agrias claudina. d, 20p, Marpesia marcella.

2007, Oct. 26   **Perf. 12½x12¾**
2213 A1218   Block of 4, #a-d   6.00 6.00

Torrijos - Carter Panama Canal Treaties, 30th Anniv. A1219

2007, Nov. 5   **Perf. 12**
2214 A1219 37p multi   4.50 4.50

America Issue, Education For All A1220

Designs: 15p, Rectangles. 37p, Squares and rectangles.

2007, Nov. 22
2215-2216 A1220 Set of 2   7.00 7.00

Naval School, Cent. — A1221

2007, Dec. 5   **Perf. 12x11¾**
2217 A1221 12p multi   1.75 1.75

Diplomatic Relations Between Uruguay and Russia, 150th Anniv. — A1223

No. 2218: a, 12p, Sacred Heart of Jesus Sanctuary, Uruguay. b, 37p, St. Basil's Cathedral, Russia.

2007, Dec. 21 Litho. Perf. 12
2218 A1223   Horiz. pair, #a-b + central label   6.00 6.00

Christmas A1224

2007, Dec. 21
2219 A1224 12p multi   1.75 1.75

Architecture A1225

Designs: 12p, House, by Julio Vilamajó. 37p, Joaquín Torres García Building, by Carlos Ott.

2007, Dec. 28
2220-2221 A1225 Set of 2   6.00 6.00

Nelly Goitiño (1924-2007), Actress and Director — A1226

2008, Mar. 24 Litho. Perf. 12
2222 A1226 12p multi   1.25 1.25

Natl. Association of Milk Producers, 75th Anniv. — A1227

2008, Apr. 23 Litho. Perf. 12
2223 A1227 12p multi   1.25 1.25

Israel, 60th Anniv. A1228

2008, May 8
2224 A1228 37p multi + label   3.75 3.75

Diplomatic Relations Between Uruguay and the People's Republic of China, 20th Anniv. — A1229

Designs: No. 2225, 12p, Terracotta warriors, China. No. 2226, 12p, The Three Chiripás, painting by J. M. Blaines.

2008, May 19 Litho. Perf. 12
2225-2226 A1229 Set of 2   2.50 2.50

Dr. Juan J. Crottogini (1908-96), Gynecologist A1230

2008, May 27 Litho. Perf. 12
2227 A1230 12p multi   1.25 1.25

     Souvenir Sheet

Uruguayan Artisans Association, 25th Anniv. — A1231

2008, May 29   **Perf. 12½x12¾**
2228 A1231 12p multi   1.25 1.25

Discount Bank, 50th Anniv. — A1232

2008, June 4   **Perf. 12**
     Self-Adhesive
2229 A1232 12p multi   1.25 1.25

Intl. Day Against Child Labor — A1233

2008, June 12
2230 A1233 12p multi   1.25 1.25

Birds
A1234

Designs: 12p, Piranga flava. 37p, Cyanocorax chrysops, vert.

2008, June 20
2231-2232 A1234   Set of 2   5.25 5.25

Salvador Allende (1908-73), President of Chile — A1235

2008, June 26
2233 A1235 37p multi   4.00 4.00

Francisco Gómez House, 120th Anniv. as Montevideo Government Building A1236

2008, July 11   *Perf. 12*
2234 A1236 12p multi   1.25 1.25

Hospital Centenaries — A1237

Designs: No. 2235, 12p, Dr. Raul Amorin Cal Hospital, Florida. No. 2236, 12p, Central Hospital of the Armed Forces. No. 2237, 12p, Pereira Rossell Hospital Center.

2008, July 15
2235-2237 A1237   Set of 3   3.75 3.75

2008 Summer Olympics, Beijing — A1238

No. 2238: a, 2p, Pole vault. b, 5p, Cycling. c, 10p, Swimming. d, 20p, Kayaking.

2008, July 22
2238 A1238   Block of 4, #a-d   4.00 4.00

Intl. Swimming Federation (FINA), Cent. A1239

2008, July 22
2239 A1239 37p multi   4.00 4.00

Club Español, Montevideo, 130th Anniv. A1240

2008, Aug. 28   Litho.   *Perf. 12*
2240 A1240 12p multi   1.25 1.25

Carlos Vaz Ferreira (1872-1958), Philosopher — A1241

2008, Sept. 25   Litho.   *Perf. 12*
2241 A1241 12p multi   1.25 1.25

Latin American and Caribbean Coalition — A1242

2008, Sept. 25
2242   Horiz. strip of 3   3.75 3.75
   a. A1242 10p Three people   .95 .95
   b. A1242 12p Three people, diff.   1.25 1.25
   c. A1242 15p Four people   1.40 1.40

Souvenir Sheet

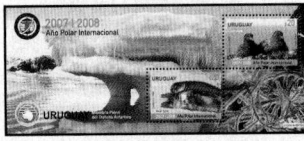

Intl. Polar Year — A1243

No. 1243: a, Skuas. b, Arctocephalus gazella.

2008, Oct. 7
2243 A1243 20p Sheet of 2, #a-b 3.75 3.75

America Issue, National Festivals A1244

Designs: 12p, Guitarist, dancers. 37p, Dancer, costumed drummers.

Perf. 12¾x12½, 12 (37p)
2008, Oct. 24
2244-2245 A1244   Set of 2   4.25 4.25

Dr. Roberto De Bellis (1938-2007), Hematologist — A1245

2008, Oct. 29   *Perf. 12*
2246 A1245 12p multi   1.10 1.10

José "Pepe" Sasía, Soccer Player A1246

2008, Nov. 20   Litho.   *Perf. 12*
2247 A1246 12p multi   1.00 1.00

Flowers A1247

Designs: 1p, Sagittaria montevidensis. 2p, Lantana camara. 10p, Calliandra parvifolia. 17p, Erythrina crista-galli. 25p, Prunus subcoriacea.

2008-09   Litho.   *Die Cut*
     Self-Adhesive
2248 A1247   1p multi   .25 .25
2249 A1247   2p multi   .25 .25
2250 A1247   10p multi   .85 .85
   a.   Dated "2009"   .90 .90

2251 A1247 17p multi   1.40 1.40
2252 A1247 25p multi   2.10 2.10
   Nos. 2248-2252 (5)   4.85 4.85

Issued: 1p, 2p, 3/12/09; 10p, 25p, 11/28; 17p, 12/18.
No. 2250a, 5/15/09.
See Nos. 2265-2266, 2287.

Occupations Type of 2007
2008, Dec. 7   *Die Cut*
     Self-Adhesive
2253 A1216 8p Pasta makers   .65 .65

Ministry of Foreign Affairs, 180th Anniv. — A1248

2008, Dec. 10   Litho.   *Perf. 12*
2254 A1248 37p multi   3.00 3.00

Christmas — A1249

2008, Dec. 24
2255 A1249 12p multi   1.00 1.00

National Flag, 180th Anniv. A1250

2008, Dec. 29
2256 A1250 37p multi   3.00 3.00

Pres. Baltasar Brum (1883-1933) — A1251

2009, Mar. 4   *Perf. 12½x12¾*
2257 A1251 12p multi   1.00 1.00

Delmira Agustini (1886-1914), Poet — A1252

2009, Mar. 26
2258 A1252 12p multi   1.00 1.00

Miguelete, Cent. — A1253

2009, Mar. 27   **Perf. 12¾x12½**
2259 A1253 12p multi   1.00 1.00

Fray Bentos, 150th Anniv. — A1254

2009, Apr. 15   **Litho.**   **Perf. 12**
2260 A1254 12p multi   1.00 1.00

City of Florida, 200th Anniv. — A1255

2009, Apr. 24   **Perf. 12¾x12½**
2261 A1255 12p multi   1.00 1.00

Carnival Costume Designed by Juan Mascheroni — A1256

2009, May 28   **Die Cut**
    Self-Adhesive
2262 A1256 37p multi   3.25 3.25

Souvenir Sheet

Intl. Year of Astronomy — A1257

No. 2263: a, 10p, Intl. Year of Astronomy emblem. b, 12p, Galileo Galilei at Inquisition. c, 25p, Head of Galileo.

2009, June 4   **Perf. 12**
2263 A1257   Sheet of 3, #a-c   4.25 4.25

Juan Carlos Onetti (1909-94), Writer — A1258

2009, July 1   **Perf. 12½x12¾**
2264 A1258 12p multi   1.10 1.10

Flowers Type of 2008-09

Designs: 30p, Tessaria absinthioides. 50p, Eichhornia crassipes.

2009, July 14   **Die Cut**
    Self-Adhesive
2265 A1247 30p multi   2.60 2.60
2266 A1247 50p multi   4.25 4.25

Souvenir Sheet

Port of Montevideo, Cent. — A1259

2009, July 21   **Perf. 12**
2267 A1259 37p multi   3.25 3.25

Charles Darwin (1809-82), Naturalist — A1260

No. 2268: a, 12p, Head of Darwin, evolution of humans. b, 37p, HMS Beagle.

2009, Aug. 31
2268 A1260   Horiz. pair, #a-b   4.50 4.50

No. 1454 Surcharged

Method, Perf. and Watermark As Before
2009, Sept. 10
2269 A639 1p on 1.80p #2269   .25 .25
    Obliterator covers the centisimos portion of the denomination.

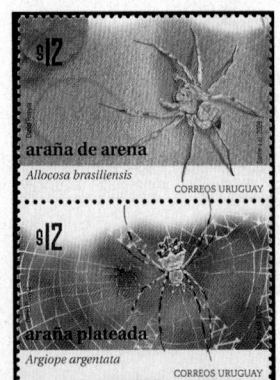

Spiders — A1261

No. 2270: a, Allocosa brasiliensis. b, Argiope argentata.

2009, Sept. 24   **Litho.**   **Perf. 12**
2270 A1261 12p Vert. pair, #a-b   — —

Acipenser Gueldenstaedtii and Caviar — A1262

Unwmk.
2009, Sept. 30   **Litho.**   **Perf. 12**
2271 A1262 37p multi   3.50 3.50

Intl. Labor Organization, 90th Anniv. — A1263

2009, Oct. 7
2272 A1263 37p multi   3.75 3.75

Butterflies and Birds — A1264

No. 2273: a, Hamadryas amphione. b, Anartia amathea. c, Tachuris rubrigasta. d, Colaptes melanochloros.

2009, Oct. 13
2273 A1264 12p Block of 4, #a-d 4.75 4.75

America Issue, Traditional Games A1265

Designs: 12p, Hand holding stone for Taba. 37p, Taba Game, painting by Juan Manuel Blanes.

2009, Oct. 23   **Perf. 12½x12¾**
2274-2275 A1265   Set of 2   4.75 4.75

Government House Museum, 10th Anniv. — A1266

2009, Nov. 6   **Perf. 12**
2276 A1266 12p multi + label   1.25 1.25

Christmas A1267

2009, Nov. 17   **Perf. 12¾x12½**
2277 A1267 12p multi   1.25 1.25

Exports — A1268

Designs: 10p, Vegetables. 25p, Fruits.

2009, Nov. 19   **Die Cut**
    Self-Adhesive
2278 A1268 10p multi   1.00 1.00
2279 A1268 25p multi   2.60 2.60

Inter-American Development Bank, 50th Anniv. — A1269

2009, Nov. 24   **Perf. 12¾x12½**
2280 A1269 37p multi   3.75 3.75

Christian Youth Association (YMCA) in Uruguay, Cent. — A1270

2009, Nov. 25
2281 A1270 12p multi   1.25 1.25

Occupations Type of 2007
2009, Nov. 27   **Die Cut**
    Self-Adhesive
2282 A1216 8p Grocer, vert.   .80 .80

Chauffeur's Protection Center, Montevideo, Cent. — A1271

2009, Dec. 3   **Perf. 12½x12¾**
2283 A1271 12p multi   1.25 1.25

Souvenir Sheet

Battle of the River Plate, 70th Anniv. — A1272

No. 2284: a, 10p, HMS Ajax. b, 12p, HMSNZ Achilles. c, 15p, HMS Exeter.

2009, Dec. 16 *Perf. 12*
2284 A1272 Sheet of 3, #a-c 3.75 3.75

Official Service of Broadcasting, Television and Entertainment, 80th Anniv. — A1273

2009, Dec. 18 *Perf. 12¾x12½*
2285 A1273 37p multi 3.75 3.75

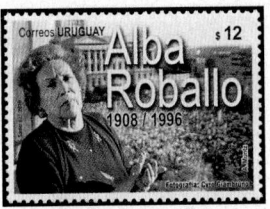

Alba Roballo (1908-96), Politician — A1274

2010, Mar. 8 **Litho.** *Perf. 12*
2286 A1274 12p multi 1.25 1.25

Flowers Type of 2008-09
2010, Apr. 12 *Die Cut*
Self-Adhesive
2287 A1247 12p Erithrina crista-galli 1.25 1.25

Historic Hotels — A1275

Designs: No. 2288, 12p, Gran Hotel Concordia, Salto. No. 2289, 12p, Hotel Colón, Piriápolis.

2010, May 26 *Perf. 12¾x12½*
2288-2289 A1275 Set of 2 2.50 2.50

Occupations Type of 2007
Designs: 5p, Street vendor with basket, vert. 7p, Candy vendor, vert. 10p, Shoemaker, vert. 17p, Cuarteador (man on horseback), vert. 25p, Fish vendor, vert. 30p, Ice cream vendor with pushcart.

2010 **Litho.** *Die Cut*
Self-Adhesive
2290 A1216 5p multi .55 .55
2291 A1216 7p multi .70 .70
2292 A1216 10p multi 1.10 1.10
2293 A1216 17p multi 1.75 1.75
2294 A1216 25p multi 2.40 2.40
2295 A1216 30p multi 3.00 3.00
Nos. 2290-2295 (6) 9.50 9.50

Issued: 5p, 10p, 5/27; 17p, 30p, 8/10; 25p, 8/19; 7p, 10/20.

First Russians in Uruguay, 150th Anniv. — A1276

Perf. 12¾x12½
2010, June 11 **Litho.**
2296 A1276 37p multi 3.75 3.75

Decade of Peace — A1277

2010, June 30
2297 A1277 12p multi 1.25 1.25

Souvenir Sheet

Frédéric Chopin (1810-49), Composer — A1278

No. 2298: a, 12p, Chopin. b, 37p, Piano.

2010, July 21 *Perf. 12*
2298 A1278 Sheet of 2, #a-b 4.75 4.75

Diplomatic Relations Between Uruguay and Romania, 75th Anniv. — A1279

2010, July 23 *Perf. 12¾x12½*
2299 A1279 37p multi 3.75 3.75

Asturian Center, Montevideo, Cent. — A1280

2010, Aug. 28
2300 A1280 37p multi 3.75 3.75

Sporting Club Uruguay, Cent. A1281

2010, Sept. 1 **Litho.** *Perf. 12*
2301 A1281 12p multi 1.25 1.25

Diplomatic Relations Between Uruguay and Greece, 135th Anniv. — A1282

2010, Sept. 8 **Litho.** *Perf. 12*
2302 A1282 37p multi 3.75 3.75

Florencio Sánchez (1875-1910), Playwright — A1283

2010, Sept. 17 *Perf. 12¼x12¾*
2303 A1283 12p multi 1.25 1.25

Restoration of Democracy in Uruguay, 25th Anniv. — A1284

Perf. 12¾x12½
2010, Sept. 21 **Litho.**
2304 A1284 12p multi 1.25 1.25

Mario Benedetti (1920-2009), Writer — A1285

No. 2305 — Benedetti at: a, Right. b, Left.

2010, Sept. 25 *Perf. 12½x12¾*
2305 A1285 12p Horiz. pair, #a-b 2.40 2.40
 c. Booklet pane of 2, #2305a-2305b 3.00 —
  Complete booklet, #2305c 3.00

No. 2305c sold for 30p.

Flowers and Birds — A1286

No. 2306: a, Bauhinia forficata var. pruinosa. b, Furnarius rufus. c, Guira guira. d, Passiflora coerulea.

2010, Sept. 30
2306 A1286 12p Block of 4, #a-d 4.75 4.75

Uruguay as Antarctic Treaty Consultative Member, 25th Anniv. — A1287

2010, Oct. 8 **Litho.** *Perf. 12½x12¾*
2307 A1287 37p multi 3.75 3.75

Christmas A1288

2010, Oct. 29 *Perf. 12¾x12½*
2308 A1288 12p multi 1.25 1.25

America Issue — A1289

No. 2309 — Flag of Uruguay and: a, 12p, National anthem. b, 37p, National coat of arms.

2010, Nov. 8
2309 A1289 Horiz. pair, #a-b 5.00 5.00

Blue Uniform of Uruguay Soccer Team, Cent. A1290

No. 2310: a, Team of 1910. b, Team of 2010, emblem of 2010 World Cup Soccer Tournament, South Africa (84x30mm).

2010, Nov. 15 *Perf. 12½x12¾*
2310 Horiz. pair 2.50 2.50
 a.-b. A1290 12p Either single 1.25 1.25

Cruise Ships and Their Ports of Call — A1291

No. 2311: a, MSC Lirica, Punta del Este. b, Veendam, Montevideo. c, Silver Whisper, Punta del Este and Casapueblo. d, Splendour of the Seas, Punta del Este and Isla de Lobos.

2010, Nov. 19   *Perf. 12*
2311 A1291 37p Block of 4,
     #a-d   15.00 15.00

Souvenir Sheet

First Airplane Flights in Uruguay, Cent. — A1292

No. 2312 — Airplane and: a, Armand Prevost, pilot of Dec. 7, 1910 flight. b, Bartolomeo Cattaneo, pilot of Dec. 16, 1910 flight.

2010, Nov. 30   *Perf. 12¾x12½*
2312 A1292 37p Sheet of 2, #a-
     b, + central la-
     bel   7.50 7.50

El Telégrafo Newspaper, Paysandu, Cent. — A1293

2010, Dec. 9   *Perf. 12¾x12½*
2313 A1293 12p multi   1.25 1.25

Socialist Party of Uruguay, Cent. A1294

2010, Dec. 10   *Perf. 12½x12¾*
2314 A1294 12p multi   1.25 1.25

Paintings by Eduardo Vernazza (1910-91) — A1295

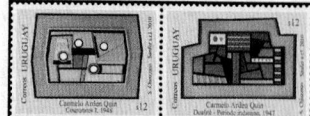

Paintings by Carmelo Arden Quin (1913-2010) — A1296

No. 2315: a, "Gato con Botas," - Ballet Ruso. b, Personaje Femenino - Opera China (Dan).
No. 2316: a, Couronnes I. b, Dualité - Periode Indienne.

2010, Dec. 22   *Perf. 12¾x12½*
2315 A1295 12p Horiz. pair, #a-b 2.40 2.40
             Perf. 12½x12¾
2316 A1296 12p Horiz. pair, #a-b 2.40 2.40

Independence, 200th Anniv. — A1297

2011, Jan. 3 Self-Adhesive   *Die Cut*
2317 A1297 1p multi   .25 .25

Artisan Crafts — A1298

Designs: 2p, Baskets, thistles and cattails. No. 2319, Handbag, wool (lana). No. 2320, Iron toy car (hierro). 12p, Wooden sheep, wood. 20p, Silver container. 22p, Bamboo sculpture, bamboo. 37p, Ceramic pot. 44p, Wire sculpture. 200p, Leather basket, cow.

2011   **Self-Adhesive**   **Die Cut**
2318 A1298   2p multi   .25 .25
2319 A1298   10p multi   1.10 1.10
2320 A1298   10p multi   1.10 1.10
2321 A1298   12p multi   1.25 1.25
2322 A1298   20p multi   2.10 2.10
2323 A1298   22p multi   2.25 2.25
2324 A1298   37p multi   4.00 4.00
         Size: 27x19mm
2325 A1298   44p multi   4.75 4.75
         Size: 42x30mm
2326 A1298 200p multi   22.00 22.00
   Nos. 2318-2326 (9)   38.80 38.80

Issed: 2p, 1/31; No. 2319, 37p, 3/23; No. 2320, 22p, 12/15; 12p, 20p, 4/12; 44p, 5/13; 200p, 5/6.

25th Gaucho Culture Festival, Tacuarembó — A1299

No. 2327: a, Cauldron, meat on grill. b, Bola, gaucho on horse. c, Spurs, gaucho on horse.

2011, Feb. 3   *Perf. 12*
2327   Horiz. strip of 3   3.75 3.75
  a.-c. A1299 12p Any single   1.25 1.25
   Uruguayan Independence, bicent.

Rabindranath Tagore (1861-1941), Poet — A1300

2011, Feb. 16   *Perf. 12¾x12½*
2328 A1300 37p multi   4.00 4.00
   Indipex 2011 Intl. Philatelic Exhibition, New Delhi.

Battle of Las Piedras, by Juan Luis and Juan Manuel Blanes — A1301

2011, Feb. 25
2329 A1301 12p multi   1.25 1.25
   Uruguayan Army, Uruguayan Independence, bicent.

Cry of Asencio, Bicent. — A1302

No. 2330: a, 12p, Hand on sword, hand on knife, spears. b, 37p, Bearded man with spear, horse, hand on knife.

2011, Feb. 28
2330 A1302   Horiz. pair, #a-b   5.00 5.00
   Uruguayan Independence, bicent.

Gen. Leandro Gómez (1811-65) A1303

2011, Mar. 3   *Perf. 12¾x12½*
2331 A1303 12p multi   1.25 1.25

Souvenir Sheet

Las Llamadas, by Carlos Páez Vilaró — A1304

2011, Mar. 4   **Litho.**
2332 A1304 37p multi   4.00 4.00

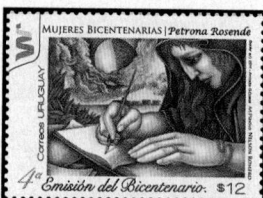

Famous Women — A1305

Designs: No. 2333, 12p, Petrona Rosende (1787-1862), writer. No. 2334, 12p, Josefa Oribe (1789-1835), independence supporter.

2011, Mar. 8   *Perf. 12*
2333-2334 A1305   Set of 2   2.50 2.50
   Uruguayan Independence, bicent.

Uruguay No. 196 — A1306

2011, Mar. 23   *Perf. 12¾x12½*
2335 A1306 37p multi   4.00 4.00
   Postal Union of the Americas, Spain and Portugal (UPAEP), cent.

Planeta Building, Atlántida A1307

2011, Apr. 8   *Perf. 12½x12¾*
2336 A1307 12p multi   1.25 1.25
   Atlántida, cent.

Mother's Day — A1308

2011, May 11   *Die Cut*
     Self-Adhesive
2337 A1308 12p multi   1.25 1.25

Monte Carlo TV Channel 4, 50th Anniv. A1309

2011, May 11   *Perf. 12½x12¾*
2338 A1309 12p multi   1.25 1.25

Battle of Las Piedras, Bicent. — A1310

2011, May 12   *Perf. 12*
2339 A1310 12p multi   1.25 1.25
Uruguayan Independence, bicent.

2011 Copa
América Soccer
Tournament,
Argentina
A1311

2011, June 15   *Perf. 12¾x12½*
2340 A1311 37p multi   4.00 4.00

Aitona, by
Ignacio
Iturria
A1312

2011, June 29   *Perf. 12½x12¾*
2341 A1312 12p multi   1.40 1.40
Basque Center, Montevideo, cent.

Campaign Against Human
Immunodeficiency Virus, 30th
Anniv. — A1313

2011, June 30   *Perf. 12¾x12½*
2342 A1313 12p multi   1.40 1.40

Natl. Physical Education Commission,
Cent. — A1314

2011, July 20   *Perf. 12½x12¾*
2343 A1314 12p multi   1.25 1.25

Uruguay,
Champions of
2011 Copa
América
Soccer
Tournament
A1315

No. 2344: a, Cristian Rodríguez. b, Alvaro
Pereira. c, Abel Hernández. d, Luis Suárez. e,
Nicolás Lodeiro. f, Sebastián Abreu. g, Diego
Pérez. h, Fernando Muslera. i, Diego Forlán. j,
Team manager Washington Tabárez. k, Edinson
son Cavani. l, Sebastián Eguren. m, Martín
Cáceres. n, Diego Godín. o, Egidio Arévalo. p,
Alvaro González. q, Maximiliano Pereira. r,
Juan Castillo. s, Diego Lugano. t, Walter Gargano.
u, Mauricio Victorino. v, Andrés Scotti.
w, Martín Silva. x, Sebastián Coates.

2011, Aug. 11   *Perf. 12*
2344   Sheet of 24   16.00 16.00
a.-x. A1315 6p Any single   .65 .65

Intl. Year of Forests — A1316

2011, Sept. 21   *Litho.*
2345 A1316 12p multi   1.25 1.25

America Issue,
Mailboxes
A1317

Designs: 12p, Cylindrical mailbox, Avenida
18 de Julio, Montevideo. 37p, Rectangular
mailbox, Plaza Independecia, Montevideo.

2011, Sept. 30   *Perf. 12¾x12½*
2346-2347 A1317   Set of 2   5.00 5.00

Diplomatic Relations Between Japan
and Uruguay, 90th Anniv. — A1318

2011, Oct. 5   *Perf. 12*
2348 A1318 37p multi + label   3.75 3.75

La Redota (Exodus of Gen. José
Artigas and Supporters),
Bicent. — A1319

2011, Oct. 13
2349 A1319 12p multi   1.25 1.25
Uruguayan Independece, bicent.

Souvenir Sheet

China Zorrilla, Actress — A1320

2011, Oct. 18   *Perf. 12½x12¾*
2350 A1320 37p multi   3.75 3.75

Whale Watching — A1321

No. 2351 — Eubalaena australis: a, 12p,
Tail above surface near boat. b, 12p, Tail below
water. c, 37p, At water's surface near land. d,
37p, Diving underwater.

2011, Nov. 16   *Litho.*
2351 A1321   Block of 4, #a-d   10.00 10.00

Isla de Flores National Park — A1322

2011, Nov. 16   *Perf. 12*
2352 A1322 12p multi   1.25 1.25

Cruise Ships — A1323

No. 2353: a, Seabourn Sojourn near José
Batlle y Ordonez Power Plant. b, Asuka II near
Joaquín Torres García Telecommunications
Tower. c, Costa Victoria in Port of Montevideo.
d, AIDAcara near Cerro de Montevideo.

2011, Nov. 22
2353 A1323 37p Block of 4,
     #a-d   15.00 15.00

PLUNA Airlines, 75th Anniv. — A1324

2011, Nov. 22
2354 A1324 12p multi   1.25 1.25

Tango
Musicians
A1325

No. 2355: a, César Zagnoli (1911-2002). b,
Juan D'Arienzo (1900-76). c, Donato Racciatti
(1918-2000).

Perf. 12½x12¾
2011, Nov. 30   *Litho.*
2355   Horiz. strip of 3   3.75 3.75
a.-c. A1325 12p Any single   1.25 1.25

Christmas — A1326

2011, Dec. 7   *Perf. 12*
2356 A1326 12p multi   1.25 1.25

Souvenir Sheet

Intl. Year of Chemistry — A1327

2011, Dec. 9   *Perf. 12½x12¾*
2357 A1327 37p multi   3.75 3.75

Diplomatic Relations Between Uruguay
and the Czech Republic and Slovakia,
90th Anniv. — A1328

2011, Dec. 13   *Perf. 12*
2358 A1328 37p multi   3.75 3.75

Paintings
A1329

Designs: No. 2359, Formas, by María
Freire. No. 2360, Composición 17 de Julio -
1968, by Freire, vert.
No. 2361, vert.: a, Crepúsculo, by Vicente
Martín. b, Dama con Mandolina, by Martín.

2011, Dec. 19   *Perf. 12½x12¾*
2359 A1329 12p multi   1.25 1.25
     Perf. 12¾x12½
2360 A1329 12p multi   1.25 1.25
2361   Horiz. pair   2.50 2.50
a.-b. A1329 12p Either single   1.25 1.25
Nos. 2359-2361 (3)   5.00 5.00

Intl. Year of
People of
African
Descent
A1330

"Año Internacional
de los Afrodescendientes"

Paintings by Mary Porto Casas: 12p, La
Lancera. 37p, Mandela, horiz.

2011, Dec. 27   **Perf. 12**
2362-2363 A1330   Set of 2   5.00 5.00

State Insurance Bank, Cent. — A1331

2011, Dec. 27
2364 A1331 12p multi   1.25 1.25

Independence, 200th Anniv. — A1332

No. 2365: a, Indigenous man with headband
holding stick. b, Man of African descent with
hat and gun.

2011, Dec. 28   **Litho.**
2365 A1332 12p Horiz. pair, #a-b 2.50 2.50

Items Made by
Artisans — A1333

No. 2366: a, Cows made of wood and wool,
by Carlos Clavelli. b, Woolen garment, by Siv
Göransson. c, Leather container and lid, by
Albertina Morelli. d, Silver pendant, bu Nilda
Echenique. e, Wire ball, by Gustavo Genta.

2012, Jan. 31   **Die Cut**
    Self-Adhesive
2366   Horiz. strip of 5   .55
   a.-e.   A1333 1p Any single   .25 .25

Written and Sign
Language
Letters and Their
Corresponding
International
Signal
Flags — A1334

Letter: 5p, A. 10p, M. 12p, O. 20p, S. 50p,
G. 60p, I.

2012   **Self-Adhesive**   **Die Cut**
2367 A1334 5p multi   .55 .55
2368 A1334 10p multi   1.10 1.10
2369 A1334 12p multi   1.25 1.25
2370 A1334 20p multi   2.00 2.00
2371 A1334 50p multi   5.00 5.00
    Size: 27x19mm
2372 A1334 60p multi   6.00 6.00
   Nos. 2367-2372 (6)   15.90 15.90

Issued: 5p, 2/9; 10p, 2/28; 12p, 50p, 60p,
4/11; 20p, 5/16.

Intl.
Women's
Day
A1335

2012, Mar. 7   **Perf. 12½x12¾**
2373 A1335 12p multi   1.25 1.25

Palacio Gandós,
Montevideo
A1336

2012, Mar. 15   **Perf. 12¾x12½**
2374 A1336 37p multi   4.00 4.00

Annual Board of Governors Meeting of the
Inter-American Development Bank and Inter-
American Investment Corporation,
Montevideo.

Enrique V.
Iglesias, Ex-
President of Inter-
American
Development
Bank — A1337

2012, Mar. 20   **Litho.**
2375 A1337 37p multi   4.00 4.00

2012 Summer Olympics,
London — A1338

No. 2376: a, Soccer, ArcelorMittal Orbit. b,
Cycling, St. Paul's Cathedral. c, Yachting,
Tower Bridge. d, Hurdler, Big Ben and
Parliament.

2012, Mar. 30   **Perf. 12**
2376 A1338 15p Block of 4, #a-d 6.00 6.00

Diplomatic Relations Between Uruguay
and Ukraine, 20th Anniv. — A1339

2012, Apr. 25
2377 A1339 37p multi   3.75 3.75

Nueva
Helvecia
Colony,
150th
Anniv.
A1340

2012, Apr. 25   **Perf. 12½x12¾**
2378 A1340 12p multi   1.25 1.25

Euskal Erria Basque Fellowship
Center, Montevideo, Cent. — A1341

2012, May 25
2379 A1341 37p multi   3.75 3.75

World Blood
Donation
Day — A1342

2012, June 14   **Die Cut**
    Self-Adhesive
2380 A1342 12p multi   1.10 1.10

Intl. Year of Cooperatives — A1343

2012, July 6   **Perf. 12½x12¾**
2381 A1343 12p multi   1.10 1.10

Uruguay
Mortgage Bank,
120th
Anniv. — A1344

    Perf. 12¾x12½
2012, Aug. 10   **Litho.**
2382 A1344 12p multi   1.10 1.10

Fauna — A1345

No. 2383: a, Paroaria coronata, Pyrocepha-
lus rubinus. b, Charadrius modestus, Caiman
latirostris. c, Pontoporia blainvilleii. d,
Xylocopa augusti, Rhinella schneideri.

    Perf. 12½x12¾
2012, Aug. 31   **Litho.**
2383 A1345 12p Block of 4, #a-d 4.50 4.50

Intl. Democracy
Day — A1346

2012, Sept. 13   **Perf. 12¾x12½**
2384 A1346 37p multi   3.75 3.75

Anibal Barrios Pintos (1918-2011),
Writer, and Sculpture of Aboriginal
People — A1347

2012, Sept. 27   **Perf. 12½x12¾**
2385 A1347 12p multi   1.25 1.25

America
Issue — A1348

Legend of: No. 2386, 12p, The Ceibo
Flower. No. 2387, 12p, The Black Shepherd.

2012, Sept. 28   **Perf. 12¾x12½**
2386-2387 A1348   Set of 2   2.40 2.40

Crops
Grown for
Alternative
Energy
Sources
A1349

Designs: No. 2388, 12p, Saccharum
officinarum. No. 2389, 12p, Helianthus
annuus.

2012, Oct. 5   **Perf. 12½x12¾**
2388-2389 A1349   Set of 2   2.50 2.50

    Souvenir Sheet

25th Universal Postal Union Congress,
Doha, Qatar — A1350

2012, Oct. 6   **Perf. 12¾x12½**
2390 A1350 37p multi   3.75 3.75

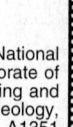

National Directorate of Mining and Geology, Cent. — A1351

2012, Oct. 22   **Litho.**
2391 A1351 12p multi   1.25 1.25

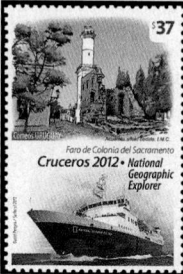

Tourist Attractions and Cruise Ships A1352

No. 2392 — Attraction and ship: a, Colonia del Sacramento Lighthouse, National Geographic Explorer. b, Yacht Club Uruguay, Puerto del Buceo, Celebrity Infinity. c, Santa Teresa Fortress, Grand Celebration. d, Argentino Hotel, Piriápolis, MSC Magnifica.

2012, Oct. 22   **Perf. 12**
2392   Horiz. strip of 4   15.00 15.00
a.-d.   A1352 37p Any single   3.75 3.75

National Road Safety Union — A1353

Designs: 5p, Stop sign. 10p, Martini glasses. 15p, Passenger with hands over seat belt. 20p, Triangular warning sign with helmeted head of person. 45p, Speed limit sign. 50p, Blue ribbon. 70p. National Road Safety Union emblem. 100p, Road Safety Decade inscription on diamond warning sign.

2012, Oct. 24   **Die Cut**
Self-Adhesive
2393 A1353 5p multi   .50 .50
2394 A1353 10p multi   1.00 1.00
2395 A1353 15p multi   1.50 1.50
2396 A1353 20p multi   2.10 2.10
2397 A1353 45p multi   4.75 4.75
a.   Vert. strip of 5, 2 #2396, 3 #2397   18.50
2398 A1353 50p multi   5.25 5.25
a.   Vert strip of 5, #2393, 2395, 2396, 2 #2398   15.00
2399 A1353 70p multi   7.25 7.25
2400 A1353 100p multi   10.00 10.00
a.   Vert. strip of 5, #2393, 2394, 2395, 2399, 2400   21.00
   Nos. 2393-2400 (8)   32.35 32.35

National Fire Fighting Directorate, 125th Anniv. — A1354

No. 2401 — Fire fighting emblem, fire fighter in protective clothing and: a, Building fire. b, Forest fire. c, Bronto Skylift F68HLA. d, Refinery fire.

2012, Oct. 26   **Perf. 12½x12¾**
2401 A1354 12p Block of 4, #a-d 5.00 5.00

Virginia Brindis de Salas (1908-58), Poet — A1355

2012, Oct. 31   **Perf. 12¾x12½**
2402 A1355 12p multi   1.25 1.25

Paintings A1356

Designs: No. 2403, 12p, Recreo, by Petrona Viera. No. 2404, 12p, Construcción, by Augusto Torres.

2012, Oct. 31   **Litho.**
2403-2404 A1356   Set of 2   2.50 2.50

National Administration of Electrical Transmission and Usage, Cent. — A1357

No. 2405: a, Rincón de Baygorria Dam, linemen working on wires. b, High tension wire tower, engineer with chart. c, Wind generators. d, Palace of Light, José Battle y Ordoñez Center, worker with hard hat.

2012, Oct. 31   **Perf. 12½x12¾**
2405 A1357 12p Horiz. strip of 4, #a-d, + 4 labels   5.00 5.00

Tango Music A1358

No. 2406: a, Double bass used in tango music. b, Francisco Canaro (1888-1964), tango orchestra leader. c, Edgardo Pedroza (1926-2000), tango orchestra leader.

2012, Nov. 23
2406   Horiz. strip of 3   11.50 11.50
a.   A1358 15p multi   1.60 1.60
b.-c.   A1358 45p Either single   4.75 4.75

Christmas A1359

2012, Nov. 23   **Perf. 12¾x12½**
2407 A1359 15p multi   1.60 1.60

Club Neptuno, Cent. — A1360

2012, Dec. 3   **Litho.**
2408 A1360 15p multi   1.60 1.60

Etchepare Colony for Psychiatric Care, Cent. A1361

2012, Dec. 4   **Perf. 12**
2409 A1361 15p multi   1.60 1.60

Independent Party, 10th Anniv. — A1362

2012, Dec. 17   **Perf. 12½x12¾**
2410 A1362 15p multi   1.60 1.60

Souvenir Sheet

National Postal Administration, 185th Anniv. — A1363

2012, Dec. 21   **Perf. 12¾x12½**
2411 A1363 15p multi   1.60 1.60

Rural Workers A1364

Designs: 1p, Farmer tending to field (agricultor). 5p, Fence builders (alambrador). 10p, Workers tending sheep (esquillador). 15p, Beekeeper and hives (apicultor). 25p, Fruit harvester (recolectora). 30p, Cattle driver (arriero). 45p, Worker processing fish (pesca). 50p, Woman milking cow (tambera). 60p, Woman moving logs (leñadora).

2013   **Litho.**   **Die Cut**
Self-Adhesive
2412 A1364 1p multi   .25 .25
2413 A1364 5p multi   .50 .50
2414 A1364 10p multi   1.10 1.10
2415 A1364 15p multi   1.50 1.50
2416 A1364 25p multi   2.75 2.75
2417 A1364 30p multi   3.25 3.25
2418 A1364 45p multi   5.00 5.00
2419 A1364 50p multi   5.25 5.25
2420 A1364 60p multi   6.00 6.00
   Nos. 2412-2420 (8)   25.10 25.10

Passage of Law No. 18,441 limiting hours of rural workers.
Issued: 1p, 10p, 2/22; 5p, 7/9; 15p, 60p, 5/17; 25p, 4/18; 30p, 50p, 3/8; 45p, 4/30.

Carnival Costume Designed by Juan Mascheroni A1365

Perf. 12¾x12½
2013, Feb. 28   **Litho.**
2421 A1365 15p multi   1.60 1.60

Souvenir Sheet

Military Aviation in Uruguay, Cent. — A1366

2013, Mar. 16   **Perf. 12**
2422 A1366 15p multi   1.60 1.60

Harald Edelstam (1913-89), Swedish Diplomat A1367

2013, Mar. 17   **Perf. 12¾x12½**
2423 A1367 45p multi   5.00 5.00

Edelstam rescued Cuban diplomats, Chilean activists and Uruguayan refugees from persecution during the 1973 Chilean coup.

Defensor Sporting Club, Cent. A1368

2013, Mar. 20   **Perf. 12½x12¾**
2424 A1368 15p multi   1.60 1.60

No. 2424 was printed in sheets of 8 + central label.

Famous Women — A1369

No. 2425: a, María "Tota" Quinteros (1918-2001) holding sign showing kidnapped daughter, Elena (1945-76). b, Jorgelina Martínez (1926-2009), labor leader. c, María Viñas Sendic (1943-2003), labor leader.

2013, Mar. 21 **Perf. 12¾x12½**
2425 Strip of 3 5.00 5.00
a.-c. A1369 15p Any single 1.60 1.60

Nibya Mariño, Pianist A1370

2013, Mar. 22 **Perf. 12½x12¾**
2426 A1370 15p multi 1.60 1.60

No. 2426 was printed in sheets of 8 + central label.

Patient Safety Day — A1371

2013, Apr. 11 **Perf. 12¾x12½**
2427 A1371 15p multi 1.60 1.60

Instructions of the Year XIII, Bicent. A1372

2013, May 3 **Perf. 12**
2428 A1372 15p multi 1.60 1.60

Souvenir Sheet

Red Cross Coach, 1897 — A1373

2013, May 30 **Litho.**
2429 A1373 15p multi 1.50 1.50

Paintings — A1374

No. 2430: a, Zíngaras, by Rafael Barradas (1890-1929). b, Bodegón (Still Life), by Augusto Torres (1913-92).

Perf. 12½x12¾
2013, June 11 **Litho.**
2430 A1374 15p Horiz. pair, #a-b 3.00 3.00

World Day of Autism Awareness A1375

2013, June 12 **Perf. 12¾x12½**
2431 A1375 15p multi 1.50 1.50

City of San Carlos II, by Daniel Arteta A1376

2013, July 8 **Perf. 12½x12¾**
2432 A1376 15p multi 1.50 1.50

San Carlos, 250th Anniv.

Amanda Rorra (1924-2005), Afro-Uruguayan Activist — A1377

2013, July 25 Litho. Perf. 12¾x12½
2433 A1377 15p multi 1.40 1.40

Intl. Year of Quinoa A1378

2013, July 26 Litho. Perf. 12½x12¾
2434 A1378 45p multi 4.25 4.25

Calabrian Association of Uruguay, 50th Anniv. — A1379

2013, Aug. 2 Litho. Perf. 12½x12¾
2435 A1379 45p multi 4.25 4.25

No. 2435 was printed in sheets of 8 + central label.

Tabernacle, Sculpture by Octavio Podestá — A1380

Perf. 12½x12¾
2013, Aug. 22 **Litho.**
2436 A1380 15p multi 1.40 1.40

Insects — A1381

No. 2437: a, Borellia bruneri. b, Diloboderus abderus. c, Sulcophanaeus menelas. d, Apis mellifera.

Perf. 12½x12¾
2013, Aug. 30 **Litho.**
2437 A1381 15p Block of 4, #a-d, 5.50 5.50
+ 2 labels

International Day of Democracy A1382

Perf. 12¾x12½
2013, Sept. 15 **Litho.**
2438 A1382 45p multi 4.25 4.25

Care Centers for Children and Families, 25th Anniv. — A1383

Perf. 12¾x12½
2013, Sept. 16 **Litho.**
2439 A1383 15p multi 1.40 1.40

Andrés Aguiar (d. 1849), Soldier for Giuseppe Garibaldi in First Italian War of Independence A1384

Perf. 12¾x12½
2013, Sept. 21 **Litho.**
2440 A1384 45p multi 4.25 4.25

Susana Dalmás (1948-2012), Politician A1385

Perf. 12¾x12½
2013, Sept. 26 **Litho.**
2441 A1385 15p multi 1.40 1.40

Tango Heritage A1386

No. 2442: a, Bandoneon. b, Musician playing violin and Romeo Gavioli (1913-57), singer. c, Microphone and Carlos Roldán (1913-73), singer.

Perf. 12½x12¾
2013, Sept. 26 **Litho.**
2442 Horiz. strip of 3 13.00 13.00
a.-c. A1386 45p Any single 4.25 4.25

Association of Chemists and Pharmacists of Uruguay, 125th Anniv. — A1387

Perf. 12¾x12½
2013, Sept. 27 **Litho.**
2443 A1387 15p multi 1.40 1.40

Montevideo, 2013 Ibero-American Cultural Capital — A1388

No. 2444: a, Eduardo Galeano, writer. b, Daniel Viglietti, musician. c, Ruben Rada, musician. d, Sara Nieto, ballerina.

2013, Oct. 2 Litho. Perf. 12¾x12½
2444 Horiz. strip of 4 5.75 5.75
a.-d. A1388 15p Any single 1.40 1.40
e. Booklet pane of 4, #2444a- 5.75 —
2444d
Complete booklet, #2444e 5.75

The Annunciation of Sarah, Painting by José Gurvich — A1389

2013, Oct. 29 Litho. Perf. 12½x12¾
2445 A1389 45p multi 4.25 4.25

Diplomatic relations between Uruguay and Israel, 65th anniv. See Israel No. 1989.

SODRE Juvenile Orchestra — A1390

No. 2446: a, Child's legs, French horn. b, Violin and bow.

2013, Nov. 4 Litho. Perf. 12¾x12½
2446 A1390 15p Horiz. pair, #a-b 3.00 3.00

Internet and Integrated Systems A1391

2013, Nov. 7 Litho. Perf. 12¾x12½
2447 A1391 45p multi   4.25 4.25

Exports — A1392

No. 2448: a, 15p, Wine grapes. b, 15p, Sides of beef. c, 45p, Wine bottle and barrels. d, 45p, Dish of beef and vegetables.

2013, Nov. 8 Litho. Perf. 12½x12¾
2448 A1392 Block of 4, #a-d 11.50 11.50

Souvenir Sheet

Brasiliana 2013 Intl. Philatelic Exhibition, Rio de Janeiro — A1393

No. 2449 — Brasiliana 2013 emblem and illustrations from song lyrics by Vinicius de Moraes (1913-80): a, 15p, Young man and woman (25x35mm). b, 45p, Woman with head covering (42x31mm).

Perf. 12, 12½x12¾ (45p)
2013, Nov. 20   Litho.
2449 A1393 Sheet of 2, #a-b 5.75 5.75

Christmas A1394

Perf. 12½x12¾
2013, Nov. 22   Litho.
2450 A1394 15p multi   1.50 1.50

Wildlife — A1395

No. 2451: a, Calidris canutus rufa. b, Chelonia mydas.

2013, Dec. 4 Litho. Perf. 12¾x12½
2451 A1395 15p Horiz. pair, #a-b 3.00 3.00
    Printed in sheets containing 4 pairs and 5 labels.

High-Speed Ferry Francisco — A1396

2013, Dec. 5   Litho.   Perf. 12
2452 A1396 45p multi   4.25 4.25

Vo Nguyên Giáp (1911-2013), Vietnamese General — A1397

Perf. 12¾x12½
2013, Dec. 10   Litho.
2453 A1397 45p multi   4.25 4.25
    Diplomatic relations between Uruguay and Viet Nam, 20th anniv.

Rampla Juniors Soccer Team, Cent. A1398

Perf. 12½x12¾
2013, Dec. 11   Litho.
2454 A1398 15p multi   1.50 1.50

Return to Uruguay of Children of Exiles, 30th Anniv. — A1399

2013, Dec. 17   Litho.   Die Cut
Self-Adhesive
2455 A1399 20p multi   1.90 1.90

Campaign Against Discrimination A1400

Perf. 12¾x12½
2013, Dec. 19   Litho.
2456 A1400 45p multi   4.25 4.25
    America issue.

New Year 2014 (Year of the Horse) — A1401

2014, Jan. 31 Litho. Perf. 12¾x12½
2457 A1401 15p multi   1.40 1.40

Carnaval Costume A1402

Perf. 12¾x12½
2014, Feb. 25   Litho.
2458 A1402 15p multi   1.40 1.40

Hugo Chávez (1954-2013), President of Venezuela — A1403

No. 2459 — Chávez: a, 15p, Waving. b, 45p, Holding map of South America.

2014, Mar. 5 Litho. Perf. 12½x12¾
2459 A1403 Horiz. pair, #a-b 5.25 5.25

Florida Infantry Batallion No. 1, 185th Anniv. A1404

2014, Mar. 6 Litho. Perf. 12½x12¾
2460 A1404 15p multi   1.40 1.40

Luisa Cuesta, Leader in Mothers and Relatives of Disappeared Uruguayans Movement — A1405

2014, Mar. 7 Litho. Perf. 12½x12¾
2461 A1405 15p multi   1.40 1.40

General José Gervasio Artigas (1764-1850) and Quotation A1406

Artigas and quotation starting with: 1p, "Sean los orientales. . ." 10p, "Que los Más infelices. . ." 30p, "La causa. . ." 50p, "Nada podemos esperar. . ." 100p, "Todas las provincias. . ."

2014   Litho.   Die Cut
Self-Adhesive
2462 A1406 1p multi   .25 .25
2463 A1406 $10 multi   .90 .90
2465 A1406 30p multi   2.60 2.60
2466 A1406 50p multi   4.50 4.50
2467 A1406 100p multi   8.75 8.75
    Nos. 2462-2467 (5)   17.00 17.00
    Issued: 1p, 6/12; 10p, 6/2; 30p, 50p, 3/7; 100p, 4/7. See No. B14.

Uruguayan Transparency Law — A1407

2014, Apr. 10 Litho. Perf. 12¾x12½
2468 A1407 15p multi   1.40 1.40

South American Athletic Institution, Cent. — A1408

2014, Apr. 22 Litho. Perf. 12¾x12½
2469 A1408 15p multi   1.40 1.40
    No. 2469 printed in sheets of 8 + central label.

Section 20 of the Communist Party of Uruguay National Historical Monument — A1409

2014, Apr. 23 Litho. Perf. 12½x12¾
2470 A1409 15p multi   1.40 1.40

University Sports League, Cent. A1410

2014, May 5 Litho. Perf. 12½x12¾
2471 A1410 15p multi   1.40 1.40
    No. 2471 was printed in sheets of 8 + central label.

Uruguay Society of Architects, Cent. — A1411

2014, May 22 Litho. Perf. 12¾x12½
2472 A1411 15p multi   1.40 1.40

Souvenir Sheet

Alcides Ghiggia, Soccer Player — A1412

No. 2473 — Uruguayan flag and: a, Ghiggia playing soccer. b, Ghiggia in 2014.

2014, May 28 Litho. Perf. 12¾x12½
2473 A1412 15p Sheet of 2, #a-b 2.60 2.60

Souvenir Sheet

Battle of Buceo, 200th Anniv. — A1413

2014, June 4 Litho. Perf. 12½x12¾
2474 A1413 45p multi 4.00 4.00

Mafalda, Comic Strip by Quino, 50th Anniv. — A1414

No. 2475 — Mafalda and: a, 15p, Globe wrapped in bandage. b, 45p, Globe with banners.

2014, June 17 Litho. Perf. 12
2475 A1414 Pair, #a-b 5.25 5.25

No. 2475 was printed in sheets containing three pairs.

Paintings — A1415

No. 2476: a, El Pozo, by Ernesto Laroche (1879-1940). b, Portrait of María de Castro de Figari, by Pedro Blanes Viale (1879-1926).

2014, July 15 Litho. Perf. 12¾x12½
2476 A1415 15p Horiz. pair, #a-b 2.60 2.60

Tranqueras, Cent. — A1416

2014, July 22 Litho. Perf. 12½x12¾
2477 A1416 15p multi 1.40 1.40

Famous People — A1417

Designs: No. 2478, 15p, Federico García Vigil, conductor. No. 2479, 15p, Cristina Morán, actress.

Perf. 12¾x12½
2014, Aug. 13 Litho.
2478-2479 A1417 Set of 2 2.60 2.60

Second Intl. Decade of the World's Indigenous Peoples — A1418

2014, Sept. 2 Litho. Perf. 12¾x12½
2480 A1418 45p multi 3.75 3.75

Miniature Sheet

A1419

No. 2481: a, 15p, La Estanzuela Experimental Station, cent. (scientist and building). b, 15p, Int'l. Day of Biodiversity (zebra and flamingo). c, 15p, World Environment Day (butterfly on flower). d, 45p, Intl. Year of Family Farming.

Perf. 12½x12¾
2014, Sept. 16 Litho.
2481 A1419 Sheet of 4, #a-d 7.50 7.50

People Doing Community Service — A1420

Perf. 12½x12¾
2014, Sept. 22 Litho.
2482 A1420 15p multi 1.25 1.25

Pinnipeds — A1421

No. 2483 — Emblem of Chile Philatelic Society and: a, Arctocephalus australis. b, Otaria flavescens.

Perf. 12½x12¾
2014, Sept. 29 Litho.
2483 A1421 15p Pair, #a-b 2.50 2.50

Diplomatic Relations Between Uruguay and South Korea, 50th Anniv. — A1422

No. 2484 — Dancers and drummers from: a, 15p, Uruguay. b, 45p, South Korea.

2014, Oct. 7 Litho. Perf. 12½x12¾
2484 A1422 Horiz. pair, #a-b 5.00 5.00

See South Korea No.

Visit of Charles de Gaulle to Uruguay, 50th Anniv. — A1423

Uruguayan and French flags, de Gaulle and: 15p, Buildings. 45p, Ship.

2014, Oct. 9 Litho. Perf. 12¾x12½
2485-2486 A1423 Set of 2 5.00 5.00

Nos. 2485-2486 were printed in sheets of 8 containing 4 of each stamp.

Souvenir Sheet

Diplomatic Relations Between Uruguay and Nicaragua — A1424

2014, Oct. 10 Litho. Perf. 12¾x12½
2487 A1424 45p multi 3.75 3.75

Souvenir Sheet

Anniversaries of Parliamentary Organizations — A1425

No. 2488: a, 15p, Interparliamentary Union, 125th anniv. b, 45p, Latin American Parliament, 50th anniv.

2014, Oct. 15 Litho. Perf. 12¾x12½
2488 A1425 Sheet of 2, #a-b 5.00 5.00

Fauna — A1427

Designs: No. 2491, 15p, Melanophryniscus sanmartini. No. 2492, 15p, Desmodus rotundus.

2014, Nov. 5 Litho. Perf. 12¾x12½
2491-2492 A1427 Set of 2 2.50 2.50

Nos. 2491-2492 were printed in sheets of 8 containing 4 of each stamp.

Christmas A1428

Perf. 12¾x12½
2014, Nov. 12 Litho.
2493 A1428 15p multi 1.25 1.25

Silvio B. Previale Intl. Accordion Festival, Salto — A1429

Perf. 12¾x12½
2014, Nov. 14 Litho.
2494 A1429 15p multi 1.25 1.25

Battle of Paysandú, 150th Anniv. — A1434

No. 2499: a, 15p, Paysandú Basilica. b, 50p, Corvette Parnahyba.

2015, Feb. 6 Litho. Perf. 12¾x12½
2499 A1434 Horiz. pair, #a-b 5.25 5.25

URUJAM 2015 Intl. Scout Jamboree, Las Cañas A1435

2015, Feb. 6 Litho. Perf. 12½x12¾
2500 A1435 50p multi 4.00 4.00

Carnaval
A1437

Perf. 12½x12¾
2015, Feb. 11 Litho.
2502 A1437 15p multi 1.25 1.25

New Year 2015
(Year of the
Goat) — A1438

Perf. 12¾x12½
2015, Feb. 19 Litho.
2503 A1438 15p multi 1.25 1.25

Prof.
Belela
Herrera,
Vice
Chancellor
of
Uruguay
A1439

2015, Mar. 6 Litho. **Perf. 12½x12¾**
2504 A1439 15p multi 1.25 1.25

SEMI-POSTAL STAMPS

Indigent Old
Man — SP1

Unwmk.
1930, Nov. 13 **Engr.** **Perf. 12**
B1 SP1 1c + 1c dark violet .30 .30
B2 SP1 2c + 2c deep green .30 .30
B3 SP1 5c + 5c red .45 .45
B4 SP1 8c + 8c gray violet .45 .45
  Nos. B1-B4 (4) 1.50 1.50

The surtax on these stamps was for a fund
to assist the aged.
For surcharge see No. 419.

Catalogue values for unused
stamps in this section, from this
point to the end of the section, are
for Never Hinged items.

Dam, Child
and Rising
Sun — SP2

Wmk. 327
1959, Sept. 29 Litho. **Perf. 11½**
B5 SP2 5c + 10c green & org .25 .25
B6 SP2 10c + 10c dk bl & org .25 .25
B7 SP2 1p + 10c purple & org .50 .50
  Nos. B5-B7,CB1-CB2 (3) 1.00 1.00

National recovery. For surcharges see Nos.
727, Q100.

Souvenir Sheet

Taipei '96, Intl. Philatelic
Exhibition — SP3

Unwmk.
1996, Oct. 21 Litho. **Perf. 12**
B8 SP3 7p +3p multi 8.00 8.00

Gen. Artigas Central Railway Station,
Montevideo, Cent. — SP4

a, Baldwin, 1889. b, Hudswell Clarke, 1895.
c, Luis Andreoni, engineer & architect. d, Hawthorn Leslie, 1914. e, General Electric, 1954.

Perf. 12½
1997, July 15 Litho. **Unwmk.**
B9 SP4 4p +1p, Strip of 5, 12.00 12.00
  #a.-e.

Diana, Princess
of Wales (1961-
97) — SP5

Designs: No. B10, In protective clothing. No.
B11, In blue blouse. No. B12, In white.

1998, Jan. 15 Litho. **Perf. 12½**
B10 SP5 2p +1p multi 2.50 2.50
B11 SP5 2p +1p multi 2.50 2.50

Souvenir Sheet
Perf. 12
B12 SP5 12p +3p multi 15.00 15.00

No. B12 contains one 35x50mm stamp.

Occupations Type of 2008
Serpentine Die Cut 11¼
2007, Nov. 18 Litho.
Self-Adhesive
B13 A1216 5p +2p Baker .90 .90

General José
Gervasio Artigas
(1764-1850) and
Quotation
SP6

2014, Apr. 28 Litho. **Die Cut**
Self-Adhesive
B14 SP6 15p+2p multi 1.50 1.50

AIR POST STAMPS

No. 91 Overprinted in
Dark Blue, Red or
Green

1921-22 **Unwmk.** **Perf. 14**
C1 A38 25c bister brn (Bl) 18.00 15.00
a. Black overprint 800.00 800.00
C2 A38 25c bister brn (R) 7.00 7.00
a. Inverted overprint 100.00 100.00
C3 A38 25c bister brn (G) 7.00 7.00
  ('22) 7.00 7.00
  Nos. C1-C3 (3) 32.00 29.00

This overprint, on No. C3, also exists in light
yellow green. Value, $85 unused and used.
No. C1a was not issued. Some authorities
consider it an overprint color trial.

AP2

Wmk. 188
1924, Jan. 2 Litho. **Perf. 11½**
C4 AP2 6c dark blue 2.50 2.00
C5 AP2 10c scarlet 3.50 3.00
C6 AP2 20c deep green 5.00 5.00
  Nos. C4-C6 (3) 11.00 10.00

Heron — AP3

1925, Aug. 24 **Perf. 12½**
Inscribed "MONTEVIDEO"
C7 AP3 14c blue & blk 35.00 25.00
Inscribed "FLORIDA"
C8 AP3 14c blue & blk 35.00 17.50

These stamps were used only on Aug. 25,
1925, the cent. of the Assembly of Florida, on
letters intended to be carried by airplane
between Montevideo and Florida, a town 60
miles north. The stamps were not delivered to
the public but were affixed to the letters and
canceled by post office clerks. Later
uncanceled stamps came on the market.
One authority believes Nos. C7-C8 served
as registration stamps on these two attempted
special flights.

Gaucho Cavalryman at Rincón — AP4

1925, Sept. 24 **Perf. 11**
C9 AP4 45c blue green 17.50

Centenary of Battle of Rincon. Used only on
Sept. 24. No. C9 was affixed and canceled by
post office clerks.

Albatross — AP5

1926, Mar. 3 **Wmk. 188** **Imperf.**
C10 AP5 6c dark blue 2.00 2.00
C11 AP5 10c vermilion 2.50 2.50
C12 AP5 20c blue green 3.00 3.00
C13 AP5 25c violet 3.50 3.50
  Nos. C10-C13 (4) 11.00 11.00

Excellent counterfeits exist.

1928, June 25 **Perf. 11**
C14 AP5 10c green 3.00 2.00
C15 AP5 20c orange 5.00 3.00
C16 AP5 30c indigo 5.00 3.00
C17 AP5 38c green 8.50 6.00
C18 AP5 40c yellow 8.50 6.00
C19 AP5 50c violet 10.00 7.50
C20 AP5 76c orange 20.00 17.50
C21 AP5 1p red 20.00 15.00
C22 AP5 1.14p indigo 45.00 35.00
C23 AP5 1.52p yellow 75.00 60.00
C24 AP5 1.90p violet 95.00 75.00
C25 AP5 3.80p red 225.00 170.00
  Nos. C14-C25 (12) 520.00 400.00

Counterfeits of No. C25 exist.

1929, Aug. 23 **Unwmk.**
C26 AP5 4c olive brown 3.00 3.00

The design was redrawn for Nos. C14-C26.
The numerals are narrower, "CENTS" is 1mm
high instead of 2½mm and imprint letters
touch the bottom frame line.

Pegasus
AP6

1929-43 **Engr.** **Perf. 12½**
Size: 34x23mm
C27 AP6 1c red lilac ('30) .40 .40
C28 AP6 1c dk blue ('32) .40 .40
C29 AP6 2c yellow ('30) .40 .40
C30 AP6 2c olive grn ('32) .40 .40
C31 AP6 4c Prus blue ('30) .70 .70
C32 AP6 4c car rose ('32) .70 .70
C33 AP6 6c dull vio ('30) .70 .70
C34 AP6 6c red brown ('32) .70 .70
C35 AP6 8c red orange 3.00 2.50
C36 AP6 8c gray ('30) 4.00 3.00
C36A AP6 8c brt green ('43) 2.50 2.00
C37 AP6 16c indigo 2.00 1.50
C38 AP6 16c rose ('30) 3.25 3.00
C39 AP6 24c claret 3.00 2.50
C40 AP6 24c brt violet ('30) 4.25 3.50
C41 AP6 30c bister 3.00 2.75
C42 AP6 30c dk green ('30) 2.00 1.50
C43 AP6 40c dk brown 5.50 5.00
C44 AP6 40c yel org ('30) 6.00 5.00
C45 AP6 60c blue green 5.00 3.25
C46 AP6 60c emerald ('30) 8.50 7.00
C47 AP6 60c dp orange ('31) 3.00 2.00
C48 AP6 80c dk ultra 8.00 7.00
C49 AP6 80c green ('30) 15.00 12.00
C50 AP6 90c light blue 8.00 6.00
C51 AP6 90c dk olive grn ('30) 15.00 12.00
C52 AP6 1p car rose ('30) 10.00 7.50
C53 AP6 1.20p olive grn 22.00 20.00
C54 AP6 1.20p dp car ('30) 30.00 26.00
C55 AP6 1.50p red brown 25.00 20.00
C56 AP6 1.50p blk brn ('30) 20.00 15.00
C57 AP6 3p deep red 40.00 35.00
C58 AP6 3p ultra ('30) 30.00 25.00
C59 AP6 4.50p black 75.00 55.00
C60 AP6 4.50p violet ('30) 45.00 35.00
C60A AP6 10p dp ultra ('43) 17.00 12.00
  Nos. C27-C60A (36) 419.40 336.40

See Nos. C63-C82. For surcharges see
Nos. C106-C112, C114.

Nos. 450, 452 Overprinted in Red

1934, Jan. 1 *Perf. 11½*

C61	A130	17c ver, gray & vio	20.00	15.00
a.		Sheet of 6	140.00	
b.		Gray omitted	150.00	
c.		Double ovrerprint	150.00	
C62	A130	36c red, blk & yel	20.00	15.00
a.		Sheet of 6	140.00	

7th Pan-American Conference, Montevideo.

Pegasus Type of 1929

1935 **Engr.** *Perf. 12½*

Size: 31½x21mm

C63	AP6	15c dull yellow	2.50	2.00
C64	AP6	22c brick red	1.50	1.40
C65	AP6	30c brown violet	2.50	2.00
C66	AP6	37c gray lilac	1.40	1.00
C67	AP6	40c rose lake	2.00	1.40
C68	AP6	47c rose	4.00	3.50
C69	AP6	50c Prus blue	1.40	.80
C70	AP6	52c dp ultra	4.00	3.50
C71	AP6	57c grnsh blue	2.00	1.75
C72	AP6	62c olive green	1.75	.80
C73	AP6	87c gray green	5.00	4.00
C74	AP6	1p olive	3.50	2.25
C75	AP6	1.12p brown red	3.50	2.25
C76	AP6	1.20p bister brn	15.00	12.00
C77	AP6	1.27p red brown	15.00	13.00
C78	AP6	1.62p rose	10.00	9.00
C79	AP6	2p brown rose	17.00	14.00
C80	AP6	2.12p dk slate grn	17.00	14.00
C81	AP6	3p dull blue	15.00	13.00
C82	AP6	5p orange	60.00	60.00
		Nos. C63-C82 (20)	184.05	161.65

Counterfeits exist.

For surcharges, see Nos. C106-C112.

Power Dam on Rio Negro — AP7

Imprint: "Imp. Nacional" at center

1937-41 **Litho.**

C83	AP7	20c lt green ('38)	5.50	4.00
C84	AP7	35c red brown	8.00	6.50
C85	AP7	62c blue grn ('38)	.80	.30
C86	AP7	68c yel org ('38)	2.00	1.50
C86A	AP7	68c pale vio brn ('41)	1.75	.70
C87	AP7	75c violet	7.50	5.00
C88	AP7	1p dp pink ('38)	2.50	1.75
C89	AP7	1.38p rose ('38)	25.00	20.00
C90	AP7	3p dk blue ('40)	17.00	12.00
		Nos. C83-C90 (9)	70.05	51.75

Imprint at left

C91	AP7	8c pale green ('39)	.60	.50
C92	AP7	20c lt green ('38)	2.00	1.50

For surcharge and overprint see Nos. 545, C120.

Plane over Sculptured Oxcart — AP8

1939-44 *Perf. 12½*

C93	AP8	20c slate	.50	.40
C94	AP8	20c lt violet ('43)	.80	.80
C95	AP8	20c blue ('44)	.60	.40
C96	AP8	35c red	1.00	.80
C97	AP8	50c brown org	1.00	.30
C98	AP8	75c deep pink	1.10	.25
C99	AP8	1p dp blue ('40)	3.25	.60
C100	AP8	1.38p brt vio	5.50	2.25
C101	AP8	1.38p yel org ('44)	5.00	4.00
C102	AP8	2p blue	8.00	1.40
a.		Perf. 11	7.00	1.10
C103	AP8	5p rose lilac	10.00	2.25
C104	AP8	5p blue grn ('44)	15.00	7.00
C105	AP8	10p rose ('40)	100.00	65.00
		Nos. C93-C105 (13)	151.75	85.45

Counterfeits exist. These differ in design detail and are perfed other than 12½.

For surcharges see Nos. C116-C119.

Nos. C68, C71, C75, C73, C77-C78, C80 Surcharged in Red or Black

1944, Nov. 22

C106	AP6	40c on 47c	1.00	1.00
C107	AP6	40c on 57c (R)	1.00	1.00
C108	AP6	74c on 1.12p	1.00	1.00
C109	AP6	79c on 87c	2.00	2.00
C110	AP6	79c on 1.27p	3.00	3.00
C111	AP6	1.20p on 1.62p	2.00	2.00
C112	AP6	1.43p on 2.12p (R)	2.00	2.00
		Nos. C106-C112 (7)	12.00	12.00

Catalogue values for unused stamps in this section, from this point to the end of the section, are for Never Hinged items.

Legislature Building AP9

Unwmk.

1945, May 11 **Engr.** *Perf. 11*

C113	AP9	2p ultra	5.00	2.00

Type of 1929, Srchd. in Violet

1945, Aug. 14 *Perf. 12½*

C114	AP6	44c on 75c brown	2.00	.55
a.		Double overprint	45.00	

Allied Nations' victory in Europe.

"La Eolo" AP10

1945, Oct. 31 *Perf. 11*

C115	AP10	8c green	4.00	1.00

Nos. C97 and C101 Srchd. in Violet, Black or Blue

1945-46 *Perf. 12½*

C116	AP8	14c on 50c (V) ('46)	1.50	.50
a.		Inverted surcharge	37.50	
C117	AP8	23c on 1.38p	1.50	.50
a.		Inverted surcharge	75.00	
C118	AP8	23c on 50c	1.50	.50
a.		Inverted surcharge	75.00	
C119	AP8	1p on 1.38p (Bl)	1.50	.50
a.		Inverted surcharge	75.00	
		Nos. C116-C119 (4)	6.00	2.00

Victory of the Allied Nations in WWII.

No. C85 Overprinted in Black

1946, Jan. 9

C120	AP7	62c blue green	2.00	1.00

Issued to commemorate the inauguration of the Black River Power Dam.

AP11

1946-49 **Black Overprint** **Litho.**

C121	AP11	8c car rose	.40	.25
a.		Inverted overprint		
C122	AP11	50c brown	.80	.25
a.		Double overprint	25.00	
C123	AP11	1p lt bl	1.60	.40
C124	AP11	2p ol ('49)	4.00	2.00
C125	AP11	3p lil rose	6.00	3.00
C126	AP11	5p rose car	12.00	6.00
		Nos. C121-C126 (6)	24.80	11.90

Four-Motored Plane — AP12

National Airport AP13

1947-49 *Perf. 11½, 12½*

C129	AP12	3c org brn ('49)	.25	.25
C130	AP12	8c car rose ('49)	.40	.25
C131	AP12	14c ultra	.70	.30
C132	AP12	23c emerald	.55	.25
C133	AP13	1p car & brn ('49)	1.60	.40
C134	AP13	3p ultra & brn ('49)	4.00	1.60
C135	AP13	5p grn & brn ('49)	9.50	4.00
C136	AP13	10p lil rose & brn	15.00	6.00
		Nos. C129-C136 (8)	32.00	13.05

Counterfeits exist, perf 11¼. Design size of genuine stamps is 34½x24mm, while forgeries are 33½x23½mm.

See Nos. C145-C164. For surcharges see Nos. C206, Q94.

AP14

Black Overprint

1948, June 9 *Perf. 12½*

C137	AP14	12c blue	.25	.25
C138	AP14	24c Prus grn	.50	.25
C139	AP14	36c slate blue	.55	.35
		Nos. C137-C139 (3)	1.30	.85

School of Architecture, University of Uruguay AP15

Designs: 27c, Medical School. 31c, Engineering School. 36c, University.

1949, Dec. 7

C141	AP15	15c carmine	.25	.25
C142	AP15	27c chocolate	.25	.25
C143	AP15	31c dp ultra	.50	.25
C144	AP15	36c dull green	.70	.35
		Nos. C141-C144 (4)	1.70	1.10

Founding of the University of Uruguay, cent.

Plane Type of 1947-49

1952-59 **Unwmk.** *Perf. 11, 12½*

C145	AP12	10c blk ('54)	.25	.25
C146	AP12	10c lt red ('58)	.25	.25
a.		Imperf., pair	30.00	
C147	AP12	15c org brn	.40	.25
a.		Vert. pair, imperf btwn.	42.50	
C148	AP12	20c lil rose ('54)	.50	.25
C149	AP12	21c purple	.55	.25
C150	AP12	27c yel grn ('57)	.55	.25
C151	AP12	31c chocolate	.70	.25
C152	AP12	36c ultra	.55	.25
C153	AP12	36c blk ('58)	.55	.25
C154	AP12	50c lt bl ('57)	.95	.50
C155	AP12	50c bl blk ('58)	.70	.25
C156	AP12	62c dl sl bl ('53)	1.25	.50
C157	AP12	65c rose ('53)	1.25	.50
C158	AP12	84c org ('59)	1.60	.70
C159	AP12	1.08p vio brn	2.40	.80
C160	AP12	2p Prus bl	3.50	1.40
C161	AP12	3p red org	5.00	1.75
C162	AP12	5p dk gray grn	9.50	4.00
C163	AP12	5p gray ('57)	5.00	2.50
C164	AP12	10p dp grn ('55)	24.00	12.50
		Nos. C145-C164 (20)	59.45	27.65

Planes and Show Emblem AP16

Unwmk.

1956, Jan. 5 **Litho.** *Perf. 11*

C166	AP16	20c ultra	.60	.40
C167	AP16	31c olive grn	.70	.30
C168	AP16	36c car rose	1.20	.40
		Nos. C166-C168 (3)	2.40	1.10

First Exposition of National Products.

Type of Regular Issue and

José Batlle y Ordonez AP17

Designs: 10c, Full-face portrait without hand. 36c, Portrait facing right.

Perf. 13½

1956, Dec. 15 **Wmk. 90** **Photo.**

C169	A178	10c magenta	.50	.25
C170	A178	20c grnsh blk	.50	.25
C171	AP17	31c brown	.60	.40
C172	A178	36c bl grn	1.00	.50
		Nos. C169-C172 (4)	2.60	1.30

Stamp of 1856 and Stagecoach — AP18

1956, Dec. 15 **Litho.**

C173	AP18	20c grn, bl & pale yel	.70	.40
C174	AP18	31c brn, bl & lt bl	.80	.40
C175	AP18	36c dp claret & bl	1.40	.40
		Nos. C173-C175 (3)	2.90	1.20

1st postage stamps of Uruguay, cent.

Organization of American States, 10th Anniv. — AP19

Perf. 11, 11½ (No. C177)

1958, June 19 **Unwmk.**

C176	AP19	23c blue & blk	.50	.25
C177	AP19	34c green & blk	.70	.25
C178	AP19	44c cerise & blk	.80	.40
		Nos. C176-C178 (3)	2.00	.90

Universal Declaration of Human Rights, 10th Anniv. — AP20

1958, Dec. 10 — Perf. 11
C179 AP20 23c blk & blue .40 .25
C180 AP20 34c blk & yel grn .60 .25
C181 AP20 44c blk & org red 1.00 .45
Nos. C179-C181 (3) 2.00 .95

"Flight" from Monument to Fallen Aviators — AP21

1959 — Litho. — Perf. 11
Size: 22x37½mm
C182 AP21 3c bis brn & blk .40 .25
C183 AP21 8c brt lil & blk .40 .25
C184 AP21 38c black .40 .25
C185 AP21 50c citron & blk .40 .25
C186 AP21 60c vio & blk .50 .25
C187 AP21 90c ol grn & blk .55 .25
C188 AP21 1p blue & blk .65 .25
C189 AP21 2p ocher & blk 2.00 .55
C190 AP21 3p grn & blk 2.75 .95
C191 AP21 5p vio brn & blk 4.00 1.50
C192 AP21 10p dp rose car & blk 12.00 4.25
Nos. C182-C192 (11) 24.05 9.00

See Nos. C211-C222. For surcharge see No. Q97.

Alberto Santos-Dumont — AP22

1959, Feb. 13 — Wmk. 327 — Perf. 11½
C193 AP22 31c multi .60 .25
C194 AP22 36c multi .60 .25

Airplane flight of Alberto Santos-Dumont, Brazilian aeronaut, in 1906 in France.

Girl and Waves AP23

Designs: 38c, 60c, 1.05p, Compass and map of Punta del Este.

1959, Mar. 6 — Perf. 11½
C195 AP23 10c ocher & lt bl .30 .25
C196 AP23 38c grn & bis .30 .25
C197 AP23 60c lilac & bister .45 .25
C198 AP23 90c red org & grn .60 .25
C199 AP23 1.05p blue & bister .90 .55
Nos. C195-C199 (5) 2.55 1.55

50th anniv. of Punta del Este, seaside resort.

Torch, YMCA Emblem and Chrismon AP24

1959, Dec. 22 — Wmk. 327 — Litho. — Perf. 11½
C200 AP24 38c emer, blk & gray .50 .25
C201 AP24 50c bl, blk & gray .50 .25
C202 AP24 60c red, blk & gray .70 .50
Nos. C200-C202 (3) 1.70 1.00

50th anniv. of the YMCA in Uruguay.

José Artigas and George Washington AP25

1960, Mar. 2 — Perf. 11½x12
C203 AP25 38c red & blk .30 .25
C204 AP25 50c brt bl & blk .40 .25
C205 AP25 60c dp grn & blk .65 .25
Nos. C203-C205 (3) 1.35 .75

Pres. Eisenhower's visit to Uruguay, Feb. 1960.

No. C204 exists imperforate, but was not regularly issued in this form.

No. C150 Surcharged

1960, Apr. 8 — Unwmk. — Perf. 11
C206 AP12 20c on 27c yel grn .50 .25
a. Perf. 12½ .50 .25

Refugees and WRY Emblem — AP26

Size: 24x35mm

1960, June 6 — Wmk. 332
C207 AP26 60c brt lil rose & blk .50 .25

World Refugee Year, 7/1/59-6/30/60.

Type of Regular Issue, 1960
Wmk. 332

1960, Nov. 4 — Litho. — Perf. 12
C208 A186 38c bl & ol grn .25 .25
C209 A186 50c bl & ver .25 .25
C210 A186 60c bl & pur .50 .25
Nos. C208-C210 (3) 1.10 .60

Type of 1959 Redrawn with Silhouette of Airplane Added

1960-61 — Litho. — Perf. 12
C211 AP21 3c blk & pale vio .30 .25
C212 AP21 20c blk & crimson .30 .25
C213 AP21 38c blk & pale bl .30 .25
C214 AP21 50c blk & buff .30 .25
C215 AP21 60c blk & dp grn .40 .25
C216 AP21 90c blk & rose .45 .25
C217 AP21 1p blk & gray .60 .25
C218 AP21 2p blk & yel grn .85 .25
C219 AP21 3p blk & red lil 1.10 .25
C220 AP21 5p blk & org ver 1.60 .50
C221 AP21 10p blk & yel 3.50 1.60
C222 AP21 20p blk & dk bl ('61) 7.50 3.25
Nos. C211-C222 (12) 17.20 7.60

Pres. Gronchi and Flag Colors AP27

1961, Apr. 17 — Wmk. 332 — Perf. 12
C223 AP27 90c multi .45 .25
C224 AP27 1.20p multi .55 .25
C225 AP27 1.40p multi .60 .40
Nos. C223-C225 (3) 1.60 .90

Visit of President Giovanni Gronchi of Italy to Uruguay, April, 1961.

Carrasco National Airport AP28

1961, May 16 — Wmk. 332 — Perf. 12
Building in Gray
C226 AP28 1p lt vio .30 .25
C227 AP28 2p ol gray .70 .25
C228 AP28 3p orange 1.25 .40
C229 AP28 4p purple 1.50 .50
C230 AP28 5p aqua 2.00 .70
C231 AP28 10p lt ultra 4.00 1.25
C232 AP28 20p maroon 6.00 2.50
Nos. C226-C232 (7) 15.75 5.85

Type of Regular "CIES" Issue, 1961

1961, Aug. 3 — Wmk. 332
C233 A189 20c blk & org .40 .25
C234 A189 45c blk & grn .40 .25
C235 A189 50c blk & gray .40 .25
C236 A189 90c blk & plum .40 .25
C237 A189 1p blk & dp rose .50 .25
C238 A189 1.40p blk & lt vio .60 .25
C239 A189 2p blk & bister .70 .25
C240 A189 3p blk & lt bl 1.10 .30
C241 A189 4p blk & yellow 1.50 .55
C242 A189 5p blk & blue 2.00 .85
C243 A189 10p blk & yel grn 3.50 1.50
C244 A189 20p blk & dp pink 7.50 2.75
Nos. C233-C244 (12) 19.00 7.70

Swiss Flag, Plow, Wheat Sheaf AP29

1962, Aug. 1 — Wmk. 332 — Perf. 12
C245 AP29 90c car, org & blk .30 .25
C246 AP29 1.40p car, bl & blk .50 .35

Cent. of the Swiss Settlement in Uruguay.

Red-crested Cardinal — AP30

Birds: 45c, White-capped tanager, horiz. 90c, Vermilion flycatcher. 1.20p, Great kiskadee, horiz. 1.40p, Fork-tailed flycatcher.

1962, Dec. 5 — Litho. — Perf. 12
C247 AP30 20c gray, blk & red .30 .25
C248 AP30 45c multi .60 .25
C249 AP30 90c crim rose, blk & lt brn 1.25 .25
C250 AP30 1.20p lt bl, blk & yel 1.60 .25
C251 AP30 1.40p blue & sepia 2.40 .30
Nos. C247-C251 (5) 6.15 1.30

No frame on #C248, thin frame on #C251. See #C258-C263. For surcharge see #C320.

Type of Regular UPAE Issue, 1963

1963, May 31 — Wmk. 332 — Perf. 12
C252 A195 90c bluish grn & blk .25 .25
C253 A195 90c magenta & blk .40 .25

Freedom from Hunger Type of Regular Issue

1963, July 9 — Wmk. 332 — Perf. 12
C254 A196 90c red & yel .25 .25
C255 A196 1.40p violet & yel .50 .50

"Alferez Campora" AP31

1963, Aug. 16 — Litho.
C256 AP31 90c dk grn & org .30 .25
C257 AP31 1.40p ultra & yel .70 .45

Voyage around the world by the Uruguayan sailing vessel "Alferez Campora," 1960-63.

Bird Type of 1962
Birds: 1p, Glossy cowbird (tordo). 2p, Yellow cardinal. 3p, Hooded siskin. 5p, Sayaca tanager. 10p, Blue and yellow tanager. 20p, Scarlet-headed marsh-bird. All horizontal.

1963, Nov. 15 — Wmk. 332 — Perf. 12
C258 AP30 1p vio bl, blk & brn org .80 .25
C259 AP30 2p lt brn, blk & yel 1.60 .30
C260 AP30 3p yel, brn & blk 2.40 .50
C261 AP30 5p emer, bl grn & blk 4.00 .70
C262 AP30 10p multi 8.00 1.25
C263 AP30 20p gray, org & blk 20.00 7.75
Nos. C258-C263 (6) 36.80 10.75

Frame on Nos. C260-C263.

Pres. Charles de Gaulle AP32

2.40p, Flags of France and Uruguay.

1964, Oct. 9 — Litho. — Perf. 12
C264 AP32 1.50p multi .50 .25
C265 AP32 2.40p multi 1.25 .35

Charles de Gaulle, Pres. of France, Oct. 1964.

Submerged Statue of Ramses II — AP33

Design: 2p, Head of Ramses II.

1964, Oct. 30 — Litho. — Wmk. 332
C266 AP33 1.30p multi .30 .25
C267 AP33 2p bis, red brn & brt bl 1.25 .50
a. Souv. sheet of 3, #713, C266-C267, imperf. 2.50 2.50

UNESCO world campaign to save historic monuments in Nubia.

National Flag AP34

1965, Feb. 18 — Wmk. 332 — Perf. 12
C268 AP34 50p gray, dk bl & yel 8.50 4.00

Kennedy Type of Regular Issue
1965, Mar. 5 — Wmk. 327 — Perf. 11½
C269 A202 1.50p gold, lil & blk .30 .30
C270 A202 2.40p gold, brt bl & blk .70 .70

Issue of
1864, No.
23 — AP35

6c, 8c, 10c denominations of 1864 issue.

Wmk. 332

1965, Mar. 19   Litho.   Perf. 12
C271   Sheet of 10   4.50 4.50
"URUGUAY" at bottom
a. AP35 1p blue & black   .35   .35
b. AP35 1p brick red & black   .35   .35
c. AP35 1p green & black   .35   .35
d. AP35 1p ocher & black   .35   .35
e. AP35 1p carmine & black   .35   .35
"URUGUAY" at top
f. AP35 1p blue & black   .35   .35
g. AP35 1p brick red & black   .35   .35
h. AP35 1p green & black   .35   .35
i. AP35 1p ocher & black   .35   .35
j. AP35 1p carmine & black   .35   .35

1st Rio de la Plata Stamp Show, sponsored
jointly by the Argentine and Uruguayan philatelic associations, Montevideo, Mar. 19-28.
No. C271 contains two horizontal rows of
stamps and two rows of labels; Nos. C271a-
C271e are in first row, Nos. C271f-C271j in
second row. Adjacent labels in top and bottom
rows.
For overprint see No. C298.

National
Arms — AP36

1965, Apr. 30   Wmk. 332   Perf. 12
C272 AP36 20p multi   2.50 1.10

Type of Regular Issue and

Artigas
Monument
AP37

Designs: 1.50p, Artigas and wagontrain.
2.40p, Artigas quotation.

Perf. 11½x12, 12x11½
1965, May 17   Litho.   Wmk. 327
C273 AP37   1p multi   .25   .25
C274 A205 1.50p multi   .50   .25
C275 A205 2.40p multi   .90   .50
    Nos. C273-C275 (3)   1.60   .95

José Artigas (1764-1850), leader of the
independence revolt against Spain.

**Olympic Games Type of Regular
Issue**

Designs: 1p, Boxing. 1.50p, Running. 2p,
Fencing. 2.40p, Sculling. 3p, Pistol shooting.
20p, Olympic rings.

1965, Aug. 3   Litho.   Perf. 12x11½
C276 A206   1p red, gray & blk   .25   .25
C277 A206 1.50p emer, bl & blk   .25   .25
C278 A206   2p dk car, bl & blk .50   .25
C279 A206 2.40p lt ultra, org &
              blk   .70   .35
C280 A206   3p lil, yel & blk   1.00   .50
C281 A206   20p dk vio bl, pink
              & lt bl   1.60   .85
    Nos. C276-C281 (6)   4.20 2.35

Souvenir Sheet

Designs: 5p, Stamp of 1924, No. 284. 10p,
Stamp of 1928, No. 389.

C282   Sheet of 2   3.00 3.00
a. 5p buff, blue & black   .95   .95
b. 10p blue, black & rose red   1.40 1.40

18th Olympic Games, Tokyo, 10/10-25/64.

ITU Emblem
and Satellite
AP38

1966, Jan. 25   Wmk. 332   Perf. 12
C283 AP38 1p bl, bluish blk & ver .50   .25
Cent. of the ITU (in 1965).

Winston
Churchill — AP39

1966, Apr. 29   Wmk. 332   Perf. 12
C284 AP39 2p car, brn & gold   .50   .25

**Rio de Janeiro Type of Regular
Issue**

1966, June 9   Wmk. 332   Perf. 12
C285 A208 80c dp org & brn   .40   .25

International
Cooperation
Year
Emblem
AP40

1966, June 9   Litho.
C286 AP40 1p bluish grn & blk   .40   .25
UN International Cooperation Year.

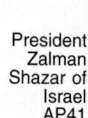

President
Zalman
Shazar of
Israel
AP41

1966, June 21   Wmk. 327
C287 AP41 7p multi   1.00   .30
Visit of Pres. Zalman Shazar of Israel.

Crested
Screamer — AP42

1966, July 7   Wmk. 327   Perf. 12
C288 AP42 100p bl, blk, red &
            gray   10.50 2.25

Jules Rimet
Cup, Soccer
Ball and
Globe
AP43

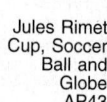

1966, July 11   Litho.
C289 AP43 10p dk pur, org & lil 1.00   .30
World Cup Soccer Championship, Wem-
bley, England, July 11-30.

Bulls
AP44

1966   Wmk. 327, 332 (10p)
C290 AP44   4p Hereford   .25   .25
C291 AP44   6p Holstein   .25   .25
C292 AP44 10p Shorthorn   .70   .25
C293 AP44 15p Aberdeen
              Angus   1.25   .35
C294 AP44 20p Norman   2.25   .55
C295 AP44 30p Jersey   3.00   .85
C296 AP44 50p Charolais   5.00 1.50
    Nos. C290-C296 (7)   12.70 4.00

Issued to publicize Uruguayan cattle.
Issued: 4p, 50p, 8/13; 6p, 30p, 8/29; 10p, 15p,
20p, 9/26.

Boiso
Lanza,
Early
Plane and
Space
Capsule
AP45

1966, Oct. 14   Litho.   Perf. 12
C297 AP45 25p ultra, blk & lt bl 1.10   .50

Issued to honor Capt. Juan Manuel Boiso
Lanza, pioneer of military aviation.

No. C271 Overprinted in Black

1966, Nov. 4   Wmk. 332
C298   Sheet of 10   4.50 4.50
"URUGUAY" at bottom
a.-e. AP35 1p each   .35   .35
"URUGUAY" at top
f.-j. AP35 1p each   .35   .35

2nd Rio de la Plata Stamp Show, Buenos
Aires, Apr. 1966, sponsored by the Argentine
and Uruguayan philatelic associations, and for
the cent. of Uruguay's 1st surcharged issue.
The addition of black numerals makes the
designs resemble the surcharged issue of
1866, Nos. 24-28.
Labels in top row are overprinted
"SEGUNDA MUESTRA 1966," in bottom row
"SEGUNDAS JORNADAS 1966" and
"CENTENARIO DEL SELLO / ESCUDO
RESELLADO" in both rows. One label each in
top and bottom rows is overprinted "BUENOS
AIRES / ABRIL 1966."

No. 613 Surcharged in Dark Blue

Perf. 12½x13
1966, Dec. 17   Engr.   Unwmk.
C299 A175 1p on 12c   .50   .25
Philatelic Club of Uruguay, 40th anniv.

Dante
Alighieri — AP46

Wmk. 332
1966, Dec. 27   Litho.   Perf. 12
C300 AP46 50c sepia & bister   .55   .25
Dante Alighieri (1265-1321), Italian poet.

Planetarium
Projector — AP47

1967, Jan. 13   Wmk. 332   Perf. 12
C301 AP47 5p dl bl & blk   .80   .30
Montevideo Municipal Planetarium, 10th
anniv.

Archbishop
Makarios
and Map of
Cyprus
AP48

1967, Feb. 14   Wmk. 332   Perf. 12
C302 AP48 6.60p rose lil & blk   .50   .25
Visit of Archbishop Makarios, president of
Cyprus, Oct. 21, 1966.

Dr. Albert
Schweitzer Holding
Fawn — AP49

1967, Mar. 31   Litho.   Wmk. 332
C303 AP49 6p grn, blk, brn & sal .85   .85
Albert Schweitzer (1875-1965), medical
missionary.

Corriedale
Ram
AP50

Various Rams: 4p, Ideal. 5p, Romney
Marsh. 10p, Australian Merino.

1967, Apr. 5
C304 AP50   3p red org, blk &
              gray   1.75   .25
C305 AP50   4p emer, blk & gray 1.75   .25
C306 AP50   5p ultra, blk & gray 1.75   .25
C307 AP50 10p yel, blk & gray   1.75   .25
    Nos. C304-C307 (4)   7.00 1.25

Uruguayan sheep raising.

Flag of
Uruguay
and Map
of the
Americas
AP51

1967, Apr. 8
C308 AP51 10p dk gray, bl & gold .85 .25

Meeting of American Presidents, Punta del Este, Apr. 10-12.

Numeral Stamps of 1866, Nos. 30-31 AP52

Design: 6p, Nos. 32-33; diff. frame.

Wmk. 332
1967, May 10   Litho.   Perf. 12
C309 AP52 3p bl, yel grn & blk .45 .25
  a. Souvenir sheet of 4 1.50 1.50
C310 AP52 6p bis, dp rose & blk .55 .30
  a. Souvenir sheet of 4 2.50 2.50

Cent. of the 1866 numeral issue. Nos. C309a-C310a each contain 4 stamps similar to Nos. C309 and C310 respectively (the arrangement of colors differs in the souvenir sheets).

Ansina, Portrait by Medardo Latorre — AP53

1967, May 17
C311 AP53 2p gray, dk bl & red .40 .25

Issued to honor Ansina, servant of Gen. José Artigas.

Plane Landing AP54

1967, May 30
C312 AP54 10p red, bl, blk & yel .70 .25

30th anniv. (in 1966) of PLUNA Airline.

Shooting for Basket — AP55

Basketball Game — AP56

Basketball Players in Action: No. C314, Driving (ball shoulder high). No. C315, About to pass (ball head high). No. C316, Ready to pass (ball held straight in front). No. C317, Dribbling with right hand.

1967, June 9
C313 AP55 5p multi .40 .25
C314 AP55 5p multi .40 .25
C315 AP55 5p multi .40 .25
C316 AP55 5p multi .40 .25
C317 AP55 5p multi .40 .25
  a. Strip of 5, Nos. C313-C317 2.75 2.75

Souvenir Sheet
C318 AP56 10p org, brt grn & blk 2.50 2.50

5th World Basketball Championships, Montevideo, May 1967.
For overprint see No. C349.

José Artigas, Manuel Belgrano, Flags of Uruguay and Argentina — AP57

Wmk. 332
1967, June 19   Litho.   Imperf.
C319 AP57 5p bl, grn & yel 1.50 1.50

3rd Rio de la Plata Stamp Show, Montevideo, Uruguay, June 18-25.
For surcharge see No. 859.

Nos. C248 and C252 Surcharged in Gold
1967, June 22   Perf. 12
C320 AP30 5.90p on 45c multi .45 .25
C321 A195 5.90p on 45c multi .45 .25

Don Quixote and Sancho Panza, Painted by Denry Torres — AP58

1967, July 10
C322 AP58 8p bister brn & brn .60 .25

Issued in honor of Miguel de Cervantes Saavedra (1547-1616), Spanish novelist.
For surcharge see No. C356.

Stone Axe — AP59

Designs: 15p, Headbreaker stones. 20p, Spearhead. 50p, Birdstone. 75p, Clay pot. 100p, Ornitholite (ritual sculpture), Balizas, horiz. 150p, Lasso weights (boleadores). 200p, Two spearheads.

1967-68   Wmk. 332   Perf. 12
C323 AP59 15p gray & blk .30 .25
C324 AP59 20p gray & blk .30 .25
C325 AP59 30p gray & lt gray .70 .25
C326 AP59 50p gray & blk 1.00 .25
C327 AP59 75p brn & blk 1.60 .35
C328 AP59 100p gray & blk 2.25 .70
C329 AP59 150p gray & blk ('68) 2.50 .70
C330 AP59 200p gray & blk ('68) 4.00 1.50
  Nos. C323-C330 (8) 12.65 4.25

Railroad Crossing AP60

1967, Dec. 4
C331 AP60 4p blk, yel & red .50 .25

10th Pan-American Highway Congress, Montevideo.

Lions Emblem and Map of South America — AP61

1967, Dec. 29
C332 AP61 5p pur, yel & emer .70 .25

50th anniversary of Lions International.

Boy Scout AP62

1968, Jan. 24   Litho.
C333 AP62 9p sepia & brick red .75 .30

Issued in memory of Robert Baden-Powell, founder of the Boy Scout organization.

Sun, UN Emblem and Transportation Means — AP63

1968, Feb. 29   Wmk. 332   Perf. 12
C334 AP63 10p gray, yel, lt & dk bl .50 .25

Issued for International Tourist Year.

Octopus AP64

Marine Fauna: 20p, Silversides. 25p, Characin. 30p, Catfish, vert. 50p, Squid, vert.

1968   Wmk. 332   Perf. 12
C335 AP64 15p lt grn, bl & blk 1.00 .25
C336 AP64 20p brn, grn & bl 1.00 .25
C337 AP64 25p multi 1.50 .25
C338 AP64 30p bl, grn & blk 1.75 .50
C339 AP64 50p dp org, grn & dk bl 2.75 .65
  Nos. C335-C339 (5) 8.00 1.90

Issued: 30p, 50p, 10/10; 15p, 20p, 25p, 11/5.

Navy Type of Regular Issue
Designs: 4p, Naval Air Force. 6p, Naval arms. 10p, Signal flags, vert. 20p, Corsair (chartered by General Artigas).

1968, Nov. 12   Litho.
C340 A226 4p bl, blk & red .30 .25
C341 A226 6p multi .30 .25
C342 A226 10p lt ultra, red & yel .30 .25
C343 A226 20p ultra & blk .50 .25
  Nos. C340-C343 (4) 1.40 .80

Rowing AP65

1969, Feb. 11   Wmk. 332   Perf. 12
C344 AP65 30p shown .60 .25
C345 AP65 50p Running 1.00 .35
C346 AP65 100p Soccer 1.75 .55
  Nos. C344-C346 (3) 3.35 1.15

19th Olympic Games, Mexico City, 10/12-27/68.

Bicycling Type of Regular Issue
Designs: 20p, Bicyclist and globe, vert.

1969, Mar. 21   Wmk. 332   Perf. 12
C347 A229 20p bl, pur & yel .60 .25

"EFIMEX 68" and Globe AP66

1969, Apr. 10   Wmk. 332   Perf. 12
C348 AP66 20p dk grn, red & bl .90 .25

EFIMEX '68, International Philatelic Exhibition, Mexico City, Nov. 1-9, 1968.

No. C318 Ovptd. with Names of Participating Countries, Emblem, Bars, etc. and "CAMPEONATO MUNDIAL DE VOLEIBOL"
1969, Apr. 25
Souvenir Sheet
C349 AP56 10p org, brt grn & blk 1.10 1.10

Issued to commemorate the World Volleyball Championships, Montevideo, Apr. 1969.

Book, Quill and Emblem — AP67

1969, Sept. 16   Litho.   Perf. 12
C350 AP67 30p grn, org & blk .75 .25

10th Congress of Latin American Notaries.

Automobile Club Emblem — AP68

1969, Oct. 7   Wmk. 332   Perf. 12
C351 AP68 10p ultra & red .50 .25

50th anniv. (in 1968) of the Uruguayan Automobile Club.

ILO Emblem AP69

1969, Oct. 29   Litho.   Perf. 12
C352 AP69 30p dk bl grn & blk .60 .25

50th anniv. of the ILO.

Exhibition Emblem — AP70

1969, Nov. 15   Wmk. 332   Perf. 12
C353 AP70 20p ultra, yel & grn   .60 .25
ABUEXPO 69 Philatelic Exhibition, San Pablo, Brazil, Nov. 15-23.

Rotary Emblem and Hemispheres AP71

1969, Dec. 6   Perf. 12
C354 AP71 20p ultra, bl & bis   1.00 .30
South American Regional Rotary Conference and the 50th anniv. of the Montevideo Rotary Club.

Dr. Luis Morquio — AP72

1969, Dec. 22   Litho.   Wmk. 332
C355 AP72 20p org red & brn   .50 .25
Centenary of the birth of Dr. Luis Morquio, pediatrician.

No. C322 Surcharged "FELIZ AÑO 1970 / 6.00 / PESOS"
1969, Dec. 24
C356 AP58 6p on 8p bis brn & brn   .50 .25
Issued for New Year 1970.

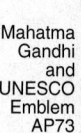

Mahatma Gandhi and UNESCO Emblem AP73

1970, Jan. 26   Wmk. 332   Perf. 12
C357 AP73 100p lt bl & brn   5.00 .90
Mohandas K. Gandhi (1869-1948), leader in India's fight for independence.

Evaristo C. Ciganda — AP74

1970, Mar. 10   Litho.
C358 AP74 6p brt grn & brn   .50 .25
Ciganda, author of the 1st law for teachers' pensions, birth cent.

Giuseppe Garibaldi — AP75

1970, Apr. 7   Unwmk.   Perf. 12
C359 AP75 20p rose car & pink   .70 .25
Centenary of Garibaldi's command of foreign legionnaires in the Uruguayan Civil War.

Fur Seal AP76

Designs: 20p, Rhea, vert. 30p, Common tegu (lizard). 50p, Capybara. 100p, Mulita armadillo. 150p, Puma. 200p, Nutria.

1970-71   Wmk. 332   Perf. 12
C361 AP76 20p pur, emer & blk   1.25 .25
C362 AP76 30p emer, yel & blk   1.25 .30
C363 AP76 50p dl yel & brn   2.50 .50
C365 AP76 100p org, sep & blk   3.25 .75
C366 AP76 150p emer & brn   2.50 .85
C367 AP76 200p brt rose, brn & blk ('71)   6.00 2.25
C368 AP76 250p gray, bl & blk   7.00 2.25
    Nos. C361-C368 (7)   23.75 7.15

Soccer and Mexican Flag AP77

1970, June 2   Litho.   Perf. 12
C369 AP77 50p multi   1.10 .50
9th World Soccer Championships for the Jules Rimet Cup, Mexico City, 5/30-6/21.

"U N" and Laurel — AP78

1970, June 26   Wmk. 332   Perf. 12
C370 AP78 32p dk bl & gold   .60 .25
25th anniversary of the United Nations.

Eisenhower and US Flag — AP79

1970, July 14   Litho.
C371 AP79 30p gray, vio bl & red   1.00 .25
Issued in memory of Gen. Dwight David Eisenhower, 34th Pres. of US (1890-1969).

Neil A. Armstrong Stepping onto Moon — AP80

1970, July 21
C372 AP80 200p multi   5.00 1.50
1st anniv. of man's 1st landing on the moon.

Flag of the "Immortals" — AP81

1970, Aug. 24   Wmk. 332   Perf. 12
C373 AP81 500p bl, blk & red   7.00 7.00
The 145th anniversary of the arrival of the 33 "Immortals," the patriots, who started the revolution for independence.

Congress Emblem with Map of South America AP82

1970, Sept. 16   Unwmk.   Perf. 12
C374 AP82 30p bl, dk bl & yel   .80 .25
Issued to publicize the 5th Pan-American Congress of Rheumatology, Punta del Este.

Souvenir Sheet

Types of First Air Post Issue — AP83

1970, Oct. 1   Wmk. 332   Perf. 12½
C375 AP83   Sheet of 3   3.00 3.00
    a.   25p brown (Bl)   .90 .90
    b.   25p brown (R)   .90 .90
    c.   25p brown (G)   .90 .90
Stamp Day. #C375 contains 3 stamps similar to #C1-C3, but with denominations in pesos.

Flags of ALALC Countries — AP84

1970, Nov. 23   Litho.   Perf. 12
C376 AP84 22p multi   .75 .25
For the Latin-American Association for Free Trade (Asociación Latinoamericana de Libre Comercio).

Yellow Fever, by J. M. Blanes AP85

1971, June 8   Wmk. 332   Perf. 12
C377 AP85 50p blk, dk red brn & yel   .80 .35
Juan Manuel Blanes (1830-1901), painter.

Racial Equality, UN Emblem AP86

1971, June 28   Litho.
C378 AP86 27p blk, pink & bis   .65 .25
Intl. Year Against Racial Discrimination.

Congress Emblem with Maps of Americas AP87

1971, July 6   Wmk. 332   Perf. 12
C379 AP87 58p dl grn, blk & org   1.00 .40
12th Pan-American Congress of Gastroenterology, Punta del Este, Dec. 5-10, 1971.

Committee Emblem AP88

1971, Nov. 29
C380 AP88 30p bl, blk & yel   .85 .25
Inter-governmental Committee for European Migration.

Llama and Mountains AP89

1971, Dec. 30
C381 AP89 37p multi   1.00 .40
EXFILIMA '71, Third Inter-American Philatelic Exposition, Lima, Peru, Nov. 6-14.

Munich Olympic Games Emblem — AP90

Designs (Munich '72 Emblem and): 100p, Torchbearer. 500p, Discobolus.

1972, Feb. 1   **Perf. 11½x12**
C382	AP90	50p blk, red & org	.35	.25
C383	AP90	100p multi	.65	.40
C384	AP90	500p multi	3.50	2.00
	Nos. C382-C384 (3)		4.50	2.65

20th Olympic Games, Munich, 8/26-9/11.

Retort and WHO Emblem — AP91

1972, Feb. 22   **Perf. 12**
C385 AP91 27p multi   .70 .25

50th anniversary of the discovery of insulin by Frederick G. Banting and Charles H. Best.

Ship with Flags Forming Sails — AP92

1972, Mar. 6   **Wmk. 332**
C386 AP92 37p multi   .70 .25

Stamp Day of the Americas.

1924 and 1928 Gold Medals, Soccer — AP93

Design: 300p, Olympic flag, Motion and Munich emblems, vert.

1972, June 12   **Litho.**   **Perf. 12**
C387	AP93	100p bl & multi	.75	.75
C388	AP93	300p multi	2.25	2.25

20th Olympic Games, Munich, 8/26-9/11.

Cross AP94

1972, Aug. 10
C389 AP94 37p vio & gold   .45 .25

Dan A. Mitrione (1920-70), slain US official.

Interlocking Squares and UN Emblem — AP95

1972, Aug. 16
C390 AP95 30p gray & multi   .60 .25

3rd UN Conf. on Trade and Development (UNCTAD III), Santiago, Chile, Apr.-May 1972.

Brazil's "Bull's-eye," 1843 — AP96

Wmk. 332
1972, Aug. 26   **Litho.**   **Perf. 12**
C391 AP96 50p grn, yel & bl   .60 .25

4th Inter-American Philatelic Exhibition, EXFILBRA, Rio de Janeiro, Aug. 26-Sept. 2.

Map of South America, Compass Rose — AP97

1972, Sept. 28
C392 AP97 37p multi   .45 .25

Uruguay's support for extending territorial sovereignty 200 miles into the sea.

Adoration of the Kings and Shepherds, by Rafael Perez Barradas — AP98

1972, Oct. 12
C393 AP98 20p lemon & multi + label   .65 .25

Christmas 1972 and first biennial exhibition of Uruguayan painting, 1970.

WPY Emblem AP99

Wmk. 332
1974, Aug. 20   **Litho.**   **Perf. 12**
C394 AP99 500p gray & red   1.10 .70

World Population Year 1974.

Soccer, Olympics and UPU Emblems AP100

Anniversaries and events: No. C398a, 17th UPU Congress, Lausanne. No. C398b, World Soccer Federation, 1st South American president. No. C398c, 1976 Summer and Winter Olympics, Innsbruck and Montreal.

1974, Aug. 30
C395	AP100	200p grn & multi	1.00	1.00
C396	AP100	300p org & multi	1.00	1.00
C397	AP100	500p multicolored	9.00	9.00

Souvenir Sheet
C398		Sheet of 3	70.00	70.00
a.-c.		AP100 500p any single	20.00	20.00

Centenary of Universal Postal Union. Nos. C397-C398 had limited distribution.

Mexico No. O1 and Mexican Coat of Arms AP101

Wmk. 332
1974, Oct. 15   **Litho.**   **Perf. 12**
C399 AP101 200p multi   .60 .25

EXFILMEX '74 5th Inter-American Philatelic Exhibition, Mexico City, Oct. 26-Nov. 3.

Christmas Type of 1974
240p, Kings following star. 2500p, Virgin & Child.

1974
C400 A315 240p multi   .60 .25

Miniature Sheet
C401 A315 2500p multi   5.00 5.00

Issued: 240p. Dec. 27; 2500p, Dec. 31.

Spain No. 1, Colors of Spain and Uruguay — AP102

1975, Mar. 4
C402 AP102 400p multi   .70 .25

Espana 75, International Philatelic Exhibition, Madrid, Apr. 4-13.

Souvenir Sheet

Nos. C253, 893 and C402 — AP103

Wmk. 332
1975, Apr. 4   **Litho.**   **Perf. 12**
C403	AP103	Sheet of 3	6.50	6.50
a.		1000p No. C253	2.00	2.00
b.		1000p No. 893	2.00	2.00
c.		1000p No. C402	2.00	2.00

Espana 75 Intl. Phil. Exhib., Madrid, Apr. 4-13.

1976 Summer & Winter Olympics, Innsbruck & Montreal AP104

1975, May 16   **Perf. 12**
C404	AP104	400p shown	1.00	.60
C405	AP104	600p Flags, Olympic rings	1.50	.95

Souvenir Sheets
C406		Sheet of 2	42.50	42.50
a.		AP104 500p Montreal emblem	12.50	12.50
b.		AP104 1000p Innsbruck emblem	27.50	27.50
C407		Sheet of 2	42.50	42.50
a.		AP104 500p Emblems, horiz.	12.50	12.50
b.		AP104 1000p Flags, horiz.	27.50	27.50

Nos. C404-C407 had limited distribution.

Floor Design for Capitol, Rome AP105

1975, Aug. 15
C408 AP105 1p multi   1.50 1.50

500th birth anniversary of Michelangelo Buonarroti (1475-1564), Italian sculptor, painter and architect.

Apollo-Soyuz Space Mission, USA & Uruguay Independence — AP106

Anniversaries and events: 15c, Apollo-Soyuz spacecraft. 20c, Apollo-Soyuz spacecraft. 25c, Artigas monument, vert. 30c, George Washington, Pres. Artigas. No. C412, Early Aircraft, vert. No. C413a, Apollo spacecraft, astronauts. No. C413b, US and Uruguayan Declarations of Independence. No. C413c, Modern aircraft. No. C413d, UN Secretaries General. No. C414c, Boiso Lanza, aviation pioneer. 1p, Flags of UN and Uruguay.

1975, Sept. 29
C409	AP106	10c multicolored	1.10	.85
C410	AP106	15c multicolored	1.60	1.25
C411	AP106	25c multicolored	2.00	1.40
C412	AP106	50c multicolored	2.75	1.75
	Nos. C409-C412 (4)		7.45	5.25

Souvenir Sheets
C413		Sheet of 4	42.50	42.50
a.-d.		AP106 40c any single	9.00	9.00
C414		Sheet of 4	42.50	42.50
a.		AP106 20c multicolored	1.75	1.75
b.		AP106 30c multicolored	4.25	4.25
c.		AP106 50c multicolored	7.25	7.25
d.		AP106 1p multicolored	16.00	16.00

Nos. C409-C414 had limited distribution.

Sun, Uruguay No. C59 and other
Stamps — AP108

Wmk. 332

1975, Oct. 13	Litho.	Perf. 12
C415 AP108 1p blk, gray & yel		3.25 1.60

Uruguayan Stamp Day.

Montreal Olympic   Flags of US and
Emblem and   Uruguay — AP110
Argentina
'78 — AP109

UPU and UPAE
Emblems
AP111

Wmk. 332

1975, Oct. 14	Litho.	Perf. 11½
C416 AP109 1p multi		2.00 .70
C417 AP110 1p multi		2.00 .70
C418 AP111 1p multi		2.00 .70
a. Souvenir sheet of 3		22.50 22.50
Nos. C416-C418 (3)		6.00 2.10

EXFILMO '75 and ESPAMER '75 Stamp
Exhibitions, Montevideo, Oct. 10-19. No.
C418a contains 3 stamps similar to Nos.
C416-C418, 2p each.

Ocelot
AP112

Orchid: #C416, Oncidium bifolium.

1976, Jan.	Litho.	Perf. 12
C419 AP112 50c vio bl & multi		.75 .35
C420 AP112 50c emer & multi		.75 .35

Souvenir Sheets

Olympics, Soccer, Telecommunications
and UPU — AP113

1976, June 3		Perf. 11½
C422	Sheet of 3	55.00 55.00
a.	AP113 30c Soccer player	6.50 6.50
b.	AP113 70c Alexander Graham Bell	15.00 15.00
c.	AP113 1p UPU emblem, UN #5	22.50 22.50

C423	Sheet of 3	55.00 55.00
a.	AP113 40c Discus thrower	6.50 6.50
b.	AP113 60c Telephone, cent.	10.00 10.00
c.	AP113 2p UPU emblem, UN #11	27.50 27.50

Nos. C422-C423 had limited distribution.

**Anniversaries and Events Type of
1976
Souvenir Sheets**

20c, Frederick Passy, Henri Dunant. 35c,
Nobel prize, 75th anniv. 40c, Viking space-
craft. 60c, 1976 Summer Olympics, Montreal.
75c, US space missions. 90c, 1976 Summer
Olympics, diff.
World Cup Soccer Championships, Argen-
tina: 1p, Uruguay, 1930 champions. 1.50p,
Uruguay, 1950 champions.

1976, Nov. 12		Perf. 12
C424	Sheet of 4	40.00 40.00
a.	A355 20c multicolored	2.75 2.75
b.	A355 40c multicolored	5.00 5.00
c.	A355 60c multicolored	7.25 7.25
d.	A355 1.50p multicolored	17.50 17.50
C425	Sheet of 4	40.00 40.00
a.	A355 35c multicolored	5.50 5.50
b.	A355 75c multicolored	7.75 7.75
c.	A355 90c multicolored	8.75 8.75
d.	A355 1p multicolored	11.00 11.00

Nos. C424-C425 had limited distribution.

**Nobel Prize Type of 1977
Souvenir Sheets**

Anniversaries and events: 10c, World Cup
Soccer Championships. 40c, Victor Hess,
Nobel Prize in Physics. 60c, Max Plank, Nobel
Prize in Physics. 80c, Graf Zeppelin, Con-
corde. 90c, Virgin and Child by Rubens. 1.20p,
World Cup Soccer Championships, diff. 1.50p,
Eduardo Bonilla, Count von Zeppelin. 2p, The
Nativity by Rubens.

1977, July 21		
C426	Sheet of 4	35.00 35.00
a.	A361 10c multicolored	1.00 1.00
b.	A361 60c multicolored	4.00 4.00
c.	A361 80c multicolored	6.00 6.00
d.	A361 2p multicolored	14.00 14.00
C427	Sheet of 4	35.00 35.00
a.	A361 40c multicolored	2.50 2.50
b.	A361 90c multicolored	6.50 6.50
c.	A361 1.20p multicolored	7.50 7.50
d.	A361 1.50p multicolored	11.00 11.00

Nos. C426-C427 had limited distribution.

Uruguay
Natl.
Postal
System,
150th
Anniv.
AP114

1977, July 27		
C428 AP114 8p multicolored		12.00 12.00

Souvenir Sheet

C429 AP114 10p multicolored	17.00 17.00

No. C428, imperf., was not valid for post-
age. Souvenir sheets sold in the package with
No. C429 were not valid for postage.
For overprint see No. C435.

Paintings Type of 1978

Paintings: 1p, St. George Slaying Dragon by
Durer. 1.25p, Duke of Lerma by Rubens. No.
432a, Madonna and Child by Durer. No. 432b,
Holy Family by Rubens. No. 432c, Flight from
Egypt by Francisco de Goya (1746-1828).

1978, June 13		Perf. 12½
C430	A374 1p brn & blk	4.25 4.25
C431	A374 1.25p blk & brn	4.50 4.50

Souvenir Sheet

C432	Sheet of 3	19.00 19.00
a.-c.	A374 1p any single	5.25 5.25

Nos. C430-C432 had limited distribution.

Souvenir Sheet

ICAO, 30th Anniv. and 1st Powered
Flight, 75th Anniv. — AP115

Designs: a, Concorde, Dornier DO-x. b,
Graf Zeppelin, Wright Brothers' Flyer. c,
Space shuttle and De Pinedo's plane.

1978, June 13		
C433	Sheet of 3	25.00 25.00
a.-c.	AP115 1p any single	6.50 6.50

No. C433 had limited distribution.

Souvenir Sheet

World Cup Soccer Championships,
Argentina — AP116

1978, June 13		Perf. 12
C434	Sheet of 3	55.00 55.00
a.	AP116 50c multicolored	5.00 5.00
b.	AP116 1.50p multicolored	13.50 13.50
c.	AP116 2p multicolored	20.00 20.00

No. C434 had limited distribution.

No. C428 Overprinted in Black

1978, Aug. 28		
C435 AP114 8p multicolored		7.50 3.00

No. C435 had limited distribution.

Madonna and Child Type of 1979

Various Madonna and Child etchings by
Albrecht Dürer with Intl. Year of the Child
emblem at: a, UL. b, UR.

Wmk. 332

1979, June 18	Litho.	Perf. 12½
C436 A390 1.50p Sheet of 2, #a-b		26.00 26.00

No. C436 had limited distribution.

Boiso
Lanza,
Wright
Brothers
AP117

75th anniv. of powered flight.

1979, June 18		Perf. 12½
C437 AP117 1.80p multicolored		3.50 1.50

No. C437 had limited distribution.
Issued in sheet of 24 containing 6 blocks of
4r with margin around. See Nos. 1040-1042.

Souvenir Sheet

1982 World Cup Soccer
Championships, Spain — AP118

1979, June 18		Perf. 12
C438 AP118 Sheet of 3		40.00 40.00
a.	50c Jules Rimet cup	3.00 3.00
b.	2.50p Uruguay flag	12.50 12.50
c.	3p Espana '82	17.00 17.00

No. C438 had limited distribution.

Souvenir Sheet

Rowland Hill Cent. — AP119

1979, June 18		
C439 AP119 Sheet of 2		40.00 40.00
a.	2p Uruguay #1, C1	20.00 20.00
b.	2p Great Britain #1, 836	20.00 20.00

No. C439 had limited distribution.

AIR POST SEMI-POSTAL STAMPS

Catalogue values for unused
stamps in this section are for
Never Hinged items.

**Type of Semi-Postal Stamps, 1959
Wmk. 327**

1959, Dec. 29	Litho.	Perf. 11½
CB1 SP2 38c + 10c brown & org		.30 .30
CB2 SP2 60c + 10c gray grn & org		.50 .50

Issued for national recovery.

SPECIAL DELIVERY STAMPS

No. 242 Overprinted

1921, Aug.	Unwmk.	Perf. 11½
E1 A97 2c fawn		.70 .25
a. Double overprint		4.25

Caduceus — SD1

Imprint: "IMP. NACIONAL."

1922, Dec. 2   Litho.   Wmk. 188
Size: 21x27mm
E2   SD1   2c light red   .50   .25

1924, Oct. 1
E3   SD1   2c pale ultra   .50   .25

1928   Unwmk.   Perf. 11
E4   SD1   2c light blue   .50   .25

Imprint: "IMPRA. NACIONAL."

1928-36   Wmk. 188
Size: 16½x19½mm.
E5   SD1   2c black, green   .25   .25
Unwmk.
E6   SD1   2c blue green ('29)   .25   .25
Perf. 11½, 12½
E7   SD1   2c blue ('36)   .25   .25
      Nos. E5-E7 (3)   .75   .75

1944, Oct. 23   Perf. 12½
E8   SD1   2c salmon pink   .25   .25

Catalogue values for unused stamps in this section, from this point to the end of the section, are for Never Hinged items.

1947, Nov. 19
E9   SD1   2c red brown   .25   .25

No. E9 Surcharged in Black

1957, Oct. 30
E10   SD1   5c on 2c red brown   .25   .25

LATE FEE STAMPS

Galleon and Modern Steamship — LF1

Wmk. Crossed Keys in Sheet
1936, May 18   Litho.   Perf. 11
I1   LF1   3c green   .25   .25
I2   LF1   5c violet   .25   .25
I3   LF1   6c blue green   .25   .25
I4   LF1   7c brown   .25   .25
I5   LF1   8c carmine   .50   .50
I6   LF1   12c deep blue   .65   .65
      Nos. I1-I6 (6)   2.15 2.15

POSTAGE DUE STAMPS

D1

1902   Unwmk.   Engr.   Perf. 14 to 15
Size: 21¼x18½mm
J1   D1   1c blue green   .75   .30
J2   D1   2c carmine   .75   .30
J3   D1   4c gray violet   .80   .30
J4   D1   10c dark blue   1.75 .70
J5   D1   20c ocher   2.50 1.25
      Nos. J1-J5 (5)   6.55 2.85

Surcharged in Red

1904
J6   D1   1c on 10c dk bl   1.25 1.25
   a.   Inverted surcharge   12.00 12.00

1913-15   Litho.   Perf. 11½
Size: 22½x20mm
J7   D1   1c lt grn   .75   .30
J8   D1   2c rose red   .75   .30
J9   D1   4c dl vio   1.00 .30
J10 D1   6c dp brn   1.00 .50
Size: 21¼x19mm
J11 D1   10c dl bl   1.50 .60
      Nos. J7-J11 (5)   5.00 2.00

Imprint: "Imprenta Nacional"

1922   Size: 20x17mm
J12 D1   1c bl grn   .50   .30
J13 D1   2c red   .50   .30
J14 D1   3c red brn   .70   .50
J15 D1   4c brn vio   .50   .50
J16 D1   5c blue   .80   .50
J17 D1   10c gray grn   1.00 .60
      Nos. J12-J17 (6)   4.00 2.50

1926-27   Wmk. 188   Perf. 11
Size: 20x17mm
J18 D1   1c bl grn ('27)   .50   .25
J19 D1   3c red brn ('27)   .50   .25
J20 D1   5c slate blue   .50   .25
J21 D1   6c light brown   .50   .50
      Nos. J18-J21 (4)   2.00 1.25

1929   Unwmk.   Perf. 10½, 11
J22 D1   1c blue green   .25   .25
J23 D1   10c gray green   .50   .25

Figure of Value Redrawn
(Flat on sides)
1932   Wmk. 188
J24 D1   6c yel brn   .50   .25

Imprint: "Casa A. Barreiro Ramos S. A."

1935   Unwmk.   Litho.   Perf. 12½
Size: 20x17mm
J25 D1   4c violet   .50   .25
J26 D1   5c rose   .50   .25

Type of 1935
Imprint: "Imprenta Nacional" at right
1938
J27 D1   1c blue green   .25   .25
J28 D1   2c red brown   .25   .25
J29 D1   3c deep pink   .25   .25
J30 D1   4c light violet   .25   .25
J31 D1   5c blue   .25   .25
J32 D1   8c rose   .25   .25
      Nos. J27-J32 (6)   1.50 1.50

OFFICIAL STAMPS

Regular Issues Handstamped in Black, Red or Blue

Many double and inverted impressions exist of the handstamped overprints on Nos. O1-O83. Prices are the same as for normal stamps or slightly more.

On Stamps of 1877-79
1880-82   Unwmk.   Rouletted 8
O1   A9   1c red brown   4.00 3.50
O2   A10   5c green   3.00 2.50
O3   A11   7c bister   3.25 3.25
O4   A11   50c black   22.00 22.00
O5   A12   1p blue   22.00 22.00
      Nos. O1-O5 (5)   54.25 53.25

On No. 44
Rouletted 6
O6   A9   1c brown ('81)   6.00 6.00

On Nos. 43-43A
Rouletted 8
O7   A11   50c black (R)   17.00 16.00
O8   A12   1p blue (R)   22.50 20.00

On Nos. 45, 41, 37a
Perf. 12½
O9   A13   7c blue (R) ('81)   4.25 3.25
Rouletted 8
O10 A11   10c ver (Bl)   2.00 2.00
Perf. 13½
O11 A8b   15c yellow (Bl)   5.00 4.50

1883   On Nos. 46-47   Perf. 12½
O12 A14   1c green   6.50 6.50
O13 A14a 2c rose   9.50 9.50

On Nos. 50-51
Perf. 12½, 12x12½, 13
O14 A17   5c blue (R)   4.00 4.00
   a.   Imperf., pair   4.50
O15 A18   10c brown (Bl)   6.50 6.50
   a.   Imperf., pair   6.00

No. 48 Handstamped

1884   Perf. 12½
O16 A15   1c green   35.00 32.50

Overprinted Type "a" in Black
On Nos. 48-49
1884   Perf. 12, 12x12½, 13
O17 A15   1c green   35.00 32.50
O18 A16   2c red   12.00 9.50

On Nos. 53-56
Rouletted 8
O19 A11   1c on 10c ver   2.00 1.60
   a.   Small "1" (No. 53a)   5.00
Perf. 12½
O20 A14a 2c rose   6.50 6.50
O21 A22   5c ultra   6.50 6.50
O22 A23   5c blue   5.00 2.00
      Nos. O17-O22 (6)   67.00 58.60

On Stamps of 1884-88
1884-89   Rouletted 8
O23 A24   1c gray   12.00 5.50
O24 A24   1c green ('88)   2.50 1.60
O25 A24   1c olive grn   3.25 1.75
O26 A24a 2c vermilion   1.00 .60
O27 A24a 2c rose ('88)   2.25 1.25
O28 A24b 5c slate blue   2.25 1.25
O29 A24b 5c slate bl, bl   6.50 5.00
O30 A24b 5c violet ('88)   6.50 5.00
O31 A24b 5c lt blue ('89)   6.50 5.00
O32 A25   7c dk brown   3.25 1.60
O33 A25   7c orange ('89)   3.25 2.25
O34 A26   10c olive brn   2.00 .90
O35 A30   10c violet ('89)   16.00 9.50
O36 A27   20c red violet   3.00 1.60
O37 A27   20c bister brn ('89) 16.00 7.00
O38 A28   25c gray violet   3.50 2.50
O39 A28   25c vermilion ('89)   16.00 7.00
      Nos. O23-O39 (17)   105.75 59.30

The OFICIAL handstamp, type "a," was also applied to No. 73, the 5c violet with "Provisorio" overprint, but it was not regularly issued.

1887   On No. 71   Rouletted 9
O40 A29   10c lilac   5.00

No. O40 was not regularly issued.

On Stamps of 1889-1899
Perf. 12½ to 15 and Compound
1890-1900
O41 A32   1c green   .80   .25
O43 A32   1c blue ('95)   2.00 2.00
O44 A33   2c rose   .80   .25
O45 A33   2c red brn ('95)   2.50 2.50
O46 A33   2c orange ('00)   .80   .80
O47 A34   5c deep blue   1.50 1.50
O48 A34   5c rose ('95)   2.00 2.00
O49 A35   7c bister brown   1.25 .80
O50 A35   7c green ('95)   25.00
O51 A36   10c blue green   1.25 .80
O52 A36   10c orange ('95)   25.00
O53 A37   20c orange   1.25 .80
O54 A37   20c brown ('95)   25.00
O55 A38   25c red brown   1.25 .80
O56 A38   25c ver ('95)   55.00
O57 A39   50c lt blue   4.50 4.50
O58 A39   50c lilac ('95)   5.50 5.50
O59 A40   1p lilac   7.00 5.00
O60 A40   1p lt blue ('95)   40.00 22.50

Nos. O50, O52, O54, O56 and O60 were not regularly issued.

1891   On No. 99   Rouletted 8
O61 A24b 5c violet   1.50 1.25
   a.   "1391"   9.00

On Stamps of 1895-99
Perf. 12½ to 15 and Compound
1895-1900
O62 A51   1c bister   .60   .60
O63 A51   1c slate blue ('97)   1.25 .55
O64 A52   2c blue   .25   .25
O65 A52   2c claret ('97)   1.25 .55
O66 A53   5c red   .80   .55
O67 A53   5c green ('97)   1.25 .55
O68 A53   5c grnsh blue ('00)   .95   .75
O69 A54   7c deep green   .50   .50
O70 A55   10c brown   .50   .50
O71 A56   20c green & blk   .80   .80
O72 A56   20c claret & blk ('97) 4.50 2.25
O73 A57   25c red brn & blk   .80   .80
O74 A57   25c pink & bl ('97)   4.50 2.25
O75 A58   50c blue & blk   .95   .95
O76 A58   50c grn & brn ('97)   5.75 2.75
O77 A59   1p org brn & blk   4.75 4.75
O78 A59   1p yel brn & bl ('97) 9.25 5.75
   a.   Inverted overprint
      Nos. O62-O78 (17)   38.65 25.10

1897, Sept.   On Nos. 133-135
O79 A62   1c brown vio & blk   1.25 1.00
O80 A63   5c pale bl & blk   1.75 1.00
O81 A64   10c lake & blk   1.75 1.10
      Nos. O79-O81 (3)   4.75 3.10

Perf. 12½ to 15 and Compound
1897-1900   On Nos. 136-137
O82 A68   10c red   2.50 1.50
O83 A68   10c red lilac ('00)   1.25 1.25

Regular Issue of 1900-01 Overprinted

1901   Perf. 14 to 16
O84 A72   1c yellow green   .50   .25
O85 A75   2c vermilion   .65   .25
O86 A73   5c dull blue   .65   .25
O87 A76   7c brown orange   .90   .50
O88 A74   10c gray violet   .95   .55
O89 A37   20c lt blue   8.00 4.00
O90 A38   25c bister brown   1.60 .80
O91 A40   1p deep green   10.50 6.00
   a.   Inverted overprint   12.50 8.00
      Nos. O84-O91 (8)   23.75 12.60

Most of the used official stamps of 1901-1928 have been punched with holes of various shapes, in addition to the postal cancellations.

Regular Issue of 1904-05 Overprinted

1905   Perf. 11½
O92 A79   1c green   .50   .25
O93 A80   2c orange red   .50   .25
O94 A81   5c deep blue   .50   .25
O95 A82   10c dark violet   1.00 .40
O96 A83   20c gray green   3.25 1.00
   a.   Inverted overprint
      Nos. O92-O97 (6)   8.00 2.95

Regular Issues of 1904-07 Overprinted

1907, Mar.
O98 A79   1c green   .25   .25
O99 A86   5c deep blue   .25   .25
O100 A86   7c orange brown   .25   .25
O101 A82   10c dark violet   .25   .25
O102 A83   20c gray green   .40   .35
   a.   Inverted overprint   4.00
O103 A84   25c olive bister   .50   .40
O104 A86   50c rose   .95   .70
      Nos. O98-O104 (7)   2.85 2.45

Regular Issues of 1900-10 Overprinted

1910, July 15 *Perf. 14½ to 16*

O105 A75 2c vermilion 8.75 4.00
O106 A73 5c slate green 5.25 3.00
O107 A74 10c gray violet 2.75 1.25
O108 A37 20c grnsh blue 2.75 1.25
O109 A38 25c bister brown 4.50 2.40

Perf. 11½

O110 A86 50c rose 6.00 2.50
a. Inverted overprint 20.00 15.00
Nos. O105-O110 (6) 30.00 14.40

Peace—O1

1911, Feb. 18 **Litho.**

O111 O1 2c red brown .40 .25
O112 O1 5c dark blue .40 .40
O113 O1 8c slate .40 .65
O114 O1 20c gray brown .55 .95
O115 O1 23c claret .80 .95
O116 O1 50c orange 1.60 1.25
O117 O1 1p red 4.00 1.50
Nos. O111-O117 (7) 8.15 5.95

Regular Issue of 1912-15 Overprinted

1915, Sept. 16

O118 A90 2c carmine .55 .40
O119 A90 5c dark blue .55 .40
O120 A90 8c ultra .55 .40
O121 A90 20c dark brown 1.25 .50
O122 A91 23c dark blue 4.00 3.50
O123 A91 50c orange 6.00 3.50
O124 A91 1p vermilion 8.00 4.00
Nos. O118-O124 (7) 20.90 12.70

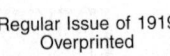

Regular Issue of 1919 Overprinted

1919, Dec. 25

O125 A95 2c red & black .80 .40
a. Inverted overprint 3.50
O126 A95 5c ultra & blk .95 .40
O127 A95 8c gray bl & lt brn .95 .40
a. Inverted overprint 3.50
O128 A95 20c brown & blk 2.00 .80
O129 A95 23c green & brn 2.00 .80
O130 A95 50c brown & bl 4.00 2.00
O131 A95 1p dull red & bl 10.00 4.00
a. Double overprint 15.00
Nos. O125-O131 (7) 20.70 8.80

Regular Issue of 1923 Overprinted

1924 **Wmk. 189** *Perf. 12½*

O132 A100 2c violet .25 .25
O133 A100 5c light blue .25 .25
O134 A100 12c deep blue .30 .25
O135 A100 20c buff .40 .25
O136 A100 36c blue green 1.75 1.25
O137 A100 50c orange 3.50 2.50
O138 A100 1p pink 6.25 5.00
O139 A100 2p lt green 12.00 10.00
Nos. O132-O139 (8) 24.70 19.75

Same Overprint on Regular Issue of 1924

1926-27 **Unwmk.** *Imperf.*

O140 A100 2c rose lilac .40 .25
O141 A100 5c pale blue .65 .25
O142 A100 8c pink ('27) .80 .25
O143 A100 12c slate blue .95 .25
O144 A100 20c brown 2.00 .40
O145 A100 36c dull rose 3.25 .95
Nos. O140-O145 (6) 8.05 2.35

Regular Issue of 1924 Overprinted

1928 *Perf. 12½*

O146 A100 2c rose lilac 1.50 .95
O147 A100 8c pink 1.50 .50
O148 A100 10c turq blue 2.00 .50
Nos. O146-O148 (3) 5.00 1.95

Since 1928, instead of official stamps, Uruguay has used envelopes with "S. O." printed on them, and stamps of many issues which are punched with various designs such as star or crescent.

NEWSPAPER STAMPS

No. 245 Surcharged

1922, June 1 **Unwmk.** *Perf. 11½*

P1 A97 3c on 4c orange .40 .40
a. Inverted surcharge 9.50 9.50
b. Double surcharge 2.50 2.50

Nos. 235-237 Surcharged

1924, June 1 *Perf. 14½*

P2 A96 3c on 2c car & blk .40 .40
P3 A96 6c on 4c red org & bl .40 .40
P4 A96 9c on 5c bl & brn .40 .40
Nos. P2-P4 (3) 1.20 1.20

Nos. 288, 291, 293 Overprinted or Surcharged in Red

1926 *Imperf.*

P5 A100 3c gray green .80 .25
a. Double overprint 1.00 1.00
P6 A100 9c on 10c turq bl .95 .40
a. Double surcharge 1.00 1.00
P7 A100 15c light violet 1.25 .50
Nos. P5-P7 (3) 3.00 1.15

PARCEL POST STAMPS

Mercury — PP1

Imprint: "IMPRENTA NACIONAL"
Inscribed "Exterior"
Size: 20x29½mm

Perf. 11½

1922, Jan. 15 **Litho.** **Unwmk.**

Q1 PP1 5c grn, *straw* .25 .25
Q2 PP1 10c grn, *bl gray* .40 .25
Q3 PP1 20c grn, *rose* 2.10 .55
Q4 PP1 30c grn, *grn* 2.10 .25
Q5 PP1 50c grn, *blue* 3.50 .40
Q6 PP1 1p grn, *org* 5.25 1.60
Nos. Q1-Q6 (6) 13.60 3.30

Inscribed "Interior"

Q7 PP1 5c grn, *straw* .25 .25
Q8 PP1 10c grn, *bl gray* .25 .25
Q9 PP1 20c grn, *rose* 1.00 .25
Q10 PP1 30c grn, *grn* 1.40 .25
Q11 PP1 50c grn, *blue* 2.25 .35
Q12 PP1 1p grn, *org* 6.00 1.25
Nos. Q7-Q12 (6) 11.15 2.60

Imprint: "IMP. NACIONAL"
Inscribed "Exterior"

1926, Jan. 20 *Perf. 11½*

Q13 PP1 20c grn, *rose* 1.75 .50

Inscribed "Interior"

Perf. 11

Q14 PP1 5c grn, *yellow* .40 .25
Q15 PP1 10c grn, *bl gray* .50 .25
Q16 PP1 20c grn, *rose* 1.00 .25
Q17 PP1 30c grn, *bl grn* 1.75 .40
Nos. Q13-Q17 (5) 5.40 1.65

Inscribed "Exterior"

1926 *Perf. 11½*

Q18 PP1 5c blk, *straw* .40 .25
Q19 PP1 10c blk, *bl gray* .65 .25
Q20 PP1 20c blk, *rose* 1.75 .25

Inscribed "Interior"

Q21 PP1 5c blk, *straw* .40 .25
Q22 PP1 10c blk, *bl gray* .50 .25
Q23 PP1 20c blk, *rose* 1.00 .25
Q24 PP1 30c blk, *bl grn* 1.75 .40
Nos. Q18-Q24 (7) 6.45 1.90

PP2

Perf. 11, 11½

1927, Feb. 22 **Wmk. 188**

Q25 PP2 1c dp bl .25 .25
Q26 PP2 2c lt grn .25 .25
Q27 PP2 4c violet .25 .25
Q28 PP2 5c red .25 .25
Q29 PP2 10c dk brn .40 .25
Q30 PP2 20c orange .65 .40
Nos. Q25-Q30 (6) 2.05 1.65

See Nos. Q35-Q38, Q51-Q54.

PP3

Size: 15x20mm

1928, Nov. 20 *Perf. 11*

Q31 PP3 5c blk, *straw* .25 .25
Q32 PP3 10c blk, *gray blue* .25 .25
Q33 PP3 20c blk, *rose* .50 .25
Q34 PP3 30c blk, *green* .80 .25
Nos. Q31-Q34 (4) 1.80 1.00

Type of 1927 Issue

1929-30 **Unwmk.** *Perf. 11, 12½*

Q35 PP2 1c violet .25 .25
Q36 PP2 1c ultra ('30) .25 .25
Q37 PP2 2c bl grn ('30) .25 .25
Q38 PP2 5c red ('30) .25 .25
Nos. Q35-Q38 (4) 1.00 1.00

Nos. Q35-Q38, and possibly later issues, occasionally show parts of a papermaker's watermark.

PP4

1929, July 27 **Wmk. 188** *Perf. 11*

Q39 PP4 10c orange .50 .50
Q40 PP4 15c slate blue .50 .50
Q41 PP4 20c ol brn .50 .50
Q42 PP4 25c rose red 1.00 .50
Q43 PP4 50c dark gray 2.00 1.00
Q44 PP4 75c violet 8.00 6.00
Q45 PP4 1p gray green 7.50 3.00
Nos. Q39-Q45 (7) 20.00 12.00

For overprints see Nos. Q57-Q63.

Ship and Train — PP5

1938-39 **Unwmk.** *Perf. 12½*

Q46 PP5 10c scarlet .40 .25
Q47 PP5 20c dk bl .60 .25
Q48 PP5 30c lt vio ('39) .95 .25
Q49 PP5 50c green 1.75 .25
Q50 PP5 1p brn org 2.50 1.10
Nos. Q46-Q50 (5) 6.20 2.10

See Nos. Q70-Q73, Q80, Q88-Q90, Q92-Q93, Q95.

Type of 1927 Redrawn

1942-55? **Litho.** *Perf. 12½*

Q51 PP2 1c vio ('55)
Q52 PP2 2c bl grn .25 .25
Q54 PP2 5c lt red ('44) .25 .25

The vertical and horizontal lines of the design have been strengthened, the "2" redrawn, etc. No. Q51 has oval "O" in CENTESIMO, 2¼mm from frame line at right; No. Q35 has round "O" 1¾mm from frame line.

Numeral of Value — PP6

1943, Apr. 28 **Engr.**

Q55 PP6 1c dk car rose .25 .25
Q56 PP6 2c grnsh blk .25 .25

Parcel Post Stamps of 1929 Overprinted in Black

1943, Dec. 15 **Wmk. 188** *Perf. 11*

Q57 PP4 10c orange 1.00 .50
Q58 PP4 15c slate blue 1.00 .50
Q59 PP4 20c olive brn 1.00 .50
Q60 PP4 25c rose red 1.50 1.00
Q61 PP4 50c dk gray 2.50 2.00
Q62 PP4 75c violet 5.00 4.00
Q63 PP4 1p gray grn 8.00 4.50
Nos. Q57-Q63 (7) 20.00 13.00

Catalogue values for unused stamps in this section, from this point to the end of the section, are for Never Hinged items.

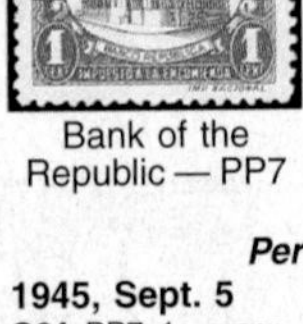

Bank of the Republic — PP7

University — PP8

Perf. 12½

1945, Sept. 5 **Litho.** **Unwmk.**

Q64 PP7 1c green .25 .25
Q65 PP8 2c brt vio .25 .25

See Nos. Q77-Q79, Q84.

Custom House — PP9

1946, Dec. 11   *Perf. 11½*
Q66 PP9 5c yel brn & bl   .25 .25

Type A141 Overprinted
in Red

1946, Dec. 27   *Perf. 12½*
Q67 A141 1p light blue   .95 .25
See Nos. Q69, Q76.

Mail Coach — PP11

1946, Dec. 23
Q68 PP11 5p red & ol brn   12.00 5.00

Type A141 Overprinted
in Black

1947
Q69 A141 2c dull violet brn   .25 .25
See Nos. Q74-Q76.

Type of 1938
1947-52   **Unwmk.**   *Perf. 12½*
   Size: 16x19.5mm (5c, 30c)
Q70 PP5 5c brown org ('52)   .25 .25
   Size: 17x20.5mm
Q71 PP5 10c violet   .25 .25
Q72 PP5 20c vermilion   .40 .25
Q73 PP5 30c blue   .55 .25
   Nos. Q70-Q73 (4)   1.45 1.00

Type of 1947
1948-49   **Black Overprint**
Q74 A141 1c rose lilac ('49)   .25 .25
Q75 A141 5c ultra   .25 .25
Q76 A141 5p rose carmine   4.00 1.75
   Nos. Q74-Q76 (3)   4.50 2.25

Types of 1945
1950
Q77 PP8 1c vermilion   .25 .25
Q78 PP7 2c chalky blue   .25 .25

1952   *Perf. 11*
Q79 PP7 10c blue green   .25 .25

Type of 1938-39
1954   *Perf. 12½*
Q80 PP5 20c carmine   .25 .25

Custom
House — PP13

1p, State Railroad Administration Building.

1955   **Unwmk.**   **Litho.**   *Perf. 12½*
Q81 PP13 5c brown   .25 .25
Q82 PP13 1p light ultra   2.10 1.60
See Nos. Q83, Q85-Q86, Q96. For
surcharge see No. Q87.

Types of 1945 and 1955
Design: 20c, Solis Theater.

1956-57   *Perf. 11*
Q83 PP13 5c gray ('57)   .30 .25
Q84 PP7 10c lt olive grn   .25 .25
Q85 PP13 20c yellow   .25 .25
Q86 PP13 20c lt red brn ('57)   .25 .25
   Nos. Q83-Q86 (4)   1.05 1.00

No. Q83 Surcharged with New Value
in Red

1957
Q87 PP13 30c on 5c gray   .25 .25

Type of 1938-39
1957-60   **Wmk. 327**   *Perf. 11*
Q88 PP5 20c lt blue ('59)   .25 .25
      Unwmk.
Q89 PP5 30c red lilac   .25 .25
      Perf. 12½
Q90 PP5 1p dk blue ('60)   .50 .50
   Nos. Q88-Q90 (3)   1.00 1.00
Nos. Q88 and Q93 are in slightly larger for-
mat-17¼x21mm instead of 16x19½mm.

National
Printing
Works
PP14

1960, Mar. 23   **Wmk. 327**   *Perf. 11*
Q91 PP14 30c yellow green   .25 .25

Type of 1938-39
1962-63   **Wmk. 332**   *Perf. 11*
Q92 PP5 50c slate green   .25 .25
      Perf. 10½
Q93 PP5 1p blue grn ('63)   .50 .50

No. C158
Surcharged

1965   **Unwmk.**   *Perf. 11*
Q94 AP12 5p on 84c orange   .35 .25
For use on regular and air post parcels.

Types of 1938-55
1p, State Railroad Administration Building.

1966   **Litho.**   *Perf. 10½*
Q95 PP5 10c blue green   .25 .25
      Wmk. 327
Q96 PP13 1p brown   .25 .25

No. C184
Surcharged in Red

1966   **Unwmk.**   *Perf. 11*
Q97 AP21 1p on 38c black   .25 .25

Plane and
Bus — PP15

Design: 20p, Plane facing left and bus;
"Encomiendas" on top.

      Wmk. 332
1969, July 8   **Litho.**   *Perf. 12*
Q98 PP15 10p blk, crim & bl grn   .25 .25
Q99 PP15 20p bl, blk & yel   .40 .25

No. B7
Surcharged

1971, Feb. 3   **Wmk. 327**   *Perf. 11½*
Q100 SP2 60c on 1p + 10c   1.25 .60

No. 761 Surcharged
in Red

1971, Nov. 12   **Wmk. 332**   *Perf. 12*
Q101 A226 60c on 6p lt grn & blk   .45 .25

Nos. 770-
771
Surcharged

1972, Nov. 6   **Litho.**   *Perf. 12*
Q102 A233 1p on 6p multi (#770)   1.40 .55
Q103 A233 1p on 6p multi (#771)   1.40 .55
   a.   Pair, #Q102-Q103   3.00 1.10
   See note after No. 771.

Parcels and
Arrows
PP16

Old Mail
Truck
PP17

Designs: Early means of mail transport.

1974   **Wmk. 332**   **Litho.**   *Perf. 12*
Q104 PP16 75p shown   .25 .25
Q105 PP17 100p shown   .40 .25
Q106 PP17 150p Steam engine   .95 .95
Q107 PP17 300p Side-wheeler   .90 .55
Q108 PP17 500p Plane   1.40 .80
   Nos. Q104-Q108 (5)   3.90 2.80
Issue dates: 75p, Feb. 13; others, Mar. 6.

UZBEKISTAN

„uz-ˌbe-ki-'stan

LOCATION — Central Asia, bounded
by Kazakhstan, Turkmenistan, Tajikistan, Afghanistan and Kyrgyzstan
GOVT. — Independent republic, member of the Commonwealth of Independent States
AREA — 172,741 sq. mi.
POP. — 25,155,064 (2001 est.)
CAPITAL — Tashkent (Toshkent)

    With the breakup of the Soviet Union
on Dec. 26, 1991, Uzbekistan and ten

---

former Soviet republics established the
Commonwealth of Independent States.

      100 Kopecks = 1 Ruble
      100 Tiyin = 1 Sum

> **Catalogue values for all unused
> stamps in this country are for
> Never Hinged items.**

Princess Nadira
(1792-1842) — A1

      Perf. 11½x12
1992, May 7   **Unwmk.**   **Photo.**
1   A1 20k multicolored   .35 .35
   For surcharge, see No. 749.

Melitaea
Acreina
A2

1992, Aug. 31   **Litho.**   *Perf. 12*
2   A2 1r multicolored   .30 .30
   For surcharge, see No. 752.

Independence from Soviet Union, 1st
Anniv. — A3

1992, Sept. 25   **Photo.**   *Perf. 12*
3   A3 1r multicolored   .30 .30

Khiva
Mosque,
19th
Cent. — A4

1992, Oct. 20   *Perf. 11½*
4   A4 50k multicolored   .30 .30
   For surcharge, see No. 750.

Samarkand — A5

1992, Oct. 28   **Litho.**   *Perf. 13x13½*
5   A5 10r multicolored   .60 .60
   Winner of 1992 Aga Khan Award for Architecture. For surcharge, see No. 753.

Samovar, 19th Cent. — A6

1992, Nov. 20   **Perf. 12x11½**
6   A6   50k multicolored   .35   .35

For surcharge, see No. 751.

Fauna A7

Designs: 1r, Teratoscincus scincus. No. 8, Naja oxiana. No. 9, Ondatra zibethica, vert. 3r, Pandion haliaetus, vert. 5r, Remiz pendulinus, vert. 10r, Dryomys nitedula, vert. 15r, Varanus griseus. 20r, Cervus elaphus baktrianus.

1993, Mar. 12   **Litho.**   **Perf. 12**
7   A7   1r multicolored   .25   .25
8   A7   2r multicolored   .25   .25
9   A7   2r multicolored   .25   .25
10   A7   3r multicolored   .25   .25
11   A7   5r multicolored   .25   .25
12   A7   10r multicolored   .25   .25
13   A7   15r multicolored   .50   .50
    Nos. 7-13 (7)   2.00 2.00

Souvenir Sheet
14   A7   20r multicolored   1.00 1.00

Russia Nos. 4596-4600, 5838, 5841-5843, 5984 Surcharged in Vio Bl, Brt Bl, Bl, Red, Blk and Grn

a

Methods and perfs as before
1993
15   A2765   2r on 1k (#5838, BB)   .60   .60
16   A2138   8r on 4k (#4599, Bl)   .55   .55
17   A2138   15r on 2k (#4597)   4.50 4.50
18   A2765   15r on 2k (#5984)   4.50 4.50
19   A2765   15r on 3k (#5839, R)   4.50 4.50
20   A2765   15r on 4k (#4520, V)   4.50 4.50
21   A2765   15r on 4k (#5840, R)   4.50 4.50
22   A2765   15r on 5k (#5841)   4.50 4.50
23   A2139   15r on 6k (#4600, R)   4.50 4.50
24   A2765   15r on 7k (#5985a, R)   4.50 4.50
25   A2765   15r on 10k (#5842)   4.50 4.50
26   A2765   15r on 15k (#5843, R)   4.50 4.50
27   A2138   20r on 4k (#4599, Bk)   .75   .75
28   A2139   30r on 3k (#4598, G)   .75   .75
28A   A2138   100r on 1k (#4596, R)   .90   .90
29   A2138   500r on 1k (#4596, Bl)   5.25 5.25
    Nos. 15-29 (16)   53.80 53.80

No. 18 exists imperf.

Flag and Coat of Arms — A8

Perf. 12x12½, 11½x12 (#33)
1993, June 10   **Litho.**
30   A8   8r multicolored   .30   .30
31   A8   15r multicolored   .35   .35
33   A8   50r multicolored   .85   .85
34   A8   100r multicolored   2.00 2.00
    Nos. 30-34 (4)   3.50 3.50

No. 33 is 19x26½mm.

Flowers — A9

No. 38, Dianthus uzbekistanicus. No. 39, Colchicum kesselringii. No. 40, Crocus alatavicus. No. 41, Salvia bucharica. No. 42, Tulipa kaufmanniana. No. 43, Tulipa greigii. No. 44, Tulip.

1993, Sept. 10   **Perf. 12**
38   A9   20r multicolored   .25   .25
39   A9   20r multicolored   .25   .25
40   A9   25r multicolored   .30   .30
41   A9   25r multicolored   .30   .30
42   A9   30r multicolored   .35   .35
43   A9   30r multicolored   .35   .35
    Nos. 38-43 (6)   1.80 1.80

Souvenir Sheet
44   A9   50r multicolored   1.00 1.00

Coat of Arms — A10

1994-95   **Litho.**   **Perf. 12**
45   A10   1t green   7.00 2.50
    Perf. 11½x12
46   A10   75s claret   .35   .35
    Issued: 1t, 3/20/95; 75s, 7/2.

1995   **Litho.**   **Perf. 14**
47   A10   2s green   1.00 1.00
    Size: 20x33mm
48   A10   3s carmine   1.00 1.00
49   A10   6s carmine   1.50 1.50
49A   A10   15s blue   2.25 2.25
    Denomination Shown with Decimal
50   A10   3s carmine   .35   .35
51   A10   6s blue   1.50 1.50
    Nos. 45-51 (8)   14.95 10.45

Issued: 15s, 12/26; others, 4/18.
See Nos. 151A-154, 167-171, 228-237, 405-415.

Statue of Tamerlane, Tashkent — A10a

1994, Sept. 1   **Litho.**   **Perf. 12½x12**
52   A10a   20t multicolored   .40   .40

Bakhouddin, 675th Anniv. — A11

1994, Aug. 1   **Perf. 12½x12**
55   A11   100s multi + label   .50   .50

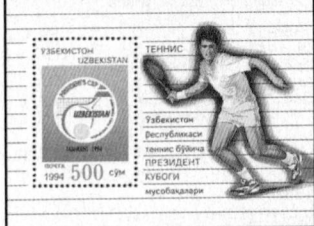

Souvenir Sheet

President's Cup Intl. Tennis Tournament, Tashkent — A12

1994, June 3   **Perf. 12x12½**
56   A12   500s multicolored   1.25 1.25

Ulugh Beg (1394-1449), Astronomer — A13

30t, Portals of Samarkand. 35t, Portals of Bukhara. 40t, Globe, astrolabe. 45t, Statue. 60t, Portrait.

1994, Sept. 15   **Litho.**   **Perf. 12x12½**
57   A13   30t multi + label   .30   .30
58   A13   35t multi + label   .30   .30
59   A13   40t multi + label   .30   .30
60   A13   45t multi + label   .70   .70
    Nos. 57-60 (4)   1.60 1.60

Souvenir Sheet
61   A13   60t multicolored   .75   .75

Russia Nos. 4596, 5113, 5839, 5840, 5843, 5984 Surcharged in Red Violet or Red

b

Methods and perfs as before
1995, Jan.
61A   A2138(a)   2s on 1k (#4596, R)   1.50 1.50
61B   A2765(a)   2s on 3k (#5839, R)   1.50 1.50
61C   A2765(b)   200s on 2k (#5984)   1.50 1.50
61D   A2765(b)   200s on 4k (#5840)   1.50 1.50
61E   A2436(b)   200s on 5k (#5113)   1.50 1.50
61F   A2765(b)   200s on 15k (#5843)   1.50 1.50
    Nos. 61A-61F (6)   9.00 9.00

No. 61C exists imperf. Value $5.

Souvenir Sheet

End of World War II, 50th Anniv. — A14

1995, May 8   **Litho.**   **Perf. 12**
62   A14   20s multicolored   3.00 3.00

Souvenir Sheet

UPU — A15

1995, Sept. 21
63   A15   20s multicolored   2.50 2.50

Capra Falconeri A16

1995, Aug. 15   **Perf. 12½**
64   A16   6s shown   .90   .50
65   A16   10s Three on mountain   1.50   .75
66   A16   10s Up close   1.50   .75
67   A16   15s Lying down   2.25 1.25
    Nos. 64-67 (4)   6.15 3.25

World Wildlife Fund.

Intl. Tennis Tournament, Tashkent '95 — A17

1995, Aug. 25   **Perf. 14**
68   A17   10s multicolored   2.25 2.25

Silk Road Architecture A19

Designs: 6s, Mosque, 15th cent. No. 71, Blue-domed mosque, ruins, 15th cent. No. 72, Mosque with 4 minarets, 19th cent. No. 73, Cylindrical-style mosque, 19th cent. 20s, Map of mosque sites, camel, mosque.

1995, Aug. 28   **Litho.**   **Perf. 12x12½**
70   A19   6s multicolored   1.25 1.25
71   A19   10s multicolored   2.50 2.50
72   A19   10s multicolored   2.50 2.50
73   A19   15s multicolored   3.75 3.75
    Nos. 70-73 (4)   10.00 10.00

Souvenir Sheet
74   A19   20s multicolored   6.00 6.00

Folktales — A20

6s, Man wrestling with creature, woman spilling bowls. #76, Man looking at stork, nest of eggs. #77, Women watching man cut into watermelon full of gold coins. #78, Creature carrying woman. 15s, Man holding beads, parrot.

1995, Aug. 24
75	A20	6s multi + label	2.40	2.40
76	A20	10s multicolored	3.25	3.25
77	A20	10s multicolored	3.25	3.25
78	A20	10s multicolored	3.25	3.25
79	A20	10s multicolored	5.00	5.00
		Nos. 75-79 (5)	17.15	17.15

Moths
A21

6s, Karanasa abramovi. #81, Colias romanovi. #82, Parnassius delphius. #83, Neohipparchia fatua. #84, Chasara staudingeri. #85, Colias wiskotti. 15s, Parnassius tianschanicus. 20s, Colias christophi.

1995, Oct. 10 Perf. 12½x12
80	A21	6s multicolored	1.40	1.40
81	A21	10s multicolored	2.25	2.25
82	A21	10s multicolored	2.25	2.25
83	A21	10s multicolored	2.25	2.25
84	A21	10s multicolored	2.25	2.25
85	A21	10s multicolored	2.25	2.25
86	A21	15s multicolored	3.00	3.00
		Nos. 80-86 (7)	15.65	15.65

Souvenir Sheet
87	A21	20s multicolored	3.75	3.75

Aircraft
A22

1995, Oct. 10
88	A22	6s JIN-2	1.25	1.25
89	A22	10s IL-76	2.00	2.00
90	A22	10s KA-22	2.00	2.00
91	A22	10s AN-8	2.00	2.00
92	A22	10s AN-22	2.00	2.00
93	A22	10s AN-12	2.00	2.00
94	A22	15s IL-114	3.00	3.00
		Nos. 88-94 (7)	14.25	14.25

Souvenir Sheet
95	A22	20s like No. 94	4.25	4.25

Wildlife from
Tashkent
Zoo — A23

Designs: 6s, Camelus ferus. No. 97, Aegypius monachus. No. 98, Ursus arctos isabellinus. No. 99, Zebra. No. 100, Macaca mulatta. No. 101, Pelecanus crispus. 15s, Loxodonta africana.
20s, Capra falconeri.

1995, Nov. 30 Perf. 12x12½
96	A23	6s multicolored	1.10	1.10
97	A23	10s multicolored	1.75	1.75
98	A23	10s multicolored	1.75	1.75
99	A23	10s multicolored	1.75	1.75
100	A23	10s multicolored	1.75	1.75
101	A23	10s multicolored	1.75	1.75
102	A23	15s multicolored	2.50	2.50
		Nos. 96-102 (7)	12.35	12.35

Souvenir Sheet
103	A23	20s multicolored	3.25	3.25

Wild
Animals
A24

Designs: 10s, Ovis ammon bocharensis. No. 105, Ovis ammon severtzov. No. 106, Cervus elaphus bactrianus. No. 107, Capra sibirica. No. 108, Ovis ammon karelini. No. 109, Ovis ammon cycloceros. 20s, Saiga tatarica.
25s, Gazella subgutturosa.

1996, Feb. 16 Perf. 12½x12
104	A24	10s multicolored	1.25	1.25
105	A24	15s multicolored	1.90	1.90
106	A24	15s multicolored	1.90	1.90
107	A24	15s multicolored	1.90	1.90
108	A24	15s multicolored	1.90	1.90
109	A24	15s multicolored	1.90	1.90
110	A24	20s multicolored	2.75	2.75
		Nos. 104-110 (7)	13.50	13.50

Souvenir Sheet
111	A24	25s multicolored	3.50	3.50

Painting
A25

1995, Oct. Litho. Perf. 12x12½
112	A25	15s multicolored	2.00	2.00

Souvenir Sheet

Save the Aral Sea — A26

a, 15s, Felis caracal. b, 15s, Salmo trutta aralensis. c, 20s, Hyaena hyaena. d, 20t, Pseudoscaphirynchus kaufmanni. e, 25t, Aspiolucius esocinus.

1996, May 15 Perf. 14
113	A26	Sheet of 5, #a.-e.	5.50	5.50

See Kazakhstan #145, Kyrgyzstan #107, Tadjikistan #91, Turkmenistan #52.

1996
Summer
Olympic
Games,
Atlanta
A27

1996, June 23 Litho. Perf. 12½x12
114	A27	6s Soccer	.60	.60
115	A27	10s Equestrian event	1.25	1.25
116	A27	15s Boxing	1.75	1.75
117	A27	20s Cycling	2.50	2.50
		Nos. 114-117 (4)	6.10	6.10

Souvenir Sheet

Tamerlane (1336-1405) — A28

1996, Aug. 31 Litho. Perf. 14
118	A28	20s multicolored	4.50	4.50
a.		Inscribed "1336-1404," perf 12x12½	6.00	6.00

Issued: No. 118a, 8/9/96.

Souvenir Sheet

Independence Day — A29

1996, Aug. 27 Litho. Perf. 12x12½
119	A29	20s multicolored	2.50	2.50

Tashkent Tennis
Cup Championship
A30

1996, Sept. 2 Litho. Perf. 14
121	A30	12s green	8.00	8.00

A31

1996, Sept. 18 Perf. 14
122	A31	15s Faizulla Khodjaev	6.00	6.00

A32

1996, Oct. 14 Litho. Perf. 14
123	A32	15s black & buff	6.00	6.00

Abdurauf Fitrat (1886-1996).

Futuristic Space Travel — A33

9s, Shuttle-type vehicle. #126, Vehicle in front of sun. #127, Sun's rays, vehicle traveling left. #128, Large vehicle, sun in distance. #129, Saucer-shaped vehicle landing on planet. 25s, Two men in cockpit.
30s, Two different space vehicles.

1997, Mar. 17
124	A33	9s multi, vert.	1.00	1.00
125	A33	15s shown	1.50	1.50
126	A33	15s multi	1.50	1.50
127	A33	15s multi	1.50	1.50
128	A33	15s multi, vert.	1.50	1.50
129	A33	15s multi, vert.	1.50	1.50
130	A33	25s multi, vert.	2.25	2.25
		Nos. 124-130 (7)	10.75	10.75

Souvenir Sheet
131	A33	30s multi, vert.	6.00	6.00

Fairy Tales
A34

#132, Genie. #133, Bird. #134, Child holding mirror in front of couple. #135, Ape. #136, Face of creature, horse. #137, Large bird attacking deer. 30s, Two people kneeling before throne.
35s, Man on horse.

1997, Apr. 18
132	A34	15s multicolored	1.10	1.10
133	A34	15s multicolored	1.10	1.10
134	A34	20s multicolored	1.40	1.40
135	A34	20s multicolored	1.40	1.40
136	A34	25s multicolored	1.60	1.60
137	A34	25s multicolored	1.60	1.60
138	A34	30s multicolored	2.25	2.25
		Nos. 132-138 (7)	10.45	10.45

Souvenir Sheet
139	A34	35s multicolored	6.50	6.50

Abdulhamid
Sulaymon, Birth
Cent. — A35

1997, June 20
140	A35	6s lilac, black & gray	2.00	2.00

Pantera
Pardus
Tullianus
A36

Designs: No. 142, Yawning. No. 143, Stretching. 25s, Walking on fallen tree.
30s, With mouth open.

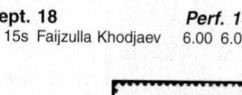

1997, May 28

141	A36	9s multicolored	.95 .95
142	A36	15s multicolored	1.75 1.75
143	A36	15s multicolored	1.75 1.75
144	A36	25s multicolored	3.25 3.25
		Nos. 141-144 (4)	7.70 7.70

Souvenir Sheet

145	A36	30s multicolored	3.75 3.75

No. 145 contains one 30x40mm stamp.

Sites on
Silk Road
A37

In Bukhara: No. 146, Ancient citadel. No. 147, Tomb of Ismail Samani, vert.
In Khiva: No. 148, Minaret, vert. No. 149, Fortress wall with open door.
No. 150, Mosque, Bukhara. No. 151, Minaret, Khiva, diff., vert.

1997   Litho.   Perf. 14

146	A37	15s multicolored	2.50 2.50
147	A37	15s multicolored	2.50 2.50
148	A37	15s multicolored	2.50 2.50
149	A37	15s multicolored	2.50 2.50
		Nos. 146-149 (4)	10.00 10.00

Souvenir Sheets

150	A37	30s multicolored	3.00 3.00
151	A37	30s multicolored	3.00 3.00

Issued: Nos. 146-147, 150, 10/7; Nos. 148-149, 151, 10/8.

Arms Type of 1994 Redrawn

1998   Litho.   Perf. 14
Size: 14x22mm

151A	A10	2s green	.40 .40
152	A10	3s carmine, "1998"	1.25 1.25
a.		Dated "1999"	.50 .50
153	A10	6s green, "1998"	3.00 3.00
a.		Dated "1999"	.70 .70
153A	A10	12s green	2.75 2.75
153B	A10	15s red	1.75 1.75
154	A10	45s blue	4.25 4.25
		Nos. 151A-154 (6)	13.40 13.40

Nos. 152-154 have country name "O'ZBEKISTON" at top and "POCHTA 1998" at bottom.
Issued: 6s, 2/25; 12s, 15s, 45s, 3/25; 2s, 4/16; 3s, 4/17.

Intl. Tennis
Tournament,
Tashkent
A38

Emblem and: No. 155, President's Cup. No. 156, Tennis player. No. 157, Camel.

1997   Litho.   Perf. 14

155	A38	6s blue & grn	3.00 3.00
156	A38	6s blue & grn	3.00 3.00
157	A38	6s blue & grn	3.00 3.00
		Nos. 155-157 (3)	9.00 9.00

Automobiles — A39

a, 9s, Tico. b, 12s, Damas. c, 15s, Nexia.

1997, Sept. 19   Litho.   Perf. 14

158	A39	Block of 3, #a.-c. + label	6.00 6.00

Tennis
Tournament — A40

1998, Aug. 17   Litho.   Perf. 14

159	A40	15s multicolored	1.50 1.50

Sharq Taronlalari
Intl. Music
Festival — A41

1998, July 15

160	A41	15s multicolored	1.00 1.00

Berdekh
Monument — A42

1998, Aug. 17

161	A42	15s blue & brown	1.00 1.00

Kamal ud-Din
Behzad,
Painter — A43

1998, Aug. 17

162	A43	15s multicolored	1.40 1.40

Imam al-
Buhkari — A44

1998, June 26

163	A44	15s multicolored	1.00 1.00

Ahmad al-Farghani,
Astronomer — A45

1998, June 26

164	A45	15s multicolored	1.50 1.50

Folktales — A46

Designs: a, 8s, Woman holding baby. b, 10s, "Alpomish" over rainbow. c, 15s, Three men seated before fire. d, 15s, Man talking to man with sword. e, 18s, Man riding horse. f, 18s, Knight with longbow, squire with arrow. g, 20s, Swordmaker at work. h, 20s, Man fighting lion. i, 25s, Man, woman walking arm in arm.

1998, Nov. 27   Litho.   Perf. 14

165	A46	Sheet of 9, #a.-i.	7.50 7.50

No. 165 is a continuous design.

Arms Type of 1994 Redrawn

1999-2001   Litho.   Perf. 14
Size: 14x23mm

167	A10	5s blue green, "2000"	.50 .50
a.		Dated "2004"	.50 .50
b.		Dated "2005"	.50 .50
168	A10	6s green	1.00 1.00
168A	A10	10s dk green	.50 .50
d.		10s emerald, dated "2004"	.50 .50
168B	A10	15s lt blue	.85 .85
168C	A10	17s dk blue	.90 .90
169	A10	30s blue	1.00 1.00
170	A10	40s rose, "2000"	1.00 1.00
b.		Dated "2001"	.90 .90
170A	A10	45s rose	1.75 1.75
c.		45s carmine, dated "2001"	2.10 2.10
171	A10	60s rose car	1.75 1.75
		Nos. 167-171 (9)	9.25 9.25

Issued: 6s, 3/22/99. 15s, 17s, 30s, 45s, 12/5/00. 5s, 60s, 1/17/01; No. 168A, 40s, 2/5/01. No. 168Ad, 6/15/04.
Nos. 167-171 have country name "O'ZBEKISTON" at top and "POCHTA" and year at bottom. Stamps issued in 2001 are inscribed "2000."
No. 168 is inscribed "6 so'm." No. 153 is inscribed "6-00."

Trains — A47

Locomotives: #172, OV steam, 1897-1917. #173, EA steam, 1931-35. 28s, FD steam, 1931-41. 36s, SO steam, 1934-52. #176, VL-22 electric. #177, KCh. 69s, TEP-6.

1999, May 11   Litho.   Perf. 14

172	A47	18s multicolored	.70 .70
173	A47	18s multicolored	.70 .70
174	A47	28s multicolored	1.00 1.00
175	A47	36s multicolored	1.10 1.10
176	A47	56s multicolored	2.00 2.00
177	A47	56s multicolored	2.00 2.00
178	A47	69s multicolored	2.25 2.25
		Nos. 172-178 (7)	9.75 9.75

A48

Designs: 18s, Horse rearing.
No. 180, horiz.: a, 36s, Robed rider on horse. b, 28s, White horse. c, 69s, Jockey on race horse.
75s, Black horse, horiz.

1999, May 25

179	A48	18s multicolored	1.50 1.50

180	A48	Vert. strip of 3, #a.-	
c.			3.50 3.50

Souvenir Sheet

181	A48	75s multicolored	6.50 6.50

No. 180 printed in sheets of 8 stamps containing 2 strips and one each of Nos. 180a and 180c.

A49

Story of Badal Qorachi — #182: a, 18s, Woman, deer. b, 18s, Two archers on horses. c, 28s, Archer on horse. d, 36s, White giant. e, 56s, Black giant. f, 56s, Troll, cat, bones. g, Man, woman.
75s, Woman on sofa, demon, horiz.

1999, June 8

182	A49	Sheet of 7, #a.-g. + label	7.50 7.50

Souvenir Sheet

183	A49	75s multicolored	3.25 3.25

A50

Reptiles: No. 184, Trapelus sanguinolentus. No. 185, horiz.: a, 18s, Eremias arguta. b, 18s, Vipera ursinii. c, 28s, Phrynocephalus mystaceus. d, 36s, Agkistrodon halys. e, 56s, Eumeces schneideri. f, 69s, Vipera lebetina.
75s, Two lizards, horiz.

1999, June 22

184	A50	56s multicolored	1.25 1.25
185	A50	Sheet of 6, #a.-f.	6.25 6.25

Souvenir Sheet

186	A50	75s multicolored	3.75 3.75

A51

1999, July 7

187	A51	45s light green & black	1.60 1.60

UPU, 125th anniv.

A52

1999, July 21

188	A52	30s green & claret	1.25 1.25

Muhammadrizo Erniyozbek ogli-Ogahiy, poet.

O'ZBEKISTON
A53

Birds of Prey: No. 189, Circaetus qallicus. No. 190, Falco tinnunculus. No. 191, Aquila chrysaetos. No. 192, Gyps fulvus. 36s, Falco cherrug. 56s, Gypaetus barbatus. 60s, Pandion haliaetus.
75s, Bird, hatchlings.

1999, Oct. 22 Litho. Perf. 14x13¾
189	A53	15s multi	.70	.70
190	A53	15s multi	.70	.70
191	A53	18s multi	.90	.90
192	A53	18s multi	.90	.90
193	A53	36s multi	1.25	1.25
194	A53	56s multi	1.75	1.75
195	A53	60s multi	2.00	2.00
		Nos. 189-195 (7)	8.20	8.20

Souvenir Sheet
196	A53	75s multi	5.00	5.00

A54

Soccer.

1999, Nov. 8
197	A54	15s Two players	.65	.65
198	A54	18s Two players, diff.	.65	.65
199	A54	28s Two players, diff.	.85	.85
200	A54	28s Player, goalie	.85	.85
201	A54	36s Player, goalie, diff.	1.50	1.50
202	A54	56s Two players, diff.	1.75	1.75
203	A54	69s Two players, diff.	2.25	2.25
		Nos. 197-203 (7)	8.50	8.50

Souvenir Sheet
Perf. 13¾x14
204	A54	75s Two players, horiz.	4.00	4.00

A55

Prehistoric Animals: a, 28s, Meqaneura. b, 28s, Mesosaurus. c, 36s, Rhamphorhynchus. d, 36s, Styracosaurus albertensis. e, 56s, Trachodon annectens. f, 56s, Tarbosaurus bataar. g, 69s, Arsinoitherium. h, 75s, Phororhacos.

1999, Dec. 13 Litho. Perf. 14x13¾
205	A55	Sheet of 8, #a.-h.	12.00	12.00

Uzbek National Circus — A56

28s, Woman and lion. # 207, 36s, Acrobat with bow and arrow. #208, 36s, Acrobat. #209,

56s, Clown on horse. #210, 56s, Two riders on horse. 69s, Wire walker.
100s, Woman, camels, llamas, horiz.

2000. Jan. 4 Perf. 14
206	A56	28s multi	.95	.95
207	A56	36s multi	.95	.95
208	A56	36s multi	.95	.95
209	A56	56s multi	1.90	1.90
210	A56	56s multi	1.90	1.90
211	A56	69s multi	2.25	2.25
		Nos. 206-211 (6)	8.90	8.90

Souvenir Sheet
212	A56	100s multi	3.25	3.25

Horses — A57

Designs: 69s, Horses pulling carriage. No. 214: a, 36s, Horse in dressage competition. b, 36s, Horse jumping fences. c, 56s, Horses in race. d, 56s, Horse jumping steeplechase fence. e, 75s, Horse with sulky. f, 75s, Race winner.

2000, Feb. 1
213	A57	69s multi	1.60	1.60
214	A57	Sheet of 6, #a.-f.	9.00	9.00

Ajiniyoz Qo'siboy, Poet — A58

2000, Mar. 31 Litho. Perf. 14
215	A58	28s multi	1.25	1.25

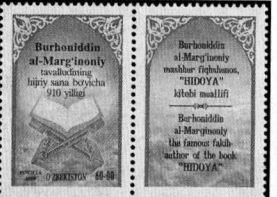

Famous Islamic Scholars — A59

Designs: No. 216, 60s, Burhan al-Din al-Marghinani. No. 217, 60s, Imam Abu Mansur al-Maturidi, horiz.

2000, Oct. 24 Stamp + label
216-217	A59	Set of 2	3.25	3.25

UN High Commissioner for Refugees, 50th Anniv. — A60

2000, Dec. 11
218	A60	125s multi + label	2.25	2.25

Bats A61

Designs: 15s, Tadarida teniotis. 30s, Otonycteris hemprichi. 45s, Nyctalus lasiopterus, vert. 50s, Myotis frater, vert. 60s, Rhinolophus hipposideros, vert. 90s, Barbastella leucomelas, vert. 125s, Nyctalus noctula, vert. 160s, Unidentified bat, vert.

2001, Feb. 23 Perf. 13¾x14, 14x13¾
219-225	A61	Set of 7	6.00	6.00

Souvenir Sheet
226	A61	160s multi	2.75	2.75

Dated 2000.

Native Costumes — A62

2001, Feb. 26 Perf. 14x13¾
227		Horiz. strip of 5 + label	6.00	6.00
a.	A62	45s multi	.50	.50
b.	A62	50s multi, diff.	.60	.60
c.	A62	60s multi, diff.	.70	.70
d.	A62	90s multi, diff.	1.00	1.00
e.	A62	125s multi, diff.	1.50	1.50

Dated 2000.

Arms Type of 1994 Redrawn
2001-05 Litho. Perf. 14
Size: 14x23mm
228	A10	15s emerald	.70	.70
229	A10	17s dull green	.70	.70
230	A10	20s dull green	.70	.70
231	A10	25s bright blue	.70	.70
232	A10	30s sky blue	.70	.70
232A	A10	30s green	.90	.90
a.		Dated "2004"	.90	.90
b.		light green, dated "2005"	.90	.90
233	A10	33s gray blue	.90	.90
234	A10	45s red	1.25	1.25
235	A10	50s rose	1.40	1.40
236	A10	60s rose pink	1.75	1.75
237	A10	100s rose, "2001"	2.10	2.10
a.		Dated "2003"	.85	.85
		Nos. 228-237 (11)	11.80	11.80

Issued: 15s, 17s, 25s, 33s, 50s, 60s, 100s, 4/3; 20s, 30s, 4/11; 45s, 6/22. No. 232A, 5/26/03; No. 232Aa, 6/15/04; No. 232Ab, 3/25/05. No. 237a, 5/26/03.

Ali Shir Nava'i (1441-1501), Poet — A63

2001, Apr. 11
238		Horiz. strip of 5 + label	8.25	8.25
a.	A63	60s Hayrat ul-abror	1.00	1.00
b.	A63	70s Farhod va Shirin	1.00	1.00
c.	A63	85s Layli va Majnun	1.25	1.25
d.	A63	90s Sab'ai sayyora	1.25	1.25
e.	A63	125s Saddi Iskandariy	1.75	1.75

World Environment Day — A64

2001, June 20
239	A64	100s multi	2.10	2.10

Avesto, 2700th Anniv. — A65

2001, June 20
240	A65	160s multi	2.50	2.50

Souvenir Sheet

Termiz, 2500th Anniv. — A66

2001, June 20
241	A66	175s multi	3.50	3.50

Souvenir Sheet

Independence, 10th Anniv. — A67

2001, June 20
242	A67	175s multi	3.50	3.50

Souvenir Sheet

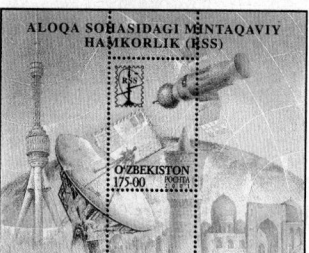

Regional Communications Cooperation — A68

2001, June 20
243	A68	175s multi	3.25	3.25

10th Anniv. of Independence Issue

Vertical Label

Horizontal Label

Tourist
Hotel — A69

Monuments — A70

Inauguration of Pres. Islam
Karimov — A71

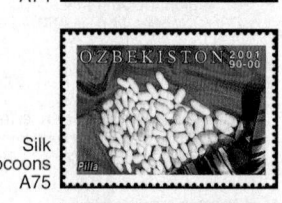

Pres.
Karimov at
United
Nations
A72

Pres.
Karimov at
Istanbul
Summit
A73

Hirmon
A74

Silk
Cocoons
A75

Fergana
Refinery
A76

Power
Station
A77

Daewoo
Auto
Factory
A78

Securities
Exchange
A79

Kamchik
Tunnel
A80

Pres.
Karimov
and US
Pres.
Clinton
A81

Pres.
Karimov
and
Russian
Pres.
Vladimir
Putin
A82

Pres.
Karimov
and
Japanese
Emperor
Akihito
A83

Pres.
Karimov
and
Chinese
Pres.
Jiang
Zemin
A84

Pres.
Karimov
and
German
Chancellor
Gerhard
Schröder
A85

Pres.
Karimov
and
French
Pres.
Jacques
Chirac
A86

Pres.
Karimov
and British
Prime
Minister
John
Major
A87

Pres. Karimov and Iranian Pres. Ali
Mohammad Khatami — A88

Pres.
Karimov
and
Egyptian
Pres.
Hosni
Mubarak
A89

Pres.
Karimov
and Italian
Pres.
Carlos
Ciampi
A90

Pres.
Karimov
and Indian
Pres.
Kocheril
Narayanan
A91

Pres.
Karimov
and Pope
John Paul
II — A92

Textile
Workers
A93

Shurtan Gas
Complex — A94

Muborak
Refinery — A95

Oil Pipeline — A96

Solar
Collector
A97

Soldiers
with Flag
A98

Missiles
A99

Soldiers
Training
A100

Kurash
Sports
Complex
A101

New Year's Celebration — A102

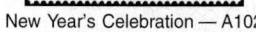

Mother and
Child — A103

Wedding
A104

Bukhara
Refinery — A105

Nuclear Power
Plant — A106

A70 Designs: No. 245, Zahriddin Bobur Monument. No. 246, Amir Temur Monument. No. 247, Al-Motorudi Mausoleum. No. 248, Al-Marginoniy Monument. No. 249, Jaloliddin Manguberdi Monument. No. 250, Al-Bukhoriy Mausoleum. No. 273, Alisher Navoi Monument. No 274, Berdakh Monument. No. 284, Alpomish Monument. No. 288, Al-Fargoni Monument.

2001   Litho.   Perf. 14x13¾, 13¾x14
Stamp + Label with Same Orientation

244	A69	60s multi	.50	.50
245	A70	60s multi	.50	.50
246	A70	70s multi	.50	.50
247	A70	75s multi	.50	.50
248	A70	75s multi	.50	.50
249	A70	85s multi	.70	.70
250	A70	90s multi	.70	.70
251	A71	90s multi	.70	.70
252	A72	90s multi	.70	.70
253	A73	90s multi	.70	.70
254	A74	90s multi	.70	.70
255	A75	90s multi	.70	.70
256	A76	90s multi	.70	.70
257	A77	90s multi	.70	.70
258	A78	90s multi	.70	.70
259	A79	90s multi	.70	.70
260	A80	90s multi	.70	.70
261	A81	95s multi	.80	.80
262	A82	95s multi	.80	.80
263	A83	95s multi	.80	.80
264	A84	95s multi	.80	.80
265	A85	95s multi	.80	.80
266	A86	95s multi	.80	.80
267	A87	95s multi	.80	.80
268	A88	95s multi	.80	.80
269	A89	95s multi	.80	.80
270	A90	95s multi	.80	.80
271	A91	95s multi	.80	.80
272	A92	95s multi	.80	.80
273	A70	115s multi	1.00	1.00
274	A70	115s multi	1.00	1.00
275	A93	115s multi	1.00	1.00
276	A94	115s multi	1.00	1.00
277	A95	115s multi	1.00	1.00
278	A96	115s multi	1.00	1.00
279	A97	115s multi	1.00	1.00
280	A98	115s multi	1.00	1.00
281	A99	115s multi	1.00	1.00
282	A100	115s multi	1.00	1.00
283	A101	115s multi	1.00	1.00
284	A70	125s multi	1.00	1.00
285	A102	125s multi	1.00	1.00
286	A103	125s multi	1.00	1.00
287	A104	125s multi	1.00	1.00
288	A70	160s multi	1.25	1.25
289	A105	160s multi	1.25	1.25
290	A106	160s multi	1.25	1.25
	Nos. 244-290 (47)		*39.25*	*39.25*

Nos. 244-290 were each printed in sheets of 2 stamps and 2 labels.
See No. 363.

Uzbekistan Arms — A107

Uzbekistan Flag — A108

Motor
Vehicles
A109

Central Bank
Building — A110

Bank Association
Building — A111

Tashkent
Khokimiyat
Building
A112

Central
Trade
Center
Building
A113

Shurtan
Gas
Complex
A114

Shurtan
Gas
Complex
A115

Couple
with Baby
A116

Children
A117

Farm Equipment
A118

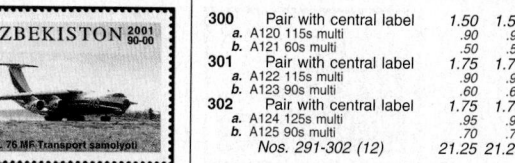

Airplanes
A119

Constitution
A120

Majlis Hall — A121

Gold
Ingots and
Coins
A122

Muruntay
Gold Mine
A123

Independence Day
Celebrations — A124

Independence Day
Celebrations — A125

A109 Designs: No. 292a, Nexia. No. 292b, Damas. No. 293a, Tico. No. 293b, Matiz.
A118 Designs: No. 298a, Case 2022 cotton picker. No. 298b, SHR-100 tractor.
A119 Designs: No. 299a, IL-76 MF cargo plane. No. 299b, IL-114-100 passenger plane.

291	Pair with central label	1.50	1.50
a.	A107 90s multi	.75	.75
b.	A108 90s multi	.75	.75
292	Pair with central label	1.50	1.50
a.-b.	A109 90s Any single	.75	.75
293	Pair with central label	1.50	1.50
a.-b.	A109 90s multi	.75	.75
294	Pair with central label	1.50	1.50
a.	A110 90s multi	.75	.75
b.	A111 90s multi	.75	.75
295	Pair with central label	1.50	1.50
a.	A112 90s multi	.75	.75
b.	A113 90s multi	.75	.75
296	Pair with central label	2.25	2.25
a.	A114 115s multi	1.10	1.10
b.	A115 115s multi	1.10	1.10
297	Pair with central label	2.25	2.25
a.	A116 125s multi	1.10	1.10
b.	A117 125s multi	1.10	1.10
298	Pair with central label	2.50	2.50
a.-b.	A118 160s Any single	1.25	1.25
299	Pair with central label	1.75	1.75
a.	A119 90s multi	.75	.75
b.	A119 115s multi	.95	.95
300	Pair with central label	1.50	1.50
a.	A120 115s multi	.90	.90
b.	A121 60s multi	.50	.50
301	Pair with central label	1.75	1.75
a.	A122 115s multi	.90	.90
b.	A123 90s multi	.60	.60
302	Pair with central label	1.75	1.75
a.	A124 125s multi	.95	.95
b.	A125 90s multi	.70	.70
	Nos. 291-302 (12)	*21.25*	*21.25*

Nos. 291-302 printed in sheets of four stamps and two labels (two pairs).
See Nos. 361-362, 364-366, 371.

Theater
A126

Theater
A127

Theater
A128

Medals — A129

Combine
A130

Combine
A131

Pres.
Karimov
and
Farmers
A132

Soldier
Taking
Oath
Before
Flag
A133

Man and
Soldier
Embracing
A134

Frontier Guards and Dog A135

Athletes — A136

Soldiers in Formation A137

Diver Training A138

Decontamination Training — A139

Modern Architecture — A140

Armed Forces — A141

Archaeology — A142

High School — A143

Uzbekistan on World Map — A144

A129 Designs: No. 304a, Dostelik. No. 304b, I Darajali "Shon-Sharaf." No. 304c, II Darajali "Shon-Sharaf." No. 305a, I Darajali Sog'lom Avlod Uchun. No. 305b, II Darajali Sog'lom Avlod Uchun. No. 305c, Mehnat Shuhrati. No. 306a, Jaloliddin Manguberdi. No. 306b, Buyuk Xizmatlari Uchun. No. 306c, El-Yurt Hurmati. No. 307a, Oltin Yildiz. No. 307b, Mustaqillik. No. 307c, Amir Temur.

A136 Designs: No. 310a, Muhammadqodir Abdullayev. No. 310b, Lina Cheryazova. No. 310c, Artur Grigoryan. No. 312a, 160s, Armen Bagdasarov. No. 312b, 160s, Rustam Qosimjonov. No. 312c, 115s, Otabek Kosimov. No. 312d, 115s, Iroda To'laganova. No. 312e, 100s, Dilshod Muxtorov. No. 312e, 115s, Oksana Chusovitina.

No. 313: a, Temuriylar Tarixi Muzeyi (Amir Temur Museum). b, Oqsaroy. c, Oliy Majlis. d, Motamsaro Ona (Monument to Grieving Mother). e, Shahidlar Xotirasi (Respect Monument). f, Interkontinental mehmonxonasi (Intercontinental Hotel). g, Milliy Bank (National Bank). h, Yunusobod Sport Majmuasi (Yunusobod Sport Complex).

No. 314: a, 60s, Infantrymen, tank. b, 70s, Airplane and crew. c, 80s, Helicopter and crew. d, 90s, Soldier directing tank with flags. e, 90s, Minesweeper. f, 115s, Soldiers in classroom. g, 160s, Tanks. h, 60s, Artillery.

No. 315: a, 75s, Pot. b, 75s, Artifact with arch. c, 75s, Artifact with hole at top and side. d, 80s, Broken pot. e, 80s, Anthropomorphic figure with arms. f, 80s, Buddha. g, 80s, Costumed figure. h, 80s, Disk. i, 80s, Anthropomorphic figure missing arm. j, 80s, Box. k, 80s, Face.

303	Strip of 3 + label	1.90	1.90
a.	A126 90s multi	.60	.60
b.	A127 90s multi	.60	.60
c.	A128 90s multi	.60	.60
304	Strip of 3 + label	3.25	3.25
a.-c.	A129 160s Any single	1.00	1.00
305	Strip of 3 + label	3.25	3.25
a.-c.	A129 160s Any single	1.00	1.00
306	Strip of 3 + label	3.25	3.25
a.-c.	A129 160s Any single	1.00	1.00
307	Strip of 3 + label	3.25	3.25
a.-c.	A129 160s Any single	1.00	1.00
308	Strip of 3 + label	3.25	3.25
a.	A130 160s multi	1.00	1.00
b.	A131 160s multi	1.00	1.00
c.	A132 160s multi	1.00	1.00
309	Strip of 3 + label	2.25	2.25
a.	A133 60s multi	.45	.45
b.	A134 80s multi	.60	.60
c.	A135 90s multi	.70	.70
310	Strip of 3 + label	3.00	3.00
a.	A136 160s multi	1.25	1.25
b.-c.	A136 115s Any single	.85	.85
311	Block of 3 + label	2.25	2.25
a.	A137 115s multi	.80	.80
b.	A138 80s multi	.60	.60
c.	A139 70s multi	.50	.50
	Nos. 303-311 (9)	25.65	25.65

Sheets

312	A136	Sheet of 6, #a-f, + 3 labels	5.50	5.50
313	A140	115s Sheet of 8, #a-h, + label	7.50	7.50
314	A141	Sheet of 8, #a-h, + label	5.50	5.50
315	A142	Sheet of 11, #a-k, + label	6.50	6.50

Souvenir Sheets

| 316 | A143 160s multi | 2.00 | 2.00 |
| 317 | A144 175s multi | 2.25 | 2.25 |

Labels have same orientation as stamps and are at left side of strips on Nos. 303-310, and at UR on No. 311. No. 312 contains three different labels.
See No. 370.

Commonwealth of Independent States, 10th Anniv. — A145

2001, Nov. 8   **Perf. 13¾x14**
318 A145 60s multi   1.40 1.40

Artwork of Oral Tansiqboyev — A146

No. 319: a, 100s, Mening Qo'shig'im (My Song). b, 125s, Angren-Qo'qon Tog'yo'li (Angren-Kokand Mountain Road).

2001, Nov. 8
319 A146   Pair, #a-b, with central label   5.00 5.00

Flowers — A147

Designs: 45s, Zygophyllum bucharicum. 50s, Viola hissarica. 60s, Bergenia hissarica. 70s, Eremurus hilariae. 85s, Salvia korolkowii. 90s, Lamyropappus schakaptaricus. 145s, Punica granatum. 175s, Undescribed flowers.

2002, May 10   **Litho.**   **Perf. 14x13¾**
320-326   A147   Set of 7   6.00 6.00

Souvenir Sheet
327 A147 175s multi   3.00 3.00

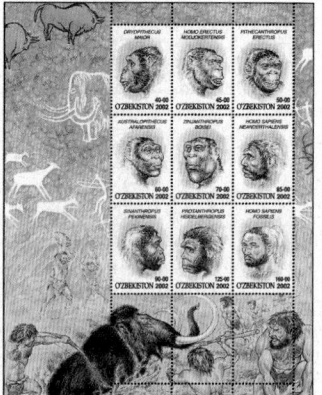

Hominids — A148

No. 328: a, 40s, Dryopithecus maior. b, 45s, Homo erectus modjokertensis. c, 50s, Pithecanthropus erectus. d, 60s, Australopithecus afarensis. e, 70s, Zinjanthropus boisei. f, 85s, Homo sapiens neanderthalensis. g, 90s, Sinanthropus pekinensis. h, 125s, Protanthropus heidelbergensis. i, 160s, Homo sapiens fossilis.

2002, May 10   **Perf. 13¾x14**
328 A148   Sheet of 9, #a-i, + 3 labels   7.50 7.50

Protection of Ozone Layer — A149

2002, June 7   **Litho.**   **Perf. 13¾x14**
329 A149 40s multi   1.25 1.25

Souvenir Sheet

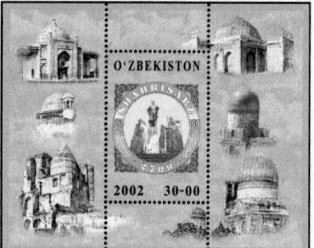

City of Shahrisabz, 2700th Anniv. — A150

2002, June 14   **Perf. 14**
330 A150 30s multi   1.00 1.00

Uzbek Sports A151

Designs: 45s, Chavgon. 50s, Poyga. 60s, Kamondan otish. 70s, Qiz quvmoq. 85s, Ro'molcha olish. 90s, Kurash. 145s, Uloq. 175s, Ro'molcha olish, diff.

2002, July 26   **Perf. 13¾x14**
331-337   A151   Set of 7   7.00 7.00

Souvenir Sheet
338 A151 175s multi   2.75 2.75

Ancient Coins — A152

No. 339: a, 30s, Silver tetradrachm of Eucratides I c. 171-135 BC, obverse. b, 45s, As "a," reverse. c, 60s, Silver coin of Buxoro, obverse. d, 90s, As "c," reverse. e, 125s, Silver miri of Tamerlane, 1370-1405, obverse. f, 160s, As "e," reverse.

2002, Aug. 1
339 A152   Block of 6, #a-f   6.00 6.00
See Nos. 367-369.

City of Nukus, 70th Anniv. — A153

2002, Oct. 2
340 A153 100s multi   1.60 1.60

Iris Varieties — A154

Designs: 15s, Qoraqum. 30s, Solnechniy zaychik. 45s, Simfoniya. 50s, Chimyon. 60s, Ikar. 90s, Babye leto. 125s, Toshkent. 160s, Askiya.

2002, Oct. 2   **Perf. 14x13¾**
341-347 A154   Set of 7   7.00 7.00

Souvenir Sheet
348 A154 160s multi   2.50 2.50

Uzbekistan postal officials have declared the following items as "illegal":
Sheets of eight stamps depicting Trains (4 different sheets with denominations of 56s, 75s, 95s and 125s);
Sheets of six stamps with various denominations depicting Birds (2 different), Animals, Year of the Snake, Chiroptera, Lizards, Chess;
Sheets of one label and five stamps with various denominations depicting Perissodactyla;
Souvenir sheets of one depicting Trains (8 different 36s sheets, 4 different 56s sheets, 2 different 75s sheets).

G'afur G'ulom (1903-66), Poet — A155

2003, May 4   Litho.   Perf. 13¾x14
349 A155 1000s brown   6.00 6.00

European Bank Annual Meeting Issue

Vertical Label

Horizontal Label

National Bank, Tashkent — A156

Kaltaminor Minaret, Khiva — A157

Aloqabank, Tashkent A158

Pres Karimov and European Bank for Reconstruction and Development Pres. Jean Lemierre — A159

Islamkhodja Minaret, Khiva — A160

East Gates, Khiva — A161

Samanid Museum, Bukhara — A162

Ark, Bukhara — A163

Women's Traditional Dress — A164

Women's Traditional Dress — A165

Women's Traditional Dress — A166

Women's Traditional Dress — A167

Women's Traditional Dress — A168

A157 Designs: 630s, Gumbazi Sayyidon Mausoleum, Shahrisabz. 920s, Go'ri Amir Mausoleum, Samarqand. 970s, Chorminor Madrasasi, Bukhara. 1330s, Registon, Samarqand, horiz.

2003, May 4   Perf. 14x13¾, 13¾x14
Stamp + Label with Same Orientation

350	A156	520s multi	6.25	6.25
351	A157	520s multi	6.25	6.25
352	A157	630s multi	7.25	7.25
353	A157	920s multi	11.00	11.00
354	A157	970s multi	12.00	12.00
355	A158	970s multi	12.00	12.00
356	A157	1330s multi	15.00	15.00
357	A159	1330s multi	15.00	15.00
358		Horiz. pair with central label	14.00	14.00
a.	A160	580s multi	6.25	6.25
b.	A161	520s multi	6.25	6.25
359		Horiz. pair with central label	21.00	21.00
a.	A162	1170s multi	12.50	12.50
b.	A163	630s multi	7.00	7.00
360		Horiz. strip of 5 with flanking label	27.50	27.50
a.	A164	240s multi	2.75	2.75
b.	A165	320s multi	4.00	4.00
c.	A166	520s multi	6.25	6.25
d.	A167	580s multi	6.25	6.25
e.	A168	630s multi	7.25	7.25

Types of 2001-02
Stamp + Label with Same Orientation

361	A110	520s multi	6.25	6.25
362	A111	580s multi	6.25	6.25
363		Horiz. pair with central label	14.00	14.00
a.	A74	170s multi	2.00	2.00
b.	A93	920s multi	11.00	11.00
364		Horiz. pair with central label	9.75	9.75
a.	A107	240s multi	2.75	2.75
b.	A108	520s multi	6.25	6.25
365		Horiz. pair with central label	10.00	10.00
a.	A114	630s multi	7.25	7.25
b.	A115	240s multi	2.75	2.75
366		Horiz. pair with central label	10.00	10.00
a.	A122	520s multi	6.25	6.25
b.	A123	320s multi	4.00	4.00
367		Horiz. pair with flanking label	14.00	14.00
a.	A152	520s Like #339a	6.25	6.25
b.	A152	520s Like #339b	6.25	6.25

368		Horiz. pair with flanking label	14.00	14.00
a.	A152	580s Like #339c	6.25	6.25
b.	A152	580s Like #339d	6.25	6.25
369		Horiz. pair with flanking label	15.00	15.00
a.	A152	630s Like #339e	7.25	7.25
b.	A152	630s Like #339f	7.25	7.25
370	A140	Sheet of 8 + central label	60.00	60.00
a.		520s Like #313a	6.25	6.25
b.		970s Like #313b	12.00	12.00
c.		580s Like #313c	6.25	6.25
d.		630s Like #313d	7.25	7.25
e.		320s Like #313e	4.00	4.00
f.		630s Like #313f	7.25	7.25
g.		920s Toshkent shahar hokimiyati (mayor's house)	11.00	11.00
h.		240s Like #313h	2.75	2.75

Type of 2001 Redrawn

371		Horiz. pair with central label	19.00	19.00
a.	A109	630s Like #292a	7.25	7.25
b.	A109	970s Like #293b	12.00	12.00
		Nos. 350-371 (22)	325.50	325.50

Famous Men — A169

Designs: 125s, Komil Yormatov, film director. 500s, Jo'raxon Sultonov, singer.

2003, July 8   Perf. 13¾x14
372-373 A169   Set of 2   5.00 5.00

Birds — A170

Designs: No. 374, 100s, Ciconia ciconia asiatica. No. 375, 100s, Ciconia nigra. No. 376, 125s, Platalea leucorodia. No. 377, 125s, Phoenicopterus ruber.

2003, Sept. 17   Perf. 14x13¾
374-377 A170   Set of 4   5.50 5.50

Caps — A171

Designs: No. 378, 100s, Kula-tung. No. 379, 100s, Erkaklar do'ppisi. No. 380, 100s, Bayram do'ppisi. No. 381, 125s, Ayollar do'ppisi. No. 382, 125s, Ayollar taxya-do'ppisi. No. 383, 155s, Erkaklar do'ppisi, diff. No. 384, 155s, Bolalar bayram do'ppisi.

2003, Oct. 7
378-384 A171   Set of 7   11.00 11.00

Paintings — A172

No. 385: a, Tong. Onalik, by R. Ahmedov. b, Baxt, by S. Ayitbayev.

2003, Nov. 19
385 A172 970s Horiz. pair, #a-
     b   13.00 13.00
       See Kazakhstan No. 434.

Abuxoliq G'ijduvoniy, Bukhara, 900th
Anniv. — A173

2003, Nov. 28   **Perf. 13¾x14**
386 A173 125s multi + label   1.60 1.60

Souvenir Sheet

2004 Summer Olympics,
Athens — A174

2004, June 15   Litho.   Perf. 14x13¾
387 A174 205s multi   3.00 3.00

Ma'murjon   Abdulla Qodiriy
Uzoqov (1904-   (1894-1938),
63),   Writer — A176
Singer — A175

2004, Oct. 11   **Perf. 14**
388 A175 100s lt blue & blk   1.50 1.50
389 A176 125s lt blue & blk   1.75 1.75

Grapes — A177

    Designs: 60s, Kaltak. No. 391, 100s, Oq
husayni. No. 392, 100s, Kattaqo'rg'on. No.
393, 125s, Echkemar. No. 394, 125s, Qizil
Xurmoni. 155s, Qora Andijon. 210s, Parkent.

2004, Oct. 11   **Perf. 14x13¾**
390-396 A177   Set of 7   12.00 12.00

Jewelry of 19th
and 20th
Centuries
A178

    Inscriptions: 60s, Tumor, Samarqand. No.
398, 100s, Tumor, Toshkent. No. 399, 100s,
Qi'ltiqtumor, Qo'qon. No. 400, 125s, Tumor,
Buxoro. No. 401, 125s, Bo'yintumor, Toshkent.
155s, Qo'ltiqtumor, Buxoro. 210s, Tumor, Buxoro, diff.

2004, Oct. 18
397-403 A178   Set of 7   14.00 14.00

Kitab State Geological Reserve, 25th
Anniv. — A179

2004, Dec. 1
404 A179 100s multi + label   2.00 2.00

Arms Type of 1994 Redrawn
2004-06   **Litho.**   **Perf. 14**
           Size: 14x23mm
405 A10   35s green   .25   .25
406 A10   60s green   .35   .35
    a.   light green, dated "2005"   .35   .35
407 A10   65s green   .40   .40
408 A10   125s dark blue   .60   .60
409 A10   200s red   .85   .85
410 A10   250s blue   1.10   1.10
411 A10   290s red   1.25   1.25
412 A10   350s blue   1.50   1.50
413 A10   430s red   1.75   1.75
414 A10   2500s red   10.00   10.00
415 A10   3700s blue   14.00   14.00
    Nos. 405-415 (11)   32.05   32.05

    Issued: No. 406, 6/15; Nos. 406a, 408,
4/15/05; others, 1/5/06. Nos. 405, 407, 409-
415 are dated "2005," though issued in 2006.

Oybek (1905-68),
Writer — A180

2005, Apr. 25   Litho.   Perf. 14x13¾
416 A180 125s multi   1.50 1.50

Miniature Sheet

End of World War II, 60th
Anniv. — A181

    No. 417: a, 60s, Veterans at war memorial.
b, 60s, Child with balloon at memorial. c, 100s,
Sculptures. d, 100s, Child looking at memorial.
e, 125s, Veterans looking at airplane sculpture. f, 125s, Woman passing soldiers. g,
155s, Soldier and floral display. h, 155s, Man
looking at scrapbook.

2005, May 6
417 A181   Sheet of 8, #a-h, +
            central label   8.50 8.50

Tashkent University of Information
Technologies, 50th Anniv. — A182

2005, May 25   **Perf. 13¾x14**
418 A182 125s multi + label   1.90 1.90

Qarshi, 2700th
Anniv. — A183

2005, Aug. 1
419 A183 125s multi   1.25 1.25

Doves — A184

    No. 420: a, 85s, Qopqon-chinni. b, 85s,
Ruyan. c, 100s, Novvoti. d, 100s, Oq kaptar. e,
125s, Juk. f, 125s, Chelkar. g, 155s, Udi. h,
155s, Gulsor.
      210s, Buxoro kaptari.

2005, Sept. 15
420 A184   Sheet of 8, #a-h   6.75 6.75
       Souvenir Sheet
421 A184 210s multi   2.75 2.75

Miniature Sheet

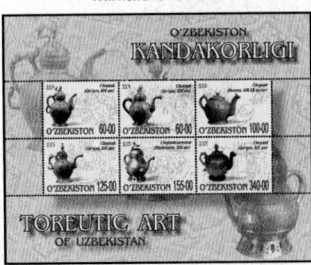

Toreutic Art — A185

    No. 422: a, 60s, Teapot with ribbed orna-
mentation. b, 60s, Teapot with round orna-
mentation. c, 100s, Teapot, diff. d, 125s, Teapot, diff. 155s, Teapot-samovar. 340s, Teapot
with square lid.

2005, Oct. 25
422 A185   Sheet of 6, #a-f   7.50 7.50

Ma'mun Academy,
1000th
Anniv. — A186

2005, Dec. 15   **Perf. 13¾x14**
423 A186 430s multi   2.75 2.75

Paintings
A187

    Designs: No. 424, 200s, Ko'i, by V. I. Yenin.
No. 425, 200s, Osuda Kun, by B. Boboyev,
vert. No. 426, 250s, Samarqand, Navro'z, by
G. Abdurahmanov, vert. No. 427, 250s,
Qo'qondagi Choyxona, by J. Umarbekov, vert.
No. 428, 300s, Oqtosh, by R. Ahmedov, vert.
No. 429, 300s, Yoz, by Y. P. Melnikov, vert.
350s, Kuz, by N. Qo'ziboyev, vert.

2006, Jan. 3   **Perf. 13¾x14, 14x13¾**
424-430 A187   Set of 7   10.00 10.00
       Dated 2005.

Rustam Qosimjonov, Intl. Chess
Federation World Champion — A188

2006, Jan. 5   **Perf. 13¾x14**
431 A188 200s multi   1.25 1.25
       Dated 2005.

Medalists at
2004 Summer
Olympics,
Athens — A189

    Designs: No. 432, 200s, Artur Taymazov,
120kg freestyle wrestling gold medalist. No.
433, 200s, Aleksandr Doxturushvili, 74kg
Greco-Roman wrestling gold medalist. 250s,
Magomed Ibragimov, 96kg freestyle wrestling
silver medalist. 350s, O'tkir Haydarov and
Bahodir Sultonov, 81kg and 54kg boxing
bronze medalists, horiz.

2006, Jan. 5   **Perf. 14x13¾, 13¾x14**
432-435 A189   Set of 4   5.50 5.50
       Dated 2005.

2006 Winter
Olympics,
Turin — A190

    Designs: 1540s, Skiing. 2155s, Figure
skating.

2006, May 19   Litho.   Perf. 14x13¾
436-437 A190   Set of 2   13.50 13.50

Musical Instruments
A191

Designs: 200s, Tanbur and Qashqar rubobi. 250s, Surnay and Tor. 290s, Surnay and Doira. 350s, Nay and Dutor. 410s, G'ijjak. 430s, Nog'om. 580s, Tanbur and Chang.

2006, May 19
438-444 A191 Set of 7   10.00 10.00

Dogs
A192

Designs: 350s, Labrador retriever. 540s, Cocker spaniel. 600s, German shepherd. 780s, Asian sheepdog.

1150s, Collie and German shepherd.

2006, May 19   **Perf. 13¾x14**
445-448 A192 Set of 4   9.00 9.00
Souvenir Sheet
449 A192 1150s multi   4.00 4.00

Souvenir Sheet

2006 World Cup Soccer Championships, Germany — A193

2006, May 19   **Perf. 14x13¾**
450 A193 720s multi   3.50 3.50

Fish — A194

No. 451: a, 45s, Salmo trutta aralensis. b, 90s, Acipenser nudiventris. c, 250s, Pseudoscaphirhynchus kaufmanni. d, 300s, Barbus brachcephalus.

1010s, Aspiolucius esocinus.

2006, July 10   **Perf. 13¾x14**
451 A194   Sheet of 4, #a-d   3.50 3.50
Souvenir Sheet
452 A194 1010s multi   4.25 4.25

Bell Tower, Tashkent
A195

Alisher Navoiy Theater
A196

2006, Aug. 10   **Perf. 14x13¾**
453 A195 55s green   .55 .55
        Perf. 13¾x14
454 A196 90s emerald   .75 .75
See Nos. 543, 545, 548, 597, 599. Compare with Type A249.

Butterflies
A197

Designs: 45s, Papilio alexanor. 90s, Parnassius mnemosyne. 200s, Parnassius apollonius. 250s, Parnassius maximinus. 300s, Parnassius honrathi. No. 460, 350s, Hypermnestra helios. No. 461, 350s, Parnassius charltonius.

1010s, Parnassius actius.

2006, Aug. 10   **Perf. 13¾x14**
455-461 A197 Set of 7   6.50 6.50
Souvenir Sheet
462 A197 1010s multi   4.75 4.75

15th Anniv. of Independence Issue

Horizontal Label

Vertical Label

Pres. Islam Karimov and Indian Prime Minister Manmohan Singh — A198

School and Children, Kokand — A199

House of Children's Creativity — A200

Senate Chamber — A201

Emblem of 2005 Intl. Cotton Fair, Tashkent, and Cotton Boll — A202

Pres. Karimov and People's Republic of China Chairman Hu Jintao — A203

Pres. Karimov and Latvian Pres. Vaire Vike-Fraiberg — A204

Qungirot Soda Factory — A205

Leaders at Shanghai Cooperation Organization Summit, Tashkent — A206

Cement Factory
A207

Railroad Construction — A208

Pres. Karimov and Graduates of Vaseda University — A209

Monument of Independence and Humanism — A210

Mine — A211

Bronze Smelter — A212

Festival — A213

Daewoo Nexia DOHC — A214

Kurash
A215

Intl. Kurash
Association
Medal
A216

Pres. Karimov and Cotton
Pickers — A217

Pres. Karimov and Cotton
Pickers — A218

Pres. Karimov and Farmers — A219

Roads — A220

Textiles — A221

Military — A222

Sports — A223

A198 Designs — Pres. Karimov and: No. 466, Malaysian King Tuanku Syed Sirajuddin. No. 470, Writer Said Akhmad. No. 474, Slovenian Pres. Janez Drnovsek. No. 477, Russian Pres. Vladimir Putin. No. 480, South Korean Pres. Roh Moo-hyun. No. 483, Uzbek labor leader.

A200 Designs: No. 469, Humanism Arch. No. 478, Medical School, Margilan. No. 484, Tashkent Railway Station. No. 486, Senate Building.

A206 Design: No. 482, Leaders at Euro-Asian Economic Union meeting.

A207 Design: No. 481, Angren Coal Mine.

A213 Design: No. 489b, 90s, Festival, diff.

A214 Design: No. 490b, 200s, Daewoo Damas II.

A215 Designs: No. 491b, 90s, Kurash, diff. No. 491c, 100s, Kurash, diff.

A216 Designs: No. 492b, 580s, FILA Wrestling medal. No. 492c, 720s, National Olympic Committee medal.

No. 494: a, 90s, Winding mountain road. b, 180s, Road construction. c, 55s, Highway.

No. 495: a, 410s, Workers and textile mill machinery. b, 580s, Women holding skeins of thread. c, 250s, Textile mill machinery.

No. 496: a, 410s, Soldiers in joint Uzbekistan-Russia anti-terrorism exercises, flags. b, 100s, Graduation of cadets. c, 250s, Soldiers at desks.

No. 497: a, 580s, Pres. Karimov and student athletes. b, 45s Stadium. c, 55s, Swimming meet. d, 90s, Athletes with medals. e, 200s, Karate. f, 250s, Soccer. g, 100s, Synchronized swimming. h, 290s, Equestrian event.

Perf. 13¾x14, 14x13¾
2006, Aug. 25
Stamp + Label With Same Orientation

463	A198	45s multi	.60	.60
464	A199	45s multi	.60	.60
465	A200	45s multi	.60	.60
466	A198	55s multi	.60	.60
467	A201	90s multi	.60	.60
468	A202	90s multi	.60	.60
469	A200	95s multi	.60	.60
470	A198	100s multi	.60	.60
471	A203	200s multi	1.00	1.00
472	A204	200s multi	1.00	1.00
473	A205	200s multi	1.00	1.00
474	A198	250s multi	1.25	1.25
475	A206	250s multi	1.25	1.25
476	A207	250s multi	1.25	1.25
477	A198	290s multi	1.50	1.50
478	A200	290s multi	1.50	1.50
479	A208	290s multi	1.50	1.50
480	A198	350s multi	1.50	1.50
481	A207	350s multi	1.50	1.50
482	A206	410s multi	2.00	2.00
483	A200	430s multi	2.10	2.10
484	A200	430s multi	2.10	2.10
485	A209	580s multi	3.00	3.00
486	A200	720s multi	3.75	3.75
487	A210	1010s multi	5.25	5.25
		Nos. 463-487 (25)	37.25	37.25

Pairs

488		Horiz. pair with central label	1.20	1.20
a.	A211	45s multi	.60	.60
b.	A212	45s multi	.60	.60
489		Horiz. pair with central label	1.20	1.20
a.	A213	45s multi	.60	.60
b.	A213	45s multi	.60	.60
490		Horiz. pair with central label	2.50	2.50
a.	A214	290s multi	1.50	1.50
b.	A214	200s multi	1.00	1.00
		Nos. 488-490 (3)	4.90	4.90

Strips

491		Strip of 3 + label	3.25	3.25
a.	A215	430s multi	2.10	2.10
b.	A215	90s multi	.60	.60
c.	A215	100s multi	.60	.60
492		Strip of 3 + label	9.00	9.00
a.	A216	410s multi	2.00	2.00
b.	A216	580s multi	3.00	3.00
c.	A216	720s multi	3.75	3.75
493		Strip of 3 + label	3.00	3.00
a.	A217	200s multi	1.00	1.00
b.	A218	250s multi	1.25	1.25
c.	A219	90s multi	.60	.60
		Nos. 491-493 (3)	15.25	15.25

Sheets

494	A220	Sheet of 3, #a-c, + label	1.60	1.60
495	A221	Sheet of 3, #a-c, + label	6.00	6.00
496	A222	Sheet of 3, #a-c, + label	3.75	3.75
497	A223	Sheet of 8, #a-h, + label	8.25	8.25
		Nos. 494-497 (4)	19.60	19.60

Nos. 463-475, 477-480, 482-486 were printed in sheets of 2 stamps and 2 labels. Nos. 476, 481 and 487 were printed in sheets of 5 stamps and 5 labels. Nos. 488-490 were printed in sheets of 4 stamps and 2 labels (2 pairs).

National Flag, 15th Anniv. — A224

2006, Nov. 1   **Perf. 13¾x14**
498   A224   600s multi + label   2.50   2.50

Miniature Sheet

Intl. Year of Deserts and Desertification — A225

No. 499: a, 45s, Oxyura leucocephala. b, 250s, Haliaeetus albicilla. c, 350s, Phalcrocorax pygmaeus. d, 350s, Marmaronetta angustirostris.

2006, Nov. 1
499   A225   Sheet of 4, #a-d   5.00   5.00

Roses — A226

Designs: 45s, Rosa divina. 90s, Rosa maracandica. 250s, Rosa persica. 350s, Rosa vassilczencoi.
600s, Rosa divina, diff.

2006, Nov. 1   **Perf. 14x13¾**
500-503   A226   Set of 4   4.25   4.25
Souvenir Sheet
504   A226   600s multi   2.00   2.00

Souvenir Sheet

Year of Charity and Medical Workers — A227

2006, Nov. 17   **Perf. 13¾x14**
505   A227   720s multi   2.75   2.75

Souvenir Sheet

Regional Communications Commonwealth, 15th Anniv. — A228

2006, Nov. 17
506   A228   1010s multi   4.75   4.75

2006 Asian Games, Doha, Qatar A229

Designs: 90s, High jump. 250s, Tennis. No. 509, 350s, Basketball. No. 510, 350s, Soccer.

2006, Dec. 27   **Litho.**   **Perf. 13¾x14**
507-510   A229   Set of 4   4.75   4.75

Diplomatic Relations Between Uzbekistan and People's Republic of China, 15th Anniv. — A230

2006, Dec. 29
511   A230   200s multi   1.25   1.25

Admission to the United Nations, 15th Anniv. — A231

2007, Mar. 1
512   A231   410s multi   1.75   1.75

Souvenir Sheet

Spring Festival — A232

2007, Mar. 1   **Perf. 14x13¾**
513 A232 1440s multi   5.75 5.75

2007 Winter Asian Games, Changchun, People's Republic of China — A233

Designs: 250s, Figure skating. 350s, Skiing.

2007, Mar. 1
514-515 A233 Set of 2   3.00 3.00

Abdulla Qahhor (1907-68), Writer — A234

No. 516: a, 350s, Scene from "Shohi So'zana." b, 420s, Qahhor.

2007, May 31   **Perf. 13¾x14**
516 A234 Horiz. pair, #a-b   3.25 3.25

Souvenir Sheets

A235

A236

A237

Architecture — A238

No. 517: a, 200s, Norbo'tabiy Madrasasi (madrassa). b, 410s, Daxmai Shohon Maqbarasi (mausoleum). c, 430s, Xudoyorxon Saroyi (palace).
No. 518: a, 250s, Modarixon Madrasasi (madrassa). b, 420s, Mir Arab Madrasasi (madrassa). c, 430s, Chor Bakr Me'moriy Majmuasi (mausoleum).
No. 519: a, 90s, Qo'shdarvoza (city gate). b, 250s, Muhammad Rahimxon Madrasasi (madrassa). c, 1010s, Pahlavon Mahmud Maqbarasi (mausoleum).
No. 520: a, 300s, Yunusxon Maqbarasi (mausoleum). b, 350s, Baroqxon Madrasasi (madrassa). c, Abulqosim Madrasasi (madrassa).

2007, May 31 **Perf. 13¾x14, 14x13¾**
517 A235 Sheet of 3, #a-c, + label   4.50 4.50
518 A236 Sheet of 3, #a-c, + label   4.50 4.50
519 A237 Sheet of 3, #a-c, + label   5.50 5.50
520 A238 Sheet of 3, #a-c, + label   5.50 5.50
          Nos. 517-520 (4)   20.00 20.00

Margilan, 2000th Anniv. — A239

2007, June 30   **Perf. 14x13¾**
521 A239 350s multi   1.40 1.40

Quddus Muhammadiy (1907-99), Poet — A240

2007, July 30   **Perf. 13¾x14**
522 A240 410s light blue & blk   1.60 1.60

Berries A241

Designs: 100s, Fragaria. 250s, Ribes nigrum. 580s, Rubus idaeus. 720s, Grossularia reclinata.

2007, July 30   **Litho.**
523-526 A241 Set of 4   6.75 6.75

Jewelry — A242

Designs: 300s, Yarim tirnoq. 350s, Ko'krak do'zi, horiz. 670s, Shovkala, horiz. 720s, Bodomoy.

2007, July 30 Perf. 14x13¾, 13¾x14
527-530 A242 Set of 4   8.25 8.25

Miniature Sheets

Samarqand, 2750th Anniv. — A243

No. 531: a, 45s, Registon Maydoni, Ulug'bel Madrasasi. b, 55s, Registon Maydoni, Sherdor Madrasasi. c, 100s, Registon Maydoni, Tillakori Madrasasi. d, 180s, Amir Temur Maqbarasi, Umumiy Ko'rinishi. e, 200s, Bibixonim Masjidi. f, 250s, Ruhobod Maqbarasi. g, 490s, Registon Maydoni, Umumiy Ko'rinishi. h, 720s, Shohisinda Majmuasi, Qo'shgumbazli Maqbara.
No. 532, vert.: a, 90s, Imom al-Moturidiy Maqbarasi. b, 100s, Imom Buxoriy Maqbarasi. c, 180s, Amir Temur Maqbarasi Kirish Peshtoqi. d, 200s, Amir Temur Haykali (statue). e, 410s, Bibixonim Maqbarasi. f, 680s, Shohizinda Majmuasi. g, 700s, Bibixonim Masjidi Kirish Peshtoqi. h, 1150s, Shohizinda Majmuasi, Tuman Oqo Maqbarasi.

2007, July 30   **Perf. 13¾x14**
531 A243 Sheet of 8, #a-h, + central label   8.00 8.00
          Perf. 14x13¾
532 A243 Sheet of 8, #a-h, + central label   14.00 14.00

Acinonyx Jubatus A244

Designs: 90s, Leaping. 490s, Resting. 680s, Walking. 780s, Standing. 1440s, Adult with juvenile, vert.

2007, Oct. 3   **Perf. 13¾x14**
533-536 A244 Set of 4   7.25 7.25
          Souvenir Sheet
          Perf. 14x13¾
537 A244 1440s multi   5.25 5.25

Souvenir Sheet

Tashkent Subway, 30th Anniv. — A245

No. 538: a, 540s, Train and system map. b, 780s, Subway emblem and station entrance.

2007, Nov. 20   **Perf. 14x13¾**
538 A245 Sheet of 2, #a-b   5.00 5.00

Constitution, 15th Anniv. — A246

2007, Dec. 5   **Litho.**
539 A246 600s multi   2.25 2.25

Miniature Sheet

Zahiruddin Muhammad Babur (1483-1530), Founder of Mughal Dynasty — A247

No. 540 — Inscriptions: a, 200s, Boburning toj kiyib Farg'ona taxtiga chiqishi (Coronation). b, 250s, Boburning Samarqandliklar tomonidan tantana bilan kutib olinishi (Samarqand people welcome Babur). c, 350s, Bobur Hirotda Sulton Huseyn xonadonida (Babur at Sultan Hussein's house). d, 350s, Bengaliya elchisi Bobur qabulida (Babur receives Bengal ambassador). e, 350s, Babur. f, 410s, Qobul qal'asining qamaldan ozod etilishi (Babur freeing Kabul fortress). g, 490s, Bobur Dehli atrofidagi maqbaralarni ziyorat qilmoqda (Babur views Delhi mausoleum). h, 540s, Qobul atrofidagi Xo'ja Seyoron chashmasi (Xo'ja Seyoron Spring near Kabul). i, 680s, Bobur Mon Sing va Bikramojit saroylarini tomosha qilmoqda (Babur views Man Singh and Bikramajit Palaces).

2008, Feb. 13
540 A247 Sheet of 9, #a-i   12.50 12.50

National Academic Drama Theater — A248

Alisher Navoiy Theater — A249

2008, Feb. 28   *Perf. 13¾x14*
541 A248 45s blue   .55   .55
542 A249 90s dark green   .55   .55

No. 542 has thicker lettering than No. 454.

Architecture Types of 2006-08
2008   Litho.   Perf. 13¾x14, 14x13¾
543 A195 30s green   .35   .35
544 A195 75s dark green   .35   .35
545 A195 85s dark green   .35   .35
546 A249 100s red   .35   .35
547 A249 150s dark green   .45   .45
548 A249 160s green   .45   .45
549 A248 200s red   .55   .55
550 A249 250s blue   .75   .75
551 A249 310s dark green   .90   .90
552 A248 350s blue   1.00 1.00
     Nos. 543-552 (10)   5.50 5.50

Issued: 75s, 85s, 150s, 310s, 350s, 4/1;
30s, 7/15; 100s, 11/25; 160s, 200s, 250s, 4/1.
See Nos. 598, 600-601.

Yahyo Gulomov
(1908-77),
Archaeologist
A250

2008, June 25   Litho.   Perf. 13¾x14
553 A250 150s multi   .65   .65

2008
Summer
Olympics,
Beijing
A251

Designs: 150s, Judo. 200s, Boxing. 250s,
Running. 310s, Rhythmic gymnastics, vert.

Perf. 13¾x14, 14x13¾
2008, June 25
554-557 A251   Set of 4   6.00 6.00

Flowers — A252

Designs: 150s, Cousinia butkovii. 200s,
Cousinia dshisakensis. 250s, Cousinia ade-
nophora. 310s, Cousinia angreni.

2008, June 25   *Perf. 14x13¾*
558-561 A252   Set of 4   3.00 3.00

Intl. Swimming Federation (FINA),
Cent. — A253

No. 562: a, 310s, Water polo. b, 450s, Synchronized swimming.
No. 563: a, 620s, Diving. b, 750s, Freestyle
swimming.

2008, July 24   *Perf. 14x13¾*
Horiz. Pairs, #a-b, + Central Label
562-563 A253   Set of 2   7.75 7.75

Souvenir Sheet

Navoi, 50th Anniv. — A254

No. 564: a, 930s, Farkhad monument, Culture Palace. b, 1250s, Gold bars.

2008, Oct. 22   *Perf. 13¾x14*
564 A254   Sheet of 2, #a-b, + 2
           labels   7.75 7.75

Writers — A255

Designs: 620s, Maqsud Shayxzoda (1908-
67). 750s, Mirzakalon Ismoiliy (1908-86).

2008, Nov. 5
565-566 A255   Set of 2   4.25 4.25

Men's Traditional
Costumes
A256

2008, Dec. 31   *Perf. 14x13¾*
567   Horiz. strip of 4 + label 9.50 9.50
  a. A256 310s Joma   1.00 1.00
  b. A256 350s Yaktak   1.10 1.10
  c. A256 750s Erkalar liboslari 2.50 2.50
  d. A256 1250s Joma, diff.   4.50 4.50

Louis Braille (1809-52), Educator of
the Blind — A257

2009, Feb. 2   Litho.   Perf. 13¾x14
568 A257 620s multi   2.00 2.00

Intl. Year of Astronomy — A258

No. 569: a, 350s, Observatory of Sultan
Ulugh Beg, Samarkand. b, 750s, Statue of
Ulugh Beg.

2009, Mar. 22   *Perf. 14x13¾*
569 A258   Horiz. pair, #a-b, +
           central label   3.50 3.50

Birds
A259

2009, Apr. 8   *Perf. 13¾x14*
570   Horiz. strip of 4   6.00 6.00
  a. A259 310s Rufibrenta ruticollis .90   .90
  b. A259 350s Cygnus cygnus   1.00 1.00
  c. A259 620s Aythya nyroca   1.75 1.75
  d. A259 750s Anser erythropus 2.25 2.25

A260

A261

A262

A263

A264

Children's
Art — A265

2009, June 1   *Perf. 13¾x14*
571 A260 200s multi   .60   .60
572 A261 200s multi   .60   .60
573 A262 200s multi   .60   .60

Perf. 14x13¾
574 A263 200s multi   .60   .60
575 A264 200s multi   .60   .60
576 A265 200s multi   .60   .60
     Nos. 571-576 (6)   3.60 3.60

2010 Youth
Olympic Games,
Singapore
A266

Designs: 450s, Basketball. 750s, Soccer,
horiz.

2009, July 1   *Perf. 14x13¾, 13¾x14*
577-578 A266   Set of 2   3.75 3.75

Miniature Sheet

Tashkent, 2200th Anniv. — A267

No. 579: a, 310s, Majlis Building (Oliy Majlis
binosi). b, 310s, Senate Building (Senat
binosi). c, 350s, Intl. Business Center (Xalqaro
biznes markazi). d, 350s, Temurids History
Museum (Temuriylar tarixi davlat muzeyi). e,
620s, Turkistan Palace (Turkiston saroyi). f,
620s, Madrassa (Hazrat Imom majmuasi
Baroqxon madrasasi). g, 750s, Museum of
Victims of Oppression. h, 750s, Map of Great
Silk Road.

2009, Aug. 17   *Perf. 13¾x14*
579 A267   Sheet of 8, #a-h   12.00 12.00

Cities Along the
Great Silk
Road — A268

Designs: 350s, Khiva. 750s, Madrassa,
Tashkent.
1250s, Samarkand Gate, Bukhara.

2009, Oct. 9   *Perf. 14x13¾*
580-581 A268   Set of 2   3.00 3.00

Souvenir Sheet
582 A268 1250s multi   3.50 3.50

Theater Types of 2009
2009, Dec. 1   Litho.   Perf. 13¾x14
583 A248 450s red   1.40 1.40
584 A249 600s blue   1.60 1.60

Circus Performers
A269

Designs: 450s, Two women on horse. 600s, Three women on two horses. 1200s, Three women on horse.

2009, Dec. 28   **Perf. 14x13¾**
585-587 A269   Set of 3   6.25 6.25

Carpet Designs A270

No. 588: a, Samarqand, 19th cent. b, Andijon, 20th cent.
No. 589: a, Bukhara, 19th cent. b, Tashkent, 20th cent.

2009, Dec. 28   **Perf. 13¾x14**
588   Horiz. pair + central label   4.00 4.00
   a. A270 450s multi   1.00 1.00
   b. A270 1200s multi   3.00 3.00
589   Horiz. pair + central label   4.00 4.00
   a. A270 600s multi   1.50 1.50
   b. A270 1000s multi   2.50 2.50

Endangered Flora — A271

Designs: 450s, Fritillaria eduardii. 1200s, Iridodictyum winklerii.

2010, Jan. 26   **Perf. 14x13¾**
590-591 A271   Set of 2   4.50 4.50

Tashkent Zoo Animals — A272

Designs: 450s, Macaca sinica. 800s, Macaca fascicularis. 1000s, Mandrillus sphinx. 1650s, Lemur catta, horiz.

2010, Feb. 12   **Perf. 14x13¾**
592-594 A272   Set of 3   3.00 3.00
Souvenir Sheet
Perf. 13¾x14
595 A272 1650s multi   2.25 2.25

Amir Temur Monument, Shahrisabz — A273

Qarshi Railroad Station A274

2010, Mar. 29   **Perf. 13¾x14**
596   Horiz. pair + central label   2.60 2.60
   a. A273 800s multi   1.00 1.00
   b. A274 1200s multi   1.60 1.60

Sites in Kashkadarya Vilayet.

Architecture Types of 2006-08
2010, Apr. 1   **Perf. 14x13¾, 13¾x14**
597 A195   25s green   .25 .25
598 A248   100s green   .25 .25
599 A195   110s green   .25 .25
600 A248   125s green   .25 .25
601 A248   200s green   .25 .25
    Nos. 597-601 (5)   1.25 1.25

Endangered Birds — A275

Designs: 400s, Chettusia gregaria. 800s, Myiophonus caeruleus. 1000s, Tichodroma muraria. 1200s, Grus leucogeranus. 1900s, Cygnus olor.

2010, Apr. 15   **Perf. 14x13¾**
602-605 A275   Set of 4   4.25 4.25
Souvenir Sheet
606 A275 1900s multi   2.40 2.40

No. 606 contains one 37x52mm stamp.

43rd Annual Meeting of the Asian Development Bank Board of Governors Issue

Horizontal Label

Vertical Label

Combine A276

Irrigation Canal A277

Bukhara Oil Refinery A278

Fergana Oil Refinery A279

Tractor Trailer A280

Train A281

Poytaxt Business Center A282

Uzbekistan Forum — A283

Sitorai Mohi Xosa Palace, Bukhara A284

Hazrati Imam Complex, Tashkent A285

Majlis A286

Conservatory Building — A287

Arch A288

Tashkent Business Center A289

Senate Building A290

White Palace A291

Highway Cloverleaf A292

Highway and Bridge A293

Two Highways A294

Bridge Over Highway A295

Seamstresses — A296

Pottery Shop A297

Water Polo A298

Parade of Competitors at Yunusabad Sports Complex — A299

Construction Vehicles — A300

Railway Bridge A301

Daewoo Automobile Plant — A302

Tashkent Tractor Factory A303

Students in Laboratory — A304

Children in Computer Class A305

Flag of Uzbekistan — A306

Coat of Arms A307

Bank Association Building — A308

Central Bank Building — A309

Man and Woman in Traditional Clothes — A310

Man, Woman and Child in Traditional Clothes — A311

Infant and Nurse — A312

Surgeons in Operating Room — A313

2010, Apr. 15   *Perf. 13¾x14*

607	Horiz. pair + central label		
		2.25	2.25
a.	A276 800s multi	1.00	1.00
b.	A277 1000s multi	1.25	1.25
608	Horiz. pair + central label		
		2.25	2.25
a.	A278 800s multi	1.00	1.00
b.	A279 1000s multi	1.25	1.25
609	Horiz. pair + central label		
		2.50	2.50
a.	A280 800s multi	1.00	1.00
b.	A281 1200s multi	1.50	1.50
610	Horiz. pair + central label		
		2.50	2.50
a.	A282 800s multi	1.00	1.00
b.	A283 1200s multi	1.50	1.50
611	Horiz. pair + central label		
		2.50	2.50
a.	A284 800s multi	1.00	1.00
b.	A285 1200s multi	1.50	1.50
612	Horiz. pair + central label		
		2.50	2.50
a.	A286 800s multi	1.00	1.00
b.	A287 1200s multi	1.50	1.50
613	Horiz. pair + central label		
		2.50	2.50
a.	A288 800s multi	1.00	1.00
b.	A289 1200s multi	1.50	1.50
614	Horiz. pair + central label		
		2.50	2.50
a.	A290 800s multi	1.00	1.00
b.	A291 1200s multi	1.50	1.50
615	Horiz. pair + central label		
		2.50	2.50
a.	A292 900s multi	1.10	1.10
b.	A293 1100s multi	1.40	1.40
616	Horiz. pair + central label		
		2.50	2.50
a.	A294 900s multi	1.10	1.10
b.	A295 1100s multi	1.40	1.40
617	Horiz. pair + central label		
		2.60	2.60
a.	A296 900s multi	1.10	1.10
b.	A297 1200s multi	1.50	1.50
618	Horiz. pair + central label		
		2.60	2.60
a.	A298 900s multi	1.10	1.10
b.	A299 1200s multi	1.50	1.50
619	Horiz. pair + central label		
		2.75	2.75
a.	A300 1000s multi	1.25	1.25
b.	A301 1200s multi	1.50	1.50
620	Horiz. pair + central label		
		2.75	2.75
a.	A302 1000s multi	1.25	1.25
b.	A303 1200s multi	1.50	1.50
621	Horiz. pair + central label		
		2.75	2.75
a.	A304 1000s multi	1.25	1.25
b.	A305 1200s multi	1.50	1.50
622	Horiz. pair + central label		
		2.75	2.75
a.	A306 1000s multi	1.25	1.25
b.	A307 1200s multi	1.50	1.50

Perf. 14x13¾

623	Horiz. pair + central label		
		2.50	2.50
a.	A308 800s multi	1.00	1.00
b.	A309 1200s multi	1.50	1.50
624	Horiz. pair + central label		
		2.60	2.60
a.	A310 900s multi	1.10	1.10
b.	A311 1200s multi	1.50	1.50
625	Horiz. pair + central label		
		2.60	2.60
a.	A312 900s multi	1.10	1.10
b.	A313 1200s multi	1.50	1.50
	Nos. 607-625 (19)	48.40	48.40

Miniature Sheet

Victory in World War II, 65th Anniv. — A314

No. 626: a, 400s, Young people giving flowers to veterans. b, 800s, Ceremony at Grieving Mother Monument. c, 1000s, Soldier, women and children. d, 1200s, Celebratory ceremony with soldiers.

2010, May 9   *Perf. 13¾x14*
626   A314   Sheet of 4, #a-d   4.25   4.25

2010 Youth Olympics, Singapore A315

2010, July 12   *Perf. 14x13¾*
627   A315   800s multi   1.00   1.00

Uzbekistan-China Gas Pipeline — A316

2010, July 15   **Litho.**
628   A316   250s multi   .30   .30

Miniature Sheet

19th Century Copperware — A317

No. 629: a, 400s, Bucket, Central Asia. b, 800s, Bowl and pitcher, Khiva. c, 1000s, Pitcher and warming plate, Kokand. d, 1200s, Tray and pitcher, Khiva and Bukhara.

2010, Aug. 25   *Perf. 13¾x14*
629   A317   Sheet of 4, #a-d   4.25   4.25

Tulips — A318

Designs: 400s, Tulipa micheliana. 800s, Tulipa dasystemon. No. 632, 1000s, Tulipa lehmaniana. No. 633, 1200s, Tulipa bifloriformis.

No. 634: a, 1000s, Three Tulipa dasystemon. b, 1900s, One Tulipa dasystemon, rock.

2010, Sept. 27   *Perf. 14x13¾*
630-633   A318   Set of 4   4.25   4.25

Souvenir Sheet
634   A318   Sheet of 2, #a-b   3.75   3.75

Fish A319

Designs: 800s, Pterois volitans. No. 636, 1000s, Trichogaster leeri. 1200s, Carassius auratus.

No. 638: a, 1000s, Pterophyllum scalare. b, 1900s, Trichogaster leeri, diff.

2010, Oct. 9   *Perf. 13¾x14*
635-637   A319   Set of 3   3.75   3.75

Souvenir Sheet
638   A319   Sheet of 2, #a-b   3.75   3.75

16th Asian Games, Guangzhou, China — A320

2010, Oct. 25   **Litho.**
639   A320   800s multi   1.00   1.00

Protection of
Polar Regions
and
Glaciers — A321

2010, Oct. 25   *Perf. 14x13¾*
640 A321 900s multi   1.10 1.10

Bobur Monument, Andijon — A322

Olympic
Sports
College,
Andijon
A323

2010, Dec. 30   *Perf. 13¾x14*
641   Horiz. pair + central label 2.60 2.60
a.   A322 900s multi   1.10 1.10
b.   A323 1200s multi   1.50 1.50

Sites in Andijon Vilayet.

Soyib Xo'jayev
(1910-82),
Actor — A324

2010, Dec. 30   *Perf. 14x13¾*
642 A324 900s multi   1.10 1.10

Seventh Asian
Winter Games,
Astana and
Almaty — A325

Designs: 800s, Figure skater. 900s, Freestyle skier.

2011, Jan. 5
643-644 A325   Set of 2   2.10 2.10

Flowers — A326

Designs: 800s, Lagochilus vevedenskyi.
900s, Echinops babtagensis. No. 647, 1000s,
Saxifraga hirculus. 1200s, Nathaliella alaica.
   No. 649: a, 1000s, Eremus korolkovii, plant
21mm tall. b, 1900s, Eremus korolkovii, plant
37mm tall.

2011, Mar. 31
645-648 A326   Set of 4   4.75 4.75
   Souvenir Sheet
649 A326   Sheet of 2, #a-b   3.50 3.50

Miniature Sheet

Carved Wood Items — A327

No. 650: a, 800s, Table, 1983. b, 900s,
Round covered box, 1984. c, 1000s, Lavh,
1990. d, 1200s, Decorative pumpkin, 1985.

2011, Apr. 12   *Perf. 13¾x14*
650 A327   Sheet of 4, #a-d   4.75 4.75

A328

A329

A330

Children's
Art — A331

2011, June 1
651 A328 500s multi   .60   .60
652 A329 500s multi   .60   .60
653 A330 500s multi   .60   .60
654 A331 500s multi   .60   .60
   Nos. 651-654 (4)   2.40 2.40

Independence, 20th Anniv. Issue

Vertical Label

Horizontal
Label

Navoiyazot Gas
Tanks — A332

Maxam-Chirchiq
Fertilizer
Plant — A333

Wedding
Hall,
Termez
A334

Archaeological Museum,
Termez — A335

Plaza,
Urgench
A336

Al-Xorazmi Monument,
Urgench — A337

Theater,
Bukhara
A338

Monument, Bukhara — A339

Jokorgi
Kenes
Building,
Nukus
A340

Berdaq
Museum,
Nukus
A341

Sports Complex, Namangan — A342

Aloqabank Building,
Namangan — A343

Daewoo Automotive Plant — A344

Captiva, Epica and Spark
Automobiles, Car Dealership — A345

Highway
Cloverleaf
A346

Highway
Overpass
A347

Regional
Pre-natal
Center,
Gulistan
A348

Denausky Medical Association
Hospital — A349

Independence Day
Celebrations — A350

Ballet
Dancers
A351

High
Jumper
Svetlana
Radzivil
A352

Judoka
Rishat
Sabirov
and
Opponent
A353

Zarafshansky
Gold Mining
Complex — A354

Bekabadsky
Metallurgical
Complex — A355

Wedding Hall, Samarkand — A356

Concert Hall, Samarkand — A357

Academic Lyceum, State University,
Karshi — A358

Fergana Branch of Tashkent University
of Information Technology — A359

Youth
Center,
Andijan
A360

College
of Light
Industry,
Andijan
A361

Worker at Control Center of MTS-
Uzbekistan Company — A362

Uztelecom Control Center — A363

Textile
Factory,
Bukhara
A364

Gulistansky Textile Factory — A365

Talimarzhdansky Power Plant — A366

Sogdiana Substation — A367

Kungradsky Soda Factory — A368

Shurtangas Oil Pumps — A369

Mountains in Winter — A370

Mountains in Spring — A371

Gissar
National
Park
A372

Gissar
National
Park
A373

Uzbekistan Forum, Tashkent — A374

Educational Center, Tashkent — A375

Buildings,
Kokand
A376

Park
Gazebos,
Kokand
A377

Isuzu Automotive Factory,
Samarqand — A378

Isuzu
Truck
A379

Bodomzor Subway Station — A380

Train on Tashguzar-Baysun-
Kumkurgan Bridge — A381

Eski
Machit
Dancers
A382

Musicians
With
Karnays
A383

National Library and Monument to
Amir Temur (Tamerlane) — A384

Perf. 14x13¾ (#655, 666), 13¾x14
2011, Aug. 29   Litho.
655		Horiz. pair + central label		
			2.40	2.40
a.	A332 800s multi		.95	.95
b.	A333 1200s multi		1.40	1.40
656		Horiz. pair + central label		
			2.40	2.40
a.	A334 800s multi		.95	.95
b.	A335 1200s multi		1.40	1.40
657		Horiz. pair + central label		
			2.40	2.40
a.	A336 800s multi		.95	.95
b.	A337 1200s multi		1.40	1.40
658		Horiz. pair + central label		
			2.40	2.40
a.	A338 800s multi		.95	.95
b.	A339 1200s multi		1.40	1.40
659		Horiz. pair + central label		
			2.40	2.40
a.	A340 800s multi		.95	.95
b.	A341 1200s multi		1.40	1.40
660		Horiz. pair + central label		
			2.40	2.40
a.	A342 800s multi		.95	.95
b.	A343 1200s multi		1.40	1.40
661		Horiz. pair + central label		
			2.40	2.40
a.	A344 800s multi		.95	.95
b.	A345 1200s multi		1.40	1.40
662		Horiz. pair + central label		
			2.40	2.40
a.	A346 800s multi		.95	.95
b.	A347 1200s multi		1.40	1.40
663		Horiz. pair + central label		
			2.40	2.40
a.	A348 800s multi		.95	.95
b.	A349 1200s multi		1.40	1.40
664		Horiz. pair + central label		
			2.40	2.40
a.	A350 800s multi		.95	.95
b.	A351 1200s multi		1.40	1.40
665		Horiz. pair + central label		
			2.40	2.40
a.	A352 800s multi		.95	.95
b.	A353 1200s multi		1.40	1.40
666		Horiz. pair + central label		
			2.50	2.50
a.	A354 900s multi		1.10	1.10
b.	A355 1200s multi		1.40	1.40
667		Horiz. pair + central label		
			2.50	2.50
a.	A356 900s multi		1.10	1.10
b.	A357 1200s multi		1.40	1.40
668		Horiz. pair + central label		
			2.50	2.50
a.	A358 900s multi		1.10	1.10
b.	A359 1200s multi		1.40	1.40
669		Horiz. pair + central label		
			2.50	2.50
a.	A360 900s multi		1.10	1.10
b.	A361 1200s multi		1.40	1.40
670		Horiz. pair + central label		
			2.50	2.50
a.	A362 900s multi		1.10	1.10
b.	A363 1200s multi		1.40	1.40
671		Horiz. pair + central label		
			2.50	2.50
a.	A364 900s multi		1.10	1.10
b.	A365 1200s multi		1.40	1.40
672		Horiz. pair + central label		
			2.50	2.50
a.	A366 900s multi		1.10	1.10
b.	A367 1200s multi		1.40	1.40
673		Horiz. pair + central label		
			2.50	2.50
a.	A368 900s multi		1.10	1.10
b.	A369 1200s multi		1.40	1.40
674		Horiz. pair + central label		
			2.50	2.50
a.	A370 900s multi		1.10	1.10
b.	A371 1200s multi		1.40	1.40
675		Horiz. pair + central label		
			2.50	2.50
a.	A372 900s multi		1.10	1.10
b.	A373 1200s multi		1.40	1.40
676		Horiz. pair + central label		
			2.75	2.75
a.	A374 1000s multi		1.25	1.25
b.	A375 1200s multi		1.40	1.40
677		Horiz. pair + central label		
			2.75	2.75
a.	A376 1000s multi		1.25	1.25
b.	A377 1200s multi		1.40	1.40
678		Horiz. pair + central label		
			2.75	2.75
a.	A378 1000s multi		1.25	1.25
b.	A379 1200s multi		1.40	1.40
679		Horiz. pair + central label		
			2.75	2.75
a.	A380 1000s multi		1.25	1.25
b.	A381 1200s multi		1.40	1.40
680		Horiz. pair + central label		
			2.75	2.75
a.	A382 1000s multi		1.25	1.25
b.	A383 1200s multi		1.40	1.40

**Litho. & Embossed With Foil
Application
Perf. 14**
681	A384 15,000s multi		17.50	17.50
	Nos. 655-681 (27)		82.65	82.65

Souvenir Sheet

Regional Communications
Commonwealth, 20th Anniv. — A385

2011, Nov. 1   Litho.   **Perf. 14x13¾**
682	A385 2000s multi		2.25	2.25

Campaign
Against AIDS,
30th
Anniv. — A386

2011, Dec. 16
683	A386 900s multi		1.00	1.00

Miniature Sheet

Uzbekistan Armed Forces, 20th
Anniv. — A387

No. 684: a, 200s, Soldier with parents. b,
550s, Soldier reading proclamation, honor
guard with flag. c, 700s, Soldier with wife and
child. d, 900s, Helicopter. e, 1000s, Soldiers in
camouflage. f, 1200s, Soldiers taking oath. g,
1900s, Military academy classroom. h, 2150s,
Tank.

2012, Jan. 3   **Perf. 13¾x14**
684	A387	Sheet of 8, #a-h, + central label	9.50	9.50

Monuments — A388

Monuments commemorating: 100s, 450s,
600s, Amir Temur (Tamerlane, 1336-1405),
conqueror. 150s, 170s, Berdaq (1827-1900),
poet. 250s, 300s, Muhammad Al-Khorezmi (c.
780-c.850), mathematician, horiz.

2012   **Perf. 14x13¾, 13¾x14**
685	A388 100s green		.25	.25
686	A388 150s green		.25	.25
687	A388 170s green		.25	.25
688	A388 250s green		.30	.30
689	A388 300s green		.35	.35
690	A388 450s green		.50	.50
691	A388 600s green		.65	.65
	Nos. 685-691 (7)		2.55	2.55

Issued: 100s, 5/5; others, 4/5. See Nos.
711-713, 723-725, 736, 754-755.

Paintings
A389

Designs: 800s, Onalik O'ylari, by Rakhim
Ahmedov. 900s, Lagan O'yini, by Dzhavlon
Umarbekov. 1000s, Bog'da, by Shorasul
Shoahmedov. 1200s, Chavgon O'yini, by
Shoahmedov.

2012, June 5   **Perf. 14x13¾**
692-695	A389	Set of 4	4.25	4.25

Flowers — A390

Designs: 800s, Hedysarum angrenicum.
900s, Cousinia glabriseta. No. 698, 1000s,
Oxytropis pseudoleptophysa. 1200s, Phlo-
moides tschimganica.
No. 700: a, 1000s, Scorzonera bungei. b,
1900s, Spirostegia bucharica.

2012, June 5
696-699	A390	Set of 4	4.25	4.25

Souvenir Sheet
700	A390	Sheet of 2, #a-b	3.25	3.25

Al-Xakim at-Termizi Mausoleum,
Termez — A391

Riders in Game of Ulok-
kupkari — A392

2012, June 20   **Perf. 13¾x14**
701		Horiz. pair + central label	2.25	2.25
a.	A391 900s multi		1.00	1.00
b.	A392 1200s multi		1.25	1.25

2012
Summer
Olympics,
London
A393

2012, July 27
702	A393 800s multi		.85	.85

Endangered
Animals — A394

Designs: 400s, Mellivora capensis indica.
800s, Falco pelegrinoides. No. 705, 1000s,
Hemiechinus hypomelas. 1200s, Lutra lutra
seistanicus.
No. 707, Lynx lynx isabellina.

2012, Aug. 27   **Perf. 14x13¾**
703-706	A394	Set of 4	3.50	3.50

Souvenir Sheet
707	A394 1000s multi		1.00	1.00

Miniature Sheet

Akhal-Teke Horses — A395

No. 708: a, 950s, Amirana. b, 950s, G'ayrat.
c, 950s, Asmanbek. d, 1050s, Go'zalli. e,
1050s, Ayg'ir. f, 1050s, Gallas. g, 2200s, Geldi
Botir. h, 2200s, Xon. i, 2200s, Potmagul.

2012, Sept. 25   **Perf. 14**
708	A395	Sheet of 9, #a-i	13.00	13.00

Miniature Sheet

Soccer in Uzbekistan, Cent — A396

No. 709 — Various soccer players: a, 600s.
b, 650s, c, 950s. d, 1050s. e, 1150s. f, 1300s.
g, 2200s. h, 2500s.

2012, Sept. 25   **Perf. 13¾x14**
709	A396	Sheet of 8, #a-h, + central label	11.00	11.00

2012
Summer
Olympics,
London
A397

2012, Oct. 25   Litho.
710	A397 900s multi		.95	.95

Monuments Type of 2012

Monument commemorating: 50s, 200s,
Berdaq. 350s, Muhammad Al-Khorezmi, horiz.

2012, Nov. 9   **Perf. 14x13¾, 13¾x14**
711	A388 50s green		.25	.25
712	A388 200s green		.25	.25
713	A388 350s green		.35	.35
	Nos. 711-713 (3)		.85	.85

Tashkent Zoo Animals — A398

Designs: 400s, Threskiornis aethiopicus. 800s, Dolichotis patagonum. 1000s, Struthio camelus. 1200s, Elephas maximus.

2012, Dec. 28   **Perf. 14x13¾**
714-716 A398   Set of 3   2.25 2.25
Souvenir Sheet
717 A398 1200s multi   1.25 1.25

Flora and Fauna of Chatkal National Biosphere Reserve A399

Designs: No. 718, 800s, Trichius fasciatus. No. 719, 900s, Juno tubergeniana. No. 720, 1000s, Bubo bubo. No. 721, 1200s, Ursus arctos isabellinus.
No. 722, vert: a, 1000s, Marmota menzbieri. b, 1900s, Marmota menzbieri, diff.

2012, Dec. 28   **Perf. 13¾x14**
718-721 A399   Set of 4   4.00 4.00
Souvenir Sheet
Perf. 14x13¾
722 A399   Sheet of 2, #a-b   3.00 3.00

Monuments Type of 2012
Monuments commemorating: 110s, Amir Temur (Tamerlane, 1336-1405), conqueror. 400s, 1500s, Muhammad Al-Khorezmi (c. 780-c. 850), mathematician, horiz.

Perf. 14x13¾, 13¾x14
2013, June 5   **Litho.**
723 A388   110s green   .25 .25
724 A388   400s green   .60 .60
725 A388   1500s green   2.25 2.25
    Nos. 723-725 (3)   3.10 3.10

Architecture of the Great Silk Road — A400

Designs: 1400s, Buildings, Bukhara. 1500s, Kutlug-Murad-inak Madrassa, Khiva.
3200s, Ota Darvoza, Khiva, and map of Great Silk Road.

2013, June 5   **Litho.**   **Perf. 14**
726-727 A400   Set of 2   4.50 4.50
Souvenir Sheet
728 A400 3200s multi   5.00 5.00

Flora — A401

Designs: 1400s, Cousinia platystegia. 1500s, Diospyros lotus.

2013, June 17   **Litho.**   **Perf. 14**
729-730 A401   Set of 2   4.75 4.75

Sports A402

Designs: No. 731, 1500s, Judo. No. 732, 1500s, Fencing.

2013, June 17   **Litho.**   **Perf. 14**
731-732 A402   Set of 2   5.00 5.00

2013 Summer Universiade, Kazan, Russia (No. 731); 2013 Asian Youth Games, Nanjing, People's Republic of China (No. 732).

Miniature Sheet

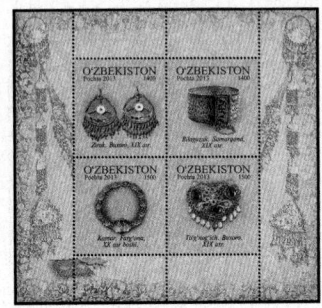

Jewelry — A403

No. 733: a, 1400s, Earrings from Bukhara, 19th cent. b, 1400s, Bracelet from Samarkand, 19th cent. c, 1500s, Round cincture from Fergana, 20th cent. d, 1500s, Heart-shaped pendant from Bukhara, 19th cent.

2013, Sept. 25   **Litho.**   **Perf. 14**
733 A403   Sheet of 4, #a-d   8.75 8.75

2014 Winter Olympics, Sochi, Russia — A404

2014, Jan. 31   **Litho.**   **Perf. 14x13¾**
734 A404 1200s multi   2.00 2.00

Yonboshqal'a Fortress — A405

Gas Complex A406

2014, Jan. 31   **Litho.**   **Perf. 13¾x14**
735   Horiz. pair + central label   5.00 5.00
   a.   A405 1500s multi   2.25 2.25
   b.   A406 2000s multi   2.75 2.75
Sites in Karakalpakstan Region.

Monuments Type of 2012
Design: 1000s, Muhammad Al-Khorezmi (c. 780-c. 850), mathematician, horiz.

2014, Apr. 10   **Litho.**   **Perf. 13¾x14**
736 A388 1000s green   1.90 1.90

Flowers A407

Designs: 1300s, Delphinium knorringianum. 1500s, Corydalis severzowii. 3200s, Juno magnifica.

2014, Apr. 10   **Litho.**   **Perf. 14**
737-738 A407   Set of 2   4.00 4.00
Souvenir Sheet
739 A407 3200s multi   4.50 4.50

A408

A409

Children's Art A410

Perf. 13¾x14, 14x13¾
2014, May 30   **Litho.**
740 A408 1200s multi   1.60 1.60
741 A409 1200s multi   1.60 1.60
742 A410 1200s multi   1.60 1.60
    Nos. 740-742 (3)   4.80 4.80

Fauna A411

Designs: 1000s, Chlamydotis undulata. 1300s, Tetrax tetrax. 3200s, Saiga tatarica.

2014, May 30   **Litho.**   **Perf. 14**
743-744 A411   Set of 2   3.25 3.25
Souvenir Sheet
745 A411 3200s multi   4.50 4.50

17th Asian Games, Incheon, South Korea A412

2014, July 30   **Litho.**   **Perf. 13¾x14**
746 A412 1200s multi   2.10 2.10

Paintings — A413

Designs: 1500s, Ilhom Parisi, by Shorasul Shoahmedov. 2100s, Teatr, by Muzaffar Polatov.

2014, Oct. 16   **Litho.**   **Perf. 14x13¾**
747-748 A413   Set of 2   4.75 4.75

Nos. 1-2, 4-6 Surcharged

Methods and Perfs. As Before
2014, Nov. 3
749 A1   300s on 20k #1   .55 .55
750 A4   300s on 50k #4   .55 .55
751 A6   300s on 50k #6   .55 .55
752 A2   500s on 1r #2   .85 .85
753 A5   1900s on 10r #5   3.25 3.25
    Nos. 749-753 (5)   5.75 5.75

Monuments Type of 2012
Monument commemorating: 290s, Berdaq. 500s, Amir Temur (Tamerlane).

2014, Nov. 6   **Litho.**   **Perf. 14x13¾**
754 A388 290s green   .50 .50
755 A388 500s green   .90 .90

VANUATU

ˌvan-ˌwä-ˈtü

LOCATION — Island group in south Pacific Ocean northeast of New Caledonia
GOVT. — Republic
AREA — 5,700 sq. mi.
POP. — 189,036 (1999 est.)
CAPITAL — Port Vila

The Anglo-French condominium of New Hebrides (Vol. 5) became the independent state of Vanuatu July 30, 1980.

Hebrides franc Vatu (1981)

Catalogue values for all unused stamps in this country are for Never Hinged items.

Watermark

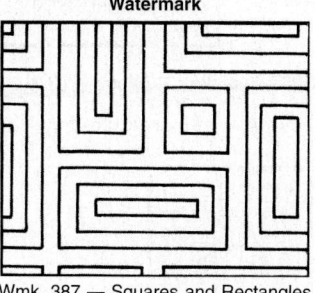

Wmk. 387 — Squares and Rectangles

Erromango Is. and Kaori Tree — A44

Designs: 10fr, Archipelago and man making copra. 15fr, Espiritu Santo Island and cattle. 20fr, Efate Island and Post Office, Vila. 25fr, Malakula Island and headdresses. 30fr, Aoba and Maewo Islands and pig tusks. 35fr, Pentecost Island and land diving. 40fr, Tanna Island and Prophet John Frum's Red Cross. 50fr, Shepherd Island and canoe with sail. 70fr, Banks Island and dancers. 100fr, Ambrym Island and carvings. 200fr, Aneityum Island and decorated baskets. 500fr, Torres Islands and fishing with bow and arrow.

Wmk. 373

1980, July 30		Litho.		Perf. 14
280	A44	5fr multicolored	.25	.25
281	A44	10fr multicolored	.25	.25
282	A44	15fr multicolored	.25	.30
283	A44	20fr multicolored	.30	.40
284	A44	25fr multicolored	.40	.45
285	A44	30fr multicolored	.50	.60
286	A44	35fr multicolored	.55	.65
287	A44	40fr multicolored	.55	.75
288	A44	50fr multicolored	.60	.90
289	A44	70fr multicolored	1.10	1.25
290	A44	100fr multicolored	1.10	1.00
291	A44	200fr multicolored	1.25	1.75
292	A44	500fr multicolored	2.25	3.75
		Nos. 280-292 (13)	9.35	12.30

Inscribed in French
Unwmk.

280a	A44	5fr multicolored	.35	.25
281a	A44	10fr multicolored	.50	.25
282a	A44	15fr multicolored	.55	.45
283a	A44	20fr multicolored	.60	.50
284a	A44	25fr multicolored	.70	.55
285a	A44	30fr multicolored	.70	.65
286a	A44	35fr multicolored	.75	.80
287a	A44	40fr multicolored	1.10	.90
288a	A44	50fr multicolored	1.20	1.10
289a	A44	70fr multicolored	1.75	1.50
290a	A44	100fr multicolored	1.75	1.60
291a	A44	200fr multicolored	2.00	2.75
292a	A44	500fr multicolored	4.75	5.25
		Nos. 280a-292a (13)	16.70	16.55

Rotary Emblem — A52

1980, Sept. 16				Wmk. 373
293	A52	10fr Emblem, horiz.	.25	.25
294	A52	40fr shown	.50	.50

Inscribed in French
Unwmk.

293a	A52	10fr multicolored	.25	.25
294a	A52	40fr multicolored	.70	.70

75th anniv. of Rotary Intl. and 8th anniv. of Port Vila Rotary Club (40fr).

Kiwanis Emblem — A53

1980, Sept. 16				Wmk. 373
295	A53	10fr shown	.25	.25
296	A53	40fr Emblem, horiz.	.75	.75

Inscribed in French
Unwmk.

295a	A53	10fr multicolored	.25	.25
296a	A53	40fr multicolored	1.00	1.00

New Zealand District Kiwanis Convention, Port Vila, Sept. 16-18.

Christmas A54

Paintings: 10fr, Virgin and Child, by Michael Pacher. 15fr, Virgin and Child, by Hans Memling. 30fr, Rest on the Flight to Egypt, by Adriaen van der Werff.

1980, Nov. 12				Wmk. 373
297	A54	10fr multicolored	.25	.25
298	A54	15fr multicolored	.25	.25
299	A54	30fr multicolored	.40	.40
		Nos. 297-299 (3)	.90	.90

Erythrura Trichroa — A55

20fr, Chalcophaps indica. 30fr, Pachycephala pectoralis. 40fr, Ptilinopus tannensis.

1981, Feb. 18				
300	A55	10fr shown	.60	.30
301	A55	20fr multicolored	1.00	.65
302	A55	30fr multicolored	1.50	1.00
303	A55	40fr multicolored	2.00	1.25
		Nos. 300-303 (4)	5.10	3.20

Duke of Edinburgh's 60th Birthday — A56

1981, June 10				Perf. 14x14½
304	A56	15v Tribesman, portrait	.25	.25
305	A56	25v Portrait	.25	.25
306	A56	35v Family	.35	.35
307	A56	45v shown	.45	.45
		Nos. 304-307 (4)	1.30	1.30

Common Design Types
pictured following the introduction.

Royal Wedding Issue
Common Design Type

1981, July 29				
308	CD331	15v Bouquet	.25	.25
309	CD331	45v Charles	.35	.35
310	CD331	75v Couple	.55	.55
		Nos. 308-310 (3)	1.15	1.15

First Anniv. of Independence — A57

1981, July 19				
311	A57	15v Map, flag, vert.	.25	.25
312	A57	25v Emblem	.25	.25
313	A57	45v Anthem	.40	.40
314	A57	75v Arms, vert.	.55	.55
		Nos. 311-314 (4)	1.45	1.45

Christmas A58

Children's drawings: 15v, Three kings. 25v, Girl holding lamb, vert. 35v, Butterfly-angel. 45v, Gift bearer, vert.

1981, Nov. 11		Litho.		Perf. 14
315	A58	15v multicolored	.25	.25
316	A58	25v multicolored	.25	.25
317	A58	35v multicolored	.40	.40
318	A58	45v multicolored	.60	.60
a.		Souvenir sheet, #315-318	2.25	2.25
		Nos. 315-318 (4)	1.50	1.50

Broadbills — A59

20v, Rainbow lories. 25v, Buff-bellied flycatchers. 45v, Fantails.

1982, Feb. 8				Perf. 14½x14
319	A59	15v shown	.60	.60
320	A59	20v multicolored	.80	.80
321	A59	25v multicolored	1.00	1.00
322	A59	45v multicolored	1.75	1.75
		Nos. 319-322 (4)	4.15	4.15

Orchids — A60

1v, Flickengeria comata. 2v, Calanthe triplicata. 10v, Dendrobium sladei. 15v, Dendrobium mohlianum. 20v, Dendrobium macrophyllum. 25v, Dendrobium purpureum. 30v, Robiquetia mimus. 35v, Dendrobium mooreanum. 45v, Spathoglottis plicata. 50v, Dendrobium seemannii. 75v, Dendrobium conanthum. 100v, Dendrobium macranthum. 200v, Coelogyne lamellata. 500v, Bulbophyllum longiscapum.

Perf. 14x13½, 13½x14

1982, June 15				
323	A60	1v multicolored	.25	.70
324	A60	2v multicolored	.25	.75
325	A60	10v multicolored	.30	.40
326	A60	15v multicolored	.40	.35
327	A60	20v multicolored	.50	.40
328	A60	25v multicolored	.75	.70
329	A60	30v multicolored	.90	1.10
330	A60	35v multicolored	1.00	1.25
331	A60	45v multicolored	1.20	1.40
332	A60	50v multicolored	1.40	1.75
333	A60	75v multicolored	2.25	2.75
334	A60	100v multicolored	2.60	2.75
335	A60	200v multicolored	3.25	4.25
336	A60	500v multicolored	6.25	9.25
		Nos. 323-336 (14)	21.30	27.80

Nos. 330-333 horiz.
For surcharges see Nos. 383, 512, 551-554, 586-589A, B1.

Scouting Year A61

			Wmk. 373	
1982, Sept. 1		Litho.		Perf. 14
337	A61	15v Around campfire	.35	.35
338	A61	20v First aid	.35	.35
339	A61	25v Signal tower	.45	.45
340	A61	45v Building raft	1.00	1.00
341	A61	75v Scout sign	1.40	1.40
		Nos. 337-341 (5)	3.55	3.55

Christmas — A62

Details from Nativity painting. 35v, 45v horiz.

1982, Nov. 16				
342	A62	15v multicolored	.35	.35
343	A62	25v multicolored	.55	.55
344	A62	35v multicolored	.80	.80
345	A62	45v multicolored	1.00	1.00
a.		Souvenir sheet of 4, #342-345	3.25	3.25
		Nos. 342-345 (4)	2.70	2.70

Hypolimnas Octocula A63

1983, Jan. 17				Perf. 14½
346		Pair	2.25	1.60
a.		A63 15v shown	1.00	.75
b.		A63 15v Euploea sylvester	1.00	.75
347		Pair	2.60	2.25
a.		A63 20v Polyura sacco	1.20	1.00
b.		A63 20v Papilio canopus	1.20	1.00
348		Pair	3.50	2.40
a.		A63 25v Parantica pumila	1.60	1.20
b.		A63 25v Luthrodes cleotas	1.60	1.20
		Nos. 346-348 (3)	8.35	6.25

A64

1983, Mar. 14   **Perf. 13½x14**
349 A64 15v Pres. Sokomanu .30 .30
350 A64 20v Fisherman .30 .30
351 A64 25v Herdsman, cattle .35 .35
352 A64 75v Flags, map .75 .75
    Nos. 349-352 (4) 1.70 1.70

Commonwealth Day. 20v, 75v inscribed in French.

Economic Zone — A65

a, Thunnus albacares. b, Map. c, Matthew Isld. d, Hunter Isld. e, Epinephelus morrhua, etelis carbunculus. f, Katsuwonus pelamis.

Perf. 14x13½
1983, May 23   **Litho.**   **Wmk. 373**
353   Sheet of 6 4.25 4.25
  a.-f. A65 25v multicolored .65 .65

Manned Flight Bicentenary — A66

Balloons or Airships: 15v, Montgolfiere, 1783. 20v, J.A.C. Charles 1st hydrogen balloon, 1783. 25v, Blanchard & Jeffries 1st English Channel crossing, 1785. 35v, H. Giffard's 1st mechanically powered airship, 1852. 40v, Renard and Krebs' airship, 1884. 45v, Graf Zeppelin's 1st transworld flight, 1929.

1983, Aug. 4   **Litho.**   **Perf. 14**
354 A66 15v multi, vert. .30 .30
355 A66 20v multi, vert. .35 .35
356 A66 25v multi, vert. .45 .45
357 A66 35v multi .60 .60
358 A66 40v multi .75 .75
359 A66 45v multi .85 .85
    Nos. 354-359 (6) 3.30 3.30

For overprint see No. 372.

World Communications Year — A67

15v, Mail transport, Bauerfield Airport. 20v, Switchboard operator. 25v, Telex operator. 45v, Satellite earth station.

1983, Oct. 10   **Litho.**   **Wmk. 373**
360 A67 15v multicolored .25 .25
361 A67 20v multicolored .40 .40
362 A67 25v multicolored .55 .55
363 A67 45v multicolored .95 .95
  a. Souv. sheet of 4, #360-363 + 3
     labels 5.50 5.50
    Nos. 360-363 (4) 2.15 2.15

No. 363a issued for WCY and 75th anniv. of New Hebrides stamps.

Local Fungi — A68

15v, Cymatoderma elegans, vert. 25v, Lignosus rhinoceros, vert. 35v, Stereum ostrea. 45v, Ganoderma boninenze, vert.

1984, Jan. 9   **Litho.**   **Perf. 14**
364 A68 15v multicolored .80 .80
365 A68 25v multicolored .90 .90
366 A68 35v multicolored 1.50 1.50
367 A68 45v multicolored 1.75 1.75
    Nos. 364-367 (4) 4.95 4.95

Lloyd's List Issue
Common Design Type

1984, Apr. 30   **Litho.**   **Perf. 14½x14**
368 CD335 15v Port Vila .35 .35
369 CD335 20v Induna .45 .45
370 CD335 25v Air Vanuatu jet .60 .60
371 CD335 45v Brahman Express 1.00 1.00
    Nos. 368-371 (4) 2.40 2.40

No. 359 Overprinted "UPU CONGRESS / HAMBURG"

1984, June 11   **Wmk. 373**   **Perf. 14**
372 A66 45v multicolored .85 .85

Cattle A69

1984, July 3   **Litho.**   **Perf. 14**
373 A69 15v Charolais .30 .30
374 A69 25v Charolais-Afrikaner .45 .45
375 A69 45v Friesian .75 .75
376 A69 75v Charolais-Brahman 1.40 1.40
    Nos. 373-376 (4) 2.90 2.90

Ausipex '84 — A70

Ships.
1984, Sept. 7
377 A70 25v Makambo .70 .50
378 A70 45v Rockton 1.25 1.00
379 A70 100v Waroonga 2.40 *4.00*
  a. Souvenir sheet of 3, #377-379 5.00 *5.25*
    Nos. 377-379 (3) 4.35 5.50

Christmas A71

25v, Father Christmas, child in hospital. 45v, Nativity. 75v, Father Christmas, children.

1984, Nov. 19   **Litho.**   **Wmk. 373**
380 A71 25v multicolored .50 .30
381 A71 45v multicolored .90 .75
382 A71 75v multicolored 1.50 1.50
    Nos. 380-382 (3) 2.90 2.55

No. 323 Surcharged

1985, Jan. 22   **Litho.**   **Perf. 14x13½**
383 A60 5v on 1v multi 1.50 1.00

Ceremonial Dance Costumes — A71a

1985, Jan. 22   **Perf. 14**
384 A71a 20v Ambrym Island .35 .35
385 A71a 25v Pentecost Island .50 .50
386 A71a 45v Women's Grade Ceremony, S.W. Malakula .80 .80
387 A71a 75v Same, men's 1.25 1.25
    Nos. 384-387 (4) 2.90 2.90

Audubon Birth Bicent. — A72

Wmk. 373
1985, Mar. 26   **Litho.**   **Perf. 14**
Peregrine falcons.
388 A72 20v multicolored 1.00 1.00
389 A72 35v multicolored 1.20 1.20
390 A72 45v multicolored 1.40 1.40
391 A72 100v multicolored 2.40 2.40
    Nos. 388-391 (4) 6.00 6.00

Queen Mother 85th Birthday
Common Design Type
Perf. 14½x14
1985, June 7   **Wmk. 384**
392 CD336 5v Wedding photo .25 .25
393 CD336 20v 80th birthday celebration .45 .45
394 CD336 35v At Ancona, Italy .60 .60
395 CD336 55v Holding Prince Henry .95 .95
    Nos. 392-395 (4) 2.25 2.25

Souvenir Sheet
396 CD336 100v At Covent Garden Opera 3.00 3.00

EXPO '85, Tsukuba — A73

35v, Mala naval patrol boat. 45v, Japanese fishing fleet, Port Vila. 55v, Mobile Force Band. 100v, Prime Minister Walter H. Lini.

1985, July 26   **Wmk. 373**   **Perf. 14**
397 A73 35v multicolored .65 .40
398 A73 45v multicolored .80 .60
399 A73 55v multicolored .90 .70
400 A73 100v multicolored 1.00 *1.60*
  a. Souvenir sheet of 4, #397-400 4.25 4.25
    Nos. 397-400 (4) 3.35 3.30

Natl. independence, 5th anniv.

Intl. Youth Year A74

Children's drawings.

1985, Sept. 16   **Wmk. 373**   **Perf. 14**
401 A74 20v Alain Lagaliu .55 .55
402 A74 30v Peter Obed .65 .65
403 A74 50v Mary Estelle 1.00 1.00
404 A74 100v Abel M rani 1.75 1.75
    Nos. 401-404 (4) 3.95 3.95

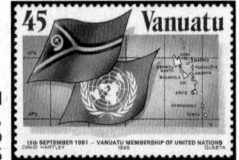
Natl. and UN Flags, Map A75

1985, Sept. 24   **Litho.**   **Perf. 14**
405 A75 45v multicolored 1.50 1.25

Admission of Vanuatu to UN, 4th anniv.

Sea Slugs — A76

20v, Chromodoris elisa bethina. 35v, Halgerda aurantiomaculata. 55v, Chromodoris kuniei. 100v, Notodoris minor.

1985, Nov. 11   **Wmk. 373**   **Perf. 14½**
406 A76 20v multicolored .40 .40
407 A76 35v multicolored .80 .80
408 A76 55v multicolored 1.10 1.10
409 A76 100v multicolored 2.10 2.10
    Nos. 406-409 (4) 4.40 4.40

Nos. 407-408 horiz. See Nos. 497-500.

Scuba Diving — A77

1986, Jan. 22   **Wmk. 384**   **Perf. 14**
410 A77 30v shown .90 .50
411 A77 35v Volcanic eruption 1.00 .60
412 A77 55v Land diving 1.00 .80
413 A77 100v Wind surfing 1.40 *2.00*
    Nos. 410-413 (4) 4.30 3.90

See No. 479.

Queen Elizabeth II 60th Birthday
Common Design Type

Designs: 20v, With Prince Charles and Princess Anne, 1951. 35v, At christening of Prince William, the Music Room, Buckingham Palace, 1982. 45v, State visit, 1985. 55v, State visit to Mexico, 1974. 100v, Visiting Crown Agents' offices, 1983.

1986, Apr. 21   **Litho.**   **Perf. 14x14½**
414 CD337 20v scar, blk & sil .25 .25
415 CD337 35v ultra & multi .45 .45
416 CD337 45v green & multi .50 .50
417 CD337 55v violet & multi .65 .65
418 CD337 100v multicolored 1.25 1.25
    Nos. 414-418 (5) 3.10 3.10

For overprints & surcharges see #465-469, B2-B6.

AMERIPEX '86 — A78

45v, SS President Coolidge. 55v, As troop ship, 1942. 135v, Site of sinking, 1942.

1986, May 19   Wmk. 373   Perf. 14
419 A78 45v multicolored   1.40 .70
420 A78 55v multicolored   1.60 .90
421 A78 135v multicolored 2.75 2.25
 a. Souvenir sheet of 3, #419-421 6.25 6.25
  Nos. 419-421 (3)   5.75 3.85

Halley's Comet A79

30v, Comet, deity statue. 45v, Family sighting comet. 55v, Comet over SW Pacific. 100v, Edmond Halley, manuscript.

1986, June 23   Wmk. 384   Perf. 14½
422 A79 30v multicolored   1.20 1.20
423 A79 45v multicolored   1.25 1.25
424 A79 55v multicolored   1.60 1.60
425 A79 100v multicolored 2.10 2.10
  Nos. 422-425 (4)   6.15 6.15

Coral A80

1986, Oct. 27   Wmk. 373   Perf. 14
426 A80 20v Daisy   .70 .70
427 A80 45v Organ pipe 1.50 1.50
428 A80 55v Sea fan   1.75 1.75
429 A80 135v Soft   4.50 4.50
  Nos. 426-429 (4)   8.45 8.45

Intl. Peace Year A81

30v, Children of the world. 45v, Child praying. 55v, UN building, negotiators. 135v, Peoples working in harmony.

1986, Nov. 3   Litho.   Perf. 14
430 A81 30v multi   .65 .65
431 A81 45v multi   1.00 1.00
432 A81 55v multi   1.25 1.25
433 A81 135v multi 3.00 3.00
  Nos. 430-433 (4)   5.90 5.90

Automotives A82

20v, Datsun 240Z, 1969. 45v, Model A Ford, 1927. 55v, Unic, 1924-25. 135v, Citroen DS19, 1975.

1987, Jan. 22
434 A82 20v multi   .35 .35
435 A82 45v multi   .65 .65
436 A82 55v multi   .80 .80
437 A82 135v multi 1.90 1.90
  Nos. 434-437 (4)   3.70 3.70

IRHO Coconut Research Station, 25th Anniv. A83

35v, Nursery. 45v, Cocos nucifera tree. 100v, Cocos nucifera fruit. 135v, Station.

1987, May 13   Perf. 14½x14
438 A83 35v multicolored   .55 .55
439 A83 45v multicolored   .85 .85
440 A83 100v multicolored 1.25 1.25
441 A83 135v multicolored 1.75 1.75
  Nos. 438-441 (4)   4.40 4.40

Fish — A84

1v, Cirrhitichthys aprinus. 5v, Zanclus cornutus. 10v, Canthigaster cinctus. 15v, Amphiprion rubrocinctus. 20v, Acanthurus lineatus. 30v, Thalassoma hardwicki. 35v, Anthias tuka. 40v, Adioryx microstomus. 45v, Balistoides conspicillum. 50v, Xyrichtys taeniouris. 55v, Hemitaurich-thys polyepis. 65v, Pterois volitans. 100v, Paracirrhites forsteri. 300v, Balistapus undulatus. 500v, Chaetodon ephippium.

Perf. 14x14½
1987, July 15   Wmk. 384
442 A84 1v multicolored   .25 .25
443 A84 5v multicolored   .25 .25
444 A84 10v multicolored   .25 .25
445 A84 15v multicolored   .30 .30
446 A84 20v multicolored   .40 .40
447 A84 30v multicolored   .55 .55
448 A84 35v multicolored   .60 .60
449 A84 40v multicolored   .65 .65
450 A84 45v multicolored   .85 .85
451 A84 50v multicolored   .90 .90
452 A84 55v multicolored   1.00 1.00
453 A84 65v multicolored   1.10 1.10
454 A84 100v multicolored 2.10 2.10
455 A84 300v multicolored 5.50 5.50
456 A84 500v multicolored 7.75 7.75
  Nos. 442-456 (15)   22.45 22.45

Insects A85

45v, Xylotrupes gideon. 55v, Phyllodes imperialis. 65v, Cyphogaster. 100v, Othreis fullonia.

1987, Sept. 22   Wmk. 373   Perf. 14
457 A85 45v multicolored   .90 .90
458 A85 55v multicolored   1.00 1.00
459 A85 65v multicolored   1.40 1.40
460 A85 100v multicolored 2.00 2.00
  Nos. 457-460 (4)   5.30 5.30

Christmas Carols — A86

1987, Nov. 10   Perf. 13½x14
461 A86 20v Away in a Manger .40 .40
462 A86 45v Once in Royal David's City .85 .85
463 A86 55v While Shepherds Watched Their Flocks 1.00 1.00
464 A86 65v We Three Kings of Orient Are 1.25 1.25
  Nos. 461-464 (4)   3.50 3.50

Nos. 414-418 Ovptd. in Silver "40TH WEDDING ANNIVERSARY"
Perf. 14x14½
1987, Dec. 9   Litho.   Wmk. 384
465 CD337 20v scar, blk & sil .45 .45
466 CD337 35v ultra & multi   .60 .60
467 CD337 45v green & multi   .75 .75
468 CD337 55v violet & multi .80 .80
469 CD337 100v multicolored 1.50 1.50
  Nos. 465-469 (5)   4.10 4.10

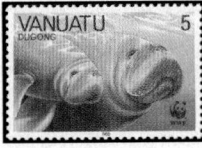

World Wildlife Fund — A87

Dugongs.

1988, Feb. 29   Perf. 13x13½
470 A87 5v Mother, calf 1.00 .40
471 A87 10v Adult   1.60 .40
472 A87 20v Two adults 2.10 1.10
473 A87 45v Herd   3.75 2.75
  Nos. 470-473 (4)   8.45 4.65

Australia Bicentennial A88

Burns Philp emblem, bicent. emblem and steamships.

1988, May 18   Wmk. 373   Perf. 12
474 A88 20v S.S. Tambo   .35 .35
475 A88 45v S.S. Induna .75 .75
476 A88 55v S.S. Morinda .90 .90
477 A88 65v S.S. Marsina 1.00 1.00
  Nos. 474-477 (4)   3.00 3.00

Capt. James Cook (1728-1779), Explorer — A89

Perf. 14 on 2 or 3 Sides
1988, July 29   Wmk. 384
478 A89 45v black & red   .90 .90

SYDPEX '88. No. 478 printed in panes of 10 plus 5 center labels picturing a map of Vanuatu, HMS Resolution, exhibition emblem, HMS Endeavour or a map of Australia.

Tourism Type of 1986
Souvenir Sheet
Wmk. 373
1988, Aug. 24   Litho.   Perf. 14
479 Sheet of 2   4.50 4.50
 a. A77 55v like No. 412 1.10 1.10
 b. A77 100v like No. 413 2.25 2.25

EXPO '88. Nos. 479a-479b are dated 1988 and "Vanuatu" is inscribed in violet blue.

1988 Summer Olympics, Seoul — A90

1988, Sept. 19   Perf. 13½x14
480 A90 20v Boxing   .25 .25
481 A90 45v Track events .70 .70
482 A90 55v Signing Olympic agreement .85 .85
483 A90 65v Soccer   1.00 1.00
  Nos. 480-483 (4)   2.80 2.80
Souvenir Sheet
484 A90 150v Tennis   3.50 3.50
Intl. Tennis Federation, 75th anniv. (150v).

Lloyds of London, 300th Anniv.
Common Design Type

Designs: 20v, Lloyds new building, 1988. 55v, Cargo ship Shirrabank, horiz. 65v, Adela, horiz. 145v, Excursion steamer General Slocum on fire in New York Harbor, 1904.

1988, Oct. 25   Wmk. 384   Perf. 14
485 CD341 20v multicolored   .45 .45
486 CD341 55v multicolored   1.20 1.20
487 CD341 65v multicolored   1.25 1.25
488 CD341 145v multicolored 3.00 3.00
  Nos. 485-488 (4)   5.90 5.90

FAO — A91

Perf. 14½x14, 14x14½
1988, Nov. 14
489 A91 45v Tending crops   .80 .80
490 A91 55v Fishing, vert.   .90 .90
491 A91 65v Animal husbandry, vert. .90 .90
492 A91 120v Produce market 1.10 1.10
  Nos. 489-492 (4)   3.70 3.70

Christmas A92

Carols: 20v, Silent Night, Holy Night. 45v, Angels From the Realms of Glory. 65v, O Come All Ye Faithful. 155v, In That Poor Stable How Charming Jesus Lies.

1988, Dec. 1   Litho.   Perf. 14½x14
493 A92 20v multicolored   .40 .40
494 A92 45v multicolored   .65 .65
495 A92 65v multicolored   .75 .75
496 A92 155v multicolored 1.90 1.90
  Nos. 493-496 (4)   3.70 3.70

Marine Life Type of 1985
Shrimp.

1989, Feb. 1   Perf. 14
497 A76 20v Periclimenes brevicarpalis .40 .40
498 A76 45v Lysmata grabhami 1.00 1.00
499 A76 65v Rhynchocinetes 1.40 1.40
500 A76 150v Stenopus hispidus 2.60 2.60
  Nos. 497-500 (4)   5.40 5.40

Economic & Social Commission for Asia and the Pacific (ESCAP) A93

20v, Consolidated Catalina. 45v, Douglas DC-3. 55v, Embraer EMB110 Bandeirante. 200v, Boeing 737-300.

Perf. 12x12½
1989, Apr. 5   Litho.   Wmk. 373
501 A93 20v multicolored   1.00 1.00
502 A93 45v multicolored   1.40 1.40
503 A93 55v multicolored   1.60 1.60
504 A93 200v multicolored 5.00 5.00
  Nos. 501-504 (4)   9.00 9.00

Inauguration of the Sydney-Noumea-Espiritu Santo Service, 1948 (20v).

PHILEXFRANCE '89 — A94

Exhibition emblem and: No. 505a, Porte de Versailles Hall Number 1. No. 505b, Eiffel Tower. No. 506, Revolt of French Troops, Nancy, 1790.

1989, July 5   Wmk. 373   Perf. 12
505 A94 Pair   5.25 5.25
 a.-b. 100v any single   2.50 2.50

Souvenir Sheet
Perf. 14
Wmk. 384

506 A94 100v multicolored   2.25 2.25
French revolution, bicent.

Moon Landing, 20th Anniv.
Common Design Type

Apollo 17: 45v, Command module in space. 55v, Harrison Schmitt, Gene Cerman and Ron Evans. 65v, Mission emblem. 120v, Liftoff. 100v, Recovery of Apollo 11 crew after spashdown.

1989, July 20   **Wmk. 384**   *Perf. 14*
Size of Nos. 508-509: 29x29mm

507	CD342	45v multicolored	1.40	1.40
508	CD342	55v multicolored	1.40	1.40
509	CD342	65v multicolored	1.60	1.60
510	CD342	120v multicolored	2.75	2.75
		Nos. 507-510 (4)	7.15	7.15

Souvenir Sheet

511 CD342 100v multicolored   2.75 2.75

No. 324
Surcharged

Perf. 14x13½
1989, Oct. 18   **Litho.**   **Wmk. 373**
512 A60 100v on 2v multi   5.50 5.50
STAMPSHOW '89, Melbourne.

World Stamp Expo '89 — A95

Perf. 14x13½
1989, Nov. 6   **Litho.**   **Wmk. 384**
513 A95 65v New Hebrides #256   3.75 3.75

Souvenir Sheet

514	Sheet of 2	9.50	9.50
a.	A95 65v New Hebrides #254	3.00	3.00
b.	A95 100v The White House (detail)	5.00	5.00

Flora — A96

45v, Alocasia macrorrhiza. 55v, Acacia spirorbis. 65v, Metrosideros collina. 145v, Hoya australis.

Perf. 12½x12
1990, Jan. 5   **Wmk. 373**

515	A96	45v multicolored	.85	.85
516	A96	55v multicolored	1.00	1.00
517	A96	65v multicolored	1.20	1.20
518	A96	145v multicolored	2.75	2.75
		Nos. 515-518 (4)	5.80	5.80

A97

Stamp World London '90 Exhibition emblem and simulated stamps or stamps on stamps: 45v, Kava (simulated stamps). 65v, Luganville P.O. exterior, interior (simulated stamps). 100v, Propeller plane, 19th cent. packet (simulated stamps). 150v, New Hebrides #187-188, first day cancellation. 200v, Great Britain #1, Vanuatu #281.

1990, Apr. 30   **Perf. 13x13½**

519	A97	45v multicolored	.90	.90
520	A97	65v multicolored	1.40	1.40
521	A97	100v multicolored	2.00	2.00
522	A97	200v multicolored	3.75	3.75
		Nos. 519-522 (4)	8.05	8.05

Souvenir Sheet

523 A97 150v multicolored   7.50 7.50
Penny Black, 150th anniv. No. 523 margin pictures first day cancel and cachet.

Independence, 10th Anniv. — A98

25v, Natl. Council of Women Emblem. 50v, Pres. Frederick Kalomuana Timakata. 55v, Preamble to Constitution. 65v, Vanuaaku Pati flag. 80v, Reserve Bank. 150v, Prime Minister Walter H. Lini.

1990, July 30   **Perf. 14**

524	A98	25v multicolored	.45	.45
525	A98	50v multicolored	.95	.95
526	A98	55v multicolored	1.10	1.10
527	A98	65v multicolored	1.20	1.20
528	A98	80v multicolored	1.50	1.50
		Nos. 524-528 (5)	5.20	5.20

Souvenir Sheet

529 A98 150v multi   5.75 5.75

Miniature Sheet

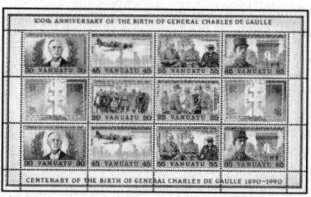

Charles De Gaulle (1890-1970) — A99

Wmk. 373
1990, Nov. 22   **Litho.**   **Perf. 14**

530	Sheet, 2 ea #530c-530f + 2 labels		22.50	22.50
a.	A99 20v At Bayeux, after D-day landing		4.00	4.00
b.	A99 25v Alsace, 1945		4.00	4.00
c.	A99 30v Portrait		1.60	1.60
d.	A99 45v Spitfire, Biggin Hill, 1942		1.75	1.75
e.	A99 55v Casablanca, 1943		1.90	1.90
f.	A99 65v Day of Glory, Paris, 1944		2.00	2.00

Christmas — A100

1990, Dec. 5   **Perf. 13**

531	Strip of 5		5.00	5.00
a.	A100 25v Angel facing right		.50	.50
b.	A100 50v Shepherds		.75	.75
c.	A100 65v Nativity		.80	.80
d.	A100 70v The Three Kings		.85	.85
e.	A100 80v Angel facing left		.85	.85

Butterflies
A101

25v, Parthenos sylvia. 55v, Euploea leucostictos. 80v, Lampides boeticus. 150v, Danaus plexippus.

Perf. 14x14½
1991, Jan. 9   **Wmk. 384**

532	A101	25v multicolored	.65	.65
533	A101	55v multicolored	1.25	1.25
534	A101	80v multicolored	1.90	1.90
535	A101	150v multicolored	3.50	3.50
		Nos. 532-535 (4)	7.30	7.30

Art Festival — A102

Wmk. 373
1991, May 2   **Litho.**   **Perf. 13½**

536	A102	25v Dance	.45	.45
537	A102	65v Weaving	1.25	1.25
538	A102	80v Carving	1.60	1.60
539	A102	150v Music	3.00	3.00
		Nos. 536-539 (4)	6.30	6.30

Elizabeth & Philip, Birthdays
Common Design Types
Wmk. 384
1991, June 17   **Litho.**   **Perf. 14½**

540	CD345	65v multicolored	1.00	1.00
541	CD346	70v multicolored	1.10	1.10
a.	Pair, #540-541 + label		2.50	2.50

Phila Nippon '91 — A103

Birds: 50v, White-collared kingfisher. 55v, Green palm loriket. 80v, Scarlet robin. 100v, Pacific swallow. 150v, Reef heron.

Wmk. 373
1991, Nov. 15   **Litho.**   **Perf. 14½**

542	A103	50v multicolored	1.00	1.00
543	A103	55v multicolored	1.00	1.00
544	A103	80v multicolored	1.50	1.50
545	A103	100v multicolored	1.75	1.75
		Nos. 542-545 (4)	5.25	5.25

Souvenir Sheet

546 A103 150v multicolored   3.75 3.75

Fight Against AIDS A104

Designs: 25v, Multiple partners, unsafe sex can spread AIDS. 65v, AIDS victim and care giver. 80v, AIDS kills, shark. 150v, Children's playground.

1991, Nov. 29   **Wmk. 384**   **Perf. 14**

547	A104	25v multicolored	.65	.65
548	A104	65v multicolored	1.20	1.20
549	A104	80v multicolored	1.50	1.50
550	A104	150v multicolored	2.75	2.75
		Nos. 547-550 (4)	6.10	6.10

Nos. 324-326 & 329 Surcharged

Perf. 14x13½
1991, June 12   **Litho.**   **Wmk. 373**

551	A60	20v on 2v #324	.70	.70
552	A60	60v on 10v #325	2.00	2.00
553	A60	70v on 15v #326	2.40	2.40
554	A60	80v on 30v #329	2.60	2.60
		Nos. 551-554 (4)	7.70	7.70

Queen Elizabeth II's Accession to the Throne, 40th Anniv.
Common Design Type
1992, Feb. 6   **Wmk. 384**   **Perf. 14**

555	CD349	20v multicolored	.35	.35
556	CD349	25v multicolored	.40	.40
557	CD349	60v multicolored	.90	.90
558	CD349	65v multicolored	1.00	1.00

Wmk. 373
559 CD349 70v multicolored   1.00 1.00
   Nos. 555-559 (5)   3.65 3.65

New Hebrides Participation in World War II — A105

Designs: 50v, Grumman F4F-4 Wildcat. 55v, Douglas SBD-3 Dauntless. 65v, Consolidated PBY-5A Catalina. 80v, USS Hornet. 200v, Vought-Sikorsky OS2U-3.

Perf. 13½x14
1992, May 22   **Litho.**   **Wmk. 373**

560	A105	50v multicolored	2.25	2.25
561	A105	55v multicolored	2.25	2.25
562	A105	65v multicolored	2.50	2.50
563	A105	80v multicolored	3.50	3.50
		Nos. 560-563 (4)	10.50	10.50

Souvenir Sheet

564 A105 200v multicolored   12.00 12.00
World Columbian Stamp Expo, Chicago (No. 564).
See Nos. 590-594, 664-667.

Vanuatu's Membership in the World Meteorological Organization, 10th Anniv. — A106

Designs: 25v, Meteorological station, Port Vila. 60v, Cyclone near Vanuatu seen by Japanese satellite GMS 4. 80v, Weather chart showing cyclone. 105v, Cyclone warning broadcast by radio.

1992, June 20   **Perf. 14**

565	A106	25v multicolored	.50	.50
566	A106	60v multicolored	1.25	1.25
567	A106	80v multicolored	1.60	1.60
568	A106	105v multicolored	1.75	1.75
		Nos. 565-568 (4)	5.10	5.10

1992 Melanesian Cup — A107

1992, July 20   *Perf. 13½x14*
569	A107	20v Soccer team, trophy	.50	.50
570	A107	65v Soccer players	1.25	1.25
571	A107	70v Men's track	1.50	1.50
572	A107	80v Women's track	1.50	1.50
		Nos. 569-572 (4)	4.75	4.75

1992 Summer Olympics, Barcelona (#571-572).
For surcharges see Nos. 621-622.

World Food Day — A108

Designs: 20v, "Breast is best." 70v, Central Hospital, Port Vila. 80v, "Give your children a healthy future." 150v, Nutritious food.

1992, Oct. 16   **Wmk. 384**   *Perf. 14*
573	A108	20v green & brown	.40	.40
574	A108	70v brown & green	1.00	1.00
575	A108	80v green & brown	1.25	1.25
576	A108	150v brown & green	2.25	2.25
		Nos. 573-576 (4)	4.90	4.90

Turtles A109

55v, Leatherback turtle. 65v, Loggerhead turtle. 70v, Hawksbill turtle. 80v, Green turtle. 200v, Green turtle hatchlings.

1992, Dec. 15   *Perf. 14x14½*
577	A109	55v multicolored	1.60	1.60
578	A109	65v multicolored	1.75	1.75
579	A109	70v multicolored	2.50	2.50
580	A109	80v multicolored	3.25	3.25
		Nos. 577-580 (4)	9.10	9.10

Souvenir Sheet
581	A109	200v multicolored	6.75	6.75

Hibiscus — A110

Designs: 25v, Light pink hibiscus rosa-sinensis. 55v, Hibiscus tiliaceus. 80v, Red hibiscus rosa-sinensis. 150v, Dark pink hibiscus rosa-sinensis.

Wmk. 384
1993, Mar. 3   **Litho.**   *Perf. 14*
582	A110	25v multicolored	.45	.45
583	A110	55v multicolored	1.00	1.00
584	A110	80v multicolored	1.25	1.25
585	A110	150v multicolored	2.40	2.40
		Nos. 582-585 (4)	5.10	5.10

Nos. 331, 333-335 Surcharged

Perf. 13½x14, 14x13½
1993, Apr. 21   **Litho.**   **Wmk. 373**
586	A60	40v on 45v #331	.85	.85
587	A60	55v on 75v #333	1.10	1.10
588	A60	65v on 100v #334	1.40	1.40
589	A60	150v on 200v #335	3.00	3.00
		Nos. 586-589 (4)	6.35	6.35

Size and location of surcharge varies.

No. 326 Surcharged

1993, June 1
589A	A60	20v on 35v #326	6.75	6.75

World War II Type of 1992

20v, Grumman F6F-3 Hellcat. 55v, Lockheed P-38F Lightning. 65v, Grumman TBF-1 Avenger. 80v, USS Essex. 200v, Douglas C-47 Dakota.

1993, June 30   *Perf. 13½*
590	A105	20v multicolored	.90	.90
591	A105	55v multicolored	2.50	2.50
592	A105	65v multicolored	3.00	3.00
593	A105	80v multicolored	3.75	3.75
		Nos. 590-593 (4)	10.15	10.15

Souvenir Sheet
594	A105	200v multicolored	9.75	9.75

Island Scenes A111

Designs: 5v, Iririki Island, Port Vila. 10v, Iririki Island, yachts. 15v, Court House, Port Vila. 20v, Two girls, Pentecost Island. 25v, Women dancers, Tanna Island. 30v, Market, Port Vila. 45v, Man with canoe, Erakor Island, vert. 50v, Coconut trees, Champagne Beach. 55v, Coconut trees, North Efate Islands. 60v, Fish (Banks Group). 70v, Sea fan, Tongoa Island, vert. 75v, Espiritu Santo Island. 80v, Sailboat at sunset, Port Vila Bay, vert. 100v, Mele Waterfall, vert. 300v, Yasur Volcano, Tanna Island, vert. 500v, Erakor Island.

1993, July 7   *Perf. 14x14½, 14½x14*
595	A111	5v multicolored	.25	.25
596	A111	10v multicolored	.25	.25
597	A111	15v multicolored	.30	.30
598	A111	20v multicolored	.40	.40
599	A111	25v multicolored	.45	.45
600	A111	30v multicolored	.55	.50
601	A111	45v multicolored	.80	.80
602	A111	50v multicolored	.90	.90
603	A111	55v multicolored	1.00	1.00
604	A111	60v multicolored	1.10	1.10
605	A111	70v multicolored	1.25	1.25
606	A111	75v multicolored	1.40	1.40
a.		Souvenir sheet, #596, 603, 604, 606 ('94)	4.75	4.75
607	A111	80v multicolored	1.40	1.40
608	A111	100v multicolored	1.75	1.75
609	A111	300v multicolored	5.25	5.25
610	A111	500v multicolored	8.75	8.75
		Nos. 595-610 (16)	25.80	25.75

No. 606a, Philakorea '94 International Stamp Exhibition.
For surcharges see Nos. 619-620, 742-745A, 745D.

Shells — A112

55v, Trochus niloticus. 65v, Lioconcha castrensis. 80v, Turbo petholatus. 150v, Pleuroploca trapezium.

Wmk. 373
1993, Sept. 15   **Litho.**   *Perf. 14½*
611	A112	55v multi	1.40	1.40
612	A112	65v multi	1.75	1.75
613	A112	80v multi	2.00	2.00
614	A112	150v multi	4.00	4.00
		Nos. 611-614 (4)	9.15	9.15

See Nos. 632-635, 654-657.

Louvre Museum, Bicent. A113

Paintings by De La Tour: 25v, St. Joseph the Carpenter. 55v, The Newborn. 80v, Adoration of the Shepherds (detail). 150v, Adoration of the Shepherds (entire).

Wmk. 373
1993, Nov. 10   **Litho.**   *Perf. 14*
615	A113	25v multicolored	.45	.45
616	A113	55v multicolored	1.00	1.00
617	A113	80v multicolored	1.50	1.50
618	A113	150v multicolored	3.00	3.00
		Nos. 615-618 (4)	5.95	5.95

Nos. 570, 572, 598, 600 Surcharged

1993, Dec. 6   **Litho.**   **Wmk. 373**
Perfs. as Before
619	A111	15v on 20v #598	.30	.30
620	A111	25v on 30v #600	.40	.40
621	A107	55v on 65v #570	1.00	1.00
622	A107	70v on 80v #572	1.25	1.25
		Nos. 619-622 (4)	2.95	2.95

Service Organizations A114

Hong Kong '94: 25v, Kiwanis Intl., Charity Races, vert. 60v, Lions Intl. Twin Otter on mercy mission. 75v, Rotary Intl. fighting malaria, vert. 150v, Red Cross blood donar service. 200v, Emblems of service organizations.

Perf. 14x15, 15x14
1994, Feb. 18   **Litho.**   **Wmk. 373**
623	A114	25v multicolored	.40	.40
624	A114	60v multicolored	1.10	1.10
625	A114	75v multicolored	1.25	1.25
626	A114	150v multicolored	2.50	2.50
		Nos. 623-626 (4)	5.25	5.25

Souvenir Sheet
627	A114	200v multicolored	3.50	3.50

Intl. Year of the Family — A115

1994, Mar. 2   *Perf. 14*
628	A115	25v vio & rose brn	.40	.40
629	A115	60v ver & dk grn	1.00	1.00
630	A115	90v green & sepia	1.40	1.40
631	A115	150v brn & vio bl	2.50	2.50
		Nos. 628-631 (4)	5.30	5.30

Shell Type of 1993

60v, Cyprea argus. 70v, Conus marmoreus. 85v, Lambis chiragra. 155v, Chicoreus brunneus.

1994, May 31   **Litho.**   *Perf. 12*
632	A112	60v multicolored	1.40	1.40
633	A112	70v multicolored	1.40	1.40
634	A112	85v multicolored	2.10	2.10
635	A112	155v multicolored	3.75	3.75
		Nos. 632-635 (4)	8.65	8.65

Tourism — A116

Designs: a, 25v, Slit gong (drum), traditional hut. b, 75v, Volcano, boats. c, 90v, Sailboats, airplane, green palm lorikeet. d, 200v, Helicopter, woman with tray of fruit.

1994, July 27   **Litho.**   *Perf. 13½*
636	A116	Strip of 4, #a.-d.	8.00	8.00

Anemonefish — A117

1994, Aug. 16   **Litho.**   *Perf. 12*
637	A117	55v Pink	2.10	2.10
638	A117	70v Clark's	2.75	2.75
639	A117	80v Red & black	2.90	2.90
640	A117	140v Orange-fin	5.25	5.25
a.		Souvenir sheet of 1	5.50	5.50
		Nos. 637-640 (4)	13.00	13.00

Philakorea '94 (#640a).

ICAO, 50th Anniv. — A118

Designs: 25v, 1950 Qantas Catalina. 60v, 1956 Tai Douglas DC3. 75v, 1966 New Herbrides Airways Drover. 90v, 1994 Air Vanuatu Boeing 737.

1994, Dec. 7
641	A118	25v multicolored	.60	.60
642	A118	60v multicolored	1.60	1.60
643	A118	75v multicolored	1.90	1.90
644	A118	90v multicolored	2.50	2.50
		Nos. 641-644 (4)	6.60	6.60

Hibiscus A119

1995, Feb. 1   **Litho.**   *Perf. 12*
645	A119	25v The Path	.45	.45
646	A119	60v Old Frankie	1.20	1.20
647	A119	90v Fijian white	1.75	1.75
648	A119	200v Surf rider	4.00	4.00
		Nos. 645-648 (4)	7.40	7.40

Lizards A120

Designs: 25v, Emoia nigromarginata. 55v, Nactus multicarinatus. 70v, Lepidodactylus. 80v, Emoia caerulocauda. 140v, Emoia sanfordi.

1995, Apr. 12
649	A120	25v multicolored	.50	.50
650	A120	55v multicolored	1.20	1.20
651	A120	70v multicolored	1.50	1.50

652	A120	80v multicolored	1.60	1.60
653	A120	140v multicolored	3.00	3.00
		Nos. 649-653 (5)	7.80	7.80

Shell Type of 1993

25v, Epitonium scalare. 55v, Strombus latissimus. 90v, Conus bullatus. 200v, Pterynotus pinnatus.

1995, June 1

654	A112	25v multicolored	.60	.60
655	A112	55v multicolored	1.25	1.25
656	A112	90v multicolored	2.00	2.00
657	A112	200v multicolored	4.75	4.75
		Nos. 654-657 (4)	8.60	8.60

Anniversaries — A121

Designs: 25v, Girls wearing traditional head pieces. 55v, Stylized picture of natives dancing, vert. 60v, Children, doves, natl. flag, UN flag, vert. 75v, Embroidered tapestry of native, vert. 90v, Troops parading. 140v, Group in traditional ceremony.

Perf. 14x13½, 13½x14

1995, July 28   Litho.

658	A121	25v multicolored	.50	.50
659	A121	55v multicolored	1.00	1.00
660	A121	60v multicolored	1.00	1.00
661	A121	75v multicolored	1.50	1.50
662	A121	90v multicolored	1.60	1.60
663	A121	140v multicolored	2.50	2.50
a.		Souvenir sheet of 1	4.25	4.25
		Nos. 658-663 (6)	8.10	8.10

UN, 50th anniv. (#660). Singapore 95 (#663a). Others, independence, 15th anniv.

World War II Type of 1992

60v, SB2C Helldiver. 70v, Spitfire Mk VIII. 75v, F4U-1A Corsair. 80v, PV1 Ventura. 140v, Japanese surrender, USS Missouri.

1995, Sept. 1   Litho.   Perf. 12½

664	A105	60v multicolored	2.75	2.75
665	A105	70v multicolored	3.00	3.00
666	A105	75v multicolored	3.00	3.00
667	A105	80v multicolored	3.50	3.50
		Nos. 664-667 (4)	12.25	12.25

Souvenir Sheet

Perf. 13½

| 667A | A105 | 140v multicolored | 9.00 | 9.00 |

No. 667A for Singapore 95.

Artifacts — A122

Ambae money mat and: a, 25v, Rambaramp mortuary effigy, Malakula. b, 60v, Wusi pot, Espiritu Santo. c, 75v, Slit gong, Efate Island. d, 90v, Tapa cloth, Erromango Island.
Nos. 668e, 668f, like No. 668d.

1995, Nov. 22   Litho.   Perf. 13½x13

668	A122	Strip of 4, #a.-d.	5.50	5.50
e.		90v Perf. 14	1.50	1.50
f.		Souvenir sheet, #668e	2.75	2.75

No. 668f, 9th Asian Intl. Philatelic Exhibition, Beijing.
Issued: Nos. 668e, 668f, Dec. 1995.
See No. 720.

Fishing
A123

1996, Feb. 1   Litho.   Perf. 14

669	A123	55v Cast net	1.00	1.00
670	A123	75v Reef	1.25	1.25
671	A123	80v Deep water, vert.	1.25	1.25
672	A123	140v Game, vert.	2.50	2.50
		Nos. 669-672 (4)	6.00	6.00

Flying Foxes
A124

No. 673, Notopteris macdonaldi, facing left. No. 674, Pteropus anetianus, green leaves on tree, vert. No. 675, Pteropus anetianus, diff., vert. No. 676, Notopteris macdonaldi, diff.
No. 677, vert: a, 90v, Pteropus tonganus. b, 140v, Pteropus tonganus, diff.

1996, Apr. 3   Litho.   Perf. 14

673	A124	25v multicolored	.70	.55
674	A124	25v multicolored	.70	.55
675	A124	25v multicolored	.70	.55
676	A124	25v multicolored	.70	.55
		Nos. 673-676 (4)	2.80	2.20

Souvenir Sheet

| 677 | A124 | Sheet of 2, #a.-b. | 5.25 | 5.25 |

World Wildlife Fund (Nos. 673-676). 9th Asian Intl. Philatelic Exhibition (No. 677).

UNICEF, 50th Anniv.
A125

Unwmk.

1996, June 5   Litho.   Perf. 14

| 678 | A125 | 55v Immunizations | 1.10 | 1.10 |
| 679 | A125 | 60v Breast feeding | 1.40 | 1.40 |

Radio, Cent.
A126

60v, Airplane, radio signal. 75v, Radio Vanuatu. 80v, Guglielmo Marconi. 90v, Ship, radio signal.

1996, June 5   Perf. 14½

680	A126	60v multicolored	1.00	1.00
681	A126	75v multicolored	1.20	1.20
682	A126	80v multicolored	1.25	1.25
683	A126	90v multicolored	1.50	1.50
a.		Block of 4, #680-683	6.50	6.50

Modern Olympic Games,
Cent. — A127

Designs: 25v, Marie Kapalu, Tawai Keiruan, Baptiste Firiam, Tava Kalo, 1996 athletes from Vanuatu. 70v, 1996 Athletes in training. 75v, 1950's Athletes. 200v, 1896 Athletes.

1996, July 17   Litho.   Perf. 14

684	A127	25v multicolored	.45	.45
685	A127	70v multicolored	1.25	1.25
686	A127	75v multicolored	1.25	1.25
687	A127	200v multicolored	3.75	3.75
		Nos. 684-687 (4)	6.70	6.70

Christmas
A128

Children of various races holding candles in front of churches: a, 25v, Presbyterian, Roman Catholic. b, 60v, Church of Christ. c, 75v, 7th Day Adventist, Apostolic. d, 90v, Anglican.

1996, Sept. 11   Litho.   Perf. 14

| 688 | A128 | Strip of 4, #a.-d. | 4.50 | 4.50 |

No. 688 is a continuous design.

Hibiscus
A129

1996, Nov. 13   Litho.   Perf. 13½

689	A129	25v Lady Cilento	.50	.50
690	A129	60v Kinchen's Yellow	1.25	1.25
691	A129	90v D.J. O'Brien	1.75	1.75
692	A129	200v Cuban Variety	3.75	3.75
a.		Sheet of 2, #689, #692	6.00	6.00
		Nos. 689-692 (4)	7.25	7.25

Hong Kong '97. No. 692a issued 2/12/97.

Diving
A130

Designs: 70v, Coral Garden. 75v, Lady of the President Coolidge. 90v, "Boris," Queensland grouper. 140v, Wreck of the President Coolidge.

1997, Jan. 15   Litho.   Perf. 14½x14

693	A130	70v multicolored	1.25	1.25
694	A130	75v multicolored	1.25	1.25
695	A130	90v multicolored	1.50	1.50
696	A130	140v multicolored	2.50	2.50
a.		Souvenir sheet, #694, 696	6.00	6.00
b.		Souvenir sheet, #693-696	12.00	12.00
		Nos. 693-696 (4)	6.50	6.50

Pacific '97 (#696a).

Birds
A131

25v, Sharp-tailed sandpiper. 55v, Crested tern. 60v, Little pied cormorant. 75v, Brown booby. 80v, Reef heron. 90v, Red-tailed tropic bird.

1997, June 4   Litho.   Perf. 13½x14

697	A131	25v multi	.55	.55
698	A131	55v multi	1.10	1.10
699	A131	60v multi	1.20	1.20
700	A131	75v multi	1.40	1.40
701	A131	80v multi, vert.	1.40	1.40
702	A131	90v multi, vert.	1.75	1.75
		Nos. 697-702 (6)	7.40	7.40

Air Vanuatu, 10th Anniv.
A132

Designs: 25v, Pilot at controls. 60v, Airplane being serviced, cargo loaded. 90v, Serving drinks to passengers. 200v, Passengers leaving plane upon arrival at Vanuatu.

1997, Apr. 2   Perf. 14½x14

703	A132	25v multicolored	.45	.45
704	A132	60v multicolored	1.10	1.10
705	A132	90v multicolored	1.75	1.75
706	A132	200v multicolored	3.75	3.75
		Nos. 703-706 (4)	7.05	7.05

No. 704 is 81x31mm.

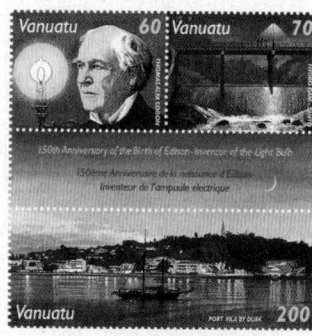

Thomas A. Edison (1847-1931) — A133

Designs: 60v, Light bulb, Edison. 70v, Hydro dam, Santo. 200v, Port Vila by dusk.

1997, Aug. 27   Litho.   Perf. 12

707		60v multicolored	1.00	1.00
708		70v multicolored	1.25	1.25
709		200v multicolored	3.50	3.50
a.	A133	Block of 3, #707-709 + label	7.25	7.25

No. 709 is 80x30mm.

Fish — A134

Designs: 25v, Yellow-faced angelfish. 55v, Flame angelfish. 60v, Lemonpeel angelfish. 70v, Emperor angelfish. 140v, Multi-barred angelfish.

1997, Nov. 12   Litho.   Perf. 14x13½

710	A134	25v multicolored	.45	.45
711	A134	55v multicolored	1.00	1.00
712	A134	60v multicolored	1.20	1.20
713	A134	70v multicolored	1.25	1.25
714	A134	140v multicolored	2.50	2.50
		Nos. 710-714 (5)	6.40	6.40

Architecture in Vanuatu
A135

Designs: 30v, Fale-Espiritu Santo. 65v, Natl. Cultural Center. 80v, University of the South Pacific. 200v, Chief's Nakamal.

1998, Feb. 11   Litho.   Perf. 14½x14

715	A135	30v multicolored	.45	.45
716	A135	65v multicolored	1.00	1.00
717	A135	80v multicolored	1.20	1.20
718	A135	200v multicolored	3.00	3.00
		Nos. 715-718 (4)	5.65	5.65

Diana, Princess of Wales (1961-97)
Common Design Type

Various portraits: a, 75v. b, 85v. c, 145v.

1998, Mar. 31   Litho.   *Perf. 14½x14*
718A CD355 95v multicolored   1.50 1.50
Sheet of 4
719 CD355 #a.-c., 718A   6.50 6.50

No. 719 sold for 400v + 50v, with surtax from international sales being donated to The Diana, Princess of Wales Memorial Fund and surtax from national sales being donated to designated local charity.

Artifacts Type of 1995

Tribal masks: a, 30v, South West Malakula. b, 65v, North Ambrym. c, 75v, Gana Island Banks. d, 85v, Uripiv Island, Malakula. e, 95v, Vao Island, Malakula, and Central South Pentecost.

1998, June 3   Litho.   *Perf. 14½*
720 A122   Strip of 5, #a.-e.   7.25 7.25

Butterflies — A136

30v, Danaus plexippus. 60v, Hypolimnas bolina. 65v, Eurema hecabe. 75v, Nymphalidae. 95v, Precis villida. 205v, Tirumala hamata.

1998, July 23   Litho.   *Die Cut*
Self-Adhesive
721 A136 30v multicolored   .55 .55
722 A136 60v multicolored   1.10 1.10
723 A136 65v multicolored   1.25 1.25
724 A136 75v multicolored   1.60 1.60
725 A136 95v multicolored   1.90 1.90
726 A136 205v multicolored   3.25 3.25
a.   Souvenir sheet of 1   5.00 5.00
   Nos. 721-726 (6)   9.65 9.65

Singpex '98 (#726a).

Volcanoes — A137

30v, Yasur, Tanna. 60v, Marum & Benbow, Ambrym. 75v, Gaua. 80v, Lopevi. 145v, Ambae.

1998, Oct. 23   Litho.   *Perf. 15x14*
728 A137 30v multicolored   .45 .45
729 A137 60v multicolored   .90 .90
730 A137 75v multicolored   1.20 1.20
731 A137 80v multicolored   1.20 1.20
732 A137 145v multicolored   2.25 2.25
   Nos. 728-732 (5)   6.00 6.00

Early Explorers A138

Explorer, ship: 34v, Pedro Fernandez de Quiros, San Pedro y Paulo, 1606. 73v, Louis-Antoine de Bougainville, Boudeuse, 1768. 84v, Capt. James Cook, HMS Resolution, 1774. 90v, Jean-Fancois de Galaup de la Perousse, Astrolabe, 1788. 96v, Jules Sebastien-Cesar Dumont d'Urville, Astrolabe, "1788."

1999, Feb. 17   Litho.   *Perf. 14*
733 A138 34v multicolored   .50 .50
734 A138 73v multicolored   1.60 1.60
735 A138 84v multicolored   1.90 1.90
a.   Souv. sheet, #733-735   3.75 3.75

736 A138 90v multicolored   1.90 1.90
737 A138 96v multicolored   2.00 2.00
a.   Souv. sheet, #734, 736-737   5.50 5.50
   Nos. 733-737 (5)   7.90 7.90

No. 735a was released for Australia '99 World Stamp Expo on 3/19/99; No. 737a for PhilexFrance 99.

Birds — A139

34v, Vanuatu kingfisher. 67v, Shining cuckoo. 73v, Peregrine falcon. 107v, Rainbow lorikeet.

1999, May 12   Litho.   *Perf. 14*
738 A139 34v multicolored   .75 .75
739 A139 67v multicolored   1.25 1.25
   Booklet, 5 #739   7.00
740 A139 73v multicolored   1.50 1.50
741 A139 107v multicolored   2.25 2.25
a.   Sheet of 1   4.75 4.75
b.   Sheet of 1 with China 1999 emblem in margin   5.75 5.75
   Nos. 738-741 (4)   5.75 5.75

Issued: #741b, 8/18.

Nos. 601, 603-605, 607, 608 Surcharged

Perf. 14½x14, 14x14½
1998-2000   Litho.
742 A111 1v on 100v #608   .25 .25
742A A111 2v on 45v #601   .25 .25
743 A111 2v on 55v #603   .25 .25
744 A111 3v on 60v #604   .25 .25
744A A111 3v on 75v #606   .25 .25
745 A111 4v on 45v #601   .25 .25
745A A111 5v on 70v #605
745B A111 34v on 20v #598   .50 .50
745C A111 67v on 300v #609   1.00 1.00
745D A111 73v on 80v #607
   Nos. 742-745D (10)   3.00 3.00

Issued: No. 742, No. 742A, 743, 744, 745, 745A, 12/18/98; No. 744A, 4/27/99; Nos. 745B, 745C, 745D, 2/17/00.

Ceremonial Dancers — A140

1v, Banks Islands. 2v, Small Nambas, Laman-Malakula. 3v, Small Nambas, Malakula. 5v, Smol Bag Theatre. 107v, South West Bay, Malakula. 200v, Big Nambas, Malakula. 500v, Pentacost.

1999, July 14   *Perf. 14*
746 A140 1v multicolored   .25 .25
747 A140 2v multicolored   .25 .25
748 A140 3v multicolored   .25 .25
749 A140 5v multicolored   .25 .25
750 A140 107v multicolored   1.60 1.60
751 A140 200v multicolored   3.25 3.25
752 A140 500v multicolored   7.75 7.75
   Nos. 746-752 (7)   13.60 13.60

See Nos. 788-791.

Poisonous Fish — A141

Designs: 34v, Pterois antennata. 84v, Pterois antennata, diff. 90v, Pterois volitans. 96v, Pterois volitans, diff.

1999, Oct. 13   Litho.   *Perf. 14¼*
753 A141 34v multi   .70 .70
754 A141 84v multi   1.75 1.75
755 A141 90v multi   2.00 2.00
756 A141 96v multi   2.25 2.25
   Nos. 753-756 (4)   6.70 6.70

Millennium A142

Designs: a, 34v, Fish. b, 68v, Girl, land diver, vert. c, 84v, Fetish, vert. d, 90v, Bird, flowers. e, 96v, Man with conch shell.

1999, Dec. 1   *Perf. 14½*
757 A142   Sheet of 5, #a.-e.   7.00 7.00

Souvenir Sheet

Queen Mother, 100th Birthday — A143

a, 107v, As child. b, 100v, As old woman.

Litho. with Foil Application
2000, May 22   *Perf. 13¼*
758 A143   Sheet of 2, #a-b   5.50 5.50

The Stamp Show 2000, London.

Intelsat A144

Designs: 10v, Launch vehicle. 34v, Port Vila ground station. 100v, Intelsat 802 over Vaunatu. 225v, Intelsat and Tam Tam drum.

Litho. with Foil Application
2000, June 21   *Die Cut Perf. 10*
Self-Adhesive
759-762 A144   Set of 4   7.00 7.00
762a   Souvenir sheet, #760, 762   5.25 5.25

World Stamp Expo 2000, Anaheim (#762a).

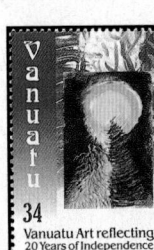

Independence, 20th Anniv., UN Peace Year — A145

Artwork: 34v, Abstract painting by Sero Kuautonga. 67v, Tapa cloth by Moses Pita. 73v, Tapestry by Juliet Pita. 84v, Natora wood carving by Emmannuel Watt. 90v, Watercolor by Joseph John.

2000, July 29   Litho.   *Perf. 13¾x13¼*
763-767 A145   Set of 5   8.00 8.00
   Booklet, 5 #764   6.50

2000 Summer Olympics, Sydney — A146

Designs: 56v, Runner. 67v, Weight lifter. 90v, High jumper. 96v, Boxer.

2000, Sept. 15   *Perf. 13¼x13*
768-771 A146   Set of 4   5.50 5.50
   Booklet, 5 #769   6.00

Dolphins — A147

34v, Common. 73v, Spotted. 84v, Spinner. 107v, Bottlenose.

2000, Nov. 30   Litho.   *Perf. 12½*
772-775 A147   Set of 4   6.50 6.50
775a   Souvenir sheet, #774-775   5.50 5.50

Hong Kong 2001 Stamp Exhibition (#775a).

Birds — A148

Designs: 35v, Cardinal honeyeater. 60v, Vanuatu white-eye. 90v, Santo Mountain starling. 100v, Royal parrotfinch. 110v, Vanuatu Mountain honeyeater.

2001, Feb. 1   Litho.   *Perf. 14*
776-780 A148   Set of 5   10.50 10.50
780a   Horiz. strip, #776-780   10.50 10.50

Exports — A149

Designs: 35v, Vanilla. 75v, Cacao. 90v, Coffee. 110v, Copra.

2001, Apr. 11   *Perf. 13¼x13*
781-784 A149   Set of 4   6.50 6.50

Whales A150

Designs: 60v, Sperm. 80v, Humpback, vert. 90v, Blue.

Perf. 14½x14¾, 14¾x14½

2001, July 18 Litho.
785-787 A150 Set of 3   6.00 6.00
787a   Souvenir sheet, #785-787,
    perf. 14½   6.25 6.25

See New Caledonia No. 874.

Ceremonial Dancers Type of 1999

Designs: 35v, Snake dance, Banks Islands, horiz. 100v, Toka Dance, Tanna, horiz. 300v, Rom Dance, Ambryn, horiz. 1000v, Brasive Dance, Futuna, horiz.

2001, Sept. 12 Litho. **Perf. 13x13¼**
788 A140   35v multi   .75 .75
789 A140   100v multi   2.10 2.10
790 A140   300v multi   6.25 6.25

Litho. With Foil Application
791 A140   1000v multi   20.00 20.00
   Nos. 788-791 (4)   29.10 29.10

Sand
Drawings — A151

Various sand drawings and: a, Four people on beach. b, Man standing in canoe in water. c, Man sitting on canoe, man rowing canoe. d, Canoe, shelter.

Perf. 12¾x13½

2001, Nov. 28 Litho.
792 A151   60v multi   1.00 1.00
792A A151   90v multi   1.50 1.50
792B A151   110v multi   1.90 1.90
792C A151   135v multi   2.40 2.40
  d.   Horiz. strip of 4 + central label   9.00 9.00

Intl. Year of
Ecotourism
A152

Designs: Nos. 793, 798a, 35v, Mount Yasur, Pentecost Island land diver, dancers. Nos. 794, 798b, 60v Dancers, man making kava. Nos. 795, 798c, 75v, Siri Falls, flowers, birds, vert. Nos. 796, 798d, 110v, Kayakers, scuba diver, vert. Nos. 797, 798e, 135v, Beach bungalows, tourists.

2002, Jan. 30 Litho. **Perf. 14**
Stamps + Label
793-797 A152   Set of 5   8.75 8.75

Souvenir Sheet
Without Labels
Perf. 14½x14¾
798 A152   Sheet of 5, #a-e   8.75 8.75

Nos. 793, 794, and 797 are 38x26mm and Nos. 795-796 are 26x38mm, while Nos. 798a, 798b, and 798e are 37x25mm and Nos. 798c-798d are 25x37mm.

Horses
A153

Designs: 35v, Working horses. 60v, Cattle roundup. 75v, Horse racing. 80v, Tourism and horses. 200v, Wild Tanna horse.

2002, Mar. 27 **Perf. 14¾x14**
799-803 A153   Set of 5   8.25 8.25
803a   Souvenir sheet of 1   4.25 4.25
803b   Souvenir sheet of 1 with Phi-
    lakorea 2002 emblem   4.25 4.25

Issued: No. 803b, 7/31/02.

Soccer
A154

Designs: 35v, Children's soccer. 80v, Under 17 soccer. 110v, Women's soccer. 135v, International soccer.

2002, May 31 Litho. **Perf. 13¾**
804-807 A154   Set of 4   7.00 7.00

Value is for stamps with surrounding selvage.

Reforestation — A155

No. 808: a, Girl with seedling of Artocarpus atilis. b, Boy and man planting seedling of Endospermum medullosum. c, Canoe carver with Gyrocarpus americanus log. d, Mother and child with Dracontomelon vitiense fruit.

Serpentine Die Cut

2002, July 31 Litho.
Self-Adhesive
808   Horiz. strip of 4   6.75
  a.   A155 35v multi   .80 .80
  b.   A155 60v multi   1.40 1.40
  c.   A155 90v multi   1.90 1.90
  d.   A155 110v multi   2.50 2.50

Dugongs
A156

Designs: 35v, Pair nuzzling. 75v, Pair swimming. 80v, One swimming. 135v, One on ocean floor.

2002, Sept. 25 Litho. **Perf. 13¾**
812-815 A156   Set of 4   6.25 6.25
815a   Souvenir sheet, #814-815   7.00 7.00

Orchids — A157

Designs: 35v, Dendrobium gouldii. 60v, Dendrobium polysema. 90v, Dendrobium spectabile. 110v, Flickingeria comata.

2002, Nov. 27 Litho. **Perf. 13¼**
816-819 A157   Set of 4   6.25 6.25

Year of
Cattle — A158

Cattle Breeds: 35v, Limousin. 80v, Charolais. 110v, Simmental. 135v, Red Brahman.

2003, Jan. 29 **Perf. 13**
820-823 A158   Set of 4   7.50 7.50

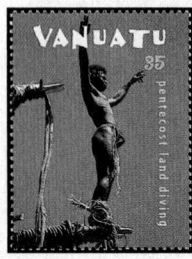

Pentecost
Island Land
Divers — A159

Designs: 35v, Diver on platform. 80v, Diver in air. 110v, Dancers, platform. 200v, Diver and platform (35x90mm).

2003, Mar. 26 **Perf. 13¾x13¼**
824-827 A159   Set of 4   9.50 9.50
827a   Souvenir sheet of 1   5.25 5.25

Snorkeling
A160

Various people snorkeling: 35v, 80v, 90v, 110v, 135v. 80v and 90v are vert.

2003, May 28 Litho. **Perf. 13¾**
828-832 A160   Set of 5   7.50 7.50
832a   Souvenir sheet, #828-832,
    perf. 13¼   8.25 8.25

Natanggura
Palm — A161

Half of palm nut and: 35v, Man planting palm tree, carved dolphins. 80v, Man weaving thatch for roof, carved turtle. 90v, Carver, carved lizard. 135v, Carvers, carved fish.

2003, July 23 **Perf. 13¾x13¼**
833-836 A161   Set of 4   5.75 5.75

Opening of
Underwater Post
Office in May
2003 — A162

2003, Sept. 24 **Perf. 13¾**
837 A162   90v multi   2.25 2.25

Sea
Horses — A163

Designs: 60v, Hippocampus kuda. 90v, Hippocampus histrix. 200v, Hippocampus bargibanti.

2003, Sept. 24
838-840 A163   Set of 3   6.00 6.00
840a   Souvenir sheet of 1   4.50 4.50

Moths
A164

Designs: 35v, Daphnis hypothous. 90v, Hippotion celerio. 110v, Euchromia creusa. 135v, Eudocima salaminia.

2003, Nov. 26 **Perf. 13½**
841-844 A164   Set of 4   6.50 6.50

Activities at
Underwater Post
Office — A165

Designs: 35v, Workers placing mail in bag. 80v, Swimmer placing mail in mail box. 110v, Swimmer at counter. 220v, Clerk at counter, swimmer near mail box.

2004, Jan. 30 **Perf. 13¾x13½**
845-848 A165   Set of 4   8.25 8.25
848a   Souvenir sheet of 1   4.50 4.50

2004 Hong Kong Stamp Expo (#848a).

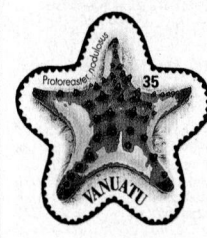

Starfish
A166

Designs: 35v, Protoreaster nodulosus. 60v, Linckia laevigata. 90v, Fromia monilis. 250v, Echinaster callosus.

Serpentine Die Cut

2004, Apr. 28 Litho.
Self-Adhesive
849-852 A166   Set of 4   8.25 8.25

Red-tailed
Tropicbird
A167

Designs: 35v, Adult and juvenile. 50v, Adult and chick, vert. 75v, Adult flying above juvenile, vert. 135v, Adult in flight. 200v, Adult pair.

2004, July 14   Litho.   Perf. 13¾
853-857 A167   Set of 5   10.50 10.50
857a   Souvenir sheet, #853-857,
       perf. 13½   11.50 11.50

Musket Cove to Port Vila Yacht Race,
25th Anniv. — A168

Various yachts: 35v, 80v, 90v, 200v. 80v
and 200v are vert.

2004, Sept. 18   Perf. 14¼
858-861 A168   Set of 4   10.00 10.00
861a   Souvenir sheet of 1   5.25   5.25

See Fiji Nos. 1024-1027.

Miniature Sheet

Marine Life — A169

No. 862: a, Red and black anemonefish. b,
Longfin bannerfish. c, Goldman's sweetlips. d,
Green turtle. e, Clark's anemonefish. f, Harlequin sweetlips. g, Yellowtail coris. h, Emperor
angelfish. i, Hairy red hermit crab, leaf oyster.
j, Spotfin lionfish. k, Yellow-lipped sea krait. l,
Clam.

Serpentine Die Cut 13¼
2004, Nov. 24   Litho.
Self-Adhesive
862 A169 35v Sheet of 12, #a-l 11.00 11.00

Christmas
A170

Serpentine Die Cut 13
2004, Nov. 24   Self-Adhesive
863 A170 80v multi   2.25   2.25

Sunsets
A171

Designs: 60v, Sailboat. 80v, Man with raised
arm, vert. 90v, Sailboats, vert. 135v, Man
blowing conch shell.

2005, Jan. 19   Perf. 14x14½, 14½x14
864-867 A171   Set of 4   9.25   9.25

Miniature Sheet

Lapita People — A172

No. 868: a, 50v, Man holding tool, vert. b,
70v, People cleaning fish. c, 110v, People
tending fire and carrying animal to fire. d,

200v, Women making baskets, mother and
child, vert.

2005, Mar. 2   Perf. 13¼
868 A172   Sheet of 4, #a-d   11.50 11.50

Pacific Explorer 2005 World Stamp Expo,
Sydney.

Volcano
Post
A173

Mail box on Mount Yasur and: 35v, Five
tourists. 80v, Native woman. 100v, Three postal workers. 250v, Postal worker removing
mail.

2005, May 31   Litho.   Perf. 14x14¼
869-872 A173   Set of 4   9.25   9.25
872a   Souvenir sheet of 1   5.50   5.50

Souvenir Sheet

Independence, 25th Anniv. — A174

No. 873: a, 35v, Vanuatu natives celebrating. b, 50v, Soldiers raising Vanuatu flag,
1980. c, 400v, Children and statue of family.

2005, July 30   Litho.   Perf. 13
873 A174   Sheet of 3, #a-c   12.50 12.50

Miniature Sheet

Corals — A175

No. 874: a, Lace coral. b, Star coral. c, Sun
coral (Tubastraea sp.). d, Plate coral. e, Brown
anthelia. f, Bubble coral. g, Flowerpot coral. h,
Cup coral. i, Daisy coral. j, Sun coral (Tubastraea diaphana). k, Mushroom-feather coral. l,
Sun coral (Tubastraea micrantha).

Serpentine Die Cut 13½x13¼
2005, Sept. 7   Litho.
Self-Adhesive
874 A175 35v Sheet of 12, #a-l 11.00 11.00

Landscapes — A176

Designs: 80v, Horse and rider on beach.
90v, Palm trees. 110v, Waterfall. 135v,
Harbor.

2005, Nov. 16   Litho.   Perf. 14¼x14
875-878 A176   Set of 4   11.00 11.00

Miniature Sheet

Reef Shells — A177

No. 879: a, Crocus clam. b, Pearl oyster. c,
Gold-ringer cowrie. d, Cock-a-comb oyster. e,
Tiger cowrie. f, Textile cone. g, Marlinspike. h,
Vibex bonnet. i, Erosa cowrie. j, Scorpion
conch. k, Honey cowrie. l, Umbilical ovula.

Serpentine Die Cut 13½
2006, Feb. 8   Self-Adhesive
879 A177 35v Sheet of 12, #a-l 11.00 11.00

Queen
Elizabeth
II, 80th
Birthday
A178

Queen: 50v, As young woman in Army uniform. 100v, Without hat. No. 882, 110v, With
blue hat. No. 883, 200v, With yellow hat.
No. 884: a, 110v, Like 100v. b, 200v, Like
No. 882.

2006, Apr. 21   Litho.   Perf. 14
With White Frames
880-883 A178   Set of 4   8.00   8.00
Souvenir Sheet
Without White Frames
884 A178   Sheet of 2, #a-b   5.75   5.75

Souvenir Sheet

Arrival in Vanuatu of Pedro Fernandez
de Quiros, 400th Anniv. — A179

2006, May 10   Perf. 13¼
885 A179 350v multi   7.50   7.50

2006 World Cup Soccer
Championships, Germany — A180

Various soccer players, 2006 World Cup
emblem on soccer jersey: 35v, 80v, 110v,
135v.

2006, June 9   Litho.   Die Cut
Self-Adhesive
886-889 A180   Set of 4   7.00   7.00
889a   Souvenir sheet, #886-889   7.00   7.00

Flowers
A181

Designs: 5v, Passiflora foetida. 10v, Hibiscus rosa-sinensis. 20v, Cereus undatus. 40v,
Strelitzia reginae. 50v, Spathodea campanulata. 70v, Delonix regia. 90v, Hibiscus
hilaceus. 100v, Nymphaea sp. 150v, Plumeria
obtusa. 500v, Allamanda cathartica. 1000v,
Thunbergia grandiflora.

Serpentine Die Cut 11¾
2006, July 1   Self-Adhesive
890 A181   5v multi   .25   .25
891 A181   10v multi   .25   .25
892 A181   20v multi   .35   .35
893 A181   40v multi   .65   .65
894 A181   50v multi   .80   .80
895 A181   70v multi   1.10   1.10
896 A181 100v multi   1.60   1.60
897 A181 150v multi   2.50   2.50
898 A181 500v multi   8.00   8.00
899 A181 1000v multi   16.50 16.50
Inscribed "International Post" at
Left
900 A181   5v multi   .25   .25
901 A181   10v multi   .25   .25
902 A181   20v multi   .35   .35
903 A181   50v multi   .80   .80
904 A181   90v multi   1.40   1.40
905 A181 100v multi   1.60   1.60
906 A181 500v multi   8.00   8.00
907 A181 1000v multi   16.50 16.50
   Nos. 890-907 (18)   61.15 61.15

Miniature Sheet

Worldwide Fund for Nature
(WWF) — A182

No. 908: a, 70v, Giant grouper and coral. b,
90v, Giant grouper and smaller fish. c, 100v,
Juvenile giant groupers. d, 150v, Giant
grouper, smaller fish, diff.

2006, Oct. 4   Litho.   Perf. 13¼
908 A182   Sheet, 2 each #a-
       d   13.50 13.50

Shipwreck of the SS President
Coolidge — A183

Designs: 90v, Diver, corals. 100v, Divers,
fish. 130v, Shipwreck, fish. 150v, Ship sinking,
sailors leaving ship (85x30mm).
No. 913: a, 90v, Like #909. b, 100v, Like
#910. c, 130v, Like #911. d, 150v, Like #912.

2006, Nov. 29   Litho.   Perf. 13¼
Stamps Inscribed "International
Post"
909-912 A183   Set of 4   8.50   8.50
Souvenir Sheet
Stamps Without "International Post"
913   A183   Sheet of 4,
                #a-d   8.50   8.50

Reef Heron
A184

Reef heron: 10v, With wings extended. 20v,
Standing on land, vert. 50v, With fish in bill,
vert. 70v, Head. 250v, Chicks.

2007, Feb. 9   Litho.   Perf. 14½
914-918 A184   Set of 5   8.00   8.00
918a   Souvenir sheet, #914-918   8.00   8.00

Diving at
Million
Dollar
Point
A185

Designs: Nos. 919, 923a, 90v, Divers near submerged jeep. Nos. 920, 923b, 100v, Divers near submerged truck, vert. (42x60mm). Nos. 921, 923c, 130v, Diver, diff. Nos. 922, 923d, 150v, Diver, lionfish.

2007, Apr. 18   Perf. 13¼

Stamps Inscribed "International Post"

919-922 A185   Set of 4   8.50 8.50

Souvenir Sheet

Stamps Without "International Post"

923 A185   Sheet of 4, #a-d   8.50 8.50

Fruit — A186

Designs: 30v, Bananas. 40v, Watermelon. 70v, Limes. 100v, Papayas. 250v, Coconuts.

2007, June 27   Serpentine Die Cut

Self-Adhesive

924-928 A186   Set of 5   9.50 9.50

James A. Michener (1907-97), Writer A187

Michener: 40v, With pen. 90v, At typewriter. 130v, With island natives. 350v, Holding book.

2007, Aug. 22   Perf. 14½

929-932 A187   Set of 4   11.50 11.50

Banded Iguana — A188

Designs: 50v, Two iguanas, two flowers. 70v, Iguana on branch. 100v, Iguana. 250v, Iguana on flower bud.

Serpentine Die Cut 15

2007, Nov. 7   Litho.

Self-Adhesive

933-936 A188   Set of 4   9.25 9.25
936a   Souvenir sheet, #935-936   7.75 7.75

Air Vanuatu, 20th Anniv. — A189

Designs: 40v, Three airplanes at airport. 90v, Boeing 737-800. 130v, Boeing 737-300. 180v, Twin Otter. 250v, ATR 42.

2007-08   Serpentine Die Cut 15

937 A189 40v multi   .75   .75
938 A189 90v multi   1.75   1.75
939 A189 130v multi   2.50   2.50
940 A189 180v multi   3.50   3.50
941 A189 250v multi   4.75   4.75
         Nos. 937-941 (5)   13.25 13.25
    First flight of Boeing 737-800 (#938). Issued: 40v, 130v, 180v, 250v, 11/23; 90v, 1/17/08.

Coconut Crabs A190

Crab on: 60v, Beach. 500v, Tree, vert.

Perf. 13½x13¼, 13¼x13½

2008, Feb. 20   Litho.

942-943 A190   Set of 2   13.00 13.00
943a   Souvenir sheet, #942-943   13.00 13.00

Miniature Sheet

2008 Summer Olympics, Beijing — A191

No. 944: a, 10v, Archery. b, 40v, Athletics. c, 60v, Table tennis. d, 90v, Weight lifting.

2008, June 18   Litho.   Perf. 12

944 A191   Sheet of 4, #a-d   4.25 4.25

Underwater Post Office — A192

Designs: 40v, Underwater postal workers carrying sacks of mail, fish with postcard. 80v, Postal worker, fish with letters. 100v, Postal workers in raft, fish with mail. 200v, Underwater post office, fish and marine life with letters.

2008, July 30   Litho.   Die Cut

Self-Adhesive

945-948 A192   Set of 4   8.50 8.50

Tourism — A193

Scenes and website addresses of: No. 949, 90v, Vanuatu Tourism. No. 950, 90v, Breakas Beach Resort. No. 951, 90v, Iririki Island Resort and Spa. No. 952, 90v, Le Lagon Resort. No. 953, 90v, The Melanesian Hotel. No. 954, 90v, Le Meridien Resort Spa and Casino. No. 955, 90v, Sebel Hotel.

2008, Aug. 27   Perf. 15x14¾

949-955 A193   Set of 7   13.00 13.00

Miniature Sheet

Nudibranchs — A194

No. 956: a, Risbecia tryoni. b, Phyllidia coelestis. c, Flabellina rubrolineata. d, Chromodoris lochi. e, Chromodoris

elisabethina. f, Jorunna funebris. g, Glossodoris rufomarginata. h, Phyllidia ocellata. i, Chromodoris geometrica. j, Phyllidia madangensis. k, Hexabranchus sanguineus. l, Glossodoris atromarginata.

Serpentine Die Cut 13¼

2008, Oct. 8   Self-Adhesive

956 A194 40v Sheet of 12, #a-l   8.50 8.50

Birds — A195

Designs: 45v, Eastern reef heron. 100v, Great crested tern. 130v, White-tailed tropicbird. 250v, Fairy tern.

2008, Nov. 26   Litho.   Perf. 14½x15

957-960 A195   Set of 4   9.00 9.00
960a   Souvenir sheet of 1 #960   5.00 5.00

Romance in Vanuatu — A196

Couples in Vanuatu, website addresses for: No. 961, 90v, Bride and groom wearing flowers (Events Vanuatu). No. 962, 90v, Bride and groom with wine glasses (Events Vanuatu). No. 963, 90v, Man and woman sitting on beach (Air Vanuatu). No. 964, 90v, Man and woman sitting on chaise lounges (Breakas Beach Resort). No. 965, 90v, Man and woman at table (White Grass Ocean Resort).

2009, Jan. 28   Litho.   Die Cut

Self-Adhesive

961-965 A196   Set of 5   7.00 7.00

Mystery (Inyeug) Island — A197

Designs: Nos. 966, 970a, 90v, Boat dock. Nos. 967, 970b, 100v, Snorkelers and boat, horiz. Nos. 968, 970c, 130v, Sailboat and trees, horiz. Nos. 969, 970d, 200v, Man and woman on outrigger canoe on beach.

2009, Mar. 28   Litho.   Perf. 14

Stamps Inscribed "International Post"

966-969 A197   Set of 4   8.25 8.25

Souvenir Sheet

Stamps Without "International Post"

970 A197   Sheet of 4, #a-d   8.25 8.25

Peonies A198

2009, Apr. 10   Litho.   Perf. 13¼

971 A198 100v multi   1.75   1.75
    Printed in sheets of 8.

Plumeria Flowers — A199

Various plumeria flowers: 90v, 100v, 130v, 150v.

2009, May 14   Perf. 14½x14

972-975 A199   Set of 4   8.00 8.00

Souvenir Sheet

Hong Kong 2009 Intl. Stamp Exhibition — A200

2009, May 14   Perf. 13½

976 A200   Sheet of 2, Pitcairn
             Islands #685a,
             Vanuatu #976a   5.50 5.50
  a.   150v Two pandas   2.50 2.50

No. 976 sold for 310v and New Zealand $5, and is identical to Pitcairn Islands No. 685.

Souvenir Sheet

First Contact Between Russia and Vanuatu, 200th Anniv. — A201

No. 977 — Map and: a, 130v, Russian Admiral V. M. Golovnin. b, 350v, Russian ship, "Diana."

2009, July 28   Perf. 13¼

977 A201   Sheet of 2, #a-b   8.50 8.50

Charles Darwin (1809-82), Naturalist — A202

No. 978 — Darwin, birds and: a, Tortoises. b, Iguanas.

2009, Sept. 2   Perf. 13¼x13½

978 A202 200v Horiz. pair, #a-b,
             + central label   7.50 7.50

Worldwide Fund for Nature (WWF) — A203

No. 979 — Beach thick-knee: a, Adult on nest, bird in flight. b, Adult and chick on ground, two birds in flight. c, Two adults at water's edge, bird in flight. d, Adult on beach, bird in flight.

	2009, Nov. 25	**Litho.**	**Perf. 13¼**
979	Horiz. strip of 4	8.00	8.00
a.	A203 50v multi	1.00	1.00
b.	A203 90v multi	1.60	1.60
c.	A203 130v multi	2.50	2.50
d.	A203 150v multi	2.75	2.75

No. 979 was printed in sheets containing two strips.

Souvenir Sheet

New Year 2010 (Year of the Tiger) — A204

	2010, Feb. 14		**Perf. 13¼**
980	A204 250v multi	5.00	5.00

Miniature Sheet

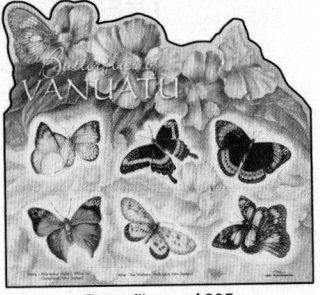

Butterflies — A205

No. 981: a, Calopsilia pomona. b, Papilio godeffroyi. c, Hypolimnas octocula. d, Doleschallia bisaltide. e, Acraea andromacha. f, Danaus affinis.

	2010, Apr. 14		**Die Cut**
	Self-Adhesive		
981	A205 100v Sheet of 6, #a-f	11.00	11.00

Tourism — A206

Designs: 40v, Dugong off Epi Island. 140v, Snake Dance, Banks Island, horiz. 160v, Iririki Resort, Efate Island. 190v, Mt. Yasur Volcano, Tanna Island, horiz.

	Perf. 13¼x13¾, 13¾x13¼		
	2010, Apr. 30		
982	A206 40v multi	.75	.75
a.	Perf. 14	.75	.75

Inscribed "International Post" at Left			
983	A206 140v multi	2.75	2.75
984	A206 160v multi	3.00	3.00
985	A206 190v multi	3.50	3.50
	Nos. 982-985 (4)	11.10	11.10

Miniature Sheet
Perf. 14

986	Sheet of 4, #982a, 986a-986c	10.50	10.50
a.	A206 140v Like #983, without "International Post" at left	2.75	2.75
b.	A206 160v Like #984, without "International Post" at left	2.90	2.90
c.	A206 190v Like #985, without "International Post" at left	3.75	3.75

Expo 2010, Shanghai (#986).

Cats — A207

Color of cat: 10v, White. 100v, Black and white. 160v, Brown and white. 190v, Gray and white.

	2010, July 14		**Perf. 14½x14**
987-990	A207 Set of 4	8.50	8.50

Souvenir Sheet

2010 Youth Olympics, Singapore — A208

	2010, Aug. 14		**Perf. 13¼**
991	A208 500v multi	8.50	8.50

"Smile With Us" A209

Designs: No. 992, 20v, Man, statues in background. No. 993, 20v, Two women. No. 994, 20v, Three children. No. 995, 20v, Fish. No. 996, 20v, Dugong. No. 997, 100v, Woman. No. 998, 100v, Divers at Underwater Post Office. No. 999, 100v, Island. No. 1000, 100v, Dolphin. No. 1001, 100v, Airplane.

	2010, Dec. 15		**Perf. 13½**
992-1001	A209 Set of 10	11.00	11.00
996a	Horiz. strip of 5, #992-996	1.75	1.75
1001a	Horiz. strip of 5, #997-1001	9.00	9.00

Turtles A210

No. 1002: a, Green turtles, "International Post" at left. b, Green turtles, "International Post" at right. c, Hawksbill turtle, "International Post" at left. d, Hawksbill turtles, "International Post" at right.

	2011, Jan. 26		**Perf. 13½x13¼**
1002	Horiz. strip of 4 + central label	7.75	7.75
a.-d.	A210 100v Any single	1.75	1.75

Tanna Coffee — A211

Designs: No. 1003, 100v, Short black. No. 1004, 100v, Long black. 140v, Latte. 160v, Cappuccino.

	2011, Mar. 23		**Perf. 14½x14**
1003-1006	A211 Set of 4	9.75	9.75

Worldwide Fund for Nature (WWF) — A212

No. 1007 — Massena's lorikeet: a, Bird facing left. b, Bird on branch. c, Two birds on branch. d, Bird on palm frond.

	2011, May 25	**Litho.**	**Perf. 14**
1007	Horiz. strip of 4	8.50	8.50
a.	A212 40v multi	.80	.80
b.	A212 60v multi	1.25	1.25
c.	A212 140v multi	2.90	2.90
d.	A212 160v multi	3.25	3.25
e.	Sheet of 8, 2 each #1007a-1007d	17.50	17.50

Green and Golden Bell Frog — A213

Designs: 45v, Frog on branch. 70v, Frog in flower. 140v, Three frogs in flower. 200v, Frog on cut branch.

	2011, July 27		**Perf. 14¼**
1008-1011	A213 Set of 4	9.00	9.00
1011a	Souvenir sheet of 2, #1010-1011	7.00	7.00

Beaches A214

Designs: No. 1012, 100v, Airplane on beach of Eratap Island, birds. No. 1013, 100v, Trees near Champagne Beach, Espiritu Santo Island, turtles. 140v, Woman on beach at Havannah Harbor, Efate Island, shells. 160v, Beach on Pele Island, fish.

	2011, Sept. 28		**Perf. 14x14½**
1012-1015	A214 Set of 4	10.00	10.00

A gritty substance has been applied to the beach portions of the stamp designs.

Flowers — A215

Designs: No. 1016, 100v, Heliconia psittacorum. No. 1017, 100v, Heliconia rostrata. 140v, Strelitzia reginae. 180v, Heliconia caribaea variety.

	2011, Dec. 7		**Perf. 14½x14**
1016-1019	A215 Set of 4	10.50	10.50

Dragonflies A216

Designs: 40v, Yellow-striped flutterer. 90v, Globe skimmer. 140v, Fiery skimmer. 250v, Painted grasshawk.

	2012, Feb. 22		**Perf. 14¼**
1020-1023	A216 Set of 4	11.00	11.00
1023a	Souvenir sheet of 2, #1021, 1023	7.00	7.00

Diplomatic Relations Between Vanuatu and People's Republic of Chin, 30th Anniv. — A217

	2012, Mar. 26		**Perf. 12**
1024	A217 90v multi	1.75	1.75

Birds — A218

Designs: 10v, Southern shrikebill. 20v, Silvereyes. 40v, Red-bellied fruit doves. 50v, Pacific imperial pigeon. 70v, Long-tailed trillers. 90v, Vanuatu scrubfowl. 100v, Streaked fantails. 140v, Dark brown honeyeater. 160v, Vanuatu petrels. 400v, Ruddy turnstones. 500v, Purple swamphens. 1000v, Striated mangove heron. 40v and 70v lack blue triangle and airplane.

	2012, May 2	**Litho.**	**Perf. 14¼**
1025	A218 10v multi	.25	.25
1026	A218 20v multi	.40	.40
1027	A218 40v multi	.80	.80
1028	A218 50v multi	1.00	1.00
1029	A218 70v multi	1.40	1.40
1030	A218 90v multi	1.75	1.75
1031	A218 100v multi	2.00	2.00
1032	A218 140v multi	3.00	3.00
1033	A218 160v multi	3.25	3.25
1034	A218 400v multi	8.00	8.00
1035	A218 500v multi	10.00	10.00
1036	A218 1000v multi	20.00	20.00
a.	Souvenir sheet of 12, #1025-1036	52.50	52.50
	Nos. 1025-1036 (12)	51.85	51.85

Reign Of Queen Elizabeth II, 60th Anniv. — A219

No. 1037 — Queen Elizabeth II: a, 250v, On horse. b, 300v, Waving.

	2012, June 1		**Perf. 13¼x13½**
1037	Horiz. pair + central label	11.00	11.00
a.	A219 250v multi	5.00	5.00
b.	A219 300v multi	6.00	6.00

Kiwanis Charity Race Day A220

Kiwanis emblem and various race horses: 35v, 50v, 150v, 250v.

Perf. 14x14¼
2012, July 12 Litho. Unwmk.
1038-1041 A220 Set of 4 10.50 10.50

Nov. 14, 2012 Partial Solar Eclipse A221

People in boats and diagram of position of Sun and Moon at various times during eclipse: 40v, 60v, 160v, 180v.

Perf. 14x14¼
2012, Oct. 31 Litho. Unwmk.
1042-1045 A221 Set of 4 9.75 9.75

Vanuatu Red Cross Society, 30th Anniv. A222

Vanuatu Red Cross Society emblem, anniversary emblem and: 60v, Workers removing boxes from small boat. 100v, Hand under water running from faucet.

Perf. 14x14¼
2012, Dec. 5 Litho. Wmk. 387
1046-1047 A222 Set of 2 3.50 3.50

Greetings A223

Designs: 80v, Children and flowers. 100v, Snorkeler, fish, coral reef. 140v, Volcano. 160v, Aerial view of islands, butterflies.

Wmk. 387
2012, Dec. 5 Litho. **Perf. 14½**
1048-1051 A223 Set of 4 10.50 10.50

Sam's Animal Welfare Association — A224

Various dogs and people: 40v, 60v, 160v, 200v.

Perf. 14x14¼
2013, Feb. 27 Litho. Wmk. 387
1052-1055 A224 Set of 4 10.00 10.00
1055a Souvenir sheet of 2, #1054-1055 8.00 8.00

Worldwide Fund for Nature (WWF) A225

Various depictions of orange spot filefish.

Wmk. 387
2013, Mar. 28 Litho. **Perf. 14**
1056 Horiz. strip of 4 9.00 9.00
a. A225 30v multi .65 .65
b. A225 70v multi 1.60 1.60
c. A225 100v multi 2.25 2.25
d. A2225 200v multi 4.50 4.50
Printed in sheets of 8 containing 2 each #1056a-1056d.

Waterfalls — A226

Designs: 40v, Siri Falls, Gaua. 100v, Big Wota Falls, Northern Maewo. 140v, Saser Twin Falls, Vanua Lava. 160v, Mele Cascades, Efate.

Perf. 14¼x14
2013, June 26 Litho. Wmk. 387
1057-1060 A226 Set of 4 9.25 9.25

Birth of Prince George of Cambridge A227

Designs: 40v, Duke of Cambridge holding Prince George. 60v, Duchess of Cambridge holding Prince George. 100v, Duke and Duchess of Cambridge, Prince George. 250v, Prince George.

Perf. 13¾x13¼
2013, Sept. 18 Litho. Unwmk.
1061-1064 A227 Set of 4 9.50 9.50

Christmas A228

Santa Claus: 40v, In hammock. 100v, Snorkeling near underwater post office, vert. 160v, In sleigh above island, vert. 250v, Looking at card in Vanuatu post office lobby.

Perf. 13½
2013, Nov. 6 Litho. Unwmk.
1065-1068 A228 Set of 4 12.00 12.00

Souvenir Sheet

Underwater Post Office, 10th Anniv. — A229

Unwmk.
2013, Dec. 11 Litho. **Perf. 14**
1069 A229 350v multi 7.50 7.50

Submarine Cable Between Fiji and Vanuatu — A230

No. 1070: a, Workers, ship and cable with floats. b, Divers examining cable. c, Electronic cables plugged into machine.

Litho. With Foil Application
2014, Jan. 15 **Perf. 14½x14**
1070 Horiz. strip of 6 + central label, #1070a-1070c, Fiji #1304a-1304c 14.50 14.50
a. A230 40v multi .65 .65
b. A230 130v multi 2.10 2.10
c. A230 190v multi 3.25 3.25
No. 1070 sold for 750v in Vanuatu and $13.30 in Fiji. See Fiji No. 1304.

Wan Smolbag International Theater Festival, 25th Anniv. — A231

Art for: 10v, 9 Long 1 Step Wan music compact disc. 40v, Film Vanua-tai. . .of Land and Sea. 120v, Television show Love Patrol. 300v, Film Las Kad.

2014, May 7 Litho. **Perf. 14x14¼**
1071-1074 A231 Set of 4 10.00 10.00

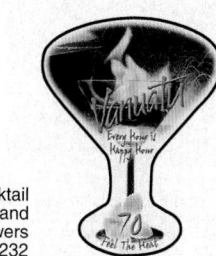

Cocktail Glasses and Flowers A232

Flower and cocktail glass containing: 70v, Fire. 100v, Underwater post office. 180v, Woman drinking at beach. 250v, Sailboat at sea.

2014, July 23 Litho. **Die Cut**
Self-Adhesive
1075-1078 A232 Set of 4 13.00 13.00

Extreme Sports — A233

Designs: 50v, Kiteboarding. 120v, People riding off-road buggies, vert. 160v, Parasailing, vert. 190v, Jet boating.

2014, Oct. 29 Litho. **Perf. 14½**
1079-1082 A233 Set of 4 10.50 10.50

Submarine Cable Between Fiji and Vanuatu — A230

Nelson Mandela (1918-2013), President of South Africa — A234

Flags of South Africa and Vanuatu, various pictures of Mandela and quotes starting with: 40v, "Action without vision. . ." 120v, "Education is the most powerful weapon. . ." 150v, "Sport has the power to inspire. . ." 200v, "Forgiveness liberates the soul. . ."

2014, Dec. 5 Litho. **Perf. 14x14¼**
1083-1086 A234 Set of 4 10.50 10.50

SEMI-POSTAL STAMPS

No. 324 Surcharged

Nos. 414-418 Surcharged

Wmk. 373 (No. B1), 384
Perf. 14x13½, 14x14½
1987, May 12 Litho.
B1 A60 20v +10v on 2v 1.00 1.00
B2 CD337 20v +10v 1.00 1.00
B3 CD337 35v +15v 1.75 1.75
B4 CD337 45v +20v 1.90 1.90
B5 CD337 55v +25v 3.75 3.75
B6 CD337 100v +50v 4.00 4.00
Nos. B1-B6 (6) 13.40 13.40
Old value of #B1 obliterated by 2 horizontal bars. Surcharge indicated by text "Surcharge +10."

VATICAN CITY

'va-ti-kən 'si-tē

LOCATION — Western Italy, directly outside the western boundary of Rome

GOVT. — Independent state subject to certain political restrictions under a treaty with Italy

AREA — 108.7 acres

POP. — 870 (1999 est.)

100 Centesimi = 1 Lira
100 Cents = 1 Euro (2002)

Catalogue values for unused stamps in this country are for Never Hinged items, beginning with Scott 68 in the regular postage section, Scott C1 in the airpost section, Scott E3 in the special delivery section, and Scott J7 in the postage due section.

Certificates for often forged or never hinged high value items are advised.

Watermarks

Wmk. 235 — Crossed Keys

Wmk. 277 — Winged Wheel

Papal Arms — A1

Pope Pius XI — A2

Unwmk.

1929, Aug. 1　Engr.　Perf. 14

Surface-Colored Paper

1	A1	5c dk brn & pink	.25	.25
2	A1	10c dk grn & lt grn	.25	.35
3	A1	20c violet & lilac	.75	.65
4	A1	25c dk bl & lt bl	.95	.75
5	A1	30c indigo & yellow	1.10	.85
6	A1	50c ind & sal buff	1.60	.90
7	A1	75c brn car & gray	2.25	1.50

Photo.

White Paper

8	A2	80c carmine rose	1.60	.50
9	A2	1.25 l dark blue	2.60	1.10
10	A2	2 l olive brown	5.25	2.25
11	A2	2.50 l red orange	4.50	3.75
12	A2	5 l dk green	5.25	12.00
13	A2	10 l olive blk	11.00	17.00
		Nos. 1-13,E1-E2 (15)	74.85	75.35
		Set, never hinged	265.00	

The stamps of Type A1 have, in this and subsequent issues, the words "POSTE VATICANE" in rows of colorless letters in the background.

For surcharges and overprints see Nos. 14, 35-40, 61-67, J1-J6, Q1-Q13.

No. 5 Surcharged in Red

1931, Oct. 1

14	A1	25c on 30c ind & yel	3.00	2.25
		Never hinged	10.00	

Arms of Pope Pius XI — A5

Vatican Palace and Obelisk — A6

Vatican Gardens — A7

Pope Pius XI A8

St. Peter's Basilica A9

1933, May 31　Engr.　Wmk. 235

19	A5	5c copper red	.25	.25
a.		Imperf., pair	600.00	825.00
20	A6	10c dk brn & blk	.25	.25
21	A6	12½c dp grn & blk	.25	.25
22	A6	20c orange & blk	.25	.25
a.		Vertical pair imperf. between and at bottom	750.00	
23	A6	25c dk olive & blk	.25	.25
a.		Imperf., pair	425.00	600.00
24	A7	30c blk & dk brn	.25	.25
25	A7	50c vio & dk brn	.25	.25
26	A7	75c brn red & dk brn	.25	.25
27	A7	80c rose & dk brn	.25	.25
28	A8	1 l violet & blk	7.50	7.50
29	A8	1.25 l dk bl & blk	22.50	13.50
30	A8	2 l dk brn & blk	52.50	37.50
31	A8	2.75 l dk vio & blk	67.50	90.00
32	A9	5 l blk brn & dk grn	.25	.25
33	A9	10 l dk bl & dk grn	.25	.30
34	A9	20 l blk & dp grn	.40	.50
		Nos. 19-34,E3-E4 (18)	153.85	152.70
		Set, never hinged	620.00	

Nos. 8-13 Surcharged in Black

No. 36

No. 36a

1934, June 16　Unwmk.

35	A2	40c on 80c	45.00	20.00
36	A2	1.30 l on 1.25 l	180.00	100.00
a.		Small figures "30" in "1.30"	24,000.	16,000.
		Never hinged	30,000.	
37	A2	2.05 l on 2 l	240.00	32.50
a.		No comma btwn. 2 & 0	550.00	40.00
		Never hinged	1,200.	
38	A2	2.55 l on 2.50 l	150.00	275.00
a.		No comma btwn. 2 & 5	200.00	300.00
		Never hinged	500.00	
39	A2	3.05 l on 5 l	500.00	450.00
40	A2	3.70 l on 10 l	450.00	600.00
a.		No comma btwn. 3 & 7	—	—
		Nos. 35-40 (6)	1,565.	1,477.
		Set, never hinged	3,680.	

A second printing of Nos. 36-40 was made in 1937. The 2.55 l and 3.05 l of the first printing and 1.30 l of the second printing sell for more.

The status of No. 40a has been questioned. The editors would like to examine an authenticated example of this variety.

Forged surcharges of Nos. 35-40 are plentiful.

Tribonian Presenting Pandects to Justinian I A10

Pope Gregory IX Promulgating Decretals A11

1935, Feb. 1　Photo.

41	A10	5c red orange	4.50	4.50
42	A10	10c purple	4.50	4.50
43	A10	25c green	25.00	35.00
44	A11	75c rose red	65.00	60.00
45	A11	80c dark brown	55.00	42.50
46	A11	1.25 l dark blue	65.00	52.50
		Nos. 41-46 (6)	219.00	199.00
		Set, never hinged	1,045.	

Intl. Juridical Congress, Rome, 1934.

Doves and Bell — A12

Allegory of Church and Bible — A13

St. John Bosco — A14

St. Francis de Sales — A15

1936, June 22

47	A12	5c blue green	1.50	1.50
48	A13	10c black	1.50	1.50
49	A14	25c yellow green	45.00	15.00
50	A12	50c rose violet	1.50	1.50
51	A13	75c rose red	47.50	60.00
52	A14	80c orange brn	2.60	3.00
53	A15	1.25 l dark blue	3.00	3.00
54	A15	5 l dark brown	3.00	7.50
		Nos. 47-54 (8)	105.60	93.00
		Set, never hinged	495.00	

Catholic Press Conference, 1936.

Crypt of St. Cecilia in Catacombs of St. Calixtus
A16

Basilica of Sts. Nereus and Achilleus in Catacombs of St. Domitilla
A17

1938, Oct. 12 ***Perf. 14***

55	A16	5c bister brown	.40	.40
56	A16	10c deep orange	.40	.40
57	A16	25c deep green	.45	.40
58	A17	75c deep rose	7.50	7.50
59	A17	80c violet	20.00	20.00
60	A17	1.25 l blue	29.00	29.00
		Nos. 55-60 (6)	57.75	57.70
		Set, never hinged	200.00	

Intl. Christian Archaeological Congress, Rome, 1938.

Interregnum Issue

Nos. 1-7 Overprinted in Black

1939, Feb. 20 ***Perf. 14***

61	A1	5c dk brn & pink	26.00	7.50
62	A1	10c dk grn & lt grn	.75	.25
63	A1	20c violet & lilac	.75	.25
64	A1	25c dk bl & lt bl	3.25	*5.00*
65	A1	30c indigo & yellow	1.25	.25
a.		Pair, one without ovpt.	*3,000.*	
66	A1	50c indigo & sal buff	1.25	.25
67	A1	75c brn car & gray	1.25	.25
		Nos. 61-67 (7)	34.50	13.75
		Set, never hinged	135.00	

Catalogue values for unused stamps in this section, from this point to the end of the section, are for Never Hinged items.

Coronation of Pope Pius XII — A18

1939, June 2 **Photo.**

68	A18	25c green	3.00	.40
69	A18	75c rose red	.70	.70
70	A18	80c violet	8.50	4.00
71	A18	1.25 l deep blue	.70	.70
		Nos. 68-71 (4)	12.90	5.80

Coronation of Pope Pius XII, Mar. 12, 1939.

Arms of Pope Pius XII — A19

Pope Pius XII
A20 A21

Wmk. 235

1940, Mar. 12 **Engr.** ***Perf. 14***

72	A19	5c dark carmine	.45	.25
a.		Imperf, pair	1,100.	
73	A20	1 l purple & blk	.45	.25
74	A21	1.25 l slate bl & blk	.45	.25
a.		Imperf., pair	*1,100.*	*1,200.*
75	A20	2 l dk brn & blk	2.00	2.00
76	A21	2.75 l dk rose vio & blk	2.50	2.50
		Nos. 72-76 (5)	5.85	5.25

See Nos. 91-98. For surcharges see Nos. 102-109.

A22

Picture of Jesus inscribed "I have Compassion on the Multitude."

1942, Sept. 1 **Photo.** **Unwmk.**

77	A22	25c dk blue green	.25	.25
78	A22	80c chestnut brown	.25	.25
79	A22	1.25 l deep blue	.25	.25
		Nos. 77-79 (3)	.75	.75

See Nos. 84-86, 99-101.

A23

Consecration of Archbishop Pacelli by Pope Benedict XV.

1942, Jan. 16

80	A23	25c myr grn & gray grn	.25	.25
81	A23	80c dk brn & yel grn	.25	.25
82	A23	1.25 l sapphire & vio bl	.25	.25
a.		Name and value panel omitted		
83	A23	5 l vio blk & gray blk	.35	.25
		Nos. 80-83 (4)	1.10	1.00

25th anniv. of the consecration of Msgr. Eugenio Pacelli (later Pope Pius XII) as Archbishop of Sardes.

Type of 1942 Inscribed MCMXLIII

1944, Jan. 31

84	A22	25c dk blue green	.25	.25
85	A22	80c chestnut brown	.25	.25
86	A22	1.25 l deep blue	.25	.25
		Nos. 84-86 (3)	.75	.75

Raphael Sanzio — A24

Designs: 80c, Antonio da Sangallo. 1.25 l, Carlo Maratti. 10 l, Antonio Canova.

1944, Nov. 21 **Wmk. 235** **Photo.**

87	A24	25c olive & green	.35	.25
88	A24	80c cl & rose vio	.60	.50
a.		Dbl. impression of center	*1,800.*	
89	A24	1.25 l bl vio & dp bl	.80	.40
a.		Imperf., pair	*1,900.*	*2,100.*
90	A24	10 l bister & ol brn	2.00	2.00
		Nos. 87-90 (4)	3.75	3.15

400th anniv. of the Pontifical Academy of the Virtuosi of the Pantheon.

Types of 1940

1945, Mar. 5 **Engr.** **Unwmk.**

91	A19	5c gray	.25	.25
a.		Imperf., pair	360.00	
92	A19	30c brown	.25	.25
a.		Imperf., pair	475.00	
93	A19	50c dark green	.25	.25
94	A21	1 l brown & blk	.25	.25
95	A21	1.50 l rose car & blk	.25	.25
a.		Imperf., pair	475.00	
96	A21	2.50 l dp ultra & blk	.25	.25
a.		Imperf, pair	475.00	
97	A20	5 l rose vio & blk	.30	*.25*
98	A20	20 l gray grn & blk	.40	*.40*
		Nos. 91-98,E5-E6 (10)	3.45	3.65

Nos. 91-96 exist in pairs imperf. between, some vertical, some horizontal. Value, each pair $150.

Type of 1942 Inscribed MCMXLIV Wmk. 277

1945, Sept. 12 **Photo.** ***Perf. 14***

99	A22	1 l dk blue green	.25	.25
100	A22	3 l dk carmine	.25	.25
a.		Jesus image omitted	225.00	225.00
101	A22	5 l deep ultra	.25	.25
a.		Jesus image omitted	225.00	225.00
		Nos. 99-101 (3)	.75	.75

Nos. 99-101 exist in pairs imperf. between, both horizontal and vertical. Value, each pair $140.

Pairs imperf. horizontally exist of 3 lire (value $150) and 5 lire (value $200).

Nos. 91 to 98 Surcharged with New Values and Bars in Black or Blue

Two types of 25c on 30c:
I — Surcharge 16mm wide.
II — Surcharge 19mm wide.

Two types of 1 l on 50c:
I — Surcharge bars 5mm wide.
II — Bars 4mm wide.

1946, Jan. 9 **Unwmk.** ***Perf. 14***

102	A19	20c on 5c	.25	.25
a.		Inverted surcharge	975.00	975.00
103	A19	25c on 30c (I)	.25	.25
a.		Type II	.40	.25
b.		Inverted surcharge (II)	975.00	975.00
104	A19	1 l on 50c (I)	.25	.25
a.		Type II	11.50	6.00
105	A21	1.50 l on 1 l (Bl)	.25	.25
a.		Double surcharge	450.00	
106	A21	3 l on 1.50 l	.25	.25
107	A21	5 l on 2.50 l	.50	.30
a.		Double surcharge	450.00	
108	A20	10 l on 5 l	1.75	.60
109	A20	30 l on 20 l	4.25	2.00
		Nos. 102-109,E7-E8 (10)	18.75	9.65

Nos. 102, 105-109 exist in horizontal pairs, imperf. between. Value, each pair $150.

Vertical pairs imperf. between exist of Nos. 102, 106-107 (value, each $150) and of No. 104a (value $250).

Nos. 102-108 exist in pairs, one without surcharge. Value, Nos. 102-105, each pair $600.; Nos. 106-108, each pair $900.

St. Vigilio Cathedral, Trent — A28

St. Angela Merici — A29

Designs: 50c, St. Anthony Zaccaria. 75c, St. Ignatius of Loyola. 1 l, St. Cajetan Thiene. 1.50 l, St. John Fisher. 2 l, Christoforo Cardinal Madruzzi. 2.50 l, Reginald Cardinal Pole. 3 l, Marello Cardinal Cervini. 4 l, Giovanni Cardinal del Monte. 5 l, Emperor Charles V. 10 l, Pope Paul III.

Perf. 14, 14x13½

1946, Feb. 21 **Photo.** **Unwmk.**

Centers in Dark Brown

110	A28	5c olive bister	.25	.25
111	A29	25c purple	.25	.25
112	A29	50c brown orange	.25	.25
113	A29	75c black	.25	.25
114	A29	1 l dk violet	.25	.25
115	A29	1.50 l red orange	.25	.25
116	A29	2 l yellow green	.25	.25
117	A29	2.50 l deep blue	.25	.25
118	A29	3 l brt carmine	.25	.25
119	A29	4 l ocher	.25	.25
120	A29	5 l brt ultra	.25	.25
121	A29	10 l dp rose car	.25	.25
a.		Imperf, pair	1,900.	
		Nos. 110-121,E9-E10 (14)	3.50	3.50

Council of Trent (1545-63), 400th anniv.

Vertical pairs imperf. between exist of Nos. 110-114, 116-118 (value, each pair $100); No. 121 (value, each pair $150).

Horizontal pairs imperf. between exist of #121 (value $325); #119 (value $275).

Basilica of St. Agnes — A40

Basilica of the Holy Cross in Jerusalem A41

Pope Pius XII A42

Basilicas: 3 l, St. Clement, 5 l, St. Prassede. 8 l, St. Mary in Cosmedin. 16 l, St. Sebastian. 25 l, St. Lawrence. 35 l, St. Paul. 40 l, St. Mary Major.

Perf. 14, 14x13½

1949, Mar. 7 **Photo.** **Wmk. 235**

122	A40	1 l dark brown	.25	.25
123	A40	3 l violet	.25	.25
124	A40	5 l deep orange	.25	.25
a.		Perf. 14x13½	18.50	7.50
125	A40	8 l dp blue grn	.25	.25

Perf. 14, 13½x14

126	A41	13 l dull green	3.25	3.25
127	A41	16 l dk olive brn	.35	.30
a.		Perf. 14	.50	.30
128	A41	25 l car rose	6.50	.65
129	A41	35 l red violet	30.00	10.00
a.		Perf. 13½x14	47.50	10.00
130	A41	40 l blue	.35	.30
a.		Perf. 13½x14	.40	.30

Engr.

Perf. 14

131	A42	100 l sepia	3.00	3.00
		Nos. 122-131,E11-E12 (12)	109.45	50.50

All values come in two perfs except the 100 l.

Nos. 127, 128 exist imperf horizontally, Nos. 125-126 exist imperf vertically. Value in pairs $200 each pair.

Nos. 130-131 exist imperf.

Jesus Giving St. Peter the Keys to Heaven — A43

Cathedrals of St. Peter, St. Paul, St. John Lateran and St. Mary Major — A44

Pope Boniface VIII Proclaiming Holy Year in 1300 — A45

Pope Pius XII in Ceremony of Opening the Holy Door — A46

Wmk. 277

1949, Dec 21		**Photo.**		**Perf. 14**	
132	A43	5 l	red brn & brn	.25	.25
133	A44	6 l	ind & yel brn	.25	.25
134	A45	8 l	ultra & dk grn	.85	.55
135	A46	10 l	green & slate	.25	.25
136	A43	20 l	dk grn & red brn	1.40	.30
137	A44	25 l	sepia & dp blue	.75	.25
138	A45	30 l	grnsh blk & rose lil	2.50	1.10
139	A46	60 l	blk brn & brn rose	1.40	1.10
		Nos. 132-139 (8)		7.65	4.05

Holy Year, 1950.

Palatine Guard and Statue of St. Peter — A47

1950, Sept. 12					
140	A47	25 l	sepia	7.50	4.50
141	A47	35 l	dark green	3.50	3.50
142	A47	55 l	red brown	2.00	3.75
		Nos. 140-142 (3)		13.00	11.75

Centenary of the Palatine Guard.

Pope Pius XII Making Proclamation A48

Crowd at St. Peter's Basilica — A49

1951, May 8				**Unwmk.**	
143	A48	25 l	chocolate	11.00	1.00
144	A49	55 l	bright blue	4.75	12.00

Proclamation of the Roman Catholic dogma of the Assumption of the Virgin Mary, Nov. 1, 1950.

A50

Pope Pius X — A51

Perf. 14x13½

1951, June 3		**Photo.**		**Wmk. 235**	
Background of Medallion in Gold					
145	A50	6 l	purple	.25	.25
146	A50	10 l	Prus green	.40	.25
147	A51	60 l	blue	7.00	5.50
148	A51	115 l	brown	22.50	22.50
		Nos. 145-148 (4)		30.15	28.50

Council of Chalcedon A52

Pope Leo I Remonstrating with Attila the Hun — A53

1951, Oct. 31		**Engr.**		**Perf. 14x13½**	
149	A52	5 l	dk gray green	.50	.40
a.		Pair, imperf. horiz.		900.00	
150	A53	25 l	red brown	3.50	2.00
a.		Horiz. pair, imperf. btwn.		2,250.	2,250.
151	A52	35 l	carmine rose	8.00	4.00
152	A53	60 l	deep blue	25.00	11.00
153	A52	100 l	dark brown	42.50	37.50
		Nos. 149-153 (5)		79.50	54.90

Council of Chalcedon, 1500th anniv.

No. 126 Surcharged with New Value and Bars in Carmine

1952, Mar. 15				**Perf. 14**	
154	A41	12 l on 13 l	dull grn	2.00	1.00
a.		Perf. 13½x14		2.00	1.00
b.		Pair, one without surcharge		750.00	750.00
c.		Surcharge inverted		750.00	
d.		As "a," surcharge double		750.00	

Roman States Stamp and Stagecoach — A54

1952, June 9		**Engr.**		**Perf. 13**	
155	A54	50 l	sep & dp bl, cr	5.00	4.50
a.		Souvenir sheet		160.00	160.00

1st stamp of the Papal States, cent.
#155a contains 4 stamps similar to #155, with papal insignia and inscription in purple. Singles from the souvenir sheet differ slightly from #155. The colors are closer to black and blue, and the cream tone of the paper is visible on the back.

St. Maria Goretti — A55

Perf. 13½x14

1953, Feb. 12		**Photo.**		**Wmk. 235**	
156	A55	15 l	dp brown & vio	4.75	2.50
157	A55	35 l	dp rose & brn	3.50	2.50

Martyrdom of St. Maria Goretti, 50th anniv.

St. Peter — A56

Designs: 5 l, Pius XII and Roman sepulcher. 10 l, St. Peter and Tomb of the Apostle. 12 l, Sylvester I and Constantine Basilica. 20 l, Julius II and Bramante's plans. 25 l, Paul III and the Apse. 35 l, Sixtus V and dome. 45 l, Paul V and facade. 60 l, Urban VIII and the canopy. 65 l, Alexander VII and colonnade. 100 l, Pius VI and the sacristy.

Perf. 13½x13, 14

1953, Apr. 23				**Engr.**	
158	A56	3 l	dk red brn & blk	.25	.25
159	A56	5 l	slate & blk	.25	.25
160	A56	10 l	dk green & blk	.25	.25
161	A56	12 l	chestnut & blk	.25	.25
162	A56	20 l	violet & blk	.25	.25
163	A56	25 l	dk brown & blk	.25	.25
164	A56	35 l	dk carmine & blk	.25	.25
165	A56	45 l	olive brn & blk	.25	.25
166	A56	60 l	dk blue & blk	.25	.25
167	A56	65 l	car rose & blk	.25	.25
168	A56	100 l	rose vio & blk	.25	.25
		Nos. 158-168,E13-E14 (13)		3.35	3.25

Nos. 158, 163 and 165 exist imperf. Value $900 each pair.

St. Clare of Assisi — A57

Unwmk.

1953, Aug. 12		**Photo.**		**Perf. 13**	
169	A57	25 l	aqua, yel brn & vio brn	2.00	1.50
170	A57	35 l	brn red, yel brn & vio brn	16.00	11.00

Death of St. Clare of Assisi, 700th anniv.

Virgin Mary and St. Bernard A58

1953, Nov. 10					
171	A58	20 l	ol grn & dk vio brn	.75	.75
172	A58	60 l	brt bl & ol grn	7.50	5.50

Death of St. Bernard of Clairvaux, 800th anniv.

Peter Lombard Medal — A59

1953, Dec. 29					
173	A59	100 l	lil rose, bl, dk grn & yel	37.50	20.00

Peter Lombard, Bishop of Paris 1159.

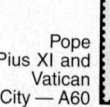

Pope Pius XI and Vatican City — A60

1954, Feb. 12				**Wmk. 235**	
174	A60	25 l	bl, red brn & cr	1.25	1.00
175	A60	60 l	yel brn & dp bl	3.50	3.00

Signing of the Lateran Pacts, 25th anniv.

Pope Pius IX A61

Portraits: (At left) - 6 l, 20 l, Pope Pius IX. (At right) — 4 l, 12 l, 35 l, Pope Pius XII.

1954, May 26		**Engr.**		**Perf. 13**	
176	A61	3 l	violet	.25	.25
177	A61	4 l	carmine	.25	.25
178	A61	6 l	plum	.25	.25
179	A61	12 l	blue green	1.00	.25
180	A61	20 l	red brown	.90	.85
181	A61	35 l	ultra	2.00	2.00
		Nos. 176-181 (6)		4.65	3.85

Marian Year; centenary of the dogma of the Immaculate Conception.

St. Pius X — A62

1954, May 29				**Photo.**	
Colors (except background): Yellow and Plum					
182	A62	10 l	dark brown	.30	.25
183	A62	25 l	violet	2.50	1.50
184	A62	35 l	dk slate gray	4.50	3.25
		Nos. 182-184 (3)		7.30	5.00

Canonization of Pope Pius X, May 20, 1954. #182-184 exist imperf. Value, each pair $800.

Basilica of St. Francis of Assisi A63

1954, Oct. 1		**Photo.**		**Perf. 14**	
185	A63	20 l	dk vio gray & cr	2.00	1.60
186	A63	35 l	dk brown & cream	1.50	1.50

Consecration of the Basilica of St. Francis of Assisi, 200th anniv.

St. Augustine A64

1954, Nov. 13
187 A64 35 l blue green 1.10 .90
188 A64 50 l redsh brown 1.75 1.75

1600th birth anniv. of St. Augustine.

Madonna of the Gate of Dawn, Vilnius — A65

1954, Dec. 7
189 A65 20 l pink & multi 1.40 .85
190 A65 35 l blue & multi 9.00 6.50
191 A65 60 l multicolored 13.50 8.50
Nos. 189-191 (3) 23.90 15.85

Issued to mark the end of the Marian Year.

St. Boniface and Fulda Abbey A66

1955, Apr. 28 Engr. Perf. 13
192 A66 10 l grnsh gray .25 .25
193 A66 35 l violet .60 .60
a. Imperf., pair 525.00
194 A66 60 l brt blue green .75 .70
Nos. 192-194 (3) 1.60 1.55

1200th death anniv. of St. Boniface. No. 193 also exists imperf horizontally and vertically. Value $275 each pair.

Pope Sixtus II and St. Lawrence — A67

Wmk. 235
1955, June 27 Photo. Perf. 14
195 A67 50 l carmine 4.25 2.00
196 A67 100 l deep blue 2.75 2.00

Fra Angelico (1387-1455), painter. Design is from a Fra Angelico fresco.

Pope Nicholas V — A68

1955, Nov. 28
197 A68 20 l grnsh bl & ol brn .30 .25
198 A68 35 l rose car & ol brn .40 .30
199 A68 60 l yel grn & ol brn .75 .40
Nos. 197-199 (3) 1.45 .95

Death of Pope Nicholas V, 500th anniv.

St. Bartholomew and Church of Grottaferrata — A69

1955, Dec. 29
200 A69 10 l brown & gray .25 .25
201 A69 25 l car rose & gray .50 .30
202 A69 100 l dk green & gray 2.00 1.50
Nos. 200-202 (3) 2.75 2.05

900th death anniv. of St. Bartholomew, abbot of Grottaferrata.

Capt. Gaspar Roust — A70

6 l, 50 l, Guardsman. 10 l, 60 l, Two drummers.

1956, Apr. 27 Engr. Perf. 13
203 A70 4 l dk carmine rose .25 .25
204 A70 6 l deep orange .25 .25
205 A70 10 l deep ultra .25 .25
206 A70 35 l brown .55 .40
207 A70 50 l violet .75 .60
208 A70 60 l blue green .85 .65
Nos. 203-208 (6) 2.90 2.40

450th anniv. of the Swiss Papal Guard.

St. Rita of Cascia — A71

1956, May 19 Photo. Perf. 14
209 A71 10 l gray green .25 .25
210 A71 25 l olive brown .55 .55
211 A71 35 l ultra .35 .35
Nos. 209-211 (3) 1.15 1.15

500th death anniv. of St. Rita of Cascia.

Pope Paul III Confirming Society of Jesus — A72

1956, July 31 Engr. Perf. 13
212 A72 35 l dk red brown .50 .50
213 A72 60 l blue gray .95 .95

400th death anniv. of St. Ignatius of Loyola, founder of the Society of Jesus.

St. John of Capistrano A73

1956, Oct. 30 Perf. 14
214 A73 25 l slate blk & grn 2.10 1.25
215 A73 35 l dk brn car & brn .75 .75

5th cent. of the death of St. John of Capistrano, leader in the war against the Turks.

Black Madonna of Czestochowa A74

1956, Dec. 20
216 A74 35 l dk blue & blk .25 .25
217 A74 60 l green & ultra .45 .45
218 A74 100 l brn & dk car rose .90 .80
Nos. 216-218 (3) 1.60 1.50

300th anniv. of the proclamation of the Madonna of Czestochowa as "Queen of Poland."

St. Domenico Savio — A75

6 l, 60 l, Sts. Domenico Savio and John Bosco.

1957, Mar. 21 Wmk. 235 Perf. 13½
219 A75 4 l red brown .25 .25
220 A75 6 l brt carmine .25 .25
221 A75 25 l green .25 .25
222 A75 60 l ultra 1.20 .95
Nos. 219-222 (4) 1.95 1.70

Death cent. of St. Domenico Savio.

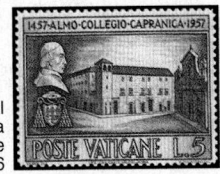

Cardinal Capranica and College A76

Design: 10 l, 100 l, Pope Pius XII.

1957, June 27 Engr. Perf. 13
223 A76 5 l dk carmine rose .25 .25
224 A76 10 l pale brown .25 .25
225 A76 35 l grnsh black .25 .25
226 A76 100 l ultra .50 .50
Nos. 223-226 (4) 1.25 1.25

500th anniv. of Capranica College, oldest seminary in the world.

Pontifical Academy of Science A77

1957, Oct. 9 Photo. Perf. 14
227 A77 35 l dk blue & green .55 .55
228 A77 60 l brown & ultra .75 .55

Pontifical Academy of Science, 20th anniv.

Mariazell A78

High Altar — A79

1957, Nov. 14 Engr. Perf. 13½
229 A78 5 l green .25 .25
230 A79 15 l slate .25 .25
231 A78 60 l ultra .70 .25
232 A79 100 l violet .90 .85
Nos. 229-232 (4) 2.10 1.60

Mariazell shrine, Austria, 800th anniv.

Apparition of the Virgin Mary — A80

Designs: 10 l, 35 l, Sick man and basilica. 15 l, 100 l, St. Bernadette.

Perf. 13x14
1958, Feb. 21 Wmk. 235
233 A80 5 l dark blue .25 .25
234 A80 10 l blue green .25 .25
235 A80 15 l reddish brown .25 .25
236 A80 25 l rose carmine .25 .25
237 A80 35 l gray brown .25 .25
238 A80 100 l violet .25 .25
Nos. 233-238 (6) 1.50 1.50

Centenary of apparition of the Virgin Mary at Lourdes and the establishment of the shrine.

Pope Pius XII — A81

60 l, 100 l, Vatican pavilion at Brussels fair.

1958, June 19 Engr. Perf. 13
239 A81 35 l claret .30 .25
Perf. 13x14
240 A81 60 l fawn .55 .55
241 A81 100 l violet 1.75 1.25
242 A81 300 l ultra 1.40 1.10
a. Souvenir sheet of 4, #239-242 20.00 15.00
Nos. 239-242 (4) 4.00 3.15

Universal and Intl. Exposition, Brussels.

Statue of Pope Clement XIII by Canova — A82

Statues: 10 l, Clement XIV. 35 l, Pius VI. 100 l, Pius VII.

1958, July 2 Perf. 14
243 A82 5 l brown .25 .25
244 A82 10 l carmine rose .25 .25
245 A82 35 l blue gray .25 .25
246 A82 100 l dark blue .85 .85
Nos. 243-246 (4) 1.60 1.60

Antonio Canova (1757-1822), sculptor.

Interregnum Issue

St. Peter's Keys and Papal Chamberlain's Insignia — A83

Wmk. 235
1958, Oct. 21   Photo.   Perf. 14
247 A83 15 l brn blk, *yel*   1.40 1.00
248 A83 25 l brown black   .25   .25
249 A83 60 l brn blk, *pale vio*   .25   .25
    Nos. 247-249 (3)   1.90 1.50

Pope John
XXIII — A84

Design: 35 l, 100 l, Coat of Arms.

1959, Apr. 2   Photo.   Perf. 14
250 A84 25 l car rose, bl & buff   .25   .25
251 A84 35 l multicolored   .25   .25
252 A84 60 l rose car, bl &
               ocher   .25   .25
253 A84 100 l multicolored   .25   .25
    Nos. 250-253 (4)   1.00 1.00
Coronation of Pope John XXIII, 11/4/58.

Pope
Pius XI — A85

1959, May 25   Wmk. 235   Perf. 14
254 A85 30 l brown   .25   .25
255 A85 100 l violet blue   .25   .25
Lateran Pacts, 30th anniversary.

St. Lawrence — A86

Portraits of Saints: 25 l, Pope Sixtus II. 50 l,
Agapitus. 60 l, Filicissimus. 100 l, Cyprianus.
300 l, Fructuosus.

1959, May 25
256 A86 15 l red, brn & yel   .25   .25
257 A86 25 l lilac, brn & yel   .25   .25
258 A86 50 l Prus bl, blk & yel   .25   .25
259 A86 60 l ol grn, brn & bis   .25   .25
260 A86 100 l maroon, brn & yel   .25   .25
261 A86 300 l bis brn & dk brn   .50   .35
    Nos. 256-261 (6)   1.75 1.60
Martyrs of Emperor Valerian's persecutions.

Radio Tower and
Archangel
Gabriel — A87

1959, Oct. 27   Photo.   Perf. 14
262 A87 25 l rose, org yel & dk brn .25 .25
263 A87 60 l multicolored   .25 .25
2nd anniv. of the papal radio station, St.
Maria di Galeria.

St. Casimir,
Tower of
Gediminas
and
Cathedral,
Vilnius
A88

1959, Dec. 14   Engr.   Wmk. 235
264 A88 50 l brown   .25   .25
265 A88 100 l dull green   .25   .25
500th anniv. (in 1958) of the birth of St.
Casimir, patron saint of Lithuania.

Nativity by
Raphael — A89

1959, Dec. 14   Engr.   Perf. 13½
266 A89 15 l dark gray   .25   .25
267 A89 25 l magenta   .25   .25
268 A89 60 l bright ultra   .25   .25
    Nos. 266-268 (3)   .75   .75

St.
Antoninus — A90

25 l, 110 l, St. Antoninus preaching.

Perf. 13x14
1960, Feb. 29   Wmk. 235
269 A90 15 l ultra   .25   .25
270 A90 25 l turquoise   .25   .25
271 A90 60 l brown   .30   .25
272 A90 110 l rose claret   .60   .35
    Nos. 269-272 (4)   1.40 1.10
5th cent. of death of St. Antoninus, bishop of
Florence.

Transept of Lateran
Basilica — A91

1960, Feb. 29   Photo.   Perf. 14
273 A91 15 l brown   .25   .25
274 A91 60 l black   .40   .25
Roman Diocesan Synod, February, 1960.

Flight into Egypt
by Fra
Angelico — A92

Designs: 10 l, 100 l, St. Peter Giving Alms to
the Poor, by Masaccio. 25 l, 300 l, Madonna of
Mercy, by Piero della Francesca.

1960, Apr. 7   Wmk. 235   Perf. 14
275 A92   5 l green   .25   .25
276 A92 10 l gray brown   .25   .25
277 A92 25 l deep carmine   .25   .25
278 A92 60 l lilac   .25   .25
279 A92 100 l ultra   1.40 1.25
280 A92 300 l Prus green   .80   .50
    Nos. 275-280 (6)   3.20 2.75
World Refugee Year, 7/1/59-6/30/60.

Cardinal Sarto's
Departure from
Venice — A93

35 l, Pope John XXIII praying at coffin of
Pope Pius X. 60 l, Body of Pope Pius X
returning to Venice.

1960, Apr. 11   Engr.   Perf. 13½
281 A93 15 l brown   .25   .25
282 A93 35 l rose carmine   .75   .60
283 A93 60 l Prus green   1.75 1.25
    Nos. 281-283 (3)   2.75 2.10
Return of the body of Pope Pius X to Venice.

Feeding the
Hungry
A94

"Acts of Mercy," by Della Robbia: 10 l, Giving drink to the thirsty. 15 l, Clothing the
naked. 20 l, Sheltering the homeless. 30 l,
Visiting the sick. 35 l, Visiting prisoners. 40 l,
Burying the dead. 70 l, Pope John XXIII.

1960, Nov. 8   Photo.   Perf. 14
Centers in Brown
284 A94   5 l red brown   .25   .25
285 A94 10 l green   .25   .25
286 A94 15 l slate   .25   .25
287 A94 20 l rose carmine   .25   .25
288 A94 30 l violet blue   .25   .25
289 A94 35 l violet brown   .25   .25
290 A94 40 l red orange   .25   .25
291 A94 70 l ocher   .25   .25
    Nos. 284-291,E15-E16 (10)   2.50 2.50

Holy
Family by
Gerard van
Honthorst
A95

1960, Dec. 6   Wmk. 235   Perf. 14
292 A95 10 l slate grn & slate blk .25   .25
293 A95 15 l sepia & ol blk   .25   .25
294 A95 70 l grnsh bl & dp bl   .30   .25
    Nos. 292-294 (3)   .80   .75

St. Vincent de
Paul — A96

Designs: 70 l, St. Louisa de Marillac. 100 l,
St. Louisa and St. Vincent.

1960, Dec. 6
295 A96 40 l dull violet   .25   .25
296 A96 70 l dark gray   .30   .25
297 A96 100 l dk red brown   .70   .30
    Nos. 295-297 (3)   1.25 .80
Death of St. Vincent de Paul, 300th anniv.

St.
Meinrad — A97

Designs: 40 l, Statue of Our Lady of Einsiedeln. 100 l, Einsiedeln monastery, horiz.

1961, Feb. 28   Perf. 14
298 A97 30 l dark gray   .40   .25
299 A97 40 l lt violet   .75   .40
300 A97 100 l brown   1.50 1.00
    Nos. 298-300 (3)   2.65 1.65
Death of St. Meinrad, 1,100th anniv.; Einsiedeln Abbey, Switzerland.

Pope Leo the
Great Defying
Attila — A98

Wmk. 235
1961, Apr. 6   Photo.   Perf. 14
301 A98 15 l rose brown   .25   .25
302 A98 70 l Prus green   .25   .25
303 A98 300 l brown black   1.75 .55
    Nos. 301-303 (3)   2.25 1.05
Death of Pope Leo the Great (St. Leo
Magnus), 1,500th anniv. The design is from a
marble bas-relief in St. Peter's Basilica.

St. Paul
Arriving in
Rome, 61
A.D. — A99

10 l, 30 l, Map showing St. Paul's journey to
Rome. 20 l, 200 l, First Basilica of St. Paul,
Rome.

1961, June 13   Wmk. 235   Perf. 14
304 A99 10 l Prus green   .25   .25
305 A99 15 l dl red brn & gray   .25   .25
306 A99 20 l red org & gray   .25   .25
307 A99 30 l blue   .25   .25
308 A99 75 l org brn & gray   .30   .30
309 A99 200 l blue & gray   1.40 1.00
    Nos. 304-309 (6)   2.70 2.30
Arrival of St. Paul in Rome, 1,900th anniv.

1861 and
1961
Mastheads
A100

70 l, Editorial offices. 250 l, Rotary press.

1961, July 4
310 A100 40 l red brn & blk   .25   .25
311 A100 70 l blue & blk   .50   .35
312 A100 250 l yellow & blk   2.00 1.25
    Nos. 310-312 (3)   2.75 1.85
Centenary of L'Osservatore Romano, Vatican's newspaper.

St. Patrick's
Purgatory, Lough
Derg — A101

10 l, 40 l, St. Patrick, marble sculpture.

Wmk. 235
1961, Oct. 6   Photo.   Perf. 14
313 A101 10 l buff & slate grn   .25   .25
314 A101 15 l blue & sepia   .25   .25
315 A101 40 l yellow & bl grn   .25   .25
316 A101 150 l Prus bl & red brn   .45   .30
    Nos. 313-316 (4)   1.20 1.05
Death of St. Patrick, 1,500th anniv.

Arms of Roncalli Family — A102

Designs: 25 l, Church at Sotto il Monte. 30 l, Santa Maria in Monte Santo, Rome. 40 l, Church of San Carlo al Corso, Rome (erroneously inscribed with name of Basilica of Sts. Ambrosius and Charles, Milan). 70 l, Altar, St. Peter's, Rome. 115 l, Pope John XXIII.

1961, Nov. 25

317	A102	10 l	gray & red brn	.25 .25
318	A102	25 l	ol bis & sl grn	.25 .25
319	A102	30 l	vio bl & pale pur	.25 .25
320	A102	40 l	lilac & dk blue	.25 .25
321	A102	70 l	gray grn & org brn	.30 .25
322	A102	115 l	choc & slate	.40 .40
		Nos. 317-322 (6)		1.70 1.55

80th birthday of Pope John XXIII.

"The Adoration" by Lucas Chen — A103

1961, Nov. 25   Center Multicolored

323	A103	15 l	bluish green	.25 .25
324	A103	40 l	gray	.25 .25
325	A103	70 l	pale lilac	.25 .25
		Nos. 323-325 (3)		.75 .75

Christmas.

Draining of Pontine Marshes Medal by Pope Sixtus V, 1588 — A104

40 l, 300 l, Map of Pontine Marshes showing 18th cent. drainage under Pope Pius VI.

1962, Apr. 6   Wmk. 235   Perf. 14

326	A104	15 l	dark violet	.25 .25
327	A104	40 l	rose carmine	.25 .25
328	A104	70 l	brown	.25 .25
329	A104	300 l	dull green	.40 .30
		Nos. 326-329 (4)		1.15 1.05

WHO drive to eradicate malaria.

"The Good Shepherd" A105

Wheatfield (Luke 10:2) — A106

1962, June 2   Photo.

330	A105	10 l	lilac & black	.25 .25
331	A106	15 l	blue & ocher	.25 .25
332	A105	70 l	lt green & blk	.25 .30
333	A106	115 l	fawn & ocher	1.40 1.00
334	A105	200 l	brown & black	1.60 1.25
		Nos. 330-334 (5)		3.75 3.05

Issued to honor the priesthood and to stress its importance as a vocation.
"The Good Shepherd" is a fourth-century statue in the Lateran Museum, Rome.

St. Catherine of Siena — A107

1962, June 12

335	A107	15 l	brown	.25 .25
336	A107	60 l	brt violet	.30 .25
337	A107	100 l	blue	.45 .40
		Nos. 335-337 (3)		1.00 .90

Canonization of St. Catherine of Siena, 500th anniv. The portrait is from a fresco by Il Sodoma, Church of St. Dominic, Siena.

Paulina M. Jaricot — A108

1962, July 5   Portrait Multicolored

338	A108	10 l	pale violet	.25 .25
339	A108	50 l	dull green	.25 .25
340	A108	150 l	gray	.45 .40
		Nos. 338-340 (3)		.95 .90

Paulina M. Jaricot (1799-1862), founder of the Society for the Propagation of the Faith.

Sts. Peter and Paul A109

Design: 40 l, 100 l, "The Invincible Cross," relief from sarcophagus.

Wmk. 235

1962, Sept. 25   Photo.   Perf. 14

341	A109	20 l	lilac & brown	.25 .25
342	A109	40 l	lt brown & blk	.25 .25
343	A109	70 l	bluish grn & brn	.25 .25
344	A109	100 l	sal pink & blk	.25 .25
		Nos. 341-344 (4)		1.00 1.00

6th Congress of Christian Archeology, Ravenna, Sept. 23-28.

"Faith" by Raphael — A110

Designs: 10 l, "Hope." 15 l, "Charity." 25 l, Arms of Pope John XXIII and emblems of the Four Evangelists. 30 l, Ecumenical Congress meeting in St. Peter's. 40 l, Pope John XXIII on throne. 60 l, Statue of St. Peter. 115 l, The Holy Ghost as a dove (symbolic design).

Photo.; Center Engr. on 30 l

1962, Oct. 30

345	A110	5 l	brt blue & blk	.25 .25
346	A110	10 l	green & blk	.25 .25
347	A110	15 l	ver & sepia	.25 .25
348	A110	25 l	ver & slate	.25 .25
349	A110	30 l	lilac & blk	.25 .25
350	A110	40 l	dk carmine & blk	.25 .25
351	A110	60 l	dk grn & dp org	.25 .25
352	A110	115 l	crimson	.25 .25
		Nos. 345-352 (8)		2.00 2.00

Vatican II, the 21st Ecumenical Council of the Roman Catholic Church, which opened Oct. 11, 1962. Nos. 345-347 show "the Three Theological Virtues" by Raphael.

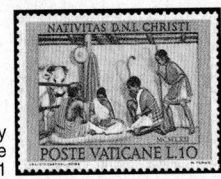

Nativity Scene A111

Set in India, following a design by Marcus Toano.

1962, Dec. 4   Center Multicolored

353	A111	10 l	gray	.25 .25
354	A111	15 l	brown	.25 .25
355	A111	90 l	dull green	.30 .25
		Nos. 353-355 (3)		.80 .75

Miracle of the Loaves and Fishes by Murillo — A112

Design: 40 l, 200 l, "The Miraculous Catch of Fishes" by Raphael.

Wmk. 235

1963, Mar. 21   Photo.   Perf. 14

356	A112	15 l	brn & dk brn	.25 .25
357	A112	40 l	rose red & blk	.25 .25
358	A112	100 l	blue & dk brn	.25 .25
359	A112	200 l	bl grn & blk	.25 .25
		Nos. 356-359 (4)		1.00 1.00

FAO "Freedom from Hunger" campaign.

Pope John XXIII — A113

1963, May 8

360	A113	15 l	red brown	.25 .25
361	A113	160 l	black	.40 .25

Awarding of the Balzan Peace Prize to Pope John XXIII.

Interregnum Issue

Keys of St. Peter and Papal Chamberlain's Insignia — A114

1963, June 15   Wmk. 235   Perf. 14

362	A114	10 l	dk brown	.25 .25
363	A114	40 l	dk brown, yel	.25 .25
364	A114	100 l	dk brown, vio	.25 .25
		Nos. 362-364 (3)		.75 .75

Pope Paul VI — A115

Design: 40 l, 200 l, Arms of Pope Paul VI.

1963, Oct. 16   Engr.   Perf. 13x14

365	A115	15 l	black	.25 .25
366	A115	40 l	carmine	.25 .25
367	A115	115 l	redsh brown	.25 .25
368	A115	200 l	slate blue	.40 .25
		Nos. 365-368 (4)		1.15 1.00

Coronation of Pope Paul VI, June 30, 1963.

St. Cyril — A116

Designs: 70 l, Map of Hungary, Moravia and Poland, 16th century. 150 l, St. Methodius.

Wmk. 235

1963, Nov. 22   Photo.   Perf. 14

369	A116	30 l	violet black	.25 .25
370	A116	70 l	brown	.30 .25
371	A116	150 l	rose claret	.40 .25
		Nos. 369-371 (3)		.95 .75

1100th anniv. of the beginning of missionary work among the Slavs by Sts. Cyril and Methodius. The pictures of the saints are from 16th century frescoes in St. Clement's Basilica, Rome.

African Nativity Scene — A117

1963, Nov. 22

372	A117	10 l	brn & pale brn	.25 .25
373	A117	40 l	ultra & brown	.25 .25
374	A117	100 l	gray olive & brn	.25 .25
		Nos. 372-374 (3)		.75 .75

The design is after a sculpture by the Burundi artist Andreas Bukuru.

Church of the Holy Sepulcher, Jerusalem A118

15 l, Pope Paul VI. 25 l, Nativity Church, Bethlehem. 160 l, Well of the Virgin Mary, Nazareth.

1964, Jan. 4   Wmk. 235   Perf. 14

375	A118	15 l	black	.25 .25
376	A118	25 l	rose brown	.25 .25
377	A118	70 l	brown	.25 .25
378	A118	160 l	ultra	.25 .25
		Nos. 375-378 (4)		1.00 1.00

Visit of Pope Paul VI to the Holy Land, Jan. 4-6.

St. Peter from Coptic Church at Wadi-es-Sebua, Sudan — A119

Design: 20 l, 200 l, Trajan's Kiosk, Philae.

1964, Mar. 10   **Photo.**

379	A119	10 l ultra & red brn	.25	.25
380	A119	20 l multicolored	.25	.25
381	A119	70 l gray & red brn	.25	.25
382	A119	200 l gray & multi	.25	.25
		Nos. 379-382 (4)	1.00	1.00

UNESCO world campaign to save historic monuments in Nubia.

Pietà by Michelangelo A120

Designs: 15 l, 100 l, Pope Paul VI. 250 l, Head of Mary from Pietà.

1964, Apr. 22   **Wmk. 235**   **Perf. 14**

383	A120	15 l violet blue	.25	.25
384	A120	50 l dark brown	.25	.25
385	A120	100 l slate blue	.25	.25
386	A120	250 l chestnut	.25	.25
		Nos. 383-386 (4)	1.00	1.00

New York World's Fair, 1964-65.

Isaiah by Michelangelo A121

10 l, Michelangelo, after Jacopino del Conte. 25 l, Isaiah. 30 l, Delphie Sibyl. 40 l, Jeremiah. 150 l, Joel.

1964, June 16   **Engr.**   **Perf. 13½x14**

387	A121	10 l multicolored	.25	.25
388	A121	25 l multicolored	.25	.25
389	A121	30 l multicolored	.25	.25
390	A121	40 l multicolored	.25	.25
391	A121	150 l multicolored	.25	.25
		Nos. 387-391 (5)	1.25	1.25

Michelangelo Buonarroti (1475-1564). Designs are from the Sistine Chapel.

The Good Samaritan A122

Perf. 14x13½

1964, Sept. 22   **Engr.**   **Wmk. 235**

392	A122	10 l red brown & red	.25	.25
393	A122	30 l dark blue & red	.25	.25
394	A122	300 l gray & red	.25	.25
		Nos. 392-394 (3)	.75	.75

Cent. (in 1963) of the founding of the Intl. Red Cross.

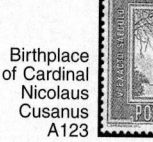

Birthplace of Cardinal Nicolaus Cusanus A123

Design: 200 l, Cardinal's sepulcher, Church of San Pietro in Vincoli, Rome.

1964, Nov. 16   **Wmk. 235**

395	A123	40 l dull blue grn	.25	.25
396	A123	200 l rose red	.30	.25

German cardinal Nicolaus Cusanus (Nicolaus Krebs of Kues) (1401-1464).

Japanese Nativity Scene by Kimiko Koseki — A124

1964, Nov. 16   **Photo.**   **Perf. 14**

397	A124	10 l multicolored	.25	.25
a.		Yellow omitted		
398	A124	15 l black & multi	.25	.25
399	A124	135 l bister & multi	.25	.25
		Nos. 397-399 (3)	.75	.75

Pope Paul VI and Map of India and Southeast Asia — A125

Designs: 15 l, Pope Paul VI at prayer. 25 l, Eucharistic Congress altar, Bombay, horiz. 60 l, Gateway of India, Bombay, horiz.

1964, Dec. 2

400	A125	15 l dull violet	.25	.25
401	A125	25 l green	.25	.25
402	A125	60 l brown	.25	.25
403	A125	200 l dull violet	.25	.25
		Nos. 400-403 (4)	1.00	1.00

Trip of Pope Paul VI to India, Dec. 2-5, 1964.

Uganda Martyrs — A126

Various groups of Martyrs of Uganda.

Perf. 13½x14

1965, Mar. 16   **Engr.**   **Wmk. 235**

404	A126	15 l Prus green	.25	.25
405	A126	20 l brown	.25	.25
406	A126	30 l ultra	.25	.25
407	A126	75 l black	.25	.25
408	A126	100 l rose red	.25	.25
409	A126	160 l violet	.25	.25
		Nos. 404-409 (6)	1.50	1.50

Canonization of 22 African martyrs, 10/18/64.

Dante by Raphael — A127

Designs: 40 l, Dante and the 3 beasts at entrance to the Inferno. 70 l, Dante and Virgil at entrance to Purgatory. 200 l, Dante and Beatrice in Paradise. (40 l, 70 l, 200 l, by Botticelli.)

Photogravure and Engraved

1965, May 18   **Perf. 13½x14**

410	A127	10 l bis brn & dk brn	.25	.25
411	A127	40 l rose & dk brn	.25	.25
412	A127	70 l lt grn & dk brn	.25	.25
413	A127	200 l pale bl & dk brn	.25	.25
		Nos. 410-413 (4)	1.00	1.00

Birth of Dante Alighieri, 700th anniv.

St. Benedict by Perugino — A128

Design: 300 l, View of Monte Cassino.

1965, July 2   **Photo.**   **Perf. 14**

414	A128	40 l brown	.25	.25
415	A128	300 l dark green	.30	.25

Conferring of the title Patron Saint of Europe upon St. Benedict by Pope Paul VI; restoring of the Abbey of Monte Cassino.

Pope Paul VI Addressing UN Assembly — A129

30 l, 150 l, UN Headquarters and olive branch.

1965, Oct. 4   **Wmk. 235**   **Perf. 14**

416	A129	20 l brown	.25	.25
417	A129	30 l sapphire	.25	.25
418	A129	150 l olive green	.25	.25
419	A129	300 l rose violet	.25	.25
		Nos. 416-419 (4)	1.00	1.00

Visit of Pope Paul VI to the UN, NYC, Oct. 4.

Peruvian Nativity Scene — A130

1965, Nov. 25   **Engr.**   **Perf. 13½x14**

420	A130	20 l rose claret	.25	.25
421	A130	40 l red brown	.25	.25
422	A130	200 l gray green	.25	.25
		Nos. 420-422 (3)	.75	.75

Cartographer A131

Designs: 5 l, Pope Paul VI. 10 l, Organist. 20 l, Painter. 30 l, Sculptor. 40 l, Bricklayer. 55 l, Carpenter. 75 l, Plowing farmer. 90 l, Blacksmith. 130 l, Scholar.

1966, Mar. 8   **Photo.**   **Perf. 14**

423	A131	5 l sepia	.25	.25
424	A131	10 l violet	.25	.25
425	A131	15 l brown	.25	.25
426	A131	20 l gray green	.25	.25
427	A131	30 l brown red	.25	.25
428	A131	40 l Prus green	.25	.25
429	A131	55 l dark blue	.25	.25
430	A131	75 l dk rose brown	.25	.25
431	A131	90 l carmine rose	.25	.25
432	A131	130 l black	.25	.25
		Nos. 423-432,E17-E18 (12)	3.00	3.00

The Pope's portrait is from a bas-relief by Enrico Manfrini; the arts and crafts designs

are bas-reliefs by Mario Rudelli from the chair in the Pope's private chapel.

King Mieszko I and Queen Dabrowka A132

Designs: 25 l, St. Adalbert (Wojciech) and Cathedrals of Wroclaw and Gniezno. 40 l, St. Stanislas, Skalka Church, Wawel Cathedral and Castle, Cracow. 50 l, Queen Jadwiga (Hedwig), Holy Gate with Our Lady of Mercy, Vilnius, and Jagellon University Library, Cracow. 150 l, Black Madonna of Czestochowa, cloister and church of Bright Mountain, Czestochowa, and St. John's Cathedral, Warsaw. 220 l, Pope Paul VI blessing students and farmers.

Perf. 14x13½

1966, May 3   **Engr.**   **Wmk. 235**

433	A132	15 l black	.25	.25
434	A132	25 l violet	.25	.25
435	A132	40 l brick red	.25	.25
436	A132	50 l claret	.25	.25
437	A132	150 l slate blue	.25	.25
438	A132	220 l brown	.25	.25
		Nos. 433-438 (6)	1.50	1.50

Millenium of Christianization of Poland.

Pope John XXIII Opening Vatican II Council — A133

Designs: 15 l, Ancient Bible on ornate display stand. 55 l, Bishops celebrating Mass. 90 l, Pope Paul VI greeting Patriarch Athenagoras I. 100 l, Gold ring given to participating bishops. 130 l, Pope Paul VI carried in front of St. Peter's.

1966, Oct. 11   **Photo.**   **Perf. 14**

439	A133	10 l red & black	.25	.25
440	A133	15 l brown & green	.25	.25
441	A133	55 l blk & brt rose	.25	.25
442	A133	90 l slate grn & blk	.25	.25
443	A133	100 l green & ocher	.25	.25
444	A133	130 l orange brn & brn	.25	.25
		Nos. 439-444 (6)	1.50	1.50

Conclusion of Vatican II, the 21st Ecumenical Council of the Roman Catholic Church, Dec. 8, 1965.

Nativity, Sculpture by Scorzelli — A134

1966, Nov. 24   **Wmk. 235**   **Perf. 14**

445	A134	20 l plum	.25	.25
446	A134	55 l slate green	.25	.25
447	A134	225 l yellow brown	.25	.25
		Nos. 445-447 (3)	.75	.75

St. Peter, Fresco, Catacombs, Rome — A135

Designs: 20 l, St. Paul, fresco from Catacombs, Rome. 55 l, Sts. Peter and Paul, glass painting, Vatican Library. 90 l, Baldachin by

Bernini, St. Peter's, Rome. 220 l, Interior of St. Paul's, Rome.

Perf. 13½x14

1967, June 15 **Photo.** **Unwmk.**
448	A135	15 l multi	.25	.25
449	A135	20 l multi	.25	.25
450	A135	55 l multi	.25	.25
451	A135	90 l multi	.25	.25
452	A135	220 l multi	.25	.25
	Nos. 448-452 (5)		1.25	1.25

Martyrdom of the Apostles Peter and Paul, 1,900th anniv.

Cross, People and Globe — A136

1967, Oct. 13 **Wmk. 235** **Perf. 14**
453	A136	40 l carmine rose	.25	.25
454	A136	130 l brt blue	.25	.25

3rd Congress of Catholic Laymen, Rome, Oct. 11-18.

Sculpture of Shepherd Children of Fatima — A137

Designs: 50 l, Basilica at Fatima. 200 l, Pope Paul VI praying before statue of Virgin of Fatima.

1967, Oct. 13 **Perf. 13½x14**
455	A137	30 l multi	.25	.25
456	A137	50 l multi	.25	.25
457	A137	200 l multi	.25	.25
	Nos. 455-457 (3)		.75	.75

Apparition of the Virgin Mary to 3 shepherd children at Fatima, 50th anniv.

Christmas Issue

Nativity, 9th Century Painting on Wood — A138

1967, Nov. 28 **Photo.** **Unwmk.**
458	A138	25 l purple & multi	.25	.25
459	A138	55 l gray & multi	.25	.25
460	A138	180 l green & multi	.25	.25
	Nos. 458-460 (3)		.75	.75

Pope Paul VI — A139

Designs: 55 l, Monstrance from fresco by Raphael. 220 l, Map of South America.

1968, Aug. 22 **Wmk. 235** **Perf. 14**
461	A139	25 l blk & dk red brn	.25	.25
462	A139	55 l blk, gray & ocher	.25	.25
463	A139	220 l blk, lt bl & sep	.25	.25
	Nos. 461-463 (3)		.75	.75

Visit of Pope Paul VI to the 39th Eucharistic Congress in Bogotá, Colombia, Aug. 22-25.

Holy Infant of Prague — A140

Engraved and Photogravure
1968, Nov. 28 **Perf. 13½x14**
464	A140	20 l plum & pink	.25	.25
465	A140	50 l vio & pale vio	.25	.25
466	A140	250 l dk bl & lt bluish gray	.25	.25
	Nos. 464-466 (3)		.75	.75

The Resurrection, by Fra Angelico de Fiesole — A141

Easter Issue
Perf. 13½x14
1969, Mar. 6 **Engr.** **Wmk. 235**
467	A141	20 l dk carmine & buff	.25	.25
468	A141	90 l green & buff	.25	.25
469	A141	180 l ultra & buff	.25	.25
	Nos. 467-469 (3)		.75	.75

Common Design Types pictured following the introduction.

Europa Issue
Common Design Type
1969, Apr. 28 **Photo.** **Wmk. 235**
Size: 36½x27mm
470	CD12	50 l gray & lt brn	.25	.25
471	CD12	90 l vermilion & lt brn	.25	.25
472	CD12	130 l olive & lt brn	.25	.25
	Nos. 470-472 (3)		.75	.75

Pope Paul VI with African Children — A142

Designs: 55 l, Pope Paul VI and African bishops. 250 l, Map of Africa with Kampala, olive branch and compass rose.

Perf. 13½x14
1969, July 31 **Photo.** **Wmk. 235**
473	A142	25 l bister & brown	.25	.25
474	A142	55 l dk red & brown	.25	.25
475	A142	250 l multicolored	.25	.25
	Nos. 473-475 (3)		.75	.75

Visit of Pope Paul VI to Uganda, 7/31-8/2.

Pope Pius IX — A143

Designs: 50 l, Chrismon, emblem of St. Peter's Circle. 220 l, Pope Paul VI.

Perf. 13½x14
1969, Nov. 18 **Engr.** **Wmk. 235**
476	A143	30 l red brown	.25	.25
477	A143	50 l dark gray	.25	.25
478	A143	220 l deep plum	.25	.25
	Nos. 476-478 (3)		.75	.75

Centenary of St. Peter's Circle, a lay society dedicated to prayer, action and sacrifice.

Mt. Fuji and EXPO '70 Emblem — A144

EXPO '70 Emblem and: 25 l, EXPO '70 emblem. 40 l, Osaka Castle. 55 l, Japanese Virgin and Child, by Domoto in Osaka Cathedral. 90 l, Christian Pavilion.

1970, Mar. 16 **Photo.** **Unwmk.**
479	A144	25 l gold, red & blk	.25	.25
480	A144	40 l red & multi	.25	.25
481	A144	55 l brown & multi	.25	.25
482	A144	90 l gold & multi	.25	.25
483	A144	110 l blue & multi	.25	.25
	Nos. 479-483 (5)		1.25	1.25

EXPO '70 Intl. Exhibition, Osaka, Japan, Mar. 15-Sept. 13.

Centenary Medal, Jesus Giving St. Peter the Keys — A145

Designs: 50 l, Coat of arms of Pope Pius IX. 180 l, Vatican I Council meeting in St. Peter's, obverse of centenary medal.

Engr. & Photo.; Photo. (50 l)
1970, Apr. 29 **Perf. 13x14**
484	A145	20 l orange & brown	.25	.25
485	A145	50 l multicolored	.25	.25
486	A145	180 l ver & brn	.30	.25
	Nos. 484-486 (3)		.80	.75

Centenary of the Vatican I Council.

Christ, by Simone Martini A146

25 l, Christ with Crown of Thorns, by Rogier van der Weyden. 50 l, Christ, by Albrecht Dürer. 90 l, Christ, by El Greco. 180 l, Pope Paul VI.

1970, May 29 **Photo.** **Perf. 14x13**
487	A146	15 l gold & multi	.25	.25
488	A146	25 l gold & multi	.25	.25
489	A146	50 l gold & multi	.25	.25
490	A146	90 l gold & multi	.25	.25
491	A146	180 l gold & multi	.25	.25
	Nos. 487-491 (5)		1.25	1.25

Ordination of Pope Paul VI, 50th anniv.

Adam, by Michelangelo; UN Emblem — A147

UN Emblem and: 90 l, Eve, by Michelangelo. 220 l, Olive branch.

1970, Oct. 8 **Photo.** **Perf. 13x14**
492	A147	20 l multi	.25	.25
493	A147	90 l multi	.25	.25
494	A147	220 l multi	.25	.25
	Nos. 492-494 (3)		.75	.75

25th anniversary of the United Nations.

Pope Paul VI — A148

Designs: 55 l, Holy Child of Cebu, Philippines. 100 l, Madonna and Child, by Georg Hamori, Darwin Cathedral, Australia. 130 l, Cathedral of Manila. 220 l, Cathedral of Sydney.

1970, Nov. 26 **Photo.** **Unwmk.**
495	A148	25 l multi	.25	.25
496	A148	55 l multi	.25	.25
497	A148	100 l multi	.25	.25
498	A148	130 l multi	.25	.25
499	A148	220 l multi	.25	.25
	Nos. 495-499 (5)		1.25	1.25

Visit of Pope Paul VI to the Far East, Oceania and Australia, Nov. 26-Dec. 5.

Angel Holding Lectern — A149

Sculptures by Corrado Ruffini: 40 l, 130 l, Crucified Christ surrounded by doves. 50 l, like 20 l.

1971, Feb. 2 **Perf. 13x14**
500	A149	20 l multicolored	.25	.25
501	A149	40 l dp orange & multi	.25	.25
502	A149	50 l purple & multi	.25	.25
503	A149	130 l multicolored	.25	.25
	Nos. 500-503 (4)		1.00	1.00

Intl. year against racial discrimination.

Madonna and Child by Francesco Ghissi — A150

Paintings: Madonna and Child, 40 l, by Sassetta (Stefano di Giovanni); 55 l, Carlo Crivelli; 90 l, by Carlo Maratta. 180 l, Holy Family, by Ghisberto Ceracchini.

1971, Mar. 26 **Photo.** **Perf. 14**
504	A150	25 l gray & multi	.25	.25
505	A150	40 l gray & multi	.25	.25
506	A150	55 l gray & multi	.25	.25
507	A150	90 l gray & multi	.25	.25
508	A150	180 l gray & multi	.25	.25
	Nos. 504-508 (5)		1.25	1.25

St. Dominic, Sienese School — A151

Portraits of St. Dominic: 55 l, by Fra Angelico. 90 l, by Titian. 180 l, by El Greco.

1971, May 25   Unwmk.   Perf. 13x14

509	A151	25 I multi	.25	.25
510	A151	55 I multi	.25	.25
511	A151	90 I multi	.25	.25
512	A151	180 I multi	.25	.25
		Nos. 509-512 (4)	1.00	1.00

St. Dominic de Guzman (1170-1221), founder of the Dominican Order.

St. Stephen, from Chasuble, 1031 — A152

180 I, Madonna as Patroness of Hungary, 1511.

1971, Nov. 25

513	A152	50 I multi	.25	.25
514	A152	180 I black & yellow	.30	.25

Millenium of the birth of St. Stephen (975?-1038), king of Hungary.

Bramante A153

Designs: 25 I, Bramante's design for dome of St. Peter's. 130 I, Design for spiral staircase.

1972, Feb. 22   Engr.   Perf. 13½x14

515	A153	25 I dull yellow & blk	.25	.25
516	A153	90 I dull yellow & blk	.25	.25
517	A153	130 I dull yellow & blk	.25	.25
		Nos. 515-517 (3)	.75	.75

Bramante (real name Donato d'Agnolo; 1444-1514), architect.

St. Mark in Storm, 12th Century Mosaic — A154

Map of Venice, 1581 — A155

Design: 180 I, St. Mark's Basilica, Painting by Emilio Vangelli.

Unwmk.
1972, June 6   Photo.   Perf. 14

518	A154	25 I lt brown & multi	.25	.25
519	A155	Block of 4	1.00	.60
a.-d.		50 I, UL, UR, LL, LR, each	.25	.25
520	A154	180 I lt blue & multi	1.10	.65
a.		Souvenir sheet, #518-520	2.50	2.50
		Nos. 518-520 (3)	2.35	1.50

UNESCO campaign to save Venice.

Gospel of St. Matthew, 13th Century, French A156

Illuminated Initials from: 50 I, St. Luke's Gospel, Biblia dell'Aracoeli 13th century, French. 90 I, Second Epistle of St. John, 14th century, Bologna. 100 I, Apocalypse of St. John, 14th century, Bologna. 130 I, Book of Romans, 14th century, Central Italy.

1972, Oct. 11   Perf. 14x13½

521	A156	30 I multi	.25	.25
522	A156	50 I multi	.25	.25
523	A156	90 I multi	.25	.25
524	A156	100 I multi	.25	.25
525	A156	130 I multi	.35	.25
		Nos. 521-525 (5)	1.35	1.25

Intl. Book Year. Illustrations are from illuminated medieval manuscripts.

Luigi Orione A157

Design: 180 I, Lorenzo Perosi and music from "Hallelujah."

1972, Nov. 28   Photo.   Perf. 14x13½

526	A157	50 I rose, lilac & blk	.25	.25
527	A157	180 I orange, grn & blk	.30	.25

Secular priests Luigi Orione (1872-1940), founder of CARITAS, Catholic welfare organization; and Lorenzo Perosi (1872-1956), composer.

Cardinal Bessarion A158

40 I, Reading Bull of Union between the Greek and Latin Churches, 1439, from bronze door of St. Peter's. 130 I, Coat of arms from tomb, Basilica of Holy Apostles, Rome.

Perf. 13x14
1972, Nov. 28   Wmk. 235   Engr.

528	A158	40 I dull green	.25	.25
529	A158	90 I carmine	.25	.25
530	A158	130 I black	.25	.25
		Nos. 528-530 (3)	.75	.75

Johannes Cardinal Bessarion (1403?-1472), Latin Patriarch of Constantinople, who worked for union of the Greek and Latin Churches. Portrait by Cosimo Rosselli in Sistine Chapel.

Eucharistic Congress Emblem — A159

Designs: 75 I, Head of Mary (Pietá), by Michelangelo. 300 I, Melbourne Cathedral.

1973, Feb. 27   Photo.   Unwmk.

531	A159	25 I violet & multi	.25	.25
532	A159	75 I olive & multi	.25	.25
533	A159	300 I multicolored	.50	.40
		Nos. 531-533 (3)	1.00	.90

40th Intl. Eucharistic Congress, Melbourne, Australia, Feb. 18-25.

St. Teresa — A160

Designs: 25 I, St. Teresa's birthplace, Alençon. 220 I, Lisieux Basilica.

1973, May 23   Engr. & Photo.

534	A160	25 I black & pink	.25	.25
535	A160	55 I black & yellow	.25	.25
536	A160	220 I black & lt blue	.75	.75
		Nos. 534-536 (3)		

St. Teresa of Lisieux and of the Infant Jesus (1873-1897), Carmelite nun.

Copernicus A161

Designs: 20 I, 100 I, View of Torun.

1973, June 19   Engr.   Perf. 14

537	A161	20 I dull green	.25	.25
538	A161	50 I brown	.25	.25
539	A161	100 I lilac	.25	.25
540	A161	130 I dark blue	.30	.25
		Nos. 537-540 (4)	1.05	1.00

Nicolaus Copernicus (1473-1543), Polish astronomer.

St. Wenceslas A162

90 I, Arms of Prague Diocese. 150 I, Spire of Prague Cathedral. 220 I, St. Adalbert.

1973, Sept. 25   Photo.   Perf. 14

541	A162	20 I shown	.25	.25
542	A162	90 I multicolored	.25	.25
543	A162	150 I multicolored	.25	.25
544	A162	220 I multicolored	.35	.25
		Nos. 541-544 (4)	1.10	1.00

Millenium of Prague Latin Episcopal See.

St. Nerses Shnorali — A163

25 I, Church of St. Hripsime. 90 I, Armenian khatchkar, a stele with cross and inscription.

Engr. & Litho.
1973, Nov. 27   Perf. 13x14

545	A163	25 I tan & dk brown	.25	.25
546	A163	90 I lt violet & blk	.25	.25
547	A163	180 I lt green & sepia	.35	.25
		Nos. 545-547 (3)	.85	.75

Armenian Patriarch St. Nerses Shnorali (1102-1173).

Noah's Ark, Rainbow and Dove (Mosaic) — A164

Design: 90 I, Lamb drinking from stream, and Tablets of the Law (mosaic).

1974, Apr. 23   Litho.   Perf. 13x14

548	A164	50 I gold & multi	.25	.25
549	A164	90 I gold & multi	.30	.25

Centenary of the Universal Postal Union.

"And There was Light" — A165

Designs: 25 I, Noah's Ark, horiz. 50 I, The Annunciation. 90 I, Nativity (African). 180 I, Hands holding grain (Spanish inscription: The Lord feeds his people), horiz. Designs chosen through worldwide youth competition in connection with 1972 Intl. Book Year.

Perf. 13x14, 14x13
1974, Apr. 23   Photo.

550	A165	15 I brown & multi	.25	.25
551	A165	25 I yellow & multi	.25	.25
552	A165	50 I blue & multi	.25	.25
553	A165	90 I green & multi	.25	.25
554	A165	180 I rose & multi	.25	.25
		Nos. 550-554 (5)	1.25	1.25

"The Bible: the Book of Books."

St. Thomas Aquinas Teaching — A166

Designs: 50 I, Students (left panel). 220 I, Students (right panel). Designs from a painting in the Convent of St. Mark in Florence, by an artist from the School of Fra Angelico.

Sizes: 50 I, 220 I, 20x36mm, 90 I, 26x36mm

Engr. & Litho.
1974, June 18   Unwmk.   Perf. 13x14

555	A166	50 I dk brown & gold	.25	.25
556	A166	90 I dk brown & gold	.25	.25
557	A166	220 I dk brown & gold	.40	.25
a.		Strip of 3, #555-557	.90	.75

St. Thomas Aquinas (1225-1274), scholastic philosopher.

St. Bonaventure A167

Woodcuts: 40 I, Civita Bagnoregio. 90 I, Tree of Life (13th century).

1974, Sept. 26 Photo. Perf. 13x14
558 A167 40 l gold & multi .25 .25
559 A167 90 l gold & multi .25 .25
560 A167 220 l gold & multi .30 .25
Nos. 558-560 (3) .80 .75

St. Bonaventure (Giovanni di Fidanza; 1221-1274), scholastic philosopher.

Christ, St. Peter's Basilica — A168

Pope Paul VI Giving his Blessing — A169

Holy Year 1975: 10 l, Christus Victor, Sts. Peter and Paul. 30 l, Christ. 40 l, Cross surmounted by dove. 50 l, Christ enthroned. 55 l, St. Peter. 90 l, St. Paul. 100 l, St. Peter. 130 l, St. Paul. 220 l, Arms of Pope Paul VI. Designs of 10 l, 25 l, are from St. Peter's; 30 l, 40 l, from St. John Lateran; 50 l, 55 l, 90 l, from St. Mary Major; 100 l, 130 l, from St. Paul outside the Walls.

1974, Dec. 19 Photo. Perf. 13x14
561 A168 10 l multi .25 .25
562 A168 25 l multi .25 .25
563 A168 30 l multi .25 .25
564 A168 40 l multi .25 .25
565 A168 55 l multi .25 .25
566 A168 90 l multi .25 .25
567 A168 100 l multi .25 .25
568 A168 130 l multi .25 .25
569 A169 220 l multi .25 .25
570 A169 250 l multi .30 .25
571 A169 250 l multi
Nos. 561-571 (11) 2.80 2.75

Pentecost, by El Greco — A170

1975, May 22 Engr. Perf. 13x14
572 A170 300 l car rose & org .60 .40

Fountain, St. Peter's Square — A171

Fountains of Rome: 40 l, Piazza St. Martha, Apse of St. Peter's. 50 l, Borgia Tower and St. Peter's. 90 l, Belvedere Courtyard. 100 l, Academy of Sciences. 200 l, Galleon.

Litho. & Engr.
1975, May 22 Perf. 14
573 A171 20 l buff & blk .25 .25
574 A171 40 l pale violet & blk .25 .25
575 A171 50 l salmon & blk .25 .25
576 A171 90 l pale citron & blk .25 .25
577 A171 100 l pale green & blk .25 .25
578 A171 200 l pale blue & blk .30 .25
Nos. 573-578 (6) 1.55 1.50

European Architectural Heritage Year.

Miracle of Loaves and Fishes, Gilt Glass A172

Designs: 150 l, Painting of Christ, from Comodilla Catacomb. 200 l, Raising of Lazarus. All works from 4th century.

Perf. 14x13½
1975, Sept. 25 Photo. Unwmk.
579 A172 30 l multi .25 .25
580 A172 150 l brown & multi .25 .25
581 A172 200 l green & multi .25 .30
Nos. 579-581 (3) .75 .80

9th Intl. Congress of Christian Archaeology.

Investiture of First Librarian Bartolomeo Sacchi by Pope Sixtus IV A173

Designs: 100 l, Pope Sixtus IV and books in old wooden press, from Latin Vatican Codex 2044, vert. 250 l, Pope Sixtus IV visiting Library, fresco in Hospital of the Holy Spirit. Design of 70 l is from fresco by Melozzo di Forli in Vatican Gallery.

Perf. 14x13½, 13½x14
1975, Sept. 25 Litho. & Engr.
582 A173 70 l gray & lilac .25 .25
583 A173 100 l lt yellow & grn .25 .25
584 A173 250 l gray & red .30 .30
Nos. 582-584 (3) .80 .80

Founding of the Vatican Apostolic Library, 500th anniv.

Mt. Argentario Monastery A174

St. Paul of the Cross, by Giovanni Della Porta — A175

Design: 300 l, Basilica of Sts. John and Paul and burial chapel of Saint.

1975, Nov. 27 Photo. Perf. 14x13½
585 A174 50 l multi .25 .25
586 A175 150 l multi .25 .25
587 A174 300 l multi .30 .25
Nos. 585-587 (3) .80 .75

Bicentenary of death of St. Paul of the Cross, founder of the Passionist religious order in 1737.

Praying Women, by Fra Angelico — A176

International Women's Year: 200 l, Seated women, by Fra Angelico.

1975, Nov. 27 Perf. 13½x14
588 A176 100 l multi .25 .25
589 A176 200 l multi .30 .25

Virgin and Child in Glory, by Titian A177

Design: 300 l, The Six Saints, by Titian. Designs from "The Madonna in Glory with the Child Jesus and Six Saints."

1976, May 13 Engr. Perf. 14x13½
590 A177 100 l rose magenta .25 .25
591 A177 300 l rose magenta .30 .25
a. Pair, #590-591 .75 .60

Titian (1477-1576), painter.

A178

Designs: 150 l, Eucharist, wheat and globe. 200 l, Hands Holding Eucharist. 400 l, Hungry mankind reaching for the Eucharist.

1976, July 2 Photo. Perf. 13½x14
592 A178 150 l gold, red & bl .25 .25
593 A178 200 l gold & blue .25 .25
594 A178 400 l gold, grn & brn .30 .25
Nos. 592-594 (3) .80 .75

41st Intl. Eucharistic Congress, Philadelphia, PA, Aug. 1-8.

A179

Details from Transfiguration by Raphael: 30 l, Moses Holding Tablets. 40 l, Transfigured Christ. 50 l, Prophet Elijah with book. 100 l, Apostles John and Peter. 150 l, Group of women. 200 l, Landscape.

1976, Sept. 30 Photo. Perf. 13½x14
595 A179 30 l ocher & multi .25 .25
596 A179 40 l red & multi .25 .25
597 A179 50 l violet & multi .25 .25
598 A179 100 l multicolored .25 .25
599 A179 150 l green & multi .25 .25
600 A179 200 l ocher & multi .25 .25
Nos. 595-600 (6) 1.50 1.50

St. John's Tower A180

Roman Views: 100 l, Fountain of the Sacrament. 120 l, Fountain at entrance to the gardens. 180 l, Basilica, Cupola of St. Peter's and Sacristy. 250 l, Borgia Tower and Sistine Chapel. 300 l, Apostolic Palace and Courtyard of St. Damasius.

Litho. & Engr.
1976, Nov. 23 Perf. 14
601 A180 50 l gray & black .25 .25
602 A180 100 l salmon & dk brn .25 .25
603 A180 120 l citron & dk grn .25 .25
604 A180 180 l pale gray & blk .25 .25
605 A180 250 l yellow & brn .25 .25
606 A180 300 l pale lilac & mag .25 .25
Nos. 601-606 (6) 1.50 1.50

The Lord's Creatures A181

70 l, Brother Sun. 100 l, Sister Moon and Stars. 130 l, Sister Water. 170 l, Praise in infirmities and tribulations. 200 l, Praise for bodily death. Designs are illustrations by Duilio Cambellotti for "The Canticle of Brother Sun," by St. Francis.

1977, Mar. 10 Photo. Perf. 14x13½
607 A181 50 l multi .25 .25
608 A181 70 l multi .25 .25
609 A181 100 l multi .25 .25
610 A181 130 l multi .25 .25
611 A181 170 l multi .25 .25
612 A181 200 l multi .25 .25
Nos. 607-612 (6) 1.50 1.50

St. Francis of Assisi, 750th death anniv.

Sts. Peter and Paul A182

Design: 350 l, Pope Gregory XI and St. Catherine of Siena. Designs are after fresco by Giorgio Vasari.

1977, May 20 Engr. Perf. 14
613 170 l black .30 .25
614 350 l black .45 .25
a. A182 Pair, #613-614 .85 .60

Return of Pope Gregory XI from Avignon, 600th anniv.

Dormition of the Virgin — A183

Design: 400 l, Virgin Mary in Heaven. Both designs after miniatures in Latin manuscripts, Vatican Library.

1977, July 5 Photo. Perf. 13½x14
615 A183 200 l multi .30 .25
616 A183 400 l multi .55 .30

Feast of the Assumption.

The Nile Deity, Roman Sculpture — A184

Sculptures: 120 l, Head of Pericles. 130 l, Roman Couple Joining Hands. 150 l, Apollo Belvedere, head. 170 l, Laocoon, head. 350 l, Apollo Belvedere, torso.

1977, Sept. 29 Perf. 14x13½
617 A184 50 l multi .25 .25
618 A184 120 l multi .25 .25
619 A184 130 l multi .25 .25
620 A184 150 l multi .25 .25
621 A184 170 l multi .25 .25
622 A184 350 l multi .25 .25
Nos. 617-622 (6) 1.50 1.50

Classical sculptures in Vatican Museums.

Creation of Man and Woman — A185

Designs: 70 l, Three youths in the furnace. 100 l, Adoration of the Kings. 130 l, Raising of Lazarus. 200 l, The Good Shepherd. 400 l, Chrismon, Cross, sleeping soldiers (Resurrection). Designs are bas-reliefs from Christian sarcophagi, 250-350 A.D., found in Roman excavations.

1977, Dec. 9   Photo.   Perf. 14x13½

623	A185	50 l	multi	.25 .25
624	A185	70 l	multi	.25 .25
625	A185	100 l	multi	.25 .25
626	A185	130 l	multi	.25 .25
627	A185	200 l	multi	.25 .25
628	A185	400 l	multi	.25 .25
	Nos. 623-628 (6)			1.50 1.50

Madonna with the Parrot and Rubens Self-portrait A186

1977, Dec. 9   Perf. 13½x14

629	A186	350 l	multi	.50 .50

Peter Paul Rubens (1577-1640).

Pope Paul VI, by Lino Bianchi Barriviera A187

Design: 350 l, Christ's Face, by Pericle Fazzini and arms of Pope Paul VI.

1978, Mar. 9   Photo.   Perf. 14

630	A187	350 l	multi	.40 .30
631	A187	400 l	multi	.45 .40

80th birthday of Pope Paul VI.

Pope Pius IX (1792-1878) A188

Designs: 130 l, Arms of Pope Pius IX. 170 l, Seal of Pius IX, used to sign definition of Dogma of Immaculate Conception.

Litho. & Engr.

1978, May 9   Perf. 13x14

632	A188	130 l	multi	.25 .25
633	A188	170 l	multi	.25 .25
634	A188	200 l	multi	.30 .25
	Nos. 632-634 (3)			.80 .75

Interregnum Issues

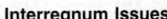

Keys of St. Peter and Papal Chamberlain's Insignia — A189

1978, Aug. 23   Photo.   Perf. 14

635	A189	120 l	purple & lt green	.25 .25
636	A189	150 l	purple & salmon	.25 .25
637	A189	250 l	purple & yellow	.25 .25
	Nos. 635-637 (3)			.75 .75

Keys of St. Peter and Papal Chamberlain's Insignia — A190

1978, Oct. 12   Photo.   Perf. 14

638	A190	120 l	black & multi	.25 .25
639	A190	200 l	black & multi	.25 .25
640	A190	250 l	black & multi	.25 .25
	Nos. 638-640 (3)			.75 .75

Pope John Paul I, Pope from Aug. 26 to Sept. 28, 1978 — A191

Pope John Paul I: 70 l, Sitting on his throne. 250 l, Walking in Vatican garden. 350 l, Giving blessing, horiz.

1978, Dec. 11   Perf. 13x14, 14x13

641	A191	70 l	multi	.25 .25
642	A191	120 l	multi	.25 .25
643	A191	250 l	multi	.25 .25
644	A191	350 l	multi	.30 .30
	Nos. 641-644 (4)			1.05 1.05

Arms of Pope John Paul II A192

Designs: 250 l, Pope John Paul II raising hand in blessing. 400 l, Jesus giving keys to St. Peter.

Litho. & Engr.

1979, Mar. 22   Perf. 14x13

645	A192	170 l	black & multi	.25 .25
646	A192	250 l	black & multi	.30 .30
647	A192	400 l	black & multi	.55 .45
	Nos. 645-647 (3)			1.10 1.00

Inauguration of pontificate of Pope John Paul II.

Martyrdom of St. Stanislas — A193

Designs: 150 l, St. Stanislas appearing to the people. 250 l, Gold reliquary, 1504, containing saint's head. 500 l, View of Cracow Cathedral.

1979, May 18   Photo.   Perf. 14

648	A193	120 l	multi	.25 .25
649	A193	150 l	multi	.25 .25
650	A193	250 l	multi	.30 .30
651	A193	500 l	multi	.50 .50
	Nos. 648-651 (4)			1.30 1.30

900th anniversary of martyrdom of St. Stanislas (1030-1079), patron saint of Poland.

St. Basil the Great Instructing Monk — A194

St. Basil the Great, 16th cent. of death: 520 l, St. Basil the Great visiting the sick.

Engr. & Photo.

1979, June 25   Perf. 13½x14

652	A194	150 l	multi	.25 .25
653	A194	520 l	multi	.55 .50

Father Secchi, Solar Protuberance, Spectrum and Meteorograph — A195

Father Angelo Secchi (1818-1878), astronomer, solar protuberance, spectrum and: 220 l, Spectroscope. 300 l, Telescope.

Litho. & Engr.

1979, June 25   Perf. 14x13½

654	A195	180 l	multi	.25 .25
655	A195	220 l	multi	.25 .25
656	A195	300 l	multi	.30 .30
	Nos. 654-656 (3)			.80 .80

Vatican City A196

Papal Arms and Portraits: 70 l, Pius XI. 120 l, Pius XII. 150 l, John XXIII. 170 l, Paul VI. 250 l, John Paul I. 450 l, John Paul II.

1979, Oct. 11   Photo.   Perf. 14x13½

657	A196	50 l	multi	.25 .25
658	A196	70 l	multi	.25 .25
659	A196	120 l	multi	.25 .25
660	A196	150 l	multi	.25 .25
661	A196	170 l	multi	.25 .25
662	A196	250 l	multi	.25 .25
663	A196	450 l	multi	.40 .40
	Nos. 657-663 (7)			1.90 1.90

Vatican City State, 50th anniversary.

Infant, by Andrea Della Robbia, IYC Emblem — A197

IYC Emblem and Della Robbia Bas Reliefs, Hospital of the Innocents, Florence.

Engr. & Photo.

1979, Nov. 27   Perf. 13½x14

664	A197	50 l	multi	.25 .25
665	A197	120 l	multi	.25 .25
666	A197	200 l	multi	.25 .25
667	A197	350 l	multi	.30 .25
	Nos. 664-667 (4)			1.05 1.00

International Year of the Child.

Abbot Desiderius Giving Codex to St. Benedict — A198

Illuminated Letters and Illustrations, Codices, Vatican Apostolic Library: 100 l, St. Benedict writing the Rule. 150 l, Page from the Rule. 220 l, Death of St. Benedict. 450 l, Montecassino (after painting by Paul Bril).

1980, Mar. 21   Photo.   Perf. 14x13½

668	A198	80 l	multi	.25 .25
669	A198	100 l	multi	.25 .25
670	A198	150 l	multi	.25 .25
671	A198	220 l	multi	.25 .25
672	A198	450 l	multi	.40 .30
	Nos. 668-672 (5)			1.40 1.30

St. Benedict of Nursia (patron saint of Europe), 1500th birth anniversary.

Bernini, Medallion Showing Baldacchino in St. Peter's — A199

Gian Lorenzo Bernini (1598-1680), Architect (Self-portrait and Medallion): 170 l, St. Peter's Square with third wing (never built). 250 l, Bronze chair, Doctors of the Church. 350 l, Apostolic Palace stairway.

1980, Oct. 16   Litho.   Perf. 14x13½

673	A199	80 l	multicolored	.25 .25
674	A199	170 l	multicolored	.25 .25
675	A199	250 l	multicolored	.30 .25
676	A199	350 l	multicolored	.35 .25
	Nos. 673-676 (4)			1.15 1.00

St. Albertus Magnus on Mission of Peace — A200

1980, Nov. 18   Litho.   Perf. 13½x14

677	A200	300 l	shown	.40 .30
678	A200	400 l	As bishop	.50 .40

St. Albertus Magnus, 700th death anniv.

Communion of the Saints — A201

1980, Nov. 18   Perf. 14x13½

679	A201	250 l	shown	.35 .25
680	A201	500 l	Christ and saints	.50 .50

Feast of All Saints.

Guglielmo Marconi and Pope Pius XI, Vatican Radio Emblem, Vatican Arms A202

Designs: 150 l, Microphone, Bible text. 200 l, St. Maria di Galeria Radio Center

antenna, Archangel Gabriel statue. 600 l,
Pope John Paul II.

1981, Feb. 12 Photo. *Perf. 14x13½*
681	A202	100 l shown	.25	.25
682	A202	150 l multicolored	.25	.25
683	A202	200 l multicolored	.25	.25
684	A202	600 l multicolored	.50	.50
		Nos. 681-684 (4)	1.25	1.25

Vatican Radio, 50th anniversary.

Virgil Seated at Podium, Vergilius
Romanus — A203

1981, Apr. 23 Litho. *Perf. 14*
685	A203	350 l multicolored	.30	.30
686	A203	600 l multicolored	.50	.50
		Set, with labels	1.75	1.75

2000th birth anniversary of Virgil.
Issued in sheets of 16 stamps plus 9 labels.

Congress
Emblem
A204

Congress Emblem and: 150 l, Virgin
appearing to St. Bernadette. 200 l, Pilgrims
going to Lourdes. 500 l, Bishop and pilgrims.

1981, June 22 Photo.
687	A204	80 l multicolored	.25	.25
688	A204	150 l multicolored	.25	.25
689	A204	200 l multicolored	.25	.30
690	A204	500 l multicolored	.50	.50
		Nos. 687-690 (4)	1.25	1.30

42nd Intl. Eucharistic Congress, Lourdes,
France, July 16-23.

Intl. Year of
the
Disabled
A205

1981, Sept. 29 Photo. *Perf. 14x13½*
691	A205	600 l multicolored	.65	.60

Jan van
Ruusbroec,
Flemish Mystic,
500th Birth
Anniv. — A206

Litho. & Engr.
1981, Sept. 29 *Perf. 13½x14*
692	A206	200 l shown	.25	.25
693	A206	300 l Portrait	.30	.25

1980 Journeys of
Pope John
Paul II — A207

50 l, Papal arms. 100 l, Map of Africa. 120 l,
Crucifix. 150 l, Baptism. 200 l, African bishop.
250 l, Visiting sick. 300 l, Notre Dame, France.
400 l, UNESCO speech. 600 l, Christ the

Andes, Brazil. 700 l, Cologne Cathedral, Germany. 900 l, John Paul II.

1981, Dec. 3 Photo. *Perf. 13½x14½*
694	A207	50 l multicolored	.25	.25
695	A207	100 l multicolored	.25	.25
696	A207	120 l multicolored	.25	.25
697	A207	150 l multicolored	.25	.25
698	A207	200 l multicolored	.25	.25
699	A207	250 l multicolored	.30	.30
700	A207	300 l multicolored	.30	.30
701	A207	400 l multicolored	.35	.35
702	A207	600 l multicolored	.50	.50
703	A207	700 l multicolored	.65	.65
704	A207	900 l multicolored	.95	.95
a.		Complete booklet, 8 each		
		#694, 695, 698, 699 ('82)	27.50	
		Nos. 694-704 (11)	4.30	4.30

700th Death
Anniv. of St.
Agnes of
Prague — A208

Designs: 700 l, Handing order to Grand
Master of the Crosiers of the Red Star. 900 l,
Receiving letter from St. Clare.

1982, Feb. 16 Photo. *Perf. 13½x14*
705	A208	700 l multicolored	.75	.75
706	A208	900 l multicolored	1.10	1.10

Pueri
Cantores — A209

Luca Della Robbia (1400-1482), Sculptor:
No. 708, Pueri Cantores, diff. No. 709, Virgin
in Prayer (44x36mm).

Photo. & Engr.
1982, May 21 *Perf. 14*
707	A209	1000 l multicolored	.80	.75
708	A209	1000 l multicolored	.80	.75
709	A209	1000 l multicolored	.80	.75
a.		Strip of 3, #707-709	3.50	3.25

St. Teresa of
Avila (1515-1582)
A210

Sketches of St. Teresa by Riccardo Tom-
masi-Ferroni.

1982, Sept. 23 Photo.
710	A210	200 l multicolored	.25	.25
711	A210	600 l multicolored	.50	.50
712	A210	1000 l multicolored	1.10	1.10
		Nos. 710-712 (3)	1.85	1.85

Christmas
A211

Nativity Bas-Reliefs: 300 l, Wit Stwosz,
Church of the Virgin Mary, Cracow. 450 l,
Enrico Manfrini.

Photo. & Engr.
1982, Nov. 23 *Perf. 14*
713	A211	300 l multicolored	.40	.40
714	A211	450 l multicolored	.55	.55

400th Anniv. of
Gregorian
Calendar — A212

Sculpture Details, Tomb of Pope Gregory XIII, St. Peter's Basilica: 200 l, Surveying
the globe. 300 l, Receiving Edict of Reform.
700 l, Presenting edict.

1982, Nov. 23 Engr. *Perf. 13½x14*
715	A212	200 l multicolored	.25	.25
716	A212	300 l multicolored	.35	.35
717	A212	700 l multicolored	.80	.80
a.		Souvenir sheet of 3, #715-717	2.25	2.25
		Nos. 715-717 (3)	1.40	1.40

Souvenir Sheets

The Papacy and Art, US 1983
Exhibition — A213

1983, Mar. 10 Litho. *Perf. 13½x14*
718		Sheet of 6	3.25	2.00
a.	A213	100 l Greek Vase	.30	.25
b.	A213	200 l Italian vase	.30	.25
c.	A213	250 l Female terra-cotta bust	.40	.35
d.	A213	300 l Marcus Aurelius bust	.40	.35
e.	A213	350 l Bird fresco	.50	.40
f.	A213	400 l Pope Clement VIII vestment	.50	.40

1983, June 14 Litho. *Perf. 13½x14*
719		Sheet of 6	3.50	3.50
a.	A213	100 l Horse's head, Etruscan terra cotta	.35	.30
b.	A213	200 l Horseman, Greek fragment	.35	.30
c.	A213	300 l Male head, Etruscan	.45	.40
d.	A213	400 l Apollo Belvedere head	.45	.40
e.	A213	500 l Moses, Roman fresco	.55	.45
f.	A213	1000 l Madonna and Child, by Bernardo Daddi	.60	.45

1983, Nov. 10 Litho. *Perf. 13½x14*
720		Sheet of 6	3.75	3.75
a.	A213	150 l Greek cup, Oedipus and the Sphinx	.40	.35
b.	A213	200 l Etruscan bronze statue of a child	.40	.35
c.	A213	350 l Emperor Augustus marble statue	.50	.45
d.	A213	400 l Good Shepherd marble statue	.50	.45
e.	A213	500 l St. Nicholas Saving a ship by G. da Fabriano	.60	.50
f.	A213	1200 l The Holy face by G. Rouault	.75	.60

Vatican Collection: The Papacy and Art - US
1983 exhibition, New York, Chicago, San
Francisco.

Extraordinary
Holy Year, 1983-
84 (1950th Anniv.
of Redemption)
A214

Sketches by Giovanni Hajnal.

1983, Mar. 10 Photo. & Engr.
721	A214	300 l Crucifixion	.30	.25
722	A214	350 l Christ the Redeemer	.30	.25
723	A214	400 l Pope	.40	.40
724	A214	2000 l Holy Spirit	2.00	1.75
		Nos. 721-724 (4)	3.00	2.65

Theology, by
Raphael (1483-
1517)
A215

Allegories, Room of the Segnatura.

1983, June 14
725	A215	50 l shown	.25	.25
726	A215	400 l Poetry	.35	.25
727	A215	500 l Justice	.50	.50
728	A215	1200 l Philosphy	1.40	1.25
		Nos. 725-728 (4)	2.50	2.25

Gregor Johann Mendel (1822-1884),
Biologist — A216

Phases of pea plant hybridization.

Photo. & Engr.
1984, Feb. 28 *Perf. 14x13½*
729	A216	450 l multicolored	.45	.40
730	A216	1500 l multicolored	1.75	1.25

St. Casimir of
Lithuania (1458-
1484) — A217

1984, Feb. 28 *Perf. 14*
731	A217	550 l multicolored	.55	.50
732	A217	1200 l multicolored	1.60	1.25

Pontifical Academy of
Sciences — A218

1984, June 18 Litho. & Engr.
733	A218	150 l shown	.25	.25
734	A218	450 l Secret Archives	.50	.40
735	A218	550 l Apostolic Library	.75	.55
736	A218	1500 l Observatory	1.75	1.50
		Nos. 733-736 (4)	3.25	2.70

Papal Journeys
A218a

1984-85 Photo. *Perf. 13½x14½*
737	A218a	50 l Pakistan	.25	.25
738	A218a	100 l Philippines	.25	.25
739	A218a	150 l Guam	.25	.25

740	A218a	250 l	Japan	.25	.25
741	A218a	300 l	Alaska	.30	.30
742	A218a	400 l	Africa	.35	.30
743	A218a	450 l	Portugal	.40	.40
a.		Bkit. pane, 4 ea #738, 741-743 + 4 labels ('85)		10.00	
		Complete booklet, #743a		10.00	
744	A218a	550 l	Grt. Britain	.80	.60
745	A218a	1000 l	Argentina	1.00	.90
746	A218a	1500 l	Switzerland	1.75	1.25
747	A218a	2500 l	San Marino	3.00	2.50
748	A218a	4000 l	Spain	6.00	4.75
		Nos. 737-748 (12)		14.60	12.00

Issued: Nos. 737-748, 10/2/84; No. 743a, 3/14/85.

St. Damasus I (b. 304) A219

St. Damasus I and: 200 l, Sepulchre of Sts. Marcellinus and Peter. 500 l, Epigraph of St. Januarius. 2000 l, Basilica, Church of the Martyrs Simplicius, Faustinus and Beatrice.

1984, Nov. 27 Photo. Perf. 14x13½

749	A219	200 l	multicolored	.35	.25
750	A219	500 l	multicolored	.70	.50
751	A219	2000 l	multicolored	2.25	2.00
		Nos. 749-751 (3)		3.30	2.75

St. Methodius (d. 885) — A220

St. Methodius and: 500 l, Madonna and Christ. 600 l, St. Cyril, carrying the body of St. Clement I. 1700 l, Sts. Benedict and Cyril, patrons of Europe.

Photo. & Engr.

1985, May 7 Perf. 13½x14

752	A220	500 l	multicolored	.50	.30
753	A220	600 l	multicolored	.70	.50
754	A220	1700 l	multicolored	2.25	1.50
		Nos. 752-754 (3)		3.45	2.30

St. Thomas More (1477-1535) — A221

St. Thomas More (from a portrait by Hans Holbein) and: 250 l, map of British Isles. 400 l, Frontispiece of Utopia. 2000 l, Frontispiece of Domenico Regi's biography of More.

Litho. & Engr.

1985, May 7 Perf. 14x13½

755	A221	250 l	multicolored	.40	.25
756	A221	400 l	multicolored	.50	.40
757	A221	2000 l	multicolored	2.60	2.00
		Nos. 755-757 (3)		3.50	2.65

St. Gregory VII (c. 1020-85) A222

Designs: 150 l, Eagle from Byzantine door, St. Paul's Basilica, Rome. 450 l, St. Gregory blessing. 2500 l, Sarcophagus.

Perf. 13½x14, 14x13½

1985, June 18 Photo.

758	A222	150 l	multi, vert.	.25	.25
759	A222	450 l	multi, vert.	.60	.45
760	A222	2500 l	multicolored	2.75	2.50
		Nos. 758-760 (3)		3.60	3.20

43rd Intl. Eucharistic Congress — A223

Emblem, host, cross and: 100 l, Outline map of Africa. 400 l, Altar and Assembly of Bishops. 600 l, African chalice. 2300 l, African Christian family.

Photo. & Engr.

1985, June 18 Perf. 13½x14

761	A223	100 l	multicolored	.25	.25
762	A223	400 l	multicolored	.45	.40
763	A223	600 l	multicolored	.55	.55
764	A223	2300 l	multicolored	2.60	2.00
		Nos. 761-764 (4)		3.85	3.20

Concordat Agreement Ratification A224

1985, Oct. 15 Photo. Perf. 14x13½

765	A224	400 l	Papal arms, map of Italy	.60	.50

Coaches A225

1985, Oct. 15 Litho. & Engr.

766	A225	450 l	dp lil rose & int bl	.45	.35
767	A225	1500 l	brt bl & dp lil rose	1.50	1.25
a.		Souvenir sheet of 2, #766-767, perf. 13½x12½		3.25	3.25

Italia '85.

Intl. Peace Year 1986 — A226

Biblical and gospel texts: 50 l, Isaiah 2:4. 350 l, Isaiah 52:7. 450 l, Matthew 5:9. 650 l, Luke 2:14. 2000 l, Message for World Peace, speech of Pope John Paul II, Jan. 1, 1986.

1986, Apr. 14 Photo. Perf. 14

768	A226	50 l	multicolored	.25	.25
769	A226	350 l	multicolored	.35	.30
770	A226	450 l	multicolored	.60	.40
771	A226	650 l	multicolored	.80	.60
772	A226	2000 l	multicolored	2.25	1.75
		Nos. 768-772 (5)		4.25	3.30

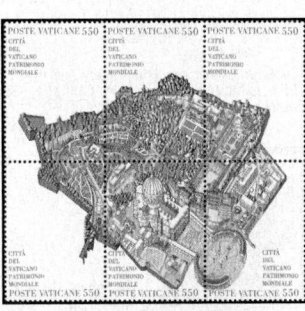

Vatican City — A227

1986, Apr. 14 Perf. 13½x14

773	A227	Block of 6		5.00	4.00
a.-f.		550 l, any single		.70	.40

UNESCO World Heritage Campaign. No. 773 has continuous design.

Patron Saints of the Sick — A228

Designs: No. 774, St. Camillus de Lellis rescuing invalid during Tiber flood, by Pierre Subleyras (1699-1749). No. 775, St. John of God with invalids, by Gomez Moreno (1834-1918). 2000 l, Pope John Paul II visiting the sick.

Litho. & Engr.

1986, June 12 Perf. 13½x14

774	A228	700 l	multicolored	.80	.60
775	A228	700 l	multicolored	.80	.60
776	A228	2000 l	multicolored	2.50	1.90
		Nos. 774-776 (3)		4.10	3.10

Pontifical Academy of Sciences, 50th Anniv. A229

School of Athens (details), by Raphael: 1500 l, Scribes. 2500 l, Students learning math.

Litho. & Engr.

1986, Oct. 2 Perf. 14x13½

777	A229	1500 l	multicolored	1.75	1.50
778	A229	2500 l	multicolored	3.00	2.50

Conversion of St. Augustine (354-430) in 387 — A230

Religious art: 300 l, St. Augustine reading St. Paul's Epistles, fresco by Benozzo Gozzoli (1420-1498), Church of St. Augustine, San Gimignano. 400 l, Baptism of St. Augustine, painting by Bartolomeo di Gentile (1470-1534), Vatican Art Gallery. 500 l, Ecstasy of St. Augustine, fresco by Benozzo Gozzoli, Church of St. Augustine. 2200 l, St. Augustine, detail of Disputa del Sacramento, fresco by Raphael (1483-1520), Room of the Segnatura, Apostolic Palace.

1987, Apr. 7 Photo. Perf. 13½x14

779	A230	300 l	multicolored	.40	.30
780	A230	400 l	multicolored	.55	.45
781	A230	500 l	multicolored	.65	.50
782	A230	2200 l	multicolored	3.00	2.50
		Nos. 779-782 (4)		4.60	3.50

A231

Seals: 700 l, Church of Riga, 1234-1269. 2400 l, Marian Basilica of the Assumption, Aglona, 1780.

1987, June 2 Photo. Perf. 13½x14

783	A231	700 l	multicolored	1.25	.95
784	A231	2400 l	multicolored	3.25	2.75

Christianization of Latvia, 800th anniv.

Christianization Anniversaries A232

Designs: 200 l, Christ, statue in the Lithuanian Chapel, Vatican Crypt. 700 l, Two Angels and Our Lady Holding the Body of Christ, by a Lithuanian artist. 3000 l, Lithuanian shrine.

1987, June 2 Perf. 13½x14

785	A232	200 l	multicolored	.30	.25
786	A232	700 l	multicolored	1.00	.75
787	A232	3000 l	multicolored	3.25	2.75
		Nos. 785-787 (3)		4.55	3.75

Christianization of Lithuania, 600th anniv.

OLYMPHILEX '87, Rome, Aug. 29-Sept. 9 — A233

Details of mosaic from the Baths of Caracalla: 400 l, Judge. 500 l, Athlete. 600 l, Athlete, diff. 2000 l, Athlete, diff.

Litho. & Engr.

1987, Aug. 29 Perf. 14

788	A233	400 l	multicolored	.40	.30
789	A233	500 l	multicolored	.50	.40
790	A233	600 l	multicolored	.60	.50
791	A233	2000 l	multicolored	3.00	2.25
		Nos. 788-791 (4)		4.50	3.45

Souvenir Sheet

792		Sheet of 4 + 4 labels		4.25	4.25
a.	A233	400 l	like No. 788	.40	.30
b.	A233	500 l	like No. 789	.50	.40
c.	A233	600 l	like No. 780	.60	.50
d.	A233	2000 l		2.75	2.25

Stamps from souvenir sheet have a Greek border in blue surrounding vignettes (pictured). Nos. 788-791 have single line border in blue. No. 792 has 4 labels picturing the papal arms, a goblet, a crown and the exhibition emblem.

Inauguration of the Philatelic and Numismatic Museum — A235

Designs: 400 l, Philatelic department, Vatican City, No. 1. 3500 l, Numismatic department, 1000-lire coin of 1986.

1987, Sept. 29 Photo. Perf. 14x13½

793	A235	400 l	multicolored	.50	.45
794	A235	3500 l	multicolored	4.50	3.75

Journeys of Pope John Paul II, 1985-86 A236

Designs: 50 l, Venezuela, Peru, Ecuador and Trinidad & Tobago, 1985. 250 l, The Netherlands, Luxembourg, Belgium, 1985. 400 l, Togo, Ivory Coast, Cameroun, Central Africa, Zaire, Kenya and Morocco, 1985. 500 l, Liechtenstein, 1986. 600 l, India, 1986. 700 l, Colombia, St. Lucia, 1986. 2500 l, France, 1986. 4000 l, Bangladesh, Singapore, Fiji, New Zealand, Australia and Seychelles, 1986.

1987, Oct. 27 Photo. *Perf. 14x13½*

795	A236	50 l multicolored	.30	.25
796	A236	250 l multicolored	.50	.30
797	A236	400 l multicolored	.60	.40
798	A236	500 l multicolored	.80	.50
799	A236	600 l multicolored	1.00	.80
800	A236	700 l multicolored	1.50	1.00
801	A236	2500 l multicolored	5.50	4.25
802	A236	4000 l multicolored	8.50	7.00
	Nos. 795-802 (8)		18.70	14.50

A237

Transfer of St. Nicholas Relics from Myra to Bari, 900th anniv.: 500 l, Arrival of relics at Bari. 700 l, Act of charity, three improverished women. 3000 l, Miraculous rescue of ship.

1987, Dec. 3 *Perf. 13½x14*

803	A237	500 l multicolored	1.00	1.00
804	A237	700 l multicolored	1.50	1.25
805	A237	3000 l multicolored	11.50	8.00
	Nos. 803-805 (3)		14.00	10.25

St. Nicholas of Bari (c. 270-352), bishop of Myra. Legend of Santa Claus originated because of his charitable works. Printed in sheets of 8 + 16 se-tenant labels picturing Santa Claus.

A238

Children and: 500 l, Sister of the Institute of the Daughters of Mary Help of Christians. 1000 l, St. John Bosco. 2000 l, Salesian lay brother. Printed in a continuous design.

1988, Apr. 19 Photo.

806		Strip of 3	5.25	4.00
a.	A238	500 l multicolored	.45	.40
b.	A238	1000 l multicolored	.75	.50
c.	A238	2000 l multicolored	1.50	1.25

St. John Bosco (1815-1888), educator.

A239

50 l, Annunciation. 300 l, Nativity. 500 l, Pentecost. 750 l, Assumption. 1000 l, Mother of the Church. 2400 l, Refuge of Sinners.

1988, June 16 Photo. *Perf. 13½x14*

807	A239	50 l multicolored	.25	.25
808	A239	300 l multicolored	.30	.25
809	A239	500 l multicolored	.50	.40
810	A239	750 l multicolored	.90	.60
811	A239	1000 l multicolored	1.25	.80
812	A239	2400 l multicolored	2.75	1.75
	Nos. 807-812 (6)		5.95	4.05

Marian Year, 1987-88.

A240

Baptism of the Rus' of Kiev, Millennium: 450 l, "Prince St. Vladimir the Great," from a 15th cent. icon. 650 l, Cathedral of St. Sophia, Kiev. 2500 l, "Mother of God in Prayer," from a mosaic at the cathedral.

1988, June 16

813	A240	450 l multicolored	.60	.45
814	A240	650 l multicolored	.85	.65
815	A240	2500 l multicolored	3.00	2.25
	Nos. 813-815 (3)		4.45	3.35

Paintings by Paolo Veronese (1528-1588) — A241

Designs: 550 l, Marriage of Cana (Madonna and Christ) the Louvre, Paris. 650 l, Self-portrait of the Artist, Villa Barbaro of Maser, Treviso. 3000 l, Marriage of Cana (woman and two men).

Perf. 13½x14, 14x13½

1988, Sept. 29 Photo. & Engr.

816	A241	550 l multi, vert.	.75	.45
817	A241	650 l multicolored	.85	.55
818	A241	3000 l multi, vert.	4.00	2.50
	Nos. 816-818 (3)		5.60	3.50

Christmas
A242

Luke 2:14 and: 50 l, Angel facing LR. 400 l, Angel facing UR. 500 l, Angel facing LL. 550 l, Shepherds. 850 l, Nativity. 1500 l, Magi.

1988, Dec. 12 Photo. *Perf. 13½x14*

819	A242	50 l multicolored	.25	.25
820	A242	400 l multicolored	.45	.30
821	A242	500 l multicolored	.60	.35
822	A242	550 l multicolored	.70	.40
823	A242	850 l multicolored	1.00	.60
824	A242	1500 l multicolored	1.50	1.00
	Nos. 819-824 (6)		4.50	2.90

Souvenir Sheet

825		Sheet of 6	5.00	5.00
a.	A242	50 l gold & multi	.25	.25
b.	A242	400 l gold & multi	.40	.30
c.	A242	500 l gold & multi	.50	.35
d.	A242	550 l gold & multi	.70	.40
e.	A242	850 l gold & multi	1.00	.60
f.	A242	1500 l gold & multi	1.50	1.00

No. 825 has continuous design.

Feast of the Visitation, 600th Anniv. — A243

Illuminations: 550 l, The Annunciation. 750 l, The Visitation (Virgin and St. Elizabeth). 2500 l, Mary, Elizabeth and infants.

1989, May 5 Photo. *Perf. 13½x14*

826	A243	550 l multicolored	.75	.40
827	A243	750 l multicolored	.90	.55
828	A243	2500 l multicolored	2.75	1.90
	Nos. 826-828 (3)		4.40	2.85

Souvenir Sheet

Gregorian Egyptian Museum, 150th Anniv. — A244

Designs: 400 l, Apis. 650 l, Isis and Apis dicephalous bust. 750 l, Statue of the physician Ugiahorresne. 2400 l, Pharaoh Mentuhotep.

1989, May 5 Litho. & Engr. *Perf. 14x13½*

829		Sheet of 4	4.75	4.75
a.	A244	400 l multicolored	.30	.25
b.	A244	650 l multicolored	.40	.25
c.	A244	750 l multicolored	.55	.45
d.	A244	2400 l multicolored	1.50	1.25

A245

Birds from engravings by Eleazar Albin in *Histoire Naturelle des Oiseaux*, 1750 — 100 l, Parrot. 150 l, Green woodpecker. 200 l, Crested and common wrens. 350 l, Kingfisher. 500 l, Red grosbeak of Virginia. 700 l, Bullfinch. 1500 l, Lapwing plover. 3000 l, French teal.

1989, June 13 Photo. *Perf. 12*
Granite Paper

830	A245	100 l multicolored	.25	.25
831	A245	150 l multicolored	.25	.25
832	A245	200 l multicolored	.25	.25
833	A245	350 l multicolored	.45	.25
834	A245	500 l multicolored	.65	.30
835	A245	700 l multicolored	.90	.45
836	A245	1500 l multicolored	2.00	1.00
837	A245	3000 l multicolored	4.00	2.00
	Nos. 830-837 (8)		8.75	4.75

A246

Symbols of the Eucharist.

Photo. & Engr.
1989, Sept. 29 *Perf. 13½x14*

838	A246	550 l shown	.70	.40
839	A246	850 l multi, diff.	1.00	.65
840	A246	1000 l multi, diff.	1.25	.75
841	A246	2500 l multi, diff.	3.25	1.90
	Nos. 838-841 (4)		6.20	3.70

44th Intl. Eucharistic Cong., Seoul, Oct. 5-8.

Ecclesiastical Hierarchy in the US, Bicent. — A247

Designs: 450 l, Basilica of the Assumption of the Blessed Virgin Mary, Baltimore. 1350 l, John Carroll (1735-1815), 1st bishop of Baltimore and the US. 2400 l, Cathedral of Mary Our Queen, Baltimore.

1989, Nov. 9 Photo. *Perf. 12*

842	A247	450 l multicolored	.60	.40
843	A247	1350 l multicolored	1.75	1.25
844	A247	2400 l multicolored	3.25	2.00
	Nos. 842-844 (3)		5.60	3.65

Papal Journeys 1988
A248

Papal arms, Pope John Paul II and maps: 50 l, Uruguay, Bolivia, Peru and Paraguay, May 7-19. 550 l, Austria, June 23-27. 800 l, Zimbabwe, Botswana, Lesotho, Swaziland and Mozambique, Sept. 10-19. 1000 l, France, Oct. 8-11. 4000 l, Pastoral visits in Italy, 1978-1988.

1989, Nov. 9 *Perf. 14x13½*

845	A248	50 l multicolored	.25	.25
846	A248	550 l multicolored	.80	.50
847	A248	800 l multicolored	1.10	.70
848	A248	1000 l multicolored	1.50	.90
849	A248	4000 l multicolored	5.75	3.50
	Nos. 845-849 (5)		9.40	5.85

St. Angela Merici (c. 1474-1540)
A249

Designs: 700 l, The vision of the mystical stair, Prophecy of the Ursulines. 800 l, Evangelical counsel. 2800 l, Ursulines mission continued.

1990, Apr. 5 Photo. *Perf. 13½x14*

850	A249	700 l multicolored	1.10	.80
851	A249	800 l multicolored	1.25	.95
852	A249	2800 l multicolored	4.25	3.25
	Nos. 850-852 (3)		6.60	5.00

Caritas Intl., 40th Anniv.
A250

Designs: 450 l, Abraham. 650 l, Three visitors. 800 l, Abraham and Sarah. 2000 l, Three visitors at Abraham's table.

1990, June 5 Photo. *Perf. 12x11½*
Granite Paper

853	A250	450 l multicolored	.75	.45
854	A250	650 l multicolored	1.25	.70
855	A250	800 l multicolored	1.50	.85
856	A250	2000 l multicolored	3.00	2.00
	Nos. 853-856 (4)		6.50	4.00

Souvenir Sheet

857		Sheet of 4	7.00	7.00
a.	A250	450 l like #853	.70	.60
b.	A250	650 l like #854	1.10	.90
c.	A250	800 l like #855	1.25	1.00
d.	A250	2000 l like #856	3.25	2.25

Nos. 853-856 have a single line border in gold. Nos. 857a-857d have no border line.

No. 857 with "Pro Terremotati 1997" overprinted in sheet margin exists in limited quantities, sold for 8000 l to assist earthquake victims in Umbria and Marche, but was not officially issued by Vatican postal authorities. Value $25.

A251

300 l, Ordination of St. Willibrord. 700 l, Stay in Antwerp. 3000 l, Leaving belongings, death.

1990, June 5   **Perf. 13½x14**
858	A251	300 l multicolored	.50	.30
859	A251	700 l multicolored	1.00	.70
860	A251	3000 l multicolored	4.00	3.25
		Nos. 858-860 (3)	5.50	4.25

1300th anniv. of ministry of St. Willibrord.

A252

Diocese of Beijing-Nanking, 300th Anniv.: 500 l, Lake Beijing. 750 l, Church of the Immaculate Conception, Beijing, 1650. 1500 l, Lake Beijing, diff. 2000 l, Church of the Redeemer, Beijing, 1703.

1990, Oct. 2
861	A252	500 l multicolored	.70	.45
862	A252	750 l multicolored	1.10	.70
863	A252	1500 l multicolored	2.25	1.40
864	A252	2000 l multicolored	2.75	1.90
		Nos. 861-864 (4)	6.80	4.45

Christmas
A253

Details from painting by Sebastiano Mainardi.

1990, Nov. 27   **Photo.**   **Perf. 13**
865	A253	50 l Choir of Angels	.25	.25
866	A253	200 l St. Joseph	.30	.30
867	A253	650 l Holy Child	1.10	1.10
868	A253	750 l Madonna	1.25	1.25
869	A253	2500 l Nativity scene, vert.	4.00	4.00
		Nos. 865-869 (5)	6.90	6.90

Paintings of the Sistine Chapel — A254

Different details from lunettes: 50 l, 100 l, Eleazar. 150 l, 250 l, Jacob. 350 l, 400 l, Josiah. 500 l, 650 l, Asa. 800 l, 1000 l, Zerubbabel. 2000 l, 3000 l, Azor.

1991, Apr. 9   **Photo.**   **Perf. 11½**
Granite Paper
870	A254	50 l multicolored	.25	.25
871	A254	100 l multicolored	.25	.25
a.		Booklet pane of 6	.75	
872	A254	150 l multicolored	.25	.25
a.		Booklet pane of 6	1.25	
873	A254	250 l multicolored	.30	.30
874	A254	350 l multicolored	.40	.40
875	A254	400 l multicolored	.50	.50
876	A254	500 l multicolored	.65	.65
877	A254	650 l multicolored	.85	.85
a.		Booklet pane of 6	5.50	
		Complete booklet, #871a, 872a, 877a	7.50	
878	A254	800 l multicolored	.90	.90
879	A254	1000 l multicolored	1.25	1.25
880	A254	2000 l multicolored	2.50	2.50
881	A254	3000 l multicolored	3.75	3.75
		Nos. 870-881 (12)	11.85	11.85

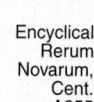

Encyclical Rerum Novarum, Cent. A255

Arms of Pope Leo XIII and: 600 l, Title page of Encyclical. 750 l, Allegory of Church's interest in workers, employers. 3500 l, Pope Leo XIII (1878-1903).

1991, May 23   **Engr.**   **Perf. 14x13½**
882	A255	600 l blue & dk grn	.90	.85
883	A255	750 l sage grn & rose car	1.10	1.00
884	A255	3500 l brt pur & dk bl	5.00	4.50
		Nos. 882-884 (3)	7.00	6.35

Vatican Observatory, Cent. — A256

Designs: 750 l, Astrograph for making photographic sky map, 1891. 1000 l, Zeiss Double Astrograph, Lake Castelgandolfo, 1935, horiz. 3000 l, New telescope, Vatican Observatory, Mt. Graham, Arizona, 1991.

Perf. 11½x12, 12x11½
1991, Oct. 1   **Photo.**
Granite Paper
885	A256	750 l multicolored	1.25	1.10
886	A256	1000 l multicolored	1.75	1.50
887	A256	3000 l multicolored	4.75	5.00
		Nos. 885-887 (3)	7.75	7.60

Canonization of St. Bridget, 600th Anniv. — A257

Designs: 1500 l, Receiving Madonna's revelations. 2000 l, Receiving Christ's revelations.

1991, Oct. 1   **Perf. 12½x13**
888	A257	1500 l multicolored	2.50	2.25
889	A257	2000 l multicolored	3.50	3.25

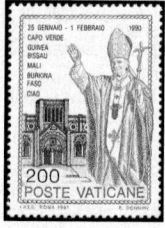

Journeys of Pope John Paul II, 1990 — A258

Pope John Paul II and: 200 l, Cathedral of Immaculate Conception, Ouagadougou, Burkina Faso. 550 l, St. Vitus' Cathedral, Prague. 750 l, Our Lady of Guadaloupe's Basilica, Mexico. 1500 l, Ta' Pinu Sanctuary, Gozo. 3500 l, Cathedral of Christ the King, Gitega, Burundi.

Litho. & Engr.
1991, Nov. 11   **Perf. 13½x14**
890	A258	200 l green & multi	.40	.40
891	A258	550 l org brn & multi	.90	.90
892	A258	750 l claret & multi	1.25	1.25
893	A258	1500 l dk brn & multi	2.50	2.50
894	A258	3500 l grn bl & multi	6.00	6.00
		Nos. 890-894 (5)	11.05	11.05

West Africa, Jan. 25-Feb. 1 (200 l); Czechoslovakia, Apr. 21-22 (550 l); Mexico, Curacao, May 6-14 (750 l); Malta, May 25-27 (1500 l); Tanzania, Burundi, Rwanda, Ivory Coast, Sept. 1-10 (3500 l).

A259

Special Assembly for Europe of Synod of Bishops: 300 l, Colonnade of St. Peter's Basilica. 500 l, St. Peter's Basilica and Square. 4000 l, Colonnade of St. Peter's Basilica, Apostolic Palace.

1991, Nov. 11   **Engr.**   **Perf. 12½x13**
895		300 l olive & blk	.50	.50
896		500 l olive & blk	.90	.90
897		4000 l olive & blk	6.00	6.00
a.	A259	Strip of 3, #895-897	8.00	8.00

No. 897a has continous design.

A260

Discovery and Evangelization of America, 500th Anniv.: 500 l, Christopher Columbus. 600 l, Saint Peter Claver. 850 l, La Virgen de los Reyes Catolicos. 1000 l, Bishop Bartolome de las Casas. 2000 l, Father Junipero Serra.

Charts: 1500 l, New World. 2500 l, Old World.

1992, Mar. 24   **Photo.**   **Perf. 11½x12**
Granite Paper
898	A260	500 l multicolored	.75	.75
899	A260	600 l multicolored	.90	.90
900	A260	850 l multicolored	1.25	1.25
901	A260	1000 l multicolored	1.50	1.50
902	A260	2000 l multicolored	3.00	3.00
		Nos. 898-902 (5)	7.40	7.40

Souvenir Sheet
Perf. 12
903	A260	Sheet of 2	8.00	8.00
a.		1500 l multicolored	2.25	2.25
b.		2500 l multicolored	3.75	3.75

Piero Della Francesca (d. 1492), Painter — A261

Frescoes: 300 l, 750 l (detail), Our Lady of Childbirth. 1000 l, 3000 l (detail), Resurrection.

1992, May 15   **Photo.**   **Perf. 13½x14**
904	A261	300 l multicolored	.40	.40
905	A261	750 l multicolored	1.10	1.10
906	A261	1000 l multicolored	1.40	1.40
907	A261	3000 l multicolored	4.25	4.25
		Nos. 904-907 (4)	7.15	7.15

St. Giuseppe Benedetto Cottolengo (1786-1842) A262

St. Giuseppe Benedetto Cottolengo: 650 l, Comforting the sick. 850 l, With Little House of Divine Providence.

1992, May 15   **Perf. 11½x12**
Granite Paper
908	A262	650 l multicolored	1.00	1.00
909	A262	850 l multicolored	1.40	1.40

A263

Plants of the New World: a, Frumentum indicum. b, Solanum pomiferum. c, Opuntia. d, Cacaos, cacavifera. e, Solanum tuberosum, capsicum, mordens. f, Ananas sagitae folio.

1992, Sept. 15   **Photo.**   **Perf. 11½x12**
Granite Paper
910		Block of 6	8.25	8.25
a.-f.	A263	850 l any single	1.10	1.10

A264

1992, Oct. 12   **Perf. 12½x13**
911	A264	700 l multicolored	1.25	1.10

4th General Conference of the Latin American Episcopacy.

Christmas
A265

Mosaics from Basilica of St. Maria Maggiore, Rome: 600 l, The Annunciation. 700 l, Nativity. 1000 l, Adoration of the Magi. 1500 l, Presentation to the Temple.

1992, Nov. 24   **Photo.**   **Perf. 11½**
Granite Paper
912	A265	600 l multicolored	1.10	.95
913	A265	700 l multicolored	1.25	1.10
914	A265	1000 l multicolored	1.50	1.40
915	A265	1500 l multicolored	3.00	2.75
		Nos. 912-915 (4)	6.85	6.20

St. Francis Healing Man from Ilerda, by Giotto di Bondone (1266-1337) — A266

1993, Jan. 9   **Litho.**   **Perf. 13½x14**
916	A266	1000 l multi + label	2.10	1.75

Prayer Meeting for Peace in Europe, Assisi.

Architecture of Vatican City and Rome — A267

Buildings: 200 l, St. Peter's Basilica, Vatican City. 300 l, St. John Lateran Basilica, Rome. 350 l, St. Mary Major's Basilica, Rome. 500 l, St. Paul's Basilica, Rome. 600 l, Apostolic Palace, Vatican. 700 l, Lateran Apostolic Palace, Rome. 850 l, Papal Palace, Castel Gandolfo.

1000 l, Chancery Palace, Rome. 2000 l, Palace of the Propagation of the Faith, Rome. 3000 l, St. Calixtus Palace, Rome.

1993, Mar. 23 Photo. *Perf. 12x11½*
Granite Paper

917	A267	200 l multicolored	.25	.25
a.		Booklet pane of 4	1.10	
918	A267	300 l multicolored	.40	.40
a.		Booklet pane of 4	1.60	
919	A267	350 l multicolored	.50	.50
a.		Booklet pane of 4	2.00	
920	A267	500 l multicolored	.65	.65
a.		Booklet pane of 4	2.75	
		Complete booklet, #917a, 918a, 919a, 920a	7.50	
921	A267	600 l multicolored	.80	.80
922	A267	700 l multicolored	.95	.95
923	A267	850 l multicolored	1.00	1.00
924	A267	1250 l multicolored	1.25	1.25
925	A267	2000 l multicolored	2.60	2.60
926	A267	3000 l multicolored	3.75	3.75
		Nos. 917-926 (10)	12.15	12.15

A268

Congress emblem, Vatican arms and: 500 l, Cross, grape vines. 700 l, Cross, hands breaking bread. 1500 l, Hands lifting chalice. 2500 l, Wheat, banner.

1993, May 22 Litho. *Perf. 14x13½*

927	A268	500 l multicolored	.60	.60
928	A268	700 l multicolored	.90	.90
929	A268	1500 l multicolored	1.90	1.90
930	A268	2500 l multicolored	3.00	3.00
		Nos. 927-930 (4)	6.40	6.40

45th Intl. Eucharistic Congress, Seville.

A269

Traditio Legis Sarcophagus, St. Peter's Basilica: a, 200 l, Sacrifice of Isaac. b, 750 l, Apostle Peter receiving law from Jesus, Apostle Paul. c, 3000 l, Christ watching servant pouring water on Pilate's hands.

1993, May 22 Engr. *Perf. 13½x14*

931	A269	Triptych, #a.-c.	5.25	5.25

Ascension Day, May 20.

Contemporary Art — A270

Europa: 750 l, Crucifixion, by Felice Casorati (1886-1963). 850 l, Rouen Cathedral, by Maurice Utrillo (1883-1955).

1993, Sept. 29 Photo. *Perf. 13*

932	A270	750 l multicolored	.95	.95
933	A270	850 l multicolored	1.00	1.00

Death of St. John of Nepomuk, 600th Anniv. — A271

2000 l, Buildings in Prague, Charles Bridge.

1993, Sept. 29 Litho. *Perf. 13½x14*

934	A271	1000 l multicolored	1.40	1.25
935	A271	2000 l multicolored	2.75	2.50

Travels of Pope John Paul II — A272

Visits to: 600 l, Senegal, Gambia, Guinea. 1000 l, Angola, St. Thomas and Prince. 5000 l, Dominican Republic.

1993, Nov. 23 Photo. *Perf. 12x11½*
Granite Paper

936	A272	600 l multicolored	.75	.75
937	A272	1000 l multicolored	1.50	1.50
938	A272	5000 l multicolored	7.00	7.00
		Nos. 936-938 (3)	9.25	9.25

Hans Holbein the Younger (1497?-1543), Painter — A273

Details or entire paintings: 700 l, 1000 l, Madonna of Solothurn. 1500 l, Self-portrait.

Litho. & Engr.
1993, Nov. 23 *Perf. 13½x14*

939	A273	700 l multicolored	.90	.90
940	A273	1000 l multicolored	1.50	1.50
941	A273	1500 l multicolored	2.25	2.25
		Nos. 939-941 (3)	4.65	4.65

Synod of Bishops, Special Assembly for Africa A274

Designs: 850 l, Stylized crosier, dome with cross, vert. 1000 l, Crucifix, dome of St. Peter's Basilica, crosiers, African landscape.

Perf. 12½x13, 13x12½
1994, Apr. 8 Photo.

942	A274	850 l multicolored	1.25	1.25
943	A274	1000 l multicolored	1.50	1.50

The Restored Sistine Chapel — A275

Frescoes, by Michelangelo: Creation of the Sun and Moon: No. 944, Sun. No. 945, God pointing toward moon. Creation of Man: No. 946, Adam. No. 947, God. Original Sin: No. 948, Adam, Eve taking apple from serpent. No. 949, Adam, Eve forced from Garden of Eden. The Flood: No. 950, People on dry ground. No. 951, People on stone outcropping.
4000 l, Detail of Last Judgment, Christ and the Virgin.

1994, Apr. 8 Photo. *Perf. 11½*

944		350 l multicolored	.40	.40
945		350 l multicolored	.40	.40
a.		A275 Pair, #944-945	1.00	1.00
946		500 l multicolored	.60	.60
947		500 l multicolored	.60	.60
a.		A275 Pair, #946-947	1.50	1.50
948		1000 l multicolored	1.50	1.50
949		1000 l multicolored	1.50	1.50
a.		A275 Pair, #948-949	2.50	2.50
950		2000 l multicolored	4.00	4.00
951		2000 l multicolored	3.00	3.00
a.		A275 Pair, 950-951	8.00	8.00
		Nos. 944-951 (8)	12.00	12.00

Souvenir Sheet
Perf. 12

952	A275	4000 l multicolored	6.25	6.25

No. 952 contains one 36x54mm stamp.

European Inventions, Discoveries — A276

Europa: 750 l, Progess from wheel to atom traced by white thread. 850 l, Galileo in center of solar system, scientific instruments.

1994, May 31 Litho. *Perf. 13x13½*

953	A276	750 l multicolored	.95	.95
954	A276	850 l multicolored	1.10	1.10

Intl. Year of the Family — A277

Stained glass: 400 l, God creating man and woman. 750 l, Family under names of four Evangelists. 1000 l, Parents teaching son. 2000 l, Young man comforting elderly couple.

1994, May 31 Photo. *Perf. 13x14*

955	A277	400 l multicolored	.50	.50
956	A277	750 l multicolored	.95	.95
957	A277	1000 l multicolored	1.40	1.40
958	A277	2000 l multicolored	2.50	2.50
		Nos. 955-958 (4)	5.35	5.35

Giovanni da Montecorvino (1247-1328), Missionary — A278

1994, Sept. 27 Litho. *Perf. 14*

959	A278	1000 l multicolored	1.75	1.75

Evangelization of China, 700th anniv.

13th Intl. Convention of Christian Archaeology, Split, Croatia — A279

Mosaics from Euphrasian Basilica, Parentium, Croatia, 6th Cent.: 700 l, Bishop Euphrasius, Archdeacon Claudius, Claudius' son. 1500 l, Madonna and Child, two angels. 3000 l, Christ, Apostles Peter & Paul.

1994, Sept. 27 *Perf. 13x14*

960	A279	700 l multicolored	1.00	1.00
961	A279	1500 l multicolored	2.00	2.00
962	A279	3000 l multicolored	4.25	4.25
		Nos. 960-962 (3)	7.25	7.25

Travels of Pope John Paul II — A280

Designs: 600 l, Benin, Uganda, Sudan. 700 l, Albania. 1000 l, Spain. 2000 l, Jamaica, Mexico, US. 3000 l, Lithuania, Latvia, Estonia.

1994, Nov. 18 Engr. *Perf. 13*

963	A280	600 l multicolored	.85	.85
964	A280	700 l multicolored	1.00	1.00
965	A280	1000 l multicolored	1.40	1.40
966	A280	2000 l multicolored	2.75	2.75
967	A280	3000 l multicolored	4.25	4.25
		Nos. 963-967 (5)	10.25	10.25

Christmas A281

The Nativity, by Il Tintoretto: 700 l, The Holy Family. No. 969, The Holy Family, two women. No. 970, Adoration of the shepherds.

1994, Nov. 18 Photo. *Perf. 11½*
Granite Paper

968	A281	700 l multicolored	1.00	1.00

Size: 45x27mm

969	A281	1000 l multicolored	1.40	1.40
970	A281	1000 l multicolored	1.40	1.40
a.		Pair, #969-970	3.00	3.00
		Nos. 968-970 (3)	3.80	3.80

Peace and Freedom A282

1995, Mar. 25 Photo. *Perf. 14x13*

971	A282	750 l shown	.90	.90
972	A282	850 l Hands clasp, dove	1.00	1.00

Europa.

Shrine of Loreto, 700th Anniv. — A283

Details of artworks from vaults of Sacristy: 600 l, St. Mark's, Angel with chalice, by Melozzo da Forli. 700 l, St. Mark's, Angel with lamb, by da Forli. 1500 l, 2500 l, St. John's, Music making angels, by Luca Signorelli.
No. 977, Marble carving showing Holy House of Loreto.

1995, Mar. 25 *Perf. 11½*

973	A283	600 l multicolored	.75	.75
974	A283	700 l multicolored	.85	.85
975	A283	1500 l multicolored	2.00	2.00
976	A283	2500 l multicolored	4.00	4.00
		Nos. 973-976 (4)	7.60	7.60

Souvenir Sheet

977	A283	3000 l multicolored	3.75	3.75

No. 977 contains one 36x36mm stamp.

Radio, Cent. A284

Designs: 850 l, Guglielmo Marconi, transmitting equipment. 1000 l, Archangel Gabriel, Pope John Paul II, Marconi broadcasting station, Vatican City.

1995, June 8   **Photo.**   *Perf. 14*
978	A284	850 l multicolored	1.25	1.25
979	A284	1000 l multicolored	1.75	1.75

See Germany No. 1990, Ireland Nos. 973-974, Italy Nos. 2038-2039, San Marino Nos. 1336-1337.

A285

European Nature Conservation Year (Scenes in Vatican Gardens & Castel Gandolfo: 200 l, Fountain of the Triton, arches of rhyncospernum jasminoides. 300 l, Avenue of roses, Palazzo Barberini. 400 l, Statue of Apollo Citaredo. 550 l, Ruins of Domitian's Villa, Avenue of roses. 750 l, Acer negundo, Viale dell'Osservatorio. 1500 l, Belvedere garden. 2000 l, Fountain of the Eagle, Quercus ilex. 3000 l, Avenue of cypresses, equestrian statue.

1995, June 8   *Perf. 12*
Granite Paper
980	A285	200 l multicolored	.25	.25
981	A285	300 l multicolored	.35	.35
a.		Booklet pane of 3	1.00	
982	A285	400 l multicolored	.50	.50
a.		Booklet pane of 3	1.50	
983	A285	550 l multicolored	.70	.70
a.		Booklet pane of 3	2.25	
984	A285	750 l multicolored	.90	.90
a.		Booklet pane of 3	2.75	
		Complete booklet, #981a, 982a, 983a, 984a	7.50	
985	A285	1500 l multicolored	1.90	1.90
986	A285	2000 l multicolored	2.50	2.50
987	A285	3000 l multicolored	3.75	3.75
		Nos. 980-987 (8)	10.85	10.85

A286

Paintings of peace, by Paolo Guiotto: 550 l, Small hearts flying from large heart. 750 l, Stylized faces. 850 l, Doves in flight. 1250 l, Lymph reaching to smallest branches. 2000 l, Explosion of colors, people.

1995, Oct. 3   **Photo.**   *Perf. 13½x13*
988	A286	550 l multicolored	.65	.65
989	A286	750 l multicolored	.85	.85
990	A286	850 l multicolored	1.00	1.00
991	A286	1250 l multicolored	1.40	1.40
992	A286	2000 l multicolored	2.25	2.25
		Nos. 988-992 (5)	6.15	6.15

UN, 50th anniv.

A287

St. Anthony of Padua (1195-1231): 750 l, St. John of God (1495-1550). 3000 l, St. Philip Neri (1515-95).

Litho. & Engr.
1995, Oct. 3   *Perf. 13½x14*
993	A287	500 l green & brown	.65	.65
994	A287	750 l violet & green	.95	.95
995	A287	3000 l magenta & black	3.75	3.75
		Nos. 993-995 (3)	5.35	5.35

A288

Scenes depicting life of Jesus Christ from illuminated manuscripts: 400 l, The Annunciation. 850 l, Nativity. 1250 l, Flight into Egypt. 2000 l, Jesus among the teachers.

1995, Nov. 20   **Photo.**   *Perf. 12x11½*
Granite Paper
996	A288	400 l multicolored	.50	.50
997	A288	850 l multicolored	1.10	1.10
998	A288	1250 l multicolored	1.60	1.60
999	A288	2000 l multicolored	2.50	2.50
		Nos. 996-999 (4)	5.70	5.70

Towards the Holy Year 2000.

Travels of Pope John Paul II A289

Designs: 1000 l, Giving greeting in Croatia, statue of Blessed Lady, Zagreb Cathedral. 2000 l, In Italy, lighthouse in Genoa, Orvieto Cathedral, Valley of Temples in Agrigento.

1995, Nov. 20   **Litho.**   *Perf. 14½x14*
1000	A289	1000 l multicolored	1.50	1.50
1001	A289	2000 l multicolored	3.00	3.00

Religious Anniversaries A290

Designs: 1250 l, Angel holding crosses, Union of Brest-Litovsk, 400th anniv. 2000 l, Cross with branches, Latin episcopal mitre, Byzantine mitre, Union of Uzhorod, 350th anniv.

1996, Mar. 16   **Photo.**   *Perf. 13½x14*
1002	A290	1250 l multicolored	1.60	1.60
1003	A290	2000 l multicolored	2.50	2.50

A291

Marco Polo's Return from China, 700th Anniv. — A292

Designs from miniatures, Bodleian Library, Oxford: 350 l, Marco Polo delivering Pope Gregory X's letter to Great Khan. 850 l, Great Khan dispensing alms to poor in Cambaluc. 1250 l, Marco Polo receiving golden book from Great Khan. 2500 l, Marco Polo in Persia listening to story of three Kings who go to Bethlehem to adore Jesus.
   2000 l, Stylized portrait of Marco Polo drawn from first printed edition of "Il Milione."

1996, Mar. 15   *Perf. 11½*
Granite Paper
1004	A291	350 l multicolored	.45	.45
1005	A291	850 l multicolored	1.10	1.10
1006	A291	1250 l multicolored	1.60	1.60
1007	A291	2500 l multicolored	3.25	3.25
		Nos. 1004-1007 (4)	6.40	6.40

Souvenir Sheet
Perf. 12x11½
1008	A292	2000 l black	2.50	2.50

A293

Famous Women: 750 l, Gianna Baretta Molla (1922-62), physician. 850 l, Sister Edith Stein (1891-1942).

1996, May 7   **Engr.**   *Perf. 13x14*
1009	A293	750 l blue	1.25	1.25
1010	A293	850 l brown	1.50	1.50

A294

Modern Olympic Games, Cent.: a, Statue of athlete. b, Athlete's torso. c, Hand. d, Statue of athlete reaching upward. e, Hercules.

1996, May 7   **Photo.**   *Perf. 13*
1011		Strip of 5	10.00	10.00
a.-e.	A294	1250 l any single	1.40	1.40

Ordination of Pope John Paul II, 50th Anniv. A295

Designs: 500 l, Wawel Cathedral, Krakow. 750 l, Pope John Paul II giving blessing. 1250 l, Basilica of St. John Lateran, Rome.

1996, Oct. 12   **Litho.**   *Perf. 14*
1012	A295	500 l multicolored	.65	.65
1013	A295	750 l multicolored	1.00	1.00
1014	A295	1250 l multicolored	2.00	2.00
		Nos. 1012-1014 (3)	3.65	3.65

Life of Jesus Christ from Illuminated Manuscripts A296

Designs: 550 l, Baptism of Jesus at River Jordan. 850 l, Temptation in the desert. 1500 l, Cure of the leper. 2500 l, Jesus the teacher.

1996, Oct. 12   **Photo.**   *Perf. 12x11½*
1015	A296	550 l multicolored	.75	.75
1016	A296	850 l multicolored	1.50	1.25
1017	A296	1500 l multicolored	3.00	2.50
1018	A296	2500 l multicolored	5.00	3.50
		Nos. 1015-1018 (4)	10.25	8.00

Christmas — A297

Nativity, by Murillo (1618-82).

1996, Nov. 20   **Litho.**   *Perf. 13½*
1019	A297	750 l multicolored	2.00	1.50

St. Celestine V (1215-96) A298

No. 1021, St. Alfonso Maria De'Liguori (1696-1787).

1996, Nov. 20   *Perf. 13½x14*
1020	A298	1250 l multicolored	1.60	1.60
1021	A298	1250 l multicolored	1.60	1.60

Travels of Pope John Paul II, 1995 A299

Designs: 250 l, Jan. 11-21, Philippines, Papua New Guinea, Australia, Sri Lanka. 500 l, May 20-22, Czech Republic, Poland. 750 l, June 3-4, Belgium. 1000 l, June 30-July 3, Slovakia. 2000 l, Sept. 14-20, Cameroun, South Africa, Kenya. 5000 l, Oct. 4-9, UN headquarters, NY, US.

1996, Nov. 20   *Perf. 14x13½*
1022	A299	250 l blue & multi	.35	.35
1023	A299	500 l blue green & multi	.65	.65
1024	A299	750 l green & multi	1.00	1.00
1025	A299	1000 l brown & multi	1.25	1.25
1026	A299	2000 l gray & multi	2.50	2.50
1027	A299	5000 l pink & multi	6.75	6.75
		Nos. 1022-1027 (6)	12.50	12.50

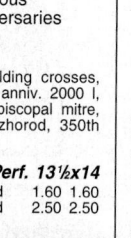

Papal Carriages and Automobiles A300

Designs: 50 l, Touring carriage. 100 l, Graham Paige. 300 l, Festive traveling carriage. 500 l, Citroen Lictoria VI. 750 l, Grand touring

carriage. 850 l, Mercedes Benz. 1000 l, Festive half carriage. 1250 l, Mercedes Benz 300SEL. 2000 l, Touring carriage, diff. 4000 l, Fiat "Pope mobile."

1997, Mar. 20   **Photo.**   **Perf. 12**
Granite Paper

1028	A300	50 l	multicolored	.25	.25
1029	A300	100 l	multicolored	.25	.25
a.		Booklet pane of 4		.75	
1030	A300	300 l	multicolored	.35	.35
a.		Booklet pane of 4		1.40	
1031	A300	500 l	multicolored	.60	.60
a.		Booklet pane of 4		2.50	
1032	A300	750 l	multicolored	.90	.90
a.		Booklet pane of 4		3.75	
		Complete booklet, #1029a, 1030a, 1031a, 1032a		8.50	
1033	A300	850 l	multicolored	1.00	1.00
1034	A300	1000 l	multicolored	1.25	1.25
1035	A300	1250 l	multicolored	1.75	1.75
1036	A300	2000 l	multicolored	2.50	2.50
1037	A300	4000 l	multicolored	5.00	5.00
		Nos. 1028-1037 (10)		*13.85*	*13.85*

A301

Swiss Guard: 750 l, Guard in traditional attire. 850 l, Guard in armor with sword in front of iron gate.

1997, Mar. 20   **Litho.**   **Perf. 13½**

1038	A301	750 l	multicolored	.90	.90
1039	A301	850 l	multicolored	1.00	1.00
a.		Strip of 2 + 2 labels		1.90	1.90

Europa.

A302

1997, Apr. 23   **Engr.**   **Perf. 14**

1040	A302	850 l	deep violet	1.60	1.60

St. Adalbert (956-997). See Germany No. 1964, Poland No. 3337, Czech Republic No. 3012, Hungary No. 3569.

A303

"Looking at the Classics," Museum Exhibition — A304

Pictures from texts of Latin and Greek classics: 500 l, Aristotle observing and describing various species from man to insect, from his "De Historia Animalium." 750 l, Bacchus riding dragon, from "Metamorphoses" by Ovid. 1250 l, General haranguing his soldiers, from "Iliad" by Homer. 2000 l, Hannibal leaving Canne, two horsemen, foot soldier, from "Ab Urbe Condita" by Titus Livius.

Masks from "Comedies," by Terence: No. 1045: a, Man, woman. b, Two women. c, Two men.

1997, Apr. 23   **Photo.**   **Perf. 14**

1041	A303	500 l	multicolored	.60	.60
1042	A303	750 l	multicolored	.90	.90
1043	A303	1250 l	multicolored	1.50	1.50
1044	A303	2000 l	multicolored	2.40	2.40
		Nos. 1041-1044 (4)		*5.40*	*5.40*

Perf. 13½

1045	A304	1000 l	Sheet of 3, #a.-c.	4.00	4.00

A305

46th Intl. Eucharistic Congress, Wroclaw, Poland: 650 l, Elements of the Eucharist, chalice, consecrated Host, arms of Wroclaw. 1000 l, The Last Supper, fish, Congress emblem. 1250 l, Wroclaw Cathedral, sheaf of wheat, holy spirit descending on church. 2500 l, "IHS" symbol of Christ on cross, doves, world with two hands on it.

1997, May 27   **Photo.**   **Perf. 13**

1046	A305	650 l	multicolored	.75	.70
1047	A305	1000 l	multicolored	1.25	1.10
1048	A305	1250 l	multicolored	1.50	1.40
1049	A305	2500 l	multicolored	3.25	2.75
		Nos. 1046-1049 (4)		*6.75*	*5.95*

A306

1997, Sept. 15   **Litho.**   **Perf. 13x14**

1050	A306	900 l	multicolored	.90	.70

Pope Paul VI (1897-1978).

No. 1050 was printed se-tenant with 4 labels. Value $2.00

St. Ambrose (d. 397) — A307

1997, Sept. 15   **Photo.**   **Perf. 13x14**

1051	A307	800 l	multicolored	1.50	1.25

Towards the Holy Year 2000 — A308

Illustrations of Christ's miracles: 400 l, Healing of paralyzed man. 800 l, Calming of the tempest. 1300 l, Multiplication of bread and fish. 3600 l, Peter's confession and conferment of primacy.

1997, Sept. 15   **Perf. 12**
Granite Paper

1052	A308	400 l	multicolored	.60	.50
1053	A308	800 l	multicolored	1.25	1.00
1054	A308	1300 l	multicolored	2.50	2.00
1055	A308	3600 l	multicolored	7.00	6.00
		Nos. 1052-1055 (4)		*11.35*	*9.50*

1996 Travels of Pope John Paul II — A309

Designs: 400 l, Central & South America, Feb. 5-12. 900 l, Tunisia, Apr. 14. 1000 l, Slovenia, May 17-19. 1300 l, Germany, June 21-23. 2000 l, Hungary, Sept. 6-7. 4000 l, France, Sept. 19-22.

1997, Nov. 11   **Litho.**   **Perf. 14x13½**

1056	A309	400 l	multicolored	.50	.50
1057	A309	900 l	multicolored	1.00	1.00
1058	A309	1000 l	multicolored	1.50	1.50
1059	A309	1300 l	multicolored	2.00	2.00
1060	A309	2000 l	multicolored	3.00	3.00
1061	A309	4000 l	multicolored	6.00	6.00
		Nos. 1056-1061 (6)		*14.00*	*14.00*

Christmas — A310

Detail from "The Nativity," by Benozzo Gozzoli (1420-97).

1997, Nov. 11   **Photo.**   **Perf. 14**

1062	A310	800 l	multicolored	1.60	1.40

Feasts of Sts. Peter and Paul, June 29th — A311

1998, Mar. 24   **Photo.**   **Perf. 13**

1063	A311	800 l	St. Peter	.90	.90
1064	A311	900 l	St. Paul	1.00	1.00

Europa.

The Popes of the Holy Years 1300-1525 — A312

Designs: 200 l, Boniface VIII, 1300. 400 l, Clement VI, 1350. 500 l, Boniface IX, 1390, 1400. 700 l, Martin V, 1423. 800 l, Nicholas V, 1450. 900 l, Sixtus IV, 1475. 1300 l, Alexander VI, 1500. 3000 l, Clement VII, 1525.

1998, Mar. 24   **Litho.**   **Perf. 14**

1065	A312	200 l	multicolored	.30	.30
1066	A312	400 l	multicolored	.50	.50
1067	A312	500 l	multicolored	.65	.65
1068	A312	700 l	multicolored	.85	.85
1069	A312	800 l	multicolored	1.00	1.00
1070	A312	900 l	multicolored	1.25	1.25
1071	A312	1300 l	multicolored	1.75	1.75
1072	A312	3000 l	multicolored	3.75	3.75
		Nos. 1065-1072 (8)		*10.05*	*10.05*

Nos. 1065-1072 were each printed se-tenant with a label picturing the respective papal arms.

See Nos. 1095-1102, 1141-1150.

Face on Shroud — A313

2500 l, Cathedral of Turin.

Litho. & Engr.
1998, May 19   **Perf. 13½x14**

1073	A313	900 l	multicolored	1.00	1.00
1074	A313	2500 l	multicolored	3.00	3.00

Exposition of the Shroud of Turin.

A314

Frescoes of Angels, by Melozzo da Forli (1438-94), Basilica of Sts. Apostles, Rome: Angels playing various musical instruments.

1998, May 19   **Photo.**   **Perf. 12**
Granite Paper

1075	A314	450 l	multicolored	.65	.65
1076	A314	650 l	multicolored	.80	.80
1077	A314	800 l	multicolored	1.00	1.00
1078	A314	1000 l	multicolored	1.25	1.25
1079	A314	1300 l	multicolored	2.00	2.00
1080	A314	2000 l	multicolored	2.75	2.75
		Nos. 1075-1080 (6)		*8.45*	*8.45*

Towards Holy Year 2000 A315

Episodes from the Life of Christ: 500 l, Triumphal entry into Jerusalem. 800 l, Washing of the feet. 1300 l, The Last Supper. 3000 l, Crucifixion.

1998, May 19   **Perf. 12**
Granite Paper

1081	A315	500 l	multicolored	.60	.60
1082	A315	800 l	multicolored	.90	.90
1083	A315	1300 l	multicolored	1.75	1.75
1084	A315	3000 l	multicolored	3.50	3.50
		Nos. 1081-1084 (4)		*6.75*	*6.75*

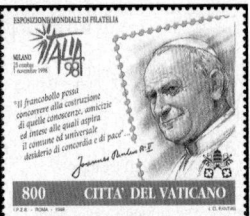

Italia '98 A316

1998, Oct. 23   **Photo.**   **Perf. 14**

1085	A316	800 l	Pope John Paul II	1.40	1.40
		Complete booklet, 5 #1085		7.50	

See Italy No. 2259 and San Marino No. 1430.

The Good
Shepherd — A317

1998, Oct. 25   *Perf. 12 Vert.*
Granite Paper
Booklet Stamp
1086 A317 900 l multicolored   1.30 1.30
   a.   Booklet pane of 5   6.50
      Complete booklet, #1086a   6.50
Italia '98.

Christian
Sculptures
A318

Designs: a, 600 l, Peter's denial. b, 900 l, Praying woman. c, 1000 l, Christ and the Cyrenean. 2000 l, Christ with the Cross and Two Apostles.

Granite Paper

1998, Oct. 25   *Perf. 12*
1087 A318 Sheet of 4, #a.-d.   6.50 6.50
Italia '98. Margin is embossed.

Christmas — A319

1998, Dec. 1   **Litho.**   *Perf. 14x13½*
1088 A319 800 l multicolored   1.10 1.00
See Croatia No. 381.

1997 Travels of
Pope John Paul
II — A320

Designs: 300 l, Sarajevo, 4/12-13/97. 600 l, Prague, 4/25-27/97. 800 l, Beirut, 5/10-11/97. 900 l, Poland, 5/21-6/10/97. 1300 l, Paris, 8/21-24/97. 5000 l, Rio de Janeiro, 10/2-6/97.

1998, Dec. 1   *Perf. 12½*
1089 A320 300 l brown   .40   .40
1090 A320 600 l green   .75   .75
1091 A320 800 l brown   1.25 1.25
1092 A320 900 l violet blue   1.50 1.50
1093 A320 1300 l org brn   1.75 1.75
1094 A320 5000 l org brn   6.50 6.50
   Nos. 1089-1094 (6)   12.15 12.15

**Popes of the Holy Years Type of
1998**

Popes: 300 l, Julius III, 1550. 600 l, Gregory XIII, 1575. 800 l, Clement VIII, 1600. 900 l, Urban VIII, 1625. 1000 l, Innocent X, 1650. 1300 l, Clement X, 1675. 1500 l, Innocent XII, 1700. 2000 l, Benedict XIII, 1725.

1999, Mar. 23   **Litho.**   *Perf. 14*
1095 A312 300 l multicolored   .55   .55
1096 A312 600 l multicolored   1.00 1.00
1097 A312 800 l multicolored   1.75 1.75
1098 A312 900 l multicolored   2.00 2.00
1099 A312 1000 l multicolored   2.25 2.25
1100 A312 1300 l multicolored   2.50 2.50

1101 A312 1500 l multicolored   3.00 3.00
1102 A312 2000 l multicolored   4.00 4.00
   Nos. 1095-1102 (8)   17.05 17.05

Nos. 1095-1102 were each printed se-tenant with a label picturing the respective papal arms.

Flowers from
Vatican Gardens
and Papal Villa,
Castelgandolfo
A321

Europa: 800 l, John Paul II Rose. 900 l, Water lilies.

1999, Mar. 23   **Litho.**   *Perf. 12½x13*
1103 A321 800 l multicolored   1.00 1.00
1104 A321 900 l multicolored   1.25 1.25
   a.   Pair, #1103-1104 + label   3.50 3.50

Padre Pio de Pietrelcina (1887-
1968) — A322

#1106: a, 1st church, San Giovanni Rotondo. b, New church, San Giovanni Rotondo. c, Like #1105.

1999, Apr. 27   **Litho.**   *Perf. 14x13*
1105 A322 800 l multicolored   1.25 1.25
Souvenir Sheet
Perf. 13x13½
1106 A322 Sheet of 3   2.10 2.10
   a.   300 l multi, vert.   .35   .35
   b.   600 l multi, vert.   .70   .70
   c.   900 l multi   1.00 1.00

Nos. 1106a-1106b are 30x40mm, No. 1106c is 60x40mm.

A323

Holy Places in Palestine — A324

Nos. 1107-1111: 19th cent. watercolors, Pontifical Lateran University Library.
Map of Holy Land from "Geographia Blaviana," 17th cent — #1112: a, Mediterranean Sea, denomination, LL. b, Mediterranean Sea, denomination LR. c, Red Sea, Holy Land. d, Inscription identifying map.

1999, May 25   *Perf. 11½*
Granite Paper
1107 A323 200 l Bethlehem   .25   .25
1108 A323 500 l Nazareth   .55   .55
1109 A323 800 l Lake of
        Tiberias   .85   .85
1110 A323 900 l Jerusalem   1.25 1.25
1111 A323 1300 l Mount Tabor   1.60 1.60
   Nos. 1107-1111 (5)   4.50 4.50
Perf. 12x11¾
1112 A324 1000 l Sheet of 4,
        #a.-d.   11.00 11.00

Towards
Holy Year
2000
A325

Events from life of Christ: 400 l, Deposition from the Cross. 700 l, Resurrection. 1300 l, Pentecost. 3000 l, Last Judgement.

1999, May 25   *Perf. 12x11¾*
Granite Paper
1113 A325 400 l multicolored   .45   .45
1114 A325 700 l multicolored   .75   .75
1115 A325 1300 l multicolored   1.40 1.40
1116 A325 3000 l multicolored   3.25 3.25
   Nos. 1113-1116 (4)   5.85 5.85

Kosovo 1999 — A326

1999, May 25   *Perf. 12¼*
Granite Paper
1117 A326 3600 l black   4.75 4.75
Proceeds from sale of stamp benefits victims of the fighting in Kosovo.

1998 Travels of
Pope John Paul
II — A327

600 l, Cuba, June 21-26. 800 l, Nigeria, Mar. 21-23. 900 l, Austria, June 19-21. 1300 l, Croatia, Oct. 2-4. 2000 l, Italy, Oct. 20.

1999, Oct. 12   **Litho.**   *Perf. 14x13½*
1118 A327 600 l multicolored   1.00 1.00
1119 A327 800 l multicolored   1.10 1.10
1120 A327 900 l multicolored   1.25 1.25
1121 A327 1300 l multicolored   2.00 2.00
1122 A327 2000 l multicolored   3.00 3.00
   Nos. 1118-1122 (5)   8.35 8.35

Council of
Europe, 50th
Anniv. — A328

1999, Oct. 12   **Photo.**   *Perf. 11¾*
Granite Paper
1123 A328 1200 l multicolored   1.50 1.50

Christmas
A329

The Birth of Christ, by Giovanni di Pietro: 500 l, Joseph (detail). 800 l, Christ (detail). 900 l, Mary (detail). 1200 l, Entire painting.

1999, Nov. 24   **Litho.**
1124 A329 500 l multi   .75   .75
1125 A329 800 l multi   1.25 1.25
1126 A329 900 l multi   1.50 1.50
1127 A329 1200 l multi   1.75 1.75
   Nos. 1124-1127 (4)   5.25 5.25

Opening of
the Holy
Door for
Holy Year
2000
A330

Various panels of Holy Door. Stamps on No. 1136 lack white border.

1999, Nov. 24   Photo.   *Perf. 11¾x12*
Granite Paper
1128 A330 200 l multi   .30   .30
1129 A330 300 l multi   .35   .35
1130 A330 400 l multi   .45   .45
1131 A330 500 l multi   .60   .60
1132 A330 600 l multi   .70   .70
1133 A330 800 l multi   .90   .90
1134 A330 1000 l multi   1.50 1.50
1135 A330 1200 l multi   2.25 2.25
   Nos. 1128-1135 (8)   7.05 7.05
Souvenir Sheet
1136   Sheet of 8, #a.-h.   10.00 10.00
   a.   A330 200 l Like #1128   .30   .30
   b.   A330 300 l Like #1129   .40   .40
   c.   A330 400 l Like #1130   .50   .50
   d.   A330 500 l Like #1131   .60   .60
   e.   A330 600 l Like #1132   .70   .70
   f.   A330 800 l Like #1133   1.00 1.00
   g.   A330 1000 l Like #1134   1.25 1.25
   h.   A330 1200 l Like #1135   1.50 1.50

Holy Year
2000 — A331

Designs: 800 l, St. Peter's Basilica. 1000 l, Basilica of St. John Lateran. 1200 l, Basilica of St. Mary Major. 2000 l, Basilica of St. Paul.

2000, Feb. 4   **Photo.**   *Perf. 11¾*
Granite Paper
1137 A331 800 l multi   1.00   .80
1138 A331 1000 l multi   1.40 1.25
1139 A331 1200 l multi   1.75 1.40
1140 A331 2000 l multi   2.50 2.25
   Nos. 1137-1140 (4)   6.65 5.70

Popes of the Holy Year Type of 1998

Designs: 300 l, Benedict XIV, 1750. 400 l, Pius VI, 1775. 500 l, Leo XII, 1825. 600 l, Pius IX, 1875. 700 l, Leo XIII, 1900. 800 l, Pius XI, 1925. 1200 l, Pius XII, 1950. 1500 l, Paul VI, 1975. No. 1149, John Paul II with miter, 2000. No. 1150, John Paul II with hand on chin, 2000.

2000, Feb. 4   **Litho.**   *Perf. 13¾*
1141 A312 300 l multi + label   .50   .50
1142 A312 400 l multi + label   .75   .75
1143 A312 500 l multi + label   1.00 1.00
1144 A312 600 l multi + label   1.25 1.25
1145 A312 700 l multi + label   1.50 1.50
1146 A312 800 l multi + label   1.75 1.75
1147 A312 1200 l multi + label   2.25 2.25
1148 A312 1500 l multi + label   2.50 2.50
1149 A312 2000 l multi + label   5.50 5.50
   Nos. 1141-1149 (9)   17.00 17.00
Souvenir Sheet
1150 A312 2000 l multi   2.00 2.00
No. 1150 contains one label.

Christianity
in Iceland,
1000th
Anniv.
A332

2000, Feb. 4   *Perf. 13¼x13¾*
1151 A332 1500 l multi   2.10 2.10
See Iceland Nos. 900-901.

Europa, 2000
Common Design Type

2000, May 9 **Litho.** **Perf. 13¼x13**
1152 CD17 1200 l multi 1.25 1.25

Printed in sheets of 10, with left and right side selvage of Priority Mail etiquettes.

Pope John Paul II, 80th Birthday — A333

800 l, Pope. 1200 l, Black Madonna of Jasna Gora. 2000 l, Pope's silver cross.

2000, May 9 **Engr.** **Perf. 13x12¾**
1153 A333 800 l purple 1.00 1.00
1154 A333 1200 l dark blue 1.75 1.50
1155 A333 2000 l green 3.00 2.50
   Nos. 1153-1155 (3) 5.75 5.00

See Poland Nos. 3520-3522.

Restored Sistine Chapel Frescoes — A334

Designs: 500 l, The Calling of St. Peter and St. Andrew, by Domenico Ghirlandaio. 1000 l, The Trials of Moses, by Sandro Botticelli. 1500 l, The Donation of the Keys, by Pietro Perugino. 3000 l, The Worship of the Golden Calf, by Cosimo Rosselli.

Perf. 11½x11¾
2000, May 9 **Photo.** **Blue Frame**
Granite Paper
1156 A334 500 l multi 1.00 .75
1157 A334 1000 l multi 1.50 1.25
1158 A334 1500 l multi 2.25 2.00
1159 A334 3000 l multi 5.00 3.50
   Nos. 1156-1159 (4) 9.75 7.50

See Nos. 1172-1175, 1215-1218.

20th World Youth Day — A335

Various photos of Pope John Paul II and youth.

Perf. 13¾x13¼
2000, June 19 **Litho.**
Color of Cross
1160 A335 800 l red 1.00 1.00
1161 A335 1000 l green 1.25 1.10
1162 A335 1200 l violet 1.50 1.25
1163 A335 1500 l green 2.25 1.75
Booklet Stamp
Self-Adhesive
Serpentine Die Cut 12
1164 A335 1000 l green 1.25 1.25
   a. Booklet of 4 + 4 labels 6.00
   Nos. 1160-1164 (5) 7.25 6.35

47th Intl. Eucharistic Congress A336

2000, June 19 **Perf. 13x12½**
1165 A336 1200 l multi 1.50 1.50

Beatification of Pope John XXIII — A337

2000, Sept. 1 **Photo.** **Perf. 13¼x14**
1166 A337 1200 l multi 1.60 1.60

1999 Travels of Pope John Paul II — A338

#1167: a, Mexico, 1/22-28. b, Romania, 5/7-9. c, Poland, 6/17. d, Slovenia, 9/19. e, India and Georgia, 11/5-9.

2000, Sept. 1 **Perf. 11¾**
Granite Paper
1167   Horiz. strip of 5 7.00 7.00
   a.-e. A338 1000 l Any single 1.00 1.00

Christmas A339

Frescoes in Basilica of St. Francis, Assisi, by Giotto: 800 l, Nativity. 1200 l, Infant Jesus. 1500 l, Mary. 2000 l, Joseph.

2000, Nov. 7 **Photo.** **Perf. 11¾x11½**
Granite Paper
1168-1171 A339 Set of 4 9.00 7.00

Sistine Chapel Restoration Type of 2000

Paintings: 800 l, The Baptism of Christ, by Pietro Perugino. 1200 l, The Passage of the Red Sea, by Biagio d'Antonio. 1500 l, The Punishment of Korah and the Stoning of Moses and Aaron, by Sandro Botticelli. 4000 l, The Sermon on the Mount, by Cosimo Rosselli.

Perf. 11½x11¾
2001, Feb. 15 **Photo.**
Granite Paper
Red Frame
1172-1175 A334 Set of 4 9.75 8.00

Christian Conversion of Armenia, 1700th Anniv. — A340

Scenes from illuminated code of 1569: 1200 l, St. Gregory prepares to give King Tiridates human features. 1500 l, St. Gregory makes Agatangel write history of Armenians. 2000 l, St. Gregory and King Tiridates meet Emperor Constantine and Pope Sylvester I.

2001, Feb. 15 **Perf. 11¾**
Granite Paper
1176-1178 A340 Set of 3 6.00 6.00

Year of Dialogue Among Civilizations A341

2001, May 22 **Litho.** **Perf. 14¼x14**
1179 A341 1500 l multi 1.75 1.75

Europa — A342

Designs: 800 l, Hands holding water above earth. 1200 l, Hand catching water.

2001, May 22 **Perf. 13½x13¼**
1180-1181 A342 Set of 2 1.75 1.75

Giuseppe Verdi (1813-1901), Composer A343

Verdi and: 800 l, Score from Nabucco. 1500 l, Costumes from Aida. 2000 l, Scenery from Othello.

2001, May 22 **Perf. 13¼x14¼**
1182-1184 A343 Set of 3 5.50 5.50

2000 Travels of Pope John Paul II — A344

Designs: 500 l, Mount Sinai, Feb. 26. 800 l, Mount Nebo, Mar. 20. 1200 l, The Last Supper, Mar. 23. 1500 l, Holy Sepulchre, Mar. 26. 5000 l, Fatima, May 12. 3000 l, Western Wall.

2001, Sept. 25 **Litho.** **Perf. 13¼**
1185-1189 A344 Set of 5 12.00 12.00
Souvenir Sheet
Perf. 13¼x14
1190 A344 3000 l multi 4.00 4.00

No. 1190 contains one 35x26mm stamp.

Remission of Debts of Poor Countries A345

Various panels by Carlo di Camerino: 200 l, 400 l, 800 l, 1000 l, 1500 l.

2001, Sept. 25 **Photo.** **Perf. 13**
1191-1195 A345 Set of 5 5.25 5.25

Giuseppe Toniolo Institute for Higher Studies, 80th Anniv. — A346

Litho. & Embossed
2001, Nov. 22 **Perf. 12¾**
1196 A346 1200 l red & blue 1.75 1.75

Etruscan Museum Gold Objects — A347

Designs: 800 l, Parade fibula. 1200 l, Earrings. 1500 l, Vulci fibula. 2000 l, Head of Medusa.

2001, Nov. 22 **Photo.** **Perf. 13½**
1197-1200 A347 Set of 4 8.00 8.00

Christmas A348

Artwork by Egino G. Weinert: 800 l, The Annunciation. 1200 l, The Nativity. 1500 l, Adoration of the Magi.

2001, Nov. 22 **Litho.** **Perf. 13x13¼**
1201-1203 A348 Set of 3 4.75 3.75
1202a   Booklet pane of 4 + 4 eti-
         quettes 7.00
         Booklet, #1202a 7.00

100 Cents = 1 Euro (€)

Depictions of Virgin Mary in Vatican Basilica — A349

Designs: 8c, Our Lady of Women in Labor. 15c, Our Lady with People Praying. 23c, Our Lady at the Tomb of Pius XII. 31c, Our Lady of the Fever. 41c, Our Lady of the Slap. 52c, Mary Immaculate. 62c, Our Lady Help of Christians. 77c, Virgin of the Deesis. €1.03, L'Addolorata. €1.55, Presentation of Mary at the Temple.

2002, Mar. 12 **Litho.** **Perf. 13¼x13**
1204 A349 8c multi .30 .30
1205 A349 15c multi .40 .40
1206 A349 23c multi .60 .50
1207 A349 31c multi .65 .60
1208 A349 41c multi 1.00 .80
1209 A349 52c multi 1.25 1.10
1210 A349 62c multi 1.60 1.25
1211 A349 77c multi 2.00 1.75
1212 A349 €1.03 multi 2.75 2.50
1213 A349 €1.55 multi 4.50 4.00
   Nos. 1204-1213 (10) 15.05 13.20

Pontifical Ecclesiastical Academy, 300th Anniv. — A350

No. 1214: a, Pope Clement XI. b, Academy building (46x33mm). c, Pope John Paul II.

2002, Mar. 12   Engr.   Perf. 13¼x13
1214   A350   Horiz. strip of 3   6.00 6.00
a.-c.   77c Any single   1.80 1.80

Sistine Chapel Restoration Type of 2000

Designs: 26c, The Temptation of Christ, by Sandro Botticelli. 41c, The Last Supper, by Cosimo Rosselli. 77c, Moses' Journey in Egypt, by Pietro Perugino. €1.55, The Last Days of Moses, by Luca Signorelli.

Perf. 11½x11¾
2002, June 13   Photo.
Granite Paper
1215-1218   A334   Set of 4   7.75 7.75

Europa — A351

Christ and the Circus, by Aldo Carpi: 41c, Entire painting. 62c, Detail.

2002, June 13   Perf. 13¼
1219-1220   A351   Set of 2   2.40 2.40

Roman States Postage Stamps, 150th Anniv. — A352

Designs: 41c, Regina Viarum, Roman States #11. 52c, Cassian Way, Roman States #25. €1.03, Vatican walls, Vatican City #2. €1.55, St. Peter's Basilica.

2002, June 13   Perf. 13x13¼
1221-1223   A352   Set of 3   5.00 5.00

Souvenir Sheet
Perf.
1224   A352   €1.55 multi   4.00 4.00

No. 1224 contains one 31mm diameter stamp.

St. Leo IX (1002-54), Pope A353

Designs: 41c, Portrait. 62c, In procession, receiving papal miter. €1.29, Reading from scroll, as prisoner of Normans.

2002, Sept. 26   Litho.   Perf. 13x13¼
1225-1227   A353   Set of 3   6.00 6.00

Cimabue (1240-1302), Artist — A354

Designs: 26c, Crucifix. 62c, Jesus Christ. 77c, Virgin Mary. €1.03, St. John.

2002, Sept. 26   Photo.   Perf. 13¼x14
1228-1231   A354   Set of 4   7.00 7.00

Nativity, by Pseudo Ambrogio di Baldese — A355

2002, Nov. 21   Photo.   Perf. 13
1232   A355   41c multi   1.10 1.10

See New Zealand No. 1834.

2001 Travels of Pope John Paul II — A356

Designs: 41c, Greece, Syria and Malta, May 4-9. 62c, Ukraine, June 23-27. €1.55, Armenia and Kazakhstan, Sept. 22-27.

2002, Nov. 21   Litho.   Perf. 13x13¼
1233-1235   A356   Set of 3   6.50 6.50
1234a   Booklet pane, 4 #1234 + 4 etiquettes   6.50
    Booklet, #1234a   6.50

A357

Pontificate of John Paul II, 25th Anniv. — A358

No. 1236: a, Election as Pope, 1978. b, In Poland, 1979. c, In France, 1980. d, Assassination attempt, 1981. e, At Fatima, Portugal, 1982. f, Extraordinary Holy Year, 1983. g, At Quirinale Palace, Rome, 1984. h, World Youth Day, 1985. i, At synagogue, Rome, 1986. j, Pentecost vigil, 1987. k, At European Parliament, Strasbourg, France, 1988. l, Meeting with Mikhail Gorbachev, 1989. m, At Guinea-Bissau leper colony, 1990. n, At European Bishops' Synod, 1991. o, Publication of Catechism of the Catholic Church, 1992. p, Praying for the Balkans in Assisi, 1993. q, At Sistine Chapel, 1994. r, At UN Headquarters for 50th anniv. celebrations, 1995. s, In Germany, 1996. t, In Sarajevo, Bosnia & Herzegovina, 1997. u, In Cuba, 1998. v, Opening Holy Doors, 1999. w, World Youth Day, 2000. x, Closing Holy Doors, 2001. y, Addressing Italian Parliament, 2002.

2003, Mar. 20   Litho.   Perf. 13x13¼
1236   Sheet of 25   27.50 27.50
a.-y.   A357 41c Any single   1.00   .95

Etched on Silver Foil
Die Cut Perf. 12½x13
Self-Adhesive
1237   A358   €2.58 Pope John Paul II   9.00 9.00

Cancels can be easily removed from No. 1237.
See Poland Nos. 3668-3669.

Martyrdom of St. George, 1700th Anniv. A359

2003, May 6   Litho. & Engr.   Perf. 13
1238   A359   62c multi   1.90 1.90

Europa — A360

Poster art for: 41c, 1975 Holy Year. 62c, Exhibition of Slav codices, incunabula and rare books at Sistine Hall, 1985.

2003, May 6   Litho.   Perf. 13¼x13
1239-1240   A360   Set of 2   2.40 2.40

Masterpieces by Beato Angelico in Niccolina Chapel — A361

Designs: 41c, Diaconal Consecration of St. Lawrence. 62c, St. Stephen Preaching. 77c, Trial of St. Lawrence. €1.03, Stoning of St. Stephen.

2003, May 6   Photo.   Perf. 13¼
1241-1244   A361   Set of 4   7.00 7.00

Beatification of Mother Teresa of Calcutta — A362

Perf. 13½x13¼
2003, Sept. 23   Litho.
1245   A362   41c multi + label   1.25 1.25

Printed in sheets of 5 + 5 different labels. Value $7.00

19th Century Artists — A363

Designs: 41c, Blessed Are the Pure at Heart, by Paul Gauguin. 62c, The Pietà, by Vincent van Gogh.

Perf. 13¼x13½
2003, Sept. 23   Photo.
1246   A363   41c multi   1.10 1.00
1247   A363   62c multi   1.75 1.50
a.   Booklet pane of 4 + 4 etiquettes   7.00 —
    Complete booklet, #1247a   7.00

Animals in Vatican Basilica Art A364

Designs: 21c, Dragon. 31c, Camel. 77c, Horse. €1.03, Leopard.

2003, Sept. 23
1248-1251   A364   Set of 4   6.00 5.50

Canonization of Josemaría Escrivá de Balaguer, Oct. 6, 2003 — A365

2003, Nov. 18   Litho.   Perf. 14x13¼
1252   A365   41c multi   1.10 1.10

2002 Travels of Pope John Paul II — A366

Designs: 62c, Bulgaria and Azerbaijan, May 22-26. 77c, Canada, Guatemala and Mexico, July 23-Aug. 2. €2.07, Poland, Aug. 16-19.

2003, Nov. 18   Perf. 13x13¼
1253-1255   A366   Set of 3   9.00 9.00

Christmas A367

2003, Nov. 18
Stamp With White Border
1256   A367   41c multi   1.60 1.60

Souvenir Sheet
Stamp Without White Border
1257   A367   41c multi   1.75 1.75

Death of Pope Paul VI, 25th anniv. (#1257).

St. Pius V (1504-72) A368

Altarpiece by Grazio Cossoli in Chapel of the Rosary, Santa Croce di Bosco Marengo: 4c, Detail depicting St. Pius V and flag. €2, Entire altarpiece.

Litho. & Silk Screened
2004, Mar. 18   Perf. 13¼x13
1258-1259   A368   Set of 2   5.50 5.50

2003 Travels of Pope John Paul II — A369

Designs: 60c, Spain, May 3-4. 62c, Bosnia & Herzegovina, June 22. 80c, Croatia, June 5-9. €1.40, Slovakia, Sept. 11-14.

2004, Mar. 18   **Litho.**
1260-1263 A369   Set of 4   9.00 9.00

EMISSIONE CONGIUNTA

Papal Visits to Poland — A370

No. 1264, 45c: a, Pope with hand on chin. b, Pope praying. c, Pope carrying crucifix. d, Pope with crucifix against head.
No. 1265, 62c: a, Pope holding crucifix, diff. b, Pope with arm raised. c, Pope, wearing white, seated. d, Pope, wearing red cape, seated.

Litho. (Labels Litho. & Embossed)
2004, Mar. 18
Sheets of 4, #a-d, + 8 Labels
1264-1265 A370   Set of 2   13.00 13.00
See Poland Nos. 3724-3725.

Children AIDS Victims — A371

2004, June 3   **Photo.**   **Perf. 13¼x13**
1266 A371 45c multi + label   1.50 1.50
Printed in sheets of 6 + 6 stamp-sized labels (with different text) and 1 large central label.

Europa — A372

Paintings of: 45c, Men on horses. 62c, People in garden.

2004, June 3   **Litho.**   **Perf. 12¾x13¼**
1267-1268 A372   Set of 2   2.60 2.60

Flags and One-Euro Coins — A373

2004, June 3   **Litho.**   **Perf. 13½**
1269	A373	4c	Austria	.25 .25
1270	A373	8c	Belgium	.25 .25
1271	A373	15c	Finland	.35 .35
1272	A373	25c	France	.60 .60
1273	A373	30c	Germany	.70 .70
1274	A373	40c	Greece	.95 .95
1275	A373	45c	Vatican City	1.10 1.10
1276	A373	60c	Ireland	1.40 1.40
1277	A373	62c	Italy	1.50 1.50
1278	A373	70c	Luxembourg	1.75 1.75
1279	A373	80c	Monaco	1.90 1.90
1280	A373	€1	Netherlands	2.40 2.40
1281	A373	€1.40	Portugal	3.50 3.50
1282	A373	€2	San Marino	4.75 4.75
1283	A373	€2.80	Spain	6.75 6.75

Nos. 1269-1283 (15)   28.15 28.15

48th Intl. Eucharistic Congress A374

Designs: 45c, Hands breaking bread over chalice. 65c, Hand raising eucharist.

2004, Sept. 16   **Litho.**   **Perf. 13x13¼**
1284-1285 A374   Set of 2   3.00 3.00

Contemporary Religious Art in Vatican Museum Collection — A375

Designs: 45c, Still Life with Bottles, by Giorgio Morandi. 60c, The Fall of an Angel, by Marino Marini. 80c, Landscape with Houses, by Ezio Pastorio. 85c, Tuscan Countryside, by Giulio Cesare Vinzio.

2004, Sept. 16   **Photo.**   **Perf. 14x13¼**
1286	A375	45c multi	1.10 1.10
1287	A375	60c multi	1.50 1.50
a.		Perf. 13½x13¼	1.75 1.75
b.		Booklet pane of 4 #1287a + 4 etiquettes	7.00
		Complete booklet, #1287b	7.00
1288	A375	80c multi	2.25 2.25
1289	A375	85c multi	2.50 2.50

Nos. 1286-1289 (4)   7.35 7.35

Petrarch (1304-74), Poet A376

2004, Nov. 18   **Photo.**   **Perf. 13¼x13**
1290 A376 60c multi   1.60 1.60

Christmas A377

2004, Nov. 18   **Litho.**   **Perf. 13¼**
1291 A377 80c multi   2.25 2.25

Interregnum Issue

Arms of St. Peter and Papal Chamberlain's Insignia — A378

Inscription colors: 60c, Blue. 62c, Red. 80c, Green.

2005, Apr. 12   **Litho.**   **Perf. 13½x13**
1292-1294 A378   Set of 3   8.25 8.25

Pope Benedict XVI — A379

Pope Benedict XVI wearing: 45c, Stole. 62c, White vestments. 80c, Miter.

2005, June 2   **Litho.**   **Perf. 13¼x13**
1295-1297 A379   Set of 3   5.25 5.25
Coronation of Pope Benedict XVI, Apr. 19, 2005.

20th World Youth Day A380

2005, June 2
1298 A380 62c multi   1.50 1.50
See Germany No. 2343.

Europa A381

Ceramic plates depicting fish painted by Pablo Picasso with background colors of: 62c, Orange. 80c, Blue.

2005, June 2   **Perf. 12½**
1299-1300 A381   Set of 2   4.00 4.00

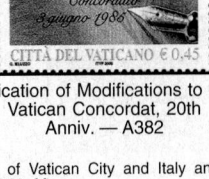

Ratification of Modifications to Italy-Vatican Concordat, 20th Anniv. — A382

Arms of Vatican City and Italy and: 45c, Pen. €2.80, Map.

2005, June 9   **Photo.**   **Perf. 13¼**
1301-1302 A382   Set of 2   8.00 8.00
See Italy Nos. 2677-2678.

Resurrection of Christ, by Perugino — A383

Various painting details: 60c, 62c, 80c, €1. €2.80, Jesus Christ.

2005, June 9   **Perf. 14x13¼**
1303-1306 A383   Set of 4   7.50 7.50
Souvenir Sheet
Perf. 13¼x13¾
1307 A383 €2.80 multi   7.25 7.25
No. 1307 contains one 29x60mm stamp.

Dinner at Emmaus, by Primo Conti A384

2005, Nov. 10   **Litho.**   **Perf. 13x13¼**
1308 A384 62c multi   1.50 1.50
Eleventh General Assembly of the Synod of Bishops.

2004 Journeys of Pope John Paul II — A385

Designs: 45c, Bern, Switzerland, June 5-6. 80c, Lourdes, France, Aug. 14-15. €2, Loreto, Italy, Sept. 5.

2005, Nov. 10
1309-1311 A385   Set of 3   8.00 8.00

The Annunciation, by Raphael — A386

Designs: Nos. 1312, 1314a, Drawing of Angel, Painting of Virgin Mary. Nos. 1313, 1314b, Painting of Angel, drawing of Virgin Mary.

Litho. & Engr.
2005, Nov. 10   **Perf. 13x13¼**
1312	A386	62c multi	1.60 1.60
1313	A386	€1 multi	2.75 2.75

Souvenir Sheet

1314 A386 €1.40 Sheet of 2,
#a-b   7.00 7.00

See France No. 3153.

Swiss Papal Guards, 500th Anniv. A387

Designs: 62c, Guard and drummers. 80c, Guards and St. Peter's Basilica.

2005, Nov. 22   Litho.   Perf. 14x14¼
1315-1316 A387   Set of 2   3.50 3.50

Nos. 1315-1316 each issued in sheets of 6. See Switzerland Nos. 1224-1225.

Christmas A388

Details from Adoration of the Shepherds, by François Le Moyne: 45c, Shepherds and sheep. 62c, Angel. 80c, Madonna and Child.

2005, Nov. 22   Perf. 13¼x13
1317-1319 A388   Set of 3   4.75 4.75
1319a   Booklet pane of 4 #1319   8.00
             Complete booklet, #1319a   8.00

Europa A389

Designs: 62c, Praying hands, church, mosque and synagogue. 80c, Handshake, classroom.

2006, Mar. 16   Litho.   Perf. 13x13¼
1320-1321 A389   Set of 2   3.50 3.50

Jesuits A390

Designs: 45c, Blessed Peter Faber (1506-46). 60c, St. Ignatius of Loyola (1491-1556). €2, St. Francis Xavier (1506-52).

2006, Mar. 16
1322-1324 A390   Set of 3   7.50 7.50

Andrea Mantegna (c. 1430-1506), Painter A391

Designs: 60c, Madonna and Child. 85c, Saints Gregory and John the Baptist. €1, Saints Peter and Paul.
No. 1328 — San Zeno Polyptych: a, Country name at right. b, Country name at left.

2006, Mar. 16   Photo.   Perf. 12¾
1325-1327 A391   Set of 3   6.00 6.00
Souvenir Sheet
Perf. 13¼x13
1328 A391 €1.40 Sheet of 2,
#a-b   7.00 7.00

No. 1328 contains two 21x37mm stamps.

Wolfgang Amadeus Mozart (1756-91), Composer A392

Litho. & Engr.
2006, June 22   Perf. 14x14¼
1329 A392 80c multi   2.25 2.25

2005 Travels of Pope Benedict XVI — A393

Designs: 62c, National Eucharistic Congress, Bari, Italy, May 21-29. €1.40, World Youth Day, Cologne, Germany, Aug. 16-21.

2006, June 22   Litho.   Perf. 13¼x13
1330-1331 A393   Set of 2   5.25 5.25

St. Peter's Basilica, 500th Anniv. — A394

No. 1332, 45c — 1506 medallion depicting: a, Allegory of architecture (denomination at LL). b, Architect Donato Bramante (denomination at UR).
No. 1333, 60c — 1506 medallion depicting: a, Pope Julius II (denomination at LL). b, Bramante's plan for St. Peter's Basilica (denomination at UR).

Litho. & Embossed
2006, June 22   Perf. 14
Horiz. Pairs, #a-b
1332-1333 A394   Set of 2   6.00 6.00

Intl. Year of Deserts and Desertification — A395

Designs: 62c, Flowers, child on parched earth. €1, Trees, child and cattle.

2006, Oct. 12   Litho.   Perf. 13½x13¼
1334-1335 A395   Set of 2   4.25 4.25

Diplomatic Relations Between Vatican City and Singapore, 25th Anniv. — A396

Designs: 85c, Merlion and St. Peter's Basilica. €2, Flags of Singapore and Vatican City.

2006, Oct. 12   Perf. 13½x13
1336-1337 A396   Set of 2   7.50 7.50

See Singapore Nos. 1232-1233.

Vatican Musum, 500th Anniv. A397

Heads from Laocoon sculpture: 60c, Son of Laocoon. 65c, Laocoon. €1.40, Son of Laocoon, diff. €2.80, Laocoon, horiz.

Litho. & Embossed
2006, Oct. 12   Perf. 13x13¼
1338-1340 A397   Set of 3   7.00 7.00
Souvenir Sheet
Perf. 13 Horiz.
1341 A397 €2.80 multi   8.00 8.00

No. 1341 contains one 80x30mm stamp.

Christmas A398

Stained glass from Pope's private chapel: 60c, Shepherds. 65c, Holy Family. 85c, Magi and Star of Bethlehem.

2006, Oct. 12   Litho.   Perf. 13¼x13
1342-1344 A398   Set of 3   5.50 5.50
1343a   Booklet pane of 4 #1343   7.00 —
             Complete booklet, #1343a   7.00

St. Francis of Paola (1416-1507) — A399

Details from sculpture: 60c, Head of St. Francis. €1, Angel.

2007, Mar. 16   Litho.   Perf. 13x13¼
1345-1346 A399   Set of 2   4.25 4.25

Pope Benedict XVI, 80th Birthday — A400

Pope Benedict XVI: 60c, Wearing zucchetto. 65c, Without head covering. 85c, Wearing miter.

2007, Mar. 16   Perf. 13¼x13
Stamp + Label
1347-1349 A400   Set of 3   5.75 5.75

Europa A401

Designs: 60c, Scouts reading map, Scout holding chick. 65c, Scouts around campfire.

2007, June 12   Perf. 13x13¼
1350-1351 A401   Set of 2   3.50 3.50

Scouting, cent.

Christian Museum, 250th Anniv. A402

Designs: 85c, Gilded glass depicting Saints Peter and Paul, silver vase. €2, Bronze lamp with monogram of Christ, silver bottle.

2007, June 12
1352-1353 A402   Set of 2   8.00 8.00

Carlo Goldoni (1707-93), Playwright A403

Goldoni and: 60c, Bridge, man, harlequin. 85c, Church, man, woman. €2.80, Goldoni holding book.

2007, June 12   Perf. 13x13¼
1354-1355 A403   Set of 2   4.00 4.00
Souvenir Sheet
Perf. 13
1356 A403 €2.80 multi   7.75 7.75

No. 1356 contains one 45x33mm stamp and was sold with side portions of the sheet folded to produce an effect like a theater curtain.

New Philatelic and Numismatic Museum — A404

No. 1357: a, Vatican City #37, 576, 1013, 1296. b, Four Vatican City coins.

Litho. & Embossed
2007, Sept. 20   Perf. 14
1357 A404 60c Horiz. pair, #a-b   3.50 3.50

Treaty of Rome, 50th Anniv. A405

Stars and: 15c, Atomium, Brussels. 30c, Eiffel Tower, Paris. 60c, Brandenburg Gate, Berlin. 65c, Plaza, Rome. €1, Castle, Luxembourg. €4, Buildings and bridges, Amsterdam. €2.80, Mother and child.

2007, Sept. 20   Litho.   Perf. 13x13¼
1358-1363 A405   Set of 6   19.00 19.00
Souvenir Sheet
Perf. 13x13¼ on 2 Sides
1364 A405   €2.80 multi   8.00 8.00
No. 1364 contains one 40x37mm stamp.

St. Elizabeth of Hungary (1207-31) A406

2007, Nov. 20   Perf. 13¾
1365 A406   65c multi   1.90 1.90

2006 Travels of Pope Benedict XVI — A407

Travels: 60c, Poland, May 25-28. 65c, Valencia, Spain, July 8-9. 85c, Germany, Sept. 9-14. €1.40, Turkey, Nov. 28-Dec. 1.

2007, Nov. 20   Perf. 13¼x13
1366-1369 A407   Set of 4   9.75 9.75
Booklet Stamp
Self-Adhesive
1370 A407 85c Like #1368   2.50 2.50
  a.   Booklet pane of 4   10.00

Christmas A408

Vatican arms and nave paintings in St. Andrew's Church, Luqa, Malta, by Giuseppe Cali: 60c, Madonna and Child. 65c, Holy Family with Women and Young Girl. 85c, Infant Jesus and Young Girl.

2007, Nov. 20
1371-1373 A408   Set of 3   6.25 6.25
See Malta Nos. 1319-1321.

Europa A409

Designs: 60c, Envelope with cachet and cancels. 85c, Handwritten letter, Pope Benedict XVI.

2008, Mar. 6   Litho.   Perf. 13¾
1374-1375 A409   Set of 2   4.00 4.00

Sistine Chapel Paintings by Michelangelo, 500th Anniv. — A410

Designs: 5c, Libyan. 10c, Eritrean. 25c, Delphic Sibyl. 60c, Sibyl Cumana. 65c, Daniel. 85c, Jonah. €2, Ezekiel. €5, Zaccharias.

2008, Mar. 6   Perf. 13x13¼
1376 A410   5c multi   .25 .25
1377 A410   10c multi   .30 .30
1378 A410   25c multi   .75 .75
1379 A410   60c multi   1.75 1.75
1380 A410   65c multi   1.90 1.90
1381 A410   85c multi   2.40 2.40
1382 A410   €2 multi   5.50 5.50
1383 A410   €5 multi   14.00 14.00
  Nos. 1376-1383 (8)   26.85 26.85

23rd World Youth Day A411

2008, May 15   Litho.   Perf. 13¾
1384 A411   €1 multi   3.25 3.25

Visit of Pope Benedict XVI to United Nations — A412

2008, May 15
1385 A412   €1.40 multi   4.25 4.25

49th Eucharistic Congress, Quebec — A413

Designs: 60c, Wedding at Cana, Washing of the Feet, Last Supper. 85c, Crucifixion, Resurrection, Disciples of Emmaus.

2008, May 15   Perf. 13¾x13¼
1386-1387 A413   Set of 2   4.50 4.50

Apparition of the Virgin Mary at Lourdes, 150th Anniv. — A414

Designs: 65c, Pilgrims at Lourdes. 85c, Virgin Mary, Lourdes.

2008, May 15   Litho.   Perf. 13x13¼
1388-1389 A414   Set of 2   9.50 9.50
Nos. 1388-1389 each were printed in sheets of 4.

2007 Travels of Pope Benedict XVI — A415

Travels: 65c, Brazil, May 9-14. 85c, Austria, Sept. 7-9.

Litho. & Engr.
2008, Sept. 17   Perf. 12¾
1390-1391 A415   Set of 2   4.75 4.75

Pauline Year — A416

Designs: 60c, Conversion of St. Paul. 65c, St. Paul preaching. 85c, St. Paul imprisoned.

2008, Sept. 17   Litho.   Perf. 13¼x13
1392-1394 A416   Set of 3   6.00 6.00

Postal Convention Between Vatican City and Sovereign Military Order of Malta A417

2008, Nov. 13   Litho.   Perf. 13¾
1395 A417   €2.50 multi + label 7.00 7.00

Andrea Palladio (1508-80), Architect — A418

Designs: 65c, San Giorgio Maggiore Church, Venice. 85c, Villa Rotonda, Vicenza, Italy. €2.80, Palladio.

2008, Nov. 13   Perf. 13¼x14
1396-1397 A418   Set of 2   4.00 4.00
Souvenir Sheet
1398 A418   €2.80 multi   7.25 7.25

Christmas A419

Designs: 60c, Adoration of the Magi, by Raphael. 65c, Nativity, by Albrecht Dürer.

2008, Nov. 13   Litho.   Perf. 13x13¼
1399-1400 A419   Set of 2   3.25 3.25
Booklet Stamp
Self-Adhesive
Serpentine Die Cut 12½
1401 A419   60c multi   1.60 1.60
  a.   Booklet pane of 4   6.50
See Germany Nos. B1008-B1009.

Gibraltar Shrine to Our Lady of Europe, 700th Anniv. — A420

2009, Feb. 10   Litho.   Perf. 14x14¾
1402 A420   85c multi   2.25 2.25
Printed in sheets of 4. See Gibraltar No. 1182.

A421

Vatican City State, 80th Anniv. — A422

Popes: No. 1403, 65c, Pius XI. No. 1404, 65c, Pius XII. No. 1405, 65c, John XXIII. No. 1406, 65c, Paul VI. No. 1407, 65c, John Paul I. No. 1408, 65c, John Paul II. No. 1409, Benedict XVI.
€2.80, Vatican City map.

2009, Feb. 10   Perf. 13½x14
1403-1409 A421   Set of 7   11.50 11.50
Souvenir Sheet
1410 A422   €2.80 gray & blk   8.00 8.00

Europa A423

Paintings from Astronomical Observations series by Donato Creti: 60c, The Sun. 65c, Saturn.

2009, May 20   Litho.   Perf. 14¼
1411-1412 A423   Set of 2   3.50 3.50
Intl. Year of Astronomy.

St. Frances of Rome (1384-1440) — A424

Designs: 85c, St. Frances healing a poor man with an injured arm. €1, Miracle of the grapes.

2009, May 20   **Perf. 13¼**
1413-1414 A424   Set of 2   5.25 5.25

World Book and Copyright Day — A425

Pontifical Biblical Institute, Cent. — A426

75th Intl. Federationo of Library Associations and Institutions General Conference, Milan — A427

2009, May 20   **Perf. 14x14¾**
1415 A425   60c multi   1.75 1.75
1416 A426   85c multi   2.40 2.40
1417 A427   €1.40 multi   4.00 4.00
   Nos. 1415-1417 (3)   8.15 8.15

Guglielmo Cardinal Massaja (1809-89), Missionary in Africa — A428

2009, Sept. 23   **Litho.**   **Perf. 13¼**
1418 A428   60c brown   1.75 1.75

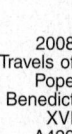 

2008 Travels of Pope Benedict XVI A429

Travels: 65c, France, Sept. 12-15. 85c, United States, Apr. 15-21. €1, Australia, July 12-21.

2009, Sept. 23
1419-1421 A429   Set of 3   8.00 8.00

A430

A431

The Disputation of the Holy Sacrament, by Raphael, 500th Anniv. — A432

Designs: Nos. 1422-1424, Various painting details. €3.30, Entire painting.

2009, Sept. 23   **Perf. 14**
1422 A430   65c multi   1.90 1.90
1423 A431   65c multi   1.90 1.90
1424 A432   65c multi   1.90 1.90
   Nos. 1422-1424 (3)   5.70 5.70

Souvenir Sheet
Perf. 13¾
1425 A432   €3.30 multi   9.75 9.75
No. 1425 contains one 35x50mm stamp.

Italian Language Day — A433

2009, Oct. 21   **Photo.**   **Perf. 13¼x13**
1426 A433   60c multi + label   1.90 1.90
Printed in sheets of 5 + 5 labels. See Italy No. 2966; San Marino No. 1801.

Composers — A434

Designs: 65c, George Frideric Handel (1685-1759). 85c, Joseph Haydn (1732-1809). €5, Felix Mendelssohn Bartholdy (1809-47).

2009, Oct. 24   **Litho.**   **Perf. 14¾x14**
1427-1429 A434   Set of 3   19.50 19.50

Convocation of Second Vatican Council, 50th Anniv. — A435

Litho. & Embossed
2009, Nov. 4   **Perf. 14**
1430 A435   60c multi   1.90 1.90

Louis Braille (1809-52), Educator of the Blind A436

2009, Nov. 4   **Perf. 14¾x14**
1431 A436   65c multi   2.00 2.00

Christmas A437

Madonna and Child Enthroned with Two Angels and Saints Joachim and Anne, by Francesco Melanzio: 60c, Detail. 65c, Entire painting.

2009, Nov. 4   **Litho.**   **Perf. 12½**
1432 A437   60c multi   1.90 1.90
1433 A437   65c multi   2.00 2.00
  a.   Booklet pane of 4   8.00 8.00
    Complete booklet, #1433a   8.00

Easter — A438

Litho. & Engr.
2010, Mar. 5   **Perf. 13x12¾**
1434 A438   65c multi   2.00 2.00

Sandro Botticelli (1445-1510), Painter — A439

Details of Sistine Chapel paintings: 60c, Women from The Temptation of Christ. 85c, Woman holding walking stick from The Life of Moses. €1.45, Woman carrying basket on head from The Life of Moses.

2010, Mar. 5   **Litho.**   **Perf. 13¾x13½**
1435-1437 A439   Set of 3   8.25 8.25

The Deposition, by Caravaggio (1573-1610) A440

2010, June 22   **Litho.**   **Perf. 13¼x14**
1438 A440   65c multi   1.75 1.75

Europa A441

Illustrations from The Bible Narrated for Children: 60c, Adam and Eve in the Garden of Eden. 65c, Jesus and children.

2010, June 22   **Perf. 13**
1439-1440 A441   Set of 2   3.25 3.25

Sacerdotal Year — A442

Designs: €1.40, St. John Vianney (1786-1859) and priests. €1.50, The Good Shepherd, sheep and wolf.

2010, June 22   **Perf. 13¾x13½**
1441-1442 A442   Set of 2   8.25 8.25

Father Matteo Ricci (1552-1610), Missionary to China — A443

Designs: 5c, Ricci and Xu Guangqi, Chinese court official. €3.30, Ricci.

2010, June 22   **Perf. 14¾x14**
1443-1444 A443   Set of 2   9.50 9.50

Pope Leo XIII (1810-1903) A444

2010, Sept. 20   **Litho.**   **Perf. 14¾x14**
1445 A444   65c multi   1.90 1.90

Composers A445

Designs: 65c, Frédéric Chopin (1810-49). €1, Robert Schumann (1810-56). €4.40, Chopin and Schumann, horiz. (65x16mm).

2010, Sept. 20   **Perf. 13x12¾**
1446 A445   65c multi   2.00 2.00
1447 A445   €1 multi   3.00 3.00
   Perf. 12¾ at Top
1448 A445   €4.40 multi + label   12.50 12.50
   Nos. 1446-1448 (3)   17.50 17.50

Reopening of the Vatican Library
A446

Designs: 65c, Crucified Christ. 85c, Sts. Cosmas and Damian. €3.90, Medallion depicting Pope Sixtus V, vert.

2010, Sept. 20   **Perf. 14x13½**
1449 A446 65c multi   2.00 2.00
1450 A446 85c multi   2.50 2.50

Imperf

1451 A446 €3.90 multi   14.00 14.00
   Nos. 1449-1451 (3)   18.50 18.50

No. 1451 is printed as a miniature book made up of two pieces of paper of different sizes. Both pieces of paper are printed on both sides, and are glued together. The cover of the book is the longer of the two pieces of paper, and is folded into three parts. The stamp, the front cover of the book, is the middle part of this piece of paper. The gum, applied to the left of the stamp, becomes the book's back cover when the longer piece of paper is folded. The title page of *De Nuptiis Philologiae et Mercurii* is to the right of the stamp, and is the book's first page. Text and illustrations are on the reverse of this picture and the stamp, and another picture depicting text and the seal of the Vatican Library is printed on the back of the gum. The second piece of paper, folded in half to constitute four pages of the book, has text and illustrations, and is glued to the back of longer sheet where the fold between the stamp and the photo is found. Values are for the complete item.

Approval of the Franciscan Rule, 800th Anniv. — A447

2010, Nov. 15   **Litho.**   **Perf. 12¾**
1452 A447 65c multi   2.00 2.00

Writers — A448

Scenes from works by: 60c, Anton Chekhov (1860-1904). 65c, Leo Tolstoy (1828-1910).

2010, Nov. 15   **Perf. 14¼x14¾**
1453-1454 A448 Set of 2   3.75 3.75

2009 Travels of Pope Benedict XVI
A449

Travels: 10c, Cameroun and Angola, Mar. 17-23. 65c, Holy Land, May 8-15. 85c, Czech Republic, Sept. 26-28.

2010, Nov. 15   **Perf. 13x13¼**
1455-1457 A449 Set of 3   4.75 4.75
   See Israel No. 1837.

Christmas
A450

Paintings: 60c, The Birth of Jesus, by Gheorghe Tattarascu. 65c, The Nativity and Adoration of the Shepherds, by the School of Murillo.

2010, Nov. 15   **Perf. 13¼**
1458 A450 60c multi   1.75 1.75
1459 A450 65c multi   1.90 1.90

Booklet Stamps
Self-Adhesive
Serpentine Die Cut 12½

1460 A450 60c multi   1.75 1.75
  a.   Booklet pane of 4   7.00
1461 A450 65c multi   1.90 1.90
  a.   Booklet pane of 4   7.75

   See Romania Nos. 5218-5219.

Easter
A451

2011, Mar. 21   **Perf. 12¾**
1462 A451 75c multi   2.25 2.25

Father Eusebio Kino (1645-1711), Missionary in Mexico — A452

2011, Mar. 21   **Perf. 14¼x14¾**
1463 A452 €1.60 maroon & black   4.75 4.75

A453

Unification of Italy, 150th Anniv. — A454

Designs: No. 1464, 60c, Milan Cathedral and Lombardy-Venetia #6. No. 1465, 60c, Modena Cathedral and Modena #3. No. 1466, 60c, Uffizi Gallery, Palazzo Vecchio, Florence and Tuscany #4. No. 1467, 60c, San Carlo Square, Turin and Sardinia #1. No. 1468, 60c, Mt. Vesuvius and Naples, Two Sicilies #3, 13. No. 1469, 60c, Baptistry, Parma and Parma #4.
€1.50, Piazza del Popolo, Rome.

2011, Mar. 21   **Perf. 12½**
1464-1469 A453 Set of 6   11.00 11.00

Souvenir Sheet

1470 A454 €1.50 multi   5.00 5.00
   See Italy No. 3046.

Beatification of Pope John Paul II — A455

2011, Apr. 12   **Perf. 13**
1471 A455 75c multi   2.50 2.50
Printed in sheets of 6. See Poland No. 4009.

World Youth Day, Madrid — A456

2011, June 21   **Perf. 14x13½**
1472 A456 75c multi   2.10 2.10
   See Spain No. 3797.

Europa — A457

Detail from The Journey of Moses into Egypt, by Perugino: a, 60c, "Europa" at UL. b, 75c, "Europa" at UR.

2011, June 21   **Perf. 13¾**
1473 A457 Horiz. pair, #a-b   4.00 4.00
   Intl. Year of Forests.

Ordination of Pope Benedict XVI, 60th Anniv. — A458

Designs: No. 1474, 75c, Shell, photograph from ordination as priest, June 29, 1951. No. 1475, 75c, Bear, photograph from installation as bishop, May 28, 1977. No. 1476, 75c, St. Corbinian, photograph from installation as cardinal, June 27, 1977. No. 1477, 75c, Papal arms, photograph from installation as pope, Apr. 19, 2005.

2011, June 21   **Perf. 13½x13¾**
1474-1477 A458 Set of 4   9.00 9.00

Miniature Sheet

L'Osservatore Romano (Official Vatican Newspaper), 150th Anniv. — A459

No. 1478 — Front pages of newspaper announcing election of Pope: a, Leo XIII. b, Pius X. c, Benedict XV. d, Pius XI. e, Pius XII. f, John XXIII. g, Paul VI. h, John Paul I. i, John Paul II. j, Benedict XVI.

2011, June 21   **Perf. 14x14¾**
1478 A459 60c Sheet fo 10, #a-j   18.50 18.50

Mater et Magistra, Encyclical by Pope John XXIII, 50th Anniv.
A460

2011, Sept. 2   **Perf. 13¾**
1479 A460 60c multi   1.75 1.75

Room of Heliodorus Frescoes by Raphael, 500th Anniv. — A461

Details from The Expulsion of Heliodorus from the Temple. 75c, Left side of fresco. €1.60, Right side of fresco.

2011, Sept. 2   **Perf. 14¼**
1480-1481 A461 Set of 2   7.00 7.00

Rudjer Boskovic (1711-87), Astronomer, and Dome of St. Peter's Basilica — A462

2011, Sept. 13
1482 A462 €3.30 multi   10.00 10.00
   See Croatia No. 810.

Composers
A463

Designs: 75c, Franz Liszt (1811-86). €1.60, Gustav Mahler (1860-1911).

2011, Nov. 18   **Litho.**   **Perf. 14x14¾**
1483-1484 A463 Set of 2   6.50 6.50

2010 Travels of Pope Benedict XVI
A464

Travels: 60c, Malta, Apr. 17-18. 75c, Portugal, May 11-14. €1.40, Cyprus, June 4-6. €1.60, United Kingdom, Sept. 16-19. €2, Spain, Nov. 6-7.

2011, Nov. 18   **Perf. 13¼**
1485-1489 A464 Set of 5   18.00 18.00

Christmas
A465

Designs: 60c, Madonna and Child, Saints Benedict and Francis. 75c, Infant Jesus and animals.

2011, Nov. 18   **Perf. 13¼**
1490 A465 60c multi   1.75 1.75
1491 A465 75c multi   2.00 2.00

Booklet Stamp
Self-Adhesive
Serpentine Die Cut 12½x12¼
1492 A465 75c multi   2.00 2.00
    a.   Booklet pane of 4   8.00

Easter — A466

2012, Mar. 1   **Perf. 14¼x14¾**
1493 A466 75c multi   2.00 2.00

Father Christopher Clavius (1538-1612), Mathematician and Astronomer A467

2012, Mar. 1   **Perf. 14¼**
1494 A467 €1.60 black & red   4.50 4.50

Madonna of Foligno, by Raphael A468

Sistine Madonna, by Raphael A469

2012, Mar. 1   **Perf. 13¼**
1495 A468 60c multi   1.75 1.75
1496 A469 75c multi   2.25 2.25

Souvenir Sheets
1497 A468 €1.40 multi   4.00 4.00
1498 A469 €2.40 multi   7.00 7.00

See Germany No. 2666.

St. Joan of Arc (c. 1412-31) — A470

Litho. & Engr.
2012, May 11   **Perf. 13**
1499 A470 75c multi   2.00 2.00

See France No. 4220.

Seventh World Meeting of Families, Milan — A471

2012, May 11   Litho.   **Perf. 13¼x14**
1500 A471 €1.50 multi   4.00 4.00

Europa — A472

Designs: No. 1501, 75c, Dome of St. Peter's Basilica. No. 1502, 75c, Dove in stained-glass window, St. Peter's Basilica.

2012, May 11
1501-1502 A472   Set of 2   4.00 4.00

50th Intl. Eucharistic Congress, Dublin A473

Designs: 75c, Celtic cross from the Rock of Cashel, Tipperary, Ireland. €1, Ardagh Chalice.

2012, May 11   **Perf. 14¾x14**
1503-1504 A473   Set of 2   4.75 4.75

Pope John Paul I (1912-78) A474

2012, Sept. 13   **Perf. 14x13¾**
1505 A474 75c multi   2.00 2.00

No. 1505 was printed in sheets of 6.

Vatican Secret Archives, 400th Anniv. — A475

No. 1506: a, Pope Benedict XVI. b, Sealed document. c, Pope Paul V.

2012, Sept. 13   **Perf. 13¾x13½**
1506 A475 75c Horiz. strip of 3,
    #a-c   6.00 6.00

No. 1506 was printed in sheets containing four strips.

Souvenir Sheet

Battle of the Milvian Bridge, 1700th Anniv. — A476

2012, Sept. 13   **Perf. 14x13½**
1507 A476 €4.40 multi   11.50 11.50

See Italy No. 3136.

2011 Travels of Pope Benedict XVI A477

Travels: 60c, Croatia, June 4-5. 75c, San Marino, June 19. €1.40, Spain, Aug. 18-21. €1.60, Germany, Sept. 22-25. €2, Benin, Nov. 18-20.

2012, Nov. 6   **Perf. 13½**
1508-1512 A477   Set of 5   17.50 17.50

Christmas A478

Stained-glass windows by János Hajnal depicting: 60c, Annunciation. 75c, Holy Family and shepherd.

2012, Nov. 6   **Perf. 13¾**
1513-1514 A478   Set of 2   3.50 3.50
  1514a   Booklet pane of 8, 4 each
    #1513-1514   14.00 —
    Complete booklet, #1514a   14.00

Souvenir Sheet

Restoration of the Colonnade of St. Peter's Square — A479

No. 1515 — Papal arms of: a, Alexander VII. b, Benedict XVI.

Litho. With Foil Application
2012, Nov. 20   **Perf. 13¾**
1515 A479 €10 Sheet of 2,
    #a-b   52.50 52.50

Inscription in sheet margin "Officium Philatelicum et Nomismaticum" could be personalized.

Sculpture of Risen Christ, by Pericle Fazzini A480

Perf. 13¼x13½
2013, Feb. 28   **Litho.**
1516 A480 85c multi   2.25 2.25

Easter.

Year of Faith — A481

No. 1517 — Details from Faith, by Raphael: a, Putto, denomination at LL (20x38mm). b, Putto, denomination at LR (20x38mm). c, Faith with chalice and host (30x38mm).

2013, Feb. 28   **Perf. 13½x13¾**
1517 A481   Horiz. strip of 3   6.00 6.00
    a.-b.   60c Either single   1.60 1.60
    c.   €1 multi   2.60 2.60

Souvenir Sheet

Mass of Bolsena, by Raphael — A482

2013, Feb. 28   **Perf. 13½x13¾**
1518 A482 €4.80 multi   12.50 12.50

Miracle of Bolsena, 750th anniv.

Interregnum Issue

Angel and Sede Vacante Arms — A483

Background colors: 70c, Blue green. 85c, Blue. €2, Gray. €2.50, Yellow.

2013, Mar. 1   **Perf. 13¼x13**
1519-1522 A483   Set of 4   16.00 16.00

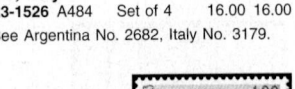

Pope Francis — A484

Various photographs of Pope Francis: 70c, 85c, €2, €2.50.

2013, May 2   **Perf. 13¼x14**
1523-1526 A484   Set of 4   16.00 16.00

See Argentina No. 2682, Italy No. 3179.

Giuseppe Gioachino Belli (1791-1863), Poet — A485

2013, May 2   **Perf. 14x14¾**
1527 A485 €1 multi   2.60 2.60

World Youth
Day — A486

2013, May 2 *Perf. 13¼x13*
1528 A486 €1.90 multi 5.00 5.00

Europa — A487

Vatican City postal van and: 70c, St. Peter's Basilica. 85c, Globe.

2013, May 2
1529-1530 A487 Set of 2 4.00 4.00

Pope John XXIII
(1881-1963)
A488

2013, June 12 *Perf. 14x13½*
1531 A488 85c multi 2.25 2.25
No. 1531 was printed in sheets of 9.

Edict of
Milan,
1700th
Anniv.
A489

Frescoes from the Oratory of St. Sylvester, Rome, depicting Pope Sylvester I and Emperor Constantine: 70c, 85c, €2.50. €1.90, Pope Sylvester I showing icon depicting Sts. Peter and Paul to Emperor Constantine.

2013, June 12 *Perf. 13x13¼*
1532-1534 A489 Set of 3 11.00 11.00
Souvenir Sheet
1535 A489 €1.90 multi 5.25 5.25
See Italy No. 3178.

Souvenir Sheet

Mission of Sts. Cyril and Methodius to
Slavic Lands, 1150th Anniv. — A490

Litho. & Engr.
2013, June 12 *Perf. 11¾*
1536 A490 €1.90 multi 5.25 5.25
See Bulgaria No. 4647, Czech Republic No. 3573, Slovakia No. 666.

Composers
A491

Designs: 70c, Giuseppe Verdi (1813-1901). 85c, Richard Wagner (1813-83).

2013, Aug. 30 Litho. *Perf. 14x14¾*
1537-1538 A491 Set of 2 4.25 4.25

Popes of the
Renaissance
A492

Designs: 70c, Pope Julius II (1443-1513). €2, Pope Leo X (1475-1521).

2013, Aug. 30 *Perf. 13¾x13½*
1539-1540 A492 Set of 2 7.25 7.25

Raoul
Follereau
(1903-77),
Journalist,
and Lepers
A493

2013, Nov. 7 Litho. *Perf. 13¾*
1541 A493 €2 multi 5.50 5.50
World Leprosy Day.

2012
Travels of
Pope
Benedict
XVI
A494

Travels: 70c, Mexico and Cuba, Mar. 23-29. 85c, Lebanon, Sept. 14-16.

2013, Nov. 7 Litho. *Perf. 14x13¾*
1542 A494 70c multi 1.90 1.90
1543 A494 85c multi 2.40 2.40
a. Booklet pane of 4, 2 each
#1542-1543 8.75 —
Complete booklet, #1543a 8.75

Santa Maria di
Nardò
Cathedral,
Lecce, Italy,
600th
Anniv. — A495

Cathedral frescoes depicting: 5c, St. Augustine. 10c, Our Lady of Health. 15c, Madonna del Giglio. 25c, St. Nicholas of Myra. 45c, Christ Pantocrator.

2013, Nov. 7 Litho. *Perf. 13x13¼*
1544-1548 A495 Set of 5 2.75 2.75

Christmas
A496

Paintings by Pinturicchio: 70c, Nativity. 85c, Adoration of the Magi.

2013, Nov. 7 Litho. *Perf. 13¼x13¾*
1549-1550 A496 Set of 2 4.25 4.25
Nos. 1549-1550 each were printed in sheets of 8 + central label. See Finland (Aland Islands) Nos. 349-350.

27th Intl. Book
Fair,
Turin — A497

2014, Mar. 21 Litho. *Perf. 13*
1551 A497 70c multi 2.00 2.00

Easter — A498

2014, Mar. 21 Litho. *Perf. 13¾*
1552 A498 85c multi 2.40 2.40

Start of Second
Year of Reign of
Pope
Francis — A499

Various photographs of Pope Francis with denomination in: 70c, Red. 85c, Blue. €2, Green. €2.50, Bister.

2014, Mar. 21 Litho. *Perf. 13½x13*
1553-1556 A499 Set of 4 17.00 17.00
See Philippines No.

Canonization of Pope John
XXIII — A500

2014, Mar. 21 Litho. *Perf. 13¼*
1557 A500 70c multi 2.00 2.00
See Italy No. 3228

Souvenir Sheet

Canonization of Popes John Paul II
and John XXIII — A501

No. 1558: a, Pope John Paul II. b, Pope John XXIII.

Perf. 11½x11¼ Syncopated
2014, Mar. 21 **Litho.**
1558 A501 €1 Sheet of 2, #a-b 5.50 5.50
See Poland No. 4112.

A502

Canonization of Pope John Paul
II — A503

Perf. 11½x11¾ Syncopated
2014, Mar. 21 **Litho.**
1559 A502 85c multi 2.40 2.40
Souvenir Sheets
Perf. 11¼x11½ Syncopated
1560 A503 €1.90 multi 5.25 5.25
Engr.
1561 A503 €2.50 bister 7.00 7.00
See Poland Nos. 4113-4115.

Charlie Chaplin
(1889-1977), Film
Actor — A504

2014, May 20 Litho. *Perf. 13½*
1562 A504 70c multi 1.90 1.90

Face of Christ, by El Greco (1541-1614) A505

2014, May 20   Litho.   Perf. 14¾x14
1563 A505 85c multi   2.40 2.40

Europa — A506

Pipe organ from: 70c, Basilica of St. John Lateran. 85c, St. Peter's Basilica.

2014, May 20   Litho.   Perf. 13¾
1564-1565 A506 Set of 2   4.25 4.25

Emperor Charlemagne (742-814) — A507

Charlemagne: 85c, On horse. €1.90, With orb and scepter.

2014, May 20   Litho.   Perf. 13¾
1566-1567 A507 Set of 2   7.50 7.50

Souvenir Sheet

Donato Bramante (1444-1514), Architect — A508

No. 1568: a, €1.20, Bramante (38mm diameter). b, €3.60, Bramante Staircase, Octagonal Courtyard of the Belvedere (30x40mm).

Perf. (#1568a), Perf. 14¼ (#1568b)
2014, May 20   Litho.
1568 A508 Sheet of 2, #a-b   13.00 13.00

Saint Camillus Amongst the Plague-Stricken, by Sebastiano Conca — A509

2014, Aug. 28   Litho.   Perf. 13¼
1569 A509 70c multi   1.90 1.90

St. Camillus de Lellis (1550-1614), founder of the Order of the Ministers of the Sick.

Richard Strauss (1864-1949), Composer A510

2014, Aug. 28   Litho.   Perf. 13¾
1570 A510 70c multi   1.90 1.90

Beatification of Pope Paul VI (1897-1978) A511

2014, Aug. 28   Litho.   Perf. 13¼x13
1571 A511 70c multi   1.90 1.90

No. 1571 was issued in sheets of 4.

Statue of St. Pius X (1835-1914), by Pier Enrico Astorri — A512

2014, Aug. 28   Litho.   Perf. 13
1572 A512 €2 multi   5.25 5.25

Synod of Ayutthaya, 350th Anniv. A513

2014, Aug. 28   Litho.   Perf. 13¾
1573 A513 €2 multi   5.25 5.25

See Thailand No. 2822.

Fall of the Berlin Wall, 25th Anniv. — A514

Designs: 85c, Old woman holding chisel against wall. €3.60, Rainbow.

2014, Aug. 28   Litho.   Perf. 14¼
1574 A514 85c multi   2.25 2.25
Souvenir Sheet
1575 A514 €3.60 multi   9.50 9.50

William Shakespeare (1564-1616), Writer — A515

2014, Nov. 21   Litho.   Perf. 13¾
1576 A515 85c multi   2.10 2.10

Pauline Chapel Paintings by Michelangelo (1475-1564) — A516

Designs: 70c, Crucifixion of Saint Peter. 85c, Conversion of Saint Paul.

Perf. 11½x11¾
2014, Nov. 21   Litho.
1577-1578 A516 Set of 2   4.00 4.00

2013 Travels of Pope Francis A517

Travels: 70c, Rio de Janeiro, Brazil, July 22-29. 85c, Lampedusa, Cagliari and Assisi, Italy, July 8, vert.

2014, Nov. 21   Litho.   Perf. 13¾
1579 A517 70c multi   1.75 1.75
1580 A517 85c multi   2.10 2.10
a.   Booklet pane of 4   8.50
      Complete booklet, #1580a   8.50

Nativity, by Raúl Soldi (1905-94) A518

2014, Nov. 21   Litho.   Perf. 13½
1581 A518 85c multi   2.10 2.10

Christmas. See Argentina No.

Easter — A519

2015, Feb. 15   Litho.   Perf. 13¾
1582 A519 80c multi   1.75 1.75

Public Display of the Shroud of Turin A520

2015, Feb. 19   Litho.   Perf. 13¾
1583 A520 95c multi   2.10 2.10

International Year of Light — A521

2015, Feb. 19   Litho.   Perf. 13¼
1584 A521 €2.15 multi   4.75 4.75

Pope Francis — A522

Various photographs of Pope Francis: 80c, 95c, €2.30, €3.

2015, Feb. 19   Litho.   Perf. 14x14¾
1585-1588 A522 Set of 4   16.00 16.00

SEMI-POSTAL STAMPS

Holy Year Issue

Cross and Orb
SP1   SP2

1933 Unwmk. Engr. Perf. 13x13½
B1	SP1	25c + 10c green	4.75	4.75
B2	SP1	75c + 15c scarlet	8.25	16.50
B3	SP2	80c + 20c red brown	30.00	22.50
B4	SP2	1.25 l + 25c ultra	9.00	17.00

Nos. B1-B4 (4)   52.00 60.75
Set, never hinged   190.00

Catalogue values for unused stamps in this section, from this point to the end of the section, are for Never Hinged items.

Shrine of Our Lady of Mentorella, Italy, 1500th Anniv. — SP3

2010, Mar. 5 Litho. Perf. 14¼x14¾
B5	SP3	65c +20c multi	2.25	2.25

Printed in sheets of 6. Surtax for Haitian earthquake relief.

AIR POST STAMPS

Catalogue values for unused stamps in this section are for Never Hinged items.

Statue of St. Peter AP1

Dove of Peace over Vatican AP2

Elijah's Ascent into Heaven AP3

Our Lady of Loreto and Angels Moving the Holy House AP4

Wmk. 235
1938, June 22 Engr. Perf. 14
C1	AP1	25c brown	.30	.25
C2	AP2	50c green	.30	.25
C3	AP3	75c lake	.30	.30
C4	AP4	80c dark blue	.30	.45
C5	AP1	1 l violet	.90	.50
C6	AP2	2 l ultra	1.60	.80
C7	AP3	5 l slate blk	3.50	2.50
C8	AP4	10 l dk brown vio	3.50	2.50

Nos. C1-C8 (8)   10.70 7.55

Dove of Peace Above St. Peter's Basilica — AP5

House of Our Lady of Loreto — AP6

Birds Circling Cross — AP7

1947, Nov. 10 Photo.
C9	AP5	1 l rose red	.25	.25
C10	AP6	4 l dark brown	.25	.25
C11	AP5	5 l brt ultra	.25	.25
C12	AP7	15 l brt purple	2.25	2.10
C13	AP6	25 l dk blue green	5.25	2.75
C14	AP7	50 l dk gray	7.50	5.25
C15	AP7	100 l red orange	35.00	9.00

Nos. C9-C15 (7)   50.75 19.85

Nos. C13-C15 exist imperf. Value, each pair $1,000.

Archangel Raphael and Young Tobias AP8

1948, Dec. 28 Engr. Perf. 14
C16	AP8	250 l sepia	55.00	10.00
C17	AP8	500 l ultra	585.00	375.00

Set, hinged   440.00

Angels and Globe AP9

1949, Dec. 3
C18	AP9	300 l ultra	30.00	12.50
C19	AP9	1000 l green	150.00	82.50

Set, hinged   95.00

UPU, 75th anniversary.

Franciscus Gratianus — AP10

1951, Dec. 20 Perf. 14x13
C20	AP10	300 l deep plum	350.00	220.00
C21	AP10	500 l deep blue	45.00	20.00

Set, hinged   240.00

Publication of unified canon laws, 800th anniv.

Dome of St. Peter's Basilica — AP11

1953, Aug. 10 Perf. 13
C22	AP11	500 l chocolate	35.00	9.00
C23	AP11	1000 l deep ultra	105.00	20.00

Set, hinged   47.50

See Nos. C33-C34.

Archangel Gabriel by Melozzo da Forli — AP12

Archangel Gabriel: 10 l, 35 l, 100 l, Annunciation by Pietro Cavallini. 15 l, 50 l, 300 l, Annunciation by Leonardo da Vinci.

1956, Feb. 12 Wmk. 235
C24	AP12	5 l gray black	.25	.25
C25	AP12	10 l blue green	.25	.25
C26	AP12	15 l deep orange	.25	.25
C27	AP12	25 l dk car rose	.25	.25
C28	AP12	35 l carmine	.25	.25
C29	AP12	50 l olive brown	.25	.25
C30	AP12	60 l ultra	2.75	2.25
C31	AP12	100 l orange brown	.25	.25
C32	AP12	300 l deep violet	.75	.75

Nos. C24-C32 (9)   5.25 4.75

Type of 1953
1958 Perf. 13½
C33	AP11	500 l grn & bl grn	7.50	4.00
a.		Perf. 14	4,000.	1,200.
C34	AP11	1000 l dp mag	.75	.75
a.		Perf. 14	.75	.75

Obelisk of St. John Lateran — AP13

Obelisks, Rome: 10 l, 60 l, St. Mary Major. 15 l, 100 l, St. Peter. 25 l, 200 l, Piazza del Popolo. 35 l, 500 l, Trinita dei Monti.

1959, Oct. 27 Engr. Perf. 13½x14
C35	AP13	5 l dull violet	.25	.25
C36	AP13	10 l blue green	.25	.25
C37	AP13	15 l dk brown	.25	.25
C38	AP13	25 l slate grn	.25	.25
C39	AP13	35 l ultra	.25	.25
C40	AP13	50 l yellow grn	.25	.25
C41	AP13	60 l rose carmine	.25	.25
C42	AP13	100 l bluish black	.25	.25
C43	AP13	200 l brown	.25	.25
C44	AP13	500 l orange brn	.30	.25

Nos. C35-C44 (10)   2.55 2.50

Archangel Gabriel by Filippo Valle — AP14

1962, Mar. 13 Wmk. 235
C45	AP14	1000 l brown	1.25	.75
C46	AP14	1500 l dark blue	1.75	1.25

Jet over St. Peter's Cathedral AP15

Designs: 40 l, 200 l, Radio tower and statue of Archangel Gabriel (like A87). 90 l, 500 l,

---

Aerial view of St. Peter's Square and Vatican City.

1967, Mar. 7 Photo. Perf. 14
C47	AP15	20 l brt violet	.25	.25
C48	AP15	40 l black & pink	.25	.25
C49	AP15	90 l sl bl & dk gray	.25	.25
C50	AP15	100 l black & salmon	.25	.25
C51	AP15	200 l vio blk & gray	.25	.25
C52	AP15	500 l dk brn & lt brn	.25	.25

Nos. C47-C52 (6)   1.50 1.50

Archangel Gabriel by Fra Angelico — AP16

1968, Mar. 12 Engr. Perf. 13½x14
C53	AP16	1000 l dk car rose, cr	1.00	.75
C54	AP16	1500 l black, cr	1.75	1.50

St. Matthew, by Fra Angelico AP17

The Evangelists, by Fra Angelico from Niccolina Chapel: 300 l, St. Mark. 500 l, St. Luke. 1000 l, St. John.

Engr. & Photo.
Perf. 14x13½
1971, Sept. 30 Unwmk.
C55	AP17	200 l blk & pale grn	.25	.25
C56	AP17	300 l black & bister	.25	.25
C57	AP17	500 l black & salmon	.85	.60
C58	AP17	1000 l black & pale lil	1.00	.75

Nos. C55-C58 (4)   2.35 1.85

AP18

Seraph, mosaic from St. Mark's Basilica, Venice.

Litho. & Engr.
1974, Feb. 21 Perf. 13x14
C59	AP18	2500 l multicolored	2.50	2.00

AP19

Last Judgment, by Michelangelo: 500 l, Angel with Trumpet. 1000 l, Ascending figures. 2500 l, Angels with trumpets.

Litho. & Engr.
1976, Feb. 19 Perf. 13x14
C60	AP19	500 l sal, bl & brn	1.25	1.10
C61	AP19	1000 l sal, bl & brn	1.50	1.10
C62	AP19	2500 l sal, bl & brn	2.00	1.50

Nos. C60-C62 (3)   4.75 3.70

Radio Waves, Antenna, Papal Arms AP20

1978, July 11   Engr.   Perf. 14x13

C63	AP20	1000 l multicolored	1.00	.70
C64	AP20	2000 l multicolored	2.00	1.40
C65	AP20	3000 l multicolored	3.00	1.90
		Nos. C63-C65 (3)	6.00	4.00

10th World Telecommunications Day.

Pope John Paul II Shaking Hands, Arms of Dominican Republic AP21

Litho. & Engr.

1980, June 24   Perf. 14x13½

C66	AP21	200 l shown	.25	.25
C67	AP21	300 l Mexico	.30	.30
C68	AP21	500 l Poland	.60	.60
C69	AP21	1000 l Ireland	1.10	1.10
C70	AP21	1500 l US	1.75	1.75
C71	AP21	2000 l UN	2.00	2.00
C72	AP21	3000 l with Dimitrios I, Turkey	3.50	3.50
		Nos. C66-C72 (7)	9.50	9.50

Issued: 3000 l, Sept. 18; others June 24.

World Communications Year — AP22

Designs: 2000 l, Moses Explaining The Law to the People by Luca Signorelli. 5000 l, Paul Preaching in Athens, Tapestry of Raphael design.

1983, Nov. 10   Perf. 14

| C73 | AP22 | 2000 l multicolored | 3.00 | 3.00 |
| C74 | AP22 | 5000 l multicolored | 6.75 | 6.75 |

Journeys of Pope John Paul II, 1983-84 AP23

Designs: 350 l, Central America, the Caribbean, 1983. 450 l, Warsaw Cathedral, Our Lady of Czestochowa, Poland, 1983. 700 l, Statue of Our Lady, Lourdes, France, 1983. 1000 l, Mariazell Sanctuary, St. Stephen's Cathedral, Austria, 1983. 1500 l, Asia, the Pacific, 1984. 2000 l, Einsiedeln Basilica, St. Nicholas of Flue, Switzerland, 1984. 2500 l, Quebec's Notre Dame Cathedral, five crosses of the Jesuit martyrs, Canada, 1984. 5000 l, Saragossa, Spain, Dominican Republic and Puerto Rico, 1984.

1986, Nov. 20   Photo.   Perf. 14x13½

C75	AP23	350 l multicolored	.50	.50
C76	AP23	450 l multicolored	.65	.65
C77	AP23	700 l multicolored	1.00	1.00
C78	AP23	1000 l multicolored	1.50	1.50
C79	AP23	1500 l multicolored	2.25	2.25
C80	AP23	2000 l multicolored	3.25	3.25
C81	AP23	2500 l multicolored	4.00	4.00
C82	AP23	5000 l multicolored	8.00	8.00
		Nos. C75-C82 (8)	21.15	21.15

Papal Journeys Type of 1986

Designs: 450 l, Horseman, shepherdess, St. Peter's Basilica, Cathedral of Santiago in Chile, and the Sanctuary of Our Lady of Lujan, Argentina. 650 l, Youths and the Cathedral of Speyer, Federal Republic of Germany. 1000 l, St. Peter's Basilica, Altar of Gdansk, flowers

---

and thorns. 2500 l, Crowd and American skyscrapers. 5000 l, Tepee at Fort Simpson, Canada, and American Indians.

1988, Oct. 27   Photo.   Perf. 14x13½

C83	AP23	450 l multicolored	.65	.65
C84	AP23	650 l multicolored	.95	.95
C85	AP23	1000 l multicolored	1.50	1.50
C86	AP23	2500 l multicolored	3.50	3.50
C87	AP23	7250 l multicolored	7.25	7.25
		Nos. C83-C87 (5)	13.85	13.85

Uruguay, Chile and Argentina, Mar. 30-Apr. 14, 1987 (450 l); Federal Republic of Germany, Apr. 30-May 4, 1987 (650 l); Poland, June 8-14, 1987 (1000 l); US, Sept. 10-19, 1987 (2500 l); and Canada, Sept. 20, 1987 (5000 l).

Journeys of Pope John Paul II, 1989 AP24

500 l, Africa. 1000 l, Scandinavia. 3000 l, Santiago de Compostela, Spain. 5000 l, Asia.

1990, Nov. 27   Photo.   Perf. 12
Granite Paper

C88	AP24	500 l multicolored	.80	.80
C89	AP24	1000 l multicolored	1.60	1.60
C90	AP24	3000 l multicolored	5.00	5.00
C91	AP24	5000 l multicolored	8.00	8.00
		Nos. C88-C91 (4)	15.40	15.40

Madagascar, Reunion, Zambia and Malawi, Apr. 28-May 6 (500 l); Norway, Iceland, Finland, Denmark and Sweden, June 1-10 (1000 l); Korea, Indonesia and Mauritius, Oct. 6-16 (5000 l).

Travels of Pope John Paul II, 1991 AP25

1992, Nov. 24   Photo.   Perf. 14

C92	AP25	500 l multicolored	.65	.65
C93	AP25	1000 l multicolored	1.40	1.40
C94	AP25	4000 l multicolored	5.25	5.25
C95	AP25	6000 l multicolored	8.00	8.00
		Nos. C92-C95 (4)	15.30	15.30

Portugal, May 10-13 (500 l); Poland, June 1-9 (1000 l); Poland, Hungary, Aug. 13-20 (4000 l); Brazil, Oct. 12-21 (6000 l).

SPECIAL DELIVERY STAMPS

Pius XI SD1

Unwmk.

1929, Aug. 1   Photo.   Perf. 14

| E1 | SD1 | 2 l carmine rose | 20.50 | 15.00 |
| E2 | SD1 | 2.50 l dark blue | 17.00 | 18.50 |

For overprints see Nos. Q14-Q15.

> Catalogue values for unused stamps in this section, from this point to the end of the section, are for Never Hinged items.

Aerial View of Vatican City SD2

1933, May 31   Wmk. 235   Engr.

| E3 | SD2 | 2 l rose red & brn | .35 | .35 |
| E4 | SD2 | 2.50 l dp blue & brn | .35 | .55 |

1945, Mar. 2   Unwmk.

| E5 | SD2 | 3.50 l dk car & ultra | .50 | .50 |
| E6 | SD2 | 5 l ultra & green | .75 | 1.00 |

Nos. E5 and E6 Srchd. with New Values and Bars in Black

1945, Dec. 29

| E7 | SD2 | 6 l on 3.50 l dk car & ultra | 5.50 | 2.75 |
| E8 | SD2 | 12 l on 5 l ultra & grn | 5.50 | 2.75 |

Vertical pairs imperf. between exist of No. E7 (value $150) and No. E8 (value $200).

Bishop Matteo Giberti SD3

Design: 12 l, Gaspar Cardinal Contarini.

1946, Feb. 21   Photo.
Centers in Dark Brown

| E9 | SD3 | 6 l dark green | .25 | .25 |
| E10 | SD3 | 12 l copper brown | .25 | .25 |

See note after No. 121.
Nos. E9-E10 exist imperf (No. E10 value pair $1,900.) and part perf. (Value, pair $150.00).

St. Peter's Basilica SD5

Design: 80 l, Basilica of St. John.

1949, Mar. 7   Wmk. 235   Perf. 14

E11	SD5	40 l slate gray	15.00	4.50
a.		Perf. 13½x14	32.50	8.00
E12	SD5	80 l chestnut brown	50.00	27.50
a.		Perf. 13½x14	55.00	32.50

St. Peter and His Tomb — SD6

85 l, Pius XII and Roman sepulcher.

Perf. 13½x13, 14

1953, Apr. 23   Engr.

| E13 | SD6 | 50 l blue grn & dk brn | .25 | .25 |
| E14 | SD6 | 85 l dp orange & dk brn | .35 | .25 |

Arms of Pope John XXIII SD7

1960   Photo.   Perf. 14

| E15 | SD7 | 75 l red & brown | .25 | .25 |
| E16 | SD7 | 100 l dk blue & brown | .25 | .25 |

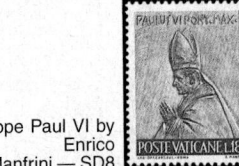

Pope Paul VI by Enrico Manfrini — SD8

Design: 150 l, Papal arms.

1966, Mar. 8   Wmk. 235   Perf. 14

| E17 | SD8 | 150 l black brown | .25 | .25 |
| E18 | SD8 | 180 l brown | .25 | .25 |

POSTAGE DUE STAMPS

Nos. 1-3 Overprinted in Black and Brown

1931, Oct. 1   Unwmk.   Perf. 14

J1	A1	5c dk brown & pink	.35	.75
a.		Double frame		
J2	A1	10c dk grn & lt grn	.35	.75
a.		Frame omitted	5,250.	
J3	A1	20c violet & lilac	1.90	2.25

No. 5 Surcharged

| J4 | A1 | 40c on 30c indigo & yel | 2.25 | 6.00 |

Nos. 10-11 Surcharged

J5	A2	60c on 2 l olive brn	40.00	30.00
J6	A2	1.10 l on 2.50 l red org	11.00	22.50
		Nos. J1-J6 (6)	55.85	62.25
		Set, never hinged	235.00	

In addition to the surcharges, #J4-J6 are overprinted with ornamental frame as on #J1-J3.

No. J5 is valued in the grade of fine.

> Catalogue values for unused stamps in this section, from this point to the end of the section, are for Never Hinged items.

Papal Arms — D1

Unwmk.

1945, Aug. 16   Typo.   Perf. 14

J7	D1	5c black & yellow	.25	.25
J8	D1	20c black & lilac	.25	.25
J9	D1	80c black & salmon	.25	.25
J10	D1	1 l black & green	.25	.25
J11	D1	2 l black & blue	.25	.25
J12	D1	5 l black & gray	.25	.25
a.		Imperf., pair	150.00	150.00
		Nos. J7-J12 (6)	1.50	1.50

A second type of Nos. J7-J12 exists, in which the colored lines of the background are thicker.

The 20c and 5 lire exist in horizontal pairs imperf. vertically. Value, each $100.

The 20c exists in horizontal pairs imperf. between. Value $275.

Papal Arms — D2

Perf. 13½x13

1954, Apr. 30   Wmk. 235   Engr.

J13	D2	4 l black & rose	.25	.25
J14	D2	6 l black & green	.30	.30
J15	D2	10 l black & yellow	.25	.25
J16	D2	20 l black & blue	.55	.55
J17	D2	50 l black & ol brn	.25	.25
J18	D2	70 l black & red brn	.25	.25
		Nos. J13-J18 (6)	1.85	1.85

Papal Arms — D3

Photo. & Engr.
1968, May 28   Wmk. 235   Perf. 14

J19	D3	10 l black, *grysh bl*	.25	.25
J20	D3	20 l black, *pale bl*	.25	.25
J21	D3	50 l black, *pale lil rose*	.25	.25
J22	D3	60 l black, *gray*	.25	.25
J23	D3	100 l black, *dull yel*	.25	.25
J24	D3	180 l black, *bluish lil*	.25	.25
		Nos. J19-J24 (6)	1.50	1.50

PARCEL POST STAMPS

Nos. 1-7 Overprinted

1931, Oct. 1   Unwmk.   Perf. 14

Q1	A1	5c dk brown & pink	.25	.55
Q2	A1	10c dk grn & lt grn	.25	.55
Q3	A1	20c violet & lilac	7.50	2.60
Q4	A1	25c dk bl & lt bl	11.00	5.50
Q5	A1	30c indigo & yel	7.50	5.50
Q6	A1	50c indigo & sal buff	7.50	5.50
Q7	A1	75c brn car & gray	1.50	5.50
a.		Inverted overprint	750.00	

Nos. 8-13 Overprinted

Q8	A2	80c carmine rose	1.10	5.50
Q9	A2	1.25 l dark blue	1.50	5.50
Q10	A2	2 l olive brown	1.10	5.50
a.		Inverted overprint	750.00	900.00
Q11	A2	2.50 l red orange	1.90	5.50
a.		Double overprint	750.00	
b.		Inverted overprint	1,350.	
Q12	A2	5 l dark green	1.90	5.50
Q13	A2	10 l olive black	1.50	5.50
a.		Double overprint	950.00	

Nos. E1-E2
Overprinted
Vertically

Q14	SD1	2 l carmine rose	1.50	5.50
Q15	SD1	2.50 l dark blue	1.50	5.50
a.		Inverted overprint	750.00	
		Nos. Q1-Q15 (15)	47.50	69.70
		Set, never hinged	160.00	

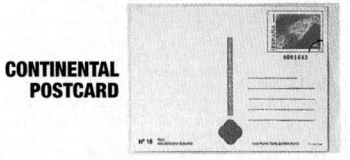

VENEZUELA

ˌve-nə-ˈzwā-lə

LOCATION — Northern coast of South America, bordering on the Caribbean Sea
GOVT. — Republic
AREA — 352,143 sq. mi.
POP. — 23,203,466 (1999 est.)
CAPITAL — Caracas

100 Centavos = 8 Reales = 1 Peso
100 Centesimos = 1 Venezolano (1879)
100 Centimos = 1 Bolivar (1880)

Watermark

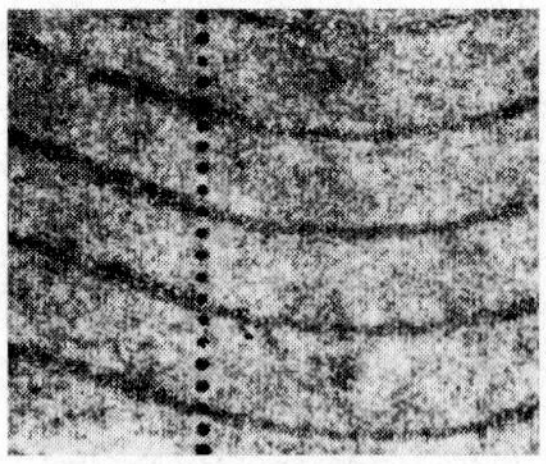

Wmk. 346

Catalogue values for unused stamps in this country are for Never Hinged items, beginning with Scott 743 in the regular postage section, Scott B2 in the semi-postal section, Scott C709 in the airpost section, and Scott E1 in the special delivery section.

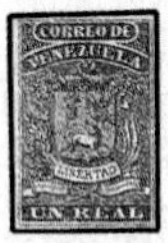

Coat of Arms — A1

Fine Impression
No Dividing Line Between Stamps

Unwmk.

1859, Jan. 1 Litho. *Imperf.*

1 A1 ½r yellow 60.00 12.00
a. ½r orange — —
b. Greenish paper *225.00*
2 A1 1r blue 450.00 15.00
a. Half used as ½r on cover *7,500.*
3 A1 2r red 42.50 15.00
a. 2r dull rose red 55.00 17.00
b. Half used as 1r on cover *1,250.*
c. Greenish paper 225.00 140.00
Nos. 1-3 (3) 552.50 42.00

Coarse Impression

1859-62 Thick Paper

4 A1 ½r orange ('61) 12.00 4.00
a. ½r yellow ('59) 500.00 30.00
b. ½r olive yellow 750.00 35.00
c. Bluish paper 575.00
d. ½r dull rose (error) 250,000. 350,000.
5 A1 1r blue ('62) 20.00 12.50
a. 1r pale blue 35.00 15.00
b. 1r dark blue 35.00 15.00
c. Half used as ½r on cover *7,500.*
d. Bluish paper 200.00
6 A1 2r red ('62) 45.00 80.00
a. 2r dull rose 55.00 80.00
b. Tête bêche pair *10,000.*
c. Half used as 1r on cover *400.00*
d. Bluish paper *225.00*
Nos. 4-6 (3) 77.00 96.50

In the fine impression, the background lines of the shield are more sharply drawn. In the coarse impression, the shading lines at each end of the scroll inscribed "LIBERTAD" are usually very heavy. Stamps of the coarse impression are closer together, and there is usually a dividing line between them.

Nos. 1-3 exist on thick paper and on bluish paper. Nos. 1-6 exist on pelure paper.

The greenish paper varieties (Nos. 1b and 3c) and the bluish paper varieties were not regularly issued.

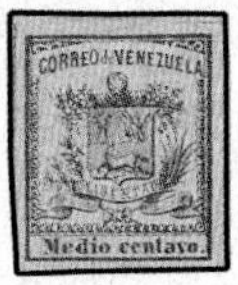

Arms — A2

1862 Litho.

7 A2 ¼c green 20.00 *200.00*
8 A2 ½c dull lilac 8.00 *240.00*
a. ½c violet 40.00 210.00
9 A2 1c gray brown 42.50 *400.00*
Nos. 7-9 (3) 70.50 *840.00*

Counterfeits are plentiful. Forged cancellations abound on Nos. 7-17.

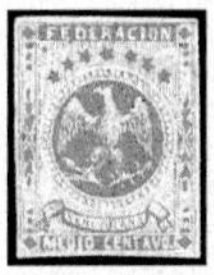

Eagle — A3

1863-64

10 A3 ½c pale red ('64) 55.00 *400.00*
a. ½c red 60.00 *400.00*
11 A3 1c slate ('64) 62.50 *160.00*
12 A3 ½r orange 7.75 3.50
13 A3 1r blue 17.00 8.50
a. 1r pale blue 30.00 13.00
b. Half used as ½r on cover *750.00*
14 A3 2r green 23.00 20.00
a. 2r deep yellow green 30.00 20.00
b. Quarter used as ½r on cover *7,500.*
c. Half used as 1r on cover *2,000.*

Counterfeits exist.

1865 Redrawn

15 A3 ½r orange 4.00 *2.50*

The redrawn stamp has a broad "N" in "FEDERACION." "MEDIO REAL" and "FEDERACION" are in thin letters. There are 52 instead of 49 pearls in the circle.

No. 15 in yellow is a postal forgery.

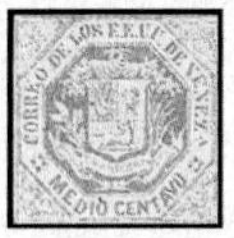

A4

1865-70

16 A4 ½c yel grn ('67) 275.00 *300.00*
17 A4 1c bl grn ('67) 275.00 *250.00*
18 A4 ½r brn vio (thin paper) 9.50 2.00
19 A4 ½r lil rose ('70) 9.50 3.25
a. ½r brownish rose 9.50 3.00
b. Tête bêche pair 200.00 *600.00*
20 A4 1r vermilion 45.00 15.00
a. Half used as ½r on cover *500.00*
21 A4 2r yellow 160.00 77.50
a. Half used as 1r on cover *3,000.*
Nos. 16-21 (6) 774.00 *647.75*

This issue is known unofficially rouletted.

Postal forgeries exist of the ½r.

One quarter of #21 used as ½r is a postal forgery.

For overprints see Nos. 37-48.

Overprinted in Very Small Upright Letters "Bolivar Sucre Miranda — Decreto de 27 de Abril de 1870", or "Decreto de 27 de Junio 1870" in Slanting Letters

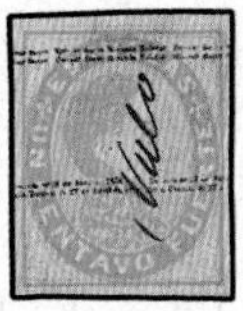

Simón Bolívar — A5

(The "Junio" overprint is continuously repeated, in four lines arranged in two pairs, with the second line of each pair inverted.)

Un	1	Siete	7
Dos	2	Nueve	9
Tres	3	Quince	15
Cuatro	4	Veinte	20
Cinco	5	Cincuenta	50

1871-76 Litho.

22 A5 1c yellow 1.50 .40
a. 1c orange 2.10 .45
b. 1c brown orange ('76) 2.10 .30
c. 1c pale buff ('76) 2.10 .45
d. Laid paper 1.00 .75
23 A5 2c yellow 2.00 .45
a. 2c orange 4.00 .45
b. 2c brown orange 3.50 .75
c. 2c pale buff ('76) 3.50 .45
d. Laid paper 3.50 .55
e. Frame inverted *4,000.* *3,000.*
24 A5 3c yellow 3.00 .75
a. 3c orange 3.00 1.40
b. 3c pale buff ('76) 5.50 1.75
25 A5 4c yellow 4.00 .75
a. 4c orange 4.50 1.25
b. 4c brown orange ('76) 4.50 1.25
c. 4c buff ('76) 4.50 1.25
26 A5 5c yellow 4.00 .75
a. 5c orange 4.00 .90
b. 5c pale buff ('76) 4.00 .90
c. Laid paper 7.50 .90
27 A5 1r rose 4.00 2.00
a. 1r pale red 4.00 2.00
b. Laid paper 6.00 2.50
c. Half used as ½r on cover *1,500.*
28 A5 2r rose 4.50 2.00
a. 2r pale red 4.50 2.00
b. Laid paper 12.00 2.50
29 A5 3r rose 6.00 2.00
a. 3r pale red 6.00 2.00
30 A5 5r rose 5.75 1.00
a. 5r pale red 5.75 1.00
31 A5 7r rose 22.50 4.00
a. 7r pale red 22.50 4.00
32 A5 9r green 22.50 4.25
a. 9r olive green 22.50 6.00
33 A5 15r green 55.00 8.50
a. 15r gray green ('76) 55.00 8.50
b. Frame inverted *8,000.* *6,500.*
34 A5 20r green 77.50 20.00
a. Laid paper 110.00 35.00
35 A5 30r green 375.00 110.00
a. 30r gray green ('76) 600.00 160.00
b. Double overprint
36 A5 50r green 1,200. 300.00
a. 50r gray green ('76)
Nos. 22-34 (13) 212.25 46.85
Nos. 22-35 (14) 587.25 156.85

These stamps were made available for postage and revenue by official decree, and were the only stamps sold for postage in Venezuela from Mar., 1871 to Aug., 1873.

Due to lack of canceling handstamps, the majority of stamps were canceled with pen marks. Fiscal cancellations were also made with the pen. The values quoted are for pen-canceled stamps.

Different settings were used for the different overprints. Stamps with the upright letters were issued in 1871. Those with the slanting letters in one double line were issued in 1872-73. Those with the slanting overprint in two double lines were issued starting in 1874 from several different settings, those of 1877-78 showing much coarser impressions of the design than the earlier issues. The 7r and 9r are not known with this overprint. Stamps on laid paper (1875) are from a separate setting.

Stamps and Types of 1866-67 Overprinted in Two Lines of Very Small Letters Repeated Continuously

Overprinted "Estampillas de Correo — Contrasena"

1873, July 1

37 A4 ½r pale rose 70.00 13.00
a. ½r rose 70.00 13.00
b. Inverted overprint 175.00 75.00
c. Tête bêche pair *3,000.* *2,000.*
38 A4 1r vermilion 85.00 25.00
a. Inverted overprint — —
b. Half used as ½r on cover *5,500.*
39 A4 2r yellow 300.00 125.00
a. Inverted overprint — —
b. Half used as 1r on cover *12,000.*
Nos. 37-39 (3) 455.00 163.00

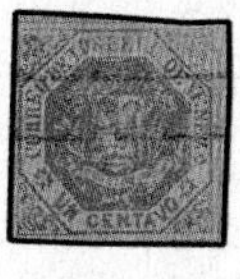

Overprinted "Contrasena — Estampillas de Correo"

1873, Nov.

40 A4 1c gray lilac 30.00 32.50
a. Inverted overprint 6.50 *17.00*
41 A4 2c green 125.00 90.00
a. Inverted overprint 40.00 50.00
b. As "a," half used as 1c on cover *7,500.*
42 A4 ½r rose 72.50 13.00
a. Inverted overprint 30.00 4.00
b. ½r pink 60.00 11.00
43 A4 1r vermilion 85.00 23.00
a. Inverted overprint 35.00 9.00
b. Half used as ½r on cover *300.00*
44 A4 2r yellow 325.00 160.00
a. Inverted overprint 110.00 50.00
b. Half used as 1r on cover *10,000.*
Nos. 40-44 (5) 637.50 318.50

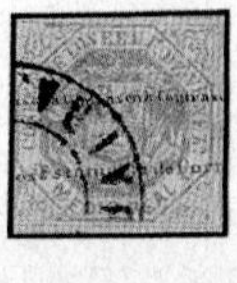

Overprinted "Contrasena — Estampilla de Correos"

1875

45 A4 ½r rose 85.00 10.00
a. Inverted overprint 125.00 25.00
b. Double overprint 160.00 90.00
46 A4 1r vermilion 160.00 15.00
a. Inverted overprint 200.00 80.00
b. Tête bêche pair *3,500.* *3,000.*
c. Half used as ½r on cover *3,500.*

Overprinted "Estampillas de correo — Contrasena"

1876-77

47 A4 ½r rose 77.50 9.25
a. ½r pink 65.00 7.50
b. Inverted overprint 65.00 7.50
c. Both lines of overprint read "Contrasena" 75.00 17.50
d. Both lines of overprint read "Estampillas de correo" 75.00 17.50
e. Double overprint 125.00 35.00
48 A4 1r vermilion ('77) 92.50 23.00
a. Inverted overprint 85.00 24.00
b. Tête bêche pair *2,250.* *2,500.*
c. Half used as ½r on cover —

On Nos. 47 and 48 "correo" has a small "c" instead of a capital. Nos. 45 and 46 have the overprint in slightly larger letters than the other stamps of the 1873-76 issues.

Overprinted "Decreto de 27 Junio 1870" Twice, One Line Inverted

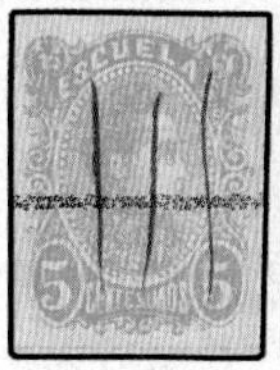 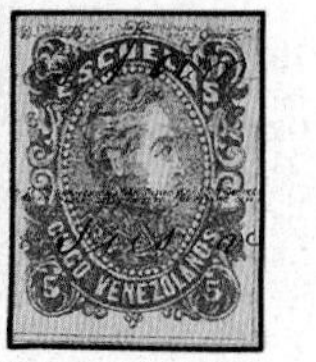

Simón Bolívar
A6 A7

1879 *Imperf.*

49 A6 1c yellow 4.00 1.00
a. 1c orange 5.00 1.50
b. 1c olive yellow 5.50 1.75
50 A6 5c yellow 3.50 .50
a. 5c orange 2.50 .75
b. Double overprint 20.00 10.00
51 A6 10c blue 5.00 .50
52 A6 30c blue 7.75 1.00
53 A6 50c blue 7.75 1.00
54 A6 90c blue 40.00 12.00
55 A7 1v rose red 77.50 18.00
56 A7 3v rose red 130.00 55.00
57 A7 5v rose red 225.00 77.50
Nos. 49-57 (9) 500.50 166.50

In 1879 and the early part of 1880 there were no regular postage stamps in Venezuela and the stamps inscribed "Escuelas" were permitted to serve for postal as well as revenue purposes. Postally canceled stamps are extremely scarce. Values quoted are for stamps with cancellations of banks or business houses or with pen cancellations. Stamps with pen marks removed are sometimes offered as unused stamps, or may have fraudulent postal cancellations added.

Nos. 49-57 exist without overprint. These are proofs.

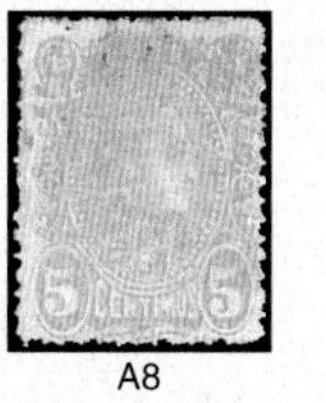 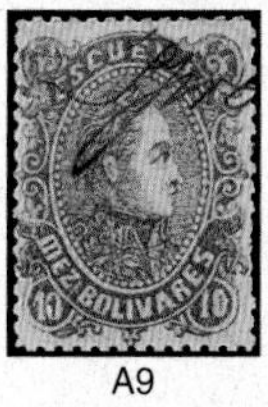

A8 A9

1880 *Perf. 11*

58 A8 5c yellow 1.50 .50
a. 5c orange 1.50 .50
b. Printed on both sides 150.00 85.00
59 A8 10c yellow 2.50 .60
a. 10c orange 2.50 .60
60 A8 25c yellow 2.50 .60
a. 25c orange 2.75 .70
b. Printed on both sides 110.00 52.50
c. Impression of 5c on back *175.00* 90.00
61 A8 50c yellow 4.75 .80
a. 50c orange 5.25 .85
b. Half used as 25c on cover —
c. Printed on both sides 150.00 90.00
d. Impression of 25c on back 150.00 90.00
62 A9 1b pale blue 12.00 1.40
63 A9 2b pale blue 17.00 1.75
64 A9 5b pale blue 40.00 5.75
a. Half used as 2½b on cover —
65 A9 10b rose red 200.00 70.00
66 A9 20b rose red 1,200. 200.00
67 A9 25b rose red *5,000.* 500.00
Nos. 58-65 (8) 280.25 81.40

See note on used values below No. 57.

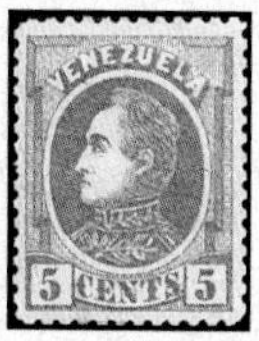
Bolívar — A10

1880 Litho. *Perf. 11*
Thick or Thin Paper

68	A10	5c blue	15.00	7.25
a.		Printed on both sides	225.00	140.00
69	A10	10c rose	20.00	12.00
a.		10c carmine	20.00	12.00
b.		Double impression	90.00	75.00
c.		Horiz. pair, imperf. btwn.	75.00	75.00
70	A10	10c scarlet	20.00	12.00
a.		Horiz. pair, imperf. btwn.	75.00	75.00
71	A10	25c yellow	15.00	7.25
b.		Thick paper	20.00	10.00
72	A10	50c brown	92.50	40.00
a.		50c deep brown	92.50	40.00
b.		Printed on both sides	225.00	140.00
c.		Half used as 25c on cover		*5,000.*
73	A10	1b green	140.00	50.00
a.		Horiz. pair, imperf. btwn.	300.00	300.00
		Nos. 68-73 (6)	302.50	128.50

Nos. 68 to 73 were used for the payment of postage on letters to be sent abroad and the Escuelas stamps were then restricted to internal use.

Counterfeits of this issue exist in a great variety of shades as well as in wrong colors. They are on thick and thin paper, white or toned, and imperf. or perforated 11, 12 and compound. They are also found téte bêche. Counterfeits of Nos. 68 to 72 inclusive often have a diagonal line across the "S" of "CENTS" and a short line from the bottom of that letter to the frame below it. Originals of No. 73 show parts of a frame around "BOLIVAR."

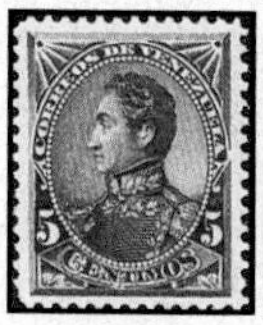
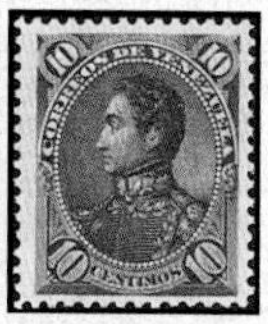
Simón Bolívar
A11 A12

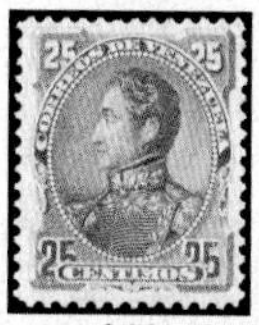
A13

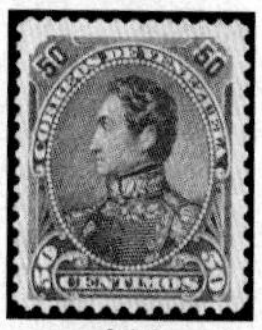
A14

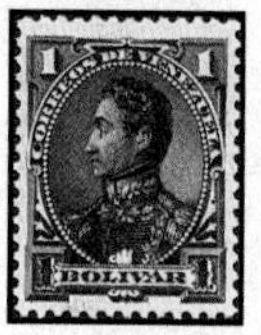
A15

1882, Aug. 1 Engr. *Perf. 12*

74	A11	5c blue	.70	.35
75	A12	10c red brown	.70	.35
76	A13	25c yellow brown	1.10	.40
a.		Printed on both sides	50.00	27.50
77	A14	50c green	2.40	.70
a.		Half used as 25c on cover		*500.00*
78	A15	1b violet	4.50	1.75
		Nos. 74-78 (5)	9.40	3.55

Nos. 75-78 exist imperf. Value, set $32.50.

See Nos. 88, 92-95. For surcharges and overprints see Nos. 100-103, 108-112.

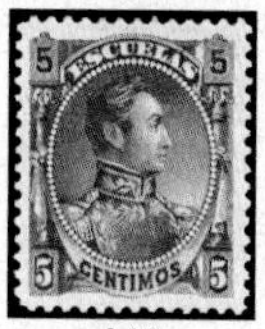
A16

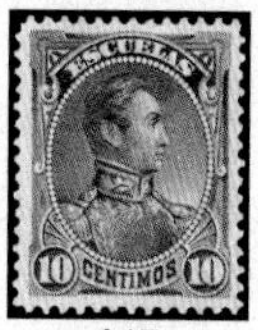
A17

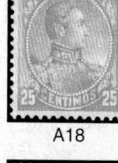

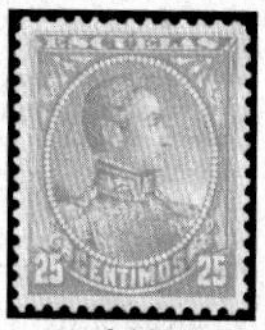
A18

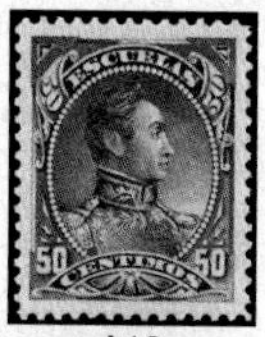
A19

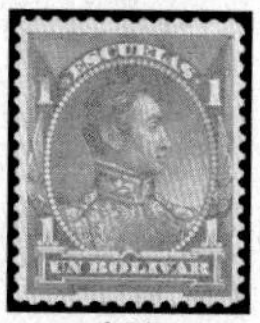
A20

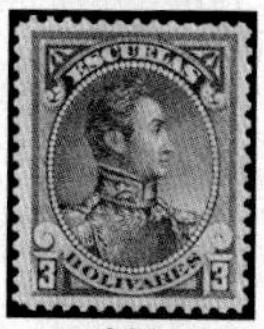
A21

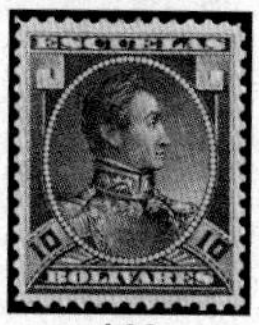
A22

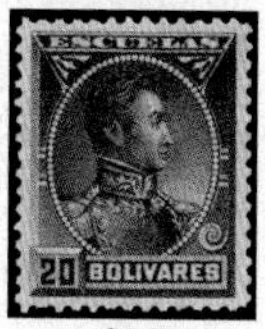
A23

1882-88

79	A16	5c blue green	.25	.25
80	A17	10c brown	.25	.25
81	A18	25c orange	.25	.25
82	A19	50c blue	.25	.25
83	A20	1b vermilion	.25	.25
84	A21	3b dull vio ('88)	.25	.25
85	A22	10b dark brn ('88)	1.25	.80
86	A23	20b plum ('88)	1.50	.95
		Nos. 79-86 (8)	4.25	3.25

By official decree, dated Apr. 14, 1882, stamps of types A11 to A15 were to be used for foreign postage and those of types A16 to A23 for inland correspondence and fiscal use.

Issue date: Nos. 79-83, Aug. 1.

See Nos. 87, 89-91, 96-99. For surcharges and overprints see Nos. 104-107, 114-122.

1887-88 Litho. *Perf. 11*

87	A16	5c gray green	.45	.30
88	A13	25c yellow brown	55.00	22.50
89	A18	25c orange	.70	.45
90	A20	1b orange red ('88)	4.75	.90
		Nos. 87-90 (4)	60.90	24.15

Perf. 14

91	A16	5c gray green	95.00	40.00

Stamps of type A16, perf. 11 and 14, are from a new die with "ESCUELAS" in smaller letters. Stamps of the 1887-88 issue, perf. 12, and a 50c dark blue, perf. 11 or 12, are believed by experts to be from printer's waste.

Counterfeits of No. 91 have been made by perforating printers waste of No. 96.

Rouletted 8

92	A11	5c blue	40.00	17.00
93	A13	25c yel brown	15.00	10.00
94	A14	50c green	15.00	10.00
95	A15	1b purple	30.00	20.00
		Nos. 92-95 (4)	100.00	57.00

1887-88

96	A16	5c green	.25	.25
97	A18	25c orange	.25	.25
98	A19	50c dark blue	1.25	1.10
99	A21	3b purple ('88)	3.50	3.50
		Nos. 96-99 (4)	5.25	5.10

The so-called imperforate varieties of Nos. 92 to 99, and the pin perforated 50c dark blue, type A19, are believed to be from printer's waste.

Stamps of 1882-88 Handstamp Surcharged in Violet

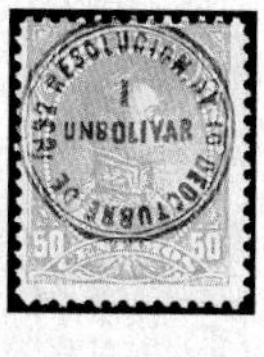

1892 *Perf. 12*

100	A11	25c on 5c blue	*40.00*	*40.00*
101	A12	25c on 10c red brn	*16.00*	*16.00*
102	A13	1b on 25c yel brn	*16.00*	*16.00*
103	A14	1b on 50c green	*20.00*	*20.00*
		Nos. 100-103 (4)	*92.00*	*92.00*

See note after No. 107.

1892

104	A16	25c on 5c bl grn	*10.00*	*6.00*
105	A17	25c on 10c brown	*10.00*	*6.00*
106	A18	1b on 25c orange	*15.00*	*12.00*
107	A19	1b on 50c blue	*23.00*	*12.00*
		Nos. 104-107 (4)	*58.00*	*36.00*

Counterfeits of this surcharge abound.

Stamps of 1882-88 Overprinted in Red or Black

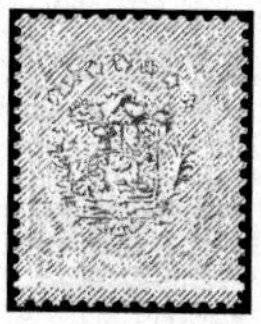

1893

108	A11	5c blue (R)	.55	.25
a.		Inverted overprint	3.25	3.25
b.		Double overprint	16.00	16.00
109	A12	10c red brn (Bk)	.90	.90
a.		Inverted overprint	4.00	4.00
b.		Double overprint	16.00	16.00
110	A13	25c yel brn (R)	.80	.50
a.		Inverted overprint	5.25	5.25
b.		Double overprint	16.00	16.00
c.		25c yel brn (Bk)	*500.00*	*500.00*
111	A14	50c green (R)	1.25	.80
a.		Inverted overprint	5.25	5.25
b.		Double overprint	27.50	27.50
112	A15	1b pur (R)	3.25	1.20
a.		Inverted overprint	10.00	10.00
		Nos. 108-112 (5)	6.75	3.65

1893

114	A16	5c bl grn (R)	.25	.25
a.		Inverted overprint	3.25	3.25
b.		Double overprint	5.25	5.25
115	A17	10c brn (R)	.25	.25
a.		Inverted overprint	3.25	3.25
116	A18	25c org (R)	.25	.25
a.		Inverted overprint	3.25	3.25
117	A18	25c org (Bk)	5.75	2.75
a.		Inverted overprint	8.25	5.00
118	A19	50c blue (R)	.25	.25
a.		Inverted overprint	3.25	3.25
119	A20	1b ver (Bk)	.60	.40
a.		Inverted overprint	4.00	4.00
120	A21	3b dl vio (R)	.90	.40
a.		Double overprint	8.25	8.25
121	A22	10b dk brn (R)	3.50	2.25
a.		Double overprint	10.00	10.00
b.		Inverted overprint	20.00	20.00
122	A23	20b plum (Bk)	3.00	3.00
a.		Double overprint	10.00	20.00
b.		Inverted overprint		
		Nos. 114-122 (9)	14.75	9.80

Counterfeits exist.

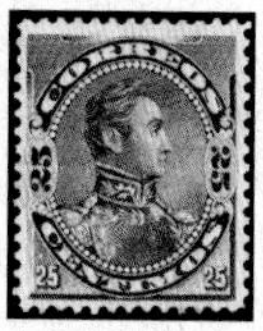
Simón Bolívar — A24

1893 Engr.

123	A24	5c red brn	.90	.25
124	A24	10c blue	3.25	1.25
125	A24	25c magenta	15.00	.50
126	A24	50c brn vio	4.25	.55
127	A24	1b green	5.75	1.25
		Nos. 123-127 (5)	29.15	3.80

Many shades exist in this issue, but their values do not vary.

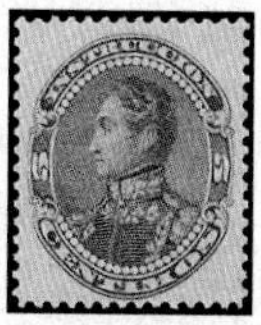
Simón Bolívar — A25

1893

128	A25	5c gray	.25	.25
129	A25	10c green	.25	.25
130	A25	25c blue	.25	.25
131	A25	50c orange	.25	.25
132	A25	1b red vio	.25	.25
133	A25	3b red	.55	.25
134	A25	10b dl vio	.90	.80
135	A25	20b red brn	4.25	2.75
		Nos. 128-135 (8)	6.95	5.05

By decree of Nov. 28, 1892, the stamps inscribed "Correos" were to be used for external postage and those inscribed "Instruccion" were for internal postage and revenue purposes.

For surcharge see No. 230.

After July 1, 1895, stamps inscribed "Escuelas" or "Instruccion" were no longer available for postage. Stamps of design A25 in shades different than those listed were printed after 1895.

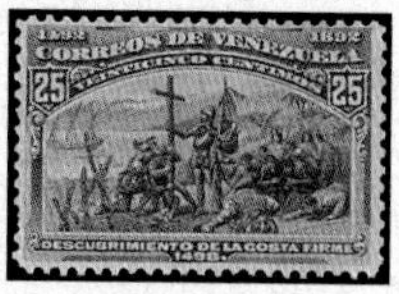
Landing of Columbus
A26

1893 *Perf. 12*

136	A26	25c magenta	11.00	.60

4th cent. of the discovery of the mainland of South America, also participation of Venezuela in the Intl. Exhib. at Chicago in 1893.

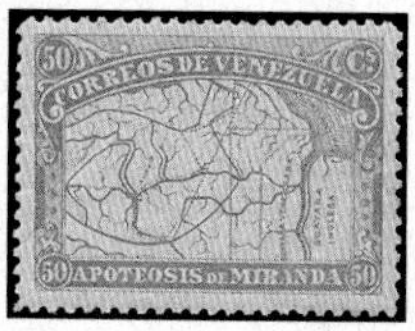
Map of Venezuela
A27

1896 Litho.

137	A27	5c yel grn	3.00	2.75
a.		5c apple green	3.00	2.75
138	A27	10c blue	4.00	5.50
139	A27	25c yellow	4.00	5.50
a.		25c orange	4.00	5.50
b.		Tête bêche pair	125.00	125.00
140	A27	50c rose red	55.00	25.00
a.		50c red	52.50	52.50
b.		Tête bêche pair	375.00	375.00
141	A27	1b violet	40.00	27.50
		Nos. 137-141 (5)	106.00	66.25

Gen. Francisco Antonio Gabriel de Miranda (1752-1816).

These stamps were in use from July 4 to Nov. 4, 1896. Later usage is known.

There are many forgeries of this issue. They include faked errors, imperforate stamps and many tête bêche. The paper of the originals is thin, white and semi-transparent. The gum is shiny and crackled. The paper of the reprints is often thick and opaque. The gum is usually dull, smooth, thin and only slightly adhesive.

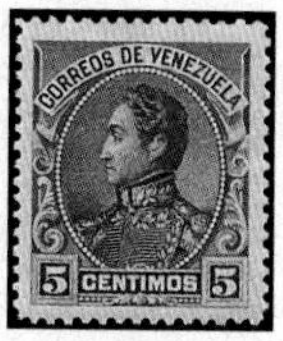
Bolívar — A28

1899-1901 Engr.

142	A28	5c dk grn	1.00	.25
143	A28	10c red	1.25	.40
144	A28	25c blue	1.50	.55
145	A28	50c gray blk	2.00	1.00
146	A28	50c org ('01)	1.75	.50
147	A28	1b yel grn	32.50	15.00
149	A28	2b orange	400.00	225.00
		Nos. 142-147,149 (7)	440.00	242.70

Stamps of 1899 Overprinted in Black

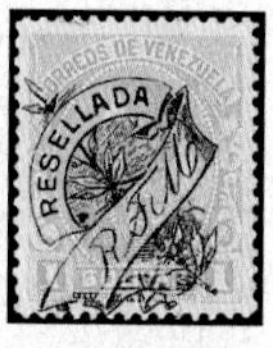

1900

150	A28	5c dk grn	1.25	.40
a.		Inverted overprint	4.75	4.75
151	A28	10c red	1.25	.40
a.		Inverted overprint	6.50	6.50
b.		Double overprint	10.50	10.50
152	A28	25c blue	7.75	1.25
a.		Inverted overprint	13.00	13.00
153	A28	50c gray blk	4.00	.55
a.		Inverted overprint	12.00	12.00
154	A28	1b yel grn	1.75	.80
a.		Double overprint	13.00	13.00
b.		Inverted overprint	12.00	12.00
155	A28	2b orange	2.75	2.25
a.		Inverted overprint	35.00	35.00
b.		Double overprint	32.50	32.50
		Nos. 150-155 (6)	18.75	5.65

Initials are those of R. T. Mendoza.

Counterfeit overprints exist, especially of inverted and doubled varieties.

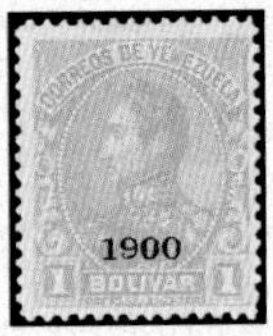

Bolivar Type of 1899-1903 Overprinted

1900

No.	Type	Description	Unused	Used
156	A28	5c dk grn	750.00	750.00
157	A28	10c red	750.00	750.00
158	A28	25c blue	600.00	600.00
159	A28	50c yel orange	23.00	1.60
160	A28	1b slate	1.25	1.00
a.		Without overprint	7,000.	—
		Nos. 156-160 (5)	2,124.	2,102.

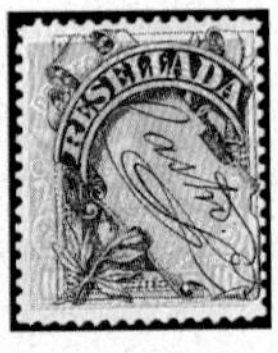

Nos. 156-158 Overprinted

1900, Aug. 14

No.	Type	Description	Unused	Used
161	A28	5c green	8.00	.55
162	A28	10c red	7.00	1.00
163	A28	25c blue	8.00	1.00
		Nos. 161-163 (3)	23.00	2.55

Inverted Overprint

No.	Type	Description	Unused	Used
161a	A28	5c	9.25	9.25
162a	A28	10c	9.25	9.25
163a	A28	25c	12.00	12.00
		Nos. 161a-163a (3)	30.50	30.50

Overprint exists on each value without "Castro" or without "1900."

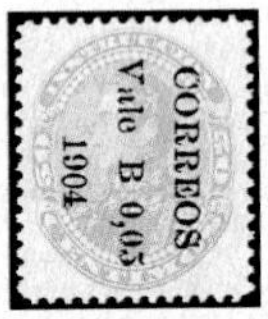

Type of 1893 Surcharged

1904, Jan. *Perf. 12*

No.	Type	Description	Unused	Used
230	A25	5c on 50c green	.80	.60
a.		"Vele"	23.00	23.00
b.		Surcharge reading up	1.00	.50
c.		Double surcharge	18.00	18.00

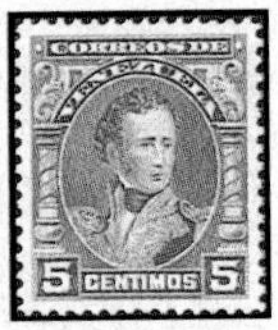

Gen. José de Sucre — A35

1904-09 **Engr.**

No.	Type	Description	Unused	Used
231	A35	5c bl grn	.50	.25
232	A35	10c carmine	.55	.25
233	A35	15c violet	.90	.40
234	A35	25c dp ultra	6.50	.40
235	A35	50c plum	1.00	.50
236	A35	1b plum	1.10	.50
		Nos. 231-236 (6)	10.55	2.30

Issue date: 15c, Dec. 1909. Others, July 1, 1904.

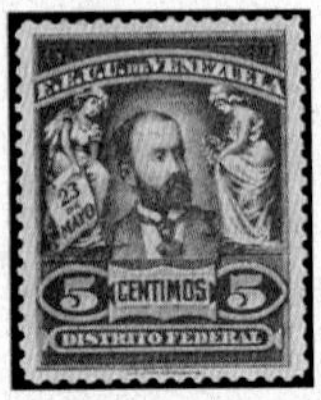

Pres. Cipriano Castro — A37

1905, July 5 **Litho.** *Perf. 11½*

No.	Type	Description	Unused	Used
245	A37	5c vermilion	3.25	3.25
a.		5c carmine	5.00	5.00
246	A37	10c dark blue	5.50	4.25
247	A37	25c yellow	2.00	1.50
		Nos. 245-247 (3)	10.75	9.00

National Congress. Issued for interior postage only. Valid only for 90 days.

Various part-perforate varieties of Nos. 245-247 exist. Value, $15-$30.

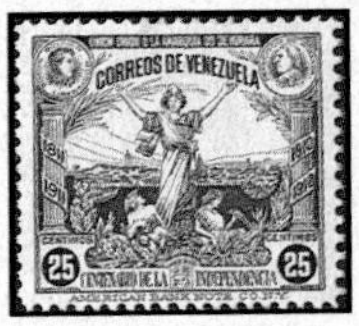

Liberty — A38

1910, Apr. 19 **Engr.** *Perf. 12*

No.	Type	Description	Unused	Used
249	A38	25c dark blue	13.00	.70

Centenary of national independence.

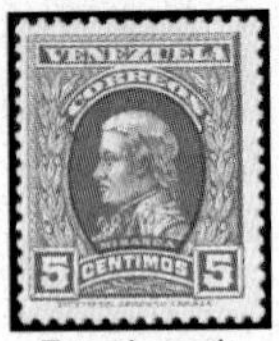

Francisco de Miranda A39

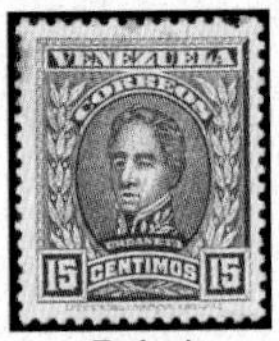

Rafael Urdaneta A40

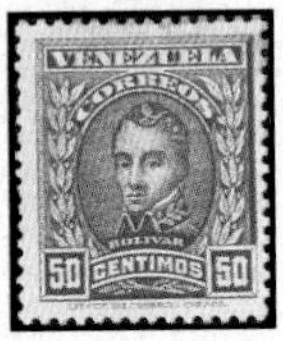

Bolívar — A41

1911 **Litho.** *Perf. 11½x12*

No.	Type	Description	Unused	Used
250	A39	5c dp grn	.50	.25
251	A39	10c carmine	.50	.25
252	A40	15c gray	5.75	.40
253	A40	25c dp bl	3.25	.60
a.		Imperf., pair	40.00	50.00
254	A41	50c purple	3.50	.40
255	A41	1b yellow	3.50	1.50
		Nos. 250-255 (6)	17.00	3.40

The 50c with center in blue was never issued although examples were postmarked by favor.

The centers of Nos. 250-255 were separately printed and often vary in shade from the rest of the design. In a second printing of the 5c and 10c, the entire design was printed at one time.

1913 **Redrawn**

No.	Type	Description	Unused	Used
255A	A40	15c gray	3.50	2.25
255B	A40	25c deep blue	2.00	.65
255C	A41	50c purple	2.00	.65
		Nos. 255A-255C (3)	7.50	3.55

The redrawn stamps have two berries instead of one at top of the left spray; a berry has been added over the "C" and "S" of "Centimos"; and the lowest leaf at the right is cut by the corner square.

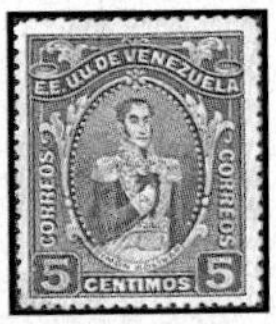

Simón Bolívar — A42

1914, July **Engr.** *Perf. 13½, 14, 15*

No.	Type	Description	Unused	Used
256	A42	5c yel grn	37.50	.55
257	A42	10c scarlet	35.00	.50
258	A42	25c dark blue	5.75	.25
		Nos. 256-258 (3)	78.25	1.30

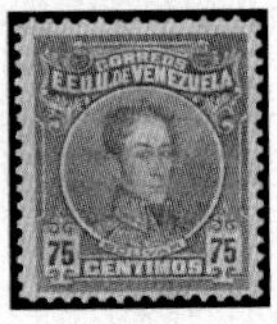

Simón Bolívar — A43

Different frames.

Printed by the American Bank Note Co.

1915-23 *Perf. 12*

No.	Type	Description	Unused	Used
259	A43	5c green	4.25	.25
260	A43	10c vermilion	10.00	.60
261	A43	10c claret ('22)	10.00	.90
262	A43	15c dull ol grn	9.25	.60
263	A43	25c ultra	6.50	.25
a.		25c blue	13.00	.60
264	A43	40c dull green	23.00	11.50
265	A43	50c dp violet	6.50	.80
266	A43	50c ultra ('23)	17.00	4.75
267	A43	75c lt blue	57.50	23.00
a.		75c greenish blue	57.50	23.00
268	A43	1b dark gray	35.00	5.25
		Nos. 259-268 (10)	179.00	47.90

See Nos. 269-285. For surcharges see Nos. 307, 309-310.

Type of 1915-23 Issue Re-engraved Printed by Waterlow & Sons, Ltd.

1924-39 *Perf. 12½*

No.	Type	Description	Unused	Used
269	A43	5c orange brn	.55	.25
a.		5c yellow brown	.55	.25
b.		Horiz. pair, imperf. between	25.00	40.00
270	A43	5c green ('39)	12.00	1.00
271	A43	7½c yel grn ('39)	1.25	.40
272	A43	10c dk green	.25	.25
273	A43	10c dk car ('39)	4.00	.25
274	A43	15c olive grn	2.25	.50
275	A43	15c brown ('27)	.30	.25
276	A43	25c ultra	2.25	.25
277	A43	25c red ('28)	.25	.25
a.		Horiz. pair, imperf. btwn.	50.00	85.00
278	A43	40c dp blue ('25)	.55	.25
279	A43	40c slate bl ('39)	7.75	1.25
280	A43	50c dk blue	.55	.25
281	A43	50c dk pur ('39)	7.75	.85
282	A43	1b black	.55	.25
283	A43	3b yel org ('25)	1.75	.95
284	A43	3b red org ('39)	12.00	4.25
285	A43	5b dull vio ('25)	16.00	8.50
		Nos. 269-285 (17)	70.00	19.95

Perf. 14

No.	Type	Description	Unused	Used
269c	A43	5c	7.00	2.00
272a	A43	10c	7.00	2.00
274a	A43	15c	8.25	2.75
276a	A43	25c	12.00	4.75
280a	A43	50c	35.00	14.00
282a	A43	1b	42.50	27.00
		Nos. 269c-282a (6)	111.75	52.50

The re-engraved stamps may readily be distinguished from the 1915 issue by the perforation and sometimes by the colors. The designs differ in many minor details which are too minute for illustration or description.

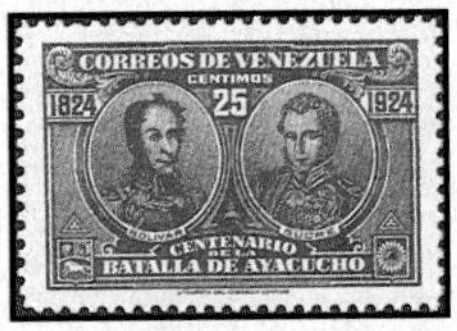

Bolívar and Sucre A44

Perf. 11½x12, 12

1924, Dec. 1 **Litho.**

No.	Type	Description	Unused	Used
286	A44	25c grayish blue	2.75	.55

Redrawn

No.	Type	Description	Unused	Used
286A	A44	25c ultra	3.50	.85

Centenary of the Battle of Ayacucho.

The redrawn stamp has a whiter effect with less shading in the faces. Bolívar's ear is clearly visible and the outline of his aquiline nose is broken.

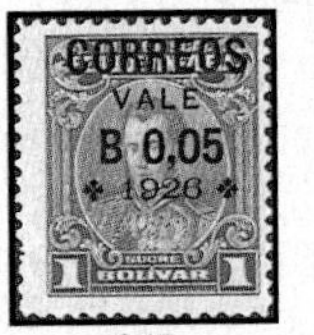

A45

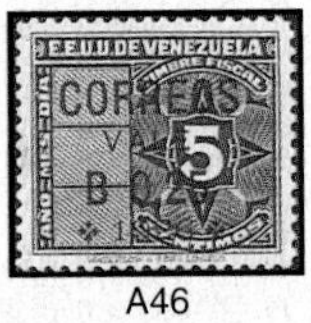

A46

Revenue Stamps Surcharged in Black or Red

1926 *Perf. 12, 12½*

No.	Type	Description	Unused	Used
287	A45	5c on 1b ol grn	.65	.40
a.		Double surcharge	8.00	8.00
b.		Pair, one without surcharge	12.00	12.00
c.		Inverted surcharge	8.00	8.00
288	A46	25c on 5c dk brn (R)	.65	.40
a.		Inverted surcharge	8.00	8.00
b.		Double surcharge	8.00	8.00

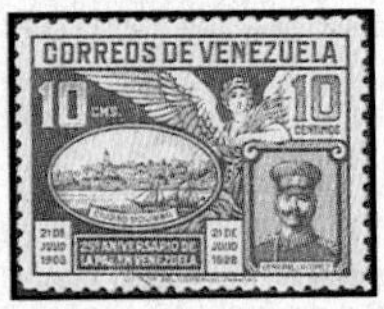

View of Ciudad Bolívar and General J.V. Gómez — A47

1928, July 21 **Litho.** *Perf. 12*

No.	Type	Description	Unused	Used
289	A47	10c deep green	1.00	.65
a.		Imperf., pair	40.00	

25th anniversary of the Battle of Ciudad Bolívar and the foundation of peace in Venezuela.

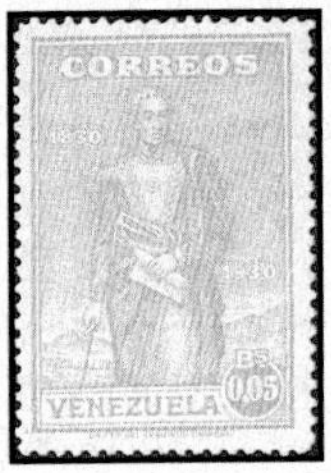

Simón Bolívar — A48

1930, Dec. 9

No.	Type	Description	Unused	Used
290	A48	5c yellow	1.00	.35
291	A48	10c dark blue	1.00	.25
292	A48	25c rose red	1.00	.25
		Nos. 290-292 (3)	3.00	.85

Imperf., Pairs

No.	Type	Description	Unused	Used
290a	A48	5c	5.25	5.25
291a	A48	10c	6.50	6.50
292a	A48	25c	10.50	10.50

Death centenary of Simón Bolívar (1783-1830), South American liberator.

Nos. 290-292 exist part-perforate, including pairs imperf. between, imperf. horiz., imperf. vert. Value range, $6-12.

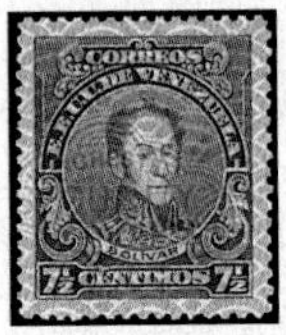

Simón Bolívar — A49

Various Frames

Bluish Winchester Security Paper

1932-38 **Engr.** *Perf. 12½*

No.	Type	Description	Unused	Used
293	A49	5c violet	.50	.25
294	A49	7½c dk green ('37)	1.10	.40
295	A49	10c green	.65	.25
296	A49	15c yellow	1.50	.25
297	A49	22½c dp car ('38)	3.50	.50
298	A49	25c red	1.25	.25
299	A49	37½c ultra ('36)	4.50	2.00
300	A49	40c indigo	4.50	.25
301	A49	50c olive grn	4.50	.40
302	A49	1b lt blue	6.00	.70
303	A49	3b brown	47.50	13.00
304	A49	5b yellow brn	65.00	17.50
		Nos. 293-304 (12)	140.50	35.75

For surcharges see Nos. 308, 318-319, C223.

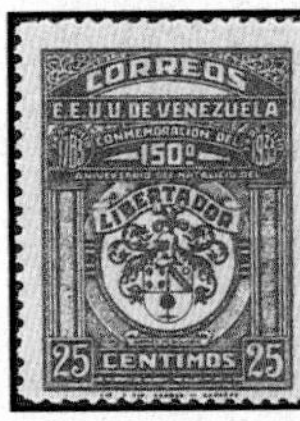

Arms of Bolívar — A50

1933, July 24 **Litho.** *Perf. 11*

No.	Type	Description	Unused	Used
306	A50	25c brown red	3.00	2.40
a.		Imperf., pair	32.50	32.50

150th anniv. of the birth of Simón Bolívar. Valid only to Aug. 21.

Stamps of 1924-32 Surcharged in Black — (Blocks of Surcharge in Color of stamps)

1933

No.	Type	Description	Unused	Used
307	A43	7½c on 10c grn	.50	.25
a.		Double surcharge	2.50	2.50
b.		Inverted surcharge	4.25	4.25
308	A49	22½c on 25c (#298)	2.00	.85
309	A43	22½c on 25c (#277)	1.50	1.50
a.		Double surcharge	10.00	10.00
310	A43	37½c on 40c dp bl	2.00	.95
a.		Double surcharge	11.50	11.50
b.		Inverted surcharge	10.00	10.00
		Nos. 307-310 (4)	6.00	3.55

Nurse and
Child — A51

River
Scene — A52

Gathering Cacao
Pods — A53

Cattle
Raising
A54

Plowing
A55

Perf. 11, 11½ or Compound

1937, July 1   Litho.

311	A51	5c deep violet	.55	.35
312	A52	10c dk slate grn	.55	.25
313	A53	15c yellow brn	1.00	.55
314	A51	25c cerise	1.00	.35
315	A54	50c yellow grn	6.50	4.25
316	A55	3b red orange	12.00	7.75
317	A51	5b lt brown	23.00	15.00
		Nos. 311-317 (7)	44.60	28.50

Nos. 311-317 exist imperforate. Value for
set $75. Nos. 311-315 exist in pairs, imperf.
between; value range, $20-$30.
For overprints and surcharges see Nos.
321-324, 345, 376-377, 380-384.

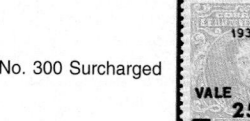

No. 300 Surcharged
in Black

1937, July   Perf. 12½

318	A49	25c on 40c indigo	7.75	.95
a.		Double surcharge	16.00	16.00
b.		Inverted surcharge	13.00	13.00
c.		Triple surcharge	32.50	32.50

No. 300 Surcharged

319	A49	25c on 40c indigo	440.00	350.00
a.		Double surcharge		

A56

1937, Oct. 28   Litho.   Perf. 10½

320	A56	25c blue	1.25	.45

Acquisition of the Port of La Guaira by the
Government from the British Corporation,
June 3, 1937. Exists imperf. See Nos. C64-
C65.
A redrawn printing of No. 320, with top
inscription beginning "Nacionalización . . ."
was prepared but not issued. Value, $40.
For surcharge see No. 385.

Stamps of 1937
Overprinted in Black

1937, Dec. 17   Perf. 11, 11½

321	A51	5c deep violet	5.75	3.25
322	A52	10c dk slate grn	1.75	.75
a.		Inverted overprint	13.00	13.00
323	A51	25c cerise	1.50	.55
a.		Inverted overprint	16.00	16.00
324	A55	3b red orange	375.00	225.00
		Nos. 321-324 (4)	384.00	229.55

Part-perforate pairs exist of Nos. 321-322
and 324. Value range, $12.50 to $125.
See Nos. C66-C78.

Gathering Coffee
Beans — A57

Simón
Bolívar — A58

Post Office,
Caracas — A59

1938   Engr.   Perf. 12

325	A57	5c green	.40	.25
326	A57	5c deep green	.40	.25
327	A58	10c car rose	.70	.25
328	A58	10c dp rose	.70	.25
329	A59	15c dk violet	1.40	.25
330	A59	15c olive grn	.85	.25
331	A58	25c lt blue	.40	.25
332	A58	25c dk blue	.40	.25
333	A58	37½c dk blue	8.50	4.00
334	A58	37½c lt blue	2.75	.85
335	A59	40c sepia	20.00	7.75
336	A59	40c black	17.00	7.75
337	A57	50c olive grn	27.50	7.75
338	A57	50c dull violet	9.25	.85
339	A58	1b dp brown	12.00	5.50
340	A58	1b black brown	17.00	1.50
341	A57	3b orange	92.50	50.00
342	A59	5b black	15.00	7.75
		Nos. 325-342 (18)	226.75	95.70

See Nos. 400, 412.

Teresa
Carreño — A60

1938, June 12   Perf. 11½x12

343	A60	25c blue	5.75	.60

Teresa Carreno, Venezuelan pianist, whose
remains were repatriated Feb. 14, 1938.
For surcharge see No. 386.

Bolívar Statue — A61

1938, July 24   Perf. 12

344	A61	25c dark blue	6.50	.60

"The Day of the Worker."
For surcharge see No. 387.

Type of 1937
Surcharged in Black

1938   Litho.   Perf. 11, 11½

345	A51	40c on 5b lt brn	8.50	4.50
a.		Inverted surcharge	21.00	21.00

Gen. José I. Paz
Castillo, Postmaster of
Venezuela, 1859 — A62

1939, Apr. 19   Engr.   Perf. 12½

348	A62	10c carmine	2.50	.70

80th anniv. of the first Venezuelan stamp.

View of
Ojeda
A63

1939, June 24   Photo.

349	A63	25c dull blue	9.25	.75

Founding of city of Ojeda.

Cristóbal
Mendoza — A64

1939, Oct. 14   Engr.   Perf. 13

350	A64	5c green	.40	.25
351	A64	10c dk car rose	.40	.25
352	A64	15c dull lilac	1.00	.25
353	A64	25c brt ultra	.80	.25
354	A64	37½c dark blue	15.00	6.25
355	A64	50c lt olive grn	16.00	4.00
356	A64	1b dark brown	6.50	3.50
		Nos. 350-356 (7)	40.10	14.75

Mendoza (1772-1839), postmaster general.

Diego Urbaneja — A65

1940-43   Perf. 12

357	A65	5c Prus green	.55	.25
357A	A65	7½c dk bl grn ('43)	.80	.30
358	A65	15c olive	.95	.30
359	A65	37½c deep blue	1.50	.70
360	A65	40c violet blue	1.10	.90
361	A65	50c violet	6.50	1.75
362	A65	1b dk violet brn	3.50	.90
363	A65	3b scarlet	9.50	3.75
		Nos. 357-363 (8)	24.40	8.30

See Nos. 399, 408, 410-411. For
surcharges see Nos. 396, C226.

Battle of
Carabobo,
1821 — A67

1940, June 13

365	A67	25c blue	6.75	.80

Birth of General JoséAntonio Páez, 150th
anniv.

"Crossing the
Andes" by Tito
Salas — A68

1940, June 13

366	A68	25c dark blue	6.75	.80

Death cent. of General Francisco Santander.

Monument and
Urn containing
Ashes of Simón
Bolívar — A69

Bed where Simón
Bolívar was
Born — A70

Designs: 15c, "Christening of Bolivar" by
Tito Salas. 20c, Bolivar's birthplace, Caracas.
25c, "Bolivar on Horseback" by Salas. 30c,
Patio of Bolivar House, Caracas. 37½c, Patio
of Bolivar's Birthplace. 50c, "Rebellion of
1812" by Salas.

1940-41

367	A69	5c turq green	.25	.25
368	A70	10c rose pink	.25	.25
369	A69	15c olive	.60	.25
370	A70	20c blue ('41)	1.00	.25
371	A69	25c lt blue	.60	.25
372	A70	30c plum ('41)	1.50	.25
373	A70	37½c dk blue	3.00	1.00
374	A70	50c purple	2.00	.50
		Nos. 367-374 (8)	9.20	3.00

110th anniv. of the death of Simón Bolívar.
See Nos. 397, 398, 403, 405-407, 409. For
surcharges see Nos. 375, 401-402, C224,
C237-C238.

No. 371 Surcharged
In Black

1941

375	A69	20c on 25c lt blue	.60	.25
a.		Inverted surcharge	10.00	10.00

Nos. 311-312
Overprinted in Black

1941   **Perf. 11½**
376 A51 5c deep violet   2.00 .50
  a. Double overprint   10.00 8.25
  b. Vert. pair, imperf. btwn.   14.00 14.00
  c. Inverted overprint   20.00 16.00
377 A52 10c dk slate grn   1.00 .30
  a. Double overprint   13.00 13.00

Symbols of
Industry — A77

1942, Dec. 17   Litho.   Perf. 12
378 A77 10c scarlet   1.10 .25
  a. Imperf., pair   22.50 22.50

Grand Industrial Exposition, Caracas.

Caracas
Cathedral — A78

1943   **Engr.**
379 A78 10c rose carmine   .75 .25

See No. 404.

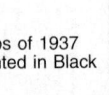

Stamps of 1937
Overprinted in Black

1943   **Perf. 11, 11½**
380 A51 5c deep violet   16.00 9.50
381 A52 10c dk slate grn   6.00 4.00
382 A54 50c yellow green   8.00 4.50
383 A55 3b red orange   45.00 22.00
  Nos. 380-383 (4)   75.00 40.00

Issued for sale to philatelists & sold only in
sets.

Stamps of 1937-38
Surcharged in Black

1943   **Perf. 11½, 10½, 12**
384 A51 20c on 25c cerise   30.00 30.00
385 A56 20c on 25c blue   77.50 77.50
386 A60 20c on 25c dk blue   15.00 15.00
387 A61 20c on 25c dk blue   15.00 15.00
  a. Inverted surcharge   42.50 42.50
  Nos. 384-387 (4)   137.50 137.50

Issued for sale to philatelists & sold only in
sets.

Souvenir Sheet

A79

1944, Aug. 22   Litho.   Perf. 12
Flags in Red, Yellow, Blue & Black
388 A79   Sheet of 4   35.00 35.00
  a. 5c Prussian green   3.00 .80
  b. 10c rose   4.50 .80
  c. 20c ultramarine   4.50 1.75
  d. 1b rose lake   6.00 2.25

80th anniv. of Intl. Red Cross and 37th
anniv. of Venezuela's joining.
No. 388 exists imperf. Value $60.

Antonio José de
Sucre — A80

1945, Mar. 3   Engr.   Unwmk.
389 A80 5c orange yellow   2.10 1.10
390 A80 10c dark blue   3.25 1.75
391 A80 20c rose pink   4.25 1.75
  Nos. 389-391,C206-C215 (13) 33.55 22.30

Birth of Antonio de Sucre, 150th anniv.

Andrés   Gen. Rafael
Bello — A81   Urdaneta — A82

1946, Aug. 24
392 A81 20c deep blue   .65 .35
393 A82 20c deep blue   .65 .35
  Nos. 392-393,C216-C217 (4)   3.50 1.20

80th anniversary of the death of Andrés
Bello (1780?-1865), educator and writer, and
the centenary of the death of Gen. Rafael
Urdaneta.

Allegory of the
Republic — A83

1946, Oct. 18   Litho.   Perf. 11½
394 A83 20c light blue   .80 .35
  Nos. 394,C218-C221 (5)   5.60 3.85

Anniversary of Revolution of October, 1945.
Exists imperf.

Anti-tuberculosis Institute,
Maracaibo — A84

1947, Jan. 12
395 A84 20c ultra & yellow   .80 .35
  Nos. 395,C228-C231 (5)   6.90 5.15

12th Pan-American Health Conf., Caracas,
Jan. 1947. Exists imperf. and part perf.

No. 362 Surcharged in
Green

396 A65 15c on 1b dk vio brn   .70 .30
  a. Inverted surcharge   6.00 5.00
  Nos. 396,C223-C227 (6)   30.50 23.95

Types of 1938-40

1947   **Engr.**
397 A69 5c green   .25 .25
398 A70 30c black   1.00 .50
399 A65 40c red violet   .95 .25
400 A59 5b deep orange   40.00 18.00
  Nos. 397-400 (4)   42.20 19.00

In 1947 a decree authorized the use
of 5c and 10c revenue stamps of the
above type for franking correspondence. Other denominations were also
used unofficially.
For surcharges see Nos. 876-883.

Nos. 398 and 373
Surcharged in Red

1947   Unwmk.   Perf. 12
401 A70 5c on 30c black   .40 .25
  a. Inverted surcharge   5.00 5.00
402 A70 5c on 37½c dk bl   .45 .25
  a. Inverted surcharge   5.00 5.00

Types of 1938-43

1947-48
403 A69 5c brt ultra   .25 .25
404 A78 10c red   .25 .25
405 A69 15c rose car   .50 .25
406 A69 25c violet   .40 .25
407 A70 30c dk vio brn ('48)   .50 .25
408 A65 40c orange ('48)   .50 .25
409 A70 50c olive green   .95 .25
410 A65 1b deep blue   1.75 .25
411 A65 3b gray   3.50 .90
412 A59 5b chocolate   13.00 5.00
  Nos. 403-412 (10)   21.60 7.90

M. S.
Republica
de
Venezuela
A85

Imprint: "American Bank Note
Company"

1948-50   Engr.   Perf. 12
413 A85 5c blue   .25 .25
414 A85 7½c red org ('49)   .70 .40
  a. Booklet pane of 20
415 A85 10c car rose   .55 .25
  a. Booklet pane of 10
416 A85 15c gray ('50)   .55 .25
417 A85 20c sepia   .40 .25
418 A85 25c violet ('49)   .55 .25
419 A85 30c orange ('50)   3.75 2.25
420 A85 37½c brown ('49)   1.75 1.40
421 A85 40c olive ('50)   2.50 1.75
422 A85 50c red violet ('49)   .70 .25
423 A85 1b gray green   1.75 .55
  Nos. 413-423 (11)   13.45 7.85

Grand Colombian Merchant Fleet. See Nos.
632-634, C256-C271, C554-C556. For
surcharges see Nos. 450-451.

Santos
Michelena — A86

1949, Apr. 25   **Perf. 12½**
424 A86 5c ultra   .25 .25
425 A86 10c carmine   .40 .25
426 A86 20c sepia   1.60 .60
427 A86 1b green   5.75 3.00
  Nos. 424-427,C272-C277 (10) 16.50 9.70

Centenary of the death of Santos
Michelena, Finance Minister, and the 110th
anniversary of the Postal Convention of
Bogota.

Christopher
Columbus — A87

1949-50   **Engr.**
428 A87 5c deep ultra   .45 .25
429 A87 10c carmine   1.50 .50
430 A87 20c dark brown   1.75 .60
431 A87 1b green   4.75 2.10
  Nos. 428-431,C278-C283 (10) 18.45 8.65

450th anniversary (in 1948) of Columbus'
discovery of the American mainland.
Issued: 5c, 10c, 1949; 20c, 1b, Jan. 1950.

Arms of
Venezuela
A88

1948
432 A88 5c blue   1.40 .70
433 A88 10c red   1.75 .80

The 20c and 1b, type A88, and six similar air
post stamps were prepared but not issued.
Value, set of 8, about $125.

Gen. Francisco de
Miranda — A89

1950, Mar. 28   Unwmk.   Perf. 12
434 A89 5c blue   .25 .25
435 A89 10c green   .40 .25
436 A89 20c sepia   .85 .35
437 A89 1b rose carmine   4.00 1.75
  Nos. 434-437 (4)   5.50 2.60

Bicentenary of birth of General Francisco de
Miranda.

Map and Population
Chart — A90

1950, Sept. 1
438 A90 5c blue   .25 .25
439 A90 10c gray   .25 .25
440 A90 15c sepia   .25 .25
441 A90 25c green   .45 .25
442 A90 30c red   .55 .25

443 A90 50c violet 1.10 .45
444 A90 1b red brown 2.75 1.40
Nos. 438-444,C302-C310 (16) 12.00 7.50

8th National Census of the Americas.

Alonso de
Ojeda — A91

1950, Dec. 18 Photo. Perf. 11½
445 A91 5c deep blue .25 .25
446 A91 10c deep red .30 .25
447 A91 15c slate gray .35 .25
448 A91 20c ultra 1.40 .25
449 A91 1b blue green 5.50 2.75
Nos. 445-449 (5) 7.80 4.05
Nos. 445-449,C316-C321 (11) 15.65 7.80

450th anniversary (in 1949) of the discovery of the Gulf of Maracaibo.

Nos. 414 and 420 Surcharged in Black

1951 Unwmk. Perf. 12
450 A85 5c on 7½c red org .30 .25
451 A85 10c on 37½c brn .30 .25
a. Inverted surcharge 16.00 16.00

Telegraph Stamps
Surcharged in
Black or Red

"Habilitado"
"Correos"
"Bs. 0,05"

Grayish Security Paper

1951, June Engr.
452 5c on 5c brown .25 .25
453 10c on 10c green .25 .25
454 20c on 1b blk (R) .50 .25
455 25c on 25c carmine .65 .25
456 30c on 2b ol grn (R) .90 .70
Nos. 452-456 (5) 2.55 1.70

The 5c and 10c surcharges include quotation marks on each line and values are expressed "Bs. 0.05" etc.

Bolivar
Statue, New
York — A92

1951, July 13 Perf. 12
457 A92 5c green .25 .25
458 A92 10c car rose .40 .25
459 A92 20c ultra .40 .25
460 A92 30c slate gray .50 .25
461 A92 40c deep green .70 .25
462 A92 50c red brown 1.50 .50
463 A92 1b gray black 4.75 2.50
Nos. 457-463 (7) 8.50 4.25
Nos. 457-463,C322-C329 (15) 21.65 9.50

Relocation of the equestrian statue of Simon Bolivar in NYC, Apr. 19, 1951.

Arms of Carabobo
and
"Industry" — A93

1951 Unwmk. Photo. Perf. 11½
464 A93 5c green .25 .25
465 A93 10c red .25 .25
466 A93 15c brown 1.40 .25
467 A93 20c ultra 2.00 .25
468 A93 25c orange brn 2.25 .25
469 A93 30c blue 5.00 2.00
470 A93 35c purple 19.00 16.00
Nos. 464-470 (7) 30.05 19.00

Issue dates: 5c, 10c, Oct. 8; others, Oct. 29.

Arms of Zulia and "Industry"
471 A93 5c green .25 .25
472 A93 10c red .95 .25
473 A93 15c brown 2.10 .95
474 A93 20c ultra 2.75 1.25
475 A93 50c brown org 16.00 12.00
476 A93 1b dp gray grn 5.50 2.10
477 A93 5b rose violet 12.00 8.00
Nos. 471-477 (7) 39.50 24.70

Issued: 5c, 10c, Sept. 8; others, Sept. 20.

Arms of Anzoategui and Globe
478 A93 5c green .25 .25
479 A93 10c red .25 .25
480 A93 15c brown 2.25 1.00
481 A93 20c ultra 3.75 .25
482 A93 40c red orange 7.75 3.75
483 A93 45c rose violet 22.50 1.25
484 A93 3b blue gray 8.75 4.25
Nos. 478-484 (7) 45.40 10.85

Issue date: Nov. 9.

Arms of Caracas and Buildings
485 A93 5c green 1.25 .25
486 A93 10c red 1.75 .25
487 A93 15c brown 4.25 1.00
488 A93 20c ultra 8.50 1.00
489 A93 25c orange brn 11.50 2.25
490 A93 30c blue 11.00 2.50
491 A93 35c purple 110.00 62.50
Nos. 485-491 (7) 148.25 69.65

Issued: 5c, 10c, June 20; others, Aug. 6.

Arms of Tachira and Agricultural Products
492 A93 5c green .25 .25
493 A93 10c red .95 .25
494 A93 15c brown 1.75 .60
495 A93 20c ultra 4.25 1.10
496 A93 50c brown org 260.00 3.25
497 A93 1b dp gray grn 4.25 1.50
498 A93 5b dull purple 10.50 6.00
Nos. 492-498 (7) 281.90 12.85

Issue date: Aug. 9.

Arms of Venezuela and Statue of Simon Bolivar
499 A93 5c green 1.00 .25
500 A93 10c red .85 .25
501 A93 15c brown 7.50 1.50
502 A93 20c ultra 7.50 1.00
503 A93 25c orange brn 12.50 2.75
504 A93 30c blue 12.50 2.75
505 A93 35c purple 65.00 50.00
Nos. 499-505 (7) 106.85 58.40

Issue date: Aug. 6.

Arms of Miranda and Agricultural Products
1952
506 A93 5c green .25 .25
507 A93 10c red .25 .25
508 A93 15c brown 1.75 .25
509 A93 20c ultra 1.90 .25
510 A93 25c orange brn 2.50 1.10
511 A93 30c blue 4.25 1.90
512 A93 35c purple 26.00 18.00
Nos. 506-512 (7) 36.80 21.80

Arms of Aragua and Stylized Farm
513 A93 5c green .25 .25
514 A93 10c red .25 .25
515 A93 15c brown 1.90 .25
516 A93 20c ultra 1.90 .25
517 A93 25c orange brn 4.25 1.10
518 A93 30c blue 4.25 1.90
519 A93 35c purple 22.50 17.50
Nos. 513-519 (7) 35.20 21.30

Issue date: 20c, 30c, Mar. 24.

Arms of Lara, Agricultural Products and Rope
520 A93 5c green .25 .25
521 A93 10c red .25 .25
522 A93 15c brown 1.00 .25
523 A93 20c ultra 2.40 .25
524 A93 25c orange brn 2.75 1.75

525 A93 30c blue 5.25 1.40
526 A93 35c purple 21.00 13.00
Nos. 520-526 (7) 32.80 16.95

Issue date: 20c, 30c, Mar. 24.

Arms of Bolivar and Stylized Design
527 A93 5c green .25 .25
528 A93 10c red .25 .25
529 A93 15c brown .95 .25
530 A93 20c ultra 2.10 .25
531 A93 40c red orange 8.00 2.75
532 A93 45c rose violet 20.00 14.00
533 A93 3b blue gray 9.50 6.25
Nos. 527-533 (7) 40.95 23.80

Issue date: 20c, Mar. 24.

Arms of Sucre, Palms and Seascape
534 A93 5c green .25 .25
535 A93 10c red .25 .25
536 A93 15c brown 2.40 .25
537 A93 20c ultra 2.40 .25
538 A93 40c red orange 8.00 2.10
539 A93 45c rose violet 27.50 17.50
540 A93 3b blue gray 7.00 4.75
Nos. 534-540 (7) 47.70 25.15

Arms of Trujillo Surrounded by Stylized Tree
541 A93 5c green .25 .25
542 A93 10c red .25 .25
543 A93 15c brown 2.50 .25
544 A93 20c ultra 2.50 .60
545 A93 50c brown orange 15.00 7.25
546 A93 1b dp gray green 3.50 1.25
547 A93 5b dull purple 9.00 4.50
Nos. 541-547 (7) 32.90 14.20

Map of Delta Amacuro and Ship
1953-54
548 A93 5c green .25 .25
549 A93 10c red .25 .25
550 A93 15c brown .90 .25
551 A93 20c ultra 1.50 .25
552 A93 40c red orange 4.75 3.00
553 A93 45c rose violet 22.50 13.50
554 A93 3b blue gray 6.00 4.50
Nos. 548-554 (7) 36.05 21.80

Arms of Falcon and Stylized Oil Refinery
555 A93 5c green .25 .25
556 A93 10c red .25 .25
557 A93 15c brown 1.40 .25
558 A93 20c ultra 1.40 .25
559 A93 50c brown orange 7.25 3.50
560 A93 1b dp gray grn 4.50 2.75
561 A93 5b dull purple 13.50 7.25
Nos. 555-561 (7) 28.45 14.30

Issue date: 20c, Feb. 13.

Arms of Guarico and Factory
562 A93 5c green .25 .25
563 A93 10c red .25 .25
564 A93 15c brown 1.10 .25
565 A93 20c ultra 1.25 .25
566 A93 40c red orange 6.50 4.00
567 A93 45c rose violet 16.00 7.75
568 A93 3b blue gray 6.50 3.50
Nos. 562-568 (7) 31.75 16.05

Issue date: 20c, Feb. 13.

Arms of Merida and Church
569 A93 5c green .25 .25
570 A93 10c red .25 .25
571 A93 15c brown .85 .25
572 A93 20c ultra 2.10 .25
573 A93 50c brown orange 9.00 4.00
574 A93 1b dp gray green 2.50 1.75
575 A93 5b dull purple 9.00 5.25
Nos. 569-575 (7) 23.85 11.80

Issue date: 20c, Feb. 2.

Arms of Monagas and Horses
576 A93 5c green .25 .25
577 A93 10c red .25 .25
578 A93 15c brown 1.10 .90
579 A93 20c ultra 1.60 .90
580 A93 40c red orange 7.50 2.75
581 A93 45c rose violet 22.50 13.50
582 A93 3b blue gray 9.25 7.50
Nos. 576-582 (7) 42.35 25.25

Arms of Portuguesa and Forest
583 A93 5c green .25 .25
584 A93 10c red .25 .25
585 A93 15c brown .65 .25
586 A93 20c ultra 1.40 .25
587 A93 50c brown org 7.25 4.75
588 A93 1b dp gray grn 1.90 .80
589 A93 5b dull purple 8.00 5.25
Nos. 583-589 (7) 19.60 11.60

Issue date: 5c, 10c, Feb. 2.

Map of Amazonas and Orchid
590 A93 5c green 1.40 .25
591 A93 10c red 1.40 .25
592 A93 15c brown 3.00 .25
593 A93 20c ultra 8.50 .85
594 A93 40c red orange 10.00 3.00
595 A93 45c rose violet 16.00 7.75
596 A93 3b blue gray 24.00 8.00
Nos. 590-596 (7) 64.30 20.70

Issue date: Jan. 1954.

Arms of Apure, Horse and Bird
597 A93 5c green .25 .25
598 A93 10c red .25 .25
599 A93 15c brown 1.60 .25
600 A93 20c ultra 8.50 .25
601 A93 50c brown org 11.00 8.50
602 A93 1b dp gray grn 3.50 3.00
603 A93 5b dull purple 21.00 12.00
Nos. 597-603 (7) 46.00 24.30

Issue date: Jan. 1954.

Arms of Barinas, Cow and Horse
604 A93 5c green .25 .25
605 A93 10c red .25 .25
606 A93 15c brown .55 .25
607 A93 20c ultra 3.75 .55
608 A93 50c brown org 4.50 2.75
609 A93 1b dp gray grn 1.10 .55
610 A93 5b dull purple 10.00 5.00
Nos. 604-610 (7) 20.30 9.45

Issue date: Jan. 1954.

Arms of Cojedes and Cattle
611 A93 5c green .25 .25
612 A93 10c red .25 .25
613 A93 15c brown .25 .25
614 A93 20c ultra .25 .25
615 A93 25c orange brown 4.00 1.10
616 A93 30c blue 6.25 1.75
617 A93 35c purple 7.75 6.25
Nos. 611-617 (7) 18.80 9.90

Issue date: Dec, 17, 1953.

Arms of Nueva Esparta and Fish
618 A93 5c green .25 .25
619 A93 10c red .25 .25
620 A93 15c brown 1.40 .25
621 A93 20c ultra 1.60 .25
622 A93 40c red orange 7.25 2.75
623 A93 45c rose vio 17.50 10.00
624 A93 3b blue gray 8.00 5.50
Nos. 618-624 (7) 36.15 19.05

Issue date: Jan. 1954.

Arms of Yaracuy and Tropical Foliage
625 A93 5c green 1.50 .25
626 A93 10c red .25 .25
627 A93 15c brown 1.10 .25
628 A93 20c ultra 1.75 .25
629 A93 25c orange brn 2.50 1.10
630 A93 30c blue 2.75 .95
631 A93 35c purple 6.50 4.25
Nos. 625-631 (7) 16.30 7.10
Nos. 464-631 (168) 1,264. 514.15

Issue date: Jan. 1954.
See Nos. C338-C553.

Ship Type of 1948-50, Redrawn
Coil Stamps
Imprint: "Courvoisier S.A."
1952 Unwmk. Photo. Perf. 11½x12
632 A85 5c green 1.50 .25
633 A85 10c car rose 2.50 .25
634 A85 15c gray 9.00 .25
Nos. 632-634,C554-C556 (6) 22.50 1.50

Juan de Villegas and
Cross of Father
Yepez — A94

1952, Sept. 14 Perf. 11½
635 A94 5c green .25 .25
636 A94 10c red 1.25 .25
637 A94 20c dk gray bl 1.90 .60
638 A94 40c dp org 9.00 3.50
639 A94 50c brown 4.75 2.00
640 A94 1b violet 9.00 2.40
Nos. 635-640 (6) 26.15 9.00
Nos. 635-640,C557-C564 (14) 38.00 13.80

Founding of the city of Barquisimeto by Juan de Villegas, 400th anniv.

Virgin of Coromoto and
Child — A95

1952-53 Perf. 11½x12
Size: 17x26mm
641 A95 1b rose pink 8.00 1.25

Size: 26½x41mm

642	A95 1b rose pink ('53)	6.00	1.25

Size: 36x55mm

643	A95 1b rose pink ('53)	2.75	.95
	Nos. 641-643 (3)	16.75	3.45

300th anniv. of the appearance of the Virgin Mary to a chief of the Coromoto Indians.
Issue date: No. 641, Oct. 6.

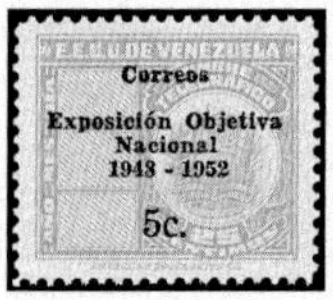

Telegraph Stamps Surcharged in Black or Red

1952, Nov. 24 Engr. *Perf. 12*
Grayish Security Paper

644	5c on 25c car	.30	.25
645	10c on 1b blk (R)	.30	.25

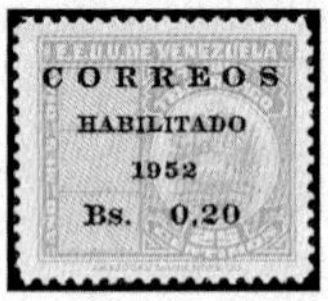

Surcharged

1952, Dec.

646	20c on 25c car	.35	.25
647	30c on 2b ol grn	2.10	1.40
648	40c on 1b blk (R)	.85	.45
649	50c on 3b red org	2.75	1.60
	Nos. 646-649 (4)	6.05	3.70

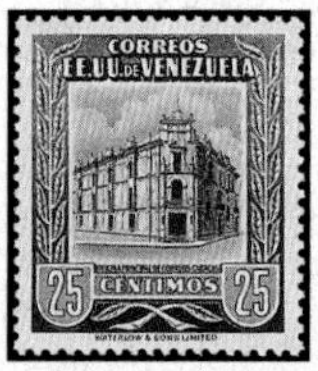

Post Office, Caracas — A96

Perf. 13x12½
1953-54 Unwmk. Photo.

650	A96 5c green	.25	.25
a.	Bklt. pane of 10		
651	A96 7½c brt green	.35	.25
652	A96 10c rose carmine	.25	.25
a.	Bklt. pane of 10		
653	A96 15c gray	.40	.25
654	A96 20c ultra	.25	.25
655	A96 25c magenta	.40	.25
656	A96 30c blue	1.90	.25
657	A96 35c brt red vio	.85	.25
658	A96 40c orange	1.25	.40
659	A96 45c violet	1.90	.65
660	A96 50c red orange	1.25	.40
	Nos. 650-660 (11)	9.05	3.45

Issued: 20c, 30c, 45c, 3/11; 7½c, 25c, 50c, 6/53; 5c, 10c, 2/54; 15c, 1954.
See Nos. C565-C575, C587-C589.

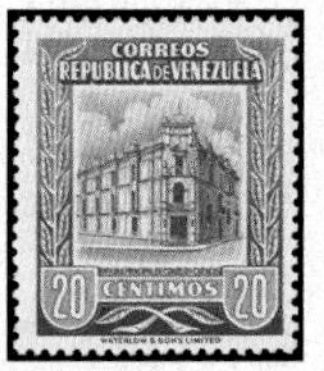

A96a

Type of 1953-54 Inscribed "Republica de Venezuela"

1955

661	A96a 5c green	.25	.25
662	A96a 10c rose car	.25	.25
663	A96a 15c gray	.25	.25
664	A96a 20c ultra	.25	.25
665	A96a 30c blue	.65	.40
666	A96a 35c brt red vio	.65	.25
667	A96a 40c orange	1.00	.25
668	A96a 45c violet	1.25	.50
	Nos. 661-668 (8)	4.55	2.40
	Nos. 661-668,C597-C606 (18)	13.65	6.55

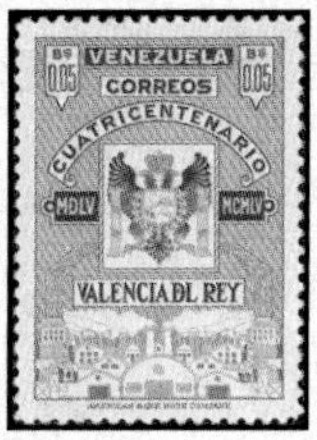

Arms of Valencia and Industrial Scene — A97

1955, Mar. 26 Engr. *Perf. 12*

669	A97 5c brt grn	.25	.25
670	A97 20c ultra	.40	.25
671	A97 25c reddish brn	.65	.25
672	A97 50c vermilion	1.00	.25
	Nos. 669-672,C590-C596 (11)	5.10	2.75

Founding of Valencia del Rey, 400th anniv.

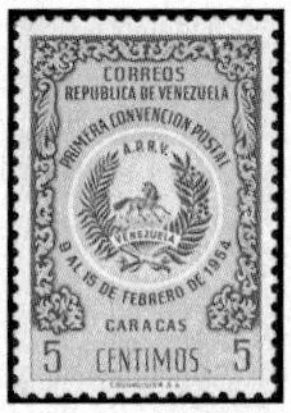

Coat of Arms — A98

1955, Dec. 9 Unwmk. *Perf. 11½*

673	A98 5c green	1.10	.25
674	A98 20c ultra	3.75	.25
675	A98 25c rose car	3.00	.25
676	A98 50c orange	3.75	.25
	Nos. 673-676,C607-C612 (10)	19.90	3.50

1st Postal Convention, Caracas, 2/9-15/54.

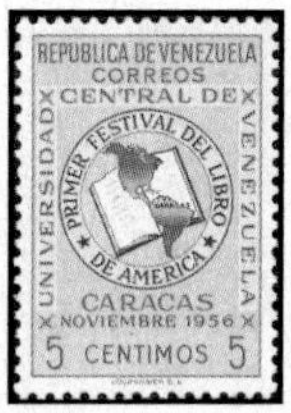

Book and Map of the Americas — A99

1956 Photo. *Perf. 11½*
Granite Paper

677	A99 5c lt grn & bluish grn	.25	.25
678	A99 10c lil rose & rose vio	.25	.25
679	A99 20c ultra & dk bl	.25	.25
680	A99 25c gray & lil gray	.55	.25
681	A99 30c lt bl & bl	.55	.25
682	A99 40c bis brn & brn	.65	.25
683	A99 50c ver & red brn	1.40	.65
684	A99 1b lt pur & vio	2.25	1.10
	Nos. 677-684 (8)	6.15	3.25
	Nos. 677-684,C629-C635 (15)	10.80	5.15

Book Festival of the Americas, 11/15-30/56.

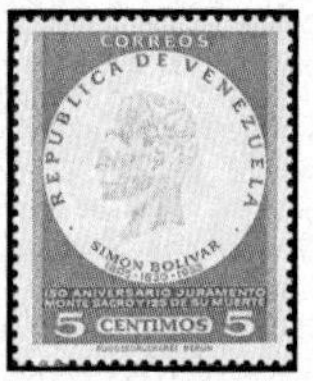

Simon Bolivar — A100

Engraved, Center Embossed
1957-58 Unwmk. *Perf. 13½*

685	A100 5c brt bl grn	.25	.25
686	A100 10c red	.25	.25
687	A100 20c lt slate bl	.40	.25
688	A100 25c rose lake	.40	.25
689	A100 30c vio blue	.50	.25
690	A100 40c red orange	.75	.25
691	A100 50c orange yel	1.10	.55
	Nos. 685-691 (7)	3.65	2.05
	Nos. 685-691,C636-C642 (14)	7.40	3.45

150th anniv. of the Oath of Monte Sacro and the 125th anniv. of the death of Simon Bolivar (1783-1830).
Issued: 10c, 50c, 1958; others, 11/15/57.

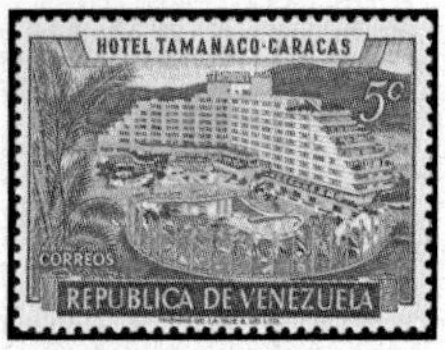

Hotel Tamanaco, Caracas A101

1957-58 Engr. *Perf. 13*

692	A101 5c green	.25	.25
693	A101 10c carmine	.25	.25
694	A101 15c black	.25	.25
695	A101 20c dark blue	.30	.25
696	A101 25c dp claret	.30	.25
697	A101 30c dp ultra	.50	.25
698	A101 35c purple	.30	.25
699	A101 40c orange	.40	.25
700	A101 45c rose violet	.50	.25
701	A101 50c yellow	.70	.25
702	A101 1b dk slate grn	1.10	.45
	Nos. 692-702 (11)	4.85	2.95
	Nos. 692-702,C643-C657 (26)	14.65	7.30

Issued: 5c, 10c, Oct. 10, 1957; others, 1958.
For surcharge see No. 878.

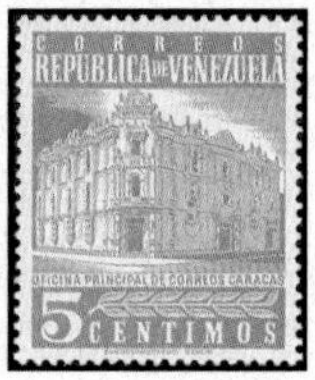

Main Post Office, Caracas — A102

1958, May 14 Litho. *Perf. 14*

703	A102 5c emerald	.25	.25
704	A102 10c rose red	.25	.25
705	A102 15c gray	.25	.25
706	A102 20c lt bl	.25	.25
707	A102 35c red lilac	.25	.25
708	A102 45c brt vio	1.25	.85
709	A102 50c yellow	.30	.25
710	A102 1b lt ol grn	.75	.40
	Nos. 703-710 (8)	3.55	2.75
	Nos. 703-710,C658-C670 (21)	15.80	10.85

See Nos. 748-750, C658-C670, C786-C792.
For surcharges see Nos. 865, C807, C856-C861.

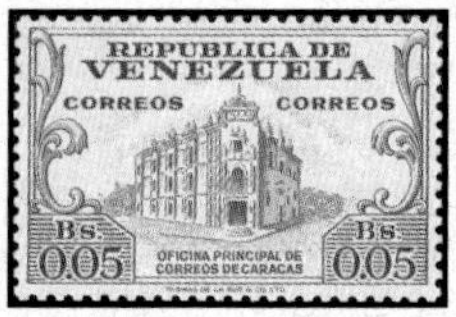

Main Post Office, Caracas A103

1958, Nov. 17 Engr. *Perf. 11½x12*

711	A103 5c green	.25	.25
712	A103 10c rose red	.40	.25
713	A103 15c black	.60	.25
	Nos. 711-713,C671-C673 (6)	2.45	1.50

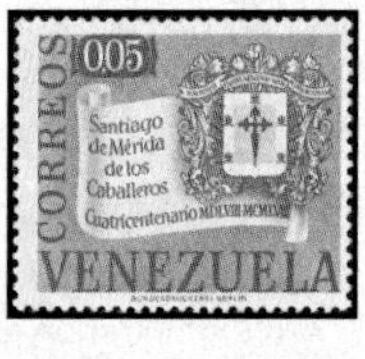

Arms of Merida — A104

1958, Oct. 9 Photo. *Perf. 14x13½*

714	A104 5c green	.25	.25
715	A104 10c bright red	.25	.25
716	A104 15c greenish gray	.25	.25
717	A104 20c blue	.25	.25
718	A104 25c magenta	.45	.25
719	A104 30c violet	.25	.25
720	A104 35c light purple	.30	.25
721	A104 40c orange	.65	.25
722	A104 45c deep rose lilac	.35	.25
723	A104 50c bright yellow	.55	.25
724	A104 1b gray green	1.60	.55
	Nos. 714-724 (11)	5.15	3.05
	Nos. 714-724,C674-C689 (27)	13.90	7.50

400th anniversary of the founding of the city of Merida. For surcharge see No. 873.

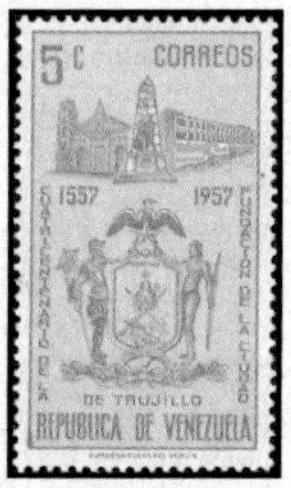

Arms of Trujillo, Bolivar Monument and Trujillo Hotel — A105

1959, Nov. 17 Unwmk. *Perf. 14*

725	A105 5c emerald	.25	.25
726	A105 10c rose	.25	.25
727	A105 15c gray	.25	.25
728	A105 20c blue	.25	.25
729	A105 25c brt pink	.35	.25
730	A105 30c lt ultra	.50	.25
731	A105 35c lt pur	.50	.25
732	A105 45c rose lilac	.65	.35
733	A105 50c yellow	.65	.25
734	A105 1b lt ol grn	1.60	.85
	Nos. 725-734 (10)	5.25	3.20
	Nos. 725-734,C690-C700 (21)	10.95	5.95

Founding of the city of Trujillo, 400th anniv.

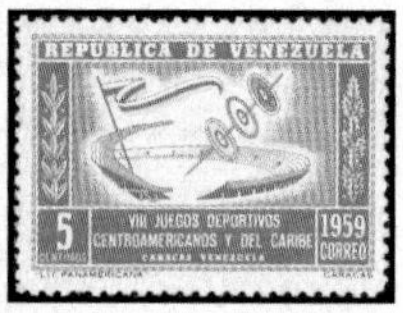

Stadium A106

1959 Mar. 10 Litho. *Perf. 13½*

735	A106 5c brt grn	.35	.25
736	A106 10c rose pink	.35	.25
737	A106 20c blue	.60	.25
738	A106 30c dk bl	.70	.25
739	A106 50c red lilac	1.10	.25
	Nos. 735-739 (5)	3.10	1.25
	Nos. 735-739,C701-C705 (10)	5.55	2.45

8th Central American and Caribbean Games, Caracas, Nov. 29-Dec. 14, 1958.
#735-739 exist imperf. Value, pair $25.

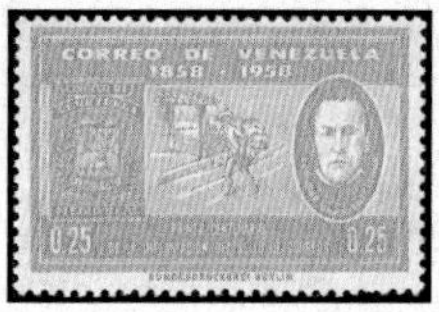

Stamp of 1859, Mailman and José Ignacio Paz Castillo A107

Stamp of 1859 and: 50c, Mailman on horseback and Jacinto Gutierrez. 1b, Plane, train and Miguel Herrera.

1959, Sept. 15 Engr. *Perf. 13½x14*

740	A107 25c org yel	.50	.25
741	A107 50c blue	.50	.25
742	A107 1b rose red	1.25	.45
	Nos. 740-742,C706-C708 (6)	3.90	1.85

Centenary of Venezuelan postage stamps.

Catalogue values for unused stamps in this section, from this point to the end of the section, are for Never Hinged items.

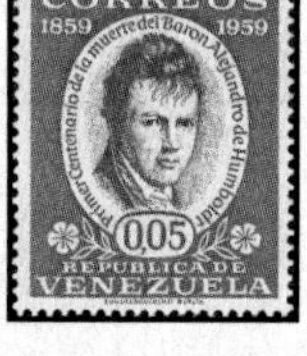

Alexander von Humboldt — A108

1960, Feb. 9 Unwmk. *Perf. 13½*

743	A108 5c grn & yel grn	.45	.25
744	A108 30c vio bl & vio	1.40	.35
745	A108 40c org & brn org	1.75	.55
	Nos. 743-745,C709-C711 (6)	7.35	2.15

Centenary of the death of Alexander von Humboldt, German naturalist and geographer.

Post Office Type of 1958

1960, July Litho. *Perf. 14*

748	A102 25c yellow	.25	.25
749	A102 30c light blue	.25	.25
750	A102 40c fawn	.55	.25
	Nos. 748-750 (3)	1.05	.75

Newspaper, 1808, and View of Caracas, 1958 — A109

1960, June 6   **Litho.**   *Perf. 14*
751 A109 10c rose & blk   .55   .25
752 A109 20c lt blue & blk   .95   .25
753 A109 35c lilac & blk   1.40   1.00
Nos. 751-753,C712-C714 (6)   9.15   3.75

150th anniv. (in 1958) of the 1st Venezuelan newspaper, Gazeta de Caracas.

Agustin Codazzi A110

1960, June 15   **Engr.**   **Unwmk.**
754 A110 5c brt green   .25   .25
755 A110 15c gray   1.10   .25
756 A110 20c blue   .85   .25
757 A110 45c purple   1.10   .50
Nos. 754-757,C715-C720 (10)   9.35   3.70

Centenary (in 1959) of the death of Agustin Codazzi, geographer.
For surcharges see Nos. 869, C884.

National Pantheon — A111

Pantheon in Bister

1960, May 9   **Litho.**
758 A111 5c emerald   .25   .25
759 A111 20c brt blue   .60   .25
760 A111 25c light olive   .95   .25
761 A111 30c dull blue   1.10   .30
762 A111 40c fawn   1.60   .55
763 A111 45c lilac   1.50   .55
Nos. 758-763 (6)   6.00   2.15
Nos. 758-763,C721-C734 (20)   27.95   7.75

For surcharges see Nos. C894-C895.

Andres Eloy Blanco, Poet (1896-1955) A112

1960, May 21   **Unwmk.**   *Perf. 14*
Portrait in Black
764 A112 5c emerald   .30   .25
765 A112 30c dull blue   .40   .25
766 A112 50c yellow   .85   .30
Nos. 764-766,C735-C737 (6)   5.25   1.85

For surcharge see No. C874.

Independence Meeting of April 19, 1810, Led by Miranda — A113

1960, Aug. 19   **Litho.**   *Perf. 13½*
Center Multicolored
767 A113 5c brt green   .65   .25
768 A113 20c blue   1.40   .35
769 A113 30c violet blue   1.75   .45
Nos. 767-769,C738-C740 (6)   8.25   2.35

150th anniversary of Venezuela's Independence.

See Nos. 812-814, C804-C806. For surcharge see No. C893.

Drilling for Oil — A114

1960, Aug. 26   **Engr.**   *Perf. 14*
770 A114 5c grn & slate grn   2.75   .95
771 A114 10c dk car & brn   .90   .35
772 A114 15c gray & dull pur   1.25   .45
Nos. 770-772,C741-C743 (6)   8.40   3.00

Issued to publicize Venezuela's oil industry.

Luisa Cáceres de Arismendi A115

Unwmk.
1960, Oct. 21   **Litho.**   *Perf. 14*
Center Multicolored
773 A115 20c light blue   1.40   .40
774 A115 25c citron   1.00   .40
775 A115 30c dull blue   1.40   .55
Nos. 773-775,C744-C746 (6)   9.50   3.40

Death of Luisa Cáceres de Arismendi, 94th anniv.

José Antonio Anzoategui — A116

1960, Oct. 29   **Engr.**
776 A116 5c emerald & gray ol   .35   .25
777 A116 15c ol gray & dl vio   .50   .25
778 A116 20c blue & gray vio   .70   .25
Nos. 776-778,C747-C749 (6)   4.35   2.05

140th anniversary (in 1959) of the death of General José Antonio Anzoategui.

Antonio José de Sucre — A117

Unwmk.
1960, Nov. 18   **Litho.**   *Perf. 14*
Center Multicolored
779 A117 10c deep rose   .45   .25
780 A117 15c gray brown   .50   .25
781 A117 20c blue   .85   .40
Nos. 779-781,C750-C752 (6)   5.85   2.40

130th anniversary of the death of General Antonio José de Sucre.

Bolivar Peak, Merida — A118

Designs: 15c, Caroni Falls, Bolivar. 35c, Guacharo caves, Monagas.

1960, Mar. 22   *Perf. 14*
782 A118 5c emerald & grn   1.00   1.00
783 A118 15c gray & dk gray   3.25   3.25
784 A118 35c rose lil & lil   2.75   2.75
Nos. 782-784,C753-C755 (6)   13.75   13.75

Buildings and People — A119

1961   **Litho.**   **Unwmk.**
Building in Orange
785 A119 5c emerald   .25   .25
786 A119 10c carmine   .25   .25
787 A119 15c gray   .25   .25
788 A119 20c blue   .25   .25
789 A119 25c lt red brown   .25   .25
790 A119 30c dull blue   .25   .25
791 A119 35c red lilac   .35   .25
792 A119 40c fawn   .55   .25
793 A119 45c brt violet   .70   .30
794 A119 50c yellow   .55   .25
Nos. 785-794 (10)   3.65   2.55

1960 national census. See #C756-C770. For surcharge see No. 866.

Rafael Maria Baralt — A120

1961, Mar. 11   **Engr.**   *Perf. 14*
795 A120 5c grn & slate grn   .25   .25
796 A120 15c gray & dull red brn   .50   .25
797 A120 35c rose lilac & lt vio   .75   .25
Nos. 795-797,C771-C773 (6)   4.30   1.95

Rafael Maria Baralt, statesman, death cent.

Yellow-headed Parrot — A121

1961, Sept. 6   **Litho.**   *Perf. 14½*
798 A121 30c shown   1.25   .50
799 A121 40c Snowy egret   1.90   .50
800 A121 50c Scarlet ibis   3.00   .90
Nos. 798-800,C776-C778 (6)   9.55   4.25

Juan J. Aguerrevere — A122

1961, Oct. 21   **Unwmk.**   *Perf. 14*
801 A122 25c dark blue   .35   .25
   a. Souvenir sheet, imperf.   2.50   2.50

Centenary of the founding of the Engineering Society of Venezuela, Oct. 28, 1861.
No. 801a sold for 1b.
No. 801a exists with "Valor: Bs 1,00" omitted at lower left corner. Value, $7.

Battle of Carabobo, 1821 — A123

1961, Dec. 1   *Perf. 14*
Center Multicolored
802 A123 5c emerald & blk   .25   .25
803 A123 40c brown & blk   .70   .25
Nos. 802-803,C779-C784 (8)   15.20   5.00

140th anniversary of Battle of Carabobo.

Oncidium Papilio Lindl. — A124

Orchids: 10c, Caularthron bilamellatum. 20c, Stanhopea Wardii Lodd. 25c, Catasetum pileatum. 30c, Masdevallia tovarensis. 35c, Epidendrum Stamfordianum Batem, horiz. 50c, Epidendrum atropurpureum Willd. 3b, Oncidium falcipetalum Lindl.

Perf. 14x13½, 13½x14
1962, May 30   **Litho.**   **Unwmk.**
Orchids in Natural Colors
804 A124 5c black & orange   .25   .25
805 A124 10c blk & brt grnsh bl   .25   .25
806 A124 20c black & yel grn   .55   .25
807 A124 25c black & lt blue   .80   .25
808 A124 30c black & olive   .90   .25
809 A124 35c black & yellow   1.00   .30
810 A124 50c black & gray   1.10   .35
811 A124 3b black & vio   6.75   2.75
Nos. 804-811 (8)   11.60   4.65
Nos. 804-811,C794-C803 (18)   28.10   10.10

For surcharges see Nos. 872, C885-C887.

Independence Type of 1960
Signing Declaration of Independence.

1962, June 11   *Perf. 13½*
Center Multicolored
812 A113 5c emerald   .25   .25
813 A113 20c blue   .50   .25
814 A113 25c yellow   .75   .30
   a. Souv. sheet, #812-814, imperf   3.25   3.25
Nos. 812-814,C804-C806 (6)   5.80   2.10

150th anniv. of the Venezuelan Declaration of Independence, July 5, 1811.
No. 814a sold for 1.50b.

Shot Put A125

1962, Nov. 30   **Litho.**   *Perf. 13x14*
815 A125 5c shown   .30   .25
816 A125 10c Soccer   .30   .25
817 A125 25c Swimming   .40   .25
   a. Souv. sheet, #815-817, imperf   3.50   3.50
Nos. 815-817,C808-C810 (6)   3.95   2.20

1st Natl. Games, Caracas, 1961. The stamps are arranged so that two pale colored edges of each stamp join to make a border around blocks of four.
No. 817a sold for 1.40b.
For surcharge see No. C899.

Vermilion Cardinal — A126

Birds: 10c, Great kiskadee. 20c, Glossy black thrush. 25c, Collared trogons. 30c, Swallow tanager. 40c, Long-tailed sylph. 3b, Black-necked stilt.

1962, Dec. 14   *Perf. 14x13½*
Birds in Natural Colors, Black Inscription

818	A126	5c brt yellow grn	.25	.25
819	A126	10c violet blue	.25	.25
820	A126	20c lilac rose	.50	.25
821	A126	25c dull brown	.60	.25
822	A126	30c lemon	.75	.25
823	A126	40c lilac	1.00	.30
824	A126	3b fawn	7.00	3.00
		Nos. 818-824 (7)	10.35	4.55
	Nos. 818-824,C811-C818 (15)		27.95	11.45

For surcharges see Nos. 868, C880-C882.

Malaria Eradication Emblem, Mosquito and Map — A127

Lithographed and Embossed
Perf. 13½x14
1962, Dec. 20   **Wmk. 346**
825 A127 50c brown & black   .80 .30

WHO drive to eradicate malaria. See Nos. C819-C819a.

White-tailed Deer A128

Designs: 10c, Collared peccary. 35c, Collared titi (monkey). 50c, Giant Brazilian otter. 1b, Puma. 3b, Capybara.

Perf. 13½x14
1963, Mar. 13   **Litho.**   **Unwmk.**
Multicolored Center; Black Inscriptions

826	A128	5c green	.25	.25
827	A128	10c orange	.25	.25
828	A128	35c red lilac	.25	.25
829	A128	50c blue	.55	.29
830	A128	1b rose brown	2.75	1.40
831	A128	3b yellow	5.50	3.50
		Nos. 826-831 (6)	9.55	5.90
	Nos. 826-831,C820-C825 (12)		23.75	11.00

For surcharges see #870-871, C888-C889.

Fisherman and Map of Venezuela — A129

1963, Mar. 21
832 A129 25c pink & ultra   .25 .25
   Nos. 832,C826-C827 (3)   1.80 1.30

FAO "Freedom from Hunger" campaign.

Cathedral of Bocono — A130

1963, May 30   **Wmk. 346**
833 A130 50c brn, red & grn, *buff*   .75 .25

400th anniversary of the founding of Bocono. See No. C828.

St. Peter's Basilica, Rome A131

1963, June 11   *Perf. 14x13½*
834 A131 35c dk bl, brn & buff   .45 .25
835 A131 45c dk grn, red brn & buff   .50 .25
   Nos. 834-835,C829-C830 (4)   3.45 1.35

Vatican II, the 21st Ecumenical Council of the Roman Catholic Church.

National Flag — A132

1963, July 29   **Unwmk.**   *Perf. 14*
836 A132 30c gray, red, yel & bl   1.00 .25

Centenary of Venezuela's flag and coat of arms. See No. C831.

Lake Maracaibo Bridge — A133

Perf. 13½x14
1963, Aug. 24   **Wmk. 346**
837 A133 30c blue & brown   .45 .25
838 A133 35c bluish grn & brn   .50 .25
839 A133 80c blue grn & brn   1.10 .45
   Nos. 837-839,C832-C834 (6)   6.65 2.55

Opening of bridge over Lake Maracaibo. For surcharge see No. 875.

Map, Soldier and Emblem — A134

1963, Sept. 10   **Unwmk.**
840 A134 50c red, bl & grn, *buff*   .75 .25

25th anniversary of the armed forces. See No. C835. For surcharge see No. C862.

Dag Hammarskjold and World Map — A135

Perf. 14x13½
1963, Sept. 25   **Unwmk.**
841 A135 25c dk bl, bl grn & ocher   .30 .25
842 A135 55c grn, grnsh bl & ocher   1.10 .40
   Nos. 841-842,C836-C837 (4)   4.40 1.85

"1st" anniv. of the death of Dag Hammarskjold, Secretary General of the UN, 1953-61.
See #C837a. For surcharges see #867, C875-C876.

Dr. Luis Razetti — A136

1963, Oct. 10   **Litho.**
843 A136 35c blue, ocher & brn   .60 .25
844 A136 45c mag, ocher & brn   .90 .25
   Nos. 843-844,C838-C839 (4)   4.50 2.40

Dr. Luis Razetti, physician, birth cent.

Dr. Francisco A. Risquez — A137

Design: 20c, Dr. Carlos J. Bello.

1963, Dec. 31   *Perf. 11½x12*
845 A137 15c multicolored   .50 .25
846 A137 20c multicolored   .70 .25
   Nos. 845-846,C840-C841 (4)   2.70 1.50

Cent. of the Intl. Red Cross.

Oil Field Workers — A138

10c, Oil refinery. 15c, Crane & building construction. 30c, Cactus, train & truck. 40c, Tractor.

1964, Feb. 5   **Litho.**   *Perf. 14x13½*
847 A138 5c multi   .25 .25
848 A138 10c multi   .25 .25
849 A138 15c multi   .30 .25
850 A138 30c multi   .50 .25
851 A138 40c multi   .55 .25
   Nos. 847-851 (5)   1.85 1.25
   Nos. 847-851,C842-C846 (10)   3.35 2.10

Department of Industrial Development, cent.

Pedro Gual — A139

1964, Mar. 20   **Unwmk.**   *Perf. 14*
852 A139 40c lt olive green   .60 .25
853 A139 50c lt red brown   .80 .30
   Nos. 852-853,C847-C848 (4)   3.50 1.40

Pedro Gual (1784-1862), statesman.

Carlos Arvelo — A140

1964, Apr. 17   **Engr.**   *Perf. 14x13½*
854 A140 1b dull bl & gray   1.50 .55

Centenary of the death of Dr. Carlos Arvelo (1784-1862), chief physician of Bolivar's revolutionary army, director of Caracas Hospital, rector of Central University and professor of pathology.

For surcharge see No. 874.

Foundry Ladle and Molds A141

1964, May 22   *Perf. 14x13½*
855 A141 20c multicolored   .40 .25
856 A141 50c multicolored   .75 .25
   Nos. 855-856,C849-C850 (4)   4.15 1.60

Orinoco Steel Mills.

Romulo Gallegos, Novelist, 80th Birthday — A142

Unwmk.
1964, Aug. 3   **Litho.**   *Perf. 12*
857 A142 5c dk & lt green   .25 .25
858 A142 10c bl & pale bl   .25 .25
859 A142 15c dk & lt red lil   .40 .25
   Nos. 857-859,C852-C854 (6)   2.90 1.55

Angel Falls, Bolivar State A143

Tourist Publicity: 10c, Tropical landscape, Sucre State. 15c, San Juan Peaks, Guarico. 30c, Net fishermen, Anzoategui. 40c, Mountaineer, Merida.

1964, Oct. 22   *Perf. 13½x14*
860 A143 5c multi   .25 .25
861 A143 10c multi   .25 .25
862 A143 15c multi   .25 .25
863 A143 30c multi   .55 .25
864 A143 40c multi   .80 .25
   Nos. 860-864 (5)   2.10 1.25

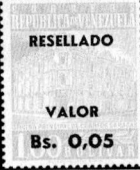

Issues of 1958-64 Surcharged in Black, Dark Blue or Lilac

1965
865 A102 5c on 1b (#710)   .60 .25
866 A119 10c on 45c (#793)   .25 .25
867 A135 15c on 55c (#842)   .25 .25
868 A126 20c on 3b (#824)   .25 .25
869 A110 25c on 45c (#757)
   (DB)   .25 .25

870	A128	25c on 1b (#830)	.40	.25
871	A128	25c on 3b (#831)	.45	.25
872	A124	25c on 3b (#811) (L)	.25	.25
873	A104	30c on 1b (#724)	.40	.25
874	A140	40c on 1b (#854)	.90	.25
875	A133	60c on 80c (#839)	1.25	.40

Nos. 865-875 (11)   5.25 2.90

Lines of surcharge arranged variously; old denomination obliterated with bars on Nos. 867, 870-872. See Nos. C856-C899.

Revenue Stamps of 1947 Surcharged in Red or Black

Imprint: "American Bank Note Co."

1965 Engr. Perf. 12, 13½ (No. 882)

876	R1	5c on 5c emerald	.30	.25
877	R1	5c on 20c red brn	.30	.25
878	R1	10c on 10c brn ol	.30	.25
879	R1	15c on 40c grn	.30	.25
880	R1	20c on 3b dk bl (R)	.50	.25
881	R1	25c on 5b vio bl (R)	1.00	.35
882	R1	25c on 5b vio bl (R) (Imprint: "Bundesdruckerei Berlin")	.50	.25
883	R1	60c on 3b dk bl (R)	1.25	.35

Nos. 876-883 (8)   4.45 2.20

Type R1 is illustrated above No. 401.

John F. Kennedy and Alliance for Progress Emblem A144

1965, Aug. 20 Photo. Perf. 12x11½

884	A144	20c gray	.50	.25
885	A144	40c bright lilac	.80	.25

Nos. 884-885,C900-C901 (4)   3.65 1.40

Map of Venezuela and Guiana by Codazzi, 1840 — A145

Maps of Venezuela and Guiana: 15c, by Juan M. Restrepo, 1827, horiz. 40c, by L. de Surville, 1778.

1965, Nov. 5 Litho. Perf. 13½

886	A145	5c multi	.25	.25
887	A145	15c multi	.40	.25
888	A145	40c multi	.70	.25
a.		Souv. sheet, #886-888, imperf	8.00	8.00

Nos. 886-888,C905-C907 (6)   3.45 1.65

Issued to publicize Venezuela's claim to part of British Guiana.
No. 888a sold for 85c.

Protesilaus Leucones — A146

Various Butterflies in Natural Colors Black Inscriptions

1966, Jan. 25 Litho. Perf. 13½x14

889	A146	20c lt olive grn	1.25	.25
890	A146	30c lt yellow grn	2.50	.25
891	A146	50c yellow	.75	.30

Nos. 889-891,C915-C917 (6)   14.50 2.30

Ship and Map of Atlantic Ocean A147

1966, Mar. 10 Litho. Perf. 13½x14

892	A147	60c brown, bl & blk	2.25	.70

Bicentenary of the first maritime mail.

"El Carite" Dance — A148

Various Folk Dances

Perf. 14x13½

1966, Apr. 5 Litho. Unwmk.

893	A148	5c gray & multi	.25	.25
894	A148	10c orange & multi	.25	.25
895	A148	15c lemon & multi	.35	.25
896	A148	20c lilac & multi	.45	.25
897	A148	25c brt pink & multi	.55	.35
898	A148	35c yel grn & multi	.70	.40

Nos. 893-898,C919-C924 (12)   11.45 4.70

Type of Air Post Stamps and

Arturo Michelena, Self-portrait A149

Paintings: 1b, Penthesileia, battle scene. 1.05b, The Red Cloak.

Perf. 12½x12, 12x12½

1966, May 12 Litho. Unwmk.

899	A149	95c sepia & buff	.90	.65
900	AP74	1b multi	1.10	.65
901	AP74	1.05b multi	1.40	.65

Nos. 899-901,C927-C929 (6)   7.05 3.60

Arturo Michelena (1863-1898), painter. Miniature sheets of 12 exist.

Construction Worker and Map of Americas — A150

Designs: 20c, as 10c. 30c, 65c, Labor monument. 35c, Machinery worker and map of Venezuela. 50c, Automobile assembly line.

1966, July 6 Litho. Perf. 14x13½

902	A150	10c yellow & blk	.25	.25
903	A150	20c lt grnsh bl & blk	.30	.25
904	A150	30c lt blue & vio	.30	.25
905	A150	35c lemon & olive	.45	.25
906	A150	60c brt rose & claret	.60	.30
907	A150	65c salmon pink & brn	.80	.35

Nos. 902-907 (6)   2.70 1.65

2nd Conference of Ministers of Labor of the Organization of American States.

Velvet Cichlid A151

1966, Aug. 31 Litho. Perf. 13½x14

908	A151	15c shown	.30	.25
909	A151	25c Perch cichlid	.40	.25
910	A151	45c Piranha	1.00	.35

Nos. 908-910,C933-C935 (6)   6.50 2.20

Nativity — A152

1966, Dec. 9 Litho. Perf. 13½x14

911	A152	65c violet & blk	1.00	.40

Christmas 1966.

Satellite, Radar, Globe, Plane and Ship A153

1966, Dec. 28 Perf. 13½x14

912	A153	45c multi	.80	.30

Ministry of Communications, 30th anniv.

Rubén Dario — A154

1967 Litho.

913	A154	70c gray bl & dk bl	1.25	.65

Rubén Dario (pen name of Felix Rubén Garcia Sarmiento, 1867-1916), Nicaraguan poet, newspaper correspondent and diplomat.

Old Building and Arms, University of Zulia A155

1967, Apr. 21 Litho. Unwmk.

914	A155	80c gold, blk & car	1.25	.65

University of Zulia founding, 75th anniv.

Front Page and Printing Press — A156

1968, June 27 Photo. Perf. 14x13½

915	A156	1.50b emer, blk & brn	1.75	.80

Newspaper Correo del Orinoco, 150th anniv.

Boll Weevil A157

Insect Pests: 20c, Corn borer, vert. 90c, Tobacco caterpillar.

Perf. 14x13½, 13½x14

1968, Aug. 30 Litho.

916	A157	20c multicolored	.50	.25
917	A157	75c olive & multi	1.50	.35
918	A157	90c multicolored	2.10	.35

Nos. 916-918,C989-C991 (6)   7.10 1.60

Guayana Substation A158

Designs: 45c, Guaira River Dam, horiz. 50c, Macagua Dam and power plant, horiz. 80c, Guri River Dam and power plant.

1968, Nov. 8 Litho.

919	A158	15c fawn & multi	.25	.25
920	A158	45c dk yel & multi	.70	.35
921	A158	50c bl grn & multi	.90	.35
922	A158	80c blue & multi	1.40	.75

Nos. 919-922 (4)   3.25 1.60

Electrification program.

House and Piggy Bank A159

1968, Dec. 6 Litho. Perf. 13½x14

923	A159	45c blue & multi	.80	.35

National Savings System.

Nursery and Child Planting Tree A160

Designs: 15c, Child planting tree (vert.; this design used as emblem on entire issue). 30c, Waterfall, vert. 45c, Logging. 55c, Fields and village, vert. 75c, Palambra (fish).

Perf. 14x13½, 13½x14

1968, Dec. 19 Litho.

924	A160	15c multicolored	.35	.25
925	A160	20c multicolored	.35	.25
926	A160	30c multicolored	.40	.25
927	A160	45c multicolored	.55	.25
928	A160	55c multicolored	1.25	.35
929	A160	75c multicolored	.85	.25

Nos. 924-929 (6)   3.75 1.60
Nos. 924-929,C1000-C1005 (12)   10.55 4.05

Issued to publicize nature conservation.

Colorada Beach, Sucre A161

Designs: 45c, Church of St. Francis of Yare, Miranda. 90c, Stilt houses, Zulia.

1969, Jan. 24   **Perf. 13½x14**
930 A161 15c multicolored   .25 .25
931 A161 45c multicolored   .75 .25
932 A161 90c multicolored   1.10 .75
   Nos. 930-932,C1006-C1008 (6)   3.55 3.85

Tourist publicity. For souvenir sheet see No. C1007a.

Bolivar Addressing Congress of Angostura — A162

1969, Feb. 15   **Litho.**   **Perf. 11**
933 A162 45c multicolored   .85 .35

Sesquicentennial of the Congress of Angostura (Ciudad Bolivar).

Martin Luther King, Jr. — A163

1969, Apr. 1   **Litho.**   **Perf. 13½**
934 A163 1b bl, red & dk brn   1.10 .30

Rev. Dr. Martin Luther King, Jr. (1929-1968), American civil rights leader and recipient of the Nobel Peace Prize, 1964.

Tabebuia A164

Trees: 65c, Erythrina poeppigiana. 90c, Platymiscium.

1969, May 30   **Litho.**   **Perf. 13½x14**
935 A164 50c multicolored   .75 .25
936 A164 65c gray & multi   1.00 .25
937 A164 90c pink & multi   1.50 .40
   Nos. 935-937,C1009-C1011 (6)   5.35 1.65

Issued to publicize nature conservation.

Still Life with Pheasant, by Rojas — A165

Paintings by Cristobal Rojas (1858-1890): 25c, On the Balcony, vert. 45c, The Christening. 50c, The Empty Place (family). 60c, The Tavern. 1b, Man's Arm, vert.

Perf. 14x13½, 13½x14
1969, June 27   **Litho.**   **Unwmk.**
   Size: 32x42mm, 42x32mm
938 A165 25c gold & multi   .25 .25
939 A165 35c gold & multi   .55 .25
940 A165 45c gold & multi   .90 .30
941 A165 50c gold & multi   1.00 .35
942 A165 60c gold & multi   1.40 .45
    Perf. 11
    Size: 26x53mm
943 A165 1b gold & multi   1.90 .70
   Nos. 938-943 (6)   6.00 2.30

ILO Emblem A166

1969, July 28   **Perf. 13½**
944 A166 2.50b fawn & blk   2.50 1.50

50th anniv. of the ILO.

Charter and Coat of Arms A167

Industrial Complex A168

1969, Aug. 26   **Litho.**   **Perf. 13½**
945 A167 45c ultra & multi   .85 .30
946 A168 1b multicolored   1.25 .40

Industrial development.

House with Arcade, Carora — A169

Designs: 25c, Ruins of Pastora Church. 55c, Chapel of the Cross. 65c, House of Culture.

1969, Sept. 8   **Perf. 13x14½**
947 A169 20c multicolored   .25 .25
948 A169 25c multicolored   .40 .25
949 A169 55c multicolored   .90 .30
950 A169 65c multicolored   1.25 .45
   Nos. 947-950 (4)   2.80 1.25

400th anniversary of city of Carora.

Simon Bolivar in Madrid — A170

Designs: 10c, Bolivar's wedding, Madrid, 1802, horiz. 35c, Bolivar monument. Madrid.

Perf. 13½x14, 14x13½
1969, Oct. 28   **Litho.**
951 A170 10c multicolored   .25 .25
952 A170 15c brn red & blk   .45 .25
953 A170 35c multicolored   .60 .25
  a.   Souvenir sheet of 2   2.50 2.50
   Nos. 951-953 (3)   1.30 .75

Bolivar's sojourn in Spain. No. 953a contains 2 imperf. stamps similar to Nos. 952-953 with simulated perforation. Sold for 75c.

"Birds in the Woods" — A171

Design: 45c, "Children in Summer Camp." Both designs are after children's paintings.

1969, Dec. 12   **Litho.**   **Perf. 12½**
954 A171 5c emerald & multi   .25 .25
955 A171 45c red & multi   .90 .40

Issued for Children's Day.

Map of Great Colombia A172

1969, Dec. 16   **Litho.**   **Perf. 11½**
956 A172 45c multicolored   .70 .25

150th anniversary of the founding of the State of Great Colombia.

St. Anthony's, Clarines A173

Churches: 30c, Church of the Conception, Caroni. 40c, St. Michael's, Burbusay. 45c, St. Anthony's, Maturin. 75c, St. Nicholas, Moruy. 1b, Coro Cathedral.

1970, Jan. 15   **Perf. 14**
957 A173 10c pink & multi   .25 .25
958 A173 30c emerald & multi   .30 .25
959 A173 40c yellow & multi   .65 .25
960 A173 45c gray bl & multi   .90 .30
  a.   Souvenir sheet of 1, imperf.   2.00 2.00
961 A173 75c yellow & multi   1.25 .45
962 A173 1b orange & multi   1.50 .55
   Nos. 957-962 (6)   4.85 2.05

Colonial architecture. No. 960a sold for 75c.

A174

Design: Seven Hills of Valera.

1970, Feb. 13   **Litho.**   **Perf. 13x14½**
963 A174 95c multicolored   1.25 .40

Sesquicentennial of the city of Valera.

A175

Flowers: 20c, Monochaetum Humboldtianum. 25c, Symbolanthus vasculosis. 45c, Cavedishia splendens. 1b, Befaria glauca.

1970, July 29   **Litho.**   **Perf. 14x13½**
964 A175 20c multicolored   .50 .25
965 A175 25c multicolored   .80 .25
966 A175 45c multicolored   1.10 .40
967 A175 1b multicolored   1.60 .55
   Nos. 964-967,C1049-C1052 (8)   8.50 2.75

Battle of Boyaca, by Martin Tovar y Tovar A176

1970, Aug. 7   **Perf. 13½x14**
968 A176 30c multicolored   .50 .25

150th anniversary of Battle of Boyaca.

Our Lady of Belén de San Mateo — A177

Designs: 35c, Pastoral Cross of Archbishop Silvestre Guevera y Lira, 1867. 40c, Our Lady of Valle. 90c, Virgin of Chiquinquira. 1b, Our Lady of Socorro de Valencia.

1970, Sept. 1   **Perf. 14x13½**
969 A177 35c gray & multi   .60 .25
970 A177 40c gray & multi   .70 .25
971 A177 60c gray & multi   1.00 .40
  a.   Souvenir sheet of 1, imperf.   1.75 1.75
972 A177 90c gray & multi   1.25 .55
973 A177 1b gray & multi   1.60 .65
   Nos. 969-973 (5)   5.15 2.10

The designs are from sculptures and paintings in various Venezuelan churches. No. 971a sold for 75c.

Venezuela No. 22 and EXFILCA Emblem — A178

Designs: 20c, EXFILCA emblem and flags of participating nations, vert. 70c, Venezuela No. C13 and EXFILCA emblem, vert.

1970, Nov. 28   **Litho.**   **Perf. 11**
974 A178 20c yellow & multi   .40 .25
975 A178 25c dk blue & multi   .45 .25
976 A178 70c brown & multi   .90 .40
  a.   Souvenir sheet of 1, imperf.   1.75 1.75
   Nos. 974-976 (3)   1.75 .90

EXFILCA 70, 2nd Interamerican Philatelic Exhibition, Caracas, Nov. 27-Dec. 6. No. 976a is a hexagon with each side 50mm long. Sold for 85c.

Guardian Angel, by Juan Pedro Lopez — A179

1970, Dec. 1   **Litho.**   **Perf. 14½x13½**
977 A179 45c dull yellow & multi   .70 .30

Christmas 1970.

Jet and 1920 Plane A180

1970, Dec. 10   **Perf. 13x14**
978 A180 5c blue & multi   .40   .25
Venezuelan Air Force, 50th anniversary.

Question Mark Full of Citizens — A181

1971, Apr. 30   **Litho.**   **Perf. 14x13½**
Light Green, Red & Black
979   Block of 4   4.00   2.25
a. A181 30c frame L & T   .95   .45
b. A181 30c frame T & R   .95   .45
c. A181 30c frame L & B   .95   .45
d. A181 30c frame B & R   .95   .45

National Census, 1971. Sheet of 20 contains 5 No. 979 and 5 blocks of 4 labels. See No. C1054.

Battle of Carabobo A182

1971, June 21   **Perf. 13½x14**
980 A182 2b blue & multi   2.10   1.25
Sesquicentennial of Battle of Carabobo.

Map of Federal District — A183

State maps. 25c, 55c, 85c, 90c, vert.

1971   **Litho.**   **Perf. 13½x14, 14x13½**
981 A183 5c shown   .40   .25
982 A183 15c Monagas   .40   .25
983 A183 20c Nueva Esparta   .40   .25
984 A183 25c Portuguesa   .40   .25
985 A183 45c Sucre   .45   .25
986 A183 55c Tachira   .55   .25
987 A183 65c Trujillo   .65   .25
988 A183 75c Yaracuy   .75   .30
989 A183 85c Zulia   .95   .30
990 A183 90c Amazonas   1.50   .30
991 A183 1b Federal Dependencies   1.60   .55
   Nos. 981-991 (11)   8.05   3.20
Nos. 981-991,C1035-C1048 (25)   19.20   6.85

Issued: 5c, 7/15; 15c, 20c, 8/16; 25c, 45c, 9/15; 55c, 65c, 10/15; 75c, 85c, 11/15; 90c, 1b, 12/15.

Madonna and Child — A184

Design: #993, Madonna & Jesus in manger.

1971, Dec. 1   **Perf. 11**
992 A184 25c multicolored   .60   .25
993 A184 25c multicolored   .60   .25
a. Pair, #992-993   1.40   .60
Christmas 1971. Printed checkerwise.

Luis Daniel Beauperthuy A185

1971, Dec. 10   **Perf. 14x13½**
994 A185 1b vio bl & multi   1.25   .60
Dr. Luis Daniel Beauperthuy, scientist.

Globe in Heart Shape — A186

1972, Apr. 7   **Litho.**   **Perf. 14x13½**
995 A186 1b red, ultra & blk   1.00   .60
"Your heart is your health," World Health Day 1972.

Flags of Americas and Arms of Venezuela A187

Designs: 4b, Venezuelan flag. 5b, National anthem. 10b, Araguaney, national tree. 15b, Map, North and South America. All show flags of American nations in background.

1972, May 16   **Litho.**   **Perf. 14x13½**
996 A187 3b multicolored   4.00   1.00
997 A187 4b multicolored   4.25   1.75
998 A187 5b multicolored   4.75   2.25
999 A187 10b multicolored   9.00   3.00
1000 A187 15b multicolored   13.00   4.25
   Nos. 996-1000 (5)   35.00   12.25
"Venezuela in America."

Parque Central Complex A188

#1002, Front view ("Parque Central" on top). #1003, Side view ("Parque Central" at right).

1972, July 25   **Perf. 11½**
1001 A188 30c yellow & multi   .25   .25
1002 A188 30c blue & multi   .25   .25
1003 A188 30c red & multi   .25   .25
a. Strip of 3, #1001-1003   1.40   1.40
Completion of "Parque Central" middle-income housing project, Caracas.

Mahatma Gandhi — A189

1972, Oct. 2   **Litho.**   **Perf. 13½x14**
1004 A189 60c multicolored   1.25   .40
103rd birthday of Mohandas K. Gandhi (1869-1948), leader in India's fight for independence, advocate of non-violence.

Children Playing Music — A190

Christmas: #1006, Children roller skating.

1972, Dec. 5   **Litho.**   **Perf. 13½x14**
1005 30c multicolored   .25   .25
1006 30c multicolored   .25   .25
a. A190 Pair, #1005-1006   1.00   1.00

Indigo Snake A191

Snake: 15c, South American chicken snake. 25c, Venezuelan lance-head. 30c, Coral snake. 60c, Casabel rattlesnake. 1b, Boa constrictor.

1972, Dec. 15   **Litho.**   **Perf. 13½x14**
1007 A191 10c black & multi   .50   .35
1008 A191 15c black & multi   .50   .35
1009 A191 25c black & multi   .70   .35
1010 A191 30c black & multi   .80   .35
1011 A191 60c black & multi   1.50   .40
1012 A191 1b black & multi   2.25   .60
   Nos. 1007-1012 (6)   6.25   2.40

Copernicus — A192

Designs: 5c, Model of solarcentric system. 15c, Copernicus' book "De Revolutionibus."

1973, Feb. 19   **Litho.**   **Perf. 13½x14**
1013 5c multicolored   .25   .25
1014 10c multicolored   .35   .25
1015 15c multicolored   .50   .25
a. A192 Strip of 3, #1013-1015   1.50   .90

Sun — A193

Designs: Planetary system.

Size: 26½x29mm

1973   **Litho.**   **Perf. 13½**
1016 A193 5c shown   .25   .25
1017 A193 5c Earth   .25   .25
1018 A193 20c Mars   .55   .25
1019 A193 20c Saturn   .40   .25
1020 A193 30c Asteroids   .45   .25
1021 A193 40c Neptune   .55   .25
1022 A193 50c Venus   .80   .40
1023 A193 60c Jupiter   .95   .45
1024 A193 75c Uranus   1.10   .55
1025 A193 90c Pluto   1.40   .80
1026 A193 90c Moon   2.00   .80
1027 A193 1b Mercury   2.25   .95

Size: 27x55mm
Perf. 12
1028 A193 10c Orbits and Saturn   .25   .25
1029 A193 15c Sun, Mercury, Venus, Earth   .40   .25
1030 A193 15c Jupiter, Uranus, Neptune, Pluto   .45   .25
a. Strip of 3, #1028-1030   1.10   1.10
   Nos. 1016-1030 (15)   12.05   6.20

10th anniversary of Humboldt Planetarium. No. 1030a has continuous design showing solar system.
Issue dates: Nos. 1016, 1018, 1021, 1023-1025, Mar. 15; others Mar. 30.

OAS Emblem, Map of Americas — A194

1973, Apr. 30   **Litho.**   **Perf. 13½x14**
1031 A194 60c multicolored   .65   .30
Organization of American States, 25th anniv.

José Antonio Paez — A195

Street of the Lancers, Puerto Cabello — A196

Designs: 10c, Paez in uniform. 30c, Paez and horse, from old print. 2b, Paez at Battle of Centauro, horiz. 10c, 2b are after contemporary paintings.

1973   **Perf. 14x13½, 13½x14**
1032 A195 10c gold & multi   .25   .25
1033 A195 30c red, blk & gold   .35   .25
1034 A195 50c blk, vio bl & dk gold   .60   .35
1035 A196 1b multicolored   1.25   .60
1036 A195 2b gold & multi   2.10   1.25
   Nos. 1032-1036 (5)   4.55   2.70

Gen. José Antonio Paez (1790-1873), leader in War of Independence, President of Venezuela. The 1b for the sesquicentenary of the fall of Puerto Cabello.
Issue dates: Nos. 1033-1034, May 6; Nos. 1032, 1036, June 13; No. 1035, Nov. 8.

José P. Padilla, Mariano Montilla, Manuel Manrique — A197

1b, Naval battle. 2b, Line-up for naval battle.

1973, July 27   Litho.   Perf. 12½
1037 A197 50c multicolored   .35   .25
1038 A197 1b multicolored   1.00   .45
1039 A197 2b multicolored   2.00   1.00
   Nos. 1037-1039 (3)   3.35   1.70

150th anniv. of the Battle of Maracaibo.

Bishop Ramos de Lora — A198

1973, Aug. 1   Photo.   Perf. 14x13½
1040 A198 75c gold & dk brn   .60   .25

Sesquicentennial of the birth of Ramos de Lora (1722-1790), first Bishop of Merida of Maracaibo and founder of the Colegio Seminario, the forerunner of the University of the Andes.

Plane, Ship, Margarita Island — A199

1973, Sept. 8   Litho.   Perf. 14x13½
1041 A199 5c multicolored   .50   .25

Establishment of Margarita Island as a free port.

Map of Golden Road and Waterfall — A200

Designs (Road Map and): 10c, Scarlet macaw. 20c, Church ruins. 50c, 60c, Indian mountain sanctuary. 90c, Colonial church. 1b, Flags of Venezuela and Brazil.

1973, Oct. 1   Litho.   Perf. 13
1042 A200 5c black & multi   .25   .25
1043 A200 10c black & multi   .25   .25
1044 A200 20c black & multi   .80   .25
1045 A200 50c black & multi   .85   .35
1046 A200 60c black & multi   .85   .35
1047 A200 90c black & multi   1.30   .40
1048 A200 1b black & multi   1.60   .55
   Nos. 1042-1048 (7)   5.90   2.40

Completion of the Golden Road from Santa Elena de Uairen, Brazil, to El Dorado, Venezuela.
   Issued: 50c, 60c, Oct. 30; others Oct. 1.

Gen. Paez Dam and Power Station — A201

1973, Oct. 14   Perf. 14x13½
1049 A201 30c multicolored   .50   .25

Opening of the Gen. José Antonio Paez Dam and Power Station.

Child on Slide — A202

Designs: No. 1051, Fairytale animals. No. 1052, Children's book. No. 1053, Children disembarking from plane for vacation.

1973, Dec. 4   Litho.   Perf. 12
1050 A202 10c multicolored   .40   .25
1051 A202 10c multicolored   .40   .25
1052 A202 10c multicolored   .40   .25
1053 A202 10c multicolored   .40   .25
   Nos. 1050-1053 (4)   1.60   1.00

Children's Foundation Festival.

King Following Star — A203

Christmas: No. 1055, Two Kings.

1973, Dec. 5   Litho.   Perf. 14x13½
1054   30c multicolored   .55   .25
1055   30c multicolored   .55   .25
   a. A203 Pair, #1054-1055   1.40   1.40

Regional Map of Venezuela A204

1973, Dec. 13   Perf. 13½x14
1056 A204 25c multicolored   .75   .25

Introduction of regionalization.

Handicraft A205

Designs: 35c, Industrial park. 45c, Cog wheels and chimney.

1973, Dec. 18   Perf. 14x13½
1057 A205 15c blue & multi   .25   .25
1058 A205 35c multicolored   .30   .25
1059 A205 45c yellow & multi   .50   .25
   Nos. 1057-1059 (3)   1.05   .75

Progress in Venezuela and jobs for the handicapped.

Map of Carupano and Revelers — A206

1974, Feb. 22   Perf. 13½x14
1060 A206 5c multicolored   .60   .25

10th anniversary of Carupano Carnival.

Congress Emblem — A207

1974, May 20   Litho.   Perf. 13½
1061 A207 50c multicolored   .60   .25

9th Venezuelan Engineering Congress, Maracaibo, May 19-25.

Waves and "M" A208

Designs: Under-water photographs of deep-sea fish and marine life.

1974, June 20   Litho.   Perf. 12½
1062 A208 15c multicolored   .50   .25
1063 A208 35c multicolored   .70   .25
1064 A208 75c multicolored   .95   .30
1065 A208 80c multicolored   .95   .40
   Nos. 1062-1065 (4)   3.10   1.20

3rd UN Conference on the Law of the Sea, Caracas, June 20-Aug. 29.

Pupil and New School — A209

"Pay your Taxes" Campaign: 10c, 15c, 20c, like 5c. 25c, 30c, 35c, 40c, Suburban housing development. 45c, 50c, 55c, 60c, Highway and overpass. 65c, 70c, 75c, 80c, Playing field (sport). 85c, 90c, 95c, 1b, Operating room. All designs include Venezuelan coat of arms, coins and banknotes.

1974   Perf. 13½
1066 A209 5c blue & multi   .25   .25
1067 A209 10c ultra & multi   .25   .25
1068 A209 15c violet & multi   .25   .25
1069 A209 20c lilac & multi   .25   .25
1070 A209 25c multicolored   .25   .25
1071 A209 30c multicolored   .65   .25
1072 A209 35c multicolored   .25   .25
1073 A209 40c olive & multi   .45   .25
1074 A209 45c multicolored   .45   .25
1075 A209 50c green & multi   .45   .25
1076 A209 55c multicolored   .80   .40
1077 A209 60c multicolored   .65   .30
1078 A209 65c bister & multi   1.50   .60
1079 A209 70c multicolored   .70   .25
1080 A209 75c multicolored   .80   .30
1081 A209 80c brown & multi   .80   .30
1082 A209 85c ver & multi   .80   .30
1083 A209 90c multicolored   1.00   .30
1084 A209 95c multicolored   1.75   .95
1085 A209 1b multicolored   1.00   .40
   Nos. 1066-1085 (20)   13.30   6.60

Bolivar at Battle of Junin A210

1974, Aug. 6   Litho.   Perf. 13½x14
1086 A210 2b multicolored   2.00   1.00

Sesquicentennial of the Battle of Junin.

Globe and UPU Emblem — A211

50c, Postrider, sailing ship, steamer and jet.

1974, Oct. 9   Perf. 12
1087 A211 45c dk blue & multi   .45   .25
1088 A211 50c black & multi   .55   .25

Centenary of Universal Postal Union.

Rufino Blanco-Fombona — A212

Portraits of Blanco-Fombona and his books.

1974, Oct. 16   Litho.   Perf. 12½
1089 A212 10c gray & multi   .25   .25
1090 A212 30c yellow & multi   .25   .25
1091 A212 45c multicolored   .45   .25
1092 A212 90c buff & multi   .70   .35
   Nos. 1089-1092 (4)   1.65   1.10

Centenary of the birth of Rufino Blanco-Fombona (1874-1944), writer.

Children A213

1974, Nov. 29   Litho.   Perf. 13½
1093 A213 70c blue & multi   .60   .25

Children's Foundation Festival.

General Sucre — A214

Globe with South American Map and Flags — A215

Battle of Ayacucho — A216

1b, Map of South America with battles marked.

1974, Dec. 9   Perf. 14x13½, 13½x14
1094	A214	30c multicolored	.25	.25
1095	A215	50c multicolored	.40	.35
1096	A215	1b multicolored	.85	.40
1097	A216	2b multicolored	1.75	.85
		Nos. 1094-1097 (4)	3.25	1.85

Sesquicentennial of the Battle of Ayacucho.

Adoration of the Shepherds, by J. B. Mayno — A217

1974, Dec. 16   Photo.   Perf. 14x13½
1098		30c Shepherd	.35	.30
1099		30c Madonna & Child	.35	.30
a.	A217	Pair, #1098-1099	1.00	1.00

Christmas 1974.

Road Building, 1905 and El Ciempies Overpass, 1972 — A219

Designs: 20c, 1b, Jesus Muñoz Tebar, first Minister of Public Works. 25c, Bridges on Caracas-La Guaira Road, 1912 and 1953. 40c, View of Caracas, 1874 and 1974. 70c, Tucacas Railroad Station, 1911, and projected terminal, 1974. 80c, Anatomical Institute, Caracas, 1911, and Social Security Hospital, 1969. 85c, Quininari River Bridge, 1804, and Orinoco River Bridge, 1967.

1974, Dec. 18   Litho.   Perf. 12½
1100	A219	5c ultra & multi	.25	.25
1101	A219	20c ocher & blk	.30	.25
1102	A219	25c blue & multi	.35	.25
1103	A219	40c yellow & multi	.35	.25
1104	A219	70c green & multi	1.75	.30
1105	A219	80c multicolored	1.40	.35

1106	A219	85c orange & multi	1.75	.35
1107	A219	1b red & black	1.90	.60
		Nos. 1100-1107 (8)	8.05	2.60

Centenary of the Ministry of Public Works.

Women and IWY Emblem — A220

1975, Oct. 8   Litho.   Perf. 13½x14
| 1108 | A220 | 90c multicolored | .60 | .35 |

International Women's Year.

Scout Emblem and Tents — A221

1975, Nov. 11   Litho.   Perf. 13½x14
| 1109 | A221 | 20c multicolored | .25 | .25 |
| 1110 | A221 | 80c multicolored | .60 | .30 |

14th World Boy Scout Jamboree, Lille-hammer, Norway, July 29-Aug. 7.

Adoration of the Shepherds — A222

1975, Dec. 5   Litho.   Perf. 13½x14
1111		30c multicolored	.40	.40
1112		30c multicolored	.40	.40
a.	A222	Pair, #1111-1112	1.40	1.40

Christmas 1975.

Bolivar's Tomb — A224

Design: 1.05b, National Pantheon.

1976, Feb. 2   Engr.   Perf. 14x13½
| 1113 | A224 | 30c gray & ultra | .25 | .25 |
| 1114 | A224 | 1.05b sepia & car | .75 | .30 |

Centenary of National Pantheon.

Bolivia Flag Colors A225

1976, Mar. 22   Litho.   Perf. 13½
| 1115 | A225 | 60c multicolored | .60 | .25 |

Sesquicentennial of Bolivia's independence.

Aerial Map Survey — A226

1976, Apr. 8   Perf. 13½x12½
| 1116 | A226 | 1b black & vio bl | 1.00 | .35 |

Natl. Cartographic Institute, 40th anniv.

Gen. Ribas' Signature A227

José Felix Ribas A228

1976, Apr. 26   Photo.   Perf. 12½x13
| 1117 | A227 | 40c red & green | .40 | .25 |

Perf. 13½
| 1118 | A228 | 55c multicolored | .60 | .25 |

Gen. José Felix Ribas (1775-1815), independence hero, birth bicentenary.

Musicians of the Chacao School, by Armandio Barrios — A229

Lamas's Colophon A230

1976, May 13   Litho.   Perf. 13½
| 1119 | A229 | 75c multicolored | 1.25 | .80 |

Photo.   Perf. 12½x13
| 1120 | A230 | 1.25b buff, red & gray | .70 | .35 |

José Angel Lamas (1775-1814), composer, birth bicentenary.

Bolivar, by José Maria Espinoza — A231

1976   Engr.   Perf. 12
Size: 18x22½mm
1121	A231	5c green	.25	.25
1122	A231	10c lilac rose	.25	.25
1123	A231	15c brown	.25	.25
1124	A231	20c black	.25	.25
1125	A231	25c yellow	.25	.25
1126	A231	30c violet bl	.25	.25
1127	A231	45c dk purple	.25	.25
1128	A231	50c orange	.25	.25
1129	A231	65c blue	.35	.25
1130	A231	1b vermilion	.45	.35

Size: 26x32mm
Perf. 12x11½
1131	A231	2b gray	.90	.35
1132	A231	3b violet blue	1.40	.55
1133	A231	4b yellow	1.75	.75
1134	A231	5b orange	2.10	1.00
1135	A231	10b dull purple	5.00	2.00
1136	A231	15b blue	7.25	2.75
1137	A231	20b vermilion	9.25	3.75
		Nos. 1121-1137 (17)	30.45	13.75

Issued: 5c-1b, May 17; 2b-20b, July 15.

Coil Stamps
1978, May 22   Perf. 13½ Horiz.
Size: 18x22½mm
1138	A231	5c green	.30	.25
1139	A231	10c lilac rose	.30	.25
1140	A231	15c brown	.30	.25
1141	A231	20c black	.30	.25
1142	A231	25c yellow	.30	.25
1143	A231	30c violet blue	.35	.25
1144	A231	45c dk purple	.45	.25
1144A	A231	50c orange	.60	.25
1144B	A231	65c blue	.75	.25
1144C	A231	1b vermilion	1.25	.25
		Nos. 1138-1144C (10)	4.90	2.50

Black control number on back of every fifth stamp.
See Nos. 1305-1307, 1362-1366, 1401-1409, 1482, 1484, 1487, 1490. Compare with designs A405-A406.

Maze A232

Central University A233

Faculty Emblems A234

1976, June 1   Litho.   Perf. 12½x13
1145	A232	30c multicolored	.25	.25
1146	A233	50c yel, org & blk	.35	.25
1147	A234	90c black & yellow	.70	.45
		Nos. 1145-1147 (3)	1.30	.95

Central University of Venezuela, 250th anniv.

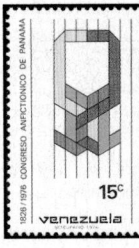

"Unity" — A235

Designs: 45c, 1.25b, similar to 15c.

1976, June 29   Litho.   Perf. 12½
1148	A235	15c multicolored	.25	.25
1149	A235	45c multicolored	.35	.25
1150	A235	1.25b multicolored	.70	.45
		Nos. 1148-1150 (3)	1.30	.95

Amphictyonic Cong. of Panama, Sesqui.

Washington, US Bicent. Emblem A236

US Bicentennial Emblem and: No. 1152, Jefferson. No. 1153, Lincoln. No. 1154, F. D. Roosevelt. No. 1155, J. F. Kennedy.

1976, July 4   Engr.   Perf. 14
1151 A236 1b red brn & blk   .70 .35
1152 A236 1b green & blk   .70 .35
1153 A236 1b purple & blk   .70 .35
1154 A236 1b blue & blk   .70 .35
1155 A236 1b olive & blk   .70 .35
 Nos. 1151-1155 (5)   3.50 1.75
American Bicentennial.

Valve — A237

Computer drawings of valves & pipelines.

1976, Nov. 8   Photo.   Perf. 12½x14
1156 A237 10c multicolored   .25 .25
1157 A237 30c multicolored   .25 .25
1158 A237 35c multicolored   .30 .25
1159 A237 40c multicolored   .30 .25
1160 A237 55c multicolored   .40 .25
1161 A237 90c multicolored   .70 .25
 Nos. 1156-1161 (6)   2.20 1.50
Nationalization of the oil industry.

Nativity, by
Barbaro
Rivas — A238

1976, Dec. 1   Litho.   Perf. 13x14
1162 A238 30c multicolored   .60 .30
Christmas 1976.

Ornament
A239

Lithographed and Embossed
1976, Dec. 15   Perf. 14x13½
1163 A239 60c yellow & black   .60 .25
Declaration of Bogota (economic agreements of Andean countries), 10th anniv.

Coat of Arms of Barinas — A240

1977, May 25   Photo.   Perf. 12½x13
1164 A240 50c multicolored   .60 .25
400th anniv. of the founding of Barinas.

Crucified Christ,
Patron Saint of
La Grita — A241

1977, Aug. 6   Litho.   Perf. 13
1165 A241 30c multicolored   .50 .25
Founding of La Grita, 400th anniv. (in 1976).

Symbolic
City — A242

1977, Aug. 26   Litho.   Perf. 13½
1166 A242 1b multicolored   .65 .30
450th anniversary of the founding of Coro.

Communications Symbols — A243

1977, Sept. 30   Litho.   Perf. 13½x14
1167 A243 85c multicolored   .65 .25
9th Interamerican Postal and Telecommunications Staff Congress, Caracas, Sept. 26-30.

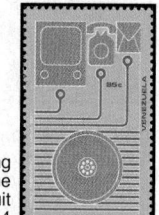
Cable Connecting
with TV, Telephone
and Circuit
Box — A244

1977, Oct. 12   Litho.   Perf. 14
1168 A244 95c multicolored   .95 .25
Inauguration of Columbus underwater cable
linking Venezuela and the Canary Islands.

"Venezuela"
A245

Designs: "Venezuela" horizontal on 50c,
1.05b; reading up on 80c, 1.25b; reading down
on 1.50b.

1977, Nov. 26   Photo.   Perf. 13½x13
1169 A245   30c brt yel & blk   .25 .25
1170 A245   50c dp org & blk   .35 .25
1171 A245   80c gray & blk   .60 .25
1172 A245 1.05b red & blk   .80 .25
1173 A245 1.25b yel & blk   .90 .25
1174 A245 1.50b gray & blk   1.10 .35
 Nos. 1169-1174 (6)   4.00 1.60
Iron industry nationalization, 1st anniv.

Juan Pablo
Duarte — A246

1977, Dec. 8   Engr.   Perf. 11x13
1175 A246 75c black & lilac   .55 .25
Duarte (1813-76), leader in liberation
struggle.

Nativity, Colonial
Sculpture — A247

1977, Dec. 15   Litho.   Perf. 13
1176 A247 30c green & multi   .40 .25
Christmas 1977.

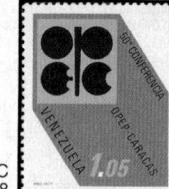
OPEC
Emblem — A248

1977, Dec. 20
1177 A248 1.05b brt & lt bl & blk   .90 .25
50th Conference of Oil Producing and
Exporting Countries, Caracas.

Bicyclist
A249

1978, Jan. 16   Litho.   Perf. 13½x13
1178 A249   5c Racing bicy-
       clists   .25 .25
1179 A249 1.25b shown   1.00 .25
World Bicycling Championships, San Cristobal, Tachira, Aug. 22-Sept. 4.

Profiles
A250

1978, Apr. 21   Litho.   Perf. 13½x14
1180 A250 70c blk, gray & lil   .65 .25
Language Day.
Issued in tete-beche pairs. Value $1.25.

Magnetic
Computer
Tape and
Satellite
A251

1978, May 17   Litho.   Perf. 14
1184 A251 75c violet blue   .75 .25
10th World Telecommunications Day.

"1777-1977" — A252

Goya's Carlos
III as Computer
Print — A253

1978, June 23   Litho.   Perf. 12
1185 A252 30c multicolored   .25 .25
1186 A253 1b multicolored   .55 .25
200th anniversary of Venezuelan unification.

Bolivar Bicentenary

Juan Vicente Bolivar y Ponte, Father
of Simon Bolivar — A254

The Oath on Monte Sacro, Rome, by
Tito Salas — A255

Designs: 30c, Bolivar as infant in nurse-
maid's arms (detail from design of No. 1189).
No. 1189, Baptism of the Liberator, by Tito
Salas, 1929.

1978, July 24   Engr.   Perf. 12½
1187 A254 30c emerald & blk   .25 .25
1188 A254 1b multicolored   .55 .25

Souvenir Sheet
Litho.
Perf. 14
1189 A255   Sheet of 5   40.00 40.00
 a.   50c, single stamp   1.50 1.50

1978, Dec. 17   Engr.   Perf. 12½
Designs: 30c, Bolivar at 25. 1b, Simon Rodriguez. No. 1192, shown. (Bolivar's tutor).
1190 A254 30c multicolored   .25 .25
1191 A254 1b rose red & blk   .45 .25

Souvenir Sheet
Litho.
Perf. 14
1192 A255   Sheet of 5   24.00 24.00
 a.   50c, single stamp   1.10 1.10

Size of souvenir sheet stamps: 20x24mm.
Size of #1189: 154x130mm; #1192:
130x155mm.

1979, July 24   Engr.   Perf. 12½
Designs: 30c, Alexander Sabes Petion,
president of Haiti. 1b, Bolivar's signature.
No. 1195: a, Partial map of Jamaica, horiz.
b, Partial map of Jamaica, vert. c, Bolivar,
1816. d, Luis Brion. e, Petion.
1193 A254 30c org, vio & blk   .30 .25
1194 A254 1b red org & blk   .45 .25

Souvenir Sheet
Litho.
Perf. 14
1195 A255   Sheet of 5   3.25 3.25
 a.-e.   50c, any single   .35 .35

Size of souvenir sheet stamps: 26x20,
20x26mm.

1979, Dec. 17   Engr.   Perf. 12½
Designs: 30c, Bolivar. 1b, Slave. No. 1198,
Freeing of the Slaves, by Tito Salas. (30c, 1b,
details from design of No. 1198.)
1196 A254 30c multicolored   .25 .25
1197 A254 1b multicolored   .30 .25

Souvenir Sheet
Litho.
Perf. 14
1198 A255   Sheet of 5   5.50 5.50
 a.   50c, single stamp   1.10 1.10

Simon Bolivar, birth centenary. Size of souvenir sheet stamps: 22x28mm.
See Nos. 1228-1230, 1264-1266, 1276-
1284, 1294-1296, 1317-1322.

"T" and
"CTV" — A256

Designs: Different arrangement of letters "T"
and "CTV" for "Confederacion de Trabajeros
Venezolanos."

1978, Sept. 27 Photo. Perf. 13x13½
1199   Strip of 5   .90   .90
   a.-e. A256 30c, single stamp   .25   .25
1200   Strip of 5   1.90   1.90
   a.-e. A256 95c, single stamp   .30   .25
     Workers' Day.

Symbolic Design — A257

1978, Oct. 3 Litho. Perf. 14
1201   A257 50c dark brown   .75   .30
   Rafael Rangel, physician and scientist, birth centenary.

Drill Head, Tachira Oil Field Map — A258

"P" as Pipeline A259

1978, Nov. 2 Litho. Perf. 13½
1202   A258 30c multicolored   .25   .25
1203   A259 1.05b multicolored   .95   .30
     Centenary of oil industry.

Star — A260

1978, Dec. 6 Litho. Perf. 14
1204   A260 30c multicolored   .60   .25
     Christmas 1978.

"P T" — A261

1979, Feb. 8 Litho. Perf. 12½
1205   A261 75c black & red   .40   .25
   Creation of Postal and Telegraph Institute.

"Dam Holding Back Water" A262

1979, Feb. 15 Photo. Perf. 13½
1206   A262 2b silver, gray & blk   .90   .45
     Guri Dam, 10th anniversary.

San Martin, by E. J. Maury — A263

60c, San Martin, by Mercedes. 70c, Monument, Guayaquil. 75c, San Martin's signature.

1979, Feb. 25 Perf. 12½x13
1207   A263 40c blue, blk & yel   .25   .25
1208   A263 60c blue, blk & yel   .30   .25
1209   A263 70c blue, blk & yel   .40   .25
1210   A263 75c blue, blk & yel   .40   .25
     Nos. 1207-1210 (4)   1.35   1.00
   José de San Martin (1778-1850), South American liberator.

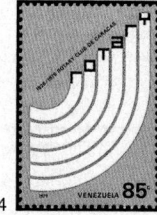

"Rotary" — A264

1979, Aug. 7 Litho. Perf. 14x13½
1211   A264 85c gold & blk   .70   .25
   Rotary Club of Caracas, 50th anniversary.

Our Lady of Coromoto Appearing to Children A265

Engraved and Lithographed
1979, Aug. 23 Perf. 13
1212   A265 55c black & dp org   .65   .25
   Canonization of Our Lady of Coromoto, 25th anniv.

London Residence, Coat of Arms, Miranda — A266

1979, Oct. 23 Litho. Perf. 14½x14
1213   A266 50c multicolored   .50   .25
   Francisco de Miranda (1750-1816), Venezuelan independence fighter.

O'Leary, Maps of South America and United Kingdom A267

1979, Nov. 6
1214   A267 30c multicolored   .50   .25
   Daniel O'Leary (1801-1854), general, writer.

A268

   IYC Emblem and: 79c, Boy holding nest. 80c, Boys in water, bridge.

1979, Nov. 20 Litho. Perf. 14½x14
1215   A268 70c lt blue & blk   .25   .25
1216   A268 80c multicolored   .40   .25
     International Year of the Child.

A269

1979, Dec. 1 Litho. Perf. 13
1217   A269 30c multicolored   .50   .25
     Christmas 1979.

Caudron Bomber, EXFILVE Emblem A270

   EXFILVE Emblem and: No. 1219, Stearman biplane. No. 1220, UH-1H helicopter. No. 1221, CF-5 jet fighter.

1979, Dec. 15 Perf. 11x11½
1218   A270 75c multicolored   .40   .25
1219   A270 75c multicolored   .40   .25
1220   A270 75c multicolored   .40   .25
1221   A270 75c multicolored   .40   .25
   a.   Block of 4, #1218-1221   1.75   1.00
   Venezuelan Air Force, 59th anniv.; EXFILVE 79, 3rd Natl. Philatelic Exhibition, Dec. 7-17.

IPOSTEL Emblem, World Map A271

1979, Dec. 27 Perf. 11½
1222   A271 75c multicolored   .50   .25
   Postal and Telegraph Institute, introduction of new logo.

Queen Victoria, Hill — A272

1980, Feb. 13 Litho. Perf. 12½
1223   A272 55c multicolored   .50   .25
   Sir Rowland Hill (1795-1879), originator of penny postage.

Dr. Augusto Pi Suner, Physiologist, Birth Centenary — A273

1980, Mar. 14 Litho. Perf. 11½
1224   A273 80c multicolored   .50   .25

Spanish Seed Leaf — A274

Lithographed and Engraved
1980, Mar. 27 Perf. 13
1225   A274 50c multicolored   .60   .25
   Pedro Loefling (1729-56), Swedish botanist.

Juan Lovera (1778-1841), Artist — A275

1980, May 25 Litho. Perf. 13½
1226   A275 60c blue & dp org   .25   .25
1227   A275 75c violet & org   .30   .25

Bolivar Types of 1978
   30c, Signing of document. 1b, House of Congress. #1230, Angostura Congress, by Tito Salas.

1980, July 24 Engr. Perf. 12½
1228   A254 30c multicolored   .25   .25
1229   A254 1b multicolored   .50   .25

Souvenir Sheet
Litho.
Perf. 14
1230   A255   Sheet of 5   4.00   4.00
   a.   50c, single stamp   .25   .25
   Simon Bolivar (1783-1830), revolutionary. Size of souvenir sheet stamps: 25x20mm, 20x25mm.

Dancing Girls, by Armando Reveron — A276

1980, Aug. 17 Litho. Perf. 13
1231   A276 50c shown   .25   .25
     Size: 25x40mm
1232   A276 65c Portrait   .55   .30
   Armando Reveron (1889-1955), artist.

Bernardo O'Higgins — A277

Lithographed and Engraved
1980, Aug. 22 Perf. 13x14
1233   A277 85c multicolored   .75   .30
   Bernardo O'Higgins (1776-1842), Chilean soldier and statesman.

School Ship Simon Bolivar A278

Frigate Mariscal Sucre
A279

Perf. 11½ (#1234), 11x11½
1980, Sept. 13   **Litho.**
1234 A278 1.50b shown   1.25 .40
1235 A279 1.50b shown   1.25 .40
1236 A279 1.50b Submarine
       Picua   1.25 .40
1237 A279 1.50b Naval Academy   1.25 .40
     Nos. 1234-1237 (4)   5.00 1.60

"Picuda" is misspelled on stamp.

Workers Holding OPEC Emblem
A280

20th Anniv. of OPEC (Organization of Petroleum Exporting Countries): #1239, Emblem.

1980, Sept. 14   Litho.   Perf. 12x11½
1238 A280 1.50b multicolored   .75 .30
1239 A280 1.50b multicolored   .75 .30

 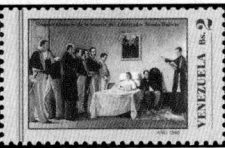

Death of Simon Bolivar
A281

1980, Dec. 17   Litho.   Perf. 11x11½
1240 A281 2b multicolored   1.60 .50

Simon Bolivar, 150th anniversary of death.

A282

Lithographed and Engraved
1980, Dec. 17   **Perf. 13x12½**
1241 A282 2b multicolored   .90 .40

Gen. José Antonio Sucre, 150th anniv. of death.

A283

1980, Dec. 19   Litho.   Perf. 14x13½
1242 A283 1b Nativity by Rubens   .60 .35

Christmas 1980.

Helen Keller's Initials (Written and Braille) — A284

Lithographed and Embossed
1981, Feb. 12   **Perf. 12½**
1243 A284 1.50b multicolored   .90 .35

Helen Keller (1880-1968), blind and deaf writer and lecturer.

John Baptiste de la Salle — A285

1981, May 15   Litho.   Perf. 11½x11
1244 A285 1.25b multicolored   .55 .25

Christian Brothers' 300th anniv.

San Felipe City, 250th Anniv. — A286

1981, May 1   **Perf. 11½**
1245 A286 3b multicolored   1.10 .50

Municipal Theater of Caracas Centenary
A287

1981, June 28   Litho.   Perf. 12
1246 A287 1.25b multicolored   2.00 .35

A288

1981, Sept. 15   Litho.   Perf. 11½
1247 A288 2b multicolored   .60 .25

UPU membership centenary.

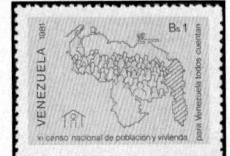

A289

1981, Oct. 14   **Litho.**
1248 A289 1b multicolored   .50 .25

11th natl. population and housing census.

A290

1981, Dec. 3   Litho.   Perf. 11½
1249 A290 95c multicolored   .50 .25

9th Bolivar Games, Barquismeto.

19th Cent. Bicycle
A291

1981, Dec. 5   Photo.   Perf. 13x14
1250 A291   1b shown   .55 .35
1251 A291 1.05b Locomotive,
       1926   .55 .35
1252 A291 1.25b Buick, 1937   .95 .50
1253 A291 1.50b Coach   1.25 .60
     Nos. 1250-1253 (4)   3.30 1.80

See Nos. 1289-1292, 1308-1311.

Christmas 1981
A292

1981, Dec. 21   Litho.   Perf. 11½
1254 A292 1b multicolored   .50 .25

50th Anniv. of Natural Science Society — A293

1982, Jan. 21   **Perf. 11½**
1255 A293   1b Mt. Autana   .45 .25
1256 A293 1.50b Sarisarinama   .70 .40
1257 A293   2b Guacharo Cave   .90 .45
     Nos. 1255-1257 (3)   2.05 1.10

20th Anniv. of Constitution
A294

1982, Jan. 28   Photo.   Perf. 13x13½
1258 A294 1.85b gold & blk   .90 .35

A295

1982, Feb. 19   Litho.   Perf. 13½
1259 A295 3b multicolored   1.40 .60

20th anniv. of agricultural reform.

A296

1982, Mar. 12   Litho.   Perf. 13½
1260 A296 1b blue & dk blue   .75 .25

Jules Verne (1828-1905), science fiction writer.

Natl. Anthem Centenary (1981)
A297

1982, Mar. 26   **Perf. 11½**
1261 A297 1b multicolored   .65 .25

1300th Anniv. of Bulgaria — A298

1982, June 2   Litho.   Perf. 13½
1262 A298 65c multicolored   .60 .35

6th Natl. 5-Year Plan, 1981-85 — A299

1982, June 11
1263 A299 2b multicolored   .50 .25

Bolivar Types of 1978

30c, Juan José Rondon. 1b, José Antonio Anzoategui.

1982, July 24   Engr.   Perf. 12½
1264 A254 30c multicolored   .50 .30
1265 A254   1b multicolored   .50 .30

Souvenir Sheet

        Litho.   **Perf. 14**
1266 A255   Sheet of 5   4.50 4.50
   a.-e.   50c, any single   .30 .30

Single stamps of No. 1266 show details from Battle of Boyaca, by Martin Tovar y Tovar. Size of souvenir sheet stamps: 19x26mm, 26x19mm.

Cecilio Acosta (1818-1881), Writer — A299a

1982, Aug. 13   Litho.   Perf. 11½
1266F A299a 3b multicolored   .65 .35

Aloe
A300

1982, Oct. 14   Photo.   Perf. 13
1267	A300	1.05b shown	.75	.40
1268	A300	2.55b Tortoise	1.90	.40
1269	A300	2.75b Tara amarilla tree	2.10	.40
1270	A300	3b Guacharo bird	2.50	.45
		Nos. 1267-1270 (4)	7.25	1.65

Andres Bello (1781-1865), Statesman and Reformer — A301

1982, Nov. 20   Litho.   Perf. 12
1271	A301	1.05b multicolored	.45	.25
1272	A301	2.55b multicolored	.95	.30
1273	A301	2.75b multicolored	.95	.30
1274	A301	3b multicolored	1.25	.35
		Nos. 1271-1274 (4)	3.60	1.20

Christmas 1982 — A302

Design: Holy Family creche figures by Francisco J. Cardozo, 18th cent.

Photogravure and Engraved
1982, Dec. 7   Perf. 13½
| 1275 | A302 | 1b multicolored | .40 | .25 |

Bolivar Types of 1978

No. 1276, Victory Monument, Carabobo. No. 1277, Monument to the Meeting plaque. No. 1278, Antonio de Sucre. No. 1279, Jose Antonio Paez. No. 1280, Sword hilt, 1824. No. 1281, Guayaquil Monument.

1982-83   Engr.   Perf. 12½
1276	A254	30c multicolored	.25	.25
1277	A254	30c multicolored	.25	.25
1278	A254	30c multicolored	.25	.25
1279	A254	1b multicolored	.35	.25
1280	A254	1b multicolored	.35	.25
1281	A254	1b multicolored	.35	.25
		Nos. 1276-1281 (6)	1.80	1.50

Souvenir Sheets
Litho.
Perf. 14
1282	A255	Sheet of 5	5.00	5.00
a.-e.		50c, any single	.30	.30
1283	A255	Sheet of 5	5.00	5.00
a.-e.		50c, any single	.30	.30
1284	A255	Sheet of 5	5.00	5.00
a.-e.		50c, any single	.30	.30

No. 1282, Battle of Carabobo by Martin Tovar y Tovar; No. 1283, Monument to the Meeting; No. 1284, Battle of Ayacucho, by Martin Tovar y Tovar.

Issue dates: Nos. 1276-1277, 1279, 1281-1283, Dec. 17; others, Apr. 18, 1983.

Gen. Jose Francisco Bermudez — A303

Antonio Nicolas Briceno, Liberation Hero A304

Perf. 13x13½, 15x14
1982, Dec. 23   Litho.
| 1285 | A303 | 3b multicolored | 1.60 | .50 |
| 1286 | A304 | 3b multicolored | 1.60 | .50 |

25th Anniv. of 1958 Reforms A305

1983, Jan. 23   Perf. 10½x10
| 1287 | A305 | 3b multicolored | 1.00 | .45 |

A306

1983, Mar. 20   Photo.   Perf. 13½x13
| 1288 | A306 | 4b olive & red | 1.00 | .45 |

25th anniv. of Judicial Police Technical Dept.

Transportation Type of 1981
Perf. 13½x14½
1983, Mar. 28   Photo.
1289	A291	75c Lincoln, 1923	1.10	.45
1290	A291	80c Locomotive, 1889	1.10	.45
1291	A291	85c Willys truck, 1927	1.40	.45
1292	A291	95c Cleveland motorcycle, 1920	1.40	.45
		Nos. 1289-1292 (4)	5.00	1.80

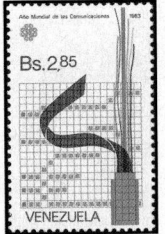

A307

1983, May 17   Photo.   Perf. 13x12½
| 1293 | A307 | 2.85b multicolored | .75 | .40 |

World Communications Year.

Bolivar Types of 1978

Designs: 30c; Flags of Colombia, Peru, Chile, Venezuela, and Buenos Aires. 1b; Equestrian Statue of Bolivar.

Photo. & Engr. (#1294), Engr. (#1295)
1983, July 25   Perf. 12½
| 1294 | A254 | 30c multicolored | .35 | .25 |
| 1295 | A254 | 1b multicolored | .50 | .25 |

Souvenir Sheet
Litho.
Perf. 14
| 1296 | A255 | Sheet of 5 | 5.00 | 4.75 |
| a.-e. | | 50c, any single | .25 | .26 |

Single stamps of No. 1296 show details of "The Liberator on the Silver Mountain of Potosi" Size of souvenir sheet stamps, 20x25mm.

 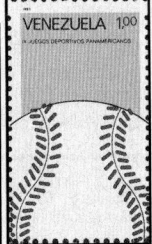

9th Pan-American Games
A308   A309

Designs: #1303a, baseball. b, cycle wheel. c, boxing glove. d, soccer ball. e, target.

Lithographed and Engraved
1983, Aug. 25   Perf. 13
1297	A308	2b shown	.50	.25
1298	A308	2b Swimming	.50	.25
1299	A308	2.70b Cycling	.60	.40
1300	A308	2.70b Fencing	.60	.40
1301	A308	2.85b Runners	.75	.50
1302	A308	2.85b Weightlifting	.75	.50
		Nos. 1297-1302 (6)	3.70	2.30

Souvenir Sheet
| 1303 | | Sheet of 5 | 16.00 | 16.00 |
| a.-e. | A309 | 1b, any single | 16.00 | 16.00 |

#1303 for Copan '83. Size: 167x121mm.

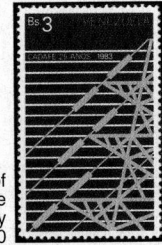

25th Anniv. of Cadafe (State Electricity Authority) — A310

1983, Oct. 27   Litho.   Perf. 14
| 1304 | A310 | 3b multicolored | 1.40 | .65 |

Redrawn Bolivar Type of 1976
1983, Sept. 29   Engr.   Perf. 12
Size: 26x32mm
1305	A231	25b blue green	11.50	5.50
1306	A231	30b brown	13.50	6.75
1307	A231	50b brt rose lilac	20.00	11.50
		Nos. 1305-1307 (3)	45.00	23.75

Transportation Type of 1981
Various views of Caracas Metro.

1983, Dec.   Photo.   Perf. 13½x14½
1308	A291	55c multicolored	.70	.45
1309	A291	75c multicolored	.70	.45
1310	A291	95c multicolored	.70	.45
1311	A291	2b multicolored	1.50	.65
		Nos. 1308-1311 (4)	3.60	2.00

Christmas 1983 A311

1983, Dec. 1   Litho.   Perf. 13x14
| 1312 | A311 | 1b Nativity | .50 | .35 |

Scouting Year (1982) A312

Lithographed and Engraved
1983, Dec. 14   Perf. 12½x13
| 1313 | A312 | 2.25p Pitching tent | .60 | .35 |

1314	A312	2.55b Planting tree	.60	.35
1315	A312	2.75b Mountain climbing	.75	.35
1316	A312	3b Camp site	.75	.35
		Nos. 1313-1316 (4)	2.70	1.40

Bolivar Types of 1978

Designs: No. 1317, Title page of "Opere de Raimondo Montecuccoli" (most valuable book in Caracas University Library). No. 1318, Pedro Gual, Congress of Panama delegate, 1826. No. 1319, Jose Maria Vargas (b. 1786), University of Caracas pres. No. 1320, José Faustino Sanchez Carrion, Congress of Panama delegate, 1826.

1984   Engr.   Perf. 12½
1317	A254	30c multicolored	.25	.25
1318	A254	30c multicolored	.25	.25
1319	A254	1b multicolored	.25	.25
1320	A254	1b multicolored	.25	.25
		Nos. 1317-1320 (4)	1.00	1.00

Souvenir Sheets
Litho.
Perf. 14
1321	A255	Sheet of 5	4.75	4.50
a.-e.		50c, any single	.30	.30
1322	A255	Sheet of 5	5.25	5.25
a.-e.		50c, any single	.30	.30

Single stamps of No. 1321 show details of Arts, Science and Education, fresco by Hector Poleo; 1322, Map of South America, 1829. Size of souvenir sheet stamps: 20x30mm; 27x20mm.

Issued: #1317, 1319, 1321, 1/19; others, 1/20.

Radio Waves — A313

1984, Jan. 30   Litho.   Perf. 14x13
| 1323 | A313 | 2.70b multicolored | .65 | .25 |

Radio Club of Venezuela, 50th anniv.

Intelligentsia for Peace — A314

1984, Jan. 31
1324	A314	1b Doves	.30	.25
1325	A314	2.70b Profile	.60	.25
1326	A314	2.85b Flower, head	.60	.25
		Nos. 1324-1326 (3)	1.50	.75

President Romulo Gallegos (1884-1969) A315

Gallegos: No. 1327, Portrait as a young man in formal dress. No. 1328, Portrait, 1948.

1984-85   Litho.   Perf. 11½
| 1327 | A315 | 1.70b royal bl, dl bl, beige & blk | .65 | .40 |
| 1328 | A315 | 1.70b ocher, org brn & buff | .65 | .40 |

Issued: #1327, 10/12/84; #1328, 1/18/85.
See Nos. 1335-1336.

Pan-American Union of Engineering Associations, 18th Convention
A316

1984, Oct. 28
1329 A316 2.55b pale buff, dk bl   .65   .25

Christmas 1984
A317

1984, Dec. 3
1330 A317 1b multicolored   .50   .25

Pope John Paul II, Statue of the Virgin of Caracas
A318

1985, Jan. 26   Litho.   Perf. 12
1331 A318 1b multicolored   1.75   .45
Papal visit, 1985.

Pascua City Bicent.
A319

1985, Feb. 10
1332 A319 1.50b multicolored   .60   .35

Dr. Mario Briceno-Iragorry (b. 1897), Historian — A320

1985, Oct.   Litho.   Perf. 12
1333 A320 1.25b silver & ver   .50   .25

Natl. St. Vincent de Paul Soc., Cent. — A321

1985, July
1334 A321 1b dk ol bis, ver & buff   .60   .25

Gallegos Memorial Type of 1984-85
Designs: Gallegos, diff.

1985, Aug. 8
1335 A315 1.70b gray grn, dk gray
              grn & dl gray grn   .35   .25
1336 A315 1.70b grn, sage grn & dl
              grn   .35   .25
Dated 1984.

Latin American Economic System, 10th Anniv.
A322

1985, Aug. 15
1337 A322 4b black & red   2.00   .85

Miniature Sheet

Virgin Mary, Birth Bimillennium — A323

Statues: a, Virgin of the Divine Shepherd. b, Chiquinquira Madonna. c, Coromoto Madonna. d, Valley Madonna. e, Virgin of Perpetual Succor. f, Virgin of Peace. g, Immaculate Conception Virgin. h, Soledad Madonna. i, Virgin of Consolation. j, Nieves Madonna.

1985, Sept. 9
1338   Sheet of 10   7.00 7.00
a.-j. A323 1b, any single   .40   .25

OPEC, 25th Anniv.
A324

1985, Sept. 13
1339 A324 6b multicolored   1.75   .80

Opening of the Museum of Contemporary Art, Caracas — A325

1985, Oct. 24   Perf. 13½
1340 A325 3b multicolored   .90   .45
Dated 1983.

UN, 40th Anniv.
A326

1985, Nov. 15   Perf. 12
1341 A326 10b brt blue & ver   2.25 1.40

Intl. Youth Year
A327

1985, Nov. 26
1342 A327 1.50b multicolored   .60   .25

Christmas 1985 — A328

Nativity: a, Sheperds. b, Holy Family, Magi. Se-tenant in a continuous design.

1985, Dec. 2
1343 A328 Pair   1.75 1.75
a.-b.   2b, any single   .85   .25

Dr. Luis Maria Drago (b. 1859), Politician
A329

1985, Dec. 20   Perf. 13½
1344 A329 2.70b tan, ver & sepia   .70   .50
Dated 1984.

Miniature Sheet

Natl. Oil Industry, 10th Anniv. — A330

Designs: a, Industry emblem. b, Isla Oil Refinery. c, Bariven oil terminal. d, Pequiven refinery. e, Corpoven drilling rig. f, Maraven offshore rig. g, Intevep labs. h, Meneven refinery. i, Lagoven refinery. j, Emblem, early drilling rig.

1985, Dec. 13   Perf. 12
1345   Sheet of 10   12.00 12.00
a.-b. A330 1b multi   .25   .25
c.-d. A330 2b multi   .55   .25
e.-f. A330 3b multi   1.00   .35
g.-h. A330 4b multi   1.25   .40
i.-j. A330 5b multi   1.50   .50

Simon Bolivar Memorial Coins — A331

1985, Dec. 18
1346 A331 2b multicolored   .50   .35
1347 A331 2.70b multicolored   .70   .45
1348 A331 3b multicolored   .80   .50
      Nos. 1346-1348 (3)   2.00 1.30
Dated 1984.

Guayana Development Corp., 25th Anniv. — A332

2b, Guayana City. 3b, Orinoco Steel Mill. 5b, Raul Leoni-Guri Hydro-electric Dam.

1985, Dec. 27
1349 A332 2b multicolored   .50   .40
1350 A332 3b multicolored   .85   .50
1351 A332 5b multicolored   1.40   .90
      Nos. 1349-1351 (3)   2.75 1.80

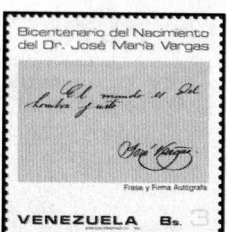

Dr. Jose Vargas (1786-1854) — A334

Designs: No. 1352a, Handwriting and signature. b, Portrait, 1874, by Martin Tovar y Tovar. c, Statue, Palace of the Academies. d, Flags, EXFILBO '86 emblem. e, Vargas do Caracas Hospital. f, Frontispiece of lectures manual, 1842. g, Portrait, 1986, by Alirio Palacios. h, Gesneria vargasii. i, Bolivar-Vargas commemorative medal, 1955, 6th Natl. Medical Sciences Cong. j, Portrait, anonymous, 19th cent.
No. 1353a, Portrait, facing front. b, Portrait, facing left, Nos. 1352a, 1352d, 1352e, 1352i and 1352i have horizontal vignettes.

Miniature Sheet
1986, Mar. 10   Litho.   Perf. 12
1352   Sheet of 10   11.00 11.00
a.-j. A333 3b, any single   .90   .40
Souvenir Sheet
Imperf
1353   Sheet of 2   13.50 13.50
a.-b. A334 15b, any single   6.00 1.00
EXFILBO '86, Mar. 10-17, Caracas, 1st Bolivarian exhibition.

Youths Painting School Wall
A335

1986, May 12   Perf. 12
1354 A335 3b shown   .75   .35
1355 A335 5b Repairing desk   1.25   .35
Founding and maintenance of educational institutions.

Francisco Miranda's Work for American Liberation, Bicent. (1981)
A336

Lithographed and Engraved
1986, Apr. 18   **Perf. 13**
1356 A336 1.05b multicolored   .50 .25
Dated 1983.

INDULAC,
45th Anniv.
A337

2.55b, Milk trucks, vert. 2.70b, Map, vert.
3.70b, Milk processing plant.

1986, June 27   **Litho.**   **Perf. 12**
1357 A337 2.55b multicolored   .60 .25
1358 A337 2.70b multicolored   .60 .25
1359 A337 3.70b multicolored   .80 .25
    Nos. 1357-1359 (3)   2.00 .75
Industria Lactea (INDULAC), Venezuelan
milk processing company.

Miniature Sheet

Viasa Venezuelan Airlines, 25th
Anniv. — A338

a, Commemorative coin. b, Douglas DC-8
ascending. c, DC-8 taxiing. d, Boeing 747 in
flight. e, DC-10 tails. f, Map of hemispheres. g,
DC-10 taking off. h, Rear of DC-10 & DC8 on
runway. i, DC-9 over mountains. j, Crew in
cockpit.

1986, Aug. 11   **Litho.**   **Perf. 12**
1360   Sheet of 10   9.00 9.00
   a.-e. A338 3b, any single   .55 .40
   f.-j. A338 3.25b, any single   .60 .40

Miniature Sheet

Romulo Betancourt (1908-1981),
President — A339

a, i, Portrait with natl. flag. b, j, Seated in
armchair, smoking pipe. c, h, Wearing hat,
text. d, f, Wearing sash of office. e, g, Reading.

1986, Sept. 28
1361   Sheet of 10   10.00 10.00
   a.-e. A339 2.70b, any single   .50 .25
   f.-j. A339 3b, any single   .60 .25

Redrawn Bolivar Type of 1976
1986, Sept. 29   **Litho.**   **Perf. 12½**
1362 A231 25c red   .50 .35
1363 A231 50c blue   .50 .35
1364 A231 75c pink   .50 .35
1365 A231 1b orange   .50 .35
1366 A231 2b brt yellow grn   .60 .35
    Nos. 1362-1366 (5)   2.60 1.75
Nos. 1362-1366 inscribed Armitano.

For surcharges see Nos. 1453-1464.

Re-opening of
Zulia University,
40th
Anniv. — A340

1986, Sept. 29
1367 A340 2.70b shown   .45 .35
1368 A340 2.70b Library en-
    trance   .45 .35
   a.   Pair, #1367-1368   1.00 1.00

11th Congress of Architects,
Engineers and Affiliated
Professionals — A341

1986, Oct. 3
1369 A341 1.40b multicolored   .40 .25
1370 A341 1.55b multicolored   .40 .25
   a.   Pair, #1369-1370   .85 .85

Fauna
and
Flora
A342

70c, Priodontes maximus. 85c, Espeletia
angustifolia. 2.70b, Crocodylus intermedius.
3b, Brownea grandiceps.

1986, Sept. 12   **Photo.**   **Perf. 13½**
1371 A342 70c multicolored   .70 .60
1372 A342 85c multicolored   .70 .60
1373 A342 2.70b multicolored   .70 .60
1374 A342 3b multicolored   .90 .65
    Nos. 1371-1374 (4)   3.00 2.45

Miniature Sheet

State Visit of Pope John
Paul II — A343

1986, Oct. 22   **Perf. 12**
1375   Sheet of 10   7.50 7.50
   a.   A343 1b, Pope, mountains   .25 .25
   b.   A343 2b Bridge   .40 .25
   c.   A343 3b Kissing the ground   .50 .25
   d.   A343 3b Statue of Our Lady   .50 .25
   e.   A343 4b Crosier, buildings   .70 .25
   f.   A343 5.25b Waterfall   .95 .30
#1375 contains 2 each #1375a-1375b,
1375e-1375f and one each #1375c-1375d.

Miniature Sheet

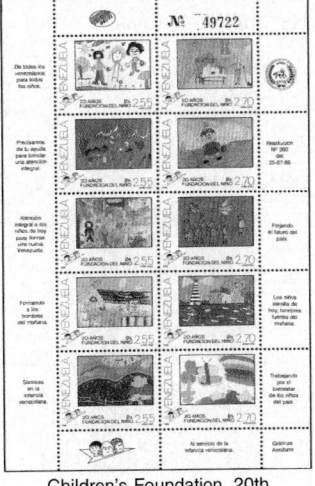

Children's Foundation, 20th
Anniv. — A344

Children's drawings: a, Three children. b,
Hearts, children, birds. c, Child, animals. d,
Animals, house. e, Landscape. f, Child, flowers on table. g, Child holding ball. h, Children,
birds. i, Lighthouse, port. j, Butterfly in flight.

1986, Nov. 10
1376   Sheet of 10   5.50 5.50
   a.-e. A344 2.55b, any single   .40 .25
   f.-j. A344 2.70b, any single   .40 .25

Christmas — A345

Creche figures carved by Eliecer Alvarez.

1986, Nov. 10
1377   2b shown   .40 .25
1378   2b Virgin and child   .40 .25
   a. A345 Pair, #1377-1378   .90 .90

City Police,
25th Anniv.
A346

Emblem and: a, Emergency medical aid,
helicopter. b, Security at sporting event. c, Bar
code. d, Cadets in front of police academy. e,
Motorcycle police.

1986, Dec. 10
1379   Strip of 5   4.00 4.00
   a.-e. A346 2.70b, any single   .50 .25

Folk Art
A347

Lithographed and Engraved
1987, Jan. 31   **Perf. 13**
1380 A347 2b Musical instrument   .70 .25
1381 A347 2b Fabric   .70 .25
1382 A347 3b Ceramic pot   .90 .25
1383 A347 3b Basket work   .90 .25
    Nos. 1380-1383 (4)   3.20 1.00
Dated 1983. Nos. 1380, 1382 show Pre-His-
panic art.

Discovery of the Tubercle Bacillus by
Robert Koch, Cent. (in 1982)
A348

Lithographed and Engraved
1987, Feb. 27   **Perf. 14x14½**
1384 A348 2.55b multicolored   1.60 .25
Dated 1983.

Miniature Sheet

Easter 1987 — A349

Paintings and sculpture: a, Arrival of Jesus
in Jerusalem. b, Christ at the Column. c, Jesus
of Nazareth. d, The Descent. e, The Solitude.
f, The Last Supper. g, Christ Suffering. h, The
Crucifixion. i, Christ Entombed. j, The
Resurrection.

1987, Apr. 2   **Litho.**   **Perf. 12**
1385   Sheet of 10   17.50 17.50
   a.-e. A349 2b, any single   1.00 .25
   f.-j. A349 2.25b, any single   1.10 .25

World
Neurochemistry
Congress — A350

3b, Bolivar and Bello, outdoor sculpture by
Marisol Escobar. 4.25b, Retinal neurons.

1987, May 8   **Litho.**   **Perf. 12**
1386 A350 3b multicolored   .50 .25
1387 A350 4.25b multicolored   .70 .25
   a.   Pair, #1386-1387   3.00 3.00

Miniature Sheet

Tourism — A351

Hotels: a, f, Barquisimeto Hilton. b, g, Lake Hotel Intercontinental, Maracaibo. c, h, Macuto Sheraton, Caraballeda. d, i, Melia Caribe, Caraballeda. e, j, Melia, Puerto la Cruz.

1987, May 29   Litho.   Perf. 12
1388	Sheet of 10	13.00	13.00
a.-e.	A351 6b, any single	.70	.25
f.-j.	A351 6.50b, any single, diff.	.70	.25

Natl. Institute of Canalization, 35th Anniv. — A352

2b, Map of Amazon territory waterways. 4.25b, Apure and Bolivar states waterways.

1987, June 25   Litho.   Perf. 12
1389	A352	2b multicolored	.30	.25
1390	A352	4.25b multicolored	.50	.30
g.		Pair, #1389-1390	1.25	1.25

Vicente Emilio Sojo (1887-1974), Composer — A352a

2b, Academy of Fine Arts, Caracas. 4b, Sojos directing choir. 5b, Hymn to Bolivar score. 6b, Sojo, score on blackboard. 7b, Portrait, signature.

1987, July 1   Litho.   Perf. 12
1390A	Strip of 5	37.50	37.50
b.	A352a 2b tan & sepia	1.25	1.25
c.	A352a 4b tan & sepia	2.00	1.40
d.	A352a 5b tan & sepia	2.00	1.40
e.	A352a 6b tan & sepia	3.25	2.00
f.	A352a 7b tan & sepia	4.00	2.00

Printed in sheets of 10 containing two strips of five, black control number (UR).

Simon Bolivar University, 20th Anniv. A353

Designs: a, Bolivar statue by Roca Rey, 1973. b, Outdoor sculpture of solar panels by

---

Alejandro Otero, 1972. c, Rectory, 1716. d, Laser. e, Owl, sculpture, 1973.

1987, July 9   Litho.   Perf. 12
1391	Strip of 5	15.00	15.00
a.	A353 2b multicolored	.50	.25
b.	A353 3b multicolored	.75	.25
c.	A353 4b multicolored	1.00	.25
d.	A353 5b multicolored	1.25	.50
e.	A353 6b multicolored	1.50	.50

Miniature Sheet

Ministry of Transportation and Communication — A354

Designs: a, Automobiles. b, Ship. c, Train, Cathedral. d, Letters, telegraph key. e, Communication towers. f, Highway. g, Airplane. h, Locomotive, rail caution signs. i, Satellite dish. j, Satellite in orbit.

1987, July 16
1392	Sheet of 10	9.00	9.00
a.-e.	A354 2b any single	.25	.25
f.-j.	A354 2.25b any single	.25	.25

Nos. 1392a and 1392f, 1392b and 1392g, 1392c and 1392h, 1392d and 1392i, 1392e and 1392j have continuous designs.

Miniature Sheet

Venezuela Navigation Company, 70th Anniv. — A355

Designs: a, Corporate headquarters. b, Fork lift. c, Ship's Superstructure. d, Engine room. e, The Zulia. f, The Guarico. g, Ship's officer on the bridge. h, Bow of supertanker. i, Loading dock. j, Map of sea routes.

1987, July 31   Litho.   Perf. 12
1393	Sheet of 10	6.25	6.25
a.-b.	A355 2b, any single	.25	.25
c.-d.	A355 3b, any single	.25	.25
e.-f.	A355 4b, any single	.30	.25
g.-h.	A355 5b, any single	.40	.25
i.-j.	A355 6b, any single	.45	.25

Nos. 1393a, 1393c, 1393e, 1393g and 1393i in vertical strip; No. 1393b, 1393d, 1393f, 1393h and 1393j in vertical strip.

Miniature Sheet

Natl. Guard, 50th Anniv. — A356

a, f, Air-sea rescue. b, g, Traffic control. c, h, Environment and nature protection. d, i, Border control. e, j, Industrial security.

1987, Aug. 6
1394	Sheet of 10	40.00	40.00
a.-e.	A356 2b, any single	.75	.25
f.-j.	A356 4b, any single	1.50	.50

Discovery of America, 500th Anniv. (in 1992) A357

20th cent. paintings (details): 2b, Departure from Port of Palos, by Jacobo Borges. 7b, Discovery of America, by Tito Salas. 11.50b, El Padre de las Casas, Protector of the Indians, by Salas. 12b, Trading in Venezuela at the Time of the Conquest, by Salas. 12.50b, Defeat of Guaicaipuro, by Borges.

1987, Oct.   Litho.   Perf. 12
1395	Strip of 5	11.00	11.00
a.	A357 2b multi	.25	.25
b.	A357 7b multi	.60	.30
c.	A357 11.50b multi	1.00	.45
d.	A357 12b multi	1.10	.55
e.	A357 12.50b multi	1.25	.55

Christmas 1987 — A358

Paintings and sculpture representing the Spanish Colonial School, 18th cent.: 2b, The Annunciation, by Juan Pedro Lopez (1724-1787). 3b, Nativity, by Jose Francisco Rodriguez (1767-1818). 5.50b, Adoration of the Magi, anonymous. 6b, Flight into Egypt, by Lopez.

1987, Nov. 17   Litho.   Perf. 12
1396	Block of 4	6.75	6.75
a.	A358 2b multi	.25	.25
b.	A358 3b multi	.30	.25
c.	A358 5.50b multi	.50	.30
d.	A358 6b multi	.60	.30

Miniature Sheet

Sidor Mills, 25th Anniv. — A359

Natl. steel production: a-d, Exterior view of steel plant (in a continuous design). e, Tower bearing the SIDOR emblem. f, Furnaces and molten steel flowing down gutters. g, Pooring steel rods. h, Slab mill. i, Steel rod production, diff. j, Anniv. emblem.

1987, Nov. 23
1397	Sheet of 10	11.00	11.00
a.	A359 2b multi	.25	.25
b.	A359 6b multi	.80	.40
c.	A359 7b multi	.95	.50
d.	A359 11.50b multi	1.50	.75
e.	A359 12b black	1.75	.80
f.	A359 2b multi	.25	.25
g.	A359 6b multi	.80	.40
h.	A359 7b multi	.95	.50
i.	A359 11.50b multi	1.50	.75
j.	A359 12b multi	1.75	.80

Meeting of 8 Latin American Presidents, 1st Anniv. — A360

1987, Nov. 26
| 1398 | A360 6b multicolored | .80 | .40 |

Pequiven Petrochemical Co., 10th Anniv. — A361

1987, Dec. 1
1399	Strip of 5	7.75	7.75
a.	A361 2b Plastics	.25	.25
b.	A361 6b Refined oil products	.60	.30
c.	A361 7b Fertilizers	.70	.30
d.	A361 11.50b Installations	1.10	.55
e.	A361 12b Expansion	1.25	.60

St. John Bosco (1815-88) A362

Portrait of Bosco and: 2b, Map, children. 3b, National Church, Caracas. 4b, Vocational training (printer's apprentice). 5b, Church of Mary Auxiliadora. 6b, Missionary school (nun teaching children).

1987, Dec. 8
1400	Strip of 5	4.00	4.00
a.	A362 2b multicolored	.25	.25
b.	A362 3b multicolored	.30	.25
c.	A362 4b multicolored	.40	.25
d.	A362 5b multicolored	.45	.25
e.	A362 6b multicolored	.60	.30

Redrawn Bolivar Type of 1976

1987, Dec. 31   Litho.   Perf. 12½
1401	A231	3b emerald grn	.35	.25
1402	A231	4b gray	.50	.25
1403	A231	5b vermilion	.65	.25
1404	A231	10b dark olive bister	1.50	.50
1405	A231	15b rose claret	2.50	.90
1406	A231	20b bright blue	3.00	1.10
1407	A231	25b olive bister	4.00	1.75
1408	A231	30b dark violet	4.75	1.90
1409	A231	50b carmine	7.75	3.00
	Nos. 1401-1409 (9)	25.00	9.90

Nos. 1401-1409 inscribed Armitano.

29th Assembly of Inter-American Development Bank Governors — A363

1988, Mar. 18   Litho.   Perf. 12
1410 A363 11.50b multi   1.50   .80

Miniature Sheet

Republic Bank, 30th Anniv. — A364

Bank functions and finance projects: a, Personal banking at branch. b, Capital for labor. c, Industrial projects. d, Financing technology. e, Exports and imports. f, Financing agriculture. g, Fishery credits. h, Dairy farming development. i, Construction projects. j, Tourism trade development.

1988, Apr. 11
1411   Sheet of 10   10.00 10.00
a.-e. A364 2b any single   .35   .25
f.-j. A364 6b any single   .50   .25

No. 1411 contains two strips of five.

Anti-Polio Campaign Day of Victory, May 25 — A365

Design: Polio victims pictured on bronze relief, Rotary and campaign emblems.

1988, May 20   Litho.   Perf. 12
1412 A365 11.50b multi   1.40   .65

Carlos Eduardo Frias (1906-1986), Founder of the Natl. Publicity Industry — A366

1988, May 27   Litho.   Perf. 12
1414 A366 Pair   3.00   3.00
a.   4b multi   .35   .25
b.   10b multi   .75   .45

Publicity Industry, 50th anniv.

Venalum Natl. Aluminum Corp., 10th Anniv. — A367

Designs: 2b, Factory interior. 6b, Electric smelter. 7b, Aluminum pipes. 11.50b, Aluminum blocks moved by crane. 12b, Soccer team, aluminum equipment on playing field.

1988, June 10
1415   Strip of 5   7.50   7.50
a.   A367 2b multi   .30   .25
b.   A367 6b multi   .80   .25
c.   A367 7b multi   .90   .25
d.   A367 11.50b multi   1.50   .55
e.   A367 12b multi   1.50   .55

Nature Conservation — A368

Birds: 2b, Carduelis cucullata. 6b, Eudocimus ruber. 11.50b, Harpia harpyja. 12b, Phoenicopterus ruber ruber. 12.50b, Pauxi pauxi.

1988, June 17   Litho.   Perf. 12
1416   Strip of 5   7.50   7.50
a.   A368 2b multi   .25   .25
b.   A368 6b multi   .60   .25
c.   A368 11.50b multi   1.10   .45
d.   A368 12b multi   1.25   .40
e.   A368 12.50b multi   1.25   .45

Army Day — A369

Military uniforms: a, Simon Bolivar in dress uniform, 1828. b, Gen.-in-Chief Jose Antonio Paez in dress uniform, 1821. c, Liberation Army division gen., 1810. d, Brig. gen., 1820. e, Artillery corpsman, 1836. f, Alferez Regiment parade uniform, 1988. g, Division Gen. No. 1 dress uniform, 1988. h, Line Infantry Regiment, 1820. i, Promenade Infantry, 1820. j, Light Cavalry, 1820.

1988, June 20
1417   Sheet of 10   15.00 15.00
a., f. A369 2b multi   .30   .25
b., g. A369 6b multi   .75   .25
c., h. A369 7b multi   .90   .25
d., i. A369 11.50b multi   1.50   .45
e., j. A369 12b multi   1.60   .45

Scabbard, Sword and Signature A370

Paintings by Tito Salas: 4.75b, The General's Wedding. 6b, Portrait. 7b, Battle of Valencia. 12b, Retreat from San Carlos.

1988, July 1   Litho.   Perf. 12
1418   Strip of 5   7.50   7.50
a.   A370 2b shown   .35   .25
b.   A370 4.75b multi   .65   .25
c.   A370 6b multi   .75   .25
d.   A370 7b multi   1.25   .30
e.   A370 12b multi   2.75   .45

General Rafael Urdaneta (b. 1788).

General Santiago Marino (b. 1788), by Martin Tovar y Tovar — A371

1988, July
1419 A371 4.75b multi   .65   .35

1988 Summer Olympics, Seoul — A372

1988, Aug. 2
1420 A372 12b multi   1.75   .70

Electric Industry, Cent. A373

Buildings, 1888: 2b, 1st Office. 4.75b, Jaime Carrillo and electrical plant. 10b, Bolivar Plaza. 11.50b, Baralt Theater. 12.50b, Central Thermoelectric Plant, Ramon Lagoon, 1988.

1988, Oct. 25   Litho.   Perf. 12
1421   Strip of 5   6.50   6.50
a.   A373 2b multi   .25   .25
b.   A373 4.75b multi   .40   .25
c.   A373 10b multi   .80   .35
d.   A373 11.50b multi   .90   .45
e.   A373 12.50b multi   1.00   .45

Christmas — A374

Designs: 4b, Nativity (left side), by Tito Salas, 1936. 6b, Christ child, anonymous, 17th cent. 15b, Nativity (right side).

1988, Dec. 9
1422   4b multi   .40   .25
1423   6b multi   .70   .30
1424   15b multi   1.90   .90
a.   A374 Strip, #1423, 2 ea #1422,
         1424   5.00   5.00

Miniature Sheet

Marian Year — A375

Icons: a, Our Lady of Copacabana, Bolivia. b, Our Lady of Chiquinquira, Colombia. c, Our Lady of Coromoto, Venezuela. d, Our Lady of the Clouds, Ecuador. e, Our Lady of Antigua, Panama. f, Our Lady of the Evangelization, Peru. g, Our Lady of Lujan, Argentina. h, Our Lady of Altagracia, Dominican Republic. i, Our Lady of Aparecida, Brazil. j, Our Lady of Guadalupe, Mexico.

1988, Aug. 15   Litho.   Perf. 12
1425   Sheet of 10   12.50 12.50
a.-e. A375 4.75b any single   .50   .25
f.-j. A375 6b any single   .55   .35

Juan Manuel Cagigal Observatory, Cent. — A376

Designs: 2b, Bardou refracting telescope. 4.75b, Universal theodolite AUZ-27. 6b, Bust of Cagigal. 11.50b, Boulton cupola and night sky over Caracas in September. 12b, Satellite photographing Hurricane Allen.

1989, Sept. 5
1426   Strip of 5   6.75   6.75
a.   A376 2b multicolored   .25   .25
b.   A376 4.75b multicolored   .45   .25
c.   A376 6b multicolored   .60   .30
d.   A376 11.50b multicolored   1.00   .50
e.   A376 12b multicolored   1.10   .60

Comptroller-General's Office, 50th Anniv. — A377

1988, Oct. 14   Litho.   Perf. 12
1427 A377 10b multi   1.10   .60

Portrait of Founder Juan Pablo Rojas Paul, by Cristobal Rojas, 1890 — A378

6b, Commemorative medal.

1989, Oct. 21   Litho.   Perf. 12
1428 A378 6b multi   .60   .35
1429 A378 6.50b shown   .65   .35
a.   Pair, #1428-1429   1.50   1.50

Natl. History Academy, cent.

Portrait of Ricardo A379

Paintings: No. 1430, Simon Bolivar and Dr. Mordechay Ricardo. No. 1430A, The Octagon. Nos. 1430-1430A printed in continuous design completing the painting The Liberator in Curacao, by John de Pool.

1989, Jan. 27   Litho.   Perf. 12
1430   A379   10b multi   .75   .40
1430A   A379   10b multi   .75   .40
1430B   A379   11.50b shown   1.10   .50
c.   Strip of 5, #1430B, 2 ea
         #1430-1430A   9.25   9.25

Convention with Holy See, 25th Anniv. — A380

Designs: a, Raul Leoni, constitutional president, 1964-69. b, Cardinal Quintero, archbishop of Caracas, 1960-80. c, Arms of Cardinal Lebrun, archbishop of Caracas since 1980. d, Arms of Luciano Storero, titular archbishop of Tigimma. e, Pope Paul VI.

1989, May 4   Litho.   *Perf. 12*
1431	Strip of 5	5.00	5.00
a.-b.	A380 4b any single	.40	.25
c.-d.	A380 12b any single	1.00	.75
e.	A380 16b any single	1.40	1.00

Bank of Venezuela, Cent. A381

Designs: a, *Cocoa Harvest,* by Tito Salas, 1946. b, *Teaching a Boy How to Grow Coffee,* by Salas, 1946. c, Bank headquarters, Caracas. d, Archive of the Liberator, Caracas. e, Aforestation campaign (seedling). f, Aforestation campaign (five youths planting seedlings). g, 50-Bolivar bank note (left side). h, 50-Bolivar bank note (right side). i, 500-Bolivar bank note (left side). j, 500-Bolivar bank note (right side).

1989, Aug. 1
1432	Sheet of 10	12.50	12.50
a.-f.	A381 4b any single	.35	.25
g.-j.	A381 8b any single	.85	.50

Nos. 1432g-1432h and 1432i-1432j printed in continuous designs.

America Issue — A382

UPAE emblem and pre-Columbian votive bisque artifacts: 6b, Vessel. 24b, Statue of a man.

1989
1433	A382 6b multicolored	.80	.25
1434	A382 24b multicolored	3.50	1.75
a.	Pair, #1433-1434	6.00	6.00

Miniature Sheet

Christmas A383

Denomination at top: a, Shepherds, sheep. c, Angel appears to 3 shepherds. e, Holy Family. g, Two witnesses. i, Adoration of the kings. Denomination at bottom: b, like a. d, like c. f, like e. h, like g. j, like i.

1989   Litho.   *Perf. 12*
1435	Sheet of 10	11.50	11.50
a.-b.	A383 5b any single	.40	.25
c.-f.	A383 6b any single	.45	.25
g.-h.	A383 12b any single	1.00	.45
i.-j.	A383 15b any single	1.10	.60

Miniature Sheets

Bank of Venezuela Foundation, 20th Anniv. — A384

Tree and arms: No. 1436: a, Tabebuia chrysantha, national. b, Ceiba pentandra, Federal District. c, Myrospermum frutescens, Anzoategui. d, Pithecellobium saman, Aragua. e, Cedrela odorata, Barinas. f, Diptenyx punctata, Bolivar. g, Licania pyrofolia, Apure. h, Sterculia apetala, Carabobo.
No. 1437: a, Tabebuia rosea, Cojedes. b, Prosopis juliflora, Falcon. c, Copernicia tectorum, Guarico. d, Erythrina poeppigiana, Merida. e, Brawnea leucantha, Miranda. f, Mauritia flexuosa, Monagas. g, Malpighia glabra, Lara. h, Guaicum officinale, Nueva Esparta.
No. 1438: a, Swietenia macrophylla, Portuguesa. b, Platymiscium diadelphum, Sucre. c, Prumnopitys montana de Laub, Tachira. d, Roystonea venezuelana, Yaracuy. e, Cocos nucifera, Zulia. f, Hevea benthamiana, Federal Territory of Amazonas. g, Erythrina fusca, Trujillo. h, Rhizophora mangle, Territory of the Amacuro Delta.

1990, June 27   Litho.   *Perf. 12*
1436	Sheet of 8 + 2 labels	22.50	22.50
a.-f.	A384 10b any single	.65	.35
g.	A384 40b multicolored	2.50	1.25
h.	A384 50b multicolored	3.25	1.60
1437	Sheet of 8 + 2 labels	22.50	22.50
a.-f.	A384 10b any single	.65	.35
g.	A384 40b multicolored	2.50	1.25
h.	A384 50b multicolored	3.25	1.60
1438	Sheet of 8 + 2 labels	22.50	22.50
a.-f.	A384 10b any single	.65	.35
g.	A384 40b multicolored	2.50	1.25
h.	A384 50b multicolored	3.25	1.60

Central Bank of Venezuela, 50th Anniv. A385

Designs: a, Santa Capilla Headquarters, 1943. b, Headquarters, 1967. c, Left half of 500b Bank Note, 1940. d, Right half of 500b Bank Note, 1940. e, Sun of Peru decoration, 1825. f, Medals Ayacucho, 1824, Boyaca, 1820 and Liberators of Quito, 1822. g, Swords of Peru, 1825. h, Cross pendant, Bucaramanga, 1830. i, Medallion of George Washington, 1826. j, Portrait of Gen. O'Leary.

1990, Oct. 15
1439	Sheet of 10	15.00	15.00
a.-f.	A385 10b any single	.70	.40
g.-h.	A385 15b any single	1.00	.50
i.	A385 40b multicolored	2.75	1.40
j.	A385 50b multicolored	3.50	1.75

University of Zulia, Cent. A386

Designs: a, Dr. Francisco Ochoa, founder. b, Dr. Jesus E. Lossada, President, 1946-47. c, Soil conservation. d, Developing alternative automotive fuels. e, Organ transplants.

1990, Sept. 18   Litho.   *Perf. 12*
1440	Strip of 5	8.00	8.00
a.-b.	A386 10b any single	.50	.30
c.-d.	A386 15b any single	.75	.35
e.	A386 20b multicolored	1.10	.55

Christmas A387

Paintings: a, St. Joseph and Child by Juan Pedro Lopez. b, The Nativity by Lopez. c, The Return from Egypt by Matheo Moreno. d, The Holy Family by unknown artist. e, The Nativity (oval painting) by Lopez.

1990, Nov. 25
1441	Strip of 5	7.50	7.50
a.-c.	A387 10b any single	.50	.30
d.-e.	A387 20b any single	1.10	.55

OPEC, 30th Anniv. — A388

a, Globe. b, Square emblem. c, Circular emblem. d, Diamond emblem. e, Flags.

1990, Dec. 21   Litho.   *Perf. 12*
1442	Strip of 5	8.00	8.00
a.-b.	A388 10b any single	.70	.40
c.	A388 20b multicolored	1.50	.75
d.	A388 30b multicolored	2.10	1.00
e.	A388 40b multicolored	2.75	1.50

America Issue — A389

1990, Dec. 12   Litho.   *Perf. 12*
1443	A389 10b Lake dwelling	1.50	.65
1444	A389 40b Coastline	4.00	2.25
a.	Pair, #1443-1444	6.00	6.00

Exfilve '90, Caracas — A389a

Designs: 40b, Bank of Venezuela 1000b note. 50b, Bank of Caracas 100b note.

1990, Nov. 16   Litho.   *Imperf.*
1444B	A389a 40b multicolored	3.50	3.50
1444C	A389a 50b multicolored	4.50	4.50

No. 1444B, Bank of Venezuela, cent. No. 1444C, Bank of Caracas, cent.

St. Ignatius of Loyola (1491-1556) A390

Designs: a, Jesuit quarters, Caracas. b, Death mask. c, Statue by Francisco de Vergara, 18th century. d, Statue of Our Lady of Montserrat, 11th century.

Venezuelan-American Cultural Center, 50th Anniv. — A391

Designs: a, Elisa Elvira Zuloaga (1900-1980), painter & engraver. b, Gloria Stolk (1912-1979), writer. c, Caroline Lloyd (1924-1980), composer. d, Jules Waldman (1912-1990), publisher. e, William Coles (1908-1978), attorney.

1991, Apr. 12   Litho.   *Perf. 12*
1445	Strip of 4 + label	12.50	12.50
a.-b.	A390 12b any single	.55	.30
c.	A390 40b multicolored	2.00	.90
d.	A390 50b multicolored	2.25	1.10

1991, July 4   Litho.   *Perf. 12*
1446	Strip of 5	12.50	12.50
a.-c.	A391 12b any single	.55	.30
d.	A391 40b multicolored	2.00	1.00
e.	A391 50b multicolored	2.25	1.10

Miniature Sheet

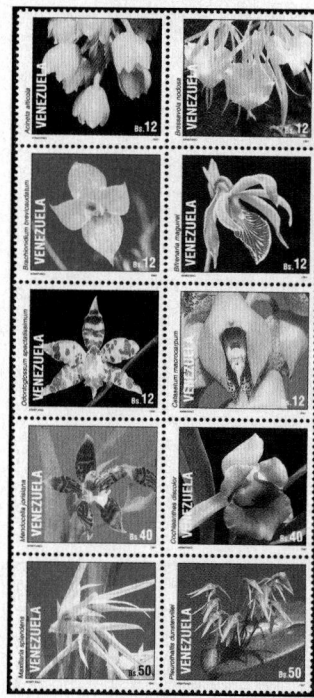

Orchids — A392

Designs: No. 1447a, 12b, Acineta alticola. b, 12b, Brassavola nodosa. c, 12b, Brachionidium brevicaudatum. d, 12b, Bifrenaria maguirei. e, 12b, Odontoglossum spectatissimum. f, 12b, Catasetum macrocarpum. g, 40b, Mendocella jorisiana. h, 40b, Cochleanthes discolor. i, 50b, Maxillaria splendens. j, 50b, Pleurothallis dunstervillei. No. 1448, Cattleya violacea.

1991, Aug. 22   Litho.   *Perf. 12*
1447	A392 Sheet of 10, #a.-j.	18.00	18.00

Souvenir Sheet
1448	A392 50b multicolored	18.00	18.00

No. 1448 contains one 42x37mm stamp. Nos. 1447-1448 exist imperf. Values: No. 1447 $55; No. 1448 $25.
See Nos. 1499-1500, 1508-1509.

Democratic Action Party, 50th Anniv. — A393

Designs: a, People voting. b, Agricultural reform. c, Students and teachers. d, Nationalization of the petroleum industry.

1991, Sept. 13   Litho.   Perf. 12
1449 A393 12b Block of 4, #a.-d.   3.25 3.25

America Issue A394

1991, Oct. 24
1450 A394 12b Terepaima Chief   .60 .30
1451 A394 40b Paramaconi Chief   2.40 1.50
  a.   Pair, #1450-1451   4.50 4.50

Nos. 1450-1451 also exist imperf.

Children's Foundation, 25th Anniv. — A395

Children's drawings: a, 12b, Children in house. b, 12b, Playground. c, 12b, Carnival. d, 12b, Woman and girl walking by pond. e, 12b, Boy in hospital. f, 12b, Five children around tree. g, 40b, Two girls in colorful room. h, 40b, Classroom. i, 50b, Three children. j, 50b, Four children dancing.

1991, Oct. 31   Litho.   Perf. 12
1452 A395 Sheet of 10, #a.-j.   17.00 17.00

Nos. 1362-1364 Surcharged

1991   Litho.   Perf. 12½
1453 A231 5b on 25c red   .30 .25
1454 A231 5b on 75c pink   .30 .25
1455 A231 10b on 25c red   .55 .30
1456 A231 10b on 75c pink   .55 .30
1457 A231 12b on 50c blue   .70 .40
1458 A231 12b on 75c pink   .70 .40
1459 A231 20b on 50c blue   1.10 .55
1460 A231 20b on 75c pink   1.10 .55
1461 A231 40b on 50c blue   2.10 1.10
1462 A231 40b on 75c pink   2.10 1.10
1463 A231 50b on 50c blue   2.75 1.40
1464 A231 50b on 75c pink   2.75 1.40
  Nos. 1453-1464 (12)   15.00 8.00

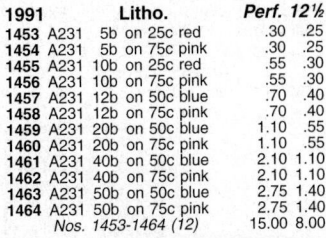

Christmas A396

Children's art work: a, 10b, Wise men. b, 12b, Holy Family. c, 20b, Statues of Holy Family. d, 25b, Shepherds. e, 30b, Holy Family, cow, donkey.

1991, Nov. 14   Litho.   Perf. 12
1465 A396 Strip of 5, #a.-e.   6.75 6.75

Souvenir Sheet

Exfilve '91, Caracas — A397

1991, Nov. 29   Litho.   Perf. 12
1466 A397 50b No. 136   3.50 3.50

Discovery of America, 500th Anniv. (in 1992) A398

a, 12b, Coat of arms of Columbus. b, 12b, Santa Maria. c, 12b, Map by Juan de la Cosa. d, 40b, Sighting land. e, 50b, Columbus with Queen Isabella and King Ferdinand II.

1991, Dec. 12   Litho.   Perf. 12
1468 A398 Strip of 5, #a.-e.   6.25 6.25

1992, Mar. 15
Designs: No. 1469a, 12b, Emblem for discovery of America Commission. b, 12b, Venezuelan pavillion, Expo '92. c, 12b, 15th century map of Spain. d, 12b, Portrait of Columbus, by Susy Dembo. e, 12b, Encounter, by Ivan Jose Rojas. f, 12b, 0x500 America, by Annella Armas. g, 40b, Imago-Mundi, by Alessandro Grechi. h, 40b, Long Journey, by Gloria Fiallo. i, 50b, Playa Dorado, by Carlos Riera. j, 50b, Irminaoro, by Erasmo Sanches Cedeno. No. 1470, Untitled work, by Mauricio Sanchez.

1469 A398   Sheet of 10, #a.-j.   18.00 18.00
1470 A398 50b multicolored   4.50 4.50

Expo '92, Seville. No. 1470 contains one 38x42mm stamp.

Protection of Nature — A399

Turtles: No. 1471a, Geochelone carbonaria, facing left. b, Geochelone carbonaria, facing right. c, Podocnemis expansa, facing left. d, Podocnemis expansa, swimming.

1992, June 12   Litho.   Perf. 12
1471 A399 12b Block of 4, #a.-d.   10.00 6.00

World Wildlife Fund. No. 1471 also exists imperf.

Miniature Sheet

Beatification of Josemaria Escriva — A400

Designs: a, 18b, Teaching in Venezuela, 1975. b, 18b, Celebrating mass. c, 18b, Parents, Jose Escriva and Dolores Albas. d, 18b, Text with autograph. e, 18b, Kissing feet of Madonna. f, 18b, Commemorative medallion. g, 60b, With Pope Paul VI. h, 60b, At desk, writing. i, 75b, Portrait. j, 75b, Portrait in St. Peter's Square, 1992.

1992, Oct. 2   Litho.   Perf. 12
1472 A400 Sheet of 10, #a.-j.   18.00 18.00

Electrification of Southern Regions A401

Designs: a, 12b, Roof of native hut. b, 12b, Transmission lines and towers. c, 12b, Horses running through pond. d, 40b, Workmen under tower. e, 50b, Baskets, crafts.

1992, July 15   Litho.   Perf. 12
1473 A401 Strip of 5, #a.-e.   6.00 6.00

Miniature Sheet

Artwork, by Mateo Manaure — A402

Color of background: a, 12b, Red. b, 12b, Red violet. c, 12b, Gray. d, 12b, Violet brown. e, 40b, Brown. f, 40b, Blue. g, 50b, Blue violet. h, 50b, Black.

1993, July 23
1474 A402   Sheet of 8, #a.-h. + 2 labels   8.50 8.50

Bank of Maracaibo, 110th anniv.

Discovery of America, 500th Anniv. — A403

Paintings: a, 18b, The Third Trip, by Elio Caldera. b, 60b, Descontextura, by Juan Pablo Nascimiento.

1992, Nov. 20   Litho.   Perf. 12
1476 A403 Pair, #a.-b.   4.00 4.00

Christmas A404

Artwork by Lucio Rivas: a, 18b, Adoration of the Shepherds. b, 75b, Adoration of the Magi. 100b, Flight into Egypt.

1992, Dec. 3   Litho.   Perf. 12
1477 A404 Pair, #a.-b.   3.50 3.50

Souvenir Sheet
1478 A404 100b multicolored   4.00 4.00

No. 1478 contains one 42x38mm stamp.

A405   A406

A407

Designs: 1b, 2b, Simon Bolivar. 5b, Natl. Pantheon. 10b, Victory Monument, Carabobo. 20b, Jose Antonio Paez. 25b, Luisa Caceres de Arismendi. 35b, Ezequiel Zamora. 40b, Cristobal Mendoza. No. 1490, Central University. No. 1491, Jose Felix Ribas. No. 1494, Manuel Piar. 200b, Simon Bolivar.

1993-94   Litho.   Perf. 12½
Size: 18x22mm
1479 A405 1b silver   .35 .25
1480 A405 2b greenish blue   .35 .25
1482 A406 5b red   .35 .25
1484 A406 10b violet   .35 .25
1487 A407 20b olive green   .75 .35
1488 A407 25b red brown   .55 .45
1488A A407 35b brt yel grn   .85 .55
1489 A407 40b lt blue   .90 .65
1490 A406 50b orange   2.00 .85
1491 A407 50b lilac rose   1.25 .90

1493	A407	100b brown	4.00	2.00
1494	A407	100b dark blue	2.50	1.40
1496	A407	200b brown	5.00	2.75
	Nos. 1479-1496 (13)		19.20	10.90

Nos. 1479-1493 inscribed Armitano.
See Nos. 1548-1562.

Orchid Type of 1991
Miniature Sheet

Designs: a, 20b, Cattleya percivaliana. b, 20b, Anguloa ruckeri. c, 20b, Chondrorhyncha flaveola. d, 20b, Stenia pallida. e, 20b, Zygosepalum lindeniae. f, 20b, Maxillaria triloris. g, 80b, Stanhopea wardii. h, 80b, Oncidium papilio. i, 100b, Oncidium hastilabium. j, 100b, Sobralia cattleya. 150b, Polycycnis muscifera.

1993, Apr. 1   Litho.   *Perf. 12*
1499 A392   Sheet of 10, #a.-j.   18.00 18.00

Souvenir Sheet
1500 A392   150b multicolored   7.50 7.50

Miniature Sheet

Settlement of Tovar Colony, 150th Anniv. — A408

Designs: a, 24b, Woman. b, 24b, Children. c, 24b, Catholic Church, 1862. d, 24b, Statue of St. Martin of Tours, 1843. e, 24b, Fruits and vegetables. f, 24b, School, 1916. g, 80b, Home of founder, Augustin Codazzi, 1845. h, 80b, House of colony director, Alexander Benitz, 1845. i, 100b, Breidenbach Mill, 1860. j, 100b, Parade.

1993, Apr. 12   Litho.   *Perf. 12*
1501 A408   Sheet of 10, #a.-j.   18.00 18.00

Miniature Sheet

19th Pan-American Railways Conference — A409

Designs: a, 24b, Tucacas steam locomotive. b, 24b, Halcon steam locomotive on Las Mostazas Bridge, 1894. c, 24b, Maracaibo locomotive. d, 24b, Tender, rail cars, Palo Grande Station. e, 24b, Fiat diesel locomotive, 1957. f, 24b, GP-9-L diesel locomotive, 1957. g, 80b, GP-15-L diesel locomotive, 1982. h, 80b, Metro subway train, Caracas. i, 100b, Electric locomotive. j, 100b, Passenger cars of electric train.

1993, May 25   Litho.   *Perf. 12*
1502 A409   Sheet of 10, #a.-j.   22.50 22.50

Nos. 1502c-1502d, 1502i-1502j are continuous designs.

A410

World Day to Stop Smoking: a, 24b, Shown. b, 80b, "No smoking" emblem.

1993, May 27   Litho.   *Perf. 12½x12*
1503 A410   Pair, #a.-b.   4.00 4.00

A411

America Issue: a, 24b, Amazona barbadensis. b, 80b, Ara macao.

1993, Oct. 7   Litho.   *Perf. 12*
1504 A411   Pair, #a.-b.   6.75 6.75

Miniature Sheets

Native Indians — A412

Designs: No. 1505a, 1b, Two Yanomami children with painted bodies, spear. b, 1b, Yanomami woman preparing food. c, 40b, Two Panare children performing in Katyayinto ceremony. d, 40b, Panare man with nose flute. e, 40b, Taurepan man in canoe. f, 40b, Taurepan girl weaving. g, 40b, Piaroa woman with infant. h, 40b, Piaroa dancers wearing war masks. i, 100b, Hoti man blowing flute. j, 100b, Hoti woman carrying baby, basket over back. 150b, Child blowing traditional whistle.

1993, Nov. 25   Litho.   *Perf. 12*
1505 A412   Sheet of 10, #a.-j.   12.00 12.00

Souvenir Sheet
1506 A412   150b multicolored   4.50 4.50

Christmas A413

Nativity scene: a, f, 24b, Joseph. b, g, 24b, Madonna and Child. c, h, 24b, Shepherd boy, wise man holding gift, lambs. d, i, 80b, Wise man with hands folded, boy. e, j, 100b, Wise man presenting gift, boy with hands folded.

1993, Nov. 30
1507 A413   Sheet of 10, #a.-j.   15.00 15.00

Nos. 1507f-1507j are black, magenta & buff.

Orchid Type of 1991
Miniature Sheet

Designs: a, 35b, Chrysocycnis schlimii. b, 35b, Galeandra minax. c, 35b, Oncidium falcipetalum. d, 35b, Oncidium lanceanum. e, 40b, Sobralia violacea linden. f, 40b, Sobralia infundibuligera. g, 80b, Mendoncella burkei. h, 80b, Phragmipedium caudatum. i, 100b, Phragmipedium kaieteurum. j, 200b, Stanhopea grandiflora. 150b, Epidendrum elongatum.

1994, May 19   Litho.   *Perf. 12*
1508 A392   Sheet of 10, #a.-j.   18.00 18.00

Souvenir Sheet
1509 A392   150b multicolored   3.75 3.75

No. 1509 contains one 42x37mm stamp.

Miniature Sheet of 10

FEDECAMARAS (Federal Council of Production & Commerce Associations), 50th Anniv. — A414

a, 35b; f, 80b, Anniversary emblem. b, 35b; e, 80b, Luis Gonzalo Marturet (1914-64), 1st president. c, 35b; d, 80b, FEDECAMARAS emblem.

1994, July 17   Litho.   *Perf. 12*
1510 A414   #c, f, 2 ea #a-b, d-e   13.50 13.50

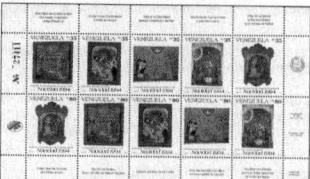

Judicial Service A415

1994, Sept. 13   Litho.   *Perf. 12*
1511 A415   100b multicolored   1.75 1.75

Miniature Sheet

Christmas — A416

Paintings: a, 35b, g, 80b, The Nativity, by follower of Jose Lorenzo de Alvarado. b, 35b, h, 80b, Birth of Christ, 19th cent. c, 35b, i, 80b, The Nativity, diff., by follower of Jose Lorenzo de Alvarado. d, 35b, j, 80b, Adoration of the Magi, 17th cent.. e, 35b, f, 80b, Birth of Christ, by School of Tocuyo.

1994, Dec. 1
1512 A416   Sheet of 10, #a.-j.   13.50 13.50

Miniature Sheet

Antonio Jose de Sucre (1795-1830) — A417

Designs: No. 1513a, 25b, Portrait. b, 25b, Dona Mariana Carcelen Y Larrea Marquesa de Solanda. c, 35b, Top of equestrian monument. d, 35b, Bottom of monument. e, 40b, Painting of Battle of Pichincha, mountains at top. f, 40b, Painting of Battle of Pichincha, battle scent. g, 80b, Painting of Battle of Ayacucho, soldiers on horseback. h, 80b, Painting of Battle of Ayacucho, dead soldiers. i, 100b, Painting of Surrender at Ayachucho, general signing document. j, 100b, Painting of Surrender at Ayachucho, seated general at right. 150b, Portion of mural, Carabobo, by Pedro Centeno Vallenilla.

1995, Feb. 2
1513 A417   Sheet of 10, #a.-j.   13.50 13.50

Souvenir Sheet
1514 A417   150b multicolored   3.50 3.50

Postal Transportation — A418

a, 35b, Post office van. b, 80b, Airplane.

1995, Mar. 22   Litho.   Perf. 12
1515 A418 Pair, #a.-b.   2.50 2.50

No. 1515 issued in sheets of 10 stamps.

Miniature Sheet

St. Jean-Baptiste de La Salle (1651-1719), Educator — A419

Denomination LR: a, 100b, Portrait. b, 35b, Students with microscope, academic education. c, 35b, Soccer players, sports education. d, 35b, Scouts at camp, citizenship education. e, 80b, La Salle College, Caracas.

Denomination LL: f, like #1516e. g, like #1516d. h, like #1516b. i, like #1516c. j, like #1516a.

1995, May 15
1516 A419 Sheet of 10, #a.-j.   11.00 11.00

Miniature Sheet

Founding of Salesian Order, Cent. — A420

Designs: a, 35b, St. John Bosco (1815-88), priest with child. b, 35b, Lonely child, Madonna and Child. c, 35b, Man running

machine tool. d, 35b, Young men working with electronic instruments. e, 35b, Baseball game. f, 35b, Basketball game. g, 80b, People working in fields. h, 80b, Man looking at chili peppers. i, 100b, Young tribal natives receiving religious training. j, 100b, Tribal native.

1995, Apr. 26
1517 A420 Sheet of 10, #a.-j.   11.00 11.00

Miniature Sheet

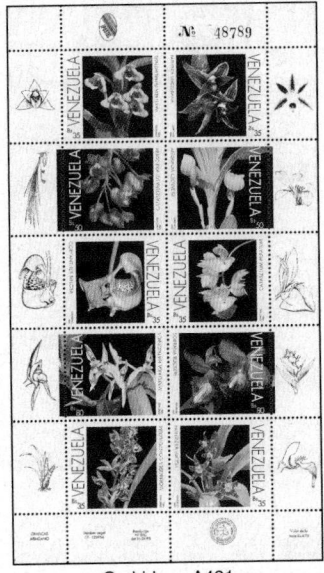

Orchids — A421

Designs: a, 35b, Maxillaria guareimensis. b, 35b, Paphinia lindeniana. c, 50b, Catasetum longifolium. d, 50b, Anguloa clowesii. e, 35b, Coryanthes biflora. f, 35b, Catasetum pileatum. g, 80b, Maxillaria histrionica. h, 80b, Sobralia ruckeri. i, 35b, Mormodes convolutum. j, 35b, Huntleya lucida.

150b, Catasetum barbatum.

1995, May 31   Litho.   Perf. 12
1518 A421 Sheet of 10, #a.-j.   12.00 12.00
Souvenir Sheet
1519 A421 150b multicolored   3.50 3.50

No. 1519 contains one 42x36mm stamp. See #1534-1535, 1563-1564, 1587-1588.

CAF (Andes Development Corporation), 25th Anniv. — A422

1995, June 7
1520 A422 80b multicolored   1.60 1.60

Miniature Sheet

Beatification of Mother Maria of San Jose — A423

Designs: a, 35b, In formal habit. b, 35b, Pope John Paul II. c, 35b, As young woman distributing Bibles. d, 35b, Doing embroidary work. e, 35b, Statue of Madonna, altar. f, 35b, Kneeling in devotions. g, 80b, Walking with Sisters in hospital. h, 80b, With patient in hospital. i, 100b, Working with children. j, 100b, Helping person seated along road.

1995, July 2
1521 A423 Sheet of 10, #a.-j.   11.00 11.00

Nos. 1521a-1521b, 1521c-1521d, 1521e-1521f, 1521g-1521h, 1521i-1521j are each continuous designs.

UN, 50th Anniv. — A424

Designs: a, People from different countries unfurling UN flag. b, Emblem on UN flag.

1995, June 26
1522 A424 50b Pair, #a.-b.   3.25 3.25

Gen. José Gregorio Monagas (1795-1858), President, Liberator of the Slaves — A425

a, Portrait. b, Slave family with opened chains.

1995, July 26   Litho.   Perf. 12
1523 A425 50b Pair, #a.-b.   2.40 2.40

Slave Rebellion, Bicent. — A426

Jose Leonardo Chirino and: a, Liberty leading the people (after Delacroix). b, Revolutionaries with weapons.

1995, Aug. 16
1524 A426 50b Pair, #a.-b.   2.50 2.50

Venezuelan Red Cross, Cent. A427

Designs: a, 100b, Red Cross flag. b, 80b, Carlos J. Bello Hospital. c, 35b, Surgery scene. d, 35b, Rescue workers carrying victim. e, 35b, Care givers with child.

1995, Aug. 30
1525 A427 Strip of 5, #a.-e.   6.00 6.00

America Issue A428

Environmental protection: a, 35b, Trees, lake. b, 80b, Flowers, hillside.

1995, Sept. 13   Litho.   Perf. 12
1526 A428 Pair, #a.-b.   3.50 3.50

No. 1526 was issued in sheets of 10 stamps. No. 1526 exists in two types: the heavy border at top is above "America" only: the heavy line extends over the denomination. Values the same.

Miniature Sheet

Native Aboriginals — A429

No. 1527: a, 25b, Kuana man seated on post. b, 25b, Kuana woman using stones to do laundry. c, 35b, Guahibo people, one playing flute. d, 35b, Guahibo shaman with child. e, 50b, Uruak man with tree branch. f, 50b, Uruak woman cooking. g, 80b, Warao woman spinning twine. h, 80b, Warao man, woman in boat. i, 100b, Bari men with bows, arrows. j, 100b, Bari man rubbing sticks to make fire.

150b, Young boy with bird.

1995, Oct. 18
1527 A429 Sheet of 10, #a.-j.   16.00 16.00
Souvenir Sheet
1528 A429 150b multicolored   5.00 5.00

See Nos. 1541-1542.

Miniature Sheet

Electricity in Caracas, Cent. — A430

Designs: a, 35b, Ricardo Zuloaga, early pioneer. b, 35b, Early electric plant. c, 35b, Substation. d, 35b, 1908 Electric trams. e, 35b, Electric lampposts mandated by Congress, 1908. f, 35b, Lampposts, Bolivar Plaza. g, 80b, Electrical repairman. h, 80b, Lighted cross, Avila. i, 100b, Teresa Carreño Cultural Complex. j, 100b, Ricardo Zuloaga main generator plant.

1995, Nov. 6
1529   A430   Sheet of 10, #a.-j.   11.00   11.00

Miniature Sheet

Christmas — A431

Designs: a, 35b, The Annunciation. b, 35b, Being turned away at the inn. c, 100b, Birth of Christ in the stable. d, 35b, Angel appearing to shepherds. e, 35b, Three Magi. f, 40b, Christmas pageant. g, 40b, Children skating. h, 100b, Christmas presents. i, 40b, Women preparing food for holidays. j, 40b, Children, mother preparing food for holidays.

1995, Nov. 15
1530   A431   Sheet of 10, #a.-j.   10.00   10.00

Nos. 1530f-1530g, and 1530i-1530j are each continuous designs.

Miniature Sheet

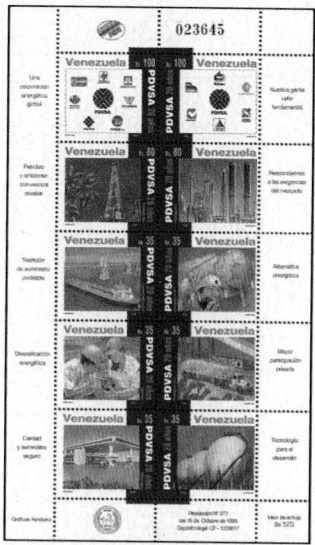

Petroleum Industries of South America (PDVSA), 20th Anniv. — A432

a, 35b, PDVSA emblem, 7 petroleum company emblems. b, PDVSA emblem, 6 petroleum company emblems. c, 80b, Oil derrick. d, 80b, Refinery. e, 35b, Oil tanker crossing under bridge. f, 35b, Worker, orimulsion tanks. g, 35b, Two people examining carbon. h, 35b, Semi truck hauling petrochemicals. i, 35b, Filling station. j, 35b, Gas storage tanks.

1995, Dec. 13   Litho.   Perf. 12
1531   A432   Sheet of 10, #a.-j.   11.00   11.00

Miniature Sheet

Town of El Tocuyo, 450th Anniv. — A433

Designs: a, 35b, City arms. b, 35b, Workers in sugar cane field. c, Church of Our Lady of Immaculate Conception. d, Statue of Madonna inside church. e, 35b, Ruins of Temple of Santa Domingo. f, 35b, House of Culture. g, 80b, Cactus, vegetation. h, 80b, Cactus up close. i, 100b, Dancers with swords. j, 100b, Man playing guitar.

1995, Dec. 5
1532   A433   Sheet of 10, #a.-j.   11.00   11.00

Miniature Sheet

Vist of Pope John Paul II — A434

Statues of various saints, Pope and: a, 25b, Children. b, 25b, Man, woman. c, 40b, Man, woman, baby. d, 40b, Elderly man. e, 50b, Woman, boy. f, 50b, Sick person. g, 60b, Man in prison. h, 60b, Working man. i, 100b, People of various career fields. j, 100b, Priests, nuns.

200b, Pope John Paul II holding crucifix.

1996, Jan. 26
1533   A434   Sheet of 10, #a.-j.   12.00   12.00

Souvenir Sheet
1533K   A434   200b multicolored   6.50   6.50

Orchid Type of 1995

Designs: a, Epidendrum fimbriatum. b, Myoxanthus reymondii. c, Catasetum pileatum. d, Ponthieva maculata. e, Maxillaria triloris. f, Scaphosepalum breve. g, Cleistes rosea. h, Maxillaria sophronitis. i, Catasetum discolor. j, Oncidium ampliatum.

200b, Odontoglossum naevium.

1996, May 31   Litho.   Perf. 12
1534   A421   60b Sheet of 10, #a.-j.   11.00   11.00

Souvenir Sheet
1535   A421   200b multicolored   6.50   6.50

1996 Summer Olympic Games, Atlanta A435

Designs: a, Emblem of Olympic Committee. b, Swimmer. c, Boxer. d, Cyclist. e, Medal winners.

1996, June 28   Litho.   Perf. 12
1536   A435   130b Strip of 5, #a.-e.   9.00   9.00

No. 1536 was issued in a sheet of 10 stamps.

Miniature Sheet

Maiquetia Intl. Airport, 25th Anniv. — A436

Designs: a, Symbol of automation. b, Map of airport flight routes. c, La Guaira Airdrome, 1929. d, Maiqueitia Airport, 1944. e, Simon Bolivar Airport, 1972. f, Interior view of terminal. g, Airport police, control tower. h, Airport firetruck. i, Airplane at terminal, Simon Bolivar Airport. j, Airplane on taxiway, Simon Bolivar Airport.

1996, Aug. 4
1537   A436   80b Sheet of 10, #a-j   12.50   12.50

America Issue A437

Traditional costumes: a, 60b, Women's. b, 130b, Men's.

1996, Sept. 10
1538   A437   Pair, #a.-b.   3.75   3.75

No. 1538 was issued in sheets of 10 stamps.

Mario Briceño-Iragorry (1897-1958) — A438

Portraits: a, As young man, Trujillo, 1913. b, At University of Mérida, 1919. c, As politician, 1944. d, As writer, 1947. e, As older man, Caracas, 1952.

1996, Sept. 24
1539   A438   80b Strip of 5, #a.-e.   6.50   6.50

No. 1539 was issued in sheets of 10 stamps.

Caracas Rotary Club, 70th Anniv. — A439

1996, Oct. 3
1540 A439 50b multicolored .85 .85

No. 1540 was issued in sheets of 10.

Native Aboriginal Type of 1995

Designs: a, 80b, Yukpa boy working in garden. b, 80b, Paraujanos girl carrying fruit. c, 80b, Kinaroes man, woman bundling cattails. d, 80b, Motilon man with bananas. e, 80b, Chaque mother carrying infant on back. f, 100b, Guajiros man, young woman fixing hair. g, 100b, Mucuchi man carrying pack on back. h, 100b, Mape man with bow and arrow. i, 100b, Macoa working with grain, painted faces. j, 100b, Yaruros man weaving.
200b, Woman breastfeeding infant.

1996, Oct. 11
1541 A429 Sheet of 10, #a.-j. 13.50 13.50
Souvenir Sheet
1542 A429 200b multicolored 3.25 3.25

Souvenir Sheet

Taipei '96, Intl. Philatelic Exhibition — A440

1996, Oct. 21 Litho. Perf. 12
1543 A440 200b Ara chloroptera 7.50 7.50

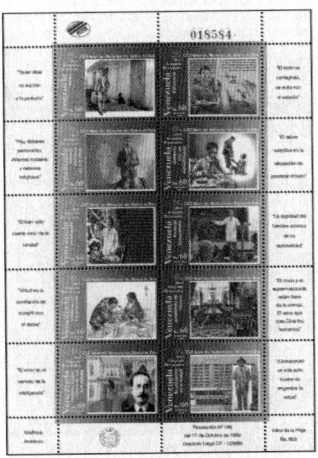

José Gregorio Hernández (1864-1908), Physician — A441

a, As young boy. b, As student, anatomy drawing. c, Praying, Madonna statue. d, Thinking of the needy. e, In research study. f, As professor of university. g, Comforting sick patient. h, Empty chair at academy. i, Vargas Hospital, statue, portrait of Hernández. j, Hospital named after Hernández, statue.
200b, Portrait of Hernández.

1996, Oct. 26 Litho. Perf. 12
1544 A441 60b Sheet of 10, #a.-j. 7.00 7.00
Souvenir Sheet
1545 A441 200b multicolored 2.75 2.75

No. 1545 contains one 42x36mm stamp.

Christmas — A442

Designs: a, 60b, Child setting up Nativity scene. b, 60b, Three men with guitars, woman. c, 60b, Rooster, people making music. d, 60b, People with painted faces dancing, singing. e, 60b, Men, woman playing drums, instruments. f, 80b, Exchanging gifts of food. g, 80b, Family at table, looking at gift of food. h, 80b, Child in hammock, presents. i, 80b, Parading replica of infant Jesus. j, 80b, Kissing feet of Christ Child.

1996, Nov. 7
1546 A442 Sheet of 10, #a.-j. 6.50 6.50

Andrés Eloy Blanco (1896-1955), Politician, Writer — A443

Designs: a, As adolescent. b, As Caracas city official, government building. c, With family. d, With democratic founders. e, As politician, building. f, As President of Constituent Assembly, building. g, As "Poet of Pueblo." h, Lincoln Memorial, as Chancellor of the Republic. i, Author of writings on Spain, sailing ship. j, Map of Spain, sailing ships, conquistador on horseback.

1997, Feb. 17 Litho. Perf. 12
1547 A443 100b Sheet of 10, #a.-j. 9.00 9.00

Simon Bolivar (1783-1830) — A444

1997, Mar. 7 Litho. Perf. 13½x13
1548 A444 15b olive .25 .25
1549 A444 20b brown org .25 .25
1550 A444 40b dark brown .40 .40
1551 A444 50b rose claret .60 .60
1552 A444 70b deep violet .85 .85
1553 A444 90b deep blue 1.25 1.25
1554 A444 200b dp grn bl 2.25 2.25
1555 A444 300b dp bl grn 3.00 3.00
1556 A444 400b gray 4.50 4.50
1557 A444 500b pale sepia 5.25 5.25
1558 A444 600b pale brown 5.75 5.75
1559 A444 800b pale vio brn 7.25 7.25
1560 A444 900b slate blue 7.50 7.50
1561 A444 1000b dk org brn 8.00 8.00
1562 A444 2000b olive bister 15.00 15.00
Nos. 1548-1562 (15) 62.10 62.10

Orchid Type of 1995

Designs: a, Phragmipedium lindleyanum. b, Zygosepalum labiosum. c, Acacallis cyanea. d, Maxillaria camaridii. e, Scuticaria steelei. f, Aspasia variegata. g, Comparettia falcata. h, Scapyglottis stellata. i, Maxillaria ruffescens. j, Vanilla pompona.
250b, Rodriguezia lanceolata.

1997, May 30 Perf. 12
1563 A421 165b Sheet of 10, #a.-j. 15.00 15.00
Souvenir Sheet
1564 A421 250b multicolored 3.50 3.50

No. 1564 contains one 42x37mm stamp.

Independence Conspiracy of Gual and España, Bicent. — A445

#1565, José María España, proclamation for independence being read. #1566, España under arrest. #1567, Manuel Gual, soldiers. #1568, Gual fleeing through door, sailing ship, standing on Trinidad. #1569, Revolutionary flag, sailing ship.

1997, July 16
1565 A445 165b multicolored 1.50 1.50
1566 A445 165b multicolored 1.50 1.50
  a. Pair, #1565-1566 3.00 3.00
1567 A445 165b multicolored 1.50 1.50
  a. Pair, #1566-1567 3.00 3.00
1568 A445 165b multicolored 1.50 1.50
  a. Pair, #1567-1568 3.00 3.00
1569 A445 165b multicolored 1.50 1.50
  a. Pair, #1565, 1569 3.00 3.00
  b. Pair, #1565, 1569 3.00 3.00

Printed in sheet of 10 containing one each #1566a, 1567a, 1568a, 1569a-1569b. Value $16.

Treaty of Tlatelolco Banning Use of Nuclear Weapons in Latin America, 30th Anniv. — A446

Various stylized designs representing devastation resulting from use of nuclear weapons: a.-e., White inscriptions. f.-j., Black inscriptions.

1997, July 31
1570 A446 140b Sheet of 10, #a.-j. 15.00 15.00

Stories for Children A447

"The Rabbit and the Tiger:" a, Rabbit, tiger carrying satchel. b, Watching rat figure digging. c, Watching turtle on his back. d, Rabbit. e. Rat in net, rabbit. f, Tiger, house, rat. g, Bird, rat, rabbit, bee, beehive. h, Rabbit, turtle. i, Tiger with stick over shoulder. j, Tiger with mouth open, bees.
250b, Rabbit, tiger.

1997, Aug. 7
1571 A447 55b Sheet of 10, #a.-j. 8.00 8.00
Souvenir Sheet
1572 A447 250b multicolored 3.25 3.25

No. 1572 contains one 42x37mm stamp.
The reverse of Nos. 1571a-1571j are each inscribed with parts of the childrens' story.

Unexpected Adventures of a Postman A448

America Issue: 110b, Giving letter to woman with dog. 280b, With motor scooter in rain.

1997, Aug. 29 Litho. Perf. 12
1573 A448 110b multicolored 2.00 2.00
1574 A448 280b multicolored 3.50 3.50
  a. Pair, #1573-1574 7.25 7.25

No. 1574a was issued in sheets of 10 stamps.

Villa of Anauco Villa, Bicent. A449

Designs: a, Inscription. b, Main entrance. c, Entrance corridor. d, Interior patio. e, Exterior corridor leading to kitchen. f, Kitchen. g, Stairs leading to balcony. h, Coach house. i, Stable. j, Outside stable, water trough.

1997, Sept. 23
1575 A449 110b Sheet of 10, #a.-j. 11.00 11.00

Independence in India, 50th Anniv. — A450

Designs: a, 165b, Jawaharlal Nehru. b, 200b, Sardar Patel, flag. c, 165b, Congressional building. d, 200b, Gandhi. e, 165b, Purification at the Ganges. f, 200b, Rabindranath Tagore. g, 165b, Motion picture industry. h, 200b, Traditional music. i, 165b, Insat-1B meteorological satellite. j, 200b, Use of modern technology.
250b, Minarets of Taj Majal.

1997, Oct. 2
1576 A450 Sheet of 10, #a.-j. 20.00 20.00
Souvenir Sheet
1577 A450 250b multicolored 3.25 3.25

Heinrich von Stephan (1831-97) A451

a, 110b, Portrait. b, 280b, UPU emblem.

1997, Oct. 9 Litho. Perf. 12
1578 A451 Pair, #a.-b. 3.75 3.75

Wicker-work
A452

No. 1579: a, Red basket, Ye'Kuana. b, With handles, Ye'Kuana. c, Round, Ye'Kuana. d, Tray, Panare. e, Backpack, Pemon. f, With carrying strap, Yanomami. g, Round (dk brown), diff., Ye'Kuana. h, Tray, Ye'Kuana. i, Oval tray, Panare. j, Wide mouth, Warao.
250b, Square box with lid, Ye'Kuana.

1997, Oct. 24   *Perf. 12*
1579 A452 140b Sheet of 10,
    #a.-j.   15.00 15.00
Souvenir Sheet
1580 A452 250b multicolored   4.00 4.00
No. 1580 contains one 42x37mm stamp.

Christmas
A453

a, Annunciation. b, Mary, St. Elizabeth. c, No room at the inn. d, Nativity. e, Annunciation to shepherds. f, Adoration of the shepherds. g, Magi following star. h, Adoration of the Magi. i, Presentation of Christ child in temple. j, Flight into Egypt.

1997, Oct. 31
1581 A453 110b Sheet of 10,
    #a.-j.   11.00 11.00

7th Summit of Latin American Chiefs of State and Government, Isla de Margarita
A454

a, 165b, j, 200b, Social justice. b, 165b, i, 200b, Free elections. c, 165b, h, 200b, Summit emblem. d, 165b, g, 200b, Truthful information. e, 165b, f, 200b, Human rights.

1997, Nov. 5
1582 A454   Sheet of 10, #a.-j.
                18.00 18.00

Diocese of Zulia, Cent.
A455

Churches: a, Convent. b, Church of St. Ann. c, Reliquary, Chiquinquira. d, Basilica of Chiquinquira and St. John of God. e, Church, Aranza. f, Cathedral, Maracaibo. g, Cathedral, Machiques. h, Archbishop's seal. i, Cathedral, Cabimas. j, Cathedral of the Virgin, San Carlos.

1997, Dec. 16
1583 A455 110b Sheet of 10,
    #a.-j.   10.00 10.00

Democracy in Venezuela, 40th Anniv. — A456

Designs: a, Commemorative emblem. b, Popular decision. c, Public education. d, Social development. e, Freedom of expression. f, Capital, constitution. g, Popular culture. h, Civil rights. i, Environmental protection. j, Social and civic participation.

1998, Feb. 19   **Litho.**   *Perf. 12*
1584 A456 110b Sheet of 10,
    #a.-j.   12.00 12.00

Discovery of Margarita Island, 500th Anniv. — A457

Map of Margarita Islands and: a, 200b, Angel Rock. b, 265b, Christopher Columbus, ship. c, 200b, Simon Bolivar. d, 200b, Pearl diver. e, 265b, Statue of the Virgin del Valle, church. f, 100b, Mending fish net, fishermen in boats. g, 200b, Gen. Santiago Marino. h, 100b, Petronila Mata, cannon. i, 200b, Gen. Juan Bautista Arismendi. j, 100b, Parrot.
250b, Women weeping at the Lagoon of Martyrs, horiz.

1998, Mar. 26   **Litho.**   *Perf. 12*
1585 A457   Sheet of 10, #a.-j. 17.00 17.00
Souvenir Sheet
1586 A457 250b multicolored   3.25 3.25
No. 1586 contains one 42x37mm stamp.

Orchid Type of 1995

a, Oncidium orthostates. b, Epidendrum praetervisum. c, Odontoglossum schilleranum. d, Bletia lansbergii. e, Caularthron bicornutum. f, Darwiniera bergoldii. g, Houlletia tigrina. h, Pleurothallis acuminata. i, Elleanthus lupulinus. j, Epidendrum ferrugineum.
250b, Pleurothallis immersa.

1998, May 29
1587 A421 185b Sheet of 10,
    #a.-j.   18.00 18.00
Souvenir Sheet
1588 A421 250b multicolored   3.25 3.25
No. 1588 contains one 42x37mm stamp.

Henri Pittier Natl. Park, 60th Anniv. — A458

Fauna: a, 140b, Crax pauxi. b, 150b, Spizaetus ornatus. c, 200b, Touit collaris. d, 200b, Trogon collaris. e, 350b, Cyanocorax yncas. f, 140b, Tersina viridis. g, 150b, Phyllomedusa trinitatis. h, 200b, Morpho peleides. i, 200b, Acrocinus longimanus. j, 350b, Dynastes hercules.

1998, July 17
1589 A453   Sheet of 10, #a.-j. 20.00 20.00

Comptroller General of the Republic, 60th Anniv. — A459

Designs: a, 140b, Gumersindo Torres Millet, founding Comptroller. b, 140b, Luis Antonio Pietri Yépez, first Comptroller of the democracy. c, 140b, View of capitol dome. d, 140b, Colors of flag (service to society). e, 200b, Simon Bolivar, coins. f, 200b, Various numbers on green background. g, 350b, Newspaper headlines (inform the public). h, 350b, Statue of justice (uphold law). i, 350b, Text of duties of the Comptroller General. j, 350b, Emblem, the 6th Assembly of the Latin American and Caribbean States Comptrollers.

1998, July 29
1590 A459   Sheet of 10, #a.-j. 20.00 20.00

Organization of the American States (OAS), 50th Anniv. — A460

a, 140b, Logo of the anniversary. b, 140b, OAS emblem. c, 350b, Flags forming double helix, US flag at center left. d, 150b, Deactivating land mine. e, 150b, Defending human rights. f, 200b, Simon Bolivar. g, 200b, Scroll, quill pen, inkwell. h, 350b, Flags forming double helix, Venezuelan flag at center right. i, 200b, Road sign with map of Americas. j, 200b, Mountain climbers.

1998, July 30
1591 A460   Sheet of 10, #a.-j. 17.50 17.50

Expo '98, Lisbon
A461

Designs: a, 140b, Bird, turtle, crab. b, 140b, Fishermen throwing net from boat. c, 150b, Seashells, turtle. d, 150b, Fish. e, 200b, Marine life, denomination UR. f, 200b, Marine life, denomination LR. g, 200b, Man riding through river on horse. h, 200b, Cattle in river, monkey. i, 350b, Two sea birds. j, 350b, Monkey, waterfall, flower.

1998, July 31
1592 A461   Sheet of 10, #a.-j. 20.00 20.00

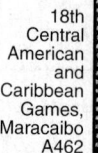

18th Central American and Caribbean Games, Maracaibo
A462

Figures: a, 150b, Running. b, 200b, Playing basketball. c, 150b, Bowling. d, 200b, Boxing. e, 150b, Cycling. f, 200b, Fencing. g, 150b, Performing gymnastics. h, 200b, Weight lifting. i, 150b, Swimming. j, 200b, Playing tennis.

1998, Aug. 4
1593 A462   Sheet of 10, #a.-j. 15.00 15.00

Discovery of Venezuela, 500th Anniv. — A463

Designs: a, 350b, Christopher Columbus. b, 200b, Juan de la Cosa (1460?-1510), map. c, 200b, Huts built on stilts in water. d, 150b, Women of three different races. e, 140b, 13th cent. artifact. f, 350b, Alonso de Ojeda (1465-1515), map. g, 200b, Detail of map of Jodocus Hondius. h, 200b, Modern city. i, 150b, Various people of modern Venezuela. j, 140b, Statues of Catholic king and queen.

1998, Aug. 10
1594 A463   Sheet of 10, #a.-j. 18.00 18.00

Landing of Christoper Columbus, and Exploration of Amerigo Vespucci, 500th Anniv.
A464

1998, Aug. 12
1595 A464 400b multicolored   3.50 3.50
See Italy No. 2252.

Treaty of Amazon Cooperation, 20th Anniv.
A465

Designs: a, Casiquiare River, denomination LR. b, Casiquiare River, denomination LL. c, Bactris gasipaes. d, Neblinaria celiae. e, Paracheidon axelrodi. f, Dendrobates leucomelas. g, Nocthocrax urumatum. h, Speothos venaticus. i, Cocuy mountain. j, Neblina Mountains.

1998, Aug. 20
1596 A465 200b Sheet of 10,
    #a.-j.   18.00 18.00

Children's Story — A466

Cockroach Martinez and Perez Rat: a, Cockroach. b, Burro. c, Parrot. d, Insects with camera, pad. e, Cat. f, Cockroach, pig. g, Goat. h, Cockroach, rat. i, Rat. j, Cockroach, bird.
350b, Cockroach.

1998, Aug. 21   **Litho.**   *Perf. 12*
1597 A466 130b Sheet of 10,
    #a.-j.   10.00 10.00
Souvenir Sheet
1598 A466 350b multicolored   4.00 4.00

State of Israel, 50th Anniv. — A467

a, 350b, Menorah. b, 350b, Moses, Ten Commandments. c, 200b, Theodore Herzl. d, 200b, King David. e, 140b, Blowing of Shofar. f, 350b, Torah. g, 350b, Praying at Wailing Wall. h, 200b, David Ben Gurion. i, 200b, Knesset. j, 140b, Book Museum.

1998, Sept. 15
1599 A467 Sheet of 10, #a.-j. 20.00 20.00

Souvenir Sheet

Comptroller General, 60th Anniv. — A468

1998, Sept.
1600 A468 480b multicolored 4.50 4.50

UPU, 125th Anniv. A469

a, 100b, Customer at window, clerks at left. b, 100b, Scanning bar code, woman at right. c, 100b, Electronic mail. d, 100b, Hybrid mail. e, 100b, Business mail. f, 300b, Like "a," clerks at right. g, 300b, Like "b," woman at left. h, 300b, Like "c," large monitor at right. i, 300b, Like "d," woman at right. j, 300b, Like "e," building with stacks at left.

1998, Sept. 29
1601 A469 Sheet of 10, #a.-j. 10.00 10.00

Legendary Caciques A470

a, Caruao. b, Manaure. c, Guacamayo. d, Tapiaracay. e, Mamacuri. f, Maniacuare. g, Mara. h, Chacao. i, Tamanaco. j, Tiuna. 500b, Indian.

1998, Oct. 9
1602 A470 420b Sheet of 10, #a.-j. 22.50 22.50

Souvenir Sheet
1603 A470 500b multicolored 4.00 4.00

Evangelism in Venezuela, 500th Anniv. A471

No. 1604: a, 100b, Fr. Francisco de Córdoba, Fr. Juan Garcés. b, 100b, Fr. Matías Ruíz Blanco. c, 100b, Fr. Vincente de Requejada. d, 100b, Fr. José Gumilla. e, 100b, Fr. Antonio Gonzáles de Acuña. f, 300b, Fr. Pedro de Córdoba. g, 300b, Fr. Francisco de

Pamplona. h, 300b, Fr. Bartolomé Díaz. i, 300b, Fr. Filipe Salvador Gilij. j, 300b, Don Mariano Martí.
350b, Emblem of Papal Nuncio.

1998, Oct. 24   Litho.   Perf. 12
1604 A471 Sheet of 10, #a.-j. 13.50 13.50

Souvenir Sheet
1605 A471 350b multicolored 3.50 3.50
No. 1605 contains one 42x37mm stamp.

Special Olympics, 30th Anniv. A472

180b: a, Carrying torch. b, Giving hug. c, Soccer players. d, Girl holding small flag. e, Girl performing gymnastics.
420b: f, Swimmer. g, Coach walking with athletes. h, Hitting volleyball. i, Particpants cheering. j, Coach instructing girl in softball.

1998, Oct. 30   Litho.   Perf. 12
1606 A472 Sheet of 10, #a.-j. 15.00 15.00

Christmas A473

Children standing in front of windows — 180b: a, Girl holding sparkler. b, Boy holding artist's brush, ornament. c, Girl with kite. d, Boy with pinwheel. e, Girls playing musical instruments.
420b: f, Boy on wagon. g, Girl with yo-yo, doll. h, Boy with bell. i, Girl with spool and thread. j, Boy on skateboard.

1998, Nov. 4
1607 A473 Sheet of 10, #a.-j. 15.00 15.00

America Issue — A474

Famous women: a, 180b, Teresa de la Parra (1889-1936), writer. b, 420b, Teresa Carreño (1853-1917), pianist.

1998, Nov. 23
1608 A474 Pair, #a.-b. 3.75 3.75

William H. Phelps (1875-1965), Ornithologist A475

Portrait of Phelps and — 200b: a, Cephalopterus ornatus. b, Topaza pella. c, Grallaria excelsa phelpsi. d, Chrysolampis mosquitus. e, Tangara xanthogastra phelpsi.
300b: f, Radio transmitter. g, Mt. Phelps. h, Baseball and glove. i, Phelps Library. j, Cash register.

1998, Dec. 4
1609 A475 Sheet of 10, #a.-j. 16.00 16.00

Msgr. Jesús Manuel Jáuregui Moreno (1848-1905) A476

Designs: a, Portrait as younger man. b, Christ on the cross. c, Our Mother of Angels Church. d, Madonna and Child. e, Portrait as older man.

1999, Jan. 30   Litho.   Perf. 12
1610 A476 500b Strip of 5, #a.-e. 12.00 12.00

Holy Sacrament for the Consecration of the Republic of Venezuela, Cent. A477

No. 1612: a, Man, elderly woman. b, Priest. c, Ostensorium (top). d, Boy with basketball, girl. e, Man, woman holding baby. f, Lady doctor. g, Woman. h, Ostensorium (base). i, Soldier. j, Native man holding spear.
500b, Hands of priest holding the Host.

1999, June 16   Litho.   Perf. 12
1611 A477 250b Sheet of 10, #a.-j. 12.00 12.00

Souvenir Sheet
1612 A477 500b multicolored 2.25 2.25
No. 1612 contains one 42x37mm stamp.

Souvenir Sheet

Andino Parliament, 20th Anniv. — A478

1999   Litho.   Perf. 12
1613 A478 500b multi 3.00 3.00

Christmas A479

a, 500b, Betrothal of Joseph, Mary. b, 500b, Annunciation. c, 500b, Elizabeth, Mary. d, 500b, The search for lodging in Bethlehem. e, 500b, Birth of Jesus. f, 300b, Vision of the shepherds. g, 300b, Magi following star. h, 300b, Adoration of the Magi. i, 300b, Flight into Egypt. j, 300b, Slaughter of the innocents.

1999, Nov. 5   Perf. 12x12¼
1614 A479 Sheet of 10, #a.-j. 24.00 24.00

Souvenir Sheet

Expo 2000, Hanover — A480

2000, July 8   Litho.   Perf. 12
1615 A480 650b multi 4.00 4.00

2nd Summit of Heads of State and Government of OPEC Countries — A481

No. 1616 — Sites in Venezuela: a, 300b, Angel Falls. b, 300b, Llanos, Cojedes. c, 300b, Quebrada Jaspe. d, 300b, Morichal Largo. e, 300b, Auyantepuy, Carrao River. f, 400b, Lake Maracaibo. g, 400b, Humboldt Peak. h, 400b, Mochima. i, 400b, Morichal Largo River. j, 400b, Auyantepuy, from Uruyen.
No. 1617, 550b: a, Saudi Arabia. b, Algeria. c, United Arab Emirates. d, Indonesia. e, Iraq. f, Iran. g, Kuwait. h, Libya. i, Nigeria. j, Qatar.

2000, Sept. 26   Litho.   Perf. 12
Sheets of 10, #a-j
1616-1617 A481 Set of 2 70.00 70.00

Christmas — A482

No. 1618: a, 300b, Angel and "Gloria." b, 300b, Angel and "a." c, 650b, Angel and "Dios." d, 300b, Angel and "en los." e, 300b, Angel and "Cielos." f, 300b, Shepherd and lamb. g, 550b, Joseph. h, 650b, Jesus. i, 550b, Mary. j, 300b, Woman with water jar.

2000, Nov. 29
1618 A482 Sheet of 10, #a-j 30.00 30.00

America Issue,
A New
Millennium
Without
Arms — A483

No. 1619: a, 300b, Finger in gun barrel. b, 650b, Man in heaven.

2000, Dec. 14

1619	A483	Vert. pair, #a-b	6.50	6.50

Educational
Building and
Endowment
Foundation,
25th
Anniv. — A484

No. 1620 — School buildings in: a, Caracas. b, Vargas State. c, Portuguesa State. d, Mérida State. e, Yaracuy State.

2001, May 9　　Litho.　　*Perf. 12*

1620		Horiz. strip of 5	9.50	9.50
a.-c.	A484	300b Any single	1.60	1.60
d.-e.	A484	400b Any single	2.10	2.10

Orchids — A485

No. 1621: a, 200b, Galeottia jorisiana. b, 200b, Lycaste longipetala. c, 300b, Coryanthes albertinae. d, 300b, Hexisea bidentata. e, 400b, Lycaste macrophylla. f, 400b, Masdevallia maculata. g, 550b, Ada aurantiaca. h, 550f, Kefersteinia graminea. i, 550b, Sobralia liliastrum. j, 550b, Gongora maculata.
650b, Masdevallia tovarensis.

2001, May 25

1621	A485	Sheet of 10, #a-j	30.00	30.00

Souvenir Sheet

1622	A485	650b multi	7.00	7.00

Blessed Josemaría Escrivá de
Balaguer (1902-75), Founder of Opus
Dei — A486

No. 1623: a, 300b, Portrait. b, 300b, Bell of Nuestra Senora de los Angeles Church. c, 300b, Figure of Infant Jesus. d, 300b, Escrivá with men. e, 550b, Escrivá with women. f, 550f, Escrivá receiving doctorate, 1972. g, 550b, Escrivá with children, 1975. h, 300b, Commemorative plaque, Caracas Cathedral. i,

550b, Color portrait. j, 300b, Beatification ceremony, St. Peter's Square, Vatican City.

2001, June 8

1623	A486	Sheet of 10, #a-j	32.50	32.50

Battle of Carabobo, 180th
Anniv. — A487

No. 1624: a, Thomas I. Ferriar. b, Bolívar in Buenavista, by Martín Tovar y Tovar. c, Quote by Simón Bolívar. d, Commemorative column. e, Pedro Camejo. f, José Antonio Páez, by Tovar y Tovar. g, Santiago Mariño, by Tovar y Tovar. h, Simón Bolívar, by M. Eberstein. i, Manuel Cedeño, by Tito Salas. j, Ambrosio Plaza, by Salas.

2001, June 22

1624	A487	Sheet of 10	32.50	32.50
a.-e.		400b Any single	1.40	1.40
f.-j.		600b Any single	1.90	1.90

Christmas — A488

Holy Family and angel with: a, 200b, Clarinet. b, 200b, Guitar. c, 220b, Lute. d, 220b, Trumpet. e, 280b, Violin. f, 280b, Harp. g, 400b, Bagpipes. h, 400b, Pan pipes. i, 500b, Drum. j, 500b, Stringed instrument.

2001, Nov. 30　　Litho.　　*Perf. 12*

1625	A488	Sheet of 10, #a-j	24.00	24.00

Navigational
Signaling,
160th
Anniv. — A489

Navigational aids: a, Margarita Aqueduct buoy. b, BNFA buoy. c, Punta Brava lighthouse. d, Punta Macolla lighthouse. e, Los Roques lighthouse. f, Isla Redonda lighthouse. g, Punta Faragoza lighthouse. h, Punta Ballena lighthouse. i, Punta Tigre lighthouse. j, Recalada de Güiria lighthouse.

2002, May 10　　Litho.　　*Perf. 12*

1626		Sheet of 10	25.00	25.00
a.-b.	A489	300b Either single	1.00	1.00
c.-f.	A489	450b Any single	1.40	1.40
g.-j.	A489	500b Any single	1.50	1.50

Symbolic Incorporation of Guacaipuro
into National Pantheon — A490

No. 1627: a, Tiaora and Caycape, sisters of Guacaipuro. b, Guacaipuro defeats Pedro de Miranda. c, Guacaipuro defeated by Juan Rodriguez Suárez. d, Killing in the gold mines. e, Death of Juan Rodriguez Suárez. f, Guacaipuro's escape from cabin fire. g, Death of Guacaipuro. h, Urquía, companion of Guacairpuro. i, Baruta, first son of Guacaipuro. j, Guacaipuro, Cacique of the Teques and Caracas people.

2002, Oct. 29　　Litho.　　*Perf. 12*

1627		Sheet of 10	14.00	14.00
a.	A490	200b multi	.60	.60
b.-g.	A490	300b any single	.75	.75
h.	A490	350b multi	.90	.90
i.	A490	400b multi	1.00	1.00
j.	A490	500b multi	1.25	1.25

Mission Robinson — A491

No. 1628: a, Toddler. b, Boy reading. c, Simón Bolívar and torch. d, Simón "Robinson" Rodriguez, Bolívar's teacher. e, Rodriguez and Eiffel Tower. f, Bolívar and flag. g, Bolívar and Rodriguez reading. h, Bolívar standing and Rodriguez seated. i, Rodriguez, men and women reading. j, Indians reading.

2003, Sept. 19　　Litho.　　*Perf. 12x12¼*

1628	A491	Sheet of 10	8.50	8.50
a.-d.		300b Any single	.40	.40
e.-f.		400b Either single	.60	.60
g.-j.		500b Any single	.75	.75

Agricultural, Fishery and Forestry
Fund (FONDAFA) — A492

No. 1629: a, Cattle drive. b, Farmer plowing field. c, Row of tractors. d, Farmer tending crops. e, Corn in field. f, Boats. g, Ear of corn. h, Farmer in tractor in field. i, Cacao pods. j, Cacao beans.

2003, Nov. 7　　　　　*Perf. 12*

1629	A492	Sheet of 10	7.50	7.50
a.-f.		300b Any single	.40	.40
g.-h.		400b Either single	.60	.60
i.-j.		500b Either single	.75	.75

National Urban Development Fund
(FONDUR), 28th Anniv. — A493

No. 1630: a, Barinas. b, Portuguesa. c, Carabobo. d, Miranda. e, Sucre. f, Trujillo. g, Táchira. h, Vargas. i, FONDUR emblem. j, Lara.

2003, Dec. 16　　Litho.　　*Perf. 14¼*

1630	A493	Sheet of 10	7.50	7.50
a.-f.		300b Any single	.50	.50
g.-h.		400b Either single	.75	.75
i.-j.		500b Either single	.90	.90

Natl. Urban Transportation Fund
(FONTUR), 12th Anniv. — A494

No. 1631: a, Av. Uruguay, Lara. b, Carretera del Páramo, Merida. c, Av. Cumanan-Cumanacoa, Sucre. d, Carratera Santa Lucia, Barinas. e, Francissco Fajardo Expressway, Caracas. f, Students. g, Paraiso Tunnel, Caracas. h, VIVEX Module. i, Row of buses. j, Av. Cruz Paredes, Barinas.

2003, Dec. 18   Litho.   Perf. 14¼
1631   A494   Sheet of 10   9.00   9.00
a.-c.   300b Any single   .60   .60
d.-f.   400b Any single   .75   .75
g.-j.   500b Any single   1.00   1.00

Natl. Telecommunications Commission
(CONATEL) — A495

No. 1632: a, Three Amazonian children, two dogs and hammock. b, Caracas and mountain. c, Amazonian children with spears. d, Snow-covered Bolivar Peak. e, Amazonian child in canoe aiming arrow. f, Medina Beach. g, Amazonian children aiming arrows skyward. h, Angel Falls. i, Amazonian children making baskets. j, Coro Dunes.

2003, Dec. 23   Litho.   Perf. 12
1632   A495   Sheet of 10   9.00   9.00
a.-d.   300b Any single   .60   .60
e.-f.   400b Either single   .80   .80
g.-h.   500b Either single   1.00   1.00
i.-j.   600b Either single   1.25   1.25

Foundation for the Development of
Community and Municipal
Reconstruction (FUNDACOMUN),
42nd Anniv. — A496

No. 1633: a, Miranda. b, Trujillo. c, Mérida. d, Falcón. e, Vargas. f, Esparta. g, Caracas, denomination at left. h, Caracas, denomination at right. i, Barinas. j, Lara.

2004, Mar. 10   Litho.   Perf. 12
1633   A496   Sheet of 10   9.00   9.00
a.-c.   300b Any single   .60   .60
d.-f.   400b Any single   .80   .80
g.-j.   500b Any single   .90   .90

Barrio Adentro Mission — A497

No. 1634: a, Houses on hillside, people in doorway. b, Woman, house, ladder, people in alley. c, Woman, mother and child. d, Family, children. e, Boys playing baseball, boat. f, People near fence, man with cap. g, Man, sand dunes. h, Man with guitar, cows. i, Mountain, woman, cross and statue. j, Indians, river.

2004, Mar. 24   Perf. 12
1634   A497   Sheet of 10   14.00   14.00
a.-b.   300b Either single   .40   .40
c.-f.   500b Any single   .60   .60
g.   750b multi   1.00   1.00
h.-i.   1500b Either single   1.90   1.90
j.   1700b multi   2.00   2.00

Souvenir Sheet
Design: 1000b, Man pushing wheelbarrow, horiz.

1634K   A497   1000b multi   3.00   3.00
No. 1634K contains one 41x36mm stamp.

National Housing Institute
(INAVI) — A498

No. 1635: a, Apartment block 6, El Silencio. b, El Pilar. c, Central section of apartment block 1, El Silencio. d, La Quiboreña. e, Apartment block 7, El Silencio. f, Santa Ana. g, Apartment block 144, El Silencio. h, La Quiracha. i, Architectural drawings of Caracas buildings. j, Los Peregrinos.

2004, May 28   Litho.   Perf. 12
1635   A498   Sheet of 10   7.50   7.50
a.-c.   300b Any single   .45   .45
d.-f.   400b Any single   .70   .70
g.-j.   500b Any single   .80   .80

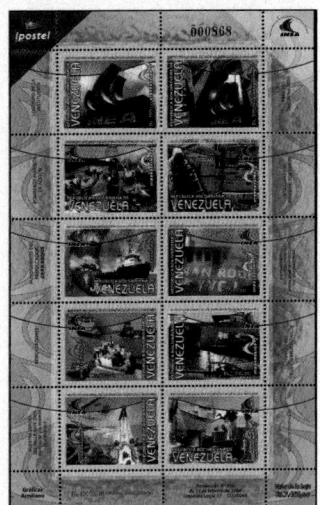

National Aquatic Areas and Islands
Institute (INEA) — A499

No. 1636: a, INEA emblem. b, INEA emblem and headquarters. c, Marine firefighters, boats. d, Firetruck, marine firefighter moving drum. e, Sunken tugboat Gran Roque. f, Underwater view of Gran Roque. g, Tugboats. h, Large ships at port. i, Starfish, religious statue. j, Boats and birds.

2004, June 15
1636   A499   Sheet of 10   15.00   15.00
a.-b.   300b Either single   .45   .45
c.-f.   500b Any single   .80   .80
g.   600b multi   1.00   1.00
h.   1000b multi   1.60   1.60
i.   1500b multi   2.40   2.40
j.   1700b multi   2.75   2.75

A500

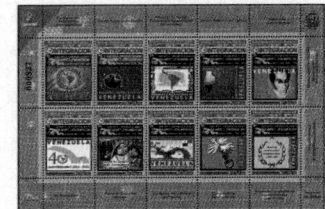

Latin American Parliament, 40th
Anniv. — A501

No. 1637: a, Latin American Parliament emblem, 40th anniversary emblem. b, 40th anniversary emblem. c, Latin American Parliament flag and 40th anniversary emblem. d, Flags of member nations. e, Flags and Andrés Townsend Ezcurra. f, Flags and Luis Beltrán Prieto Figueroa. g, Flags and Nelson Carneiro. h, Plenary meeting room, Venezuela. i, Assembly hall, Sao Paolo. j, Latin American Parliament Building, Sao Paolo.
No. 1638: a, Latin American Parliament emblem. b, 40th Anniversary emblem. c, Mérida Session emblem. d, Charter of Social Rights. e, Flags and map of Latin America. f, Flag and map of Panama. g, Táchira Session emblem. h, Bird with ball and chain (social

debt). i, Simón Bolivar. j, Constitutional Hypothesis.

2004, July 12
1637   A500   Sheet of 10   12.50   12.50
a.-c.   300b Any single   .45   .45
d.-e.   450b Either single   .75   .75
f.-g.   500b Either single   .80   .80
h.-i.   1500b Either single   2.25   2.25
j.   1700b multi   2.40   2.40
1638   A501   Sheet of 10   12.50   12.50
a.-c.   300b Any single   .45   .45
d.-e.   450b Either single   .75   .75
f.-g.   500b Either single   .80   .80
h.-i.   1500b Either single   2.25   2.25
j.   1700b multi   2.40   2.40

CVG Edelca, 40th Anniv. — A502

No. 1639: a, Macagua Hydroelectric Station and Dam,, Ciudad Guayana. b, Electric transmission towers and lines. c, Electrical power equipment. d, Room, Guri. e, Native people. f, Guri Hydroelectric Station and Dam. g, Streetlights near Macagua Hydroelectric Station and Dam. h, Solar tower, by Alejandro Otero. i, Dam, Ecomuseum, Caroní. j, Gran Sabana.
No. 1640, Guri Hydroelectric Station and Dam.

2004, July 29
1639   A502   Sheet of 10   10.00   10.00
a.-b.   300b Either single   .45   .45
c.   400b multi   .70   .70
d.-g.   500b Any single   .80   .80
h.   600b multi   .90   .90
i.   1000b multi   1.40   1.40
j.   1500b multi   2.25   2.25

Souvenir Sheet
1640   A502   1000b multi   4.50   4.50
No. 1640 contains one 41x36mm stamp.

United Nations Population
Fund — A503

No. 1641 — Inscriptions: a, Los y las adolescentes . . . b, El comporttmiento . . . Las niñas tienen . . . d, Los seres humanos . . . e, Promovamos el empoderamiento . . . f, Los derechjos reproductivos . . . g, Por una maternidad sin riesgo. h, El derecho al desarrollo . . . i, Eliminemos la violencia . . . j, El condón protege vidas.

2004, Sept. 15

1641	A503	Sheet of 10	12.50	12.50
a.-d.		500b Any single	.80	.80
e.-j.		1000b Any single	1.40	1.40

National Parks Institute
(INPARQUES) — A504

No. 1642 — Parks and: a, Food. b, Education. c, Recreation. d, Water. e, Landscapes. f, Biodiversity. g, Conservation. h, Electricity. i, Tourism. j, Ethnic people.

2004, Oct. 11   Litho.   Perf. 14¼x14½

1642	A504	Sheet of 10	10.00	10.00
a.-b.		300b Either single	.45	.45
c.		400b multi	.70	.70
d.-g.		500b Any single	.80	.80
h.		600b multi	.90	.90
i.		1000b multi	1.60	1.60
j.		1500b multi	2.25	2.25

National Tax and Customs
Administration (SENIAT) — A505

No. 1643 — Inscriptions: a, Aporte a la educación, cultura y deporte (children). b, Aporte a la salud. c, Dile no al contrabando. d, Con tus tributos . . . e, Aporte a la educación, cultura y deporte (baseball players). f, Construcción de futuras . . . g, Aporte a la vialidad. h, Bienvenidos a un país . . . i, Aporte a la educación, cultura y deporte (building and palm tree). j, Aporte a la educación, cultura y deporte (modern building and sculpture).

2004, Oct. 15   Litho.   Perf. 12

1643	A505	Sheet of 10	13.00	13.00
a.-d.		500b Any single	.90	.90
e.-j.		1000b Any single	1.40	1.40

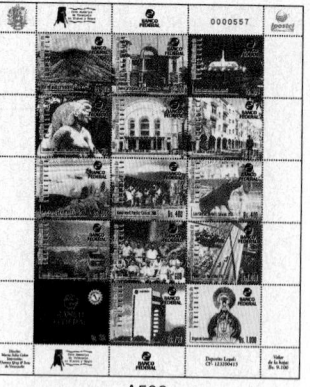

A506

Banco Federal — A507

No. 1644: a, Cerro El Avila, Caracas, 1945. b, Nuevo Circo, Caracas, 1970. c, Plaza Venezuela, Caracas, 1943. d, Sculpture by Francisco Narváez, Caracas, 1940. e, Baralt Theater, Maracaibo, 1883. f, Los Próceres, Caracas, 1956. g, El Paraíso Horse Track, Caracas, 1908. h, Bullfighter Luis Sánchez Olivares, Caracas, 1950. i, Funicular, Mérida, 1954. j, Angel Falls, Bolivar State, 1937. k, Banco Federal emblem, gold star. l, Banco Federal Building (sepia). m, Lake Bridge, Maracaibo, 1962. n, Virgin of Coromoto (sepia). o, El Silencio, Caracas, 1945.

No. 1645: a, San Fernando de Apure Church. b, Caracas Cathedral. c, Coro Cathedral. d, Santa Inés de Cumaná Cathedral. e, Our Lady of Chiquinquirá Basilica. f, Our Lady of Coromoto Basilica. g, St. Rose of Lima Church, Ortíz. h, Mérida Cathedral. i, Our Lady of the Assumption Cathedral. j, San Cristóbal Cathedral. k, Banco Federal emblem, silver star. l, Banco Federal Building (full color). m, Barquisimeto Cathedral. n, Virgin of Coromoto (full color). o, Valencia Cathedral.

2005, Jan. 20   Litho.   Perf. 14¼x14½

1644	A506	Sheet of 15	15.00	15.00
a.-e.		300b Any single	.45	.45
f.-h.		400b Any single	.60	.60
i.-j.		600b Either single	.90	.90
k.-l.		750b Either single	1.20	1.20
m.-n.		1000b Either single	1.60	1.60
o.		1700b multi	2.40	2.40
1645	A507	Sheet of 15	15.00	15.00
a.-e.		300b Any single	.45	.45
f.-h.		400b Any single	.60	.60
i.-j.		600b Either single	.90	.90
k.-l.		750b Either single	1.20	1.20
m.-n.		1000b Either single	1.60	1.60
o.		1700b multi	2.40	2.40

Christmas — A508

No. 1646 — Creche figures from various states: a, Bolívar. b, Falcón. c, Mérida. d, Aragua. e, Miranda. f, Miranda, diff. g, Falcón, diff. h, Zulia. i, Bolívar, diff. j, Trujillo.

2004, Dec. 23   Perf. 12

1646	A508	Sheet of 10	12.50	12.50
a.-b.		300b Either single	.50	.50
c.-d.		400b Either single	.60	.60
e.		600b multi	.90	.90
f.-g.		750b Either single	1.20	1.20
h.-i.		1000b Either single	1.60	1.60
j.		1700b multi	2.40	2.40

Souvenir Sheet

Incan and Modern Mail
Deliverers — A509

2004   Perf. 12

1647	A509	1000b multi	4.50	4.50

Petróleos de Venezuela, S. A. — A510

No. 1648: a, Crane above turbines, Puerto La Cruz Refinery. b, Night view of tower Puerto La Cruz Refinery. c, Aerial view of Puerto La Cruz refinery. d, Man inspecting pipes. e, Crane and Venezuelan flag. f, Storage tanks. g, Oil wells. h, Refinery towers. i, Oil tanker and pipes. j, Tankers at Guaraguao Marine Terminal.

2004, Nov. 24   Litho.   Perf. 14¼

1648	A510	Sheet of 10	10.00	10.00
a.-b.		300b Either single	.50	.50
c.-d.		450b Either single	.65	.65
e.-f.		500b Either single	.75	.75
g.-h.		600b Either single	1.00	1.00
i.		750b multi	1.20	1.20
j.		1000b multi	1.60	1.60

Mountains — A511

Designs: No. 1649, Bolivar Peak, Venezuela. No. 1650, Mt. Damavand, Iran.

2004   Litho.   Perf. 13

1649	A511	1700b multi	3.00	3.00
1650	A511	1700b multi	3.00	3.00
a.		Horiz. pair, #1649-1650	6.50	6.50

No. 1650 has "Republica Bolivariana de Venezuela" overprinted in black over vignette. No. 1650 exists without overprint.

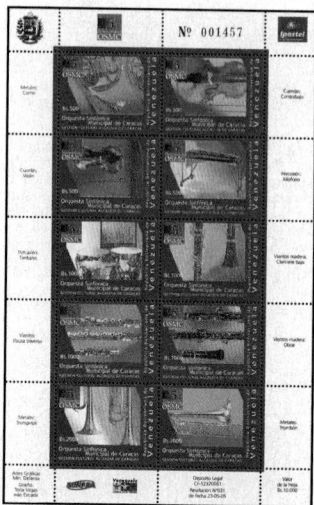

Caracas Municipal Symphony
Orchestra, 25th Anniv. — A512

No. 1651: a, French horns. b, Bass (in blue) and bow. c, Violin and bow. d, Marimba. e, Timpani. f, Clarinets. g, Flutes. h, Oboes. i, Trumpets. j, Trombone.

2005   Perf. 12

1651	A512	Sheet of 10	18.00	18.00
a.-d.		500b Any single	.75	.75
e.-h.		1000b Any single	1.60	1.60
i.-j.		2000b Either single	3.00	3.00

16th World Youth and Student
Festival — A513

No. 1652: a, Festival emblems from 1947-59. b, Festival emblems from 1962-2005. c, Festival emblem and joined arms. d, Festival emblem and text of Simón Bolívar's Vow of Monte Sacro. e, Festival emblem and Bolívar with outstretched arm, signature of Bolívar. f, Festival emblem and broken chain. g, Festival emblem, Bolívar. h, Festival emblem, dove. i, Festival emblem, dove, globe and hands. j, Festival emblem and hands.

1000b, Festival emblem and Bolívar with outstretched arm, horiz.

2005, Aug. 5   Litho.   Perf. 12

1652	A513	Sheet of 10	8.50	8.50
a.-d.		300b Any single	.50	.50
e.-i.		500b Any single	.75	.75
j.		1500b multi	2.25	2.25

**Souvenir Sheet
Perf. 12x11¾**

1653	A513	1000b multi	4.00	4.00

No. 1653 contains one 41x36mm stamp.

IPOSTEL — A514

No. 1654: a, IPOSTEL emblem, flag, Caracas Post Office. b, Postal vans. c, IPOSTEL emblem on envelope, Caracas Post Office. d, Postal motorcycles. e, Carmelitas Post Office. f, Airplane, postal bicycles. g, Falcón Post Office. h, Mail carriers. i, Zulia Post Office. j, Postal workers in San Martín.

No. 1655: a, Man, IPOSTEL emblem, letters. b, Postal worker, mail sacks. c, Mail on conveyor belt. d, Mail carriers with parcels. e, Postal workers sorting mail. f, Postal workers at Ribas Mission. g, Mail sacks. h, Doctor, medical equipment at Barrio Adentro Mission. i, Postal worker and postal machinery. j, Forklift and Mercal emblem.

2005, Oct. 10			**Perf. 12**	
1654	A514	Sheet of 10	15.00	15.00
a.-b.		300b Either single	.50	.50
c.-d.		400b Either single	.60	.60
e.-f.		600b Either single	.85	.85
g.-i.		1700b Any single	2.40	2.40
j.		2000b multi	2.90	2.90
1655	A514	Sheet of 10	15.00	15.00
a.-b.		300b Either single	.50	.50
c.-d.		400b Either single	.60	.60
e.-f.		600b Either single	.85	.85
g.-i.		1700b Any single	2.40	2.40
j.		2000b multi	2.90	2.90

Central Bank of Venezuela, 65th Anniv. — A515

No. 1656: a, Bank emblem. b, Caracas branch. c, Maracaibo branch. d, Venezuela Mint. e, Children's economic educational program. f, Numismatic Museum. g, Plaza Juan Pedro López. h, Gold bars. i, Bank notes and printing plates. j, Coins.

2005, Oct. 20			**Perf. 12½x13½**	
1656	A515	Sheet of 10	15.00	15.00
a.-b.		300b Either single	.50	.50
c.-d.		400b Either single	.60	.60
e.-f.		600b Either single	.85	.85
g.-h.		1500b Either single	2.10	2.10
i.-j.		1700b Either single	2.40	2.40

Christmas — A516

No. 1657 — Angel with: a, h, Long-necked stringed instrument with bow. b, j, Lute. c, Harp. d, g, Maracas. e, i, Stringed instrument with bow. f, Horn.

2005, Dec. 1			**Perf. 12**	
1657	A516	Sheet of 10	15.00	15.00
a.-c.		400b Any single	.65	.65
d.-f.		600b Any single	1.00	1.00
g.-h.		1000b Either single	1.60	1.60
i.		1500b multi	2.25	2.25
j.		2000b multi	3.25	3.25

National Guard — A517

No. 1658: a, Villa Zoila. b, Troops and building with ornate roof. c, Troops and automobiles. d, Troops saluting. e, Helicopter. f, Troops in inflatable raft. g, Three guardsmen at industrial site. h, Two guardsmen inspecting boxes. i, Guardsman with drug-sniffing dog. j, Guardsman, children.

2006, Feb. 23				
1658	A517	Sheet of 10	15.00	15.00
a.-d.		300b Any single	.50	.50
e.-f.		400b Either single	.60	.60
g.-h.		1500b Either single	2.25	2.25
i.-j.		2000b Either single	3.00	3.00

Banco Guayana, 50th Anniv. — A518

No. 1659 — Shimaraña people: a, People with painted faces. b, Archer and man with spear. c, Canoes on water. d, Women near dock. e, Man in canoe, woman's face. f, Children. g, Bow fishermen. h, Men, child, waterfall. i, Child. j, Women, dancer and river.

2006, Mar. 16				
1659	A518	Sheet of 10	17.00	17.00
a.-b.		300b Either single	.50	.50
c.-f.		500b Any single	.75	.75
g.-h.		1700b Either single	2.50	2.50
i.-j.		2000b Either single	2.90	2.90

National Tax and Customs Administration (SENIAT) — A519

No. 1660 — Customs buildings in: a, Valencia. b, Puerto Cabello. c, Paraguachón. d, Santa Elena de Uairén. e, Maiquetía (in day). f, Maiquetía (at night). g, Ureña. h, Táchira. i, Barcelona. j, La Guaira.

2006, Mar. 22				
1660	A519	Sheet of 10	17.00	17.00
a.-b.		400b Either single	.60	.60
c.-d.		500b Either single	.75	.75
e.-f.		700b Either single	1.00	1.00
g.-h.		1000b Either single	1.40	1.40
i.-j.		2000b Either single	3.00	3.00

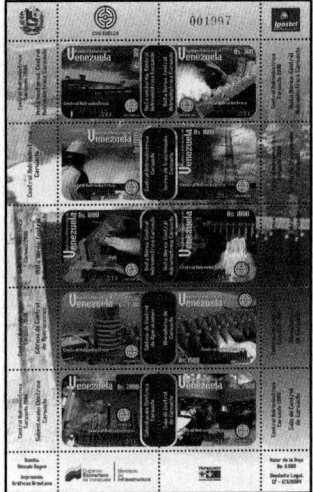

Carauchi Hydroelectric Dam Project — A520

No. 1661: a, Dam at night. b, Aerial view of dam. c, Worker at dam. d, Power lines. e, Aerial view of dam, water flowing to right. f, Aerial view of dam, water flowing straight ahead, descriptive text at left. g, Control tower. h, Spillway. i, Electrical substation. j, Control room.

No. 1662 — Rescued animals: a, Iguana iguana. b, Caluromys philander. c, Paleosuchus palpebrosus. d, Geochelone carbonaria. e, Cebus olivaceus. f, Choloepus didactylus. g, Tupinambis teguixin. h, Lora bejuca. i, Coendou prehensilis. j, Tamandua tetradactyla.

No. 1663, Aerial view of dam, water flowing straight ahead, descriptive text at top.

2006, Apr. 6				
1661	A520	Sheet of 10	20.00	20.00
a.-b.		300b Either single	.50	.50
c.-f.		1000b Any single	1.60	1.60
g.-h.		1500b Either single	2.25	2.25
i.-j.		2000b Either single	3.50	3.50
1662	A520	Sheet of 10	20.00	20.00
a.-b.		300b Either single	.50	.50
c.-f.		1000b Any single	1.60	1.60
g.-h.		1500b Either single	2.25	2.25
i.-j.		2000b Either single	3.25	3.25

Souvenir Sheet

1663	A520	1000b multi	4.50	4.50

No. 1663 contains one 42x37mm stamp.

141st Extraordinary Meeting of OPEC — A521

No. 1664 — Petroleum facilities, meeting emblem and: a, "OPEP". b, Flag of United Arab Emirates flag. c, Flag of Libya. d, Flag of Iraq. e, Flag of Saudi Arabia. f, Flag of Indonesia. g, Flag of Nigeria. h, Flag of Algeria. i, Flag of Iran. j, Flag of Qatar. k, Flag of Venezuela. l, Flag of Kuwait.

2006, June 1				
1664		Sheet of 12	20.00	20.00
a.-b.	A521	300b Either single	.60	.60
c.-h.	A521	500b Any single	.75	.75
i.-j.	A521	1500b Either single	2.25	2.25
k.-l.	A521	2000b Either single	3.00	3.00

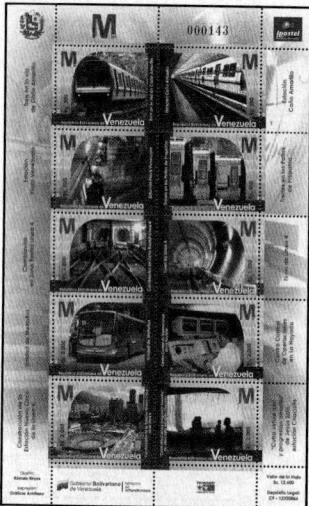

Caracas Mass Transit — A522

No. 1665: a, Train on Yellow line. b, Yellow line station. c, Plaza Venezuela Station. d, Three trains. e, Train switches. f, Line 4 Tunnel. g, Metro bus. h, Control room. i, Construction of Line 4 Nuevo Circo Station. j, Art by Jesús Soto, Chacaíto Station.

2006, July 2

1665	A522	Sheet of 10	25.00	25.00
a.-b.		300b Either single	.60	.60
c.-d.		500b Either single	.90	.90
e.-f.		1500b Either single	2.50	2.50
g.-j.		2000b Any single	3.25	3.25

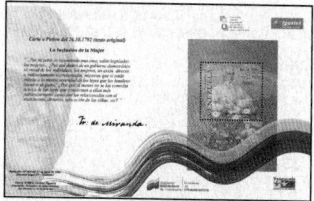

Francisco de Miranda University — A523

No. 1666, vert.: a, Miranda on horse. b, Miranda facing left. c, Nose, mouth and hand of Miranda. d, Statue of Miranda, Venezuelan flag. e, Miranda holding flag. f, Miranda at Venezuelan independence ceremonies. g, Miranda. h, Statues of Miranda. i, Miranda facing right. j, Miranda writing letter, ship.
No. 1667, Like #1666j.

2006, July 28

1666	A523	Sheet of 10	17.50	17.50
a.-d.		300b Any single	.60	.60
e.-f.		500b Either single	.90	.90
g.-h.		1500b Either single	2.50	2.50
i.-j.		2000b Either single	3.25	3.25

Souvenir Sheet

1667	A523	1500b multi	2.50	2.50

No. 1666 contains ten 35x45mm stamps.

Children's Art — A524

No. 1668: a, Flag of Liberty, by Elimar Sanchez. b, Miranda (Miranda and broken chain), by Gabriel Solano. c, Miranda and Catalina, by Elikarina Sánchez. d, Musical Aspects of Miranda (G clef), by Josmelys Díaz. e, Miranda Playing, by Nasser Sultan. f, Miranda and His Dreams, by Cynthia Urbina. g, Flag of Miranda, by Janem Sultan. h, Miranda Thinking, by Luis Miguel Martínez. i, Miranda and His Family, by Vianny Gonella. j, Diary of Miranda, by José A. Martínez.

2006

1668	A524	Sheet of 10	17.50	17.50
a.-d.		300b Any single	.60	.60
e.-f.		500b Either single	.80	.80
g.-h.		1500b Either single	2.40	2.40
i.-j.		2000b Either single	3.25	3.25

Souvenir Sheet

CVG EDELCA, 43rd Anniv. — A525

2006

1669	A525	3500b multi	6.50	6.50

Central University, Caracas — A526

No. 1670: a, Exterior of Engineering Library. b, Interior of Engineering Library. c, Electrical Engineering Building. d, School of Engineering, Metallurgy and Material Sciences, Sculpture by Harry Abend. e, School of Civil Engineering. f, School of Chemical Engineering, Petroleum and Geology, Mines and Geophysics. g, Mural by Alejandro Otero at School of Engineering. h, Machinery at Institute of Materials and Structural Models. i, Fluid Mechanics Institute. j, Aulas Auditorium.

2006

1670	A526	Sheet of 10	32.50	32.50
a.-d.		400b Any single	.60	.60
e.-f.		600b Either single	.90	.90
g.-h.		3000b Either single	4.50	4.50
i.-j.		5000b Either single	7.50	7.50

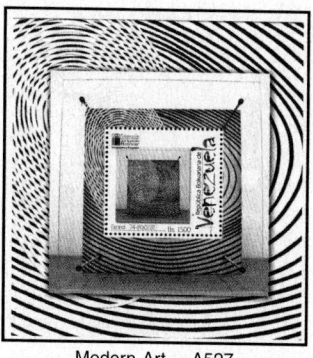

Modern Art — A527

No. 1671: a, Esfera Japón. b, Biface Naranja. c, Repetición y Progresión. d, Repetición Optica No. 2. e, Composición Dinámica. f,

Muro Optico. g, Pardelas Interferentes. h, Espiral. i, Ambivalencia Dicembre. j, Estructura Cinética.
1500b, Espiral, diff.

2006

1671	A527	Sheet of 10	14.00	14.00
a.-b.		300b Either single	.60	.60
c.-f.		500b Any single	.80	.80
g.-j.		1000b Any single	1.75	1.75

Souvenir Sheet

1672	A527	1500b multi	4.25	4.25

No. 1671 contains ten 45x35mm stamps.

Transportation — A528

No. 1673: a, Airplane in flight. b, Simón Bolívar Intl. Airport, Maiquetía. c, Highway, Ayacucho. d, Highway, Barquisimeto. e, José Antonio Páez Highway. f, Caracas — La Guaira Viaduct. g, Line 3, Caracas Metro. h, Line 4, Caracas Metro. i, Maracaibo Metro. j, Teques Metro. k, Valencia Metro. l, Caracas — Tuy Medio tram.

2006

1673	A528	Sheet of 12	27.50	27.50
a.-g.		300b Any single	.60	.60
h.-j.		2000b Any single	3.25	3.25
k.-l.		3000b Either single	4.50	4.50

A529

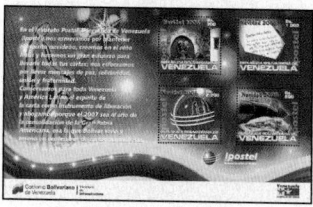

Christmas — A530

No. 1674: a, Musicians. b, Toy. c, Top. d, Holiday table setting. e, Food. f, Letter to Baby Jesus. g, Illuminated cross. h, Yo-yo. i, Yo-yo, top and toy. j, Envelope with Holy Family.
No. 1675: a, Nativity. b, Food. c, Letter to Baby Jesus. d, IPOSTEL emblem with Holy Family.

2006

1674	A529	Sheet of 10	16.00	16.00
a.-b.		300b Either single	.50	.50
c.-d.		450b Either single	.70	.70
e.-f.		550b Either single	.85	.85
g.-h.		1000b Either single	1.50	1.50
i.		2000b multi	2.90	2.90
j.		3000b multi	4.25	4.25
1675	A530	Sheet of 4	7.50	7.50
a.-b.		300b Either single	.50	.50
c.		1000b multi	1.50	1.50
d.		2000b multi	2.90	2.90

Miniature Sheets

A531

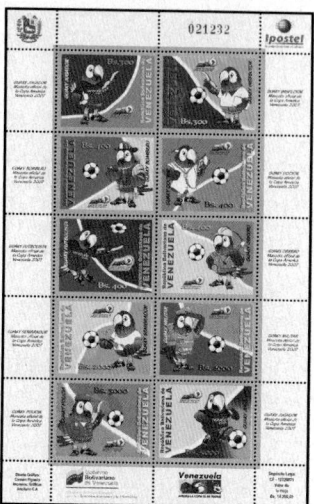

A532

2007 Copa America Soccer Tournament, Venezuela — A533

No. 1676: a, Mascot Guaky and soccer ball. b, City University Olympic Stadium, Caracas. c, José E. Pachencho Stadium, Maracaibo. d, Metropolitan Stadium, Lara. e, Agustín Tovar "La Carolina" Stadium, Barinas. f, General J. A. Anzoátegui Stadium, Puerto La Cruz. g, Cachamay Total Entertainment Center, Ciudad Guayana. h, Metropolitan Stadium, Mérida. i, Monumental Stadium, Maturin. j,

Multisport Stadium, Pueblo Nuevo San Cristóbal.

No. 1677 — Mascots: a, Guaky Jugador. b, Guaky Inspector. c, Guaky Bombero. d, Guaky Doctor. e, Guaky Futbolista. f, Guaky Obrero. g, Guaky Sembrador. h, Guaky Militar. i, Guaky Policia. j, Guaky Jugador, diff.

No. 1678 — Mascot Guaky and emblem of soccer governing body of: a, Venezuela. b, Brazil. c, Argentina. d, Mexico. e, Colombia. f, Chile. g, Peru. h, Uruguay. i, Ecuador. j, Bolivia. k, Paraguay. l, United States.

2007, June 18	Litho.	Perf. 12	
1676 A531	Sheet of 10	25.00	25.00
a.-b.	300b Either single	.50	.50
c.-f.	400b Any single	.65	.65
g.-h.	2000b Either single	3.00	3.00
i.	3000b multi	4.00	4.00
j.	5000b multi	7.00	7.00
1677 A532	Sheet of 10	25.00	25.00
a.-b.	300b Either single	.50	.50
c.-f.	400b Any single	.65	.65
g.-h.	2000b Either single	3.00	3.00
i.	3000b multi	4.00	4.00
j.	5000b multi	7.00	7.00
1678 A533	Sheet of 12	25.00	25.00
a.-d.	300b Any single	.50	.50
e.-h.	400b Any single	.65	.65
i.-j.	2000b Either single	2.50	2.50
k.	3000b multi	4.00	4.00
l.	5000b multi	6.50	6.50
	Nos. 1676-1678 (3)	75.00	75.00

Intelligence and Prevention Service (DISIP), 38th Anniv. — A534

No. 1679 — DISIP emblem and: a, El Helicoide (Headquarters Building), denomination in red, "Venezuela" in dark blue. b, Model of El Helicoide, denomination in dark blue, "Venezuela" in orange. c, Model of El Helicoide, denomination in yellow. d, El Helicoide being built, denomination in red, "Venezuela" in green. e, Cupola of El Helicoide, denomination in orange. f, Auditorium of El Helicoide, denomination in light blue, "Venezuela" in red. g, El Helicoide, denomination in green. h, El Helicoide, denomination in red. i, Garden outside El Helicoide. j, Plaza Bolívar.

3500b, El Helicoide, denomination in yellow.

2007, June 21			
1679 A534	Sheet of 10	25.00	25.00
a.-f.	300b Any single	.50	.50
g.-h.	2000b Either single	3.00	3.00
i.	3000b multi	4.00	4.00
j.	5000b multi	7.00	7.00
	Souvenir Sheet		
1680 A534	3500b multi	6.00	6.00

No. 1680 contains one 42x37mm stamp.

Miniature Sheet

Simón Bolívar Center, Caracas — A535

No. 1681: a, Muses de los Niños. b, Juan Pablo II buildings. c, Torres del Silencio. d, Palacio de Justicia. e, Parque Central building. f, Museo de Arte Contemporaneo de Caracas. g, Avenida Bolívar. h, Paseo Vargas. i, Teresa Carreño Theater. j, Cristobal Rojas.

2007, July 19			
1681 A535	Sheet of 10	20.00	20.00
a.-d.	300b Any single	.40	.40
e.-f.	450b Either single	.55	.55
g.-h.	2000b Either single	2.75	2.75
i.	3000b multi	3.75	3.75
j.	5000b multi	6.75	6.75

Miniature Sheet

Christmas — A536

No. 1682 — Art: a, Resplendent God, by Hugo Rivero. b, Creole Christmas, by Vidalia González. c, Christmas Door, by Soccoro Peraza. d, Christmas, wood carvings by Orlando Campos. e, Christmas, wood carving by Tomás Flores. f, Christmas Wish, by Alberto Allup. g, St. Joseph, Virgin and Child, by Baldomero Higuera. h, Christmas, by Edgar Vegas. i, Holy Family, by Margarita Pérez de Lamanna. j, Merry Christmas, by Ana Teresa Pesce.

2007, Dec. 10			
1682 A536	Sheet of 10	12.50	12.50
a.-d.	500b Any single	.65	.65
e.-h.	1000b Any single	1.40	1.40
i.-j.	1500b Either single	1.95	1.95

Miniature Sheet

Venezuelan Institute for Scientific Investigations (IVIC) — A537

No. 1683 — IVIC emblem and: a, Quimbiotec Blood Products Plant. b, Beatriz Roche Children's Band. c, Academic medal. d, Cubagua gargoyle. e, Advance Studies Center graduates. f, Bolívar and Bello Plaza. g, Molecular model. h, Investigative laboratory. i, Marcel Roche Library. j, Samuel Robinson Apartments.

2007, Dec. 14			
1683 A537	Sheet of 10	15.00	15.00
a.-d.	500b Any single	.65	.65
e.-h.	1000b Any single	1.40	1.40
i.-j.	2000b Either single	2.75	2.75

Miniature Sheet

Coins and Banknotes of Revalued Currency — A538

No. 1685: a, Coins and banknotes. b, 1 centimo coin. c, 5 centimo coin. d, 10 centimo coin. e, 12½ centimo coin. f, 25 centimo coin. g, 50 centimo coin. h, 1 bolivar coin. i, Francisco de Miranda and Inia geoffrensis from 2 bolivar banknote. j, Pedro Camejo and Priodontes maximus from 5 bolivar banknote. k, Guaicaipuro and Harpia harpyja from 10 bolivar banknote. l, Luisa Cáceres de Arismendi and Eretmochelys imbricata from 20 bolivar banknote. m, Simón Rodríguez and Tremarctos ornatus from 50 bolivar banknote. n, Simon Bolivar and Carduelis cucullata from 100 bolivar banknote.

2008, May 7	Litho.	Perf. 12	
1685 A538	Sheet of 14	13.50	13.50
a.-d.	40c Any single	.45	.45
e.-f.	50c Either single	.50	.50
g.-h.	60c Either single	6.00	6.00

i.-j.	1b Either single	1.00	1.00
k.-l.	1.50b Either single	1.50	1.50
m.-n.	2b Either single	2.10	2.10

Miniature Sheet

2008 Summer Olympics, Beijing — A539

No. 1686: a, Swimming. b, Weight lifting. c, Women's wrestling. d, Fencing.

2008, June 20		Perf. 12	
1686 A539 1b Sheet of 4, #a-d		4.50	4.50

Miniature Sheet

Sites in Caracas — A540

No. 1687: a, Palacio de las Academias. b, Sabana Grande Boulevard. c, Plaza El Venezolano. d, Abra Solar. e, Carmelitas Post Office. f, Plaza O'Leary. g, City Hall (Palacio Municipal). h, Reflecting pool (Paseo Monumental Los Próceres). i, Casona Anauco Arriba. j, Plaza Bolívar.

3b, Reflecting pool (Paseo Monumental Los Próceres).

2008, Oct. 9	Litho.	Perf. 12	
1687 A540	Sheet of 10	24.00	24.00
a.-b.	30c Either single	.40	.40
c.-d.	40c Either single	.50	.50
e.-f.	60c Either single	.70	.70
g.-h.	1.50b Either single	1.60	1.60
i.	5b multi	5.50	5.50
j.	10b multi	11.00	11.00
	Souvenir Sheet		
1688 A540	3b multi	4.00	4.00

Miniature Sheet

Portraits of Simon Bolivar — A541

No. 1689 — Portraits by: a, José M. Espínosa. b, Pierre Colf. c, Tito Salas. d, José Gil de Castro. e, Angel Zeballos. f, Gil de Castro, diff. g, Salas, diff. h, Juan Lovera. i, Unknown artist. j, Salas, diff. k, Salas, diff. l, Daniel Hernández.

2008	Litho.	Perf. 12	
1689 A541	Sheet of 12	25.00	25.00
a.-d.	30c Any single	.40	.40
e.-g.	50c Any single	.60	.60
h.-j.	1.50b Any single	1.60	1.60
k.	3b multi	3.50	3.50
l.	10b multi	11.00	11.00

Miniature Sheet

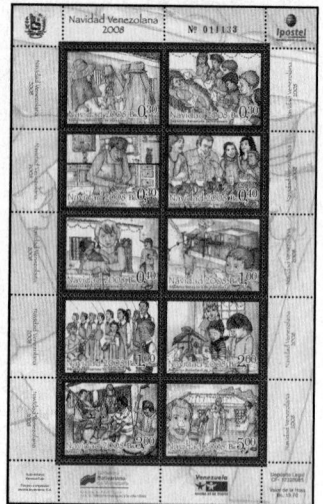

Christmas — A542

No. 1690: a, Four people wearing hats, baby. b, Children giving letters to baby Jesus. c, Woman in kitchen. d, Family eating holiday meal. e, Boy and girl with toys. f, Boys flying kite. g, Choir and musicians. h, Three children at small creche. i, Musicians. j, Children playing, house decorated with Christmas lights.

2008, Dec. 1   Litho.   Perf. 12
1690	A542	Sheet of 10	16.00	16.00
a.-c.		30c Any single	.35	.35
d.-e.		40c Either single	.45	.45
f.-g.		1b Either single	1.10	1.10
h.		2b multi	2.10	2.10
i.		3b multi	3.00	3.00
j.		5b multi	5.00	5.00

Miniature Sheet

Simón Bolívar Satellite — A543

No. 1691: a, Parts of satellite. b, Arm of satellite folded up. c, Satellite on scaffolds. d, Scaffolds and sign. e, Launch pad. f, Satellite dishes. g, Lift-off. h, Satellite dishes and control building. i, Satellite dish and control room. j, Satellite in space.

2009, Jan. 8
1691	A543	Sheet of 10	25.00	25.00
a.-b.		30c Either single	.40	.40
c.-d.		60c Either single	.65	.65
e.-f.		1b Either single	1.10	1.10
g.		2b multi	2.10	2.10
h.-i.		3b Either single	3.00	3.00
j.		8b multi	8.50	8.50

Miniature Sheet

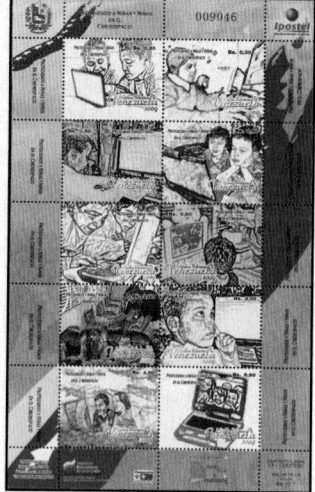

Protection of Children on the Internet — A544

No. 1692: a, Two boys at laptop computer. b, Two children at desktop computers. c, Man at computer. d, Two children at laptop computer, diff. (children at right). e, Two boys at laptop computer, diff. (children at left). f, Child at computer with adult watching. g, Group of children in computer classroom. h, Boy with finger at ear near computer. i, Man and woman in field with computer. j, Laptop computer showing children on screen.

2009, May 15
1692	A544	Sheet of 10	20.00	20.00
a.-b.		30c Either single	.35	.35
c.-f.		50c Any single	.50	.50
g.-h.		2b Either single	2.10	2.10
i.		4b multi	4.00	4.00
j.		6.50b multi	7.00	7.00

Francisco de Miranda (1750-1816), Revolutionist in Venezuela and France — A545

2009, Oct. 15
1693	A545	1.50b multi	1.60	1.60
a.		Souvenir sheet of 1, imperf.	3.00	3.00

See France No. 3729.

Miniature Sheets

Venezuelan Declaration of Independence, 200th Anniv. (in 2011) — A546

A547

Signers of the Venezuelan Declaration of Independence — A548

No. 1694: a, Part 7 of Declaration of Independence. b, Part 8. c, Part 9. d, Part 4. e, Part 5. f, Part 6. g, Part 2. h, Part 3. i, Part 1. j, Signatures. k, Signatures, diff. l, Simon Bolivar and map of North and South America.

No. 1695: a, Francisco de Miranda. b, Francisco Hernández. c, Salvador Delgado. d, Juan José de Maya. e, Juan Antonio Díaz Argote. f, Felipe Fermín Paul. g, Manuel Vicente Maya. h, Juan Toro. i, Francisco Policarpo Ortiz. j, Gabriel Pérez de Pagola. k, José María Ramírez. l, Fernando Toro.

No. 1696: a, Gabriel de Ponte. b, Lino de Clemente. c, Ramón Ignacio Méndez. d, Francisco Javier Ustáriz. e, Isidoro Antonio López Méndez. f, El Marqués del Toro. g, Juan Antonío Rodríguez Domínguez. h, José de Sata y Busy. i, José Vicente de Unda. j, Antonio Nicolás Briceño.

2009   Litho.   Perf. 12
1694	A546	Sheet of 12	24.00	24.00
a.-c.		30c Any single	.35	.35
d.-f.		50c Any single	.50	.50
g.-h.		1b Either single	1.10	1.10
i.-j.		2b Either single	2.10	2.10
k.		3.50b multi	3.50	3.50
l.		9.50b multi	10.00	10.00
1695	A547	Sheet of 12	24.00	24.00
a.-c.		30c Any single	.35	.35
d.-f.		50c Any single	.50	.50
g.-h.		1b Either single	1.10	1.10
i.-j.		2b Either single	2.10	2.10
k.		3.50b multi	3.50	3.50
l.		9.50b multi	10.00	10.00
1696	A548	Sheet of 10	24.00	24.00
a.		30c multi	.35	.35
b.-c.		50c Either single	.50	.50
d.-f.		1b Any single	1.10	1.10
g.-h.		2b Either single	2.10	2.10
i.		3.50b multi	3.50	3.50
j.		9.50b multi	10.00	10.00
		Nos. 1694-1696 (3)	72.00	72.00

Miniature Sheets

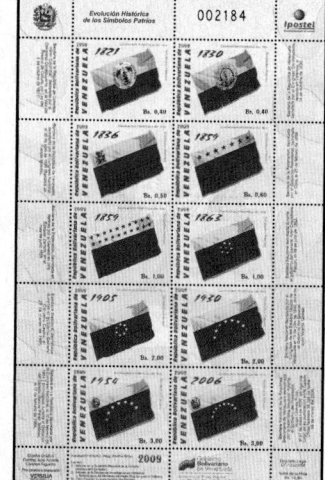

History of the Venezuelan Flag — A549

No. 1697 — Flag from: a, 1797. b, 1800. c, 1806 (Sun and Moon). d, 1806 (yellow, blue and red stripes). e, 1810. f, 1811. g, 1817 (7 stars). h, 1817 (8 stars). i, 1819. j, 1821 (arms in upper left corner).

No. 1698 — Flag from: a, 1821. b, 1830. c, 1836. d, 1859 (7 stars). e, 1859 (20 stars). f, 1863. g, 1905. h, 1930. i, 1954. j, 2006.

2009   Litho.   Perf. 12
1697	A549	Sheet of 10	15.00	15.00
a.-b.		40c Either single	.45	.45
c.		50c multi	.50	.50
d.		60c multi	.60	.60
e.-f.		1b Either single	1.10	1.10
g.-h.		2b Either single	2.10	2.10
i.-j.		3b Either single	2.90	2.90
1698	A549	Sheet of 10	15.00	15.00
a.-b.		40c Either single	.45	.45
c.		50c multi	.50	.50
d.		60c multi	.60	.60
e.-f.		1b Either single	1.10	1.10
g.-h.		2b Either single	2.10	2.10
i.-j.		3b Either single	2.90	2.90

Miniature Sheets

History of the Venezuelan Coat of Arms — A550

No. 1699 — Arms from: a, 1591. b, 1811 (sun and banner). c, 1811 (dated 19 Abril de 1810). d, 1811 (dated 1811). e, 1812 (with 7 stars). f, 1812 (eagle with shield). g, 1819. h, 1821 (with eagle). i, 1821 (fasces and cornucopias). j, 1822.

No. 1700 — Arms from: a, 1830. b, 1834. c, 1836. d, 1856. e, 1863. f, 1871. g, 1905. h, 1930. i, 1954. j, 2006.

2009   Litho.   Perf. 12
1699	A550	Sheet of 10	15.00	15.00
a.-b.		40c Either single	.45	.45
c.		50c multi	.50	.50
d.		60c multi	.60	.60
e.-f.		1b Either single	1.10	1.10
g.-h.		2b Either single	2.10	2.10
i.-j.		3b Either single	2.90	2.90
1700	A550	Sheet of 10	15.00	15.00
a.-b.		40c Either single	.45	.45
c.		50c multi	.50	.50
d.		60c multi	.60	.60
e.-f.		1b Either single	1.10	1.10
g.-h.		2b Either single	2.10	2.10
i.-j.		3b Either single	2.90	2.90

Miniature Sheet

Ayacucho Library, 35th Anniv. — A551

No. 1701 — Map color: a, Bister. b, Dark green. c, Dark blue. d, Lilac. e, Gray brown. f, Light blue. g, Yellow. h, Apple green. i, Brownish lilac. j, Gray.

2009   Litho.   Perf. 12
1701	A551	Sheet of 10	22.50	22.50
a.-d.		30c Any single	.35	.35
e.-f.		2b Either single	2.10	2.10
g.-h.		3.50b Either single	3.50	3.50
i.-j.		4b Either single	4.00	4.00

Miniature Sheet

Christmas — A552

No. 1702 — Religious art by: a, Lidoska Pirela. b, Miguel MarSán. c, Thays Arteaga. d, Gustavo Martínez. e, Orlando Campos. f, Daniel Sanseviero. g, Hugo Rivero. h, Edgar Vegas. i, Liliana Benítez. j, Alberto Allup.

2009
1702	A552	Sheet of 10	30.00	30.00
a.-d.		30c Any single	.50	.50
e.-g.		50c Any single	.80	.80

h.	3.10b multi	5.00	5.00
i.	4.20b multi	7.00	7.00
j.	6.50b multi	10.00	10.00

Miniature Sheets

A553

Signers of the Venezuelan Declaration of Independence — A554

No. 1703: a, Juan Germán Roscio. b, Fernando Peñalver. c, Martín Tovar Ponte. d, Ignacio Fernández. e, José Angel Alamo. f, Luis Ignacio Mendoza. g, Nicolás de Castro. h, Ignacio Ramón Briceño. i, Francisco Javier Yánes. j, Gabriel de Alcalá.

No. 1704: a, Mariano de la Cova. b, Juan Bermúdez. c, Francisco Isnardi. d, Manuel Plácido Maneiro. e, Juan Pablo Pacheco. f, José Luis Cabrera. g, Manuel Palacio. h, Juan Nepomuceno Quintana. i, Luis José de Cazorla. j, Francisco Javier de Mayz.

2009   *Perf. 12*

1703	A553	Sheet of 10	30.00	30.00
a.-b.		30c Either single	.45	.45
c.		50c multi	.65	.65
d.-f.		1b Any single	1.25	1.25
g.-h.		2b Either single	2.50	2.50
i.		3.50b multi	4.50	4.50
j.		9.50b multi	12.50	12.50
1704	A554	Sheet of 10	30.00	30.00
a.-b.		30c Either single	.45	.45
c.-d.		50c Either single	.65	.65
e.-f.		1b Either single	1.25	1.25
g.-h.		2b Either single	2.50	2.50
i.		3.50b multi	4.50	4.50
j.		9.50b multi	12.50	12.50

Miniature Sheet

Bolivarian Militia — A555

No. 1705 — General Command Building: a, Domed and crenellated tower. b, Columns and balcony. c, Flag above main entrance. d, Round crenellated tower in foreground. e, Rectangular tower. g, Columns and Plaza of Honor. h, Militia members, round crenellated tower in background. i, Building. j, Building and flag.

2010, Apr. 21

1705	A555	Sheet of 10	19.00	19.00
a.-c.		1b Any single	.55	.55
d.-f.		2b Any single	1.10	1.10
g.-h.		4.50b Either single	2.25	2.25
i.		6b multi	3.00	3.00
j.		10.50b multi	6.00	6.00

Miniature Sheet

Prominent Figures of the First Republic of Venezuela — A556

No. 1706: a, Juan Germán Roscio (1763-1821). b, José Félix Ribas (1775-1815). c, Francisco Espejo (1758-1814). d, Isidoro López Méndez (1751-1814). e, Lino de Clemente (1767-1834). f, José Félix Sosa (1773-1814). g, Martín Tovar Ponte (1772-1843). h, Francisco Javier Ustáriz (1772-1814). i, Francisco Salias (1785-1834). j, José Cortés de Madariaga (1766-1826).

2010, Apr. 28

1706	A556	Sheet of 10	21.00	21.00
a.-b.		1b Either single	.60	.60
c.-f.		2.50b Any single	1.50	1.50
g.-i.		4b Any single	2.25	2.25
j.		12b multi	7.00	7.00

Manuela Sáenz (c. 1797-1856), Mistress of Simón Bolívar — A557

2010, May 24

1707	A557	2.50b multi	2.50	2.50

See Ecuadoe No. 2007.

Miniature Sheet

Scenes From Independence Day Military Parade — A558

No. 1708: a, National flag (Bandera Nacional). b, Athletes on float (Atletas). c, Women from cultural group wearing yellow and green dresses (Agrupaciones Culturales). d, People from cultural group wearing masks, red and white costumes (Agrupaciones Culturales). e, Women from cultural group wearing headdresses and white blouses (Agrupaciones Culturales). f, Indigenous people (Etnias Indigenas). g, People carrying flags (Estandartes FANB). h, Two uniformed men and white horse (Réplica de la Espada del Libertador). i, Soldiers from Venezuela Military Academy marching (Academia Militar de Venezuela). j, Sailors from Naval School (Escuela Naval). k, Students from Military Aviation School (Escuela de Aviación Militar). l, Students from National Guard Officer's Training School (EFOFAC). m, Students from Military Technical School (Escuela Técnica Militar). n, Male members of Bolivarian Militia wearing red pants (Milicia Bolivariana). o, Female members of Bolivarian Militia wearing white boots (Milicia Bolivariana). p, Rural militia (Milicia Campesina). q, AMX-30 tank. r, C-90 Escorpión tank. s, Dragón 300 armored fighting vehicle. t, E-11 Urutu armored personnel carrier. u, Oto Melara armored personnel carrier. v, Sultán tank. w, AMX-13 tank. x, Tank of Mechanized Infantry with banner (Infantería Mecanizada del Ejército). y, Members of Brazil delegation. z, Members of Cuba delegation. aa, Members of Bolivia delegation. ab, Members of Nicaragua delegation. ac, Members of Argentina delegation. ad, Members of Ecuador delegation. ae, Members of Belarus delegation. af, Members of Dominican Republic delegation. ag, Members of Parachute battalion (Batallón de Paracaidistas). ah, Members of Caribbean Batallion (Batallón de Caribes). ai, Members of Forest Batallion (Batallón de Selva). aj, Special Forces wearing jungle camouflage with hoods (Fuerzas Especiales). ak, Special Forces members, man with black ski cap at right (Fuerzas Especiales). al, Special Forces members with open mouths and camouflage painted faces, white gun straps (Fuerzas Especiales). am, Special Forces members wearing red berets (Fuerzas Especiales). an, Special Forces members with fully-painted faces, black gun straps (Fuerzas Especiales). ao, Sukhoi 30MK2 jet. ap, F-16 jet. aq, K-8 jet. ar, MI-26T Panare helicopter. as, MI-35M Caribe helicopter. at, MI-17V5

Pemón helicopter. au, Sikorsky AS-61D helicopter. av, Mounted sqadron (Escuadrón de Caballería.

2010, Aug. 9

1708		Sheet of 48	25.00	25.00
a.-x.		A558 30c Any single	.35	.35
y.-av.		A558 1b Any single	.65	.65

Organization of Petroleum Exporting Countries (OPEC), 50th Anniv. — A559

No. 1709 — Paintings: a, Sembradores, by Ender Cepeda. b, Y Por Fin Nos Tocó Un Chorrito de Petróleo, by Soccorro Salinas. c, Cartografía Soberana, by Saúl Huerta. d, Serie Atardecer en Campos Petroleros, by Ernesto León. e, Como Caída del Cielo, by Rosa Contreras. f, Marea, by Morella Jurado. g, Julio, by Omar Carreño. h, Del Reventón al Barril Dorado, by Gabriel Bracho. i, Petróleo Nuestro de Cada Día, by Manuel Quintana Castillo. j, El Pozo y Las Ocho Estrellas, by Paúl Del Río.

12p, 50th anniversary emblem, horiz.

2010, Sept. 14

1709		Sheet of 10	21.00	21.00
a.-c.		30c Any single	.30	.30
d.-e.		50c Either single	.30	.30
f.-g.		3b Either single	1.50	1.50
h.		8b multi	4.00	4.00
i.-j.		10b Either single	5.00	5.00

Souvenir Sheet

1710	A559	12b multi	7.50	7.50

No. 1710 contains one 42x37mm stamp.

Miniature Sheet

Central Bank of Venezuela Art Collection, 70th Anniv. — A560

No. 1711 — Paintings: a, Venezuela, by Armando Reverón. b, Formas en Equilibio N-1, by Angel Hurtado. c, Bananeros, by Camille Pissarro. d, La Pareja, by Armando Barrias. e, Left half of El Avila Visto Desde el Country Club (trees at left), by Manuel Cabré. f, Right half of El Avila Visto Desde el Country Club (trees at right), by Cabré.

2010, Nov. 24

1711	A560	Sheet of 6	21.00	21.00
a.-b.		30c Either single	.30	.30
c.		5b multi	2.50	2.50
d.		8b multi	4.00	4.00
e.-f.		12.50b Either single	6.50	6.50

Miniature Sheet

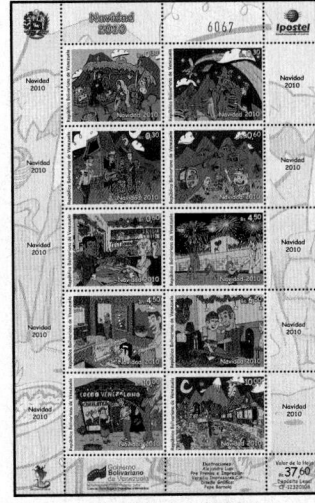

Christmas — A561

No. 1712: a, Nativity. b, Satellite over the three Magi. c, Musicians. d, Cable car, buildings on mountainside, children playing. e, Woman and man at market. f, Fireworks over building. g, Teacher and children in school room, boy working at computer. h, Father and son opening Christmas gift. i, Father and son outside of candy store. j, Child on blanket in plaza, people, bus.

2010, Dec. 7

1712	A561	Sheet of 10	21.00	21.00
a.-c.		30c Any single	.30	.30
d.-e.		60c Either single	.35	.35
f.-g.		4.50b Either single	2.25	2.25
h.		6.50b multi	3.25	3.25
i.-j.		10b Either single	5.00	5.00

Miniature Sheet

Venezuelan Antarctic Program — A562

No. 1713: a, Members of first expedition, 2008. b, Scientists taking measurements. c, Members of third expedition, 2010. d, Line of expedition members in snowstorm. e, Iceberg adrift. f, Antarctic base buildings, iceberg. g, Members of second expedition, 2009. h, Giant petrel. i, Penguins and ship, Barrientos Island. j, Whale at surface.

2010, Dec. 21   *Perf. 12¼x12*

1713	A562	Sheet of 10	27.50	27.50
a.-b.		30c Either single	.40	.40
c.-d.		40c Either single	.40	.40
e.-f.		60c Either single	.60	.60
g.		6.50b multi	4.00	4.00
h.-i.		8.50b Either single	5.00	5.00
j.		13.50b multi	7.50	7.50

America Issue (National Symbols) — A563

2011, Feb. 21   **Perf. 14¼**
1714 A563 2b multi   1.25 1.25

Miniature Sheet

Army Day — A564

No. 1715 — Uniform of: a, Batallón Bravos de Apure. b, Guardia de Honor del Libertador. c, Soldado Llanero. d, Batallón de Rifles. e, Batallón Tiradores de la Guardia. f, Cazadores Britanicos. g, Dragones de la Guardia. h, Husares de Páez. i, General de División Patriota. j, Campaña del Libertador.

2011, June 27   **Perf. 12**
1715 A564   Sheet of 10   24.00 24.00
a.-b.	30c Either single	.30	.30
c.-e.	40c Any single	.30	.30
f.-g.	1.50b Either single	.90	.90
h.	6.50b multi	4.00	4.00
i.	10b multi	6.00	6.00
j.	15.60b multi	9.00	9.00

Reunion of the Patriotic Society, by Tito Salas — A565

The Pantheon of Heroes, by Arturo Michelena — A566

No. 1716: a, Woman in black dress at right (left fifth of painting). b, Three men seated on bench at right, man at lectern in foreground (fourth fifth of painting). c, Bearded man standing at right (right fifth of painting). d, Woman with white dress in foreground at table (second fifth of painting). e, As "a." f, As "b." g, Three men seated on bench at left, lectern in foreground (middle fifth of painting). h, As "d." i, As "b." j, As "g."

2011, June 27   **Perf. 12**
1716 A565   Sheet of 10   30.00 30.00
a.-c.	30c Any single	.30	.30
d.-e.	60c Either single	.40	.40
f.	1.50b multi	.90	.90
g.-h.	8.50b Either single	5.00	5.00
i.-j.	12.50b Either single	7.00	7.00

Souvenir Sheet
1717 A566 18b multi   11.00 11.00

Miniature Sheet

Central Bank of Venezuela Gold Coin Collection — A567

No. 1718: a, Reverse of 1975 Venezuela 1000b coin depicting arms. b, Reverse of 1886 Venezuela 100b coin depicting arms. c, Obverse of 1851 United States $20 coin depicting Liberty. d, Reverse of 1851 United States $20 coin depicting Great Seal. e, Obverse of 1886 Venezuela 100b coin depicting Simón Bolívar. f, Obverse of 1975 1000b coin depicting bird.

2011, Oct. 25
1718 A567   Sheet of 6   30.00 30.00
a.	40c multi	.35	.35
b.	60c multi	.40	.40
c.-d.	5.50b Either single	2.75	2.75
e.	13b multi	7.50	7.50
f.	20b multi	11.00	11.00

Stained Glass Windows at Supreme Justice Tribunal, by Alirio Rodríguez — A568

No. 1719 — Detail from window numbered: a, 1/10. b, 6/10. c, 2/10. d, 7/10. e, 3/10. f, 8/10. g, 4/10. h, 9/10. i, 5/10. j, 10/10. 25b, Detail from different window.

2011, Dec. 14
1719 A568   Sheet of 10   30.00 30.00
a.-b.	30c Either single	.35	.35
c.-d.	40c Either single	.35	.35
e.-f.	1.50b Either single	1.00	1.00
g.-h.	6.50b Either single	4.00	4.00
i.	12b multi	9.00	9.00
j.	15.60b multi	12.00	12.00

Souvenir Sheet
1720 A568 25b multi   17.50 17.50

Souvenir Sheet

Simón Bolívar (1783-1830) — A569

2012, Sept. 27
1721 A569 25b multi   17.50 17.50

New Bolívar Mausoleum, Caracas.

Miniature Sheet

Luis Zambrano (1901-90), Inventor — A570

No. 1722 — Zambrano: a, Facing forward, wearing hat. b, Facing left, without hat. c, Fancing forward, without hat. d, Facing right, without hat. e, Working on machine with two men. f, Standing in front of machine. g, Touching wheel. h, Putting rod in machine. i, Wearing cap. j, Standing next to machine.

2012
1722 A570   Sheet of 10   25.00 25.00
a.-b.	30c Either single	.35	.35
c.-d.	40c Either single	.35	.35
e.-f.	1.50b Either single	1.00	1.00
g.	4b multi	3.00	3.00
h.-i.	6.50b Either single	5.00	5.00
j.	12.50b multi	10.00	10.00

Miniature Sheet

Pres. Hugo Chávez (1954-2013) — A571

No. 1723 — Pres. Chávez: a, Touching crucifix. b, Wearing beret and uniform, saluting. c, Hugging Venezuelan flag. d, Visiting school children. e, Hugging elderly woman. f, Holding flagpole. g, Shaking hands with person in crowd. h, Pointing finger. i, Wearing beret and uniform. j, Holding microphone.
20b, Wearing sash and necklace, vert.

2013, Apr. 9
1723 A571   Sheet of 10   15.00 15.00
a.-d.	30c Any single	.35	.35
e.	40c multi	.35	.35
f.-g.	1.50b Either single	.60	.60
h.	4.20b multi	1.60	1.60
i.	11.70b multi	4.25	4.25
j.	14b multi	5.00	5.00

Souvenir Sheet
1724 A571 20b multi   8.00 8.00

No. 1724 contains one 37x42mm stamp.

Miniature Sheet

Correos Carmelitas Building, Caracas — A572

No. 1725: a, 50c, Black-and-white photograph. b, 50c, Color photograph of builing painted yellow. c, 20b, Black-and-white photograph of different corner of building. d, 34b, Color photograph of building painted red.

2014, Jan. 28   **Litho.**   **Perf. 12**
1725 A572   Sheet of 4   18.00 18.00
a.-b.	50c Either single	.25	.25
c.	20b multi	6.50	6.50
d.	34b multi	11.00	11.00

America Issue — A573

No. 1726 — Pres. Hugo Chávez (1954-2013): a, Waving. b, Holding map of South America.

2014, Mar. 5   **Litho.**   **Perf. 12**
1726 A573   Pair   4.25 4.25
a.	1b multi	.25	.25
b.	12.50b multi	4.00	4.00

Works of the Revolution — A574

No. 1727: a, Estadio Monumental de Maturín (soccer stadium). b, Tractor in field. c, Latin American Infantile Cardiological Hospital. d, Metrocable cable car. e, Bridge over Orinoco River. f, Buildings, Ciudad Caribia. g, Miranda Satellite. h, Children with computers (Canaima Education Project).

2014, Dec. 18   **Litho.**   **Perf. 12**
1727   Horiz. strip of 8   57.00 57.00
a.	A574 30c multi	.25	.25
b.	A574 40c multi	.25	.25
c.	A574 50c multi	.25	.25
d.	A574 3.50b multi	1.10	1.10
e.	A574 15.60b multi	5.00	5.00
f.	A574 25b multi	8.00	8.00
g.	A574 31.50b multi	10.00	10.00
h.	A574 100b multi	32.00	32.00

SEMI-POSTAL STAMPS

A 5c green stamp of the Cruzada Venezolana Sanitaria Social portraying Simon Bolivar was overprinted "EE. UU. DE VENEZUELA CORREOS" in 1937.
It is stated that 50,000 stamps without control numbers on back were sold by post offices and 147,700 with control numbers on back were offered for sale by the Society at eight times face value.

Bolívar
Funeral
Carriage
SP1

Unwmk.

1942, Dec. 17   Engr.   Perf. 12
B1   SP1   20c + 5c blue   6.00   .65

Cent. of the arrival of Simón Bolívar's remains in Caracas. The surtax was used to erect a monument to his memory. See Nos. CB1-CB2.

Catalogue values for unused stamps in this section, from this point to the end of the section, are for Never Hinged items.

Red Cross
Nurse — SP2

1975, Dec. 15   Litho.   Perf. 14
B2   SP2   30c + 15c multi   .40   .25
B3   SP2   50c + 25c multi   .60   .40

Surtax for Venezuelan Red Cross.

Carmen América
Fernandez de
Leoni — SP3

Children in
Home — SP4

1976, June 7   Litho.   Perf. 13½
B4   SP3   30c + 15c multi   .30   .25
B5   SP4   50c + 25c multi   .50   .35

Surtax was for the Children's Foundation, founded by Carmen América Fernandez de Leoni in 1966.

Patient — SP5

1976, Dec. 8   Litho.   Perf. 14
B6   SP5   10c + 5c multi   .25   .25
B7   SP5   30c + 10c multi   .25   .25

Surtax was for Anti-tuberculosis Society.

AIR POST STAMPS

Air post stamps of 1930-42 perforated "GN" (Gobierno Nacional) were for official use.

Airplane and Map
of
Venezuela — AP1

1930   Unwmk.   Litho.   Perf. 12
C1   AP1   5c bister brn   .25   .25
C2   AP1   10c yellow   .25   .25
a.   10c salmon   32.50   32.50
C3   AP1   15c gray   .25   .25
C4   AP1   25c lilac   .25   .25
C5   AP1   40c olive grn   .25   .25
a.   40c slate blue   45.00
b.   40c slate green   45.00
C6   AP1   75c dp red   .30   .25
C7   AP1   1b indigo   .45   .25
C8   AP1   1.20b blue grn   .70   .35
C9   AP1   1.70b dk blue   .90   .45
C10   AP1   1.90b blue grn   .90   .50
C11   AP1   2.10b dk blue   1.75   .65
C12   AP1   2.30b vermilion   1.75   .50
C13   AP1   2.50b dk blue   1.75   .50
C14   AP1   3.70b blue grn   1.75   1.10
C15   AP1   10b dull vio   5.25   2.40
C16   AP1   20b gray grn   8.00   4.50
    Nos. C1-C16 (16)   24.75   12.70

Issued: 10b, 6/8; 20b, 6/16; others, 4/5.
Nos. C1-C16 exist imperforate or partly perforated. Value, imperf set $200.
See Nos. C119-C126.

Airplane and Map
of
Venezuela — AP2

Bluish Winchester Security Paper

1932, July 12   Engr.   Perf. 12½
C17   AP2   5c brown   .40   .25
C18   AP2   10c org yel   .40   .25
C19   AP2   15c gray lilac   .40   .25
C20   AP2   25c violet   .40   .25
C21   AP2   40c ol grn   .80   .25
C22   AP2   70c rose   .55   .25
C23   AP2   75c red org   1.00   .25
C24   AP2   1b dk bl   1.10   .25
C25   AP2   1.20b green   2.40   .85
C26   AP2   1.70b red brn   4.75   .55
C27   AP2   1.80b ultra   2.40   .35
C28   AP2   1.90b green   6.00   3.50
C29   AP2   1.95b blue   6.50   2.75
C30   AP2   2b blk brn   4.00   2.25
C31   AP2   2.10b blue   9.50   6.00
C32   AP2   2.30b red   4.00   2.40
C33   AP2   2.50b dk bl   6.00   1.40
C34   AP2   3b dk vio   6.00   .85
C35   AP2   3.70b emerald   8.00   6.00
C36   AP2   4b red org   6.00   1.40
C37   AP2   5b black   6.50   2.40
C38   AP2   8b dk car   13.00   4.75
C39   AP2   10b dk vio   26.00   8.00
C40   AP2   20b grnsh slate   60.00   20.00
    Nos. C17-C40 (24)   176.10   65.45

Pairs imperf. between exist of the 1b (value $150); the 25c and 4b (value $300 each).

Air Post Stamps of
1932 Surcharged
in Black

1937, June 4
C41   AP2   5c on 1.70b red
            brn   11.00   7.00
C42   AP2   10c on 3.70b em-
            er   11.00   7.00
C43   AP2   15c on 4b red org   5.00   3.50
C44   AP2   25c on 5b blk   5.00   3.50
C45   AP2   1b on 8b dk car   4.00   3.50
C46   AP2   2b on 2.10b bl   30.00   23.00
    Nos. C41-C46 (6)   66.00   47.50

Various varieties of surcharge exist, including double and triple impressions. No. C43 exists in pair imperf. between; value $30 unused, $50 used.

Allegory of
Flight
AP3

Allegory of
Flight
AP4

National
Pantheon
at Caracas
AP5

Airplane — AP6

Perf. 11, 11½ and Compound
1937, July 1   Litho.
C47   AP3   5c brn org   .30   .40
C48   AP4   10c org red   .25   .25
C49   AP5   15c gray blk   .60   .40
C50   AP6   25c dk vio   .60   .40
C51   AP4   40c yel grn   1.10   .55
C52   AP3   70c red   1.10   .40
C53   AP3   75c bister   2.50   1.30
C54   AP3   1b dk gray   1.50   .55
C55   AP4   1.20b pck grn   6.50   4.25
C56   AP3   1.80b dk ultra   3.25   2.00
C57   AP5   1.95b lt ultra   10.00   7.75
C58   AP6   2b chocolate   4.25   2.75
C59   AP6   2.50b gray bl   11.50   11.50
C60   AP4   3b lt vio   6.50   4.50
C61   AP6   3.70b rose red   11.50   15.00
C62   AP5   10b red vio   25.00   15.00
C63   AP3   20b gray   30.00   23.00
    Nos. C47-C63 (17)   116.45   90.00

All values exist imperf, and all except the 3.70b part-perf.
Counterfeits exist.
For overprints & surcharges see Nos. C66-C78, C114-C118, C164-C167, C169-C172, C174-C180.

AP7

1937, Oct. 28   Perf. 11
C64   AP7   70c emerald   1.40   .55
C65   AP7   1.80b ultra   2.25   1.00

Acquisition of the Port of La Guaira by the Government from the British Corporation, June 3, 1937. Nos. C64-C65 exist imperf. Value, set $275.
A redrawn printing of Nos. C64-C65, with lower inscription beginning "Nacionalización..." was prepared but not issued. Value, $40 each.
For overprints see Nos. C168, C173.

**Air Post Stamps of 1937
Overprinted in Black**

1937, Dec. 17   Perf. 11, 11½
C66   AP4   10c org red   1.00   .70
a.   Inverted overprint   15.00   12.00

C67   AP6   25c dk vio   2.00   1.00
C68   AP4   40c yel grn   2.00   1.40
C69   AP3   70c red   1.50   1.00
a.   Inverted overprint   15.00   14.00
b.   Double overprint   20.00   16.00
C70   AP3   1b dk gray   2.00   1.40
a.   Inverted overprint   16.00   13.00
b.   Double overprint   13.00
C71   AP4   1.20b pck grn   30.00   20.00
a.   Inverted overprint   77.50
C72   AP3   1.80b dk ultra   5.75   2.40
C73   AP5   1.95b lt ultra   7.75   4.25
a.   Inverted overprint   60.00   40.00
C74   AP6   2b chocolate   50.00   23.00
a.   Inverted overprint   100.00   90.00
b.   Double overprint   82.50   82.50
C75   AP6   2.50b gray bl   50.00   19.00
a.   Double overprint   70.00
b.   Inverted overprint   100.00   82.50
C76   AP4   3b lt vio   30.00   12.00
C77   AP5   10b red vio   72.50   40.00
C78   AP3   20b gray   77.50   47.50
a.   Double overprint   150.00   150.00
    Nos. C66-C78 (13)   332.00   173.65

Counterfeit overprints exist on #C77-C78.

View of La
Guaira
AP8

National
Pantheon
AP9

Oil Wells
AP10

1938-39   Engr.   Perf. 12
C79   AP8   5c green   1.00   .50
C80   AP8   5c dk grn   .25   .25
C81   AP9   10c car rose   1.40   .25
C82   AP9   10c scarlet   .25   .25
C83   AP8   12½c dull vio   .60   .55
C84   AP10   15c slate vio   3.00   1.25
C85   AP10   15c dk bl   .85   .25
C86   AP8   25c dk bl   3.00   1.25
C87   AP8   25c bis brn   .35   .25
C88   AP10   30c vio ('39)   2.00   .25
C89   AP9   40c dk vio   3.50   1.25
C90   AP9   40c redsh brn   2.50   .25
C91   AP8   45c Prus grn
            ('39)   1.00   .25
C92   AP9   50c blue ('39)   1.25   .25
C93   AP10   70c car rose   .85   .25
C94   AP8   75c bis brn   6.00   2.00
C95   AP8   75c ol bis   1.40   .25
C96   AP10   90c red org
            ('39)   1.00   .25
C97   AP8   1b ol & bis   7.00   2.75
C98   AP9   1b dk vio   1.25   .25
C99   AP10   1.20b orange   20.00   5.75
C100   AP10   1.20b green   2.00   .55
C101   AP8   1.80b ultra   2.00   .55
C102   AP9   1.90b black   5.50   2.75
C103   AP10   1.95b lt bl   4.25   2.50
C104   AP8   2b ol grn   45.00   15.00
C105   AP8   2b car rose   1.75   .70
C106   AP9   2.50b red brn   45.00   20.00
C107   AP9   2.50b orange   10.00   2.75
C108   AP10   3b bl grn   20.00   4.75
C109   AP10   3b ol gray   5.50   2.00
C110   AP8   3.70b gray blk   7.75   5.50
C111   AP10   5b red brn
            ('39)   7.75   2.00
C112   AP9   10b vio brn   20.00   2.40
C113   AP10   20b red org   57.50   25.00
    Nos. C79-C113 (35)   292.35   105.55

See Nos. C227a, C235-C236, C254-C255.
For surcharge see No. C227.

**Nos. C51, C56, C58-C59, C61
Surcharged**

1938, Apr. 15   Perf. 11, 11½
C114   AP3   5c on 1.80b   .85   .60
a.   Inverted surcharge   12.50   7.50

C115	AP6	10c on 2.50b	3.00	1.40
a.		Inverted surcharge	10.00	7.50
C116	AP6	15c on 2b	1.40	1.10
C117	AP4	25c on 40c	1.75	1.40
C118	AP6	40c on 3.70b	3.50	3.25
		Nos. C114-C118 (5)	10.50	7.75

Plane & Map Type of 1930

White Paper; No Imprint

1938-39 Engr. ***Perf. 12½***

C119	AP1	5c dk grn ('39)	.25	.25
C120	AP1	10c org yel ('39)	.55	.25
C121	AP1	12½c rose vio ('39)	1.10	.85
C122	AP1	15c dp bl	.95	.25
C123	AP1	25c brown	1.10	.25
C124	AP1	40c olive ('39)	2.75	.40
C125	AP1	70c rose car ('39)	20.00	7.75
C126	AP1	1b dk bl ('39)	7.75	3.00
		Nos. C119-C126 (8)	34.45	13.00

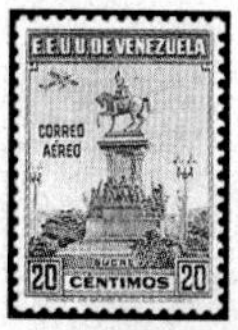

Monument to Sucre — AP11

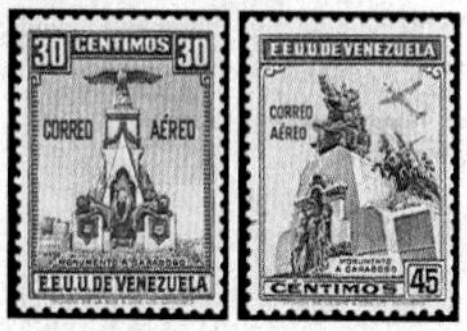

Monuments at Carabobo
AP12 AP13

1938, Dec. 23 ***Perf. 13½***

C127	AP11	20c brn blk	.80	.30
C128	AP12	30c purple	1.20	.30
C129	AP13	45c dk bl	1.75	.25
C130	AP11	50c lt ultra	1.50	.25
C131	AP13	70c dk car	26.00	7.50
C132	AP12	90c red org	2.50	.75
C133	AP13	1.35b gray blk	3.00	1.00
C134	AP11	1.40b slate gray	12.00	2.75
C135	AP12	2.25b green	6.00	2.00
		Nos. C127-C135 (9)	54.75	15.10

For surcharge see No. C198.

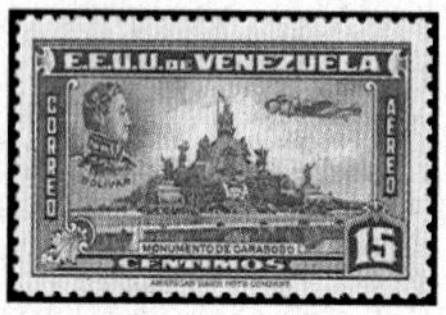

Simón Bolívar and Carabobo Monument AP14

1940, Mar. 30 ***Perf. 12***

C136	AP14	15c blue	.75	.25
C137	AP14	20c olive bis	.75	.25
C138	AP14	25c red brn	2.75	.40
C139	AP14	40c blk brn	2.25	.25
C140	AP14	1b red lilac	5.00	.55
C141	AP14	2b rose car	11.00	1.40
		Nos. C136-C141 (6)	22.50	3.10

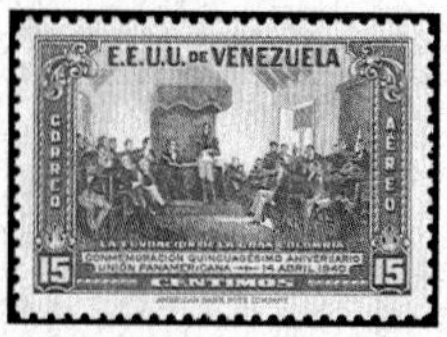

"The Founding of Grand Colombia" AP15

1940, June 13

C142	AP15	15c copper brown	1.25	.45

Founding of the Pan American Union, 50th anniv.

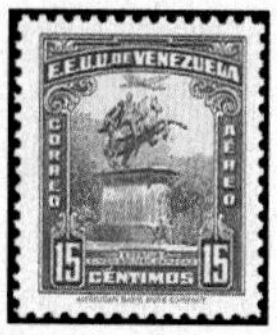

Statue of Simón Bolívar, Caracas — AP16

1940-44

C143	AP16	5c dk grn ('42)	.25	.25
C144	AP16	10c scar ('42)	.25	.25
C145	AP16	12½c dull purple	.75	.30
C146	AP16	15c blue ('43)	.50	.25
C147	AP16	20c bis brn ('44)	.50	.25
C148	AP16	25c bis brn ('42)	.50	.25
C149	AP16	30c dp vio ('43)	.50	.25
C150	AP16	40c blk brn ('43)	.65	.25
C151	AP16	45c turq grn ('43)	.65	.25
C152	AP16	50c blue ('44)	.65	.25
C153	AP16	70c rose pink	2.00	.30
C154	AP16	75c ol bis ('43)	7.75	1.60
C155	AP16	90c red org ('43)	1.25	.30
C156	AP16	1b dp red lil ('42)	.65	.25
C157	AP16	1.20b dp yel grn ('43)	2.50	.75
C158	AP16	1.35b gray blk ('42)	10.50	3.50
C159	AP16	2b rose pink ('43)	2.00	.25
C160	AP16	3b ol blk ('43)	3.25	.75
C161	AP16	4b black	2.50	.75
C162	AP16	5b red brn ('44)	20.00	8.00
		Nos. C143-C162 (20)	57.60	19.00

See Nos. C232-C234, C239-C253. For surcharges see Nos. C225, C873.

Nos. C48, C50-C65 Overprinted

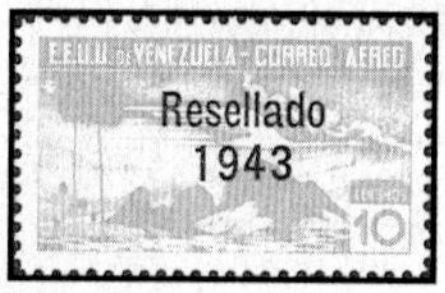

Perf. 11, 11½ & Compound

1943, Dec. 21

C164	AP4	10c orange red	2.00	.90
C165	AP6	25c dk violet	2.00	.90
C166	AP4	40c yellow grn	2.00	.90
C167	AP3	70c red	2.00	.90
C168	AP7	70c emerald	2.00	.90
C169	AP5	75c bister	2.00	.90
C170	AP3	1b dk gray	2.00	.90
C171	AP4	1.20b peacock grn	5.00	1.60
C172	AP3	1.80b dk ultra	5.00	1.60
C173	AP7	1.80b dk ultra	5.00	2.50
C174	AP5	1.95b lt ultra	6.00	3.25
C175	AP6	2b chocolate	6.00	3.25
C176	AP6	2.50b gray blue	5.00	3.25
C177	AP4	3b lt violet	6.00	3.25
C178	AP6	3.70b rose red	52.50	45.00
C179	AP5	10b red violet	12.00	10.00
C180	AP3	20b gray	27.50	20.00
		Nos. C164-C180 (17)	144.00	100.00
		Set, never hinged	275.00	

Issued for sale to philatelists. Nos. C164-C169 were sold only in sets.

Nearly all are known with invtd. ovpt.

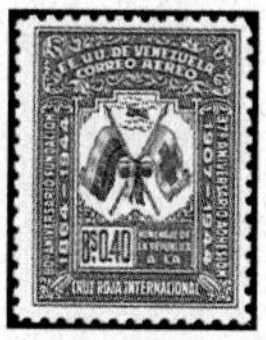

Flags of Venezuela and the Red Cross — AP17

Flags in red, yellow, blue and black

1944, Aug. 22 Litho. ***Perf. 12***

C181	AP17	5c gray green	.25	.25
C182	AP17	10c magenta	.25	.25
C183	AP17	20c brt blue	.25	.25
C184	AP17	30c violet bl	.40	.25
C185	AP17	40c chocolate	.55	.25
C186	AP17	45c apple green	1.75	.45
C187	AP17	90c orange	1.60	.45
C188	AP17	1b gray black	2.40	.45
		Nos. C181-C188 (8)	7.45	2.60
		Set, never hinged	12.00	

80th anniv. of the Intl. Red Cross and 37th anniv. of Venezuela's joining the organization. Nos. C181-C188 exist imperf. and part perf. Value, imperf set $30.

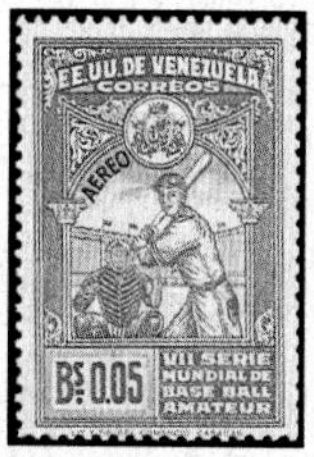

Baseball Players — AP18

"AEREO" in dark carmine

1944, Oct. 12

C189	AP18	5c dull vio brn	.30	.25
C190	AP18	10c gray green	.50	.25
C191	AP18	20c ultra	.50	.25
C192	AP18	30c dull rose	1.00	.40
C193	AP18	45c rose violet	2.00	.70
C194	AP18	90c red orange	3.50	1.40
C195	AP18	1b dark gray	4.00	1.40
C196	AP18	1.20b yellow grn	9.25	7.25
C197	AP18	1.80b ocher	12.00	9.25
		Nos. C189-C197 (9)	33.05	21.15
		Set, never hinged	55.00	

7th World Amateur Baseball Championship Games, Caracas.

Nos. C189-C197 exist imperf, and all but 1b exist part perf. Value, imperf set $75.

Various errors of "AEREO" overprint exist.

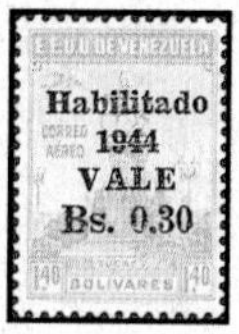

No. C134 Surcharged in Black

1944, Nov. 17 ***Perf. 13½***

C198	AP11	30c on 1.40b	.50	.50
a.		Double surcharge	35.00	35.00
b.		Inverted surcharge	13.50	13.50

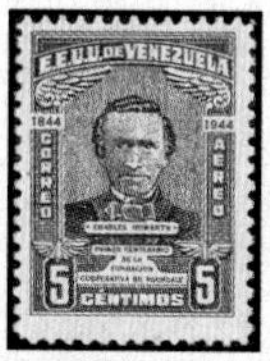

Charles Howarth — AP19

1944, Dec. 21 Unwmk. ***Perf. 12***

C199	AP19	5c black	.25	.25
C200	AP19	10c purple	.25	.25
C201	AP19	20c sepia	.40	.25
C202	AP19	30c dull green	.55	.25
C203	AP19	1.20b bister	2.50	2.40
C204	AP19	1.80b deep ultra	4.50	2.90
C205	AP19	3.70b rose	6.00	4.75
		Nos. C199-C205 (7)	14.45	11.05
		Set, never hinged	20.00	

Cent. of founding of 1st cooperative shop in Rochdale, England, by Charles Howarth.

Nos. C199-C205 exist imperf. and part perf.

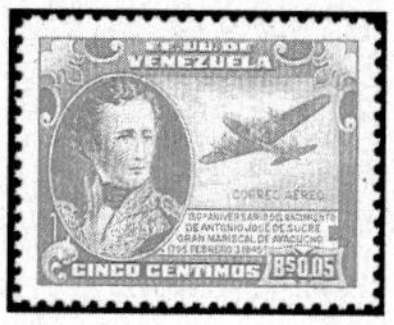

Antonio José de Sucre — AP20

1945, Mar. 3 Engr.

C206	AP20	5c orange	.25	.25
C207	AP20	10c violet	.25	.25
C208	AP20	20c grnsh blk	.25	.25
C209	AP20	30c brt green	.25	.25
C210	AP20	40c olive	1.10	1.10
C211	AP20	45c black brn	1.60	1.10
C212	AP20	90c redsh brn	2.10	1.10
C213	AP20	1b dp red lil	2.10	1.10
C214	AP20	1.20b black	6.25	5.25
C215	AP20	2b yellow	10.00	7.25
		Nos. C206-C215 (10)	24.15	17.90
		Set, never hinged	40.00	

150th birth anniv. of Antonio Jose de Sucre, Grand Marshal of Ayacucho.

Type of 1946

1946, Aug. 24 ***Perf. 12***

C216	A81	30c Bello	1.10	.25
C217	A82	30c Urdaneta	1.10	.25
		Set, never hinged	2.75	

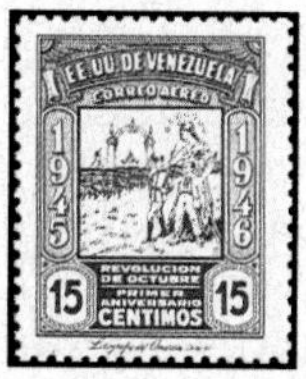

Allegory of Republic — AP23

Perf. 11½

1946, Oct. 18 Litho. Unwmk.

C218	AP23	15c dp violet bl	.40	.25
C219	AP23	20c bister brn	.40	.25
C220	AP23	30c dp violet	.50	.35
C221	AP23	1b brt rose	3.50	2.75
		Nos. C218-C221 (4)	4.80	3.60
		Set, never hinged	8.00	

Anniversary of the Revolution of October, 1945. Exist imperf. and part perf.

Nos. 297, 371, C152 and 362 Surcharged in Black

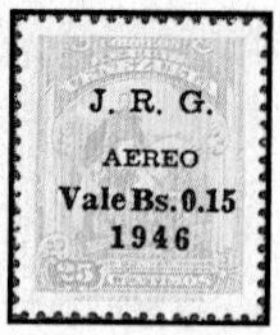

1947, Jan. ***Perf. 12***

C223	A49	10c on 22½c dp car	.25	.25
a.		Inverted surcharge	7.00	5.00
C224	A69	15c on 25c lt bl	.40	.25
C225	AP16	20c on 50c blue	.40	.25
a.		Inverted surcharge	9.00	7.00
C226	A65	70c on 1b dk vio brn	.75	.45
a.		Inverted surcharge	9.00	5.00

Type of 1938 Surcharged in Black

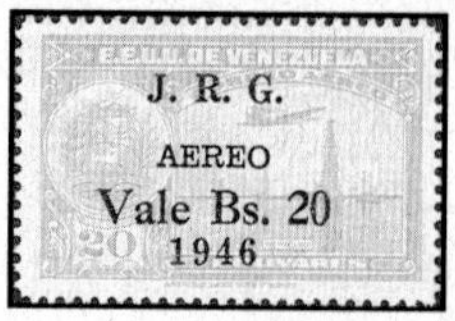

C227	AP10	20b on 20b org red	28.00	22.50
a.		Surcharge omitted	92.50	40.00
		Nos. C223-C227 (5)	29.80	23.70
		Set, never hinged	40.00	

"J. R. G." are the initials of "Junta Revolucionaria de Gobierno."

Also exist: 20c on #C143, 10c on #371.

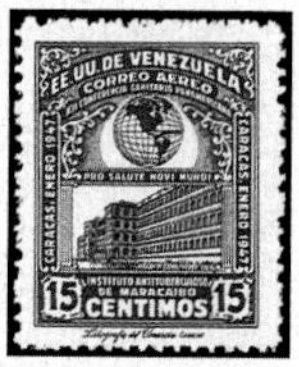

Anti-tuberculosis Institute, Maracaibo — AP24

1947, Jan. 12 Litho.

Venezuela Shown on Map in Yellow

C228	AP24	15c dark blue	.45	.35
C229	AP24	20c dark brown	.45	.35
C230	AP24	30c violet	.45	.35
C231	AP24	1b carmine	4.75	3.75
		Nos. C228-C231 (4)	6.10	4.80
		Set, never hinged	16.00	

12th Pan-American Health Conf., Caracas, Jan. 1947.

Nos. C228-C231 exist imperf., part perf. and with yellow omitted.

Types of 1938-40

1947, Mar. 17 Engr.

C232	AP16	75c orange	7.50	4.50
C233	AP16	1b brt ultra	.70	.25
C234	AP16	3b red brown	17.50	8.00
C235	AP10	5b scarlet	15.00	5.00
C236	AP9	10b violet	20.00	7.50
		Nos. C232-C236 (5)	60.70	25.25
		Set, never hinged	100.00	

On Nos. C235 and C236 the numerals of value are in color on a white table.

No. 370 Surcharged in Black

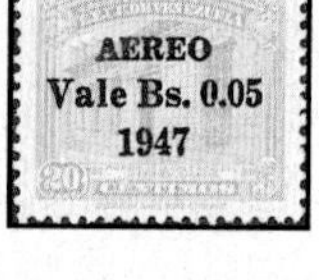

1947, June 20

C237	A70	5c on 20c blue	.40	.25
C238	A70	10c on 20c blue	.40	.25
a.		Inverted surcharge	5.00	5.00
		Set, never hinged	1.00	

Types of 1938-44

1947-48 Engr.

C239	AP16	5c orange	.25	.25
C240	AP16	10c dk green	.25	.25
C241	AP16	12½c bister brn	.45	.45
C242	AP16	15c gray	.25	.25
C243	AP16	20c violet	.25	.25
C244	AP16	25c dull green	.25	.25
C245	AP16	30c brt ultra	.45	.25
C246	AP16	40c green ('48)	.25	.25
C247	AP16	45c vermilion	.45	.25
C248	AP16	50c red violet	.25	.25
C249	AP16	70c dk car	1.00	.45
C250	AP16	75c purple ('48)	.65	.25
C251	AP16	90c black	1.00	.30
C252	AP16	1.20b red brn ('48)	1.25	.50

C253	AP16	3b dp blue	1.75	.50
C254	AP10	5b olive grn	9.25	5.00
C255	AP9	10b yellow	8.25	4.75
		Nos. C239-C255 (17)	26.25	14.45
		Set, never hinged	60.00	

On Nos. C254 and C255 the numerals of value are in color on a white tablet.

Issue dates: 5c, 10c, Oct. 8. 15c, Dec. 2, 40c, 75c, 1.20b, May 10, 1948. Others, Oct. 27, 1947.

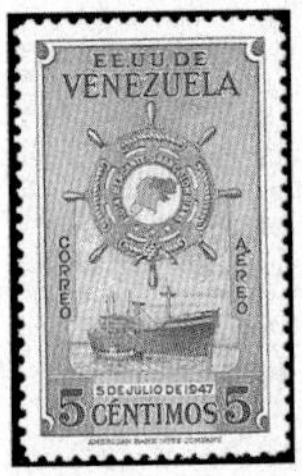

M. S. Republica de Venezuela — AP25

Imprint: "American Bank Note Company"

1948-50 Unwmk. *Perf. 12*

C256	AP25	5c red brown	.25	.25
C257	AP25	10c deep green	.25	.25
C258	AP25	15c brown	.25	.25
C259	AP25	20c violet brn	.35	.25
C260	AP25	25c brown black	.35	.25
C261	AP25	30c olive green	.35	.25
C262	AP25	45c blue green	.65	.35
C263	AP25	50c gray black	1.00	.55
C264	AP25	70c orange	1.75	.55
C265	AP25	75c brt ultra	3.00	.75
C266	AP25	90c car lake	1.75	1.75
C267	AP25	1b purple	2.40	1.10
C268	AP25	2b gray	2.50	1.75
C269	AP25	3b emerald	9.75	5.50
C270	AP25	4b deep blue	4.50	5.50
C271	AP25	5b orange red	18.00	8.25
		Nos. C256-C271 (16)	47.10	27.55

Issued to honor the Grand-Colombian Merchant Fleet. See Nos. C554-C556.

Issued: 5c, 10c, 15c, 25c, 30c, 1b, 7/9/48; 45c, 75c, 5b, 5/11/50; others, 3/9/49.

For surcharges see Nos. C863-C864.

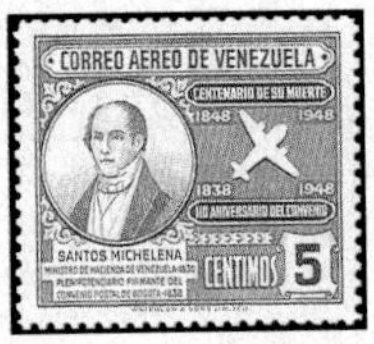

Santos Michelena AP26

1949, Apr. 25

C272	AP26	5c orange brn	.25	.25
C273	AP26	10c gray	.25	.25
C274	AP26	15c red orange	.50	.50
C275	AP26	25c dull green	1.00	.80
C276	AP26	30c plum	1.00	.80
C277	AP26	1b violet	5.50	3.00
		Nos. C272-C277 (6)	8.50	5.60
		Set, never hinged	12.00	

See note after No. 427.

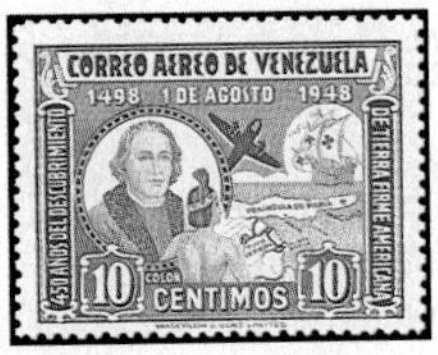

Christopher Columbus AP27

1948-49 Unwmk. *Perf. 12½*

C278	AP27	5c brown ('49)	.30	.25
C279	AP27	10c gray	.30	.30
C280	AP27	15c orange ('49)	.65	.30
C281	AP27	25c green ('49)	1.25	.65
C282	AP27	30c red vio ('49)	1.50	.95
C283	AP27	1b violet ('49)	6.00	2.75
		Nos. C278-C283 (6)	10.00	5.20
		Set, never hinged	16.00	

See note after No. 431.

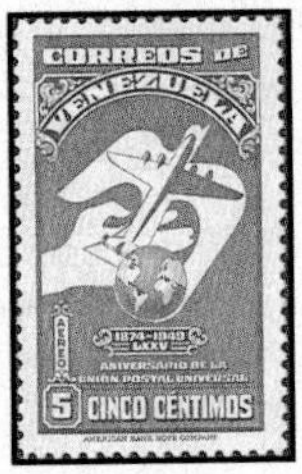

AP28

Symbols of global air mail.

1950 *Perf. 12*

C284	AP28	5c red brown	.25	.25
C285	AP28	10c dk green	.25	.25
C286	AP28	15c olive brn	.25	.25
C287	AP28	25c olive gray	.40	.30
C288	AP28	30c olive grn	.55	.30
C289	AP28	50c black	.40	.25
C290	AP28	60c brt ultra	1.10	.60
C291	AP28	90c carmine	1.40	.75
C292	AP28	1b purple	1.90	.50
		Nos. C284-C292 (9)	6.50	3.45
		Set, never hinged	10.50	

75th anniv. of the UPU.

Issue dates: 5c, Jan. 28. Others, Feb. 19.

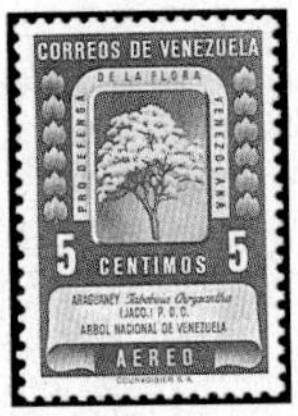

AP29

Araguaney, Venezuelan national tree.

Foliage in Yellow

1950, Aug. 25 Photo. *Perf. 11½*

C293	AP29	5c orange brn	.45	.25
C294	AP29	10c blue grn	.45	.25
C295	AP29	15c deep plum	.90	.25
C296	AP29	25c dk gray grn	5.50	1.60
C297	AP29	30c red orange	7.00	2.00
C298	AP29	50c dark gray	3.50	.45
C299	AP29	60c deep blue	5.50	1.00
C300	AP29	90c red	9.00	2.00
C301	AP29	1b rose violet	13.50	2.50
		Nos. C293-C301 (9)	45.80	10.30
		Set, never hinged	160.00	

Issued to publicize Forest Week, 1950.

Census Type of 1950

1950, Sept. 1 Engr. *Perf. 12*

C302	A90	5c olive gray	.25	.25
C303	A90	10c green	.25	.25
C304	A90	15c olive green	.25	.25
C305	A90	25c gray	.45	.45
C306	A90	30c orange	.65	.30
C307	A90	50c lt brown	.45	.25
C308	A90	60c ultra	.45	.25
C309	A90	90c rose carmine	1.40	.65
C310	A90	1b violet	1.75	1.75
		Nos. C302-C310 (9)	5.90	4.40
		Set, never hinged	10.00	

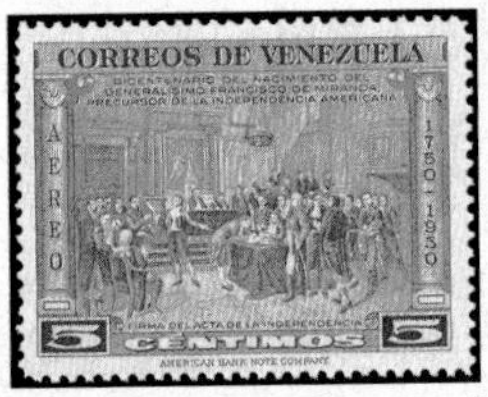

Signing Act of Independence — AP31

1950, Nov. 17

C311	AP31	5c vermilion	.60	.25
C312	AP31	10c red brown	.60	.25
C313	AP31	15c violet	.85	.25
C314	AP31	30c brt blue	1.00	.40
C315	AP31	1b green	5.00	2.40
		Nos. C311-C315 (5)	8.05	3.55
		Set, never hinged	10.00	

200th anniversary of the birth of Gen. Francisco de Miranda.

Alonso de Ojeda Type of 1950

1950, Dec. 18 Photo. *Perf. 11½*

C316	A91	5c orange brn	.25	.25
C317	A91	10c cerise	.30	.25
C318	A91	15c black brn	.55	.25
C319	A91	25c violet	.60	.30
C320	A91	30c orange	1.25	.50
C321	A91	1b emerald	5.00	2.50
		Nos. C316-C321 (6)	7.95	4.05
		Set, never hinged	12.00	

Bolivar Statue Type of 1951

1951, July 13 Engr. *Perf. 12*

C322	A92	5c purple	.70	.25
C323	A92	10c dull green	.80	.25
C324	A92	20c olive gray	.80	.25
C325	A92	25c olive green	.90	.25
C326	A92	30c vermilion	1.10	.55
C327	A92	40c lt brown	1.10	.55
C328	A92	50c gray	2.50	1.00
C329	A92	70c orange	3.50	2.50
		Nos. C322-C329 (8)	11.40	5.60
		Set, never hinged	15.00	

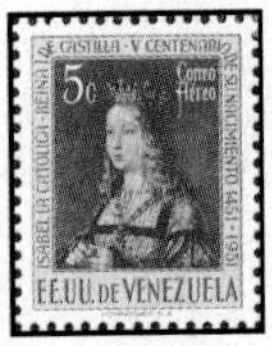

Queen Isabella I — AP34

1951, Oct. 12 Photo. *Perf. 11½*

C330	AP34	5c dk green & buff	.45	.25
C331	AP34	10c dk red & cream	.45	.25
C332	AP34	20c dp blue & gray	.75	.25
C333	AP34	30c dk blue & gray	.75	.25
a.		Souv. sheet of 4, #C330-C333	14.00	*15.00*
		Never hinged	24.00	
		Nos. C330-C333 (4)	2.40	1.00
		Set, never hinged	8.00	

500th anniv. of the birth of Queen Isabella I of Spain.

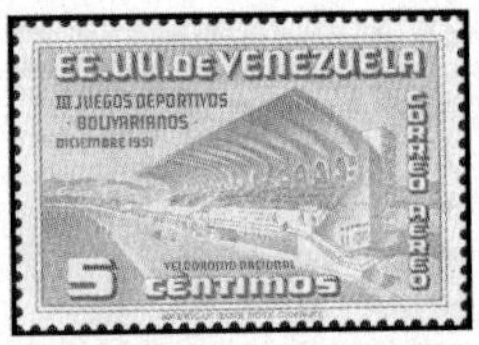

Bicycle Racecourse — AP35

1951, Dec. 18 Engr. *Perf. 12*

C334	AP35	5c green	.80	.25
C335	AP35	10c rose carmine	.80	.25
C336	AP35	20c redsh brown	1.00	.70
C337	AP35	30c blue	1.30	1.00
a.		Souv. sheet, #C334-C337	20.00	*24.00*
		Never hinged	32.50	
		Nos. C334-C337 (4)	3.90	2.20
		Set, never hinged	6.50	

3rd Bolivarian Games, Caracas, Dec. 1951.

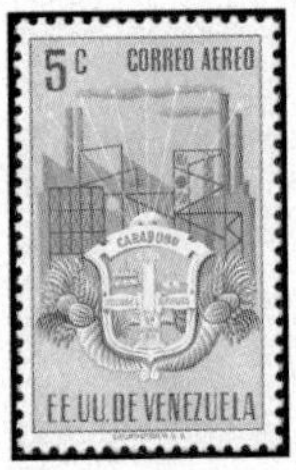

Arms of Carabobo and "Industry" — AP36

1951 Photo. *Perf. 11½*

C338	AP36	5c blue green	2.50	1.10
C339	AP36	7½c gray green	3.25	1.90
C340	AP36	10c car rose	2.50	1.10
C341	AP36	15c dark brown	3.25	1.10
C342	AP36	20c gray blue	3.50	1.10
C343	AP36	30c deep blue	9.50	1.60
C344	AP36	45c magenta	4.75	1.60
C345	AP36	60c olive brown	9.00	3.50
C346	AP36	90c rose brown	20.00	11.00
		Nos. C338-C346 (9)	58.25	24.00

Issue date: Oct. 29.

Arms of Zulia and "Industry"

C347	AP36	5c blue green	1.25	.60
C348	AP36	10c car rose	1.25	.60
C349	AP36	15c dark brown	1.90	.60
C350	AP36	30c deep blue	12.50	4.00
C351	AP36	60c olive brown	7.50	1.25
C352	AP36	1.20b brown car	25.00	16.00
C353	AP36	3b blue gray	8.75	2.40
C354	AP36	5b purple brn	12.50	6.25
C355	AP36	10b violet	20.00	12.50
		Nos. C347-C355 (9)	90.65	44.20

Issued: 5b, 9/8; 5c, 3b, 10b, 10/8; others, 10/29.

Arms of Anzoategui

C356	AP36	5c blue green	1.50	.85
C357	AP36	10c car rose	1.50	.85
C358	AP36	15c dk brown	2.00	.85
C359	AP36	25c sepia	2.40	.85
C360	AP36	30c deep blue	6.25	3.50
C361	AP36	50c henna brn	6.25	1.75
C362	AP36	60c olive brn	9.00	1.10
C363	AP36	1b purple	11.00	3.50
C364	AP36	2b violet gray	19.00	7.75
		Nos. C356-C364 (9)	58.90	21.00

Issue date: Nov. 9.

Arms of Caracas and Buildings

C365	AP36	5c blue green	2.75	1.10
C366	AP36	7½c gray green	8.00	3.50
C367	AP36	10c car rose	1.90	1.10
C368	AP36	15c dk brown	19.00	2.50
C369	AP36	20c gray blue	12.50	2.50
C370	AP36	30c deep blue	21.00	4.75
C371	AP36	45c magenta	12.50	2.75
C372	AP36	60c olive brn	42.50	5.75
C373	AP36	90c rose brn	25.00	20.00
		Nos. C365-C373 (9)	145.15	43.95

Issue date: Aug. 6.

Arms of Tachira and Agricultural Products

C374	AP36	5c blue green	.90	.90
C375	AP36	10c car rose	.90	.90
C376	AP36	15c dk brown	2.50	.90
C377	AP36	30c deep blue	32.50	3.75
C378	AP36	60c olive brn	26.00	3.75
C379	AP36	1.20b brown car	26.00	18.00
C380	AP36	3b blue gray	8.50	3.75
C381	AP36	5b purple brn	15.00	7.75
C382	AP36	10b violet	20.00	15.00
		Nos. C374-C382 (9)	132.30	54.70

Issue date: Aug. 9.

Arms of Venezuela and Bolivar Statue

C383	AP36	5c blue green	1.75	.90
C384	AP36	7½c gray grn	4.50	2.75
C385	AP36	10c car rose	13.50	.90
C386	AP36	15c dk brown	10.00	2.75
C387	AP36	20c gray blue	13.50	2.25
C388	AP36	30c deep blue	24.50	4.75
C389	AP36	45c magenta	11.00	2.00
C390	AP36	60c olive brn	50.00	10.00
C391	AP36	90c rose brn	32.50	22.50
		Nos. C383-C391 (9)	161.25	48.80

Issue date: Aug. 6.

Arms of Miranda and Agricultural Products

1952

C392	AP36	5c blue green	1.00	.70
C393	AP36	7½c gray grn	1.75	1.00
C394	AP36	10c car rose	1.00	.70
C395	AP36	15c dark brown	2.10	.70
C396	AP36	20c gray blue	3.00	.85
C397	AP36	30c deep blue	6.00	1.40
C398	AP36	45c magenta	5.50	.70
C399	AP36	60c olive brn	10.50	1.90
C400	AP36	90c rose brn	45.00	27.50
		Nos. C392-C400 (9)	75.85	35.45

Issue date: 7½c, 15c, 20c, 30c, Mar. 24.

Arms of Aragua and Stylized Farm

C401	AP36	5c blue green	2.50	.90
C402	AP36	7½c gray grn	2.25	1.25
C403	AP36	10c car rose	1.25	.90
C404	AP36	15c dk brown	7.75	1.10
C405	AP36	20c gray blue	3.75	1.10
C406	AP36	30c deep blue	11.00	1.25
C407	AP36	45c magenta	8.50	1.10
C408	AP36	60c olive brn	18.00	1.75
C409	AP36	90c rose brn	67.50	35.00
		Nos. C401-C409 (9)	122.50	44.35

Issue date: 7½c, 15c, 20c, 30c, Mar. 24.

Arms of Lara, Agricultural Products and Rope

C410	AP36	5c blue green	2.25	.80
C411	AP36	7½c gray grn	2.00	1.10
C412	AP36	10c car rose	1.10	.80
C413	AP36	15c dk brown	3.50	.80
C414	AP36	20c gray blue	5.50	.80
C415	AP36	30c deep blue	11.00	1.60
C416	AP36	45c magenta	5.50	1.40
C417	AP36	60c olive brn	11.00	2.50
C418	AP36	90c rose brn	60.00	40.00
		Nos. C410-C418 (9)	101.85	49.80

Issue date: 7½c, 15c, 20c, Mar. 24.

Arms of Bolivar and Stylized Design

C419 AP36 5c blue green 11.50 1.25
C420 AP36 10c car rose 1.00 .70
C421 AP36 15c dark brown 1.75 .70
C422 AP36 25c sepia 1.40 .70
C423 AP36 30c deep blue 8.00 3.25
C424 AP36 50c henna brn 5.40 1.40
C425 AP36 60c olive brn 9.00 1.75
C426 AP36 1b purple 8.00 1.40
C427 AP36 2b violet gray 18.00 6.25
Nos. C419-C427 (9) 64.05 17.40

Issue date: 15c, 30c, Mar. 24.

Arms of Sucre, Palms and Seascape

C428 AP36 5c blue green 1.00 .65
C429 AP36 10c car rose .65 .65
C430 AP36 15c dk brown 1.40 .65
C431 AP36 25c sepia 27.50 .65
C432 AP36 30c deep blue 9.25 2.75
C433 AP36 50c henna brn 4.25 1.00
C434 AP36 60c olive brn 5.25 2.10
C435 AP36 1b purple 6.75 1.60
C436 AP36 2b violet gray 15.00 7.50
Nos. C428-C436 (9) 71.05 17.55

Issue date: 15c, 30c, Mar. 24.

Arms of Trujillo Surrounded by Stylized Tree

C437 AP36 5c blue green 11.00 .70
C438 AP36 10c car rose .80 .40
C439 AP36 15c dk brown 3.00 .40
C440 AP36 30c deep blue 13.50 2.25
C441 AP36 60c olive brn 9.75 2.10
C442 AP36 1.20b rose red 8.75 5.00
C443 AP36 3b blue gray 4.25 3.10
C444 AP36 5b purple brn 9.25 3.50
C445 AP36 10b violet 16.00 8.25
Nos. C437-C445 (9) 76.30 25.70

Issue date: 5c, 30c, Mar. 24.

Map of Delta Amacuro and Ship

1953-54

C446 AP36 5c bl grn 1.25 .85
C447 AP36 10c car rose .85 .85
C448 AP36 15c dk brn 1.90 .96
C449 AP36 25c sepia 2.75 1.25
C450 AP36 30c dp bl 11.00 3.25
C451 AP36 50c hn brn 5.50 1.25
C452 AP36 60c ol brn 8.25 2.50
C453 AP36 1b purple 10.50 3.50
C454 AP36 2b vio gray 17.50 13.00
Nos. C446-C454 (9) 59.50 27.41

Issue date: 15c, 30c, Feb. 13.

Arms of Falcon and Stylized Oil Refinery

C455 AP36 5c bl grn 1.00 .50
C456 AP36 10c car rose .50 .50
C457 AP36 15c dk brn 1.00 .50
C458 AP36 30c dp bl 8.25 2.25
C459 AP36 60c ol brn 6.25 1.75
C460 AP36 1.20b rose red 7.75 7.25
C461 AP36 3b bl gray 8.25 4.50
C462 AP36 5b pur brn 13.50 9.25
C463 AP36 10b violet 13.50 10.50
Nos. C455-C463 (9) 60.00 37.00

Issue date: 10c, 15c, 30c, Feb. 13.

Arms of Guarico and Factory

C464 AP36 5c blue grn 1.10 .80
C465 AP36 10c car rose .80 .80
C466 AP36 15c dk brn 1.75 .80
C467 AP36 25c sepia 2.50 1.10
C468 AP36 30c dp bl 11.00 4.25
C469 AP36 50c hn brn 5.50 1.75
C470 AP36 60c ol brn 6.25 2.50
C471 AP36 1b purple 11.00 2.50
C472 AP36 2b vio gray 16.00 8.25
Nos. C464-C472 (9) 55.90 22.75

Issue date: 15c, 30c, Feb. 13.

Arms of Merida and Church

C473 AP36 5c bl grn .95 .80
C474 AP36 10c car rose .80 .80
C475 AP36 15c dk brn 1.50 .80
C476 AP36 30c dp bl 14.00 3.25
C477 AP36 60c ol brn 7.00 1.90
C478 AP36 1.20b rose red 12.00 7.00
C479 AP36 3b bl gray 7.00 3.25
C480 AP36 5b pur brn 13.50 7.00
C481 AP36 10b violet 19.00 12.00
Nos. C473-C481 (9) 75.75 36.80

Issue date: 10c, Feb. 2.

Arms of Monagas and Horses

C482 AP36 5c bl grn 1.10 .85
C483 AP36 10c car rose .85 .85
C484 AP36 15c dk brn 1.75 .85
C485 AP36 25c sepia 1.25 .85
C486 AP36 30c dp bl 16.00 4.25
C487 AP36 50c hn brn 6.50 2.10
C488 AP36 60c ol brn 7.50 2.10
C489 AP36 1b purple 11.00 2.75
C490 AP36 2b vio gray 15.00 7.50
Nos. C482-C490 (9) 60.95 22.10

Issue date: 10c, Feb. 2.

Arms of Portuguesa and Forest

C491 AP36 5c bl grn 4.00 1.25
C492 AP36 10c car rose .95 .95
C493 AP36 15c dk brn 2.40 .95
C494 AP36 30c dp bl 12.00 5.50
C495 AP36 60c ol brn 8.75 2.25
C496 AP36 1.20b rose red 20.00 12.00
C497 AP36 3b bl gray 7.00 4.00
C498 AP36 5b pur brn 12.50 7.00
C499 AP36 10b violet 18.00 15.00
Nos. C491-C499 (9) 85.60 48.90

Issue date: 5c, 10c, 30c, Feb. 2.

Map of Amazonas and Orchid

C500 AP36 5c bl grn 9.25 2.10
C501 AP36 10c car rose 2.10 2.10
C502 AP36 15c dk brn 9.25 2.10
C503 AP36 25c sepia 19.00 2.10
C504 AP36 30c dp bl 47.50 4.75
C505 AP36 50c hn brn 37.50 8.25
C506 AP36 60c ol brn 47.50 8.25
C507 AP36 1b purple 190.00 27.50
C508 AP36 2b vio gray 75.00 32.50
Nos. C500-C508 (9) 437.10 89.65

Issue date: Jan. 1954

Arms of Apure, Horse and Bird

C509 AP36 5c bl grn 1.60 .80
C510 AP36 10c car rose .80 .80
C511 AP36 15c dk brn 1.60 .80
C512 AP36 30c dp bl 6.25 2.75
C513 AP36 60c ol brn 5.75 1.40
C514 AP36 1.20b brn car 9.75 7.00
C515 AP36 3b bl gray 5.75 3.00
C516 AP36 5b pur brn 11.50 5.50
C517 AP36 10b violet 16.00 11.50
Nos. C509-C517 (9) 59.00 33.55

Issue date: Jan. 1954.

Arms of Barinas, Cow and Horse

C518 AP36 5c bl grn .50 .50
C519 AP36 10c car rose .50 .50
C520 AP36 15c dk brn 1.90 .50
C521 AP36 30c dp blue 6.50 2.50
C522 AP36 60c ol brn 6.50 1.25
C523 AP36 1.20b brn car 9.00 4.75
C524 AP36 3b bl gray 5.75 3.50
C525 AP36 5b pur brn 9.75 3.25
C526 AP36 10b violet 14.00 10.00
Nos. C518-C526 (9) 54.40 26.75

Issue date: Jan. 1954.

Arms of Cojedes and Cattle

C527 AP36 5c bl grn 7.75 1.10
C528 AP36 7½c gray grn 2.00 1.10
C529 AP36 10c car rose .60 .60
C530 AP36 15c dk brn .60 .60
C531 AP36 20c gray bl 1.50 .60
C532 AP36 30c dp blue 10.50 1.50
C533 AP36 45c mag 3.75 .90
C534 AP36 60c ol brn 7.75 1.25
C535 AP36 90c rose brn 9.25 5.25
Nos. C527-C535 (9) 43.70 12.90

Issue date: Dec.

Arms of Nueva Esparta and Fish

C536 AP36 5c bl grn 1.25 .65
C537 AP36 10c car rose .65 .65
C538 AP36 15c dk brn 2.10 .65
C539 AP36 25c sepia 3.50 .85
C540 AP36 30c dp bl 7.50 1.60
C541 AP36 50c hn brn 7.50 1.60
C542 AP36 60c ol brn 7.50 1.00
C543 AP36 1b purple 11.00 2.50
C544 AP36 2b vio gray 15.00 7.50
Nos. C536-C544 (9) 56.00 17.00

Issue date: Jan. 1954.

Arms of Yaracuy and Tropical Foliage

C545 AP36 5c bl grn 2.00 .75
C546 AP36 7½c gray grn 24.50 22.50
C547 AP36 10c car rose 1.10 .75
C548 AP36 15c dk brn 2.25 .75
C549 AP36 20c gray bl 3.75 .75
C550 AP36 30c dp bl 7.50 1.90
C551 AP36 45c mag 5.25 1.10
C552 AP36 60c ol brn 5.25 1.90
C553 AP36 90c rose brn 14.00 9.50
Nos. C545-C553 (9) 65.60 39.90
Nos. C338-C553 (216) 2,271. 841.61

Issue date: Jan. 1954.

Ship Type of 1948-50 Redrawn

Coil Stamps

Imprint: "Courvoisier S.A."

1952 Unwmk. *Perf. 12x11½*

C554 AP25 5c rose brn 2.00 .25
C555 AP25 10c org red 3.25 .25
C556 AP25 15c ol brn 4.25 .25
Nos. C554-C556 (3) 9.50 .75

Barquisimeto Type of 1952

1952, Sept. 14 Photo. *Perf. 11½*

C557 A94 5c blue green .25 .25
C558 A94 10c car rose .25 .25
C559 A94 20c dk blue .40 .25
C560 A94 25c black brn .60 .25
C561 A94 30c ultra .75 .25
C562 A94 40c brown org 3.50 1.50
C563 A94 50c dk ol grn 1.40 .40
C564 A94 1b purple 4.75 2.00
Nos. C557-C564 (8) 11.90 5.15

Caracas Post Office Type of 1953-54

1953, Mar. 11 *Perf. 12½*

C565 A96 7½c yellow grn .25 .25
C566 A96 15c dp plum .25 .25
C567 A96 20c slate .25 .25
C568 A96 25c sepia .50 .25
C569 A96 40c plum .50 .25
C570 A96 45c rose vio .50 .25
C571 A96 50c red orange .75 .25
C572 A96 70c dk sl grn 1.50 .75
C573 A96 75c dp ultra 5.25 1.10
C574 A96 90c brown org 1.25 .60
C575 A96 1b violet blue 1.25 .60
Nos. C565-C575 (11) 12.25 4.80

See Nos. C587-C589, C597-C606.

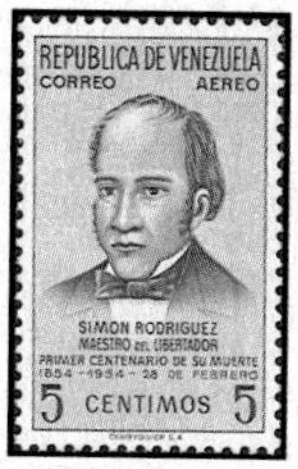

Simon Rodriguez — AP39

1954, Feb. 28 *Perf. 11½*

C576 AP39 5c blue green 1.50 .25
C577 AP39 10c car rose 1.50 .25
C578 AP39 20c gray blue 1.50 .25
C579 AP39 45c magenta 1.50 1.50
C580 AP39 65c gray green 3.50 6.00
Nos. C576-C580 (5) 9.50 8.25
Set, never hinged 24.00

Centenary of the death of Simon Rodriguez, scholar and tutor of Bolivar.

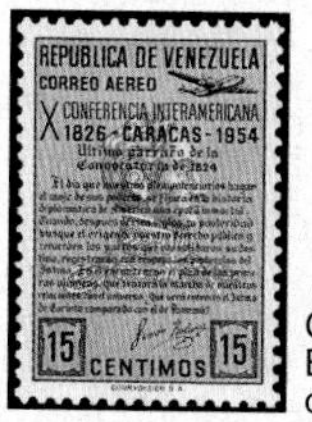

Quotation from Bolivar's Manifesto of 1824 — AP40

1954, Mar. 1 Unwmk.

C581 AP40 15c blk & brn buff 1.50 .25
C582 AP40 25c dk red brn & gray 1.50 .25
C583 AP40 40c dk red brn & red org 1.50 .25
C584 AP40 65c black & blue 1.50 1.00
C585 AP40 80c dk red brn & rose 1.50 .65
C586 AP40 1b pur & rose lil 3.50 .50
Nos. C581-C586 (6) 11.00 2.90
Set, never hinged 27.50

10th Inter-American Conf., Caracas, Mar. 1954.

P.O. Type of 1953

1954, Feb. Photo. *Perf. 12½*

C587 A96 5c orange .25 .25
C588 A96 30c red brown 1.25 1.25
C589 A96 60c bright red 1.25 2.00
Nos. C587-C589 (3) 2.75 3.50
Set, never hinged 7.00

Valencia Arms Type of 1955

1955, Mar. 26 Engr. *Perf. 12*

C590 A97 5c blue green .25 .25
C591 A97 10c rose pink .25 .25
C592 A97 20c ultra .25 .25
C593 A97 25c gray .25 .25
C594 A97 40c violet .35 .25
C595 A97 50c vermilion .35 .25
C596 A97 60c olive green .50 .25
Nos. C590-C596 (7) 2.20 1.75
Set, never hinged 6.00

P.O. Type of 1953 Inscribed: "Republica de Venezuela"

1955 Photo. *Perf. 12½*

C597 A96a 5c orange .25 .25
C598 A96a 10c olive brn .25 .25
C599 A96a 15c deep plum .25 .25
C600 A96a 20c slate .25 .25
C601 A96a 30c red brn .25 .25
C602 A96a 40c plum .75 .40
C603 A96a 45c rose violet .75 .60
C604 A96a 70c dk slate grn 1.75 1.25
C605 A96a 75c deep ultra 1.00 .75
C606 A96a 90c brown org .75 .40
Nos. C597-C606 (10) 6.25 4.65
Set, never hinged 9.50

Caracas Arms Type of 1955

1955, Dec. 9 Unwmk. *Perf. 11½*

C607 A98 5c yellow org .60 .25
C608 A98 15c claret brn .60 .25
C609 A98 25c violet blk .60 .25
C610 A98 40c red 1.75 .25
C611 A98 50c red orange 1.75 .25
C612 A98 60c car rose 1.75 1.25
Nos. C607-C612 (6) 7.05 2.50
Set, never hinged 16.00

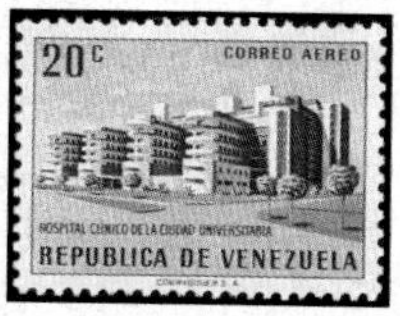

University Hospital, Caracas AP43

5c, 10c, 15c, 70c, O'Leary School, Barinas. 25c, 30c, 80c, University Hospital, Caracas. 40c, 45c, 50c, 1b, Caracas-La Guaira Highway. 60c, 65c, 75c, 2b, Towers of Simon Bolivar Center.

1956-57 Unwmk. *Perf. 11½*

C613 AP43 5c orange 1.00 .25
C614 AP43 10c sepia 1.00 .25
C615 AP43 15c claret brown 1.00 .25
C616 AP43 20c dark blue 1.00 .25
C617 AP43 25c gray black 1.00 .25
C618 AP43 30c henna brown 1.50 .25
C619 AP43 40c bright crimson 1.50 .30
C620 AP43 45c brown violet 1.50 .30
C621 AP43 50c deep orange 1.50 .30
C622 AP43 60c olive green 1.50 .30
C623 AP43 65c bright blue 2.50 .30
C624 AP43 70c blue green 2.50 .30
C625 AP43 75c ultra 2.50 .45
C626 AP43 80c carmine rose 2.50 .25
C627 AP43 1b plum 2.50 .30
C628 AP43 2b dark car rose 2.50 .95
Nos. C613-C628 (16) 27.50 5.25
Set, never hinged 42.50

Issued: 20c, 40c, 45c, 50c, 1b, 11/5/56; others, 1957.

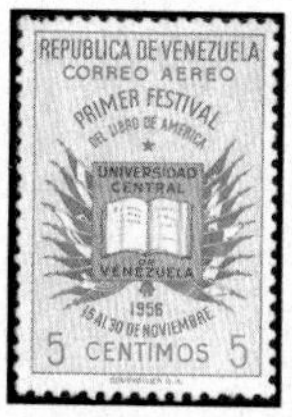

Book and Flags of American Nations — AP44

1956-57 Granite Paper

C629 AP44 5c orange & brn .35 .25
C630 AP44 10c brn & pale brn .35 .25
C631 AP44 20c blue & sapphire .35 .25
C632 AP44 25c gray vio & gray .35 .25
C633 AP44 40c rose red & pale pur .35 .25

C634 AP44 45c vio brn & gray brn .35 .25
C635 AP44 60c olive & gray ol .85 .80
Nos. C629-C635 (7) 2.95 2.30
Set, never hinged 17.50

Book Festival of the Americas, 11/15-30/56.
Issued: 5c, 40c, 11/15; others, 2/7/57.

Bolivar Type of 1957-58
Engraved; Center Embossed

1957-58 Unwmk. *Perf. 13½*

C636 A100 5c orange .25 .25
C637 A100 10c olive gray .25 .25
C638 A100 20c blue .35 .25
C639 A100 25c gray black .40 .25
C640 A100 40c rose red .35 .25
C641 A100 45c rose lilac .40 .25
C642 A100 65c yellow brn .75 .45
Nos. C636-C642 (7) 2.75 1.95
Set, never hinged 6.00

Issued: 45c, 1958; others, Nov. 15, 1957.

Tamanaco Hotel Type of 1957-58

1957-58 Engr. *Perf. 13*

C643 A101 5c dull yellow .25 .25
C644 A101 10c brown .25 .25
C645 A101 15c chocolate .25 .25
C646 A101 20c gray blue .25 .25
C647 A101 25c sepia .25 .25
C648 A101 30c violet bl .25 .25
C649 A101 40c car rose .25 .25
C650 A101 45c claret .25 .25
C651 A101 50c red org .25 .25
C652 A101 60c yellow grn .25 .25
C653 A101 65c orange brn 1.10 .90
C654 A101 70c slate .60 .45
C655 A101 75c grnsh blue .65 .55
C656 A101 1b dk claret .65 .55
C657 A101 2b dk gray 1.10 .70
Nos. C643-C657 (15) 6.60 5.65
Set, never hinged 13.00

Issue dates: 5c, 10c, Oct. 10; others, 1958.
For surcharge see No. C878.

Post Office Type of 1958

1958, May 14 Litho. *Perf. 14*

C658 A102 5c dp yellow .25 .25
C659 A102 10c brown .25 .25
C660 A102 15c red brn .25 .25
C661 A102 20c lt blue .25 .25
C662 A102 25c lt gray .25 .25
C663 A102 30c lt ultra .25 .25
C664 A102 40c brt yel grn .25 .25
C665 A102 50c red orange .25 .25
C666 A102 60c rose pink .25 .25
C667 A102 65c red .25 .25
C668 A102 90c violet .40 .25
C669 A102 1b lilac .50 .25
C670 A102 1.20b bister brn 6.50 6.00
Nos. C658-C670 (13) 9.90 9.00
Set, never hinged 23.00

See Nos. C786-C792. For surcharges see Nos. C856-C861.

Post Office Type of 1958
Coil Stamps

1958 Engr. *Perf. 11½x12*

C671 A103 5c deep yellow .25 .25
C672 A103 10c brown .25 .25
C673 A103 15c dark brown .35 .25
Nos. C671-C673 (3) .85 .75
Set, never hinged 1.25

Merida Type of 1958

1958, Oct. 9 Photo. *Perf. 13½*

C674 A104 5c orange yellow .25 .25
C675 A104 10c gray brown .25 .25
C676 A104 15c dull red brn .25 .25
C677 A104 20c chalky blue .25 .25
C678 A104 25c brown gray .25 .25
C679 A104 30c violet bl .25 .25
C680 A104 40c rose car .25 .25
C681 A104 45c brt lilac .25 .25
C682 A104 50c red orange .35 .25
C683 A104 60c lt olive grn .25 .25
C684 A104 65c hennna brn .85 .75
C685 A104 70c gray black .50 .50
C686 A104 75c brt grnsh bl 1.00 1.20
C687 A104 80c brt vio bl .60 .55
C688 A104 90c blue green .60 .60
C689 A104 1b lilac .75 .75
Nos. C674-C689 (16) 6.90 6.85
Set, never hinged 13.00

Trujillo Type of 1959

1958, Nov. 17 Photo. *Perf. 14*

C690 A105 5c orange yel .25 .25
C691 A105 10c lt brown .25 .25
C692 A105 15c redsh brown .25 .25
C693 A105 20c lt blue .25 .25
C694 A105 25c pale gray .25 .25
C695 A105 30c lt vio blue .25 .25
C696 A105 40c brt yel grn .35 .25
C697 A105 50c red orange .35 .25
C698 A105 60c lilac rose .50 .35
C699 A105 65c vermilion 1.50 1.25
C700 A105 1b lilac 1.00 .65
Nos. C690-C700 (11) 5.20 4.25
Set, never hinged 10.00

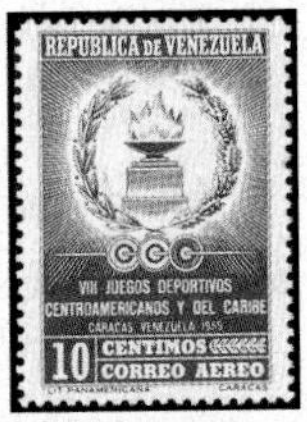
Emblem — AP45

1959, Mar. 10 Litho. *Perf. 13½*

C701 AP45 5c yellow .25 .25
C702 AP45 10c red brown .25 .25
C703 AP45 15c orange .25 .25
C704 AP45 30c gray .50 .45
C705 AP45 50c green .75 .55
Nos. C701-C705 (5) 2.00 1.75
Set, never hinged 3.75

8th Central American and Caribbean Games, Caracas, Nov. 29-Dec. 14, 1958.
Exist imperf. Value, pair $25.

Stamp Centenary Type of 1959

Stamp of 1859 and: 25c, Mailman and José Ignacio Paz Castillo. 50c, Mailman on horseback and Jacinto Gutierrez. 1b, Plane, train and Miguel Herrera.

1959, Sept. 15 Engr. *Perf. 13½*

C706 A107 25c orange yel .30 .25
C707 A107 50c blue .45 .25
C708 A107 1b rose red .90 .45
Nos. C706-C708 (3) 1.65 .95
Set, never hinged 6.00

Catalogue values for unused stamps in this section, from this point to the end of the section, are for Never Hinged items.

Alexander von Humboldt Type of 1960

1960, Feb. 9 Unwmk.

C709 A108 5c ocher & brn .45 .25
C710 A108 20c brt bl & turq bl 1.40 .25
C711 A108 40c ol & ol grn 2.00 .50
Nos. C709-C711 (3) 3.85 1.00

Newspaper Type of 1960

1960, June 11 Litho. *Perf. 14*

C712 A109 5c yellow & blk 2.75 1.10
C713 A109 15c lt red brn & blk 1.40 .40
C714 A109 65c salmon & blk 2.10 .75
Nos. C712-C714 (3) 6.25 2.25

Agustin Codazzi Type of 1960

1960, June 15 Engr.

C715 A110 5c yel org & brn .25 .25
C716 A110 10c brn & dk brn .40 .25
C717 A110 25c gray & blk .55 .25
C718 A110 30c vio bl & sl 1.25 .25
C719 A110 50c org brn & brn 2.00 .50
C720 A110 70c gray ol & ol gray 3.25 .95
Nos. C715-C720 (6) 7.70 2.45

For surcharge see No. C884.

National Pantheon Type of 1960

1960, May 9 Litho.
Pantheon in Bister

C721 A111 5c dp bister .25 .25
C722 A111 10c red brown .25 .25
C723 A111 15c fawn .40 .25
C724 A111 20c lt blue .55 .25
C725 A111 25c gray 3.25 .40
C726 A111 30c lt vio bl 3.25 .65
C727 A111 40c brt yel grn .55 .25
C728 A111 45c lt violet .85 .25
C729 A111 60c deep pink 1.20 .45
C730 A111 65c salmon 1.20 .45
C731 A111 70c gray 1.75 .65
C732 A111 75c chalky blue 4.75 1.20
C733 A111 80c lt ultra 2.40 .95
C734 A111 1.20b bister brn 2.75 1.25
Nos. C721-C734 (14) 23.40 7.50

For surcharges see Nos. C894-C895.

Andres Eloy Blanco Type of 1960

1960, May 21 *Perf. 14*
Portrait in Black

C735 A112 20c blue .50 .25
C736 A112 75c grnsh blue 1.75 .40
C737 A112 90c brt violet 1.60 .40
Nos. C735-C737 (3) 3.85 1.05

For surcharge see No. C874.

Independence Type of 1960

1960, Aug. 19 Litho. *Perf. 13½*
Center Multicolored

C738 A113 50c orange .80 .40
C739 A113 75c brt grnsh blue 2.00 .65
C740 A113 90c purple 1.60 .75
Nos. C738-C740 (3) 4.40 1.80

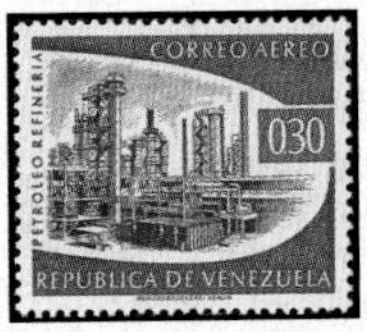
Oil Refinery AP46

Unwmk.

1960, Aug. 26 Engr. *Perf. 14*

C741 AP46 30c dk bl & sl bl 1.40 .40
C742 AP46 40c yel grn & ol 1.60 .45
C743 AP46 50c org & red brn 1.75 .60
Nos. C741-C743 (3) 4.75 1.45

Issued to publicize Venezuela's oil industry.

Luisa Cáceres de Arismendi Type of 1960

1960, Oct. 21 Litho. *Perf. 14*
Center Multicolored

C744 A115 5c bister 1.10 .40
C745 A115 10c redsh brown 1.50 .65
C746 A115 60c rose carmine 2.75 .80
Nos. C744-C746 (3) 5.35 1.85

José Antonio Anzoategui Type of 1960

1960, Oct. 29 Engr.

C747 A116 25c gray & brown .75 .25
C748 A116 40c yel grn & ol gray 1.25 .35
C749 A116 45c rose cl & dl pur 1.25 .45
Nos. C747-C749 (3) 3.25 1.05

Antonio José de Sucre Type of 1960

Unwmk.

1960, Nov. 18 Litho. *Perf. 14*
Center Multicolored

C750 A117 25c gray 1.00 .40
C751 A117 30c violet blue 1.40 .55
C752 A117 50c brown orange 1.75 .75
Nos. C750-C752 (3) 4.15 1.70

Type of Regular Issue, 1960

Designs: 30c, Bolivar Peak. 50c, Caroni Falls. 65c, Guacharo caves.

1960, Mar. 22 *Perf. 14*

C753 A118 30c vio bl & blk bl 2.75 2.75
C754 A118 50c brn org & brn 2.75 2.75
C755 A118 65c red org & red brn 2.75 2.75
Nos. C753-C755 (3) 8.25 8.25

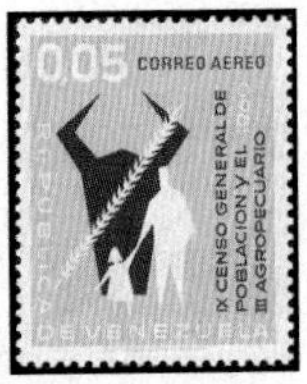
Cow's Head, Grain, Man and Child — AP47

1961, Feb. 6 Litho. Unwmk.
Cow and Inscription in Black

C756 AP47 5c yellow .25 .25
C757 AP47 10c brown .25 .25
C758 AP47 15c redsh brn .25 .25
C759 AP47 20c dull blue .25 .25
C760 AP47 25c gray .25 .25
C761 AP47 30c violet bl .25 .25
C762 AP47 40c yellow grn .45 .25
C763 AP47 45c lilac .45 .25
C764 AP47 50c orange .45 .25
C765 AP47 60c cerise .65 .25
C766 AP47 65c red orange .80 .40
C767 AP47 70c gray 1.20 .55
C768 AP47 75c brt grnsh bl 1.00 .45
C769 AP47 80c brt violet 1.20 .40
C770 AP47 90c violet 1.60 .80
Nos. C756-C770 (15) 9.30 5.10

9th general census & 3rd agricultural census.
Issued: 5-15c, 30c, 60-65c, 75-80c, 2/6; others, 4/6.
For surcharges see Nos. C865-C866.

Rafael Maria Baralt Type of 1961

1961, Mar. 11 Engr. *Perf. 14*

C771 A120 25c gray & sepia .80 .40
C772 A120 30c dk blue & vio .90 .45
C773 A120 40c yel grn & ol grn 1.25 .55
Nos. C771-C773 (3) 2.95 1.40

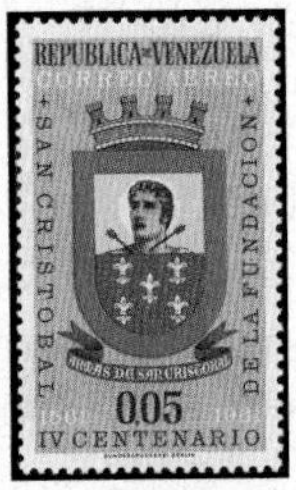
Arms of San Cristobal — AP48

1961, Apr. 10 Litho.
Arms in Original Colors

C774 AP48 5c orange & blk .25 .25
C775 AP48 55c yel grn & blk .85 .30

400th anniversary of San Cristobal.
For surcharge see No. C879.

Bird Type of 1961

Birds: 5c, Troupial. 10c, Golden cock of the rock. 15c, Tropical mockingbird.

1961, Sept. 6 Unwmk. *Perf. 14½*

C776 A121 5c multicolored 1.60 1.10
C777 A121 10c multicolored .80 .60
C778 A121 15c multicolored 1.00 .65
Nos. C776-C778 (3) 3.40 2.35

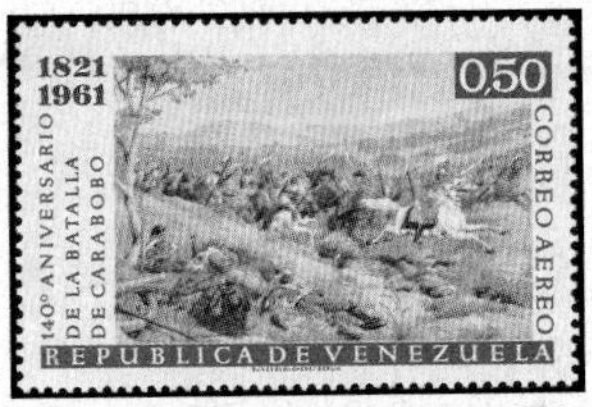
Charge, Battle of Carabobo — AP49

1961, Dec. 1 Litho. *Perf. 14*
Center Multicolored

C779 AP49 50c black & ultra .75 .25
C780 AP49 1.05b black & org 1.75 .50
C781 AP49 1.50b blk & lil rose 2.00 .50
C782 AP49 1.90b black & lilac 2.50 1.00
C783 AP49 2b black & gray 3.25 1.00
C784 AP49 3b black & grnsh bl 4.00 1.25
Nos. C779-C784 (6) 14.25 4.50

140th anniversary of Battle of Carabobo.
For surcharges see Nos. C867-C870.

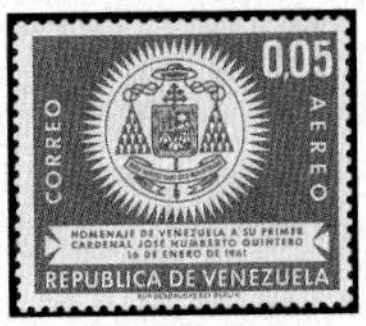
Arms of Cardinal Quintero AP50

1962, Mar. 1 Unwmk.

C785 AP50 5c lilac rose .50 .25
a. Souv. sheet of 1, imperf. 4.00 3.50

1st Venezuelan Cardinal, José Humberto Quintero.
No. C785a, issued Mar. 23, sold for 1b.

Post Office Type of 1958

1962, Apr. 12 Litho. *Perf. 13½x14*

C786 A102 35c citron .25 .25
C787 A102 55c gray olive .45 .25
C788 A102 70c bluish green .75 .30
C789 A102 75c brown orange .90 .25
C790 A102 80c fawn .90 .35
C791 A102 85c deep rose 1.40 .50
C792 A102 95c lilac rose .95 .45
Nos. C786-C792 (7) 5.60 2.35

For surcharges see Nos. C856-C861.

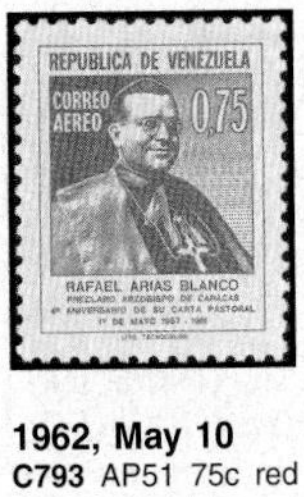
Archbishop Rafael Arias Blanco — AP51

1962, May 10 *Perf. 10½*

C793 AP51 75c red lilac .80 .30

4th anniversary (in 1961) of the anti-communist pastoral letter of the Archbishop of Caracas, Rafael Arias Blanco.

Orchid Type of 1962

Orchids: 5c, Oncidium volvox. 20c, Cycnoches chlorochilon. 25c, Cattleya Gaskelliana. 30c, Epidendrum difforme, horiz. 40c, Catasetum callosum Lindl, horiz. 50c, Oncidium bicolor Lindl. 1b, Brassavola nodosa Lindl, horiz. 1.05b, Epidendrum lividum Lindl. 1.50b, Schomburgkia undulata Lindl. 2b, Oncidium zebrinum.

Perf. 14x13½, 13½x14
1962, May 30   Litho.   Unwmk.
Orchids in Natural Colors

C794	A124	5c blk & lt grn	.25	.25
C795	A124	20c black	.25	.25
C796	A124	25c black & fawn	.60	.25
C797	A124	30c black & pink	.55	.25
C798	A124	40c black & yel	.60	.25
C799	A124	50c black & lil	.95	.40
C800	A124	1b blk & pale rose	1.25	.60
C801	A124	1.05b blk & dp org	4.75	2.00
C802	A124	1.50b blk & pale vio	4.50	2.25
C803	A124	2b blk & org brn	5.00	2.75
		Nos. C794-C803 (10)	18.70	9.25

For surcharges see Nos. C885-C887.

Independence Type of 1960
Signing Declaration of Independence.

1962, June 11   Perf. 13½
Center Multicolored

C804	A113	55c olive	.65	.25
C805	A113	1.05b brt rose	2.10	.85
C806	A113	1.50b purple	1.75	.80
a.		Souv. sheet of 3, #C804-C806, imperf.	5.00	5.00
		Nos. C804-C806 (3)	4.50	1.90

No. C806a, issued Oct. 13, sold for 4.10b.
A buff cardboard folder exists with impressions of Nos. 812-814, C804-C806. Perforation is simulated. Sold for 5.60b. Value $10.
For surcharge see No. C893.

No. 710 Srchd. in Rose Carmine "BICENTENARIO DE UPATA 1762-1962 RESELLADO AEREO VALOR Bs. 2,00"

1962, July 7   Perf. 13½x14
C807	A102	2b on 1b lt ol grn	2.50	1.20

Upata, a village in the state of Bolivar, 200th anniv.

National Games Type of 1962
Perf. 13x14
1962, Nov. 30   Unwmk.   Litho.

C808	A125	40c Bicycling	.50	.30
C809	A125	75c Baseball	.95	.40
C810	A125	85c Woman athlete	2.00	.95
a.		Souv. sheet of 3, #C808-C810 imperf.	4.50	4.50
		Nos. C808-C810 (3)	3.45	1.65

See note after No. 817.
No. C810a sold for 3b.
For surcharge see No. C899.

Bird Type of 1962

Birds: 5c, American kestrel. 20c, Black-bellied tree duck, horiz. 25c, Amazon kingfisher. 30c, Rufous-tailed chachalaca. 50c, Black-and-yellow troupial. 55c, White-naped nightjar. 2.30b, Red-crowned woodpecker. 2.50b, Black-moustached quail-dove.

1962, Dec. 14   Perf. 14x13½, 13½x14
Birds in Natural Colors; Black Inscription

C811	A126	5c car rose	.25	.25
C812	A126	20c brt blue	.60	.25
C813	A126	25c lt gray	.70	.25
C814	A126	30c lt olive	.80	.30
C815	A126	50c violet	1.25	.45
C816	A126	55c dp orange	2.10	.80
C817	A126	2.30b dl red brn	6.00	3.50
C818	A126	2.50b orange yel	6.00	4.00
		Nos. C811-C818 (8)	17.70	9.80

For surcharges see Nos. C880-C882.

Malaria Eradication Emblem, Mosquito and Map — AP52

Lithographed and Embossed
Perf. 13½x14
1962, Dec. 20   Wmk. 346

C819	AP52	30c green & blk	.75	.35
a.		Souv. sheet of 2, #825, C819, imperf.	4.00	4.00

WHO drive to eradicate malaria. No. C819a sold for 2b.

Animal Type of Regular Issue

5c, Spectacle bear, vert. 40c, Paca. 50c, Three-toed sloths. 55c, Great anteater. 1.50b, South American tapirs. 2b, Jaguar.

Multicolored Center; Black Inscriptions
Perf. 14x13½, 13½x14
1963, Mar. 13   Litho.   Unwmk.

C820	A128	5c yellow	.25	.25
C821	A128	40c brt green	.80	.25
C822	A128	50c lt violet	1.10	.40
C823	A128	55c brown olive	1.40	.45
C824	A128	1.50b gray	4.00	2.00
C825	A128	2b ultra	6.75	3.25
		Nos. C820-C825 (6)	14.30	6.60

For surcharges see Nos. C888-C889.

Freedom from Hunger Type of 1963
40c, Map, shepherd. 75c, Map, farmer.

1963, Mar. 21
C826	A129	40c lt yel grn & dl red	.65	.40
C827	A129	75c yellow & brown	.90	.65

Arms of Bocono — AP53

1963, May 30   Wmk. 346
C828	AP53	1b multicolored	2.00	.65

400th anniversary of the founding of Bocono.
For surcharge see No. C892.

Papal and Venezuelan Arms AP54

1963, June 11   Perf. 14x13½
Arms Multicolored

C829	AP54	80c light green	1.25	.35
C830	AP54	90c gray	1.25	.50

Vatican II, the 21st Ecumenical Council of the Roman Catholic Church.
For surcharges see Nos. C871-C872.

Arms of Venezuela — AP55

1963, July 29   Unwmk.   Perf. 14
C831	AP55	70c gray, red, yel & bl	1.25	.50

Cent. of Venezuela's flag and coat of arms.
For surcharge see No. C883.

Lake Maracaibo Bridge AP56

Wmk. 346
1963, Aug. 24   Litho.   Perf. 14

C832	AP56	90c grn, brn & ocher	1.50	.50
C833	AP56	95c blue, brn & och	1.50	.60
C834	AP56	1b ultra, brn & och	1.25	.50
		Nos. C832-C834 (3)	4.25	1.60

Opening of bridge over Lake Maracaibo.
For surcharges see Nos. C897-C898.

Armed Forces Type of 1963
1963, Sept. 10   Unwmk.
C835	A134	1b red & bl, buff	2.00	1.00

For surcharge see No. C862.

Hammarskjold Type of 1963
1963, Sept. 25   Unwmk.   Perf. 14

C836	A135	80c dk bl, lt ultra & ocher	1.25	.50
C837	A135	90c dk bl, bl & ocher	1.75	.70
a.		Souv. sheet of 4, #841-842, C836-C837, imperf.	5.25	5.25

No. C837a sold for 3b.
For surcharges see Nos. C875-C876.

Dr. Luis Razetti, Physician, Birth Cent. — AP57

1963, Oct. 10   Engr.
C838	AP57	95c dk blue & mag	1.50	.90
C839	AP57	1.05b dk brn & grn	1.50	1.00

For surcharges see Nos. C890-C891.

Red Cross Type of 1963
Designs: 40c, Sir Vincent K. Barrington. 75c, Red Cross nurse and child.

1963, Dec. 31   Litho.   Perf. 11½x12
C840	A137	40c multicolored	.55	.40
C841	A137	75c multicolored	.95	.60

Development Type of 1964
Designs: 5c, Loading cargo. 10c, Tractor and corn. 15c, Oil field workers. 20c, Oil refinery. 50c, Crane and building construction.

1964, Feb. 5   Unwmk.   Perf. 14x13½

C842	A138	5c multicolored	.25	.25
C843	A138	10c multicolored	.25	.25
C844	A138	15c multicolored	.25	.25
C845	A138	20c multicolored	.25	.25
C846	A138	50c multicolored	.65	.25
		Nos. C842-C846 (5)	1.65	1.40

Cent. of the Dept. of Industrial Development and to publicize the Natl. Industrial Expo.

Pedro Gual Type of 1964
1964, Mar. 20   Perf. 14x13½
C847	A139	75c dull blue green	.85	.40
C848	A139	1b bright pink	1.25	.45

Blast Furnace and Map of Venezuela AP58

1964, May 22   Litho.   Perf. 13½x14
C849	AP58	80c multi	1.25	.45
C850	AP58	1b multi	1.75	.65

Issued to publicize the Orinoco steel mills.

Arms of Ciudad Bolivar — AP59

1964, May 22   Perf. 10½
C851	AP59	1b multi	1.75	1.00

Bicentenary of Ciudad Bolivar.

AP60

1964, Aug. 3   Unwmk.   Perf. 11½
C852	AP60	30c bister brn & yel	.45	.25
C853	AP60	40c plum & pink	.70	.25
C854	AP60	50c brn & tan	1.00	.40
		Nos. C852-C854 (3)	2.15	.90

80th birthday of novelist Romulo Gallegos.

AP61

1964, Nov. 11   Litho.   Perf. 14x13½
C855	AP61	1b orange & dk vio	1.50	.65

Eleanor Roosevelt and 15th anniv. (in 1963) of the Universal Declaration of Human Rights.
For surcharge see No. C896.

Issues of 1947-64 Srchd. in Black, Dark Blue, Red, Carmine or Lilac with New Value and "RESELLADO / VALOR"

1965

C856	A102	5c on 55c (#C787)	.55	.25
C857	A102	5c on 70c (#C788)	.55	.25
C858	A102	5c on 80c (#C790)	.55	.25
C859	A102	5c on 85c (#C791)	.55	.25
C860	A102	5c on 90c (#C668)	.55	.25
C861	A102	5c on 95c (#C792)	.55	.25
C862	A134	5c on 1b (#C835)	.75	.25
C863	AP25	10c on 3b (#C269)	.55	.25
C864	AP25	10c on 4b (#C270) (C)	.95	.25
C865	AP47	10c on 70c (#C767) (C)	.60	.25
C866	AP47	10c on 90c (#C770) (C)	.55	.25
C867	AP49	10c on 1.05b (#C780)	.80	.25
C868	AP49	10c on 1.90b (#C782)	.55	.25
C869	AP49	10c on 2b (#C783)	.60	.25
C870	AP49	10c on 3b (#C784)	.60	.25
C871	AP54	10c on 80c (#C829)	.55	.25
C872	AP54	10c on 90c (#C830)	.55	.25
C873	AP16	15c on 3b (#C253)	.60	.25
C874	A112	15c on 70c (#C737)	.55	.25
C875	A135	15c on 80c (#C836)	.55	.25
C876	A135	15c on 90c (#C837)	.55	.25
C877	AP59	15c on 1b (#C851)	.60	.25
C878	A101	20c on 2b (#C657) (R)	.75	.25
C879	AP48	20c on 55c (#C775) (DB)	.60	.25
C880	A126	20c on 55c (#C816)	.80	.25
a.		25c on 55c (#C816)		
C881	A126	20c on 2.30b (#C817)	.60	.25

C882	A126 20c on 2.50b		
	(#C818)	.80	.25
C883	AP55 20c on 70c		
	(#C831)	.80	.25
C884	A110 25c on 70c		
	(#C720) (DB)	.85	.25
C885	A124 25c on 1.05b		
	(#C801) (L)	.60	.25
C886	A124 25c on 1.50b		
	(#C802) (L)	.60	.25
C887	A124 25c on 2b (#C803)		
	(L)	.80	.25
C888	A128 25c on 1.50b		
	(#C824)	.80	.25
C889	A128 25c on 2b (#C825)	.80	.25
C890	AP57 25c on 95c		
	(#C838)	.75	.25
C891	AP57 25c on 1.05b		
	(#C839)	.80	.25
C892	AP53 30c on 1b (#C828)	1.00	.25
C893	A113 40c on 1.05b		
	(#C805) (DB)	.80	.25
C894	A111 50c on 65c		
	(#C730) (DB)	.55	.25
C895	A111 50c on 1.20b		
	(#C734) (DB)	1.00	.25
C896	AP61 50c on 1b (#C855)	.60	.25
C897	AP56 60c on 90c		
	(#C832)	1.40	.40
C898	AP56 60c on 95c		
	(#C833)	1.10	.25
C899	A125 75c on 85c		
	(#C810)	1.25	.40
	Nos. C856-C899 (44)	31.25	11.30

Lines of surcharge arranged variously on Nos. C856-C899. Old denominations obliterated with bars on Nos. C862, C871-C873, C875-C877, C883, C885-C887, C889, C892, C896-C898. Vertical surcharge on Nos. C865-C866, C871-C872, C874, C878, C896.

Kennedy Type of 1965

1965, Aug. 20   Photo.   Perf. 12x11½

C900	A144 60c lt grnsh bl	1.10	.40
C901	A144 80c red brn	1.25	.50

Medical Federation Emblem — AP62

1965, Aug. 24   Litho.   Perf. 13½x14

C902	AP62 65c red org & blk	1.60	.75

20th anniversary of the founding of the Medical Federation of Venezuela.

Unisphere and Venezuela Pavilion AP63

1965, Aug. 31   Perf. 14x13½

C903	AP63 1b multi	1.25	.35

New York World's Fair, 1964-65.

Andrés Bello (1780?-1865), Educator and Writer — AP64

Perf. 14x13½

1965, Oct. 15   Litho.   Unwmk.

C904	AP64 80c dk brn & org	1.50	.75

Map Type of 1965

Maps of Venezuela and Guiana: 25c, Map of Venezuela and Guiana by J. Cruz Cano, 1775. 40c, Map stamp of 1896 (No. 140). 75c, Map by the Ministry of the Exterior, 1965 (all horiz.).

1965, Nov. 5   Perf. 13½

C905	A145 25c multi	.45	.25
C906	A145 40c multi	.70	.25

C907	A145 75c multi	1.00	.40
a.	Souv. sheet of 3, #C905-C907, imperf.	14.00	14.00
	Nos. C905-C907 (3)	2.15	.90

#C907a, issued June 7, 1966, sold for 1.65b.

ITU Emblem and Telegraph Poles AP65

1965, Nov. 19   Litho.   Perf. 13½x14

C908	AP65 75c blk & ol grn	1.00	.40

Cent. of the ITU.

Simon Bolivar and Quotation AP66

1965, Dec. 9   Perf. 14x13½

C909	AP66 75c lt bl & dk brn	1.00	.40

Sesquicentennial of Bolivar's Jamaica letter, Sept. 6, 1815.

Children Riding Magic Carpet and Three Kings on Camels — AP67

1965, Dec. 16   Perf. 13½x14

C910	AP67 70c yel & vio bl	1.50	.75

Children's Festival, 1965 (Christmas).

Fermin Toro — AP68

1965, Dec. 22   Perf. 14x13½

C911	AP68 1b blk & org	1.25	.55

Death centenary of Fermin Toro (1808-1865), statesman and writer.

Winston Churchill — AP69

1965, Dec. 29   Perf. 14½x13

C912	AP69 1b lilac & blk	1.50	.55

Sir Winston Spencer Churchill (1874-1965), statesman and World War II leader.

ICY Emblem, Arms of Venezuela and UN Emblem AP70

1965, Dec. 30   Perf. 13½x14

C913	AP70 85c gold & vio blk	1.50	.55

International Cooperation Year, 1965.

OAS Emblem and Map of America — AP71

1965, Dec. 31   Perf. 14x13½

C914	AP71 50c bl, blk & gold	1.25	.45

Organization of American States, 75th anniv.

Butterfly Type of 1966

1966, Jan. 25   Litho.   Perf. 13½x14

Various Butterflies in Natural Colors; Black Inscriptions

C915	A146 65c lilac	1.75	.40
C916	A146 85c blue	2.50	.50
C917	A146 1b salmon pink	2.75	.60
	Nos. C915-C917 (3)	7.00	1.50

Farms of 1936 and 1966 — AP72

1966, Mar. 1   Perf. 14x13½

C918	AP72 55c blk, yel & emer	1.10	.40

30th anniversary of the Ministry for Agriculture and Husbandry.

Dance Type of 1966

Various folk dances.

1966, Apr. 5   Litho.   Perf. 14

C919	A148 40c bl & multi	.85	.35
C920	A148 50c multi	1.00	.40
C921	A148 60c vio & multi	.70	.25
C922	A148 70c multi	1.60	.50
C923	A148 80c red & multi	1.75	.65
C924	A148 90c ocher & multi	1.90	.80
	Nos. C919-C924 (6)	7.80	2.95

Title Page "Popule Meus" AP73

1966, Apr. 15   Perf. 13½x14

C925	AP73 55c yel grn, blk & bis	.80	.45
C926	AP73 95c dp mag, blk & bis	1.00	.60

150th anniv. (in 1964) of the death of José Angel Lamas, composer of natl. anthem.

Circus Scene, by Michelena — AP74

Paintings by Michelena: 1b, Miranda in La Carraca. 1.05b, Charlotte Corday.

Perf. 12x12½

1966, May 12   Litho.   Unwmk.

C927	AP74 95c multi	1.00	.75
C928	AP74 1b multi	1.25	.75
C929	AP74 1.05b multi	1.40	.75
	Nos. C927-C929 (3)	3.65	2.25

Cent. of the birth of Arturo Michelena (1863-1898), painter. Miniature sheets of 12 exist. See Nos. 900-901.

Abraham Lincoln — AP75

1966, May 31   Perf. 13½x14

C930	AP75 1b gray & blk	1.25	.75

Dr. José Gregorio Hernandez AP76

1966, July 29   Litho.   Perf. 14x13½

C931	AP76 1b brt bl & vio bl	1.60	.65

Centenary (in 1964) of the birth of Dr. José Gregorio Hernandez, physician.

Dr. Manuel Dagnino and Hospital AP77

1966, Aug. 16   Litho.   Perf. 13½x14

C932	AP77 1b sl grn & yel grn	1.50	.55

Founding of Chiquinquira Hospital, cent.

Fish Type of 1966

Fish: 75c, Pearl headstander, vert. 90c, Swordtail characine. 1b, Ramirez's dwarf cichlid.

Perf. 14x13½, 13½x14

1966, Aug. 31

C933	A151 75c multi	1.60	.50
C934	A151 90c grn & multi	1.60	.50
C935	A151 1b multi	1.60	.50
	Nos. C933-C935 (3)	4.80	1.50

Rafael Arevalo Gonzalez — AP78

1966, Sept. 13   Litho.   Perf. 13½x14

C936	AP78 75c yel bis & blk	1.40	.55

Centenary of the birth of Rafael Arevalo Gonzalez, journalist.

Simon Bolivar, 1816 — AP79

Bolivar Portraits: 25c, 30c, 35c, by José Gil de Castro, 1825. 40c, 50c, 60c, Anonymous painter, 1825. 80c, 1.20b, 4b, Anonymous painter, c. 1829.

Imprint: "Bundesdruckerei Berlin 1966"

1966			Multicolored Center	
C937	AP79	5c lem & blk	.25	.25
C938	AP79	10c lt ol grn & blk	.25	.25
C939	AP79	20c grn & blk	.25	.25
C940	AP79	25c salmon & blk	.25	.25
C941	AP79	30c pink & blk	.25	.25
C942	AP79	35c dl rose & blk	.30	.25
C943	AP79	40c bis brn & blk	.25	.25
C944	AP79	50c org brn & blk	.45	.25
C945	AP79	60c brn red & blk	.45	.25
C946	AP79	80c brt bl & blk	.90	.35
C947	AP79	1.20b dl bl & blk	1.40	.65
C948	AP79	4b vio bl & blk	4.50	2.75
		Nos. C937-C948 (12)	9.50	6.00

Issued to honor Simon Bolivar.
Issue dates: Nos. C937-C939, Aug. 15; Nos. C940-C942, Sept. 29; others, Oct. 14.
See Nos. C961-C972.

"Justice" — AP80

1966, Nov. 3   Litho.   Perf. 14x13½
C949 AP80 50c pale lil & red lil   1.00   .40

50th anniversary of the Academy of Political and Social Sciences.

Angostura Bridge, Orinoco River — AP81

1967, Jan. 6   Litho.   Perf. 13½x14
C950 AP81 40c multi   .50   .25

Issued to commemorate the opening of the Angostura Bridge over the Orinoco River.

Pavilion of Venezuela AP82

1967, Apr. 28   Litho.   Perf. 11x13½
C951 AP82 1b multi   1.25   .40

EXPO '67, International Exhibition, Montreal, Apr. 28-Oct. 27, 1967.

Statue of Chief Guaicaipuro AP83

Constellations over Caracas, 1567 and 1967 — AP84

Designs: 45c, Captain Francisco Fajardo. 55c, Diego de Losada, the Founder. 65c, Arms of Caracas. 90c, Map of Caracas, 1578. 1b, Market on Plaza Mayor, 1800.

1967   Litho.   Perf. 14x13½, 13½x14
C952	AP83	15c multi	.25	.25
C953	AP83	45c gold, car & brn	.45	.25
C954	AP83	55c multi	.55	.25
C955	AP84	60c blk, ultra & sil	.60	.25
C956	AP84	65c multi	.80	.30
C957	AP84	90c multi	.95	.35
C958	AP84	1b multi	1.10	.45
		Nos. C952-C958 (7)	4.70	2.10

400th anniv. of the founding of Caracas (1st issue). See Nos. C977-C982 (2nd issue).
Two souvenir sheets each contain single stamps similar to Nos. C952-C953, but with simulated perforation. Sold for 1b each. Size: 80x119mm. Value $45 each.
Issued: 55c, 65c, July 28; others, July 12.

Gen. Francisco Esteban Gomez — AP85

1967, July 31   Litho.   Perf. 14x13½
C959 AP85 90c multi   1.25   .55

150th anniversary, Battle of Matasiete.

Juan Vicente González — AP86

1967, Oct. 18   Litho.   Perf. 14x13½
C960 AP86 80c ocher & blk   1.25   .40

Centenary of the death (in 1866) of Juan Vicente González, journalist.

Bolivar Type of 1966
Imprint: "Druck Bruder Rosenbaum. Wien"

1967-68   Litho.   Perf. 13½x14
Multicolored Center
C961	AP79	5c lemon & blk	.25	.25
C962	AP79	10c lemon & blk	.25	.25
C963	AP79	20c grn & blk	.35	.25
C964	AP79	25c salmon & blk	.30	.25
C965	AP79	30c pink & blk	.35	.25
C966	AP79	35c dl rose & blk	.35	.25
C967	AP79	40c bis brn & blk	.60	.25
C968	AP79	50c org brn & blk	4.75	.35
C969	AP79	60c brn red & blk	2.10	.90
C970	AP79	80c brt bl & blk	1.25	.50
C971	AP79	1.20b dl bl & blk	1.75	.35
C972	AP79	4b vio bl & blk	4.75	1.90
		Nos. C961-C972 (12)	17.05	5.75

Issue dates: 20c, 30c, 50c, Nov. 24; 5c, 25c, 40c, Feb. 5, 1968; others, Aug, 28, 1967.

Child with Pinwheel AP87

1967, Dec. 15   Litho.   Perf. 14x13½
C973	AP87	45c multi	.60	.25
C974	AP87	75c multi	.80	.30
C975	AP87	90c multi	1.00	.35
		Nos. C973-C975 (3)	2.40	.90

Children's Festival.

Madonna with the Rosebush, by Stephan Lochner AP88

1967, Dec. 19
C976 AP88 1b multi   1.60   .70

Christmas 1967.

Palace of the Academies, Caracas — AP89

Views of Caracas: 50c, St. Theresa's Church, vert. 70c, Federal Legislature. 75c, University City. 85c, El Pulpo highways crossing. 2b, Avenida Libertador.

1967, Dec. 28   Perf. 13½x14, 14x13½
C977	AP89	10c multi	.25	.25
C978	AP89	50c lil & multi	.35	.25
C979	AP89	70c multi	.65	.25
C980	AP89	75c multi	.75	.25
C981	AP89	85c multi	.80	.30
C982	AP89	2b multi	2.25	.85
		Nos. C977-C982 (6)	5.05	2.15

400th anniv. of Caracas (2nd issue).

Dr. José Manuel Nuñez Ponte (1870-1965), Educator — AP90

1968, Mar. 8   Litho.   Perf. 14
C983 AP90 65c multi   .75   .35

De Miranda and Printing Press AP91

Designs (Miranda Portraits and): 35c, Parliament, London. 45c, Arc de Triomphe, Paris. 70c, Portrait, vert. 80c, Portrait bust and Venezuelan flags, vert.

Perf. 13½x14, 14x13½
1968, June 20   Litho.
C984	AP91	20c yel brn, grn & brn	.35	.25
C985	AP91	35c multi	.55	.25
C986	AP91	45c lt bl & multi	1.00	.40
C987	AP91	70c multi	1.25	.35
C988	AP91	80c multi	1.50	.55
		Nos. C984-C988 (5)	4.65	1.80

General Francisco de Miranda (1750?-1816), revolutionist, dictator of Venezuela.

Insect Type of 1968
Insect Pests: 5c, Red leaf-cutting ant, vert. 15c, Sugar cane beetle, vert. 20c, Leaf beetle.

Perf. 14x13½, 13½x14
1968, Aug. 30   Litho.
C989	A157	5c multi	.50	.25
C990	A157	15c multi	1.00	.25
C991	A157	20c gray & multi	1.50	.25
		Nos. C989-C991 (3)	3.00	.75

Three Keys — AP92

1968, Oct. 17   Litho.   Perf. 14x13½
C992 AP92 95c yel, vio & dk grn   1.40   .50

Natl. Comptroller's Office, 30th anniv.

Fencing — AP93

Designs: 5c, Pistol shooting, vert. 15c, Running. 75c, Boxing. 5b, Sailing, vert.

Perf. 14x13½, 13½x14
1968, Nov. 6   Litho.   Unwmk.
C993	AP93	5c vio, bl & blk	.50	.30
C994	AP93	15c multi	.60	.30
C995	AP93	30c yel grn, dk grn & blk	.75	.30
C996	AP93	75c multi	1.40	.40
C997	AP93	5b multi	5.25	1.90
		Nos. C993-C997 (5)	8.50	3.20

19th Olympic Games, Mexico City, 10/12-27.

Holy Family, by Francisco José de Lerma — AP94

1968, Dec. 4   Litho.   Perf. 14x13½
C998 AP94 40c multi   .75   .25

Christmas 1968.

Dancing Children and Stars — AP95

1968, Dec. 13   Litho.   Perf. 14x13½
C999 AP95 80c vio & org   1.10   .50

Issued for the 5th Children's Festival.

Conservation Type of 1968
Designs: 15c, Marbled wood-quail, vert. 20c, Water birds, vert. 30c, Woodcarvings and tools, vert. 90c, Brown trout. 95c, Valley and road. 1b, Red-eyed vireo feeding young bronzed cowbird.

Perf. 13½x14, 14x13½
1968, Dec. 19   Litho.
C1000	A160	15c multi	.45	.35
C1001	A160	20c multi	.45	.35
C1002	A160	30c multi	.55	.35
C1003	A160	90c multi	1.50	.45
C1004	A160	95c multi	2.25	.65
C1005	A160	1b multi	1.60	.55
		Nos. C1000-C1005 (6)	6.80	2.70

Tourist Type of 1969
Designs: 15c, Giant cactus and desert, Falcon. 30c, Hotel Humboldt, Federal District. 40c, Cable car and mountain peaks, Merida.

1969, Jan. 24   Perf. 13½x14
C1006 A161 15c multi   .30   .25

C1007 A161 30c multi .... .35 .25
  a.   Souv. sheet of 2, #931,
        C1007, imperf. 2.10 2.10
C1008 A161 40c multi .... .60 .25
  Nos. C1006-C1008 (3) .... 1.25 .75

Tree Type of 1969

Trees: 5c, Cassia grandis. 20c, Triplaris
caracasana. 25c, Samanea saman.

1969, May 30   Litho.   Perf. 13½x14
C1009 A164 5c lt grn & multi .... .50 .25
C1010 A164 20c org & multi .... .75 .25
C1011 A164 25c lt vio & multi .... .85 .25
  Nos. C1009-C1011 (3) .... 2.10 .75

Alexander von
Humboldt, by
Joseph
Stieler — AP96

1969, Sept. 12   Photo.   Perf. 14
C1012 AP96 50c multi .... .80 .25

Alexander von Humboldt (1769-1859), naturalist and explorer.

Map of
Maracaibo,
1562 — AP97

20c, Ambrosio Alfinger, Alfonso Pacheco,
Pedro Maldonado, horiz. 40c, Maracaibo coat
of arms. 70c, University Hospital. 75c, Monument to the Indian Mara. 1b, Baralt Square,
horiz.

Perf. 13½x13, 13x13½
1969, Sept. 30   Litho.
C1013 AP97 20c lil & multi .... .35 .25
C1014 AP97 25c org & multi .... .40 .25
C1015 AP97 40c multi .... .45 .25
C1016 AP97 70c grn & multi .... 1.00 .35
C1017 AP97 75c brn & multi .... 1.25 .40
C1018 AP97 1b multi .... 1.40 .50
  Nos. C1013-C1018 (6) 4.85 2.00

400th anniversary of Maracaibo.

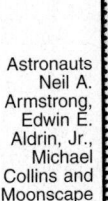

Astronauts
Neil A.
Armstrong,
Edwin E.
Aldrin, Jr.,
Michael
Collins and
Moonscape
AP98

1969, Nov. 18   Litho.   Perf. 12½
C1019 AP98 90c multi .... 1.60 .65
  a.   Souv. sheet of 1, imperf. ... 3.25 3.25
  See note after US No. C76.

Virgin with the
Rosary, 17th
Century
AP99

Christmas: 80c, Holy Family, Caracas, 18th
Cent.

1969, Dec. 1   Litho.   Perf. 12½
C1020 AP99 75c gold & multi .... .90 .35
C1021 AP99 80c gold & multi .... 1.10 .45
  a.   Pair, #C1020-C1021 .... 2.40 2.40

Simon Bolivar,
1819, by M. N.
Bate — AP100

Bolivar Portraits: 45c, 55c, like 15c. 65c,
70c, 75c Drawing by Francois Roulin, 1828.
85c, 90c, 95c, Charcoal drawing by José
Maria Espinoza, 1828. 1b, 1.50b, 2b, Drawing
by Espinoza, 1830.

1970, Mar. 16   Litho.   Perf. 14x13½
C1022 AP100 15c multi .... .25 .25
C1023 AP100 45c bl & multi .... .45 .25
C1024 AP100 55c org & multi .... .60 .25
C1025 AP100 65c multi .... .60 .30
C1026 AP100 70c bl & multi .... .70 .40
C1027 AP100 75c org & multi .... .95 .40
C1028 AP100 85c multi .... 1.10 .40
C1029 AP100 90c bl & multi .... 1.10 .45
C1030 AP100 95c org & multi .... 1.25 .50
C1031 AP100 1b multi .... 1.25 .50
C1032 AP100 1.50b bl & multi ..... 1.40 .55
C1033 AP100 2b multi 3.00 1.75
  Nos. C1022-C1033 (12) 12.65 6.00

Issued to honor Simon Bolivar (1783-1830),
liberator and father of his country.

General
Antonio
Guzmán
Blanco and
Dr. Martin
J. Sanabria
AP101

1970, June 26   Litho.   Perf. 13
C1034 AP101 75c brt grn & multi .80 .35

Free obligatory elementary education, cent.

Map of Venezuela with Claim to Part
of Guyana — AP102

State map and arms. 55c, 90c, vert.

Perf. 13½x14, 14x13½
1970-71   Litho.
C1035 AP102 5c shown .... .35 .25
C1036 AP102 15c Apure .... .35 .25
C1037 AP102 20c Aragua .... .40 .25
C1038 AP102 20c Anzoategui ...... .45 .25
C1039 AP102 25c Barinas .... .45 .25
C1040 AP102 25c Bolivar .... .45 .25
C1041 AP102 45c Carabobo .... .65 .25
C1042 AP102 55c Cojedes .... .70 .25
C1043 AP102 65c Falcon .... .75 .25
C1044 AP102 75c Guárico .... .90 .25
C1045 AP102 85c Lara .... 1.10 .30
C1046 AP102 90c Mérida .... 1.10 .30
C1047 AP102 1b Miranda .... 1.10 .40
C1048 AP102 2b Delta
              Amacuro
              Territory .... 2.40 .95
  Nos. C1035-C1048 (14) 11.15 4.45

Issued: 5c, 7/15; 15c, #C1037, 1/18;
#C1038-C1039, 2/15/71; #C1040, 45c,
3/15/71; 55c, 65c, 4/15; 75c, 85c, 5/15/71;
90c, 1b, 6/15/71; 2b, 7/15/71.

Flower Type of 1970

Flowers: 20c, Epidendrum secundum. 25c,
Oyedaea verbesinoides. 45c, Heliconia villosa. 1b, Macleania nitida.

1970, July 29   Litho.   Perf. 14x13½
C1049 A175 20c multi .... .50 .25
C1050 A175 25c multi .... .60 .25
C1051 A175 45c multi .... 1.50 .25
C1052 A175 1b multi .... 1.90 .45
  Nos. C1049-C1052 (4) 4.50 1.30

Caracciolo
Parra Olmedo
AP104

1970, Nov. 16   Photo.   Perf. 12½
C1053 AP104 20c bl & multi .... .30 .25

Sesquicentennial of birth of Caracciolo
Parra Olmedo (1819-1900), professor of law,
rector of University of Merida.

Census Chart — AP105

1971, Apr. 30   Litho.   Perf. 13½x14
C1054   Block of 4 .... 5.00 2.50
  a.   AP105 70c, frame L & T ..... .90 .35
  b.   AP105 70c, frame T & R ..... .90 .35
  c.   AP105 70c, frame L & B ..... .90 .35
  d.   AP105 70c, frame B & R ..... .90 .35
  See note after No. 979.

Cattleya Gaskelliana — AP106

Orchids: 20c, Cattleya percivaliana, vert.
75c, Cattleya mossiae, vert. 90c, Cattleya violacea. 1b, Cattleya lawrenciana.

Perf. 14x13½, 13½x14
1971, Aug. 25
C1055 AP106 20c blk & multi .... .55 .25
C1056 AP106 25c blk & multi .... .80 .25
C1057 AP106 75c blk & multi .... 1.50 .50
C1058 AP106 90c blk & multi .... 2.10 .80
C1059 AP106 1b blk & multi .... 2.25 .90
  Nos. C1055-C1059 (5) 7.20 2.70

40th anniversary of Venezuelan Society of
Natural History. Issued in sheets of 5 stamps
and one label with Society emblem in blue.
Value $37.50.

Draft of
Constitution
Superimposed
on Capitol
AP107

1971, Dec. 29   Litho.   Perf. 13½
C1060 AP107 90c multi .... .80 .40

Anniversary of 1961 Constitution.

AIR POST SEMI-POSTAL STAMPS

King Vulture
SPAP1

Unwmk.
1942, Dec. 17   Engr.   Perf. 12
CB1 SPAP1 15c + 10c org brn ..... 2.25 .60
CB2 SPAP1 30c + 5c violet .... 2.25 .75
  Set, never hinged 7.50
  See note after No. B1.

SPECIAL DELIVERY STAMPS

Catalogue values for unused
stamps in this section are for
Never Hinged items.

SD1

Perf. 12½
1949, Mar. 9   Unwmk.   Engr.
E1 SD1 30c red .... .75 .30

SD2

Wmk. 116
1961, Apr. 7   Litho.   Perf. 13½
E2 SD2 30c orange .... .75 .25

REGISTRATION STAMPS

Bolívar — R1

1899, May   Unwmk.   Engr.   Perf. 12
F1 R1 25c yellow brown 3.25 2.75

No. F1 Overprinted

1900
F2 R1 25c yellow brown 2.00 2.00
  a.   Inverted overprint 32.50 32.50
  b.   Double overprint 40.00 40.00

Counterfeit overprints exist, especially of the
varieties.

OFFICIAL STAMPS

Coat of Arms — O1

Lithographed, Center Engraved
1898, May 1   **Unwmk.**   **Perf. 12**

O1	O1	5c bl grn & blk	.80	.55
O2	O1	10c rose & blk	.95	.85
O3	O1	25c bl & blk	1.50	1.40
O4	O1	50c yel & blk	2.50	2.25
O5	O1	1b vio & blk	2.75	2.50
		Nos. O1-O5 (5)	8.50	7.55

Nos. O4 and O5
Handstamp
Surcharged in
Magenta or Violet

1899, Nov.

O6	O1	5c on 50c yel & blk	4.75	4.50
O7	O1	5c on 1b vio & blk	20.00	18.00
O8	O1	25c on 50c vio & blk	20.00	18.00
O9	O1	25c on 1b vio & blk	12.00	11.00
		Nos. O6-O9 (4)	56.75	51.50

Inverted Surcharge

O6a	O1	5c on 50c	15.00	15.00
O7a	O1	5c on 1b	40.00	40.00
O8a	O1	25c on 50c	32.50	32.50
O9a	O1	25c on 1b	32.50	32.50
		Nos. O6a-O9a (4)	120.00	120.00

Nos. O6-O9 exist with double surcharge.
Value each $18.50-$37.50.

Many of the magenta overprints have
become violet. There are intermediate
shades.

Counterfeit overprints exist.

Coat of Arms — O3

1900   Litho., Center Engr.

O14	O3	5c bl grn & blk	.40	.40
O15	O3	10c rose & blk	.55	.55
O16	O3	25c bl & blk	.55	.55
O17	O3	50c yel & blk	.55	.55
O18	O3	1b dl vio & blk	.65	.65
		Nos. O14-O18 (5)	2.70	2.70

O4

Imprint: "American Bank Note Co.,
N.Y."

1904, July   Engr.

O19	O4	5c emerald & blk	.25	.25
O20	O4	10c rose & blk	.65	.65
O21	O4	25c blue & blk	.65	.65
O22	O4	50c red brn & blk	4.25	4.25
a.		50c claret & black	4.25	4.25
O23	O4	1b red brn & blk	2.00	2.00
a.		1b claret & black	2.00	2.00
		Nos. O19-O23 (5)	7.80	7.80

No Stars Above
Shield — O5

1912   Lithographed in Caracas

O24	O5	5c grn & blk	.55	.30
O25	O5	10c car & blk	.55	.30
O26	O5	25c dk bl & blk	.55	.30
O27	O5	50c pur & blk	.55	.40
a.		Center double	19.00	
O28	O5	1b yel & blk	1.30	.80
		Nos. O24-O28 (5)	3.50	2.10

Perforated Initials
After 1925, Venezuela's official
stamps consisted of regular postage
stamps, some commemoratives and air
post stamps of 1930-42 punched with
"GN" (Gobierno Nacional) in large perforated initials.

LOCAL STAMPS FOR THE PORT OF CARUPANO

In 1902 Great Britain, Germany and
Italy, seeking compensation for revolutionary damages, established a block-
ade of La Guaira and seized the custom
house. Carúpano, a port near Trinidad,
was isolated and issued the following
provisionals. A treaty effected May 7,
1903, referred the dispute to the Hague
Tribunal.

A1

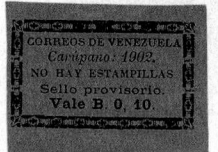

A2

1902   Typeset   *Imperf.*

1	A1	5c purple, *orange*	27.00
2	A2	10c black, *orange*	40.00
a.		Tête bêche pair	82.50
3	A1	25c purple, *green*	32.50
4	A1	50c green, *yellow*	85.00
5	A1	1b blue, *rose*	120.00
		Nos. 1-5 (5)	304.50

```
o o o o o o o o o o o o o o o
o  INSTRUCCIÓN  o
o  SELLO PROVISIONAL  o
o  CARÚPANO : 1902  o
o  Vale un Bolivar.  o
o o o o o o o o o o o o o o o
```

A3

1902

6	A3	1b black, *yellow*	200.00
a.		Tête bêche pair	

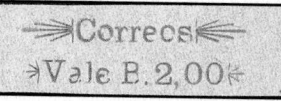

A4

1903   Handstamped

7	A4	5c carmine, *yellow*	45.00	45.00
8	A4	10c green, *yellow*	92.50	92.50
9	A4	25c green, *orange*	45.00	45.00
10	A4	50c blue, *rose*	45.00	45.00
11	A4	1b violet, *gray*	45.00	45.00
12	A4	2b carmine, *green*	45.00	45.00
13	A4	5b violet, *blue*	45.00	45.00
		Nos. 7-13 (7)	362.50	362.50

Dangerous counterfeits exist of Nos. 1-13.

LOCAL STAMPS FOR THE STATE OF GUAYANA

Revolutionary
Steamship
"Banrigh" — A1

Control Mark

Control Mark on Block of 4

1903   Typo.   Perf. 12

1	A1	5c black, *gray*	19.00	19.00
2	A1	10c black, *orange*	47.50	47.50
3	A1	25c black, *pink*	19.00	19.00
4	A1	50c black, *blue*	30.00	30.00
5	A1	1b black, *straw*	25.00	25.00
		Nos. 1-5 (5)	140.50	140.50

Nos. 1-5 can be found with or without the
illustrated control mark which covers four
stamps.

Counterfeits include the 10c and 50c in red
and are from different settings from the originals. They are on papers differing in colors
from the originals. All 5c on granite paper are
bogus.

Coat of
Arms
A2

1903

11	A2	5c black, *pink*	40.00
12	A2	10c black, *orange*	50.00
13	A2	25c black, *gray blue*	40.00
a.		25c black, *blue*	40.00
14	A2	50c black, *straw*	40.00
15	A2	1b black, *gray*	30.00
		Nos. 11-15 (5)	200.00

Postally used examples are very scarce, as
are examples having 9 ornaments in horizontal borders. Nos. 11-15 pen canceled sell for
same values as unused.

See note on controls after No. 5.

Counterfeits exist of Nos. 11-15. Stamps
with 10 ornaments in horizontal borders are
counterfeits.

Nos. 1-5, 11-15 were issued by a group of
revolutionists and had a limited local use. The
dates on the stamps commemorate the declaration of Venezuelan independence and a
compact with Spain against Joseph
Bonaparte.

VIET NAM

vē-'et-'näm

LOCATION — In eastern Indo-China
GOVT. — Kingdom
AREA — 123,949 sq. mi.
POP. — 77,311,210 (1999 est.)
CAPITAL — Hanoi

Viet Nam, which included the former
French territories of Tonkin, Annam and
Cochin China, became an Associated
State of the French Union in 1949. The
Communist Viet Minh obtained control
of Northern Viet Nam in 1954, and the
republic of South Viet Nam was estab-
lished in October, 1955.

100 Cents (Xu) = 1 Piaster (Dong)

> Catalogue values for unused
> stamps in this country are for
> Never Hinged items, beginning
> with Scott 27 in the regular post-
> age section, Scott B2 in the semi-
> postal section, Scott C1 in the air-
> post section, Scott J1 in the post-
> age due section, and Scott M1 in
> the military section.

Bongour
Falls,
Dalat — A1

Emperor Bao-
Dai — A2

Designs: 20c, 2pi, 10pi, Imperial palace,
Hué. 30c, 15pi, Lake, Hanoi. 50c, 1pi, Temple,
Saigon.

Perf. 13x13½, 13½x13
Unwmk.
1951, June 6-Oct. 23   **Photo.**

1	A1	10c olive green	.25	.25
2	A1	20c deep plum	.25	.25
3	A1	30c blue	.30	.40
4	A1	50c red	.50	.25
5	A1	60c brown	.40	.25
6	A1	1pi chestnut brn	.40	.25
7	A2	1.20pi yellow brn	4.00	5.00
8	A1	2pi purple	1.50	.25
9	A2	3pi dull blue	4.00	.25
10	A1	5pi green	5.00	.70
11	A1	10pi crimson	14.00	1.00
12	A1	15pi red brown	60.00	6.00
13	A2	30pi blue green	35.00	7.00
		Nos. 1-13 (13)	125.60	21.85
		Set, never hinged	200.00	

Souvenir booklets exist comprising five
gummed sheets of 1 containing Nos. 1, 2, 6, 9,
12, together with commemorative inscriptions.
Value, $175.

Empress Nam-
Phuong — A3

1952, Aug. 15   Perf. 12½

14	A3	30c dk pur, yel & brn	.60	.35
15	A3	50c blue, yel & brn	1.25	.65
16	A3	1.50pi ol grn, yel & brn	2.40	.30
		Nos. 14-16 (3)	4.25	1.30
		Set, never hinged	8.00	

For surcharge see No. B1.

Globe and Lightning Bolt — A4

1952, Aug. 24   Engr.   Perf. 13
17 A4 1pi greenish blue   2.50 1.75
    Never hinged   9.00

Viet Nam's admission to the ITU, 1st anniv.

Coastal Scene and UPU Emblem A5

1952, Sept. 12
18 A5 5pi red brown   2.75 1.60
    Never hinged   4.75

Viet Nam's admission to the UPU, 1st anniv.

Bao-Dai and Pagoda of Literature, Hanoi — A6

1952, Nov. 10   Perf. 12
19 A6 1.50pi rose violet   2.50 1.25
    Never hinged   4.50

39th birthday of Emperor Bao-Dai.

Crown Prince Bao-Long in Annamite Costume — A7

70c, 80c, 100pi, Prince in Annamite costume. 90c, 20pi, 50pi, Prince in Western uniform.

1954, June 15   Perf. 13
20 A7 40c aqua   .25   .40
21 A7 70c claret   .25   .40
22 A7 80c black brown   .25   .40
23 A7 90c dark green   .40 1.25
24 A7 20pi rose pink   1.25 2.25
25 A7 50pi violet   4.00 7.00
26 A7 100pi blue violet   6.00 17.50
    Nos. 20-26 (7)   12.40 29.20
    Set, never hinged, brown
    gum   20.00
    Set, never hinged, white
    gum   45.00

REPUBLIC OF VIET NAM

(South Viet Nam)

(Viet Nam Cong Hoa)

GOVT. — Republic
AREA — 66,280 sq. mi.
POP. — 19,600,000 (est. 1973)
CAPITAL — Saigon

Catalogue values for unused stamps in this section, from this point to the end of the section, are for Never Hinged items. Because of the tropical conditions, never hinged stamps must also be free of wrinkles, toning, and any other disturbance.

Mythological Turtle — A8

Unwmk.
1955, July 20   Engr.   Perf. 13
27 A8 30c claret   2.50   .25
28 A8 50c dark green   6.00 1.50
29 A8 1.50pi bright blue   6.00   .60
    Nos. 27-29 (3)   14.50 2.35

Refugees on Raft — A9

1955, Oct. 11
30 A9 70c crimson rose   1.00 1.00
31 A9 80c brown violet   3.00 3.00
32 A9 10pi indigo   5.50 5.50
33 A9 20pi vio, red brn &
        org   17.50 17.50
34 A9 35pi dk bl, blk brn
        & yel   30.00 30.00
35 A9 100pi dk grn, brn vio
        & org   72.50 72.50
    Nos. 30-35 (6)   129.50 129.50

1st anniv. of the flight of the North Vietnamese.
No. 34 is inscribed "Chiên-Dich-Huynh-Dê" (Operation Brotherhood) below design. See No. 54.

Post Office, Saigon — A10

1956, Jan. 10   Perf. 12
36 A10 60c bluish green   1.90 1.50
37 A10 90c violet   3.50 2.00
38 A10 3pi red brown   6.75 4.00
    Nos. 36-38 (3)   12.15 7.50

5th anniv. of independent postal service.
For overprints see Nos. 51-53.

Pres. Ngo Dinh Diem — A11

1956   Engr.   Perf. 13x13½
39 A11 20c orange ver   .40   .25
40 A11 30c rose lilac   .75   .40
41 A11 50c brt carmine   .40   .40
42 A11 1pi violet   .80   .50
43 A11 1.50pi violet   1.60   .50
44 A11 3pi black brown   1.60   .60
45 A11 4pi dark blue   2.40   .70
46 A11 5pi red brown   3.25   .80
47 A11 10pi blue   3.75 1.25
48 A11 20pi gray black   10.00 2.25
49 A11 35pi green   25.00 4.00
50 A11 100pi brown   50.00 20.00
    Nos. 39-50 (12)   99.95 31.65

Nos. 36-38 Overprinted

1956, Aug. 6   Perf. 12
51 A10 60c bluish green   1.10   .80
52 A10 90c violet   2.50   .80
53 A10 3pi red brown   3.25 1.25
    Nos. 51-53 (3)   6.85 2.85

The overprint reads: "Government Post Office Building."

No. 34 Overprinted

1956, Aug. 6
54 A9 35pi dk bl, blk brn & yel 11.00 6.00

Bamboo — A12

1956, Oct. 26   Litho.   Perf. 13x13½
55 A12 50c scarlet   .95   .95
56 A12 1.50pi rose violet   1.25 1.25
57 A12 2pi brt green   1.60 1.60
58 A12 4pi deep blue   4.25 4.25
    Nos. 55-58 (4)   8.05 8.05

1st anniv. of the Republic.

Children — A13

1956, Nov. 7   Engr.   Perf. 13½x14
59 A13 1pi lilac rose   .80   .40
60 A13 2pi blue green   1.25   .40
61 A13 6pi purple   2.00   .40
62 A13 35pi violet blue   11.00 2.75
    Nos. 59-62 (4)   15.05 3.95

"Operation Brotherhood."

Hunters on Elephants — A14

Design: 90c, 2pi, 3pi, Mountain dwelling.

1957, July 7   Photo.   Perf. 13
63 A14 20c yellow grn & pur   1.25   .50
64 A14 30c bister & dp mag   1.50   .55
65 A14 90c yel grn & dk brn   1.75   .65
66 A14 2pi green & ultra   2.40   .70
67 A14 3pi blue vio & brn   3.00   .80
    Nos. 63-67 (5)   9.90 3.20

Loading Cargo — A15

1957, Oct. 21   Perf. 13½x13
68 A15 20c rose violet   .25   .25
69 A15 40c lt olive grn   .25   .25
70 A15 50c lt carmine rose   .50   .40

71 A15 2pi ultra   1.60   .45
72 A15 3pi brt green   2.25   .55
    Nos. 68-72 (5)   4.85 1.90

9th Colombo Plan Conference, Saigon.

Torch, Map and Constitution — A16

1957, Oct. 26   Litho.   Perf. 13x13½
73 A16 50c black, green & sal   .25   .25
74 A16 80c black, brt bl & mag   .25   .25
75 A16 1pi black, bl grn & brt
         car   .50   .40
76 A16 4pi blk, ol grn & fawn   .70   .45
77 A16 5pi blk, grnsh bl & cit 1.00   .55
78 A16 10pi black, ultra & rose 2.10   .75
    Nos. 73-78 (6)   4.80 2.65

Republic of South Viet Nam, 2nd anniv.

Farmers, Tractor and Village — A17

1958, July 7   Engr.   Perf. 13½
79 A17 50c yellow green   .40   .25
80 A17 1pi deep violet   .60   .25
81 A17 2pi ultra   1.25   .60
82 A17 10pi brick red   2.50   .90
    Nos. 79-82 (4)   4.75 2.00

4th anniv. of the government of Ngo Dinh Diem.

Girl and Lantern — A18

1958, Sept. 27
83 A18 30c yellow   .45   .25
84 A18 50c dk carmine rose   .50   .25
85 A18 2pi dp carmine   .60   .40
86 A18 3pi blue green   1.25   .50
87 A18 4pi lt olive green   2.10   .55
    Nos. 83-87 (5)   4.90 1.95

Children's Festival.

A19

1958, Oct. 26   Perf. 13½
88 A19 1pi dull red brown   .60   .25
89 A19 2pi bluish green   .75   .25
90 A19 4pi rose carmine   1.10   .45
91 A19 5pi rose lilac   2.40   .75
    Nos. 88-91 (4)   4.85 1.70

Issued for United Nations Day.

Most South Viet Nam stamps from 1958 onward exist imperforate in issued and trial colors, and also in small presentation sheets in issued colors.

UNESCO Building, Paris — A20

1958, Nov. 3   **Perf. 12½x13**
92	A20	50c ultra	.55 .25
93	A20	2pi bright red	.70 .25
94	A20	3pi lilac rose	1.40 .40
95	A20	6pi violet	2.25 .60
		Nos. 92-95 (4)	4.90 1.50

UNESCO Headquarters in Paris opening, 11/3.

Torch and UN Emblem — A21

1958, Dec. 10   **Engr.**   **Perf. 13½**
96	A21	50c dark blue	.25 .25
97	A21	1pi brown carmine	.45 .25
98	A21	2pi yellow green	.75 .40
99	A21	6pi rose violet	1.60 .65
		Nos. 96-99 (4)	3.05 1.55

Signing of the Universal Declaration of Human Rights, 10th anniv.

Cathedral of Hué — A22

Thien Mu Pagoda, Hué — A23

National Museum A24

50c, 2pi, Palace of Independence, Saigon.

1958-59   **Perf. 13½**
100	A22	10c dk blue gray	.25 .40
101	A23	30c green ('59)	.60 .85
102	A24	40c dk green ('59)	.85 .70
103	A24	50c green ('59)	.85 .85
104	A22	2pi grnsh blue ('59)	2.50 2.00
105	A23	4pi dull purple ('59)	2.75 2.25
106	A24	5pi dk carmine ('59)	3.00 2.25
107	A22	6pi orange brown	4.25 2.25
		Nos. 100-107 (8)	15.05 11.55

Trung Sisters on Elephants A25

1959, Mar. 14   **Photo.**   **Perf. 13**
108	A25	50c multicolored	1.25 .75
109	A25	2pi ocher, grn & bl	2.50 1.20
110	A25	3pi emerald, vio & bis	4.00 1.50
111	A25	6pi multicolored	7.50 2.25
		Nos. 108-111 (4)	15.25 5.70

Sisters Trung Trac and Trung Nhi who resisted a Chinese invasion in 40-44 A.D.

Symbols of Agrarian Reforms A26

1959, July 7   **Engr.**   **Perf. 13**
112	A26	70c lilac rose	.60 .25
113	A26	2pi dk grn & Prus bl	.70 .25
114	A26	3pi olive	1.25 .40
115	A26	6pi dark red & red	2.50 1.25
		Nos. 112-115 (4)	5.05 2.15

5th anniv. of Ngo Dinh Diem's presidency.

Diesel Engine and Map of North and South Viet Nam — A27

1959, Aug. 7
116	A27	1pi lt violet & grn	1.25 .75
117	A27	2pi gray & green	1.40 1.25
118	A27	3pi grnsh bl & grn	1.90 1.50
119	A27	4pi maroon & grn	3.25 2.25
		Nos. 116-119 (4)	7.80 5.75

Re-opening of the Saigon-Dongha Railroad.

Volunteer Road Workers A28

1959, Oct. 26
120	A28	1pi org brn, ultra & grn	.95 .25
121	A28	2pi violet, org & grn	1.25 .25
122	A28	4pi dk bl, bl & bis	3.00 .45
123	A28	5pi bister, brn & ocher	3.00 .95
		Nos. 120-123 (4)	8.20 1.90

4th anniv. of the constitution, stressing communal development.

Boy Scout — A29

1959, Dec.   **Engr.**   **Perf. 13**
124	A29	3pi brt yellow grn	.50 .25
125	A29	4pi deep lilac rose	1.25 .25
126	A29	8pi dk brn & lil rose	2.25 .65
127	A29	20pi Prus bl & bl grn	5.50 1.25
		Nos. 124-127 (4)	9.50 2.40

National Boy Scout Jamboree.

Symbols of Family and Justice A30

1960
128	A30	20c emerald	.40 .85
129	A30	30c brt grnsh blue	.50 .95
130	A30	2pi orange & maroon	1.10 1.75
131	A30	6pi car & rose vio	4.20 1.75
		Nos. 128-131 (4)	6.20 5.30

Issued to commemorate the family code.

Refugee Family and WRY Emblem A31

1960, Apr. 7   **Engr.**   **Perf. 13**
132	A31	50c brt lilac rose	.40 .25
133	A31	3pi brt green	.70 .25
134	A31	4pi scarlet	.85 .40
135	A31	5pi dp violet blue	1.25 .65
		Nos. 132-135 (4)	3.20 1.55

World Refugee Year, 7/1/59-6/30/60.

Henri Dunant — A32

1960, May 8   **Cross in Carmine**
136	A32	1pi dark blue	.70 .25
137	A32	3pi green	2.25 .25
138	A32	4pi crimson rose	2.25 .50
139	A32	6pi dp lilac rose	2.75 .70
		Nos. 136-139 (4)	7.95 1.70

Centenary (in 1959) of the Red Cross idea.

Model Farm A33

1960, July 7   **Perf. 13**
140	A33	50c ultra	.50 .25
141	A33	1pi dark green	.60 .25
142	A33	3pi orange	1.25 .40
143	A33	7pi bright pink	2.40 .65
		Nos. 140-143 (4)	4.75 1.55

Establishment of communal rice farming.

Girl With Basket of Rice and Rice Plant A34

1960, Nov. 21
144	A34	2pi emerald & green	1.00 .40
145	A34	4pi blue & ultra	2.25 .65

Conf. of the UN FAO, Saigon, Nov. 1960.

Map and Flag of Viet Nam — A35

1960, Oct. 26   **Engr.**   **Perf. 13**
146	A35	50c grnsh bl, car & yel	.55 .25
147	A35	1pi ultra, car & yel	.75 .30
148	A35	3pi purple, car & yel	1.25 .40
149	A35	7pi yel grn, car & yel	2.25 .65
		Nos. 146-149 (4)	4.80 1.60

Fifth anniversary of the Republic.

Agricultural Development Center, Tractor and Plow — A36

1961, Jan. 3   **Perf. 13**
150	A36	50c red brown	.45 .25
151	A36	70c rose lilac	.85 .30
152	A36	80c rose red	.95 .40
153	A36	10pi bright pink	4.75 1.00
		Nos. 150-153 (4)	7.00 1.95

Plant and Child — A37

1961, Mar. 23   **Perf. 13**
154	A37	70c light blue	.45 .25
155	A37	80c ultra	.55 .30
156	A37	4pi olive bister	.75 .50
157	A37	7pi grnsh bl & yel grn	2.00 .75
		Nos. 154-157 (4)	3.75 1.80

Child protection.

Pres. Ngo Dinh Diem — A38

1961, Apr. 29   **Perf. 13**
158	A38	50c brt ultra	.60 .55
159	A38	1pi red	1.00 1.00
160	A38	2pi lilac rose	2.00 1.20
161	A38	4pi brt violet	4.00 2.00
		Nos. 158-161 (4)	7.60 4.75

Second term of Pres. Ngo Dinh Diem.

Boy, Girl and Flaming Torch A39

1961, July 7   **Engr.**   **Perf. 13**
162	A39	50c red	.25 .25
163	A39	70c bright pink	.65 .30
164	A39	80c ver & maroon	.80 .40
165	A39	8pi dp claret & mag	2.25 .80
		Nos. 162-165 (4)	3.95 1.75

Issued for Youth Day.

Saigon-Bien Hoa Highway Bridge — A40

1961, July 28
166	A40	50c yellow green	.55 .25
167	A40	1pi orange brown	.80 .30
168	A40	2pi dark blue	1.25 .40
169	A40	5pi brt red lilac	2.40 .50
		Nos. 166-169 (4)	5.00 1.45

Opening of Saigon-Bien Hoa Highway.

Alexandre de Rhodes A41

1961, Sept. 5

170	A41	50c rose carmine	.35	.25
171	A41	1pi claret	.50	.30
172	A41	3pi bister brown	.55	.40
173	A41	6pi emerald	1.60	.65
		Nos. 170-173 (4)	3.00	1.60

Alexandre de Rhodes (1591-1660), Jesuit missionary who introduced Roman characters to express the Viet Nam language.

Young Man with Torch, Sage, Pagoda — A42

1961, Oct. 26 — *Perf. 13*

174	A42	50c orange ver	.40	.25
175	A42	1pi brt green	.85	.30
176	A42	3pi rose red	1.00	.40
177	A42	8pi rose lilac & brn	3.25	.75
		Nos. 174-177 (4)	5.50	1.70

Moral Rearmament of Youth Movement.

Temple Dedicated to Confucius — A43

1961, Nov. 4 — *Engr.*

178	A43	1pi brt green	.60	.25
179	A43	2pi rose red	.90	.30
180	A43	5pi olive	2.50	.50
		Nos. 178-180 (3)	4.00	1.05

15th anniversary of UNESCO.

Earth Scraper Preparing Ground for Model Village — A44

1961, Dec. 11 — *Perf. 13*

181	A44	50c dark green	.60	.25
182	A44	1pi Prus bl & car lake	.70	.30
183	A44	2pi olive grn & brn	.90	.40
184	A44	10pi Prus blue	3.25	.65
		Nos. 181-184 (4)	5.45	1.60

Agrarian reform program.

Man Fighting Mosquito and Emblem — A45

1962, Apr. 7 — *Perf. 13*

185	A45	50c brt lilac rose	.45	.25
186	A45	1pi orange	.65	.30
187	A45	2pi emerald	.85	.40
188	A45	6pi ultra	2.00	.65
		Nos. 185-188 (4)	3.95	1.60

WHO drive to eradicate malaria.

Postal Check Center, Saigon — A46

1962, May 15 — *Engr.* — *Perf. 13*

189	A46	70c dull green	.25	.25
190	A46	80c chocolate	.40	.30
191	A46	4pi lilac rose	1.25	.40
192	A46	7pi rose red	3.00	.65
		Nos. 189-192 (4)	4.90	1.60

Inauguration of postal checking service.

Madonna of Vang — A47

1962, July 7

193	A47	50c violet & rose red	.40	.25
194	A47	1pi red brn & indigo	.55	.30
195	A47	2pi brown & rose car	1.00	.40
196	A47	8pi green & dk blue	5.25	.65
		Nos. 193-196 (4)	7.20	1.60

Catholic shrine of the Madonna of Vang.

Armed Guards and Village A48

1962, Oct. 26

197	A48	50c bright red	.55	.25
198	A48	1pi yellow green	.85	.30
199	A48	1.50pi lilac rose	1.10	.40
200	A48	7pi ultra	3.00	.65
		Nos. 197-200 (4)	5.50	1.60

"Strategic village" defense system.

Gougah Waterfall, Dalat — A49

1963, Jan. 3

201	A49	60c orange red	1.25	.30
202	A49	1pi bluish black	2.00	.45

62nd birthday of Pres. Ngo Dinh Diem; Spring Festival.

Trung Sisters' Monument and Vietnamese Women — A50

1963, Mar. 1 — *Engr.*

203	A50	50c green	.25	.25
204	A50	1pi dk carmine rose	.50	.30
205	A50	3pi lilac rose	.60	.45
206	A50	8pi violet blue	1.75	.65
		Nos. 203-206 (4)	3.10	1.65

Issued for Women's Day.

Farm Woman with Grain A51

1963, Mar. 21 — *Perf. 13*

207	A51	50c red	.50	.25
208	A51	1pi dk car rose	.55	.30
209	A51	3pi lilac rose	.80	.45
210	A51	5pi violet	1.40	.75
		Nos. 207-210 (4)	3.25	1.75

FAO "Freedom from Hunger" campaign.

Common Defense Emblem — A52

1963, July 7 — *Engr.* — *Perf. 13*

211	A52	30c bister	.65	.25
212	A52	50c lilac rose	.80	.25
213	A52	3pi brt green	1.25	.30
214	A52	8pi red	2.10	.65
		Nos. 211-214 (4)	4.80	1.45

Common defense effort. The inscription says: "Personalism-Common Progress."

Emblem — A53

1963, Oct. 26 — *Perf. 13*

215	A53	50c rose red	.40	.25
216	A53	1pi emerald	.65	.30
217	A53	4pi purple	1.40	.40
218	A53	5pi orange	2.50	.95
		Nos. 215-218 (4)	4.95	1.90

The fighting soldiers of the Republic.

Centenary Emblem and Map — A54

1963, Nov. 17 — *Engr.*

Cross in Deep Carmine

219	A54	50c Prus blue	.50	.25
220	A54	1pi deep carmine	1.00	.30
221	A54	3pi orange yellow	1.40	.40
222	A54	6pi brown	3.25	.65
		Nos. 219-222 (4)	6.15	1.60

Centenary of International Red Cross.

Constitution and Scales — A55

1963, Dec. 10 — *Perf. 13*

223	A55	70c orange	.25	.25
224	A55	1pi brt rose	.50	.30
225	A55	3pi green	.65	.40
226	A55	8pi ocher	1.75	.65
		Nos. 223-226 (4)	3.15	1.60

15th anniv. of the Universal Declaration of Human Rights.

Danhim Hydroelectric Station — A56

1964, Jan. 15 — *Engr.*

227	A56	40c rose red	.65	.25
228	A56	1pi bister brown	.65	.30
229	A56	3pi violet blue	.95	.40
230	A56	8pi olive green	1.75	.70
		Nos. 227-230 (4)	4.00	1.65

Inauguration of the Danhim Hydroelectric Station.

Atomic Reactor A57

1964, Feb. 3 — *Perf. 13*

231	A57	80c olive	.60	.25
232	A57	1.50pi brown orange	.60	.30
233	A57	3pi chocolate	1.25	.45
234	A57	7pi brt blue	1.60	.75
		Nos. 231-234 (4)	4.05	1.75

Peaceful uses of atomic energy.

Compass Rose, Barograph and UN Emblem — A58

1964, Mar. 23 — *Engr.*

235	A58	50c bister	.25	.25
236	A58	1pi vermilion	.40	.30
237	A58	1.50pi rose claret	.60	.40
238	A58	10pi emerald	1.90	.70
		Nos. 235-238 (4)	3.15	1.65

4th World Meteorological Day, Mar. 23.

South Vietnamese Gesturing to North Vietnamese; Map — A59

1964, July 20 — *Perf. 13*

239	A59	30c dk grn, ultra & mar	1.60	.25
240	A59	50c dk car rose, yel & blk	1.60	.30
241	A59	1.50pi dk bl, dp org & blk	1.60	.65
		Nos. 239-241 (3)	4.80	1.20

10th anniv. of the Day of National Grief, July 20, 1954, when the nation was divided into South and North Viet Nam.

Hatien Beach — A60

1964, Sept. 7   Engr.   Perf. 13½
242 A60 20c bright ultra   .50   .50
243 A60 3pi emerald   1.75   .55

Revolutionists and "Nov. 1" — A61

Designs: 80c, Soldier breaking chain. 3pi,
Broken chain and date: "1-11 1963," vert.

1964, Nov. 1   Engr.   Perf. 13
244 A61 50c red lilac & indigo   .65   .25
245 A61 80c violet & red brn   .70   .30
246 A61 3pi dk blue & red   1.10   .70
     Nos. 244-246 (3)   2.45 1.25

Anniv. of November 1963 revolution.

Temple,
Saigon
A62

Designs: 1pi, Royal tombs, Hué. 1.50pi,
Fishermen and sailboats at Phan-Thiet beach.
3pi, Temple, Gia-Dhin.

1964-66   Size: 35½x26mm   Perf. 13
247 A62 50c fawn, grn & dl
          vio   .70   .25
248 A62 1pi olive bis & ind   1.10   .30
249 A62 1.50pi ol gray & dk sl
          grn   1.00   .40
250 A62 3pi vio, dk sl grn &
          cl   2.00   .65
     Nos. 247-250 (4)   4.80 1.60

**Coil Stamp
Size: 23x17mm**
250A A62 1pi ol bis & ind
         ('66)   6.00 3.50

Issue date: Nos. 247-250, Dec. 2, 1964.

Hung
Vuong and
Au Co with
their
Children
A63

1965, Apr.   Engr.   Perf. 13
251 A63 3pi car lake & org
          red   1.50   .45
252 A63 100pi brown vio & vio   19.00 3.50

Mythological founders of Viet Nam, c. 2000
B.C.

ITU Emblem,
Insulator and TV
Mast — A64

1965, May 17   Engr.
253 A64 1pi olive, dp car & bister   .75   .30
254 A64 3pi henna brn, car & lil   1.75   .45

ITU, centenary.

Buddhist Wheel
of Life and
Flames — A65

1.50pi, Wheel, lotus blossom and world
map, horiz. 3pi, Wheel and Buddhist flag.

Inscribed: "Phat-Giao" (Buddhism)

1965, May 15   Perf. 13
255 A65 50c dark carmine   1.50   .25
256 A65 1.50pi dk blue & ocher   1.50   .30
257 A65 3pi org brn & dk brn   2.25   .45
     Nos. 255-257 (3)   5.25 1.00

Anniversary of Buddha's birth.

ICY Emblem and
Women of
Various
Races — A66

1965, June 26
258 A66 50c bluish blk & bis   1.00   .25
259 A66 1pi dk brn & brn   1.00   .30
260 A66 1.50pi dark red & gray   1.60   .45
     Nos. 258-260 (3)   3.60 1.00

International Cooperation Year.

Ixora — A67

Flowers: 80c, Orchid. 1pi, Chrysanthemum.
1.50pi, Lotus, horiz. 3pi, Plum blossoms.

1965, Sept. 10   Engr.   Perf. 13
261 A67 70c grn, slate grn &
          red   .40   .25
262 A67 80c dk brn, lil & sl grn   .55   .30
263 A67 1pi dk blue & yellow   .70   .40
264 A67 1.50pi sl grn, dl grn &
          gray   1.00   .45
265 A67 3pi slate grn & org   2.10   .75
     Nos. 261-265 (5)   4.75 2.15

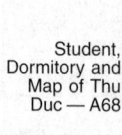

Student,
Dormitory and
Map of Thu
Duc — A68

1965, Oct. 15   Perf. 13
266 A68 50c dark brown   .25   .25
267 A68 1pi bright green   .25   .25
268 A68 3pi crimson   .75   .30
269 A68 7pi dark blue violet   2.00   .65
     Nos. 266-269 (4)   3.25 1.45

Issued to publicize higher education.

Farm Boy
and Girl,
Pig and 4-T
Emblem
A69

4pi, Farm boy with chicken, village and 4-T
flag.

1965, Nov. 25   Engr.   Perf. 13
270 A69 3pi emerald & dk red   1.50   .25
271 A69 4pi dull violet & plum   2.50   .50

10th anniv. of the 4-T Clubs and the
National Congress of Young Farmers.

Basketball
A70

Designs: 1pi, Javelin. 1.50pi, Hand holding
torch, athletic couple. 10pi, Pole vault.

1965, Dec. 14   Engr.   Perf. 13
272 A70 50c dk car & brn org   .60   .25
273 A70 1pi brn org & red brn   .75   .30
274 A70 1.50pi brt green   1.10   .40
275 A70 10pi red lil & brn org   3.00   .75
     Nos. 272-275 (4)   5.45 1.70

Radio
Tower — A71

Radio tower, telephone dial, map of Viet
Nam.

1966, Apr. 24   Engr.   Perf. 13
276 A71 3pi brt blue & brn   .45   .25
277 A71 4pi purple, red & blk   .55   .30

Saigon microwave station.

Loading Hook
and Globe — A72

1966, June 22   Engr.   Perf. 13
278 A72 3pi gray & dk car rose   .40   .25
279 A72 4pi olive & dk purple   .60   .30
280 A72 6pi brt grn & dk blue   1.00   .40
     Nos. 278-280 (3)   2.00   .95

Appreciation of the help given by the free
world.

Hands
Reaching
for
Persecuted
Refugees
A73

1966, July 20
281 A73 3pi brn, vio brn & olive   .50   .25
282 A73 7pi claret, vio brn & dk
          pur   1.25   .30

Refugees from communist oppression.

Paper
Soldiers,
Votive
Offering
A74

Designs: 1.50pi, Man and woman making
offerings. 3pi, Floating candles in paper boats.
5pi, Woman burning paper offerings.

1966, Aug. 30   Engr.   Perf. 13
283 A74 50c red, blk & bis brn   .75   .25
284 A74 1.50pi brown, emer &
          grn   1.25   .30
285 A74 3pi rose red & lake   1.75   .40
286 A74 5pi org brn, bis & dk
          brn   2.50   .65
     Nos. 283-286 (4)   6.25 1.60

Wandering Souls Festival.

Oriental
Two-string
Violin
A75

Vietnamese Instruments: 3pi, Woman playing 16-string guitar. 4pi, Musicians playing
two-string guitars. 7pi, Woman and boy playing flutes.

**1966   Engr.   Perf. 13
Size: 35½x26mm**
287 A75 1pi brown red & brn   .95   .25
288 A75 3pi rose lilac & pur   .95   .30
289 A75 4pi rose brown & brn   1.60   .40
290 A75 7pi dp blue & vio bl   3.50   .65
     Nos. 287-290 (4)   7.00 1.60

**Coil Stamp
Size: 23x17mm**
290A A75 3pi rose lil & pur   3.50 2.50
  b. Booklet pane of 5   30.00
      Complete booklet, 2 #290Ab   70.00

Nos. 287-290 were issued Sept. 28.
Complete booklet contains two vertical
strips of 5 with selvage at either end. These
strips were also sold loose without booklet
cover.

WHO Building,
Geneva, and
Flag — A76

Designs: 50c, WHO Building and emblem,
horiz. 8pi, WHO flag and building.

1966, Oct. 12
291 A76 50c purple & carmine   .25   .25
292 A76 1.50pi red brn, vio bl &
          blk   .25   .30
293 A76 8pi grnsh bl, vio bl &
          brn   2.50 1.10
     Nos. 291-293 (3)   3.00 1.65

Opening of WHO Headquarters, Geneva.

Hand
Holding
Spade,
and
Soldiers
A77

Soldier and
Workers — A78

Designs: 1.50pi, Flag, workers. 4pi, Soldier
and cavalryman.

1966, Nov. 1   Engr.   Perf. 13
294 A77 80c dull brn & red brn   .40   .25
295 A77 1.50pi car rose, yel &
          brn   .85   .30

296 A78 3pi brown & slate grn .85 .40
297 A78 4pi lilac, black & brn 3.00 .65
Nos. 294-297 (4) 5.10 1.60

3rd anniv. of the revolution against the government of Pres. Ngo Dinh Diem.

Symbolic Tree
and UNESCO
Emblem — A79

Designs: 3pi, Globe and olive branches. 7pi, Symbolic temple, horiz.

1966, Dec. 15 Engr. Perf. 13
298 A79 1pi pink, brn & dk car 1.10 .40
299 A79 3pi dp bl, grn & brn org 1.10 .30
300 A79 7pi grnsh bl, dk bl & red 2.75 .65
Nos. 298-300 (3) 4.95 1.20

20th anniv. of UNESCO.

Bitter
Melon
A80

1967, Jan. 12 Engr. Perf. 13
301 A80 50c Cashew, vert. 1.40 .25
302 A80 1.50pi shown 2.10 .30
303 A80 3pi Sweetsop 2.40 .40
304 A80 20pi Areca nuts 6.00 .65
Nos. 301-304 (4) 11.90 1.60

Phan-Boi-Chau — A81

Designs: 20pi, Phan-Chau-Trinh portrait and addressing crowd.

1967, Mar. 24 Engr. Perf. 13
305 A81 1pi mar, red brn & dk brn .75 .25
306 A81 20pi vio, slate grn & blk 2.00 .80

Issued to honor Vietnamese patriots.

Woman
Carrying
Produce
A82

Labor Day: 1pi, Market scene. 3pi, Two-wheeled horse cart. 8pi, Farm scene with water buffalo.

1967, May 1 Engr. Perf. 13
307 A82 50c vio bl, dk bl & ultra .25 .25
308 A82 1pi sl grn & dull pur .30 .30
309 A82 3pi dk carmine .60 .40
310 A82 8pi brt car rose & pur 1.25 .65
Nos. 307-310 (4) 2.40 1.60

Potter, Vases
and
Lamp — A83

Weavers
and
Potters
A84

Designs: 1.50pi, Vase and basket. 35d, Bag and lacquerware.

1967, July 22 Engr. Perf. 13
311 A83 50c red brn, grn & ultra .25 .25
312 A83 1.50pi grnsh bl, car & blk .55 .30
313 A84 3pi red, vio & org brn 1.40 .40
314 A83 35pi bis brn, blk & dk red 4.25 1.40
Nos. 311-314 (4) 6.45 2.35

Issued to publicize Vietnamese handicrafts.

Wedding
Procession
A85

1967, Sept. 18 Engr. Perf. 13
315 A85 3pi rose cl, dk vio & red 1.25 .45

Symbols of
Stage,
Music and
Art — A86

Litho. & Engr.
1967, Oct. 27 Perf. 13
316 A86 10pi bl gray, blk & red 1.50 .55

Issued to publicize the Cultural Institute.

"Freedom and
Justice"
A87

Balloting
A88

"Establishment of Democracy" — A89

1967, Nov. 1 Photo.
317 A87 4pi mag, brn & ocher .95 .25
318 A88 5pi brown, yel & blk 1.25 .30
319 A89 30pi dl lil, indigo & red 3.50 .65
Nos. 317-319 (3) 5.70 1.20

National Day; general elections.

Pagoda and
Lions Emblem
A90

1967, Dec. 5 Photo. Perf. 13½x13
320 A90 3pi multicolored 1.75 1.00

50th anniversary of Lions International.

Teacher with Pupils and Globe — A91

1967, Dec. 10 Perf. 13x13½
321 A91 3pi tan, blk, yel & car 1.75 .65

International Literacy Day, Sept. 8, 1967.

Tractor and
Village — A92

Rural Construction Program: 9pi, Bulldozer and home building. 10pi, Wheelbarrow, tractor and new building. 20pi, Vietnamese and Americans working together.

1968, Jan. 26 Photo. Perf. 13½
322 A92 1pi multicolored .25 .25
323 A92 9pi lt blue & multi 1.00 .25
324 A92 10pi multicolored 1.60 .30
325 A92 20pi yel, red lil & blk 2.10 .65
Nos. 322-325 (4) 4.95 1.45

WHO Emblem — A93

1968, Apr. 7 Photo. Perf. 13½
326 A93 10pi gray grn, blk & yel 2.00 1.00

WHO, 20th anniversary.

Flags of Viet
Nam's
Allies — A94

Designs: 1.50pi, Flags surrounding SEATO emblem. 3pi, Flags, handclasp, globe and map of Viet Nam. 50pi, Flags and handclasp.

1968, June 22 Photo. Perf. 13½
327 A94 1pi multicolored .60 .25
328 A94 1.50pi multicolored 1.25 .30
329 A94 3pi multicolored 2.40 .40
330 A94 50pi multicolored 7.75 .95
Nos. 327-330 (4) 12.00 1.90

Issued to honor Viet Nam's allies.

Three-wheeled Truck and
Tractor — A95

Private Property Ownership: 80c, Farmer, city man and symbols of property. 2pi, Three-wheeled cart, taxi and farmers. 30pi, Taxi, three-wheeled cart and tractor in field.

Inscribed: "HUU-SAN-HOA CONG-NHAN VA NONG-DAN"

1968, Nov. 1 Photo. Perf. 13½
331 A95 80c multicolored .25 .25
332 A95 2pi steel blue & multi .25 .30
333 A95 10pi orange brn & multi 1.10 .45
334 A95 30pi gray blue & multi 3.50 1.25
Nos. 331-334 (4) 5.10 2.25

Human Rights
Flame — A96

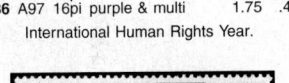

Men of Various
Races — A97

1968, Dec. 10 Photo. Perf. 13½
335 A96 10pi multicolored .90 .30
336 A97 16pi purple & multi 1.75 .40

International Human Rights Year.

UNICEF Emblem, Mother and
Child — A98

6pi, Children flying kite with UNICEF emblem.

1968, Dec. 11
337 A98 6pi multicolored 1.00 .50
338 A98 16pi multicolored 2.00 .80

Workers and
Train — A99

1.50pi, 3pi, Crane, train, map of Viet Nam.

1968, Dec. 15
339 A99 1.50pi multicolored 1.00 .25
340 A99 3pi org, vio bl & grn 1.10 .30
341 A99 9pi multicolored 1.50 .40
342 A99 20pi multicolored 2.75 .65
Nos. 339-342 (4) 6.35 1.60

Reopening of Trans-Viet Nam Railroad.

Farm
Woman — A100

Vietnamese Women: 1pi, Merchant. 3pi, Nurses, horiz. 20pi, Three ladies.

1969, Mar. 23　　Engr.　　Perf. 13
343　A100　50c vio bl, lil & ocher　.25　.25
344　A100　1pi grn, bis & dk brn　.25　.30
345　A100　3pi brown, blk & bl　.55　.40
346　A100　20pi lilac & multi　2.50　1.00
　　　Nos. 343-346 (4)　3.55　1.95

Soldiers and Civilians A101

Family Welcoming Soldier A102

1969, June 1　　Photo.　　Perf. 13
347　A101　2pi multicolored　.25　.25
348　A102　50pi multicolored　3.25　.75

Pacification campaign.

Man Reading Constitution, Scales of Justice A103

Voters, Torch and Scales A104

1969, June 9
349　A103　1pi yel org, yel & blk　.25　.25
350　A104　20pi multicolored　3.00　.50

Constitutional democracy. Phrase on both stamps: "Democratic and Governed by Law."

Mobile Post Office — A105

Mobile Post Office: 3pi, Window service. 4pi, Child with letter. 20pi, Crowd at window and postmark: "15, 12, 67."

1969, July 10
351　A105　1pi multicolored　.25　.25
352　A105　3pi multicolored　.60　.30
353　A105　4pi multicolored　.75　.45
354　A105　20pi ocher & multi　1.50　.75
　　　Nos. 351-354 (4)　3.10　1.75

Installation of the first mobile post office in Viet Nam.

Mnong-gar Woman A106

1pi, Djarai woman. 50pi, Bahnar man.

1969, Aug. 29　　Photo.　　Perf. 13
355　A106　1pi brt pink & multi　.90　.40
356　A106　6pi sky blue & multi　2.10　.65
357　A106　50pi gray & multi　9.00　.95
　　　Nos. 355-357 (3)　12.00　2.00

Ethnic minorities in Viet Nam.

Civilians Becoming Soldiers A107

General Mobilization: 3pi, Bayonet training. 5pi, Guard duty. 10pi, Farewell.

Inscribed: "TONG BONG VIEN"
1969, Sept. 20
358　A107　1.50pi orange & multi　.80　.25
359　A107　3pi purple & multi　1.75　.30
360　A107　5pi blk, red & ocher　2.50　.40
361　A107　10pi pink & multi　3.50　.65
　　　Nos. 358-361 (4)　8.55　1.60

ILO Emblem and Globe — A108

1969, Oct. 29　　Photo.　　Perf. 13
362　A108　6pi blue grn, blk & gray　.60　.30
363　A108　20pi red, blk & gray　1.90　.45

ILO, 50th anniversary.

Pegu House Sparrow — A109

Birds: 6pi, Moluccan munia. 7pi, Great hornbill. 30pi, Old world tree sparrow.

1970, Jan. 15　Photo.　Perf. 12½x14
364　A109　2pi blue & multi　1.00　.35
365　A109　6pi orange & multi　3.00　.70
366　A109　7pi org brn & multi　4.00　.70
367　A109　30pi blue & multi　14.00　2.10
　　　Nos. 364-367 (4)　22.00　3.85

Burning House and Family — A110

Design: 20pi, Family fleeing burning house and physician examining child.

1970, Jan. 31　　Photo.　　Perf. 13
368　A110　10pi multicolored　1.25　.25
369　A110　20pi multicolored　2.00　.30

Mau Than disaster, 1968.

Vietnamese Costumes — A111

Traditional Costumes: 1pi, Man, woman and priest, vert. 2pi, Seated woman with fan. 100pi, Man and woman.

Inscribed: "Y-PHUC CO TRUYEN"
1970, Mar. 13　　Photo.　　Perf. 13
370　A111　1pi lt brown & multi　.25　.25
371　A111　2pi pink & multi　.30　.30
372　A111　3pi ultra & multi　.40　.40
373　A111　100pi multicolored　8.00　2.00
　　　Nos. 370-373 (4)　8.95　2.95

Issued for the Trung Sisters' Festival.

Building Workers, Pagodas and Bridge A112

Rebuilding of Hue: 20pi, Concrete mixers and scaffolds.

1970, June 10　　Litho. & Engr.
374　A112　6pi multicolored　1.00　.30
375　A112　20pi rose lil, brn & bis　1.50　.50

Plower in Rice Field — A113

1970, Aug. 29　　　　Perf. 13
376　A113　6pi multicolored　1.75　.45

"Land to the Tiller" agricultural reform program.

New Building and Scaffold A114

Construction Work — A115

1970, Sept. 15　　Engr.　　Perf. 13
377　A114　8pi pale ol & brn org　1.25　.30
378　A115　16pi brn, indigo & yel　2.75　.45

Reconstruction after 1968 Tet Offensive.

Productivity Year Emblem A116

1970, Oct. 3
379　A116　10pi multicolored　1.75　.45

Asian Productivity Year.

Nguyen-Dinh-Chieu — A117

1970, Nov. 16　　Engr.　　Perf. 13½
380　A117　6pi dull vio, red & brn　1.25　.30
381　A117　10pi grn, red & dk brn　2.00　.45

Nguyen-Dinh-Chieu (1822-1888), poet.

Education Year Emblem — A118

Litho. & Engr.
1970, Nov. 30　　　　　Perf. 13
382　A118　10pi pale brn, yel & blk　1.75　.65

International Education Year.

Parliament Building A119

Design: 6pi, Senate Building.

1970, Dec.
383　A119　6pi lt bl, cit & dk brn　.75　.30
384　A119　10pi multicolored　1.50　.45

6pi issued Dec. 8 for the 6th Cong.; 10pi issued Dec. 9 for the 9th General Assembly of the Asian Interparliamentary Union.

Dancers — A120

Designs: Various Vietnamese dancers and musicians. 6pi and 7pi horizontal.

1971, Jan. 12
385　A120　2pi ultra & multi　.85　.30
386　A120　6pi pale green & multi　2.40　.35
387　A120　7pi pink & multi　2.75　.45
388　A120　10pi brown org & multi　3.00　.50
　　　Nos. 385-388 (4)　9.00　1.60

For surcharge see No. 500.

Farmers and Law — A121

Agrarian Reform Law: 3pi, Tractor and law, dated 26.3.1970. 16pi, Farmers, people rejoicing and law book.

1971, Mar. 26　　Engr.　　Perf. 13
389　A121　2pi vio bl, dk brn & dl org　.25　.25
　a.　Dated "1970"　30.00
390　A121　3pi pale grn, brn & dk bl　.80　.30
391　A121　16pi multicolored　3.50　.45
　　　Nos. 389-391 (3)　4.55　1.00

No. 389 is dated "1971."

For surcharge see No. 482.

Courier on Horseback A122

Design: 6pi, Mounted courier with flag.

Engr. & Photo.
1971, June 6　　　　　Perf. 13
392　A122　2pi violet & multi　.50　.30
393　A122　6pi tan & multi　2.25　.45

Postal history.

Military and Naval Operations on Vietnamese Coast — A123

1971, June 19
394　A123　3pi multi + label　1.00　.45
395　A123　40pi multi + label　5.00　1.00

Armed Forces Day.

Deer — A124

1971, Aug. 20 Engr.
396 A124 9pi shown 1.25 .35
397 A124 30pi Tiger 3.75 .90

Rice Harvest A125

30pi, Threshing and winnowing rice and rice plants. 40pi, Bundling and carrying rice.

1971, Sept. 28 Litho. & Engr. Perf. 13
398 A125 1pi multicolored .25 .30
399 A125 30pi sal pink, dk pur & blk 3.00 .75
400 A125 40pi sepia, yel & grn 3.50 .80
Nos. 398-400 (3) 6.75 1.85

For surcharge see No. 496.

Inauguration of UPU Building, Bern — A126

1971, Nov. 9 Engr. Perf. 13
401 A126 20pi green & multi 2.50 .75

Fish — A127

Various Fish; 2pi vertical.

1971, Nov. 16 Photo. & Engr.
402 A127 2pi multicolored 2.00 .30
403 A127 10pi violet & multi 4.00 .45
404 A127 100pi lilac & multi 27.50 2.40
Nos. 402-404 (3) 33.50 3.15

Mailman and Woman on Water Buffalo A128

Rural Mail: 10pi, Bird carrying letter. 20pi, Mailman with bicycle delivering mail to villagers.

Inscribed: "PHAT TRIEN BUU-CHINH NONG THON"

1971, Dec. 20 Engr. Perf. 13
405 A128 5pi multicolored .65 .30
406 A128 10pi multicolored 1.10 .45
407 A128 20pi multicolored 2.00 .65
Nos. 405-407 (3) 3.75 1.40

Trawler Fishermen, and Fish — A129

Publicity for Fishing Industry: 7pi, Net fishing from boat. 50d, Trawler with seine.

1972, Jan. 2 Engr. Perf. 13
408 A129 4pi pink, blk & blue .40 .25
409 A129 7pi lt blue, blk & red .65 .30
410 A129 50pi multicolored 3.50 1.60
Nos. 408-410 (3) 4.55 2.15

King Quang Trung (1752-1792) — A130

1972, Jan. 28 Perf. 13½
411 A130 6pi red & multi 1.10 .35
a. Booklet pane of 10 100.00
412 A130 20pi black & multi 3.50 1.20

No. 411a is imperf. horizontally.

Road Workers A131

1972, Feb. 4
413 A131 3pi multicolored .50 .30
414 A131 8pi multicolored 1.50 .45

Community development.

Rice Farming A132

1972, Mar. 26 Engr. Perf. 13½
415 A132 1pi shown .25 .25
416 A132 10pi Wheat farming 2.00 .30

Farmers' Day.

Plane over Dalat — A133

1972, Apr. 18 Engr. & Photo.
417 A133 10pi shown 2.00 .50
418 A133 10pi over Ha-tien 2.00 .50
419 A133 10pi over Hue 2.00 .50
420 A133 10pi over Saigon 2.00 .50
a. Block of 4, #417-420 18.00 4.00
421 A133 25pi like No. 417 4.50 .75
422 A133 25pi like No. 418 4.50 .75
423 A133 25pi like No. 419 5.00 .75
424 A133 25pi like No. 420 5.00 .75
a. Block of 4, #421-424 40.00 10.00
Nos. 417-424 (8) 27.00 5.00

20 years Air Viet Nam.

Scholar A134

20pi, Teacher, pupils. 50pi, Scholar, scroll.

1972, May 5 Engr. & Litho.
425 A134 5pi multicolored .40 .30

Engr.
426 A134 20pi lt green & multi 1.75 .50
427 A134 50pi pink & multi 4.75 .90
Nos. 425-427 (3) 6.90 1.70

Ancient letter writing art.

Armed Farmer — A135

6pi, Civilian rifleman & Self-defense Forces emblem, horiz. 20pi, Man, woman training with rifles.

Engr. & Litho.
1972, June 15 Perf. 13
428 A135 2pi brt rose & multi 1.25 .35
429 A135 6pi multicolored 2.00 .50
430 A135 20pi lt violet & multi 2.75 .60
Nos. 428-430 (3) 6.00 1.45

Civilian Self-defense Forces.

Hands Holding Safe — A136

1972, July 10
431 A136 10pi lt blue & multi 1.75 .30
432 A136 25pi lt green & multi 3.25 .45

Treasury Bonds campaign.

Frontier Guard — A137

Designs: 10pi, 3 guards and horse, horiz. 40pi, Marching guards, horiz.

Engr. & Litho.
1972, Aug. 14 Perf. 13
433 A137 10pi olive & multi 1.00 .30
434 A137 30pi buff & multi 2.50 .50
435 A137 40pi lt blue & multi 3.25 .70
Nos. 433-435 (3) 6.75 1.50

Historic frontier guards.

Soldier Helping Wounded Man — A138

Designs: 16pi, Soldier on crutches and flowers. 100pi, Veterans' memorial, map and flag.

1972, Sept. 1
436 A138 9pi olive & multi 1.00 .35
437 A138 16pi yellow & multi 1.40 .45
438 A138 100pi lt blue & multi 7.50 1.40
Nos. 436-438 (3) 9.90 2.20

For surcharge see No. 483.

Tank, Memorial, Flag and Map — A139

Soldiers and Map of Viet Nam — A140

1972, Nov. 25 Litho. Perf. 13
439 A139 5pi multicolored 8.00 .30
440 A140 10pi ultra & multi 12.00 .45

Victory at Binh-Long.

Book Year Emblem and Globe — A141

Designs: 4pi, Emblem, books circling globe. 5pi, Emblem, books and globe.

1972, Nov. 30
441 A141 2pi dp carmine & multi 1.00 .25
442 A141 4pi blue & multi 1.60 .30
443 A141 5pi yellow bister & multi 2.50 .45
Nos. 441-443 (3) 5.10 1.00

International Book Year.

Liberated Vietnamese Family — A142

1973, Feb. 18 Litho. Perf. 13
444 A142 10pi yellow & multi 2.25 1.20

To celebrate the 200,000th returnee.

Soldiers Raising Vietnamese Flag — A143

Design: 10pi, Victorious soldiers and map of demilitarized zone, horiz.

1973, Feb. 24 Litho. Perf. 13
445 A143 3pi lilac & multi 1.75 .75
446 A143 10pi yellow grn & multi 2.25 1.50

Victory at Quang Tri.

Satellite, Storm over Viet Nam — A144

1973, Mar. 23 Litho. Perf. 12½x12
447 A144 1pi lt blue & multi 1.25 .60

World Meteorological Day.
For surcharge see No. 497.

Farmers with Tractor, Symbol of Law — A145

Farmer Plowing with Water Buffalos A146

Pres. Thieu Holding Agrarian Reform Law A147

1973, Mar. 26 *Litho.* *Perf. 12½x12*
448 A145 2pi lt green & multi 3.00 .60
449 A146 5pi orange & multi 3.00 .60
Perf. 11
450 A147 10pi blue & multi 90.00 30.00
Nos. 448-450 (3) 96.00 31.20

3rd anniv. of the agrarian reform law; 5-year plan for rural development.
Value for No. 450 is for stamp with first day cancel. Commercially used examples are worth substantially more.
See No. 475.

INTERPOL Emblem and Headquarters A148

2pi, INTERPOL emblem. 25pi, INTERPOL emblem, side view of Headquarters.

1973, Apr. 8 *Litho.* *Perf. 12½x12*
451 A148 1pi olive & multi .25 .25
452 A148 2pi yellow & multi .30 .30
453 A148 25pi ocher, lilac & brn 4.75 .45
Nos. 451-453 (3) 5.30 1.00

Intl. Criminal Police Org., 50th anniv.
For surcharge see No. 498.

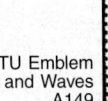

ITU Emblem and Waves A149

2pi, Globe and waves. 3pi, ITU emblem.

1973, May 17
454 A149 1pi dull blue & multi .40 .25
455 A149 2pi brt blue & multi .85 .30
456 A149 3pi orange & multi 1.25 .45
Nos. 454-456 (3) 2.50 1.00

World Telecommunications Day.
For surcharge see No. 499.

Globe, Hand Holding House — A150

Men Building Pylon — A151

Design: 10pi, Fish in net, symbols of agriculture, industry and transportation.

1973, Nov. 6 *Litho.* *Perf. 12x12½*
457 A150 8pi gray & multi 1.00 .25
458 A150 10pi vio bl, blk & gray 1.25 .30
459 A151 15pi blk, org & lil rose 2.10 .45
Nos. 457-459 (3) 4.35 1.00

National development.

For surcharge see No. 514.

Water Buffalos A152

1973, Dec. 20 *Litho.* *Perf. 12½x12*
460 A152 5pi shown 1.50 .50
461 A152 10pi Water buffalo 2.50 .75

Human Rights Flame, Three Races A153

Design: 100pi, Human Rights flame, scales and people, vert.

1973, Dec. 29 *Perf. 12½x12, 12x12½*
462 A153 15pi ultra & multi 1.00 .25
463 A153 100pi green & multi 3.25 .50

25th anniv. of Universal Declaration of Human Rights.

"25" and WHO Emblem A154

Design: 15pi, WHO emblem, diff.

1973, Dec. 31 *Perf. 12½x12*
464 A154 8pi orange, bl & brn 1.00 .30
465 A154 15pi lt brn, bl & brt pink 1.50 .45

25th anniversary of WHO.
For surcharge see No. 515.

Sampan Ferry A155

Design: 10pi, Sampan ferry (different).

1974, Jan. 13 *Litho.* *Perf. 14x13½*
466 A155 5pi lt blue & multi 1.75 .30
467 A155 10pi yellow grn & multi 2.50 .70

Sampan ferry women.

Soldiers of 7 Nations A156

American War Memorial A157

Map of South Viet Nam and Allied Flags — A158

Design: No. 469, Soldiers and flags of South Viet Nam, Korea, US, Australia New Zealand, Thailand and Philippines. Same flags shown on 8pi and 60pi.

1974, Jan. 28 *Perf. 12½x12, 12x12½*
468 A156 8pi multicolored .65 .25
469 A156 15pi lt brown & multi 1.40 .30
470 A157 15pi multicolored 1.40 .30
471 A158 60pi multicolored 4.00 .60
Nos. 468-471 (4) 7.45 1.45

In honor of South Viet Nam's allies.
For surcharge see No. 516.

Trung Sisters on Elephants Fighting Chinese A159

1974, Feb. 27 *Litho.* *Perf. 12½x12*
472 A159 8pi green, citron & blk 1.50 .25
473 A159 15pi dp orange & multi 2.00 .30
474 A159 80pi ultra, pink & blk 3.75 .45
Nos. 472-474 (3) 7.25 1.00

Trung Trac and Trung Nhi, queens of Viet Nam, 39-43 A.D. Day of Vietnamese Women.

Pres. Thieu Type of 1973 and

Farmers Going to Work — A160

Woman Farmer Holding Rice — A161

1974, Mar. 26 *Litho.* *Perf. 14*
475 A147 10pi blue & multi 1.50 .30
Perf. 12½x12, 12x12½
476 A160 20pi yellow & multi 1.50 .45
477 A161 70pi blue & multi 12.00 1.50
Nos. 475-477 (3) 15.00 2.25

Agriculture Day. Size of No. 475 is 31x50mm, No. 450 is 34x54mm and printed on thick paper. No. 475 has been extensively redrawn and first line of inscription in bottom panel changed to "26 THANG BA."
Value for No. 477 is for stamp with first day cancel. Commercially used examples are worth substantially more.

Hung Vuong with Bamboo Tallies A162

Flag Inscribed: Hung Vuong, Founder of Kingdom A163

1974, Apr. 2 *Perf. 14x13½*
478 A162 20pi yellow & multi 1.60 .45
479 A163 100pi olive & multi 5.50 .80

Hung Vuong, founder of Vietnamese nation and of Hông-Bang Dynasty (2879-258 B.C.).

National Library A164

New National Library Building: 15pi, Library, right facade and Phoenix.

1974, Apr. 14
480 A164 10pi orange, brn & blk 1.25 .75
481 A164 15pi multicolored 1.50 1.20

Nos. 391 and 437 Srchd. with New Value and Two Bars in Red
1974 *Perf. 13*
482 A121 25pi on 16pi multi 10.00 2.75
483 A138 25pi on 16pi multi 5.00 2.25

Memorial Tower, Saigon — A165

Globe, Crane Lifting Crate — A167

Crane with Flags, Globe and Map of Viet Nam — A166

Perf. 12x12½, 12½x12
1974, June 22 *Litho.*
484 A165 10pi blue & multi .75 .35
485 A166 20pi multicolored 1.75 .45
486 A167 60pi yellow & multi 5.50 .60
Nos. 484-486 (3) 8.00 1.40

International Aid Day.

Sun and Views of Saigon, Dalat Hué A168

Cau-Bong Bridge, Nha Trang A169

Thien-Mu Pagoda, Hué — A170

1974, July 12 *Perf. 14x13½, 13½x14*
487 A168 5pi blue & multi 1.10 .30
488 A169 10pi blue & multi 1.10 .60
489 A170 15pi red, yellow & multi 1.90 1.00
Nos. 487-489 (3) 4.10 1.90

Tourist publicity.

Rhynchostylis Gigantea — A171

Orchids: 20pi, Cypripedium caliosum, vert. 200pi, Dendrobium nobile.

1974, Aug. 18
490 A171 10pi blue & multi .35 .40
491 A171 20pi yellow & multi .40 .45
492 A171 200pi bister & multi 6.50 1.25
Nos. 490-492 (3) 7.25 2.10

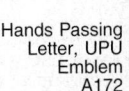

Hands Passing
Letter, UPU
Emblem
A172

UPU Emblem and
Woman — A173

UPU Cent.: 30pi, World map, bird, UPU
emblem.

Perf. 12½x12, 12x12½
1974, Oct. 9 | | | **Litho.**
493 | A172 | 20pi ultra & multi | .30 | .30
494 | A172 | 30pi orange & multi | .65 | .45
495 | A173 | 300pi gray & multi | 4.25 | 1.25
 | | Nos. 493-495 (3) | 5.20 | 2.00

**Nos. 398, 447, 451, 454, 387 Srchd.
with New Value and Two Bars in
Red**

1974-75
496 | A125 | 25pi on 1pi multi | 16.00 | 5.00
497 | A144 | 25pi on 1pi multi | 16.00 | 5.00
498 | A148 | 25pi on 1pi multi | 16.00 | 5.00
499 | A149 | 25pi on 1pi multi | 22.50 | 9.00
500 | A120 | 25pi on 1pi multi | 19.00 | 5.00
 | | Nos. 496-500 (5) | 89.50 | 29.00

Issued: #496, 498, 1/1/75; others, 11/18/74.

Hien Lam
Pavilion,
Hué
A174

Throne,
Imperial
Palace,
Hué
A175

Water
Pavilion,
Hué
A176

1975, Jan. 5 Litho. Perf. 14x13½
501 | A174 | 25pi multicolored | 1.50 | 1.50
502 | A175 | 30pi multicolored | 2.25 | 2.00
503 | A176 | 60pi multicolored | 2.75 | 2.25
 | | Nos. 501-503 (3) | 6.50 | 5.75

Historic sites.

Symbol of Youth,
Children Holding
Flower — A177

Family and
Emblem
A178

1975, Jan. 14 **Perf. 11½**
504 | A177 | 20pi blue & multi | 3.50 | .35
 | | **Perf. 12½x12** | |
505 | A178 | 70pi yellow & multi | 3.50 | .35

Intl. Conf. on Children & Natl. Development.

Unicorn
Dance
A179

Boy Lighting
Firecracker
A180

Bringing New
Year Gifts and
Wishes — A181

Perf. 14x13½, 13½x14
1975, Jan. 26 **Litho.**
506 | A179 | 20pi multicolored | 2.50 | .35
507 | A180 | 30pi blue & multi | 3.00 | .50
508 | A181 | 100pi bister & multi | 7.00 | 1.00
 | | Nos. 506-508 (3) | 12.50 | 1.85

Lunar New Year, Tet.

A182

A183

A184

Designs: 25pi, Military chief from play "San
Hau." 40pi, Scene from "Tam Ha Nam Duong."
100pi, Warrior Luu-Kim-Dinn.

1975, Feb. 23
509 | A182 | 25pi rose & multi | 1.25 | .45
510 | A183 | 40pi lt green & mul-
 | | ti | 2.00 | .45
511 | A184 | 100pi violet & multi | 6.75 | .75
 | | Nos. 509-511 (3) | 10.00 | 1.65

National theater.

Produce, Map
of Viet Nam,
Ship — A185

Irrigation
Project
A186

1975, Mar. 26 Litho. Perf. 12½x12
512 | A185 | 10pi multicolored | 1.75 | .75
513 | A186 | 50pi multicolored | 5.25 | 1.20

Agriculture Day; 5th anniv. of Agrarian
Reform Law.

**Nos. 457, 464, 468 Srchd. with New
Value and Two Bars in Red**

1975
514 | A150 | 10pi on 8pi multi | 30.00 | 10.00
515 | A154 | 10pi on 8pi multi | 19.00 | 6.00
516 | A156 | 25pi on 8pi multi | 9.00 | 4.00
 | | Nos. 514-516 (3) | 58.00 | 20.00

In the 1980's a number of South Viet
Nam stamps appeared on the market.
These apparently had been printed
before the collapse of the Republic but
saw no postal use. These include, but
are not limited to, sets of two for western electric and for rural electric, one
each for history, library, New Year and
cows, a set of three for transportation
and a set of four for economic
development.

SEMI-POSTAL STAMPS

Type of 1952
Surcharged in
Carmine

Perf. 12x12½
1952, Nov. 10 **Unwmk.**
B1 | A3 | 1.50pi + 50c bl, yel &
 | | brn | 4.00 | 3.25
 | Never hinged | | 10.00

The surtax was for the Red Cross.

> Catalogue values for unused
> stamps in this section, from this
> point to the end of the section, are
> for Never Hinged items. Because
> of the tropical conditions, never
> hinged stamps must also be free
> of wrinkles, toning, and any other
> disturbance.

Sabers and
Flag — SP1

1952, Dec. 21 Engr. Perf. 13
B2 | SP1 | 3.30pi + 1.70pi dp clar-
 | | et | 2.50 | 2.25

The surtax was for the Wounded Soldiers'
Aid Organization.

X-ray
Camera
and Patient
SP2

1960, Aug. 1 **Perf. 13**
B3 | SP2 | 3pi + 50c bl grn & red | 1.50 | .90

The surtax was for the Anti-Tuberculosis
Foundation.

AIR POST STAMPS

> Catalogue values for unused
> stamps in this section, from this
> point to the end of the section, are
> for Never Hinged items. Because
> of the tropical conditions, never
> hinged stamps must also be free
> of wrinkles, toning, and any other
> disturbance.

AP1

AP2

Perf. 13½x12½
1952-53 | | **Unwmk.** | **Photo.**
C1 | AP1 | 3.30pi dk brn red & pale
 | | yel grn | 1.00 | .50
C2 | AP1 | 4pi brown & yellow | 1.50 | .35
C3 | AP1 | 5.10pi dk vio bl & sal
 | | pink | 1.50 | .75
C4 | AP2 | 6.30pi yellow & car | 1.50 | .85
 | | Nos. C1-C4 (4) | 5.50 | 2.45

Issued: #C2, 11/24/53; others, 3/8/52.

Dragon
AP3

Fish — AP4

1952, Sept. 3 Engr. Perf. 13
C5 | AP3 | 40c red | 1.40 | .35
C6 | AP3 | 70c green | 2.40 | .50
C7 | AP3 | 80c ultra | 2.40 | .50
C8 | AP3 | 90c brown | 2.40 | .50
C9 | AP4 | 3.70pi deep magenta | 5.25 | .75
 | | Nos. C5-C9 (5) | 13.85 | 2.60

Nos. C5-C9 exist imperforate in a souvenir
booklet. Value, $175.

South Viet Nam

Phoenix — AP5

1955, Sept. 7

C10	AP5	4pi violet & lil rose	3.25	2.25

Crane
Carrying
Letter
AP6

1960, Dec. 20.   *Perf. 13*

C11	AP6	1pi olive	.90	.45
C12	AP6	4pi green & dk blue	2.10	.60
C13	AP6	5pi ocher & purple	2.50	.75
C14	AP6	10pi deep magenta	4.50	1.20
		Nos. C11-C14 (4)	10.00	3.00

POSTAGE DUE STAMPS

Catalogue values for unused stamps in this section, from this point to the end of the section, are for Never Hinged items. Because of the tropical conditions, never hinged stamps must also be free of wrinkles, toning, and any other disturbance.

Temple Lion — D1

Perf. 13x13½

1952, June 16   Typo.   Unwmk.

J1	D1	10c red & green	.85	.60
J2	D1	20c green & yellow	1.10	.80
J3	D1	30c purple & orange	1.40	1.00
J4	D1	40c dk grn & sal rose	1.90	1.25
J5	D1	50c dp carmine & gray	2.50	1.75
J6	D1	1pi blue & silver	4.25	3.00
		Nos. J1-J6 (6)	12.00	8.40

South Viet Nam

Dragon — D2

1955-56

J7	D2	2pi red vio & org	.40	.30
J8	D2	3pi violet & grnsh bl	.55	.40
J9	D2	5pi violet & yellow	.60	.45
J10	D2	10pi dk green & car	.90	.65
J11	D2	20pi red & brt grn ('56)	2.00	1.50
J12	D2	30pi brt grn & yel ('56)	3.00	2.25
J13	D2	50pi dk red brn & yel ('56)	6.00	4.50
J14	D2	100pi pur & yel ('56)	12.00	9.00
		Nos. J7-J14 (8)	25.45	19.05

Nos. J11-J14 inscribed "BUU-CHINH" instead of "TIMBRE-TAXE."

Atlas Moth — D3

Design: 3pi, 5pi, 10pi, Three butterflies.

1968, Aug. 20   Photo.   *Perf. 13½x13*

J15	D3	50c multicolored	3.00	.90
J16	D3	1pi multicolored	3.00	1.00
J17	D3	2pi multicolored	6.00	2.00
J18	D3	3pi multicolored	8.00	3.00
J19	D3	5pi multicolored	14.00	4.75
J20	D3	10pi multicolored	18.00	6.75
		Nos. J15-J20 (6)	52.00	18.40

Nos. J15-J18 Srchd. with New Value and Two Bars in Red

1974, Oct. 1

J21	D3	5pi on 3pi multi	2.00	1.50
J22	D3	10pi on 50c multi	2.00	1.50
J23	D3	40pi on 1pi multi	2.00	1.50
J24	D3	60pi on 2pi multi	2.00	1.50
		Nos. J21-J24 (4)	8.00	6.00

MILITARY STAMPS

Catalogue values for unused stamps in this section, from this point to the end of the section, are for Never Hinged items. Because of the tropical conditions, never hinged stamps must also be free of wrinkles, toning, and any other disturbance.

Soldier
Guarding
Village
M1

Rouletted 7½

1961, June   Unwmk.   Litho.

M1	M1	och, brn, dk grn & blk	4.00	1.50

1961, Sept.   Typo.

M2	M1	org yel, dk grn & brn	4.00	1.50

Bottom inscription on No. M1 is black, brown on No. M2.

Battle and
Refugees
M2

1969, Feb. 22   Litho.   *Imperf.*

M3	M2	red & green	65.00	60.00
a.		Booklet pane of 10	700.00	

VIET NAM, DEMOCRATIC REPUBLIC

(North Viet Nam)

LOCATION — In eastern Indo-China
GOVT. — Republic
AREA — 61,293 sq. mi.
POP. — 18,800,000 (1968 est.)
CAPITAL — Hanoi

Beginning in 1946, the Communist Viet Minh fought the French in a guerrilla war that ended with the French defeat at Dien Bien Phu in 1954. In an agreement signed in Geneva on July 21, 1954, Viet Nam was partitioned at the 17th parallel. The government in Hanoi controlled the north, and engaged in another protracted military campaign against American and South Vietnamese forces that led to the official reunification of the country under Communist control on July 2, 1976.

100 cents = 1 Dong
100 Xu = 1 Dong (1959)

All stamps are without gum unless otherwise indicated. Values for stamps with gum are for Never Hinged items.

Watermark

Wmk. 376 — "R de C"

VIET MINH ISSUES

Stamps and Types of Indo-China Overprinted or Surcharged

No. 236 Overprinted

Printing Methods and Perfs as Before

1945-46   Without Gum

1L1	A41	1pi yel grn (Yersin)	8.00	20.00

Nos. 238-239 (Rhodes) Ovptd.

1L2	A43	15c dk vio brn, perf. 11½	2.25	3.00
a.		Perf. 12	2.25	3.00
b.		Perf. 11½, green overprint	8.00	8.00
1L3	A43	30c org brn, perf. 11½	2.25	2.25
a.		Perf. 13½	4.00	4.00
b.		Perf. 12	24.00	—

No. 242 Overprinted

1L4	A44	50c dl red (Athlete)	16.00	20.00

No. 241 Ovptd.

1L5	A44	10c dk vio brn & yel (Athlete)	6.50	8.00

Nos. 218-222 (Petain) Overprinted

1L6	A32	3c olive brn, perf. 11½	8.00	8.00
a.		Perf. 12x14	5.00	
b.		Perf. 14	24.00	
1L7	A32	6c rose red	2.40	2.40
1L8	A32	10c dull grn (R)	5.00	
1L9	A32	40c dk bl (R)	4.00	8.00
1L10	A32	40c slate bl (R)	8.00	16.00
		Nos. 1L6-1L10 (5)	27.40	34.40

Nos. 245-246 and Type (Pavie) Overprinted

1L11	A46	4c org yel	2.40	2.40
1L12	A46	10c dl grn	4.00	4.75
1L13	A46	20c dark red	2.40	2.40
		Nos. 1L11-1L13 (3)	8.80	9.55

No. 165A Overprinted "VIET NAM DAN CHU CONG HOA" with "BUU CHINH" and Slanted Lines Obliterator

1L14	A22	25c dk bl (Planting Rice, R), top line 18 mm wide	80.00	90.00
a.		Top line 20 mm wide	67.50	9.00

Nos. 1L14-1L14a issued with gum.

No. 232 (Courbet) Overprinted

1L15	A39	3c lt brn	1.60	1.60
1L16	A39	6c car rose	1.60	1.60

No. 261 (Lagree) Overprinted Vertically

1L17	A52	40c brt bl	4.00	12.00

Nos. 253-255 (Doumer) Overprinted

1L18	A50	2c red vio	1.60	1.60
1L19	A50	4c lt brn	1.60	1.60
1L20	A50	10c yel grn	4.00	12.00
a.		"HANH-PHUC" inverted	22.00	
		Nos. 1L18-1L20 (3)	7.20	15.20

No. 217 (Petain)
Overprinted

Nos. 256-258
(Charner)
Overprinted

1L21	A32	1c blk brn	1.60	1.60
1L22	A51	10c green	4.00	12.00
1L23	A51	20c brn red	4.00	12.00
1L24	A51	1pi pale yel grn	8.00	20.00
		Nos. 1L21-1L24 (4)	17.60	45.60

**No. 230 and Type (Genouilly)
Overprinted**

| 1L25 | A37 | 5c dull brown | 1.60 | 1.60 |
| 1L26 | A37 | 6c carmine rose | 2.75 | 2.75 |

No. 210-212
(Sihanouk)
Surcharged

1L27	A28	5d on 1c red org (Bl)	35.00	35.00
1L28	A28	10d on 6c violet (R)	40.00	40.00
1L29	A28	15d on 25c dp ultra (R)	40.00	40.00
		Nos. 1L27-1L29 (3)	115.00	115.00

Nos. 225-226
(Sihanouk)
Surcharged

| 1L30 | A34 | 50xu on 1c brown | 3.25 | 4.00 |
| 1L31 | A35 | 2d on 6c car rose | 24.00 | 24.00 |

Nos. 213-214
(Elephant)
Surcharged

| 1L32 | A29 | 2d on 3c reddish brn (G) | 35.00 | 35.00 |
| 1L33 | A29 | 4d on 6c crim (G) | 35.00 | 35.00 |

Nos. 247-248
(Pasquier)
Surcharged
Vertically

| 1L34 | A47 | 1d on 5c brn vio | 2.40 | 3.25 |
| 1L35 | A47 | 2d on 10c dl grn | 3.25 | 4.00 |

No. B30 (Cathedral) Surcharged

| 1L36 | SP7 | 5d on 15c+60c brn vio | 32.50 | 32.50 |

Nos. 259-260
(Lagree)
Surcharged
Vertically

| 1L37 | A52 | 30xu on 1c dl gray brn (R) | 2.40 | 2.75 |
| 1L38 | A52 | 3d on 15c dl rose vio | 4.75 | 5.50 |

**Nos. 243-244 (La Grandiere)
Surcharged**

| 1L39 | A45 | 1d on 5c dk brn (Bl) | 6.50 | 6.50 |
| 1L40 | A45 | 4d on 1c dull brn | 3.25 | 4.75 |

Type of
1943
(Garnier)
Srchd.

| 1L41 | A42 | 30xu on 15c brn vio (R) | 1.60 | 2.40 |

**No. 242 (Garnier) Surcharged with
New Value, "VIET-NAM DAN CHU
CONG HOA BUU-CHINH," Wavy &
Straight Line Obliterators**

| 1L42 | A42 | 5d on 1c dull ol bis | 4.75 | 5.50 |

**Nos. 249-252 (De Lanessan, Van
Vollenhoven) Surcharged**

No. 1L43

No. 1L44

No. 1L45

No. 1L46

1L43	A49	50xu on 1c dl gray brn	4.00	4.75
1L44	A48	60xu on 1c ol brn	4.00	4.00
1L45	A48	1.60d on 10c green	2.40	3.25
1L46	A49	3d on 15c dl rose vio (Bl)	3.25	4.00
		Nos. 1L43-1L46 (4)	13.65	16.00

**Nos. B30-B31 (Cathedral)
Surcharged**

| 1L47 | SP7 | 2d on 15c+60c brn vio | 20.00 | 20.00 |
| 1L48 | SP7 | 3d on 40c+1.10pi blue | 20.00 | 20.00 |

No. 234 (Yersin)
Surcharged

| 1L49 | A41 | +2d on 6c car rose | 4.00 | 5.50 |

No. 233 (Behaine)
Surcharged

| 1L50 | A40 | +3d on 20c dull red | 7.00 | 7.00 |

**No. 215 (Saigon Fair) Surcharged
with Added Value, "VIET-NAM DAN
CHU CONG HOA Chong nan mu
chu" & Wavy Line**

| 1L51 | A30 | +4d on 6c car rose | 4.00 | 4.75 |

**No. 229 (Natl. Revolution)
Surcharged with Added Value,
"VIET-NAM DAN-CHU CONGHOA
Doi song moi," and "X" Obliterator**

| 1L52 | A36 | +4d on 6c car rose | 8.00 | 8.00 |

Nos. 213-214
Surcharged

| 1L53 | A29 | +5d on 3c reddish brown | 6.50 | 8.00 |
| 1L54 | A29 | +10d on 6c crimson | 6.50 | 8.00 |

Nos. 216, 224
Surcharged

| 1L55 | A31 | 30xu +3d on 6c (Nam-Phuong) | 1.60 | 2.40 |

Perf. 13½

| 1L56 | A33 | 30xu +3d on 6c (Bao-Dai) | 2.00 | 2.40 |
| a. | | Perf. 12 | 25.00 | |

Ho Chi Minh — VM1

1946		Litho.	Unwmk.	*Perf. 11½*
			Without Gum	
1L57	VM1	1h green	.75	.75
1L58	VM1	3h rose	.75	.75
1L59	VM1	9h yellow bister	.75	.75

With Added Inscription

1L60	VM1	4h +6h Prussian blue	2.60	4.00
1L61	VM1	6h +9h brown violet	2.60	4.00
		Nos. 1L57-1L61 (5)	7.45	10.25

Ho Chi
Minh — VM2

1948		Typo.	*Perf. 7 Rough*	
		Thin, Rough, Brown Paper		
1L62	VM2	2d brown	20.00	160.00
1L63	VM2	5d red	20.00	160.00

For surcharge and overprints see Nos. 50,
O6-O7.

DEMOCRATIC REPUBLIC
OF VIET NAM

From 1945-2002, all stamps are
without gum unless otherwise
indicated. Values for stamps with
gum are for Never Hinged items.

Many North Vietnamese stamps
are roughly perforated, especially
issues before 1958.

Ho Chi
Minh, Map
of Vietnam
A1

1951-55 Unwmk. Litho. Imperf.
1	A1	100d brown	26.00	26.00
a.		Perf. 11¼ ('55)	26.00	26.00
2	A1	100d green	26.00	26.00
a.		Perf. 11¼ ('55)	26.00	26.00
3	A1	200d red	26.00	26.00
a.		Imperf. ('55)	26.00	26.00
		Nos. 1-3 (3)	78.00	78.00

Nos. 1-3 printed on thin semi-transparent paper.

Nos. 1-3 used values are for cto. Postally used examples are worth about 5 times these values.

Counterfeits exist.

For surcharges, see Nos. 9-14, 36-38, and note before No. J1.

Blacksmith — A2

1953-55 Perf. 11¼
4	A2	100d violet	4.00	3.00
5	A2	500d brown	6.00	8.00

Issued: 100d, 6/53. 500d, 2/55.

Georgi Malenkov, Ho Chi Minh, Mao Tse-tung and Flags — A3

1954-55 Perf. 11¼
6	A3	50d brown & red, brnish	25.00	35.00
7	A3	100d red	25.00	30.00
8	A3	100d yellow & red, brnish	37.50	37.50
		Nos. 6-8 (3)	87.50	102.50

Issued: 50d, 10/54; #7, 1/54; #8, 4/55.

No. 7 printed on thin, white paper.

Nos. 1-3 Surcharged in Red or Blue

1954, Oct. Imperf.
9	A1	10d on 100d brown	22.50	32.50
10	A1	10d on 100d green	22.50	32.50

Perf. 11
11	A1	20d on 200d red (Bl)	22.50	42.50
		Nos. 9-11 (3)	67.50	107.50

Nos. 1-3 Surcharged in Black, Red or Blue

1954, Oct. Imperf.
12	A1	10d on 100d brown (Bk, R or Bl)	26.00	35.00
13	A1	10d on 100d green (Bk, R or Bl)	26.00	35.00

Perf. 11
14	A1	20d on 200d red (Bk or Bl)	60.00	75.00
		Nos. 12-14 (3)	112.00	145.00

Nos. 9-14 exist with counterfeit surcharges, counterfeit surcharges on counterfeit stamps, and with fantasy surcharges.

Victory at Dien Bien Phu A4

1954-56 Perf. 11¼
17	A4	10d red brn & yel brn	25.00	30.00
a.		Imperf	110.00	110.00
18	A4	50d red & org yel	25.00	30.00
a.		Imperf	25.00	40.00
19	A4	150d brown & blue	25.00	35.00
a.		Imperf	25.00	40.00
		Nos. 17-19 (3)	75.00	95.00

Issued: Imperfs, 10/54; others, 1956. See #O5.

Used values for Nos. 17-19 are for postally used examples. The 10d exists cto, perf or imperf. Value about 1/10 those shown above.

Liberation of Hanoi — A5

1955, Jan. 1 Perf. 11½
20	A5	10d lt blue & bl	6.50	6.50
21	A5	50d dk grn & grn	8.00	8.00
22	A5	150d rose & brn red	10.00	12.00
		Nos. 20-22 (3)	24.50	26.50

Nos. 20-22 used values are for postally used examples. Cto stamps are worth about $1 each.

Land Reform A6

1955-56 Perf. 11¼
23	A6	5d lt green	18.00	4.75
24	A6	10d gray	18.00	4.75
25	A6	20d orange	18.00	6.00
26	A6	50d rose	18.00	6.00
27	A6	100d lt brown	37.50	6.00
		Nos. 23-27 (5)	109.50	27.50

Issued: 100d, 12/55; 20d, 50d, 2/56; others, 6/56. See Nos. O8-O9.

Return of Government to Hanoi — A7

1956, Mar. 1 Perf. 11¼
28	A7	1000d violet	47.50	12.00
29	A7	1500d dk blue	65.00	12.00
30	A7	2000d turquoise	65.00	12.00
31	A7	3000d blue green	80.00	12.00
		Nos. 28-31 (4)	257.50	48.00

Counterfeits exist, often imperf and offered as proofs.

Re-opening of Hanoi-China Railroad — A8

1956, Mar. 1
32	A8	100d dark blue	20.00	6.00
33	A8	200d blue green	20.00	6.00
34	A8	300d violet	40.00	6.00
35	A8	500d lilac brown	47.50	6.00
		Nos. 32-35 (4)	127.50	24.00

Counterfeits exist, often imperf and offered as proofs.

Nos. 1-3 Surcharged

1954, Oct. Imperf.
36	A1	10d on 100d brown	25.00	40.00
37	A1	10d on 100d green	25.00	—

Perf. 11
38	A1	20d on 200d red	15.00	15.00
		Nos. 36-38 (3)	65.00	55.00

Nos. 36-38 exist with counterfeit surcharges, counterfeit surcharges on counterfeit stamps, and with fantasy surcharges.

Tran Dang Ninh (1910-55), Guerrilla Leader A9

1956, July Litho. Perf. 11¼
39	A9	5d bl grn & pale grn	4.50	2.00
40	A9	10d lilac & rose	4.50	2.00
41	A9	20d gr brn & dk gray	5.50	3.00
42	A9	100d dk blue pale bl	6.50	3.50
		Nos. 39-42 (4)	21.00	10.50

Nos. 39-42 used values are for postally used. CTO value, set $2.50.

Mac Thi Buoi (1927-51), Guerrilla Leader A10

1956, Nov. 3 Perf. 11½
43	A10	1000d rose & lilac rose	47.50	15.00
44	A10	2000d brown & bister	90.00	24.00
45	A10	4000d bl grn & green	190.00	35.00
46	A10	5000d ultra & lt blue	240.00	60.00
		Nos. 43-46 (4)	567.50	134.00

Nos. 43-46 used values are for postally used. Cto value, set $40.

Counterfeits exist, often imperf and offered as proofs.

Bai Thuong Dam — A11

1956-58 Perf. 11¼
47	A11	100d vio bl & lil brn	10.00	6.50
a.		Perf 13	11.00	9.50
48	A11	200d lilac & gr grn	11.00	6.50
a.		Perf 13	12.50	11.00
49	A11	300d rose & lil brn	16.00	12.00
a.		Perf 13	12.50	11.00
		Nos. 47-49 (3)	37.00	25.00

Nos. 47-49 used values are for postally used. CTO values: Nos. 47-49, set $4; Nos. 47a-49a, set $5.50.

Issued: #47-49, 12/15/56; #47a-49a, 1958.

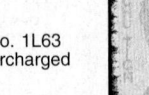 

No. 1L63 Surcharged

1956, Dec. Typo. Perf. 7 Rough
50	VM2	50d on 5d org red, brnish	40.00	50.00
a.		50d on 5d dp red, brnish	90.00	100.00

Reprints and counterfeits exist.

Nam Dinh Textile Mill — A13

1957, Mar. Litho. Perf. 12½
51-53	A13	100d, 200d, 300d, set of 3	25.00	2.50
51a		Perf. 11½	6.00	6.00
51b		Imperf	12.00	12.00
51c		Perf. 11½x12½	6.50	6.50
51d		Imperf x perf 11½	12.00	12.00

Nos. 51-53 used values are for cto. Postally used value, set $25.

Ho Chi Minh — A14

1957 Perf. 12½
54-57	A14	20d, 60d, 100d, 300d, set of 4	20.00	2.00

Nos. 54-57 used values are for cto. Postally used value, set $8.

Issued: 20d, 60d, 12/13; others, 5/19.

Fourth World Trade Union Congress, Leipzig A15

1957, Aug. 1 Perf. 12½
58	A15	300d red violet	8.00	.75

No. 58 used value is for cto. Postally used value $5.50.

See Nos. O17-O20.

Democratic Republic, 12th Anniv. A16

1957, Sept. 2 Perf. 13
59-60	A16	20d, 100d, set of 2	10.00	2.00

Nos. 59-60 used values are for cto. Postally used value, set $5.50.

Presidents Voroshilov, Ho Chi Minh — A17

1957, Nov. 7   **Perf. 12½**
61-63 A17   100d, 500d, set of
     1000d, 3   40.00   30.00
     Russian revolution, 40th anniv.

> Used values from No. 64 on are for cto stamps. Postally used examples are worth substantially more.

Anti-illiteracy Campaign — A18

1958, Jan. 6   **Perf. 12½**
64-66 A18   50d, 150d, 1000d,
     set of 3   30.00   2.00

A19

1958, Mar. 8
67-68 A19   150d, 500d, set of 2   30.00   2.50
     Physical education.

A20

1958, May 1
69-70 A20   50d, 150d, set of 2   10.00   1.10
     May Day.

Fourth Intl.
Congress of
Democratic
Women,
Vienna
A21

1958, May   **Typo.**
71   A21   150d blue   8.00   .75

A22

A22a

    A22: #72, 150d, #75, 2000d, Basket, lace &
cup, vert.
    A22a: #73, 150d, #74, 1000d, Potter.

1958   **Litho.**
72-75 A22, A22a   Set of 4   25.00   2.00
     Arts & Crafts Fair, Hanoi.
    Issued: Nos. 72, 75, 6/26; others, 8/19.

Building the Reunification
Railway — A23

1958, July 20
76-77 A23   50d, 150d, set of 2   8.00   .75

August
Revolution,
13th Anniv.
A24

1958, Aug. 19
78-79 A24   150d, 500d, set of 2   7.00   1.10

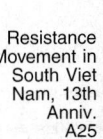 Resistance
Movement in
South Viet
Nam, 13th
Anniv.
A25

1958, Sept. 23
80-81 A25   50d, 150d, set of 2   12.00   .75

A26

1958, Oct.
82   A26   150d grnsh blue & blk   3.00   .40
     Tran Hung Dao (1253-1300).

A27

    Hanoi Engineering Plant.

1958, Nov. 7   **Engr.**   **Perf. 11½**
83   A27   150d brown   3.50   .40

Mutual Aid
Teams — A28

1958, Nov. 7
84-85 A28   150d, 500d, set of 2   12.00   2.75

Ngoc Son
Temple
(Temple of
Jade) — A29

1958, Dec. 1   **Photo.**   **Perf. 12**
86-87 A29   150d, 2000d, set of
     2   32.50   4.00

Rattanware
Cooperative
A30

1958, Dec. 31
88   A30   150d greenish blue   3.50   .65

Ha Long
Bay — A31

1959, Feb. 8
89-90 A31   150d, 350d, set of 2   7.00   2.00

Cam Pha Coal
Mines — A32

1959, Mar. 3   **Engr.**   **Perf. 11½**
91   A32   150d blue   8.00   .40

Trung
Sisters — A33

1959, Mar. 14   **Litho.**   **Perf. 11**
92-93 A33   5xu, 8xu, set of 2   9.00   1.25

World Peace Movement, 10th
Anniv. — A34

1959, Apr. 15
94   A34   12xu purple, *rose*   1.50   .60

Xuan
Quang
Dam
A35

1959, May 1
95-96 A35   6xu, 12xu, set of 2   7.50   .80

Phu Loi
Massacre
A36

1959, May 15
97-98 A36   12xu, 20xu, set of 2   7.00   .80

Hien Luong
Bridge — A37

1959, July 20
99   A37   12xu black & carmine   3.00   .75

Me Tri Radio
Station — A38

1959, Aug. 10
100-101 A38   3xu, 12xu, set of 2   5.00   1.10

Sports
A39

    Designs: 1xu, Shooting. 6xu, Swimming.
12xu, Wrestling.

1959, Sept. 2
102-104 A39   Set of 3   8.00   1.20
     Size of No. 103 is 43x31mm.

People's
Republic of
China, 10th
Anniv. — A40

1959, Oct. 1
105   A40   12xu multicolored   5.00   .70

Fruits — A41

    Designs: 3xu, Coconuts. 12xu, Bananas.
30xu, Pineapple.

1959, Nov. 20
106-108 A41   Set of 3   8.00   1.20

People's
Army, 15th
Anniv.
A42

1959, Dec. 22
109   A42   12xu multicolored   3.00   .40

A43

1960, Jan. 6
110-111 A43 2xu, 12xu, set of 2　5.50　.80
Vietnamese Workers' Party, 30th Anniv.

A44

Ethnic costumes: 2xu, Ede. 10xu, Meo. No. 114, 12xu, Tay. No. 115, 12xu, Thai.

1960, Jan. 6
112-115 A44　Set of 4　9.00　2.25

Census
A45

Designs: 1xu, People. 12xu, Transmitting tower, dam, buildings, workers.

1960, Feb. 20
116-117 A45　Set of 2　4.00　1.25
No. 117 is 37x26mm.

Intl. Women's Day, 50th Anniv. A46

1960, Mar. 8
118 A46 12xu multicolored　2.50　.80

A47

1960, Apr. 5
119-120 A47 4xu, 12xu, set of 2　62.50　30.00
Hung Vuong Temple.

A48

1960, Apr. 22
121-122 A48 5xu, 12xu, set of 2　6.50　1.25
121a　Souv. sheet of 1, olive brown & blue, imperf.　75.00　65.00
Lenin. No. 121a exists on brownish paper.

Election of National Assembly Delegates — A49

1960, May 3　　**Perf. 11**
123 A49 12xu multicolored, *rose*　2.00　.45

A50

1960, May 8
124-125 A50 8xu, 12xu, set of 2　6.00　.75
Viet Nam Red Cross.

A51

Ho Chi Minh, 70th Birthday: Nos. 128, 130, Ho with children.

1960, May 19
126 A51　4xu　green & purple　2.00　.40
127 A51　12xu　pink & brown　3.00　.40
128 A51　12xu　multicolored　3.00　.40
　　Nos. 126-128 (3)　8.00　1.20
Souvenir Sheets
Imperf
129 A51 10xu yel bis & brn, *rose*　12.00　10.00
130 A51 10xu multicolored　11.00　8.00
No. 128 is 25x39mm.

New Constitution A52

1960, July 7
131 A52 12xu lemon & gray　3.00　1.25

National Day, 15th Anniv. A53

1960, Sept. 2
132-133 A53 4xu, 12xu, set of 2　7.50　.80

Development — A54

Designs: No. 134, Classroom. No. 135, Plowing. No. 136, Factory.

1960, Sept. 2
134-136 A54 12xu Set of 3　13.50　1.20

3rd Vietnamese Communist Party Congress — A55

1960, Sept. 4
137-138 A55 1xu, 12xu, set of 2　6.50　.75

World Federation of Trade Unions, 15th Anniv. — A56

1960, Oct. 3
139 A56 12xu black & vermilion　5.00　.40

Hanoi, 950th Anniv. A57

1960, Oct. 10　**Litho.**　**Perf. 11**
140-141 A57 8xu, 12xu, set of 2　6.75　.80
141a　Souv. sheet of 1, imperf.　15.00　12.00
No. 141a exists on brownish paper.

15 Years' Achievements Exhibition — A58

1960, Oct. 20
142-143 A58 2xu, 12xu, set of 2　4.00　.80

World Federation of Democratic Youth, 15th Anniv. — A59

1960, Nov. 10
144 A59 12xu multicolored　3.50　.40

Trade Unions, 2nd Natl. Congress A60

1961, Feb. 10
145 A60 12xu multicolored, *rose*　2.50　.80

Vietnamese Women's Union, 3rd Natl. Congress — A61

1961, Mar. 8　　**Tinted Paper**
146-147 A61 6xu, 12xu, set of 2　5.00　1.25

Animals — A62

Designs: 12xu, Rusa unicolor. 20xu, Helarctos malynus. 50xu, Elephas maximus. 1d, Hylobates leucogenys.

1961, Mar. 8
148-151 A62　Set of 4　30.00　4.00
　　Imperf., #148-151　60.00　60.00

Ly Tu Trong — A63

1961, Mar. 18
152-153 A63 2xu, 12xu, set of 2　3.75　1.00
Youth Labor Union, 3rd Congress.

Young Pioneers, 20th Anniv. — A64

1961, May 2
154-155 A64 1xu, 12xu, set of 2　4.00　1.00

Intl. Red Cross — A65

1961, May 8
156-157 A65 6xu, 12xu, set of 2　6.50　1.00

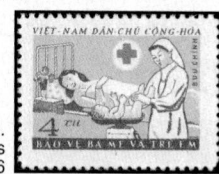

Intl. Children's Day — A66

1961, June 1 *Perf. 11*
158-159 A66 4xu, 12xu, set of 2 6.00 .80

Yuri Gagarin's Space Flight A67

1961, June 15
160-161 A67 6xu, 12xu, set of
2 24.00 2.50
Imperf., #160-161 27.50 27.50

Hanoi, Hue and Saigon A68

1961, July 20
162-163 A68 12xu, 3d, set of 2 11.00 1.25

A69

1961, July 20
164-165 A69 12xu, 2d, set of 2 10.00 1.25
Imperf., #164-165 — —

Reunification campaign.

A70

1961, Aug. 21
166-167 A70 2xu, 12xu, set of 2 5.00 .80
Geological exploration.

Savings Campaign A71

1961, Aug. 21
168-169 A71 3xu, 12xu, set of 2 5.00 .80

Ancient Towers — A72

Designs: 6xu, Thien Mu, Hue. 10xu, Pen Brush, Bac Ninh. No. 172, 12xu, Binh Son, Vinh Phuc. No. 173, 12xu, Cham, Phan Rang.

1961, Sept. 12
170-173 A72 Set of 4 10.00 3.75
Imperf., #170-173 12.00 12.00

A73

6xu, 12xu, Gherman Titov's Space Flight.

1961, Oct. 17
174-175 A73 Set of 2 8.00 .80
Imperf., #174-175 12.00 12.00

A74

1961, Oct. 17
176 A74 12xu vermilion & black 3.50 .40
22nd Communist Party Congress, Moscow.

Port of Haiphong — A75

1961, Nov. 7
177-178 A75 5xu, 12xu, set of 2 9.50 .80

A76

Musicians: No. 179, 12xu, Flutist. No. 180, 12xu, Cymbalist. 30xu, Dancer with fan. 50xu, Guitarist.

1961, Nov. 18 *Perf. 13½*
179-182 A76 Set of 4 16.00 2.00
Imperf., #179-182 20.00 20.00
182a Souvenir sheet, #179-182 50.00 50.00

Stamps on No. 182a are se-tenant and perfed on outside edges of the strip of 4.

5th World Trade Union Congress, Moscow A77

1961, Dec. 4 *Perf. 11*
183 A77 12xu dp red lil & gray 2.00 .45

Natl. Resistance, 15th Anniv. A78

1961, Dec. 4
184-185 A78 4xu, 12xu, set of 2 2.25 .65

Tet Holiday — A79

Designs: 6xu, Sow, piglets. 12xu, Poultry.

1962, Jan. 16 *Litho.*
186-187 A79 Set of 2 9.00 1.50

Tet Tree-Planting Festival — A80

1962, Jan. 16
188-189 A80 12xu, 40xu, set of 2 5.00 .80

Crops — A81

Designs: 2xu, Camellia sinensis. 6xu, Illicium verum. No. 192, 12xu, Coffea arabica. No. 193, 12xu, Ricinus communis. 30xu, Rhus succedanea.

1962, Mar. 1
190-194 A81 Set of 5 15.00 3.25

Folk Dances — A82

Designs: No. 195, 12xu, Rong Chieng. No. 196, 12xu, Bamboo. 30xu, Hat. 50xu, Parasol.

1962, Mar. 20 *Photo.* *Perf. 11½x12*
195-198 A82 Set of 4 20.00 2.25
Imperf., #195-198 20.00 20.00
Souvenir Sheet
199 A82 30xu like #195 20.00 20.00

First Five Year Plan — A83

Designs: 1xu, Kim Lien Apartments, Hanoi. 3xu, State farm. 8xu, Natl. Institute of Hydraulics.

1962, Apr. 10 *Litho.* *Perf. 11*
200-202 A83 Set of 3 4.00 1.25

A84

Flowers: No. 203, 12xu, Hibiscus rosa sinensis. No. 204, 12xu, Plumeria acutifolia. 20xu, Chrysanthemum indicum. 30xu, Nelumbium nuciferum. 50xu, Ipomoea pulchella.

Perf. 12½x11½
1962, Apr. 10 *Photo.*
203-207 A84 Set of 5 21.00 4.00
Imperf., #203-207 30.00 30.00
206a Souvenir sheet of 1 12.00 12.00

A85

1962, May 4 *Litho.* *Perf. 11*
208 A85 12xu multicolored 3.00 .55

3rd Natl. Heroes of Labor Congress.

Harrow A86

Dai Lai Lake A87

1962, May 25
209-210 A86-A87 6xu, 12xu, set of 2 4.00 .80

Visit by Gherman Titov A88

Titov: 12xu, Waving at children. 20xu, Receiving medal from Ho Chi Minh. 30xu, Wearing space suit.

1962, June 12
211-213 A88 Set of 3 8.00 1.50
Imperf., #211-213 12.00 12.00

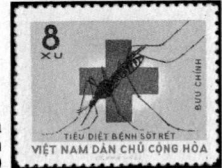

Anti-Malaria Campaign A89

1962, July 9
214-216 A89   8xu, 12xu, 20xu, set of 3   7.50   1.50

War for Reunification — A90

1962, July 20
217 A90 12xu multicolored   2.50   .40

Ba Be Lake — A91

Design: No. 219, Ban Gioc Falls, vert.

1962, Aug. 14
218-219 A91 12xu Set of 2   4.00   .90

A stamp picturing a weight lifter exists, but was not released. Values: mint $120; used $130.

King Quang Trung (1752-92) — A92

1962, Sept. 16
220-221 A92   3xu, 12xu, set of 2   3.50   .70

Nguyen Trai (1380-1442) — A93

1962, Sept. 19
222-223 A93   3xu, 12xu, set of 2   3.50   .70

Food Crops A94

Designs: 1xu, Peanuts. 4xu, Beans. 6xu, Sweet potatoes. 12xu, Corn. 30xu, Cassava.

1962, Oct. 10
224-228 A94   Set of 5   9.00   4.75
    Imperf., #224-228

Animal Husbandry A95

Designs: 2xu, Feeding poultry. No. 230, 12xu, Feeding pigs. No. 231, 12xu, Cattle grazing. No. 232, 12xu, Tending water buffalo.

1962, Nov. 28
229-232 A95 Set of 4   8.00   1.75

A stamp commemorating the 45th anniversary of the Russian Revolution exists, but was not issued. Value $200.

First Five Year Plan A96

#233, Evening classes. #234, Clearing land.

1962, Dec. 28
233-234 A96 12xu Set of 2   5.00   .80

Flights of Vostok 3 and 4 — A97

12xu, Pavel Popovich, Vostok 4. 20xu, Andrian Nikolayev, Vostok 3. 30xu, Rockets lifting-off, vert.

1962, Dec. 28   *Perf. 11*
235-237 A97   Set of 3   6.00   1.25
    Imperf., #235-237   12.00   12.00

Guerrilla — A98

1963, Jan. 15
238-239 A98   5xu, 12xu, set of 2   3.00   .70

Hoang Hoa Tham (1846-1913) A99

1963, Feb. 10
240-241 A99   6xu, 12xu, set of 2   3.00   .90

A100

First Five Year Plan A100a

Designs: No. 242, Fertilizing rice paddy. No. 243, Lam Thao superphosphate plant.

1963, Feb. 25
242-243 A100-A100a 12xu Set of 2   3.50   .75

Karl Marx — A101

1963, Mar. 14
244-245 A101 3xu, 12xu, set of 2   3.25   .70
    Nos. 244-245 are printed on greenish and rose toned paper respectively.

Fidel Castro, Vietnamese Soldiers A102

1963, Apr. 17
246 A102 12xu multicolored   2.25   .50

May Day A103

1963, May 8
247 A103 12xu multicolored   2.25   .45

A104   Intl. Red Cross, Cent. — A105

Design: No. 249, Child, syringe.

1963, May 8
248 A104 12xu grn, blk & red   2.00   .40
249 A104 12xu grn, red & blk   2.00   .40
250 A105 20xu multicolored   3.00   .40
    Nos. 248-250 (3)   7.00   1.20

Mars 1 Spacecraft — A106

6xu, 12xu (#252), Mars 1 approaching Mars. 12xu (#253), 20xu, Mars 1 entering orbit, vert.

1963, May 21
251-254 A106   Set of 4   7.50   1.50
    Imperf., #251-254   15.00   15.00

Fishing Industry A107

Designs: No. 255, Trawler, offshore fish. No. 256, Freshwater fish.

1963, July 3
255-256 A107 12xu Set of 2   10.50   .75

Ho Chi Minh, Nguyen Van Hien — A108

1963, July 20
257 A108 12xu multicolored   2.50   .40

Flights of Vostok 3, 4 A109

Designs: 12xu, Rockets in orbit. 20xu, Nikolayev. 30xu, Popovich.

1963, Aug. 11
258-260 A109   Set of 3   7.00   1.25
    Imperf., #258-260   15.00   15.00

First Five Year Plan for Chemical Industry A110

Designs: 3xu, Viet Tri Insecticide Factory. 12xu, Viet Tri Chemical Factory.

1963, Aug. 11
261-262 A110   Set of 2   3.00   .60

Fish A111

Designs: No. 263, 12xu, Cyprinus carpio. No. 264, 12xu, Myloharyngodon piceus. No. 265, 12xu, Hypophthalmichthys molitrix. 20xu, Ophiocephalus caqua. 30xu, Tilapia mossambica.

1963, Sept. 10
263-267 A111   Set of 5   17.00   3.50
    Imperf., #263-267   20.00   20.00
    a. Souvenir Sheet Of 1, #266   67.50

A112

Birds: #268, 12xu, Francolinus stephenson. #269, 12xu, Acridotheres cristatellus. #270, 12xu, Halcyon smyrneusis. 20xu, Diardigallus diardi, horiz. 30xu, Egretta. 40xu, Psittacula alexandri.

    Perf. 11½x12, 12x11½
1963, Oct. 15   *Photo.*
268-273 A112   Set of 6   35.00   4.00
    Imperf., #268-273   45.00   45.00
    Souvenir Sheet
274 A112 50xu Sheet of 1, like #272   80.00   80.00

A113

1963, Oct. 20   Litho.   Perf. 11
275 A113 12xu multicolored   2.00   .40
World Federation of Trade Unions Congress
for Viet Nam.

GANEFO
Games
A114

#276, 12xu, Swimming. #277, 12xu, Volley-
ball, vert. #278, 12xu, Soccer, vert. 30xu, High
jump.

1963, Nov. 10
276-279 A114 Set of 4   5.00 1.50
    Imperf., #276-279   6.00 6.00

A115

Flowers: 6xu, Rauwolfia verticillata. No. 281,
12xu, Sophora japonica. No. 282, 12xu,
Fibraurea tinctoria. No. 283, 12xu, Cheno-
podium ambrosioides. 20xu, Momordica
cochinchinensis.

1963, Dec. 3
280-284 A115 Set of 5   7.50 2.00
    Imperf., #280-284   10.00 10.00

A116

1963, Dec. 20
285 A116 12xu multicolored   2.50   .40
World Day for Viet Nam.

First Five-Year
Plan — A118

6xu, Molten cast iron. #287, 12xu, Thai
Nguyen Steel & Iron Works. #288, 12xu,
Power lines.

1964, Jan. 25
286-288 A117-A118 Set of 3   4.50 1.60

Intl. Quiet Sun
Year — A119

1964, Jan. 25
289-290 A119 12xu, 50xu, set
    of
    2   5.00   .80
    Imperf., #289-290   17.50 17.50

Flights
of
Vostok
5 and
6
A120

#291, 12xu, Rockets in orbit. #292, 12xu,
Valery Bykovsky. 30xu, Valentina Tereshkova.

1964, Mar. 25
291-293 A120 Set of 3   6.00 1.25
    Imperf., #291-293   12.00 12.00

A stamp commemorating the anniversary of the founding of the People's
Democratic Republic of Korea was
printed but not issued.

A121

Flowers: No. 294, 12xu, Persica vulgaris.
No. 295, 12xu, Hibiscus mutabilis. No. 296,
12xu, Passiflora hispida. No. 297, 12xu,
Saraca dives. 20xu, Michelia champaca. 30xu,
Camellia amplexicaulis.

1964, Apr. 10   Perf. 11½x12
294-299 A121 Set of 6   13.00 2.40
    Imperf., #294-299   15.00 15.00

A122

Costumes: 6xu, Peasant, 19th cent. No.
301, 12xu, Woman wearing large hat, 19th
cent. No. 302, 12xu, Woman carrying hat.

1964, Apr. 27   Perf. 11
300-302 A122 Set of 3   5.00 1.25

Battle of
Dien Bien
Phu, 10th
Anniv.
A123

Designs: 3xu, Artillery. 6xu, Machine gun
emplacement. Nos. 305, 307c, Bomb dispo-
sal. Nos. 306, 307d, Farmer on tractor.

1964, May 7
303 A123 3xu red & black
304 A123 6xu blue & black
305 A123 12xu yel org & blk
306 A123 12xu red lilac &
    black
    Nos. 303-306
    (4)   7.50 1.60
    Imperf., #303-306   12.00 12.00

Souvenir Sheet
Imperf
307   Sheet of 4   13.00 13.00
 a.   A123 3xu orange & black
 b.   A123 6xu yellow green &
    black
 c.   A123 12xu red, black & or-
    ange
 d.   A123 12xu blue & black

Ham Rong Bridge — A124

1964, May 17
308 A124 12xu multicolored   2.50   .40

Wild
Animals
A125

Designs: No. 309, 12xu, Panthera tigris,
vert. No. 310, 12xu, Pseudaxis axis, vert. No.
311, 12xu, Tapirus indicus. 20xu, Bubalus
bubalis. 30xu, Rhinoceros bicornis. 40xu,
Bibos banteng.

1964, June 2   Perf. 10½
309-314 A125 Set of 6   16.00 2.40
    Imperf., #309-314   15.00 15.00

Geneva
Agreement
on Viet
Nam, 10th
Anniv.
A126

Intl. Labor
Federation
Committee United
with People of
South Viet
Nam — A127

1964, July 20   Perf. 11
315-316 A126-A127 12xu Set of
    2   3.00   .80

Nam Bac
Ninh
Pumping
Station
A128

1964, Aug. 25
317 A128 12xu blue gray & black   1.75   .40

Liberation of Hanoi, 10th
Anniv. — A129

6xu, People cheering soldiers in truck. 12xu,
Construction, hammerhead crane.

1964, Oct. 10
318-319 A129 Set of 2   3.50   .80

Natl. Defense Games — A130

Designs: 5xu, Rowing. No. 321, 12xu, Para-
chuting, vert. No. 322, 12xu, Gliders, vert. No.
323, 12xu, Shooting.

1964, Oct. 18
320-323 A130 Set of 4   6.50 2.50

Fruits — A131

Designs: No. 324, 12xu, Mangifera indica.
No. 325, 12xu, Guarcinia mangostana. No.
326, 12xu, Nephelium litchi. 20xu, Anona
squamosa. 50xu, Citrus medica.

1964, Oct. 31   Photo.   Perf. 11½x12
324-328 A131 Set of 5   10.00 2.00
    Imperf., #324-328   15.00 15.00

World Solidarity Conference — A132

Designs: a, Ba Dinh Hall. b, Vietnamese soldier shaking hands with foreign people. c, Fist,
planes, submarine.

1964, Nov. 25   Litho.   Perf. 11
329 A132 12xu Strip of 3, #a.-c.   6.50 1.25

People's
Army,
20th
Anniv.
A133

Designs: No. 330, Soldiers, flag. No. 331a,
Coast guards. No. 331b, Mounted border
guards, vert.

1964, Dec. 22
330 A133 12xu multicolored   1.50   .40
331 A133 12xu Pair, #a.-b.   3.00 3.00
    Nos. 330-331 (2)   4.50 3.40

Cuban Revolution, 6th Anniv. — A134

Designs: a, Vietnamese, Cuban flags. b, Cuban revolutionaries.

1965, Jan. 1
332 A134 12xu Pair, #a.-b.　　4.50 2.50

Economic & Cultural Development of Mountain Region — A135

Designs: 2xu, 3xu, Women pollinating corn. 12xu, Girls walking to school.

1965, Feb. 28
333-335 A135 Set of 3　　　　3.00 1.25
　　Imperf., #333-335

A136

Vietnamese Worker's Party, 35th Anniv. — A137

Politicians: No. 336a, Le Hong Phong. b, Tran Phu. c, Hoang Van Thu. d, Ngo Gia Tu. e, Nguyen Van Cu.
No. 337a, Party flag. b, Worker, soldier.

1965, Feb. 3　　Litho.　　Perf. 11
336 A136　6xu Strip of 5, #a.-e.　2.00 2.00
337 A137　12xu Pair, #a.-b.　　3.00 1.50
　　Nos. 336-337 (2)　　　　　5.00 3.50

　　Issued: No. 336, 2/3; No. 337, 1/30.

Transportation Ministers Conference, Hanoi — A138

12xu, 30xu, Nguyen Van Troi, locomotive.

1965, Mar. 23
338-339 A138　Set of 2　　　　7.50 .80
　　Imperf., #338-339

　　Vignette on No. 339 is mirror image of No. 338.

Flight of Voskhod 1 — A139

20xu, Cosmonauts Komarov, Feoktistov, Yegorov, rocket, globe. 1d, Cosmonauts, rocket.

1965, Mar. 30
340-341 A139　Set of 2　　　　9.00 .80
　　Imperf., #340-341　　　　11.00 11.00

Lenin, 95th Birth Anniv. A140

1965, Apr. 22　　　　　　Litho.
342-343 A140 8xu, 12xu, set of 2 3.00 .80

A141

1965, May 19
344-345 A141 6xu, 12xu, set of 2 2.50 .80
　　Ho Chi Minh, 75th birthday.

A142

1965, May 19
346 A142 12xu multicolored　　2.50 .40
　　Afro-Asian Conference, 10th anniv.

Trade Union Conference, Hanoi — A143

Designs: No. 347, Workers solidarity. No. 348, Soldiers, vert. No. 349, Naval battle.

1965, June 2
347-349 A143 12xu Set of 3　　4.50 1.25

Wild Animals — A144

Designs: No. 350, 12xu, Martes flavigula. No. 351, 12xu, Chrotogale owstoni. No. 352, 12xu, Manis pentadactyla. No. 353, 12xu,

Presbytis delacouri, vert. 20xu, Petaurista lylei, vert. 50xu, Nycticebus pygmaeus, vert.

1965, June 24　Photo.　　Perf. 12
350-355 A144　Set of 6　　　17.00 2.50
　　Imperf., #350-355　　　　25.00 25.00

A145

1965, July 1　　　　Perf. 11½x11
356 A145 12xu multicolored　　3.50 .40
　　6th Socialist Postal Ministers Conference.

A146

Nguyen Van Troi (1940-64). Denominations: 12xu, 50xu, 4d.

1965, July 20　Litho.　　Perf. 11
357-359 A146　Set of 3　　　　9.00 2.40

A147

Insects — A148

Designs: No. 360, 12xu, Tessaratoma papillosa. No. 361, 12xu, Rhynchocoris humeralis. No. 362, 12xu, Poeciliocoris latus.
　　No. 363, 12xu, Tosena melanoptera. 20xu, Cicada. 30xu, Fulgora candelaria.

1965, July 24　　　　　　Photo.
360-362 A147　Set of 3　　　4.00 1.25
363-365 A148　Set of 3　　　8.00 1.25
　　Nos. 360-365 (6)　　　12.00 2.50
　　Imperf., #360-365　　　18.00 18.00

August Revolution, 20th Anniv. — A149

1965, Aug. 19　　　　　　Litho.
366-367 A149 6xu, 12xu, set of 2 3.00 .80

Crustaceans — A150

Designs: No. 368, 12xu, Penaeus indicus. No. 369, 12xu, Scylla serrata. No. 370, 12xu, Metapenaeus joyneri. No. 371, 12xu, Neptunus. 20xu, Palinurus japonicus. 50xu, Uca marionis.

1965, Aug. 19
368-373 A150　Set of 6　　　19.00 2.50
　　Imperf., #368-373　　　21.00 21.00

500th US Warplane Shot Down — A151

1965, Aug. 30
374 A151 12xu gray green & lilac 7.00 4.50

A152

Completion of 1st Five-Year Plan — A153

#375, Foundry worker. #376, Electricity, irrigation. #377, Public health, education. #378, Students, children playing. #379, Factory worker. #380, Agricultural workers.

1965
375-377 A152 12xu Set of 3　　3.50 1.75
378-380 A153 12xu Set of 3　　3.50 1.75
　　Imperf., #375-380

　　Issued: #375-377, 9/2; #378-380, 12/25.

Nghe An, Ha Tinh Uprising, 35th Anniv. — A154

1965, Sept. 12
381-382 A154 10xu, 12xu, set of
　　　　　　　　　　　　　　2　2.50 .80
　　Imperf., #381-382

Friendship Between Viet Nam, People's Republic of China, 16th Anniv. — A155

Designs: No. 383, Youth holding flags, Friendship Gate. No. 384, Children waving flags, walking through Gate, vert.

1965, Oct. 1
383-384 A155 12xu Set of 2   10.00 1.75

Flight of Voskhod 2 — A156

#385, 12xu, Konstantin Tsiolkovsky, Sputnik I. #386, 12xu, Voskhod 2, A. Leonov, P. Belyayev. #387, 50xu, Yuri Gagarin. #388, 50xu, Leonov walking in space.

1965, Oct. 5
385-388 A156 Set of 4   8.00 3.25
　　　Imperf., #385-388

A157

Norman R. Morrison, US anti-war demonstration.

1965, Nov. 22
389 A157 12xu black & red   3.00 .40

A158

Nguyen Du (1765-1820), poet: No. 390, 12xu, Birthplace. No. 391, 12xu, Museum. 20xu, Volume of poems entitled Kieu. 1d, Scene from Kieu.

1965, Nov. 25
390-393 A158 Set of 4   6.00 1.50

A159

Designs: No. 394, Ho Chi Minh. No. 395, 12xu, Karl Marx. No. 396, 12xu, Lenin. 50xu, Frederich Engels.

Litho. & Engr. (#394), Litho.
1965, Nov. 28   **Perf. 11½**
394-397 A159 Set of 4   6.00 1.50
　　　Nos. 395-397 have white border.

Butterflies
A160

#398, 12xu, Cethosia cyane. #399, 12xu, Zelides sarpedon. #400, 12xu, Cethosia. #401, 12xu, Apatura ambica. 20xu, Papilio paris. 30xu, Tros aristolochiae.

1965, Nov. 18   **Litho.**   **Perf. 11**
398-403 A160 Set of 6   22.50 2.50
　　　Imperf., #398-403   55.00 55.00

South Viet Nam Natl. Liberation Front, 5th Anniv. — A161

1965, Dec. 20
404 A161   12xu lilac   2.50 .40
　　　Imperf.

1st General Elections, 20th Anniv. — A162

1966, Jan. 6
405 A162 12xu black & red   2.50 .50

A163

Orchids: No. 406, 12xu, Vanda teres. No. 407, 12xu, Dendrobium meschatum. No. 408, 12xu, Dendrobium nobile. No. 409, 12xu, Dendrobium crystallinum. 20xu, Vandopsis gigantea. 30xu, Dendrobium.

1966, Jan. 10   **Perf. 12**
406-411 A163 Set of 6   12.00 2.50
　　　Imperf., #406-411   20.00 20.00

A164

1966, Jan. 18   **Perf. 11**
412 A164 12xu multicolored   2.50 .40
　　　Imperf.

New Year 1966 (Year of the Horse).

Reptiles
A165

#413, 12xu, Physignathus cocincinus. #414, 12xu, Gekko gecko. #415, 12xu, Trionyx sinensis. #416, 12xu, Testudo elongata. 20xu, Varanus salvator. 40xu, Eretmochelys imbricata.

1966, Feb. 25   **Perf. 12x11½**
413-418 A165 Set of 6   12.00 2.50
　　　Imperf., #413-418   20.00 20.00

Natl. Sports
A166

Designs: No. 419, Archery. No. 420, Wrestling. No. 421, Spear fighting.

1966, Mar. 25   **Perf. 11**
419-421 A166 12xu Set of 3   5.00 1.25

6xu, 12xu, 1d stamps for running, swimming and shooting were printed but not issued.

Youth Labor Union, 35th Anniv. — A167

1966, Mar. 26
422 A167 12xu multicolored   2.00 .50

1000th US Warplane Shot Down — A168

1966, Apr. 29
423 A168 12xu multicolored   7.50 4.00

May Day — A169

1966, May 1
424 A169 6xu multicolored   2.00 .40

Defending Con Co Island — A170

1966, June 1
425 A170 12xu multicolored   2.50 .40

A171

1966, June 1
426 A171 12xu red & black   1.75 .40
　　　Young Pioneers, 25th anniv.

A172

Designs: 3xu, View of Yenan. 12xu, Ho Chi Minh, Mao Tse-Tung.

1966, July 1
427-428 A172 Set of 2   4.00 .80
　　　Imperf., #427-428

Chinese Communist Party, 45th anniv.

A173

Luna 9: 12xu, Flight path to moon. 50xu, In lunar orbit.

1966, Aug. 5
429-430 A173 Set of 2   6.50 1.50
　　　Imperf., #429-430   10.00 10.00

A174

1966, Oct. 14
431 A174 12xu multicolored   10.00 3.00
With Additional Inscription: "NGAY 14.10.1966"
431A A174 12xu multicolored   15.00 3.75
　　　Imperf., #431-431A

1500th US warplane shot down.

Victory in Dry Season
Campaign — A175

Designs: 1xu, 12xu (No. 433), Woman guerrilla carrying guns. 12xu (No. 434), Soldier escorting prisoners of war.

1966, Oct. 15
432-434 A175 Set of 3   5.00 1.50
          Imperf., #432-434

See also No. 618A.

Vietnamese
Women's
Union, 20th
Anniv.
A176

1966, Oct. 20
435 A176 12xu orange & black   2.25 .40
          Imperf.

Birds
A177

Designs: No. 436, 12xu, Pitta moluccensis. No. 437, 12xu, Psarisomus dolhousiae. Nos. 438, 12xu, Alcedo atthis, vert. No. 439, 12xu, Oriolus chinensis, vert. 20xu, Upupa epops, vert. 30xu, Oriolus traillii.

1966, Oct. 31 Perf. 12x12½, 12½x12
436-441 A177 Set of 6   10.00 2.50
          Imperf., #436-441   25.00 25.00

GANEFO Asian
Games — A178

Designs: No. 442, Soccer. No. 443, Shooting. No. 444, Swimming. No. 445, Running.

1966, Nov. 25   Perf. 11
442-445   Set of 4   7.00 1.50
          Imperf., #442-445   10.00 10.00
443a A178   12xu Pair, #442-443   3.50
445a A178   30xu Pair, #444-445   4.50
      Nos. 443a-445a (2)   8.00

Ho Chi Minh's Appeal for Natl.
Resistance, 20th Anniv. — A179

Designs: No. 446, Flags, workers. No. 447, Soldiers, workers, ships.

1967, Jan. 30
446-447 A179 12xu Set of 2   2.25 .80
See Nos. 501-504.

Rice
Harvest
A180

1967, Jan. 30
448 A180 12xu multicolored   1.75 .40

Bamboo
A181

No. 449, 12xu, Bambusa arundinaceu. No. 450, 12xu, Arundinaria rolleana. No. 451, 12xu, Arundinaria racemosa. No. 452, 12xu, Bambusa bingami. 30xu, Bambusa nutans. 50xu, Dendrocalamus patellaris.

1967, Feb. 2   Perf. 12x11½
449-454 A181 Set of 6   9.00 2.40
          Imperf., #449-454   12.00 12.00

Wild Animals — A182

Designs: No. 455, 12xu, Cuon rutilans. No. 456, 12xu, Arctictis binturong. No. 457, 12xu, Arctonyx collaris. 20xu, Viverra zibetha. 40xu, Macaca speciosa. 50xu, Neofelis nebulosa.

1967, Mar. 26   Litho.   Perf. 12
455-460 A182 Set of 6   11.00 2.50
          Imperf., #455-460   13.00 13.00

2000th US
Aircraft Shot
Down — A183

1967, June 5   Perf. 11
461-462 A183 6xu, 12xu, set
                     of 2   8.00 3.25

Fish
A184

#463, 12xu, Saurida filamentosa. #464, 12xu, Scomberomorus niphonius. #465, 12xu, Haplogenys mucronatus. 20xu, Lethrinus haematopterus. 30xu, Formio niger. 50xu, Lutianus erythropterus.

1967, July 25   Perf. 12
463-468 A184 Set of 6   11.00 2.50
          Imperf., #463-468   13.00 13.00

A185

Launch of 1st Chinese ballistic missile: 12xu, Missile, flag, agricultural scene. 30xu, Missile, Gate of Heavenly Peace.

1967, July 25   Perf. 11
469-470 A185 Set of 2   7.00 3.00
          Imperf., #469-470

A186

Russian October Revolution, 50th anniv.: 6xu, Lenin, revolutionary soldiers. No. 472a, 12xu, Lenin, armed mob. No. 472b, 12xu, Lenin, Marx, Vietnamese soldiers. 20xu, Cruiser Aurora.

1967, Oct. 15
471-473 A186 Set of 4   4.00 1.50
No. 472 is printed se-tenant.

2500th US Warplane Shot
Down — A187

Design: No. 475, Plane in flames, vert.

1967, Nov. 6
474-475 A187 12xu Set of 2   8.00 4.00
Nos. 474-475 exist imperf. Value, set $50.

1st Chinese Hydrogen Bomb
Test — A188

Designs: 12xu, Atomic symbol, Gate of Heavenly Peace. 20xu, Chinese lantern, atomic symbol, dove.

1967, Nov. 20
476-477 A188 Set of 2   5.00 1.50
          Imperf., #476-477   30.00 30.00
No. 477 is 30x35mm.

A189

#478, 12xu, Rifle fire from trenches. #479, 12xu, Militia with captured US pilot. #480, 12xu, Factory anti-aircraft unit. #481, 12xu,

Naval anti- aircraft unit. 20xu, Aerial dog-fight. 30xu, Heavy anti-aircraft battery.

1967, Dec. 19   Perf. 12
478-483 A189 Set of 6   6.00 2.50

Chickens — A190

Designs: No. 484, 12xu, White spotted cock, hen. No. 485, 12xu, Black hens. No. 486, 12xu, Bantam cock, hen. No. 487, 12xu, Bantam cocks. 20xu, Fighting cocks. 30xu, Exotic hen. 40xu, Hen, chicks from Ho region. 50xu, Dong Cao's cock, hen.

1968, Feb. 29
484-491 A190 Set of 8   11.00 3.25
          Imperf., #484-491   17.50 17.50

Victories of 1966-67 — A191

No. 492: a, Soldier attacking US tank. b, Gunner firing on US ships. c, Burning stockade. d, Soldier firing mortar.
No. 493: a, Attacking US artillery. b, Escorting US prisoners. c, Interrogating refugees. d, Civilian demonstration.

1968, Mar. 5   Perf. 11
492-493 A191 12xu 2 blocks of 4 6.00 6.00
          Imperf., #492-493

Maxim Gorki (1868-1936) — A192

1968, Mar. 5
494 A192 12xu brown & black   1.75 .40
          Imperf.

Roses — A193

Designs: No. 495, 12xu, Pale red. No. 496, 12xu, Orange. No. 497, 12xu, Yellow, 30xu, Dark red. 40xu, Lilac.

1968, Apr. 25 Photo. Perf. 11½x12
495-500 A193 Set of 6   9.00 2.50
          Imperf., #495-500   15.00 15.00

**Ho Chi Minh's Appeal for
Resistance Type**

Values and colors: No. 501, 6xu, greenish blue and yellow. No. 502, 12xu, vermilion. No. 503, 12xu, bright blue. No. 504, 12xu, brownish lilac.

**1968, Apr. 25 Litho. Perf. 11
Size: 25x17mm**
501-504 A179 6xu, 12xu Set of 4 6.00 1.00
          Imperf., #501-504

Ho Chi Minh, Flag A195

1968, May 19
505 A195 12xu brown & red   1.60   .50
   Imperf.

Karl Marx — A196

1968, May 19
506 A196 12xu olive grn & blk   1.75   .40

3000th US Warplane Shot Down A197

#507: a, 12xu, Anti-aircraft machine gunners. b, 12xu, Women firing anti-aircraft gun. #508: a, 40xu, Vietnamese plane shooting down US plane. b, 40xu, Anti-aircraft missile.

1968, June 25
507-508 A197 Set of 2 pairs   12.00   4.50
   Imperf., #507-508

Handicrafts — A198

6xu, Rattan products. #510, 12xu, Ceramics. #511, 12xu, Bamboo products. 20xu, Ivory carving. 30xu, Lacquerware. 40xu, Silverware.

1968, July 5   **Perf. 12**
509-514 A198 Set of 6   6.50   2.50
   Imperf., #509-514   15.00   15.00

Martial Arts A199

Designs: No. 515, 12xu, Saber fencing. No. 516, 12xu, Stick fighting. No. 517, 12xu, Dagger fighting. 30xu, Unarmed combat. 40xu, Chinese war sword fighting. 50xu, Duel with swords, shields.

1968, Oct. 25
515-520 A199 Set of 6   10.00   2.50
   Imperf., #515-520   16.00   16.00

Architecture — A200

Designs: No. 521, 12xu, Khue Van tower, vert. No. 522, 12xu, Bell tower, Keo pagoda, vert. 20xu, Covered bridge, Thay pagoda. 30xu, One-pillar pagoda, Hanoi, vert. 40xu, Gateway, Ninh Phuc pagoda. 50xu, Tay Phuong pagoda.

1968, Nov. 15
521-526 A200 Set of 6   6.00   2.50
   Imperf., #521-526   10.00   10.00

Foreign Solidarity with Viet Nam — A201

#527, 12xu, Latin American guerrilla, vert. #528, 12xu, Cuban, Vietnamese militia. 20xu, Asian, African, Latin American soldiers, vert.

1968, Dec. 15   Wmk. 376   Perf. 12½
With Gum
527-529 A201 Set of 3   4.00   2.50

Scenes of War A202

Artworks: No. 530, 12xu, Defending the mines. No. 531, 12xu, Plowman with rifle, vert. 30xu, Repairing railway track. 40xu, Wreckage of US aircraft.

1968, Dec. 15   Wmk. 376   Perf. 12½
With Gum
530-533 A202 Set of 4   4.00   2.50

Victories in South Viet Nam — A203

#534, 12xu, Tay Nguyen throwing grenade. #535, 12xu, Gun crews, Tri Thien. #536, 12xu, Nam Ngai shooting down US aircraft. 40xu, Insurgents, Tay Ninh, destroyed US armor. 50xu, Guerrillas preparing bamboo spike booby traps.

1969, Feb. 16   Unwmk.   Perf. 11½
534-538 A203 Set of 5   6.00   2.00

Timber Industry A204

Designs: 6xu, Loading timber trucks. No. 540, 12xu, Log raft running rapids. No. 541,

---

12xu, Launch towing log raft. No. 542, 12xu, Elephant hauling timber. No. 543, 12xu, Forest protection. 20xu, Water buffalo hauling log. 30xu, Hauling logs by overhead cable.

1969, Apr. 10
539-545 A204 Set of 7   7.50   2.75
   Imperf., #539-545   15.00   15.00

Scenes of War — A205

Designs: No. 546, 12xu, Young guerrilla. No. 547, 12xu, Scout on patrol. 20xu, Female guerrilla, vert. 30xu, Halt at way station. 40xu, After a skirmish. 50xu, Liberated hamlet.

Perf. 12½x11½, 11½x12½
1969, June 20
546-551 A205 Set of 6   8.00   2.50
   Imperf., #546-551   15.00   15.00

Tet Offensive Battles — A206

Designs: 8xu, 12xu (No. 553), Ben Tre. No. 554, 12xu, Mortar crew, Khe Sanh, vert. No. 555, 12xu, Two soldiers, flag, Hue, vert. No. 556, 12xu, Soldier running toward US Embassy, Saigon, vert.

1969, Sept. 20   **Perf. 11**
552-556 A206 Set of 5   3.50   2.25
   Imperf., #552-556

Liberation of Hanoi, 15th Anniv. A207

#557, Soldier with flamethrower. #558, Children constructing toy buildings.

1969, Oct. 10
557-558 A207 12xu Set of 2   4.00   .80
   Imperf., #557-558

A208

1969, Nov. 20
559 A208 12xu brn, blk & red   2.50   .40
   Imperf.

Bertrand Russell Intl. War Crimes Tribunal, Stockholm and Roskilde.

A209

Fruits: No. 560, 12xu, Papaya. No. 561, 12xu, Grapefruit. 20xu, Tangerines. 30xu, Oranges. 40xu, Lychee nuts. 50xu, Persimmons.

1969, Nov. 20   **Perf. 12**
560-565 A209 Set of 6   5.50   2.75
   Imperf., #560-565   8.50   8.50

Viet Nam Labor Party, 40th Anniv. — A210

Designs: No. 566, Nguyen Ai Quoc. No. 567, Ho Chi Minh. No. 568, Le Hong Phong. No. 569, Tran Phu. No. 570, Nguyen Van Cu.

1970, Feb. 3   **Perf. 11**
566-570 A210 12xu Set of 5   4.00   3.25
   Imperf., #566-570

Nos. 568-570 are 40x25mm. Nos. 566-567 issued in vert. or horiz. se-tenant pairs. Nos. 568-570 issued in horizontal strips of 3.

Children's Activities — A211

Designs: No. 571, 12xu, Playing with toys. No. 572, 12xu, Three boys at kindergarten. No. 573, 20xu, Tending a garden. No. 574, 20xu, Tending water buffaloes. 30xu, Feeding chickens. 40xu, Piano, violin duet. 50xu, Flying model airplane. 60xu, Walking to school.

1970, Mar. 8   **Perf. 12**
571-578 A211 Set of 8   6.50   3.00

For overprints see Nos. 2181-2188.

Lenin, Birth Centenary A212

Designs: 12xu, Making speech. 1d, Portrait.

1970, Apr. 22   **Perf. 11**
579-580 A212 Set of 2   4.00   .80
   Imperf., #579-580

Shells A213

No. 581, 12xu, On con lon. No. 582, 12xu, Oc xa cu. 20xu, Oc tien. 1d, Oc tu va.

1970, Apr. 26   **Perf. 12½x12**
581-584 A213 Set of 4   6.50   1.50
   Imperf., #581-584   11.50   10.00

Ho Chi
Minh — A214

12xu (#585, 588c, 588g), In 1930 (full face, no beard). 12xu (#586, 588b, 588f), In 1945 (facing right, beard). 2d, 6xu, (#587, 588a, 588e), In 1969 (full face, beard).

1970, May 19   **Perf. 11**
585-587 A214 Set of 3   4.75 1.25
       Imperf., #585-587

Souvenir Sheets of 3
Imperf

588   Types of #585-587, #a.-c.,
       orange background   8.00 7.00
588D   Types of #585-587, #e.-g.,
       pale lilac background   8.00 7.00

Stamps in souvenir sheets have white backgrounds. The 6xu stamp is larger than the 2d stamp. Nos. 588a and 588e, 588c and 588g are different colors.

Vietcong
Flag
A215

1970, June 6
589   A215 12xu multicolored   1.50 .40

Formation of Revolutionary Provisional Government of South Viet Nam, 1st anniv.

Fruits and
Vegetables
A216

#590, 12xu, Watermelon. #591, 12xu, Pumpkin. 20xu, Cucumber. 50xu, Zucchini. 1d, Melon.

1970, July 15   **Perf. 12**
590-594 A216 Set of 5   4.50 2.00
       Imperf., #590-594   12.00 12.00

Consumer Industries — A217

#595, Coal miners, truck. #596, Power linesman, vert. #597, Textile worker, soldier, vert. #598, Stoker, power plant, vert.

Perf. 12x11½, 11½x12
1970, Aug. 25   **Litho. & Engr.**
595-598 A217 12xu Set of 4   4.00 1.50

Agriculture
A218

1970, Aug. 25   **Litho.**   **Perf. 11**
599   A218 12xu multicolored   2.00 .40

Democratic Republic of Viet Nam, 25th Anniv. — A219

Famous people: #600, 12xu, Vo Thi Sau facing firing squad. #601, 12xu, Nguyen Van Troi, captors. #602, 12xu, Phan Din Giot attacking pillbox. #603, 12xu, Ho Chi Minh. 20xu, Nguyen Viet Xuan, troops in battle. 1d, Nguyen Van Be attacking tank with mine.

1970-71
600-605 A219 Set of 6   4.00 4.00
       Imperf., #600-605

       No. 603 is 41x28mm.
       Issued 9/2-71: Nos. 600, 603, 604; 3/71: Nos. 601, 602, 605.

Indo-Chinese People's Summit
Conf. — A220

1970, Oct. 25
606   A220 12xu multicolored   2.50 .40
       Imperf.

Bananas
A221

Designs: No. 607, 12xu, Tay. No. 608, 12xu, Tieu. 50xu, Ngu. 1d, Mat.

1970, Oct. 25   **Perf. 12**
607-610 A221 Set of 4   6.00 1.50
       Imperf., #607-610   12.00 12.00

Friedrich Engels — A222

1970, Nov. 28   **Perf. 11**
611-612 A222 12xu, 1d set of 2   2.50 .80

Snakes
A223

Designs: 12xu, Akistrodon ciatus. 20xu, Calliophis macclellandii. 50xu, Bungarus faciatus. 1d, Trimeresurus gramineus.

1970, Nov. 30 Photo.   Perf. 12x11½
613-616 A223 Set of 4   6.00 .80
       Imperf., #613-616   20.00 20.00

Natl. Liberation Front of South Viet Nam, 10th Anniv. — A224

Design: 6xu, Mother and child, flag, vert.

1970, Dec. 20   Litho.   Perf. 11
617-618 A224 Set of 2   2.50 .80
       Imperf., #617-618

Victory Type of 1966
1971, Mar.?
618A   A175 2xu black & orange   2.00 .40

Launching of 1st Chinese Satellite, 1st
Anniv. — A225

1971, Apr. 10
619-620 A225 12xu, 50xu Set of
                                   2   4.00 .80
       Imperf., #619-620

Ho Chi
Minh
A226

Denominations: 1xu, 3xu, 10xu, 12xu.

1971, May 19
621-624 A226 Set of 4   2.00 1.50
       Imperf., #621-624
624a   Souvenir sheet of 1, imperf.   6.00 5.00

No. 624a contains one 52x52mm stamp.

Tay Son Uprising, Bicent. — A227

1971, May 25
625-626 A227 6xu, 12xu, set of 2 3.00 .80
       Imperf., #625-626

Marx, Music for The
Internationale — A228

1971, June 20   **Perf. 12½**
627   A228 12xu org, blk & red   1.50 .40
       Imperf.

Paris Commune, cent.

Hai
Thuong
Lan Ong,
Physician,
250th Birth
Anniv.
A229

1971, July 1
628-629 A229 12xu, 50xu Set of
                                   2   3.50 .80
       Imperf., #628-629

Statues from
Tay Phuong
Pagoda
A230

Designs: No. 630, 12xu, Vasumitri. No. 631, 12xu, Kapimala. No. 632, 12xu, Dhikaca. No. 633, 12xu, Sangkayasheta. 30xu, Bouddha Nandi. 40xu, Rahulata. 50xu, Sangha Nandi. 1d, Cakyamuni.

1971, July 30   Photo.   Perf. 12
630-637 A230 Set of 8   12.00 3.00
       Imperf., #630-637   20.00 20.00

Ho Chi Minh
Working Youth
Union, 40th
Anniv.
A231

1971, Sept. 7   Litho.   Perf. 11
638   A231 12xu multicolored   1.50 .40
       Imperf.

Flight of Luna
16 — A232

Luna 16: No. 639a, 12xu, Return from Moon. No. 639b, 12xu, Flight to Moon. 1d, On Moon.

1971, Sept. 17
639-640 A232 Set of 3   4.00 1.25
       Imperf., #639-640   15.00 15.00

       No. 639 is se-tenant.

Flight
of
Luna
17
A233

Designs: No. 641, 12xu, Landing on Moon,
vert. No. 642 12xu, On Moon. 1d, Lunakhod 1
crossing lunar crevasse.

1971, Oct. 15
641-643 A233 Set of 3   5.00 1.25
   Imperf., #641-643   15.00 15.00

Five Tigers
A234

Folk paintings: No. 644, 12xu, White tiger.
No. 645, 12xu, Red tiger. No. 646, 12xu, Yellow tiger. 40xu, Green tiger. 50xu, Black tiger.
1d, Five tigers.

1971, Nov. 25   **Perf. 12**
644-649 A234 Set of 6   10.00 2.50
   Imperf., #644-649   18.00 18.00
           Size: 90x119mm
              Imperf
650 A234 1d multicolored   14.00 12.00

Chinese
Communist
Party, 50th
Anniv.
A235

1971, Dec. 1   **Perf. 11**
651 A235 12xu multicolored   1.50   .40

Mongolian
People's Republic,
50th
Anniv. — A236

1971, Dec. 25
652 A236 12xu multicolored   1.50   .40

Folk Engravings from Dong
Ho — A237

#653a, 12xu, Traditional wrestling. #653b,
12xu, Drum procession. #654a, 12xu, Gathering coconuts, vert. #654b, 12xu, Jealousy,
vert. 40xu, Wedding of mice. 50xu, Frog
school.

1972, Jan. 30
653-656 A237 Set of 6   10.00 5.00
   Imperf., #653-656   12.00 12.00
     No. 653 is tete-beche.
The 30xu in design of #654a is a proof.

3rd Natl.
Trade
Unions
Congress
A238

Designs: 1xu, Workers facing right. 12xu,
Workers facing left.

1972, May 1
657-658 A238 Set of 2   2.00   .80
   Imperf., #657-658   10.00 10.00

Natl.
Resistance,
25th
Anniv. — A239

Designs: No. 659, Munitions worker. No.
660, Soldier in battle. No. 661, Woman in
paddy field. No. 662, Text of Ho Chi Minh's
appeal.

1972, May 5
659-662 A239 12xu Set of 4   3.00 1.50
   Imperf., #659-662   20.00 20.00

Ho Chi
Minh's
Birthplace
A240

Design: No. 664, Home in Hanoi.

1972, May 19
663-664 A240 12xu Set of 2   2.50   .80
   Imperf., #663-664   5.00 5.00

A241

1972, June 20
665-666 A241 12xu Set of 2   5.00 2.50
   Imperf., #665-666
   3500th US warplane shot down.
Added inscription on No. 666 reads "NGAY
20.4.1972."

A242

Georgi Dimitrov (1882-1949), Bulgarian politician: No. 668, Dimitrov at Leipzig Court,
1933.

1972, Aug. 15
667-668 A242 12xu Set of 2   2.50   .80
   Imperf., #667-668   5.00 5.00

Birds — A243

Designs: No. 669, 12xu, Lobivanellus
indicus. No. 670, 12xu, Anas falcata. 30xu,
Bubulcus ibis. 40xu, Gallicrex cinerea. 50xu,
Prophyria porphyrio. 1d, Leptoptilos dubius.

1972, Oct. 12   **Perf. 12**
669-674 A243 Set of 6   10.00 2.50
   Imperf., #669-674   22.50 22.50

A244

4000th US warplane shot down: No. 676,
Gunner holding rocket.

1972, Oct. 17   **Perf. 11**
675-676 A244 12xu Set of 2   8.00 1.50
   Imperf., #675-676   9.00

A245

Tay Nguyen folk dances: #677, 12xu, Drum.
#678, 12xu, Umbrella. #679, 12xu, Shield.
20xu, Horse. 30xu, Ca Dong. 40xu, Rice
pounding. 50xu, Khaen. 1d, Cham rong.

1972, Dec. 20   **Perf. 12**
677-684 A245 Set of 8   8.00 3.00
   Imperf., #677-684   10.00 10.00

Flight
of
Soyuz
11
A246

Designs: 12xu, Soyuz 11 docking with
Salyut laboratory. 1d, Soyuz 11 cosmonauts.

1972, Dec. 30   **Perf. 11**
685-686 A246 Set of 2   3.00   .80
   Imperf., #685-686   8.00 8.00

Wild Animals — A247

Designs: 12xu, Cuon alpinus. 30xu,
Panthera pardus. 50xu, Felis bengalensis. 1d,
Lutra lutra.

Copernicus
A248

Copernicus and: No. 691a, 12xu, Armillary
sphere. No. 691b, 12xu, Sun. 30xu, Signature,
vert.

1973, Feb. 19   **Perf. 11**
691-692 A248 Set of 3   4.00 2.00
   Imperf., #691-692

1973, Feb. 15   **Perf. 12½**
687-690 A247 Set of 4   7.00 1.50
   Imperf., #687-690   20.00 20.00

Engravings on Ngoc Lu Bronze
Drums — A249

Designs: No. 693, Drummers (Nha Danh
Trong). No. 694, Pounding rice (Nha Gia Gao).
No. 695, Dancers (Mua). No. 696, War canoe
(Thuyen). No. 697, Birds (Chim, Thu).

1973, Apr. 12
693-697 A249 12xu Set of 5   4.00 2.00
   Imperf., #693-697

Wild
Animals — A250

Designs: 12xu, Tragulus javanicus. 30xu,
Capricornis sumatraensis. 50xu, Sus scrofa.
1d, Moschus moschiferus.

1973, May 25   **Perf. 12x12½**
698-701 A250 Set of 4   5.00 1.50
   Imperf., 698-701   12.00 12.00

Birds
A251

#702, 12xu, Pycnonotus jocosus. #703,
12xu, Megalurus palustris. 20xu, Capsychus
saularis. 40xu, Rhipidura albicollis. 50xu,
Parus major. 1d, Zosterops japonica.

1973, July 15   **Perf. 12**
702-707 A251 Set of 6   7.00 2.50
   Imperf., 702-707   15.00 15.00

Disabled Soldiers
A252   A252a

1973, July 27   *Perf. 11*
708-709 A252, A252a 12xu Set
         of 2   .80   .80
     Imperf., #708-709

Nos. 708-709 were issued for the use of disabled soldiers.

Three Readiness Youth Movement A253

Designs: No. 710, Road building. No. 711, Open-air class. No. 712, On the march.

1973, Sept. 2
710-712 A253 12xu Set of 3   2.00   1.25
     Imperf., #710-712

Democratic People's Republic of Korea, 25th Anniv. — A254

1973, Sept. 9
713 A254 12xu multicolored   1.50   .40
     Imperf.

4181st US Warplane Shot Down A255

Designs: No. 714, 12xu, US B-52 hit by air attack. No. 715, 12xu, US B-52, fighter crashing over Haiphong Harbor. No. 716, 12xu, Anti-aircraft battery. 1d, Aircraft wreckage caught in fishing net.

1973, Oct. 10
714-717 A255   Set of 4   9.00   2.00
     Imperf., #714-717

Flowers — A256

6xu, 12xu (#719), Chrysanthemum (Cuc). #720, 12xu, Rose. #721, 12xu, Dahlia. #722, 12xu, Chrysanthemum (Bach mi). #723, 12xu, Chrysanthemum (Dai doa).

1974, Jan. 15
718-723 A256   Set of 6   40.00
     Imperf., #718-723   70.00

Nos. 718-723 may not have been officially released.

Elephants A257

#724, 12xu, Hauling logs. #725, 12xu, War elephant. 40xu, Setting logs in place. 50xu, Circus elephant. 1d, Carrying war supplies.

1974, Feb. 10   *Perf. 11½*
724-728 A257   Set of 5   7.50   2.00
     Imperf., #724-728   12.00   12.00

Victory at Dien Bien Phu, 20th Anniv. — A258

Designs: a, Dien Bien Phu soldier's badge. b, Soldier waving victory flag.

1974, May 7   *Perf. 11*
729 A258 12xu Pair, #a.-b.   2.50   .70
     Imperf.   5.00   5.00

Three Responsibilities Women's Movement — A259

Designs: a, Armed worker, peasant. b, Female textile worker.

1974, June 1
730 A259 12xu Pair, #a.-b.   2.50   1.25
     Imperf.

A260

Chrysanthemums: No. 731, 12xu, Brown. No. 732, 12xu, Yellow (Vang). 20xu, Ngoc Khong Tuoc. 30xu, White. 40xu, Kim. 50xu, Hong mi. 60xu, Gam. 1d, Lilac.

1974, June 20   *Perf. 12x12½*
731-738 A260   Set of 8   7.00   4.00
     Imperf., #731-738   10.00   10.00

A261

Industrial plants: No. 739, 12xu, Corchorus capsularis. No. 740, 12xu, Cyperus tojet jormis. 30xu, Morus alba.

1974, Aug. 15   *Perf. 11*
739-741 A261   Set of 3   4.00   1.25
     Imperf., #739-741   10.00   10.00

Liberation of Hanoi, 20th Anniv. — A262

Designs: a, Woman laying bricks. b, Soldier holding child waving flag.

1974, Oct. 10
742 A262 12xu Pair, #a.-b.   2.50   .80
     Imperf.

Solidarity with Chilean Revolution A263

Designs: No. 743, Pres. Salvador Allende, flag. No. 744, Pablo Neruda, poet.

1974, Oct. 15
743-744 A263 12xu Set of 2   2.50   .70
     Imperf., #743-744   5.00   5.00

Marine Life — A264

Designs: No. 745, 12xu, Rhizostoma. No. 746, 12xu, Loligo. 30xu, Haleotis. 40xu, Pteria martensii. 50xu, Sepia officinalis. 1d, Palinurus japonicus.

1974, Oct. 25   *Perf. 12½*
745-750 A264   Set of 6   7.00   2.50
     Imperf., #745-750   12.00   12.00

People's Republic of Albania, 30th Anniv. — A265

Designs: a, Natl. arms. b, Albanian, Vietnamese flags, women.

1974, Nov. 29   *Perf. 11*
752 A265 12xu Pair, #a.-b.   2.25   .75
     Imperf.

Paris Agreement on Vietnam, 2nd Anniv. — A266

Designs: No. 753, Intl. Conference on Viet Nam in session, 5-line inscription. No. 754, Signing of Paris Agreement, 4-line inscription.

1975, Jan. 27
753-754 A266 12xu Set of 2   2.50   .75
     Imperf.

Medicinal Plants — A267

Designs: No. 755, 12xu, Costus speciosus. No. 756, 12xu, Curcuma zedoaria. No. 757, 12xu, Rosa laevigata. 30xu, Erythrina indica. 40xu, Lilium brownii. 50xu, Hibiscus sagittifolius. 60xu, Papaver somniferum. 1d, Belamcanda chinensis.

1975, Feb. 8   *Perf. 11½x12*
755-762 A267   Set of 8   8.00   3.00
     Imperf., #755-762   12.50   12.50

Vietnamese Labor Party, 45th Anniv. — A268

Designs: No. 763, 12xu, Tran Phu. No. 764, 12xu, Le Hong Phong. No. 765, 12xu, Nguyen Van Cu. No. 766, 12xu, Ngo Gia Tu. 60xu, Ho Chi Minh in 1924, vert.

1975, Feb. 3   *Perf. 11*
763-767 A268   Set of 5   2.50   1.50
     Imperf., #763-767   10.00   10.00

A269

Fruit: No. 768, 12xu, Achras sapota. No. 769, 12xu, Persica vulgaris. 20xu, Eugenia jambos. 30xu, Chrysophyllum cainito. 40xu, Lucuma mamosa. 50xu, Prunica granitum. 60xu, Durio ziberthinus. 1d, Prunus salicina.

1975, Apr. 25   *Perf. 12x12½*
768-775 A269   Set of 8   6.50   3.00
     Imperf., 768-775   12.00   12.00

A270

No. 776, 12xu. No. 777, 60xu.

1975, May 19   *Perf. 11*
776-777 A270   Set of 2   3.50   1.25
     Imperf., #776-777   10.00   10.00

Ho Chi Minh, 85th birthday.

People's Republic of Poland, 30th Anniv. A271

1975, July 5
778-781 A271 1xu, 2xu, 3xu,
12xu, set of 4   3.00   .80
Imperf., #778-781

Flags
A272

Natl. Arms — A273

Flag of North Viet Nam and: No. 782,
Draped flag. No. 783, Flag with star & cresent.
No. 784, DDR flag and handshake.

1975
782-785 A272-A273 12xu Set of
4   7.00   .80
Imperf., #782-784

People's Republic of China, 25th anniv.
(#782), Republic of Algeria, 20th anniv.
(#783), German Democratic Republic, 25th
anniv. (#784), liberation of Hungary, 30th
anniv. (#785).
Issued: No. 782, 7/5. Nos. 783-785, 8/15.

Independence, 30th Anniv. — A274

#786, Flag. #787, Natl. arms. #788-789, Ho
Chi Minh proclaiming independence.

1975, Sept. 2
786-788 A274 12xu Set of 3   3.50 1.25
Souvenir Sheet
Imperf
789   A274 20xu multi   20.00 15.00

No. 789 contains one 45x30mm stamp.

Reptiles
A275

#790, 12xu, Dermochelys coriacea. #791,
12xu, Physignathus cocincinus. 20xu,
Hydrophis brookii. 30xu, Platysternum
megacephalum. 40xu, Leiolepis belliana.
50xu, Python molurus. 60xu, Naja hannah. 1d,
Draco maculatus.

1975, Nov. 25   *Perf. 12*
790-797 A275 Set of 8   9.00 3.00
Imperf., #790-797   15.00 15.00

Butterflies — A276

#798, 12xu, Pathysa antiphates. #799,
12xu, Danaus plexippus. 20xu, Cynautocera
papilionaria. 30xu, Maenas salaminia. 40xu,
Papilio machaon. 50xu, Ixias pyrene. 60xu,
Eusemia vetula. 1d, Eriboea.

1976, Jan. 6
798-805 A276 Set of 8   9.00 3.00
Imperf., #798-805   25.00 25.00

No. 799 misspelled "Danais."

Lan Hoang
Thao Orchid
A277

1976, Jan. 25   *Perf. 11*
806-807 A277 6xu, 12xu, set of 2 4.00 1.50

See Nos. 854-855.

Wild Animals
A278

#808, 12xu, Callosciurus erythraeus. #809,
12xu, Paguma larvata. 20xu, Macaca mulatta.
30xu, Hystrix hodgsoni. 40xu, Nyctereutes
procyonoides. 50xu, Selenarctos thibetanus.
60xu, Panthera pardus. 1d, Cynocephalus
variegatus.

1976, Mar. 20   *Perf. 12*
808-815 A278 Set of 8   7.00 2.50
Imperf., #808-815   15.00 15.00

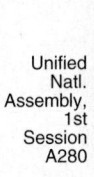

1st
Elections
to Unified
Natl.
Assembly
A279

6xu (#816), Map, hand placing ballot in ballot box. 6xu (#817), 12xu, Map, voters.

1976, Apr. 10   *Perf. 11*
816-818 A279 Set of 3   3.50 1.25
Imperf., #816-818

Size of Nos. 817-818 is 35x22mm.
Identical stamps inscribed "Mien Nam Viet
Nam" are National Front issues. Same values.

Unified
Natl.
Assembly,
1st
Session
A280

Design: 12xu, Inscribed "Doc Lap Thong
Nhat Chu Nghia Xa Hoi."

1976, June 24
819-820 A280 6xu, 12xu, set of 2 2.50 .80

Identical stamps inscribed "Mien Nam Viet
Nam" are National Front issues. Same values.

A281

1976, June 24   *Perf. 12x12½*
821   A281 12xu multicolored   1.50   .40

Reunification of Viet Nam.

A282

Orchids: No. 822, 12xu, Habenaria
rhodocheila. No. 823, 12xu, Dendrobium
devonianum. 20xu, Dendrobium tortile. 30xu,
Doritis pulcherrima. 40xu, Dendrobium
farmeri. 50xu, Dendrobium aggregatum. 60xu,
Eria pannea. 1d, Paphiopedilum concolor.

1976, June 24   *Perf. 12*
822-829 A282 Set of 8   9.00 2.00
Imperf., #822-829   12.00 12.00

DEMOCRATIC REPUBLIC OF VIET NAM
(After Unification)

AREA — 128,000 sq. mi.
POP. — 77,311,210 (1999 est.)
CAPITAL — Hanoi

Vietnamese Red Cross, 30th
Anniv. — A283

1976, July 27   *Perf. 11*
830   A283 12xu multicolored   2.50   .40
Imperf.

Fish — A284

#831, 12xu, Lutjanus sebae. #832, 12xu,
Dampieria melanotaenia. 20xu, Therapon
theraps. 30xu, Amphiprion bifasciatus. 40xu,
Abudefduf sexfasciatus. 50xu, Heniochus
acuminatus. 60xu, Amphiprion macrostoma.
1d, Symphorus spilurus.

1976, Aug. 15   *Perf. 12*
831-838 A284 Set of 8   8.00 3.00
Imperf., #831-838   10.00 10.00

Viet Nam
Worker's
Party, 4th
Natl.
Congress
A285

1976, Nov. 12   *Perf. 11*
839-844 A285 2, 3, 5, 10, 12,
20xu, set of 6   3.50 2.50

Viet Nam Communist Party, 4th Natl.
Congress — A286

Designs: a, Agriculture, industry. b, Ho Chi
Minh, worker, farmer, soldier, scientist.

Design size: 24.5mmx35mm

1976, Dec. 10
845   A286 12xu Pair, #a.-b.   2.50   .80
Imperf.

See Nos. 951-954.

Unification of Viet
Nam — A287

1976, Dec. 14
846-847 A287 6xu, 12xu, set of 2 2.50 .80
Imperf., #846-847   4.50

General Offensive, 1975 — A288

Designs: 2xu, 50xu, Liberation of Buon Me
Thuot. 3xu, 1d, Tanks liberating Da Nang. 6xu,
2d, Tank, soldiers liberating Presidential palace, Saigon.

1976, Dec. 14
848-853 A288 Set of 6   4.50 2.50

**Lan Hoang Thao Orchid Type of
1976 Inscribed "VIET NAM" and
"1976"**

1976, Dec.   *Litho.*   *Perf. 11*
854-855 A277 6xu, 12xu Set of
2   12.00 10.00

Dragonflies — A289

#856, 12xu, Ho. #857, 12xu, Bao. 20xu,
Canh dom. 30xu, Nuong. 40xu, Suoi. 50xu,
Canh vang. 60xu, Canh khoang. 1d, Canh
den.

1977, Jan. 25   *Perf. 12*
856-863   A289   Set of 8   7.00   1.50
    Imperf., #856-863   15.00   15.00

A290

Rare Birds: 12xu (#864), 60xu, Buceros bicornis. 12xu (#865), Ptilolaemus tickelli. 20xu, Berenicornis comatus. 30xu, Aceros undulatus. 40xu, Anthracoceros malabaricus. 50xu, Anthracoceros malayanus. 1d, Aceros nipalensis.

1977, Apr. 15
864-871   A290   Set of 8   6.00   2.00
    Imperf., #864-871   10.00   10.00

A291

Bronze drum and: 4xu, Thang Long Tower. 5xu, Map. 12xu, Lotus blossom. 50xu, Flag.

1977, Apr. 25   *Perf. 11*
872-875   A291   Set of 4   4.50   2.00
    Imperf., #872-875

Natl. Assembly general elections, 1st anniv.

Beetles
A292

#876, 12xu, Black-spotted (Dom den). #877, 12xu, Yellow-spotted (Lang vang). 20xu, Veined (Van gach). 30xu, Green (Nhung xanh). 40xu, Green-spotted (Hoa xanh). 50xu, Black (Van den). 60xu, Leopard skin (Da bao). 1d, Nine-spotted (Chin cham).

1977, June 15   *Perf. 12½x12*
876-883   A292   Set of 8   7.00   1.75
    Imperf., #876-883   12.00   12.00

Wildflowers
A293

Designs: No. 884, 12xu, Thevetia peruviana. No. 885, 12xu, Broussonetia papvrifera. 20xu, Aleurites montana. 30xu, Cerbera manghes. 40xu, Cassia multijuga. 50xu, Cassia nodosa. 60xu, Hibiscus schizopetalus. 1d, Lagerstroesnia speciosa.

1977, Aug. 19   *Perf. 12x12½*
884-891   A293   Set of 8   5.00   1.75
    Imperf., #884-891   10.00   10.00

A294

Dahlias: 6xu (#892), 12xu (#894), Pink. 6xu (#893), 12xu (#895), Orange.

1977, Sept. 10   *Perf. 11*
892-895   A294   Set of 4   4.00   .60
    See Nos. 921-924.

A295

Children drawing map of unified Viet Nam. Denominations: 4xu, 5xu, 10xu, 12xu, 30xu each have different colored border.

1977, Sept. 10
896-900   A295   Set of 5   5.00   2.00

Goldfish
A296

Designs: No. 901, 12xu, Dong nai. No. 902, 12xu, Velvet (Hoa nhung). 20xu, Blue Chinese (Tau xanh). 30xu, Dragon-eyed (Mat bong). 40xu, Cam trang. 50xu, Five-colored (Ngu sac). 60xu, Dong nai. 1d, Thap cam.

1977, Oct. 20   *Perf. 12*
901-908   A296   Set of 8   7.50   1.50
    Imperf., #901-908   10.00   10.00

A297

Russian October Revolution, 60th anniv.: 12xu (No. 909, olive background), 12xu (No. 910, blue background), Ho Chi Minh, Lenin banner. 50xu, Mother holding child with flag. 1d, Workers, farmers, Moscow Kremlin, cruiser Aurora.

1977, Nov. 7
909-912   A297   Set of 4   3.25   1.50

A298

Songbirds: 12xu, Gracula religiosa. No. 914, 20xu, Garrulax canorus. No. 915, 20xu, Streptopelia chinensis. 30xu, Linius schach. 40xu, Garrulax formosus. 50xu, Garrulax chinensis. 60xu, Acridotheres cristatellus. 1d, Garrulax yersini.

1978, Jan. 25
913-920   A298   Set of 8   6.00   1.75
    Imperf., #913-920   12.00   12.00

Cultivated Flower Type of 1977

5xu, 10xu, Sunflower. 6xu, 12xu, Pansy.

1978, Mar. 20   *Perf. 11*
921-924   A294   Set of 4   4.25   .60

Intl. Children's Day (June 1977) — A299

1978, Mar. 20
925   A299   12xu multicolored   1.75   .40

Sports
A300

#926, 12xu, Discus. #927, 12xu, Long jump. 20xu, Hurdles. 30xu, Hammer throw. 40xu, Shot put. 50xu, Javelin. 60xu, Running. 1d, High jump.

1978, Apr. 10   *Perf. 11½*
926-933   A300   Set of 8   4.50   1.50
    Imperf., #926-933   10.00   10.00

A301

4th Viet Nam Trade Union Cong.: #934, Trade Union emblem. #935, Ho Chi Minh, workers.

1978, May 1   *Perf. 11*
934-935   A301   10xu Set of 2   2.50   .80

A302

10xu, Ho Chi Minh conducting orchestra. 12xu, Ho Chi Minh's mausoleum, horiz.

1978, May 15
936-937   A302   Set of 2   2.25   .80
    No. 937 is 39x23mm.

Young Pioneers' Cultural Palace, Hanoi — A303

1978, May 29
938   A303   10xu multicolored   1.50   .40
    Intl. Children's Day.

Sculptures from Tay Phuong Pagoda — A304

Designs: No. 939, 12xu, Sanakavasa. No. 940, 12xu, Parsva. No. 941, 12xu, Punyasas. No. 942, 20xu, Kumarata. No. 943, 20xu, Nagarjuna. 30xu, Yayata. 40xu, Cadiep. 50xu, Ananda. 60xu, Buddhamitra. 1d, Asvagmosa.

1978, July 1   *Perf. 12*
939-948   A304   Set of 10   7.00   1.50
    Imperf., #939-948   20.00   20.00

Cuban Revolution, 25th Anniv. — A305

1978, July 20   *Perf. 11*
949-950   A305   6xu, 12xu Set of 2   2.50   .80

Types of 1976

6xu (No. 951), 12xu (No. 953), like #845a. 6xu (No. 952), 12xu (No. 952), like #845b.

Design size: 18.5mmx23mm

1978, Aug. 15
951-954   A286   Set of 4   4.00   2.00

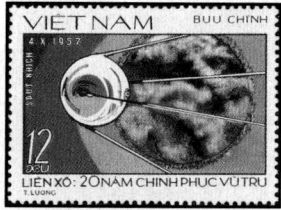
Space Exploration, 20th Anniv. — A306

#955, 12xu, Sputnik. #956, 12xu, Venera 1. 30xu, Spacecraft docking. 40xu, Molniya 1. 60xu, Soyuz. 2d, Cosmonauts Gubarev, Grechko.

1978, Aug. 28   *Perf. 12½x12*
955-960   A306   Set of 6   5.00   1.75
    Imperf., #955-960   10.00   10.00

World Telecommunications Day — A307

Designs: a, Printed circuit. b, ITU emblem.

1978, Sept. 25   **Perf. 11**
962 A307 12xu Pair, #a.-b.   2.50   .80
    Imperf.   18.00   18.00

20th Congress of Socialist Postal
Ministers — A308

1978, Sept. 25
963 A308 12xu multicolored   1.50   .40

Chrysanthemums — A309

No. 964, 12xu, Tim. No. 965, 12xu, Kim tien.
20xu, Hong. 30xu, Van tho. 40xu, Vang. 50xu,
Thuy tim. 60xu, Hong. 1d, Nau do.

1978, Oct. 1   **Perf. 12**
964-971 A309 Set of 8   5.50   1.50
    Imperf., #964-971   12.00   12.00

Dinosaurs
A310

Designs: No. 972, 12xu, Plesiosaurus. No.
973, 12xu, Brontosaurus. 20xu, Iguanodon.
30xu, Tyrannosaurus rex. 40xu, Stegosaurus.
50xu, Mosasaurus. 60xu, Triceratops. 1d,
Pteranodon.

1979, Jan. 1   **Litho.**   **Perf. 11½**
972-979 A310 Set of 8   10.00   1.25
    Imperf., #972-979   17.00   17.00

No. 977 misspelled "Mozasaurus."

A311

1979, Jan. 1   **Perf. 11**
980 A311 12xu multicolored   1.50   .40
    Imperf.   5.00   5.00

Socialist Republic of Cuba, 20th anniv.

A312

Quang Trung's victory over the Chinese,
190th Anniv.: #981, Battle plan. #982, Quang
Trung.

1979, Feb. 1
981-982 A312 12xu Set of 2   2.50   .80
    a.   Perf 12, #981-982   20.00

Albert Einstein,
Physicist
A313

Designs: No. 983, 12xu, Einstein. No. 984,
60xu, Equation, sun, planets.

1979, Mar. 14
983-984 A313 12xu, 60xu, set of
          2   4.00   .50

Domestic Animals — A314

10xu, Ram. 12xu, Ox. 20xu, Ewe, lamb.
30xu, White water buffalo, vert. 40xu, Cow.
50xu, Goat. 60xu, Water buffalo, calf. 1d,
Young goat, vert.

1979, Mar. 20   **Perf. 12**
985-992 A314 Set of 8   5.00   1.25
    Imperf., #985-992   8.00   8.00

Five Year Plan (1976-
80) — A315

#993, 998, Map, emblem. #994, 999, Fac-
tory worker. #995, 1000, Peasant woman,
tractor. #996, 1001, Soldier. #997, 1002, Man,
atom, compass.

1979   **Perf. 11**
993-997 A315   6xu Set of 5   5.00   2.00
998-1002 A315 12xu Set of 5   5.00   5.00
  1000a   Perf. 12
    Nos. 993-1002 (2)   10.00   7.00

Issued: Nos. 993-997, 5/1. Nos. 998-1002,
6/1. Nos. 993, 996-1002 on toned paper.

Philaserdica
'79, Intl.
Stamp
Exhibition,
Sofia,
Bulgaria
A316

1979, May 27   **Perf. 12**
1003-1004   12xu, 30xu Set of 2   2.50   .80

Intl. Year of the
Child — A317

2xu, Ho Chi Minh, children. 20xu, Nurse,
mother, child. 50xu, Children with glider, painting supplies. 1d, Girls of different races.

1979, June 1   **Perf. 11**
1005-1008 A317   Set of 4   4.00   1.50

Ornamental Birds — A318

#1009, 12xu, Lophura diardi. #1010, 12xu,
Tragopan temminckii. 20xu, Phasianus
colchicus. 30xu, Lophura edwardsi. 40xu,
Lophura nycthemera, vert. 50xu, Polyplectron
germaini, vert. 60xu, Rheinhardia ocellata,
vert. 1d, Pavo muticus, vert.

1979, June 16   **Perf. 12**
1009-1016 A318 Set of 8   6.50   1.75
    Imperf., #1009-1016   12.00   12.00

Orchids
A319

Designs: No. 1017, 12xu, Dendrobium
heterocacpum. No. 1018, 12xu, Cymbidium
hybridum. 20xu, Rhynchostylis gigantea.
30xu, Dendrobium mobile. 40xu, Aerides falcatum. 50xu, Paphiopedilum callosum. 60xu,
Vanda teres. 1d, Dendrobium phalaenopsis.

1979, Aug. 10   **Perf. 12**
1017-1024 A319 Set of 8   6.50   1.75
    Imperf., #1017-1024   12.00   12.00

Cats
A320

Designs: No. 1025, 12xu, Meo tam the. No.
1026, 12xu, Meo muop, vert. 20xu, Meo
khoang, vert. 30xu, Meo dom van. 40xu, Meo
muop dom, vert. 50xu, Meo vang, vert. 60xu,
Meo xiem. 1d, Meo van am.

1979, Nov. 10
1025-1032 A320   Set of 8   5.50   3.00
    Imperf., #1025-1032   12.00   12.00

Vietnamese People's Army, 25th
Anniv. — A321

a, People greeting soldiers. b, Frontier
guards.

1979, Dec. 22   **Perf. 11**
1033 A321 12xu Pair, #a.-b.   1.00   1.00

Roses — A322

Designs: 1xu, 12xu (No. 1036), Red, pink
roses. 2xu, 12xu (No. 1037), Single pink rose.

1980, Jan. 1
1034-1037 A322   Set of 4   4.50   1.50
     See Nos. 1084-1085.

Aquatic
Flowers
A323

#1038, 12xu, Nelumbium nuciferum. #1039,
12xu, Nymphala stellata. 20xu, Ipomola
reptans. 30xu, Nymphoides indicum. 40xu,
Jussiala repens. 50xu, Eichhornia crassipes.
60xu, Monochoria voginalis. 1d, Nelumbo
nucifera.

1980, Jan. 15   **Perf. 12½**
1038-1045 A323   Set of 8   4.75   1.25
    Imperf., #1038-1045   9.00   9.00

Vietnamese Communist Party, 50th
Anniv. — A324

Designs: No. 1046a, Ho Chi Minh proclaiming independence, 1945. No. 1046b, Peasants
with banner, improvised weapons. No. 1047a,
Map, soldiers, tanks storming palace. No.
1047b, Soldiers waving flag at Dien Bien Phu.
2d, Ho Chi Minh, soldiers and workers.

1980, Feb. 3   **Perf. 11**
1046 A324 12xu Pair, #a.-b.   1.00   .75
1047 A324 20xu Pair, #a.-b.   1.00   .75
1048 A324   2d multicolored   2.00   .40
    Nos. 1046-1048 (3)   4.00   1.90

Lenin,
110th
Anniv.
of Birth
A325

1980, Apr. 22   **Perf. 12**
1049-1051 A325   6xu, 12xu, 1d,
     set of 3   3.25   2.00

1980
Summer
Olympics,
Moscow
A326

#1052, 12xu, Hurdles. #1053, 12xu, Run-
ning. 20xu, Team handball. 30xu, Soccer.
40xu, Wrestling. 50xu, Gymnastics, horiz.
60xu, Swimming, horiz. 1d, Sailing, horiz.

1980, May 1   **Perf. 12x12½, 12½x12**
1052-1059 A326 Set of 8   6.00   1.25
    Imperf., #1052-1059   10.00   10.00

A327

Ho Chi Minh, 90th anniv. of birth: 12xu, In 1924. 40xu, As president.

1980, May 19   **Perf. 11**
1060-1061 A327 Set of 2   2.25 1.25

A328

1980, June 15
1062 A328 5xu multicolored   1.25 .40

Intl. Children's Day.

Intercosmos '80, Soviet-Vietnamese Space Mission — A329

Designs: No. 1063, 12xu, Cosmonauts. No. 1064, 12xu, Soyuz 37 atop booster. 20xu, Soyuz 37. 40xu, Soyuz docking with Salyut space station. 1d, Soyuz firing retro-rockets. 2d, Parachute landing. 3d, Cosmonauts, Soyuz-Salyut station.

1980, July 24   **Perf. 12x12½**
1063-1068 A329 Set of 6   5.50 1.00
     Imperf., #1063-1068   10.00 10.00
Souvenir Sheet
1069 A329 3d multicolored   8.00 8.00
     Imperf.   9.00 9.00

Saltwater Fish — A330

Designs: No. 1070, 12xu, Rhincodon typus. No. 1071, 12xu, Galeocerdo cuvier. 20xu, Orectolobus japonicus. 30xu, Heterodontus zebra. 40xu, Dasyatis uarnak. 50xu, Pristis microdon. 60xu, Sphyrna lewini. 1d, Myliobatis tobijei.

1980, Aug. 1   **Perf. 12**
1070-1077 A330 Set of 8   6.50 1.75
     Imperf., #1070-1077   10.00 10.00

A331

Post and Telecommunications Office, 35th Anniv.: 12xu, Ho Chi Minh reading newspaper. 20xu, Ho Chi Minh talking on telephone. 50xu, Kim Dong carrying bird in cage. 1d, Dish antenna.

1980, Aug. 15   **Litho.**   **Perf. 12½**
1078-1081 A331 Set of 4   3.50 1.50

A332

Natl. Telecommunications Day: No. 1082, Telephone switchboard operator. No. 1083, Train, map.

1980, Aug. 25   **Perf. 11, 12 (#1083)**
1082-1083 A332 12xu Set of 2   2.75 .80

Rose Type of 1980

No. 1084, Pink. No. 1085, Red and pink.

1980, Aug. 25   **Perf. 11**
       Size: 20x24mm
1084-1085 A322 12xu Set of 2   4.25 .40
     For surcharge see Nos. 1384A-1385.

Republic of Vietnam, 35th Anniv. — A333

Designs: No. 1086, 12xu, Ho Chi Minh. No. 1087, 12xu, Natl. arms. 40xu, Pac Bo Cave. 1d, Source of Lenin River, horiz.

1980, Sept. 2   **Perf. 12½**
1086-1089 A333 Set of 4   4.00 1.50

A334

Natl. emblems: 6xu, Arms. No. 1091, 12xu, Flag, horiz. No. 1092, 12xu, Anthem.

1980, Sept. 20   **Perf. 12**
1090-1092 A334 Set of 3   3.50 1.25

A335

Nguyen Trai, 600th birth anniv.: 12xu, Nguyen Trai. 50xu, Books, horiz. 1d, Ho Chi Minh reading commemorative stele, Con Son.

1980, Oct. 6   **Perf. 11**
1093-1095 A335 Set of 3   4.50 1.25
     For surcharge see No. 1386.

A336

Natl. Women's Union, 50th Anniv.: #1096, Ho Chi Minh, women. #1097, Group of 4 women.

1980, Oct. 20
1096-1097 A336 12xu Set of 2   1.50 .80

A337

Flowers: No. 1098, 12xu, Ipomoea pulchella. No. 1099, 12xu, Biguoniaceae venusta. 20xu, Petunia hybrida. 30xu, Trapaeolum majus. 40xu, Thunbergia grandiflora. 50xu, Anlamanda cathartica. 60xu, Campsis radicans. 1d, Bougainivillaea spectabilis.

1980, Nov. 20   **Perf. 12½**
1098-1105 A337 Set of 8   6.25 1.25
     Imperf., #1098-1105   10.00 10.00

Ornamental Fish — A338

Designs: No. 1106, 12xu, Betta splendens. No. 1107, 12xu, Symphysodon aequifasciata. 20xu, Poecilobrycon eques. 30xu, Gyrinochei-lus aymonieri. 40xu, Barbus tetrazona. 50xu, Pterophyllum eimekei. 60xu, Xiphophorus helleri. 1d, Trichopterus sumatranus.

1981, Jan. 15   **Perf. 12**
1106-1113 A338 Set of 8   6.25 3.00
     Imperf., #1106-1113   10.00 9.00

26th Soviet Communist Party Congress A339

20xu, Rocket, book. 50xu, Young people, flag.

1981, Feb. 23   **Perf. 11**
1114-1115 A339 Set of 2   2.50 .80

Animals from Cuc Phuona Natl. Forest — A340

#1116, 12xu, Hylobates concolor. #1117, 12xu, Macaca speciosa. 20xu, Selenarctos thibetanus. 30xu, Cuon alpinus. 40xu, Sus scrofa. 50xu, Cervus unicolor. 60xu, Panthera pardus. 1d, Panthera tigris.

1981, Apr. 10   **Perf. 12½x12**
1116-1123 A340 Set of 8   7.50 1.50
     Imperf., #1116-1123   11.00 11.00

Doves A341

#1124, 12xu, Treron sieboldi. #1125, 12xu, Ducula aenea, vert. 20xu, Streptopelia tran-quebarica, vert. 30xu, Macropygia unchall, vert. 40xu, Ducula badia, vert. 50xu, Treron apicauda. 60xu, Chalcophaps indica. 1d, Seimun treron seimundi.

1981, June 5   **Perf. 12**
1124-1131 A341 Set of 8   6.00 3.00
     Imperf., #1124-1131   10.00 9.00

Nectar-sucking Birds — A342

Designs: No. 1132, 20xu, Aethopyga siparaja. No. 1133, 20xu, Anthreptes singalensis. 30xu, Aethopyga saturata. 40xu, Aethopyga gouldiae. No. 1136, 50xu, Nectarinia chalcostetha. No. 1137, 50xu, Nectarinia hypogrammica. 60xu, Nectarinia sperata. 1d, Aethopyga nipalensis.

1981, Aug. 5   **Perf. 12½x12**
1132-1139 A342 Set of 8   5.00 1.75
     Imperf., #1132-1139   10.00 10.00

A343

1981, Aug. 5   **Perf. 11**
1140 A343 12xu Lotus flower   1.00 .40

A343a

Design: Factory militiawoman.

1981, Aug. 5
1140A A343a 12xu yel & multi   20.00 .75
     See Nos. M30-M31.

A344

Fruit: No. 1141, 20xu, Elaeagnus latifolia. No. 1142, 20xu, Fortunella japonica. 30xu, Nephelium lappaceum. 40xu, Averrhoa bilimbi. No. 1145, 50xu, Ziziphus mauritiana. No. 1146, 50xu, Fragaria vesca. 60xu, Bouea oppositifolia. 1d, Syzygium aqueum.

1981, Oct. 12   **Perf. 12**
1141-1148 A344 Set of 8   5.75 1.25
   Imperf., #1141-1148   10.00

A345

Planting trees: No. 1149, Ho Chi Minh. No. 1150, Three people.

1981, Nov. 15   **Perf. 11**
1149-1150 A345 30xu Set of 2   2.00 .50
   Tree planting festival.

Bulgaria, 1300th Anniv. A346

1982, May 7   **Perf. 11**
1151-1153 A346   30xu, 50xu, 2d, set of 3   4.00 1.25

Wild Animals — A347

Designs: No. 1154, 30xu, Orangutan. No. 1155, 30xu, Bison bonasus. No. 1156, 40xu, Kangaroo. No. 1157, 40xu, Hippopotamus. No. 1158, 50xu, Rhinoceros sondaicus. No. 1159, 50xu, Giraffe. 60xu, Zebra. 1d, Lion.

1981, Dec. 9   **Perf. 12½x12**
1154-1161 A347 Set of 8   5.00 1.50
   Imperf., #1154-1161   10.00 10.00

A348

World Food Day: 30xu, 50xu, Woman holding sheaf of rice. 2d, FAO emblem, horiz.

1982, Jan. 26   **Perf. 11**
1162-1164 A348 Set of 3   3.00 1.25

A349

1982, Feb. 19
1165-1166 A349 50xu, 5d, set of 2   4.00 2.00
   10th World Trade Unions Congress, Havana, Cuba.

5th Vietnamese Communist Party Congress — A350

Designs: No. 1167, 30xu, Ho Chi Minh. No. 1168, 30xu, Hammer, sickle. No. 1169, 30xu, Worker, dam. 50xu, Women harvesting rice. 1d, Ho Chi Minh.

1982
1167-1170 A350   Set of 4   4.50 1.50
    Imperf
    Size: 99x61 mm
1171 A350 1d multicolored   60.00 60.00
   Issued: Nos. 1167-1168, 1171, 2/15; Nos. 1169-1170, 3/27.

Bees & Wasps A351

Designs: No. 1172, 20xu, Ong bove. No. 1173, 20xu, Ong van xanh. 30xu, To vo nau. 40xu, Ong vang. No. 1176, 50xu, Ong dau nau. No. 1177, 50xu, To vo xanh. 60xu, Ong bau. 1d, Ong mat.

1982, Feb. 20   **Perf. 12**
1172-1179 A351 Set of 8   5.00 1.50
   Imperf., #1172-1179   10.00 10.00

Soccer A352

#1180, 30xu, 3 players. #1181, 30xu, 2 players. #1182, 40xu, Striped background. #1183, 40xu, grass background. #1184, 50xu, Vertically striped background. #1185, 50xu, Horizontally striped background. 60xu, 1d, Various soccer scenes.

1982, Apr. 15
1180-1187 A352 Set of 8   5.00 1.40
   Imperf., #1180-1187   10.00 10.00
   For overprints see Nos. 2142-2149.

A353

Vietnamese Red Cross, 35th Anniv.: 1d, Red Cross emblem.

1982, May 15   **Perf. 11**
1188-1189 A353 Set of 2   3.00 .75

A354

5th Natl. Women's Congress: No. 1191, Congress emblem, three women.

1982, May 19   **Perf. 12**
1190-1191 A354 12xu Set of 2   2.50 .75

A355

Birds of Prey: No. 1192, 30xu, Microhierax melanoleucos. No. 1193, 30xu, Falco tinnunculus. 40xu, Aviceda leuphotes. No. 1195, 50xu, Icthyophaga nana. No. 1196, 50xu, Milvus korschun. 60xu, Neohierax harmandi, horiz. No. 1198, 1d, Elanus caeruleus, horiz. No. 1199, 1d, Circaetus gallicus.

1982, June 10
1192-1199 A355 Set of 8   8.00 1.75
   Imperf., #1192-1199   16.00 16.00

A356

1982, May 16   **Perf. 11**
1200-1201 A356 30xu, 3d, set of 2   4.00 2.00
   Georgi Dimitrov (1882-1949), Bulgarian Communist leader.

Dahlias A357

Designs (last word or two of Vietnamese inscription): No. 1202, 30xu, Da cam. No. 1203, 30xu, Do. 40xu, Canh se. No. 1205, 50xu, Do nhung. No. 1206, 50xu, Vang. 60xu, Do tuoi. No. 1208, 1d, Bien. No. 1209, 1d, Trang. Various flowers.

1982, July 15   **Perf. 12x12½**
1202-1209 A357 Set of 8   7.00 2.25
   Imperf., #1202-1209   14.00 14.00

1982 World Cup Soccer Championships, Spain — A358

#1210, 50xu, Ball at bottom right. #1211, 50xu, Ball at right in air. #1212, 50xu, Ball at bottom center. #1213, 1d, 1 player. #1214, 1d, 3 players. 2d, 2 players.

1982, July 25   **Perf. 12x12½**
1210-1215 A358 Set of 6   6.00 2.50
   Imperf., #1210-1215   12.00 12.00

A359

1982, Apr. 22   **Perf. 11**
1216 A359 30xu Natl. defense   1.50 .80
   See No. M32.

A360

1982, Aug. 15
1217 A360 30xu multicolored   1.50 .40
   Cuban victory at Giron (Bay of Pigs), 20th anniv.

World Environment Day — A361

#1219, Ho Chi Minh, children planting tree.

1982, Aug. 15
1218-1219 A361 30xu Set of 2   2.00 .80
   Imperf., #1218-1219   40.00

A362

1982, Sept. 20
1220 A362 30xu multicolored   1.50 .40
   Rabindranath Tagore (1861-1941), poet.

A363

Insects: No. 1221, 30xu, Catacanthus incarnatus. No. 1222, 30xu, Sycanus falleni. 40xu, Nezara viridula. No. 1224, 50xu, Lohita grandis. No. 1225, 50xu, Helcomeria spinosa. 60xu, Chrysocoris stollii. No. 1227, 1d, Pterygamia srayi. No. 1228, 1d, Tiarodes ostentans.

1982, Sept. 25   *Perf. 12x12½*
1221-1228 A363 Set of 8   6.00   2.00
    Imperf., #1221-1228   12.00   12.00

Russian Revolution, 65th Anniv. — A364

Design: No. 1230, Lenin, workers.

1982, Nov. 7   *Perf. 11*
1229-1230 A364 30xu Set of 2   2.00   .80

9th South East Asian Games, New Delhi, India A365

#1231, 30xu, Table tennis. #1232, 30xu, Swimming. 1d, Wrestling. 2d, Shooting.

1982, Nov. 19
1231-1234 A365 Set of 4   4.75   1.50

Fish A366

Designs: No. 1235, 30xu, Samaris cristatus. No. 1236, 30xu, Tephrinectes sinensis. No. 1237, 40xu, Psettodes erumei. No. 1238, 40xu, Zebrias zebra. No. 1239, 50xu, Cynoglossus puncticeps. No. 1240, 50xu, Pardachirus pavoninus. 60xu, Brachirus orientalis. 1d, Psettina iijimae.

1982, Dec. 15   *Perf. 12*
1235-1242 A366 Set of 8   6.00   1.50
    Imperf., #1235-1242   12.00   12.00

Socialist Ideals — A367

#1243, 30xu, Agriculture. #1244, 30xu, Industry. 1d, Natl. defense. 2d, Health & education.

1982, Dec. 25   *Perf. 11*
1243-1246 A367 Set of 4   5.50   1.50

Founding of Soviet Union, 60th Anniv. A368

1982, Dec. 30
1247 A368 30xu multicolored   2.50   .40

Sampans A369

Designs: 30xu, Docked. 50xu, With striped sails. 1d, Sampans on Red River. 3d, With white sails. 5d, With patched sail. 10d, Fast sampan, horiz.

1983, Jan. 10   *Perf. 12½*
1248-1253 A369 Set of 6   6.00   2.00
    Imperf., #1248-1253   12.00   12.00

Locomotives — A370

30xu, Class 231-300. 50xu, Class 230-000. 1d, Class 140-601. 2d, Class 241-000. 3d, Class 141-500. 5d, Class 150-000. 8d, Class 40-300.

1983, Feb. 20   *Perf. 13*
1254-1260 A370 Set of 7   7.50   2.50
    Imperf., #1254-1260   15.00   15.00

1st Manned Balloon Flight, Bicent. A371

Balloons: 30xu, Montgolfier. 50xu, Yellow. 1d, CA-11. 2d, Hot-air. 3d, Over harbor. 5d, Le Geant. 8d, Ascending. 10d, Montgolfier, diff.

1983, Mar. 25   *Litho.*   *Perf. 12½*
1261-1267 A371 Set of 7   8.00   2.00
    Imperf., #1261-1267   16.00   16.00
Souvenir Sheet
Perf. 13
1268 A371 10d Sheet of 1   5.50   1.50

No. 1268 contains one 32x40mm stamp.

Discovery of Tubercle Bacillus, Cent. — A372

1983, Mar. 25   *Perf. 11*
1269 A372 5d multicolored   3.00   .75

Laos-Cambodia-Viet Nam Summit — A373

1983, Mar. 25
1270-1271 A373 50xu, 5d Set of 2   2.75   .75

Cosmonauts — A374

Designs: 30xu, Gubarev, Remek. No. 1273, 50xu, Klimuk, Hermaszewski. No. 1274, 50xu, Bykovsky, Jahn. No. 1275, 1d, Rukavishnikov, Ivanov. No. 1276, 1d, Farcas, Kubasov. No. 1277, 2d, Mendez, Romanenko. No. 1278, 2d, Gorbatko, Tuan. 5d, Dzhanibekov, Gurragcha. 8d, Popov, Prunariu. No. 1281, Gagarin.

1983, Apr. 1   *Perf. 12½x12*
1272-1280 A374 Set of 9   7.50   2.00
    Imperf., #1272-1280   15.00   15.00
Souvenir Sheet
1281 A374 10d multicolored   6.00   1.50

No. 1281 contains one 36x28mm stamp.

Reptiles A375

Designs: No. 1282, 30xu, Teratolepis fasciata. No. 1283, 30xu, Chamaeleo jacksoni. No. 1284, 50xu, Uromastyx acanthinurus. No. 1285, 80xu, Heloderma suspectum. 1d, Cameleo menle. 2d, Amphibolurus barbatus. 5d, Chlamydosaurus kingi. 10d, Phrynosoma coronatum.

1983, Apr. 5   *Perf.*
1282-1289 A375 Set of 8   7.50   3.00
    Imperf., #1282-1289   15.00   15.00

Raphael (1483-1520), Painter — A375a

Designs: 30xu, Virgin Mother Seated on Chair. 50xu, Granduca, the Virgin Mother. 1d, Sistine Madonna. 2d, Marriage of Maria. 3d,

The Gardener. 5d, Woman with Veil. 8d, 10d, Self-Portrait.

1983, Apr. 30   *Perf. 12½*
1289A-1289G A375a Set of 7   7.50   2.00
    Imperf., #1289A-1289G   15.00   15.00
Souvenir Sheet
Perf. 13
1289H A375a 10d multicolored   12.00   1.50

Chess Pieces — A376

Designs: 30xu, Vietnamese pawns. 50xu, Indian elephant. 1d, Scottish knight, bishop. 2d, Indian elephant, diff. 3d, Knight. 5d, Sailing ship. 8d, Jester, elephant. 10d, Modern pawns.

1983, May 9   *Perf. 13*
1290-1296 A376 Set of 7   6.50   2.00
    Imperf., #1290-1296   13.00   13.00
Souvenir Sheet
1297 A376 10d multicolored   7.25   1.50

No. 1297 contains one 28x36mm stamp.

Souvenir Sheet

TEMBAL '83 World Stamp Exhibition, Basel — A377

1983, May 21   *Perf. 13*
1298 A377 10d multicolored   5.00   1.50

1984 Summer Olympics, Los Angeles A378

Designs: 30xu, Long jump. 50xu, Running. 1d, Javelin. 2d, High jump, horiz. 3d, Hurdles, horiz. 5d, Shot put. 8d, Pole vault. 10d, Discus.

1983, June 13   *Litho.*   *Perf. 13*
1299-1305 A378 Set of 7   7.50   2.00
Souvenir Sheet
1306 A378 10d Sheet of 1   6.25   1.50

No. 1306 contains one 32x40mm stamp.
The issuance of this set has been questioned.

Souvenir Sheet

Brasiliana '83, Rio de Janeiro — A379

1983, July 20 *Perf. 13*
1307 A379 10d Rhamphastos
toco 15.00 2.50

Butterflies
A380

Designs: No. 1308, 30xu, Leptocircus meges. No. 1309, 30xu, Terias hecabe. No. 1310, 40xu, Zetides agamemnon. No. 1311, 40xu, Nyctalemon patroclus. No. 1312, 50xu, Papilio chaon. No. 1313, 50xu, Precis almana. 60xu, Thauria lathyi. 1d, Kallima inachus.

1983, July 30 *Litho.* *Perf. 12*
1308-1315 A380 Set of 8 8.00 3.00
 Imperf., #1308-1315 16.00 16.00

Souvenir Sheet

Bangkok '83 — A381

1983, Aug. 4 *Perf. 13*
1316 A381 10d multicolored 10.00 1.50

Karl Marx
(1818-1883)
A382

No. 1317, 50xu. No. 1318, 10d,

1983, Oct. 10 *Perf. 11*
1317-1318 A382 Set of 2 5.00 1.25
 Imperf., #1317-1318 50.00

Phu Dong Sports Festival — A383

1983, Oct. 10
1319-1320 A383 30xu, 1d, Set of
2 2.75 .80

World
Food Day
A384

Design: 50xu, Infant, fish. 4d, Family.

1983, Oct. 10 *Perf. 12½*
1321-1322 A384 Set of 2 2.50 .80
 Imperf., #1321-1322 7.00

Mushrooms
A385

#1323, 50xu, Flammulina velutipes. #1324, 50xu, Pleurotus ostreatus. #1325, 50xu, Cantharellus cibarius. #1326, 50xu, Coprinus atramentarius. 1d, Volvariella volvacea. 2d, Agaricus silvaticus. 5d, Morchella esculenta. 10d, Amanita caesarea.

1983, Oct. 10 *Perf. 12x12½*
1323-1330 A385 Set of 8 11.00 3.00
 Imperf., #1323-1330 14.50

For overprints see Nos. 2150-2157.

World Communications Year — A386

50xu, Letter carrier. 2d, Mail sorting room. 8d, Switchboard operators. #1334, 10d, Radio operator, antenna. #1335, 10d, Telephone, letter, dish antenna, ship.

1983, Sept. 30 *Perf. 12½*
1331-1334 A386 Set of 4 5.75 1.50
Souvenir Sheet
Perf. 13
1335 A386 10d Sheet of 1 4.00 1.50

5th Natl. Trade Unions
Congress — A387

50xu, Woman with flowers, Vietnam-Soviet Union Friendship Cultural Building. 2d, 30d, Welder.

1983, Nov. 16 *Perf. 11*
1336-1338 A387 Set of 3 7.50 1.50

Water Birds
A388

Designs: No. 1339, 50xu, Ciconia nigra. No. 1340, 50xu, Ardea cinerea. No. 1341, 50xu, Ardea purpurea. No. 1342, 50xu, Ibis leucocephalus. 1d, Grus grus. 2d, Platalea minor. 5d, Nycticorax nycticorax. 10d, Anastomus oscitans.

1983, Nov. 20 *Perf. 12x12½*
1339-1346 A388 Set of 8 9.00 3.00
 Imperf., #1339-1346 18.00 18.00

No. 1343 inscribed "Grus grue."

World Peace
Conference,
Prague — A389

Designs: 50xu, Shown. 3d, 5d, 20d, Hands, globe, dove.

1983, Dec. 19 *Perf. 11*
1347-1350 A389 Set of 4 9.00 2.00

1984 Winter Olympics, Sarajevo,
Yugoslavia — A390

#1351, 50xu, Cross-country skiing, vert. #1352, 50xu, Biathlon, vert. 1d, Speed skating, vert. 2d, Bobsled, vert. 3d, Hockey. 5d, Ski jumping. 6d, Slalom skiing. 10d, Pairs figure skating.

1984, Jan. 30 *Perf. 12½*
1351-1357 A390 Set of 7 7.50 2.00
 Imperf., #1351-1357 15.00 15.00
Souvenir Sheet
1358 A390 10d multicolored 4.50 1.50

No. 1358 contains one 40x32mm stamp.

Soviet Union-Vietnamese Projects,
1978-83 — A391

Designs: 20xu (No. 1359), 4d, Hoa Binh Hydro-electric project. 20xu (No. 1360), Vietnamese-Soviet Cultural Palace. 50xu, Thang Long Bridge.

1984, Jan. 31 *With Gum* *Perf. 11*
1359-1362 A391 Set of 4 55.00

Endangered Animals — A392

Designs: No. 1363, 50xu, Felis marmorata. No. 1364, 50xu, Panthera tigris. No. 1365, 50xu, Panthera pardus. No. 1366, 1d, Hylobates lar. No. 1367, 1d, Nycticebus coucang. No. 1368, 2d, Elephas indidus. No. 1369, 2d, Bos gaurus.

1984, Feb. 26 *Perf. 12½x12*
1363-1369 A392 Set of 7 6.00 1.00
 Imperf., #1363-1369 12.00 12.00

A393

Wildflowers: No. 1370, 50xu, Banhinia variegata. No. 1371, 50xu, Caesalpinia pulcherrima. 1d, Cassia fistula. 2d, Delonix regia. 3d, Artagotrys uncinatus. 5d, Corchorus olitorius. 8d, Banhinia grandiflora.

1984, Mar. 15 *Perf. 12½x12½*
1370-1376 A393 Set of 7 6.50 2.50
 Imperf., #1370-1376 13.00 13.00
Souvenir Sheet
1377 A393 10d Delonix regia 4.50 1.50

Location of inscriptions differs on Nos. 1373, 1377.

A394

Orchids: No. 1378, 50xu, Cymbidium. No. 1379, 50xu, Brasse cattleya. 1d, Cattleya Dianx. 2d, Cymbidium, diff. 3d, Cymbidium hybridum. 5d, Phoenix winged orchids. 8d, Yellow Queen orchids.

1984, Mar. 28 *Perf. 13*
1378-1384 A394 Set of 7 8.00 2.00
 Imperf., #1378-1384 16.00 16.00

Nos. 1084-1085, 1093 Surcharged

 a b

1984, Apr. 25 *Perfs. as before*
1384A A322(a) 50xu on 12xu
 #1084 3.00 3.00
1385 A322(a) 50xu on 12xu
 #1085 3.00 3.00
1386 A335(b) 50xu on 12xu
 #1093 2.00 2.00

Souvenir Sheet

Espana '84, Madrid — A395

1984, Apr. 27   *Perf. 12½*
1387 A395 10d Ciconia ciconia   8.00 2.50

Victory at Dien Bien Phu, 30th Anniv. A396

#1388, 50xu; #1395, 10d, Ho Chi Minh, generals, battle map. #1389, 50xu, Troops, truck. 1d, Civilians carrying provisions. 2d, Man-hauling artillery. 3d, Anti-aircraft battery. 5d, Troops attacking enemy base. 8d, Troops waving flag.

1984, May 7   *Perf. 12½*
1388-1394 A396   Set of 7   5.00 2.00
Souvenir Sheet
1395   A396 10d multicolored 4.50 1.50

Souvenir Sheet

UPU Congress, Hamburg '84 — A397

1984, June 19   *Perf. 13*
1396 A397 10d Junkers JU-52 3M   5.00 1.50

Fish A398

Designs: No. 1397, 30xu, Cypselurus spilopterus. No. 1398, 30xu, Ostracion cornutus. 50xu, Diodon hystrix. 80xu, Chelmon rostratus. 1d, Antennarius tridens. 2d, Pterois russelli. 5d, Mola mola. 10d, Minous monodactylus.

1984, June 25   Litho.   *Perf. 12*
1397-1404 A398   Set of 8   7.25 3.00
    Imperf., #1397-1404   14.50 14.50

Ornamental Fish — A399

Designs: No. 1405, 50xu, Trichogaster trichopterus. No. 1406, 50xu, Brachydanio rerio. 1d, Macropodus opercularis. 2d, Gymnocorymbus ternetzi. 3d, Hyphessobrycon serpae. 5d, Labeo bicolor. 8d, Batta splendens.

1984, June 29   *Perf. 12½*
1405-1411 A399   Set of 7   6.00 3.00
    Imperf., #1405-1411   12.00 12.00

Vietnamese Trade Union Movement, 55th Anniv. — A400

Designs: No. 1412a, 50xu, House at 15 Hang Non St., Hanoi, vert. No. 1412b, 50xu, Nguyen Duc Canh, vert. 1d, Striking workers. 2d, Ho Chi Minh visiting factory. 3d, Hanoi Mechanical Engineering plant. 5d, Intl. trade union movement.

1984, July 20   *Perf. 11*
1412-1416 A400   Set of 6   4.50 2.25
Souvenir Sheet
Imperf
1417   A400 2d like #1414 11.00 11.00

No. 1412 printed se-tenant. No. 1417 contains one 45x38mm stamp.

Rock Formations, Ha Long Bay — A401

#1418, 50xu, Hang-Bo Nau. #1419, 50xu, Nui Yen Ngua. #1420, 50xu, Hon Dua. #1421, 50xu, Hang Con Gai. 1d, Hon Coc. #1423, 1d, Hon Ga Choi. 2d, Hon Dinh Huong. 3d, Hon Su Tu. 5d, Hon Am. 8d, Nui Bai Tho.

1984, July 30   *Perf. 12½x12*
1418-1427 A401   Set of 10   7.00 2.50
    Imperf., #1418-1427   14.00 14.00

Dinosaurs — A402

#1428, 50xu, Styracosaurus. #1429, 50xu, Diplodocus. #1430, 1d, Corythosaurus. #1431, 1d, Rhamphyorhynchus. 2d, Seymouria. 3d, Allosaurus. 5d, Dimetrodon. 8d, Brachiosaurus.

1984, Aug. 30   *Perf. 12½*
1428-1435 A402   Set of 8   13.50 3.00
    Imperf., #1428-1435   27.00 27.00

Viet Nam-Laos-Cambodia Friendship — A403

1984, Aug. 30   *Perf. 11*
1436-1437 A403 50xu, 10d, set of 2 6.00 .80

Souvenir Sheet

Ausipex '84, Melbourne, Australia — A404

1984, Sept. 20   *Perf. 13*
1438 A404 10d Koala   12.00 1.50

Viet Nam-Cambodia Friendship Agreement, 5th Anniv. — A405

50xu, 3d, People, pagoda, statue. 50d, Dancers.

1984, Sept. 30   *Perf. 11*
1439-1441 A405   Set of 3   12.00 4.00

Liberation of Hanoi, 30th Anniv. A406

Designs: 50xu, Thang Long Bridge. 1d, Khue Van Gateway. 2d, Ho Chi Minh mausoleum.

1984, Oct. 5
1442-1444 A406   Set of 3   3.50 1.25

Vintage Automobiles — A407

#1445, 50xu, Vis-a-Vis, vert. #1446, 50xu, Duc. 1d, Tonneau. 2d, Double phaeton. 3d, Landaulet. 5d, Torpedo. 6d, Coupe de Ville.

1984, Oct. 30   *Perf. 12½x13, 13x12½*
1445-1451 A407   Set of 7   5.00 2.50
    Imperf., #1445-1451   10.00 10.00

Lenin (1870-1924) A408

Paintings of Lenin: 50xu, At his desk. 1d, Standing with revolutionaries. 3d, Speaking at factory. 5d, Meeting with farmers.

1984, Nov. 15   *Perf. 12x12½*
1452-1455 A408 Set of 4   3.00 1.50
    Imperf., #1452-1455   6.00 6.00

UNICEF A409

Paintings: 30xu, Woman, soldiers. 50xu, Mother, children. 1d, Miner, family. 3d, Young girl, vert. 5d, Children playing on ground. 10d, Women, child, vert.

1984, Dec. 7   *Perf. 12*
1456-1461 A409 Set of 6   5.50 2.75
    Imperf., #1456-1461   11.00 11.00

A410

50xu, 30d. Frontier Forces, 25th anniv.

1984, Dec. 15   *Perf. 11*
1462-1463 A410 Set of 2   10.00 1.90
    Imperf., #1462-1463
    See No. M39.

A411

Flora and Fauna: 20xu, Bubalus bubalis. 30xu, Felis marmorata. No. 1466, 50xu, Hibiscus rosa-sinensis. No. 1467, 50xu, Ailurus fulgens. No. 1468, 50xu, Rosa centifolia. No. 1469, 50xu, Betta splendens. No. 1470, 1d, Chrysanthemum sinense. No. 1471, 1d, Nymphaea ampla. No. 1472, 1d, Pelecanus onocrotalus. No. 1473, 1d, Panthera tigris. No. 1474, 2d, Nycticebus coucang. No. 1475, 2d, Macaca fascicularis. No. 1476, 2d, Dalia coccinea. 5d, Gekko gecko. 10d, Rhytidoceros bicornis.

1984, Dec.   *Perf. 12½x12*
1464-1478 A411 Set of 15   11.00 4.00
    Imperf., #1464-1478   15.00

No. 1466 inscribed "Hybiscus." No. 1470 inscribed "Chrysanthemun."

A412

1985   *Perf. 11*
1479-1480 A412 3d, 5d, set of 2   2.75 .80
    Imperf., #1479-1480   30.00

New Year 1985 (Year of the Buffalo). Issued: 3d, 1/21; 5d, 4/30.

A413

1985, Apr. 26 *Perf. 11*
1481 A413 2d Ho Chi Minh 1.10 .40
Vietnamese Communist Party, 55th anniv.

Military Victory in South Viet Nam, 10th Anniv. A414

Designs: 1d, Soldiers advancing forward. 2d, 10d, Ho Chi Minh, tank, soldiers. 4d, Construction worker. 5d, Map, women.

1985, Apr. 30 *Perf. 12½*
1482-1485 A414 Set of 4 3.50 1.50
Souvenir Sheet
Perf. 13
1486 A414 10d multicolored 3.75 1.75

Cactus A415

Designs: No. 1487, 50xu, Echinocereus knippelianus. No. 1488, 50xu, Lemaireocereus thurberi. 1d, Notocactus haselbergii. 2d, Parodia chrysacanthion. 3d, Pelecyphora pseudopectinata. 5d, Rebutia frebrighii. 8d, Lobivia aurea.

1985, Mar. 30 *Perf. 11½*
1487-1493 A415 Set of 7 7.00 2.50
Imperf., #1487-1493 15.00 15.00

Vietnamese People's Army, 40th Anniv. — A416

Designs: No. 1494, 50xu, Ho Chi Minh. No. 1495, 50xu, Taking oath on flag. 1d, Anti-aircraft missile. 2d, Soldiers, civilians working together. 3d, Tank entering grounds of presidential palace, Saigon. 5d, Soldier demonstrating use of rifle. 8d, Officers, soldiers, map. 10d, Four soldiers representing branches of military.

1984, Dec. 22 *Perf. 12½*
1494-1500 A416 Set of 7 5.50 3.00
Souvenir Sheet
1501 A416 10d multi 4.00 1.50

End of World War II, 40th Anniv. — A417

Designs: 1d, 10d, Victory Monument. 2d, Vietnamese soldier. 4d, Dove, falling American eagle. 5d, Child, doves.

1985, June 5 *Perf. 12x12½*
1502-1505 A417 Set of 4 3.50 1.50
Imperf., #1502-1505 15.00 15.00
Souvenir Sheet
1506 A417 10d multicolored 3.25 1.50

Liberation of Haiphong, 30th Anniv. — A418

Designs: 2d, Long Chau Lighthouse. 5d, An Duong Bridge, horiz. 10d, To Hieu (1912-44), vert.

1985, May 13 *Perf. 11*
1507-1508 A418 Set of 2 2.50 .80
Souvenir Sheet
Imperf
1509 A418 10d multicolored 3.50 1.50

Ho Chi Minh, 95th Birth Anniv. — A419

Ho Chi Minh: 1d, At battlefield. 2d, Reading. 4d, 10d, Portrait, vert. 5d, Writing.

1985, July 6 *Perf. 12½*
1510-1513 A419 Set of 4 4.00 2.00
Souvenir Sheet
Perf. 13
1514 A419 10d multicolored 5.00 1.40
No. 1514 contains one 30x36mm stamp.

Motorcycles, Cent. — A420

Designs: No. 1515, 1d, 1895, Germany. No. 1516, 1d, 1898 tricycle, France. No. 1517, 2d, 1913 Harley-Davidson, US. No. 1518, 2d, 1918 Cleveland, US. 3d, 1935 Simplex, US. 4d, 1984 Minarelli, Italy. 6d, 1984 Honda, Japan. 10d, 1984 Honda racing bike.

1985, June 28 *Perf. 13*
1515-1521 A420 Set of 7 5.50 2.75
Imperf., #1515-1521 13.00 13.00
Souvenir Sheet
1522 A420 10d multicolored 5.00 1.40
No. 1522 contains one 32x40mm stamp.

Argentina '85, Buenos Aires — A421

Wild animals: No. 1523, 1d, Aptenodytes pennati, vert. No. 1524, 1d, Dolichotis patagonum, vert. No. 1525, 2d, Panthera onca. No. 1526, 2d, Hydrochoerys capibara.

3d, Peterocnemia pennata, vert. 4d, Priodontes giganteus. 6d, Voltur gryphus. 10d, Lama glama, horiz.

1985, July 5 *Perf. 12½*
1523-1529 A421 Set of 7 10.00 2.50
Imperf., #1523-1529 18.00 18.00
Souvenir Sheet
With Gum
Perf. 13
1530 A421 10d multicolored 12.50 1.50
No. 1530 contains one 40x32mm stamp.

12th World Youth and Students Festival, Moscow A422

No. 1531, 2d, Youth carrying flags, globe. No. 1532, 2d, Workers, power transmission lines. 4d, Lighthouse, coastal defense. 5d, Intl. festival.

1985, June 20 *Perf. 12½*
1531-1534 A422 Set of 4 5.00 1.50
Imperf., #1531-1534 17.50 17.50
Souvenir Sheet
With Gum
Perf. 13
1535 A422 10d like #1531 5.00 1.25

Marine Life A423

#1536, 3d, Nadoa tuberculata. #1537, 3d, Luidia maculata. #1538, 3d, Stichopus chloronotus. #1539, 3d, Holothuria monacaria. #1540, 4d, Astropyga radiata. #1541, 4d, Astropecten scoparius. #1542, 4d, Linckia laevigata.

1985, July 30 *Perf. 12*
1536-1542 A423 Set of 7 8.00 2.75
Imperf., #1536-1542 19.00 19.00

Socialist Republic of Viet Nam, 40th Anniv. — A424

Designs: 2d, Construction. 3d, Hands shaking, doves. 5d, Flag, military forces. No. 1567, 10d, Flag, Ho Chi Minh.

1985, Aug. 28 *Perf. 12½*
1543-1546 A424 Set of 4 4.50 1.90
Imperf., #1543-1546 20.00 20.00
Souvenir Sheet
Perf. 13
1547 A424 10d like #1543 3.00 3.00
No. 1547 contains one 32x40mm stamp.

Vietnamese Police Force, 40th Anniv. — A425

1985, Aug. 30 *Perf. 11*
1548 A425 10d multicolored 4.00 .40
See No. M41.

1st Natl. Sports Festival A426

Designs: 5d, Gymnastics. 10d, Gymnastics, running, swimming.

1985, Aug. 30
1549-1550 A426 Set of 2 4.50 .80

German Railways, 150th Anniv. — A427

Various locomotives: #1551, 1d, Facing left. #1552, 1d, Facing right. #1553, 2d, Facing left. #1554, 2d, Facing right. 3d, 4d, 6d.

1985, Sept. 13 *Perf. 12½*
1551-1557 A427 Set of 7 6.25 2.50
Imperf., #1551-1557 10.00 10.00
Souvenir Sheet
With Gum
Perf. 13
1558 A427 10d multicolored 4.50 1.50
No. 1558 contains one 32x40mm stamp.

Vietnamese Geological Survey, 30th Anniv. — A428

#1559, Drilling rigs. #1560, Aerial survey.

1985, Oct. 5 *Perf. 11*
1559-1560 A428 1d Set of 2 2.50 .80

Italia '85 A429

Vintage Italian cars: No. 1561, 1d, 1922 Alfa Romeo. No. 1562, 1d, 1932 Bianchi Berlina. No. 1563, 2d, 1928 Isotta Fraschini. No. 1564, 2d, 1930 Bugatti. No. 1565, 3d, 1912 Itala. 4d, 1934 Lancia Augusta. 6d, 1927 Fiat Convertable (top up). 10d, 1927 Fiat Convertable (top down).

1985, Oct. 25 *Perf. 13*
1561-1567 A429 Set of 7 5.50 2.25
Imperf., #1561-1567 17.50 17.50
Souvenir Sheet
With Gum
1568 A429 10d multicolored 6.00 1.25
No. 1568 contains one 40x32mm stamp.

Whales A430

Designs: No. 1569, 1d, Balaenoptera musculus. No. 1570, 1d, Balaena borealis. No. 1571, 2d, Orcinus orca. No. 1572, 2d, Delphinus. 3d, Megaptera boops. 4d, Balaenoptera physalus. 6d, Eubalaena glacialis.

1985, Nov. 15
1569-1575 A430 Set of 7   8.00   2.50
        Imperf., #1569-1575   20.00   20.00

1986 World Cup Soccer
Championships, Mexico City — A431

Various soccer plays: No. 1576, 1d, From
behind goal. No. 1577, 1d, Goalie from side.
No. 1578, 2d, From behind goal. No. 1579, 2d,
From in front of goal, vert. 3d, vert. 4d, vert.
6d, vert.

1985, Nov. 30
1576-1582 A431 Set of 7   5.00   1.75
        Imperf., #1576-1582   10.00   10.00
        Souvenir Sheet
            Perf. 13
1583 A431 10d multicolored   5.00   1.25
  No. 1583 contains one 40x32mm stamp.

People's
Democratic
Republic of
Laos, 10th
Anniv. — A432

a, Woman, dove. b, Woman dancing, natl.
arms.

1985, Dec. 2   **Perf. 11**
1584 A432 1d Pair, #a.-b.   3.00   1.50

Traditional Musical
Instruments — A433

#1585, 1d, Stone chimes. #1586, 1d, Large
bronze drum. #1587, 2d, Flutes. #1588, 2d,
Large red drum. 3d, Monochord. 4d, Moon-
shaped lute. 6d, Vietnamese two-string violin.

1985, Dec. 5   **Perf. 12½x12**
1585-1591 A433 Set of 7   5.75   2.75
        Imperf., #1585-1591   12.00   12.00

A434

Socialist Republic of Viet Nam, 40th Anniv.:
No. 1592, 10d, Industry. No. 1593, 10d, Agriculture. 20d, Public health. 30d, Education.

1985, Dec. 6   **Perf. 11**
1592-1595 A434 Set of 4   30.00   15.00

A435

1986, Jan. 6   Litho.   Perf. 11
1596-1597 A435 50xu, 1d Set of
                2   2.25   .80
    1st Natl. Elections, 40th anniv.

A436

1986, Jan. 6
1598 A436 1d multicolored   1.50   .45
        UN 40th anniv.

A437

Halley's Comet: No. 1599, 2d, Edmond Halley. No. 1600, 2d, Isaac Newton. 3d, Rocket,
flags. 5d, Comet.

1986, Feb. 24   **Perf. 12½**
1599-1602 A437 Set of 4   5.00   1.50
        Imperf., #1599-1602   10.00   10.00

A438

Soviet Communist Party, 27th Congress:
50xu, Kremlin, map. 1d, Lenin banner.

1986, Feb. 25   **Perf. 11**
1603-1604 A438 Set of 2   2.50   .80
        Imperf., #1603-1604   40.00

A439

1986, Mar. 1
1605 A439 1d Map of Battle of
                Xuong Giang   1.50   .40
        Le Loi, 600th birth anniv.

1986 World
Cup Soccer
Championships,
Mexico
City — A440

Various soccer players in action: No. 1606,
1d, Viet Nam at left. No. 1607, 1d, Viet Nam at
right. 2d, Viet Nam at left. No. 1609, 3d, Viet
Nam at left. No. 1610, 3d, Viet Nam at right.
No. 1611, 5d, Viet Nam at left. No. 1612, 5d,
Viet Nam at right.

1986, Mar. 3   **Perf. 12½**
1606-1612 A440 Set of 7   4.50   2.50
        Imperf., #1606-1612   9.00   9.00
        Souvenir Sheet
            Perf. 13
1613 A440 10d multicolored   4.50   1.25
  No. 1613 contains one 40x32mm stamp.

1st
Manned
Space
Flight,
25th
Anniv.
A441

#1614, 1d, Konstantin Tsiolkovsky. #1615,
1d, Rocket on transporter. 2d, Yuri Gagarin.
#1617, 3d, Valentina Tereshkova, vert. #1618,
3d, Alexei Leonov. #1619, 5d, Apollo-Soyuz,
crews. #1620, 5d, Soyuz, Salut space station.
10d, Cosmonauts, vert.

1986, Apr. 12   **Perf. 13**
1614-1620 A441 Set of 7   4.50   2.25
        Imperf., #1614-1620   10.00   10.00
        Souvenir Sheet
1621 A441 10d multicolored   5.00   1.25
  No. 1621 contains one 32x40mm stamp.

Ernst Thalmann (1886-1944), German
Politician — A442

1986, Apr. 16   **Perf. 11**
1622 A442 2d red & black   1.50   .40

May Day — A443

1986, May 1
1623-1624 A443 1d, 5d, set of 2 2.25   .40

Vancouver Expo '86 — A444

Airplanes: No. 1625, 1d, Hawker Hart. No.
1626, 1d, Curtiss Jenny. 2d, PZL-P23. No.
1628, 3d, Yakovlev Yak-11. No. 1629, 3d, Fokker Dr.1. No. 1630, 5d, Boeing P-12 (1920).

No. 1631, 5d, Nieuport-Delage NiD.29C1
(1929).

1986, Sept. 30   **Perf. 13**
1625-1631 A444 Set of 7   5.50   2.00
        Imperf., #1625-1631   10.00   10.00

Dam-Strengthening Committee, 40th
Anniv. — A445

1986, May 22   **Perf. 11**
1632 A445 1d carmine   1.50   .45

Bonsai — A446

Designs: No. 1633, 1d, Ficus glomerata. No.
1634, 1d, Ficus benjamina. 2d, Ulmus
tonkinensis. No. 1636, 3d, Persica vulgaris.
No. 1637, 3d, Streblus asper. No. 1638, 5d,
Pinus khasya. No. 1639, 5d, Podocarpus
macrophyllus. 10d, Serissa foetida, horiz.

1986, Dec. 10   **Perf. 12x12½**
1633-1639 A446 Set of 7   6.00   2.75
        Imperf., #1633-1639   15.00   15.00
        Souvenir Sheet
            Perf. 12½x12
1640 A446 10d multicolored   4.00   4.00

Domestic Cats — A447

Various cats (Background colors): No. 1641,
1d, blue green. No. 1642, 1d, red. 2d, blue.
No. 1644, 3d, brown. No. 1645, 3d, blue. No.
1646, 5d, violet. No. 1647, 5d, red, vert.

Perf. 13x12½, 12½x13
1986, June 16
1641-1647 A447 Set of 7   7.50   2.75
        Imperf., #1641-1647   16.00   16.00

Traditional
Houses
A448

Designs: No. 1648, 1d, Thai den. No. 1649,
1d, Nung. 2d, Thai trang. No. 1651, 3d, Tay.
No. 1652, 3d, Hmong. No. 1653, 5d, Dao. No.
1654, 5d, Tay nguyen, vert.

Perf. 12½x12, 12x12½
1986, June 20
1648-1654 A448 Set of 7   6.00   2.75
        Imperf., #1648-1654   15.00   15.00
        Souvenir Sheet
            Perf. 12x12½
1655 A448 10d like #1654   3.50   1.25

Postal Service, 40th Anniv. — A449

Designs: No. 1656, 2d, Telecommunications. No. 1657, 2d, Map, letter carrier. 4d, Soldiers, Nguyen Thi Nghia. 5d, Dish antenna.

1986, Aug. 15			Perf. 13	
1656-1659	A449	Set of 4	3.25	1.25
	Imperf., #1656-1659		22.50	22.50

A450

Birds: No. 1660, 1d, Merops apiaster. No. 1661, 1d, Cissa chinensis. 2d, Pteruthius erythropterus. No. 1663, 3d, Garrulax leucolophus. No. 1664, 3d, Psarisomus dalhousiae, horiz. No. 1665, 5d, Cyanopica cyanus, horiz. No. 1666, 5d, Motacilla alba. 10d, Copsychus malabaricus.

1986, Aug. 28			Perf. 13	
1660-1666	A450	Set of 7	5.00	2.50
	Imperf. #1660-1666		12.00	12.00

Souvenir Sheet
Perf. 12½

1667	A450	10d multicolored	5.25	1.25

No. 1667 contains one 32x40mm stamp. Stockholmia '86.

A451

Domestic fowl: No. 1668, 1d, Plymouth Rock. No. 1669, 1d, Maleagris gallopavo. No. 1670, 2d, Ri. No. 1671, 2d, White Plymouth rock. No. 1672, 3d, Leghorn. No. 1673, 3d, Rhode Island red. No. 1674, 3d, Rhode ri. 5d, Gray Plymouth rock hen.

1986, Sept. 15			Perf. 12x12½	
1668-1675	A451	Set of 8	6.00	3.00
	Imperf., #1668-1675		13.50	13.50

11th Intl. Trade Unions Congress — A452

1986, Sept. 16			Perf. 12½	
1676	A452	1d blue & red	1.50	.40

Artifacts, Hung-Voung Period — A453

Designs: No. 1677, 1d, Seated figure, vert. No. 1678, 1d, Knife hilt in form of female figure, vert. 2d, Bronze axe. No. 1680, 3d, Bronze axe, diff. No. 1681, 3d, Bronze bowl. No. 1682, 5d, Bronze pot (round). No. 1683, 5d, Bronze vase (open top).

1986, Oct. 15			Perf. 12x12½, 12½x12	
1677-1683	A453	Set of 7	5.00	2.75
	Imperf., #1677-1683		11.00	11.00

Souvenir Sheet
Perf. 12x12½

1684	A453	10d like #1677	4.25	4.25

Vietnamese Red Cross, 40th Anniv. — A454

1986, Oct. 20			Perf. 12½	
1685	A454	3d rose & greenish blue	1.50	.40

Sailing Ships — A455

Various sail and oar-powered ships (sail colors): #1686, 1d, bl, grn, yel. #1687, 1d, org. 2d, yel. #1689, 3d, pur & red. #1690, 3d, bl. #1691, 5d, bl, brn, org. #1692, 5d, org.

Perf. 12½x12, 12½x13 (#1688)				
1986, Oct. 20				
1686-1692	A455	Set of 7	6.00	1.50

No. 1688 is 38x47mm.

Butterflies — A456

Designs: No. 1693, 1d, Catopsilia scylla. No. 1694, 1d, Euploea midamus. 2d, Appias nero. No. 1696, 3d, Danaus chrysippus. No. 1697, 3d, Papilio polytes stichius. No. 1698, 5d, Euploea diocletiana. No. 1699, 5d, Charaxes polyxena.

1987, June 30			Perf. 12½	
1693-1699	A456	Set of 7	6.00	2.00
	Imperf., #1693-1699		13.00	

No. 1696 misspelled "Danais."

Vietnamese Communist Party, 6th Congress — A457

1d, Construction projects. 2d, Natl. defense. 4d, Ho Chi Minh. 5d, Intl. cooperation.

1986, Nov. 20			Perf. 11	
1700-1703	A457	Set of 4	5.50	1.50
1700a-1703a		Perf. 12½	50.00	50.00
1702b		Perf. 11x12½	27.50	27.50

Souvenir Sheet
Imperf

1704	A457	10d like #1700	4.50	1.25

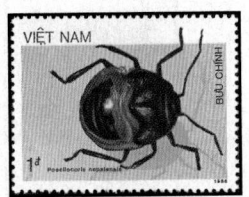

Insects A458

Designs: No. 1705, 1d, Poecilocoris nepalensis. No. 1706, 1d, Bombus americanorum. 2d, Romalea microptera. No. 1708, 3d, Chalcocoris rutilans. No. 1709, 3d, Chrysocoris sellatus. No. 1710, 5d, Paranthrene palmi. No. 1711, 5d, Crocisa crucifera. 10d, Anabrus simplex.

1987, June 30			Perf. 12½	
1705-1711	A458	Set of 7	5.50	2.75
	Imperf., #1705-1711		12.50	12.50

Souvenir Sheet

1712	A458	10d multicolored	5.00	1.25

No. 1712 contains one 32x40mm stamp.

Intl. Peace Year — A459

1986, Dec. 7			Perf. 11	
1713-1714	A459	1d, 3d, set of 2	2.50	.80

Handicrafts — A460

Designs: No. 1715, 1d, Round dish. No. 1716, 1d, Rattan handbag. 2d, Rattan foot stool. No. 1718, 3d, Bamboo hand basket. No. 1719, 3d, Muong pannier. No. 1720, 5d, Rattan basket with shoulder straps. No. 1721, 5d, Rattan basket with lid. 10d, Tall rattan basket.

1986, Dec. 10			Perf. 11½	
1715-1721	A460	Set of 7	5.00	2.75
	Imperf., #1715-1721		9.00	9.00

Souvenir Sheet

1722	A460	10d multicolored	3.50	3.50

A461

1986, Dec. 18			Perf. 11	
1723	A461	2d blue green & fawn	1.50	.40

Natl. Resistance, 40th anniv.

A462

Endangered flora: No. 1724, 1d, Fokienia hodginsii. No. 1725, 1d, Amentotaxus yunnanensis. 2d, Pinus kwangtungensis. No. 1727, 3d, Taxus chinensis. No. 1728, 3d, Cupressus torulosa. No. 1729, 5d, Ducampopinus krempfii. No. 1730, 5d, Tsuga yunnanensis. 10d, Abies nukiangensis.

1986, Dec. 26			Perf. 12x12½	
1724-1730	A462	Set of 7	5.00	2.75
	Imperf., #1724-1730		12.00	12.00

Souvenir Sheet

1731	A462	10d multicolored	4.25	1.25

Elephants — A463

#1732, 1d, Two elephants. #1733, 1d, Female, calf. #1734, 3d, Elephant. #1735, 1d, Elephant facing, vert. #1736, 5d, Man riding elephant, vert. #1737, 5d, Four elephants.

1987, Mar. 10			Perf. 12½	
1732-1737	A463	Set of 6	7.50	1.50
	Imperf., #1732-1737		15.00	15.00

No. 1737 is 68x27mm.

Vietnamese Legends A464

Designs: a, Son Tinh. b, My Nuong. c-e, Battle between Mountain Genie and Water Genie. f-h, Celebration.

1987, Jan. 20			Perf. 12	
1738	A464	3d Strip of 8, #a.-h.	7.00	3.50
	Imperf.		13.50	13.50

New Year 1987
(Year of the
Cat) — A465

1987, Jan. 6   *Perf. 11*
1739 A465 3d red lilac
                1.50   .45

Natl.
Events
A466

Ho Chi Minh and: 10d, August revolution, Aug. 19, 1945. 20d, Proclaiming independence, Sept. 9, 1945. 30d, Victory at Dien Bien Phu, July 7, 1954. 50d, Capture of Saigon, Apr. 30, 1975.

1987, Apr. 12   *Perf. 11*
1740-1743 A466 Set of 4   6.25 1.50

A467

Champa art: 3d, Temple, Da Nang. 10d, Tower, Na Trang. 15d, Temple, Da Nang (side view). 20d, Dancing girl. 25d, Bust of woman. 30d, Girl playing flute. 40d, Dancing girl, diff.

1987, June 30   *Perf. 12x12½*
1744-1750 A467 Set of 7   7.25 2.75
     Imperf., #1744-1750   9.50 9.50
Souvenir Sheet
1751 A467 50d like #1749   4.00 4.00

A468

Various flowering cacti: 5d, 10d, 15d, 20d, 25d, 30d, 40d.

1987, Dec. 30   *Perf. 12½*
1752-1758 A468 Set of 7   5.00 2.00
Souvenir Sheet
        Perf. 13
1759 A468 50d multicolored   5.00 1.25

Global Population Reaches 5
Billion — A469

1987, July 11   *Perf. 13*
1760 A469 5d multicolored   1.50   .45

World Wildlife
Fund — A470

Designs: No. 1761, 5d, Concolor gibbon. No. 1762, 5d, Douc monkeys. 15d, Black concolor gibbon. 40d, Douc monkey.

1987, Sept. 23   *Perf. 12½*
1761-1764 A470 Set of 4   9.00 2.00
     Imperf., #1761-1764   40.00

A471

Western high plateau costumes: 5d, Male Bana. No. 1766, 20d, Female Bana. No. 1767, 20d, Female Gia Rai. No. 1768, 30d, Male Gia Rai. No. 1769, 30d, Male Ede. 40d, Female Ede.

1987, July 25   *Perf. 12x12½*
1765-1770 A471 Set of 6   7.00 2.50
     Imperf., #1765-1770   12.50

A472

1987, July 27   *Perf. 13*
1771 A472 5d multicolored   1.60   .40
    Day of the Invalids, 40th anniv.

Postal
Trade
Union,
40th
Anniv.
A473

Designs: 5d, Letter carrier, jet, truck, train. 30d, Switchboard operator.

1987, Aug. 30
1772-1773 A473 Set of 2   2.10 1.20

A474

Paintings by Picasso: No. 1774, 3d, *The Three Musicians*. No. 1775, 20d, War. No. 1776, 20d, Peace. No. 1777, 30d, Child with Dove, vert. No. 1778, 30d, Portrait of Gertrude Stein, vert. 40d, Guernica. 50d, Child as Harlequin.

1987, Dec. 30   *Perf. 12½*
1774-1779 A474 Set of 6   5.75 1.75
     Imperf., #1774-1779   12.00
Souvenir Sheet
1780 A474 50d multicolored   5.00 1.50
    No. 1779 is 44x27mm. No. 1780 contains one 40x32mm stamp.

Coral — A475

Designs: 5d, Epanouis. 10d, Acropora. 15d, Rhizopsammia. 20d, Acropora, diff. 25d, Alcyone, 30d, Corollum. 40d, Cristatella.

1987, Oct. 30   *Perf. 12x12½*
1781-1787 A475 Set of 7   7.50 2.75
     Imperf., #1781-1787   12.50

Intl. Year
for
Housing
for the
Homeless
A476

1987, Sept. 23   *Perf. 13*
1788 A476 5d greenish bl & blk   1.50   .40

Russian
Revolution, 70th
Anniv. — A477

Designs: 5d, 65d, Industry, agriculture. 20d, Lenin. 30d, Construction. 50d, Ho Chi Minh.

1987, Oct. 6   *Perf. 13*
1789-1792 A477 Set of 4   3.50 1.50
Souvenir Sheet
1793 A477 65d multicolored   4.00 4.00

Hafnia
'87
A478

Seaplanes: 5d, PBY-5. 10d, LeO H-246. 15d, Dornier DO-18. 20d, Short Sunderland. 25d, Rohrbach Rostra. 30d, Chetverikov ARK-3. 40d, CANT Z-509. 50d, Curtiss H-16.

1987, Dec. 30   *Perf. 13*
1794-1800 A478 Set of 7   5.00 2.00
     Imperf., #1794-1800   12.50
Souvenir Sheet
1801 A478 50d multicolored   4.50 1.25
    No. 1801 contains one 40x32mm stamp.

Czechoslovakia-Viet Nam Friendship
Agreement, 10th Anniv. — A479

10d, Handshake. 50d, Flags, buildings.

1987, Oct. 31
1802-1803 A479 Set of 2   3.25   .80
     Imperf., 1802-1803   17.50

Viet Nam-Soviet Union
Cooperation — A480

Designs: 5d, Industry. 50d, Buildings.

1987, Nov. 3
1804-1805 A480 Set of 2   3.50   .80

Mushrooms
A481

Designs: 5d, Polyporellus squamosus. 10d, Clitocybe geotropa. 15d, Tricholoma terreum. 20d, Russula aurata. 25d, Collybia fusipes. 30d, Cortinarius violaceus. 40d, Boletus aereus.

1987, Dec. 30   *Perf. 12½*
1806-1812 A481 Set of 7   5.00 2.00
     Imperf., #1806-1812   11.50

Peace
A482

1987, Nov. 10   *Perf. 13*
1813 A482 10d multicolored   1.40   .40

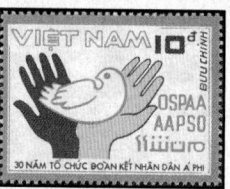

Afro-Asian Solidarity Committee
(AAPSO), 30th Anniv. — A483

10d, Hands, dove. 30d, Map, hands, vert.

1987, Nov. 30
1814-1815 A483 Set of 2   2.25   .80
     Imperf., #1814-1815   20.00

Victory Over US Bombing Campaign, 15th Anniv. — A484

Designs: 10d, B-52 wreckage. 30d, Children with flowers, wreckage.

1987, Dec. 26
1816-1817 A484 Set of 2   2.75   .80
    Imperf., #1816-1817   27.50

Productivity A485

Designs: 5d, Consumer goods. 20d, Agriculture. 30d, Export products.

1987, Dec. 30
1818-1820 A485 Set of 3   3.25 1.20

Hoang Sa, Truong Sa Islands A486

Designs: 10d, Ship, sailor. 100d, Maps.

1988, Jan. 19
1821-1822 A486 Set of 2   5.25   .90

Roses — A487

Various roses: 5d, 10d, 15d, 20d, 25d, 30d, 40d.

1988, Jan. 20   **Perf. 12½**
1823-1829 A487 Set of 7   6.00 2.75
    Imperf., #1823-1829   15.00
    Souvenir Sheet
    Perf. 13
1830 A487 50d multicolored   5.00 1.25

Tropical Fish A488

Designs: 5d, Red betta splendens. 10d, Labeo bicolor. 15d, Puntis tetrazona. 20d, Brachydania albolineatus. 25d, Puntis conchonius. 30d, Betta splendens, diff. 40d, Botia lecontei.

1988, Jan. 20   **Perf. 13**
1831-1837 A488 Set of 7   5.00 2.00
    Imperf., #1831-1837   12.00

Intl. Red Cross, Red Crescent, 125th Anniv. — A489

1988, Feb. 17
1838 A489 10d multicolored   1.25   .40

Battle of Bach Dang, 700th Anniv. A490

80d, Fleet of ships. 200d, Battle scene.

1988, Apr. 8
1839-1840 A490 Set of 2   5.00   .80

Tourism A491

5d, One-pillar pagoda. 10d, Bach Dang River. 15d, Thien Mu Tower, Hue. 20d, Hgu Hanh Mountain, Da Nang. 25d, Nha Trang beach. 30d, Pren Waterfalls. 40d, Market, Ben Thanh. 50d, Cleft Rocks, Quang Ninh.

1988, Apr. 20   **Perf. 12½x12**
1841-1847 A491 Set of 7   5.50 2.00
    Imperf., #1841-1847   9.00
    Souvenir Sheet
1848 A491 50d multicolored   3.50 1.25

Water Lilies — A492

Designs: 5d, Nymphaea lotus. No. 1850, 10d, Nymphaea pubescens. No. 1851, 10d, Nymphaea nouchali. No. 1852, 20d, Nymphaea rubra. No. 1853, 20d, Nymphaea gigantea. 30d, Nymphaea laydekeri. 50d, Nymphaea capensis.

1988, Apr. 24   **Perf. 12x12½**
1849-1855 A492 Set of 7   5.75 2.00
    Imperf., #1849-1855   12.00

Offshore Oil Drilling — A493

1988, Apr. 28   **Perf. 13**
1856 A493 1000d multicolored   8.50 8.50

A494

Parrots: No. 1857, 10d, Ara araruna. No. 1858, 10d, Psittacula himalayana. No. 1859, 20d, Aprosmictus erythropterus. No. 1860, 20d, Ara chloroptera. No. 1861, 30d, Ara militaris. No. 1862, 30d, Psittacula alexandri. 50d, Loriculus vernalis. 80d, Ara chloroptera, diff.

1988, May 5   **Perf. 12x12½**
1857-1863 A494 Set of 7   6.00 2.75
    Imperf., #1857-1863   16.00
    Souvenir Sheet
1864 A494 80d multicolored   4.00 1.25

A495

Membership in Council of Mutual Economic Assistance, 10th Anniv.: 200d, Map. 300d, Headquarters building.

1988, May 29
1865-1866 A495 Set of 2   5.50 1.25

A496

1988, June 1
1867 A496 60d multicolored   1.25   .80
Vaccinations against disease.

Problems of Peace and Socialism Magazine, 30th Anniv. — A497

1988, July 20
1868 A497 20d multicolored   1.25   .40

A498

1988, Aug. 20
1869 A498 150d multicolored   2.00   .40
Pres. Ton Duc Thang, birth cent.

A499

6th Vietnamese Trade Union Congress: 50d, Emblem. 100d, Workers.

1988, Aug. 28
1870-1871 A499 Set of 2   2.25   .80

Children's Paintings A500

#1872, 10d, My Family. #1873, 10d, My House. #1874, 20d, Fishing. #1875, 20d, Flying Kites. #1876, 30d, Girl playing guitar, animals. #1877, 30d, Children in rain, vert. 50d, Girl holding dove, vert. 80d, Family, diff., vert.

Perf. 12½x12, 12x12½

1988, Sept. 25 Set of 7   6.00 2.50
1872-1878 A500
    Imperf., #1872-1878   11.50
    Souvenir Sheet
    Perf. 12x12½
1879 A500 80d multicolored   4.00 1.25

Hydroelectric Plants — A501

Designs: 2000d, Tri An. 3000d, Hoa Binh.

1988, Sept. 27   **Perf. 13**
1880-1881 A501 Set of 2   11.00 5.50

A502

1988, Nov. 3   **Perf. 13½x13**
1882 A502 50d multicolored   2.00   .45
Viet Nam-USSR Friendship Agreement, 10th anniv.

A503

Designs: 100d, Fidel Castro. 300d, Flags, Vietnamese, Cuban people.

1988, Dec. 27
1883-1884 A503 Set of 2   2.25   .80
Cuban revolution, 30th anniv.

Wild Animals A504

Designs: No. 1885, 10d, Bos banteng. No. 1886, 10d, Bos gaurus. No. 1887, 20d, Axis porcinus. No. 1888, 20d, Tapirus indicus. No. 1889, 30d, Capricornis sumatrensis. No. 1890, 30d, Sus scrofa. 50d, Bubalus bubalus. 80d, Rhinoceros sodaicus.

1988, Dec. 30   **Perf. 12½**
1885-1891 A504 Set of 7   5.00 2.00
Imperf., #1885-1891   15.00
Souvenir Sheet
1892 A504 80d multicolored   7.25 4.00
Imperf.   20.00

Locomotives — A505

Designs: No. 1893, 20d, Kiha 80, Japan. No. 1894, 20d, LRC, Canada. No. 1895, 20d, Hitachi, Japan. No. 1896, 20d, BL-85, USSR. No. 1897, 30d, RC-1, Sweden. No. 1898, 30d, DR-1A, USSR. 50d, T3-136, USSR. 80d, SCNF Z6400.

1988, Dec. 30   **Perf. 13**
1893-1899 A505 Set of 7   5.00 2.25
Imperf., #1893-1899   12.50
Souvenir Sheet
1900 A505 80d multicolored   4.75 1.25
Imperf.   7.00

No. 1900 contains one 40x32mm stamp.

A506

Fruits, vegetables: No. 1901, 10d, Lagenaria siceraria. No. 1902, 10d, Momordica charantia. No. 1903, 20d, Solanum melongena. No. 1904, 20d, Cucurbita moschata. No. 1905, 30d, Luffa cylindrica. No. 1906, 30d, Benincasa hispida. 50d, Lycopercicon esculentum.

1988, Dec. 30   **Perf. 12x12½**
1901-1907 A506 Set of 7   5.50 2.75
Imperf., #1901-1907   10.50

A507

Various project spacecraft: No. 1908, 10d, Mars. No. 1909, 10d, Moon. No. 1910, 20d, Saturn. No. 1911, 20d, Inter-planetary. No. 1912, 30d, Venus. No. 1913, 30d, Earth orbital space station. 50d, Cosmos house. 80d, Lander docking with orbiter.

1988, Dec. 30   **Perf. 13**
1908-1914 A507 Set of 7   4.75 1.50
Imperf., #1908-1914   17.00
Souvenir Sheet
1915 A507 80d multicolored   4.50 1.25
Cosmos Day.
No. 1915 contains one 32x40mm stamp.

Shells A508

Designs: No. 1916, 10d, Conus miles. No. 1917, 10d, Strombus lentiginosus. No. 1918, 20d, Nautilus. No. 1919, 20d, Bursa rana. No. 1920, 30d, Turbo petholatus. No. 1921, 30d, Oliva erythros. 50d, Mitra eriscopalis. 80d, Tonna tessellata.

1988, Dec. 30   **Perf. 12½x12**
1916-1922 A508 Set of 7   5.75 2.50
Imperf., #1916-1922   13.50
Souvenir Sheet
1923 A508 80d multicolored   5.00 1.25

India '89 — A509

Butterflies: No. 1924, 50d, Anaea echemus. No. 1925, 50d, Ascia monuste. No. 1926, 50d, Juniona evarete. No. 1927, 100d, Phoebis avellaneda. No. 1928, 100d, Eurema proterpia. 200d, Papilio palamedes. 300d, Danaus plexippus. 400d, Parides gundlachiamus.

1989, Jan. 7   **Perf. 12½**
1924-1930 A509 Set of 7   6.50 2.75
Imperf., #1924-1930   11.00
Souvenir Sheet
1931 A509 400d multicolored   4.75 1.25

No. 1931 contains one 40x32mm stamp. Nos. 1924-1930 printed with se-tenant label.

Natl. Day of Cambodia, 10th Anniv. — A510

Designs: 100d, Soldiers, women working in field. 500d, Viet Nam-Cambodia friendship.

1989, Jan. 7   **Perf. 13x13½**
1932-1933 A510 Set of 2   2.75 1.20
Imperf., #1932-1933   21.00

India '89 — A511

Designs: No. 1934, 100d, Science, technology. No. 1935, 100d, Agriculture, industry. 300d, Asoka pillar. 600d, Nehru (1889-1964).

1989, Jan. 20   **Perf. 13**
1934-1937 A511 Set of 4   3.00 1.50

Battle of Dong Da, Bicent. — A512

Designs: 100d, Festival. 1000d, Quang Trung defeating Qing invaders.

1989, Feb. 10   **Perf. 13**
1938-1939 A512 Set of 2   3.00 1.50

Inter-Parliamentary Union, Cent. — A513

Designs: 100d, Vietnamese membership, 10th anniv. 200d, Centennial emblem.

1989, Mar. 1
1940-1941 A513 Set of 2   2.25 .60

Fishing Boats — A513a

Boats from: No. 1942, 10d, Quang Nam. No. 1943, 10d, Quang Tri. No. 1944, 20d, Thua Thien. No. 1945, 20d, Da Nang (sail furled). No. 1946, 30d, Da Nang (under sail). No. 1947, 30d, Quang Tri (under sail). 50d, Hue.

1989, Mar. 20   **Perf. 12½x12**
1942-1948 A513a Set of 7   5.50 2.25
Imperf., #1942-1948   12.00

Helicopters — A514

#1949, 10d, Kamov KA-26. #1950, 10d, Boeing Vertol 234. #1951, 20d, Mil MI-10(V10). #1952, 20d, MBB BO 105. #1953, 30d, Kawasaki Hughes 369HS. #1954, 30d, Bell 206B Jet Ranger, 50d, Mil MI-8. 80d, Puma SA330.

1989, Apr. 12   **Perf. 12½**
1949-1955 A514 Set of 7   4.75 1.90
Imperf., #1949-1955   14.00
Souvenir Sheet
1956 A514 80d multicolored   3.00 1.25
Imperf.   10.00

No. 1956 contains one 40x32mm stamp.

Bicycles A515

#1957, 10d, Bowden Spacelander. #1958, 10d, Rabasa Derbi. #1959, 20d, Huffy. #1960, 20d, Rabasa Derbi. #1961, 30d, VMX-PL. #1962, 30d, Premier. 50d, Columbia RX5.

1989, May 1   **Perf. 13**
1957-1963 A515 Set of 7   5.50 1.90
Imperf., #1957-1963   10.00

Turtles — A516

No. 1964, 10d, Cuora trifasciata. No. 1965, 10d, Testudo elegans. No. 1966, 20d, Eretmochelys imbricata. No. 1967, 20d, Platysternon megacephalum. No. 1968, 30d, Dermochelys coriacea. No. 1969, 30d, Chelonia mydas. 50d, Caretta caretta. 80d, Caretta caretta, diff.

1989, May 1   **Perf. 12½**
1964-1970 A516 Set of 7   7.00 2.25
Imperf., #1964-1970   13.50
Souvenir Sheet
1971 A516 80d multicolored   6.00 1.25
Imperf.   17.00
Finlandia '88 (#1971).

Poisonous Snakes — A517

Designs: No. 1972, 10d, Trimeresurus popeorum. No. 1973, 10d, Trimeresurus mucrosquamatus. No. 1974, 20d, Bungarus fasciatus. No. 1975, 20d, Bungarus candidus. No. 1976, 30d, Calliophis maclellandii. No. 1977, 30d, Ancistrodon acutus. 50d, Ophiophagus hannah, vert.

1989, May 1
1972-1978 A517 Set of 7   5.75 1.90
Imperf., #1972-1978   13.50

Pairs Figure Skating — A518

Various figure skaters: No. 1979, 10d, "Viet Nam" at left. No. 1980, 10d, "Viet Nam" at right. No. 1981, 20d, "Viet Nam" at left. No. 1982, 20d, "Viet Nam" at right, horiz. No. 1983, 30d, "Viet Nam" at left. No. 1984, 30d, "Viet Nam" at right, horiz. 50d, "Viet Nam" at left, horiz.

1989, May 29   **Perf. 13**
1979-1985 A518 Set of 7   5.00 1.50
Imperf., #1979-1985   11.00
Souvenir Sheet
With Gum
1986 A518 80d multi, horiz.   4.25 1.25

No. 1986 contains one 40x32mm stamp.

A519

1989, June 5   **Perf. 13**
1987 A519 100d buff   1.40 .25
Post & Telecommunications.

A520

Ceramics, Li-Tran Period: 50d, Pitcher. No. 1989, 100d, Bowl. No. 1990, 100d, Jug. 200d, Jug, diff. 300d, Vase.

1989, July 1   **Perf. 12**
1988-1992 A520   Set of 5   3.75 1.50
    Imperf., #1988-1992   8.00

Legend of Giong
A521

Designs: 50d, Mother nursing infant. No. 1994, Giong meets imperial messenger. No. 1995, 100d, Giong riding iron horse, people following. 200d, Giong pulling up bamboo trees. 300d, Giong flying into sky.

1989, July 1   **Perf. 12½x12**
1993-1997 A521   Set of 5   3.50 1.50
    Imperf., #1993-1997   7.25

French Revolution, Bicent. — A522

Designs: 100d, Emblem. 500d, Liberty leading the people, after Delacroix.

1989, July 14   **Perf. 13½x13**
1998-1999 A522   Set of 2   2.50 .80

PHILEXFRANCE '89 — A523

Paintings: No. 2000, 50d, Oath of the Tennis Court, by David. No. 2001, 50d, Capture of Louis XVI, horiz. No. 2002, 50d, Liberty, Equality, Fraternity, horiz. No. 2003, 100d, Storming the Bastille. No. 2004, 100d, Death of Marat, by David. 200d, Child and Rabbit, by Prud'hon. 300d, Slave Market, by Gerome, horiz. 400d, Liberty Leading the People, by Delacroix.

1989, July 14   **Perf. 13**
2000-2006 A523   Set of 7   5.00 2.25
    Imperf., #2000-2006   10.00
    Souvenir Sheet
2007 A523   400d multicolored   3.50 1.25
No. 2007 contains one 33x44mm stamp.

1989 World Cup Soccer Championships, Italy — A524

Soccer plays: No. 2008, 50d, Dribbling. No. 2009, 50d, Tackling. No. 2010, 50d, Goalie. No. 2011, 100d, Dribbling, diff. No. 2012, 100d, Dribbling, diff., vert. 200d, Preparing to kick, vert. 300d, Heading ball, vert. 400d, Heading ball, diff., vert.

Perf. 13x12½, 12½x13
1989, Aug. 27
2008-2014 A524   Set of 7   4.50 1.75
    Imperf., #2008-2014   11.00
    Souvenir Sheet
    Perf. 13
2015 A524   400d multicolored   3.50 1.25
No. 2015 contains one 32x40mm stamp.

Dogs
A525

#2016, 50d, Dachshund. #2017, 50d, Beagle. #2018, 50d, English setter, vert. #2019, 100d, German short-haired pointer, vert. #2020, 100d, Basset hounds. 200d, German sheperd, vert. 300d, Beagle, diff.

1989, Aug. 20   **Perf. 12½**
2016-2022 A525   Set of 7   5.50 1.75
    Imperf., #2016-2022   10.00
No. 2020 is 68x28mm.

Horses
A526

#2023, 50d, Tennessee Walking. #2024, 50d, Appaloosa. #2025, 50d, Tersky. #2025, 100d, Kladruber. #2026, 100d, Welsh cob. 200d, Pinto. 300d, Pony and bridle.

1989, Sept. 23   **Perf. 13**
2023-2029 A526   Set of 7   5.50 1.75
    Imperf., #2023-2029   12.50
No. 2029 is 68x28mm.

Flowers — A527

No. 2030, 50d, Paphiopedilum siamense. No. 2031, 50d, Fuchsia fulgens. No. 2032, 100d, Hemerocallis fulva. No. 2033, 100d, Gloriosa superba. 200d, Strelitzia reginae. 300d, Iris.

1989, Sept. 23   **Perf. 12½**
2030-2035 A527   Set of 6   5.50 1.50
    Imperf., #2030-2035   11.50

German Democratic Republic, 40th Anniv. — A528

1989, Oct. 7   **Perf. 13**
2036 A528   200d multicolored   1.25 .40

Immunization Campaign — A529

#2037, Woman receiving vaccination. #2038, Child receiving oral vaccine. #2039, Clinic.

1989, Oct. 20
2037-2039 A529 100d Set of 3   2.50 .90

Drawings of Everyday Life, 19th Cent. — A530

Designs: 50d, Assembling plow. No. 2041, 100d, Harrowing. No. 2042, 100d, Irrigating. 200d, Fertilizing. 300d, Harvesting.

1989, Oct. 28   **Perf. 12x12½**
2040-2044 A530   Set of 5   3.75 1.50
    Imperf., #2040-2044   8.50

Horse Paintings, by Xu Beihong (1895-1953) A531

Various horses: 100d, 200d, 300d, 500d horiz., 800d, 1000d, 1500d.

1989, Dec. 22   **Perf. 13**
2045-2051 A531   Set of 7   4.25 1.50
    Imperf., #2045-2051   9.00
    Imperf
    Size: 117x72mm
2052 A531   2000d multicolored   7.50 1.25
    Imperf.   14.00

Vietnamese Communist Party, 60th Anniv. — A532

Designs: 100d, Ho Chi Minh, tank. 500d, Workers, refinery, field.

1990, Feb. 3   **Litho.**   **Perf. 13**
2053-2054 A532   Set of 2   3.00 1.20
    Imperf., #2053-2054   6.50

Ducks — A533

a, 100d, Anas platyrhynchos hybrid. b, 300d, Anas penelope. c, 500d, Anas platyrhynchos. d, 1000d, Anas erythrorhyncha. e, 2000d, Anas platyrhynchos, diff. f, 3000d, Anas undulata.

1990, Feb. 15
2055 A533   Block of 6, #a.-f.   4.75 1.50

Trucks
A534

100d, Mack. 200d, Volvo F89. 300d, Tatra 915 S1. 500d, Hino KZ30000. 1000d, Iveco. 2000d, Leyland DAF Super Comet. 3000d, Kamaz 53212.

1990, Feb. 20
2056-2062 A534   Set of 7   3.75 1.50
    Imperf., #2056-2062   6.25

Architectural Sites, Hue — A535

#2063, 100d, Tu Duc's Mausoleum. #2064, 100d, Hien Nhon Arch. 200d, Ngo Mon Gate. 300d, Thien Mu Temple. 400d, Palace, gateway.

1990, Feb. 20   **Perf. 12½x12**
2063-2066 A535   Set of 4   3.50 1.50
    Souvenir Sheet
2067 A535   400d multicolored   4.00 1.20

Goldfish — A536

100d, Bulging-eyed, horiz. 300d, Telescopic-eyed, horiz. 500d, Red-headed, horiz. 1000d, Double-tailed. 2000d, Rainbow. 3000d, Comet.

1990, Mar. 20   **Perf. 13**
2068-2073 A536   Set of 6   4.50 1.50
    Imperf., #2068-2073   7.50

Paintings
A537

London '90: 100d, Antonia Zarate, by Goya. 200d, Girl Holding a Paper Fan, by Renoir. 300d, Janet Grizel, by John Russell. 500d,

Love Untieing the Belt of Beauty, by Sir Joshua Reynolds. 1000d, Portrait of a Woman, by George Romney. 2000d, Portrait of Madame Ginoux, by Van Gogh. 3000d, Woman in Blue, by Gainsborough. 3500d, Woman in a Straw Hat, by Van Gogh.

1990, Apr. 10
2074-2080 A537 Set of 7 4.50 1.50
Imperf., #2074-2080 9.00
Souvenir Sheet
2081 A537 3500d multicolored 3.00 1.50

1990 World Cup Soccer Championships, Italy — A538

Various soccer players in action: 100d, 200d, 300d, 500d, 1000d, 2000d, 3000d.

1990, Apr. 19
2082-2088 A538 Set of 7 4.00 1.50
Imperf., #2082-2088 20.00
Souvenir Sheet
2089 A538 3500d multicolored 3.25 1.25
No. 2089 contains one 32x40mm stamp. For overprints see Nos. 2189-2196.

Cats — A539

Various cats: 100d, horiz., 200d, 300d, horiz., 500d, 1000d, horiz., 2000d, 3000d.

1990, May 5
2090-2096 A539 Set of 7 5.00 1.50
Souvenir Sheet
2097 A539 3500d multicolored 4.00 1.25
Imperf. 5.00
No. 2097 contains one 44x33mm stamp. Belgica '90 (#2097).

Dogs — A540

Various dogs: 100d, 200d, 300d, 500d, 1000d, 2000d, 3000d.

1990, May 15
2098-2104 A540 Set of 7 4.25 1.50
Souvenir Sheet
2105 A540 3500d Collies 3.25 1.25
Imperf. 7.50
New Zealand '90.

Ho Chi Minh (1890-1969) A541

Ho Chi Minh and: 100d, Lenin. 300d, Soldiers waving flag. 500d, Hand holding rifle,

dove. 1000d, Map. 2000d, Child, dove. 3000d, Stylized globe. 3500d, Flag.

1990, May 17 *Perf. 13*
2106-2111 A541 Set of 6 4.00 4.00
Imperf., #2106-2111 6.00
Souvenir Sheet
Perf. 12½x13
2112 A541 3500d multicolored 4.00 4.00
No. 2112 contains one 33x44mm stamp.

Dinosaurs — A542

100d, Gorgosaurus. 500d, Ceratosaurus. 1000d, Ankylosaurus. 2000d, Ankylosaurus, diff. 3000d, Edaphosaurus.

1990, June 1 *Perf. 13*
2113-2117 A542 Set of 5 5.25 2.25

Columbus' Discovery of America, 500th Anniv. — A543

Designs: 50d, Fleet. No. 2119, 100d, Columbus presenting gifts to natives. No. 2120, 100d, Columbus, priest at Rabida. No. 2121, 100d, Columbus at Court of Ferdinand, Isabella. No. 2122, 200d, Map of Caribbean. No. 2123, 200d, Columbus, arms. 300d, Map of Atlantic. 500d, Teotihuacan pot.

1990, June 10 *Perf. 12½*
2118-2124 A543 Set of 7 5.75
Imperf., #2118-2124 20.00
Souvenir Sheet
2125 A543 500d multicolored 3.50
No. 2125 contains one 40x32mm stamp. For overprints see Nos. 2313-2320.

Sailing Ships A544

Designs: 100d, Viking longship. 500d, Caravel. No. 2128, 1000d, Carrack, 14th-15th cent. No. 2129, 1000d, Flit. No. 2130, 1000d, Carrack, 15th cent., vert. 2000d, Galleon, vert. 3000d, Galleon, diff. 4200d, Egyptian barge.

1990, June 10 *Perf. 13*
2126-2132 A544 Set of 7 4.00
Imperf., #2126-2132 10.50
Souvenir Sheet
Perf. 13x12½
2133 A544 4200d multicolored 4.50
No. 2133 contains one 44x33mm stamp.

11th Asian Games, Beijing — A545

Designs: 100d, High jump. 200d, Basketball. 300d, Table tennis. 500d, Volleyball. 1000d, Rhythmic gymnastics. 2000d, Tennis. 3000d, Judo. 3500d, Hurdles.

1990, June 20 *Perf. 13*
2134-2140 A545 Set of 7 4.00 4.00
Imperf., #2134-2140 12.00
Souvenir Sheet
Perf. 12½x13
2141 A545 3500d multicolored 3.00 3.00
No. 2141 contains one 33x44mm stamp.

Nos. 1180-1187 Ovptd. in Red, Green and Black

1990, June 22 *Perf. 12*
2142-2149 A352 Set of 8 10.00
1990 World Cup Soccer Championships, Italy.

Nos. 1323-1330 Ovptd. in Black and Red

1990, June 22 *Perf. 12x12½*
2150-2157 A385 Set of 8 10.00
Tourism.

Modern Ships A546

100d, Freighter. 300d, Container ship. 500d, Cruise ship. 1000d, Liquified natural gas tanker. 2000d, Ro-Ro ship. 3000d, Ferry.

1990, July 20 *Perf. 13*
2158-2163 A546 Set of 6 4.25
Imperf., #2158-2163 7.50

Post & Telecommunications Dept., 45th Anniv. — A547

Designs: 100d, Dove, ship, plane. 1000d, Satellite antenna.

1990, Aug. 15 *Perf. 13x13½*
2164-2165 A547 Set of 2 2.00
Imperf., #2164-2165 4.00

Socialist Republic of Viet Nam, 45th Anniv. — A548

Designs: 100d, Flag, construction projects. 500d, Map, tank, soldiers. 1000d, "VI," ship, communications network. 3000d, Workers, oil rigs. 3500d, Ho Chi Minh.

1990, Sept. 1 *Perf. 13*
2166-2169 A548 Set of 4 4.00
Imperf., #2166-2169 6.00
Souvenir Sheet
Perf. 12½x13
2170 A548 3500d multicolored 3.00
No. 2170 contains one 33x44mm stamp. Sixth Vietnamese Communist Party Congress (#2168).

Airships A549

Designs: 100d, Henry Gifford, 1871. 200d, Lebandy, 1910. 300d, Graf Zeppelin. 500d, R-101, 1930. 1000d, Soviet, 1936. 2000d, Tissandier, 1883. 3000d, US Navy. 3500d, "Zodiac," 1931.

1990, Sept. 10 *Perf. 12½*
2171-2177 A549 Set of 7 5.00
Imperf., #2171-2177 9.50
Souvenir Sheet
2178 A549 3500d multicolored 2.50 1.00
No. 2178 contains one 40x32mm stamp. Helvetia '90, Stamp World London '90.

Fable of Thach Sanh — A550

Designs: a, 100d, Thach Sanh carrying bundles of wood. b, 300d, Ly Thong. c, 500d, Thach Sanh killing python. d, 1000d, Thach Sanh shooting arrow at eagle. e, 2000d, Thach Sanh in prison. f, 3000d, Thach Sanh, princess.

1990, Sept. 20 *Perf. 13*
2179 A550 Block of 6, #a.-f. 6.00
Imperf. 8.00

Asian-Pacific Postal Training Center, 20th Anniv. — A551

1990, Sept. 25
2180 A551 150d multicolored 1.00

Nos. 571-578 Ovptd. with Red Cross in Red & "FOR THE FUTURE GENERATION" in various Languages in Black

Language: No. 2181, 12xu, Japanese. No. 2182, 12xu, Italian. No. 2183, 20xu, German. No. 2184, 20xu, Vietnamese. 30xu, English. 40xu, Russian. 50xu, French. 60xu, Spanish.

1990, Sept. 25 *Perf. 12*
2181-2188 A211 Set of 8 10.00
Position of overprint varies. Use of these stamps at stated face value is unlikely.

Nos. 2082-2089 Ovptd.

1990, Sept. 25   **Perf. 13**
2189-2195 A538 Set of 7   10.00
Souvenir Sheet
2196 A538 3500d multicolored   8.00

Vietnamese Women's Federation, 60th
Anniv. — A552

Designs: 100d, Woman carrying rifle. 500d,
Women working in field, laboratory.

1990, Oct. 10
2197-2198 A552 Set of 2   2.00
   Imperf., #2197-2198   5.00

Correggio
(1494-1534),
Painter — A553

Various paintings of the Madonna and Child:
No. 2199, 50xu, shown. No. 2200, 50xu, diff.
1d, 2d, 3d, 5d, 6d.

1990, Nov. 13   **Perf. 12½**
2199-2205 A553 Set of 7   4.50
Souvenir Sheet
2206 A553 10d multicolored   4.50
No. 2206 contains one 32x40mm stamp.
Dated "1984." Use of these stamps at stated
face value is unlikely.

Protection of Forests — A554

Designs: 200d, Water conservation, healthy
forest. 1000d, SOS, prevent forest fires.

1990, Nov. 15   **Perf. 13**
2207-2208 A554 Set of 2   1.50 .30
   Imperf., #2207-2208   6.00

A555

Poisonous mushrooms: 200d, Amanita
pantherina. 300d, Amanita phalloides. 1000d,
Amanita virosa. 1500d, Amanita muscaria.

2000d, Russula emetica. 3000d, Boletus
satanas.

1991, Jan. 21
2209-2214 A555 Set of 6   5.00 2.00
   Imperf., #2209-2214   9.50

A555a

1992 Summer Olympics, Barcelona: 200d,
Sailing. 300d, Boxing. 400d, Cycling. 1000d,
High jump. 2000d, Equestrian. No. 2220,
3000d, Judo. No. 2221, 3000d, Wrestling,
horiz. 5000d, Soccer, horiz.

1991, Jan. 31
2215-2221 A555a Set of 7   4.00 2.00
   Imperf., #2215-2221   7.00
Souvenir Sheet
2222 A555a 5000d multicolored   3.00 1.25
   Imperf., #2222   7.00
No. 2222 contains one 44x33mm stamp.

Nguyen Binh Khiem (1491-1585),
Writer — A556

1991, Feb. 15
2223 A556 200d multicolored   1.50 .25
   Imperf.   3.25

Discovery of America, 500th
Anniv. — A557

Sailing ships: 200d, Marisiliana. No. 2225,
400d, Venetian. No. 2226, 400d, Cromster,
vert. No. 2227, 2000d, Nina. No. 2228, 2000d,
Pinta. 3000d, Howker, vert. 5000d, Santa
Maria.
6500d, Portrait of Columbus.

1991, Feb. 22
2224-2230 A557 Set of 7   5.75 2.00
   Imperf., #2224-2230   6.00
Souvenir Sheet
2231 A557 6500d multicolored   2.75 1.25
   Imperf.   7.00

Golden Heart
Charity — A558

Women wearing traditional costumes: 200d,
500d, 1000d, 5000d.

1991, Feb. 26
2232-2235 A558 Set of 4   3.75 1.25
   Imperf., #2232-2235   7.50

Sharks
A559

Designs: 200d, Carcharhinus melanopterus.
300d, Carcharhinus amblyrhynchos. 400d,
Triakis semifasciata. 1000d, Sphyrna mokar-
ran. 2000d, Triaenodon obesus. No. 2241,
3000d, Carcharias taurus. No. 2242, 3000d,
Carcharhinus leucas.

1991, Apr. 6
2236-2242 A559 Set of 7   9.00 2.00
   Imperf., #2236-2242   13.00

Endangered Birds — A560

World Wildlife Fund: 200d, Grus vipio. 300d,
Grus antigone chick, vert. 400d, Grus
japonensis, vert. 1000d, Grus antigone,
adults, vert. 2000d, Grus nigricollis, vert. No.
2248, 3000d, Balearica regulorum, vert. No.
2249, 3000d, Bugeranus leucogerranus.

1991, Apr. 20
2243-2249 A560 Set of 7   8.50 2.00
   Imperf., #2243-2249   20.00

Shellfish
A561

Designs: 200d, 1000d, 2000d, Palinurus, all
diff. 300d, Alpheus bellulus. 400d, Per-
iclemenes brevicarpalis. No. 2255, 3000d,
Astacus. No. 2256, 3000d, Palinurus, diff.

1991, Apr. 20
2250-2256 A561 Set of 7   5.00 2.00
   Imperf., #2250-2256   10.00

Young Pioneers,
50th
Anniv. — A562

Designs: 200d, shown. 400d, UN Convention on Children's Rights.

1991, May 15
2257-2258 A562 Set of 2   2.00 .65
   Imperf., #2257-2258   4.50

Rally
Cars
A563

#2259, 400d, Lada. #2260, 400d, Nissan.
500d, Ford Sierra RS Cosworth. 1000d,
Suzuki. 2000d, Mazda 323 4WD. #2264,
3000d, Lancia. #2265, 3000d, Peugeot.
5000d, Peugeot 405.

1991, May 24
2259-2265 A563 Set of 7   5.00 2.25
   Imperf.   7.50
Souvenir Sheet
2266 A563 5000d multicolored   2.25 1.25
   Imperf.   5.00
No. 2266 contains one 44x33mm stamp.

Locomotives — A564

#2267, 400d, Puffing Billy, 1811, vert.
#2268, 400d, Fusee, 1829, vert. 500d, Ste-
vens, 1825. 1000d, Crampton #80, 1852.
2000d, Locomotion, 1825. #2272, 3000d,
Saint-Lo, 1844. #2273, 3000d, Coutances,
1855. 5000d, Atlantic, 1843.

1991, May 25
2267-2273 A564 Set of 7   5.00
   Imperf., #2267-2273   8.00
Souvenir Sheet
2274 A564 5000d multicolored   3.75
   Imperf.   6.50
No. 2274 contains one 33x44mm stamp.

Frogs
A565

World Wildlife Fund: 200d, Dendrobates
leucomelas. 400d, Rana esculenta. 500d,
Mantella aurantiaca. 1000d, Dendrobates
tinctorius. 2000d, Hyla halowelli. No. 2280,
3000d, Agalychnis callidryas. No. 2281,
3000d, Hyla aurea.

1991, June 12
2275-2281 A565 Set of 7   8.50 2.50
   Imperf., #2275-2281   25.00

7th Vietnamese
Communist
Party Congress
A566

Designs: 200d, Ho Chi Minh, buildings.
300d, Workers. 400d, Mother, children.

1991, May 15
2282-2284 A566 Set of 3   1.25 .65
   Imperf., #2282-2284   4.50

Vietnamese
Communist
Party, 60th
Anniv. — A566a

1991, June 24   **Litho.**   **Perf. 13**
2284A A566a 100d red   2.00 2.00

1992 Winter Olympics, Albertville A567

Designs: 200d, Speed skating, vert. 300d, Free-style skiing, vert. 400d, Bobsled. 1000d, Biathlon. 2000d, Slalom skiing. No. 2290, 3000d, Cross-country skiing, vert. No. 2291, 3000d, Ice dancing, vert. 5000d, Hockey, vert.

1991, July 15
2285-2291 A567 Set of 7   5.00 2.00
    Imperf., #2285-2291   5.00
     Souvenir Sheet
2292 A567 5000d multicolored   2.50 1.25
   Imperf.

No. 2292 contains one 33x44mm stamp.

Prehistoric Animals — A568

Designs: a, 200d, Arsinoitherium zitteli. b, 500d, Elephas primigenius. c, 1000d, Baluchitherium. d, 2000d, Deinotherium giganteum. e, 3000d, Brontops. f, 3000d, Uinatherium.

1991, July 26
2293 A568 Block of 6, #a.-f.   5.00 4.00
   Imperf., #2293   5.00

A569

Golden Heart Charity: 200d, Eye, folded hands. 3000d, Tennis player in wheelchair.

1991, Dec. 19
2294-2295 A569 Set of 2   2.00 .70

A570

Chess pieces: 200d, Pawn. 300d, Knight. 1000d, Rook. 2000d, Queen. No. 2300, 3000d, Bishop. No. 2301, 3000d, King. 5000d, Pawn, Knight, King.

1991, Aug. 20
2296-2301 A570 Set of 6   5.50 2.00
   Imperf., #2296-2301   6.75
     Souvenir Sheet
2302 A570 5000d multicolored   2.25 1.25
   Imperf.   5.00

No. 2302 contains one 33x44mm stamp.

PHILANIPPON '91 — A571

Butterflies: 200d, Attacus atlas. 400d, Morpho cypris. 500d, Troides rotschildi. No. 2306, 1000d, Papilio demetrius. No. 2307, 1000d, Vanessa atalanta. 3000d, Papilio weiskei. 5000d, Apatura ilia substituta. 5500d, Heliconius melpomene.

1991, Aug. 29
2303-2309 A571 Set of 7   4.50 2.25
   Imperf., #2303-2309   5.00
     Souvenir Sheet
2310 A571 5500d multicolored   4.50 1.25
   Imperf.   7.00

No. 2310 contains one 44x33mm stamp.

Post and Telecommunications Research Institute, 25th Anniv. — A572

3500d, Communications network, horiz.

1991, Aug.
2311 A572 200d multicolored   1.25 .25
   Imperf.   4.50
     Souvenir Sheet
2312 A572 3500d multicolored   2.25 1.25
   Imperf.   5.00

No. 2312 contains one 44x33mm stamp.

Nos. 2118-2125 Ovptd. in Red

1992, Jan. 15   **Perf. 12½**
2313-2319 A543 Set of 7   7.50 2.75
     Souvenir Sheet
2320 A543 500d multicolored   4.50 1.40

7th Vietnamese Communist Party Congress A574

200d, Workers, industry, agriculture, atomic energy symbol. 2000d, Map of Asia, hands clasped.

1992, Feb. 3   **Litho.**   **Perf. 13**
2322-2323 A574 Set of 2   2.00 1.75

1992 Winter Olympics, Albertville — A575

Designs: 200d, Biathlon. 2000d, Hockey. 4000d, Slalom skiing. 5000d, Pairs figure skating. 6000d, Downhill skiing.

1992, Feb. 5
2324-2328 A575 Set of 5   4.50 1.75

    Miniature Sheet

Columbus' Discovery of America, 500th Anniv. — A576

Designs: a, 4000d, Columbus, flag. b, 6000d, Columbus, natives. c, 8000d, Aboard ship. d, 3000d, Two sailing ships. e, 400d, Columbus' fleet setting sail. 11,000d, Columbus with Ferdinand and Isabella.

1992, Feb. 12
2329 A576 #a.-f. + label   4.25 2.00
     Imperf
     Size: 102x70mm
2330 A576 11,000d multicolored   3.75 1.25

Airplanes — A577

Designs: 400d, Tupolev TU-154M. 500d, Concorde. 1000d, Airbus A-320. 3000d, Airbus A340-300. 4000d, Boeing Dash 8-400. 5000d, Boeing 747-200. 6000d, McDonnell-Douglas MD-11CF.

1992, Mar. 6   **Perf. 13**
2331-2337 A577 Set of 7   4.25 2.25

A578

Intl. Decade for Natural Disaster Reduction: 400d, Storm system, weather forecasting equipment. 4000d, Man taking water depth readings.

1992, Mar. 23
2338-2339 A578 Set of 2   2.00 .50

A579

1992 Summer Olympics, Barcelona: 400d, Archery. 600d, Volleyball. 1000d, Wrestling. 3000d, Fencing. 4000d, Running. 5000d, Weight lifting. 6000d, Field hockey. 10,000d, Basketball.

1992, Mar. 28
2340-2346 A579 Set of 7   4.50 2.00
     Souvenir Sheet
2347 A579 10,000d multicolored   3.00 1.25

No. 2347 contains one 32x43mm stamp.

Motorcycles — A580

Designs: 400d, 5000d, Suzuki 500F. 500d, Honda CBR 600F. 1000d, Honda HRC 500F. 3000d, Kawasaki 250F, vert. 4000d, Suzuki RM 250F, vert. 6000d, BMW 1000F. 10,000d, Suzuki RM 250F, diff.

1992, Apr. 8
2348-2354 A580 Set of 7   4.50 2.00
     Souvenir Sheet
2355 A580 10,000d multicolored   3.50 1.25

No. 2355 contains one 33x44mm stamp.

Intl. Space Year A581

400d, Space shuttle launch, vert. 500d, Launch of shuttle Columbia, vert. 3000d, Columbia in space. 4000d, Space station, shuttle Hermes. 5000d, Shuttle Hermes. 6000d, Astronauts, Hubble space telescope, vert.

1992, Apr. 12
2356-2361 A581 Set of 6   4.25 2.00

Saigon Post Office, Cent. A582

200d, Main entrance. 10,000d, Facade.

1992, Apr. 30   **Perf. 13**
2362 A582 200d multicolored   1.00 .25
     Souvenir Sheet
      Perf. 13½
2363 A582 10,000d multicolored   3.00 1.25

No. 2363 contains one 43x32mm stamp.

European Cup Soccer Championships A583

Various soccer players in action: 200d, 2000d, 4000d, 5000d, 6000d.

1992, May 14   **Perf. 13**
2364-2368 A583 Set of 5   4.75 2.00

Souvenir Sheet

2369 A583 9000d multicolored   3.00 1.25

No. 2369 contains one 44x33mm stamp.

Spanish Paintings A584

Designs: 400d, Childhood of the Virgin, by Zurbaran. 500d, Woman with a Jug, by Murillo. 1000d, Portrait of Maria Aptrickaia, by Velazquez. 3000d, Holy Family with St. Katherine, by de Ribera. 4000d, Madonna and Child with Saints Agnes and Thekla, by El Greco. 5000d, Woman with a Jug, by Goya. 6000d, The Naked Maja, by Goya, horiz. 10,000d, Three Women, by Picasso, horiz.

1992, May 30
2370-2376 A584 Set of 7   4.25 2.00

Souvenir Sheet

2377 A584 10,000d multicolored   3.50 1.25

No. 2377 contains one 44x33mm stamp. Expo '92, Seville (#2377).

UN Conference on Environmental Protection, 20th Anniv. — A585

Designs: 200d, Clean, polluted water. 4000d, Graph comparing current development pattern with environmentally safe pattern.

1992, June 1
2378-2379 A585 Set of 2   2.00 .50

A586

Lighthouses: 200d, Cu Lao Xanh. 3000d, Can Gio. 5000d, Vung Tau. 6000d, Long Chau.

1992, June 14   **Perf. 13½x13**
2380-2383 A586 Set of 4   10.00 1.40

Genoa '92.

Flowers — A587

Designs: 200d, Citrus maxima. 2000d, Nerium indicum. 4000d, Ixora coccinea. 5000d, Cananga oborata. 6000d, Cassia surattensis.

1992, June 28   **Perf. 13**
2384-2388 A587 Set of 5   4.00 1.40

Birds — A588

Designs: 200d, Ducula spilorrhoa. 2000d, Petrophassa ferruginea. 4000d, Columba livia. 5000d, Lopholaimus antareticus. 6000d, Streptopelia senegalensis, horiz.

1992, July 3
2389-2393 A588 Set of 5   4.50 1.40

Rodents — A589

Designs: 200d, 500d, Cavia porcellus, horiz. 3000d, Hystrix indica, horiz. 4000d, Gerbillus gerbillus. 5000d, Petaurista petaurista. 6000d, Oryctolagus cuniculus.

1992, July 26
2394-2399 A589 Set of 6   4.50 2.00

Disabled Soldiers Day, 45th Anniv. A590

1992, July 27
2400 A590 200d multicolored   1.00 .25

3rd Phu Dong Games A591

1992, Aug. 1
2401 A591 200d multicolored   1.00 .25

Betta Splendens — A592

Various fish: 200d, 500d, 3000d, 4000d, 5000d, 6000d.

1992, Aug. 15
2402-2407 A592 Set of 6   4.50 2.00

1984 Summer Olympics, Los Angeles A592a

Designs: No. 2407A, 50xu, Gymnastics. No. 2407B, 50xu, Soccer, vert. 1d, Wrestling. 2d, Volleyball, vert. 3d, Hurdles. 5d, Basketball, vert. 8d, Weight lifting. 10d, Running, vert.

1992, Sept. 1   **Litho.**   **Perf. 12½**
2407A-2407G A592a Set of 7   5.00 5.00

Souvenir Sheet

2407H A592a 10d multi   5.00 5.00

Nos. 2407A-2407G were prepared in 1984 but were not released at that time, because of Viet Nam's boycott of the 1984 Summer Olympics.

Intl. Planned Parenthood Federation, 40th Anniv. — A593

Designs: 200d, Map showing member's locations, vert. 4000d, Anniv. emblem, map.

1992, Oct. 1
2408-2409 A593 Set of 2   2.00 .50

Hanoi Medical School, 90th Anniv. A594

Designs: 200d, Medical students. 5000d, Alexandre Yersin, school.

1992, Nov. 20
2410-2411 A594 Set of 2   2.50 .50

SOS Children's Villages — A595

Designs: 200d, Adult sheltering child. 5000d, Women, children inside house.

1992, Dec. 22
2412-2413 A595 Set of 2   2.00 .50

17th Southeast Asian Games, Singapore — A596

1993, Jan. 1
2414 A596 200d multicolored   1.00 .25

Bees A597

Designs: 200d, Apis dorsata. 800d, Apis koschevnikovi. 1000d, Apis laboriosa. 2000d, Apis cerana japonica. 5000d, Apis cerana cerana. 10,000d, Apis mellifera, vert.

1993, Jan. 15
2415-2420 A597 Set of 6   5.00 2.00

Fable of Tam Cam — A598

Designs: 200d, Returning from river. 800d, Vision of old man by goldfish pool. 1000d, With unsold rice at market. 3000d, Trying on slipper for prince. 4000d, Rising from lotus flower. 10,000d, Royal couple.

1993, Jan. 18
2421-2426 A598 Set of 6   6.50 2.00

New Year 1993 (Year of the Rooster) A599

200d, 5000d, Rooster, hen and chicks.

1993, Jan. 20
2427-2428 A599 Set of 2   2.50 .50

Medicinal Plants A600

Designs: 200d, Atractylodes macrocephala. No. 2430, 1000d, Lonicera japonica. No. 2431, 1000d, Quisqualis indica. 3000d, Rehmannia glutinosa. 12,000d, Gardenia jasminoides.

1993, Feb. 27
2429-2433 A600 Set of 5   5.50 1.50

Communications A601

200d, Map, communications equipment. 2500d, Map, Hong Kong-Sri Racha Cable route.

1993, Mar. 1
2434-2435 A601 Set of 2   1.50 .30

Asian
Animals
A602

200d, Ailuropoda melanoleuca. 800d,
Panthera tigris. 1000d, Elephas maximus.
3000d, Rhinoceros unicornis. 4000d, Hylobates leucogenys. #2441, 10,000d, Neofelis
nebulosa. #2442, 10,000d, Bos sauveli.

1993, Mar. 10
2436-2441 A602 Set of 6   6.50 2.00
Souvenir Sheet
Perf. 13½
2442 A602 10,000d multicolored   4.00 1.25

1994 World Cup Soccer
Championships, U.S. — A603

Various soccer players in action.

1993, Mar. 30   *Perf. 13*
2443-2445 A603 200d, 1500d,
7000d, set of
3   3.00 .65

Transportation — A604

Designs: 200d, Wheelbarrow. 800d, Buffalo
cart. 1000d, Rickshaw, top up. 2000d, Rickshaw with passenger. 5000d, Rickshaw, top
down. 10,000d, Horse-drawn carriage.

1993, Apr. 6
2446-2451 A604 Set of 6   5.00 2.00

500Kv Electricity
Lines — A605

1993, May 1
2452-2453 300d, 400d, set of 2   1.75 .30

Polska
'93 — A606

Paintings: 200d, Sunflowers, by Van Gogh.
No. 2455, 1000d, Young Woman, by Mogid-
liani. No. 2456, 1000d, Couple in Forest, by
Rousseau. 5000d, Harlequin with Family, by
Picasso. No. 2458, 10,000d, Female Model,
by Matisse, horiz. No. 2459, 10,000d, Portrait
of Dr. Gachet, by Van Gogh.

1993, May 7
2454-2458 A606 Set of 5   *Perf. 13*
                                   5.00 1.25
Souvenir Sheet
Perf. 12½
2459 A606 10,000d multicolored   5.00 1.25
No. 2459 contains one 32x43mm stamp.

Da Lat,
Cent.
A607

Orchids: 400d, Paphiopedilum hirsutissimum. No. 2461, 1000d, Paphiopedilum mali-
poense. No. 2462, 1000d, Paphiopedilum gratrixianum. 12,000d,   Paphiopedilum
hennisianum.

1993, June 15   *Perf. 13*
2460-2463 A607 Set of 4   5.00 1.50

Asian Architecture — A608

Landmark buildings from: 400d, Thailand,
vert. 800d, Indonesia, vert. 1000d, Singapore,
vert. No. 2467, 2000d, Malaysia. No. 2468,
2000d, Cambodia. 6000d, Laos. 8000d,
Brunei.
10,000d, Thai Binh, Viet Nam, vert.

1993, July 10   *Litho.*
2464-2470 A608 Set of 7   4.75 1.50
Souvenir Sheet
Perf. 14x13½
2471 A608 10,000d multicolored   4.00 1.50

7th Trade Union Congress — A608a

Designs: 400d, Industry, communications.
5000d, Hand holding hammer, doves, flowers.

1993, July 28   *Litho.* *Perf. 13*
2471A-2471B A608a Set of 2   4.50 .40

Crabs
A609

Designs: 400d, Scylla serrata. 800d, Portunus sanguinotentus. 1000d, Charybdis
bimaculata. 2000d, Paralithodes brevipes.
5000d, Portunus pelagicus. 10,000d, Lithodes
turritus.

1993, July 30
2472-2477 A609 Set of 6   6.50 1.50

Stamp
Day
A610

5000d, Hand holding stamped envelope.

1993, Aug. 15
2478-2479 A610 Set of 2   2.25 .40

Miniature Sheet

Tennis — A611

Women tennis players: a, 400d. c, 1000d.
Male tennis players: b, 1000d. d, 12,000d.

1993, Sept. 20
2480 A611 #a.-d. + 2 labels   5.50 3.50

A613

Costumes: 400d, Lo Lo. 800d, Thai. 1000d,
Dao Do. 2000d, H'mong. 5000d, Kho Mu. No.
2488, 10,000d, Kinh.
No. 2489, 10,000d, Precious gem stones.

1993, Oct. 1   *Perf. 13*
2483-2488 A613 Set of 6   4.00 1.75
Souvenir Sheet
Perf. 13½
2489 A613 10,000d multicolored   5.25 1.25
Bangkok '93. Issued: Nos. 2483-2488,
10/1/93. No. 2489, 10/10/93.
No. 2489 contains one 43x32mm stamp.

New Year 1994 (Year of the Dog): Various
dogs.

1994, Jan. 1
2490-2491 A614 400d, 6000d,
set of 2   2.50 .45
Imperf., #2490-2491   4.00

Flowers
A615

#2492, 400d, Prunus persica. #2493, 400d,
Chrysanthemum morifolium. #2494, 400d,
Rosa chinensis. 15,000d, Delonix regia.

1994
2492-2495 A615 Set of 4   5.50 1.60
Issued: #2492, 1/4; 15,000d, 4/30; #2493,
7/30; #2494, 10/10.

Chess
A616

Designs: 400d, Anatoly Karpov. 1000d,
Gary Kasparov. 2000d, Bobby Fischer. 4000d,
Emanuel Lasker. No. 2500, 10,000d, Jose
Capablanca.
No. 2501, 10,000d, King.

1994, Jan. 20
2496-2500 A616 Set of 5   4.50 1.50
Imperf., #2496-2500   8.00
Souvenir Sheet
2501 A616 10,000d multicolored   3.25 1.25
Imperf.   5.25

Hong Kong
'94 — A617

Festivals: 400d, Hoi Lim. 800d, Cham.
1000d, Tay Nguyen. 12,000d, Nam Bo.

1994, Feb. 18
2502-2505 A617 Set of 4   3.75 1.25
Imperf., #2502-2505   6.75

A618

Various opera masks: 400d, 500d, 2000d,
3000d, 4000d, 7000d.

1994, Mar. 15
2506-2511 A618 Set of 6   4.25 1.50
Imperf., #2506-2511   8.50

A619

Various gladiolus hybridus: 400d, 2000d,
5000d, 8000d.

1994, Mar. 30
2512-2515 A619 Set of 4   3.75 1.25
Imperf., #2512-2515   6.75

Japanese Paintings — A620

Paintings by: 400d, Utamaro. 500d, Haru-nobu. 1000d, Hokusai. 2000d, Hiroshige. 3000d, Hokusai, diff. 4000d, Utamaro, diff. 8000d, Choki.

1994, Apr. 9
2516-2522 A620 Set of 7   6.50 1.75
   Imperf., #2516-2522   11.00

Insects — A621

Designs: 400d, Cicindela aurulenta. 1000d, Harmonia octomaculata. 6000d, Cicindela ten-nipes. 7000d, Collyris.

1994, June 15
2523-2526 A621 Set of 4   4.00 1.25
   Imperf., #2523-2526   6.75

Victory at Dien Bien Phu, 40th Anniv. A622

Designs: 400d, Soldiers dragging equipment. 3000d, Celebration.

1994, May 7
2527-2528 A622 Set of 2   1.00 .45
   Imperf., #2527-2528   1.40

Newspaper "Young Pioneers," 40th Anniv. A623

1994, May 15   *Perf. 13x13½*
2529 A623 400d red & black   .50 .25

Crocodiles — A625

Designs: 400d, Crocodylus porosus. 600d, Alligator mississippiensis. 2000d, Crocodylus niloticus. 3000d, Alligator sinensis. 4000d, Caiman yacare. 9000d, Crocodylus johnsoni. 10,000d, Caiman crocodilus.

1994, June 1   *Perf. 13x13½*
2532-2537 A625 Set of 6   5.00 1.75
   Imperf., #2532-2537   7.50
   Souvenir Sheet
         Perf. 13½
2538 A625 10,000d multicolored   3.50 1.25
   Imperf.   6.00

No. 2538 contains one 43x32mm stamp.

1994 World Cup Soccer Championships, US — A626

Various soccer players in action: 400d, 600d, 1000d, 2000d, 3000d, 11,000d.

1994, Apr. 20   *Perf. 13*
2539-2544 A626 Set of 6   4.75 1.10
   Imperf., #2539-2544   8.00
   Souvenir Sheet
         Perf. 13½
2545 A626 10,000d multicolored   3.00 1.10
   Imperf.   4.75

No. 2545 contains one 32x43mm stamp.

Yersin's Discovery of Plague Bacillus, Cent. A627

1994, June 15   *Perf. 13x13½*
2546 A627 400d multicolored   .75 .25

UPU, 120th Anniv. A629

Designs: 400d, UPU emblem, "120." 5000d, World map. 10,000d, UPU emblem, "P," vert.

1994, Aug. 10   *Perf. 13*
2551-2552 A629 Set of 2   1.50 .45
   Souvenir Sheet
         Perf. 14x13½
2553 A629 10,000d multicolored   4.25 1.25

PHILAKOREA '94 — A630

Birds: 400d, Numenius arquata. 600d, Oceanites oceanicus. 1000d, Fregata minor. 2000d, Morus capensis. 3000d, Lunda cirrhata. 11,000d, Larus belcheri. 10,000d, Collocalia fuciphaga.

1994, Aug. 16   *Perf. 13x13½*
2554-2559 A630 Set of 6   5.00 1.50
   Souvenir Sheet
         Perf. 13½
2560 A630 10,000d multicolored   4.00 1.25

No. 2560 contains one 43x32mm stamp.

A631

Bamboo: 400d, Bambusa blumeana. 1000d, Phyllostachys aurea. 2000d, Bambusa vulgaris. 4000d, Tetragonocalamus quadrangularis. 10,000d, Bambusa venticosa.

1994, Aug. 17   *Perf. 13½x13*
2561-2565 A631 Set of 5   5.00 1.50

   Singpex '94.

A632

Various bridges: 400d, 900d, 8000d.

1994, Sept. 20   *Perf. 13x13½*
2566-2568 A632 Set of 3   2.75 .90

Children's Future A634

Designs: 400d+100d, Boy helping girl in wheelchair with kite. 2000d, Children dancing, vert.

1994, Oct. 10   *Litho.*   *Perf. 13*
2572-2573 A634 Set of 2   1.00 .40

A636

People's Army, 50th Anniv.: 400d, People in formation. 1000d, Soldiers, battle map. 2000d, Ho Chi Minh, child. 4000d, Anti-aircraft battery.

1994, Dec. 22
2576-2579 A636 Set of 4   2.25 .75

A637

Intl. Olympic Committee, Cent.: 400d, Flags. 6000d, Pierre de Coubertin.

1994, June 25   *Perf. 13*
2580-2581 A637 Set of 2   2.75 .90

ICAO, 50th Anniv. A638

Jets: 400d, In flight. 3000d, On ground.

1994, Dec. 7
2582-2583 A638 Set of 2   1.25 .40

Trams A639

Designs: 400d, With overhead conductor. 900d, Paris tram. 8000d, Philadelphia mail.

1994, Oct. 10 *Litho.*   *Perf. 13x13½*
2584-2586 A639 Set of 3   2.25 .75

Liberation of Hanoi, 40th Anniv. A640

Designs: 400d, Greeting soldiers. 2000d, Workers, students, modern technology.

1994, Oct. 10
2587-2588 A640 Set of 2   1.00 .40

New Year 1995 (Year of the Boar) A641

Stylized boars: 400d, Adult, five young. 8000d, One eating.

1995, Jan. 2 *Litho.*   *Perf. 13*
2589-2590 A641 Set of 2   2.50 .65

A642

Birds: No. 2591, 400d, Pluvialis apricaria, horiz. No. 2592, 400d, Philetairus socius, horiz. No. 2593, 400d, Oxyruncus cristatus, horiz. No. 2594, 400d, Pandion haliaetus. No. 2595, 5000d, Cariama cristata.

1995, Jan. 20 *Perf. 13x13½, 13½x13*
2591-2595 A642 Set of 5   2.00 .75

A number has been reserved for a souvenir sheet with this set.

A643

Traditional women's attire: 400d, Young women, bicycle. 3000d, Bride. 5000d, Girl in formal dress holding hat.

1995, Feb. 1   *Perf. 13*
2597-2599 A643 Set of 3   2.50 .75

Vietstampex '95 — A644

1995, Feb. 18
2600 A644 5500d multicolored   2.00 .50

Owls — A645

Designs: 400d, Ketupa zeylonensis. 1000d, Strix aluco. 2000d, Strix nebulosa. 5000d, Strix seloputo. 10,000d, Otus leucotis. 12,500d, Tyto alba.

1995, Mar. 1　　**Perf. 13½x13**
2601-2605　A645　Set of 5　　5.00　1.50
Souvenir Sheet
Perf. 14x13½
2606　A645　12,500d multicolored　5.50　1.10
Imperf.　　　6.75

Fish
A646

Designs: 400d, Pomacanthus arcuatus. 1000d, Rhinecanthus rectangulus. 2000d, Pygoplites diacanthus. 4000d, Pomacanthus ciliaris. 5000d, Balistes vetula. 9000d, Balistes conspicillum.

1995, Mar. 20　　**Perf. 13**
2607-2612　A646　Set of 6　　4.00　1.50

Lenin, 125th Birth Anniv. — A647

1995, Apr. 22　**Litho.**　**Perf. 13**
2613　A647　400d red & black　　.50　.25

End of World War II, 50th Anniv. A648

1995, May 2　**Litho.**　**Perf. 13**
2614　A648　400d multicolored　　1.00　.25

A649

1996 Summer Olympics, Atlanta: 400d, Hammer throw. 3000d, Cycling. 4000d, Running. 10,000d, Pole vault. 12,500d, Basketball.

1995, Apr. 5　**Litho.**　**Perf. 13**
2615-2618　A649　Set of 4　　4.00　1.40
Souvenir Sheet
2619　A649　12,500d multicolored　3.50　1.10

A650

Various balloons: 500d, 1000d, 2000d, 3000d, 4000d, 5000d, 7000d.

1995, May 5
2620-2626　A650　Set of 7　　6.50　1.50
Finlandia '95, Intl. Philatelic Exhibition, Helsinki.

Miniature Sheets

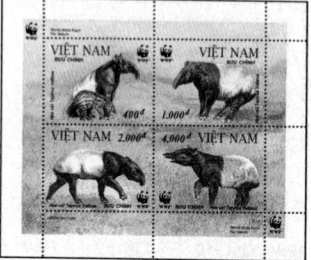

Tapirus Indicus — A651

No. 2627a, 400d, With young. b, 1000d, Facing left. c, 2000d, Walking right. d, 4000d, Mouth open, left.
No. 2528a, 4000d, Facing right. b, 4000d, Eating leaves. c, 5000d, In water. d, 6000d, Head protruding out of water.

1995, Apr. 25
2627　A651　Sheet of 4, #a.-d.　4.25　3.00
2628　A651　Sheet of 4, #a.-d.　6.00　3.50
World Wildlife Fund (#2627).

Miniature Sheet

Parachutes — A652

No. 2629: a, 400d, One parachutist descending from sky. b, 2000d, Two descending. c, 3000d, One about to touch ground. d, 9000d, Three men on ground with open parachute.

1995, May 24
2629　A652　Sheet of 4, #a.-d.　4.00　2.00

Rhododendrons — A653

Designs: 400d, Fleuryi. 1000d, Sulphoreum. 2000d, Sinofalconeri. 3000d, Lyi. 5000d, Ovatum. 9000d, Tanastylum.

1995, June 30
2630-2635　A653　Set of 6　　4.50　1.50

Miniature Sheet

Native Folktale — A654

a, 400d, Brothers and their parents. b, 1000d, Mother saying farewell to her departing sons. c, 3000d, One brother is transformed into a statue. d, 10,000d, Both brothers transformed into statues.

1995, July 20　**Litho.**　**Perf. 13**
2636　A654　Sheet of 4, #a.-d.　4.25　2.75

A655

400d, Statue of a woman holding child. 3000d, Three women of different races, emblem, horiz.

1995, Aug. 5
2637-2638　A655　Set of 2　　1.00　.40
Women's Federation of Viet Nam: 65th anniv. (#2637), 1995 Intl. Women's Conf., Beijing (#2638).

A656

1995, July 26
2639　A656　400d multicolored　　.35　.25
Admission to Assoc. of Southeast Asian Nations (ASEAN).

Natl. Day — A657

#2640, 400d, Ho Chi Minh, people waving flags, dove of peace. #2641, 400d, Ho Chi Minh holding child. #2642, 1000d, Communist symbol, bridge, electrical wire, Ho Chi Minh Mausoleum. #2643, 1000d, Ho Chi Minh, silhouettes of soldiers, building with flags flying. #2644, 2000d, Soldiers, natl. flag. #2645, 2000d, Antenna, satellite dish, van, olive branch, people on motorcycles.

1995, Aug. 14
2640-2645　A657　Set of 6　　3.00　.90
Viet Nam Labor Party, 65th anniv. (No. 2640). Ho Chi Minh, 105th birth anniv. (No. 2641). Evacuation of French troops from North Viet Nam, 40th anniv. (No. 2642). End of war in Viet Nam, 20th anniv. (No 2643). Natl.

army, 50th anniv. (No. 2644). Post and Telecommunications Service, 50th anniv. (No. 2645).

Sir Rowland Hill (1795-1879) A658

Design: 4000d, Hill, "penny black."

1995, Aug. 15
2646　A658　4000d multicolored　1.25　.25

Natl. Sports Games — A659

1995, Aug. 30
2647　A659　400d multicolored　　.50　.25

Singapore '95 — A660

Orchids: 400d, Paphiopedilum druryi. 2000d, Dendrobium orcraceum. 3000d, Vanda. 4000d, Cattelya. 5000d, Paphiopedilum hirsutissimum. 6000d, Christenosia vietnamica haeger.
12,500d, Angraecum sesquipedale.

1995, Sept. 1
2648-2653　A660　Set of 6　　6.50　1.40
Souvenir Sheet
2654　A660　12,500d multicolored　5.50　1.25
No. 2654 contains one 32x43mm stamp.

Asian Sites — A661

Designs: 400d, Buildings, monuments, tombs, Hue, Viet Nam. 3000d, Zigzag bridge, West Lake, Hangzhou, China. 4000d, Temple, Macao. 5000d, Peak tram, Hong Kong. 6000d, Pagoda, Peace Memorial Park, Taipei, Taiwan.

1995, Sept. 6
2655-2659　A661　Set of 5　　4.75　1.25

UN, 50th Anniv. A662

1995, Oct. 10
2660　A662　2000d multicolored　　.75　.25

Total Solar Eclipse, Oct. 10, 1995
A663

1995, Dec. 23   Litho.   Perf. 13
2661 A663 400d multicolored   1.00 .30

Paintings of Women
A664

Designs: 400d, Woman in white dress, flowers, by To Ngoc Van (1906-54) (4-1). 2000d, Washing hair, by Tran Van Can (1906-94) (4-2). 6000d, Standing beside vase of flowers, by To Ngoc Van (4-3). 8000d, Two women, by Tran Van Can (4-4).

1995, Nov. 15   Litho.   Perf. 13
2662-2665 A664 Set of 4   3.50 3.00

New Year 1996 (Year of the Rat) — A665

Stylized rats: 400d, One carrying fan, one riding horse. 8000d, Four carrying one in palanquin.
13,000d, Marching in parade, carrying banner.

1996, Jan. 2   Litho.   Perf. 13
2666 A665 400d multicolored   .35 .25
2667 A665 8000d multicolored   1.00 1.25

Souvenir Sheet
2668 A665 13,000d multi, vert.   2.50 1.50
No. 2668 contains one 32x43mm stamp.

Dinosaurs — A666

Designs: 400d, Tsintaosaurus. 1000d, Archaeopteryx. 2000d, Psittacosaurus. 3000d, Hypsilophodon. 13,000d, Parasaurolophus.

1996, Mar. 6
2669-2673 A666 Set of 5   4.25 3.00

Kingfishers
A667

Designs: 400d, Halcyon smyrnensis. 1000d, Megaceryle alcyon. 2000d, Alcedo Atthis. 4000d, Halcyon coromanda. 12,000d, Ceryle rudis.

1996, Mar. 11
2674-2678 A667 Set of 5   4.50 3.00

Flowers
A668

Various flowers: No. 2679, 400d, brown (5-1). No. 2680, 400d, claret (5-2). No. 2681, 400d, green (5-3). No. 2682, 400d, blue (5-4). No. 2683, 5000d, red (5-5), vert.

Perf. 13x13½, 13½x13
1996, Jan. 10   Litho.
2679-2683 A668 Set of 5   1.50 1.10

8th Vietnamese Communist Party Congress — A669

Designs: 400d, Ho Chi Minh (2-1). 3000d, Stylized dove, satellite dish, electrical towers, hammer & sickle, building, olive branch (2-2).

1996, Feb. 3   Perf. 13
2684-2685 A669 Set of 2   .75 .60

Asian Sites — A670

Monuments and statues in: 400d, Hanoi. 2000d, Thailand. 3000d, Bhubanesvar, India. 4000d, Kyoto, Japan. 10,000d, Borobudur, Java.

1996, Apr. 10   Litho.   Perf. 13
2686-2690 A670 Set of 5   4.00 3.00
See Nos. 2773-2777.

Statues — A671

Various statues of men in traditional costumes of early warriors: 400d, 600d, 1000d, 2000d, 3000d, 5000d, 6000d, 8000d.

1996, Feb. 10   Litho.   Perf. 13½x13
2691-2698 A671 Set of 8   5.00 4.00

Central Committee, 50th Anniv. — A672

1996, May 22   Perf. 13
2699 A672 400d multicolored   .30 .25

UNICEF, 50th Anniv.
A673

Designs: 400d, Children of different races, cultures. 7000d, Plant, emblem, water droplets containing representations of education, drinking water, medicine, food.

1996, May 15
2700-2701 A673 Set of 2   2.00 1.50

Red Cross of Viet Nam, 50th Anniv.
A674

1996, May 8   Perf. 13½
2702 A674 3000d Quotation, Ho Chi Minh   .75 .50

A675

Traditional Musical Instruments: a, 400d, Mandolin. b, 3000d, Bow and string instrument. c, 4000d, Square-shaped guitar-like instrument. d, 9000d, Zither.

1996, Apr. 24   Perf. 13½x13
2703 A675 Sheet of 4, #a.-d.   3.50 1.75
China '96 Intl. Philatelic Exhibition.

A676

Insects: 400d, Cincindela japonica. 500d, Calodema wallacei. 1000d, Mylabris oculata. 4000d, Chrysochroa buqueti. 5000d, Ophioniea nigrofasciata. 12,000d, Carabus tauricus.

1996, May 20   Perf. 13
2704-2709 A676 Set of 6   5.00 3.50

1996 Summer Olympic Games, Atlanta
A677

Designs: 2000d, Soccer. 4000d, Sailing. 5000d, Field hockey.

1996, July 8
2710-2712 A677 Set of 3   2.75 1.50

Euro '96, European Soccer Championships, Great Britain — A678

Designs: a, 400d, Net, goalie. b, 8000d, Player making shot on goal.

1996, June 1
2713 A678 Pair, #a.-b.   2.00 1.00
No. 2713 is a continuous design.

Aircraft
A679

400d, Airbus A320. 1000d, AN-72. 2000d, MD-11F. 6000d, RJ-85. 10,000d, B747-400F. 13,000d, Space shuttle carried by Boeing 747.

1996, June 1
2714-2718 A679 Set of 5   4.50 3.00

Souvenir Sheet
Perf. 13½
2719 A679 13,000d multicolored   2.75 2.00

Stamp Day
A680

1996, Aug. 15   Perf. 13
2720 A680 400d No. 1L57 (1-1)   .30 .25

Paintings by Nguyen Sáng (1923-88)
A681

400d, Woman, vase of flowers (2-1). 8000d, Soldiers returning from battle (2-2).

1996, Sept. 10   Perf. 13
2721-2722 A681 Set of 2   1.75 1.00

Hue School, Cent. — A682

400d, Women walking beside entrance (2-1). 3000d, View of portals, building (2-2).

1996, Sept. 5
2723-2724 A682 Set of 2   .75 .45

Mushrooms
A683

Designs: 400d, Aleuria aurantia. 500d, Morchella conica. 1000d, Anthurus archeri. 4000d, Laetiporus serlphureus. 5000d, Filoboletus manipularis. 12,000d, Tremiscus helvelloides.

1996, Aug. 26   Litho.   Perf. 13
2725-2730 A683 Set of 6   5.00 4.00

Wild Animals — A684

Designs: a, 400d, Pygathrix nemacus. b, 2000d, Panthera tigris. c, 4000d, Rhinoceros sondaicus. d, 10,000d, Balearica regulorum.

1996, Oct. 10   Litho.   Perf. 13
2731 A684 Sheet of 4, #a.-d.   3.50 4.00
          Taipei '96.

Campaign Promoting Iodized Salt — A685

1996, Nov. 2   Litho.   Perf. 13
2732 A685 400d multicolored   .55 .30

Natl. Liberation Movement, 50th Anniv. — A686

1996, Dec. 19
2733 A686 400d multicolored   .40 .30

Fruit — A687

Designs: No. 2734, Hylocereus undatus. No. 2735, Durio zibethinus. No. 2736, Persea americana. No. 2737, Garcinia mangostana. No. 2738, Nephelium lappaceum.

1997, Jan. 2   Perf. 13x13½
2734-2738 A687 400d Set of 5   1.50 1.00

New Year 1997 (Year of the Ox) — A688

Stylized oxen: 400d, Adult, calf. 8000d, Adult.

1997, Jan. 8   Litho.   Perf. 13
2739-2740 A688 Set of 2   2.00 1.50

8th Vietnamese Communist Party Congress — A689

1997, Feb. 3
2741 A689 400d multicolored   .50 .30

Goldfish
A690

Various carassius auratus: 400d, 1000d, 5000d, 7000d, 8000d.

1997, Feb. 5
2742-2746 A690 Set of 5   4.00 3.00
Souvenir Sheet
Perf. 13½x14
2747 A690 14,000d multicolored   3.00 1.50
No. 2747 contains one 43x32mm stamp. Hong Kong '97 (#2747).

Sculptures from Ly Dynasty — A691

Designs: 400d, Serpents in round figure, vert. 1000d, Dragon head, vert. 3000d, People playing instruments. 5000d, Gargoyle. 10,000d, Dragon-head bowl.

1997, Mar. 5
2748-2752 A691 Set of 5   4.00 2.50

Scenes — A692

Designs: 400d, Lake, people in park, Hà Tay. 5000d, Footbridge over river, Lai Chau. 7000d, Houses, fog, trees, Lào Cai.

1997, Mar. 20
2753-2755 A692 Set of 3   3.00 2.00

Huynh Thuc Khang (1876-1947)
A693

1997, Apr. 21   Litho.   Perf. 13½x13
2756 A693 400d multi   .35 .30

Disabled People in Sports — A694

1000d, Tennis. 6000d, Shooting.

1997, Apr. 27   Perf. 13
2757-2758 A694 Set of 2   1.60 1.20

Wild Animals
A695

400d, Chrotogale owstoni. 3000d, Lutra lutra. 4000d, Callosciurus erythraeus. 10,000d, Felis bangalensis.

1997, May 2
2759-2762 A695 Set of 4   3.75 2.75

A696

1997, May 19
2763 A696 400d Women's Union   .50 .30

A697

Lilium longiflorum (Lilies): 400d, Red. 1000d, White. 5000d, Pink & white. 10,000d, Orange.

1997, Apr. 15   Litho.   Perf. 13
2764-2767 A697 Set of 4   3.50 2.50

PACIFIC 97 — A698

Suspension bridges: 400d, Golden Gate, San Francisco. 5000d, Raippaluoto. 10,000d, Seto.

1997, May 12
2768-2770 A698 Set of 3   3.25 2.50

Children
A699

400d, UN Convention on the Rights of the Child. 5000d, Breast milk is better.

1997, June 1   Litho.   Perf. 13
With Gum
2771-2772 A699 Set of 2   1.25 1.00

Asian Sites Type of 1996

Designs: 400d, Pagoda, Hanoi, Viet Nam. 1000d, Ruins of Persepolis, Iran. 3000d, Statue of woman, Iraq. 5000d, Sacred Rock, Kyaikto, Burma. 10,000d, Statue of Buddha lying down, Sr. Lanka.

1997, June 20   Litho.   Perf. 13
2773-2777 A670 Set of 5   4.25 3.00

Women's Costumes
A700

Various costumes: 400d, Woman holding umbrella, San Chay. 2000d, Woman sewing, wearing jacket tied with sash, Dao quain trang. 5000d, Woman pumping water from well provided by UNICEF, Phù Lá. 10,000d, Woman holding hands in air, Kho Me.

1997, July 8
2778-2781 A700 Set of 4   3.75 2.50

A701

1997, July 11
2782 A701 400d multicolored   1.50 .40
          Prevention of AIDS.

A702

1997, Aug. 8   Litho.   *Perf. 13*
2783 A702 400d multicolored   .35   .25
ASEAN, 30th anniv.

Monument to War Martyrs & Invalids,
50th Anniv. — A703

1997, July 25
2784 A703 400d multicolored   .35   .35

Hibiscus — A704

a, 1000d, Hibiscus rosa sinensis. b, 3000d,
Hibiscus schizopetalus. c, 5000d, Hibiscus
syriacus (pink). d, 9000d, Hibiscus syriacus
(yellow).

1997, Aug. 1
2785 A704 Sheet of 4, #a.-d.   3.50 2.50

A705

1997, Aug. 26   Litho.   *Perf. 13*
2786 A705 400d multicolored   .40   .30
Post and Telecommunications Union, 50th
anniv.

A706

Sea horses: 400d, 1000d, Hippocampus
(diff.). 3000d, Hippocampus guttulatus. 5000d,
Hippocampus kelloggi. 6000d, Hippocampus
japonicus. 7000d, Hippocampus
hippocampus.

1997, Sept. 4
2787-2792 A706 Set of 6   4.50 4.00

19th Southeast
Asian
Games — A707

1997, Oct. 11   Litho.   *Perf. 13*
2793 A707 5000d multicolored   1.10   .90

Handicrafts
A708

Designs: No. 2794, 400d, Lamp. No. 2795,
400d, Two baskets. No. 2796, 400d, Swan-
shaped basket. No. 2797, 400d, Deer-shaped
basket. 2000d, Basket with handle.

1998, Jan. 1   Litho.   *Perf. 13*
2794-2798 A708 Set of 5   1.10   .80

7th Francophone Summit,
Hanoi — A709

1997, Sept. 24   Litho.   *Perf. 13½x13*
2799 A709 5000d multicolored   2.75 2.00

Birds
A710

400d, Syrmaticus ellioti. 3000d, Lophura
diardi. 5000d, Phasianus cholchicus. 6000d,
Chrysolophus amherstiae. 8000d, Polyplectron germaini.
14,000d, Lophura imperialis.

1997, Oct. 15   *Perf. 13*
2800-2804 A710 Set of 5   4.75 4.00
Souvenir Sheet
Perf. 13½
2805 A710 14,000d multicolored   2.75 2.50
No. 2805 contains one 43x30mm stamp.

New Year
1998 (Year of
the Tiger)
A711

Stylized tigers: 400d, Adult with young.
8000d, Adult.

1998, Jan. 5   *Perf. 13*
2806-2807 A711 Set of 2   2.00 1.50

Sites in
Vietnam
A712

Designs: No. 2808, 400d, Rocks, lake, Ninh
Thuan. No. 2809, 400d, Lake, cavern, Quang
Binh. 10,000d, Village of Quang Nam.

1998, Feb. 2
2808-2810 A712 Set of 3   2.10 1.50

Communist
Manifesto, 150th
Anniv. — A713

1998, Feb. 3
2811 A713 400d multicolored   .40   .30

Bonsai
A714

#2812, 400d, Limonia acidissima. #2813,
400d, Deeringia polysperma. #2814, 400d,
Pinus merkusii, vert. 4000d, Barringtonia
acutangula, vert. 6000d, Ficus elastica, vert.
10,000d, Wrightia religiosa, vert.
No. 2818, Adenium obesum.

1998, Mar. 2
2812-2817 A714 Set of 6   4.25 3.00
Souvenir Sheet
Perf. 13½
2818 A714 14,000d multicolored   2.50 2.00
No. 2818 contains one 43x32mm stamp.

Tet Offensive,
30th
Anniv. — A715

1998, Jan. 30   Litho.   *Perf. 13*
2819 A715 400d multicolored   .40   .30

Opera — A716

Designs: a, 400d, Thi kính bi oan. b, 1000d,
Thi mầu lên chùa. c, 2000d, Thi mầu-gia nô. d,
4000d, Thi me dộp-Xa trưởng. e, 6000d, Thi
kính bi phạt va. f, 9000d, Thi kính xin sua.

1998, Apr. 20
2820 A716   Sheet of 6, #a.-f   4.50 3.50

Raptors
A717

Designs: No. 2821, 400d, Pernis apivorus.
No. 2822, 400d, Spizaetus ornatus. No. 2823,
400d, Accipiter gentilis. 3000d, Buteo buteo.
5000d, Circus melanoleucas. 12,000d,
Haliaeetus albicilla.

1998, May 4   Litho.   *Perf. 13*
2821-2826 A717 Set of 6   4.25 3.00

Ho Chi Minh
City (Saigon),
300th
Anniv. — A718

400d, Tank, natl. flag, Ho Chi Minh as young
man, building. 5000d, Monument to Ho Chi
Minh, symbols of industry, communications,
and transportation.
14,000d, Statue of Nguyen Huu Canh
(1650-1700), general.

1998, Apr. 30
2827-2828 A718 Set of 2   1.10   .90
Souvenir Sheet
Perf. 14x13½
2828A A718 14,000d multi   — —

Orchids
A719

Designs: 400d, Paphiopedilum appletoni-
anum. 6000d, Paphiopedilum helenae.

1998, May 18   Litho.   *Perf. 13½*
2829-2830 A719 Set of 2   2.00 1.00

Children's
Paintings
A720

UNICEF: 400d, Children, mother in front of
home. 5000d, Children on playground.

1998, June 1   *Perf. 13*
2831-2832 A720 Set of 2   1.25   .90

1998 World Cup Soccer
Championships, France — A721

Various soccer plays: 400d, 5000d, 7000d.

1998, June 10
2833-2835 A721 Set of 3   2.50 2.00

Sculptures of
the Tran
Dynasty
A722

Ornate designs: No. 2836, 400d, Serpent.
No. 2837, 400d, Two people. 1000d, Shown.
8000d, Person. 9000d, Face.

1998, June 15   Litho.   Perf. 13
2836-2840 A722   Set of 5   3.50 2.75

Martial
Arts
A723

1998, July 13
2841 A723 2000d multicolored   .70 .50

Intl. Year
of the
Ocean
A724

1998, Aug. 1   Litho.   Perf. 13
2842 A724 400d multicolored   1.00 .30

Stamp
Day — A725

1998, Aug. 15
2843 A725 400d Bell's telephone   .40 .30

Ton Duc Thang
(1888-1980)
A726

1998, Aug. 20
2844 A726 400d multicolored   .40 .30

Moths
A727

Designs: No. 2845, 400d, Antheraea helferi.
No. 2846, 400d, Attacus atlas. 4000d, Argema
mittrei, vert. 10,000d, Argema maenas, vert.

1998, Aug. 22
2845-2848 A727   Set of 4   3.25 2.50

Paintings by Te
Bach Thach (Qi
Baishi; 1863-
1957)
A728

Various paintings: 400d, Dragonfly & Lotus.
1000d, Chrysanthemum, Cock & Hens.
2000d, Shrimps, 1948. 4000d, Crabs. 6000d,
Lotus & Mandarin Ducks. 9000d, Shrimps,
1949.

1998, Sept. 16
2849-2854 A728   Set of 6   4.25 3.25

Legend
of the
Lake
A729

Designs: No. 2855, Turtle with sword leading boat. No. 2856, Lake.

1998, Oct. 10
2855-2856 A729 400d Set of 2   .70 .50

Le Thanh Tong (1442-1497) — A730

1998, Oct. 12
2857 A730 400d multicolored   .40 .30

Souvenir Sheet

Italia '98, Intl. Philatelic
Exhibition — A731

Milan Cathedral.

1998, Oct. 6   Perf. 13½
2858 A731 16,000d multicolored 3.25 2.00

8th Trade
Union
Congress
A732

1998, Oct. 15   Litho.   Perf. 13
2859 A732 400d multicolored   .40 .30

Quy Nhon City, 396th Anniv., Binh
Dinh Province, Cent. — A733

1998, Oct. 20
2860 A733 400d multicolored   .40 .30

Buoi-Chu Van An Secondary School,
90th Anniv. — A734

Designs: 400d, Students outside school.
5000d, Students listening to speaker.

1998, Nov. 20
2861-2862 A734 Set of 2   1.25 .90

6th ASEAN
Congress,
Hanoi — A735

1998, Dec.   Litho.   Perf. 13
2863 A735 1000d multicolored   .75 .40

Cuban Revolution, 40th Anniv. (in
1999) — A736

1998, Dec.   Litho.   Perf. 13
2864 A736 400d multicolored   .30 .30

A737

Paintings: 400d, Birds, tree, flowers
(Spring). 1000d, Flowers, ducks (Summer).
3000d, Flowers, rooster (Fall). 12,000d, Tree,
flowers, deer & fawn (Winter).

1999, Jan. 4   Litho.   Perf. 13½x13
2865-2868 A737   Set of 4   3.50 2.00

A738

New Year 1999 (Year of the Cat): 400d, Cat
holding tree branch. 8000d, Two cats.
13,000d, Kittens, ball.

1999, Jan. 6   Perf. 13½
2869-2870 A738   Set of 2   1.75 1.40

Souvenir Sheet
2871 A738 13,000d multicolored 2.50 2.00

No. 2871 contains one 32x43mm stamp.

Kites — A739

400d, Large bird with long tail. 5000d, Crescent-shaped. 7000d, Bird with long legs.

1999, Feb. 16   Litho.   Perf. 13½x13
2872-2874 A739   Set of 3   2.25 1.50

Australia
'99,
World
Stamp
Expo
A740

Various sailing vessels: #2875, 400d, (4-1).
#2876, 400d, (4-2). 7000d, (4-3). 9000d, (4-4).

1999, Mar. 10   Litho.   Perf. 13
2875-2878 A740   Set of 4   3.00 2.00

Medicinal
Plants
A741

Designs: No. 2879, 400d, Kaempferia
galanga. No. 2880, 400d, Tacca chantrieri,
vert. No. 2881, Alpinia galanga, vert. 6000d,

Typhonium trilobatum, vert. 13,000d, Asarum maximum, vert.

1999, Mar. 15
2879-2883 A741 Set of 5   3.75 2.25

Opera Masks
A742

Various masks: 400d (6-1). 1000d (6-2). 2000d (6-3). 5000d (6-4). 6000d (6-5). 10,000d (6-6).

1999, Apr. 16   **Perf. 13½**
2884-2889 A742 Set of 6   4.25 3.50

IBRA '99,
World
Philatelic
Exhibition,
Nuremberg
A743

Octopuses: No. 2890, 400d, Octopus gibertianus. No. 2891, 400d, Philonexis catenulata. 4000d, Paroctopus yendol. 12,000d, Octopus vulgaris.

1999, Apr. 20
2890-2893 A743 Set of 4   3.00 2.25

Landscape Paintings of Southern Viet Nam — A744

#2894, 400d, Sun over lake, Cà Mau. #2895, 400d, Rocks protruding out of water, Kien Giang. 12,000d, Traditional huts, Bac Lieu.

1999, May 4   **Perf. 13**
2894-2896 A744 Set of 3   2.25 1.50

Asia-Pacific Telecommunity, 20th
Anniv. — A745

1999, May 10   **Litho.**   **Perf. 13x13¼**
2897 A745 400d multi   2.00 1.50

Woodpeckers
A746

Designs: 400d, Chrysocolaptes lucidus. 1000d, Picumnus innominatus. 3000d, Picus rabieri. 13,000d, Blythipicus pyrrhotis.

1999, May 18   **Litho.**   **Perf. 13**
2898-2901 A746 Set of 4   4.00 2.50

UNICEF
A747

Designs: 400d, Girl, hand. 5000d, Boy carrying factory.

1999, June 1   **Litho.**   **Perf. 13**
2902-2903 A747 Set of 2   1.00 .50

Architecture of Late 19th and Early
20th Centuries — A748

Designs: No. 2904, 400d, Government Office Building, Hanoi (3-1). No. 2905, 400d, History Museum, Ho Chi Minh City (3-2). 12,000d, Duc Ba Cathedral (3-3). 15,000d, Theater, Hanoi.

1999, June 10   **Perf. 13**
2904-2906 A748 Set of 3   2.25 1.50
Souvenir Sheet
Perf. 13½x14
2907 A748 15,000d multi   2.75 2.00

PhilexFrance '99 (No. 2907). No. 2907 contains one 44x32mm stamp.

Intl.
Day to
Stop
Drug
Abuse
A749

1999, June 24   **Litho.**   **Perf. 13**
2908 A749 400d multicolored   .35 .25

Da
Rang
Bridge,
Phu
Yen
A750

1999, July 1   **Litho.**   **Perf. 13**
2909 A750 400d multi   .40 .30

Le Dynasty Sculptures — A751

Designs: No. 2910, 1000d, Man Against Tiger (5-1). No. 2911, 1000d, Phoenix (5-2). 3000d, Playing Chess, vert. (5-3). 7000d, Hostler, vert. (5-4). 9000d, Dragon (5-5).

1999, July 1
2910-2914 A751 Set of 5   3.75 5.00

Birth of World's
Six Billionth
Person — A752

1999, Aug. 2
2915 A752 400d multi   .50 .25

Chinese Landscapes — A753

Designs: 400d, Park, Beijing (4-1). 2000d, Scenic overlook, Anhwei (4-2). 3000d, Park, Shandong, (4-3). 10,000d, Park, Beijing, diff. (4-4).
14,000d, Great Wall of China.

1999, Aug. 16   **Perf. 13**
2916-2919 A753 Set of 4   3.50 2.50
Souvenir Sheet
Perf. 13½x14
2920 A753 14,000d multi   3.50 2.50

China 1999 World Philatelic Exhibition (No. 2920). No. 2920 contains one 43x32mm stamp.

Boat
Races
A754

Races from regions: 400d, North (3-1). 2000d, Central (3-2). 10,000d, South (3-3).

1999, Sept. 10   **Perf. 13**
2921-2923 A754 Set of 3   2.50 2.00

Women's
Costumes
A755

Various costumes. #2924, 400d (3-1). #2925, 400d (3-2). #2926, 12,000d (3-3).

1999, Sept. 10
2924-2926 A755 Set of 3   3.00 2.00

Buffalo
Fighting
Festivals
A756

Fighting buffaloes: 400d, (2-1). 5000d, (2-2).

1999, Sept. 15
2927-2928 A756 Set of 2   1.50 .75

Ngo Quyen (898-944),
General — A757

1999, Oct. 21
2929 A757 400d multi   .75 .30

Nguyen Van
Sieu (1799-
1872), Teacher,
Writer — A758

1999, Nov. 2   **Litho.**   **Perf. 13**
2930 A758 400d multi   .75 .30

Tran Xuan Soan (1849-1923), Anti-
colonial Leader — A759

1999, Nov. 24
2931 A759 400d multi   .75 .30

United Nations Development
Program — A760

Designs: 400d, Mother and child, farmer, fisherman. 8000d, Villagers, buildings.

1999, Dec. 3
2932-2933 A760 Set of 2   2.00 1.00

Viet Nam in the
20th
Century — A761

Designs; No. 2934, 400d, Founding of Viet Nam Communist Party (6-1). No. 2935, 400d, Ho Chi Minh's declaration of country's independence (6-2). No. 2936, 1000d, Conquest of South Viet Nam (6-3). No. 2937, 1000d, People, dam, high tension wire tower, atom (6-4). 8000d, People, satellite, satellite dish, dam, high tension wire tower (6-5). 12,000d, Organizations Viet Nam belongs to (6-6).

2000, Jan. 1   **Litho.**   **Perf. 13**
With Gum
2934-2939 A761 Set of 6   5.00 3.00
2939a   Sheet, #2934-2939, without gum   8.00 4.00

New Year 2000 (Year of the Dragon) A762

Dragon: 400d, Facing right (2-1). 8000d, Facing right (2-2).

2000, Jan. 3   With Gum   Perf. 13½
2940-2941 A762 Set of 2   2.50 1.50

Intl. Year of Culture and Peace A763

2000, Jan. 18   With Gum
2942 A763 400d multi   .50 .30

Viet Nam Communist Party, 70th Anniv. — A764

#2943, Ho Chi Minh (1890-1969), Pres. (8-1). #2944, Tran Phu (1904-31), 1st Gen. Sec. (8-2). #2945, Le Hong Phong (1902-42), Gen. Sec. (8-3). #2946, Ha Huy Tap (1902-41), Gen. Sec. (8-4). #2947, Nguyen Van Cu (1912-41), Gen. Sec. (8-5). #2948, Truong Chinh (1907-88), Gen. Sec. (8-6). #2949, Le Duan (1907-86), Gen. Sec. (8-7). #2950, Nguyen Van Linh (1915-98), Gen. Sec. (8-8).

2000, Feb. 2   With Gum   Perf. 13
2943-2950 A764 400d Set of 8   2.50 1.00

Cockfighting — A765

Postures: No. 2951, 400d, Song long cuoc (4-1). No. 2952, 400d, Long vu da dao (4-2). 7000d, Song long phuong hoang (4-3). 9000d, Nhan u giap chien (4-4).

2000, Feb. 8   Litho.   Perf. 13
2951-2954 A765 Set of 4   3.50 2.50
    Imperf., #2951-2954   5.75

Bangkok 2000 Stamp Exhibition A766

Palanquins: 400d, Imperial court roofed palanquin (3-1). 7000d, Palanquin without roof (3-2). 8000d, Roofed palanquin (3-3). 15,000d, Palanquin in procession.

2000, Mar. 10   With Gum
2955-2957 A766 Set of 3   3.50 2.50
    Souvenir Sheet
2958 A766 15,000d multi   3.50 2.50

Legend of Lac Long Quan and Au Co — A767

Designs: No. 2959, 400d, Lang Long Quan and Au Co marry (6-1). No. 2960, 400d, Au Co, gives birth to 100 sons (6-2). 500d, Au Co takes 50 children to forest (6-3). 3000d, Lac Long Quan takes 50 children to sea (6-4). 4000d, Eldest son, Hung Vuong ascends to throne (6-5). 11,000d, Vietnamese ethnic groups as descendents (6-6).

2000, Apr. 4   Perf. 13½
2959-2964 A767 Set of 6   4.50 3.50

Souvenir Sheet

The Stamp Show 2000, London — A768

No. 2965 — Fire engines: a, 400d, Iveco Magirus, Germany. b, 1000d, Hino, Japan. c, 5000d, ZIL 103E, Russia. d, 12,000d, FPS.32 Camiva, France.

2000, May 15   Perf. 13
2965 A768 Sheet of 4, #a-d   4.00 3.00

Worldwide Fund for Nature A769

Pseudoryx nghetinhensis: No. 2966, 400d, Head, vine (4-1). No. 2967, 400d, In grass (4-2). 5000d, Near pond (4-3). 10,000d, Head, mountains (4-4).

2000, May 18   With Gum   Perf. 13½
2966-2969 A769 Set of 4   4.50 2.50
2969a   Sheet, 2 each #2966-2969 9.75 5.00

Ho Chi Minh (1890-1969) A770

2000, May 19   With Gum   Perf. 13
2970 A770 400d multi   .50 .30

World Stamp Expo 2000, Anaheim A771

Water puppets: No. 2971, 400d, Chu teu (6-1). No. 2972, 400d, Fairy (6-2). No. 2973, 400d, Man plowing field (6-3). 3000d, Female peasant (6-4). 9000d, Drummer (6-5). 11,000d, Fisherman (6-6).

2000, June 28   Perf. 13½
2971-2976 A771 Set of 6   4.50 3.50

50th Vietnam Youth Volunteers' Day — A772

2000, July 15   With Gum   Perf. 13
2977 A772 400d multi   .50 .30

Phu Dong Natl. Youth Sports Festival A773

2000, July 20   With Gum
2978 A773 400d multi   .50 .30

Fish A774

Designs: No. 2979, 400d, Cephalopholis miniatus (6-1). No. 2980, 400d, Pomacanthus imperator (6-2). No. 2981, 400d, Epinephelus merra (6-3). 4000d, Zancius cornutus, vert. (6-4). 6000d, Chaetodon ephippium, vert. (6-5). 12,000d, Heniochus acuminatus, vert. (6-6). 15,000d, Chaetodon lunula.

2000, Aug. 7   Perf. 13
2979-2984 A774 Set of 6   4.00 3.00
    Souvenir Sheet
    Perf. 13½x13¾
2985 A774 15,000d multi   2.75 2.00

Post and Telegraph Dept., 55th Anniv. A775

2000, Aug. 15   With Gum   Perf. 13
2986 A775 400d multi   .50 .30

People's Police, 50th Anniv. A776

Designs: 400d, Ho Chi Minh, five policemen. 2000d, Policeman checking documents, vert.

2000, Aug. 19   Litho.   Perf. 13
                 With Gum
2987-2988 A776 Set of 2   1.00 .55

Gen. Nguyen Tri Phuong, 200th Anniv. of Birth — A777

2000, Aug. 31   With Gum   Perf. 13½
2989 A777 400d multi   .60 .30

UN Right of the Child Conference, 10th Anniv. — A778

Emblem and: 400d, Boy and girl. 5000d, Five children, vert.

2000, Sept. 8   Perf. 13
2990-2991 A778 Set of 2   1.50 1.00

2000 Summer Olympics, Sydney — A779

Designs: 400d, Running. 6000d, Shooting. 7000d, Taekwondo, vert.

2000, Sept. 15
2992-2994 A779 Set of 3   2.50 2.25

Gen. Tran Hung Dao, 700th Anniv. of Death. — A780

2000, Sept. 17   With Gum
2995 A780 400d multi   .60 .30

Birds — A781

Designs: No. 2996, 400d, Leiothrix argentauris. No. 2997, 400d, Pitta ellioti. No. 2998, 400d, Pomatorinus ferruginosus. 5000d, Dicrurus paradiceus, vert. 7000d, Melanochlora sultanea, vert. 10,000d, Stachyris striolata, vert.

2000, Sept. 28   Perf. 13½
2996-3001 A781 Set of 6   4.50 4.00
    Souvenir Sheet
    Perf. 13½x13¾
3002 A781 15,000d Trena puella 3.50 2.50

No. 3002 contains one 42x31mm stamp. España 2000 Intl. Philatelic Exhibition (No. 3002).

Vietnam Philately Association, 40th Anniv. — A782

2000, Oct. 6   With Gum   Perf. 13
3003 A782 400d No. 821   .60   .30

Farmer's Association, 70th Anniv. — A783

2000, Oct. 14   With Gum
3004 A783 400d multi   .60   .30

Women's Union, 70th Anniv. A784

2000, Oct. 14   With Gum
3005 A784 400d multi   .60   .30

Hanoi, 990th Anniv. A785

Designs: 400d, Building, and Ly Thai To, founder of Hanoi. 3000d, Temple, two people, monuments. 10,000d, Peasants with goods, building.
15,000d, People and doves.

2000, Oct. 15   Perf. 13
3006-3008 A785 Set of 3   2.50   2.25
Souvenir Sheet
Perf. 13½x13¾
3009 A785 15,000d multi   3.00   2.50

Bats — A786

Designs: No. 3010, 400d, Scotomanes ornatus. No. 3011, 400d, Pteropus lylei. 2000d, Rhinolophus paradoxolophus. 6000d, Eonycteris spelaea. 11,000d, Cynopterus sphinx.

2000, Oct. 14   Perf. 13
3010-3014 A786 Set of 5   3.50   3.00

Fatherland Front, 70th Anniv. — A787

2000, Oct. 18   With Gum
3015 A787 400d multi   .60   .30

6th Natl. Emulation Congress A788

Designs: 400d, People at work. 3000d, Symbols of industry, vert.

2000, Nov. 10   With Gum
3016-3017 A788 Set of 2   .90   .90

Flowers A789

Designs: 400d, Oxyspora sp. 5000d, Melanstoma villosa, vert.

With Gum
2000, Nov. 15   Perf. 13½
3018-3019 A789 Set of 2   1.50   1.00

Hon Khoai Uprising, 60th Anniv. A790

2000, Dec. 13   With Gum   Perf. 13
3020 A790 400d multi   .60   .30

Advent of New Millennium A791

2001, Jan. 1   With Gum
3021 A791 400d multi   .60   .30

New Year 2001 (Year of the Snake) A792

Snake and: 400d, Pink flowers. 8000d, Yellow flowers.

2001, Jan. 1   With Gum   Perf. 13½
3022-3023 A792 Set of 2   1.60   1.60

Hong Kong 2001 Stamp Exhibition — A793

Fish: 400d, Toxotes microlepis. 800d, Cosmocheilus harmandi. 2000d, Anguilla bicolor pacifica. 3000d, Chitala ornata. 7000d, Megalops cyprinoides. 8000d, Probarbus jullieni.

2001, Jan. 18   Litho.   Perf. 13
3024-3029 A793   Set of 6   4.00 3.00

Nobel Prize, Cent. A794

2001, Jan. 27   With Gum   Perf. 13½
3030 A794 400d multi   .60   .30

Four Seasons — A795

No. 3031: a, 400d, Peach blossoms and birds (spring). b, 800d, Cotton rose and pheasant (summer). c, 4000d, Chrysanthemum and phoenix (autumn). d, 10,000d, Pine tree and cranes (winter).

With Gum
2001, Feb. 1   Perf. 13¼x13
3031 A795   Sheet of 4, #a-d   4.00 2.25

Wild Fruits — A796

Designs: No. 3032, 400d, Rubus cochinchinensis. No. 3033, 400d, Rhizophora mucronata. No. 3034, 400d, Podocarpus neriifolius. No. 3035, 400d, Magnolia pumila. 15,000d, Taxus chinensis.

2001, Feb. 8   With Gum   Perf. 13½
3032-3036 A796   Set of 5   3.50 2.25

Landscapes — A797

Designs: No. 3037, 400d, Co Tien Mountain (3-1). No. 3038, 400d, Dong Pagoda, Yen Tu Mountain (3-2). 10,000d, King Dinh Temple (3-3).

2001, Feb. 23   Perf. 13
3037-3039 A797   Set of 3   3.00 1.50

Nhan Dan Newspaper, 50th Anniv. — A798

2001, Mar. 11   With Gum
3040 A798 400d multi   .60   .30

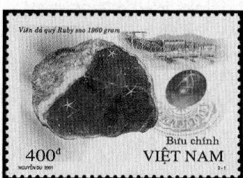

Rubies Found in Tan Huong A799

Designs: 400d, 1960-gram ruby. 6000d, 2160-gram "Viet Nam Star."

2001, Mar. 20   With Gum
3041-3042 A799   Set of 2   2.00 1.00

Ho Chi Minh Youth Union, 70th Anniv. — A800

2001, Mar. 26   Litho.   Perf. 13
With Gum
3043 A800 400d multi   .60   .30

9th Communist Party Congress — A801

Designs: 400d, Ho Chi Minh, flag, map (2-1). 3000d, Hammer and sickle, Ngoc Lu bronze drum head, symbols of technology, vert (2-2).

2001, Apr. 18   With Gum
3044-3045 A801   Set of 2   .75   .55

Fauna in Cat Tien Natl. Park — A802

Designs: 400d, Arborophila davidi (4-1). 800d, Stichophthalma uemurai (4-2). 3000d, Rhinoceros sondaicus (4-3). 5000d, Crocodylus siamensis (4-4).

2001, Apr. 3   Perf. 13½
3046-3049 A802   Set of 4   3.00 2.00

Mushrooms A803

Designs: No. 3050, 400d, Phallus indusiatus (7-1). No. 3051, 400d, Aseroe arachnoidea (7-2). No. 3052, 400d, Phallus tenuis (7-3). 2000d, Phallus impudicus (7-4). 5000d, Phallus rugulosus (7-5). 6000d, Simblum periphragmoides (7-6). 7000d, Mutinus bambusinus (7-7).

2001, May 2
3050-3056 A803 Set of 7 4.50 3.50

Mushrooms Type of 2001

Design: 13,000d, Pseudocolus schellenbergiae.

2001, May 2 Litho. Perf. 13½x13¾
3057 A803 13,000d multi 4.00 2.50

No. 3057 contains one 42x31mm stamp.

Ho Chi Minh Young Pioneer's League, 60th Anniv. — A804

2001, May 15 Litho. Perf. 13
With Gum
3058 A804 400d multi .60 .30

Viet Minh Front, 60th Anniv. A805

2001, May 19 With Gum
3059 A805 400d multi .60 .30

Campaign Against Smoking — A806

2001, May 30 Perf. 13¼x13½
With Gum
3060 A806 800d multi .75 .45

Children A807

Designs: 400d, Two children, UNICEF emblem. 5000d, Five children, UN emblem.

2001, June 1 Perf. 13½
3061-3062 A807 Set of 2 1.50 1.00

Children's safety day (#3061); UN Special Session on Children, Washington, DC (#3062).

Diesel Locomotives — A808

Designs: No. 3063, 400d, D18E (6-1). No. 3064, 400d, D4H (6-2). 800d, D11H (6-3).

2000d, D5H (6-4). 6000d, D9E (6-5). 7000d, D12E (6-6).

2001, June 5 Perf. 13
3063-3068 A808 Set of 6 4.50 3.00

Souvenir Sheet
Perf. 13½x13¾
3069 A808 13,000d D11H, diff. 3.50 2.25

No. 3069 contains one 43x32mm stamp.

Orchids A809

Designs: No. 3070, 800d, Vanda sp. (6-1). No. 3071, 800d, Dendrobium lowianum (6-2). No. 3072, 800d, Phajus wallichii (6-3). No. 3073, 800d, Habenaria medioflexa (6-4). No. 3074, 800d, Arundina graminifolia, vert. (6-5). 12,000d, Calanthe clavata, vert. (6-6).

Perf. 13½x13¼, 13¼x13½
2001, July 5 With Gum
3070-3075 A809 Set of 6 3.50 2.75

Phila Nippon '01 — A810

Butterflies: No. 3076, 800d, Troides aeacus (6-1). No. 3077, 800d, Inachis io (6-2). No. 3078, 800d, Ancyluris formosissima (6-3). 5000d, Cymothoe sanguris (6-4). 7000d, Taenaris selene (6-5). 10,000d, Trogonoptera brookiana (6-6).

13,000d, Atrophaneura horishanus, vert.

2001, July 16 Perf. 13½x13¼
3076-3081 A810 Set of 6 5.00 3.50

Souvenir Sheet
Perf. 13¾x13½
3082 A810 13,000d multi 4.00 2.25

No. 3082 contains one 32x42mm stamp.

2002 World Cup Soccer Championships, Japan and Korea — A811

No. 3083: a, 800d, Player with red shirt. b, 3000d, Player with white shirt.

2001, July 24 With Gum Perf. 13
3083 A811 Horiz. pair, #a-b 2.50 1.50

Musical Instruments — A812

Designs: No. 3084, 800d, Ho gáo (6-1). No. 3085, 800d, Kenh (6-2). No. 3086, 800d, Dàn tú, vert. (6-3). 2000d, Dàn t'rung, vert. (6-4). 6000d, Trong kinang, vert . (6-5). 9000d, Tính tau, vert. (6-6).

Perf. 13x13¼, 13¼x13
2001, Aug. 4 Litho.
3084-3089 A812 Set of 6 4.50 3.00

Year of Dialogue Among Civilizations — A813

2001, Oct. 9 Litho. Perf. 13¼x13½
With Gum
3090 A813 800d multi 1.00 .40

Tran Huy Lieu (1901-69), Writer — A814

2001, Nov. 5 Perf. 13x12¾
With Gum
3091 A814 800d multi .75 .40

Nam Cao (1917-51), Writer A815

2001, Nov. 30 Perf. 13x13¼
With Gum
3092 A815 800d multi .75 .45

A816  A817

2001 With Gum Perf. 13½
3093 A816 800d multi .30 .25
3094 A817 3000d multi 1.00 .45

New Year 2002 (Year of the Horse) A818

Horse facing: 800d, Right. 8000d, Left. 14,000d, Horse galloping.

2002, Jan. 2 With Gum Perf. 13½
3095-3096 A818 Set of 2 2.50 1.10

Souvenir Sheet
Perf. 13½x13¼
3097 A818 14,000d multi 3.50 2.50

No. 3097 contains one 42x31mm stamp.

Opera Costumes A819

Designs: No. 3098, 1000d, Giáp Tuong Nam (6-1). No. 3099, 1000d, Giáp Tuong Nu (6-2). 2000d, Giáp Tuong Phan Dien (6-3). 3000d, Long Chan (6-4). 5000d, Giáp Tuong Phien (6-5). 9000d, Lung Xiem Quan Giáp (6-6).

2002, Jan. 15 Perf. 13
3098-3103 A819 Set of 6 5.00 3.25

Vo Thi Sáu, Heroine, 50th Anniv. of Death A820

2002, Jan. 23 Perf. 13x13¼
3104 A820 1000d multi .75 .40

Program Implementation of 9th Communist Party Congress A821

Designs: 800d, Map, satellite, buildings, dam, power lines, bridge, computer keyboard (2-1). 3000d, Flag, building, doves, people (2-2).

2002, Feb. 1 Perf. 13¼x13
With Gum
3105-3106 A821 Set of 2 1.25 .65

Cacti — A822

Designs: No. 3107, 1000d, Echinocereus albatus (5-1). No. 3108, 1000d, Echinocereus delaetii (5-2). No. 3109, 1000d, Cylindropuntia bigelowii (5-3). 5000d, Echinocereus triglochidatus (5-4). 10,000d, Epiphyllum truncatum (5-5).

2002, Feb. 18 Perf. 13¼x13½
3107-3111 A822 Set of 5 3.50 2.50

Victor Hugo (1802-85), French Writer A823

2002, Feb. 26 Perf. 13x13¼
With Gum
3112 A823 1000d multi .75 .45

A824

2002, Feb. 21 Litho. Perf. 13x13¼
With Gum
3113 A824 800d multi .75 .45

Birds — A825

Designs: 600d, Actinodura sodangorum (6-1). No. 3115, 800d, Garrulax ngoclinhensis (6-2). No. 3116, 800d, Garrulax pectoralis (6-3). No. 3117, 800d, Pomatorhinus hypoleucos (6-4). 5000d, Minla ignotincta (6-5). 8000d, Minla cyanouroptera (6-6).

2002, Mar. 15   Litho.   Perf. 13½
With Gum
3114-3119 A825   Set of 6   4.00 2.75

Landscapes
A826

Designs: No. 3120, 800d, Ganh Son, Binh Thuan (3-1). No. 3121, 800d, Dawn over Tung Estuary, Quang Tri (3-2). 10,000d, Sa Huynh Harbor, Quang Ngai (3-3).

2002, Mar. 15   With Gum
3120-3122 A826   Set of 3   3.00 2.00

Primates — A827

Designs: 600d, Trachypithecus poliocephalus (8-1). 800d, Trachypithecus delacouri (8-2). 1000d, Rhinopithecus avunculus (8-3). 2000d, Pygathrix cinerea (8-4). 4000d, Nomascus concolor (8-5). 5000d, Trachypithecus laotum hatinhensis (8-6). 7000d, Trachypithecus phayrei (8-7). 9000d, Pygathrix nemaeus (8-8).

2002, Apr. 10
3123-3130 A827   Set of 8   5.25 4.50
3130a   Souvenir sheet, #3123-   6.00 4.50
          3130 + label

Bui Thi Xuan,
200th Anniv. of
Death — A828

2002, Apr. 13   With Gum   Perf. 13
3131 A828 1000d multi   .75 .45

Souvenir Sheet

2002 World Cup Soccer
Championships, Japan and
Korea — A829

Color of player or players: a, 1000d, Blue. b, 2000d, Red. c, 5000d, Red violet. d, 7000d, Green.

2002, June 1   With Gum   Litho.
3132 A829   Sheet of 4, #a-d   3.25 2.75

Flowers — A830

Designs: 600d, Paphiopedilum concolor (7-1). 800d, Sterculia lanceolata (7-2). 1000d, Schefflera alongensis (7-3). 2000d, Hibiscus tiliaceus (7-4). 3000d, Mussaenda glabra (7-5). 5000d, Boniodendron parviflorum (7-6). 9000d, Bauhinia ornata.

2002, June 5
3133-3139 A830   Set of 7   4.00 3.25

Chau Van Liem, Communist Party
Leader, Cent. of Birth — A831

2002, June 28   Litho.   Perf. 13
With Gum
3140 A831 800d multi   .75 .45

Stamp Day — A832

2002, July 1   Perf. 13x12¾
With Gum
3141 A832 800d multi + label   .75 .45

Tay
Nguyen
Province
A833

2002, July 10   Litho.   Perf. 13
With Gum
3142 A833 800d multi   .75 .40

Soft-shell
Turtles
A834

Designs: 800d, Pelochelys bibroni (4-1). 2000d, Pelodiscus sinensis. 5000d, Palea steindachneri. 9000d, Trionyx cartilagineus.

2002, July 15   Litho.   Perf. 13½
3143-3146 A834   Set of 4   4.00 2.60
3146a   Souvenir sheet, 2 each   7.50 5.25
          #3143-3146

Viet Nam
— Laos
Diplomatic
Relations,
40th
Anniv.
A835

2002, July 18   With Gum   Perf. 13
3147 A835 800d multi   .65 .45

Civil
Aircraft
A836

Designs: 800d, Super King Air B200 in air (4-1). 2000d, Fokker 70 (4-2). 3000d, ATR-72 (4-3). 8000d, Boeing 767-300 (4-4). 14,000d, Super King Air B200 on ground.

2002, Aug. 1   With Gum   Perf. 13
3148-3151 A836   Set of 4   3.50 2.25
Souvenir Sheet
Perf. 13½x13¾
3152 A836 14,000d multi   3.50 2.25

Autumn
Festival
Lanterns
A837

Designs: No. 3153, 800d, Den Ong Sao (4-1). No. 3154, 800d, Den Ong Su (4-2). 2000d, Den Con Tho Om Trang (4-3). 7000d, Den Xep (4-4).

2002, Aug. 16   With Gum   Perf. 13½
3153-3156 A837   Set of 4   2.50 1.50

Designs: No. 3153, 800d, Den Ong Sao...

Viet Nam Posts and
Telecommunications Trade Union, 55th
Anniv. — A838

2002, Aug. 23   With Gum   Perf. 13
3157 A838 800d multi   .75 .40

Bridges — A839

Designs: No. 3158, 800d, Cau Long Bien (4-1). No. 3159, 800d, Cau Song Han (4-2). 2000d, Cau Truong Tien (4-3). 10,000d, Cau My Thuan (4-4).

2002, Sept. 27   Perf. 13x13¼
With Gum
3158-3161 A839   Set of 4   3.00 2.00

Communist Party's Ideology and
Culture Commission, 72nd
Anniv. — A840

2002, Oct. 10   With Gum   Perf. 13
3162 A840 800d multi   .75 .40

Hanoi
Medical
University,
Cent.
A841

2002, Nov. 15   With Gum
3163 A841 800d multi   .75 .40

Teachers'
Day — A842

2002, Nov. 20   With Gum
3164 A842 800d multi   .75 .40

New Year
2003 (Year of
the
Ram) — A843

Various goats with background colors of: 800d, Rose pink (2-1). 8000d, Orange (2-2).

2002, Dec. 15   Perf. 13½
With Gum
3165-3166 A843   Set of 2   2.00 1.25

Viet Nam —
South Korea
Diplomatic
Relations, 10th
Anniv. — A844

Pagoda from: No. 3167, 800d, Viet Nam (2-1). No. 3168, 800d, South Korea (2-2).

2002, Dec. 21   With Gum
3167-3168 A844   Set of 2   .90 .65

Starting with the 2003 issues, stamps are gummed unless otherwise indicated.

Landscapes — A845

Designs: 800d, Rung Cao Su, Bình Phuoc (3-1). 3000d, Ao Bà Om, Trà Vinh (3-2). 7000d, Mot nhahn song Rach Gam-Xoài Mút, Tien Giang (3-3).

2003, Feb. 1   Litho.   Perf. 13
3169-3171 A845 Set of 3   2.25 1.40

Viet Nam Culture Program, 60th Anniv. — A846

2003, Feb. 3
3172 A846 800d multi   .60 .30

Viet Nam Cinema Association, 50th Anniv. — A847

2003, Mar. 1
3173 A847 1000d multi   .75 .40

Khanh Hoa Province, 350th Anniv. A848

2003, Mar. 25
3174 A848 800d multi   .65 .30

Cycle Rickshaws A849

Cycle rickshaws from: 800d, Hanoi. 3000d, Ho Chi Minh City. 8000d, Haiphong.

2003, Apr. 1
3175-3177 A849 Set of 3   2.50 1.60

Adventures of the Cricket — A850

2003, May 1   Perf. 13¼x13½
3178   Horiz. strip of 6   3.50 2.60
a. A850 800d Toi là út...   .25 .25
b. A850 1000d Chang bao...   .25 .25

---

c. A850 2000d Toi an han...   .30 .25
d. A850 3000d Toi và Trui...   .45 .40
e. A850 5000d Mot ngày...   .85 .70
f. A850 8000d Tu nay the...   1.40 1.10

Animals in Ba Vi National Park — A851

Designs: No. 3179, 800d, Manis pentadactyla (4-1). No. 3180, 800d, Petaurista petaurista (4-2). 5000d, Selenarctos thibetanus (4-3). 10,000d, Capricornis suma-traensis (4-4).

2003, June 5   Perf. 13½
3179-3182 A851 Set of 4   3.50 2.25

22nd South East Asian Games, Viet Nam — A852

Designs: 800d, Soccer (4-1). 2000d, Hurdles (4-2). 3000d, Kayaking (4-3). 7000d, Wrestling (4-4). 10,000d, Games emblem, mascot, stadium.

2003, July 1   Perf. 13
3183-3186 A852 Set of 4   3.00 1.75
Souvenir Sheet
Perf. 13½x13¾
3187 A852 10,000d multi   3.25 1.50

Ninth Congress of Viet Nam Federation of Trade Unions — A853

2003, July 28   Perf. 13
3188 A853 800d multi   .65 .25

Camellias — A854

Designs: 800d, Camellia petelotii (4-1). 1000d, Camellia rubriflora (4-2). 5000d, Camellia vietnamensis (4-3). 6000d, Camellia gilberti (4-4).

2003, Sept. 1   Perf. 13½
3189-3192 A854 Set of 4   2.50 1.75
Bangkok 2003 World Philatelic Exhibition.

Orchids A855

Designs: 800d, Paphiopedilum dianthum (2-1). 8000d, Pleione bulbocodioides (2-2).

2003, Oct. 1   Perf. 13
3193-3194 A855 Set of 2   2.50 1.10

Asian Elephants A856

Designs: 800d, Elephant with trunk extended (4-1). 1000d, Elephants and riders (4-2). 2000d, Elephant with trunk down (4-3). 8000d, Two elephants (4-4)

2003, Oct. 1   Perf. 13½
3195-3198 A856 Set of 4   3.00 1.50
3198a   Miniature sheet, 2 each
            #3195-3198   6.50 3.00

My Son World Heritage Site — A857

Various ruins: 800d, (3-1). 3000d, (3-2). 8000d (3-3). 10,000d, Temple (43x32mm).

2003, Dec. 1   Perf. 13x13¼
3199-3201 A857 Set of 3   3.50 2.00
Souvenir Sheet
Perf. 13½x13¾
3202 A857 10,000d multi   2.75 2.00

New Year 2004 (Year of the Monkey) A858

Monkeys and: 800d, Apple tree (2-1). 8000d, Palm leaf (2-2).

2003, Dec. 1   Perf. 13½
3203-3204 A858 Set of 2   1.50 1.10

Ngo Gia Tu (1908-35), Leader of 1926 Strike — A859

2003, Dec. 30   Perf. 13¼x13
3205 A859 800d multi   .60 .25

Congratulations A860

Designs: 800d, Flowers (2-1). 8000d, Bird with envelope (2-2).

2004, Jan. 1   Perf. 13 Syncopated
3206-3207 A860 Set of 2   1.75 1.10

Shells A861

Designs: 800d, Murex trocheli (3-1). 3000d, Murex haustellum (3-2). 8000d, Chicoreus ramosus (3-3).

2004, Feb. 1   Perf. 13
3208-3210 A861 Set of 3   3.25 1.50

Bamboo Lamps — A862

Various lamps with background colors of: 400d, Yellow (3-1). 1000d, Pale green (3-2). 7000d, Buff (3-3).

Perf. 13 Syncopated
2004, Mar. 1   Litho.
3211-3213 A862 Set of 3   2.25 1.10
See Nos. 3352-3363.

Hué, UNESCO World Heritage Site — A863

Designs: 800d, Pavilion of Edicts (3-1). 4000d, Ngo Mon Gate (3-2). No. 3216, 8000d, Hien Lam Pavilion (3-3). No. 3217, 8000d, Thai Hoa Palace.

2004, Apr. 1   Perf. 13
Stamp + Label
3214-3216 A863 Set of 3   2.00 1.75
Souvenir Sheet
Perf. 13½x13¾
3217 A863 8000d multi   2.50 1.00
No. 3217 contains one 42x31mm stamp.

Tran Phu (1904-31), Communist Leader — A864

2004, May 1   Perf. 13
3218 A864 800d multi   .60 .25

Battle of Dien Bien Phu, 50th Anniv. A865

Designs: 800d, Soldier, flowers (2-1). 5000d, Dancer, flowers. 8000d, Three dancers, flowers.

2004, May 4   Perf. 13
3219-3220 A865 Set of 2   1.90 .75
Souvenir Sheet
Perf. 13½x13¾
3221 A865 8000d multi   2.40 1.00

FIFA (Fédération Internationale de Football Association), Cent. — A866

2004, May 21 *Perf. 13*
3222 A866 800d multi .90 .25

Thieu Nien Newspaper, 50th Anniv. — A867

2004, June 1
3223 A867 800d multi .60 .25

Bonsai — A868

Designs: 800d, Ficus microcarpa (4-1). 2000d, Premna serratifolia (4-2). 3000d, Ficus pilosa (4-3). 8000d, Ficus religiosa (4-4).

2004, July 1
3224-3227 A868 Set of 4 3.50 1.75
2004 World Stamp Championship, Singapore.

2004 Summer Olympics, Athens — A869

Designs: 800d, Hurdles (4-1). 1000d, Swimming, horiz. (4-2). 6000d, Shooting, horiz. (4-3). 7000d, Taekwondo (4-4).

2004, Aug. 1
3228-3231 A869 Set of 4 3.25 1.90

Naming of Country as Viet Nam, Bicent. — A870

Designs: 800d, Citadel, Hué, lotus flower (2-1). 5000d, Ho Chi Minh, flag (2-2).

2004, Sept. 2
3232-3233 A870 Set of 2 1.50 .75

World Summit on the Information Society, Geneva — A871

2004, Oct. 9
3234 A871 1000d multi .60 .25

Liberation of Hanoi From French, 50th Anniv. — A872

2004, Oct. 10
3235 A872 800d multi .60 .25

Dak Lak Province, Cent. — A873

2004, Nov. 22
3236 A873 800d multi 1.00 .25

Hoi An, UNESCO World Heritage Site — A874

Designs: 800d, Chua Cau. 8000d, Hoi Quán Phúc Kien.

Perf. 13¼x13¾ Syncopated
2004, Dec. 1
3237 A874 800d multi 1.00 .25
Souvenir Sheet
Perf. 13½x13¾
3238 A874 8000d multi 2.50 1.50
No. 3238 contains one 42x31mm stamp.

New Year 2005 (Year of the Rooster) A875

Designs: 800d, Rooster (2-1). 8000d, Hen and chicks.

2004, Dec. 15 *Perf. 13*
3239-3240 A875 Set of 2 2.25 1.10
3240a Souvenir sheet, #3239-3240 2.25 1.50

Viet Nam Communist Party, 75th Anniv. — A876

2005, Feb. 3
3241 A876 800d multi .60 .25

Gia Lai Province A877

Perf. 13¼x13¾ Syncopated
2005, Mar. 16 *Litho.*
3242 A877 800d multi .75 .25

Nha Trang Bay — A878

Designs: 800d, Boat near shore (2-1). 8000d, Road near shore (2-2).

2005, Apr. 2 *Perf. 13x12¾*
Stamp + Label
3243-3244 A878 Set of 2 1.75 1.40

Worldwide Fund for Nature (WWF) A879

Various views of Chrotogale owstoni: 800d, (4-1). 3000d, (4-2). 5000d, (4-3). 8000d, (4-4).

2005, May 2 *Perf. 13½*
3245-3248 A879 Set of 4 3.25 3.25
3248a Souvenir sheet, #3245-3248, perf. 13x13½ 3.50 3.50

Liberation of Haiphong, 50th Anniv. — A880

Designs: 800d, Burning airplanes at Cat Bi Airport, Haiphong harbor (2-1). 5000d, Nam Trieu Port (2-2).

2005, May 6 *Perf. 13x12¾*
Stamp + Label
3249-3250 A880 Set of 2 1.75 .75

People's Police, 60th Anniv. A881

Medals and: 800d, Marching police, statue of Ho Chi Minh (2-1). 10,000d, Police helping civilians (2-2).

2005, Aug. 10 *Perf. 13*
3251-3252 A881 Set of 2 1.75 1.40

Posts and Telecommunications Dept., 60th Anniv. — A882

2005, Aug. 15 *Perf. 13*
Background Color
3253 A882 800d beige .75 .25
Souvenir Sheet
Perf. 13½x13¾
3254 A882 8000d gray 1.75 1.25

August Revolution, 60th Anniv. — A883

Crowd with flags in: 1000d, Hanoi (3-1). 2000d, Hué (3-2). 4000d, Saigon (3-3).

2005, Aug. 19 *Perf. 13*
3255-3257 A883 Set of 3 1.50 .90
3257a Souvenir sheet, #3255-3257 1.50 .90

Traditional Dress and Houses of Ethnic Groups — A884

No. 3258: a, Ba-na (54-1). b, Bo Y (54-2). c, Brau (54-3). d, Bru-Van Kieu (54-4). e, Cham (54-5). f, Cho-ro (54-6). g, Chu-ru (54-7). h, Chut (54-8). i, Co (54-9). j, Cong (54-10). k, Co-ho (54-11). l, Co Lao (54-12). m, Co-tu (54-13). n, Dao (54-14). o, E-de (54-15). p, Gia-rai (54-16). q, Giay (54-17). r, Gie-Trieng (54-18). s, Ha Nhi (54-19). t, Hoa (54-20). u, Hre (54-21). v, Khang (54-22). w, Khmer (54-23). x, Kho-mu (54-24). y, Kinh (54-25). z, La Chi (54-26). aa, La Ha (54-27). ab, La Hu (54-28). ac, Lao (54-29). ad, Lo Lo (54-30). ae, Lu (54-31). af, Ma (54-32). ag, Mang (54-33). ah, Mnong (54-34). ai, Mong (54-35). aj, Muong (54-36). ak, Ngai (54-37). al, Nung (54-38). am, O Du (54-39). an, Pa Then (54-40). ao, Phu La (54-41). ap, Pu Peo (54-42). aq, Ra-glai (54-43). ar, Ro-mam (54-44). as, San Chay (54-45). at, San Diu (54-46). au, Si La (54-47). av, Ta-oi (54-48). aw, Tay (54-49). ax, Thai (54-50). ay, Tho (54-51). az, Xinh-mun (54-52). ba, Xo-dang (54-53). bb, Xtieng (54-54).

Perf. 13¾x13¼ Syncopated
2005, Aug. 30
3258 Sheet of 54 + 2 labels 15.00 15.00
a.-bb. A884 800d Any single .25 .25
Complete booklet, #3258a-3258bb 15.00

Thang Long (Hanoi), 1000th Anniv. A885

People reenacting battles and: 800d, Statue of Gen. Quang Trung, building (3-1). 5000d, Statue of Independence Fighters, building (3-2). No. 3261, 8000d, Statue of Victory Against B-52's, Long Bien Bridge (3-3). No. 3262, Government officials on dais in Ba Dinh Square.

2005, Oct. 10   **Litho.**   *Perf. 13*
3259-3261 A885   Set of 3   2.50   1.75
Souvenir Sheet
Perf. 13½x13¾
3262 A885 8000d multi   2.25   1.50

New Year 2006 (Year of the Dog) A886

Designs: 800d, Dog and puppies (2-1). 8000d, Dog (2-2).

2005, Dec. 1   *Perf. 13*
3263-3264 A886   Set of 2   1.75   1.10
3264a   Souvenir sheet, #3263-3264   1.75   1.25

National Coat of Arms, 50th Anniv. A887

2006, Jan. 16   *Perf. 13*
3265 A887 1000d multi   .60   .25

10th Vietnamese Communist Party Congress A888

2006, Feb. 3
3266 A888 800d multi   .60   .25

Prime Minister Pham Van Dong (1906-2000) — A889

2006, Mar. 1
3267 A889 800d multi   .60   .25

Wolfgang Amadeus Mozart (1756-91), Composer — A890

2006, Mar. 1
3268 A890 2000d multi   1.00   .35

Léopold Senghor (1906-2001), First President of Senegal — A891

2006, Mar. 20   **Litho.**   *Perf. 13*
3269 A891 800d multi   .75   .25

BirdLife International A892

Designs: 800d, Lophura edwardsi (5-1). 2000d, Arborophila davidi (5-2). 3000d, Lophura hatinhensis (5-3). 5000d, Polyplectron germaini (5-4, 49x23mm). 8000d, Rheinardia ocellata (5-5, 49x23mm).

Perf. 13¼x14 Syncopated, 13¼x13½ Syncopated (#3273-3274)
2006, Apr. 1
3270-3274 A892   Set of 5   4.50   4.50
3274a   Souvenir sheet, #3270-3274   4.50   4.50

2006 World Cup Soccer Championships, Germany — A893

Designs: 800d, One player (1-2). 10,000d, Two players (2-2).

2006, May 1   **Litho.**   *Perf. 13¼x13*
3275-3276 A893   Set of 2   2.50   2.50

Phong Nha - Ke Bang National Park World Heritage Site — A894

Designs: 800d, Bi Ky Cave (3-1). 4000d, Xuyen Son Cave (3-2). 8000d, Nuoc Moc Stream (3-3).
12,000d, Tien Cave, vert.

2006, June 1   *Perf. 13x12¾*
3277-3279 A894   Set of 3   4.00   2.50
Souvenir Sheet
Perf. 13¾x13½
3280 A894 12,000d multi   4.00   2.50
No. 3280 contains one 32x43mm stamp.

Animals in Ben En Botanical Gardens A895

Designs: 800d, Nycticebus bengalensis (4-1). 1000d, Neofelis nebulosa, horiz. (4-2). 7000d, Cuon alpinus, horiz. (4-3). 10,000d, Nomascus leucogenys (4-4).
12,000d, Physignathus cocincinus, horiz.

2006, July 1   *Perf. 13¼x13, 13x13¼*
3281-3284 A895   Set of 4   3.50   3.50
Souvenir Sheet
Perf. 13½x13¾
3285 A895 12,000d multi   2.75   2.50

Flowers — A896

Designs: 800d, Momordica cochinchinensis (4-1). 3000d, Telosma cordata (4-2). 5000d, Momordica charantia (4-3). 8000d, Luffa cylindrica (4-4).

2006, Aug. 1   *Perf. 13*
3286-3289 A896   Set of 4   3.25   3.25

Asia-Pacific Economic Cooperation Summit — A897

2006, Sept. 16
3290 A897 8000d multi   2.00   2.00

Cooperation Between Viet Nam and European Union — A898

2006, Oct. 1   *Perf. 13x13¼*
3291 A898 800d multi   .50   .25

New Year 2007 (Year of the Pig) A899

Designs: 800d, Pig and piglets (2-1). 8000d, Pig (2-2).

2006, Dec. 15   *Perf. 13*
3292-3293 A899   Set of 2   2.00   2.00

Tran Te Xuong (1870-1907), Poet — A900

2007, Jan. 20   **Litho.**   *Perf. 13x13¼*
3294 A900 1000d multi   .60   .40

Implementation of Resolutions of 10th Communist Party Congress — A901

Perf. 13½x13¼ Syncopated
2007, Feb. 3
3295 A901 800d multi   .60   .40

Truong Chinh (1907-88), General Secretary of Communist Party — A902

2007, Feb. 9   *Perf. 13x13¼*
3296 A902 800d multi   .60   .40

Le Duan (1907-86), First Secretary of Communist Party — A903

2007, Apr. 7
3297 A903 800d multi   .60   .40

Dugong Dugon — A904

Various depictions of Dugong dugon: 800d, (4-1). 1000d, (4-2). 7000d, (4-3). 9000d, (4-4).

2007, Aug. 1   **Litho.**   *Perf. 13*
3298-3301 A904   Set of 4   3.00   2.25

Association of South East Asian Nations (ASEAN), 40th Anniv. — A905

Designs: No. 3302, 800d, Secretariat Building, Bandar Seri Begawan, Brunei (10-1). No. 3303, 800d, National Museum of Cambodia (10-2). No. 3304, 800d, Fatahillah Museum, Jakarta, Indonesia (10-3). No. 3305, 800d, Typical house, Laos (10-4). No. 3306, 800d, Malayan Railway Headquarters Building, Kuala Lumpur, Malaysia (10-5). No. 3307, 800d, Yangon Post Office, Myanmar (Burma) (10-6). No. 3308, 800d, Malacañang Palace, Philippines (10-7). No. 3309, 800d, National Museum of Singapore (10-8). No. 3310, 800d, Vimanmek Mansion, Bangkok, Thailand (10-9). No. 3311, 800d, Presidential Palace, Hanoi, Viet Nam (10-10).

2007, Aug. 8   **Litho.**   *Perf. 13x13¼*
3302-3311 A905   Set of 10   3.00   1.25
3311a   Miniature sheet of 10, #3302-3311   3.25   1.25

See Brunei No. 607, Burma No. 370, Cambodia No. 2339, Indonesia Nos. 2120-2121, Laos Nos. 1717-1718, Malaysia No. 1170, Philippines Nos. 3103-3105, Singapore No. 1265, and Thailand No. 2315.

Tay Nguyen Tribal Gongs A906

Various tribal members using gongs: 800d, (3-1). 5000d, (3-2). 8000d, (3-3). 12,000d, Man holding gong.

2007, Nov. 21 Litho. Perf. 13x13¼
3312-3314 A906 Set of 3 2.00 1.75
Souvenir Sheet
3314A A906 12,000d multi 2.50 1.50

New Year 2008 (Year of the Rat) — A907

Designs: 800d, Rat at left (2-1). 8000d, Rat at right (2-2).

2007, Dec. 1 Perf. 13½
3315-3316 A907 Set of 2 1.75 1.10

Ho Chi Minh (1890-1969) A908

Perf. 13¼x13½
2007, Dec. 31 Litho.
3317 A908 1000d dk red & pink .30 .25
3318 A908 3000d dk & lt green .50 .30
3319 A908 4000d dk & lt blue .90 .50
Nos. 3317-3319 (3) 1.70 1.05

Vietnamese Cuisine — A909

Designs: 800d, Nem rán (2-1). 9000d, Pho bò (2-2).

2008, Feb. 1 Perf. 13x13¼
3320-3321 A909 Set of 2 1.75 1.25

Orchids A910

Designs: 800d, Calanthe densiflora (4-1). 2000d, Ludisia discolor (4-2). 6000d, Spathoglottis affinis (4-3). 8000d, Calanthe argenteo-striata (4-4).

2008, Mar. 1 Litho. Perf. 13½
3322-3325 A910 Set of 4 2.75 2.10

2008 Summer Olympics, Beijing — A911

Designs: 800d, Wushu (4-1). 3000d, Swimming (4-2). 5000d, Taekwondo (4-3). 9000d, Canoeing (4-4).

Perf. 14x13½ Syncopated
2008, Mar. 15 Litho.
3326-3329 A911 Set of 4 2.75 2.25

Cyprinus Carpio — A912

Various depictions of Cyprinus carpio: 800d, (3-1). 6000d, (3-2). 8000d, (3-3).

2008, Apr. 1 Perf. 13
3330-3332 A912 Set of 3 2.75 1.90

Vinasat-1 Satellite A913

2008, Apr. 19 Perf. 13½
3333 A913 800d multi .60 .25

Vietnamese Court Music, UNESCO Masterpiece of Intangible Heritage — A914

Inscriptions: 800d, Dai nhac, Bien khanh (3-1). 4000d, Tieu nhac, Dàn Nguyet và Nhi (3-2). 8000d, Luc cúng hoa dang, Kèn Bóp và Sáo (3-3).
9000d, Dai nhac trong le te.

2008, June 3 Litho. Perf. 13x12¾
3334-3336 A914 Set of 3 2.75 1.60
Souvenir Sheet
Perf. 13x12¾ Syncopated
3337 A914 9000d multi 1.75 1.10
No. 3337 contains one 40x28mm stamp.

Tran Quy Cáp (1870-1908), Progressive Movement Leader — A915

2008, June 8 Litho. Perf. 13
3338 A915 1000d multi .50 .25

Binh Thuan Province A916

2008, Sept. 1 Perf. 13x12¾
3339 A916 800d multi .50 .25

Seascapes of France and Viet Nam — A917

Designs: 800d, Strait of Bonifacio, France (2-1). 14,000d, Along Bay, Viet Nam (2-2).

2008, Oct. 15
3340-3341 A917 Set of 2 2.50 1.75
See France Nos. 3519-3520.

Lady Trieu's Rebellion, A.D. 248 — A918

Perf. 13¼x13½ Syncopated
2008, Oct. 20
3342 A918 1000d multi .50 .25

Flowers A919

Designs: 800d, Ceiba chodatii (2-1). 10,000d, Nelumbo nucifera (2-2).

2008, Oct. 25 Perf. 13
3343-3344 A919 Set of 2 2.00 1.40
See Argentina Nos. 2508-2509.

Fruit — A920

Designs: 2000d, Durio zibetinus (2-1). 8000d, Hylocereus undatus (2-2).

2008, Nov. 18 Litho. Perf. 13½
3345-3346 A920 Set of 2 2.00 1.25
See Singapore Nos. 1352-1353.

New Year 2009 (Year of the Ox) — A921

Designs: 2000d, Ox (2-1). 9000d, Ox and calf (2-2).

2008, Dec. 1 Litho. Perf. 13½
3347-3348 A921 Set of 2 2.00 1.40
3348a Souvenir sheet, #3347-3348 2.50 1.40

Nguyen Khuyen (1835-1909), Poet — A922

2009, Feb. 2 Litho. Perf. 13¼x13
3349 A922 2000d multi .50 .50

Charles Darwin (1809-82), Naturalist A923

2009, Feb. 12 Perf. 13
3350 A923 2000d multi .60 .50

Border and Coast Guard's Day — A924

2009, Mar. 3 Perf. 13¼x13
3351 A924 2000d multi .50 .50

Bamboo Lamps Type of 2004
Perf. 13 Syncopated
2009, May 15 Litho.
Background Color
Design of No. 3211
3352 A862 1200d yellow (12-1) .25 .25
3353 A862 2000d lt green (12-2) .25 .25
3354 A862 2500d blue (12-3) .30 .30
3355 A862 4500d gray blue (12-4) .50 .50
Design of No. 3212
3356 A862 5000d gray green (12-5) .55 .55
3357 A862 6500d brn vio (12-6) .75 .75
3358 A862 9500d violet (12-7) 1.10 1.10
3359 A862 10,500d red (12-8) 1.25 1.25
Design of No. 3213
3360 A862 13,500d fawn (12-9) 1.50 1.50
3361 A862 14,500d brn yel (12-10) 1.75 1.75
3362 A862 17,500d drab (12-11) 2.00 2.00
3363 A862 18,500d olive grn (12-12) 2.10 2.10
Nos. 3352-3363 (12) 12.30 12.30

Opening of the Ho Chi Minh Trail, 50th Anniv. A925

2009, May 19 Perf. 13
3364 A925 2000d multi .60 .30

Praying Mantises
A926

Designs: 1500d, Mantis religiosa (2-1). 12,500d, Tenodera aridiforia (2-2).

2009, July 1   Litho.   *Perf. 13½*
3365-3366 A926   Set of 2   2.00 1.60

Rhododendrons — A927

Designs: 500d, Rhododendron fortunei (4-1). 1200d, Rhododendron simsii (4-2). 4500d, Rhododendron sp. (4-3). 14,500d, Enkianthus quinqueflorus (4-4).

Perf. 13¼x13¾ Syncopated
2009, Aug. 1
3367-3370 A927   Set of 4   2.75 2.40

Fish
A928

Designs: 2000d, Botia macracanthus (4-1). 3000d, Trichopsis pumila (4-2). 6500d, Cynolebias elongatus (4-3). 10,500d, Centropyge flavissima (4-4). 14,500d Scleropages formosus.

2009, Sept. 1   *Perf. 13*
3371-3374 A928   Set of 4   2.75 2.75
Souvenir Sheet
Perf. 13½x13¾
3375 A928 14,500d multi   1.75 1.75

New Year 2010 (Year of the Tiger)
A929

Tiger: 2000d, Walking (2-1). 8500d, Sitting (2-2).

2009, Dec. 1   Litho.   *Perf. 13x13¼*
3376-3377 A929   Set of 2   1.25 1.25

Viet Nam Communist Party, 80th Anniv. — A930

2010, Feb. 2   Litho.   *Perf. 13¼x13*
3378 A930 2000d multi   .25 .25

Frédéric Chopin (1810-49), Composer — A931

2010, Feb. 22   Litho.   *Perf. 13*
3379 A931 2000d multi   .40 .25

Intl. Women's Day
A932

2010, Mar. 3   Litho.   *Perf. 13x13¼*
3380 A932 3000d multi   .65 .40

Pres. Ho Chi Minh (1890-1969)
A933

2010, May 16   Litho.   *Perf. 13*
3381 A933 2000d multi   .40 .30

BirdLife International — A934

Birds: 2000d, Tringa guttifer. 6500d, Calidris pygmeus. 8500d, Larus saundersi. 14,500d, Rynchops albicollis.

2010, May 25   Litho.   *Perf. 13x13¼*
3382-3384 A934   Set of 3   2.50 2.00
Souvenir Sheet
Perf. 13½x13¾
3385 A934 14,500d multi   1.60 1.60

Nguyen Huu Tho (1910-96), Acting President — A935

2010, July 10   *Perf. 13x13¼*
3386 A935 2000d multi   .40 .40

Fairy Lilies — A937

Designs: 3500d, Zephyranthes carinata. 10,500d, Zephyranthes ajax.

Perf. 14x13½ Syncopated
2010, July 30
3388-3389 A937   Set of 2   2.50 2.50
Bangkok 2010 Intl. Philatelic Exhibition.

Worldwide Fund for Nature (WWF) — A938

Prionailurus viverrinus: 2000d, At water's edge, facing right. 2500d, In water with fish in mouth. 4500d, Standing on rocks, facing left. 10,500d, Sitting.

2010, Aug. 1   Litho.   *Perf. 13*
3390-3393 A938   Set of 4   3.25 3.25
3393a   Miniature sheet of 8, 2 each #3390-3393   7.00 7.00

Hanoi, 1000th Anniv.
A939

Dragon and: 2000d, Banner, Hanoi Flag Tower. 2500d, Quan Chuong City Gate, National Conference Center, apartment buildings. 4500d, Long Biên Bridge, Nhật Tân Bridge. 6500d, Hanoi Train Station, Noi Bài Airport. 14,000d, Highways, graduate, computer operators, vert.

2010, Oct. 2   *Perf. 13x13¼*
3394-3397 A939   Set of 4   2.75 2.75
Souvenir Sheet
Perf. 13¾x13½
3398 A939 14,000d multi   2.50 2.50

Viet Nam Stamp Association, 50th Anniv. — A940

2010, Oct. 3   *Perf. 13x13¼*
3399 A940 2000d multi   .40 .40

Viet Nam Membership in Association of South East Asian Nations (ASEAN), 15th Anniv. — A941

2010, Oct. 27
3400 A941 8500d multi   1.50 1.50

New Year 2011 (Year of the Cat) — A942

Cat: 2000d, Sitting. 10,500d, Lying down.

2010, Dec. 1   *Perf. 13½*
3401-3402 A942   Set of 2   2.25 2.25

Diplomatic Relations Between Viet Nam and Cuba, 50th Anniv.
A943

2010, Dec. 2
3403 A943 2000d multi   .40 .40

11th Congress of Vietnamese Communist Party — A944

2011, Jan. 5   *Perf. 13¼x13*
3404 A944 2000d multi   .40 .40

UNESCO Intangible Heritage Quan Ho Bac Ninh Folk Songs — A945

Singers: 3000d, Two men with umbrella, two women with hats. 4500d, Two men and two women seated, horiz. 10,500d, Two men with umbrella in boat, two women holding hats. 12,500d, Men and women in boat, horiz.

2011, Jan. 15   *Perf. 13¼x13, 13x13¼*
3405-3407 A945   Set of 3   1.90 1.90
Souvenir Sheet
Perf. 13½x13¾
3408 A945 12,500d multi   1.40 1.40

Ho Chi Minh Communist Youth Union, 80th Anniv. — A946

2011, Mar. 26   Litho.   *Perf. 13*
3409 A946 2000d multi   .30 .30

Ta Quang Buu (1910-86), Minister of Higher and Secondary Professional Education — A936

2010, July 27
3387 A936 2000d multi   .40 .40

Phú Yên, 400th Anniv. — A947

2011, Mar. 31   *Perf. 13x12¾*
3410 A947 2000d multi   .30 .30

Fauna in Ba Be National Park A948

Designs: 2000d, Muntiacus muntjac (4-1). 3500d, Gorsachius magnificus (4-2). 6000d, Acanthosaura lepidogaster (4-3). 8500d, Pyxidea mouhoti (4-4).
14,500d, Catopuma temminckii.

2011, May 15   *Perf. 13*
3411-3414 A948   Set of 4   2.50 2.50
Souvenir Sheet
Perf. 13½x13¾
3415 A948 14,500d multi   1.50 1.50

Ho Chi Minh 's Departure From Viet Nam, Cent. — A949

2011, June 5   *Perf. 13*
3416 A949 2000d multi   .30 .30

Ernest Hemingway (1899-1961), Writer A950

2011, July 2   *Perf. 13½*
3417 A950 10,500d multi   1.25 1.25

Dragonflies A951

Designs: 2000d, Lyriothemis mortoni (4-1). 2500d, Trithemis aurora (4-2). 6500d, Rhyothemis obsolescens (4-3). 10,500d, Ictinogomphus decoratus (4-4).

2011, July 11   *Perf. 13½*
3418-3421 A951   Set of 4   2.75 2.75
PhilaNippon '11 Intl. Philatelic Exhibition, Yokohama.

Tran Van Giau (1911-2010), Revolutionary Activist — A952

2011, Sept. 6   *Perf. 13*
3422 A952 2000d multi   .30 .30

Decade for Road Safety — A953

Designs: 2000d, Traffic light, police officer teaching students traffic signs (2-1). 6500d, People crossing street in crosswalk (2-2).

2011, Oct. 1   *Litho.*
3423-3424 A953   Set of 2   1.25 1.25

Mikhail Lomonosov (1711-65), Scientist — A954

2011, Nov. 19
3425 A954 8500d multi   1.25 1.25

New Year 2012 (Year of the Dragon) A955

Dragon with background color of: 2000d, Bright pink (2-1). 10,500d, Olive green (2-2).

2011, Dec. 1   *Perf. 13x13¼*
3426-3427 A955   Set of 2   1.75 1.75

One-Pillar Pagoda, Hanoi — A956   Keo Pagoda, Vu Thu — A957

Bridge Pagoda, Hoi An — A958

Perf. 13¾x13½ Syncopated
2012, Jan. 16
3428 A956 2000d rose carmine   .25 .25
3429 A956 3000d green   .35 .35
3430 A957 3500d brn orange   .40 .40
3431 A957 4500d red lilac   .60 .60

Perf. 13½x13¾ Syncopated
3432 A958 6500d blue   .80 .80
3433 A958 10,500d red   1.25 1.25
   Nos. 3428-3433 (6)   3.00 3.00

Ao Dais — A959

Designs: 2500d, Woman in brown ao dai with hat (4-1). 3000d, Woman in orange ao dai, woman in red ao dai (4-2). 6000d, Woman in red ao dai holding hat, woman in blue ao dai (4-3). 10,500d, Woman in blue ao dai standing, woman in purple ao dai seated (4-4).

2012, Mar. 8   *Perf. 13*
3434-3437 A959   Set of 4   3.00 3.00

Campaign Against Tuberculosis — A960

2012, Mar. 24
3438 A960 2000d multi   .30 .30

Asian Pacific Postal Union, 50th Anniv. A961

2012, Apr. 1
3439 A961 3000d multi   .40 .40

Bears A962

Designs: 2000d, Ursus thibetanus (4-1). 4500d, Ursus malayanus (4-2). 8500d, Ursus malayanus, diff. (4-3). 10,500d, Ursus thibetanus, diff. (4-4).
14,500d, Ursus thibetanus, diff.

2012, Apr. 1   *Perf. 13x13¼*
3440-3443 A962   Set of 4   3.00 3.00
Souvenir Sheet
Perf. 13½x13¾
3444 A962 14,500d multi   1.75 1.75

Tiled Covered Bridges — A963

Bridge in: 2000d, Huong Thuy (3-1). 3000d, Kim Son (3-2). 12,000d, Hai Hau (3-3).

2012, Apr. 8   *Perf. 13*
3445-3447 A963   Set of 3   2.00 2.00

Nguyen Huy Tuong (1912-60), Writer — A964

2012, May 6   *Perf. 13x13¼*
3448 A964 2000d multi   .30 .30

Ton That Tung (1912-82), Physician — A965

2012, May 10
3449 A965 2000d multi   .30 .30

Plumeria Flowers A966

Designs: 2500d, Plumeria rubra (2-1). 8500d, Plumeria obtusa (2-2).

2012, May 15
3450-3451 A966   Set of 2   1.50 1.50

Pham Hung (1912-88), Politician — A967

2012, June 11   *Perf. 13*
3452 A967 2000d multi   .30 .30

Nguyen Van Cu (1912-41), Communist Party General Secretary — A968

2012, July 9
3453 A968 2000d multi   .30 .30

2012 Summer Olympics, London A969

Designs: 2000d, Weight lifting (4-1). 3500d, Fencing (4-2). 8500d, Gymnast on pommel horse (4-3). 12,000d, Taekwondo (4-4).

2012, July 12   *Perf. 13½*
3454-3457 A969   Set of 4   3.00 3.00

Flags, Laotian Prime Minister Kaysone Phomivane and Vietnamese President Ho Chi Minh — A970

Buildings in Laos and Viet Nam — A971

2012, July 18   **Perf. 13**
3458 A970   2000d multi   .25   .25
3459 A971   12,000d multi   1.60   1.60
See Laos Nos. 1860-1861.

Monument to Heroic Mothers, Thach Phu — A972

2012, July 27   **Perf. 13¼x13**
3460 A972 2000d multi   .30   .30

Vo Chi Cong (1912-2011), Politician — A973

2012, Aug. 7   **Perf. 13**
3461 A973 2000d multi   .30   .30

Vu Trong Phung (1912-39), Writer — A974

2012, Oct. 20   **Perf. 13¼x13**
3462 A974 2000d multi   .30   .30

Nguyen Thi Minh Khai (1910-41), Communist Party Leader — A975

2012, Nov. 23   **Perf. 13x13¼**
3463 A975 2000d multi   .30   .30

New Year 2013 (Year of the Snake) A976

Various snakes and flowers in: 2000d, Orange (2-1). 10,500d, Red violet (2-2).

2012, Dec. 1   **Perf. 13½**
3464-3465 A976   Set of 2   1.25   1.25

Huynh Tan Phat (1913-89), Politician — A977

2013, Feb. 15   **Litho.**   **Perf. 13**
3466 A977 2000d multi   .25   .25

Vovinam (Vietnamese Martial Arts) — A978

Various combatants with frame color of: 2000d, Orange yellow (3-1). 6500d, Lilac (3-2). 8500d, Green (3-3).

2013, Mar. 1   **Litho.**   **Perf. 13**
3467-3469 A978   Set of 3   1.75   1.75

Orchids — A979

Designs: 2000d, Dendrobium aphyllum (3-1). 2500d, Dendrobium chrysotoxum (3-2). 17,500d, Dendrobium draconis (3-3).

2013, Apr. 1   **Litho.**   **Perf. 13**
3470-3472 A979   Set of 3   2.10   2.10

Lighthouses A980

Designs: 2000d, Diêm Diên Lighthouse (4-1). 3000d, Quang Ngai Lighthouse (4-2). 6000d, Dai Lanh Lighthouse (4-3). 14,500d, Kê Gà Lighthouse (4-4).

2013, May 15   **Litho.**   **Perf. 13¼x13**
3473-3476 A980   Set of 4   2.50   2.50

Birds in Xuân Thuy National Park A981

Designs: 2000d, Platalea minor (4-1). 3500d, Limnodromus semipalmatus (4-2). 6500d, Anas clypeata (4-3). 10,500d, Vanellus cinereus (4-4). 15,000d, Pelecanus philippensis.

2013, June 1   **Litho.**   **Perf. 13**
3477-3480 A981   Set of 4   2.25   2.25
Souvenir Sheet
3481 A981 15,000d multi   1.50   1.50

Musical Instruments A982

Designs: 2000d, Ta lu (3-1). 4500d, Kloong put, horiz. (3-2). 12,000d, Goong (3-3).

2013, July 15   **Litho.**   **Perf. 13**
3482-3484 A982   Set of 3   1.75   1.75

Birds A983

Designs: 2000d, Gallus gallus (2-1). 10,500d, Polyplectron bicalcaratum (2-2).

2013, Sept. 12   **Litho.**   **Perf. 13x13¼**
3485-3486 A983   Set of 2   1.25   1.25
Diplomatic relations between Viet Nam and Singapore, 40th anniv. See Singapore Nos. 1626-1627.

Tran Dai Nghia (1913-97), Military Engineer — A984

2013, Sept. 13   **Litho.**   **Perf. 13**
3487 A984 2000d multi   .25   .25

Alexandre Yersin (1863-1943), Bacteriologist — A985

Yersin as: 2000d, Young man (2-1). 18,500d, Older man (2-2).

2013, Sept. 22   **Litho.**   **Perf. 13**
3488-3489 A985   Set of 2   2.00   2.00
See France Nos. 4480-4481.

Rudolf Diesel (1858-1913), Inventor — A986

2013, Sept. 29   **Litho.**   **Perf. 13¼x13**
3490 A986 2000d multi   .25   .25

Tran Huu Tuóc (1913-83), Physician — A987

2013, Oct. 13   **Litho.**   **Perf. 13x13¼**
3491 A987 2000d multi   .25   .25

New Year 2014 (Year of the Horse) A988

Horse with background color of: 2000d, Orange (2-1). 10,500d, Red violet (2-2).

2013, Dec. 1   **Litho.**   **Perf. 13½**
3492-3493 A988   Set of 2   1.25   1.25

This stamp depicting Nguyen Chi Thanh, released Dec. 31, 2013, was a gift for standing order customers. It was not made available for sale.

Tree Frogs A989

Designs: 3000d, Rhacophorus puerensis (5-1). 4500d, Rhacophorus annamensis (5-2). 6000d, Rhacophorus robertingeri (5-3). 8000d, Rhacophorus kio (5-4). 10,000d, Rhacophorus rhodopus (5-5).

2014, Apr. 1   **Litho.**   **Perf. 13**
3494-3498 A989   Set of 5   3.00   3.00

Battle of Dien Bien Phu, 60th Anniv. A990

2014, May 5   **Litho.**   **Perf. 13**
3499 A990 3000d multi   .30   .30

Ca Trù Singing, UNESCO Intangible Cultural Heritage A991

Various musicians and singers: 3000d, (3-1). 3500d, (3-2). 10,500d (3-3). 16,000d, Ca trù musicians and singers, diff.

2014, June 1 **Litho.** **Perf. 13**
3500-3502 A991 Set of 3 1.60 1.60
Souvenir Sheet
Perf. 13½x13¾
3503 A991 16,000d multi 1.50 1.50

Ngo Mon (Gate of Noon), Hué — A992

Opera House, Ho Chi Minh City — A993

Main Post Office, Ho Chi Minh City — A994

Perf. 13½x13¾ Syncopated
2014, July 1 **Litho.**
3504 A992 3000d purple .30 .30
3505 A992 6000d emerald .55 .55
3506 A993 6500d blue .60 .60
3507 A993 8000d brown .75 .75
3508 A994 10,000d red .95 .95
3509 A994 12,000d ol brn 1.10 1.10
Nos. 3504-3509 (6) 4.25 4.25

Endangered Primates A995

Designs: 3000d, Rhinopithecus avunculus (4-1). 5500d, Trachypithecus poliocephalus (4-2). 8500d, Pygathrix cinerea (4-3). 12,500d, Trachypithecus delacouri (4-4). 18,000d, Nomascus nasutus.

2014, Aug. 11 **Litho.** **Perf. 13**
3510-3513 A995 Set of 4 2.75 2.75
Souvenir Sheet
Perf. 13¾x13½
3514 A995 18,000d multi 1.75 1.75
25th Intl. Primatological Society Congress, Hanoi.

Truong Dinh (1820-64), Anti-Colonial Military Leader — A996

2014, Aug. 20 **Litho.** **Perf. 13**
3515 A996 3000d multi .30 .30

Lê Trong Tan (1914-86), General — A997

2014, Oct. 1 **Litho.** **Perf. 13**
3516 A997 3000d multi .30 .30

New Year 2015 (Year of the Goat) A998

Goats and flowers with background color of: 3000d, Yellow (2-1). 10,500d, Pink (2-2).

2014, Dec. 1 **Litho.** **Perf. 13½**
3517-3518 A998 Set of 2 1.25 1.25

SEMI-POSTAL STAMPS

World Communications Year — SP1

#B1, Hands holding envelope with ITU emblem. #B2, Satellite dish antenna.

Unwmk.
1983, Nov. 1 **Litho.** **Perf. 11**
B1-B2 SP1 50xu +10xu Set of 2 3.75 .80

AIR POST STAMP

AP1

Unwmk.
1959, Nov. 20 **Litho.** **Perf. 11**
C1 AP1 20xu blue & black 10.00 2.00

POSTAGE DUE STAMPS

Democratic Republic of Viet Nam Nos. 1-4 exist with handstamps of "TT" in a diamond. It is unclear to the editors if these stamps were used.

D1

1955 **Typo.** **Perf. 11½**
J14 D1 50d brown & yellow 10.00 6.00

D2

1958, Dec. 1 **Litho.** **Perf. 12½**
J15 D2 10d purple & red .65 .60
J16 D2 20d orange & aqua 1.50 1.00
J17 D2 100d gray blue & red 3.00 2.50
J18 D2 300d olive grn & red 4.50 3.50
Nos. J15-J18 (4) 9.65 7.60

MILITARY STAMPS

M1

Perf. 12½
1958, May 1 **Litho.** **Unwmk.**
M1 M1 multicolored 12.00 4.50

Invalids in Field Paddy M2

1959-60 **Litho.** **Perf. 11**
M2 M2 org brn & brown 4.00 1.00
M3 M2 grey blue & olive 6.00 1.75
Nos. M2-M3 (2) 10.00 2.75
Issued: No. M2, 3/14/59; No. M3, 7/27/60.

Soldier, Train — M3

1959, July 1
M4 M3 bluish green 4.00 1.50

Frontier Guard — M4

1961, Jan. 3
M5 M4 multicolored 13.50 8.00

Naval Patrol M5

1962, June 15
M6 M5 multicolored 4.75 2.00

Military Medal, Invalid's Badge — M6

1963, Sept. 10
M7 M6 12xu multicolored 4.00 4.00

Rifleman M7

1964, Aug.
M8 M7 multicolored 4.00 4.00

Rifleman Jumping Wall — M8

1965
M9 M8 red & black 4.00 4.00
M10 M8 yellow green & black 4.00 4.00
Nos. M9-M10 (2) 8.00 8.00
Issued: No. M9, 7/1; No. M10, 12/25.

Soldier, Guerrilla Woman M9

1966-67
M11 M9 greenish blue & vio bl 8.00 8.00
Redrawn with two boats at right
M12 M9 olive & brown bl 13.50 12.00
Issued: No. M11, 9/25; No. M12, 6/26/67.

Badge of People's Army — M10

1967, Oct. 10
M13 M10 multicolored 2.75 1.50

M11

1968, Nov. 10
M14 M11 lilac 3.00 1.25

M12

1969, Nov. 15
M15 M12   red & brown red   2.00 1.25

M13

1971, Apr. 27
M16 M13   yellow, brown & red   2.00 1.25

Nguyen
Van Be
M14

Design: No. M18, Nguyen Viet Xuan.

1971, Oct. 30   **Perf. 11**
M17 M14   multicolored
                      1.75 1.25
            Perf. 12½
M18 M14   black, pink & buff   2.50 1.10
M19 M14   black & green   2.50 1.10

M15

M16

1973, Dec. 22   **Perf. 11**
M20 M15   blue, black & buff   1.25 .50
  a.   Perf. 12½   4.50 4.50
M22 M16   olive, red & black   1.25 .50
  a.   Perf. 12½   4.50 4.50

Disabled
Veteran in
Factory
M17

No. M24, Invalid's Badge, open book, vert.

1976, July 27
M23-M24 M17   Set of 2   3.50 1.50

Soldier,
Map — M18

1976, Oct. 21
M25 M18   red & black
                        1.25 1.25

Pilot — M19

No. M27, Tank driver. No. M28, Seaman.

1978
M26-M28 M19   Set of 3   5.00 2.00
  Issued: No. M26, 6/3; others, 10/10.

M20

Designs: a, Pilot. b, Badge of People's
Army.

1979, Dec. 22
M29 M20   Vertical pair, #a.-b.   3.50 3.50

Types A343a, A359 and

Ho Chi
Minh — M21

#M30, Factory militiawoman. #M31, Soldier,
woman pointing. #M32, Militiawoman.

1981, Aug. 5
M30 A343a   salmon & multi   1.25 .75
M31 A343a   green & multi   1.25 .75
M32 A359   blue & multi   1.25 .75
M33 M21   blue & tan   1.25 .75
  Nos. M30-M33 (4)   5.00 3.00
  Size of No. M32: 13x18mm.

M22

1982, Nov. 9
M34 M22   pink & greenish blue   1.75 1.00

M23

1983, Apr. 30
M35 M23   multicolored   2.25 1.10

Victory at
Dien Bien
Phu, 30th
Anniv.
M24

1984, May 5   **Litho.**
M37 M24   multicolored   1.75 .75

Disabled
Soldier
Teaching
Class — M25

1984, Nov. 10
M38 M25   tan & brown   1.25 .75

Frontier Forces Type of 1984

1984, Dec. 15
M39 A410   multicolored   1.50 .75

M26

1984, Dec. 22
M40 M26   multicolored   2.50 .50

Policemen
and
Women
M27

1985, Aug. 30
M41 M27   multicolored   2.00 .60

M28

1986, Oct. 1
M42 M28   olive brown & black   1.50 .75

M29

1987, Sept. 23
M43 M29   carmine and tan   2.00 1.00

OFFICIAL STAMPS

Harvesting
Rice — O1

Denominations in grams or kilograms of
rice. Dated 1952.

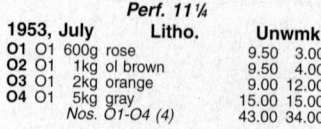

1953, July		**Litho.**	**Unwmk.**
O1	O1	600g rose	9.50 3.00
O2	O1	1kg ol brown	9.50 4.00
O3	O1	2kg orange	9.00 12.00
O4	O1	5kg gray	15.00 15.00

           Perf. 11¼

  Nos. O1-O4 (4)   43.00 34.00

Dien Bien Phu Type of 1954

1954-56   **Perf. 11**
O5 A4   600g sepia & ocher   18.00 12.50

  No. O5 exists perf 6, Value $60; and also
imperf, Value $18.
  Issued: #O5, 10/54; perf 6, 12/54; imperf,
1956.

Nos. 1L62-1L63
Overprinted

1955   **Typo.**   **Perf. 7 Rough**
O6-O7 VM2   100g on 2d,
                   100g on
                   5d, set of
                   2   400.00 300.00

Land Reform Type of 1955-56
Inscribed "SU VU" Above Value

1955   **Litho.**   **Perf. 11**
O8-O9 A6   40d, 80d, set of 2   35.00 20.00

Cu Chinh
Lan (1930-
1952)
O3

Denominations: 20d, 80d, 100d, 500d,
1000d, 2000d, 3000d.

1956, June   **Litho.**   **Perf. 11½**
O10-O16 O3   Set of 7   250.00 225.00

4th World Trade Union Congress
Type of 1957
Inscribed "SU VU" Above Value

1957, Aug. 1   **Perf. 12½**
O17-O20 A15   20d, 40d, 80d,
                100d, set of 4   20.00 16.00

One-Pillar
Pagoda — O4

1957-58
O21 O4   150d green and brown
O22 O4   150d orange and slate
  Nos. O21-O22 (2)   26.00 11.00

  Nos. O21-O22 exist with and without imprint
and designer's name. Issued: No. O21,
12/22/57; No. O22, 3/12/58.

Craft Fair,
Hanoi — O5

1958, May 30
O23-O24 O5   150d, 200d, set of
                 2   8.00 6.00

1st World
Congress of
Young
Workers,
Prague —
O6

1958, June 26
O25 O6 150d lt olive green & red 3.50 1.75

Soldier,
Factory,
Crops — O7

1958, Aug. 19
O26-O28 O7 50, 150, 200d, set
of 3 11.00 7.00

Opening of
New Hanoi
Stadium
O8

1958, Dec. 31
O29-O32 O8 10d, 20d, 80d,
150d, set of 4 9.50 4.75

Planting Rice — O9

1962, Sept. 1 **Perf. 11**
O33-O35 O9 3, 6, 12xu, set of 3 3.00 2.50

Rural
Mail
Service
O10

1966, July 1 **Perf. 11**
O36-O37 O10 3xu, 6xu, set of 2 3.00 1.00

VIRGIN ISLANDS

ˈvər-jən ˈī-ləndz

LOCATION — West Indies, southeast
of Puerto Rico
GOVT. — British colony
AREA — 59 sq. mi.
POP. — 19,107 (1997)
CAPITAL — Road Town

The British Virgin Islands constituted
one of the presidencies of the former
Leeward Islands colony until it became
a colony itself in 1956. For many years
stamps of Leeward Islands were used
concurrently.

The Virgin Islands group is divided
between Great Britain and the United
States. See Danish West Indies.

12 Pence = 1 Shilling
20 Shillings = 1 Pound
100 Cents = 1 Dollar (1951)
100 Cents = 1 US Dollar (1962)

Values for unused stamps are for
examples with original gum as defined
in the catalogue introduction. However,
Nos. 1-2c are valued without gum as
the vast majority of examples are found
thus.

Virgin and
Lamps — A1

St. Ursula — A2

A3

A4

1866 Litho. Unwmk. Perf. 12
Toned or White Paper
1 A1 1p green 50.00 65.00
a. Toned paper 52.50 65.00
c. Perf. 15x12, toned paper 12,000. 7,750.
2 A3 6p rose 65.00 100.00
a. Large "V" in "VIRGIN" 375.00 475.00
b. White paper 100.00 120.00
c. As "a," white paper 425.00 525.00

Examples offered as No. 1c frequently have
forged perfs.

1867-70 Perf. 15
3 A1 1p blue grn
('70) 65.00 75.00
4 A1 1p yel grn ('68) 80.00 80.00
a. Toned paper 92.50 85.00
5 A2 4p lake, buff 45.00 65.00
a. 4p lake, rose 55.00 75.00
6 A3 6p rose 650.00 650.00
a. Toned paper ('68) 325.00 375.00
7 A4 1sh rose & blk 300.00 400.00
a. Toned paper 300.00 400.00
b. Double lined frame 300.00 400.00
c. As "b," bluish paper 400.00 400.00

Colored Margins
8 A4 1sh rose & blk 70.00 82.50
a. White paper 85.00 95.00
b. Bluish paper 825.00 1,000.
c. Central figure omitted 225,000.
Nos. 3-8 (6) 1,210. 1,352.

Examples of No. 8c have perfs. trimmed on
one or two sides.

1878 Wmk. 1 Perf. 14
9 A1 1p green 90.00 110.00
See #16-17, 19-20. For surcharge see #18.

Queen Victoria — A5

1880 Typo.
10 A5 1p green 80.00 95.00
11 A5 2½p red brown 110.00 130.00

1883-84 Wmk. 2
12 A5 ½p yellow 92.50 92.50
13 A5 ½p green 6.50 13.00
a. Imperf., pair 1,750.
14 A5 1p rose 37.50 40.00
15 A5 2½p ultra ('84) 3.00 17.50
Nos. 12-15 (4) 139.50 163.00

No. 13a probably is a plate proof.

1887 Litho.
16 A2 4p brick red 40.00 70.00
a. 4p brown red 50.00 80.00
17 A3 6p violet 19.00 50.00

No. 8 Handstamp
Surcharged in Violet

1888 Unwmk. Perf. 15
18 A4 4p on 1sh dp rose &
blk, toned paper 140.00 175.00
a. Double surcharge 8,500.
b. Inverted surcharge 55,000.
c. White paper 200.00 250.00

1889 Wmk. 2 Perf. 14
19 A1 1p carmine 2.75 8.25
20 A4 1sh brown 50.00 80.00
a. 1sh black brown 90.00 110.00

St. Ursula with Sheaf of
Lilies — A7

1899 Engr.
21 A7 ½p yellow grn 3.75 .60
a. "PFNNY" 92.50 140.00
b. "F" without cross bar 92.50 140.00
c. Horiz. pair, imperf. between 13,000.
22 A7 1p red 5.00 2.75
23 A7 2½p ultra 13.00 3.00
24 A7 4p chocolate 4.50 20.00
d. "PENCF" 825. 1,200.
25 A7 6p dark violet 6.50 3.50
26 A7 7p slate green 12.00 6.50
27 A7 1sh ocher 25.00 37.50
28 A7 5sh dark blue 80.00 95.00
Nos. 21-28 (8) 149.75 168.85

Edward VII — A8

1904 Typo. Wmk. 3
29 A8 ½p violet & bl grn 1.00 .60
30 A8 1p violet & scar 3.25 .55
31 A8 2p violet & bis 7.75 4.75
32 A8 2½p violet & ultra 3.25 2.75
33 A8 3p violet & blk 4.75 3.25
34 A8 6p violet & brn 3.50 3.25
35 A8 1sh green & scar 6.00 6.50
36 A8 2sh6p green & blk 35.00 72.50
37 A8 5sh green & ultra 62.50 87.50
Nos. 29-37 (9) 127.00 181.65

Numerals of 2p, 3p, 1sh and 2sh6p of type
A8 are in color on plain tablet.

George V — A9

Die I

For description of dies I and II see "Dies of
British Colonial Stamps" in Table of Contents.

1913 Ordinary Paper
38 A9 ½p green 3.75 6.00
39 A9 1p scarlet 2.75 17.50
a. 1p carmine 57.50 32.50
40 A9 2p gray 5.50 30.00
41 A9 2½p ultra 7.00 11.00

Chalky Paper
42 A9 3p vio, yel 3.25 8.00
43 A9 6p dl vio & red
vio 8.00 17.00
44 A9 1sh blk, green 3.75 11.00
45 A9 2sh6p blk & red, bl 57.50 60.00
46 A9 5sh grn & red, yel 45.00 140.00
Nos. 38-46 (9) 136.50 300.50

Numerals of 2p, 3p, 1sh and 2sh6p of type
A9 are in color on plain tablet.

1921 Die II Wmk. 4
47 A9 ½p green 9.50 47.50
48 A9 1p carmine 6.50 30.00

For overprints see Nos. MR1-MR2.

Colony Seal — A10

1922 Wmk. 3
49 A10 3p violet, yel 1.10 21.00
50 A10 1sh black, emerald 1.00 17.50
51 A10 2sh6p blk & red, bl 7.25 14.00
52 A10 5sh grn & red, yel 42.50 125.00
Nos. 49-52 (4) 51.85 177.50

1922-28 Wmk. 4
53 A10 ½p green 1.25 3.50
54 A10 1p rose red .80 .80
55 A10 1p violet ('27) 1.40 5.00
56 A10 1½p rose red
('27) 2.10 3.25
57 A10 1½p fawn ('28) 2.25 1.90
58 A10 2p gray 1.40 7.75
59 A10 2½p ultra 3.25 24.00
60 A10 2½p orange ('23) 1.75 2.10
61 A10 3p dl vio, yel
('28) 3.25 15.00
62 A10 5p dl lil & ol grn
('28) 7.75 60.00
63 A10 6p dl vio & red
vio 2.10 9.00
a. 6p brown lilac & red violet 2.10 9.00
64 A10 1sh blk, emer
('28) 3.50 19.00
65 A10 2sh6p blk & red, bl
('28) 27.50 62.50
66 A10 5sh grn & red,
yel ('23) 27.50 95.00
Nos. 53-66 (14) 85.80 308.80

The ½, 1, 2 and 2½p are on ordinary paper,
the others on chalky.

Numerals of 1½p of type A10 are in color on
plain tablet.

Common Design Types
pictured following the introduction.

Silver Jubilee Issue
Common Design Type

1935, May 6 Engr. Perf. 11x12
69 CD301 1p car & dk blue 1.10 7.00
70 CD301 1½p black & ultra 1.10 6.00
71 CD301 2½p ultra & brn 3.00 5.50
72 CD301 1sh brn vio & ind 17.00 29.00
Nos. 69-72 (4) 22.20 47.50
Set, never hinged 32.50

Coronation Issue
Common Design Type

1937, May 12 Perf. 11x11½
73 CD302 1p dark carmine .40 2.00
74 CD302 1½p brown .40 2.00
75 CD302 2½p deep ultra .40 1.00
Nos. 73-75 (3) 1.20 5.00
Set, never hinged 1.75

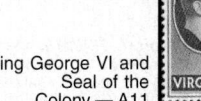

King George VI and
Seal of the
Colony — A11

1938-47 Photo. Perf. 14
76 A11 ½p green .90 .90
77 A11 1p scarlet 1.25 1.00
78 A11 1½p red brown 1.50 1.25
79 A11 2p gray 1.50 1.25
80 A11 2½p ultra 2.00 1.50
81 A11 3p orange 1.25 1.00
82 A11 6p deep violet 3.50 1.00
83 A11 1sh olive bister 2.50 2.00
84 A11 2sh6p sepia 11.00 5.00
85 A11 5sh rose lake 11.00 6.00
86 A11 10sh brt blue ('47) 6.00 11.00
87 A11 £1 gray blk ('47) 10.00 25.00
Nos. 76-87 (12) 49.40 56.90
Set, never hinged 70.00

Peace Issue
Common Design Type

Perf. 13½x14
1946, Nov. 1 Engr. Wmk. 4
88 CD303 1½p red brown .25 .25
89 CD303 3p orange .25 .25

Silver Wedding Issue
Common Design Types

1949, Jan. 3 Photo. *Perf. 14x14½*
90 CD304 2½p brt ultra .35 .35

Engr.; Name Typo.
Perf. 11½x11
91 CD305 £1 gray black 18.50 21.00

UPU Issue
Common Design Types
Engr.; Name Typo. on Nos. 93 & 94
1949, Oct. 10 *Perf. 13½, 11x11½*
92 CD306 2½p ultra .40 *1.75*
93 CD307 3p deep orange 1.25 *2.00*
94 CD308 6p red lilac .50 .40
95 CD309 1sh olive .45 .45
Nos. 92-95 (4) 2.60 4.60

University Issue
Common Design Types
1951 Engr. *Perf. 14x14½*
96 CD310 3c red brn & gray blk .40 *2.00*
97 CD311 12c purple & black 1.10 *1.40*

Map of the Islands A12

1951, Apr. 2 Wmk. 4 *Perf. 14½x14*
98 A12 6c red orange .50 1.25
99 A12 12c purple 1.00 .50
100 A12 24c olive grn .65 1.00
101 A12 $1.20 carmine 2.50 1.50
Nos. 98-101 (4) 4.65 4.25

Restoration of the Legislative Council, 1950.

Sombrero Lighthouse — A13

Map of Jost van Dyke — A14

Designs: 3c, Sheep. 4c, Map, Anegada. 5c, Cattle. 8c, Map, Virgin Gorda. 12c, Map, Tortola. 24c, Badge of the Presidency. 60c, Dead Man's Chest. $1.20, Sir Francis Drake Channel. $2.40, Road Town. $4.80, Map, Virgin Islands.

1952, Apr. 15 *Perf. 12½x13, 13x12½*
102 A13 1c gray black .40 2.00
103 A14 2c deep green .85 .25
104 A14 3c choc & gray blk .45 1.25
105 A14 4c red .70 1.60
106 A14 5c gray blk & rose lake 1.40 .70
107 A14 8c ultra .85 *1.25*
108 A14 12c purple 1.25 *1.60*
109 A13 24c dk brown 1.00 .25
110 A14 60c blue & ol grn 4.00 11.00
111 A14 $1.20 ultra & blk 6.00 12.00
112 A14 $2.40 hn brn & dk grn 15.00 *16.00*
113 A14 $4.80 rose car & bl 19.00 19.00
Nos. 102-113 (12) 50.90 66.90

Coronation Issue
Common Design Type
1953, June 2 *Perf. 13½x14*
114 CD312 2c dk green & blk .40 *1.00*

Map of Tortola — A15

Brown Pelican A16

Designs: 1c, Virgin Islands sloop. 2c, Nelthrop Red Poll bull. 3c, Road Harbor. 4c, Mountain travel. 5c, St. Ursula. 8c, Beach scene. 12c, Boat launching. 24c, White Cedar tree. 60c, Skipjack tuna. $1.20, Treasury Square. $4.80, Magnificent frigatebird.

Perf. 13x12½
1956, Nov. 1 Engr. Wmk. 4
115 A15 ½c claret & blk .45 .25
116 A15 1c dk bl & grnsh bl 1.90 1.10
117 A15 2c black & ver .40 .25
118 A15 3c olive & brt bl .40 .45
119 A15 4c blue grn & brn .45 .45
120 A15 5c gray .50 .25
121 A15 8c dp ultra & org .75 .65
122 A15 12c car & brt ultra 2.50 1.10
123 A15 24c dull red & grn 1.25 1.00
124 A15 60c yel org & dk bl 10.00 12.00
125 A15 $1.20 car & yel grn 2.75 11.00

Perf. 12x11½
126 A16 $2.40 vio brn & dl yel 37.50 16.00
127 A16 $4.80 grnsh bl & dk brn 40.00 16.00
Nos. 115-127 (13) 98.85 60.50

Types of 1956 Surcharged

Perf. 13x12½
1962, Dec. 10 Wmk. 314
128 A15 1c on ½c .25 .25
129 A15 2c on 1c 1.25 .25
130 A15 3c on 2c .25 .25
131 A15 4c on 3c .25 .25
132 A15 5c on 4c .25 .25
133 A15 8c on 8c .35 .35
134 A15 10c on 12c .45 .45
135 A15 12c on 24c .65 .65
136 A15 25c on 60c 3.25 1.25
137 A15 70c on $1.20 .70 3.25

Perf. 12x11½
138 A16 $1.40 on $2.40 12.50 10.50
139 A16 $2.80 on $4.80 12.50 8.00
Nos. 128-139 (12) 32.65 25.70

Freedom from Hunger Issue
Common Design Type
1963, June 4 Photo. *Perf. 14x14½*
140 CD314 25c lilac .50 .50

Red Cross Centenary Issue
Common Design Type
Wmk. 314
1963, Sept. 2 Litho. *Perf. 13*
141 CD315 2c black & red .25 .25
142 CD315 25c ultra & red .55 .55

Shakespeare Issue
Common Design Type
1964, Apr. 23 Photo. *Perf. 14x14½*
143 CD316 10c ultramarine .45 .45

Bonito — A17

Map of Tortola Island — A18

2c, Seaplane at Soper's Hole. 3c, Brown pelican. 4c, Dead Man's Chest (mountain). 5c, Road Harbor. 6c, Fallen Jerusalem Island. 8c, The Baths, Virgin Gorda. 10c, Map of Virgin Islands. 12c, Ferry service, Tortola—St. Thomas. 15c, The Towers. 25c, Plane at Beef Island Airfield. $1, Virgin Gorda Island. $1.40, Yachts, Tortola. $2.80, Badge.

Perf. 13x12½
1964, Nov. 2 Engr. Wmk. 314
144 A17 1c gray ol & dk bl .35 2.40
145 A17 2c rose red & ol .35 .45
146 A17 3c grnsh bl & sep 4.25 2.40
147 A17 4c carmine & blk 1.10 2.40
148 A17 5c green & blk .90 1.60
149 A17 6c orange & blk .35 1.40
150 A17 8c pink & blk .35 1.00
151 A17 10c lt violet & mar 1.60 .45
152 A17 12c vio bl & Prus grn 2.75 3.50
153 A17 15c gray & yel grn .45 3.50
154 A17 25c pur & yel grn 13.00 3.50

Perf. 13x13½
Size: 27x30½mm
155 A18 70c bister brn & blk 5.25 8.00
156 A18 $1 red brn & yel grn 4.25 3.00
157 A18 $1.40 pink & blue 24.00 13.00

Perf. 11½x12
Size: 27x37mm
158 A18 $2.80 rose lilac & blk 26.00 13.00
Nos. 144-158 (15) 84.95 59.60

For surcharges & overprints see Nos. 173-175, 190-191.

ITU Issue
Common Design Type
Perf. 11x11½
1965, May 17 Litho. Wmk. 314
159 CD317 4c yellow & bl grn .25 .25
160 CD317 25c blue & org yel .70 .70

Intl. Cooperation Year Issue
Common Design Type
1965, Oct. 25 Wmk. 314 *Perf. 14½*
161 CD318 1c blue grn & cl .25 .25
162 CD318 25c lt violet & grn .55 .55

Churchill Memorial Issue
Common Design Type
1966, Jan. 24 Photo. *Perf. 14*
Design in Black, Gold and Carmine Rose
163 CD319 1c brt blue .25 .25
164 CD319 2c green .25 .25
165 CD319 10c brown .40 .40
166 CD319 25c violet 1.00 1.00
Nos. 163-166 (4) 1.90 1.90

Royal Visit Issue
Common Design Type
1966, Feb. 22 Litho. *Perf. 11x12*
167 CD320 4c violet blue .25 .25
168 CD320 70c dk car rose 2.00 2.00

Stamps of 1866 — A19

Designs: 5c, R.M.S. Atrato, 1866. 25c, Beechcraft mail plane on Beef Island Airfield and 6p stamp (No. 2). 60c, Landing mail at Road Town, 1866, and 1p stamp (No. 1).

Perf. 12½x13
1966, Apr. 25 Wmk. 314
169 A19 5c grn, yel, red & blk .25 .25
170 A19 10c yel, grn, red, blk & rose .25 .25
171 A19 25c lt grn, bl, red, blk & rose .75 .75
172 A19 60c bl, red, blk, & grn 1.50 1.50
Nos. 169-172 (4) 2.75 2.75

Centenary of Virgin Islands postage stamps.

Nos. 155, 157-158 Srchd. with New Value and Two Bars
Perf. 13x12½, 11½x12
1966, Sept. 15 Engr. Wmk. 314
173 A18 50c on 70c 2.00 2.00
174 A18 $1.50 on $1.40 3.75 3.75
175 A18 $3 on $2.80 3.75 3.75
Nos. 173-175 (3) 9.50 9.50

UNESCO Anniversary Issue
Common Design Type
1966, Dec. 1 Litho. *Perf. 14*
176 CD323 2c "Education" .25 .25
177 CD323 12c "Science" .25 .25
178 CD323 60c "Culture" .80 .80
Nos. 176-178 (3) 1.30 1.30

Map and Seal of Virgin Islands A20

Wmk. 314
1967, Apr. 18 Photo. *Perf. 14½*
179 A20 2c gold, grn & org .25 .25
180 A20 10c gold, rose red, grn & org .25 .25
181 A20 25c gold, red brn, grn & org .25 .25
182 A20 $1 gold, bl, grn & org .45 .45
Nos. 179-182 (4) 1.20 1.20

Introduction of new constitution.

Map of Virgin Islands, Bermuda and C.S. Mercury — A21

10c, Communications center, Chalwell, Virgin Islands. 50c, Cable ship Mercury.

1967, Sept. 14 Wmk. 314 *Perf. 14½*
183 A21 4c green & multi .25 .25
184 A21 10c dp plum & multi .25 .25
185 A21 50c bister & multi .60 .60
Nos. 183-185 (3) 1.10 1.10

Completion of the Bermuda-Tortola, Virgin Islands, telephone link.

Blue Marlin A22

Designs: 10c, Sergeant fish (cobia). 25c, Peto fish (Wahoo). 40c, Fishing boat, map of Virgin Islands and fishing records.

Perf. 12½x12
1968, Jan. 2 Photo. Wmk. 314
186 A22 2c multicolored .25 .25
187 A22 10c multicolored .30 .30
188 A22 25c multicolored .50 .50
189 A22 40c multicolored .90 .90
Nos. 186-189 (4) 1.95 1.95

Game fishing in Virgin Islands waters.

Nos. 151 and 154 Ovptd. "1968 / INTERNATIONAL / YEAR FOR / HUMAN RIGHTS"
1968, July 1 Engr. *Perf. 13x12½*
190 A17 10c lt violet & maroon .25 .25
191 A17 25c purple & green .40 .40

Martin Luther King, Bible and Sword A23

1968, Oct. 15 Litho. *Perf. 14*
192 A23 4c dl org, vio & blk .35 .35
193 A23 25c dl org, gray grn & blk .45 .45

Martin Luther King, Jr. (1929-68), American civil rights leader.

DHC-6 Twin Otter A24

Designs: 10c, Hawker Siddeley 748. 25c, Hawker Siddeley Heron. $1, Badge from cap of Royal Engineers.

1968, Dec. 16   Unwmk.   Perf. 14

194	A24	2c brn red & multi	.25	1.00
195	A24	10c grnsh bl, blk & red	.25	.25
196	A24	25c ultra, lt bl, org & blk	.30	.25
197	A24	$1 green & multi	1.40	2.25
		Nos. 194-197 (4)	2.20	3.75

Opening of enlarged Beef Island Airport.

Long John Silver and Jim Hawkins — A25

Scenes from Treasure Island: 10c, Jim's escape from the pirates, horiz. 40c, The fight with Israel Hands. $1, Treasure trove, horiz.

Perf. 13½x13, 13x13½

1969, Mar. 18   Photo.   Wmk. 314

198	A25	4c dp car & multi	.35	.25
199	A25	10c multicolored	.40	.25
200	A25	40c ultra & multi	.50	.65
201	A25	$1 black & multi	1.10	1.75
		Nos. 198-201 (4)	2.35	2.90

Robert Louis Stevenson (1850-94). The Virgin Islands were used as the setting for "Treasure Island."

Tourist and Rock Grouper — A26

Tourist Publicity: 10c, Yachts in Road Harbor, Tortola, horiz. 20c, Tourists on beach in Virgin Gorda National Park, horiz. $1, Pipe organ cactus and woman tourist.

1969, Oct. 20   Litho.   Perf. 12½

202	A26	2c multicolored	.25	.55
203	A26	10c multicolored	.25	.25
204	A26	20c multicolored	.35	.25
205	A26	$1 multicolored	1.25	2.00
		Nos. 202-205 (4)	2.10	3.05

Carib Canoe A27

Ships: 1c, Santa Maria. 2c, H.M.S. Elizabeth Bonaventure. 3c, Dutch buccaneer, 1660. 4c, Thetis (1827 merchant ship). 5c, Henry Morgan's ship. 6c, Frigate Boreas. 8c, Schooner L'Eclair, 1804. 10c, H.M.S. Formidable. 12c, H.M.S. Nymph burning. 15c, Packet Windsor Castle fighting French privateer. 25c, Frigate Astrea, 1808. 50c, H.M.S. Rhone. $1, Tortola sloop. $2, H.M.S. Frobisher. $3, Booker Line Viking (cargo ship). $5, Hydrofoil Sun Arrow.

Wmk. 314 Sideways

1970, Feb. 16   Perf. 14½

206	A27	½c brn & ocher	.25	.25
207	A27	1c bl, lt grn & vio	.25	.25
208	A27	2c red brn, org & gray	.25	.25
209	A27	3c ver, bl & brn	.25	.25
210	A27	4c brn, bl & vio bl	.25	.25
211	A27	5c grn, pink & blk	.25	.25
212	A27	6c lil, grn & blk	.25	.25
213	A27	8c lt ol, yel & brn	.30	.30
214	A27	10c ocher, bl & brn	.35	.40
215	A27	12c sep, yel & dp cl	.50	.60
216	A27	15c org, grnsh bl & brn	.45	.55
217	A27	25c bl, grnsh gray & pur	.65	.85
218	A27	50c rose car, lt grn & brn	1.40	1.60
219	A27	$1 brn, sal pink & dk grn	2.75	3.00
220	A27	$2 gray & yel	5.50	6.25
221	A27	$3 brn, ol bis & dk bl	8.50	9.50
222	A27	$5 lil & gray	14.00	15.00
		Nos. 206-222 (17)	36.15	39.80

For overprints see Nos. 235-236.

1973, Oct. 17   Wmk. 314 Upright

206a	A27	½c	.85	5.75
209a	A27	3c	2.00	2.25
210a	A27	4c	2.00	4.25
211a	A27	5c	2.00	2.10
214a	A27	10c	2.40	2.40
215a	A27	12c	3.25	3.25
		Nos. 206a-215a (6)	12.50	20.00

Wmk. 314 Sideways

1974, Nov. 11   Perf. 13½

207a	A27	1c	1.25	1.90
214b	A27	10c	2.25	2.10
215b	A27	12c	2.25	3.00
216a	A27	15c	3.25	3.00
		Nos. 207a-216a (4)	9.00	10.00

"A Tale of Two Cities," by Dickens A28

Charles Dickens: 10c, "Oliver Twist." 25c, "Great Expectations."

1970, May 4   Litho.   Perf. 14½

223	A28	5c blk, gray & pink	.25	.25
224	A28	10c blk, pale yel grn & blue	.35	.35
225	A28	25c blk, yel & lt yel grn	.50	.95
		Nos. 223-225 (3)	1.10	1.55

Hospital Visitor A29

10c, Girl Scouts receiving 1st aid training at lake side. 25c, Red Cross & Virgin Islands coat of arms.

1970, Aug. 10   Wmk. 314   Perf. 14

226	A29	4c multicolored	.25	.25
227	A29	10c multicolored	.45	.25
228	A29	25c multicolored	1.10	1.10
		Nos. 226-228 (3)	1.80	1.60

Centenary of British Red Cross.

Mary Read — A30

Pirates: 10c, George Lowther. 30c, Edward Teach (Blackbeard). 60c, Henry Morgan.

1970, Nov. 16   Wmk. 314   Perf. 14

229	A30	½c dp rose & multi	.25	.25
230	A30	10c blue grn & multi	.40	.40
231	A30	30c ultra & multi	1.20	1.20
232	A30	60c multicolored	1.60	1.60
		Nos. 229-232 (4)	3.45	3.45

Children Spelling out "UNICEF" A31

1971, Dec. 13

233	A31	15c tan & multi	.25	.25
234	A31	30c lt blue & multi	.30	.30

25th anniv. of UNICEF.

Nos. 210 and 217 Dated "1972" and Ovptd. "VISIT OF / H.R.H. / THE / PRINCESS MARGARET"

1972, Mar. 7   Perf. 14½

235	A27	4c multicolored	.40	.40
236	A27	25c multicolored	1.00	1.00

Seaman, 1800 — A32

10c, Boatswain, 1787-1807. 30c, Captain, 1795-1812. 60c, Admiral in full dress uniform, 1787-95.

1972, Mar. 17   Perf. 14x13½

237	A32	½c yellow & multi	.25	.25
238	A32	10c brt pink & multi	.40	.40
239	A32	30c orange & multi	1.10	1.10
240	A32	60c blue & multi	2.25	2.25
		Nos. 237-240 (4)	4.00	4.00

INTERPEX, 14th Intl. Stamp Exhib., NYC, Mar. 17-19.

Silver Wedding Issue, 1972
Common Design Type

Design: Queen Elizabeth II, Prince Philip, sailfish and "Sir Winston Churchill" yacht.

1972, Nov. 24   Photo.   Perf. 14x14½

241	CD324	15c ultra & multi	.25	.25
242	CD324	25c Prus blue & multi	.25	.25

Allison Tuna A33

1972, Dec. 12   Litho.   Perf. 13½x14

243	A33	½c Wahoo	.25	.25
244	A33	½c Blue marlin	.25	.25
a.		Horiz. or vert. pair, #243-244	.25	
245	A33	15c shown	.45	.45
246	A33	25c White marlin	.70	.70
247	A33	50c Sailfish	1.15	1.15
248	A33	$1 Dolphin	3.00	3.00
a.		Souvenir sheet of 6, #243-248	13.50	13.50
		Nos. 243-248 (6)	5.80	5.80

Game fish.

Lettsom House and Medal — A34

Themes from Quaker History: ½c, Dr. John Coakley Lettsom, vert. 15c, Dr. William Thornton, vert. 30c, US Capitol, Washington, DC,

---

and Dr. Thornton who designed it. $1, Library Hall, Philadelphia, and William Penn.

1973, Mar. 9   Litho.   Perf. 13½

249	A34	½c rose & multi	.25	.25
250	A34	10c multicolored	.25	.25
251	A34	15c multicolored	.25	.25
252	A34	30c ultra & multi	.35	.35
253	A34	$1 multicolored	1.10	1.10
		Nos. 249-253 (5)	2.20	2.20

INTERPEX, 15th Intl. Phil. Exhib., NYC, Mar. 9-11.

Hummingbirds on 1c Coin — A35

Coins and Beach Scenes: 5c, Zenaida doves. 10c, Kingfisher. 25c, Mangrove cuckoos. 50c, Brown pelicans. $1, Magnificent frigate birds.

1973, June 30   Wmk. 314   Perf. 14½

254	A35	1c orange & multi	.25	.45
255	A35	5c lt blue & multi	.70	.25
256	A35	10c pale ultra & multi	1.00	.25
257	A35	25c yellow & multi	1.25	.25
258	A35	50c lt violet & multi	1.40	1.60
259	A35	$1 ultra & multi	1.75	3.00
		Nos. 254-259 (6)	6.35	5.80

New Virgin Islands coinage.

Princess Anne's Wedding Issue
Common Design Type

1973, Nov. 16   Wmk. 314   Perf. 14

260	CD325	5c citron & multi	.25	.25
261	CD325	50c blue grn & multi	.25	.25

Virgin and Child, by Bernardino Pintoricchio — A36

Christmas (Paintings of the Virgin and Child by): 3c, Lorenzo Credi. 25c, Carlo Crivelli. 50c, Bernardino Luini.

1973, Dec. 7   Perf. 14x14½

262	A36	½c lt green & multi	.25	.25
263	A36	3c rose & multi	.25	.25
264	A36	25c ocher & multi	.30	.30
265	A36	50c lt blue & multi	.60	.60
		Nos. 262-265 (4)	1.40	1.40

Arms of French Minesweeper Canopus — A37

1974, Mar. 22   Wmk. 314   Perf. 14

266	A37	5c shown	.25	.25
267	A37	18c USS Saginaw	.35	.35
268	A37	25c HMS Rothesay	.40	.40
269	A37	50c HMCS Ottawa	.85	.85
a.		Souvenir sheet of 4, #266-269	2.50	2.50
		Nos. 266-269 (4)	1.85	1.85

INTERPEX Phil. Exhib., NYC, Mar. 22-24.

Famous Explorers — A38

1974, Aug. 19 *Perf. 14½*

270	A38	5c Columbus	.30	.30
271	A38	10c Sir Walter Raleigh	.40	.40
272	A38	25c Sir Martin Frobisher	.45	.45
273	A38	40c Sir Francis Drake	.85	.85
a.		Souvenir sheet of 4, #270-273	2.50	2.50
		Nos. 270-273 (4)	2.00	2.00

Sea Shells A39

1974, Sept. 30 *Perf. 13x13½*

274	A39	5c Trumpet triton	.45	.45
275	A39	18c West Indian murex	1.00	1.00
276	A39	25c Bleeding tooth	1.25	1.25
277	A39	75c Virgin Island latirus	3.00	3.00
a.		Souvenir sheet of 4, #274-277	7.00	7.00
		Nos. 274-277 (4)	5.70	5.70

St. Mary, Aldermanbury, London, — A40

Design: 50c, St. Mary, Fulton, Missouri.

1974, Nov. 30 **Wmk. 373** *Perf. 14*

278	A40	10c multicolored	.25	.25
279	A40	50c multicolored	.45	.45
a.		Souvenir sheet of 2, #278-279	.90	.90

Sir Winston Churchill (1874-1965).

Figurehead from "Boreas" — A41

Figureheads: 18c, The Golden Hind. 40c, Crowned lion from the "Superb." 85c, Warrior, from the "Formidable."

Perf. 13½x13

1975, Mar. 14 **Wmk. 314**

280	A41	5c multicolored	.25	.25
281	A41	18c multicolored	.50	.50
282	A41	40c multicolored	.70	.70
283	A41	85c multicolored	1.40	1.40
a.		Souv. sheet of 4, #280-283, perf. 14	3.25	3.25
		Nos. 280-283 (4)	2.85	2.85

INTERPEX, 17th Phil. Exhib., NYC, Mar. 14-16.

Rock Beauty A42

Fish: 1c, Squirrelfish. 3c, Queen triggerfish. 5c, Blue angelfish. 8c, Stoplight parrotfish. 10c, Queen angelfish. 12c, Nassau grouper. 13c, Blue tang. 15c, Sergeant major. 18c, Jewfish. 20c, Bluehead wrasse. 25c, Gray angelfish. 60c, Glasseye snapper. $1, Blue chromis. $2.50, French angelfish. $3, Queen parrotfish. $5, Four-eye butterflyfish.

1975 **Wmk. 373** *Perf. 14*

Inscribed "1975" Below Design

284	A42	½c shown	.25	.25
285	A42	1c multicolored	.55	.65
286	A42	3c multicolored	1.50	1.75
287	A42	5c multicolored	.35	.45
288	A42	8c multicolored	.35	.45
289	A42	10c multicolored	.35	.45
290	A42	12c multicolored	.55	.65
291	A42	13c multicolored	.55	.65
292	A42	15c multicolored	.55	.65
293	A42	18c multicolored	1.25	1.50
294	A42	20c multicolored	.75	.95
295	A42	25c multicolored	1.60	1.90
296	A42	60c multicolored	1.90	2.40
297	A42	$1 multicolored	2.75	3.25
298	A42	$2.50 multicolored	4.50	5.50
299	A42	$3 multicolored	6.25	7.25
300	A42	$5 multicolored	6.75	8.00
		Nos. 284-300 (17)	30.75	36.70

Issue dates: $5, Aug. 15. Others, June 16.

1977

Inscribed "1977" Below Design

284a	A42	½c multicolored	.55	.55
287a	A42	5c multicolored	1.00	1.00
288a	A42	8c multicolored	1.00	1.00
289a	A42	10c multicolored	1.00	1.00
290a	A42	12c multicolored	1.40	1.40
291a	A42	13c multicolored	1.40	1.40
292a	A42	15c multicolored	1.40	1.40
294a	A42	20c multicolored	2.00	2.00
		Nos. 284a-294a (8)	9.75	9.75

St. Georges Parish School A43

Designs: 25c, Legislative Council Building. 40c, Mace and gavel of Legislative Council. 75c, Scroll with dates of historical events.

1975, Nov. 27 **Litho.** **Wmk. 373**

301	A43	5c ultra & multi	.25	.25
302	A43	25c green & multi	.25	.25
303	A43	40c ocher & multi	.25	.25
304	A43	75c ultra & multi	.35	.35
		Nos. 301-304 (4)	1.10	1.10

Restoration of Legislative Council, 25th anniv.

Copper Mine Point A44

Historic Sites: 18c, Dr. Thornton's Ruin, Pleasant Valley. 50c, Callwood distillery. 75c, The Dungeon.

1976, Mar. 12 **Litho.** *Perf. 14½*

305	A44	5c red & multi	.25	.25
306	A44	18c red & multi	.25	.25
307	A44	50c red & multi	.40	.40
308	A44	75c red & multi	.60	.60
		Nos. 305-308 (4)	1.50	1.50

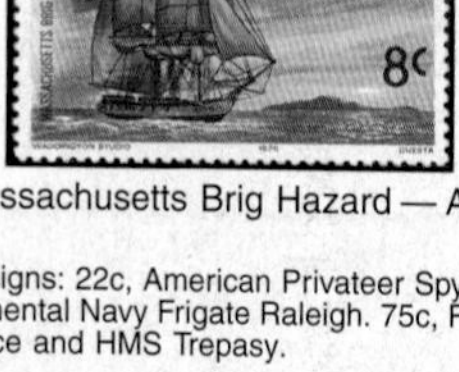

Massachusetts Brig Hazard — A45

Designs: 22c, American Privateer Spy. 40c, Continental Navy Frigate Raleigh. 75c, Frigate Alliance and HMS Trepasy.

1976, May 29 **Wmk. 373** *Perf. 14*

309	A45	8c multicolored	.30	.25
310	A45	22c multicolored	.65	.45
311	A45	40c multicolored	1.20	1.00
312	A45	75c multicolored	2.40	1.75
a.		Souvenir sheet of 4, #309-312	9.00	9.00
		Nos. 309-312 (4)	4.55	3.45

American Bicentennial.

Government House, Tortola — A46

Designs: 15c, Government House, St. Croix, vert. 30c, Flags of US and British Virgin Islands, vert. 75c, Arms of British and US Virgin Islands.

1976, Oct. 29 **Litho.** *Perf. 14*

313	A46	8c green & multi	.25	.25
314	A46	15c green & multi	.25	.25
315	A46	30c green & multi	.25	.25
316	A46	75c green & multi	.55	.55
		Nos. 313-316 (4)	1.30	1.30

US and British Virgin Islands Friendship Day, 5th anniversary.

Holy Bible — A47

8c, Queen visiting Agricultural Station, Tortola, 1966. 60c, Presentation of Holy Bible.

1977, Feb. 7 *Perf. 14x13½*

317	A47	8c silver & multi	.25	.25
318	A47	30c silver & multi	.25	.25
319	A47	60c silver & multi	.25	.25
		Nos. 317-319 (3)	.75	.75

25th anniv. of the reign of Elizabeth II. For overprints see Nos. 324-326.

Virgin Islands Chart, 1739 — A48

18th Century Maps of Virgin Islands: 22c, 1758. 30c, 1775. 75c, 1779.

1977, June 12 **Wmk. 373** *Perf. 13½*

320	A48	8c multicolored	.30	.25
321	A48	22c multicolored	.65	.60
322	A48	30c multicolored	.90	.80
323	A48	75c multicolored	1.90	1.90
		Nos. 320-323 (4)	3.75	3.55

Type of 1977 Inscribed "ROYAL VISIT"

Designs: 5c, Queen visiting Agricultural Station, Tortola, 1966. 25c, Holy Bible. 50c, Presentation of Holy Bible.

1977, Oct. 26 **Litho.** *Perf. 14x13½*

324	A47	5c yel brn & multi	.25	.25
325	A47	25c dk blue & multi	.25	.25
326	A47	50c purple & multi	.40	.40
		Nos. 324-326 (3)	.90	.90

Caribbean visit of Queen Elizabeth II.

Divers Checking Equipment — A49

Tourist publicity: 5c, Cup coral inside bow of "Rhone." 8c, Sponge growing on superstructure of "Rhone." 22c, Sponge and cup coral. 30c, Scuba diver searching for sponges in cave. 75c, Marine life.

1977, Dec. 15 **Wmk. 373** *Perf. 13½*

327	A49	½c multicolored	.25	.25
328	A49	5c multicolored	.25	.25
329	A49	8c multicolored	.25	.25
330	A49	22c multicolored	.65	.65
331	A49	30c multicolored	.85	.85
332	A49	75c multicolored	1.60	1.60
		Nos. 327-332 (6)	3.85	3.85

Corals A50

1978, Feb. 10 *Perf. 14*

333	A50	8c Fire	.35	.35
334	A50	15c Staghorn	.55	.55
335	A50	40c Brain	1.00	1.00
336	A50	75c Elkhorn	2.10	2.10
		Nos. 333-336 (4)	4.00	4.00

Elizabeth II Coronation Anniversary Issue

Common Design Types

Souvenir Sheet

1978, June 2 **Unwmk.** *Perf. 15*

337	Sheet of 6	2.25	2.25
a.	CD326 50c Falcon of the Plantagenets	.35	.35
b.	CD327 50c Elizabeth II	.35	.35
c.	CD328 50c Iguana	.35	.35

No. 337 contains 2 se-tenant strips of Nos. 337a-337c, separated by horizontal gutter.

Lignum Vitae A51

Flowering Trees: 22c, Ginger thomas. 40c, Dog almond. 75c, White cedar.

1978, Sept. 4 **Litho.** *Perf. 13x13½*

338	A51	8c multicolored	.30	.30
339	A51	22c multicolored	.45	.45
340	A51	40c multicolored	.60	.60
341	A51	75c multicolored	.90	.90
a.		Souvenir sheet of 4, #338-341	2.00	2.00
		Nos. 338-341 (4)	2.25	2.25

Eurema Lisa A52

Butterflies: 22c, Dione vanillae. 30c, Heliconius charitonius. 75c, Hemiargus hanno.

1978, Dec. 4 **Wmk. 373** *Perf. 14*

342	A52	5c multicolored	.35	.25
343	A52	22c multicolored	1.25	1.00
a.		Sheet of 9, 6 #342, 3 #343	5.00	5.00
344	A52	30c multicolored	1.60	1.40
345	A52	75c multicolored	4.00	3.50
		Nos. 342-345 (4)	7.20	6.15

Spiny Lobsters A53

Conservation: 15c, Iguana, vert. 22c, Hawksbill turtle. 75c, Black coral, vert.

1979, Feb. 10 **Litho.**

346	A53	5c multicolored	.25	.25
347	A53	15c multicolored	.45	.45
348	A53	22c multicolored	.80	.80
349	A53	75c multicolored	1.75	1.75
a.		Souvenir sheet of 4, #346-349	4.50	4.50
		Nos. 346-349 (4)	3.25	3.25

British Virgin Islands ½c USCy Strawberry Cactus — A54

Native Cacti: 5c, Snowy cactus. 13c, Barrel cactus. 22c, Tree cactus. 30c, Prickly pear. 75c, Dildo cactus.

1979, May 7   **Wmk. 373**   **Perf. 14**
350	A54	½c multicolored	.25	.25
351	A54	5c multicolored	.25	.25
352	A54	13c multicolored	.35	.35
353	A54	22c multicolored	.50	.50
354	A54	30c multicolored	.55	.55
355	A54	75c multicolored	.90	.90
		Nos. 350-355 (6)	2.80	2.80

West Indies Girl and Church — A55

Children and IYC Emblem: 10c, African boy and dancers. 13c, Asian girl and children playing. $1, European girl and bicycle.

1979, July 9   **Perf. 14x14½**
356	A55	5c multicolored	.25	.25
357	A55	10c multicolored	.25	.25
358	A55	13c multicolored	.25	.25
359	A55	$1 multicolored	.40	.40
a.		Souvenir sheet of 4, #356-359	1.25	1.25
		Nos. 356-359 (4)	1.15	1.15

International Year of the Child.

No. 118 — A56

Rowland Hill's Signature and: 13c, Virgin Islands No. 11, horiz. 75c, Unissued Great Britain 2d stamp, 1910, horiz. $1, Virgin Islands No. 8c.

1979, Oct. 1   **Photo.**   **Perf. 13½**
360	A56	5c multicolored	.25	.25
361	A56	13c multicolored	.25	.25
362	A56	75c multicolored	.60	.60
		Nos. 360-362 (3)	1.10	1.10

Souvenir Sheet
363	A56	$1 multicolored	.90	.90

Sir Rowland Hill (1795-1879), originator of penny postage.
For overprints see Nos. 389-390.

Pencil Urchin — A57

½c, Calcified algae. 1c, Purple-tipped sea anemone. 3c, Starfish. 8c, Triton's trumpet. 10c, Christmas tree worms. 13c, Flamingo tongue snails. 15c, Spider crab. 18c, Sea squirts. 20c, True tulip. 25c, Rooster tail conch. 30c, Fighting conch. 60c, Mangrove crab. $1, Coral polyps. $2.50, Peppermint shrimp. $3, West Indian murex. $5, Carpet anemone.

"1979" or "1980" Below Design

1979-80   **Litho.**   **Perf. 14**
364	A57	½c multicolored	.25	.25
365	A57	1c multicolored	.25	.25
366	A57	3c multicolored	.25	.25
367	A57	5c shown	.25	.25
368	A57	8c multicolored	.25	.25
369	A57	10c multicolored	.25	.25
370	A57	13c multicolored	.25	.25
371	A57	15c multicolored	.35	.35
372	A57	18c multicolored	.35	.35
373	A57	20c multicolored	.40	.40
374	A57	25c multicolored	.50	.55
375	A57	30c multicolored	.70	.75
376	A57	60c multicolored	1.50	1.60
377	A57	$1 multicolored	2.25	2.40
378	A57	$2.50 multicolored	5.50	6.00
379	A57	$3 multicolored	6.75	7.25
380	A57	$5 multicolored	11.50	12.50
		Nos. 364-380 (17)	31.55	33.90

Issued: 5, 8, 10, 15, 20, 25c, $2.50, $3, 12/17/79; others, 4/1/80. Date of year of issue below design.
For overprints see Nos. O1-O15.

"1982" Below Design

1982, Aug. 27   **Chalky Paper**
367a	A57	5c multicolored	.95	.95
368a	A57	8c multicolored	.95	.95
370a	A57	13c multicolored	1.90	1.90
371a	A57	15c multicolored	1.90	1.90
373a	A57	20c multicolored	1.60	1.60
375a	A57	30c multicolored	2.60	2.60
		Nos. 367a-375a (6)	9.90	9.90

Rotary Athletic Meet, Tortola, Emblem A58

22c, Paul P. Harris. 60c, Mount Sage National Park. $1, Anniversary emblem.

1980, Mar. 3   **Litho.**   **Perf. 13½x14**
381	A58	8c shown	.25	.25
382	A58	22c multicolored	.25	.25
383	A58	60c multicolored	.50	.50
384	A58	$1 multicolored	.80	.80
a.		Souvenir sheet of 4, #381-384	2.00	2.00
		Nos. 381-384 (4)	1.80	1.80

Rotary International, 75th anniv.

Brown Booby, London 1980 Emblem A59

25c, Magnificent frigatebird. 50c, White-tailed tropic bird. 75c, Brown pelican.

1980, May 6   **Wmk. 373**   **Perf. 14**
385	A59	20c shown	.35	.35
386	A59	25c multicolored	.45	.45
387	A59	50c multicolored	.70	.70
388	A59	75c multicolored	.95	.95
a.		Souvenir sheet of 4, #385-388	2.50	2.50
		Nos. 385-388 (4)	2.45	2.45

London 80 Intl. Stamp Exhib., May 6-14.

Nos. 361-362 Overprinted

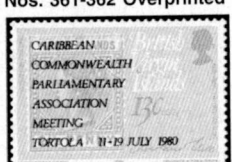

CARIBBEAN COMMONWEALTH PARLIAMENTARY ASSOCIATION MEETING TORTOLA 11-19 JULY 1980

1980, July 7   **Photo.**   **Perf. 13½**
389	A56	13c multicolored	.25	.25
390	A56	75c multicolored	.55	.55

Sir Francis Drake — A60

1980, Sept. 26   **Litho.**   **Perf. 14½**
391	A60	8c shown	.45	.45
392	A60	15c Queen Elizabeth I	.75	.75
393	A60	30c Drake knighted	.90	.90
394	A60	75c Golden Hinde	1.90	1.90
a.		Souvenir sheet of 4, #391-394	4.25	4.25
		Nos. 391-394 (4)	4.00	4.00

400th anniv. of circumnavigation of the world.

Jost Van Dyke A61

1980, Dec. 1   **Wmk. 373**   **Perf. 14**
395	A61	2c shown	.25	.25
396	A61	5c Peter Island	.25	.25
397	A61	13c Virgin Gorda	.25	.25
398	A61	22c Anegada	.35	.35
399	A61	30c Norman Island	.40	.40
400	A61	$1 Tortola	1.25	1.25
a.		Souvenir sheet of 1	1.60	1.60
		Nos. 395-400 (6)	2.75	2.75

Dancing Lady — A62

1981, Mar. 3   **Litho.**   **Perf. 11**
401	A62	5c shown	.30	.30
402	A62	20c Love in the mist	.35	.35
403	A62	22c Red pineapple	.35	.35
404	A62	75c Dutchman's pipe	1.10	1.10
405	A62	$1 Maiden apple	1.25	1.25
		Nos. 401-405 (5)	3.35	3.35

Royal Wedding Issue
Common Design Type

1981, July 22   **Litho.**   **Perf. 14**
406	CD331	10c Bouquet	.25	.25
407	CD331	35c Charles, Queen Mother	.25	.25
408	CD331	$1.25 Couple	.80	.80
		Nos. 406-408 (3)	1.30	1.30

#406-408 each se-tenant with decorative label.

Duke of Edinburgh's Awards, 25th Anniv. — A63

1981, Sept. 16   **Wmk. 373**   **Perf. 14**
409	A63	10c Stamp collecting	.25	.25
410	A63	15c Running	.25	.25
411	A63	50c Camping	.30	.30
412	A63	$1 Duke of Edinburgh	.60	.60
		Nos. 409-412 (4)	1.40	1.40

Intl. Year of the Disabled A64

1981, Oct. 19   **Litho.**   **Perf. 14**
413	A64	15c Children	.25	.25
414	A64	20c Fort Charlotte Children's Center	.30	.30
415	A64	30c Playing music	.35	.35
416	A64	$1 Center, diff.	1.15	1.15
		Nos. 413-416 (4)	2.05	2.05

A65

Virgin and Child (Christmas): Details from Adoration of the Shepherds, by Rubens. 50c, horiz.

1981, Nov. 30   **Litho.**   **Perf. 14**
417	A65	5c multicolored	.25	.25
418	A65	15c multicolored	.25	.25
419	A65	30c multicolored	.50	.50
420	A65	$1 multicolored	2.00	2.00
		Nos. 417-420 (4)	3.00	3.00

Souvenir Sheet
421	A65	50c multicolored	3.00	3.00

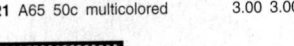

A66

Hummingbirds on local flora: 15c, Green-throated carib, erythrina. 30c, Same, bougainvillea. 35c, Antillean crested hummingbird, granadilla passiflora. $1.25, Same, hibiscus.

1982, Apr. 15   **Litho.**   **Perf. 14x14½**
422	A66	15c multicolored	.50	.50
423	A66	30c multicolored	1.00	1.00
424	A66	35c multicolored	1.25	1.25
425	A66	$1.25 multicolored	3.75	3.75
		Nos. 422-425 (4)	6.50	6.50

10th Anniv. of Lions Club of Tortola — A67

1982, May 3   **Perf. 13½x14**
426	A67	10c Helping disabled	.25	.25
427	A67	20c Headquarters	.30	.30
428	A67	30c Map	.40	.40
429	A67	$1.50 Emblem	2.25	2.25
a.		Souvenir sheet of 4, #426-429	4.00	4.00
		Nos. 426-429 (4)	3.20	3.20

Princess Diana Issue
Common Design Type

1982, July 1   **Litho.**   **Perf. 14**
430	CD333	10c Arms	.25	.25
431	CD333	35c Diana	.45	.45
432	CD333	50c Wedding	.60	.60
433	CD333	$1.50 Portrait	2.25	2.25
		Nos. 430-433 (4)	3.55	3.55

10th Anniv. of Air BVI (Natl. Airline)
A68

1982, Sept. 10 Wmk. 373 *Perf. 14*

434 A68 10c Douglas DC-3 .30 .30
435 A68 15c Britten-Norman Islander .55 .55
436 A68 60c Hawker-Siddeley 2.40 2.40
437 A68 75c Planes 2.75 2.75
Nos. 434-437 (4) 6.00 6.00

Scouting Year
A69

8c, Emblem, Flag raising. 20c, Cub scout, nature study. 50c, Kayak, sea scout. $1, Camp Brownsea Is., Baden-Powell.

1982, Nov. 18

438 A69 8c multicolored .25 .25
439 A69 20c multicolored .35 .35
440 A69 50c multicolored .90 .90
441 A69 $1 multicolored 1.90 1.90
Nos. 438-441 (4) 3.40 3.40

Commonwealth Day — A70

1983, Mar. 14 *Perf. 13½x14*

442 A70 10c Legislature in session .25 .25
443 A70 30c Wind surfing .50 .50
444 A70 35c Globe .60 .60
445 A70 75c Flags 1.25 1.25
Nos. 442-445 (4) 2.60 2.60

Nursing Week
A71

10c, Florence Nightingale (1820-1910), vert. 30c, Nurse, assistant, vert. 60c, Public health. 75c, Peebles Hospital.

1983, May 9 Litho. *Perf. 14½*

446 A71 10c multicolored .50 .50
447 A71 30c multicolored 1.10 1.10
448 A71 60c multicolored 2.40 2.40
449 A71 75c multicolored 3.00 3.00
Nos. 446-449 (4) 7.00 7.00

Boat Building
A72

1983, July 25 *Perf. 14*

450 A72 15c First stage .35 .35
451 A72 25c 2nd stage .55 .55
452 A72 50c Launching 1.10 1.10
453 A72 $1 First voyage 2.25 2.25
a. Souvenir sheet of 4, #450-453 4.00 4.00
Nos. 450-453 (4) 4.25 4.25

Manned Flight Bicentenary — A73

1983, Sept. 15 Wmk. 373 *Perf. 14*

454 A73 10c Grumman Goose .25 .25
455 A73 30c De Havilland Heron .50 .50
456 A73 60c EMB Bandeirante 1.15 1.15
457 A73 $1.25 Hawker-Siddeley 748 2.10 2.10
Nos. 454-457 (4) 4.00 4.00

Christmas — A74

Raphael Paintings: 8c, Madonna & Child with Infant Baptist. 15c, La Belle Jardiniere. 50c, Madonna del Granduca. $1, Terranuova Madonna.

1983, Nov. 7 Litho. *Perf. 14½*

458 A74 8c multicolored .25 .25
459 A74 15c multicolored .25 .25
460 A74 50c multicolored .80 .80
461 A74 $1 multicolored 1.60 1.60
a. Souvenir sheet of 4, #458-461 4.25 4.25
Nos. 458-461 (4) 2.90 2.90

World Chess Federation, 60th Anniv. — A75

10c, Local tournament. 35c, Chess pieces, vert. 75c, 1980 Olympiad, Winning board, vert. $1, Gold medal.

1984, Feb. 20 Litho. *Perf. 14*

462 A75 10c multicolored .55 .55
463 A75 35c multicolored 1.75 1.75
464 A75 75c multicolored 4.25 4.25
465 A75 $1 multicolored 6.75 6.75
Nos. 462-465 (4) 13.30 13.30

Lloyd's List Issue

Common Design Type

15c, Port Purcell, Tortola. 25c, Boeing 747. 50c, Shipwreck of RMS Rhone. $1, Booker Viking.

1984, Apr. 16 Litho. *Perf. 14½x14*

466 CD335 15c multicolored .35 .35
467 CD335 25c multicolored .65 .65
468 CD335 50c multicolored 1.25 1.25
469 CD335 $1 multicolored 2.75 2.75
Nos. 466-469 (4) 5.00 5.00

Souvenir Sheet

UPU Congress — A76

1984, May 16 Wmk. 373 *Perf. 14*

470 A76 $1 Emblem, jet, mailboat 3.25 3.25

1984 Summer Olympics
A77

1984, July 3

471 A77 15c Runners .40 .40
472 A77 15c Runner .40 .40
a. Pair, #471-472 1.25 1.25
473 A77 20c Wind surfers .50 .50
474 A77 20c Wind surfer .50 .50
a. Pair, #473-474 1.50 1.50
475 A77 30c Yachts .75 .75
476 A77 30c Yacht .75 .75
a. Pair, #475-476 2.25 2.25
Nos. 471-476 (6) 3.30 3.30

Souvenir Sheet

477 A77 $1 Torch bearer, vert. 2.75 2.75

Festival (Slavery Abolition Sesquicentennial) — A78

Designs: No. 478: a, Steel band. b, Calypso dancers. c, Dancers (men). d, Woman in traditional dress. e, Parade float.

No. 479 (Sail color of boat(s) in foreground): a, Green & white. b, Red & white, white, purple & white. c, white, yellow & white, blue & white. d, Yellow, red & white. e, Purple & white, white.

Nos. 478 and 479 each in continuous design.

1984, Aug. 14 *Perf. 13½x14*

478 Strip of 5, Parade 1.50 1.50
a.-e. A78 10c, any single .25 .25
479 Strip of 5, Regatta 3.75 3.75
a.-e. A78 30c, any single .60 .60

Local Boats
A79

1984, Nov. 15 Wmk. 373 *Perf. 13*

480 A79 10c Sloop .25 .25
481 A79 35c Fishing boat 1.10 1.10
482 A79 60c Schooner 2.00 2.00
483 A79 75c Cargo boat 2.40 2.40
a. Souvenir sheet of 4, #480-483 6.00 6.00
Nos. 480-483 (4) 5.75 5.75

Four stamps picturing Michael Jackson were printed. The designs were not acceptable to the Virgin Islands so they were not issued. A number of stamps had been distributed in advance for publicity purposes.

New Coinage
A80

1985, Jan. 15 Litho. *Perf. 14½*

484 A80 1c Hawksbill Turtle .25 .25
485 A80 5c Bonito .25 .25
486 A80 10c Great Barricuda .25 .25
487 A80 25c Blue Marlin .75 .75
488 A80 50c Dolphin 1.50 1.50
489 A80 $1 Spotfin Butterfly Fish 2.75 2.75
a. Miniature sheet of 6, #484-489 6.50 6.50
Nos. 484-489 (6) 5.75 5.75

Birds — A81

1985, July 3 Wmk. 373 *Perf. 14*

490 A81 1c Boatswain bird .30 .30
491 A81 2c Night gaulin .30 .30
492 A81 5c Rain bird .30 .30
493 A81 8c Mockingbird .30 .30
494 A81 10c Chinchary .35 .40
495 A81 12c Wild pigeon .50 .50
496 A81 15c Bittlin .60 .55
497 A81 18c Blach witch .65 *.65*
498 A81 20c Pond shakey .75 .75
499 A81 25c Killy-killy .95 .90
500 A81 30c Thrushie 1.20 1.25
501 A81 35c Marmi dove 1.30 *1.40*
502 A81 40c Little gaulin 1.60 *1.75*
503 A81 50c Ground dove 1.90 2.00
504 A81 60c Blue gaulin 3.00 2.75
505 A81 $1 Pimleco 4.75 4.25
506 A81 $2 White booby 9.50 9.50
507 A81 $3 Cow bird 13.00 13.00
508 A81 $5 Turtle dove 21.00 22.50
Nos. 490-508 (19) 62.25 63.35

For overprints see Nos. O16-O34.

1987, Oct. 28 Wmk. 384

494a A81 10c .70 .70
496a A81 15c 1.05 1.05
498a A81 20c 1.50 1.50
499a A81 25c 1.75 1.75
501a A81 35c 2.40 2.40
505a A81 $1 7.25 7.25
507a A81 $3 21.00 21.00
Nos. 494a-507a (7) 35.65 35.65

Queen Mother, 85th Birthday — A82

Portraits.

1985, Aug. 26 Litho. *Perf. 12½*

509 A82 10c Facing right .25 .25
510 A82 10c Facing left .25 .25
a. Pair, #509-510 .30 .30
511 A82 25c Facing right .25 .25
512 A82 25c Facing left .25 .25
a. Pair, #511-512 .55 .55
513 A82 50c Facing right .55 .55
514 A82 50c Facing forward .55 .55
a. Pair, #513-514 1.10 1.10
515 A82 75c Facing right .75 .75
516 A82 75c Facing forward .75 .75
a. Pair, #515-516 1.50 1.50
Nos. 509-516 (8) 3.60 3.60

Souvenir Sheets

1985-86 Litho. *Perf. 13x12½*

517 Sheet of 2 2.25 2.25
a.-b. A82 $1 dull grn & multi 1.10 1.10
518 Sheet of 2 3.00 3.00
a.-b. A82 $1 orange & multi 1.50 1.50
519 Sheet of 2 7.50 7.50
a.-b. A82 $2.50 dl yel & multi 3.75 3.75

Issued: #517, 12/18/85; #518-519, 2/18/86.

For overprints see Nos. 528-531.

Audubon Birth Bicent. — A83

1985, Dec. 17 *Perf. 15*

520 A83 5c Seaside sparrow .25 .25
521 A83 30c Passenger pigeon .50 .50
522 A83 50c Yellow-breasted chat .85 .85
523 A83 $1 American kestrel 1.75 1.75
Nos. 520-523 (4) 3.35 3.35

Cruise Ships
A84

1986, Jan. 27

524 A84 35c Flying Cloud .75 .75
525 A84 50c Newport Clipper 1.10 1.10
526 A84 75c Cunard Countess 1.75 1.75
527 A84 $1 Sea Goddess 2.50 2.50
Nos. 524-527 (4) 6.10 6.10

Nos. 511-512, 515-516 Ovptd.

1986, Apr. 17   Litho.   Perf. 12½
528 A82 25c on No. 511   .50   .50
529 A82 25c on No. 512   .50   .50
530 A82 75c on No. 515   1.75   1.75
531 A82 75c on No. 516   1.75   1.75
    Nos. 528-531 (4)   4.50   4.50

Queen Elizabeth II, 60th Birthday — A85

12c, Portrait, 1958. 35c, Maundy service. $1.50, Contemporary photograph. $2, Canberra, 1982, vert.
$3, Contemporary photograph, diff.

Perf. 13x12½, 12½x13
1986, Apr. 21   Litho.
532 A85 12c multicolored   .25   .25
533 A85 35c multicolored   .25   .25
534 A85 $1.50 multicolored   .85   .85
535 A85 $2 multicolored   1.20   1.20
    Nos. 532-535 (4)   2.55   2.55

Souvenir Sheet
536 A85 $3 multicolored   5.75   5.75

Stamps with blue ribbons and frames omitted were from stock sold when the printer was liquidated.

Wedding of Prince Andrew and Sarah Ferguson — A86

1986, July 23   Perf. 12½
537 A86 35c Couple, vert.   .45   .45
538 A86 35c Sarah, vert.   .45   .45
539 A86 $1 Andrew   1.25   1.25
540 A86 $1 Sarah, diff.   1.25   1.25
    Nos. 537-540 (4)   3.40   3.40

Stamps of the same denomination exist setenant.

Nos. 537-540 overprinted "Congratulations to T.R.H. The Duke & Duchess of York" were not issued.

Traditional Rum Production — A87

1986, July 30   Perf. 14
541 A87 12c Harvesting sugar
             cane   .50   .50
542 A87 40c Grinding   2.00   2.00
543 A87 60c Distillery   3.25   3.25
544 A87 $1 Transport   5.25   5.25
    Nos. 541-544 (4)   11.00 11.00

Souvenir Sheet
545 A87 $2 Up Spirits cere-
             mony, 19th cent.   9.25   9.25

Souvenir Sheet

Wedding of Prince Andrew and Sarah Ferguson — A88

1986, Oct. 15   Litho.   Perf. 13x12½
546 A88 $4 multicolored   4.50   4.50

Cable-Laying Ships — A89

1986, Oct. 15   Wmk. 380   Perf. 12½
547 A89 35c Sentinel   .65   .65
548 A89 35c Retriever   .65   .65
    a.   Pair, #547-548   1.30   1.30
549 A89 60c Cable Enterprise 1.10   1.10
550 A89 60c Mercury   1.10   1.10
    a.   Pair, #549-550   2.25   2.25
551 A89 75c Recorder   1.25   1.25
552 A89 75c Pacific Guardian 1.25   1.25
    a.   Pair, #551-552   2.50   2.50
553 A89 $1 Great Eastern   1.75   1.75
554 A89 $1 Cable Venture   1.75   1.75
    a.   Pair, #553-554   3.50   3.50
    Nos. 547-554 (8)   9.50   9.50

Souvenir Sheets
555   Sheet of 2   1.30   1.30
a.-b. A89 40c, like #547-548   .65   .65
556   Sheet of 2   1.60   1.60
a.-b. A89 50c, like #549-550   .80   .80
557   Sheet of 2   2.50   2.50
a.-b. A89 80c, like #551-552 1.25   1.25
558   Sheet of 2   4.75   4.75
a.-b. A89 $1.50, like #553-554 2.25   2.25

Cable and wireless in the islands, 20th anniv.

Souvenir Sheets

Statue of Liberty, Cent. — A90

Various views of the statue.

1986, Dec. 15   Litho.   Perf. 14
559 A90 50c multicolored   .60   .60
560 A90 75c multicolored   1.00   1.00
561 A90 90c multicolored   1.10   1.10
562 A90 $1 multicolored   1.30   1.30
563 A90 $1.25 multicolored   1.60   1.60
564 A90 $1.50 multicolored   1.90   1.90
565 A90 $1.75 multicolored   2.25   2.25
566 A90 $2 multicolored   2.40   2.40
567 A90 $2.50 multicolored   3.25   3.25
    Nos. 559-567 (9)   15.40 15.40

A91

Shipwrecks — A92

12c, Spanish galleon, 18th cent. 35c, HMS Astrea, 1808. 75c, RMS Rhone, 1867. $1.50, SS Rocus, 1929.
$2.50, Brig Volvart, 1918.

1987, Apr. 15   Perf. 14
572 A91 12c multicolored   .85   .85
573 A91 35c multicolored   2.40   2.40
574 A91 75c multicolored   4.75   4.75
575 A91 $1.50 multicolored   10.00 10.00
    Nos. 572-575 (4)   18.00 18.00

Souvenir Sheet
576 A92 $2.50 multicolored   19.00 19.00

Natl. Flags, Outline Maps — A93

1987, May 28
577 A93 10c Montserrat   .25   .25
578 A93 15c Grenada   .55   .55
579 A93 20c Dominica   .80   .80
580 A93 25c St. Kitts-Nevis   1.00   1.00
581 A93 35c St. Vincent and
             Grenadines   1.25   1.25
582 A93 50c Virgin Isls.   1.90   1.90
583 A93 75c Antigua & Barbu-
             da   2.75   2.75
584 A93 $1 St. Lucia   4.00   4.00
    Nos. 577-584 (8)   12.50 12.50

11th Meeting of the Organization of Eastern Caribbean States.

Botanical Gardens — A94

1987, Aug. 12   Wmk. 384
585 A94 12c Spider lily   .75   .75
586 A94 35c Barrel cactus   2.25   2.25
587 A94 $1 Wild plantain   6.25   6.25
588 A94 $1.50 Little butterfly
             orchid   9.25   9.25
    Nos. 585-588 (4)   18.50 18.50

Souvenir Sheet
589 A94 $2.50 White cedar   6.25   6.25

Postal Service Bicent. A95

Designs: 10c, 18th Cent. packet, #7 canceled "A13." 20c, Map of the islands, #22 canceled "A91." 35c, Tortola Post Office and Customs House, and #5 canceled "Tortola De 20 61." $1.50, Mail plane and #154 canceled "Road town No 2 64 Tortola W.I." $2.50, Late 19th cent. steam packet and #10 canceled "A Tortola Ap 12 70."

1987, Dec. 17   Litho.   Perf. 14½
590 A95 10c multicolored   .70   .70
591 A95 20c multicolored   1.40   1.40
592 A95 35c multicolored   2.25   2.25
593 A95 $1.50 multicolored   10.00 10.00
    Nos. 590-593 (4)   14.35 14.35

Souvenir Sheet
594 A95 $2.50 multicolored   8.00   8.00

Paintings by Titian — A96

10c, Salome, 1512. 12c, Man with the Glove, c. 1520-22. 20c, Fabrizio Salvaresio, 1558. 25c, Daughter of Roberto Strozzi, 1542. 40c, Pope Julius II. 50c, Bishop Ludovico Beccadelli, 1552. 60c, Philip II. $1, Empress Isabella of Portugal, 1548. #603, Emperor Charles V at Muhlberg, 1548. #604, Pope Paul III & His Grandsons, 1546.

Perf. 13½x14
1988, Aug. 11   Unwmk.
595 A96 10c multicolored   .35   .35
596 A96 12c multicolored   .50   .50
597 A96 20c multicolored   .80   .80
598 A96 25c multicolored   1.00   1.00
599 A96 40c multicolored   1.75   1.75
600 A96 50c multicolored   2.10   2.10
601 A96 60c multicolored   2.75   2.75
602 A96 $1 multicolored   4.75   4.75
    Nos. 595-602 (8)   14.00 14.00

Souvenir Sheet
603 A96 $2 multicolored   10.00 10.00
604 A96 $2 multicolored   10.00 10.00

1st Annual Open Chess Tournament — A97

35c, Pawn & Transporter aircraft over Sir Francis Drake Channel. $1, King & Jose Raul Capablanca (1888-1942), Cuban chess master and world champion from 1921-27. $2, Match scene.

1988, Aug. 25   Unwmk.   Perf. 14
605 A97 35c multicolored   4.00   4.00
606 A97 $1 multicolored   11.50 11.50

Souvenir Sheet
607 A97 $2 multicolored   12.50 12.50

1988 Summer Olympics, Seoul A98

1988, Sept. 8
608 A98 12c Hurdling   .65   .65
609 A98 20c Windsurfing   1.10   1.10
610 A98 75c Basketball   3.75   3.75
611 A98 $1 Tennis   5.00   5.00
    Nos. 608-611 (4)   10.50 10.50

Souvenir Sheet
612 A98 $2 Running   5.25   5.25

Intl. Red
Cross,
125th
Anniv.
A99

Safety warnings and steps in administering
cardiopulmonary resuscitation (CPR): 12c,
"Don't swim alone." 30c, "No swimming during
electrical storms." 60c, "Don't eat before swimming." $1, "Proper equipment for boating." No.
617a, Turn victim on back. No. 617b, Position
victim's chin so breathing passages are not
blocked. No. 617c, Mouth-to-mouth resuscitation. No. 617d, Chest compressions. Nos.
617a-617d vert.

1988, Sept. 26
613 A99 12c multicolored   .80   .80
614 A99 30c multicolored   2.00   2.00
615 A99 60c multicolored   3.75   3.75
616 A99 $1 multicolored   6.50   6.50
     Nos. 613-616 (4)   13.05 13.05

Souvenir Sheet
617   Sheet of 4   8.75   8.75
a.-d.   A99 50c any single   1.10   1.10

#617a-617d has a continuous design.

Visit of Princess
Alexandra — A100

Various photographs of the princess.

1988, Nov. 9   Litho.   Perf. 14
618 A100 40c shown   2.00   2.00
619 A100 $1.50 multi, diff.   8.00   8.00

Souvenir Sheet
620 A100 $2 multi, diff.   9.00   9.00

World Wildlife
Fund — A101

Brown pelicans, Pelecanus Occidentalis:
10c, Pelican in flight. 12c, Perched. 15c,
Close-up of head. 35c, Swallowing fish.

1988, Nov. 15
621 A101 10c multicolored   1.50   1.50
622 A101 12c multicolored   1.75   1.75
623 A101 15c multicolored   2.00   2.00
624 A101 35c multicolored   4.75   4.75
     Nos. 621-624 (4)   10.00 10.00

Reptiles, Marine Mammals and
Birds — A102

20c, Anegada rock iguana. 40c, Virgin
gorda dwarf gecko. 60c, Hawksbill turtle. $1,
Humpback whale. #629, Northern shoveler,
American widgeon & ring-necked ducks. #630,
Trunk turtle.

1988, Nov. 15
625 A102 20c multicolored   1.50   1.50
626 A102 40c multicolored   2.75   2.75
627 A102 60c multicolored   4.25   4.25
628 A102 $1 multicolored   7.00   7.00
     Nos. 625-628 (4)   15.50 15.50

Souvenir Sheets
629 A102 $2 multicolored   9.50   9.50
630 A102 $2 multicolored   7.50   7.50

Spring
Regatta
A103

Various yachts.

1989, Apr. 7   Litho.   Perf. 14
631 A103 12c multi, diff., vert.   .45   .45
632 A103 40c shown   1.40   1.40
633 A103 75c multi, diff., vert. 2.25   2.25
634 A103 $1 multi, diff.   3.25   3.25
     Nos. 631-634 (4)   7.35   7.35

Souvenir Sheet
635 A103 $2 multi, diff., vert. 8.25   8.25

Pre-Columbian Societies and Their
Customs — A104

1989, May 18
636 A104 10c Hammock   .45   .45
637 A104 20c Making a fire   .95   .95
638 A104 25c Carvers   1.10   1.10
639 A104 $1.50 Arawak family 7.00   7.00
     Nos. 636-639 (4)   9.50   9.50

Souvenir Sheet
640 A104 $2 Ritual   11.00 11.00
Discovery of America 500th anniv. (in 1992).

1st Moon
Landing,
20th
Anniv.
A105

Highlights of the Apollo 11 mission: 15c,
Lunar surface, mission emblem. 30c, Buzz
Aldrin conducting solar wind experiment. 65c,
Raising American flag. $1, Recovery of crew
after splashdown. $2, Portrait of crew.

1989, Sept. 28   Litho.   Perf. 14
641 A105 15c multicolored   1.00   1.00
642 A105 30c multicolored   1.75   1.75
643 A105 65c multicolored   3.50   3.50
644 A105 $1 multicolored   5.75   5.75
     Nos. 641-644 (4)   12.00 12.00

Souvenir Sheet
Perf. 13½x14
645 A105 $2 multicolored   11.00 11.00
No. 645 contains one 37x46mm stamp.

Methodist
Church,
200th
Anniv.
A106

Designs: 12c, Black Harry, Nathaniel Gilbert
preaching. 25c, Book symbolizing role of the
church in education. 35c, East End Methodist
Church, 1810. $1.25, John Wesley, modern
youth choir. $2, Thomas Coke.

1989, Oct. 24   Perf. 14
646 A106 12c multicolored   .50   .50
647 A106 25c multicolored   1.10   1.10
648 A106 35c multicolored   1.60   1.60
649 A106 $1.25 multicolored   5.75   5.75
     Nos. 646-649 (4)   8.95   8.95

Souvenir Sheet
650 A106 $2 multicolored   8.00   8.00

1990 World Cup
Soccer
Championships,
Italy — A107

Various athletes.

1989, Nov. 6
651 A107 5c shown   .65   .65
652 A107 10c multi, diff.   .65   .65
653 A107 20c multi, diff.   1.25   1.25
654 A107 $1.75 multi, diff. 10.50 10.50
     Nos. 651-654 (4)   13.05 13.05

Souvenir Sheet
655 A107 $2 Natl. team   10.00 10.00

Princess Alexandra, Sunset
House — A108

Royal Yacht Britannia — A109

b, Princess Margaret, Government House.
c, Hon. Angus Ogilvy, Little Dix Bay Hotel. d,
Princess Diana & her children, Necker Island
Resort.

1990, May 3   Litho.   Perf. 14
656   Min. sheet of 4   13.00 13.00
a.-d.   A108 50c any single   1.25   1.25

Souvenir Sheet
657 A109 $2 multicolored   14.00 14.00
Stamp World London '90.

Audubon's Shearwater — A110

12c, Red-necked pigeon. 20c, Common gallinule. 25c, Green heron. 40c, Yellow warbler.
60c, Smooth-billed ani. $1, Antillean crested
hummingbird. $1.25, Black-faced grassquit.
No. 666, Egg of royal tern. No. 667, Egg of
red-billed tropicbird.

1990, May 15
658 A110 5c shown   .35   .35
659 A110 12c multicolored   .55   .55
660 A110 20c multicolored   1.00   1.00
661 A110 25c multicolored   1.25   1.25
662 A110 40c multicolored   2.00   2.00
663 A110 60c multicolored   3.25   3.25
664 A110 $1 multicolored   5.00   5.00
665 A110 $1.25 multicolored 6.25   6.25
     Nos. 658-665 (8)   19.65 19.65

Souvenir Sheets
666 A110 $2 multicolored   6.75   6.75
667 A110 $2 multicolored   6.75   6.75

Blue
Tang
A111

1990, June 18
668 A111 10c shown   .60   .60
669 A111 35c Glasseye   2.40   2.40
670 A111 50c Slippery Dick 3.50   3.50
671 A111 $1 Porkfish   6.75   6.75
     Nos. 668-671 (4)   13.25 13.25

Souvenir Sheet
672 A111 $2 Yellowtail snap-
            per   8.00   8.00

A112

1990, Aug. 30   Litho.   Perf. 14
673 A112 12c multicolored   .40   .40
674 A112 25c multi, diff.   .85   .85
675 A112 60c multi, diff.   2.25   2.25
676 A112 $1 multi, diff.   4.00   4.00
     Nos. 673-676 (4)   7.50   7.50

Souvenir Sheet
677 A112 $2 multi, diff.   6.00   6.00
Queen Mother, 90th birthday.

A113

Various soccer players.

1990, Dec. 10   Litho.   Perf. 14
678 A113 12c multicolored   .45   .45
679 A113 20c multi, diff.   .80   .80
680 A113 50c multi, diff.   1.90   1.90
681 A113 $1.25 multi, diff. 5.25   5.25
     Nos. 678-681 (4)   8.40   8.40

Souvenir Sheet
682 A113 $2 multi, diff.   7.25   7.25
World Cup Soccer Championships, Italy.

1992
Summer
Olympics,
Barcelona
A114

1990, Dec. 20   Litho.   Perf. 14
683 A114 12c Judo   .65   .65
684 A114 40c Yachting   2.10   2.10
685 A114 60c Hurdles   3.25   3.25
686 A114 $1 Show jumping   5.50   5.50
     Nos. 683-686 (4)   11.50 11.50

Souvenir Sheet
687 A114 $2 Windsurfing   6.50   6.50

Copper Mine Ruins A115

10c, Cyathea arborea, vert. 35c, Mt. Healthy windmill ruin, vert. $2, Baths, Virgin Gorda.

1991, Mar. 1 Litho. *Perf. 14*

688	A115	10c multicolored	.50	.50
689	A115	25c shown	1.25	1.25
690	A115	35c multicolored	2.00	2.00
691	A115	$2 multicolored	9.25	9.25
		Nos. 688-691 (4)	13.00	13.00

National Park Trust.

Flowers — A116

1c, Haiti Haiti. 2c, Lobster claw. 5c, Frangipani. 10c, Autograph tree. 12c, Yellow allamanda. 15c, Lantana. 20c, Jerusalem thorn. 25c, Turk's cap. 30c, Swamp immortelle. 35c, White cedar. 40c, Mahoe tree. 45c, Pinguin. 50c, Christmas orchid. 70c, Lignum vitae. $1, African tulip tree. $2, Beach morning glory. $3, Organ pipe cactus. $5, Tall ground orchid. $10, Ground orchid.

1991-92 Litho. *Perf. 14*

No Date Imprint Below Design

692	A116	1c multicolored	.25	.25
693	A116	2c multicolored	.25	.25
694	A116	5c multicolored	.25	.25
695	A116	10c multicolored	.25	.25
696	A116	12c multicolored	.25	.25
697	A116	15c multicolored	.40	.40
698	A116	20c multicolored	.55	.55
699	A116	25c multicolored	.65	.65
700	A116	30c multicolored	.75	.75
701	A116	35c multicolored	.85	.85
702	A116	40c multicolored	1.00	1.00
703	A116	45c multicolored	1.10	1.10
704	A116	50c multicolored	1.25	1.25
a.		Perf 12	2.00	2.00
705	A116	70c multicolored	1.75	1.75
706	A116	$1 multicolored	2.50	2.50
a.		Perf 12	3.25	3.25
707	A116	$2 multicolored	5.00	5.00
a.		Perf 12	6.50	6.50
708	A116	$3 multicolored	7.25	7.25
a.		Perf 12½x11½	10.00	10.00
709	A116	$5 multicolored	12.50	12.50
710	A116	$10 multicolored	24.00	24.00
		Nos. 692-710 (19)	60.80	60.80

Issued: 1c-$5, 5/1/91; $10, 5/92; Nos. 704a, 706a, 707a, 708a, 8/95.

For overprints see Nos. O37-O51.

1995, June 1 Wmk. 373 Sideways

Inscribed "1995" Below Design

695b	A116	10c multicolored	.60	*1.60*
697b	A116	15c multicolored	.80	.50
700b	A116	30c multicolored	.85	.60
701b	A116	35c multicolored	1.00	.65
703b	A116	45c multicolored	1.20	1.00
704b	A116	50c multicolored	2.75	2.10
707b	A116	$2 multicolored	3.75	*6.00*
709b	A116	$5 multicolored	10.50	*14.00*
		Nos. 695b-709b (8)	21.45	*26.45*

Butterflies — A117

5c, Cloudless sulphur. 10c, Flambeau. 15c, Caribbean buckeye. 20c, Gulf fritillary. 25c, Polydamus swallowtail. 30c, Little sulphur. 35c, Zebra. $1.50, Malachite.

No. 719, Monarch, horiz. No. 720, Red rim, horiz.

Unwmk.

1991, June 28 Litho. *Perf. 14*

711	A117	5c multicolored	.50	.50
712	A117	10c multicolored	.50	.50
713	A117	15c multicolored	.85	.85
714	A117	20c multicolored	1.25	1.25
715	A117	25c multicolored	1.40	1.40
716	A117	30c multicolored	1.75	1.75
717	A117	35c multicolored	2.10	2.10
718	A117	$1.50 multicolored	8.75	8.75
		Nos. 711-718 (8)	17.10	17.10

Souvenir Sheets

719	A117	$2 multicolored	10.00	10.00
720	A117	$2 multicolored	10.00	10.00

Voyages of Discovery A118

Ships of explorers: 12c, Ferdinand Magellan, 1519-1521. 50c, Rene-Robert de la Salle, 1682. 75c, John Cabot, 1497-1498. $1, Jacques Cartier, 1534. $2, Columbus' ship, 1493 woodcut, vert.

1991, Sept. 20 Litho. *Perf. 14*

721	A118	12c multicolored	.55	.55
722	A118	50c multicolored	2.25	2.25
723	A118	75c multicolored	3.75	3.75
724	A118	$1 multicolored	5.00	5.00
		Nos. 721-724 (4)	11.55	11.55

Souvenir Sheet

725	A118	$2 multicolored	10.00	10.00

Vincent Van Gogh (1853-1890), Painter — A119

Paintings: 15c, Cottage with Decrepit Barn and Stooping Woman. 30c, Paul Gauguin's Armchair, vert. 75c, Breton Women. $1, Vase with Red Gladioli, vert. $2, The Dance Hall in Arles (detail).

1991, Nov. 1 *Perf. 13*

726	A119	15c multicolored	.90	.90
727	A119	30c multicolored	1.75	1.75
728	A119	75c multicolored	4.50	4.50
729	A119	$1 multicolored	6.25	6.25
		Nos. 726-729 (4)	13.40	13.40

Souvenir Sheet

730	A119	$2 multicolored	12.50	12.50

Christmas A120

Entire paintings or details by Quinten Massys: 15c, The Virgin and Child Enthroned. 30c, The Virgin and Child Enthroned, diff. 60c, The Adoration of the Magi. $1, Virgin in Adoration. No. 735, The Virgin Standing with Angels. No. 736, The Adoration of the Magi.

1991, Dec. 12 Litho. *Perf. 12*

731	A120	15c multicolored	.80	.80
732	A120	30c multicolored	1.75	1.75
733	A120	60c multicolored	3.50	3.50
734	A120	$1 multicolored	5.75	5.75
		Nos. 731-734 (4)	11.80	11.80

Souvenir Sheets

Perf. 14½

735	A120	$2 multicolored	7.00	7.00
736	A120	$2 multicolored	7.00	7.00

Mushrooms — A121

12c, Agaricus bisporus, vert. 30c, Lentinus edodes. 45c, Hyrocybe acutoconica, vert. $1, Gymnopilus chrysopellus.

$2, Pleurotus ostreatus.

1992, Jan. 15 *Perf. 14*

737	A121	12c multicolored	.90	.90
738	A121	30c multicolored	2.10	2.10
739	A121	45c multicolored	3.25	3.25
740	A121	$1 multicolored	6.75	6.75
		Nos. 737-740 (4)	13.00	13.00

Souvenir Sheet

741	A121	$2 multicolored	15.00	15.00

Queen Elizabeth II's Accession to the Throne, 40th Anniv.

Common Design Type

1992, Feb. 6 Litho. *Perf. 14*

742	CD348	12c multicolored	.40	.40
743	CD348	45c multicolored	1.50	1.50
744	CD348	60c multicolored	2.10	2.10
745	CD348	$1 multicolored	3.50	3.50
		Nos. 742-745 (4)	7.50	7.50

Souvenir Sheet

746	CD348	$2 multicolored	8.00	8.00

Discovery of America, 500th Anniv. A122

10c, Queen Isabella. 15c, Columbus' fleet. 20c, Columbus' second coat of arms. 30c, Landing Monument on Watling Island, Columbus' signature. 45c, Columbus. 50c, Flag of Ferdinand & Isabella, Columbus landing on Watling Island. 70c, Convent at La Rabida. $1.50, Replica of Santa Maria at New York World's Fair, 1964-65. #755, Columbus' 2nd fleet. #756, Map.

1992, May 26 Litho. *Perf. 14*

747	A122	10c multi, vert.	.50	.50
748	A122	15c multi	.70	.70
749	A122	20c multi, vert.	.95	.95
750	A122	30c multi	1.25	1.25
751	A122	45c multi, vert.	1.75	1.75
752	A122	50c multi	2.10	2.10
753	A122	70c multi, vert.	3.00	3.00
754	A122	$1.50 multi	6.75	6.75
		Nos. 747-754 (8)	17.00	17.00

Souvenir Sheet

755	A122	$2 multicolored	7.50	7.50
756	A122	$2 multicolored	7.50	7.50

1992 Summer Olympics, Barcelona — A123

1992, Aug. Litho. *Perf. 14*

757	A123	15c Basketball	.80	.80
758	A123	30c Tennis	1.75	1.75
759	A123	60c Volleyball	3.50	3.50
760	A123	$1 Soccer	5.75	5.75
		Nos. 757-760 (4)	11.80	11.80

Souvenir Sheet

761	A123	$2 Olympic flame	14.00	14.00

Ministerial Government, 25th Anniv. — A124

Designs: 12c, Social progress and development. 15c, Map of Virgin Islands. 45c, Administration complex. $1.30, International finance.

1993, Apr. Litho. *Perf. 14*

762	A124	12c multicolored	.35	.35
763	A124	15c multicolored	.40	.40
764	A124	45c multicolored	1.25	1.25
765	A124	$1.30 multicolored	4.00	4.00
		Nos. 762-765 (4)	6.00	6.00

Tourism A125

15c, Swimming from anchored yacht. 30c, Sailboat. 60c, Scuba diver in pink wetsuit. $1, Snorkelers, anchored boat.

#770: a, Trimaran, vert. b, Scuba diver, vert.

1993, Apr. Litho. *Perf. 14*

766	A125	15c multi	.50	.50
767	A125	30c multi, vert.	1.25	1.25
768	A125	60c multi	2.75	2.75
769	A125	$1 multi, vert.	4.50	4.50
		Nos. 766-769 (4)	9.00	9.00

Souvenir Sheet

770	A125	$1 Sheet of 2, #a.-b.	9.00	9.00

Miniature Sheet

Coronation of Queen Elizabeth II, 40th Anniv. A126

No. 771: a, 12c, Official coronation photograph. b, 45c, Dove atop Rod of Equity and Mercy. c, 60c, Royal family. d, $1, Recent color photo.

1993, June 2 Litho. *Perf. 13½x14*

771	A126	Sheet, 2 each #a.-d.	14.00	14.00

A souvenir sheet containing a $2 stamp was not an authorized issue. Value $18.

Discovery of Virgin Islands, 500th Anniv. A127

3c, Ferdinand and Isabella supporting Columbus. 12c, Departure of Columbus. 15c, Departure of second voyage. 25c, Arms, flag of British Virgin Islands. 30c, Columbus, Santa Maria. 45c, Columbus' second fleet at sea. 60c, Rowing ashore. $1, Landing of Columbus. #781, Natives watching ships. #782, Columbus, two ships of his fleet.

1993, Sept. 24 Litho. *Perf. 14*

773	A127	3c multicolored	.30	.30
774	A127	12c multicolored	.40	.40
775	A127	15c multicolored	.55	.55
776	A127	25c multicolored	.85	.85
777	A127	30c multicolored	1.10	1.10
778	A127	45c multicolored	1.50	1.50
779	A127	60c multicolored	2.10	2.10
780	A127	$1 multicolored	3.50	3.50
		Nos. 773-780 (8)	10.30	10.30

Souvenir Sheets

781	A127	$2 multicolored	7.50	7.50
782	A127	$2 multicolored	7.50	7.50

Secondary Education and Library Services, 50th Anniv. — A128

Designs: 5c, Historical documents. 10c, Sporting activities. 15c, Stanley W. Nibbs, educator, vert. 20c, Bookmobile. 30c, Norwell E. Harrigan, educator, vert. 35c, Public library's annual summer program. 70c, Text. $1, High school.

Perf. 14x13½, 13½x14

		1993, Dec.		Litho.
783	A128	5c multicolored	.50	.50
784	A128	10c multicolored	.50	.50
785	A128	15c multicolored	.70	.70
786	A128	20c multicolored	1.00	1.00
787	A128	30c multicolored	1.60	1.60
788	A128	35c multicolored	1.90	1.90
789	A128	70c multicolored	3.25	3.25
790	A128	$1 multicolored	5.00	5.00
		Nos. 783-790 (8)	14.45	14.45

Anegada Ground Iguana — A129

5c, Crawling right. 10c, Head up to right. 15c, View from behind. 45c, Head up to left. $2, Head.

		1994, Jan.		Litho.	Perf. 14
791	A129	5c multicolored	.90	.90
792	A129	10c multicolored	.90	.90
793	A129	15c multicolored	1.25	1.25
794	A129	45c multicolored	4.00	4.00
		Nos. 791-794 (4)	7.05	7.05

Souvenir Sheet

795	A129	$2 multicolored	6.25	6.25

World Wildlife Fund.

Rotary Club of Virgin Islands, 25th Anniv. A130

Designs: 15c, Disaster relief airlift. 45c, Kids, Sea "Kats." 50c, Donated hospital equipment. 90c, Paul P. Harris (1868-1947), founder of Rotary Intl.

		1994, June 3		Litho.	Perf. 14
796	A130	15c multicolored	.60	.60
797	A130	45c multicolored	1.60	1.60
798	A130	50c multicolored	1.90	1.90
799	A130	90c multicolored	3.25	3.25
		Nos. 796-799 (4)	7.35	7.35

Miniature Sheet of 6

First Manned Moon Landing, 25th Anniv. — A131

Designs: No. 800a, Anniversary emblem. b, Lunar landing training vehicle. c, Apollo 11 lift-off, July 16, 1969. d, Lunar module Eagle in flight. e, Moon landing site approached by Eagle. f, 1st step on Moon, July 20, 1969. No. 801, Mission patch, crew signatures.

		1994, Sept. 30		Litho.	Perf. 14
800	A131	50c #a.-f.	15.00	15.00

Souvenir Sheet

801	A131	$2 multicolored	13.00	13.00

A132

Previous champions: 15c, Argentina, 1978. 35c, Italy, 1982. 50c, Argentina, 1986. $1.30, W. Germany, 1990.
$2, US flag, World Cup trophy, horiz.

		1994, Dec. 16		Litho.	Perf. 14
802	A132	15c multicolored	.85	.85
803	A132	35c multicolored	1.90	1.90
804	A132	50c multicolored	2.25	2.25
805	A132	$1.30 multicolored	7.00	7.00
		Nos. 802-805 (4)	12.00	12.00

Souvenir Sheet

806	A132	$2 multicolored	14.00	14.00

1994 World Cup Soccer Championships, US.

UN, 50th Anniv.
Common Design Type

Designs: 15c, Peugeot P4 all-purpose light vehicle. 30c, Foden medium tanker. 45c, Sisu all-terrain vehicle. $2, Westland Lynx AH7 helicopter.

Wmk. 373

		1995, Oct. 24		Litho.	Perf. 14
807	CD353	15c multicolored	.45	.45
808	CD353	30c multicolored	.90	.90
809	CD353	45c multicolored	1.60	1.60
810	CD353	$2 multicolored	6.50	6.50
		Nos. 807-810 (4)	9.45	9.45

A133

Anegada Flamingos.

Wmk. 373

		1995, Nov. 15		Litho.	Perf. 13
811	A133	15c Juveniles	.50	.50
812	A133	20c Adults	.75	.75
813	A133	60c Adult feeding	2.25	2.25
814	A133	$1.45 Adult feeding chick	5.50	5.50
		Nos. 811-814 (4)	9.00	9.00

Souvenir Sheet

815	A133	$2 Chicks	9.00	9.00

Christmas — A134

Children's paintings: 12c, House with palm trees. 50c, Santa in boat. 70c, Red house, Christmas tree, presents. $1.30, Dove of peace.

Wmk. 384

		1995, Dec. 1		Litho.	Perf. 14
816	A134	12c multicolored	.65	.65
817	A134	50c multicolored	2.75	2.75
818	A134	70c multicolored	3.75	3.75
819	A134	$1.30 multicolored	7.00	7.00
		Nos. 816-819 (4)	14.15	14.15

Island Scenes A135

Designs: 15c, Seine fishing. 35c, Sandy Spit, Jost Van Dyke. 90c, Map of Jost Van Dyke. $1.50, Foxy's wooden boat regatta.

Perf. 13½x13

		1996, Feb. 14		Litho.	Wmk. 373
820	A135	15c multicolored	.65	.65
821	A135	35c multicolored	1.60	1.60
822	A135	90c multicolored	3.50	3.50
823	A135	$1.50 multicolored	6.25	6.25
		Nos. 820-823 (4)	12.00	12.00

See Nos. 892-896.

Queen Elizabeth II, 70th Birthday
Common Design Type

Queen in various attire, scenes of Virgin Islands: 10c, Government House, Tortola. 30c, Legislative Council Chambers. 45c, Road Harbor. $1.50, Map of Virgin Islands.
$2, Wearing royal crown.

Perf. 13½x14

		1996, Apr. 22		Litho.	Wmk. 373
824	CD354	10c multicolored	.30	.30
825	CD354	30c multicolored	1.00	1.00
826	CD354	45c multicolored	1.50	1.50
827	CD354	$1.50 multicolored	4.25	4.25
		Nos. 824-827 (4)	7.05	7.05

Souvenir Sheet
Perf. 13x13½

828	CD354	$2 multicolored	5.25	5.25

Modern Olympic Games, Cent. A136

Wmk. 373

		1996, May 22		Litho.	Perf. 13
829	A136	20c Hurdles	.65	.65
830	A136	35c Volleyball	1.25	1.25
831	A136	50c Swimming	1.60	1.60
832	A136	$1 Sailing	3.50	3.50
		Nos. 829-832 (4)	7.00	7.00

CAPEX '96 A137

Vintage automobiles: 15c, 1934 Mercedes-Benz 500KA Cabriolet. 40c, 1934 Citroen 12. 60c, 1932 Cadillac V-8 Sport Phaeton. $1.35, 1934 Rolls Royce Phantom II.
$2, 1932 Ford Sport Coupe.

Wmk. 373

		1996, June 8		Litho.	Perf. 13½
833	A137	15c multicolored	.35	.35
834	A137	40c multicolored	1.00	1.00
835	A137	60c multicolored	1.75	1.75
836	A137	$1.35 multicolored	3.75	3.75
		Nos. 833-836 (4)	6.85	6.85

Souvenir Sheet

837	A137	$2 multicolored	5.00	5.00

UNICEF, 50th Anniv. A138

Goals of UNICEF for the year 2000: 10c, Educate the child. 15c, Children first. 30c, Children have rights. 45c, No more polio.

Perf. 14x14½

		1996, Sept. 16		Litho.	Wmk. 373
838	A138	10c multicolored	.45	.45
839	A138	15c multicolored	.70	.70
840	A138	30c multicolored	1.60	1.60
841	A138	45c multicolored	2.25	2.25
		Nos. 838-841 (4)	5.00	5.00

Girl Guiding in Virgin Islands, 25th Anniv. — A139

Designs: 10c, Rainbows, arts and crafts. 15c, Brownies, community service. 30c, Guides, campfire. 45c, Rangers, H.M. Queen's birthday parade. $2, Lady Baden-Powell, world chief guide.

Wmk. 373

		1996, Dec. 30		Litho.	Perf. 13½
842	A139	10c multicolored	.25	.25
843	A139	15c multicolored	.40	.40
844	A139	30c multicolored	.70	.70
845	A139	45c multicolored	1.00	1.00
846	A139	$2 multicolored	4.50	4.50
		Nos. 842-846 (5)	6.85	6.85

Game Fish A140

		1997, Jan. 6		Wmk. 384	Perf. 14
847	A140	1c Mackerel	.25	.25
848	A140	10c Wahoo	.25	.25
849	A140	15c Barracuda	.35	.35
850	A140	20c Tarpon	.50	.50
851	A140	25c Tiger shark	.60	.60
852	A140	35c Sailfish	.85	.85
853	A140	40c Dolphin	.95	.95
854	A140	50c Blackfin tuna	1.25	1.25
855	A140	60c Yellowfin tuna	1.50	1.50
856	A140	75c Kingfish	1.75	1.75
857	A140	$1.50 White marlin	3.50	3.50
a.		Souvenir sheet of 1, wmk. 373	4.50	4.50
858	A140	$1.85 Amberjack	4.50	4.50
859	A140	$2 Bonito	4.75	4.75
860	A140	$5 Bonefish	12.00	12.00
861	A140	$10 Blue marlin	24.00	24.00
		Nos. 847-861 (15)	57.00	57.00

No. 857a, Hong Kong '97.
See Nos. 1020-1023.

Queen Elizabeth II and Prince Philip, 50th Wedding Anniv. — A141

#862, Prince with horse. #863, Queen Elizabeth II. #864, Queen riding in open carriage. #865, Prince Philip. #866, Queen holding hat down, Prince. #867, Prince Charles on polo pony.
$2, Queen, Prince riding in open carriage, horiz.

Wmk. 373

		1997, July 10		Litho.	Perf. 13
862		30c multicolored	.70	.70
863		30c multicolored	.70	.70
a.	A141	Pair, #862-863	1.75	1.75
864		45c multicolored	1.00	1.00
865		45c multicolored	1.00	1.00
a.	A141	Pair, #864-865	2.50	2.50
866		70c multicolored	1.50	1.50
867		70c multicolored	1.50	1.50
a.	A141	Pair, #866-867	4.00	4.00
		Nos. 862-867 (6)	6.40	6.40

Souvenir Sheet

868	A141	$2 multicolored	6.50	6.50

Crabs
A142

Wmk. 373

1997, Sept. 11	Litho.		Perf. 13	
869	A142	12c Fiddler	.40	.40
870	A142	15c Coral	.60	.60
871	A142	35c Blue	1.50	1.50
872	A142	$1 Giant hermit	4.50	4.50
		Nos. 869-872 (4)	7.00	7.00

Souvenir Sheet

873	A142	$2 Arrow	7.00	7.00

Orchids
A143

Designs: a, 20c, Psychilis macconnelliae. b, 50c, Tolumnia prionochila. c, 60c, Tetramicra canaliculata. d, 75c, Liparis elata.
$2, Dendrobium crumenatum, vert.

Wmk. 373

1997, Nov. 26	Litho.		Perf. 14	
874	A143	Strip of 4, #a.-d.	7.00	7.00

Souvenir Sheet

875	A143	$2 multicolored	6.00	6.00

World Voyage of Sir Francis Drake
A144

Portions of map and: No. 876: a, Francis Drake. b, Drake Coat of Arms. c, Queen Elizabeth I. d, Christopher & Marigold. e, Golden Hinde. f, Swan. g, Cacafuego. h, Elizabeth. i, Maria. j, Drake's Astrolabe. k, Golden Hinde beakhead. l, 16th cent. compass rose.
$2, Modern ship named, "Sir Francis Drake."

1997, Dec. 13			Perf. 14½	
876	A144	40c Sheet of 12, #a.-l.	19.00	19.00

Souvenir Sheet

877	A144	$2 multicolored	7.00	7.00

Diana, Princess of Wales (1961-97)
Common Design Type

Portraits: a, 15c. b, 45c. c, 70c. d, $1.

Perf. 14½x14

1998, Mar. 31	Litho.		Wmk. 373	
878	CD355	Sheet of 4, #a.-d.	5.50	5.50

No. 878 sold for $2.30 + 20c, with surtax from international sales being donated to the Princess Diana Memorial Fund and surtax from national sales being donated to designated local charity.

Royal Air Force, 80th Anniv.
Common Design Type of 1993 Reinscribed

Designs: 20c, Fairey IIIF. 35c, Supermarine Scapa. 50c, Westland Sea King HAR3. $1.50, BAe Harrier GR7.
No. 883: a, Curtiss H.12 Large America. b, Curtiss JN-4A. c, Bell Airacobra. d, Boulton-Paul Defiant.

Perf. 13½x14

1998, Apr. 1	Litho.		Wmk. 373	
879	CD350	20c multicolored	.50	.50
880	CD350	35c multicolored	1.00	1.00
881	CD350	50c multicolored	1.50	1.50
882	CD350	$1.50 multicolored	4.50	4.50
		Nos. 879-882 (4)	7.50	7.50

Souvenir Sheet

883	CD350	75c Sheet of 4, #a.-d.	9.50	9.50

Marine Life — A145

Designs: 15c, Fingerprint cyphoma. 30c, Long spined sea urchin. 45c, Split crown feather duster worm. $1, Upside down jelly. $2, Giant anemone.

1998, May 20	Wmk. 384		Perf. 14½	
884	A145	15c multicolored	.65	.65
885	A145	30c multicolored	1.40	1.40
886	A145	45c multicolored	2.10	2.10
887	A145	$1 multicolored	4.50	4.50
		Nos. 884-887 (4)	8.65	8.65

Souvenir Sheet

888	A145	$2 multicolored	8.50	8.50

No. 888 is a continuous design.

Childrens' Art Festival
A146

Wmk. 373

1998, Aug. 25	Litho.		Perf. 14	
889	A146	30c Girl in yellow & red, vert.	1.00	1.00
890	A146	45c Dancer, vert.	1.60	1.60
891	A146	$1.30 shown	4.50	4.50
		Nos. 889-891 (3)	7.10	7.10

Island Scenes Type of 1996

Designs: 12c, Salt pond. 30c, Shipwreck, HMS Rhone. 70c, Traditional house. $1.45, Salt Island.
$2, Gathering salt.

1998, Oct. 28				
892	A135	12c multicolored	.55	.55
893	A135	30c multicolored	1.10	1.10
894	A135	70c multicolored	2.50	2.50
895	A135	$1.45 multicolored	5.75	5.75
		Nos. 892-895 (4)	9.90	9.90

Souvenir Sheet

896	A135	$2 multicolored	9.00	9.00

Anniversaries and Events — A147

5c, Classes in computer training, woodworking, electronics. 15c, Students playing musical instruments. 30c, Chapel, Mona Campus, Jamaica. 45c, Plaque on wall, university crest. 50c, Dr. John Coakley Lettsom, map of Little Jost Van Dyke island. $1, Crest of the Medical Society of London, building.

Wmk. 384

1998, Dec. 14	Litho.		Perf. 14	
897	A147	5c multicolored	.25	.25
898	A147	15c multicolored	.40	.40
899	A147	30c multicolored	.90	.90
900	A147	45c multicolored	1.25	1.25
901	A147	50c multicolored	1.50	1.50
902	A147	$1 multicolored	2.75	2.75
		Nos. 897-902 (6)	7.05	7.05

Comprehensive education in Virgin Islands, 30th anniv. (#897-898). University of West Indies, 50th anniv. (#899-900). Founding of the Medical Society of London by Dr. John Coakley Lettsom, 225th anniv. (#901-902).

Lizards
A148

Designs: 5c, Rock iguana. 35c, Pygmy gecko. 60c, Slippery back skink. $1.50, Wood slave gecko.

No. 907: a, Doctor lizard. b, Yellow-bellied lizard. c, Man lizard. d, Ground lizard.

Perf. 14½x14

1999, Apr. 30	Litho.		Wmk. 373	
903	A148	5c multicolored	.30	.30
904	A148	35c multicolored	1.10	1.10
905	A148	60c multicolored	2.00	2.00
906	A148	$1.50 multicolored	4.75	4.75
		Nos. 903-906 (4)	8.15	8.15

Sheet of 4

907	A148	75c #a.-d.	9.00	9.00

Wedding of Prince Edward and Sophie Rhys-Jones
Common Design Type

Perf. 13¾x14

1999, June 15	Litho.		Wmk. 384	
908	CD356	20c Separate portraits	.55	.55
909	CD356	$3 Couple	7.75	7.75

1st Manned Moon Landing, 30th Anniv.
Common Design Type

Designs: 10c, Apollo 11 on launch pad. 40c, Second stage fires. 50c, Artist's rendition of Apollo 11 on moon. $2, Astronauts transfer to lunar module.
$2.50, Looking at earth from moon.

Perf. 14x13¾

1999, July 20	Litho.		Wmk. 384	
910	CD357	10c multicolored	.25	.25
911	CD357	40c multicolored	1.10	1.10
912	CD357	50c multicolored	1.40	1.40
913	CD357	$2 multicolored	5.50	5.50
		Nos. 910-913 (4)	8.25	8.25

Souvenir Sheet
Perf. 14

914	CD357	$2.50 multicolored	6.75	6.75

No. 914 contains one 40mm circular stamp.

Shells — A149

Designs: 25c, Measle cowrie. 35c, West Indian top shell. 75c, Zigzag scallop. $1, West Indian fighting conch.
No. 919: a, 5c, Sunrise tellin. b, 10c, King helmet. c, 25c, Like No. 915. d, 35c, Like No. 916. e, 75c, Like No. 917. f, $1, Like No. 918.

Wmk. 373

1999, Nov. 1	Litho.		Perf. 14¼	
915	A149	25c multi	.90	.90
916	A149	35c multi	1.50	1.50
917	A149	75c multi	3.00	3.00
918	A149	$1 multi	3.75	3.75
919	A149	Strip of 6, #a.-f.	17.50	17.50
		Nos. 915-919 (5)	26.65	26.65

Vignette extends to the top perforations on Nos. 915-918, but does not on stamps from No. 919.

Christmas
A150

Churches: 20c, Zion Hill Methodist. 35c, Fat Hogs Bay Seventh Day Adventist. 50c, Ruins of Kingstown St. Philip's Anglican. $1, Road Town St. William's Catholic.

Perf. 13¼x13

1999, Dec. 16	Litho.		Wmk. 373	
920	A150	20c multi	.50	.50
921	A150	35c multi	.85	.85
922	A150	50c multi	1.25	1.25
923	A150	$1 multi	2.60	2.60
		Nos. 920-923 (4)	5.20	5.20

British Monarchs — A151

a, Henry VII. b, Lady Jane Grey. c, Charles I. d, William III. e, George III. f, Edward VII.

Wmk. 373

2000, Feb. 29	Litho.		Perf. 14	
924	A151	60c Sheet of 6, #a.-f.	9.00	9.00

The Stamp Show 2000, London.

Prince William, 18th Birthday
Common Design Type

William: 20c, As toddler, on chest. 40c, As toddler, standing. 50c, With ski cap & goggles. 60c, Wearing suits & striped shirts. $1, Wearing sweater & bow tie.

Perf. 14¼x13¾, 13¾x14¼

2000, June 21	Litho.		Wmk. 373	
	Stamps With White Border			
925	CD359	20c multi	.50	.50
926	CD359	40c multi, vert.	1.00	1.00
927	CD359	50c multi, vert.	1.50	1.50
928	CD359	$1 multi	2.75	2.75
		Nos. 925-928 (4)	5.75	5.75

Souvenir Sheet
Stamps Without White Border
Perf. 14¼

929		Sheet of 5	9.00	9.00
a.	CD359	20c multi	.50	.50
b.	CD359	40c multi	1.00	1.00
c.	CD359	50c multi	1.25	1.25
d.	CD359	60c multi	1.60	1.60
e.	CD359	$1 multi	2.50	2.50

Queen Mother, 100th Birthday — A152

Various photos. Frame color: 15c, Lilac. 35c, Light green. 70c, Pink. $1.50, Light blue.

Wmk. 373

2000, Aug. 4	Litho.		Perf. 13¾	
930-933	A152	Set of 4	9.00	9.00

Flowering Plants and Trees — A153

10c, Red hibiscus. 15c, Pink oleander. 35c, Yellow bell. 50c, Yellow & white frangipani. 75c, Flamboyant. $2, Bougainvillea.

2000, Sept. 7			Perf. 13½x13¾	
934-939	A153	Set of 6	10.00	10.00

Millennium — A154

Virgin Islands history: 5c, Site of Emancipation Proclamation. 20c Nurse Mary Louise Davies. 30c, Cheyney University, US, founded by Richard Humphries. 45c, Enid Leona Scatliffe, former chief education officer. 50c, H. Lavity Stoutt Community College. $1 Sir J. Olva Georges.
$2, Victoria Cross of Pvt. Samuel Hodge, vert.

Wmk. 373

2000, Nov. 16	**Litho.**		**Perf. 14**
940-945 A154	Set of 6	6.75	6.75

Souvenir Sheet

946 A154	$2 multi	5.50	5.50

Restoration of the Legislative Council,
50th Anniv. — A155

Virgin Islands Councilmen: 10c, Dr. Q. William Osbourne & Arnando Scatliffe. 15c, H. Robinson O'Neal & A. Austin Henley. 20c, Wilfred W. Smith & John C. Brudenell-Bruce. 35c, Howard R. Penn & I. G. Fonseca. 50c, Carlton L. de Castro & Theodolph H. Faulkner. 60c, Willard W. Wheatley. $1, H. Lavity Stoutt.

2000, Nov. 22

947-953 A155	Set of 7	9.00	9.00

Souvenir Sheet

New Year 2001 (Year of the
Snake) — A156

No. 954: a, 50c, White-crowned dove. b, 50c, Bar-tailed cuckoo dove.

2001, Feb. 1			**Perf. 14½**
954 A156	Sheet of 2, #a-b	6.00	6.00

Hong Kong 2001 Stamp Exhibition.

Visiting
Royal
Navy
Ships
A157

Designs: 35c, HMS Wistaria, 1923-30. 50c, HMS Dundee, 1934-35. 60c, HMS Eurydice, 1787. 75c, HMS Pegasus, 1787. $1, HMS Astrea, 1807. $1.50 HM Yacht Britannia, 1966.

Wmk. 373

2001, Sept. 28	**Litho.**		**Perf. 14**
955-960 A157	Set of 6	19.00	19.00

Nobel Prizes,
Cent. — A158

Nobel laureates: 10c, Fridtjof Nansen, Peace, 1922. 20c, Albert Einstein, Physics, 1921. 25c, Sir Arthur Lewis, Economics, 1979. 40c, Saint-John Perse, Literature, 1960. 70c, Mother Teresa, Peace, 1979. $2, Christian Lous Lange, Peace, 1921.

2001, Oct. 5

961-966 A158	Set of 6	16.00	16.00

**Reign Of Queen Elizabeth II, 50th
Anniv. Issue**

Common Design Type

Designs: Nos. 967, 971a, 15c, Princess Elizabeth in uniform. Nos. 968, 971b, 50c, In 1977. Nos. 969, 971c, 60c, Holding flowers. Nos. 970, 971d, 75c, In 1996. No. 971e, $1, 1955 portrait by Annigoni (38x50mm).

Perf. 14¼x14½, 13¾ (#971e)

2002, Feb. 6	**Litho.**		**Wmk. 373**	
With Gold Frames				
967 CD360	15c multicolored		.60	.60
968 CD360	50c multicolored		1.90	1.90
969 CD360	60c multicolored		2.25	2.25
970 CD360	75c multicolored		2.75	2.75
Nos. 967-971 (4)			7.50	7.50

Souvenir Sheet

Without Gold Frames

971 CD360	Sheet of 5, #a-e	11.50	11.50

Reptiles in
Guinness
Book Of
World
Records
A159

Designs: 5c, Estuarine crocodile. 20c, Reticulated python. 30c, Komodo dragon. 40c, Boa constrictor. $1, Dwarf caiman. $2, Sphaerodactylus parthenopion. $1.50, Head of Sphaerodactylus parthenopion.

Perf. 13¼x13

2002, June 10	**Litho.**	**Wmk. 373**	
972-977 A159	Set of 6	13.00	13.00
977a	Sheet of 6, #972-977	13.00	13.00

Souvenir Sheet

978 A159	$1.50 multi	7.50	7.50

Queen Mother Elizabeth (1900-2002)

Common Design Type

Designs: 20c, Wearing tiara (black and white photograph). 60c, Wearing dark blue hat. Nos. 981, 983a, $2, Wearing hat (black and white photograph). Nos. 982, 983b, $3, Wearing pink hat.

Perf. 13¾x14¼

2002, Aug. 5	**Litho.**		**Wmk. 373**	
With Purple Frames				
979 CD361	20c multicolored		.50	.50
980 CD361	60c multicolored		1.50	1.50
981 CD361	$2 multicolored		5.00	5.00
982 CD361	$3 multicolored		7.50	7.50
Nos. 979-982 (4)			14.50	14.50

Souvenir Sheet

Without Purple Frames

Perf. 14½x14¼

983 CD361	Sheet of 2, #a-b	12.00	12.00

Royal
Navy
Ships
A160

Designs: 20c, HMS Invincible and HMS Argo. 35c, HMS Boreas and HMS Solebay. 50c, HMS Coventry. $3, HMS Argyll.

Wmk. 373

2002, Aug. 30	**Litho.**		**Perf. 14**
984-987 A160	Set of 4	16.00	16.00

Island Scenes Type of 1996

Designs: 5c, Spring Bay. 40c, Devils Bay. 60c, The Baths. 75c, St. Thomas Bay. $1, Savannah and Pond Bay. $2, Trunk Bay.

2002, Sept. 13

988-993 A135	Set of 6	11.00	11.00

West Indian
Whistling
Duck — A161

Designs: Nos. 994, 998a, 10c, Duckling and eggs. Nos. 995, 998b, 35c, Duck standing on rock, vert. Nos. 996, 998c, 40c, Duck in water, vert. Nos. 997, 998d, 70c, Two ducks. No. 998e, $2, Duck's head.

Perf. 14¼x13¾, 13¾x14¼

2002, Dec.	**Litho.**		**Wmk. 373**	
Stamps With Brown Border				
994-997 A161	Set of 4		4.25	4.25

Souvenir Sheet

Stamps Without Brown Border

**Perf. 14¼x14½ (Horiz. stamps), 14½
(Vert. stamps)**

998 A161	Sheet of 5, #a-e	10.00	10.00

Birdlife International.

Anniversaries and Events — A162

No. 999, 10c: a, Sprinters. b, Cyclists.
No. 1000, 35c: a, Laser class sailboats. b, Women's long jump.
No. 1001, 50c: a, Bareboat class sailboats. b, Racing Cruiser class sailboats.
No. 1002, $1.35: a, Carlos and Esme Downing, founders of Island Sun newspaper. b, Island Sun newspaper and emblem.

Wmk. 373

2003, Mar. 13	**Litho.**		**Perf. 13½**	
Horiz. pairs, #a-b				
999-1002 A162	Set of 4		13.00	13.00

2002 Commonwealth Games (#999); Admission to Olympic Games, 20th anniv. (#1000); Spring Regatta, 30th anniv. (#1001); Island Sun newspaper, 40th anniv. (#1002).

Head of Queen Elizabeth II

Common Design Type

Wmk. 373

2003, June 2	**Litho.**		**Perf. 13¾**	
1003 CD362	$5 multi		10.00	10.00

**Coronation of Queen Elizabeth II,
50th Anniv.**

Common Design Type

Designs: Nos. 1004, 1006a, 15c, Queen in gown. Nos. 1005, 1006b, $5, Royal Family on Buckingham Palace balcony.

Perf. 14¼x14½

2003, June 2	**Litho.**		**Wmk. 373**	
Vignettes Framed, Red Background				
1004 CD363	15c multi		.50	.50
1005 CD363	$5 multi		12.00	12.00

Souvenir Sheet

**Vignettes Without Frame, Purple
Panel**

1006 CD363	Sheet of 2, #a-b	12.50	12.50

Prince William, 21st Birthday

Common Design Type

Designs: 50c, William in polo uniform at right. $2, William on polo pony at left.

Wmk. 373

2003, June 21	**Litho.**		**Perf. 14¼**	
With Gray Frames				
1007 CD364	50c multi		1.00	1.00
1008 CD364	$2 multi		4.00	4.00
Without Gray Frames				
1009	Horiz. pair		5.00	5.00
a.	CD364 50c multi		1.00	1.00
b.	CD364 $2 multi		4.00	4.00
Nos. 1007-1009 (3)			10.00	10.00

Powered Flight, Cent. — A163

Designs: 15c, Douglas DC-4. 20c, Boeing Stearman "Kaydet." 35c, B-25 J Mitchell. 40c, F-4B Phantom. 70c, CH-47 Chinook helicopter. $2, AH-64 Apache helicopter.

Perf. 13¼x13¾

2003, Nov. 15	**Litho.**	**Wmk. 373**	
Stamp + Label			
1010-1015 A163	Set of 6	13.00	13.00

Christmas — A164

Details from Arrival of the English Ambassadors, by Vittore Carpaccio: 20c, Men standing near railing and pillar. 40c, Men, ships in background. $2.50, Seated man.
No. 1019a (36x36mm), Kneeling man delivering message.

Perf. 13¾x13½

2003, Dec. 15	**Litho.**	**Wmk. 373**	
1016-1018 A164	Set of 3	8.00	8.00

Souvenir Sheet

1019 A164	Sheet, #1016-1018, 1019a	11.50	11.50
a.	$1 multi, perf. 13½x13¼		

Game Fish Type of 1997

Serpentine Die Cut 12½ on 3 Sides

2004, July 1	**Litho.**		**Unwmk.**
Self-Adhesive			
Booklet Stamps			
Size: 21x17mm			
1020 A140	15c Barracuda	.30	.30
a.	Booklet pane of 4	1.20	
1021 A140	20c Tarpon	.40	.40
a.	Booklet pane of 4	1.60	
1022 A140	35c Sailfish	.70	.70
a.	Booklet pane of 4	2.80	
	Complete booklet, #1020a, 1022a	4.00	
1023 A140	40c Dolphin	.80	.80
a.	Booklet pane of 3 + label	2.40	
	Complete booklet, #1021a, 1023a	5.25	
Nos. 1020-1023 (4)		2.20	2.20

Fruit — A165

2004, July 20	**Wmk. 373**		**Perf. 13¾**
Inscribed "2004" Below Design			
1024 A165	15c Pomegranates	.30	.30
1025 A165	20c Cashews	.40	.40
1026 A165	35c Tamarinds	.70	.70
1027 A165	40c Soursop	.80	.80
1028 A165	50c Mangos	1.00	1.00
1029 A165	$2 Guavaberries	4.00	4.00
1030 A165	$5 Mamee apples	4.00	4.00
Nos. 1024-1030 (7)		17.20	17.20

See Nos. 1042-1049.

2007

Inscribed "2007" Below Design

1025a A165	20c multicolored	.40	.40
1026a A165	35c multicolored	.70	.70
1028a A165	50c multicolored	1.00	1.00
1029a A165	$2 multicolored	4.00	4.00
Nos. 1025a-1029a (4)		6.10	6.10

Virgin Islands
Festival, 50th
Anniv. — A166

Designs: 10c, Parade. 60c, Horse race. $1, Kayak race. $2.35, Festival Queen.

Wmk. 373

2004, Oct. 26	**Litho.**		**Perf. 13¼**
1031-1034 A166	Set of 4	11.50	11.50

Sports — A167

Designs: 75c, Women soccer players. $1, Runner.

2004, Dec. 30   **Perf. 14**
1035-1036 A167   Set of 2   6.00 6.00

FIFA (Fédération Internationale de Football Association), cent.; 2004 Summer Olympics, Athens.

Caribbean Endemic Bird Festival A168

Designs: 5c, Black and white warbler. 25c, Worm-eating warbler. 35c, Yellow warbler. 50c, Prothonotary warbler.
No. 1041: a, 10c, Prairie warbler. b, 15c, Yellow-rumped warbler. c, 40c, Black-throated blue warbler. d, 60c, Cape May warbler. e, 75c, Northern parula. f, $2.75, Palm warbler.

Wmk. 373
2005, July 8   **Litho.**   **Perf. 13¾**
1037-1040 A168   Set of 4   3.50 3.50
1041 A168   Miniature sheet, #1037-1040, 1041a-1041f   14.00 14.00

Fruit Type of 2004
2005, Aug. 25   **Wmk. 373**
Inscribed "2005" Below Design
1042	A165	1c Hog plum	.25	.25
a.		Inscribed "2007"	.25	.25
1043	A165	10c Coco plum	.25	.25
1044	A165	25c Sugar apple	.50	.50
1045	A165	60c Papaya	1.25	1.25
1046	A165	75c Custard apple	1.50	1.50
1047	A165	$1 Otaheite gooseberry	2.00	2.00
1048	A165	$1.50 Guava	3.00	3.00
1049	A165	$10 Passion fruit	20.00	20.00
		Nos. 1042-1049 (8)	28.75	28.75

Pope John Paul II (1920-2005) A169

Wmk. 373
2005, Aug. 18   **Litho.**   **Perf. 14**
1050 A169   75c multi   3.25 3.25

Worldwide Fund for Nature (WWF) — A170

Various depictions of Virgin Islands tree boa: 20c, 30c, 70c, $1.05.

Wmk. 373
2005, Sept. 15   **Litho.**   **Perf. 14**
1051-1054 A170   Set of 4   4.50 4.50
1054a   Miniature sheet, 2 each #1051-1054   10.50 10.50

Battle of Trafalgar, Bicent. — A171

Designs: 5c, HMS Colossus. 25c, HMS Boreas. 75c, HMS Victory. $3, Admiral Horatio Nelson, vert.
$2.50, HMS Colossus and French ship.

2005, Oct. 18   **Perf. 14x14¾, 14¾x14**
1055-1058 A171   Set of 4   19.00 19.00
Souvenir Sheet
Perf. 13½
1059 A171 $2.50 multi   12.50 12.50
No. 1059 contains one 44x44mm stamp.

Christmas A172

Flora: 15c, Century plant. 35c, Poinsettia, horiz. 60c, Inkberry. $2.50, Snow on the mountain, horiz.

2005, Nov. 3   **Perf. 14¾x14, 14x14¾**
1060-1063 A172   Set of 4   10.00 10.00

Anniversaries A173

Designs: 20c, Social Security, 25th anniv. 40c, ZBVI radio station, 40th anniv. 50c, Beef Island Airstrip, 50th anniv. $1, Rotary International, cent.

Wmk. 373
2005, Nov. 16   **Litho.**   **Perf. 13¾**
1064-1067 A173   Set of 4   6.00 6.00

Queen Elizabeth II, 80th Birthday A174

Queen: 15c, As young woman, in uniform. 75c, Wearing white hat. No. 1070, $1.50, Wearing large earrings. No. 1071, $2, Wearing gray hat with large brim.
No. 1072: a, $1.50, Like 75c. b, $2, Like #1070.

Perf. 14¼x14
2006, July 17   **Litho.**   **Wmk. 373**
Stamps With White Frames
1068-1071 A174   Set of 4   12.50 12.50
Souvenir Sheet
Stamps Without White Frames
1072 A174   Sheet of 2, #a-b   10.00 10.00

Red Cross Buildings A175

Designs: 20c, New building. $3, Previous building.

Wmk. 373
2007, Aug. 1   **Litho.**   **Perf. 14**
1073-1074 A175   Set of 2   7.00 7.00

Royal Air Force, 90th Anniv. A176

Designs: 18c, Supermarine Spitfire. 20c, Avro Lancaster. 35c, Douglas C-47 Dakota. 60c, Handley Page Halifax. $1.25 Westland Lysander.
$2.50, Spitfire patrolling D-Day beaches.

Wmk. 373
2008, Apr. 1   **Litho.**   **Perf. 14**
1075-1079 A176   Set of 5   5.25 5.25
Souvenir Sheet
1080 A176 $2.50 multi   5.00 5.00

Princess Diana (1961-97) A177

Princess Diana in: 60c, Black dress. $3.50, Red dress.

2008, Apr. 7   **Perf. 13¾**
1081 A177   60c multi   1.25 1.25
Souvenir Sheet
Perf. 14¼
1082 A177 $3.50 multi   7.25 7.25
No. 1082 contains one 42x57mm stamp.

Rev. Charles Wesley (1707-88), Hymn Writer — A178

Designs: 20c, Arms. 50c, Wesley. $1.75, Wesley, diff.

2008, May 1   **Perf. 14**
1083-1085 A178   Set of 3   5.00 5.00

2008 Summer Olympics, Beijing A179

Designs: 15c, Bamboo, runner. 18c, Dragon, yachting. 20c, Lanterns, runner. $1, Fish, yachting.

2008, Aug. 1   **Perf. 13½**
1086-1089 A179   Set of 4   4.00 4.00

Ministerial Government — A180

Arms and: 18c, Mace in House of Assembly, mace head. 35c, House of Assembly, entrance arch. 60c, Henry O. Creque, Ivan Dawson. $2, Paul Wattley, Terrance B. Lettsome.

2008, Aug. 21   **Perf. 14x14¾**
1090-1093 A180   Set of 4   6.50 6.50

End of World War I, 90th Anniv. — A181

Designs: 75c, Sanctuary Wood Cemetery, Ypres, Belgium. 80c, Somme Battlefield, France, horiz. 90c, Lone Pine Cemetery, Gallipoli, Turkey, horiz. $1, War Memorial, Vauquois, France. $1.15, Theipval Memorial, France, horiz. $1.25, Menin Gate, Ypres, Belgium, horiz.
$2, Wreath of Remembrance.

Wmk. 406
2008, Sept. 16   **Litho.**   **Perf. 14**
1094-1099 A181   Set of 6   13.00 13.00
Souvenir Sheet
1100 A181 $2 multi   5.00 5.00

J. R. O'Neal Botanic Gardens — A182

Designs: 20c, Climbing pandanus. 35c, True aloe. 50c, Crown of thorns. $1, Red-eared slider (turtle).
$2.50, Fountain.

Wmk. 373
2009, Mar. 27   **Litho.**   **Perf. 14**
1101-1104 A182   Set of 4   6.00 6.00
Souvenir Sheet
1105 A182 $2.50 multi   7.00 7.00

Ships and Explorers A183

Designs: 15c HMS Ark Royal. 20c, Whydah. 60c, Santa Maria. 70c, RMS Rhone. 90c, Golden Hind. $1.95, HMY Britannia.
$2, Christopher Columbus, vert.

Wmk. 406
2009, May 25   **Litho.**   **Perf. 14**
1106-1111 A183   Set of 6   11.00 11.00
Souvenir Sheet
1112 A183 $2 multi   5.50 5.50

Naval Aviation, Cent. A184

Victoria Cross recipients: 18c, Lieutenant Robert Hampton Gray. 35c, Lieutenant Commander Eugene Esmonde. 60c, Flight Squadron Lieutenant Rex Warneford. 90c, Squadron Commander Richard Bell Davies. $2, HMS Illustrious.

2009, June 30
1113-1116 A184 Set of 4 6.00 6.00
Souvenir Sheet
1117 A184 $2 multi 5.50 5.50

Nos. 1113-1116 each were printed in sheets of 8 + central label.

Space Exploration A185

Designs: 50c, Goddard Rocket Shop, Roswell, New Mexico, 1940. 75c, Vertol VZ-2, 1960. $1, Apollo 11 on launch pad, 1969. $1.25, Space Shuttle flight STS-126 on launch pad, 2008. $2.30, Docking procedure, International Space Station.
$3, Lunar Rover on Moon, painting by Capt. Alan Bean, vert.

2009, July 20 *Perf. 13¼*
1118-1122 A185 Set of 5 15.00 15.00
Souvenir Sheet
Perf. 13x13¼
1123 A185 $3 multi 7.50 7.50

No. 1123 contains one 40x60mm stamp. Nos. 1118-1122 each were printed in sheets of 6.

Scouting in the Virgin Islands, 75th Anniv. (in 2007) — A185a

2009 Litho. **Wmk. 373** *Perf. 14*
1123A A185a 40c multi — —

Coral Reefs A186

Designs: 20c, Sea turtle. 35c, Fish. 50c, Seahorse, vert. 60c, Shell. $1.50, Coral reef.

2010, Mar. 29 **Wmk. 406** Litho. *Perf. 12½*
1124-1128 A186 Set of 5 7.50 7.50

Construction of New North Sound Post Office Substation A187

Designs: 20c, John E. George, Sub-postmaster. 50c, New post office substation, horiz. $2, Old post office substation, horiz.

Wmk. 406
2010, May 3 Litho. *Perf. 12½*
1129-1131 A187 Set of 3 5.50 5.50

East End Methodist Church, 200th Anniv. A188

Designs: 20c, Church bell. 50c, Church in 2010. 60c, Church in 1977. $2, Church in early 19th cent.

Wmk. 406
2010, Nov. 10 Litho. *Perf. 13¼*
1132-1135 A188 Set of 4 6.75 6.75

Sailability — A189

Various sailors and sailboats with country name and lower panels in: 5c, Dark red. 20c, Violet blue. 25c, Purple. 40c, Green. 50c, Red. $1.50, Orange red.

Wmk. 406
2011, Feb. 24 Litho. *Perf. 12½*
1136-1141 A189 Set of 6 6.00 6.00

2011 Spring Regatta A190

Various sailboats with country name and lower panels in: 15c, Green. 35c, Blue, vert. 50c, Olive green, vert. $2, Olive brown.

2011, Mar. 1
1142-1145 A190 Set of 4 6.00 6.00

Souvenir Sheet

Wedding of Prince William and Catherine Middleton — A191

Perf. 14¾x14
2011, Apr. 29 **Wmk. 406**
1146 A191 $5 multi 10.00 10.00

Coronation of Queen Elizabeth II, 60th Anniv. — A192

Queen Elizabeth II: 20c, And Prince Philip at coronation, 1953. 50c, With Prince Philip on

1966 Virgin Islands visit. $1.50, Walking in Virgin Islands, 1977. $2, With Prince Philip, 2013.

2013, Oct. 1 *Perf. 13¼x13¾*
1147-1150 A192 Set of 4 8.50 8.50

Worldwide Fund for Nature (WWF) — A193

Antillean crested hummingbird: Nos. 1151, 1155a, 35c, Two birds on branch. Nos. 1152, 1155b, 40c, Bird in nest. Nos. 1153, 1155c, 75c, Bird in flight near flowers. Nos. 1154, 1155d, $1.50, Head of bird.
$5, Bird in flight near flowers, diff.

Unwmk.
2014, Jan. 30 Litho. *Perf. 14*
Stamps With White Frames
1151-1154 A193 Set of 4 6.00 6.00
Stamps Without White Frames
1155 A193 Strip of 4, #a-d 6.00 6.00
Souvenir Sheet
Perf. 14x14¾
1156 A193 $5 multi 10.00 10.00

No. 1156 contains one 48x32mm stamp.

Royal Christenings A194

Photographs of British royalty with christened infants: 50c, Queen Elizabeth II, 1926. 75c, Prince Charles, 1948. $2, Prince William, 1982. $2.50, Prince George, 2013.

2014, Sept. 25 Litho. *Perf. 13x13¼*
1157-1160 A194 Set of 4 11.50 11.50

WAR TAX STAMPS

Regular Issue of 1913 Overprinted

1916-17 **Wmk. 3** *Perf. 14*
Die I
MR1 A9 1p scarlet .55 8.00
 a. 1p carmine 2.50 21.00
MR2 A9 3p violet, *yellow* 4.50 26.00

OFFICIAL STAMPS

Catalogue values for unused stamps in this section are for Never Hinged items.

Nos. 365-368, 370-380 Overprinted "OFFICIAL" in Silver

1985, July		Litho.	*Perf. 14*	
O1	A57	1c multi	.30	1.25
O2	A57	3c multi	.45	1.25
O3	A57	5c multi	.45	.45
O4	A57	8c multi	.55	.60
O5	A57	13c multi	.80	.75
O6	A57	15c multi	.80	.75
O7	A57	18c multi	.90	1.50
O8	A57	20c multi	.90	.80
O9	A57	25c multi	1.25	2.00
O10	A57	30c multi	1.40	1.00
O11	A57	60c multi	2.00	2.50
O12	A57	$1 multi	3.25	3.75
O13	A57	$2.50 multi	5.75	8.00
O14	A57	$3 multi	8.75	10.00
O15	A57	$5 multi	11.50	11.50
		Nos. O1-O15 (15)	39.05	46.10

Nos. 364-380 overprinted in gold and Nos. 364, 369 overprinted in silver exist but were not issued by the Virgin Islands.

Nos. 490-508 Ovptd. "OFFICIAL"

1986		Litho.	*Perf. 14*	
O16	A81	1c multicolored	.40	.40
O17	A81	2c multicolored	.40	.40
O18	A81	5c multicolored	.40	.40
O19	A81	8c multicolored	.40	.40
O20	A81	10c multicolored	.40	.40
O21	A81	12c multicolored	.50	.50
O22	A81	15c multicolored	.60	.60
O23	A81	18c multicolored	.70	.70
O24	A81	20c multicolored	.85	.85
O25	A81	25c multicolored	1.00	1.00
O26	A81	30c multicolored	1.25	1.25
O27	A81	35c multicolored	1.40	1.40
O28	A81	40c multicolored	1.60	1.60
O29	A81	50c multicolored	1.75	1.75
O30	A81	60c multicolored	2.10	2.10
O31	A81	$1 multicolored	3.50	3.50
O32	A81	$2 multicolored	7.50	7.50
O33	A81	$3 multicolored	11.00	11.00
O34	A81	$5 multicolored	20.00	20.00
		Nos. O16-O34 (19)	55.75	55.75

Issue: 1, 5, 10, 15, 20-35c, $5, 7/3; others, 1/28.

Nos. 694-695, 698, 701-706, 708 Ovptd. "OFFICIAL"

1991, Sept.		Litho.	*Perf. 14*	
O37	A116	5c multicolored	.25	.25
O38	A116	10c multicolored	.25	.25
O41	A116	20c multicolored	.75	.75
O44	A116	35c multicolored	1.40	1.40
O45	A116	40c multicolored	1.50	1.50
O46	A116	45c multicolored	1.75	1.75
O47	A116	50c multicolored	1.90	1.90
O48	A116	70c multicolored	2.75	2.75
O49	A116	$1 multicolored	3.75	3.75
O51	A116	$3 multicolored	11.50	11.50
		Nos. O37-O51 (10)	25.80	25.80

Ovpt. on Nos. O37-O51 is 19mm long.
Used values are for c-t-o examples.
Nos. O37-O38, O41, O44-O49, O51 were not available unused until mid-1992.
This set was never used in the Virgin Islands.

Nos. 694-695, 698, 700-706, 708 Ovptd. "OFFICIAL"

1992		Litho.	*Perf. 14*	
O55	A116	5c multicolored	.25	.25
O56	A116	10c multicolored	.25	.25
O59	A116	20c multicolored	.75	.75
O61	A116	30c multicolored	1.25	1.25
O62	A116	35c multicolored	1.40	1.40
O63	A116	40c multicolored	1.50	1.50
O64	A116	45c multicolored	1.75	1.75
O65	A116	50c multicolored	1.90	1.90
O66	A116	70c multicolored	2.75	2.75
O67	A116	$1 multicolored	3.75	3.75
O69	A116	$3 multicolored	11.50	11.50
		Nos. O55-O69 (11)	27.05	27.05

Ovpt. on Nos. O55-O56, O59, O61-O67, O69 is 15½mm long.

WALLIS & FUTUNA ISLANDS

ˈwä-ləs and fə-ˈtü-nə

ˈī-lənds

LOCATION — Group of islands in the South Pacific Ocean, northeast of Fiji
GOVT. — French Overseas Territory
AREA — 106 sq. mi.
POP. — 15,129 (1999 est.)
CAPITAL — Mata-Utu, Wallis Island

100 Centimes = 1 Franc

Catalogue values for unused stamps in this country are for Never Hinged items, beginning with Scott 127 in the regular postage section, Scott B9 in the semi-postal section, Scott C1 in the airpost section, and Scott J37 in the postage due section.

New Caledonia Stamps of 1905-28 Overprinted in Black or Red

1920-28 Unwmk. *Perf. 14x13½*

1	A16	1c black, *green*	.30	.30
a.		Double overprint	175.00	
2	A16	2c red brown	.30	.30
3	A16	4c blue, *org*	.50	.50
4	A16	5c green	.50	.50
5	A16	5c dull blue ('22)	.40	*.55*
6	A16	10c rose	.65	.65
7	A16	10c green ('22)	.90	.90
8	A16	10c red, *pink* ('25)	2.25	2.25
9	A16	15c violet	1.10	1.10
10	A17	20c gray brown	1.00	*1.25*
11	A17	25c blue, *grn*	1.50	1.50
12	A17	25c red, *yel* ('22)	1.00	1.00
13	A17	30c brown, *org*	1.60	*2.00*
14	A17	30c dp rose ('22)	1.50	*1.75*
15	A17	30c red orange ('25)	.85	.85
16	A17	30c lt green ('27)	2.40	*3.25*
17	A17	35c black, *yel* (R)	1.00	1.00
18	A17	40c rose, *grn*	1.25	*1.50*
19	A17	45c violet brn, *pnksh*	1.60	*2.00*
20	A17	50c red, *org*	1.75	*2.10*
21	A17	50c dark blue ('22)	2.00	*2.40*
22	A17	50c dark gray ('25)	2.60	*3.25*
23	A17	65c deep blue ('28)	7.50	*7.50*
24	A17	75c olive green	2.50	*2.60*

Nos. 113, 115-116 Overprinted

25	A18	1fr blue, *yel grn*	5.25	*5.25*
a.		Triple overprint	200.00	
b.		Double overprint	200.00	
c.		Pair, one stamp without overprint	525.00	
26	A18	1.10fr orange brn ('28)	5.50	*7.25*
27	A18	2fr carmine, *bl*	8.50	*8.50*
28	A18	5fr black, *org* (R)	17.00	*17.00*
		Nos. 1-28 (28)	73.20	*79.00*

No. 9 Surcharged in Various Colors

1922

29	A16	0.01c on 15c violet (Bk)	.75	*.95*
30	A16	0.02c on 15c violet (Bl)	.75	*.95*
31	A16	0.04c on 15c violet (G)	.75	*.95*
32	A16	0.05c on 15c violet (R)	.75	*.95*
		Nos. 29-32 (4)	3.00	*3.80*

Stamps and Types of 1920 Surcharged in Black or Red

1924-27

33	A18	25c on 2fr car, *bl*	1.00	1.00
34	A18	25c on 5fr black, *org*	1.00	1.00
35	A17	65c on 40c rose red, *grn* ('25)	1.75	*2.00*
36	A17	85c on 75c ol grn ('25)	1.40	*1.60*
37	A17	90c on 75c dp rose ('27)	2.25	*2.75*
38	A18	1.25fr on 1fr dp bl (R; '26)	1.10	*1.40*
39	A18	1.50fr on 1fr dp bl, *bl* ('27)	5.50	*5.50*
a.		Double surcharge	300.00	
b.		Surcharge omitted	290.00	
40	A18	3fr on 5fr red vio ('27)	9.00	*8.00*
a.		Surcharge omitted	240.00	
b.		Double surcharge	325.00	
41	A18	10fr on 5fr ol, *lav* ('27)	42.50	42.50
42	A18	20fr on 5fr vio rose, *yel* ('27)	50.00	50.00
		Nos. 33-42 (10)	115.50	*115.75*

New Caledonia Stamps and Types of 1928-40 Overprinted as in 1920

1930-40 *Perf. 13½, 14x13, 14x13½*

43	A19	1c brn vio & indigo	.25	.25
a.		Double overprint	200.00	
44	A19	2c dk brn & yel grn	.25	.25
45	A19	3c brn vio & ind ('40)	.25	.25
46	A19	4c org & Prus grn	.25	.25
47	A19	5c Prus bl & dp ol	.30	*.40*
48	A19	10c gray lil & dk brn	.30	*.40*
49	A19	15c yel brn & dp bl	.30	*.40*
50	A19	20c brn red & dk brn	.60	*.70*
51	A19	25c dk grn & dk brn	1.10	*1.25*
52	A20	30c gray grn & bl grn	1.10	*1.25*
53	A20	35c Prus grn & dk grn ('38)	1.10	*1.25*
a.		Without overprint	200.00	
54	A20	40c brt red & olive	1.10	1.10
55	A20	45c dp bl & red org	1.10	*1.25*
56	A20	45c bl grn & dl grn ('40)	.90	*1.00*
57	A20	50c violet & brn	1.10	1.10
58	A20	55c bl vio & rose red ('38)	2.40	*2.75*
59	A20	60c vio bl & car ('40)	.75	*.90*
60	A20	65c org brn & bl	2.00	2.00
61	A20	70c dp rose & brn ('38)	1.40	*1.60*
62	A20	75c Prus bl & ol gray	3.00	3.00
63	A20	80c dk cl & grn ('38)	1.40	*1.60*
64	A20	85c green & brown ('38)	3.75	*4.00*
65	A20	90c dp red & brt red	2.40	*2.75*
66	A20	90c ol grn & rose red ('39)	1.10	*1.25*
67	A21	1fr dp ol & sal red	4.00	*4.75*
68	A21	1fr rose red & dk car ('38)	2.40	*2.75*
69	A21	1fr brn red & grn ('40)	.80	.80
70	A21	1.10fr dp grn & brn	40.00	*40.00*
71	A21	1.25fr brn red & grn ('33)	3.75	*3.50*
72	A21	1.25fr rose red & dk car ('39)	1.10	*1.25*
73	A21	1.40fr dk bl & red org ('40)	1.10	*1.40*
74	A21	1.50fr dp bl & bl	1.25	*1.50*
75	A21	1.60fr dp grn & brn ('40)	1.60	*2.00*
76	A21	1.75fr dk bl & red org ('33)	16.00	*16.00*
77	A21	1.75fr vio bl ('38)	2.50	*2.75*
78	A21	2fr red org & brn	2.00	*1.90*
79	A21	2.25fr vio bl ('39)	2.50	*2.40*
80	A21	2.50fr brn & lt brn ('40)	2.00	*2.40*
81	A21	3fr magenta & brn	2.00	*2.00*
82	A21	5fr dk bl & brn	2.50	*2.60*
83	A21	10fr vio & brn, *pnksh*	3.50	*3.50*
84	A21	20fr red & brn, *yel*	5.25	*5.25*
		Nos. 43-84 (42)	122.45	*127.70*

For overprints see Nos. 94-126.

For types A19 and A21 of New Caledonia, with "RF," overprinted as above, see Nos. 126A-126F.

Common Design Types pictured following the introduction.

Colonial Exposition Issue

Common Design Types

1931, Apr. 13 Engr. *Perf. 12½*
Name of Country Typo. in Black

85	CD70	40c deep green	8.75	8.75
86	CD71	50c violet	8.75	8.75
87	CD72	90c red orange	8.75	8.75
88	CD73	1.50fr dull blue	8.75	8.75
		Nos. 85-88 (4)	35.00	35.00

Colonial Arts Exhibition Issue

Common Design Type
Souvenir Sheet

1937 *Imperf.*

89	CD78	3fr red violet	28.50	*37.50*
		Never hinged	45.00	

New York World's Fair Issue

Common Design Type

1939, May 10 Engr. *Perf. 12½x12*

90	CD82	1.25fr carmine lake	3.00	3.00
91	CD82	2.25fr ultramarine	3.00	3.00

Petain Issue

New Caledonia Nos. 216A-216B Overprinted "WALLIS ET FUTUNA" in Lilac or Red

1941 Engr. *Perf. 12½x12*

92	A21a	1fr bluish green (L)	1.40	
93	A21a	2.50fr dark blue (R)	1.40	

Nos. 92-93 were issued by the Vichy government in France, but were not placed on sale in Wallis & Futuna.

For surcharges, see Nos. B8A-B8B.

Nos. 43-69, 71, 74, 77-78, 80-84 with Additional Overprint in Black

1941-43 *Perf. 14x13½*

94	A19	1c	2.75	2.75
95	A19	2c	2.75	2.75
96	A19	3c	100.00	100.00
97	A19	4c	3.75	3.75
98	A19	5c	3.75	3.75
99	A19	10c	3.75	3.75
100	A19	15c	3.75	3.75
101	A19	20c	5.00	5.00
102	A19	25c	5.00	5.00
103	A20	30c	5.00	5.00
104	A20	35c	3.75	3.75
105	A20	40c	4.50	4.50
106	A20	45c #55	4.50	4.50
107	A20	45c #56	110.00	110.00
108	A20	50c	3.75	3.75
109	A20	55c	3.75	3.75
110	A20	60c	90.00	90.00
111	A20	65c	3.75	3.75
112	A20	70c	3.75	3.75
113	A20	75c	5.00	5.00
114	A20	80c	3.75	3.75
115	A20	85c	4.50	4.50
116	A20	90c #65	3.75	3.75
117	A21	1fr #68	4.50	4.50
118	A21	1.25fr #71	4.50	4.50
119	A21	1.50fr	3.75	3.75
120	A21	1.75fr #77	3.75	3.75
121	A21	2fr	4.50	4.50
122	A21	2.50fr	175.00	175.00
123	A21	3fr	3.75	3.75
124	A21	5fr	10.00	10.00
125	A21	10fr	65.00	65.00
126	A21	20fr	110.00	110.00
		Nos. 94-126 (33)	765.00	765.00

Types of New Caledonia Without "RF" overprinted as in 1920

1944

126A	A19	10c gray lil & dk brn	1.10
126B	A19	15c yel brn & dp bl	1.25
126C	A21	1fr brn red & grn	1.90
126D	A21	1.50fr blue	2.10
126E	A21	10fr vio & brn, *pnksh*	2.10
126F	A21	20fr red & brn, *yel*	2.60
		Nos. 126A-126F (6)	11.05

Nos. 126A-126F were issued by the Vichy government in France, but were not placed on sale in Wallis & Futuna.

Catalogue values for unused stamps in this section, from this point to the end of the section, are for Never Hinged items.

Ivi Poo, Bone Carving in Tiki Design
A1

1944 Unwmk. Photo. *Perf. 11½x12*

127	A1	5c lt brown	.40	.30
128	A1	10c dp gray blue	.40	.30
129	A1	25c emerald	.40	.30
130	A1	30c dull orange	.40	.30
131	A1	40c dk slate grn	1.10	.90
132	A1	80c brown red	1.10	.90
133	A1	1fr red violet	.50	.40
134	A1	1.50fr red	.65	.40
135	A1	2fr gray black	.65	.50
136	A1	2.50fr brt ultra	.90	.65
137	A1	4fr dark purple	1.10	.90
138	A1	5fr lemon yellow	1.40	1.10
139	A1	10fr chocolate	1.80	1.40
140	A1	20fr deep green	1.90	1.50
		Nos. 127-140 (14)	12.70	9.85

Nos. 127, 129 and 136 Surcharged with New Values and Bars in Black or Carmine

1946

141	A1	50c on 5c lt brown	.90	.65
142	A1	60c on 5c lt brown	1.00	.75
143	A1	70c on 5c lt brown	1.00	.75
144	A1	1.20fr on 5c lt brown	1.00	.75
145	A1	2.40fr on 25c emerald	1.10	.90
146	A1	3fr on 25c emerald	1.10	.90
147	A1	4.50fr on 25c emerald	2.40	1.75
148	A1	15fr on 2.50fr (C)	2.50	1.75
		Nos. 141-148 (8)	11.00	8.20

Military Medal Issue

Common Design Type

Engraved and Typographed

1952, Dec. 1 *Perf. 13*

149	CD101	2fr multicolored	9.50	7.00

Wallis Islander
A2

Unwmk.

1957, June 11 Engr. *Perf. 13*

150	A2	3fr dk purple & lil rose	1.50	1.10
151	A2	9fr bl, dl lil & vio brn	2.75	2.25

See Nos. 753a, 753c

Imperforates

Most Wallis and Futuna stamps from 1957 onward exist imperforate in issued and trial colors, and also in small presentation sheets in issued colors.

Flower Issue

Common Design Type

Design: 5fr, Montrouziera, horiz.

1958, Aug. 4 Photo. *Perf. 12½x12*

152	CD104	5fr multicolored	4.50	2.50

Human Rights Issue

Common Design Type

1958, Dec. 10 Engr. *Perf. 13*

153	CD105	17fr brt bl & dk bl	5.75	4.00

Women Making Tapa Cloth — A3

Kava Ceremony
A4

17fr, Dancers. 19fr, Dancers with paddles.

1960, Sept. 19   Engr.   Perf. 13
154 A3 5fr dk brown, grn & org
       brn   1.50   1.10
155 A4 7fr dk brown & Prus
       grn   2.25   1.90
156 A4 17fr ultra, claret & grn   3.00   2.25
157 A3 19fr claret & slate   3.25   2.50
     Nos. 154-157 (4)   10.00   7.75

For No. 157 with surcharge, see No. 174.
See No. 753b.

Map of South Pacific — A4a

1962, July 18   Photo.   Perf. 13x12
158 A4a 16fr multicolored   4.50   4.00

5th South Pacific Conf., Pago Pago, 1962.

Sea Shells — A5

1962-63   Engr.   Perf. 13
Size: 22x36mm
159 A5 25c Triton   1.10   1.10
160 A5 1fr Mitra episcopalis   1.10   1.10
161 A5 2fr Cypraecassis rufa   2.10   2.10
162 A5 4fr Murex tenuspina   3.00   3.00
163 A5 10fr Oliva erythrostoma   7.00   7.00
164 A5 20fr Cyprae tigris   10.50   10.50
    Nos. 159-164,C18 (7)   37.30   31.80

Red Cross Centenary Issue
Common Design Type
1963, Sept. 2   Unwmk.   Perf. 13
165 CD113 12fr red lil, gray & car 4.00 3.50

Human Rights Issue
Common Design Type
1963, Dec. 10   Engr.
166 CD117 29fr dk red & ocher   8.00   7.50

Philatec Issue
Common Design Type
1964, Apr. 15   Unwmk.   Perf. 13
167 CD118 9fr dk sl grn, grn &
        red   3.50   3.50

Queen Amelia and Ship "Queen Amelia" A6

1965, Feb. 15   Photo.   Perf. 12½x13
168 A6 11fr multicolored   8.00   7.50

WHO Anniversary Issue
Common Design Type
1968, May 4   Engr.   Perf. 13
169 CD126 17fr bl grn, org & lil   6.50   4.50

Human Rights Year Issue
Common Design Type
1968, Aug. 10   Engr.   Perf. 13
170 CD127 19fr dk pur, org brn &
         brt mag   3.75   3.75

Outrigger Canoe A7

1969, Apr. 30   Photo.   Perf. 13
171 A7 1fr multicolored   1.10   1.10
    Nos. 171,C31-C35 (6)   40.60   18.85

ILO Issue
Common Design Type
1969, Nov. 24   Engr.   Perf. 13
172 CD131 9fr orange, brn & bl   3.00   2.90

UPU Headquarters Issue
Common Design Type
1970, May 20   Engr.   Perf. 13
173 CD133 21fr lil rose, ind & ol
         bis   4.00   4.00

No. 157 Surcharged with New Value and Two Bars
1971   Perf. 13
174 A3 12fr on 19fr   1.25   1.25

Weight Lifting — A8

1971, Oct. 25
175 A8 24fr shown   6.00   5.25
176 A8 36fr Basketball   7.00   6.50
    Nos. 175-176,C37-C38 (4)   27.25   19.75

4th South Pacific Games, Papeete, French Polynesia, Sept. 8-19.

De Gaulle Issue
Common Design Type
Designs: 30fr, Gen. de Gaulle, 1940. 70fr, Pres. de Gaulle, 1970.
1971, Nov. 9   Engr.   Perf. 13
177 CD134 30fr blue & black   9.50   6.25
178 CD134 70fr blue & black   14.50   10.00

Child's Outrigger Canoe A9

Designs: 16fr, Children's canoe race. 18fr, Outrigger racing canoe.

1972, Oct. 16   Photo.   Perf. 13x12½
Size: 35½x26½mm
179 A9 14fr dk green & multi   10.00   4.25
180 A9 16fr dk plum & multi   10.00   4.25
181 A9 18fr blue & multi   15.00   6.25
    Nos. 179-181,C41 (4)   80.00   39.75

Outrigger sailing canoes.

Rhinoceros Beetle A10

Insects: 25fr, Cosmopolities sordidus (beetle). 35fr, Ophideres fullonica (moth). 45fr, Dragonfly.

1974, July 29   Photo.   Perf. 13
182 A10 15fr ol & multi   3.75   2.10
183 A10 25fr ol & multi   4.50   3.00
184 A10 35fr gray bl & multi   7.00   4.00
185 A10 45fr multicolored   10.00   6.00
    Nos. 182-185 (4)   25.25   15.10

Georges Pompidou (1911-74), Pres. of France — A11

1975, Dec. 1   Engr.   Perf. 13
186 A11 50fr ultra & slate   8.00   5.50

Battle of Yorktown and George Washington — A12

American Bicentennial: 47fr, Virginia Cape Battle and Lafayette.

1976, June 28   Engr.   Perf. 13
187 A12 19fr blue, red & olive   3.00   1.40
188 A12 47fr blue, red & maroon 4.50   4.00

For overprints see Nos. 205-206.

Conus Ammiralis — A13

Sea Shells: 23fr, Cyprae assellus. 43fr, Turbo petholatus. 61fr, Mitra papalis.

1976, Oct. 1   Engr.   Perf. 13
189 A13 20fr multicolored   2.75   2.00
190 A13 23fr multicolored   2.75   2.00
191 A13 43fr multicolored   6.00   4.00
192 A13 61fr ultra & multi   8.50   6.50
    Nos. 189-192 (4)   20.00   14.50

Father Chanel and Poi Church — A14

32fr, Father Chanel and map of islands.

1977, Apr. 28   Litho.   Perf. 12
193 A14 22fr multicolored   2.25   1.40
194 A14 32fr multicolored   2.50   1.50

Return of the ashes of Father Chanel, missionary.

Bowl, Mortar and Pestle A15

Handicrafts: 25fr, Wooden bowls and leather bag. 33fr, Wooden comb, club, and boat model. 45fr, War clubs, Futuna. 69fr, Lances.

1977, Sept. 26   Litho.   Perf. 12½
195 A15 12fr multicolored   1.30   .75
196 A15 25fr multicolored   2.00   1.00
197 A15 33fr multicolored   2.25   1.25
198 A15 45fr multicolored   3.50   1.75
199 A15 69fr multicolored   4.50   3.00
    Nos. 195-199 (5)   13.55   7.75

Post Office, Mata Utu — A16

50fr, Sia Hospital, Mata Utu. 57fr, Administration Buildings, Mata Utu. 63fr, St. Joseph's Church, Sigave. 120fr, Royal Palace, Mara Utu.

1977, Dec. 12   Litho.   Perf. 13
200 A16 27fr multicolored   1.80   1.40
201 A16 50fr multicolored   2.50   1.80
202 A16 57fr multicolored   3.50   1.80
203 A16 63fr multicolored   4.50   2.75
204 A16 120fr multicolored   9.00   4.50
    Nos. 200-204 (5)   21.30   12.25

Nos. 187-188 Overprinted

1978, Jan. 20   Engr.   Perf. 13
205 A12 19fr multicolored   3.50   2.50
206 A12 47fr multicolored   7.00   4.00

Bicentenary of the arrival of Capt. Cook in the Hawaiian Islands.

Cruiser Triomphant — A17

Warships: 200fr, Destroyers Cap des Palmes and Chevreuil. 280fr, Cruiser Savorgnan de Brazza.

1978, June 18   Photo.   Perf. 13x12½
207 A17 150fr multicolored   10.50   6.25
208 A17 200fr multicolored   14.00   9.00
209 A17 280fr multicolored   18.00   12.50
    Nos. 207-209 (3)   42.50   27.75

Free French warships serving in the Pacific, 1940-1944.

Solanum Seaforthianum — A18

Flowers: 24fr, Cassia alata. 29fr, Gloriosa superba. 36fr, Hymenocallis littoralis.

1978, July 11   Photo.   Perf. 13
210 A18 16fr multicolored   1.50   .90
211 A18 24fr multicolored   1.75   1.00
212 A18 29fr multicolored   2.50   1.40
213 A18 36fr multicolored   3.50   1.80
    Nos. 210-213 (4)   9.25   5.10

Gray
Egret — A19

Birds: 18fr, Red-footed booby. 28fr, Brown booby. 35fr, White tern.

1978, Sept. 5   Photo.   Perf. 13
214 A19 17fr multicolored   1.75   .90
215 A19 18fr multicolored   1.80 1.00
216 A19 28fr multicolored   2.50 1.40
217 A19 35fr multicolored   3.50 1.60
    Nos. 214-217 (4)   9.55 4.90

Traditional Patterns — A20

Designs: 55fr, Corpus Christi procession. 59fr, Chief's honor guard.

1978, Oct. 3
218 A20 53fr multicolored   3.00 1.80
219 A20 55fr multicolored   4.00 2.10
220 A20 59fr multicolored   3.50 2.50
    Nos. 218-220 (3)   10.50 6.40

Human
Rights
Flame
A21

1978, Dec. 10   Litho.   Perf. 12½
221 A21 44fr multicolored   1.80 1.30
222 A21 56fr multicolored   2.75 1.80

30th anniversary of Universal Declaration of Human Rights.

Fishing Boat — A22

Designs: 30fr, Weighing young tuna. 34fr, Stocking young tunas. 38fr, Measuring tuna. 40fr, Angler catching tuna. 48fr, Adult tuna.

1979, Mar. 19   Litho.   Perf. 12
223 A22 10fr multicolored   .90   .50
224 A22 30fr multicolored   1.40   .90
225 A22 34fr multicolored   1.50 1.00
226 A22 38fr multicolored   2.40 1.40
227 A22 40fr multicolored   2.75 2.00
228 A22 48fr multicolored   3.75 2.00
    a.   Souv. sheet of 6, #223-228 +
         3 labels   30.00 30.00
    Nos. 223-228 (6)   12.70 7.80

Tuna tagging by South Pacific Commission.
For surcharge see No. 261.

Boy with Raft and IYC Emblem — A23

Design: 58fr, Girl on horseback.

1979, Apr. 9   Photo.   Perf. 13
229 A23 52fr multicolored   2.25 1.30
230 A23 58fr multicolored   2.25 1.70

International Year of the Child.

Bombax
Ellipticum — A24

64fr, Callophyllum. 76fr, Pandanus odoratissimus.

1979, Apr. 23   Litho.   Perf. 13
231 A24 50fr multicolored   2.25 1.40
232 A24 64fr multicolored   3.00 1.80
233 A24 76fr multicolored   4.25 2.50
    Nos. 231-233 (3)   9.50 5.70

Green and Withered
Landscapes — A25

1979, May 28   Photo.   Perf. 13
234 A25 22fr multicolored   1.80 1.10

Anti-alcoholism campaign.

Flowers — A26

1979, July 16   Photo.   Perf. 12½x13
235 A26 20fr Crinum   .90   .65
236 A26 42fr Passiflora   2.10 1.10
237 A26 62fr Canna indica   3.00 1.75
    Nos. 235-237 (3)   6.00 3.50

See Nos. 279-281.

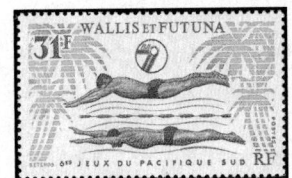

Swimming — A27

1979, Aug. 27   Engr.   Perf. 13
238 A27 31fr shown   2.25 1.40
239 A27 39fr High jump   3.00 1.80

6th South Pacific Games, Suva, Fiji, Aug. 27-Sept. 8.

Flower Necklaces — A28

Design: 140fr, Coral necklaces.

1979, Aug. 27   Litho.
240 A28 110fr multicolored   4.25 2.75
241 A28 140fr multicolored   5.25 3.50

Trees and Birds, by Sutita — A29

Paintings by Local Artists: 65fr, Birds and Mountain, by M. A. Pilioko, vert. 78fr, Festival Procession, by Sutita.

1979, Oct. 8   Perf. 13x12½, 12½x13
242 A29 27fr multicolored   1.40 1.10
243 A29 65fr multicolored   2.25 1.50
244 A29 78fr multicolored   4.00 2.25
    Nos. 242-244 (3)   7.65 4.85

Marine
Mantis
A30

Marine Life: 23fr, Hexabranchus sanguineus. 25fr, Spondylus barbatus. 43fr, Gorgon coral. 45fr, Linckia laevigata. 63fr, Tridacna squamosa.

1979, Nov. 5   Photo.   Perf. 13x12½
245 A30 15fr multicolored   1.40   .75
246 A30 23fr multicolored   1.40   .90
247 A30 25fr multicolored   1.80 1.00
248 A30 43fr multicolored   2.25 1.10
249 A30 45fr multicolored   2.40 1.25
250 A30 63fr multicolored   4.50 2.50
    Nos. 245-250 (6)   13.75 7.50

See #294-297. For surcharge see #272.

Transportation Type of 1979
1980, Feb. 29   Litho.   Perf. 13
251 AP32 1fr like No. C87   .35   .25
252 AP32 3fr like No. C88   .35   .25
253 AP32 5fr like No. C89   .40   .35
    Nos. 251-253 (3)   1.10   .85

Radio Station
and Tower — A31

1980, Apr. 21   Litho.   Perf. 13
254 A31 47fr multicolored   2.75 1.40

Radio station FR3, 1st anniversary.

Jesus Laid in the Tomb, by Maurice
Denis — A32

1980, Apr. 28   Perf. 13x12½
255 A32 25fr multicolored   1.80   .90

Easter 1980.

Gnathodentex Mossambicus — A33

27fr, Pristipomoides filamentosus. 32fr, Etelis carbunculus. 51fr, Cephalopholis wallisi. 59fr, Aphareus rutilans.

1980, Aug. 25   Litho.   Perf. 12½x13
256 A33 23fr multi   1.40   .90
257 A33 27fr multi   1.80 1.00
258 A33 32fr multi   2.50 1.40
259 A33 51fr multi   3.50 2.40
260 A33 59fr multi   5.75 2.75
    a.   Vert. strip of 5, Nos. 256-260
                                16.00 15.00

No. 228 Surcharged

1980, Sept. 29   Litho.   Perf. 12
261 A22 50fr on 48fr multi   3.00 1.80

Sydpex 80 Philatelic Exhibition, Sydney.

13th World Telecommunications
Day — A34

1981, May 17   Litho.   Perf. 12½
262 A34 49fr multicolored   1.80 1.10

Pierre Curie and Laboratory
Equipment — A35

1981, May 25   Litho.   Perf. 13
263 A35 56fr multicolored   2.25 1.40

Pierre Curie (1859-1906), discoverer of radioactivity.

Conus Textile A36

Marine life: 28fr, Favites. 30fr, Cyanophycees. 31fr, Ceratium vultur. 35fr, Amphiprion frenatus. 55fr, Comatule.

1981, June 22   *Perf. 12½x13*
264	A36	28fr multicolored	1.10	.90
265	A36	30fr multicolored	1.40	.90
266	A36	31fr multicolored	1.50	.90
267	A36	35fr multicolored	2.25	1.10
268	A36	40fr shown	2.25	1.40
269	A36	55fr multicolored	2.75	1.60
a.		Vert. strip of 6, Nos. 264-269	11.50	11.00

No. 269a is from sheet of 24.

60th Anniv. of Anti-tuberculin Vaccine (Developed by Calmette and Guerin) — A37

1981, July 28   **Litho.**   *Perf. 13*
270	A37	27fr multicolored	1.10	.90

Intl. Year of the Disabled — A38

1981, Aug. 17
271	A38	42fr multicolored	2.25	1.20

No. 245 Surcharged in Red

1981, Sept.   **Photo.**   *Perf. 13x12½*
272	A30	5fr on 15fr multi	.65	.35

Thomas Edison (1847-1931) and his Phonograph, 1878 — A39

1981, Sept. 5   **Engr.**   *Perf. 13*
273	A39	59fr multicolored	2.50	1.40

Battle of Yorktown, 1781 (American Revolution) — A40

1981, Oct. 19   **Engr.**   *Perf. 13*
274	A40	66fr Admiral de Grasse	2.75	1.80
275	A40	74fr Sea battle, vert.	3.50	2.75

200-Mile Zone Surveillance — A41

60fr, Patrol boat Dieppoise. 85fr, Protet.

1981, Dec. 4   **Litho.**   *Perf. 13*
276	A41	60fr multicolored	1.80	1.40
277	A41	85fr multicolored	2.75	2.10

TB Bacillus Centenary — A42

1982, Mar. 24   **Litho.**   *Perf. 13*
278	A42	45fr multicolored	3.00	1.40

Flower Type of 1979 in Changed Colors

1982, May 3   **Photo.**   *Perf. 12½x13*
279	A26	1fr like No. 235	.30	.25
280	A26	2fr like No. 236	.40	.25
281	A26	3fr like No. 237	.40	.30
		Nos. 279-281 (3)	1.10	.80

PHILEXFRANCE '82 Intl. Stamp Exhibition, Paris, June 11-21 — A43

1982, May 12   **Engr.**   *Perf. 13*
282	A43	140fr like No. 25	3.50	2.75

Acanthe Phippium A44

68fr, Acanthe phippium, diff. 70fr, Spathoglottis pacifica. 83fr, Mussaenda raiateensis, Orchids and rubiaceae.

1982, May 24   **Litho.**   *Perf. 12½x13*
283	A44	34fr shown	1.10	.90
284	A44	68fr multicolored	2.25	1.75
285	A44	70fr multicolored	2.50	1.75
286	A44	83fr multicolored	3.00	2.25
		Nos. 283-286 (4)	8.85	6.65

Scouting Year A45

1982, June 21   *Perf. 12½*
287	A45	80fr Baden-Powell	2.25	1.75

Cypraea Talpa A46

Porcelaines shells.

1982, June 28   *Perf. 12½x13*
288	A46	10fr shown	.30	.30
289	A46	15fr Cypraea vitellus	.70	.30
290	A46	25fr Cypraea argus	.85	.65
291	A46	27fr Cypraea carneola	1.10	.75
292	A46	40fr Cypraea mappa	1.40	1.10
293	A46	50fr Cypraea tigris	1.75	1.25
		Nos. 288-293 (6)	6.10	4.35

Marine Life Type of 1979

1982, Oct. 1   **Photo.**   *Perf. 13x12½*
294	A30	32fr Gorgones milithea	1.40	.75
295	A30	35fr Linckia laevigata	1.75	1.10
296	A30	46fr Hexabranchus sanguineus	2.10	1.50
297	A30	63fr Spondylus barbatus	3.00	2.25
		Nos. 294-297 (4)	8.25	5.60

St. Teresa of Jesus of Avila (1515-1582) — A48

1982, Nov. 8   **Engr.**   *Perf. 13*
298	A48	31fr multicolored	1.40	.75

See No. 315.

Traditional House A49

1983, Jan. 20   **Litho.**   *Perf. 13*
299	A49	19fr multicolored	.90	.50

Gustave Eiffel (1832-1923), Architect — A50

1983, Feb. 14   **Engr.**   *Perf. 13*
300	A50	97fr multicolored	3.50	2.75

Thai Dancer, 19th Cent. — A51

1983, June 28   **Engr.**   *Perf. 13*
301	A51	92fr multicolored	3.00	1.80

BANGKOK '83 Intl. Stamp Show, Aug. 4-13.

A52

1983, Aug. 25   **Litho.**   *Perf. 13x13½*
302	A52	20fr multicolored	.70	.50

World Communications Year.

Cone Shells A53

10fr, Conus tulipa. 17fr, Conus capitaneus. 21fr, Conus virgo. 22fr, Strombus lentiginosus. 25fr, Lambis chiragra. 35fr, Strombus dentatus. 39fr, Conus vitulinus. 43fr, Lambis scorpius. 49fr, Strombus aurisdianae. 52fr, Conus marmoreus. 65fr, Conus leopardus. 76fr, Lambis crocata.

1983-84   **Litho.**   *Perf. 13½x13*
303	A53	10fr multicolored	.50	.30
304	A53	17fr multicolored	.75	.50
305	A53	21fr multicolored	.75	.50
306	A53	22fr multicolored	.65	.50
307	A53	25fr multicolored	.75	.60
308	A53	35fr multicolored	1.40	.75
309	A53	39fr multicolored	1.40	.90
310	A53	43fr multicolored	1.75	.90
311	A53	49fr multicolored	2.00	1.40
312	A53	52fr multicolored	1.80	1.40
313	A53	65fr multicolored	2.40	1.75
314	A53	76fr multicolored	3.00	1.60
		Nos. 303-314 (12)	17.15	11.10

Issued: 22, 25, 35, 43, 49, 76fr, 3/23/84; others, 10/14/83.

No. 298 Redrawn with Espana '84 Emblem

1984, Apr. 27   **Engr.**   *Perf. 13*
315	A48	70fr multicolored	2.25	1.40

Denis Diderot (1713-1784), Philosopher A54

100fr, Portrait, encyclopedia title page.

1984, May 11
316	A54	100fr multicolored	3.00	1.75

Nature Protection (Whale) A55

1984, June 5   **Litho.**   *Perf. 13x12½*
317	A55	90fr Orcina orca	3.00	1.75

4th Pacific Arts Festival — A56

1984, Nov. 30   **Litho.**   *Perf. 13*
318 A56 160fr Islanders   3.75 2.50

Lapita Pottery — A57

Ethno-Archaeological Museum: Excavation site, reconstructed ceramic bowl.

1985, Jan. 16   **Litho.**   *Perf. 13*
319 A57 53fr multicolored   1.50 .90

Seashells A58

1985, Feb. 11
320 A58 2fr Nautilus pompilius   .25 .25
321 A58 3fr Murex bruneus   .25 .25
322 A58 41fr Casmaria erinaceus   1.40 .90
323 A58 47fr Conus vexillum   1.75 1.00
324 A58 56fr Harpa harpa   2.10 1.10
325 A58 71fr Murex ramosus   2.50 1.60
   Nos. 320-325 (6)   8.25 5.10

Victor Hugo, Author (1802-1885) A59

1985, Mar. 7   **Engr.**
326 A59 89fr multicolored   3.00 1.60

Bat — A60

1985, Apr. 29   **Litho.**
327 A60 38fr multicolored   2.00 1.10

Intl. Youth Year — A61

1985, May 20   **Litho.**   *Perf. 12½x13*
328 A61 64fr Children   1.75 1.10

UN, 40th Anniv. — A61a

1985, July 12   **Engr.**   *Perf. 13*
328A A61a 49fr Prus grn, dk ultra & red   1.50 .90

Pierre de Ronsard (1524-1585), Poet — A62

1985, Sept. 16   **Engr.**   *Perf. 13*
329 A62 170fr brt bl, sep & brn   5.00 3.50

Dr. Albert Schweitzer — A63

1985, Nov. 22   **Engr.**   *Perf. 13*
330 A63 50fr blk, dk red lil & org brn   2.00 1.25

World Food Day — A64

1986, Jan. 23   **Litho.**   *Perf. 12½x13*
331 A64 39fr Breadfruit   1.25 .75

Flamboyants — A65

1986, Feb. 13   *Perf. 13x12½*
332 A65 38fr multicolored   2.00 1.00

Seashells A66

1986, Apr. 24   **Litho.**   *Perf. 13½x13*
333 A66 4fr Lambis truncata   .35 .35
334 A66 5fr Charonia tritonis   .35 .35
335 A66 10fr Oliva miniacea   .50 .50
336 A66 18fr Distorsio anus   .80 .70
337 A66 25fr Mitra mitra   1.20 1.20
338 A66 107fr Conus distans   3.75 2.25
   Nos. 333-338 (6)   6.95 4.75

Also exists in se-tenant strips of 6 from sheet of 24.

1986 World Cup Soccer Championships, Mexico — A67

1986, May 20   *Perf. 13x12½*
339 A67 95fr multicolored   3.25 1.80

   UNICEF.

Discovery of Horn Islands, 370th Anniv. — A68

No. 340: a, 8fr, William Schouten, ship. b, 9fr, Jacob LeMaire, ship. c, 155fr, Map of Alo & Alofi.

1986, June 19   **Engr.**   *Perf. 13*
340 A68   Strip of 3, #a.-c.   6.50 4.75

James Watt (1736-1819), Inventor, and Steam Engine — A69

1986, July 11
341 A69 74fr blk & dk red   2.40 1.50

Minesweeper La Lorientaise — A70

7fr, Corvette Commandant Blaison, vert. 120fr, Frigate Balny.

1986, Aug. 7
342 A70 6fr shown   .70 .50
343 A70 7fr multicolored   .75 .50
344 A70 120fr multicolored   4.25 2.75
   Nos. 342-344 (3)   5.70 3.75

Rose Laurel — A71

1986, Oct. 2   **Litho.**   *Perf. 13x12½*
345 A71 97fr multi   3.25 2.00

Virgin and Child, by Sandro Botticelli A72

1986, Dec. 12   **Litho.**   *Perf. 12½x13*
346 A72 250fr multicolored   7.50 4.50

   Christmas.

Butterflies — A73

1987, Apr. 2   **Litho.**   *Perf. 12½*
347 A73 2fr Papilio montrouzieri   .50 .35
348 A73 42fr Belenois java   1.25 .70
349 A73 46fr Delias ellipsis   1.40 .75
350 A73 50fr Danaus pumila   1.60 .95
351 A73 52fr Luthrodes cleotas   2.00 1.00
352 A73 59fr Precis villida   2.40 1.50
   Nos. 347-352 (6)   9.15 5.25

World Wrestling Championships — A74

1987, May 26   **Litho.**   *Perf. 12½*
353 A74 97fr multi   3.25 1.90

   For overprint see No. 360.

Seashells A75

1987, June 24   **Litho.**   *Perf. 13*
354 A75 3fr Cymatium pileare   .35 .35
355 A75 4fr Conus textile   .35 .35
356 A75 28fr Cypraea mauritiana   1.25 .75
357 A75 44fr Bursa bubo   1.50 1.00
358 A75 48fr Cypraea testudinaria   1.60 1.10
359 A75 78fr Cypraecassis rufa   2.75 1.50
   Nos. 354-359 (6)   7.80 5.05

Also exists in se-tenant strips of 6 from sheet of 24.

No. 353 Overprinted

1987, Aug. 29   **Litho.**   *Perf. 12½*
360 A74 97fr multicolored   3.75 2.40

   OLYMPHILEX '87, Rome.

Bust of a Girl, by
Auguste Rodin
(1840-1917)
A76

1987, Sept. 15 **Engr.** *Perf. 13*
361 A76 150fr plum   4.50 2.75

See No. 390.

World Post Day — A77

1987, Oct. 9 **Litho.** *Perf. 13*
362 A77 116fr multicolored   3.25 1.80

Birds — A78

1987, Oct. 28 *Perf. 13x12½*
363 A78 6fr Anas superciliosa   .35 .35
364 A78 19fr Pluvialis dominica   .70 .50
365 A78 47fr Gallicolumba stairi   1.25 .95
366 A78 56fr Arenaria interpres   1.60 1.00
367 A78 64fr Rallus philippensis   1.75 1.10
368 A78 68fr Limosa lapponica   2.25 1.30
Nos. 363-368 (6)   7.90 5.20

Francis Carco (1886-1958),
Poet — A79

Design: Carco and views of the Moulin de la
Galette and Place du Tertre, Paris.

1988, Jan. 29 **Litho.** *Perf. 13*
369 A79 40fr multicolored   1.40 .95

Jean-Francois de Galaup (1741-
c.1788), Comte de La Perouse,
Explorer — A80

Design: Ships L'Astrolabe and La Boussole,
portrait of La Perouse.

1988, Mar. 21 **Engr.** *Perf. 13*
370 A80 70fr org brn, dark blue &
olive grn   3.25 2.40

Intl. Red Cross
and Red
Crescent
Organizations,
125th
Annivs. — A81

1988, July 4 **Engr.** *Perf. 13*
371 A81 30fr blk, dark red & brt
blue grn   2.00 1.00

1988 Summer Olympics, Seoul — A82

1988, Sept. 1 **Engr.** *Perf. 13*
372 A82 11fr Javelin   .70 .50
373 A82 20fr Women's volleyball   .95 .70
374 A82 60fr Windsurfing   2.00 1.50
375 A82 80fr Yachting   2.90 1.90
a.   Souv. sheet of 4, #372-375 + 2
labels, gutter between   8.25 8.25
Nos. 372-375 (4)   6.55 4.60

Intl. Maritime Organization Emblem
and Frigate F727 Admiral
Charner — A83

1989, Jan. 26 **Litho.** *Perf. 13*
376 A83 26fr multi   1.00 .70

Jean Renoir (1894-1979), Film
Director, and Scene from The Grand
Illusion — A84

1989, Feb. 16 **Engr.** *Perf. 13*
377 A84 24fr brt lil rose, dark vio
brn & brt org   1.25 .75

Antoine Becquerel (1788-1878),
Physicist — A85

Perf. 13x12½
1988, Nov. 9 **Engr.** **Unwmk.**
378 A85 18fr blk & dark ultra   .95 .50

Futuna Hydroelectric Plant — A86

Wmk. 385
1989, Apr. 13 **Litho.** *Perf. 13½*
379 A86 25fr multi   .95 .50

A87

Unwmk.
1988, Oct. 26 **Litho.** *Perf. 13*
380 A87 17fr multi   .95 .50

World Post Day.

A88

1989, May 17 *Perf. 12½x13*
381 A88 21fr multi   .95 .50

World Telecommunications Day.

Fresco
A89

1989, June 8 *Perf. 12½*
382 A89 22fr multi   .95 .50

PHILEXFRANCE '89 — A90

Declaration of Human Rights and
Citizenship, Bicent. — A91

1989, July 7 **Litho.** *Perf. 13*
383 A90 29fr multi   1.00 .70
384 A91 900fr multi   22.00 14.00
a.   Souv. sheet of 2, #383-384 +
label   30.00 30.00

No. 384 is airmail. No. 384a sold for 1000fr.

World Cycling Championships — A92

1989, Sept. 14 **Engr.** *Perf. 13*
385 A92 10fr blk, red brn & emer   .60 .45

World Post Day — A93

Unwmk.
1989, Oct. 18 **Litho.** *Perf. 13*
386 A93 27fr multicolored   .95 .50

Landscape — A94

1989, Nov. 23 **Litho.** *Perf. 13*
387 A94 23fr multicolored   .95 .70

Star of
Bethlehem
A95

1990, Jan. 9 **Litho.** *Perf. 12½*
388 A95 44fr multicolored   1.50 1.00

Fossilized
Tortoise
A96

1990, Feb. 15 **Litho.** *Perf. 12½x13*
389 A96 48fr multicolored   2.75 1.40

Sculpture by
Auguste Rodin
(1840-1917)
A97

1990, Mar. 15 **Engr.** *Perf. 13*
390 A97 200fr royal blue   6.00 4.00

1990 World Cup Soccer
Championships, Italy — A98

1990, Apr. 16   **Litho.**
391 A98 59fr multicolored   1.60 1.10

Orchids
A99

1990, May 17   **Litho.**   **Perf. 12½**
392 A99 78fr multicolored   2.75 1.50

Mother's Day

Phaeton — A100

1990, July 16   **Perf. 13**
393 A100 300fr multicolored   8.00 4.50
394 A100 600fr Island   17.50 8.50

Moana II — A101

1990, Aug. 16   **Engr.**   **Perf. 13**
395 A101 40fr shown   1.25 .95
396 A101 50fr Moana III   1.75 1.00

Native Huts
A102

1990, Sept. 17   **Litho.**   **Perf. 13x12½**
397 A102 28fr multicolored   .95 .50

Stamp Day
A103

1990, Oct. 16   **Litho.**   **Perf. 12½**
398 A103 97fr multicolored   3.25 1.90

Wallis Island
Pirogue — A104

1990, Nov. 16   **Litho.**   **Perf. 13x12½**
399 A104 46fr multicolored   1.50 .95

Best Wishes — A105

1990, Dec. 17   **Litho.**   **Perf. 13x12½**
400 A105 100fr multicolored   3.25 1.90

Patrol Boats — A106

1991   **Engr.**   **Perf. 13**
401 A106 42fr La Moqueuse   1.40 .95
402 A106 52fr La Glorieuse   1.75 1.00
   Issue dates: 42fr, Jan. 7; 52fr, Mar. 4.

A107

1991, Feb. 4   **Litho.**   **Perf. 13**
403 A107 7fr Breadfruit picker   .35 .35
404 A107 54fr Taro planter   1.60 1.00
405 A107 62fr Spear fisherman   1.75 1.20
406 A107 72fr Native warrior   2.40 1.30
407 A107 90fr Kailao dancer   3.00 1.75
   a.   Souv. sheet of 5, #403-407   10.00 10.00
     Nos. 403-407 (5)   9.10 5.60
   Issued: 7fr, 9/2; 54fr, 5/13; 62fr, 4/1; 72fr,
2/4; 90fr, 11/4.
   No. 407a sold for 300fr.

Doctors
Without
Borders,
20th Anniv.
A108

1991, Feb. 18   **Litho.**   **Perf. 13½**
408 A108 55fr multicolored   1.60 1.00

Ultralight Aircraft — A108a

1991, June 24
409 A108a 85fr multicolored   2.75 1.80

Portrait of Jean by Auguste Renoir
(1841-1919) — A109

1991, July 8   **Photo.**   **Perf. 12½x13**
410 A109 400fr multicolored   11.00 8.00
     Litho.
     Die Cut
     Self-Adhesive
411 A109 400fr multicolored   11.00 8.00

Overseas Territorial Status, 30th
Anniv. — A110

1991, July 29   **Litho.**   **Perf. 13**
412 A110 102fr multicolored   2.75 1.80

Feast of the Assumption — A111

1991, Aug. 15   **Perf. 13x12½**
413 A111 30fr multicolored   1.00 .70

Amnesty
Intl., 30th
Anniv.
A113

1991, Oct. 7   **Perf. 13x12½**
414 A113 140fr bl, vio & yel   4.50 2.75

Central Bank for Economic
Cooperation, 50th Anniv. — A114

1991, Dec. 2   **Litho.**   **Perf. 13**
415 A114 10fr multicolored   .50 .35

Flowers
A115

   1fr, Monette allamanda cathartica. 4fr,
Hibiscus rosa sinensis. 80fr, Ninuphar.

1991, Dec. 2   **Perf. 12½x13, 13x12½**
416 A115 1fr multi   .50 .25
417 A115 4fr multi, vert.   .50 .35
418 A115 80fr multi   2.40 1.50
     Nos. 416-418 (3)   3.40 2.10

Christmas — A116

1991, Dec. 16   **Litho.**   **Perf. 13**
419 A116 60fr multicolored   2.00 1.20

Maritime Surveillance — A117

1992, Jan. 20   **Litho.**   **Perf. 13**
420 A117 48fr multicolored   2.00 1.00

1992 Winter Olympics,
Albertville — A118

1992, Feb. 17   **Litho.**   **Perf. 13**
421 A118 150fr multicolored   4.00 2.75

Canada '92, Intl. Philatelic Exposition,
Montreal — A119

1992, Mar. 25   **Engr.**   **Perf. 13**
422 A119 35fr blk, violet & red   1.25 .70

1992 Summer Olympics, Barcelona — A120

1992, Apr. 15   Engr.   Perf. 13
423 A120 106fr bl grn, grn & bl   3.25 2.25

Granada '92, Intl. Philatelic Exposition — A121

1992, Apr. 17   Engr.   Perf. 12½x12
424 A121 100fr multicolored   3.25 2.00

Expo '92, Seville — A122

1992, Apr. 20   Perf. 13
425 A122 200fr bl grn, ol & red brn   5.50 3.75

Chaetodon Ephippium — A123

Designs: 22fr, Chaetodon auriga. 23fr, Heniochus monoceros. 24fr, Pygoplites diacanthus. 25fr, Chaetodontoplus conspicillatus. 26fr, Chaetodon unimaculatus. 27fr, Siganus punctatus. 35fr, Zebrasoma veliferum. 45fr, Paracanthurus hepatus. 53fr, Siganus vulpinus.

1992-93   Litho.   Perf. 13
426 A123 21fr multicolored   .70 .50
427 A123 22fr multicolored   .70 .50
428 A123 23fr multicolored   .70 .50
429 A123 24fr multicolored   .80 .70
430 A123 25fr multicolored   1.00 .70
431 A123 26fr multicolored   1.00 .70
432 A123 27fr multicolored   1.00 .80
433 A123 35fr multicolored   1.00 .80
434 A123 45fr multicolored   1.25 .95
435 A123 53fr multicolored   1.60 1.25
    Nos. 426-435 (10)   9.75 7.40

Issued: 21fr, 26fr, 5/18; 22fr, 7/27; 25fr, 7/27; 23fr, 24fr, 9/14; 35fr, 45fr, 6/21/93; 27fr, 53fr, 9/6/93.

Natives — A125

a, 3 warriors. b, 2 warriors. c, Warrior, 2 boats. d, 2 spear fisherman. e, 3 fisherman.

1992, June 15   Litho.   Perf. 12
436 A125 70fr Strip of 5, #a.-e.   12.50 9.00
    f.   Souvenir sheet of 5, #a.-e.   13.00 13.00

#436 has continuous design. #436f sold for 450fr.

Support Ship, "La Garonne" A126

1992, Oct. 12   Litho.   Perf. 12
437 A126 20fr multicolored   .75 .50

L'Idylle D'Ixelles, by Auguste Rodin (1840-1917) A127

1992, Nov. 17   Engr.   Perf. 13
438 A127 300fr lilac & dk blue   8.50 6.00

Miribilis Jalapa A128

1992, Dec. 7   Litho.   Perf. 12½
439 A128 200fr multicolored   5.50 3.75

Maritime Forces of the Pacific — A129

1993, Jan. 27   Litho.   Perf. 13x12½
440 A129 130fr multicolored   3.75 2.75

School Art — A130

1993, Feb. 22   Litho.   Perf. 12
441 A130 56fr multicolored   1.80 1.40

See Nos. 451-452.

Birds A131

Designs: 50fr, Rallus philippensis swindellsi. 60fr, Porphyrio porphyrio. 110fr, Ptilinopus greyi.

1993, Mar. 20   Perf. 13½
442 A131 50fr multicolored   1.60 1.00
443 A131 60fr multicolored   1.90 1.50
444 A131 110fr multicolored   3.25 1.90
    Nos. 442-444 (3)   6.75 4.40

Mother's Day A132

1993, May 30   Litho.   Perf. 12½
445 A132 95fr Hibiscus   2.75 1.75
446 A132 120fr Siale   3.50 2.75

Admiral Antoine d'Entrecasteaux (1737-1793), French Navigator — A133

1993, July 12   Engr.   Perf. 13
447 A133 170fr grn bl, red brn & blk   5.00 3.25

Taipei '93 — A134

1993, Aug. 14   Litho.   Perf. 13x12½
448 A134 435fr multicolored   12.50 10.00

Churches — A135

1993, Aug. 15   Perf. 13
449 A135 30fr Tepa, Wallis   1.00 .80
450 A135 30fr Vilamalia, Futuna   1.00 .80

School Art Type of 1993
1993   Litho.   Perf. 13x13½, 13½x13
451 A130 28fr Stylized trees   .80 .55
452 A130 52fr Family, vert.   1.60 1.00

    Issue dates: 28fr, Oct. 18. 52fr, Nov. 8.

Christmas A136

1993, Dec. 6   Perf. 13
453 A136 80fr multicolored   2.40 1.60

Traditional Arts and Crafts Exhibition A137

1994, Mar. 24   Litho.   Perf. 12½
454 A137 80fr multicolored   2.40 1.60

Liberation of Paris, 50th Anniv. — A138

1994, Apr. 21   Engr.   Perf. 13
455 A138 110fr black, blue & red   3.50 2.00

Satellite Communications — A139

1994, June 23   Litho.
456 A139 10fr multicolored   2.40 1.75

1994 World Cup Soccer Championships, U.S. — A140

1994, June 23
457 A140 105fr multicolored   3.25 2.00

Princesses Ouveennes, 1903 — A141

1994, July 21   Engr.   Perf. 13
458 A141 90fr blue grn, blk & red 2.50 1.50

Symbols of Playing Cards Suits — A142

1994, Aug. 25   Litho.   Perf. 13
459 A142 40fr multicolored   1.40 .70

Ultra-Light Aircraft — A143

1994, Aug. 25
460 A143 5fr multicolored   .35 .35

Coconut — A144

1994, Oct. 13   Litho.   Perf. 13
461 A144 36fr multicolored   1.25 .70

Parrots
A145

1994, Nov. 17   Litho.   Perf. 13x13½
462 A145 62fr multicolored   2.00 1.25

Grand Lodge of France, Cent. — A146

1994, Nov. 24   Engr.   Perf. 13
463 A146 250fr multicolored   6.50 4.50

Preparing Traditional Meal — A147

1995, Jan. 25   Litho.   Perf. 13
464 A147 80fr multicolored   2.40 1.40

Aerial View
of Islands
A148

1995, Feb. 21   Perf. 13x13½, 13½x13
465 A148   85fr Nukulaelae   2.25 1.25
466 A148   90fr Nukufetau, vert.   2.50 1.40
467 A148 100fr Nukufotu,
        Nukuloa,   2.75 1.90
     Nos. 465-467 (3)   7.50 4.55

Mua
College — A149

1995, Apr. 11   Perf. 12
468 A149 35fr multicolored   1.10 .70

UN, 50th Anniv. — A150

1995, June 26   Litho.   Perf. 13½
469 A150 55fr multicolored   1.60 1.00

10th South Pacific Games — A151

1995, Aug. 1   Litho.   Perf. 13
470 A151 70fr multicolored   1.90 1.40

Local
Plants — A152

1995, Oct. 24   Litho.   Perf. 13½x13
471 A152 20fr Breadfruit tree   .70 .55
472 A152 60fr Tarot   1.60 1.00
473 A152 65fr Kava   2.00 1.40
    Nos. 471-473 (3)   4.30 2.95
   See Nos. 478-481, 484-485.

Tapa — A153

1995, Dec. 12   Litho.   Perf. 13
474 A153 25fr Native life, vert.   .80 .70
475 A153 26fr Fish, sea shells   1.00 .70

Mothers from the
Islands — A154

1996, Jan. 14   Litho.   Perf. 13½x13
476 A154 80fr multicolored   2.25 1.50

Golf
A155

1996, Jan. 24   Perf. 13
477 A155 95fr multicolored   3.50 2.00

Local Plant Type of 1995
1996   Litho.   Perf. 13½x13
478 A152 27fr Cananga odorata   .80 .70
479 A152 28fr Mahoaa   .90 .70
480 A152 45fr Hibiscus   1.25 .80
481 A152 52fr Ufi   1.60 1.00
    Nos. 478-481 (4)   4.55 3.20
  Issued: #479, 481, 3/14; #478, 480, 6/20.

Sanglants Swamp — A156

1996, June 26   Perf. 13
482 A156 53fr multicolored   1.60 1.00

Chess — A157

1996, July 17
483 A157 110fr multicolored   3.25 2.00

Local Plant Type of 1995
Designs: 30fr, 48fr, Calladium.

1996, Sept. 17   Litho.   Perf. 13½x13
Background Color
484 A152 30fr blue green   1.00 .70
485 A152 48fr lilac   1.40 .90

Francoise Perroton,
Missionary — A158

1996, Oct. 25   Perf. 13
486 A158 50fr multicolored   1.50 1.00

UNICEF,
50th Anniv.
A159

1996, Dec. 4   Litho.   Perf. 13
487 A159 25fr multicolored   .90 .70

CPS, 50th
Anniv.
A160

1997, Feb. 6   Litho.   Perf. 13
488 A160 7fr multicolored   .35 .35

Royal
Standards
A161

1997, Feb. 14   Litho.   Perf. 13x13½
489 A161 56fr King Lavelua   1.40 1.00
490 A161 60fr King Tuiagaifo   1.40 1.00
491 A161 70fr King Tuisigave   1.90 1.00
    Nos. 489-491 (3)   4.70 3.00

Brasseur de
Kava — A162

1997, Apr. 17   Perf. 13½x13
492 A162 170fr multicolored   4.00 2.75

Island
Scenes
A163

Designs: 10fr, Old man telling stories to children seated around campfire. 36fr, Braiding mat, vert. 40fr, Preparing "Kai'umu" (feast).

Perf. 13x13½, 13½x13
1997, May 20   Litho.
493 A163 10fr multicolored   .35 .35
494 A163 36fr multicolored   1.00 .80
495 A163 40fr multicolored   1.10 .80
    Nos. 493-495 (3)   2.45 1.95

Green
Lagoon
Turtles
A164

1997, June 18   Perf. 13x13½
496 A164 62fr Crawling ashore   1.75 1.00
497 A164 80fr Swimming   2.25 1.40

Festival of Avignon — A165

1997, July 31   Litho.   Perf. 13
498 A165 160fr multicolored   4.50 2.40

Berlin Handicapped Sports Festival — A166

1997, Aug. 12
499 A166 35fr multicolored   1.10 .70

D'Uvéa Karate Club — A167

1997, Oct. 15   **Litho.**   *Perf. 13x13½*
500 A167 24fr multicolored   1.00 .50

Fight Against AIDS — A168

1997, Dec. 1   **Litho.**   *Perf. 13*
501 A168 5fr multicolored   1.50 .35

Christmas — A169

1997, Dec, 24
502 A169 85fr Nativity   2.25 1.50

Preparation of UMU — A170

1998, Jan. 26
503 A170 800fr multicolored   16.50 11.00

Orchids — A171

70fr, Vanda T.M.A.. 85fr, Cattleya bow bells. 90fr, Arachnis. 105fr, Cattleya.

1998, Feb. 18   **Litho.**   *Perf. 13*
504 A171 70fr multi, vert.   1.90 1.00
505 A171 85fr multi   2.25 1.25
506 A171 90fr multi, vert.   2.40 1.25
507 A171 105fr multi   2.75 1.50
   Nos. 504-507 (4)   9.30 5.00

Telecom 2000 — A172

1998, Mar. 24   **Litho.**   *Perf. 13*
508 A172 7fr multicolored   .40 .40

Fishing — A173

Designs: 50fr, Fisherman casting net into lagoon. 52fr, Fisherman sorting catch.

1998, May 26   **Litho.**   *Perf. 13*
509 A173 50fr multicolored   1.40 .70
510 A173 52fr multicolored   1.40 .70

1998 World Cup Soccer Championships, France — A174

1998, June 10
511 A174 80fr multicolored   2.10 1.40

Insects A175

1998, July 21   **Litho.**   *Perf. 13x13½*
512 A175 36fr Dragonfly   1.00 .50
513 A175 40fr Cicada   1.10 .70

Coral — A176

Various corals: a, 4fr. b, 5fr. c, 10fr. d, 15fr.

1998   **Litho.**   *Perf. 13x13½*
514 A176   Strip of 4, #a.-d.   1.50 1.50

52nd Autumn Philatelic Salon — A177

1998, Nov. 5   **Litho.**   *Perf. 13½*
515 A177 175fr multicolored   4.75 2.50

World Fight Against AIDS A178

1998, Dec. 1   *Perf. 13*
516 A178 62fr multicolored   1.60 1.00

Islet of Nuku Taakimoa A179

1999, Mar. 22   **Litho.**   *Perf. 13*
517 A179 130fr multicolored   3.50 1.80
   See No. 594.

Souvenir Sheet

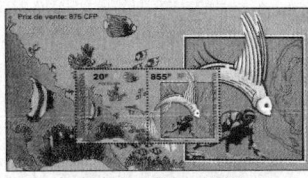

Lagoon Life — A180

a, 20fr, Various fish. b, 855fr, Fish, diver.

1999, May 17   **Litho.**   *Perf. 13*
518 A180   Sheet of 2, #a.-b.   24.00 22.50

PhilexFrance '99, World Philatelic Exhibition — A181

1999, July 2   **Litho.**   *Perf. 13*
519 A181 200fr multicolored   5.50 3.25

French Senate, Bicent. — A182

1999, Sept. 20   **Engr.**   *Perf. 13*
520 A182 125fr multicolored   3.50 2.00

Territorial Assembly Building — A183

1999, Aug. 23   **Litho.**
521 A183 17fr multicolored   .45 .35

Pandanus A184

1999, Oct. 18
522 A184 25fr multicolored   .70 .45

Man Making Canoe A185

1999, Nov. 8
523 A185 55fr multicolored   1.50 .80

French Postage Stamps, 150th Anniv. — A186

1999, Dec. 1
524 A186 65fr Wallis & Futuna #86   1.75 1.00

Millennium — A187

2000, Jan. 1   **Litho.**   *Perf. 13*
525 A187 350fr multicolored   9.50 4.50

Mata'utu Cathedral A188

2000, Apr. 28   Photo.   Perf. 13x13¼
526 A188 300fr multicolored   8.00 3.75

Patrol Boat "La Glorieuse" — A189

2000, June 5   Engr.   Perf. 13x12¾
527 A189 155fr multicolored   4.25 2.40

Sosefo Papilio Makape, First Senator — A190

2000, June 19   Perf. 12¾x13
528 A190 115fr multicolored   3.00 1.50

Overseas Broadcasting Institute — A191

2000, July 3   Perf. 13x12½
529 A191 200fr multicolored   5.50 2.50

Taro Cultivation A192

2000, July 27   Litho.   Perf. 13
530 A192 275fr multicolored   7.50 3.50

Souvenir Sheet

2000 Summer Olympics, Sydney — A193

Traditional games, 85fr: a, Spear throwing. b, Sailing. c, Rowing. d, Volleyball.

2000, Sept. 15   Litho.   Perf. 13
531 A193 #a-d + 2 labels   9.00 9.00

8th Pacific Arts Festival A194

2000, Oct. 23   Perf. 13x13¼
532 A194 330fr multicolored   9.00 4.50

Fish — A195

No. 533: a, Coryphaena hippurus. b, Caranx melanpygyus. c, Thunnus albacares.

2000, Nov. 9   Litho.   Perf. 13
533   Vert. strip of 3 + 2 la-
          bels   9.25 9.25
a.-c. A195 115fr Any single   3.10 1.75

Canonization of St. Marcellin Champagnat, 1st Anniv. — A196

2000, Nov. 13
534 A196 380fr multicolored   10.00 5.00

Talietumu Archaeological Site — A197

2000, Dec. 1   Perf. 13x13½
535 A197 205fr multicolored   5.50 2.75

Christmas A198

2000, Dec. 25   Perf. 13
536 A198 225fr multicolored   6.00 2.75

Ship "Jacques Cartier" — A199

2001, Feb. 26   Engr.   Perf. 13
537 A199 225fr multicolored   6.00 2.75

Campaign Against Alcoholism A200

2001, Mar. 14   Litho.   Perf. 13¼x13
538 A200 75fr multicolored   2.00 1.00

Souvenir Sheet

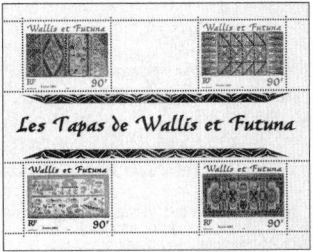

Tapas — A201

Tapa with: a, Large diamond, shells, map of islands. b, Triangles and diamonds. c, Scenes of native life, fish, shells, boat. d, Overlapping ovals.

2001, Apr. 14   Perf. 13
539 A201 90fr Sheet of 4, #a-d, +
          2 labels   9.75 9.75

Children's Drawings of Flowers — A202

2001, May 31
540   Horiz. strip of 4   8.25 8.25
a.   A202 50fr multi   1.40 1.40
b.   A202 55fr multi   1.50 1.50
c.   A202 95fr multi   2.50 2.50
d.   A202 100fr multi   2.75 2.75

Territorial Status, 40th Anniv. A203

2001, July 29   Litho.   Perf. 13
541 A203 165fr multicolored   4.50 2.00

Installation of Mediator, 1st Anniv. A204

2001, Sept. 26
542 A204 800fr multicolored   22.00 10.00

Year of Dialogue Among Civilizations A205

2001, Oct. 9
543 A205 390fr multicolored   10.50 5.00

5th Autumn Salon — A206

Birds: a, Dacula pacifica. b, Vini australis. c, Tyto alba.

2001, Nov. 8
544   Vert. strip of 3 + 2
          labels   12.00 12.00
a.-c. A206 150fr Any single   4.00 3.00

Children's Drawings of Fruit A207

No. 545, 65fr: a, Custard apple (pomme canelle). b, Breadfruit (fruit de pain).
No. 546, 65fr: a, Pineapple. b, Mango.

2001, Aug. 22   Litho.   Perf. 13
Vert. Pairs, #a-b
545-546 A207 Set of 2 pairs   7.00 5.00

Tomb of Futuna King Fakavelikele — A208

2001, Dec. 28   Litho.   Perf. 13
547 A208 325fr multicolored   9.00 3.75

Finemui-Teesi College — A209

2002, Jan. 29   **Perf. 13x13½**
548 A209 115fr multicolored   3.00 1.40

Intl. Women's Day — A210

2002, Mar. 5   **Litho.**   **Perf. 13**
549 A210 800fr Queen Aloisia   22.00 10.00

Arms of Bishop Pompallier A211

2002, Apr. 19   **Engr.**   **Perf. 13¼**
550 A211 500fr multicolored   13.50 6.50

Uvea Firefighters A212

Serpentine Die Cut
2002, Apr. 28   **Photo.**
Self-Adhesive
551 A212 85fr multicolored   2.25 1.40

2002 World Cup Soccer Championships, Japan and Korea — A213

2002, May 31   **Litho.**   **Perf. 13**
552 A213 65fr multicolored   1.75 1.00

World Environment Day — A214

2002, June 5   **Perf. 13x13½**
553 A214 330fr multicolored   9.00 4.00

Traditional Buildings A215

Designs: No. 554, 50fr, Building with overhanging roof. No. 555, 50fr, Open-air shelter, vert. No. 556, 55fr, Building with two entry ways. No. 557, 55fr, Building with ladder to roof, vert.

2002, Aug. 9   **Engr.**   **Perf. 13¼**
554-557 A215   Set of 4   5.75 2.50

Discovery of the Horn Islands, 1616 A216

No. 558: a, Jacob Lemaire and compass rose. b, Map of Futuna and Alofi Islands. c, William Schouten and ship.

2002, Aug. 30   **Litho.**   **Perf. 13x13¼**
558   Horiz. strip of 3   10.00 10.00
   a.-c.   A216 125fr any single   3.25 3.25
   d.   Souvenir sheet, #558   10.00 10.00

Landscapes A217

No. 559: a, Utua Bay. b, Liku Bay. c, Kingfisher at Vele. d, Aka'Aka Bay.

2002, Sept. 20
559   Horiz. strip of 4   11.50 11.50
   a.   A217 95fr multi   2.50 1.50
   b.   A217 100fr multi   2.75 1.50
   c.   A217 105fr multi   2.75 1.60
   d.   A217 135fr multi   3.50 1.75

Enygrus Bibroni — A218

2002, Oct. 28   **Litho.**   **Perf. 13¼x13**
560 A218 75fr multicolored   2.00 .75

Fish A219

No. 561: a, Dendrochirus biocellatus. b, Discordipina griessingeri. c, Antennacius nummifer. d, Novaculichthys taeniourus.

2002, Nov. 7   **Perf. 13x13¼**
561   Vert. strip of 4 + 3   10.00 9.00
     labels
   a.-d.   A219 110fr Any single   3.00 1.75

Best Wishes A220

2002, Dec. 5
562 A220 140fr multicolored   3.75 1.40

Last Avro Lancaster Flight to Wallis, 40th Anniv. A221

2003, Jan. 26   **Perf. 13**
563 A221 135fr multicolored   3.60 1.75

St. Valentine's Day — A222

2003, Feb. 14   **Perf. 13**
564 A222 85fr multicolored   2.25 1.00

Introduction of the Euro, 1st Anniv. A223

2003, Feb. 17   **Perf. 12½x12¾**
565 A223 125fr multicolored   3.25 1.80
Values are for examples with surrounding selvage.

Alain Gerbault (1893-1941), Circumnavigator, Aboard Boat "Firecrest" — A224

2003, Mar. 6   **Engr.**   **Perf. 13¼**
566 A224 600fr grn & ol grn   16.00 8.00

Postal Art — A225

Various designs.

2003, Mar. 31   **Litho.**   **Perf. 13**
567   Horiz. strip of 5   2.40 2.40
   a.   A225 5fr multi   .25 .25
   b.   A225 10fr multi   .25 .25
   c.   A225 15fr multi   .40 .40
   d.   A225 20fr multi   .55 .25
   e.   A225 40fr multi   1.10 .40

Coral Reefs A226

Various views.

2003, Apr. 10   **Perf. 13x13¼**
568   Horiz. strip of 4   10.00 10.00
   a.   A226 95fr multi   1.75 1.75
   b.   A226 105fr multi   1.90 1.90
   c.   A226 110fr multi   2.00 2.00
   d.   A226 115fr multi   2.10 2.10

St. Pierre Chanel (1803-41), Martyred Missionary A227

2003, Apr. 28   **Engr.**   **Perf. 12¼**
569 A227 130fr multicolored   3.50 1.80

2003 Census — A228

2003, June 12   **Litho.**   **Perf. 13**
570 A228 55fr multicolored   1.50 .70

Pacific Legends A229

Legend of the Coconut Palm: 30fr, Eel. 50fr, Coconut palms, split coconut. 60fr, Split and whole coconuts. 70fr, Coconut palms and clouds.

2003, July 28   **Litho.**   **Perf. 13x13¼**
571   Horiz. strip of 4   5.75 5.75
   a.   A229 30fr multi   .80 .40
   b.   A229 50fr multi   1.40 .75
   c.   A229 60fr multi   1.60 .85
   d.   A229 70fr multi   1.90 .95
   e.   Souvenir sheet, #571a-571d   6.00 6.00

Still Life with Maori Statuette, by Paul Gauguin (1848-1903) A230

No. 573a: Study of Heads of Tahitian Women, by Gauguin.

2003   **Perf. 13**
572 A230 100fr multicolored   2.75 1.60
Souvenir Sheet
573   Sheet, #572, 573a   5.50 5.50
   a.   A230 100fr multi   2.75 2.25
Issued: No. 572, 7/31; No. 573, 8/20. See New Caledonia No. 929.

Futuna Waterfalls — A231

2003, Aug. 6   **Perf. 13¼x13**
574 A231 115fr multicolored   3.00 1.75

Frigate Le Nivose
A232

2003, Sept. 15 Engr. **Perf. 13¼**
575 A232 325fr multicolored 8.75 4.00

Bishop Alexandre Poncet (1884-1973)
A233

2003, Sept. 18 Engr. **Perf. 13¼**
576 A233 205fr multicolored 5.50 3.00

Arms of Bishop Pierre Bataillon (1810-77) — A234

2003, Oct. 1 Litho. **Perf. 13¼**
577 A234 500fr multicolored 13.50 7.00

2003 Rugby World Cup, Australia A235

2003, Oct. 10 **Perf. 13**
578 A235 65fr multicolored 1.75 .85

Parinari Insularum
A236

2003, Nov. 6 Litho. **Perf. 13¼x13**
579 A236 250fr multicolored 6.75 3.50

Goddess Havea Hikule'o — A237

2004, Jan. 8
580 A237 85fr multicolored 2.25 1.40

People in Canoe
A238

2004, Jan. 13 **Perf. 13**
581 A238 75fr multicolored 2.00 1.25

Miniature Sheet

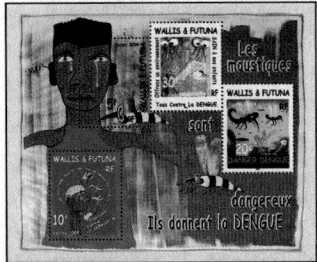

Campaign Against Dengue Fever — A239

No. 582: a, 5fr, Mosquito, crying man. b, 10fr, Mosquitos, man. c, 20fr, Mosquitos, trash. d, 30fr, Mosquitos, sleeping child.

Perf. 13¼x12¾
2004, Feb. 18 Litho.
582 A239 Sheet of 4, #a-d 2.25 2.25

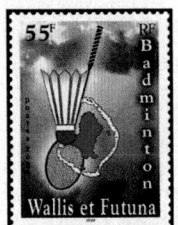

Badminton A240

2004, Mar. 12 **Perf. 13¼x13**
583 A240 55fr multicolored 1.50 1.25

Kava Drinkers A241

2004, Mar. 31 **Perf. 13x13¼**
584 A241 205fr multicolored 5.50 4.25

Flora A242

2004, Apr. 22 **Perf. 13**
585 Horiz. strip of 4 + central label 3.25 3.25
a. A242 15fr Colocasia esculenta .40 .30
b. A242 25fr Carrica papaya .65 .50
c. A242 35fr Artocarpus altilus .95 .70
d. A242 40fr Dioscorea sp. 1.10 .80

Dispatch Boat Savorgnan de Brazza A243

Gourdou-Leseurre GL 832 Hy No. 5 and Wallis Island — A244

2004, May 12 Engr. **Perf. 13¼**
586 A243 300fr multi 8.00 6.00
587 A244 380fr multi 10.25 7.75

Souvenir Sheet
Litho.
588 Sheet of 2 18.50 18.50
a. A243 300fr multi 8.00 6.00
b. A244 380fr multi 9.50 7.75

First flight over Wallis Island, 68th anniv.

Seaweeds — A245

2004, June 26 Litho. **Perf. 13**
589 Horiz. strip of 3 + 2 alternating labels 17.50 17.50
a. A245 105fr Turbinaria ornata 2.90 2.90
b. A245 155fr Padina melemele 4.25 4.25
c. A245 175fr Tubinaria concoides 4.75 4.75

Miniature Sheet

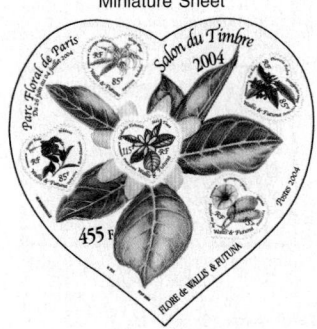

Flowers — A246

No. 590: a, Hibiscus rosa-sinensis. b, Cananga odorata. c, Plumeria rubra. d, Ipomeapes caprae. e, Gardenia taitensis.

Serpentine Die Cut 14
2004, June 26 Photo.
Self-Adhesive
590 A246 Sheet of 5 12.50 12.50
a.-d. 85fr Any single 2.25 2.25
e. 115fr multi 3.00 3.00

Salon du Timbre 2004, Paris.

Ninth Pacific Arts Festival, Palau A247

2004, July 22 Litho. **Perf. 13x13¼**
591 A247 200fr multicolored 5.50 4.25

Pili'uli Lizard — A248

2004, July 26 **Perf. 13**
592 A248 100fr multicolored 2.75 2.10

Arms of Monsignor Louis Elloy (1829-78) A249

2004, Sept. 6 Engr. **Perf. 13¼**
593 A249 500fr multicolored 13.50 10.50

No. 517 Redrawn
2004, Nov. 10 Litho. **Perf. 13**
594 A179 115fr multi 3.10 2.50

No. 594 shows a 115fr denomination below an obliterated 130fr denomination, the denomination shown on No. 517. This new denomination is not overprinted. No. 594 also has a 2004 year date, rather than an obliterated 1999 year date.

A250

Traditional Houses — A251

2004, Nov. 11 **Perf. 13¼x13**
595 A250 95fr multicolored 2.50 2.10
596 A251 130fr multicolored 3.50 3.00

Nos. 595-596 were printed in sheets containing four of each stamp plus a large central label.

Miniature Sheet

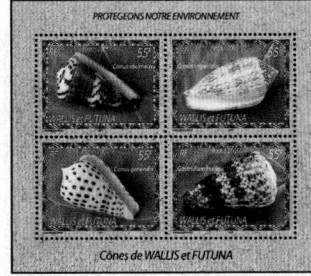

Cone Shells — A252

No. 597: a, Conus eburneus. b, Conus imperialis. c, Conus generalis. d, Gastridium textile.

2005, Jan. 26 **Perf. 13x13¼**
597 A252 55fr Sheet of 4, #a-d 6.00 5.00

Miniature Sheet

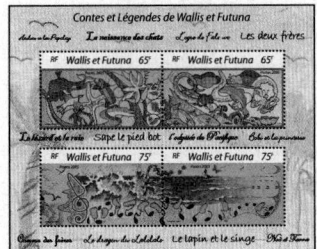

Stories and Legends — A253

No. 598: a, 65fr, Whale, bird, crab, eel, turtle. b, 65fr, Fish, octopus, dolphin, butterfly. c,

75fr, Boy, waves, G clef and musical notes. d, 75fr, Musical notes, butterflies.

2005, Jan. 31   **Perf. 13**
598 A253   Sheet of 4, #a-d   7.50 7.50

Pirogue
A254

2005, Feb. 25   **Litho.**   **Perf. 13x13¼**
599 A254 330fr multicolored   9.00 7.50

Francophone Week — A255

2005, Mar. 17
600 A255 135fr multicolored   3.60 3.00
Printed in sheets of 10 + 5 labels. See New Caledonia No. 959.

Family
Budget
Inquiry
A256

2005, Mar. 31   **Perf. 12¾**
601 A256 205fr multicolored   5.50 4.50
Values are for stamps with surrounding selvage.

Warriors — A257

2005, Apr. 19   **Perf. 13½x13**
602   Horiz. strip of 5   3.25 3.25
   a.   A257 5fr blk, red & maroon   .25 .25
   b.   A257 10fr blk, bl & vio blue   .25 .25
   c.   A257 20fr blk, pur & indigo   .55 .40
   d.   A257 30fr blk & red   .80 .65
   e.   A257 50fr blk, lt grn & emerald   1.40 1.10

Traditional
Cricket
A258

2005, May 16   **Perf. 13**
603 A258 190fr multicolored   5.00 4.00

Butterflies — A259

No. 604: a, 40fr, Papilio montrouzieri. b, 60fr, Danaus pumila.

2005, June 30   **Perf. 13x13¼**
604 A259   Horiz. pair, #a-b   2.75 2.75

Warrior With
Spear — A260

Serpentine Die Cut 11
2005, July 14   **Self-Adhesive**
     Booklet Stamp
605 A260 115fr multicolored   3.00 2.40
   a.   Booklet pane of 10   30.00

Historical Images of Wallis
Island — A261

2005, July 14   **Engr.**   **Perf. 13x13¼**
606   Horiz. pair + central label   9.00 9.00
   a.   A261 155fr Village scene   4.25 3.25
   b.   A261 175fr Family, house   4.75 3.75

First Noumea to Hihifo Flight, 58th
Anniv. — A262

2005, Aug. 19
607 A262 380fr multi   10.00 8.00

     Souvenir Sheet

Chelomia Mydas — A263

No. 608 — Green turtle: a, Adult entering water. b, Hatchlings entering water. c, Head. d, Swimming underwater.
2005, Aug. 19   **Litho.**   **Perf. 13x13¼**
608 A263   Sheet of 4, #a-d   9.25 9.25

Arms of
Monsignor Jean
Armand Lamaze
(1833-1906)
A264

2005, Oct. 5   **Engr.**   **Perf. 13¼**
609 A264 500fr multi   13.50 10.00

Spattoglottis Cinguiculata — A265

2005, Oct. 30   **Litho.**   **Perf. 13**
610 A265 100fr multi   2.75 2.00
Printed in sheets of 10 + 5 labels.

Design of Wallis
and Futuna Islands
No. 4 — A266

Design of
Wallis and
Futuna
Islands No.
87 — A267

2005, Nov. 10   **Litho.**   **Perf. 13x13¼**
611 A266 150fr multi   4.00 3.00
612 A267 150fr multi   4.00 3.00
59th Autumn Philatelic Show.

Native
Child
A268

2006, Mar. 29   **Litho.**   **Perf. 13x13¼**
613 A268 75fr multi   2.00 1.60

Monarchical
Flags — A269

Designs: 55fr, Kingdom of Uvea. 65fr, Kingdom of Sigave. 85fr, Kingdom of Alo.

     Self-Adhesive
     Booklet Stamps
2006   **Litho.**   ***Serpentine Die Cut 11***
614 A269 55fr multi   1.50 1.25
   a.   Booklet pane of 10   15.00
615 A269 65fr multi   1.75 1.40
   a.   Booklet pane of 10   17.50
616 A269 85fr multi   2.25 1.75
   a.   Booklet pane of 10   22.50
Issued: 55fr, 6/17; 65fr, 4/18; 85fr, 3/29.

Haka Mai — A270

2006   **Perf. 13¼x13**
617 A270 190fr multi   5.00 4.25

Removal of
Christ from the
Cross, by Jean
Soane Michon
(1926-68)
A271

2006, May 31   **Litho.**   **Perf. 13¼x13**
618 A271 400fr multi   11.00 8.50

2006 World Cup
Soccer
Championships,
Germany
A272

2006, June 9
619 A272 100fr multi   2.75 2.10

Mata Vai
A273

Mata Tai
A274

2006, June 17   **Perf. 13x13¼**
620 A273 140fr multi   3.75 3.00
621 A274 200fr multi   5.50 4.25

Historical Images From the 19th
Century — A275

2006, July 13   **Engr.**   **Perf. 13x13¼**
622   Horiz. pair + central la-
     bel   19.50 19.50
   a.   A275 330fr Girls dancing   9.00 7.00
   b.   A275 380fr Mua Church   10.00 8.00

Stamp Day — A276

2006, Aug. 5 Litho. Perf. 13¼x13
623 A276 150fr multi 4.00 3.25

Twin Otter Airplane "Ville de Paris", 20th Anniv. — A277

2006, Aug. 7 Perf. 13
624 A277 30fr multi .80 .65

Territorial Rugby Committee — A278

2006, Sept. 9 Perf. 12¾x13½
625 A278 10fr multi .25 .25

Uhilamoafa Gravesite A279

2006, Sept. 12 Perf. 13x13¼
626 A279 290fr multi 7.75 6.25

Arms of Monsignor Joseph Félix Blanc (1872-1962) A280

2006, Oct. 5 Engr. Perf. 13¼
627 A280 500fr multi 13.50 10.50

Tagaloa, Polynesian Deity — A281

2006, Nov. 8 Litho. Perf. 13½x13
628 A281 150fr multi 4.00 3.50

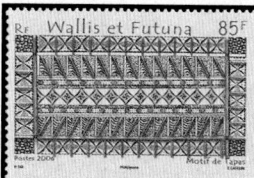

Tapas A282

No. 629: a, Tapas design (shown). b, Mako à Ono. c, Tauasu à Leava. d, Tapas design, diff.

Litho. & Engr.
2006, Nov. 8 Perf. 13x13¼
629 Vert. strip of 4 + central label 9.25 9.25
a.-d. A282 85fr Any single 2.25 1.90

Souvenir Sheet

Christmas — A283

2006, Nov. 8 Litho. Perf. 13
630 A283 225fr multi 6.00 6.00

Pio Cardinal Taofinu'u (1923-2006) A284

2007, Jan. 19 Engr. Perf. 12½x13
631 A284 800fr multi 21.50 17.50

Telemedicine A285

2007, Feb. 28 Litho. Perf. 13¼x13
632 A285 5fr multi .25 .25

Audit Office, Bicent. A286

2007, Mar. 19 Engr. Perf. 13¼
633 A286 105fr multi 2.75 2.40

Woman A287

2007, Mar. 22 Litho. Perf. 13
634 A287 75fr multi 2.00 1.75

First Noumea-Hihifo Air Service, 50th Anniv. — A288

2007, Apr. 30 Engr. Perf. 13x12½
635 A288 290fr multi 6.75 6.75

Fish — A289

2007, May 22 Litho. Perf. 12¾x13¼
636 Horiz. pair 2.00 2.00
a. A289 40fr Eviota .90 .90
b. A289 50fr Trimma 1.10 1.10

Secretary General of the Pacific Community, 60th Anniv. — A290

2007, June 28 Litho. Perf. 13
637 A290 155fr multi 3.50 3.50

Lolesio Tuita, Javelin Thrower A291

2007, July 30 Engr. Perf. 12½x13
638 A291 330fr purple & red 7.50 7.50

Buildings — A292

No. 639: a, House, Tamana. b, Sanctuary of Pierre Chanel, Poi.

2007, July 31 Engr. Perf. 13x13¼
639 Horiz. pair with central label 9.00 9.00
a. A292 190fr brown 4.25 4.25
b. A292 200fr brown 4.75 4.75

Discovery of Uvea Island by Samuel Wallis, 240th Anniv. — A293

2007, Aug. 3 Litho.
640 A293 225fr multi 5.25 5.25
a. Souvenir sheet of 1 5.50 5.50
No. 640a sold for 240fr.

Legends of Lomipeau A294

No. 641 — People and: a, Togitapu Island. b, Uvea Island.

2007, Aug. 3 Horiz. pair 1.25 1.25
641 Horiz. pair 1.25 1.25
a. A294 20fr multi .50 .50
b. A294 30fr multi .75 .75

Arms of Monsignor Armand Olier (1851-1911) A295

2007, Oct. 22 Engr. Perf. 13¼
642 A295 500fr multi 12.50 12.50

Emblem of Handisport A296

2007, Oct. 11 Photo. Perf. 12¾
643 A296 10fr multi .25 .25
Values are for stamps with surrounding selvage.

2007 Rugby World Cup Championships, France — A297

2007, Oct. 20 Litho. Perf. 13
644 A297 205fr multi 5.00 5.00
Printed in sheets of 10 + label.

Dances — A298

Designs: No. 645, 100fr, Mio dance, Futuna. No. 646, 100fr, Kailao Tokotoko dance, Wallis.

2007, Nov. 10 Litho. Perf. 13¼x13
645-646 A298 Set of 2 5.00 5.00

Connection to the Internet, 10th Anniv. A299

2008, Mar. 3　Litho.　Perf. 13x13¼
647　A299　55fr multi　　　　1.50　1.50
Printed in sheets of 10 + central label.

Coral Reef A300

2008, Mar. 7
648　A300　95fr multi　　　　2.50　2.50

Islands — A301

No. 649: a, Uvea. b, Futuna and Alofi, horiz.

Perf. 13¼x13 (#649a), 13x13¼
(#649b)
2008, Mar. 7
649　A301　85fr Pair, #a-b　　4.50　4.50
Printed in sheets containing four of each stamp.

Women and Hibiscus Flowers — A302

2008, Mar. 7　　　　Perf. 13
650　A302　65fr multi　　　　1.75　1.75
Printed in sheets of 10 + 5 labels.

2008 Summer Olympics, Beijing A303

2008, June 14　　Perf. 13x13¼
651　A303　75fr multi　　　　2.00　2.00

Intl. Year of Planet Earth — A304

2008, June 14　　　Perf. 13
652　A304　190fr multi　　　5.00　5.00

Souvenir Sheet
653　A304　200fr multi　　　5.25　5.25

King Tomasi Kulimoetoke II (1918-2007) A305

2008, July 29　Engr.　Perf. 13¼
654　A305　380fr orange brown　9.75　9.75

Aglaia Psilopetala A306

2008, July 30　Litho.　Perf. 13
655　A306　105fr multi　　　　2.75　2.75

Historical Images of Futuna — A307

No. 656: a, Women braiding straw. b, Boats returning to island.

2008, July 30　Engr.　Perf. 13x13¼
656　　Horiz. pair with central　6.75　6.75
　　　　label
　a.　A307　110fr brown　　2.75　2.75
　b.　A307　155fr brown　　4.00　4.00

Stained-glass Windows of Lano Church — A308

Designs: 100fr, St. Theresa. 140fr, St. Peter Chanel.

2008, July 31　Litho.　Perf. 13
657-658　A308　Set of 2　　6.00　6.00

Pirogue Hulls A309

Various painted pirogue hulls.

2008, Aug. 18　　　Perf. 13x13¼
659　　Horiz. strip of 4　　2.75　2.75
　a.　A309　5fr multi　　　.25　.25
　b.　A309　20fr multi　　.50　.50
　c.　A309　40fr multi　　.95　.95
　d.　A309　50fr multi　1.10　1.10

Lolesio Tuita Stadium A310

2008, Oct. 28
660　A310　55fr multi　　　　1.25　1.25

Arms of Monsignor Alexandre Poncet (1884-1973) A311

2008, Oct. 28　Engr.　Perf. 13¼
661　A311　500fr multi　　11.00　11.00

World Youth Day — A312

2008, Nov. 8　Litho.　Perf. 13¼x13
662　A312　10fr multi　　　　.25　.25

Pigs — A313

No. 663 — Pigs on farm with denomination at: a, UL. b, UR.

2008, Nov. 8　　　Perf. 13x13¼
663　A313　115fr Horiz. pair, #a-b　5.00　5.00

Fifth French Republic, 50th Anniv. A314

2008, Nov. 8　Engr.　Perf. 13¼
664　A314　225fr multi　　　5.00　5.00

Louis Braille (1809-52), Educator of the Blind — A315

2009, Mar. 7　Engr.　Perf. 12¾x13
665　A315　330fr multi　　　7.50　7.50

Bougainvillea Spectabilis — A316

Flowers with background colors of: No. 666, 55fr, Black. No. 667, 55fr, Green. No. 668, 55fr, Red. No. 669, 55fr, White.

2009, May 4　Litho.　Perf. 13
666-669　A316　Set of 4　　5.25　5.25

Gobies — A317

No. 670: a, Akihito futuna. b, Stiphodon rubromaculatus.

2009, May 7　　　Perf. 12¾x13¼
670　　Horiz. pair　　　　3.00　3.00
　a.-b.　A317　65fr Either single　1.50　1.50

St. Theresa of Lisieux (1873-97) A318

Phil@poste at bottom in: No. 671, White (brown border at bottom). No. 672, Black (brown border at top).

2009, June 9　　　Perf. 13½x13
671　A318　140fr multi　　　3.25　3.25
672　A318　140fr multi　　　3.25　3.25

New Year 2009, (Year of the Ox) — A319

2009, June 27　　Perf. 13¼x13
673　A319　95fr multi　　　2.25　2.25

Pétanque Playing in Wallis & Futuna Islands — A320

2009, July 31
674　A320　105fr multi　　　2.50　2.50

Arms of Bishop Michel Darmancier (1918-84) A321

2009, Oct. 30   Engr.   Perf. 13¼
675 A321 500fr multi   12.50 12.50

Historical Images — A322

No. 676: a, France House. b, Army of Wallisians.

2009, Nov. 5   Perf. 13x13¼
676   Horiz. pair + central label   9.50 9.50
  a.-b. A322 190fr Either single   4.75 4.75

Man Preparing Kava — A323

2009, Nov. 12   Litho.   Perf. 13¼x13
677 A323 115fr multi   3.00 3.00

Eiffel Tower on Tapa Cloth — A324

2009, Dec. 8   Perf. 13x13¼
678 A324 85fr brown & black   2.10 2.10

Wallis & Futuna Islands as French Overseas Territory, 50th Anniv. — A325

2009, Dec. 27   Engr.   Perf. 13¼
679 A325 205fr multi   5.00 5.00

Arrival of First Doctors on Futuna Island, 50th Anniv. — A326

2010, Jan. 3   Litho.   Perf. 13
680 A326 800fr multi   18.50 18.50

Gobies — A327

2010, Feb. 19   Perf. 12¾x13¼
681   Horiz. pair   2.75 2.75
  a. A327 50fr Sicyopus sasali   1.25 1.25
  b. A327 65fr Stenogobius keletaona 1.50 1.50

A328

A329

A330

Coral Reefs A331

2010, Mar. 12   Litho.   Perf. 13x13¼
682   Horiz. strip of 4   2.40 2.40
  a. A328 10fr multi   .25 .25
  b. A329 20fr multi   .45 .45
  c. A330 30fr multi   .70 .70
  d. A331 40fr multi   .95 .95

Easter — A332

2010, Apr. 2
683 A332 135fr multi   3.25 3.25

Mother's Day A333

2010, May 28   Perf. 13
684 A333 105fr multi   2.25 2.25

Renewable Energy — A334

No. 685: a, Solar panels on ground. b, Solar panels on roof.

2010, June 11
685   Horiz. pair + central label   16.50 16.50
  a.-b. A334 400fr Either single   8.25 8.25

Arms of Bishop Lolesio Fuahea — A335

2010, July 16   Engr.   Perf. 13¼
686 A335 500fr multi   11.00 11.00

Traditional Group Fishing — A337

2010, Sept. 24
688 A337 205fr brown   4.75 4.75

Depictions of the Elements — A338

No. 689: a, Water. b, Fire.

2010, Oct. 15   Perf. 13
689 A338 150fr Horiz. pair, #a-b   7.00 7.00

Souvenir Sheet

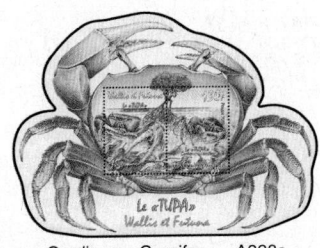

Cardisoma Carnifex — A338a

No. 689C: d, 95fr, Denomination at LL. e, 130fr, Denomination at UR.

2010, Nov. 6   Litho.   Perf. 13¼x13
689C A338a Sheet of 2, #d-e   5.25 5.25

Christmas A339

2010, Dec. 24   Litho.   Perf. 13
690 A339 95fr multi   2.25 2.25

Cicada — A340

2011, Jan. 17
691 A340 55fr multi   1.25 1.25

Arms of Bishop Ghislain Marie Raoul Suzanne de Rasilly — A341

2011, Feb. 19   Engr.   Perf. 13¼
692 A341 500fr multi   12.00 12.00

French Navy Ship Jacques Cartier, Relief Ship for Victims of Tropical Cyclone Tomas A342

2011, Mar. 31   Litho.   Perf. 13
693 A342 600fr multi   14.50 14.50

St. Peter Chanel (1803-41) — A343

2011, Apr. 28
694 A343 75fr multi   1.75 1.75

Birds — A344

No. 695: a, 5fr, Vini australis (30x40mm). b, 20fr, Melipphage foulehaio (30x40mm). c, 115fr, Lalage maculosa futunae (60x40mm).

2011, May 28   *Perf. 13¼x13*
695 A344   Horiz. strip of 3, #a-c   3.50   3.50

Campaign Against Alcohol — A345

2011, June 28
696 A345 130fr multi   3.25   3.25

Georges Pompidou (1911-74), President of France A346

2011, July 5   *Perf. 13x13¼*
697 A346 1000fr multi   24.00   24.00

Territorial Statute, 50th Anniv. — A347

2011, July 16
698 A347 380fr multi   9.25   9.25

Souvenir Sheet

Pacific Games, Noumea, New Caledonia — A348

No. 699: a, 10fr, Track. b, 190fr, Sailing.

2011, Aug. 24
699 A348   Sheet of 2, #a-b   4.75   4.75

Tapa Cloth Designs — A349

Designs: 40fr, Flowers and diamonds. 50fr, Shells.

2011, Sept. 24
700-701 A349   Set of 2   2.10   2.10

Wallis Open Air Market, 1st Anniv. — A350

2011, Oct. 2
702 A350 30fr multi   .70   .70

Historical Images — A351

No. 703: a, Marriage in Mua. b, Marist Sisters, Sofala.

2011, Nov. 4
703   Horiz. pair + central label   6.25   6.25
   a. A351 110fr brown   2.50   2.50
   b. A351 155fr brown   3.75   3.75

Ninth Pacific Mini-Games, Wallis and Futuna Islands — A352

2012, Jan. 25
704 A352 65fr multi   1.50   1.50

Tekena — A353

Fai Koka A354

2012, Feb. 17
705 A353 75fr multi   1.75   1.75
706 A354 115fr multi   2.60   2.60

First Territorial Assembly — A355

2012, Mar. 4
707 A355 200fr multi   4.50   4.50

Corals A356

Various corals.

2012, Apr. 17   *Perf. 13x13¼*
708   Horiz. strip of 4   3.25   3.25
   a. A356 10fr multi   .25   .25
   b. A356 30fr multi   .70   .70
   c. A356 40fr multi   .90   .90
   d. A356 55fr multi   1.25   1.25

Arrival of Americans, 70th Anniv. — A357

2012, May 28   *Perf. 13*
709 A357 55fr multi   1.25   1.25

Lavelua, King of Uvea, and Chieftains, Circa 1900 — A358

2012, June 21   *Engr.*   *Perf. 13x13¼*
710 A358 380fr bl grn & blk   8.00   8.00

Poetry of the Seas — A359

2012, July 16   *Litho.*   *Perf. 13*
711 A359 35fr multi   .75   .75

Opening of New Payment Office — A360

2012, July 27
712 A360 135fr multi   3.00   3.00

Reconstruction of Futuna Upper Administration Delegation Building — A361

2012, Sept. 5
713 A361 95fr multi   2.10   2.10

2013 Oceania Pétanque Tournament, Wallis & Futuna Islands — A362

2012, July 7   *Litho.*
714 A362 25fr multi   .55   .55

Arms of Bishop Guillaume Douarre (1810-53) — A363

2012, Oct. 18   *Engr.*   *Perf. 13¼*
715 A363 500fr multi   11.00   11.00

Second Vatican Council, 50th Anniv. — A364

2012, Oct. 11   *Litho.*   *Perf. 13*
716 A364 290fr multi   6.25   6.25

Shells A365

Various shells.

2012, Nov. 8   *Perf. 13x13¼*
717   Horiz. strip of 4   3.50   3.50
   a. A365 5fr multi   .25   .25
   b. A365 25fr multi   .55   .55
   c. A365 35fr multi   .75   .75
   d. A365 85fr multi   1.90   1.90

Bishop Lolesio Fuahea (1927-2011), First Wallis & Futuna Islands Bishop Born in Oceania A366

2012, Dec. 2   **Engr.**   *Perf. 13¼x13*
718   A366   1000fr multi   22.00   22.00

A367

Ocean Garden — A368

2013, Jan. 17   **Litho.**   *Perf. 13*
719   A367   85fr multi   2.00   2.00
720   A368   85fr multi   2.00   2.00

Bats — A369

2013, Feb. 20   **Litho.**   *Perf. 13*
721   A369   55fr multi   1.25   1.25

Hervé Loste (1926-94), Politician — A370

2013, Mar. 5   **Litho.**   *Perf. 13*
722   A370   800fr multi   17.50   17.50

State High School, 20th Anniv. — A371

2013, Mar. 10   **Litho.**   *Perf. 13*
723   A371   65fr multi   1.40   1.40

First Session of Mata-Utu Tribunal, 50th Anniv. — A372

2013, Apr. 5   **Litho.**   *Perf. 13*
724   A372   190fr multi   4.25   4.25

Discovery of Horn Island (Futuna Island), 400th Anniv. (in 2016) — A373

2013, May 19   **Litho.**   *Perf. 13*
725   A373   330fr multi   7.50   7.50

Story Telling A374

Traditional Dancers A375

2013, June 14   **Litho.**   *Perf. 13x13¼*
726   A374   105fr multi   2.40   2.40
727   A375   140fr multi   3.25   3.25

Petelo Sanele Vakalima, Javelin Thrower — A376

2013, July 3   **Litho.**   *Perf. 13*
728   A376   75fr multi   1.75   1.75

Sister Marie Françoise Perroton (1796-1873), Missionary A377

2013, Aug. 10   **Engr.**   *Perf. 13¼x13*
729   A377   400fr beige & blk   9.00   9.00

2013 Pacific Mini-Games, Mata-Utu — A378

No. 730 — Red lizard mascot: a, Serving volleyball, map of Wallis Island. b, Diving for volleyball, map of Futuna Island. c, Sailing, map of Futuna Island, horiz. d, Weight lifting, map of Futuna Island, horiz. e, Playing rugby, map of Wallis Island. f, Making Taekwondo kick, map of Wallis Island. g, Paddling outrigger canoe, map of Futuna Island, horiz. h, Throwing javelin, map of Wallis Island.

Litho. & Silk-screened
2013, Sept. 2   *Serpentine Die Cut 11*
Self-Adhesive
730   Booklet pane of 8   15.50
a.-h.   A378 85fr Any single   1.90   1.90

Bishop Alexandre Poncet (1884-1973) — A379

2013, Sept. 18   **Engr.**   *Perf. 13x13¼*
731   A379   150fr black   3.50   3.50

Landscapes of Shores of Wallis Island — A380

Designs: 55fr, Fisherman in surf. 65fr, Beach, tree at right.

2013, Oct. 25   **Litho.**   *Perf. 13*
732-733   A380   Set of 2   2.75   2.75

Flowers — A381

Designs: No. 734, 165fr, Hyacinth (jacinth). No. 735, 165fr, Red jasmine (frangipanier).

2013, Nov. 5   **Litho.**   *Perf. 13*
734-735   A381   Set of 2   7.50   7.50

Christmas A382

2013, Dec. 1   **Litho.**   *Perf. 13*
736   A382   175fr multi   4.00   4.00

New Banknotes — A383

Designs: 50fr, 500-franc banknote. 90fr, 1000-franc banknote. 115fr, 5000-franc banknote. 800fr, 10,000-franc banknote.

2014, Jan. 24   **Litho.**   *Perf. 13*
737-740   A383   Set of 4   24.00   24.00

Cyrthandra Futunae — A384

2014, Feb. 18   **Litho.**   *Perf. 13*
741   A384   95fr multi   2.25   2.25

Fai Koka — A385

2014, Mar. 5   **Litho.**   *Perf. 13*
742   A385   95fr multi   2.25   2.25

Canonization of Popes — A386

Designs: No. 743, 100fr, Pope John XXIII. No. 744, 100fr, Pope John Paul II.

2014, Apr. 27   **Litho.**   *Perf. 13¼x13*
743-744   A386   Set of 2   4.75   4.75

Chapel and Shrine to St. Peter Chanel, Poi — A387

2014, Apr. 28   Litho.   Perf. 13
745 A387 130fr multi   3.00 3.00

Mother's Day — A388

2014, May 23   Litho.   Perf. 13¼x13
746 A388 115fr multi   2.60 2.60

2014 Oceania Weight Lifting Championships, Noumea, New Caledonia — A389

2014, May 27   Litho.   Perf. 13
747 A389 20fr multi   .45   .45

Turtles In Water — A390

2014, June 16   Litho.   Perf. 13
748 A390 65fr multi   1.50 1.50

2014 World Cup Soccer Championships, Brazil — A391

2014, July 12   Litho.   Perf. 13
749 A391 330fr multi   7.50 7.50

Talietumu Archaeological Site — A392

2014, Aug. 6   Litho.   Perf. 13
750 A392 75fr multi   1.75 1.75

American Village Near Gahi A394

2014, Oct. 3   Litho.   Perf. 13x13¼
752 A394 400fr brown   8.50 8.50

Miniature Sheet

Old Stamps — A395

No. 753 — Old stamps redrawn in different sizes: a, Stamp like #150. b, Stamp like #155. c, Stamp like #151. d, Stamp like #B9

2014, Nov. 6   Litho.   Perf. 13x13¼
753 A395   Sheet of 9, #753a-
              753c, 6 #753d   30.00 30.00
 a.   3fr multi   .25   .25
 b.   7fr multi   .25   .25
 c.   9fr multi   .25   .25
 d.   225fr red   4.75 4.75

Benjamin Brial (1923-2004), Politician — A397

2014, Nov. 12   Litho.   Perf. 13
755 A397 340fr multi   7.00 7.00

SEMI-POSTAL STAMPS

French Revolution Issue
Common Design Type
Unwmk.
1939, July 5   Photo.   Perf. 13
Name and Value Typo. in Black
B1   CD83   45c + 25c
                green   19.00 19.00
B2   CD83   70c + 30c
                brown   19.00 19.00
B3   CD83   90c + 35c red
                org   19.00 19.00
B4   CD83   1.25fr + 1fr rose
                pink   19.00 19.00
B5   CD83   2.25fr + 2fr blue 19.00 19.00
     Nos. B1-B5 (5)   95.00 95.00
     Set, never hinged   150.00

New Caledonia Nos. B10 and B12 Ovptd. "WALLIS ET FUTUNA" in Blue or Red, and Common Design Type
1941   Photo.   Perf. 13½
B6   SP2   1fr + 1fr red   2.40
B7   CD86 1.50fr + 3fr maroon   2.40
B8   SP3   2.50fr + 1fr dark
                blue   2.40
     Nos. B6-B8 (3)   7.20
     Set, never hinged   10.00

Nos. B6-B8 were issued by the Vichy government in France, but were not placed on sale in Wallis & Futuna.

Nos. 92-93 Srchd. in Black or Red

1944   Engr.   Perf. 12x12½
B8A   50c + 1.50fr on 2.50fr
           deep blue (R)   1.90
B8B   + 2.50fr on 1fr green   1.90
      Colonial Development Fund.
Nos. B8A-B8B were issued by the Vichy government in France, but were not placed on sale in Wallis & Futuna.

> Catalogue values for unused stamps in this section, from this point to the end of the section, are for Never Hinged items.

Red Cross Issue
Common Design Type
1944   Photo.   Perf. 14½x14
B9   CD90 5fr + 20fr red orange 4.50 3.25
The surtax was for the French Red Cross and national relief. See No. 753d.

AIR POST STAMPS

> Catalogue values for unused stamps in this section are for Never Hinged items.

Victory Issue
Common Design Type
Perf. 12½
1946, May 8   Unwmk.   Engr.
C1   CD92 8fr dark violet   2.50 1.90

Chad to Rhine Issue
Common Design Types
1946
C2   CD93   5fr dark violet   1.40 1.10
C3   CD94 10fr dk slate grn   1.60 1.30
C4   CD95 15fr violet brn   1.60 1.30
C5   CD96 20fr brt ultra   2.40 1.75
C6   CD97 25fr brown orange   2.75 2.10
C7   CD98 50fr carmine   4.00 2.90
     Nos. C2-C7 (6)   13.75 10.45

New Caledonia Nos. C21-C22 Overprinted in Blue

1949, July 4   Perf. 13x12½, 12½x13
C8   AP2   50fr yel & rose red   9.50 7.00
C9   AP3 100fr yel & red brn   15.00 12.00
The overprint on No. C9 is in three lines.

UPU Issue
Common Design Type
1949, July 4   Engr.   Perf. 13
C10 CD99 10fr multicolored   12.50 8.25

Liberation Issue
Common Design Type
1954, June 6
C11 CD102 3fr sepia & vio brn 12.50 8.25

Father Louis Marie Chanel — AP1

1955, Nov. 21   Unwmk.   Perf. 13
C12 AP1 14fr dk grn, grnsh bl &
            ind   4.00 1.40
Issued in honor of Father Chanel, martyred missionary to the Islands.

View of Mata-Utu, Queen Amelia and Msgr. Bataillon — AP2

33fr, Map of islands and sailing ship.

1960, Sept. 19   Engr.   Perf. 13
C13 AP2 21fr blue, brn & grn   5.25 4.00
C14 AP2 33fr ultra, choc & bl grn 9.00 6.00
For No. C14 with surcharge, see No. C36.

Shell Diver — AP3

1962, Sept. 20   Unwmk.   Perf. 13
C16 AP3 100fr bl, grn & dk red
            brn   21.00 15.00

Telstar Issue
Common Design Type
1962, Dec. 5
C17 CD111 12fr dk pur, mar & bl 3.50 3.50

Sea Shell Type of Regular Issue
1963, Apr. 1   Engr.
Size: 26x47mm
C18 A5 50fr Harpa ventricosa 12.50 7.00

Javelin Thrower — AP4

1964, Oct. 10   Engr.   Perf. 13
C19 AP4 31fr emer, ver & vio
            brn   22.50 14.50
18th Olympic Games, Tokyo, Oct. 10-25.

ITU Issue
Common Design Type
1965, May 17   Unwmk.   Perf. 13
C20 CD120 50fr multicolored   21.00 15.00

Mata-Utu Wharf — AP5

1965, Nov. 26   Engr.   Perf. 13
C21 AP5 27fr brt bl, sl grn & red
            brn   5.25 3.50

French Satellite A-1 Issue
Common Design Type
Designs: 7fr, Diamant rocket and launching installations. 10fr, A-1 satellite.

1966, Jan. 17   Engr.   Perf. 13
C22 CD121 7fr crim, red & car
            lake   4.00 4.00
C23 CD121 10fr car lake, red &
            crim   4.50 4.50
a.   Strip of 2, #C22-C23 + label 9.25 9.25

French Satellite D-1 Issue
Common Design Type

1966, June 2   Engr.   Perf. 13
C24 CD122 10fr lake, bl grn &
            red   3.50 3.50

WHO Headquarters, Geneva, and
Emblem — AP6

1966, July 5   Photo.   Perf. 12½x13
C25 AP6 30fr org, maroon & bl   3.75 3.75
New WHO Headquarters, Geneva.

Girl and Boy Reading; UNESCO
Emblem — AP7

1966, Nov. 4   Engr.   Perf. 13
C26 AP7 50fr green, org & choc 6.25 4.25
20th anniv. of UNESCO.

Athlete and
Pattern
AP8

Design: 38fr, Woman ballplayer and pattern.

1966, Dec. 8   Engr.   Perf. 13x12½
C27 AP8 32fr bl, dp car & blk   4.75 3.00
C28 AP8 38fr emer & brt pink   6.75 4.00
2nd South Pacific Games, Nouméa, 12/8-18.

Samuel Wallis' Ship and Coast of
Wallis Island — AP9

1967, Dec. 16   Photo.   Perf. 13
C29 AP9 12fr multicolored   8.00 4.75
Bicentenary of the discovery of Wallis Island.

Concorde Issue
Common Design Type

1969, Apr. 17   Engr.   Perf. 13
C30 CD129 20fr black & plum   15.00 10.00

Man Climbing Coconut Palm — AP10

32fr, Horseback rider. 38fr, Men making
wooden stools. 50fr, Spear fisherman & man

holding basket with fish. 100fr, Women sorting
coconuts.

1969, Apr. 30   Photo.   Perf. 13
C31 AP10 20fr multi   3.00 1.50
C32 AP10 32fr multi   5.25 2.00
C33 AP10 38fr multi   6.00 2.50
C34 AP10 50fr multi   9.25 4.50
C35 AP10 100fr multi   16.00 7.25
        Nos. C31-C35 (5)   39.50 17.75

**No. C14 Surcharged with New Value
and Three Bars**

1971   Engr.   Perf. 13
C36 AP2 21fr on 33fr multi   5.25 4.25

Pole Vault — AP11

1971, Oct. 25   Engr.   Perf. 13
C37 AP11 48fr shown   6.25 3.00
C38 AP11 54fr Archery   8.00 5.00
4th South Pacific Games, Papeete, French
Polynesia, Sept. 8-19.

South Pacific Commission
Headquarters, Noumea — AP12

1972, Feb. 5   Photo.   Perf. 13
C39 AP12 44fr blue & multi   7.25 4.25
South Pacific Commission, 25th anniv.

Round House
and Festival
Emblem — AP13

1972, May 15   Engr.   Perf. 13
C40 AP13 60fr dp car, grn &
            pur   9.25 5.00
South Pacific Festival of Arts, Fiji, May 6-20.

Canoe Type of Regular Issue

Design: 200fr, Outrigger sailing canoe race,
and island woman.

**1972, Oct. 16   Photo.   Perf. 13x12½
Size: 47½x28mm**
C41 A9 200fr multicolored   45.00 25.00

La Pérouse and "La
Boussole" — AP14

Explorers and their Ships: 28fr, Samuel
Wallis and "Dolphin." 40fr, Dumont D'Urville
and "Astrolabe." 72fr, Bougainville and "La
Boudeuse."

1973, July 20   Engr.   Perf. 13
C42 AP14 22fr brn, slate & car 11.00 6.00
C43 AP14 28fr sl grn, dl red &
            bl   13.50 6.00
C44 AP14 40fr brn, ind & ultra 17.50 9.25
C45 AP14 72fr brown, bl & pur   25.00 12.50
        Nos. C42-C45 (4)   67.00 33.75

Charles de Gaulle — AP15

1973, Nov. 9   Engr.   Perf. 13
C46 AP15 107fr brn org & dk
            brn   18.00 11.00
Pres. Charles de Gaulle (1890-1970).

Red
Jasmine
AP16

Flowers from Wallis: 17fr, Hibiscus tiliaceus.
19fr, Phaeomeria magnifica. 21fr, Hibiscus
rosa sinensis. 23fr, Allamanda cathartica. 27fr,
Barringtonia. 39fr, Flowers in vase.

1973, Dec. 6   Photo.   Perf. 13
C47 AP16 12fr shown   1.90 1.40
C48 AP16 17fr multicolored   2.25 1.90
C49 AP16 19fr multicolored   3.00 1.90
C50 AP16 21fr multicolored   4.50 2.10
C51 AP16 23fr multicolored   4.75 2.50
C52 AP16 27fr multicolored   5.50 3.00
C53 AP16 39fr multicolored   8.75 6.25
        Nos. C47-C53 (7)   30.65 19.05

UPU Emblem
and Symbolic
Design — AP17

1974, Oct. 9   Engr.   Perf. 13
C54 AP17 51fr multicolored   8.00 4.75
Centenary of Universal Postal Union.

Holy
Family,
Primitive
Painting
AP18

1974, Dec. 9   Photo.   Perf. 13
C55 AP18 150fr multicolored   15.00 10.00
Christmas 1974.

Tapa Cloth — AP19

Tapa Cloth: 24fr, Village scene. 36fr, Fish &
marine life. 80fr, Marine life, map of islands,
village scene.

1975, Feb. 3   Photo.   Perf. 13
C56 AP19 3fr multicolored   .95 .65
C57 AP19 24fr multicolored   2.40 1.50
C58 AP19 36fr multicolored   4.00 2.25
C59 AP19 80fr multicolored   8.50 5.25
        Nos. C56-C59 (4)   15.85 9.65

DC-7 in
Flight — AP20

1975, Aug. 13   Engr.   Perf. 13
C60 AP20 100fr multicolored   7.25 5.50
First regular air service between Nouméa,
New Caledonia, and Wallis.

Volleyball
AP21

1975, Nov. 10   Photo.   Perf. 13
C61 AP21 26fr shown   2.10 1.20
C62 AP21 44fr Soccer   3.00 1.90
C63 AP21 56fr Javelin   5.00 2.90
C64 AP21 105fr Spear fishing   10.50 6.50
        Nos. C61-C64 (4)   20.60 12.50
5th South Pacific Games, Guam, Aug. 1-10.

Lalolalo Lake, Wallis — AP22

Landscapes: 29fr, Vasavasa, Futuna. 41fr,
Sigave Bay, Futuna. 68fr, Gahi Bay, Wallis.

1975, Dec. 1   Litho.   Perf. 13
C65 AP22 10fr grn & multi   1.40 .95
C66 AP22 29fr grn & multi   3.00 1.75
C67 AP22 41fr grn & multi   4.50 2.40
C68 AP22 68fr grn & multi   6.25 3.75
        Nos. C65-C68 (4)   15.15 8.85

Concorde, Eiffel Tower and Sugar Loaf
Mountain — AP23

1976, Jan. 21　Engr.　Perf. 13
C69　AP23　250fr multi　　　　27.50 20.00
1st commercial flight of supersonic jet Concorde from Paris to Rio, Jan. 21.
For overprint see No. C73.

Hammer Throw and Stadium — AP24

39fr, Diving, Stadium and maple leaf.

1976, Aug. 2　Engr.　Perf. 13
C70　AP24　31fr multi　　　　3.00 2.25
C71　AP24　39fr multi　　　　4.75 3.50
21st Olympic Games, Montreal, Canada,
July 17-Aug. 1.

De Gaulle
Memorial
AP25

Photogravure and Embossed
1977, June 18　Perf. 13
C72　AP25　100fr gold & multi　10.50 7.50
5th anniversary of dedication of De Gaulle
Memorial at Colombey-les-Deux-Eglises.

No. C69 Ovptd. in Dark Brown
"PARIS NEW-YORK / 22.11.77 / 1er
VOL COMMERCIAL"
1977, Nov. 22　Engr.　Perf. 13
C73　AP23　250fr multicolored　27.50 17.50
Concorde, 1st commercial flight, Paris-NY.

Balistes Niger — AP26

Fish: 35fr, Amphiprion akindynos. 49fr,
Pomacanthus imperator. 51fr, Zanclus
cornutus.

1978, Jan. 31　Litho.　Perf. 13
C74　AP26　26fr multi　　　　1.40　.75
C75　AP26　35fr multi　　　　2.10 1.00
C76　AP26　49fr multi　　　　2.40 1.25
C77　AP26　51fr multi　　　　4.50 3.25
　　Nos. C74-C77 (4)　　　　10.40 6.25

Map of Wallis and Uvea
Islands — AP27

300fr, Map of Futuna and Alofi Islands, horz.

1978, Mar. 7　Engr.
C78　AP27　300fr vio bl & grnsh
　　　　　　　　bl　　　　　17.50 12.50
C79　AP27　500fr multi　　　23.00 19.00

Father Bataillon, Churches on Wallis
and Futuna Islands — AP28

72fr, Monsignor Pompallier, map of Wallis,
Futuna and Alofi Islands, outrigger canoe.

1978, Apr. 28　Litho.　Perf. 13x12½
C80　AP28　60fr multi　　　　2.75 1.75
C81　AP28　72fr multi　　　　3.50 2.00
First French missionaries on Wallis and
Futuna Islands.

ITU Emblem — AP29

1978, May 17　Litho.　Perf. 13
C82　AP29　66fr multi　　　　3.50 2.25
10th World Telecommunications Day.

Nativity and Longhouse — AP30

1978, Dec. 4　Photo.　Perf. 13
C83　AP30　160fr multi　　　　9.75 5.50
　　　　Christmas 1978.

Popes Paul VI, John Paul I, St.
Peter's, Rome — AP31

37fr, Pope Paul VI. 41fr, Pope John Paul I.

Perf. 12½x13, 13x12½
1979, Jan. 31　Litho.
C84　AP31　37fr multi, vert.　　2.25 1.40
C85　AP31　41fr multi, vert.　　2.40 1.75
C86　AP31　105fr multi　　　　5.00 3.50
　　Nos. C84-C86 (3)　　　　9.65 6.65
In memory of Popes Paul VI and John Paul I.

Monoplane
of UTA
Airlines
AP32

68fr, Freighter Muana. 80fr, Hihifo Airport.

1979, Feb. 28　Perf. 13x12½
C87　AP32　46fr multi　　　　1.50　.95
C88　AP32　68fr multi　　　　2.00 1.50
C89　AP32　80fr multi　　　　3.50 2.00
　　Nos. C87-C89 (3)　　　　7.00 4.45
　　Inter-Island transportation.
　　See Nos. 251-253.

France No. 67 and Eole Weather
Satellite — AP33

70fr, Hibiscus & stamp similar to #25. 90fr,
Rowland Hill & Penny Black. 100fr, Birds,
Kano School, Japan 17th cent. & Japan #9.

1979, May 7　Photo.　Perf. 13
C90　AP33　5fr multi　　　　1.10　.65
C91　AP33　70fr multi, vert.　3.50 1.90
C92　AP33　90fr multi　　　　4.50 2.50
C93　AP33　100fr multi　　　6.00 3.75
　　Nos. C90-C93 (4)　　　15.10 8.80
Sir Rowland Hill (1795-1879), originator of
penny postage.

Cross of Lorraine and People — AP34

1979, June 18　Engr.　Perf. 13
C94　AP34　33fr multi　　　　2.75 1.75

Map of
Islands,
Arms of
France
AP35

1979, July 19　Photo.　Perf. 13
C95　AP35　47fr multi　　　　3.00 2.00
Visit of Pres. Valery Giscard d'Estaing of
France.

Capt. Cook, Ships and Island — AP36

1979, July 28
C96　AP36　130fr multi　　　7.25 4.25
Capt. James Cook (1728-1779).

Telecom Emblem, Satellite, Receiving
Station — AP37

1979, Sept. 20　Litho.　Perf. 13
C97　AP37　120fr multi　　　5.25 3.50
3rd World Telecommunications Exhibition,
Geneva, Sept. 20-26.

Virgin of
the
Crescent
Moon, by
Albrecht
Durer
AP38

1979, Dec. 17　Engr.　Perf. 13
C98　AP38　180fr red & blk　9.25 6.25
Christmas 1979. See No. C163.

Rotary International, 75th
Anniversary — AP39

1980, Feb. 29　Litho.　Perf. 13
C99　AP39　86fr multi　　　　5.25 3.50

Rochambeau
and Troops, US
Flag,
1780 — AP40

1980, May 27　Engr.　Perf. 13
C100　AP40　102fr multi　　　5.25 3.50
Rochambeau's landing at Newport, RI
(American Revolution), bicentenary.

National Day, 10th
Anniversary — AP41

1980, July 15   Litho.   *Perf. 13*
C101 AP41 71fr multi   2.25 1.50

Transatlantic Airmail Flight, 50th
Anniversary — AP42

1980, Sept. 22   Engr.   *Perf. 13*
C102 AP42 122fr multi   4.75 3.50

Fleming,
Penicillin
Bacilli — AP43

1980, Oct. 20
C103 AP43 101fr multi   4.00 2.50

Alexander Fleming (1881-1955), discoverer
of penicillin, 25th death anniversary.

Charles De Gaulle, 10th Anniversary
of Death — AP44

1980, Nov. 9   Engr.   *Perf. 13*
C104 AP44 200fr sep & dk ol
grn   10.00 7.25

Virgin and Child with St. Catherine, by
Lorenzo Lotto — AP45

1980, Dec. 20   Litho.   *Perf. 13x12½*
C105 AP45 150fr multi   4.50 3.50
Christmas 1980.

Alan B. Shepard
and Spacecraft
AP46

20th Anniv. of Space Flight: 44fr, Yuri
Gagarin.

1981, May 11   Litho.   *Perf. 13*
C106 AP46 37fr multi   1.40 .95
C107 AP46 44fr multi   1.75 1.40

Vase of Flowers, by Paul Cezanne
(1839-1906) — AP47

Design: 135fr, Harlequin, by Pablo Picasso.

1981, Oct. 22   Litho.   *Perf. 12½x13*
C108 AP47 53fr multi   2.25 1.40
C109 AP47 135fr multi   4.50 3.00

Espana '82 World Cup
Soccer — AP48

1981-82   Engr.   *Perf. 13*
C110   AP48 120fr blk, brn & grn 3.75 2.25
C110A AP48 120fr lil, brn & ol
grn   3.75 3.00
Issued: #C110, 11/16/81; #C110A,5/13/82.
For overprint see No. C115.

Christmas 1981 — AP49

1981, Dec. 21   Litho.   *Perf. 12½*
C111 AP49 180fr multi   6.75 4.25

Tapestry,
by Pilioho
Aloi
AP50

1982, Feb. 22   Litho.   *Perf. 12½x13*
C112 AP50 100fr multi   4.50 2.50

Boats at Collioure, by George Braque
(1882-1963) — AP51

1982, Apr. 13   Litho.   *Perf. 12½x13*
C113 AP51 300fr multi   9.25 5.25

Alberto Santos-Dumont (1873-1932),
Aviation Pioneer — AP52

1982, July 24
C114 AP52 95fr multi   3.75 2.40

**No. C110 Overprinted with Winner's
Name in Blue**

1982, Aug. 26   Engr.   *Perf. 13*
C115 AP48 120fr multi   4.00 3.00

Italy's victory in 1982 World Cup.

French Overseas Possessions Week,
Sept. 18-25 — AP53

1982, Sept. 17   Litho.
C116 AP53 105fr Beach   3.00 2.25

Day of the
Blind — AP54

1982, Oct. 18   Engr.
C117 AP54 130fr red & blue   3.75 2.00

Christmas
1982
AP55

Adoration of the Virgin, by Correggio.

1982, Dec. 20   Litho.   *Perf. 12½x13*
C118 AP55 170fr multi   4.50 3.00

Wind Surfing
(1984 Olympic
Event) — AP56

1983, Mar. 4   Litho.   *Perf. 13*
C119 AP56 270fr multi   6.50 4.75

World UPU Day — AP57

1983, Mar. 30   Litho.   *Perf. 13*
C120 AP57 100fr multi   2.75 1.75

Manned Flight
Bicentenary
AP58

1983, Apr. 25   Litho.   *Perf. 13*
C121 AP58 205fr Montgolfiere   5.75 4.00

Cat, 1926,
by Foujita
(d. 1968)
AP59

1983, May 20   Litho.   *Perf. 12½x13*
C122 AP59 102fr multi   3.75 2.00

Pre-Olympic
Year — AP60

1983, July 5 Engr. Perf. 13
C123 AP60 250fr Javelin
6.50 4.50

Alfred Nobel (1833-1896) — AP61

1983, Aug. 1 Engr. Perf. 13
C124 AP61 150fr multi
4.00 2.75

Nicephore Niepce (1765-1833),
Photography Pioneer — AP62

1983, Sept. 20 Engr. Perf. 13
C125 AP62 75fr dk grn & rose
vio
2.75 1.75

Raphael (1483-1520), 500th Birth
Anniv. — AP63

1983, Nov. 10 Litho. Perf. 12½x13
C126 AP63 167fr The Triumph of
Galatea
4.50 3.00

Pandanus
AP64

1983, Nov. 30 Litho. Perf. 13
C127 AP64 137fr multi
4.00 3.00

Christmas
1983
AP65

Sistine Madonna, by Raphael.

1983, Dec. 22 Litho. Perf. 12½x13
C128 AP65 200fr multi
5.50 4.00

Steamer Commandant Bory — AP66

1984, Jan. 9 Perf. 13
C129 AP66 67fr multi
2.25 1.40

1984 Summer Olympics — AP67

1984, Feb. 3 Litho. Perf. 13
C130 AP67 85fr Weight lifting
2.40 1.75

Frangipani
Blossoms
AP68

1984, Feb. 28 Perf. 12½
C131 AP68 130fr multi
4.00 2.25

Easter
1984
AP69

1984, Apr. 17 Litho. Perf. 12½x13
C132 AP69 190fr Descent from
the Cross
5.00 3.25

Homage to
Jean
Cocteau
AP70

1984, June 30 Litho. Perf. 13
C133 AP70 150fr Portrait
4.00 2.90

Soano Hoatau
Tiki Sculpture
AP71

1984, July 26
C134 AP71 175fr multi
4.75 3.50

Portrait of Alice,
by Modigliani
(1884-1920)
AP72

1984, Aug. 20
C135 AP72 140fr multi
3.75 2.50

Ausipex
'84 — AP73

1984, Sept. 21 Litho. Perf. 12½x13
C136 AP73 180fr Pilioko Tapestry 4.00 3.00
Se-tenant with label showing exhibition
emblem.

Local Dances, by Jean
Michon — AP74

1984, Oct. 11 Photo. Perf. 13
C137 AP74 110fr multi
3.50 2.00

Altar
AP75

1984, Nov. 5 Litho. Perf. 13x12½
C138 AP75 52fr Mount Lulu
Chapel
1.50 1.10

Christmas 1984 — AP76

1984, Dec. 21 Litho. Perf. 13x12½
C139 AP76 260fr Tropical Nativity 7.00 4.00

Pilioko Tapestry — AP77

1985, Apr. 3 Litho. Perf. 13x12½
C140 AP77 500fr multi
13.50 6.50

The Post in
1926, by
Utrillo
AP78

1985, June 17 Litho. Perf. 12½x13
C141 AP78 200fr multi
6.00 4.00

Wallis Island Pirogue — AP79

1985, Aug. 9 Perf. 13
C142 AP79 350fr multi
9.50 5.00

Ship Jacques
Cartier — AP80

1985, Oct. 2   Engr.   Perf. 13x13½
C143 AP80 51fr Prus bl, brt bl &
dk bl   1.75 1.10

Portrait of a
Young
Woman, by
Patrice
Nielly
AP81

1985, Oct. 28   Litho.   Perf. 12½x13
C144 AP81 245fr multi   6.75 4.50

Nativity, by
Jean
Michon
AP82

1985, Dec. 19   Litho.   Perf. 12½x13
C145 AP82 330fr multi   10.00 6.50

Halley's Comet — AP83

1986, Mar. 6   Litho.   Perf. 13
C146 AP83 100fr multi   3.25 1.75

Cure of Ars, Birth
Bicent. — AP84

1986, Mar. 28   Litho.   Perf. 12½x13
C147 AP84 200fr multi   5.75 4.25

French Overseas Territory Status, 25th
Anniv. — AP85

90fr, Queen Amelia. 137fr, July 30 Law,
Journal of the Republic.

1986, July 29   Engr.   Perf. 13
C148 AP85 90fr multicolored   2.75 2.25
C149 AP85 137fr multicolored   4.50 3.25
  a.   Strip of 2, #C148-C149 + label   7.25 6.00
  Queen Amelia's request to France for pro-
tection, cent.

World Post Day — AP86

1986, Oct. 9   Litho.
C150 AP86 270fr multi   7.25 4.00

Statue of Liberty,
Cent. — AP87

1986, Oct. 31   Engr.
C151 AP87 205fr multi   8.00 5.00

Poi Basilica, 1st
Anniv. — AP88

230fr, Fr. Chanel, basilica.

1987, Apr. 30   Litho.   Perf. 13
C152 AP88 230fr multicolored   7.00 3.75

Telstar Transmitting to Pleumeur-
Bodou, France — AP89

1987, May 17   Engr.   Perf. 13
C153 AP89 200fr gray, brt bl &
brn org   7.00 3.75
  World Communications Day, 25th anniv. of
Telstar.

Piccard,
Bathyscaphe
Trieste and
Stratospheric
Balloon — AP90

1987, Aug. 21   Engr.   Perf. 13
C154 AP90 135fr brt ol grn, dk bl
& brt bl   4.50 3.00
  Auguste Piccard (1884-1962), physicist.

Arrival of First Missionary, 150th
Anniv. — AP91

Design: 260fr, Monsignor Bataillon's arrival
in 1837, ship and the islands.

1987, Nov. 8   Engr.   Perf. 13
C155 AP91 260fr brt blue, blk &
blue grn   7.50 5.00

Christmas 1987 — AP92

1987, Dec. 15   Litho.   Perf. 13x12½
C156 AP92 300fr multi   8.00 5.00

Garros and Bleriot Aircraft — AP93

1988, Feb. 18   Engr.   Perf. 13
C157 AP93 600fr multi   19.00 10.50
  Roland Garros (1888-1918), aviator and
tennis player.

Self-portrait
with Lace
Cravat, by
Maurice
Quentin de
La Tour
(1704-88)
AP94

1988, Apr. 8   Litho.
C158 AP94 500fr multi   15.00 9.50

World Telecommunications
Day — AP95

1988, May 5   Litho.   Perf. 12½x13
C159 AP95 100fr multi   3.00 1.90

South Pacific Episcopal
Conference — AP96

1988, June 1   Litho.   Perf. 13
C160 AP96 90fr Map, bishop   2.75 1.75

Christmas — AP97

Unwmk.
1988, Dec. 15   Litho.   Perf. 13
C161 AP97 400fr multi   13.00 7.00

Royal
Throne — AP98

1989, Mar. 11
C162 AP98 700fr multi   19.00 10.50

Type of 1979
  Virgin of the Crescent Moon, by Albrecht
Durer

1989, Dec. 21   Engr.   Perf. 13½x13
C163 AP38 800fr plum   22.00 13.00
  Christmas 1989.

Clement Ader (1841-1926), Aviation
Pioneer — AP100

1990, June 9   Engr.   Perf. 13
C164 AP100 56fr multicolored   2.00 1.40
  First anniversary of Wallis-Tahiti air link.

Gen. Charles de Gaulle (1890-
1979) — AP101

1990, Nov. 22   Perf. 12½x13
C165 AP101 1000fr multi   27.50 19.00

Father Louis Marie Chanel, 150th
Death Anniv. — AP102

1991, Apr. 28   Litho.   *Perf. 13*
C166 AP102 235fr multicolored   6.50 4.25

French Open Tennis Championships,
Cent. — AP103

1991, May 24   Engr.   *Perf. 13x12½*
C167 AP103 250fr blk, grn & org 8.00 5.50

Wolfgang
Amadeus
Mozart,
Death
Bicent.
AP104

1991, Sept. 23   Engr.   *Perf. 13*
C168 AP104 500fr multicolored   15.00 9.50

World Columbian Stamp Expo '92,
Chicago — AP105

1992, May 22   Litho.   *Perf. 13x12½*
C169 AP105 100fr multicolored   3.00 2.25

1992, July 15   *Perf. 13*
C170 AP105 800fr multicolored 22.00 13.00
      Genoa '92.

First French Republic,
Bicent. — AP106

1992, Aug. 17   Engr.   *Perf. 13*
C171 AP106 350fr blk, bl & red   9.75 7.50

Louvre Museum, Bicent. — AP107

1993, Apr. 12   Engr.   *Perf. 13*
C172 AP107 315fr blue, dk blue
      & red   9.00 5.50

Nicolaus Copernicus, Heliocentric
Solar System — AP108

1993, May 7   Engr.   *Perf. 13*
C173 AP108 600fr multicolored 16.00 9.25
      Polska '93.

Second Year of First French Republic,
Bicent. — AP109

1993, Sept. 22   Engr.   *Perf. 13*
C174 AP109 400fr bl, blk & red 11.00 7.50

Wallis Island Landscape — AP110

1994, Jan. 26   Litho.   *Perf. 13*
C175 AP110 400fr multicolored 11.00 7.50

Hong Kong '94 — AP111

1994, Feb. 18   Litho.   *Perf. 14x13½*
C176 AP111 700fr multicolored 19.00 12.00

South Pacific Geography
Day — AP112

1994, May 4   Litho.   *Perf. 13*
C177 AP112 85fr multicolored   2.50 1.75
      See New Caledonia No. C259.

European Stamp
Salon,
Paris — AP113

1994, Sept. 22   Litho.   *Perf. 13*
C178 AP113 300fr multicolored   9.00 5.00

Antoine de Saint-Exupery (1900-44),
Aviator, Author — AP114

1994, Oct. 27   Engr.   *Perf. 13*
C179 AP114 800fr multicolored 22.00 15.00

Christmas
AP115

1994, Dec. 15   Litho.   *Perf. 13*
C180 AP115 150fr multicolored   4.00 3.00

Louis Pasteur (1822-95) — AP116

1995, Mar. 25   Litho.   *Perf. 13*
C181 AP116 350fr multicolored   9.50 4.75

AP117

1995, Apr. 19   *Perf. 13½x13*
C182 AP117 115fr multicolored   3.50 1.90
      University Teacher's Training Institute of the
Pacific. See French Polynesia No. 656.

AP118

1995, May 17   *Perf. 13*
C183 AP118 200fr Painting of
      Cocoa Nuts   5.50 3.00

Intl. Youth Year, 10th Anniv. — AP119

1995, July 25   Litho.   *Perf. 13*
C184 AP119 450fr multicolored 12.50 6.25

Singapore '95 — AP120

1995, Aug. 24   Litho.   *Perf. 13*
C185 AP120 500fr multicolored 13.50 6.75

Motion Pictures, Cent. — AP121

      Lumiere Brothers, film strip.

1995, Sept. 19
C186 AP121 600fr multicolored 16.00 8.50

Charles de Gaulle (1890-
1970) — AP122

1995, Nov. 14   Engr.   *Perf. 13*
C187 AP122 315fr multicolored   8.50 5.50

7th Va'a (Outrigger Canoe) World Championship, Noumea, New Caledonia — AP123

1996, Apr. 24　Litho.　Perf. 13
C188　AP123　240fr multicolored　6.50 4.25

Sisia College — AP124

1996, May 22　Litho.　Perf. 13½x13
C189　AP124　235fr multicolored　6.50 4.25

Radio, Cent. — AP125

1996, July 25　Engr.　Perf. 13
C190　AP125　550fr multicolored　15.00 9.25

Modern Olympic Games, Cent. — AP126

1996, Aug. 20　Engr.　Perf. 13
C191　AP126　1000fr blk & dk bl　27.50 17.00

50th Autumn Stamp Salon AP127

1996, Oct. 24　Litho.　Perf. 13
C192　AP127　175fr multicolored　4.75 3.00

Campaign to Control Alcoholism AP128

1996, Nov. 19　　　Perf. 13x13½
C193　AP128　260fr multicolored　7.00 4.25

Natl. Center for Scientific Research AP129

1997, Mar. 14　Litho.　Perf. 13
C194　AP129　400fr Lapita pottery　11.00 5.50

HIHIFO Air Service — AP130

1997, July 8　Litho.　Perf. 13
C195　AP130　130fr multicolored　3.25 2.10

Sundown Over the Lagoon — AP131

1997, Sept. 22　Litho.　Perf. 13½x13
C196　AP131　300fr multicolored　8.00 4.25

51st Autumn Stamp Salon — AP132

350fr, #C194, 492, 497, 486, C184, C185, 475, C192, C188, 464, 493.
1000fr, Hemispheres, #486, 475, 464, C185, C175, 493, C184, 492, C192, 497, C188, C194, Winged Victory of Samothrace.

1997, Nov. 6　Litho.　Perf. 13
C197　AP132　350fr multi　9.50 4.75
Imperf
C198　AP132　1000fr multi　27.50 24.00

Marshal Jacques Leclerc (1902-47) — AP133

1997, Nov. 28　Litho.　Perf. 13
C199　AP133　800fr multicolored　22.00 11.50

Alphonse Daudet (1840-97), Writer — AP134

1997, Dec. 16　Litho.　Perf. 13
C200　AP134　710fr multi　19.00 10.00

Alofi Beach — AP135

1998, Apr. 21　Litho.　Perf. 13
C201　AP135　315fr multicolored　8.50 4.25

Cricket AP136

1998, Sept. 22　Litho.　Perf. 13x13½
C202　AP136　106fr multicolored　2.90 1.40

Paul Gauguin (1848-1903) — AP137

1998, Oct. 27　Litho.　Perf. 13
C203　AP137　700fr multicolored　19.00 9.25

Garden of Happiness — AP138

1998, Nov. 17
C204　AP138　460fr multicolored　12.50 7.25

Polynesian Dancing AP139

1998, Dec. 15　Litho.　Perf. 13
C205　AP139　250fr multicolored　6.75 3.50

Kava Porter AP140

1999, Jan. 18
C206　AP140　600fr multicolored　16.00 8.00

Shells AP141

95fr, Epitonium scalare. 100fr, Cassis cornuta. 110fr, Charonia tritonis. 115fr, Lambis lambis.

1999, Feb. 15
C207　AP141　95fr multi, vert.　2.50 1.75
C208　AP141　100fr multi, vert.　2.75 1.75
C209　AP141　110fr multi　3.00 1.75
C210　AP141　115fr multi　3.10 1.75
　Nos. C207-C210 (4)　11.35 7.00

Finemui — AP142

1999, Apr. 19　Engr.　Perf. 12¾
C211　AP142　900fr multicolored　24.00 11.50

Birds of Nuku Fotu AP143

a, 10fr, Airgrettes. b, 20fr, Audubon's. c, 26fr, Fregates. d, 54fr, Paille en queue.

1999, June 14　Litho.　Perf. 13x13¾
C212　AP143　Strip of 4, #a.-d.　3.00 2.50

Wind Song — AP144

1999, Nov. 22　Engr.　Perf. 13
C213　AP144　325fr multi　8.75 4.50

Sunrise Over a Lagoon AP145

1999, Dec. 20　　　Litho.
C214　AP145　500fr multi　13.50 7.50

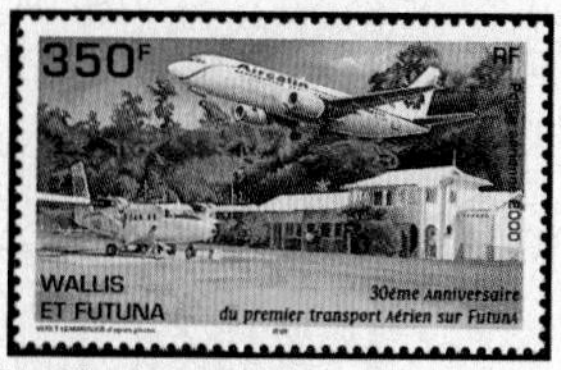

First Transport Flight to Futuna, 30th Anniv. — AP146

2000, Aug. 24 Litho. *Perf. 13*

C215	AP146	350fr multi	9.50	4.50

AIR POST SEMI-POSTAL STAMPS

New Caledonia Nos. CB2-CB3 overprinted "ILES WALLIS ET FUTUNA"

1942, June 22 Engr. *Perf. 13*

CB1	SPAP1	1.50fr + 3.50fr green	2.25
CB2	SPAP1	2fr + 6fr yellow brown	2.25

Native children's welfare fund.

Nos. CB1-CB2 were issued by the Vichy government in France, but were not placed on sale in Wallis & Futuna.

Colonial Education Fund

New Caledonia No. CB4 Common Design Type overprinted "ILES WALLIS ET FUTUNA"

1942, June 22

CB3	CD86a	1.20fr + 1.80fr blue & red	2.25

No. CB3 was issued by the Vichy government in France, but was not placed on sale in Wallis & Futuna.

POSTAGE DUE STAMPS

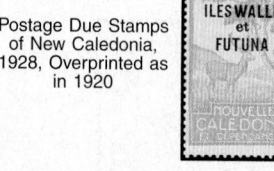

Postage Due Stamps of New Caledonia, 1906, Overprinted in Black or Red

1920 Unwmk. *Perf. 13½x14*

J1	D2	5c ultra, *azure*	1.00	1.00
J2	D2	10c brn, *buff*	1.10	1.10
J3	D2	15c grn, *grnsh*	1.10	1.10
J4	D2	20c blk, *yel* (R)	1.50	1.50
a.		Double overprint	200.00	
J5	D2	30c carmine rose	1.50	1.50
J6	D2	50c ultra, *straw*	2.40	2.40
J7	D2	60c olive, *azure*	2.90	2.90
a.		Double overprint	200.00	
J8	D2	1fr grn, *cream*	3.75	3.75
		Nos. J1-J8 (8)	15.25	15.25

Type of 1920 Issue Surcharged

1927

J9	D2	2fr on 1fr brt vio	17.50	17.50
J10	D2	3fr on 1fr org brn	17.50	17.50

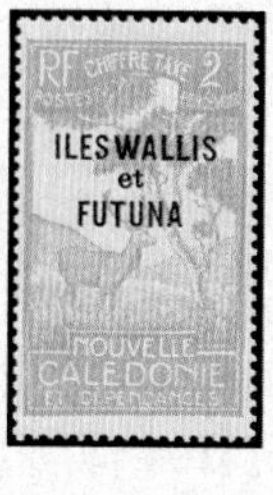

Postage Due Stamps of New Caledonia, 1928, Overprinted as in 1920

1930

J11	D3	2c sl bl & dp brn	.25	.25
J12	D3	4c brn red & bl grn	.25	.25
J13	D3	5c red org & bl blk	.25	.25
J14	D3	10c mag & Prus bl	.25	.25
J15	D3	15c dl grn & scar	.35	.35
J16	D3	20c maroon & ol grn	.75	.75
J17	D3	25c bis brn & sl bl	.75	.75
J18	D3	30c bl grn & ol grn	1.40	1.40
J19	D3	50c lt brn & dk red	.85	.85
J20	D3	60c mag & brt rose	1.40	1.40
J21	D3	1fr dl bl & Prus grn	1.40	1.40
J22	D3	2fr dk red & ol grn	1.40	1.40
J23	D3	3fr vio & brn	1.40	1.40
		Nos. J11-J23 (13)	10.70	10.70

Postage Due Stamps of 1930 with Additional Overprint in Black

1943

J24	D3	2c sl bl & dp brn	37.50	37.50
J25	D3	4c brn red & bl grn	37.50	37.50
J26	D3	5c red org & bl blk	37.50	37.50
J27	D3	10c mag & Prus bl	37.50	37.50
J28	D3	15c dl grn & scar	40.00	40.00
J29	D3	20c mar & ol grn	40.00	40.00
J30	D3	25c bis brn & sl bl	40.00	40.00
J31	D3	30c bl grn & ol grn	40.00	40.00
J32	D3	50c lt brn & dk red	40.00	40.00
J33	D3	60c mag & brt rose	42.50	42.50
J34	D3	1fr dl bl & Prus grn	42.50	42.50
J35	D3	2fr dk red & ol grn	42.50	42.50
J36	D3	3fr violet & brn	42.50	42.50
		Nos. J24-J36 (13)	520.00	520.00

Catalogue values for unused stamps in this section, from this point to the end of the section, are for Never Hinged items.

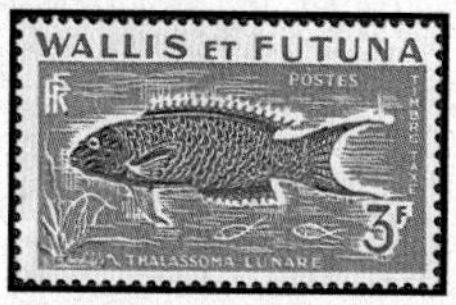

Thalassoma Lunare — D1

Fish: 1fr, Zanclus cornutus, vert. 5fr, Amphiprion percula.

Perf. 13x13½

1963, Apr. 1 Typo. Unwmk.

J37	D1	1fr yel org, bl & blk	.95	.95
J38	D1	3fr red, grnsh bl & grn	1.90	2.40
J39	D1	5fr org, bluish grn & blk	3.00	3.50
		Nos. J37-J39 (3)	5.85	6.85

WESTERN UKRAINE

'wes-tərn yü-'krān

LOCATION — In Eastern Central Europe

GOVT. — A former short-lived independent State

A provisional government was established in 1918 in the eastern part of Austria-Hungary but the area later came under Polish administration.

100 Shahiv (Sotykiv) = 1 Hryvnia
100 Heller = 1 Krone

Forgeries of almost all Western Ukraine stamps are plentiful. Particularly dangerous forgeries have been noted for the Kolomyia Issue and for the First and Second Stanyslaviv Issues.

Lviv Issue

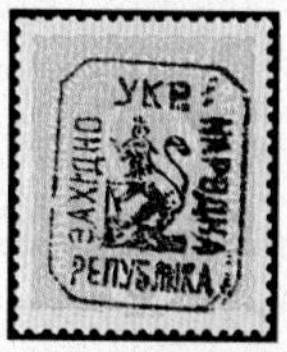

Austria Nos. 145-146, 148, 169 Overprinted

Nos. 1-4A are handstamped with an octagonal overprint that reads "ZAKHIDNO UKR. NARODNA REPUBLYKA" ("Western Ukrainian National Republic"), framing the image of a rearing crowned lion.

1918, Nov. 20

1	A37	3h	55.00	425.00
a.		Inverted overprint	150.00	
2	A37	5h light green	50.00	325.00
a.		Inverted overprint	150.00	
3	A37	10h magenta	50.00	325.00
a.		Inverted overprint	150.00	
4	A42	20h dark green	35.00	350.00
a.		Inverted overprint	150.00	
4A	A42	20h light green	240.00	900.00
		Nos. 1-4A (5)	430.00	2,325.

This issue was in circulation for only two days before Lviv was captured by the Poles on Nov. 22. No examples of Nos. 1-4A used in Lviv are known.

The Western Ukrainian National Republic (ZUNR) government evacuated to the city of Ternopil, which became the provisional capital. ZUNR postal operations were set up in other Western Ukrainian cities, and the Lviv Issue was used in Stanyslaviv (earliest known cancellation date, Dec. 8), Khodoriv and Kolomyia.

Nos. 1-4 exist in pairs with both normal and inverted overprints. Value $325.

Overprints in other colors (green, red and violet) are known, but these are probably proofs. Violet-black overprints are likely transitional color impressions.

Kolomyia Issue

Austria Nos. 168, 145, 147, 149 Surcharged

Kolomyia is the main town of the Pokutia region of southwestern Ukraine. Cut off from ZUNR postal officials by wartime conditions and in urgent need of basic value stamps, the Kolomyia postmaster obtained permission from the District Military Command to surcharge remaining Austrian postage stamps to either 5 or 10 sotyks, the equivalent of 5 or 10 heller. These stamps were produced on Dec. 10, under very strict security, by preparing two distinct plates (one for each value) that overprinted 25 stamps at a time (5x5 quarter sections of the Austrian 100-stamp panes). The stamps were placed on sale two days later.

1918, Dec. 12 Unwmk. *Perf. 12½*

5	A42	5sot on 15h dl red	90.00	120.00
a.		Inverted overprint	600.00	725.00
b.		Double overprint	1,500.	1,600.
6	A37	10sot on 3h vio	90.00	120.00
7	A37	10sot on 6h dp org	1,650.	1,250.
8	A37	10sot on 12h lt bl	1,750.	1,500.
		Nos. 5-8 (4)	3,580.	2,990.

10 sotyk on 15 heller values are essays; only six were produced.

All inverted surcharges on Nos. 6-8 are forgeries. Double surcharges are forgeries.

First Stanyslaviv Issue

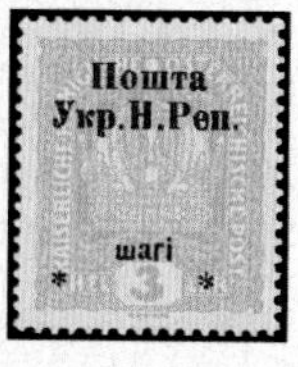

Austrian Stamps of 1916-18 Surcharged in Shahiv (shown) and Hryvnia Currency

At the end of December, 1918, the national government again moved, this time to the city of Stanyslaviv (present-day Ivano-Frankivsk). A shortage of qualified postal personnel resulted in a considerable delay in the creation of new ZUNR postage stamps. In the interim, remaining unoverprinted Austrian stamps were used. Finally, on March 18, 1919, 20 different available Austrian definitive stamps were typograph surcharged at the Weidenfeld Printing Shop in Stanyslaviv.

1919, Mar. 18

9	A37	3sh on 3h bright vio	17.00	22.50
10	A37	5sh on 5h light green	17.00	22.50
11	A37	6sh on 6h deep orange	32.50	55.00
12	A37	10sh on 10h mag	27.50	37.50
13	A37	12sh on 12h lt blue	27.50	37.50
a.		Double overprint	300.00	425.00
b.		Double overprint, one on reverse	500.00	210.00
14	A42	15sh on 15h dull red	27.50	37.50
15	A42	20sh on 20h dp grn	27.50	37.50
16	A42	30sh on 30h dull violet	100.00	100.00
17	A39	40sh on 40h ol green	27.50	37.50
18	A39	50sh on 50h dk grn	27.50	37.50
19	A39	60sh on 60h deep blue	27.50	37.50
20	A39	80sh on 80h org brown	27.50	37.50
a.		Inverted overprint	300.00	425.00
21	A39	1hr on 1k car, *yel*	40.00	45.00
22	A40	2hr on 2k lt blue	40.00	50.00
23	A40	3hr on 3k claret (on #161)	3,250.	3,250.
24	A40	3hr on 3k car rose (on #165)	100.00	82.50
25	A40	3hr on 3k car rose (on #173)	80.00	80.00
26	A40	4hr on 4k dk grn (on #162)	800.00	700.00
27	A40	4hr on 4k yel grn (on #166)	75.00	55.00
28	A40	10hr on 10k deep violet	800.00	800.00
a.		Double overprint	3,000.	3,500.
		Nos. 9-28 (20)	5,571.	5,562.

The 25sh on 25h, type A42, in both light and dull blue shades, never received this overprint. All such stamps are fantasies.

Second Stanyslaviv Issue

The overprinting of a second issue of postage stamps in Stanyslaviv was undertaken in early May. Stamps from several different Austrian stamp series were utilized to create four distinct sets. Most of the stamps available were Austrian postage due, charity or field post stamps.

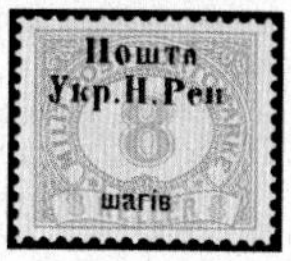

Postage Due Stamps of Bosnia, 1904 Surcharged but without Asterisks

1919, May 5

29	D1	1sh on 1h blk, red & yel	32.50	40.00
a.		Inverted overprint	100.00	65.00
b.		Double overprint	90.00	90.00
30	D1	2sh on 2h blk, red & yel	15.00	15.00
a.		Inverted overprint	85.00	150.00
31	D1	3sh on 3h blk, red & yel	17.50	35.00
a.		Inverted overprint	25.00	45.00
32	D1	4sh on 4h blk, red & yel	125.00	125.00
a.		Inverted overprint	175.00	175.00
b.		Double overprint	300.00	300.00
33	D1	5sh on 5h blk, red & yel	3,250.	3,500.
34	D1	6sh on 6h blk, red & yel	600.00	600.00
a.		Inverted overprint	900.00	900.00
b.		Double overprint	750.00	750.00
35	D1	7sh on 7h blk, red & yel	25.00	27.50
a.		Inverted overprint	37.50	42.50
36	D1	8sh on 8h blk, red & yel	25.00	30.00
a.		Inverted overprint	50.00	60.00
b.		Vertical overprint	750.00	950.00
c.		As "b," double overprint	950.00	1,100.
37	D1	10sh on 10h blk, red & yel	1,250.	1,400.
38	D1	15sh on 15h blk, red & yel	625.00	625.00
a.		Inverted overprint	750.00	800.00
39	D1	20sh on 20h blk, red & yel	6,250.	
a.		Double overprint	7,750.	17,000.
40	D1	50sh on 50h blk, red & yel	350.00	375.00
a.		Inverted overprint	550.00	600.00

Nos. 29-40 were created by overprinting Bosnian 1904 postage due stamps, which had been brought to Stanyslaviv by a Ukrainian military officer returning from the Serbian front. The same printing cliché was used as for the First Stanyslaviv Issue, but the asterisk obliterators were removed.

Most of the overprinting was made using 50-stamp panes (half of a sheet). After one half of the pane (25 positions) was overprinted, it would apparently be turned over and its second half overprinted with the same 25-position block, but as an inverted impression. After overprinting, the pane was torn into two equal 25-stamp halves.

A corrected block was utilized in overprinting, resulting in two types of surcharges on No. 29 (shahiv to shaha) and on Nos. 32, 34 and 38 (shahiv to shahi).

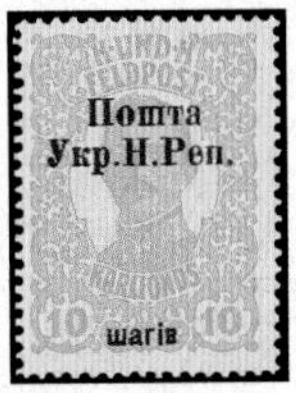

Austrian Military Semipostal Stamps of 1918 Srchd.

41 MSP7 10sh on 10h gray green 150.00 *150.00*
a. Inverted overprint 150.00 *160.00*
b. Double overprint 175.00 *210.00*
42 MSP8 20sh on 20h mag 125.00 *110.00*
a. Inverted overprint 125.00 *120.00*
b. Double overprint 160.00 *180.00*
43 MSP7 45sh on 45h blue 100.00 *110.00*
a. Inverted overprint 100.00 *120.00*

Nos. 41-43 were printed in the same manner as Nos. 29-40.

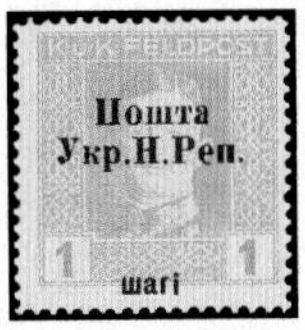

Austrian Military Stamps of 1917 Srchd.

44 M3 1sh on 1h grnsh blue *950.00* *950.00*
45 M3 2sh on 2h red orange 100.00 100.00
a. Inverted overprint 125.00 125.00
b. Double overprint 210.00 210.00
46 M3 3sh olive gray 175.00 *190.00*
a. Double overprint *750.00* *750.00*
47 M3 5sh on 5h olive grn 275.00 275.00
48 M3 6sh on 6h vio 150.00 *175.00*
49 M3 10sh on 10h org brn *900.00* *1,000.*
50 M3 12sh on 12h blue 550.00 *600.00*
a. Inverted overprint 650.00 *725.00*
51 M3 15sh on 15h brt rose 500.00 *600.00*
a. Inverted overprint 625.00 *725.00*
52 M3 20sh on 20h red brown 16.50 *20.00*
a. Inverted overprint 82.50 *140.00*
b. Double overprint 47.50 *55.00*
53 M3 25sh on 25h ultra *3,250.* *3,900.*
54 M3 30sh on 30h slate *1,000.* *1,200.*
55 M3 40sh on 40h ol bister *850.00* *850.00*
56 M3 50sh on 50h dp grn 9.00 9.00
a. Inverted overprint 20.00 20.00
b. Double overprint 55.00 55.00
57 M3 60sh on 60h car rose 950.00 950.00
58 M3 80sh on 80h dull blue 47.50 47.50
a. Inverted overprint 80.00 *85.00*
59 M3 90sh on 90h dk vio *950.00* *1,000.*
60 M4 2hr on 2k rose, *straw* 15.00 *17.50*
a. Inverted overprint 27.50 *35.00*
b. Imperforate 3,000.
61 M4 3hr on 3k blue, *grn* 22.50 *25.00*
a. Inverted overprint 27.50 *30.00*
b. Double overprint 60.00 *65.00*
62 M4 4hr on 4k rose, *grn* 22.50 *25.00*
a. Inverted overprint 50.00 *30.00*
b. Double overprint 60.00 *65.00*
63 M4 10hr on 10k dl vio, *gray* *35,000.* *35,000.*

Two examples of No. 63 were printed, and neither was ever postally used. The "used" example was cut from a document prepared by the Western Ukrainian economic bureau (Ekonomat) to display the stamps that made up the First, Second and Third Stanyslaviv issues. The specimen stamps on this document were tied with a double-ring bureau cancel that somewhat resembles a regular double-ring postal cancellation.

About half of this issue, where several sheets were available for printing, was overprinted in the manner of Nos. 29-43.

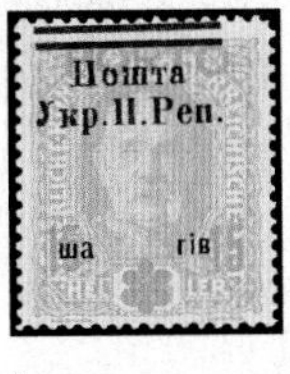

Austrian Stamps of 1916-18 Surcharged

64 A38 15sh on 36h vio (on #J61) 350.00 *450.00*
a. Double overprint 450.00 *500.00*
65 A38 50sh on 42h choc (on #J63) 5,000. *5,500.*
66 A37 3sh on 3h brt violet (on #145) 190.00 190.00
67 A37 5sh on 5h lt green (on #146) 190.00 190.00
a. Inverted overprint 290.00 290.00
68 A37 6sh on 6h deep org (on #147) 725.00 725.00
69 A37 10sh on 10h mag (on #148) 210.00 210.00
a. Inverted overprint 250.00 250.00
70 A37 12sh on 12h lt blue (on #149) 425.00 425.00
71 A38 15sh on 15h rose red (on #150) (on #149) 190.00 190.00
a. Inverted overprint 225.00 225.00
72 A42 15sh on 15h dull red (on #168) 210.00 210.00
73 A42 30sh on 30h dull vio (on #171) 190.00 190.00
a. Double overprint 350.00 350.00
74 A39 40sh on 40h ol grn (on #154) 300.00 300.00
75 M3 50sh on 50h dp grn (on #M61) 475.00 475.00

The two bars in the surcharge were originally created to obliterate the "PORTO" on Nos. 64 and 65 but were subsequently retained for Nos. 66-75.

Third Stanyslaviv Issue

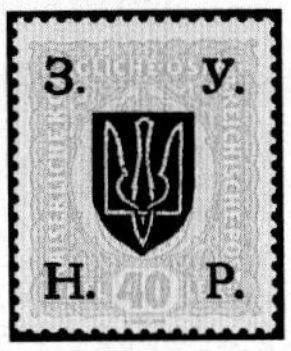

Austrian Stamps of 1916-18 Overprinted

1919, May

76 A37 3h brt violet .50 *1.00*
77 A37 5h light green .50 *1.00*
78 A37 6h deep orange .50 *1.00*
79 A37 10h magenta .50 *1.00*
80 A37 12h light blue .50 *1.00*
81 A42 15h dull red .50 *1.00*
82 A42 20h deep green .50 *1.00*
83 A42 25h blue .50 *1.00*
84 A42 30h dull vio .50 *1.00*
85 A39 40h olive green .75 *1.25*
86 A39 50h dark green .75 *1.25*
87 A39 60h deep blue .75 *1.25*
88 A39 80h orange brn 1.00 *1.25*
89 A39 90h red violet 1.00 *1.60*
90 A39 1k car, *yel* 1.25 *4.00*
91 A40 2k light blue 2.00 *6.00*
92 A40 3k carmine rose 2.50 *7.50*
93 A40 4k yellow grn 12.00 *16.00*
94 A40 10k deep violet 16.00 *50.00*
Nos. 76-94 (19) 42.50 *99.10*

Issued: 3h-10h, 15h, 25h-40h, 60h-1k, 5/8; balance of set, 5/13.

A definitive set for Western Ukraine was ordered from the Austrian State Printing Office in March, 1919. Because of the time involved in designing and printing these stamps, Nos. 76-94 were overprinted in Vienna as a provisional issue and were delivered in two shipments. Because travel into and out of Stanyslaviv was becoming more difficult as the month wore on, it was not known whether or not the second shipment, which included the higher values, would arrive. Because of this, the Fourth Stanyslaviv Issue, Nos. 95-103, were overprinted locally.

Fourth Stanislaviv Issue

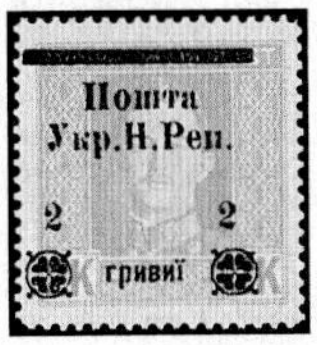

Austrian Military Stamps of 1917-18 Surcharged in Black

1919, May *Perf. 12½*

95 M3 2hr on 2k rose, *straw* 15.00 *15.00*
a. Perf 11½ 130.00 *150.00*
96 M3 3hr on 2k rose, *straw* 13.00 *16.00*
a. Perf 11½ 130.00 *160.00*
97 M3 3hr on 3k grn, *blue* 125.00 *175.00*
a. "5" instead of "3" at left in overprint *1,500.*
98 M3 4hr on 2k rose, *straw* 15.00 *16.00*
99 M3 4hr on 4k rose, *grn* 1,300. *1,900.*
100 M3 5hr on 2k rose, *straw* 20.00 *22.50*
a. Inverted surcharge 300.00
101 M3 10hr on 50h dp grn 30.00 *40.00*
a. Double surcharge 175.00

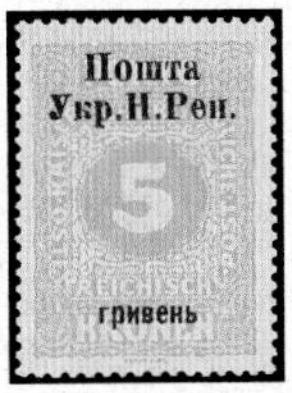

Austrian Postage Due Stamps of 1916 Srchd., but without Rosettes and Numerals

102 D5 1hr ultra 140.00 *210.00*
103 D5 5hr ultra 1,400. *2,100.*

REGISTRATION STAMPS

Kolomyia Issue

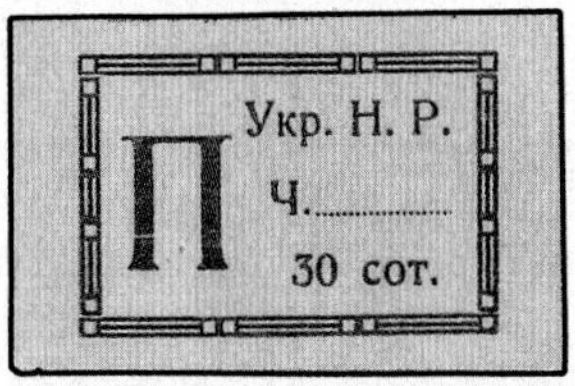

RS1

Without Gum

1918-19 Unwmk. Typeset *Imperf.*
F1 RS1 30sot black, *rose* 250.00 175.00
F2 RS1 50sot black, *rose* ('19) 120.00 *150.00*

No. F1 was printed on Dec. 10 and issued Dec. 12, 1918, along with the regular Kolomyia Issue (Nos. 5-8). On Dec. 19, the ZUNR government approved an increase in the registered letter rate to 50 sotyks, effective January 1, 1919. Because of communication disruptions, the Kolomyia post office did not learn of this decree until about January 7, when it ordered new values in the higher denomination (No. F2). F1 continued to be used, usually in combination with 20h of Austrian stamps, until supplies were exhausted, at which point No. F2 was put into use. A second printing of the 50sot value was made in late March. Variations in paper color — from light pink to deep rose — as well as paper thickness occurred in the 30-sot and both of the 50-sot printings.

Nos. F1-F2a were typographed in vertical panes of five stamps by the Wilhelm Brauner Print Ship in Kolomyia.

Forgeries exist.

OCCUPATION STAMPS

Romanian Occupation of Pokutia

Only the stamps listed below were officially created. Soon after the Romanian occupation ended on Aug. 20, 1919, the C.M.T. handstamps fell into the hands of speculators, and some 37 other Austrian stamps were overprinted. None of these privately-created stamps are known on authentic covers.

Austrian Stamps Surcharged in Dark Violet Blue

1919, June 14 Unwmk. *Perf. 12½*
On Stamps of 1916-18

N1 A37 40h on 5h lt grn 4.50 *5.50*
N2 A42 60h on 15h dl red 5.50 *6.50*
N3 A42 60h on 20h dp grn 2.25 *3.25*
a. Inverted overprint 3,000.
b. Double overprint 25.00
N4 A42 60h on 25h blue 12.00 *13.00*
a. Inverted overprint 60.00
b. Double overprint 82.50
N5 A42 60h on 30h dl vio 14.00 15.00
N6 A39 1k 20h on 50h dk grn 5.50 *6.50*
N7 A39 1k 20h on 60h dp bl 10.00 *12.00*
N8 A39 1k 20h on 1k car, *yel* 19.00 21.00

On Austrian Postage Due Stamps of 1910-1917

N9 D4 40h on 5h rose red 21.00 *22.50*
N10 D3 1k 20h on 25h car 175.00 *350.00*
N11 D4 1k 20h on 25h rose red 175.00 *350.00*
N12 D4 1k 20h on 30h rose red 1,400. 1,400.
N13 A38 1k 20h on 50h on 42h choc 1,500. 1,500.

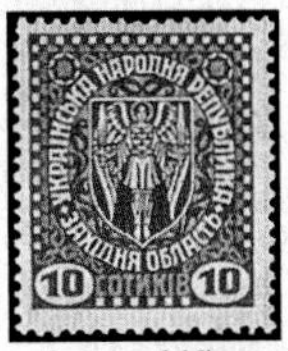

Arms of Kiev

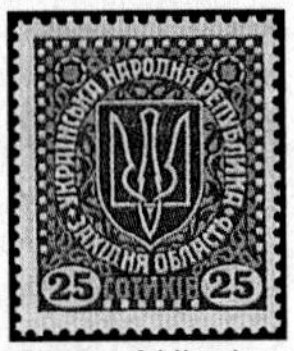

Arms of Ukraine

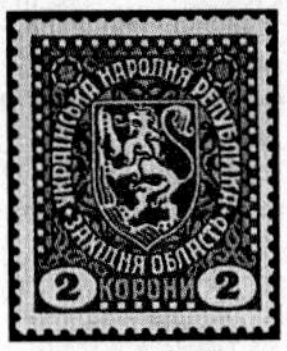

Arms of Galicia

First Definitive Issue, May 1919: Lithographed at the Austrian State Printing Office on unwatermarked white paper. Inscribed: "Ukrainska Narodnia Republyka Zakhidnia Oblast." ("Ukrainian National Republic Western Province"). Set of 12 values (four of each design), perf 11½ or imperf. Not issued. Value, set of 12: perf $350; imperf $550.

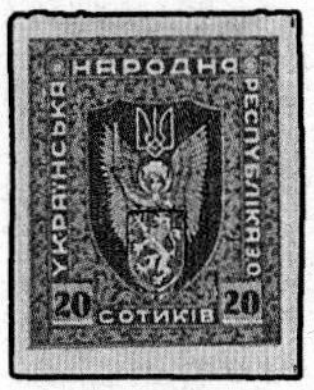

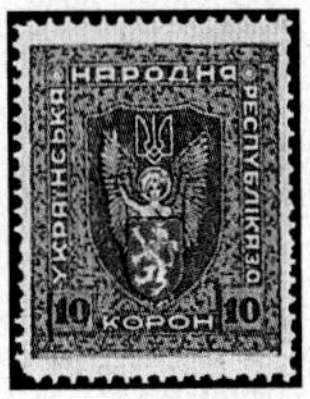

Second Definitive Issue, May 1919: Lithographed at the Austrian State Printing Office on unwatermarked white paper. Inscribed: "Ukrainska Narodnia Respublika Z.O." ("Ukrainian National Republic W(estern) P(rovince)"). Design incorporates the heraldic arms of Ukraine (trident), Kiev (Archangel Michael) and Lviv (lion rampant). 10, 20 and 50 sotyk values imperf; 1 and 10 krone values perf 11½. Not issued. Value, set of 5, $6. Also exists on cream-colored paper.

WEST IRIAN
(Irian Barat)
(West New Guinea)

Stamps formerly listed under West Irian now appear in Volume 1, following United Nations, and Volume 3, following Indonesia.

YEMEN
ˈye-mən

LOCATION — Arabian Peninsula, south of Saudi Arabia and bordering on the Red Sea
GOVT. — Republic
AREA — 204,000 sq. mi. (est.)
POP. — 16,942,230 (1999 est.)
CAPITAL — Sana'a (San'a)

40 Bogaches = 1 Imadi
40 Bogaches = 1 Riyal (1962)
100 Fils = 1 Riyal (1975)

The Yemen Arab Republic and the People's Republic of Yemen planned a 30-month unification process scheduled for completion by November 1992. While government ministries merged, both currencies remained valid.

> Catalogue values for unused stamps in this country are for Never Hinged items, beginning with Scott 44 in the regular postage section, Scott C1 in the airpost section.

Watermarks

Wmk. 127 — Quatrefoils

Wmk. 258 — Arabic Characters and Y G Multiple

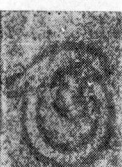

Wmk. 277 — Winged Wheel

For Domestic Postage

A1

Crossed Daggers and Arabic Inscriptions
A2

1926   Unwmk.   Typo.   *Imperf.*
Laid Paper
Without Gum

1	A1	2½b black	60.00	60.00
2	A1	2½b black, *orange*	60.00	60.00
3	A2	5b black	60.00	60.00
		Nos. 1-3 (3)	180.00	180.00

No. 2 is known rouletted 7½ or 9.
Type A1 differs from A2 primarily in the inscription in the left dagger blade.
All come on wove paper. Beware of forgeries, especially those on wove paper.
Replica sheets of Nos. 1-3 exist on horizontally laid, watermarked paper. The sheets are marked on the reverse with "CRC / FAC" in san-serif font. Any stamps removed from these replica sheets will contain this marking from 1-4 times on the reverse.

For Foreign and Domestic Postage

Arabic Inscriptions
A3   A4

1930-31   Wmk. 127   Perf. 14

7	A3	½b orange ('31)	.30	.25
8	A3	1b green	.40	.30
9	A3	1b yellow grn ('31)	.35	.25
10	A3	2b olive grn	.40	.35
11	A3	2b olive brn ('31)	.35	.25
12	A3	3b dull vio ('31)	.40	.35
13	A3	4b red	.60	.50
14	A3	4b deep rose ('31)	.50	.40
15	A3	5b slate gray ('31)	.90	.50
16	A4	6b dull blue	1.25	1.00
17	A4	6b dp ultra ('31)	1.00	.75
18	A4	8b lilac rose ('31)	1.40	1.00
19	A4	10b lt brown	2.00	1.40
20	A4	10b brn org ('31)	1.75	1.00
21	A4	20b yel grn ('31)	4.50	2.50
22	A4	1i red brn & lt bl	8.00	6.00
23	A4	1i lil rose & yel grn ('31)	8.00	6.00
		Nos. 7-23 (17)	32.10	22.80

Some values exist imperforate.
For surcharges and overprints see Nos. 30, 59-62, 166-167, 169-171, 174-176, 246-246Q.

Flags of Saudi Arabia, Yemen and Iraq — A5

1939   Litho.   Wmk. 258   Perf. 12½

24	A5	4b dl rose & ultra	.80	.50
25	A5	6b slate bl & ultra	.80	.50
26	A5	10b fawn & ultra	1.40	.75
27	A5	14b olive & ultra	2.25	1.25
28	A5	20b yel grn & ultra	3.25	1.75
29	A5	1i claret & ultra	6.50	3.50
		Nos. 24-29 (6)	15.00	8.25

2nd anniv. of the Arab Alliance. Nos. 24-29 exist imperforate. Value set, $20.
For overprints see Nos. C29-C29D.

a   b

c    d

e

Five types of surcharge:
All genuine surcharges are 12-13mm x 15-16mm and were made from steel handstamps.
a. "YEMEN" ½mm from left frameline and ½mm above bottom frameline.
b. "YEMEN" ½mm from left frameline and 1½mm above bottom frameline.
c. "YEMEN" 1½mm from left frameline and ½mm above bottom frameline. Found only on Types A13 and D1.
d. Arabic "4" at the center of the surcharge has been replaced with two vertical strokes. Usually blurred and found only on Type A9.
e. Arabic "4" has been replaced by a pair of crescents. Found only on Type A13.
Values of surcharged stamps are for ordinary examples. Clear, legible surcharges command a premium. Beware of fraudulent rubber-stamped surcharges in violet or grey black ink.

1939   Wmk. 127   Perf. 14
No. 7 Handstamped Type "a" in Black

30	A3	4b on ½b orange	15.00	12.50

See Nos. 44-48, 59-67, 82, 86-87.

A6

A7

1940   Wmk. 258   Litho.   Perf. 12½

31	A6	½b ocher & ultra	.25	.25
32	A6	1b lt grn & rose red	.25	.25
33	A6	2b bis brn & vio	.25	.25
34	A6	3b dl vio & ultra	.25	.25
35	A6	4b rose & yel grn	.35	.30
36	A6	5b dk gray grn & bis brn	.40	.35
37	A7	6b ultra & yel org	.45	.45
38	A7	8b claret & dull bl	.55	.50
39	A7	10b brn org & yel grn	.75	.75
40	A7	14b gray grn & vio	.95	.80
41	A7	18b emerald & blk	1.10	.90
42	A7	20b yel ol & cerise	1.50	1.50
43	A7	1i vio rose, yel grn & brn red	2.75	2.50
		Nos. 31-43 (13)	9.80	9.05
		Set, never hinged	20.00	

No. 36 was used as a 4b stamp in 1957.
For surcharges see Nos. 44-47.

> Catalogue values for unused stamps in this section, from this point to the end of the section, are for Never Hinged items.

Nos. 31-34, 36 Handstamped Type "a" in Black

1945-48   Perf. 12½

44	A6	4b on ½b	3.50	2.50
45	A6	4b on 1b ('48)	4.00	3.00
46	A6	4b on 2b ('48)	4.50	3.50
47	A6	4b on 3b ('48)	5.00	3.50
48	A6	4b on 5b ('46)	4.00	3.00

1949-51
Handstamp Type "b" in Black

44a	A6	4b on ½b ('51)	4.00	3.00
45a	A6	4b on 1b ('49)	4.00	3.50
46a	A6	4b on 2b ('49)	4.50	3.50
47a	A6	4b on 3b ('49)	5.00	3.50

Forged surcharges exist.

A8

1946   Frames in Emerald

49	A8	4b black	1.75	.85
50	A8	6b lilac rose	2.50	1.50
51	A8	10b ultra	3.50	1.90
52	A8	14b olive green	6.00	3.25
		Nos. 49-52 (4)	13.75	7.50

Opening of Mutawakkili Hospital. Exist imperforate. Value, set $15.
For overprints see Nos. 168, 172-173.

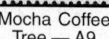

Mocha Coffee Tree — A9   Palace, San'a — A10

1947-58   Unwmk.   Engr.   Perf. 12½

53	A9	½b yellow brown	.25	.25
54	A9	1b purple	.70	.40
55	A9	2b ultra	1.40	.90
56	A10	4b red	2.25	1.25
57	A10	5b gray blue	2.50	1.50
58	A9	6b yellow green ('58)	3.50	2.00
		Nos. 53-58 (6)	10.60	6.30

No. 58 was printed in 1947 but not officially issued until June, 1958.
Additional values, prepared but not issued, were 10b, 20b and 1i, with views of palaces superimposed on flag, and palace square. These were looted from government storehouses during the 1948 revolution and a number of copies later reached collectors. Values, set: unused $20; used (cto) $15.
For surcharges see Nos. 63-65.

Admission of Yemen to the U.N.
10 postage, 5 airmail and 5 postage due stamps for the Admission of Yemen to the UN were not officially issued for use on domestic mail. Pictured on some of the stamps were Truman, Roosevelt, Churchill and the Statue of Liberty. Value, unused: 10v postage, $35; 5v air post, $22; 5v postage due, $14. Covers, scarce and all philatelic, exist to foreign destinations. A few local-use covers are also known.

Nos. 9, 11, 12 and 15 Handstamped Type "a" in Black

1949   Wmk. 127   Perf. 14

59	A3	4b on 1b yellow grn	10.00	8.00
60	A3	4b on 2b olive brn	35.00	30.00
61	A3	4b on 3b dull vio	12.00	10.00
62	A3	4b on 5b slate gray	12.00	10.00

Handstamped type "b" were unauthorized.

Nos. 53-55 Handstamped Types "a" and "b" in Black

1949		Unwmk.		Perf. 12½	
63	A9(b)	4b on ½b yel brn		6.00	6.00
64	A9(a)	4b on 1b purple		5.00	5.00
a.		Handstamp type "b"		5.00	5.00
b.		Handstamp type "d"		20.00	15.00
65	A9(a)	4b on 2b ultra		6.00	6.00
a.		Handstamp type "b"		6.00	6.00
b.		Handstamp type "d"		20.00	10.00

Nos. J1-J2 Handstamped Type "b" in Black

1953			Wmk. 258	
66	D1	4b on 1b org & yel grn	20.00	25.00
a.		Handstamp type "c"	35.00	40.00
67	D1	4b on 2b org & yel grn	20.00	25.00
a.		Handstamp type "c"	25.00	30.00

Types "a" and "b" exist inverted, double or horizontal.
Forged surcharges exist.

Parade Ground, San'a — A13

Mosque, San'a A14

Designs: 5b, Flag of Yemen. 6b, Flag & eagle. 8b, Mocha coffee branch. 14b, Walled city of San'a. 20b, 1i, Ta'iz & its citadel.

1951		Wmk. 277 Photo.		Perf. 14	
68	A13	1b dark brown		.30	.25
69	A13	2b red brown		.60	.25
70	A13	3b lilac rose		.75	.35
71	A14	5b blue & red		1.25	.60
72	A13	6b dk pur & red		1.40	.65
73	A13	8b dk bl & gray grn		1.50	.75
74	A14	10b rose lilac		1.25	.85
75	A14	14b blue green		2.25	1.00
76	A14	20b rose red		3.25	1.75
77	A14	1i violet		7.50	3.00
		Nos. 68-77 (10)		20.05	9.45
		Nos. 68-77,C3-C9 (17)		44.70	17.70

No. 71 was used as a 4b stamp in 1956. For surcharges see Nos. 82, 86-87.

Palace of the Rock, Wadi Dhahr — A15

Design: 20b, Walls of Ibb.

Engraved and Photogravure

1952		Unwmk.	Perf. 14½, Imperf.	
78	A15	12b choc, bl & dl grn	6.00	6.00
79	A15	20b dp car, bl & brn	9.00	9.00
		Nos. 78-79,C10-C11 (4)	35.00	35.00

Flag and View of San'a (Palace in Background) — A16

1952
80	A16	1i red brn, car & gray	12.50	12.50

4th anniv. of the accession of King Ahmed, Feb. 18, 1948. See Nos. 81, C12-C13.

1952   Palace in Foreground
81	A16	30b red brn, car & dk grn	11.00	11.00

Victory of Mar. 13, 1948. See No. C13.

No. 69 Handstamped Type "b" in Black

1951 (?)		Wmk. 277	Perf. 14	
82	A13	4b on 2b red brown	5.00	5.00
a.		Handstamp type "c"	10.00	6.00

Surcharge exists without left frameline. Forged surcharges exist. See Nos. 86-87.

Leaning Minaret, Mosque of Ta'iz — A17

1954		Photo.	Unwmk.	
83	A17	4b deep orange	1.25	.40
84	A17	6b deep blue	2.00	.60
85	A17	8b deep blue green	2.50	1.50
		Nos. 83-85,C14-C16 (6)	19.50	6.65

Accession of King Ahmed I, 5th anniv.

Nos. 68 and 70 Handstamped Type "b" in Black

1955		Wmk. 277	Perf. 14	
86	A13	4b on 1b dk brown	5.00	5.00
a.		Handstamp type "c"	20.00	10.00
b.		Handstamp type "e"	—	—
87	A13	4b on 3b lilac rose	7.50	6.00

Yemen Gate, San'a — A18

1956-57		Wmk. 277	Perf. 14	
87A	A18	1b lt brown	1.00	.75
87B	A18	5b blue green	1.25	.75
87C	A18	10b dark blue ('57)	1.50	.85
		Nos. 87A-87C (3)	3.75	2.35

Nos. 87A-87C were prepared for official use, but issued for regular postage. The 1b and 5b were used as 4b stamps. A 20b and 1-imadi of type A18 were not issued. Value unused $25., used (CTO) $15.

Arab Postal Union Issue

Globe — A19

Perf. 13½x13
1957-58		Wmk. 195	Photo.	
88	A19	4b yellow brown	1.00	.90
89	A19	6b green ('58)	1.40	1.10
90	A19	16b violet ('58)	2.00	1.50
		Nos. 88-90 (3)	4.40	3.50

Arab Postal Union founding, July 1, 1954.

Telecommunications Issue

Globe, Radio and Telegraph A20

1959, Mar.		Wmk. 318	Perf. 13x13½	
91	A20	4b vermilion	1.75	1.25

Arab Union of Telecommunications.
Exists imperf, Value $6.

United Arab States Issue

Flags of UAR and Yemen A21

1959, Mar. 13
92	A21	1b dl red brn & blk	.35	.25
93	A21	2b dk blue & blk	.45	.35
94	A21	4b sl grn, car & blk	.65	.50
		Nos. 92-94,C17-C19 (6)	6.55	5.05

First anniversary of United Arab States. No. 94 exists imperf. Value $50.

In 1959 four special sets of stamps were distributed abroad. They honored Human Rights (4v), Yemeni stamps (6v), Automatic Telephone Service (5v) and King Ahmed's Reign (4v). They were overprinted on stamps of either the 1940 issue (type A6) or the 1931 issue (type A4). Although not regularly sold at post offices in Yemen, several values from these sets do appear on covers that passed through normal postal channels. Some values are known with inverted or doubled overprints.

Arab League Center Issue

Arab League Center, Cairo A22

Perf. 13x13½
1960, Mar. 22		Wmk. 328		
95	A22	4b dull green & blk	.90	.90

Opening of the Arab League Center and the Arab Postal Museum in Cairo.
Exists imperf. Value $10.

Refugees Pointing to Map of Palestine A23

1960, Apr. 7			Photo.	
96	A23	4b brown	1.10	.90
97	A23	6b yellow green	1.75	1.25

World Refugee Year, 7/1/59-6/30/60.
Exist imperf. Value, set $25.
In 1961 a souvenir sheet was issued containing a 4b gray and 6b sepia in type A18, imperf. Black marginal inscription, "YEMEN 1960," repeated in Arabic. Size: 103x85mm. Value $50.

Torch and Olympic Rings A24

1960, Dec.		Unwmk.	Perf. 14x14½	
98	A24	2b black & lil rose	.55	.35
99	A24	4b black & yellow	.85	.50
100	A24	6b black & orange	1.20	.75
101	A24	8b brn blk & bl grn	2.10	1.40
102	A24	20b dk bl, org & vio	5.00	3.00
		Nos. 98-102 (5)	9.70	6.00

17th Olympic Games, Rome, 8/25-9/11.
Exist imperf. Value, set $75.
An imperf. souvenir sheet exists, containing one example of No. 99. Size: 100x60mm. Value $80.

UN Emblem Breaking Chains — A25

1961		Unwmk.	Perf. 14x14½	
103	A25	1b violet	.35	.25
104	A25	2b green	.40	.30
105	A25	3b grnsh blue	.50	.35
106	A25	4b brt ultra	.55	.40
107	A25	6b brt lilac	.70	.50
108	A25	14b rose brown	1.00	.60
109	A25	20b brown	2.00	1.60
		Nos. 103-109 (7)	5.50	4.00

15th anniversary (in 1960) of UN.
Exist imperf. Value, set $14.
An imperf. souvenir sheet exists, containing one example of No. 106. Blue marginal inscription. Size: 100x60mm. Value $15.
For overprints see Nos. 137-143.

Cranes and Ship, Hodeida A26

1961, June		Litho.	Perf. 13x13½	
110	A26	4b multicolored	.85	.40
111	A26	6b multicolored	1.40	.75
112	A26	16b multicolored	2.75	1.60
		Nos. 110-112 (3)	5.00	2.75

Opening of deepwater port at Hodeida.
An imperf. souvenir sheet exists, containing one each of Nos. 110-112. Size: 160x130mm. Value $7.
For overprints see Nos. 177, 180.

Alabaster Funerary Mask — A27

Designs (ancient sculptures from Marib, Sheba): 2b, Horned animal's head, symbolizing Moon God (limestone). 4b, Bronze head of an Emperor 1st or 2nd century. 8b, Statue of Emperor Dhamar Ali. 10b, Statue of a child, 2nd or 3rd century (alabaster). 12b, Stairs in court of Temple of the Moon God. 20b, Alabaster relief, boy riding monster. 1i, Woman with grapes, relief.

1961, Oct. 14		Photo.	Perf. 11½	
		Granite Paper		
113	A27	1b salmon, blk & gray	.35	.25
114	A27	2b purple & gray	.60	.25
115	A27	4b pale brn, gray & blk	.80	.25
116	A27	8b brt pink & blk	1.00	.25
117	A27	10b yellow & blk	1.00	.35
118	A27	12b lt vio bl & blk	2.00	.50

119	A27	20b gray & blk	2.40	.60
120	A27	1i gray ol & blk	5.00	1.25
		Nos. 113-120,C20-C21 (10)	16.90	5.45

Exist imperf. Value, set (10), $25.

For overprints see Nos. 144-145, 147, 151, 153, 156-158, C24, C25.

Imam's New Palace, San'a — A28

8b, Side view of Imam's palace, San'a, horiz. 10b, Palace of the Rock (Dar al-Hajar).

1961, Nov. 15   **Unwmk.**

121	A28	4b black & lt bl grn	.35	.25
122	A28	8b blk, brt pink & grn	.75	.45
123	A28	10b black, sal & grn	.85	.50
		Nos. 121-123,C22-C23 (5)	3.90	2.05

Exist imperf. Value, set (5) $6.

For overprints see #148, 152, 154, C24A, C25A.

Hodeida-San'a Road — A29

1961, Dec. 25   **Litho.**   **Perf. 13½x13**

124	A29	4b multicolored	.75	.25
125	A29	6b multicolored	.90	.40
126	A29	10b multicolored	1.50	.50
		Nos. 124-126 (3)	3.15	1.15

Opening of the Hodeida-San'a highway. A miniature sheet exists containing one each of Nos. 124-126, imperf. Size: 159x129mm. Value $7.

For overprints see Nos. 178-179.

Trajan's Kiosk, Philae, Nubia — A30

1962, Mar. 1   **Photo.**   **Perf. 11x11½**

127	A30	4b dk red brown	3.50	1.00
128	A30	6b blue green	6.25	2.00

Issued to publicize UNESCO's help in safeguarding the monuments of Nubia. Exist imperf. on toned paper with printer's imprint. Value, set $10.

A souvenir sheet exists, containing one each of #127-128, imperf. on white paper with printer's imprint at the bottom of the sheet. Size: 100x88½mm. Value $12.50.

Arab League Building, Cairo, and Emblem — A31

1962, Mar. 22   **Perf. 13½x13**

129	A31	4b dark green	.70	.25
130	A31	6b deep ultra	.85	.40

Arab League Week, Mar. 22-28. A souvenir sheet exists, containing one each of Nos. 129-130, imperf. Size: 94x80mm. Value $3.50.

For overprints see Nos. 164-165.

Nurses, Mother and Child — A32

Designs: 4b, Nurse weighing child. 6b, Vaccination. 10b, Weighing infant.

1962, June 20   **Unwmk.**   **Perf. 11½**

131	A32	2b multicolored	.60	.25
132	A32	4b multicolored	.85	.30
133	A32	6b multicolored	1.00	.40
134	A32	10b multicolored	1.75	.50
		Nos. 131-134 (4)	4.20	1.45

Issued for Child Welfare. Exist imperf. Value, set $8.

For overprints see Nos. 146, 149-150, 155.

Malaria Eradication Emblem — A33

1962, July 20   **Perf. 13½x13**

135	A33	4b black & dp org	.70	.25
136	A33	6b dk brown & grn	1.00	.40

WHO drive to eradicate malaria. An imperf. souvenir sheet contains one each of Nos. 135-136. Size: 95x79mm. Value $15.

No. 136 has laurel leaves added and inscription rearranged.

For overprints see Nos. 189-190.

Nos. 103-109 Overprinted

Perf. 14x14½

1962, Nov. 7   **Photo.**   **Unwmk.**

137	A25	1b violet	1.50	1.50
138	A25	2b green	1.50	1.50
139	A25	3b greenish blue	1.50	1.50
140	A25	4b brt ultra	1.50	1.50
141	A25	6b brt lilac	1.50	1.50
142	A25	14b rose brown	1.50	1.50
143	A25	20b brown	1.50	1.50
		Nos. 137-143 (7)	10.50	10.50

Exist imperf. and with inverted overprint.

Yemen Arab Republic
Nos. 113-123 and 131-134 Ovptd. in Dark Green or Dark Red

a

b

1963, Jan. 1   **Perf. 11½**

144	A27 (a)	1b No. 113 (G)	.25	.25
145	A27 (a)	2b No. 114	.25	.25
146	A32 (b)	2b No. 131	.35	.35
147	A27 (b)	4b No. 115 (G)	.35	.35
148	A28 (a)	4b No. 121	.50	.50
149	A32 (b)	4b No. 132	.50	.50
150	A32 (b)	6b No. 133	.65	.65
151	A27 (a)	8b No. 116	.65	.65
152	A28 (b)	8b No. 122 (G)	.90	.90

153	A27 (a)	10b No. 117	.90	.90
154	A28 (a)	10b No. 123	1.60	1.60
155	A32 (b)	10b No. 134 (G)	1.60	1.60
156	A27 (a)	12b No. 118	1.25	1.25
157	A27 (a)	20b No. 119	1.80	1.80
158	A27 (a)	1i No. 120	5.00	5.00
		Nos. 144-158,C24-C25A (19)	22.60	22.60

Nos. 144-158, C24-C25A exist imperf. Value, set $45.

Proclamation of the Republic — A34

1963, Mar. 15   **Perf. 11x11½**

159	A34	4b shown	.55	.55
160	A34	6b Flag, tank	.85	.85

An imperf. souvenir sheet containing Nos. 159-160 exists. Value $10.

See Nos. C26-C28.

UN Freedom From Hunger Campaign — A35

1963, Mar. 21   **Perf. 11½x11, 11x11½**

162	A35	4b Milk cow, horiz.	.90
163	A35	6b shown	1.25

An imperf. souvenir sheet of 2 containing one each Nos. 162-163 exists. Value $12.

For overprints see Nos. 218-218A.

Nos. 129-130 Ovptd. in Dark Red

1963, Sept. 1   **Perf. 13½x13**

164	A31	4b dark green	6.00	6.00
165	A31	6b deep ultra	6.00	6.00

Nos. 98-100 Overprinted in Black or Red

1963   **Unwmk.**   **Perf. 14x14½**

165A	A24	2b black & lil rose	5.00	5.00
165B	A24	4b black & yellow		
		(R)	5.00	5.00
165C	A24	6b black & orange		
		(R)	5.00	5.00
		Nos. 165A-165C (3)	15.00	15.00

Nos. 15-16, 18-23, 50-52 Ovptd. in Black

     a   b

1963, Sept. 1

166	A3 (a)	5b No. 15	1.25	1.25
167	A4 (a)	6b No. 16	1.60	1.60
168	A8 (b)	6b No. 50	1.60	1.60
169	A4 (a)	8b No. 18	1.80	1.80
170	A4 (a)	10b No. 19	2.25	2.25
171	A4 (a)	10b No. 20	2.25	2.25
172	A8 (b)	10b No. 51	2.25	2.25
173	A8 (b)	14b No. 52	6.25	6.25
174	A4 (a)	20b No. 21	2.50	2.50
175	A4 (a)	1i No. 22	6.25	6.25
176	A4 (a)	1i No. 23	4.75	4.75
		Nos. 166-176 (11)	32.75	32.75

Nos. 111-112 and 125-126 Ovptd. in Black

Perf. 13x13½, 13½x13

1963, Sept. 1   **Litho.**   **Unwmk.**

177	A26	6b No. 111	1.75	1.75
178	A29	6b No. 125	1.75	1.75
179	A29	10b No. 126	2.50	2.50
180	A26	16b No. 112	2.50	2.50
		Nos. 177-180 (4)	8.50	8.50

On Nos. 178-179 the bars eliminate old inscription with text of overprint positioned below and to the right of them, on Nos. 177 and 180, the text is slightly left below the bars.

Imperf. souvenir sheets of 2 exist containing Nos. 177 and 180 or Nos. 178-179. Value $20 each.

1st Anniv. of the Revolution — A36

2b, Flag, torch, candle, vert. 6b, Flag, grain, chain, vert.

Perf. 11½x11, 11x11½

1963, Sept. 26   **Photo.**

186	A36	2b multicolored	.35	.30
187	A36	4b shown	.55	.45
188	A36	6b multicolored	.90	.70
		Nos. 186-188 (3)	1.80	1.45

Imperf. souvenir sheet exists containing one each Nos. 186-188. Value $5.

Red Cross, Centennial — A36a

1963, October   **Photo.**   **Perf. 13½x13**

188A	A36a	¼b bl, blk & red	.25	.25
188B	A36a	½b lil brn, blk & red	.25	.25
188C	A36a	½b ol grey, blk & red	.25	.25
188D	A36a	4b vio, black & red	.75	.35

188E A36a 8b ocher, blk & red 1.00 .50
188F A36a 20b grn, blk & red 2.00 1.00
Nos. 188A-188F (6) 4.50 2.60

Nos. 188A-188F exist imperf. Value $12. An imperf. souvenir sheet of 2 exists containing one each Nos. 188D-188E. Value $9.

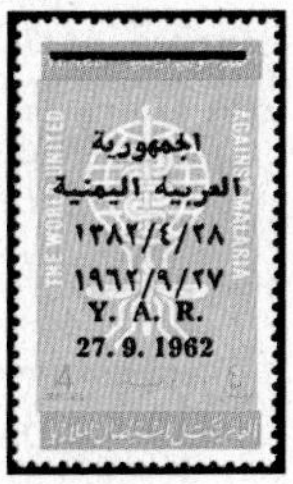

Nos. 135-136 Ovptd. in Black

1963, Nov. 25 ***Perf. 13½x13***
189 A33 4b black & dp orange 3.00 3.00
190 A33 6b dk brown & green 4.00 4.00

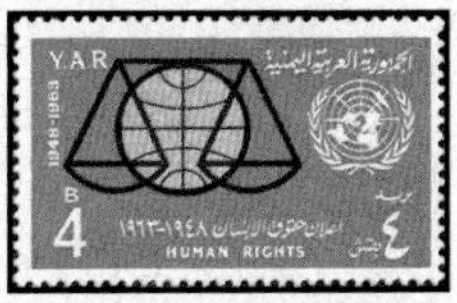

UN Declaration of Human Rights, 15th Anniv. — A37

1963, Dec. 10 ***Perf. 13½***
191 A37 4b orange & dk brn vio .55 .55
192 A37 6b blue grn & blk .75 .75

Nos. 191-192 exist imperf. Value $7.50. An imperf. souvenir sheet of 2 exists containing one each Nos. 191-192. Value $10.

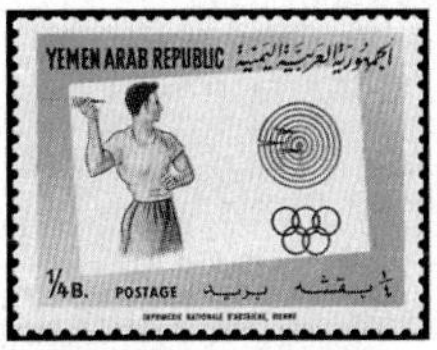

Olympic Sports — A37a

1964, Mar. 30 **Photo.** ***Perf. 12***
192A A37a ¼b Darts .25 .25
192B A37a ⅓b Table tennis .25 .25
192C A37a ½b Running, vert. .25 .25
192D A37a 1b Volleyball, vert. .45 .40
192E A37a 1½b Soccer, vert. .45 .40
192F A37a 4b Horse racing .65 .50
192G A37a 20b Pole vault 1.35 1.25
i. Souvenir sheet of 1 3.00 3.00
192H A37a 1r Basketball, vert. 2.75 1.50
Nos. 192A-192H (8) 6.40 4.80

Nos. 192F-192H are airmail. Nos. 192A-192H exist imperf. Value $25. An imperf. souvenir sheet containing 1 No. 192F exists. Value $4.

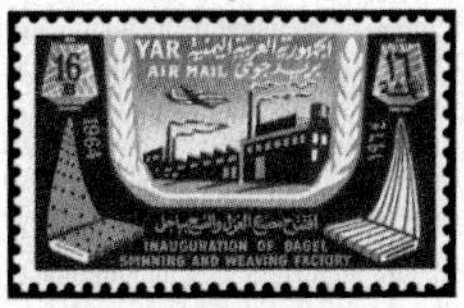

Bagel Spinning and Weaving Factory Inauguration — A38

2b, Factory, bobbin, spool, cloth. 4b, Loom machine. 6b, Factory, spool, bolt of cloth.

1964, Apr. 10 ***Perf. 11x11½, 11½x11***
193 A38 2b multicolored .30 .25
193A A38 4b mutlicolored .40 .30
193B A38 6b multicolored .55 .35
193C A38 16b shown 1.50 1.40
Nos. 193-193C (4) 2.75 2.30

Nos. 193-193B vert. An imperf. souvenir sheet of one exists containing No. 193C. Value $4.
No. 193C is air mail.

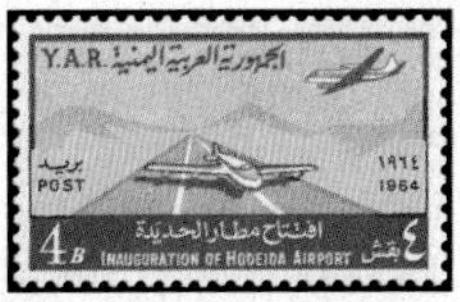

Hodeida Airport Inauguration — A39

1964, Apr. 30 ***Perf. 11½x11***
194 A39 4b Runway .40 .35
194A A39 6b Runway, terminal .55 .50
194B A39 10b Aircraft, terminal, ship at sea .75 .55
Nos. 194-194B (3) 1.70 1.40

An imperf. souvenir sheet of one exists containing No. 194B. Value $3.

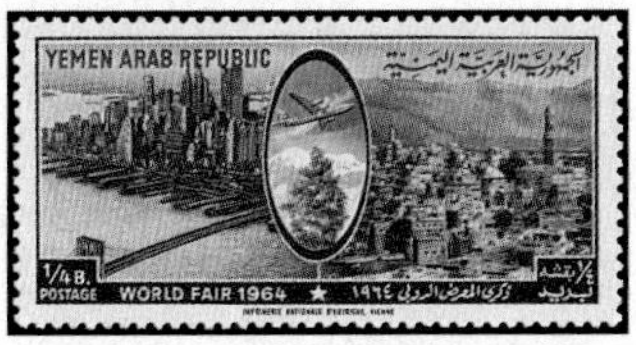

1964 New York World's Fair — A39a

Designs: ¼b, 1b, 20b, Manhattan skyline, Sana'a. ⅓b, 4b, Empire State Building, minaret. ½b, 16b, Statue of Liberty, ship loading cranes.

1964, May 10 ***Perf. 12***
195 A39a ¼b brown & multi .25 .25
195A A39a ⅓b grey & multi .25 .25
195B A39a ½b dk bl green & multi .30 .25
195C A39a 1b dk grey & multi .45 .35
195D A39a 4b dk grey & multi .80 .50
195E A39a 16b brown & multi 1.50 1.00
195F A39a 20b red vio & multi 2.00 1.50
Nos. 195-195F (7) 5.55 4.10

Nos. 195E-195F are airmail. An imperf. souvenir sheet containing 1 No. 195F exists. Value $4.
For overprints see Nos. 220-220F.

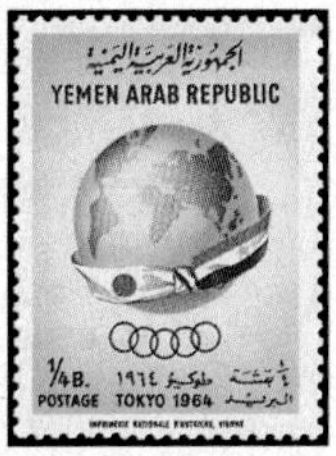

1964 Summer Olympic Games, Tokyo — A39b

Designs: ¼b, 12b, Globe and flags. ⅓b, 6b, Torch. ½b, 20b, Discus thrower. 1b, Yemen flag. 1½b, 4b, Swimmers, horiz.

1964, June 1 ***Perf. 12***
196 A39b ¼b multicolored .25 .25
196A A39b ⅓b multicolored .25 .25
196B A39b ½b multicolored .30 .25
196C A39b 1b multicolored .40 .30
196D A39b 1½b multicolored .50 .35
196E A39b 4b multicolored .70 .60
196F A39b 6b multicolored .80 .75
196G A39b 12b multicolored 1.50 1.25
196H A39b 20b multicolored 2.25 2.00
i. Souvenir sheet of 1 4.00 4.00
Nos. 196-196H (9) 6.95 6.00

Exist imperf. Value, set $25.
Nos. 196E-196H are airmail.

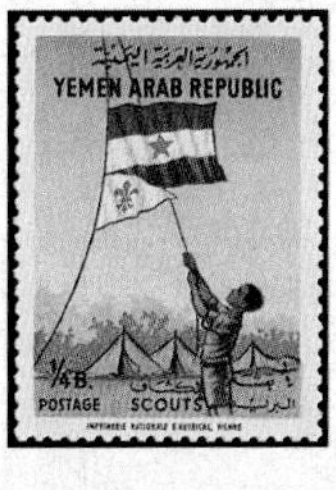

Boy Scouts A39c

Designs: ¼b, 4b, Raising flag. ⅓b, 1b, 6b, Scouts, tents. ½b, 16b, Bugler. 1½b, 20b, Campfire.

1964, June 20
197 A39c ¼b multicolored .25 .25
197A A39c ⅓b multicolored .25 .25
197B A39c ½b multicolored .30 .25
197C A39c 1b multicolored .40 .30
197D A39c 1½b multicolored .50 .35
197E A39c 4b multicolored .85 .60
197F A39c 6b multicolored 1.00 .75
197G A39c 16b multicolored 1.75 1.25
i. Souvenir sheet of 1 4.00 4.00
197H A39c 20b multicolored 2.75 2.00
Nos. 197-197H (9) 8.05 6.00

Exist imperf. Value, set $20. An imperf. souvenir sheet containing 1 No. 197H exists. Value, $5.
Nos. 197E-197H are airmail.

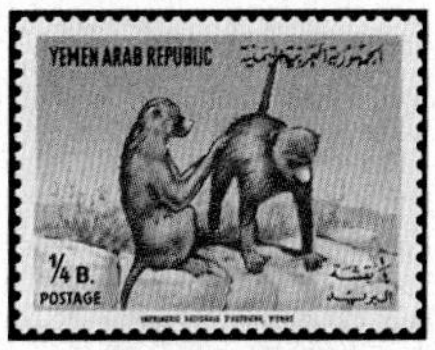

Animals — A39d

Designs: ¼b, Baboons. ⅓b, Arabian horses. ½b, 12b, Zebu. 1b, 20b, Lions. 1½b, 4b, Gazelles.

1964, Aug. 15 **Photo.** ***Perf. 12x11½***
198 A39d ¼b lilac & brown .25 .25
198A A39d ⅓b blue & dk brn .25 .25
198B A39d ½b org & brn .30 .25
198C A39d 1b blue & brn .40 .30
198D A39d 1½b multicolored .50 .35
198E A39d 4b multicolored .85 .60
198F A39d 12b multicolored 1.00 .75
198G A39d 20b multicolored 1.75 1.25
Nos. 198-198G (8) 5.30 4.00

Exist imperf. Value, set $15.
Nos. 198E-198G are airmail. See Nos. J9-J11.

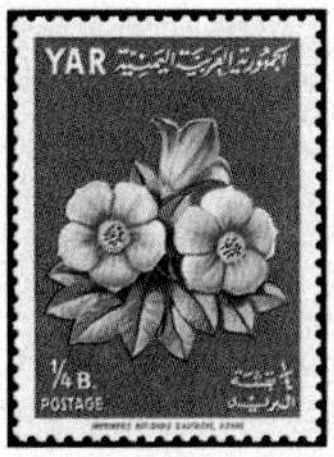

Flowers — A39e

Designs: ¼b, shown. ⅓b, Crinum. ½b, 12b, Poinsettia. 1b, 4b, Hybrid tea. 1½b, 20b, Peppermint.

1964, Aug. 15 **Photo.** ***Perf. 11½x12***
199 A39e ¼b multicolored .25 .25
199A A39e ⅓b multicolored .25 .25
199B A39e ½b grn, red & yel .30 .25
199C A39e 1b multicolored .40 .30
199D A39e 1½b red, grn & blk .50 .35
199E A39e 4b multicolored .85 .60
199F A39e 12b dk grn, red & yel 1.00 .75
199G A39e 20b multicolored 1.75 1.25
Nos. 199-199G (8) 5.30 4.00

Exist imperf. Value, set $12. Nos. 199E-199G are airmail. See Nos. J12-J14.

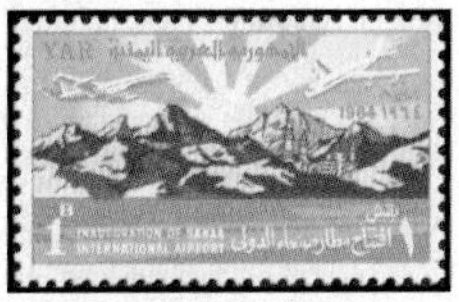

Sana'a Intl. Airport Inauguration — A40

1964, Oct. 1
200 A40 1b shown .35 .35
201 A40 2b Terminal, runway, aircraft .35 .35
202 A40 4b like 2b .35 .35
203 A40 8b like 1b .70 .70
Nos. 200-203 (4) 1.75 1.75

An imperf. souvenir sheet of two exists containing one each Nos. 202 and C30. Value $4.
See No. C30.

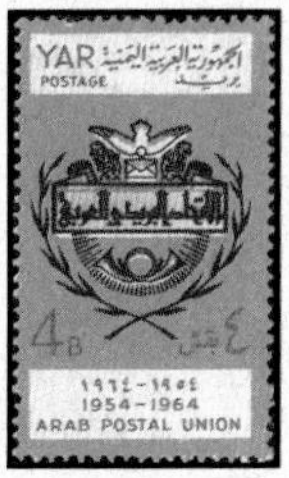

Arab Postal Union, 10th Anniv. — A41

1964, Oct. 15 ***Perf. 13½***
204 A41 4b multicolored .75 .65

See No. C31.

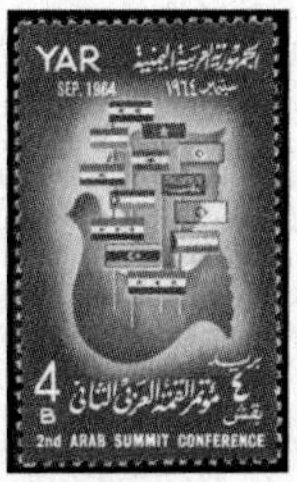

2nd Arab Summit Conference — A42

1964, Nov. 30
205 A42 4b shown .75 .65
206 A42 6b Conference emblem, map 1.00 .80

An imperf. souvenir sheet of 2 exists containing one each Nos. 205-206. Value $3.
For overprints see Nos. 222-222A.

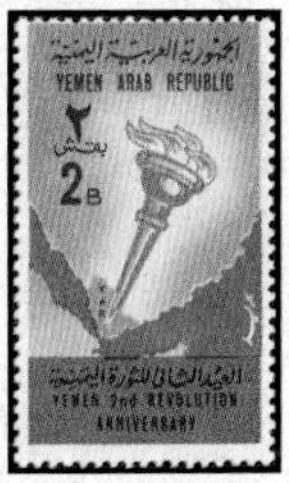

2nd Anniv. of the Revolution — A43

1964, Dec. 30
207 A43 2b Torch, map .35 .30
208 A43 4b Revolutionary .70 .50
209 A43 6b Flag, 2 candles, map .70 .50
Nos. 207-209 (3) 1.75 1.30

An imperf. souvenir sheet of one exists containing No. 209. Value $3.

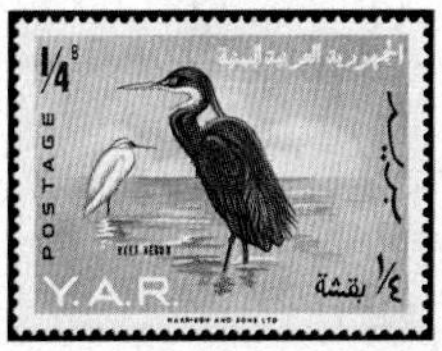

Birds — A43a

Designs: ¼b, Reef Heron. ½b, Arabian red-legged partridge. ¾b, Eagle owl, vert. 1b, Hammer kop. 1½b, Yemen linnets. 4b, Hoopoes. 6b, Amethyst starlings. 8b, Bald ibis, vert. 12b, Arabian woodpecker, vert. 20b, Bateleur, vert. 1r, Bruce's green pigeon.

Perf. 15x14½, 14½x15
1965, Jan. 30 **Photo.**

Background Color

209A A43a ¼b light violet .50 .25
209B A43a ½b brown olive .75 .25
209C A43a ¾b grey .75 .25
209D A43a 1b olive green 1.00 .40
209E A43a 1½b rose 1.00 .40
209F A43a 4b light blue 2.00 .75
209G A43a 6b blue 2.00 .75
209H A43a 8b bistre 2.00 1.00
209I A43a 12b green 3.00 1.50
209J A43a 20b orange 4.00 2.00
209K A43a 1r blue green 6.00 3.00
Nos. 209A-209K (11) 23.00 10.55

Souvenir Sheet

Imperf

209L A43a 20b rose *15.00 15.00*

Nos. 209A-209K exist imperf. Value, set $60.
Nos. 209H-209L are airmail. For overprints see Nos. 221-221B.

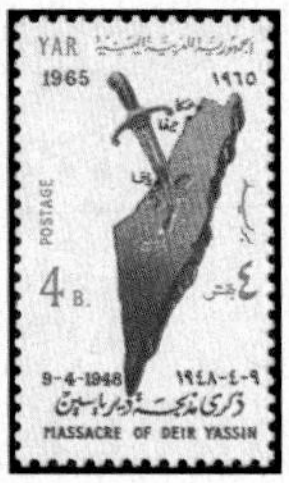

Deir Yassin Massacre — A44

1965, Apr. 30 *Perf. 11x11½*
210 A44 4b red lil & deep blue .80 .60

See No. C32.

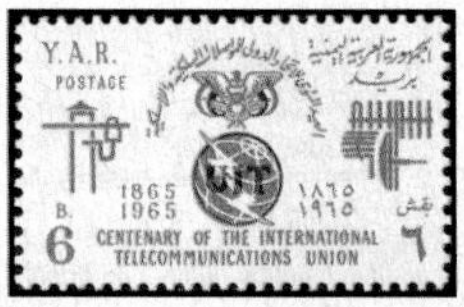

Intl. Telecommunications Union (ITU), Cent. — A45

1965, May 17 *Perf. 11x11½, 11½x11*
211 A45 4b red & pale blue, vert. .65 .35
212 A45 6b org brn & grn .90 .50

A souvenir sheet of 1 exists containing #212. Value $4.

Burning of Algiers Library, 3rd Anniv. A46

1965, July 7 *Perf. 11½x11*
213 A46 4b sepia, red & grn .65 .45

See No. C33.

3rd Anniv. of the Revolution A47

1965, Sept. 26
214 A47 4b Tractor, corn, grain .70 .45
214A A47 6b Tractor, tower, buildings .90 .50

An imperf. souvenir sheet of one exists containing No. 214A. Value $4.

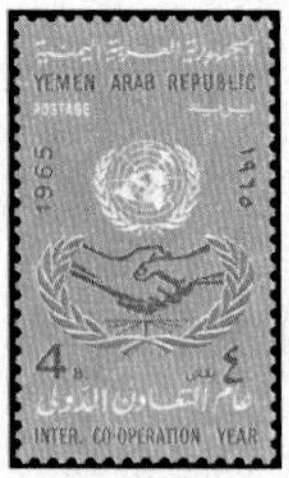

Intl. Cooperation Year — A48

1965, Oct. 15 *Perf. 11x11½*
215 A48 4b shown .70 .55
215A A48 6b UN building, New York 1.00 .60

Nos. 215-215A exist imperf. Value $5. An imperf. souvenir sheet of one exists containing No. 215A. Value $4.

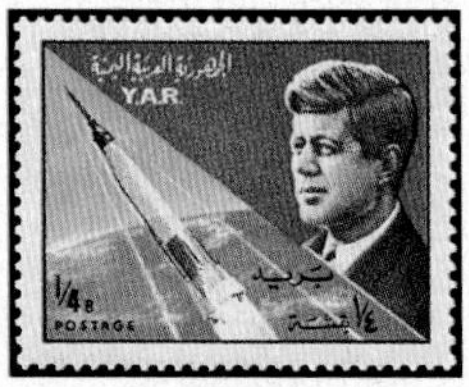

Pres. John F. Kennedy — A48a

Kennedy and: Nos. 216, 216D, Rocket in flight. Nos. 216A, 216G, Launch pads. Nos. 216B-216C, Lift-off. 4b, Capsule in space. 8b, Splash down.

1965, Nov. 29 Photo. *Perf. 12x11½*
216 A48a ¼b multicolored .25 .25
216A A48a ¼b multicolored .25 .25
216B A48a ¼b multicolored .25 .25
216C A48a ½b multicolored .25 .25
216D A48a ½b multicolored .25 .25
216E A48a 4b multicolored 1.35 .75
216F A48a 8b multicolored 2.25 1.25
216G A48a 12b multicolored 5.50 3.00
Nos. 216-216G (8) 10.35 6.25

Nos. 216F-216G are airmail. Nos. 216-216G exist imperf. Value $12.50. Imperf. souvenir sheets of Nos. 216E-216F exist. Value $5 each.

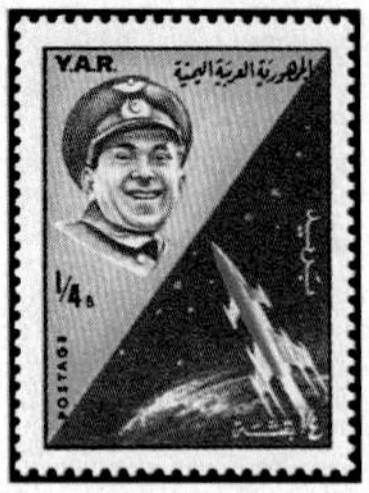

Astronauts and Cosmonauts — A48b

Spacecraft and: Nos. 217, 8b, Pavel Belyayev. Nos. 217A, 4b, Alexei Leonov. Nos. 217B, 217D, M. Scott Carpenter. Nos. 217C, 16b, Virgil I. "Gus" Grissom. No. 217H, James McDivitt, Edward White.

1965, Dec. 29 Photo. *Perf. 11½x12*
217 A48b ¼b multicolored .25 .25
217A A48b ¼b multicolored .25 .25
217B A48b ¼b multicolored .25 .25
217C A48b ⅓b multicolored .25 .25
217D A48b ½b multicolored .25 .25
217E A48b 4b multicolored .75 .35
217F A48b 8b multicolored 2.75 1.40
217G A48b 16b multicolored 6.25 3.25
Nos. 217-217G (8) 11.00 6.25

Souvenir Sheet

Imperf

217H A48b 16b multicolored *12.50 12.50*

Exist imperf. Value, set $15.

Nos. 217E-217H are airmail. For overprints see Nos. 225-225H, 229-229D.

Nos. 162-163 Overprinted in Black

a

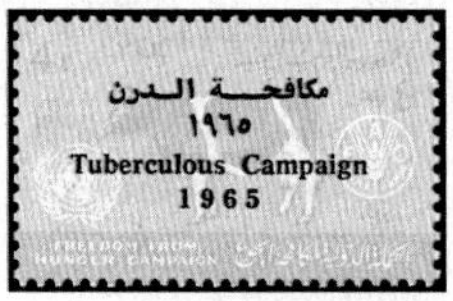

b

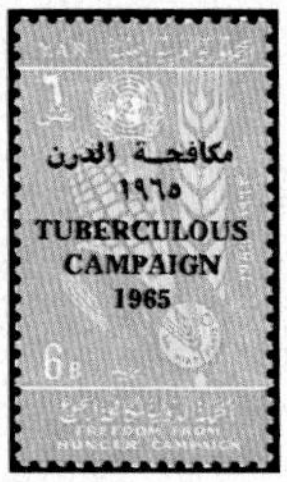

1966, Jan. 15 *Perf. 11½x11, 11x11½*
218 A35 (a) 4b sal rose & gold-en brn 1.00 .75
218A A35 (b) 6b brt pur & yel 1.75 1.00

An imperf. souvenir sheet of two exists containing Nos. 218-218A. Value $10.

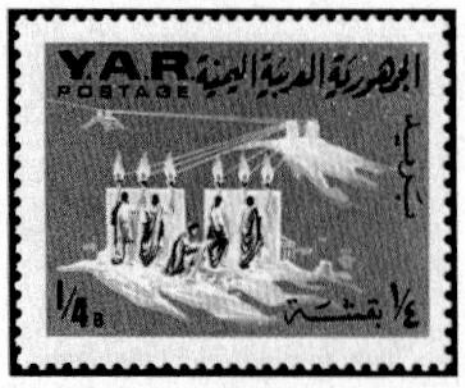

Telecommunications — A48c

Designs: No. 219, Light signals. No. 219A, Samuel F.B. Morse, telegraph. No. 219B, Early telephone. No. 219C, Philipp Reis, Thomas Edison, ealry telephone system. No. 219D, Television camera, antenna. No. 219E, Radar dish. No. 219F, Fax machine. No. 219G, Satellite.

1966, Jan. 29 Photo. *Perf. 12x11½*
219 A48c ¼b red & black .25 .25
219A A48c ¼b grnish bl & blk .25 .25
219B A48c ¼b yel brn & blk .25 .25
219C A48c ⅓b org red & blk .25 .25
219D A48c ½b violet & black .25 .25
219E A48c 4b yel grn & blk .75 .35
219F A48c 6b drab & black 1.25 .65
219G A48c 20b blue & black 2.50 1.25
Nos. 219-219G (8) 5.75 3.50

Nos. 219E-219G are airmail. Nos. 291-219G exist imperf. Value $10. An imperf. souvenir sheet containing 1 No. 219G exists. Value $6.

Nos. 195-195F Overprinted in Black

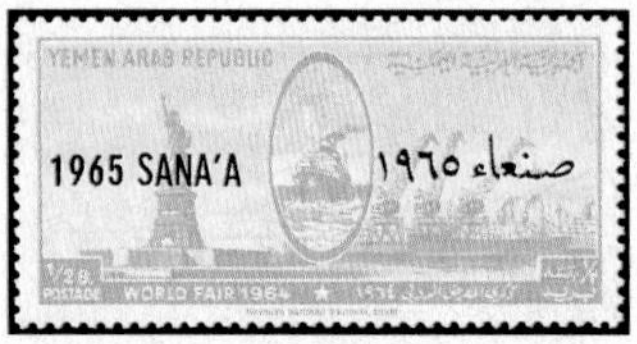

1966, Feb. 10 Photo. *Perf. 12*
220 A39a ¼b brown & multi .50 .50
220A A39a ⅓b grey & multi .50 .50
220B A39a ½b dk bl grn & multi .60 .50
220C A39a 1b dk grey & multi .90 .70
220D A39a 4b dk grey & multi 1.60 1.00
220E A39a 16b brown & multi 3.00 2.00
220F A39a 20b red vio & multi 4.00 3.00
Nos. 220-220F (7) 11.10 8.20

Nos. 220E-220F are airmail. An imperf. souvenir sheet containing 1 No. 220F exists. Value $10.

Nos. 209A-209C Overprinted in Black or Red

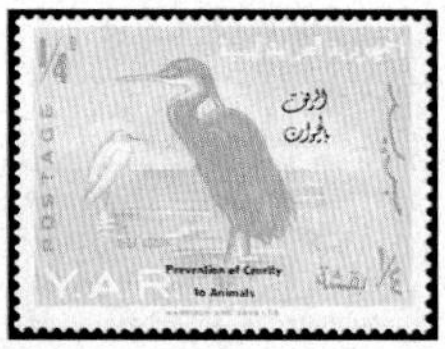

1966, Mar. 5 Photo. *Perf. 12x11½*

Background Color

221 A43a ¼b light violet 1.00 .75
221A A43a ½b brown olive 1.00 .75
221B A43a ¾b grey (R) 1.25 1.00
Nos. 221-221B (3) 3.25 2.50

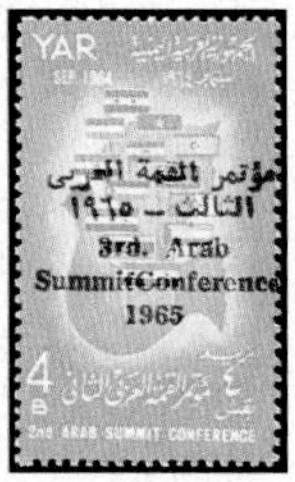

Nos. 205-206 Ovptd. in Red or Black

1966, Mar. 20 *Perf. 13½*
222 A42 4b dark green (R) .75 .50
222A A42 6b orange brown .85 .55

An imperf. souvenir sheet of two exists containing Nos. 222-222A ovptd. in bright pink (4b) or black (6b) with additional inscription at bottom "CASABLANCA / 1965." Value $4.

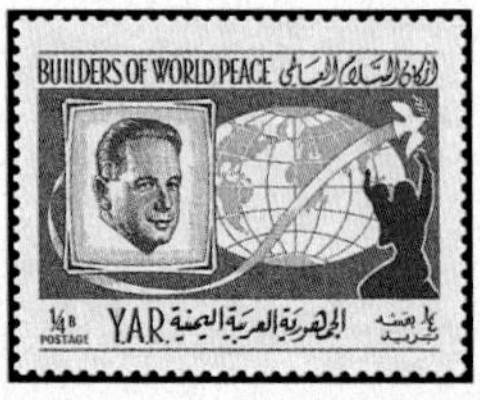

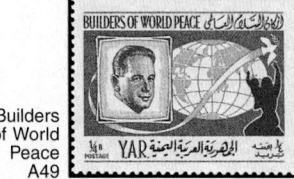

Builders of World Peace A49

Designs: Nos. 223, 223C, Dag Hammerskjold. Nos. 223A, 4b, John F. Kennedy. Nos. 223B, 223D, Jawaharlal Nehru. 6b, Mohammed Abdel Khaliq Hassuna. 10b, U Thant. 12b, Pope Paul VI.

1966, Mar. 25 Photo. *Perf. 12*
223 A49 ¼b green .25 .25
223A A49 ¼b orange brown .25 .25
223B A49 ¼b dark grey .25 .25
223C A49 ⅓b red brown .25 .25
223D A49 ½b violet brown .25 .25
223E A49 4b claret .75 .35

Size:51x38mm

223F A49 6b bl grn & brn 1.00 .50
223G A49 10b blue & brown 1.25 .65
223H A49 12b red lilac & brn 2.00 1.00
Nos. 223-223H (9) 6.25 3.75

Exist imperf. Value, set $9. Nos. 223F-223H are airmail.

Two imperf. souvenir sheets, 4b and 8b, exist. Values $4 and $6, respectively.

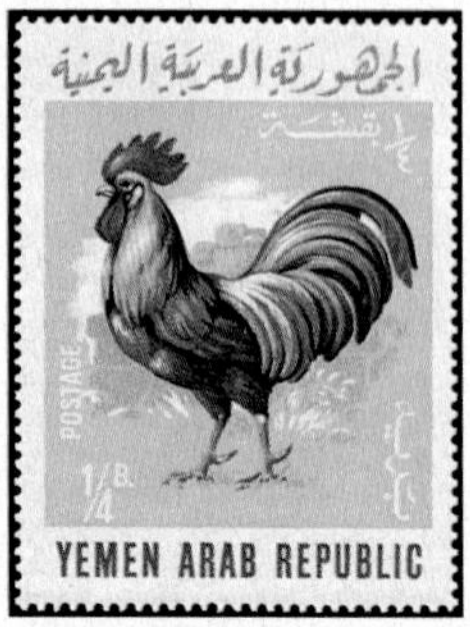

Domesticated Animals — A50

1966, May 5 Photo. *Perf. 12½*
224 A50 ¼b Rooster .30 .25
224A A50 ¼b Rabbit .30 .25
224B A50 ¼b Donkey .30 .25
224C A50 ⅓b Cat .40 .25
224D A50 ½b Sheep .40 .25
224E A50 4b Camel 1.00 .50
Nos. 224-224E (6) 2.70 1.75

Souvenir Sheet

Imperf

224F A50 22b Sheep, chick-ens, geese 4.00 3.00

Nos. 224-224E exist imperf. Value, set $10. No. 224F is airmail.

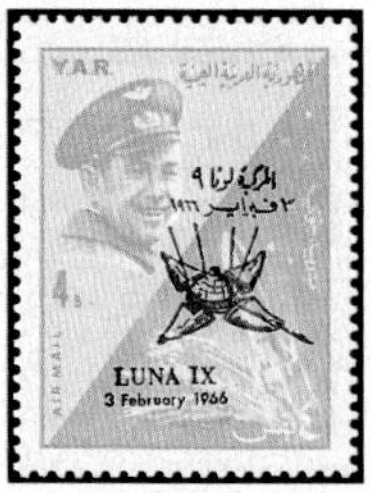

Nos. 217-217H Overprinted in Black and Red

Luna IX

1966, May 20 Photo. *Perf. 11½x12*
225 A48b ¼b multicolored .25 .25
225A A48b ¼b multicolored .25 .25
225B A48b ¼b multicolored .25 .25
225C A48b ⅓b multicolored .25 .25
225D A48b ½b multicolored .25 .25
225E A48b 4b multicolored .75 .35
225F A48b 8b multicolored 2.50 1.40
225G A48b 16b multicolored 5.75 3.25
Nos. 225-225G (8) 10.25 6.25

Souvenir Sheet

Imperf

225H A48b 16b multicolored *11.00 11.00*

Nos. 225-225G exist imperf. Value, set $15. Nos. 225E-225H are airmail.

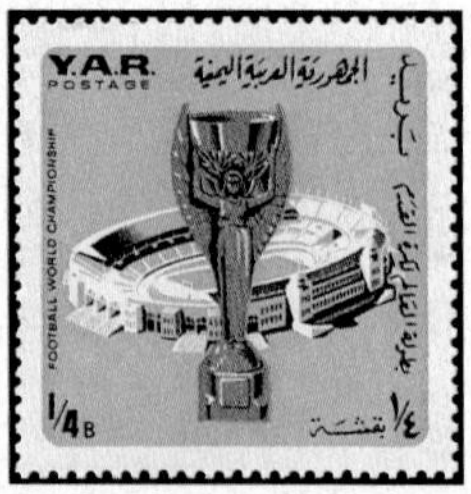

World Cup Soccer Championship, London — A51

1966, May 29 Photo. *Perf. 11*

Background Color

226	A51	¼b light green	.25	.25
226A	A51	¼b violet	.25	.25
226B	A51	¼b dull rose	.25	.25
226C	A51	⅓b green	.25	.25
226D	A51	½b orange red	.25	.25
226E	A51	4b blue	.45	.25
226F	A51	5b bistre	.60	.30
226G	A51	20b gold	1.90	1.00
		Nos. 226-226G (8)	4.20	2.80

Nos. 226-226G exist imperf. Value $8. An imperf souvenir sheet containing 1 No. 226G exists. Value $6.

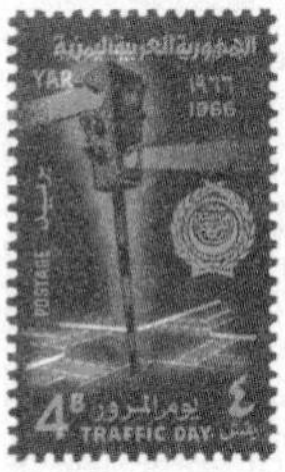

Traffic Day — A52

1966, June 30 *Perf. 11x11½*

227	A52 4b green & ver	.65	.45
228	A52 6b green & ver	.75	.50

Nos. 227-228 exist imperf. Value $3. An imperf. souvenir sheet of No. 228 exists. Value $3.50.

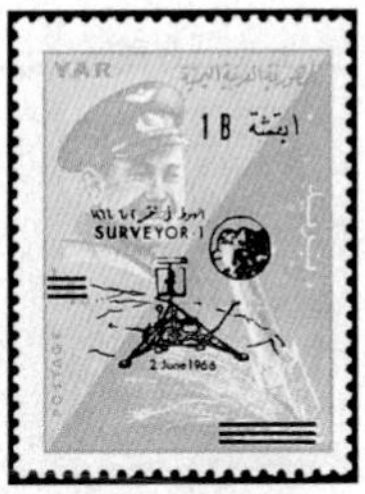

Nos. 217-217D Surcharged in Black

Surveyor I.

1966, Aug. 15 Photo. *Perf. 11½x12*

229	A48b	1b on ¼b multi	1.00	1.00
229A	A48b	¼b multicolored	1.00	1.00
229B	A48b	¼b multicolored	1.00	1.00
229C	A48b	⅓b multicolored	1.00	1.00
229D	A48b	½b multicolored	1.00	1.00
		Nos. 229-229D (5)	5.00	5.00

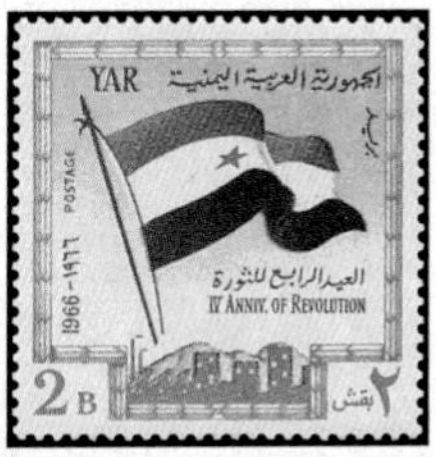

A53

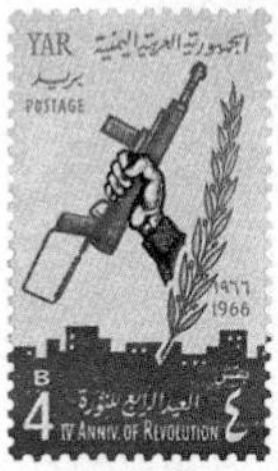

Revolution, 6th Anniv. — A53a

1966, Sept. Photo. *Perf. 11½*

230	A53	2b multicolored	2.50	2.00

Perf. 11x11¼

230A	A53a	4b multicolored	3.00	2.00
230B	A53a	6b Factory, tractor, wheat, corn	4.50	3.00
		Nos. 230-230B (3)	10.00	7.00

An imperf. souvenir sheet containing 1 each of Nos. 230A-230B exists. Value $20.

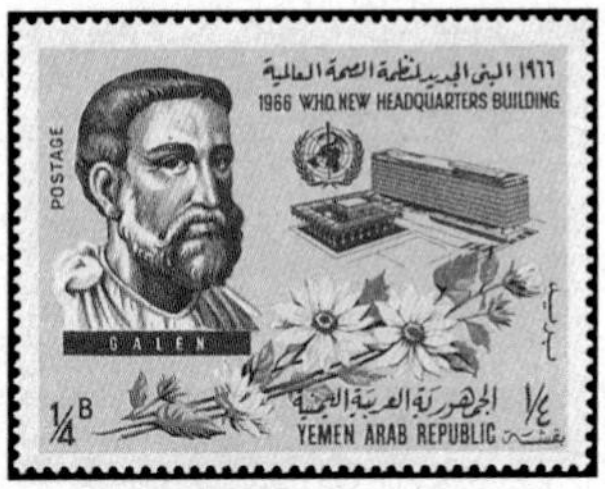

New WHO Headquarters, Geneva — A54

WHO Headquarters, flowers and: Nos. 231, 4b, Galen (129-199). Nos. 231A, 8b, Hippocrates (460-370 BC). Nos. 231B, 16b, Ibn Sina (Avicenna) (980-1037).

1966, Nov. 1 Litho. *Perf. 12½*

231	A54	¼b multicolored	.25	.25
231A	A54	¼b multicolored	.25	.25
231B	A54	¼b multicolored	.25	.25
231C	A54	4b multicolored	.50	.25
231D	A54	8b multicolored	1.00	.50
231E	A54	16b multicolored	2.00	1.00
		Nos. 231-231E (6)	4.25	2.50

Nos. 231C-231E are airmail. Nos. 231-231E exist imperf. Value $10 An imperf. souvenir sheet of 1 No. 231E exists. Value $8.

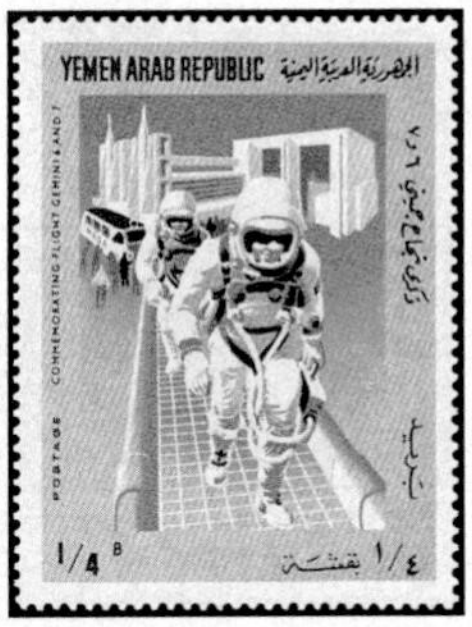

Gemini 6 and 7 Flights A55

Designs: No. 232, Astronauts. No. 232A, Lift off. No. 232B, Spacecraft, Earth. ⅓b, 2b, Spacecraft in orbit. ½b, 8b, Splash down. 12b, Rendevous.

1966, Dec. 1 Photo. *Perf. 12½*

Background Color

232	A55	¼b rose	.25	.25
232A	A55	¼b olive bistre	.25	.25
232B	A55	¼b blue	.25	.25
232C	A55	⅓b light blue	.25	.25
232D	A55	½b blue green	.25	.25
232E	A55	2b bistre	.50	.25
232F	A55	8b blue	1.00	.50
232G	A55	12b violet	1.50	.75
		Nos. 232-232G (8)	4.25	2.75

Nos. 232F-232G are airmail. Nos. 232-232G exist imperf. Value $9. An imperf. souvenir sheet containing 1 No. 232G exists. Value $6.

Nos. 232-232G Overprinted in Red

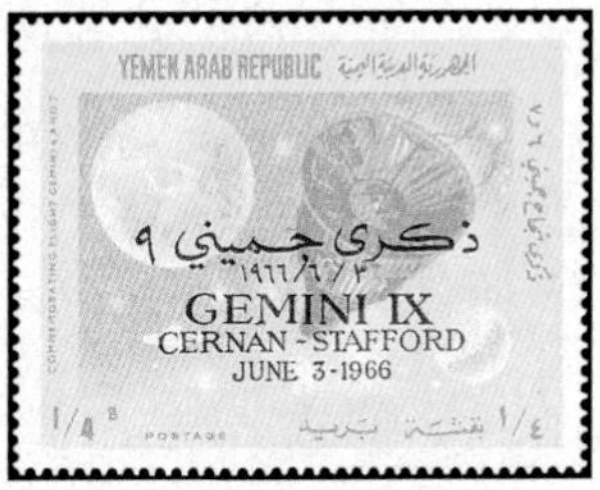

1966, Dec. 25 Photo. *Perf. 12½*

Background Color

233	A55	¼b rose	.25	.25
233A	A55	¼b olive bistre	.25	.25
233B	A55	¼b blue	.25	.25
233C	A55	⅓b light blue	.25	.25
233D	A55	½b blue green	.25	.25
233E	A55	2b bistre	.50	.25
233F	A55	8b blue	1.00	.50
233G	A55	12b violet	1.50	.75
		Nos. 233-233G (8)	4.25	2.75

Nos. 233F-233G are airmail. Nos. 233-233G exist imperf. Value $8. An imperf. souvenir sheet containing 1 No. 233G exists. Value $6.

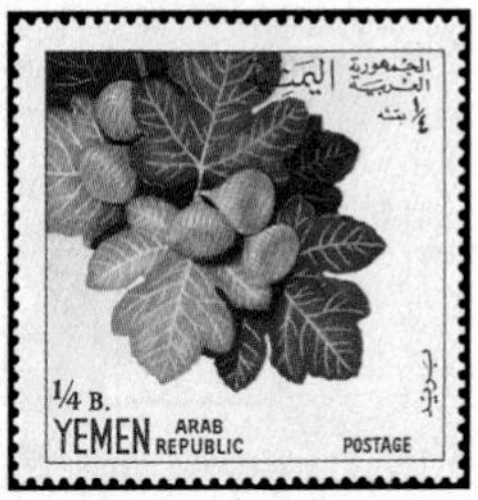

Fruit A56

1967, Feb. 10 Litho. *Perf. 12½x12*

234	A56	¼b Figs	.25	.25
234A	A56	¼b Red apples	.25	.25
234B	A56	¼b Purple grapes	.25	.25
234C	A56	⅓b Dates	.25	.25
234D	A56	½b Apricots	.25	.25
234E	A56	2b Yellow apples	.55	.30
234F	A56	4b Oranges	.70	.40
234G	A56	6b Bananas	.90	.50
234H	A56	8b Green figs	1.10	.65
234I	A56	10b Green grapes	1.35	.75
		Nos. 234-234I (10)	5.85	3.85

Exist imperf. Value, set $9. Nos. 234G-234I are airmail. See Nos. J23-J25.

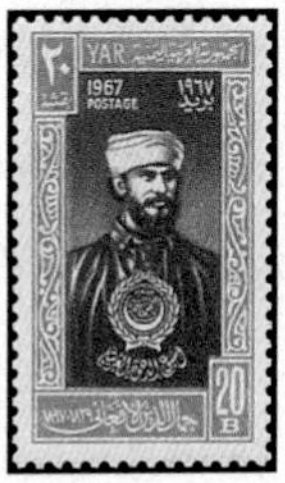

Arab League Day — A57

1967, July Photo. *Perf. 11x11½*

235	A57	4b violet & brown	.50	.25
235A	A57	6b dk violet & brown	.75	.40
235B	A57	8b violet & brown	1.25	.65
235C	A56	20b dk bl grn & brn	2.00	1.00
235D	A57	40b dk bl grn & blk	4.00	2.00
		Nos. 235-235D (5)	8.50	4.30

Gamal el-Din el-Afghani (1839-97), advocate of Arab unity.

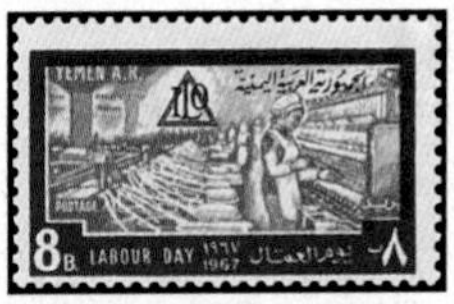

Intl. Labor Organization (ILO) — A58

1968, Aug. Photo. *Perf. 11½x11*

236	A58	2b vio & dk blue	.40	.25
236A	A58	4b car & dk bl grn	.60	.30
236B	A58	6b grn & dp red lilac	1.00	.50
236C	A58	8b vio bl & ol bis	1.50	.75
		Nos. 236-236C (4)	3.50	1.80

An imperf. souvenir sheet containing 1 10b No. 236C exists. Value $6.

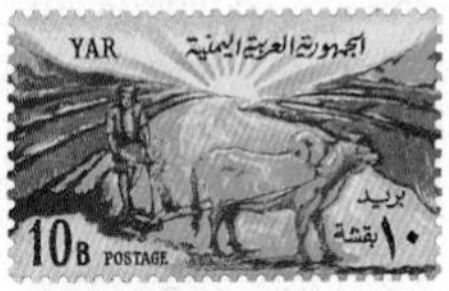

Agriculture — A59

1967, Sept. Photo. *Perf. 11½x11*

237	A59	1b multicolored	.25	.25
237A	A59	2b multicolored	.30	.25
237B	A59	4b multicolored	.35	.25
237C	A59	6b multicolored	.50	.25
237D	A59	8b multicolored	.85	.45
237E	A59	10b multicolored	1.25	.65
237F	A59	12b multicolored	1.50	.75
237G	A59	16b multicolored	1.75	.85
237H	A59	20b multicolored	2.50	1.25
237I	A59	40b multicolored	4.00	2.00
		Nos. 237-237I (10)	13.25	6.95

Nos. 237-237E Overprinted in Black

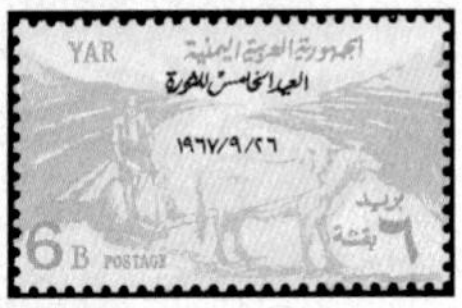

1967, Sept.

238	A59	1b multicolored	.40	.25
238A	A59	2b multicolored	.60	.30
238B	A59	4b multicolored	1.00	.50
238C	A59	6b multicolored	1.50	.75
238D	A59	8b multicolored	2.00	1.00
238E	A59	10b multicolored	2.50	1.25
		Nos. 238-238E (6)	8.00	4.05

Fifth Anniv. of the Revolution.

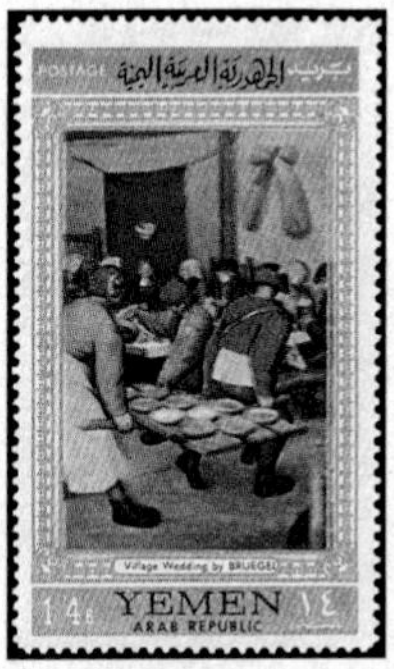

Paintings by Flemish Masters A60

Designs: ¼b, Village Wedding by Bruegel. ⅓b, The Doctor G. Zeile by Van Orley. ½b, H. Fourment and Her Children by Rubens. 3b, The King is Drinking by Jordaens. 6b, Self-Portrait by Van Dyck.

1967, Oct. Photo. *Perf. 13½*

239	A60	¼b gold & multi	.25	.25
239A	A60	⅓b gold & multi	.25	.25
239B	A60	½b gold & multi	.25	.25
239C	A60	3b gold & multi	.50	.25
239D	A60	6b gold & multi	1.10	.55
		Nos. 239-239D (5)	2.35	1.55

Nos. 239C-239D are airmail. An imperf. souvenir sheet containing 1 No. 239D exists. Nos. 239-239D exist imperf. with silver frames.

Flemish Painting Type

Paintings by Florentine Masters: ¼b, Portrait of a Young Man by Raphael. ⅓b, E. de Toledo and Her Son by A. Bronzino. ½b, Simoneta Vespucci by P. Di Cosimo. 3b, The Delphic Sibyl by Michelangelo. 6b, Spring by Botticelli.

1967, Nov. 17 Photo. *Perf. 13½*

240	A60	¼b gold & multi	.25	.25
240A	A60	⅓b gold & multi	.25	.25
240B	A60	½b gold & multi	.25	.25
240C	A60	3b gold & multi	.60	.25
240D	A60	6b gold & multi	1.35	.55
		Nos. 240-240D (5)	2.70	1.55

Nos. 240C-240D are airmail. An imperf. souvenir sheet containing 1 No. 240D exists. Nos. 240-240D exist imperf. with silver frames.

Flemish Painting Type

Paintings by Spanish Masters: ¼b, The Infanta Margarita by Velazquez. ⅓b, The Knock-Kneed Man by Ribera. ½b, The Beggar by Murillo. 3b, A Knight by El Greco. 6b, The Grape Gathering by Goya.

1967, Nov. 17 Photo. *Perf. 13½*

241	A60	¼b gold & multi	.25	.25
241A	A60	⅓b gold & multi	.25	.25
241B	A60	½b gold & multi	.25	.25
241C	A60	3b gold & multi	.60	.25
241D	A60	6b gold & multi	1.35	.55
		Nos. 241-241D (5)	2.70	1.55

Nos. 241C-241D are airmail. An imperf. souvenir sheet containing 1 No. 241D exists. Nos. 241-241D exist imperf. with silver frames.

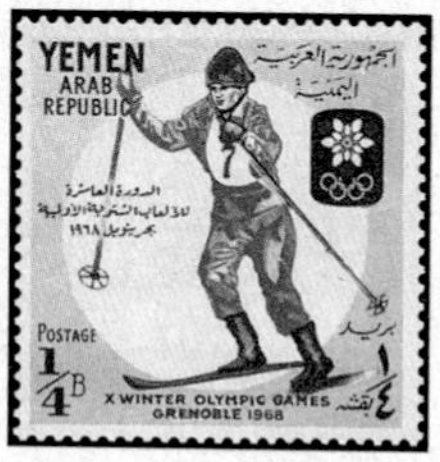

1968 Winter Olympic Games, Grenoble
A61

Sports: ¼b, Cross-country skiing. ⅓b, Figure skating. ½b, Bobsled. 3b, Ice hockey. 6b, Slalom skiing.

1967, Dec. 9 Photo. *Perf. 11½*

242	A61	¼b multicolored	.25	.25
242A	A61	⅓b multicolored	.25	.25
242B	A61	½b multicolored	.25	.25
242C	A61	3b multicolored	.60	.25
242D	A61	6b multicolored	1.35	.55
		Nos. 242-242D (5)	2.70	1.55

An imperf. souvenir sheet containing 1 No. 242D exists. Nos. 242-242D exist imperf. with different colors.

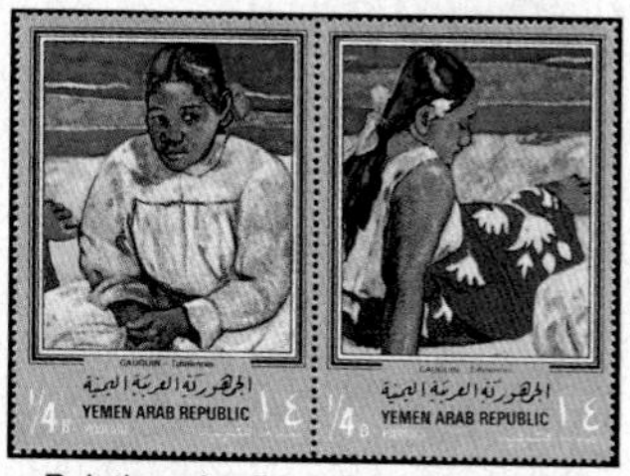

Paintings by Paul Gauguin — A62

Paintings: No. 243e, Woman in white dress. No. 243f, Woman lying on beach. No. 243g, Self-portrait. No. 243h, Nevermore. No. 243i, Girls from Pouldu. No. 243j, Girls from Bretagne. No. 243k, La Lune et la Terre. No. 243l, Angela. No. 243m, Woman. No. 243n, Two women.

1968, June Litho. *Perf. 13½*

243	A62	¼b Pair, #e.-f.	.40	.25
243A	A62	⅓b Pair, #g.-h.	.40	.25
243B	A62	½b Pair, #i.-j.	.40	.25
243C	A62	3b Pair, #k.-l.	1.00	.50
243D	A62	6b Pair, #m.-n.	2.00	1.00
		Nos. 243-243D (5)	4.20	2.25

Nos. 243C-243D are airmail. Nos. 243-243D exist imperf. with gold frames. An imperf. souvenir sheet containing 1 No. 243D exists with either silver or gold frame.

Paintings by Gaugin Type

Paintings by Van Gogh: No. 244e, Julien Tanguy. No. 244f, Joseph Roulin. No. 244g, Sunflowers. No. 244h, Church in Auvers. No. 244i, Arnand Roulin. No. 244j, La Berceuse (Madam Roulin). No. 244k, Une Arlésienne an Mouemé. No. 244l, Marguerite Gachet at piano.. No. 244m, L'Arlésienne. No. 244n, Self-portrait.

1968, June Litho. *Perf. 13½*

244	A62	¼b Pair, #e.-f.	.40	.25
244A	A62	⅓b Pair, #g.-h.	.40	.25
244B	A62	½b Pair, #i.-j.	.40	.25
244C	A62	3b Pair, #k.-l.	1.00	.50
244D	A62	6b Pair, #m.-n.	2.00	1.00
		Nos. 244-244D (5)	4.20	2.25

Nos. 244C-244D are airmail. Nos. 244-244D exist imperf. with gold frames. An imperf. souvenir sheet containing 1 No. 244D exists with either silver or gold frame.

Paintings by Gaugin Type

Paintings by Rubens: No. 245e, Head of a little girl. No. 245f, Child's head (Holy Family detail). No. 245g, Portrait of a Negro. No. 245h, Thomas, Count of Arundel. No. 245i, Self-Portrait. No. 245j, Isabelle Brandt. No. 245k, Woman in a Hat. No. 245l, Helene Fourment. No. 245m, Rubens' sons. No. 245n, The Holy Family.

1968, June Litho. *Perf. 13½*

245	A62	¼b Pair, #e.-f.	.40	.25
245A	A62	⅓b Pair, #g.-h.	.40	.25
245B	A62	½b Pair, #i.-j.	.40	.25
245C	A62	3b Pair, #k.-l.	1.00	.50
245D	A62	6b Pair, #m.-n.	2.00	1.00
		Nos. 245-245D (5)	4.20	2.25

Nos. 245C-245D are airmail. Nos. 245-245D exist imperf. with gold frames. An imperf. souvenir sheet containing 1 No. 245D exists with either silver or gold frame.

Nos. 7-23 Overprinted in Black or Red

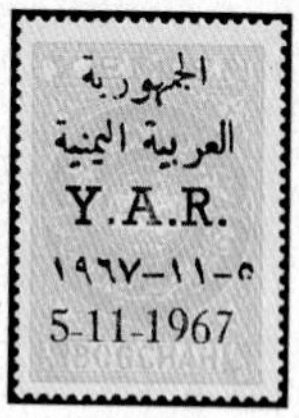

1968 Wmk. 127 *Perf. 14*

246	A3	½b on No. 7	.75
246A	A3	1b On No. 8 (R)	.75
246B	A3	1b On No. 9 (R)	.75
246C	A3	2b On No. 10 (R)	1.00
246D	A3	2b On No. 11	1.00
246E	A3	3b On No. 12	1.25
246F	A3	4b On No. 13	1.25
246G	A3	4b On No. 14	1.25
246H	A3	5b On No. 15 (R)	2.00
246I	A4	6b On No. 16 (R)	2.00
246J	A4	6b On No. 17 (R)	2.00
246K	A4	8b On No. 18	*10.00*
246L	A4	10b On No. 19	3.00
246M	A4	10b On No. 20	3.00
246N	A4	20b On No. 21	4.00
246O	A4	1i On No. 22	7.00
246P	A4	1i On No. 23	7.00
		Nos. 246-246P (17)	48.00

No. 246 exists with a red overprint. No. 246H is known with an inverted overprint.

Flemish Painting Type of 1967

Paintings of Horses: ¼b, Righteous Judge and Warrior of God by Hugo Van Eyck. ⅓b, The Virgin and the Unicorn by Zampieri (Domenichino). ½b, The Prince Baltsar Carlos by Velazquez. 3b, Roman Slave with Horses by Gericault. 6b, The Hunt by Ucello.

1968, July 10 Photo. *Perf. 13½*

247	A60	¼b gold & multi	.25	.25
247A	A60	⅓b gold & multi	.25	.25
247B	A60	½b gold & multi	.25	.25
247C	A60	3b gold & multi	.75	.35
247D	A60	6b gold & multi	1.25	.65
		Nos. 247-247D (5)	2.75	1.75

Nos. 247C-247D are airmail. An imperf. souvenir sheet containing 1 No. 247D exists. Nos. 247-247D exist imperf. with silver frames.

Flemish Painting Type of 1967

Paintings by Raphael: ¼b, La Velata. ⅓b, Angelo Doni. ½b, Plato and Aristotle. 3b, A Man. 6b, A Young Woman.

1968, July 10 Photo. *Perf. 13½*

248	A60	¼b gold & multi	.25	.25
248A	A60	⅓b gold & multi	.25	.25
248B	A60	½b gold & multi	.25	.25
248C	A60	3b gold & multi	.50	.25
248D	A60	6b gold & multi	1.10	.55
e.		Souvenir sheet of 1	4.00	
		Nos. 248-248D (5)	2.35	1.55

Nos. 248C-248D are airmail. An imperf. souvenir sheet of No. 248De exists. Nos. 248-248D exist imperf. with silver frames.

Flemish Painting Type of 1967

Paintings by Rembrandt: ¼b, Jan Six. ⅓b, Saskia. ½b, Mars. 3b, H. Stoffels. 6b, Self-portrait.

1968, July 10 Photo. *Perf. 13½*

249	A60	¼b gold & multi	.25	.25
249A	A60	⅓b gold & multi	.25	.25
249B	A60	½b gold & multi	.25	.25
249C	A60	3b gold & multi	.50	.25
249D	A60	6b gold & multi	1.10	.55
e.		Souvenir sheet of 1	4.00	
		Nos. 249-249D (5)	2.35	1.55

Nos. 249C-249D are airmail. An imperf. souvenir sheet of No. 249De exists. Nos. 249-249D exist imperf. with silver frames.

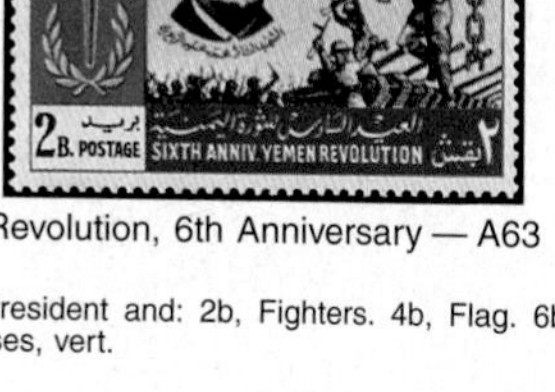

Revolution, 6th Anniversary — A63

President and: 2b, Fighters. 4b, Flag. 6b, Roses, vert.

1968, July Litho. *Perf. 12¾*

250	A63	2b multicolored	.40	.25
250A	A63	4b multicolored	.60	.30
250B	A63	6b multicolored	1.00	.50
		Nos. 250-250B (3)	2.00	1.05

Nos. 250-250B exist imperf. Value $2. An imperf souvenir sheet of No. 250B exists. Value $3.50.

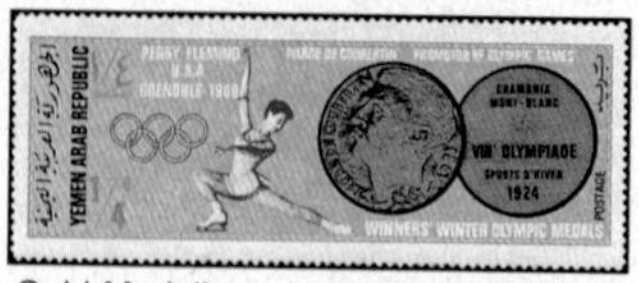

Gold Medalists, 1968 Winter Olympic Games — A64

Various Olympic Gold Medals and: ¼b, Peggy Fleming, USA. ⅓b, Franco Nones, Italy. ½b, Jiri Raska, Czechosovakia. 2b, Hockey Team, USSR. 3b, Jean Claude Killy, France. 4b, Erhard Keller, Germany.

1968, Sept. 10 Litho. *Perf. 13½*

251	A64	¼b multicolored	.25	.25
251A	A64	⅓b multicolored	.25	.25
251B	A64	½b multicolored	.25	.25
251C	A64	2b multicolored	.35	.25
251D	A64	3b multicolored	.45	.25
251E	A64	4b multicolored	.60	.30
		Nos. 251-251E (6)	2.15	1.55

Nos. 251D-251E are airmail. No. 251E exists in perf. and imperf. souvenir sheets of one. Nos. 251-251E exist imperf. with light blue borders.

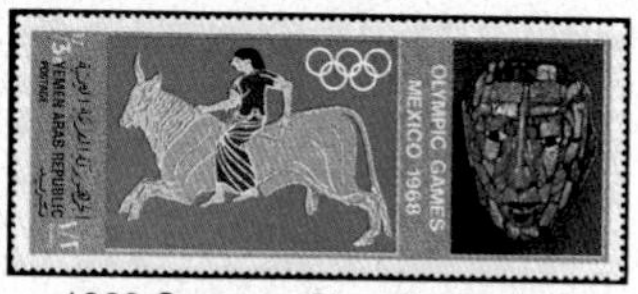

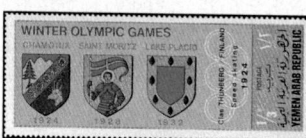

1968 Summer Olympic Games, Mexico City — A65

Ancient Greek art and artifacts of Mexico: ¼b, Greek man, sculpture. ⅓b, Woman on bull, jade mask. ½b, Three people, jaguar. 2b, Two warriors, large carving. 3b, Chariot, mask. 4b, Rider and 2 people, sculpture. No. 252F, Three warriors, Central University City Campus site.

1968, Sept. 30 Litho. *Perf. 13½*

252	A65	¼b multicolored	.25	.25
252A	A65	⅓b multicolored	.25	.25
252B	A65	½b multicolored	.25	.25
252C	A65	2b multicolored	.35	.25
252D	A65	3b multicolored	.45	.25
252E	A65	4b multicolored	.60	.30
		Nos. 251-251E (6)	2.15	1.55

Souvenir Sheet

252F	A65	4b multicolored	3.00	1.50

Nos. 252D-252F are airmail. No. 252F contains one 88x35mm stamp. Nos. 252-252F exist imperf. with silver frames.

Olympic Medals Type of 1968

Olympic Gold Medals from: ¼b, 1896, 1908, 1912. ⅓b, 1920, 1924. ½b, 1928, 1932. 2b, 1936, 1948, 1952. 3b, 1956, 1960, 1964. 4b, 1968, 1972.

1968, Oct. 18 Litho. *Perf. 13½*

253	A64	¼b multicolored	.25	.25
253A	A64	⅓b multicolored	.25	.25
253B	A64	½b multicolored	.25	.25
253C	A64	2b multicolored	.35	.25
253D	A64	3b multicolored	.45	.25
253E	A64	4b multicolored	.60	.30
		Nos. 253-253E (6)	2.15	1.55

Nos. 253D-253E are airmail. No. 253E exists in perf. and imperf. souvenir sheets of one. Nos. 253-253E exist imperf. with light blue borders.

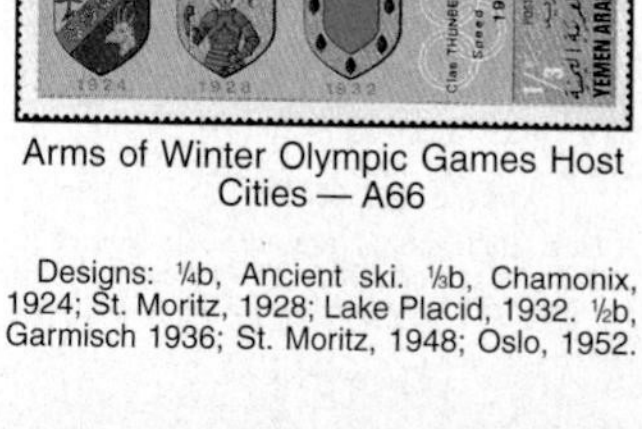

Arms of Winter Olympic Games Host Cities — A66

Designs: ¼b, Ancient ski. ⅓b, Chamonix, 1924; St. Moritz, 1928; Lake Placid, 1932. ½b, Garmisch 1936; St. Moritz, 1948; Oslo, 1952. 2b, Cortina, 1956; Squaw Valley, 1960; Innsbruck, 1964. 3b, Grenoble, 1968. 4b,Sapporo, 1972.

1968, Nov. 23 Litho. *Perf. 13½*

254	A66	¼b multicolored	.25	.25
254A	A66	⅓b multicolored	.25	.25
254B	A66	½b multicolored	.25	.25
254C	A66	2b multicolored	.35	.25
254D	A66	3b multicolored	.45	.25
254E	A66	4b multicolored	.60	.30
		Nos. 254-254E (6)	2.15	1.55

Nos. 254D-254E are airmail. A perf. and imperf. souvenir sheet containing one each of Nos. 254D-254E exist. Nos. 254-254E exist perf. and imperf. with light blue borders.

Arms of Olympic Host Cities Type

Arms of Summer Olympic Games Host Cities: ¼b, Athens, 1896; London, 1908; Stockholm, 1912. ⅓b, Antwerp, 1920; Paris, 1924. ½b, Amsterdam, 1928; Los Angeles, 1932; Berlin, 1936. 2b, London, 1948; Helsinki, 1952. 3b, Melbourne, 1956; Rome, 1960; Tokyo, 1964. 4b, Mexico City, 1968; Munich, 1972.

1968, Dec. 22 Litho. *Perf. 13½*

255	A66	¼b multicolored	.25	.25
255A	A66	⅓b multicolored	.25	.25
255B	A66	½b multicolored	.25	.25
255C	A66	2b multicolored	.35	.25
255D	A66	3b multicolored	.45	.25
255E	A66	4b multicolored	.60	.30
		Nos. 255-255E (6)	2.15	1.55

Nos. 255D-255E are airmail. A perf. and imperf. souvenir sheet containing one No. 255E exists. Nos. 255-255E exist perf. and imperf. with light blue borders.

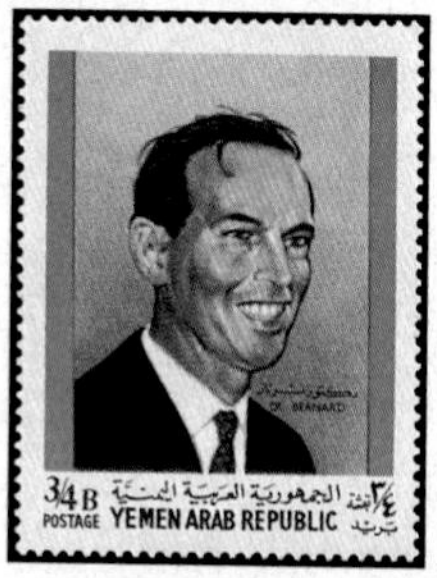

Intl. Human Rights Figures
A67

Designs: ¼b, 10b, Dr. Christian Bernhard with patient, horiz. ½b, 2b, Dag Hammarskjold. ¾b, Dr. Bernhard. 1b, 4b, Rev. Martin Luther King. 6b, 14b, Robert F. and John F. Kennedy, horiz. 8b, Dr. Bernhard with heart, horiz. 12b, 16b, Dr. King and Abraham Lincoln, horiz.

1968 Litho. *Perf. 12½*

256	A67	¼b multicolored	.25	.25
256A	A67	½b multicolored	.25	.25
256B	A67	¾b multicolored	.35	.25
256C	A67	1b multicolored	.35	.25
256D	A67	2b multicolored	.40	.25
256E	A67	4b multicolored	.50	.25
256F	A67	6b multicolored	.65	.35
256G	A67	8b multicolored	.75	.35
256H	A67	10b multicolored	1.00	.50
256I	A67	12b multicolored	1.10	.55
256J	A67	14b multicolored	1.25	.65
256K	A67	16b multicolored	1.25	.65
		Nos. 256-256K (12)	8.10	4.55

Nos. 256-256K exist imperf. Three imperf. souvenir sheets exist; a 10b with Robert and John Kennedy, a 16b with King and LIncoln and a 20b with Dr. Bernhard.

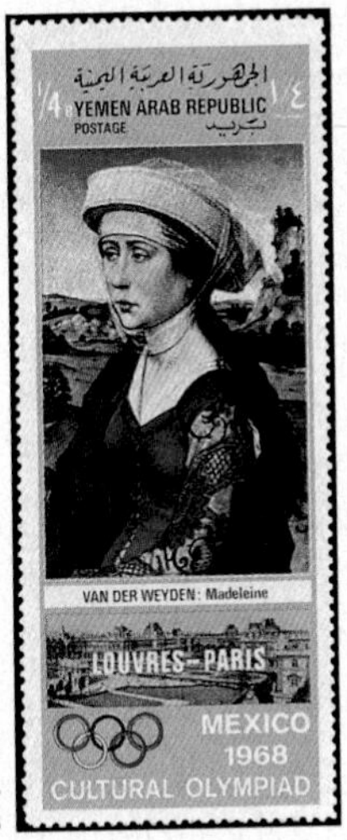

Cultural Olympiad, Mexico City — A68

Paintings in the Louvre, Paris: ¼b, Madeleine by Van Der Weyden. ⅓b, The Gypsy by Frans Hals. ½b, Balthasar Castiglionne by Raphael. 2b, The Lacemaker by Vermeer. 3b, Women and Child by Da Vinci. 4b, Madonna and Child by Botticelli. No. 257F, Mona Lisa by Da Vinci.

1969, Feb. 19 Litho. *Perf. 13½*

257	A68	¼b silver & multi	.25	.25
257A	A68	⅓b silver & multi	.25	.25
257B	A68	½b silver & multi	.25	.25
257C	A68	2b silver & multi	.35	.25
257D	A68	3b silver & multi	.45	.25
257E	A68	4b silver & multi	.60	.30
		Nos. 257-257E (6)	2.15	1.55

Souvenir Sheet

257F	A68	4b gold & multi	*3.50*	*3.50*

Nos. 257D-257F are airmail. Nos. 257-257E exist with gold frames. No. 257F has an orange yellow background and exists imperf., as well as both perf and imperf with a blue green background. No. 257C is iinscribed The Embroiderer. No. 257E is inscribed Woman and Child.

Cultural Olympiad Type

Paintings in the Uffizi Gallery, Florence: ¼b, Battista Sforza by Piero Della Francesca. ⅓b, Francesco delle Opere by Perugino. ½b, Francesco Maria della Rovere by Raphael. 2b, Isabel Brandt by Rubens. 3b, Don Garcia de Médicis by Bronzino. 4b, The Birth of Venus (detail) by Botticelli No. 257F, Alegoria della Primavera by Botticelli.

1969, Mar. 29 Litho. *Perf. 13½*

258	A68	¼b gold & multi	.25	.25
258A	A68	⅓b gold & multi	.25	.25
258B	A68	½b gold & multi	.25	.25
258C	A68	2b gold & multi	.35	.25
258D	A68	3b gold & multi	.45	.25
258E	A68	4b gold & multi	.60	.30
		Nos. 258-258E (6)	2.15	1.55

Souvenir Sheet

258F	A68	4b gold & multi	*3.50*	*3.50*

Nos. 258D-258F are airmail. Nos. 258-258E exist with gold frames. No. 258F has a red background and exists imperf, as well as perf and imperf with a red orange frame.

Cultural Olympiad Type

Paintings in the Prado, Madrid: ¼b, Charles the First, of England by Van Dyck. ⅓b, The Story of Nastaglio by Botticelli. ½b, Maria Ruthwen by Van Dyck. 2b, Portrait of a Man by Dürer. 3b, Young Girl by Raphael. 4b, Selfportrait by Dürer. No. 257F, A Maja Vestida by Goya.

1969, May 2 Litho. *Perf. 13½*

259	A68	¼b silver & multi	.25	.25
259A	A68	⅓b silver & multi	.25	.25
259B	A68	½b silver & multi	.25	.25
259C	A68	2b silver & multi	.35	.25
259D	A68	3b silver & multi	.45	.25
259E	A68	4b silver & multi	.60	.30
		Nos. 259-259E (6)	2.15	1.55

Souvenir Sheet

259F	A68	4b gold & multi	*3.50*	*3.50*

Nos. 259D-259F are airmail. Nos. 259-259E exist with bronze frames. No. 258F exists imperf.

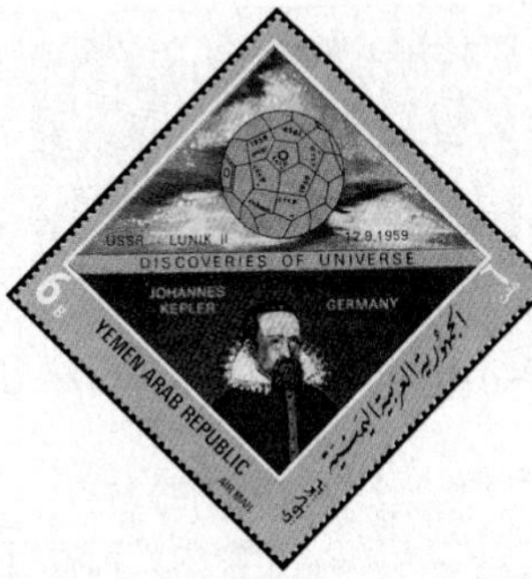

Discoveries of the Universe — A69

Spacecraft and Astronomers: No. 260, Vanguard, Ptolemy. No. 260A, Sputknik III, Copernicus. No. 260B, Lunik, Michelangelo. No. 260C, Explorer VI, Tycho Brahe. 3b, Lunik III, Galileo. 6b, Lunik II, Kepler. 10b, Explorer VII, Newton. 14b, Apollo 8.

1969, May 26 Litho. *Perf. 13½*

260	A69	¼b silver & multi	.25	.25
260A	A69	¼b silver & multi	.25	.25
260B	A69	⅓b silver & multi	.25	.25
260C	A69	⅓b silver & multi	.25	.25
260D	A69	3b silver & multi	.75	.35
260E	A69	6b silver & multi	1.25	.65
260F	A69	10b silver & multi	2.00	1.00
		Nos. 260-260F (7)	5.00	3.00

Souvenir Sheet

260G	A69	14b multicolored	6.00	3.00

Nos. 260E-260G are airmail. Nos. 260-260F exist imperf. with lilac-silver frames. A 14b imperf. souvenir sheet with Soyuz 4-5 and Apollo 8 exists.

Discoveries of the Universe Type

Old and New Space Travel: No. 261, Wan Pou, Pioneer IV, Pioneer V. No. 261A, Lucion di Samosa, Sputnik V, Explorer 10, Venus I. No. 261B, Cyrano de Bergerac, Mariner II, Mariner III. No. 261C, Jules Verne, Mariner IV. 2b, Nicolar Kibaltchich, Zond II. 4b, Rocket Lift-off, Venus II, Venus III, Luna X. 22b, Lunar lander, Venus IV. No. 261G, Apollo 9.

1969, July 3 Litho. *Perf. 13½*

261	A69	¼b silver & multi	.25	.25
261A	A69	¼b silver & multi	.25	.25
261B	A69	⅓b silver & multi	.25	.25
261C	A69	⅓b silver & multi	.25	.25
261D	A69	2b silver & multi	.50	.35
261E	A69	4b silver & multi	.75	.35
261F	A69	22b silver & multi	2.25	1.10
		Nos. 261-261F (7)	4.50	2.80

Souvenir Sheet

261G	A69	6b multicolored	*4.00*	*2.00*

Nos. 261D-261G are airmail. Nos. 261-261F exist imperf. with gold frames. A 6b imperf. souvenir sheet with Apollo 9 and a space station exists.

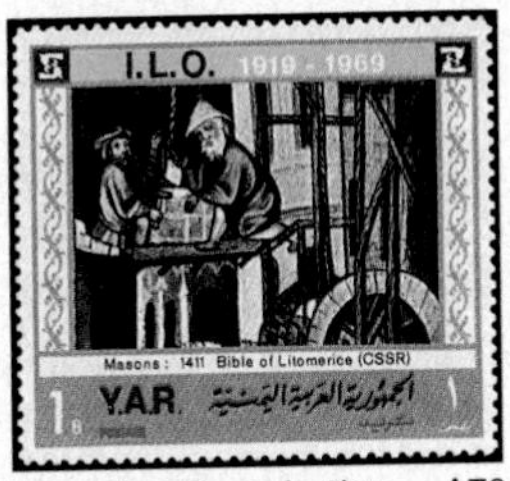

Intl. Labor Organization — A70

1969, Aug. 4 Litho. *Perf. 13½*

262	A70	1b Stonemason	.25	.25
262A	A70	2b Blacksmith	.35	.25
262B	A70	3b Teacher	.50	.25
262C	A70	4b Printer	.60	.30
262D	A70	6b Polisher	.75	.35
262E	A70	8b Foundry worker	1.00	.50
262F	A70	10b Farrier	1.25	.60
		Nos. 262-262F (7)	4.70	2.50

Nos. 262D-262F are airmail. Nos. 262-262F exist imperf.

Discoveries of the Universe Type

Spacecraft: No. 263, Mercury Atlas 3, Vostok I, Vostok II, Mercury Atlas 6. No. 263A, Mercury Atlas 8, Vostok III & IV, Mercury Atlas 9, Vostok VI. No. 263B, Voskhod II, Voskhod I, Gemini 3, Gemini 4. No. 263C, Gemini 5-9. 3b, Apollo 8-9. 6b, Soyuz III, Soyuz I, Apollo 7-8. 10b, Gemini 10-12, Apollo 7. No. 263G, Vostok I, Mercury.

1969, Aug. 25 Litho. *Perf. 13½*

263	A69	¼b multicolored	.25	.25
263A	A69	¼b multicolored	.25	.25
263B	A69	⅓b multicolored	.25	.25
263C	A69	⅓b multicolored	.25	.25
263D	A69	3b multicolored	.50	.35
263E	A69	6b multicolored	1.00	.50
263F	A69	10b multicolored	1.50	.75
		Nos. 263-263F (7)	4.00	2.60

Souvenir Sheet

263G	A69	6b multicolored	*6.00*	*3.00*

Nos. 263D-263G are airmail. No. 263G contains one 82x43mm stamp. Nos. 263-263F exist imperf. with light yellow green frames. A 6b imperf. souvenir sheet with Apollo 10 exists.

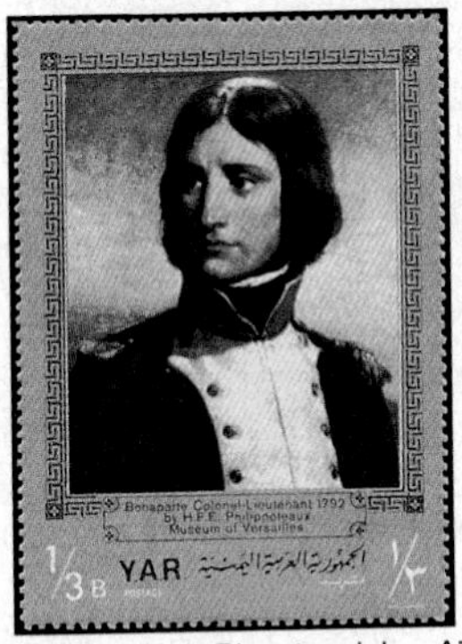

Napoleon, Birth Bicentennial — A71

Napoleon: ¼b, As artillery lieutenant. ⅓b, As lieutenant colonel, 1792. ½b, As consul. ¾b, On his way to Augsburg. 4b, Crossing over the St. Bernard. 8b, In 1814. 10b, At the height of his career. No. 264G, At his coronation, 1804.

1969, Sept. 16 Litho. *Perf. 13½*

264	A71	¼b silver & multi	.35	.25
264A	A71	⅓b silver & multi	.35	.25
264B	A71	b silver & multi	.40	.25
264C	A71	¾b silver & multi	.40	.25
264D	A71	4b silver & multi	1.50	.75
264E	A71	8b silver & multi	2.00	1.00
264F	A71	10b silver & multi	2.50	1.25
		Nos. 264-264F (7)	7.50	4.00

Souvenir Sheet

264G	A71	4b multicolored	*6.00*	2.00

Nos. 264D-264G are airmail. No. 264G contains one 46x69mm stamp. An imperf. 4b souvenir sheet showing a Napoleon bicentennial medal exists. Nos. 264-264F exist imperf. with lilac-silver frames.

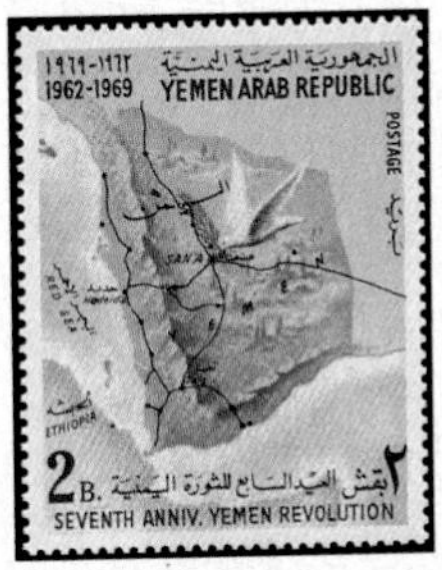

Revolution, 7th Anniv. — A71a

Designs: 2b, Map of Yemen, vert. 4b, Parliament. 6b, Worker, soldier, farmer and student.

1969, Sept. 26 *Perf. 13*

264H	A71a	2b multicolored	.30	.30
264I	A71a	4b multicolored	.60	.60
264J	A71a	6b multicolored	1.25	1.25
		Nos. 264H-264J (3)	2.15	2.15

Nos. 264H-264J exist imperf. Nos. 264J also exists in an imperf. souvenir sheet.

Discoveries of the Universe Type

Lunar Research: No. 265, Soyuz IV & V, Apollo 10. No. 265A, Apollo 11. No. 265B, Planned Lunar trips. No. 265C, Lunar surface vehicles. 2b, Lunar vehicles, diff. 4b, Moon base and vehicles. 22b, Soviet lunar project, Apollo 11. No. 265G, Apollo 11.

1969, Oct. 10 Litho. *Perf. 13½*

265	A69	¼b multicolored	.25	.25
265A	A69	¼b multicolored	.25	.25
265B	A69	⅓b multicolored	.25	.25
265C	A69	⅓b multicolored	.25	.25
263D	A69	2b multicolored	.40	.25
265E	A69	4b multicolored	.60	.30
265F	A69	22b multicolored	2.00	1.00
		Nos. 265-265F (7)	4.00	2.55

Souvenir Sheet

265G	A69	14b multicolored	*5.00*	2.00

Nos. 265D-265G are airmail. No. 263G contains one 63x49mm stamp. Nos. 265-265F exist imperf. with light orange frames. A 14b imperf. souvenir sheet with Apollo 11 plaque and astronauts exists.

Cultural Olympiad Type

Paintings in the National Gallery, Washington, DC: ¼b, David by Del Castagno. ⅓b, Elena Grimaldi by Van Dyck. ½b, Girl with her Dueña by Murillo. 2b, Agostina by Corot. 3b, Ginevra Bentivoglio by Ercole Roberti. 4b, Balthasar Coymans by Frans Hals. No. 266F, Ginevra de Benci by Da Vinci.

1969, Nov. Litho. *Perf. 13½*

266	A68	¼b lilac silver & multi	.25	.25
266A	A68	⅓b lilac silver & multi	.25	.25
266B	A68	½b lilac silver & multi	.25	.25
266C	A68	2b lilac silver & multi	.35	.25
266D	A68	3b lilac silver & multi	.45	.25
266E	A68	4b lilac silver & multi	.60	.30
		Nos. 266-266E (6)	2.15	1.55

Souvenir Sheet

266F	A68	4b gold & multi	*4.00*	*2.00*

Nos. 266D-266F are airmail. Nos. 266-266E exist with gold frames. No. 266F contains one 36x69mm stamp. No. 266F exists with a red background instead of blue green and also exists imperf.

Cultural Olympiad Type

Paintings in the National Gallery, London: ¼b, Portrait of a Woman by Van Der Weyden. ⅓b, Portrait of a Young Man by Antonello da Messina. ½b, Portrait of a Young Girl by Mabuse. 2b, The Crab Saleswoman by Hogarth. 3b, Baron Schwiter by Delacroix. 4b, Portrait of an Old Woman by Cézanne. No. 266F, Morning Promenade by Gainsborough.

1969, Dec. Litho. *Perf. 13½*

267	A68	¼b bluish sil & multi	.25	.25
267A	A68	⅓b bluish sil & multi	.25	.25
267B	A68	½b bluish sil & multi	.25	.25
267C	A68	2b bluish sil & multi	.35	.25
267D	A68	3b bluish sil & multi	.45	.25
267E	A68	4b bluish sil & multi	.60	.30
		Nos. 267-267E (6)	2.15	1.55

Souvenir Sheet

267F	A68	4b gold & multi	*4.00*	*2.00*

Nos. 267D-267F are airmail. Nos. 267-267E exist with bronze frames. No. 267F contains one 35x74mm stamp. No. 267F exists with an orange yellow background instead of greenish blue and also exists imperf.

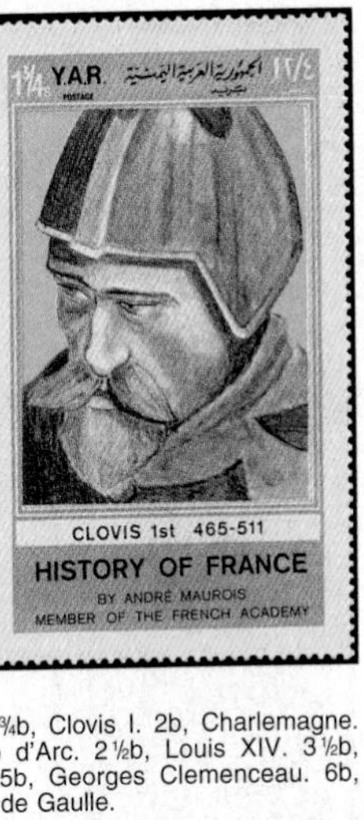

Famous French Leaders A72

Designs: 1¾b, Clovis I. 2b, Charlemagne. 2¼b, Jeanne d'Arc. 2½b, Louis XIV. 3½b, Napoleon I. 5b, Georges Clemenceau. 6b, 10b, Charles de Gaulle.

1969 Litho. *Perf. 13½*

268	A72	1¾b gold & multi	.50	.25
268A	A72	2b gold & multi	.50	.25
268B	A72	2¼b gold & multi	.50	.25
268C	A72	2½b gold & multi	.50	.25
268D	A74	3½b gold & multi	.60	.30
268E	A72	5b gold & multi	.75	.35
268F	A72	6b gold & multi	.90	.45
		Nos. 268-268F (7)	4.25	2.10

Souvenir Sheet

268G	A72	10b multicolored	*6.00*	*2.00*

Nos. 268-268F exist imperf. with silver frames. Value $7.50. Nos. 268D-268G are airmail. No. 268G contains one 50x83mm stamp. A 10b imperf. souvenir sheet exists depicting

DeGaulle, Jeanne d'Arc and Napoleon. Value $12.

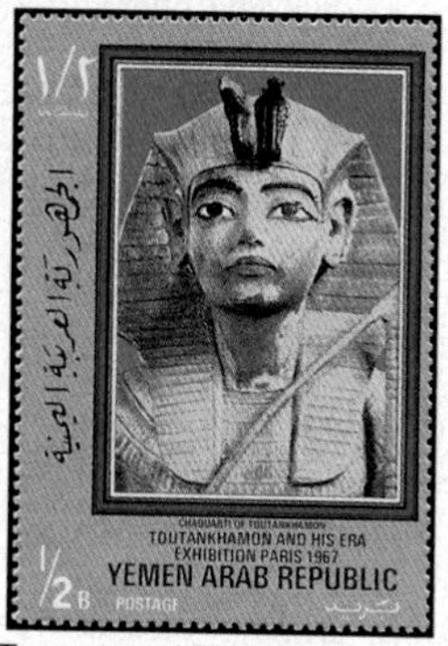

Art Treasures of Tutankhamen — A73

Tutankhamun: ¼b, Stone bust. ⅓b, Alabaster bust. ½b, Painted bust. 2b, Painted statue. 3b, Gold Mask. 4b, Painted head.

1970, May 20 Litho. *Perf. 13½*

269 A73 ¼b lilac silver & multi .25 .25
269A A73 ⅓b lilac silver & multi .25 .25
269B A73 ½b lilac silver & multi .25 .25
269C A73 2b lilac silver & multi .60 .30
269D A73 3b lilac silver & multi .75 .35
269E A73 4b lilac silver & multi .90 .45
Nos. 269-269E (6) 3.00 1.85

Nos. 269D-269E are airmail. Perf. and imperf. souvenir sheets containing 1 No. 269E exist. These sheets were also overprinted in Red or Green for Roma '70. Nos. 269-269E exist imperf with silver frames.

Art Treasures Type

Treasures of Siam: ¼b, Bronze Buddha head. ⅓b, Stone Buddha head. ½b, Statue from Angkor. 2b, Spirit of Echiffre. 3b, King Pisei. 4b, Buddha on Naga.

1970 Litho. *Perf. 13½*

270 A73 ¼b lilac silver & multi .25 .25
270A A73 ⅓b lilac silver & multi .25 .25
270B A73 ½b lilac silver & multi .25 .25
270C A73 2b lilac silver & multi .60 .30
270D A73 3b lilac silver & multi .75 .35
270E A73 4b lilac silver & multi .90 .45
Nos. 270-270E (6) 3.00 1.85

Nos. 270D-270E are airmail. Perf. and imperf. souvenir sheets containing 1 No. 270E exist. Nos. 270-270E exist imperf with silver frames.

Art Treasures Type

Treasures of Japan: Various paintings.

1970 Litho. *Perf. 13½*

271 A73 ¼b lilac silver & multi .25 .25
271A A73 ⅓b lilac silver & multi .25 .25
271B A73 ½b lilac silver & multi .25 .25
271C A73 2b lilac silver & multi .60 .30
271D A73 3b lilac silver & multi .75 .35
271E A73 4b lilac silver & multi .90 .45
f. Souvenir sheet of 1, silver & multi *5.00 2.00*
Nos. 271-271E (6) 3.00 1.85

Nos. 271D-271E, 271Ef are airmail. No. 271Ef has red Expo '70 imprint in the sheet margin. Nos. 271-271E exist imperf with silver frames. No. 271Ef exists imperf.

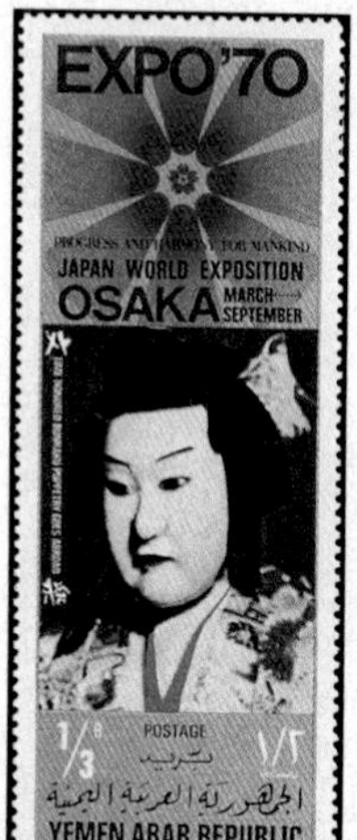

Expo '70, Osaka, Japan — A74

Various traditional Japanese puppets.

1970, Mar. 15 Litho. *Perf. 13½*

272 A74 ¼b gold & multi .35 .25
272A A74 ⅓b gold & multi .35 .25
272B A74 ½b gold & multi .35 .25
272C A74 2b gold & multi .70 .35
272D A74 3b gold & multi .90 .45
272E A74 4b gold & multi 1.10 .55
Nos. 272-272E (6) 3.75 2.10

Nos. 272D-272E are airmail. Nos. 272-272E exist with silver frames, and imperf. with gold frames. Perf. and imperf. souvenir sheets containing 1 No. 272E exist.

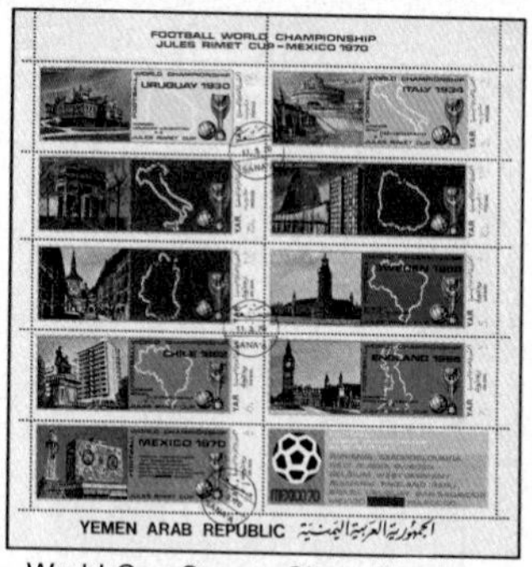

World Cup Soccer Championships, Mexico — A75

1970, Apr. 4 Litho. *Perf. 13½*

273 A75 Sheet of 9 + label 5.50 2.75
c. 1¾b Uruguay 1930 .50 .25
d. 2b Italy 1934 .50 .25
e. 2¼b France 1938 .50 .25
f. 2½b Brazil 1950 .50 .25
g. 3½b Switzerland 1954 .60 .30
h. 5b Sweden 1968 .60 .30
i. 6b Chile 1962 .60 .30
j. 7b England 1966 .70 .35
k. 8b Mexico 1970 .80 .40

Souvenir Sheets

273A A75 4b Pele *5.00*
273B A75 4b Beckenbauer *7.50*

Nos. 273g-273k, 273A-273B are airmail. No. 273B exists imperf.

No. 273k and the adjacent label exist with the name ISRAEL showing and also with the name covered with a black overprint.

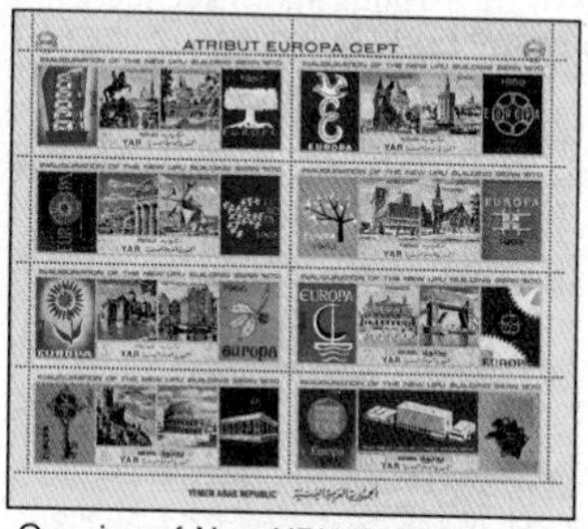

Opening of New UPU Headquarters, Bern, Switzerland — A76

Country Views and Europa Stamp Designs: 1½b, Austria, Luxembourg, 1956-57 designs. 1¾b, Belgium, Spain, 1958-59 designs. 2¼b, Greece, Portugal, 1960-61 designs. 2½b, Norway, Denmark, 1962-63 designs. 5b, Switzerland, Netherlands, 1964-65 designs. 7b, France, England, 1965-66 Designs. 8b, Germany, Italy, 1968-69 designs. 10b, New UPU Headquarters, 1970 design, UPU emblem.

1970, May 5 Litho. *Perf. 13½*

274 A76 Sheet of 8 4.50 2.25
b. 1½b multicolored .40 .25
c. 1¾b multicolored .40 .25
d. 2¼b multicolored .40 .25
e. 2½b multicolored .40 .25
f. 5b multicolored .50 .30
g. 7b multicolored .65 .30
h. 8b multicolored .75 .35
i. 10b multicolored 1.00 .50

Souvenir Sheet

274A A76 10b Liechtenstein 356 *5.00* 2.00

Nos. 274g-274i, 274A are airmail. No. 274 exists imperf with light orange borders. No. 274A contains one 50x50mm stamp. An imperf. 10b souvenir sheet showing Luxembourg 320 exists.

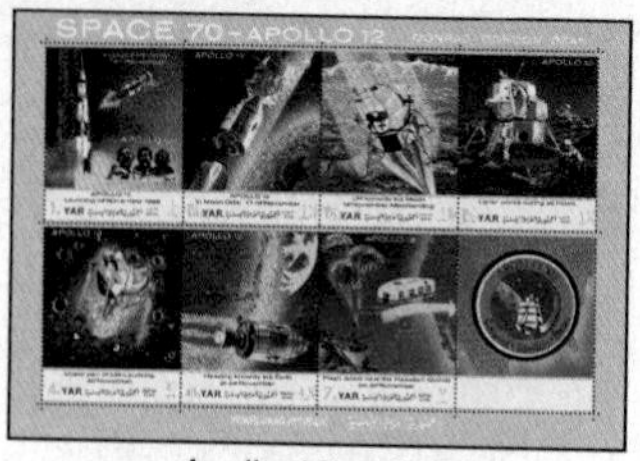

Apollo 12 — A77

Stages of Apollo 12 Mission: 1b, Lift-off. 1¼b, In Lunar orbit. 1⅓b, LM approaches landing site. 1½b, 32 hours on Lunar surface. 4b, Lift-off from the Moon. 4½b, Return to Earth. 7b, Splash down. No. 275A, Astronauts on Lunar surface.

1970, May 11 Litho. *Perf. 13½*

275 A77 Sheet of 7 + label 4.50 2.25
b. 1b multicolored .40 .25
c. 1¼b multicolored .40 .25
d. 1⅓b multicolored .40 .25
e. 1½b multicolored .40 .25
f. 4b multicolored .65 .30
g. 4½b multicolored .75 .30
h. 7b multicolored 1.25 .65

Souvenir Sheet

275A A77 4b multicolored *5.00*

Nos. 274f-275h, 275A are airmail. No. 275 exists imperf with yellow and gold borders. No. 275A contains one 72x56mm stamp. An imperf 4b souvenir sheet exists with the lunar scene reflected in astronaut's helmet.

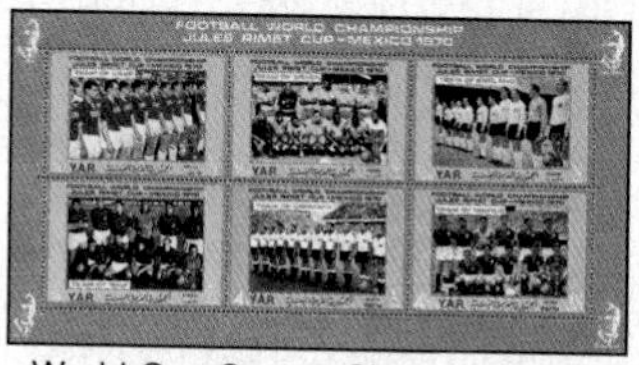

World Cup Soccer Championships, Mexico — A78

1970, May 20 Litho. *Perf. 13½*

276 A78 Sheet of 6 4.00 2.00
c. ¼b Soviet team .50 .25
d. ⅓b Brazilian team .50 .25
e. ½b English team .50 .25
f. ¾b Italian team .50 .25
g. 4b German team .60 .30
h. 4½b Mexican team .60 .30

Souvenir Sheets

276A A78 6b Stadium *5.00*
276B A78 6b Two players *7.50*

Nos. 276g-276h, 276A-276B are airmail. Nos. 276A-276B each contain a 57x58mm stamp, and exist imperf. No. 276 exists imperf. with silver borders.

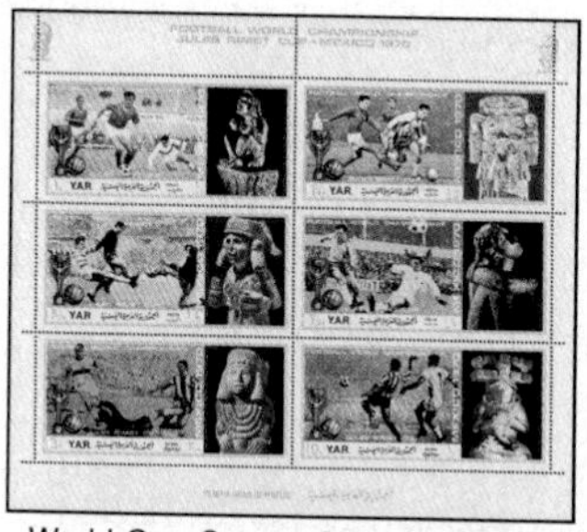

World Cup Soccer Championships, Mexico — A79a

No. 277: Various soccer players, pre-Columbian sculptures. Nos. 277A-277B, Players, World Cup trophy, soccer ball.

1970, May 31 Litho. *Perf. 13½*

277 A79a Sheet of 6 4.00 2.00
c. 1b olive grn & multi .50 .25
d. 1¼b blue & multi .50 .25
e. 1½b red lil & multi .50 .25
f. 1½b grn & multi .50 .25
g. 3b pink & multi .60 .30
h. 10b org & multi .60 .30

Souvenir Sheets

277A A79a 10b grn & multi *6.00*
277B A79a 10b red & multi *8.50*

Nos. 277g-277h, 277A-277B are airmail. Nos. 277A contains an 85x30mm stamp. No. 277B contains a 49x62mm stamp and exists imperf. No. 277 exists imperf. with light orange background. Value $5. No. 277B also exists imperf. Value $15.

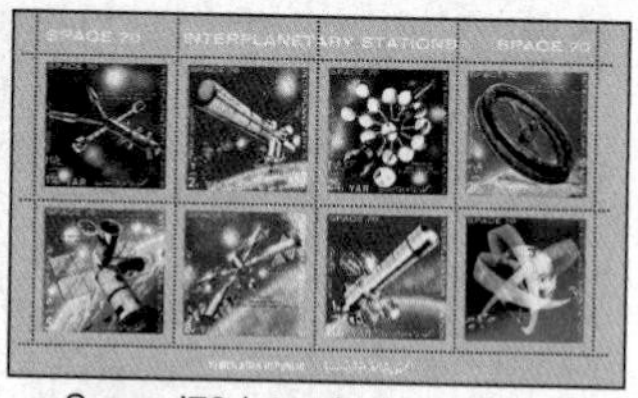

Space '70 Interplanetary Travel A79b

Interplanetary Stations: 1¾b, McDonnel Douglas project 1975-80. 2b, McDonnel Douglas project, diff. 2¼b, Boeing project 1980. 2½b, McDonnel Douglas project 1980-85. 5b, Earth-Moon relay station. 8b, Boeing project 1980-85. 10b, Space telescope. No. 278A, Skylab.

1970, July 21 Litho. *Perf. 13½*

278 A79b Sheet of 7 + label 4.50 2.25
b. 1¾b silver & multi .40 .25
c. 2b silver & multi .40 .25
d. 2¼b silver & multi .40 .25
e. 2½b silver & multi .40 .25
f. 5b silver & multi .60 .30
g. 8b silver & multi .80 .40
h. 10b silver & multi 1.00 .50

Souvenir Sheet

278A A79b 10b multicolored *5.00*

Nos. 278f-278h, 278A are airmail. No. 278 exists imperf with gold borders. No. 278A contains one 67x43mm stamp. An imperf 10b souvenir sheet exists with the a space workshop 1975 design.

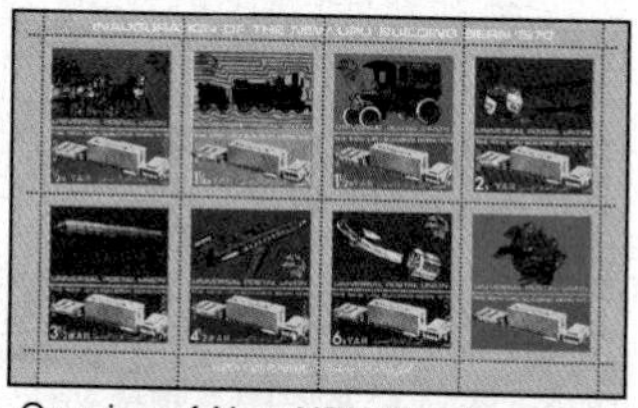

Opening of New UPU Headquarters, Bern, Switzerland — A79c

New UPU Headquarters and: ⅓b, Post coach. 1¼b, Train. 1½b, Early mail truck. 2b, Biplane. 3½b, Zeppelin. 4½b, Jet plane. 6b, Satellite. No. 279A, Zeppelin and post coach.

1970, Aug. 25 Litho. *Perf. 13½*

279 A79c Sheet of 7 + label 4.50 2.25
b. ⅓b silver & multi .40 .25
c. 1¼b silver & multi .40 .25
d. 1½b silver & multi .40 .25
e. 2b silver & multi .40 .25
f. 3½b silver & multi .60 .30
g. 4½b silver & multi .80 .40
h. 6b silver & multi 1.00 .50

Souvenir Sheet

279A A79c 6b multicolored *5.00*

Nos. 279f-279h, 279A are airmail. No. 279 exists imperf with gold borders. No. 279A contains one 44x64mm stamp. An imperf 6b souvenir sheet exists with the a satellite design.

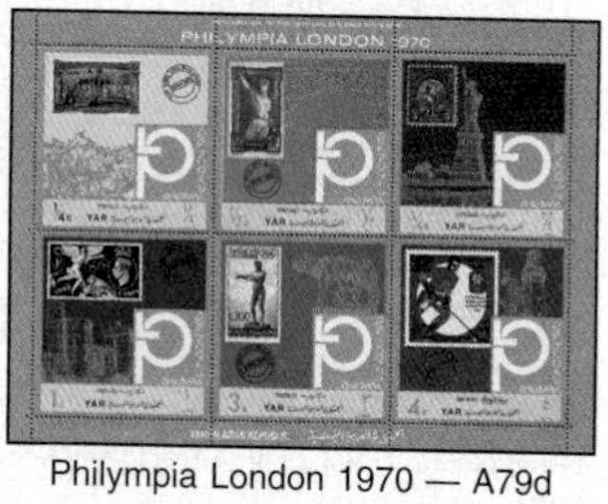

Philympia London 1970 — A79d

Landmarks and stamps: ¼b, Ruins, Greece 163. ⅓b, Stadium, France 201. ¾b, Statue of Liberty, US719. 1b, Windsor Castle, Great Britain 274. 3b, Statue of She wolf suckling Romulus and Remus, Italy 807. 4b, Tower, Yemen 242C. No. 280A, UPU Headquarters, Germany B89.

1970, Sept. 10 Litho. *Perf. 13½*

280 A79d Sheet of 6 3.50 2.25
b. ¼b greenish silver & multi .30 .25
c. ⅓b greenish silver & multi .35 .25
d. ¾b greenish silver & multi .40 .25
e. 1b greenish silver & multi .50 .25
f. 3b greenish silver & multi .85 .40
g. 4b greenish silver & multi 1.10 .55

Souvenir Sheet

280A A79d 4b multicolored *5.00*

Nos. 280g, 280A are airmail. No. 280 exists imperf with brownish silver borders. No. 280A contains one 45x51mm stamp, and also exists

imperf. An imperf 4b souvenir sheet exists with Mexico C311.

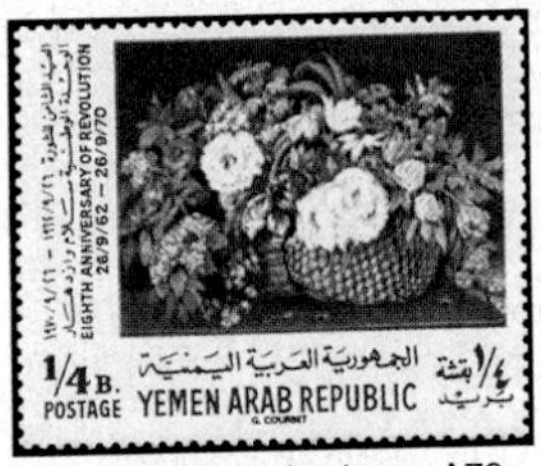

Revolution, 8th Anniv. — A79e

Still Life Paintings by: No. 281b, Courbet. c, No. 281A, Linared. d, Fantin-Latour. e, Renoir, vert. f, Beert, vert.

1970, Sept. 26 Litho. *Perf. 13*

281 Strip of 5 3.00
b.-f. A79e ¼b any single .60

Souvenir Sheet

281A A79e 10b multicolored *4.50*

No. 281 was issued in sheets of 4 strips and also exists imperf.

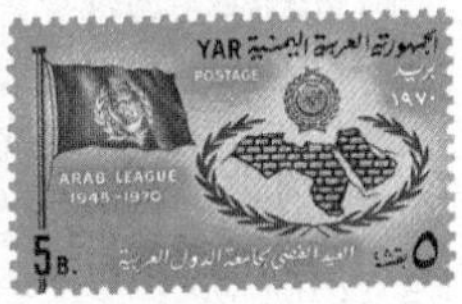

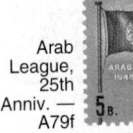

Arab League, 25th Anniv. — A79f

1970, Oct. 5 Photo. *Perf. 11½x11*

282 A79f 5b org, grn & dark pur .35 —
282A A79f 7b blue, grn & brn .75 —
282B A79f 16b dark olive grn, grn & chalky blue 1.75 —

Nos. 282-282B exist imperf. A perf. souvenir sheet of one exists containing No. 282B. Value, $4.

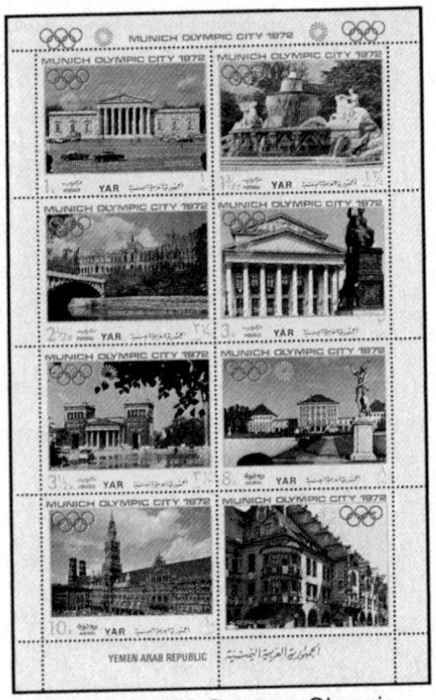

Munich, 1972 Summer Olympic Games Host City — A79g

City Landmarks: 1b, Glyptothek. 1¾b, Wittelsbach Fountain. 2½b, Maximilianeum. 3b, National Theater. 3½b, Propylaea. 8b, Nymphenburg Castle. 10b, City Hall. No. 283A, Munich Olympic Tower, vert.

1970, Oct. 15 Litho. *Perf. 13½*

283 A79g Sheet of 7 + label 4.50 2.25
b. 1b multicolored .40 .25
c. 1¾b multicolored .45 .25
d. 2½b multicolored .45 .25
e. 3b multicolored .50 .25
f. 3½b multicolored .50 .25
g. 8b multicolored .80 .40
h. 10b multicolored .90 .45

Souvenir Sheet

283A A79g 10b multicolored *3.50*

Nos. 283g-283h, 283A are airmail. No. 283 exists imperf with olive inscriptions at top. No. 283A contains one 30x96mm stamp. An imperf 10b souvenir sheet exists with the Marienplatz.

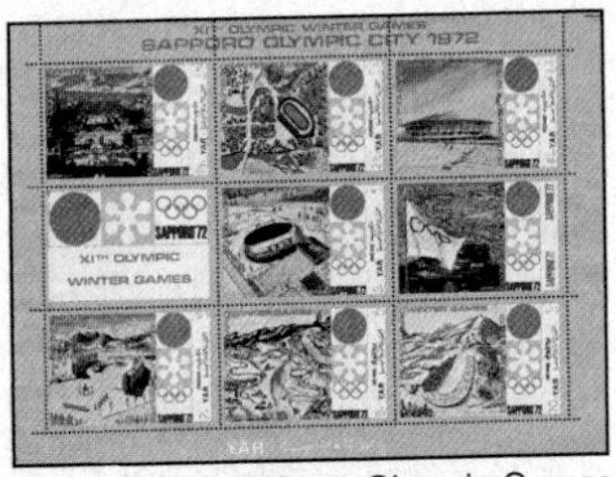

Sapporo, 1972 Winter Olympic Games Host City — A79h

City Landmarks: 1½b, Sapporor City. 2½b, Olympic Skating Center. 4½b, Makomanai Indoor Ice Arena. 5b, Main Stadium. 7b, Olympic Village. 8b, Bobsled and Luge Courses. 10b, Olympic Jump Hill. No. 283A, Ski Jumper, vert.

1970, Nov. 16 Litho. *Perf. 13½*

284 A79h Sheet of 7 + 2 labels 4.00 2.25
b. 1½b silver & multi .30 .25
c. 2½b silver & multi .30 .25
d. 4½b silver & multi .45 .25
e. 5b silver & multi .45 .25
f. 7b silver & multi .60 .30
g. 8b silver & multi .60 .30
h. 10b multicolored .80 .40

Souvenir Sheet

284A A79h 4b multicolored *5.00*

Nos. 284g-284h, 284A are airmail. No. 284 exists imperf with gold frames and inscriptions. No. 284A contains one 54x74mm stamp. An imperf 4b souvenir sheet exists with a map and speed skater.

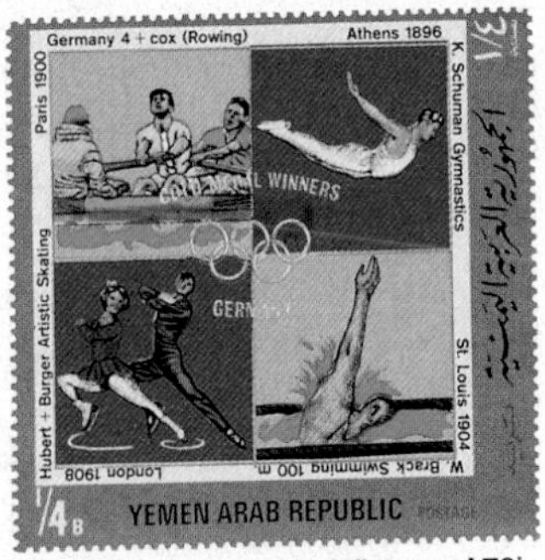

German Olympic Medalists — A79i

Medalists: No. 285, 1896-1908 medalists. No. 285A, 1908-1932 medalists. No. 285B, 1936-1956 medalists. No. 285C, 1956-1964 medalists. No. 285D, 1968 medalists, Sapporo & Munich emblems. No. 285E, Summer Olympic medals.

1970, Dec. 15 Litho. *Perf. 13½*

285 A79i ¼b red lilac & multi .25 .25
285A A79i ¼b red lilac & multi .25 .25
285B A79i ⅓b red lilac & multi .25 .25
285C A79i ⅓b red lilac & multi .25 .25
285D A79i 6b red lilac & multi 2.50 1.25
Nos. 285-285D (5) 3.50 2.25

Souvenir Sheet

285E A79i 6b multicolored 3.50 1.75

Nos. 285D-285E are airmail. No. 285E contains 1 54x54mm stamp and exists imperf. Nos. 285-285D exist imperf.

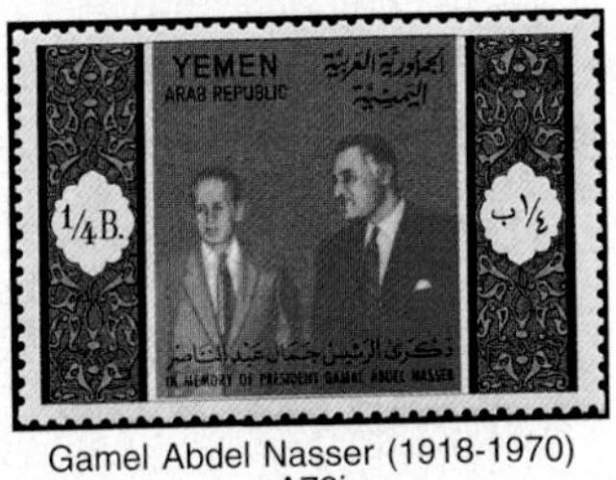

Gamel Abdel Nasser (1918-1970) A79j

Nassar and: No. 286, Sukarno. No. 286A, Nehru. No. 286B, Arif. No. 286C, Hammarskjold. No. 286D, Eisenhower. No. 286E, Abdarrahman al-Iryani. No. 286F, Farmer. No. 286G, Suez Canal. No. 286H, Industrial site. No. 286I, Aswan High Dam. No. 286J, Oil field. No. 286K, Abu Simbel. No. 286L, World map.
No. 286M, Nassar.

1971, Jan. 6 Litho. *Perf. 11*

286 A79j ¼b multicolored .25 .25
286A A79j ¼b multicolored .25 .25
286B A79j ¼b multicolored .25 .25
286C A79j ¼b multicolored .25 .25
286D A79j ½b multicolored .25 .25
286E A79j ½b multicolored 1.00 .50
286F A79j 1b multicolored .35 .25
286G A79j 2b multicolored .40 .25
286H A79j 5b multicolored .50 .25
286I A79j 7b multicolored .65 .30
286J A79j 10b multicolored 1.00 .50
286K A79j 16b multicolored 1.35 .75
Nos. 286-286K (12) 6.50 4.05

Souvenir Sheets

286L A79i 5b multicolored 3.00 1.00
286M A79i 16b multicolored 7.50

No. 286E is 85x81mm. Nos. 286F-286K, 286M are airmail. Nos. 286-286K exist imperf. No. 286M contains one 59x40mm stamp.

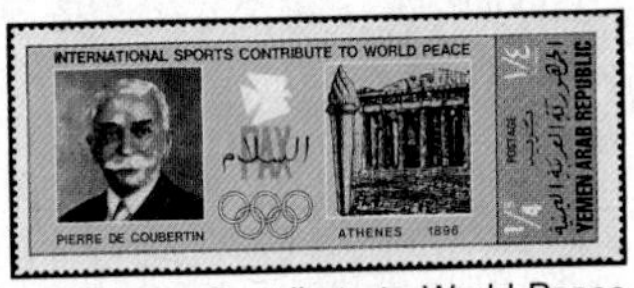

Intl. Sports Contribute to World Peace A79k

Sports: ¼b, No. 287, Athens, Pierre de Coubertin. ⅓b, No. 287A, Skier, hurdler. ½b, No. 287B, Figure skater, weightlifter. 2b, Biathlon, Equestrian. 3b, Speed skater, high jump. Nos. 287E-287Ef, Ski jumping, gymnastics.

1971, Jan. 15 Litho. *Perf. 13½*

287 A79k ¼b blk, yel & gold .25 .25
287A A79k ⅓b blk, grn & gold .25 .25
287B A79k ½b blk, pink & gold .25 .25
287C A79k 2b blk, pur & gold .50 .25
287D A79k 3b blk, yel grn & gold .75 .35
287E A79k 4b blk, blue & gold 1.00 .50
f. Souvenir sheet of 1 *5.00 1.50*
Nos. 287-287E (6) 3.00 1.85

Nos. 287D-287E are airmail. No. 287Ef exists imperf. Nos. 287-287E, 287Ef exist imperf with silver borders.

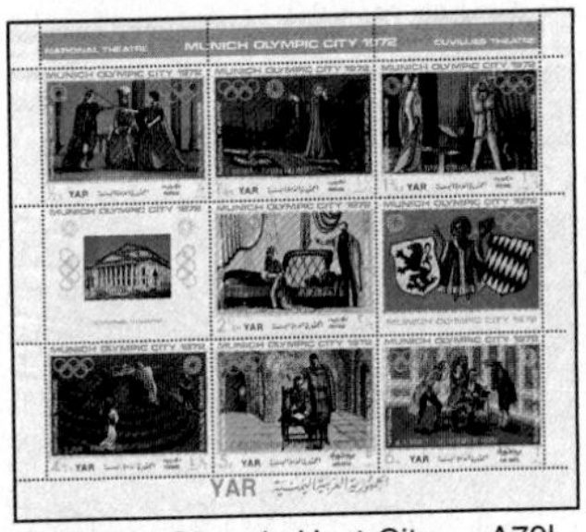

Munich, Olympic Host City — A79l

Composer, opera scenes — No. 288: ⅓b, Handel, Agrippina. 1¼b, Wagner, Tristan & Isolde. 1¾b, Verdi, Othello. 2¼b, Berg, Lulu. 4½b, Orff, Prometheus. 5b, Wagner, Die Meistersinger. 6b, Mozart, Marriage of Figaro. No. 288A, Richard Wagner (1813-1883), vert.

1971, Feb. 15 Litho. *Perf. 13½*

288 A79l Sheet of 7 + 2 labels 3.75 2.00
b. ½b multicolored .40 .25
c. 1¼b multicolored .40 .25
d. 1¾b multicolored .50 .25
e. 2¼b multicolored .50 .25
f. 4½b multicolored .60 .30
g. 5b multicolored .60 .30
h. 6b multicolored .75 .35

Souvenir Sheet

288A A79l 6b multicolored *5.00 1.50*

Nos. 288g-288h, 288A are airmail. No. 288 exists with light green inscription at top. No. 288A contains one 50x56mm stamp. A 6b imperf. souvenir sheet exists with a portrait of Mozart.

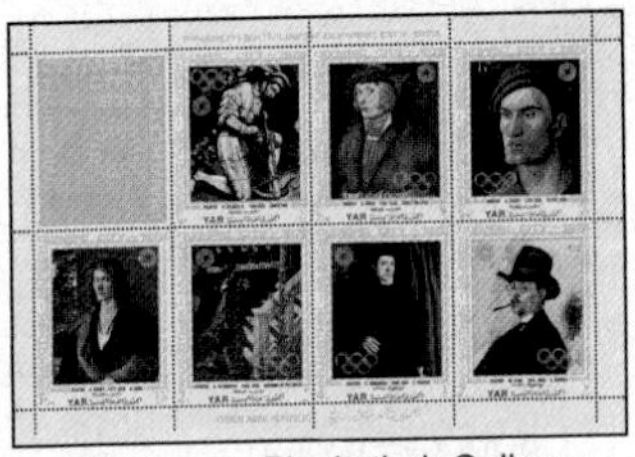

Paintings in Pinakothek Gallery, Munich — A79m

Paintings — No. 289: ¼b, Sebastian by Holbein. ⅓b, Count Philippe by Grein. ¾b, Young Man by Dürer. 1½b, O. Krel by Dürer. 2b, Susanna in the Bath by Altdorfer. 4b, C. Fugger by Amberger. 7b, C. Schuch by Leibl. No. 289A, Count Otto von Wittelsbach, horiz.

1971, Mar. 15 Litho. *Perf. 13½*

289 A79m Sheet of 7 + label 4.00
b. ¼b multicolored .40 .25
c. ⅓b multicolored .40 .25
d. ¾b multicolored .50 .25
e. 1½b multicolored .45 .25
f. 2b multicolored .45 .25
g. 4b multicolored .70 .35
h. 7b multicolored .90 .45

Souvenir Sheet

289A A79m 4b multicolored *5.00 2.00*

Nos. 289g-289h, 289A are airmail. No. 289A contains one 66x46mm stamp. No. 288 exists imperf with inscriptions in light red. A 4b imperf. souvenir sheet exists with Suzanne in the Bath.

Art Type of 1970

Chinese Paintings: ¼b, The Hall of Green Country by Yuan Kiang. ⅓b, Lady at Her Dressing Table by Sou Han. ½b, The Bodhisattva Wen Tchou. 2b, Gatherer of Simples at Tchen Wei by Wou Li. 3b, Buddha by Ting Yun.4b, Li T'ie Kouai by Yen Houei.

1971, Apr. 8 Litho. *Perf. 13½*

290 A73 ¼b lilac silver & multi .25 .25
290A A73 ⅓b lilac silver & multi .25 .25
290B A73 ½b lilac silver & multi .25 .25
290C A73 2b lilac silver & multi .50 .25
290D A73 3b lilac silver & multi .75 .35
290E A73 4b lilac silver & multi 1.00 .50
f. Souvenir sheet of 1 *5.00 1.50*
Nos. 290-290E (6) 3.00 1.85

Nos. 290D-290E, 290Ef are airmail. Stamp in No. 290Ef has white borders. No. 290Ef exists imperf.

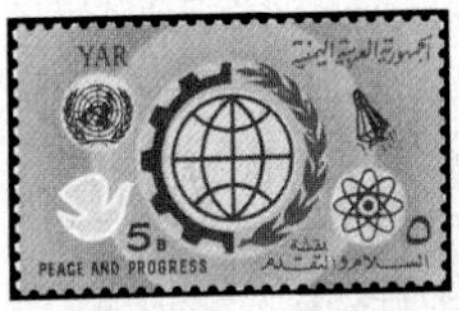

UN, 25th Anniv. A79n

1971, Apr. 4 Photo. *Perf. 11½x11*

291 A79n 5b dk ol grn, grn & dk vio .55 .45
291A A79n 7b bl, grn & dk bl .90 .75

Exist imperf. Value $6.

Souvenir Sheet

Imperf

291B A79n 16b multicolored 2.00 1.50

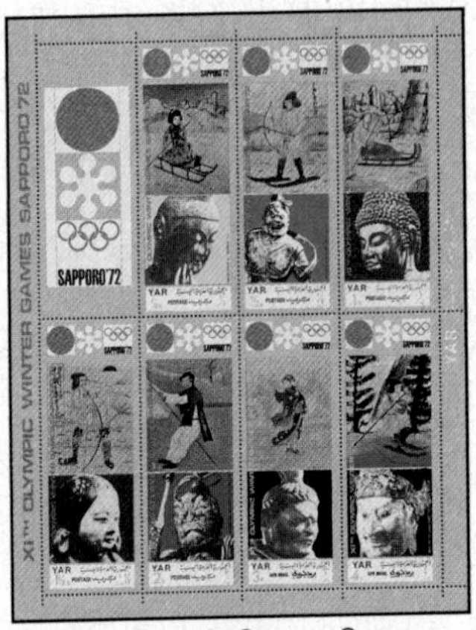

Winter Olympic Games, Sapporo A79o

Early Winter Sports: ¼b, Woman on sled. ½b, Skier with bow. 1b, Woman on sled, diff.

1⅓b, Archer on ice skates. 2b, Man on ice skates. 3b, Woman on ice skates. 4b, Man on skis. No. 292A, Sapporo Games emblem, snowflakes, horiz.

1971, Apr. 15 Litho. *Perf. 13¼*

292	A79o	Sheet of 7 + label	3.75	2.25
b.		¼b silver & multi	.40	.25
c.		⅓b silver & multi	.40	.25
d.		1b silver & multi	.40	.25
e.		1⅓b silver & multi	.50	.25
f.		2b silver & multi	.60	.30
g.		3b silver & multi	.80	.40
h.		4b silver & multi	.80	.40

Souvenir Sheet

292A	A79o	10b multicolored	5.00	1.25

Nos. 292g-292h, 292A are airmail. No. 292A contains one 66x61mm stamp. No. 292 exists imperf with grayish green borders. A 10b imperf. souvenir sheet exists with Snow Festival.

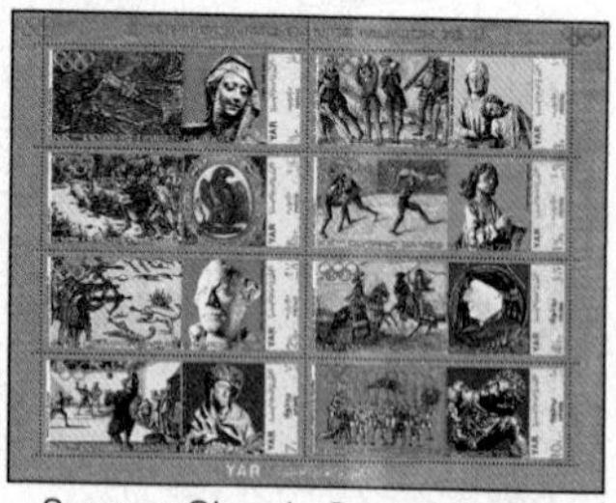

Summer Olympic Games, Munich A79p

Early Summer Sports: ⅓b, Swimming. 1b, Stone throwing. 1⅓b, Walking, diff. 1¾b, Wrestling. 2¼b, Crossbow. 4½b, Jousting. 7b, Handball. 10b, Gymnastics. No. 293A, Stone throwing, vert.

1971, May 15 Litho. *Perf. 13½*

293	A79p	Sheet of 8	4.50	2.25
b.		⅓b gold & multi	.30	.25
c.		1b gold & multi	.30	.25
d.		1⅓b gold & multi	.30	.25
e.		1¾b gold & multi	.40	.25
f.		2¼b gold & multi	.40	.30
g.		4½b gold & multi	.70	.35
h.		7b gold & multi	.90	.45
i.		10b gold & multi	1.25	.65

Souvenir Sheet

293A	A79p	10b multicolored	5.00	1.50

Nos. 293g-293i, 293A are airmail. No. 293A contains one 44x78mm stamp. No. 293 exists imperf with silver borders. A 10b imperf. souvenir sheet exists with swimmers.

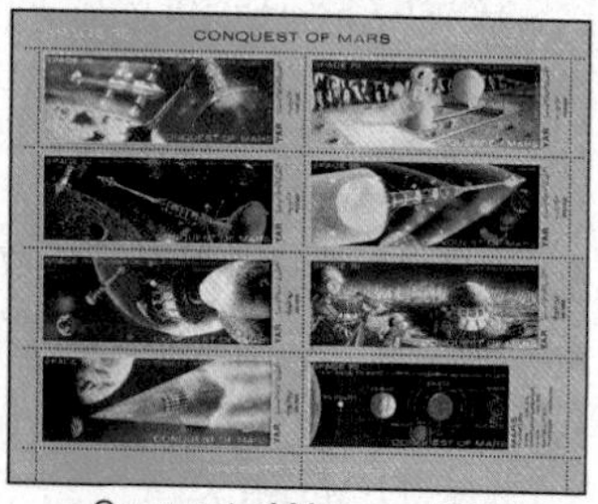

Conquest of Mars — A79q

Stages of Mars exploration: ¼b, Assembly of Photon rocket in Earth orbit. ⅓b, Lunar Base, preparations for Mars mission. ½b, Photon rocket in Lunar orbit. ¾b, Departure for Mars. 3b, In orbit around Phobos. 3½b, Three men on Mars. 6b, Upper stage of Photon rocket returns to Earth. No. 294A, Daedalus, rocket shuttle, Phobos, Mars.

1971, June 15 Litho. *Perf. 13½*

294	A79q	Sheet of 7 + label	4.00	2.25
b.		¼b orange & multi	.40	.25
c.		⅓b orange & multi	.40	.25
d.		½b orange & multi	.40	.25
e.		¾b orange & multi	.40	.25
f.		3b orange & multi	.60	.30
g.		3½b orange & multi	.70	.35
h.		6b orange & multi	.90	.45

Souvenir Sheet

294A	A79q	6b multicolored	5.00	1.50

Nos. 294f-294h, 294A are airmail. No. 294A contains one 70x51mm stamp. No. 294 exists imperf with light blue borders. A 6b imperf. souvenir sheet exists with Galileo.

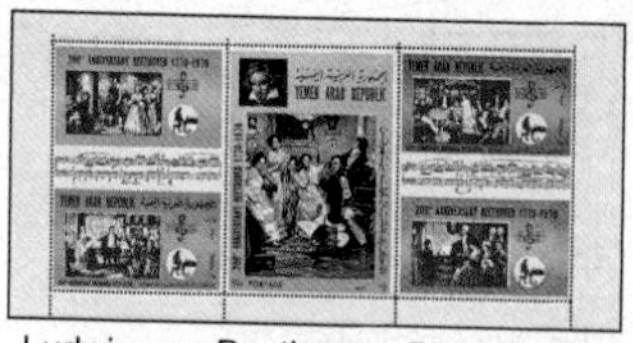

Ludwig van Beethoven, Birth Bicent. A79r

Designs: No. 295h, Recital with Beethoven. No. 295i, Chamber music evening. No. 295j, Portrait of Beethoven, Schubert at piano. No. 295k, View of Bonn. No. 295l, View of Vienna. No. 295m, Beethoven's study. 1b, Birth of Beethoven. 2b, Josephine von Brunswick. 5b, Young Beethoven. 7b, 10b, 16b, Beethoven at piano, various.

1971, June 23 Litho. *Perf. 12*

295	A79r	Sheet of 3	1.50
h.		¼b bl, blk & grn	.50
i.		¼b org, blk & pink	.50
j.		½b blue & multi	.50
295A	A79r	Sheet of 3 + 3 labels	1.50
k.		¼b multicolored	.50
l.		¼b multicolored	.50
m.		½b multicolored	.50
295B	A79r	1b multicolored	.40
295C	A79r	2b multicolored	.50
295D	A79r	5b multicolored	.60
295E	A79r	7b multicolored	.80
295F	A79r	10b multicolored	.80
295G	A79r	16b multicolored	1.00
		Nos. 295-296G (8)	7.10

No. 295A contains 2 80x49mm stamps and 1 40x49mm stamp. Imperf. 5b and 16b souvenir sheets exist.

Nos. 295B-295G are airmail.

Art Type of 1970

Indian Paintings: ¼b, Ibrahim Adil Shah II of Bijapur. ⅓b, Head of Apsaras. ½b, Kamodi Ragini. 2b, Virahini. 3b, Krishna and Radha. 4b, Girls Swimming in a Lotus Pond.

1971, Apr. 8 Litho. *Perf. 13½*

296	A73	¼b lilac silver & multi	.25	.25
296A	A73	⅓b lilac silver & multi	.25	.25
296B	A73	½b lilac silver & multi	.25	.25
296C	A73	2b lilac silver & multi	.50	.25
296D	A73	3b lilac silver & multi	.75	.35
296E	A73	4b lilac silver & multi	1.00	.50
f.		Souvenir sheet of 1	*5.00*	*1.50*
		Nos. 296-296E (6)	3.00	1.85

Nos. 296D-296E, 296Ef are airmail. Stamp in No. 296Ef has white borders. No. 296Ef exists imperf.

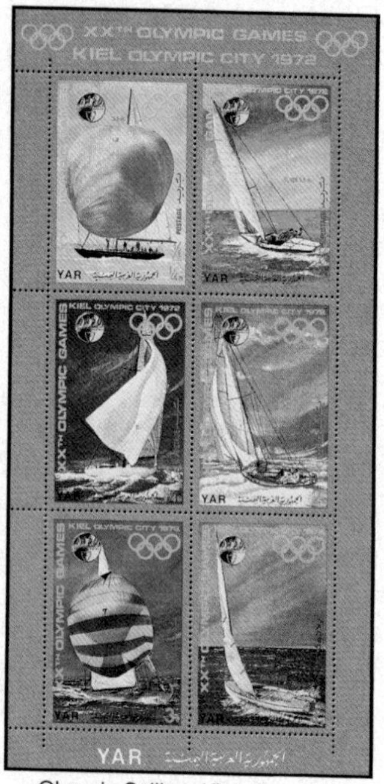

Olympic Sailing, Kiel, Germany A79s

Olympic sailing yachts: ¼b, 16.5m class, blue spinnaker. ⅓b, 5.5m class. 1¼b, 16.5m class, white spinnaker.2b, Belouga class. 3b, Flying Dutchman class. 4b, Finn class. No. 297A, Finn class, diff.

1971, Sept. 1 Litho. *Perf. 13½*

297	A79s	Sheet of 6	3.25	1.65
b.		¼b lilac silver & multi	.40	.25
c.		⅓b lilac silver & multi	.40	.25
d.		1¼b lilac silver & multi	.40	.25
e.		2b lilac silver & multi	.60	.30
f.		3b lilac silver & multi	.65	.30
g.		4b lilac silver & multi	.80	.40

Souvenir Sheet

297A	A79s	4b multicolored	5.00	1.50

Nos. 297g, 297A are airmail. No. 297A contains one 42x64mm stamp and also exists imperf. No. 297exists imperf with gold borders.

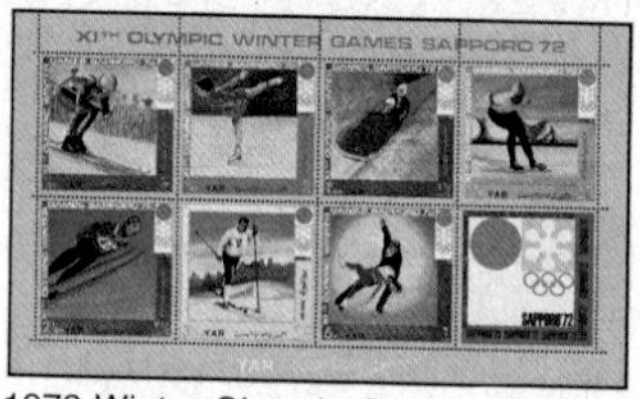

1972 Winter Olympic Games, Sapporo A79t

Olympic Sports: ⅓b, Downhill skiing. ¾b, Women's figure skating. 1¼b, 2-man bobsled. 1¾b, Speed skating. 2¼b, Ski jumping. 3½b, Cross-country skiing. 6b, Pairs figure skating. No. 298A, Ski jumping, diff.

1971, Oct. 2 Litho. *Perf. 13½*

298	A79t	Sheet of 7 + label	4.50
b.		⅓b silver & multi	.45
c.		¾b silver & multi	.45
d.		1¼b silver & multi	.45
e.		1¾b silver & multi	.60
f.		2¼b silver & multi	.60
g.		3½b silver & multi	.75
h.		6b silver & multi	1.00

Souvenir Sheet

298A	A79t	6b multicolored	5.00	1.25

Nos. 298g-298h, 298A are airmail. No. 298A contains one 73x50mm stamp. No. 298 exists imperf with gray violet borders. A 6b imperf. souvenir sheet exists with Sapporo emblems.

Art Type of 1970

Persian Paintings: ¼b, Murakka Gulshan. ⅓b, Shanname de Baisonghor. ½b, Djami al Tawarikh (drummers). 2b, Murakka Gulshan (fighting bear) . 3b, Djami al Tawarikh (kneeling). 4b, Shanname de Baisonghor (musicians).

1971, Oct. 15 Litho. *Perf. 13½*

299	A73	¼b lilac silver & multi	.25	.25
299A	A73	⅓b lilac silver & multi	.25	.25
299B	A73	½b lilac silver & multi	.25	.25
299C	A73	2b lilac silver & multi	.50	.25
299D	A73	3b lilac silver & multi	.75	.35
299E	A73	4b lilac silver & multi	1.00	.50
f.		Souvenir sheet of 1	*5.00*	*1.50*
		Nos. 299-299E (6)	3.00	1.85

Nos. 299D-299E, 299Ef are airmail. Stamp in No. 299Ef has white borders and exists imperf.

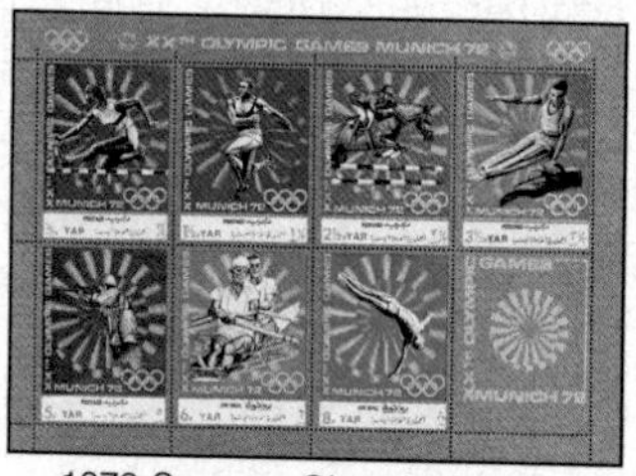

1972 Summer Olympic Games, Munich — A79u

Olympic Sports: ¾b, Women's hurdles. 1½b, Discus. 2½. Equestrian. 3½b, Gymnastics. 5b, Shooting. 6b, Rowing. 8b, Diving. No. 300A, Sprinter at start.

1971, Nov. 4 Litho. *Perf. 13½*

300	A79u	Sheet of 7 + label	4.00	2.25
b.		¾b gold & multi	.40	.25
c.		1½b gold & multi	.40	.25
d.		2½b gold & multi	.50	.25
e.		3½b gold & multi	.50	.25
f.		5b gold & multi	.60	.30
g.		6b gold & multi	.60	.30
h.		8b gold & multi	.75	.35

Souvenir Sheet

300A	A79u	6b multicolored	5.00	1.25

Nos. 300g-300h, 300A are airmail. No. 300A contains one 44x59mm stamp. No. 300 exists imperf with silver gray borders. A 6b imperf. souvenir sheet exists with equestrian design.

Olympic Medalists Type of 1970 in Diamond Shape

Italian Medalists: No. 301, 1908-1924 medalists. No. 301A, 1928-1936 medalists. No. 301B, 1952-1956 medalists. No. 301C, 1960-1968 medalists. No. 301D, 1968 medalists, Sapporo, Munich emblems. No. 301E, Emblesm of Rome, Tokyo and Munich Games.

1971, Dec. 3 Litho. *Perf. 13½*

301	A79i	¼b silver & multi	.25	.25
301A	A79i	¼b silver & multi	.25	.25
301B	A79i	⅓b silver & multi	.25	.25
301C	A79i	⅓b silver & multi	.25	.25
301D	A79i	22b silver & multi	2.50	1.25
		Nos. 301-301D (5)	3.50	2.25

Souvenir Sheet

301E	A79i	14b multicolored	3.50	1.75

Nos. 301D-301E are airmail. No. 301E contains 1 54x54mm stamp. Nos. 301-301D exist imperf. with light green borders. A 14b imperf. souvenir sheet with different Olympic emblems exists.

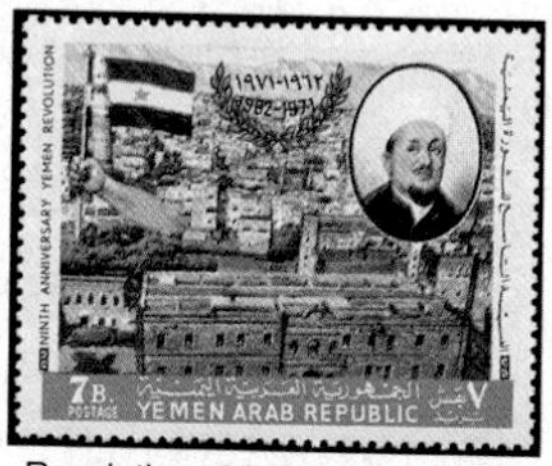

Revolution, 9th Anniv. — A79v

Designs: 7b, View of Sana'a. 18b, Military parade. 24b, Mosque in Sana'a.

1972, Feb. 29 *Perf. 13*

302	A79v	7b multi	1.10
302A	A79v	18b multi	2.25
302B	A79v	24b multi	3.25
		Nos. 302-302B (3)	6.60

An imperf souvenir sheet containing No. 302B exists. Value $3.50.

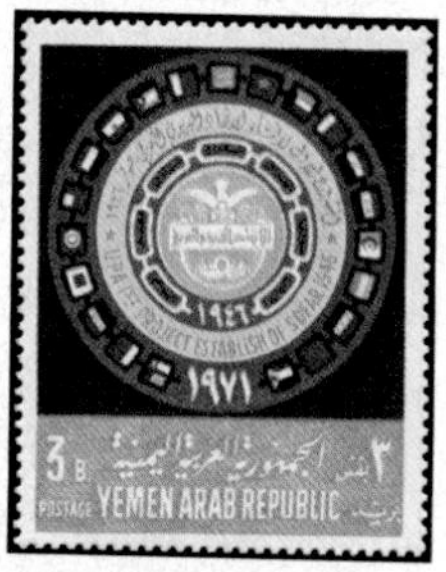

Arab Postal Union, 25th Anniv. — A79w

1972, Mar. 18 *Perf. 13*

303	A79v	3b multi	.50
303A	A79w	7b multi	1.00
303B	A79w	10b multi	1.50
		Nos. 303-303B (3)	3.00

A 16b souvenir sheet also exists. Value $2.50.

Olympic Medalists Type of 1970 in Diamond Shape

French Medalists: 2b, 1896-1912 medalists. 3b, 1920-1932 medalists. 4b, 1936-1964 medalists. 10b, 1968 medalists, Sapporo, Munich emblems. No. 304D, Olympic Stadia from Tokyo, Mexico City and Munich Games.

1972, Apr. 4 Litho. *Perf. 13½*

304	A79i	2b bl grey & multi	.50	.25
304A	A79i	3b bl grey & multi	.60	.30
304B	A79i	4b bl grey & multi	.65	.35
304C	A79i	10b bl grey & multi	1.50	.75
		Nos. 304-304C (4)	3.25	1.65

Souvenir Sheet

304D	A79i	4b multicolored	5.00	1.50

Nos. 304B-304D are airmail. No. 304D contains 1 50x33mm stamp. Nos. 304-304C exist imperf. with light blue borders. A 4b imperf. souvenir sheet with different Olympic venues exists.

Art Treasures — A79x

Designs: 1b, Azure stone vase, 1583. 1¼b, Siren of the "Nautilus Cup," 1822. 1½b, Neptune vase. 1½b, Emperor Rudolph II's crown, 1602. 3b, Statue of Balthazar, 1724. 4½b, Catherine the Great's carriage, 1779. 7b, Statue of St. George.

6b, The Bath of Diana.

1972, July 31   Litho.   Perf. 13x13½
305	A79x	1b bluish sil & multi	.35	.25
305A	A79x	1¼b bluish sil & multi	.35	.25
305B	A79x	1½b bluish sil & multi	.40	.25
305C	A79x	1½b bluish sil & multi	.50	.25
305D	A79x	3b bluish sil & multi	.60	.30
305E	A79x	4½b bluish sil & multi	.80	.40
305F	A79x	7b bluish sil & multi	1.00	.50
		Nos. 305-305F (7)	4.00	2.20

Souvenir Sheet
305G	A79x	6b multicolored	4.00	2.00

Nos. 305D-305F are airmail. An imperf 6b souvenir sheets with a Jasper Cup, Florence, exists.

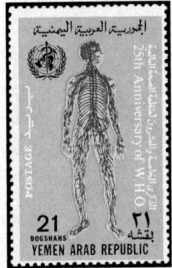

10th anniv. of Revolution A80

1972, Nov. 25   Photo.   Perf. 13
306	A80	7b lt blue, blk & multi	.65	.50
307	A80	10b gray, blk & multi	1.00	.65
		Nos. 306-307,C40 (3)	6.65	4.65

For surcharge see No. 318.

25th Anniv. of WHO — A81

1972, Dec. 1   Litho.
308	A81	2b lt yel grn & multi	.60	.35
308A	A81	21b sky blue & multi	1.75	1.40
308B	A81	37b red lilac & multi	2.75	2.25
		Nos. 308-308B (3)	5.10	4.00

For surcharge see No. 341A.

Burning of Al-Aqsa Mosque, 2nd Anniv. — A82

1972, Jan. 1   Photo.   Perf. 13½
309	A82	7b lt bl, blk & multi	1.50	.60
309A	A82	18b lt bl, blk & multi	2.50	1.10
		Nos. 309-309A,C41 (3)	9.00	4.20

For surcharges see Nos. 319, 341.

25th Anniv. of UNICEF — A83

1973, Jan. 15   Photo.   Perf. 13
310	A83	7b lt bl, blk & multi	1.10	.65
310A	A83	10b lt bl, blk & multi	1.60	.80
		Nos. 310-310A,C42 (3)	4.60	2.95

For surcharge see No. C46.

UPU Cent. — A84

1974, Nov. 20   Photo.   Perf. 14
311	A84	10b multicolored	.75	.40
311A	A84	30b multicolored	2.25	1.50
311B	A84	40b multicolored	3.25	1.90
		Nos. 311-311B (3)	6.25	3.80

For surcharge see No. 341B.

10th World Hunger Program A85

1975, Feb. 5   Litho.   Perf. 13½
313	A85	10b multicolored	.25	.25
314	A85	30b multicolored	1.00	1.00
315	A85	63b multicolored	1.75	1.75
		Nos. 313-315 (3)	3.00	3.00

12th Anniv. of Revolution A86

1975, Sept. 25
316	A86	25f Janad Mosque	.50	.35
317	A86	75f Althawra Hospital	1.00	.65

Nos. 306, 309 Surcharged in Black with New Values and Bars

1975, Nov. 15   Photo.   Perf. 13½
318	A80	75f on 7b	2.00	.65
319	A82	278f on 7b	3.50	1.25
		Nos. 318-319,C46-C48 (6)	22.75	15.40

Telephone Cent. — A87

1976
341	A82	75f on 7b	1.00	.65

1976, Mar. 10   Litho.   Perf. 14½
320	A87	25f brt pink & blk	.65	.65
321	A87	75f lt grn & blk	2.00	2.00
322	A87	160f lt bl & blk	3.25	3.25
a.		Souvenir sheet of 1	4.00	4.00
		Nos. 320-322 (3)	5.90	5.90

No. 322a exists both perf. and imperf.

Coffee Bean Branch — A88

1976, Apr. 25   Perf. 14
323	A88	1f dull lilac	.25	.25
324	A88	3f pale gray	.25	.25
325	A88	5f lt bl grn	.25	.25
326	A88	10f bis brn	.25	.25
327	A88	25f golden brn	.25	.25
328	A88	50f brt plum	.55	.40
329	A88	75f dull pink	.95	.60

Size: 22x30mm

Perf. 14½
330	A88	1r sky blue	1.75	.70
331	A88	1.50r red lilac	2.50	1.40
332	A88	2r light grn	3.00	1.40
333	A88	5r yel org	6.75	3.00
		Nos. 323-333 (11)	16.75	8.75

For surcharges see Nos. 403-407, 592.

2nd Anniv. of Reformation Movement — A89

1976, June 13   Photo.   Perf. 12x12½
334	A89	75f Industrial Park	1.60	1.60
335	A89	135f Forestry	2.75	2.75

Souvenir Sheet
336	A89	135f Forestry	5.00	5.00

No. 336 contains one stamp (32x47mm).

14th Anniv. of Revolution — A90

Designs: 25f, Natl. Institute of Public Administration. 75f, Housing and population census. 160f, Sanaa University emblem.

1976, Sept. 26   Photo.   Perf. 12x12½
337	A90	25f buff & multi	.65	.65
338	A90	75f yel bis & multi	1.75	1.75
339	A90	160f pale grn & multi	3.25	3.25
		Nos. 337-339 (3)	5.65	5.65

Souvenir Sheet
340	A90	160f pale grn & multi	5.00	5.00

No. 340 contains one stamp (33x49mm).

No. 309 Surcharged in Black

1976
341	A82	75f on 7b	1.00	.65

Nos. 308A, 311B Surcharged in Black or Red

1976   Photo.   Perf. 14
341A	A81	75f on 21b (R)	2.00	1.50
341B	A84	160f on 40b	3.00	2.50

Size and location of surcharge varies.

3rd Anniv. of Correction Movement — A91

1977   Photo.   Perf. 14
342	A91	25f Dish antenna	.45	.30
343	A91	75f Computer, technician	1.25	.65
a.		Miniature sheet of 1	4.00	4.00

15th Anniv. of September Revolution — A92

1977   Photo.   Perf. 13½
344	A92	25f Sa'ada-San'a Road	.45	.35
345	A92	75f Television, Transmitting tower	1.25	.85
346	A92	160f like 25f	2.50	2.00
a.		Souvenir sheet of 1	5.00	5.00
		Nos. 344-346 (3)	4.20	3.20

25th Anniv. of Arab Postal Union — A93

1978   Perf. 14
347	A93	25f lt yel grn & multi	.90	.75
348	A93	60f bis & multi	2.25	1.60
a.		Miniature sheet of 1	5.00	4.50

Pres. Hamdi — A94

1978   Perf. 11½
349	A94	25f dk grn & blk	.35	.35
350	A94	75f ultra & blk	1.25	1.10
351	A94	160f brn & blk	2.50	1.90
a.		Miniature sheet of 1	5.00	5.00
		Nos. 349-351 (3)	4.10	3.35

30th
Anniv.
of
ICAO
(1977)
A95

1979, Nov. 15   Photo.   Perf. 13½
352 A95 75f multi   2.10 1.00
353 A95 135f multi   3.25 1.60
  a. Miniature sheet of 1   5.00 4.50

Book, World Map, Arab
Achievements — A96

1979, Dec. 1   Perf. 14
354 A96 25f multi   .60   .35
355 A96 75f multi   1.50 1.00
  a. Souvenir sheet of 1   3.75 3.25

A97

1980, Jan. 1
356 A97 75f multi   2.00 1.00
357 A97 135f multi, horiz.   3.00 1.60
  a. Miniature sheet of 1   3.00 1.60

12th World Telecommunications Day, May
17, 1979.

A98

Dome of the Rock.

1980   Photo.   Perf. 14
358 A98 5f brt bl & multi   .50   .35
359 A98 10f yel & multi   1.00   .65

Palestinian fighters and their families.

Argentina World Cup — A99

World Cup emblem and various players.

1980, Mar. 30
360 A99 25f gold & multi   .60   .40
361 A99 30f gold & multi   .60   .30
362 A99 35f gold & multi   .75   .40
363 A99 50f gold & multi   1.05   .50
      Nos. 360-363,C49-C52 (8)   9.80 4.80

      Issued in sheets of 8.
Exist imperf. (Value, set $20) and in souve-
nir sheets (Value, set $60).

International Year of the Child — A100

1980, Apr. 1   Perf. 13½
364 A100 25f Girl, bird   1.75   .50
365 A100 50f Girl, bird, diff.   2.50   .80
366 A100 75f Boy, butterfly,
                flower   2.60 1.25
      Nos. 364-366,C53-C55 (6)   18.85 6.80

      Issued in sheets of 6.
Exist imperf. (Value, set $25) and in souve-
nir sheets (Value, set $45).

World Scouting Jamboree — A101

25f, Fishing. 35f, Troup, aircraft. 40f,
Mounted bugler, flag. 50f, Telescope, night
sky.

1980, May 1   Perf. 13½x14
367 A101 25f multicolored   .60   .30
368 A101 35f multicolored   1.40   .50
369 A101 40f multicolored   1.40   .50
370 A101 50f multicolored   1.50   .65
      Nos. 367-370,C56-C58 (7)   13.05 5.35

      Issued in sheets of 6.
Exist imperf. (Value, set $25) and in souve-
nir sheets (Value, set $50).

Argentina 1978 World Cup
Winners — A102

World cup emblem and various soccer
players.

1980, June 1   Perf. 14
371 A102 25f gold & multi   .60   .25
372 A102 30f gold & multi   .90   .30
373 A102 35f gold & multi   .90   .40
374 A102 50f gold & multi   1.35   .40
      Nos. 371-374,C59-C62 (8)   12.00 4.35

Exist imperf. (Value, set $20) and in souve-
nir sheets (Value, set $60).

Hegira, 1400th Anniv. — A102a

Designs: 160f, Outside view.

1980, July 1   Perf. 13½
375 A102a 25f blk & multi   .30   .25
376 A102a 75f car rose & multi   .90   .60
377 A102a 160f blk & multi   1.90   .75
  a. Miniature sheet of 1   4.00 4.00
      Nos. 375-377 (3)   3.10 1.60

18th Anniv.
of
September
Revolution
A103

A104

1980, Sept. 26   Perf. 13½
378 A103 25f multi   .35   .25
379 A104 75f multi   1.10   .65

Souvenir Sheet
380   100f multi   2.00 2.00

No. 380 contains one stamp combining
designs A103 and A104 (42x34mm).

Al Aqsa
Mosque
A105

Mosques: 25f, Al-Rawda entrance. 100f, Al-
Nabwi. 160f, Al-Haram.

1980, Nov. 6   Photo.   Perf. 13½
381 A105 25f multi   .40   .25
382 A105 75f multi   .90   .50
383 A105 100f multi   2.25   .65
384 A105 160f multi   3.00 1.00
      Nos. 381-384 (4)   6.55 2.40

Souvenir Sheet
385   160f multi   6.00 3.25

Islamic Postal Systems Week and Hegira.
No. 385 contains one stamp (109x47mm)
combining designs of Nos. 382-384.

Intl. Palestinian
Solidarity
Day — A106

1980, Nov. 29
386 A106 25f lt bl & multi   .40   .25
387 A106 75f ver & multi   1.10   .90

      Inscribed 1979.

9th Arab Archaeological
Conference — A107

1981, Mar. 1   Perf. 13½
388 A107 75f Al Aamiriya
                Mosque   1.10   .60
389 A107 125f Al Hadi Mosque   1.75   .85
  a. Souvenir sheet of 2, #388-389   3.25 3.25

1980 World
Tourism
Conference,
Manila
A108

1981, Apr. 1
390 A108 25f shown   .25   .25
391 A108 75f Mosque, houses   .60   .30
392 A108 100f Columns, horiz.   .80   .45
393 A108 135f Bridge   1.10   .60
394 A108 160f View of San'a,
                horiz.   1.40   .60
  a. Miniature sheet of 1   4.50 4.50
      Nos. 390-394 (5)   4.15 2.20

Sir Rowland Hill (1795-1879), Postage
Stamp Inventor — A109

25f, Portrait, UPU emblem. 30f, Emblem,
stamp of 1963. 50f, Portrait, stamps. 75f, Portrait, globe, jet. 100f, Portrait, stamp collection.
150f, Jets, No. 322.
No. 401, Portrait, vert. No. 402, Portrait, diff.

1981, Sept. 15   Litho.   Perf. 14
395 A109 25f multicolored   .90
396 A109 30f multicolored   1.05
397 A109 50f multicolored   1.50
398 A109 75f multicolored   2.40
399 A109 100f multicolored   3.25
400 A109 150f multicolored   6.00
      Nos. 395-400 (6)   15.10

Souvenir Sheets
401 A109 200f multicolored   7.50

Imperf
402 A109 200f multicolored   7.50

      Nos. 398-402 are airmail.
Nos. 395-400 exist imperf. (Value, set $20)
and in souvenir sheets (Value, set $45).

Nos. 323-327 Surcharged
1981
403 A88 125f on 1f   1.00
404 A88 150f on 3f   1.25
405 A88 325f on 5f   2.75
406 A88 350f on 10f   3.25
407 A88 375f on 25f   3.50
      Nos. 403-407 (5)   11.75

20th Anniv. of Yemen Airways — A110

1983, Apr. 1 — Litho. — Perf. 14
408	A110	75f yel & multi	.75	.50
409	A110	125f red & multi	1.25	.80
410	A110	325f bl & multi	3.00	2.00
		Nos. 408-410 (3)	5.00	3.30

Folk Costumes — A111

No. 411, Woman carrying waterjar. No. 412, Women, sheep. No. 413, Man, donkeys. No. 414, Man in town square. No. 415, Women, child, well. No. 416, Scholar. No. 417, Woman on beach. No. 418, Camel-drawn plow. No. 419, Woman. No. 420, Man.

1983, May 1
411	A111	50f multicolored	2.50
412	A111	50f multicolored	2.50
413	A111	50f multicolored	2.50
414	A111	50f multicolored	2.50
415	A111	75f multicolored	3.75
416	A111	75f multicolored	3.75
417	A111	75f multicolored	3.75
418	A111	75f multicolored	3.75
		Nos. 411-418 (8)	25.00

Souvenir Sheets
419	A111	200f multicolored	8.00

Imperf
420	A111	200f multicolored	8.00

#411-414 vert. #415-420 are airmail. Nos. 411-418 exist imperf. (Value, set $25) and in souvenir sheets (Value, set $60).

Sept. 26th Revolution, 20th Anniv. (1982) — A112

1983, Sept. 26 — Litho. — Perf. 14
421	A112	100f Communications	1.25
422	A112	150f Literacy	1.75
423	A112	325f Educational development	3.50
a.		Souvenir sheet of 2, #422, 423	6.00
424	A112	400f Independence	5.00

World Communications Year — A113

1983, Dec. 15
425	A113	150f lt bl & multi	2.25
426	A113	325f lt grn & multi	3.50
a.		Souvenir sheet of 1	6.00

Sept. 26 Revolution, 21st Anniv. — A114

1984, Apr. 1 — Litho. — Perf. 14
427	A114	100f shown	1.50
428	A114	150f Fist, statue	2.00
429	A114	325f Gate, tank	3.50
a.		Souvenir sheet of 1	6.00

Israel Aggression Day — A115

1984, Sept. 7
430	A115	150f multi	1.50
431	A115	325f multi	4.00

Size: 91x120mm
Imperf
432	A115	325f multi	25.00
		Nos. 430-432 (3)	30.50

Sept. 26 Revolution, 22nd Anniv. — A116

1985, Oct. 1
433	A116	50f Triumphal Arch	.75
434	A116	150f San'a Castle walls	1.75
435	A116	325f Stadium, Govt. Palace, San'a	3.50
a.		Souvenir sheet of 1	6.00

Intl. Anti-Apartheid Year (1978) — A117

1985, Jan. 1
436	A117	150f dp ver & multi	1.75
437	A117	325f grn & multi	3.50
a.		Souvenir sheet of 1	6.00

Intl. Civil Aviation Org., 40th Anniv. A118

1985, Sept. 20
438	A118	25f multi	.40
439	A118	50f multi	.60
440	A118	150f multi	1.50
441	A118	325f multi	3.50
a.		Souvenir sheet of 1	6.00

Arabsat Satellite, 1st Anniv. A119

1986, Apr. 15 — Litho. — Perf. 14
442	A119	150f multi	2.75
443	A119	325f multi	6.00
a.		Souvenir sheet of 1	9.50

World Telecommunications, 120th Anniv. — A120

1986, May 1
444	A120	150f multi	2.75
445	A120	325f multi	6.00
a.		Souvenir sheet of 1	9.00

General People's Conference, 2nd Anniv. — A121

1986, May 1
446	A121	150f multi	2.75
447	A121	325f multi	5.00
a.		Souvenir sheet of 1	6.00

A122

1986, July 1
448	A122	150f multi	7.25
449	A122	325f multi	5.00
a.		Souvenir sheet of 1	6.00

15th Islamic Foreign Ministers' Conference, San'a, Dec. 18-22, 1984.

A123

1986, Oct. 1
450	A123	150f multi	2.50
451	A123	325f multi	4.50
a.		Souvenir sheet of 1	6.00

UN 40th anniv.

Arab League, 39th Anniv. A124

1986, Nov. 15
452	A124	150f multi	2.75
453	A124	325f multi	5.00

Natl. Arms A125

1987, Sept. 26 — Litho. — Perf. 14
454	A125	100f multi	1.00
455	A125	150f multi	1.40
456	A125	425f multi	4.00
a.		Souvenir sheet of 1	4.50
457	A125	450f multi	4.50
		Nos. 454-457 (4)	10.90

Sept. 26th Revolution, 25th anniv. For surcharge see No. 593.

Intl. Youth Year (1985) A126

1987, Oct. 15 — Perf. 13x13½
458	A126	150f multi	1.75
459	A126	325f multi	3.75
a.		Souvenir sheet of 1	5.00

For surcharge see No. C150.

Drilling of the Republic's First Oil Well, 1984 A127

1987, Nov. 1 — Perf. 14
460	A127	150f Oil derrick	1.75
461	A127	425f Derrick, refinery	3.75
a.		Souvenir sheet of 1	5.00

For surcharge see No. C151.

General Population and Housing Census, 1986 A128

1987, Dec. 1
462	A128	150f multi	2.50
463	A128	425f multi	4.50
a.		Souvenir sheet of 1	5.50

For surcharge see No. C152.

1986 World Cup Soccer Championships, Mexico — A129

Designs: 100f, 150f, Match scenes, vert. 425f, Match scene and Pique, character trademark.

1988, Jan. 1 — Litho. — Perf. 14
464	A129	100f multi	1.00
465	A129	150f multi, diff.	1.50
466	A129	425f multi	3.50
a.		Souvenir sheet of 1	5.00
		Nos. 464-466 (3)	6.00

For surcharge see No. C153.

17th Scouting Conference, San'a — A130

1988, Mar. 1 — Litho. — Perf. 14
467	A130	25f Skin diving	.35
468	A130	30f Table tennis	.45
469	A130	40f Tennis	.55
470	A130	50f Two scouts, flag	.65

471 A130 60f Volleyball .75
472 A130 100f Tug-of-war 1.10
473 A130 150f Basketball 1.75
474 A130 425f Archery 4.00
  Nos. 467-474 (8) 9.60
Souvenir Sheet
475 A130 425f Scout, emblem,
        hand sign 5.00

For surcharge see No. C154.

San'a Preservation — A131

1988, May 1   Litho.   Perf. 14
476 A131 25f multicolored .45
477 A131 50f multicolored .85
478 A131 100f multicolored 1.40
479 A131 150f multicolored 1.90
480 A131 425f multicolored 4.50
  a. Souvenir sheet of 1 6.00
  Nos. 476-480 (5) 9.10

For surcharge see No. 594.

Battle of
Hattin,
800th
Anniv. in
1987
A132

1988   Litho.   Perf. 14
482 A132 150f multicolored 2.75
483 A132 425f multicolored 6.75
  a. Souvenir sheet 10.00

For surcharge see No. C155.

Arab Telecommunication Day,
1987 — A133

1988
484 A133 100f multicolored 1.50
485 A133 150f multicolored 2.25
486 A133 425f multicolored 5.25
  a. Souvenir sheet 7.50
  Nos. 484-486 (3) 9.00

For surcharge see No. C156.

A134

Sept. 26
Revolution, 26th
Anniv. — A134a

1989, Sept. 30
487 A134 300f multicolored 1.25
488 A134 375f multicolored 1.5
489 A134a 850f multicolored 3.00
490 A134a 900f multicolored 3.50
  Nos. 487-490 (4) 9.25

A souvenir sheet containing one #488 exists.
For surcharges see Nos. 595, 605.

A135

October 14
Revolution, 25th
Anniv. — A135a

1989, Oct. 14
491 A135 300f multicolored 1.25
492 A135 375f multicolored 1.50
493 A135a 850f multicolored 3.00
494 A135a 900f multicolored 3.50
  Nos. 491-494 (4) 9.25

A souvenir sheet containing one #492 exists.
For surcharges see Nos. 596, 606.

1988
Summer
Olympics,
Seoul
A136

Game emblem and various events: 300f,
Table tennis, basketball, track, boxing. 375f,
Soccer game. 850f, Soccer, judo, vert. 900f,
Torch bearer.

1989, Nov. 10   Litho.   Perf. 13x13½
495 A136 300f multicolored 1.50
496 A136 375f multicolored 1.75
  a. Souvenir sheet 8.50
497 A136 850f multicolored 3.50
498 A136 900f multicolored 4.25
  Nos. 495-498 (4) 11.00

For surcharges see Nos. 597, 607.

Palestinian
Uprising
A137

375f, Flag raising, vert. 850f, Burning barri-
cades. 900f, Man waving flag, vert.

1989, Dec. 9   Perf. 13x13½, 13½x13
499 A137 300f shown 2.00
500 A137 375f multicolored 3.00
  a. Souvenir sheet of 1 15.00
501 A137 850f multicolored 5.50
502 A137 900f multicolored 7.00
  Nos. 499-502 (4) 17.50

For surcharges see Nos. 598, 608.

Arab Cooperation Council — A138

1990, Feb. 16   Litho.   Perf. 13x13½
504 A138 300f multicolored 1.00
505 A138 375f multicolored 1.25
  a. Souvenir sheet 7.50
506 A138 850f multicolored 2.75
507 A138 900f multicolored 3.00
  Nos. 504-507 (4) 8.00

For surcharges see Nos. 599, 609.

First
Exported
Oil — A139

1990, Mar. 15   Perf. 14
508 A139 300f multicolored 1.00
509 A139 375f multicolored 1.25
  a. Souvenir sheet 7.50
510 A139 850f multi, diff. 2.75
511 A139 900f like 850f 3.00
  Nos. 508-511 (4) 8.00

For surcharges see Nos. 600, 610.

Arab Scout
Movement,
75th Anniv.
A140

300f, Scouts holding globe. 850f, Oil rig,
scouts, globe.

1990, June 15   Litho.   Perf. 13x13½
512 A140 300f multicolored 1.00
513 A140 375f like No. 512 1.25
  a. Souvenir sheet of 1 4.50
514 A140 850f multicolored 2.75
515 A140 900f like No. 514 3.00
  Nos. 512-515 (4) 8.00

For surcharges see Nos. 601, 611.

Arab Board for
Medical
Specializations,
10th
Anniv. — A141

1990, Apr. 15   Photo.   Perf. 13½x13
516 A141 300f brt grn & multi 1.00
517 A141 375f lt bl & multi 1.25
  a. Sheet of 1, perf. 12½ 4.50
518 A141 850f lt org & multi 2.75
519 A141 900f lt vio & multi 3.00
  Nos. 516-519 (4) 8.00

For surcharges see Nos. 602, 612.

Immunization Campaign — A142

300f, 375f, Mother feeding infant, vert.

1990, May 15   Perf. 13½x13, 13x13½
520 A142 300f lt bl & multi 1.00
521 A142 375f lt org & multi 1.25
  a. Sheet of 1, perf. 12½ 5.00
522 A142 850f lt bl grn & multi 2.75
523 A142 900f lt lake & multi 3.00
  Nos. 520-523 (4) 8.00

No. 521a contains one 26x37mm stamp.
For surcharges see Nos. 603, C157.

UN Development
Program, 40th
Anniv. — A144

1990, Oct. 24   Litho.   Perf. 12
532 A144 150f multicolored 1.00

For surcharge see No. 622.

Ducks
A145

1990, Sept. 18   Litho.   Perf. 12
533 A145 10f Pintail swimming .25
534 A145 20f Wigeon .25
535 A145 25f Ruddy shelduck .25
536 A145 40f Gadwall .30
537 A145 75f Shelduck, male .50
538 A145 150f Shoveler .90
539 A145 600f Teal 2.75
  Nos. 533-539 (7) 5.20

Souvenir Sheet
540 A145 460f Pintail in flight 5.00

For surcharge see No. 623.

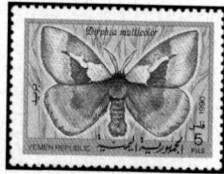

Moths and
Butterflies
A146

5f, Dirphia multicolor. 20f, Automeris io. 25f,
Papilio machaon. 40f, Bhutanitis lidderdalii.
55f, Prepona demophon muson. 75f, Agarista
agricola. 700f, Attacus edwardsii.
460f, Daphnis nerii, vert.

1990, Nov. 3   Perf. 12½x12
541 A146 5f   multicolored .25
542 A146 20f multicolored .25
543 A146 25f multicolored .25
544 A146 40f multicolored .35
545 A146 55f multicolored .45
546 A146 75f multicolored .55
547 A146 700f multicolored 3.75
  Nos. 541-547 (7) 5.85

Souvenir Sheet
Perf. 12x12½
548 A146 460f multicolored 7.50

Prehistoric
Animals
A147

Perf. 12x12½, 12½x12
1990, Nov. 27
549 A147 5f   Protembolotheri-
            um, vert. .25
550 A147 10f Diatryma, vert. .25
551 A147 35f Mammuthus .25
552 A147 40f Edaphosaurus .30
553 A147 55f Dimorphodon .40
554 A147 75f Phororhacos .50
555 A147 700f Ichthyosaurus,
            vert. 3.25
  Nos. 549-555 (7) 5.20

Size: 61x90mm
Imperf
556 A147 460f Tyrannosaurus,
            vert. 4.00

A148

Various domestic cats.

1990, Dec. 26   *Perf. 12x12½*
557	A148	5f multicolored	.25
558	A148	15f multicolored	.25
559	A148	35f multicolored	.25
560	A148	55f multicolored	.35
561	A148	60f multicolored	.35
562	A148	150f multicolored	.75
563	A148	600f multicolored	2.75
	Nos. 557-563 (7)		4.95

Size: 70x90mm

Imperf
564	A148	460f multicolored	5.00

A149

Mushrooms: 50f, Boletus aestivalis. 60f, Suillus luteus. 80f, Gyromitra esculenta. 100f, Leccinum scabrum. 130f, Amanita muscaria. 200f, Boletus erythropus. 300f, Leccinum testaceoscabrum.
460f, Stropharia aeruginosa.

1991, Mar. 18   *Litho.*   *Perf. 12x12½*
565	A149	50f multicolored	.30
566	A149	60f multicolored	.40
567	A149	80f multicolored	.50
568	A149	100f multicolored	.60
569	A149	130f multicolored	.70
570	A149	200f multicolored	1.00
571	A149	300f multicolored	1.50
	Nos. 565-571 (7)		5.00

Size: 70x90mm

Imperf
572	A149	460f multicolored	3.00

Unified
Yemen
Republic,
1st Anniv.
A150

Designs: 300f, 375f, Eagle crest. 850f, 900f, Hand holding flag, map, sun.

1991, May 22   *Perf. 13x13½*
573	A150	300f pink & multi	.60
574	A150	375f grn bl multi	.75
a.	Sheet of 1, perf. 12½		2.00
575	A150	850f lt bl & multi	1.50
576	A150	900f bl grn & multi	1.75
	Nos. 573-576 (4)		4.60

No. 574a contains one 37x27mm stamp.
For surcharges see #604, 613, 624, 627.

Unity Agreement
Signed Nov. 30,
1989 — A151

Designs: 300f, 375f, Fist, flag, map.

1991, May 22   *Perf. 13½x13*
577	A151	225f multicolored	.50
578	A151	300f multicolored	.60
579	A151	375f multicolored	.75
a.	Sheet of 1, perf. 12½		2.00
580	A151	650f multicolored	1.25
581	A151	850f multiccolored	1.50
	Nos. 577-581 (5)		4.60

No. 579a contains one 27x37mm stamp.
For surcharges see #614, 617-619, 625.

World Anti-Smoking Day — A153

Designs: 300f, 375f, 850f, Man facing skull smoking cigarette.

1991, May 31   *Perf. 13x13½*
582	A153	225f multicolored	.55
583	A153	300f multicolored	.65
584	A153	375f multicolored	.80
a.	Sheet of 1, perf. 12½		2.50
585	A153	650f multicolored	1.40
586	A153	850f multicolored	1.75
	Nos. 582-586 (5)		5.15

No. 584a contains one 36x26mm stamp.
For surcharges see Nos. 615, 620, 626.

United
Nations,
45th Anniv.
A154

1991, June 26   *Perf. 13x13½*
587	A154	5r multicolored	.90
588	A154	6r multicolored	1.50
589	A154	10r multicolored	1.75
590	A154	12r multicolored	2.40
	Nos. 587-590 (4)		6.55

Souvenir Sheet

Perf. 12½
591	A154	6r multicolored	2.00

No. 591 contains one 37x28mm stamp.

Nos. 329, 456, 480, 489-490, 493-494, 497-498, 501-502, 506-507, 510-511, 514-515, 518-519, 523, 575-576, 581 & 586 Surcharged, "Rials" Spelled Out

1993, Jan. 1   *Perfs., Etc. as Before*
592	A88	5r on 75f #329	5.75
593	A125	8r on 425f #456	6.50
594	A131	8r on 425f #480	6.50
595	A134a	10r on 900f #490	6.50
596	A135a	10r on 900f #494	6.50
597	A136	10r on 900f #498	6.50
598	A137	10r on 900f #502	6.50
599	A138	10r on 900f #507	6.50
600	A139	10r on 900f #511	6.50
601	A140	10r on 900f #515	6.50
602	A141	10r on 900f #519	6.50
603	A142	10r on 900f #523	6.50
604	A150	10r on 900f #576	6.50
605	A134a	12r on 850f #489	7.25
606	A135a	12r on 850f #493	7.25
607	A136	12r on 850f #497	7.25
608	A137	12r on 850f #501	7.25
609	A138	12r on 850f #506	7.25
610	A139	12r on 850f #510	7.25
611	A140	12r on 850f #514	7.25
612	A141	12r on 850f #518	7.25
613	A150	12r on 850f #575	7.25
614	A151	12r on 850f #581	7.25
615	A153	12r on 850f #586	7.25
	Nos. 592-615 (24)		163.50

Size and location of surcharge varies.

Yemen (PDR)
Nos. 441, 443,
447, and Yemen
Nos. 577-578,
583 Srchd. Type
a or — c

1993   *Perfs., Etc. as Before*
616	A139(a)	50r on 500f #447	100.00	
617	A151(a)	50r on 225f #577	175.00	
618	A151(c)	50r on 225f #577	—	
a.	Pair, #617-618			
619	A151(a)	100r on 300f #578	175.00	
620	A153(a)	100r on 300f #583	225.00	
621	A139(a)	200r on 5f #441	250.00	
a.	3-Line surcharge			
621B	A139(a)	200r on 20f #443	250.00	

Size and location of surcharge varies.

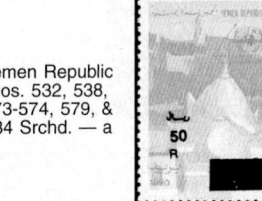

Yemen Republic
Nos. 532, 538,
573-574, 579, &
584 Srchd. — a

1993, Sept. 1   *Perfs., Etc. as Before*
622	A144(a)	50r on 150f #532	25.00	20.00
623	A145(a)	50r on 150f #538	25.00	20.00
623A	A153(a)	50r on 225f #582	300.00	200.00
624	A150(a)	50r on 375f #574	27.50	20.00
625	A151(a)	50r on 375f #579	27.50	25.00
626	A153(a)	50r on 375f #584	27.50	25.00
627	A150(a)	100r on 300f #573	50.00	25.00

Size and location of surcharge varies.
No. 623 exists with a surcharge similar to
surcharge "c."

**Yemen People's Democratic
Republic Nos. 75, 84B, 204, 208,
216, 232, 235, 244, 267, 335-336,
347, 425, 436-437, 439 & Types
Surcharged Type a and**

b

1993, Sept. 1   *Perfs., Etc. as Before*
628	A25(a)	8r on 110f #84B	4.75	
629	A63(a)	8r on 110f #204	4.75	
630	A64(a)	8r on 110f #208	4.75	
631	A66(a)	8r on 110f #216	4.75	
632	A72(a)	8r on 110f #232	4.75	
633	A74(a)	8r on 110f #235	4.75	
634	A76(a)	8r on 110f #244	16.00	
635	A86(a)	8r on 110f #267	4.75	
636	A105(a)	100r on 2d #347	60.00	
637	A137(a)	100r on 300f #439	60.00	
638	A24(a)	200r on 5f #75	100.00	
639	(b)	200r on 15f Soyuz 10 & Salyut 1	100.00	
640	A105(b)	200r on 15f #335	100.00	
641	(b)	200r on 20f Apollo 8	100.00	
642	A105(b)	200r on 20f #336	100.00	
643	A131(a)	200r on 20f #425	240.00	
644	A134(a)	200r on 75f #436	100.00	
645	A135(a)	200r on 250f #437	100.00	

Size and location of surcharge varies.
No. 582 exists with a 50r type "b" surcharge.
No. 636 exists with a surcharge similar to
surcharge "c."
Nos. 639, 641 without surcharge have not
been listed in the Scott Catalogue.

Yemen Unity,
4th
Anniv. — A155

Various views of govt. building, San'a.

1994, Sept. 27   *Litho.*   *Perf. 13½x14*
646	A155	3r multicolored	.60
647	A155	5r multicolored	.90
648	A155	8r multicolored	1.50
649	A155	20r multicolored	3.25
	Nos. 646-649 (4)		6.25

Souvenir Sheet
650	A155	20r multi, diff.	4.00

1994 World Cup
Soccer
Championships,
US — A156

2r, Player in yellow shirt dribbling ball, vert.
6r, Player in striped shirt dribbling, vert. 10r,
Goal keeper. No. 654, Heading ball, vert.
No. 655, Tackling.

1994, Oct. 1   *Perf. 14x13½, 13½x14*
651	A156	2r multicolored	.50
652	A156	6r multicolored	1.25
653	A156	10r multicolored	2.00
654	A156	12r multicolored	2.50
	Nos. 651-654 (4)		6.25

Souvenir Sheet
655	A156	12r multicolored	3.50

World Day of
Environmental
Protection — A157

Perf. 14x13½, 13½x14

1995, Oct. 15   *Litho.*
656	A157	15r Arabian leopard	1.25
657	A157	20r Caracal lynx	1.50
658	A157	30r Guinea fowl, horiz.	2.50
	Nos. 656-658 (3)		5.25

Souvenir Sheet
659	A157	50r Partridge, horiz.	4.50

FAO, 50th
Anniv. — A158

Emblem, field, hand holding: 10r, Plant. 25r,
Seed. 30r, Fish. 50r, Grain.

1995, Oct. 16   *Perf. 14x13½*
660	A158	10r violet & multi	.80
661	A158	25r claret & multi	1.60
662	A158	30r light blue & multi	2.00
	Nos. 660-662 (3)		4.40

Souvenir Sheet
663	A158	50r dark blue & multi	3.75

A159

UN, 50th anniv.: Various views of Aden
Dam.

1995, Oct. 24   *Perf. 14x13½, 13½x14*
664	A159	10r multi	1.00
665	A159	20r multi	2.00
666	A159	25r multi, horiz.	2.50
		Nos. 664-666 (3)	5.50

Souvenir Sheet
667	A159	50r multi, horiz.	5.00

A160

Naseem Hamed Kashmem, world boxing champion: 10r, With champion belts. 20r, Up close. 25r, Boxing opponent, horiz. 30r, Holding up arm as winner, trainer.
50r, Boxing opponent, diff., horiz.

Perf. 14x13½, 13½x14

1995, Nov. 29
668	A160	10r multicolored	1.00
669	A160	20r multicolored	2.00
670	A160	25r multicolored	2.50
671	A160	30r multicolored	3.00
		Nos. 668-671 (4)	8.50

Souvenir Sheet
672	A160	50r multicolored	5.00

Souvenir Sheet

CHINA '96, 9th Asian Intl. Philatelic Exhibition — A161

1996, May 18   **Litho.**   *Perf. 11½*
673	A161	80r Shanghai	7.50

1996 Summer Olympic Games, Atlanta — A162

1996, July 19   *Perf. 14x13½, 13½x14*
674	A162	20r Wrestling, vert.	.90
675	A162	50r High jump	1.90
676	A162	60r Running, vert.	2.10
677	A162	70r Gymnastics, vert.	2.75
678	A162	100r Judo, vert.	4.50
		Nos. 674-678 (5)	12.15

Souvenir Sheet
679	A162	150r Javelin, vert.	7.50

Landmarks
A163

10r, 70r, 250r, Popular Heritage Museum, Seiyoan. 15r, 40r, 60r, 500r, Rock Palace, Wadi Dhahr, vert. 20r, 100r, 200r, Old Sana'a City. 30r, 50r, 150r, 300r, Al-Mohdhar Minaret, Tarim, vert.

Perf. 13½x14, 14x13½

1996, Sept. 26   **Litho.**
680	A163	10r org yel & multi	.50
681	A163	15r grn yel & multi	.75
682	A163	20r lt blue & multi	1.00
683	A163	30r blue & multi	1.25
684	A163	40r salmon & multi	1.75
685	A163	50r green & multi	2.25
686	A163	60r lilac & multi	3.00
687	A163	70r violet & multi	3.50
688	A163	100r yellow & multi	4.50
689	A163	150r orange & multi	6.00
690	A163	200r rose & multi	8.00
691	A163	250r gray & multi	10.00
692	A163	300r red & multi	12.50
693	A163	500r yellow & multi	20.00
		Nos. 680-693 (14)	75.00

Birds — A164

Designs: 20r, Tyto alba. 50r, Alectoris philbyi. 60r, Gypaetus barbatus. 70r, Alectoris melanocephala. 100r, Chlamydotis undulata. 150r, Ixobrychus minutus, vert.

1996, Oct. 14   **Litho.**   *Perf. 13½x14*
694	A164	20r multicolored	.60
695	A164	50r multicolored	1.50
696	A164	60r multicolored	1.80
697	A164	70r multicolored	2.10
698	A164	100r multicolored	3.00
		Nos. 694-698 (5)	9.00

Souvenir Sheet
Perf. 14x13½
699	A164	150r multicolored	5.00

Rare Plants in Yemen — A165

Designs: 20r, Parodia masii. 50r, Notocatus cristata. 60r, Adenium obesum socotranum. 70r, Dracaena cinnabari. 100r, Mammillaria erythrosperma. 150r, Parodia maasii, diff.

1996, Nov. 30   *Perf. 13½x14*
700	A165	20r multicolored	.60
701	A165	50r multicolored	1.50
702	A165	60r multicolored	1.80
703	A165	70r multicolored	2.10
704	A165	100r multicolored	3.00
		Nos. 700-704 (5)	9.00

Souvenir Sheet
705	A165	150r multicolored	5.00

A166

Fish: 20r, Heniochus acuminatus. 50r, 150r, Cheilinus undulatus. 60r, Zebrasoma xanthurum. 70r, Pomacanthus imperator. 100r, Pomacanthus vanthometopon.

1996, Nov. 30
706	A166	20r multicolored	.60
707	A166	50r multicolored	1.50
708	A166	60r multicolored	1.80
709	A166	70r multicolored	2.10
710	A166	100r multicolored	3.00
		Nos. 706-710 (5)	9.00

Souvenir Sheet
711	A166	150r multicolored	5.00

A167

UNICEF, 50th Anniv.: 20r, Children with books. 50r, Girls clapping hands. 60r, Mother, child. 70r, Mother, three children.
150r, Child making jewelry, horiz.

1996, Dec. 11   *Perf. 14x13½*
712	A167	20r multicolored	.60
713	A167	50r multicolored	1.50
714	A167	60r multicolored	1.80
715	A167	70r multicolored	2.10
		Nos. 712-715 (4)	6.00

Souvenir Sheet
Perf. 13½x14
716	A167	150r multicolored	5.00

1998 World Cup Soccer Championships, France — A168

Various soccer plays.

1998, June 10   **Litho.**   *Perf. 13x13½*
717	A168	10r multicolored	.35
718	A168	15r multicolored	.45
719	A168	35r multicolored	.85
720	A168	65r multicolored	1.40
721	A168	75r multicolored	1.60
a.		Souvenir sheet, #717-721	6.00
		Nos. 717-721 (5)	4.65

Birds A169

Designs: 10r, Ardeotis arabs. 15r, Neophron percnopterus. 35r, Coracias abyssinicus. 65r, Cinnyricinclus leucogaster. 75r, Melierax metabates.

1998, Sept. 26   **Litho.**   *Perf. 13*
722-726	A169	Set of 5	6.00	6.00
726a		Sheet of 5, #722-726	6.00	6.00

Universal Declaration of Human Rights, 50th Anniv. A170

15r, Hands in air. 35r, Hands clasped in handshake. 100r, Hands reaching out.

1998, Oct. 12
727-729	A170	Set of 3	4.50	4.50
729a		Sheet of 3, #727-729	4.50	4.50

First General Conference of Yemeni Immigrants (in 1999) A171

Emblem &: 60r, Dhows. 90r, Fort, camel.

2000, May 16   **Litho.**   *Perf. 14½x14*
730-731	A171	Set of 2	4.00	4.00
731a		Souvenir sheet, #730-731	4.00	4.00

Tenth National Day — A172

Background colors: 30r, Light green. 50r, Rose lilac. 70r, Light blue. 150r, Orange.

2000, May 22   *Perf. 14x14½*
732-734	A172	Set of 3	4.00	4.00

Souvenir Sheet
735	A172	150r multi	4.00	4.00

Plants of Socotra — A173

Designs: 30r, Euphorbia abdalkuri. 70r, Dendrosicyos socotranus. 80r, Caralluma socotrana. 120r, Dracaena cinnabari. 300r, Exacum affine.

2000, July 15
736-739	A173	Set of 4	8.00	8.00

Souvenir Sheet
740	A173	300r multi	8.00	8.00

2000 Summer Olympics, Sydney — A174

Designs: 50r, Judo. 70r, Runner. 80r, Hurdler. 100r, Shooting. 300r, Tennis.

2000, Sept. 15
741-744	A174	Set of 4	8.00	8.00

Souvenir Sheet
745	A174	300r multi	8.00	8.00

Antiquities — A175

Designs: 30r, Stone idols, 3000 B.C. 70r, Statue of Ma'adi Karib, 800 B.C. 100r, Horned griffin, Royal Palace of Shabwa, 300. 120r, Statue of King of Awsan Yasduq Eil, 100 B.C. 320r, Stele with bull's head, 100 B.C., horiz.

2002, June 15   **Litho.**   *Perf. 13x12¾*
746-749	A175	Set of 4	8.50	8.50

Souvenir Sheet
Imperf
750	A175	320r multi	8.50	8.50

No. 750 contains one 41x26mm stamp.

2002 World Cup Soccer Championships, Japan and Korea — A176

Soccer players with background colors of: 30r, Bister, vert. 70r, Green. 100r, Blue, vert. 120r, Red brown, vert.
No. 755: a, Player's foot and ball. b, World Cup trophy.

2002, May 31   *Perf. 13x12¾, 12¾x13*
751-754 A176   Set of 4   8.50 8.50

Souvenir Sheet
Perf.

755 A176 160r Sheet of 2, #a-b   8.50 8.50

No. 755 contains two 28mm diameter stamps.

Scouting in Yemen, 75th Anniv. A177

Designs: 30r, Scout escorting man across street. 60r, Scout digging. 70r, Scouts in rowboat.
160r, Scout saluting, vert.

2002, Apr. 30   *Perf. 12¾x13*
756-758 A177   Set of 3   4.25 4.25

Souvenir Sheet
Perf. 13x13¼

759 A177 160r multi   4.25 4.25

No. 759 contains one 16x26mm stamp.

Palestinian Intifada — A178

Designs: 30r, Frightened child. 60r, Bleeding child.
90r, Dome of the Rock, horiz.

2002, Apr. 27   *Perf. 13x12¾*
760-761 A178   Set of 2   2.50 2.50
Imperf
Size: 111x78mm

762 A178 90r multi   2.50 2.50

Poets — A179

Designs: Nos. 763, 30r, 765, 60r, 767a, 70r, Hussain Al-Muhdhar (1931-2000). Nos. 764, 30r, 766, 60r, 767b, 70r, Abdullah Al-Baradony (1929-99).

2002, June 30   Litho.   *Perf. 13x12¾*
763-766 A179   Set of 4   4.50 4.50

Souvenir Sheet
Perf. 13x13¼

767 A179 70r Sheet of 2, #a-b   3.50 3.50

No. 767 contains two 16x28mm stamps.

Revolution, 40th Anniv. — A180

Background colors: 30r, Dull green. 60r, Rose.
90r, Lilac.

2002, Sept. 26   *Perf. 13x12¾*
768-769 A180   Set of 2   2.25 2.25
Imperf
Size: 110x76mm

770 A180 90r multi   2.25 2.25

World Under-17 Soccer Championships, Finland — A181

Various soccer players with background color of: 30r, Red violet. 50r, Golden brown. 70r, Blue. 100r, Green.
250r, Soccer team and stadium.

2003, Aug. 13   Litho.   *Perf. 12¾x13*
771-774 A181   Set of 4   6.00 6.00
Imperf
Size: 109x74mm

775 A181 250r multi   6.00 6.00

Antiquities — A182

Various sculptures with background colors of: 20r, Pale yellow. 40r, Lilac. 50r, Light green. 150r, Pink.
260r, Black, horiz.

2003, Sept. 26   *Perf. 13x12¾*
776-779 A182   Set of 4   6.00 6.00

Souvenir Sheet
Perf. 12¾x13

780 A182 260r multi   6.00 6.00

Traditional Women's Clothing — A183

Various women with panel colors of: 30r, Purple. 60r, Yellow green. 70r, Dark green. 100r, Red violet. 150r, Brown.
410r, Purple background, horiz.

2003, Oct. 14   *Perf. 13x12¾*
781-785 A183   Set of 5   9.00 9.00

Souvenir Sheet
Perf. 12¾x13

786 A183 410r multi   9.00 9.00

Children's Art — A184

Designs: 20r, Girl with flower on globe, vert. 30r, Dove over buildings, vert. 40r, Dove holding swing, vert. 50r, Children in field. 60r, Animals in field. 70r, Street and park.

2003, Oct. 15   *Perf. 13x12¾, 12¾x13*
787-792 A184   Set of 6   6.00 6.00

Sana'a, 2004 Arabic Cultural Capital — A185

Various buildings with frame colors of: 30r, White. 50r, Purple. 70r, Black. 100r, Dark brown. 150r Red brown.
400r, Buildings, horiz.

2003, Nov. 30   *Perf. 13x12¾*
793-797 A185   Set of 5   9.00 9.00

Souvenir Sheet
Perf. 12¾x13

798 A185 400r multi   9.00 9.00

FIFA (Fédération Internationale de Football Association), Cent. — A186

2004, May 21   Litho.   *Perf. 13x12¾*
799 A186 100r multi   2.25 2.25

Dated 2005. Stamps did not appear in marketplace until 2005.

2004 Summer Olympics, Athens — A187

Designs: 70r, Running. 80r, Shooting. 100r, Swimming.
250r, Equestrian.

2004, Aug. 13
800-802 A187   Set of 3   5.50 5.50

Souvenir Sheet

803 A187 250r multi   5.50 5.50

Dated 2005. Stamps did not appear in marketplace until 2005.

Telecommunications and Technology — A188

Designs: 60r, Computer chips, "@" symbol, keyboard. 70r, Computer and stylized people, vert. 100r, Yemen Mobile emblem, vert.
400r, Like 70r, vert.

Perf. 12¾x13, 13x12¾
2004, Sept. 26
804-806 A188   Set of 3   5.00 5.00

Souvenir Sheet

807 A188 400r multi   9.00 9.00

Dated 2005. Stamps did not appear in marketplace until 2005.

Spiders A189

No. 808: a, Tidarren argo. b, Scelidomachus socotranus. c, Habrocestum albopunctatum. d, Rafalus insignipalpis. e, Latrodectus hystrix. f, Atrophothele socotrana.
300r, Like No. 808b.

2004, Oct. 14   *Perf. 12¾x13*
808   Horiz. strip of 6   6.50 6.50
  a.-f.   A189 50r Any single   1.00 1.00

Souvenir Sheet

809 A189 300r multi   6.50 6.50

Dated 2005. Stamps did not appear in marketplace until 2005.

Traditional Men's Clothing — A190

Men wearing various outfits with background colors of: 50r, Light yellow. 60r, Green. 70r, Pink. 100r, Blue.
360r, Orange brown.

2004, Oct. 30   *Perf. 13x12¾*
810-813 A190   Set of 4   6.50 6.50

Souvenir Sheet

814 A190 360r multi   8.00 8.00

Dated 2005. Stamps did not appear in marketplace until 2005.

Handicrafts A191

No. 815: a, Knife maker holding hammer. b, Textile worker piecing fabric. c, Jeweler. d, Weaver at loom.
3004, Like No. 815a.

2004, Nov. 30
815   Horiz. strip of 4   6.50 6.50
  a.-d.   A191 70r multi   1.60 1.60

Souvenir Sheet

816 A191 300r multi   6.50 6.50

Dated 2005. Stamps did not appear in marketplace until 2005.

15th National Day — A192

Emblem and: 30r, Industrial plant. 60r, Dam and reservoir. 70r, Man holding flag.
90r, Buildings.

2005, May 22
817-819 A192   Set of 3   3.50 3.50

Souvenir Sheet

820 A192 90r multi   2.00 2.00

United Nations,
60th
Anniv. — A193

Symbols of eight goals for a better Yemen:
No. 821, 40r, Pregnant woman and doctor.
No. 822, 40r, Woman, infant and doctor. No.
823, 40r, Woman reading book. No. 824, 40r,
Mosquito, AIDS ribbon, medicine and bottle.
No. 825, 40r, Man depositing trash in can,
tree, smiling sun. 80r, Goats, hat seller and
child. 100r, Woman, man and balance. 120r,
Handshake.
130r, UN anniversary emblem.

2005, Oct. 24　Litho.　Perf. 13x12¾
821-828　A193　Set of 8　　11.00　11.00
　　　　　Size: 111x83mm
　　　　　　　Imperf
829　A193　130r multi　　　　3.00　3.00
No. 829 contains one perforated label lacking a denomination.

Flowers
A194

Various flowers: 50r, 80r, 110r, 130r, 140r,
150r, 300r.

**　　　　　Perf. 13¼x13¾**
2007, Sept. 26　　　　　Litho.
830-835　A194　Set of 6　　13.50　13.50
　　　Souvenir Sheet
836　A194　300r multi　　　　6.00　6.00

Insects
A195

Designs: No. 837, 50r, Cheilomenes lunata
yemenensis. No. 838, 50r, Pharoscymnus c-
luteus. No. 839, 50r, Hippodamia variegata.
No. 840, 50r, Cheilomenes propinqua vicina.
No. 841, 50r, Brumoides nigrifrons. No. 842,
50r, Serangium buettikeri.
250r, Pharoscymnus c-luteus, diff.

2007, Sept. 26　　　　Perf. 13¾x13¼
837-842　A195　Set of 6　　6.00　6.00
　　　Souvenir Sheet
843　A195　250r multi　　　　5.00　5.00

Mosques
A196

Designs: 50r, Mosque of Prophethood,
Hadhramaut. 80r, Al Ameria Mosque, Radaa.
100r, Queen Arwa Mosque, Jebla. 110r, Al
Ashrafiah Mosque, Taiz. 120r, Al Aidarous
Mosque, Aden. 200r, Al Bukiriah Mosque,
Sana'a.
300r, Unidentified mosque.

2007, Oct. 14　　　　Perf. 13¼x13¾
844-849　A196　Set of 6　　13.50　13.50
　　　Souvenir Sheet
850　A196　300r multi　　　　6.00　6.00

Citadels
and
Castles
A197

Designs: 50r, Thulaa Citadel, Amran. 80r, Al
Tawama Citadels, Hadhramaut. 100r, Serah
Castle, Aden. 110r, Sumarah Castle, Ibb.
130r, Al Qahira Castle, Taiz.
300r, Unidentified castle.

2007, Oct. 14
851-855　A197　Set of 5　　9.50　9.50
　　　Souvenir Sheet
856　A197　300r multi　　　　6.00　6.00

Marine
Life
A198

Designs: 50r, Parupeneus marconema. 80r,
Sarda orientalis. 100r, Carcharhinus melanopterus. 110r, Plectorhinchus schotaf. 130r,
Panulirus homarus. 160r, Seriola rivoliana.
300r, Panulirus homarus, diff.

2007, Nov. 30
857-862　A198　Set of 6　　13.00　13.00
　　　Souvenir Sheet
863　A198　300r multi　　　　6.00　6.00

Yemeni Onyx
A199

Various set and unset onyx stones: 50r, 80r,
100r, 110r, 120r, 130r, 140r, 160r.
250r, Set and unset onyx stones.

2007, Nov. 30　　　　Perf. 13¾x13¼
864-871　A199　Set of 8　　18.00　18.00
　　　Souvenir Sheet
872　A199　250r multi　　　　5.00　5.00

Natl. Day
of Human
Rights
A200

Globe, flag, dove, human rights emblem
with background color of: 110r, Red violet.
130r, Blue.
250r, Dove and flag, vert.

2007, Dec. 10　　　　Perf. 13¼x13¾
873-874　A200　Set of 2　　5.00　5.00
　　　Souvenir Sheet
　　　Perf. 13¾x13¼
875　A200　250r multi　　　　5.00　5.00

Yasser Arafat
(1929-2004),
Palestinian
Leader — A201

Palestinian Authority flag and Arafat: 120r,
With hand raised. 300fr, With hands not
shown, horiz.

2008, Nov. 4　Litho.　Perf. 13x12¾
876　A201　120r multi　　　　2.50　2.50
　　　Size: 110x70mm
　　　　　Imperf
877　A201　300r multi　　　　6.00　6.00

Opening of
Al-Saleh
Mosque,
Sana'a
A202

Mosque: 80r, Pillars, ceiling and chande-
liers. 100r, Interior wall. 120r, Exterior.
300r, Exterior, diff.

2008, Nov. 22　　　　Perf. 12¾x13
878-880　A202　Set of 3　　6.00　6.00
　　　Size: 109x70mm
　　　　　Imperf
881　A202　300r multi　　　　6.00　6.00

Gaza — A203

Designs: 60r, Man, boy carrying Palestinian
flag. 100r, Barbed wire, children looking
through hole in wall, horiz.
120r, Dove and chain.

2009, May 22　Perf. 13¼x13, 13x13¼
882-883　A203　Set of 2　　3.25　3.25
　　　Souvenir Sheet
884　A203　120r multi　　　　2.50　2.50

Ancient
Coins
A204

Various ancient coins: 50r, 60r, 70r, 80r,
100r, 120r. 60r and 80r are vert. 120r is
50x50mm diamond-shaped stamp.

2009, May 22　Perf. 13x13¼, 13¼x13
885-889　A204　Set of 5　　7.50　7.50
　　　Souvenir Sheet
　　　Perf. 13¼
890　A204　120r multi　　　　2.50　2.50

Ancient
Jewelry — A205

Designs: 50r, Bracelet and ring. 60r, Bracelet, horiz. 80r, Necklace and earrings. 100r,

Bracelets, horiz. 120r, Necklace. 140r, Bracelets, diff., horiz.
150r, Belt, horiz.

2009, May 22　Perf. 13¼x13, 13x13¼
891-896　A205　Set of 6　　11.00　11.00
　　　Souvenir Sheet
897　A205　150r multi　　　　3.00　3.00

Horses
A206

Designs: 60r, Head of brown horse with
white blaze. 80r, Black horse. 100r, Brown
horse with white blaze. 120r, Brown horse
with white mane. 140r, White horse. 150r, Head of
brown horse with white blaze, diff.
200r, Dappled gray horse, vert.

2009, May 22　　　　Perf. 13x13¼
898-903　A206　Set of 6　　13.00　13.00
　　　Souvenir Sheet
　　　Perf. 13¼x13
904　A206　200r multi　　　　4.25　4.25

　　　Souvenir Sheet

Arab Postal Day — A207

No. 905 — Emblem and: a, World map, pigeon. b, Camel caravan.

2009, May 22　　　　　Perf. 12¾
905　A207　100r Sheet of 2, #a-b　4.25　4.25

Tarim, 2010
Capital of
Islamic
Culture
A208

Designs: 50r, Palace, yellow and red panel.
60r, Minaret, yellow and green panel. 80r, Al
Kaff Palace, orange panel. 100r, Qasr al-
Qubba Hotel, black panel.
200r, Palace at night, yellow and brown
frame.

2010, Mar. 1　　　Litho.　Perf. 13¼
906-909　A208　Set of 4　　3.50　3.50
　　　Souvenir Sheet
910　A208　200r multi　　　　4.75　4.75

National
Day — A209

20th anniversary emblem and background
colors of: 60r, Brown and red brown. 80r, Yellow and brown. 200r, Emblem, horiz.

2010, May 22　　　Litho.　Perf. 13
911-912　A209　Set of 2　　3.00　3.00
　　　Souvenir Sheet
913　A209　200r multi　　　　4.25　4.25

2010 World Cup Soccer Championships, South Africa — A210

2010 World Cup emblem, World Cup and various South African stadiums hosting matches: 50r, 60r, 80r, 100r.
No. 918, vert.: a, 50r, 2010 World Cup emblem. b, 100r, World Cup.

2010, June 11

914-917 A210	Set of 4	7.75	7.75

Souvenir Sheet

918 A210	Sheet of 2, #a-b	4.75	4.75

Yemeni Janbiahs (Daggers) A211

Various daggers in sheaths: 50r, 60r, 80r, 100r, 120r. 60r and 100r are vert.
200r, Dagger, diff.

2010, July 21 ***Perf. 12¾***

919-923 A211	Set of 5	8.50	8.50

Souvenir Sheet

924 A211 200r multi		4.25	4.25

20th Gulf Cup of Nations Soccer Tournament, Aden — A212

Soccer player at LL and: 60r, Emblem depicting soccer ball, map of Arabian Peninsula. 80r, Soccer players in posed photograph. 100r, Gulf Cup, ring of flags. 120r, Stadium. 150r, Tournament emblem.
250r, Soccer ball with tournament emblem depicting soccer ball and map of Arabian Peninsula.

2010, Nov. 22 ***Perf. 13¼***

925-929 A212	Set of 5	7.25	7.25

Souvenir Sheet

930 A212 250r multi		3.50	3.50

AIR POST STAMPS

Catalogue values for unused stamps in this section are for Never Hinged items.

Plane over San'a AP1

1947 Unwmk. Engr. ***Perf. 12½***

C1 AP1 10b bright blue		6.00	2.00
C2 AP1 20b olive green		10.00	2.50

Views Type of Regular Issue

6b, 8b, View of San'a. 10b, Mocha coffee tree. 12b, Palace of the Rock, Wadi Dhahr. 16b, Palace, Ta'iz. 20b, 1i, Parade Ground, San'a.

1951 Wmk. 277 Photo. ***Perf. 14***

C3 A14 6b blue	1.40	.50
C4 A14 8b dark brown	1.75	.60
C5 A14 10b dark green	2.25	1.40
C6 A13 12b dark blue	2.50	.80
C7 A14 16b lilac rose	3.00	.80
C8 A13 20b orange brown	3.75	1.25
C9 A13 1i dark red	10.00	3.00
Nos. C3-C9 (7)	24.65	8.35

Nos. C3 and C4 were used provisionally in 1957 for registry and foreign ordinary mail.

Type of Regular Issue

Designs: 12b, Palace of the Rock, Wadi Dhahr. 20b, Walls of Ibb.

Engraved and Photogravure

1952 Unwmk. ***Perf. 14½, Imperf.***

C10 A15 12b grnsh blk, bl & brn	10.00	10.00
C11 A15 20b indigo, bl & brn	10.00	10.00

Flag-and-View Type

1952

C12 A16 1i dk brn, car & brt ultra	18.00	18.00

1952 Palace in Foreground

C13 A16 30b yel grn, car & gray	11.00	11.00

Leaning Minaret, Mosque of Ta'iz — AP6

1954 Photo. ***Perf. 14***

C14 AP6 10b scarlet	3.25	.90
C15 AP6 12b dull blue	4.00	1.25
C16 AP6 20b olive bister	6.50	2.00
Nos. C14-C16 (3)	13.75	4.15

Accession of King Ahmed I, 5th anniv.

Type of Regular Issue

1959 Wmk. 318 ***Perf. 13x13½***

C17 A21 6b orange & blk	1.00	.70
C18 A21 10b red & blk	1.60	1.25
C19 A21 16b brt violet & red	2.50	2.00
Nos. C17-C19 (3)	5.10	3.95

In 1959, four values of the 1931 issue and three values of the 1930 issue overprinted Air Mail 1959 were distributed. Although these stamps were not regularly sold in Yemeni post offices, several values of these sets were used on air-mail cover going abroad. Several of these stamps exist with inverted or doubled overprints.

Antiquities of Marib Type

Designs: 6b, Columns, Temple of the Moon God. 16b, Control tower and spillway of 2,700-year-old dam of Marib.

Perf. 11½

1961, Oct. 14 Unwmk. Photo.

C20 A27 6b lt bl grn & blk	1.00	.25
C21 A27 16b lt blue & blk	2.75	1.50

Exist imperf.
For overprints see Nos. C24, C25.

Buildings Type

6b, Bab al-Yemen, main gate of San'a, horiz. 16b, Palace of the Rock (Dar al-Hajar).

1961, Nov. 15

C22 A28 6b blk, lt bl & grn	.55	.25
C23 A28 16b blk, rose & grn	1.40	.60

For overprints see Nos. C24A, C25A.

Nos. C20-C23 Ovptd. Like Nos. 144-158 in Dark Red or Black

Perf. 11½

1963, Jan. 1 Photo. Unwmk.

C24 A27 (a) 6b No. C20	.70	.70
C24A A28 (b) 6b No. C22	.85	.85
C25 A27 (a) 16b No. C21	1.75	1.75
C25A A28 (a) 16b No. C23 (B)	2.75	2.75

Proclamation of the Republic Type

1963, Mar. 15 ***Perf. 11x11½, 11½x11***

C26 A34 8b Bayonette, torch	1.50	1.50
C27 A34 10b Jet, torch, tank	2.00	2.00
C28 A34 16b Flag, chain, torch	2.75	2.75

Nos. C27-C28 horiz.

An imperf. souvenir sheet containing one No. C28 exists. Value $10.

Nos. 25-29 Ovptd. in Black

Wmk. 258

1963, Sept. 1 Litho. ***Perf. 12½***

C29 A5 6b slate blue & ultra	1.50	1.50
C29A A5 10b fawn & ultra	1.90	1.90
C29B A5 14b olive & ultra	2.25	2.25
C29C A5 20b yel grn & ultra	3.00	3.00
C29D A5 1i claret & ultra	6.50	6.50
Nos. C29-C29D (5)	15.15	15.15

Exist imperf. Value, set $25.

Spacecraft — AP6a

Various spacecraft.

1963, Dec. 5 Photo. ***Perf. 13***

C29E AP6a ¼b multicolored	.50	.50
C29F AP6a ⅓b multicolored	.50	.50
C29G AP6a ½b multicolored	.50	.50
C29H AP6a 4b multicolored	1.00	1.00
C29I AP6a 20b multicolored	5.00	5.00
Nos. C29E-C29I (5)	7.50	7.50

Exist imperf. Value, set $15. An imperf. souvenir sheet containing C29I also exists. Value $7.

Nos. C29E-C29G Overprinted in Black, Red Brown or Brown

1964-1966 Photo. ***Perf. 13***

C29J AP6a ¼b On No. C29E	1.00	1.00
C29K AP6a ¼b On No. C29E (RB)	2.50	2.50
C29L AP6a ⅓b On No. C29F	1.00	1.00
C29M AP6a ⅓b On No. C29F (RB)	2.50	2.50
C29N AP6a ½b On No. C29G	1.00	1.00
C29O AP6a ½b On No. C29G (Br)	5.00	5.00
Nos. C29J-C29O (6)	13.00	13.00

Issued: Nos. C29J, C29L, C29N, 12/6/64. Nos. C29K, C29M, 1965. No. C29O, 1966.
Imperf. examples of Nos. C29H-C29I exist with the red brown overprint.

San'a Intl. Airport Type

Perf. 11½x11

1964, Oct. 1 Photo. Unwmk.

C30 A40 6b Sun, buildings, aircraft	.70	.70

See note after No. 203.

APU 10th Anniv. Type

1964, Oct. 15 ***Perf. 13½***

C31 A41 6b blue grn & blk	1.00	.80

An imperf. souvenir sheet of one exists containing No. C31. Value $3.

Deir Yassin Massacre Type

1965, Apr. 30 ***Perf. 11x11½***

C32 A44 6b ver & brt org	1.00	

Library Type

1965, July 7 ***Perf. 11½x11***

C33 A46 6b sepia, red & int blue	.75	.50

An imperf. souvenir sheet of one exists containing No. C33. Value $2.50.

Butterflies — AP6b

Various butterflies.

1966, May 5 Photo. ***Perf. 12½***

C33A AP6b 6b multicolored	1.50	.75
C33B AP6b 8b multicolored	2.00	1.00
C33C AP6b 10b multicolored	3.00	1.50
C33D AP6b 16b multicolored	4.00	2.00
Nos. C33A-C33D (4)	10.50	5.25

Nos. C33A-C33D exist imperf. Value $20.

1968 Winter Olympic Games, Grenoble — AP6c

1967, Nov. 11 Litho. ***Perf. 13¼***

C33E AP6c 5b gold & multi	1.05
C33F AP6c 10b gold & multi	2.10
C33G AP6c 15b gold & multi	3.25
Nos. C33E-C33G (3)	6.40

Exist imperf. in silver. Perf. and imperf. souvenir sheets containing one No. C33G exist in both gold and silver.

Konrad Adenauer (1876-1967) AP6d

1968, June Litho. ***Perf. 11***

C33H AP6d 5b gold & black	1.90
C33I AP6d 10b gold, blk & grn	3.75
C33J AP6d 15b gold, blk & blue	5.50
Nos. C33H-C33J (3)	11.15

Exist imperf. in silver. Perf. and imperf. souvenir sheets containing one No. C33J exist in both gold and silver.

Red Crescent Organization — AP6e

1968 **Litho.** **Perf. 11**
C33K AP6e 5b gold & multi 1.50
C33L AP6e 10b gold & multi 3.00
C33M AP6e 15b gold & multi 4.50
Nos. C33K-C33M (3) 9.00

Exist imperf. in silver. An imperf. souvenir sheet containing one No. C33M exists in silver.
For surcharge see No. C39A.

Vladimir Komarov (1927-1967), Soviet Cosmonaut — AP6f

1968 **Litho.** **Perf. 13½**
C33N AP6f 5b gold & multi 1.00
C33O AP6f 10b gold & multi 2.00
C33P AP6f 15b gold & multi 3.00
Nos. C33N-C33P (3) 6.00

Exist imperf. in silver. An imperf. souvenir sheet containing one No. C33P exists in gold.

Nos. C33H-C33J Overprinted in Black for Refugees

1968 **Litho.** **Perf. 11**
C33Q AP6d 5b gold & black 1.00
C33R AP6d 10b gold, blk & grn 2.00
C33S AP6d 15b gold, blk & blue 3.00
Nos. C33Q-C33S (3) 6.00

Exist imperf. in silver. Perf. and imperf. souvenir sheets containing one No. C33S exist in both gold and silver.

1968 Summer Olympic Games, Mexico City — AP6g

1968, July 2 **Litho.** **Perf. 13½**
C33T AP6g 5b gold & multi 1.00
C33U AP6g 10b gold & multi 2.00
C33V AP6g 15b gold & multi 3.00
Nos. C33T-C33V (3) 6.00

Exist imperf. in silver. Imperf. souvenir sheets containing one No. C33V exists in gold and silver.
For surcharge see No. C39B.

Universal Declaration of Human Rights, 20th Anniv. — AP6h

1968, Oct. 20 **Litho.** **Perf. 13½**
C33W AP6g 5b gold & multi 1.00
C33X AP6g 10b gold & multi 2.00
C33Y AP6g 15b gold & multi 3.00
Nos. C33W-C33Y (3) 6.00

Exist imperf. in silver. An imperf. souvenir sheet containing one No. C33Y exists in gold.
For surcharge see No. C39C.

Lenin's Birth Centenary AP7

1970, Aug. 15 **Litho.** **Perf. 12x12½**
C34 AP7 6b Public speech 1.40 1.10
C35 AP7 16b Meeting with Arab delegates 3.00 1.90

8th Anniv. of the Revolution — AP8

1971, Jan. 24 **Perf. 13**
C36 AP8 5b Country estate .75
C37 AP8 7b Workers 1.10
C38 AP8 16b Handshake, flag, flowers, open book 1.50
Nos. C36-C38 (2) 2.25

A souv. sheet of 1 exists containing. No. C38. Value $5.

No. C38 Overprinted in Black

1971, Jan. 24
C39 AP8 16b multicolored 5.00 3.00

Nos. C33L, C33V and C33X Surcharged in Black

1971, Jan. 24 **Perf. 13**
C39A AP6e 40b On 10b #C33L, "40" is 4.5mm high
d. "40" is 3.5mm high
C39B AP6g 60b on 15b #C33V
C39C AP6h 80b On 10b #C33X
e. Missing "B" in surcharge

Revolution Type
1972, Nov. 25 **Photo.** **Perf. 13**
C40 A80 21b lilac, blk & multi 5.00 3.50

For surcharge see No. C46A.

Al-Aqsa Mosque Type
1973, Jan. 1 **Photo.** **Perf. 13½**
C41 A82 24b lt bl, blk & multi 5.00 2.50
a. Min. sheet of 1, imperf. 5.00 2.50

UNICEF Type
1973, Jan. 15 **Photo.** **Perf. 13**
C42 A83 18b lt bl, blk & multi 1.90 1.50
a. Min. sheet of 1, imperf. 3.25 2.50

For surcharge see No. C46.

11th Anniv. of Revolution AP10

1973, Sept. 26 **Photo.** **Perf. 14**
C43 AP10 7b Bank .50 .35
C44 AP10 10b Cement factory .65 .55
C45 AP10 18b Hospital 1.50 1.10
Nos. C43-C45 (3) 2.65 2.00

For surcharges see Nos. C47-C48.

Nos. C40, C42, C43, C45 Surcharged in Black or Red with New Value and Bars
1975, Nov. 15
C46 A83 75f on 18b lt bl, blk & multi 2.50 2.50
C46A A80 75f on 21b #C40 (R) 5.00 4.00
C47 AP10 90f on 7b multi 5.50 2.75
C48 AP10 120f on 18b multi 4.25 4.25
a. Overprinted in black (R)

Argentina 1978 World Cup Type
World cup emblem and various soccer players.

1980, Mar. 30 **Photo.** **Perf. 14**
C49 A99 60f gold & multi 1.25 .60
C50 A99 75f gold & multi 1.50 .70
C51 A99 80f gold & multi 1.80 .90
C52 A99 100f gold & multi 2.25 1.00
Nos. C49-C52 (4) 4.55 3.20

Two 225f souvenir sheets exist. Value, perf. $12, imperf. $15.

IYC Type
1980, Apr. 1 **Perf. 13½**
C53 A100 80f Girl, bird 3.50 1.25
C54 A100 100f Boy, butterfly, flower 3.50 1.25
C55 A100 150f Boy, butterfly, flower, diff. 5.00 1.75
Nos. C53-C55 (3) 10.50 4.25

Two 200f souvenir sheets exist. Value $12 each.

Scouting Type of 1980
1980, May 1 **Photo.** **Perf. 13½x14**
C56 A101 60f Bicycling 2.00 .80
C57 A101 75f Fencing 2.40 1.10
C58 A101 120f Butterfly catching 3.75 1.50
Nos. C56-C58 (3) 8.15 3.40

Two 300f souvenir sheets exist. Value $15 each.

Argentina 1978 Winners' Type
World cup emblem and various soccer players.

1980, June 1 **Photo.** **Perf. 14**
C59 A102 60f gold & multi 1.50 .50
C60 A102 75f gold & multi 2.10 .65
C61 A102 80f gold & multi 2.25 .75
C62 A102 100f gold & multi 2.40 1.10
Nos. C59-C62 (4) 5.50 3.00

Two 225f souvenir sheets exist. Value $12 each.

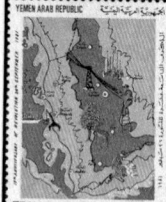

19th Anniv. of Sept. 26th Revolution (1981) — AP11

1982, Jan. 25 **Litho.** **Perf. 14**
C63 AP11 75f Map .45 .25
C64 AP11 125f Map in sunset .70 .40
C65 AP11 325f Dove in natl. colors 2.00 1.25
a. Souvenir sheet of 1 5.00 5.00
C66 AP11 400f Jets 2.25 1.40
Nos. C63-C66 (4) 5.40 3.30

Al-Hasan Ibn Al-Hamadani, Writer — AP12

1982, Feb. 1
C67 AP12 125f green & multi 1.25 .60
C68 AP12 325f blue & multi 2.75 1.40

Souvenir Sheet
C69 AP12 375f multi 3.50 3.50

No. C69 contains one stamp (36x46mm).
For surcharge see No. C138.

World Food Day — AP13

Designs: No. C76a, Eggplants. No. C76b, Tomatoes. No. C76c, Beets, peas. No. C76d, Cauliflower, carrots. No. C77a, Dove. No. C77b, Water birds. No. C77c, Fish. No. C77d, Geese.

1982, Mar. 1 **Litho.** **Perf. 14**
C70 AP13 25f Rabbits 1.25
C71 AP13 50f Rooster, Hens 1.50
C72 AP13 60f Turkeys 1.75
C73 AP13 75f Sheep 2.50
C74 AP13 100f Cattle 3.50
C75 AP13 125f Deer 4.00
Nos. C70-C75 (6) 14.50

Souvenir Sheets
C76 Sheet of 4 8.00
a.-d. AP13 100f, any single 2.00
C77 Sheet of 4 10.00
a.-d. AP13 125f, any single 2.50

For surcharges see Nos. C139, C144.
Nos. C70-C75 exist imperf. (Value, set $20) and in souvenir sheets (Value, set $45).

1980 Summer Olympics, Moscow AP14

1982, Apr. 1
C78 AP14 25f Gymnastics 1.25
C79 AP14 50f Pole vault 1.50
C80 AP14 60f Javelin 1.75

C81 AP14 75f Running 2.50
C82 AP14 100f Basketball 3.50
C83 AP14 125f Soccer 4.00
    Nos. C78-C83 (6) 14.50

Nos. C78-C81 exist imperf. (Value, set $25) and in souvenir sheets (Value, set $45).
Two souvenir sheets of 4 exist: 100f, picturing boxing, wrestling, canoeing, swimming (Value $12.50), and 125f, picturing weight lifting, discus, long jump, fencing (Value $15).
For surcharges see Nos. C140, C145.

Aviation — AP15

Various space and aircraft.

1982, May 21
C86 AP15 25f multi 1.25
C87 AP15 50f multi 1.50
C88 AP15 60f multi 1.75
C89 AP15 75f multi 2.50
C90 AP15 100f multi 3.50
C91 AP15 125f multi 4.00
    Nos. C86-C91 (6) 14.50

Nos. C86-C91 exist imperf. (Value set, $25) and in souvenir sheets (Value, set $45).
Two souvenir sheets of 4 exist, 100f and 125f, picturing various aircraft and satellites. Values $12.50 and $15, respectively.
For surcharges see Nos. C141, C146.

Intl. Year of the Disabled — AP16

Designs: Nos. C94-C99, Diff. flowers.
No. C100a, Emblem, natl. flag. b, Emblem on globe. c, Natl. colors, UN emblems. d, Disabled man, gifts, nurse.
No. C101a, Flags, globe and nurse. b, UN emblems, natl. flag. c, Emblem, disabled man. d, UN emblem, nurse.

1982, June 1
C94 AP16 25f multi 1.25
C95 AP16 50f multi 1.50
C96 AP16 60f multi 1.75
C97 AP16 75f multi 2.50
C98 AP16 100f multi 3.50
C99 AP16 125f multi 4.00
    Nos. C94-C99 (6) 14.50

Souvenir Sheets
C100   Sheet of 4 12.50
 a.-d.   AP16 100f, any single 3.00
C101   Sheet of 4 15.00
 a.-d.   AP16 125f, any single 3.50

Nos. C94-C99 exist imperf. (Value, set $25) and in souvenir sheets (Value, set $45).
For surcharge see No. C147.

Telecommunications Progress — AP17

Designs: 25f, FNRR communication center. 50f, Dish receivers, satellite, globe. 60f, Broadcast towers, dish receivers. 75f, Receivers, birds over plain. 100f, Receivers, satellite, telegraph key. No. C107, Receivers, passenger jet, Earth.
No. C108a, Receivers, Earth. b, Earth, television, flag and camera. c, Computer. d, Skyscraper, Earth, telephone.

No. C109a, Receivers, satellite, ship. b, Communication center, bolts of energy, receivers. c, Receivers, jet, ship, train, car, carriage. d, Radar.

1982, July 1   Litho.   *Perf. 14*
C102 AP17 25f multi 1.00
C103 AP17 50f multi 1.25
C104 AP17 60f multi 1.50
C105 AP17 75f multi 2.25
C106 AP17 100f multi 3.25
C107 AP17 125f multi 3.75
    Nos. C102-C107 (6) 13.00

Souvenir Sheets
C108   Sheet of 4 10.00
 a.-d.   AP17 100f any single 2.50
C109   Sheet of 4 12.00
 a.-d.   AP17 100f any single 3.00

Nos. C102-C107 exist imperf. (Value, set $20) and in souvenir sheets (Value, set $45).
For surcharges see Nos. C142, C148.

TB Bacillus Centenary — AP18

1982, Aug. 1   Litho.   *Perf. 14*
C110 AP18 25f multi 1.00
C111 AP18 50f multi 1.25
C112 AP18 60f multi 1.50
C113 AP18 75f multi 2.25
C114 AP18 100f multi 3.25
C115 AP18 125f multi 3.75
    Nos. C110-C115 (6) 13.00

Souvenir Sheets
C116   Sheet of 4, Fruit 14.00
 a.   AP18 100f, any single 3.50
C117   Sheet of 4, Flowers 14.00
 a.   AP18 125f, any single 3.50

Nos. C110-C115 exist imperf. (Value, set $20) and in souvenir sheets (Value, set $40).
For surcharges see Nos. C143, C149.

1982 World Cup Soccer Championships, Spain — AP19

Various soccer plays.

1982, Sept. 1   *Perf. 14*
C118 AP19 25f multi 1.25
C119 AP19 50f multi 1.50
C120 AP19 60f multi 1.75
C121 AP19 75f multi 2.50
C122 AP19 100f multi 3.50
C123 AP19 125f multi 4.00
    Nos. C118-C123 (6) 14.50

Nos. C118-C123 exist imperf. (Value, set $25) and in souvenir sheets (Value, set $72).

Palestinian Children's Day — AP20

1982, Oct. 20
C126 AP20 75f Boy 1.50 1.00
C127 AP20 125f Girl 2.50 2.00
C128 AP20 325f Boy and girl 6.00 4.00
 a.   Souvenir sheet of 1 8.00 8.00
    Nos. C126-C128 (3) 10.00 7.00

Arab Postal Union, 30th Anniv. — AP21

1982, Dec. 1
C129 AP21 75f yellow & multi 1.25 1.00
C130 AP21 125f green & multi 2.25 1.75
C131 AP21 325f magenta & multi 4.00 2.00
 a.   Souvenir sheet of 1 8.00 8.00
    Nos. C129-C131 (3) 7.50 4.75

1984 Summer Olympics, Los Angeles — AP22

1984, Nov. 15
C132 AP22 20f Wrestling .60
C133 AP22 30f Boxing .90
C134 AP22 40f Running 1.25
C135 AP22 60f Hurdling 1.50
C136 AP22 150f Pole vault 2.25
C137 AP22 325f Javelin throw 3.50
    Nos. C132-C137 (6) 10.00

Nos. C132-C137 exist imperf. (Value, set $20) and in souvenir sheets (Value, set $45).
Two souvenir sheets of four 75f stamps exist picturing water sports, gymnastics, weightlifting, shot put and discus throwing. Value $12.50 each.

No. C67 Surcharged Nos. 459, 461, 463, 466, 474, 483, 486, 522, C73, C75, C81, C83, C89, C91, C97, C105, C107, C113 & C115 Surcharged with New Value and "AIR MAIL"

1993, Jan. 1   *Perfs, etc. as Before*
C138 AP12 3r on 125f #C67
C139 AP13 3r on 125f #C75
C140 AP14 3r on 125f #C83
C141 AP15 3r on 125f #C91
C142 AP17 3r on 125f #C107
C143 AP18 3r on 125f #C115
C144 AP13 5r on 75f #C73
C145 AP14 5r on 75f #C81
C146 AP15 5r on 75f #C89
C147 AP16 5r on 75f #C97
C148 AP17 5r on 75f #C105
C149 AP18 5r on 75f #C113
C150 A126 8r on 425f #459
C151 A127 8r on 425f #461
C152 A128 8r on 425f #463
C153 A129 8r on 425f #466
C154 A130 8r on 425f #474
C155 A132 8r on 425f #483
C156 A133 8r on 425f #486
C157 A142 12r on 850f #522

Size and location of surcharge varies.

POSTAGE DUE STAMPS

D1

1942   Litho.   Wmk. 258   *Perf. 12½*
J1 D1 1b org & yel grn .25 .25
J2 D1 2b org & yel grn .25 .25
J3 D1 4b org & yel grn .45 .45
J4 D1 6b org & brt ultra .55 .55
J5 D1 8b org & brt ultra .80 .80
J6 D1 10b org & brt ultra 1.00 1.00

J7 D1 12b org & brt ultra 1.50 1.50
J8 D1 20b org & brt ultra 3.00 3.00
    Nos. J1-J8 (8) 7.80 7.80

Yemen had no postage due system. Nos. J1-J8 were used for regular postage.
See Nos. 66-67 for surcharges.

Animals Type of Regular Issue Inscribed "Postage Due"

1964, Aug. 15   Photo.   *Perf. 12x11½*
J9 A39d 4b Gazelles 1.35 .45
J10 A39d 12b Buffalo 3.00 1.00
J11 A39d 20b Arabian horse 5.25 1.75
    Nos. J9-J11 (3) 9.60 3.20

Flower Type of Regular Issue Inscribed "Postage Due"

1964, Sept. 1   Photo.   *Perf. 11½x12*
J12 A39e 4b Like No. 199C 1.40 1.00
J13 A39e 12b Like No. 199B 3.50 2.00
J14 A39e 20b Like No. 199D 5.00 3.50
    Nos. J12-J14 (3) 9.90 6.50

Nos. 209G-209K Overprinted in Black

Perf. 14x14½, 14½x15
1966, Mar. 5   Photo.
J15 A43a 6b On No. 209G 2.75 2.00
J16 A43a 8b On No. 209H 3.50 2.50
J17 A43a 12b On No. 209I 4.50 3.50
J18 A43a 20b On No. 209J 6.00 4.00
J19 A43a 1r On No. 209K 11.00 8.00
    Nos. J15-J19 (5) 27.75 20.00

World Cup Soccer Type of Regular Issue Inscribed "Postage Due"

Designs: No. J20, Goalie defending shot on goal. No. J21, Three players. No. J22, Jules Rimet Cup emblem.

1966, May 29   Litho.   *Perf. 11*
J20 A51 4b multicolored 1.50 1.25
J21 A51 5b multicolored 2.50 1.50
J22 A51 20b multicolored 5.00 3.50
    Nos. J20-J22 (3) 9.00 6.25

Fruit Type of Regular Issue Inscribed "Postage Due"

1967, Feb. 10   Litho.   *Perf. 12½x12*
J23 A56 6b Bananas 1.60 1.25
J24 A56 8b Figs 2.25 1.75
J25 A56 10b Green grapes 2.75 2.25
    Nos. J23-J25 (3) 6.60 5.25

Two stamps of this design were released in the late 1960s or early 1970s. While they have been called postal tax stamps, questions about their status and use exist. The editors would like more information about these stamps and would like to examine unused and on cover examples.

YEMEN, PEOPLE'S DEMOCRATIC REPUBLIC OF

'pē-pəls ri-'pə-blik of 'ye-mən

LOCATION — Southern Arabia
GOVT. — Republic
AREA — 111,074 sq. mi.
POP. — 2,030,000 (est. 1981)
CAPITAL — Aden

The People's Republic of Southern Yemen was proclaimed Nov. 30, 1967, when the Federation of South Arabia achieved independence. It consisted of the former British colony of Aden and the protectorates. The name was changed to People's Democratic Republic of Yemen on Nov. 30, 1970. See South Arabia.

The Yemen Arab Republic and the People's Republic of Yemen planned a 30-month unification process scheduled for completion by November 1992. While government ministries merged, both currencies remained valid. A civil war in 1994 delayed the merger.

1,000 Fils = 1 Dinar

Catalogue values for all unused stamps in this country are for Never Hinged items.

People's Republic of Southern Yemen

South Arabia Nos. 3-16 Overprinted in Red or Blue

Nos. 1-10

Nos. 11-14

Perf. 14½x14

		1968, Apr. 1	Photo.	Unwmk.	
1	A1	5f blue		.25	.25
2	A1	10f lt vio bl		.25	.25
3	A1	15f bl grn		.25	.25
4	A1	20f green		.25	.25
5	A1	25f org brn (B)		.25	.25
6	A1	30f lemon		.25	.25
7	A1	35f red brn (B)		.35	.25
8	A1	50f rose red (B)		.45	.35
9	A1	65f lt yel grn		.60	.40
10	A1	75f rose car (B)		.75	.55
11	A2	100f multi (B)		1.10	.70
12	A2	250f multi		2.25	1.40
13	A2	500f multi (B)		4.50	2.75
14	A2	1d vio & multi		10.00	7.00
		Nos. 1-14 (14)		21.50	14.90

Globe and Flag A1

Designs: 15f, Revolutionist with broken chain and flames, vert. 50f, Aden Harbor. 100f, Cotton picking.

		1968, May 25	Litho.	Perf. 13x12½	
15	A1	10f multi		.25	.25
16	A1	15f multi		.25	.25
17	A1	50f multi		.55	.55
18	A1	100f multi		1.50	1.50
		Nos. 15-18 (4)		2.55	2.55

Independence Day, Nov. 30, 1967.

Girl Scouts at Campfire A2

Designs: 25f, Three Girl Scouts, vert. 50f, Three Girl Scout leaders.

Perf. 13½

		1968, Sept. 21	Litho.	Unwmk.	
19	A2	10f ultra & sepia		.50	.50
20	A2	25f org brn & Prus bl		.75	.75
21	A2	50f yel, bl & brn		1.40	1.40
		Nos. 19-21 (3)		2.65	2.65

Girl Scout movement in Southern Yemen, established 1966 (in Aden).

Revolutionary — A3

"Freedom-Socialism-Unity" — A4

Design: 30f, Radfan Mountains where first revolutionary fell.

		1968, Oct. 14	Unwmk.	Perf. 13	
22	A3	20f brn & lt bl		.30	.30
23	A3	30f grn & brn		.45	.45
24	A4	100f ver & yel		1.10	1.10
		Nos. 22-24 (3)		1.85	1.85

Revolution Day (revolution of Oct. 14, 1963).

King of Ausan, Alabaster Statue — A5

Antiquities of Southern Yemen: 35f, African-type sculpture of a man. 50f, Winged bull, Assyrian-type bas-relief, horiz. 65f, Bull's head (Moon God), alabaster plaque, 230 B.C., horiz.

		1968, Dec. 28	Litho.	Perf. 13	
25	A5	5f olive & bister		.25	.25
26	A5	35f maroon & lt bl		.50	.50
27	A5	50f bister & blue		1.10	1.10
28	A5	65f lt grnsh bl & lilac		1.40	1.40
		Nos. 25-28 (4)		3.25	3.25

A6

Martyr Monument, Steamer Point, Aden.

		1969, Feb. 11	Litho.	Perf. 13	
29	A6	15f yellow & multi		.25	.25
30	A6	35f emerald & multi		.25	.25
31	A6	100f orange & multi		1.50	1.50
		Nos. 29-31 (3)		2.00	2.00

Issued for Martyr Day.

A7

Albert Thomas Monument, Geneva, and ILO emblem.

		1969, June 1	Litho.	Perf. 13	
32	A7	10f brt grn, blk & lt brn		.25	.25
33	A7	35f car rose, blk & lt brn		.60	.60

50th anniv. of the ILO, and to honor founder Albert Thomas.

Classroom — A8

		1969, Sept. 8	Litho.	Perf. 13	
34	A8	35f orange & multi		.65	.65
35	A8	100f yellow & multi		1.50	1.50

International Literacy Day, Sept. 8.

Mahatma Gandhi — A9

		1969, Sept. 27	Litho.	Perf. 13	
36	A9	35f lt ultra & vio brn		1.75	.60

Mohandas K. Gandhi (1869-1948), leader in India's fight for independence.

Family A10

		1969, Oct. 1			
37	A10	25f lt grn & multi		.65	.60
38	A10	75f car rose & multi		1.50	.90

Issued for Family Day.

UN Headquarters, NYC — A11

		1969, Oct. 24		Perf. 13	
39	A11	20f rose red & multi		.60	.25
40	A11	65f emer & multi		1.25	.60

Issued for United Nations Day.

Map and Flag of Southern Yemen — A12

40f, 50f, Tractors, flag (agricultural progress).

		1969, Nov. 30	Litho.	Unwmk.	
		Size: 41x24½mm			
41	A12	15f multi		.25	.25
42	A12	35f multi		.45	.25
		Size: 37x37mm			
43	A12	40f blue & multi		.55	.45
44	A12	50f brown & multi		.90	.60
		Nos. 41-44 (4)		2.15	1.55

Second anniversary of independence.

Map of Arab League Countries, Flag and Emblem — A13

		1970, Mar. 22	Unwmk.	Perf. 13	
45	A13	35f lt bl & multi		.75	.35

25th anniversary of the Arab League.

Lenin — A14

		1970, Apr. 22	Litho.	Perf. 13	
46	A14	75f multi		1.50	.60

Lenin (1870-1924), Russian communist leader.

Fighter — A15

Designs: 35f, Underground soldier and plane destroyed on ground. 50f, Fighting people hailing Arab liberation flag, horiz.

		1970, May 15			
47	A15	15f grn, red & blk		.25	.25
48	A15	35f bl, red & blk		.55	.55
49	A15	50f grn, blk & red		.85	.70
		Nos. 47-49 (3)		1.65	1.50

Issued for Palestine Day.

UPU Headquarters, Bern — A16

1970, May 22   Litho.   Perf. 13
50	A16 15f org & brt grn	.60	.25
51	A16 65f yel & car rose	1.40	.60

New UPU Headquarters in Bern.

Yemeni Costume — A17

Regional Costumes: 15f, 20f, Women's costumes. 50f, Three men of Aden.

1970, July 2   Litho.   Perf. 13
52	A17 10f yel & multi	.40	.25
53	A17 15f lt lil & multi	.40	.25
54	A17 20f lt bl & multi	.65	.25
55	A17 50f multi	1.25	.45
	Nos. 52-55 (4)	2.70	1.20

Camel and Calf — A18

Designs: 25f, Goats. 35f, Arabian oryx. 65f, Socotra dwarf cows.

1970, Aug. 31   Litho.   Perf. 13
56	A18 15f dk brn & multi	.40	.25
57	A18 25f car rose & multi	.65	.45
58	A18 35f ultra & multi	1.20	.75
59	A18 65f brt grn & multi	2.00	1.25
	Nos. 56-59 (4)	4.25	2.70

A19

35f, Natl. Front Organization Headquarters. 50f, Farm worker, 1970, battle scene, 1963.

1970, Oct. 14   Litho.   Perf. 13
Size: 41½x29½mm
60	A19 25f multi	.50	.25

Size: 56½x27mm
61	A19 35f multi	.65	.45

Size: 41x24½mm
62	A19 50f multi	1.00	.60
	Nos. 60-62 (3)	2.15	1.30

7th anniversary of Oct. 14 Revolution.

UN Headquarters, Emblem — A20

1970, Oct. 24   Litho.   Perf. 13
63	A20 10f org & bl	.55	.25
64	A20 65f brt pink & bl	1.75	.80

25th anniversary of the United Nations.

People's Democratic Republic of Yemen

Temples at Philae — A21

1971, Feb. 1   Litho.   Perf. 13½x13
65	A21 5f violet & multi	.25	.25
66	A21 35f blue & multi	.65	.40
67	A21 65f green & multi	1.60	.90
	Nos. 65-67 (3)	2.50	1.55

UNESCO campaign to save the monuments in Nubia.

Scales, Book and Sword A22

1971, Mar. 1   Perf. 13x12½
68	A22 10f brt pink & multi	.25	.25
69	A22 15f brt grn & multi	.25	.25
70	A22 35f lt ultra & multi	.65	.65
71	A22 50f rose & multi	.85	.85
	Nos. 68-71 (4)	2.00	2.00

First Constitution, 1971.

Men of 3 Races, Human Rights Emblem A23

1971, Mar. 21
72	A23 20f lt bl & multi	.25	.25
73	A23 35f grn & multi	.75	.75
74	A23 75f lt vio & multi	1.10	1.10
	Nos. 72-74 (3)	2.10	2.10

Intl. year against racial discrimination.

Map and Flag — A24

"Brothers' Blood" Tree, Socotra Island — A25

1971-77   Litho.   Perf. 13½
75	A24 5f yel & multi	.25	.25
76	A24 10f grn & multi	.25	.25
77	A24 15f yel & multi	.25	.25
78	A24 20f org & multi	.25	.25
79	A24 25f bl & multi	.25	.25
80	A24 35f red org & multi	.35	.25
81	A24 40f vio & multi	.50	.25
82	A24 50f yel grn & multi	.65	.45
82A	A24 60f red & multi	1.40	.60
83	A24 65f pale vio & multi	.90	.65
84	A24 80f org brn & multi	1.00	.80
84A	A24 90f ol & multi	1.40	.75

Perf. 13
84B	A25 110f brn & multi	2.00	.95
85	A25 125f ultra & multi	1.60	1.50
86	A25 250f org & multi	2.90	2.00
87	A25 500f multi	6.00	4.00
88	A25 1d grn & multi	13.50	8.00
	Nos. 75-88 (17)	33.45	21.45

Issued: #82A, 84A-84B, 10/17/77; others, 4/1/71.

See Nos. 332-333. For surcharges see Yemen Nos. 628, 638.

Machine Gun and Map — A26

Designs: 45f, Woman fighter and flame, horiz. 50f, Fighter, factories and rainbow.

1971, June 9   Litho.   Perf. 12½x13
89	A26 15f multi	.25	.25
90	A26 45f green & multi	.65	.45
91	A26 50f multi	1.10	.75
	Nos. 89-91 (3)	2.00	1.45

Armed revolution in the Arabian Gulf.

Arms with Wrench and Cogwheel — A27

25f, Torch, factories, symbols. 65f, Windmill.

1971, June 22
92	A27 15f blue & multi	.25	.25
93	A27 25f multi	.75	.55
94	A27 65f multi	1.25	.75
	Nos. 92-94 (3)	2.25	1.55

2nd anniversary of the revolution of June 22, 1969 (Corrective Movement).

A 20f picturing a fighter holding rifle and flag, with flag colors transposed, was withdrawn on day of issue.

Revolutionary Emblem — A28

40f, Map of southern Arabia & flag of republic.

1971, Sept. 26
95	A28 10f yellow & multi	.25	.25
96	A28 40f lt grn & multi	.75	.55

9th anniv. of the revolution of Sept. 26.

Gamal Abdel Nasser — A29

1971, Sept. 28   Litho.   Perf. 12½x13
97	A29 65f multi	1.25	.75

1st anniv. of the death of Gamal Abdel Nasser (1918-1970), President of Egypt.

UNICEF Emblem, Children of the World — A30

1971, Dec. 11   Perf. 13x13½
98	A30 15f org, car & blk	.25	.25
99	A30 40f lt ultra, car & blk	.40	.35
100	A30 50f yel grn, car & blk	.70	.55
	Nos. 98-100 (3)	1.35	1.15

25th anniv. of UNICEF.

Pigeons A31

Birds: 40f, Partridge. 65f, Partridge and guinea fowl. 100f, European kite.

1971, Dec. 22   Perf. 13½x13
101	A31 5f bl, blk & car	.35	.25
102	A31 40f salmon & multi	1.25	.60
103	A31 65f brt grn, blk & car	3.00	1.10
104	A31 100f yel, blk & car	5.25	2.25
	Nos. 101-104 (4)	9.85	4.20

Dhow under Construction A32

Design: 80f, Dhow under sail, vert.

1972, Feb. 15   Perf. 13½x13, 13x13½
105	A32 25f bl, brn & yel	.75	.45
106	A32 80f lt bl & multi	2.40	1.60

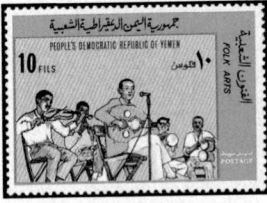

Band — A33

Designs: 25f, 40f, 80f, Various folk dances.

1972, Apr. 8   Litho.   Perf. 13
107	A33 10f lt grn & multi	.25	.25
108	A33 25f org & multi	.35	.25
109	A33 40f red & multi	.80	.45
110	A33 80f blue & multi	1.50	.90
	Nos. 107-110 (4)	2.90	1.85

Palestinian Fighter and Barbed Wire — A34

1972, May 15
111	A34 5f emerald & multi	.30	.25
112	A34 20f blue & multi	.60	.35
113	A34 65f org ver & multi	1.50	.85
	Nos. 111-113 (3)	2.40	1.45

Struggle for Palestine liberation.

Militia Women on Parade
A35

Design: 25f, Policemen on parade.

1972, June 20   **Litho.**   **Perf. 13½**
114 A35 25f lt bl & multi   .60   .25
115 A35 80f bl grn & multi   2.50   1.50
   a.   Souv. sheet of 2, #114-115   9.00   9.00

Police Day. No. 115a sold for 150f.

Start of Bicycle Race
A36

15f Parade of young women. 40f, Yemeni Guides & Scouts on parade. 80f, Acrobats, vert.

1972, July 20   **Litho.**   **Perf. 13½**
116 A36 10f lt bl & multi   .40   .25
117 A36 15f multi   .55   .25
118 A36 40f buff & multi   1.00   .60
119 A36 80f lt ultra & multi   1.60   .90
   Nos. 116-119 (4)   3.55   2.00

Turtle
A37

1972, Sept. 2   **Litho.**   **Perf. 13**
120 A37 15f shown   .90   .50
121 A37 40f Sailfish   1.10   .70
122 A37 65f Kingfish   1.75   .90
123 A37 125f Spiny lobster   3.25   1.60
   Nos. 120-123 (4)   7.00   3.45

Book Year Emblem
A38

1972, Sept. 9
124 A38 40f red, ultra & yel   .75   .50
125 A38 65f org, ultra & yel   1.25   .80

International Book Year 1972.

Farm Couple and Fields
A39

1972, Nov. 23   **Litho.**   **Perf. 13**
126 A39 10f orange & multi   .25   .25
127 A39 25f rose lilac & multi   .70   .45
128 A39 40f red & multi   1.25   .80
   Nos. 126-128 (3)   2.20   1.50

Lands Day, publicizing land reforms.

Militia — A40

20f, Soldier guarding village. 65f, Industrial, agricultural and educational progress, vert.

1972, Dec. 2   **Litho.**   **Perf. 13**
129 A40 5f multi   .25   .25
130 A40 20f multi   .25   .25
131 A40 65f multi   1.60   1.60
   a.   Souv. sheet of 3, #129-131, imperf.   4.00   4.00
   Nos. 129-131 (3)   2.10   2.10

5th anniversary of independence.

Census Chart
A41

1973, Apr. 3   **Litho.**   **Perf. 12½x13½**
132 A41 25f org, emer & ol   .25   .25
133 A41 40f rose, bl & vio   1.25   1.25

Population census 1973.

WHO Emblem and "25" — A42

5f, "25" and WHO emblem, vert. 125f, "25" and WHO emblem.

1973, Apr. 7   **Perf. 14x12½, 12½x14**
134 A42 5f multicolored   .25   .25
135 A42 20f shown   .25   .25
136 A42 125f multicolored   2.10   2.10
   Nos. 134-136 (3)   2.60   2.60

25th anniv. of the WHO.

Elephant Bay
A43

Tourist Publicity: 20f, Taweels Tanks Reservoir, vert. 25f, Shibam Town. 100f, Al-Mohdar Mosque, Tarim.

1973, June 9   **Litho.**   **Perf. 13**
137 A43 20f multi   .25   .25
138 A43 25f multi   .25   .25
139 A43 40f multi   1.50   1.50
140 A43 100f multi   1.75   1.75
   Nos. 137-140 (4)   3.75   3.75

Office Buildings and Slum, Aden — A44

Design: 80f, Intersection, Aden, vert.

1973, Aug. 4   **Litho.**   **Perf. 13**
141 A44 20f multi   .25   .25
142 A44 80f multi   1.75   1.75

Nationalization of buildings.

Army Unit
A45

People's Army: 20f, Four marching soldiers. 40f, Sailors on parade. 80f, Tanks.

1973, Sept. 1
143 A45 10f multi   .25   .25
144 A45 20f multi   .25   .25
145 A45 40f multi   1.00   1.00
146 A45 80f multi   1.40   1.40
   Nos. 143-146 (4)   2.90   2.90

FAO Emblem, Loading Food
A46

Design: 80f, Workers and grain sacks.

1973, Dec. 19   **Litho.**   **Perf. 13**
147 A46 20f blue & multi   .25   .25
148 A46 80f blue & multi   1.50   .90

World Food Program, 10th anniversary.

Letter and UPU Emblem
A47

UPU Emblem and Yemeni Flag — A48

Map of Yemen, UPU Emblem — A49

UPU cent.: 20f, "100" formed by people, and UPU emblem.

1974, Oct. 9   **Litho.**   **Perf. 12½x13½**
149 A47 5f multi   .25   .25
150 A47 20f multi   .25   .25
151 A48 40f multi   .70   .70
152 A49 125f multi   1.25   1.25
   Nos. 149-152 (4)   2.45   2.45

Irrigation System — A50

Progress in Agriculture: 20f, Bulldozer pushing soil. 100f, Tractors plowing field.

1974   **Litho.**   **Perf. 13**
153 A50 10f multi   .25   .25
154 A50 20f multi   .25   .25
155 A50 100f multi   1.50   1.50
   Nos. 153-155 (3)   2.00   2.00

Lathe Operator — A51

Industrial progress: 40f, Printers. 80f, Women textile workers, horiz.

1975, May 1   **Litho.**   **Perf. 13**
156 A51 10f multi   .25   .25
157 A51 40f multi   .60   .60
158 A51 80f multi   1.00   1.00
   Nos. 156-158 (3)   1.85   1.85

Yemeni Woman — A52

Designs: Various women's costumes.

1975, Nov. 15   **Litho.**   **Perf. 11½x12**
159 A52 5f blk & ocher   .25   .25
160 A52 10f blk & vio   .25   .25
161 A52 15f blk & olive   .25   .25
162 A52 25f blk & rose lil   .45   .45
163 A52 40f blk & Prus bl   .75   .75
164 A52 50f blk & org brn   1.10   1.10
   Nos. 159-164 (6)   3.05   3.05

Women Factory Workers, IWY Emblem
A53

1975, Dec. 30   **Litho.**   **Perf. 12x11½**
165 A53 20f blk & salmon   .60   .60
166 A53 50f blk & yel grn   1.00   1.00

International Women's Year 1975.

Soccer Player and Field — A54

Designs: Different scenes from soccer.

1976, Apr. 1   **Litho.**   **Perf. 11½x12**
167 A54 5f lt bl & brn   .25   .25
168 A54 40f yel & green   .70   .70
169 A54 80f salmon & vio   1.10   1.10
   Nos. 167-169 (3)   2.05   2.05

Rocket Take-off from Moon — A55

15f, Alexander Satalov. 40f, Lunokhod on moon, horiz. 65f, Valentina Tereshkova, rocket.

Perf. 11½x12, 12x11½

1976, Apr. 17		Litho.	
170	A55 10f multi	.25	.25
171	A55 15f multi	.25	.25
172	A55 40f multi	1.00	1.00
173	A55 65f multi	1.25	1.25
	Nos. 170-173 (4)	2.75	2.75

Soviet cosmonauts and space program.

Traffic Policemen A56

1977, Apr. 16		Litho.	Perf. 14
174	A56 25f red & blk	.60	.60
175	A56 60f yel & blk	1.25	1.25
176	A56 75f grn & blk	1.50	1.50
177	A56 110f dp bl & blk	2.00	2.00
	Nos. 174-177 (4)	5.35	5.35

Traffic change to right side of road.

APU Emblem — A57

1977, Apr. 12		Litho.	Perf. 13½
178	A57 20f lt bl & multi	.25	.25
179	A57 60f gray & multi	.80	.80
180	A57 70f lt grn & multi	1.00	1.00
181	A57 90f bl grn & multi	1.10	1.10
	Nos. 178-181 (4)	3.15	3.15

Arab Postal Union, 25th anniversary.

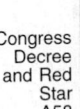

Congress Decree and Red Star A58

Designs: 25f, Pres. Salim Rubi'a Ali, Council members Ali Nasser Muhamed and Abdul Farta Ismail. 65f, Women's militia on parade. 95f, Aerial view of textile mill.

1977, May		Photo.	Perf. 13
182	A58 25f grn, gold & dk brn	.25	.25
183	A58 35f red, gold & lt bl	.50	.50
184	A58 65f bl, gold & lil	1.00	1.00
185	A58 95f org, gold & grn	1.10	1.10
	Nos. 182-185 (4)	2.85	2.85

Unification Congress, 1st anniversary.

Afrivoluta Pringlei A59

Shells: 60f, Festilyria duponti, vert. 110f, Conus splendidulus. 180f, Cypraea 4broderipii.

1977, July 16		Litho.	Perf. 13½
186	A59 60f multi	.95	.70
187	A59 90f multi	1.40	.70
188	A59 110f multi	2.40	1.40
189	A59 180f multi	3.25	2.40
	Nos. 186-189 (4)	8.00	5.20

Emblem and Flag — A60

Designs: 20f, Man with broken chain. 90f, Pipeline, agriculture and industry. 110f, Flag, symbolic tree and hands holding tools.

1977, Nov. 30		Litho.	Perf. 13½
190	A60 5f blk & multi	.25	.25
191	A60 20f blk & multi	.25	.25
192	A60 90f blk & multi	.50	.25
193	A60 110f blk & multi	.85	.40
	Nos. 190-193 (4)	1.85	1.15

10th anniversary of independence.

Dome of the Rock A61

1978, May 15			Perf. 12
194	A61 5f multi		.70 .40

Palestinian fighters & families. See #264A.

Festival Emblem and "CUBA" — A62

Designs: 60f, Festival emblem. 90f, Festival emblem as flower. 110f, Festival emblem, dove, young man and woman.

1978, June 22		Litho.	Perf. 14
195	A62 5f multi	.25	.25
196	A62 60f multi	.65	.40
197	A62 90f multi	.85	.45
198	A62 110f multi	1.10	.70
	Nos. 195-198 (4)	2.85	1.80

11th World Youth Festival, Havana.

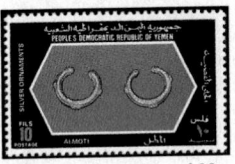

Silver Ornaments — A63

Designs: Various silver ornaments.

1978, July 22		Litho.	Perf. 13½
199	A63 10f blk & multi	.25	.25
200	A63 15f blk & multi	.25	.25
201	A63 20f blk & multi	.25	.25
202	A63 60f blk & multi	.25	.25
203	A63 90f blk & multi	1.00	.65
204	A63 110f blk & multi	1.50	.75
	Nos. 199-204 (6)	3.50	2.40

For surcharge see Yemen No. 629.

Yemeni Musical Instruments — A64

1978, Aug. 26			Perf. 14
205	A64 35f Almarfaai	.40	.25
206	A64 60f Almizmar	.90	.35
207	A64 90f Alqnboos	1.60	.45
208	A64 110f Simsimiya	2.00	.80
	Nos. 205-208 (4)	4.90	1.85

For surcharge see Yemen No. 630.

"V" for Vanguard A65

1978, Oct. 11		Litho.	Perf. 14
209	A65 5f multi	.25	.25
210	A65 20f multi	.25	.25
211	A65 60f multi	.40	.25
212	A65 180f multi	.85	.50
	Nos. 209-212 (4)	1.75	1.25

1st Conf. of Vanguard Party, Oct. 11-13.

Man with Palm, Factories — A66

Designs: 10f, Palm branches, broken chains, horiz. 60f, Candle and "15." 110f, Woman and man with rifle, "15."

1978, Oct. 14			
213	A66 10f multi	.25	.25
214	A66 35f multi	.25	.25
215	A66 60f multi	.45	.25
216	A66 110f multi	.75	.45
	Nos. 213-216 (4)	1.70	1.20

15th Revolution Day.
For surcharge see Yemen No. 631.

Child, Map of Arabia and IYC Emblem — A67

1979, Mar. 20		Litho.	Perf. 13½
217	A67 15f multi	.25	.25
218	A67 20f multi	.25	.25
219	A67 60f multi	.50	.25
220	A67 90f multi	.70	.25
	Nos. 217-220 (4)	1.70	1.00

International Year of the Child.

Sickle, Star, Tractor, Wheat and Dove — A68

Designs: 35f, Pylon, star, compass, wheat and hammer. 60f, Students, worker and clock. 90f, Woman with raised arms, doves and star.

1979, June 22		Litho.	Perf. 14
221	A68 20f multi	.25	.25
222	A68 35f multi	.25	.25
223	A68 60f multi	.40	.25
224	A68 90f multi	.55	.25
	Nos. 221-224 (4)	1.45	1.00

Corrective Movement, 10th anniversary.

Yemen #52, Hill A69

Hill and: 110f, Yemen #56. 250f, Aden #12.

1979, Aug. 27		Litho.	Perf. 14
225	A69 90f multi	.60	.25
226	A69 110f multi	.75	.45

Souvenir Sheet

227	A69 250f multi		2.25 2.25

Sir Rowland Hill (1795-1879), originator of penny postage.

Book, World Map, Arab Achievements — A70

1979, Sept. 26		Litho.	Perf. 14
228	A70 60f multi		.70 .25

Party Emblem — A71

1979, Oct. 13			Perf. 14½x14
229	A71 60f multi		.70 .25

Yemeni Socialist Party, 1st anniversary.

Cassia Adenesis — A72

Flowers: 90f, Nerium oleander. 110f, Calligonum comosum. 180f, Adenium obesium.

1979, Nov. 30   **Litho.**   *Perf. 13½*
230 A72	20f multi	.25	.25
231 A72	90f multi	.90	.50
232 A72	110f multi	1.50	.75
233 A72	180f multi	1.90	.90
	Nos. 230-233 (4)	4.55	2.40

For surcharge see Yemen No. 632.

First Anniv. of
Iranian
Revolution — A73

1980, Feb. 12   **Litho.**   *Perf. 13½*
| 234 A73 | 60f multi | 1.10 | 1.10 |

Dido
A74

1980, Mar. 5   **Litho.**   *Perf. 13½*
235 A74	110f shown	1.10	.50
236 A74	180f Anglia	1.50	.70
237 A74	250f India	2.10	.90
	Nos. 235-237 (3)	4.70	2.10

For surcharge see Yemen No. 633.

Basket Maker,
London 1980
Emblem — A75

1980, May 6   **Litho.**   *Perf. 14*
238 A75	60f shown	.25	.25
239 A75	90f Hubble bubble pipe maker	.65	.25
240 A75	110f Weaver	.90	.55
241 A75	250f Potter	2.00	1.10
	Nos. 238-241 (4)	3.80	2.15

London 1980 Intl. Stamp Exhib., May 6-14.

Hemprich's Skink — A76

1980, May 8   **Litho.**   *Perf. 14*
242 A76	20f shown	.25	.25
243 A76	35f Mole viper	.60	.25
244 A76	110f Carter's day gecko	1.50	.60
245 A76	180f Cobra	2.50	1.25
	Nos. 242-245 (4)	4.85	2.35

For surcharge see Yemen No. 634.

Misha and
Olympic
Emblem — A77

1980, July 19   **Litho.**   *Perf. 12½x12*
| 246 A77 | 110f multi | 1.10 | .65 |

For overprint see No. 287.

Farmers
Armed — A78

50f, Armed farmers working, horiz. 110f,
Sickle (wheat) and fist.

1980, Oct. 17   *Perf. 13½*
247 A78	50f multicolored	.50	.25
248 A78	90f shown	.75	.50
249 A78	110f multicolored	1.00	.70
	Nos. 247-249 (3)	2.25	1.45

10th anniversary of farmers' uprising.

110th Birth
Anniversary of
Lenin — A79

1980, Nov. 7   **Litho.**   *Perf. 12*
| 250 A79 | 35f multi | .50 | .50 |

Douglas DC-3 — A80

1981, Mar. 11   **Litho.**   *Perf. 13½*
251 A80	60f shown	.25	.25
252 A80	90f Boeing 707	1.50	.25
253 A80	250f DHC Dash 7	3.50	1.60
	Nos. 251-253 (3)	5.25	2.10

Democratic Yemen Airlines, 10th anniv.

Ras
Boradli
Earth
Satellite
Station
A82

1981, June 22   **Litho.**   *Perf. 12*
| 257 A82 | 60f multi | .90 | .65 |

Conocarpus
Lancifolius — A83

1981, Aug. 1   **Litho.**   *Perf. 12*
258 A83	90f shown	.85	.25
259 A83	180f Ficus vasta	2.00	1.10
260 A83	250f Maerua crassifolia	3.00	1.75
	Nos. 258-260 (3)	5.85	3.10

Supreme People's
Council, 10th
Anniv. — A84

1981, Aug. 18   **Litho.**   *Perf. 15x14½*
| 261 A84 | 180f multi | 1.50 | .90 |

Desert Fox — A85

1981, Sept. 26   **Litho.**   *Perf. 14½*
262 A85	50f shown	.70	.25
263 A85	90f South Arabian leopard	1.40	.70
264 A85	250f Ibex	3.25	1.60
	Nos. 262-264 (3)	5.35	2.55

No. 194 Redrawn

1981, Oct. 15   **Litho.**   *Perf. 12*
Size: 25x27mm
| 264A A61 | 5f multi | .45 | .45 |

Denomination in upper right.

Tephrosia
Apollinea — A86

1981, Nov. 30   **Litho.**   *Perf. 13½*
265 A86	50f shown	.25	.25
266 A86	90f Citrullus colocynthis	1.00	.25
267 A86	110f Aloe sqarrosa	1.40	.25
268 A86	250f Lawsonia inermis	3.50	2.00
	Nos. 265-268 (4)	6.15	2.75

For surcharge see Yemen No. 635.

Intl. Year
of the
Disabled
A87

1981, Dec. 12   **Litho.**   *Perf. 14½*
269 A87	50f multi	.25	.25
270 A87	100f multi	1.00	.25
271 A87	150f multi	1.50	1.00
	Nos. 269-271 (3)	2.75	1.50

TB Bacillus Centenary — A88

1982, Mar. 24   **Litho.**   *Perf. 14½*
| 272 A88 | 50f multi | 1.10 | .25 |

30th
Anniv. of
Arab
Postal
Union
A89

1982, Apr. 12   **Litho.**   *Perf. 14*
| 273 A89 | 100f multi | 1.25 | .75 |

1982
World Cup
A90

Designs: Various soccer players.

1982, June 13   **Litho.**   *Perf. 14*
274 A90	50f multi	.70	.25
275 A90	100f multi	1.40	.90
276 A90	150f multi	2.00	1.25
277 A90	200f multi	3.00	1.75
a.	Souv. sheet of 4, #274-277	7.00	7.00
	Nos. 274-277 (4)	7.10	4.15

For overprints see Nos. 281-284.

60th
Anniv. of
USSR
A93

1982, Dec. 22   **Litho.**   *Perf. 12½x12*
| 280 A93 | 50f Flags, arms | .65 | .45 |

**Nos. 274-277, 277a Ovptd. with
Emblem and "WORLD CUP /
WINNERS / 1982 / 1st ITALY / 2nd
W-GERMANY / 3rd POLAND / 4th
FRANCE" in Blue**

1982, Dec. 30   **Litho.**   *Perf. 14*
281 A90	50f multi	.25	.25
282 A90	100f multi	1.50	1.50
283 A90	150f multi	2.25	2.25
284 A90	200f multi	2.50	2.50
a.	Souvenir sheet of 4, #281-284	7.00	7.00
	Nos. 281-284 (4)	6.50	6.50

Palestinian
Solidarity
A94

1983, Apr. 10   *Perf. 13½x14½*
285 A94	50f Yasser Arafat	.25	.25
286 A94	100f Arafat, Dome of the Rock	3.00	3.00
a.	Souvenir sheet of 1, imperf.	3.00	3.00

**No. 246 Ovptd. with TEMBAL '83
Emblem in Yellow**

1983, May 21   *Perf. 12½x12*
| 287 A94 | 110f multi | 4.75 | 4.75 |

World Communications Year — A95

Designs: 50f, Correspondent, postrider,
ship. 100f, Postman, coach, telegraph. No.
290, Telephones, bus. 200f, Telecommunications. No. 292, Montage.

1983, June 10   *Perf. 13x13½*

288	A95	50f blk & brt bl	.25 .25
289	A95	100f multi	1.50 1.50
290	A95	150f multi	2.40 2.40
291	A95	200f multi	2.75 2.75
		Nos. 288-291 (4)	6.90 6.90

Souvenir Sheet

292	A95	150f multi	3.00 3.00

Pablo Picasso (1881-1973),
Painter — A96

Paintings: No. 293, The Poor Family, 1903. No. 294, Woman with Crow. No. 295a, The Gourmet. No. 295b, Woman with Child on Beach. No. 295c, Sitting Beggar. No. 296, The Soler Family, horiz.

1983, July 25   *Perf. 14*

293	A96	50f multi	.25 .25
294	A96	100f multi	2.00 2.00

Souvenir Sheets

295		Sheet of 3	13.50 13.50
a.	A96	50f multi	1.75 1.75
b.	A96	100f multi	4.50 4.50
c.	A96	150f multi	6.50 6.50
296	A96	150f multi	8.00 8.00

23rd Pre-Olympics Games,
1984 — A97

1983, July 30

297	A97	25f Show jumping	.25 .25
298	A97	50f Show jumping, diff.	.25 .25
299	A97	100f Three-day event	2.50 2.50
		Nos. 297-299 (3)	3.00 3.00

Souvenir Sheets

300		Sheet of 4	13.50 13.50
a.	A97	20f Bay, vert.	2.50 2.50
b.	A97	40f Gray, vert.	2.50 2.50
c.	A97	60f Bay, diff., vert.	3.25 3.25
d.	A97	80f Arabian	4.50 4.50
301	A97	200f Show jumping, diff., vert.	9.75 9.75

Locomotives — A98

1983, Aug. 24   *Perf. 14½x15*

302	A98	25f P8 steam engine, 1905	.25 .25
303	A98	50f 880 steam, 1915	.25 .25
304	A98	100f GT 2-4-4, 1923	4.00 4.00
		Nos. 302-304 (3)	4.50 4.50

Souvenir Sheets

305		Sheet of 3	20.00 20.00
a.	A98	40f D51 steam, 1936	4.75 4.75
b.	A98	60f 45 Series, 1937	4.75 4.75
c.	A98	100f PT 47, 1948	9.00 9.00
306	A98	200f P36, 1950	20.00 20.00

Ships — A99

1983, Sept. 15   *Perf. 14*

307	A99	50f Europa	.25 .25
308	A99	100f World Discoverer	3.00 1.75

Miniature Sheet

309		Sheet of 4	18.00 18.00
a.	A99	20f Kruzenstern	1.75 1.75
b.	A99	40f Grossherzogin Elisabeth	3.50 3.50
c.	A99	60f Sedov	5.50 5.50
d.	A99	80f Dar Pomorza	7.50 7.50

Souvenir Sheet

310	A99	200f Gorch Foch	16.00 15.00

Natl. Revolution, 20th Anniv. A100

1983, Oct. 15   Litho.   *Perf. 13½x13*

312	A100	50f shown	.25 .25
313	A100	100f Flag, freedom fighter	2.75 2.75

1st Manned Flight, Bicent. — A101

Balloons: 100f, La Montgolfiere prototype. No. 316a, Lunardi's. No. 316b, Charles and Robert's. No. 316c, Wiseman's. No. 316d, Blanchard and Jeffries's. 200f, Five-balloon craft.

1983, Oct. 25   *Perf. 14*

314	A101	50f shown	.25 .25
315	A101	100f multi	2.50 2.50

Souvenir Sheets

316		Sheet of 4	13.50 13.50
a.	A101	20f multi	3.00 3.00
b.	A101	40f multi	3.00 3.00
c.	A101	60f multi	3.00 3.00
d.	A101	80f multi	4.00 4.00
317	A101	200f multi	13.50 13.50

1984 Winter Olympics, Sarajevo A102

50f, Men's downhill skiing. 100f, Two-man bobsled.

1983, Dec. 28   Litho.   *Perf. 14*

318	A102	50f multicolored	.25 .25
319	A102	100f multicolored	2.50 2.50

Souvenir Sheets

320		Sheet of 3	10.00 10.00
a.	A102	40f Ski jumping	3.00 3.00
b.	A102	60f Figure skating	3.00 3.00
c.	A102	100f Two-man bobsled	3.00 3.00
321	A102	200f Ice hockey	10.00 10.00

1984 Summer Olympics, Los Angeles — A103

1984, Jan. 24

322	A103	25f Fencing	.45 .25
323	A103	50f Fencing, diff.	.90 .45
324	A103	100f Fencing, diff.	1.40 .75
		Nos. 322-324 (3)	2.75 1.45

Souvenir Sheets

325		Sheet of 4	11.00 11.00
a.	A103	20f Gymnastics	2.75 2.75
b.	A103	40f Water polo	2.75 2.75
c.	A103	60f Wrestling	2.75 2.75
d.	A103	80f Show jumping	2.75 2.75
326	A103	200f Show jumping, diff.	11.00 11.00

Space Flights — A104

Designs: 15f, Soyuz 10 and Salyut 1 docking, 1971. 20f, Apollo 8 circling Moon, 1968. 50f, Apollo 11 Moon landing, 1969. 100f, Apollo-Soyuz mission, 1975.

1984, Apr. 16   Litho.   *Perf. 14*

327-330	A104	Set of 4	— —

An additional souvenir sheet was issued with this set. The editors would like to examine any example of it.

Nos. 83 and 84B Surcharged with Black Squares

1984, May 26   Litho.   *Perf. 13½, 13*

332	A24	50f on 65f multi	
333	A25	100f on 110f multi	

Fish — A105

10f, Abalistes stellaris. 15f, Caranx speciocus. 20f, Pomadasys maculatus. 25f, Chaetodon fasciatus. 35f, Pomacanthus imperator. 50f, Rastrelliger kanagurta. 100f, Euthynnus affinis. 150f, Heniochus acuminatus. 200f, Pomacanthus maculosus. 250f, Pterois russellii. 400f, Argyrops spinifer. 500f, Dasyatis uarnak. 1d, Epinephalus chlorostigma. 2d, Drepane longimana.

1984, Nov. 25   Litho.   *Perf. 11½*

334	A105	10f multicolored	.25 .25
335	A105	15f multicolored	.25 .25
336	A105	20f multicolored	.30 .25
337	A105	25f multicolored	.45 .25
338	A105	35f multicolored	.70 .25
339	A105	50f multicolored	1.00 .25
340	A105	100f multicolored	2.00 .45
341	A105	150f multicolored	3.00 .90
342	A105	200f multicolored	4.00 1.00
343	A105	250f multicolored	5.50 1.75
344	A105	400f multicolored	9.00 2.40
345	A105	500f multicolored	11.00 3.25
346	A105	1d multicolored	24.00 7.50
347	A105	2d multicolored	52.50 15.00
		Nos. 334-347 (14)	113.95 33.75

For surcharges see Yemen Nos. 636, 640, 642.

Natl. Literacy Campaign A106

1985, Feb. 27   *Perf. 12*

350	A106	50f Girls writing	1.40 .75
351	A106	100f Hand, fountain pen, vert.	2.90 1.20

Victory Parade, Red Square, Moscow, 1945 — A107

1985, May 9   *Perf. 12x12½*

352	A107	100f multi	1.75 .80

Defeat of Nazi Germany, end of World War II, 40th anniv.

12th World Youth and Students Festival — A108

1985, Aug. 3   *Perf. 12*

353	A108	50f Emblem	1.50 .70
354	A108	100f Hand holding emblem	3.00 1.25

UNESCO World Heritage Campaign — A109

1985, Aug. 29

355	A109	50f Shibam city	.90 .50
356	A109	50f Close-up of buildings	.90 .50
357	A109	100f Windows	1.90 1.90
358	A109	100f Door	1.90 1.90
		Nos. 355-358 (4)	5.60 4.80

Nos. 355-357 horiz.

Natl. Socialist Party, 3rd Gen. Cong. — A110

1985, Oct. 10

359	A110	25f Energy	.70 .45
360	A110	50f Industry	1.25 .60
361	A110	100f Agriculture	2.40 1.00
		Nos. 359-361 (3)	4.35 2.05

UN Child Survival
Campaign — A111

1985, Nov. 28
362	A111	50f Mother feeding child	.90	.70
363	A111	50f Holding child	.90	.70
364	A111	100f Feeding child, diff.	1.90	1.25
365	A111	100f Breastfeeding	1.90	1.25
		Nos. 362-365 (4)	5.60	3.90

World Food
Day — A112

1986, Jan. 30
366	A112	20f Almihdar Mosque, Aden	.90	.25
367	A112	180f Palm trees	4.00	1.75

UN Food and Agriculture Org., 40th anniv.

Lenin, Red
Square,
Moscow
A113

1986, Feb. 25 **Perf. 12x12½**
368	A113	75f multi	1.75	.70
369	A113	250f multi	4.00	2.00

27th Soviet Communist Party Cong.,
Moscow.

Costumes Worn at
the 1984 Brides
Dance
Festival — A114

Designs: No. 370, Bride wearing red and
green costume, face markings. No. 371, Violet costume. No. 372, Veiled bride. No. 373,
Unveiled bride. No. 374, Groom holding dagger. No. 375, Groom holding rifle.

1986, Feb. 27
370	A114	50f multi	.80	.50
371	A114	50f multi	.80	.50
372	A114	50f multi	.80	.50
373	A114	100f multi	1.50	1.25
374	A114	100f multi	1.50	1.25
375	A114	100f multi	1.50	1.25
		Nos. 370-375 (6)	6.90	5.25

Revolution
Martyrs
A115

1986, Oct. 15 **Litho.** **Perf. 12**
376	A115	75f Abdul Fattah Ismail	1.10	.70
377	A115	75f Ali Shayaa Hadi	1.10	.70
378	A115	75f Saleh Musleh Kasim	1.10	.70
379	A115	75f Ali Ahmed N. Antar	1.10	.70
		Nos. 376-379 (4)	4.40	2.80

UN Child
Survival
Campaign
A116

Infant Immunization Program: 20f, Immunizing pregnant woman. 75f, Immunizing infant.
140f, Oral immunization. 150f, Infant, girl,
pregnant woman.

1987, Apr. 7 **Litho.** **Perf. 12**
380	A116	20f multicolored	.35	.25
381	A116	75f multicolored	1.10	.70
382	A116	140f multicolored	2.25	1.00
383	A116	150f multicolored	2.25	1.25
		Nos. 380-383 (4)	5.95	3.20

1st Socialist Party General
Conference — A117

1987, July 30 **Litho.** **Perf. 12**
384	A117	75fr multi	1.10	.45
385	A117	150fr multi	2.25	1.00

October Revolution,
Russia, 70th
Anniv. — A118

1987, Nov. 7 **Litho.** **Perf. 12½x12**
386	A118	250f multi		4.50	2.25

Monuments,
Ancient City of
Shabwa — A119

25f, Royal palace and court. 75f, Palace,
diff. 140f, Winged lion bas-relief on stone capital. 150f, The Moon, legend on bronze tablet.

1987, Nov. 18 **Perf. 12**
387	A119	25f multicolored	.45	.24
388	A119	75f multicolored	1.10	.55
389	A119	140f multicolored	2.00	1.10
390	A119	150f multicolored	2.25	1.25
		Nos. 387-390 (4)	5.80	3.15

Nos. 387-388 horiz.

Natl. Independence, 20th
Anniv. — A120

Designs: 5f, Students walking to school. 75f,
Family, apartments. 140f, Workers, oil derrick,
thermal plant. 150f, Workers, soldier, Workers'
Party headquarters.

1987, Nov. 29 **Perf. 12x12½**
391	A120	25f multi	.35	.25
392	A120	75f multi	1.00	.45
393	A120	140f multi	2.00	.90
394	A120	150f multi	2.25	1.00
		Nos. 391-394 (4)	5.60	2.60

September
26th
Revolution,
25th Anniv.
A121

1988, Feb. 27 **Litho.** **Perf. 13**
395	A121	75f Revolution monu-ment, San'a	1.10	.45

WHO, 40th
Anniv.
A122

40f, Sanitary public water supply, vert. 75f,
No smoking. 140f, Child immunization. 250f,
Health care for all by the year 2000.

1988, Apr. 7 **Litho.** **Perf. 12**
396	A122	40f multicolored	.45	.30
397	A122	75f multicolored	1.00	.35
398	A122	140f multicolored	1.75	.70
399	A122	250f multicolored	2.75	1.25
		Nos. 396-399 (4)	5.95	2.60

1988
Summer
Olympics,
Seoul
A125

1988, Sept. 17 **Litho.** **Perf. 12x12½**
406	A125	40f Weight lifting	.55	.25
407	A125	75f Running	1.00	.45
408	A125	140f Boxing	2.25	1.10
409	A125	150f Soccer	2.40	1.25
		Nos. 406-409 (4)	6.20	3.05

1st Freedom
Fighter Killed
at the
Liberation
Front, Radfan
Mountains
A126

25f, Freedom fighters, flag, vert. 300f,
Anniv. emblem, vert.

Perf. 12½x12, 12x12½
1988, Oct. 12 **Litho.**
410	A126	25f multicolored	.35	.25
411	A126	75f shown	1.00	.35
412	A126	300f multicolored	4.00	1.75
		Nos. 410-412 (3)	5.35	2.35

October 14th Revolution, 25th anniv.

Indigenous
Birds
A127

40f, Treron waalia. 50f, Coracias caudatus
lorti, vert. 75f, Upupa epops, vert. 250f,
Chlamydotis undulata macqueenii.

1988, Nov. 5 **Perf. 12x12½, 12½x12**
413	A127	40f multicolored	.60	.60
414	A127	50f multicolored	.80	.55
415	A127	75f multicolored	1.40	.80
416	A127	250f multicolored	3.75	2.00
		Nos. 413-416 (4)	6.55	3.95

Handicrafts — A128

Designs: 25f, Incense brazier. 75f, Cage-
shaped dress form. 150f, Shell and wicker lidded basket. 250f, Wicker basket.

1988, Nov. 29 **Litho.** **Perf. 12½x12**
417	A128	25f multi	.25	.25
418	A128	75f multi	1.00	.45
419	A128	150f multi	1.75	1.00
420	A128	250f multi	3.25	1.75
		Nos. 417-420 (4)	6.25	3.45

Aden Harbor
and Yemen
Port
Authority,
Cent.
A129

1988, Dec. 5 **Perf. 12x12½**
421	A129	75f Old harbor facility	1.50	.50
422	A129	300f New facility	4.50	2.10

Preservation of San'a City, a Site on
the UNESCO World Heritage
List — A130

1988, Dec. 15 **Perf. 12x12½, 12½x12**
423	A130	75f shown	1.00	.70
424	A130	250f City view, diff., vert.	4.00	1.75

World Wildlife Fund — A131

1989, May 18 **Litho.** **Perf. 12½x12**
425	A131	20f Sand cat	1.50	.25
426	A131	25f Cat's head	1.50	.30
427	A131	50f Fennec fox	3.00	.50
428	A131	75f Fox's head	4.00	.80
		Nos. 425-428 (4)	10.00	1.85

For surcharge see Yemen No. 643.

Military
Forces — A132

Developments of the corrective movement.

1989, Aug. 15 **Perf. 12x12½**
429	A132	25f shown	.35	.25
430	A132	35f Industry	.45	.25
431	A132	40f Agriculture	.55	.25
		Nos. 429-431 (3)	1.35	.75

June 22 Corrective Movement, 20th anniv.

Abdul Fattah
Ismail — A133

1989, Aug. 28
432 A133 75f multi   .75   .75
433 A133 150f multi   1.50 1.25

50th Birthday of Abdul Fattah Ismail, 1st secretary-general of the natl. Socialist Party.

Ali Anter Yemeni
Pioneer
Organization,
15th
Anniv. — A134

10f, Drawing by Abeer Anwer. 25f, Girl in pioneer uniform. 75f, Parade, Aden.

Perf. 12x12½, 12½x12
1989, Sept. 29   **Litho.**
434 A134 10f multicolored   .25   .25
435 A134 25f multicolored   .35   .25
436 A134 75f multicolored   .90   .55
       Nos. 434-436 (3)   1.50 1.05

Nos. 434-435 vert.
For surcharge see Yemen No. 644.

Nehru and the Taj
Mahal — A135

1989, Nov. 14   Photo.   Perf. 14
437 A135 250f blk & golden brn   3.50 1.50

Jawaharlal Nehru, 1st prime minister of independent India.
For surcharge see Yemen No. 645.

Seventy-Day
Siege of San'a,
1967-68 — A136

1989, Oct. 25   Litho.   Perf. 12x12½
438 A136 150f multicolored   4.50 2.50

Coffee
Plant — A137

1989, Dec. 20
439 A137 300f multicolored   5.00 2.50

For surcharge see Yemen No. 637.

Seera
Rock,
Aden, and
the Arc de
Triomphe,
Paris
A138

1989, Dec. 29   Litho.   Perf. 12½x12
440 A138 250f multicolored   4.25 2.50

French Revolution, bicent.

World Cup Soccer Championships,
Italy — A139

Character trademark, soccer plays and flags of participants: 5f, US, Belgium, 1930. 10f, Switzerland, Holland, 1934. 20f, Italy, France, 1938. 35f, Sweden, Spain, 1950. 50f, Federal Republic of Germany, Austria, 1954. Brazil, England, 1958. 500f, Russia, Uruguay, 1962. No. 448, Soccer game.

1990, Apr. 30   Litho.   Perf. 12½x12
441 A139 5f multicolored   .25   .25
442 A139 10f multicolored   .25   .25
443 A139 20f multicolored   .25   .25
444 A139 35f multicolored   .30   .30
445 A139 50f multicolored   .35   .35
446 A139 60f multicolored   .40   .40
447 A139 500f multicolored 4.00 1.00
       Nos. 441-447 (7)   5.80 2.80

Souvenir Sheet
448 A139 340f multicolored   3.00 3.00

For surcharges see Yemen Nos. 616, 621-621B.

YUGOSLAVIA

ỳü-gō-'slä-vē-ə

LOCATION — Southern Europe, bordering on the Adriatic Sea
GOVT. — Republic
AREA — 39,500 sq. mi. (est)
POP. — 11,206,847 (1999 est.)
CAPITAL — Belgrade

On December 1, 1918, Bosnia and Herzegovina, Croatia, Dalmatia, Montenegro, Serbia and Slovenia united to form a kingdom which was later called Yugoslavia. A republic was proclaimed November 29, 1945. Other listings may be found under all.

100 Heller = 1 Krone (Bosnia & Herzegovina)
100 Filler = 1 Krone (Croatia-Slavonia)
100 Paras = 1 Dinar (General Issues)

> Catalogue values for unused stamps in this country are for Never Hinged items, beginning with Scott 410 in the regular postage section, Scott C50 in the airpost section, Scott F1 in the registered letter section, Scott J67 in the postage due section, Scott RA1 in the postal tax section, and Scott RAJ1 in the postal tax due section.

> Counterfeits exist of most of the 1918-19 overprints for Bosnia and Herzegovina, Croatia-Slavonia and Slovenia.

BOSNIA AND HERZEGOVINA

Stamps of Bosnia and Herzegovina, 1910, Overprinted or Surcharged in Black or Red

a

b

c

1918		Unwmk.		Perf. 12½
1L1	A4(a)	3h olive green	.40	.80
1L2	A4(b)	5h dk grn (R)	.40	.40
1L3	A4(a)	10h carmine	.40	.40
1L4	A4(a)	20h dk brn (R)	.40	.40
1L5	A4(a)	25h deep blue (R)	.40	.40
1L6	A4(b)	30h green	.40	.40
1L7	A4(b)	40h orange	.40	.40
1L8	A4(b)	45h brown red	.40	.40
1L9	A4(b)	50h dull violet	.55	.80
1L10	A4(a)	60h on 50h dl vio	.40	.40
1L11	A4(b)	80h on 6h org brown	.40	.40
1L12	A4(b)	90h on 35h myr green	.40	.40
1L13	A5(c)	2k gray green	.40	.40
1L14	A4(b)	3k on 3h ol grn	2.00	2.75
1L15	A5(c)	4k on 1k mar	4.00	4.75
1L16	A4(b)	10k on 2h vio	6.00	6.75
		Nos. 1L1-1L16 (16)	17.35	20.25

Inverted and double overprints and assorted varieties exist on the stamps for Bosnia and Herzegovina.

Bosnian Girl — A1

1918		Typo.		Perf. 11½
1L17	A1	2h ultramarine		.40 .40
1L18	A1	6h violet		.80 1.20
1L19	A1	10h rose		.40 .40
1L20	A1	20h green		.40 .40
		Nos. 1L17-1L20 (4)		2.00 2.40

Imperforate stamps of this type (A1) are newspaper stamps of Bosnia.
See Nos. 1L21-1L22, 1L43-1L45.

Bosnia and Herzegovina Nos. P1-P2 (Nos. 1L17-1L18, Imperf.) Srchd.

1918				Imperf.
1L21	A1	3h on 2h ultra		.40 .40
a.		Double surcharge		14.00
1L22	A1	5h on 6h violet		.40 .40
a.		Double surcharge		14.00

Stamps of Bosnia and Herzegovina, 1906-17, Ovptd. or Srchd. in Black or Red

d

e

f

1919				Perf. 12½
1L25	A23(d)	3h claret		.40 .80
1L26	A23(e)	5h green		.40 .40
1L27	A23(e)	10h on 6h dark gray		.40 .40
1L28	A24(d)	20h on 35h myr green		.40 .40
1L29	A23(e)	25h ultra		.40 .40
1L30	A23(e)	30h orange red		.40 .40
1L31	A24(d)	45h olive brn		.40 .40
1L32	A27(e)	45h on 80h org brown		.40 .40
a.		Perf. 11½		1.40 1.60
1L33	A23(e)	50h slate blue		100.00 100.00
1L34	A24(e)	50h on 72h dk blue (R)		.40 .40
1L35	A24(d)	60h brown violet		.40 .40
1L36	A27(e)	80h orange brown		.40 .40
a.		Perf. 11½		35.00 30.00
1L37	A27(d)	90h dark violet		.40 .40
a.		Perf. 11½		3.50 2.75
1L38	A17(f)	2k gray green		.40 .40
a.		Imperf.		35.00
b.		Perf. 9½		4.50 5.00
1L39	A26(3)	3k car, green		.40 .55
1L40	A28(e)	4k car, green		1.75 2.50
1L41	A26(3)	5k dk vio, gray		1.75 2.75
1L42	A28(3)	10k dk vio, gray		3.25 4.00
		Nos. 1L25-1L42 (18)		112.35 115.40

Nos. 1L32, 1L36, 1L37, 1L40 and 1L42 have no bars in the overprint.
Nos. 1L25 to 1L42 exist with inverted overprint or surcharge.

Bosnia and Herzegovina Nos. P2-P4 (Nos. 1L18-1L20, Imperf.) Srchd.

1920				Imperf.
1L43	A1	2h on 6h violet		200.00 180.00
1L44	A1	2h on 10h rose		50.00 50.00
1L45	A1	2h on 20h green		10.00 10.00
		Nos. 1L43-1L45 (3)		260.00 240.00

SEMI-POSTAL STAMPS ISSUES FOR BOSNIA AND HERZEGOVINA

Leading Blind Soldier — SP1

Wounded Soldier — SP2

Semi-Postal Stamps of Bosnia and Herzegovina, 1918 Overprinted

1918		Unwmk.		Perf. 12½, 13
1LB1	SP1	10h greenish bl		.80 1.00
a.		Overprinted as No. 1LB2		52.50 52.50
1LB2	SP2	15h red brown		2.00 2.00
a.		Overprinted as No. 1LB1		47.50 47.50

Bosnian Semi-Postal Stamps of 1916 Overprinted like No. 1LB2

1918				
1LB3	SP1	5h green		125.00 175.00
a.		Overprinted as No. 1LB1		375.00 375.00
1LB4	SP2	10h magenta		100.00 125.00
		Nos. 1LB1-1LB4 (4)		227.80 303.00

Inverted and double overprints exist on Nos. 1LB1-1LB4.

Regular Issue of Bosnia, 1906 Surcharged in Black

Mail Wagon SP3

Bridge at Mostar SP4

Scene near Sarajevo — SP5

1919				
1LB5	SP3	10h + 10h on 40h org red		1.25 2.00
1LB6	SP4	20h + 10h on 20h dk brown		.60 1.75
1LB7	SP5	45h + 15h on 1k mar		4.75 4.75
		Nos. 1LB5-1LB7 (3)		6.60 8.50

Nos. 1LB5-1LB7 exist with surcharge inverted. Value each $7.50.

SPECIAL DELIVERY STAMPS ISSUES FOR BOSNIA AND HERZEGOVINA

SD1　　　　　　SD2
Lightning

Bosnian Special Delivery Stamps Overprinted in Black

1918		Unwmk.		Perf. 12½, 13
1LE1	SD1	2h vermilion		6.00 6.00
a.		Inverted overprint		35.00
b.		Overprinted as No. 1LE2		47.50 47.50
1LE2	SD2	5h deep green		3.25 3.25
a.		Inverted overprint		18.00
b.		Overprinted as No. 1LE1		47.50 47.50

POSTAGE DUE STAMPS ISSUES FOR BOSNIA AND HERZEGOVINA

Postage Due Stamps of Bosnia and Herzegovina, 1916, Overprinted in Black or Red

a　　　　　　　　b

1918		Unwmk.		Perf. 12½, 13
1LJ1	D2 (a)	2h red		.25 .25
1LJ2	D2 (b)	4h red		.55 .55
1LJ3	D2 (a)	5h red		.25 .25
1LJ4	D2 (b)	6h red		.90 .90
1LJ5	D2 (a)	10h red		.25 .25
1LJ6	D2 (b)	15h red		6.75 6.75
1LJ7	D2 (a)	20h red		.25 .25
1LJ8	D2 (b)	25h red		.55 .55
1LJ9	D2 (a)	30h red		.55 .55
1LJ10	D2 (b)	40h red		.25 .25
1LJ11	D2 (a)	50h red		1.20 1.20

c　　　　　　　　d

1LJ12	D2 (c)	1k dark blue (R)		.55 .55
1LJ13	D2 (d)	3k dark blue (R)		.40 .40
		Nos. 1LJ1-1LJ13 (13)		12.70 12.70

Nos. 1LJ1-1LJ13 exist with overprint double or inverted. Value $3 to $7.
Nos. 1LJ1-1LJ11 exist with type "b" overprint instead of type "a," and vice versa. Value, each $10.

Stamps of Bosnia and Herzegovina, 1900-04, Surcharged

e　　　　　　　　f

1919				
1LJ14	A2 (e)	2h on 35h blue		.55 .80
1LJ15	A2 (e)	5h on 45h grnsh bl		.95 1.20
1LJ16	A2 (f)	10h on 10 red		.25 .25
1LJ17	A2 (e)	10h on 40h org		.40 .50
1LJ18	A2 (f)	20h on 5h green		.25 .25
1LJ19	A2 (e)	25h on 20h pink		.40 .55

1LJ20	A2 (f)	30h on 30h bis brn		.40	.55
1LJ21	A2 (e)	1k on 50h red lil		.25	.55
1LJ22	A2 (e)	3k on 25h blue		.50	.55

Postage Due Stamps of Bosnia and Herzegovina, 1904 Surcharged

g   h

1LJ23	D1 (g)	40h on 6h blk, red & yel		.25	.25
1LJ24	D1 (h)	50h on 8h blk, red & yel		.25	.25
1LJ25	D1 (h)	200h blk, red & grn		8.00	6.75
1LJ26	D1 (h)	4k on 7h blk, red & yel		.40	.55
		Nos. 1LJ14-1LJ26 (13)		12.85	13.00

Nos. 1LJ14-1LJ26 exist with overprint double or inverted. Value, $3 to $6.

CROATIA-SLAVONIA

Stamps of Hungary Overprinted in Blue

A1

1918		**Wmk. 137**		**Perf. 15**
		On Stamps of 1913		
2L1	A1	6f olive green	1.10	2.00
2L2	A1	50f lake, blue	1.20	2.00

A2   A3

		On Stamps of 1916		
2L3	A2	10f violet	100.00	140.00
2L4	A3	15f red	100.00	140.00

A4

		On Hungary Nos. 106-107 White Numerals		
2L4A	A4	10f rose	1,600.	1,600.
2L5	A4	15f violet	150.00	150.00
a.		Inverted overprint		

		On Stamps of 1916-18 Colored Numerals		
2L6	A4	2f brown orange	.40	.40
2L7	A4	3f red lilac	.40	.40
2L8	A4	5f green	.40	.40
2L9	A4	6f greenish blue	.40	.40
2L10	A4	10f rose red	16.00	12.00
2L11	A4	15f violet	.40	.40
2L12	A4	20f gray brown	.40	.40
2L13	A4	25f dull blue	.40	.40
2L14	A4	35f brown	.40	.40
2L15	A4	40f olive green	.40	.80

The overprints and surcharges for Croatia-Slavonia exist inverted, double, double inverted, in wrong colors, on wrong stamps, on back, in pairs with one lacking overprint, etc.

A5

A6

2L16	A5	50f red vio & lilac	.40	.40
2L17	A5	75f brt bl & pale bl	.40	.40
2L18	A5	80f grn & pale grn	.40	.40
2L19	A6	1k red brown & cl	.40	.40
2L20	A6	2k olive brn & bis	.40	.40
2L21	A6	3k dark vio & ind	.40	.40
2L22	A6	5k dk brn & lt brn	2.50	3.00
2L23	A6	10k vio brn & vio	16.00	16.00

Stamps of Hungary Overprinted in Blue, Black or Red

A7   A8

2L24	A7	10f scarlet (Bl)	.40	.40
2L25	A7	20f dark brown (Bk)	.40	.40
2L26	A7	25f deep blue (R)	.40	.80
2L27	A8	40f olive green (Bl)	.40	.40
		Nos. 2L6-2L27 (22)	42.10	39.40

Many other stamps of the 1913-18 issues of Hungary, the Semi-Postal Stamps of 1915-16 and Postage Due Stamps were surreptitiously overprinted but were never sold through the post office.

Freedom of Croatia-Slavonia
A9

1919		**Unwmk.** **Litho.**		**Perf. 11½**
2L28	A9	10f rose	6.50	4.00
2L29	A9	20f violet	6.50	4.00
2L30	A9	25f blue	12.00	8.00
2L31	A9	45f greenish blk	95.00	55.00
		Nos. 2L28-2L31 (4)	120.00	71.00

Independence of Croatia, Slavonia and Dalmatia.
#2L28-2L31 exist imperforate, but were not officially issued in this condition.
Excellent counterfeits of #2L28-2L31 exist.

Allegory of Freedom
A10   Youth with Standard
A11

Falcon, Symbol of Liberty — A12

1919				**Perf. 11½**
2L32	A10	2f brn orange	.25	.40
2L33	A10	3f violet	.25	.50
2L34	A10	5f green	.25	.25
2L35	A11	10f red	.25	.25
2L36	A11	20f black brown	.25	.25
2L37	A11	25f deep blue	.25	.25
2L38	A11	45f dark ol grn	.25	.25
2L39	A12	1k carmine rose	.25	.25
2L40	A12	3k dark violet	.80	.95
2L41	A12	5k deep brown	1.20	4.15
		Nos. 2L32-2L41 (10)	4.00	4.15

				Perf. 12½
2L32a	A10	2f	2.90	2.90
2L33a	A10	3f	2.90	2.90
2L34a	A10	5f	15.00	15.00
2L35a	A11	10f	2.90	2.90
2L36a	A11	20f	2.90	2.90
		Nos. 2L32a-2L36a (5)	26.60	26.60

#2L32-2L41 exist imperf. Value, set $25.

SEMI-POSTAL STAMPS ISSUES FOR CROATIA-SLAVONIA

SP1   SP2

SP3

1918		**Wmk. 137**		**Perf. 15**
2LB1	SP1	10f + 2f rose red	.40	2.75
2LB2	SP2	15f + 2f dull violet	.40	.40
2LB3	SP3	40f + 2f brn carmine	.40	.85
		Nos. 2LB1-2LB3 (3)	1.20	4.00

SPECIAL DELIVERY STAMP ISSUE FOR CROATIA-SLAVONIA

SD1

Hungary No. E1 Overprinted in Black

1918		**Wmk. 137**		**Perf. 15**
2LE1	SD1	2f gray green & red	.25	.25

POSTAGE DUE STAMPS ISSUES FOR CROATIA-SLAVONIA

D1

Postage Due Stamps of Hungary Overprinted in Blue

1918		**Wmk. Crown (136)**		**Perf. 15**
2LJ1	D1	50f green & blk	650.00	650.00
		Wmk. Double Cross (137)		
2LJ2	D1	1f green & red	40.00	40.00
a.		Inverted overprint		
2LJ3	D1	2f green & red	1.20	1.20
2LJ4	D1	10f green & red	1.20	1.20
2LJ5	D1	12f green & red	160.00	160.00
2LJ6	D1	15f green & red	.80	.80
2LJ7	D1	20f green & red	.80	.80
2LJ8	D1	30f green & red	2.00	2.00
2LJ9	D1	50f green & blk	65.00	65.00
		Nos. 2LJ2-2LJ9 (8)	271.00	271.00

NEWSPAPER STAMPS ISSUES FOR CROATIA-SLAVONIA

N1

Hungary No. P8 Overprinted in Black

1918		**Wmk. 137**		**Imperf.**
2LP1	N1	(2f) orange	.40	.40

N2

1919		**Litho.**		**Unwmk.**
2LP2	N2	2f yellow orange	.25	1.20

SLOVENIA

Chain Breaker
A1   A2

3, 5, 10, 15f: Chain on right wrist is short, extending only about half way to the frame.
10f: Numerals are 8½mm high.
20, 25, 30, 40f: Distant mountains show faintly between legs of male figure.
40f: Numerals 7mm high. The upright strokes of the "4" extend to the same height; the "0" is 3mm wide.

1919		**Unwmk.**		**Perf. 11½**
		Lithographed at Ljubljana Fine Impression		
3L1	A1	3f violet	.25	.25
3L2	A1	5f green	.25	.25
3L3	A1	10f carmine rose	.40	.25
3L4	A1	15f blue	.25	.25
3L5	A2	20f brown	.65	.25
3L6	A2	25f blue	.30	.25
3L7	A2	30f lilac rose	.30	.25
3L8	A2	40f bister	.30	.25
		Nos. 3L1-3L8 (8)	2.70	2.00

Various stamps of this series exist imperforate and part perforate. Many shades exist.
See Nos. 3L9-3L17, 3L24-3L28. For surcharges see Nos. 3LJ15-3LJ32.

Allegories of Freedom
A3   A4

King Peter I — A5

3, 5, 15f: The chain on the right wrist touches the bottom tablet.
10f: Numerals are 7½mm high.
15f: Curled end of loin cloth appears above letter "H" in the bottom tablet.
20, 25, 30, 40f: The outlines of the mountains have been redrawn and they are more distinct than on the lithographed stamps.
40f: Numerals 8mm high. The left slanting stroke of the "4" extends much higher than the main vertical stroke. The "0" is 2½mm wide and encloses a much narrower space than on the lithographed stamp.

1919-20				**Perf. 11½**
		Typographed at Ljubljana and Vienna		
		Coarse Impression		
3L9	A1	3f violet	.25	.25
3L10	A1	5f green	.30	.25
3L11	A1	10f red	.25	.25
3L12	A1	15f blue	1.60	.25
3L13	A2	20f brown	.55	.25

3L14 A2 25f blue .50 .25
3L15 A2 30f carmine rose .55 .25
3L16 A2 30f dp red 2.75 .90
3L17 A2 40f orange .55 .25
3L18 A3 50f green .55 .25
a. 50f dark green .55 .25
b. 50f olive green 3.50 1.10
3L19 A3 60f dark blue .85 .25
a. 60f violet blue .85 .25
3L20 A4 1k vermilion .55 .25
a. 1k red orange .55 .25
3L21 A4 2k blue .55 .25
a. 2k dull ultramarine .90 .25
3L22 A5 5k brown lake .80 .25
a. 5k lake 12.00 1.60
b. 5k dull red .60 .25
3L23 A5 10k deep ultra 3.25 .90
Nos. 3L9-3L23 (15) 13.85 5.05

Nos. 3L9-3L23 exist imperf. Value, set $90.
Many of the series exist part perforate.
Many shades exist of lower values.
See Nos. 3L29-3L32, 3L40-3L41.

Serrate Roulette 13½

3L24 A1 5f light grn .25 .25
3L25 A1 10f carmine .25 .25
3L26 A1 15f slate blue .30 .25
3L27 A2 20f dark brown .65 .25
a. Serrate x straight roul. .65 .25
3L28 A2 30f car rose .30 .25
a. Serrate x straight roul. .70 .25
3L29 A3 50f green .30 .25
3L30 A3 60f dark blue .95 .40
a. 60f violet blue 2.25 1.10
3L31 A4 1k vermilion 1.40 .40
a. 1k rose red 1.40 .40
3L32 A4 2k blue 9.00 2.75
Nos. 3L24-3L32 (9) 13.40 5.05

Roulette x Perf. 11½

3L24a A1 5f 150.00 150.00
3L25a A1 10f 55.00 55.00
3L26a A1 15f 175.00 175.00
3L28b A2 30f 55.00 55.00
3L29a A3 50f 5.25 4.00
3L30b A3 60f 55.00 55.00
3L31b A4 1k 55.00 55.00

Thick Wove Paper

1920 Litho. *Perf. 11½*
3L40 A5 15k gray green 7.25 14.50
3L41 A5 20k dull violet 1.40 2.40

On Nos. 3L40-3L41 the horizontal lines have been removed from the value tablets. They are printed over a background of pale brown wavy lines.

Chain Breaker A7

Freedom A8

King Peter I — A9

Pale red wavy lines

Dinar Values:
Type I — Size: 21x30½mm.
Type II — Size: 22x32½mm.

Thin to Thick Wove Paper

1920 *Serrate Roulette 13½*
3L42 A7 5p olive green .25 .25
3L43 A7 10p green .25 .25
3L44 A7 15p brown .25 .25
3L45 A7 20p carmine .40 .40
3L46 A7 25p chocolate .40 .25
3L47 A8 40p dark violet .25 .25
3L48 A8 45p yellow .25 .25
3L49 A8 50p dark blue .25 .25
3L50 A8 60p red brown .25 .25
3L51 A9 1d dark brown (I) .25 .25

Perf. 11½

3L52 A9 2d gray vio (II) .25 .25
3L53 A9 4d grnsh black (I) .30 .30
3L54 A9 6d olive brn (II) .25 .25
3L55 A9 10d brown red (II) .30 .80
Nos. 3L42-3L55 (14) 3.90 4.25

The 2d and 6d have a background of pale red wavy lines, the 10d of gray lines.
Counterfeits exist of No. 3L45.

POSTAGE DUE STAMPS ISSUES FOR SLOVENIA

D1

Ljubljana Print
Numerals 9½mm high

1919 Litho. Unwmk. *Perf. 11½*
3LJ1 D1 5f carmine .25 .25
3LJ2 D1 10f carmine .25 .25
3LJ3 D1 20f carmine .25 .25
3LJ4 D1 50f carmine .25 .25

Nos. 3LJ1-3LJ4 were also printed in scarlet and dark red.

Numerals 8mm high

3LJ5 D1 1k dark blue .45 .30
3LJ6 D1 5k dark blue .65 .50
3LJ7 D1 10k dark blue .90 .75
Nos. 3LJ1-3LJ7 (7) 3.00 2.55

Vienna Print

1920 Numerals 11 to 12 mm high
3LJ8 D1 5f red .25 .25
3LJ9 D1 10f red .25 .25
3LJ10 D1 20f red .25 .25
3LJ11 D1 50f red 1.25 .85

Numerals 7mm high

3LJ12 D1 1k Prussian blue 1.10 .70
a. 1k dark blue 5.00 4.50
3LJ13 D1 5k Prussian blue 1.60 1.25
a. 5k dark blue 8.00 6.75
3LJ14 D1 10k Prussian blue 3.75 3.25
a. 10k dark blue 14.00 15.00
Nos. 3LJ8-3LJ14 (7) 8.45 6.80

Nos. 3LJ8-3LJ14 exist imperf. Value, set $40.

No. 3L4 Surcharged in Red

1920 On Litho. Stamps *Perf. 11½*
3LJ15 A1 5p on 15f blue .25 .25
3LJ16 A1 10p on 15f blue .60 .80
3LJ17 A1 20p on 15f blue .25 .25
3LJ18 A1 50p on 15f blue .25 .25
Nos. 3LJ15-3LJ18 (4) 1.35 1.55

Nos. 3L7, 3L12, 3L26, 3L28, 3L28a Surcharged in Dark Blue

3LJ19 A2 1d on 30f lil rose .25 .25
3LJ20 A2 3d on 30f lil rose .25 .25
3LJ21 A2 8d on 30f lil rose 1.60 .80
Nos. 3LJ19-3LJ21 (3) 2.10 1.30

On Typographed Stamps

3LJ22 A1 5p on 15f pale bl 12.00 2.50
3LJ23 A1 10p on 15f pale bl 35.00 25.00
3LJ24 A1 20p on 15f pale bl 11.00 4.00
3LJ25 A1 50p on 15f pale bl 6.00 7.00
Nos. 3LJ22-3LJ25 (4) 64.00 38.50

3LJ26 A1 5p on 15f slate bl 2.75 .50
3LJ27 A1 10p on 15f slate bl 8.50 3.25
3LJ28 A1 20p on 15f slate bl 2.75 .50
3LJ29 A1 50p on 15f slate bl 2.75 .50
3LJ30 A2 1d on 30f dp rose 2.75 .65
a. Serrate x straight roulette 7.00 4.50
3LJ31 A2 3d on 30f dp rose 5.75 1.75
a. Serrate x straight roulette 8.00 5.50
3LJ32 A2 8d on 30f dp rose 125.00 6.50
a. Serrate x straight roulette 125.00 7.50
Nos. 3LJ26-3LJ32 (7) 150.25 13.65

The para surcharges were printed in sheets of 100, ten horizontal rows of ten. There were: 5p three rows, 10p one row, 20p three rows, 50p three rows. The dinar surcharges were in a setting of 50, arranged in vertical rows of five. There were: 1d five rows, 3d three rows, 8d two rows.

NEWSPAPER STAMPS ISSUES FOR SLOVENIA

Eros — N1

Ljubljana Print

1919 Unwmk. Litho. *Imperf.*
3LP1 N1 2f gray .25 .25
3LP2 N1 4f gray .25 .40
3LP3 N1 6f gray 3.50 4.00
3LP4 N1 10f gray .25 .25
3LP5 N1 30f gray .25 .40
Nos. 3LP1-3LP5 (5) 4.50 5.30

See Nos. 3LP6-3LP13. For surcharges see Nos. 3LP14-3LP23, 4LB1-4LB5.

N2

1920 Vienna Print
3LP6 N2 2f gray .25 .25
3LP7 N2 4f gray 6.50 10.00
3LP8 N2 6f gray 1.75 2.75
3LP9 N2 10f gray 14.00 21.00
3LP10 N2 2f blue .25 .30
3LP11 N2 4f blue .25 .25
3LP12 N2 6f blue 125.00 125.00
3LP13 N2 10f blue .25 .25
Nos. 3LP6-3LP13 (8) 148.25 159.80

Nos. 3LP1, 3LP10 Surcharged

a

b

On Ljubljana Print

3LP14 N1 (a) 2p on 2f gray .25 .40
3LP15 N1 (a) 4p on 2f gray .25 .40
3LP16 N1 (a) 6p on 2f gray .40 .65
3LP17 N1 (b) 10p on 2f gray .65 .80
3LP18 N1 (b) 30p on 2f gray .65 .85

On Vienna Print

3LP19 N1 (a) 2p on 2f blue .25 .25
3LP20 N1 (a) 4p on 2f blue .25 .25
3LP21 N1 (a) 6p on 2f blue .25 .25
3LP22 N1 (b) 10p on 2f blue .25 .25
3LP23 N1 (b) 30p on 2f blue .25 .25
Nos. 3LP14-3LP23 (10) 3.45 4.35

The five surcharges were arranged in a setting of 100, in horizontal rows of ten. There were: 2p three rows, 4p three rows, 6p two rows, 10p one row and 30p one row. The sheets were perforated 11½ horizontally between the groups of the different values.

SEMI-POSTAL STAMPS ISSUE FOR CARINTHIA PLEBISCITE

SP1

Nos. 3LP2, 3LP1 Surcharged With Various Designs in Dark Red

1920
4LB1 SP1 5p on 4f gray .25 .25
4LB2 SP1 15p on 4f gray .25 .25
4LB3 SP1 25p on 4f gray .25 .55
4LB4 SP1 45p on 2f gray .25 1.20
4LB5 SP1 50p on 2f gray .25 1.40
4LB6 SP1 2d on 2f gray 2.00 6.00
Nos. 4LB1-4LB6 (6) 3.25 9.65

Nos. 4LB1 to 4LB6 have a different surcharge on each stamp but each includes the letters "K.G.C.A." which signify Carinthian Governmental Commission, Zone A.
Sold at three times face value for the benefit of the Plebiscite Propaganda Fund.

GENERAL ISSUES

For Use throughout the Kingdom

King Alexander — A1

King Peter I — A2

Unwmk.
1921, Jan. 16 Engr. *Perf. 12*
1 A1 2p olive brown .25 .25
2 A1 5p deep green .25 .25
3 A1 10p carmine .25 .25
4 A1 15p violet .25 .25
5 A1 20p black .25 .25
6 A1 25p dark blue .25 .25
7 A1 50p olive green .25 .25
8 A1 60p vermilion .25 .25
9 A1 75p purple .25 .25
10 A2 1d orange .25 .25
11 A2 2d olive bister .30 .25
12 A2 4d dark green .60 .25
13 A2 5d carmine rose 2.50 .25
14 A2 10d red brown 12.00 .55
Nos. 1-14 (14) 17.90 3.80
Set, never hinged 32.50

Exist imperf. Value, set $125.
For surcharge see No. 27.

Nos. B1-B3 Surcharged in Black, Brown, Green or Blue

a

b

1922-24
15 SP1(a) 1d on 10p .25 .25
16 SP2(b) 1d on 15p ('24) .25 .25
17 SP3(a) 1d on 25p (Br) .25 .25
18 SP2(b) 3d on 15p (G) .80 .25
a. Blue surcharge 1.20 1.20
19 SP2(b) 8d on 15p (G) 1.60 .25
a. Double surcharge 35.00 30.00
b. 9d on 15p (error) 130.00
20 SP2(b) 20d on 15p 10.00 1.00
21 SP2(b) 30d on 15p (Bl) 27.50 2.50
Nos. 15-21 (7) 40.65 4.75
Set, never hinged 60.00

A3

1923, Jan. 23 **Engr.**

22	A3	1d red brown	2.00	.25
23	A3	5d carmine	3.75	.25
24	A3	8d violet	6.75	.25
25	A3	20d green	27.50	.75
26	A3	30d red orange	72.50	2.75
		Nos. 22-26 (5)	112.50	4.25
		Set, never hinged	250.00	

For surcharge see No. 28.

Nos. 8 and 24 Surcharged in Black or Blue

1924, Feb. 18

27	A1	20p on 60p ver	.25	.25
28	A3	5d on 8d violet (Bl)	8.00	.60
		Set, never hinged	17.50	

The color of the surcharge on No. 28 varies, including blue, blue black, greenish black and black.

A4

A5

1924, July 1 ***Perf. 14***

29	A4	20p black	.25	.25
30	A4	50p dark brown	.25	.25
31	A4	1d carmine	.25	.25
32	A4	2d myrtle green	.25	.25
33	A4	3d ultramarine	.25	.25
34	A4	5d orange brown	1.40	.25
35	A5	10d dark violet	12.50	.25
36	A5	15d olive green	7.50	.25
37	A5	20d vermilion	7.50	.25
38	A5	30d dark green	7.50	1.25
		Nos. 29-38 (10)	37.65	3.50
		Set, never hinged	80.00	

No. 33 Surcharged

1925, June 5

39	A4	25p on 3d ultramarine	.35	.25
40	A4	50p on 3d ultramarine	.35	.25
		Set, never hinged	1.60	

King Alexander — A6

1926-27 **Typo.** ***Perf. 13***

41	A6	25p deep green	.25	.25
42	A6	50p olive brown	.25	.25
43	A6	1d scarlet	.25	.25
44	A6	2d slate black	.25	.25
45	A6	3d slate blue	.30	.25
46	A6	4d red orange	.50	.25
47	A6	5d violet	.80	.25
48	A6	8d black brown	5.25	.25
49	A6	10d olive brown	4.00	.25
50	A6	15d brown ('27)	15.00	.25
51	A6	20d dark vio ('27)	17.50	.25
52	A6	30d orange ('27)	65.00	.45
		Nos. 41-52 (12)	109.35	3.20
		Set, never hinged	240.00	

For overprints and surcharges see Nos. 53-62, 87-101, B5-B16.

Nos. B7-B16 Overprinted over the Red Surcharge

1928, July

53	A6	1d scarlet	.25	.25
a.		Surcharge "0.50" inverted		
54	A6	2d black	.50	.25
55	A6	3d deep blue	.80	.50
56	A6	4d red orange	2.00	.60
57	A6	5d bright vio	1.60	.25
58	A6	8d black brown	6.50	.95
59	A6	10d olive brown	12.50	.25
60	A6	15d brown	95.00	3.00
61	A6	20d violet	47.50	3.00
62	A6	30d orange	125.00	9.50
		Nos. 53-62 (10)	291.65	18.55
		Set, never hinged	725.00	

King Alexander — A7

With Imprint at Foot

1931-34 ***Perf. 12½***

63	A7	25p black	.25	.25
64	A7	50p green	.25	.25
65	A7	75p slate green	.40	.25
66	A7	1d red	.25	.25
67	A7	1.50d pink	.80	.25
68	A7	1.75d dp rose ('34)	1.60	.35
69	A7	3d slate blue	6.00	.25
70	A7	3.50d ultra ('34)	2.40	.35
71	A7	4d deep orange	3.00	.25
72	A7	5d purple	3.00	.25
73	A7	10d dark olive	12.00	.25
74	A7	15d deep brown	12.00	.25
75	A7	20d dark violet	24.00	.25
76	A7	30d rose	12.00	.45
		Nos. 63-76 (14)	77.95	3.90
		Set, never hinged	175.00	

Type of 1931 Issue Without Imprint at Foot

1932-33

77	A7	25p black	.25	.25
78	A7	50p green	.25	.25
79	A7	1d red	.25	.25
80	A7	3d slate bl ('33)	1.00	.25
81	A7	4d deep org ('33)	3.50	.25
82	A7	5d purple ('33)	5.25	.25
83	A7	10d dk olive ('33)	17.00	.25
84	A7	15d deep brn ('33)	27.50	.25
85	A7	20d dark vio ('33)	35.00	.25
86	A7	30d rose ('33)	45.00	.35
		Nos. 77-86 (10)	135.00	2.60
		Set, never hinged	225.00	

See Nos. 102-115.

Nos. 41 to 52 Overprinted

1933, Sept. 5 ***Perf. 13***

87	A6	25p deep green	.25	.25
88	A6	50p olive brown	.25	.25
89	A6	1d scarlet	.75	.25
90	A6	2d slate black	3.25	.70
91	A6	3d slate blue	3.00	.25
92	A6	4d red orange	2.00	.25
93	A6	5d violet	4.00	.25
94	A6	8d black brown	9.25	1.40
95	A6	10d olive brown	16.00	.25
96	A6	15d brown	24.00	1.75
97	A6	20d dark violet	32.50	.80
98	A6	30d orange	32.50	.80
		Nos. 87-98 (12)	127.75	7.20
		Set, never hinged	240.00	

Semi-Postal Stamps of 1926 Overprinted like Nos. 87 to 98 and Four Bars over the Red Surcharge of 1926

1933, Sept. 5

99	A6	25p green	.80	.25
100	A6	50p olive brown	.80	.25
101	A6	1d scarlet	2.40	.50
		Nos. 99-101 (3)	4.00	1.00
		Set, never hinged	8.00	

Nos. 99-101 exist with double impression of bars. Value, each $5.50 unused, $4.50 used.

King Alexander Memorial Issue

Type of 1931-34 Issues

Borders in Black

1934, Oct. 17

102	A7	25p black	.25	.25
103	A7	50p green	.25	.25
104	A7	75p slate green	.25	.25
105	A7	1d red	.25	.25
106	A7	1.50d pink	.25	.25
107	A7	1.75d deep rose	.25	.25
108	A7	3d slate blue	.25	.25
109	A7	3.50d ultramarine	.25	.25
110	A7	4d deep orange	.40	.25
111	A7	5d purple	.60	.25
112	A7	10d dark olive	2.00	.25
113	A7	15d deep brown	4.00	.25
114	A7	20d dark violet	12.00	.25
115	A7	30d rose	10.00	.40
		Nos. 102-115 (14)	31.00	3.65
		Set, never hinged	50.00	

Cyrillic Characters

Latin and Cyrillic inscriptions are transposed within some sets. In some sets some stamps are inscribed in Latin, others in Cyrillic. This will be mentioned only if it is necessary to identify otherwise identical stamps.

King Peter II — A10

1935-36 ***Perf. 13x12½***

116	A10	25p brown black	.25	.25
117	A10	50p yel orange	.25	.25
118	A10	75p turq green	.25	.25
119	A10	1d brown red	.25	.25
120	A10	1.50d scarlet	.25	.25
121	A10	1.75d cerise	.25	.25
122	A10	2d magenta ('36)	.25	.25
123	A10	3d brn orange	.25	.25
124	A10	3.50d ultramarine	.40	.25
125	A10	4d yellow grn	1.20	.25
126	A10	4d slate blue ('36)	.25	.25
127	A10	10d bright vio	1.20	.25
128	A10	15d brown	1.20	.25
129	A10	20d bright blue	4.75	.25
130	A10	30d rose pink	2.40	.25
		Nos. 116-130 (15)	13.40	3.75
		Set, never hinged	25.00	

For overprints see Nos. N12, N14, N29.

King Alexander — A11

1935, Oct. 9 ***Perf. 12½x11½, 11½***

131	A11	75p turq green	.30	.40
132	A11	1.50d scarlet	.30	.40
133	A11	1.75d dark brown	.35	.80
134	A11	3.50d ultramarine	2.00	2.40
135	A11	7.50d rose carmine	1.25	2.00
		Nos. 131-135 (5)	4.20	6.00

Death of King Alexander, 1st anniv.

Nikola Tesla — A12

1936, May 28 **Litho.** ***Perf. 12½x11½***

136	A12	75p yel grn & dk brn	.40	.25
137	A12	1.75d dull blue & indigo	.40	.25
		Set, never hinged	2.00	

80th birthday of Nikola Tesla (1856-1943), electrical inventor.

Memorial Church, Oplenac — A13

1937, July 1

138	A13	3d Prussian grn	1.00	.50
a.		Perf. 12½	15.00	24.00
		Never hinged	30.00	
139	A13	4d dark blue	1.00	1.20
		Set, never hinged	4.00	

"Little Entente," 16th anniversary.

Coats of Arms of Yugoslavia, Greece, Romania and Turkey — A14

Perf. 11, 11½, 12½

1937, Oct. 29 **Photo.**

140	A14	3d peacock grn	1.25	.40
141	A14	4d ultramarine	1.75	1.25
		Set, never hinged	5.50	

Balkan Entente.

King Peter II — A16

1939-40 **Typo.** ***Perf. 12½***

142	A16	25p black ('40)	.25	.25
143	A16	50p orange ('40)	.25	.25
144	A16	1d yellow grn	.25	.25
145	A16	1.50d red	.25	.25
146	A16	2d dp mag ('40)	.25	.25
147	A16	3d dull red brn	.25	.25
148	A16	4d ultra	.25	.25
148A	A16	5d dk blue ('40)	.25	.25
148B	A16	5.50d dk vio brn ('40)	.50	.25
149	A16	6d slate blue	1.00	.25
150	A16	8d sepia	1.20	.25
151	A16	12d bright vio	1.75	.25
152	A16	16d dull violet	2.40	.25
153	A16	20d blue ('40)	2.40	.25
154	A16	30d brt pink ('40)	5.50	.55
		Nos. 142-154 (15)	16.75	4.05
		Set, never hinged	35.00	

For overprints and surcharges see Nos. N1-N11, N13, N15-N28, N30-N35, Croatia 1-25, Serbia 2N1-2N30.

Arms of Yugoslavia, Greece, Romania and Turkey

A17 A18

1940, June 1

155	A17	3d ultramarine	.80	.50
156	A18	3d ultramarine	.80	.50
a.		Pair, #155-156	6.00	12.00
157	A17	4d dark blue	.80	.50
158	A18	4d dark blue	.80	.50
a.		Pair, #157-158	6.00	12.00
		Nos. 155-158 (4)	3.20	2.00
		Set, never hinged	7.50	
		Pairs, never hinged	30.00	

Balkan Entente.

Bridge at Obod
A19

1940, Sept. 29   Litho.
159   A19 5.50d slate grn & dull
     grn   2.00 3.25
     Never hinged   3.75

Zagreb Phil. Exhib.; 500th anniv. of Johann Gutenberg's invention of printing. The first press in the Yugoslav area was located at Obod in 1493.

Issues for Federal Republic

Serbia Nos. 2N37, 2N39 Srchd. in Green or Vermilion

Overprinted with Pale Green Network

1944, Dec.   Unwmk.   Perf. 11½
159A   OS4   5d (3d + 2d) rose
      pink   .25   .25
159B   OS4   10d (7d + 3d) dk sl
      grn (V)   .25   .25

Similar Srch. on Serbia Nos. 2N37-2N39

1945, Jan. 24   Without Network
159C   OS4   5d (3d + 2d) rose
      pink   .25   .25
159D   OS4   10d (7d + 3d) dk sl
      grn (V)   .25   .25
159E   OS4   25d (4d + 21d) ultra
      (Bk)   .25   .25
     Nos. 159C-159E (3)   .75   .75

Marshal Tito (Josip Broz) — A20

1945   Photo.   Perf. 12½
160   A20   25p bright bl grn   .25   .25
161   A20   50p deep green   .25   .25
162   A20   1d crimson rose   1.20   .25
163   A20   2d dark car rose   .25   .25
164   A20   4d deep blue   .25   .25
165   A20   5d deep green   .25   .40
166   A20   6d dark purple   .25   .25
167   A20   9d orange brown   .35   .25
168   A20   10d deep rose   .25   .40
169   A20   20d orange   1.75 1.60
170   A20   25d dark purple   .25   .25
171   A20   30d deep blue   .25   .25
     Nos. 160-171 (12)   5.55 4.65
     Set, never hinged   9.00

Prohor Pcinski Monastery — A21

1945, Aug. 2   Typo.   Perf. 11½
172   A21   2d red   2.00 2.00
     Never hinged   4.00

Formation of the Popular Antifascist Chamber of Deputies of Macedonia, Aug. 2, 1944.

Partisans
A22   A23

Marshal Tito — A24   City of Jajce — A25

Partisan Girl and Flag — A26

1945, Oct. 10   Litho.   Perf. 12½
173   A22   50p olive gray   .25   .25
174   A22   1d blue green   .25   .25
175   A23   1.50d orange brown   .25   .25
176   A24   2d scarlet   .25   .25
177   A25   3d red brown   1.75   .25
178   A24   4d dark blue   .30   .25
179   A25   5d dark yel grn   1.00   .25
180   A26   6d black   .45   .25
181   A26   9d deep plum   .40   .25
182   A23   12d ultramarine   .90   .25
183   A23   16d blue   .70   .25
184   A23   20d orange ver   1.60   .25
     Nos. 173-184 (12)   8.10 3.00
     Set, never hinged   17.50

See Nos. 211-214. For surcharges and overprints see Nos. 202-203, 273-292, 286-289, Istria 42, 44, 46, 48, 50, Trieste 5-14.

"Labor" and "Agriculture"
A27   A28

1945, Nov. 29   Photo.   Perf. 12
185   A27   2d brn carmine   1.60 3.25
186   A28   2d brn carmine   1.60 3.25
187   A27   4d deep blue   1.60 3.25
188   A28   4d deep blue   1.60 3.25
189   A27   6d dk slate grn   1.60 3.25
190   A28   6d dk slate grn   1.60 3.25
191   A27   9d red orange   1.60 3.25
192   A28   9d red orange   1.60 3.25
193   A27   16d bright ultra   1.60 3.25
194   A28   16d bright ultra   1.60 3.25
195   A27   20d dark brown   1.60 3.25
     a.   Souv. sheet of 2, #191, 195,
        perf. 11½   12.00 24.00
196   A28   20d dark brown   1.60 3.25
     a.   Souv. sheet of 2, #192, 196,
        perf. 11½   12.00 24.00
     Nos. 185-196 (12)   19.20 39.00
     Set, never hinged   40.00
     Se-tenant pairs, #185-196 (6)   22.50 22.50
     Se-tenant pairs, never
       hinged   45.00

Constitution for the Democratic Federation of Yugoslavia, Nov. 29, 1945.

Parade of Armed Forces — A31

1946, May 9   Unwmk.   Perf. 12½
199   A31   1.50d org yel & red   .40   .55
200   A31   2.50d cerise & red   .80   .80
201   A31   5d blue & red   2.75 1.60
     Nos. 199-201 (3)   3.95 2.95

Victory over fascism, 1st anniv.

Type of 1945 Surcharged with New Values in Black

1946, Apr. 1
202   A26   2.50d on 6d bright red   .40   .25
203   A26   8d on 9d orange   .50   .25
     Set, never hinged   1.75

Svetozar Markovic — A32

1946, Sept. 22
204   A32   1.50d blue green   .75   .35
205   A32   2.50d dp red lilac   .85   .50
     Set, never hinged   2.50

Markovic, Serbian socialist, birth cent.

People's Theater, Sofia A33

Sigismund Monument, Warsaw — A35

Designs: 1d, Prague. 2½d, Victory Monument, Belgrade. 5d, Spassky Tower, Kremlin.

1946, Dec. 8   Litho.   Perf. 11½
206   A33   ½d dk brn & yel brn   2.00 4.00
207   A33   1d grnsh blk & emer   2.00 4.00
208   A35   1½d dk car rose &
      rose   2.00 4.00
209   A35   2½d hn brn & brn org   2.00 4.00
210   A35   5d dark bl & blue   2.00 4.00
     Nos. 206-210 (5)   10.00 20.00
     Set, never hinged   20.00

Pan-Slavic Congress, Belgrade, Dec. 1946.

Types of 1945

1947, Jan. 15   Litho.   Perf. 12½
211   A26   2.50d red orange   .35   .25
212   A25   3d dull red   .50   .25
213   A25   5d dark blue   1.40   .25
214   A26   8d orange   .90   .25
     Nos. 211-214 (4)   3.15 1.00
     Set, never hinged   6.00

Gorski Vijenac — A38   Peter P. Nyegosh — A39

1947, June 8   Typo.
215   A38   1.50d Prus grn & blk   .40   .80
216   A39   2.50d ol bis & dk car   .40   .80
217   A38   5d blue & black   .40   .80
     Nos. 215-217 (3)   1.20 2.40
     Set, never hinged   2.40

Centenary of the Montenegrin national epic "Gorski Vijenac" (Wreath of Mountains) by Nyegosh.

Girls' Physical Training Classes — A40

Girl Runner — A41

Physical Culture Parade A42

1947, June 15   Litho.   Perf. 11
218   A40   1.50d brown   1.00 1.00
219   A41   2.50d red   1.00 1.00
220   A42   4d violet blue   1.00 1.00
     Nos. 218-220 (3)   3.00 3.00
     Set, never hinged   6.00

Natl. sports meet, Belgrade, 6/15-22/47.

Map and Star — A43

1947, Sept. 16   Typo.
231   A43   2.50d dp car & dark bl   .40   .80
232   A43   5d org brn & dk grn   .40   .80
     Set, never hinged   1.60

Annexation of Julian Province.

Music and One-string Gusle A44

Vuk Karadzic — A45

1947, Sept. 27   Perf. 11½x12, 12½
233   A44   1.50d green   .40   .80
234   A45   2.50d orange red   .40   .80
235   A44   5d violet blue   .40   .80
     Nos. 233-235 (3)   1.20 2.40
     Set, never hinged   2.40

Centenary of Serbian literature.

Symbols of Industry and Agriculture, Map and Flag — A46

1948, Apr. 8   Litho.   Perf. 12½
236 A46 1.50d grn, bl & salmon 1.40 2.00
237 A46 2.50d red brn, bl &
         salmon 1.40 2.00
238 A46 5d dk bl, bl & salmon 1.40 2.00
     Nos. 236-238 (3) 4.20 6.00
     Set, never hinged 8.00
     International Fair, Zagreb, May 8-17.

Danube River Scene — A47

1948, July 30   Unwmk.
239 A47 2d green 2.25 4.00
240 A47 3d carmine 2.25 4.00
241 A47 5d blue 2.25 4.00
242 A47 10d brown orange 2.25 4.00
     Nos. 239-242 (4) 9.00 16.00
     Set, never hinged 16.00
     Danube Conference, Belgrade.

Marchers with Party Flag — A48

1948, July 21   Perf. 11½, 12½
243 A48 2d dark green .40 .40
244 A48 3d dark red .60 1.20
245 A48 10d dark blue vio .60 .80
     Nos. 243-245 (3) 1.60 2.40
     Set, never hinged 3.25
     5th Congress of the Communist Party in Yugoslavia, July 21, 1948.

Laurent Kosir — A49

1948, Aug. 21   Perf. 12½
246 A49 3d claret .40 .40
247 A49 5d blue .40 .40
248 A49 10d red orange .40 .40
249 A49 12d dull green .40 .40
     Nos. 246-249 (4) 1.60 1.60
     Set, never hinged 3.25
     80th death anniv. of Laurent Kosir, recognized by Yugoslavia as inventor of the postage stamp.

Arms of Bosnia and Herzegovina A50

Arms of Yugoslavia A51

1948, Nov. 29   Perf. 12½, 12x11½
Arms of Yugoslav Peoples Republics
250 A50 3d green .40 .80
251 A50 3d rose lil (Macedonia) .40 .80
252 A50 3d gray bl (Serbia) .40 .80
253 A50 3d gray (Montenegro) .40 .80
254 A50 3d rose (Croatia) .40 .80
255 A50 3d orange (Slovenia) .40 .80
256 A51 10d deep carmine .60 1.40
     Nos. 250-256 (7) 3.00 6.20
     Set, never hinged 6.00
     The Cyrillic and Latin inscriptions are transposed on Nos. 252, 253 and 255.

Franc Presern — A52

1949, Feb. 8   Photo.   Perf. 11½
257 A52 3d dark blue .30 .25
258 A52 5d brown orange .30 .25
259 A52 10d olive black 1.00 .80
     Nos. 257-259 (3) 1.60 1.30
     Set, never hinged 2.75
     Death cent. of Franc Presern, poet.

Ski Jump, Planica — A53

Ski Jumper — A54

Perf. 12½x11½
1949, Mar. 20   Litho.
260 A53 10d magenta .40 1.00
261 A54 12d slate gray .80 1.10
     Set, never hinged 2.40
     Intl. Ski Championships, Planica, Mar. 13-20.

Soldiers — A55

Farmers — A56

Arms and Flags of Macedonia and Yugoslavia — A57

1949, Aug. 2   Perf. 12½
262 A55 3d carmine rose .30 .65
263 A56 5d dull blue .40 .80
264 A57 12d red brown 2.00 2.75
     Nos. 262-264 (3) 2.70 4.20
     Set, never hinged 4.00
     Liberation of Macedonia, 5th anniv.
     It is reported that No. 264 was not sold to the public at post offices.
     For overprints see Nos. C30-C32.

Postal Communications A58

UPU, 75th anniversary: 5d, Plane, locomotive and stagecoach, horiz.

1949, Sept. 8   Unwmk.
265 A58 3d red 1.60 3.25
266 A58 5d blue .40 .80
267 A58 12d brown .40 .80
     Nos. 265-267 (3) 2.40 4.85
     Set, never hinged 4.75
     For overprints see Trieste Nos. 15-16.

Locomotives A60

1949, Dec. 15   Photo.
269 A60 2d Early steam 1.00 2.00
270 A60 3d Modern steam 1.00 2.00
271 A60 5d Diesel 1.00 2.00
272 A60 10d Electric 22.50 24.00
     Nos. 269-272 (4) 25.50 30.00
     Set, never hinged 50.00
     Centenary of Yugoslav railroads.
     For overprints see Trieste Nos. 17-20.

Official Stamps Nos. O7 and O8 Surcharged

1949   Typo.
272A O1 3d on 8d chocolate .50 .40
272B O1 3d on 12d violet .50 .40
     Set, never hinged 2.00

Stamps of 1945 and 1947 Overprinted or Surcharged in Black

a   b

c   d

1949   Litho.
273 A22 (a) 50p olive gray .25 .25
274 A22 (a) 1d blue green .25 .25
275 A24 (b) 2d scarlet .25 .25
276 A26 (c) 3d on 8d orange .25 .25
277 A25 (d) 3d dull red .25 .25
278 A25 (d) 5d dark blue .25 .25
279 A23 (a) 10d on 20d org ver .45 .25
280 A23 (a) 12d ultramarine .40 .25
281 A22 (a) 16d blue .60 .25
282 A23 (a) 20d orange ver .60 .25
     Nos. 273-282 (10) 3.55 2.50
     Set, never hinged 6.00
     On No. 279 the surcharge includes a rule below "JUGOSLAVIJA" and "D 10" with two bars over "20D."
     See Nos. 286-289.

Surveying for Highway A61

Bridge, Map and Automobile A62

Highway Completion Symbolized A63

1950, Jan. 16   Photo.   Perf. 12½
283 A61 2d blue green .55 .80
284 A62 3d rose brown .55 .80
285 A63 5d violet blue .80 1.20
     Nos. 283-285 (3) 1.90 2.80
     Set, never hinged 3.75
     Completion of Belgrade-Zagreb highway, Dec. 1949.

Types of 1945 Overprinted in Black
1950   Unwmk.   Perf. 12½
286 A22 (a) 1d brownish org .40 .25
287 A24 (b) 2d blue green .40 .25
288 A25 (d) 3d rose pink .60 .25
289 A25 (d) 5d blue .60 .25
     Nos. 286-289 (4) 2.00 1.00
     Set, never hinged 4.00

Marshal Tito — A64

1950, Apr. 30   Engr.
290 A64 3d red 1.00 .80
291 A64 5d dull blue 1.00 .80
292 A64 10d red orange 10.00 20.00
293 A64 12d olive black 1.25 2.40
     Nos. 290-293 (4) 13.25 24.00
     Set, never hinged 24.00
     Labor Day, May 1.

Child Eating — A65

1950, June 1   Photo.
294 A65 3d brown red .80 .45
     Never hinged 1.60
     Issued to publicize Children's Day, June 1.

Boy and Model Plane — A66

Designs: 3d, Glider aloft. 5d, Parachutists. 10d, Aviatrix. 20d, Glider on field.

1950, July 2   Engr.
295 A66 2d dark green 1.60 3.25
296 A66 3d brown red 1.60 3.25
297 A66 5d violet 1.60 3.25
298 A66 10d chocolate 1.60 3.25
299 A66 20d ultramarine 12.00 24.00
     Nos. 295-299 (5) 18.40 37.00
     Set, never hinged 37.50
     Third Aviation Meet, July 2-11.

Map and Chess Symbols — A67

3d, Rook and ribbon. 5d, Globe and chess board. 10d, Allegory of international chess. 20d, View of Dubrovnik, knight and ribbon.

1950, Aug. 20　　Photo.　　Perf. 11½
300	A67	2d red brn & rose brown	.45	.80
301	A67	3d blk brn, gray brn & dl yellow	.45	.80
302	A67	5d dk grn, bl & buff	1.10	.80
303	A67	10d cl, bl & org yel	1.10	2.00
304	A67	20d dk bl, bl & org yellow	22.00	22.50
		Nos. 300-304 (5)	25.10	26.90
		Set, never hinged	50.00	

Intl. Chess Matches, Dubrovnik, Aug. 1950.

Electrification — A68

Designs: 50p, Metallurgy. 2d, Agriculture. 3d, Construction. 5d, Fishing. 7d, Mining. 10d, Fruitgrowing. 12d, Lumbering. 16d, Gathering sunflowers. 20d, Livestock raising. 30d, Book manufacture. 50d, Loading ship.

1950-51　　Unwmk.　Engr.　　Perf. 12½
305	A68	50p dk brn ('51)	.25	.25
306	A68	1d blue green	.25	.25
307	A68	2d orange	.25	.25
308	A68	3d rose red	.25	.25
309	A68	5d ultramarine	.60	.25
310	A68	7d gray	.60	.25
311	A68	10d chocolate	.60	.25
312	A68	12d vio brn ('51)	2.00	.25
313	A68	16d vio bl ('51)	1.75	.30
314	A68	20d ol grn ('51)	1.75	.25
314A	A68	30d red brn ('51)	4.00	.55
315	A68	50d violet ('51)	21.00	24.00
		Nos. 305-315 (12)	33.30	27.10
		Set, never hinged	55.00	

See Nos. 343-354, 378-384A. For overprints see Trieste Nos. 68-75, 90-92.

Coal and Logs for Export — A69

1950, Sept. 23　　Photo.
316	A69	3d red brown	.80	.25
		Never hinged	1.60	

Zagreb International Fair, 1950.

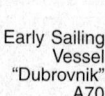

Early Sailing Vessel "Dubrovnik" A70

Designs: 3d, Partisans in boat. 5d, Loading freighter. 10d, Transatlantic ship "Zagreb." 12d, Sailboats. 20d, Naval gun and ship.

1950, Nov. 29
317	A70	2d brown violet	.25	.25
318	A70	3d orange brown	.25	.25
319	A70	5d dull green	.25	.25
320	A70	10d chalky blue	.30	.25
321	A70	12d dark blue	.80	.30
322	A70	20d red brown	10.00	2.90
		Nos. 317-322 (6)	11.85	4.20
		Set, never hinged	20.00	

Yugoslav navy.

Partisans with Flag — A71

1951, Mar. 27　　　　　　Engr.
323	A71	3d red & red brn	3.50	3.50
		Never hinged	7.50	

Yugoslavia's resistance to Nazi Germany, 10th anniv.

Stane Rozman A72

5d, Post-boy during Slovene insurrection.

1951, Apr. 27　　　　　Photo.
324	A72	3d brown red	.25	.25
325	A72	5d dark blue	.60	.40
		Set, never hinged	1.60	

Slovene insurrection, 10th anniv.

Children Painting A73

1951, June 3
326	A73	3d red	.80	.25
		Never hinged	1.60	

Issued to publicize Children's Day, June 3.

Zika Jovanovich — A74

Serbian Revolutionists A75

1951, July 7
327	A74	3d brown red	.30	.45
328	A75	5d deep blue	.55	.90
		Set, never hinged	1.60	

Serbian insurrection, 10th anniv.

Sava Kovacevich A76

Kovacevich Leading Revolutionists A77

1951, July 13
329	A76	3d rose pink	.40	.50
330	A77	5d light blue	1.00	1.10
		Set, never hinged	2.60	

Montenegrin insurrection, 10th anniv.

Monument to Marko Oreskovich A78

1951, July 27
331	A78	3d shown	.45	.50
332	A78	5d Monument to wounded	.70	.90
		Set, never hinged	2.00	

Croatian insurrection, 10th anniv.

Sium Bolaj — A79

Revolutionists A80

1951, July 27
333	A79	3d rose brown	.40	.50
334	A80	5d blue	.75	.90
		Set, never hinged	2.00	

Revolution in Bosnia and Herzegovina, 10th anniv.

Primoz Trubar — A81

12d, Marko Marulic. 20d, Tsar Stefan Duschan.

1951, Sept. 9　　　　　　Engr.
335	A81	10d slate gray	3.25	6.50
336	A81	12d brown orange	3.25	6.50
337	A81	20d violet	10.00	20.00
		Nos. 335-337 (3)	16.50	33.00
		Set, never hinged	32.50	

Yugoslav cultural anniversaries. For overprints see Trieste Nos. 40-41.

National Handicrafts — A82

1951, Sept. 15　　Litho.　　Perf. 11½
338	A82	3d multicolored	1.75	1.20
		Set, never hinged	2.50	

Zagreb International Fair, 1951.

Mirce Acev — A83

Monument at Skopje A84

1951, Oct. 11
339	A83	3d deep plum	.40	.40
340	A84	5d indigo	.80	1.20
		Set, never hinged	2.50	

Macedonian insurrection, 10th anniv.

Soldier and Emblem — A85

1951, Dec. 22　　Photo.　　Perf. 12½
341	A85	15d deep carmine	.25	.25
		Never hinged	.50	

Army Day. See No. C54.

Peter P. Nyegosh — A86

1951, Nov. 29　　　　　　Engr.
342	A86	15d deep claret	2.00	.80
		Never hinged	3.25	

Death centenary of Nyegosh. See note after No. 217.

Types of 1950-51

Designs: 15d, Gathering sunflowers. 25d, Agriculture. 35d, Construction. 75d, Lumbering. 100d, Metallurgy.

1951-52　　　　　　　　　　Engr.
343	A68	1d gray ('52)	.25	.25
344	A68	2d rose car ('52)	.25	.25
345	A68	5d orange ('52)	.80	.25
346	A68	10d emerald ('52)	4.00	.25
347	A68	15d rose car ('52)	20.00	.25
348	A68	20d purple	2.00	.25
349	A68	25d yel brn ('52)	8.75	.25
350	A68	30d blue	1.00	.25
351	A68	35d red brn ('52)	1.50	.25
352	A68	50d greenish bl	.80	.25
353	A68	75d purple ('52)	2.00	.25
354	A68	100d sepia ('52)	4.00	.25
		Nos. 343-354 (12)	45.35	3.00
		Set, never hinged	90.00	

No. 349 exists with and without printer's inscriptions at bottom, with stamps differing slightly.

Marshal Tito

A87　　　　　　　　　A88

1952, May 25   Photo.   Perf. 11½

355	A87	15d shown	.40	.80
356	A88	28d shown	.40	.80
357	A87	50d Tito facing left	19.00	30.00
		Nos. 355-357 (3)	19.80	31.60
		Set, never hinged	40.00	

60th birthday of Marshal Tito.

Child with Ball — A89

1952, June 1   Litho.   Perf. 12½

358	A89	15d bright rose	3.00	3.00
		Never hinged	6.00	

Issued to publicize Children's Day, June 1.
For overprint see Trieste No. 60.

Girl Gymnast — A90

1952, July 10   Perf. 12½

359	A90	5d shown	.40	.25
360	A90	10d Runner	.60	.25
361	A90	15d Swimmer	.60	.25
362	A90	28d Boxer	1.40	.80
363	A90	50d Basketball	2.00	4.50
364	A90	100d Soccer	24.00	27.50
		Nos. 359-364 (6)	29.00	33.55
		Set, never hinged	55.00	

15th Olympic Games, Helsinki, 1952.
Nos. 359-364 exist imperf. Value $800.
For overprints see Trieste Nos. 51-56.

Split, Dalmatia — A91

1952, Sept. 10   Litho.

365	A91	15d shown	.40	.80
366	A91	28d Naval scene	.80	1.75
367	A91	50d St. Stefan	9.00	14.00
		Nos. 365-367 (3)	10.20	16.55
		Set, never hinged	20.00	

Yugoslav navy, 10th anniv.
For overprints see Trieste Nos. 57-59.

Belgrade, 16th Century A92

1952, Sept. 14   Engr.   Perf. 11½

368	A92	15d violet brn	6.00	10.00
		Never hinged	10.00	

1st Yugoslav Phil. Exhib., Sept. 14-20. Sold only at the exhibition.

Marching Workers and Congress Flag — A93

1952, Nov. 2   Perf. 11½

369	A93	15d red brown	.60	1.20
370	A93	15d dark vio blue	.60	1.20
371	A93	15d dark brown	.60	1.20
372	A93	15d blue green	.60	1.20
		Nos. 369-372 (4)	2.40	4.80
		Set, never hinged	5.00	

6th Yugoslav Communist Party Congress, Zagreb.
For overprints see Trieste Nos. 61-64.

Nikola Tesla — A94

1953, Jan. 7   Unwmk.

373	A94	15d brown carmine	.40	.25
374	A94	30d chalky blue	2.00	.65
		Set, never hinged	4.00	

Death of Nikola Tesla, 10th anniv.
For overprints see Trieste Nos. 66-67.

Woman Pouring Water — A95

Designs: 30d, Hands holding two birds. 50d, Woman holding Urn.

1953, Mar. 24   Litho.   Perf. 11½

375	A95	15d dk olive green	.40	.65
376	A95	30d chalky blue	.90	.65
377	A95	50d henna brown	8.75	4.50
		Nos. 375-377 (3)	10.05	5.80
		Set, never hinged	20.00	

Issued to honor the United Nations.
See Nos. RA19 and RAJ16. For overprints see Trieste Nos. 76-78.

Types of 1950-52

1953-55   Litho.   Perf. 12½

8d, Mining. 17d, Livestock raising.

378	A68	1d dull gray	.40	.25
379	A68	2d carmine	1.00	.25
380	A68	5d orange	3.50	.25
381	A68	8d blue	2.50	.25
382	A68	10d yellow green	4.00	.25
383	A68	12d lt vio brown	20.00	.25
384	A68	15d rose red	8.00	.25
384A	A68	17d vio brn ('55)	1.50	.25
		Nos. 378-384A (8)	40.90	2.00
		Set, never hinged	75.00	

For overprints see Trieste Nos. 68-75, 90-92.

Automobile Climbing Mt. Lovcen — A96

30d, Motorcycle & auto at Opatija. 50d, Racers leaving Belgrade. 70d, Auto near Mt. Triglav.

1953, May 10   Photo.   Perf. 12½

385	A96	15d sal & dp plum	.25	.25
386	A96	30d bl & dark blue	.25	.25
387	A96	50d ocher & choc	.60	.40
388	A96	70d lt bl grn & ol grn	15.00	4.75
		Nos. 385-388 (4)	16.10	5.65
		Set, never hinged	35.00	

Intl. Automobile & Motorcycle Races, 1953.

President Tito — A97

1953, June 28   Engr.   Unwmk.

389	A97	50d deep purple	6.00	8.00
		Never hinged	12.00	

Marshal Tito's election to the presidency, Jan. 14, 1953.
For overprint see Trieste No. 83.

Star and Flag-encircled Globe — A98

1953, July 25   Engr.; Star Typo.

390	A98	15d gray & green	1.50	2.40
		Never hinged	3.00	

38th Esperanto Cong., Zagreb, 7/25-8/1.
For overprint see Trieste No. 84.

Macedonian Revolutionary A99

Nicolas Karev A100

1953, Aug. 2   Litho.

391	A99	15d dark red brown	.30	.65
392	A100	30d dull green	1.75	3.50
		Set, never hinged	4.00	

Macedonian Insurection of 1903, 50th anniv.

Family — A101

1953, Sept. 6   Photo.

393	A101	15d deep green	40.00	40.00
		Never hinged	100.00	

Liberation of Istria and the Slovene coast, 10th anniv.
For overprint see Trieste No. 85.

Branko Radicevic — A102

1953, Oct. 1   Engr.

394	A102	15d lilac	2.50	2.00
		Never hinged	5.00	

10th death anniv. of Branko Radicevic, poet.
For overprint see Trieste No. 86.

View of Jajce — A103

Designs: 30d, First meeting place. 50d, Marshal Tito addressing Assembly.

1953, Nov. 29   Perf. 12½x12

395	A103	15d dark green	.40	.80
396	A103	30d rose car	.60	1.20
397	A103	50d dark brown	4.00	8.00
		Nos. 395-397 (3)	5.00	10.00
		Set, never hinged	10.00	

2nd Assembly of the Natl. Republic of Yugoslavia, 10th anniv.
For overprints see Trieste Nos. 87-89.

Wildlife A104

Lammergeier A105

1954, June 30   Photo.   Perf. 11½

398	A104	2d Ground squirrel	.25	.25
399	A104	5d Lynx	.25	.25
400	A104	10d Red deer	.40	.25
401	A104	15d Brown bear	.50	.25
402	A104	17d Chamois	.80	.25
403	A104	25d White pelican	1.20	.40
404	A105	30d shown	1.20	.40
405	A105	35d Black beetle	1.60	.55
406	A105	50d Bush cricket	6.00	2.00
407	A105	65d Adriatic lizard	10.00	10.00
408	A105	70d Salamander	8.00	10.00
409	A105	100d Trout	24.00	32.50
		Nos. 398-409 (12)	54.20	57.10
		Set, never hinged	125.00	

See Nos. 497-505. For overprints see Trieste Nos. 93-104.

Ljubljana, 17th Century A106

1954, July 29   Engr.

410	A106	15d multicolored	13.00	13.00

2nd Yugoslav Phil. Exhib., July 29-Aug. 8.
Sold for 50d, which included admission to the exhibition.

Revolutionary Flag — A107

1954, Oct. 3   Engr. & Typo.   Perf. 12½

411	A107	15d shown	1.60	.45
412	A107	30d Cannon	2.25	.80
413	A107	50d Revolutionary seal	5.00	1.10
414	A107	70d Karageorge	32.50	15.00
		Nos. 411-414 (4)	41.35	17.35

1st Serbian insurrection, 150th anniv.
For overprints see Trieste Nos. 105-108.

Vatroslav
Lisinski — A108

30d, Andrea Kacic-Miosic. 50d, Jure Vega.
70d, Jovan Jovanovic-Zmaj. 100d, Philip
Visnic.

1954, Dec. 25   **Engr.**
415	A108	15d dark green	2.75	1.00
416	A108	30d chocolate	2.75	1.60
417	A108	50d dp claret	3.75	3.00
418	A108	70d indigo	7.50	7.00
419	A108	100d purple	19.00	19.00
		Nos. 415-419 (5)	35.75	31.60

Scene from
"Robinja" — A109

"A
Midsummer
Night's
Dream"
A110

1955   **Photo.**   **Perf. 12x11½, 12½**
Glazed Paper
420	A109	15d brown lake	1.00	.55
421	A110	30d dark blue	3.50	2.00

Festival at Dubrovnik.

Dragon Emblem
of
Ljubljana — A111

1955   **Engr.**   **Perf. 12½**
422	A111	15d dk grn & brn	6.00	4.00

1st Intl. Exhib. of Graphic Arts, Ljubljana,
July 3-Sept. 3.

Symbol of Sign
Language
A112

1955, Aug. 23
423	A112	15d rose lake	2.00	.45

2nd World Congress of Deaf Mutes, Zagreb,
Aug. 23-27.

Hops — A113

Medicinal Plants.

1955, Sept. 24   **Photo.**   **Perf. 11½**
424	A113	5d shown	.25	.25
425	A113	10d Tobacco	.25	.25
426	A113	15d Poppy	.25	.25
427	A113	17d Linden	.25	.25
428	A113	25d Chamomile	.25	.25
429	A113	30d Salvia	.55	.30
430	A113	50d Dog rose	3.00	2.00
431	A113	70d Gentian	5.00	2.75
432	A113	100d Adonis	25.00	17.50
		Nos. 424-432 (9)	34.80	23.80

"Peace" Statue,
New York — A114

1955, Oct. 24   **Litho.**   **Perf. 12½**
433	A114	30d lt bl & blk	1.50	1.10

United Nations, 10th anniversary.

Woman and
Dove — A115

1955, Nov. 29   **Engr.**
434	A115	15d dull violet	.80	.55

10th anniv. of the "New Yugoslavia."

St. Donat,
Zadar — A116

Cornice,
Cathedral
at Sibenik
A117

Yugoslav Art: 10d, Relief of a King, Split.
15d, Griffin, Studenica Monastery. 20d,
Figures, Trogir Cathedral. 25d, Fresco, Sopocani Monastery. 30d, Tombstone, Radimlje.
40d, Ciborium, Kotor Cathedral. 50d, St. Martin from Tryptich, Dubrovnik. 70d, Figure,
Belec Church. 100d, Rihard Jakopic, self-portrait. 200d, "Peace" Statue, New York.

1956, Mar. 24   **Photo.**   **Perf. 11½**
435	A116	5d blue vio	.45	.25
436	A116	10d slate grn	.45	.25
437	A116	15d olive brn	.45	.25
438	A116	20d brown car	.45	.25
439	A116	25d black brn	.45	.25
440	A116	30d dp claret	.45	.25
441	A117	35d olive grn	1.00	.25
442	A117	40d red brown	1.75	.50
443	A116	50d olive brn	2.50	.70
444	A116	70d dk green	9.25	6.75
445	A116	100d dark pur	32.50	20.00
446	A116	200d deep blue	77.50	32.50
		Nos. 435-446 (12)	127.20	62.20

13th
Century
Tower,
Zagreb
A118

1956, Apr. 20   **Engr.**   **Perf. 11½**
Chalky Paper
447	A118	15d vio brn, bis brn & gray	1.00	.25
a.		Miniature sheet of 4	9.00	—

3rd Yugoslavia Phil. Exhib. (JUFIZ III),
Zagreb, May 20-27. No. 447a was sold at the
exhibition, tipped into a folder, for 75 dinars.
See No. C56.

Induction
Motor — A119

Perf. 11½x12½
1956, July 10   **Photo.**
448	A119	10d shown	.50	.25
449	A119	15d Transformer	.60	.25
450	A119	30d Electronic controls	1.10	.50
451	A119	50d Nikola Tesla	4.00	2.00
		Nos. 448-451 (4)	6.20	3.00

Birth cent. of Nikola Tesla, inventor.

Sea Horse — A120

Paper
Nautilus
A121

Designs: 20d, European rock lobster. 25d,
"Sea Prince." 30d, Sea perch. 35d, Red mul-
let. 50d, Scorpion fish. 70d, Wrasse. 100d,
Dory.

1956, Sept. 10   **Perf. 11½**
Granite Paper
Animals in Natural Colors
452	A120	10d bright grn	.50	.30
453	A121	15d ultra & blk	.50	.30
454	A121	20d deep blue	.50	.30
455	A121	25d violet blue	.80	.30
456	A121	30d brt grnsh bl	.85	.30
457	A121	35d dk bl green	1.75	.30
458	A121	50d indigo	6.50	1.90
459	A121	70d slate grn	8.00	4.00
460	A121	100d dark blue	32.50	20.00
		Nos. 452-460 (9)	51.90	27.70

Runner
A122

Designs: 15d, Paddling kayak. 20d, Skiing.
30d, Swimming. 35d, Soccer. 50d, Water
polo. 70d, Table tennis. 100d, Sharpshooting.

1956, Oct. 24   **Litho.**   **Perf. 12½**
Design and Inscription in Bister
461	A122	10d dk carmine	.80	.35
462	A122	15d dark blue	.80	.35
463	A122	20d ultramarine	1.50	.70
464	A122	30d olive grn	1.50	.70
465	A122	35d dark brown	1.50	.70
466	A122	50d green	1.50	.70
467	A122	70d brn violet	*50.00*	22.50
468	A122	100d dark red	*50.00*	22.50
		Nos. 461-468 (8)	107.60	48.50

16th Olympic Games, Melbourne, 11/22-
12/8.

Centaury — A123

Medicinal Plants: 15d, Belladonna. 20d,
Autumn crocus. 25d, Marsh mallow. 30d,
Valerian. 35d, Woolly Foxglove. 50d,
Aspidium. 70d, Green Winged Orchid. 100d,
Pyrethrum.

Granite Paper
Flowers in Natural Colors
1957, May 25   **Photo.**   **Perf. 11½**
469	A123	10d dk bl & grn	.25	.25
470	A123	15d violet	.25	.25
471	A123	20d lt ol grn & brn	.25	.25
472	A123	25d dp cl & dk bl	.50	.25
473	A123	30d lil rose & claret	.90	.25
474	A123	35d dk gray & dl pur	1.50	.25
475	A123	50d dp grn & choc	2.50	.75
476	A123	70d pale brn & grn	4.50	1.60
477	A123	100d gray & brown	14.00	6.00
		Nos. 469-477 (9)	24.65	9.85

See #538-546, 597-605, 689-694, 772-777.

Hand
Holding
Factory
A124

1957, June 25   **Engr.**   **Perf. 12½**
478	A124	15d dark car rose	.40	.25
479	A124	30d dark violet blue	1.40	.80

Congress of Workers' Councils, Belgrade,
June 25. Exist imperf.

2nd Gymnastic
Meet, Zagreb,
July 10-
14 — A125

Various gymnastic positions.

1957, July 1   **Photo.**
480	A125	10d ol grn & blk	.25	.25
481	A125	15d brn red & blk	.25	.25
482	A125	30d Prus bl & blk	.80	.25
483	A125	50d brn & black	3.75	1.25
		Nos. 480-483 (4)	5.05	2.00

Montenegro
A126

Natl. Costumes: 15d, Macedonia. 30d,
Croatia. 50d, Serbia. 70d, Bosnia and Herzegovina. 100d, Slovenia. 50d, 70d, 100d vert.

1957, Sept. 24   **Typo.**   **Perf. 12½**
Background in Bister Brown
484	A126	10d dk brn, ultra & red	.40	.25
485	A126	15d dk brn, blk & red	.40	.25
486	A126	30d dk brn, grn & red	.40	.25
487	A126	50d dk brn & green	1.00	.25
488	A126	70d dk brn & black	1.40	.50
489	A126	100d dk brn, grn & red	6.50	3.25
		Nos. 484-489 (6)	10.10	4.75

Revolutionists
A127

Lithographed and Engraved
1957, Nov. 7   **Perf. 11½x12½**
490 A127 15d ocher & red   .65 .45
Russian Revolution, 40th anniv.

Simon
Gregorcic — A128

Famous Yugoslavs: 30d, Anton Linhart, dramatist and historian. 50d, Oton Kucera, physicist. 70d, Stevan Mokranjac, composer. 100d, Jovan Sterija Popovic, writer

1957, Dec. 3   **Engr.**   **Perf. 12½**
491 A128 15d sepia   .45 .40
492 A128 30d indigo   .60 .40
493 A128 50d reddish brn   1.25 .40
494 A128 70d dl violet   9.00 4.75
495 A128 100d olive grn   15.00 8.00
    Nos. 491-495 (5)   26.30 13.95

"Young Man on
Fire" — A129

1958, Apr. 22   **Photo.**
496 A129 15d deep plum   .80 .25
Union of Yugoslav Communists, 7th congress, Ljubljana, Apr. 22.

Types of 1954
Game birds.

1958, May 25   **Perf. 11½**
Granite Paper
Birds in Natural Colors
497 A104 10d Mallard   .30 .25
498 A104 15d Capercaillie   .30 .25
499 A104 20d Ring-necked
         pheasant   .30 .25
500 A105 25d Coot   .30 .25
501 A105 30d Water rail   .70 .25
502 A105 35d Great bustard   1.25 .45
503 A105 50d Rock partridge   4.50 1.25
504 A104 70d Woodcock   8.25 3.25
505 A105 100d Eurasian crane   17.50 7.50
    Nos. 497-505 (9)   33.40 13.50

Stylized
Bird — A130

1958, June 14   **Engr.**   **Perf. 12½**
506 A130 15d bluish black   .80 .25
Opening of Postal Museum, Belgrade. Exists imperf.

Flag and
Laurel
A131

1958, July 1   **Unwmk.**
507 A131 15d brn carmine   .50 .30
15th anniv. of victory over Germans at Sutjeska, Bosnia.

Onufrio Well,
Dubrovnik
A132

1958, Aug. 10   **Litho.**   **Perf. 12½**
508 A132 15d black & brn   1.50 .30
Marin Drzic, dramatist, 450th birth anniv.

Sisak Steel
Works — A133

Titograd Hotel and
Open-Air
Theater — A134

Industrial Progress Designs: 2d, Crude oil production. 5d, Shipbuilding. 10d, Sisak steel works. 15d, Jablanica hydroelectric works. 17d, Lumber industry. 25d, Overpass, Zagreb-Ljubljana highway. 30d, Litostroy turbine factory. 35d, Lukavac coke plant. 50d, Bridge at Skopje. 70d, Railroad station, Sarajevo. 100d, Triple bridge, Ljubljana. 200d, Mestrovic station, Zagreb. 500d, Parliament, Belgrade.

1958   **Typo.**   **Perf. 12½ Horiz.**
509 A133 10d green   14.00 6.00
510 A133 15d orange ver   14.00 6.00

                  Engr.   **Perf. 12½**
511 A133 2d olive   .25 .25
512 A133 5d brown red   .25 .25
513 A133 10d green   .40 .25
514 A133 15d orange ver   .40 .25
515 A133 17d deep claret   .40 .25
516 A133 25d slate   .40 .25
517 A133 30d blue black   .40 .25
518 A133 35d rose red   .40 .25
519 A134 40d car rose   .45 .25
520 A134 50d bright bl   .50 .25
521 A134 70d orange ver   1.25 .25
522 A134 100d green   4.75 .25
523 A134 200d red brown   4.50 .25
524 A134 500d intense bl   8.50 .30
    Nos. 511-524 (14)   22.85 3.55

Nos. 509-510 are coil stamps.
See #555-562, 627-645, 786-789, 830-840.

Ocean
Exploration
A135

1958, Oct. 24   **Unwmk.**
525 A135 15d brown violet   .50 .25
Intl. Geophysical Year, 1957-58. Exists imperf. See #C58.

White and
Black Hands
Holding
Scales
A136

1958, Dec. 10   **Perf. 12½**
526 A136 30d steel blue   1.10 .80
Universal Declaration of Human Rights, 10th anniv.

Dubrovnik
A137

Tourist attractions: #528, Bled. #529, Postojna grotto. #530, Ohrid. #531, Opatija. #532, Plitvice National Park. #533, Split. #534, Sveti Stefan. #535, Exhibition Hall, Belgrade.

1959, Feb. 16   **Litho.**   **Perf. 12½**
527 A137 10d crim rose & cit   .25 .25
528 A137 10d lt grn & lt vio bl   .25 .25
529 A137 15d grnsh bl & pur   .25 .25
530 A137 15d grn & bright bl   .25 .25
531 A137 20d lt grn & grnsh bl   .25 .25
532 A137 20d ol bis & brt grn   .25 .25
533 A137 30d yel org & purple   1.40 .25
534 A137 30d lt vio bl & gray ol   1.40 .25
535 A137 70d gray & grnsh bl   4.50 2.25
    Nos. 527-535 (9)   8.80 4.25

Nos. 527, 530, 532 and 534 are inscribed in Cyrillic characters. See #650-658, 695-700.

Red
Flags — A138

1959, Apr. 20   **Unwmk.**   **Perf. 12½**
536 A138 20d multicolored   .50 .25
Yugoslav Communist Party, 40th anniv.

Dubrovnik,
15th
Century
A139

1959, May 24   **Engr.**   **Perf. 11½**
537 A139 20d yel grn, dk grn &
         bl   10.00 3.50
4th Yugoslavia Phil. Exhib. (JUFIZ IV), Dubrovnik.

Flower Type of 1957

Medicinal Plants: 10d, Lavender. 15d, Black Alder. 20d, Scopolia. 25d, Monkshood. 30d, Bilberry. 35d, Juniper. 50d, Primrose. 70d, Pomegranate. 100d, Jimson weed.

1959, May 25   **Photo.**
Granite Paper
Flowers in Natural Colors
538 A123 10d lt bl & dk blue   .25 .25
539 A123 15d brt yel & car   .25 .25
540 A123 20d dk ol bis & mar   .25 .25
541 A123 25d ap grn & dk pur   .25 .25
542 A123 30d pink & dk bl   .25 .25
543 A123 35d bis brn & vio bl   1.25 .25
544 A123 50d brn & green   3.00 .40
545 A123 70d yel & ocher   4.00 .65
546 A123 100d lt brn & brn   8.50 4.00
    Nos. 538-546 (9)   18.00 6.55

Tug of
War — A140

Sports: 15d, High jump and runners. 20d, Ring and parallel bar exercises. 35d, Women gymnasts. 40d, Sailors doing gymnastics. 55d, Field ball and basketball. 80d, Swimming. 100d, Festival emblem, vert.

1959, June 26   **Litho.**   **Perf. 12½**
547 A140 10d dk sl grn &
         ocher   .25 .25
548 A140 15d vio bl & sepia   .25 .25
549 A140 20d ol bis & dl lil   .25 .25
550 A140 35d deep cl & gray   .25 .25
551 A140 40d violet & gray   .25 .25
552 A140 55d sl grn & ol bis   .50 .25
553 A140 80d indigo & olive   3.25 .50
554 A140 100d pur & bister   7.00 3.50
    Nos. 547-554 (8)   12.00 5.50

Physical Culture Festival. Exist imperf.

Types of 1958; Designs as before

Designs: 8d, Lumber industry. 15d, Overpass, Zagreb-Ljubljana highway. 20d, Jablanica hydroelectric works. 40d, Titograd Hotel. 55d, Bridge at Skopje. 80d, Railroad Station, Sarajevo.

1959   **Typo.**   **Perf. 12½ Horizontally**
555 A133 15d green   2.50 1.10
556 A133 20d orange ver   3.00 1.10

                  Engr.   **Perf. 12½**
557 A133 8d deep claret   .40 .25
558 A133 15d green   .55 .25
559 A133 20d orange ver   .95 .25
560 A134 40d bright blue   2.25 .25
561 A134 55d carmine rose   3.50 .25
562 A134 80d orange ver   6.00 .25
    Nos. 557-562 (6)   13.65 1.50

Nos. 555-556 are coil stamps.

Fair
Emblem — A141

1959, Sept. 5   **Litho.**   **Unwmk.**
563 A141 20d lt vio bl & blk   2.00 1.00
50th International Fair at Zagreb.

Athletics — A142

1960, Apr. 25   **Perf. 12½**
564 A142 15d shown   .40 .40
565 A142 20d Swimming   .40 .40
566 A142 30d Skiing   .40 .40
567 A142 35d Wrestling   .40 .40
568 A142 40d Bicycling   .40 .40
569 A142 55d Yachting   .40 .40
570 A142 80d Horseback rid-
         ing   5.00 3.50
571 A142 100d Fencing   5.00 3.50
    Nos. 564-571 (8)   12.40 9.40

17th Olympic Games.

Hedgehog
A143

1960, May 25 Photo. Perf. 12x11½
Animals in Natural Colors

572	A143	15d shown	.30	.30
573	A143	20d Red squirrel	.30	.30
574	A143	25d Pine marten	.30	.30
575	A143	30d Hare	.70	.70
576	A143	35d Red fox	.70	.70
577	A143	40d Badger	.70	.70
578	A143	55d Wolf	1.50	1.50
579	A143	80d Roe deer	1.50	1.50
580	A143	100d Wild boar	4.00	4.00
		Nos. 572-580 (9)	10.00	10.00

See Nos. 663-671.

Lenin, 90th Birth
Anniv. — A144

1960, June 22 Engr. Perf. 12½
581 A144 20d dk grn & slate grn .25 .25

Atomic
Accelerator
A145

1960, Aug. 23   Unwmk.

582	A145	15d shown	8.00	8.00
583	A145	20d Generator	8.00	8.00
584	A145	40d Nuclear reactor	8.00	8.00
		Nos. 582-584 (3)	24.00	24.00

Nuclear energy exposition, Belgrade. Exist imperf.

Serbian National
Theater, Novi
Sad — A146

Designs: 20d, Woman from Croatian play. 40d, Edward Rusijan and early plane. 55d, Symbolic hand holding fruit. 80d, Atom and UN emblem.

1960, Oct. 24   Perf. 12½

585	A146	15d gray black	.75	.75
586	A146	20d brown	.75	.75
587	A146	40d dark gray blue	.75	.75
588	A146	55d dull claret	1.00	1.00
589	A146	80d dark green	1.00	1.00
		Nos. 585-589 (5)	4.25	4.25

Serbian Natl. Theater, Novi Sad, cent. (#585); Croatian Natl. Theater, Zagreb, cent. (#586); 1st flight in Yugoslavia, 50th anniv. (#587); 15th anniv. of the Yugoslav Republic (#588); UN, 15th anniv. (#589). Exist imperf.

Ivan Cankar,
Writer — A147

Famous Yugoslavs: 20d, Silvije Strahimir Kranjcevic, poet. 40d, Paja Jovanovic, painter. 55d, Dura Jaksic, writer and painter. 80d, Mihajlo Pupin, electro-technician. 100d, Rudjer Boscovich, mathematician.

1960, Dec. 24   Engr.   Perf. 12½

590	A147	15d dark green	.35	.30
591	A147	20d henna brown	.35	.30
592	A147	40d olive bister	.35	.30

593	A147	55d magenta	.35	.30
594	A147	80d dark blue	.35	.30
595	A147	100d Prussian bl	.35	.30
		Nos. 590-595 (6)	2.10	1.80

Exist imperf.

International
Atomic Energy
Commission
Emblem — A148

Engr. & Litho.
1961, May 15   Perf. 12½
596 A148 25d multicolored .50 .25

Intl. Nuclear Electronic Conf., Belgrade.

Flower Type of 1957

Medicinal plants: 10d, Yellow foxglove. 15d, Marjoram. 20d, Hyssop. 25d, Scarlet haw. 40d, Rose mallow. 50d, Soapwort. 60d, Clary. 80d, Blackthorn. 100d, Marigold.

1961, May 25 Photo. Perf. 11½
Granite Paper
Flowers in Natural Colors

597	A123	10d lt bl & grnsh bl	.30	.30
598	A123	15d gray & chnt	.30	.30
599	A123	20d buff & green	.30	.30
600	A123	25d lt vio & vio	.30	.30
601	A123	40d lt ultra & ultra	.30	.30
602	A123	50d lt bl & blue	.30	.30
603	A123	60d beige & dk car rose	.30	.30
604	A123	80d lt grn & green	.30	.30
605	A123	100d redsh brn & choc	12.00	9.00
		Nos. 597-605 (9)	14.40	11.40

Victims' Monument,
Kragujevac — A149

Monuments: 15d, Stevan Filipovic, Valjevo. 20d, Relief from Insurrection, Bozansko Grahovo. 60d, Victory, Nova Gradiska. 100d, Marshal Tito, Titovo Uzice.

Granite Paper
Gold Frames and Inscriptions
1961, July 3   Perf. 12x12½

606	A149	15d crimson & brn	.25	.25
607	A149	20d brn & ol bis	.25	.25
608	A149	25d bl grn & gray olive	.25	.25
609	A149	60d violet	.25	.25
610	A149	100d indigo & black	.25	.25
		Nos. 606-610 (5)	1.25	1.25

Souvenir Sheet
Imperf
611 A149 500d indigo & black 125.00 125.00

Natl. Insurrection, 20th anniv.

Men of
Five
Races
A150

National Assembly Building,
Belgrade — A151

1961, Sept. 1   Litho.   Perf. 11½
613 A150 25d brown .25 .25
Engr.
614 A151 50d blue green .25 .25
Nos. 613-614,C59-C60 (4) 3.40 2.35

Miniature Sheet
Imperf
615 A150 1000d claret 20.00 17.50

Conference of Non-aligned Nations, Belgrade, Sept. 1961.

St. Clement, 14th
Century Wood
Sculpture — A152

1961, Sept. 10   Engr.   Perf. 12½
616 A152 25d sepia & olive 2.00 .65

12th Intl. Congress for Byzantine Studies.

Serbian
Women
A153

Regional Costumes: 25d, Montenegro. 30d, Bosnia and Herzegovina. 50d, Macedonia. 65d, Croatia. 100d, Slovenia.

1961, Nov. 28   Litho.

617	A153	15d beige, brn & red	.25	.25
618	A153	25d beige, red brn & black	.25	.25
619	A153	30d beige, brn & dk red	.25	.25
620	A153	50d multicolored	.25	.25
621	A153	65d brn, red & yel	.60	.25
622	A153	100d multicolored	1.60	.75
		Nos. 617-622 (6)	3.20	2.00

Luka
Vukalovic — A154

1961, Dec. 15   Engr.
623 A154 25d slate blue .25 .25

Centenary of Herzegovina insurrection.

Hands with
Flower and
Rifle — A155

1961, Dec. 22
624 A155 25d red & vio blue .25 .25

20th anniversary of Yugoslav army.

Miladinov
Brothers
A156

1961, Dec. 25   Litho.
625 A156 25d buff & claret .25 .25

Centenary of Macedonian folksong "Koder"; Dimitri and Konstantin Miladinov, brothers who collected and published folksongs. Monument is at Struga.

Types of 1958; Designs as before

Designs: 5d, Shipbuilding. 8d, Lumber industry. 10d, Sisak steel works. 15d, Overpass. 20d, Jablanica hydroelectric works. 25d, Cable factory, Svetozarevo. 30d, Litostroy turbine factory. 40d, Lukavac coke plant. 50d, Zenica steel works. 65d, Sevojno copper works. 100d, Crude oil production. 150d, Titograd hotel. 200d, Bridge, Skopje. 300d, Railroad station, Sarajevo. 500d, Triple bridge, Ljubljana. 1000d, Mestrovic station, Zagreb. 2000d, Parliament, Belgrade.

1961-62   Typo.   Perf. 12½ Horiz.

627	A133	10d dark red brn	7.50	.55
628	A133	15d emerald	12.00	.30

Engr.   Perf. 12½

629	A133	5d dull orange	.25	.25
630	A133	8d gray	.25	.25
631	A133	10d dk red brn	.25	.25
632	A133	15d emerald	.25	.25
633	A133	20d violet blue	.50	.25
634	A133	25d vermilion	.25	.25
635	A133	30d red brown	6.50	.25
636	A133	40d dp cl ('62)	.25	.25
637	A133	50d gray blue	1.60	.25
638	A133	65d green	.25	.25
639	A133	100d yel olive	3.25	.25
640	A134	150d carmine ('62)	.75	.25
641	A134	200d slate grn ('62)	.75	.25
642	A134	300d olive ('62)	1.50	.25
643	A134	500d dull violet	1.25	.25
644	A134	1000d bister brn	4.50	.25
645	A134	2000d claret	10.00	.40
		Nos. 629-645 (17)	32.35	4.40

Nos. 627-628 are coil stamps. For surcharges see Nos. 786, 789.

Isis of
Kalabsha — A157

Design: 50d, Ramses II, Abu Simbel.

1962, Apr. 7   Engr.   Perf. 12½

646	A157	25d grnsh blk, cream	.25	.25
647	A157	50d brown, buff	.25	.25

15th anniv. (in 1961) of UNESCO.

Joy of
Motherhood by
Frano
Krsinic — A158

1962, Apr. 7
648 A158 50d black, cream .30 .25

15th anniv. (in 1961) of UNICEF.

Anopheles
Mosquito — A159

1962, Apr. 7   **Unwmk.**
649 A159 50d black, *gray*   .40 .25
WHO drive to eradicate malaria.

Scenic Type of 1959

Tourist attractions: #650, Portoroz. #651, Jajce. #652, Zadar. #653, Popova Sapka. #654, Hvar. #655, Bay of Kotor. #656, Danube, Iron Gate. #657, Rab. #658, Zagreb.

1962, Apr. 24   **Litho.**
650 A137 15d ol & chlky bl   .25 .25
651 A137 15d blue & bis   .25 .25
652 A137 15d blue & red brn   .25 .25
653 A137 25d dk bl & pale bl   .25 .25
654 A137 30d blue & brn org   .25 .25
655 A137 30d gray & chlky bl   .25 .25
656 A137 50d ol & grnsh bl   .90 .25
657 A137 50d blue & olive   .90 .25
658 A137 100d dk grn & gray bl   7.50 3.00
   Nos. 650-658 (9)   10.80 5.00

#651, 653, 655-656 are inscribed in Cyrillic. Exist imperf.

Marshal Tito, by
Augustincic
A160

Design: 50d, 200d, Sideview of bust by Antun Augustincic.

1962, May 25   **Engr.**   **Perf. 12½**
659 A160 25d dark green   1.00 .80
660 A160 50d dark brown   1.00 .80
661 A160 100d dark blue   1.00 .80
662 A160 200d greenish blk   1.00 .80
  a. Souv. sheet of 4, #659-662, imperf.   35.00 35.00
   Nos. 659-662 (4)   4.00 3.20

70th birthday of Pres. Tito (Josip Broz).

Animal Type of 1960

Designs: 15d, Crested newt. 20d, Fire salamander. 25d, Yellow-bellied toad. 30d, Pond frog. 50d, Pond turtle. 65d, Lizard. 100d, Emerald lizard. 150d, Leopard snake. 200d, European viper (adder).

1962, June 8   **Photo.**   **Perf. 12x11½**
Animals in Natural Colors
663 A143 15d green   .50 .50
664 A143 20d purple   .50 .50
665 A143 25d chocolate   .50 .50
666 A143 30d violet blue   .50 .50
667 A143 50d dark red   .50 .50
668 A143 65d bright grn   .50 .50
669 A143 100d black   1.25 1.25
670 A143 150d brown   1.25 1.25
671 A143 200d car rose   12.50 7.00
   Nos. 663-671 (9)   18.00 12.50

Pole
Vault — A161

Sports: 25d, Woman discus thrower, horiz. 30d, Long distance runners. 50d, Javelin thrower, horiz. 65d, Shot put. 100d, Women runners, horiz. 150d, Hop, step and jump. 200d, High jump, horiz.

Athletes in Black

1962, July 10   **Litho.**   **Perf. 12½**
672 A161 15d blue   .35 .25
673 A161 25d magenta   .35 .25
674 A161 30d emerald   .35 .25
675 A161 50d red   .35 .25

676 A161 65d vio blue   .35 .25
677 A161 100d green   .70 .25
678 A161 150d orange   3.50 .40
679 A161 200d orange brn   9.50 .80
   Nos. 672-679 (8)   15.45 2.70

7th European Athletic Championships, Belgrade, Sept. 12-16. See No. C61.

Child at
Play — A162

Litho. & Engr.
1962, Oct. 1   **Perf. 12½**
680 A162 25d red & black   .30 .25
Issued for Children's Week.

Gold Mask,
Trebeniste, 5th
Century
B.C. — A163

Bathing the Infant
Christ, Fresco,
Decani
Monastery — A164

Yugoslav Art Treasures: 25d, Horseman and bird, bronze vase (5th cent. B.C.). 50d, God Kairos, marble relief. 65d, "The Pigeons of Nerezi," fresco (12th cent.). 150d, Archangel Gabriel, icon (14th cent.).

1962, Nov. 28   **Photo.**
681 A163 25d Prus bl, blk & gold   .25 .25
682 A163 30d gold, saph & blk   .25 .25
683 A164 50d dk grn, brn & gold   .25 .25
684 A164 65d multicolored   .25 .25
685 A164 100d multicolored   .50 .50
686 A163 150d multicolored   1.00 1.00
   Nos. 681-686 (6)   2.50 2.50

Parched Earth
and
Wheat — A165

1963, Mar. 21   **Engr.**   **Perf. 12½**
687 A165 50d dark brn, *tan*   .40 .40
FAO "Freedom from Hunger" campaign.

Dr. Andrija
Mohorovicic and
UN
Emblem — A166

1963, Mar. 23   **Unwmk.**
688 A166 50d dk blue, *gray*   .40 .40
UN 3rd World Meteorological Day, Mar. 23. Dr. Mohorovicic (1857-1936) was director of the Zagreb meteorological observatory.

Flower Type of 1957

Medicinal Plants: 15d, Lily of the valley. 25d, Iris. 30d, Bistort. 50d, Henbane. 65d, St. John's wort. 100d, Caraway.

1963, May 25   **Photo.**   **Perf. 11½**
Granite Paper
Flowers in Natural Colors
689 A123 15d gray grn & grn   .25 .25
690 A123 25d lt bl, ultra & pur   .25 .25
691 A123 30d gray & black   .25 .25
692 A123 50d redsh brn & red brn   .25 .25
693 A123 65d pale brn & brn   .65 .65
694 A123 100d slate & blk   3.50 2.75
   Nos. 689-694 (6)   5.15 4.40

Scenic Type of 1959

Tourist attractions: 15d, Pula. 25d, Vrnjacka Banja. 30d, Crikvenica. 50d, Korcula. 65d, Durmitor mountain. 100d, Ljubljana.

1963, June 6   **Litho.**   **Perf. 12½**
695 A137 15d multicolored   .25 .25
696 A137 25d multicolored   .25 .25
697 A137 30d multicolored   .25 .25
698 A137 50d multicolored   .25 .25
699 A137 65d multicolored   .25 .25
700 A137 100d multicolored   1.50 .40
   Nos. 695-700 (6)   2.75 1.65

Partisans on the March, by Djordje
Andrejevic-Kun — A167

Sutjeska
(Gorge) — A168

Design: No. 702A, As 15d, but inscribed "Vis 1944-1964." 50d, Partisans in battle.

Engr. & Litho.; Litho. (No. 702)
1963-64   **Perf. 12½, 11½**
701 A167 15d gray & dk sl grn   .25 .25
702 A168 25d dark slate grn   .25 .25
702A A167 25d gray & dark car rose   .45 .45
703 A167 50d tan & purple   .25 .25
   Nos. 701-703 (4)   1.20 1.20

20th anniv. of the Partisan Battle of Sutjeska (Nos. 701, 702-703); 20th anniv. of the arrival of the Yugoslav General Staff on the island of Vis (No. 702A).
Issued: #702A, 7/27/64; others, 7/3/63.

Gymnast on
Vaulting
Horse — A169

1963, July 6   **Litho.**   **Perf. 12½**
704 A169 25d shown   .40 .40
705 A169 50d Parallel bars   .80 .40
706 A169 100d Rings   1.20 .40
   Nos. 704-706 (3)   2.40 1.20

5th Gymnastics Europa Prize.

Mother, by Ivan
Mestrovic
A170

Sculptures by Mestrovic (1883-1962): 50d, "Reminiscences" (woman). 65d, Head of Kraljevic Marko. 100d, Indian on Horseback.

1963, Sept. 28   **Engr.**
707 A170 25d brown, *buff*   .25 .25
708 A170 50d sl green, *grnsh*   .25 .25
709 A170 65d grnsh blk, *grysh*   .25 .25
710 A170 100d black, *grayish*   1.00 .75
   Nos. 707-710 (4)   1.75 1.50

Children with
Toys — A171

1963, Oct. 5   **Litho.**
711 A171 25d multicolored   .40 .25
Issued for Children's Week.

Soldier with
Gun and
Flag — A172

Litho. & Engr.
1963, Oct. 20   **Perf. 12½**
712 A172 25d ver, tan & gold   .25 .25
Yugoslavian Democratic Federation, 20th anniv.

Relief from
Tombstone,
Herzegovina
A173

Art through the centuries: 30d, Horseback trio, Split Cathedral. 50d, King & queen on horseback, Beram Church, Istria. 65d, Archangel Michael, Dominican monastery, Dubrovnik. 100d, Man pouring water, fountain, Ljubljana. 150d, Archbishop Eufrasie, mosaic, Porec Basilica, Istria.

1963, Nov. 29   **Photo.**
713 A173 25d multi   .25 .25
714 A173 30d multi, horiz.   .25 .25
715 A173 50d multi, horiz.   .25 .25
716 A173 65d multi   .25 .25
717 A173 100d multi   .25 .25
718 A173 150d multi   .95 .75
   Nos. 713-718 (6)   2.20 2.00

Issued for the Day of the Republic.

Dositej Obradovic
A174

Famous Yugoslavians: 30d, Vuk Stefanovic Karadzic, reformer of Serbian language. 50d, Franc Miklosic, Slovenian philologist. 65d, Ljudevit Gaj, reformer of Croatian language. 100d, Peter Petrovich Nyegosh, Montenegrin prince, bishop and poet.

Variously Toned Paper

1963, Dec. 10   **Engr.**
719 A174 25d black   .25 .25
720 A174 30d black   .25 .25
721 A174 50d black   .25 .25
722 A174 65d black   1.00 .85
723 A174 100d black   1.00 .50
   Nos. 719-723 (5)   2.75 1.50

Vanessa Io — A175

Butterflies & Moths: 30d, Vanessa antiopa. 40d, Daphnis nerii. 50d, Parnassius apollo. 150d, Saturnia pyri. 200d, Papilio machaon.

1964, May 25   Photo.   Perf. 12½

724	A175	25d multicolored	.40	.40
725	A175	30d multicolored	.40	.40
726	A175	40d multicolored	.40	.40
727	A175	50d multicolored	.40	.40
728	A175	150d multicolored	4.00	4.00
729	A175	200d multicolored	4.00	4.00
	Nos. 724-729 (6)		9.60	9.60

Fireman Rescuing Child — A176

1964, June 14   Litho.

730	A176	25d red & black	.25	.25

Centenary of voluntary firemen. Exists imperf.

Runner A177

1964, July 1   Unwmk.   Perf. 12½

731	A177	25d shown	.25	.25
732	A177	30d Boxing	.25	.25
733	A177	40d Rowing	.25	.25
734	A177	50d Basketball	.25	.25
735	A177	150d Soccer	5.00	1.00
736	A177	200d Water polo	5.00	1.00
	Nos. 731-736 (6)		11.00	3.00

18th Olympic Games, Tokyo, Oct. 10-25.

UN Flag over Scaffolding A178

25d, Upheaval of the earth & scaffolding.

1964, July 26   Engr.

737	A178	25d red brown	.25	.25
738	A178	50d blue	.25	.25

Earthquake at Skopje; 1st anniv.

Serbian Women — A179

Regional Costumes: 30d, Slovenia. 40d, Bosnia and Herzegovina. 50d, Croatia. 150d, Macedonia. 200d, Montenegro.

Costumes Multicolored

1964, Aug. 5   Litho.

740	A179	25d violet & brn	.65	.65
741	A179	30d slate & green	.65	.65
742	A179	40d redsh brn & blk	.65	.65
743	A179	50d blue & black	.65	.65
744	A179	150d dl grn & sepia	2.75	2.75
745	A179	200d tan, red & brn	2.75	2.75
	Nos. 740-745 (6)		8.10	8.10

Exist imperf.

Friedrich Engels — A180

Litho. & Engr.

1964, Sept. 27   Perf. 11½

746	A180	25d shown	.25	.25
747	A180	50d Karl Marx	.25	.25

1st Socialist Intl., London, Sept. 28, 1864. Exist imperf.

Children at Play — A181

1964, Oct. 4   Litho.   Perf. 12½

748	A181	25d ver, pink & gray grn	.40	.40

Issued for Children's Week. Exists imperf.

The Victor by Ivan Mestrovic — A182

1964, Oct. 20   Engr.   Perf. 11½

749	A182	25d gold & blk, *pnksh*	.25	.25

Liberation of Belgrade, 20th anniv.

Initial from Evangel of Hilandar — A183

Art through the centuries: 30d, Initial from Evangel of Miroslav (musician). 40d, Detail from Cetigne octavo, 1494 (saint with scroll). 50d, Miniature from Evangel of Trogir, 13th cent. (female saint). 150d, Miniature from Hrovoe Missal, 15th cent. (knight on horseback). 200d, Miniature from 14th cent. manuscript (symbolic fight), horiz.

Perf. 11½x12, 12x11½

1964, Nov. 29   Photo.   Unwmk.

750	A183	25d multicolored	.25	.25
751	A183	30d multicolored	.25	.25
752	A183	40d multicolored	.25	.25
753	A183	50d multicolored	.25	.25
754	A183	150d multicolored	.25	.25
755	A183	200d multicolored	.25	.25
	Nos. 750-755 (6)		1.50	1.50

Issued for Day of the Republic.

Hand, "Liberty and Equality" — A184

50d, Dove over factory, "Peace and Socialism." 100d, Smokestacks, "Building Socialism."

1964, Dec. 7   Perf. 12

756	A184	25d multicolored	.25	.25
757	A184	50d multicolored	.25	.25
758	A184	100d multicolored	.40	.25
	Nos. 756-758 (3)		.90	.75

Yugoslav Communist League, 8th congress.

Table Tennis Player — A185

1965, Apr. 15   Litho.   Perf. 12½

759	A185	50d shown	4.00	4.00
760	A185	150d Player at left	4.00	4.00

28th Table Tennis Championships, Ljubljana, Apr. 15-25. Exist imperf.

Titograd — A186

1965, May 8   Engr.

761	A186	25d shown	.25	.25
762	A186	30d Skopje	.25	.25
763	A186	40d Sarajevo	.25	.25
764	A186	50d Ljubljana	.50	.50
765	A186	150d Zagreb	.50	.50
766	A186	200d Belgrade	.65	.65
	Nos. 761-766 (6)		2.40	2.40

Liberation of Yugoslavia from the Nazis, 20th anniv. Exist imperf.

Young Pioneer — A187

1965, May 10   Litho. & Engr.

767	A187	25d blk & tan, *buff*	.25	.25

Young Pioneer Games "20 Years of Freedom." Exists imperf.

ITU Emblem and Television Tower — A188

1965, May 17   Engr.

768	A188	50d dark blue	.25	.25

ITU, centenary.

Iron Gate, Danube — A189

Arms of Yugoslavia and Romania and Djerdap Dam — A190

50d, Iron Gate hydroelectric plant and dam.

1965, May 20   Litho.   Perf. 12½x12

769	A189	25d (30b) lt bl & grn	.25	.25
770	A189	50d (55b) lt bl & dk red	.40	.25

Miniature Sheet

Perf. 13½x13

771	A190	Sheet of 4	4.25	4.25
a.		100d multicolored	.35	.35
b.		150d multicolored	.70	.70

Nos. 769-771 were issued simultaneously by Yugoslavia and Romania to commemorate the start of the construction of the Iron Gate hydroelectric plant. Nos. 769-770 were valid for postage in both countries.

No. 771 contains one each of Nos. 771a, 771b and Romania Nos. 1747a and 1747b. Only Nos. 771a and 771b were valid in Yugoslavia. Sold for 500d.

See Romania Nos. 1745-1747.

Flower Type of 1957

Medicinal Plants: 25d, Milfoil. 30d, Rosemary. 40d, Inula. 50d, Belladonna. 150d, Mint. 200d, Foxglove.

1965, May 25   Photo.   Perf. 11½
Granite Paper
Flowers in Natural Colors

772	A123	25d deep carmine	.30	.30
773	A123	30d olive bister	.30	.30
774	A123	40d red brown	.30	.30
775	A123	50d dark blue	.30	.30
776	A123	150d violet blue	.35	.35
777	A123	200d purple	2.00	2.00
	Nos. 772-777 (6)		3.55	3.55

Intl. Cooperation Year Emblem A191

1965, June 26   Litho.   Perf. 12½

778	A191	50d dk bl & dull bl	.25	.25

Sibenik — A192

1965, July 6   Unwmk.   Perf. 12½

779	A192	25d Rogaska Slatina	.40	.40
780	A192	30d shown	.40	.40
781	A192	40d Prespa Lake	.40	.40
782	A192	50d Prizren	.40	.40
783	A192	150d Scutari	1.20	1.20
784	A192	200d Sarajevo	2.00	2.00
	Nos. 779-784 (6)		4.80	4.80

Cat — A193

1965, Oct. 3   Litho.   Perf. 12½

785	A193	30d maroon & brt yel	.45	.25

Issued for Children's Week. Exists imperf.

Nos. 630 and 634 Surcharged in Maroon and Type of 1958

Designs: 20d, Jablanica hydroelectric works. 30d, Litostroy turbine factory.

1965		Engr.	Perf. 12½
786	A133	5d on 8d gray	.60	.25
787	A133	20d emerald	.50	.25
788	A133	30d red orange	.80	.25
789	A133	50d on 25d vermilion	.60	.25
		Nos. 786-789 (4)	2.50	1.00

Branislav Nusic — A194

Famous Yugoslavs: 50d, Antun Gustav Matos, poet. 60d, Ivan Mazuranic, writer. 85d, Fran Levstik, writer. 200d, Josif Pancic, physician and botanist. 500d, Dimitrije Tucovic, political writer.

1965, Nov. 28			Engr.
Variously Toned Paper			
790	A194	30d dull red	.25	.25
791	A194	50d indigo	.25	.25
792	A194	60d brown	.25	.25
793	A194	85d dark blue	.25	.25
794	A194	200d dk olive grn	.25	.25
795	A194	500d deep claret	.60	.45
		Nos. 790-795 (6)	1.85	1.70

Marshal Tito — A195

1966, Feb. 4		Litho.	Perf. 12½
796	A195	20p bluish grn	.40	.25
797	A195	30p rose pink	.55	.25

Exists imperf.

Rowing A196

30p, Long jump. 50p, Ice hockey. 3d, Hockey sticks, puck. 5d, Oars, scull.

1966, Mar. 1			Engr.
798	A196	30p dk car rose	.25	.25
799	A196	50p dk purple	.25	.25
800	A196	1d gray green	.25	.25
801	A196	3d dk red brn	1.75	1.75
802	A196	5d dark blue	1.75	1.75
		Nos. 798-802 (5)	4.25	4.25

25th Balkan Games; World ice hockey championship; 2nd rowing championships.

"T" from 15th Century Psalter — A197

Art through the Centuries (Initials from Medieval Manuscripts): 50p, Cyrillic "V," Divosh Evangel, 14th cent. 60p, "R," Gregorius I, Libri moralium, 12th cent. 85p, Cyrillic "P," Miroslav Evangel, 12th cent. 2d, Cyrillic "B," Radomir Evangel, 13th cent. 5d, "F," Passional, 11th cent.

1966, Apr. 25		Photo.	Perf. 12
803	A197	30p multicolored	.25	.25
804	A197	50p multicolored	.25	.25
805	A197	60p multicolored	.25	.25
806	A197	85p multicolored	.25	.25

807	A197	2d multicolored	.25	.25
808	A197	5d multicolored	.80	.40
		Nos. 803-808 (6)	2.05	1.65

Radio Amateurs' Emblem — A198

1966, May 23	Engr.	Perf. 12½x12
809	A198	85p dark blue	2.50	1.20

Union of Yugoslav Radio Amateurs, 20th anniv.; Intl. Congress of Radio Amateurs, Opatija, 5/23-28.

Stag Beetle — A199

Beetles: 50p, Floral beetle. 60p, Oil beetle. 85p, Ladybird. 2d, Rosalia alpina. 5d, Aquatic beetle.

1966, May 25	Photo.	Perf. 12x12½
810	A199	30p gray, blk & bis	.30	.25
811	A199	50p gray, emer & blk	.30	.25
812	A199	60p bluish blk, sl grn & gray	.30	.25
813	A199	85p dl org, dp org & black	.30	.25
814	A199	2d gray, ultra & blk	.30	.25
815	A199	5d tan, brn & blk	.55	.25
		Nos. 810-815 (6)	2.05	1.50

Serbia No. 2, 1866 — A200

	Litho. & Engr.	
1966, June 25		Perf. 12½
816	A200	30p shown	.25	.25
817	A200	50p No. 3	.25	.25
818	A200	60p No. 4	.25	.25
819	A200	85p No. 5	.25	.25
820	A200	2d No. 6	.45	.39
		Nos. 816-820 (5)	1.45	1.35

Souvenir Sheet
Imperf

| 821 | A200 | 10d No. 1 | 2.00 | 2.00 |

Serbia's first postage stamps, cent.

Leather Shield with Farmer, Soldier and Woman — A201

1966, July 2		Perf. 12½
822	A201	20p pale grn, gold & red brown	.25	.25
823	A201	30p buff, gold & dp mag	.25	.25
824	A201	85p lt gray, gold & Prus bl	.25	.25
825	A201	2d lt bl, gold & vio	.25	.25
		Nos. 822-825 (4)	1.00	1.00

25th anniversary of National Revolution.

Bishop Strossmayer and Franjo Racki — A202

1966, July 15		
826	A202	30p dl ol, blk & buff	.25	.25

Centenary of Academy of Arts and Sciences, founded by Bishop Josip Juraj Strossmayer with Racki as first president.

Mostar Bridge, Neretva River — A203

1966, Sept. 24	Engr.	Perf. 12½
827	A203	30p rose claret	4.00	1.60

400th anniversary of Mostar Bridge.

Medieval View of Sibenik A204

1966, Sept. 24		
828	A204	30p deep plum	.25	.25

900th anniversary of Sibenik.

Girl — A205

1966, Oct. 2		Litho.
829	A205	30p ultra, org, red & blk	1.50	1.50

Issued for Children's Week.

Shipbuilding — A206

Designs: 10p, Sisak steel works. 15p, Overpass. 20p, Jablonica hydroelectric works. 30p, Litostroy turbine factory. 40p, Lukavac coke factory. 50p, Zenica steel works. 60p, Cable factory, Svetozarevo. 65p, Sevojno copper works. 85p, Lumber industry. 1d, Crude oil production.

1966		Engr.	Perf. 12½
830	A206	5p dull orange	1.00	1.00
831	A206	10p brown	1.00	1.00
832	A206	15p vio blue	1.00	1.00
833	A206	20p emerald	.25	.25
834	A206	30p vermilion	.75	.29
835	A206	40p dp claret	1.00	1.00
836	A206	50p gray blue	1.00	1.00
837	A206	60p red brown	1.00	1.00
838	A206	65p green	1.00	1.00
839	A206	85p dl purple	1.00	1.00
840	A206	1d yel olive	2.00	2.00
		Nos. 830-840 (11)	11.00	10.50

Issued: 5, 15p, 6/10; 10, 40, 50p, 6/8; 20, 30p, 4/28; 60, 65, 85p, 5/12; 1d, 6/18.
Nos. 830, 832 and 840 exist imperf.
For surcharge see No. 1322.

UNESCO Emblem — A207

1966, Nov. 4		Litho.
841	A207	85p violet blue	.25	.25

20th anniversary of UNESCO.

Santa Claus — A208

Designs: 15p, Stylized winter landscape. 30p, Stylized Christmas tree.

1966, Nov. 25		Litho.	Perf. 12½
842	A208	15p org & dk bl	.25	.25
843	A208	20p org & purple	.25	.25
844	A208	30p org & sl grn	.25	.25
1966, Dec. 23		Photo.	Perf. 12½
845	A208	15p gold & dk bl	.30	.25
846	A208	20p gold & red	.30	.25
847	A208	30p gold & green	.30	.25
		Nos. 842-847 (6)	1.65	1.50

Nos. 842-847 issued for New Year, 1967.

Wolf's Head Coin of Durad I, 1373 — A209

Medieval Coins: 50p, ½d of King Stefan, c. 1461 (arms of Bosnia). 60d, Dinar of Serbia (portrait of Durad Brankovic). 85p, Dinar of Ljubljana, c. 1250 (heraldic eagle). 2d, Dinar of Split, c. 1403-1413 (shield with arms of Duke Hrvoje Vukcic). 5d, Dinar of Emperor Stefan Dusan, c. 1346-1355 (Emperor on horseback).

1966, Nov. 28			Photo.
Coins in Silver, Gray and Black			
848	A209	30p ver & blk	.25	.25
849	A209	50p ultra & blk	.25	.25
850	A209	60p magenta & blk	.25	.25
851	A209	85p violet & blk	.25	.25
852	A209	2d dk ol bis & blk	.25	.25
853	A209	5d brt grn & blk	.55	.35
		Nos. 848-853 (6)	1.80	1.60

Medicinal Plants — A210

1967, May 25		Photo.	Perf. 11½
Granite Paper			
854	A210	30p Arnica	.25	.25
855	A210	50p Flax	.25	.25
856	A210	85p Oleander	.25	.25
857	A210	1.20d Gentian	.25	.25
858	A210	3d Laurel	.25	.25
859	A210	5d African rue	.80	.80
		Nos. 854-859 (6)	2.05	2.05

Youth Day, May 25.

Marshal Tito — A211

Size: 20x27½mm

		1967, May 25	Engr.	Perf. 12½	
860	A211	5p orange		.25	.25
861	A211	10p dk red brown		.25	.25
862	A211	15p dk vio blue		.25	.25
863	A211	20p green		.25	.25
864	A211	30p vermilion		.25	.25
865	A211	40p black		.25	.25
866	A211	50p Prussian grn		.25	.25
867	A211	60p lilac		.25	.25
868	A211	85p deep blue		.25	.25
869	A211	1d plum		.25	.25
		Nos. 860-869 (10)		2.50	2.50

75th birthday of Pres. Tito. Sheets of 15. Nos. 860-869 were reissued in 1967 with slight differences including thinner paper and slightly darker shades.
See #924-939. For surcharge see #1414.

Coil Stamps

		1968-69	Photo.	Perf. 12½ Horiz.	
869A	A211	20p green		.30	.25
869B	A211	30p vermilion		.40	.25
869C	A211	50p vermilion ('69)		.30	.25
		Nos. 869A-869C (3)		1.00	.75

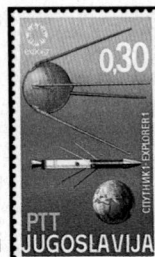

EXPO Emblem, Sputnik 1 and Explorer 1 — A212

Spacecraft: 50p, Tiros, Telstar and Molniya. 85p, Luna 9 and lunar satellite. 1.20d, Mariner 4, and Venera 3. 3d, Vostok, Gemini and Agena Rocket. 5d, Astronaut walking in space.

		1967, June 26	Photo.	Perf. 11½	
870	A212	30p ultra & multi		.25	.25
871	A212	50p yel & multi		.25	.25
872	A212	85p slate & multi		.25	.25
873	A212	1.20d multicolored		.25	.25
874	A212	3d vio & multi		.25	.25
875	A212	5d blue & multi		2.75	2.75
		Nos. 870-875 (6)		4.00	4.00

EXPO '67, Montreal, Apr. 28-Oct. 27; 18th Congress of the Intl. Astronautical Federation, Belgrade. Exist imperf.

ITY Emblem, St. Tripun's Church, Kotor — A213

Designs (ITY Emblem and): 50p, Municipal Building, Maribor. 85p, Cathedral, Trogir. 1.20d, Fortress gate, Nis. 3d, Drina Bridge, Visegrad. 5d, Daut-pasha's Bath, Skopje.

		1967, July 17		Engr.	
876	A213	30p slate bl & lt ol		.25	.25
877	A213	50p brn & dl vio		.25	.25
878	A213	85p dk bl & dp claret		.25	.25
879	A213	1.20d dp claret & brn		.25	.25
880	A213	3d brn & slate grn		.35	.25
881	A213	5d slate grn & brn		3.00	.45
		Nos. 876-881 (6)		4.35	1.70

Issued for International Tourist Year, 1967.

Partridge — A214

1967, Sept. 22		Photo.	Perf. 14	
882	A214	30p shown	.30	.30
883	A214	50p Pike	.30	.30
884	A214	1.20d Red deer	.50	.50
885	A214	5d Peregrine falcon	1.25	1.25
		Nos. 882-885 (4)	2.35	2.35

Intl. Fishing and Hunting Exposition and Fair, Novi Sad.

Congress Emblem with Sputnik 1 A215

Litho. & Engr.

1967, Sept. 25			Perf. 12½	
886	A215	85p dk bl, lt bl & gold	.25	.25

18th Congress of the Intl. Astronautical Federation, Belgrade, Sept. 25-30.

Old Theater and Castle, Ljubljana — A216

1967, Sept. 29		Engr.	Perf. 12½	
887	A216	30p sepia & dk grn	.25	.25

Centenary of Slovene National Theater.

Child's Drawing: Winter Scene — A217

1967, Oct. 2			Litho.	
888	A217	30p multicolored	.50	.25

International Children's Week, Oct. 2-8.

Lenin by Mestrovic A218

1967, Nov. 7		Engr.	Perf. 12½	
889	A218	30p dark purple	.25	.25
890	A218	85p olive gray	.25	.25

Souvenir Sheet
Imperf

891	A218	10d magenta	8.00	8.00

Russian October Revolution, 50th anniv. Nos. 889-890 exist imperf.

4-Leaf Clover — A219

30p, Chimney sweep. 50p, Horseshoe & flower.

Dated "1968"

1967, Nov. 15		Photo.	Perf. 14	
892	A219	20p shown	.25	.25
893	A219	30p Chimney sweep	.25	.25
894	A219	50p Horseshoe, flower	.25	.25
		Nos. 892-894 (3)	.75	.75

New Year 1968. See Nos. 957-959.

The Young Sultana, by Vlaho Bucovac — A220

Paintings: 85p, The Watchtower, by Dura Jaksic. 2d, Visit to the Family, by Josip Petkovsek. 3d, The Cock Fight, by Paja Jovanovic. 5d, "Spring" (woman and children), by Ivana Kobilca.

Perf. 11½x12, 12x11½

1967, Nov. 28		Engr. & Litho.		
895	A220	85p multi, vert.	1.50	.35
896	A220	1d multi	1.50	.35
897	A220	2d multi	1.50	.35
898	A220	3d multi	1.50	.35
899	A220	5d multi, vert.	6.00	3.00
		Nos. 895-899 (5)	12.00	4.40

Issued for the Day of the Republic, Nov. 29. See Nos. 942-946, 995-1000.

Ski Jump — A221

Sport: 1d, Figure skating pair. 2d, Downhill skiing. 5d, Ice hockey.

1968, Feb. 5		Engr.	Perf. 12½	
900	A221	50p dk bl & dk pur	.40	.25
901	A221	1d brn & sl green	.40	.25
902	A221	2d sl grn & lake	.70	.40
903	A221	5d sl grn & dk bl	5.50	3.00
		Nos. 900-903 (4)	7.00	3.90

10th Winter Olympic Games, Grenoble, France, Feb. 6-18.

Annunciation A222

Medieval Icons: 50p, Madonna, St. George's Church, Prizren. 1.50d, St. Sava and St. Simeon. 2d, Christ's descent into hell, Ohrid. 3d, Crucifixion, St. Clement's Church, Ohrid. 5d, Madonna, Church of Our Lady of the Bell Tower, Split.

1968, Apr. 20		Photo.	Perf. 13½	
906	A222	50p gold & multi	.25	.25
907	A222	1d gold & multi	.25	.25
908	A222	1.50d gold & multi	.25	.25
909	A222	2d gold & multi	.35	.25
910	A222	3d gold & multi	.50	.40
911	A222	5d gold & multi	1.10	1.00
		Nos. 906-911 (6)	2.70	2.40

European Bullfinch — A223

Finches: 1d, Goldfinch. 1.50d, Chaffinch. 2d, European greenfinch. 3d, Red crossbill. 5d, Hawfinch.

Birds in Natural Colors

1968, May 25		Photo.	Perf. 11½	
912	A223	50p bister	.40	.40
913	A223	1d rose lake	.40	.40
914	A223	1.50d gray blue	.40	.40
915	A223	2d deep orange	.40	.40
916	A223	3d olive green	.45	.45
917	A223	5d pale violet	6.50	3.25
		Nos. 912-917 (6)	8.55	5.30

Issued for Youth Day. Exist imperf.

800-meter Race for Women — A224

1d, Basketball. 1.50d, Gymnast on vaulting horse. 2d, Rowing. 3d, Water polo. 5d, Wrestling.

Litho. & Engr.

1968, June 28			Perf. 12½	
918	A224	50p dk brn & dk red brown	.40	.40
919	A224	1d Prus bl & blk	.40	.40
920	A224	1.50d slate & dk brn	.40	.40
921	A224	2d bis & sl grn	1.50	.40
922	A224	3d blk brn & ind	1.50	.40
923	A224	5d dk grn & vio blk	16.00	5.00
		Nos. 918-923 (6)	20.20	7.00

19th Olympic Games, Mexico City, 10/12-27.

Tito Type of 1967

1968-72		Engr.	Perf. 12½	

Size: 20x27½mm

924	A211	20p dark blue	1.25	.25
925	A211	25p lake	.25	.25
926	A211	30p green	.25	.25
927	A211	50p vermilion	.75	.25
928	A211	70p black	.30	.25
929	A211	75p slate grn	.40	.25
930	A211	80p olive	2.00	.25
930A	A211	80p red org ('72)	.40	.25
931	A211	90p olive	.30	.25
932	A211	1.20d dark blue	.50	.25
932A	A211	1.20d sl grn ('72)	.40	.25
933	A211	1.25d deep blue	.25	.25
934	A211	1.50d slate grn	.40	.25

Size: 20x30½mm

935	A211	2d sepia	2.50	.25
936	A211	2.50d Prussian grn	1.60	.25
937	A211	5d deep plum	1.40	.25
938	A211	10d violet blk	3.00	.35
939	A211	20d bluish black	4.25	.45
		Nos. 924-939 (18)	20.20	4.80

The shading of the background of Nos. 924-939 has been changed from the 1967 issue to intensify the contrast around the portrait.

Cannon and Laurel Wreath — A225

1968, Aug. 2		Photo.	Perf. 12½	
940	A225	50p org brn & gold	.25	.25

65th anniversary of the Ilinden uprising.

Mother Nursing Twins, Fresco by Jan of Kastav — A226

1968, Sept. 9   **Litho.**
941 A226 50p black & multi   .25 .25

Annexation of Istria and the Slovene Coast to Yugoslavia, 25th anniv. Exists imperf.

Painting Type of 1967

Paintings: 1d, Lake Klansko, by Marko Pernhart. 1.50d, Bavarian Landscape, by Milan Popovic. 2d, Porta Terraferma, Zadar, by Ferdo Quiquerez. 3d, Mt. Triglav seen from Bohinj, by Anton Karinger. 5d, Studenica Monastery, by Djordje Krstic.

Engr. & Litho.

1968, Oct. 3   **Perf. 14x13½**
942 A220 1d gold & multi   .25 .25
943 A220 1.50d gold & multi   .25 .25
944 A220 2d gold & multi   .25 .25
945 A220 3d gold & multi   .30 .25
946 A220 5d gold & multi   2.40 .70
    Nos. 942-946 (5)   3.45 1.70

Exist imperf.

Aleksa Santic (1868-1924), Poet — A227

1968, Oct. 5   **Engr.**   **Perf. 12½**
947 A227 50p dark blue   .25 .25

"Going for a Walk" — A228

1968, Oct. 6   **Litho.**
948 A228 50p multicolored   .25 .25

Issued for Children's Week.

Karl Marx (1818-1883), by N. Mitric — A229

1968, Oct. 11   **Engr.**
949 A229 50d dk car rose   .25 .25

Old Theater and Belgrade Castle — A230

1968, Nov. 22   **Engr.**   **Perf. 12½**
950 A230 50p ol brn & sl grn   .25 .25

Serbian National Theater, Belgrade, cent.

Hasan Brkic — A231

Portraits: 75p, Ivan Milutinovic. 1.25d, Rade Koncar. 2d, Kuzman Josifovski. 2.50d, Tone Tomsic. 5d, Mosa Pijade.

1968, Nov. 28   **Perf. 12½**
951 A231 50p violet black   .25 .25
952 A231 75p black   .25 .25
953 A231 1.25d red brown   .25 .25
   a.   Souv. sheet, 2 ea #951-953   15.00 15.00
954 A231 2d bluish black   .25 .25
955 A231 2.50d slate green   .25 .25
956 A231 5d claret   1.25 .50
   a.   Souv. sheet, 2 ea #954-956   15.00 15.00
    Nos. 951-956 (6)   2.50 1.75

2nd Assembly of the National Republic of Yugoslavia, 25th anniv.
No. 954 exists imperf. Value $100.
Nos. 953a and 956a exist imperf.

New Year's Type of 1967

1968, Nov. 25   **Photo.**   **Perf. 14**
    Dated "1969"
957 A219 20p Four-leaf clover   .25 .25
958 A219 30p Chimney sweep   .25 .25
959 A219 50p Horseshoe, flower   .25 .25
    Nos. 957-959 (3)   .75 .75

Issued for New Year 1969.

The Family, by J. Soldatovic A232

1968, Dec. 10   **Engr.**   **Perf. 12½**
960 A232 1.25d dark blue   .25 .25

International Human Rights Year.

ILO Emblem — A233

Litho. & Engr.

1969, Jan. 27   **Perf. 12½**
961 A233 1.25d red & black   .25 .25

ILO, 50th anniv.

Dove, Hammer and Sickle Emblem — A234

75p, Graffiti "TITO" & 5-pointed star. 1.25d, 5-pointed crystal. 10d, Marshal Tito in 1943.

Engr. & Photo.

1969, Mar. 11   **Perf. 12½**
962 A234 50p black & red   .25 .25
963 A234 75p ol bis & blk   .25 .25
964 A234 1.25d red & black   .25 .25
    Nos. 962-964 (3)   .75 .75

Souvenir Sheet

964A   Sheet of 9   9.00 9.00
   b.   A234 10d brown, engr.   5.00 5.00

Communist Federation of Yugoslavia, 50th anniv.; 9th party congress.

#964A contains 4 #962, 2 each #963-964, 964b.
Nos. 962-964A exist imperf.

St. Nikita, from Manasija Monastery A235

Frescoes from Monasteries: 75p, Apostles, Zakopani. 1.25d, Crucifixion, Studenica. 2d, Wedding at Cana, Kalenic. 3d, Angel at the Grave, Milseva. 5d, Pietá, Nerezi.

1969, Apr. 7   **Photo.**   **Perf. 13½**
965 A235 50p gold & multi   .25 .25
966 A235 75p gold & multi   .25 .25
967 A235 1.25d gold & multi   .25 .25
968 A235 2d gold & multi   .25 .25
969 A235 3d gold & multi   .45 .45
970 A235 5d gold & multi   2.00 .90
    Nos. 965-970 (6)   3.45 2.35

Roman Memorial and View of Ptuj A236

1969, Apr. 23   **Engr.**   **Perf. 11½**
971 A236 50p violet brown   .25 .25

1900th anniv. of Ptuj, the Roman Petovio. Issued in sheets of 9 (3x3).

Vasil Glavinov — A237

1969, May 8   **Perf. 12x12½**
972 A237 50p ocher & rose lilac   .25 .25

Vasil Glavinov, Macedonian socialist, birth cent. Issued in sheets of 9 (3x3).

Thin-leafed Peony — A238

Medicinal Plants: 75p, Coltsfoot. 1.25d, Primrose. 2d, Hellebore. 2.50d, Violets. 5d, Anemones.

Flowers in Natural Colors

1969, May 25   **Photo.**   **Perf. 11½**
973 A238 50p yellow brn   .25 .25
974 A238 75p dull purple   .25 .25
975 A238 1.25d blue   .25 .25
976 A238 2d brown   .25 .25
977 A238 2.50d plum   .25 .25
978 A238 5d green   2.75 2.75
    Nos. 973-978 (6)   4.00 4.00

Exist imperf.
See Nos. 1056-1061, 1140-1145.

Eber, by Vasa Ivankovic — A239

Paintings of Sailing Ships: 1.25d, Tare, by Franasovic. 1.50d, Brig Sela, by Vasa Ivankovic. 2.50d, Dubrovnik galleon, 16th century. 3.25d, Madre Mimbelli, by Antoine Roux. 5d, The Virgin Saving Seamen from Disaster, 16th century ikon.

1969, July 10   **Photo.**   **Perf. 11½**
979 A239 50p gold & multi   .25 .25
980 A239 1.25d gold & multi   .25 .25
981 A239 1.50d gold & multi   .25 .25
982 A239 2.50d gold & multi   .25 .25
983 A239 3.25d gold & multi   .55 .30
984 A239 5d gold & multi   2.75 2.25
    Nos. 979-984 (6)   4.30 3.55

Dubrovnik Summer Festival, 20th anniv. Exist imperf.

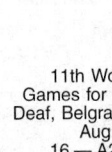

11th World Games for the Deaf, Belgrade, Aug. 9-16 — A240

1969, Aug. 9   **Engr.**   **Perf. 12½**
985 A240 1.25d dp claret & dl vio   .40 .25

Lipice Horse A241

Horses: 75p, Bosnian mountain horse. 3.25d, Ljutomer trotter. 5d, Half-breed.

1969, Sept. 26   **Photo.**   **Perf. 11½**
986 A241 75p multicolored   .25 .25
987 A241 1.25d olive & multi   .25 .25
988 A241 3.25d brn & multi   .30 .25
989 A241 5d multicolored   3.00 1.50
    Nos. 986-989 (4)   3.80 2.25

Zagreb Veterinary College, 50th anniv. Exist imperf.

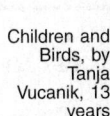 

Children and Birds, by Tanja Vucanik, 13 years A242

1969, Oct. 5   **Litho.**   **Perf. 12½**
990 A242 50p org, blk & gray   .25 .25

Issued for Children's Week.

Arms of Belgrade — A243

Arms: #992, Skopje (bridge & mountain). #993, Titograd (bridge & fortifications).

1969   Litho.   Perf. 12½
991 A243 50p gold & multi .25 .25
992 A243 50p gold & multi .25 .25
993 A243 50p gold & multi .25 .25
Nos. 991-993 (3) .75 .75

Liberation of capitals of the Federated Republics, 25th anniv. See Nos. 1017-1020.

Josip Smodlaka
A244

1969, Nov. 9   Engr.
994 A244 50p dark blue .25 .25

Smodlaka (1869-1956), leader in Yugoslavia's fight for independence.

Painting Type of 1967

Paintings of Nudes: 50p, The Little Gypsy with the Rose, by Nikola Martinoski. 1.25d, Girl on a Red Chair, by Sava Sumanovic. 1.50d, Woman Combing her Hair, by Marin Tartaglia. 2.50d, Olympia, by Miroslav Kraljevic. 3.25d, The Bather, by Jovan Bijelic. 5d, Woman on a Couch, by Matej Sternen.

Photo. & Engr.
1969, Nov. 29   Perf. 13½
995 A220 50p multi, vert. .25 .25
996 A220 1.25d multi, vert. .25 .25
997 A220 1.50d multi, vert. .25 .25
998 A220 2.50d multi .30 .30
999 A220 3.25d multi, vert. .40 .40
1000 A220 5d multi 2.50 2.50
Nos. 995-1000 (6) 3.95 3.95

Exist imperf.

University of Ljubljana, 50th Anniv.
A245

1969, Dec. 9   Engr.   Perf. 11½
1001 A245 50p slate grn .25 .25

Seal of Zagreb University
A246

Photo. & Engr.
1969, Dec. 17   Perf. 12½
1002 A246 50p gold, bl & brn .25 .25

University of Zagreb, 300th anniv.

Common Design Types pictured following the introduction.

Europa Issue, 1969
Common Design Type
1969, Dec. 20   Photo.   Perf. 11½
1003 CD12 1.25d grnsh gray, buff & brn 1.25 1.25
1004 CD12 3.25d rose lil, gray & dk bl 2.75 2.75

Yugoslavia's admission to CEPT. Exist imperf.

Jovan Cvijic, Geographer
A247

Famous Yugoslavs: 1.25d, Dr. Andrija Stampar, hygienist. 1.50d, Joakim Krcovski, author. 2.50d, Marko Miljanov, Montenegrin patriot-hero. 3.25d, Vaca Pelagic, socialist. 5d, Oton Zupancic, Slovenian poet.

1970, Feb. 16   Engr.   Perf. 12½
1005 A247 50p reddish brn .25 .25
1006 A247 1.25d brnsh black .25 .25
1007 A247 1.50d lilac .25 .25
1008 A247 2.50d slate grn .25 .25
1009 A247 3.25d reddish brn .25 .25
1010 A247 5d blue vio .25 .25
Nos. 1005-1010 (6) 1.50 1.50

Punishment of Dirce,
Pulj — A248

Mosaics from the 1st-4th Centuries: 1.25d, Cerberus, Bitola, horiz. 1.50d, Angel of the Annunciation, Porec. 2.50d, Hunters, Gamzigard. 3.25d, Bull and cherry tree, horiz. 5d, Virgin and Child enthroned, Porec.

1970, Mar. 16   Photo.   Perf. 13½
1011 A248 50p gold & multi .25 .25
1012 A248 1.25d gold & multi .25 .25
1013 A248 1.50d gold & multi .25 .25
1014 A248 2.50d gold & multi .30 .25
1015 A248 3.25d gold & multi .55 .35
1016 A248 5d gold & multi 1.50 1.50
Nos. 1011-1016 (6) 3.10 2.85

Exist imperf.

Arms Type of 1969

#1017, Sarajevo (arcade). #1018, Zagreb (castle). #1019, Ljubljana (dragon and tower). #1020a, Yugoslavia (embossed coat of arms.)

1970   Litho.   Perf. 12½
1017 A243 50p gold & multi .25 .25
1018 A243 50p gold & multi .25 .25
1019 A243 50p gold & multi .25 .25
Nos. 1017-1019 (3) .75 .75

Souvenir Sheet
1020   Sheet of 7 15.00 15.00
  a.   A243 12d gold & black 12.50 12.50

Liberation of Yugoslavia, 25th anniv. No. 1020 contains Nos. 991-993, 1017-1019, 1020a + 2 labels.
Issued: #1017, Apr. 6; #1018, May 8; #1019, May 9; #1020, May 15.

Lenin (1870-1924), by S. Stojanovic
A249

Design: 1.25d, Lenin sculpture facing left.

1970, Apr. 22   Engr.
1021 A249 50p rose lilac .25 .25
1022 A249 1.25d blue gray .25 .25

Basketball
A250

1970, Apr. 25
1023 A250 1.25d plum .25 .25

6th World Basketball Championships, Ljubljana, May 10-23. Exists imperf.

Europa Issue, 1970
Common Design Type
1970, May 4   Photo.   Perf. 11½
Size: 32½x23mm
1024 CD13 1.25d lt bl, dk bl & lt grnsh bl .40 .40
1025 CD13 3.25d rose lil, plum & gray .40 .40

Exist imperf.

Istrian Shorthaired Hound
A251

Yugoslav Breeds of Dogs: 1.25d, Yugoslav tricolor hound. 1.50d, Istrian hard-haired hound. 2.50d, Balkan hound. 3.25d, Dalmatian. 5d, Shara mountain dog.

1970, May 25   Photo.   Perf. 11½
Granite Paper
1026 A251 50p tan & multi .25 .25
1027 A251 1.25d olive & multi .25 .25
1028 A251 1.50d violet & multi .25 .25
1029 A251 2.50d slate & multi .25 .25
1030 A251 3.25d multi .45 .25
1031 A251 5d multi 2.00 2.00
Nos. 1026-1031 (6) 3.45 3.25

Exist imperf.

Telegraph Circuit — A252

1970, June 20   Litho.   Perf. 12½
1032 A252 50p henna brn, gold & blk .25 .25

Telegraph service in Montenegro, cent.

Bird — A253

1970, Oct. 5
1033 A253 50p multicolored .25 .25

Issued for Children's Week, Oct. 5-11.

Stylized Gymnast — A254

1970, Oct. 22   Engr.
1034 A254 1.25d car & slate .25 .25

17th World Gymnastics Championships, Ljubljana, Oct. 22-27.

UN Emblem and Hand Holding Dove, by Makoto
A255

Litho. & Engr.
1970, Oct. 24   Perf. 11½
1035 A255 1.25d dk brn, blk & gold .25 .25

25th anniversary of the United Nations.

Ascension, by Teodor D. Kracum
A256

Baroque Paintings: 75p, Abraham's Sacrifice, by Federiko Benkovic. 1.25d, Holy Family, by Francisek Jelovsek. 2.50d, Jacob's Ladder, by Hristofor Zefarovic. 3.25d, Baptism of Christ, by unknown Serbian painter. 5.75d, The Coronation of Mary, by Tripo Kokolja.

Engr. & Photo.
1970, Nov. 28   Perf. 13½x14
1036 A256 50p gold & multi .25 .25
1037 A256 75p gold & multi .25 .25
1038 A256 1.25d gold & multi .25 .25
1039 A256 2.50d gold & multi .25 .25
1040 A256 3.25d gold & multi .45 .25
1041 A256 5.75d gold & multi .75 .70
Nos. 1036-1041 (6) 2.20 1.95

Exist imperf.

Alpine Rhododendron — A257

European Nature Protection Year emblem and: 3.25d, Bearded vulture.

1970, Dec. 14   Photo.   Perf. 11½
1042 A257 1.25d multi 3.00 3.00
1043 A257 3.25d multi 10.00 10.00

Sheets of 9.

Frano Supilo — A258

Litho. & Engr.

1971, Jan. 25 **Perf. 12½**
1044 A258 50p black & buff .25 .25

Supilo (1870-1917), Croat leader for independence from Austria-Hungary. Sheets of 9.

British, French, Canadian, Italian Satellites A259

75p, Satellite. 1.25d, Automated moon exploration. 2.50d, Various spacecraft. 3.25d, 1st experimental space station. 5.75d, Astronauts on moon.

1971, Feb. 8 **Photo.** **Perf. 13½**
1045 A259 50p multi .25 .25
1046 A259 75p multi .25 .25
1047 A259 1.25d multi .25 .25
1048 A259 2.50d multi, horiz. .25 .25
1049 A259 3.25d multi, horiz. .25 .25
1050 A259 5.75d multi, horiz. 1.10 1.10
    Nos. 1045-1050 (6) 2.35 2.35

"Space in the service of science." Sheets of 9.

Proclamation of the Commune, Town Hall, Paris — A260

Litho. & Engr.

1971, Mar. 18 **Perf. 11½**
1051 A260 1.25d bis brn & gray brn .25 .25

Centenary of the Paris Commune. Exist imperf.

Europa Issue, 1971
Common Design Type

1971, May 4 **Photo.** **Perf. 11½**
Size: 33x23mm
1052 CD14 1.50d Prus bl, pale
    grn & dk bl .25 .25
1053 CD14 4d mag, pink & dk
    mag .25 .25

Exist imperf.

Circles — A261

1971, May 5 **Perf. 13½**
1054 A261 50p shown .50 .25
1055 A261 1.25d 20 circles 1.40 .70

2nd Congress of Managers of Autonomous States.

Flower Type of 1969
Medicinal Plants: 50p, Common mallow. 1.50d, Common buckthorn. 2d, Water lily. 2.50d, Poppy. 4d, Wild chicory. 6d, Physalis.

1971, May 25 **Photo.** **Perf. 11½**
Flowers in Natural Colors
1056 A238 50p lt ultra .25 .25
1057 A238 1.50d olive bis .25 .25
1058 A238 2d dull blue .25 .25
1059 A238 2.50d dark car .30 .25
1060 A238 4d dp bister .65 .65
1061 A238 6d org brown 4.00 4.00
    Nos. 1056-1061 (6) 5.70 5.65

Exist imperf.

Prince Lazar, Fresco, Lazarica Church — A262

1971, June 28 **Photo.** **Perf. 13½**
1062 A262 50p gray & multi .25 .25

600th anniversary of founding of Krusevac by Prince Lazar Hrebeljanovic (1329-1389).

View of Krk — A263

Views: 5p, Krusevo. 10p, Castle & mosque, Gradacac. 20p, Church & bridge, Bohinj. 35p, Shore & mountains, Omis. 40p, Peje. 50p, Memorial column, Krusevac. 60p, Logar Valley. 75p, Bridge & church, Bohinj. 80p, Church, Piran. 1d, Street, Bitolj. 1.20d, Minaret, Pocitelj. 1.25d, 1.50d, Gate tower, Hercegnovi. 2d, Cathedral & City Hall Square, Novi Sad. 2.50d, Crna River.

1971-73 **Engr.** **Perf. 13**
1063 A263 5p orange ('73) .25 .25
1064 A263 10p brown ('72) .25 .25
1065 A263 20p vio blk ('73) .25 .25
1066 A263 30p ol gray ('72) .25 .25
    a. 30p green 1.00 .25
1067 A263 35p brn car ('73) .25 .25
1068 A263 40p black ('72) .25 .25
1069 A263 50p vermilion 1.50 .25
1070 A263 50p green ('72) .25 .25
1071 A263 60p purple ('72) .25 .25
1072 A263 75p slate green .25 .25
1073 A263 80p rose red
    ('72) 1.50 .25
1073A A263 1d violet brn 1.50 .45
1073B A263 1.20d sl grn ('72) 2.00 .25
1073C A263 1.25d deep blue 1.10 .25
1073D A263 1.50d bluish blk
    ('73) 1.00 .25
1073E A263 2d blue ('72) 1.00 .25
1073F A263 2.50d dl pur ('73) 1.00 .25
    Nos. 1063-1073F (17) 12.10 4.45

Issued with and without fluorescent bars. See type A323. See Nos. 1482-1486, 1599-1600, 1602-1603, 1717. For surcharges see Nos. 1413, 1711-1712, 1765-1766, 1769.

Tourist Issue

Emperor Constantine, 4th Century — A264

Antique Bronzes excavated in Yugoslavia: 1.50d, Boy with fish. 2d, Hercules, replica after Lysippus. 2.50d, Satyr. 4d, Head of Aphrodite. 6d, Citizen of Emona, 1st century tomb.

1971, Sept. 20 **Photo.** **Perf. 13½**
1074 A264 50p rose & multi .25 .25
1075 A264 1.50d multicolored .25 .25
1076 A264 2d multicolored .25 .25
1077 A264 2.50d lem & multi .25 .25

1078 A264 4d ocher & multi .25 .25
1079 A264 6d multicolored .25 .25
    Nos. 1074-1079 (6) 1.50 1.50

Sheets of 9.

UNICEF Emblem, Children in Balloon — A265

1971, Oct. 4 **Litho.** **Perf. 13x13½**
1080 A265 50p multicolored .25 .25

Children's Week, Oct. 3-10.

Woman in Serbian Costume, by Katarina Ivanovic A266

Portraits, 19th Century: 1.50d, The Merchant Ivanisevic, by Anastasije Bocaric. 2d, Ana Kresic, by Vjekoslav Karas. 2.50d, Pavle Jagodic, by Konstantin Danil. 4r, Luiza Pesjakova, by Mihael Stroj. 6d, Old Man and view of Ljubljana, by Matevz Langus.

Engraved and Photogravure
1971, Nov. 29 **Perf. 13½x14**
1081 A266 50p gold & multi .25 .25
1082 A266 1.50d gold & multi .25 .25
1083 A266 2d gold & multi .25 .25
1084 A266 2.50d gold & multi .25 .25
1085 A266 4d gold & multi .25 .25
1086 A266 6d gold & multi .80 .80
    Nos. 1081-1086 (6) 2.05 2.05

See Nos. 1120-1125.

Letter with Postal Code, Map of Yugoslavia — A267

1971, Dec. 15 **Photo.** **Perf. 13½x14**
1087 A267 50p ultra & multi .25 .25

Introduction of postal code system.

Damjan Gruev (1871-1906), Macedonian Revolutionist A268

1971, Dec. 22 **Engr.** **Perf. 12½**
1088 A268 50p dark blue .25 .25

11th Winter Olympic Games, Sapporo, Japan, Feb. 3-13 A269

Engr. & Typo.

1972, Feb. 3 **Perf. 11½**
1089 A269 1.25d Speed skating .25 .25
1090 A269 6d Slalom 2.50 1.25

Sheets of 9.

First Page of Statute of Dubrovnik A270

Lithographed and Engraved
1972, Mar. 15 **Perf. 13½**
1091 A270 1.25d gold & multi .25 .25

700th anniversary of the Statute of Dubrovnik, a legal code given by Prince Marko Justiniani.

Ski Jump Track, Planica — A271

1972, Mar. 21 **Perf. 11½**
1092 A271 1.25d blk, lt bl & grn .25 .25

World Ski Jump Championships, Planica, Mar. 22-26.

Water Polo and Olympic Rings — A272

1972, Apr. 17 **Litho.** **Perf. 12½x12**
1093 A272 50p shown .25 .25
1094 A272 1.25d Basketball .25 .25
1095 A272 2.50d Butterfly stroke .25 .25
1096 A272 3.25d Boxing .25 .25
1097 A272 5d Running .25 .25
1098 A272 6.50d Yachting .40 .40
    Nos. 1093-1098 (6) 1.65 1.65

20th Olympic Games, Munich, Aug. 26-Sept. 10. Sheets of 9.

Europa Issue 1972
Common Design Type

1972, May 4 **Photo.** **Perf. 11½**
1100 CD15 1.50d bl, grn & yel .60 .60
1101 CD15 5d brt rose, mag
    & org .60 .60

Wall Creeper — A275

Birds: 1.25d, Little bustard. 2.50d, Red-billed chough. 3.25d, Spoonbill. 5d, Eagle owl. 6.50d, Rock ptarmigan.

1972, May 8
Birds in Natural Colors
1102 A275 50p gray violet .25 .25
1103 A275 1.25d ocher .25 .25
1104 A275 2.50d gray olive .25 .25
1105 A275 3.25d light plum .35 .35

1106 A275 5d red brown .65 .65
1107 A275 6.50d violet 2.50 2.50
Nos. 1102-1107 (6) 4.25 4.25
Nature protection.

Marshal Tito, by Bozidar Jakac — A276

1972, May 25 Litho. Perf. 12½
1108 A276 50p cream & dk brn .25 .25
1109 A276 1.25d gray & indigo .50 .25

Souvenir Sheet
Imperf
1110 A276 10d gray & blk brn 2.75 2.75
80th birthday of Pres. Tito. Sheets of 9. No. 1110 printed in blocks of 4.

First Locomotive Built in Serbia, 1882 — A277

5d, Modern Yugoslavian electric locomotive.

1972, June 12 Photo. Perf. 11½
1111 A277 1.50d multicolored .25 .25
1112 A277 5d multicolored .80 .30
Intl. Railroad Union, 50th anniv. Exist imperf.

Glider A278

1972, July 8 Photo. Perf. 12½
1113 A278 2d bl gray, gold & blk .25 .25
13th World Gliding Championships, Vrsac Airport, July 9-23. Sheets of 9. Exists imperf.

Pawn on Chessboard — A279

6d, Chessboard, emblems of King and Queen.

1972, Sept. 18 Perf. 11½
1114 A279 1.50d multi .25 .25
1115 A279 6d multi 1.25 .70
20th Men's and 5th Women's Chess Olympiad, Skopje, Sept.-Oct. Sheets of 9.

Boy on Rocking Horse — A280

1972, Oct. 2 Litho. Perf. 12½
1116 A280 80p org & multi .25 .25
Children's Week, Oct. 2-8.

Goce Delchev — A281

1972, Oct. 16 Perf. 13
1117 A281 80p yel grn & blk .25 .25
Delchev (1872-1903), Macedonian freedom fighter.

Grga Martic, by Ivan Mestrovic A282

1972, Nov. 3 Perf. 12½
1118 A282 80p red, yel grn & blk .25 .25
Brother Grga Martic (1822-1905), Franciscan administrator, educator and poet.

Serbian National Library, Belgrade A283

1972, Nov. 25 Engr. Perf. 11½x12
1119 A283 50p chocolate .25 .25
140th anniversary of the Serbian National Library and opening of new building.

Painting Type of 1971
Still-Life Paintings: 50p, by Milos Tenkovic, horiz. 1.25d, by Jozef Pekovsek. 2.50d, by Katarina Jovanovic, horiz. 3.25d, by Konstantin Danil, horiz. 5d, by Nikola Masic. 6.50d, by Celestin Medovic, horiz.

Perf. 14x13½, 13½x14
1972, Nov. 28 Engr. & Photo.
1120 A266 50p gold & multi .25 .25
1121 A266 1.25d gold & multi .25 .25
1122 A266 2.50d gold & multi .25 .25
1123 A266 3.25d gold & multi .25 .25
1124 A266 5d gold & multi .25 .25
1125 A266 6.50d gold & multi .70 .50
Nos. 1120-1125 (6) 1.95 1.75
Exist imperf.

Battle of Stubica, by Krsto Hegedusic — A284

6d, Battle of Krsko, by Gojmir Anton Kos.

1973, Jan. 29 Photo. Perf. 11½
1126 A284 2d gold & multi .30 .25
1127 A284 6d gold & multi 1.25 .70
Croatian-Slovenian Rebellion, 400th anniv. (2d); Beginning of the peasant rebellions in Slovenia, 500th anniv. (6d). Sheets of 9.

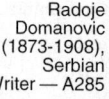

Radoje Domanovic (1873-1908), Serbian Writer — A285

1973, Feb. 3 Litho. Perf. 12½
1128 A285 80p tan & brn .40 .25
Sheets of 9.

Skofja Loka A286

1973, Feb. 15 Perf. 11½
1129 A286 80p brown & buff .30 .25
Millennium of the founding of Skofja Loka. Sheets of 9.

Novi Sad, by Peter Demetrovic — A287

Old Engravings: 1.25d, Zagreb, by Josef Szeman. 2.50d, Kotor, by Pierre Mortier. 3.25d, Belgrade, by Mancini. 5d, Split, by Louis-Francois Cassas. 6.50d, Kranj, by Matthaus Merian.

Engraved and Photogravure
1973, Mar. 15 Perf. 13½
1130 A287 50p gold, buff & blk .25 .25
1131 A287 1.25d gold, gray & black .25 .25
1132 A287 2.50d gold & blk .25 .25
1133 A287 3.25d gold & blk .25 .25
1134 A287 5d gold, buff & blk .25 .25
1135 A287 6.50d gold & blk .25 .25
Nos. 1130-1135 (6) 1.50 1.50
Nos. 1130-1131, 1133-1135 exist imperf.

Championship Poster A288

1973, Apr. 5 Litho. Perf. 13½x13
1136 A288 2d multicolored .40 .40
32nd Intl. Table Tennis Championships, Sarajevo, Apr. 5-15. Sheets of 9.

Europa Issue, 1973
Common Design Type
1973, Apr. 30 Photo. Perf. 11½
Size: 32½x23mm
1138 CD16 2d dk bl, lil & lt grn .35 .30
1139 CD16 5.50d pur, cit & sal pink .80 .80
Sheets of 9.

Flower Type of 1969
Medicinal Plants: 80p, Birthwort. 2d, Globe thistles. 3d, Olive branch. 4d, Corydalis. 5d, Mistletoe. 6d, Comfrey.

1973, May 25 Photo. Perf. 11½
Flowers in Natural Colors
1140 A238 80p orange & grn .25 .25
1141 A238 2d dl bl & blue .25 .25
1142 A238 3d olive & blk .25 .25
1143 A238 4d yel grn & grn .25 .25

1144 A238 5d org & sepia .40 .40
1145 A238 6d lilac & grn 1.75 1.75
Nos. 1140-1145 (6) 3.15 3.15

Anton Jansa (1734-1773), Teacher, Apiculturist and Bee — A291

1973, Aug. 25 Engr. Perf. 12½
1147 A291 80p black .40 .25
Sheets of 9.

Championship Badge A292

1973, Sept. 1 Litho. Perf. 13½x13
1148 A292 2d multicolored .25 .25
World water sport championships (swimming, water polo, water jumps, figure swimming), Belgrade, Sept. 1-9. Sheets of 9.

"Greeting the Sun," by Ivan Vucovic A293

1973, Oct. 1 Perf. 12½
1149 A293 80p multicolored 1.20 .80
Children's Week, Oct. 1-7. Sheets of 9.

Post Horn — A294

Coil Stamps
1973-77 Photo. Perf. 14½x14
1150 A294 30p brown .25 .25
1151 A294 50p gray blue .25 .25
1152 A294 80p rose red ('74) .40 .25
1153 A294 1d yel grn ('77) .40 .25
1154 A294 1.20d pink ('74) .30 .25
1155 A294 1.50d rose ('77) .40 .25
Nos. 1150-1155 (6) 2.00 1.50

Juraj Dalmatinac, Sculptor, Architect, 500th Anniv. of Death — A295

1973, Oct. 8 Litho. Perf. 12½
1158 A295 80p grnsh gray & ol blk .25 .25
Sheets of 9.

Nadezda Petrovic (1873-1915), Self-Portrait — A296

Lithographed and Engraved
1973, Oct. 12   Perf. 11½
1159 A296 2d gold & multi   .30 .25
Sheets of 9.

Interior, by Marko Celebonovic — A297

Paintings of Interiors by Yugoslav artists: 2d, St. Duja, by Emanuel Vidovic. 3d, Room with Slovak Woman, by Marino Tartaglia. 4d, Painter with Easel, by Miljenko Stancic. 5d, Studio, by Milan Konjovic. 6d, Tavern in Stara Loka, by France Slana.

1973, Oct. 20   Photo.   Perf. 13½
1160 A297 80p gold & multi   .25 .25
1161 A297 2d gold & multi   .25 .25
1162 A297 3d gold & multi   .25 .25
1163 A297 4d gold & multi   .25 .25
1164 A297 5d gold & multi   .25 .25
1165 A297 6d gold & multi   .45 .40
     Nos. 1160-1165 (6)   1.70 1.65
Sheets of 9.

Dragojlo Dudic — A298

Lithographed and Engraved
1973, Nov. 29   Perf. 12½
Gray and Indigo
1166 A298 80p shown   .25 .25
1167 A298 80p Strahil Pindzur   .25 .25
1168 A298 80p Boris Kidric   .25 .25
1169 A298 80p Radoje Dakic   .25 .25
Gray and Plum
1170 A298 2d Josip Mazar-Sosa   .25 .25
1171 A298 2d Zarko Zrenjanin   .25 .25
1172 A298 2d Emin Duraku   .25 .25
1173 A298 2d Ivan-Lola Ribar   .25 .25
     a.   Sheet of 8, #1166-1173   2.00 2.00
Republic Day, Nov. 29, honoring national heroes who perished during WWII.

Memorial, by O. Boljka, Ljubljana A299

Winged Globe, by D. Dzamonja, at Podgaric A300

Sculptures: 4.50d, Tower by D. Dzamonja, at Kozara. 5d, Memorial, by B. Grabulovski, at Belcista. 10d, Abstract, by M. Zivkovic, at Sutjeska. 50d, Stone "V," by Zivkovic, at Kragujevac.

1974   Engr.   Perf. 12½
1174 A299 3d slate grn   .65 .25
1175 A299 4.50d brn lake   1.00 .25
1176 A299 5d dark vio   .90 .25
     b.   Perf. 13½   6.00 .40
1177 A300 10d slate grn   1.60 .40
1178 A300 20d dull pur   3.25 .25
1179 A300 50d indigo   4.00 1.00
     Nos. 1174-1179 (6)   11.40 2.40
Exist imperf.

1978-82   Litho.
1176a A299 5d   2.25
1177a A300 10d ('81)   2.25 .50
1178a A300 20d ('81)   3.25 .50
1179a A300 50d ('82)   4.00 1.00
     Nos. 1176a-1179a (4)   11.75 2.25

Metric Measure A301

1974, Jan. 10   Litho.   Perf. 13
1180 A301 80p plum & multi   .25 .25
Centenary of introduction of metric system.

European Ice Skating Championships, Jan. 29-Feb. 2, Zagreb — A302

1974, Jan. 29
1181 A302 2d multicolored   .65 .25
Exists imperf.

Diligence, 1874 A303

Litho. & Engr.
1974, Feb. 25   Perf. 11½
1182 A303 80p shown   .25 .25
1183 A303 2d New UPU headquarters   .25 .25
1184 A303 8d Jet plane   .25 .25
     Nos. 1182-1184 (3)   .75 .75
Centenary of the Universal Postal Union.

Montenegro No. 1 — A304

Litho. & Engr.
1974, Mar. 11   Perf. 13
1185 A304 80p shown   .25 .25
1186 A304 6d Montenegro No. 7   .30 .25
Centenary of first Montenegrin postage stamps.

Marshal Tito — A305

1974   Litho.   Perf. 13
1193 A305 50p green   .25 .25
     a.   Perf. 13x12½   .40 .25
1196 A305 80p vermilion   .25 .25
1198 A305 1.20d slate green   .25 .25
1201 A305 2d gray blue   .25 .25
     a.   Perf. 13x12½   .40 .25
     b.   Perf. 13¼x13½   .40 .25
     Nos. 1193-1201 (4)   1.00 1.00
Issued with and without fluorescence. For surcharge see No. 1415.

Lenin, by Nandor Glid — A306

1974, Apr. 20   Litho.   Perf. 13
1204 A306 2d blk & silver   .25 .25
50th death anniv. of Lenin.

Lepenski Vir Statue, c. 4950 B.C. — A307

Europa: 6d, Widow & Child, by Ivan Mestrovic.

1974, Apr. 29   Photo.   Perf. 11½
1205 A307 2d multicolored   .40 .40
1206 A307 6d multicolored   1.20 1.20
Exist imperf.

Great Tit — A308

1974, May 25   Photo.   Perf. 11½
1207 A308 80p shown   .25 .25
1208 A308 2d Rose   .25 .25
1209 A308 6d Cabbage butterfly   1.40 1.10
     Nos. 1207-1209 (3)   1.90 1.60
Youth Day. Issued in sheets of 9.

Congress Poster — A309

1974, May 27   Litho.   Perf. 11½
1210 A309 80p gold & multi   .25 .25
1211 A309 2d silver & multi   .25 .25
1212 A309 6d ocher & multi   .40 .40
     Nos. 1210-1212 (3)   .90 .90
10th Congress of Yugoslav League of Communists, Belgrade, May 27-30.

Radar Ground Station, Ivanjica — A311

1974, June 7   Engr.   Perf. 13
1214 A311 80p shown   .25 .25
1215 A311 6d Intelsat IV   .50 .25
Opening of first satellite ground station in Yugoslavia at Ivanjica. Sheets of 9.

Games Emblem and Soccer Cup — A312

1974, June 13   Litho.   Perf. 13
1216 A312 4.50d vio bl & multi   1.25 .90
World Cup Soccer Championship, Munich, June 13-July 7. Sheets of 9.

Klek Mountain, Edelweiss, Mountaineers' Emblem — A313

1974, June 15
1217 A313 2d grn & multi   .25 .25
Mountaineering in Yugoslavia, cent. Sheets of 9. Exists imperf. Value $40.

Children's Dance, by Jano Knjazovic — A314

Paintings: 2d, "Crucified Rooster," by Ivan Generalic, vert. 5d, Laundresses, by Ivan Lackovic, vert. 8d, Dance, by Janko Brasic.

1974, Sept. 9   Photo.   Perf. 11½
1218 A314 80p multi   .30 .30
1219 A314 2d multi   .30 .30
1220 A314 5d multi   .30 .30
1221 A314 8d multi   .75 .75
     Nos. 1218-1221 (4)   1.65 1.65
Yugoslav primitive art.

Cock and Flower, by Kaca Milinojsin A315

Designs (Children's Paintings): 3.20d, Girl and Boy, by Ewa Medrzecka, vert. 5d, Cat and Kitten, by Jelena Anastasijevic.

1974, Oct. 7   Litho.   Perf. 13
1222 A315 1.20d multi   .25 .25
1223 A315 3.20d multi   .25 .25
1224 A315 5d multi   .25 .25
     Nos. 1222-1224 (3)   .75 .75
Children's Week, Oct. 1-7, and Joy of Europe meeting in Belgrade. Sheets of 9.

Library and Primoz Trubar Statue
A316

1974, Oct. 21   Engr.   Perf. 13
1225 A316 1.20d black   .25 .25
Natl. University Library, Ljubljana, 200th anniv. Exists imperf.

White Peonies, by Petar Dobrovic
A317

Paintings of Flowers by Yugoslav artists: 2d, Carnations, by Vilko Gecan. 3d, Flowers, still-life, by Milan Konjovic. 4d, White Vase, by Sava Sumanovic. 5d, Larkspur, by Stane Kregar. 8d, Roses, by Petar Lubarda.

1974, Nov. 28   Photo.   Perf. 11½
1226 A317 80p gold & multi   .25 .25
1227 A317   2d gold & multi   .25 .25
1228 A317   3d gold & multi   .25 .25
1229 A317   4d gold & multi   .25 .25
1230 A317   5d gold & multi   .25 .25
1231 A317   8d gold & multi   .80 .80
       Nos. 1226-1231 (6)   2.05 2.05
Sheets of 9.

Title Page and View of Belgrade
A318

1975, Jan. 8   Litho.   Perf. 13
1232 A318 1.20d citron   .25 .25
  a.   Perf. 12½   30.00 30.00
Sesquicentennial of the first publication of Matica Srpska, literary journal.

Map of Europe and Dove — A319

1975, Jan. 30   Perf. 12x11½
1233 A319 3.20d bl & multi   .25 .25
1234 A319   8d multi   .50 .25
Interparliamentary Union for European Cooperation and Security, 2nd Conference, Belgrade, Jan. 31-Feb. 6. Exist imperf.

Gold-plated Bronze Earring
A320

Antique jewelry in Yugoslav museums: 2.10d, Silver bracelet, 18th cent. 3.20d, Silver belt buckle, 18th cent. 5d, Silver ring with Nike cameo, 14th cent. 6d, Silver necklace, 17th cent. 8d, Bronze gilt bracelet, 14th cent.

1975, Feb. 25   Photo.   Perf. 14x13
1235 A320 1.20d multi   .25 .25
1236 A320 2.10d multi   .25 .25
1237 A320 3.20d multi   .25 .25
1238 A320   5d multi   .25 .25
1239 A320   6d multi   .25 .25
1240 A320   8d multi   .40 .40
       Nos. 1235-1240 (6)   1.65 1.65

Svetozar Markovic, by Stevan Bodnarov
A321

1975, Feb. 26   Engr.   Perf. 13
1241 A321 1.20d blue blk   .50 .25
Markovic (1846-1875), writer and poet.

Fettered Woman, by Frano Krsinic
A322

1975, Mar. 8   Photo.   Perf. 14½x14
1242 A322 3.20d gold & sepia   .25 .25
International Women's Year.

Street, Ohrid — A323

Views: 25p, Budva. 75p, City Hall, Rijeka (Fiume). Nos. 1245, 1246, Street, Ohrid. 1.50d, Church, Bihac. 2.10d, Street and fountain, Hvar. 3.20d, Skofja Loka. 3.40d, Main Square, Vranje. 4.90d, Mosque, Perast.

No Inscription at Bottom
1975-77   Litho.   Perf. 13
1243 A323   25p carmine ('76)   1.20 .25
1244 A323   75p purple ('76)   .80 .25
1245 A323   1d dull purple   .25 .25
1246 A323   1d dl grn ('76)   .40 .25
  a.   Perf. 13x12½   .40 .25
1247 A323 1.50d rose red ('76)   .25 .25
  a.   Perf. 13x12½   24.00 24.00
1248 A323 2.10d gray green   .25 .25
1249 A323 3.20d dull blue   .25 .25
1250 A323 3.40d gray grn ('77)   .80 .25
  a.   Perf. 13x12½   1.60
1251 A323 4.90d dl bl ('76)   2.75 .25
       Nos. 1243-1251 (9)   7.90 2.25

See Nos. 1487-1491, 1598, 1601, 1603A, 1713, 1718-1719. For surcharges see Nos. 1382-1383, 1481, 1502, 1545, 1550, 1594-1597A, 1764, 1767-1768, 1770-1771, 1964, 1973.
Nos. 1243, 1246, 1247 exist imperf. Value each, $20.

Europa Issue

Still Life with Eggs, by Mosa Pijade
A325

Painting: 8d, Three Graces, by Ivan Radovic.

1975, Apr. 28
1252 A325 3.20d gold & multi   .40 .40
1253 A325   8d gold & multi   .40 .40
Exist imperf.

Srem Front Fighters' Monument, by Dusan Dzamonja
A326

1975, May 9   Litho.   Perf. 13½
1254 A326 3.20d red & multi   .30 .25
Victory over Fascism in WWII; liberation of Yugoslavia, 30th anniv.

Garland Flower — A327

1975, May 24   Photo.   Perf. 14x14½
1255 A327 1.20d shown   .25 .25
1256 A327 2.10d Garden balsam   .25 .25
1257 A327 3.20d Rose mallow   .25 .25
1258 A327   5d Geranium   .25 .25
1259 A327   6d Crocus   .25 .25
1260 A327   8d Oleander   1.00 1.00
       Nos. 1255-1260 (6)   2.25 2.25
Youth Day.

Kayak — A328

1975, June 20   Litho.   Perf. 13½
1261 A328 3.20d grnsh bl & multi   .25 .25
9th World Championship of Wild Water Racing, Radika River, June 24-25, and 14th World Championship of Canoe-Slalom, Treska River, June 28-29.

Ambush, Herzegovinian Insurgents, by Ferdo Quiquerez — A329

1975, July 9   Photo.   Perf. 13½x14½
1262 A329 1.20d gold & multi   .25 .25
Bosnian & Herzegovinian Uprising, cent.

Stjepan Mitrov Ljubisa (1824-1878)
A330

Yugoslav writers: 2.10d, Ivan Prijatelj (1875-1937). 3.20d, Jakov Ignjatovic (1824-89). 5d, Dragojla Jarnevic (1813-75). 6d, Svetozar Corovic (1875-1919). 8d, Ivana Brlic-Mazuranic (1874-1938).

1975, Sept. 16   Litho.   Perf. 13
1263 A330 1.20d brick red & blk   .25 .25
1264 A330 2.10d dl grn & blk   .25 .25
1265 A330 3.20d ol bis & blk   .25 .25
1266 A330   5d brn org & blk   .25 .25
1267 A330   6d yel grn & blk   .25 .25
1268 A330   8d Prus bl & blk   .30 .30
       Nos. 1263-1268 (6)   1.55 1.55

"Joy of Europe" Children's Meeting, Oct. 2-7, Belgrade
A331

Children's drawings.

1975, Oct. 1   Litho.   Perf. 13½
1269 A331 3.20d Young Lion   .25 .25
1270 A331   6d Baby Carriage   .70 .65

Peace Dove
A332

1975, Oct. 10
1271 A332 3.20d multi   .25 .25
1272 A332   8d multi   .45 .45
European Security and Cooperation Conference, Helsinki, July 30-Aug. 1. Exist imperf.

Red Cross, "100", Map of Yugoslavia
A333

8d, Red Cross, people seeking help.

1975, Nov. 1   Litho.   Perf. 13½x13
1273 A333 1.20d red & multi   .25 .25
1274 A333   8d red & multi   .25 .25
Centenary of Red Cross in Yugoslavia.

Soup Kitchen, by Dorde Andrejevic-Kun
A334

Social paintings by 20th century Yugoslav artists: 2.10d, People at the Door, by Vinko Grdan. 3.20d, Drunks in Coach, by Marijan Detoni, horiz. 5d, Workers' Lunch, by Tone Kralj, horiz. 6d, Water Wheel, by Lazar Licenoski. 8d, The Hanging, by Krsto Hegedusic.

Perf. 14½x13½, 13½x14½
1975, Nov. 28   Photo.
1275 A334 1.20d gold & multi   .25 .25
1276 A334 2.10d gold & multi   .25 .25
1277 A334 3.20d gold & multi   .25 .25
1278 A334   5d gold & multi   .25 .25
1279 A334   6d gold & multi   .25 .25
1280 A334   8d gold & multi   .30 .30
       Nos. 1275-1280 (6)   1.55 1.55
Sheets of 9. No. 1277 exists imperf.

Diocletian's Palace, 304 A.D. — A335

3.20d, House of Ohrid, 19th cent., vert. 8d, Gracanica Monastery, Kosovo, 1321.

1975, Dec. 10   Engr.   Perf. 13½
1281 A335 1.20d dark brown   .25 .25
1282 A335 3.20d bluish black   .25 .25
1283 A335 8d dk vio brown   .25 .25
     Nos. 1281-1283 (3)   .75 .75
European Architectural Heritage Year 1975.
Sheets of 9. Exist imperf.

12th Winter Olympic Games, Feb. 4-15, Innsbruck, Austria A336

1976, Feb. 4   Engr.   Perf. 13½
1284 A336 3.20d Ski jump   .25 .25
1285 A336 8d Pair figure skating .70 .40
     Exist imperf.

Red Flag — A337

1976, Feb. 14   Litho.
1286 A337 1.20d red & multi   .25 .25
"Red Flag" workers demonstration, Kragujevac, Feb. 15, 1876.
Exists imperf. Value $32.50.

Svetozar Miletic (1826-1901), Lawyer, Founder of United Serbian Youth — A338

1976, Feb. 23   Perf. 13½x13
1287 A338 1.20d grnsh gray & dl grn   .25 .25

Borislav "Bora" Stankovic, (1876-1927), Writer A339

1976, Mar. 31   Litho.   Perf. 13½x13
1288 A339 1.20d lem, ol & mar   .25 .25
     Sheets of 9.

Europa Issue

King Matthias, by Jakob Pogorelec, 1931 — A340

1976, Apr. 26   Photo.   Perf. 11½
1289 A340 3.20d shown   .25 .25
1290 A340 8d Bowl, 14th cent   .25 .25

Ivan Cankar (1876-1918), Slovenian Writer A341

1976, May 8   Litho.   Perf. 13½x13
1291 A341 1.20d orange & plum   .25 .25

Train on Viaduct in Bosnia A342

Design: 8d, Train on viaduct in Montenegro.

1976, May 15   Engr.   Perf. 13½
1292 A342 3.20d deep magenta   .25 .25
1293 A342 8d deep blue   .40 .40
Inauguration of the Belgrade-Bar railroad.

Hawker Dragonfly A343

Fresh-water Fauna: 2.10d, Winkle. 3.20d, Rudd. 5d, Green frog. 6d, Ferruginous duck. 8d, Muskrat.

1976, May 25   Litho.
1294 A343 1.20d yel & multi   .40 .40
1295 A343 2.10d bl & multi   .40 .40
1296 A343 3.20d vio & multi   .40 .40
1297 A343 5d multicolored   .80 .80
1298 A343 6d multicolored   .80 .80
1299 A343 8d multicolored   2.75 2.75
     Nos. 1294-1299 (6)   5.55 5.55
Youth Day. Exist imperf.

Vladimir Nazor, Croatian Writer, Birth Cent. — A344

1976, May 29   Perf. 13
1300 A344 1.20d pale lil & dl bl .25 .25

Battle of Vucji Dol, 1876 A345

1976, June 16   Litho.   Perf. 13
1301 A345 1.20d gold, brn & buff .25 .25
Liberation of Montenegro from Turkey, cent. Exists imperf.

Serbian Pitcher A346

Water Pitchers: 2.10d, Slovenia. 3.20d, Bosnia-Herzegovina. 5d, Vojvodina 6d, Macedonia. 8d, Kosovo.

1976, June 22   Photo.   Perf. 14x13
1302 A346 1.20d dk car & multi   .25 .25
1303 A346 2.10d olive & multi   .25 .25
1304 A346 3.20d red & multi   .25 .25
1305 A346 5d brown & multi   .25 .25
1306 A346 6d dk grn & multi   .25 .25
1307 A346 8d dk bl & multi   .35 .35
     Nos. 1302-1307 (6)   1.60 1.60
     Exist imperf.

Tesla Monument, Belgrade, and Niagara Falls — A347

1976, July 10   Engr.   Perf. 13
1308 A347 5d slate grn & indigo   .50 .25
Nikola Tesla (1856-1943), electrical engineer and inventor. Sheets of 9. Exists imperf.

21st Olympic Games, July 17-Aug. 1, Montreal, Canada, A348

1976, July 17
1309 A348 1.20d Long jump   .25 .25
1310 A348 3.20d Team handball   .25 .25
1311 A348 5d Target shooting   .25 .25
1312 A348 8d Single scull rowing 2.00 1.50
     Nos. 1309-1312 (4)   2.75 2.25
     Sheets of 9.

World Map and Peace Dove A349

1976, Aug. 16   Litho.   Perf. 13
1313 A349 4.90d multi   .30 .25
5th Summit Conference of Non-Aligned Countries, Colombo, Sri Lanka, Aug. 9-19. Sheets of 9.
Exists imperf. Value $25.

Children's Train — A350

Children's drawings: 4.90d, Navy Day (submarine).

1976, Oct. 2   Litho.   Perf. 13
1314 A350 4.90d multi   .25 .25
1315 A350 8d multi   .30 .30
"Joy of Europe" Children's Meeting, Belgrade, Oct. 2-7.
No. 1315 exists imperf.

Herzegovinian Fugitives, by Uros Predic — A351

Historical paintings by 19th-20th century Yugoslav painters: 1.20d, Battle of the Montenegrins, by Djura Jaksic, vert. 2.10d, Nikola S. Zrinjski at Siget, by Oton Ivekovic, vert. 5d, Uprising at Razlovci, by Borko Lazeski. 6d, Enthroning of Slovenian Duke at Gospovetsko Field, by Anton Gojmir Kos. 8d, Break-through at Solun Front, by Veljko Stanojevic.

Perf. 13½x12½, 12½x13½
1976, Nov. 29   Photo.
1316 A351 1.20d gold & multi   .25 .25
1317 A351 2.10d gold & multi   .25 .25
1318 A351 3.20d gold & multi   .25 .25
1319 A351 5d gold & multi   .25 .25

1320 A351 6d gold & multi   .25 .25
1321 A351 8d gold & multi   .80 .80
     Nos. 1316-1321 (6)   2.05 2.05
     Sheets of 9.

No. 839 Surcharged with New Value and 3 Bars in Rose

1976, Dec. 8   Engr.   Perf. 12½
1322 A206 1d on 85p dl pur   .40 .25

Mateja Nenadovic A352

1977, Feb. 4   Photo.   Perf. 13½x14
1323 A352 4.90d multicolored   .30 .25
Prota Mateja Nenadovic (1777-1854), Serbian Duke, archbishop and writer.

Rajko Zinzifov — A353

1977, Feb. 10   Litho.   Perf. 13x13½
1324 A353 1.50d brn & sepia   .25 .25
Rajko Zinzifov (1839-1877), writer.

Phlox — A354

Flowers: 3.40d, Lily. 4.90d, Bleeding heart. 6d, Zinnia. 8d, Spreading marigold. 10d, Horseshoe geranium.

1977, Mar. 8   Perf. 13½x13
1325 A354 1.50d multi   .25 .25
1326 A354 3.40d multi   .25 .25
1327 A354 4.90d multi   .25 .25
1328 A354 6d multi   .30 .25
1329 A354 8d multi   .30 .25
1330 A354 10d multi   1.00 .80
     Nos. 1325-1330 (6)   2.35 2.05
     Exists imperf.

Croatian Music Institute, Zagreb, 150th Anniv. A355

1977, Apr. 4   Engr.   Perf. 13
1331 A355 4.90d bl & sepia   .40 .40

Alojz Kraigher — A356

1977, Apr. 11   Litho.   Perf. 13½
1332 A356 1.50d lemon & brn   .30 .25
Kraigher (1877-1959), Slovenian writer.

Boka
Kotorska, by
Milo Milunovic
A357

10d, Zagorje in November, by Ljubo Babie.

1977, May 4　　Photo.　　Perf. 11½
1333 A357 4.90d gold & multi　.40　.40
1334 A357 10d gold & multi　.40　.40
Europa. Issued in sheets of 9.

Marshal Tito,
by Omer
Mujadzic
A358

1977, May 25　　　　Perf. 11½x12
1335 A358 1.50d gold & multi　.25　.25
1336 A358 4.90d gold & multi　.25　.25
1337 A358 8d gold & multi　.30　.30
　　Nos. 1335-1337 (3)　.80　.80
85th birthday of Pres. Tito. Sheets of 9.
Exists imperf.

Mountain Range
and
Gentian — A359

Design: 10d, Plitvice Lakes Falls, trees,
robin and environmental protection emblem.

1977, June 6　　Litho.　　Perf. 13x13½
1338 A359 4.90d multicolored　.25　.25
1339 A359 10d multicolored　.70　.50
World Environment Day.

Petar Kocic
(1877-1916),
Writer
A360

1977, June 15　　　　Perf. 13½
1340 A360 1.50d pale grn & brn　.30　.25

Map of
Europe and
Peace Dove
A361

1977, June 15　　Litho.　　Perf. 13½
1341 A361 4.90d multi　.25　.25
1342 A361 10d multi　1.00　1.00
Security and Cooperation Conference, Belgrade, June 15.

Child on
Float — A362

Children's drawings: 10d, Fruit picking.

1977, Oct. 3　　Litho.　　Perf. 13½
1343 A362 4.90d multi　.25　.25
1344 A362 10d multi　.50　.40
"Joy of Europe" Children's Meeting.

Sava
Congress
Center,
Belgrade
A363

1977, Oct. 4　　Litho.　　Perf. 13½
1345 A363 4.90d bl & multi　.25　.25
1346 A363 10d car & multi　1.00　1.00
European Security and Cooperation Conference, Belgrade.
Exist imperf. Value, each $125.

Exhibition
Emblem — A364

1977, Oct. 20　　Litho.　　Perf. 13½
1347 A364 4.90d gold & multi　.30　.25
Balkanfila 1977, 6th Intl. Phil. Exhib. of Balkan Countries, Belgrade, Oct. 24-30.

Double Flute
and
Shepherd
A365

Landscape and Musician: 3.40d, 4.90d, 6d,
Various string instruments. 8d, Bagpipes.
10d, Panpipes.

1977, Oct. 25　　Engr.　　Perf. 13½
1348 A365 1.50d och & red brn　.25　.25
1349 A365 3.40d green & brn　.25　.25
1350 A365 4.90d dk brn & yel　.25　.25
1351 A365 6d bl & red brn　.25　.25
1352 A365 8d brick red & sep　.25　.25
1353 A365 10d sl grn & bis　.50　.50
　　Nos. 1348-1353 (6)　1.75　1.75
Musical instruments from Belgrade Ethno-
graphical Museum.

Ivan Vavpotic,
Self-portrait
A366

Self-portraits of Yugoslav artists: 3.40d,
Mihailo Vukotic. 4.90d, Kosta Hakman. 6d,
Miroslav Kraljevic. 8d, Nikola Martinovski.
10d, Milena Pavlovic-Barili.

**　　　Perf. 13½x12½**
1977, Nov. 26　　　　　Photo.
1354 A366 1.50d gold & multi　.25　.25
1355 A366 3.40d gold & multi　.25　.25
1356 A366 4.90d gold & multi　.25　.25
1357 A366 6d gold & multi　.25　.25
1358 A366 8d gold & multi　.25　.25
1359 A366 10d gold & multi　.65　.65
　　Nos. 1354-1359 (6)　1.90　1.90

Festival of
Testaccio, by
Klovic — A367

Julija Klovic, by
El
Greco — A368

1978, Jan. 14　　Photo.　　Perf. 13½
1360 A367 4.90d multicolored　.25　.25
1361 A368 10d multicolored　.25　.25
Julija Klovic (1498-1578), Croat miniaturist.

Stampless Cover,
Banaviste to
Kubin,
1869 — A369

Designs: 3.40d, Mailbox. 4.90d, Ericsson
telephone, 1900. 10d, Morse telegraph, 1844.

1978, Jan. 28　　　　Perf. 13x14
1362 A369 1.50d multicolored　.25　.25
1363 A369 3.40d multicolored　.25　.25
1364 A369 4.90d multicolored　.25　.25
1365 A369 10d multicolored　.25　.25
　　Nos. 1362-1365 (4)　1.00　1.00
Post Office Museum, Belgrade.

Battle of
Pirot
A370

1978, Feb. 20　　Litho.　　Perf. 13½
1366 A370 1.50d gold, blk & sl
　　grn　1.75　1.75
Centenary of Serbo-Turkish War.
Exists imperf. Value $40.

Airplanes
A371

1978, Apr. 24　　Litho.　　Perf. 13½
1367 A371 1.50d S-49A, 1949　.25　.25
1368 A371 3.40d Galeb, 1961　.25　.25
1369 A371 4.90d Utva-75, 1976　.25　.25
1370 A371 10d Orao, 1974　.80　.80
　　Nos. 1367-1370 (4)　1.55　1.55
Aeronautical Day.
Exist imperf. Value, each $35.

Europa Issue

View of
Golubac
A372

10d, St. Naum Monastery, Ohrid.

1978, May 3　　Photo.　　Perf. 11½
1371 A372 4.90d shown　.25　.25
1372 A372 10d multicolored　.40　.40
Exist imperf.

Boxing
Glove — A373

1978, May 5　　Litho.　　Perf. 13½
1373 A373 4.90d multicolored　.35　.25
Amateur Boxing Championships.
Exists imperf. Value $35.

Honeybee — A374

Bees of Yugoslavia: 3.40d, Halictus scabi-
osae. 4.90d, Blue carpenter bee. 10d, Large
earth bumblebee.

1978, May 25　　Photo.　　Perf. 11½
1374 A374 1.50d multi　.25　.25
1375 A374 3.40d multi　.25　.25
1376 A374 4.90d multi　.25　.25
1377 A374 10d multi　.95　.95
　　Nos. 1374-1377 (4)　1.70　1.70
Exist imperf.

Filip Filipovic (1878-1938), Radovan
Radovic (1878-1906),
Revolutionaries — A375

1978, June 19　　Litho.　　Perf. 13½
1378 A375 1.50d dk pur & dl ol　.25　.25

Marshal
Tito — A376

Congress
Emblem — A377

1978, June 20
1379 A376 2d red & multi　.25　.25
1380 A377 4.90d red & multi　.30　.25
Souvenir Sheet
Imperf
1381 A376 15d red & multi　3.00　3.00
11th Congress of Yugoslav League of Communists, Belgrade, June 20-23.

Nos. 1379-1380 exist imperf. Value, each $35.

Nos. 1246, 1248 Surcharged with New Value and Two Bars in Brown

1978   **Litho.**   *Perf. 13*
1382 A323   2d on 1d   10.00   .25
1383 A323   3.40d on 2.10d   .40   .25

Issue dates: #1382, July 17; #1383, Aug. 1.

Conference Emblem over Belgrade — A378

1978, July 25   **Photo.**   *Perf. 13½*
1384 A378   4.90d bl & lt blue   .30   .25

Conference of Foreign Ministers of Nonaligned Countries, Belgrade, July 25-29. Exists imperf. Value $35.

Championship Emblem — A379

1978, Aug. 10   **Litho.**   *Perf. 13½x13*
1385 A379   4.90d multicolored   .30   .25

14th Kayak and Canoe Still Water Championships, Lake Sava, Aug. 10-14.

Mt. Triglav, North Rock — A380

1978, Aug. 26   **Photo.**   *Perf. 14*
1386 A380   2d multicolored   .25   .25

Bicentenary of first ascent of Mt. Triglav by Slovenian climbers.

Black Lake, Mt. Durmitor A381

1978, Sept. 20
1387 A381   4.90d shown   .25   .25
1388 A381   10d Tara River   .55   .30

Protection of the environment.

Night Sky A382

1978, Sept. 30   **Litho.**   *Perf. 13x12½*
1389 A382   4.90d bl blk, blk & gold   .30   .25

29th Congress of International Astronautical Federation, Dubrovnik, Oct. 1-8.

People in Forest A383

Children's drawings: 10d, Family around pond.

1978, Oct. 2   *Perf. 13½x13*
1390 A383   4.90d multi   .35   .25
1391 A383   10d multi   .65   .45

"Joy of Europe" Children's Meeting.

Seal on Insurrection Declaration A384

1978, Oct. 5   *Perf. 13½*
1392 A384   2d gold, brn & blk   .25   .25

Centenary of Kresna uprising. Exists imperf. Value $40.

Teachers' Training Institute, Sombor, Bicent. A385

1978, Oct. 16
1393 A385   2d multicolored   .25   .25

Exists imperf.

Croatian Red Cross, Cent. A386

1978, Oct. 21
1394 A386   2d lt bl, blk & red   .25   .25

Metallic Sculpture XXII, by Dusan Dzamonja A387

Modern Sculptures: 3.40d, Circulation in Space I, by Vojin Bakic, vert. 4.90d, Tectonic Octopode, by Olga Jevric, vert. 10d, Tree of Life, by Drago Trsar.

Perf. 13½x13, 13x13½
1978, Nov. 4   **Litho.**
1395 A387   2d multicolored   .25   .25
1396 A387   3.40d multicolored   .25   .25
1397 A387   4.90d multicolored   .25   .25
1398 A387   10d multicolored   .35   .35
    Nos. 1395-1398 (4)   1.10   1.10

Crossing of Neretva Pass, by Ismet Mujezinovic A388

1978, Nov. 10   **Litho.**   *Perf. 13*
1399 A388   2d multicolored   .25   .25

35th anniversary of Battle of Neretva. Exists imperf.

Workers Leaving Factory, by Marijan Detoni — A389

Engravings: 3.40d, Workers, by Maksim Sedej. 4.90d, Lumberjacks, by Daniel Ozmo. 6d, Meal Break, by Pivo Karamatijevic. 10d, Hanged Man and Raped Woman, by Djordje Andrejevic Kun.

1978, Nov. 28   **Photo.**   *Perf. 14x13½*
1400 A389   2d gold, blk & buff   .25   .25
1401 A389   3.40d gold & black   .25   .25
1402 A389   4.90d gold, yel & blk   .25   .25
1403 A389   6d gold, buff & blk   .25   .25
1404 A389   10d gold, cr & blk   .70   .50
    Nos. 1400-1404 (5)   1.70   1.50

Republic day.

Larch Cone — A390

1978, Dec. 11   **Photo.**   *Perf. 13x12½*
1405 A390   1.50d shown   .25   .25
1406 A390   1.50d Red squirrel   .25   .25
1407 A390   2d Sycamore leaves   .25   .25
1408 A390   2d Red deer   .25   .25
  a.   Bklt. pane of 8   1.25
1409 A390   3.40d Alder leaves   .25   .25
1410 A390   3.40d Partridge   .25   .25
1411 A390   4.90d Oak leaves   .25   .25
1412 A390   4.90d Grouse   .25   .25
  a.   Bklt. pane of 8   3.25
    Nos. 1405-1412 (8)   2.00   2.00

New Year 1979. Nos. 1405-1412 printed se-tenant in sheets of 25.

No. 1408a contains 4 each of Nos. 1407-1408; No. 1412a 2 each of Nos. 1409-1412, with background colors changed. Exist imperf.

Nos. 1064, 868, 1198 Surcharged with New Value and Bars

1978   **Engr.; Litho.**   *Perf. 12½, 13½*
1413 A263   35p on 10p brown   1.60   .30
1414 A211   60p on 85p dp bl   1.60   .30
1415 A305   80p on 1.20d sl grn   1.60   .30
    Nos. 1413-1415 (3)   4.80   .90

First Masthead of Politika A391

1979, Jan. 25   **Litho.**   *Perf. 13½*
1416 A391   2d gold & black   .25   .25

Politika daily newspaper, 75th anniv. Exists imperf. Value $35.

Red Flags and Emblem — A392

1979, Feb. 15
1417 A392   2d red & gold   .25   .25

11th Meeting of Self-managers, Kragujevac, Feb. 15-16. Exists imperf. Value $40.

Child and IYC Emblem — A393

1979, Mar. 1   **Photo.**   *Perf. 11½x12*
1418 A393   4.90d gold vio & bl   .45   .30

International Year of the Child. Exists imperf.

Sabre, Mace, Koran Pouch A394

Old Weapons: 3.40d, Pistol and ramrod, Montenegro. 4.90d, Short carbine and powder horn, Slovenia and Croatia. 10d, Oriental rifle and cartridge pouch.

1979, Mar. 26   **Photo.**   *Perf. 14*
1419 A394   2d multicolored   .25   .25
1420 A394   3.40d multicolored   .25   .25
1421 A394   4.90d multicolored   .25   .25
1422 A394   10d multicolored   .50   .50
    Nos. 1419-1422 (4)   1.25   1.25

5-Pointed Star, Hammer and Sickle — A395

1979, Apr. 20   **Photo.**   *Perf. 13½*
1423 A395   2d multicolored   .25   .25
1424 A395   4.90d multicolored   .25   .25

Communist and Communist Youth Leagues, 60th anniversary. Exist imperf. Value, each used, $25.

Cyril and Methodius University and Emblem A396

1979, Apr. 24   **Litho.**
1425 A396   2d multicolored   .25   .25

Sts. Cyril and Methodius University, Skopje, 30th anniv.

19th Century Belgrade, by C. Goebel A397

Europa: 10d, Postilion and Ljubljana, 17th century, by Jan van der Heyden.

1979, Apr. 30   **Photo.**   *Perf. 11½*
1426 A397   4.90d multicolored   .40   .40
1427 A397   10d multicolored   .40   .40

Blue Sow Thistles — A398

Flowers: 3.40d, Anemones. 4.90d, Astragalus. 10d, Alpine trifolium.

1979, May 25   **Photo.**   *Perf. 13½*
1428 A398   2d multicolored   .25   .25
1429 A398   3.40d multicolored   .25   .25
1430 A398   4.90d multicolored   .25   .25
1431 A398   10d multicolored   .75   .75
    Nos. 1428-1431 (4)   1.50   1.50

Milutin Milankovic, by Paja Jovanovic — A399

1979, May 28
1432 A399 4.90d multi   .35   .25
Milutin Milankovic (1879-1958), scientist.

Kosta Abrasevic (1879-1898), Poet — A400

1979, May 29   **Litho.**   *Perf. 13½x13*
1433 A400 2d org, blk & gray   .25   .25
Exists imperf. Value, used $40.

Eight-Oared Shell A401

1979, Aug. 28   **Litho.**   *Perf. 13*
1434 A401 4.90d multicolored   .40   .25
9th World Rowing Championship, Lake Bled. Exist imperf. Value $40.

8th Mediterranean Games, Sept. 15-29, Split — A402

1979, Sept. 10
1435 A402   2d Games Emblem   .25   .25
1436 A402 4.90d Mascot   .25   .25
1437 A402   10d Map, Flags   .30   .30
    Nos. 1435-1437 (3)   .80   .80
Exist imperf. Value, each $30.

Seal, 15th Century A403

1979, Sept. 14   *Perf. 12½*
1438 A403 2d multicolored   .25   .25
Zagreb Postal Service, 450th anniversary. Exists imperf. Value $35.

Lake Palic — A404

Environment Protection: 10d, Lakefront, Prokletije Mountains.

1979, Sept. 20   **Photo.**   *Perf. 14x13½*
1439 A404 4.90d multicolored   .25   .25
1440 A404   10d multicolored   .65   .40

Bank and Fund Emblems A405

Engr. & Photo.
1979, Oct. 1   *Perf. 13½*
1441 A405 4.90d multicolored   .25   .25
1442 A405   10d multicolored   .40   .40
Meeting of the World Bank and International Monetary Fund, Belgrade, Oct. 2-5. Exist imperf. Value, each $25.

"Joy of Europe" A406

Children's drawings.

1979, Oct. 2   **Litho.**
1443 A406 4.90d shown   .25   .25
1444 A406   10d Child in yard   .45   .45
Exist imperf. Value, each $40.

Mihailo Pupin (1854-1935), Physicist, Inventor — A407

1979, Oct. 9   *Perf. 13x13½*
1445 A407 4.90d multicolored   .40   .25

Marko Cepenkov A408

1979, Nov. 15   **Litho.**   *Perf. 13½*
1446 A408 2d multicolored   .25   .25
Cepenkov (1829-1920), Macedonian folklorist. Exists imperf.

Pristina University, 10th Anniversary A409

1979, Nov. 17
1447 A409 2d multicolored   .25   .25
Exists imperf. Value, used $40.

Radovan Portal, Trogir Cathedral A410

Romanesque Sculptures: 3.40d, Choir stall, Cathedral of Split. 4.90d, Triforium, Church of

---

the Resurrection, Decani. 6d, Buvina Portal, Cathedral of Split. 10d, Western portal, Church of Our Lady, Studenica.

1979, Nov. 28   **Photo.**
1448 A410   2d multi   .25   .25
1449 A410 3.40d multi   .25   .25
1450 A410 4.90d multi   .25   .25
1451 A410   6d multi   .25   .25
1452 A410   10d multi   .35   .35
    Nos. 1448-1452 (5)   1.35   1.35
    Exist imperf.

Sarajevo University, 30th Anniversary A411

1979, Dec. 1   **Litho.**
1453 A411 2d multicolored   .25   .25
Exists imperf. Value, used $40.

Duro Dakovic and Nikola Hecimovic, Communist Revolutionaries, 50th Death Anniv. — A412

1979, Dec. 10
1454 A412 2d multicolored   .25   .25
Exists imperf. Value, used $40.

Sidewheeler Deligrad, 1862-1914 — A413

10d, Sidewheeler Serbia, 1917-72.

1979, Dec. 14
1455 A413 4.90d shown   .50   .60
1456 A413   10d multicolored   1.00   1.00
    Danube Conference.
Exist imperf. Value, each $60.

Milton Manaki and Camera A414

1980, Jan. 21   **Litho.**   *Perf. 13½*
1457 A414 2d deep bister & plum   .25   .25
Manaki (1880-1964), photographer and documentary film maker.

Edward Kardelj, by Zdenko Kalin — A415

1980, Jan. 26
1458 A415 2d multicolored   .25   .25
Kardelj (1910-1979), labor movement leader. Exists imperf. Value, used $40.

No. 1458 Overprinted in Red

1980, Jan. 26
1459 A415 2d multicolored   .25   .25
Ploce renamed Kardeljevo. Exists imperf. Value, used $40.

13th Winter Olympic Games, Feb. 12-24, Lake Placid, NY — A416

1980, Feb. 13
1460 A416 4.90d Speed skating   .25   .25
1461 A416   10d Cross-country skiing   1.40   1.40
    Exist imperf.

University of Belgrade, 75th Anniversary A417

1980, Feb. 27
1462 A417 2d multicolored   .25   .25

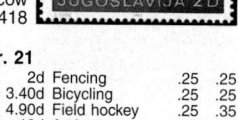

22nd Summer Olympic Games, July 19-Aug. 3, Moscow A418

1980, Apr. 21
1463 A418   2d Fencing   .25   .25
1464 A418 3.40d Bicycling   .25   .25
1465 A418 4.90d Field hockey   .25   .35
1466 A418   10d Archery   .50   .50
    Nos. 1463-1466 (4)   1.25   1.35

Marshal Tito, by Antun Augustincic A419

Europa: 13d, Tito, by Djordje Prudnikov.

1980, Apr. 28   **Photo.**   *Perf. 11½*
                   Granite Paper
1467 A419 4.90d multi   .25   .25
1468 A419   13d multi   1.00   1.00
    Exist imperf. Value, each $15.

Marshal Tito, by Bozidar Jakac — A420

1980, May 4   **Litho.**   *Perf. 13½*
1469 A420 2.50d purplish blk   .25   .25
   a.   Perf. 10½   .30   .30
1470 A420 4.90d gray black   .60   .60
Marshal Tito (1892-1980) memorial. Issued in sheets of 8 plus label. Exist imperf. Value, each $25.

Sava Kovacevic (1905-1943), Revolutionary — A421

1980, May 11   Litho.   Perf. 13½
1471 A421 2.50d multicolored   .25 .25

Wood Baton and Letter A422

1980, May 14
1472 A422 2d multicolored   .25 .25
1st Tito Youth Relay Race, 35th anniv. Exists imperf. Value $35.

Flying Gunard — A423

1980, May 24   Photo.   Perf. 12
1473 A423   2d shown   .25 .25
1474 A423   3.40d Loggerhead tur-
             tle   .25 .25
1475 A423   4.90d Sea swallow   .30 .30
1476 A423   10d Dolphin   2.25 2.25
     Nos. 1473-1476 (4)   3.05 3.05

Emperor Trajan Decius Coin, 3rd Cent. — A424

3rd Century Roman Coins (Illyrian Emperors): 3.40d, Aurelianus. 4.90d, Probus. 10d, Diocletianus.

1980, June 10
1477 A424   2d multicolored   .25 .25
1478 A424   3.40d multicolored   .25 .25
1479 A424   4.90d multicolored   .30 .25
1480 A424   10d multicolored   .50 .30
     Nos. 1477-1480 (4)   1.30 1.05

No. 1247 Surcharged with New Value and Bars

1980, June 17   Litho.   Perf. 13½
1481 A323 2.50d on 1.50d   .40 .25

Types of 1971-77

Views: 5p, Krusevac. 10p, Gradacac. 20p, Church and bridge, Bohinj. 30p, Krk. 35p, Omis. 40p, Pec. 60p, Logar Valley. 2.50d, Kragujevac. 3.50d, Vrsac. 5.60d, Travnik. 8d, Dubrovnik.

Perf. 13½, 13¼x12½ (#1487), 13¼ (#1486A)

1978-81
1482 A263   5p deep orange   .40 .25
1483 A263   10p brown   .40 .40
1483A A263   20p purple ('78)   .80 .55
1484 A263   30p olive gray   .40 .25
1485 A263   35p brown red   .80 .55
1486 A263   40p gray   .40 .25
1486A A263   60p purple   .40 .25
1487 A323   2.50d rose red   .80 .25
1488 A323   2.50d bl gray ('81) .35 .25
1489 A323   3.50d red org ('81) .25 .25
1490 A323   5.60d gray grn ('81) .25 .25
1491 A323   8d gray ('81)   .25 .25
     Nos. 1482-1491 (12)   5.50 3.75

No. 1483A has all three numerals in denomination the same size. On No. 1065 "20" is taller than first "0."

Perf. 13¼x12½
1482a A263   5p   1.25 .25
1483b A263   10p   .60   .60
1483Ac A263   20p   .80   .55
1484a A263   30p   .80   .40
1485a A263   35p   1.25   .80
1486b A263   40p   .55   .25
1486Ac A263   60p   .55   .40
1487a A323   2.50d   .50   .25
1488a A323   2.50d   .25   .25
1489a A323   3.50d   .25   .25
1490a A323   5.60d   .25   .25
1491a A323   8d   .60   .25
     Nos. 1482a-14891a (12)   7.65 4.50

400th Anniversary of Lipica Stud Farm — A425

1980, June 25
1493 A425 2.50d black   .25 .25

A426

1980, June 27   Perf. 13½
1494 A426 2.50d magenta & red   .25 .25
Tito, Basic Law of Self-management, 30th anniv.

A427

1980, June 28   Perf. 13
1495 A427 2.50d light green   .25 .25
University of Novi Sad, 20th anniv.

Mljet National Park — A428

1980, Sept. 5   Photo.   Perf. 14
1496 A428 4.90d shown   .25 .25
1497 A428 13d Galicica Natl.
          Park   .25 .25
European Nature Protection Year.

Minerals — A429

1980, Sept. 10   Litho.   Perf. 13½
1498 A429 2.50d Pyrrhotine   .35 .35
1499 A429 3.40d Dolomite   .35 .35
1500 A429 4.90d Sphalerite   .35 .35
1501 A429 13d Wulfenite   .80 .80
     Nos. 1498-1501 (4)   1.85 1.85

No. 1244 Surcharged with New Value and Bars

1980, Oct. 15   Litho.   Perf. 13
1502 A323 5d on 75p purple   2.00 .25

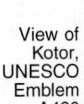

View of Kotor, UNESCO Emblem A430

1980, Sept. 23   Perf. 13½
1503 A430 4.90d multicolored   .25 .25
21st UNESCO General Conf., Belgrade,

Children in Garden A431

Joy of Europe Children's Festival: 13d, 3 faces.

1980, Oct. 2   Perf. 13½x13
1504 A431 4.90d multi   .25 .25
1505 A431 13d multi   .35 .35

Dove over Madrid Meeting Hall — A432

Lithographed and Engraved
1980, Nov. 11   Perf. 13½
1506 A432 4.90d dk grn & bl grn   .25 .25
1507 A432 13d dk brn & yel
          brown   .40 .40
European Security Conference, Madrid.

Federal Flag of Yugoslavia A433

Republic Day: Socialist Republic flags. Nos. 1508-1515 se-tenant. No. 1511 has Latin letters.

1980, Nov. 28   Litho.   Perf. 12½
1508 A433 2.50d Bosnia & Her-
          zegovina   .25 .25
1509 A433 2.50d Croatia   .25 .25
1510 A433 2.50d shown   .25 .25
1511 A433 2.50d Yugoslavia   .25 .25
1512 A433 2.50d Macedonia   .25 .25
1513 A433 2.50d Montenegro   .25 .25
1514 A433 2.50d Serbia   .25 .25
1515 A433 2.50d Slovenia   .25 .25
     Nos. 1508-1515 (8)   2.00 2.00

Woman with Straw Hat — A434

Paintings: 3.40d, Atelier No. 1, by Gabriel Stupica. 4.90d, To the Glory of the Sutjeska Fighters, by Ismet Mujezinovic. 8d, Serenity, by Marino Tartaglia. 13d, Complaint, by Milos Vuskovic.

1980, Dec. 16   Perf. 13½
1516 A434 2.50d multi   .25 .25
1517 A434 3.40d multi   .25 .25
1518 A434 4.90d multi   .25 .25
1519 A434 8d multi, vert.   .25 .25
1520 A434 13d multi, vert.   .80 .80
     Nos. 1516-1520 (5)   1.80 1.80

Ivan Ribar (1881-1968), Politician — A435

1981, Jan. 21   Litho.   Perf. 13½
1521 A435 2.50d rose red & blk   .25 .25

Cementusa Hand Bomb A436

Partisan Weapons: 5.60d, Rifle. 8d, 52-mm Cannon. 13d, Man-powered tank.

1981, Feb. 16
1522 A436 3.50d brick red & blk   .25 .25
1523 A436 5.60d grn & blk   .25 .25
1524 A436 8d bis brn & blk   .25 .25
1525 A436 13d rose vio & blk   .50 .50
     Nos. 1522-1525 (4)   1.25 1.25

Monastery of the Virgin, Eleousa, 900th Anniversary A437

1981, Mar. 3
1526 A437 3.50d multicolored   1.10 1.10
Exists imperf. Value $35.

36th World Table Tennis Championship, Novi Sad, Apr. 14-26 — A438

1981, Apr. 14   Litho.   Perf. 13½
1527 A438 8d multicolored   .25 .25
Exists imperf.

Europa Issue

Wedding in Herzegovina, by Nikola Arsenovic A439

Paintings by Nikola Arsenovic (1823-85): 13d, Witnesses at a Wedding.

1981, May 5   Photo.   Perf. 12
Granite Paper
1528 A439 8d multicolored   .30 .25
1529 A439 13d multicolored   .30 .25

Dimitrije Tucovic and Slavija Square, Belgrade A440

1981, May 13   Litho.   Perf. 13½
1530 A440 3.50d bl vio & red   .25 .25
Tucovic (1881-1914), Socialist leader. Exists imperf.

Marshal Tito, by Milivoje Unkovic — A441

1981, May 25　　Photo.　　Perf. 11½x12
Granite Paper
1531　A441　3.50d gold & dk brn　　.40　.40
Marshal Tito's 89th birth anniversary. Exists imperf.

Sunflower — A442

1981, May 28　　Photo.　　Perf. 11½
Granite Paper
1532　A442　3.50d shown　　　　.25　.25
1533　A442　5.60d Hops　　　　.25　.25
1534　A442　　8d Corn　　　　.30　.25
1535　A442　13d Wheat　　　　.55　.35
　　Nos. 1532-1535 (4)　　1.35　1.10
Exist imperf.

3rd Autonomous Enterprises Cong. — A443

1981, June 16　　Litho.　　Perf. 13½
1536　A443　3.50d multicolored　　.25　.25

Djordje Petrov (1864-1921), Macedonian Revolutionary A444

1981, June 22
1537　A444　3.50d bister & black　　.25　.25

National Insurrection, 40th Anniv. A445

1981, July 4　　　　　　Perf. 12½
1538　A445　3.50d red org & tan　　.25　.25
1539　A445　　8d red org & tan　　.25　.25

Souvenir Sheet
Imperf
1540　A445　30d Tito monument　1.25　1.25

800th Anniv. of Varazdin A446

1981, Aug. 20　　Litho.　　Perf. 13½
1541　A446　3.50d multicolored　　.25　.25

Parliament Building, Belgrade — A447

1981, Sept. 1
1542　A447　8d red & blue　　　.25　.25
Belgrade Conference of Non-Aligned Countries, 20th anniv.

Serbian Printing Office, 150th Anniv. A448

1981, Sept. 15
1543　A448　3.50d pale rose & dk bl　.25　.25

Fran Levstik (1831-1887), Writer A449

1981, Sept. 28　　　　　Perf. 12x11½
1544　A449　3.50d dl red & gray　　.25　.25

No. 1251 Surcharged with New Value and Bars

1981, Oct.　　　　　　　Perf. 13
1545　A323　5d on 4.90d dl bl　　.80　.25
　　a.　Perf. 13x12½　　　1.60　.40

Joy of Europe Children's Festival A450

1981, Oct. 2
1546　A450　8d Barnyard　　　.25　.25
1547　A450　13d Skiers　　　.25　.25

125th Anniv. of European Danube Commission — A451

8d, Tugboat Karlovac. 13d, Train hauling boat, Sip Canal.
1981, Oct. 28　　Litho.　　Perf. 13½
1548　A451　8d multicolored　　.25　.25
1549　A451　13d multicolored　　.70　.70
Nos. 1548-1549 exist imperf. Value, set $75.

No. 1250a Surcharged with New Value and Bars

1981, Oct. 9　　Litho.　　Perf. 13x12½
1550　A323　3.50d on 3.40d gray
　　　　　　　　grn　　　1.75　.30
　　a.　　on #1250　　　.40　.25

Savings Bank of Yugoslavia, 60th Anniv. — A452

1981, Oct. 31　　　　　Perf. 11½x12
1551　A452　3.50d multicolored　　.25　.25

Intl. Inventions Conference A453

1981, Nov. 4　　　　　　Perf. 13½
1552　A453　8d red & gold　　　.25　.25

Nature Protection — A454

8d, Plant, Ruguvo Gorge. 13d, Lynx, Prokletjie Mountains.
1981, Nov. 14
1553　A454　8d multicolored　　.25　.25
1554　A454　13d multicolored　　.75　.75

August Senoa (1838-1881), Writer — A455

1981, Dec. 12　　　　　Perf. 11½x12
1555　A455　3.50d dl gray vio & gldn
　　　　　　　brn　　　　　.25　.25

Still Life with a Fish, by Jovan Bijelic (1886-1964) — A456

Paintings of Animals: 5.60d, Raven, by Milo Milunovic (1897-1967). 8d, Bird on Blue Background, by Marko Celebonovic (b. 1902). 10d, Horses, by Peter Lubarda (1907-1974). 13d, Sheep, by Nikola Masic (1852-1902).

1981, Dec. 29　　Photo.　　Perf. 13½
1556　A456　3.50d multi　　　.25　.25
1557　A456　5.60d multi　　　.25　.25
1558　A456　　8d multi　　　.25　.25
1559　A456　10d multi　　　.25　.25
1560　A456　13d multi　　　.55　.55
　　Nos. 1556-1560 (5)　1.55　1.55

40th Anniv. of Foca Regulations A457

1982, Jan 14　　Litho.　　Perf. 13½
1561　A457　3.50d Mosa Pijade　　.25　.25

60th Anniv. of Communist Newspaper Borba A458

1982, Feb. 19　　　　　　　Litho.
1562　A458　3.50d red & blk　　.25　.25

500th Anniv. of City of Cetinje — A459

1982, Mar. 10
1563　A459　3.50d dull red brn　　.25　.25

Capt. Ivo Visin (1806-1868), Boka Kotorska's Map — A460

1982, May 5　　Photo.　　Perf. 11½
1564　A460　8d shown　　　　.40　.40
1565　A460　15d Ship Splendido　.40　.40
Europa, 1st Yugoslavian circumnavigation, 1852-1859.

Male House Sparrow A461

5.60d, Female house sparrow. 8d, Male field sparrow. 15d, Female field sparrow.

1982, May 24　　Litho.　　Perf. 13½
1566　A461　3.50d shown　　　.25　.25
1567　A461　5.60d multicolored　.25　.25
1568　A461　　8d multicolored　.25　.25
1569　A461　15d multicolored　2.40　2.40
　　Nos. 1566-1569 (4)　3.15　3.15
See Nos. 1687-1690.

90th Birth Anniv. of Marshal Tito — A462

1982, May 25　　Photo.　　Perf. 11½x12
Granite Paper
1570　A462　3.50d multicolored　　.25　.25

1982 World
Cup — A463

Designs: Soccer ball in various positions.

1982, June 12   **Perf. 11½**
Granite Paper

1571		Sheet of 4	1.60	1.60
a.	A463	3.50d multicolored	.25	.25
b.	A463	5.60d multicolored	.25	.25
c.	A463	8d multicolored	.25	.25
d.	A463	15d multicolored	.25	.25

12th
Congress of
Yugoslavian
Communists'
League,
Belgrade,
June 26-29
A464

1982 June 26   **Litho.**   **Perf. 13½**

1572	A464	3.50d orange & red	.25	.25
1573	A464	8d gray & red	.25	.25

Souvenir Sheet
Perf. 12½

1574		Sheet of 2	.80	.80
a.	A464	10d like 3.50d	.25	.25
b.	A464	20d like 8d	.55	.55

Exists imperf. Value $250.

Dura Jaksic
(1832-1878),
Writer, Painter
A465

1982, July 27   **Litho.**   **Perf. 14**
1575 A465 3.50d Self-portrait   .25 .25

1982 World Championships Held in
Yugoslavia — A466

1982, July 30   **Perf. 13½**

1576	A466	8d Gymnastics	.80	.25
1577	A466	8d Kayak	.80	.25
1578	A466	8d Weightlifting	.80	.25
		Nos. 1576-1578 (3)	2.40	.75

Ivan Zajc (1832-
1914), Composer
and Conductor
A467

1982, Aug. 3
1579 A467 4d brown   .25 .25

Breguet
XIX and
Potez XXV
A468

6.10d, Super Galeb G-4. 8.80d, Armed
boat. 15d, Rocket gun boat.

1982, Sept. 1   **Litho.**   **Perf. 13½**

1580	A468	4d shown	.25	.25
1581	A468	6.10d multicolored	.25	.25
1582	A468	8.80d multicolored	.25	.25
1583	A468	15d multicolored	.50	.50
		Nos. 1580-1583 (4)	1.25	1.25

40th anniv. of Air Force/Anti-aircraft
Defense and Navy.

Spruce
Branch,
Tara
Natl.
Park
A469

15d, Mediterranean monk seal, Kornati.

1982, Sept. 3

1584	A469	8.80d shown	.25	.25
1585	A469	15d multicolored	.60	.60

14th Joy of Europe Children's
Festival — A470

1982, Oct. 2

1586	A470	8.80d Traffic	.25	.25
1587	A470	15d In the Bath	.55	.55

Small
Onofrio's
Fountain,
15th Cent.
A471

1982, Oct. 23
1588 A471 8.80d multi   .25 .25

16th Universal Federation of Travel Agents'
Assoc. Cong., Dubrovnik, Oct. 24-30.

600th Anniv.
of
Hercegnovi
A472

1982, Oct. 28
1589 A472 4d multicolored   .50 .50

14th Winter
Olympic
Games,
Sarajevo,
Feb. 8-19,
1984 — A473

4d, Bridge, Miljacka River. 6.10d, Minaret,
Mosque. 8.80d, Evangelical Church. 15d,
Street.

1982, Nov. 20   **Perf. 12½**

1590	A473	4d multicolored	.25	.25
1591	A473	6.10d multicolored	.25	.25
1592	A473	8.80d multicolored	.50	.50
1593	A473	15d multicolored	1.10	1.10
		Nos. 1590-1593 (4)	2.10	2.10

**Nos. 1488a and 1489a Surcharged
In Red, Blue, Black or Red Violet
with Two Bars or Shield**

1982-83   **Litho.**   **Perf. 13x12½**

1594	A323	30p on 2.50d (R)	.50	.25
1595	A323	50p on 2.50d (Bl)	1.20	.25
1596	A323	60p on 2.50d ('83)	.50	.25

1597	A323	1d on 3.50d	.25	.25
1597A	A323	2d on 2.50d (RV)	1.60	.25
		Nos. 1594-1597A (5)	4.05	1.25

Perf. 13

1594a	A323	30p on #1488	.40	.25
1595a	A323	50p on #1488	.25	.25
1596a	A323	60p on #1488	1.00	.25
1597b	A323	1d on #1489	.65	.25
		Nos. 1594a-1597b (4)	2.30	1.00

Types of 1971-77

Designs: 3d, Skofja Loka. 4d, Pocitelj. 5d,
Osijek. 6.10d, like 2.10d. 8.80d, Hercegnovi.
10d, Sarajevo. 16.50d, Ohrid.

1982-83   **Litho.**   **Perf. 13x12½**

1598	A323	3d gray bl	.25	.25
1599	A263	4d red org	.25	.25
1600	A263	5d grnsh bl ('83)	.40	.25
1601	A323	6.10d olive grn	.60	.25
1602	A263	8.80d gray	.40	.25

Perf. 13½

1603	A263	10d red lil ('83)	.25	.25
1603A	A323	16.50d dl bl ('83)	.25	.25
		Nos. 1598-1603A (7)	2.40	1.75

Type styles of Nos. 1600, 1603-1603A differ
somewhat from illustrations.
No. 1600 exists imperf. Value $35.

Perf. 13

1598a	A323	3d	.50	.25
1599a	A323	4d	.50	.25
1600a	A323	5d	.40	.25
1601a	A323	6.10d	.80	.25
1602a	A323	8.80d	1.20	.25
1603b	A323	10d	1.10	.25
1603c	A323	16.50d	1.25	.30
		Nos. 1598a-1603c (7)	5.75	1.80

40th Anniv.
of Anti-
Fascist
Council
A474

1982, Nov. 26   **Perf. 13½**
1604 A474 4d Bihac, 1942   .25 .25

The Manuscript, by Janez Bernik (b.
1933) — A475

4d, Prophet on Golden Background, by Joze
Ciuha (b. 1924). 6.10d, Journey to the West,
by Andrej Jemec (b. 1934). 8.80d, Black Comb
with Red Band, by Riko Debenjak (b. 1908).
15d, The Vitrine, by Adriana Maraz (b. 1931).

1982, Nov. 27

1605	A475	4d multi, vert.	.25	.25
1606	A475	6.10d multi, vert.	.25	.25
1607	A475	8.80d multi, vert.	.25	.25
1608	A475	10d multi	.25	.25
1609	A475	15d multi	.55	.55
		Nos. 1605-1609 (5)	1.55	1.55

Uros Predic
(1857-1953),
Painter — A476

1982, Dec. 7
1610 A476 4d multicolored   .25 .25

Union of Pioneers,
40th Anniv. — A477

1982, Dec. 27   **Perf. 12**
1611 A477 4d multicolored   .25 .25

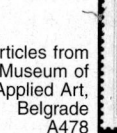

Articles from
Museum of
Applied Art,
Belgrade
A478

Designs: 4d, Lead pitcher, Gnjilane, 16th
cent. 6.10d, Silver-plated jug, Macedonia, 18th
cent. 8.80d, Goblet, 16th cent., Dalmatia. 15d,
Mortar, 15th cent., Kotor.

1983, Feb. 19

1612	A478	4d multicolored	.25	.25
1613	A478	6.10d multicolored	.25	.25
1614	A478	8.80d multicolored	.25	.25
1615	A478	15d multicolored	.40	.30
		Nos. 1612-1615 (4)	1.15	1.05

Mount
Jalovec — A479

1983, Feb. 26
1616 A479 4d blue & lt bl   .25 .25

Slovenian Mountaineering Soc., 90th anniv.

Serbian
Telephone
Service
Centenary
A480

1983, Mar. 15
1617 A480 3d Ericsson phone   .25 .25

25th Anniv. of
Intl. Org. for
Maritime
Navigation
(OMI) — A481

1983, Mar. 17   **Perf. 13½x14**
1618 A481 8.80d multi   .25 .25

Edible
Mushrooms
A482

4d, Agaricus campestris. 6.10d, Morchella
vulgaris. 8.80d, Boletus edulis. 15d,
Cantharellus cibarius.

1983, Mar. 21   **Perf. 14**

1619	A482	4d multi	.30	.30
1620	A482	6.10d multi	.30	.30
1621	A482	8.80d multi	.30	.30
1622	A482	15d multi	1.20	1.20
		Nos. 1619-1622 (4)	2.10	2.10

Rijeka Railway, 110th Anniv. — A483

No. 1623, Steam engine series 401. No. 1624, Thyristor locomotive 442.

1983, Apr. 5
1623	A483	4d multi	.25	.25
1624	A483	23.70d on 8.80d multi	.50	.50

No. 1624 not issued without surcharge.

Boro and Ramiz Monument, Landovica A484

1983, Apr. 10
1625	A484	4d multi	.25	.25

Boro Vukmirovic and Ramiz Sadiku, revolutionary martyrs, 40th death anniv.

Ivo Andric (1892-1975), Poet, 1961 Nobel Prize Winner A485

8.80d, Medal, Travnik Chronicle text. 20d, Portrait, Bridge, Drina River.

1983, May 5   Photo.   Perf. 11½
Granite Paper
1626	A485	8.80d multicolored	.40	.40
1627	A485	20d multicolored	.40	.40

Europa.

50th Intl. Agricultural Fair, Novi Sad — A486

1983, May 13   Litho.   Perf. 14
1628	A486	4d Combine harvester	.25	.25

40th Anniv. of Battle of Sutjeska A487

3d, Assault, by Pivo Karamatijevic.

1983, May 14   Perf. 12½
1629	A487	3d multicolored	.25	.25

A488

1983, May 25   Perf. 13½
1630	A488	4d Tito, Parliament	.25	.25
a.		Perf. 12½	1.00	1.00

30th anniv. of election of Pres. Tito.

A489

4d, First mail and passenger car. 16.50d, Mountain road, Kotor.

1983, May 27
1631	A489	4d multi	.25	.25
1632	A489	16.50d multi	.25	.25

80th anniv. of automobile service in Montenegro.

A490

1983, June 5   Perf. 14
1633	A490	23.70d multi	.25	.25

UN Conference on Trade and Development, 6th session, Belgrade, June 6-30.

Engraving by Valvasor — A491

1983, June 7   Perf. 12½
1634	A491	4d multicolored	.25	.25

Town of Pazin millennium.

Triumphal Arch, Titograd A492

100d, Memorial to S. Filipovic, Valjevo, vert.

1983, June 9   Perf. 12½
1635	A492	100d multicolored	2.50	.25
a.		Perf. 13x13½	1.40	.25
1636	A492	200d shown	2.00	.95
a.		Perf. 13½x13	3.75	.95

Skopje Earthquake, 20th Anniv. — A493

1983, July 26   Litho.   Perf. 12½
1637	A493	23.70d deep magenta	.25	.25
a.		Perf. 13½	.80	.45

For surcharge, see No. 1715.

Sculpture by Ivan Mestrovic — A494

1983, Aug. 15
1638	A494	6d multicolored	.25	.25

European Nature Protection — A495

16.50d, Gentian, Kopaonik National Park. 23.70d, Chamois, Perucica Gorge.

1983, Sept. 10   Litho.   Perf. 13
1639	A495	16.50d multi	.35	.35
1640	A495	23.70d multi	.65	.65

See Nos. 1685-1686.

Joy of Europe — A496

Children's Paintings: 16.50d, Bride and Bridegroom by Verna Paunkonik. 23.70d, Andres and his Mother by Marta Lopez-Ibor.

1983, Oct. 3   Litho.   Perf. 13½
1641	A496	16.50d multi	.25	.25
1642	A496	23.70d multi	.65	.65

A497

1983, Oct. 17   Litho.   Perf. 12½
1643	A497	5d multicolored	.25	.25

Kragujevac High School sesquicentenary.

A498

1983, Oct. 17   Litho.   Perf. 13½
1644	A498	5d multicolored	.25	.25

Timok Uprising centenary.

14th Winter Olympic Games, Sarajevo, Feb. 8-19, 1984 A499

1983, Nov. 25   Engr.   Perf. 13½
1645	A499	4d Ski jump	.25	.25
1646	A499	4d Slalom	.25	.25
1647	A499	16.50d Bobsledding	.25	.25
1648	A499	16.50d Downhill skiing	.25	.25
1649	A499	23.70d Speed skating	.50	.50
1650	A499	23.70d Hockey	.50	.50
		Nos. 1645-1650 (6)	2.00	2.00

Souvenir Sheet
Imperf
1651	A499	50d Emblem	1.75	1.75

Nos. 1645-1651 exist imperf.

Jovan Jovanovic Zmaj (1833-1904), Poet, Neven Masthead A500

1983, Nov. 24   Litho.   Perf. 12½
1652	A500	5d multicolored	.25	.25

Peasant Wedding, by Pieter Brueghel A501

Paintings: No. 1654, Susanna with the Old Men, by the "Master of the Prodigal Son." No. 1655, Allegory of Wisdom and Strength, by Paolo Veronese (1528-1588). No. 1656, Virgin Mary from Salamanca, by Robert Campin (1375-1444). No. 1657, St. Ann with Madonna and Jesus, by Albrecht Dürer (1471-1528).

1983, Nov. 26   Perf. 14
1653	A501	4d multi	.25	.25
1654	A501	16.50d multi	.25	.25
1655	A501	16.50d multi	.25	.25
1656	A501	23.70d multi	.55	.55
1657	A501	23.70d multi	.80	.80
		Nos. 1653-1657 (5)	2.10	2.10

View of Jajce — A502

1983, Nov. 28   Perf. 13x12½
1658	A502	5d multicolored	.25	.25

Souvenir Sheet
Imperf
1659	A502	30d Tito	.80	.80

40th anniv. of Second Session of the Antifascist Council of the Natl. Liberation of Yugoslavia, Jajce, Nov. 29-30.

World Communications Year — A503

1983, Dec. 10   Perf. 13½
1660	A503	23.70d multi	.25	.25

Koco Racin (1908-1943), Writer — A504

1983, Dec. 22
1661	A504	5d multicolored	.25	.25

Politika Front Page, Oct. 28, 1944 — A505

1984, Jan. 25   Litho.   Perf. 12½
1662	A505	5d red & black	.25	.25

80th anniv. of Politika newspaper and 40th anniv. in Yugoslavia.

Veljko Petrovic (1884-1967), Poet — A506

1984, Feb. 4   Litho.   Perf. 13½
1663	A506	5d multicolored	.25	.25

1984
Winter
Olympics
A507

1984, Feb. 8
1664	A507	4d	Biathlon	.25 .25
1665	A507	4d	Giant slalom	.25 .25
1666	A507	5d	Bobsledding	.25 .25
1667	A507	5d	Slalom	.25 .25
1668	A507	16.50d	Speed skating	.25 .25
1669	A507	16.50d	Hockey	.25 .25
1670	A507	23.70d	Ski jumping	.25 .25
1671	A507	23.70d	Downhill skiing	.25 .25

Nos. 1664-1671 (8)   2.00 2.00

Souvenir Sheets
Imperf

1672	A507	50d	Flame, rings	1.40 1.40
1673	A507	100d	Flame, map	2.75 2.75

No. 1664-1671 exist imperf.

Natl. Heroines
A508

Designs: a, Marija Bursac (1902-43). b, Jelena Cetkovic (1916-43). c, Nada Dimic (1923-42). d, Elpida Karamandi (1920-42). e, Toncka Cec Olga (1896-1943). f, Spasenija Babovic Cana (1907-77). g, Jovanka Radivojevic Kica (1922-43). h, Sonja Marinkovic (1916-41).

1984, Mar. 8   **Litho.**   **Perf. 14**
1674   Sheet of 8 + label   3.50 3.50
   a.-h.   A508 5d any single   .25 .25

Slovenia
Monetary
Institute,
40th Anniv.
A509

1984, Mar. 12   **Perf. 12½**
1675 A509 5d Bond, note   .25 .25

Railroad Service in Serbia (Belgrade-Nis) Centenary — A510

5d, Train, Central Belgrade Station.

1984, Apr. 9   **Perf. 13**
1676 A510 5d multicolored   .25 .25

Jure Franko,
Giant Slalom
Silver Medalist,
1984 — A511

1984, Apr. 28
1677 A511 23.70d multi   .80 .80
Yugoslavia's first Winter Olympic medalist.

Europa (1959-84)
A512

1984, Apr. 30   **Perf. 13½**
1678	A512	23.70d	multi	.40 .40
1679	A512	50d	multi	.80 .80

1984 Summer
Olympics, Los
Angeles
A513

1984, May 14
1680	A513	5d	Basketball	.55 .55
1681	A513	16.50d	Diving	.55 .55
1682	A513	23.70d	Equestrian	.55 .55
1683	A513	50d	Running	2.00 2.00

Nos. 1680-1683 (4)   3.65 3.65

Marshal
Tito — A514

1984, May 25   **Perf. 13**
1684 A514 5d brown red   .25 .25

Nature Type of 1983

Designs: 26d, Centaurea gloriosa (flower), Biokovo Mountain Park. 40d, Anophthalmus (insect), Pekel Cave, Savinja Valley.

1984, June 11   **Litho.**   **Perf. 13½**
1685	A495	26d	multicolored	.50 .25
1686	A495	40d	multicolored	.80 .40

Bird Type of 1982

4d, Great black-backed gull. 5d, Black-headed gull. 16.50d, Herring gull. 40d, Common tern.

1984, June 28
1687	A461	4d	multicolored	.40 .40
1688	A461	5d	multicolored	.40 .40
1689	A461	16.50d	multicolored	.40 .40
1690	A461	40d	multicolored	3.50 1.50

Nos. 1687-1690 (4)   4.70 2.70

19th Cent.
Cradles
A515

1984, Sept. 1   **Litho.**   **Perf. 12½**
1691	A515	4d	Bosnia & Herzegovina	.25 .25
1692	A515	5d	Montenegro	.25 .25
1693	A515	26d	Macedonia	.40 .40
1694	A515	40d	Serbia	.65 .65

Nos. 1691-1694 (4)   1.55 1.55

Olive Tree,
Mirovica
A516

1984, Sept. 1
1695 A516 5d multi   .25 .25

Joy of
Europe — A517

Children's Drawings: 26d, Traditional costumes. 40d, Girl with doll carriage.

1984, Oct. 2   **Litho.**   **Perf. 14**
1696	A517	26d	multicolored	.35 .35
1697	A517	40d	multicolored	.90 .90

City of
Virovitica,
750th
Anniv.
A518

5d, Engraving, 17th cent.

1984, Oct. 4   **Perf. 13½**
1698 A518 5d multicolored   .25 .25

Map, Concentric
Waves — A519

1984, Oct. 10
1699 A519 6d Prus bl & brt grn   .25 .25
Radio and telegraph service in Montenegro, 80th anniv.

Veterans
Conference
A520

1984, Oct. 18
1700	A520	26d	multicolored	.90 .90
1701	A520	40d	multicolored	1.20 1.20

Conf. of Veterans on Security, Disarmament & Cooperation in Europe, Belgrade, 10/18-20.

Liberation of
Belgrade, 40th
Anniv. — A521

1984, Oct. 20
1702 A521 6d "40," arms   .25 .25

Miloje Milojevic
(1884-1946),
Composer
A522

1984, Oct. 27
1703 A522 6d Portrait, score   .25 .25

Medals Events,
1984 Summer
Olympics
A522a

Designs: a, Wrestling. b, Running. c, Field hockey. d, Shot put. e, Soccer. f, Basketball. g, Netball. h, Rowing.

1984, Nov. 14   **Litho.**   **Perf. 13½**
1704   Sheet of 8   4.00 4.00
   a.-h.   A522a 26d any single   .25 .25

The Tahitians, by Gauguin — A523

Paintings by Foreign Artists in Yugoslav Museums: 6d, Portrait of Madame Tatichek, by Ferdinand Waldmuller (1793-1865). No. 1706, The Bathers, by Renoir (1841-1919). No. 1707, At the Window, by Henri Matisse (1869-1954). 40d, Ballerinas, by Edgar Degas (1834-1917).

Perf. 13½x14, 14x13½
1984, Nov. 15
1705	A523	6d	multi, vert.	.25 .25
1706	A523	26d	multi, vert.	.25 .25
1707	A523	26d	multi, vert.	.25 .25
1708	A523	38d	multi	.50 .50
1709	A523	40d	multi	.80 .80

Nos. 1705-1709 (5)   2.05 2.05

Nova
Macedonia
Newspaper,
40th Anniv.
A523a

1984, Nov. 29   **Perf. 13½**
1710 A523a 6d 1st & recent editions   .25 .25

Nos. 1602, 1599 and
1637 Surcharged in
Red Brown or Black

Types of 1975 and

Exhibition
Center,
Zagreb
A524

Bird, Jet,
Landscape
A525

Designs: 6d, Kikinda. 26d, Korcula. 38d, Maribor. 70d, Trumpeter monument, riverside buildings in Zagreb. 1000d, bird, tail of jet on airfield.

Perf. 13½x12½, 13 (#1713, 1717), 12½ (#1715)
1984-86   **Litho.**
1711	A263	2d on 8.80d	1.75	1.75
a.		on #1602a	.40	.25
1712	A263	6d on 4d (RBr)	.40	.25
a.		on #1599a	.55	.40
1713	A323	6d lt red brn	.40	.25
a.		Perf. 13x12½	.80	.25
1715	A493	20d on 23.70d	.40	.25
1717	A263	26d dp ultra	.40	.25
a.		Perf. 13x12½	.50	.25

1718	A323	38d dp lil rose	1.60	.25
a.		Perf. 13	.40	.25
1719	A323	70d brt ultra ('85)	1.25	.55
b.		Perf. 13	.55	.45

Perf. 14

| 1719A | A524 | 100d brt org yel & vio | .65 | .35 |

Perf. 12½

1720	A525	500d redsh brn & multi ('85)	3.75	1.40
a.		Perf. 13¼	1.75	.65
1721	A525	1000d org brn & multi ('85)	5.50	2.90
a.		Perf. 13½	2.10	1.25
	Nos. 1711-1721 (10)		16.10	8.20

Type styles for Nos. 1717-1718 differ somewhat from illustration.
For surcharge, see No. 1973.

Museum
Exhibits -
Fossils
A526

5d, Aturia aturi. 6d, Pachyophis woodwardi.
33d, Chaetodon hoeferi. 60d, Homo sapiens
neanderthalensis.

1985, Feb. 4   Litho.   Perf. 12½

1722	A526	5d multi	.25	.25
1723	A526	6d multi	.25	.25
1724	A526	33d multi	.40	.40
1725	A526	60d multi	.90	.90
	Nos. 1722-1725 (4)		1.80	1.80

40th Anniv.,
Monument
Protection
A527

1985, Feb. 20   Litho.   Perf. 12½

| 1726 | A527 | 6d Hopovo church | .25 | .25 |

Ski Jumping at
Planica, 50th
Anniv. — A528

1985, Mar. 15   Litho.   Perf. 13½

| 1727 | A528 | 6d Three herons in flight | 4.75 | 2.40 |

European Nature
Conservation
A529

1985, Mar. 30   Perf. 14

| 1728 | A529 | 42d Pandion haliaetus | 1.25 | .80 |
| 1729 | A529 | 60d Upupa epops | 2.40 | 1.25 |

Audubon birth bicentenary, European Information Center for Nature Protection.

A530

Fresco of St. Methodius, St. Naum Monastery, Ohrid.

1985, Apr. 6   Litho.   Perf. 11½x12

| 1730 | A530 | 10d multicolored | 1.75 | .80 |

St. Methodius (d. 885), archbishop of Pannonia and Moravia.

A531

1985, Apr. 16   Litho.   Perf. 12½

| 1731 | A531 | 6d Clasped hands | .25 | .25 |

Osimo Agreements, 10th anniv. Yugoslavia-Italy political and economic cooperation.

Josip
Slavenski
(1896-1955),
Composer
A532

Europa: 60d, Portrait, block flute, darabukka. 80d, Balkanophonia score, signature.

1985, Apr. 29   Perf. 14

| 1732 | A532 | 60d multi | .40 | .40 |
| 1733 | A532 | 80d multi | .80 | .80 |

Joachim
Vujic, by
Dimitrije
Avramovic
(1815-1855)
A533

1985, May 8   Perf. 12x11½

| 1734 | A533 | 10d multi | .25 | .25 |

Joachim Vujic Theater, Kragujevac, 150th anniv.

Liberation from German Occupation
Forces, 40th Anniv. — A534

1985, May 9   Perf. 13½

| 1735 | A534 | 10d shown | .25 | .25 |
| 1736 | A534 | 10d Order of Natl. Liberation | .25 | .25 |

Franjo Kluz
(1912-1944), Rudi
Cajavec (1911-
1942), Breguet-19
Fighter — A535

1985, May 21   Perf. 13x12½

| 1737 | A535 | 10d multi | .25 | .25 |

Air Force Day.

Pres. Tito (1892-
1980)
A536

1985, May 25   Perf. 13½

| 1738 | A536 | 10d Portrait | .50 | .25 |

Cres-Losinj
Municipal
Tourism Bureau,
Cent. — A537

1985, June 12

| 1739 | A537 | 10d Map, town arms, villa | .65 | .65 |

UN 40th
Anniv. — A538

1985, June 26   Litho.   Perf. 12½

| 1740 | A538 | 70d Emblem, rainbow | .25 | .25 |

Rowing — A539

1985, June 29   Litho.   Perf. 13½

| 1741 | A539 | 70d multicolored | .40 | .40 |

Souvenir Sheet

| 1742 | A539 | 100d Course map, arms | 1.40 | 1.40 |

Intl. European-Danube Rowing Regatta, 30th anniv.

Nautical
Tourism — A540

1985, July 1   Litho.

1743	A540	8d Sailboat	.80	.80
1744	A540	10d Windsurfing	.80	.80
1745	A540	50d Sailboat, diff.	.80	.80
1746	A540	70d Sailboat, diff.	2.50	2.50
	Nos. 1743-1746 (4)		4.90	4.90

F1B Class
Motorized
Model Plane
A541

1985, Aug. 10   Litho.   Perf. 12½x13

| 1747 | A541 | 70d multicolored | .50 | .40 |

Free Flight World Championships, Livno, Aug. 12-18.

Algae — A542

8d, Corallina officinalis. 10d, Desmarestia viridis. 50d, Fucus vesiculosus. 70d, Padina pavonia.

1985, Sept. 20   Perf. 14

1748	A542	8d multicolored	.25	.25
1749	A542	10d multicolored	.25	.25
1750	A542	50d multicolored	.30	.30
1751	A542	70d multicolored	1.50	1.50
	Nos. 1748-1751 (4)		2.30	2.30

Intl. Federation of Stomatologists, 73rd
Congress, Belgrade, Sept. 21-
28 — A543

1985, Sept. 21   Perf. 12x11½

| 1752 | A543 | 70d multicolored | .40 | .40 |

Children's
Drawings
A544

Designs: 50d, Children in a Horse-drawn Cart, by Branka Lukic, age 14, Yugoslavia. 70d, Children in Field, by Suzanne Straathof, age 9, Netherlands.

1985, Oct. 2   Perf. 14

| 1753 | A544 | 50d multicolored | .40 | .40 |
| 1754 | A544 | 70d multicolored | 1.25 | 1.25 |

Croatian
Natl.
Theater,
Zagreb,
125th Anniv.
A545

1985, Nov. 23   Perf. 12½

| 1755 | A545 | 10d Facade detail | .25 | .25 |

Miladin
Popovic — A546

1985, Nov. 26   Perf. 11½x12

| 1756 | A546 | 10d Portrait | .25 | .25 |

Popovic (1910-1945), revolutionary.

Natl. Coat of Arms — A547

1985, Nov. 28   **Perf. 13½**
1757 A547 10d multicolored .25 .25

Souvenir Sheet
Imperf
1758 A547 100d multicolored 1.00 1.00

Socialist Federal Republic of Yugoslavia, 40th anniv. No. 1758 contains one stamp 18x27mm.

Royal Procession, by Iromie Wijewardena, Sri Lanka — A548

Paintings from the Art Gallery of Non-aligned Countries, Titograd: 10d, Return from Hunting, by Mama Cangare, Mali. No. 1761, Drum of Coca, by Agnes Ovando Sanz De Franck, Bolivia. No. 1762, The Cock, by Mariano Rodriguez, Cuba. 70d, Three Women, by Quamrul Hassan, Bangladesh.

1985, Dec. 2   **Perf. 14**
1759 A548 8d multicolored .25 .25
1760 A548 10d multicolored .25 .25
1761 A548 50d multicolored .25 .25
1762 A548 50d multicolored .25 .25
1763 A548 70d multicolored 1.40 1.40
   Nos. 1759-1763 (5) 2.40 2.40

Nos. 1243, 1482, 1485a, 1490, 1491, 1713a, 1717a, 1603A and 1718 Srchd. in Light Red Brown, Brown or Dark Brown

1985-86   **Litho.**   **Perf. 13½, 13½x12½**
1764 A323 1d on 25p (B) .80 .25
1765 A263 2d on 5p (DB) .40 .25
  a.   on #1482a .40 .25
1766 A263 3d on 35p (DB) .25 .25
  a.   on #1485a .25 .25
1767 A323 4d on 5.60d (B) .25 .25
  b.   on #1490 .80 .50
1767A A323 5d on 8d (B) .40 .25
  c.   on #1491a .80 .80
1768 A323 8d on 6d .25 .25
  a.   on #1713 .25 .25
1769 A263 20d on 26d .25 .25
  a.   on #1717 7.00 4.00
1770 A323 50d on 16.50d (B) .80 .40
  a.   on #1603c .80 .40
1771 A323 70d on 38d .80 .50
   Nos. 1764-1771 (9) 4.20 2.65

Issued: #1767A, 3/17/86; others, 12/85.

Natl. Automobile Assoc., 40th Anniv. A549

1986, Feb. 25   **Perf. 12½**
1772 A549 10d Car .25 .25
1773 A549 70d Helicopter .80 .80

Tara River, Montenegro A550

1986, Mar. 3   **Perf. 14**
1774 A550 100d Canyon .40 .40
1775 A550 150d Bridge .80 .80
European nature protection. Sheets of 9.

Studenica Monastery, 800th Anniv. — A551

1986, Mar. 15   **Perf. 13½**
1776 A551 10d Chapel of Our Lady .55 .40

A552

Various soccer plays.

1986, Apr. 5   **Litho.**   **Perf. 14**
1777 A552 70d multi .65 .65
1778 A552 150d multi .80 .80

1986 World Cup Soccer Championships, Mexico.

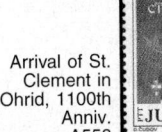

Arrival of St. Clement in Ohrid, 1100th Anniv. A553

1986, Apr. 12   **Perf. 12½**
1779 A553 10d Township model 5.00 5.00

Europa Issue

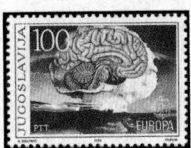

Brain, Mushroom Cloud — A554

1986, Apr. 28   **Perf. 14**
1780 A554 100d shown .40 .40
1781 A554 200d Injured deer 1.20 .80

European Men's Senior Judo Championships, Belgrade, May 8-11 — A555

1986, May 7   **Perf. 12½**
1782 A555 70d multi .50 .40

A559

Natl. Costumes — A556

a, Slovenia. b, Vojvodina. c, Croatia. d, Macedonia. e, Serbia. f, Montenegro. g, Kosovo. h, Bosnia & Herzegovina.

1986, May 22   **Litho.**   **Perf. 12x13**
Booklet Stamps
1783   Bklt. pane of 8 4.50
  a.-h.   A556 50d any single .55 .55

Yachts, Moscenika Draga Bay — A557

1986, May 23   **Perf. 14**
1784 A557 50d multi .25 .25
1785 A557 80d multi, diff. .40 .40

Souvenir Sheet
Imperf
1786 A557 100d multi 3.25 3.25

European Sailing Championships, Croatia, May 29-June 7, Flying Dutchman Class. No. 1786 contains one stamp 22x28mm.

Marshal Tito — A557a

1986, May 24   **Perf. 13x12½**
1787 A557a 10d multicolored .25 .25

Moths and Butterflies A558

1986, May 26   **Perf. 14**
1788 A558 10d Eudia pavonia .80 .80
1789 A558 20d Inachis io .80 .80
1790 A558 50d Parnassius apollo .80 .80
1791 A558 100d Apatura iris 1.60 1.60
   Nos. 1788-1791 (4) 4.00 4.00

Ancient Manuscripts A558a

Designs: 10d, Evangelical, 18th cent. 20d, Leontijevo Evangelical, 16th cent. 50d, Astrological, Mesopotamia, 15th cent. 100d, Hebrew Haggadah, Spain, 14th cent.

1986, June 12   **Litho.**   **Perf. 14**
1792 A558a 10d multicolored .25 .25
1793 A558a 20d multicolored .25 .25
1794 A558a 50d multicolored .40 .40
1795 A558a 100d multicolored .80 .65
   Nos. 1792-1795 (4) 1.70 1.55

A559

A560

Designs: 20d, Postman on motorcycle. 30d, Postman, resident. 40d, Forklift, mail pallets. 50d, Mail train. 60d, Man posting letters in mailbox. 93d, Open envelope and greetings telegram form. 100d, Postman, mail van. No. 1803, Computer operator facing right. No. 1804, 140d, Computer operator facing left. 120d, Woman sending love letter. 200d, Freighter in high seas. 500d, Postal employee sorting mail. 1000d, Woman at telephone station. 2000d, Aircraft, hemispheres on world map. 30d, 60d, 93d, 106d, 120d, 140d, 500d, 1000d vert.

Perf. 13½, 12½x13½ (20d, 40d, 50d), 14 (100d)

1986-88			Litho.
1796	A559	20d brt pink	.40	.25
a.		Perf. 13	.40	.25
1797	A559	30d lt brn vio	.40	.25
a.		Perf. 13x12½	.80	.25
1798	A559	40d brt red	.40	.25
a.		Perf. 13	.40	.25
1799	A559	50d violet	.40	.25
a.		Perf. 13	.25	.25
1800	A559	60d lt sage grn	.40	.25
1801	A559	93d ultra	.40	.25
1802	A559	100d dl magenta	.80	.30
1803	A559	106d rose red	.40	.25
1804	A559	106d brn org	.40	.25
1805	A559	120d dull blue grn	.25	.25
1806	A559	140d dull rose	.25	.25
1807	A559	200d greenish bl	1.00	.40
a.		Perf. 12½	2.00	1.60
b.		Perf. 12½x13½	6.00	2.00
1808	A559	500d deep blue & beige	.40	.40
1809	A559	500d chalky blue & yel	.25	.25
1810	A559	1000d vio & blue grn	.25	.25
b.		Perf. 12½	.55	.50
1810A	A560	2000d brt blue, red & brt vio	1.00	.50
	Nos. 1796-1810A (16)		7.40	4.60

Size of No. 1802: 19½x18mm.
Issued: 20d, 3/17; 50d, 200d, 6/4; 40d, 7/17; 100d, 6/12; 30d, 7/26; 60d, 6/5/87; #1803, 12/10/87; 93d, 12/16/87; #1804, 1/22/88; #1808, 4/29/88; 1000d, 7/21/88; 20d, 140d, 2000d, #1809, 9/5/88.
See Nos. 1935-1945, 2004-2007, 2013-2015, 2021. For surcharges see Nos. 1877, 1912-1913, 1947-1948, 1972, 1974-1975, 2017, 2019, 2048-2051, 2053.

13th Communist Federations Congress (SKJ) A561

1986, June 25   **Perf. 12½**
1811 A561 10d shown .25 .25
1812 A561 20d Star .25 .25

Souvenir Sheet
Imperf
1813 A561 100d Tito .80 .80

Trubar, Abecedarian Manuscript Title Page A562

1986, June 28   **Litho.**   **Perf. 12½x13**
1814 A562 20d multi .55 .40

Primoz Trubar (1508-1568), Slovenian philologist and religious reformer.

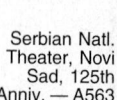

Serbian Natl. Theater, Novi Sad, 125th Anniv. — A563

1986, July 28 *Perf. 14*
1815 A563 40d Thalia .25 .25

Rugovo Dance, Kosovo Province — A564

1986, Sept. 10
1816 A564 40d multi .25 .25

1987 Universiade Games, Zagreb, July 8-19 — A565

1986, Sept. 22 *Perf. 13½*
1817 A565 30d Volleyball .35 .35
1818 A565 40d Canoeing .35 .35
1819 A565 100d Gymnastics .55 .55
1820 A565 150d Fencing .80 .80
Nos. 1817-1820 (4) 2.05 2.05

18th Joy of Europe Youth Conference A566

Children's drawings: 100d, Dove, by Tanja Faletic, 14. 150d, Buildings, by Johanna Kraus, 12, DDR.

1986, Oct. 2 *Perf. 14*
1821 A566 100d multicolored .55 .55
1822 A566 150d multicolored .80 .80

Rotary Switching Apparatus, Village of Bled — A567

1986, Oct. 4 *Perf. 13½*
1823 A567 40d multicolored .25 .25

Telephone exchanges connected with automatic switching equipment, 50th anniv.

INTERPOL 55th General Assembly, Belgrade, Oct. 6-13 — A568

1986, Oct. 6 *Perf. 14*
1824 A568 150d multicolored .40 .40

Intl. Brigades, 50th Anniv. — A569

1986, Oct. 21 *Perf. 13½*
1825 A569 40d multicolored .25 .25

Intl. Peace Year — A570

1986, Nov. 20
1826 A570 150d multicolored .50 .50

Serbian Academy of the Arts and Sciences, Cent. A571

1986, Nov. 1 *Photo.* *Perf. 13½*
1827 A571 40d multicolored .25 .25

Paintings by Foreign Artists in the Museum of Contemporary Art, Skopje — A572

No. 1828, Still Life, by Frantisek Muzika, Czechoslovakia. #1829, Disturance, by Rafael Canogar, England. #1830, Iol, by Victor Vasarely, France. #1831, Portrait, by Bernard Buffet, France. #1832, Woman's Head, by Pablo Picasso, Spain.

1986, Dec. 10 *Litho.* *Perf. 14*
1828 A572 30d multi .25 .25
1829 A572 40d multi .25 .25
1830 A572 100d multi, vert. .40 .40
1831 A572 100d multi, vert. .40 .40
1832 A572 150d multi, vert. .65 .65
Nos. 1828-1832 (5) 1.95 1.95

Wildlife Conservation A573

30d, Lutra lutra. 40d, Ovis musimon. 100d, Cervus elaphus. 150d, Ursus arctos.

1987, Jan. 22 *Litho.* *Perf. 13½x14*
1833 Strip of 4 + label 8.00 8.00
a. A573 30d multi .65 .65
b. A573 40d multi .65 .65
c. A573 100d multi .65 .65
d. A573 150d multi .65 .65

Label pictures nature reserve.

Rudjer Boscovich (1711-1787), Scientist, and Solar Eclipse over Brera Observatory, Italy — A574

1987, Feb. 13 *Perf. 14*
1834 A574 150d multicolored .50 .40

European Nature Protection — A575

1987, Mar. 9
1835 A575 150d shown 1.00 1.00
1836 A575 400d Triglav glacial lake 1.50 1.50

1987 World Alpine Skiing Championships, Crans Montana — A576

1987, Mar. 20 *Litho.* *Perf. 14*
1837 A576 200d multicolored 2.40 2.40

No. 1837 printed in sheets of 8 plus center label.

Natl. Civil Aviation, 60th Anniv. A577

1987, Mar. 20 *Perf. 14*
1838 A577 150d POTEZ-29 .55 .55
1839 A577 400d DC-10 1.20 1.20

Each printed in sheets of 8 plus center label.

Kole Nedelkovski (1912-1941), Poet, Revolutionary A578

1987, Apr. 2 *Perf. 13½*
1840 A578 40d multicolored .25 .25

Liberation of Montenegro from Turkey, 125th Anniv. A579

1987, Apr. 16 *Perf. 13½*
1841 A579 40d Battle flags, folk guitar .25 .25

Slovenian Communist Party, Cebine, 50th Anniv. — A580

1987, Apr. 18 *Perf. 14*
1842 A580 40d multicolored .25 .25

Europa Issue

Tito Bridge, Krk — A581

1987, Apr. 30 *Litho.* *Perf. 14*
1843 A581 200d shown .40 .40
1844 A581 400d Bridges over canal .80 .80

Fruit Trees — A582

1987, May 15 *Litho.* *Perf. 14*
1845 A582 60d Almond .25 .25
1846 A582 150d Pear .65 .65
1847 A582 200d Apple .80 .80
1848 A582 400d Plum 1.60 1.60
Nos. 1845-1848 (4) 3.30 3.30

Tito, 1930, by Mosa Pijade — A583

1987, May 25
1849 A583 60d multi .30 .25

50th anniv. of Tito's assumption of Yugoslavian communist party leadership.

Vuk Stefanovik Karadzic (1787-1864), Linguist and Historian — A584

60d, Bust by Petar Ubavkic, his Trsic residence & Vienna. 200d, Portrait by Uros Knezevic, & alphabet from Karadzic's Serbian Dictionary, 1818.

1987, June 10
1850 A584 60d multi .25 .25
1851 A584 200d multi .40 .40

Zrenjanin Postal Service, 250th Anniv. A585

1987, June 22 *Perf. 13½*
1852 A585 60d multi .25 .25

UNIVERSIADE '87, Zagreb, July 8-19 — A586

1987, July 8   **Litho.**   *Perf. 13½*
1853 A586   60d Hurdling   .25   .25
1854 A586   150d Basketball   .40   .40
1855 A586   200d Balance beam   .55   .55
1856 A586   400d Swimming   1.25   1.25
    Nos. 1853-1856 (4)   2.45   2.45
Each printed in sheets of eight plus label.

Fire Fighting A587

1987, July 20   *Perf. 14*
1857 A587   60d Canadair CL-215   spraying forest   .25   .25
1858 A587   200d Fire boat   .25   .25
Each printed in sheets of eight plus label.

Monument, Anindol Park, Samobor — A588

1987, Aug. 1   *Perf. 13½*
1859 A588   60d multi   .25   .25
Communist Party of Croatia, 50th anniv.

Sabac High School, 150th Anniv. A589

1987, Sept. 10   **Litho.**   *Perf. 13½*
1860 A589   80d multi   .25   .25

Exhibition Emblem, Balkan Peninsula, Flowers A590

Clock Tower, Petrovaradin Fortress and Novi Sad — A591

1987, Sept. 19   *Perf. 14*
1861 A590   250d multi   .40   .40

Souvenir Sheet
Imperf
1862 A591   400d multi   1.00   1.00
BALKANFILA XI, Novi Sad, Sept. 19-26.

19th Joy of Europe Conference A592

Children's drawings: 250d, Girls in forest, by Bedic Aranka, Juguoslavia. 400d, Scarecrow, by Schaffer Ingeborg, Austria.

1987, Oct. 2   **Litho.**   *Perf. 14*
1863 A592   250d multi   .75   .75
1864 A592   400d multi   .80   .80
Printed in sheets of nine.

Bridges A593

80d, Arslanagica, Trebinje, 16th cent. 250d, Terzija, Djakovica, 15th cent.

1987, Oct. 15
1865 A593   80d multi   .40   .40
1866 A593   250d multi   .40   .40

Ship, Dunav-Tisa Channel A594

1987, Oct. 20   *Perf. 13½*
1867 A594   80d multi   .25   .25
City of Titov Vrbas, 600th anniv.

Astronomical and Meteorological Observatory, Belgrade, Cent. — A595

1987, Nov. 21   *Perf. 14*
1868 A595   80d multi   .25   .25

St. Luke the Evangelist, by Raphael A596

Paintings by foreign artists in national museums: 200d, Infanta Maria Theresa, by Velazquez. 250d, Nicholas Rubens, Painter's Son, by Rubens. 400d, Louis Laure Sennegon, Painter's Niece, by Jean-Baptiste-Camille Corot (1796-1875).

1987, Nov. 28
1869 A596   80d shown   .25   .25
1870 A596   200d multi   .40   .40
1871 A596   250d multi   .40   .40
1872 A596   400d multi   1.10   1.10
    Nos. 1869-1872 (4)   2.15   2.15

Traditional Competitions A597

80d, Bull fighting. 200d, Ljubicevo Horse Games. 250d, Moresca game. 400d, Sinj iron ring.

1987, Dec. 10
1873 A597   80d multi   .25   .25
1874 A597   200d multi   .40   .40
1875 A597   250d multi   .40   .40
1876 A597   400d multi   1.50   1.50
    Nos. 1873-1876 (4)   2.55   2.55

No. 1800 Surcharged

1987, Sept. 22   *Perf. 13½*
1877 A559   80d on 60d sg grn   .40   .25

Vinodol Codex, City of Vinodolski, Coat of Arms — A598

1988, Jan. 6   **Litho.**   *Perf. 14*
1878 A598   100d multi   .25   .25
Vinodol Codex, 700th anniv.

Intl. Women's Golden Fox Skiing Championships, 25th Anniv. — A599

1988, Jan. 30
1879 A599   350d Slalom, emblem,   Mirobor City   .25   .25
Printed in sheets of eight plus center label.

World Wildlife Fund — A600

Brown bears (Ursus arctos).

1988, Feb. 1
1880 A600   70d Cub   2.40   1.60
1881 A600   80d Cubs   2.40   1.60
1882 A600   200d Adult, head   2.40   1.60
1883 A600   350d Adult   9.00   4.75
    Nos. 1880-1883 (4)   16.20   9.55

1988 Winter Olympics, Calgary — A601

1988, Feb. 13   *Perf. 14x13½*
1884 A601   350d Slalom   .85   .85
1885 A601   1200d Ice hockey   1.25   1.25
Each printed in sheets of 8 plus center label.

Souvenir Sheet

Map of Europe Highlighting Balkan Nations — A602

1988, Feb. 24   **Litho.**   *Imperf.*
1886 A602   1500d multi   1.75   1.75
Congress of Foreign Affairs Ministers from the Balkan Countries, Belgrade, Feb. 24-26.

1988 Summer Olympics, Seoul — A603

South Korean Landscape — A604

1988, Mar. 21 — Perf. 14x13½
1887	A603	106d Basketball	.55	.55
1888	A603	450d High jump	.55	.55
1889	A603	500d Pommel horse	.55	.55
1890	A603	1200d Boxing	.55	.55
		Nos. 1887-1890 (4)	2.20	2.20

Souvenir Sheet
Imperf
1891	A604	1500d multi	2.00	2.00

Nos. 1887-1890 printed in sheets of 8 plus center label.

Europa Issue

Telecommunications — A605

1988, Apr. 30 Litho. Perf. 13½x14
1892	A605	450d shown	.45	.45
1893	A605	1200d Transportation	.80	.80

Sea Shells — A606

106d, Gibbula magus. 550d, Pecten jacobaeus. 600d, Tonna galea. 1000d, Argonauta argo.

1988, May 14
1894	A606	106d multicolored	.65	.50
1895	A606	550d multicolored	.65	.50
1896	A606	600d multicolored	1.00	.80
1897	A606	1000d multicolored	1.50	.80
		Nos. 1894-1897 (4)	3.80	2.60

Trial of Tito and Five Comrades, 60th Anniv. — A607

1988, May 25
1898	A607	106d black & brn	.25	.25

Palace of Princess Ljubica of Serbia, 1st University Building A608

1988, June 14 Litho. Perf. 13½
1899	A608	106d multi	.25	.25

Belgrade University, 150th anniv.

Flowers — A609

600d, Phelypaea boissieri. 1000d, Campanula formanekiana.

1988, July 2 Perf. 14
1900	A609	600d multicolored	.80	.80
1901	A609	1000d multicolored	1.25	1.25

European Nature Protection.

Esperanto, Cent. — A610

1988, July 14 Perf. 13½
1902	A610	600d dull vio & ol grn	.80	.55

Printed in sheets of 8 plus center label.

Cargo Ships — A611

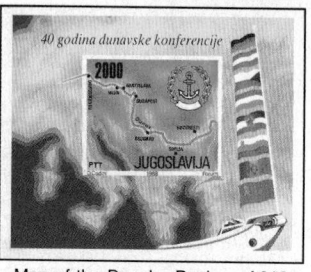

Map of the Danube Basin — A612

1988, Aug. 18 Litho. Perf. 14
1903	A611	1000d multi	.50	.50

Souvenir Sheet
Imperf
1904	A612	2000d multi	3.25	3.25

Danube Conference, 40th anniv.

13th European Junior Basketball Championships, Aug. 21-28 — A613

1988, Aug. 20 Perf. 14
1905	A613	600d multi	.40	.40

1st Horse Race in Belgrade, 125th Anniv. — A614

1988, Aug. 27
1906	A614	140d Thoroughbred racing	.40	.40
1907	A614	600d Steeplechase	.80	.80
1908	A614	1000d Harness racing	1.20	1.20
		Nos. 1906-1908 (3)	2.40	2.40

Museum of Bosnia and Herzegovina, Sarajevo, Cent. A615

140d, Museum, Bosnian bellflower.

1988, Sept. 10 Perf. 13½
1909	A615	140d multicolored	.25	.25

Anti-Cancer and AIDS Campaigns A616

140d, Arm, lobster claw. 1000d, Blood, scream.

1988, Sept. 24 Perf. 14
1910	A616	140d multicolored	.25	.25
1911	A616	1000d multicolored	.65	.65

Nos. 1801 and 1804 Surcharged
1988, July Litho. Perf. 13½
1912	A559	120d on 93d ultra	.25	.25
1913	A559	140d on 106d brn org	.25	.25

Joy of Europe Youth Conference A617

Portraits of girls by: 1000d, P. Ranosovic. 1100d, Renoir.

1988, Oct. 1 Litho. Perf. 14
1914	A617	1000d multi	.65	.65
1915	A617	1100d multi	.80	.80

See Nos. 1987-1988.

Slovenski Academy, 50th Anniv. — A618

1988, Oct. 13 Litho. Perf. 14
1916	A618	200d multi	.25	.25

Museum Exhibits and Places of Origin A618a

200d, Wood bassinet, traditional wedding (Galicka). #1918, Embroidery, man and woman wearing folk costumes of Vojvodina. #1919, Scimitar, flintlock, man & woman wearing folk costumes of Kotor (Bokelji). 1100d, Masks (Kurenti).

1988, Oct. 18
1917	A618a	200d multi, vert.	.65	.65
1918	A618a	1000d shown	.65	.65
1919	A618a	1000d multi, vert.	.65	.65
1920	A618a	1100d multi	.65	.65
		Nos. 1917-1920 (4)	2.60	2.60

Woman with Lyre, 4th Cent. B.C. — A618b

Grecian terra cotta figurines: #1922, Eros & Psyche, 2nd cent. BC. #1923, Seated woman, 3rd cent. BC. 1100d, Woman by Stele, 3rd cent. BC.

1988, Oct. 28
1921	A618b	200d multi	.50	.50
1922	A618b	1000d multi	.50	.50
1923	A618b	1000d multi	.50	.50
1924	A618b	1100d multi	.50	.50
		Nos. 1921-1924 (4)	2.00	2.00

Peter II (1813-1851), Prince Bishop and Poet — A618c

Portraits and: 200d, Cetinje Monastery and frontispiece of his principal work. 1000d, Njegos Mausoleum.

1988, Nov. 1
1925	A618c	200d multi	.25	.25
1926	A618c	1000d multi	.55	.55

Postal Service Types of 1986 and

Telephone Receiver and Telephone Card — A619

Bird, Posthorn, Simulated Stamp — A620

Propeller Plane, Two Arrows and Map — A621

Designs: 170d, 300d, Flower, envelope, mailbox and simulated stamp. 220d, PTT emblem on simulated stamp, mail coach. 800d, Postman on motorcycle. No. 1941, Postman, resident. No. 1942, Mail train. No. 1943, Envelopes, satellite dish. No. 1944, Earth, telecommunications satellite. 100,000d, Bird, open envelope, flower. 170d, 220d, 300d, 2000d, 5000d, No. 1941 vert.

1988-89 Litho. Perf. 13¼
1935	A559	170d dl grn	.40	.25
1936	A559	220d brn org	.40	.25
1937	A559	300d ver	.40	.25
1938	A559	800d brt ultra	.25	.25
1939	A619	2000d multi	.25	.25
1940	A620	5000d dk red & ultra	.80	.40
1941	A559	10,000d org & brt lil	.55	.55
1942	A559	20,000d lt ol grn & lt red brn	.55	.55

Perf. 13½
1943	A560	10,000d multi	1.25	.55
1944	A560	20,000d multi	.80	.55
1944A	A621	50,000d org & dl bl	1.00	.40
1945	A560	100,000d org & dl grn	.25	.25
		Nos. 1935-1945 (12)	6.90	4.50

Perf. 12½
1937a	A559	300d	.40	.25
1938a	A559	800d	.25	.25
1939a	A619	2000d	.25	.25
1940a	A620	5000d	.80	.40
1941a	A559	10,000d	.25	.25
1942a	A559	20,000d	.25	.25
		Nos. 1937a-1941a (5)	1.95	1.40

Issued: 1988 — 170d, 11/17; 220d, 12/6; 1989 — 300d, 5/11; 800d, 2000d, 7/20; 5000d, 1/20; #1941, 11/28; #1942, 12/8; #1943, 3/20; #1944, 7/19; 50,000d, 11/8; 100,000d, 12/4.
See Nos. 2008-2009, 2017, 2052. For surcharges see Nos. 1972, 1974, 2048.

Yugoslavia, 70th Anniv. — A622

1988, Dec. 1   Litho.   Perf. 14
1946 A622 200d Krsmanovic Hall,
Belgrade .25 .25

Nos. 1805-1806 Surcharged
1988   Litho.   Perf. 13½
1947 A559 170d on 120d .80 .25
1948 A559 220d on 140d .80 .25

Issued: #1947, Dec. 21; #1948, Dec. 15.

Miniature Sheet

Victory of Yugoslavian Athletes at the
1988 Summer Olympics,
Seoul — A623

Medals and events: a, Women's air pistol.
b, Team handball. c, Table tennis. d, Wrestling.
e, Double sculls. f, Basketball. g, Water polo.
h, Boxing.

1988, Dec. 31   Litho.   Perf. 14
1949   Sheet of 8 + label   3.00 3.00
a.-h. A623 500d any single   .30 .25

Ivan Gundulic (1589-1638), Poet — A624

1989, Jan. 7   Perf. 13½
1950 A624 220d multi   .40 .25

World Wildlife Fund — A625

Ducks.

1989, Feb. 23   Litho.   Perf. 14
1951   Strip of 4 + label   14.00 8.00
a. A625 300d Anas platyrhynchos   1.25 .50
b. A625 2100d Anas crecca   3.50 1.75
c. A625 2200d Anas acuta   3.50 1.75
d. A625 2200d Anas clypeata   3.50 1.75

Printed in sheets of 20+5 labels. Label pictures WWF emblem.

Publication of The Glory of the Duchy of Kranjska, by Johann Valvasor (1641-1693), 300th Anniv. A626

1989, Mar. 10   Perf. 13½
1952 A626 300d Portrait   .25 .25

Flowering Plants — A627

300d, Bulbocodium vernum. 2100d, Nymphaea alba. 2200d, Fritillaria degeniana, vert. 3000d, Orchis simia, vert.

1989, Mar. 20   Perf. 14
1953 A627 300d multi   1.00 1.00
1954 A627 2100d multi   1.00 1.00
1955 A627 2200d multi   1.00 1.00
1956 A627 3000d multi   1.00 1.00
Nos. 1953-1956 (4)   4.00 4.00

6th World Air-Gun Championships, Sarajevo, Apr. 27-30 — A628

1989, Apr. 26
1957 A628 3000d multi   .50 .50

Europa 1989 — A629

1989, Apr. 29
1958 A629 3000d shown   .80 .80
1959 A629 6000d Marbles   .80 .80

15th European Trophy for Natl. Athletic Club Champions, Belgrade, June 3-4 — A630

1989, June 1   Litho.   Perf. 13½
1960 A630 4000d Pole vault   .80 .80

Printed in sheets of 8+label picturing flags of participating nations.

Yugoslavia Motorcycle Grand Prix, Rijeka, June 9-11 — A631

Various race scenes.

1989, June 9   Perf. 14
1961 A631 500d multi   .25 .25
1962 A631 4000d multi   .40 .40

Souvenir Sheet
Perf. 14x13½
1963 A631 6000d multi   1.50 1.50

No. 1963 contains one 54x35 stamp.

No. 1246 Surcharged
1989, Apr. 6   Litho.   Perf. 13
1964 A323 100d on 1d dull grn   .40 .25
a.   Perf. 13x12½   .40 .40

Tito — A632

1989, May 25   Perf. 13½x14
1965 A632 300d multi   .25 .25

Early Adriatic Ships A633

a, Ancient Greek galley. b, Roman galley. c, Crusade galleon, 13th cent. d, Nava of Dubrovnik, 16th cent. e, French ship, 17th cent. f, Vessels, 18th cent. 3000d, View of Dubrovnik seaport, called Ragusa in Italian, from a 17th cent. engraving.

1989, June 10   Perf. 13½
1966   Block of 6   2.00 1.50
a.-f. A633 1000d any single   .30 .25
Souvenir Sheet
1967 A633 3000d multi   .75 .35

No. 1967 contains one 75x32mm stamp. Nos. 1966-1967 printed se-tenant and sold folded in booklet cover.

26th European Basketball Championships — A634

Map of Europe, basketball and flags of: No. 1968, France, Yugoslavia, Greece, Bulgaria. No. 1969, Netherlands, Italy, Russia, Spain.

1989, June 20   Litho.   Perf. 13½x14
1968 A634 2000d multi   .25 .25
1969 A634 2000d multi   .25 .25

Nos. 1968-1969 exist with setenant label.

Defeat of the Serbians at the Battle of Kosovo, 1389 — A635

1989, June 28
1970 A635 500d multi   .25 .25

Danilovgrad Library, Cent. A636

1989, July 15   Litho.   Perf. 13½
1971 A636 500d multi   .25 .25

Nos. 1797, 1719, 1935, 1936 Surcharged
1989
1972 A559 400d on 30d lt brn vio   .80 .25
1973 A323 700d on 70d brt ultra   .80 .25
1974 A559 700d on 170d dull green   .80 .25
1975 A559 700d on 220d brn org   .80 .25
Nos. 1972-1975 (4)   3.20 1.00

Issued: #1975, 7/19; #1974, 8/10; #1972, 8/23; #1973, 12/13.

Kulin Ban Charter, 800th Anniv. A638

1989, Aug. 29   Litho.   Perf. 14
1976 A638 500d multi   .25 .25

World Rowing Championships A639

1989, Sept. 2   Perf. 13½
1977 A639 10,000d multi   .50 .50

Interparliamentary Union, Cent. — A640

Architecture: No. 1978, Parliament, London (emblem at R). No. 1979, Notre Dame Cathedral (emblem at L).

1989, Sept. 4   Perf. 13½x14
1978 A640 10,000d multi   .40 .40
1979 A640 10,000d multi   .40 .40

A641

View of Belgrade and Maps BEOGRAD '89 — A642

Architecture & antiquities of non-aligned summit host cities: #1980, Belgrade '61, Cairo

'64. #1981, Lusaka '70, Algiers '73. #1982, Colombo '76, Havana '79. #1983, New Delhi '83, Harare '76.

1989, Sept. 4
1980	A641	10,000d multi	.25	.25
1981	A641	10,000d multi	.25	.25
1982	A641	10,000d multi	.25	.25
1983	A641	10,000d multi	.25	.25
		Nos. 1980-1983 (4)	1.00	1.00

Souvenir Sheet
Perf. 14
1984	A642	20,000d multi	1.25	1.25

European Nature Protection A643

8000d, Paeonia officinalis, Brezovica-Jazinac Lake. 10,000d, Paeonia corallina, Mirusa Canyon.

1989, Sept. 11   *Perf. 14*
1985	A643	8000d multi	.40	.40
1986	A643	10,000d multi	.40	.40

Joy of Europe Type of 1988
Portraits of children: No. 1987, Child with Lamb, by Jovan Popovic. No. 1988, Girl Feeding Dog, by Albert Cuyp (1620-1691).

1989, Oct. 2   Litho.   *Perf. 14*
1987	A617	10,000d multi	.50	.50
1988	A617	10,000d multi	.50	.50

Karpos Uprising, 300th Anniv. — A644

1989, Oct. 20   Litho.   *Perf. 13½*
1989	A644	1200d ver & dark brn	.25	.25

No. 1833c, Cancellation, Quill Pen, Wax Seals and Seal Device on Parchment A645

1989, Oct. 31   *Perf. 14*
1990	A645	1200d multicolored	.25	.25

Stamp Day.

Museum Exhibits A646

1989, Nov. 2
1991	A646	1200d Pack-saddle maker	.25	.25
1992	A646	14,000d Cooper	.55	.55
1993	A646	15,000d Winegrower	.80	.80
1994	A646	30,000d Weaver	1.40	1.40
		Nos. 1991-1994 (4)	3.00	3.00

Religious Paintings — A647

2100d, Apostle Matthew, vert. 21,000d, St. Barbara, vert. 30,000d, The Fourth Day of Creation. 50,000d, The Fifth Day of Creation.

1989, Nov. 28   Litho.   *Perf. 14*
1997	A647	2100d multicolored	.25	.25
1998	A647	21,000d multicolored	.40	.40
1999	A647	30,000d multicolored	.80	.80
2000	A647	50,000d multicolored	1.25	1.25
		Nos. 1997-2000 (4)	2.70	2.70

A648

League of Communists 14th Congress — A649

1990, Jan. 20   Litho.   *Perf. 13½x14*
2001	A648	10,000d Star	.30	.25
2002	A648	50,000d Computer	.55	.55

Souvenir Sheet
Imperf
2003	A649	100,000d Star, diff.	1.25	1.25

Postal Service Types of 1986-88
10p, Man posting letters in mailbox. 20p, Postal employee sorting mail. 30p, Postman, resident. 40p, Woman at telephone station. 1d, Mail train. 2d, Ship & envelope. 3d, Flower, mailbox, envelope & simulated stamp. 5d, Airplane, letters, map of Europe. 10d, Bird, open envelope, flower. 20d, Woman at telephone station.
Designs for other values as before.
10p, 20p, 30p, 40p, 3d, 5d vert.

1990   *Perf. 12½*
2004	A559	10p br yel grn & vio	.50	.25
2005	A559	20p red vio & org	.50	.25
2006	A559	30p org & yel grn	.25	.25
2007	A559	40p blue grn & red vio		
2008	A620	50p pur & blue grn	.25	.25
2009	A619	60p red org & brt vio	.30	.25
2013	A559	1d rose lil & greenish bl	.30	.25
2014	A559	2d red lil & blue	.50	.25
2015	A559	3d org & dl blue	.90	.25
2017	A619	5d ultra & grnsh blue	.90	.30
2019	A559	10d red org & vio bl	.90	.45
		Nos. 2004-2019 (11)	1.75	1.40
			7.05	4.15

Issued: 10p, 20p, 2/9; 30p, 40p, 1/24; 50p, 1/29; 60p, 2/6; 2d, 2/14; 3d, 2/22; 5d, 1/31; 1d, 5/24; 10d, 6/12.
For surcharges see Nos. 2049-2053, 2168//2176.

1990-92   *Perf. 13¼*
2004a	A559	10p br yel grn & vio	.50	.25
2005a	A559	20p red vio & org	1.40	.70
2006a	A559	30p org & yel grn	.25	.25
2007a	A559	40p blue grn & red vio	.25	.25

2008a	A620	50p pur & blue grn	.30	.25
2009a	A619	60p red org & brt vio	.30	.30
2013a	A559	1d rose lil & greenish bl	1.75	1.25
2014a	A559	2d red lil & blue	.65	.45
2015a	A559	3d org & dl blue>	2.50	2.25
2017a	A619	5d ultra & grnsh blue	1.25	1.00
2019a	A559	10d red org & vio bl	7.50	5.50
2021	A559	20d car rose & org	.45	.25
		Nos. 2004a-2021 (12)	17.10	12.70

Issued: 30p, 40p, 1/24; 50p, 1/29; 5d, 1/31; 60p, 2/6; 10p, 20p, 2/9; 2d, 2/14; 3d, 2/22; 10d, 6/12; 1d, 7/2; 20d, 1/27/92.
For surcharges see Nos. 2049a-2053a, 2168//2176.

Anti-smoking Campaign A650

1990, Jan. 31   Litho.   *Perf. 13½x13*
2034	A650	10d gry & yel brn	.90	.90

Protected Fish — A651

1990, Feb. 15   *Perf. 13½*
2035		Strip of 4 + label	8.00	8.00
a.	A651	1d Esox lucius	1.25	1.25
b.	A651	5d Silurus glanis	1.25	1.25
c.	A651	10d Lota lota	1.25	1.25
d.	A651	15d Perca fluviatilis	1.25	1.25

Zabljak Fortress, Illuminated Manuscript, Coat of Arms — A652

1990, Mar. 9   *Perf. 14x13½*
2036	A652	50p multicolored	1.20	1.20

Enthronement of Djuradj Crnojevic, 500th anniv.

ITU, 125th Anniv. A653

1990, Mar. 23
2037	A653	6.50d Telegrapher, computer	.90	.90

1990 World Cup Soccer Championships, Italy — A654

1990, Apr. 16
2038	A654	6.50d shown	1.40	1.40
2039	A654	10d multi, diff.	1.40	1.40

Europa 1990 — A655

Post offices: 6.50d, PTT Central, Skopje. 10d, Telecommunications Central, Belgrade.

1990, Apr. 23   *Perf. 13½x14*
2040	A655	6.50d multicolored	1.60	1.60
2041	A655	10d multicolored	1.60	1.60

A656

1990, Apr. 30   Litho.   *Perf. 13½*
2042	A656	6.50d multicolored	1.00	1.00

Labor Day, cent.

A657

Eurovision Song Contest: 10d, Conductor, musical score.

1990, May 5   *Perf. 14x13½*
2043	A657	6.50d multicolored	1.10	1.10
2044	A657	10d multicolored	1.20	1.20

No. 2043 exists with setenant label.

Tennis — A658

1990, May 15   Litho.   *Perf. 14*
2045	A658	6.50d multicolored	1.40	1.40
2046	A658	10d multicolored	1.40	1.40

Tito — A659

1990, May 25   *Perf. 13½x14*
2047	A659	50p multicolored	.30	.30

Nos. 1938, 2004-2009a Surcharged

No. 2048   No. 2049

1990-91   Litho.   *Perf. 12½*
2048	A559	50p on 800d (#1938a)	.45	.25
a.		Perf 13¼ (#1938)	.45	.25
2049	A559	50p on 20p (#2005)	.45	.25
a.		Perf 13¼ (#2005a) ('91)	3.50	2.75

2050 A559 1d on 30p (#2006) .45 .25
   a. Perf 13¼ (#2006a) 3.50 3.25
2051 A559 2d on 40p (#2007), I .90 .45
   a. Type II, perf. 13¼ (#2007a) 1.40 .90
   b. Type I, perf. 13¼ (#2007a) 2.25 2.25
2052 A619 5d on 60p (#2009) .45 .25
   a. Perf 13¼ (#2009a) 4.50 1.75
2053 A559 10d on 10p (#2004) .45 .25
   a. Perf 13¼ (#2004a) 1.00 .55
   Nos. 2048-2053 (6) 3.15 1.70

Type II surcharge has 3 instead of 2 bars obliterating old value, new denomination is at bottom of stamp.
Issued: #2048, 2048a, 5/24; #2050, 8/7; #2049, 2049a, 9/18; #2051-2051b, 10/2; #2050a, 1/4/91; #2053, 2053a, 12/12/91; #2052, 2052a, 12/17/91.

Public Postal Service in Serbia, 150th Anniv. A660

1990, May 25
2056 A660 50p multicolored 2.25 1.50

Pigeons A661

1990, June 8   *Perf. 13½*
2057 A661 50p multicolored .55 .55
2058 A661 5d multicolored 1.10 1.10
2059 A661 6.50d multi, vert. 1.10 1.10
2060 A661 10d multi, vert. 2.75 2.75
   Nos. 2057-2060 (4) 5.50 5.50

Mercury Mine at Idrija, 500th Anniv. — A662

Designs: 6.50d, Miners at work, ca. 1490.

1990, June 22   *Perf. 13½x14*
2061 A662 50p multicolored .25 .25
2062 A662 6.50d multicolored 1.00 1.00

Newspaper "Vjesnik," 50th Anniv. — A663

1990, June 23   *Perf. 13½*
2063 A663 60p multicolored .70 .70

Serbian Migration, 300th Anniv. — A664

1990, Sept. 20   *Perf. 14*
2064 A664 1d shown .25 .25
2065 A664 6.50d Caravan .90 .90

European Track & Field Championships, Split — A665

1990, Aug. 27   *Perf. 13½*
2067 A665 1d Start of race .60 .60
2068 A665 6.50d Runners' feet .90 .90

Souvenir Sheet
2069 A665 10d Runners 2.25 2.25

No. 2069 contains one 54x35mm stamp. A 50p exists but no information on its postal category is available.

Joy of Europe A666

Paintings: 6.50d, Children by I. Kobilca. 10d, William III of Orange as a Child by A. Hanneman, vert.

1990, Oct. 2   *Litho.*   *Perf. 14*
2070 A666 6.50d multicolored 1.10 1.10
2071 A666 10d multicolored 1.50 1.50

Souvenir Sheets

29th Chess Olympics, Novi Sad — A667

1990, Oct. 2   *Perf. 11½*
Granite Paper
2072 Sheet of 4 8.00 8.00
   a. A667 1d shown 1.10 1.10
   b. A667 5d Rook, bishop, knight 1.10 1.10
   c. A667 6.50d King, bishop, knght, pawn 1.10 1.10
   d. A667 10d Chess pieces 1.10 1.10

Imperf
2073 Sheet of 4 8.00 8.00
   a. A667 1d like No. 2072a 1.10 1.10
   b. A667 5d like No. 2072b 1.10 1.10
   c. A667 6.50d like No. 2072c 1.10 1.10
   d. A667 10d like No. 2072d 1.10 1.10

No. 2073 has blue margin inscriptions. Emblems on Nos. 2072a-2072d are in silver, those on Nos. 2073a-2073d are in gold.

Stamp Day A668

1990, Oct. 2   *Perf. 14*
2074 A668 2d multicolored .60 .55

150th anniv. of the Penny Black.

European Nature Protection A669

1990, Nov. 16   *Litho.*   *Perf. 14*
2075 A669 6.50d Vransko Lake 1.10 1.10
2076 A669 10d Gyps fulvus 1.50 1.50

Frescoes — A670

Designs: 2d, King Milutin, Monastery of Our Lady, Ljeviska. 5d, Saint Sava, Mileseva Monastery. 6.50d, Saint Elias, Moraca Monastery. 10d, Jesus Christ, Sopocani Monastery.

1990, Nov. 28
2077 A670 2d multicolored .45 .45
2078 A670 5d multicolored .95 .95
2079 A670 6.50d multicolored .95 .95
2080 A670 10d multicolored 1.40 1.40
   Nos. 2077-2080 (4) 3.75 3.75

Dr. Bozo Milanovic (1890-1980), Religious and Political Leader A671

1990, Nov. 28   *Litho.*   *Perf. 13½*
2081 A671 2d multicolored .30 .30

Religious Carvings A672

Designs: 2d, Christ in the temple. 5d, Nativity scene. 6.50d, Flight from Egypt, horiz. 10d, Entry into Jerusalem, horiz.

1990, Dec. 24   *Perf. 13½x14, 14x13½*
2082 A672 2d gld, brn, & blk .45 .45
2083 A672 5d gld, brn, & blk .70 .70
2084 A672 6.50d gld, brn, & blk .90 .90
2085 A672 10d gld, brn, & blk 1.10 1.10
   Nos. 2082-2085 (4) 3.15 3.15

Protected Birds — A673

1991, Jan. 31   *Litho.*   *Perf. 14x13½*
2086 Strip of 4 + label 9.00 9.00
   a. A673 2d Vanellus vanellus 1.10 1.10
   b. A673 5d Lanius senator 1.10 1.10
   c. A673 6.50d Grus grus 1.10 1.10
   d. A673 10d Mergus merganser 1.10 1.10

Flora — A674

2d, Crocus kosaninii. 6d, Crocus scardicus. 7.50d, Crocus rujanesis. 15d, Crocus adamii.

1991, Feb. 20
2087 A674 2d multicolored .45 .45
2088 A674 6d multicolored .55 .55
2089 A674 7.50d multicolored .60 .60
2090 A674 15d multicolored 2.00 2.00
   Nos. 2087-2090 (4) 3.60 3.60

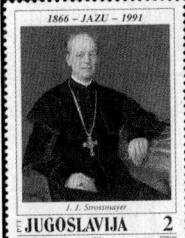

Bishop Josip J. Strossmayer (1815-1905), Founder of Academy of Arts and Sciences A675

1991, Mar. 4   *Litho.*   *Perf. 13½x14*
2091 A675 2d multicolored 1.10 .60

Academy of Arts and Sciences, 125th Anniv.

Wolfgang Amadeus Mozart, Composer A676

1991, Mar. 20   *Perf. 14*
2092 A676 7.50d multicolored .90 .60

Otto Lilienthal's First Glider Flight, Cent. — A677

Designs: 7.50d, Edvard Rusjan (1886-1911), pilot, aircraft designer. 15d, Otto Lilienthal (1848-1896), aviation pioneer.

1991, Apr. 1
2093 A677 7.50d multicolored 1.10 1.10
2094 A677 15d multicolored 1.40 1.40

Printed in sheets of 8 plus label.

Lhotse I, Himalayas, South Face First Climbed by Tomo Cesen, 1990 — A678

1991, Apr. 24   *Perf. 14x13½*
2095 A678 7.50d multicolored .90 .55

Europa A679

Designs: 7.50d, Telecommunications satellite. 15d, Satellite, antenna, telephone.

1991, May 6   *Perf. 14*
2096 A679 7.50d multicolored .90 .90
2097 A679 15d multicolored 1.75 1.75

Franciscan Monastery, Trsat, 700th Anniv. — A680

1991, May 10   Litho.   Perf. 13½x14
2098 A680 3.50d multicolored   .80   .25

Governments of Danube River Region Conf., Belgrade — A681

15d, Danube River shipping. 20d, Course of Danube, landmarks, regional animals.

1991, May 15   Perf. 13½
2099 A681 7.50d multicolored   1.00   1.00
2100 A681 15d multicolored   1.50   1.50
Souvenir Sheet
2101 A681 20d multicolored   9.00   9.00
No. 2101 contains one 55x35mm stamp.

Opening of Karavanke Tunnel — A682

Designs: 4.50d, Passage Over Karavanke by J. Valvasor, 17th century. 11d, Entrance to new Karavanke Tunnel.

1991, June 1   Perf. 14x13½
2102 A682 4.50d multicolored   .60   .60
2103 A682 11d multicolored   .90   .90

Basketball, Cent. — A683

1991, June 15   Perf. 13½x14
2104 A683 11d shown   1.10   1.10
2105 A683 15d Nets, "100"   1.10   1.10

Yugoslavian Insurrection, 50th Anniv. — A684

Designs: 4.50d, Partisan Memorial Medal, 1941. 11d, Medal for Courage.

1991, July 4   Litho.   Perf. 14
2106 A684 4.50d multicolored   .35   .35
2107 A684 11d multicolored   .70   .70
Yugoslav Natl. Army, 50th Anniv.

Tin Ujevic (1891-1955), Writer — A685

1991, July 5   Perf. 13½
2108 A685 4.50d multicolored   .60   .45

Jacobus Gallus (1550-1591), Composer A686

1991, July 18
2109 A686 11d multicolored   .60   .60

Lighthouses of Adriatic and Danube — A687

Designs: a, Savudrija, 1818. b, Sveti Ivan na pucini, 1853. c, Porer, 1833. d, Stoncica, 1865. e, Olipa, c. 1842. f, Glavat, 1884. g, Veli rat, 1849. h, Vir, 1881. i, Tajerske sestrice, 1876. j, Razanj, 1875. k, Derdap-Danube. l, Tamis-Danube.

1991, July 25   Litho.   Perf. 13½
2110 A687 10d Bklt. pane of 12, #a.-l.   12.00   12.00

Sremski Karlovci High School, Bicent. — A688

1991, Sept. 12   Litho.   Perf. 14
2111 A688 4.50d multicolored   .45   .30

European Nature Protection A689

11d, Palingenia longicauda. 15d, Phalacrocorax pygmaeus.

1991, Sept. 24   Perf. 13½x14
2112 A689 11d multicolored   .90   .90
2113 A689 15d multicolored   .90   .90

A690

1991, Sept. 28   Perf. 14
2114 A690 4.50d multicolored   .45   .30
Town of Subotica, 600th anniv.

A691

Paintings: 15d, Little Dubravka, by Jovan Bijelic (1886-1964). 30d, Little Girl with a Cat by Mary Cassatt (1845-1926).

1991, Oct. 2
2115 A691 15d multicolored   .70   .70
2116 A691 30d multicolored   1.10   1.10
Joy of Europe.

33rd Intl. Apicultural Congress, APIMONDIA '91 — A692

1991, Sept. 28   Litho.   Perf. 13½x14
2117 A692 11d multicolored   1.10   .90

Stamp Day, Monument to Prince Michael Obrenovich, Serbia #1 — A693

1991, Oct. 31   Perf. 14
2118 A693 4.50d multicolored   .60   .25
First Serbia Postage Stamps, 125th Anniv.

Museum Exhibits A694

Flags and medals: 20d, Vucjido battle flag, medal for courage. 30d, Grahovac battle flag and medal. 40d, Montenegrin state flag, medal for bravery. 50d, Montenegrin court flag, medal of Petrovich Nyegosh Dynasty.

1991, Nov. 28   Perf. 13½x14
2119 A694 20d multicolored   .25   .25
2120 A694 30d multicolored   .45   .45
2121 A694 40d multicolored   .60   .60
2122 A694 50d multicolored   .90   .90
Nos. 2119-2122 (4)   2.20   2.20

Illustrations from Ancient Manuscripts A695

Designs: 20d, Angel carrying Sun around Earth, 17th cent. 30d, Celnica Gospel, menology for April, 14th cent. 40d, Angel from the Annunciation, 13th cent. 50d, Mary Magdalene, 12th cent.

1991, Dec. 12
2123 A695 20d multicolored   .25   .25
2124 A695 30d multicolored   .45   .45
2125 A695 40d multicolored   .60   .60
2126 A695 50d multicolored   .90   .90
Nos. 2123-2126 (4)   2.20   2.20

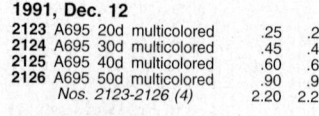

Gotse Deltchev (1872-1903), Macedonian Revolutionary A696

1992, Jan. 29   Litho.   Perf. 13½
2127 A696 5d multicolored   2.25   2.25

Red Star, European and World Soccer Champions A697

1992, Jan. 29   Litho.   Perf. 14x13½
2128 A697 17d multicolored   2.00   2.00

A698

1992, Feb. 8   Perf. 14x13½
2129 A698 80d Ski jumping   1.75   1.75
2130 A698 100d Freestyle skiing   1.75   1.75
1992 Winter Olympics, Albertville.

A699

Protected Animals: a, 50d, Lepus europaeus. b, 60d, Pteromys volans. c, 80d, Dryomys nitedula. d, 100d, Cricetus cricetus.

1992, Mar. 10   Litho.   Perf. 14
2131 A699 Strip of 4, #a.-d. + label   8.00   8.00

Madonna and Child, 14th century, Pec — A700

1992, Mar. 14   Perf. 13½x14
2132 A700 80d multicolored   1.00   1.00
Promotion of Breastfeeding.

Ski Association of Montenegro — A701

1992, Mar. 25   **Perf. 14x13½**
2133 A701 8d multicolored   5.00 5.00

Skiing in Montenegro, cent.

1860 Fountain, Belgrade — A702    A702a

A702b    A702c

A702d    A702e

A702f    A702g

A702h    A702i

A702j

5d, Griffins, 14th cent. #2136, #2139, Fisherman Fountain, Belgrade. #2138, like #2137. 300d, Kalemgdan Fountain, Belgrade. 500d, Fountain, Sremski Karlovci. #2142, Symbols of Miroslav-Evangelium, 12th cent. 3000d, Fountain, Studenica. 5000d, Fountain, Oplenzu. 10,000d, 500,000d, Health spa, Vrnjacka Banja. 50,000d, Envelopes over map of Europe. #2147, Airplane. #2148, Health spa, Bukovacka Banja.

Inscribed "1992" or "1993"

			Litho.	Perf. 13¼	
1992-93					
2135	A702a		5d brn & olive	1.00	.25
2136	A702		50d dk bl & lt bl	.45	.25
2137	A702		50d violet	.45	.35
2138	A702		100d lil rose & pink	.45	.25
2139	A702		100d dk grn & lt grn	.25	.25
2140	A702b		300d brn & red brn	.45	.25
2141	A702c		500d dk ol & pale org	.90	.25
a.		Perf. 12½		1.75	1.75
2142	A702d	(A) red, 18x22mm		1.75	.45
a.		Perf. 12½		4.00	.45
b.		Inscribed "1996," Perf. 13¼		2.25	2.25
c.		Inscribed "1996," perf. 12½		.90	.25
d.		Inscribed "1997," perf. 12½		1.50	.25
e.		Inscribed "2002," perf. 12½		5.00	1.50
2143	A702e		3000d red brn	.45	.25
a.		Perf. 12½		2.75	2.25
2144	A702f		5000d vio & yel brn	.45	.25
a.		Perf 12½		3.50	2.75
2145	A702g		10,000d vio bl & grn bl	1.00	.25
2146	A702h		50,000d gray & gray bl	.45	.25
a.		Perf. 12½		1.10	.90
2147	A702i		100,000d red & bl	.90	.45
a.		Perf. 12½		1.10	.90
2148	A702j		100,000d brn red & brn	.90	.25
2149	A702g		500,000d bl & vio	.45	.25
			Nos. 2135-2149 (15)	10.30	4.25

Issued: #2137, 4/1/92; #2139, 5/6/92; 5d, 11/24/92; #2136, 12/15/92; #2138, 12/22/92; 300d, 12/3/92; 500d, 1/14/93; #2142, 4/5/93; #2142a, 1993; #2143, 4/23/93; 5000d, 3/18/93; 10,000d, 11/9/93; 50,000d, 6/10/93; 100,000d, 6/28/93; 100,000d, 12/6/93; 500,000d, 8/10/93.

No. 2142 was valued at 3000d on day of issue.

See No. 2386. For surcharges see Nos. 2220A-2220I, 2253-2254.

Sinking of the Titanic, 80th Anniv. — A703

1992, Apr. 14   **Perf. 14**
2152 A703 150d multicolored   .90 .90

Expo '92, Seville A704

1992, Apr. 20
2153 A704 150d multicolored   .90 .90

Discovery of America, 500th Anniv. — A705

300d, Columbus, ship. 500d, Columbus' fleet. 1200d, Ships in port.

1992, May 5   **Litho.**   **Perf. 13½x14**
2154 A705 300d multicolored   4.50 4.50
2155 A705 500d multicolored   4.50 4.50

Souvenir Sheet
Perf. 14x13½
2156 A705 1200d multicolored 13.50 13.50

Europa. No. 2156 contains one 54x34mm stamp.

1992 Summer Olympics, Barcelona — A706

1992, May 20   **Perf. 14x13½**
2157 A706 500d Pistol shooting   .90 .90
2158 A706 500d Water polo   .90 .90
2159 A706 500d Tennis   .90 .90
2160 A706 500d Handball   .90 .90
   Nos. 2157-2160 (4)   3.60 3.60

European Soccer Championships — A707

Various soccer plays.

1992, June 1   **Perf. 13½**
2161 A707 1000d shown   1.60 1.60
2162 A707 1000d multicolored   1.60 1.60

Domestic Cats — A708

Designs: No. 2163, Red Persian. No. 2164, White Persian. No. 2165, Yellow tabby. No. 2166, British blue short-hair.

1992, June 25   **Litho.**   **Perf. 13½x14**
Background Color
Cyrillic Letters
2163 A708 1000d blue   1.60 1.60
2164 A708 1000d purple   1.60 1.60
Latin Letters
2165 A708 1000d dark purple   1.60 1.60
2166 A708 1000d brown   1.60 1.60
   Nos. 2163-2166 (4)   6.40 6.40

Steam Locomotives A709

Designs: a, JDZ 162. b, JDZ 151. c, JDZ 73. d, JDZ 83. e, JDZ 16. f, Prince Nicholas' coach.

1992, July 3   **Litho.**   **Perf. 14**
2167 A709 1000d Booklet pane of 6, #a.-f.   15.00 15.00

Nos. 2005//2017a Surcharged

1992		Perfs., Etc. as Before		
2168	A559	2d on 30p #2006	.90	.50
a.		Perf 13¼ (#2006a)	1.75	1.00
2169	A559	5d on 20p #2005	1.75	.25
2170	A559	5d on 40p #2007	.90	.50
a.		Perf 13¼ (#2007a)	1.75	1.00
2171	A620	10d on 50p #2008	1.75	.25
2172	A621	10d on 5d #2017a	.90	.25
2173	A559	20d on 1d #2013	3.00	.90
a.		Perf 13¼ (#2013a)	1.75	.90
2174	A621	20d on 5d type of #2017, yel, bl & grn bl	1.00	.50
2175	A559	50d on 2d #2014	10.00	5.00
a.		Perf 13¼ (#2014a)	1.75	.25
2176	A559	100d on 3d #2015	6.00	2.00
a.		Perf 13¼ (#2015a)	3.75	.25
		Nos. 2168-2176 (9)	26.20	10.15

Issued: #2168, 2170, 10/26; #2169, 9/12; #2171, 9/17; #2172, 10/29; #2173, 2175-2176, 8/6; #2174, 11/9.

World Chess Champions A710

1992, Sept. 14   **Litho.**   **Perf. 14**
2177 A710 500d Bobby Fischer   1.75 1.75
2178 A710 500d Boris Spassky   1.75 1.75

Telephone Service in Vojvodina, Cent. A711

1892 Telephone, buildings of Novi Sad, Subotica and Zrenjanin.

1992, Oct. 1
2179 A711 10d multicolored   1.40 1.40

Stamp Day A712

Design: Montenegro #7, musician.

1992, Oct. 2
2180 A712 50d multicolored   1.00 .90

European Art — A713

Europa: No. 2181, Ballet Dancer, by Edgar Degas (1834-1917). No. 2182, Painting of young man, by U. Knezevic.

1992, Oct. 2
2181 A713 500d multicolored   1.40 1.40
2182 A713 500d multicolored   1.40 1.40

European Nature Protection A714

1992, Nov. 14   **Perf. 13½**
2183 A714 500d Tetrao urogallus 4.00 4.00
2184 A714 500d Pelecanus onocrotalus 4.00 4.00

Publisher Srpska Knjizevna Zadruga, Cent. — A715

1992, Nov. 20   **Perf. 14**
2185 A715 100d multicolored   1.00 1.00

Traditional Architecture — A716

Designs: No. 2186, Ancient hut, Zlatibor region. No. 2187, Round house, Morava region. No. 2188, House, on stone cliff, Metohija region. No. 2189, Large estate house, Vojvodina region.

1992, Dec. 12
2186	A716	500d multicolored	.80	.80
2187	A716	500d multicolored	.80	.80
2188	A716	500d multicolored	.80	.80
2189	A716	500d multicolored	.80	.80
		Nos. 2186-2189 (4)	3.20	3.20

Icons, Mosaics — A717

#2190, St. Petka, St. Petka Church, Belgrade. #2191, St. Vasilije-Ostronoski, St. Vasilije-Ostronoski Church, Montenegro. #2192, Mosaic of Simeon Nemanja with model of Blessed Virgin Church, Studenica. #2193, Mosaic of St. Lazar with model of Ravanica Monastery.

1992, Dec. 15
2190	A717	500d multi	1.00	1.00
2191	A717	500d multi	1.00	1.00
2192	A717	500d multi, vert.	1.00	1.00
2193	A717	500d multi, vert.	1.00	1.00
		Nos. 2190-2193 (4)	4.00	4.00

Aviation in Yugoslavia, 80th Anniv. — A718

1992, Dec. 24
2194	A718	500d Bleriot XI	1.10	1.10

Diocletian's Reformation of the Roman Empire, 1700th Anniv. — A719

Design: Detail of Roman fresco.

1993, Jan. 28   Litho.   Perf. 13½
2195	A719	1500d multicolored	1.10	1.10

State Museum, Cetinje, Cent. — A720

1993, Feb. 12   Perf. 14
2196	A720	2500d multicolored	1.10	1.10

Marine Life — A721

Designs: a, Acipenser sturio. b, Scorpaena scrofa. c, Xiphias gladius. d, Tursiops truncatus.

1993, Mar. 20   Perf. 13½
2197	A721	10,000d Strip of 4, #a.-d. + label	8.00	8.00

Serbian Money — A722

#2198, Ancient document, 10 para coins. #2199, 5 dinar banknotes, 5 dinar coins.

1993, Mar. 30
2198	A722	10,000d multicolored	1.40	1.40
2199	A722	10,000d multicolored	1.40	1.40

Restablishment of Serbian monetary system, 125th anniv. (No. 2198). Restoring dinars as Serbian currency, 120th anniv. (No. 2199).

Famous People A723

Designs: No. 2200, Milos Crnjanski (1893-1977), writer, journalist. No. 2201, Nicola Tesla (1856-1943), physicist. No. 2202, Mihailo Petrovic (1868-1943), mathematician. No. 2203, Aleksa Santic (1868-1924), poet.

1993, Apr. 1
2200	A723	40,000d multicolored	1.40	1.40
2201	A723	40,000d multicolored	1.40	1.40
2202	A723	40,000d multicolored	1.40	1.40
2203	A723	40,000d multicolored	1.40	1.40
		Nos. 2200-2203 (4)	5.60	5.60

Joy of Europe — A724

Children's paintings: No. 2204, Girl holding flowers, children, dove, by M. Markovski. No. 2205, Angels, birds, by J. Rugovac.

1993, Apr. 5
2204	A724	50,000d multicolored	1.40	1.40
2205	A724	50,000d multicolored	1.75	1.75

Contemporary Art — A725

Europa: No. 2206, Nude with a Mirror, by M. Milunovic. No. 2207, Composition, by M.P. Barili.

1993, May 5
2206	A725	95,000d multicolored	2.75	2.75
2207	A725	95,000d multicolored	2.75	2.75

A726

A727

A728

A729

A730

Ancient Fortresses: No. 2208, Sutorina, Montenegro. No. 2209, Kalemegdan, Belgrade. No. 2210, Medun, Montenegro. No. 2211, Petrovaradin, near Novi Sad. No. 2212, Bar, Montenegro. No. 2213, Golubac.

1993, July 9   Booklet Stamps
2208	A726	900,000d multi	1.00	1.00
2209	A727	900,000d multi	1.00	1.00
2210	A728	900,000d multi	1.00	1.00
2211	A729	900,000d multi	1.00	1.00
2212	A730	900,000d multi	1.00	1.00
2213	A730	900,000d multi	1.00	1.00
a.		Booklet pane, #2208-2213	6.00	
		Complete booklet, #2213a	6.00	

Flowers A731

Colors of various flowers in vases: No. 2214, Yellow, white. No. 2215, Orange, red. No. 2216, Purple, pink, white. No. 2217, Mixed.

1993, July 10   Perf. 14
2214	A731	1,000,000d multi	1.40	1.40
2215	A731	1,000,000d multi	1.40	1.40
2216	A731	1,000,000d multi	1.40	1.40
2217	A731	1,000,000d multi	1.40	1.40
		Nos. 2214-2217 (4)	5.60	5.60

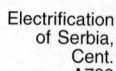

Electrification of Serbia, Cent. A732

1993, July 28   Perf. 13½
2218	A732	2,500,000d multi	.70	.65

European Nature Protection A733

Designs: No. 2219, Garrulus glandarius. No. 2220, Oriolus oriolus.

1993, Sept. 30
2219	A733	300,000,000d multi	6.25	6.25
2220	A733	300,000,000d multi	6.25	6.25

Nos. 2147a, 2135, 2144, 2136 and 2140 Srchd.

No. 2143 Surcharged

1993   Perf. 13¼
2220A	A702i	10d on 100,000d	.90	.90
b.		Perf 12½	1.75	.25
2220B	A702a	50d on 5d	1.00	.25
2220C	A702f	100d on 5000d	1.00	.25
2220D	A702	500d on 50d	1.00	.60
2220E	A702e	1000d on 3000d	1.00	.60
b.		Perf 12½	1.00	.25
2220F	A702b	10,000d on 300d	1.00	.25
2220G	A702a	50,000d on 50d on 5d	2.75	.75
		Nos. 2220A-2220G (7)	8.65	3.25

Issued: 50,000d, 11/9/93; others, 10/18/93. Size and location of surcharge varies.

No 2220G was created by applying three additional "0"s to the "50" surcharge on No. 2220B.

A734

Cooperation on the Danube River — A735

Designs: No. 2221, Ships on river. No. 2222, Ship going down river. 20,000d, Map showing location of Danube River.

1993, Oct. 20   Perf. 14
2221	A734	15,000d multicolored	1.40	1.40
2222	A734	15,000d multicolored	1.40	1.40

Souvenir Sheet
2223	A735	20,000d multicolored	2.75	2.75

Post Office in Jagodina, 150th Anniv. A736

1993, Oct. 30   Perf. 13½
2224	A736	12,000d multicolored	1.50	1.00

Stamp Day.

Joy of Europe — A737

Paintings: No. 2225, Boy with Cat, by Sava Sumanovic (1896-1942). No. 2226, Circus Rider, by Georges Rouault (1871-1958).

1993, Nov. 26
2225	A737	2,000,000d multi	1.40	1.40
2226	A737	2,000,000d multi	1.40	1.40

Icons in Monasteries A738

Designs: No. 2227, The Annunciation, Mileseva. No. 2228, Nativity, Studenica. No. 2229, Madonna and Child, Bogorodica Ljeviska. No. 2230, Flight into Egypt, Oplenac.

1993, Dec. 15
2227	A738	400,000,000d multi	1.00	1.00
2228	A738	400,000,000d multi	1.00	1.00
2229	A738	400,000,000d multi	1.00	1.00
2230	A738	400,000,000d multi	1.00	1.00
	Nos. 2227-2230 (4)		4.00	4.00

Traditional Houses — A739

#2231, A-frame huts, Savardak, horiz. #2232, Watchtower. #2233, Stone house on edge of river. #2234, Crmnicka house, Bar, horiz.

1993, Dec. 31
2231	A739	50d multicolored	1.00	1.00
2232	A739	50d multicolored	1.00	1.00
2233	A739	50d multicolored	1.00	1.00
2234	A739	50d multicolored	1.00	1.00
	Nos. 2231-2234 (4)		4.00	4.00

Publication of Oktoechos, 500th Anniv. — A740

1994, Jan. 17   **Litho.**   **Perf. 13½**
2235	A740	1000d Text	.80	.80
2236	A740	1000d Liturgists	.80	.80

Raptors A741

Designs: a, Neophron percnopterus. b, Falco cherrug. c, Buteo rufinus. d, Falco naumanni.

1994, Feb. 7
2237	A741	80p Strip of 4, #a.-d. + label	22.50	22.50

Intl. Mimosa Festival, Herceg-Novi A742

1994, Feb. 28
2238	A742	80p multicolored	1.40	1.40

Natl. Museum, Belgrade, 150th Anniv. A743

Design: No. 2240, National Theater, Belgrade, 125th anniv., portrait of Prince Milos Obrenovic.

1994, Mar. 19
2239	A743	80p multicolored	1.40	1.40
2240	A743	80p multicolored	1.40	1.40

1994 Winter Olympics, Lillehammer — A744

a, Speed skater. b. Olympic rings, flame. c, Skier.

1994, Apr. 11
2241	A744	60p Strip of 3, #a.-c.	3.25	3.25

Europa A745

Map of flight route and: 60p, Kodron C61, automobile. 1.80d, Kodron C61 in air over Belgrade.

1994, May 5
2242	A745	60p multicolored	1.75	1.75
2243	A745	1.80d multicolored	2.25	2.25

First night flight Paris-Belgrade-Bucharest-Istanbul, piloted by Louis Guidon, 1923.

Burning of Relics of Holy Sava, 400th Anniv. A746

1994, May 10   **Perf. 14**
2244	A746	60p multicolored	1.75	1.75

1994 World Cup Soccer Championships, U.S. — A747

60p, Three players with arms raised in victory. 1d, Three players down on ground.

1994, June 10   **Perf. 13½**
2245	A747	60p multicolored	1.40	1.40
2246	A747	1d multicolored	1.40	1.40

A748

1994, July 8
2247	A748	60p Basset hound	1.40	1.40
2248	A748	60p Maltese	1.40	1.40
2249	A748	60p Welsh terrier	1.40	1.40
2250	A748	1d Husky	1.40	1.40
	Nos. 2247-2250 (4)		5.60	5.60

A749

1994, July 20
2251	A749	60p multicolored	1.40	1.40

Assembly of Eastern Orthodox Christian nations.

Protecting the Ecology of Montenegro A750

1994, July 28
2252	A750	50p Tcherna Gora Park	1.40	1.40

Nos. 2148, 2145 Surcharged

1994, July 15   **Perf. 13½**
2253	A702j	10p on 100,000d	.50	.50
2254	A702g	50p on 10,000d	.90	.65

A751

Monasteries: 1p, Moraca, 13th cent. 5p, Gracanica, 14th cent. 10p, Ostrog. No. 2258-2259, Lazarica, 14th cent. 50p, Studenica, 12th cent. 1d, Sopocani, 13th cent.

Inscribed "1994"

1994   **Litho.**   **Perf. 13¼**
2255	A751	1p bister & purple	1.40	.25
a.		Perf 12½, Inscr. "1997"	1.40	.25
2256	A751	5p yel brn & blue	1.40	.25
a.		Perf 12½, Inscr. "1998"	1.40	.25
2257	A751	10p magenta & slate	.55	.25
a.		Perf 12½, Inscr. "1998"	.55	.25
2258	A751	20p lil rose & pale vio	.90	.25
2259	A751	20p pale org & gray	35.00	.25
a.		Perf 12½, Inscr. "1998"	1.75	.25
2260	A751	50p deep pur & mag	.55	.25
a.		Inscribed "1997"	.55	.25
b.		As "a," perf 12½	.55	.25
2261	A751	1d blue & org brown	1.40	.50
a.		Perf 12½, Inscr. "1997"	1.40	.50
	Nos. 2255-2261 (7)		41.20	2.00

UNESCO (#2260-2261).

Issued: 1p, 5p, #2258, 1d, 8/15; #2259, 9/10; 10p, 50p, 11/10.
Nos. 2262-2271 are unassigned.
For surcharges, see Serbia Nos. 195, 260-261.

A752

1994, Sept. 10
2272	A752	50p multicolored	.90	.90

St. Arsenius Seminary, Sremski Karlovci, bicent.

European Nature Protection A753

Designs: 1d, Fishing pier, Reka Bojana. 1.50d, Lake, Belgrade.

1994, Sept. 20
2273	A753	1d multicolored	2.75	2.75
2274	A753	1.50d multicolored	2.75	2.75

Painting by U. Knezevic — A754

1994, Oct. 5   **Perf. 14**
2275	A754	1d multicolored	1.75	1.75

Joy of Europe.

Sailing Ships in Bottles — A755

a, Revenge, 1585. b, Grand yacht, 1678. c, Santa Maria, 15th cent. d, Nava, 15th cent. e, Mayflower, 1615. f, Carrack, 14th cent.

1994, Oct. 27   **Perf. 13½**
2276	A755	50p Bklt. pane of 6, #a.-f.	6.00	6.00
	Complete booklet, #2276		6.00	

Stamp Day — A756

1994, Oct. 31
2277	A756	50p multicolored	4.00	4.00

Drawings on Gravestones
A757

#2278, Man holding umbrella, purse. #2279, 2 men. #2280, Cemetery, stone with man on horse, inscriptions. #2281, Fence, 2 gravestones, cross, man.

1994, Nov. 25
2278	A757	50p multicolored	.80 .80
2279	A757	50p multicolored	.80 .80
2280	A757	50p multicolored	.80 .80
2281	A757	50p multicolored	.80 .80
	Nos. 2278-2281 (4)		3.20 3.20

Religious Art — A758

#2282, The Annunciation, by D. Bacevic. #2283, Adoration of the Magi, by N. Neskovic. #2284, Madonna and Child, by T.N. Cesljar. #2285, St. John Baptizing Christ, by T. Kracun.

1994, Dec. 15
2282	A758	60p multicolored	.80 .80
2283	A758	60p multicolored	.80 .80
2284	A758	60p multicolored	.80 .80
2285	A758	60p multicolored	.80 .80
	Nos. 2282-2285 (4)		3.20 3.20

Natl. Symbols A759

1995, Jan. 26   Litho.   Perf. 13½
2286	A759	1d Flag	1.50 1.50
2287	A759	1d Arms	1.50 1.50

Sheets of 8

World Chess Champions — A760

#2288: a, Wilhelm Steinitz (1836-1900), Austria. b, Silhouettes of chessman. c, Emmanuel Lasker (1868-1941), Germany. d, Knight. e, Chessman, row of pawns at top. f, José Raúl Capablanca (1888-1942), Cuba. g, Chessman, rook at left. h, Alexander Alekhine (1892-1946), Russia.
#2289: a, Max Euwe, Netherlands. b, Board, pawn in center. c, Mikhail M. Botvinik, Soviet Union. d, Board, queen in middle. e, Board, bishop, knight. f, Vassili Smyslov, Soviet Union. g, Silhouette of knight, rook queen, chessboard. h, Mikhail N. Tal, Soviet Union.

1995
2288	A760	60p #a.-h. + label	10.00 10.00
2289	A760	60p #a.-h. + label	10.00 10.00
	Issued: No. 2288, 2/28; No. 2289, 9/1.		

Red Star Army Sport Club, 50th Anniv. A761

1995, Mar. 4
2290	A761	60p bl, red & bister	1.75 1.75

Protection of Nature A762

a, Salamandra salamandra. b, Triturus alpestris. c, Rana graeca. d, Pelobates syriacus balcanicus.

1995, Mar. 23
2291	A762	60p Strip of 4, #a.-d. + label	10.00 10.00

A763

1995, Apr. 20
2292	A763	60p multicolored	1.50 1.50
	Radnicki Soccer Club, Belgrade, 75th anniv.		

A764

Europa: 60p, Eagle, mountains. 1.90d, Girl on tricycle, elderly man, woman on park bench, horiz.

1995, May 6
2293	A764	60p multicolored	3.00 2.50
2294	A764	1.90d multicolored	3.00 2.50

A765

1995, May 9
2295	A765	60p multicolored	1.50 1.50
	End of World War II, 50th anniv.		

A766

1995, May 28
2296	A766	60p multicolored	2.00 2.00
	Opening of Vukov-Denkmal Subway Station, Belgrade.		

Draba Bertiscea A767

a, shown. b, Plants, diff. c, Flowers, mountain. d, Plants on rock, stems at right.

1995, June 12
2297	A767	60p Strip of 4, #a.-d. + label	10.00 10.00

European Nature Protection A768

Designs: 60p, Eremophila alpestris balcanica. 1.90d, Rhinolophus blasii.

1995, July 10
2298	A768	60p multicolored	2.00 2.00
2299	A768	1.90d multicolored	2.50 2.50

Slovakian Folk Festival, by Zuzka Medvedova (1897-1985), Painter — A769

1995, Aug. 3
2300	A769	60p multicolored	1.25 1.25

Volleyball, Cent. — A770

1995, Sept. 10
2301	A770	90d multicolored	1.25 1.25

Church of St. Luke, Kotor, 800th Anniv. — A771

1995, Sept. 20
2302	A771	80p multicolored	1.25 1.25

Motion Pictures, Cent. A772

Designs: 1.10d, Newsreel showing coronation of King Peter II. 2.20d, Auguste and Louis Jean Lumière, film projector.

1995, Oct. 3
2303	A772	1.10d dk brn, lt red brn	1.50 1.50
2304	A772	2.20d dk brn, lt red brn	1.50 1.50

Army Sports Club "Partisan," 50th Anniv. — A773

1995, Oct. 4
2305	A773	80p multi + label	1.25 1.25

UN, 50th Anniv. — A774

1995, Oct. 24
2306	A774	1.10d multicolored	1.25 1.25

Stamp Day — A775

1995, Oct. 31
2307	A775	1.10d multicolored	1.00 1.00

Joy of Europe — A776

Paintings: 1.10d, Young boy by Milos Tenkovic. 2.20d, Young girl by Pierre Bonnard.

1995, Nov. 26
2308	A776	1.10d multicolored	1.50 1.50
2309	A776	2.20d multicolored	1.50 1.50
	Children's Day.		

Souvenir Sheet

JUFIZ VIII, Natl. Philatelic Exhibition, Budva — A777

Design: Montenegro #37, Serbia #6.

1995, Dec. 13   Perf. 14
2310	A777	2.50d Sheet of 1 + label	2.00 2.00

Christmas
A778

Contemporary religious paintings: No. 2311, Flight into Egypt, by Z. Halupova. No. 2312, Nativity, by D. Milojevic, vert. No. 2313, Outdoor Christmas scene, by M. Rasic, vert. No. 2314, Indoor traditional Christmas scene, by J. Brasic.

1995, Dec. 26   **Perf. 13½**
2311	A778	1.10d multicolored	.50	.50
2312	A778	1.10d multicolored	.50	.50
2313	A778	2.20d multicolored	1.00	1.00
2314	A778	2.20d multicolored	1.00	1.00
		Nos. 2311-2314 (4)	3.00	3.00

Airplanes
A779

1995, Dec. 26
2315	A779	1.10d Saric No. 1	.50	.50
2316	A779	1.10d Douglas DC-3	.50	.50
2317	A779	2.20d Fizir FN	1.00	1.00
2318	A779	2.20d Caravelle	1.00	1.00
		Nos. 2315-2318 (4)	3.00	3.00

Battle of Mojkovac, 80th Anniv. — A780

Design: Montenegrins on mountain.

1996, Jan. 6
2319	A780	1.10d multicolored	.50	.50

Birth of Sava Sumanovic, Cent. A781

Design: 1927 Painting, "Drink Boat."

1996, Jan. 22
2320	A781	1.10d multicolored	.50	.50

Insects — A782

a, Pyrgomorphela serbica. b, Calosoma sycopanta. c, Formica rufa. d, Ascalaphus macaronius.

1996, Feb. 15
2321	A782	2.20d Strip of 4, #a.-d. + label	7.00	7.00

Protection of nature.

A783

Churches.

1996, Feb. 29   **Litho.**   **Perf. 12½**
2322	A783	5d Ljeviska	2.00	1.50
2323	A783	10d Zica	4.00	3.00
2324	A783	20d Decani	8.00	6.00
		Nos. 2322-2324 (3)	14.00	10.50

Chess Champions — A784

Designs: a, Tigran Petrosian, Soviet Union. b, Chess pieces, sundial, chess board. c, Boris Spassky, Soviet Union. d, Chess pieces, board, clock showing two time zones. e, Garry Kasparov, Soviet Union. f, Chess pieces, hand holding hour glass. g, Bobby Fischer, US. h, Chess pieces, six clocks. i, Anatoly Karpov, Soviet Union.

1996, Mar. 15   **Litho.**   **Perf. 13½**
2325	A784	1.50d Sheet of 9, #a.-i.	6.00	6.00

Olympic Games, Cent. A786

1.50d, Discus throwers. 2.50d, Runners.

Perf. 13½x13¼
1996, Mar. 30   **Litho.**
2326	A786	1.50d multi	.75	.75
2327	A786	2.50d multi	1.25	1.25

1996 Summer Olympics, Atlanta — A787

1996, Apr. 12
2328	A787	1.50d shown	1.50	1.50
2329	A787	1.50d Basketball	1.50	1.50
2330	A787	1.50d Handball	1.50	1.50
2331	A787	1.50d Volleyball	1.50	1.50
2332	A787	1.50d Shooting	1.50	1.50
2333	A787	1.50d Water polo	1.50	1.50
		Nos. 2328-2333 (6)	9.00	9.00

1996 Summer Olympic Games, Atlanta — A787a

1996, Apr. 12   **Litho.**   **Perf. 13**
2334	A787	5d Sheet of 1 + label	2.00	2.00

Stamp Day — A788

1996, Apr. 30   **Litho.**   **Perf. 13½**
2335	A788	1.50d Railway mail car	.60	.60

Famous Women Writers — A789

Europa: 2.50d, Isidora Sekulic (1877-1958). 5d, Desanka Maksimovic (1898-1993).

1996, May 7   **Litho.**   **Perf. 13½**
2336	A789	2.50d multicolored	2.00	2.00
2337	A789	5d multicolored	2.00	2.00

Serbian Red Cross, 120th Anniv. A790

1996, May 8
2338	A790	1.50d Dr. Vladan Djordjevic	.60	.60

Architectural Education in Yugoslavia, 150th Anniv. — A791

1996, June 1   **Litho.**   **Perf. 13½**
2339	A791	1.50d multicolored	.60	.60

European Nature Protection A792

2.50d, Platalea leucorodia. 5d, Plegadis falcinellus.

1996, June 28
2340	A792	2.50d multicolored	1.00	1.00
2341	A792	5d multicolored	2.00	2.00

Prince Peter I Petrovic at Battle of Martinici, 1796 — A793

Design: 2.50d, Prince's Guard at Battle of Kruse (1796), by Valerio, vert.

1996, July 22
2342	A793	1.50d multicolored	.50	.50
2343	A793	2.50d multicolored	1.00	1.00

Horse Racing, Ljubicevo A794

1996, Sept. 2   **Litho.**   **Perf. 13½**
2344	A794	1.50d shown	.50	.50
2345	A794	2.50d 3 horses racing	1.00	1.00

Fauna — A795

Designs: a, 1.50d, Probosciger aterrimus. b, 2.50d, Goura scheepmakeri. c, 1.50d, Equus burchelli. d, 2.50d, Panthera tigris.

1996, Sept. 25
2346	A795	Strip of 4, #a.-d. + label	8.00	8.00

Belgrade Zoo, 60th anniv.

Children's Day — A796

1996, Oct. 2
2347	A796	1.50d multicolored	.70	.70
2348	A796	2.50d Bird	1.25	1.25

Medalists, 1996 Summer Olympic Games A797

Designs: No. 2349, Shooting, bronze. No. 2350, Shooting, bronze. No. 2351, Volleyball, bronze. No. 2352, Basketball, silver.

1996, Oct. 31   **Litho.**   **Perf. 13½**
2349	A797	2.50d multicolored	1.40	1.40
2350	A797	2.50d multicolored	1.40	1.40
2351	A797	2.50d multicolored	1.40	1.40
2352	A797	2.50d multicolored	1.40	1.40
		Nos. 2349-2352 (4)	5.60	5.60

Savings Accounts, 75th Anniv. — A798

1996, Oct. 31   **Litho.**   **Perf. 13½**
2353	A798	1.50d multicolored	.70	.70

Soccer in Yugoslavia, Cent. — A799

1996, Nov. 8   **Litho.**   **Perf. 13½**
2354	A799	1.50d multicolored	.70	.70

Archaeological Finds — A800

Sculptures: No. 2355, God of Autumn. No. 2356, Mother with child. No. 2357, Head of woman. No. 2358, Redheaded goddess.

1996, Nov. 25
2355	A800	1.50d multicolored	.60	.50
2356	A800	1.50d multicolored	.60	.50
2357	A800	2.50d multicolored	1.00	.75
2358	A800	2.50d multicolored	1.00	.75
		Nos. 2355-2358 (4)	3.20	2.50

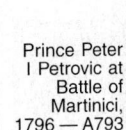

A801

Christmas (Paintings): No. 2359, Annunciation. No. 2360, Mother of God with Christ. No. 2361, Birth of Christ. No. 2362, Palm Sunday.

1996, Dec. 10
2359	A801	1.50d multicolored	.60	.50
2360	A801	1.50d multicolored	.60	.50
2361	A801	2.50d multicolored	1.00	.75
2362	A801	2.50d multicolored	1.00	.75
		Nos. 2359-2362 (4)	3.20	2.50

A802

1997, Jan. 24   Litho.   Perf. 13½
2363 A802 1.50d multicolored   .60   .60

Radomir Putnik Voivode, 150th birth anniv.

25th Intl. Film Festival, Belgrade
A803

1997, Jan. 31
2364 A803 1.50d multicolored   .70   .70

Protected Birds — A804

Designs: No. 2365, Dendrocopos major. No. 2366, Nucifraga caryocatactes. No. 2367, Parus cristatus. No. 2368, Erithacus rubecula.

1997, Feb. 21
2365	A804	1.50d multicolored	.60	.60
2366	A804	2.50d multicolored	.60	.60
2367	A804	1.50d multicolored	.90	.90
2368	A804	2.50d multicolored	.90	.90
a.		Strip of 4, #2365-2368 + label	7.00	7.00

A805

1997, Mar. 17   Litho.   Perf. 13
2369 A805 1.50d multicolored   1.00   1.00

St. Achilleus Church, 700th Anniv.

A806

Design: Prince Peter I Petrovic (1747-1830), Bishop of Montenegro.

1997, Apr. 3   Perf. 13½
2370 A806 1.50d multicolored   1.00   1.00

A807

1997, Apr. 19
2371 A807 2.50d multicolored   1.25   1.25

10th Belgrade Marathon.

A808

1997, Apr. 22   Litho.   Perf. 13½
2372 A808 2.50d multicolored   1.25   1.25

Serbian Medical Assoc., 125th anniv.

Air Mail Being Loaded at Night
A809

1997, May 3
2373 A809 2.50d multicolored   1.25   1.25

Stamp Day.

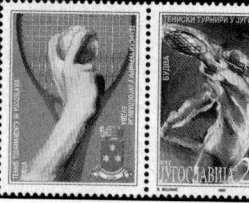

Tennis Tournaments in Yugoslavia — A810

Stylized designs: No. 2374, Player, large racket overhead, Budva. No. 2375, Player with ball flying from racket, Belgrade. No. 2376, Player with racket out in front, Novi Sad.

1997, May 8
2374	A810	2.50d multi + label	1.25	1.25
2375	A810	2.50d multi + label	1.25	1.25
2376	A810	2.50d multi + label	1.25	1.25
		Nos. 2374-2376 (3)	3.75	3.75

Stories and Legends
A811

Europa: 2.50d, Shackled Bach Chelik surrounded by creatures. 6d, Bach Chelik in chains, prince fighting with him, princess, castle.

1997, May 30   Perf. 11½
2377 A811 2.50d multicolored   2.00   2.00
2378 A811 6d multicolored   2.00   2.00

Each issued in sheets of 8 + label.

European Nature Protection
A812

2.50d, Cerambyx cerdo. 6d, Quercus robur.

1997, June 5
2379 A812 2.50d multicolored   1.00   1.00
2380 A812 6d multicolored   2.00   2.00

Stanislav Binicki (1872-1947) — A813

1997, June 7   Perf. 13½
2381 A813 2.50d multicolored   1.00   1.00

Printing of Gorski Vijenac, 150th Anniv. — A814

1997, June 7
2382 A814 2.50d multicolored   1.00   1.00

Flowers — A815

Designs: a, 1.50d, Pelargonium grandiflorum. b, 2.50d, Saintpaulia ionantha. c, 1.50d, Hydrangea macrophylla. d, 2.50d, Oncidium varicosum.

1997, Sept. 10   Litho.   Perf. 13
2383 A815 Strip of 4, #a.-d. + label   7.00   7.00

Souvenir Sheet

JUFIZ IX, 9th Natl. Philatelic Exhibition — A816

Design: Sculpture, by Dragomir Arambasic, in front of art gallery.

1997, Sept. 10   Perf. 14
2384 A816 5d multicolored   2.50   2.50

A817

1997, Sept. 24   Perf. 13½x14
2385 A817 2.50d multicolored   1.00   1.00

Serbian Chemical Society, cent.

Type of 1993
Size: 18x18mm

1997, Oct. 2   Perf. 14
2386 A702d (A) like #2142   1.00   .25
a. Dated "1999"   1.00   .25

A818

Joy of Europe children's art works: 2.50d, 5d, Busts of people formed from collage of various food products.

1997, Oct. 2
2387 A818 2.50d multicolored   1.00   1.00
2388 A818 5d multicolored   2.00   2.00

"May Assembly in Sremski Karlivoci," by Pavle Simic — A819

1997, Oct. 10   Litho.   Perf. 14
2389 A819 2.50d multicolored   1.00   1.00

Matica Srpska Gallery, 150th anniv.

A820

Museum exhibits: No. 2390, Two-headed statuette. No. 2391, Parade helmet. No. 2392, Terra cotta statuette. No. 2393, Virgin icon.

1997, Nov. 12
2390	A820	1.50d multicolored	.50	.50
2391	A820	1.50d multicolored	.50	.50
2392	A820	2.50d multicolored	1.00	1.00
2393	A820	2.50d multicolored	1.00	1.00
		Nos. 2390-2393 (4)	3.00	3.00

A821

Icons (Chelandari Serbian Monastery, Mount Athos): No. 2394, Christ. No. 2395, Madonna and Child, 12th cent. No. 2396, Madonna and Child, 13th cent. No. 2397, 3-handed Madonna.

Granite Paper

1997, Dec. 2   *Perf. 11½*
2394 A821 1.50d multicolored .50 .50
2395 A821 1.50d multicolored .50 .50
2396 A821 2.50d multicolored 1.00 1.00
2397 A821 2.50d multicolored 1.00 1.00
Nos. 2394-2397 (4) 3.00 3.00

A822

1998, Jan. 20   Litho.   *Perf. 13½*
2398 A822 1.50d Savina 1.00 1.00
2399 A822 2.50d Donji Brceli 1.00 1.00

Monasteries of Montenegro.

A823

1998, Feb. 6   *Perf. 14*
2400 A823 2.50d Figure skater 2.00 2.00
2401 A823 6d Skier 2.00 2.00

1998 Winter Olympic Games, Nagano.

Horses
A824

Designs: a, 1.50d, Two running. b, 2.50d, Arabian up close. c, 1.50d, Thoroughbred. d, 2.50d, Thoroughbred running on race track.

1998, Feb. 26   Litho.   *Perf. 12x11½*
2402 A824 Strip of 4, #a.-d. +
    label 10.00 10.00

Intl.
Women's
Day
A825

1998, Mar. 7   *Perf. 13½*
2403 A825 2.50d multicolored 1.00 1.00

Yugoslav
Airlines
Assoc., 50th
Anniv.
A826

1998, Apr. 24
2404 A826 2.50d multicolored 1.00 1.00

Europa — A827

Paintings: 6d, "Dressing the Bride," by Paja Jovanovic (1859-1957). 9d, "Bishop's Congratulations," by Pero Pocek (1878-1963).

1998, May 4   *Perf. 12*
     Granite Paper
2405 A827 6d multicolored 3.00 3.00
2406 A827 9d on 2.50d, multi 3.00 3.00

No. 2406 was not issued without the silver surcharge.

1998 World Cup
Soccer
Championships,
France — A828

1998, May 15   Litho.   *Perf. 13½*
2407 A828 6d shown 1.75 1.75
2408 A828 9d Soccer players,
    diff. 2.75 2.75

Souvenir Sheet

Danube Commission, 50th
Anniv. — A829

1998, May 19   *Perf. 14*
2409 A829 9d multicolored 4.00 4.00

European
Nature
Protection
A830

Designs: 6d, Heracium blecicii. 9d, Mola mola, vert.

1998, June 17   Litho.   *Perf. 13¾*
2410 A830 6d multi 1.25 1.25
2411 A830 9d multi 1.75 1.75

Each stamp was printed in sheets of 8 + label.

Famous People of
Serbia — A831

a, Djura Jaksic (1832-78), poet, painter. b, Nadezda Petrovic (1873-1915), painter. c, Radoje Domanovic (1873-1908), writer. d, Vasilije Mokranjac (1923-1984), composer. e, Streten Stojanovic (1898-1960), sculptor. f, Milan Konjovic (1898-1993), painter. g, Desanka Maksimovic (1898-1993), poet. h, Ivan Tabakovic (1898-1977), painter.

1998, June 30   *Perf. 12*
     Granite Paper
     Sheet of 8
2412 A831 1.50d #a.-h. + label 3.25 3.25

Souvenir Sheet

Yugoslavia, Winner of World
Basketball Championships — A832

1998, Aug. 21   *Perf. 13½*
2413 A832 10d multicolored 8.00 8.00

Protected Animals — A833

a, 2d, Martes martes. b, 2d, Anthropoides virgo. c, 5d, Lynx lynx. d, 5d, Loxia curvirostra.

1998, Sept. 2
2414 A833 Strip of 4, #a.-d. +
    label 9.00 9.00

Breaking of
the
Thessaloniki
Front, 80th
Anniv.
A834

Designs: No. 2415, 5d, Soldiers and cannons. No. 2416, 5d, Soldiers with machine guns, binoculars.

1998, Sept. 15   Engr.   *Perf. 13½*
2415-2416 A834 Set of 2 3.50 3.50

Stamp
Day — A835

1998, Sept. 28
2417 A835 6d Prussian blue 1.40 1.40

Serbian Philatelic Society, 50th anniv.

Joy of Europe
Children's
Drawings
A836

Designs: 6d, Fish. 9d, Fish, diff.

1998, Oct. 2   Litho.   *Perf. 13¾*
2418-2419 A836 Set of 2 3.50 3.50

Development of the Railway — A837

Souvenir Sheet

Trains: a, 1847. b, 1900. c, 1920. d, 1930. e, Diesel locomotive. f, 1990.

1998, Nov. 3   Litho.   *Perf. 13½*
2420 A837 2.50d Booklet pane of
    6, #a.-f. 9.00 9.00
    Complete booklet, #2420 9.50

Paintings of
Sailing
Ships,
Maritime
Museum,
Kotor
A838

#2421, Veracruz, 1873. #2422, Pierino, 1883. #2423, Draghetto, 1865. #2424, Group of ships.

1998, Nov. 11   *Perf. 12*
     Granite Paper
2421 A838 2d multicolored .50 .50
2422 A838 5d multicolored .50 .50
2423 A838 5d multicolored 1.50 1.50
2424 A838 5d multicolored 1.50 1.50
Nos. 2421-2424 (4) 4.00 4.00

Chelandari Monastery, 800th
Anniv. — A839

Views of monastery: No. 2425, Looking from center of complex, two trees. No. 2426, Group of taller buildings. No. 2427, Aerial view. No. 2428, Looking across group of buildings, crosses on turrets.

1998, Dec. 9   *Perf. 14*
2425 A839 2d multicolored .50 .50
2426 A839 2d multicolored .50 .50
2427 A839 5d multicolored 1.25 1.25
2428 A839 5d multicolored 1.25 1.25
Nos. 2425-2428 (4) 3.50 3.50

Third Meeting
of Southeast
European
Postal
Ministers
A840

1998, Dec. 17   Litho.   *Perf. 14*
2429 A840 5d multicolored 3.00 3.00

Souvenir Sheet

Yugoslavia, Silver Medalists at 1998
World Volleyball
Championships — A841

1998, Dec. 19   *Perf. 13½*
2430 A841 10d multicolored *50.00 50.00*

Post and Telecommunications
Museum, Belgrade, 75th
Anniv. — A842

#2431, Postrider. #No. 2432, Antique tele-
graph equipment, museum building.

1998, Dec. 21   **Engr.**
2431 A842 5d olive brown & slate 1.00 1.00
2432 A842 5d red & brown   1.00 1.00

Serbian
Monasteries
A843

1999, Jan. 14   **Litho.**   **Perf. 13¾**
2433 A843 2d Visoki Decani   .60 .60
2434 A843 5d Grachanica   1.60 1.60

Farm Animals
A844

Designs: a, 2d, Pigs. b, 6d, Goat. c, 2d,
Oxen. d, 6d, Long-horn sheep.

1999, Feb. 5   **Litho.**   **Perf. 13½**
2435 A844 Strip of 4, #a.-d. +
     label   7.00 7.00

A845

1999, Feb. 24   **Litho.**   **Perf. 13¼**
2436 A845 6d Scouting   2.00 2.00

A846

1999, Mar. 27
2437 A846 6d brown & buff   1.40 1.40
Yugoslav Bar Association, 70th anniv.

Target
A847   A848

1999   **Perf. 12¼x12½**
2438 A847 (A) black   5.00 3.00
2439 A848 (A) black & red   20.00 12.00
Issued: No. 2438, 3/27; No. 2439, 4/7. Nos.
2438-2439 sold for 2.04d when issued.

World Table Tennis Championships,
Belgrade — A849

1999, Apr. 9   **Perf. 13¼**
Player colors
2440 A849 6d blue & red   2.00 2.00
2441 A849 6d green & red   2.00 2.00

A850

Europa, National Parks and Reserves: 6d,
Falcon, trees, mountains, Kopaonik Natl. Park.
15d, Flowers, mountains, Lovcen Natl. Park.

1999, May 5   **Photo.**   **Perf. 11¾**
Granite Paper
2442 A850 6d multicolored   6.00 6.00
2443 A850 15d multicolored   6.00 6.00
Each printed in shhets of 8 + 1 central label.

A851

European Nature Protection: 6d, Shovel,
spider web. 15d, Thumb squeezing earth.

1999, May 13   **Perf. 11¾x12**
2444 A851 6d multicolored   2.50 2.50
2445 A851 15d multicolored   2.50 2.50

Mushrooms
A852

Designs: a, Amanita virosa. b, Amanita
pantherina. c, Hypholoma fasciculare. d,
Ramaria pallida.

1999, June 18   **Litho.**   **Perf. 11¾x12**
Granite Paper
2446 A852 6d Strip of 4, #a.-
     d., + central la-
     bel   10.00 10.00
Central labels differ on sheet.

Famous Montenegrins — A853

Designs: a, Stjepan Mitrov Ljubisa (1824-
78). b, Marko Milanov (1833-1901). c, Pero
Pocek (1878-1963). d, Risto Stijovic (1894-
1974). e, Milo Milunovic (1897-1967). f, Petar
Lubarda (1907-74). g, Vuko Radovic (1911-
96). h, Mihailo Lalic (1914-92).

1999, June 30   **Perf. 13¼**
2447 A853 2d Sheet of 8, #a.-h.,
     + central label   3.25 3.25

UPU, 125th
Anniv.
A854

1999, Sept. 15   **Perf. 13¼**
2448 A854 6d shown   1.00 1.00
2449 A854 12d Envelopes cir-
     cling globe   2.00 2.00

Joy of Europe
Children's
Drawings
A855

1999, Oct. 1   **Perf. 13¾**
2450 A855 6d Lion   1.00 1.00
2451 A855 15d Family, vert.   2.50 2.50

Frédéric Chopin
(1810-49),
Composer
A856

1999, Oct. 15   **Perf. 13¼**
2452 A856 10d multi   2.25 2.25

No. 2438,
Mastheads of
"Filatelista"
A857

1999, Oct. 18
2453 A857 10d multi   1.50 1.50
Stamp Day.

A858

Bridges
Destroyed by
NATO Air
Strikes
A859

Bridges: #2454, Varadinski. #2455,
Ostruznica. #2456, Murino. #2457, Grdelica.
#2458, Bistrica. #2459, Zezeljev.

1999, Oct. 29   **Perf. 13¾**
2454 A858 2d shown   .90 .90
2455 A859 2d shown   .90 .90
2456 A859 2d multi   .90 .90
2457 A859 6d multi   .90 .90
2458 A859 6d multi   .90 .90
2459 A859 6d multi   .90 .90
     Nos. 2454-2459 (6)   5.40 5.40

Millennium
A860

a, 6d, Roman altars, statue of Jupiter. b, 6d,
Sculpture of Emperor Trajan and army leaders, mosaic, lamp, lead mirror. c, 6d, Mosaic
of Dionysius, arch. d, 6d, Hagia Sophia,
mosaic of Madonna and Child, Emperor Constantine. e, 6d, Large cross, candle, fibula,
pot. f, 6d, Church, boats, manuscript. g, 15d,
Nativity and crucifixion of Christ, boats,
farmers.

1999, Nov. 19
2460 A860 Booklet pane of 7,
     #a.-g., + 2 labels   9.00 9.00
   Complete booklet, #2460   9.00
     Size of #2460g: 105x55mm.

A861

Bomb Damage
A862

#2461, Bolnice. #2462, Telecommunications
complex. #2463, Refinery. #2464, Bolnice,
diff. #2465, Telecommunications complex, diff.
#2466, Television complex.

1999, Nov. 27   **Litho.**   **Perf. 13¾**
2461 A861 2d shown   .50 .50
2462 A862 2d shown   .50 .50
2463 A862 2d multi   .50 .50
2464 A862 6d multi   1.00 1.00
2465 A862 6d multi   1.00 1.00
2466 A862 6d multi   1.00 1.00
     Nos. 2461-2466 (6)   4.50 4.50

A863

Frescoes of Poganovo Monastery,
500th Anniv. — A864

Design A863 has Latin letters, A864 has
Cyrillic letters.

1999, Dec. 23
2467	A863	6d shown	.80	.80
2468	A864	6d shown	.80	.80
2469	A863	6d Fresco, diff.	.80	.80
2470	A864	6d Fresco, diff.	.80	.80
		Nos. 2467-2470 (4)	3.20	3.20

A865

Gold Prospectors in Pec River — A866

Design A865 has Latin letters, A866 has Cyrillic letters.

1999, Dec. 30
2471	A865	6d shown	.80	.80
2472	A866	6d shown	.80	.80
2473	A865	6d Prospectors, diff.	.80	.80
2474	A866	6d Prospectors, diff.	.80	.80
		Nos. 2471-2474 (4)	3.20	3.20

Krusedol Monastery A867

2000, Jan. 13   **Perf. 13¼**
2475	A867	10d shown	1.50	1.50
2476	A867	10d Rakovac Monastery	1.50	1.50

Yugoslavian Archives, 50th Anniv. A868

2000, Jan. 21
2477	A868	10d multi	25.00 25.00

Butterflies — A869

No. 2478: a, Nymphalis antiopa. b, Parnalius polyxena. c, Limenitis populi. d, Melanargia galathea.

2000, Feb. 25   **Litho.**   **Perf. 13¾**
2478		Horiz. strip of 4 + central label	18.00 18.00
a.-d.	A869	10d Any single	2.50 2.50

Worldwide Fund for Nature — A870

Perdix perdix: a, Pair in snow. b, Pair facing right. c, Bird on nest. d, Pair, one facing left.

2000, Mar. 14   **Litho.**   **Perf. 12x11¾**
2479	A870	10d Strip of 4, #a.-d., + central label	12.00 12.00

Damage from NATO Airstrikes A871

Various destroyed buildings. Colors: 10d, Blue. 20d, Brown.

2000, Mar. 24   **Engr.**   **Perf. 13¼**
2480-2481	A871	Set of 2	5.00 5.00

Souvenir Sheet

JUFIZ X Philatelic Exhibition, Belgrade — A872

2000, May 2   **Litho.**
2482	A872	15d multi	50.00 50.00

Nature Protection A873

Designs: No. 2483, 30d, Feeding chicks by hand. No. 2484, 30d, Map of Europe in tree's leaves, vert.

Perf. 12x11¾, 11¾x12
2000, May 4   **Litho.**
2483-2484	A873	Set of 2	4.00 4.00

Europa — A874

"2000" and: No. 2485, 30d, Astronaut on moon. No. 2486, 30d, Star and mountains.

2000, May 9   **Perf. 11¾x12**
2485-2486	A874	Set of 2	8.00 8.00

European Soccer Championships A875

Inscriptions in: No. 2487, 30d, Cyrillic letters. No. 2488, 30d, Latin letters.

2000, May 20   **Litho.**   **Perf. 13¾**
2487-2488	A875	Set of 2	6.00 6.00

Postal Services in Serbia, 160th Anniv. — A876

2000, June 7   **Litho.**   **Perf. 13¾**
2489	A876	10d multi	2.00 2.00

2000 Summer Olympics, Sydney — A877

Map of Australia and: 6d, Kangaroo. 12d, Emu. 24d, Koala and soccer ball. 30d, Parrot.

2000, June 28
2490-2493	A877	Set of 4	7.00 7.00

Stamp Day — A878

2000, Sept. 26   **Perf. 13¼**
2494	A878	10d multi	4.50 4.50

"Joy of Europe" A879

Children's art: 30d, Cows. 40d, Cranes, vert.

2000, Oct. 2
2495-2496	A879	Set of 2	3.50 3.50

World Teachers' Day — A880

2000, Oct. 5
2497	A880	10d multi	20.00 20.00

13th Apiarists Congress A881

2000, Oct. 6
2498	A881	10d multi	5.00 5.00

Medals Won at 2000 Summer Olympics A882

Designs: No. 2499, 20d, Water polo (bronze). No. 2500, 20d, Shooting (silver). 30d, Volleyball, vert.

2000, Oct. 23   **Perf. 13¾**
2499-2500	A882	Set of 2	3.00 3.00

Souvenir Sheet
2501	A882	30d multi	20.00 20.00

No. 2501 contains one 35x46mm stamp.

Millennium — A883

No. 2502: a, Ships. b, Papermaking. c, Galileo and telescopes. d, Steam locomotive and steamship. e, Nikola Tesla, invention of the telephone. f, Astronaut, outer space settlement. g, Ships, airplanes, balloons, horses.

2000, Nov. 2   **Litho.**   **Perf. 13¾**
2502	A883	Booklet pane of 7 + 2 labels	6.00 —
a.-f.		12d Any single	.60 .60
g.		40d multi	2.00 2.00
		Booklet, #2502	6.00

Size of No. 2502g: 105x55mm.

Nativity Fresco, Pec — A884

2000, Nov. 7   **Litho.**   **Perf. 13¾**
2503	A884	A multi	3.50 .50

No. 2503 sold for 3.56d on day of issue.

Serb Clothing From the 1900s — A885

Designs: 6d, Vest, Jagodina. 12d, Dresses, Metochija. 24d, Blouse, Pec. 30d, Vest, Kupres.

2000, Dec. 7
2504-2507	A885	Set of 4	3.00 3.00

Montenegrin Religious Art — A886

Designs: 6d, Madonna and Child, 1573-74. 12d, Nativity, 1666-67. 24d, St. Luke, 1672-73. 30d, Madonna and Child, 1642.

2000, Dec. 19
2508-2511	A886	Set of 4	3.00 3.00

A887

A887a

2000, Dec. 29   **Litho.**   **Perf. 13¾**
2512 A887   6d multi   .50 .50
2513 A887a   12d multi   .50 .50

Resumption of Yugoslavia's membership in Organization for Security and Cooperation in Europe (#2512), and United Nations (#2513).

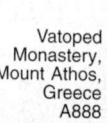

Vatoped Monastery, Mount Athos, Greece
A888

Esfigmen Monastery, Mount Athos, Greece
A889

2001, Jan. 26   **Litho.**   **Perf. 13¼**
2514 A888   10d multi   .55 .55
2515 A889   27d multi   1.60 1.60

Matica Srpska, 175th Anniv. — A890

2001, Feb. 16   **Perf. 13¾**
2516 A890   15d multi   1.10 1.10

Animals — A891

No. 2517: a, Felis leo. b, Ursus maritimus. c, Macaca fuscata. d, Spheniscus humboldti.

2001, Feb. 23
2517   Horiz. strip of 4 + central label   7.25 7.25
   a.   A891 6d multi   .45 .45
   b.   A891 12d multi   .90 .90
   c.   A891 24d multi   1.10 1.10
   d.   A891 30d multi   1.40 1.40

Women's World Chess Champions — A892

No. 2518: a, Vera Menchik (1927-44). b, Lyudmila Rudenko (1950-53). c, Yelisavyeta

Bykova (1953-56, 1958-62). d, Olga Rubtsova (1956-58). e, Nona Gaprindashvili (1962-78). f, Maia Chiburdanidze (1978-91). g, Zsuzsa Polgar (1996-99). h, Xie Jun (1991-96, 1999-2000).

2001, Mar. 8   **Perf. 13¼**
2518 A892   10d Sheet of 8, #a-h, + label   4.50 4.50

Famous Men — A893

Designs: 50d, Stevan Mokranjac (1856-1914), composer. 100d, Nikola Tesla (1856-1943), inventor.

2001, Mar. 19   **Perf. 13¾**
2519-2520 A893   Set of 2   7.25 7.25

Flowers
A894

No. 2521: a, Hibiscus syriacus. b, Nerium oleander. c, Lapageria rosea. d, Sorbus aucuparia.

2001, Apr. 13   **Perf. 12x11¾**
2521   Horiz. strip of 4 + central label   6.50 6.50
   a.   A894 6d multi   .35 .35
   b.   A894 12d multi   .55 .55
   c.   A894 24d multi   1.00 1.00
   d.   A894 30d multi   1.40 1.40

Europa — A895

Designs: 30d, Vratna River. 45d, Jerme Canyon.

2001, May 4   **Perf. 11¾x12**
2522-2523 A895   Set of 2   5.50 5.50

Serbian Mountaineering Association, Cent. — A896

2001, June 8   **Perf. 13¼**
2524 A896   15d multi   1.25 1.25

European Nature Protection
A897

Designs: 30d, Bird on branch, Lake Ludasko. 45d, Stork flying above Begej River.

2001, June 22   **Perf. 12x11¾**
2525-2526 A897   Set of 2   3.75 3.75

14th Cent. Book Illumination
A898

2001, July 2   **Perf. 13¼**
2527 A898   E multi   1.60 1.60

Sold for 28.70d on day of issue.

Souvenir Sheet

Yugoslavian Victory in European Water Polo Championships — A899

2001, July 5   **Perf. 13¾**
2528 A899   30d multi   6.50 6.50

Souvenir Sheet

Serbiafila XII Stamp Exhibition — A900

2001, Sept. 8
2529 A900   30d multi   2.50 2.50

Solar Energy — A901

2001, Sept. 19   **Perf. 13¼**
2530 A901   15d multi   1.60 1.60

Danube Commission
A902

Designs: 30d, Ships, hands raising bridge. 45d, Ship, hand, clock.

2001, Sept. 20   **Perf. 13¾**
2531-2532 A902   Set of 2   5.50 5.50

Joy of Europe — A903

Paintings: 30d, Child, by Marko Chelebonovic. 45d, Girl Under a Fruit Tree, by Beta Vukanovic.

2001, Oct. 2   **Perf. 13¼**
2533-2534 A903   Set of 2   5.50 5.50

Yugoslavian Victories in European Sports Championships
A904

Designs: No. 2535, 30d, Men's basketball. No. 2536, 30d, Men's volleyball.

2001, Oct. 11
2535-2536 A904   Set of 2   45.00 45.00

Intl. Federation of Philately (FIP), 75th Anniv.
A905

2001, Oct. 24
2537 A905   15d multi   1.60 1.60

Stamp Day.

Minerals
A906

2001, Nov. 2   **Perf. 13¾**
2538   Horiz. strip of 4 + central label   5.00 5.00
   a.   A906 7d Antimonite   1.10 1.10
   b.   A906 14d Calcite   1.10 1.10
   c.   A906 26.20d Quartz   1.10 1.10
   d.   A906 28.70d Calcite and galenite   1.10 1.10

Pljevlja Gymnasium, Cent. — A907

2001, Nov. 18   **Perf. 13¼**
2539 A907   15d multi   2.25 2.25

Public Telephone Booths in Serbia, Cent. — A908

2001, Nov. 20
2540 A908   15d multi   1.40 1.40

Christmas
A910

Paintings of the Birth of Jesus Christ: 7d, 14d, 26.20d, 28.70d.

2001, Dec. 1   **Perf. 13¾**
2541-2544 A910   Set of 4   4.50 4.50

Junior World Ice Hockey Championships, Belgrade — A911

2002, Jan. 5 *Perf. 13¼*
2545 A911 14d multi 10.00 10.00

2002 Winter Olympics, Salt Lake City — A912

Designs: 28.70d, Skier. 50d, Four-man bobsled, vert.

2002, Jan. 25 *Perf. 13¼*
2546-2547 A912 Set of 2 25.00 25.00

Jovan Karamata (1902-67), Mathematician A913

2002, Feb. 1
2548 A913 14d multi 10.00 10.00

Birds — A914

No. 2549: a, Saxicola torquata. b, Saxicola rubetra. c, Parus caeruleus. d, Turdus philomelos.

2002, Feb. 22
2549 Horiz. strip of 4 + central label 10.00 10.00
  a. A914 7d multi .65 .65
  b. A914 14d multi 1.50 1.50
  c. A914 26.20d multi 3.00 3.00
  d. A914 28.70d multi 3.50 3.50

Easter — A915

Designs: 7d, Crucifixion, fresco from Studenica Monastery, 1208. 14d, King Milutin's Veil, 1300. 26.20d, Christ's Descent to Hell, silverwork, 1540. 28.70d, Easter egg, Pec Patriarchy, 1980.

2002, Mar. 7 *Perf. 13¾*
2550-2553 A915 Set of 4 9.00 9.00

Bunjevac Women's Clothing — A916

Woman with: 7d, White blouse. 28.70d, Kerchief.

2002, Mar. 29 *Perf. 13¼*
2554-2555 A916 Set of 2 4.50 4.50

Zarko Tomic-Sremac (b. 1900), World War II Hero — A917

2002, Apr. 15
2556 A917 14d multi 12.50 12.50

Danube Fish — A918

No. 2557: a, Rutilus rutilus. b, Acipenser ruthenus. c, Huso huso. d, Stizostedion lucioperca.

2002, Apr. 25 *Litho.* *Perf. 13¼*
2557 Horiz. strip of 4 + central label 18.00 18.00
  a. A918 7d multi 1.50 1.50
  b. A918 14d multi 2.50 2.50
  c. A918 26.20d multi 5.00 5.00
  d. A918 28.70d multi 5.00 5.00

Europa A919

Designs: 28.70d, Trapeze artists. 50d, Tiger trainer.

2002, May 3 *Perf. 13¾*
2558-2559 A919 Set of 2 11.00 11.00

Europa Type
Souvenir Sheet

Design: 45d, Trained horse act.

2002, May 3 *Litho.* *Perf. 13¾*
2560 A919 45d multi 60.00 60.00

No. 2560 contains one 46x35mm stamp.

Civil Aviation in Yugoslavia, 75th Anniv. A920

Designs: 7d, Potez-29. 28.70d, Boeing 737-300.

Perf. 13¼ Syncopated
2002, June 17 *Litho.*
2561-2562 A920 Set of 2 30.00 30.00

Types of 1993 and 2001
Size: 19x21mm (#2563)

2002, July 25 *Litho.* *Perf. 12½*
2563 A702d A blue 3.00 1.50

Perf. 13¼
"E" in Green
2564 A898 E multi 7.50 4.50

Nos. 2563-2564 were intended for use in Montenegro and were sold there for 13c and 52c in euro currency respectively. The stamps were valid for use in the Serbian section of Yugoslavia.

European Nature Protection A921

Designs: 28.70d, Tara National Park. 50d, Golija Nature Park.

Perf. 13¼ Syncopated
2002, June 28 *Litho.*
2565-2566 A921 Set of 2 9.00 9.00

Mills — A922

Designs: 7d, Windmill, Melenci. 28.70d, Water mill, Lyuberada.

2002, Sept. 14
2567-2568 A922 Set of 2 9.00 9.00

Liberation of Niskic, 125th Anniv. — A923

2002, Sept. 18 *Perf. 13¾*
2569 A923 14d multi 10.00 9.00

Souvenir Sheet

Victory in 2002 World Basketball Championships — A924

2002, Sept. 20
2570 A924 30d multi 10.00 10.00

Souvenir Sheet

JUFIZ XI Philatelic Exhibition — A925

2002, Sept. 23
2571 A925 30d multi 8.00 8.00

Joy of Europe — A926

Children's art: 28.70d, Boat. 50d, Bird.

2002, Oct. 2
2572-2573 A926 Set of 2 8.50 8.50

Moraca Monastery, 750th Anniv. — A927

2002, Oct. 10
2574 A927 16d multi 20.00 12.00

Nos. 2255-2256 Srchd. in Black or Violet

2002 *Perfs, etc., as Before*
2575 A751 50p on 5p #2256 multi 2.50 1.25
2576 A702g 10d on 10,000d #2145 7.50 6.00
2577 A751 12d on 1p #2255 multi (V) 6.00 4.00
Nos. 2575-2577 (3) 16.00 11.25

Issued: No. 2575, 10/17; No. 2576, 11/28; No. 2577, 12/19.

For stamp like No. 2577, but with black surcharge, see Serbia and Montenegro No. 260.

Intl. Federation of Stamp Dealers Associations, 50th Anniv. — A928

2002, Oct. 24 *Litho.* *Perf. 13¾*
2578 A928 16d multi 7.50 7.50

Serbian Folk Costumes — A929

Paintings of costumes by Olga Benson in Ethnographic Institute of Serbian Academy of Sciences and Arts: a, Man, Kusadak. b, Woman with red headdress, Belgrade. c, Man, Novo Selo. d, Woman in profile, Belgrade.

2002, Nov. 8 *Perf. 13¾*
2579 Horiz. strip of 4, + central label 8.00 8.00
  a. A929 16d multi 1.00 1.00
  b. A929 24d multi 2.00 2.00
  c. A929 26.20d multi 2.00 2.00
  d. A929 28.70d multi 2.00 2.00

Christmas A930

Religious art: 12d, Nativity, Stavronikita Monastery, Mount Athos, Greece, 1546. 16d, Nativity, Chilandari Monastery, Mount Athos, Greece, c. 1618. 26.20d, Nativity, Tretyakov

Gallery, Moscow, 15th cent. 28.70d, Adoration of the Magi, by Sandro Botticelli.

2002, Dec. 2
2580-2583　A930　Set of 4　7.00　7.00

Abandoned Dogs — A931

Various dogs.

2003, Jan. 31　　　Perf. 13¾
2584	Horiz. strip of 4, + central label	5.00	5.00
a.	A931 16d multi	.50	.50
b.	A931 24d multi	1.25	1.25
c.	A931 26.20d multi	1.25	1.25
d.	A931 28.70d multi	1.25	1.25

Yugoslavia became Serbia & Montenegro on Feb. 4, 2003. See Serbia & Montenegro for subsequent issues.

SEMI-POSTAL STAMPS

Giving Succor to Wounded SP1

Wounded Soldier SP2

Symbolical of National Unity — SP3

Unwmk.
1921, Jan. 30　Engr.　Perf. 12
B1	SP1	10p carmine	.25	.25
B2	SP2	15p violet brown	.25	.25
B3	SP3	25p light blue	.25	.25
		Nos. B1-B3 (3)	.75	.75

Nos. B1-B3 were sold at double face value, the excess being for the benefit of invalid soldiers.
Exist imperf. Value $35.
For surcharges see Nos. 15-21.

This overprint was applied to 500,000 examples of No. B1 in 1923 and they were given to the Society for Wounded Invalids (Uprava Ratnih Invalida) which sold them for 2d a piece. These overprinted stamps had no franking power, but some were used through ignorance.

Regular Issue of 1926-27 Surcharged in Dark Red

Cathedral at Duvno SP4

King Tomislav SP6

Kings Tomislav and Alexander SP5

Perf. 12½, 11½x12
1929, Nov. 1　　　　　Typo.
B17	SP4	50p (+ 50p) olive green	.25	.25
B18	SP5	1d (+ 50p) red	.60	.40
B19	SP6	3d (+ 1d) blue	1.60	1.10
		Nos. B17-B19 (3)	2.45	1.75
		Set, never hinged	4.75	

Millenary of the Croatian kingdom. The surtax was used to create a War Memorial Cemetery in France and to erect a monument to Serbian soldiers who died there.
No. B18 exists imperf. Value $400.

View of Dobropolje SP7

War Memorial — SP8

View of Kajmaktchalan SP9

1931, Apr. 1　　　Perf. 12½, 11½
B20	SP7	50p + 50p blue grn	.25	.25
B21	SP8	1d + 1d scarlet	.25	.25
B22	SP9	3d + 3d deep blue	.25	.25
		Nos. B20-B22 (3)	.75	.75

The surtax was added to a fund for a War Memorial to Serbian soldiers who died in France during World War I.

1926, Nov. 1　　　　　Perf. 13
B5	A6	25p + 25p green	.25	.25
B6	A6	50p + 50p olive brn	.25	.25
B7	A6	1d + 50p scarlet	.25	.25
B8	A6	2d + 50p black	.25	.25
B9	A6	3d + 50p slate blue	.25	.25
B10	A6	4d + 50p red org	.30	.25
B11	A6	5d + 50p brt vio	.50	.25
B12	A6	8d + 50p black brn	1.00	.25
B13	A6	10d + 1d olive brn	2.00	.25
B14	A6	15d + 1d brown	8.00	1.00
B15	A6	20d + 1d dark vio	12.00	.55
B16	A6	30d + 1d orange	27.50	3.25
a.		Double surcharge		
		Nos. B5-B16 (12)	52.55	7.05
		Set, never hinged	105.00	

The surtax on these stamps was intended for a fund for relief of sufferers from floods. For overprints see Nos. 99-101.

SP10

SP12

SP11

Black Overprint
1931, Nov. 1　　　Perf. 12½, 11½x12
B23	SP10	50p (+ 50p) olive grn	.25	.25
B24	SP11	1d (+ 50p) red	.25	.25
B25	SP12	3d (+ 1d) blue	.30	.30
		Nos. B23-B25 (3)	.80	.80

Surtax for War Memorial fund.

Rower on Danube at Smederevo SP13

Bled Lake SP14

Danube near Belgrade SP15

View of Split Harbor SP16

Zagreb Cathedral — SP17

Prince Peter — SP18

1932, Sept. 2　Litho.　Perf. 11½
B26	SP13	75p + 50p dl grn & lt blue	.60	1.20
B27	SP14	1d + ½d scar & lt blue	.60	1.20
B28	SP15	1½d + ½d rose & green	.80	1.60
B29	SP16	3d + 1d bl & lt bl	1.60	2.40
B30	SP17	4d + 1d red org & lt blue	8.00	17.00

B31	SP18	5d + 1d dl vio & lilac	8.00	14.00
		Nos. B26-B31 (6)	19.60	37.40
		Set, never hinged	37.50	

European Rowing Championship Races, Belgrade.

King Alexander — SP19

1933, May 25　Typo.　Perf. 12½
B32	SP19	50p + 25p black	6.00	12.00
B33	SP19	75p + 25p yel grn	6.00	12.00
B34	SP19	1.50d + 50p rose	6.00	12.00
B35	SP19	3d + 1d bl vio	6.00	12.00
B36	SP19	4p + 1d dk grn	6.00	12.00
B37	SP19	5d + 1d orange	6.00	12.00
		Nos. B32-B37 (6)	36.00	72.00
		Set, never hinged	72.50	

11th Intl. Congress of P.E.N. (Poets, Editors and Novelists) Clubs, Dubrovnik, May 25-27.
The labels at the foot of the stamps are printed in either Cyrillic or Latin letters and each bears the amount of a premium for the benefit of the local P.E.N. Club at Dubrovnik.

Prince Peter — SP20

1933, June 28
B38	SP20	75p + 25p slate grn	.25	.25
B39	SP20	1½d + ½d deep red	.25	.25

60th anniv. meeting of the National Sokols (Sports Associations) at Ljubljana, July 1.

Eagle Soaring over City — SP22

1934, June 1　　　　　Perf. 12½
B40	SP22	75p + 25p green	4.00	9.00
B41	SP22	1.50d + 50p car	6.00	9.50
B42	SP22	1.75d + 25p brown	10.00	9.50
		Nos. B40-B42 (3)	20.00	28.00
		Set, never hinged	40.00	

20th anniversary of Sokols of Sarajevo.

Athlete and Eagle — SP23

1934, June 1
B43	SP23	75p + 25p Prus grn	2.40	4.75
B44	SP23	1.50d + 50p car	2.40	4.75
B45	SP23	1.75d + 25p choc	10.00	14.50
		Nos. B43-B45 (3)	14.80	24.00
		Set, never hinged	27.50	

60th anniversary of Sokols of Zagreb.

Mother and Children
SP24　　　SP25

Perf. 12½x11½

1935, Dec. 25   Photo.
B46 SP24 1.50d + 1d dk brn & brown   1.25   1.20
  a.   Perf. 11½   12.00   14.50
B47 SP25 3.50d + 1.50d bright ultra & bl   2.00   2.90
Set, never hinged   6.50

The surtax was for "Winter Help."

Queen Mother Marie — SP26

1936, May 3   Litho.
B48 SP26 75p + 25p grnsh bl   .25   .40
B49 SP26 1.50d + 50p rose pink   .25   .45
B50 SP26 1.75d + 75p brown   1.25   1.25
B51 SP26 3.50d + 1d brt bl   1.60   2.75
  Nos. B48-B51 (4)   3.35   4.85
Set, never hinged   6.50

Prince Regent Paul — SP27

1936, Sept. 20   Typo.
B52 SP27 75p + 50p turq grn & red   .40   .35
B53 SP27 1.50d + 50p cer & red   .40   .35
Set, never hinged   1.60

Surtax for the Red Cross.

Princes Tomislav and Andrej SP28   SP29

Perf. 11½x12½, 12½x11½

1937, May 1
B54 SP28 25p + 25p red brn   .25   .25
B55 SP28 75p + 75p emerald   .25   .40
B56 SP29 1.50d + 1d org red   .30   .65
B57 SP29 2d + 1d magenta   1.20   1.20
  Nos. B54-B57 (4)   1.40   2.50
Set, never hinged   2.40

Souvenir Sheet

National Costumes — SP30

1937, Sept. 12   **Perf. 14**
B57A SP30 Sheet of 4   4.75   10.00
    Never hinged   9.50
  b.   1d blue green   1.00   1.75
  c.   1.50d bright violet   1.00   1.75
  d.   2d rose red   1.00   1.75
  e.   4d dark blue   1.00   1.75

1st Yugoslavian Phil. Exhib., Belgrade. Sold only at the exhibition post office at 15d each.

SP31   SP32

Perf. 11½x12½, 12½x11½

1938, May 1   Photo.
B58 SP31 50p + 50p dark brn   .25   .30
B59 SP32 1d + 1d dk green   .25   .35
B60 SP31 1.50d + 1.50d scar   .50   .40
B61 SP32 2d + 2d magenta   1.25   .80
  Nos. B58-B61 (4)   2.25   1.85
Set, never hinged   4.00

Surtax for the benefit of Child Welfare. For overprints see Nos. B75-B78.

Bridge and Anti-aircraft Lights — SP33

1938, May 28   **Perf. 11½x12½**
B62 SP33 1d + 50p dk grn   .40   .80
B63 SP33 1.50d + 1d scarlet   .60   1.20
  a.   Perf. 11½   17.50   27.50
B64 SP33 2d + 1d rose vio   1.25   2.40
  a.   Perf. 11½   18.00   35.00
B65 SP33 3d + 1.50d dp bl   2.00   4.00
  Nos. B62-B65 (4)   4.25   8.40
Set, never hinged   8.00

Intl. Aeronautical Exhib., Belgrade.

Cliff at Demir-Kapiya — SP34

Modern Hospital SP35

Runner Carrying Torch — SP36   Alexander I — SP37

Perf. 11½x12½, 12½x11½

1938, Aug. 1
B66 SP34 1d + 1d slate grn & dp grn   .45   .40
B67 SP35 1.50d + 1.50d scar   .70   .55
B68 SP36 2d + 2d claret & dp rose   1.60   3.25
B69 SP37 3d + 3d dp bl   1.60   3.25
  Nos. B66-B69 (4)   4.35   7.45
Set, never hinged   9.00

The surtax was to raise funds to build a hospital for railway employees.

Runner SP38   Shot-Putter SP41

Hurdlers SP39

Pole Vaulter SP40

1938, Sept. 11
B70 SP38 50p + 50p org brn   1.40   2.50
B71 SP39 1d + 1d sl grn & dp grn   1.40   2.50
B72 SP40 1.50d + 1.50d rose & dk mag   1.40   2.50
B73 SP41 2d + 2d dk blue   2.75   5.00
  Nos. B70-B73 (4)   6.95   12.50
Set, never hinged   15.00

Ninth Balkan Games.

Stamps of 1938 Overprinted in Black

a   b

1938, Oct. 1
B75 SP31(a) 50p + 50p dk brn   .40   .55
B76 SP32(b) 1d + 1d dk grn   .40   .80
B77 SP31(a) 1.50d + 1.50d scar   .60   1.20
B78 SP32(b) 2d + 2d mag   1.25   2.40
  Nos. B75-B78 (4)   2.65   4.95
Set, never hinged   5.25

Surtax for the benefit of Child Welfare.

Postriders SP43

1d+1d, Rural mail delivery. 1.50d+1.50d, Mail train. 2d+2d, Mail bus. 4d+4d, Mail plane.

1939, Mar. 15   Photo.   **Perf. 11½**
B79 SP43 50p + 50p buff, bis & brown   .30   .55
B80 SP43 1d + 1d sl grn & dp green   .30   .55
B81 SP43 1.50d + 1.50d red, cop red & brn car   2.00   2.00
B82 SP43 2d + 2d dp plum & rose lilac   2.00   2.75
B83 SP43 4d + 4d ind & sl bl   2.40   4.00
  Nos. B79-B83 (5)   7.00   9.85
Set, never hinged   14.00

Centenary of the present postal system in Yugoslavia. The surtax was used for the Railway Benevolent Association.
The Cyrillic and Latin inscriptions are transposed on Nos. B82 and B83.

Child Eating SP48

Children at Seashore — SP49

Boy Planing Board SP50

Children in Crib — SP51

1939, May 1   **Perf. 12½**
B84 SP48 1d + 1d blk & dp bl green   .50   1.00
B85 SP49 1.50d + 1.50d org brn & sal   2.00   3.25
  a.   Perf. 11½   80.00   160.00
B86 SP50 2d + 2d mar & vio rose   1.40   2.90
B87 SP51 4d + 4d ind & royal blue   1.40   2.90
  Nos. B84-B87 (4)   5.30   10.05
Set, never hinged   10.50

The surtax was for the benefit of Child Welfare.

Czar Lazar of Serbia — SP52

Milosh Obilich — SP53

1939, June 28   **Perf. 11½**
B88 SP52 1d + 1d sl grn & bl grn   1.60   1.60
B89 SP53 1.50d + 1.50d mar & brt car   1.60   1.60
Set, never hinged   6.50

Battle of Kosovo, 550th anniversary.

Training Ship "Jadran" SP54

Designs: 1d+50p, Steamship "King Alexander." 1.50d+1d, Freighter "Triglan." 2d+1.50d, Cruiser "Dubrovnik."

1939, Sept. 6   **Engr.**
B90	SP54	50p + 50p brn org	.40	.80
B91	SP54	1d + 50p dull grn	.80	1.60
B92	SP54	1.50d + 1d dp rose	1.25	2.40
B93	SP54	2d + 1.50d dark bl	2.00	4.00
		Nos. B90-B93 (4)	4.45	8.80
		Set, never hinged		9.00

Yugoslav Navy and Merchant Marine. The surtax aided a Marine Museum.

Nos. B90-B93 also exist with a small "S" engraver's mark. Set value NH, $160. Location of the mark: On No. B90, above the base of the bowsprit. On No. B91, at the top of the smoke plume just below the "B" in the country name. On No. B92, at the top left of the large numeral "1". On No. B93, in the curve of the numeral "2".

Motorcycle and Sidecar — SP58

Racing Car SP59

Motorcycle SP60

Racing Car SP61

1939, Sept. 3   **Photo.**
B94	SP58	50p + 50p multi	.50	.80
B95	SP59	1d + 1d multi	1.00	1.60
B96	SP60	1.50d + 1.50d multi	1.40	2.40
B97	SP61	2d + 2d multi	2.50	4.00
		Nos. B94-B97 (4)	5.40	8.80
		Set, never hinged		10.50

Automobile and Motorcycle Races, Belgrade. The surtax was for the Race Organization and the State Treasury.

Unknown Soldier Memorial SP62

1939, Oct. 9   **Perf. 12½**
B98	SP62	1d + 50p sl grn & green	1.00	1.60
B99	SP62	1.50d + 1d red & rose red	1.00	1.60
B100	SP62	2d + 1.50d dp cl & vio rose	1.25	2.40
B101	SP62	3d + 2d dp bl & bl	2.50	4.00
		Nos. B98-B101 (4)	5.75	9.60
		Set, never hinged		11.00

Assassination of King Alexander, 5th anniv. The surtax was used to aid World War I invalids.

Postman Delivering Mail — SP64

Postman Emptying Mail Box — SP65

Parcel Post Delivery Wagon SP66

Parcel Post SP67

Repairing Telephone Wires — SP68

1940, Jan. 1
B102	SP64	50p + 50p brn & deep org	.60	1.00
B103	SP65	1d + 1d sl grn & blue grn	.60	1.00
B104	SP66	1.50d + 1.50d red brn & scar	1.00	2.40
B105	SP67	2d + 2d dl vio & red lilac	1.25	2.40
B106	SP68	4d + 4d sl bl & bl	4.00	6.50
		Nos. B102-B106 (5)	7.45	13.30
		Set, never hinged		14.50

The surtax was used for the employees of the Postal System in Belgrade.

Croats' Arrival at Adriatic in 640 SP69

King Tomislav — SP70

Death of Matija Gubec — SP71

Anton and Stjepan Radic SP72

Map of Yugoslavia SP73

1940, Mar. 1   **Typo.**   **Perf. 11½**
B107	SP69	50p + 50p brn org	.40	.55
B108	SP70	1d + 1d green	.40	.55
B109	SP71	1.50d + 1.50d brt red	1.25	.55
B110	SP72	2d + 2d dk cerise	2.00	2.40
B111	SP73	4d + 2d dark blue	2.00	2.75
		Nos. B107-B111 (5)	6.05	6.80
		Set, never hinged		12.00

The surtax was used for the benefit of postal employees in Zagreb.

Children Playing in Snow SP74

Children at Seashore — SP75

1940, May 1   **Photo.**   **Perf. 11½, 12½**
B112	SP74	50p + 50p brn org & org yellow	.25	.40
B113	SP75	1d + 1d sl grn & dk green	.25	.40
B114	SP74	1.50d + 1.50d brn red & scarlet	.60	.80
B115	SP75	2d + 2d mar & vio rose	1.00	1.60
		Nos. B112-B115 (4)	2.10	3.20
		Set, never hinged		4.00

The surtax was for Child Welfare.

Nos. C11-C14 Surcharged in Carmine

Perf. 11½x12½, 12½x11½
1940, Dec. 23
B116	AP6	50p + 50p on 5d	.25	.25
B117	AP7	1d + 1d on 10d	.25	.40
a.		Perf. 12½	40.00	40.00
B118	AP8	1.50d + 1.50d on 20d	.80	1.40
B119	AP9	2d + 2d on 30d	.90	1.75
		Nos. B116-B119 (4)	2.20	3.80
		Set, never hinged		4.00

The surtax was used to fight tuberculosis. For surcharges see Nos. NB1-NB4.

St. Peter's Cemetery, Ljubljana — SP76

Croatian, Serbian and Slovenian SP77

Chapel at Kajmaktchalan SP78

Memorial at Brezje SP79

1941, Jan. 1   **Perf. 12½**
B120	SP76	50p + 50p gray grn & yel green	.25	.40
B121	SP77	1d + 1d brn car & dl rose	.25	.40
B122	SP78	1.50d + 1.50d myr grn & bl green	.60	1.25
B123	SP79	2d + 2d gray bl & pale lilac	1.00	2.00
		Nos. B120-B123 (4)	2.10	4.05
		Set, never hinged		4.00

Surtax for the Ljubljana War Veterans Assoc.

Kamenita Gate, Zagreb — SP80

13th Century Cathedral, Zagreb — SP81

1941, Mar. 16   **Engr.**   **Perf. 11½**
B124	SP80	1.50d + 1.50d choc	.60	1.25
B125	SP81	4d + 3d blue blk	.60	1.25
		Set, never hinged		2.75

2nd Philatelic Exhibition of Croatia, at Zagreb, Mar. 16-27.

Nos. B124-B125 exist perf. 9½ on right side. Value, each $32.50.

No. B124 exists with "S" engraver's mark located next to the lower left window of the building. Value NH $80.

1941, Apr.
B126	SP80	1.50d + 1.50d bl black	12.00	24.00
B127	SP81	4d + 3d choc	12.00	24.00
		Set, never hinged		55.00

Regional philatelic exhibition at Slavonski Brod. Nos. B126-B127 with gold overprint, "Nezavisna Drzava Hrvatska," are Croatia Nos. B1-B2.

Nos. B126-B127 exist perf. 9½ on right side. Value, each $40 unused, $80 never hinged, $80 used.

No. B126 exists with "S" engraver's mark located next to the lower left window of the building. Value NH $425.

Issues for Federal Republic

Carrying Wounded Soldier — SP82

Child — SP83

1945, Sept. 15   **Typo.**   **Perf. 11½**

B131	SP82	1d + 4d deep ultra	.50 .80
B132	SP83	2d + 6d scarlet	.50 .80
			1.90

The surtax was for the Red Cross.

Russia, Yugoslavia Flags SP84

1945, Oct. 20   **Photo.**   **Unwmk.**

B133	SP84	2d + 5d multi	.80 1.60
		Never hinged	1.60

Liberation of Belgrade, 1st anniv. Exist imperf. Value $50 unused, $100 never hinged.

Communications Symbols — SP85

1946, May 10   **Perf. 12½**

B134	SP85	1.50d + 1d emer	1.60 3.25
B135	SP85	2.50d + 1.50d car rose	1.60 3.25
B136	SP85	5d + 2d gray bl	1.60 3.25
B137	SP85	8d + 3.50d dl brn	1.60 3.25
		Nos. B134-B137 (4)	6.40 13.00
		Set, never hinged	12.00

1st PTT Congress since liberation, May 10.

Flag and Young Laborers — SP86

Flag in Red or Carmine and Deep or Dark Blue

1946, Aug. 1   **Litho.**

B138	SP86	50p + 50p brn & buff	1.00 1.60
B139	SP86	1.50d + 1d dk grn & lt green	1.00 1.60
B140	SP86	2.50d + 2d rose vio & rose lilac	1.00 1.60
B141	SP86	5d + 3d gray bl & blue	1.00 1.60
		Nos. B138-B141 (4)	4.00 6.40
		Set, never hinged	8.00

The surtax aided railroad reconstruction carried out by Yugoslav youths.

Handstand on Horizontal Bar — SP87

1947, Sept. 5   **Perf. 11½**

B142	SP87	1.50d + 50p dark grn	2.00 4.00
B143	SP87	2.50d + 50p carmine	2.00 4.00
B144	SP87	4d + 50p brt blue	2.00 4.00
		Nos. B142-B144 (3)	6.00 12.00
		Set, never hinged	12.00

1947 Balkan Games, Sept. 5-7, Ljubljana.

Young Railway Laborers SP88

1947, Sept. 25   **Typo.**   **Perf. 11½x12**

B145	SP88	1d + 50p orange	.50 1.00
B146	SP88	1.50d + 1d yel green	.50 1.00
B147	SP88	2.50d + 1.50d car lake	.50 1.00
B148	SP88	5d + 2d deep blue	.50 1.00
		Nos. B145-B148 (4)	2.00 4.00
		Set, never hinged	4.00

The surtax was for youth brigades employed in the construction of the Samac-Sarajevo railway.

Symbolizing Protection of "B.C.G." Vaccine SP89

Dying Serpent SP91

"Illness" and "Recovery" SP90

1948, Apr. 1   **Litho.**   **Perf. 12½**

B149	SP89	1.50d + 1d sl blk & red	.40 .80
B150	SP90	2.50d + 2d grnsh gray, ol blk & red	.40 .80
B151	SP91	5d + 3d dk bl & car	.40 .80
		Nos. B149-B151 (3)	1.20 2.40
		Set, never hinged	2.40

Fight against tuberculosis. The surtax was for the Yugoslav Red Cross.

Juro Danicic SP92

Portraits: 2.50d+1d, Franjo Racki. 4d+2d, Josip J. Strossmayer.

1948, July 28   **Perf. 11**

B152	SP92	1.50d + 50p blk green	.40 .80
B153	SP92	2.50d + 1d dark red	.40 .80
B154	SP92	4d + 2d dark blue	.40 .80
		Nos. B152-B154 (3)	1.20 2.40
		Set, never hinged	2.40

Yugoslav Academy of Arts and Sciences, Zagreb, 80th anniv. The surtax was for the Academy.

Shot Put — SP93

1948, Sept. 10   **Perf. 12½**

B155	SP93	2d + 1d shown	.40 .80
B156	SP93	3d + 1d Hurdles	.40 .80
B157	SP93	5d + 2d Pole vault	1.00 1.25
		Nos. B155-B157 (3)	1.80 2.85
		Set, never hinged	3.50

Balkan and Central Europe Games, 1948. On sale 4 days.

AIR POST STAMPS

Dubrovnik AP1

Lake Bled AP2

Falls of Jaice — AP3

Church at Oplenac — AP4

Bridge at Mostar — AP5

Perf. 12½

1934, June 15   **Typo.**   **Unwmk.**

C1	AP1	50p violet brown	.25 .25
C2	AP2	1d green	.25 .25
C3	AP3	2d rose red	.50 .30
C4	AP4	3d ultramarine	1.10 .45
C5	AP5	10d vermilion	2.50 4.00
		Nos. C1-C5 (5)	4.60 5.25
		Set, never hinged	8.50

Border in Black

King Alexander Memorial Issue

1935, Jan. 1

C6	AP4	3d ultramarine	3.25 4.75
		Never hinged	6.50

St. Naum Convent — AP6

Port of Rab — AP7

Sarajevo AP8

Ljubljana AP9

Perf. 11½x12½, 12½x11½

1937, Sept. 12   **Photo.**

C7	AP6	50p brown	.25 .25
a.		Perf. 12½	.25 .25
C8	AP7	1d yellow grn	.25 .25
a.		Perf. 12½	.25 .25
C9	AP8	2d blue gray	.25 .25
a.		Perf. 12½	.25 .25
C10	AP9	2.50d rose red	.25 .25
a.		Perf. 12½	.25 .25
C11	AP6	5d brn violet	.25 .25
a.		Perf. 12½	.25 .25
C12	AP7	10d brown lake	.50 .25
a.		Perf. 12½	.70 .25
C13	AP8	20d dark green	5.25 8.00
a.		Perf. 12½	.70 .70
C14	AP9	30d ultramarine	18.00 27.50
a.		Perf. 12½	1.00 1.75
		Nos. C7-C14 (8)	25.00 37.00
		Nos. C7-C14, never hinged	47.50
		Nos. C7a-C14a, never hinged	5.50

For surcharges see Nos. B116-B119, NB1-NB4, NC1-NC8.

Cathedral of Zagreb AP10

Bridge at Belgrade AP11

1940, Aug. 15   **Litho.**   **Perf. 12½**

C15	AP10	40d Prus grn & pale green	4.50 3.50
C16	AP11	50d slate bl & gray bl	4.50 5.00
		Set, never hinged	17.50

For overprints see Nos. NC9-NC10.

Issues for Federal Republic

Plane over Terrace of Kalimegdan, Belgrade AP12

Plane over Dubrovnik AP13

1947, Apr. 21   **Typo.**   **Perf. 11½**

Cyrillic Inscription at Top

C17	AP12	50p ol gray & brn vio	.25 .25
C18	AP13	1d mag & ol gray	.25 .25
C19	AP12	2d blue & black	.25 .25
C20	AP13	5d green & gray	.25 .25
C21	AP12	10d olive bis & choc	.25 .25
C22	AP13	20d ultra & olive	.60 1.25

Roman Inscription at Top

C23	AP12	50p ol gray & brn vio	.25 .25
C24	AP13	1d mag & ol gray	.25 .25
C25	AP12	2d blue & black	.25 .25
C26	AP13	5d green & gray	.25 .25
C27	AP12	10d olive bis & choc	.25 .25
C28	AP13	20d ultra & olive	.60 1.25
		Nos. C17-C28 (12)	3.70 5.00
		Set, never hinged	4.75

Sheets of each denomination contain alternately stamps with Cyrillic or Roman inscription at top. Value, 6 se-tenant pairs: unused $24; never hinged $47.50.

Laurent Kosir and Birthplace AP14

1948, Aug. 27   **Engr.**
C29 AP14 15d red violet   .60   1.25
     Never hinged   1.25

Kosir, recognized by Yugoslavia as inventor of the postage stamp, 80th death anniv. Issued in sheets of 25 stamps and 25 labels.

Nos. 262 to 264
Overprinted in
Blue or Carmine

1949, Aug. 25   **Unwmk.**   **Perf. 12½**
C30 A55   3d carmine rose   5.50   8.00
C31 A56   5d dull blue (C)   5.50   8.00
C32 A57   12d red brown   5.50   8.00
     Nos. C30-C32 (3)   16.50   24.00
     Never hinged   32.50

Liberation of Macedonia, 5th anniv.
It is reported that No. C32 was not sold to the public at the post office.

Souvenir Sheet

Electric
Train
AP15

Perf. 11½x12½
1949, Dec. 15   **Photo.**
C33 AP15 10d lilac rose   90.00   105.00
     Never hinged   175.00
   a.   Imperf.   90.00   105.00
     Never hinged   175.00

Centenary of Yugoslav railroads.
For overprint see Trieste No. C17.

Iron Gate,
Derdap
AP16

Belgrade
AP17

Designs: 2d, Cascades, Plitvice. 3d, Carniola. 6d, Roman bridge, Mostar. 10d, Ohrid. 20d, Gulf of Kotor. 30d, Dubrovnik. 50d, Bled.

Perf. 12½
1951, June 16   **Unwmk.**   **Engr.**
C34 AP16   1d deep org   .25   .25
C35 AP16   2d dk green   .25   .25
C36 AP16   3d dark red   .25   .25
C37 AP16   6d ultra   2.00   4.00
C38 AP16   10d dark brn   .25   .25
C39 AP16   20d grnsh blk   .40   .25
C40 AP16   30d dp claret   1.00   .25
C41 AP16   50d dk purple   1.40   .25
C42 AP16   100d dk gray bl   27.50   9.00
     Nos. C34-C42 (9)   33.30   14.75
     Set, never hinged   65.00
Souvenir Sheet
Imperf

C43 AP17 100d red brn   90.00   175.00
     Never hinged   175.00

See Nos. C50-C53. For overprints see Nos. C44, C49, Trieste C22-C32.

**Roman Bridge Type of 1951
Overprinted "ZEFIZ 1951" in
Carmine**

1951, June 16   **Perf. 12½**
C44 AP16 6d dark green   4.00   3.75
     Never hinged   8.00

Nos. C43-C44 were issued for Zagreb Philatelic Exhibition, June 16-26.

View on Mt.
Kopaonik — AP18

Perf. 12½
1951, July   **Unwmk.**   **Photo.**
C45 AP18   3d shown   1.00   2.00
C46 AP18   5d Mt. Triglav   1.00   2.00
C47 AP18   20d Mt. Kalnik   32.50   47.50
     Nos. C45-C47 (3)   34.50   51.50
     Set, never hinged   65.00

Intl. Union of Mountaineers, 12th Assembly, Bled, July 13-18.

Plane and
Parachutists — AP19

1951, Aug. 16   **Engr.**
C48 AP19 6d carmine   2.00   2.00

Type of
1951
Overprinted
in Carmine

C49 AP16 50d blue   32.50   40.00

First World Parachute Championship, Bled, Aug. 16-20.
Nos. C48-C49, never hinged $65.

> **Catalogue values for unused stamps in this section, from this point to the end of the section, are for Never Hinged items.**

Types of 1951

Designs: 5d, Cascades, Plitvice. 100d, Carniola. 200d, Roman bridge, Mostar.

1951-52
C50 AP16   5d yel brn ('52)   .40   .25
C51 AP16   100d green   1.75   .25
C52 AP16   200d deep car ('52)   2.50   .30
C53 AP17   500d blue vio ('52)   8.00   .40
     Nos. C50-C53 (4)   12.65   1.20

Marshal Tito,
Tank, Factory
and Planes
AP20

1951, Dec. 22   **Unwmk.**
C54 AP20 150d deep blue   11.00   11.00

Army Day, Dec. 22; 10th anniv. of the formation of the 1st military unit of "New" Yugoslavia.

Star and Flag-
encircled
Globe — AP21

1953, July 30   **Engr.**
C55 AP21 300d bl & grn   175.00   175.00

38th Esperanto Congress, Zagreb, 7/25-8/1.
For overprint see Trieste No. C21.

13th
Century
Tower,
Zagreb
AP22

1956, May 20   **Perf. 11½**
Chalky Paper
C56 AP22 30d gray, vio bl & org
     red   3.25   1.40

Yugoslav Intl. Phil. Exhib., JUFIZ III, Zagreb, May 20-27.

Workers and
Cogwheel — AP23

1956, June 15   **Photo.**
Glossy Paper
C57 AP23 30d car rose & blk   3.25   1.60

10th anniversary of technical education.

Moon and Earth
with
Satellites — AP24

1958, Oct. 24   **Engr.**   **Perf. 12½**
C58 AP24 300d dark blue   7.50   3.50

Intl. Geophysical Year, 1957-58.

Types of Regular Issue, 1961

1961, Sept. 1   **Perf. 11½**
C59 A150 250d dark purple   .90   .60
C60 A151 500d violet blue   2.00   1.25

Type of Athletic Regular Issue, 1962
Souvenir Sheet

Design: Army Stadium, Belgrade.

1962, Sept. 12   **Litho.**   **Imperf.**
C61 A161 600d vio & blk   16.00   16.00

7th European Athletic Championships, Belgrade, Sept. 12-16.

REGISTERED LETTER STAMPS

> **Catalogue values for unused stamps in this section are for Never Hinged items.**

RL1

1993, June 28   **Litho.**   **Perf. 13¼**
F1 RL1 (R) ultra   1.60   .40
   a.   Perf. 12½   6.50   .55
   b.   Dated "1997"   6.50   .40

No. F1 was valued at 11,000d on day of issue. No. F1b issued 2/97.
For surcharge, see Serbia Nos. 194, 274.

Type of 1993
2002, July 25   **Litho.**   **Perf. 12½**
F2 RL1 R red   2.00   1.50

No. F2 was intended for use in Montenegro and was sold there for 39c in euro currency. The stamp was valid for use in the Serbian section of Yugoslavia.

POSTAGE DUE STAMPS

King
Alexander — D1

1921   **Typo.**   **Unwmk.**   **Perf. 11½**
Red or Black Surcharge
J1 D1 10p on 5p green (R)   .25   .25
J2 D1 30p on 5p green (Bk)   .25   .25
     Set, never hinged   .65

D2   D3

1921-22   **Typo.**   **Perf. 11½, Rough**
J3 D2 10p rose   .25   .25
J4 D2 30p yellow green   .25   .25
J5 D2 50p violet   .25   .25
J6 D2 1d brown   .30   .25
J7 D2 2d blue   .40   .25
J8 D3 5d orange   2.00   .25
J9 D3 10d violet brown   6.00   .45
   a.   Cliche of 10p in sheet of
      10d   190.00   —
J10 D3 25d pink   35.00   1.60
J11 D3 50d green   30.00   1.60
     Nos. J3-J11 (9)   74.45   5.15
     Set, never hinged   140.00

1924   **Perf. 9, 10½, 11½, Clean-cut**
J12 D3 10p rose red   .25   .25
J13 D3 30p yellow green   .35   .40
J14 D3 50p violet   .25   .25
J15 D3 1d brown   .25   .25
J16 D3 2d deep blue   .50   .25
J17 D3 5d orange   1.60   .25
J18 D3 10d violet brown   10.00   .25
J19 D3 25d pink   65.00   1.25
J20 D3 50d green   47.50   1.25
     Nos. J12-J20 (9)   125.70   4.40
     Set, never hinged   240.00

Nos. J19-J20 do not exist perf 9. Nos. J18-J20 do not exist perf 11½.

Nos. J19-J20
Surcharged

1928
J21 D3 10d on 25d pink   3.25   .40
J22 D3 10d on 50d green   3.25   .40
   a.   Inverted surcharge   30.00   18.00
     Set, never hinged   13.00

A second type of "1" in surcharge has flag projecting horizontally. Value, each: $24 never hinged; $12 unused; $3.25 used.

Coat of Arms — D4

1931   **Typo.**   *Perf. 12½*
With Imprint at Foot

J23 D4 50p violet	1.40	.25
J24 D4 1d deep magenta	3.00	.25
J25 D4 2d deep blue	9.50	.25
J26 D4 5d orange	2.00	.25
J27 D4 10d chocolate	10.00	1.25
Nos. J23-J27 (5)	25.90	2.25
Set, never hinged	47.50	

For overprints see Nos. NJ1-NJ13, Croatia 26-29, J1-J5.

1932   **Without Imprint at Foot**

J28 D4 50p violet	.25	.25
J29 D4 1d deep magenta	.25	.25
J30 D4 2d deep blue	.25	.25
J31 D4 5d orange	.25	.25
J32 D4 10d chocolate	.25	.25
Nos. J28-J32 (5)	1.25	1.25

Numeral of Value — D5

Overprint in Green, Blue or Maroon

1933   *Perf. 9, 10½, 11½*

J33 D5 50p vio (G)	.25	.25
a. Perf. 10½	.30	
J34 D5 1d brown (Bl)	.25	.25
a. Perf. 10½	2.00	1.40
J35 D5 2d blue (M)	.25	.25
a. Perf. 10½	1.00	1.25
J36 D5 5d orange (Bl)	.80	.25
J37 D5 10d violet brn (Bl)	4.00	1.25
Nos. J33-J37 (5)	5.55	1.25
Set, never hinged	10.50	

Issues for Federal Republic

Redrawn Type OD5, German Occupation of Serbia, Overprinted in Black

1945   **Unwmk.**   *Perf. 12½*

J37A OD5 10d red	.60	.55
J37B OD5 20d ultramarine	.60	.55
Set, never hinged	2.40	

In the redrawn design the eagle is replaced by a colorless tablet.

Coat of Arms — D6

1945   **Litho.**   *Perf. 12½*
Numerals in Black

J38 D6 2d brown violet	.25	.25
J39 D6 3d violet	.25	.25
J40 D6 5d green	.25	.25
J41 D6 7d orange brown	.25	.25
J42 D6 10d rose lilac	.25	.25
J43 D6 20d blue	.25	.25
J44 D6 30d light bl grn	.40	.35
J45 D6 40d rose red	.40	.40

Numerals in Color of Stamp

J46 D6 1d blue green	.25	.25
J47 D6 1.50d blue	.25	.25
J48 D6 2d vermilion	.40	.25
J49 D6 3d violet brown	.40	.25
J50 D6 4d rose violet	.60	.25
Nos. J38-J50 (13)	4.20	3.50
Set, never hinged	6.50	

For overprints see Nos. J64-J66.

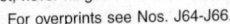

Torches and Star — D7

1946-47   **Typo.**   **Unwmk.**

J51 D7 50p dp orange ('47)	.25	.25
J52 D7 1d orange	.25	.25
J53 D7 2d dark blue	.25	.25
J54 D7 3d yellow green	.25	.25
J55 D7 5d bright purple	.25	.25
J56 D7 7d crimson	.80	.25
J57 D7 10d brt pink ('47)	.80	.25
J58 D7 20d rose lake ('47)	2.00	.55
Nos. J51-J58 (8)	4.85	2.30
Set, never hinged	8.00	

See Nos. J67-J79. For overprints see Trieste Nos. J1-J5, J11-J18.

Nos. J47, J49 and J50 Overprinted in Black

1950   **Litho.**

J64 D6 1.50d blue	.25	.25
J65 D6 3d violet brown	.25	.25
J66 D6 4d rose violet	.25	.30
Nos. J64-J66 (3)	.75	.80
Set, never hinged	1.25	

> Catalogue values for unused stamps in this section, from this point to the end of the section, are for Never Hinged items.

Type of 1946-47

1951-52   **Typo.**   *Perf. 12½*

J67 D7 1d brown ('52)	.40	.25
J68 D7 2d emerald	.40	.25
J69 D7 5d blue	.55	.25
J70 D7 10d scarlet	1.25	.25
J71 D7 20d purple	2.00	.25
J72 D7 30d org yel ('52)	4.00	.25
J73 D7 50d ultramarine	16.00	.40
J74 D7 100d dp plum ('52)	55.00	2.00
Nos. J67-J74 (8)	79.60	3.90

For overprints see Istria Nos. J20-J24, Trieste J11-J18.

1962   **Litho.**   *Perf. 12½*

J75 D7 10d red orange	3.25	.25
J76 D7 20d purple	3.25	.25
J77 D7 30d orange	6.75	.25
J78 D7 50d ultramarine	32.50	.80
J79 D7 100d rose lake	20.00	1.25
Nos. J75-J79 (5)	65.75	2.80

OFFICIAL STAMPS

Issues for Federal Republic

Arms of the Federated People's Republic — O1

Perf. 12½

1946, Nov. 1   **Unwmk.**   **Typo.**

O1 O1 50p orange	.25	.25
O2 O1 1d blue green	.25	.25
O3 O1 1.50d olive green	.25	.25
O4 O1 2.50d red	.25	.25
O5 O1 4d yellow brown	.40	.25
O6 O1 5d deep blue	.60	.25
O7 O1 8d chocolate	1.25	.25
O8 O1 12d violet	1.40	.25
Nos. O1-O8 (8)	4.65	2.00
Set, never hinged	8.00	

For surcharges see Nos. 272A-272B, Istria 43, 45, 47, 49, 51.

POSTAL TAX STAMPS

> Catalogue values for unused stamps in this section are for Never Hinged items.

The tax was for the Red Cross or The Olympic Fund unless otherwise noted.

Red Cross Emblem — PT1

Unwmk.
1933, Sept. 17   **Litho.**   *Perf. 13*
RA1   PT1 50p dark blue & red   .65   .25

Obligatory on inland letters during Red Cross Week, Sept. 17-23.
See No. RAJ1.

Dr. Vladen Djordjevic — PT2

1936, Sept. 20   **Typo.**   *Perf. 12*
RA2   PT2 50p brn blk & red   .40   .25

Obligatory on inland letters during Red Cross Week, Sept. 20-26.

Aiding the Wounded PT3

1938, Sept. 18   **Litho.**   *Perf. 12½*
RA3   PT3 50p dk bl, red, yel & grn   .40   .25

1940, Sept. 15   **Redrawn**
RA4   PT3 50p slate blue & red   .55   .25

The inscription at the upper right of this stamp and the numerals of value are in smaller characters.
Obligatory on all letters during the second week of September.

Issues for Federal Republic

Ruined Dwellings — PT4

1947, Jan. 1   **Litho.**   *Perf. 12½*
RA5   PT4 50p brn & scarlet   .25   .25

See No. RAJ2. For overprints see Trieste Nos. RA1, RAJ1.

Red Cross Nurse — PT5

1948, Oct. 1
RA6   PT5 50p dk vio bl & red   .25   .25

See No. RAJ3.

Nurse and Child — PT6

1949, Nov. 5
RA7   PT6 50p red & brown   .25   .25

See No. RAJ4. For overprints see Trieste Nos. RA2, RAJ2.

Nurse Holding Book — PT7

1950, Oct. 1
RA8   PT7 50p dark green & red   .25   .25

Obligatory Oct. 1-8, 1950.
See No. RAJ6.

Hands Raising Red Cross Flag — PT8

1951, Oct. 7
RA9   PT8 50p vio bl & red   .25   .25

Obligatory Oct. 7-14.
For overprints see Trieste Nos. RA3, RAJ3.

Nurse — PT9

1952, Oct. 5   **Photo.**   *Perf. 12½*
RA10   PT9 50p gray & carmine   .25   .25

For overprint see Trieste No. RA4.

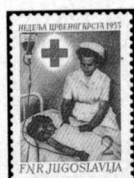

Child Receiving Blood Transfusion — PT10

1953, Oct. 25   **Litho.**
RA11   PT10 2d rose vio & red   .40   .25

See No. RAJ8. For overprints see Trieste Nos. RA5, RAJ5.

Youths Carrying Flags — PT11

1954, Nov. 1
RA12   PT11 2d gray grn & red   .40   .25

See Nos. RAJ9.

Infant — PT11a

1954, Oct. 4
RA12A PT11a 2d brn & salmon   1.25   .65
     The tax was for Children's Week.

Girl — PT12

1955, Oct. 2   Unwmk.   Perf. 12½
RA13 PT12 2d dull red   .40   .25
     The tax was for child welfare.
     See No. RAJ10.

Nurse Opening
Window — PT13

1955, Oct. 31
RA14 PT13 2d vio blk & red   .25   .25
     See No. RAJ11.

Ruins in the
Snow — PT14

1956, May 6   Perf. 12½
RA15 PT14 2d sepia & red   .30   .25
     See No. RAJ12.

Children and
Goose — PT15

1956, Sept. 30
RA16 PT15 2d gray green   .40   .25
     The tax was for child welfare.
     See No. RAJ13.

Plane over
Temporary
Shelter — PT16

1957, May 5   Litho.
RA17 PT16 2d lt bl, blk & car   .30   .25
     See No. RAJ14.

Girl and Boy
Pioneers
PT17

1957, Sept. 30   Unwmk.   Perf. 12½
RA18 PT17 2d rose & gray   .30   .25
     Children's Week. Obligatory Oct. 2-6.
     See No. RAJ15.

Redrawn Type of Regular Issue, 1953

1958, May 4   Perf. 12½x12
RA19 A95 2d multicolored   .40   .25
     On No. RA19 the UN emblem has been left
out, Cyrillic inscriptions at left added, country
name in Latin letters.

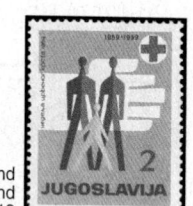

Playing
Children — PT18

1958, Oct. 5   Litho.   Perf. 12½
RA20 PT18 2d brt yel & black   .25   .25
     Children's Week, Oct. 5-11.

Helping Hand
and
Family — PT19

1959, May 3
RA21 PT19 2d blue vio & red   .30   .25
     Red Cross centenary. Obligatory May 3-9.
     See No. RAJ18.

Blackboard,
Flower and
Fish — PT20

1959, Oct. 5   Unwmk.
RA22 PT20 2d ocher & Prus grn   .30   .25
     Children's Week. Obligatory on domestic
mail, Oct. 5-11.
     See No. RAJ19.

"Reconstruction"
PT21

1960, May 8   Perf. 12½
RA23 PT21 2d slate & red   .30   .25
     Obligatory May 8-14. See No. RAJ20.

Girl and
Toys — PT22

1960, Oct. 2   Litho.   Perf. 12½
RA24 PT22 2d red   .25   .25
     Issued for Children's Week. Obligatory on
domestic mail Oct. 2-8.
     See No. RAJ21.

Blood Donor
Symbolism
PT23

1961, May 7
RA25 PT23 2d multicolored   .30   .25
     Obligatory May 7-13. Exists imperf. Value
$14.
     See No. RAJ22.

Bird Holding
Flower
PT24

1961, Oct. 1
RA26 PT24 2d orange & violet   .25   .25
     Children's Week. Exists imperf. Obligatory
on domestic mail, Oct. 1-7.
     See No. RAJ23.

Bandages and Symbols of Home,
Industry, Weather, Transportation, Fire
and Flood — PT25

1962, Apr. 30   Perf. 12½
RA27 PT25 5d red brn, gray &
            red   .25   .25
     Obligatory on domestic mail May 6-12.
     See No. RAJ24.

Centenary
Emblem — PT26

1963, May 5   Unwmk.   Perf. 12½
RA28 PT26 5d dl yel, red & gray   .30   .25
     Intl. Red Cross, centenary. Exists imperf.
Obligatory on all domestic mail during Red
Cross Week, May 5-11.
     See No. RAJ25.

Parachute Drop of
Supplies,
Yugoslav
Flag — PT27

1964, Apr. 27   Litho.
RA29 PT27 5d blue, rose & dk bl   .25   .25
     Obligatory on domestic mail, May 3-9.

Children in
Circle — PT28

1965, May 2   Litho.   Perf. 12½
RA30 PT28 5d tan & red   .25   .25
     Obligatory on domestic mail, May 2-8.

Arrows
PT29

1966, Apr. 28   Litho.   Perf. 12½
RA31 PT29 5p gray & multi   .25   .25
     Obligatory on domestic mail, May 1-7.

Crosses and
Flower
PT30

1967, Apr. 28   Litho.   Perf. 12½
RA32 PT30 5p vio, red & yel grn   .25   .25
     Exists imperf.

Honeycomb and
Red
Cross — PT31

1968, Apr. 30   Litho.   Perf. 12
RA33 PT31 5p multicolored   .25   .25
     Obligatory on all domestic mail May 5-11.

Aztec Calendar
Stone and
Olympic
Rings — PT32

1968, Oct. 12   Perf. 12½
RA34 PT32 10p black & multi   .25   .25

Red Cross, Hands and Globe — PT33

1969, May 18 **Litho.** *Perf. 12*
RA35 PT33 20p red org, dl red & blk .25 .25

Globe, Olympic Torch and Rings — PT34

1969, Nov. 24 **Litho.** *Perf. 11¼*
RA36 PT34 10p gold & multi 4.50 .25
a. Perf. 9 12.00 1.90
Yugoslav Olympic Committee, 50th anniv. Exists imperf. Value $125.

Symbolic Flower and People PT35

1970, Apr. 27 **Litho.** *Perf. 13*
RA37 PT35 20p vio bl, org & red .25 .25

Olympic Flag — PT36

1970, June 10 **Litho.** *Perf. 13x13½*
RA38 PT36 10p multicolored .25 .25

Red Cross Encircling Globe PT37

1971, Apr. 26 **Litho.** *Perf. 12½*
RA39 PT37 20p blue, yel & red .25 .25

Olympic Rings and Disk — PT38

1971, June 15 **Litho.** *Perf. 12½*
RA40 PT38 10p blue & black .25 .25

Red Cross and Hemispheres PT39

1972, Apr. 27 *Perf. 13½x13*
RA41 PT39 20p red & multi .25 .25

Olympic Rings, TV Tower, Munich and Sapporo Emblems — PT40

1972, May *Perf. 13x13½*
RA42 PT40 10p ultra & multi .25 .25

Red Cross, Crescent and Lion Emblems — PT41

1973, Apr. 24 **Litho.** *Perf. 13x13½*
RA43 PT41 20p blue & multi .25 .25

Globe and Olympic Rings — PT42

1973, June 1 **Litho.** *Perf. 13x13½*
RA44 PT42 10p multicolored .25 .25

Drop of Blood, Red Cross Emblems PT43

1974, Apr. 25 **Litho.** *Perf. 13*
RA45 PT43 20p red & multi .25 .25

Olympic Rings PT44

1974, June 1 **Litho.** *Perf. 13*
RA46 PT44 10p blue & multi .25 .25

Red Cross, Hands PT45

1975, Apr. 23 **Photo.** *Perf. 11½*
RA47 PT45 20p blue, car & blk .25 .25

Olympic Rings — PT46

1975, June 2 **Litho.** *Perf. 13½*
RA48 PT46 10p multicolored .25 .25

Ruin and Clock — PT47

1975, July 26 **Litho.** *Perf. 13x13½*
RA49 PT47 30p blk & dk bl .25 .25
Solidarity Week, July 26-Aug. 1. See Nos. RA61-RA62.

Red Crescent, Red Cross, Red Lion — PT48

1976, May 8 **Photo.** *Perf. 12½x13*
RA50 PT48 20p multicolored .80 .55

1984 Olympics PT49

1976, July 26 **Litho.** *Perf. 13½*
RA51 PT49 10p intense blue .25 .25

Fight Tuberculosis, Red Cross — PT50

1977, Sept. 14 **Photo.**
RA52 PT50 50p multicolored 2.00 .80
RA53 PT50 1d multicolored 2.00 .80
Exist imperf.

1984 Olympics PT51

1977, Dec. 17 *Perf. 13½x13*
RA54 PT51 10p multicolored .25 .25

Postal Tax Stamps for use in a particular republic or republics fall beyond the scope of this catalogue and are not listed. These stamps, issued since 1977, were not intended for nationwide use. Some of these issues have designs which are similar to stamps used nationwide, most notably those using variations of the Ruin and Clock (PT47) design. Most others show the Red Cross or the Tuberculosis Cross.

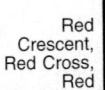

Red Crescent, Red Cross, Red Lion — PT52

1978, May 7 **Litho.** *Perf. 13½*
RA55 PT52 20p on 1d bl & red .50 .25
RA56 PT52 1d blue & red .30 .25

1984 Olympics PT53

1978, Sept.
RA57 PT53 30p multicolored .35 .25

8th Mediterranean Games, Split, Sept. 15-29 — PT54

1979, Mar. 1 **Photo.** *Perf. 13½x13*
RA58 PT54 1d violet .25 .25
RA59 PT54 1d greenish blue .25 .25

Red Cross Week PT55

1979, May 6 *Perf. 13½*
RA60 PT55 1d multicolored .25 .25

Ruin and Clock Type of 1975 Inscribed "1.-7.VI"
1979, June 1
RA61 PT47 30p blk & intense bl .25 .25
Solidarity Week.

Ruin and Clock Type of 1975 Inscribed "1.-7.VI"
1980, June 1 **Litho.** *Perf. 13x13½*
RA62 PT47 1d black & blue .25 .25
Solidarity Week, June 1-7.

Olympic Week — PT57

1979, Oct. 15 **Photo.** *Perf. 14*
RA63 PT57 30p blue & red .25 .25

Sculpture, Red Cross — PT58

1980, May 4 **Litho.** *Perf. 13½*
RA64 PT58 1d multicolored .35 .30

Olympic Week — PT59

1980, Oct. 20   **Perf. 14**
RA65 PT59 50p multicolored   .40   .25

SPENS '81, Novi Sad — PT60

1980, Dec. 20   **Perf. 13½**
RA66 PT60 1d multicolored   .25   .25

Red Cross — PT61

1981, May 4   **Photo.**
RA67 PT61 1d multicolored   .25   .25

Fight Tuberculosis, Red Cross — PT62

1981, Sept. 14
RA68 PT62 1d multicolored   .25   .25

Handshake PT63

1982, May   **Litho.**   **Perf. 13**
RA69 PT63 1d black & red   .25   .25

Robert Koch PT64

1983, Sept. 18   **Litho.**   **Perf. 13**
RA70 PT64 1d multicolored   .25   .25

For surcharge see No. RA76.

Fight Tuberculosis, Red Cross — PT65

1983, Sept. 14   **Litho.**   **Perf. 13½**
RA71 PT65 1d bluish grn, blk & red   .25   .25
RA72 PT65 2d bluish grn, blk & red   .25   .25

1984 Winter Olympics, Sarajevo PT66

1983, Oct. 20   **Litho.**   **Perf. 12½**
RA73 PT66 2d greenish blue   .25   .25

PLANICA 50 — PT67

1985, Apr. 1   **Photo.**   **Perf. 14**
RA74 PT67 2d brt ultra & blue   .25   .25

Ruin, Clock and Red Cross — PT68

1987, June 1   **Litho.**   **Perf. 10**
RA75 PT68 30d multicolored   .25   .25

Solidarity Week, June 1-7.

No. RA70 Surcharged in Silver

1988, Sept. 14   **Litho.**   **Perf. 13**
RA76 PT64 12d on 1d multi   8.00   8.00

Intl. Red Cross, 125th Anniv. — PT69

1989, May 8   **Litho.**   **Perf. 12x11**
Without Gum
RA77 PT69 20d bl, sil & red   .40   .40
RA78 PT69 80d bl, sil & red   .40   .40
RA79 PT69 150d bl, sil & red   .40   .40
RA80 PT69 160d bl, sil & red   .40   .40
   Nos. RA77-RA80 (4)   1.60   1.60

Souvenir folders with perf. or imperf. miniature sheets of 4 sold for 3200d.

Ruin, Clock and Red Cross — PT70

Building, Clock and Red Cross — PT71

1989, June 1   **Perf. 10**
Without Gum
RA81 PT70 250d red & silver   .55   .40

Roulette 10
RA82 PT71 400d brt bl gray & red   1.00   .50

Souvenir folders with perf. or imperf. miniature sheets containing one 45x65mm stamp like RA81 sold for 3200d.

Fight TB, Red Cross — PT72

1989, Sept. 14   **Rough Perf. 10½**
Without Gum
RA83 PT72 20d black & red   .30   .30
RA84 PT72 200d black & red   .30   .30
RA85 PT72 250d black & red   .30   .30
RA86 PT72 400d black & red   .30   .30
RA87 PT72 650d black & red   .30   .30
   Nos. RA83-RA87 (5)   1.50   1.50

Red Cross — PT73

1990, May 8   **Perf. 13½**
Without Gum
RA88 PT73 10p green & red   .80   .25
     Perf. 12½
RA89 PT73 20p green & red   .80   .25
   a.   Perf. 13½   .80   .25
RA90 PT73 30p green & red   .80   .25
   Nos. RA88-RA90 (3)   2.40   .75

Flowers — PT74

Macedonian Red Cross, 45th Anniv. — PT75

1990, May 8   **Perf. 10**
Without Gum
RA91 PT74 20p shown   .25   .25
RA92 PT74 20p multi, diff.   .25   .25
RA93 PT75 20p multicolored   .25   .25
   a.   Block of 3 + label, #RA91-RA93   .80   .80

Souvenir folders with perf. or imperf. miniature sheets of 3 + label sold for 4d.

PT76

1990, Sept. 14   **Litho.**   **Perf. 10**
Without Gum
RA94 PT76 20p blue, org & red   .40   .40
RA95 PT76 25p blue, yel & red   .40   .40
RA96 PT76 50p blue, yel & red   .40   .40
   Nos. RA94-RA96 (3)   1.20   1.20

Fight tuberculosis, Red Cross.

PT77

1991, Sept. 14   **Litho.**   **Perf. 12½**
Without Gum
RA97 PT77 1.20d dk bl, yel & red   .30   .30
RA98 PT77 2.50d multicolored   .30   .30

Required on mail 9/14-21/91.

PT78

1994, May 8   **Litho.**   **Perf. 13½**
RA99 PT78 10p multicolored   1.00   .50

No. RA99 was required on mail 5/8-15/94.

PT79

1994, Sept. 14   **Litho.**   **Perf. 13x13½**
RA100 PT79 10p multicolored   1.00   .50

No. RA100 was required on mail 9/14-21/94.

PT80

1995, May 8   **Litho.**   **Perf. 13½x13**
RA101 PT80 10p multicolored   1.00   .50

No. RA101 was required on mail 5/8-15/95.

PT81

1995, Sept. 9   **Litho.**   **Perf. 13½x13**
RA102 PT81 10p Wilhelm Röntgen   1.00   .50

Fight Tuberculosis. No. RA102 was required on mail 9/9-14/95.

PT82

1996, May 8   **Litho.**   **Perf. 12x12½**
RA103 PT82 15p multicolored   .40   .30

No. RA103 was required on mail 5/8-15/96.

PT83

1996, Sept.   **Litho.**   **Perf. 12x12½**
RA104 PT83 20p multicolored   2.00   .40

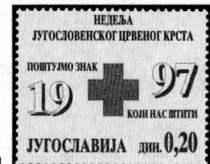

PT84

1997, May 8   Litho.   Perf. 13
RA105 PT84 20p multicolored   5.00 1.00
No. RA105 was required on mail 5/8-15/97.

Milutin Rankovic (1880-1967), Artist — PT85

1997, Sept. 14   Litho.   Perf. 14
RA106 PT85 20p multicolored   .40 .40
Fight Tuberculosis. No. RA106 was required on mail 9/14-21/97.

PT86

1998, May 8   Litho.   Perf. 13¾
RA107 PT86 20p multicolored   .40 .40
No. RA107 was required on mail 5/8-15/98.

Red Cross — PT87

1999, May 8   Litho.   Perf. 13¾
RA108 PT87 1d multi   2.00 .50
No. RA108 was required on mail 5/8-5/15/99.

Red Cross — PT88

1999, Sept. 14
RA109 PT88 1d multi   7.00 .70
No. RA109 was required on mail 9/14-9/21/99.

POSTAL TAX DUE STAMPS

Catalogue values for unused stamps in this section are for Never Hinged items.

The tax of Nos. RAJ1-RAJ9, RAJ11-RAJ12, RAJ14 and RAJ18 was for the Red Cross.

Inscribed "PORTO."

Type of Postal Tax Stamp, 1933
1933   Unwmk.   Litho.   Perf. 12½
RAJ1 PT1 50p dull grn & red   1.00 .25
  a.   Perf. 11½   20.00 8.00

Type of Postal Tax Stamp, 1947
1947
RAJ2 PT4 50p blue grn & scar   .50 .25
For surcharge see Trieste No. RAJ1.

Type of Postal Tax Stamp, 1948
1948
RAJ3 PT5 50p dark grn & red   .40 .25

Type of Postal Tax Stamp, 1949
1949
RAJ4 PT6 50p red & violet   .55 .25
For overprint see Trieste No. RAJ2.

Cross and Map of Yugoslavia — PTD2

1950   Unwmk.   Perf. 12½
RAJ5 PTD2 50p red brown & red   .40 .25
Exists imperf.

Type of Postal Tax Stamp, 1951
1951
RAJ6 PT8 50p emerald & red   .40 .25
For overprint see Trieste No. RAJ3.

Red Cross — PTD3

1952   Unwmk.   Photo.   Perf. 12½
RAJ7 PTD3 50p gray & car   .65 .25
For overprint see Trieste No. RAJ4.

Type of Postal Tax Stamp, 1953
1953   Litho.
RAJ8 PT10 2d yel brown & red   .80 .40
For overprints see Trieste Nos. RAJ5.

Type of Postal Tax Stamp, 1954
1954   Litho.
RAJ9 PT11 2d lilac & red ('54)   .75 .30

Types of Postal Tax Stamps, 1955
1955   Litho.
RAJ10 PT12 2d yel grn ('55)   .55 .25
RAJ11 PT13 2d dk vio brn & red ('55)   .80 .25

Types of Postal Tax Stamps, 1956
1956   Litho.
RAJ12 PT14 2d blue grn & red ('56)   .55 .25
RAJ13 PT15 2d violet brn ('56)   .55 .25

Types of Postal Tax Stamps, 1957
1957   Litho.
RAJ14 PT16 2d gray, blk & car ('57)   .55 .25
RAJ15 PT17 2d lt bl, bis & grn ('57)   .55 .25

Redrawn Type of Regular Issue, 1953
1958   Perf. 12½x12
RAJ16 A95 2d multicolored   .80 .40

Child With Toy — PTD4

1958   Litho.   Perf. 12½
RAJ17 PTD4 2d lt ultra & blk   .55 .25
Issued for Children's Week, Oct. 5-11.

Type of Postal Tax Stamp, 1959
1959
RAJ18 PT19 2d yel org & red   .55 .25

Type of Postal Tax Stamp, 1959
Design: Tree, cock and wheat.
1959
RAJ19 PT20 2d ocher & mar   .40 .25

Type of Postal Tax Stamp, 1960
1960
RAJ20 PT21 2d vio brn & red   .50 .25

Type of Postal Tax Stamp, 1960
Design: Boy, tools and ball.
1960
RAJ21 PT22 2d Prussian blue   .30 .25

Type of Postal Tax Stamp, 1961
1961, May 7
RAJ22 PT23 2d multicolored   .30 .25

Type of Postal Tax Stamp, 1961
1961, Oct. 1
RAJ23 PT24 2d apple grn & brn   .30 .25

Type of Postal Tax Stamp, 1962
1962, Apr. 30
RAJ24 PT25 5d brn red, bl & red   .30 .25

Type of Postal Tax Stamp, 1963
1963, May 5
RAJ25 PT26 5d red org, red & gray   .50 .25

OFFICES ABROAD

Catalogue values for unused stamps in this section are for Never Hinged items.

King Peter II — A1

1943   Unwmk.   Typo.   Perf. 12½
1K1 A1 2d dark blue   .40 4.00
1K2 A1 3d slate   .40 4.00
1K3 A1 5d carmine   .40 4.00
1K4 A1 10d black   .40 4.00
  Nos. 1K1-1K4 (4)   1.60 16.00
For surcharges see Nos. 1KB1-1KB4.

V. Vodnik — A2   Peter Nyegosh — A3

3d, Ljudovit Gaj. 4d, Vuk Stefanovic Karadzic. 5d, Bishop Joseph Strossmayer. 10d, Karageorge.

1943, Dec. 1   Engr.   Perf. 12½x13
1K5 A2 1d red org & black   .40 8.25
1K6 A3 2d yel green & blk   .80 8.50
1K7 A2 3d dp ultra & blk   .80 8.75
1K8 A2 4d dk pur & brn blk   1.60 9.25
1K9 A2 5d brn vio & brn blk   1.60 9.75
1K10 A3 10d brn & brown blk   5.50 10.00
  Nos. 1K5-1K10 (6)   10.70 54.50

Souvenir Sheet
Center in Black
1K11   Sheet of 6, #1K5-1K10   65.00
25th anniv. of the Union of Liberated Yugoslavia. Valid on ships of the Yugoslav Navy and Mercantile Marine.
Nos. 1K5-1K10 overprinted diagonally "1945" in London were not issued. In 1950, they were sold by the Yugoslav Government without postal validity. Later they appeared

---

with the additional overprint of the outline of a plane at upper left in carmine or black.

OFFICES ABROAD SEMI-POSTAL STAMPS

Nos. 1K1-1K4 Surcharged in Orange or Black

1943   Unwmk.   Perf. 12½
1KB1 A1 2d + 12.50d dk bl   2.40 8.25
1KB2 A1 3d + 12.50d slate   2.40 8.25
1KB3 A1 5d + 12.50d car   2.40 8.25
        (Bk)   2.40 8.25
1KB4 A1 10d + 12.50d black   2.40 8.25
  Nos. 1KB1-1KB4 (4)   9.60 33.00
The surtax was for the Red Cross.

LJUBLJANA
(Lubiana, Laibach)
Italian Occupation

Under Italian occupation in 1941, the western half of Slovenia was known as the Province of Ljubljana (Lubiana to the Italians, Laibach to the Germans) and a quisling administration was set up under the profascist General Rupnik.

100 Centesimi = 1 Lira

Yugoslavia Nos. 127, 128, 142-154 Overprinted in Black

Co. Ci.

1941   Unwmk.   Perf. 12½, 13x12½
N1 A16 25p black   3.25 4.00
N2 A16 50p orange   3.25 4.00
N3 A16 1d yellow grn   3.25 4.00
N4 A16 1.50d red   3.25 4.00
N5 A16 2d dp magenta   3.25 4.00
N6 A16 3d dl red brn   3.25 4.00
N7 A16 4d ultra   3.25 4.00
N8 A16 5d dark blue   3.25 4.00
N9 A16 5.50d dk vio brn   3.25 4.00
N10 A16 6d slate blue   4.75 9.50
N11 A16 8d sepia   4.75 9.50
N12 A16 10d bright vio   4.75 9.50
N13 A16 12d brt violet   12.00 14.50
N14 A10 15d brown   325.00 525.00
N15 A16 16d dl violet   12.00 14.50
N16 A16 20d blue   24.00 32.50
N17 A16 30d brt pink   52.50 95.00
  Nos. N1-N17 (17)   469.00 746.00
  Set, never hinged   1,100.

Yugoslavia Nos. 127, 142-154 Overprinted in Black

1941
N18 A16 25p black   3.25 3.25
N19 A16 50p orange   3.25 3.25
N20 A16 1d yellow grn   3.25 3.25
N21 A16 1.50d red   3.25 3.25
N22 A16 2d dp magenta   3.25 3.25
N23 A16 3d dl red brn   3.25 3.25
N24 A16 4d ultra   3.25 3.25
N25 A16 5d dark blue   3.25 3.25
N26 A16 5.50d dk vio brn   3.25 3.25
N27 A16 6d slate blue   3.25 3.25
N28 A16 8d sepia   3.25 3.25
N29 A10 10d brt violet   6.50 4.00
N30 A16 12d bright vio   3.25 3.25
N31 A16 16d dl violet   6.50 4.00
N32 A16 20d blue   20.00 27.50
N33 A16 30d brt pink   110.00 140.00

Yugoslavia Nos. 145, 148 Surcharged in Black

N34	A16	50p on 1.50d red	1.60	2.00
N35	A16	1d on 4d ultra	1.60	2.00
		Nos. N18-N35 (18)	185.20	218.50
		Set, never hinged	400.00	

German Occupation

Stamps of Italy, 1929-42, Overprinted or Surcharged in Blue, Carmine, Black or Green

a

b

c

1944		**Wmk. 140**		***Perf. 14***
N36	A90(a)	5c ol brown	.25	*5.50*
N37	A92(b)	10c dark brn	.25	*5.50*
N38	A93(a)	15c sl grn (C)	.25	*5.50*
N39	A91(b)	20c rose red	.25	*5.50*
N40	A94(a)	25c dp grn (C)	.25	*5.50*
N41	A95(b)	30c ol brown	.25	*5.50*
N42	A93(a)	35c dp bl (C)	.40	*5.50*
N43	A95(b)	50c purple (C)	.25	*7.00*
N44	A94(a)	75c rose red	.25	*10.50*
N45	A91(b)	1 l deep vio	.25	*10.50*
N46	A94(a)	1.25 l dp bl (C)	.25	*4.00*
N47	A92(b)	1.75 l red org	6.00	*24.00*
N48	A93(a)	2 l car lake	.25	*7.00*
N49	A90(c)	2.55 l on 5c ol brn (Bk)	2.40	*12.00*
N50	A94(a)	5 l on 25c dp grn	2.40	*20.00*
N51	A93(b)	10 l purple	10.00	*55.00*
N52	A91(a)	20 l on 20c rose red (G)	12.00	*65.00*
N53	A93(b)	25 l on 2 l car lake (G)	10.00	*125.00*
N54	A92(a)	50 l on 1.75 l red org (C)	40.00	*400.00*
		Nos. N36-N54 (19)	85.95	*778.50*
		Set, never hinged	175.00	

Krizna Jama — A1

Cerknica Lake — A2

Designs: 20c, Railroad Bridge, Borovnica. 25c, Landscape near Ljubljana. 50c, Church, Ribnica. 75c, View, Ljubljana. 1 l, Old Castle, Ljubljana. 1.25 l, Kocevje (Gottschee). 1.50 l, Borovnica Falls. 2 l, Castle, Konstanjevica. 2.50 l, Castle, Turjak. 3 l, Castle, Zuzemperk. 5 l, View of Krk. 10 l, View of Otolac. 20 l, Farm, Carniola. 30 l, Castle and church, Tabor.

Perf. 10½x11½, 11½x10½

1945		**Photo.**		**Unwmk.**
N55	A1	5c black	.40	*4.00*
N56	A2	10c red orange	.40	*4.00*
N57	A2	20c brn carmine	.40	*4.00*
N58	A2	25c dk sl green	.40	*4.00*
N59	A1	50c deep violet	.40	*4.00*
N60	A2	75c vermilion	.40	*4.00*
N61	A2	1 l dark ol grn	.40	*4.00*
N62	A1	1.25 l dark blue	.40	*8.00*
N63	A1	1.50 l olive black	.40	*8.00*
N64	A2	2 l ultramarine	.60	*9.50*
N65	A2	2.50 l brown	.60	*9.50*
N66	A1	3 l brt red vio	1.50	*16.00*
N67	A2	5 l dk red brn	1.60	*16.00*
N68	A2	10 l slate green	3.25	*72.50*
N69	A2	20 l sapphire	20.00	*250.00*
N70	A1	30 l rose pink	95.00	*950.00*
		Nos. N55-N70 (16)	126.15	*1,367.*
		Set, never hinged	240.00	

SEMI-POSTAL STAMPS

Italian Occupation

Yugoslavia Nos. B116-B119 with Additional Ovpt. in Black

Perf. 11½x12½, 12½x11½

1941				**Unwmk.**
NB1	AP6	50p + 50p on 5d	9.50	14.50
NB2	AP7	1d + 1d on 10d	9.50	14.50
NB3	AP8	1.50d + 1.50d on 20d	9.50	14.50
NB4	AP9	2d + 2d on 30d	9.50	14.50
		Nos. NB1-NB4 (4)	38.00	58.00
		Set, never hinged	90.00	

German Occupation

Italy Nos. E14 & E15 Srchd. in Red

1944				**Wmk. 140**
NB5	SD4	1.25 l + 50 l green	35.00	*600.00*
NB6	SD4	2.50 l + 50 l dp org	35.00	*600.00*

The surtax aided the Red Cross.

Italy Nos. E4 & E15 Srchd. in Blue or Green

NB7	SD4	1.25 l + 50 l grn (B)	35.00	*600.00*
NB8	SD4	2.50 l + 50 l dp org	35.00	*600.00*
		Nos. NB5-NB8 (4)	140.00	*2,400.*
		Set, never hinged	275.00	

The surtax aided the Homeless Relief Fund.

The German and Slovenian inscriptions in the surcharges are transposed on Nos. NB6 and NB8.

Italy Nos. C12-C14, C16-C18 Srchd. in Blue or Red

Nos. NB9, NB11

Nos. NB10, NB12, NB14

No. NB13

1944				**Wmk. 140**
NB9	AP4	25c + 10 l dk grn	14.00	*400.00*
NB10	AP3	50c + 10 l ol brn	14.00	*400.00*
NB11	AP5	75c + 20 l org brn	14.00	*400.00*
NB12	AP5	1 l + 20 l pur	14.00	*400.00*
NB13	AP6	2 l + 20 l dp bl (R)	14.00	*400.00*
NB14	AP3	5 l + 20 l dk grn	14.00	*400.00*
		Nos. NB9-NB14 (6)	84.00	*2,400.*
		Set, never hinged	175.00	

The surcharge aided orphans.

Italy Nos. C12-C14, C16-C18 Srchd. in Blue or Red

Nos. NB15, NB17

Nos. NB16, NB18, NB20

No. NB19

NB15	AP4	25c + 10 l dk grn	14.00	*400.00*
NB16	AP3	50c + 10 l ol brn	14.00	*400.00*
NB17	AP5	75c + 20 l org brn	14.00	*400.00*
NB18	AP5	1 l + 20 l pur	14.00	*400.00*
NB19	AP6	2 l + 20 l dp bl (R)	14.00	*400.00*
NB20	AP3	5 l + 20 l dk grn	14.00	*400.00*
		Nos. NB15-NB20 (6)	84.00	*2,400.*
		Set, never hinged	175.00	

The surcharge was for winter relief.

AIR POST STAMPS

Italian Occupation

Yugoslavia Nos. C7-C16 Ovptd. like Nos. NB1-NB4

Perf. 12½, 12½x11½, 11½x12½

1941				**Unwmk.**
NC1	AP6	50p brown	11.00	11.00
NC2	AP7	1d yel grn	11.00	11.00
NC3	AP8	2d bl gray	12.50	12.50
NC4	AP9	2.50d rose red	12.50	12.50
NC5	AP6	5d brn vio	20.00	20.00
NC6	AP7	10d brn lake	20.00	20.00
NC7	AP8	20d dark grn	55.00	55.00
NC8	AP9	30d ultra	87.50	95.00
NC9	AP10	40d Prus grn & pale grn	300.00	360.00
NC10	AP11	50d sl bl & gray bl	240.00	240.00
a.		Inverted overprint	950.00	
		Nos. NC1-NC10 (10)	769.50	837.00
		Set, never hinged	1,800.	

German Occupation

Italy Nos. C12-C14, C16-C19 Overprinted Types "a" and "b" in Carmine, Green or Blue

1944		**Wmk. 140**		***Perf. 14***
NC11	AP4(a)	25c dk grn (C)	10.00	*40.00*
NC12	AP3(b)	50c ol brn (C)	10.00	*125.00*
NC13	AP5(a)	75c org brn (G)	10.00	*40.00*
NC14	AP5(b)	1 l pur (C)	10.00	*125.00*
NC15	AP6(a)	2 l dp bl (Bl)	10.00	*87.50*
NC16	AP3(b)	5 l dk grn (C)	10.00	*125.00*
NC17	AP3(a)	10 l dp car (G)	10.00	*87.50*
		Nos. NC11-NC17 (7)	70.00	*630.00*

AIR POST SPECIAL DELIVERY STAMP

German Occupation

Italy #CE3 Ovptd. Type "b" in Blue

1944		**Wmk. 140**		***Perf. 14***
NCE1	APSD2	2 l gray blk	10.00	*87.50*

SPECIAL DELIVERY STAMP

German Occupation

Italy #E14 Ovptd. Type "b" in Green

1944		**Wmk. 140**		***Perf. 14***
NE1	SD4	1.25 l green	10.00	*24.00*

POSTAGE DUE STAMPS

Italian Occupation

Yugoslavia Nos. J28-J32 Overprinted in Black Like Nos. N1-N17

1941		**Unwmk.**		***Perf. 12½***
NJ1	D4	50p violet	4.00	4.00
NJ2	D4	1d rose	4.00	4.00
NJ3	D4	2d deep blue	4.00	4.00
NJ4	D4	5d orange	12.00	22.50
NJ5	D4	10d chocolate	12.00	22.50
		Nos. NJ1-NJ5 (5)	36.00	57.00
		Set, never hinged	80.00	

Same Overprinted in Black

NJ6	D4	50p violet	4.00	8.00
NJ7	D4	1d deep magenta	4.00	8.00
NJ8	D4	2d deep blue	8.00	9.50
NJ9	D4	5d orange	55.00	110.00
NJ10	D4	10d chocolate	21.00	40.00
		Nos. NJ6-NJ10 (5)	92.00	175.50

Same Overprinted in Black

NJ11	D4	50p violet	4.00	4.00
NJ12	D4	1d deep magenta	6.50	6.50
NJ13	D4	2d deep blue	55.00	110.00
		Nos. NJ11-NJ13 (3)	65.50	120.50

German Occupation

Postage Due Stamps of Italy, 1934, Overprinted or Surcharged in Various Colors

d

e

f

g

1944		**Wmk. 140**		***Perf. 14***
NJ14	D6(d)	5c brown (Br)	2.40	*80.00*
NJ15	D6(e)	10c blue (Bl)	2.40	*80.00*
NJ16	D6(d)	20c rose red (R)	1.25	*8.00*
NJ17	D6(e)	25c green (G)	1.25	*8.00*
NJ18	D6(f)	30c on 50c vio (Bk)	1.25	*8.00*
NJ19	D6(g)	40c on 5c brn (Bl)	1.25	*8.00*
NJ20	D6(d)	50c violet (V)	1.25	*8.00*
NJ21	D7(e)	1 l red orange (R)	2.40	*80.00*
NJ22	D7(d)	2 l green (Bl)	2.40	*80.00*
		Nos. NJ14-NJ22 (9)	15.85	*360.00*

Fiume-Kupa Zone

Italian Occupation

Four issues of 1941-42 consist of overprints on Yugoslav stamps of 1939-41: (a.) 14 stamps overprinted "ZONA OCCUPATO FIUMANO KUPA" and "ZOFK ZOFK ZOFK." (b.) 3 stamps overprinted as illustrated. (c.) 1 stamp surcharged "MEMENTO AVDERE SEMPER." "L1," etc. (d.) 3 stamps overprinted in arch: "Pro Maternite e Infanzia."

ISSUES FOR ISTRIA AND THE SLOVENE COAST (ZONE B)

Grapes — A1

Olive Branch — A2

Sailboat, Pola — A3

Designs: 50c, Donkey. Nos. 25-26, Ruined home. 2 l, Duino Castle. 5 l, Birthplace of Vladimir Gortan. 10 l, Plowing. Nos. 33-34, Tuna. 30 l, Viaduct at Solkan, Soca River.

Perf. 11½, 12, 10½x11½

				Photo.
1945-46				
23	A1	25c dark green	.40	1.00
24	A1	50c red brown	.25	.25
25	A1	1 l green	.25	.25
26	A1	1 l red	.25	.25
27	A2	1.50 l olive brown	.25	.25
28	A2	2 l dk Prus grn	.25	.25
29	A3	4 l red	.25	.25
30	A3	4 l bright blue	.25	.40
31	A3	5 l gray black	.25	.25
32	A3	10 l brown	.25	.25
33	A3	20 l blue	1.60	.85
34	A3	20 l dark violet	3.50	5.25
35	A3	30 l magenta	1.40	.80
		Nos. 23-35 (13)	9.15	10.30
		Set, never hinged	16.00	

The first (Ljubljana) printing is perf. 10½x11½ and consists of Nos. 23-24, 26-28, 30-32, 34-35. The second (Zagreb) printing is perf. 12 and consists of Nos. 23-25, 27-29, 31-33, 35. The third (Belgrade) printing is perf. 11½ and consists of Nos. 25, 28, 40-41.

See Nos. 40-41. For surcharges see Nos. 36-37, J1-J19.

Nos. 33 and 35 Surcharged with New Values and Bars in Black

1946		Unwmk.	Perf. 11½	
36	A3	1 l on 20 l blue	.60	1.25
37	A3	2 l on 30 l magenta	.60	1.25
		Set, never hinged	2.40	

Types of 1945

Design: 3 l, Duino Castle.

1946, Nov. 30				
40	A2	3 l crimson	1.50	1.75
41	A3	6 l ultra	3.25	4.00
		Set, never hinged	9.25	

Types of Yugoslavia & Official Stamps of 1946 Surcharged in Black

On A26

On O1

1947		Unwmk.	Perf. 12½	
42	A26	1 l on 9d lilac rose	.25	.40
43	O1	1.50 l on 50p blue	.25	.40
44	A26	2 l on 9d lilac rose	.25	.40
45	O1	3 l on 50p blue	.25	.40
46	A26	5 l on 9d lilac rose	.25	.40
47	O1	6 l on 50p blue	.25	.40
48	A26	10 l on 9d lilac rose	.25	.40
49	O1	15 l on 50p blue	.25	.55
50	A26	35 l on 9d lilac rose	.25	.90
51	O1	50 l on 50p blue	.25	.90
		Nos. 42-51 (10)		5.15
		Set, never hinged	2.00	

POSTAGE DUE STAMPS

Nos. 23, 24, 34 and 35 Surcharged in Black

1945		Unwmk.	Perf. 10½x11½	
J1	A3	50c on 20 l dk vio	.30	1.00
J2	A1	1 l on 25c dk grn	6.00	2.00
J3	A3	2 l on 30 l magenta	.90	2.40
J4	A1	4 l on 50c red brn	.70	.65
J5	A1	8 l on 50c red brn	.70	.65
J6	A1	10 l on 50c red brn	4.00	1.90
J7	A1	20 l on 50c red brn	4.50	3.25
		Nos. J1-J7 (7)	17.10	11.85
		Set, never hinged	32.50	

Nos. 25 and 35 Surcharged in Black

1945			Perf. 12	
J8	A1	1 l on 1 l green	.25	.40
J9	A1	2 l on 1 l green	.25	.40
J10	A1	4 l on 1 l green	.30	.40
J11	A3	10 l on 30 l magenta	2.50	2.00
J12	A3	20 l on 30 l magenta	4.00	4.50
J13	A3	30 l on 30 l magenta	4.00	4.50
		Nos. J8-J13 (6)	11.30	12.20

The surcharges are arranged to fit the designs of the stamps.

No. 23 Surcharged in Black

1946				
J14	A1	1 l on 25c dark green	.40	.55
J15	A1	2 l on 25c dark green	.70	.80
J16	A1	4 l on 25c dark green	.40	.55

No. 33 Surcharged in Black

J17	A3	10 l on 20 l blue	2.25	1.75
J18	A3	20 l on 20 l blue	5.50	4.50
J19	A3	30 l on 20 l blue	5.25	5.25
		Nos. J14-J19 (6)	14.50	13.40
		Set, never hinged	25.00	

Type of Yugoslavia Postage Due Stamps, 1946, Surcharged in Black

1947				
J20	D7	1 l on 1d brt blue grn	.25	.50
J21	D7	2 l on 1d brt blue grn	.25	.50
J22	D7	6 l on 1d brt blue grn	.25	.50
J23	D7	10 l on 1d brt blue grn	.25	.50
J24	D7	30 l on 1d brt blue grn	.25	.65
		Nos. J20-J24 (5)	1.25	2.65
		Set, never hinged	1.75	

TRIESTE, ZONE A
See listing under Italy, Vol. 3.

TRIESTE

A free territory (1947-1954) on the Adriatic Sea between Italy and Yugoslavia. In 1954 the territory was divided, Italy acquiring the northern section and seaport, Yugoslavia the southern section (Zone B).

Catalogue values for all unused stamps in this country are for Never Hinged items.

ZONE B

Issued by the Yugoslav Military Government
100 Centesimi = 1 Lira
100 Paras = 1 Dinar (1949)

See Istria and the Slovene Coast (Zone B) for preceding issues of 1945-47.

Stylized Gymnast and Arms of Trieste — A1

1948		Unwmk.	Litho.	Perf. 10½x11
Inscriptions in:				
1	A1	100 l Italian	8.00	4.00
2	A1	100 l Croatian	8.00	4.00
3	A1	100 l Slovene	8.00	4.00
a.		Strip of 3, #1-3	95.00	65.00
		Nos. 1-3 (3)	24.00	12.00

May Day.

Clasped Hands, Hammer and Sickle — A2

1949		Photo.	Perf. 11½x12½	
4	A2	10 l grnsh blk & ol grn	.80	.80

Labor Day, May 1, 1949.
"V.U.J.A. S.T.T." are the initials of "Vojna Uprava Jugoslovenske Armije, Slobodna Teritorija Trsta" (Military Administration Yugoslav Army, Free Territory of Trieste).

Stamps of Yugoslavia, 1945-47 Overprinted in Carmine or Ultramarine

---

1949, Aug. 15			Perf. 12½	
5	A22	50p ol gray	.40	.30
6	A22	1d bl grn	.40	.30
7	A24	2d scar (U)	.40	.30
8	A25	3d dl red (U)	.40	.30
9	A24	4d dk bl	.80	.30
10	A25	5d dk bl	.80	.30
11	A26	9d rose vio (U)	5.50	.80
12	A23	12d ultra	5.50	4.00
13	A22	16d blue	8.00	4.75
14	A23	20d org ver (U)	16.00	6.50
		Nos. 5-14 (10)	38.20	17.85

The letters of the overprint are set closer and in one line on Nos. 7 and 9.

Yugoslavia Nos. 266 and 267 Overprinted in Carmine

Burelage in Color of Stamp

1949				
15	A58	5d blue	10.50	8.00
16	A58	12d brown	10.50	8.00

75th anniv. of the UPU.

Yugoslavia, Nos. 269 to 272, Overprinted in Carmine

1950				
17	A60	2d bl grn	4.00	.80
18	A60	3d car rose	4.00	.80
19	A60	5d blue	4.00	2.40
20	A60	10d dp org	16.00	8.00
		Nos. 17-20 (4)	28.00	12.00

Workers Carrying Tools and Flag — A3

1950, May 1				Photo.
21	A3	3d violet	.55	.55
22	A3	10d carmine	1.00	1.00

Labor Day, May 1, 1950.

Peasant on Ass — A4

Designs: 1d, Cockerel. 2d, Goose. 3d, Bees and honeycomb. 5d, Oxen. 10d, Turkey. 15d, Goats. 20d, Silkworms.

1950		Unwmk.	Perf. 12½	
23	A4	50p dk gray	.40	.40
24	A4	1d brn car	.40	.40
25	A4	2d dp bl	.40	.40
26	A4	3d org brn	.40	.40
27	A4	5d aqua	3.25	.40
28	A4	10d brown	3.25	.40
29	A4	15d violet	20.00	8.00
30	A4	20d dk grn	8.00	4.00
		Nos. 23-30 (8)	36.10	14.40

1951				
31	A4	1d orange brown	1.25	.40
32	A4	3d rose brown	1.60	.40

Worker A5

1951, May 1

33	A5	3d dark red	.80	.40
34	A5	10d brown olive	1.25	.80

Labor Day.

Pietro Paolo
Vergerio — A7

1951, Oct. 21   Litho.

37	A7	5d blue	1.00	1.00
38	A7	10d claret	1.00	1.00
39	A7	20d sepia	1.00	1.00
		Nos. 37-39 (3)	3.00	3.00

Types of Yugoslavia, 1951, Overprinted "STT VUJA"

1951, Nov.

40	A81	10d brn org (V)	1.00	.70
41	A81	12d grnsh blk (C)	1.00	.70

Bicycle
Race — A8

1952   Photo.

42	A8	5d shown	.40	.40
43	A8	10d Soccer	.40	.40
44	A8	15d Rowing	.40	.40
45	A8	28d Sailing	1.60	1.25
46	A8	50d Volleyball	3.25	2.40
47	A8	100d Diving	10.00	4.00
		Nos. 42-47 (6)	16.05	8.85

Marshal Tito
A9   A10

1952, May 25   Perf. 11½

48	A9	15d dk brn	2.50	1.25
49	A10	28d red brn	2.50	2.00
50	A9	50d dk gray grn	4.75	2.75
		Nos. 48-50 (3)	9.75	6.00

60th birthday of Marshal Tito.

Types of Yugoslavia 1952 Overprinted in Carmine "STT VUJNA"

1952, July 26   Perf. 12½

51	A90	5d dk brn & sal, cr	1.60	.40
52	A90	10d dk grn & grn	1.60	.40
53	A90	15d dk brn & bl, lil	1.60	.40
54	A90	28d dk brn & buff, cr	1.60	1.60
55	A90	50d dk brn & buff, yel	14.00	9.50
56	A90	100d ind & lil, pink	32.50	27.50
		Nos. 51-56 (6)	52.90	39.80

15th Olympic Games, Helsinki, 1952. Nos. 52, 54, 56 inscribed in Cyrillic characters.
The added "N" in "VUJNA" stands for "Narodna" (Peoples'). See note after No. 4.
Nos. 51-56 exist imperf. Value of set, $950, unused or used.

Yugoslavia Nos. 365 to 367 Overprinted in Carmine "STT VUJNA"

1952, Sept. 13

57	A91	15d deep claret	3.25	2.75
58	A91	28d dark brown	4.00	2.75
59	A91	50d gray	4.75	2.75
		Nos. 57-59 (3)	12.00	8.25

Formation of the Yugoslav navy, 10th anniv.

Yugoslavia No. 358 Overprinted "STT VUJA" in Blue

1952, June 22

60	A89	15d bright rose	1.60	.80

Children's Week.

Yugoslavia Nos. 369-372 Overprinted "VUJNA STT" in Blue or Carmine

1952, Nov. 4

61	A93	15d red brn (Bl)	1.00	.65
62	A93	15d dk vio bl	1.00	.65
63	A93	15d dk brn	1.00	.65
64	A93	15d bl grn	1.00	.65
		Nos. 61-64 (4)	4.00	2.60

Issued to publicize the 6th Yugoslavia Communist Party Congress, Zagreb, 1952.

Anchovies and Starfish — A11

1952   Unwmk.   Photo.   Perf. 11x11½

65	A11	15d red brown	4.00	4.00
a.		Souvenir sheet, imperf.	55.00	55.00

Capodistria Phil. Exhib., Nov. 29-Dec. 7.
No. 65a contains a 50d dark blue green stamp. Sold for 85d.

Stamps or Types of Yugoslavia Overprinted "STT VUJNA" in Various Colors

1953, Feb. 3   Perf. 12½

66	A94	15d brn carmine (Bl)	.40	.40
67	A94	30d chalky blue (R)	1.60	1.60

10th anniv. of the death of Nikola Tesla.

1953

68	A68	1d gray	9.50	7.25
69	A68	2d car (V)	.80	.40
70	A68	3d rose red (R)	.80	.40
71	A68	5d orange	.40	.40
72	A68	10d emerald (G)	.80	.40
73	A68	15d rose red (V)	1.60	.80
74	A68	30d blue (Bl)	4.00	2.40
75	A68	50d grnsh bl (Bl)	8.00	4.00
		Nos. 68-75 (8)	25.90	16.05

Nos. 69, 71 and 73 are lithographed.
See Nos. 90-92.

1953, Apr. 21   Perf. 11½

76	A95	15d dk ol grn (O)	.25	.25
77	A95	30d chalky blue (O)	.40	.40
78	A95	50d henna brown	1.10	1.10
		Nos. 76-78 (3)	1.75	1.75

Issued in honor of the United Nations.

Automobile
Climbing Mt.
Lovcen — A12

Various automobiles and motorcycles.

1953, June 2   Perf. 12½

79	A12	15d ocher & choc	.40	.40
80	A12	30d lt bl grn & ol grn	.40	.40
81	A12	50d salmon & dp plum	.40	.40
82	A12	70d bl & dk bl	2.75	2.00
		Nos. 79-82 (4)	3.95	3.20

Intl. Automobile and Motorcycle Races, 1953.

Stamps or Types of Yugoslavia Overprinted "STT VUJNA" in Various Colors

1953, July 8   Engr.

83	A97	50d grnsh gray (C)	4.00	4.00

Tito's election to the presidency, 1/14/53.

1953, July 31

84	A98	15d gray & grn (C)	2.00	2.00

38th Esperanto Cong., Zagreb, July 25-Aug. 1, 1953. See No. C21.

1953, Sept. 5

85	A101	15d blue (C)	4.00	4.00

Liberation of Istria & the Slovene coast, 10th anniv.

1953, Oct. 3

86	A102	15d gray	1.60	1.25

Cent. of the death of Branko Radicevic, poet.

1953, Nov. 29   Perf. 12½x12

87	A103	15d gray vio (V)	1.10	.80
88	A103	30d claret (Br)	1.10	.80
89	A103	50d dl bl grn (Dk Bl)	1.10	.80
		Nos. 87-89 (3)	3.30	2.40

10th anniv. of the 1st republican legislative assembly of Yugoslavia.

1954, Mar. 5   Perf. 12½

90	A68	5d org (V)	1.00	.40
91	A68	10d yel grn (C)	.80	.40
92	A68	15d rose red (G)	1.00	.40
		Nos. 90-92 (3)	2.80	1.20

Overprinted in Carmine

1954   Photo.   Perf. 11½

93	A104	2d red brn, sl & cr	.80	.40
94	A104	5d gray & dk yel brn	.80	.40
95	A104	10d ol grn & dk org brn	.80	.40
96	A104	15d dp bl grn & dk org brn	.80	.40
97	A104	17d gray brn, dk brn & cr	.80	.40
98	A104	25d bis, gray bl & org yel	.80	.40
99	A105	30d lil & dk brn	.80	.40
100	A105	35d rose vio & bl blk	.80	.40
101	A105	50d yel grn & vio brn	1.60	1.25
102	A105	65d org brn & gray blk	4.75	3.25
103	A105	70d bl & org brn	12.00	6.50
104	A105	100d brt bl & blk brn	32.50	25.00
		Nos. 93-104 (12)	57.25	39.60

Overprinted in Various Colors

1954, Oct. 8   Perf. 12½

105	A107	15d mar, red, ocher & dk bl (Bk)	.80	.55
106	A107	30d dk bl, grn, sal buff & choc (G)	.80	.55
107	A107	50d brn, bis & red (G)	.80	.55
108	A107	70d dk grn, gray grn & choc (R)	1.60	1.25
		Nos. 105-108 (4)	4.00	2.90

150th anniv. of the 1st Serbian insurrection.

AIR POST STAMPS

AP1

Perf. 12½x11½

1948, Oct. 17   Photo.   Unwmk.

C1	AP1	25 l gray	1.10	.80
C2	AP1	50 l orange	1.10	.80

Economic Exhib. at Capodistria, Oct. 17-24.

Fishermen — AP2   Farmer and Pack Mule — AP3

Mew over
Chimneys
AP4

1949, June 1   Perf. 11½

C3	AP2	1 l grnsh bl	.40	.40
C4	AP3	2 l red brn	.80	.40
C5	AP2	5 l blue	.80	.40
C6	AP3	10 l purple	2.40	2.00
C7	AP2	25 l brown	6.50	4.00
C8	AP3	50 l ol brn	8.00	4.00
C9	AP4	100 l dk vio brn	14.50	6.50
		Nos. C3-C9 (7)	33.40	17.70

Italian inscriptions on Nos. C5 and C6, Croatian on No. C7, Slavonic on No. C8.
Nos. C3-C4 exist imperf. Value, each $150.

Nos. C3-C9 Surcharged "DIN," or New Value and "DIN" in Various Colors

1949, Nov. 5

C10	AP2	1d on 1 l (Bk)	.40	.40
C11	AP3	2d on 2 l (Br)	.80	.40
C12	AP2	5d on 5 l (Bl)	.80	.40
C13	AP3	10d on 10 l (V)	.80	.40
C14	AP2	15d on 25 l (Br)	16.00	9.50
C15	AP3	20d on 50 l (Gr)	8.00	3.25
C16	AP4	30d on 100 l (Bk)	9.50	4.00
		Nos. C10-C16 (7)	36.30	18.35

On Nos. C14 and C15 the original value is obliterated by a framed block, on No. C16 by four parallel lines.

Yugoslavia No. C33 Overprinted in Carmine and Lilac Rose Network
Souvenir Sheet

1950   Perf. 11½x12½

C17	AP15	10d lilac rose	200.00	160.00
a.		Imperf.	200.00	160.00

Main Square,
Capodistria
AP5

Lighthouse,
Pirano — AP6

Design: 25d, Hotel, Portorose.

1952		**Unwmk.**	**Photo.**	**Perf. 12½**
C18	AP5	5d brown	12.00	12.00
C19	AP5	15d brt bl	8.00	8.00
C20	AP5	25d green	8.00	8.00
		Nos. C18-C20 (3)	28.00	28.00

75th anniv. (in 1949) of the UPU.

Type of Yugoslavia, 1953
Overprinted "STT VUJNA" in
Carmine

1953, July 31				
C21	AP21	300d vio & grn	250.00	250.00

38th Esperanto Cong., Zagreb, 7/25-8/1.
Sheets of 12 (12,000 stamps) and sheets of 8 (3,000 stamps in light violet and green).
A private red overprint was applied marginally to 250 sheets of 8: "Esperantski Kongres — 38 — a Universala Kongreso de Esperanto — Congresso del Esperanto."

Air Post Stamps of Yugoslavia in
New Colors Overprinted "STT
VUJNA" in Various Colors

1954			**Engr.**	
C22	AP16	1d dp pur gray	.80	.40
C23	AP16	2d brt grn (G)	.80	.40
C24	AP16	3d red brn (Br)	.80	.40
C25	AP16	5d chocolate	.80	.40
C26	AP16	10d bl grn	.80	.40
C27	AP16	20d brn (Br)	.80	.40
C28	AP16	30d blue	.80	.40
C29	AP16	50d olive blk	.80	.60
C30	AP16	100d scar (R)	2.50	2.50
C31	AP16	200d dk bl vio (Bl)	4.75	4.00
				11x11½
C32	AP17	500d orange (Br)	27.50	20.00
		Nos. C22-C32 (11)	41.15	29.90

POSTAGE DUE STAMPS

Yugoslavia Nos. J51 to J55
Overprinted "S T T VUJA" in Two
Lines in Ultramarine or Carmine

1949		**Unwmk.**	**Perf. 12½**	
J1	D7	50p dp org	.80	.40
J2	D7	1d orange	.80	.40
J3	D7	2d dk bl (C)	.80	.40
J4	D7	3d yel grn (C)	1.60	.40
J5	D7	5d brt pur (C)	4.00	1.60
		Nos. J1-J5 (5)	8.00	3.20

Croakers
D1

Anchovies
D2

1950			**Photo.**	
J6	D1	50p brn org	4.00	.80
J7	D1	1d dp ol grn	4.00	1.60
J8	D2	2d dk grnsh bl	4.00	1.60
J9	D2	3d dk vio bl	4.00	1.60
J10	D2	5d plum	20.00	6.50
		Nos. J6-J10 (5)	36.00	12.10

Yugoslavia Nos. J67-J74
Overprinted "STT VUJNA" in Blue
or Carmine

1952				
J11	D7	1d brown (Bl)	.40	.40
J12	D7	2d emerald	.40	.40
J13	D7	5d blue	.40	.40
J14	D7	10d scar (Bl)	.40	.40
J15	D7	20d purple	.40	.40
J16	D7	30d org yel (Bl)	.40	.40
J17	D7	50d ultra	.40	.40
J18	D7	100d dp plum (Bl)	13.50	8.00
		Nos. J11-J18 (8)	16.30	10.80

POSTAL TAX STAMPS

Yugoslavia No.
RA5 Surcharged
in Blue

1948		**Unwmk.**	**Perf. 12½**	
RA1	PT4	2 l on 50p brn & scar	32.50	*32.50*

Obligatory on all mail from May 22-30.

Yugoslavia No. RA7 Overprinted
"VUJA STT" in Black

1950, July 3				
RA2	PT6	50p red & brn	2.40	1.25

Yugoslavia No. RA9 Overprinted
"STT VUJA" in Black

1951				
RA3	PT8	50p vio bl & red	24.00	16.00

Yugoslavia No. RA10 Overprinted
"STT VUJNA" in Carmine

1952				
RA4	PT9	50p gray & carmine	1.60	.80

Type of Yugoslavia, 1953
Overprinted "STT VUJNA" in Blue

1953				
RA5	PT10	2d org brn & red	1.60	.80

The tax of Nos. RA1-RA5 was for the Red Cross.

POSTAL TAX DUE STAMPS

Yugoslavia No. RAJ2 Surcharged
Like No. RA1 in Scarlet

1948		**Unwmk.**	**Perf. 12½**	
RAJ1	PT4	2 l on 50p bl grn & scar	260.00	240.00

Yugoslavia No. RAJ4 Overprinted
"VUJA STT" in Black

1950, July 3				
RAJ2	PT6	50p red & vio	2.40	1.25

Yugoslavia No. RAJ6 Overprinted
"STT VUJA" in Black

1951				
RAJ3	PT8	50p emer & red	240.00	225.00

Yugoslavia No. RAJ7 Overprinted
"STT VUJNA" in Carmine

1952				
RAJ4	PTD3	50p gray & car	1.60	1.00

Type of Yugoslavia, 1953,
Overprinted "STT VUJNA" in Blue

1953				
RAJ5	PT10	2d lilac rose & red	1.60	1.00

ZAIRE

zä-'ir

(Congo Democratic Republic)

LOCATION — Central Africa
GOVT. — Republic
AREA — 905,365 sq. mi.
POP. — 50,481,305 (1999 est.)
CAPITAL — Kinshasa

Congo Democratic Republic changed its name to Republic of the Zaire in November 1971. Issues before that date are listed in Vol. 2 under Congo Democratic Republic.

100 Sengi = 1 Li-Kuta
100 Ma-Kuta = 1 Zaire
100 Centimes = 1 Franc (July 1998)

Catalogue values for all unused stamps in this country are for Never Hinged items.

From 1971 through 1997, imperforates exist of almost all issues. Exceptions are Nos. 756-772, 850-860, 991-999 and 1259-1442.

UNICEF Emblem,
Child
Care — A143

UNICEF Emblem and: 14k, Map of Africa showing Zaire. 17k, Boy in African village.

Perf. 14x13½			
1971, Dec. 18		**Unwmk.**	
750	A143	4k gold & multi	.50 .25
751	A143	14k lt bl, gold, red & grn	1.25 .75
752	A143	17k gold & multi	2.00 1.10
		Nos. 750-752 (3)	3.75 2.10

25th anniv. of UNICEF. For surcharge see No. 1327.

Pres.
Mobutu,
MPR
Emblem
A144

1972		**Photo.**	**Perf. 11½**
753	A144	4k multi	4.00 2.50
754	A144	14k multi	4.00 2.50
755	A144	22k multi	4.00 2.50
		Nos. 753-755 (3)	12.00 7.50

5th anniv. of the People's Revolutionary Movement (MPR). For surcharge see #1308.

Zaire
Arms — A145

Pres. Joseph D.
Mobutu — A146

1972		**Litho.**	**Perf. 14**
756	A145	10s red org & blk	.25 .25
757	A145	40s brt bl & multi	.25 .25
758	A145	50s citron & multi	.25 .25
		Perf. 13	
759	A146	1k sky bl & multi	.25 .25
760	A146	2k org & multi	.25 .25
761	A146	3k multi	.25 .25
762	A146	4k emer & multi	.25 .25
763	A146	5k multi	.25 .25
764	A146	6k multi	.25 .25
765	A146	8k cit & multi	.40 .25
766	A146	9k multi	.50 .25
767	A146	10k lt lil & multi	.55 .25
768	A146	14k multi	.75 .30
769	A146	17k multi	.90 .40
770	A146	20k yel & multi	1.25 .50
771	A146	50k multi	3.00 1.00
772	A146	100k fawn & multi	6.00 2.50
		Nos. 756-772 (17)	15.60 7.70

For surcharges and overprints see Nos. 860, 1328, O1-O11.

Same, Denominations in Zaires

1973, Feb. 21			
773	A146	0.01z sky bl & multi	.25 .25
774	A146	0.02z org & multi	.25 .25
775	A146	0.03z multi	.25 .25
776	A146	0.04z multi	.25 .25
777	A146	0.10z multi	.40 .25
778	A146	0.14z multi	.60 .55
		Nos. 773-778 (6)	2.00 1.80

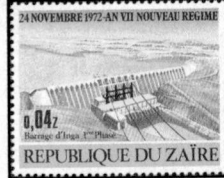

Inga Dam
A147

1973, Jan. 25		**Litho.**	**Perf. 13½**
790	A147	0.04z multi	.35 .25
791	A147	0.14z pink & multi	.45 .35
792	A147	0.18z yel & multi	.80 .55
		Nos. 790-792 (3)	1.60 1.15

Completion of first section of Inga Dam Nov. 24, 1972.

World
Map
A148

1973, June 23		**Photo.**	**Perf. 12½x12**
793	A148	0.04z lil & multi	.25 .25
794	A148	0.07z multi	.35 .25
795	A148	0.18z multi	.85 .50
		Nos. 793-795 (3)	1.45 1.00

3rd Intl. Fair at Kinshasa, June 23-July 8.
The dark brown ink of the inscription was applied by a thermographic process and varnished, producing a shiny, raised effect.

Hand and
INTERPOL
Emblem — A149

1973, Sept. 28		**Litho.**	**Perf. 12½**
796	A149	0.06z multi	.45 .25
797	A149	0.14z multi	.95 .50

50th anniversary of International Criminal Police Organization.

Leopard
with Soccer
Ball on
Globe
A150

1974, July 17		**Photo.**	**Perf. 11½x12**
798	A150	1k multi	.25 .25
799	A150	2k multi	.25 .25
800	A150	3k multi	1.00 .35
801	A150	4k multi	1.25 .50
802	A150	5k multi	1.50 .65
803	A150	14k multi	4.50 1.40
a.		Souvenir sheet, 1 #803	37.50
		Nos. 798-803 (6)	8.75 3.40

World Cup Soccer Championship, Munich, June 13-July 7.

Foreman-Ali
Fight — A151

1974, Nov. 9   Litho.   Perf. 12x12½
804 A151 1k multi   .25   .25
805 A151 4k multi   .25   .25
806 A151 6k multi   .35   .30
807 A151 14k multi   .75   .50
808 A151 20k multi   1.10   .90
    Nos. 804-808 (5)   2.70 2.20

World Heavyweight Boxing Championship match between George Foreman and Muhammad Ali, Kinshasa, Oct. 30 (postponed from Sept. 25).

Same, Type of 1974, Denominations in Zaires and Inscribed in Various Colors

1975, Aug.   Litho.   Perf. 12x12½
809 A151 0.01z multi (R)   .25   .25
810 A151 0.04z multi (Br) .25   .25
811 A151 0.06z multi (Bk) .30   .30
812 A151 0.14z multi (G)   .65   .50
813 A151 0.20z multi (Bk) 1.25   .90
    Nos. 809-813 (5)   2.70 2.20

Judge, Lawyers, IWY Emblem A152

1975, Dec.   Photo.   Perf. 11½
814 A152 1k dull blk & multi   .40   .25
815 A152 2k dp rose & multi   .50   .25
816 A152 4k dull grn & multi   1.00   .35
817 A152 14k violet & multi   2.25   .50
    Nos. 814-817 (4)   4.15 1.35

International Women's Year 1975.

Waterfall — A153

1975   Photo.   Perf. 11½
818 A153 1k multicolored   .30   .25
819 A153 2k lt blue & multi .40   .25
820 A153 3k multicolored   .50   .30
821 A153 4k salmon & multi 1.40   .65
822 A153 5k green & multi   1.50   .65
    Nos. 818-822 (5)   4.10 2.10

12th General Assembly of the Intl. Union for Nature Preservation (U.I.C.N.), Kinshasa, Sept. 1975.

Okapis A154

1975
823 A154 1k blue & multi   .60   .25
824 A154 2k yellow grn & multi .90   .25
825 A154 3k brown red & multi 1.50   .30
826 A154 4k green & multi   2.40   .50
827 A154 5k yellow & multi   3.25   .60
    Nos. 823-827 (5)   8.65 1.90

Virunga National Park, 50th anniversary.

Siderma Maluku Industry A155

Designs: 1k, Sozacom apartment building, vert. 3k, Matadi flour mill, vert. 4k, Women parachutists. 8k, Pres. Mobutu visiting Chairman Mao, vert. 10k, Soldiers working along the Salongo. 14k, Pres. Mobutu addressing UN Gen. Assembly, Oct. 1974. 15k, Celebrating crowd.

1975
828 A155 1k ocher & multi   .50   .25
829 A155 2k yel grn & multi .75   .25
830 A155 3k multi   1.00   .25
831 A155 4k multi   1.50   .25
832 A155 8k dk brn & multi 1.75   .25
833 A155 10k sep & multi   2.00   .50
834 A155 14k bl & multi   5.00   .75
835 A155 15k org & multi   7.00 1.00
    Nos. 828-835 (8)   19.50 3.60

10th anniversary of new government.

Tshokwe Mask — A156

Designs: 2k, 4k, Seated woman, Pende. 7k, like 5k. 10k, 14k, Antelope mask, Suku. 15k, 18k, Kneeling woman, Kongo. 20k, 25k, Kuba mask.

1977, Jan. 8   Photo.   Perf. 11½
836 A156 2k multi   .25   .25
837 A156 4k multi   .25   .25
838 A156 5k gray & multi   .25   .25
839 A156 7k multi   .25   .25
840 A156 10k multi   .30   .25
841 A156 14k multi   .45   .25
842 A156 15k multi   .55   .25
843 A156 18k multi   .65   .35
844 A156 20k multi   1.25   .40
845 A156 25k vio & multi 1.50   .80
    Nos. 836-845 (10)   5.70 3.30

Wood carving and masks of Zaire.

Map of Zaire, UPU Emblem — A157

1977, Apr.   Litho.   Perf. 13½
846 A157 1k org & multi   .35   .25
847 A157 4k dk bl & multi 1.00   .25
848 A157 7k ol grn & multi 1.75   .30
849 A157 50k brn & multi 6.50 4.00
    Nos. 846-849 (4)   9.60 4.80

Cent. of UPU (in 1974).

Congo Stamps of 1968-1971 Srchd. with New Value, Bars and "REPUBLIQUE DU ZAIRE"

1977
850 A126 1k on 10s (#642)   .70   .35
851 A122 2k on 9.6k (#618)   .70   .35
852 A140 10k on 10s (#735) 2.50   .75
853 A134 25k on 10s (#703) 2.75   .50
854 A127 40k on 9.6k (#652) 3.75 2.00
855 A135 48k on 10s (#713) 7.50 3.00
    Nos. 850-855 (6)   17.90 6.95

Congo Nos. 644, 643, 635, 746 Srchd. with New Value, Bars and "REPUBLIQUE DU ZAIRE" in Black or Carmine, Zaire No. 757 Srchd.

1977
856 A126 5k on 30s   1.00   .35
857 A126 10k on 15s (C)   1.00   .35
858 A124 20k on 9.60k   2.25   .75
859 A141 30k on 12k   3.75   .75
860 A145 100k on 40s (C)   9.50 3.00
    Nos. 856-860 (5)   17.50 5.20
    Nos. 850-860 (11)   29.15 17.70

Nos. 850-860 exist with a number of overprint color varieties, as well as with inverted and double overprint errors.

Souvenir Sheet

Adoration of the Kings, by Rubens — A158

1977, Dec. 19   Photo.   Perf. 13½
861 A158 5z multi   140.00 110.00

Christmas 1977.

Pantodon Buchholzi A159

Fish: 70s, Aphyosemion striatum. 55, Ctenopoma fasciolatum. 8k, Malapterurus electricus. 10k, Hemichromis bimaculatus. 30k, Marcusenius isidori. 40k, Synodontis nigriventris. 48k, Julidochromis ornatus. 100k, Nothobranchius brieni. 250k, Micralestes interruptus.

1978, Jan. 23   Litho.   Perf. 14
862 A159 30s multi   .25   .25
863 A159 70s multi   .25   .25
864 A159 5k multi   .25   .25
865 A159 8k multi   .35   .30
866 A159 10k multi   .55   .35
867 A159 30k multi   1.25   .75
868 A159 40k multi   1.75 1.00
869 A159 48k multi   2.00 1.25
870 A159 100k multi   5.50 2.75
    Nos. 862-870 (9)   12.15 7.15

Souvenir Sheet
Perf. 13½
871 A159 250k multi   14.00 14.00

No. 871 contains one 46x35mm stamp. For surcharges see Nos. 1294, 1311.

Soccer Game, Argentina-France A160

Various Soccer Games and Jules Rimet Cup: 3k, Austria-Brazil. 7k, Scotland-Iran. 9k, Netherlands-Peru. 10k, Hungary-Italy. 20k, Fed. Rep. of Germany-Mexico. 50k, Tunisia-Poland. 100k, Spain-Sweden. 500k, Rimet Cup, Games' emblem and cartoon of soccer player, horiz.

1978, Aug. 7   Litho.   Perf. 12½
872 A160 1k multi   .25   .25
873 A160 3k multi   .25   .25
874 A160 7k multi   .25   .25
875 A160 9k multi   .25   .25
876 A160 10k multi   .25   .25
877 A160 20k multi   .40   .25
878 A160 50k multi   1.10   .60
879 A160 100k multi   2.25 1.25
    Nos. 872-879 (8)   5.00 3.35

Souvenir Sheets
880 A160 500k blue & multi 25.00 25.00
881 A160 500k red & multi   25.00 25.00

11th World Cup Soccer Championship, Argentina, June 1-25. Nos. 880-881 contain one stamp each (47x36mm). Stamp of No. 880 has blue frameline. Stamp of No. 881 has red frame line.
For surcharge see No. 1259.

Mama Mobutu — A161

1978, Oct. 23   Photo.   Perf. 12
882 A161 8k multi   .30   .30

Mama Mobutu (1941-77), wife of Pres. Mobutu.

Pres. Joseph D. Mobutu — A162

Frame Color
Granite Paper
1978   Photo.   Perf. 12
883 A162 2k blue   .25   .25
884 A162 5k bister   .25   .25
885 A162 6k Prussian blue .25   .25
886 A162 8k red brown   .25   .25
887 A162 10k emerald   .25   .25
888 A162 25k red   .25   .25
889 A162 48k purple   .40   .30
890 A162 1z green   .80   .50
    Nos. 883-890 (8)   2.70 2.30

See Nos. 1053, 1055-1056. For surcharges see Nos. 1313, 1333-1336.

Souvenir Sheet

Elizabeth II in Westminster Abbey — A163

1978, Dec. 11   Photo.   Perf. 13½
891 A163 5z multi   12.00 12.00

Coronation of Queen Elizabeth II, 25th anniv.

Souvenir Sheet

Albrecht Dürer, Self-portrait — A164

1978, Dec. 18 **Perf. 13**
892 A164 5z multi 12.00 12.00
Albrecht Dürer (1471-1528), German painter and engraver.

Leonardo da Vinci and his Drawings — A165

History of Aviation: 70s, Planes of Wright Brothers, 1905, and Santos Dumont, 1906. 1k, Bleriot XI, 1909, and Farman F-60, 1909. 5k, Junkers G-38, 1929, and Spirit of St. Louis, 1927. 8k, Sikorsky S-42B, 1934 and Macchi-Castoldi MC-72, 1934. 10k, Boeing 707, 1960, and Fokker F-VII, 1935. 50k, Apollo XI, 1969, and Concorde, 1976. 75k, Helicopter and Douglas DC-10, 1971. 5z, Giffard's balloon, 1852, and Hindenburg LZ 129, 1936.

1978, Dec. 28 **Litho.** **Perf. 13**
893 A165 30s multi .25 .25
894 A165 70s multi .25 .25
895 A165 1k multi .25 .25
896 A165 5k multi .35 .25
897 A165 8k multi .40 .25
898 A165 10k multi .75 .25
899 A165 50k multi 3.25 1.00
900 A165 75k multi 4.25 1.25
Nos. 893-900 (8) 9.75 3.75

Souvenir Sheet
Perf. 11½
901 A165 5z multi 16.00 16.00
For overprint and surcharges see Nos. 993, 1173-1181, 1291, 1295.

Pres. Mobutu, Map of Zaire, N'tombe Dancer — A166

Pres. Mobutu & Map: 3k, Bird. 4k, Elephant. 10k, Diamond and cotton boll. 14k, Hand holding torch. 17k, Leopard's head and Victoria Regia lily. 25k, Finzia waterfall. 50k, Wagenia fishermen.

1979, Feb. **Litho.** **Perf. 14x13½**
902 A166 1k multicolored .25 .25
903 A166 3k multicolored .25 .25
904 A166 4k multicolored .25 .25
905 A166 10k multicolored .25 .25
  a. Souvenir sheet of 4, #902-905 13.00
906 A166 14k multicolored .25 .25
907 A166 17k multicolored .40 .25
908 A166 25k multicolored .60 .40
909 A166 50k multicolored 1.25 .85
  a. Souvenir sheet of 4, #906-909 13.00 —
Nos. 902-909 (8) 3.50 2.75
Zaire (Congo) River expedition.

A stamp similar to design No. A166, depicting Pres. Mobutu and a flag and printed on gold foil, exists. Value, $50.

Phylloporus Ampliporus A167

Mushrooms: 5k, Engleromyces goetzei. 8k, Scutellinia virungae. 10k, Pycnoporus sanguineus. 30k, Cantharellus miniatescens. 40k, Lactarius phlebonemus. 48k, Phallus indusiatus. 100k, Ramaria moelleriana.

1979, Mar. **Photo.** **Perf. 13½x13**
910 A167 30s multicolored .30 .25
911 A167 5k multicolored .35 .30
912 A167 8k multicolored .55 .40
913 A167 10k multicolored .85 .50
914 A167 30k multicolored 1.75 1.25
915 A167 40k multicolored 2.50 1.50
916 A167 48k multicolored 4.25 2.00
917 A167 100k multicolored 6.25 3.50
Nos. 910-917 (8) 16.80 9.70

For surcharges see Nos. 1296, 1298, 1312, 1361-1362, 1365-1366, 1368-1369, 1372, 1375.

Souvenir Sheets

Pope John XXIII (1881-1963) — A168

Popes: No. 919, Paul VI (1897-1978). No. 920, John Paul I (1912-78).

1979, June 25 **Litho.** **Perf. 11½**
918 A168 250k multi 5.00 5.00
919 A168 250k multi 5.00 5.00
920 A168 250k multi 5.00 5.00
Nos. 918-920 (3) 15.00 15.00

Boy Beating Drum — A169

IYC Emblem on Map of Zaire and: 10k, 20k, Girl, diff. 50k, Boy. 100k, Boys. 300k, Mother and child. 10z, Mother and children, horiz.

1979, July 23 **Litho.** **Perf. 12½**
921 A169 5k multi .25 .25
922 A169 10k multi .25 .25
923 A169 20k multi .40 .25
924 A169 50k multi .90 .50
925 A169 100k multi 1.90 1.00
926 A169 300k multi 5.25 2.50
Nos. 921-926 (6) 8.95 4.75

Souvenir Sheet
927 A169 10z multi 14.00 10.50
International Year of the Child.
For surcharges see Nos. 997, 999, 1299, 1306.

Globe and Drummer A170

1979, July 23
928 A170 1k multi .25 .25
929 A170 9k multi .25 .25
930 A170 90k multi .70 .50
931 A170 100k multi .80 .55
Nos. 928-931 (4) 2.00 1.55

Souvenir Sheet
932 A170 500k multi 5.00 5.00
6th International Fair, Kinshasa. No. 932 contains one 52x31mm stamp.
For overprint & surcharge see #996, 1320.

Globe and School Desk — A171

1979, Dec. 24 **Litho.** **Perf. 13**
933 A171 10k multi .30 .25
Intl. Bureau of Education, Geneva, 50th anniv.

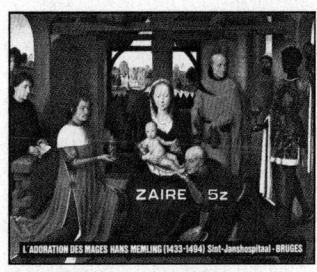

Adoration of the Kings, by Memling — A172

1979, Dec. 24 **Imperf.**
934 A172 5z multi 6.00 6.00
Christmas 1979.

"Puffing Billy," 1814, Gt. Britain A173

1.50k, Buddicom No. 33, 1843, France. 5k, "Elephant," 1835, Belgium. 8k, No. 601, 1906, Zaire. 50k, "Slieve Gullion 440," Ireland. 75k, "Black Elephant," Germany. 2z, Type 1-15, Zaire. 5z, "Golden State," US. 10z, Type E.D.75, Zaire.

1980, Jan. 14 **Litho.** **Perf. 13½x13**
935 A173 50s shown .25 .25
936 A173 1.50k multicolored .25 .25
937 A173 5k multicolored .25 .25
938 A173 8k multicolored .25 .25
939 A173 50k multicolored .75 .25
940 A173 75k multicolored 1.10 .75
941 A173 2z multicolored 2.25 1.90
942 A173 5z multicolored 6.00 6.00
Nos. 935-942 (8) 11.10 9.90

Souvenir Sheet
943 A173 10z multicolored 15.00 15.00
For overprints and surcharges see Nos. 991-992, 994, 1325.

Hill, Belgian Congo No. 257 A174

1980, Jan. 28 **Perf. 13½x14**
944 A174 2k No. 5 .25 .25
945 A174 4k No. 13 .25 .25
946 A174 10k No. 24 .25 .25
947 A174 20k No. 38 .25 .25
948 A174 40k No. 111 .40 .25
949 A174 150k No. B29 1.25 1.00
950 A174 200k No. 198 1.50 1.25
951 A174 250k shown 1.90 1.50
Nos. 944-951 (8) 6.05 5.00

Souvenir Sheet
952 A174 10z No. 198 11.00 11.00
Sir Rowland Hill (1795-1879), originator of penny postage.
For overprint and surcharge see Nos. 998, 1329.

Albert Einstein (1879-1955), Theoretical Physicist A175

1980, Feb. 18 **Perf. 13**
953 A175 40s multi .25 .25
954 A175 2k multi .25 .25
955 A175 4k multi .25 .25
956 A175 15k multi .25 .25
957 A175 50k multi .40 .40
958 A175 300k multi 1.60 1.00
Nos. 953-958 (6) 3.00 2.40

Souvenir Sheet
959 A175 5z multi, diff. 4.50 4.50
For surcharges see Nos. 1285, 1290, 1304.

Salvation Army Brass Players — A176

50s, Booth Memorial Hospital, NYC. 4.50k, Commissioner George Railton sailing for US mission. 10k, Mobile dispensary, Masina. 20k, Gen. Evangeline Booth, officer holding infant, vert. 75k, Outdoor well-baby clinic. 1.50z, Disaster relief. 2z, Parade, vert. 10z, Gen. & Mrs. Arnold Brown.

1980, Mar. 3 **Perf. 11**
960 A176 50s multi .25 .25
961 A176 4.50k multi .25 .25
962 A176 10k multi .25 .25
963 A176 20k multi .25 .25
964 A176 40k multi .35 .25
965 A176 75k multi .55 .25
966 A176 1.50z multi 1.10 .55
967 A176 2z multi 1.60 .80
Nos. 960-967 (8) 4.60 2.85

Souvenir Sheet
968 A176 10z multi 9.00 9.00
Salvation Army cent. in US. No. 968 contains one 53x38mm stamp and 2 labels.

A set of nine stamps for the 1980 Olympic Games in Moscow was prepared but not issued. Value, set $140.

Souvenir Sheets

Visite de Sa Sainteté le Pape Jean Paul II
au Zaïre — Mai 1980

Pope John Paul II — A177

1980, May 2   Litho.   Perf. 11½
969 A177 10z multi   17.50 17.50

Visit of Pope John Paul II to Zaïre, May.

Baia Castle, by Antonio Pitloo — A178

1980, May 5
970 A178 10z multi   6.00 6.00

20th International Philatelic Exhibition,
Europa '80, Naples, Apr. 26-May 4.

A179

50k, Woman, line-drawing. 100k, Plutiarch.
500k, Kneeling man, sculpture, vert.

Perf. 12½x13, 13x12½
1980, May 24   Litho.
971 A179 50k multicolored   .25   .25
972 A179 100k multicolored   .50   .40
973 A179 500k multicolored   2.50 1.75
  a.   Souvenir sheet of 3   6.00 6.00
        Nos. 971-973 (3)   3.25 2.40

Rotary Intl., 75th anniv. No. 973a contains 3
stamps similar to Nos. 971-973, size: 55x35,
35x55mm. Exists imperf.
For surcharge see No. 1313.

Tropical Fish — A180

1k, Chaetodon collaris. 5k, Zebrasoma
veliferum. 10k, Euxiphipops xanthometapon.
20k, Pomacanthus annularis. 50k, Centropyge
oriculus. 150k, Oxymonacanthus longirostris.
200k, Balistoides niger. 250k, Rhinecanthus
aculeatus.
5z, Baliste ondule.

1980, Oct. 20   Litho.   Perf. 14x13½
974 A180 1k multicolored   .25   .25
975 A180 5k multicolored   .25   .25
976 A180 10k multicolored   .25   .25
977 A180 20k multicolored   .25   .25
978 A180 50k multicolored   .60   .40
979 A180 150k multicolored   1.40   .55
980 A180 200k multicolored   1.90   .70
981 A180 250k multicolored   2.25 1.00
        Nos. 974-981 (8)   7.15 3.65

Souvenir Sheet

981A A180 5z multicolored   4.75 4.75

For surcharge see No. 1307.

Exhibition Emblem, Congo
#365 — A181

1980, Dec. 6   Litho.   Perf. 13
982   Block or strip of 4   2.00 1.75
  a.   A181 1z denomination at UR,
        shown   .45   .35
  b.   A181 1z denomination at UL,
        Belgium #511   .45   .35
  c.   A181 1z denomination at UR,
        like #982b   .45   .35
  d.   A181 1z denomination at UL,
        like #982a   .45   .35
983   Block or strip of 4   4.00 3.00
  a.   A181 2z denomination at UR,
        Congo #432   .95   .60
  b.   A181 2z denomination at UL,
        Belgium # B835   .95   .60
  c.   A181 2z denomination at UR,
        like #983b   .95   .60
  d.   A181 2z denomination at UL,
        like #983a   .95   .60
984   Block or strip of 4   6.00 4.50
  a.   A181 3z denomination at UR,
        Zaïre #755   1.40   .90
  b.   A181 3z denomination at UL,
        Belgium # B878   1.40   .90
  c.   A181 3z denomination at UR,
        like #984b   1.40   .90
  d.   A181 3z denomination at UL,
        like #984a   1.40   .90
985   Block or strip of 4   8.50 6.00
  a.   A181 4z denomination at UR,
        Congo #572   1.75 1.10
  b.   A181 4z denomination at UL,
        Belgium # B996   1.75 1.10
  c.   A181 4z denomination at UR,
        like #985b   1.75 1.10
  d.   A181 4z denomination at UL,
        like #985a   1.75 1.10
        Nos. 982-985 (4)   20.50 15.25

PHIBELZA, Belgium-Zaïre Phil. Exhib.
For surcharge see No. 1342.

Map of
Africa,
King
Leopold I
A182

Belgian independence sesquicentennial:
75k, Stanley expedition, Leopold II. 100k,
Colonial troops, Albert I. 145k, Protected animals, Leopold III. 270k, Visit of King Baudouin
and Queen Fabiola.

1980, Dec. 13   Photo.   Perf. 14
986 A182 10k multi   .45   .25
987 A182 75k multi   1.40   .45
988 A182 100k multi   2.00   .60
989 A182 145k multi   2.50   .80
990 A182 270k multi   4.50 1.25
        Nos. 986-990 (5)   10.85 3.35

For surcharges see Nos. 1326, 1331, 1345,
1357, 1408-1412, 1426.

Nos. 935, 936, 898, 939, 900, 931, 925, 951, Overprinted in Red, Silver or Black: 20e Anniversaire-Independence / 1960-1980

1980, Dec. 13   Litho.
991 A173 50s multi   .25   .25
992 A173 1.50k multi   .25   .25
993 A165 10k multi   .25   .25
994 A173 50k multi   .40   .25
995 A165 75k multi   .60   .25
996 A170 100k multi (S)   .90   .50
997 A169 1z on 5z on 100k
              multi (B)   1.00   .50
998 A174 250k multi   2.00 1.00

---

999 A169 5z on 100k multi
              (B)   4.75 2.50
        Nos. 991-999 (9)   10.40 5.75

20th anniversary of independence. For
surcharges see Nos. 1300, 1316.

Nativity
A183

1980, Dec. 24   Perf. 13
1000 A183 10k Shepherds and
              angels   .25   .25
1001 A183 75k Flight into Egypt   1.00   .40
1002 A183 80k Three kings   1.00   .40
1003 A183 145k shown   1.75   .60
        Nos. 1000-1003 (4)   4.00 1.65

Souvenir Sheet

1004 A183 10z Church, nativity   5.50 5.50

Christmas 1980. No. 1004 contains one
49x33mm stamp. Exists imperf. For
surcharges see Nos. 1301, 1317-1318.

Postal Clerk
Sorting Mail,
by Norman
Rockwell
A184

Designs: Saturday Evening Post covers by
Norman Rockwell.

1981, Apr. 27   Litho.   Perf. 14
1005 A184 10k multi   .25   .25
1006 A184 20k multi   .25   .25
1007 A184 50k multi   .40   .25
1008 A184 80k multi   .65   .35
1009 A184 100k multi   .70   .40
1010 A184 125k multi   1.10   .45
1011 A184 175k multi   1.25   .65
1012 A184 200k multi   1.40   .75
        Nos. 1005-1012 (8)   6.00 3.35

For surcharges see Nos. 1262, 1265, 1269,
1275, 1281, 1354.

First
Anniv.
of Visit
of Pope
John
Paul II
A185

Scenes of Pope's visit. 50k, 500k, vert.

1981, May 2   Perf. 13
1013 A185 5k multi   .25   .25
1014 A185 10k multi   .25   .25
1015 A185 50k multi   .35   .30
1016 A185 100k multi   1.00   .50
1017 A185 500k multi   5.50 2.50
1018 A185 800k multi   7.75 4.25
        Nos. 1013-1018 (6)   15.10 8.05

For surcharges see #1190-1194, 1292,
1302, 1343.

Soccer
Players — A186

Designs: Soccer scenes.

1981, July 6   Litho.   Perf. 12½
1019 A186 2k multi   .25   .25
1020 A186 5k multi   .25   .25
1021 A186 25k multi   .25   .25
1022 A186 90k multi   .50   .25
1023 A186 2z multi   1.00   .55
1024 A186 3z multi   1.60   .85
1025 A186 6z multi   2.75 1.50
1026 A186 8z multi   4.50 3.00
        Nos. 1019-1026 (8)   11.10 6.90

Souvenir Sheet

1027   Sheet of 2   6.00 6.00
  a.   A186 5z like #1019   2.75 2.75
  b.   A186 5z like #1025   2.75 2.75

ESPANA '82 World Cup Soccer Championship. For surcharges see Nos. 1287, 1303,
1309, 1321.

Intl. Year of the Disabled — A187

2k, Archer. 5k, Ear, sound waves. 10k,
Amputee. 18k, Cane braille, sunglasses. 50k,
Boy with leg braces. 150k, Sign language.
500k, Hands. 800k, Dove.

1981, Nov. 2   Litho.   Perf. 14x14½
1028 A187 2k multicolored   .25   .25
1029 A187 5k multicolored   .25   .25
1030 A187 10k multicolored   .25   .25
1031 A187 18k multicolored   .25   .25
1032 A187 50k multicolored   .25   .25
1033 A187 150k multicolored   .60   .30
1034 A187 500k multicolored   1.50 1.25
1035 A187 800k multicolored   2.75 2.00
        Nos. 1028-1035 (8)   6.10 4.80

For surcharges see Nos. 1288, 1293, 1305,
1314.

Souvenir Sheet

Birth Sesqui. of Heinrich von
Stephan, UPU Founder — A188

Photogravure and Engraved

1981, Dec. 21   Perf. 11½x12
1036 A188 15z purple   8.00 8.00

Christmas
1981 — A189

Designs: 25k, 1z, 1.50z, 3z, 5z, Various
children. 10z, Holy Family, horiz.

1981, Dec. 21   Litho.   Perf. 14
1037 A189 25k multi   .25   .25
1038 A189 1z multi   .70   .25
1039 A189 1.50z multi   .80   .35

1040	A189	3z multi	1.75	.75
1041	A189	5z multi	2.75	1.25
		Nos. 1037-1041 (5)	6.25	2.85

Souvenir Sheet

1042	A189	10z multi	5.50	5.50

13th World Telecommunications Day (1981) — A190

Designs: Symbols of communications and health care delivery.

1982, Feb. 8   Litho.   Perf. 13

1043	A190	1k multi	.25	.25
1044	A190	25k multi	.25	.25
1045	A190	90k multi	.30	.25
1046	A190	1z multi	.30	.25
1047	A190	1.70z multi	.55	.45
1048	A190	3z multi	1.10	.75
1049	A190	4.50z multi	1.60	1.10
1050	A190	5z multi	1.75	1.25
		Nos. 1043-1050 (8)	6.10	4.55

For surcharges see Nos. 1270, 1282.

**Pres. Mobutu Type of 1978
Frame Color
Granite Paper**

1982   Photo.   Perf. 12

1053	A162	50k purple	.25	.25
1055	A162	2z bister	.75	.25
1056	A162	5z Prussian blue	2.25	1.25
		Nos. 1053-1056 (3)	3.25	1.75

20th Anniv. of African Postal Union (1981) — A191

1982, Mar. 8   Litho.   Perf. 13

1057	A191	1z yel grn & gold	.50	.40

For surcharges see Nos. 1348, 1352.

1982 World Cup A192

Designs: Flags and players of finalists.

1982

1058	A192	2k multi	.25	.25
1059	A192	8k multi	.25	.25
1060	A192	25k multi	.25	.25
1061	A192	50k multi	.25	.25
1062	A192	90k multi	.30	.25
1063	A192	1z multi	.45	.30
1064	A192	1.45z multi	.55	.45
1065	A192	1.70z multi	.85	.70
1066	A192	3z multi	1.40	1.10
1067	A192	3.50z multi	1.90	1.40
1068	A192	5z multi	3.00	2.10
1069	A192	6z multi	3.25	2.50
		Nos. 1058-1069 (12)	12.70	9.80

Souvenir Sheet

1070	A192	10z multi	7.50	7.50

Issued: #1058-1069, July 6; #1070, Sept. 21.
For surcharges see #1289, 1315, 1322, 1344, 1435 and footnote after #1336.

9th Conference of Heads of State of Africa and France, Kinshasa, Oct. — A193

1982, Oct. 8   Litho.   Perf. 13

1071	A193	75k multi	.25	.25
1072	A193	90k multi	.25	.25
1073	A193	1z multi	.25	.25
1074	A193	1.50z multi	.25	.25
1075	A193	3z multi	.75	.60
1076	A193	5z multi	1.75	1.25
1077	A193	8z multi	2.00	1.75
		Nos. 1071-1077 (7)	5.50	4.60

For surcharges see Nos. 1268, 1271, 1280, 1283, 1347, 1351.

Animals from Virunga Natl. Park — A194

1982, Nov. 5

1078	A194	1z Lions	.30	.25
1079	A194	1.70z Buffalo	1.00	.75
1080	A194	3.50z Elephants	2.25	1.50
1081	A194	6.50z Antelope	4.00	2.75
1082	A194	8z Hippopotamus	5.75	3.25
1083	A194	10z Monkeys	6.50	4.00
1084	A194	10z Leopard	6.50	4.25
a.		Pair, #1083-1084 + label	18.00	18.00
		Nos. 1078-1084 (7)	26.30	16.75

#1084a has continuous design.
For surcharge see No. 1430.

Scouting Year — A195

**1982, Nov. 29   Photo.   Perf. 11½
Granite Paper**

1085	A195	90k Camp	.35	.30
1086	A195	1.70z Campfire	.90	.55
1087	A195	3z Scout	1.50	1.00
1088	A195	5z First aid	3.25	1.75
1089	A195	8z Flag signals	6.00	3.25
		Nos. 1085-1089 (5)	12.00	6.85

Souvenir Sheet

1090	A195	10z Baden-Powell	11.00	11.00

For surcharges see Nos. 1207-1214.

Local Birds — A196

25k, Quelea quelea. 50k, Ceyx picta. 90k, Tauraco persa. 1.50z, Charadrius tricollaris. 1.70z, Cursorius temminckii. 2z, Campethera bennettii. 3z, Podiceps ruficollis. 3.50z, Kaupifalco monogrammicus. 5z, Limnocorax flavirostris. 8z, White-headed vulture.

1982, Dec. 6   Litho.   Perf. 13

1091	A196	25k multicolored	.25	.25
1092	A196	50k multicolored	.25	.25
1093	A196	90k multicolored	.60	.25
1094	A196	1.50z multicolored	.65	.40
1095	A196	1.70k multicolored	.70	.40
1096	A196	2z multicolored	.95	.60
1097	A196	3z multicolored	1.50	.80
1098	A196	3.50z multicolored	1.60	.85
1099	A196	5z multicolored	2.50	1.25
1100	A196	8z multicolored	3.75	2.10
		Nos. 1091-1100 (10)	12.75	7.15

All except 3.50z, 8z horiz.
For surcharges see Nos. 1263, 1266, 1272, 1276, 1278, 1284, 1425, 1432, 1438, 1440.

Souvenir Sheet

Christmas — A197

15z, Adoration of the Magi, by van der Goes.

1982, Dec. 20   Photo.   Perf. 13½

1101	A197	15z multicolored	8.00	8.00

Quartz A198

2k, Malachite, vert. 75k, Gold. 1z, Uraninite. 1.50z, Bournonite, vert. 3z, Cassiterite. 6z, Dioptase, vert. 8z, Cuprite, vert. 10z, Diamonds.

**1983, Feb. 13   Photo.   Perf. 11½
Granite Paper**

1102	A198	2k multicolored	.30	.25
1103		45k shown	.40	.25
1104	A198	75k multicolored	.75	.25
1105	A198	1z multicolored	1.25	.25
1106	A198	1.50z multicolored	1.75	.80
1107	A198	3z multicolored	3.50	1.50
1108	A198	6z multicolored	6.00	3.00
1109	A198	8z multicolored	8.00	4.00
		Nos. 1102-1109 (8)	21.95	10.30

Souvenir Sheet

1110	A198	10z multicolored	10.00	10.00

For surcharges see Nos. 1324, 1330, 1332, 1346.

TB Bacillus Centenary — A199

1983, Feb. 21   Litho.   Perf. 13

1111	A199	80k multi	.25	.25
1112	A199	1.20z multi	.40	.35
1113	A199	3.60z multi	1.40	1.00
1114	A199	9.60z multi	4.00	2.25
		Nos. 1111-1114 (4)	6.05	3.85

For surcharges see Nos. 1319, 1356, 1358, 1360, 1433, 1436, 1441.

Kinshasa Monuments — A200

50k, Zaire Diplomat, vert. 1z, Echo of Zaire. 1.50z, Messengers, vert. 3z, Shield of Revolution, vert. 5z, Weeping Woman. 10z, Militant, vert.

1983, Apr. 25

1115	A200	50k multicolored	.25	.25
1116	A200	1z multicolored	.25	.25
1117	A200	1.50z multicolored	.35	.25
1118	A200	3z multicolored	.65	.50
1119	A200	5z multicolored	1.10	.90
1120	A200	10z multicolored	2.40	2.00
		Nos. 1115-1120 (6)	5.00	4.15

For surcharges see Nos. 1267, 1279, 1349-1350.

ITU Plenipotentiaries Conference, Nairobi, Sept. 1982 — A201

Various satellites, dish antennae and maps.

1983, June 13   Litho.   Perf. 13

1121	A201	2k multi	.25	.25
1122	A201	4k multi	.25	.25
1123	A201	25k multi	.25	.25
1124	A201	1.20z multi	.40	.25
1125	A201	2.05z multi	.65	.35
1126	A201	3.60z multi	1.00	.60
1127	A201	6z multi	1.75	1.00
1128	A201	8z multi	2.50	1.40
		Nos. 1121-1128 (8)	7.05	4.35

For surcharges see Nos. 1260-1261, 1264, 1273-1274, 1277, 1355, 1359, 1429, 1434, 1437, 1439, 1442.

Christmas 1983 — A202

Raphael Paintings; No. 1129: a, Virgin and Child. b, Holy Family. c, Esterhazy Madonna. d, Sistine Madonna. No. 1130: a, La Belle Jardiniere. b, Virgin of Alba. c, Holy Family, diff. d, Virgin and Child, diff.

1983, Dec. 26   Photo.   Perf. 13½x13

1129		Sheet of 4	4.50	4.50
a.-d.		A202 10z, any single	.85	.75
1130		Sheet of 4	5.00	5.00
a.-d.		A202 15z, any single	1.00	.75

Garamba Park — A203

10k, Darby's Eland. 15k, Eagles. 3z, Servals. 10z, White rhinoceros. 15z, Lions. 37.50z, Warthogs. No. 1137, Koris bustards. No. 1138, Crowned cranes.

1984, Apr. 2   Litho.   Perf. 13

1131	A203	10k multi	.25	.25
1132	A203	15k multi	.35	.25
1133	A203	3z multi	.60	.25
1134	A203	10z multi	2.25	1.25
1135	A203	15z multi	2.75	1.75
1136	A203	37.50z multi	6.25	4.25
1137	A203	40z multi	7.00	4.50
1138	A203	40z multi	7.00	4.50
a.		Pair, #1137-1138 + label	16.00	16.00
		Nos. 1131-1138 (8)	26.45	17.00

Nos. 1137-1138 are narrower, 49x34mm, with continuous design.
For surcharge see No. 1428.

World Communications Year — A204

Designs: 10k, Computer operator, Congo River ferry. 15k, Communications satellite. 8.50z, Engineer, Congo River Bridge. 10z, Satellite, ground receiving station. 15z, TV camerawoman filming crowed crane. 37.50z, Satellite, dish antennas. 80z, Switchboard operator, bus.

1984, May 14　Litho.　Perf. 13x12½
1139	A204	10k multi	.25	.25
1140	A204	15k multi	.25	.25
1141	A204	8.50z multi	.65	.65
1142	A204	10z multi	.70	.70
1143	A204	15z multi	1.10	1.10
1144	A204	37.50z multi	2.75	2.75
1145	A204	80z multi	5.75	5.75
		Nos. 1139-1145 (7)	11.45	11.45

Hypericum Revolutum A205

Local flowers: 15k, Borreria dibrachiata. 3z, Disa erubescens. 8.50z, Scaevola plumieri. 10z, Clerodendron thompsonii. 15z, Thumbergia erecta. 37.50z, Impatiens niamniamensis. 100z, Canarina eminii.

1984, May 28　Photo.　Perf. 14x13½
1146	A205	10k multi	.25	.25
1147	A205	15k multi	.25	.25
1148	A205	3z multi	.25	.25
1149	A205	8.50z multi	.80	.80
1150	A205	10z multi	.90	.90
1151	A205	15z multi	1.25	1.25
1152	A205	37.50z multi	3.25	3.25
1153	A205	100z multi	9.00	9.00
		Nos. 1146-1153 (8)	15.95	15.95

1984 Summer Olympics A206

1984, June 5　Litho.　Perf. 13
1154	A206	2z Basketball	.25	.25
1155	A206	3z Equestrian	.35	.35
1156	A206	10z Running	1.10	1.10
1157	A206	15z Long jump	1.60	1.60
1158	A206	20z Soccer	2.75	2.75
		Nos. 1154-1158 (5)	6.05	6.05

Souvenir Sheet
Perf. 11½
1159	A206	50z Kayak	5.50	5.50

No. 1159 contains one 31x49mm stamp. For surcharge see No. 1427.

Manned Flight Bicent. — A207

10k, Montgolfiere, 1783. 15k, Charles & Robert, 1783. 3z, Gustave, 1783. 5z, Santos-Dumont III, 1899. 10z, Stratospheric balloon,

1934. 15z, Zeppelin LZ-129, 1936. 37.50z, Double Eagle II, 1978. 80z, Hot air balloons.

1984, June 28　Litho.　Perf. 14
1160	A207	10k multi	.25	.25
1161	A207	15k multi	.25	.25
1162	A207	3z multi	.25	.25
1163	A207	5z multi	.50	.40
1164	A207	10z multi	.90	.75
1165	A207	15z multi	1.40	1.00
1166	A207	37.50z multi	3.25	2.75
1167	A207	80z multi	7.25	6.50
		Nos. 1160-1167 (8)	14.05	12.15

For surcharges see Nos. 1413-1420.

Okapi — A208

1984, Oct. 15　Litho.　Perf. 13
1168	A208	2z Grazing	1.25	.60
1169	A208	3z Resting	2.00	.70
1170	A208	8z Mother and		
		young	3.75	2.25
1171	A208	10z In water	6.00	4.25
		Nos. 1168-1171 (4)	13.00	7.80

Souvenir Sheet
Perf. 11½
1172	A208	50z like 10z	5.25	5.25

World Wildlife Fund. No. 1172 contains one 36x51mm stamp, margin continues the design of the 10z without emblem.

Nos. 893-900 Surcharged in Silver Over Black Bar and With One of Three Different Sabena Airlines Emblems and "1925 1985" in Silver

1985, Feb. 19　Perf. 13
1173	A165	2.50z on 30s		
		#893	.35	.25
1174	A165	5z on 5k #896	.90	.50
1175	A165	6z on 70s		
		#894	1.00	.60
1176	A165	7.50z on 1k #895	1.10	.70
1177	A165	8.50z on 10k		
		#898	1.40	.90
1178	A165	10z on 8k #897	1.75	1.25
1179	A165	12.50z on 75k		
		#900	2.00	1.75
1180	A165	30z on 50k		
		#899	3.75	3.25
		Nos. 1173-1180 (8)	12.25	9.20

No. 901 Surcharged in Silver Over Black Bar and With Silver Text "60e ANNIVERSAIRE/1re LIASON AERIENNE/BRUXELLES-KINSHASAL/PAR EDMOND THIEFFRY"
Souvenir Sheet

1985, Feb. 19　Perf. 11½
1181	A165	50z on 5z #901	70.00	70.00

OLYMPHILEX '85, Lausanne — A209

1985, Apr. 19　Perf. 13
1182	A209	1z Swimming	.25	.25
1183	A209	2z Soccer, vert.	.25	.25
1184	A209	3z Boxing	.25	.25
1185	A209	4z Basketball, vert.	.25	.25
1186	A209	5z Equestrian	.40	.40
1187	A209	10z Volleyball, vert.	.85	.85
1188	A209	15z Running	1.25	1.25
1189	A209	30z Cycling, vert.	2.50	2.50
		Nos. 1182-1189 (8)	6.00	6.00

Nos. 1013-1018, 969 Ovptd. and Surcharged with 1 or 2 Gold Bars and "AOUT 1985" in Gold or Black

1985, Aug. 15　Perf. 13, 11½
1190	A185	2z on 5k	.25	.25
1191	A185	3z on 10k	.35	.35
1192	A185	5z on 50k	.60	.60
1192A	A185	10z on 100k	1.40	1.40
1192B	A185	15z on 500k	1.90	1.90
1193	A185	40z on 800k	5.50	5.50
		Nos. 1190-1193 (6)	10.00	10.00

Souvenir Sheet
1194	A177	50z on 10z (B)	12.00	12.00

Second visit of Pope John Paul II.

Audubon Birth Bicent. — A210

Illustrations of North American bird species by John Audubon: 5z, Great egret. 10z, Yellow-beaked duck. 15z, Small heron. 25z, White-fronted duck.

1985, Oct. 1　Perf. 13
1195	A210	5z multicolored	1.25	.60
1196	A210	10z multicolored	1.90	1.10
1197	A210	15z multicolored	4.00	1.50
1198	A210	25z multicolored	6.50	3.00
		Nos. 1195-1198 (4)	13.65	6.20

For surcharges see Nos. 1421-1424.

Natl. Independence, 25th Anniv. — A211

1985, Oct. 23　Photo.　Perf. 12
Granite Paper
1200	A211	5z multi	.25	.25
1201	A211	10z multi	.45	.45
1202	A211	15z multi	.70	.70
1203	A211	20z multi	1.10	1.10
		Nos. 1200-1203 (4)	2.50	2.50

Souvenir Sheet
Perf. 11½
1204	A211	50z multi	2.50	2.50

UN, 40th Anniv. A212

1985, Nov. 26
1205	A212	10z Flags, vert.	.50	.50
1206	A212	50z Emblem, UN		
		building	2.75	2.75

Nos. 1087-1088, 1085-1086, 1089-1090 Surcharged

1985, Dec. 2　Perf. 11½
Granite Paper
1207	A195	3z on 3z multi	.60	.60
1208	A195	5z on 5z multi	.85	.85
1209	A195	7z on 90k multi	1.10	1.10
1210	A195	10z on 90k multi	1.60	1.60
1211	A195	15z on 1.70z multi	2.50	2.50

1212	A195	20z on 8z multi	3.50	3.50
1213	A195	50z on 90k multi	8.75	8.75
		Nos. 1207-1213 (7)	18.90	18.90

Souvenir Sheet
1214	A195	50z on 10z multi	12.00	12.00

Intl. Youth Year.

Souvenir Sheet

Virgin and Child, by Titian — A213

Photogravure and Engraved
1985, Dec. 23　Perf. 13½
1215	A213	100z brown	7.00	7.00

Christmas 1985.

Natl. Transit Authority, 50th Anniv. — A214

1985, Dec. 31　Perf. 13
1216	A214	7z Kokolo mail ship	.25	.25
1217	A214	10z Steam locomotive	.40	.40
1218	A214	15z Luebo ferry	.60	.60
1219	A214	50z Stanley locomotive	2.00	1.50
		Nos. 1216-1219 (4)	3.25	2.75

Postage Stamp, Cent. A215

Stamps on stamps: 7z, Belgian Congo No. 30. 15z, Belgian Congo No. B28. 20z, Belgian Congo No. 226. 25z, Congo No. 1059. 40z, Zaire No. 1152. 50z, Zaire No. 883 and Belgium No. 1094.

1986, Feb. 23　Perf. 13
1220	A215	7z multi	.40	.30
1221	A215	15z multi	.65	.50
1222	A215	20z multi	1.00	.75
1223	A215	25z multi	1.10	1.00
1224	A215	40z multi	1.75	1.25
		Nos. 1220-1224 (5)	4.90	3.80

Souvenir Sheet
Perf. 11½
1225	A215	50z multi	3.25	3.25

No. 1225 contains one 50x35mm stamp.

Beatification of Sister Anuarite Nengapeta, Aug. 15, 1985 — A216

1986, Feb. 21 Litho. *Perf. 13*

1226 A216 10z Pope John Paul II .80 .50
1227 A216 15z Sr. Anuarite 1.10 .70
1228 A216 25z Both portraits 1.60 1.10
Nos. 1226-1228 (3) 3.50 2.30

Souvenir Sheet

Imperf

1229 A216 100z Both portraits, triangular 5.00 5.00

Nos. 1226-1227 vert. No. 1229 contains one quadrilateral stamp, size: 30x36x60mm.
For surcharges see Nos. 1370-1371, 1373, 1376-1377.

Congo Stamp Cent. — A217

1986, Feb. 22 Litho. *Perf. 13*

1230 A217 25z Belgian Congo No. 3 1.25 1.00

Imperfs exist. Value $5.
See Belgium No. 1236.

Indigenous Reptiles A218

2z, Dasypeltis scaber. 5z, Agama agama. 10z, Python regius. 15z, Chamaeleo dilepis. 25z, Dendroaspis jamesoni. 50z, Naja nigricolis.

1987, Feb. 11 Litho. *Perf. 13*

1231 A218 2z multicolored .25 .25
1232 A218 5z multicolored .25 .25
1233 A218 10z multicolored .50 .50
1234 A218 15z multicolored 1.00 .65
1235 A218 25z multicolored 1.40 1.00
1236 A218 50z multicolored 2.50 2.50
Nos. 1231-1236 (6) 5.90 5.15

Christmas 1987 — A219

Paintings (details) by Fra Angelico: 50z, Virgin and Child, center panel of the Triptych of Cortona, 1435. 100z, The Nativity. 120z, Virgin and Child with Angels and Four Saints, Fiesole Retable. 180z, Virgin and Child with Six Saints, Annalena Retable.

1987, Dec. 24 Litho. *Perf. 13*

1237 A219 50z multi .75 .75
1238 A219 100z multi 1.75 1.75
1239 A219 120z multi 2.25 2.25
1240 A219 180z multi 3.25 3.25
Nos. 1237-1240 (4) 8.00 8.00

French Revolution, Bicent. — A220

Designs: 50z, Declaration of the Rights of Man and Citizen. 100z, Abstract art. 120z, Globe showing Africa, South America.

1989 Litho. *Perf. 13½x14½*

1241 A220 40z multicolored .55 .50
1242 A220 50z multicolored .65 .60
1243 A220 100z multicolored 1.40 1.25
1244 A220 120z multicolored 2.00 1.60
Nos. 1241-1244 (4) 4.60 3.95

REGIDESCO, 50th Anniv. — A221

40z, Administration bldg. 50z, Modern factory. 75z, Water works. 120z, Woman drawing water.

1989

1245 A221 40z multicolored .40 .40
1246 A221 50z multicolored .50 .50
1247 A221 75z multicolored .75 .75
1248 A221 120z multicolored 1.40 1.25
Nos. 1245-1248 (4) 3.05 2.90

Fight Against AIDS — A222

Designs: 40z, Bowman firing arrow through SIDA. 80z, "SIDA" on Leopard. 150z, World map with AIDS symbols.

1989

1249 A222 30z multicolored 1.00 .90
1250 A222 40z multicolored 1.25 1.25
1251 A222 80z multicolored 2.75 2.50
Nos. 1249-1251 (3) 5.00 4.65

Souvenir Sheet

Perf. 14

1252 A222 150z multicolored 4.75 4.75

Tourist Attractions — A223

40z, Waterfalls of Venus. 60z, Rural village. 100z, Kivu Lake. 120z, Niyara Gongo Volcano. 300z, Kisantu Botanical Gardens, vert.

1990 Litho. *Perf. 13½x14½*

1253 A223 40z multicolored .55 .55
1254 A223 60z multicolored .85 .85
1255 A223 100z multicolored 1.40 1.40
1256 A223 120z multicolored 1.75 1.75
Nos. 1253-1256 (4) 4.55 4.55

Souvenir Sheet

Perf. 14½

1257 A223 300z multicolored 4.50 4.50

Souvenir Sheet

Christmas — A224

1990 Litho. *Perf. 14*

1258 A224 500z multicolored 5.00 5.00

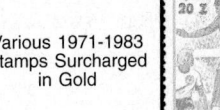

Various 1971-1983 Stamps Surcharged in Gold

1990 *Perfs., Etc. as Before*

1259 A160 20z on 20k #877 .60 .60
1260 A201 40z on 2k #1121 .60 .60
1261 A201 40z on 4k #1122 .60 .60
1262 A184 40z on 10k #1005 .60 .60
1263 A196 40z on 25k #1091 .60 .60
1264 A201 40z on 25k #1123 .60 .60
1265 A184 40z on 50k #1007 .60 .60
1266 A196 40z on 50k #1092 .60 .60
1267 A200 40z on 50k #1115 .60 .60
1268 A193 40z on 75k #1071 .60 .60
1269 A184 40z on 80k #1008 .60 .60
1270 A190 40z on 90k #1045 .60 .60
1271 A193 40z on 90k #1072 .60 .60
1272 A196 40z on 90k #1093 .60 .60
1273 A201 80z on 2k #1121 1.50 1.50
1274 A201 80z on 4k #1122 1.50 1.50
1275 A184 80z on 10k #1005 1.50 1.50
1276 A196 80z on 25k #1091 1.50 1.50
1277 A201 80z on 25k #1123 1.50 1.50
1278 A196 80z on 50k #1092 1.50 1.50
1279 A200 80z on 50k #1115 1.50 1.50
1280 A193 80z on 75k #1071 1.50 1.50
1281 A184 80z on 80k #1008 1.50 1.50
1282 A190 80z on 90k #1045 1.50 1.50
1283 A193 80z on 90k #1072 1.50 1.50
1284 A196 80z on 90k #1093 1.50 1.50
1285 A175 100z on 40s #953 2.10 2.10
1287 A186 100z on 2k #1019 2.10 2.10
1288 A187 100z on 2k #1028 2.10 2.10
1289 A192 100z on 2k #1058 2.10 2.10
1290 A175 100z on 4k #955 2.10 2.10
1291 A165 100z on 5k #896 2.10 2.10
1292 A185 100z on 5k #1013 2.10 2.10
1293 A187 100z on 5k #1029 2.10 2.10
1294 A159 100z on 8k #865 2.10 2.10
1295 A165 100z on 8k #897 2.10 2.10
1296 A167 100z on 8k #912 2.10 2.10
1298 A167 100z on 10k #913 2.10 2.10
1299 A169 100z on 10k #922 2.10 2.10
1300 A165 100z on 10k #993 2.10 2.10
1301 A183 100z on 10k #1000 2.10 2.10
1302 A185 100z on 10k #1014 2.10 2.10
1303 A186 100z on 10k #1020 2.10 2.10
1304 A175 100z on 15k #956 2.10 2.10
1305 A187 100z on 18k #1031 2.10 2.10
1306 A169 100z on 20k #923 2.10 2.10
1307 A180 100z on 20k #977 2.10 2.10
1308 A144 100z on 22k #755 2.10 2.10
1309 A186 100z on 25k #1021 2.10 2.10
1311 A159 100z on 48k #869 2.10 2.10
1312 A167 100z on 48k #916 2.10 2.10
1313 A179 100z on 50k #971 2.10 2.10
1314 A187 100z on 50k #1032 2.10 2.10
1315 A192 100z on 50k #1061 2.10 2.10
1316 A165 100z on 75k #995 2.10 2.10
1317 A183 100z on 75k #1001 2.10 2.10
1318 A183 100z on 80k #1002 2.10 2.10
1319 A199 100z on 80k #1111 2.10 2.10
1320 A170 100z on 90k #930 2.10 2.10
1321 A186 100z on 90k #1022 2.10 2.10
1322 A192 100z on 90k #1062 2.10 2.10
1324 A198 300z on 2k #1102 6.50 6.50
1325 A173 300z on 8k #938 6.50 6.50
1326 A182 300z on 10k #986 6.50 6.50
1327 A143 300z on 14k #751 6.50 6.50
1328 A146 300z on 17k #769 6.50 6.50
1329 A174 300z on 20k #947 6.50 6.50
1330 A198 300z on 45k #1103 6.50 6.50
1331 A182 300z on 75k #987 6.50 6.50
1332 A198 300z on 75k #1104 6.50 6.50
1333 A162 500z on 8k #886 11.50 11.50
1334 A162 500z on 10k #887 11.50 11.50
1335 A162 500z on 25k #888 11.50 11.50
1336 A162 500z on 48k #889 11.50 11.50
Nos. 1259-1336 (74) 204.40 204.40

Size and location of surcharge varies. Some surcharges show "z" before numeral.
100z on #1060 was surcharged in error. Value, $20.

Various 1980-1983 Stamps Surcharged

1991 *Perfs., Etc., as Before*

1342 A181 1000z on 1z #982a-982d 2.00 2.00
1343 A185 1000z on 100k #1016 .35 .35
1344 A192 1000z on 1z #1063 .35 .35
1345 A182 2000z on 100k #988 .70 .70
1346 A198 2000z on 1z #1105 .70 .70
1347 A193 2500z on 1z #1073 1.40 1.40
1348 A191 3000z on 1z #1057 2.00 2.00
1349 A200 4000z on 1z #1116 2.75 2.75
1350 A200 5000z on 1z #1116 4.00 4.00
1351 A193 10,000z on 1z #1073 5.25 5.25
1352 A191 15,000z on 1z #1057 8.00 8.00
Nos. 1342-1352 (11) 27.50 27.50

Size and location of surcharge varies.

The editors have received from a collector mint stamps bearing the surcharges shown below. There is conflicting data as to the validity of these surcharges, and anyone with information on them is asked to contact the new issues editor.

12 - 6 - 92
6ᵉ ANNIVERSAIRE DE
OFFICE NATIONAL
DU TOUR.SME

1.000 000 Z

Du 8 au 15 - 6 - 92
2ᵉ Conférence Addis - Abeba
Virus VIH 1 - et VIH 2
EN AFRIQUE

10.000.000 Z

Nos. 989,
1010, 1112,
1124 Srchd.

1992, Aug. 18   Perfs., Etc. as Before
1354 A184 50th z on 125k
          #1010   .60   .60
1355 A201 100th z on 1.20z
          #1124   .80   .80
1356 A199 150th z on 1.20z
          #1112   1.40   1.40
1357 A182 200th z on 145k
          #989   1.75   1.75
1358 A199 250th z on 1.20z
          #1112   2.25   2.25
1359 A201 300th z on 1.20z
          #1124   2.75   2.75
1360 A199 500th z on 1.20z
          #1112   4.50   4.50
    Nos. 1354-1360 (7) 14.05 14.05
Size and location of surcharge varies.

#1361-1366

#1368-1374

1993, Oct. 29   Photo.   Perf. 13½x13
1361 A167 500th z on 30s
          #910   .75   .75
1362 A167 500th z on 5k
          #911   .90   .90
1365 A167 750th z on 8k
          #912   1.00   1.00
1366 A167 750th z on 10k
          #913   1.25   1.25
1368 A167 1 mil z on 30k
          #914   1.50   1.50
1369 A167 1 mil z on 40k
          #915   1.50   1.50
1370 A167 5 mil z on 48k
          #916   7.50   7.50
1371 A167 10 mil z on 100k
          #917   15.00 15.00
    Nos. 1361-1371 (8) 29.40 29.40

Nos. 1226-
1229 Srchd. in
Black or Red

1993, Oct. 29   Litho.   Perf. 13
1373 A216 3 mil z on 10z
          #1226   3.00   3.00
1374 A216 3 mil z on 10z
          #1226 (R)   4.75   4.75
1375 A216 5 mil z on 15z
          #1227   4.75   4.75
1376 A216 10 mil z on 25z
          #1228   9.25   9.25

Souvenir Sheet
Imperf
1377 A216 10 mil z on 100z
          #1229   13.00 13.00
Size and location of surcharge varies.

Natl.
Game
Parks,
50th
Anniv.
A225

1993   Litho.   Perf. 13
1403 A225 30k Cape eland   .30   .25
1404 A225 50k Elephants   .30   .25
1405 A225 1.50z Giant eland   1.25   1.00
1406 A225 3.50z White rhinocer-
           os   3.00   2.00
1407 A225   5z Bongo   4.00   2.50
    Nos. 1403-1407 (5)   8.85   6.00

For surcharge see No. 1431.

Nos. 986-900 Surcharged

1994, Apr. 23   Photo.   Perf. 14
1408 A182 30k on 10k   .75   .75
1409 A182 50k on 75k   1.25   1.25
1410 A182 1.50z on 100k   3.75   3.75
1411 A182 3.50z on 145k   7.50   7.50
1412 A182   5z on 270k   11.50 11.50
    Nos. 1408-1412 (5)   24.75 24.75

Nos. 1160-1167 Surcharged

1994, Apr. 23   Litho.   Perf. 14
1413 A207 30k on 10k   .75   .75
1414 A207 50k on 10k   1.00   1.00
1415 A207 1.50z on 3z   2.50   2.50
1416 A207 2.50z on 5z   3.75   3.75
1417 A207 3.50z on 10z   5.50   5.50
1418 A207   5z on 15z   8.00   8.00
1419 A207 7.50z on 37.50z 12.50 12.50
1420 A207 10z on 80z   17.50 17.50
    Nos. 1413-1420 (8)   51.50 51.50

Nos. 1195-1198 Surcharged

1994, Apr. 23   Litho.   Perf. 13
1421 A210 50k on 5z   1.75   1.75
1422 A210 1.50z on 10z   5.00   5.00
1423 A210 3.50z on 15z   9.50   9.50
1424 A210   5z on 25z   19.00 19.00
    Nos. 1421-1424 (4)   35.25 35.25

**Nos. 990, 1079, 1094, 1097, 1113,
1125-1126, 1133, 1155, & 1404
Surcharged in Gold**

1994, Aug. 31   Perfs., Etc. as Before
1425 A196 20z on 3z #1097   .40   .40
1426 A182 40z on 270k #990 .40   .40
1427 A203 50z on 3z #1133   .50   .50
1428 A206 75z on 3z #1155   .60   .60
1429 A201 100z on 2.05z
          #1125   .75   .75
1430 A194 150z on 1.70z
          #1079   1.25   1.25
1431 A225 200z on 50k #1404 1.50   1.50
1432 A196 250z on 1.50z
          #1094   1.75   1.75
1433 A199 300z on 3.60z
          #1113   2.00   2.00
1434 A201 500z on 3.60z
          #1126   3.25   3.25
    Nos. 1425-1434 (10)   12.40 12.40
Size and location of surcharge varies.

**Nos. 1067, 1094, 1113, 1125-1126
Surcharged in Gold**

No.
1435

No. 1437

1996   Perfs., Etc. as Before
1435 A192 100z on 3.50z
           #1067   .50   .50
1436 A199 500z on 3.60z
           #1113   .50   .50
1437 A201 1000z on 2.05z
           #1125   .50   .50
1438 A196 2500z on 1.50z
           #1094   1.75   1.75
1439 A201 5000z on 3.60z
           #1126   3.25   3.25
1440 A196 6000z on 1.50z
           #1094   3.50   3.50
1441 A199 15,000z on 3.60z
           #1113   9.00   9.00
1442 A201 25,000z on 3.60z
           #1126   17.50 17.50
    Nos. 1435-1442 (8)   36.50 36.50

1996
Summer
Olympic
Games,
Atlanta
A226

1000z, Equestrian. 12,500z, Boxing.
25,000z, Table tennis. 35,000z, Basketball,
vert. 50,000z, Tennis.

1996, July 29   Litho.   Perf. 11½
1444 A226 1000z multi   .25   .25
1445 A226 12,500z multi   1.00   1.00
1446 A226 25,000z multi   3.00   3.00
1447 A226 35,000z multi   4.00   4.00
1448 A226 50,000z multi   4.75   4.75
    Nos. 1444-1448 (5)   13.00 13.00

Insects &
Spiders
A227

No. 1449: a, Lasius niger. b, Caloptery-
gides. c, Peucetia. d, Sphecides.

1996   Litho.   Perf. 13½
1449 A227 15,000z Sheet of 4,
          #a.-d.   15.00 15.00

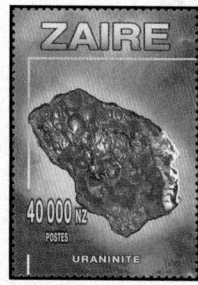

Minerals
A228

No. 1450: a, Uraninite. b, Malachite. c,
Ruby. d, Diamond.
No. 1452, Uranotile, cuprosklodowskite,
horiz.

1996
1450 A228 40,000z Sheet of
           4, #a.-d.   27.50 27.50

Souvenir Sheet
1452 A228 105,000z multi 20.00 20.00

No. 1452 exists overprinted in silver for
Hong Kong Exposition '97. Value, $50.
A number has been reserved for an addi-
tional sheet with this set.

Raptors
A229

No. 1453: a, Congo eagle. b, Crowned eagle. c, Melierax metabates. d, Urotriorchis macrourus.

1996
1453	A229	50,000z Sheet of 4,	
		#a.-d.	30.00 30.00

Butterflies
A230

No. 1454: a, Cymothoe sangaris. b, Colotis zoe. c, Physcaeneura leda. d, Charaxes candiope.

1996   **Sheet of 4**
1454	A230	70,000z #a.-d.	37.50 37.50

The validity of Nos. 1455-1481 and other stamps from the same time period has been questioned. The editors are attempting to find out more about these stamps.

1998 World Cup Soccer Championships, France — A231

Numbers on players: No. 1455, #12. No. 1456, none. No. 1457, #7. No. 1458, #3.
No. 1459: a, British player. b, Brazilian player.
No. 1460: a-d, Like #1455-1458, but with part of World Cup Trophy behind each player.

1996
1455-1458	A231	35,000z Set of 4	14.00 14.00

Souvenir Sheets
1459	A231	105,000z Sheet of 2, #a.-b.	20.00 20.00
1460	A231	35,000z Sheet of 4, #a.-d.	14.00 14.00

No. 1459 contains 2 42x39mm stamps. See Nos. 1467-1476.

World Wildlife Fund — A231a

No. 1466 — Pan paniscus: a, With young. b, Two in trees. c, Holding vines. d, Head.

1997
1466	A231a	20,000z Block of 4, #a.-d.	20.00 20.00

1998 World Cup Soccer Championships Type of 1996

African soccer players: No. 1467, 20,000z, Soccer ball at his right. No. 1468, 20,000z, Ball at head. No. 1469, 20,000z, Yellow uniform. No. 1470, 20,000z, Ball on knee.
German soccer players, soccer ball on stamp at: No. 1471, 50,000z, UR. No. 1472, 50,000z, LL. No. 1473, 50,000z, LR. No. 1474, 50,000z, UL.
Nos. 1475a-1475d, 1476a-1476d are like Nos. 1467-1474 but with part of World Cup Trophy behind each player.

1996   **Litho.**   **Perf. 13½**
1467-1470	A231	Set of 4	9.00 9.00
1471-1474	A231	Set of 4	20.00 20.00

Souvenir Sheets
1475	A231	20,000z Sheet of 4, #a.-d.	9.00 9.00
1476	A231	50,000z Sheet of 4, #a.-d.	20.00 20.00

Boy Scouts and Lions Intl. Clubs
A232

No. 1477 — Diceros bicornis: a, Walking forward. b, Walking left, left leg up. c, Facing left. d, Holding head up.
No. 1478 — Panthera leo: a, Cubs. b, Adult male. c, Adult male facing forward, mouth open. d, Adult female on fallen tree.
No. 1479 — Loxodonta africana: a, Walking right, trunk in air. b, Reaching up to tree limb with trunk. c, Walking right, trunk down. d, Mother with calf.
105,000z, Hippopotamus amphibius.

1997   **Litho.**   **Perf. 13x13½**
1477	A232	40,000z Sheet of 4, #a.-d.	13.00 13.00
1478	A232	50,000z Sheet of 4, #a.-d.	17.50 17.50
1479	A232	70,000z Sheet of 4, #a.-d.	24.00 24.00

Souvenir Sheet
1480	A232	105,000z multi	12.00 12.00

Boy Scouts (#1477, 1479-1480). Lions Intl. Clubs (#1478).

Jacqueline Kennedy Onassis (1929-94)
A233

Various portraits.

1997   **Litho.**   **Perf. 13½**
1481	A233	15,000z Sheet of 9, #a.-i.	17.50 17.50

No. 1481 also exists imperf.

Stamps from this country are now being released under the previous name, "Republique Democratique du Congo," or Congo Democratic Republic, despite the resumption of civil war. We will continue to list these stamps under the country's name of Zaire until the situation is resolved.

Diana, Princess of Wales (1961-97) — A234

No. 1482: a, Wearing tiara. b, In white jacket. c, In white hat. d, In polka dotted dress. e, Scarf around neck. f, Low cut evening dress.
No. 1483: a, Wearing tiara. b, Hand under chin. c, Leaning chin on both hands. d, One-shoulder-covered outfit.
No. 1484: a, Red & black dress. b, White jacket, pearls. c, Profile view. d, Wearing tiara.
No. 1485, 400,000z, In black evening dress. No. 1486, 400,000z, Holding flowers.

1998, Aug. 6   **Litho.**   **Perf. 14**
1482	A234	50,000z Sheet of 6, #a.-f.	13.50 7.75
1483	A234	100,000z Sheet of 4, #a.-d.	17.50 10.50
1484	A234	125,000z Sheet of 4, #a.-d.	24.00 14.50

Souvenir Sheets
1485-1486	A234	Set of 2	50.00 25.00

Mother Teresa (1910-97) — A235

1998, Aug. 6
1487	A235	50,000z shown	2.25 1.50

Souvenir Sheet
1488	A235	325,000z Portrait, diff.	11.50 7.50

No. 1487 was issued in sheets of 6.

100 Centimes = 1 Franc (1998)

Native Dwelling — A236

Arms — A237

Inauguration of Pres. Laurent Kabila — A238

Designs: 1.25fr, Troops and civilians in Kinshasa. 3fr, Flag, crowd, Pres. Kabila breaking chain with sword, horiz.
2.50fr, Gun, arrow, handshake, tractor. 3.50fr, Pres. Kabila.

1999, May 12   **Litho.**   **Perf. 14**
1489	A236	25c multi	.25 .25
1490	A237	50c multi	.55 .55
1491	A238	75c multi	.80 .80
1492	A238	1.25fr multi	1.75 1.75
1493	A238	3fr multi	3.25 3.25
		Nos. 1489-1493 (5)	6.60 6.60

Souvenir Sheets
1494	A238	2.50fr multi	2.60 2.60
1495	A238	3.50fr multi	3.75 3.75

Conquest of Kinshasa by troops of Laurent Kabila, 2nd anniv.

Chinese Zodiac Animals — A239

No. 1496: a, Rat. b, Ox. c, Tiger. d, Rabbit. e, Dragon. f, Snake. g, Horse. h, Ram. i, Monkey. j, Cock. k, Dog. l, Boar.

1999, Aug. 20   **Perf. 13¼x13½**
1496	A239	78c Sheet of 12, #a-l	27.50 17.50

A240

A241

A242

A243

Outlaws of the Marsh — A244

No. 1497 — Sheet with text starting with "The historical novel. . .": a, 1.45fr, Men fighting. b, 1.50fr, Man uprooting tree. c, 1.60fr, Man with sword in snowstorm. d, 1.70fr, Man with sword, other men at bridge. e, 1.80fr, Three men at table.
No. 1498 — Sheet with text starting with "The main theme. . .": a, 1.45fr, Men and baskets. b, 1.50fr, Man threatening another man with sword. c, 1.60fr, Man attacking tiger. d, 1.70fr, People watching men in martial arts battle. e, 1.80fr, Battling horsemen.

No. 1499 — Sheet with text starting with "The common people. . .": a, 1.45fr, Men fighting in boat. b, 1.50fr, Man with sword fighting man with hatchets. c, 1.60fr, Men near fortified wall. d, 1.70fr, Men fighting on cobblestone street. e, 1.80fr, Archer on horseback at doorway.

No. 1500 — Sheet with text starting with "Today, it is thought. . .": a, 1.45fr, Man seated and other man standing near table. b, 1.50fr, Man setting fire to building. c, 1.60fr, Man in room. d, 1.70fr, Man lifting another man in a battle. e, 1.80fr, Man holding torn scroll.

1999, Aug. 20 *Perf. 13¼*

Sheets of 5, #a-e

1497-1500	A240	Set of 4	60.00	45.00

Souvenir Sheets

Perf. 13¼x13½

1501	A241	10fr multi	17.50	17.50
1502	A242	10fr multi	17.50	17.50
1503	A243	10fr multi	17.50	17.50
1504	A244	10fr multi	17.50	17.50

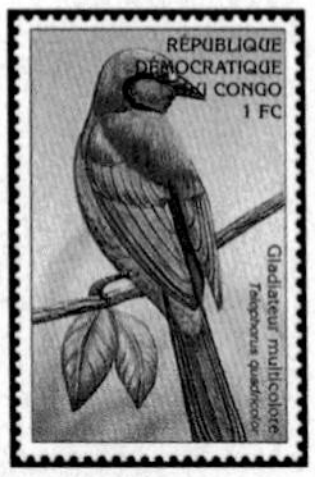

A245

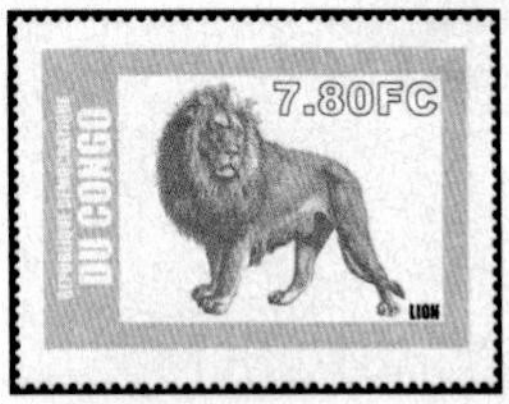

A246

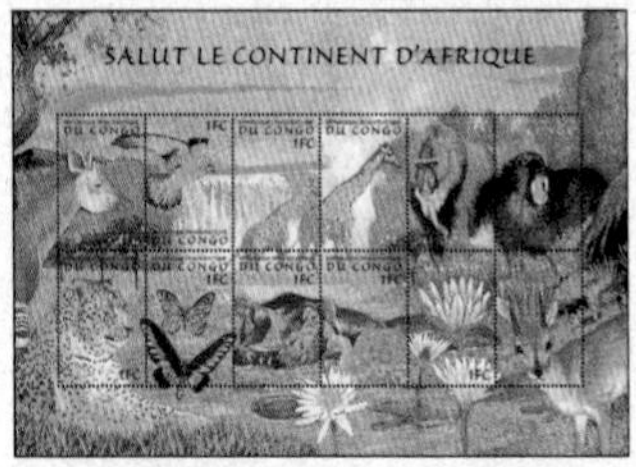

African Flora and Fauna — A247

Designs: 1fr, Telophorus quadricolor. 1.50fr, Panthera pardus. No. 1507, 2fr, Colotis protomedia. No. 1508, 2fr, Kobus vardoni. No. 1509, 3fr, Canarina abyssinica. No. 1510, 3fr, Smutsia temminckii.

7.80fr, Lion.

No. 1512: a, Okapi. b, Bird, rainbow, waterfalls. c, Giraffe, rainbow, waterfalls. d, Giraffe, waterfall mist. e, Mandrill. f, Chimpanzee. g, Leopard. h, Butterflies. i, Hippopotamus. j, Bird in water. k, Flowers. l, Antelope.

No. 1513: a, Sun. b, Pieris citrina. c, Merops apiaster. d, Lanius collurio. e, Ploceus cucullatus. f, Charaxes pelias. g, Charaxes eupale. h, Giraffa camelopardalis. i, Galago moholi. j, Strelitzia reginae. k, Gazella thomsoni. l, Upupa epops.

No. 1514, 10fr, Taurotragus oryx. No. 1515, 10fr, Hippopotamus amphibus.

No. 1516, 10fr, Warthog.

Perf. 14, 14¼x14¾ (#1511), 14¼x14 (#1516)

2000, Feb. 28

1505-1510	A245	Set of 6	14.50	14.50
1511	A246	7.80fr multi	8.00	8.00
1512	A247	1fr Sheet of 12, #a-l	12.50	12.50
1513	A245	1.50fr Sheet of 12, #a-l	20.00	20.00

Souvenir Sheets

1514-1515	A245	Set of 2	20.00	20.00
1516	A247	10fr multi	10.00	10.00

No. 1516 contains one 42x57mm stamp.

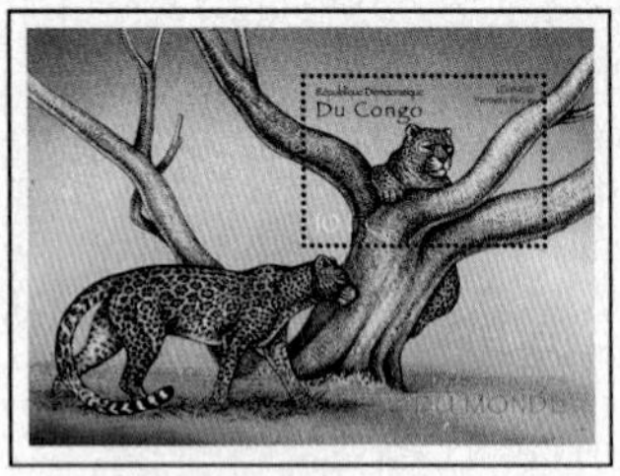

Wild Felines and Canines — A248

No. 1517, 1.50fr: a, Felis bengalensis. b, Felis aurata. c, Felis caracal. d, Felis conoclor. e, Felis nigripes. f, Panthera leo. g, Neofelis nebulosa. h, Felis wiedii. i, Acinonyx jubatus. j, Felis pardina. k, Felis yagouaroundi. l, Felis serval.

No. 1518, 2fr: a, Canis mesomelas. b, Otocyon megalotis. c, Speothos venaticus. d, Canis latrans. e, Cuon alpinus. f, Fennecus zerda. g, Urocyon cinereoargenteus. h, Canis lupus. i, Vulpes macrotis. j, Chrysocyon brachyurus. k, Nyctereutes procyonoides. l, Vulpes vulpes.

No. 1519, 10fr, Panthera pardus. No. 1520, 10fr, Alopex lagopus.

2000, Feb. 28 *Perf. 14*

Sheets of 12, #a-l

1517-1518	A248	Set of 2	40.00	40.00

Souvenir Sheets

1519-1520	A248	Set of 2	17.00	17.00

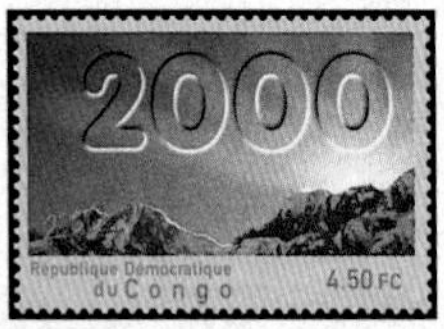

Millennium A249

2000, June 10

1521	Horiz. strip of 3	12.00	12.00
a.	A249 4.50fr multi	1.25	1.25
b.	A249 9fr multi	3.25	3.25
c.	A249 15fr multi	5.00	5.00

Printed in sheets containing two strips.

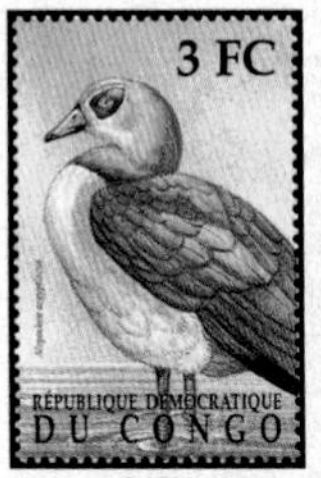

A250

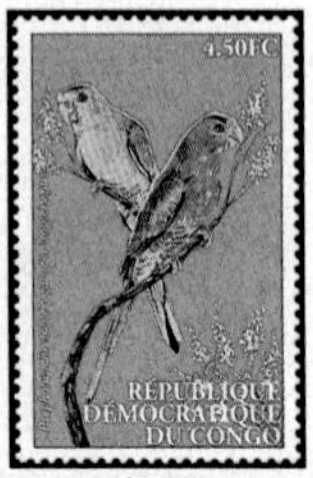

A251

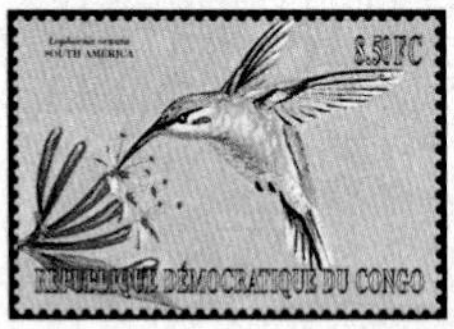

Birds A252

Designs: No. 1522, 3fr, Alopochen aegyptiacus. No. 1523, 3fr, Ardeola ibis. No. 1524, 4.50fr, Oena capensis. No. 1525, 4.50fr, Lybius torquatus. No. 1526, 9fr, Falco tinnunculus. No. 1527, 9fr, Corythaelo cristata.

No. 1528, 4.50fr, Psephotus chrysopterygius chrysopterygius. 8fr, Amazona aestiva. No. 1530, 8.50fr, Are nobilis cumanensis. No. 1531, 9fr, Agapornis roseicollis.

No. 1532, 8.50fr, Lophornis ornata. No. 1533, 9fr, Polytrus guauvunibi.

No. 1534, 9fr: a, Euplectes orix. b, Euplectes ardens. c, Oriolus auratus. d, Plocens cucullatus. e, Amandava subflava. f, Nectarina senegalensis.

No. 1535, 9fr: a, Halcyon malimbicus. b, Tachymarptis melba. c, Haliaeetus vocifer. d, Ardea purpurea. e, Balaeniceps rex. f, Balearica regulorum.

No. 1536: a, Ertoxeres aquila. b, Aglaiolepus kinde. c, Archilochus calobris. d, Trochlus polytaus. e, Chaliostigna herrani. f, Ensifera. g, Chrysolampus mosquitus. h, Phorethornus syrmatophorus. i, Calypre hetervare.

No. 1537, 5fr: a, Eos squamata squamata. b, Aratinga guarouba. c, Aratinga aurea. d, Psuedeos fuscata. e, Agapornis fischeri. f, Aratinga nana nana. g, Aratinga mitrata. h, Trichoglossus haematodus rubitorquis. i, Cacatua galerita galerita.

No. 1538, 5fr: a, Ara macao. b, Neophema elegans. c, Loriculus vernalis. d, Aratinga solstitialis. e, Pionites melancephala. f, Bolborhynchus lineola. g, Ara severa. h, Psephotus chrysopterygius dissimilis. i, Ara militaris.

No. 1539, 15fr, Actophilornis africanus, horiz. No. 1540, 20fr, Ceryle rudis, horiz.

No. 1541, 15fr, Opopsitta diophthalma. No. 1542, 15fr, Ara ararrauna, horiz.

No. 1543, 15fr, Coeligena torgoata. No. 1544, 20fr, Campylopterus hemileicurus.

2000, Aug. 16 *Perf. 14*

1522-1527	A250	Set of 6	*15.00*	*15.00*
1528-1531	A251	Set of 4	*13.50*	*13.50*
1532-1533	A252	Set of 2	*7.75*	*7.75*

Sheets of 6, #a-f

1534-1535	A250	Set of 2	*47.50*	*47.50*
1536	A252	4.50fr Sheet of 9, #a-i	*18.00*	*18.00*

Sheets of 9, #a-i

1537-1538	A251	Set of 2	*40.00*	*40.00*

Souvenir Sheets

1539-1540	A250	Set of 2	*16.00*	*16.00*
1541-1542	A251	Set of 2	*13.50*	*13.50*
1543-1544	A252	Set of 2	*16.00*	*16.00*

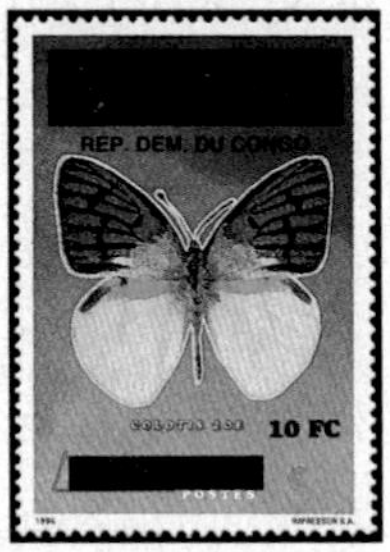

Surcharges on Unissued Stamps A253

Designs: 10fr on 70,000z, Colotis zoe. 15fr on 25,000z, Bulbophyllum falcatum. 25fr on 20,000z, Scutellosaurus. 35fr on 15,000z, Sphecides. 45fr on 100,000z, Diamond. 50fr on 35,000z, Termitomyces aurantiacus. 70fr on 50,000z, Melierax metabates. 100fr on 40,000z, Malachite. 150fr on 25,000z, Panda.

2000 **Litho.** *Perf. 13¼*

1545	A253	10fr on 70,000z multi	7.25	7.25
1546	A253	15fr on 25,000z multi	7.25	7.25
1547	A253	25fr on 20,000z multi	7.25	7.25
1548	A253	35fr on 15,000z multi	7.25	7.25
1549	A253	45fr on 100,000z multi	7.25	7.25
1550	A253	50fr on 35,000z multi	7.25	7.25
1551	A253	70fr on 50,000z multi	7.25	7.25
1552	A253	100fr on 40,000z multi	7.25	7.25
1553	A253	150fr on 25,000z multi	7.25	7.25

Location of surcharges varies. All surcharged stamps have white margins.

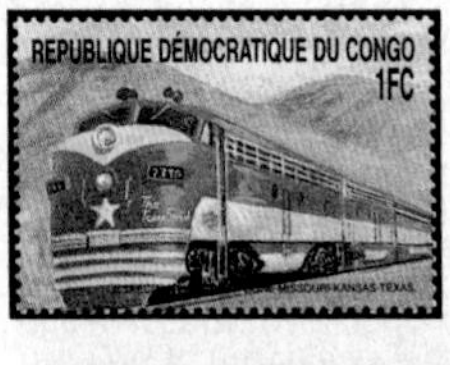

A254

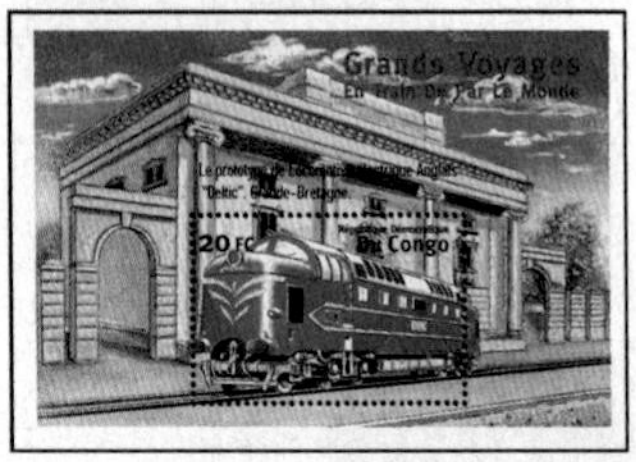

Trains — A255

Designs: 1fr, Missouri-Kansas-Texas Line locomotive. 2fr, Spremberg steam locomotive. No. 1556, 3fr, King Class, Great Western Railway. No. 1557, 3fr, Crocodile locomotive. 5fr, Inner-city trains, Great Britain. 6fr, Big Boy, Union Pacific.

No. 1560, 4.50fr: a, Class SU, 2-6-2, Russia. b, Prussian locomotive. c, Zimbabwe locomotive. d, Hunslet 2-8-2, Peru. e, London, Midland & Scottish Railway locomotive. f, London Northeastern Railway locomotive.

No. 1561, 8fr: a, Denver & Rio Grande Western Railroad locomotive. b, Mikado 2-8-2, Louisville & Nashville. c, Mogul, Rio Grande. d, New York Central Railway locomotive. e, Sumpter Valley Railway steam locomotive. f, Three-truck Shay No. 7.

No. 1562, 9.50fr: a, Compagnie du Nord locomotive, France. b, Union Pacific locomotive. c, Great Northern Railway locomotive. d, Liverpool & Manchester Railway locomotive. e, Patentee 2-2-2, London & Birmingham. f, Puffing Billy.

No. 1563, 10fr: a, Chicago, Rock Island & Pacific Railway locomotive. b, Powhattan Arrow, Norfolk & Western. c, Class S-1, New York Central Hudson River Railway. d, Reading Railroad locomotive. e, Great Bear, Great Western Railway. f, Bi-polar, Chicago, Milwaukee, St. Paul & Pacific Railway.

No. 1564, 5fr: a, Beyer-Garratt 50 4-8-2+2-8-4 locomotive. b, Locomotive Express 4-6-2. c, 780CV electric locomotive. d, Electric locomotive on curve. e, Class 2-10-0 Locomotive 56001. f, Electric locomotive on straight track. g, Class 2-8-4 Locomotive 284. h, Class G 6/6 electric locomotive.

No. 1565, 8.50fr: a, Class B-B electric locomotive AE4/4. b, Class EX, Paris-Lyon-Mediterranean. c, Big Boy. d, Tourist car. e, Class 4-8-4 GS-4. f, Class 46 electric locomotive. g, Class-4-6-0 County. h, Class DA Diesel-electric locomotive.

No. 1566, 15fr, New York Central & Hudson River Railway locomotive. No. 1567, 20fr, Mohawk & Hudson Railroad locomotive. No. 1568, 20fr, Broadway Limited, Pennsylvania Railroad. No. 1569, 20fr, Trans-Europe Express.

No. 1570, 20fr, Deltic electric locomotive, Great Britain. No. 1571, 20fr, Diesel-electric locomotive, Canada Pacific.

2001, Jan. 15 **Litho.** *Perf. 14*

1554-1559	A254	Set of 6	11.50	11.50

Sheets of 6, #a-f

1560-1563	A254	Set of 4	65.00	65.00

Sheets of 8, #a-h

1564-1565	A255	Set of 2	45.00	45.00

Souvenir Sheets

1566-1569	A254	Set of 4	32.50	32.50
1570-1571	A255	Set of 2	14.00	14.00

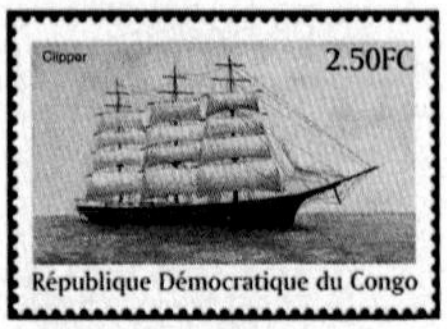

Ships A256

Designs: 2.50fr, Clipper. 5fr, Arab bum. 20fr, Flemish galley. 21.70fr, Trabaccolo, vert. 30fr, Dutch galliot. 45.80fr, Japanese coaster.

No. 1578, 10fr: a, Trireme. b, Roman caudicaria. c, 13th cent. warship. d, Byzantine galley. e, Lateneer. f, 14th century cog. g, Arab dhow. h, Hanseatic cog. i, Portuguese galley.

No. 1579, 10fr: a, Egyptian sailing ship. b, Egyptian rowing craft. c, Egyptian seagoing ship. d, Greek galley. e, Etruscan merchantman f, Etruscan fishing skiff. g, Greek merchantman. h, Minoan passenger ship. i, Roman harbor boat.

No. 1580, 10fr: a, Flemish galleon. b, English galleon. c, Carrack. d, Chinese war galley. e, Venetian galley. f, Polacre. g, Hemmena. h, Venetian bragozzo. i, Schooner.

No. 1581, 25fr, Viking drakkar. No. 1582, 25fr, Portuguese caravel, vert. No. 1583, 25fr, HMS Endeavour, vert.

2001, June 22 *Perf. 14*

1572-1577	A256	Set of 6	14.00	14.00

Sheets of 9, #a-i

1578-1580	A256	Set of 3	30.00	30.00

Souvenir Sheets

Perf. 13¾

1581-1583	A256	Set of 3	16.00	16.00

No. 1581 contains one 50x38mm stamp; Nos. 1582-1583 each contain one 38x50mm stamp.

History of Aviation — A257

No. 1584: a, Montgolfier balloon (36x61mm). b, Boxkite and Tiger Moth airplanes (36x61mm). c, Gladiator. d, Eurofighter. e, Mosquito. f, Chipmunk.
No. 1585: a, Blackburn and Spartan Arrow airplanes (36x61mm). b, Tiger Moth. c, Lightning. d, Vulcan B2. e, Tornado.
No. 1586, 25fr, Fox Moth and Avro 540K airplanes. No. 1587, 25fr, Avro 504K and Fox Moth airplanes.

2001, June 22   *Perf. 14¼*
1584 A257 10fr Sheet of 6, #a-
   f   10.00 10.00
1585 A257 10fr Sheet of 6,
   #1584a,
   1585a-1585e 10.00 10.00
Souvenir Sheets
Perf. 14¼x14½
1586-1587 A257   12.00 12.00

First Zeppelin Flight, Cent. — A258

No. 1588: a, LZ-6. b, LZ-7. c, US Navy airship Akron. c, Lindstrand HS-110 Pittsburgh Tribune-Review airship.
No. 1589, 100fr, LZ-130 Graf Zeppelin II. No. 1590, 100fr, LZ-1.

2001, June 22   *Perf. 14*
1588 A258 60fr Sheet of 4, #a-
   d   27.50 27.50
Souvenir Sheets
1589-1590 A258 Set of 2 22.50 22.50

Butterflies — A259

Designs: 5fr, Striped policeman. 21.70fr, Brown-veined white. 45fr, Common dotted border. 45.80fr, Cabbage. 50fr, African migrant. 51.80fr, Mocker swallowtail.
No. 1597, 6fr, horiz.: a, Common grass blue. b, Golden tiger. c, Palla. d, Blue diadem. e, African giant swallowtail. f, African leaf. g, Gold-banded forester. h, Small harvester.
No. 1598, 6fr, horiz.: a, Guinea fowl. b, Forest queen. c, Sweet potato acraea. d, Wanderer. e, Evening brown. f, African ringlet. g, Plain tiger. h, Monarch.
No. 1599, 8fr, horiz.: a, Broad-bordered grass yellow. b, Crimson tip. c, Orange-banded protea. d, Azure hairstreak. e, Marshall's false monarch. f, Blue swallowtail. g, Figtree blue. h, Grass jewel.
No. 1600, 25fr, Long-tailed blue, horiz. No. 1601, 25fr, Chief, horiz. No. 1602, 25fr, Large spotted acraea, horiz.

2001, June 22
1591-1596 A259 Set of 6 25.00 25.00
Sheets of 8, #a-h
1597-1599 A259 Set of 3 37.50 37.50
Souvenir Sheets
1600-1602 A259 Set of 3 17.50 17.50

Flowers and Insects — A260

Designs; 20fr, Aconite, Brazilian frog-hopper. 21.70fr, Larkspur, Mexican cicada. 25fr, Blue orchid, dragonfly. 45.80fr, Spotted blossom orchid, buck moth.
No. 1607, 10fr, horiz.: a, Rein orchids, tiger moth. b, Ivy, Siamese wasp. c, Pink lady's slipper, goat weed emperor. d, Gletscherpetersbart, velvet ant. e, Licorice, viceroy butterfly. f, Grass pink, aphid. g, Ranunculus, spider wasp. h, Clamshell orchid, tropical bee. i, Bog orchids, mayfly.
No. 1608, 10fr, horiz.: a, Common lantana, red-spotted purple butterfly. b, Deep purple lilac, zebra swallowtail. c, Mt. Fujiyama, ruddy copper butterfly. d, Pinafore pink, red admiral butterfly. e, Argemone mexicana, purple hairstreak butterfly. f, Soapwort, sulphur butterfly. g, Lungwort, Buckeye butterfly. h, Wild thyme, pipevine swallowtail. i, Loeselia mexicana, banded purple butterfly.
No. 1609, 10fr, horiz.: a, Cymbidium Stanley Fouraker Highlander, scarlet tiger moth. b, Cymbidium Sparkle "Ruby Lips," Sumatran carpenter bee. c, Dendrobium Sussex, ant lion. d, Cymbidium Vieux Rose Loch Lomond, nachahmend butterfly. e, Cymbidium, cicada-killer wasp. f, Dendrobium Mousmee, spechosoma wasp. g, Arachnis flos-aeris, green lacewing. h, Paphiopedilum, seven-spot ladybug. i, Eulophia quartiniana, damselfly.
No. 1610, 25fr, Jolly Jocker pansy, monarch butterfly, horiz. No. 1611, 25fr, Pink peony, wasp (inscribed erroneously like No. 1610), horiz. No. 1612, 25fr, Plumbago capensis, honey bee, horiz.

2001, June 22   *Perf. 14*
1603-1606 A260 Set of 4 13.00 13.00
Sheets of 9, #a-i
Perf. 14¼x14½
1607-1609 A260 Set of 3 32.50 32.50
Souvenir Sheets
1610-1612 A260 Set of 3 16.00 16.00
Nos. 1607-1609 each contain nine 37x30mm stamps; Nos. 1610-1612 each contain one 50x37mm stamp.

Tintin in Africa — A261

Designs: 190fr, Tintin with hand above eyes. 461fr, Tintin in car with dog and native.

2001, Dec. 31   **Photo.**   *Perf. 11½*
1613 A261 190fr multi   2.50 2.50
Souvenir Sheet
1614 A261 461fr multi   7.00 7.00
No. 1614 contains one 48x38mm stamp. Imperfs exist. Value: 1613, $15; 1614, $30. See Belgium Nos. 1875-1876.

Native Handicrafts A262

Designs: 10fr, Tabwa buffalo mask. 50fr, Kongo bedpost. 60fr, Loi drum. 150fr, Kuba royal statue, vert. 200fr, Tshokwe mask, vert. 300fr, Luba mask, vert.

2002, Mar. 7   **Litho.**   *Perf. 11½*
1615-1620 A262 Set of 6 13.00 13.00

Lions A263

Designs: 50fr, Lioness and cub. 75fr, Lion and dead animal. 150fr, Lioness and cubs at water's edge. 250fr, Lion and lioness. 300fr, Lion leaping in water.

2002, Mar. 7   **Litho.**   *Perf. 11½*
1621-1625 A263 Set of 5 13.50 13.50

Flowers — A264

Designs: 25fr, Gloriosa rothschildiana. 50fr, Aworthia cooperi. 125fr, Lithops aucampiae. 250fr, Angraecum sesquipedale. 500fr, Lampranthus coccineus.

2002   **Litho.**   *Perf. 11½*
1626-1629 A264 Set of 4 4.75 4.75
Souvenir Sheet
1630 A264 500fr multi   5.75 5.75

Minerals A265

Designs: 190fr, Beryl, vert. 340fr, Willemite mimetite. 410fr, Quartz chlorite. 445fr, Allophane copper. 455fr, Rhodochrosite, vert. 480fr, Zircon.

Perf. 11½x11¼
2002, Aug. 30   **Litho.**
1631 A265 190fr multi 2.25 2.25
1632 A265 340fr multi 4.00 4.00
1633 A265 410fr multi 5.00 5.00
1634 A265 445fr multi 5.25 5.25
1635 A265 455fr multi 5.25 5.25
1636 A265 480fr multi 5.75 5.75
An additional stamp was issued in the set. The editors would like to examine it.

Worldwide Fund for Nature (WWF) — A266

Designs: 20fr, Head of gorilla. 190fr, Adult and juvenile gorillas. 390fr, Gorilla in grass, vert. 455fr, Gorilla eating grass, vert.

2002, Aug. 30   **Litho.**   *Perf. 11¾*
1638-1641 A266 Set of 4 15.00 15.00
An additional stamp was issued in this set. The editors would like to examine any example of it.

Pres. Joseph Kabila A267

Background color: 195fr, Blue green. 350fr, 800fr, Light blue. 1500fr, Gold.

2002, Dec. 10   **Litho.**   *Perf. 13¼*
1643-1644 A267 Set of 2 5.00 2.00
Souvenir Sheets
1645 A267 800fr multi   7.50 7.50
Litho. & Embossed With Foil Application
1646 A267 1500fr gold & multi 16.00 16.00
Nos. 1645-1646 each contain one 42x50mm stamp.

OFFICIAL STAMPS

Nos. 756-772 Overprinted

1975   **Litho.**   *Perf. 14*
O1 A145 10s red org & blk .25 .25
O2 A145 40s multi .25 .25
O3 A145 50s multi .25 .25
     Perf. 13
O4 A146 1k multi .25 .25
O5 A146 2k multi .25 .25
O6 A146 3k multi .25 .25
O7 A146 4k multi .30 .25
O8 A146 5k multi .30 .25
O9 A146 6k multi .45 .25
O10 A146 8k multi .65 .25
O11 A146 9k multi .65 .25
O12 A146 10k multi .80 .25
O13 A146 14k multi 1.25 .40
O14 A146 17k multi 1.50 .45
O15 A146 20k multi 1.50 .60
O16 A146 50k multi 3.75 1.50
O17 A146 100k multi 12.50 4.00
Nos. O1-O17 (17) 25.15 9.95
"SP" are the initials of "Service Public."

ZAMBEZIA

zam-ˈbē-zē-ə

LOCATION — A former district of the Mozambique Province in Portuguese East Africa

GOVT. — Part of the Portuguese East Africa Colony

The districts of Quelimane and Tete were created from Zambezia. Eventually stamps of Mozambique came into use. See Quelimane and Tete.

1000 Reis = 1 Milreis

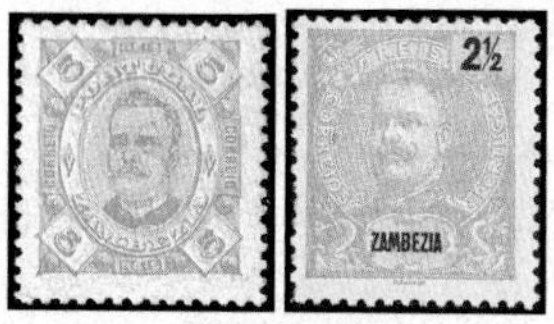

King Carlos
A1 A2

Perf. 11½, 12½, 13½

1894 Typo. Unwmk.

1	A1	5r yellow	.25	.25
2	A1	10r red violet	.75	.45
3	A1	15r chocolate	1.50	.65
a.		Perf. 12½	27.50	19.00
4	A1	20r lavender	1.50	.65
5	A1	25r blue green	2.00	1.25
a.		Perf. 11½	*30.00*	*30.00*
6	A1	50r lt blue	2.50	1.25
7	A1	75r carmine	5.00	3.25
a.		Perf. 11½	50.00	35.00
8	A1	80r yellow grn	7.00	2.50
9	A1	100r brown, *buff*	6.00	1.75
10	A1	150r car, *rose*	8.00	3.00
11	A1	200r dk blue, *bl*	9.00	3.00
a.		Perf. 11½	200.00	150.00
b.		Perf. 13½	32.50	24.00
12	A1	300r dk bl, *salmon*	15.00	4.50
a.		Perf. 11½	25.00	20.00
		Nos. 1-12 (12)	58.50	22.50

For surcharges and overprints see Nos. 36-47, 73-74, 77-81, 84-88.

1898-1903 ***Perf. 11½***

Name and Value in Black or Red (500r)

13	A2	2½r gray	.45	.45
14	A2	5r orange	.45	.45
15	A2	10r lt green	.75	.50
16	A2	15r brown	1.25	1.00
17	A2	15r gray grn ('03)	1.60	1.40
18	A2	20r gray violet	1.25	1.00
19	A2	25r sea green	1.25	1.00
20	A2	25r carmine ('03)	1.00	.85
21	A2	50r blue	1.25	1.10
22	A2	50r brown ('03)	4.00	2.25
23	A2	65r dull bl ('03)	10.00	5.50
24	A2	75r rose	20.00	5.25
25	A2	75r lilac ('03)	3.25	2.75
26	A2	80r violet	5.00	3.00
27	A2	100r dk bl, *bl*	2.00	2.00
28	A2	115r org brn, *pink* ('03)	15.00	7.25
29	A2	130r brn, *straw* ('03)	15.00	7.25
30	A2	150r brn, *buff*	6.00	3.50
31	A2	200r red vio, *pnksh*	6.00	3.50
32	A2	300r dk bl, *rose*	8.00	3.50
33	A2	400r dull bl, *straw* ('03)	12.00	8.50
34	A2	500r blk, *bl* ('01)	20.00	6.75
35	A2	700r vio, *yelsh* ('01)	30.00	8.75
		Nos. 13-35 (23)	165.50	77.50

For surcharges and overprints see Nos. 49-68, 72, 82-83, 93-107.

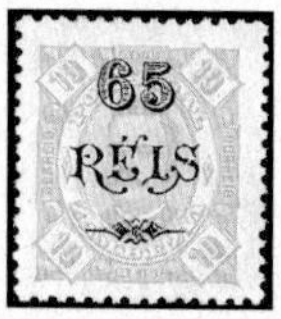

Stamps of 1894 Surcharged

1902 ***Perf. 11½, 12½***

36	A1	65r on 10r red vio	10.00	7.00
37	A1	65r on 15r choc	10.00	7.00
38	A1	65r on 20r lav	10.00	7.00
39	A1	65r on 300r bl, *sal*	10.00	7.00
40	A1	115r on 5r yel	10.00	7.00
41	A1	115r on 25r bl grn	10.00	7.00
42	A1	115r on 80r yel grn	10.00	7.00
43	A1	130r on 75r car	7.00	7.00
44	A1	130r on 150r car, *rose*	5.25	5.25
45	A1	400r on 50r lt bl	3.00	3.25
46	A1	400r on 100r brn, *buff*	3.00	3.50
47	A1	400r on 200r bl, *bl*	3.00	3.50

Same Surcharge on No. P1

48	N1	130r on 2½r brn	9.00	7.00
		Nos. 36-48 (13)	100.25	78.50

Stamps of 1898 Overprinted

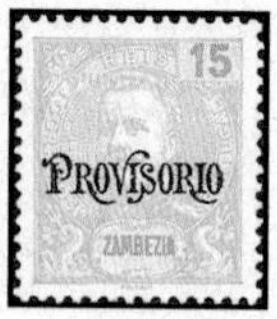

1902 ***Perf. 11½***

49	A2	15r brown	3.00	1.40
50	A2	25r sea green	3.00	1.40
51	A2	50r blue	3.00	1.40
52	A2	75r rose	8.00	3.75
		Nos. 49-52 (4)	17.00	7.95

No. 23 Surcharged in Black

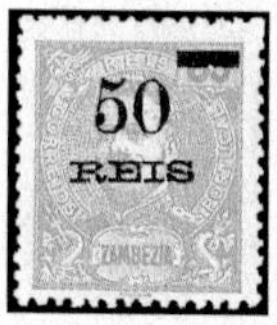

1905

53	A2	50r on 65r dull blue	6.50	4.00

Stamps of 1898-1903 Overprinted in Carmine or Green

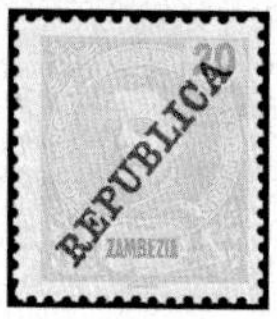

1911

54	A2	2½r gray	.35	.25
55	A2	5r orange	.35	.25
56	A2	10r light green	.40	.25
a.		Inverted overprint	15.00	12.50
57	A2	15r gray green	.40	.25
58	A2	20r gray violet	.50	.30
59	A2	25r carmine (G)	1.50	.50
60	A2	50r brown	.40	*.35*
61	A2	75r lilac	1.25	.90
62	A2	100r dk bl, *bl*	1.25	.90
63	A2	115r org brn, *pink*	1.25	.90
64	A2	130r brown, *straw*	1.25	.90
65	A2	200r red vio, *pnksh*	1.25	.90
66	A2	400r dull bl, *straw*	2.10	1.10
67	A2	500r blk & red, *bl*	2.10	1.10
68	A2	700r violet, *yelsh*	2.25	1.50
		Nos. 54-68 (15)	16.60	*10.35*

Stamps of 1902-05 Overprinted in Carmine or Green

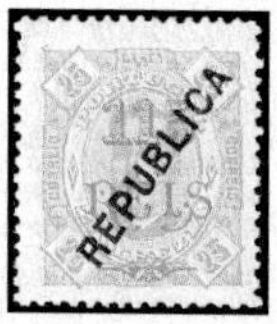

1914 **Without Gum**

72	A2	50r on 65r dl bl	*4,000.*	*1,200.*
73	A1	115r on 5r yellow	2.00	1.50
74	A1	115r on 25r bl grn	2.00	1.50
75	A1	115r on 80r yel grn	2.00	1.50
76	N1	130r on 2½r brn (G)	2.00	1.50
a.		Carmine overprint	22.50	22.50
77	A1	130r on 75r car	2.50	1.50
a.		Perf. 12½	5.50	7.00
78	A1	130r on 150r car, *rose*	2.50	1.50
79	A1	400r on 50r lt bl	3.00	3.00
a.		Perf. 12½	11.00	11.00
80	A1	400r on 100r brn, *buff*	3.00	2.50
81	A1	400r on 200r bl, *bl*	3.00	2.50

On Nos. 51-52

82	A2	50r blue	1.50	1.50
83	A2	75r rose	1.50	1.50
		Nos. 73-83 (11)	25.00	20.00

Preceding Issues Overprinted in Carmine

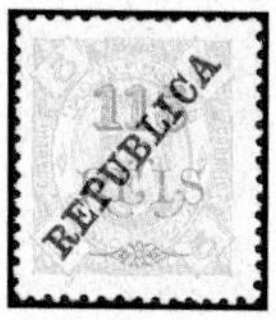

1915

On Surcharged Issue of 1902

84	A1	115r on 5r yellow	.85	.45
85	A1	115r on 25r bl grn	.85	.45
86	A1	115r on 80r lt grn	.85	.45
87	A1	130r on 75r carmine	.85	.45
a.		Perf. 12½	4.50	2.25
88	A1	130r on 150r car, *rose*	.85	.45
92	N1	130r on 2½r (down)	.85	.45

On Nos. 51, 53

93	A2	50r blue	.85	.50
a.		"Republica" inverted	15.00	15.00
94	A2	50r on 65r dull bl	3.50	*4.50*
		Nos. 84-94 (8)	9.45	*7.70*

Stamps of 1898-1903 Overprinted Locally in Carmine

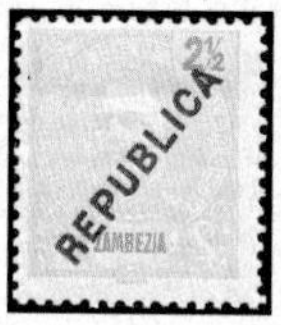

1917 **Without Gum**

95	A2	2½r gray	1.50	*3.00*
96	A2	5r orange	9.00	6.50
97	A2	10r light green	9.00	6.00
98	A2	15r gray green	8.00	6.50
99	A2	20r gray violet	9.00	6.50
100	A2	25r sea green	13.50	15.00
101	A2	100r blue, *blue*	5.00	2.75
102	A2	115r org brn, *pink*	5.00	2.75
103	A2	130r brown, *straw*	5.00	2.75
104	A2	200r red vio, *pnksh*	5.00	2.75
105	A2	400r dull bl, *straw*	5.00	3.50
106	A2	500r blk & red, *bl*	6.00	3.75
107	A2	700r vio, *yelsh*	10.00	5.25
		Nos. 95-107 (13)	91.00	67.00

NEWSPAPER STAMP

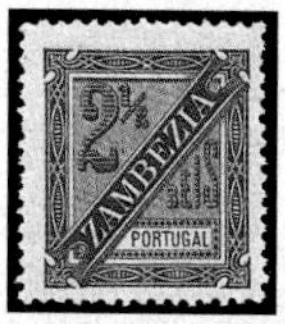

N1

1894 Unwmk. Typo. ***Perf. 12½***

P1	N1	2½r brown	.60	.35

For overprints and surcharges see Nos. 76, 92.

ZAMBIA

ˈzam-bē-ə

LOCATION — Southern Africa

GOVT. — Republic

AREA — 290,586 sq. mi.

POP. — 9,663,535 (1999 est.)

CAPITAL — Lusaka

The former British protectorate of Northern Rhodesia became an independent republic Oct. 24, 1964, taking the name Zambia. See Northern Rhodesia; see Rhodesia and Nyasaland.

12 Pence = 1 Shilling
20 Shillings = 1 Pound
100 Ngwee = 1 Kwacha (1968)

Catalogue values for all unused stamps in this country are for Never Hinged items.

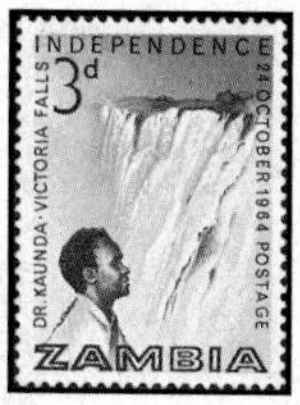

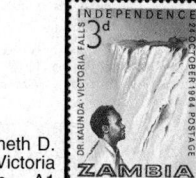

Pres. Kenneth D. Kaunda, Victoria Falls — A1

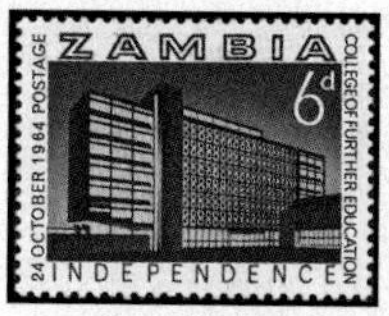

College of Further Education, Lusaka — A2

Perf. 14½x14, 14x14½

1964, Oct. 24 Photo. Unwmk.

1	A1	3p shown	.25	.25
2	A2	6p shown	.30	.25
3	A1	1sh3p Barotse dancer	.50	.30
		Nos. 1-3 (3)	1.05	.80

Zambia's independence, Oct. 24, 1964.

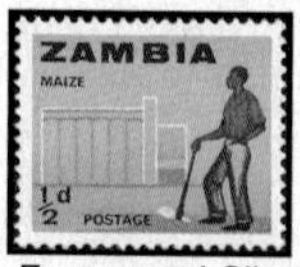

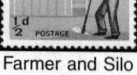

Farmer and Silo A3

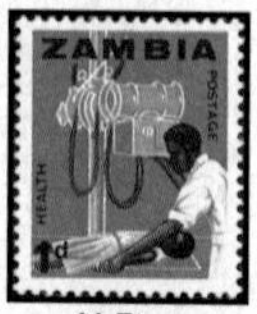

X-Ray Technician A4

Designs: 2p, Chinyau dancer. 3p, Woman picking cotton. 4p, Angoni bull. 6p, Communications by drum and teletype. 9p, Redwood blossoms and factory. 1sh, Night fishing on Lake Tanganyika. 1sh3p, Woman tobacco worker. 2sh, Tonga basket maker and child. 2sh6p, Elephants in Luangwa Valley Game Reserve. 5sh, Child and school. 10sh, Copper mining. £1, Makishi dancer.

1964, Oct. 24 Photo. ***Perf. 14½***

Size: 23x19mm, 19x23mm

4	A3	½p emerald, blk & red	.25	.25
5	A4	1p ultra, blk & brn	.25	.25
6	A4	2p orange, brn & red	.25	.25
7	A4	3p red & black	.25	.25
8	A3	4p orange & black	.25	.25

Perf. 13½x14½, 14½x13½

Size: 32x23mm, 23x32mm

9	A3	6p Prus grn, brn & org	.25	.25
10	A3	9p ultra, brn & dk car rose	.25	.25
11	A3	1sh blue, bis & blk	.25	.25
12	A4	1sh3p dk bl, ver, blk & yel	.25	.25
13	A4	2sh org, blk, brn & ultra	.30	.25
14	A3	2sh6p org yel & blk	.75	.40
15	A3	5sh emerald, blk & yel	1.20	.55
16	A3	10sh orange & blk	3.50	3.50
17	A4	£1 red, blk, brn & yel	2.60	3.50
		Nos. 4-17 (14)	10.60	10.45

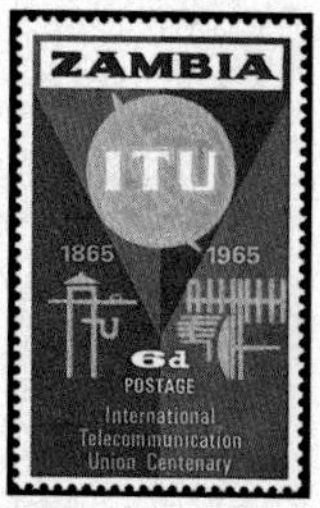

ITU Emblem, Old and New Communication Equipment — A5

1965, July 26 Photo. ***Perf. 14***

18	A5	6p brt lilac & gold	.25	.25
19	A5	2sh6p gray & gold	1.15	1.50

Cent. of the ITU.

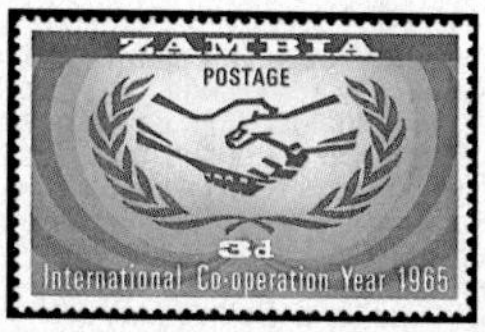

ICY Emblem A6

1965, July 26 ***Perf. 14***

20	A6	3p grnsh blue & gold	.25	.25
21	A6	1sh3p ultra & gold	.60	.65

International Cooperation Year, 1965.

Pres. Kaunda and State House, Lusaka — A7

Clematopsis — A8

Designs: 6p, Fireworks over Independence Stadium. 2sh6p, Tithonia diversifolia.

Perf. 13½x14½

1965, Oct. 18   Unwmk.
| 22 | A7 | 3p multicolored | .25 | .25 |
| 23 | A7 | 6p ind, yel & brt pink | .25 | .25 |

Perf. 14
24	A8	1sh3p pink, yel & brn	.25	.25
25	A8	2sh6p brt grn, dp org & brn	.25	.25
		Nos. 22-25 (4)	1.00	1.00

1st anniv. of independence, Oct. 24.

Inauguration of WHO Headquarters, Geneva — A9

1966, May 18   **Perf. 14**
| 26 | A9 | 3p rose brn, brt bl & gold | .25 | .25 |
| 27 | A9 | 1sh3p vio bl, brt bl & gold | 1.10 | 1.00 |

University of Zambia — A10

1966, July 12   **Photo.**   **Perf. 14**
| 28 | A10 | 3p brt green & gold | .25 | .25 |
| 29 | A10 | 1sh3p brt purple & gold | .30 | .25 |

University of Zambia opening, Mar. 17.

National Assembly Building — A11

1967, May 2   Unwmk.   **Perf. 14**
| 30 | A11 | 3p slate & bronze | .25 | .25 |
| 31 | A11 | 6p yellow grn & bronze | .30 | .25 |

Completion of National Assembly Building.

Lusaka Airport — A12

1967, Oct. 2   **Photo.**   **Perf. 13½x14½**
| 32 | A12 | 6p vio blue & bronze | .25 | .25 |
| 33 | A12 | 2sh6p brown & bronze | .75 | .75 |

Opening of Lusaka International Airport.

Symbols of Agriculture A13

Radio, Telephone and Television — A14

Designs: 4p, Emblem of Zambia Youth Service. 1sh, Map showing locations of Zambia coalfields. 1sh6p, Map showing Zambia-Tanzania Road.

Perf. 14½x13½, 13½x14½

1967, Oct. 23
34	A14	4p gray, red & gold	.25	.25
35	A13	6p lt vio bl, gold & blk	.25	.25
36	A14	9p dull blue, sil & blk	.30	.35
37	A14	1sh gold, red, blk & vio bl	.50	.25
38	A13	1sh6p bl grn, ultra, gold & blk	.75	1.25
		Nos. 34-38 (5)	2.05	2.35

Issued to publicize National Development.

Lusaka Cathedral — A15   Baobab Tree — A16

Designs: 3n, Zambia Airways plane. 5n, National Museum, Livingstone. 8n, Vimbuza dancer. 10n, Woman tobacco picker. 15n, Nudaurelia zambesina butterfly. 20n, Crowned cranes. 25n, Angoni warrior. 50n, Chokwe dancer. 1k, Railroad bridge, Kafue River. 2k, Eland.

Perf. 13½x14½, 14½x13½

1968, Jan. 16   **Photo.**
Size: 26x22mm, 22x26mm
39	A15	1n bronze & multi	.25	.25
a.		Booklet pane of 6	1.40	
b.		Booklet pane of 4	1.40	
40	A16	2n bronze & multi	.25	.25
41	A15	3n bronze & multi	.25	.25
a.		Booklet pane of 6	1.40	
b.		Booklet pane of 4	1.40	
42	A16	5n sepia & bronze	.25	.25
43	A16	8n bronze & multi	.25	.25
44	A16	10n bronze & multi	.25	.25

Size: 32x26mm, 26x32mm
45	A15	15n bronze & multi	2.50	.25
46	A16	20n bronze & multi	4.00	.25
47	A16	25n bronze & multi	.50	.25
48	A16	50n bronze, org & blk	.45	.25
49	A15	1k dk blue & brnz	4.00	.30
50	A15	2k copper & blk	3.00	1.25
		Nos. 39-50 (12)	15.95	4.05

Used values of Nos. 48-50 are for canceled-to-order stamps. Postally used examples sell for more.

Map of Zambia, Arrow Pointing to Ndola — A17

Perf. 14½x14

1968, June 29   **Photo.**   Unwmk.
| 51 | A17 | 15n brt green & gold | .35 | .35 |

Zambia Trade Fair at Ndola.

Children and Human Rights Flame — A18

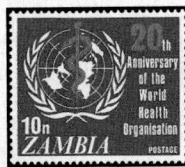

WHO Emblem A19

Children A20

Photogravure; Gold Impressed

1968, Oct. 23   **Perf. 14½x14**
52	A18	3n ultra, dk bl & gold	.30	.30
53	A19	10n brt violet & gold	.30	.30
54	A20	25n brt blue, blk & gold	.40	.60
		Nos. 52-54 (3)	1.00	1.20

Intl. Human Rights Year; 20th anniv. of WHO; 21st anniv. of UNICEF (25n).

Copper Miner — A21

Design: 25n, Worker poling furnace, horiz.

Perf. 14½x13½

1969, June 18   **Photo.**
| 55 | A21 | 3n dp violet & copper | .30 | .25 |
| 56 | A21 | 25n yellow, blk & copper | 1.25 | 1.10 |

50th anniv. of the ILO.

Map of Africa with Zambia — A22

10n, Waterbucks, Kafue National Park, horiz. 15n, Golden perch, Kasaba Bay, horiz. 25n, Carmine bee-eater, Luangwa Valley.

Perf. 13½x14, 14x13½

1969, Oct. 23   **Photo.**
57	A22	5n ultra, yel & copper	.25	.25
58	A22	10n copper & multi	.30	.25
59	A22	15n copper & multi	.55	.35
60	A22	25n copper & multi	1.40	1.40
		Nos. 57-60 (4)	2.50	2.25

International Year of African Tourism.

Nimbus III Weather Satellite — A23

1970, Mar. 23   **Litho.**   **Perf. 13x11**
| 61 | A23 | 15n multicolored | .65 | .65 |

Issued for World Meteorological Day.

"Clean Water" — A24

Designs: 15n, "Nutrition" (infant on scale). 25n, Children's immunization and Edward Jenner, M.D.

1970, July 4   **Litho.**   **Perf. 13x12½**
62	A24	3n multicolored	.25	.25
63	A24	15n multicolored	.55	.55
64	A24	25n multicolored	1.00	1.00
		Nos. 62-64 (3)	1.80	1.80

Issued to publicize preventive medicine and the "Under Five" children's clinics.

Mural by Gabriel Ellison A25

1970, Sept. 8   **Litho.**   **Perf. 14x14½**
| 65 | A25 | 15n multicolored | .55 | .55 |

Opening of the Conf. of Non-Aligned Nations in Mulungushi Hall (decorated with murals by Mrs. Ellison) in Zambia.

Ceremonial Axe — A26

Traditional Crafts: 5n, Clay pipe bowl with antelope head. 15n, Makishi mask, vert. 25n, The Kuomboka Ceremony (dancers and ceremonial boat).

1970, Nov. 30   **Litho.**   **Perf. 14x14½**
Size: 34x25mm
| 66 | A26 | 3n dp lil rose & multi | .25 | .25 |
| 67 | A26 | 5n dp org, blk & sepia | .25 | .25 |

Perf. 13x13½
Size: 30x45½mm
| 68 | A26 | 15n brt lil rose & multi | .60 | .60 |

Perf. 12½
Size: 71½x23½mm
69	A26	25n violet, blue & multi	.95	.95
a.		Souvenir sheet of 4, #66-69	10.50	10.50
		Nos. 66-69 (4)	2.05	2.05

Dag Hammarskjold and UN General Assembly — A27

Hammarskjold and: 10n, Downed plane. 15n, Dove with olive branch. 25n, Plaque and flowers.

1971, Sept. 18   **Perf. 13½**
70	A27	4n brown & multi	.25	.25
71	A27	10n yellow grn & multi	.25	.25
72	A27	15n blue & multi	.35	.35
73	A27	25n plum & multi	.55	.55
		Nos. 70-73 (4)	1.40	1.40

10th anniv. of the death of Dag Hammarskjold, (1905-61) Secretary-General of the UN, near Ndola, Zambia.

Red-Breasted Bream — A28

10n, Green-headed bream. 15n, Tiger fish.

1971, Dec. 10
74	A28	4n shown	.30	.30
75	A28	10n multicolored	.85	.80
76	A28	15n multicolored	2.00	1.10
		Nos. 74-76 (3)	3.15	2.20

Christmas.

Cheetah — A29

Soil Conservation A30

1972, Mar. 15   **Perf. 13½x14**
77	A29	4n shown	.25	.25
78	A29	10n Lechue	.55	.55

Perf. 14x13½
79	A30	15n Cape porcupine	.80	.85
80	A30	25n Elephant	2.00	1.40
		Nos. 77-80 (4)	3.60	3.05

Conservation Year.

1972, June 30 Litho. Perf. 14x13½

10n, Forest conservation. 15n, Water conservation (river view). 25n, Woman in corn field.

Size: 18½x45mm
81	A30	4n shown	.25	.25
82	A30	10n multicolored	.35	.35

Perf. 13½x14
83	A29	15n multicolored	.60	.60
84	A29	25n multicolored	1.10	1.10
		Nos. 81-84 (4)	2.30	2.30

Souvenir Sheet
85		Sheet of 4	10.00	13.50
a.	A30	10n Giraffe and zebra	1.40	1.90
b.	A30	10n Rhinoceros	1.40	1.90
c.	A30	10n Hippopotamus and deer	1.40	1.90
d.	A30	10n Lion	1.40	1.90

Conservation Year. Stamp size: 27x50mm.

1972, Sept. 22   **Perf. 13½x14**

4n, Zambian flowers. 10n, Citrus swallowtails and roses. 15n, Bee. 25n, Locusts in corn field.
All horizontal.

Size: 48x35mm
86	A30	4n multicolored	.75	.75
87	A30	10n multicolored	2.10	2.10
88	A30	15n multicolored	3.00	3.00
89	A30	25n multicolored	4.50	4.50
		Nos. 86-89 (4)	10.35	10.35

Conservation Year.

Mary and Joseph Going to Bethlehem — A31

9n, Holy Family. 15n, Adoration of the shepherds. 25n, Kings following the star.

1972, Dec. 1 Litho. Perf. 14
90	A31	4n shown	.25	.25
91	A31	9n multicolored	.25	.25
92	A31	15n multicolored	.25	.25
93	A31	25n multicolored	.35	.35
		Nos. 90-93 (4)	1.10	1.10

Christmas.

Broken Hill Man A32

Designs: 4n, Oudenodon and rubidgea (artist's conception; vert.). 10n, Zambiasaurus. 15n, Skull of Luangwa Drysdalli. 25n, Glossoptoris (seed).

Perf. 14x13½, 14
1973, Feb. 1   **Litho.**
Size: 29x45mm
94	A32	4n org ver & multi	.65	.35

Size: 37½x21mm
95	A32	9n org ver & multi	.95	.75
96	A32	10n apple grn & multi	1.10	.95
97	A32	15n lilac & multi	1.50	1.25
98	A32	25n orange brn & multi	2.40	2.40
		Nos. 94-98 (5)	6.60	5.70

Fossils from Luangwa area (except 9n), over 200 million years old.

Meeting of Stanley and Livingstone at Ujiji — A33

4n, Livingstone, the missionary. 9n, Livingstone at Victoria Falls. 10n, Livingstone stopping slave traders. 15n, Livingstone, the physician. 25n, Portrait & tree in Chitumbu, marking burial place of heart.

1973, May 1   **Perf. 13x13½**
99	A33	3n multicolored	.25	.25
100	A33	4n multicolored	.25	.25
101	A33	9n multicolored	.40	.40
102	A33	10n multicolored	.45	.45
103	A33	15n multicolored	.70	.70
104	A33	25n multicolored	1.10	1.10
		Nos. 99-104 (6)	3.15	3.15

Dr. David Livingstone (1813-73), medical missionary and explorer.

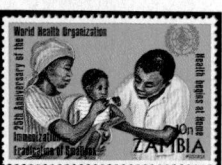

Parliamentary Mace — A34

1973, Sept. 24 Litho. Perf. 13½x14
105	A34	9n tan & multi	.40	.40
106	A34	15n gray & multi	.75	.75
107	A34	25n brt green & multi	1.00	1.00
		Nos. 105-107 (3)	2.15	2.15

Third Commonwealth Conference of Speakers and Presiding Officers, Lusaka.

Vaccination — A35

WHO Emblem and: 4n, Mother washing infant, vert. 9n, Nurse weighing infant, vert. 15n, Child eating cereal and fruit.

1973, Oct. 16   **Litho.**   **Perf. 14**
108	A35	4n blue & multi	57.50	40.00
109	A35	9n orange & multi	.30	.30
110	A35	10n brt grn & multi	.40	.40
111	A35	15n violet & multi	.50	.50
		Nos. 108-111 (4)	58.70	41.20

WHO, 25th anniv.

A36

A37

Birth of the Second Republic: 4n, UNIP flag. 9n, United National Independence Party Headquarters, Lusaka. 10n, Army band. 15n, Women dancing and singing. 25n, President's parliamentary chair.

1973, Dec. 13 Litho. Perf. 14x13½
112	A36	4n multicolored	12.00	7.50
113	A36	9n multicolored	.25	.25
114	A36	10n multicolored	.30	.30
115	A36	15n multicolored	.45	.45
116	A37	25n multicolored	.75	.75
		Nos. 112-116 (5)	13.75	9.25

Pres. Kaunda and his Home During Struggle for Independence — A38

4n, Pres. Kaunda at Mulungushi. 15n, Pres. Kaunda holding torch of freedom.

1974, Apr. 28 Litho. Perf. 14½x14
117	A38	4n multi, vert.	.50	.50
118	A38	9n multi	.60	.60
119	A38	15n multi	.90	.90
		Nos. 117-119 (3)	2.00	2.00

50th birthday of Pres. Kenneth Kaunda.

Nakambla Sugar Estate — A39

Designs: 4n, Local market. 9n, Kapiri glass factory. 10n, Kafue hydroelectric plant. 15n, Kafue Bridge. 25n, Conference of Non-aligned Nations, Lusaka, 1970.

1974, Oct. 24 Litho. Perf. 13½x14
120	A39	3n multicolored	.25	.25
121	A39	4n multicolored	.25	.25
122	A39	9n multicolored	.30	.30
123	A39	10n multicolored	.35	.35
124	A39	15n multicolored	.50	.50
125	A39	25n multicolored	.80	.80
		Nos. 120-125 (6)	2.45	2.45

Souvenir Sheet
126		Sheet of 4	6.00	10.00
a.	A39	15n Academic education	1.20	1.90
b.	A39	15n Teacher Training College	1.20	1.90
c.	A39	15n Technical education	1.20	1.90
d.	A39	15n University of Zambia	1.20	1.90

10th anniversary of indepencence.

Mobile Post Office — A40

UPU Emblem and: 9n, Rural mail service by Zambia Airways. 10n, Modern Post Office, Chipata. 15n, Ndola Postal Training Center.

1974, Nov. 15
127	A40	4n multicolored	.25	.25
128	A40	9n multicolored	.25	.25
129	A40	10n multicolored	.25	.25
130	A40	15n multicolored	.30	.30
		Nos. 127-130 (4)	1.05	1.05

Centenary of Universal Postal Union.

Radar by Day A41

1974, Dec. 16
131	A41	4n shown	.25	.25
132	A41	9n Radar by night	.45	.40
133	A41	15n Radar at dawn	.75	.70
134	A41	25n Radar station	1.20	1.20
		Nos. 131-134 (4)	2.65	2.55

Inauguration of Mwembeshi Earth Station, Oct. 21, 1974.

Rhinoceros and Calf — A42

Peanut Harvest — A43

2n, Guinea fowl. 3n, Zambian dancers. 4n, Fish eagle. 5n, Bridge, Victoria Falls. 8n, Sitatunga. 9n, Elephant, Kasaba Bay Resort. 10n, Giant pangolin. 15n, Zambezi River source, Monument. 25n, Tobacco field. 50n, Flying doctor service. 1k, Lady Ross's touraco. 2k, Village scene.

1975, Jan. 3 Litho. Perf. 13½x14
135	A42	1n shown	.55	.55
136	A42	2n multicolored	.55	.55
137	A42	3n multicolored	.25	.40
138	A42	4n multicolored	1.00	.40
139	A42	5n multicolored	1.00	1.00
140	A42	8n multicolored	1.00	.90
141	A42	9n multicolored	1.25	.85
142	A42	10n multicolored	.25	.25

Perf. 13
143	A43	15n multicolored	.35	.25
144	A43	20n shown	1.00	1.40
145	A43	25n multicolored	1.60	.65
146	A43	50n multicolored	4.00	3.00
147	A43	1k multicolored	5.75	2.50
148	A43	2k multicolored	4.00	6.00
		Nos. 135-148 (14)	22.55	18.55

For surcharges see #188-191, 319.

Map of Namibia
(South-West
Africa) — A44

1975, Aug. 26   Litho.   Perf. 14x13½
149 A44 4n green & dk green   .25 .25
150 A44 9n dk blue & gray bl   .25 .25
151 A44 15n yellow & orange   .35 .55
152 A44 25n orange & dp orange   .40 1.10
    Nos. 149-152 (4)   1.25 2.15
Namibia Day.

Sprinkler Irrigation — A45

Designs: 9n, Sprinkler irrigation over rows of vegetables. 15n, Furrow irrigation.

1975, Dec. 16   Litho.   Perf. 13
153 A45 4n multicolored   .25 .25
154 A45 9p multicolored   .35 .50
155 A45 15n multicolored   .60 1.10
    Nos. 153-155 (3)   1.20 1.85
Intl. Commission on Irrigation and Drainage, 25th anniv.

Julbernardia Paniculata — A46

Trees of Zambia: 4n, Sycamore fig. 9n, Baikiaea plurijuga. 10n, Colophospermum. 15n, Uapaca kirkiana. 25n, Pterocarpus angolensis.

1976, Mar. 22   Litho.   Perf. 13
156 A46 3n multicolored   .30 .30
157 A46 4n multicolored   .30 .30
158 A46 9n multicolored   .45 .45
159 A46 10n multicolored   .45 .45
160 A46 15n multicolored   .70 .70
161 A46 25n multicolored   .85 .85
    Nos. 156-161 (6)   3.05 3.05
World Forestry Day, Mar. 21.

TAZARA Passenger Train — A47

9n, Train carrying copper. 10n, Clearing the bush. #164, Train carrying heavy machinery. #166b, Track laying. 20n, Reinforcing railroad track. #165, Train carrying various goods. #166d, Completed tracks.

1976, Dec. 10   Litho.   Perf. 13
162 A47 4n multicolored   .25 .25
163 A47 9n multicolored   .55 .55
164 A47 15n multicolored   .90 .90
165 A47 25n multicolored   1.50 1.50
    Nos. 162-165 (4)   3.20 3.20

Souvenir Sheet
Perf. 13½x14
166   Sheet of 4   3.75 3.75
  a. A47 10n multicolored   .35 .35
  b. A47 15n multicolored   .55 .50
  c. A47 20n multicolored   .65 .55
  d. A47 25n multicolored   .90 .70
Completion of Tanzania-Zambia Railroad.

Kayowe Dance — A48

1977, Jan. 18   Litho.   Perf. 13½x14
167 A48 4n shown   .25 .25
168 A48 9n Lilombola dance   .25 .25
169 A48 15n Initiation ceremony .40 .40
170 A48 25n Munkhwele dance   .50 .50
    Nos. 167-170 (4)   1.40 1.40
2nd World Black and African Festival, Lagos, Nigeria, Jan. 15-Feb. 12.

Grimwood's
Longclaw — A49

Birds of Zambia: 9n, Shelley's sunbird. 10n, Black-cheeked lovebird. 15n, Locust finch. 20n, White-chested tinkerbird. 25n, Chaplin's barbet.

1977, July 1   Litho.   Perf. 14½
171 A49 4n multicolored   .40 .25
172 A49 9n multicolored   .65 .60
173 A49 10n multicolored   .80 .60
174 A49 15n multicolored   1.60 1.90
175 A49 20n multicolored   1.75 2.25
176 A49 25n multicolored   2.00 2.75
    Nos. 171-176 (6)   7.20 8.35

Children
Playing
with Blocks
A50

Designs: 9n, Women of various races dancing in circle. 15n, Black and white girls with young bird.

1977, Oct. 20   Litho.   Perf. 14x14½
177 A50 4n multicolored   .25 .25
178 A50 9n multicolored   .25 .25
179 A50 15n multicolored   .35 .35
    Nos. 177-179 (3)   .85 .85
Combat racism and racial discrimination.

"Glory to
God in the
Highest"
A51

Christmas: 9n, Nativity. 10n, Three Kings and camel. 15n, Presentation at the Temple.

1977, Dec. 20   Litho.   Perf. 14
180 A51 4n multicolored   .25 .25
181 A51 9n multicolored   .25 .25
182 A51 10n multicolored   .25 .25
183 A51 15n multicolored   .25 .25
    Nos. 180-183 (4)   1.00 1.00

Elephant
and Road
Check
A52

Designs: 18n, Waterbuck and Kafue River boat patrol. 28n, Warthog and helicopter surveillance of National Parks. 32n, Cheetah and armed wildlife guards in Parks and Game Management Areas.

1978, Aug. 1   Litho.   Perf. 14x14½
184 A52 8n multicolored   .30 .30
185 A52 18n multicolored   .60 .60
186 A52 28n multicolored   .95 .95
187 A52 32n multicolored   1.15 1.15
    Nos. 184-187 (4)   3.00 3.00
Anti-poaching Campaign of Zambia Wildlife Conservation Society, Aug. 1978.

**Nos. 141, 137, 145 and 143 Srchd.
with New Value and 2 Bars**
1979, Mar. 15   Perf. 13½x14, 13
188 A42 8n on 9n multi   .60 .25
189 A42 10n on 3n multi   .25 .25
190 A43 18n on 25n multi   .25 .25
191 A43 28n on 15n multi   .25 .25
    Nos. 188-191 (4)   1.35 1.00

Kayowe
Dance
A53

Designs: 32n, Kutambala dance. 42n, Chitwansombo drummers. 58n, Lilombola dance.

1979, Aug. 1
192 A53 18n multicolored   .30 .30
193 A53 32n multicolored   .35 .35
194 A53 42n multicolored   .35 .35
195 A53 58n multicolored   .50 .50
    Nos. 192-195 (4)   1.50 1.50
Commonwealth Summit Conf., Lusaka, Aug. 1-9.

"Why the Zebra is
Hornless" — A54

Children's Stories: 18n, Kalulu and the Tug of War. 42n, How the Tortoise got his Shell. 58n, Kalulu and the Lion.

1979, Sept. 21   Litho.   Perf. 14
196 A54 18n multicolored   .25 .25
197 A54 32n multicolored   .40 .55
198 A54 42n multicolored   .45 .75
199 A54 58n multicolored   .55 1.00
  a. Souvenir sheet of 4, #196-199 2.50 2.50
    Nos. 196-199 (4)   1.65 2.55
International Year of the Child.

Girls of
Different
Races
Holding
Emblem
A55

Anti-Apartheid Year (1978): 32n, Boys and toy car. 42n, Infants and butterfly. 58n, Children and microscope.

1979, Nov. 16   Litho.   Perf. 14½x15
200 A55 18n multicolored   .25 .25
201 A55 32n multicolored   .35 .35
202 A55 42n multicolored   .55 .55
203 A55 58n multicolored   .70 .70
    Nos. 200-203 (4)   1.85 1.85

Hill,
Zambia
No. 13
A56

Hill and: 32n, Mailman & bicycle. 42n, No. Rhodesia #75. 58n, Mailman & oxcart.

1979, Dec. 20   Litho.   Perf. 14½
204 A56 18n multicolored   .30 .30
205 A56 32n multicolored   .40 .50
206 A56 42n multicolored   .40 .65
207 A56 58n multicolored   .45 1.10
  a. Souvenir sheet of 4, #204-207 2.40 3.25
    Nos. 204-207 (4)   1.55 2.50
Sir Rowland Hill (1795-1879), originator of penny postage.

**Nos. 204-207a Overprinted
"LONDON 1980"**
1980, Mar 6   Litho.   Perf. 15
208 A56 18n multicolored   .25 .40
209 A56 32n multicolored   .30 .55
210 A56 42n multicolored   .40 .70
211 A56 58n multicolored   .60 .85
  a. Souvenir sheet of 4   3.00 4.00
    Nos. 208-211 (4)   1.55 2.50
London 80 Intl. Stamp Exhib., May 6-14.

Anniverary Emblem on Map of
Zambia — A57

1980, June 18   Litho.   Perf. 14
212 A57 8n multicolored   .25 .25
213 A57 32n multicolored   .45 .45
214 A57 42n multicolored   .55 .55
215 A57 58n multicolored   .70 .70
  a. Souvenir sheet of 4, #212-215 2.40 2.40
    Nos. 212-215 (4)   1.95 1.95
Rotary International, 75th anniversary.

Running
A58

1980, July 19   Litho.   Perf. 13
216 A58 18n shown   .25 .25
217 A58 32n Boxing   .45 .45
218 A58 42n Soccer   .55 .55
219 A58 58n Swimming   .75 .75
  a. Souvenir sheet of 4, #216-219 2.75 2.75
    Nos. 216-219 (4)   2.00 2.00
22nd Summer Olympic Games, Moscow, July 19-Aug. 3.

Zaddach's Forester — A59

1980, Sept. 22
220 A59 18n shown   .40 .25
221 A59 32n Northern highflier .65 .60
222 A59 42n Zambezi skipper   .95 .95
223 A59 58n Modest blue   1.30 2.10
  a. Souvenir sheet of 4, #220-223 8.00 8.00
    Nos. 220-223 (4)   3.30 3.90

Coat of
Arms — A60

1980, Sept. 27   Litho.   Perf. 14½
224 A60 18n multicolored   .25   .25
225 A60 32n multicolored   .40   .45
226 A60 42n multicolored   .50   .65
227 A60 58n multicolored   .60   1.25
    Nos. 224-227 (4)   1.75   2.60

26th Commonwealth Parliamentary Association Conference, Lusaka.

A61

Nativity and St. Francis of Assisi (stained glass window), Ndola Church.

1980, Oct.   Litho.   Perf. 14
228 A61   8n multicolored   .25   .25
229 A61 28n multicolored   .60   .90
230 A61 32n multicolored   .60   .90
231 A61 42n multicolored   .80   1.25
    Nos. 228-231 (4)   2.25   3.30

Christmas and 50th anniv. of Catholic Church in Copperbelt (central Zambia).

Trichilia
Emetica
Seed
Pods,
Musikili
A62

Seed Pods: 18n, Afzelia quanzensis, Mupapa. 28n, Erythrina abyssinica, Mulunguti. 32n, Combretum collinum, Mulama.

1981, Mar. 21   Litho.   Perf. 14
232 A62   8n shown   .25   .25
233 A62 18n multicolored   .30   .35
234 A62 28n multicolored   .35   .70
235 A62 32n multicolored   .35   1.15
    Nos. 232-235 (4)   1.25   2.45

World Forestry Day.

ITU
Emblem — A63

Designs: 18n, 32n, WHO emblem.

1981, May 15   Litho.   Perf. 14½
236 A63   8n multicolored   .50   .50
237 A63 18n multicolored   .65   .65
238 A63 28n multicolored   .75   .75
239 A63 32n multicolored   .85   .85
    Nos. 236-239 (4)   2.75   2.75

13th World Telecommunications Day (8n, 28n).

Mask Maker — A64

2n, Blacksmiths. 5n, Potter. 8n, Straw basket fishing. 10n, Roof thatching. 12n, Picking mushrooms ('83). 18n, Millet grinding. 28n, Royal Barge paddler. 30n, Makishi tightrope dancer. 35n, Tonga-ila granary, house. 42n, Cattle herding. 50n, Traditional healer. 75n, Carrying water jugs ('83). 1k, Grinding corn ('83). 2k, Woman smoking pipe.

1981-83
240 A64   1n shown   .25   .25
241 A64   2n multicolored   .25   .25
242 A64   5n multicolored   .25   .25
243 A64   8n multicolored   .25   .25
244 A64 10n multicolored   .25   .25
244A A64 12n multicolored   3.50   2.75
245 A64 18n multicolored   .50   .25
246 A64 28n multicolored   .70   .25
247 A64 30n multicolored   .70   .25
248 A64 35n multicolored   .75   .25
249 A64 42n multicolored   .75   1.50
             Perf. 14
             Size: 37x25mm
250 A64 50n multicolored   .75   .25
251 A64 75n multicolored   .75   .90
252 A64   1k multicolored   .75   .90
253 A64   2k multicolored   .75   .90
    Nos. 240-253 (15)   11.15   9.45

For surcharges see Nos. 358, 372, 499-506, 596.

Kankobele — A65

Designs: Traditional musical instruments.

1981, Sept. 30   Litho.   Perf. 14½
254 A65   8n shown   .45   .25
255 A65 18n Inshingili   .55   .45
256 A65 28n Ilimba   .80   1.40
257 A65 32n Bango   .80   1.60
    Nos. 254-257 (4)   2.60   3.70

Bornite — A66

Designs: Rocks and minerals.

1982, Jan. 5   Litho.   Perf. 14
258 A66   8n Banded Ironstone   1.30   .30
259 A66 18n Cobaltocalcite   2.60   1.10
260 A66 28n Amazonite   3.50   3.00
261 A66 32n Tourmaline   3.75   4.00
262 A66 42n Uranium ore   4.00   5.25
    Nos. 258-262 (5)   15.15 13.65

1982, July 1   Litho.   Perf. 14
263 A66   8n shown   1.05   .35
264 A66 18n Chalcopyrite   2.50   1.40
265 A66 28n Malachite   3.00   3.75
266 A66 32n Azurite   3.00   3.75
267 A66 42n Vanadinite   3.75   4.50
    Nos. 263-267 (5)   13.30 13.75

Scouting
Year
A67

8n, Scouts, flag. 18n, Baden-Powell. 28n, Horned buffalo, patrol pennant. 1k, Eagle, conservation badge.

1982, Mar. 30   Litho.   Perf. 14
268 A67   8n multicolored   .35   .35
269 A67 18n multicolored   .35   .35
270 A67 28n multicolored   .35   .35
271 A67   1k multicolored   2.10   2.60
  a.   Souvenir sheet of 4, #268-271 4.75   5.50
    Nos. 268-271 (4)   3.15   3.65

Drilling Rig,
1926
A68

Steam locomotives.

1983, Jan. 26   Perf. 14x14½
272 A68   8n shown   .55   .30
273 A68 18n Class B6, 1910   .85   .85
274 A68 28n Borsig engine, 1925 1.35   2.00
275 A68 32n 7th class, 1900   1.75   2.50
    Nos. 272-275 (4)   4.50   5.65

Commonwealth Day — A68a

1983, Mar. 10   Litho.   Perf. 14
276 A68a 12n Cotton picking   .25   .25
277 A68a 18n Miners   .25   .25
278 A68a 28n Ritual pot, dancers .25   .35
279 A68a   1k Victoria Falls, purple-crested lorie 2.75   3.75
    Nos. 276-279 (4)   3.50   4.60

Local
Flowers — A69

1983, May 26   Litho.   Perf. 14
280 A69 12n Eulophia cucullata   .25   .25
281 A69 28n Kigelia africana   .45   .60
282 A69 35n Protea gaguedi   .55   .75
283 A69 50n Leonotis nepotifolia 1.05   2.25
  a.   Souvenir sheet of 4, #280-283,
       perf. 12x12½   2.75   4.00
    Nos. 280-283 (4)   2.30   3.85

Thornicroft's Giraffes — A70

28n, Cookson's wildebeest. 35n, Black lechwe. 1k, Yellow-backed duiker.

1983, July 21   Litho.   Perf. 14
284 A70 12n shown   .65   .65
285 A70 28n multicolored   .85   .85
286 A70 35n multicolored   1.20   1.20
287 A70   1k multicolored   2.40   3.25
    Nos. 284-287 (4)   5.10   5.95

Tiger Fish
A71

1983, Sept. 29   Litho.   Perf. 14
288 A71 12n shown   .55   .25
289 A71 28n Silver Barbel   .85   .70
290 A71 35n Spotted Squeaker   .95   2.00
291 A71 38n Red Breasted
             Bream   1.10   2.00
    Nos. 288-291 (4)   3.45   4.95

For surcharge see No. 597.

Christmas — A72

1983, Dec. 12   Litho.   Perf. 14x14½
292 A72 12n Annunciation   .25   .25
293 A72 28n Shepherds   .30   .30
294 A72 35n Three Kings   .35   .75
295 A72 38n Flight into Egypt   .40   1.00
    Nos. 292-295 (4)   1.30   2.30

40th Anniv.
of Intl. Civil
Aviation
Org. — A73

1984, Jan. 26   Litho.   Perf. 14
296 A73 12n Boeing 737, 1983   .25   .25
297 A73 28n Beaver, 1954   .45   .45
298 A73 35n Short Solent Flying
             Boat, 1948   .55   .55
299 A73   1k DH-66, 1931   1.75   2.50
    Nos. 296-299 (4)   3.00   3.75

60th
Birthday of
Pres.
Kaunda
A74

12n, Receiving greetings. 28n, Swearing in, 1983, vert. 60n, Planting cherry tree. 1k, Opening Natl. Assembly, vert.

Perf. 14½x14, 14x14½
1984, Apr. 28   Litho.
300 A74 12n multicolored   .30   .30
301 A74 28n multicolored   .45   .45
302 A74 60n multicolored   .90   2.00
303 A74   1k multicolored   1.10   2.50
    Nos. 300-303 (4)   2.75   5.25

1984 Summer
Olympics — A75

1984, July 18   Litho.   Perf. 14
304 A75 12n Soccer   .25   .25
305 A75 28n Running   .50   .50
306 A75 35n Hurdles   .55   .65
307 A75 50n Boxing   .75   1.25
    Nos. 304-307 (4)   2.05   2.65

Reptiles
A76

1984, Sept. 5   Litho.   Perf. 14
308 A76 12n Gabon viper   .35   .30
309 A76 28n Chameleon   .65   .55
310 A76 35n Nile crocodile   .75   .65

311 A76 1k Blue-headed agama 1.75 2.25
  a. Souvenir sheet of 4, #308-311 4.75 4.75
    Nos. 308-311 (4) 3.50 3.75

20th Anniv. of Independence — A77

1984, Oct. 22 Litho. *Perf. 14*
312 A77 12n Pres. Kaunda,
         Mulungushi Rock .30 .30
313 A77 28n Freedom Statue .40 .50
314 A77 1k Produce 1.30 2.00
    Nos. 312-314 (3) 2.00 2.80

Local Mushrooms
A78

12n, Amanita flammeola. 28n, Amanita zambiana. 32n, Termitomyces letestui. 75n, Cantharellus miniatescens.

1984, Dec. 12 Litho. *Perf. 14x14½*
315 A78 12n multicolored 1.25 1.25
316 A78 28n multicolored 1.35 1.35
317 A78 32n multicolored 2.10 2.10
318 A78 75n multicolored 4.00 4.00
    Nos. 315-318 (4) 8.70 8.70

For surcharge see No. 600.

No. 146 Surcharged with New Value and Two Bars

1985, Mar. 5 Litho. *Perf. 13½*
319 A43 5k on 50n multi 2.50 3.00

Primates
A79

1985, Apr. 25 Litho. *Perf. 14*
320 A79 12n Chacma baboon .60 .60
321 A79 20n Moloney's monkey .80 .80
322 A79 45n Blue monkey 1.75 1.75
323 A79 1k Vervet monkey 2.60 3.25
    Nos. 320-323 (4) 5.75 6.40

For surcharge see No. 604.

SADCC,
5th Anniv.
A80

1985, July 9 Litho. *Perf. 14*
324 A80 20n Map .80 .80
325 A80 45n Mining 2.10 2.10
326 A80 1k Mulungushi Hall 2.10 2.60
    Nos. 324-326 (3) 5.00 5.50

Southern African Development Coordination Conference.
For surcharge see No. 605.

Queen Mother, 85th Birthday — A81

25n, Portrait in blue, age 80. 45n, Queen Consort at Clarence House, 1963. 55n, With Elizabeth II and Princess Margaret. 5k, With royal family, christening of Prince Henry, 1984.

1985, Aug. 2
327 A81 25n multi, vert. .25 .25
328 A81 45n multi, vert. .25 .25
329 A81 55n multi .25 .25
330 A81 5k multi 1.25 2.00
    Nos. 327-330 (4) 2.00 2.75

For surcharges see Nos. 401, 406, 410, 414, 595, 606, 611.

National Anniversaries — A81a

#330A, Pres. Kenneth Kaunda, Mulungushi Rock. #330B, Kaunda, agricultural products. #330C, Freedom statue, flags.

Die Cut Perf. 10
1985, Oct. 23   Embossed
330A-330C A81a 5k gold 18.00 18.00

United National Independence Party, 26th anniv. (No. 330A); Independence, 20th anniv. (Nos. 330B-330C).

Postal and Telecommunications Corp., 10th Anniv. — A82

20n, Lusaka P.O., 1958. 45n, Livingstone P.O., 1950. 55n, Kalomo P.O., 1902. 5k, Transcontinental Telegraph, 1900.

1985, Dec. 12   *Perf. 13½x13*
331 A82 20n multicolored .60 .60
332 A82 45n multicolored .90 .90
333 A82 55n multicolored 1.00 1.00
334 A82 5k multicolored 3.25 4.25
    Nos. 331-334 (4) 5.75 6.75

For surcharges see Nos. 590-593.

UN, 40th Anniv. — A83

1985, Dec. 19   *Perf. 14*
335 A83 20n Boy in cornfield .35 .35
336 A83 45n Emblem .60 .60
337 A83 1k Pres. Kaunda, 1970 1.15 1.50
338 A83 2k Charter signing,
         1945 1.75 2.25
    Nos. 335-338 (4) 3.85 4.70

For surcharges see #594, 607.

Beetles
A84

35n, Mylabris tricolor. 1k, Phasgonocnema melanianthe. 1.70k, Amaurodes passerinii. 5k, Ranzania petersiana.

1986, Mar. 20
339 A84 35n multicolored .25 .25
340 A84 1k multicolored .40 .45
341 A84 1.70k multicolored .65 .75
342 A84 5k multicolored 2.10 2.25
    Nos. 339-342 (4) 3.40 3.70

For surcharges see #609, 612.

Common Design Types
pictured following the introduction.

Queen Elizabeth II 60th Birthday
Common Design Type

Designs: 35n, At the Flower Ball, Savoy Hotel, London, 1951. 1.25k, With Prince Andrew at Lusaka Airport, Commonwealth Conf., 1979. 1.70k, With Dr. Kaunda observing natl. anthem. 1.95k, Wearing Queen Mary tiara, state visit to Luxembourg, 1976. 5k, Visiting Crown Agents' offices, 1983.

1986, Apr. 21 Wmk. 384 *Perf. 14*
343 CD337 35n scar, blk & sil .25 .25
344 CD337 1.25k ultra & multi .30 .30
345 CD337 1.70k grn, blk & sil .35 .35
346 CD337 1.95k vio & multi .35 .35
347 CD337 5k rose vio & multi .50 .50
    Nos. 343-347 (5) 1.75 1.75

For surcharges see Nos. 402, 405, 407, 411, 415.

Royal Wedding Issue, 1986
Common Design Type

Designs: 1.70k, Sarah Ferguson kissing Prince Andrew. 5k, Andrew in informal dress.

1986, July 23 Litho. *Perf. 14*
348 CD338 1.70k multicolored .30 .30
349 CD338 5k multicolored .80 1.00

1986 World Cup Soccer Championships, Mexico — A85

Various soccer plays.

1986, June 27 Litho. *Perf. 14½*
350 A85 35n multicolored .90 .90
351 A85 1.25k multicolored 2.00 2.00
352 A85 1.70k multicolored 2.40 2.40
353 A85 5k multicolored 3.50 3.50
    Nos. 350-353 (4) 8.80 8.80

For surcharges see Nos. 403, 408, 412, 416.

Halley's Comet
A86

Designs: 1.25k, Edmond Halley (1656-1742), by Henry Pegram. 1.70k, Giotto space probe approaching comet. 2k, Youth, astronomer. 5k, Halley's map of the southern constellations.

1986, July 4
354 A86 1.25k multicolored .90 .90
355 A86 1.70k multicolored 1.05 1.05
356 A86 2k multicolored 1.50 1.50
357 A86 5k multicolored 3.00 3.00
    Nos. 354-357 (4) 6.45 6.45

For surcharges see Nos. 404, 409, 413, 417.

#244A Surcharged in Light Red Brown
1986, July Litho. *Perf. 14½*
358 A64 20n on 12n multi 15.00 .50

Christmas
A87

Children's drawings.

1986, Dec. 15 Litho. *Perf. 14*
359 A87 35n Nativity .40 .40
360 A87 1.25k Magi 1.40 1.40
361 A87 1.75k Nativity 1.75 1.75
362 A87 5k Angel, house, tree 3.50 3.50
    Nos. 359-362 (4) 7.05 7.05

For surcharges see #602, 608.

Tazara Railroad, 10th Anniv. A88

Locomotive traveling various railway lines.

1986, Dec. 22
363 A88 35n Overpass,
         Kasama .25 .25
364 A88 1.25k Tunnel 21 vicinity .40 .40
365 A88 1.70k Tunnels 6-7 .55 .55
366 A88 5k Mpika Station
         grade separation 1.05 1.05
    Nos. 363-366 (4) 2.25 2.25

University of Zambia
A89

Designs: 35n, Pres. Kaunda shaking council member's hand. 1.25k, University crest, vert. 1.60k, University statue. 5k, Kaunda laying university building cornerstone, vert.

1987, Jan. 27 Litho. *Perf. 14*
367 A89 35n multicolored .35 .35
368 A89 1.25k multicolored .75 .75
369 A89 1.60k multicolored .85 .85
370 A89 5k multicolored 3.00 4.25
    Nos. 367-370 (4) 4.95 6.20

No. 137 Surcharged in Blue
1987   *Perf. 14½*
372 A64 25n on 8n multi .65 .45

Municipal Arms — A90

1987, Mar. 26   *Perf. 14*
373 A90 35n Kitwe .25 .25
374 A90 1.25k Ndola .30 .30
375 A90 1.70k Lusaka .40 .40
376 A90 20k Livingstone 3.00 3.00
    Nos. 373-376 (4) 3.95 3.95

For surcharge see No. 603.

Birds — A91

25n, Long-toed fluff tail. 30n, Miombo pied barbet. 35n, Black-and-rufous swallow. 50n, Slaty egret. 1k, Bradfield's hornbill. 1.25k, Margaret's batis. 1.60k, Red-and-blue sunbird. 1.70k, Boehm's bee-eater. 1.95k, Gorgeous bush shrike. 2k, Shoebill. 5k, Taita falcon.

1987-88   *Perf. 11x13*
    Size: 20x25½mm
377 A91 25n multicolored 3.50 3.50
378 A91 30n multicolored .30 .30
379 A91 35n multicolored 3.50 3.50

Size: 25x38½mm
Perf. 14

380	A91	50n multicolored	.30	.30
381	A91	1k multicolored	3.50	3.50
382	A91	1.25k multicolored	3.50	3.50
383	A91	1.60k multicolored	3.50	3.50
384	A91	1.70k multicolored	3.75	3.75
385	A91	1.95k multicolored	3.75	3.75
386	A91	2k multicolored	.50	.50
387	A91	5k multicolored	4.50	4.50
		Nos. 377-387 (11)	30.60	30.60

Surcharged

No. 390   No. 392

No. 388, Yellow swamp warbler. No. 389, Olive-flanked robin.

Size: 20x25½mm

388	A91	20n on 1n multi	.35	.35
389	A91	75n on 2n multi	.35	.35
390	A91	1.65n on 30n #378	.35	.35

Size: 25x38½mm
Perf. 14

391	A91	10k on 50n #380	2.25	2.25
392	A91	20k on 2k #386	3.00	3.00
		Nos. 388-392 (5)	6.30	6.30

Issued: #377, 379, 381-385, 387, 9/14/87; #391-392, 3/10/88; others 10/8/87.
Nos. 388-389 not issued without overprint.
See Nos. 433-435, 527-540. For surcharges see Nos. 490, 492-498.

Look-out Tree, Livingstone — A92

1.25k, Rafting, Zambezi River. 1.70k, Walking safari, Luangwa Valley. 10k, White pelicans.

1987, June 30   Perf. 14

393	A92	35n shown	.35	.35
394	A92	1.25k multicolored	.40	.40
395	A92	1.70k multicolored	1.75	1.75
396	A92	10k multicolored	6.00	6.00
		Nos. 393-396 (4)	8.50	8.50

Zambia Airways, 20th Anniv. A93

1987, Sept. 21

397	A93	35n De Havilland Beaver	.80	.80
398	A93	1.70k DC-10	1.75	1.75
399	A93	5k DC-3	4.00	4.00
400	A93	10k Boeing 707	6.25	6.25
		Nos. 397-400 (4)	12.80	12.80

Issues of 1985-86 Surcharged in Gold or Black

1987, Sept. 14   Perfs. as Before

401	A81	3k on 25n #327		
		(G)	1.40	1.40
402	CD337	3k on 35n #343	1.05	1.05
403	A85	3k on 35n #350	1.40	1.40
404	A86	3k on 1.25k #354		
		(G)	2.40	2.40
405	CD337	4k on 1.25k #344	1.30	1.30
406	A81	6k on 45n #328	2.40	2.40
407	CD337	6k on 1.70k #345	1.90	1.90
408	A85	6k on 1.25k #351	2.40	2.40
409	A86	6k on 1.70k #355		
		(G)	3.75	3.75
410	A81	10k on 55n #329		
		(G)	3.50	3.50
411	CD337	10k on 1.95k #346	3.50	3.50
412	A85	10k on 1.70k #352	3.50	3.50

413	A86	10k on 2k #356		
		(G)	6.50	6.50
414	A81	20k on 5k #330		
		(G)	6.75	6.75
415	CD337	20k on 5k #347	6.75	6.75
416	A85	20k on 5k #353	6.75	6.75
417	A86	20k on 5k #357		
		(G)	12.00	12.00
		Nos. 401-417 (17)	67.25	67.25

World Food Day — A94

Cattle.

1987, Oct. 1   Perf. 14½x15

418	A94	35n Friesian-Holstein	.25	.25
419	A94	1.25k Simmental	.40	.40
420	A94	1.70k Sussex	.40	.40
421	A94	20k Brahma	1.90	1.90
		Nos. 418-421 (4)	2.95	2.95

Traditional Heritage — A95

Zambian people.

1987, Oct. 20   Perf. 13x12½

422	A95	35n Mpoloto Ne Mikobango	.25	.25
423	A95	1.25k Zintaka	.30	.30
424	A95	1.70k Mufuluhi	.45	.45
425	A95	10k Ntebwe	1.15	1.15
426	A95	20k Kubangwa Aa Mbulunga	2.10	2.10
		Nos. 422-426 (5)	4.25	4.25

World Wildlife Fund — A96

Wild Cats — A97

50n, Black lechwe drinking water. 2k, Adults and young, horiz. 2.50k, Running, horiz. 10k, Male, diff.
No. 431, Cheetah. No. 432, Caracal.

1987, Dec. 21   Litho.   Perf. 14

427	A96	50n multicolored	1.50	1.50
428	A96	2k multicolored	2.75	2.75
429	A96	2.50k multicolored	2.75	2.75
430	A96	10k multicolored	6.00	6.00
		Nos. 427-430 (4)	13.00	13.00

Souvenir Sheets

431	A97	20k multicolored	9.00	9.00
432	A97	20k multicolored	9.00	9.00

Bird Type of 1987

1987		**Litho.**	**Perf. 11x13**	
433	A91	5n Black-tailed cisticola	.35	.35
434	A91	10n White-winged starling	.35	.35
435	A91	40n Wattled crane	.35	.35
		Nos. 433-435 (3)	1.05	1.05

For surcharge see No. 491.

Intl. Fund for Agricultural Development (IFAD), 10th Anniv. — A98

1988, Apr. 2   Perf. 14

436	A98	50n Cassava crop	.25	.25
437	A98	2.50k Net fishing	.55	.55
438	A98	2.85k Cattle breeding	.65	.65
439	A98	10k Coffee picking	2.10	2.10
		Nos. 436-439 (4)	3.55	3.55

A99

1988, Sept. 12   Litho.   Perf. 12½

440	A99	50n Breast-feeding	.25	.25
441	A99	2k Growth monitoring	.55	.55
442	A99	2.85k Immunization	.65	.65
443	A99	10k Oral rehydration	2.10	2.10
		Nos. 440-443 (4)	3.55	3.55

UN child survival campaign.

A100

1988, Oct. 10   Litho.   Perf. 12½x13

444	A100	50n Asbestos cement	.25	.25
445	A100	2.35k Textiles	.50	.50
446	A100	2.50k Tea	.55	.55
447	A100	10k Poultry	2.00	2.00
		Nos. 444-447 (4)	3.30	3.30

Preferential Trade Area Fair.

Intl. Red Cross and Red Crescent Organizations, 125th Annivs. — A101

1988, Oct. 20   Perf. 14

448	A101	50n Famine relief	.25	.25
449	A101	2.50k Giving first aid	.55	.55
450	A101	2.85k Teaching first aid	.70	.70
451	A101	10k Jean-Henri Dunant	2.60	2.60
		Nos. 448-451 (4)	4.10	4.10

Endangered Species — A102

1988, Dec. 5   Litho.   Perf. 14

452	A102	50n Aardvark	.30	.30
453	A102	2k Pangolin	.65	.65
454	A102	2.85k Wild dog	.85	.85
455	A102	20k Black rhinoceros	7.00	7.00
		Nos. 452-455 (4)	8.80	8.80

1988 Summer Olympics, Seoul
A103

1988, Dec. 30   Litho.   Perf. 14

456	A103	50n Boxing	.25	.25
457	A103	2k Running	.45	.45
458	A103	2.50k Hurdling	.55	.55
459	A103	20k Soccer	4.00	4.00
		Nos. 456-459 (4)	5.25	5.25

Souvenir Sheets

460	A103	30k Tennis	5.25	5.25
461	A103	30k Martial arts	5.25	5.25

Frogs and Toads A104

1989, Jan. 25   Litho.   Perf. 12½

462	A104	50n Red toad	.25	.25
463	A104	2.50k Puddle frog	.70	.70
464	A104	2.85k Marbled reed frog	.85	.85
465	A104	10k Young reed frogs	2.75	2.75
		Nos. 462-465 (4)	4.55	4.55

Bats A105

50n, Common slit-faced. 2.50k, Little free-tailed. 2.85k, Hildebrandt's horseshoe. 10k, Peters' epauletted fruit.

1989, Mar. 22   Litho.   Perf. 12½x13

466	A105	50n multi	.25	.25
467	A105	2.50k multi	.70	.70
468	A105	2.85k multi	.85	.85
469	A105	10k multi	2.75	2.75
		Nos. 466-469 (4)	4.55	4.55

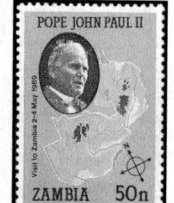

A106

1989, May 2   Litho.   Perf. 12½

470	A106	50n Map of Zambia	.90	.25
471	A106	6.85k Peace dove	3.50	3.50
472	A106	7.85k Papal arms	4.00	4.00
473	A106	10k Victoria Falls	6.00	6.00
		Nos. 470-473 (4)	14.40	13.75

State visit of Pope John Paul II, May 2-4.
For surcharges see #614, 616.

Edible Wild Fruits — A107

50n, Parinari curatellifolia. 6.50k, Uapaca kirkiana. 6.85k, Ficus capensis. 10k, Borassus aethiopum.

1989, July 26   Litho.   Perf. 14½x15

474	A107	50n multicolored	.25	.25
475	A107	6.50k multicolored	1.60	2.10
476	A107	6.85k multicolored	1.60	2.10
477	A107	10k multicolored	3.00	3.50
		Nos. 474-477 (4)	6.45	7.95

For surcharges see #613, 615.

Grasshoppers — A108

1989, Nov. 8   Litho.   Perf. 14x13½
478	A108	70n Phamphagid	.25	.25
479	A108	10.40k Pyrgomorphid	2.10	2.25
480	A108	12.50k Brown katydid	2.50	2.75
481	A108	15k Bush locust	3.00	3.75
		Nos. 478-481 (4)	7.85	9.00

No. 480 misspelled "Catydid."

Christmas — A109

Flowers.

1989, Dec. 6   Litho.   Perf. 14½
482	A109	70n Fireball	.25	.25
483	A109	10.40k Flame lily	1.30	1.40
484	A109	12.50k Foxglove lily	1.90	2.10
485	A109	20k Vlei lily	3.00	3.50
		Nos. 482-485 (4)	6.45	7.25

Stamp World London '90 A110

Designs: 1.20k, Lusaka Main P.O., van, mailman, bicycle. 19.50k, Zambia #220. 20.50k, Rhodesia and Nyasaland #164A, Northern Rhodesia #1. 50k, Great Britain #1, Maltese Cross cancel in red.

Unwmk.

1990, May 2   Litho.   Perf. 14
486	A110	1.20k multicolored	.30	.30
487	A110	19.50k multicolored	3.25	3.25
488	A110	20.50k multicolored	3.25	3.25
489	A110	50k multicolored	6.50	6.50
		Nos. 486-489 (4)	13.30	13.30

Nos. 379, 381-387, 433 Surcharged

No. 492   No. 497

1989, July 1   Perf. 11x13
490	A91	70n on 35n #379	1.00	.25
491	A91	3k on 5n #433	1.25	.40

Size: 25x38½mm
Perf. 14
492	A91	8k on 1.25k #382	1.50	1.00
493	A91	9.90k on 1.70k #384	1.75	1.75
494	A91	10.40k on 1.60k #383	1.75	1.75
495	A91	12.50k on 1k #381	2.00	2.00
496	A91	15k on 1.95k #385	2.00	2.00
497	A91	20k on 2k #386	3.00	3.00
498	A91	20.35k on 5k #387	3.00	3.00
		Nos. 490-498 (9)	17.25	15.15

Nos. 242, 244-245, 247-248 251, 253 Surcharged in Black, Orange Brown, Red Brown, or Violet

a   b

c

1989   Perf. 14½
Size: 22x26mm
499	A64(a)	1.20k on 35n #248 (OB)	.25	.25
500	A64(b)	3.75k on 5n #242	.40	.40
501	A64(b)	8.11k on 10n #244	1.00	1.00
502	A64(b)	9k on 30n #247	1.00	1.00

Size: 37x25mm
Perf. 14
503	A64(b)	10k on 75n #251	1.00	1.00
504	A64(c)	18.50k on 2k #253	2.00	2.00

Size: 22x26mm
Perf. 14½
505	A64(a)	19.50k on 12n #244A (RB)	4.00	4.00
506	A64(a)	20.50k on 18n #245 (V)	2.00	1.75
		Nos. 499-506 (8)	11.65	11.40

Issued: #500-504, 7/1; others, 11/1.

World Cup Soccer Championships, Italy — A111

Soccer players in various positions.

1990, July 7   Litho.   Perf. 14
507	A111	1.20k multicolored	.25	.25
508	A111	18.50k multicolored	2.50	2.50
509	A111	19.50k multicolored	2.50	2.50
510	A111	20.50k multicolored	2.50	2.50
		Nos. 507-510 (4)	7.75	7.75

Souvenir Sheet
510A	A111	50k multicolored	13.00	13.00

Southern African Development Co-ordination Conf. (SADCC), 10th Anniv. — A112

Map of SADCC members and: 1.20k, Truck. 19.50k, Telecommunications. 20.50k, Regional cooperation. 50k, Coal transport by cable car.

1990, July 23   Perf. 12½
511	A112	1.20k multicolored	.30	.25
512	A112	19.50k multicolored	2.25	2.25
513	A112	20.50k multicolored	2.25	2.25
514	A112	50k multicolored	7.50	7.50
		Nos. 511-514 (4)	12.30	12.25

Independence, 26th Anniv. — A113

1.20k, Agriculture. 19.50k, Shoe factory. 20.50k, Satellite communications. 50k, Mother and child statue.

1990, Oct. 23   Litho.   Perf. 14
515	A113	1.20k multicolored	.25	.25
516	A113	19.50k multicolored	1.25	1.25
517	A113	20.50k multicolored	1.40	1.40
518	A113	50k multicolored	3.00	3.00
		Nos. 515-518 (4)	5.90	5.90

Small Carnivores — A114

1990, Nov. 12
519	A114	1.20k Genet	.30	.30
520	A114	18.50k Civet	3.00	3.00
521	A114	19.50k Serval	3.25	3.25
522	A114	20.50k African wild cat	3.50	3.50
		Nos. 519-522 (4)	10.05	10.05

Intl. Literacy Year — A115

Children's stories — 1.20k, Bird and the Snake. 18.50k, Hare and the Leopard. 19.50k, Mouse and Lion. 20.50k, Hare and the Hippo.

1991, Jan. 11   Litho.   Perf. 14
523	A115	1.20k multi	.30	.30
524	A115	18.50k multi	1.90	1.90
525	A115	19.50k multi	2.75	2.75
526	A115	20.50k multi	3.00	3.00
		Nos. 523-526 (4)	7.95	7.95

Bird Type of 1987

10n, Livingstone's flycatcher. 15n, Bar-winged weaver. 30n, Purple-throated cuckoo shrike. No. 530, Red-billed helmet shrike. 1.20k, Western bronze-naped pigeon. 15k, Corn crake. 20k, Dickinson's grey kestrel. 50k, Denham's bustard.

1990-91   Litho.   Perf. 11x13
527	A91	10n multicolored	1.00	.50
528	A91	15n multicolored	1.00	.50
529	A91	30n multicolored	1.75	.50
530	A91	50n multicolored	1.75	.50
531	A91	50n like #527	1.75	.70
532	A91	1k like #528	2.00	.30
533	A91	1.20k multicolored	2.00	.30
534	A91	2k like #529	2.00	.75
535	A91	3k like #530	2.00	.75
536	A91	5k like #533	2.25	.75

Size: 25x38½mm
Perf. 14
537	A91	15k multicolored	1.75	.70
538	A91	20k multicolored	3.25	1.00
539	A91	20.50k like #538	1.75	1.00
540	A91	50k multicolored	2.75	2.25
		Nos. 527-540 (14)	27.00	11.50

Issued: #533, 1k, 2k, 3k, 5k, 20k, 5/7/91; others, 10/30.

Soy Beans — A116

1k, Woman cooking. 2k, Soy bean seed. 5k, Woman feeding child. 20k, Malnourished, healthy children. 50k, Pres. Kaunda, child.

1991, June 28   Litho.   Perf. 13½
548	A116	1k multicolored	.25	.25
549	A116	2k multicolored	.25	.25
550	A116	5k multicolored	.25	.25
551	A116	20k multicolored	1.75	1.75
552	A116	50k multicolored	3.25	3.25
		Nos. 548-552 (5)	5.75	5.75

United Church of Zambia / Rotary Foundation Project.

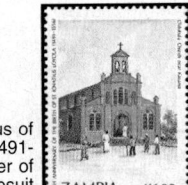

St. Ignatius of Loyola (1491-1556), Founder of Jesuit Order — A117

1k, Chilubula Church near Kasama. 2k, Chikuni Church near Monze. 20k, Bishop Joseph Du Pont. 50k, St. Ignatius of Loyola.

1991, July 18   Litho.   Perf. 13½
553	A117	1k multicolored	.30	.30
554	A117	2k multicolored	.30	.30
555	A117	20k multicolored	2.75	2.75
556	A117	50k multicolored	5.00	5.00
		Nos. 553-556 (4)	8.35	8.35

Flowering Trees A118

1k, Baobab. 2k, Dichrostachys cinerea. 10k, Sterospermum kunthianum. 30k, Azanza garckeana.

1991, Nov. 29   Litho.   Perf. 13½
557	A118	1k multicolored	.25	.25
558	A118	2k multicolored	.35	.25
559	A118	10k multicolored	2.00	1.50
560	A118	30k multicolored	3.75	3.75
		Nos. 557-560 (4)	6.35	5.75

Queen Elizabeth II's Accession to the Throne, 40th Anniv.
Common Design Type
Perf. 14x13½

1992, Feb. 2   Litho.   Wmk. 373
561	CD349	4k multicolored	.25	.25
562	CD349	32k multicolored	1.10	1.10
563	CD349	35k multicolored	1.25	1.25
564	CD349	38k multicolored	1.25	1.25
565	CD349	50k multicolored	1.75	1.75
		Nos. 561-565 (5)	5.60	5.60

For surcharges see Nos. 690-692.

Orchids — A119

1k, Disa hamatopetala. 2k, Eulophia paivae-ana. 5k, Eulophia quartiniana. 20k, Aerangis verdickii.

Perf. 13x13½

1992, Feb. 28   **Unwmk.**
566	A119	1k multi	.60	.25
567	A119	2k multi	.60	.25
568	A119	5k multi	1.00	.60
569	A119	20k multi	4.75	4.75
		Nos. 566-569 (4)	6.95	5.85

Masks — A120

1992, Mar. 10
570	A120	1k Kasinja	.30	.30
571	A120	2k Chizaluke	.30	.30
572	A120	10k Mwanapweu	1.25	1.00
573	A120	30k Maliya	3.25	3.75
		Nos. 570-573 (4)	5.10	5.35

Antelopes
A121

1992, Sept. 14   **Litho.**   **Perf. 14**
574	A121	4k Bushbuck	.25	.25
575	A121	40k Eland	1.40	.85
576	A121	45k Roan antelope	1.40	.85
577	A121	100k Sable antelope	2.75	3.75
		Nos. 574-577 (4)	5.80	5.70

Airmail
Services,
75th
Anniv.
A122

1992, Nov. 24   **Litho.**   **Perf. 14**
578	A122	4k DH66 Hercules	.35	.30
579	A122	40k VC10	2.25	.95
580	A122	45k C Class flying boat	2.25	.95
581	A122	100k DC10	3.75	5.00
		Nos. 578-581 (4)	8.60	7.20

1992 Summer
Olympics,
Barcelona — A123

1992, Dec. 28
582	A123	10k 400-meter hurdles	.25	.25
583	A123	40k Boxing	.85	.55
584	A123	80k Judo	1.75	1.75
585	A123	100k Cycling	4.25	4.25
		Nos. 582-585 (4)	7.10	6.80

Christmas — A124

1992, Dec. 23   **Litho.**   **Perf. 14**
586	A124	10k Wise men	.25	.25
587	A124	80k Nativity scene	1.75	1.75
588	A124	90k Angels singing	2.00	2.00

589	A124	100k Angel, shepherds	2.00	2.00
a.		Souvenir sheet of 4, #586-589	12.00	12.00
		Nos. 586-589 (4)	6.00	6.00

For surcharges see Nos. 658-659.

Nos. 331-334 Surcharged

1991, Mar. 4   **Litho.**   **Perf. 13½x13**
590	A82	2k on 20n #331	35.00	5.75
591	A82	2k on 45n #332	.75	5.75
592	A82	2k on 55n #333	—	5.75
593	A82	2k on 5k #334	17.50	5.75

Stamps of 1981-89
Surcharged in
Black or Gold

Perfs. as Before

1991, July 5   **Litho.**
594	A83	2k on 20n #335	10.00	6.00
595	A81	2k on 25n #327 (G)	10.00	6.00
596	A64	2k on 28n #246		—
597	A71	2k on 28n #289		—
598	A73	2k on 28n #297		—
600	A78	2k on 32n #317	30.00	8.00
601	CD337	2k on 35n #343		20.00
602	A87	2k on 35n #359	75.00	6.00
603	A90	2k on 35n #373	45.00	6.00
604	A79	2k on 45n #322	45.00	6.00
605	A80	2k on 45n #325	60.00	6.00
606	A81	2k on 45n #328	90.00	6.00
607	A83	2k on 45n #336	47.50	6.00
608	A87	2k on 1.60k #361	80.00	6.00
609	A84	2k on 1.70k #341	47.50	6.00
611	A81	2k on 5k #330	17.50	6.00
612	A84	2k on 5k #342	17.50	6.00
613	A107	2k on 6.50k #475	47.50	6.00
614	A106	2k on 6.85k #471	62.50	6.00
615	A107	2k on 6.85k #476	17.50	6.00
616	A106	2k on 7.85k #472	47.50	6.00

Numbers have been reserved for additional surcharges in this set.

Waterfalls
A125

1993, Sept. 30   **Litho.**   **Perf. 13½**
617	A125	50k Nkundalila	.35	.35
618	A125	200k Chishimba	1.40	1.40
619	A125	250k Chipoma	1.75	1.75
620	A125	300k Lumangwe	2.50	2.50
		Nos. 617-620 (4)	6.00	6.00

For surcharges, see Nos. 1011-1014.

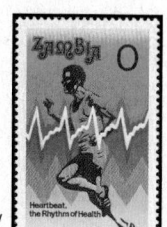

Healthy
Hearts — A126

1993, Oct. 20   **Litho.**   **Perf. 14½**
| 621 | A126 | O Runner | 1.10 | 1.10 |
| 622 | A126 | P Heart | 1.10 | 1.10 |

No. 621 sold for 50k and No. 622 sold for 80k on date of issue.

Sunbirds
A127

Designs: 20k, Bronze. 50k, Violet-backed. No. 625, Marico. No. 626, Eastern double-collared. 100k, Scarlet-chested. 150k, Bannerman's blue-headed. 200k, Oustalet's. 250k, Red and blue. 300k, Olive. 350k, Green-headed. 400k, Scarlet tufted malachite. 500k, Yellow-bellied. 800k, Copper. 1000k, Orange-tufted. 1500k, Black. 2000k, Green-throated.

1993, May 30   **Litho.**   **Perf. 13**
623	A127	20k multicolored	.25	.25
624	A127	50k multicolored	.25	.25
625	A127	O multicolored	.25	.25
626	A127	P multicolored	.30	.30
627	A127	100k multicolored	.35	.35
628	A127	150k multicolored	.55	.55
629	A127	200k multicolored	.65	.65
630	A127	250k multicolored	.80	.80
631	A127	300k multicolored	.90	.90
632	A127	350k multicolored	1.10	1.10
633	A127	400k multicolored	1.25	1.25
634	A127	500k multicolored	1.50	1.50
635	A127	800k multicolored	2.50	2.50
636	A127	1000k multicolored	3.25	3.25
637	A127	1500k multicolored	5.00	5.00
638	A127	2000k multicolored	6.75	6.75
		Nos. 623-638 (16)	25.65	25.65

Nos. 625 sold for 50k and 626 sold for 80k on date of issue.
For surcharge, see Nos. 997, 1090.

Snakes — A128

1994, Sept. 28   **Litho.**   **Perf. 14**
639	A128	50k Tiger snake	.25	.25
640	A128	200k Egyptian cobra	1.60	1.60
641	A128	300k African python	2.50	2.50
642	A128	500k Green mamba	4.25	4.25
		Nos. 639-642 (4)	8.60	8.60

For surcharges, see Nos. 996, 1007-1010.

ILO, 75th
Anniv.
A129

1995, Apr. 3   **Litho.**   **Perf. 14**
| 643 | A129 | 100k Road rehabilitation | .50 | .50 |
| 644 | A129 | 450k Block making | 2.50 | 2.50 |

For surcharge see No. 781A.

Christmas Angels — A130

1995, Aug. 29   **Perf. 14½x14**
645	A130	100k shown	.45	.45
646	A130	300k With animals	1.25	1.25
647	A130	450k Blowing horn, birds	1.90	1.90
648	A130	500k Playing drum	2.10	2.10
		Nos. 645-648 (4)	5.70	5.70

For surcharge, see No. 998.

UN, 50th
Anniv.
A131

1995, Dec. 30   **Litho.**   **Perf. 11½**
Granite Paper
| 649 | A131 | 700k multicolored | 2.25 | 2.25 |

For surcharges, see Nos. 1038, 1121, 1152.

Natl. Monuments
A132

Designs: 100k, David Livingstone. 300k, Mbereshi Mission. 450k, Von Lettow-Vorbeck. 500k, Niamkolo Church.

1996, Feb. 21   **Litho.**   **Perf. 14**
650	A132	100k multicolored	.40	.40
651	A132	300k multicolored	1.25	1.25
652	A132	450k multicolored	1.60	1.60
653	A132	500k multicolored	1.90	1.90
		Nos. 650-653 (4)	5.15	5.00

For surcharges, see Nos. 870A, 1015-1018.

World
Wildlife
Fund
A133

Designs: 200k, Saddle-billed stork. 300k, Black-cheeked lovebird. 500k, Two black-cheeked lovebirds. 900k, Saddle-billed stork with young.

1996, Nov. 27   **Litho.**   **Perf. 14x14½**
654	A133	200k multicolored	.70	.70
655	A133	300k multicolored	1.00	1.00
656	A133	500k multicolored	1.30	1.30
657	A133	900k multicolored	2.00	2.00
a.		Sheet of 4, #654-657	140.00	140.00
		Nos. 654-657 (4)	5.00	5.00

For surcharges, see Nos. 1003-1006.

Nos. 587-588 Surcharged

1996   **Litho.**   **Perf. 14**
| 658 | A124 | (0) on 90k #588 | 1.75 | 1.75 |
| 659 | A124 | 900k on 80k #587 | 3.00 | 3.00 |

No. 658 was valued at 500k on day of issue.
Size and location of surcharge varies.

New Year 1997 (Year of the Ox) — A134

Disney characters posing for portrait in Chinese scene, vert.: #660: a, Clarabelle seated. b, Holding scroll. c, Playing musical instrument. d, On bicycle. e, Minnie, Mickey, Clarabelle. f, Holding mirror.

No. 661: a, 250k, Faces of Minnie, Mickey, Clarabelle Cow. b, 400k, Clarabelle seated. c, 500k, Clarabelle standing. d, 600k, Mickey, Clarabelle, Minnie dressed in Chinese outfits. e, 750k, Minnie, Clarabelle, Mickey dancing. f, 1000k, Clarabelle with parasol.

1997, Jan. 28   Litho.   Perf. 14x13½
660 A134 500k Sheet of 6, #a.-f.   9.00 9.00
661 A134   Sheet of 6, #a.-f.   9.00 9.00

No. 660 contains six 35x61mm stamps.

Endangered Species — A135

Species of the world, each 500k: No. 662: a, Spider monkey. b, Manatee. c, Jaguar. d, Puerto Rican parrot. d, Green sea turtle. e, Harpy eagle.

Species of Africa, each 1000k: No. 663a, Black rhinoceros. b, Leopard. c, Chimpanzee. d, Zebra (Grants). e, Mountain gorilla. f, African elephant.

Each, 3000k: No. 664, Lion (African). No. 665, Margay cat.

1997, Feb. 12   Perf. 14
662 A135 Sheet of 6, #a.-f.   8.00 8.00
663 A135 Sheet of 6, #a.-f.   16.00 16.00
Souvenir Sheets
664-665 A135 Set of 2   11.50 11.50

Deng Xiaoping (1904-97) — A136

Various portraits of Deng Xiaoping and: 800k, Flags, map of Hong Kong. 1000k, Flag, Hong Kong harbor. 2000k, Hong Kong at night, countdown clock. 2500k, World map with China highlighted.

1997, May 26   Litho.   Perf. 14
666 A136 800k multicolored   2.50 2.50
667 A136 1000k multicolored   3.50 3.50
Souvenir Sheets
668 A136 2000k multicolored   5.00 5.00
669 A136 2500k multicolored   6.00 6.00

Nos. 666-667 were issued in sheets of 3 each. No. 669 contains one 72x47mm stamp.

Trains — A137

Locomotives: 200k, Suburban tank, Eastern Railway, France. 300k, Streamlined express, Belgian Natl. Railways. 500k, "Mountain" type express, Union Pacific Railroad. 900k, 2-8-2 "Mikado," Kenya & Uganda Railway. 1000k, 4-6-0 "Royal Scot," LM & S Railway. 1500k, 4-6-0 "Lord Nelson" type, Southern Railway.

No. 676, each 500k: a, Express, German State Railways. b, Express, "Duke of Abercorn," NCC (LMSR), Ireland. c, Heavy freight tank, Netherlands Railways. d, Express, Austrian Federal Railways. e, "Governor" class, Gold Coast Railways. f, 4-8-4 Express, Canadian Natl. Railways.

Each 3000k: No. 677, Diesel-electric passenger, Royal Siamese State Railways. No. 678, "Pacific" type, South African Railways.

1997, June 2
670-675 A137 Set of 6   7.25 7.25
676 A137 Sheet of 6, #a.-f.   7.00 7.00
Souvenir Sheets
677-678 A137 Set of 2   11.50 11.50

Butterflies and Moths — A138

300k, No. 683a, Gaudy commodore. 500k, No. 683b, African moon moth. 700k, No. 683c, Emperor moth. No. 682, 900k, Emperor swallowtail.

1997, Aug. 8   Litho.   Perf. 14
679-682 A138 Set of 4   11.00 11.00
683 A138 900k Sheet of 4, #a.-c., #682   17.50 17.50

Queen Elizabeth II and Prince Philip, 50th Wedding Anniv. — A139

No. 684, each 500k: a, Queen Elizabeth II. b, Royal arms. c, Queen wearing crown, Prince in uniform. d, Queen, Prince riding in open carriage. e, Buckingham Palace. f, Prince waving.

3200k, Queen, Prince waving from balcony.

1997, Aug. 26   Litho.   Perf. 14
684 A139 Sheet of 6, #a.-f.   8.50 8.50
Souvenir Sheet
685 A139 3200k multicolored   8.50 8.50

Paul P. Harris (1868-1947), Founder of Rotary, Intl. — A140

1000k, First Rotarians, Silvester Schiele, Harris, Hiram Shorey, Gus Loehr, portrait of Harris.

3200k, Zambian interactors with retirees.

1997, Aug. 27
686 A140 1000k multicolored   4.75 4.75
Souvenir Sheet
687 A140 3200k multicolored   6.25 6.25

Heinrich von Stephan (1831-97), Founder of UPU — A141

Each 1000k, Portrait of Von Stephan and: #688a, World Postal Congress, Berne, 1874. #688b, UPU emblem. #688c, Savannah, paddle steamer, 1819.

3200k, Von Stephan, Prussian postilion, 1715.

1997, Aug. 28
688 A141 Sheet of 3, #a.-c.   7.25 7.25
Souvenir Sheet
689 A141 3200k multicolored   6.25 6.25

Nos. 562-564 Surcharged

1997, Sept. 19   Litho.   Perf. 14x13½
690 CD349 500k on 35k   1.75 .75
691 CD349 (0) on 32k   1.75 .90
692 CD349 900k on 38k   3.50 3.50
  Nos. 690-692 (3)   7.00 5.15

No. 691 was valued at 600k on day of issue.

Owls — A142

300k, #697b, Verreaux's eagle owl. 500k, #697c, Pel's fishing owl. 700k, #697a, Barn owl. #696, Spotted eagle owl.

1997, Dec. 18   Litho.   Perf. 14
693 A142 300k multicolored   .80 .80
694 A142 500k multicolored   1.40 1.40
695 A142 700k multicolored   2.00 2.00
696 A142 900k multicolored   2.40 2.40
  Nos. 693-696 (4)   6.60 6.60
Sheet of 4
697 A142 900k #a.-c., #696   10.00 10.00

Christmas A143

Entire paintings or details, sculpture: No. 698, 50k, Winged Victory of Samothrace. No. 699, 50k, Ognissanti Madonna, by Giotto. No. 700, 100k, Angel, by Antonio Pollaiuolo. No. 701, 100k, Angel of the Annunciation, by Jacopo da Pontormo. No. 702, 500k, No. 703, 1000k, The Virgin and Child Enthroned Among Angels and Saints, by Benozzo Gozzoli.

Each 3200k: No. 704, All of the Rebel Angels, detail, by Rubens. No. 705, The Resurrection of the Dead, by Joseph Christian.

1997, Dec. 18   Litho.   Perf. 14
698-703 A143 Set of 6   5.75 5.75
Souvenir Sheets
704-705 A143 Set of 2   11.50 11.50

No. 704 incorrectly inscribed "The Virgin and Child Enthroned Among Angels and Saints, by Bonozzo Gozzoli."

Diana, Princess of Wales (1961-97) — A144

Various portraits with color of sheet margin: No. 706, Pale green. No. 707, Pale yellow.

Each 2500k: No. 708, Touching hand of blind man (in sheet margin). No. 709, With Barbara Bush (in sheet margin).

1997
706 A144 500k Sheet of 6, #a.-f.   9.00 9.00
707 A144 700k Sheet of 6, #a.-f.   11.00 11.00
Souvenir Sheets
708-709 A144 Set of 2   10.50 10.50

PAPU (Pan African Postal Union), 18th Anniv. A145

Designs: 500k, Kobus leche kafuensis. (O), Dove carrying letter over map. 900k, Emblem of dove carrying letter.

1998   Perf. 14½
710 A145 500k multicolored   1.40 1.40
711 A145 (O) multicolored   1.75 1.75
712 A145 900k multicolored   2.25 2.25
  Nos. 710-712 (3)   5.40 5.40

No. 711 was valued at 600k on day of issue. For surcharges, see Nos. 1019-1021.

Mahatma Gandhi (1869-1948) — A146

Portraits of Gandhi: 250k, As law student in London, 1888. 500k, With Nehru, 1946. No. 715, (O), In front of Red Fort, New Delhi. 900k, At prayer.

2000k, Gandhi at 2nd Round Table Conference, London, 1931.

1998, Jan. 30   Litho.   Perf. 13½
713-716 A146 Set of 4   16.00 16.00
Souvenir Sheet
717 A146 2000k multicolored   13.00 13.00

No. 715 was valued at 600k on day of issue. Nos. 713, 715-717 are vert.

For surcharges, see Nos. 911-912.

Flowers — A147

Designs: No. 718, Lantana camara. No. 719, Clusia rosea. No. 720, Nymphaea hybrids. No. 721, Portulaca grandiflora.

No. 722: a, Hibiscus rosa-sinensis. b, Plumeria. c, Erythrina variegata. d, Bauhinia blakeana. e, Carissa grandiflora. f, Cordia sebestena. g, Couroupita guianensis. h, Eustoma grandiflorum. i, Passiflora.

3200k, Strelitzia reginae, horiz.

1998, Feb. 27		Litho.	Perf. 14	
718-721	A147	500k Set of 4	5.00	5.00
722	A147	500k Sheet of 9, #a.-i.	11.00	11.00

Souvenir Sheet

| 723 | A147 | 3200k multicolored | 16.00 | 16.00 |

New Year 1998 (Year of the Tiger) — A148

Chinese symbols and stylized tigers, each 700k: No. 724: a, Looking right. b, Looking left. c, Facing forward, denomination UL. d, Facing forward, denomination UR.

1500k, Tiger, symbols on both sides.

1998		Litho.	Perf. 14	
724	A148	Sheet of 4, #a.-d.	6.25	6.25

Souenir Sheet

| 725 | A148 | 1500k multicolored | 4.00 | 4.00 |

Sites of India — A149

Designs: a, Taj Mahal, Agra. b, Gateway to India, Calcutta. c, Great Imambara Mosque, Lucknow.

1998

| 726 | A149 | 900k Sheet of 3, #a.-c. | 7.25 | 7.25 |

Art of India — A150

No. 727, each 700k: a, Ragmala, School of Mewar, 17th cent. b, Babur Nama, Mogul

School, 16th cent. c, Hamza Nama, Mogul School, 16th cent. d, Meghamallar, School of Mewar, 16th cent.

2500k, Hindola Raga, School of Deccan, 17th-18th cent.

1998

| 727 | A150 | Sheet of 4, #a.-d. | 8.25 | 8.25 |

Souvenir Sheet

| 728 | A150 | 2500k multicolored | 8.00 | 8.00 |

1998 World Cup Soccer Championships, France — A151

No. 729, each 450k: a, Albert, Belgium. b, Bebeto, Brazil. c, Beckenbauer, W. Germany. d, Littbarski, W. Germany. e, Juninho, Brazil. f, Lineker, England. g, Lato, Poland. h, McCoist, Scotland.

No. 730, each 500k: a, Maier, W. Germany, 1974. b, Bellini, Brazil, 1958. c, Kempes, Argentina, 1978. d, Nazassi, Uruguay, 1930. e, Pele, Brazil, 1970. f, Beckenbauer, W. Germany, 1974. g, Combi, Italy, 1934. h, Zoff, Italy, 1982.

No. 731, each 500k: a, Keane, Rep. of Ireland. b, Seaman, England. c, Like #729b. d, Futre, Portugal. e, Ravanelli, Italy. f, Weah, Liberia. g, Bergkamp, Holland. h, Raducioiu, Romania.

Each 3200k: No. 732, Juninho, Brazil. No. 733, Romario, Brazil, horiz. No. 734, McCoist, Scotland, horiz.

1998, Apr. 17		Perf. 13½x14, 14x13½		

Sheets of 8, #a-h, + Label

| 729 | A151 | multi | 5.25 | 5.25 |
| 730-731 | A151 | Set of 2 | 13.00 | 13.00 |

Souvenir Sheets

| 732-734 | A151 | Set of 3 | 13.50 | 13.50 |

Parrots — A152

No. 735, each 500k: a, Rainbow lorikeet. b, Budgerigar, blossom-headed parakeet. c, Blue-yellow macaw. d, Blue-crowned parrot. e, Golden conure. f, Sulphur-crested cockatoo.

No. 736, each 1000k: a, Ara ararauna. b, Ara chloropterd. c, Pale-headed rosellas. d, Northern rosella. e, Gang-gang cockatoo. f, Palm cockatoo.

Each 3200k: No. 737, Mulga parakeet. No. 738, Major Mitchell cockatoo, horiz.

1998, June 1		Litho.	Perf. 14	
735	A152	Sheet of 6, #a.-f.	6.00	6.00
736	A152	Sheet of 6, #a.-f.	12.00	12.00

Souvenir Shets

| 737-738 | A152 | Set of 2 | 18.00 | 18.00 |

Mushrooms — A153

No. 739, 250k, Red-tufted wood tricholoma. No. 740, 250k, Chlorophyllum molybdites. No. 741, 450k, Stuntz's psilocybe. No. 742, 450k, Lepista sordida. No. 743, 500k, Lepiota. No. 744, 500k, Rosy gomphidius. No. 745, 900k, Cantharellus cybrina. No. 746, 900k, Olive-capped boletus. No. 747, 1000k, Showy

volvaria. No. 748, 1000k, Sooty brown waxy cap.

No. 749, each 900k: a, Leller's boletus. b, Short-stemmed russula. c, Anise-scented clitocybe. d, Dung roundhead. e, Oak-loving collybia. f, Wine-red stropharia.

No. 750, each 900k: a, Flat-topped mushroom. b, Alice Eastwood's boletus. c, Pitted milky cap. d, Short-stemmed slippery jask. e, Rose-red russula. f, Zeller's tricholoma.

Each 3200k: No. 751, Honey mushroom. No. 752, Velvet-stemmed flammulina.

1998, July 1				
739-748	A153	Set of 10	22.50	22.50

Sheets of 6

| 749-750 | A153 | Set of 2 | 22.50 | 22.50 |

Souvenir Sheets

| 751-752 | A153 | Set of 2 | 18.00 | 18.00 |

Nos. 749-752 are continuous designs.

Traditional Stories — A154

No. 755, each 2000k: a, like #753. b, like #754.

1998, Dec. 2		Litho.	Perf. 14	
753	A154	300k Luchela nganga	.90	.90
754	A154	500k Kasuli	1.40	1.40

Souvenir Sheet

| 755 | A154 | Sheet of 2, #a.-b. | 6.00 | 6.00 |

Christmas.

Orchids A155

Designs, vert: No. 756, 100k, Paphiopedilum callosum. No. 757, 100k, Phaius tankervilleae. No. 758, 500k, Paphiopedilum fairrieanum. No. 759, 500k, Barkeria lindleyana. No. 760, 1000k, Laelia flava. No. 761, 1000k, Masdervallia unifloria, masdervallia angulifera.

No. 762, each 900k: a, Acacallis cyanea. b, Miltoniopsis phalaenopsis. c, Dendrobium bellatulum. d, Polystachya campyloglossa. e, Pleione bulbocodioides. f, Rhynchostylis gigantea. g, Cattleya lawrenceana. h, Sobrolaelia. i, Laelia tenebrosa.

No. 763, each 900k: a, Acacallis cyanea, diff. b, Epidendrum gastropodium. c, Laelia rubescens. d, Paphiopedilum dayanum. e, Laelia lobata. f, Dendrobium crepidatum. g, Cattleya nobilior. h, Dendrobium johnsoniae. i, Trichopilia fragrans.

Each 4000k: No. 764, Cattleya maxima, vert. No. 765, Cattleya violacea.

1998, Dec. 23				
756-761	A155	Set of 6	5.50	5.50

Sheets of 9

| 762-763 | A155 | Set of 2 | 17.50 | 17.50 |

Souvenir Sheets

| 764-765 | A155 | Set of 2 | 13.00 | 13.00 |

Classic Cars A156

Designs: 300k, Ferrari Daytona 365 GTB/4. 500k, Austin Healey Sprite. 900k, Gordon Keeble. 1000k, Alvis TD.

No. 770: a, Mercedes-Benz 300Sl. b, Chevrolet Corvair. c, AC Cobra 427. d, Aston Martin DB5. e, BMW 2002 Turbo. f, Cadillac Eldorado Brougham.

No. 771: a, Mercedes-Benz 280SE 3.5. b, Aston Martin DB2. c, Volkswagen Beetle. d, Lancia Aurelia B20 GT. e, Lamborghini 350 GT. f, Cisitalia 202 Coupe.

No. 771G: h, 1995 Ferrari 750 Pinnafarina. i, 1997 Federrari 312T2/77. j, 1983 Ferrari 208 Turbo. k, 1962 Ferrari Dino 268 SP. l, 1994 Ferrari F355 Berlinetta. m, Ferrari 250 GTE Coupe 2+2 California.

Each 4000k: No. 772, Citroen Light 15. No. 773, Austin Healey MKII 3000.

1998, Dec. 23				
766-769	A156	Set of 4	5.00	5.00

Sheets of 6, #a-f

| 770-771G | A156 | 900k Set of 3 | 17.50 | 17.50 |

Souvenir Sheets

| 772-773 | A156 | Set of 2 | 17.50 | 17.50 |

New Year 1999 (Year of the Rabbit) — A157

Various rabbits, denomination at — #774 (each 700k): a, LL. b, LR. c, LL (scratching). d, LR (nose near ground).

2000k, Rabbit, vert.

1999, Jan. 4				
774	A157	Sheet of 4, #a.-d.	4.75	4.75

Souvenir Sheet

| 775 | A157 | 2000k multicolored | 4.50 | 4.50 |

Trains A158

Locomotives: No. 776, (0), U2OC Diesel electric, 1967. No. 777, 800k, 7th Class No. 70, 1900. No. 778, 800k, 15A Class Beyer-Garrat No. 401, 1950. No. 779, 900k, HP diesel electric, 1966. No. 780, 900k, 20th Class No. 708, 1954.

4000k, 7th Class No. 955, 1892.

1999, Feb. 1		Litho.	Perf. 14½	
776-780	A158	Set of 5	6.25	6.25

Souvenir Sheet

| 781 | A158 | 4000k multicolored | 4.50 | 4.50 |

No. 776 was valued at 600k on day of issue.

No. 643 Surcharged

Methods and Perfs as Before

1999, June 1			
781A	A129	500k on 100k multi	

Queen Mother (b. 1900) — A159

No. 782: a, With Princess Elizabeth, 1936. b, Lady of the Garter. c, With Prince Andrew, 1960. d, At Ascot.
5000k, Wedding photograph, 1923.

1999, Sept. 1   **Perf. 14**
782 A159 2000k Sheet of 4, #a.- d., + label   9.50 9.50

Souvenir Sheet
Perf. 13¾
783 A159 5000k multicolored   6.50 6.50
No. 783 contains one 38x51mm stamp.

Dinosaurs
A160

Designs: 50k, Dimetrodon. 100k, Deinonychus. 500k, Protoceratops. 900k, Heterodontosaurus. 1000k, Oviraptor. 1800k, Psittacosaurus.
No. 790, each 900k: a, Stegosaurus. b, Triceratops. c, Brontosaurus. d, Gallimimus. e, Saurolophus. f, Lambeosaurus. g, Centrosaurus. h, Edmontonia. i, Parasaurolophus.
No. 791, each 900k: a, Ceratosaurus. b, Daspletosaurus. c, Baryonyx. d, Ornitholestes. e, Troodon. f, Coelophysis. g, Tyrannosaurus. h, Allosaurus. i, Compsognathus.
Each 4000k: No. 792, Saltasaurus, vert. No. 793, Stygimoloch, vert.

1999, Sept. 27   **Litho.**   **Perf. 14**
784-789 A160 Set of 6   4.50 4.50
Sheets of 9
790-791 A160 Set of 2   14.50 14.50
Souvenir Sheets
792-793 A160 Set of 2   9.00 9.00

Johann Wolfgang von Goethe (1749-1832), German Poet — A161

No. 794, each 2000k: a, A drinking party in Amerbach's cellar. b, Goethe and Friedrich von Schiller. c, Faust falls in love with Margaret.
5000k, Angel.

1999, Oct. 4   **Litho.**   **Perf. 14**
794 A161 Sheet of 3, #a.-c.   5.00 5.00
Souvenir Sheet
795 A161 5000k org brn & brn   4.50 4.50

A162

Cats: 50k, White Devon Rex. 100k, Red Persian. 500k, Chartreux. 900k, Brown tabby Maine Coon.
No. 800, each 1000k, horiz.: a, Tortie point Himalayan. b, Blue mackerel tabby Scottish Fold. c, Chocolate lynx point Balinese. d, Havana Brown. e, Seal point Ragdoll. f, Silver shaded Persian.
No. 801, each 1000k, horiz.: a, Red spotted tabby Exotic Shorthair. b, Blue tortie smoke Persian. c, Brown classic tabby longhaired Scottish Fold. d, Spotted tabby American Bobtail. e, Silver spotted tabby Ocicat. f, Blue British Shorthair.
Each 4000k: No. 802, Silver tabby longhair Persian, horiz. No. 803, Tabby point Siamese.

1999, Oct. 18
796-799 A162 Set of 4   1.60 1.60
Sheets of 6, #a.-f.
800-801 A162 Set of 2   9.50 9.50
Souvenir Sheets
802-803 A162 Set of 2   7.00 7.00

A163

Dogs: 100k, Welsh corgi. 500k, Shetland sheepdog. 900k, Italian greyhound. 1000k, Tibetan spaniel.
No. 808, each 1000k, horiz.: a, Dalmatian. b, Shetland sheepdogs. c, Bearded collie. d, Eskimo. e, Basenji. f, Saluki.
No. 809, each 1000k, horiz.: a, Norwegian elkhound. b, Flat-coated retriever. c, St. Bernard. d, Basset hound, Pembroke Welsh corgi. e, Pembroke Welsh corgi, Pointer. f, Petit Basset Griffon Vendeen.
Each 4000k: No. 810, Whippet. No. 811, Rottweiler.

1999, Oct. 18
804-807 A163 Set of 4   2.25 2.25
Sheets of 6, #a.-f.
808-809 A163 Set of 2   9.50 9.50
Souvenir Sheets
810-811 A163 Set of 2   7.00 7.00

11th Intl. Conference on AIDS in Africa, Lusaka — A164

Designs: 500k, Emblem, waterfalls. 900k, Emblem, close-up view of waterfalls.

1999, Oct. 20
812-813 A164 Set of 2   2.00 2.00

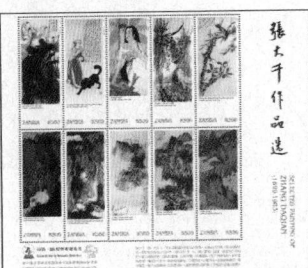

Paintings by Zhang Daqian (1899-1983) — A165

No. 814, each 500k: a, Water Lily in the Rain. b, Chinghai Tribal Girl and a Black Hound. c, Taking a Nap. d, Monkey and Old Tree. e, Bird and Tree of Chin-Chang Mountain. f, Watching Waterfalls. g, On the Way to Switzerland and Austria. h, A Boat Brings the Wine. i, Brown Landscape. j, Nice Autumn.
No. 815: a, 1000k, White Water Lily, horiz. b, 2000k, Cloudy Waterfalls and Summer Mountain, horiz.

1999, Oct. 21   **Perf. 13**
814 A165 Sheet of 10, #a.-j.   3.75 3.75
815 A165 Sheet of 2, #a.-b.   2.10 2.10
China 1999 World Philatelic Exhibition, 22nd UPU Congress, Beijing. #815 contains two 52x39mm stamps.

A166

Flora & Fauna
A167

Designs: 50k, Leatherback turtle. 100k, American kestrel. No. 818, 500k, Great blue heron. 900k, Mesene phareus. 1000k, Laeliocattleya. 1800k, Papilio cresphontes.
Each 500k: No. 822, Cairn's birdwing. No. 823, Pintail. No. 824, Rose. No. 825, Gray tree frog.
No. 826, each 700k: a, White-tailed tropicbird. b, Sooty tern. c, Laughing gull. d, Black skimmer. e, Brown pelican. f, Bottle-nosed dolphin. g, Common dolphin. h, Man in sailboat. i, Blue tang. j, Southern stingray. k, Hammerhead shark. l, Mako shark.
No. 827, each 700k: a, Heliconia. b, Purple-throated Carib. c, St. Vincent parrot. d, Bananaquit. e, prepona meander. f, Unidentified butterfly. g, Hawksbill turtle. h, Black-necked stilt. i, Banded butterflyfish. j, Porkfish. k, Seahorse. l, Chain moray eel.
No. 828: a, Baltimore oriole. b, Chipmunk. c, Blue jay. d, Monarch butterfly. e, Gray heron. f, Mallard. g, Canadian otter. h, American lotus. i, Fowler's toad. j, Bluegill sunfish. k, Rainbow trout. l, Terrapin.
Each 4000k: No. 829, Amazona guildingii. No. 830, Bottle-nosed dolphin, diff. No. 831, Fuchsia. No. 832, Red-banded pereute.

1999, Oct. 27
816-821 A166 Set of 6   4.25 4.25
822-825 A167 Set of 4   2.00 2.00
Sheets of 12, #a.-l.
826-827 A166 Set of 2   12.00 12.00
828 A167 700k multi   6.00 6.00
Souvenir Sheets
829-830 A166 Set of 2   7.50 7.50
831-832 A167 Set of 2   7.50 7.50

IBRA '99 — A168

Trains: 1000k, Crampton. 3200k, Post standard 2-8-4 tank locomotive.

1999   **Perf. 14x14¾**
833-834 A168 Set of 2   3.00 3.00

Souvenir Sheets

PhilexFrance '99 — A169

Each 5000k: #835, Paris-Orleans Railway 4-4-0. #836, paris, Lyon & Mediterranean Railway 2-4-2.

1999   **Perf. 14¼**
835-836 A169 Set of 2   7.50 7.50

Wedding of Prince Edward and Sophie Rhys-Jones — A170

No. 837: a, 500k, Sophie. b, 900k, Couple. c, 100k, Edward.
3000k, Couple kissing.

1999   **Perf. 14**
837 A170 Sheet of 3, #a.-c.   1.75 1.75
Souvenir Sheet
838 A170 3000k multi   2.10 2.10

Birds — A171

Designs: 50k, Blacksmith plover. 100k, Sacred ibis. 200k, Purple gallinule. 250k, Purple heron. 300k, Glossy ibis. 400k, Marabou stork. 450k, African spoonbill. 500k, African finfoot. O, No. 847, Knot-billed duck. 600k, Darter. 700k, African skimmer. 800k, Spur-winged goose. 900k, Hammerkop. 1000k, White pelican. 1500k, Black-winged stilt. 2000k, Black-crowned night heron.

1999, Dec. 20   **Litho.**   **Perf. 14½x15**
839-854 A171 Set of 16   14.00 14.00
No. 847 sold for 500k on day of issue. Design size of No. 847 is 30½mm wide. See Nos. 927-930.

Flowers — A172

Various flowers making up a photomosaic of Princess Diana, each 1000k.

1999, Dec. 31   **Perf. 13¾**
855 A172 Sheet of 8, #a.-h.   8.00 8.00

Millennium — A173

Highlights of 1950-2000: a, Venice Biennale shows Jackson Pollock and Abstract Expressionism. b, James Watson and Francis Crick piece together the structure of DNA. c, Edmund Hillary reaches the summit of Mount Everest. d, Jonas Salk's polio vaccine. e, Ghana achieves independence. f, Yuri Gagarin becomes 1st man in space. g, Rachel Carson and the beginning of the environmental movement. h, Indira Gandhi becomes Prime Minister of India. i, 1st successful heart transplant. j, Apollo 11 lands on moon. k, Microprocessor developed. l, Richard Nixon visits People's Republic of China. m, Qin Shi Huang Mausoleum discovered. n, Stephen Hawking proposes new ideas about the universe and black holes. o, Margaret Thatcher elected 1st female Prime Minister of Great Britain. p, Mikhail Gorbachev becomes leader of Soviet Union. q, Fall of the Berlin Wall. r, Nelson Mandela elected Pres. of South Africa.

2000, Feb. 7   **Perf. 12¾x12½**
856   A173   500k Sheet of 18, #a.-
     r., + label   8.00   8.00

Butterflies A174

400k, Papilio antimachus. 450k, Amauris niavius. 500k, Charaxes smaragdalis. 800k, Charaxes zelica. 900k, Cymothoe confusa. 1000k, #862, Labobunea ansorgei.
No. 863, each 1000k: a, Palla ussheri. b, Euphaedra aureola. c, Graphium cyrnus nuscyrus. d, Salamis cacta. e, Salamis parhassus. f, Charaxes pelias.
No. 864, each 1000k: a, Large Spotted Acraea. b, Palla (orange wings). c, Palla (blue wings). d, Gold-banded Forester (white wings). e, Figtree blue. f, Gold-banded Forester (pink wings).
No. 865, each 1500k: a, Colotis ione. b, Charaxes acraeoides. c, Euphaedra edwardsi. d, Colotis phisadia. e, Charaxes lydiae. f, Euphaedra eupaulus.
No. 866, each 1500k: a, Papilio zalmoxis. b, Amauris niavius. c, Salamis cytora. d, Salamis temora. e, Charaxes eupale. f, Cymothoe hypatha.
Each 5000k: No. 867, Euphaedra ceres. No. 868, Cymothoe fumana. No. 869, Euphaedra spatiosa. No. 870, Euryphene gambiae.

2000, Feb. 8   **Perf. 14**
857-862   A174   Set of 6   5.00   5.00
Sheets of 6, #a.-f.
863-864   A174   Set of 2   8.50   8.50
865-866   A174   Set of 2   12.50   12.50
Souvenir Sheets
867-870   A174   Set of 4   16.00   16.00

No. 650 Surcharged

Method and Perf. as Before
2000, Apr. 11
870A   A132   700k on 100k multi

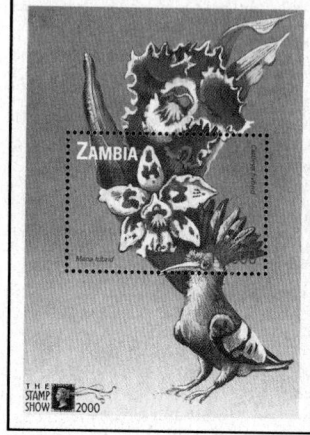

Orchids — A175

No. 871, each 1500k: a, Paphiopedilum sioux. b, Phalaenopsis amabilis hybrid. c, Thelymitza ixioides. d, Phalaenopsis schilleriana.
No. 872, each 1500k: a, Miltoniopsis pansy orchid. b, Paphiopedilum venustum. c, Odontoglossum grande. d, Vanda sanderiana alba. e, Phalaenopsis violacea. f, Pleione alishan.
No. 873, each 1500k: a, Cyrtorchis arcuata. b, Cymbioiella rhodochila. c, Unidentified orchid. d, Eulophia quartiana. e, Augraecum montanum. f, Polystacha vulcanica.
No. 874, each 1500k, vert.: a, Catasetum splendens. b, Miltonia spectabilis. c, Stenia pallida. d, Cozacias spatulata. e, Eriopsis sceptzum. f, Paphinia cristata.
Each 6000k: No. 875, Cattleya hybrid. No. 876, Brachycorythis kalbreyeri.

2000, May 16   **Litho.**   **Perf. 14**
871   A175   Sheet of 4, #a.-d.   5.00   5.00
Sheets of 6, #a.-f.
872-874   A175   Set of 3   20.00   20.00
Souvenir Sheets
875-876   A175   Set of 2   9.00   9.00
The Stamp Show 2000, London.

Popes — A176

No. 877: a, Liberius, 352-66. b, Linus, 67-76. c, Lucius I, 253-54. d, Marcellinus, 296-304. e, Mark, 336. f, Pius I, 140-155.
No. 878: a, Simplicius, 468-83. b, Siricius, 384-99. c, Stephen I, 254-57. d, Urban I, 222-30. e, Zephyrinus, 199-217. f, Zosimus, 417-18.
No. 879, Silverius, 536-37. No. 880, Vigilius, 537-55.

2000, July 7   **Litho.**   **Perf. 13¾**
Sheets of 6, #a-f
877-878   A176   1500k Set of 2   11.00   11.00
Souvenir Sheets
879-880   A176   5000k Set of 2   8.00   8.00

Birds — A177

400k, Great Indian hornbill. 500k, Cockatiel. 600k, Amazonian umbrellabird. 1000k, Unidentified bird. 2000k, Rainbow lorikeet.
No. 886: a, Green aracari. b, Eclectus parrot. c, Crimson topaz. d, King bird of paradise. e, keel-billed toucan. f, Australian king parrot. g, Sailboat. h, Hyacinth macaw.
No. 887: a, Resplendent quetzal. b, Carmine bee-eater. c, Wattled false sunbird. d, Palm trees. e, Sulphur-crested cockatoo. f, Great blue turaco. g, Crimson rosella. h, Malabar pied hornbill.
No. 888: a, Yellow-crowned amazon. b, Green turaco. c, Butterfly and palm trees. d, Plate-billed mountain toucan. e, Scarlet macaw. f, Blue and yellow macaw. g, Guianan cock of the rock. h, Palm cockatoo.
No. 889, Red-crested pochard. No. 890, Toco toucan, horiz. No. 891, Blue and yellow macaw, horiz.

2000, Sept. 8   **Perf. 14**
881-885   A177   Set of 5   3.25   3.25
Sheets of 8, #a-h
886-888   A177   1500k Set of 3   25.00   25.00
Souvenir Sheets
889-891   A177   5000k Set of 3   10.50   10.50

Birds — A178

Designs: 700k, Red-backed shrike. 800k, Golden pipet. No. 894, 1200k, Orange-breasted sunbird. No. 895, 1400k, Eurasian goldfinch. 1500k, Red-crested turaco. 3000k, Carmine bee-eater.
No. 898, 1000k: a, Gouldian finch. b, Parrot finch. c, Purple grenadier. d, Red bishop. e, Red-crested cardinal. f, Spectacled monarch. g, Crimson chat. h, Necklaced laughing thrush. i, Chestnut-backed jewel babbler.
No. 899, 1200k: a, Lovely cotinga. b, Andean cock-of-the-rock. c, Orange-bellied leafbird. d, Pin-tailed manakin. e, Pin-tailed broadbill. f, Rufous motmot. g, American goldfinch. h, Double-barred finch. i, Golden-breasted starling.
No. 900, 1400k: a, Campo oriole. b, Hooded warbler. c, Purple honeycreeper. d, Blue-faced honeyeater. e, Scarlet tanager. f, Green-headed tanager. g, Blue-breasted fairy wren. h, Banded pitta. i, Wire-tailed manakin.
No. 901, 5000k, Pin-tailed sandgrouse. No. 902, 5000k, Black bustard.

2000, Sept. 8   **Litho.**   **Perf. 14**
892-897   A178   Set of 6   5.75   5.75
Sheets of 9, #a-i
898-900   A178   Set of 3   21.50   21.50
Souvenir Sheets
901-902   A178   Set of 2   7.00   7.00

African Creation Legends A179

Designs: Nos. 903, 906a, 600k, Creation in Clay. Nos. 904, 906b, 1000k, The Chameleon and the Lizard. Nos. 905, 906c, 1400k, Why the Stones Do Not Die.

Perf. 14¼x14½
2000, Nov. 10   **Litho.**
903-905   A179   Set of 3   1.60   1.60
With Brown Frame
906   A179   Horiz. strip of 3, #a-c 1.60 1.60
Souvenir Sheet
No Frame Around Stamp
907   A179   3500k The Rooster in
     the Sky   1.90   1.90

No. 906 issued in sheets of 9 stamps. For surcharge, see No. 1106.

Common Market for Eastern and Southern Africa A180

Designs: 600k, Map of member nations. 700k, Truck crossing border. 1000k, Exchange of money and sale of goods at border.

2000
908-910   A180   Set of 3   2.25   2.25

Nos. 713-714 Surcharged

2000   **Method and Perf. as Before**
911   A146   1200k on 250k multi
912   A146   1500k on 500k multi

UN High Commissioner for Refugees, 50th Anniv. — A181

Designs: 700k, Children receiving food. 1500k, Woman carrying child.

Perf. 13¾x14¼
2001, Mar. 13   **Litho.**
915-916   A181   Set of 2   1.60   1.60

A182

Animals — A183

Designs: 500k, African buffalo. 1000k, Cheetah, vert. No. 919, 2000k, Female elephant. 3200k, Ruffed lemur, vert.

No. 921, 2000k: a, Crimson-breasted shrike. b, Common bee-eater. c, Blue monkey. d, Chimpanzee. e, Bush baby. f, Genet.

No. 922, 2000k, horiz.: a, Defassa waterbuck. b, Crowned crane. c, Red hartebeest. d, Pygmy hippopotamus. e, White rhinoceros. f, Giant forest hog.

No. 923, 2000k, horiz.: a, Cheetah. b, Three adult, one young impala. c, Four adult impalas. d, Warthog. e, Two lions. f, Four lions.

No. 924, 6000k, Bull elephant. No. 925, 6000k, Black rhinoceros. No. 926, 6000k, Zebras, vert.

Perf. 13¼x13½, 13½x13¼

2001, Mar. 30
917-920 A182 Set of 4 4.75 4.75
Sheets of 6, #a-f
921-923 A183 Set of 3 22.50 22.50
Souvenir Sheets
924-926 A182 Set of 3 11.00 11.00

Bird Type of 1999

Designs: No. 927, O, Knob-billed duck. No. 928, A, Blacksmith plover. No. 929, B, Sacred ibis. No. 930, C, Purple gallinule.

Perf. 14½x14¾

2001, Mar. 19 **Litho.**
927-930 A171 Set of 4 3.50 3.50

Nos. 927-930 each sold for 700k, 1200k, 1400k, and 1500k respectively on day of issue. No. 927 is dated "2000" and has a design width of 31½mm. No. 847 has no date and has a design width of 30½mm.

For surcharges, see Nos. 1119, 1120, 1147, 1148.

Total Solar Eclipse, June 21 — A184

Eclipse and: 1000k, Woman. 1500k, Bird. 1700k, Lizard. 1800k, Elephant and man. 2200k, Man.

2001, June 1 **Litho.** **Perf. 13¾**
931-935 A184 Set of 5 5.00 5.00

Phila Nippon '01, Japan — A185

Designs: No. 936, 500k, Senya Nakamura as Toknatsu, by Kiyomasu Torii I. No. 937, 500k, Kantaro Sanjo II and Monosuke Ichikawa I, by Okumura Masanobu, 1720. No. 938, 1000k, Kantaro Sanjo and Monosuke Ichikawa, by Masanobu, c. 1730. No. 939, 1000k, Standing Figure of a Woman, by Kiyomasu Torii I. 1500k, Ono no Komachi, by Masanobu. 1800k, Dog Bringing a Love Letter, by Shigenaga.

No. 942, 3200k: a, Matsue Nakamura as a Cat Woman, by Shunsho. b, Kantaro Sanjo With Branch of Bamboo, by Kiyomasu Torii I. c, Kinsaku Yamashika I as Peddler, by Kiyomasu Torii I. d, Portrait of an Actor, by Shunsho.

No. 943, 3200k: a, Kumetaro Nakamura I, by Shunsho. b, Actor in Female Role, by Kiyomasu Torii I. c, Kikunojo Segawa Leaning on Sugoroku Board, by Kiyomasu Torii I. d, Gennosuke Ichikawa as a Wakashu, by Kiyomasu Torii I.

No. 944, 6000k, Akashi of the Tamaya, by Ryukoku Hishikawa. No. 945, 6000k, Events of Year in the Floating World, by Moroshige, horiz.

2001, July 4 **Perf. 14**
936-941 A185 Set of 6 4.00 4.00
Sheets of 4, #a-d
942-943 A185 Set of 2 14.00 14.00
Souvenir Sheets
944-945 A185 Set of 2 6.50 6.50

SOS Children's Village A186

2001, July 30
946 A186 2500k multi 1.60 1.60

Royal Navy Submarines, Cent. — A187

No. 947, horiz.: a, HMS Tabard. b, HMS Opossum. c, HMS Unicorn. d, HMS Churchill. e, HMS Victorious. f, HMS Triumph.
6000k, Lieutenant Commander Malcolm David Wanklyn.

2001, July 30
947 A187 2000k Sheet of 6, #a-f 8.00 8.00
Souvenir Sheet
948 A187 6000k multi 4.25 4.25

Giuseppe Verdi (1813-1901), Opera Composer — A188

No. 949 — Actors in Falstaff : a, Benjamin Luxon (without hat). b, Luxon (with hat). c, Paul Plishka. d, Anne Collin.
8000k, Falstaff.

2001, July 30
949 A188 4000k Sheet of 4, #a-d 9.50 9.50
Souvenir Sheet
950 A188 8000k multi 5.50 5.50

Monet Paintings — A189

No. 951, horiz.: a, The Promenade at Argenteuil. b, View of the Argenteuil Plain from the Sannois Hills. c, The Seine at Argenteuil. d, The Basin at Argenteuil.
6000k, Rouen Cathedral Portal, Overcast Weather.

2001, July 30 **Perf. 13¾**
951 A189 1500k Sheet of 4, #a-d 6.50 6.50
Souvenir Sheet
952 A189 6000k multi 6.50 6.50

Mao Zedong (1893-1976) — A190

No. 953 — Mao in: a, 1918. b, 1945. c, 1937.
4000k, Portrait.

2001, July 30
953 A190 3200k Sheet of 3, #a-c 7.00 7.00
Souvenir Sheet
954 A190 4000k multi 5.00 5.00

Queen Victoria (1819-1901) — A191

No. 955: a, As child. b, Wearing black dress. c, With child. d, With Prince Albert. e, Wearing crown and red sash. f, Wearing red dress.
7000k, Portrait.

2001, July 30 **Perf. 14**
955 A191 2000k Sheet of 6, #a-f 7.25 7.25
Souvenir Sheet
956 A191 7000k multi 6.00 6.00

Queen Elizabeth II, 75th Birthday — A192

No. 957: a, As infant. b, As child. c, As child, in garden. d, Wearing hat.
8000k, Wearing green and black hat.

2001, July 30
957 A192 4000k Sheet of 4, #a-d 8.00 8.00
Souvenir Sheet
958 A192 8000k multi 6.00 6.00
No. 957 contains four 28x42mm stamps.

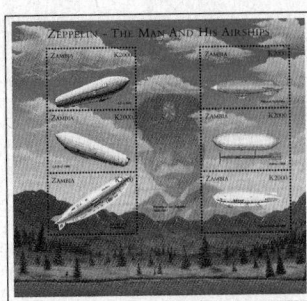

First Zeppelin Flight, Cent. — A193

No. 959: a, LZ-1. b, Parseval PL25. c, LZ-3. d, Baldwin. e, LZ-129. f, Norge Nobile N1.
No. 960, 700k, Graf Zeppelin, vert.

2001, July 30
959 A193 2000k Sheet of 6, #a-f 7.50 7.50
Souvenir Sheet
960 A173 700k multi .40 .40
No. 960 contains one 38x51mm stamp.

Pres. F. J. T.
Chiluba — A194

Chiluba: 1000k, Recieving Master's degree.
1500k, Signing forms. 1700k, With arm raised,
horiz.
6000k, Receiving Master's degree, diff.

2001   Litho.   **Perf. 14**
961-963 A194   Set of 3   3.75 3.75
Souvenir Sheet
964 A194 6000k multi   5.50 5.50

Nobel Prizes, Cent. (in 2001) — A195

No. 965, 2000k — Peace laureates: a, Nor-
man E. Borlaug, 1970. b, Lester B. Pearson,
1957. c, Intl. Red Cross, 1944. d, Anwar
Sadat, 1978. e, Georges Pire, 1958. f, Linus
Pauling, 1962.
No. 966, 2000k — Literature laureates: a,
Isaac Bashevis Singer, 1978. b, Gao Xingjian,
2000. c, Claude Simon, 1985. d, Naguib
Mahfouz, 1988. e, Camilo Jose Cela, 1989. f,
Czeslaw Milosz, 1980.
No. 967, 2000k — Literature laureates: a,
Seamus Heaney, 1995. b, Toni Morrison,
1993. c, Günter Grass, 1999. d, Wislawa
Szymborska, 1996. e, Dario Fo, 1997. f, José
Saramago, 1998.
No. 968, 6000k, George C. Marshall, Peace,
1953. No. 969, 6000k, Gerard Debreu, Eco-
nomics, 1983. No. 970, 6000k, Robert W.
Fogel, Economics, 1993.

2002, Feb. 11   Litho.   **Perf. 14**
Sheets of 6, #a-f
965-967 A195   Set of 3   17.50 17.50
Souvenir Sheets
968-970 A195   Set of 3   9.00 9.00

Souvenir Sheet

New Year 2002 (Year of the
Horse) — A196

2002, Feb. 18   **Perf. 13¼**
971 A196 5000k multi   3.00 3.00

2002 World Cup Soccer
Championships, Japan and
Korea — A197

No. 972, 2000k: a, Poster from 1954 World
Cup, Switzerland. b, Stanly Matthews and
English flag. c, Scottish player and flag. d, Bel-
gian player and flag. e, Player and Daejon
World Cup Stadium, Korea, horiz.
No. 973, 2000k: a, Ferenc Puskas and Hun-
garian flag. b, Poster from 1962 World Cup,
Chile. c, Spanish player and flag. d, English
player and flag. e, Player and Jeonju World
Cup Stadium, Korea, horiz.
No. 974, 8000k, Bryan Robson's goal
against France, 1982. No. 975, 8000k,
Salenko's fifth goal against Cameroon, 1994,
horiz.

2002, Feb. 26   **Perf. 14**
Sheets of 5, #a-e
972-973 A197   Set of 2   9.75 9.75
Souvenir Sheets
974-975 A197   Set of 2   8.00 8.00
   Size of Nos. 972a-972d, 973a-973d:
28x42mm.

United We
Stand — A198

2002, Feb.   **Perf. 13½x13¼**
976 A198 3200k multi   1.60 1.60
   Issued in sheets of 4.

Reign of Queen Elizabeth, 50th
Anniv. — A199

No. 977: a, Wearing blue and white hat. b,
Without hat. c, Wearing scarf. d, Wearing
tiara.
7500k, With Prince Philip.

2002, July 15   Litho.   **Perf. 14¼**
977 A199 3200k Sheet of 4, #a-d 6.50 6.50
Souvenir Sheet
978 A199 7500k multi   4.00 4.00

2002
Winter
Olympics,
Salt Lake
City
A200

Designs: 1000k, Ice hockey. 3200k, Cross-
country skiing.

2002, July 30   **Perf. 13¼x13¾**
979-980 A200   Set of 2   2.50 2.50

20th World Scout Jamboree,
Thailand — A201

No. 981, horiz.: a, Troop hiking. b, Knot
tying. c, Archery. d, Fire making.
8000k, Camping.

2002, July 30   **Perf. 14**
981 A201 3200k Sheet of 4, #a-d 6.75 6.75
Souvenir Sheet
982 A201 8000k multi   4.50 4.50

Intl. Year of Mountains — A202

No. 983: a, Mt. Whitney, US. b, Mt. Aconca-
gua, Argentina and Chile. c, Mt. Mönch, Switzerland. d, Mt. Ararat, Turkey.
9000k, Mt. Everest, Nepal and China.

2002, July 30
983 A202 1500k Sheet of 4, #a-d 3.75 3.75
Souvenir Sheet
984 A202 9000k multi   5.00 5.00

Birds — A203

Designs: 700k, Bee-eater. 1200k, Blue-
cheeked bee-eater. 1400k, Boehn's bee-eater.
1500k, Little bee-eater.

2002, Aug. 12
985-988 A203   Set of 4   4.25 4.25
   See Nos. 1027-1030. For surcharge, see
No. 1091.

Flowers, Butterflies and
Mushrooms — A204

No. 989, 2500k — Flowers: a, Camel's foot.
b, Christmas bells. c, Impala lily. d, Everlasting. e, Anomatheca grandiflora. f, Soldier lily.
No. 990, 2500k — Butterflies: a, False monarch. b, Golden piper. c, Blue pansy. d, Christmas tree acraea. e, Grass yellow. f, Gold-spot-
ted sylph.
No. 991, 2500k — Mushrooms: a, Copper
trumpet. b, King bolete. c, Death cap. d, Fly
agaric. e, Chanterelle. f, Deadly fiber cap.
No. 992, 8000k, Arum lily. No. 993, 8000k,
African monarch butterfly. No. 994, 8000k,
Stump brittle-head mushrooms.

2002, Sept. 9   Litho.
Sheets of 6, #a-f
989-991 A204   Set of 3   20.00 20.00
Souvenir Sheets
992-994 A204   Set of 3   15.00 15.00

Nos. 624, 629, 645 Surcharged

Methods & Perfs as Before
2002, July 1
996 A128 250k on 50k #639   —   —
997 A127 300k on 50k #624   —   —
998 A130 1000k on 100k #645   —   —

Coronation of Queen Elizabeth II, 50th
Anniv. — A205

No. 999: a, Wearing crown and pearl necklace. b, Wearing tiara and jeweled necklace. c,
Wearing pink and black hat.
10,000k, Wearing flowered dress and hat.

2003, May 19   Litho.   **Perf. 14**
999 A205 5000k Sheet of 3,
              #a-c   7.25 7.25
Souvenir Sheet
1000 A205 10,000k multi   5.00 5.00

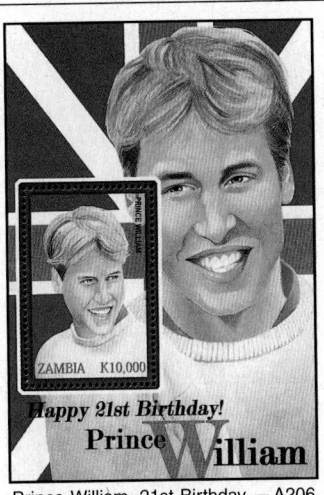

Prince William, 21st Birthday — A206

No. 1001: a, Wearing bow tie. b, Wearing blue shirt and tie. c, Wearing yellow and black sports shirt.
10,000k, Wearing sweater.

2003, May 19
1001 A206 5000k Sheet of 3, #a-c   7.25 7.25

Souvenir Sheet
1002 A206 10,000k multi   5.00 5.00

Nos. 654-657 Srchd.

Nos. 639-642 Surcharged

K1700

Nos. 617-620 Surcharged

K1800

Nos. 650-653 Surcharged

K2200

Nos. 710-712 Surcharged

K2500

Methods & Perfs. as Before
2003, June 26
1003	A133	1000k on 200k #654	25.00	25.00
1004	A133	1000k on 300k #655	25.00	25.00
1005	A133	1000k on 500k #656	25.00	25.00

1006	A133	1000k on 900k #657	25.00	25.00
1007	A128	1700k on 50k #639	1.00	1.00
1008	A128	1700k on 200k #640	1.00	1.00
1009	A128	1700k on 300k #641	1.00	1.00
1010	A128	1700k on 500k #642	1.00	1.00
1011	A125	1800k on 50k #617	1.10	1.10
1012	A125	1800k on 200k #618	1.10	1.10
1013	A125	1800k on 250k #619	1.10	1.10
1014	A125	1800k on 300k #620	1.10	1.10
1015	A132	2200k on 100k #650	1.25	1.25
1016	A132	2200k on 300k #651	1.25	1.25
1017	A132	2200k on 450k #652	1.25	1.25
1018	A132	2200k on 500k #653	1.25	1.25
1019	A145	2500k on 500k #710	1.50	1.50
1020	A145	2500k on (O) #711	1.50	1.50
1021	A145	2500k on 900k #712	1.50	1.50
Nos. 1003-1021 (19)			117.90	117.90

Location of surcharges vary on Nos. 1019-1021.

Miniature Sheet

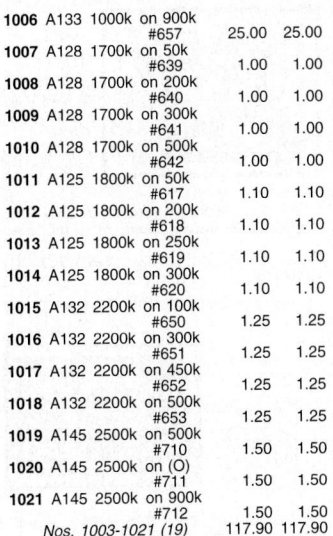

New Year 2003 (Year of the Ram) — A207

No. 1022 — Background colors: a, Green. b, Blue violet. c, Maroon. d, Purple.

2003, July 30   **Litho.**   *Perf. 13¼*
1022 A207 3200k Sheet of 4, #a-d   6.50 6.50

Intl. Year of Fresh Water — A208

No. 1023: a, Cabora Bassa Dam. b, Lake Kariba. c, Mana Pools National Park.
10,000k, Victoria Falls.

2003, July 30   *Perf. 13½x13¼*
1023 A208 5000k Sheet of 3, #a-c   7.50 7.50

Souvenir Sheet
1024 A208 10,000k multi   5.00 5.00

Powered Flight, Cent. — A209

No. 1025: a, Avro 547A. b, Avro 504O with floats. c, Avro 584 Avrocet. d, Avro 504M.
10,000k, Avro 621 Tutor Replica.

2003, July 30   *Perf. 14*
1025 A209 4000k Sheet of 4, #a-d   7.75 7.75

Souvenir Sheet
1026 A209 9000k multi   5.00 5.00

Bird Type of 2002

Designs: 1000k, White-fronted bee-eaters. 1200k, Little bee-eaters. 1500k, Blue-cheeked bee-eater. 1800k, Boehn's bee-eater.

2003, Dec. 26   *Perf. 13¼*
Size: 25x20mm
1027-1030 A203   Set of 4   2.50 2.50
For surcharges, see Nos. 1089, 1109, 1143.

Rotary International in Zambia, 50th Anniv. — A210

Design: 1000k, Rotary emblem and hands. 1200k, Rotary emblem.

2003, Nov. 21   **Litho.**   *Perf. 13*
1031 A210 1000k multi   — —
1032 A210 1200k multi   — —
For surcharges, see Nos. 1107, 1123, 1154.

Miniature Sheet

Birds — A211

No. 1033: a, 500k, African fish eagles, national bird of Zimbabwe. b, 750k, Cattle egrets, national bird of Botswana. c, 1000k, African fish eagles, national bird of Zambia. d, 1100k, Peregrine falcons, national bird of Angola. e, 1500k, Bar-tailed trogons. f, 1700k, African fish eagles, national bird of Namibia. g, 1800k, Purple-crested louries, national bird of Swaziland. h, 2200k, Blue cranes, national bird of South Africa.

2004, Oct. 11   **Litho.**   *Perf. 14*
1033 A211   Sheet of 8, #a-h   4.50 4.50
See Botswana Nos. 792-793, Namibia No. 1052, South Africa No. 1342, Swaziland Nos. 727-735, and Zimbabwe No. 975.

Independence, 40th Anniv. — A212

Design: 1500k, Vimbuza dancer. 1800k, Kayowe dancer. 2700k, Ngoma dancer. 3300k, Ukishi dancer.

2004, Oct. 23   **Litho.**   *Perf. 13x13¼*
1034 A212 1500k multi   — —
1035 A212 1800k multi   — —
1036 A212 2700k multi   — —
1037 A212 3300k multi   — —
For surcharges, see Nos. 1112, 1144.

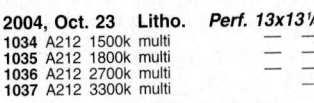

No. 649 Surcharged

Methods and Perfs As Before
2004, Dec. 28
Granite Paper
1038 A131 1000k on 700k #649   *1.50* 1.50

Mammals A213

Designs: No. 1039, 2250k, Acionyx jubatus. No. 1040, 2250k, Phacochoerus aethiopicus. No. 1041, 2250k, Giraffa camelopardalis. 2700k, Syncerus caffer.
No. 1043, vert.: a, Panthera pardus. b, Pan troglodytes. c, Lycaon pictus. d, Equus burchelli.
10,000k, Diceros bicornis, vert.

2005, June 27   **Litho.**   *Perf. 14*
1039-1042 A213   Set of 4   4.25 4.25
1043 A213 3300k Sheet of 4, #a-d   5.75 5.75

Souvenir Sheet
1044 A213 10,000k multi   4.50 4.50

Insects — A214

Designs: 1500k, Fornasinius russus. No. 1046, 2250k, Goliathus giganteus. No. 1047, 2250k, Macrorhina. 2700k, Chelorrhina polyphemus.
No. 1048: a, Sternotomis virescens. b, Cicindela regalis. c, Goliathus meleagris. d, Mecosasms explanta.
10,000k, Meloid.

2005, June 27
1045-1048 A214   Set of 4   3.75 3.75
1049 A214 3300k Sheet of 4, #a-d   5.75 5.75

Souvenir Sheet
1050 A214 10,000k multi   4.50 4.50

Butterflies — A215

Designs: No. 1051, 2250k, Ropalo ceres. No. 1052, 2250k, Morpho portis nymphalidae. No. 1053, 2250k, Phyllocnistis citrella. 2700k, H. misippus.
No. 1055: a, Colotis evippe. b, Papilio lormieri. c, Papilio dardanus. d, Papilio zalmoxis.
10,000k, Epiphora albida druce.

2005, June 27
1051-1054 A215   Set of 4   4.25 4.25

1055 A215　3300k Sheet of 4,
　　　　　#a-d　　　　5.75 5.75
　　　Souvenir Sheet
1056 A215　10,000k multi　　4.50 4.50

Orchids — A216

Designs: No. 1057, 1500k, Disa draconis.
No. 1058, 1500k, Disa uniflora. No. 1059,
1500k, Disa uniflora orange. 2700k, Phalaenopsis penetrate.
　No. 1061: a, Ansellia africana (yellow
flower). b, Ansellia africana (spotted flower). c,
Cattleya lueddemanniana. d, Laelia
tenebrosa.
　10,000k, Cymbidium.

2005, June 27
1057-1060 A216　Set of 4　　3.25 3.25
1061 A216　3300k Sheet of 4,
　　　　　#a-d　　　　5.75 5.75
　　　Souvenir Sheet
1062 A216　10,000k multi　　4.50 4.50

Jesuits in
Zambia,
Cent.
A217

Designs: 1500k, Bishop Paul Lungu, Map of
Zambia. 2550k, Father Torrend, Kasisi
Church. 2700k, Father Moreau, Chikuni
Church. 3300k, St. Ignatius of Loyola.

2005, June 25　Litho.　Perf. 13¼x13
1063-1066 A217　Set of 4　　4.50 4.50
1066a　Souvenir sheet, #1063-1066　4.50 4.50

Dag
Hammarskjöld
(1905-61), UN
Secretary
General
A218

Background color: 1500k, Dark blue. 2700k,
Blue green.

2005, July 29　Litho.　Perf. 13½
1067-1068 A218　Set of 2　　6.50 6.50
1068a　Souvenir sheet of 2,
　　　#1067-1068　　　6.50 6.50

For surcharge, see No. 1145.

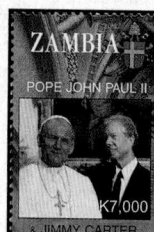

Pope John Paul II
(1920-2005) and
Pres. Jimmy
Carter — A219

Pope John Paul II — A220

No. 1070: a, With Sri Chinmoy. b, With boy
and dove. c, With Schneider brothers. d, Visiting Ukraine.

2005, Aug. 22　Litho.　Perf. 12¾
1069 A219　7000k multi　　3.00 3.00
1070 A220　3300k Sheet of 4, #a-
　　　　d　　　　5.75 5.75

No. 1069 was printed in sheets of 4.

A221

Railroads, 200th Anniv. — A222

No. 1071: a, Chinese Class KF 4-8-4. b,
Indian Class WP 4-6-2. c, Irish 800 Class 4-6-
0. d, French 241A Class 4-8-2.
　No. 1072, 1700k: a, British Rail Class 4MT
2-6-4T. b, South African Railways Class 12A.
c, Cuban sugar plantation locomotive. d,
LNER A4 Pacific facing right. e, LNER A4
Pacific facing left. f, GWR City of Truro 4-4-0.
g, British Rail HST Intercity 125. h, Eurostar. i,
LNER A3 Flying Scotsman.
　No. 1073, 1700k: a, Southern Railway King
Arthur Class 4-6-0. b, Berkshire at Kaiiman's
Bridge. c, Indian Railways WT Class 2-84
Suburban Tank steam locomotive. d, Ladders
on shell of railway car being built. e, Worker on
knees inside railway car. f, Yellow staircase
next to railway car. g, Workers looking at
undercarriage of raised railway car. h, Railway
car between blue machinery. i, Model of steam
locomotive.
　No. 1074, 1700k: a, Great Western Hall
Class 4-6-0. b, Argentinian 15B Class 4-8-0. c,
Mallet Meter Gauge steam locomotive. d,
Worker cutting track. e, Worker and pulley. f,
Workers in cherrypicker. g, Workers on tracks
and in cherrypickers. h, Workers pouring
cement. i, Track workers.
　No. 1075, Finnish Class HV2 4-6-0.
　No. 1076, 8000k, Orient Express. No. 1077,
8000k, Edinburgh to London train. No. 1078,
800k, Bernina Express.

2005, Aug. 22
1071 A221　4200k Sheet of 4,
　　　　　#a-d　　　　7.50 7.50
　　　Sheets of 9, #a-i
1072-1074 A222　Set of 3　　20.00 20.00
　　　Souvenir Sheets
1075 A221　8000k multi　　3.50 3.50
1076-1078 A222　Set of 3　　10.50 10.50

David
Livingstone
at Victoria
Falls,
150th
Anniv.
A223

Designs: 1500k, Livingstone, Victoria Falls.
2700k, Statue of Livingstone, railroad bridge.

2006, Jan. 20　Litho.　Perf. 13x13¼
1079-1080 A223　Set of 2　　2.60 2.60

For surcharges, see Nos. 1113, 1150.

Franciscan
Conventuals
in Zambia,
75th Anniv.
A224

Design: 2250k, Sister Moon. 2700k, Brother
Sun. 3300k, Sister Water.

2006, July 8　Litho.　Perf. 13¼x13
1082 A224　2250k multi　　—
1083 A224　2700k multi　　—
1084 A224　3300k multi　　—

An additional stamp was issued in this set.
The editors would like to examine any
examples.

Queen Elizabeth II, 80th
Birthday — A225

No. 1085 — Queen: a, Wearing crown. b,
Wearing necklace. c, Wearing necklace and
jacket. d, With Princess Anne.
　6500k, Wearing green hat.

2006, Aug. 8　Litho.　Perf. 13¼
1085 A225　3200k Sheet of 4, #a-
　　　　d　　　　6.50 6.50
　　　Souvenir Sheet
1086 A225　6500k multi　　3.25 3.25

Scouting, Cent. (in 2007) — A226

No. 1087, vert. — Scouting emblem, doves,
Lord Robert Baden-Powell and background
colors of: a, Pink and lilac. b, Yellow and
orange. c, Blue and light blue. d, Light green
and green.
　6500k, Purple and red.

2006, Aug. 8
1087 A226　3200k Sheet of 4, #a-
　　　　d　　　　6.50 6.50
　　　Souvenir Sheet
1088 A226　6500k multi　　3.25 3.25

Nos. 623, 987 and
1028 Surcharged

Methods and Perfs As Before
2007
1089 A203　1500k on 1200k
　　　　#1028　　　.70　.70
1090 A127　1850k on 20k #623　.95　.95
1091 A203　3300k on 1400k #987　1.60 1.60
　　Nos. 1089-1091 (3)　　3.25 3.25

Issued: Nos. 1089, 1091, 3/19; No. 1090,
5/30.

Miniature Sheet

Tazara Railway, 30th Anniv. (in
2006) — A227

No. 1092: a, Map of Tanzania and Zambia,
waterfall, mountain, people waving, and men
signing agreement. b, Men and train, elephant
and antelope. c, Dar es Salaam Station, sign
and wreaths with Chinese inscriptions. d, New
Kapiri Mposhi Station, people near train. e,
Train, bridge and tunnel, zebra and giraffe. f,
Train on bridge, lion and lioness.

2007, May 28　Litho.　Perf. 12
1092 A227　1500k Sheet of 6, #a-
　　　　f　　　　4.75 4.75

Mammals
A228

Designs: 1500k, Bat-eared fox. 2250k, Spotted hyena. 2700k, Aardwolf. 3300k, Side-
striped jackal.

2007, June 29　　　Perf. 13¼x13
1093-1096 A228　Set of 4　　5.25 5.25
1096a　Souvenir sheet, #1093-1096　5.25 5.25

For surcharges, see Nos. 1110, 1114, 1122,
1146, 1149, 1151, 1153.

National
Animals
A229

Designs: 1500k, Buffalo (Zambia). 1800k,
Nyala (Malawi). 2250k, Nyala (Zimbabwe).
2700k, Burchell's zebra (Botswana). 3300k,
Oryx (Namibia).

Litho. With Foil Application
2007, Oct. 9　　　Perf. 13¾
1097-1101 A229　Set of 5　　6.25 6.25

See Botswana No. 838, Malawi No. 752,
Namibia Nos. 1141-1142, Zimbabwe Nos.
1064-1068.

Miniature Sheet

2008 Summer Olympics,
Beijing — A230

No. 1102: a, Soccer. b, Hurdles. c, Boxing.
d, Swimming.

2008, June 8	**Litho.**		**Perf. 12**
1102	A230	2000k Sheet of 4, #a-d	5.00 5.00

Worldwide Fund for Nature
(WWF) — A231

No. 1103 — Greater kudu: a, Two males battling. b, Female and calf. c, Male drinking. d, Female and tree branches.

2008, June 30			**Perf. 13¼**
1103		Horiz. strip or block of 4	7.25 7.25
a.-d.	A231	3000k Any single	1.75 1.75
e.		Miniature sheet of 8, 2 each #1103a-1103d	14.50 14.50

Muhammad Ali, Boxer — A232

No. 1104 — Ali: a, In fighting stance without boxing gloves. b, Looking right. c, With gloved fist at chest level. d, With gloved fist near head. e, Pointing. f, Holding Olympic torch.
3200k, Ali wearing crown, with arms raised, and boxing.

2008			**Perf. 14**
1104	A232	500k Sheet of 6, #a-f	1.90 1.90

Souvenir Sheet
Perf. 13½x13¾

1105	A232	3200k multi	1.90 1.90

No. 1105 contains one 38x50mm stamp. Nos. 1104-1105 were said to have been released in 1998, but did not appear in the marketplace until 2008.

No. 905
Surcharged

Method and Perf. As Before
2008, July 22
1106 A179 1500k on 1400k #905 .90 .90

No. 1032
Surcharged

Method and Perf. As Before
2009, Feb. 17
1107	A210	1500k on 1200k #1032	1.50 1.50

Peonies
A233

2009, Apr. 10	**Litho.**		**Perf. 13¼**
1108	A233	2000k multi	.75 .75

Printed in sheets of 8.

No. 1030
Surcharged

Method and Perf. As Before
2009, May 29
1109	A203	1500k on 1800k #1030	1.50 1.50

No. 1094
Surcharged

No. 1068
Surcharged

No. 1036
Surcharged

No. 1080
Srchd.

No. 1095
Surcharged

2009   Method and Perf. As Before
1110	A228	3300k on 2250k #1094	7.75 7.75
1111	A218	3500k on 2700k #1068	—

1112	A212	3800k on 2700k #1036	— —
1113	A223	4050k on 2700k #1080	— —
1114	A228	4950k on 2700k #1095	— —

Issued: Nos. 1110-1111, 1113, 5/29, Nos. 1112, 1114, 12/1.
For surcharges, see Nos. 1150, 1151.

2010 World Cup Soccer
Championships, South Africa — A234

Soccer players, ball, 2010 World Cup mascot and flag of: Nos. 1115, 1118e, 2500k, Zambia. Nos. 1116, 1118h, 4050k, Namibia. Nos. 1117, 1118i, 4950k, South Africa.
No. 1118: a, 900k, Lesotho. b, 1000k, Mauritius. c, 2050k, Botswana. d, 2250k, Zimbabwe. f, 3500k, Malawi. g, 3800k, Swaziland.

2010, Apr. 9	**Litho.**		**Perf. 13½**

On Plain Paper With Olive Brown Background
1115-1117	A234	Set of 3	5.00 5.00

On Gold-faced Paper
1118	A234	Sheet of 9, #a-i	11.00 11.00

See Botswana Nos. 896-905, Lesotho No. , Malawi No. 753, Mauritius No. , Namibia No. 1188, South Africa No. 1403, Swaziland Nos. 794-803, and Zimbabwe Nos.1112-1121.

Nos. 649, 928, 929, 1032 and 1094 Surcharged

Methods and Perfs As Before
2010 ?
1119	A171	2500k on A #928	— —
1120	A171	2500k on B #929	— —
1121	A131	5000k on 700k #649	— —
1122	A228	10,000k on 2250k #1094	— —
1123	A210	10,000k on 1200k #1032	— —

Issued: No. 1120, 11/12/10.
For surcharges, see Nos. 1147, 1148, 1152, 1153, 1154.

Miniature Sheet

Dr. David Livingstone (1813-73),
African Missionary and
Explorer — A237

No. 1142: a, 25k, Livingstone. b, 30k, Map of northern Zambia, rhinoceros. c, 40k, Map of southwestern Zambia, hippopotamus, antelope. d, 50k, Map of southeastern Zambia, lion.

2013, Mar. 19	**Litho.**		**Perf. 13¼x13**
1142	A237	Sheet of 4, #a-d	54.00 54.00

Nos. 1028, 1036, 1068, 1095-1096, 1113-1114, 1119-1123 Surcharged

Methods and Perfs As Before
2013
1143	A203	1.50k on 1200k #1028	— —
1144	A212	1.50k on 2700k #1036	— —
1145	A218	1.50k on 2700k #1068	— —
1146	A228	1.50k on 2700k #1095	— —
1147	A171	2.50k on 2500k on A #1119	— —
1148	A171	2.50k on 2500k on B #1120	— —
1149	A228	3.80k on 2475k on 3300k #1096	— —
1150	A223	4.05k on 4050k on 2700k #1113	— —
1151	A228	4.95k on 4950k on 2700k #1114	— —
1152	A131	5k on 5000k on 700k #1121	— —
1153	A228	10k on 10,000k on 2250k #1122	— —
1154	A210	10k on 10,000k on 1200k #1123	— —

POSTAGE DUE STAMPS

Type of Northern Rhodesia
Perf. 12½

1964, Oct. 24		**Litho.**		**Unwmk.**
J1	D2	1p orange	.25	1.10
J2	D2	2p dark blue	.25	1.10
J3	D2	3p rose claret	.25	1.40
J4	D2	4p violet blue	.35	1.75
J5	D2	6p purple	.50	2.25
J6	D2	1sh emerald	1.50	8.00
		Nos. J1-J6 (6)	3.10	15.60

ZANZIBAR

'zan-zə-,bär

LOCATION — Group of islands about twenty miles off the coast of Tanganyika in East Africa
GOVT. — Republic
AREA — 1,044 sq. mi. (approx.)
POP. — 354,360 (est. 1967)
CAPITAL — Zanzibar

Before 1895, unoverprinted stamps of India were used in Zanzibar.

Zanzibar was a British protectorate until Dec. 10, 1963, when it became independent. After a revolt in January, 1964, a republic was established. Zanzibar joined Tanganyika Apr. 26, 1964, to form the United Republic of Tanganyika and Zanzibar (later renamed Tanzania). See Tanzania.

12 Pies = 1 Anna
16 Annas = 1 Rupee
100 Cents = 1 Rupee (1908)
100 Cents = 1 Shilling (1935)

Catalogue values for unused stamps in this country are for Never Hinged items, beginning with Scott 201 in the regular postage section and Scott J18 in the postage due section.

Watermarks

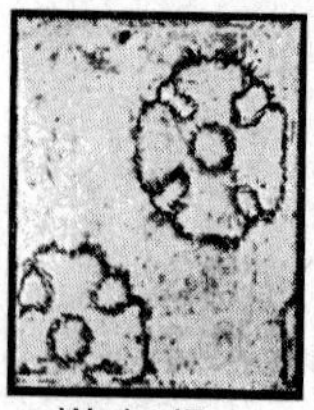

Wmk. 47 — Multiple Rosette

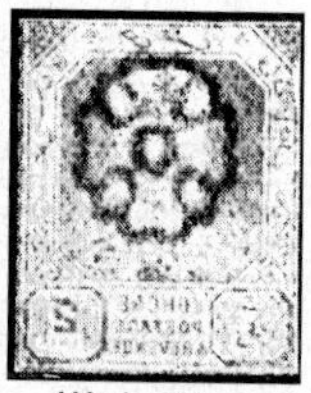

Wmk. 71 — Rosette

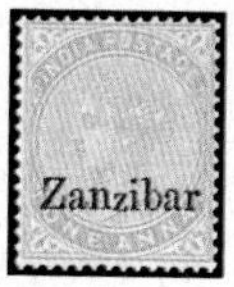

Stamps of British India Overprinted

On Stamps of 1882-95

1895 Wmk. Star (39) *Perf. 14*

Blue Overprint

No.	Type	Description	Unused	Used
1	A17	½a green	30,000.	6,250.
2	A19	1a violet brn	3,500.	600.
a.		"Zanzidar"		28,500.

1895-96 Black Overprint

No.	Type	Description	Unused	Used
3	A17	½a green	5.00	5.00
a.		"Zanzidar"	1,450.	800.00
b.		"Zanibar"	1,450.	1,900.
c.		"Zapzibar"		
4	A19	1a violet brn	5.25	4.25
a.		"Zanzidar"	—	4,000.
b.		"Zanibar"	1,900.	2,250.
5	A20	1a6p bister brn	5.50	4.25
a.		"Zanzidar"	4,500.	1,200.
b.		"Zanizbar"	2,000.	
c.		"Zanibar"	1,800.	1,750.
d.		"Zapzibar"	125.00	125.00
6	A21	2a ultra	10.00	9.00
a.		"Zanzidar"	8,500.	3,500.
b.		"Zanibar"	6,750.	2,500.
c.		"Zapzibar"	150.00	160.00
d.		Double overprint	310.00	
7	A28	2a6p green	10.00	5.50
a.		"Zanzidar"	8,500.	1,800.
b.		"Zanibar"	800.00	1,400.
c.		"Zapzibar"		
d.		"Zanzipar"	1,250.	
8	A22	3a orange	13.50	17.50
a.		"Zanzidar"	1,150.	2,150.
b.		"Zanizbar"	7,500.	8,000.
9	A23	4a olive grn	22.50	20.00
a.		"Zanzidar"	11,500.	4,750.
10	A25	8a red vio	36.00	30.00
a.		"Zanzidar"	11,500.	9,000.
11	A26	12a vio, *red*	20.00	11.50
a.		"Zanzidar"	11,500.	5,000.
12	A27	1r gray	125.00	100.00
a.		"Zanzidar"	10,500.	6,750.
13	A29	1r car rose & grn	22.50	30.00
a.		Vertical overprint	475.00	
14	A30	2r brn & rose	125.00	135.00
a.		"Zanziba"	32,500.	—
b.		Inverted "r"	4,500.	5,500.
c.		Pair, one without overprint		
15	A30	3r grn & brn	95.00	105.00
a.		"Zanziba"	32,500.	
b.		Inverted "r"	6,750.	6,750.
16	A30	5r vio & blue	105.00	97.50
a.		"Zanziba"	32,500.	
b.		Inverted "r"	5,000.	6,000.
c.		Dbl. ovpt., one invtd.	950.00	

On Stamp of 1873-76

Wmk. Elephant's Head (38)

No.	Type	Description	Unused	Used
17	A14	6a bister	22.50	12.50
a.		"Zanzidar"	11,500.	4,000.
b.		"Zanzibarr"	7,240.	4,400.
c.		"Zanibar"	900.00	1,400.
d.		"Zapzibar"		
e.		Double overprint		
		Nos. 3-17 (15)	622.75	587.00

Double and triple overprints, with one overprint albino, and color varieties exist for most of the 1-17 overprints. For detailed listings, see *Scott Classic Specialized Catalogue.*

Nos. 4-6 Surcharged

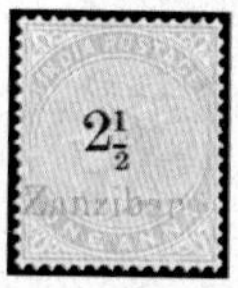

a

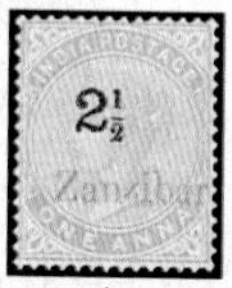

b

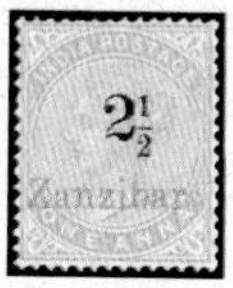

c

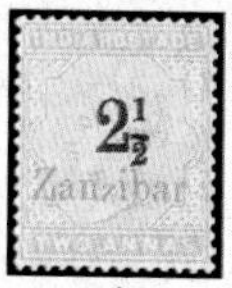

d

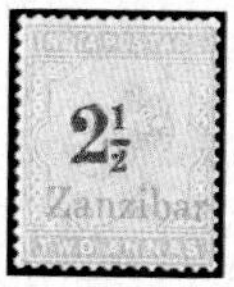

e

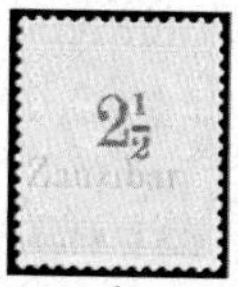

f

1896 Wmk. Star (39)

Black Surcharge

No.	Type	Description	Unused	Used
18	(a)	2½a on 1a	200.00	110.00
19	(b)	2½a on 1a	525.00	350.00
20	(c)	2½a on 1a	225.00	125.00

Red Surcharge

No.	Type	Description	Unused	Used
21	(a)	2½a on 1a	275.00	725.00
22	(b)	2½a on 1a	500.00	1,050.
23	(c)	2½a on 1a	310.00	725.00
24	(a)	2½a on 1a6p	85.00	60.00
a.		"Zanzidar"	1,700.	1,450.
b.		"Zanizbar"	5,250.	2,250.
24C	(b)	2½a on 1a6p	250.00	550.00
25	(c)	2½a on 1a6p	145.00	350.00
26	(d)	2½a on 1a6p	200.00	175.00
27	(e)	2½a on 1a6p	475.00	400.00
27A	(f)	2½a on 1a6p	27,500.	18,000.
28	(a)	2½a on 2a	160.00	360.00
28A	(b)	2½a on 2a	340.00	625.00
29	(c)	2½a on 2a	180.00	425.00
30	(d)	2½a on 2a	80.00	47.50
31	(e)	2½a on 2a	225.00	125.00
31A	(f)	2½a on 2a	5,750.	2,800.

Certain type varieties are found in the word "Zanzibar" on Nos. 1 to 31A viz: Inverted "q" for "b," broken "p" for "n," "i" without dot, small second "z" and tall second "z." These varieties are found on all values from ½a to 1r inclusive and the tall "z" is also found on the 2r, 3r and 5r.

Double and triple "Zanzibar" with one or two overprints albino exist for most of the 18-31 overprints. For detailed listings, see *Scott Classic Specialized Catalogue.*

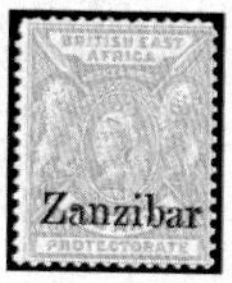

Stamps of British East Africa, 1896, Overprinted in Black or Red

1896 Wmk. Crown and C A (2)

No.	Type	Description	Unused	Used
32	A8	½a yellow grn	42.50	25.00
33	A8	1a carmine	42.50	19.00
a.		Double overprint	825.00	1,000.
34	A8	2½a dk blue (R)	100.00	52.50
35	A8	4½a orange	55.00	65.00
36	A8	5a dark ocher	70.00	45.00
37	A8	7½a lilac	60.00	70.00
		Nos. 32-37 (6)	370.00	276.50

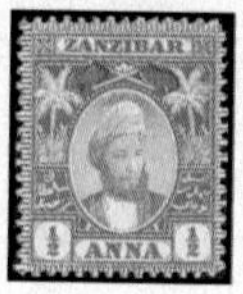

A2

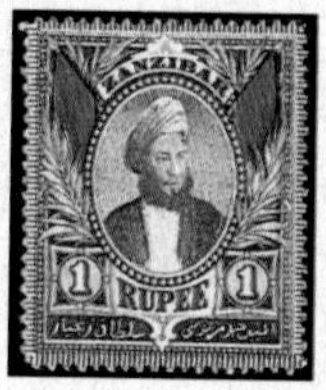

Sultan Seyyid Hamed-bin-Thwain A3

1896, Sept. 20 Engr. Wmk. 71

No.	Type	Description	Unused	Used
38	A2	½a yel grn & red	4.50	2.00
39	A2	1a indigo & red	4.00	1.75
40	A2	2a red brn & red	3.75	.85
41	A2	2½a ultra & red	17.50	1.60
42	A2	3a slate & red	19.00	10.00
43	A2	4a dk green & red	12.00	6.00
44	A2	4½a orange & red	8.75	7.00
45	A2	5a bister & red	9.25	4.00
a.		Half used as 2½a on cover		4,900.
46	A2	7½a lilac & red	6.50	6.50
47	A2	8a ol gray & red	13.50	9.00
48	A3	1r ultra & red	24.00	12.00
49	A3	2r green & red	32.50	13.00
50	A3	3r violet & red	36.00	13.00
51	A3	4r lake & red	27.50	20.00
52	A3	5r blk brn & red	38.00	20.00
		Nos. 38-52 (15)	256.75	126.70

No. 43 Surcharged in Red

1897

No.	Type	Description	Unused	Used
53	A2 (a)	2½a on 4a	100.00	55.00
54	A2 (b)	2½a on 4a	325.00	300.00
55	A2 (c)	2½a on 4a	120.00	82.50
		Nos. 53-55 (3)	545.00	437.50

1898 Engr. Wmk. 47

No.	Type	Description	Unused	Used
56	A2	½a yel grn & red	1.75	.45
57	A2	1a indigo & red	6.00	1.40
58	A2	2a red brn & red	9.25	2.25
58A	A2	2½a ultra & red	5.50	.45
59	A2	3a slate & red	8.25	.75
60	A2	4a dk grn & red	4.25	1.25
60A	A2	4½a orange & red	15.00	1.25
61	A2	5a bister & red	22.50	2.25
61A	A2	7½a lilac & red	17.50	3.50
61B	A2	8a ol gray & red	22.00	3.25
		Nos. 56-61B (10)	112.00	16.80

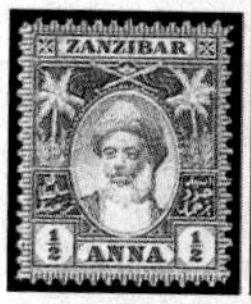

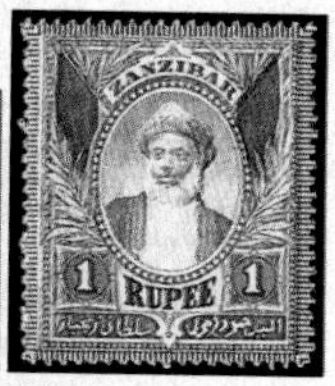

Sultan Seyyid Hamoud-bin-Mahommed-bin-Said
A4 A5

1899-1901

No.	Type	Description	Unused	Used
62	A4	½a yel grn & red	3.00	.65
63	A4	1a indigo & red	5.00	.25
64	A4	1a car & red ('01)	3.75	.25
65	A4	2a red brn & red	4.50	.75
66	A4	2½a ultra & red	4.50	.75
67	A4	3a slate & red	6.50	3.00
68	A4	4a dk green & red	6.00	3.25
69	A4	4½a orange & red	20.00	9.25
70	A4	4½a ind & red ('01)	22.00	14.50
71	A4	5a bister & red	6.50	2.40
72	A4	7½a lilac & red	6.50	7.00
73	A4	8a ol gray & red	6.50	5.50

Wmk. 71

No.	Type	Description	Unused	Used
74	A5	1r ultra & red	24.00	17.50
75	A5	2r green & red	27.50	24.00
76	A5	3r violet & red	50.00	52.50
77	A5	4r lilac rose & red	75.00	77.50
78	A5	5r gray brown & red	85.00	95.00
		Nos. 62-78 (17)	356.25	314.05

For surcharges see Nos. 94-98.

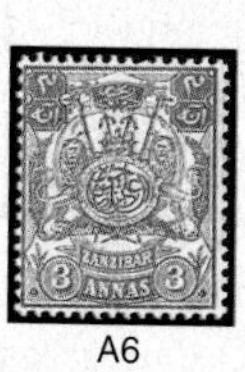

A6

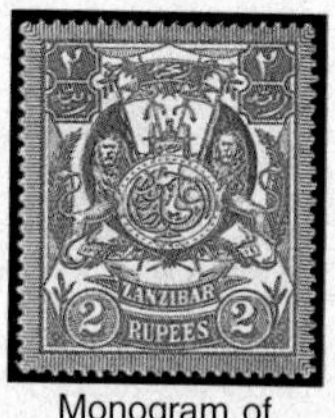

Monogram of Sultan Ali bin Hamoud — A7

1904, June 8 Typo. Wmk. 47

No.	Type	Description	Unused	Used
79	A6	½a emerald	3.00	1.00
80	A6	1a rose red	3.00	.25
81	A6	2a bister brown	5.00	.50
82	A6	2½a ultra	5.00	.40
83	A6	3a gray	6.00	2.50
84	A6	4a blue green	4.50	1.75
85	A6	4½a black	5.00	2.75
86	A6	5a ocher	7.50	1.90
87	A6	7½a violet	9.25	8.75
88	A6	8a olive green	6.50	5.50
89	A7	1r ultra & red	37.50	27.50
90	A7	2r green & red	45.00	55.00
91	A7	3r violet & red	65.00	100.00
92	A7	4r magenta & red	75.00	120.00
93	A7	5r olive & red	75.00	120.00
		Nos. 79-93 (15)	352.25	447.80

Nos. 69-70, 72-73 Surcharged in Black or Lake

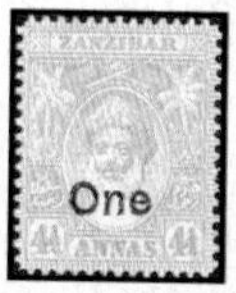

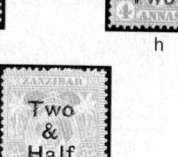

g

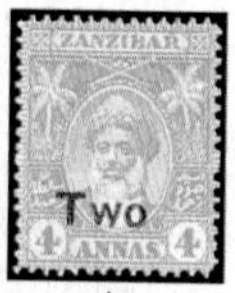

h

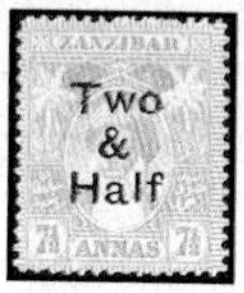

i

1904

No.	Type	Description	Unused	Used
94	A4 (g)	1a on 4½a	5.00	6.00
95	A4 (g)	1a on 4½a (L)	6.00	24.00
96	A4 (h)	2a on 4a (L)	19.00	24.00
97	A4 (i)	2½a on 7½a	17.50	25.00
a.		"Hlaf"	16,000.	
98	A4 (i)	2½a on 8a	29.00	40.00
a.		"Hlaf"	15,000.	10,000.
		Nos. 94-98 (5)	76.50	119.00

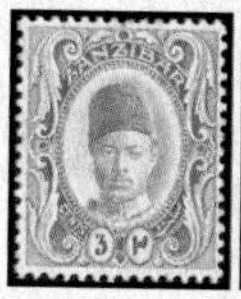

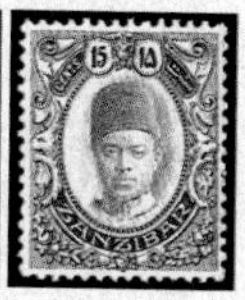

Sultan Ali bin Hamoud
A8 A9

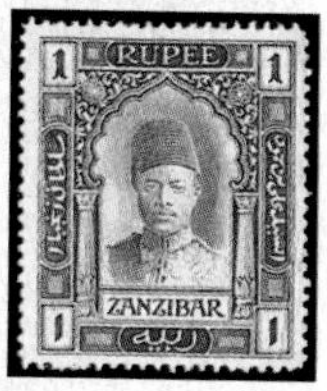

A10

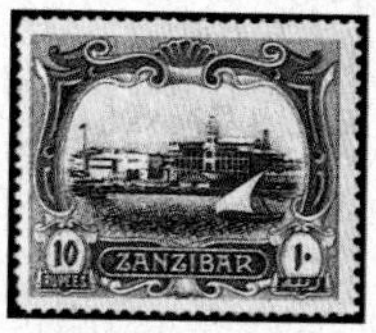

Palace of the Sultan — A11

1908-09 Engr. Wmk. 47

No.	Type	Description	Unused	Used
99	A8	1c gray ('09)	2.75	.35
100	A8	3c yellow grn	9.00	.25
101	A8	6c carmine	11.00	.25
102	A8	10c org brn ('09)	7.00	2.25
103	A8	12c violet	19.00	3.25
104	A9	15c ultra & pur	18.00	.45
105	A9	25c brown	8.50	1.10
106	A9	50c dp green	10.00	7.00
107	A9	75c slate ('09)	16.00	17.50
108	A10	1r yellow green	42.50	14.00
109	A10	2r violet	21.00	18.00
110	A10	3r yellow brown	35.00	57.50
111	A10	4r red	75.00	100.00
112	A10	5r blue	65.00	90.00
113	A11	10r brn & dk grn	200.00	350.00
114	A11	20r yel grn & blk	550.00	800.00
115	A11	30r dk brn & blk	650.00	950.00
116	A11	40r org brn & blk	850.00	
117	A11	50r lilac & blk	750.00	
118	A11	100r blue & blk	1,100.	
119	A11	200r black & brn	1,500.	
		Nos. 99-112 (14)	339.75	311.90

It is probable that Nos. 118 and 119 were used only for fiscal purposes.

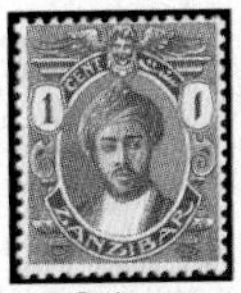

Sultan Khalifa bin Harub — A12

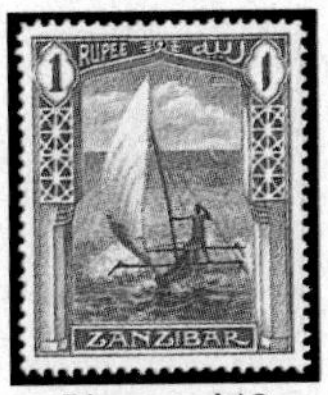

Dhow — A13

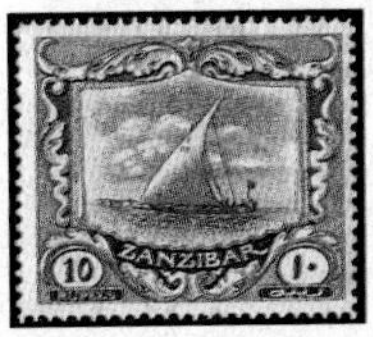

Dhow — A14

1913 *Perf. 14*

120	A12	1c gray	.50	.50
121	A12	3c yellow grn	1.50	.60
122	A12	6c carmine	1.75	.25
123	A12	10c brown	1.25	*3.25*
124	A12	12c violet	1.40	.40
125	A12	15c ultra	3.25	.40
126	A12	25c black brn	1.40	*2.50*
127	A12	50c dk green	3.75	*7.00*
128	A12	75c dk gray	2.75	*5.00*
129	A13	1r yellow grn	19.00	*16.00*
130	A13	2r dk violet	15.00	*32.50*
131	A13	3r orange	22.50	*50.00*
132	A13	4r red	35.00	*80.00*
133	A13	5r blue	50.00	*50.00*
134	A14	10r brown & grn	190.00	*375.00*
135	A14	20r yel grn & blk	350.00	*650.00*
136	A14	30r dk brn & blk	375.00	*800.00*
137	A14	40r orange & blk	600.00	*1,000.*
138	A14	50r dull vio & blk	600.00	*1,100.*
139	A14	100r blue & blk	750.00	
140	A14	200r black & brn	1,100.	
		Nos. 120-134 (15)	349.05	*623.40*

1914-22 **Wmk. 3**

141	A12	1c gray	.90	.30
142	A12	3c yellow grn	1.40	.25
143	A12	6c carmine	1.00	.25
144	A12	8c vio, *yel* ('22)	1.00	*6.50*
145	A12	10c dk grn, *yel* ('22)	.85	.40
146	A12	15c ultra	1.50	*7.50*
148	A12	50c dark green	5.00	*6.50*
149	A12	75c deep gray	3.50	*35.00*
150	A13	1r yellow grn	5.50	4.00
151	A13	2r dark violet	12.00	*13.00*
152	A13	3r brown org	25.00	*50.00*
153	A13	4r red	22.50	*95.00*
154	A13	5r blue	19.00	*72.50*
155	A14	10r brown & grn	200.00	*700.00*
		Nos. 141-155 (14)	299.15	*991.20*

1921-29 **Wmk. 4**

156	A12	1c gray	.30	*9.00*
157	A12	3c yellow grn	3.25	*5.50*
158	A12	3c orange ('22)	.40	.25
159	A12	4c green ('22)	.60	*2.50*
160	A12	6c carmine	.40	*.55*
161	A12	6c vio, *bl* ('22)	.45	.25
162	A12	10c lt brown	.80	*15.00*
163	A12	12c violet	.50	.35
164	A12	12c carmine ('22)	.50	.50
165	A12	15c ultra	.80	*14.00*
166	A12	20c dk blue ('22)	1.25	.40
167	A12	25c black brn	.90	*26.00*
168	A12	50c blue green	2.75	*6.50*
169	A12	75c dark gray	3.25	*65.00*
170	A13	1r yellow grn	7.00	4.00
171	A13	2r dk violet	4.50	*15.00*
172	A13	3r ocher	5.50	*8.50*
173	A13	4r red	17.50	*45.00*
174	A13	5r blue	24.00	*75.00*
175	A14	10r brown & grn	190.00	*450.00*
176	A14	20r green & blk	400.00	*750.00*
177	A14	30r dk brn & blk ('29)	350.00	*750.00*
		Nos. 156-175 (20)	264.65	743.30

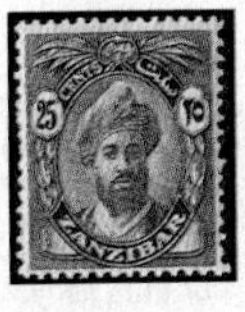

Sultan Khalifa bin Harub ("CENTS" with Serifs) — A15

1926-27

184	A15	1c brown	1.00	.25
185	A15	3c yellow org	.30	.25
186	A15	4c deep green	.30	.35
187	A15	6c dark violet	.35	.25
188	A15	8c slate	1.10	*5.50*
189	A15	10c olive green	1.10	.45
190	A15	12c deep red	3.00	.25
191	A15	20c ultra	.65	.40
192	A15	25c violet, *yel*	12.00	3.00
193	A15	50c claret	4.50	.50
194	A15	75c olive brown	30.00	*40.00*
		Nos. 184-194 (11)	54.30	51.20

Catalogue values for unused stamps in this section, from this point to the end of the section, are for Never Hinged items.

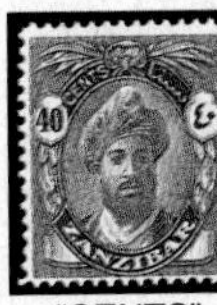

"CENTS" without Serifs — A16

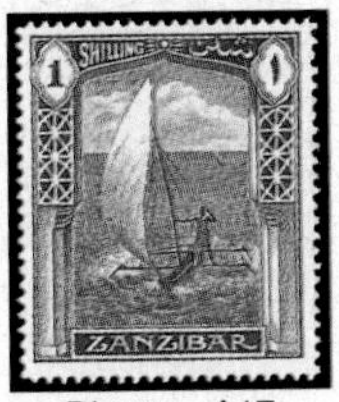

Dhow — A17

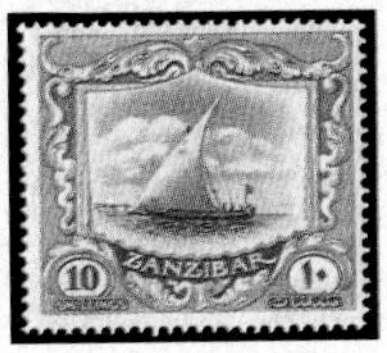

Dhow — A18

1936 *Perf. 14*

201	A16	5c deep green	.25	.25
202	A16	10c black	.25	.25
203	A16	15c carmine	.30	1.25
204	A16	20c brown org	.25	.25
205	A16	25c violet, *yel*	.25	.25
206	A16	30c ultra	.25	.25
207	A16	40c black brown	.25	.25
208	A16	50c claret	.50	.25
209	A17	1sh yellow grn	.75	.25
210	A17	2sh dark violet	2.50	2.50
211	A17	5sh red	24.00	8.00
212	A17	7.50sh blue	40.00	35.00
213	A18	10sh brn & grn	40.00	30.00
		Nos. 201-213 (13)	109.55	78.75

For overprints see Nos. 222-223.

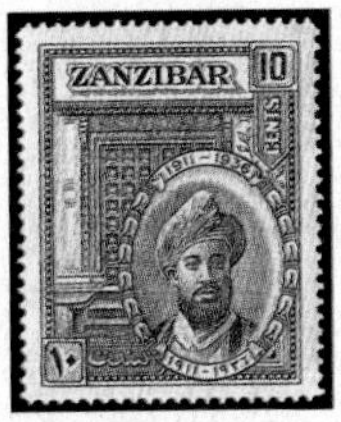

A19

1936, Dec. 9

214	A19	10c olive grn & blk	4.25	.35
215	A19	20c red violet & blk	6.50	2.75
216	A19	30c deep ultra & blk	19.00	.65
217	A19	50c red orange & blk	20.00	5.50
		Nos. 214-217 (4)	49.75	9.25

Reign of Sultan Khalifa bin Harub, 25th anniv.

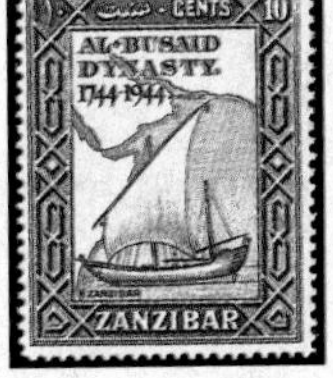

A20

Dhow & Map Showing Zanzibar & Muscat.

Perf. 14

1944, Nov. 20 **Engr.** **Wmk. 4**

218	A20	10c violet blue	1.00	*5.00*
219	A20	20c brown orange	1.50	*3.75*
220	A20	50c Prus green	1.50	.40
221	A20	1sh dull purple	1.50	1.00
		Nos. 218-221 (4)	5.50	10.15

200th anniv. of the Al Busaid Dynasty.

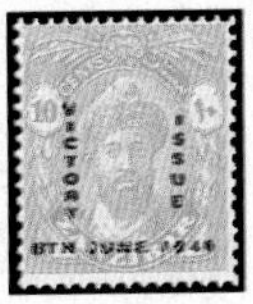

Nos. 202 and 206 Overprinted in Red

1946, Nov. 11

222	A16	10c black	.25	.50
223	A16	30c ultra	.40	.50

Victory of the Allied Nations in WW II.

Common Design Types pictured following the introduction.

Silver Wedding Issue
Common Design Types

1949, Jan. 10 **Photo.** ***Perf. 14x14½***

224	CD304	20c orange	.60	1.50

Engraved; Name Typographed
Perf. 11½x11

225	CD305	10sh light brown	29.00	36.50

UPU Issue
Common Design Types
Engr.; Name Typo. on 30c, 50c
Perf. 13½, 11x11½

1949, Oct. 10 **Wmk. 4**

226	CD306	20c red orange	.45	*3.75*
227	CD307	30c indigo	2.50	2.00
228	CD308	50c red lilac	1.25	*3.25*
229	CD309	1sh blue green	1.25	*4.50*
		Nos. 226-229 (4)	5.45	13.50

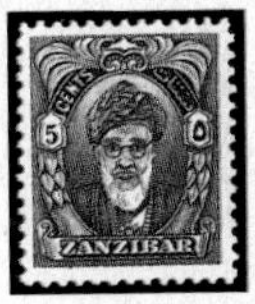

Sultan Khalifa bin Harub — A21

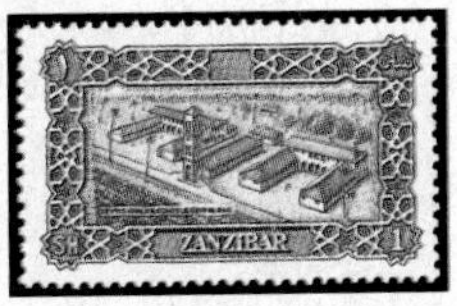

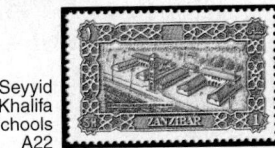

Seyyid Khalifa Schools A22

Perf. 12x12½, 13x12½

1952, Aug. 26 **Engr.**

230	A21	5c black	.25	.25
231	A21	10c red orange	.25	.25
232	A21	15c green	2.00	*3.00*
233	A21	20c carmine	.75	.75
234	A21	25c plum	1.10	.25
235	A21	30c blue green	1.10	.25
236	A21	35c ultra	1.00	*5.00*
237	A21	40c chocolate	1.00	*2.00*
238	A21	50c purple	3.25	.25
239	A22	1sh choc & bl grn	.75	.25
240	A22	2sh claret & ultra	3.00	*2.75*
241	A22	5sh carmine & blk	3.00	*6.50*
242	A22	7.50sh emer & gray	27.50	*27.50*
243	A22	10sh gray blk & rose red	12.00	*15.00*
		Nos. 230-243 (14)	56.95	64.00

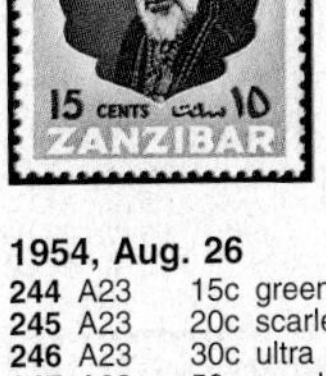

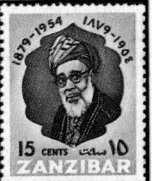

Sultan Khalifa bin Harub — A23

1954, Aug. 26 ***Perf. 12½x12***

244	A23	15c green	.25	.25
245	A23	20c scarlet	.25	.25
246	A23	30c ultra	.25	.25
247	A23	50c purple	.30	.30
248	A23	1.25sh brown orange	.50	*.75*
		Nos. 244-248 (5)	1.55	1.80

The frames differ on Nos. 245 and 247. Sultan Khalifa bin Harub, 75th birth anniv.

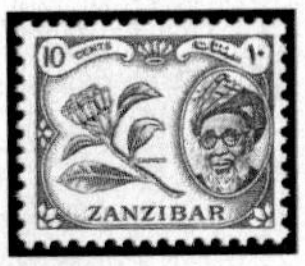

Cloves — A24

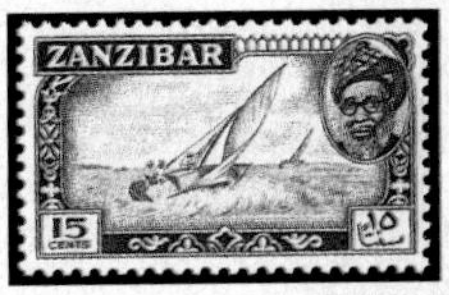

Dhows A25

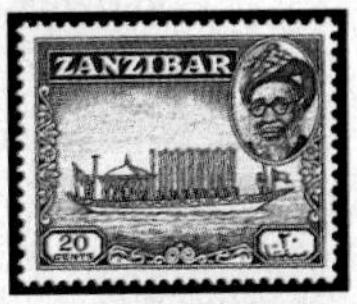

Sultan's Barge — A26

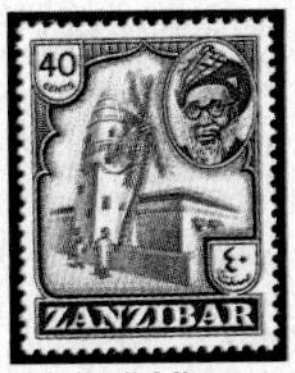

Malindi Minaret Mosque — A27

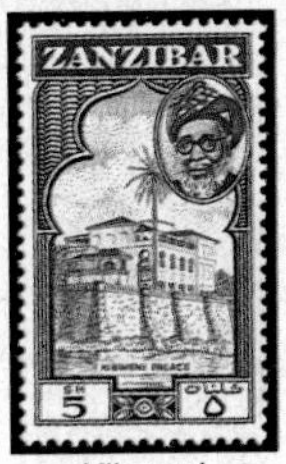

Kibweni Palace — A28

Sultan Khalifa bin Harub and: 25c, 35c, and 50c Map showing location of Zanzibar. 1sh, 2sh, Dimbani Mosque.

Perf. 11½ (A24), 11x11½ (A25), 14x13½ (A26), 13½x14 (A27), 13x13½ (A28)

1957, Aug. 26 **Engr.** **Wmk. 314**

249	A24	5c dull grn & org	.25	.25
250	A24	10c rose car & brt grn	.25	.25
251	A25	15c dk brn & grn	.25	*3.25*
252	A26	20c ultra	.25	.25
253	A26	25c blk & brn org	.25	*1.50*
254	A25	30c int blk & rose car	.25	*1.50*
255	A26	35c brt grn & ind	.30	.25
256	A27	40c int blk & redsh brn	.25	.25
257	A26	50c dull grn & bl	.35	.30
258	A27	1sh int blk & brt car	.30	.30
259	A25	1.25sh rose car & dk grn	4.00	.45
260	A27	2sh dull grn & org	4.00	2.50
261	A28	5sh ultra	6.00	2.50
262	A28	7.50sh green	15.00	4.50
263	A28	10sh rose carmine	16.00	6.50
		Nos. 249-263 (15)	47.70	24.55

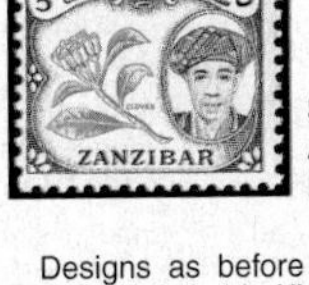

Sultan Seyyid Abdulla bin Khalifa — A29

Designs as before with portrait of Sultan Seyyid Abdulla bin Khalifa.

Perf. 11½ (A29), 11x11½ (A25), 14x13½ (A26), 13½x14 (A27)

1961, Oct. 17 **Engr.** **Wmk. 314**

264	A29	5c dull grn & org	.40	*1.10*
265	A29	10c rose car & brt grn	.40	.25
266	A25	15c dk brn & grn	.90	*3.75*
267	A26	20c ultra	.40	.45
268	A26	25c blk & brn org	1.75	1.75
269	A25	30c int blk & rose car	3.25	3.00
270	A26	35c brt grn & indigo	3.00	*5.00*
271	A27	40c int blk & redsh brn	.40	.25
272	A26	50c dull grn & bl	3.25	.25
273	A27	1sh int blk & brt car	.50	*1.50*
274	A25	1.25sh rose car & dk grn	3.00	*6.50*
275	A27	2sh dull grn & org	1.00	*3.75*

Perf. 13x13½

276	A28	5sh ultra	4.00	10.00
277	A28	7.50sh green	3.75	19.00
278	A28	10sh rose carmine	3.75	11.00
279	A28	20sh dk brown	19.00	30.00
		Nos. 264-279 (16)	48.75	97.55

For overprints see Nos. 285-300.

Freedom from Hunger Issue
Common Design Type with Portrait of
Sultan Seyyid Abdulla bin Khalifa

1963, June 4   Photo.   Perf. 14x14½

280	CD314	1.30sh sepia	1.50	.80

Independent State

Sultan Seyyid
Jamshid bin
Abdulla and
Zanzibar
Clove — A30

Designs: 50c, "To Prosperity," arch and sun.
1.30sh, "Religious Tolerance," composite view
of churches and mosques, horiz. 2.50sh,
"Towards the Light," Mangapwani Cave.

Perf. 12½

1963, Dec. 10   Photo.   Unwmk.

281	A30	30c multicolored	.25	.25
282	A30	50c multicolored	.30	.30
283	A30	1.30sh multicolored	.40	2.00
284	A30	2.50sh multicolored	.50	2.00
		Nos. 281-284 (4)	1.45	4.55

Zanzibar's independence, Dec. 10, 1963.
For overprints see Nos. 301-304.

Republic

Nos. 264-279
Overprinted

1964, Feb. 28   As Before

285	A29	5c dull grn & org	.25	.25
286	A29	10c rose car & brt grn	.25	.25
287	A25	15c dk brn & grn	.25	.25
288	A26	20c ultra	.25	.25
289	A26	25c blk & brn org	.35	.25
290	A25	30c int blk & rose car	.25	.25
291	A27	35c brt grn & ind	.35	.25
292	A27	40c int blk & redsh brn	.25	.25
293	A26	50c dull grn & blue	.35	.25
294	A27	1sh int blk & brt car	.30	.25
295	A25	1.25sh rose car & dk grn	2.25	.90
296	A27	2sh dull grn & org	.85	.45
297	A28	5sh ultra	.85	.50
298	A28	7.50sh green	1.25	7.00
299	A28	10sh rose carmine	2.00	7.00
300	A28	20sh dark brown	2.00	8.50
		Nos. 285-300 (16)	13.05	26.85

The overprint was applied in England. It is in
2 lines on 40c and 1sh to 20sh. "Jamhuri"
means "republic."

Overprint Handstamped

285a	A29	5c	1.00	.60
286a	A29	10c	1.00	.25
287a	A25	15c	1.50	2.00
288a	A26	20c	1.00	.50
289a	A26	25c	1.75	.25
290a	A25	30c	1.00	.50
291a	A26	35c	1.75	1.00
292a	A27	40c	1.00	1.00
293a	A26	50c	1.75	.25
294a	A27	1sh	1.50	1.25
295a	A25	1.25sh	1.25	1.50
296a	A27	2sh	2.50	1.50
297a	A28	5sh	2.00	1.75
298a	A28	7.50sh	2.50	1.75

299a	A28	10sh	2.50	2.50
300a	A28	20sh	3.00	6.00
		Nos. 285a-300a (16)	27.00	22.60

This overprint was applied locally. It has one
line of serifed letters. These are found diagonal, vertical, horizontal, double and inverted.
See Nos. 301a-304b. Other stamps with this
overprint, including postage dues, were
unofficial.

Nos. 281-284
Overprinted

1964, Feb. 28   As Before

301	A30	30c multi	.25	.25
302	A30	50c multi	.25	.25
303	A30	1.30sh multi	.30	.25
304	A30	2.50sh multi	.40	.60
a.		Green omitted	150.00	
		Nos. 301-304 (4)	1.20	1.35

One-line overprint on 1.30sh.

Overprint
Handstamped

301a	A30	30c	1.00	1.00
302a	A30	50c	.40	.35
303a	A30	1.30sh	1.00	.80
304b	A30	2.50sh	1.50	1.50
c.		Green omitted	350.00	
		Nos. 301a-304b (4)	3.90	3.65

See note after No. 300a.

Moorish Arch, Ax,
Sword and
Spear — A31

Designs: 10c, 20c, Arch and arrow piercing
chain. 25c, 40c, Man with rifle. 30c, 50c, Man
breaking chain. 1sh, Man, flag and sun.
1.30sh, Hands breaking chain and cloves,
horiz. 2sh, Hands waving flag, horiz. 5sh, Map
of Zanzibar and Pemba and flag, horiz. 10sh,
Flag and map of Zanzibar and Pemba. 20sh,
Flag of Zanzibar, horiz

Perf. 13x13½, 13½x13

1964, June 21   Litho.   Unwmk.

305	A31	5c multicolored	.40	.25
306	A31	10c multicolored	.40	.25
307	A31	15c multicolored	.40	.25
308	A31	20c multicolored	.50	.25
309	A31	25c multicolored	.50	.25
310	A31	30c multicolored	.40	.25
311	A31	40c multicolored	.60	.25
312	A31	50c multicolored	.40	.25
313	A31	1sh multicolored	.50	.25
314	A31	1.30sh multicolored	.30	1.25
315	A31	2sh multicolored	.50	.50
316	A31	5sh multicolored	1.25	3.00
317	A31	10sh multicolored	5.25	4.00
318	A31	20sh multicolored	5.00	20.00
		Nos. 305-318 (14)	16.40	31.00

Soldier and
Maps of
Zanzibar and
Pemba
A32

Reconstruction
A33

Perf. 13½x13, 13x13½

1965, Jan. 12   Unwmk.

319	A32	20c green & yel grn	.25	.25
320	A33	30c dk brn & ocher	.25	.25
321	A32	1.30sh vio blue & blue	.25	.25
322	A33	2.50sh purple & rose	.75	.50
		Nos. 319-322 (4)	1.50	1.25

First anniversary of the revolution.

Zanzibar and Tanzania

Rice
Planting
A34

Design: 30c, 1.30sh, Hands holding rice.

Perf. 13x12½

1965, Oct. 17   Unwmk.

323	A34	20c blue & blk brn	.25	1.00
324	A34	30c brt pink & blk brn	.25	1.00
325	A34	1.30sh org & blk brn	.35	2.25
326	A34	2.50sh emer & blk brn	.55	4.00
		Nos. 323-326 (4)	1.40	8.25

Issued to publicize agricultural development.

Symbols of Trade,
Agriculture, Industry
and
Education — A35

Designs: 50c, 2.50sh, Soldier and sunburst.

1966, Jan. 12   Litho.   Perf. 12½x13

327	A35	20c ultra, red & gray	.25	.25
328	A35	50c black & yel	.25	.25
329	A35	1.30sh multicolored	.30	.35
330	A35	2.50sh black & org	.60	1.00
		Nos. 327-330 (4)	1.40	1.85

2nd anniv. of the revolution of Jan. 12, 1964.

Pres. Abeid Amani
Karume and Vice-
Pres. Abdulla
Kassim
Hanga — A36

Design: 50c, 1.30sh, Flag, laurel and hands
holding Flame of the Union (inscribed:
Jamhuri Tanzania Zanzibar).

1966, Apr. 26   Photo.   Perf. 13½x13

331	A36	30c multicolored	.25	.25
332	A36	50c multicolored	.25	.25
333	A36	1.30sh multicolored	.35	.30
334	A36	2.50sh multicolored	.60	1.25
		Nos. 331-334 (4)	1.45	2.05

Union of Tanganyika and Zanzibar, 2nd
anniv.

Logging
A37

10c, 1sh, Clove trees & man. 15c, 40c, Cab-
inetmaker. 20c, 5sh, Lumumba College &
book. 25c, 1.30sh, Farmer & tractor. 30c, 2sh,
Volunteer farm workers. 50c, 10sh, Street
scene, vert.

Perf. 13x12½, 12½x13

1966, June 5   Litho.

335	A37	5c lemon & vio brn	.70	.80
336	A37	10c brt grn & vio brn	.70	.80
337	A37	15c vio brn & bl	.70	.80
338	A37	20c vio bl & org	.70	.25
339	A37	25c vio brn & yel	.70	.30
340	A37	30c vio brn & dl yel	.80	.25
341	A37	40c vio brn & rose	.90	.25
342	A37	50c green & yel	.90	.25
343	A37	1sh ultra & vio brn	.90	.25
344	A37	1.30sh lt bl grn & vio brn	1.00	3.25
345	A37	2sh brt grn & vio brn	1.00	.60
346	A37	5sh ver & gray	1.50	6.00
347	A37	10sh red brn & yel	2.50	20.00
348	A37	20sh brt pink & vio brn	5.00	35.00
		Nos. 335-348 (14)	18.00	68.80

Symbols of Education — A38

1966, Sept. 25   Perf. 13½x13

349	A38	50c blue, blk & org	.25	1.00
350	A38	1.30sh blue, blk & yel grn	.30	1.75
351	A38	2.50sh blue, blk & pink	.80	4.00
		Nos. 349-351 (3)	1.35	6.75

Introduction of free education.

People
and Flag
A39

Design: 50c, 1.30sh, Vice-President Abdulla
Kassim Hanga, flag and crowd, vert.

Perf. 14x14½, 14½x14

1967, Feb. 5   Litho.   Unwmk.

352	A39	30c multicolored	.25	1.00
353	A39	50c multicolored	.25	1.00
354	A39	1.30sh multicolored	.25	1.25
355	A39	2.50sh multicolored	.40	3.00
		Nos. 352-355 (4)	1.15	6.25

10th anniversary of Afro-Shirazi Party.

Volunteer
Workers
A40

Perf. 12½x12

1967, Aug. 20   Photo.   Unwmk.

356	A40	1.30sh multicolored	.30	2.50
357	A40	2.50sh multicolored	.55	6.50

Volunteer (Young) Workers Brigade.
All Zanzibar stamps were withdrawn July 1,
1968, and replaced with current Kenya,
Uganda and Tanzania stamps.

POSTAGE DUE STAMPS

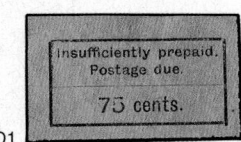

D1

Rouletted 10

1931   Typeset   Unwmk.
Thin Paper
Without Gum

J1	D1	1c blk, *orange*	12.50	150.00
J2	D1	2c blk, *orange*	5.50	80.00
J3	D1	3c blk, *orange*	5.75	65.00
J3A	D1	6c blk, *orange*		8,000.
J4	D1	9c blk, *orange*	3.25	35.00
J4A	D1	12c blk, *orange*	15,000.	12,000.
J4B	D1	12c blk, *green*	1,600.	675.00
J5	D1	15c blk, *orange*	3.25	42.50
J6	D1	18c blk, *orange*	27.50	90.00
a.		18c black, *salmon*	5.00	75.00
J7	D1	20c blk, *orange*	4.50	80.00
J8	D1	21c blk, *orange*	4.00	80.00
J8A	D1	25c blk, *orange*	19,000.	17,000.
J8B	D1	25c blk, *magenta*	3,250.	1,500.
J9	D1	31c blk, *orange*	11.00	110.00
J10	D1	50c blk, *orange*	24.00	250.00
J11	D1	75c blk, *orange*	80.00	600.00

The variety "cent.s" occurs once on each sheet of Nos. J3 to J11 inclusive.

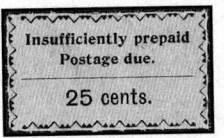

D2

1931-33   Rouletted 5
Thick Paper

J12	D2	2c blk, *salmon*	25.00	37.50
J13	D2	3c blk, *rose*	4.00	65.00
J14	D2	6c blk, *yellow*	4.00	40.00
J15	D2	12c blk, *blue*	5.00	32.50
J16	D2	25c blk, *pink*	11.00	130.00
J17	D2	25c blk, *dull violet*	25.00	80.00
		Nos. J12-J17 (6)	74.00	385.00

Catalogue values for unused stamps in this section, from this point to the end of the section, are for Never Hinged items.

D3

1936   Typo.   Wmk. 4   Perf. 14

J18	D3	5c violet	8.50	14.00
J19	D3	10c carmine	6.50	3.25
J20	D3	20c green	2.50	6.50
J21	D3	30c brown	16.00	24.00
J22	D3	40c ultra	10.00	30.00
J23	D3	1sh gray	15.00	37.50
		Nos. J18-J23 (6)	58.50	115.25

Chalky paper was introduced in 1956 for the 5c, 30c, 40c, 1sh, and in 1962 for the 10c, 20c. Value for set of 6, unused $3.25, used $110. See note after No. 300a.

ZIMBABWE

zim-'bä-bwē

LOCATION — Southeastern Africa, bordered by Zambia, Mozambique, South Africa, and Botswana
GOVT. — Republic
AREA — 150,872 sq. mi.
POP. — 11,163,160 (1999 est.)
CAPITAL — Harare

Formerly Rhodesia, the Republic of Zimbabwe was established April 18, 1980.

---

100 Cents = 1 Dollar

Catalogue values for all unused stamps in this country are for Never Hinged items.

Morganite
A69

Black Rhinoceros
A70

Odzani
Falls — A71

Perf. 14½, 14½x14 (A70)

1980   Litho.

414	A69	1c shown	.25	.35
415	A69	3c Amethyst	.40	.25
416	A69	4c Garnet	.40	.25
417	A69	5c Citrine	.40	.25
418	A69	7c Blue topaz	.40	.25
419	A70	9c shown	.25	.25
420	A70	11c Lion	.25	.25
421	A70	13c Warthog	.25	.25
422	A70	15c Giraffe	.25	.25
423	A70	17c Zebra	.25	.25
424	A71	21c shown	.25	.25
425	A71	25c Goba Falls	.35	.35
426	A71	30c Inyangombe Falls	.30	.45
426A	A71	40c Bundi Falls	5.25	4.75
427	A71	$1 Bridal Veil Falls	.45	2.00
428	A71	$2 Victoria Falls	.60	3.50
		Nos. 414-428 (16)	10.30	14.00

Rotary International, 75th Anniversary — A72

1980, June 18   Perf. 14½

429	A72	4c multicolored	.25	.25
430	A72	13c multicolored	.25	.30
431	A72	21c multicolored	.25	.50
432	A72	25c multicolored	.35	.75
a.		Souvenir sheet of 4, #429-432	1.40	1.40
		Nos. 429-432 (4)	1.10	1.80

Olympic
Rings
A73

1980, July 19

433	A73	17c multicolored	.35	.35

22nd Summer Olympic Games, Moscow, July 19-Aug. 3.

Gatooma Post Office, 1912 — A74

Post Offices: 7c, Salisbury, 1912. 9c, Umtali, 1901. 17c, Bulawayo, 1895.

1980   Litho.   Perf. 14½

434	A74	5c multicolored	.25	.25
435	A74	7c multicolored	.25	.25
436	A74	9c multicolored	.25	.25
437	A74	17c multicolored	.25	.25
a.		Souvenir sheet of 4, #434-437	1.00	1.25
		Nos. 434-437 (4)	1.00	1.00

Post Office Savings Bank, 75th anniv.

Intl. Year of the Disabled — A75

Designs: Various disabilities. Nos. 438-441 form a continuous design.

1981, Sept. 23   Litho.   Perf. 14½

438	A75	5c multicolored	.25	.25
439	A75	7c multicolored	.25	.25
440	A75	11c multicolored	.25	.25
441	A75	17c multicolored	.50	.50
		Nos. 438-441 (4)	1.25	1.25

Natl. Tree Day — A76

1981, Dec. 4

442	A76	5c Msasa	.25	.25
443	A76	7c Mopane	.25	.25
444	A76	21c Flat-crowned acacia	.70	.70
445	A76	30c Pod mahogany	.90	.90
		Nos. 442-445 (4)	2.10	2.10

Rock Paintings A77

Designs: 9c, Khoisan figures, Gwamgwadza Cave. 11c, Kudus, human figures, Epworth Mission. 17c, Diana's Vow, Rusape. 21c, Giraffes, Gwamgwadza Cave. 25c, Warthog, Mucheka Cave. 30c, Hunters, Shinzwini Shelter.

1982, Mar. 17   Litho.   Perf. 14½

446	A77	9c multicolored	.75	.75
447	A77	11c multicolored	.90	.90
448	A77	17c multicolored	1.25	1.25
449	A77	21c multicolored	1.75	1.75
450	A77	25c multicolored	1.75	1.75
451	A77	30c multicolored	2.75	2.75
		Nos. 446-451 (6)	9.15	9.15

Scouting Year — A78

1982, July 21

452	A78	9c Emblem	.35	.35
453	A78	11c Campfire	.40	.40
454	A78	21c Map reading	.75	.75
455	A78	30c Baden Powell	1.00	1.00
		Nos. 452-455 (4)	2.50	2.50

TB
Bacillus
Centenary
A79

1982, Nov. 17   Perf. 14½

456	A79	11c Koch	1.00	1.25
457	A79	30c Scientist examining slide	2.00	2.25

Commonwealth Day — A80

Sculptures: 9c, Wing Woman, by Henry Mudzengerere, vert. 11c, Telling Secrets, by Joseph Ndandarika. 30c, Hornbill Man, by John Takawira. $1, The Chief, by Nicholas Mukomberanwa, vert.

1983, Mar. 14   Perf. 14½

458	A80	9c multicolored	.25	.25
459	A80	11c multicolored	.25	.25
460	A80	30c multicolored	.30	.35
461	A80	$1 multicolored	.80	1.50
		Nos. 458-461 (4)	1.60	2.35

World Plowing Contest, May — A81

No. 463, mechanized plowing.

1983, May 13   Litho.   Perf. 14½

462	A81	Pair	.70	.70
a.-b.		21c, any single	.35	.35
463	A81	Pair	.90	.90
a.-b.		30c, any single	.45	.45

World Communications Year — A82

Means of communication and transportation. Nos. 464-467 vert.

1983, Oct. 12   Litho.   Perf. 14½

464	A82	9c Mailman	.25	.25
465	A82	11c Signaling airplane	.30	.30
466	A82	15c Telephone operators	.45	.45
467	A82	17c Reading newspapers	.60	.60
468	A82	21c Truck on highway	.70	.70
469	A82	30c Train	1.00	1.00
		Nos. 464-469 (6)	3.30	3.30

Zimbabwe Intl. Trade Fair, Bulawayo, May 5-13 — A83

1984, Apr. 11   Litho.   Perf. 14½

470	A83	9c shown	.25	.25
471	A83	11c Globe	.25	.25
472	A83	30c Emblem	.70	.70
		Nos. 470-472 (3)	1.20	1.20

1984 Summer Olympics A84

Children's Drawings.

1984, July 18   Litho.   Perf. 14½
473	A84	11c Bicycling	.30	.25
474	A84	21c Swimming	.65	.65
475	A84	30c Running	1.00	1.00
476	A84	40c Hurdles	1.40	2.25
		Nos. 473-476 (4)	3.35	4.15

Heroes' Day A85

1984, Aug. 8   Litho.   Perf. 14½
477	A85	9c Heroes	.25	.25
478	A85	11c Monument, vert.	.25	.25
479	A85	17c Statue, vert.	.45	.45
480	A85	30c Bas-relief	.75	.75
		Nos. 477-480 (4)	1.70	1.70

Fish Eagle — A86

1984, Oct. 10   Litho.   Perf. 14½
481	A86	9c shown	.75	.75
482	A86	11c Long crested eagle	.80	.80
483	A86	13c Bateleur	.90	.90
484	A86	17c Black eagle	1.25	1.25
485	A86	21c Martial eagle	1.50	1.50
486	A86	30c African hawk eagle	2.10	2.10
		Nos. 481-486 (6)	7.30	7.30

Superheat Engine No. 86, Mashonaland Railways, 1918 — A87

Steam locomotives: 11c, Engine No. 190, North British Locomotive Co., 1926. 17c, Engine No. 424, Beyer Peacock & Co., 1950. 26c, Engine No. 726, Beyer Peacock & Co., 1957.

1985, May 15   Litho.
487	A87	9c multicolored	1.00	1.00
488	A87	11c multicolored	1.40	1.40
489	A87	17c multicolored	2.10	2.10
490	A87	30c multicolored	3.75	3.75
		Nos. 487-490 (4)	8.25	8.25

INTELSAT V A88

57c, Mazowe Earth Satellite Station.

Perf. 14½x14, 14½
1985, July 8   Litho.
491	A88	26c multicolored	2.10	2.40

Size: 62x23mm
492	A88	57c multicolored	4.25	4.75

Zimbabwe Bird and Tobacco — A89

Agriculture and industry.

Perf. 14¾x14½
1985, Aug. 21   Litho.
493	A89	1c shown	.25	.25
a.		Perf 14¼x13¾ ('88)	—	2.00
494	A89	3c Corn	.25	.25
a.		Perf 14¼x13¾ ('88)	—	2.00
495	A89	4c Cotton	.25	.25
a.		Perf 14¼x13¾ ('88)	—	2.00
496	A89	5c Tea	.45	.25
497	A89	10c Cattle	.45	.25
a.		Perf 14¼x13¾ ('88)	—	2.00
498	A89	11c Birchenough Bridge	1.10	.25
499	A89	12c Stamp mill	1.90	.25
500	A89	13c Gold production	3.50	.25
a.		Perf 14¼x13¾ ('88)	—	4.00
501	A89	15c Coal mining	2.75	.25
a.		Perf 14¼x13¾ ('88)	—	4.00
502	A89	17c Amethyst mining	3.50	.45
503	A89	18c Electric train	3.50	.45
504	A89	20c Kariba Dam	2.50	.25
a.		Perf 14¼x13¾ ('88)	—	4.00
505	A89	23c Elephants	4.75	.45
506	A89	25c Zambezi River sunset	.90	.45
a.		Perf 14¼x13¾ ('88)	—	5.00
507	A89	26c Baobab tree	.90	.30
508	A89	30c Great Zimbabwe ruins	1.25	.45
509	A89	35c Folk dancing	.90	.45
510	A89	45c Crushing corn	1.25	.60
511	A89	57c Wood carving	1.25	1.00
512	A89	$1 Mbira drum	1.75	1.25
a.		Perf 14¼x13¾ ('88)	—	25.00
513	A89	$2 Mule-drawn scotch cart	3.00	4.00
514	A89	$5 Natl. coat of arms	5.50	7.00
		Nos. 493-514 (22)	41.85	19.35

Natl. Archives, 50th Anniv. A90

Designs: 12c, Gatsi Rusere (c. 1589-1623), ruler of Mashonaland and Zambezi area; mutapa, 17th cent. 18c, Lobengula, ruler of Ndebele State (1870-94), sketch by E. A. Maund, 1889; 1888 Moffat Treaty and elephant seal. 26c, Archives exhibition hall. 35c, Archives building.

1985, Sept. 18   Perf. 14½
515	A90	12c multicolored	.25	.25
516	A90	18c multicolored	.30	.30
517	A90	26c multicolored	.45	.45
518	A90	35c multicolored	.65	.65
		Nos. 515-518 (4)	1.65	1.65

UN Decade for Women A91

1985, Nov. 13
519	A91	10c Computer operator	.70	.70
520	A91	17c Nurse, child	1.00	1.00
521	A91	26c Engineer	1.75	1.75
		Nos. 519-521 (3)	3.45	3.45

Harare Conference Center — A92

1986, Jan. 29   Litho.   Perf. 14½
523	A92	26c Facade	.90	.90
524	A92	35c Interior	1.60	1.60

Southern African Development Coordination Conference — A93

1986, Apr. 1   Perf. 14½
525	A93	12c Grain elevators	.50	.50
526	A93	18c Rhinoceros	2.60	2.60
527	A93	26c Map, jet	2.60	2.60
528	A93	35c Map, flags	2.75	2.75
		Nos. 525-528 (4)	8.45	8.45

Moths — A94

12c, Jackson's emperor. 18c, Oleander hawk. 26c, Zaddach's emperor. 35c, Southern marbled emperor.

1986, June 18   Litho.   Perf. 14½x14
529	A94	12c multicolored	1.60	1.60
530	A94	18c multicolored	2.10	2.10
531	A94	26c multicolored	2.75	2.75
532	A94	35c multicolored	3.25	3.25
		Nos. 529-532 (4)	9.70	9.70

8th Non-aligned Summit Conference A95

1986, Aug. 28   Litho.   Perf. 14½x14
533	A95	26c Victoria Falls	2.75	2.75

Size: 66x26mm
Perf. 14½
534	A95	$1 Great Zimbabwe Enclosure	6.50	6.50

Motoring Cent. A96

1986, Oct. 8   Perf. 14½
535	A96	10c Sopwith, 1921	.75	.75
536	A96	12c Gladiator, 1902	.75	.75
537	A96	17c Douglas, 1920	1.10	1.10
538	A96	26c Ford Model-A, 1930	1.75	1.75
539	A96	35c Schacht, 1909	2.25	2.25
540	A96	40c Benz Velocipede, 1886	2.25	2.25
		Nos. 535-540 (6)	8.85	8.85

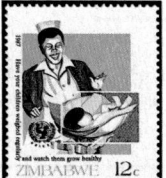

A97

UN Child Survival Campaign: a, Growth monitoring. b, Breast-feeding. c, Oral rehydration. d, Immunization.

1987, Feb. 11   Litho.   Perf. 14x14½
541		Block of 4	8.50	8.50
a.-d.		A97 12c any single	1.90	1.90

A98

Indigenous owls.

1987, Apr. 15   Perf. 14½
542	A98	12c Barred	2.75	2.75
543	A98	18c Pearl-spotted	3.50	3.50
544	A98	26c White-faced	4.00	4.00
545	A98	35c Scops	6.25	6.25
		Nos. 542-545 (4)	16.50	16.50

Natl. Girl Guides Movement, 75th Anniv. — A99

1987, June 24
546	A99	15c Commitment	.75	.75
547	A99	23c Adventure	.90	.90
548	A99	35c Service	1.10	1.10
549	A99	$1 Intl. friendship	2.60	2.60
		Nos. 546-549 (4)	5.35	5.35

Duikers and Population Maps — A100

1987, Oct. 7   Perf. 14½x14
550	A100	15c Common gray	1.00	1.00
551	A100	23c Zebra	1.10	1.10
552	A100	25c Yellow-backed	1.10	1.10
553	A100	30c Blue	1.40	1.40
554	A100	35c Jentink's	1.40	1.40
555	A100	38c Red	1.40	1.40
		Nos. 550-555 (6)	7.40	7.40

Insects A101

1988, Jan. 12   Litho.   Perf. 14½
556	A101	15c Praying mantis	.90	.25
557	A101	23c Scarab beetle	1.25	.50
558	A101	35c Short-horned grasshopper	1.75	1.50
559	A101	45c Giant shield bug	2.00	3.75
		Nos. 556-559 (4)	5.90	6.00

Natl. Gallery of Art, 30th Anniv. — A102

Sculpture and paintings: 15c, Cockerel, by Arthur Azevedo. 23c, Changeling, by Bernard Matemera. 30c, Spirit Python, by Henry Munyaradzi. 35c, Spirit Bird Carrying People, by Thomas Mukarobgwa, horiz. 38c, The Song of the Shepherd Boy, by George Nene, horiz. 45c, War Victim, by Joseph Muzondo, horiz.

Perf. 14x14½, 14½x14
1988, Apr. 14   Litho.
560	A102	15c multicolored	.25	.25
561	A102	23c multicolored	.40	.40
562	A102	30c multicolored	.50	.50
563	A102	35c multicolored	.70	.70

564	A102	38c multicolored	.70 .70
565	A102	45c multicolored	.85 .85
		Nos. 560-565 (6)	3.40 3.40

Aloes and
Succulents
A103

15c, Aloe cameronii bondana. 23c, Orbeopsis caudata. 25c, Euphorbia wildii. 30c, Euphorbia fortissima. 35c, Aloe aculeata. 38c, Huernia zebrina.

1988, July 14   *Perf. 14½*

566	A103	15c multicolored	.40 .40
567	A103	23c multicolored	.75 .75
568	A103	25c multicolored	.75 .75
569	A103	30c multicolored	.85 .85
570	A103	35c multicolored	.85 .85
571	A103	38c multicolored	1.10 1.10
		Nos. 566-571 (6)	4.70 4.70

A104

1988, Oct. 6   **Litho.**   *Perf. 14½x14*

572	A104	15c White-faced duck	1.00 .25
573	A104	23c Pygmy goose	1.10 .45
574	A104	30c Hottentot teal	1.25 1.25
575	A104	35c Knob-billed duck	1.40 1.40
576	A104	38c White-backed duck	1.50 1.50
577	A104	45c Maccoa	2.10 3.00
		Nos. 572-577 (6)	8.35 7.85

Geckos
A105

1989, Jan. 10   **Litho.**   *Perf. 14½*

578	A105	15c O'Shaughnessy's banded	1.10 1.10
579	A105	23c Tiger rock	1.25 1.25
580	A105	35c Tasman's	2.00 2.00
581	A105	45c Bibron's	2.25 2.25
		Nos. 578-581 (4)	6.60 6.60

Wildflowers
A106

1989, Apr. 12   **Litho.**   *Perf. 14½*

582	A106	15c Spotted-leaved arum-lily	.60 .60
583	A106	23c Grassland vlei-lily	.75 .75
584	A106	30c Manica protea	.75 .75
585	A106	35c Flame lily	.90 .90
586	A106	38c Poppy hibiscus	1.00 1.00
587	A106	45c Blue sesbania	1.10 1.10
		Nos. 582-587 (6)	5.10 5.10

Fish
A107

15c, Red-breasted bream. 23c, Chessa. 30c, Eastern bottle-nose. 35c, Vundu. 38c, Largemouth black bass. 45c, Tiger fish.

1989, July 12   **Litho.**   *Perf. 14½*

588	A107	15c multicolored	.90 .25
589	A107	23c multicolored	1.10 .25
590	A107	30c multicolored	1.25 1.00
591	A107	35c multicolored	1.25 1.00
592	A107	38c multicolored	1.50 1.50
593	A107	45c multicolored	2.00 2.40
		Nos. 588-593 (6)	8.00 6.40

See Nos. 696-701.

Endangered
Species
A108

1989   **Litho.**   *Perf. 14½x14*

594	A108	15c Black rhinoceros	1.75 1.75
595	A108	23c Cheetah	2.10 2.10
596	A108	30c Wild dog	2.25 2.25
597	A108	35c Pangolin	2.25 2.25
598	A108	38c Brown hyena	2.25 2.25
599	A108	45c Roan antelope	2.50 2.50
		Nos. 594-599 (6)	13.10 13.10

Achievements,
1980-1990
A109

1990, Apr. 17   **Litho.**   *Perf. 14½x14*

600	A109	15c Unity accord	.60 .25
601	A109	23c Conference center	.70 .25
602	A109	30c Education	.80 .80
603	A109	35c Satellite dish	.90 .90
604	A109	38c Sports stadium	.90 .90
605	A109	45c Agriculture	1.40 2.50
		Nos. 600-605 (6)	5.30 5.60

City of
Harare,
Cent.
A110

15c, Runhare house, 1986. 23c, Market hall, 1894. 30c, Charter house, 1959. 35c, Supreme Court, 1927. 38c, Standard Chartered Bank, 1911. 45c, Town house, 1933.

1990, July 11   **Litho.**   *Perf. 14½*

606	A110	15c multicolored	.55 .55
607	A110	23c multicolored	.80 .80
608	A110	30c multicolored	.85 .85
609	A110	35c multicolored	.90 .90
610	A110	38c multicolored	.90 .90
611	A110	45c multicolored	1.30 1.30
		Nos. 606-611 (6)	5.30 5.30

36th
Commonwealth
Parliamentary
Conf. — A111

1990, Sept. 17

612	A111	35c Speaker's mace	.75 .75
613	A111	$1 Speaker's chair	2.25 2.25

Animals — A112

Hand
Crafts — A113

Transportation — A114

1c, Tiger fish. 2c, Helmeted guineafowl. 3c, Scrub hare. 4c, Pangolin. 5c, Greater kudu. 9c, Black rhinoceros. 15c, Head rest. 20c, Hand axe. 23c, Gourd, water pot. 25c, Snuff box. 26c, Winnowing basket. 30c, Grinding stone. 33c, Riding bicycles. 35c, Buses. 38c, Train. 45c, Motorcycle, trailer. $1, Jet. $2, Tractor-trailer truck.

Perf. 14, 14½x14 (#620-625), 14¼ (#626-631)

1990, Jan. 2   **Litho.**

614	A112	1c multicolored	.25 .25
a.		Perf 14¾x14½	1.25 .25
615	A112	2c multicolored	1.50 .25
a.		Perf 14¾x14½	1.75 .25
616	A112	3c multicolored	.25 .25
a.		Perf 14¾x14½	1.25 .25
617	A112	4c multicolored	.75 .25
a.		Perf 14x13½	.90 .25
b.		Perf 14¾x14½	
618	A112	5c multicolored	.75 .75
a.		Perf 14¾x14½	1.25 .25
619	A112	9c multicolored	2.50 .40
a.		Perf 14¾x14½	2.50 .40
620	A113	15c multicolored	.50 .25
621	A113	20c multicolored	.25 .25
622	A113	23c multicolored	.25 .25
623	A113	25c multicolored	.25 .25
624	A113	26c multicolored	1.00 .60
625	A113	30c multicolored	.60 .60
626	A114	33c multicolored	2.00 .65
627	A114	35c multicolored	2.25 .70
628	A114	38c multicolored	2.75 .70
629	A114	45c multicolored	2.00 .70
630	A114	$1 multicolored	3.50 1.50
631	A114	$2 multicolored	3.00 2.50
		Nos. 614-631 (18)	24.35 11.10

Animals
A115

1991, Jan. 15   **Litho.**   *Perf. 14½x14*

632	A115	15c Small-spotted genet	1.40 1.40
633	A115	23c Red squirrel	1.50 1.50
634	A115	35c Night ape	2.10 2.10
635	A115	45c Bat-eared fox	3.00 3.00
		Nos. 632-635 (4)	8.00 8.00

A116

Traditional musical instruments.

1991, Apr. 16   **Litho.**   *Perf. 14½*

636	A116	15c Hosho	.80 .25
637	A116	23c Mbira	.85 .25
638	A116	30c Ngororombe	.95 .95
639	A116	35c Chipendani	1.25 1.25
640	A116	38c Marimba	1.25 1.25
641	A116	45c Ngoma	1.40 1.90
		Nos. 636-641 (6)	6.50 5.85

Wild
Fruits — A117

1991, July 17   **Litho.**   *Perf. 14x14½*

642	A117	20c Snot-apple	.75 .75
643	A117	39c Marula	.90 .90
644	A117	51c Mobola plum	1.00 1.00
645	A117	60c Water berry	1.10 1.10
646	A117	65c Northern dwaba berry	1.25 1.25
647	A117	77c Mahobohobo	1.50 1.50
		Nos. 642-647 (6)	6.50 6.50

See Nos. 870-875.

A118

20c, Bridal Veil Falls. 39c, Conference Emblem. 51c, Chinhoyi Caves. 60c, Kariba Dam Wall. 65c, Victoria Falls. 77c, Balancing Rocks.

1991, Oct. 16   **Litho.**   *Perf. 14½*

648	A118	20c multi	1.15 1.15
649	A118	39c multi	1.15 1.15
650	A118	51c multi	1.50 1.50
651	A118	60c multi	1.75 1.75
652	A118	65c multi	1.90 1.90
653	A118	77c multi	1.90 1.90
		Nos. 648-653 (6)	9.35 9.35

Commonwealth Heads of Government meeting, Harare.

Wild Cats
A119

1992, Jan. 8   **Litho.**   *Perf. 14½*

654	A119	20c Lion	1.25 .25
655	A119	39c Leopard	2.00 .90
656	A119	60c Cheetah	3.00 3.00
657	A119	77c Serval	4.00 3.75
		Nos. 654-657 (4)	10.25 7.90

Mushrooms
A120

Designs: 20c, Amanita zambiana. 39c, Boletus edulis. 51c, Termitomyces. 60c, Cantharellus densifolius. 65c, Cantharellus longisporus. 77c, Cantharellus cibarius.

1992, Apr. 8   **Litho.**   *Perf. 14x14½*

658	A120	20c multicolored	1.10 1.10
659	A120	39c multicolored	1.40 1.40
660	A120	51c multicolored	1.50 1.50
661	A120	60c multicolored	1.60 1.60
662	A120	65c multicolored	2.00 2.00
663	A120	77c multicolored	2.50 2.50
		Nos. 658-663 (6)	10.10 10.10

Birds — A121

25c, Blackeyed bulbul. 59c, Fiscal shrike. 77c, Forktailed drongo. 90c, Cardinal woodpecker. 98c, Yellowbilled hornbill. $1.16, Crested francolin.

1992, July 17 Litho. *Perf. 14½*

664	A121	25c	multi	1.10	1.10
665	A121	59c	multi	1.50	1.50
666	A121	77c	multi	1.60	1.60
667	A121	90c	multi	1.90	1.90
668	A121	98c	multi	1.90	1.90
669	A121	$1.16	multi	2.00	2.00
			Nos. 664-669 (6)	10.00	10.00

Butterflies A122

25c, Foxy charaxes. 59c, Orange & lemon. 77c, Emperor swallowtail. 90c, Blue pansy. 98c, African monarch. $1.16, Gaudy commodore.

1992, Oct. 15 Litho. *Perf. 14½x14*

670	A122	25c	multicolored	1.30	1.30
671	A122	59c	multicolored	2.25	2.25
672	A122	77c	multicolored	2.75	2.75
673	A122	90c	multicolored	3.25	3.25
674	A122	98c	multicolored	3.50	3.50
675	A122	$1.16	multicolored	4.00	4.00
			Nos. 670-675 (6)	17.05	17.05

Minerals A123

1993, Jan. 12 Litho. *Perf. 14½x14*

676	A123	25c	Autunite	2.00	2.00
677	A123	59c	Chromite	2.75	2.75
678	A123	77c	Azurite	2.50	2.50
679	A123	90c	Coal	4.00	4.00
680	A123	98c	Gold	4.25	4.25
681	A123	$1.16	Emerald	5.50	5.50
			Nos. 676-681 (6)	21.00	21.00

Owls — A124

25c, Wood owl. 59c, Pels fishing owl. 90c, Spotted eagle owl. $1.16, Giant eagle owl.

1993, Apr. 6 Litho. *Perf. 14½*

682	A124	25c	multicolored	2.40	2.40
683	A124	59c	multicolored	3.00	3.00
684	A124	90c	multicolored	4.50	4.50
685	A124	$1.16	multicolored	5.50	5.50
			Nos. 682-685 (4)	15.40	15.40

Household Pottery A125

1993, July 13 Litho. *Perf. 14½x14*

686	A125	25c	Hadyana	.80	.80
687	A125	59c	Chirongo	1.00	1.00
688	A125	77c	Mbiya	1.20	1.20
689	A125	90c	Pfuko	1.40	1.40
690	A125	98c	Tsaya	1.60	1.60
691	A125	$1.16	Gate	1.90	1.90
			Nos. 686-691 (6)	7.90	7.90

Orchids — A126

35c, Polystachya dendrobiflora. $1, Diaphananthe subsimplex. $1.50, Ansellia gigantea. $1.95, Vanilla polyepis.

1993, Oct. 12 Litho. *Perf. 14½*

692	A126	35c	multicolored	1.00	1.00
693	A126	$1	multicolored	2.10	2.10
694	A126	$1.50	multicolored	3.25	3.25
695	A126	$1.95	multicolored	4.25	4.25
			Nos. 692-695 (4)	10.60	10.60

Fish Type of 1989

1994, Jan. 20 Litho. *Perf. 14½*

696	A107	35c	Hunyani salmon	.45	.45
697	A107	$1	Barbel	.85	.85
698	A107	$1.30	Rainbow trout	1.10	1.10
699	A107	$1.50	Mottled eel	1.30	1.30
700	A107	$1.65	Mirror carp	1.50	1.50
701	A107	$1.95	Robustus bream	1.75	1.75
			Nos. 696-701 (6)	6.95	6.95

City of Bulawayo, Cent. A127

1994, Apr. 5 Litho. *Perf. 14½*

702	A127	35c	City Hall	.50	.50
703	A127	80c	Cresta Churchill Hotel	.50	.50
704	A127	$1.15	High Court	.80	.80
705	A127	$1.75	Douslin House	1.00	1.00
706	A127	$1.95	Goldfields Building	1.25	1.25
707	A127	$2.30	Parkade Centre	1.40	1.40
			Nos. 702-707 (6)	5.45	5.45

Export Flowers — A128

1994, July 12 Litho. *Perf. 14½*

708	A128	35c	Strelitzia	.65	.65
709	A128	80c	Protea	.65	.65
710	A128	$1.15	Phlox	1.10	1.10
711	A128	$1.75	Chrysanthemum	1.60	1.60
712	A128	$1.95	Lillum	1.75	1.75
713	A128	$2.30	Rose	2.00	2.00
			Nos. 708-713 (6)	7.75	7.75

Christmas — A129

Designs: 35c, Archangel Gabriel, Virgin Mary. 80c, Mary, Joseph on way to Bethlehem. $1.15, Nativity scene. $1.75, Angel pointing way to shepherds. $1.95, Magi following star. $2.30, Madonna and child.

1994, Oct. 11 Litho. *Perf. 14½*

714	A129	35c	multicolored	.70	.70
715	A129	80c	multicolored	.70	.70
716	A129	$1.15	multicolored	1.05	1.05
717	A129	$1.75	multicolored	1.30	1.30
718	A129	$1.95	multicolored	1.75	1.75
719	A129	$2.30	multicolored	1.90	1.90
			Nos. 714-719 (6)	7.40	7.40

A130

1c, Corn. 2c, Sugar cane. 3c, Sunflowers. 4c, Sorghum. 5c, Mine workers. 10c, Underground mining. 20c, Coal mining. 30c, Chrome smelting. 40c, Opencast mining. 45c, Underground drilling. 50c, Gold smelting. 70c, Boggie Clock Tower. 80c, Masvingo Watchtower. $1, Hanging tree. $2, Cecil House. $5, The Toposcope. $10, Paper House.

1995-96 Litho. *Perf. 14*

720	A130	1c	multicolored	.40	.40
721	A130	2c	multicolored	.40	.40
722	A130	3c	multicolored	.40	.40
723	A130	4c	multicolored	.40	.40
724	A130	5c	multicolored	.40	.40
725	A130	10c	multicolored	.40	.40
726	A130	20c	multicolored	.40	.40
727	A130	30c	multicolored	.40	.40
728	A130	40c	multicolored	.40	.40
728A	A130	45c	multicolored	.40	.40
729	A130	50c	multicolored	.40	.40
730	A130	70c	multicolored	.40	.40
731	A130	80c	multicolored	.40	.40
732	A130	$1	multicolored	.50	.50
733	A130	$2	multicolored	.95	.95
734	A130	$5	multicolored	2.40	2.40
735	A130	$10	multicolored	4.75	4.75
			Nos. 720-735 (17)	13.80	13.80

Issued: 45c, 6/3/96; others, 1/17/95.

Insects A131

35c, Spider-hunting wasp. $1.15, Emperor dragonfly. $1.75, Foxy charaxes. $2.30, Antlion.

1995, Apr. 4 Litho. *Perf. 14½*

736	A131	35c	multicolored	1.00	1.00
737	A131	$1.15	multicolored	1.50	1.50
738	A131	$1.75	multicolored	2.00	2.00
739	A131	$2.30	multicolored	2.75	2.75
			Nos. 736-739 (4)	7.25	7.25

6th All Africa Games, Harare — A132

1995, July 11 Litho. *Perf. 14x14½*

740	A132	35c	Soccer	.70	.70
741	A132	80c	Track	.70	.70
742	A132	$1.15	Boxing	1.05	1.05
743	A132	$1.75	Swimming	1.40	1.40
744	A132	$1.95	Field hockey	1.60	1.60
745	A132	$2.30	Volleyball	2.00	2.00
			Nos. 740-745 (6)	7.45	7.45

UN, 50th Anniv. — A133

1995, Oct. 17 Litho. *Perf. 14½*

746	A133	35c	Health	.35	.35
747	A133	$1.15	Environment	.60	.60
748	A133	$1.75	Food distribution	.70	.70
749	A133	$2.30	Education	.95	.95
			Nos. 746-749 (4)	2.60	2.60

Flowering Trees — A134

1996, Jan. 24 Litho. *Perf. 14½*

750	A134	45c	Fernandoa	.40	.40
751	A134	$1	Round leaf mukwa	.40	.40
752	A134	$1.50	Luckybean tree	.80	.80
753	A134	$2.20	Winter cassia	1.25	1.25
754	A134	$2.50	Sausage tree	1.40	1.40
755	A134	$3	Sweet thorn	1.75	1.75
			Nos. 750-755 (6)	6.00	6.00

Dams of Zimbabwe A135

1996, Apr. 9 Litho. *Perf. 14½*

756	A135	45c	Mazvikadei	.45	.45
757	A135	$1.50	Mutirikwi	.80	.80
758	A135	$2.20	Ncema	1.25	1.25
759	A135	$3	Odzani	1.50	1.50
			Nos. 756-759 (4)	4.00	4.00

Scenic Views A136

Designs: 45c, Matusadonha Natl. Park. $1.50, Juliasdale Rocky Outcrops. $2.20, Honde Valley. $3, Finger Rocks, Morgenster Mission.

1996, July 18 Litho. *Perf. 14½*

760	A136	45c	multicolored	.45	.45
761	A136	$1.50	multicolored	.65	.65
762	A136	$2.20	multicolored	1.00	1.00
763	A136	$3	multicolored	1.40	1.40
			Nos. 760-763 (4)	3.50	3.50

Wood Carvings A137

1996, Oct. 15 Litho. *Perf. 14½*

764	A137	45c	Frog	.35	.35
765	A137	$1.50	Tortoise	.50	.50
766	A137	$1.70	Kudu	.60	.60
767	A137	$2.20	Chimpanzee	.75	.75
768	A137	$2.50	Porcupine	.90	.90
769	A137	$3	Rhinoceros	1.00	1.00
			Nos. 764-769 (6)	4.10	4.10

Cattle A138

1997, Jan. 7 Litho. *Perf. 14½*

770	A138	45c	Mashona cow	.50	.50
771	A138	$1.50	Tuli cow	.75	.75
772	A138	$2.20	Nkoni bull	.95	.95
773	A138	$3	Brahman bull	1.35	1.35
			Nos. 770-773 (4)	3.55	3.55

Convention on Intl. Trade in Endangered Species of Flora and Fauna (CITES) — A139

1997, Apr. 15 **Litho.** ***Perf. 14½***

774	A139	45c	Cycad	.55	.55
775	A139	$1.50	Peregrine falcon	.70	.70
776	A139	$1.70	Pangolin	.80	.80
777	A139	$2.20	Black rhinoceros	1.10	1.10
778	A139	$2.50	Elephant	1.25	1.25
779	A139	$3	Python	1.50	1.50
			Nos. 774-779 (6)	5.90	5.90

Aspects of Rural Life A140

1997, July 22 **Litho.** ***Perf. 14½***

780	A140	65c	Carving	.25	.25
781	A140	$1	Winnowing	.25	.25
782	A140	$2.40	Dancing	.60	.60
783	A140	$2.50	Plowing	.70	.70
784	A140	$3.10	Stamping	.90	.90
785	A140	$4.20	Fetching water	1.30	1.30
			Nos. 780-785 (6)	4.00	4.00

Zimbabwe Railway, Cent. A141

65c, Passenger coach. $1, 12th Class, No. 257. $2.40, 16A Class, No. 605. $2.50, El 1, No. 4107. $3.10, Jack Tar. $4.20, DE 2, No. 1211.

1997, Oct. 28 **Litho.** ***Perf. 14½***

786	A141	65c	multicolored	.35	.35
787	A141	$1	multicolored	.35	.35
788	A141	$2.40	multicolored	.80	.80
789	A141	$2.50	multicolored	.80	.80
790	A141	$3.10	multicolored	1.00	1.00
791	A141	$4.20	multicolored	1.25	1.25
			Nos. 786-791 (6)	4.55	4.55

Wildlife A142

65c, Aardwolf. $2.40, Large gray mongoose. $3.10, Clawless otter. $4.20, Antbear (Aardvark).

1998, Jan. 20 **Litho.** ***Perf. 14½***

792	A142	65c	multicolored	.55	.55
793	A142	$2.40	multicolored	.70	.70
794	A142	$3.10	multicolored	1.00	1.00
795	A142	$4.20	multicolored	1.25	1.25
			Nos. 792-795 (4)	3.50	3.50

Apiculture A143

Designs: $1.20, Honeybee on flower. $4.10, Queen, worker, drone. $4.70, Queen, retinue. $5.60, Rural beekeeper. $7.40, Commercial beekeepers. $9.90, Products of the hive.

1998, Apr. 14 **Litho.** ***Perf. 14***

796	A143	$1.20	multicolored	.35	.35
797	A143	$4.10	multicolored	.90	.90
798	A143	$4.70	multicolored	1.00	1.00
799	A143	$5.60	multicolored	1.25	1.25
800	A143	$7.40	multicolored	1.50	1.50
801	A143	$9.90	multicolored	2.00	2.00
			Nos. 796-801 (6)	7.00	7.00

Fossils A144

1998, July 21 **Litho.** ***Perf. 14½***

802	A144	$1.20	Fossil fish	1.10	.45
803	A144	$5.60	Allosaurus footprints	1.60	.95
804	A144	$7.40	Massospondylus	1.90	1.60
805	A144	$9.90	Fossil wood	2.40	2.40
			Nos. 802-805 (4)	7.00	5.40

Birds — A145

Designs: $1.20, Yellow-bellied sunbird. $4.10, Lesser blue-eared starling. $4.70, Greyhooded kingfisher. $5.60, Mombo gray tit. $7.40, Chirinda apalis. $9.90, Swynnerton's robin.

1998, Oct. 20 **Litho.** ***Perf. 14***

806	A145	$1.20	multicolored	.85	.85
807	A145	$4.10	multicolored	1.00	1.00
808	A145	$4.70	multicolored	1.25	1.25
809	A145	$5.60	multicolored	1.60	1.60
810	A145	$7.40	multicolored	1.90	1.90
811	A145	$9.90	multicolored	2.40	2.40
			Nos. 806-811 (6)	9.00	9.00

UPU, 125th Anniv. — A146

$1.20, Counter services at Post Office and Philatelic Bureau. $5.60, Postman delivering mail on bicycle. $7.40, 19th cent. runner, EMS, PTC delivery today. $9.90, Harare Central Sorting Office.

1999, Jan. 19 **Litho.** ***Perf. 14***

812	A146	$1.20	multicolored	.45	.45
813	A146	$5.60	multicolored	.65	.65
814	A146	$7.40	multicolored	.85	.85
815	A146	$9.90	multicolored	1.05	1.05
			Nos. 812-815 (4)	3.00	3.00

A147

Wild cats of Zimbabwe.

1999, Mar. 16 **Litho.** ***Perf. 14***

816	A147	$1.20	Serval	.50	.50
817	A147	$5.60	Cheetah	.75	.75
818	A147	$7.40	Caracal	1.05	1.05
819	A147	$9.90	Leopard	1.40	1.40
			Nos. 816-819 (4)	3.70	3.70

A148

Owls.

1999, June 8 **Litho.** ***Perf. 14¼***

820	A148	$1.20	Cape eagle owl	.85	.85
821	A148	$5.60	Grass owl	1.35	1.35
822	A148	$7.40	Barn owl	1.75	1.75
823	A148	$9.90	Marsh owl	2.10	2.10
			Nos. 820-823 (4)	6.05	6.05

Tourist Activities A149

1999, Aug. 10 **Litho.** ***Perf. 14¼x14***

824	A149	$2	Canoeing	.40	.40
825	A149	$6.70	Rock climbing	.65	.65
826	A149	$7.70	Microlighting	.75	.75
827	A149	$9.10	White water rafting	.90	.90
828	A149	$12	Scenic view	1.25	1.25
829	A149	$16	Viewing game	1.75	1.75
			Nos. 824-829 (6)	5.70	5.70

A150

Christmas: $2, Christmas time — Family time. $6.70, Christmas tree in Africa. $7.70, Joy to you this Christmas. $9.10, Christmas time — Flame lily time. $12, Glory to God & Peace on Earth. $16, The House of Christmas.

1999, Oct. 12 **Litho.** ***Perf. 14x14¼***

830	A150	$2	multi	.35	.35
831	A150	$6.70	multi	.65	.65
832	A150	$7.70	multi	.70	.45
833	A150	$9.10	multi	.95	.95
834	A150	$12	multi	1.25	1.25
835	A150	$16	multi	1.60	1.60
			Nos. 830-835 (6)	5.50	5.25

A151

Designs: 1c, Nyala. 10c, Construction. 30c, Timber. 50c, Tobacco auction floors. 70c, Harare Central Sorting Office. 80c, New international airport, Harare. $1, Westgate Shopping Complex. $2, Nile crocodile. $3, Pungwe water project. $4, Zebra. $5, Mining. $7, National University of Science and Technology. $10, Ostrich. $15, Cape parrot. $20, Leather products. $30, Lilac-breasted roller. $50, Victoria Falls. $100, Tokwe Mukorsi Dam.

2000, Jan. 25 **Litho.** ***Perf. 14¾***

836	A151	1c	multi	.25	.25
837	A151	10c	multi	.25	.25
838	A151	30c	multi	.25	.25
839	A151	50c	multi	.25	.25
840	A151	70c	multi	.25	.25
841	A151	80c	multi	.75	.25
842	A151	$1	multi	.25	.25
843	A151	$2	multi	.75	.25
844	A151	$3	multi	.25	.25
845	A151	$4	multi	.65	.25
846	A151	$5	multi	1.00	.30
847	A151	$7	multi	.40	.40
848	A151	$10	multi	1.75	.65
849	A151	$15	multi	1.75	1.10
850	A151	$20	multi	1.25	1.25
851	A151	$30	multi	2.25	1.90
852	A151	$50	multi	3.00	3.00
853	A151	$100	multi	6.25	6.25
			Nos. 836-853 (18)	21.55	17.35

Sports — A152

2000, Apr. 25 **Litho.** ***Perf. 14***

854	A152	$2	Basketball	.40	.40
855	A152	$6.70	Lawn tennis	.65	.65
856	A152	$7.70	Netball	.85	.85
857	A152	$9.10	Weight lifting	.95	.95
858	A152	$12	Taekwondo	1.25	1.25
859	A152	$16	Diving	1.75	1.75
			Nos. 854-859 (6)	5.85	5.85

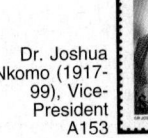

Dr. Joshua Nkomo (1917-99), Vice-President A153

Designs: $2, $12, Wearing suit. $9.10, $16, Wearing headdress.

2000, June 27 **Litho.** ***Perf. 14x14¼***

Background Color

860	A153	$2	blue	.55	.55
861	A153	$9.10	green	1.40	1.40
862	A153	$12	red	1.75	1.75
863	A153	$16	orange	2.25	2.25
			Nos. 860-863 (4)	5.95	5.95

Organizations Combatting Disease A154

Designs: $2, Ministry of Health. $6.70, Rehabilitation and Prevention of Tuberculosis (RAPT). $7.70, New Start centers. $9.10, Riders for Health. $12, Natl. Aids Coordination Program (NACP). $16, Rotary Intl.

2000, July 18 **Litho.** ***Perf. 14¼x14***

864	A154	$2	multi	.30	.30
865	A154	$6.70	multi	.55	.55
866	A154	$7.70	multi	.65	.65
867	A154	$9.10	multi	.90	.90
868	A154	$12	multi	1.05	1.05
869	A154	$16	multi	1.50	1.50
			Nos. 864-869 (6)	4.95	4.95

Wild Fruits Type of 1991

$2, Masawu. $6.70, Spiny monkey orange. $7.70, Bird plum. $9.10, Shakama plum. $12, Wild medlar. $16, Wild custard apple.

2000, Oct. 24 **Litho.** ***Perf. 14x14½***

870-875 A117 Set of 6 4.50 4.50

Aviation A155

Designs: $8, Boeing 737-200. $12, BAe Hawk MK 60. $14, Hawker Hunter FGA-9. $16, Cessna/Reims F-337. $21, Aerospatiale Alouette III helicopter. $28, Boeing 767-200ER.

2001, Jan. 31 **Litho.** ***Perf. 14¼***

876-881 A155 Set of 6 6.50 6.50

Total Solar Eclipse, June 21, 2001 — A156

Designs: $8, Solar prominences. $21, Eclipse path over Africa. $28, Eclipse phases (62x24mm).

Perf. 14¼x14, 14½ ($28)

2001, Apr. 24 **Litho.**

882-884 A156 Set of 3 4.50 4.50

Folklore — A157

Designs: $8, The Hare Who Rode Horseback. $12, The Hippo Who Lost His Hair. $13, The Lion Who Was Saved by a Mouse. $16, The Bush Fowl Who Wakes the Sun. $21, The Chameleon Who Came Too Late. $28, The Tortoise Who Collected Wisdom.

2001, July 24   **Litho.**   **Perf. 14x14¼**
885-890 A157   Set of 6   6.00 6.00
   a.   Souvenir sheet, #885-890   8.00 8.00

Heroes' Acre — A158

Designs: $8, Main entrance gate. $16, Statue of the Unknown Soldier. $21, General view. $28, Aerial view.

2001, Aug. 7   **Litho.**   **Perf. 14¼x14**
891-894 A158   Set of 4   5.00 5.00

Year of Dialogue Among Civilizations A159

Winning stamp design entry in: $8, National competition (Three Faces, by Nation Mandla Mguni). $21, International competition.

2001, Oct. 16   **Litho.**   **Perf. 14¼**
895-896 A159   Set of 2   4.00 4.00

Butterflies A160

Designs: $12, Large blue charaxes. $20, Painted lady. $25, Yellow pansy. $30, Gold-banded forester. $35, Sapphire. $45, Clear-spotted acrea.

2001, Dec. 6   **Litho.**   **Perf. 14¼x14**
897-902 A160   Set of 6   12.00 12.00
902a   Souvenir sheet, #897-902   12.00 12.00

Craftsmanship A161

Designs: $12, Knitting and crocheting. $20, Art and design. $25, Basket making. $30, Pottery. $35, Wood carving. $45, Sculpture.

2002, Jan. 22
903-908 A161   Set of 6   10.00 10.00

Gemstones A162

Designs: $12, Agate. $25, Aquamarine. $35, Diamond. $45, Emerald.

2002, Apr. 23   **Litho.**   **Perf. 14¼x14**
909-912 A162   Set of 4   12.00 12.00

Childline A163

Children's art: $12, Children embracing. $25, Girl on phone. $35, Teddy bear. $45, Arm with phone receiver.

2002, June 4   **Litho.**   **Perf. 14¼x14**
913-916 A163   Set of 4   7.75 7.75

First Lady Sally Mugabe (1931-92) — A164

Various portraits: $20, $50, $70, $90.

2002, Aug. 6   **Perf. 14x14¼**
917-920 A164   Set of 4   12.00 12.00

Children's Stamp Design Contest Winners A165

Designs: $20, Mail runner and bicycle at post office, by Agreement Ngwenya. $70, Mail runner and airplane, by Kudzai Chikomo.

2002, Oct. 8   **Litho.**   **Perf. 14¼**
921-922 A165   Set of 2   6.00 6.00

Wild Flowers A166

Designs: $20, Dissotis princeps. $35, Leonotis nepetifolia. $40, Hibiscus vitifolius. $50, Boophane disticha. $70, Pycnostachys urticifolia. $90, Gloriosa superba.

2002, Oct. 22   **Perf. 14¼x14**
923-928 A166   Set of 6   16.50 16.50
928a   Souvenir sheet, #923-928   18.00 18.00

History Society of Zimbabwe, 50th Anniv. — A167

Map of Zimbabwe and: $30, Society emblem. $80, Hourglass, books, diploma. $110, People listening to speaker. $140, Old building.

2003, Jan. 28   **Litho.**   **Perf. 14x14¼**
929-932 A167   Set of 4   8.50 8.50

Harare Intl. Festival of the Arts — A168

Designs: $30, Festival emblem. $80, Emblem and flower. $110, Eye and flowers. $140, Emblem and flowers.

2003, Apr. 22   **Litho.**   **Perf. 14x14¼**
933-936 A168   Set of 4   4.25 4.25

Type of 2000

Designs: ($100), Bateleur eagle. $500, Goliath heron. $1000, White rhinoceros. $5000, Cheetah.

2003, June 24   **Litho.**   **Perf. 14¾**
937 A151 ($100) multi   .25 .25
938 A151 $500 multi   1.00 1.00
939 A151 $1000 multi   2.00 2.00
940 A151 $5000 multi   10.00 10.00
   Nos. 937-940 (4)   13.25 13.25

Spiders A169

Designs: $150, Baboon spider. $200, Rain spider. $600, Black widow spider. $900, Wolf spider. $1250, Violin spider. $1600, Wall spider.

2003, July 30   **Perf. 14¼**
941-946 A169   Set of 6   8.50 8.50
946a   Souvenir sheet, #941-946   8.50 8.50

Women Empowerment A170

Woman in cap and gown with: $300, Globe, hoe and briefcase. $2100, Traditional woman.

2003, Oct. 14   **Litho.**   **Perf. 14¼**
947-948 A170   Set of 2   4.75 4.75

Endangered Medicinal Herbs — A171

Designs: $200, Wild verbena. $500, Pimpernel. $1000, African arrowroot. $3000, Bird pepper. $4200, Wild garlic. $5400, Cleome.

2003, Oct. 28   **Perf. 14x14¼**
949-954 A171   Set of 6   24.50 24.50
   a.   Miniature sheet, #949-954   24.50 24.50

Environmental Awareness A172

Designs: $500, Environment Africa. $3000, Sondela. $4200, Water Africa. $5400, Tree Africa.

2004, Feb. 17   **Litho.**   **Perf. 14x14¼**
955-958 A172   Set of 4   22.50 22.50

Medals — A173

Designs: $1500, Zimbabwe Independence Medal. $9000, Bronze Cross of Zimbabwe. $13,000, Silver Cross of Zimbabwe. $16,500, Gold Cross of Zimbabwe.

2004, Apr. 6   **Litho.**   **Perf. 14¼**
959-962 A173   Set of 4   65.00 65.00

Aloes — A174

Designs: $1500, Aloe ballii. $3,000, Aloe rhodesiana. $9000, Aloe greatheadii. $10,000, Aloe ortholopha. $13,000, Aloe inyangensis. $16,500, Aloe arborescens.

2004, July 20   **Litho.**   **Perf. 14x14¼**
963-968 A174   Set of 6   22.50 22.50
968a   Miniature sheet, #963-968   27.50 27.50

Co-Vice President Simon Vengai Muzenda (1922-2003) A175

Background colors: $2300, Red. $12,000, Yellow. $17,000, Green. $22,000, Gray.

2004, Sept. 20   **Litho.**   **Perf. 14x14¼**
969-972 A175   Set of 4   17.50 17.50

Conservation A176

Winning art in conservation stamp design contest: $4600, Butterfly, by Kingston Chigidhani. $33,500, Hands and wildlife, by Kudzai Chikomo.

2004, Oct. 26   **Litho.**   **Perf. 14¼x14**
973-974 A176   Set of 2   11.00 11.00

Miniature Sheet

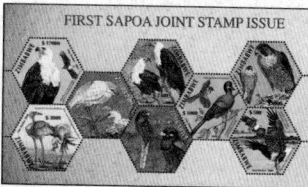

Birds — A177

No. 975: a, $500, African fish eagles, national bird of Zambia. b, $1000, Purple-crested louries, national bird of Swaziland. c, $2300, African fish eagles, national bird of Zimbabwe. d, $3000, Blue cranes, national bird of South Africa. e, $5000, Cattle egrets, national bird of Botswana. f, $9000, Peregrine falcons, national bird of Angola. g, $12,000,

Bar-tailed trogons. h, $17,000, African fish eagles, national bird of Namibia.

2004, Oct. 11 Litho. Perf. 14
975 A177 Sheet of 8, #a-h 70.00 70.00

See Botswana Nos. 792-793, Namibia No. 1052, South Africa No. 1342, Swaziland Nos. 727-735, and Zambia No. 1033.

Birds — A178

Designs: $500, Black-collared barbet. $5000, Gray-headed bush shrike. Z, Red-headed weaver. $10,000, Golden-breasted bunting. $20,000, Cut-throat finch. A, Cabanis's bunting. E, Miombo double-collared sunbird. R, Crested barbet. $50,000, Heuglin's robin. $100,000, Giant kingfisher.

2005, Feb. 8 Litho. Perf. 14¾x14½
976 A178 $500 multi .25 .25
977 A178 $5000 multi 1.40 1.40
978 A178 Z multi 1.75 1.75
979 A178 $10,000 multi 2.75 2.75
980 A178 $20,000 multi 5.50 5.50
981 A178 A multi 8.00 8.00
982 A178 E multi 10.50 10.50
983 A178 R multi 13.00 13.00
984 A178 $50,000 multi 13.00 13.00
985 A178 $100,000 multi 26.00 26.00
Nos. 976-985 (10) 82.15 82.15

On day of issue No. 978 sold for $6900, No. 981 sold for $30,000, No. 982 sold for $40,000, and No. 983 sold for $50,000.

Clouds A179

Designs: $6900, Cirrus. $13,800, Nimbostratus. $30,000, Altocumulus. $40,000, Cumulonimbus.

2005, Apr. 26 Perf. 14¼
986-989 A179 Set of 4 17.50 17.50

Snakes A180

Designs: $6900, Banded Egyptian cobra. $13,800, Puff adder. $20,000, Boomslang. $25,000, Mozambique spitting cobra. $30,000, Gaboon viper. $40,000, Black mamba.

2005, July 12 Litho. Perf. 14¼x14
990-995 A180 Set of 6 18.00 18.00
995a Miniature sheet, #990-995 25.00 25.00

Governmental Officials — A181

Designs: $6900, Josiah Tongogara (1940-79), Chief of Defense. $13,800, Herbert Chitepo (1923-75), Director of Public Prosecutions. $30,000, Bernard Chidzero (1927-2002), Minister of Economic Planning. $50,000, Moven Mahachi (1948-2001), Minister of various departments.

2005, Aug. 4 Litho. Perf. 14x14¼
996-999 A181 Set of 4 10.00 10.00

UNESCO World Heritage Sites A182

Designs: Z, Soapstone Zimbabwe bird, Great Zimbabwe National Park. $15,500, Wall, Khami Ruins. $52,000, Elephant, Mana Pools National Park. $62,000, Victoria Falls.

2005, Oct. 6 Litho. Perf. 14¼
1000-1003 A182 Set of 4 20.00 20.00
1003a Souvenir sheet, #1000-1003 20.00 20.00

No. 1000 sold for $10,250 on day of issue.

World AIDS Day — A183

Designs: $18,000, Cooking pot, field tender, care for the ill. $80,000, Children teaching AIDS prevention.

2005, Dec. 1 Litho. Perf. 14¼x14
1004-1005 A183 Set of 2 10.00 10.00

Food — A184

Designs: $25,000, Mushrooms. $35,000, Rapoko, corn and sorghum. $50,000, Pumpkin, watermelon, spiny cucumber. $150,000, Wild fruits. $250,000, Herbs. $300,000, Sweet potato, cassava, peanuts.

2006, Jan. 17 Litho. Perf. 14x14¼
1006-1011 A184 Set of 6 16.50 16.50
1011a Miniature sheet, #1006-1011 16.50 16.50

Pope John Paul II (1920-2005) A185

Pope: $25,000, Wearing crucifix. $250,000, Holding crucifix.

2006, Feb. 9
1012-1013 A185 Set of 2 15.00 15.00
1013a Souvenir sheet, #1012-1013 15.00 15.00

Water Conservation A186

Designs: $30,000, Faucet and pail. $225,000, Flood irrigation system. $375,000, Lions at waterhole. $450,000, Kariba Dam.

2006, Apr. 25 Litho. Perf. 14x14¼
1014-1017 A186 Set of 4 21.00 21.00

National Heroes — A187

Flag and: $60,000, Leopold T. Takawira (1916-70), first vice-president of Zimbabwe African National Union. $350,000, Simon C. Mazorodze (1933-81), health minister. $500,000, Herbert M. Ushewokunze (1933-95), government minister. $650,000, Tichafa S. Parirenyatwa (1927-62), deputy president of Zimbabwe African People's Union.

2006, July 25 Litho. Perf. 14x14¼
1018-1021 A187 Set of 4 17.50 17.50

Huts — A188

Designs: $100, One hut. $800, Three huts.

2006, Oct. 24 Litho. Perf. 14¼x14
1022-1023 A188 Set of 2 12.00 12.00
1023a Souvenir sheet, #1022-1023 7.25 7.25

Bridges A189

Designs: Z, Mpudzi River Bridge. $450, Victoria Falls Bridge. $600, Limpopo River Bridge. $750, Otto Beit Bridge. $800, Kariba Barrage Bridge. $1000, Birchenough Bridge.

2006, Oct. 24
1024-1029 A189 Set of 6 22.50 22.50
1029a Souvenir sheet, #1024-1029 30.00 30.00

No. 1024 sold for $100 on day of issue.

Trees — A190

Designs: $150, Ziziphuus mauritania. $600, Schlerochra birrea. $750, Jatropha carcus. $1000, Uaparca kirkiana.

2006, Dec. 1 Litho. Perf. 14x14¼
1030-1033 A190 Set of 4 15.00 15.00
1033a Souvenir sheet, #1030-1033 15.00 15.00

Birds — A191

Designs: $50, Hoopoe. $100, Cattle egret. $500, Malachite kingfisher. $1000, Little bee-eater. $2000, Purple-crested lorie. $5000, Purple gallinule. $10,000, African jacana. $20,000, Ground hornbill. $50,000, Gorgeous bush shrike. $100,000, Secretary bird.

Perf. 14¾x14½
2007, Feb. 20 Litho.
1034 A191 $50 multi .25 .25
1035 A191 $100 multi .25 .25
1036 A191 $500 multi .25 .25
1037 A191 $1000 multi .35 .35
1038 A191 $2000 multi .65 .65
1039 A191 $5000 multi 1.75 1.75
1040 A191 $10,000 multi 3.25 3.25
1041 A191 $20,000 multi 6.75 6.75
1042 A191 $50,000 multi 17.00 17.00
1043 A191 $100,000 multi 35.00 35.00
a. Souvenir sheet, #1034-1043 67.50 67.50
Nos. 1034-1043 (10) 65.50 65.50

Scouting, Cent. — A192

Scouting emblem and: $400, Great Zimbabwe Ruins. $1500, Map of Zimbabwe. $2000, Centenary emblem. $2500, Map of Africa.

2007, Feb. 20 Perf. 14x14¼
1044-1047 A192 Set of 4 15.00 15.00

Women A193

Designs: $7500, Mbuya Nehanda (?-1898), colonial resistance organizer. $29,000, Queen Lozikeyi (c. 1855-1919). $35,000, Mother Patrick (1863-1900), educator. $45,000, Amai Sally Mugabe (1932-92), First Lady.

2007, July 10 Perf. 14¼
1048-1051 A193 Set of 4 7.75 7.75

Beginning in 2007, Zimbabwean currency began to experience extreme hyperinflation. Starting with Nos. 1052-1055, most stamps are non-denominated, inscribed "Z" for surface-rate letters sent within Zimbabwe, "A" for letters sent to the rest of Africa by air, "E" for letters sent to Europe by air, and "R" for letters sent to the rest of the world by air, with letters being up to 20 grams in weight. Press release information about these stamps probably was printed in advance of their issuance, so it is unknown if the stamps were actually sold to local customers for the rates implied by the release on the stated day of issue at post offices in Zimbabwe. As the Zimbabwean dollar and denominated stamps daily became more and more worthless (with a reissuance of new Zimbabwe dollars eliminating 10 zeroes on Aug. 1, 2008, and yet again eliminating 12 zeroes on Feb. 2, 2009), the editors cannot easily determine selling prices for these stamps.

National Heroes — A194

Designs: Z, Jason Ziyaphapha Moyo (1927-77), second vice-president of Zimbabwe African People's Union. A, Maurice T. Nyagumbo (1924-89), Zimbabwe African National Union senior minister of political affairs. E, Guy Clutton-Brock (1906-95), founder of Cold Comfort Farm Society. R, Chief Rekayi Tangwena (c. 1910-84), senator.

2007, Aug. 9 Litho. Perf. 14x14¼
1052-1055 A194 Set of 4 — —

On day of issue, Nos. 1052-1055 reportedly sold for $3,000, $12,000, $17,000, and $20,000, respectively.

Butterflies
A195

Designs: Z, Mother-of-pearl. A, Citrus swallowtail. E, Orange tip. R, Blue charaxes. $50,000, Crimson tip. $100,000, Painted lady.

2007, Sept. 18
1056-1061 A195   Set of 6   —   —

On day of issue, Nos. 1056-1059 reportedly sold for $7,500, $29,000, $35,000, and $45,000, respectively.

Life of
Children — A196

Winning art in stamp design contest: Z, Boy studying, by John Ndhlovu. $100,000, Mother feeding baby, by Fungai Madzima.

2007, Oct. 9
1062-1063 A196   Set of 2   —   —

On day of issue, Nos. 1062 reportedly sold for $7,500.

National
Animals
A197

Designs: Z, Buffalo (Zambia). A, Nyala (Malawi). E, Burchell's zebra (Botswana). R, Oryx (Namibia). $100,000, Nyala (Zimbabwe).

Litho. With Foil Application
2007, Oct. 9   **Perf. 13¾**
1064-1068 A197   Set of 5   —   —

On day of issue, Nos. 1064-1067 reportedly sold for $7,500, $29,000, $35,000, and $45,000, respectively. See Botswana No. 838, Malawi No. 752, Namibia Nos. 1141-1142, Zambia Nos. 1097-1101.

St. Valentine's
Day — A198

Designs: Z, Heart. A, Cupid. E, Card (5 hearts). R, Rose.

2008, Jan. 24   Litho.   Perf. 14x14¼
1069-1072 A198   Set of 4   —   —
1072a   Souvenir sheet, #1069-
          1072   —   —

On day of issue, Nos. 1069-1072 reportedly sold for $25,000, $100,000, $170,000, and $240,000, respectively.

Rodents
A199

Designs: Z, Striped mouse. A, Water rat. E, Angoni vlei rat. R, Woodland dormouse.

$5,000,000, Bushveld gerbil. $10,000,000, Namaqua rock mouse.

2008, Apr. 24   **Perf. 14¼**
1073-1078 A199   Set of 6

On day of issue, Nos. 1073-1076 reportedly sold for $550,000, $1,900,000, $3,150,000, and $4,600,000, respectively.

National
Heroes — A200

Designs: Z, Johanna Nkomo (1927-2003), wife of Joshua Nkomo. A, Ruth Lottie Nomonde Chinamano (1925-2005), political activist. E, Dr. Swithun Tachiona Mombeshora (1945-2003), National president of Red Cross. R, Willie Dzawanda Musarurwa (1927-90), journalist.

2008, Aug. 5   **Perf. 14x14¼**
1079-1082 A200   Set of 4   —   —

On day of issue, release information states that Nos. 1079-1082 were to be sold for $250,000,000, $50,000,000,000, $90,000,000,000, and $110,000,000,000, respectively, but the stamps were issued after the Aug. 1 revaluation of the currency eliminating 10 zeroes from the denominations.

In December 2008, Zimbabwe's hyperinflation was calculated by *Forbes Asia* at 6.5 times 10 to the 108th power. By the middle of January 2009, virtually all transactions in Zimbabwe were being conducted in foreign currencies, despite law that mandated that the Zimbabwe dollar be used in transactions between parties not having a government license allowing them to conduct transactions in foreign currencies. On January 29, Zimbabwe's finance minister finally made the use of foreign currencies legal for any transactions in Zimbabwe. On February 2, the government revalued the Zimbabwe dollar for the final time, and finally suspended its use on April 12. Selling prices for stamps listed below are stated in US currency, the primary foreign currency used in the country, as well as the currency used in philatelic press releases.

2008
Summer
Olympics,
Beijing
A201

Emblem of the Zimbabwe Olympic Committee and: Z, Water Cube. A, National Stadium (Bird's Nest). E, Olympic pool. R, Flag of Zimbabwe, medals won by Zimbabwe Olympic athletes.

2009, Jan. 20   Litho.   Perf. 14¼
1083-1086 A201   Set of 4   10.00 10.00

On day of issue, Nos. 1083-1086 reportedly sold in US currency for 50c, $1, $1.50, and $2. respectively.

Paintings
A202

Designs: Zb, Cardoor Scape, bu Cosmos Shiridzinomwa. Zs, Countryside, by James Jali. No. 1089, A, Mountains, by George Churu. No. 1090, A, Barn, by Hilary Kashiri. E, Backyard 1, by Freddy Tauro. R, X in the Land, by Admire Kamudzengere.

2009, Apr. 21
1087-1092 A202   Set of 6   6.50 6.50
1092a   Souvenir sheet of 6,
          #1087-1092   6.50 6.50

On day of issue, Nos. 1087-1092 sold in US currency for 20c, 25c, 50c, 50c, 75c and $1, respectively.

Wildlife
A203

Designs: Zb, Leopard. Zs, Black rhinonceros. No. 1095, A, African buffalo. No. 1096, A, Lion. E, African elephant. R, All five animals.

2009, June 23
1093-1098 A203   Set of 6   6.50 6.50
1098a   Souvenir sheet of 6,
          #1093-1098   6.50 6.50

On day of issue, Nos. 1093-1098 sold in US currency for 20c, 25c, 50c, 50c, 75c and $1, respectively.

National
Heroes — A204

Flag of Zimbabwe and: Zb, Vitalis Musungwa Gava Zvinashe (1943-2009), commander of Zimbabwe Defense Forces. Zs, Garikayi Hlomayi Settled Magadzire (1937-96), leader of Zimbabwe National Farmers' Union. A, George Bodzo Nyandoro (1926-94), Minister of Lands, Natural Resources and Rural Development. E, Border "Madzibaba" Gezi (1964-2001), Minister of Youth, Gender and Employment Creation. R, Seugeant Masotsha Ndlovu (1890-1982), union leader.

2009, Aug. 4   **Perf. 14x14¼**
1099-1103 A204   Set of 5   5.50 5.50

On day of issue, Nos. 1099-1103 sold in US currency for 20c, 25c, 50c, 75c and $1, respectively.

Christmas
A205

Rural churches: Z, St. Barbara's Catholic Church, Kariba. A, Regina Coeli Catholic Church. E, Elim Evangelical Church, Katerere. R, Free Presbyterian Church, Mbuma.

2009, Dec. 15   **Perf. 14¼**
1104-1107 A205   Set of 4   5.00 5.00

On day of issue, Nos. 1104-1107 sold in US currency for 25c, 50c, 75c, and $1, respectively.

Zimbabwe, Africa's Paradise — A206

Winning art in stamp design contest by: Z, Fredy Tembo. A, Munashe M. Patsanza. E, Methembe Dhlamini. R, Kudzai Chikomo.

2010, Jan. 19
1108-1111 A206   Set of 4   5.00 5.00
1111a   Souvenir sheet of 4,
          #1108-1111   5.00 5.00

On day of issue, Nos. 1108-1111 sold in US currency for 25c, 50c, 75c and $1 respectively.

Railroad
Stations
A210

Station in: 25c, Harare. 30c, Kadoma. 85c, Bulawayo. $1, Mutare.

2011, May 26   **Perf. 14¼x14**
1127-1130 A210   Set of 4   5.00 5.00

National
Heroes — A211

Designs: 25c, Tarcissius Malan George Silundika (1929-81), governmental minister. 30c, Julia Zvobgo (1937-2004), politician. 85c, Ariston Maguranyanga Chambati (1934-95), politician. $1, Joseph Luke Culverwell (1918-93), governmental minister.

2011, July 27   **Perf. 14x14¼**
1131-1134 A211   Set of 4   5.00 5.00

Huts — A212

Designs: 25c, Shona hut. 30c, Ndebele hut. 85c, Manyika hut. $1, Tonga hut.

2011, Nov. 29   **Perf. 14½x14**
1135-1138 A212   Set of 4   5.00 5.00
1138a   Sheet of 4, #1135-1138   5.00 5.00

A213

Sculptures — A214

Designs: 5c, 50c, Tobacco Wither, by Henry Munyaradzi. 25c, Family, by Bernard Matemera. 30c, Mother and Daughters, by Victor Mutongwizo. 75c, $1.50, Bird Carrying Spirit People, by Thomas Mukarobgwa. 85c, Wounded Kudu, by Bakali Manzi. $1, Witch and Her Mate, by Sylvester Mubayi.

2012, Mar. 27   Litho.   Perf. 14¼
1139 A213   5c multi   .25   .25
1140 A213   25c multi   .50   .50
1141 A213   30c multi   .60   .60
1142 A213   50c multi   1.00 1.00
a.   Souvenir sheet of 4, #1139-
       1142   2.40 2.40

Perf. 14¼x14
1143 A214   75c multi   1.50 1.50
1144 A214   85c multi   1.75 1.75
1145 A214 $1 multi   2.00 2.00
1146 A214 $1.50 multi 3.00 3.00
a.   Souvenir sheet of 4, #1143-
       1146   8.25 8.25
       Nos. 1139-1146 (8)   10.60 10.60

National Heroes — A215

Designs: 30c, Solomon Tapfunmaneyi Ruzambo Mujuru (1945-2011), army officer and politician. 75c, Eddison Jonas Mudadirwa Zvobgo (1935-2004), governmental minister. 85c, Welshman Mabhena (1924-2010), politician. $1, Robson Dayford Manyika (1936-85), governmental minister.

2012, July 24   **Perf. 14x14¼**
1147-1150   A215   Set of 4   6.00 6.00

Road Safety Campaign A216

Inscriptions: 30c, Light up 5:30 PM. 75c, Speed/drunk driving. 85c, Obey the code. $1, Visibility.

2012, Aug. 28   **Perf. 14¼x14**
1151-1154   A216   Set of 4   6.00 6.00

Ants and Termites A217

Designs: 5c, Honeydew ant. No. 1156, 30c, Philidris ant. No. 1157, 30c, Leaf cutter ant. 75c, Termite and Matabele soldier ant. 85c, Carpenter ant. $1, Termite habitat.

2012, Nov. 20
1155-1160   A217   Set of 6   6.50 6.50
1160a   Souvenir sheet of 6,
       #1155-1160   6.50 6.50

Children's Art — A218

Designs: 30c, Children and rainbow. $1, Corn, mortar, pestle, bowl, head.

2013, Mar. 26
1161-1162   A218   Set of 2   2.60 2.60

Landa John Nkomo (1934-2013), Co-Vice-President A219

Sculpture at Heroes Acre, national flag and: 30c, Nkomo as young man. 75c, Nkomo as older man. 85c, Like 30c. $1, Like 75c.

2013, July 30   **Perf. 14x14¼**
1163-1166   A219   Set of 4   6.00 6.00

Women's Hairstyles A220

Designs: 30c, Tonga-Musila. 75c, Shona-Bumhu. 85c, Ndebele-Isicholo. $1, Shangaan-Bhibho.

2013, Dec. 17   **Litho.**   **Perf. 14¼x14**
1167-1170   A220   Set of 4   6.00 6.00
1170a   Souvenir sheet of 4,
       #1167-1170   6.00 6.00

Export Crops — A221

Designs: 30c, Flowers. 75c, Cotton. 85c, Tea. $1, Tobacco.

2014, Mar. 11   **Litho.**   **Perf. 14¼x14**
1171-1174   A221   Set of 4   6.00 6.00
1174a   Souvenir sheet of 4,
       #1171-1174   6.00 6.00

Transportation History — A222

Designs: 25c, Donkey-drawn sled, 1890s. No. 1176, 30c, Winston Churchill Train, 1929. No. 1177, 30c, 1928 Model A Ford Phaeton. 75c, De Havilland DH Fox Moth, 1932. 85c, 1946 Bristol Bus. $1, Ox-drawn cart, 1964.

2014, June 3   **Litho.**   **Perf. 14¼**
1175-1180   A222   Set of 6   7.00 7.00

National Heroes — A223

Designs: 30c, Sabrina Gabriel Mugabe (1929-2010), politician and sister of Pres. Robert Mugabe. 75c, Kumbirai Manyika Kangai (1938-2013), governmental minister. 85c, Stephen Kenneth Sesulelo Vuma (1936-97), politician. $1, Eric Nyakudya Gwanzura (1924-2013), politician.

2014, July 29   **Litho.**   **Perf. 14x14¼**
1181-1184   A223   Set of 4   6.00 6.00

World Post Day — A224

Designs: 30c, Ancient post runner. 75c, Post rider on horse. 85c, Harare Main Post Office. $1, Post bus.

2014, Oct. 9   **Litho.**   **Perf. 14¼x14**
1185-1188   A224   Set of 4   6.00 6.00

Frogs A225

Designs: 30c, Swynnerton's reed frog. 75c, Giant bullfrog. 85c, Bushveld rain frog. $1, Inyanga river frog.

2014, Dec. 9   **Litho.**   **Perf. 14¼**
1189-1192   A225   Set of 4   6.00 6.00
1192a   Souvenir sheet of 4, imperf.   6.00 6.00

POSTAGE DUE STAMPS

D1

1981   **Litho.**   **Perf. 14½**
J20   D1   1c emerald   .40 1.10
J21   D1   2c ultramarine   .40 1.10
J22   D1   5c lilac   .50 1.40
J23   D1   6c yellow   .65 2.00
J24   D1   10c red   1.40 4.25
     Nos. J20-J24 (5)   3.35 9.85

For surcharge see No. J30.

D2

1985, Aug. 21   **Litho.**   **Perf. 14½**
J25   D2   1c pale orange   .40 .75
J26   D2   2c lilac rose   .40 .75
J27   D2   6c light green   .40 .75
J28   D2   10c tan   .40 .75
J29   D2   13c bright blue   .40 .75
     Nos. J25-J29 (5)   2.00 3.75

No. J24 Surcharged

1990, Jan. 2   **Litho.**   **Perf. 14½**
J30   D1   25c on 10c #J24   11.00 11.00

D3

1995, Jan. 17   **Litho.**   **Perf. 14½**
J31   D3   1c yellow   .35 .35
J32   D3   2c yellow orange   .35 .35
J33   D3   5c rose lilac   .35 .35
J34   D3   10c pale blue   .35 .35
J35   D3   25c violet   .35 .35
J36   D3   40c green   .35 .35
J37   D3   60c orange   .35 .35
J38   D3 $1 brown   .55 .55
     Nos. J31-J38 (8)   3.00 3.00

D4

Bird sculpture.

2000, Jan. 25   **Litho.**   **Perf. 14½**
J39   D4   1c blk, lt grn & grn   .25 .25
J40   D4   10c blk, lt blue & blue   .25 .25
J41   D4   50c blk, lt brn & brn   .25 .25
J42   D4 $1 blk, pink & red   .25 .25
J43   D4 $2 blk, lt yel & yel   .25 .25
J44   D4 $5 blk, lil & red vio   .25 .25
J45   D4 $10 blk, lt ver & ver   .55 .55
     Nos. J39-J45 (7)   2.05 2.05

ZULULAND

ˈzü-ˌlü-ˌland

LOCATION — Northeastern part of Natal, South Africa
GOVT. — British Colony, 1887-1897
AREA — 10,427 sq. mi.
POP. — 230,000 (estimated 1900)
CAPITAL — Eshowe

12 Pence = 1 Shilling
20 Shillings = 1 Pound

Stamps of Great Britain Overprinted

ZULULAND

1888-93   **Wmk. 30**   **Perf. 14**
1   A54   ½p vermilion   7.50 3.00
2   A40   1p violet   30.00 6.00
3   A56   2p green & red   26.00 50.00
4   A57   2½p vio, bl ('91)   40.00 22.50
5   A58   3p violet, yel   30.00 25.00
6   A59   4p green & brn   60.00 75.00
7   A61   5p lil & bl ('93)   100.00 150.00
8   A62   6p vio, rose   20.00 20.00
9   A63   9p blue & lil
          ('92)   120.00 130.00
10   A65   1sh green ('92)   150.00 170.00
          Wmk. 31
11   A51   5sh rose ('92)   700.00 800.00
     Nos. 1-10 (10)   583.50 651.50

Dangerous forgeries exist.

Natal No. 66 Overprinted

1888-94   **Wmk. 2**
12   A14   ½p green, no period   28.50 47.50
  a.   Period after "Zululand"   62.50 95.00
  b.   As "a," double overprint   1,600. 1,750.
  c.   As "a," invtd. overprint   1,400.
  d.   As "a," pair, one without
      ovpt.   7,500.
  e.   As No. 12, double overprint   1,600. 1,750.

Natal No. 71 Ovptd. Like Nos. 1-11
13   A11   6p violet ('94)   70.00 62.50

A1

1891
14   A1   1p lilac   3.75 3.50

By proclamation of the Governor of Zululand, dated June 27th, 1891, No. 14 was declared to be a postage stamp.

A2

1894-96   **Typo.**
15   A2   ½p lilac & grn   6.50 6.00
16   A2   1p lilac & rose   6.00 3.00
17   A2   2½p lilac & blue   16.00 9.75
18   A2   3p lilac & brn   10.00 4.00
19   A2   6p lilac & blk   22.50 25.00
20   A2   1sh green   50.00 45.00
21   A2   2sh6p grn & blk
          ('96)   90.00 110.00
22   A2   4sh grn & car
          rose   150.00 225.00
23   A2   £1 violet, red   600.00 650.00
24   A2   £5 vio & blk,
          red   5,750. 1,900.
     Nos. 15-23 (9)   951.00 1,077.

Numerals of Nos. 19-24 are in color on plain tablet. Dangerous forgeries of No. 24 exist. **Purple or violet cancellations are not necessarily revenue cancels.** 14 of the 17 post offices and agencies used violet as well as black postal cancellations.

Zululand was annexed to Natal in Dec. 1897 and separate stamps were discontinued June 30, 1898.

Datz Guides Available Now!

Well-known author Stephen Datz has written across the philatelic spectrum with works ranging from invaluable collector's resources to amazing inside views of the world of stamp collecting. Datz himself was a stamp dealer with decades of experience. Enjoy a selection from the always-interesting Datz collection today!

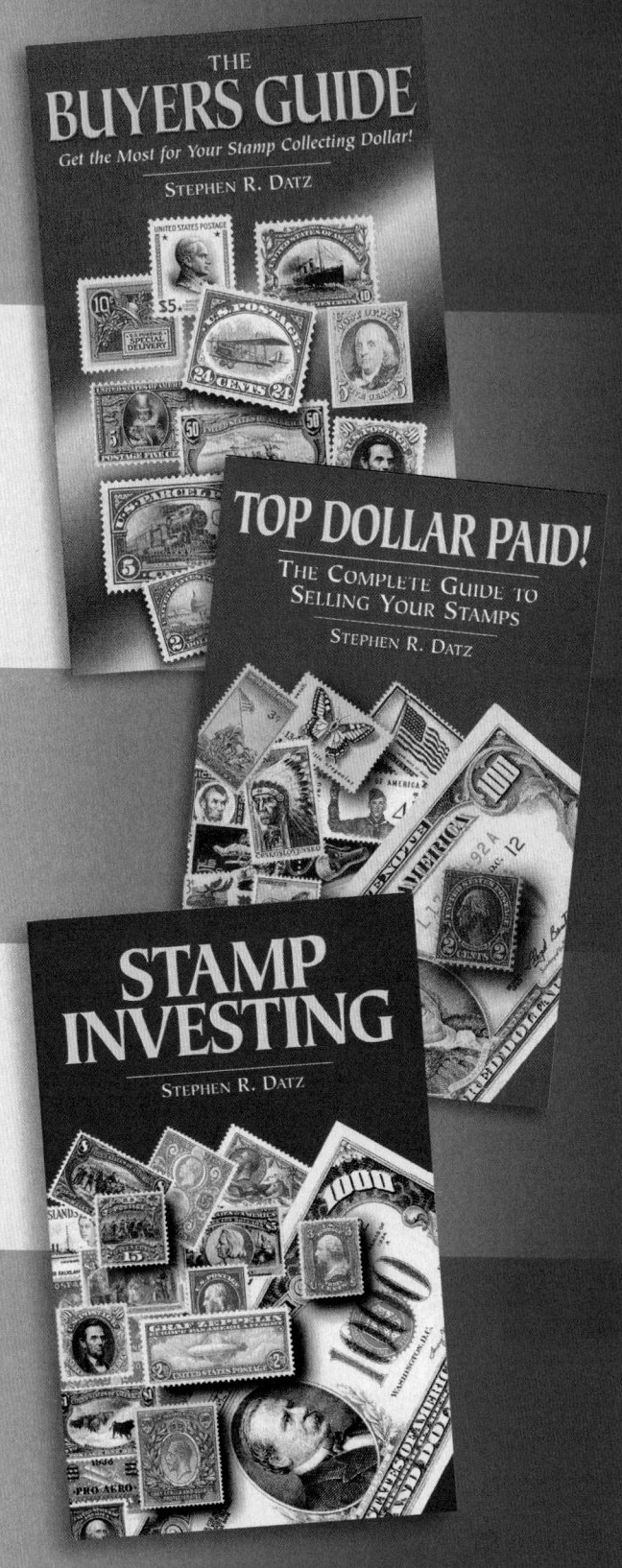

THE BUYERS GUIDE: AN ANALYSIS OF SELECTED U.S. POSTAGE STAMPS

An excellent reference for any collector actively purchasing premium quality U.S. stamps, The Buyer's Guide covers more than 600 important stamps providing a stamp-by-stamp analysis of premium characteristics: gum and hinging; centering and margins; color and freshness; faults and imperfections; warnings about fakes and problems; when to expertize; quantities NH vs. hinged; frequency at auction. Completely illustrated with b&w photos.

Item #	Retail	AA*
LIN70	14.95	13.99

TOP DOLLAR PAID: THE COMPLETE GUIDE TO SELLING YOUR STAMPS

This revealing behind-the-scenes narrative about the real-life world of stamp dealing is a must-read for anyone who buys, collects, or invests in postage stamps, as well as anyone thinking about selling a stamp collection.

Item #	Retail	AA*
LIN72	14.95	13.99

STAMP INVESTING: THE GUIDE TO PROFIT IN STAMPS

An essential guide to profit in stamp investing, covering subjects include: economics of the stamp market; basic strategies and tactics; speculative strategies; growth strategies; understanding technical analysis; spotting profit opportunities; how & when to buy right; how & when to sell; scams & rip-offs to avoid; condition and grading; protecting your investment. A resource guide is also provided.

Item #	Retail	AA*
LIN73	14.95	13.99

Call **1-800-572-6885**

Outside U.S. & Canada Call: **937-498-0800**

Visit **www.AmosAdvantage.com**

P.O. Box 4129, Sidney, OH 45365

Shipping & Handling:
United States: Orders under $10 are only 3.99 - 10% of order total. Minimum charge $7.99 Maximum Charge $45.00. Canada: 20% of order total. Minimum charge $19.99 Maximum charge $200.00. Foreign orders are shipped via FedEx Intl. or USPS and billed actual freight.

ORDERING INFORMATION
*AA prices apply to paid subscribers of Amos Media titles, or for orders placed online.
Prices, terms and product availability subject to change. Taxes will apply in CA, OH, & IL.

AMOS ADVANTAGE

Vol. 6 Number Additions, Deletions & Changes

Number in 2015 Catalogue	Number in 2016 Catalogue

Serbia
new.............................355a

Singapore
new.............................265a
new.............................345a

Solomon Islands
1142-1143 1163-1164
1144-1167 1165-1188

South Africa
new.............................39d
new.............................48q
new.............................48r
new.............................62j
new.............................64C
new.............................64Cd
new.............................64Ce

South Russia
new.............................2b
new.............................7a

Stellaland
new............................. 2c

Tanzania
1367-1371 1367-1370
1372............................. 1371

Tonga
new.............................1148a

Tripolitania
new.............................2a
new.............................2b
new.............................9a
new.............................13a
new.............................24a
new.............................26b

Turks Islands
new.............................8Bd
new.............................8Be

Viet Nam, Democratic Republic
new.............................1L20a

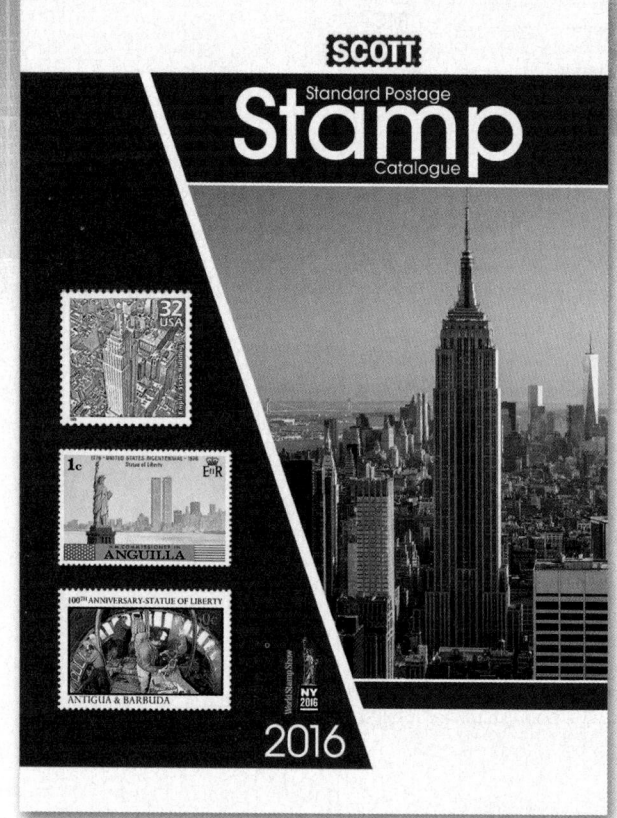

Illustrated Identifier

This section pictures stamps or parts of stamp designs that will help identify postage stamps that do not have English words on them.

Many of the symbols that identify stamps of countries are shown here as well as typical examples of their stamps.

See the Index and Identifier on the previous pages for stamps with inscriptions such as "sen," "posta," "Baja Porto," "Helvetia," "K.S.A.", etc.

Linn's Stamp Identifier is now available. The 144 pages include more than 2,000 inscriptions and more than 500 large stamp illustrations. Available from Linn's Stamp News, P.O. Box 4129, Sidney, OH 45365-4129.

1. HEADS, PICTURES AND NUMERALS

GREAT BRITAIN

Great Britain stamps never show the country name, but, except for postage dues, show a picture of the reigning monarch.

Victoria

Edward VII   George V   Edward VIII

George VI

George VI

Elizabeth II

Some George VI and Elizabeth II stamps are surcharged in annas, new paisa or rupees. These are listed under Oman.

Silhouette (sometimes facing right, generally at the top of stamp)

The silhouette indicates this is a British stamp. It is not a U.S. stamp.

VICTORIA

Queen Victoria

INDIA

Other stamps of India show this portrait of Queen Victoria and the words "Service" (or "Postage") and "Annas."

AUSTRIA

YUGOSLAVIA

(Also BOSNIA & HERZEGOVINA if imperf.)

BOSNIA & HERZEGOVINA

Denominations also appear in top corners instead of bottom corners.

HUNGARY

Another stamp has posthorn facing left

BRAZIL

AUSTRALIA

Kangaroo and Emu

GERMANY

Mecklenburg-Vorpommern

SWITZERLAND

PALAU

2. ORIENTAL INSCRIPTIONS

CHINA

Any stamp with this one character is from China (Imperial, Republic or People's Republic). This character appears in a four-character overprint on stamps of Manchukuo. These stamps are local provisionals, which are unlisted. Other overprinted Manchukuo stamps show this character, but have more than four characters in the overprints. These are listed in People's Republic of China.

Some Chinese stamps show the Sun.

Most stamps of Republic of China show this series of characters.

Stamps with the China character and this character are from People's Republic of China.

Calligraphic form of People's Republic of China

（一）	（二）	（三）	（四）	（五）	（六）
1	2	3	4	5	6
（七）	（八）	（九）	（十）	（一十）	（二十）
7	8	9	10	11	12

Chinese stamps without China character

REPUBLIC OF CHINA

PEOPLE'S REPUBLIC OF CHINA

Mao Tse-tung

MANCHUKUO

Temple   Emperor Pu-Yi

The first 3 characters are common to many Manchukuo stamps.

The last 3 characters are common to other Manchukuo stamps.

Orchid Crest

Manchukuo stamp without these elements

JAPAN

Chrysanthemum Crest   Country Name

Japanese stamps without these elements

The number of characters in the center and the design of dragons on the sides will vary.

RYUKYU ISLANDS

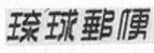

Country Name

PHILIPPINES
(Japanese Occupation)

Country Name

NETHERLANDS INDIES
(Japanese Occupation)

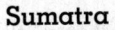

Indicates Japanese Occupation

Java   Sumatra

   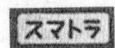

Country Name   Country Name

Moluccas, Celebes and South Borneo

Country Name

NORTH BORNEO
(Japanese Occupation)

Indicates Japanese   Country
Occupation   Name

MALAYA
(Japanese Occupation)

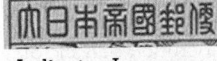   

Indicates Japanese   Country
Occupation   Name

BURMA
Union of Myanmar

প্রযেষ্টাত্তর্মিন্তিন্দির্দেন্ত

Union of Myanmar
(Japanese Occupation)

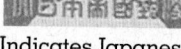

Indicates Japanese   Country
Occupation   Name

Other Burma Japanese Occupation stamps
without these elements

Burmese Script

KOREA

These two characters, in any order,
are common to stamps from the
Republic of Korea (South Korea) or of
the People's Democratic Republic of
Korea (North Korea).

This series of four characters can be found
on the stamps of both Koreas.
Most stamps of the Democratic People's
Republic of Korea (North Korea)
have just this inscription.

Indicates Republic of Korea (South Korea)

South Korean postage stamps issed after
1952 do not show currency expressed
in Latin letters. Stamps wiith "
HW," "HWAN," "WON,"
"WN," "W" or "W" with two lines through it,
if not illustrated in listings of stamps
before this date, are revenues.
North Korean postage stamps do not have
currency expressed in Latin letters.

Yin Yang appears on some stamps.

South Korean stamps show Yin Yang and
starting in 1966, 'KOREA' in Latin letters

Example of South Korean stamps lacking
Latin text, Yin Yang and standard Korean
text of country name. North Korean stamps
never show Yin Yang and starting in 1976
are inscribed "DPRK" or "DPR KOREA" in
Latin letters.

THAILAND

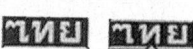

Country Name

King Chulalongkorn

King Prajadhipok and
Chao P'ya Chakri

3. CENTRAL AND EASTERN ASIAN INSCRIPTIONS

INDIA - FEUDATORY STATES

Alwar

Bhor

Bundi

Similar stamps come with
different designs in corners
and differently drawn daggers
(at center of circle).

Dhar   Duttia

Faridkot

Hyderabad

Similar stamps exist with
different central design which is
inscribed "Postage"
or "Post & Receipt."

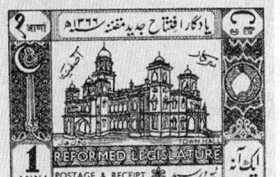

Indore

Jammu & Kashmir

Text varies.

Jasdan

Jhalawar

Kotah

Size and text varies

Nandgaon

Nowanuggur

 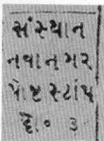

Poonch

Similar stamps exist
in various sizes with different text

Rajasthan

Rajpeepla

Soruth

Tonk

BANGLADESH

বাংলাদেশ

Country Name

NEPAL

Similar stamps are smaller, have squares in
upper corners and have five or nine
characters in central bottom panel.

TANNU TUVA   ISRAEL

GEORGIA

This inscription
is found on other
pictorial stamps.

Country Name

ARMENIA

The four characters are found somewhere
on pictorial stamps. On some stamps only
the middle two are found.

4. AFRICAN INSCRIPTIONS

ETHIOPIA

5. ARABIC INSCRIPTIONS

AFGHANISTAN

Many early Afghanistan stamps show Tiger's head, many of these have ornaments protruding from outer ring, others show inscriptions in black.

Arabic Script

Crest of King Amanullah

Mosque Gate & Crossed Cannons

The four characters are found somewhere on pictorial stamps. On some stamps only the middle two are found.

BAHRAIN

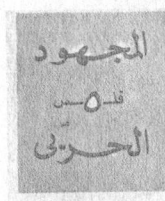 

EGYPT

Postage

IRAN

Country Name

Royal Crown

Lion with Sword

Symbol

Emblem

IRAQ

JORDAN

LEBANON

Similar types have denominations at top and slightly different design.

LIBYA

Country Name in various styles

Other Libya stamps show Eagle and Shield (head facing either direction) or Red, White and Black Shield (with or without eagle in center).

Without Country Name

SAUDI ARABIA

Tughra (Central design)

← Palm Tree and Swords

SYRIA

Arab Government Issues

THRACE   **YEMEN**

PAKISTAN

PAKISTAN - BAHAWALPUR

Country Name in top panel,
star and crescent

TURKEY

Star & Crescent is a
device found on many
Turkish stamps, but is
also found on stamps
from other Arabic
areas (see Pakistan-
Bahawalpur)

Tughra (similar tughras can be found on stamps of Turkey in Asia, Afghanistan and Saudi Arabia)

Mohammed V

Mustafa Kemal

Plane, Star and Crescent

TURKEY IN ASIA

Other Turkey in Asia pictorials show star & crescent. Other stamps show tughra shown under Turkey.

6. GREEK INSCRIPTIONS

GREECE

Country Name in various styles
(Some Crete stamps overprinted with the Greece country name are listed in Crete.)

Lepta

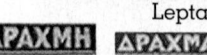
Drachma   Drachmas   Lepton

Abbreviated Country Name

Other forms of Country Name

No country name

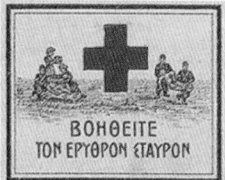

CRETE

Country Name

Crete stamps with a surcharge that have the year "1922" are listed under Greece.

EPIRUS

Similar stamps have text above the eagle.

IONIAN IS.

7. CYRILLIC INSCRIPTIONS

RUSSIA

Postage Stamp   Imperial Eagle

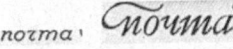

Postage in various styles

Abbreviation   Abbreviation   Russia
for Kopeck   for Ruble

Abbreviation for Russian Soviet Federated Socialist Republic RSFSR stamps were overprinted (see below)

Abbreviation for Union of Soviet Socialist Republics

This item is footnoted in Latvia

RUSSIA - Army of the North

"OKCA"

RUSSIA - Wenden

RUSSIAN OFFICES IN THE TURKISH EMPIRE

These letters appear on other stamps of the Russian offices.

The unoverprinted version of this stamp and a similar stamp were overprinted by various countries (see below).

ARMENIA

BELARUS

FAR EASTERN REPUBLIC

Country Name

FINLAND

Circles and Dots
on stamps similar
to Imperial
Russia issues

SOUTH RUSSIA

Country Name

BATUM

Forms of Country Name

TRANSCAUCASIAN
FEDERATED REPUBLICS

 Abbreviation for
Country Name

KAZAKHSTAN

Country Name

KYRGYZSTAN

Country
Name

ROMANIA

TAJIKISTAN

Country Name & Abbreviation

UKRAINE

Country Name in various forms

The trident appears
on many stamps,
usually as
an overprint.

Abbreviation for
Ukrainian
Soviet
Socialist
Republic

WESTERN UKRAINE

Abbreviation for
Country Name

AZERBAIJAN

AZƏRBAYCAN

Country Name

A.C.C.P. Abbreviation for Azerbaijan Soviet Socialist Republic

MONTENEGRO

ЦРНА ГОРА

Country Name in various forms

Abbreviation for country name

No country name
(A similar Montenegro stamp without country name has same vignette.)

SERBIA

СРПСКА   **СРБИЈА**

Country Name in various forms

Abbreviation for country name

No country name

MACEDONIA

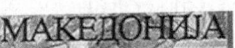

МАКЕДОНИЈА

Country Name

МАКЕДОНСКИ

Different form of Country Name

SERBIA & MONTENEGRO

YUGOSLAVIA

ЈУГОСЛАВИЈА

Showing country name

No Country Name

BOSNIA & HERZEGOVINA
(Serb Administration)

РЕПУБЛИКА СРПСКА

Country Name

РЕПУБЛИКЕ СРПСКЕ

Different form of Country Name

No Country Name

BULGARIA

Country Name   Postage

Stotinka

Stotinki (plural)   Abbreviation for
Stotinki

Country Name in various forms and styles

No country name

 Abbreviation
for Lev, leva

MONGOLIA

ШУУДАН   тѳгрѳг

Country name in   Tugrik in Cyrillic
one word

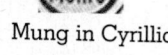

МОНГОЛ   Мѳнгѳ
ШУУДАН

Country name in   Mung in Cyrillic
two words

Mung
in Mongolian

Tugrik
in Mongolian

Arms

No Country Name

ScottMounts

PRE-CUT SINGLE MOUNTS

ITEM	W x H (MM)	DESCRIPTION	MOUNTS	RETAIL	AA*
901	40 x 25	U.S. Standard Comm. Hor. Water Activated	40	$3.50	$2.39
902	25 x 40	U.S. Standard Comm. Vert. Water Activated	40	$3.50	$2.39
903	25 x 22	U.S. Regular Issue – Hor. Water Activated	40	$3.50	$2.39
904	22 x 25	U.S. Regular Issue – Vert. Water Activated	40	$3.50	$2.39
905	41 x 31	U.S. Semi-Jumbo – Horizontal	40	$3.50	$2.39
906	31 x 41	U.S. Semi-Jumbo – Vertical	40	$3.50	$2.39
907	50 x 31	U.S. Jumbo – Horizontal	40	$3.50	$2.39
908	31 x 50	U.S. Jumbo – Vertical	40	$3.50	$2.39
909	25 x 27	U.S. Famous Americans/Champions Of Liberty	40	$3.50	$2.39
910	33 x 27	United Nations	40	$3.50	$2.39
911	40 x 27	United Nations	40	$3.50	$2.39
976	67 x 25	Plate Number Coils, Strips of Three	40	$6.25	$3.99
984	67 x 34	Pacific '97 Triangle	10	$6.25	$2.39
985	111 x 25	Plate Number Coils, Strips of Five	25	$6.25	$3.99
986	51 x 36	U.S. Hunting Permit/Express Mail	40	$6.25	$3.99
1045	40 x 26	U.S. Standard Comm. Hor. Self-Adhesive	40	$3.50	$2.39
1046	25 x 41	U.S. Standard Comm. Vert. Self-Adhesive	40	$3.50	$2.39
1047	22 x 26	U.S. Definitives Vert. Self Adhesive	40	$3.50	$2.39
966		Value Pack (Assortment pre-cut sizes)	320	$23.25	$15.25
975 B		Best Pack (Assortment pre-cut sizes - Black Only)	160	$14.75	$9.99

PRE-CUT PLATE BLOCK, FDC, POSTAL CARD MOUNTS

ITEM	W x H (MM)	DESCRIPTION	MOUNTS	RETAIL	AA*
912	57 x 55	Regular Issue Plate Block	25	$6.25	$3.99
913	73 x 63	Champions of Liberty	25	$6.25	$3.99
914	106 x 55	Rotary Press Standard Commemorative	20	$6.25	$3.99
915	105 x 57	Giori Press Standard Commemorative	20	$6.25	$3.99
916	127 x 70	Giori Press Jumbo Commemorative	10	$6.25	$3.99
917	165 x 94	First Day Cover	10	$6.25	$3.99
918	140 x 90	Postal Card Size/Submarine Booklet Pane	10	$6.25	$3.99
1048	152 x 107	Large Postal Cards	8	$10.25	$6.99

STRIPS 215MM LONG

ITEM	W x H (MM)	DESCRIPTION	MOUNTS	RETAIL	AA*
919	20	U.S. 19th Century, Horizontal Coil	22	$7.99	$5.25
920	22	U.S. Early Air Mail	22	$7.99	$5.25
921	24	U.S. Vertical Coils, Christmas (#2400, #2428 etc.)	22	$7.99	$5.25
922	25	U.S. Commemorative and Regular	22	$7.99	$5.25
1049	26	U.S. Commemorative and Regular	22	$7.99	$5.25
923	27	U.S. Famous Americans	22	$7.99	$5.25
924	28	U.S. 19th Century, Liechtenstein	22	$7.99	$5.25
925	30	U.S. 19th Century; Jamestown, etc; Foreign	22	$7.99	$5.25
926	31	U.S. Horizontal Jumbo and Semi-Jumbo	22	$7.99	$5.25
927	33	U.S. Stampin' Future, UN	22	$7.99	$5.25
928	36	U.S. Hunting Permit, Canada	15	$7.99	$5.25
929	39	U.S. Early 20th Century	15	$7.99	$5.25
930	41	U.S. Vert. Semi-Jumbo ('77 Lafayette, Pottery, etc.)	15	$7.99	$5.25
931		Multiple Assortment: One strip of each size 22-41 above (SMKB) (2 x 25mm strips)	12	$7.99	$5.25
932	44	U.S. Vertical Coil Pair Garden Flowers Booklet Pane	15	$7.99	$5.25
933	48	U.S. Farley, Gutter Pair	15	$7.99	$5.25
934	50	U.S. Jumbo (Lyndon Johnson, '74 U.P.U., etc.)	15	$7.99	$5.25
935	52	U.S. Standard Commemorative Block (Butterflies)	15	$7.99	$5.25
936	55	U.S. Standard Plate Block - normal margins	15	$7.99	$5.25
937	57	U.S. Standard Plate Block - wider margins	15	$7.99	$5.25
938	61	U.S. Blocks, Israel Tabs, '99 Christmas Madonna Pane	15	$7.99	$5.25

STRIPS 240MM LONG

ITEM	W x H (MM)	DESCRIPTION	MOUNTS	RETAIL	AA*
939	63	U.S. Jumbo Commemorative Horizontal Block	10	$9.25	$5.99
940	66	U.S. CIPEX Souvenir Sheet, Self-Adhesive Booklet Pane (#2803a, 3012a)	10	$9.25	$5.99
941	68	U.S. ATM Booklet Pane, Farley Gutter Pair & Souvenir Sheet	10	$9.25	$5.99
942	74	U.S. TIPEX Souvenir Sheet	10	$9.25	$5.99
943	80	U.S. Standard Commemorative Vertical Block	10	$9.25	$5.99
944	82	U.S. Blocks of Four, U.N. Chagall	10	$9.25	$5.99
945	84	Israel Tab Block, Mars Pathfinder Sheetlet	10	$9.25	$5.99
946	89	Submarine Booklet, Souvenir Sheet World Cup, Rockwell	10	$9.25	$5.99
947	100	U.S. '74 U.P.U. Block, U.N. Margin Inscribed Block	7	$9.25	$5.99
948	120	Various Souvenir Sheets and Blocks	7	$9.25	$5.99

STRIPS 265MM LONG

ITEM	W x H (MM)	DESCRIPTION	MOUNTS	RETAIL	AA*
1035	25	U.S. Coils Strips of 11	12	$9.25	$5.99
949	40	U.S. Postal People Standard Standard & Semi-Jumbo Commemorative Strip	10	$9.25	$5.99
981	44	U.S. Long self-adhesive booklet panes	10	$9.25	$5.99
1030	45	Various (Canada Scott #1725-1734)	10	$9.25	$5.99
1036	46	U.S. Long self adhesive booklet panes of 15	10	$9.25	$5.99

STRIPS 265MM LONG - CONTINUED

ITEM	W x H (MM)	DESCRIPTION	MOUNTS	RETAIL	AA*
950	55	U.S. Regular Plate Block or Strip of 20	10	$9.25	$5.99
951	59	U.S. Double Issue Strip	10	$9.25	$5.99
952	70	U.S. Jumbo Commemorative Plate Block	10	$12.50	$8.50
1031	72	Various (Canada Scott #1305a-1804a)	10	$12.50	$8.50
1032	75	Plate Blocks: Lance Armstrong, Prehistoric Animals, etc.	10	$12.50	$8.50
953	91	U.S. Self-Adhesive Booklet Pane '98 Wreath, '95 Santa	10	$12.50	$8.50
1033	95	Mini-Sheet Plate Blocks w/top header	10	$12.50	$8.50
954	105	U.S. Standard Semi-Jumbo Commemorative Plate Number Strip	10	$12.50	$8.50
955	107	Same as above—wide margin	10	$12.50	$8.50
956	111	U.S. Gravure-Intaglio Plate Number Strip	10	$14.75	$9.99
957	127	U.S. 2000 Space S/S, World War II S/S	10	$17.50	$11.99
958	137	Great Britain Coronation	10	$17.50	$11.99
959	158	American Glass, U.S. Football Coaches Sheets	10	$17.99	$12.50
960	175	Large Block, Souvenir Sheet	5	$12.50	$8.50
961	231	U.S. Full Post Office Pane Regular and Commemorative	5	$17.99	$12.50

SOUVENIR SHEETS/SMALL PANES

ITEM	W x H (MM)	DESCRIPTION	MOUNTS	RETAIL	AA*
962	204 x 153	New Year 2000, U.S. Bicentennial S/S	4	$9.25	$5.99
963	187 x 144	55c Victorian Love Pane, U.N. Flag Sheet	9	$15.50	$10.25
964	160 x 200	U.N., Israel Sheet	10	$15.50	$10.25
965	120 x 207	U.S. AMERIPEX Presidential Sheet	4	$6.25	$5.99
968	229 x 131	World War II S/S Plate Block Only	5	$6.25	$4.75
970	111 x 91	Columbian Souvenir Sheet	6	$6.25	$5.25
972	148 x 196	Apollo Moon Landing/Carnivorous Plants	4	$7.99	$5.25
989	129 x 122	U.S. Definitive Sheet: Harte, Hopkins, etc.	8	$10.25	$6.99
990	189 x 151	Chinese New Year	5	$10.25	$6.99
991	150 x 185	Breast Cancer/Fermi/Soccer/'96 Folk Heroes	5	$10.25	$6.99
992	198 x 151	Cherokee Strip Sheet	5	$10.25	$6.99
993	185 x 151	Bernstein/NATO/Irish/Lunt/Gold Rush Sheets	5	$10.25	$6.99
994	198 x 187	Postal Museum	4	$10.25	$6.99
995	156 x 187	Sign Language/Statehood	5	$10.25	$6.99
996	188 x 197	Illustrators, '98 Music: Folk, Gospel; Country/Western	4	$10.25	$6.99
997	151 x 192	Olympic	5	$10.25	$6.99
998	174 x 185	Buffalo Soldiers	5	$10.25	$6.99
999	130 x 198	Silent Screen Stars	5	$10.25	$6.99
1000	190 x 199	Stars Stripes/Baseball/Insects & Spiders/ Legends West/ Aircraft, Comics, '96 Olympics, Civil War	4	$10.25	$6.99
1001	178 x 181	Cranes	4	$10.25	$6.99
1002	183 x 212	Wonders of the Sea, We the People	3	$10.25	$6.99
1003	156 x 264	$14 Eagle	4	$10.25	$6.99
1004	159 x 270	$9.95 Moon Landing	4	$10.25	$6.99
1005	159 x 259	$2.90 Priority/$9.95 Express Mail	4	$10.25	$6.99
1006	223 x 187	Hubble, Hollywood Legends, O'Keefe Sheets	3	$10.25	$6.99
1007	185 x 181	Deep Sea Creatures, Olmsted Sheets	4	$10.25	$6.99
1008	152 x 228	Indian Dances/Antique Autos	5	$10.25	$6.99
1009	165 x 150	River Boat/Hanukkah	6	$10.25	$6.99
1010	275 x 200	Dinosaurs/Large Gutter Blocks	2	$10.25	$6.99
1011	161 x 160	Pacific '97 Triangle Mini Sheets	6	$10.25	$6.99
1012	174 x 130	Road Runner, Daffy, Bugs, Sylvester & Tweety	6	$10.25	$6.99
1013	196 x 158	Football Coaches	4	$10.25	$6.99
1014	184 x 184	American Dolls, Flowering Trees Sheets	4	$10.25	$6.99
1015	186 x 230	Classic Movie Monsters	3	$10.25	$6.99
1016	187 x 160	Trans-Mississippi Sheet	4	$10.25	$6.99
1017	192 x 230	Celebrate The Century	3	$10.25	$6.99
1018	156 x 204	Space Discovery	5	$10.25	$6.99
1019	182 x 209	American Ballet	5	$10.25	$6.99
1020	139 x 151	Christmas Wreaths	5	$10.25	$6.99
1021	129 x 126	Justin Morrill, Henry Luce	8	$10.25	$6.99
1022	184 x 165	Baseball Fields, Bright Eyes	4	$10.25	$6.99
1023	185 x 172	Shuttle Landing Pan Am Invert Sheets	4	$10.25	$6.99
1024	172 x 233	Sonoran Desert	3	$10.25	$6.99
1025	150 x 166	Prostate Cancer	5	$10.25	$6.99
1026	201 x 176	Famous Trains	4	$10.25	$6.99
1027	176 x 124	Canada - Historic Vehicles	5	$10.25	$6.99
1028	245 x 114	Canada - Provincial Leaders	5	$10.25	$6.99
1029	177 x 133	Canada - Year of the Family	5	$10.25	$6.99
1034	181 x 213	Arctic Animals	3	$10.25	$6.99
1037	179 x 242	Louise Nevelson	3	$10.25	$6.99
1038	179 x 217	Library Of Congress	3	$10.25	$6.99
1039	182 x 232	Youth Team Sports	3	$10.25	$6.99
1040	183 x 216	Lucille Ball Scott #3523	3	$10.25	$6.99
1041	182 x 244	American Photographers	3	$10.25	$6.99
1042	185 x 255	Andy Warhol	3	$10.25	$6.99
1043	165 x 190	American Film Making	4	$10.25	$6.99
1044	28 x 290	American Eagle PNC Strips of 11 Available in clear or black backgrounds. Please specify color choice when ordering.	12	$9.25	$5.99

ACCESSORIES

ITEM	W x H (MM)	DESCRIPTION	MOUNTS	RETAIL	AA*
LH180MC		Stamp Mount Cutter 7"		$23.99	$19.99
980RMC		Rotary Mount Cutter		$89.99	$79.99
SG622		Hawid Glue Pen		$7.95	$7.25

Call **1-800-572-6885**
Outside U.S. & Canada Call:
1-937-498-0800
Visit **AmosAdvantage.com**
P.O. Box 4129, Sidney, OH 45365-4129

ORDERING INFORMATION

1. *AA prices apply to paid subscribers of Amos Media titles, or for orders placed online.
2. Prices, terms and product availability subject to change.
3. Shipping & Handling: United States: Orders under $10 are only 3.99 - 10% of order total. Minimum charge $7.99 Maximum Charge $45.00. Canada: 20% of order total. Minimum charge $19.99 Maximum charge $200.00. Foreign orders are shipped via FedEx! Intl. or USPS and billed actual freight. Taxes will apply in CA, OH, & IL.

INDEX AND IDENTIFIER

All page numbers shown are
those in this Volume 6.

Postage stamps that do not have
English words on them are shown
in the Illustrated Identifier.

SHOWGARD MOUNTS

Showgard mounts are manufactured with the highest archival qualities in mind. The foil used to produce the mounts is acid free and stronger than other mounts for maximum protection and durability. Selecting the right size mount for your stamp is easy. Simply use a millimeter ruler to measure the stamps width then the height. Showgard incorporates these measurements into their product numbers to insure you get the right size. Mounts available with clear (c) or black (b) backgrounds. Please specify background preference when ordering.

Item	Description	Mounts	Retail	AA*
SGC50/31	50/31 U.S. Jumbo Singles - Horizontal	40	$3.95	$2.85
SGCV31/50	31/50 U.S. Jumbo Singles - Vertical	40	$3.95	$2.85
SGJ40/25	40/25 U.S. Commem. - Horizontal	40	$3.95	$2.85
SGJV25/40	25/40 U.S. Commem. - Vertical	40	$3.95	$2.85
SGE22/25	22/25 U.S. Regular Issues - Vertical	40	$3.95	$2.85
SGEH25/22	25/22 U.S. Regular Issues - Horizontal	40	$3.95	$2.85
SGT25/27	25/27 U.S. Famous Americans	40	$3.95	$2.85
SGU33/27	33/27 U.N., Germany	40	$3.95	$2.85
SGN40/27	40/27 United Nations	40	$3.95	$2.85
SGAH41/31	41/31 U.S. Semi Jumbo - Horizontal	40	$3.95	$2.85
SGAV31/41	31/41 U.S. Semi Jumbo - Vertical	40	$3.95	$2.85
SGDH52/36	52/36 U.S. Duck Stamps	30	$3.95	$2.85
SGS31/31	31/31 U.S. Celebrate the Century	30	$3.95	$2.85
SGUS2	Cut Style with Tray-8 Sizes	320	$31.50	$22.52
SGUS3	Strip Style w/Tray-No. 22 thru No. 52	75	$47.50	$33.96
SGUS1	U.S. Strip Sizes No. 22 thru No. 52	50	$24.50	$17.52
SG50VPB	50th Anniversary Value Pack	50	$24.95	$19.95
SG67/25	67/25 U.S. Coil Strips of 3	40	$7.95	$5.79
SG57/55	57/55 U.S. Regular Issue	25	$7.95	$5.79
SG106/55	106/55 U.S. 3¢, 4¢ Commemoratives	20	$7.95	$5.79
SG105/57	105/57 U.S. Giori Press Issues	20	$7.95	$5.79
SG127/70	127/70 U.S. Jumbo Issues	10	$7.95	$5.79
SG140/89	140/89 Postcards, Souvenir Sheets	10	$7.95	$5.79
SG165/94	165/94 First Day Covers	10	$7.95	$5.79
SG20	215/20 U.S. Mini Stamps, etc.	22	$9.25	$6.79
SG22	215/22 Narrow U.S. Airs	22	$9.25	$6.79
SG24	215/24 U.K. and Canada, early U.S.	22	$9.25	$6.79
SG25	215/25 U.S. Commem. & Regular Issues	22	$9.25	$6.79
SG27	215/27 U.S. Famous Americans, U.N.	22	$9.25	$6.79
SG28	215/28 Switzerland, Liechtenstein	22	$9.25	$6.79
SG30	215/30 U.S. Special Stamps, Jamestown	22	$9.25	$6.79
SG31	315/31 U.S. Squares & Semi Jumbo	22	$9.25	$6.79
SG33	215/33 U.K. Issues, Misc. Foreign	22	$9.25	$6.79
SG36	215/36 Duck Stamps, Misc. Foreign	15	$9.25	$6.79
SG39	215/39 U.S. Magsaysay, Misc. Foreign	15	$9.25	$6.79
SG41	215/41 U.S. Vertical Commem. Israel Tabs	15	$9.25	$6.79
SG44	215/44 Booklet Panes, Hatteras Quartet	15	$9.25	$6.79
SG48	215/48 Canada Reg. Issue & Comm Blocks	15	$9.25	$6.79
SG50	215/50 U.S. Plain Blocks of 4	15	$9.25	$6
SG52	215/52 France Paintings, Misc. Foreign	15	$9.25	$6.79
SG57	215/57 U.S. Commem. Plate Blocks	15	$9.25	$6.79
SG61	215/61 Souvenir Sheets, Tab Singles, etc.	15	$9.25	$6.79
SG63	240/63 U.S. Semi Jumbo Blocks	10	$11.50	$8.50
SG66	240/66 U.S. ATM Panes, SA Duck Panes	10	$11.50	$8.50
SG68	240/68 Canadian Plate Blocks, etc.	10	$11.50	$8.50
SG74	240/74 U.N. Inscription Blocks of 4	10	$11.50	$8.50
SG80	240/80 U.S. Commem. Blocks	10	$11.50	$8.50
SG82	240/82 U.N. Chagall SS, Canada Plate Blocks	10	$11.50	$8.50
SG84	240/84 Israel Plate Blocks, etc.	10	$11.50	$8.50
SG89	240/89 U.N. Inscription Blocks of 6	10	$11.50	$8.50
SG100	240/100 U.S. Squares Plate Blocks	7	$11.50	$8.50
SG120	240/120 Miniature Sheets	7	$11.50	$8.50
SG70	264/70 U.S. Jumbo Plate Blocks	10	$15.50	$11.10
SG91	264/91 U.K. Souvenir Sheets	10	$15.50	$11.10
SG105	264/105 U.K. Blocks, Covers, etc.	10	$15.50	$11.10
SG107	264/107 U.S. Plate No. Strip of 20	10	$15.50	$11.10
SGMPK	Assortment No. 22 thru No. 41	12	$7.25	$5.29
SGMPK2	Assortment No. 76 thru No. 171	15	$31.75	$23.25
SGAB	U.S. SS to 1975-except White Plains	11	$8.25	$5.99
SGWSE	World Stamp Expo Souvenir Sheets	3	$2.50	$1.75
SG265/231	265/231 U.S. Full Sheets & Souvenir Cards	5	$21.25	$15.25
SGRP94	U.S. 1994 Souvenir Sheets	5	$9.75	$6.95
SGRPAC97	Pacific 97 Issues	7	$5.50	$3.99
SGDC2006	Washington 2006 Souvenir Sheets (4)	11	$7.75	$5.50
SGTM	Trans-Mississippi Issues	11	$5.50	$3.99
SGSPC	Space Exploration Sheets	5	$6.95	$4.99
SG111	264/111 U.S. Floating Plate No. Strips of 20	5	$10.25	$7.29
SG127	264/127 Modern U.S. Definitive Sheets of 20	5	$11.50	$8.25

Item	Description	Mounts	Retail	AA*
SG137	264/137 U.N. SS, U.K. Coronation	5	$12.50	$8.99
SG158	264/158 Miniature Sheets, Apoll Soyuz PB	5	$13.75	$9.85
SG175	264/175 U.S. Sheets-Pan American Reissues	5	$15.25	$11.25
SG188	264/188 U.S. Miniature Sheets-Hollywood, etc.	5	$15.95	$11.50
SG198	264/198 U.S. Miniature Sheets	5	$16.50	$11.85
SG260/25	260/25 U.S. Coil Strips of up to 11 stamps	25	$12.25	$8.75
SG293/30	293/30 U.S. American Eagle Coil Strips of up to 11 stamps	5	$3.95	$2.85
SG260/40	260/40 U.S. Postal People Full Strip	10	$9.95	$7.10
SG260/46	260/46 U.S. Vending Booklets	10	$9.95	$7.10
SG260/55	260/55 U.S. 13¢ Eagle Full Strip	10	$9.95	$7.10
SG260/59	260/59 U.S. Double Press Reg. Iss. Strips of 20	10	$9.75	$6.95
SG111/91	111/91 U.S. Columbian Souvenir Sheets	6	$5.25	$3.75
SG229/131	229/131 U.S. WWII Sheets, Looney Tunes	5	$10.25	$7.29
SG187/144	187/144 U.N. Flag Sheetlets	10	$17.50	$12.50
SG204/153	204/153 U.S. Commem. Sheets, Bicentennial	5	$10.75	$7.75
SG120/207	120/207 U.S. Ameripex Presidential Sheetlets	4	$7.50	$5.36
SG192/201	192/201 U.S. Classics Mini-Sheets	5	$12.75	$9.15
SG280/228	280/228 U.S. Greetings From America Sheets	5	$19.50	$13.99
SG191/229	191/229 U.S. Celebrate The Century Sheets	5	$14.50	$10.50
SG76	264/76 BEP SS, Booklets, Plate Blocks	5	$11.50	$8.35
SG96	264/96 Souvenir Sheets, Panes	5	$11.50	$8.35
SG109	264/109 Foreign Miniature Sheets	5	$11.50	$8.35
SG115	264/115 Foreign Miniature Sheets	5	$11.50	$8.35
SG117	264/117 Foreign Miniature Sheets	5	$11.50	$8.35
SG121	264/121 Foreign Miniature Sheets	5	$11.50	$8.35
SG131	264/131 Looney Toons, Misc. Sheetlets	5	$11.50	$8.35
SG135	264/135 Foreign Miniature Sheets	5	$11.50	$8.35
SG139	264/139 White House Pane, etc.	5	$11.50	$8.35
SG143	264/143 Victorian Love, Misc. Sheets	5	$11.50	$8.35
SG147	264/147 Cinco de Mayo, etc.	5	$14.50	$10.37
SG151	264/151 Antique Auto, Communication, etc.	5	$14.50	$10.37
SG163	264/163 Tropical Flowers, UN Human Rights	5	$14.50	$10.37
SG167	264/167 Misc. U.S. Sheetlets	5	$14.50	$10.37
SG171	264/171 Helping Children Learn, etc.	5	$14.50	$10.37
SG181	264/181 U.S. Sheets– Calder, All Aboard, etc.	5	$17.75	$12.75
SG201	264/201 Dinosaurs, etc.	5	$17.75	$12.75
SG215	264/215 U.S. Sheets–Arctic Animals, Ballet, etc.	5	$17.75	$12.75

7" LIGHTHOUSE STAMP MOUNT CUTTER

This affordable and versatile mount cutter features an attachable measuring scale up to 7" (180mm) with an adjustable stop for accurate and clean cuts every time.

Item	Retail	AA
LH180MC	$23.99	$19.99

AMOS ADVANTAGE

Call **1-800-572-6885**

Outside U.S. & Canada: (937) 498-0800

Visit **AmosAdvantage.com**

Mail orders to: P.O. Box 4129, Sidney, OH 45365

Ordering Information: *AA prices apply to paid subscribers of Amos Media titles, or orders placed online. Prices, terms and product availability subject to change.

Shipping & Handling: United States: Orders under $10 are only 3.99 - 10% of order total.Minimum charge $7.99 Maximum Charge $45.00. Canada: 20% of order total. Minimum charge $19.99 Maximum charge $200.00. Foreign orders are shipped via FedExl Intl. or USPS and billed actual freight. Taxes will apply in CA, OH, & IL.

Pronunciation Symbols

ə .... banana, collide, abut

'ə, ˌə .... humdrum, abut

ə .... immediately preceding \l\, \n\, \m\, \ŋ\, as in battle, mitten, eaten, and sometimes open \'ō-pᵊm\, lock and key \-ᵊŋ-\; immediately following \l\, \m\, \r\, as often in French table, prisme, titre

ər .... further, merger, bird

'ər-
'ə-r } .... as in two different pronunciations of hurry \'hər-ē, 'hə-rē\

a .... mat, map, mad, gag, snap, patch

ā .... day, fade, date, aorta, drape, cape

ä .... bother, cot, and, with most American speakers, father, cart

à .... father as pronounced by speakers who do not rhyme it with bother; French patte

aù .... now, loud, out

b .... baby, rib

ch .... chin, nature \'nā-chər\

d .... did, adder

e .... bet, bed, peck

'ē, ˌē .... beat, nosebleed, evenly, easy

ē .... easy, mealy

f .... fifty, cuff

g .... go, big, gift

h .... hat, ahead

hw .... whale as pronounced by those who do not have the same pronunciation for both whale and wail

i .... tip, banish, active

ī .... site, side, buy, tripe

j .... job, gem, edge, join, judge

k .... kin, cook, ache

ḳ .... German ich, Buch; one pronunciation of loch

l .... lily, pool

m .... murmur, dim, nymph

n .... no, own

ⁿ .... indicates that a preceding vowel or diphthong is pronounced with the nasal passages open, as in French un bon vin blanc \œⁿ-bōⁿ-vaⁿ-bläⁿ\

ŋ .... sing \'siŋ\, singer \'siŋ-ər\, finger \'fiŋ-gər\, ink \'iŋk\

ō .... bone, know, beau

ȯ .... saw, all, gnaw, caught

œ .... French boeuf, German Hölle

œ̄ .... French feu, German Höhle

ȯi .... coin, destroy

p .... pepper, lip

r .... red, car, rarity

s .... source, less

sh .... as in shy, mission, machine, special (actually, this is a single sound, not two); with a hyphen between, two sounds as in grasshopper \'gras-ˌhä-pər\

t .... tie, attack, late, later, latter

th .... as in thin, ether (actually, this is a single sound, not two); with a hyphen between, two sounds as in knighthood \'nīt-ˌhùd\

t̲h̲ .... then, either, this (actually, this is a single sound, not two)

ü .... rule, youth, union \'yün-yən\, few \'fyü\

ù .... pull, wood, book, curable \'kyùr-ə-bəl\, fury \'fyùr-ē\

ᴜe .... German füllen, hübsch

ᴜ̄e .... French rue, German fühlen

v .... vivid, give

w .... we, away

y .... yard, young, cue \'kyü\, mute \'myüt\, union \'yün-yən\

ʸ .... indicates that during the articulation of the sound represented by the preceding character the front of the tongue has substantially the position it has for the articulation of the first sound of yard, as in French digne \dēnʸ\

z .... zone, raise

zh .... as in vision, azure \'a-zhər\ (actually, this is a single sound, not two); with a hyphen between, two sounds as in hogshead \'hȯgz-ˌhed, 'hägz-\

\ .... slant line used in pairs to mark the beginning and end of a transcription: \'pen\

' .... mark preceding a syllable with primary (strongest) stress: \'pen-mən-ˌship\

ˌ .... mark preceding a syllable with secondary (medium) stress: \'pen-mən-ˌship\

- .... mark of syllable division

( ) .... indicate that what is symbolized between is present in some utterances but not in others: factory \'fak-t(ə-)rē\

÷ .... indicates that many regard as unacceptable the pronunciation variant immediately following: cupola \'kyü-pə-lə, ÷-ˌlō\

INDEX TO ADVERTISERS
2016 VOLUME 6

2016
VOLUME 6
DEALER DIRECTORY
YELLOW PAGE LISTINGS

This section of your Scott Catalogue contains
advertisements to help you conveniently find
what you need, when you need it...!

Accessories

BROOKLYN GALLERY COIN & STAMP, INC.
8725 4th Ave.
Brooklyn, NY 11209
PH: 718-745-5701
FAX: 718-745-2775
info@brooklyngallery.com
www.brooklyngallery.com

Appraisals

COLONIAL STAMP COMPANY
5757 Wilshire Blvd. PH #8
Los Angeles, CA 90036
PH: 323-933-9435
FAX: 323-939-9930
Toll Free in North America
PH: 877-272-6693
FAX: 877-272-6694
info@colonialstampcompany.com
www.colonialstampcompany.com

DR. ROBERT FRIEDMAN & SONS STAMP & COIN BUYING CENTER
2029 W. 75th St.
Woodridge, IL 60517
PH: 800-588-8100
FAX: 630-985-1588
drbobstamps@comcast.net
www.drbobfriedmanstamps.com

Asia

MICHAEL ROGERS, INC.
Suite 4-1
415 S. Orlando Ave.
Winter Park, FL 32789-3683
PH: 407-644-2290
PH: 800-843-3751
FAX: 407-645-4434
Stamps@michaelrogersinc.com
www.michaelrogersinc.com

THE STAMP ACT
PO Box 1136
Belmont, CA 94002
PH: 650-703-2342
PH: 650-592-3315
FAX: 650-508-8104
thestampact@sbcglobal.net

Auctions

COLONIAL STAMP COMPANY
5757 Wilshire Blvd. PH #8
Los Angeles, CA 90036
PH: 323-933-9435
FAX: 323-939-9930
Toll Free in North America
PH: 877-272-6693
FAX: 877-272-6694
info@colonialstampcompany.com
www.colonialstampcompany.com

DANIEL F. KELLEHER AUCTIONS LLC
PMB 44
60 Newtown Rd
Danbury, CT 06810
PH: 203-297-6056
FAX: 203-297-6059
info@kelleherauctions.com
www.kelleherauctions.com

DUTCH COUNTRY AUCTIONS
4115 Concord Pike
Wilmington, DE 19803
PH: 302-478-8740
FAX: 302-478-8779
auctions@dutchcountryauctions.com
www.dutchcountryauctions.com

R. MARESCH & SON LTD.
5th Floor - 6075 Yonge St.
Toronto, ON M2M 3W2
CANADA
PH: 416-363-7777
FAX: 416-363-6511
www.maresch.com

Auctions - Public

ALAN BLAIR AUCTIONS, L.L.C.
Suite 1
5405 Lakeside Ave.
Richmond, VA 23228-6060
PH: 800-689-5602
FAX: 804-262-9307
alanblair@verizon.net
www.alanblairstamps.com

British Commonwealth

ARON R. HALBERSTAM PHILATELISTS, LTD.
PO Box 150168
Van Brunt Station
Brooklyn, NY 11215-0168
PH: 718-788-397
arh@arhstamps.com
www.arhstamps.com

Buying

DR. ROBERT FRIEDMAN & SONS STAMP & COIN BUYING CENTER
2029 W. 75th St.
Woodridge, IL 60517
PH: 800-588-8100
FAX: 630-985-1588
drbobstamps@comcast.net
www.drbobfriedmanstamps.com

Canada

CANADA STAMP FINDER
54 Soccavo Crescent
Brampton, ON L6Y 0W3
PH: 905-488-6109
Toll Free in North America
PH: 877-412-3106
FAX: 323-215-2635
info@canadastampfinder.com
www.canadastampfinder.com

China

MICHAEL ROGERS, INC.
Suite 4-1
415 S. Orlando Ave.
Winter Park, FL 32789-3683
PH: 407-644-2290
PH: 800-843-3751
FAX: 407-645-4434
Stamps@michaelrogersinc.com
www.michaelrogersinc.com

Collections

DR. ROBERT FRIEDMAN & SONS STAMP & COIN BUYING CENTER
2029 W. 75th St.
Woodridge, IL 60517
PH: 800-588-8100
FAX: 630-985-1588
drbobstamps@comcast.net
www.drbobfriedmanstamps.com

Ducks

MICHAEL JAFFE
PO Box 61484
Vancouver, WA 98666
PH: 360-695-6161
PH: 800-782-6770
FAX: 360-695-1616
mjaffe@brookmanstamps.com
www.brookmanstamps.com

German Colonies

COLONIAL STAMP COMPANY
5757 Wilshire Blvd. PH #8
Los Angeles, CA 90036
PH: 323-933-9435
FAX: 323-939-9930
Toll Free in North America
PH: 877-272-6693
FAX: 877-272-6694
info@colonialstampcompany.com
www.colonialstampcompany.com

Germany

HENRY GITNER PHILATELISTS, INC.
PO Box 3077-S
Middletown, NY 10940
PH: 845-343-5151
PH: 800-947-8267
FAX: 845-343-0068
hgitner@hgitner.com
www.hgitner.com

JAMES F TAFF
PO Box 19549
Sacramento, CA 95819
PH: 916-454-9007
FAX: 916-454-9009

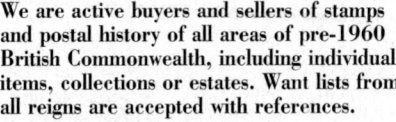

  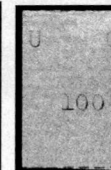 
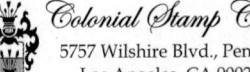

Japan

MICHAEL ROGERS, INC.
Suite 4-1
415 S. Orlando Ave.
Winter Park, FL 32789-3683
PH: 407-644-2290
PH: 800-843-3751
FAX: 407-645-4434
Stamps@michaelrogersinc.com
www.michaelrogersinc.com

Korea

MICHAEL ROGERS, INC.
Suite 4-1
415 S. Orlando Ave.
Winter Park, FL 32789-3683
PH: 407-644-2290
PH: 800-843-3751
FAX: 407-645-4434
Stamps@michaelrogersinc.com
www.michaelrogersinc.com

Manchukuo

MICHAEL ROGERS, INC.
Suite 4-1
415 S. Orlando Ave.
Winter Park, FL 32789-3683
PH: 407-644-2290
PH: 800-843-3751
FAX: 407-645-4434
Stamps@michaelrogersinc.com
www.michaelrogersinc.com

Middle East-Arab

MICHAEL ROGERS, INC.
Suite 4-1
415 S. Orlando Ave.
Winter Park, FL 32789-3683
PH: 407-644-2290
PH: 800-843-3751
FAX: 407-645-4434
Stamps@michaelrogersinc.com
www.michaelrogersinc.com

New Issues

**DAVIDSON'S STAMP
SERVICE**
PO Box 36355
Indianapolis, IN 46236-0355
PH: 317-826-2620
ed-davidson@earthlink.net
www.newstampissues.com

South Africa

**ARON R. HALBERSTAM
PHILATELISTS, LTD.**
PO Box 150168
Van Brunt Station
Brooklyn, NY 11215-0168
PH: 718-788-397
arh@arhstamps.com
www.arhstamps.com

Sri Lanka

COLONIAL STAMP COMPANY
5757 Wilshire Blvd. PH #8
Los Angeles, CA 90036
PH: 323-933-9435
FAX: 323-939-9930
Toll Free in North America
PH: 877-272-6693
FAX: 877-272-6694
info@colonialstampcompany.com
www.colonialstampcompany.com

Stamp Stores

California

**BROSIUS STAMP, COIN &
SUPPLIES**
2105 Main St.
Santa Monica, CA 90405
PH: 310-396-7480
FAX: 310-396-7455
brosius.stamp.coin@hotmail.com

COLONIAL STAMP COMPANY
5757 Wilshire Blvd. PH #8
Los Angeles, CA 90036
PH: 323-933-9435
FAX: 323-939-9930
Toll Free in North America
PH: 877-272-6693
FAX: 877-272-6694
info@colonialstampcompany.com
www.colonialstampcompany.com

Georgia

**STAMPS UNLIMITED OF
GEORGIA, INC.**
Suite 1460
100 Peachtree St. NW
Atlanta, GA 30303
PH: 404-688-9161
tonyroozen@yahoo.com
www.stampsunlimitedofga.com

Illinois

**DR. ROBERT FRIEDMAN &
SONS STAMP & COIN
BUYING CENTER**
2029 W. 75th St.
Woodridge, IL 60517
PH: 800-588-8100
FAX: 630-985-1588
drbobstamps@comcast.net
www.drbobfriedmanstamps.com

Indiana

KNIGHT STAMP & COIN CO.
237 Main St.
Hobart, IN 46342
PH: 219-942-4341
PH: 800-634-2646
knight@knightcoin.com
www.knightcoin.com

Missouri

DAVID SEMSROTT STAMPS
11235 Manchester Rd.
St. Louis Kirkwood, MO 63122
PH: 314-984-8361
fixodine@sbcglobal.net
www.DavidSemsrott.com

New Jersey

**BERGEN STAMPS &
COLLECTIBLES**
306 Queen Anne Rd.
Teaneck, NJ 07666
PH: 201-836-8987

TRENTON STAMP & COIN CO
Thomas DeLuca
Store: Forest Glen Plaza
1804 Highway 33
Hamilton Square, NJ 08690
Mail: PO Box 8574
Trenton, NJ 08650
PH: 609-584-8100
PH: 800-446-8664
FAX: 609-587-8664
TOMD4TSC@aol.com

New York

CHAMPION STAMP CO., INC.
432 W. 54th St.
New York, NY 10019
PH: 212-489-8130
FAX: 212-581-8130
championstamp@aol.com
www.championstamp.com

Ohio

HILLTOP STAMP SERVICE
Richard A. Peterson
PO Box 626
Wooster, OH 44691
PH: 330-262-8907 (0)
PH: 330-262-5378
hilltop@bright.net
www.hilltopstamps.com

Virginia

LATHEROW & CO., INC.
5054 Lee Hwy.
Arlington, VA 22207
PH: 703-538-2727
PH: 800-647-4624
FAX: 703-538-5210
latherows@gmail.com

Straits Settlements

COLONIAL STAMP COMPANY
5757 Wilshire Blvd. PH #8
Los Angeles, CA 90036
PH: 323-933-9435
FAX: 323-939-9930
Toll Free in North America
PH: 877-272-6693
FAX: 877-272-6694
info@colonialstampcompany.com
www.colonialstampcompany.com

Supplies

**BROOKLYN GALLERY COIN &
STAMP, INC.**
8725 4th Ave.
Brooklyn, NY 11209
PH: 718-745-5701
FAX: 718-745-2775
info@brooklyngallery.com
www.brooklyngallery.com

IHOBB.COM
PO Box 6502
Oceanside, CA 92052
PH: 800-978-5333
sales@ihobb.com
www.ihobb.com

Thailand

THE STAMP ACT
PO Box 1136
Belmont, CA 94002
PH: 650-703-2342
PH: 650-592-3315
FAX: 650-508-8104
thestampact@sbcglobal.net

Togo

COLONIAL STAMP COMPANY
5757 Wilshire Blvd. PH #8
Los Angeles, CA 90036
PH: 323-933-9435
FAX: 323-939-9930
Toll Free in North America
PH: 877-272-6693
FAX: 877-272-6694
info@colonialstampcompany.com
www.colonialstampcompany.com

Tonga

COLONIAL STAMP COMPANY
5757 Wilshire Blvd. PH #8
Los Angeles, CA 90036
PH: 323-933-9435
FAX: 323-939-9930
Toll Free in North America
PH: 877-272-6693
FAX: 877-272-6694
info@colonialstampcompany.com
www.colonialstampcompany.com

Topicals

E. JOSEPH McCONNELL, INC.
PO Box 683
Monroe, NY 10949
PH: 845-783-9791
FAX: 845-782-0347
ejstamps@gmail.com
www.EJMcConnell.com

**HENRY GITNER
PHILATELISTS, INC.**
PO Box 3077-S
Middletown, NY 10940
PH: 845-343-5151
PH: 800-947-8267
FAX: 845-343-0068
hgitner@hgitner.com
www.hgitner.com

Topicals-Columbus

MR. COLUMBUS
PO Box 1492
Fennville, MI 49408
PH: 269-543-4755
David@MrColumbus1492.com
MrColumbus1492.com

Transvaal

COLONIAL STAMP COMPANY
5757 Wilshire Blvd. PH #8
Los Angeles, CA 90036
PH: 323-933-9435
FAX: 323-939-9930
Toll Free in North America
PH: 877-272-6693
FAX: 877-272-6694
info@colonialstampcompany.com
www.colonialstampcompany.com

Uganda

COLONIAL STAMP COMPANY
5757 Wilshire Blvd. PH #8
Los Angeles, CA 90036
PH: 323-933-9435
FAX: 323-939-9930
Toll Free in North America
PH: 877-272-6693
FAX: 877-272-6694
info@colonialstampcompany.com
www.colonialstampcompany.com

United Nations

BRUCE M. MOYER
Box 99
East Texas, PA 18046
PH: 610-395-8410
FAX: 610-395-8537
moyer@unstamps.com
www.unstamps.com

United States

ACS STAMP COMPANY
13650 Via Varra #210
Broomfield, CO 80020
PH: 303-841-8666
ACS@ACSStamp.com
www.acsstamp.com

United States

BROOKMAN STAMP CO.
PO Box 90
Vancouver, WA 98666
PH: 360-695-1391
PH: 800-545-4871
FAX: 360-695-1616
info@brookmanstamps.com
www.brookmanstamps.com

U.S.-Collections Wanted

DR. ROBERT FRIEDMAN & SONS STAMP & COIN BUYING CENTER
2029 W. 75th St.
Woodridge, IL 60517
PH: 800-588-8100
FAX: 630-985-1588
drbobstamps@comcast.net
www.drbobfriedmanstamps.com

DUTCH COUNTRY AUCTIONS
4115 Concord Pike
Wilmington, DE 19803
PH: 302-478-8740
FAX: 302-478-8779
auctions@dutchcountryauctions.com
www.dutchcountryauctions.com

Want Lists-British Empire 1840-1935 German Cols./Offices

COLONIAL STAMP COMPANY
5757 Wilshire Blvd. PH #8
Los Angeles, CA 90036
PH: 323-933-9435
FAX: 323-939-9930
Toll Free in North America
PH: 877-272-6693
FAX: 877-272-6694
info@colonialstampcompany.com
www.colonialstampcompany.com

Wanted-Worldwide Collections

DANIEL F. KELLEHER AUCTIONS LLC
PMB 44
60 Newtown Rd
Danbury, CT 06810
PH: 203-297-6056
FAX: 203-297-6059
info@kelleherauctions.com
www.kelleherauctions.com

DR. ROBERT FRIEDMAN & SONS STAMP & COIN BUYING CENTER
2029 W. 75th St.
Woodridge, IL 60517
PH: 800-588-8100
FAX: 630-985-1588
drbobstamps@comcast.net
www.drbobfriedmanstamps.com

DUTCH COUNTRY AUCTIONS
4115 Concord Pike
Wilmington, DE 19803
PH: 302-478-8740
FAX: 302-478-8779
auctions@dutchcountryauctions.com
www.dutchcountryauctions.com

Websites

ACS STAMP COMPANY
13650 Via Varra #210
Broomfield, CO 80020
PH: 303-841-8666
ACS@ACSStamp.com
www.acsstamp.com

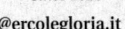

Scott International Album

Prices have never been so low on selected album parts. It is a wonderful opportunity to collect internationally. The Ultimate Album for Worldwide Collectors! Pick a period in history and embark on a philatelic adventure. With the International Album, the whole world is divided chronologically into more than 40 parts. From the classic era of philately to present day, the International is one of the broadest and far reaching worldwide albums available. *Binders are sold separately.*

- More than 16,000 pages with spaces for over 220,000 stamps.
- Pages printed on 2 sides.

Item	Part	Binder		Retail	AA*
801A140	1A1	(1840-1940)	Regular	$150.00	$120.00
801A240	1A2	(1840-1940)	Regular	$150.00	$120.00
801B140	1B1	(1840-1940)	Regular	$150.00	$120.00
801B240	1B2	(1840-1940)	Regular	$150.00	$120.00
802P149	2A	(1940-49)	Regular	$150.00	$120.00
802P249	2B	(1940-49)	Regular	$150.00	$120.00
803P155	3A	(1949-55)	Regular	$150.00	$120.00
803P255	3B	(1949-55)	Regular	$150.00	$120.00
804P159	4A	(1956-60)	Regular	$150.00	$120.00
804P259	4B	(1956-60)	Regular	$150.00	$120.00
805P063	5	(1960-63)	Jumbo	$150.00	$120.00
805P165	5A	(1963-65)	Jumbo	$150.00	$120.00
806P066	6	(1965-66)	Jumbo	$75.00	$55.00
806P168	6A	(1966-68)	Jumbo	$75.00	$55.00
807P171	7A	(1968-71)	Jumbo	$75.00	$55.00
807P271	7B	(1968-71)	Jumbo	$75.00	$55.00
808P173	8A	(1971-73)	Regular	$150.00	$120.00
808P273	8B	(1971-73)	Regular	$150.00	$120.00
809P074	9	(1973-74)	Regular	$150.00	$120.00
810P075	10	(1974-75)	Jumbo	$150.00	$120.00
811P076	11	(1975-76)	Jumbo	$150.00	$120.00
812P077	12	(1976-77)	Jumbo	$150.00	$120.00
813P078	13	(1977-78)	Jumbo	$150.00	$120.00
814P078	14	(1978)	Regular	$150.00	$120.00
815P079	15	(1979)	Regular	$150.00	$120.00
816P080	16	(1980)	Jumbo	$150.00	$120.00
817P081	17	(1981)	Regular	$150.00	$120.00
818P082	18	(1982)	Regular	$150.00	$120.00
819P083	19	(1983)	Regular	$150.00	$120.00
820P084	20	(1984)	Jumbo	$60.00	$44.00
821P085	21	(1985)	Jumbo	$150.00	$120.00
822P186	22A	(1986)	Regular	$60.00	$44.00
822P286	22B	(1986)	Regular	$60.00	$44.00
823P187	23A	(1987)	Regular	$60.00	$44.00
823P287	23B	(1987)	Regular	$150.00	$120.00
824P188	24A	(1988)	Regular	$60.00	$44.00
824P288	24B	(1988)	Regular	$60.00	$44.00
825P189	25A	(1989)	Regular	$60.00	$44.00
825P289	25B	(1989)	Regular	$60.00	$44.00
826P190	26A	(1990)	Regular	$150.00	$120.00
826P290	26B	(1990)	Regular	$60.00	$44.00
827P191	27A	(1991)	Regular	$60.00	$44.00
827P291	27B	(1991)	Regular	$60.00	$44.00
828P192	28A	(1992)	Regular	$60.00	$44.00
828P292	28B	(1992)	Regular	$60.00	$44.00
829P193	29A	(1993)	Regular	$60.00	$44.00
829P293	29B	(1993)	Regular	$60.00	$44.00
830P194	30A	(1994)	Regular	$60.00	$44.00
830P294	30B	(1994)	Regular	$60.00	$44.00
831P195	31A	(1995)	Regular	$60.00	$44.00
831P295	31B	(1995)	Regular	$60.00	$44.00
832P196	32A	(1996)	Regular	$60.00	$44.00
832P296	32B	(1996)	Regular	$60.00	$44.00
833P197	33A	(1997)	Regular	$60.00	$44.00
833P297	33B	(1997)	Regular	$60.00	$44.00
834P198	34A	(1998)	Regular	$60.00	$44.00
834P298	34B	(1998)	Regular	$60.00	$44.00
835P199	35A	(1999)	Regular	$150.00	$120.00
835P299	35B	(1999)	Regular	$150.00	$120.00
836P100	36A	(2000)	Regular	$150.00	$120.00
836P200	36B	(2000)	Regular	$150.00	$120.00
837P101	37A	(2001)	Regular	$150.00	$120.00
837P201	37B	(2001)	Regular	$150.00	$120.00
838P102	38A	(2002)	Regular	$60.00	$44.00

Item	Part	Binder		Retail	AA*
838P202	38B	(2002)	Regular	$60.00	$44.00
839P103	39A	(2003)	Regular	$60.00	$44.00
839P203	39B	(2003)	Regular	$60.00	$44.00
840P104	40A	(2004)	Regular	$60.00	$44.00
840P204	40B	(2004)	Regular	$60.00	$44.00
841P105	41A	(2005)	Regular	$60.00	$44.00
841P205	41B	(2005)	Regular	$60.00	$44.00
842P106	42A	(2006)	Regular	$135.00	$99.99
842P206	42B	(2006)	Regular	$135.00	$99.99
843P107	43A	(2007)	Regular	$99.99	$72.50
843P207	43B	(2007)	Regular	$99.99	$72.50
844P108	44A	(2008)	Jumbo	$135.00	$99.99
844P208	44B	(2008)	Jumbo	$135.00	$99.99
845P109	45A	(2009)	Jumbo	$135.00	$99.99
845P209	45B	(2009)	Jumbo	$135.00	$99.99
846P110	46A	(2010)	Regular	$135.00	$99.99
846P210	46B	(2010)	Regular	$135.00	$99.99
847P111	47A	(2011)	Regular	$135.00	$99.99
847P211	47B	(2011)	Regular	$135.00	$99.99
848P112	48A	(2012)	Regular	$135.00	$99.99
848P212	48B	(2012)	Regular	$135.00	$99.99
849P113	49A	(2013)	Regular	$135.00	$99.99
849P213	49B	(2013)	Regular	$135.00	$99.99
800PC72	People's Republic of China			$49.99	$39.99
800BOH	Bosnia & Herzegovina 1879-2007			$49.99	$39.99

INTERNATIONAL SERIES BINDERS AND SLIPCASES

Attractive, blue two-post binder is available in two sizes. Features distinctive silver embossed spine. **Binder will hold International pages only.** Labels available for all parts. For a complete list see amosadvantage.com

Item		Retail	AA*
800B001	Regular Binder Holds 300 pages	$52.99	$40.99
800B002	Jumbo Binder Holds 400 pages.	$52.99	$40.99
800BC01	Regular Binder Slipcase	$32.99	$26.99
800BC02	Jumbo Binder Slipcase	$32.99	$26.99
8__LB01	International Label(s)	$2.29	$1.69

Call: **1-800-572-6885**

Outside U.S. & Canada Call:

1-800-572-6885

Visit:

www.amosadvantage.com

ORDERING INFORMATION

*AA prices apply to paid subscribers of Amos Hobby titles, or for orders placed online.

Prices, terms and product availability subject to change.